# 2025
# STANDARD POSTAGE STAMP CATALOGUE

ONE HUNDRED AND EIGHTY-FIRST EDITION IN SIX VOLUMES

## Volume 1A
### U.S., U.N., A-Australia

| | |
|---:|:---|
| EDITOR-IN-CHIEF | Jay Bigalke |
| EDITOR-AT-LARGE | Donna Houseman |
| CONTRIBUTING EDITOR | Charles Snee |
| EDITOR EMERITUS | James E. Kloetzel |
| SENIOR EDITOR /NEW ISSUES AND VALUING | Martin J. Frankevicz |
| ASSOCIATE EDITOR | David Hartwig |
| CATALOGUE COORDINATOR | Eric Wiessinger |
| SENIOR GRAPHIC DESIGNER | Cinda McAlexander |
| SALES DIRECTOR | David Pistello |
| SALES DIRECTOR | Eric Roth |
| SALES DIRECTOR | Brenda Wyen |
| SALES REPRESENTATIVE | Julie Dahlstrom |

JOHNSTON PUBLIC LIBRARY
6700 MERLE HAY ROAD
JOHNSTON, IOWA 50131

*WITHDRAWN*

### Released April 2024
Includes New Stamp Listings through the February 2024 *Scott Stamp Monthly* Catalogue Update

Copyright© 2024 by

## AMOS MEDIA

1660 Campbell Road, Suite A, Sidney, OH 45365
Publishers of *Linn's Stamp News, Scott Stamp Monthly, Coin World* and *Coin World Monthly.*

**Scott catalog editorial team contact information**
scottstamp.com | scottcatalogueeditorial@amosmedia.com

**Scott catalog customer service contact information**
amosadvantage.com | cuserv@amosmedia.com | 800-572-6885 | Monday-Thursday 9 a.m. to 5 p.m.; Friday 9 a.m. to noon, Eastern Standard Time

# Table of contents

| | |
|---|---|
| Letter from the editor | 3A |
| Acknowledgments | 4A |
| 2025 Volume 1A-1B catalogue number additions, deletions and changes | 5A |
| Information on philatelic societies | 6A |
| Information on catalogue values, grade and condition | 9A |
| Grading illustrations | 10A |
| Gum chart | 12A |
| Catalogue listing policy | 13A |
| Understanding the listings | 14A |
| Special notices | 16A |
| Abbreviations | 16A |
| Basic stamp information | 18A |
| Terminology | 25A |
| Currency conversion | 27A |
| Pronunciation Symbols | 28A |
| The British Commonwealth of Nations | 48A |
| Colonies, former colonies, offices, territories controlled by parent states | 50A |
| Dies of British Colonial stamps referred to in the catalogue | 51A |
| British Colonial and Crown Agents watermarks | 52A |
| **United States** | 1 |
| Subject Index of Regular, Commemorative and Air Post Issues | 160 |
| **United Nations** | 1 |
| Countries of the World Abu Dhabi-Australia | 254 |
| **Index and Identifier** | **801** |
| Dealer directory yellow pages | 810 |
| Index to advertisers | 812 |

See the following volumes for other country listings:
Volume 1B through 6B for Countries of the World, Austria-Z
Volume 1B: Austria-B
Volume 2A: C-Cur; Volume 2B: Cyp-F
Volume 3A: G; Volume 3B: H-I
Volume 4A: J-L; Volume 4B: M
Volume 5A: N-Phil; Volume 5B: Pit-Sam
Volume 6A: San-Tete; Volume 6B: Thai-Z

---

### Scott Catalogue Mission Statement

The Scott Catalogue Team exists to serve the recreational, educational and commercial hobby needs of stamp collectors and dealers.
We strive to set the industry standard for philatelic information and products by developing and providing goods that help collectors identify, value, organize and present their collections.
Quality customer service is, and will continue to be, our highest priority.
We aspire toward achieving total customer satisfaction.

---

## Copyright Notice

The contents of this book are owned exclusively by Amos Media Co. and all rights thereto are reserved under the Pan American and Universal Copyright Conventions.

Copyright ©2024 by Amos Media Co., Sidney, Ohio. Printed in U.S.A.

COPYRIGHT NOTE
Permission is hereby given for the use of material in this book and covered by copyright if:
(a) The material is used in advertising matter, circulars or price lists for the purpose of offering stamps for sale or purchase at the prices listed therein; and
(b) Such use is incidental to the business of buying and selling stamps and is limited in scope and length, i.e., it does not cover a substantial portion of the total number of stamps issued by any country or of any special category of stamps of any country; and
(c) Such material is not used as part of any catalogue, stamp album or computerized or other system based upon the Scott catalogue numbers, or in any updated valuations of stamps not offered for sale or purchase; and
(d) Such use is not competitive with the business of the copyright owner; and
(e) Such use is for editorial purposes in publications in the form of articles and commentary, except for computer software or the serialization of books in such publications, for which separate written permission is required.
Any use of the material in this book which does not satisfy all the foregoing conditions is forbidden in any form unless permission in each instance is given in writing by the copyright owner.

## Trademark Notice

The terms SCOTT, SCOTT'S, SCOTT CATALOGUE NUMBERING SYSTEM, SCOTT CATALOGUE NUMBER, SCOTT NUMBER and abbreviations thereof, are trademarks of Amos Media Co., used to identify its publications and its copyrighted system for identifying and classifying postage stamps for dealers and collectors. These trademarks are to be used only with the prior consent of Amos Media Co.

No part of this work may be reproduced in any form or by any means, electronic or mechanical, including photocopying, without permission in writing from Amos Media Co., P.O. Box 4129, Sidney, OH 45365-4129.

ISBN 978-0-89487-719-3

Library of Congress Card No. 2-3301

# What's new for 2025 Scott Standard Volume 1

Another catalog season is upon us as we continue the journey of the 156-year history of the Scott catalogs. The 2025 volumes are the 181st edition of the Scott *Standard Postage Stamp Catalogue*. Volume 1A includes listings for the United States, United Nations, and countries of the world Aden through Australia. Listings for Austria through B countries of the world can be found in Vol. 1B.

This year's covers feature a postal theme, a nod to the United States Postal Service's 250th anniversary in 2025 with a photograph of a letter carrier courtesy of the Library of Congress Prints and Photographs Division. The United States 1985 21.1¢ Envelopes coil stamp (Scott 2150) is shown on the Vol. 1A catalog, and the Boznia and Herzegovina Serb Administration 2018 90-pfennig Mail Carrier and Steps of Mail Delivery stamp (600) is featured on the Vol. 1B catalog.

Because Vol. 1B is a continuation of the first part of the Vol. 1 catalog, the introduction pages are not repeated in each volume this year.

The market in classic U.S. stamps in the second half of 2023 was a bit erratic. Whereas prices at auction for very fine stamps were quite consistent in the first half of 2023, prices in the second half of the year were sometimes very strong in one auction and clearly lagging in another auction. Such price fluctuations occured even in auctions conducted by the same auction house.

One consistent trend seen since the release of the 2024 Scott U.S. Specialized catalog is the somewhat lackluster performances of the unused 1875 special printings of the 1873 issue (Scott 167-177), the 1880 unused special printings of the 1879 issue (192-204), the 1882 special printing (205C) and the 1883 special printing (211D). All of these very expensive stamps have dropped in catalog value by approximately 5 percent. The 1875 unused Special printings (180 and 181) produced a mixed valuing situation. Scott 180, the 2¢ carmine vermilion stamp, dropped from $70,000 to $65,000, but the 5¢ bright blue (181) rose slightly in value, from $450,000 to $460,000.

On the bright side, several very scarce classic stamps and varieties thereof that are seldom seen for sale appeared at auction in late 2023, and they did very well, indeed. No. 25A unused is a stamp not often seen in true very fine grade. That 3¢ rose type II stamp with gum moved from $9,000 in the 2024 U.S. Specialized catalog to $12,500 in the 2025 Vol. 1A, and the same stamp without gum jumped from $4,000 to $5,000. The 1861 3¢ rose with double impression (65f), known only used, moved smartly from $11,000 to $17,500. The used vertical pair imperforate horizontally of the 1861 10¢ green (68b) skyrocketed from $30,000 to $67,500, after the finer of the two known examples sold at auction in late 2023.

In 20th century issues, the 1901 1¢ Pan American with inverted center (Scott 294a) drops slightly from $12,500 to $11,500 in unused condition. On the upside, the $5 dark green definitive (313) in mint, never-hinged condition moves from $8,500 to $10,000. Scott 406b, the 1912 2¢ carmine type I Washington stamp with a double impression had been valued used with a dash prior to the 2025 Vol. 1A. It is now valued at $650. Other 20th-century stamp varieties that show very large value increases include No. 515c unused and mint, never-hinged, No. 527c unused, and No. 528Ag unused.

Back-of-the-book issues were quiet in the last half of 2023, but it should be mentioned that a great many very high grade examples of postage due and Official stamps were sold at auction. Though a large majority of those offerings were stamps in grades higher than very fine, the Scott catalog benchmark, the interest in and sale results for stamps in very high grades bodes well also for the general market for very fine examples.

In the Confederate States of America listings, the rare unused example of the New Orleans red postmaster's provisional (Scott 62X6) is valued for the first time, at $18,500.

The very important new listing of the 5¢ postmaster's provisional stamp from Millbury, Mass., on white print paper (Scott 7X2), rather than the bluish letter paper of the other unique Millbury variety (7X1), has been brought forward from the 2024 U.S. Specialized catalog into the Vol. 1A listings, so that both catalogs now list these two extremely scarce major numbers.

In the 1909 bluish paper stamps, a new note has been added for the 8¢ olive green (Scott 363) indicating that the Scott value for mint, never-hinged is for a stamp in the grade of fine-very fine. At the present time, it has been determined that no never-hinged examples of the 8¢ on bluish paper in the grades of very fine or higher are recorded. That fact is unlikely to change in the future.

In an interesting twist, an example of the 1912 carmine type I Washington definitive with double impression has been authenticated as being in the lake shade, rather than the normal carmine shade. The new lake variety with double impression is now listed as Scott 406d, while the carmine variety of the error remains as Scott 406b. The possible twist is that the Scott editors now feel that all of the scarce double impressions of Scott 406 should be reexamined to confirm that this double impression variety indeed appears on both shades of the stamp, or whether perhaps all double impressions come only in the lake shade. Only time and examination will tell.

Values also increased for modern U.S. forever stamps, nonmachinable-rate stamps, and global forever stamps because of the continued uptick in cost for the rates that these stamps satisfy.

Angola received a thorough review. More than 700 value changes were made, with approximately half increases

*Continued on page 4A*

*Continued from page 3A*

and half decreases. Of those changes, around 400 were for the classic time period. One such example is the 1913 Vasco da Gama common design set of eight (Scott 184-191), which moved from $24.90 in unused condition to $27.90, and from $15.50 to $20.05 in used condition.

Armenia was reviewed, and more than 650 changes were made. In the classic period, almost 60 value changes were recorded. In the modern era, the 2011 Joint United Nations Program on AIDS souvenir sheet of two (Scott 886) advanced from $3.75 unused and used to $4.25 both ways in this year's catalog.

Approximately 475 value changes, a mix of increases and decreases, were made for the nation of Azerbaijan. One of the increases was for the 2014 Winter Sports sheet of two (Scott 1069) that went from $4 in unused and used condition to $5.

Modern Bolivia overprints were the focus for this year's catalog, with almost 40 values being assigned that were previously dashed. It is also important to note that a number of new Bolivia overprint listings were added this year through the Scott New Issues update in *Scott Stamp Monthly*.

Abu Dhabi, Algeria, Bahrain and Batum were also examined, and a handful of value changes were made for each of those countries.

Other countries received reviews that are not noted in this letter. We encourage you to pay special attention to the Number Additions, Deletions and Changes listing in this volume. We also suggest reading the catalog introduction, which includes an abundance of useful information.

A digital subscription is also available for the Scott catalogs, and information about the subscription can be found online at www.amosadvantage.com.

Best wishes in your collecting pursuits!

Jay Bigalke, Scott catalog editor-in-chief

# Acknowledgments

Our appreciation and gratitude go to the following individuals who have assisted us in preparing information included in this year's Scott catalogues. Some helpers prefer anonymity. These individuals have generously shared their stamp knowledge with others through the medium of the Scott catalogue.

Those who follow provided information that is in addition to the hundreds of dealer price lists and advertisements and scores of auction catalogues and realizations that were used in producing the catalogue values. It is from those noted here that we have been able to obtain information on items not normally seen in published lists and advertisements. Support from these people goes beyond data leading to catalogue values, for they also are key to editorial changes.

Roland Austin
Michael & Cecilia Ball (A To Z Stamps)
Jim Bardo (Bardo Stamps)
Brian M. Bleckwenn
   (The Philatelic Foundation)
Les Bootman
John D. Bowman
   (Carriers and Locals Society)
Roger S. Brody
Tom Brougham
   (Canal Zone Study Group)
Paul and Josh Buchsbayew
   (Cherrystone Auctions, Inc.)
Timothy Bryan Burgess
Tina and John Carlson (JET Stamps)
Jay T. Carrigan
Carlson Chambliss
Bob Coale
Tony L. Crumbley
   (Carolina Coin and Stamp, Inc.)
Christopher Dahle
Charles Deaton
Bob and Rita Dumaine
   (Sam Houston Duck Co.)
Charles Epting
   (Robert A. Siegel Auction Galleries)
Mike Farrell
David Feldman International Auctioneers
Robert A. Fisher
Jeffrey M. Forster

Robert S. Freeman
Henry L. Gitner
   (Henry Gitner Philatelists, Inc.)
Stan Goldfarb
Marc E. Gonzales
Daniel E. Grau
Alexander Haimann
Bruce Hecht (Bruce L. Hecht Co.)
Daniel Hill
Eric Jackson
Michael Jaffe (Michael Jaffe Stamps, Inc.)
William A. (Bill) Jones
Allan Katz (Ventura Stamp Co.)
Patricia A. Kaufmann
   (Civil War Philatelic Society)
Jon Kawaguchi
   (Ryukyu Philatelic Specialist Society)
Han Ki Kim
Ingert Kuzych
Ulf Lindahl (Ethiopian Philatelic Society)
Ignacio Llach (Filatelia Llach, S.L.)
William K. McDaniel
Pat McElroy
Brian Metz
Mark S. Miller (India Study Circle)
Gary Morris (Pacific Midwest Co.)
Bruce M. Moyer
   (Moyer Stamps & Collectables)
Scott Murphy
   (Professional Stamp Experts)

Dr. Tiong Tak Ngo
Nik and Lisa Oquist
Don Peterson
   (International Philippine Philatelic
   Society)
Todor Drumev Popov
Dr. Charles Posner
Peter W. W. Powell
Ed Reiser (Century Stamp Co.)
Ghassan D. Riachi
Robert G. Rufe
Theodosios D. Sampson Ph.D.
Dennis W. Schmidt
Joyce and Chuck Schmidt
Guy Shaw
   (Mexico-Elmhurst Philatelic Society
   International)
J. Randall Shoemaker
   (Philatelic Stamp Authentication and
   Grading, Inc.)
Jay Smith
Telah Smith
Mark Stelmacovich
Scott R. Trepel
   (Robert A. Siegel Auction Galleries)
Dan Undersander
Steven Unkrich
Herbert R. Volin
Val Zabijaka (Zabijaka Auctions)

# Vols. 1A-1B number additions, deletions and changes

| Number in 2024 Catalogue | Number in 2025 Catalogue |
|---|---|

**United States**
| | |
|---|---|
| new | 406d |
| new | 1787c |
| new | 2429d |
| 2429d | 2429e |
| 2429e | 2429f |
| new | 2492l |
| new | 2520e |
| new | 2871Ad |
| new | 5788a |
| new | 5789Ab |

**Stock Transfer Stamps**
| | |
|---|---|
| new | RD24a |

**Angola**
| | |
|---|---|
| new | RA17a |

**Australian States – New South Wales**
| | |
|---|---|
| new | 66h |
| new | 66i |

**Barbuda**
| | |
|---|---|
| new | 495g |

**Belgium**
| | |
|---|---|
| Q11a | deleted |

**Bolivia**
| | |
|---|---|
| 1505A | 1506A |

**Botswana**
| | |
|---|---|
| 586a | 586 |
| 586b | 586A |
| 586c | 586B |
| 586d | 586C |
| 586 | 586Cd |

**Brunei**
| | |
|---|---|
| 14b | 14B |
| 16a | 16A |
| 18b | 18B |
| 20a | 20A |
| 23a | 23A |
| 28a | 28A |
| 30a | 30A |
| 35a | 35A |
| 37a | 37A |

# Addresses, telephone numbers, web sites, email addresses of general and specialized philatelic societies

Collectors can contact the following groups for information about the philately of the areas within the scope of these societies, or inquire about membership in these groups. Aside from the general societies, we limit this list to groups that specialize in particular fields of philately, particular areas covered by the Scott *Standard Postage Stamp Catalogue*, and topical groups. Many more specialized philatelic society exist than those listed below. These addresses are updated yearly, and they are, to the best of our knowledge, correct and current. Groups should inform the editors of address changes whenever they occur. The editors also want to hear from other such specialized groups not listed.

Unless otherwise noted all website addresses begin with http://

## General Societies

**American Philatelic Society,** 100 Match Factory Place, Bellefonte, PA 16823-1367; (814) 933-3803; https://stamps.org; apsinfo@stamps.org

**International Society of Worldwide Stamp Collectors,** Joanne Murphy, M.D., P.O. Box 19006, Sacramento, CA 95819; www.iswsc.org; executivedirector@iswsc.org

**Royal Philatelic Society of Canada,** P.O. Box 69080, St. Clair Post Office, Toronto, ON M4T 3A1 Canada; (888) 285-4143; www.rpsc.org; info@rpsc.org

**Royal Philatelic Society London,** 15 Abchurch Lane, London EX4N 7BW, United Kingdom; +44 (0) 20 7486 1044; www.rpsl.org.uk; secretary@rpsl.org.uk

## Libraries, Museums, and Research Groups

**American Philatelic Research Library,** 100 Match Factory Place, Bellefonte, PA 16823; (814) 933-3803; www.stamplibrary.org; library@stamps.org.

**V. G. Greene Philatelic Research Foundation,** P.O. Box 69100, St. Clair Post Office, Toronto, ON M4T 3A1, Canada; (416) 921-2073; info@greenefoundation.ca

## Aero/Astro Philately

**American Air Mail Society,** Stephen Reinhard, P.O. Box 110, Mineola, NY 11501; www.americanairmailsociety.org; sreinhard1@optonline.net

## Postal History

**Auxiliary Markings Club,** Jerry Johnson, 6621 W. Victoria Ave., Kennewick, WA 99336; www.postal-markings.org; membership-2010@postal-markings.org

**Postage Due Mail Study Group,** Bob Medland, Camway Cottage, Nanny Hurn's Lane, Cameley, Bristol BS39 5AJ, United Kingdom; 01761 45959; www.postageduemail.org.uk; secretary.pdmsg@gmail.com

**Postal History Society,** Yamil Kouri, 405 Waltham St. #347, Lexington, MA 02421; www.postalhistorysociety.org; yhkouri@massmed.org

**Post Mark Collectors Club,** Bob Milligan, 7014 Woodland Oaks Drive, Magnolia, TX 77354; (281) 259-2735; www.postmarks.org; bob.milligan0@gmail.com

**U.S. Cancellation Club,** Roger Curran, 18 Tressler Blvd., Lewisburg, PA 17837; rdcnrc@ptd.net

## Revenues and Cinderellas

**American Revenue Association,** Lyman Hensley, 473 E. Elm St., Sycamore, IL 60178-1934; www.revenuer.org; ilrno2@netzero.net

**Christmas Seal and Charity Stamp Society,** John Denune Jr., 234 E. Broadway, Granville, OH 43023; (740) 814-6031; www.seal-society.org

**National Duck Stamp Collectors Society,** Anthony J. Monico, P.O. Box 43, Harleysville, PA 19438-0043; www.ndscs.org; ndscs@ndscs.org

**State Revenue Society,** Kent Gray, P.O. Box 67842, Albuquerque, NM 87193; www.staterevenue.org; srssecretary@comcast.net

## Thematic Philately

**Americana Unit,** Dennis Dengel, 17 Peckham Road, Poughkeepsie, NY 12603-2018; www.americanaunit.org; ddengel@americanaunit.org

**American Topical Association,** Jennifer Miller, P.O. Box 2143, Greer, SC 29652-2143; (618) 985-5100; americantopical.org; ata@americantopical.org

**Astronomy Study Unit,** Leonard Zehr, 1411 Chateau Ave., Windsor, ON N8P 1M2, Canada; (416) 833-9317; www.astronomystudyunit.net; lenzehr@gmail.com

**Bicycle Stamps Club,** Corey Hjalseth, 1102 Broadway, Suite 200, Tacoma, WA 98402; (253) 318-6222; www.bicyclestampsclub.org; coreyh@evergreenhomeloans.com

**Biology Unit,** Chris Dahle, 1401 Linmar Drive NE, Cedar Rapids, IA 52402-3724; www.biophilately.org; chris-dahle@biophilately.org

**Bird Stamp Society,** Mr. S. A. H. (Tony) Statham, Ashlyns Lodge, Chesham Road, Berkhamsted, Herts HP4 2ST United Kingdom; www.bird-stamps.org/bss; tony.statham@sky.com

**Captain Cook Society,** Jerry Yucht, 8427 Leale Ave., Stockton, CA 95212; www.captaincooksociety.com; us@captaincooksociety.com

**The CartoPhilatelic Society,** Marybeth Sulkowski, 2885 Sanford Ave., SW, #32361, Grandville, MI 49418-1342; www.mapsonstamps.org; secretary@mapsonstamps.org

**Casey Jones Railroad Unit,** Jeff Lough, 2612 Redbud Land, Apt. C, Lawrence, KS 66046; www.uqp.de/cjr; jeffydplaugh@gmail.com

**Cats on Stamps Study Unit,** Robert D. Jarvis, 2731 Teton Lane, Fairfield, CA 94533; www.catstamps.info; catmews1@yahoo.com

**Chemistry and Physics on Stamps Study Unit,** Dr. Roland Hirsch, 13830 Metcalf Ave., Apt. 15218, Overland Park, KS 66223-8017; (301) 792-6296; www.cpossu.org; rfhirsch@cpossu.org

**Chess on Stamps Study Unit,** Barry Keith, 511 First St. N., Apt. 106; Charlottesville, VA 22902; www.chessonstamps.org; keithfam@embarqmail.com

**Cricket Philatelic Society,** A. Melville-Brown, 11 Weppons, Ravens Road, Shorham-by-Sea, West Sussex BN43 5AW, United Kingdom; www.cricketstamp.net; mel.cricket.100@googlemail.com

**Earth's Physical Features Study Group,** Fred Klein, 515 Magdalena Ave., Los Altos, CA 94024; http://epfsu.jeffhayward.com; epfsu@jeffhayward.com

**Ebony Society of Philatelic Events and Reflections (ESPER),** Don Neal, P.O. Box 5245, Somerset, NJ 08875-5245; www.esperstamps.org; esperdon@verizon.net

**Europa Study Unit,** Tonny E. Van Loij, 3002 S. Xanthia St.; Denver, CO 80231-4237; (303) 752-0189; www.europastudyunit.org; tvanloij@gmail.com

**Fire Service in Philately,** John Zaranek, 81 Hillpine Road, Cheektowaga, NY 14227-2259; (716) 668-3352; jczaranek@roadrunner.com

**Gastronomy on Stamps Study Unit,** David Wolfersburger, 5062 NW 35th Lane Road, Ocala, FL 34482; (314) 494-3795; www.gastronomystamps.org

**Gay and Lesbian History on Stamps Club,** Joe Petronie, P.O. Box 190842, Dallas, TX 75219-0842; www.glhsonline.org; glhsc@aol.com

**Gems, Minerals and Jewelry Study Unit,** Fred Haynes, 10 Country Club Drive, Rochester, NY 14618-3720; fredmhaynes55@gmail.com

**Graphics Philately Association,** Larry Rosenblum. 1030 E. El Camino Real, PMB 107, Sunnyvale, CA 94087-3759; www.graphics-stamps.org; larry@graphics-stamps.org

**Journalists, Authors and Poets on Stamps,** Christopher D. Cook, 7222 Hollywood Road, Berrien Springs, MI 49103; cdcook2@gmail.com

**Lighthouse Stamp Society,** www.lighthousestampsociety.org

**Lions International Stamp Club,** David McKirdy, s-Gravenwetering 248, 3062 SJ Rotterdam, Netherlands; 31(0) 10 212 0313; www.lisc.nl; davidmckirdy@aol.com

**Masonic Study Unit,** Gene Fricks, 25 Murray Way, Blackwood, NJ 08012-4400; genefricks@comcast.net

**Medical Subjects Unit,** Dr. Frederick C. Skvara, P.O. Box 6228, Bridgewater, NJ 08807; fcskvara@optonline.net

**Napoleonic Age Philatelists,** Ken Berry, 4117 NW 146th St., Oklahoma City, OK 73134-1746; (405) 748-8646; www.nap-stamps.org; krb4117@att.net

**Old World Archaeological Study Unit,** Caroline Scannell, 14 Dawn Drive, Smithtown, NY 11787-176; www.owasu.org; editor@owasu.org

**Petroleum Philatelic Society International,** Feitze Papa, 922 Meander Drive, Walnut Creek, CA 94598-4239; www.ppsi.org.uk; oildad@astound.net

**Rotary on Stamps Fellowship,** Gerald L. Fitzsimmons, 105 Calle Ricardo, Victoria, TX 77904; www.rotaryonstamps.org; glfitz@suddenlink.net

**Scouts on Stamps Society International,** Woodrow (Woody) Brooks, 498 Baldwin Road, Akron, OH 44312; (330) 612-1294; www.sossi.org; secretary@sossi.org

**Ships on Stamps Unit,** Erik Th. Matzinger, Voorste Havervelden 30, 4822 AL Breda, Netherlands; www.shipsonstamps.org; erikships@gmail.com

**Space Topic Study Unit,** David Blog, P.O. Box 174, Bergenfield, NJ 07621; www.space-unit.com; davidblognj@gmail.com

**Stamps on Stamps Collectors Club,** Michael Merritt, 73 Mountainside Road, Mendham, NJ 07945; www.stampsonstamps.org; michael@mischu.me

**Windmill Study Unit,** Walter J. Hallien, 607 N. Porter St., Watkins Glenn, NY 14891-1345; (607) 229-3541; www.windmillworld.com

**Wine On Stamps Study Unit,** David Wolfersburger, 5062 NW 35th Lane Road, Ocala, FL 34482; (314) 494-3795; www.wine-on-stamps.org;

## United States

**American Air Mail Society,** Stephen Reinhard, P.O. Box 110, Mineola, NY 11501; www.americanairmailsociety.org; sreinhard1@optonline.net

**American First Day Cover Society,** P.O. Box 246, Colonial Beach VA 22443-0246; (520) 321-0880; www.afdcs.org; afdcs@afdcs.org

# INTRODUCTION

**Auxiliary Markings Club,** Jerry Johnson, 6621 W. Victoria Ave., Kennewick, WA 99336; www.postal-markings.org; membership-2010@postal-markings.org

**American Plate Number Single Society,** Rick Burdsall, APNSS Secretary, P.O. BOX 1023, Palatine, IL 60078-1023; www.apnss.org; apnss.sec@gmail.com

**American Revenue Association,** Lyman Hensley, 473 E. Elm St., Sycamore, IL 60178-1934; www.revenuer.org; ilrno2@netzero.net

**American Society for Philatelic Pages and Panels,** Ron Walenciak, P.O. Box 1042, Washington Township, NJ 07676; www.asppp.org; ron.walenciak@asppp.org

**Canal Zone Study Group,** Mike Drabik, P.O. Box 281, Bolton, MA 01740, www.canalzonestudygroup.com; czsgsecretary@gmail.com

**Carriers and Locals Society,** John Bowman, 14409 Pentridge Drive, Corpus Christi, TX 78410; (361) 933-0757; www.pennypost.org; jbowman@stx.rr.com

**Christmas Seal & Charity Stamp Society,** John Denune Jr., 234 E. Broadway, Granville, OH 43023; (740) 814-6031; www.seal-society.org; john@christmasseals.net

**Civil War Philatelic Society,** Patricia A. Kaufmann, 10194 N. Old State Road, Lincoln, DE 19960-3644; (302) 422-2656; www.civilwarphilatelicsociety.org; trishkauf@comcast.net

**Error, Freaks, and Oddities Collectors Club,** Scott Shaulis, P.O. Box 549, Murrysville, PA 15668-0549; (724) 733-4134; www.efocc.org; scott@shaulisstamps.com

**National Duck Stamp Collectors Society,** Anthony J. Monico, P.O. Box 43, Harleysville, PA 19438-0043; www.ndscs.org; ndscs@ndscs.org

**Plate Number Coil Collectors Club (PNC3),** Gene Trinks, 16415 W. Desert Wren Court, Surprise, AZ 85374; (623) 322-4619; www.pnc3.org; gctrinks@cox.net

**Post Mark Collectors Club,** Bob Milligan, 7014 Woodland Oaks Drive, Magnolia, TX 77354; (281) 259-2735; www.postmarks.org; bob.milligan0@gmail.com

**Souvenir Card Collectors Society,** William V. Kriebel, www.souvenircards.org; kriebewv@drexel.edu

**United Postal Stationery Society,** Dave Kandziolka, 404 Sundown Drive, Knoxville, TN 37934; www.upss.org; membership@upss.org

**U.S. Cancellation Club,** Roger Curran, 18 Tressler Blvd., Lewisburg, PA 17837; rdcnrc@ptd.net

**U.S. Philatelic Classics Society,** Rob Lund, 2913 Fulton St., Everett, WA 98201-3733; www.uspcs.org; membershipchairman@uspcs.org

**US Possessions Philatelic Society,** Daniel F. Ring, P.O. Box 113, Woodstock, IL 60098; http://uspps.tripod.com; danielfring@hotmail.com

**United States Stamp Society,** Rod Juell, P.O. Box 3508, Joliet, IL 60434-3508; www.usstamps.org; execsecretary@usstamps.org

## Africa

**Bechuanalands and Botswana Society,** Otto Peetoom, Roos, East Yorkshire HU12 OLD, United Kingdom; 44(0)1964 670239; www.bechuanalandphilately.com; info@bechuanalandphilately

**Egypt Study Circle,** Mike Murphy, 11 Waterbank Road, Bellingham, London SE6 3DJ United Kingdom; (44) 0203 6737051; www.egyptstudycircle.org.uk; secretary@egyptstudycircle.org.uk

**Ethiopian Philatelic Society,** Ulf Lindahl, 21 Westview Place, Riverside, CT 06878; (203) 722-0769; https://ethiopianphilatelicsociety.weebly.com; ulindahl@optonline.net

**Liberian Philatelic Society,** P.O. Box 1570, Parker, CO 80134; www.liberiastamps.org, liberiastamps@comcast.net

**Orange Free State Study Circle,** J. R. Stroud, RDPSA, 24 Hooper Close, Burnham-on-sea, Somerset TA8 1JQ United Kingdom; 44 1278 782235; www.orangefreestatephilately.org.uk; richard@richardstroud.plus.com

**Philatelic Society for Greater Southern Africa,** David McNamee, 15 Woodland Drive, Alamo, CA 94507; www.psgsa.org; alan.hanks@sympatico.ca

**Rhodesian Study Circle,** William R. Wallace, P.O. Box 16381, San Francisco, CA 94116; (415) 564-6069; www.rhodesianstudycircle.org.uk; bwall8rscr@earthlink.net

**Society for Moroccan and Tunisian Philately,** S.P.L.M., 206, Bld Pereire, 75017 Paris, France; http://splm-philatelie.com; splm206@aol.com

**South Sudan Philatelic Society,** William Barclay, 1370 Spring Hill Road, South Londonderry, VT 05155; barclayphilatelics@gmail.com

**Sudan Study Group,** Andy Neal, Bank House, Coedway, Shrewsbury SY5 9AR United Kingdom; www.sudanstamps.org; andywneal@gmail.com

**Transvaal Study Circle,** c/o 9 Meadow Road, Gravesend, Kent DA11 7LR United Kingdom; www.transvaalstamps.org.uk; transvaalstudycircle@aol.co.uk

**West Africa Study Circle,** Martin Bratzel, 1233 Virginia Ave., Windsor, ON N8S 2Z1 Canada; www.wasc.org.uk; marty_bratzel@yahoo.ca

## Asia

**Aden & Somaliland Study Group,** Malcom Lacey, 108 Dalestorth Road, Sutton-in-Ashfield, Nottinghamshire NG17 3AA, United Kingdom; www.stampdomain.com/aden; neil53williams@yahoo.co.uk

**Burma (Myanmar) Philatelic Study Circle,** Michael Whittaker, 1, Ecton Leys, Hillside, Rugby, Warwickshire CV22 5SL United Kingdom; https://burmamyanmarphilately.wordpress.com/burma-myanmar-philatelic-study-circle; manningham8@mypostoffice.co.uk

**Ceylon Study Circle,** Rodney W. P. Frost, 42 Lonsdale Road, Cannington, Bridgwater, Somerset TA5 2JS United Kingdom; 01278 652592; www.ceylonsc.org; rodney.frost@tiscali.co.uk

**China Stamp Society,** H. James Maxwell, 1050 W. Blue Ridge Blvd., Kansas City, MO 64145-1216; www.chinastampsociety.org; president@chinastampsociety.org

**Hong Kong Philatelic Society,** John Tang, G.P.O. Box 446, Hong Kong; www.hkpsociety.com; hkpsociety@outlook.com

**Hong Kong Study Circle,** Robert Newton, www.hongkongstudycircle.com/index.html; newtons100@gmail.com

**India Study Circle,** John Warren, P.O. Box 7326, Washington, DC 20044; (202) 488-7443; https://indiastudycircle.org; jw-kbw@earthlink.net

**International Philippine Philatelic Society,** James R. Larot, Jr., 4990 Bayleaf Court, Martinez, CA 94553; (925) 260-5425; www.theipps.info; jlarot@ccwater.com

**International Society for Japanese Philately,** P.O. Box 1283, Haddonfield NJ 08033; www.isjp.org; secretary@isjp.org

**Iran Philatelic Study Circle,** Nigel Gooch, Marchwood, 56, Wickham Ave., Bexhill-on-Sea, East Sussex TN39 3ER United Kingdom; www.iranphilately.org; nigelmgooch@gmail.com

**Korea Stamp Society,** Peter Corson, 1109 Gunnison Place, Raleigh, NC 27609; (919) 787-7611, koreastampsociety.org; pbcorson@aol.com

**Nepal & Tibet Philatelic Study Circle,** Colin Hepper, 12 Charnwood Close, Peterborough, Cambs PE2 9BZ United Kingdom; http://fuchs-online.com/ntpsc; ntpsc@fuchs-online.com

**Pakistan Philatelic Study Circle,** Jeff Siddiqui, P.O. Box 7002, Lynnwood, WA 98046; jeffsiddiqui@msn.com

**Society of Indo-China Philatelists,** Ron Bentley, 2600 N. 24th St., Arlington, VA 22207; (703) 524-1652; www.sicp-online.org; ron.bentley@verizon.net

**Society of Israel Philatelists, Inc.,** Sarah Berezenko, 100 Match Factory Place, Bellefonte, PA 16823-1367; (814) 933-3803 ext. 212; www.israelstamps.com; israelstamps@gmail.com

## Australasia and Oceania

**Australian States Study Circle of the Royal Sydney Philatelic Club,** Ben Palmer, G.P.O. 1751, Sydney, NSW 2001 Australia; http://club.philas.org.au/states

**Fellowship of Samoa Specialists,** Trevor Shimell, 18 Aspen Drive, Newton Abbot, Devon TQ12 4TN United Kingdom; www.samoaexpress.org; trevor.shimell@gmail.com

**Malaya Study Group,** Michael Waugh, 151 Roker Lane, Pudsey, Leeds LS28 9ND United Kingdom; http://malayastudygroup.com; mawpud43@gmail.com

**New Zealand Society of Great Britain,** Michael Wilkinson, 121 London Road, Sevenoaks, Kent TN13 1BH United Kingdom; 01732 456997; www.nzsgb.org.uk; mwilkin799@aol.com

**Pacific Islands Study Circle,** John Ray, 24 Woodvale Ave., London SE25 4AE United Kingdom; www.pisc.org.uk; secretary@pisc.org.uk

**Papuan Philatelic Society,** Steven Zirinsky, P.O. Box 49, Ansonia Station, New York, NY 10023; (718) 706-0616; www.papuanphilatelicsociety.com; szirinsky@cs.com

**Pitcairn Islands Study Group,** Dr. Everett L. Parker, 207 Corinth Road, Hudson, ME 04449-3057; (207) 573-1686; www.pisg.net; eparker@hughes.net

**Ryukyu Philatelic Specialist Society,** Laura Edmonds, P.O. Box 240177, Charlotte, NC 28224-0177; (336) 509-3739; www.ryukyustamps.org; secretary@ryukyustamps.org

**Society of Australasian Specialists / Oceania,** Steve Zirinsky, P.O. Box 230049, New York, NY 10023-0049; www.sasoceania.org; president@sosoceania.org

**Sarawak Specialists' Society,** Stephen Schumann, 2417 Caballo Drive, Hayward, CA 94545; (510) 785-4794; www.britborneostamps.org.uk; vpnam@s-s-s.org.uk

**Western Australia Study Group,** Brian Pope, P.O. Box 423, Claremont, WA 6910 Australia; (61) 419 843 943; www.wastudygroup.com; wastudygroup@hotmail.com

## Europe

**American Helvetia Philatelic Society,** Richard T. Hall, P.O. Box 15053, Asheville, NC 28813-0053; www.swiss-stamps.org; secretary2@swiss-stamps.org

**American Society for Netherlands Philately,** Hans Kremer, 50 Rockport Court, Danville, CA 94526; (925) 820-5841; www.asnp1975.com; hkremer@usa.net

**Andorran Philatelic Study Circle,** David Hope, 17 Hawthorn Drive, Stalybridge, Cheshire SK15 1UE United Kingdom; www.andorranpsc.org.uk; andorranpsc@btinternet.com

**Austria Philatelic Society,** Ralph Schneider, P.O. Box 978, Iowa Park, TX 76376; (940) 213-5004; www.austriaphilatelicsociety.com; rschneiderstamps@gmail.com

7A

**Channel Islands Specialists Society,** Richard Flemming, Burbage, 64 Falconers Green, Hinckley, Leicestershire, LE102SX, United Kingdom; www.ciss.uk; secretary@ciss.uk

**Cyprus Study Circle,** Rob Wheeler, 47 Drayton Ave., London W13 0LE United Kingdom; www.cyprusstudycircle.org; robwheeler47@aol.com

**Danish West Indies Study Unit of Scandinavian Collectors Club,** Arnold Sorensen, 7666 Edgedale Drive, Newburgh, IN 47630; (812) 480-6532; www.scc-online.org; valbydwi@hotmail.com

**Eire Philatelic Association,** John B. Sharkey, 1559 Grouse Lane, Mountainside, NJ 07092-1340; www.eirephilatelicassoc.org; jsharkeyepa@me.com

**Faroe Islands Study Circle,** Norman Hudson, 40 Queen's Road, Vicar's Cross, Chester CH3 5HB United Kingdom; www.faroeislandssc.org; jntropics@hotmail.com

**France & Colonies Philatelic Society,** Edward Grabowski, 111 Prospect St., 4C, Westfield, NJ 07090; (908) 233-9318; www.franceandcolsps.org; edjjg@alum.mit.edu

**Germany Philatelic Society,** P.O. Box 6547, Chesterfield, MO 63006-6547; www.germanyphilaticusa.org; info@germanyphilatelicsocietyusa.org

**Gibraltar Study Circle,** Susan Dare, 22, Byways Park, Strode Road, Clevedon, North Somerset BS21 6UR United Kingdom; www.gibraltarstudycircle.wordpress.com; smldare@yahoo.co.uk

**International Society for Portuguese Philately,** Clyde Homen, 1491 Bonnie View Road, Hollister, CA 95023-5117; www.portugalstamps.com; ispp1962@sbcglobal.net

**Italy and Colonies Study Circle,** Richard Harlow, 7 Duncombe House, 8 Manor Road, Teddington, Middlesex TW118BE United Kingdom; 44 208 977 8737; www.icsc-uk.com; richardharlow@outlook.com

**Liechtenstudy USA,** Paul Tremaine, 410 SW Ninth St., Dundee, OR 97115-9731; (503) 538-4500; www.liechtenstudy.org; tremaine@liechtenstudy.org

**Lithuania Philatelic Society,** Audrius Brazdeikis, 9915 Murray Landing, Missouri City, TX 77459; (281) 450-6224; www.lithuanianphilately.com/lps; audrius@lithuanianphilately.com

**Luxembourg Collectors Club,** Gary B. Little, 7319 Beau Road, Sechelt, BC V0N 3A8 Canada; (604) 885-7241; http://lcc.luxcentral.com; gary@luxcentral.com

**Plebiscite-Memel-Saar Study Group of the German Philatelic Society,** Clayton Wallace, 100 Lark Court, Alamo, CA 94507; claytonwallace@comcast.net

**Polonus Polish Philatelic Society,** Daniel Lubelski, P.O. Box 2212, Benicia, CA 94510; (419) 410-9115; www.polonus.org; info@polonus.org

**Rossica Society of Russian Philately,** Alexander Kolchinsky, 1506 Country Lake Drive, Champaign, IL 61821-6428; www.rossica.org; alexander.kolchinsky@rossica.org

**Scandinavian Collectors Club,** Alan Warren, Scandinavian Collectors Club, P.O. Box 39, Exton PA 19341-0039; (612) 810-8640; www.scc-online.org; alanwar@att.net

**Society for Czechoslovak Philately,** Tom Cossaboom, P.O. Box 4124, Prescott, AZ 86302; (928) 771-9097; www.csphilately.org; klfck1@aol.com

**Society for Hungarian Philately,** Alan Bauer, P.O. Box 4028, Vineyard Haven, MA 02568; (617) 645-4045; www.hungarianphilately.org; alan@hungarianstamps.com

**Spanish Study Circle,** Edith Knight, www.spaincircle.wixsite.com/spainstudycircle; spaincircle@gmail.com

**Ukrainian Philatelic & Numismatic Society,** Martin B. Tatuch, 5117 8th Road N., Arlington, VA 22205-1201; www.upns.org; treasurer@upns.org

**Vatican Philatelic Society,** Dennis Brady, 4897 Ledyard Drive, Manlius NY 13104-1514; www.vaticanphilately.org; dbrady7534@gmail.com

**Yugoslavia Study Group,** Michael Chant, 1514 N. Third Ave., Wausau, WI 54401; 208-748-9919; www.yugosg.org; membership@yugosg.org

## Interregional Societies

**American Society of Polar Philatelists,** Alan Warren, P.O. Box 39, Exton, PA 19341-0039; (610) 321-0740; www.polarphilatelists.org; alanwar@att.net

**First Issues Collector's Club,** Kurt Streepy, 3128 E. Mattatha Drive, Bloomington, IN 47401; www.firstissues.org; secretary@firstissues.org

**Former French Colonies Specialist Society,** Col.fra, BP 628, 75367 Paris, France; www.colfra.org; postmaster@colfra.org

**France & Colonies Philatelic Society,** Edward Grabowski, 111 Prospect St., 4C, Westfield, NJ 07090; (908) 233-9318; www.franceandcolsps.org; edjjg@alum.mit.edu

**Joint Stamp Issues Society,** Richard Zimmermann, 29A, Rue Des Eviats, 67220 Lalaye, France; www.philarz.net; richard.zimmermann@club-internet.fr

**The King George VI Collectors Society,** Brian Livingstone, 21 York Mansions, Prince of Wales Drive, London SW11 4DL United Kingdom; www.kg6.info; livingstone484@btinternet.com

**International Society of Reply Coupon Collectors,** Peter Robin, P.O. Box 353, Bala Cynwyd, PA 19004; peterrobin@verizon.net

**Italy and Colonies Study Circle,** Richard Harlow, 7 Duncombe House, 8 Manor Road, Teddington, Middlesex TW118BE United Kingdom; 44 208 977 8737; www.icsc-uk.com; richardharlow@outlook.com

**St. Helena, Ascension & Tristan Da Cunha Philatelic Society,** Dr. Everett L. Parker, 207 Corinth Road, Hudson, ME 04449-3057; (207) 573-1686; www.shatps.org; eparker@hughes.net

**United Nations Philatelists,** Blanton Clement, Jr., P.O. Box 146, Morrisville, PA 19067-0146; www.unpi.com; bclemjunior@gmail.com

## Latin America

**Asociación Filatélica de Panamá,** Edward D. Vianna B. ASOFILPA, 0819-03400, El Dorado, Panama; http://asociacionfilatelicadepanama.blogspot.com; asofilpa@gmail.com

**Asociacion Mexicana de Filatelia (AMEXFIL),** Alejandro Grossmann, Jose Maria Rico, 129, Col. Del Valle, 3100 Mexico City, DF Mexico; www.amexfil.mx; amexfil@gmail.com

**Associated Collectors of El Salvador,** Pierre Cahen, Vipsal 1342, P.O. Box 02-5364, Miami FL 33102; www.elsalvadorphilately.org; sfes-aces@elsalvadorphilately.org

**Association Filatelic de Costa Rica,** Giana Wayman (McCarty), #SJO 4935, P.O. Box 025723, Miami, FL 33102-5723; 011-506-2-228-1947; scotland@racsa.co.cr

**Brazil Philatelic Association,** William V. Kriebel, www.brazilphilately.org, info@brazilphilately.org

**Canal Zone Study Group,** Mike Drabik, P.O. Box 281, Bolton, MA 01740; www.canalzonestudygroup.com; czsgsecretary@gmail.com

**Colombia-Panama Philatelic Study Group,** Allan Harris, 26997 Hemmingway Ct, Hayward CA 94542-2349; www.copaphil.org; copaphilusa@aol.com

**Falkland Islands Philatelic Study Groups,** Morva White, 42 Colton Road, Shrivenham, Swindon SN6 8AZ United Kingdom; 44(0) 1793 783245; www.fipsg.org.uk; morawhite@supanet.com

**Federacion Filatelica de la Republica de Honduras,** Mauricio Mejia, Apartado Postal 1465, Tegucigalpa, D.C. Honduras; 504 3399-7227; www.facebook.com/filateliadehonduras; ffrh@hotmail.com

**International Cuban Philatelic Society (ICPS),** Ernesto Cuesta, P.O. Box 34434, Bethesda, MD 20827; (301) 564-3099; www.cubafil.org; ecuesta@philat.com

**International Society of Guatemala Collectors,** Jaime Marckwordt, 449 St. Francis Blvd., Daly City, CA 94015-2136; (415) 997-0295; www.guatemalastamps.com; president@guatamalastamps.com

**Mexico-Elmhurst Philatelic Society International,** Eric Stovner, P.O. Box 10097, Santa Ana, CA 92711-0097; www.mepsi.org; treasurer@mepsi.org

**Nicaragua Study Group,** Erick Rodriguez, 11817 S. W. 11th St., Miami, FL 33184-2501; nsgsec@yahoo.com

## North America (excluding United States)

**British Caribbean Philatelic Study Group,** Bob Stewart, 7 West Dune Lane, Long Beach Township, NJ 08008; (941) 379-4108; www.bcpsg.com; bcpsg@comcast.net

**British North America Philatelic Society,** Andy Ellwood, 10 Doris Ave., Gloucester, ON K1T 3W8 Canada; www.bnaps.org; secretary@bnaps.org

**British West Indies Study Circle,** Steve Jarvis, 5 Redbridge Drive, Andover, Hants SP10 2LF United Kingdom; 01264 358065; www.bwisc.org; info@bwisc.org

**Bermuda Collectors Society,** John Pare, 405 Perimeter St., Mount Horeb, WI 53572; (608) 852-7358; www.bermudacollectorssociety.com; pare16@mhtc.net

**Haiti Philatelic Society,** Ubaldo Del Toro, 5709 Marble Archway, Alexandria, VA 22315; www.haitiphilately.org; u007ubi@aol.com

**Hawaiian Philatelic Society,** Gannon Sugimura, P.O. Box 10115, Honolulu, HI 96816-0115, www.hpshawaii.com; hiphilsoc@gmail.com

## Stamp Dealer Associations

**American Stamp Dealers Association, Inc.,** P.O. Box 513, Centre Hall PA 16828; (800) 369-8207; www.americanstampdealer.com; asda@americanstampdealer.com

**National Stamp Dealers Association,** Sheldon Ruckens, President, 3643 Private Road 18, Pinckneyville, IL 62274-3426; (618) 357-5497; www.nsdainc.org; nsda@nsdainc.org

## Youth Philately

**Young Stamp Collectors of America,** 100 Match Factory Place, Bellefonte, PA 16823; (814) 933-3803; https://stamps.org/learn/youth-in-philately; ysca@stamps.org

# Information on catalogue values, grade and condition

## Catalogue value

The Scott Catalogue value is a retail value; that is, an amount you could expect to pay for a stamp in the grade of Very Fine with no faults. Any exceptions to the grade valued will be noted in the text. The general introduction on the following pages and the individual section introductions further explain the type of material that is valued. The value listed for any given stamp is a reference that reflects recent actual dealer selling prices for that item.

Dealer retail price lists, public auction results, published prices in advertising and individual solicitation of retail prices from dealers, collectors and specialty organizations have been used in establishing the values found in this catalogue. Amos Media Co. values stamps, but Amos Media is not a company engaged in the business of buying and selling stamps as a dealer.

Use this catalogue as a guide for buying and selling. The actual price you pay for a stamp may be higher or lower than the catalogue value because of many different factors, including the amount of personal service a dealer offers, or increased or decreased interest in the country or topic represented by a stamp or set. An item may occasionally be offered at a lower price as a "loss leader," or as part of a special sale. You also may obtain an item inexpensively at public auction because of little interest at that time or as part of a large lot.

Stamps that are of a lesser grade than Very Fine, or those with condition problems, generally trade at lower prices than those given in this catalogue. Stamps of exceptional quality in both grade and condition often command higher prices than those listed.

Values for pre-1900 unused issues are for stamps with approximately half or more of their original gum. Stamps with most or all of their original gum may be expected to sell for more, and stamps with less than half of their original gum may be expected to sell for somewhat less than the values listed. On rarer stamps, it may be expected that the original gum will be somewhat more disturbed than it will be on more common issues. Post-1900 unused issues are assumed to have full original gum. From breakpoints in most countries' listings, stamps are valued as never hinged, due to the wide availability of stamps in that condition. These notations are prominently placed in the listings and in the country information preceding the listings. Some countries also feature listings with dual values for hinged and never-hinged stamps.

## Grade

A stamp's grade and condition are crucial to its value. The accompanying illustrations show examples of Very Fine stamps from different time periods, along with examples of stamps in Fine to Very Fine and Extremely Fine grades as points of reference. When a stamp seller offers a stamp in any grade from fine to superb without further qualifying statements, that stamp should not only have the centering grade as defined, but it also should be free of faults or other condition problems.

**FINE** stamps (illustrations not shown) have designs that are quite off center, with the perforations on one or two sides very close to the design but not quite touching it. There is white space between the perforations and the design that is minimal but evident to the unaided eye. Imperforate stamps may have small margins, and earlier issues may show the design just touching one edge of the stamp design. Very early perforated issues normally will have the perforations slightly cutting into the design. Used stamps may have heavier than usual cancellations.

**FINE-VERY FINE** stamps will be somewhat off center on one side, or slightly off center on two sides. Imperforate stamps will have two margins of at least normal size, and the design will not touch any edge. For perforated stamps, the perfs are well clear of the design, but are still noticeably off center. However, early issues of a country may be printed in such a way that the design naturally is very close to the edges. In these cases, the perforations may cut into the design very slightly. Used stamps will not have a cancellation that detracts from the design.

**VERY FINE** stamps will be just slightly off center on one or two sides, but the design will be well clear of the edge. The stamp will present a nice, balanced appearance. Imperforate stamps will be well centered within normal-sized margins. However, early issues of many countries may be printed in such a way that the perforations may touch the design on one or more sides. Where this is the case, a boxed note will be found defining the centering and margins of the stamps being valued. Used stamps will have light or otherwise neat cancellations. This is the grade used to establish Scott Catalogue values.

**EXTREMELY FINE** stamps are close to being perfectly centered. Imperforate stamps will have even margins that are slightly larger than normal. Even the earliest perforated issues will have perforations clear of the design on all sides.

**Amos Media Co. recognizes that there is no formally enforced grading scheme for postage stamps, and that the final price you pay or obtain for a stamp will be determined by individual agreement at the time of transaction.**

## Condition

*Grade* addresses only centering and (for used stamps) cancellation. *Condition* refers to factors other than grade that affect a stamp's desirability.

Factors that can increase the value of a stamp include exceptionally wide margins, particularly fresh color, the presence of selvage, and plate or die varieties. Unusual cancels on used stamps (particularly those of the 19th century) can greatly enhance their value as well.

Factors other than faults that decrease the value of a stamp include loss of original gum, regumming, a hinge remnant or foreign object adhering to the gum, natural inclusions, straight edges, and markings or notations applied by collectors or dealers.

Faults include missing pieces, tears, pin or other holes, surface scuffs, thin spots, creases, toning, short or pulled perforations, clipped perforations, oxidation or other forms of color changelings, soiling, stains, and such man-made changes as reperforations or the chemical removal or lightening of a cancellation.

## Grading illustrations

On the following two pages are illustrations of various stamps from countries appearing in this volume. These stamps are arranged by country, and they represent early or important issues that are often found in widely different grades in the marketplace. The editors believe the illustrations will prove useful in showing the margin size and centering that will be seen on the various issues.

In addition to the matters of margin size and centering, collectors are reminded that the very fine stamps valued in the Scott catalogues also will possess fresh color and intact perforations, and they will be free from defects.

Examples shown are computer-manipulated images made from single digitized master illustrations.

## Stamp illustrations used in the catalogue

It is important to note that the stamp images used for identification purposes in this catalogue may not be indicative of the grade of stamp being valued. Refer to the written discussion of grades on this page and to the grading illustrations on the following two pages for grading information.

10A INTRODUCTION

# INTRODUCTION

11A

# Gum Conditions

For purposes of helping to determine the gum condition and value of an unused stamp, Scott presents the following chart which details different gum conditions and indicates how the conditions correlate with the Scott values for unused stamps. Used together, the Illustrated Grading Chart on the previous pages and this Illustrated Gum Chart should allow catalogue users to better understand the grade and gum condition of stamps valued in the Scott catalogues.

**Never Hinged (NH; ★★):** A never-hinged stamp will have full original gum that will have no hinge mark or disturbance. The presence of an expertizer's mark does not disqualify a stamp from this designation.

**Original Gum (OG; ★):** Pre-1900 stamps should have approximately half or more of their original gum. On rarer stamps, it may be expected that the original gum will be somewhat more disturbed than it will be on more common issues. Post-1900 stamps should have full original gum. Original gum will show some disturbance caused by a previous hinge(s) which may be present or entirely removed. The actual value of a post-1900 stamp will be affected by the degree of hinging of the full original gum.

**Disturbed Original Gum:** Gum showing noticeable effects of humidity, climate or hinging over more than half of the gum. The significance of gum disturbance in valuing a stamp in any of the Original Gum categories depends on the degree of disturbance, the rarity and normal gum condition of the issue and other variables affecting quality.

**Regummed (RG; (★)):** A regummed stamp is a stamp without gum that has had some type of gum privately applied at a time after it was issued. This normally is done to deceive collectors and/or dealers into thinking that the stamp has original gum and therefore has a higher value. A regummed stamp is considered the same as a stamp with none of its original gum for purposes of grading.

| Gum Categories: | MINT N.H. | ORIGINAL GUM (O.G.) ||||| NO GUM |
|---|---|---|---|---|---|---|
| |  **Mint Never Hinged** *Free from any disturbance* |  **Lightly Hinged** *Faint impression of a removed hinge over a small area* |  **Hinge Mark or Remnant** *Prominent hinged spot with part or all of the hinge remaining* |  **Large part o.g.** *Approximately half or more of the gum intact* |  **Small part o.g.** *Approximately less than half of the gum intact* | **No gum** *Only if issued with gum* |
| **Commonly Used Symbol:** | ★★ | ★ | ★ | ★ | ★ | (★) |
| **Pre-1900 Issues** (Pre-1881 for U.S.) | *Very fine pre-1900 stamps in these categories trade at a premium over Scott value* ||| Scott Value for "Unused" | | Scott "No Gum" listings for selected unused classic stamps |
| From 1900 to breakpoints for listings of never-hinged stamps | Scott "Never Hinged" listings for selected unused stamps | Scott Value for "Unused" (Actual value will be affected by the degree of hinging of the full o.g.) |||||
| From breakpoints noted for many countries | Scott Value for "Unused" ||||||

# Catalogue listing policy

It is the intent of Amos Media Co. to list all postage stamps of the world in the Scott *Standard Postage Stamp Catalogue*. The only strict criteria for listing is that stamps be decreed legal for postage by the issuing country and that the issuing country actually have an operating postal system. Whether the primary intent of issuing a given stamp or set was for sale to postal patrons or to stamp collectors is not part of our listing criteria. Scott's role is to provide basic comprehensive postage stamp information. It is up to each stamp collector to choose which items to include in a collection.

It is Scott's objective to seek reasons why a stamp should be listed, rather than why it should not. Nevertheless, there are certain types of items that will not be listed. These include the following:

1. Unissued items that are not officially distributed or released by the issuing postal authority. If such items are officially issued at a later date by the country, they will be listed. Unissued items consist of those that have been printed and then held from sale for reasons such as change in government, errors found on stamps or something deemed objectionable about a stamp subject or design.

2. Stamps "issued" by non-existent postal entities or fantasy countries, such as Nagaland, Occusi-Ambeno, Staffa, Sedang, Torres Straits and others. Also, stamps "issued" in the names of legitimate, stamp-issuing countries that are not authorized by those countries.

3. Semi-official or unofficial items not required for postage. Examples include items issued by private agencies for their own express services. When such items are required for delivery, or are valid as prepayment of postage, they are listed.

4. Local stamps issued for local use only. Postage stamps issued by governments specifically for "domestic" use, such as Haiti Scott 219-228, or the United States nondenominated stamps, are not considered to be locals, since they are valid for postage throughout the country of origin.

5. Items not valid for postal use. For example, a few countries have issued souvenir sheets that are not valid for postage. This area also includes a number of worldwide charity labels (some denominated) that do not pay postage.

6. Egregiously exploitative issues such as stamps sold for far more than face value, stamps purposefully issued in artificially small quantities or only against advance orders, stamps awarded only to a selected audience such as a philatelic bureau's standing order customers, or stamps sold only in conjunction with other products. All of these kinds of items are usually controlled issues and/or are intended for speculation. These items normally will be included in a footnote.

7. Items distributed by the issuing government only to a limited group, club, philatelic exhibition or a single stamp dealer or other private company. These items normally will be included in a footnote.

8. Stamps not available to collectors. These generally are rare items, all of which are held by public institutions such as museums. The existence of such items often will be cited in footnotes.

The fact that a stamp has been used successfully as postage, even on international mail, is not in itself sufficient proof that it was legitimately issued. Numerous examples of so-called stamps from non-existent countries are known to have been used to post letters that have successfully passed through the international mail system.

There are certain items that are subject to interpretation. When a stamp falls outside our specifications, it may be listed along with a cautionary footnote.

A number of factors are considered in our approach to analyzing how a stamp is listed. The following list of factors is presented to share with you, the catalogue user, the complexity of the listing process.

**Additional printings** — "Additional printings" of a previously issued stamp may range from an item that is totally different to cases where it is impossible to differentiate from the original. At least a minor number (a small-letter suffix) is assigned if there is a distinct change in stamp shade, noticeably redrawn design, or a significantly different perforation measurement. A major number (numeral or numeral and capital-letter combination) is assigned if the editors feel the "additional printing" is sufficiently different from the original that it constitutes a different issue.

**Commemoratives** — Where practical, commemoratives with the same theme are placed in a set. For example, the U.S. Civil War Centennial set of 1961-65 and the Constitution Bicentennial series of 1989-90 appear as sets. Countries such as Japan and Korea issue such material on a regular basis, with an announced, or at least predictable, number of stamps known in advance. Occasionally, however, stamp sets that were released over a period of years have been separated. Appropriately placed footnotes will guide you to each set's continuation.

**Definitive sets** — Blocks of numbers generally have been reserved for definitive sets, based on previous experience with any given country. If a few more stamps were issued in a set than originally expected, they often have been inserted into the original set with a capital-letter suffix, such as U.S. Scott 1059A. If it appears that many more stamps than the originally allotted block will be released before the set is completed, a new block of numbers will be reserved, with the original one being closed off. In some cases, such as the U.S. Transportation and Great Americans series, several blocks of numbers exist. Appropriately placed footnotes will guide you to each set's continuation.

**New country** — Membership in the Universal Postal Union is not a consideration for listing status or order of placement within the catalogue. The index will tell you in what volume or page number the listings begin.

**"No release date" items** — The amount of information available for any given stamp issue varies greatly from country to country and even from time to time. Extremely comprehensive information about new stamps is available from some countries well before the stamps are released. By contrast some countries do not provide information about stamps or release dates. Most countries, however, fall between these extremes. A country may provide denominations or subjects of stamps from upcoming issues that are not issued as planned. Sometimes, philatelic agencies, those private firms hired to represent countries, add these later-issued items to sets well after the formal release date. This time period can range from weeks to years. If these items were officially released by the country, they will be added to the appropriate spot in the set. In many cases, the specific release date of a stamp or set of stamps may never be known.

**Overprints** — The color of an overprint is always noted if it is other than black. Where more than one color of ink has been used on overprints of a single set, the color used is noted. Early overprint and surcharge illustrations were altered to prevent their use by forgers.

**Personalized Stamps** — Since 1999, the special service of personalizing stamp vignettes, or labels attached to stamps, has been offered to customers by postal administrations of many countries. Sheets of these stamps are sold, singly or in quantity, only through special orders made by mail, in person, or through a sale on a computer website with the postal administrations or their agents for which an extra fee is charged, though some countries offer to collectors at face value personalized stamps having generic images in the vignettes or on the attached labels. It is impossible for any catalogue to know what images have been chosen by customers. Images can be 1) owned or created by the customer, 2) a generic image, or 3) an image pulled from a library of stock images on the stamp creation website. It is also impossible to know the quantity printed for any stamp having a particular image. So from a valuing standpoint, any image is equivalent to any other image for any personalized stamp having the same catalogue number. Illustrations of personalized stamps in the catalogue are not always those of stamps having generic images.

Personalized items are listed with some exceptions. These include:

1. Stamps or sheets that have attached labels that the customer cannot personalize, but which are nonetheless marketed as "personalized," and are sold for far more than the franking value.

2. Stamps or sheets that can be personalized by the customer, but where a portion of the print run must be ceded to the issuing country for sale to other customers.

3. Stamps or sheets that are created exclusively for a particular commercial client, or clients, including stamps that differ from any similar stamp that has been made available to the public.

4. Stamps or sheets that are deliberately conceived by the issuing authority that have been, or are likely to be, created with an excessive number of different face values, sizes, or other features that are changeable.

5. Stamps or sheets that are created by postal administrations using the same system of stamp personalization that has been put in place for use by the public that are printed in limited quantities and sold above face value.

6. Stamps or sheets that are created by licensees not directly affiliated or controlled by a postal administration.

Excluded items may or may not be footnoted.

**Se-tenants** — Connected stamps of differing features (se-tenants) will be listed in the format most commonly collected. This includes pairs, blocks or larger multiples. Se-tenant units are not always symmetrical. An example is Australia Scott 508, which is a block of seven stamps. If the stamps are primarily collected as a unit, the major number may be assigned to the multiple, with minors going to each component stamp. In cases where continuous-design or other unit se-tenants will receive significant postal use, each stamp is given a major Scott number listing. This includes issues from the United States, Canada, Germany and Great Britain, for example.

# Understanding the listings

On the opposite page is an enlarged "typical" listing from this catalogue. Below are detailed explanations of each of the highlighted parts of the listing.

**1 Scott number** — Scott catalogue numbers are used to identify specific items when buying, selling or trading stamps. Each listed postage stamp from every country has a unique Scott catalogue number. Therefore, Germany Scott 99, for example, can only refer to a single stamp. Although the Scott catalogue usually lists stamps in chronological order by date of issue, there are exceptions. When a country has issued a set of stamps over a period of time, those stamps within the set are kept together without regard to date of issue. This follows the normal collecting approach of keeping stamps in their natural sets.

When a country issues a set of stamps over a period of time, a group of consecutive catalogue numbers is reserved for the stamps in that set, as issued. If that group of numbers proves to be too few, capital-letter suffixes, such as "A" or "B," may be added to existing numbers to create enough catalogue numbers to cover all items in the set. A capital-letter suffix indicates a major Scott catalogue number listing. Scott generally uses a suffix letter only once. Therefore, a catalogue number listing with a capital-letter suffix will seldom be found with the same letter (lower case) used as a minor-letter listing. If there is a Scott 16A in a set, for example, there will seldom be a Scott 16a. However, a minor-letter "a" listing may be added to a major number containing an "A" suffix (Scott 16Aa, for example).

Suffix letters are cumulative. A minor "b" variety of Scott 16A would be Scott 16Ab, not Scott 16b.

There are times when a reserved block of Scott catalogue numbers is too large for a set, leaving some numbers unused. Such gaps in the numbering sequence also occur when the catalogue editors move an item's listing elsewhere or have removed it entirely from the catalogue. Scott does not attempt to account for every possible number, but rather attempts to assure that each stamp is assigned its own number.

Scott numbers designating regular postage normally are only numerals. Scott numbers for other types of stamps, such as air post, semi-postal, postal tax, postage due, occupation and others have a prefix consisting of one or more capital letters or a combination of numerals and capital letters.

**2 Illustration number** — Illustration or design-type numbers are used to identify each catalogue illustration. For most sets, the lowest face-value stamp is shown. It then serves as an example of the basic design approach for other stamps not illustrated. Where more than one stamp use the same illustration number, but have differences in design, the design paragraph or the description line clearly indicates the design on each stamp not illustrated. Where there are both vertical and horizontal designs in a set, a single illustration may be used, with the exceptions noted in the design paragraph or description line.

When an illustration is followed by a lower-case letter in parentheses, such as "A2(b)," the trailing letter indicates which overprint or surcharge illustration applies.

Illustrations normally are 70 percent of the original size of the stamp. Oversized stamps, blocks and souvenir sheets are reduced even more. Overprints and surcharges are shown at 100 percent of their original size if shown alone, but are 70 percent of original size if shown on stamps. In some cases, the illustration will be placed above the set, between listings or omitted completely. Overprint and surcharge illustrations are not placed in this catalogue for purposes of expertizing stamps.

**3 Paper color** — The color of a stamp's paper is noted in italic type when the paper used is not white.

**4 Listing styles** — There are two principal types of catalogue listings: major and minor.

Major listings are in a larger type style than minor listings. The catalogue number is a numeral that can be found with or without a capital-letter suffix, and with or without a prefix.

Minor listings are in a smaller type style and have a small-letter suffix or (if the listing immediately follows that of the major number) may show only the letter. These listings identify a variety of the major item. Examples include perforation and shade differences, multiples (some souvenir sheets, booklet panes and se-tenant combinations), and singles of multiples.

Examples of major number listings include 16, 28A, B97, C13A, 10N5, and 10N6A. Examples of minor numbers are 16a and C13Ab.

**5 Basic information about a stamp or set** — Introducing each stamp issue is a small section (usually a line listing) of basic information about a stamp or set. This section normally includes the date of issue, method of printing, perforation, watermark and, sometimes, some additional information of note. *Printing method, perforation and watermark apply to the following sets until a change is noted.* Stamps created by overprinting or surcharging previous issues are assumed to have the same perforation, watermark, printing method and other production characteristics as the original. Dates of issue are as precise as Scott is able to confirm and often reflect the dates on first-day covers, rather than the actual date of release.

**6 Denomination** — This normally refers to the face value of the stamp; that is, the cost of the unused stamp at the post office at the time of issue. When a denomination is shown in parentheses, it does not appear on the stamp. This includes the nondenominated stamps of the United States, Brazil and Great Britain, for example.

**7 Color or other description** — This area provides information to solidify identification of a stamp. In many recent cases, a description of the stamp design appears in this space, rather than a listing of colors.

**8 Year of issue** — In stamp sets that have been released in a period that spans more than a year, the number shown in parentheses is the year that stamp first appeared. Stamps without a date appeared during the first year of the issue. Dates are not always given for minor varieties.

**9 Value unused and Value used** — The Scott catalogue values are based on stamps that are in a grade of Very Fine unless stated otherwise. Unused values refer to items that have not seen postal, revenue or any other duty for which they were intended. Pre-1900 unused stamps that were issued with gum must have at least most of their original gum. Later issues are assumed to have full original gum. From breakpoints specified in most countries' listings, stamps are valued as never hinged. Stamps issued without gum are noted. Modern issues with PVA or other synthetic adhesives may appear ungummed. Unused self-adhesive stamps are valued as appearing undisturbed on their original backing paper. Values for used self-adhesive stamps are for examples either on piece or off piece. For a more detailed explanation of these values, please see the "Catalogue Value," "Condition" and "Understanding Valuing Notations" sections elsewhere in this introduction.

In some cases, where used stamps are more valuable than unused stamps, the value is for an example with a contemporaneous cancel, rather than a modern cancel or a smudge or other unclear marking. For those stamps that were released for postal and fiscal purposes, the used value represents a postally used stamp. Stamps with revenue cancels generally sell for less.

Stamps separated from a complete se-tenant multiple usually will be worth less than a pro-rated portion of the se-tenant multiple, and stamps lacking the attached labels that are noted in the listings will be worth less than the values shown.

**10 Changes in basic set information** — Bold type is used to show any changes in the basic data given for a set of stamps. These basic data categories include perforation gauge measurement, paper type, printing method and watermark.

**11 Total value of a set** — The total value of sets of three or more stamps issued after 1900 are shown. The set line also notes the range of Scott numbers and total number of stamps included in the grouping. The actual value of a set consisting predominantly of stamps having the minimum value of 25 cents may be less than the total value shown. Similarly, the actual value or catalogue value of se-tenant pairs or of blocks consisting of stamps having the minimum value of 25 cents may be less than the catalogue values of the component parts.

# INTRODUCTION

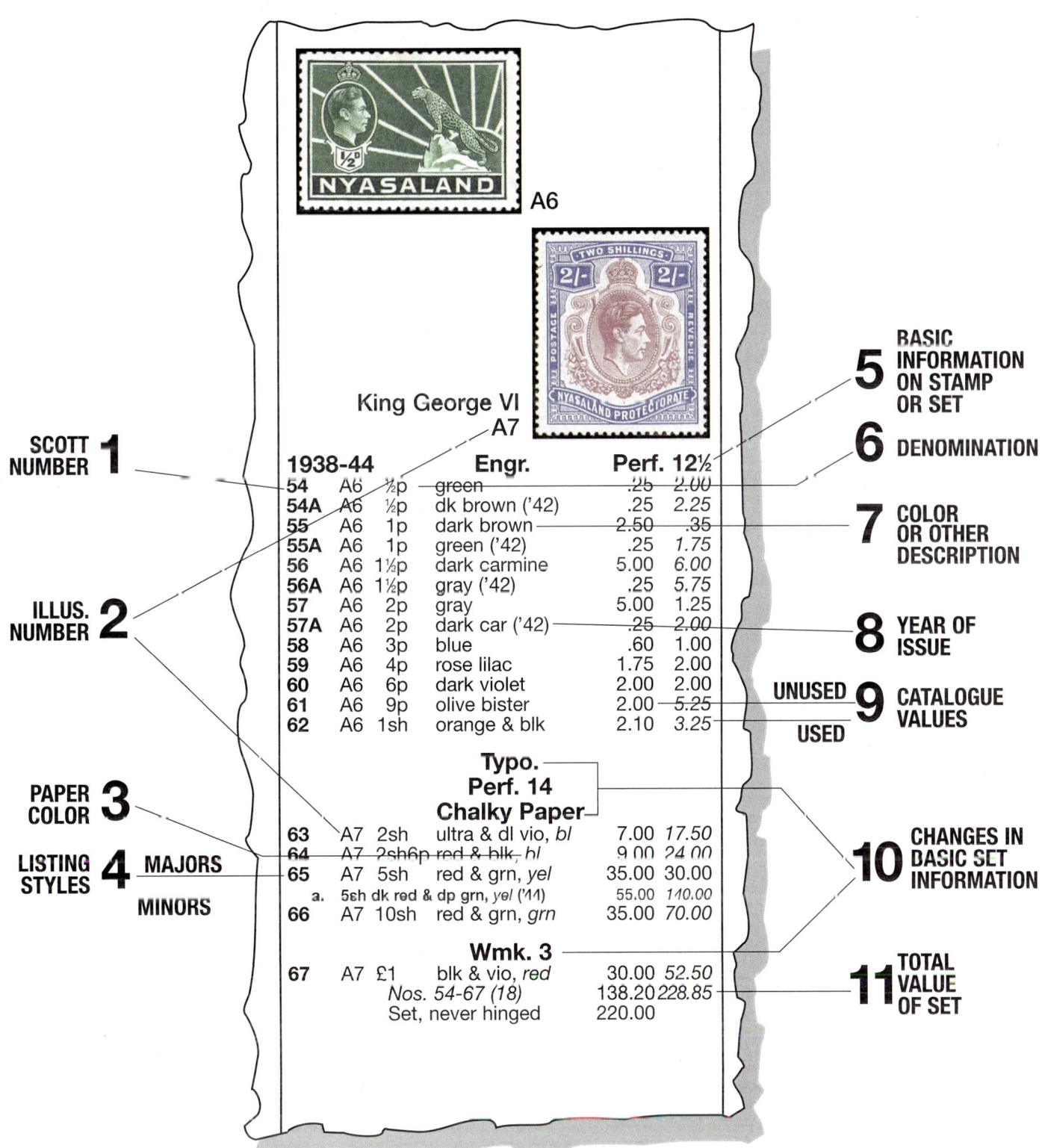

# Special notices

## Classification of stamps

The Scott Standard Postage Stamp Catalogue lists stamps by country of issue. The next level of organization is a listing by section on the basis of the function of the stamps. The principal sections cover regular postage, semi-postal, air post, special delivery, registration, postage due and other categories. Except for regular postage, catalogue numbers for all sections include a prefix letter (or number-letter combination) denoting the class to which a given stamp belongs. When some countries issue sets containing stamps from more than one category, the catalogue will at times list all of the stamps in one category (such as air post stamps listed as part of a postage set).

The following is a listing of the most commonly used catalogue prefixes.

Prefix......Category
- C..........Air Post
- M..........Military
- P..........Newspaper
- N..........Occupation - Regular Issues
- O..........Official
- Q..........Parcel Post
- J..........Postage Due
- RA........Postal Tax
- B..........Semi-Postal
- E..........Special Delivery
- MR........War Tax

Other prefixes used by more than one country include the following:
- H..........Acknowledgment of Receipt
- I...........Late Fee
- CO........Air Post Official
- CQ........Air Post Parcel Post
- RAC......Air Post Postal Tax
- CF........Air Post Registration
- CB........Air Post Semi-Postal
- CBO.....Air Post Semi-Postal Official
- CE........Air Post Special Delivery
- EY........Authorized Delivery
- S..........Franchise
- G..........Insured Letter
- GY........Marine Insurance
- MC........Military Air Post
- MQ........Military Parcel Post
- NC........Occupation - Air Post
- NO........Occupation - Official
- NJ........Occupation - Postage Due
- NRA......Occupation - Postal Tax
- NB........Occupation - Semi-Postal
- NE........Occupation - Special Delivery
- QY........Parcel Post Authorized Delivery
- AR........Postal-fiscal
- RAJ.......Postal Tax Due
- RAB......Postal Tax Semi-Postal
- F..........Registration
- EB........Semi-Postal Special Delivery
- EO........Special Delivery Official
- QE........Special Handling

## New issue listings

Updates to this catalogue appear each month in the *Linn's Stamp News* monthly magazine. Included in this update are additions to the listings of countries found in the Scott *Standard Postage Stamp Catalogue* and the *Specialized Catalogue of United States Stamps and Covers,* as well as corrections and updates to current editions of this catalogue.

From time to time there will be changes in the final listings of stamps from the *Linn's Stamp News* magazine to the next edition of the catalogue. This occurs as more information about certain stamps or sets becomes available.

The catalogue update section of the *Linn's Stamp News* magazine is the most timely presentation of this material available. Annual subscriptions to *Linn's Stamp News* are available from Linn's Stamp News, Box 4129, Sidney, OH 45365-4129.

## Number additions, deletions and changes

A listing of catalogue number additions, deletions and changes from the previous edition of the catalogue appears in each volume. See Catalogue Number Additions, Deletions & Changes in the table of contents for the location of this list.

## Understanding valuing notations

The *minimum catalogue value* of an individual stamp or set is 25 cents. This represents a portion of the cost incurred by a dealer when he prepares an individual stamp for resale. As a point of philatelic-economic fact, the lower the value shown for an item in this catalogue, the greater the percentage of that value is attributed to dealer mark up and profit margin. In many cases, such as the 25-cent minimum value, that price does not cover the labor or other costs involved with stocking it as an individual stamp. The sum of minimum values in a set does not properly represent the value of a complete set primarily composed of a number of minimum-value stamps, nor does the sum represent the actual value of a packet made up of minimum-value stamps. Thus a packet of 1,000 different common stamps — each of which has a catalogue value of 25 cents — normally sells for considerably less than $250!

The *absence of a retail value* for a stamp does not necessarily suggest that a stamp is scarce or rare. A dash in the value column means that the stamp is known in a stated form or variety, but information is either lacking or insufficient for purposes of establishing a usable catalogue value.

Stamp values in *italics* generally refer to items that are difficult to value accurately. For expensive items, such as those priced at $1,000 or higher, a value in italics indicates that the affected item trades very seldom. For inexpensive items, a value in italics represents a warning. One example is a "blocked" issue where the issuing postal administration may have controlled one stamp in a set in an attempt to make the whole set more valuable. Another example is an item that sold at an extreme multiple of face value in the marketplace at the time of its issue.

One type of warning to collectors that appears in the catalogue is illustrated by a stamp that is valued considerably higher in used condition than it is as unused. In this case, collectors are cautioned to be certain the used version has a genuine and contemporaneous cancellation. The type of cancellation on a stamp can be an important factor in determining its sale price. Catalogue values do not apply to fiscal, telegraph or non-contemporaneous postal cancels, unless otherwise noted.

Some countries have released back issues of stamps in canceled-to-order form, sometimes covering as much as a 10-year period. The Scott Catalogue values for used stamps reflect canceled-to-order material when such stamps are found to predominate in the marketplace for the issue involved. Notes frequently appear in the stamp listings to specify which items are valued as canceled-to-order, or if there is a premium for postally used examples.

Many countries sell canceled-to-order stamps at a marked reduction of face value. Countries that sell or have sold canceled-to-order stamps at *full* face value include United Nations, Australia, Netherlands, France and Switzerland. It may be almost impossible to identify such stamps if the gum has been removed, because official government canceling devices are used. Postally used examples of these items on cover, however, are usually worth more than the canceled-to-order stamps with original gum.

## Abbreviations

Scott uses a consistent set of abbreviations throughout this catalogue to conserve space, while still providing necessary information.

## Color Abbreviations

| | | | | | |
|---|---|---|---|---|---|
| amb | amber | crim | crimson | ol | olive |
| anil | aniline | cr | cream | olvn | olivine |
| ap | apple | dk | dark | org | orange |
| aqua | aquamarine | dl | dull | pck | peacock |
| az | azure | dp | deep | pnksh | pinkish |
| bis | bister | db | drab | Prus | Prussian |
| bl | blue | emer | emerald | pur | purple |
| bld | blood | gldn | golden | redsh | reddish |
| blk | black | grysh | grayish | res | reseda |
| bril | brilliant | grn | green | ros | rosine |
| brn | brown | grnsh | greenish | ryl | royal |
| brnsh | brownish | hel | heliotrope | sal | salmon |
| brnz | bronze | hn | henna | saph | sapphire |
| brt | bright | ind | indigo | scar | scarlet |
| brnt | burnt | int | intense | sep | sepia |
| car | carmine | lav | lavender | sien | sienna |
| cer | cerise | lem | lemon | sil | silver |
| chlky | chalky | lil | lilac | sl | slate |
| cham | chamois | lt | light | stl | steel |
| chnt | chestnut | mag | magenta | turq | turquoise |
| choc | chocolate | man | manila | ultra | ultramarine |
| chr | chrome | mar | maroon | Ven | Venetian |
| cit | citron | mv | mauve | ver | vermilion |
| cl | claret | multi | multicolored | vio | violet |
| cob | cobalt | mlky | milky | yel | yellow |
| cop | copper | myr | myrtle | yelsh | yellowish |

When no color is given for an overprint or surcharge, black is the color used. Abbreviations for colors used for overprints and surcharges include: "(B)" or "(Blk)," black; "(Bl)," blue; "(R)," red; and "(G)," green.

Additional abbreviations in this catalogue are shown below:

| | |
|---|---|
| Adm. | Administration |
| AFL | American Federation of Labor |
| Anniv. | Anniversary |
| APS | American Philatelic Society |
| Assoc. | Association |
| ASSR. | Autonomous Soviet Socialist Republic |
| b | Born |
| BEP | Bureau of Engraving and Printing |
| Bicent. | Bicentennial |
| Bklt. | Booklet |
| Brit. | British |
| btwn. | Between |
| Bur. | Bureau |
| c. or ca. | Circa |
| Cat. | Catalogue |
| Cent. | Centennial, century, centenary |
| CIO | Congress of Industrial Organizations |
| Conf. | Conference |
| Cong. | Congress |
| Cpl. | Corporal |
| CTO | Canceled to order |
| d | Died |
| Dbl. | Double |
| EDU | Earliest documented use |
| Engr. | Engraved |
| Exhib. | Exhibition |
| Expo. | Exposition |
| Fed. | Federation |
| GB | Great Britain |
| Gen. | General |
| GPO | General post office |
| Horiz. | Horizontal |
| Imperf. | Imperforate |
| Impt. | Imprint |
| Intl. | International |
| Invtd. | Inverted |
| L | Left |
| Lieut., lt. | Lieutenant |
| Litho. | Lithographed |
| LL | Lower left |
| LR | Lower right |
| mm | Millimeter |
| Ms. | Manuscript |
| Natl. | National |
| No. | Number |
| NY | New York |
| NYC | New York City |
| Ovpt. | Overprint |
| Ovptd. | Overprinted |
| P | Plate number |
| Perf. | Perforated, perforation |
| Phil. | Philatelic |
| Photo. | Photogravure |
| PO | Post office |
| Pr. | Pair |
| P.R. | Puerto Rico |
| Prec. | Precancel, precanceled |
| Pres. | President |
| PTT | Post, Telephone and Telegraph |
| R | Right |
| Rio | Rio de Janeiro |
| Sgt. | Sergeant |
| Soc. | Society |
| Souv. | Souvenir |
| SSR | Soviet Socialist Republic, see ASSR |
| St. | Saint, street |
| Surch. | Surcharge |
| Typo. | Typographed |
| UL | Upper left |
| Unwmkd. | Unwatermarked |
| UPU | Universal Postal Union |
| UR | Upper Right |
| US | United States |
| USPOD | United States Post Office Department |
| USSR | Union of Soviet Socialist Republics |
| Vert. | Vertical |
| VP | Vice president |
| Wmk. | Watermark |
| Wmkd. | Watermarked |
| WWI | World War I |
| WWII | World War II |

## Examination

Amos Media Co. will not comment upon the genuineness, grade or condition of stamps, because of the time and responsibility involved. Rather, there are several expertizing groups that undertake this work for both collectors and dealers. Neither will Amos Media Co. appraise or identify philatelic material. The company cannot take responsibility for unsolicited stamps or covers sent by individuals.

All letters, emails, etc. are read attentively, but they are not always answered because of time considerations.

## How to order from your dealer

When ordering stamps from a dealer, it is not necessary to write the full description of a stamp as listed in this catalogue. All you need is the name of the country, the Scott catalogue number and whether the desired item is unused or used. For example, "Japan Scott 422 unused" is sufficient to identify the unused stamp of Japan listed as "422 A206 5y brown."

# Basic stamp information

A stamp collector's knowledge of the combined elements that make a given stamp issue unique determines his or her ability to identify stamps. These elements include paper, watermark, method of separation, printing, design and gum. On the following pages each of these important areas is briefly described.

## Paper

Paper is an organic material composed of a compacted weave of cellulose fibers and generally formed into sheets. Paper used to print stamps may be manufactured in sheets, or it may have been part of a large roll (called a web) before being cut to size. The fibers most often used to create paper on which stamps are printed include bark, wood, straw and certain grasses. In many cases, linen or cotton rags have been added for greater strength and durability. Grinding, bleaching, cooking and rinsing these raw fibers reduces them to a slushy pulp, referred to by paper makers as "stuff." Sizing and, sometimes, coloring matter is added to the pulp to make different types of finished paper.

After the stuff is prepared, it is poured onto sieve-like frames that allow the water to run off, while retaining the matted pulp. As fibers fall onto the screen and are held by gravity, they form a natural weave that will later hold the paper together. If the screen has metal bits that are formed into letters or images attached, it leaves slightly thinned areas on the paper. These are called watermarks.

When the stuff is almost dry, it is passed under pressure through smooth or engraved rollers — dandy rolls — or placed between cloth in a press to be flattened and dried.

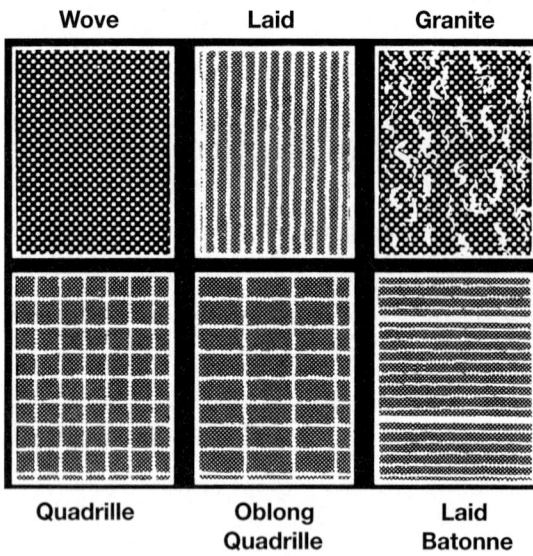

Stamp paper falls broadly into two types: wove and laid. The nature of the surface of the frame onto which the pulp is first deposited causes the differences in appearance between the two. If the surface is smooth and even, the paper will be of fairly uniform texture throughout. This is known as wove paper. Early papermaking machines poured the pulp onto a continuously circulating web of felt, but modern machines feed the pulp onto a cloth-like screen made of closely interwoven fine wires. This paper, when held to a light, will show little dots or points very close together. The proper name for this is "wire wove," but the type is still considered wove. Any U.S. or British stamp printed after 1880 will serve as an example of wire wove paper.

Closely spaced parallel wires, with cross wires at wider intervals, make up the frames used for what is known as laid paper. A greater thickness of the pulp will settle between the wires. The paper, when held to a light, will show alternate light and dark lines. The spacing and the thickness of the lines may vary, but on any one sheet of paper they are all alike. See Russia Scott 31-38 for examples of laid paper.

**Batonne,** from the French word meaning "a staff," is a term used if the lines in the paper are spaced quite far apart, like the printed ruling on a writing tablet. Batonne paper may be either wove or laid. If laid, fine laid lines can be seen between the batons.

**Quadrille** is the term used when the lines in the paper form little squares. Oblong quadrille is the term used when rectangles, rather than squares, are formed. Grid patterns vary from distinct to extremely faint. See Mexico-Guadalajara Scott 35-37 for examples of oblong quadrille paper.

Paper also is classified as thick or thin, hard or soft, and by color. Such colors may include yellowish, greenish, bluish and reddish.

Brief explanations of other types of paper used for printing stamps, as well as examples, follow.

**Colored** — Colored paper is created by the addition of dye in the paper-making process. Such colors may include shades of yellow, green, blue and red. Surface-colored papers, most commonly used for British colonial issues in 1913-14, are created when coloring is added only to the surface during the finishing process. Stamps printed on surface-colored paper have white or uncolored backs, while true colored papers are colored through. See Jamaica Scott 71-73.

**Pelure** — Pelure paper is a very thin, hard and often brittle paper that is sometimes bluish or grayish in appearance. See Serbia Scott 169-170.

**Native** — This is a term applied to handmade papers used to produce some of the early stamps of the Indian states. Stamps printed on native paper may be expected to display various natural inclusions that are normal and do not negatively affect value. Japanese paper, originally made of mulberry fibers and rice flour, is part of this group. See Japan Scott 1-18.

**Manila** — This type of paper is often used to make stamped envelopes and wrappers. It is a coarse-textured stock, usually smooth on one side and rough on the other. A variety of colors of manila paper exist, but the most common range is yellowish-brown.

**Silk** — Introduced by the British in 1847 as a safeguard against counterfeiting, silk paper contains bits of colored silk thread scattered throughout. The density of these fibers varies greatly and can include as few as one fiber per stamp or hundreds. U.S. revenue Scott R152 is a good example of an easy-to-identify silk paper stamp.

Silk-thread paper has uninterrupted threads of colored silk arranged so that one or more threads run through the stamp or postal stationery. See Great Britain Scott 5-6 and Switzerland Scott 14-19.

**Granite** — Filled with minute cloth or colored paper fibers of various colors and lengths, granite paper should not be confused with either type of silk paper. Austria Scott 172-175 and a number of Swiss stamps are examples of granite paper.

**Chalky** — A chalk-like substance coats the surface of chalky paper to discourage the cleaning and reuse of canceled stamps, as well as to provide a smoother, more acceptable printing surface. Because the designs of stamps printed on chalky paper are imprinted on what is often a water-soluble coating, any attempt to remove a cancellation will destroy the stamp. Do not soak these stamps in any fluid. To remove a stamp printed on chalky paper from an envelope, wet the paper from underneath the stamp until the gum dissolves enough to release the stamp from the paper. See St. Kitts-Nevis Scott 89-90 for examples of stamps printed on this type of chalky paper.

**India** — Another name for this paper, originally introduced from China about 1750, is "China Paper." It is a thin, opaque paper often used for plate and die proofs by many countries.

**Double** — In philately, the term double paper has two distinct meanings. The first is a two-ply paper, usually a combination of a thick and a thin sheet, joined during manufacture. This type was used experimentally as a means to discourage the reuse of stamps.

The design is printed on the thin paper. Any attempt to remove a cancellation would destroy the design. U.S. Scott 158 and other Banknote-era stamps exist on this form of double paper.

The second type of double paper occurs on a rotary press, when the end of one paper roll, or web, is affixed to the next roll to save time feeding the paper through the press. Stamp designs are printed over the joined paper and, if overlooked by inspectors, may get into post office stocks.

**Goldbeater's Skin** — This type of paper was used for the 1866 issue of Prussia, and was a tough, translucent paper. The design was printed in reverse on the back of the stamp, and the gum applied over the printing. It is impossible to remove stamps printed on this type of paper from the paper to which they are affixed without destroying the design.

**Ribbed** — Ribbed paper has an uneven, corrugated surface made by passing the paper through ridged rollers. This type exists on some copies of U.S. Scott 156-165.

Various other substances, or substrates, have been used for stamp manufacture, including wood, aluminum, copper, silver and gold foil, plastic, and silk and cotton fabrics.

# INTRODUCTION

## Watermarks

Watermarks are an integral part of some papers. They are formed in the process of paper manufacture. Watermarks consist of small designs, formed of wire or cut from metal and soldered to the surface of the mold or, sometimes, on the dandy roll. The designs may be in the form of crowns, stars, anchors, letters or other characters or symbols. These pieces of metal — known in the paper-making industry as "bits" — impress a design into the paper. The design sometimes may be seen by holding the stamp to the light. Some are more easily seen with a watermark detector. This important tool is a small black tray into which a stamp is placed face down and dampened with a fast-evaporating watermark detection fluid that brings up the watermark image in the form of dark lines against a lighter background. These dark lines are the thinner areas of the paper known as the watermark. Some watermarks are extremely difficult to locate, due to either a faint impression, watermark location or the color of the stamp. There also are electric watermark detectors that come with plastic filter disks of various colors. The disks neutralize the color of the stamp, permitting the watermark to be seen more easily.

**Multiple watermarks of Crown Agents and Burma**

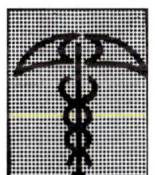 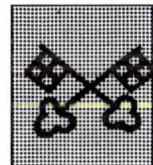 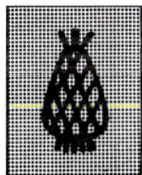

**Watermarks of Uruguay, Vatican City and Jamaica**

**WARNING:** Some inks used in the photogravure process dissolve in watermark fluids (Please see the section on Soluble Printing Inks). Also, see "chalky paper."

Watermarks may be found normal, reversed, inverted, reversed and inverted, sideways or diagonal, as seen from the back of the stamp. The relationship of watermark to stamp design depends on the position of the printing plates or how paper is fed through the press. On machine-made paper, watermarks normally are read from right to left. The design is repeated closely throughout the sheet in a "multiple-watermark design." In a "sheet watermark," the design appears only once on the sheet, but extends over many stamps. Individual stamps may carry only a small fraction or none of the watermark.

"Marginal watermarks" occur in the margins of sheets or panes of stamps. They occur on the outside border of paper (ostensibly outside the area where stamps are to be printed). A large row of letters may spell the name of the country or the manufacturer of the paper, or a border of lines may appear. Careless press feeding may cause parts of these letters and/or lines to show on stamps of the outer row of a pane.

## Soluble printing inks

**WARNING:** Most stamp colors are permanent; that is, they are not seriously affected by short-term exposure to light or water. Many colors, especially of modern inks, fade from excessive exposure to light. There are stamps printed with inks that dissolve easily in water or in fluids used to detect watermarks. Use of these inks was intentional to prevent the removal of cancellations. Water affects all aniline inks, those on so-called safety paper and some photogravure printings - all such inks are known as fugitive colors. Removal from paper of such stamps requires care and alternatives to traditional soaking.

## Separation

"Separation" is the general term used to describe methods used to separate stamps. The three standard forms currently in use are perforating, rouletting and die-cutting. These methods are done during the stamp production process, after printing. Sometimes these methods are done on-press or sometimes as a separate step. The earliest issues, such as the 1840 Penny Black of Great Britain (Scott 1), did not have any means provided for separation. It was expected the stamps would be cut apart with scissors or folded and torn. These are examples of imperforate stamps. Many stamps were first issued in imperforate formats and were later issued with perforations. Therefore, care must be observed in buying single imperforate stamps to be certain they were issued imperforate and are not perforated copies that have been altered by having the perforations trimmed away. Stamps issued imperforate usually are valued as singles. However, imperforate varieties of normally perforated stamps should be collected in pairs or larger pieces as indisputable evidence of their imperforate character.

## PERFORATION

The chief style of separation of stamps, and the one that is in almost universal use today, is perforating. By this process, paper between the stamps is cut away in a line of holes, usually round, leaving little bridges of paper between the stamps to hold them together. Some types of perforation, such as hyphen-hole perfs, can be confused with roulettes, but a close visual inspection reveals that paper has been removed. The little perforation bridges, which project from the stamp when it is torn from the pane, are called the teeth of the perforation.

As the size of the perforation is sometimes the only way to differentiate between two otherwise identical stamps, it is necessary to be able to accurately measure and describe them. This is done with a perforation gauge, usually a ruler-like device that has dots or graduated lines to show how many perforations may be counted in the space of two centimeters. Two centimeters is the space universally adopted in which to measure perforations.

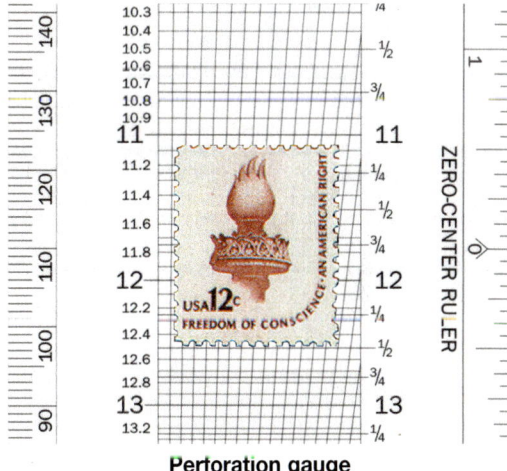

**Perforation gauge**

To measure a stamp, run it along the gauge until the dots on it fit exactly into the perforations of the stamp. If you are using a graduated-line perforation gauge, simply slide the stamp along the surface until the lines on the gauge perfectly project from the center of the bridges or holes. The number to the side of the line of dots or lines that fit the stamp's perforation is the measurement. For example, an "11" means that 11 perforations fit between two centimeters. The description of the stamp therefore is "perf. 11." If the gauge of the perforations on the top and bottom of a stamp differs from that on the sides, the result is what is known as compound perforations. In measuring compound perforations, the gauge at top and bottom is always given first, then the sides. Thus, a stamp that measures 11 at top and bottom and 10½ at the sides is "perf. 11 x 10½." See U.S. Scott 632-642 for examples of compound perforations.

Stamps also are known with perforations different on three or all four sides. Descriptions of such items are clockwise, beginning with the top of the stamp.

A perforation with small holes and teeth close together is a "fine perforation." One with large holes and teeth far apart is a "coarse perforation." Holes that are jagged, rather than clean-cut, are "rough perforations." *Blind perforations* are the slight impressions left by the perforating pins if they fail to puncture the paper. Multiples of stamps showing blind perforations may command a slight premium over normally perforated stamps.

The term *syncopated perfs* describes intentional irregularities in the perforations. The earliest form was used by the Netherlands from 1925-33, where holes were omitted to create distinctive patterns. Beginning in 1992, Great Britain has used an oval perforation to help prevent counterfeiting. Several other countries have started using the oval perfs or other syncopated perf patterns.

A new type of perforation, still primarily used for postal stationery, is known as microperfs. Microperfs are tiny perforations (in some cases hundreds of holes per two centimeters) that allows items to be intentionally separated very easily, while not accidentally breaking apart as easily as standard perforations. These are not currently measured or differentiated by size, as are standard perforations.

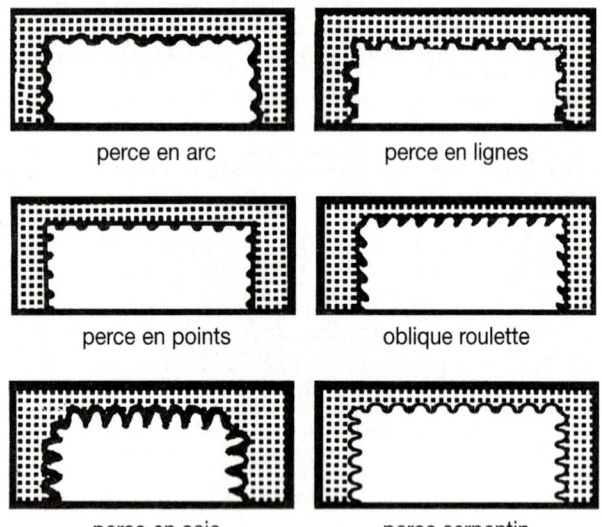

## ROULETTING

In rouletting, the stamp paper is cut partly or wholly through, with no paper removed. In perforating, some paper is removed. Rouletting derives its name from the French roulette, a spur-like wheel. As the wheel is rolled over the paper, each point makes a small cut. The number of cuts made in a two-centimeter space determines the gauge of the roulette, just as the number of perforations in two centimeters determines the gauge of the perforation.

The shape and arrangement of the teeth on the wheels varies. Various roulette types generally carry French names:

*Perce en lignes* — rouletted in lines. The paper receives short, straight cuts in lines. This is the most common type of rouletting. See Mexico Scott 500.

*Perce en points* — pin-rouletted or pin-perfed. This differs from a small perforation because no paper is removed, although round, equidistant holes are pricked through the paper. See Mexico Scott 242-256.

*Perce en arc and perce en scie* — pierced in an arc or saw-toothed designs, forming half circles or small triangles. See Hanover (German States) Scott 25-29.

*Perce en serpentin* — serpentine roulettes. The cuts form a serpentine or wavy line. See Brunswick (German States) Scott 13-18.

Once again, no paper is removed by these processes, leaving the stamps easily separated, but closely attached.

## DIE-CUTTING

The third major form of stamp separation is die-cutting. This is a method where a die in the pattern of separation is created that later cuts the stamp paper in a stroke motion. Although some standard stamps bear die-cut perforations, this process is primarily used for self-adhesive postage stamps. Die-cutting can appear in straight lines, such as U.S. Scott 2522, shapes, such as U.S. Scott 1551, or imitating the appearance of perforations, such as New Zealand Scott 935A and 935B.

# Printing processes

### ENGRAVING (Intaglio, Line-engraving, Etching)

**Master die** — The initial operation in the process of line engraving is making the master die. The die is a small, flat block of softened steel upon which the stamp design is recess engraved in reverse.

Photographic reduction of the original art is made to the appropriate size. It then serves as a tracing guide for the initial outline of the design. The engraver lightly traces the design on the steel with his graver, then slowly works the design until it is completed. At various points during the engraving process, the engraver hand-inks the die and makes an impression to check his progress. These are known as progressive die proofs. After completion of the engraving, the die is hardened to withstand the stress and pressures of later transfer operations.

**Transfer roll**

**Transfer roll** — Next is production of the transfer roll that, as the name implies, is the medium used to transfer the subject from the master die to the printing plate. A blank roll of soft steel, mounted on a mandrel, is placed under the bearers of the transfer press to allow it to roll freely on its axis. The hardened die is placed on the bed of the press and the face of the transfer roll is applied to the die, under pressure. The bed or the roll is then rocked back and forth under increasing pressure, until the soft steel of the roll is forced into every engraved line of the die. The resulting impression on the roll is known as a "relief" or a "relief transfer." The engraved image is now positive in appearance and stands out from the steel. After the required number of reliefs are "rocked in," the soft steel transfer roll is hardened.

Different flaws may occur during the relief process. A defective relief may occur during the rocking in process because of a minute piece of foreign material lodging on the die, or some other cause. Imperfections in the steel of the transfer roll may result in a breaking away of parts of the design. This is known as a relief break, which will show up on finished stamps as small, unprinted areas. If a damaged relief remains in use, it will transfer a repeating defect to the plate. Deliberate alterations of reliefs sometimes occur. "Altered reliefs" designate these changed conditions.

**Plate** — The final step in pre-printing production is the making of the printing plate. A flat piece of soft steel replaces the die on the bed of the transfer press. One of the reliefs on the transfer roll is positioned over this soft steel. Position, or layout, dots determine the correct position on the plate. The dots have been lightly marked on the plate in advance. After the correct position of the relief is determined, the design is rocked in by following the same method used in making the transfer roll. The difference is that this time the image is being transferred from the transfer roll, rather than to it. Once the design is entered on the plate, it appears in reverse and is recessed. There are as many transfers entered on the plate as there are subjects printed on the sheet of stamps. It is during this process that double and shifted transfers occur, as well as re-entries. These are the result of improperly entered images that have not been properly burnished out prior to rocking in a new image.

Modern siderography processes, such as those used by the U.S. Bureau of Engraving and Printing, involve an automated form of rocking designs in on preformed cylindrical printing sleeves. The same process also allows for easier removal and re-entry of worn images right on the sleeve.

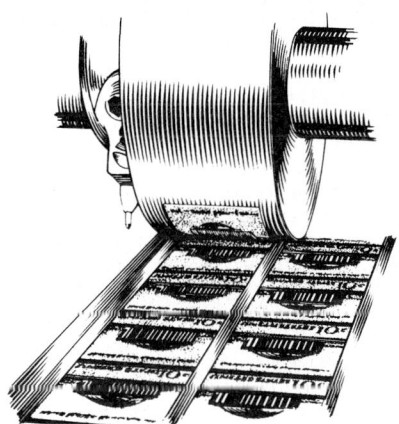

**Transferring the design to the plate**

Following the entering of the required transfers on the plate, the position dots, layout dots and lines, scratches and other markings generally are burnished out. Added at this time by the siderographer are any required guide lines, plate numbers or other marginal markings. The plate is then hand-inked and a proof impression is taken. This is known as a plate proof. If the impression is approved, the plate is machined for fitting onto the press, is hardened and sent to the plate vault ready for use.

On press, the plate is inked and the surface is automatically wiped clean, leaving ink only in the recessed lines. Paper is then forced under pressure into the engraved recessed lines, thereby receiving the ink. Thus, the ink lines on engraved stamps are slightly raised, and slight depressions (debossing) occur on the back of the stamp. Prior to the advent of modern high-speed presses and more advanced ink formulations, paper had to be dampened before receiving the ink. This sometimes led to uneven shrinkage by the time the stamps were perforated, resulting in improperly perforated stamps, or misperfs. Newer presses use drier paper, thus both *wet and dry printings* exist on some stamps.

**Rotary Press** — Until 1914, only flat plates were used to print engraved stamps. Rotary press printing was introduced in 1914, and slowly spread. Some countries still use flat-plate printing.

After approval of the plate proof, older rotary press plates require additional machining. They are curved to fit the press cylinder. "Gripper slots" are cut into the back of each plate to receive the "grippers," which hold the plate securely on the press. The plate is then hardened. Stamps printed from these bent rotary press plates are longer or wider than the same stamps printed from flat-plate presses. The stretching of the plate during the curving process is what causes this distortion.

**Re-entry** — To execute a re-entry on a flat plate, the transfer roll is re-applied to the plate, often at some time after its first use on the press. Worn-out designs can be resharpened by carefully burnishing out the original image and re-entering it from the transfer roll. If the original impression has not been sufficiently removed and the transfer roll is not precisely in line with the remaining impression, the resulting double transfer will make the re-entry obvious. If the registration is true, a re-entry may be difficult or impossible to distinguish. Sometimes a stamp printed from a successful re-entry is identified by having a much sharper and clearer impression than its neighbors. With the advent of rotary presses, post-press re-entries were not possible. After a plate was curved for the rotary press, it was impossible to make a re-entry. This is because the plate had already been bent once (with the design distorted).

However, with the introduction of the previously mentioned modern-style siderography machines, entries are made to the preformed cylindrical printing sleeve. Such sleeves are dechromed and softened. This allows individual images to be burnished out and re-entered on the curved sleeve. The sleeve is then rechromed, resulting in longer press life.

**Double Transfer** — This is a description of the condition of a transfer on a plate that shows evidence of a duplication of all, or a portion of the design. It usually is the result of the changing of the registration between the transfer roll and the plate during the rocking in of the original entry. Double transfers also occur when only a portion of the design has been rocked in and improper positioning is noted. If the worker elected not to burnish out the partial or completed design, a strong double transfer will occur for part or all of the design.

It sometimes is necessary to remove the original transfer from a plate and repeat the process a second time. If the finished re-worked image shows traces of the original impression, attributable to incomplete burnishing, the result is a partial double transfer.

With the modern automatic machines mentioned previously, double transfers are all but impossible to create. Those partially doubled images on stamps printed from such sleeves are more than likely re-entries, rather than true double transfers.

**Re-engraved** — Alterations to a stamp design are sometimes necessary after some stamps have been printed. In some cases, either the original die or the actual printing plate may have its "temper" drawn (softened), and the design will be re-cut. The resulting impressions from such a re-engraved die or plate may differ slightly from the original issue, and are known as "re-engraved." If the alteration was made to the master die, all future printings will be consistently different from the original. If alterations were made to the printing plate, each altered stamp on the plate will be slightly different from each other, allowing specialists to reconstruct a complete printing plate.

**Dropped Transfers** — If an impression from the transfer roll has not been properly placed, a dropped transfer may occur. The final stamp image will appear obviously out of line with its neighbors.

**Short Transfer** — Sometimes a transfer roll is not rocked its entire length when entering a transfer onto a plate. As a result, the finished transfer on the plate fails to show the complete design, and the finished stamp will have an incomplete design printed. This is known as a "short transfer." U.S. Scott No. 8 is a good example of a short transfer.

## TYPOGRAPHY (Letterpress, Surface Printing, Flexography, Dry Offset, High Etch)

Although the word "Typography" is obsolete as a term describing a printing method, it was the accepted term throughout the first century of postage stamps. Therefore, appropriate Scott listings in this catalogue refer to typographed stamps. The current term for this form of printing, however, is "letterpress."

As it relates to the production of postage stamps, letterpress printing is the reverse of engraving. Rather than having recessed areas trap the ink and deposit it on paper, only the raised areas of the design are inked. This is comparable to the type of printing seen by inking and using an ordinary rubber stamp. Letterpress includes all printing where the design is above the surface area, whether it is wood, metal or, in some instances, hardened rubber or polymer plastic.

For most letterpress-printed stamps, the engraved master is made in much the same manner as for engraved stamps. In this instance, however, an additional step is needed. The design is transferred to another surface before being transferred to the transfer roll. In this way, the transfer roll has a recessed stamp design, rather than one done in relief. This makes the printing areas on the final plate raised, or relief areas.

For less-detailed stamps of the 19th century, the area on the die not used as a printing surface was cut away, leaving the surface area raised. The original die was then reproduced by stereotyping or electrotyping. The resulting electrotypes were assembled in the required number and format of the desired sheet of stamps. The plate used in printing the stamps was an electroplate of these assembled electrotypes.

Once the final letterpress plates are created, ink is applied to the raised surface and the pressure of the press transfers the ink impression to the paper. In contrast to engraving, the fine lines of letterpress are impressed on the surface of the stamp, leaving a debossed surface. When viewed from the back (as on a typewritten page), the corresponding line work on the stamp will be raised slightly (embossed) above the surface.

## PHOTOGRAVURE (Gravure, Rotogravure, Heliogravure)

In this process, the basic principles of photography are applied to a chemically sensitized metal plate, rather than photographic paper. The design is transferred photographically to the plate through a halftone, or dot-matrix screen, breaking the reproduction into tiny dots. The plate is treated chemically and the dots form depressions, called cells, of varying depths and diameters, depending on the degrees of shade in the design. Then, like engraving, ink is applied to the plate and the surface is wiped clean. This leaves ink in the tiny cells that is lifted out and deposited on the paper when it is pressed against the plate.

Gravure is most often used for multicolored stamps, generally using the three primary colors (red, yellow and blue) and black. By varying the dot matrix pattern and density of these colors, virtually any color can be reproduced. A typical full-color gravure stamp will be created from four printing cylinders (one for each color). The original multicolored image will have been photographically separated into its component colors.

Modern gravure printing may use computer-generated dot-matrix screens, and modern plates may be of various types including metal-coated plastic. The catalogue designation of Photogravure (or "Photo") covers any of these older and more modern gravure methods of printing.

For examples of the first photogravure stamps printed (1914), see Bavaria Scott 94-114.

### LITHOGRAPHY (Offset Lithography, Stone Lithography, Dilitho, Planography, Collotype)

The principle that oil and water do not mix is the basis for lithography. The stamp design is drawn by hand or transferred from engraving to the surface of a lithographic stone or metal plate in a greasy (oily) substance. This oily substance holds the ink, which will later be transferred to the paper. The stone (or plate) is wet with an acid fluid, causing it to repel the printing ink in all areas not covered by the greasy substance.

Transfer paper is used to transfer the design from the original stone or plate. A series of duplicate transfers are grouped and, in turn, transferred to the final printing plate.

**Photolithography** — The application of photographic processes to lithography. This process allows greater flexibility of design, related to use of halftone screens combined with line work. Unlike photogravure or engraving, this process can allow large, solid areas to be printed.

**Offset** — A refinement of the lithographic process. A rubber-covered blanket cylinder takes the impression from the inked lithographic plate. From the "blanket" the impression is offset or transferred to the paper. Greater flexibility and speed are the principal reasons offset printing has largely displaced lithography. The term "lithography" covers both processes, and results are almost identical.

### EMBOSSED (Relief) Printing

Embossing, not considered one of the four main printing types, is a method in which the design first is sunk into the metal of the die. Printing is done against a yielding platen, such as leather or linoleum. The platen is forced into the depression of the die, thus forming the design on the paper in relief. This process is often used for metallic inks.

Embossing may be done without color (see Sardinia Scott 4-6); with color printed around the embossed area (see Great Britain Scott 5 and most U.S. envelopes); and with color in exact registration with the embossed subject (see Canada Scott 656-657).

### HOLOGRAMS

For objects to appear as holograms on stamps, a model exactly the same size as it is to appear on the hologram must be created. Rather than using photographic film to capture the image, holography records an image on a photoresist material. In processing, chemicals eat away at certain exposed areas, leaving a pattern of constructive and destructive interference. When the photoresist is developed, the result is a pattern of uneven ridges that acts as a mold. This mold is then coated with metal, and the resulting form is used to press copies in much the same way phonograph records are produced.

A typical reflective hologram used for stamps consists of a reproduction of the uneven patterns on a plastic film that is applied to a reflective background, usually a silver or gold foil. Light is reflected off the background through the film, making the pattern present on the film visible. Because of the uneven pattern of the film, the viewer will perceive the objects in their proper three-dimensional relationships with appropriate brightness. The first hologram on a stamp was produced by Austria in 1988 (Scott 1441).

### FOIL APPLICATION

A modern technique of applying color to stamps involves the application of metallic foil to the stamp paper. A pattern of foil is applied to the stamp paper by use of a stamping die. The foil usually is flat, but it may be textured. Canada Scott 1735 has three different foil applications in pearl, bronze and gold. The gold foil was textured using a chemical-etch copper embossing die. The printing of this stamp also involved two-color offset lithography plus embossing.

### THERMOGRAPHY

In the 1990s stamps began to be enhanced with thermographic printing. In this process, a powdered polymer is applied over a sheet that has just been printed. The powder adheres to ink that lacks drying or hardening agents and does not adhere to areas where the ink has these agents. The excess powder is removed and the sheet is briefly heated to melt the powder. The melted powder solidifies after cooling, producing a raised, shiny effect on the stamps. See Scott New Caledonia C239-C240.

### COMBINATION PRINTINGS

Sometimes two or even three printing methods are combined in producing stamps. In these cases, such as Austria Scott 933 or Canada 1735 (described in the preceding paragraph), the multiple-printing technique can be determined by studying the individual characteristics of each printing type. A few stamps, such as Singapore Scott 684-684A, combine as many as three of the four major printing types (lithography, engraving and typography). When this is done it often indicates the incorporation of security devices against counterfeiting.

### INK COLORS

Inks or colored papers used in stamp printing often are of mineral origin, although there are numerous examples of organic-based pigments. As a general rule, organic-based pigments are far more subject to varieties and change than those of mineral-based origin.

The appearance of any given color on a stamp may be affected by many aspects, including printing variations, light, color of paper, aging and chemical alterations.

Numerous printing variations may be observed. Heavier pressure or inking will cause a more intense color, while slight interruptions in the ink feed or lighter impressions will cause a lighter appearance. Stamps printed in the same color by water-based and solvent-based inks can differ significantly in appearance. This affects several stamps in the U.S. Prominent Americans series. Hand-mixed ink formulas (primarily from the 19th century) produced under different conditions (humidity and temperature) account for notable color variations in early printings of the same stamp (see U.S. Scott 248-250, 279B, for example). Different sources of pigment can also result in significant differences in color.

Light exposure and aging are closely related in the way they affect stamp color. Both eventually break down the ink and fade colors, so that a carefully kept stamp may differ significantly in color from an identical copy that has been exposed to light. If stamps are exposed to light either intentionally or accidentally, their colors can be faded or completely changed in some cases.

Papers of different quality and consistency used for the same stamp printing may affect color appearance. Most pelure papers, for example, show a richer color when compared with wove or laid papers. See Russia Scott 181a, for an example of this effect.

The very nature of the printing processes can cause a variety of differences in shades or hues of the same stamp. Some of these shades are scarcer than others, and are of particular interest to the advanced collector.

## Luminescence

All forms of tagged stamps fall under the general category of luminescence. Within this broad category is fluorescence, dealing with forms of tagging visible under longwave ultraviolet light, and phosphorescence, which deals with tagging visible only under shortwave light. Phosphorescence leaves an afterglow and fluorescence does not. These treated stamps show up in a range of different colors when exposed to UV light. The differing wavelengths of the light activates the tagging material, making it glow in various colors that usually serve different mail processing purposes.

Intentional tagging is a post-World War II phenomenon, brought about by the increased literacy rate and rapidly growing mail volume. It was one of several answers to the problem of the need for more automated mail processes. Early tagged stamps served the purpose of triggering machines to separate different types of mail. A natural outgrowth was to also use the signal to trigger machines that faced all envelopes the same way and canceled them.

Tagged stamps come in many different forms. Some tagged stamps have luminescent shapes or images imprinted on them as a form of security device. Others have blocks (United States), stripes, frames (South Africa and Canada), overall coatings (United States), bars (Great Britain and Canada) and many other types. Some types of tagging are even mixed in with the pigmented printing ink (Australia Scott 366, Netherlands Scott 478 and U.S. Scott 1359 and 2443).

The means of applying taggant to stamps differs as much as the intended purposes for the stamps. The most common form of tagging is a coating applied to the surface of the printed stamp. Since the taggant ink is frequently invisible except under UV light, it does not interfere with the appearance of the stamp. Another common application is the use of phosphored papers. In this case the paper itself either has a coating of taggant applied before the stamp is printed, has taggant applied during the papermaking process (incorporating it into the fibers), or has the taggant mixed into the coating of the paper. The latter method, among others, is currently in use in the United States.

Many countries now use tagging in various forms to either expedite mail handling or to serve as a printing security device against counterfeiting. Following the introduction of tagged stamps for public use in 1959 by Great Britain, other countries have steadily joined the parade. Among those are Germany (1961); Canada and Denmark (1962); United States, Australia, France and Switzerland (1963); Belgium and Japan (1966); Sweden and Norway (1967); Italy (1968); and Russia (1969). Since then, many other countries have begun using forms of tagging, including Brazil, China, Czechoslovakia, Hong Kong, Guatemala, Indonesia, Israel, Lithuania, Luxembourg, Netherlands, Penrhyn Islands, Portugal, St. Vincent, Singapore, South Africa, Spain and Sweden to name a few.

In some cases, including United States, Canada, Great Britain and Switzerland, stamps were released both with and without tagging. Many of these were released during each country's experimental period. Tagged and untagged versions are listed for the aforementioned countries and are noted in some other countries' listings. For at least a few stamps, the experimentally tagged version is worth far more than its untagged counterpart, such as the 1963 experimental tagged version of France Scott 1024.

In some cases, luminescent varieties of stamps were inadvertently created. Several Russian stamps, for example, sport highly fluorescent ink that was not intended as a form of tagging. Older stamps, such as early U.S. postage dues, can be positively identified by the use of UV light, since the organic ink used has become slightly fluorescent over time. Other stamps, such as Austria Scott 70a 82a (varnish bars) and Obock Scott 46-64 (printed quadrille lines), have become fluorescent over time.

Various fluorescent substances have been added to paper to make it appear brighter. These optical brightners, as they are known, greatly affect the appearance of the stamp under UV light. The brightest of these is known as Hi-Brite paper. These paper varieties are beyond the scope of the Scott Catalogue.

Shortwave UV light also is used extensively in expertizing, since each form of paper has its own fluorescent characteristics that are impossible to perfectly match. It is therefore a simple matter to detect filled thins, added perforation teeth and other alterations that involve the addition of paper. UV light also is used to examine stamps that have had cancels chemically removed and for other purposes as well.

## Gum

The Illustrated Gum Chart in the first part of this introduction shows and defines various types of gum condition. Because gum condition has an important impact on the value of unused stamps, we recommend studying this chart and the accompanying text carefully.

The gum on the back of a stamp may be shiny, dull, smooth, rough, dark, white, colored or tinted. Most stamp gumming adhesives use gum arabic or dextrine as a base. Certain polymers such as polyvinyl alcohol (PVA) have been used extensively since World War II.

The *Scott Standard Postage Stamp Catalogue* does not list items by types of gum. The *Scott Specialized Catalogue of United States Stamps and Covers* does differentiate among some types of gum for certain issues.

Reprints of stamps may have gum differing from the original issues. In addition, some countries have used different gum formulas for different seasons. These adhesives have different properties that may become more apparent over time.

Many stamps have been issued without gum, and the catalogue will note this fact. See, for example, United States Scott 40-47. Sometimes, gum may have been removed to preserve the stamp. Germany Scott B68, for example, has a highly acidic gum that eventually destroys the stamps. This item is valued in the catalogue with gum removed.

## Reprints and reissues

These are impressions of stamps (usually obsolete) made from the original plates or stones. If they are valid for postage and reproduce obsolete issues (such as U.S. Scott 102-111), the stamps are reissues. If they are from current issues, they are designated as *second*, *third*, etc., *printing*. If designated for a particular purpose, they are called *special printings*.

When special printings are not valid for postage, but are made from original dies and plates by authorized persons, they are *official reprints*. *Private reprints* are made from the original plates and dies by private hands. An example of a private reprint is that of the 1871-1932 reprints made from the original die of the 1845 New Haven, Conn., postmaster's provisional. *Official reproductions* or imitations are made from new dies and plates by government authorization. Scott will list those reissues that are valid for postage if they differ significantly from the original printing.

The U.S. government made special printings of its first postage stamps in 1875. Produced were official imitations of the first two stamps (listed as Scott 3-4), reprints of the demonetized pre-1861 issues (Scott 40-47) and reissues of the 1861 stamps, the 1869 stamps and the then-current 1875 denominations. Even though the official imitations and the reprints were not valid for postage, Scott lists all of these U.S. special printings.

Most reprints or reissues differ slightly from the original stamp in some characteristic, such as gum, paper, perforation, color or watermark. Sometimes the details are followed so meticulously that only a student of that specific stamp is able to distinguish the reprint or reissue from the original.

## Remainders and canceled to order

Some countries sell their stock of old stamps when a new issue replaces them. To avoid postal use, the remainders usually are canceled with a punch hole, a heavy line or bar, or a more-or-less regular-looking cancellation. The most famous merchant of remainders was Nicholas F. Seebeck. In the 1880s and 1890s, he arranged printing contracts between the Hamilton Bank Note Co., of which he was a director, and several Central and South American countries. The contracts provided that the plates and all remainders of the yearly issues became the property of Hamilton. Seebeck saw to it that ample stock remained. The "Seebecks," both remainders and reprints, were standard packet fillers for decades.

Some countries also issue stamps *canceled-to-order (CTO)*, either in sheets with original gum or stuck onto pieces of paper or envelopes and canceled. Such CTO items generally are worth less than postally used stamps. In cases where the CTO material is far more prevalent in the marketplace than postally used examples, the catalogue value relates to the CTO examples, with postally used examples noted as premium items. Most CTOs can be detected by the presence of gum. However, as the CTO practice goes back at least to 1885, the gum inevitably has been soaked off some stamps so they could pass as postally used. The normally applied postmarks usually differ slightly from standard postmarks, and specialists are able to tell the difference. When applied individually to envelopes by philatelically minded persons, CTO material is known as *favor canceled* and generally sells at large discounts.

## Cinderellas and facsimiles

*Cinderella* is a catch-all term used by stamp collectors to describe phantoms, fantasies, bogus items, municipal issues, exhibition seals, local revenues, transportation stamps, labels, poster stamps and many other types of items. Some cinderella collectors include in their collections local postage issues, telegraph stamps, essays and proofs, forgeries and counterfeits.

A *fantasy* is an adhesive created for a nonexistent stamp-issuing authority. Fantasy items range from imaginary countries (Occusi-Ambeno, Kingdom of Sedang, Principality of Trinidad or Torres Straits), to non-existent locals (Winans City Post), or nonexistent transportation lines (McRobish & Co.'s Acapulco-San Francisco Line).

On the other hand, if the entity exists and could have issued stamps (but did not) or was known to have issued other stamps, the items are considered bogus stamps. These would include the Mormon postage stamps of Utah, S. Allan Taylor's Guatemala and Paraguay inventions, the propaganda issues for the South Moluccas and the adhesives of the Page & Keyes local post of Boston.

*Phantoms* is another term for both fantasy and bogus issues.

*Facsimiles* are copies or imitations made to represent original stamps, but which do not pretend to be originals. A catalogue illustration is such a facsimile. Illustrations from the Moens catalogue of the last century were occasionally colored and passed off as stamps. Since the beginning of stamp collecting, facsimiles have been made for collectors as space fillers or for reference. They often carry the word "facsimile," "falsch" (German), "sanko" or "mozo" (Japanese), or "faux" (French) overprinted on the face or stamped on the back. Unfortunately, over the years a number of these items have had fake cancels applied over the facsimile notation and have been passed off as genuine.

## Forgeries and counterfeits

Forgeries and counterfeits have been with philately virtually from the beginning of stamp production. Over time, the terminology for the two has been used interchangeably. Although both forgeries and counterfeits are reproductions of stamps, the purposes behind their creation differ considerably.

Among specialists there is an increasing movement to more specifically define such items. Although there is no universally accepted terminology, we feel the following definitions most closely mirror the items and their purposes as they are currently defined.

Forgeries (also often referred to as Counterfeits) are reproductions of genuine stamps that have been created to defraud collectors. Such spurious items first appeared on the market around 1860, and most old-time collections contain one or more. Many are crude and easily spotted, but some can deceive experts.

An important supplier of these early philatelic forgeries was the Hamburg printer Gebruder Spiro. Many others with reputations in this craft included S. Allan Taylor, George Hussey, James Chute, George Forune, Benjamin & Sarpy, Julius Goldner, E. Oneglia and L.H. Mercier. Among the noted 20th-century forgers were Francois Fournier, Jean Sperati and the prolific Raoul DeThuin.

Forgeries may be complete replications, or they may be genuine stamps altered to resemble a scarcer (and more valuable) type. Most forgeries, particularly those of rare stamps, are worth only a small fraction of the value of a genuine example, but a few types, created by some of the most notable forgers, such as Sperati, can be worth as much or more than the genuine. Fraudulently produced copies are known of most classic rarities and many medium-priced stamps.

In addition to rare stamps, large numbers of common 19th- and early 20th-century stamps were forged to supply stamps to the early packet trade. Many can still be easily found. Few new philatelic forgeries have appeared in recent decades. Successful imitation of well-engraved work is virtually impossible. It has proven far easier to produce a fake by altering a genuine stamp than to duplicate a stamp completely.

Counterfeit (also often referred to as Postal Counterfeit or Postal Forgery) is the term generally applied to reproductions of stamps that have been created to defraud the government of revenue. Such items usually are created at the time a stamp is current and, in some cases, are hard to detect. Because most counterfeits are seized when the perpetrator is captured, postal counterfeits, particularly used on cover, are usually worth much more than a genuine example to specialists. The first postal counterfeit was of Spain's 4-cuarto carmine of 1854 (the real one is Scott 25). Apparently, the counterfeiters were not satisfied with their first version, which is now very scarce, and they soon created an engraved counterfeit, which is common. Postal counterfeits quickly followed in Austria, Naples, Sardinia and the Roman States. They have since been created in many other countries as well, including the United States.

An infamous counterfeit to defraud the government is the 1-shilling Great Britain "Stock Exchange" forgery of 1872, used on telegraph forms at the exchange that year. The stamp escaped detection until a stamp dealer noticed it in 1898.

## Fakes

*Fakes* are genuine stamps altered in some way to make them more desirable. One student of this part of stamp collecting has estimated that by the 1950s more than 30,000 varieties of fakes were known. That number has grown greatly since then. The widespread existence of fakes makes it important for stamp collectors to study their philatelic holdings and use relevant literature. Likewise, collectors should buy from reputable dealers who guarantee their stamps and make full and prompt refunds should a purchased item be declared faked or altered by some mutually agreed-upon authority. Because fakes always have some genuine characteristics, it is not always possible to obtain unanimous agreement among experts regarding specific items. These students may change their opinions as philatelic knowledge increases. More than 80 percent of all fakes on the philatelic market today are regummed, reperforated (or perforated for the first time), or bear forged overprints, surcharges or cancellations.

Stamps can be chemically treated to alter or eliminate colors. For example, a pale rose stamp can be re-colored to resemble a blue shade of high market value. In other cases, treated stamps can be made to resemble missing color varieties. Designs may be changed by painting, or a stroke or a dot added or bleached out to turn an ordinary variety into a seemingly scarcer stamp. Part of a stamp can be bleached and reprinted in a different version, achieving an inverted center or frame. Margins can be added or repairs done so deceptively that the stamps move from the "repaired" into the "fake" category.

Fakers have not left the backs of the stamps untouched either. They may create false watermarks, add fake grills or press out genuine grills. A thin India paper proof may be glued onto a thicker backing to create the appearance an issued stamp, or a proof printed on cardboard may be shaved down and perforated to resemble a stamp. Silk threads are impressed into paper and stamps have been split so that a rare paper variety is added to an otherwise inexpensive stamp. The most common treatment to the back of a stamp, however, is regumming.

Some in the business of faking stamps have openly advertised fool-proof application of "original gum" to stamps that lack it, although most publications now ban such ads from their pages. It is believed that very few early stamps have survived without being hinged. The large number of never-hinged examples of such earlier material offered for sale thus suggests the widespread extent of regumming activity. Regumming also may be used to hide repairs or thin spots. Dipping the stamp into watermark fluid, or examining it under longwave ultraviolet light often will reveal these flaws.

Fakers also tamper with separations. Ingenious ways to add margins are known. Perforated wide-margin stamps may be falsely represented as imperforate when trimmed. Reperforating is commonly done to create scarce coil or perforation varieties, and to eliminate the naturally occurring straight-edge stamps found in sheet margin positions of many earlier issues. Custom has made straight-edged stamps less desirable. Fakers have obliged by perforating straight-edged stamps so that many are now uncommon, if not rare.

Another fertile field for the faker is that of overprints, surcharges and cancellations. The forging of rare surcharges or overprints began in the 1880s or 1890s. These forgeries are sometimes difficult to detect, but experts have identified almost all. Occasionally, overprints or cancellations are removed to create non-overprinted stamps or seemingly unused items. This is most commonly done by removing a manuscript cancel to make a stamp resemble an unused example. "SPECIMEN" overprints may be removed by scraping and repainting to create non-overprinted varieties. Fakers use inexpensive revenues or pen-canceled stamps to generate unused stamps for further faking by adding other markings. The quartz lamp or UV lamp and a high-powered magnifying glass help to easily detect removed cancellations.

The bigger problem, however, is the addition of overprints, surcharges or cancellations — many with such precision that they are very difficult to ascertain. Plating of the stamps or the overprint can be an important method of detection.

Fake postmarks may range from many spurious fancy cancellations to a host of markings applied to transatlantic covers, to adding normally appearing postmarks to definitives of some countries with stamps that are valued far higher used than unused. With the increased popularity of cover collecting, and the widespread interest in postal history, a fertile new field for fakers has come about. Some have tried to create entire covers. Others specialize in adding stamps, tied by fake cancellations, to genuine stampless covers, or replacing less expensive or damaged stamps with more valuable ones. Detailed study of postal rates in effect at the time a cover in question was mailed, including the analysis of each handstamp used during the period, ink analysis and similar techniques, usually will unmask the fraud.

## Restoration and repairs

Scott bases its catalogue values on stamps that are free of defects and otherwise meet the standards set forth earlier in this introduction. Most stamp collectors desire to have the finest copy of an item possible. Even within given grading categories there are variances. This leads to a controversial practice that is not defined in any universal manner: stamp *restoration*.

There are broad differences of opinion about what is permissible when it comes to restoration. Carefully applying a soft eraser to a stamp or cover to remove light soiling is one form of restoration, as is washing a stamp in mild soap and water to clean it. These are fairly accepted forms of restoration. More severe forms of restoration include pressing out creases or removing stains caused by tape. To what degree each of these is acceptable is dependent upon the individual situation. Further along the spectrum is the freshening of a stamp's color by removing oxide build-up or the effects of wax paper left next to stamps shipped to the tropics.

At some point in this spectrum the concept of *repair* replaces that of restoration. Repairs include filling thin spots, mending tears by reweaving or adding a missing perforation tooth. Regumming stamps may have been acceptable as a restoration or repair technique many decades ago, but today it is considered a form of fakery.

Restored stamps may or may not sell at a discount, and it is possible that the value of individual restored items may be enhanced over that of their pre-restoration state. Specific situations dictate the resultant value of such an item. Repaired stamps sell at substantial discounts from the value of sound stamps.

# Terminology

**Booklets** — Many countries have issued stamps in small booklets for the convenience of users. This idea continues to become increasingly popular in many countries. Booklets have been issued in many sizes and forms, often with advertising on the covers, the panes of stamps or on the interleaving.

The panes used in booklets may be printed from special plates or made from regular sheets. All panes from booklets issued by the United States and many from those of other countries contain stamps that are straight edged on the sides, but perforated between. Others are distinguished by orientation of watermark or other identifying features. Any stamp-like unit in the pane, either printed or blank, that is not a postage stamp, is considered to be a *label* in the catalogue listings.

Scott lists and values booklet panes. Modern complete booklets also are listed and valued. Individual booklet panes are listed only when they are not fashioned from existing sheet stamps and, therefore, are identifiable from their sheet stamp counterparts.

Panes usually do not have a used value assigned to them because there is little market activity for used booklet panes, even though many exist used and there is some demand for them.

**Cancellations** — The marks or obliterations put on stamps by postal authorities to show that they have performed service and to prevent their reuse are known as cancellations. If the marking is made with a pen, it is considered a "pen cancel." When the location of the post office appears in the marking, it is a "town cancellation." A "postmark" is technically any postal marking, but in practice the term generally is applied to a town cancellation with a date. When calling attention to a cause or celebration, the marking is known as a "slogan cancellation." Many other types and styles of cancellations exist, such as duplex, numerals, targets, fancy and others. See also "precancels," below.

**Coil Stamps** — These are stamps that are issued in rolls for use in dispensers, affixing and vending machines. Those coils of the United States, Canada, Sweden and some other countries are perforated horizontally or vertically only, with the outer edges imperforate. Coil stamps of some countries, such as Great Britain and Germany, are perforated on all four sides and may in some cases be distinguished from their sheet stamp counterparts by watermarks, counting numbers on the reverse or other means.

**Covers** — Entire envelopes, with or without adhesive postage stamps, that have passed through the mail and bear postal or other markings of philatelic interest are known as covers. Before the introduction of envelopes in about 1840, people folded letters and wrote the address on the outside. Some people covered their letters with an extra sheet of paper on the outside for the address, producing the term "cover." Used airletter sheets, stamped envelopes and other items of postal stationery also are considered covers.

**Errors** — Stamps that have some major, consistent, unintentional deviation from the normal are considered errors. Errors include, but are not limited to, missing or wrong colors, wrong paper, wrong watermarks, inverted centers or frames on multicolor printing, inverted or missing surcharges or overprints, double impressions, missing perforations, unintentionally omitted tagging and others. Factually wrong or misspelled information, if it appears on all examples of a stamp, are not considered errors in the true sense of the word. They are errors of design. Inconsistent or randomly appearing items, such as misperfs or color shifts, are classified as freaks.

**Color-Omitted Errors** — This term refers to stamps where a missing color is caused by the complete failure of the printing plate to deliver ink to the stamp paper or any other paper. Generally, this is caused by the printing plate not being engaged on the press or the ink station running dry of ink during printing.

**Color-Missing Errors** — This term refers to stamps where a color or colors were printed somewhere but do not appear on the finished stamp. There are four different classes of color-missing errors, and the catalog indicates with a two-letter code appended to each such listing what caused the color to be missing. These codes are used only for the United States' color-missing error listings.

**FO** = A *foldover* of the stamp sheet during printing may block ink from appearing on the face of a stamp. Instead, the color will appear on the back of the foldover (where it might fall on the back of the selvage or perhaps a bit on the back of the stamp or on the back of another stamp. FO also will be used in the case of foldunders, where the paper may fold underneath the other stamp paper and the color will print on the platen.

**EP** = When the extraneous paper is removed, an unprinted area of stamp paper remains and may show a color or colors to be totally missing on the finished stamp.

**CM** = A misregistration of the printing plates during printing will result in a *color misregistration*, and such a misregistraion may result in a color not appearing on the finished stamp.

**PS** = A *perforation shift* after printing may remove a color from the finished stamp. Normally, this will occur on a row of stamps at the edge of the stamp pane.

**Measurements** – When measurements are given in the Scott catalogues for stamp size, grill size or any other reason, the first measurement given is always for the top and bottom dimension, while the second measurement will be for the sides (just as perforation gauges are measured). Thus, a stamp size of 15mm x 21mm will indicate a vertically oriented stamp 15mm wide at top and bottom, and 21mm tall at the sides. The same principle holds for measuring or counting items such as U.S. grills. A grill count of 22x18 points (B grill) indicates that there are 22 grill points across by 18 grill points down.

**Overprints and Surcharges** — Overprinting involves applying wording or design elements over an already existing stamp. Overprints can be used to alter the place of use (such as "Canal Zone" on U.S. stamps), to adapt them for a special purpose ("Porto" on Denmark's 1913-20 regular issues for use as postage due stamps, Scott J1-J7) or to commemorate a special occasion (United States Scott 647-648).

A *surcharge* is a form of overprint that changes or restates the face value of a stamp or piece of postal stationery.

Surcharges and overprints may be handstamped, typeset or, occasionally, lithographed or engraved. A few hand-written overprints and surcharges are known.

**Personalized Stamps** — In 1999, Australia issued stamps with se-tenant labels that could be personalized with pictures of the customer's choice. Other countries quickly followed suit, with some offering to print the selected picture on the stamp itself within a frame that was used exclusively for personalized issues. As the picture used on these stamps or labels vary, listings for such stamps are for any picture within the common frame (or any picture on a se-tenant label), be it a "generic" image or one produced especially for a customer, almost invariably at a premium price.

**Precancels** — Stamps that are canceled before they are placed in the mail are known as precancels. Precanceling usually is done to expedite the handling of large mailings and generally allow the affected mail pieces to skip certain phases of mail handling.

In the United States, precancellations generally identified the point of origin; that is, the city and state. This information appeared across the face of the stamp, usually centered between parallel lines. More recently, bureau precancels retained the parallel lines, but the city and state designations were dropped. Recent coils have a service inscription that is present on the original printing plate. These show the mail service paid for by the stamp. Since these stamps are not intended to receive further cancellations when used as intended, they are considered precancels. Such items often do not have parallel lines as part of the precancellation.

In France, the abbreviation *Affranchts* in a semicircle together with the word *Postes* is the general form of precancel in use. Belgian precancellations usually appear in a box in which the name of the city appears. Netherlands precancels have the name of the city enclosed between concentric circles, sometimes called a "lifesaver." Precancellations of other countries usually follow these patterns, but may be any arrangement of bars, boxes and city names.

Precancels are listed in the Scott catalogues only if the precancel changes the denomination (Belgium Scott 477-478); if the precanceled stamp is different from the non-precanceled version (such as untagged U.S. precancels); or if the stamp exists only precanceled (France Scott 1096-1099, U.S. Scott 2265).

**Proofs and Essays** — Proofs are impressions taken from an approved die, plate or stone in which the design and color are the same as the stamp issued to the public. Trial color proofs are impressions taken from approved dies, plates or stones in colors that vary from the final version. An essay is the impression of a design that differs in some way from the issued stamp. "Progressive die proofs" generally are considered to be essays.

**Provisionals** — These are stamps that are issued on short notice and intended for temporary use pending the arrival of regular issues. They usually are issued to meet such contingencies as changes in government or currency, shortage of necessary postage values or military occupation.

During the 1840s, postmasters in certain American cities issued stamps that were valid only at specific post offices. In 1861, postmasters of the Confederate States also issued stamps with limited validity. Both of these examples are known as "postmaster's provisionals."

**Se-tenant** — This term refers to an unsevered pair, strip or block of stamps that differ in design, denomination or overprint.

Unless the se-tenant item has a continuous design (see U.S. Scott 1451a, 1694a) the stamps do not have to be in the same order as shown in the catalogue (see U.S. Scott 2158a).

**Specimens** — The Universal Postal Union required member nations to send samples of all stamps they released into service to the International Bureau in Switzerland. Member nations of the UPU received these specimens as samples of what stamps were valid for postage. Many are overprinted, handstamped or initial-perforated "Specimen," "Canceled" or "Muestra." Some are marked with bars across the denominations (China-Taiwan), punched holes (Czechoslovakia) or back inscriptions (Mongolia).

Stamps distributed to government officials or for publicity purposes, and stamps submitted by private security printers for official approval, also may receive such defacements.

The previously described defacement markings prevent postal use, and all such items generally are known as "specimens."

**Tete-Beche** — This term describes a pair of stamps in which one is upside down in relation to the other. Some of these are the result of intentional sheet arrangements, such as Morocco Scott B10-B11. Others occurred when one or more electrotypes accidentally were placed upside down on the plate, such as Colombia Scott 57a. Separation of the tete-beche stamps, of course, destroys the tete beche variety.

# Currency conversion

| Country | Dollar | Pound | S Franc | Yen | HK $ | Euro | Cdn $ | Aus $ |
|---|---|---|---|---|---|---|---|---|
| Australia | 1.5117 | 1.9103 | 1.7249 | 0.0102 | 0.1935 | 1.6439 | 1.1171 | — |
| Canada | 1.3532 | 1.7100 | 1.5440 | 0.0091 | 0.1732 | 1.4715 | — | 0.8952 |
| European Union | 0.9196 | 1.1621 | 1.0493 | 0.0062 | 0.1177 | — | 0.6796 | 0.6083 |
| Hong Kong | 7.8136 | 9.8740 | 8.9156 | 0.0527 | — | 8.4967 | 5.7742 | 5.1688 |
| Japan | 148.14 | 187.26 | 169.08 | — | 18.964 | 161.14 | 109.50 | 98.022 |
| Switzerland | 0.8764 | 1.1075 | — | 0.0059 | 0.1122 | 0.9530 | 0.6477 | 0.5797 |
| United Kingdom | 0.7913 | — | 0.9029 | 0.0053 | 0.1013 | 0.8605 | 0.5848 | 0.5235 |
| United States | — | 1.2637 | 1.1410 | 0.0067 | 0.1280 | 1.0874 | 0.7390 | 0.6615 |

| Country | Currency | U.S. $ Equiv. |
|---|---|---|
| Afghanistan | afghani | .0143 |
| Aitutaki | New Zealand dollar | .6165 |
| Albania | lek | .0107 |
| Algeria | dinar | .0074 |
| Andorra (French) | euro | 1.0874 |
| Andorra (Spanish) | euro | 1.0874 |
| Angola | kwanza | .0012 |
| Anguilla | East Caribbean dollar | .3704 |
| Antigua | East Caribbean dollar | .3704 |
| Argentina | peso | .0028 |
| Armenia | dram | .0025 |
| Aruba | guilder | .5587 |
| Ascension | British pound | 1.2637 |
| Australia | dollar | .6615 |
| Australian Antarctic Territory | dollar | .6615 |
| United Nations-New York | U.S. dollar | 1.00 |
| United Nations-Geneva | Swiss franc | 1.1410 |
| United Nations-Vienna | euro | 1.0874 |
| United States | dollar | 1.00 |

Source: xe.com Dec. 1, 2023. Figures reflect values as of Dec. 1, 2023.

# Pronunciation Symbols

| | | | | |
|---|---|---|---|---|
| ə | banana, collide, abut | | ȯ | saw, all, gnaw, caught |
| ˈə, ˌə | humdrum, abut | | œ | French bœuf, German Hölle |
| ə | immediately preceding \l\, \n\, \m\, \ŋ\, as in battle, mitten, eaten, and sometimes open \ˈō-pᵊm\, lock and key \-ᵊŋ-\; immediately following \l\, \m\, \r\, as often in French table, prisme, titre | | œ̄ | French feu, German Höhle |
| | | | ȯi | coin, destroy |
| | | | p | pepper, lip |
| ər | further, merger, bird | | r | red, car, rarity |
| ˈər-, ˈə-r | as in two different pronunciations of hurry \ˈhər-ē, ˈhə-rē\ | | s | source, less |
| | | | sh | as in shy, mission, machine, special (actually, this is a single sound, not two); with a hyphen between, two sounds as in grasshopper \ˈgras-ˌhä-pər\ |
| a | mat, map, mad, gag, snap, patch | | | |
| ā | day, fade, date, aorta, drape, cape | | t | tie, attack, late, later, latter |
| ä | bother, cot, and, with most American speakers, father, cart | | th | as in thin, ether (actually, this is a single sound, not two); with a hyphen between, two sounds as in knighthood \ˈnīt-ˌhu̇d\ |
| ȧ | father as pronunced by speakers who do not rhyme it with bother; French patte | | th | then, either, this (actually, this is a single sound, not two) |
| au̇ | now, loud, out | | ü | rule, youth, union \ˈyün-yən\, few \ˈfyü\ |
| b | baby, rib | | u̇ | pull, wood, book, curable \ˈkyu̇r-ə-bəl\, fury \ˈfyu̇r-ē\ |
| ch | chin, nature \ˈnā-chər\ | | | |
| d | did, adder | | ue | German füllen, hübsch |
| e | bet, bed, peck | | ūe | French rue, German fühlen |
| ˈē, ˌē | beat, nosebleed, evenly, easy | | v | vivid, give |
| ē | easy, mealy | | w | we, away |
| f | fifty, cuff | | y | yard, young, cue \ˈkyü\, mute \ˈmyüt\, union \ˈyün-yən\ |
| g | go, big, gift | | | |
| h | hat, ahead | | ʸ | indicates that during the articulation of the sound represented by the preceding character the front of the tongue has substantially the position it has for the articulation of the first sound of yard, as in French digne \dēnʸ\ |
| hw | whale as pronounced by those who do not have the same pronunciation for both whale and wail | | | |
| i | tip, banish, active | | z | zone, raise |
| ī | site, side, buy, tripe | | zh | as in vision, azure \ˈa-zhər\ (actually, this is a single sound, not two); with a hyphen between, two sounds as in hogshead \ˈhȯgz-ˌhed, ˈhägz-\ |
| j | job, gem, edge, join, judge | | | |
| k | kin, cook, ache | | \ | slant line used in pairs to mark the beginning and end of a transcription: \ˈpen\ |
| k̲ | German ich, Buch; one pronunciation of loch | | ˈ | mark preceding a syllable with primary (strongest) stress: \ˈpen-mən-ˌship\ |
| l | lily, pool | | | |
| m | murmur, dim, nymph | | ˌ | mark preceding a syllable with secondary (medium) stress: \ˈpen-mən-ˌship\ |
| n | no, own | | | |
| ⁿ | indicates that a preceding vowel or diphthong is pronounced with the nasal passages open, as in French un bon vin blanc \œⁿ -bōⁿ -vaⁿ -bläⁿ\ | | - | mark of syllable division |
| | | | ( ) | indicate that what is symbolized between is present in some utterances but not in others: factory \ˈfak-t(ə-)rē\ |
| ŋ | sing \ˈsiŋ\, singer \ˈsiŋ-ər\, finger \ˈfiŋ-gər\, ink \ˈiŋk\ | | | |
| ō | bone, know, beau | | ÷ | indicates that many regard as unacceptable the pronunciation variant immediately following: cupola \ˈkyü-pə-lə, ÷-ˌlō\ |

The system of pronunciation is used by permission from Merriam-Webster's Collegiate® Dictionary, Tenth Edition ©1993 by Merriam-Webster Inc., publisher of the Merriam-Webster® dictionaries.

# COMMON DESIGN TYPES

## COMMON DESIGN TYPES

Pictured in this section are issues where one illustration has been used for a number of countries in the Catalogue. Not included in this section are overprinted stamps or those issues which are illustrated in each country. Because the location of Never Hinged breakpoints varies from country to country, some of the values in the listings below will be for unused stamps that were previously hinged.

### EUROPA
### Europa, 1956

The design symbolizing the cooperation among the six countries comprising the Coal and Steel Community is illustrated in each country.

| | |
|---|---|
| Belgium | 496-497 |
| France | 805-806 |
| Germany | 748-749 |
| Italy | 715-716 |
| Luxembourg | 318-320 |
| Netherlands | 368-369 |

| | | |
|---|---|---|
| Nos. 496-497 (2) | 9.00 | .50 |
| Nos. 805-806 (2) | 5.25 | 1.00 |
| Nos. 748-749 (2) | 7.40 | 1.10 |
| Nos. 715-716 (2) | 9.25 | 1.25 |
| Nos. 318-320 (3) | 65.50 | 42.00 |
| Nos. 368-369 (2) | 25.75 | 1.50 |
| Set total (13) Stamps | 122.15 | 47.35 |

### Europa, 1958

"E" and Dove — CD1

European Postal Union at the service of European integration.

### 1958, Sept. 13

| | |
|---|---|
| Belgium | 527-528 |
| France | 889-890 |
| Germany | 790-791 |
| Italy | 750-751 |
| Luxembourg | 341-343 |
| Netherlands | 375-376 |
| Saar | 317-318 |

| | | |
|---|---|---|
| Nos. 527-528 (2) | 3.75 | .60 |
| Nos. 889-890 (2) | 1.65 | .55 |
| Nos. 790-791 (2) | 2.95 | .60 |
| Nos. 750-751 (2) | 1.05 | .60 |
| Nos. 341-343 (3) | 1.35 | .90 |
| Nos. 375-376 (2) | 1.25 | .75 |
| Nos. 317-318 (2) | 1.05 | 2.30 |
| Set total (15) Stamps | 13.05 | 6.30 |

### Europa, 1959

6-Link Enless Chain — CD2

### 1959, Sept. 10

| | |
|---|---|
| Belgium | 536-537 |
| France | 929-930 |
| Germany | 805-806 |
| Italy | 791-792 |
| Luxembourg | 354-355 |
| Netherlands | 379-380 |

| | | |
|---|---|---|
| Nos. 536-537 (2) | 1.55 | .60 |
| Nos. 929-930 (2) | 1.40 | .80 |
| Nos. 805-806 (2) | 1.35 | .60 |
| Nos. 791-792 (2) | .80 | .50 |
| Nos. 354-355 (2) | 2.65 | 1.00 |
| Nos. 379-380 (2) | 2.10 | 1.85 |
| Set total (12) Stamps | 9.85 | 5.35 |

### Europa, 1960

19-Spoke Wheel — CD3

First anniverary of the establishment of C.E.P.T. (Conference Europeenne des Administrations des Postes et des Telecomunications.) The spokes symbolize the 19 founding members of the Conference.

### 1960, Sept.

| | |
|---|---|
| Belgium | 553-554 |
| Denmark | 379 |
| Finland | 376-377 |
| France | 970-971 |
| Germany | 818-820 |
| Great Britain | 377-378 |
| Greece | 688 |
| Iceland | 327-328 |
| Ireland | 175-176 |
| Italy | 809-810 |
| Luxembourg | 374-375 |
| Netherlands | 385-386 |
| Norway | 387 |
| Portugal | 866-867 |
| Spain | 941-942 |
| Sweden | 562-563 |
| Switzerland | 400-401 |
| Turkey | 1493-1494 |

| | | |
|---|---|---|
| Nos. 553-554 (2) | 1.25 | .55 |
| No. 379 (1) | .55 | .50 |
| Nos. 376-377 (2) | 1.80 | 1.40 |
| Nos. 970-971 (2) | .50 | .50 |
| Nos. 818-820 (3) | 1.90 | 1.35 |
| Nos. 377-378 (2) | 7.00 | 2.75 |
| No. 688 (1) | 4.25 | 1.75 |
| Nos. 327-328 (2) | 1.30 | 1.85 |
| Nos. 175-176 (2) | 47.50 | 27.50 |
| Nos. 809-810 (2) | .50 | .50 |
| Nos. 374-375 (2) | 1.00 | .80 |
| Nos. 385-386 (2) | 2.00 | 2.00 |
| No. 387 (1) | 1.00 | .80 |
| Nos. 866-867 (2) | 3.05 | 1.75 |
| Nos. 941-942 (2) | 1.50 | .75 |
| Nos. 562-563 (2) | 1.05 | .75 |
| Nos. 400-401 (2) | 1.75 | .75 |
| Nos. 1493-1494 (2) | 2.10 | 1.35 |
| Set total (34) Stamps | 80.00 | 47.40 |

### Europa, 1961

19 Doves Flying as One — CD4

The 19 doves represent the 19 members of the Conference of European Postal and Telecommunications Administrations C.E.P.T.

### 1961-62

| | |
|---|---|
| Belgium | 572-573 |
| Cyprus | 201-203 |
| France | 1005-1006 |
| Germany | 844-845 |
| Great Britain | 382-384 |
| Greece | 718-719 |
| Iceland | 340-341 |
| Italy | 845-846 |
| Luxembourg | 382-383 |
| Netherlands | 387-388 |
| Spain | 1010-1011 |
| Switzerland | 410-411 |
| Turkey | 1518-1520 |

| | | |
|---|---|---|
| Nos. 572-573 (2) | .75 | .50 |
| Nos. 201-203 (3) | .90 | .75 |
| Nos. 1005-1006 (2) | .50 | .50 |
| Nos. 844-845 (2) | .60 | .75 |
| Nos. 382-384 (3) | .75 | .75 |
| Nos. 718-719 (2) | .80 | .50 |
| Nos. 340-341 (2) | 1.10 | 1.60 |
| Nos. 845-846 (2) | .50 | .50 |
| Nos. 382-383 (2) | .55 | .55 |
| Nos. 387-388 (2) | .50 | .50 |
| Nos. 1010-1011 (2) | .60 | .50 |
| Nos. 410-411 (2) | 1.90 | .90 |
| Nos. 1518-1520 (3) | 1.55 | .90 |
| Set total (29) Stamps | 11.00 | 8.90 |

### Europa, 1962

Young Tree with 19 Leaves — CD5

The 19 leaves represent the 19 original members of C.E.P.T.

### 1962-63

| | |
|---|---|
| Belgium | 582-583 |
| Cyprus | 219-221 |
| France | 1045-1046 |
| Germany | 852-853 |
| Greece | 739-740 |
| Iceland | 348-349 |
| Ireland | 184-185 |
| Italy | 860-861 |
| Luxembourg | 386-387 |
| Netherlands | 394-395 |
| Norway | 414-415 |
| Switzerland | 416-417 |
| Turkey | 1553-1555 |

| | | |
|---|---|---|
| Nos. 582-583 (2) | .65 | .65 |
| Nos. 219-221 (3) | 21.35 | 6.75 |
| Nos. 1045-1046 (2) | .60 | .50 |
| Nos. 852-853 (2) | .65 | .75 |
| Nos. 739-740 (2) | 2.00 | 1.15 |
| Nos. 348-349 (2) | .85 | .85 |
| Nos. 184-185 (2) | 2.00 | .50 |
| Nos. 860-861 (2) | 1.00 | .55 |
| Nos. 386-387 (2) | .75 | .55 |
| Nos. 394-395 (2) | 1.35 | .90 |
| Nos. 414-415 (2) | 1.75 | 1.70 |
| Nos. 416-417 (2) | 1.65 | 1.00 |
| Nos. 1553-1555 (3) | 2.05 | 1.10 |
| Set total (28) Stamps | 36.65 | 16.95 |

### Europa, 1963

Stylized Links, Symbolizing Unity — CD6

### 1963, Sept.

| | |
|---|---|
| Belgium | 598-599 |
| Cyprus | 229-231 |
| Finland | 419 |
| France | 1074-1075 |
| Germany | 867-868 |
| Greece | 768-769 |
| Iceland | 357-358 |
| Ireland | 188-189 |
| Italy | 880-881 |
| Luxembourg | 403-404 |
| Netherlands | 416-417 |
| Norway | 441-442 |
| Switzerland | 429 |
| Turkey | 1602-1603 |

| | | |
|---|---|---|
| Nos. 598-599 (2) | 1.60 | .55 |
| Nos. 229-231 (3) | 18.30 | 8.65 |
| No. 419 (1) | 1.25 | .55 |
| Nos. 1074-1075 (2) | .60 | .50 |
| Nos. 867-868 (2) | .50 | .55 |
| Nos. 768-769 (2) | 4.65 | 1.65 |
| Nos. 357-358 (2) | 1.20 | 1.20 |
| Nos. 188-189 (2) | 4.75 | 3.25 |
| Nos. 880-881 (2) | .50 | .50 |
| Nos. 403-404 (2) | .75 | .55 |
| Nos. 416-417 (2) | 1.30 | 1.00 |
| Nos. 441-442 (2) | 2.60 | 2.40 |
| No. 429 (1) | .90 | .60 |
| Nos. 1602-1603 (2) | 1.20 | .50 |
| Set total (27) Stamps | 40.10 | 22.45 |

### Europa, 1964

Symbolic Daisy — CD7

5th anniversary of the establishment of C.E.P.T. The 22 petals of the flower symbolize the 22 members of the Conference.

### 1964, Sept.

| | |
|---|---|
| Austria | 738 |
| Belgium | 614-615 |
| Cyprus | 244-246 |
| France | 1109-1110 |
| Germany | 897-898 |
| Greece | 801-802 |
| Iceland | 367-368 |
| Ireland | 196-197 |
| Italy | 894-895 |
| Luxembourg | 411-412 |
| Monaco | 590-591 |
| Netherlands | 428-429 |
| Norway | 458 |
| Portugal | 931-933 |
| Spain | 1262-1263 |
| Switzerland | 438-439 |
| Turkey | 1628-1629 |

| | | |
|---|---|---|
| No. 738 (1) | 1.10 | .25 |
| Nos. 614-615 (2) | 1.40 | .60 |
| Nos. 244-246 (3) | 10.95 | 5.00 |
| Nos. 1109-1110 (2) | .50 | .50 |
| Nos. 897-898 (2) | .50 | .50 |
| Nos. 801-802 (2) | 4.15 | 1.55 |
| Nos. 367-368 (2) | 1.40 | 1.15 |
| Nos. 196-197 (2) | 17.00 | 4.25 |
| Nos. 894-895 (2) | .50 | .50 |
| Nos. 411-412 (2) | .75 | .55 |
| Nos. 590-591 (2) | 2.50 | .70 |
| Nos. 428-429 (2) | .75 | .60 |
| No. 458 (1) | 3.50 | 3.50 |
| Nos. 931-933 (3) | 10.00 | 2.00 |
| Nos. 1262-1263 (2) | 1.15 | .50 |
| Nos. 438-439 (2) | 1.65 | .50 |
| Nos. 1628-1629 (2) | 2.00 | .80 |
| Set total (34) Stamps | 59.80 | 23.75 |

### Europa, 1965

Leaves and "Fruit" — CD8

### 1965

| | |
|---|---|
| Belgium | 636-637 |
| Cyprus | 262-264 |
| Finland | 437 |
| France | 1131-1132 |
| Germany | 934-935 |
| Greece | 833-834 |
| Iceland | 375-376 |
| Ireland | 204-205 |
| Italy | 915-916 |
| Luxembourg | 432-433 |
| Monaco | 616-617 |
| Netherlands | 438-439 |
| Norway | 475-476 |
| Portugal | 958-960 |
| Switzerland | 469 |
| Turkey | 1665-1666 |

| | | |
|---|---|---|
| Nos. 636-637 (2) | .50 | .50 |
| Nos. 262-264 (3) | 10.80 | 7.45 |
| No. 437 (1) | 1.25 | .55 |
| Nos. 1131-1132 (2) | .70 | .55 |
| Nos. 934-935 (2) | .50 | .50 |
| Nos. 833-834 (2) | 2.25 | 1.15 |
| Nos. 375-376 (2) | 2.50 | 1.75 |
| Nos. 204-205 (2) | 16.00 | 3.35 |
| Nos. 915-916 (2) | .50 | .50 |
| Nos. 432-433 (2) | .75 | .55 |
| Nos. 616-617 (2) | 3.25 | 1.65 |
| Nos. 438-439 (2) | .55 | .50 |
| Nos. 475-476 (2) | 2.40 | 1.90 |
| Nos. 958-960 (3) | 16.00 | 2.75 |
| No. 469 (1) | 1.15 | .50 |
| Nos. 1665-1666 (2) | 2.00 | 1.25 |
| Set total (32) Stamps | 61.10 | 25.40 |

### Europa, 1966

Symbolic Sailboat — CD9

### 1966, Sept.

| | |
|---|---|
| Andorra, French | 172 |
| Belgium | 675-676 |
| Cyprus | 275-277 |
| France | 1163-1164 |
| Germany | 963-964 |
| Greece | 862-863 |
| Iceland | 384-385 |
| Ireland | 216-217 |
| Italy | 942-943 |
| Liechtenstein | 415 |
| Luxembourg | 440-441 |
| Monaco | 639-640 |
| Netherlands | 441-442 |
| Norway | 496-497 |
| Portugal | 980-982 |
| Switzerland | 477-478 |
| Turkey | 1718-1719 |

| | | |
|---|---|---|
| No. 172 (1) | 3.00 | 3.00 |
| Nos. 675-676 (2) | .80 | .50 |
| Nos. 275-277 (3) | 3.10 | 3.25 |
| Nos. 1163-1164 (2) | .55 | .50 |
| Nos. 963-964 (2) | .50 | .50 |
| Nos. 862-863 (2) | 2.10 | 1.05 |
| Nos. 384-385 (2) | 4.50 | 3.50 |
| Nos. 216-217 (2) | 6.75 | 2.00 |
| Nos. 942-943 (2) | .50 | .50 |
| No. 415 (1) | .40 | .35 |
| Nos. 440-441 (2) | .70 | .55 |
| Nos. 639-640 (2) | 2.00 | .65 |
| Nos. 441-442 (2) | .85 | .50 |
| Nos. 496-497 (2) | 2.35 | 2.15 |
| Nos. 980-982 (3) | 15.90 | 2.25 |
| Nos. 477-478 (2) | 1.40 | .60 |
| Nos. 1718-1719 (2) | 3.35 | 1.75 |
| Set total (34) Stamps | 48.75 | 23.65 |

## COMMON DESIGN TYPES

### Europa, 1967

Cogwheels — CD10

**1967**

| | |
|---|---|
| Andorra, French | 174-175 |
| Belgium | 688-689 |
| Cyprus | 297-299 |
| France | 1178-1179 |
| Germany | 969-970 |
| Greece | 891-892 |
| Iceland | 389-390 |
| Ireland | 232-233 |
| Italy | 951-952 |
| Liechtenstein | 420 |
| Luxembourg | 449-450 |
| Monaco | 669-670 |
| Netherlands | 444-447 |
| Norway | 504-505 |
| Portugal | 994-996 |
| Spain | 1465-1466 |
| Switzerland | 482 |
| Turkey | B120-B121 |

| | | |
|---|---|---|
| Nos. 174-175 (2) | 10.75 | 6.25 |
| Nos. 688-689 (2) | 1.05 | .55 |
| Nos. 297-299 (3) | 2.55 | 2.90 |
| Nos. 1178-1179 (2) | .55 | .50 |
| Nos. 969-970 (2) | .55 | .55 |
| Nos. 891-892 (2) | 3.05 | .85 |
| Nos. 389-390 (2) | 3.00 | 2.00 |
| Nos. 232-233 (2) | 5.90 | 2.30 |
| Nos. 951-952 (2) | .60 | .50 |
| No. 420 (1) | .45 | .40 |
| Nos. 449-450 (2) | 1.00 | .70 |
| Nos. 669-670 (2) | 2.75 | .70 |
| Nos. 444-447 (4) | 2.70 | 2.05 |
| Nos. 504-505 (2) | 2.00 | 1.80 |
| Nos. 994-996 (3) | 16.10 | 1.85 |
| Nos. 1465-1466 (2) | .50 | .50 |
| No. 482 (1) | .60 | .30 |
| Nos. B120-B121 (2) | 2.50 | 2.50 |
| Set total (38) Stamps | 56.60 | 26.70 |

### Europa, 1968

Golden Key with C.E.P.T. Emblem — CD11

**1968**

| | |
|---|---|
| Andorra, French | 182-183 |
| Belgium | 705-706 |
| Cyprus | 314-316 |
| France | 1209-1210 |
| Germany | 983-984 |
| Greece | 916-917 |
| Iceland | 395-396 |
| Ireland | 242-243 |
| Italy | 979-980 |
| Liechtenstein | 442 |
| Luxembourg | 466-467 |
| Monaco | 689-691 |
| Netherlands | 452-453 |
| Portugal | 1019-1021 |
| San Marino | 687 |
| Spain | 1526 |
| Switzerland | 488 |
| Turkey | 1775-1776 |

| | | |
|---|---|---|
| Nos. 182-183 (2) | 16.50 | 10.00 |
| Nos. 705-706 (2) | 1.25 | .50 |
| Nos. 314-316 (3) | 1.70 | 2.90 |
| Nos. 1209-1210 (2) | .85 | .55 |
| Nos. 983-984 (2) | .50 | .55 |
| Nos. 916-917 (2) | 3.10 | 1.45 |
| Nos. 395-396 (2) | 3.00 | 2.20 |
| Nos. 242-243 (2) | 3.30 | 2.25 |
| Nos. 979-980 (2) | .50 | .50 |
| No. 442 (1) | .45 | .40 |
| Nos. 466-467 (2) | .80 | .70 |
| Nos. 689-691 (3) | 5.40 | .95 |
| Nos. 452-453 (2) | 1.05 | .70 |
| Nos. 1019-1021 (3) | 15.90 | 2.10 |
| No. 687 (1) | .55 | .35 |
| No. 1526 (1) | .25 | .25 |
| No. 488 (1) | .40 | .25 |
| Nos. 1775-1776 (2) | 2.50 | 1.25 |
| Set total (35) Stamps | 58.00 | 27.85 |

### Europa, 1969

"EUROPA" and "CEPT" — CD12

Tenth anniversary of C.E.P.T.

**1969**

| | |
|---|---|
| Andorra, French | 188-189 |
| Austria | 837 |
| Belgium | 718-719 |
| Cyprus | 326-328 |
| Denmark | 458 |
| Finland | 483 |
| France | 1245-1246 |
| Germany | 996-997 |
| Great Britain | 585 |
| Greece | 947-948 |
| Iceland | 406-407 |
| Ireland | 270-271 |
| Italy | 1000-1001 |
| Liechtenstein | 453 |
| Luxembourg | 475-476 |
| Monaco | 722-724 |
| Netherlands | 475-476 |
| Norway | 533-534 |
| Portugal | 1038-1040 |
| San Marino | 701-702 |
| Spain | 1567 |
| Sweden | 814-816 |
| Switzerland | 500-501 |
| Turkey | 1799-1800 |
| Vatican | 470-472 |
| Yugoslavia | 1003-1004 |

| | | |
|---|---|---|
| Nos. 188-189 (2) | 18.50 | 12.00 |
| No. 837 (1) | .55 | .25 |
| Nos. 718-719 (2) | .75 | .50 |
| Nos. 326-328 (3) | 1.60 | 2.70 |
| No. 458 (1) | .75 | .75 |
| No. 483 (1) | 2.50 | .60 |
| Nos. 1245-1246 (2) | .55 | .50 |
| Nos. 996-997 (2) | .70 | .50 |
| No. 585 (1) | .25 | .25 |
| Nos. 947-948 (2) | 4.00 | 1.25 |
| Nos. 406-407 (2) | 4.20 | 2.40 |
| Nos. 270-271 (2) | 3.50 | 2.00 |
| Nos. 1000-1001 (2) | .50 | .50 |
| No. 453 (1) | .45 | .45 |
| Nos. 475-476 (2) | .95 | .50 |
| Nos. 722-724 (3) | 10.50 | 2.00 |
| Nos. 475-476 (2) | 1.35 | 1.00 |
| Nos. 533-534 (2) | 2.20 | 1.95 |
| Nos. 1038-1040 (3) | 17.75 | 2.40 |
| Nos. 701-702 (2) | .90 | .90 |
| No. 1567 (1) | .25 | .25 |
| Nos. 814-816 (3) | 4.00 | 2.85 |
| Nos. 500-501 (2) | 1.85 | 1.00 |
| Nos. 1799-1800 (2) | 2.50 | 1.65 |
| Nos. 470-472 (3) | .75 | .75 |
| Nos. 1003-1004 (2) | 4.00 | 4.00 |
| Set total (51) Stamps | 85.80 | 43.90 |

### Europa, 1970

Interwoven Threads — CD13

**1970**

| | |
|---|---|
| Andorra, French | 196-197 |
| Belgium | 741-742 |
| Cyprus | 340-342 |
| France | 1271-1272 |
| Germany | 1018-1019 |
| Greece | 985, 987 |
| Iceland | 420-421 |
| Ireland | 279-281 |
| Italy | 1013-1014 |
| Liechtenstein | 470 |
| Luxembourg | 489-490 |
| Monaco | 768-770 |
| Netherlands | 483-484 |
| Portugal | 1060-1062 |
| San Marino | 729-730 |
| Spain | 1607 |
| Switzerland | 515-516 |
| Turkey | 1848-1849 |
| Yugoslavia | 1024-1025 |

| | | |
|---|---|---|
| Nos. 196-197 (2) | 20.00 | 8.50 |
| Nos. 741-742 (2) | 1.10 | .55 |
| Nos. 340-342 (3) | 1.70 | 2.75 |
| Nos. 1271-1272 (2) | .65 | .50 |
| Nos. 1018-1019 (2) | .60 | .50 |
| Nos. 985, 987 (2) | 6.35 | 1.60 |
| Nos. 420-421 (2) | 6.00 | 4.00 |
| Nos. 279-281 (3) | 7.50 | 2.50 |
| Nos. 1013-1014 (2) | .50 | .50 |
| No. 470 (1) | .45 | .45 |
| Nos. 489-490 (2) | .80 | .55 |
| Nos. 768-770 (3) | 6.35 | 2.10 |
| Nos. 483-484 (2) | 1.30 | 1.15 |
| Nos. 1060-1062 (3) | 18.95 | 2.35 |
| Nos. 729-730 (2) | .90 | .55 |
| No. 1607 (1) | .25 | .25 |
| Nos. 515-516 (2) | 1.85 | .70 |
| Nos. 1848-1849 (2) | 2.50 | 1.50 |
| Nos. 1024-1025 (2) | .80 | .80 |
| Set total (40) Stamps | 78.55 | 31.80 |

### Europa, 1971

"Fraternity, Cooperation, Common Effort" — CD14

**1971**

| | |
|---|---|
| Andorra, French | 205-206 |
| Belgium | 803-804 |
| Cyprus | 365-367 |
| Finland | 504 |
| France | 1304 |
| Germany | 1064-1065 |
| Greece | 1029-1030 |
| Iceland | 429-430 |
| Ireland | 305-306 |
| Italy | 1038-1039 |
| Liechtenstein | 485 |
| Luxembourg | 500-501 |
| Malta | 425-427 |
| Monaco | 797-799 |
| Netherlands | 488-489 |
| Portugal | 1094-1096 |
| San Marino | 749-750 |
| Spain | 1675-1676 |
| Switzerland | 531-532 |
| Turkey | 1876-1877 |
| Yugoslavia | 1052-1053 |

| | | |
|---|---|---|
| Nos. 205-206 (2) | 20.00 | 7.75 |
| Nos. 803-804 (2) | 1.30 | .55 |
| Nos. 365-367 (3) | 1.80 | 2.75 |
| No. 504 (1) | 2.50 | .50 |
| No. 1304 (1) | .45 | .40 |
| Nos. 1064-1065 (2) | .60 | .50 |
| Nos. 1029-1030 (2) | 4.00 | 1.80 |
| Nos. 429-430 (2) | 5.00 | 3.75 |
| Nos. 305-306 (2) | 4.50 | 1.50 |
| Nos. 1038-1039 (2) | .65 | .50 |
| No. 485 (1) | .45 | .45 |
| Nos. 500-501 (2) | 1.00 | .65 |
| Nos. 425-427 (3) | .80 | .70 |
| Nos. 797-799 (3) | 15.00 | 2.80 |
| Nos. 488-489 (2) | 1.20 | .95 |
| Nos. 1094-1096 (3) | 16.15 | 1.75 |
| Nos. 749-750 (2) | .65 | .55 |
| Nos. 1675-1676 (2) | .75 | .55 |
| Nos. 531-532 (2) | 1.85 | .65 |
| Nos. 1876-1877 (2) | 2.50 | 1.25 |
| Nos. 1052-1053 (2) | .50 | .50 |
| Set total (43) Stamps | 81.65 | 30.90 |

### Europa, 1972

Sparkles, Symbolic of Communications CD15

**1972**

| | |
|---|---|
| Andorra, French | 210-211 |
| Andorra, Spanish | 62 |
| Belgium | 825-826 |
| Cyprus | 380-382 |
| Finland | 512-513 |
| France | 1341 |
| Germany | 1089-1090 |
| Greece | 1049-1050 |
| Iceland | 439-440 |
| Ireland | 316-317 |
| Italy | 1065-1066 |
| Liechtenstein | 504 |
| Luxembourg | 512-513 |
| Malta | 450-453 |
| Monaco | 831-832 |
| Netherlands | 494-495 |
| Portugal | 1141-1143 |
| San Marino | 771-772 |
| Spain | 1718 |
| Switzerland | 544-545 |
| Turkey | 1907-1908 |
| Yugoslavia | 1100-1101 |

| | | |
|---|---|---|
| Nos. 210-211 (2) | 21.00 | 7.00 |
| No. 62 (1) | 60.00 | 60.00 |
| Nos. 825-826 (2) | .95 | .55 |
| Nos. 380-382 (3) | 2.45 | 3.25 |
| Nos. 512-513 (2) | 4.00 | 1.00 |
| No. 1341 (1) | .50 | .35 |
| Nos. 1089-1090 (2) | 1.10 | .50 |
| Nos. 1049-1050 (2) | 2.00 | 1.55 |
| Nos. 439-440 (2) | 2.90 | 2.65 |
| Nos. 316-317 (2) | 13.00 | 4.50 |
| Nos. 1065-1066 (2) | .55 | .50 |
| No. 504 (1) | .45 | .45 |
| Nos. 512-513 (2) | .95 | .65 |
| Nos. 450-453 (4) | 1.05 | 1.40 |
| Nos. 831-832 (2) | 5.00 | 1.40 |
| Nos. 494-495 (2) | 1.20 | .90 |
| Nos. 1141-1143 (3) | 15.85 | 1.50 |
| Nos. 771-772 (2) | .70 | .50 |
| No. 1718 (1) | .50 | .40 |
| Nos. 544-545 (2) | 1.65 | .60 |
| Nos. 1907-1908 (2) | 4.00 | 2.00 |
| Nos. 1100-1101 (2) | 1.20 | 1.20 |
| Set total (44) Stamps | 141.00 | 92.85 |

### Europa, 1973

Post Horn and Arrows — CD16

**1973**

| | |
|---|---|
| Andorra, French | 219-220 |
| Andorra, Spanish | 76 |
| Belgium | 839-840 |
| Cyprus | 396-398 |
| Finland | 526 |
| France | 1367 |
| Germany | 1114-1115 |
| Greece | 1090-1092 |
| Iceland | 447-448 |
| Ireland | 329-330 |
| Italy | 1108-1109 |
| Liechtenstein | 528-529 |
| Luxembourg | 523-524 |
| Malta | 469-471 |
| Monaco | 866-867 |
| Netherlands | 504-505 |
| Norway | 604-605 |
| Portugal | 1170-1172 |
| San Marino | 802-803 |
| Spain | 1753 |
| Switzerland | 580-581 |
| Turkey | 1935-1936 |
| Yugoslavia | 1138-1139 |

| | | |
|---|---|---|
| Nos. 219-220 (2) | 20.00 | 11.00 |
| No. 76 (1) | 1.25 | .85 |
| Nos. 839-840 (2) | 1.00 | .65 |
| Nos. 396-398 (3) | 1.80 | 2.40 |
| No. 526 (1) | 1.25 | .55 |
| No. 1367 (1) | 1.25 | .75 |
| Nos. 1114-1115 (2) | .85 | .50 |
| Nos. 1090-1092 (3) | 2.10 | 1.40 |
| Nos. 447-448 (2) | 6.65 | 3.35 |
| Nos. 329-330 (2) | 5.25 | 2.00 |
| Nos. 1108-1109 (2) | .50 | .50 |
| Nos. 528-529 (2) | .60 | .60 |
| Nos. 523-524 (2) | .90 | .75 |
| Nos. 469-471 (3) | .90 | 1.20 |
| Nos. 866-867 (2) | 15.00 | 2.40 |
| Nos. 504-505 (2) | 1.20 | .95 |
| Nos. 604-605 (2) | 4.00 | 1.80 |
| Nos. 1170-1172 (3) | 24.95 | 2.15 |
| Nos. 802-803 (2) | 1.00 | .60 |
| No. 1753 (1) | .35 | .25 |
| Nos. 580-581 (2) | 1.55 | .60 |
| Nos. 1935-1936 (2) | 4.15 | 2.25 |
| Nos. 1138-1139 (2) | 1.15 | 1.10 |
| Set total (46) Stamps | 97.65 | 38.60 |

### Europa, 2000

CD17

**2000**

| | |
|---|---|
| Albania | 2621-2622 |
| Andorra, French | 522 |
| Andorra, Spanish | 262 |
| Armenia | 610-611 |
| Austria | 1814 |
| Azerbaijan | 698-699 |
| Belarus | 350 |
| Belgium | 1818 |
| Bosnia & Herzegovina (Moslem) | 358 |
| Bosnia & Herzegovina (Serb) | 111-112 |
| Croatia | 428-429 |
| Cyprus | 959 |
| Czech Republic | 3120 |
| Denmark | 1189 |
| Estonia | 394 |
| Faroe Islands | 376 |
| Finland | 1129 |
| Aland Islands | 166 |
| France | 2771 |
| Georgia | 228-229 |

# COMMON DESIGN TYPES 31A

| | |
|---|---|
| Germany | 2086-2087 |
| Gibraltar | 837-840 |
| Great Britain (Jersey) | 935-936 |
| Great Britain (Isle of Man) | 883 |
| Greece | 1959 |
| Greenland | 363 |
| Hungary | 3699-3700 |
| Iceland | 910 |
| Ireland | 1230-1231 |
| Italy | 2349 |
| Latvia | 504 |
| Liechtenstein | 1178 |
| Lithuania | 668 |
| Luxembourg | 1035 |
| Macedonia | 187 |
| Malta | 1011-1012 |
| Moldova | 355 |
| Monaco | 2161-2162 |
| Poland | 3519 |
| Portugal | 2358 |
| Portugal (Azores) | 455 |
| Portugal (Madeira) | 208 |
| Romania | 4370 |
| Russia | 6589 |
| San Marino | 1480 |
| Slovakia | 355 |
| Slovenia | 424 |
| Spain | 3036 |
| Sweden | 2394 |
| Switzerland | 1074 |
| Turkey | 2762 |
| Turkish Rep. of Northern Cyprus | 500 |
| Ukraine | 379 |
| Vatican City | 1152 |

| | | |
|---|---|---|
| Nos. 2621-2622 (2) | 9.50 | 9.50 |
| No. 522 (1) | 2.00 | 1.00 |
| No. 262 (1) | 1.75 | .80 |
| Nos. 610-611 (2) | 4.75 | 4.75 |
| No. 1814 (1) | 1.25 | 1.25 |
| Nos. 698-699 (2) | 6.00 | 6.00 |
| No. 350 (1) | 1.75 | 1.75 |
| No. 1818 (1) | 1.40 | .60 |
| No. 358 (1) | 4.75 | 4.75 |
| Nos. 111-112 (2) | 110.00 | 110.00 |
| Nos. 428-429 (2) | 6.25 | 6.25 |
| No. 959 (1) | 2.10 | 1.40 |
| No. 3120 (1) | 1.20 | .40 |
| No. 1189 (1) | 3.50 | 2.25 |
| No. 394 (1) | 1.25 | 1.25 |
| No. 376 (1) | 2.40 | 2.40 |
| No. 1129 (1) | 2.00 | .60 |
| No. 166 (1) | 1.10 | 1.20 |
| No. 2771 (1) | 1.25 | .40 |
| Nos. 228-229 (2) | 9.00 | 9.00 |
| Nos. 2086-2087 (2) | 4.35 | 2.10 |
| Nos. 837-840 (4) | 5.50 | 5.30 |
| Nos. 935-936 (2) | 2.40 | 2.40 |
| No. 883 (1) | 1.75 | 1.75 |
| No. 363 (1) | 1.90 | 1.90 |
| Nos. 3699-3700 (2) | 6.50 | 2.50 |
| No. 910 (1) | 1.60 | 1.60 |
| Nos. 1230-1231 (2) | 4.35 | 4.35 |
| No. 2349 (1) | 1.50 | .40 |
| No. 504 (1) | 5.00 | 2.40 |
| No. 1178 (1) | 2.25 | 1.75 |
| No. 668 (1) | 1.50 | 1.50 |
| No. 1035 (1) | 1.40 | .85 |
| No. 187 (1) | 3.00 | 3.00 |
| Nos. 1011-1012 (2) | 4.35 | 4.35 |
| No. 355 (1) | 3.50 | 3.50 |
| Nos. 2161-2162 (2) | 2.80 | 1.40 |
| No. 3519 (1) | 1.25 | .75 |
| No. 2358 (1) | 1.95 | .65 |
| No. 455 (1) | 2.00 | .50 |
| No. 208 (1) | 2.25 | .50 |
| No. 4370 (1) | 2.50 | 1.25 |
| No. 6589 (1) | 4.00 | .85 |
| No. 1480 (1) | 1.00 | 1.00 |
| No. 355 (1) | 1.60 | .80 |
| No. 424 (1) | 3.25 | 3.25 |
| No. 3036 (1) | 1.00 | .40 |
| No. 2394 (1) | 3.00 | 1.50 |
| No. 1074 (1) | 2.10 | 1.05 |
| No. 2762 (1) | 2.75 | 2.00 |
| No. 500 (1) | 2.50 | 2.50 |
| No. 379 (1) | 4.50 | 3.00 |
| No. 1152 (1) | 1.75 | 1.75 |
| Set total (68) Stamps | 264.25 | 228.35 |

The Gibraltar stamps are similar to the stamp illustrated, but none have the design shown above. All other sets listed above include at least one stamp with the design shown, but some include stamps with entirely different designs. Bulgaria Nos. 4131-4132, Guernsey Nos. 802-803 and Yugoslavia Nos. 2485-2486 are Europa stamps with completely different designs.

## PORTUGAL & COLONIES
### Vasco da Gama

Fleet Departing
CD20

Fleet Arriving at Calicut
CD21

Embarking at Rastello
CD22

San Gabriel, da Gama and Camoens
CD24

Flagship San Gabriel
CD26

Muse of History
CD23

Archangel Gabriel, the Patron Saint
CD25

Vasco da Gama
CD27

Fourth centenary of Vasco da Gama's discovery of the route to India.

### 1898

| | |
|---|---|
| Azores | 93-100 |
| Macao | 67-74 |
| Madeira | 37-44 |
| Portugal | 147-154 |
| Port. Africa | 1-8 |
| Port. Congo | 75-98 |
| Port. India | 189-196 |
| St. Thomas & Prince Islands | 170-193 |
| Timor | 45-52 |

| | | |
|---|---|---|
| Nos. 93-100 (8) | 113.50 | 73.50 |
| Nos. 67-74 (8) | 250.25 | 170.25 |
| Nos. 37-44 (8) | 60.55 | 37.25 |
| Nos. 147-154 (8) | 249.05 | 84.90 |
| Nos. 1-8 (8) | 44.00 | 29.25 |
| Nos. 75-98 (24) | 78.50 | 64.65 |
| Nos. 189-196 (8) | 25.25 | 15.50 |
| Nos. 170-193 (24) | 60.40 | 44.75 |
| Nos. 45-52 (8) | 33.50 | 23.25 |
| Set total (104) Stamps | 915.00 | 543.30 |

### Pombal
### POSTAL TAX
### POSTAL TAX DUES

Marquis de Pombal — CD28

Planning Reconstruction of Lisbon, 1755 — CD29

Pombal Monument, Lisbon — CD30

Sebastiao Jose de Carvalho e Mello, Marquis de Pombal (1699-1782), statesman, rebuilt Lisbon after earthquake of 1755. Tax was for the erection of Pombal monument. Obligatory on all mail on certain days throughout the year. Postal Tax Dues are inscribed "Multa."

### 1925

| | |
|---|---|
| Angola | RA1-RA3, RAJ1-RAJ3 |
| Azores | RA9-RA11, RAJ2-RAJ4 |
| Cape Verde | RA1-RA3, RAJ1-RAJ3 |
| Macao | RA1-RA3, RAJ1-RAJ3 |
| Madeira | RA1-RA3, RAJ1-RAJ3 |
| Mozambique | RA1-RA3, RAJ1-RAJ3 |
| Nyassa | RA1-RA3, RAJ1-RAJ3 |
| Portugal | RA11-RA13, RAJ2-RAJ4 |
| Port. Guinea | RA1-RA3, RAJ1-RAJ3 |
| Port. India | RA1-RA3, RAJ1-RAJ3 |
| St. Thomas & Prince Islands | RA1-RA3, RAJ1-RAJ3 |
| Timor | RA1-RA3, RAJ1-RAJ3 |

| | | |
|---|---|---|
| Nos. RA1-RA3,RAJ1-RAJ3 (6) | 6.60 | 5.40 |
| Nos. RA9-RA11,RAJ2-RAJ4 (6) | 6.60 | 6.60 |
| Nos. RA1-RA3,RAJ1-RAJ3 (6) | 7.80 | 7.65 |
| Nos. RA1-RA3,RAJ1-RAJ3 (6) | 36.50 | 17.25 |
| Nos. RA1-RA3,RAJ1-RAJ3 (6) | 7.95 | 14.70 |
| Nos. RA1-RA3,RAJ1-RAJ3 (6) | 3.75 | 3.60 |
| Nos. RA11-RA13,RAJ2-RAJ4 (6) | 85.50 | 76.50 |
| Nos. RA1-RA3,RAJ1-RAJ3 (6) | 8.75 | 8.55 |
| Nos. RA1-RA3,RAJ1-RAJ3 (6) | 5.85 | 5.40 |
| Nos. RA1-RA3,RAJ1-RAJ3 (6) | 4.05 | 4.05 |
| Nos. RA1-RA3,RAJ1-RAJ3 (6) | 4.95 | 3.45 |
| Nos. RA1-RA3,RAJ1-RAJ3 (6) | 3.90 | 3.45 |
| Set total (72) Stamps | 182.20 | 156.60 |

Vasco da Gama
CD34

Mousinho de Albuquerque
CD35

Dam
CD36

Prince Henry the Navigator
CD37

Affonso de Albuquerque
CD38

Plane over Globe
CD39

### 1938-30

| | |
|---|---|
| Angola | 274-291, C1-C9 |
| Cape Verde | 234-251, C1-C9 |
| Macao | 289-305, C7-C15 |
| Mozambique | 270-287, C1-C9 |
| Port. Guinea | 233-250, C1-C9 |
| Port. India | 439-453, C1-C8 |
| St. Thomas & Prince Islands | 302-319, 323-340, C1-C18 |
| Timor | 223-239, C1-C9 |

| | | |
|---|---|---|
| Nos. 274-291,C1-C9 (27) | 121.45 | 20.95 |
| Nos. 234-251,C1-C9 (27) | 122.40 | 38.30 |
| Nos. 289-305,C7-C15 (26) | 800.60 | 800.55 |
| Nos. 270-287,C1-C9 (27) | 95.71 | 15.95 |
| Nos. 233-250,C1-C9 (27) | 130.20 | 49.15 |
| Nos. 439-453,C1-C8 (23) | 98.15 | 34.70 |
| Nos. 302-319,323-340,C1-C18 (54) | 468.30 | 263.80 |
| Nos. 223-239,C1-C9 (26) | 213.85 | 104.90 |
| Set total (237) Stamps | 2,140. | 866.30 |

### Lady of Fatima

Our Lady of the Rosary, Fatima, Portugal — CD40

### 1948-49

| | |
|---|---|
| Angola | 315-318 |
| Cape Verde | 266 |
| Macao | 336 |
| Mozambique | 325-328 |
| Port. Guinea | 271 |
| Port. India | 480 |
| St. Thomas & Prince Islands | 351 |
| Timor | 254 |

| | | |
|---|---|---|
| Nos. 315-318 (4) | 68.00 | 20.60 |
| No. 266 (1) | 8.50 | 9.00 |
| No. 336 (1) | 90.00 | 30.00 |
| Nos. 325-328 (4) | 73.25 | 27.50 |
| No. 271 (1) | 6.50 | 6.00 |
| No. 480 (1) | 4.50 | 4.75 |
| No. 351 (1) | 8.50 | 7.00 |
| No. 254 (1) | 6.00 | 12.50 |
| Set total (14) Stamps | 265.25 | 117.35 |

A souvenir sheet of 9 stamps was issued in 1951 to mark the extension of the 1950 Holy Year. The sheet contains: Angola No. 316, Cape Verde No. 266, Macao No. 336, Mozambique No. 325, Portuguese Guinea No. 271, Portuguese India Nos. 480, 485, St. Thomas & Prince Islands No. 351, Timor No. 254. The sheet also contains a portrait of Pope Pius XII and is inscribed "Encerramento do Ano Santo, Fatima 1951." It was sold for 11 escudos.

### Holy Year

Church Bells and Dove
CD41

Angel Holding Candelabra
CD42

Holy Year, 1950.

### 1950-51

| | |
|---|---|
| Angola | 331-332 |
| Cape Verde | 268-269 |
| Macao | 339-340 |
| Mozambique | 330-331 |
| Port. Guinea | 273-274 |
| Port. India | 490-491, 496-503 |
| St. Thomas & Prince Islands | 353-354 |
| Timor | 258-259 |

| | | |
|---|---|---|
| Nos. 331-332 (2) | 7.60 | 1.35 |
| Nos. 268-269 (2) | 7.35 | 4.75 |
| Nos. 339-340 (2) | 110.00 | 34.00 |
| Nos. 330-331 (2) | 3.00 | 1.60 |
| Nos. 273-274 (2) | 8.50 | 5.05 |
| Nos. 490-491,496-503 (10) | 14.50 | 7.30 |
| Nos. 353-354 (2) | 10.50 | 7.25 |
| Nos. 258-259 (2) | 8.75 | 5.00 |
| Set total (24) Stamps | 170.20 | 66.30 |

A souvenir sheet of 8 stamps was issued in 1951 to mark the extension of the Holy Year. The sheet contains: Angola No. 331, Cape Verde No. 269, Macao No. 340, Mozambique No. 331, Portuguese Guinea No. 275, Portuguese India No. 490, St. Thomas & Prince Islands No. 354, Timor No. 258, some with colors changed. The sheet contains doves and is inscribed 'Encerramento do Ano Santo, Fatima 1951.' It was sold for 17 escudos.

### Holy Year Conclusion

Our Lady of Fatima — CD43

Conclusion of Holy Year. Sheets contain alternate vertical rows of stamps and labels bearing quotation from Pope Pius XII, different for each colony.

### 1951

| | |
|---|---|
| Angola | 357 |
| Cape Verde | 270 |
| Macao | 352 |
| Mozambique | 356 |
| Port. Guinea | 275 |
| Port. India | 506 |
| St. Thomas & Prince Islands | 355 |
| Timor | 270 |

| | | |
|---|---|---|
| No. 357 (1) | 4.50 | 1.60 |
| No. 270 (1) | 1.75 | 1.25 |
| No. 352 (1) | 110.00 | 23.00 |
| No. 356 (1) | 3.25 | 1.75 |
| No. 275 (1) | 2.00 | 1.00 |
| No. 506 (1) | 2.50 | 1.60 |
| No. 355 (1) | 3.50 | 2.75 |
| No. 270 (1) | 3.75 | 2.75 |
| Set total (8) Stamps | 131.25 | 35.70 |

## Common Design Types

### Medical Congress

CD44

First National Congress of Tropical Medicine, Lisbon, 1952. Each stamp has a different design.

**1952**

| | |
|---|---|
| Angola | 358 |
| Cape Verde | 287 |
| Macao | 364 |
| Mozambique | 359 |
| Port. Guinea | 276 |
| Port. India | 516 |
| St. Thomas & Prince Islands | 356 |
| Timor | 271 |

| | | |
|---|---|---|
| No. 358 (1) | 1.35 | .45 |
| No. 287 (1) | .95 | .75 |
| No. 364 (1) | 20.00 | 7.00 |
| No. 359 (1) | 1.90 | .90 |
| No. 276 (1) | .75 | .65 |
| No. 516 (1) | 7.50 | 3.25 |
| No. 356 (1) | .75 | .30 |
| No. 271 (1) | 2.00 | 1.60 |
| Set total (8) Stamps | 35.20 | 14.90 |

### Postage Due Stamps

 CD45

**1952**

| | |
|---|---|
| Angola | J37-J42 |
| Cape Verde | J31-J36 |
| Macao | J53-J58 |
| Mozambique | J51-J56 |
| Port. Guinea | J40-J45 |
| Port. India | J47-J52 |
| St. Thomas & Prince Islands | J52-J57 |
| Timor | J31-J36 |

| | | |
|---|---|---|
| Nos. J37-J42 (6) | 3.15 | 2.95 |
| Nos. J31-J36 (6) | 2.80 | 2.30 |
| Nos. J53-J58 (6) | 27.80 | 12.05 |
| Nos. J51-J56 (6) | 2.40 | 1.95 |
| Nos. J40-J45 (6) | 2.70 | 2.55 |
| Nos. J47-J52 (6) | 6.10 | 6.10 |
| Nos. J52-J57 (6) | 2.85 | 2.70 |
| Nos. J31-J36 (6) | 4.00 | 2.35 |
| Set total (48) Stamps | 51.80 | 32.95 |

### Sao Paulo

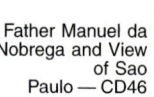

Father Manuel da Nobrega and View of Sao Paulo — CD46

Founding of Sao Paulo, Brazil, 400th anniv.

**1954**

| | |
|---|---|
| Angola | 385 |
| Cape Verde | 297 |
| Macao | 382 |
| Mozambique | 395 |
| Port. Guinea | 291 |
| Port. India | 530 |
| St. Thomas & Prince Islands | 369 |
| Timor | 279 |

| | | |
|---|---|---|
| No. 385 (1) | .80 | .30 |
| No. 297 (1) | .95 | .80 |
| No. 382 (1) | 30.00 | 6.00 |
| No. 395 (1) | .75 | .30 |
| No. 291 (1) | .50 | .35 |
| No. 530 (1) | 1.00 | .55 |
| No. 369 (1) | .70 | .50 |
| No. 279 (1) | 2.00 | 1.40 |
| Set total (8) Stamps | 36.70 | 10.20 |

### Tropical Medicine Congress

CD47

Sixth International Congress for Tropical Medicine and Malaria, Lisbon, Sept. 1958. Each stamp shows a different plant.

**1958**

| | |
|---|---|
| Angola | 409 |
| Cape Verde | 303 |
| Macao | 392 |
| Mozambique | 404 |
| Port. Guinea | 295 |
| Port. India | 569 |
| St. Thomas & Prince Islands | 371 |
| Timor | 289 |

| | | |
|---|---|---|
| No. 409 (1) | 3.50 | 1.00 |
| No. 303 (1) | 6.75 | 3.25 |
| No. 392 (1) | 13.00 | 6.00 |
| No. 404 (1) | 3.50 | 1.50 |
| No. 295 (1) | 4.50 | 2.00 |
| No. 569 (1) | 1.75 | .75 |
| No. 371 (1) | 2.75 | 2.00 |
| No. 289 (1) | 5.50 | 4.25 |
| Set total (8) Stamps | 41.25 | 20.75 |

### Sports

CD48

Each stamp shows a different sport.

**1962**

| | |
|---|---|
| Angola | 433-438 |
| Cape Verde | 320-325 |
| Macao | 394-399 |
| Mozambique | 424-429 |
| Port. Guinea | 299-304 |
| St. Thomas & Prince Islands | 374-379 |
| Timor | 313-318 |

| | | |
|---|---|---|
| Nos. 433-438 (6) | 5.55 | 3.20 |
| Nos. 320-325 (6) | 16.05 | 7.40 |
| Nos. 394-399 (6) | 129.85 | 28.95 |
| Nos. 424-429 (6) | 6.55 | 2.45 |
| Nos. 299-304 (6) | 6.00 | 3.00 |
| Nos. 374-379 (6) | 6.80 | 3.20 |
| Nos. 313-318 (6) | 11.65 | 5.90 |
| Set total (42) Stamps | 182.45 | 54.10 |

### Anti-Malaria

Anopheles Funestus and Malaria Eradication Symbol — CD49

World Health Organization drive to eradicate malaria.

**1962**

| | |
|---|---|
| Angola | 439 |
| Cape Verde | 326 |
| Macao | 400 |
| Mozambique | 430 |
| Port. Guinea | 305 |
| St. Thomas & Prince Islands | 380 |
| Timor | 319 |

| | | |
|---|---|---|
| No. 439 (1) | 2.25 | .90 |
| No. 326 (1) | 1.90 | 1.60 |
| No. 400 (1) | 12.00 | 4.00 |
| No. 430 (1) | 2.00 | .50 |
| No. 305 (1) | 1.50 | .60 |
| No. 380 (1) | 2.25 | 1.25 |
| No. 319 (1) | 2.25 | 1.40 |
| Set total (7) Stamps | 24.15 | 10.25 |

### Airline Anniversary

Map of Africa, Super Constellation and Jet Liner — CD50

Tenth anniversary of Transportes Aereos Portugueses (TAP).

**1963**

| | |
|---|---|
| Angola | 490 |
| Cape Verde | 327 |
| Mozambique | 434 |
| Port. Guinea | 318 |
| St. Thomas & Prince Islands | 381 |

| | | |
|---|---|---|
| No. 490 (1) | 1.35 | .35 |
| No. 327 (1) | 1.50 | 1.10 |
| No. 434 (1) | .55 | .25 |
| No. 318 (1) | 1.25 | .60 |
| No. 381 (1) | .80 | .50 |
| Set total (5) Stamps | 5.45 | 2.80 |

### National Overseas Bank

Antonio Teixeira de Sousa — CD51

Centenary of the National Overseas Bank of Portugal.

**1964, May 16**

| | |
|---|---|
| Angola | 509 |
| Cape Verde | 328 |
| Port. Guinea | 319 |
| St. Thomas & Prince Islands | 382 |
| Timor | 320 |

| | | |
|---|---|---|
| No. 509 (1) | .90 | .45 |
| No. 328 (1) | 1.50 | 1.30 |
| No. 319 (1) | .95 | .60 |
| No. 382 (1) | .95 | .50 |
| No. 320 (1) | 1.50 | 1.30 |
| Set total (5) Stamps | 5.80 | 4.15 |

### ITU

ITU Emblem and the Archangel Gabriel — CD52

International Communications Union, Cent.

**1965, May 17**

| | |
|---|---|
| Angola | 511 |
| Cape Verde | 329 |
| Macao | 402 |
| Mozambique | 464 |
| Port. Guinea | 320 |
| St. Thomas & Prince Islands | 383 |
| Timor | 321 |

| | | |
|---|---|---|
| No. 511 (1) | 1.25 | .65 |
| No. 329 (1) | 2.90 | 2.25 |
| No. 402 (1) | 9.00 | 3.00 |
| No. 464 (1) | .65 | .25 |
| No. 320 (1) | 2.50 | 1.00 |
| No. 383 (1) | 2.00 | 1.00 |
| No. 321 (1) | 2.20 | 1.40 |
| Set total (7) Stamps | 20.50 | 9.55 |

### National Revolution

CD53

40th anniv. of the National Revolution. Different buildings on each stamp.

**1966, May 28**

| | |
|---|---|
| Angola | 525 |
| Cape Verde | 338 |
| Macao | 403 |
| Mozambique | 465 |
| Port. Guinea | 329 |
| St. Thomas & Prince Islands | 392 |
| Timor | 322 |

| | | |
|---|---|---|
| No. 525 (1) | .50 | .25 |
| No. 338 (1) | .85 | .65 |
| No. 403 (1) | 9.00 | 3.75 |
| No. 465 (1) | .65 | .30 |
| No. 329 (1) | .85 | .65 |
| No. 392 (1) | .80 | .50 |
| No. 322 (1) | 2.40 | 1.40 |
| Set total (7) Stamps | 15.05 | 7.60 |

### Navy Club

CD54

Centenary of Portugal's Navy Club. Each stamp has a different design.

**1967, Jan. 31**

| | |
|---|---|
| Angola | 527-528 |
| Cape Verde | 339-340 |
| Macao | 412-413 |
| Mozambique | 478-479 |
| Port. Guinea | 330-331 |
| St. Thomas & Prince Islands | 393-394 |
| Timor | 323-324 |

| | | |
|---|---|---|
| Nos. 527-528 (2) | 2.35 | 1.20 |
| Nos. 339-340 (2) | 2.70 | 2.30 |
| Nos. 412-413 (2) | 18.00 | 4.70 |
| Nos. 478-479 (2) | 1.75 | .65 |
| Nos. 330-331 (2) | 1.65 | .90 |
| Nos. 393-394 (2) | 3.30 | 1.30 |
| Nos. 323-324 (2) | 4.25 | 2.40 |
| Set total (14) Stamps | 34.00 | 13.45 |

### Admiral Coutinho

CD55

Centenary of the birth of Admiral Carlos Viegas Gago Coutinho (1869-1959), explorer and aviation pioneer. Each stamp has a different design.

**1969, Feb. 17**

| | |
|---|---|
| Angola | 547 |
| Cape Verde | 355 |
| Macao | 417 |
| Mozambique | 484 |
| Port. Guinea | 335 |
| St. Thomas & Prince Islands | 397 |
| Timor | 335 |

| | | |
|---|---|---|
| No. 547 (1) | .85 | .35 |
| No. 355 (1) | .60 | .25 |
| No. 417 (1) | 7.50 | 2.25 |
| No. 484 (1) | .30 | .25 |
| No. 335 (1) | .50 | .25 |
| No. 397 (1) | .70 | .35 |
| No. 335 (1) | 2.50 | 1.40 |
| Set total (7) Stamps | 12.95 | 5.10 |

### Administration Reform

Luiz Augusto Rebello da Silva — CD56

Centenary of the administration reforms of the overseas territories.

**1969, Sept. 25**

| | |
|---|---|
| Angola | 549 |
| Cape Verde | 357 |
| Macao | 419 |
| Mozambique | 491 |
| Port. Guinea | 337 |
| St. Thomas & Prince Islands | 399 |
| Timor | 338 |

| | | |
|---|---|---|
| No. 549 (1) | .30 | .25 |
| No. 357 (1) | .65 | .40 |
| No. 419 (1) | 12.50 | 2.00 |
| No. 491 (1) | .30 | .25 |
| No. 337 (1) | .35 | .25 |
| No. 399 (1) | .60 | .45 |
| No. 338 (1) | 1.40 | .70 |
| Set total (7) Stamps | 16.10 | 4.30 |

### Marshal Carmona

CD57

Birth centenary of Marshal Antonio Oscar Carmona de Fragoso (1869-1951), President of Portugal. Each stamp has a different design.

**1970, Nov. 15**

| | |
|---|---|
| Angola | 563 |
| Cape Verde | 359 |
| Macao | 422 |
| Mozambique | 493 |
| Port. Guinea | 340 |
| St. Thomas & Prince Islands | 403 |
| Timor | 341 |

| | | |
|---|---|---|
| No. 563 (1) | .45 | .25 |
| No. 359 (1) | .70 | .50 |
| No. 422 (1) | 5.00 | 1.75 |
| No. 493 (1) | .40 | .25 |
| No. 340 (1) | .45 | .25 |

## COMMON DESIGN TYPES 33A

| | | |
|---|---|---|
| No. 403 (1) | .90 | .40 |
| No. 341 (1) | 1.00 | .50 |
| Set total (7) Stamps | 8.90 | 3.90 |

### Olympic Games

CD59

20th Olympic Games, Munich, Aug. 26-Sept. 11. Each stamp shows a different sport.

**1972, June 20**

| | |
|---|---|
| Angola | 569 |
| Cape Verde | 361 |
| Macao | 426 |
| Mozambique | 504 |
| Port. Guinea | 342 |
| St. Thomas & Prince Islands | 408 |
| Timor | 343 |

| | | |
|---|---|---|
| No. 569 (1) | .65 | .25 |
| No. 361 (1) | .85 | .40 |
| No. 426 (1) | 2.50 | 1.50 |
| No. 504 (1) | .30 | .25 |
| No. 342 (1) | .95 | .25 |
| No. 408 (1) | .60 | .25 |
| No. 343 (1) | 1.60 | .80 |
| Set total (7) Stamps | 7.45 | 3.70 |

### Lisbon-Rio de Janeiro Flight

OD00

50th anniversary of the Lisbon to Rio de Janeiro flight by Arturo de Sacadura and Coutinho, March 30-June 5, 1922. Each stamp shows a different stage of the flight.

**1972, Sept. 20**

| | |
|---|---|
| Angola | 570 |
| Cape Verde | 362 |
| Macao | 427 |
| Mozambique | 505 |
| Port. Guinea | 343 |
| St. Thomas & Prince Islands | 409 |
| Timor | 344 |

| | | |
|---|---|---|
| No. 570 (1) | .35 | .25 |
| No. 362 (1) | .85 | .40 |
| No. 427 (1) | 40.00 | 12.00 |
| No. 505 (1) | .30 | .25 |
| No. 343 (1) | .35 | .25 |
| No. 100 (1) | .50 | .25 |
| No. 344 (1) | 1.25 | .90 |
| Set total (7) Stamps | 43.60 | 14.30 |

### WMO Centenary

WMO Emblem — CD61

Centenary of international meterological cooperation.

**1973, Dec. 15**

| | |
|---|---|
| Angola | 571 |
| Cape Verde | 363 |
| Macao | 429 |
| Mozambique | 500 |
| Port. Guinea | 344 |
| St. Thomas & Prince Islands | 410 |
| Timor | 345 |

| | | |
|---|---|---|
| No. 571 (1) | .45 | .25 |
| No. 363 (1) | .85 | .40 |
| No. 429 (1) | 15.00 | 2.50 |
| No. 509 (1) | .40 | .25 |
| No. 344 (1) | .55 | .40 |
| No. 410 (1) | .80 | .50 |
| No. 345 (1) | 3.75 | 2.75 |
| Set total (7) Stamps | 21.80 | 7.05 |

### FRENCH COMMUNITY

Upper Volta can be found under Burkina Faso in Vol. 1
Madagascar can be found under Malagasy in Vol. 3

### Colonial Exposition

People of French Empire — CD70

Women's Heads — CD71

France Showing Way to Civilization CD72

"Colonial Commerce" CD73

International Colonial Exposition, Paris.

**1931**

| | |
|---|---|
| Cameroun | 213-216 |
| Chad | 60-63 |
| Dahomey | 97-100 |
| Fr. Guiana | 152-155 |
| Fr. Guinea | 116-119 |
| Fr. India | 100-103 |
| Fr. Polynesia | 76-79 |
| Fr. Sudan | 102-105 |
| Gabon | 120-123 |
| Guadeloupe | 138-141 |
| Indo-China | 140-142 |
| Ivory Coast | 92-95 |
| Madagascar | 169-172 |
| Martinique | 129-132 |
| Mauritania | 65-68 |
| Middle Congo | 61-64 |
| New Caledonia | 176-179 |
| Niger | 73-76 |
| Reunion | 122-125 |
| St. Pierre & Miquelon | 132-135 |
| Senegal | 138-141 |
| Somali Coast | 135-138 |
| Togo | 254-257 |
| Ubangi-Shari | 82-85 |
| Upper Volta | 66-69 |
| Wallis & Futuna Isls. | 85-88 |

| | | |
|---|---|---|
| Nos. 213-216 (4) | 23.00 | 18.25 |
| Nos. 60-63 (4) | 22.00 | 22.00 |
| Nos. 97-100 (4) | 26.00 | 26.00 |
| Nos. 152-155 (4) | 22.00 | 22.00 |
| Nos. 116-119 (4) | 19.75 | 19.75 |
| Nos. 100-103 (4) | 18.00 | 18.00 |
| Nos. 76-79 (4) | 30.00 | 30.00 |
| Nos. 102-105 (4) | 19.00 | 19.00 |
| Nos. 120-123 (4) | 17.50 | 17.50 |
| Nos. 138-141 (4) | 19.00 | 19.00 |
| Nos. 140-142 (3) | 12.00 | 11.50 |
| Nos. 92-95 (4) | 22.50 | 22.50 |
| Nos. 169-172 (4) | 9.25 | 6.50 |
| Nos. 129-132 (4) | 21.00 | 21.00 |
| Nos. 65-68 (4) | 22.00 | 22.00 |
| Nos. 61-64 (4) | 20.00 | 18.50 |
| Nos. 176-179 (4) | 24.00 | 24.00 |
| Nos. 73-76 (4) | 20.50 | 20.50 |
| Nos. 122-125 (4) | 22.00 | 22.00 |
| Nos. 132-135 (4) | 24.00 | 24.00 |
| Nos. 138-141 (4) | 20.00 | 20.00 |
| Nos. 135-138 (4) | 22.00 | 22.00 |
| Nos. 254-257 (4) | 22.00 | 22.00 |
| Nos. 82-85 (4) | 21.00 | 21.00 |
| Nos. 66-69 (4) | 19.00 | 19.00 |
| Nos. 85-88 (4) | 31.00 | 35.00 |
| Set total (103) Stamps | 548.50 | 543.00 |

### Paris International Exposition
### Colonial Arts Exposition

"Colonial Resources"
CD74    CD77

Overseas Commerce CD75

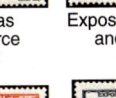
Exposition Building and Women CD76

"France and the Empire" — CD78

Cultural Treasures of the Colonies — CD79

Souvenir sheets contain one imperf. stamp.

**1937**

| | |
|---|---|
| Cameroun | 217-222A |
| Dahomey | 101-107 |
| Fr. Equatorial Africa | 27-32, 73 |
| Fr. Guiana | 162-168 |
| Fr. Guinea | 120-126 |
| Fr. India | 104-110 |
| Fr. Polynesia | 117-123 |
| Fr. Sudan | 106-112 |
| Guadeloupe | 148-154 |
| Indo-China | 193-199 |
| Inini | 41 |
| Ivory Coast | 152-158 |
| Kwangchowan | 132 |
| Madagascar | 191-197 |
| Martinique | 179-185 |
| Mauritania | 69-75 |
| New Caledonia | 208-214 |
| Niger | 77-83 |
| Reunion | 167-173 |
| St. Pierre & Miquelon | 165-171 |
| Senegal | 172-178 |
| Somali Coast | 139-145 |
| Togo | 258-264 |
| Wallis & Futuna Isls. | 89 |

| | | |
|---|---|---|
| Nos. 217-222A (7) | 18.80 | 20.30 |
| Nos. 101-107 (7) | 23.60 | 27.60 |
| Nos. 27-32, 73 (7) | 28.10 | 32.10 |
| Nos. 162-168 (7) | 22.50 | 24.50 |
| Nos. 120-126 (7) | 24.00 | 28.00 |
| Nos. 104-110 (7) | 21.15 | 36.50 |
| Nos. 117-123 (7) | 58.50 | 75.00 |
| Nos. 106-112 (7) | 23.60 | 27.60 |
| Nos. 148-154 (7) | 19.55 | 21.05 |
| Nos. 193-199 (7) | 17.70 | 19.70 |
| No. 41 (1) | 21.00 | 27.50 |
| Nos. 152-158 (7) | 22.20 | 26.20 |
| No. 132 (1) | 9.25 | 11.00 |
| Nos. 191-197 (7) | 19.25 | 21.75 |
| Nos. 179-185 (7) | 19.95 | 21.70 |
| Nos. 69-75 (7) | 20.50 | 24.50 |
| Nos. 208-214 (7) | 39.00 | 50.50 |
| Nos. 73-83 (11) | 40.60 | 45.10 |
| Nos. 107-173 (7) | 21.70 | 23.20 |
| Nos. 165-171 (7) | 49.60 | 64.00 |
| Nos. 172-178 (7) | 21.00 | 23.80 |
| Nos. 139-145 (7) | 25.60 | 32.60 |
| Nos. 258-264 (7) | 20.40 | 20.40 |
| No. 89 (1) | 19.00 | 37.50 |
| Set total (154) Stamps | 606.55 | 742.10 |

### Curie

Pierre and Marie Curie — CD80

40th anniversary of the discovery of radium. The surtax was for the benefit of the Intl. Union for the Control of Cancer.

**1938**

| | |
|---|---|
| Cameroun | B1 |
| Cuba | B1-B2 |
| Dahomey | B2 |
| France | B76 |
| Fr. Equatorial Africa | B1 |
| Fr. Guiana | B3 |
| Fr. Guinea | B2 |
| Fr. India | B6 |
| Fr. Polynesia | B5 |
| Fr. Sudan | B1 |
| Guadeloupe | B3 |
| Indo-China | B14 |
| Ivory Coast | B2 |
| Madagascar | B2 |
| Martinique | B2 |
| Mauritania | B3 |
| New Caledonia | B4 |
| Niger | B1 |
| Reunion | B4 |
| St. Pierre & Miquelon | B3 |
| Senegal | B3 |
| Somali Coast | B2 |
| Togo | B1 |

| | | |
|---|---|---|
| No. B1 (1) | 10.00 | 10.00 |
| Nos. B1-B2 (2) | 12.00 | 3.35 |
| No. B2 (1) | 9.50 | 9.50 |
| No. B76 (1) | 21.00 | 12.50 |
| No. B1 (1) | 24.00 | 24.00 |
| No. B3 (1) | 13.50 | 13.50 |
| No. B2 (1) | 8.75 | 8.75 |
| No. B6 (1) | 10.00 | 10.00 |
| No. B5 (1) | 20.00 | 20.00 |
| No. B1 (1) | 12.50 | 12.50 |
| No. B3 (1) | 11.00 | 10.50 |
| No. B14 (1) | 12.00 | 12.00 |
| No. B2 (1) | 11.00 | 7.50 |
| No. B2 (1) | 11.00 | 11.00 |
| No. B2 (1) | 13.00 | 13.00 |
| No. B3 (1) | 7.75 | 7.75 |
| No. B4 (1) | 16.50 | 17.50 |
| No. B1 (1) | 16.50 | 16.50 |
| No. B4 (1) | 14.00 | 14.00 |
| No. B3 (1) | 21.00 | 22.50 |
| No. B3 (1) | 10.50 | 10.50 |
| No. B2 (1) | 7.75 | 7.75 |
| No. B1 (1) | 20.00 | 20.00 |
| Set total (24) Stamps | 313.25 | 294.60 |

### Caillie

Rene Caillio and Map of Northwestern Africa — CD81

Death centenary of Rene Caillie (1799-1838), French explorer. All three denominations exist with colony name omitted.

**1939**

| | |
|---|---|
| Dahomey | 108-110 |
| Fr. Guinea | 161-163 |
| Fr. Sudan | 113-115 |
| Ivory Coast | 160-162 |
| Mauritania | 109-111 |
| Niger | 84-86 |
| Senegal | 188-190 |
| Togo | 265-267 |

| | | |
|---|---|---|
| Nos. 108-110 (3) | 1.20 | 3.60 |
| Nos. 161-163 (3) | 1.20 | 3.20 |
| Nos. 113-115 (3) | 1.20 | 3.20 |
| Nos. 160-162 (3) | 1.05 | 2.55 |
| Nos. 109-111 (3) | 1.05 | 3.80 |
| Nos. 84-86 (3) | 2.35 | 2.35 |
| Nos. 188-190 (3) | 1.05 | 2.90 |
| Nos. 265-267 (3) | 1.05 | 3.30 |
| Set total (24) Stamps | 10.15 | 24.90 |

### New York World's Fair

Natives and New York Skyline — CD82

**1939**

| | |
|---|---|
| Cameroun | 223-224 |
| Dahomey | 111-112 |
| Fr. Equatorial Africa | 78-79 |
| Fr. Guiana | 169-170 |
| Fr. Guinea | 164-165 |
| Fr. India | 111-112 |
| Fr. Polynesia | 124-125 |
| Fr. Sudan | 116-117 |
| Guadeloupe | 155-156 |
| Indo-China | 203-204 |
| Inini | 42-43 |
| Ivory Coast | 163-164 |
| Kwangchowan | 133-134 |
| Madagascar | 209-210 |
| Martinique | 186-187 |
| Mauritania | 112-113 |
| New Caledonia | 215-216 |
| Niger | 87-88 |
| Reunion | 174-175 |
| St. Pierre & Miquelon | 205-206 |
| Senegal | 191-192 |
| Somali Coast | 179-180 |
| Togo | 268-269 |
| Wallis & Futuna Isls. | 90-91 |

| | | |
|---|---|---|
| Nos. 223-224 (2) | 2.80 | 2.40 |
| Nos. 111-112 (2) | 1.60 | 3.20 |
| Nos. 78-79 (2) | 1.60 | 3.20 |
| Nos. 169-170 (2) | 2.60 | 2.60 |
| Nos. 164-165 (2) | 1.60 | 3.20 |
| Nos. 111-112 (2) | 3.00 | 8.00 |
| Nos. 124-125 (2) | 4.80 | 4.80 |
| Nos. 116-117 (2) | 1.60 | 3.20 |
| Nos. 155-156 (2) | 2.50 | 2.50 |
| Nos. 203-204 (2) | 2.05 | 2.05 |
| Nos. 42-43 (2) | 7.50 | 9.00 |
| Nos. 163-164 (2) | 1.50 | 3.00 |
| Nos. 133-134 (2) | 2.50 | 2.50 |
| Nos. 209-210 (2) | 1.50 | 2.50 |

# COMMON DESIGN TYPES

| | | |
|---|---|---|
| Nos. 186-187 (2) | 2.35 | 2.35 |
| Nos. 112-113 (2) | 1.40 | 2.80 |
| Nos. 215-216 (2) | 3.35 | 3.35 |
| Nos. 87-88 (2) | 1.60 | 2.80 |
| Nos. 174-175 (2) | 2.80 | 2.80 |
| Nos. 205-206 (2) | 4.80 | 6.00 |
| Nos. 191-192 (2) | 1.40 | 2.80 |
| Nos. 179-180 (2) | 1.40 | 2.80 |
| Nos. 268-269 (2) | 1.40 | 2.80 |
| Nos. 90-91 (2) | 5.00 | 6.00 |
| Set total (48) Stamps | 62.65 | 86.65 |

## French Revolution

Storming of the Bastille — CD83

French Revolution, 150th anniv. The surtax was for the defense of the colonies.

### 1939

| | |
|---|---|
| Cameroun | B2-B6 |
| Dahomey | B3-B7 |
| Fr. Equatorial Africa | B4-B8, CB1 |
| Fr. Guiana | B4-B8, CB1 |
| Fr. Guinea | B3-B7 |
| Fr. India | B7-B11 |
| Fr. Polynesia | B6-B10, CB1 |
| Fr. Sudan | B2-B6 |
| Guadeloupe | B4-B8 |
| Indo-China | B15-B19, CB1 |
| Inini | B1-B5 |
| Ivory Coast | B3-B7 |
| Kwangchowan | B1-B5 |
| Madagascar | B3-B7, CB1 |
| Martinique | B3-B7 |
| Mauritania | B4-B8 |
| New Caledonia | B5-B9, CB1 |
| Niger | B2-B6 |
| Reunion | B5-B9, CB1 |
| St. Pierre & Miquelon | B4-B8 |
| Senegal | B4-B8, CB1 |
| Somali Coast | B3-B7 |
| Togo | B2-B6 |
| Wallis & Futuna Isls. | B1-B5 |

| | | |
|---|---|---|
| Nos. B2-B6 (5) | 60.00 | 60.00 |
| Nos. B3-B7 (5) | 47.50 | 47.50 |
| Nos. B4-B8,CB1 (6) | 120.00 | 120.00 |
| Nos. B4-B8,CB1 (6) | 79.50 | 79.50 |
| Nos. B3-B7 (5) | 47.50 | 47.50 |
| Nos. B7-B11 (5) | 28.75 | 32.50 |
| Nos. B6-B10,CB1 (6) | 122.50 | 122.50 |
| Nos. B2-B6 (5) | 50.00 | 50.00 |
| Nos. B4-B8 (5) | 50.00 | 50.00 |
| Nos. B15-B19,CB1 (6) | 85.00 | 85.00 |
| Nos. B1-B5 (5) | 80.00 | 100.00 |
| Nos. B3-B7 (5) | 43.75 | 43.75 |
| Nos. B1-B5 (5) | 46.25 | 46.25 |
| Nos. B3-B7,CB1 (6) | 65.50 | 65.50 |
| Nos. B3-B7 (5) | 52.50 | 52.50 |
| Nos. B4-B8 (5) | 42.50 | 42.50 |
| Nos. B5-B9,CB1 (6) | 101.50 | 101.50 |
| Nos. B2-B6 (5) | 60.00 | 60.00 |
| Nos. B5-B9,CB1 (6) | 87.50 | 87.50 |
| Nos. B4-B8 (5) | 67.50 | 72.50 |
| Nos. B4-B8,CB1 (6) | 56.50 | 56.50 |
| Nos. B3-B7 (5) | 45.00 | 45.00 |
| Nos. B2-B6 (5) | 42.50 | 42.50 |
| Nos. B1-B5 (5) | 80.00 | 110.00 |
| Set total (128) Stamps | 1,562. | 1,621. |

Plane over Coastal Area — CD85

All five denominations exist with colony name omitted.

### 1940

| | |
|---|---|
| Dahomey | C1-C5 |
| Fr. Guinea | C1-C5 |
| Fr. Sudan | C1-C5 |
| Ivory Coast | C1-C5 |
| Mauritania | C1-C5 |
| Niger | C1-C5 |
| Senegal | C12-C16 |
| Togo | C1-C5 |

| | | |
|---|---|---|
| Nos. C1-C5 (5) | 4.00 | 4.00 |
| Nos. C1-C5 (5) | 4.00 | 4.00 |
| Nos. C1-C5 (5) | 4.00 | 4.00 |
| Nos. C1-C5 (5) | 3.80 | 3.80 |
| Nos. C1-C5 (5) | 3.50 | 3.50 |
| Nos. C1-C5 (5) | 3.50 | 3.50 |
| Nos. C12-C16 (5) | 3.50 | 3.50 |
| Nos. C1-C5 (5) | 3.15 | 3.15 |
| Set total (40) Stamps | 29.45 | 29.45 |

## Defense of the Empire

Colonial Infantryman — CD86

### 1941

| | |
|---|---|
| Cameroun | B13B |
| Dahomey | B13 |
| Fr. Equatorial Africa | B8B |
| Fr. Guiana | B10 |
| Fr. Guinea | B13 |
| Fr. India | B13 |
| Fr. Polynesia | B12 |
| Fr. Sudan | B12 |
| Guadeloupe | B10 |
| Indo-China | B19B |
| Inini | B7 |
| Ivory Coast | B13 |
| Kwangchowan | B7 |
| Madagascar | B9 |
| Martinique | B9 |
| Mauritania | B14 |
| New Caledonia | B11 |
| Niger | B12 |
| Reunion | B11 |
| St. Pierre & Miquelon | B8B |
| Senegal | B14 |
| Somali Coast | B9 |
| Togo | B10B |
| Wallis & Futuna Isls. | B7 |

| | |
|---|---|
| No. B13B (1) | 1.60 |
| No. B13 (1) | 1.20 |
| No. B8B (1) | 3.50 |
| No. B10 (1) | 1.40 |
| No. B13 (1) | 1.40 |
| No. B13 (1) | 1.25 |
| No. B12 (1) | 3.50 |
| No. B12 (1) | 1.40 |
| No. B10 (1) | 1.00 |
| No. B19B (1) | 3.00 |
| No. B7 (1) | 1.75 |
| No. B13 (1) | 1.25 |
| No. B7 (1) | .85 |
| No. B9 (1) | 1.50 |
| No. B9 (1) | 1.40 |
| No. B14 (1) | .95 |
| No. B11 (1) | 1.60 |
| No. B12 (1) | 1.40 |
| No. B11 (1) | 1.60 |
| No. B8B (1) | 4.50 |
| No. B14 (1) | 1.25 |
| No. B9 (1) | 1.60 |
| No. B10B (1) | 1.10 |
| No. B7 (1) | 1.75 |
| Set total (23) Stamps | 40.15 |

Each of the CD86 stamps listed above is part of a set of three stamps. The designs of the other two stamps in the set vary from country to country. Only the values of the Common Design stamps are listed here.

## Colonial Education Fund

CD86a

### 1942

| | |
|---|---|
| Cameroun | CB3 |
| Dahomey | CB4 |
| Fr. Equatorial Africa | CB5 |
| Fr. Guiana | CB4 |
| Fr. Guinea | CB4 |
| Fr. India | CB3 |
| Fr. Polynesia | CB4 |
| Fr. Sudan | CB4 |
| Guadeloupe | CB3 |
| Indo-China | CB5 |
| Inini | CB3 |
| Ivory Coast | CB4 |
| Kwangchowan | CB4 |
| Malagasy | CB5 |
| Martinique | CB3 |
| Mauritania | CB4 |
| New Caledonia | CB4 |
| Niger | CB4 |
| Reunion | CB4 |
| St. Pierre & Miquelon | CB3 |
| Senegal | CB5 |
| Somali Coast | CB3 |
| Togo | CB3 |
| Wallis & Futuna | CB3 |

| | | |
|---|---|---|
| No. CB3 (1) | 1.10 | |
| No. CB4 (1) | .80 | 5.50 |
| No. CB5 (1) | .80 | |
| No. CB4 (1) | 1.10 | |
| No. CB4 (1) | .40 | 5.50 |
| No. CB3 (1) | .90 | |
| No. CB4 (1) | 2.00 | |
| No. CB4 (1) | .40 | 5.50 |
| No. CB3 (1) | 1.10 | |
| No. CB5 (1) | 2.00 | |
| No. CB3 (1) | 1.25 | |
| No. CB4 (1) | 1.00 | 5.50 |
| No. CB4 (1) | 1.00 | |
| No. CB5 (1) | .65 | |
| No. CB3 (1) | 1.00 | |
| No. CB4 (1) | .80 | |
| No. CB4 (1) | 2.25 | |
| No. CB4 (1) | .35 | |
| No. CB4 (1) | .90 | |
| No. CB3 (1) | 7.00 | |
| No. CB5 (1) | .80 | 6.50 |
| No. CB3 (1) | .70 | |
| No. CB3 (1) | .35 | |
| No. CB3 (1) | 2.00 | |
| Set total (24) Stamps | 30.65 | 28.50 |

Cross of Lorraine & Four-motor Plane — CD87

### 1941-5

| | |
|---|---|
| Cameroun | C1-C7 |
| Fr. Equatorial Africa | C17-C23 |
| Fr. Guiana | C9-C10 |
| Fr. India | C1-C6 |
| Fr. Polynesia | C3-C9 |
| Fr. West Africa | C1-C3 |
| Guadeloupe | C1-C2 |
| Madagascar | C37-C43 |
| Martinique | C1-C2 |
| New Caledonia | C7-C13 |
| Reunion | C18-C24 |
| St. Pierre & Miquelon | C1-C7 |
| Somali Coast | C1-C7 |

| | | |
|---|---|---|
| Nos. C1-C7 (7) | 6.30 | 6.30 |
| Nos. C17-C23 (7) | 10.40 | 6.35 |
| Nos. C9-C10 (2) | 3.80 | 3.10 |
| Nos. C1-C6 (6) | 9.30 | 15.00 |
| Nos. C3-C9 (7) | 13.75 | 10.00 |
| Nos. C1-C3 (3) | 9.50 | 3.90 |
| Nos. C1-C2 (2) | 3.75 | 2.50 |
| Nos. C37-C43 (7) | 5.60 | 3.80 |
| Nos. C1-C2 (2) | 3.00 | 1.60 |
| Nos. C7-C13 (7) | 8.85 | 7.30 |
| Nos. C18-C24 (7) | 7.05 | 5.00 |
| Nos. C1-C7 (7) | 11.60 | 9.40 |
| Nos. C1-C7 (7) | 13.95 | 11.10 |
| Set total (71) Stamps | 106.85 | 85.35 |

Somali Coast stamps are inscribed "Djibouti".

Transport Plane — CD88

Caravan and Plane — CD89

### 1942

| | |
|---|---|
| Dahomey | C6-C13 |
| Fr. Guinea | C6-C13 |
| Fr. Sudan | C6-C13 |
| Ivory Coast | C6-C13 |
| Mauritania | C6-C13 |
| Niger | C6-C13 |
| Senegal | C17-C25 |
| Togo | C6-C13 |

| | |
|---|---|
| Nos. C6-C13 (8) | 7.15 |
| Nos. C6-C13 (8) | 5.75 |
| Nos. C6-C13 (8) | 8.00 |
| Nos. C6-C13 (8) | 11.15 |
| Nos. C6-C13 (8) | 9.75 |
| Nos. C6-C13 (8) | 6.20 |
| Nos. C17-C25 (9) | 9.45 |
| Nos. C6-C13 (8) | 6.75 |
| Set total (65) Stamps | 64.20 |

## Red Cross

Marianne CD90

The surtax was for the French Red Cross and national relief.

### 1944

| | |
|---|---|
| Cameroun | B28 |
| Fr. Equatorial Africa | B38 |
| Fr. Guiana | B12 |
| Fr. India | B14 |
| Fr. Polynesia | B13 |
| Fr. West Africa | B1 |
| Guadeloupe | B12 |
| Madagascar | B15 |
| Martinique | B11 |
| New Caledonia | B13 |
| Reunion | B15 |
| St. Pierre & Miquelon | B13 |
| Somali Coast | B13 |
| Wallis & Futuna Isls. | B9 |

| | | |
|---|---|---|
| No. B28 (1) | 2.00 | 1.60 |
| No. B38 (1) | 1.60 | 1.20 |
| No. B12 (1) | 1.75 | 1.25 |
| No. B14 (1) | 1.50 | 1.25 |
| No. B13 (1) | 2.00 | 1.60 |
| No. B1 (1) | 6.50 | 4.75 |
| No. B12 (1) | 1.40 | 1.00 |
| No. B15 (1) | .90 | .90 |
| No. B11 (1) | 1.20 | 1.20 |
| No. B13 (1) | 1.50 | 1.50 |
| No. B15 (1) | 1.60 | 1.10 |
| No. B13 (1) | 2.60 | 2.60 |
| No. B13 (1) | 1.75 | 2.00 |
| No. B9 (1) | 3.00 | 3.00 |
| Set total (14) Stamps | 29.30 | 24.95 |

## Eboue

CD91

Felix Eboue, first French colonial administrator to proclaim resistance to Germany after French surrender in World War II.

### 1945

| | |
|---|---|
| Cameroun | 296-297 |
| Fr. Equatorial Africa | 156-157 |
| Fr. Guiana | 171-172 |
| Fr. India | 210-211 |
| Fr. Polynesia | 150-151 |
| Fr. West Africa | 15-16 |
| Guadeloupe | 187-188 |
| Madagascar | 259-260 |
| Martinique | 196-197 |
| New Caledonia | 274-275 |
| Reunion | 238-239 |
| St. Pierre & Miquelon | 322-323 |
| Somali Coast | 238-239 |

| | | |
|---|---|---|
| Nos. 296-297 (2) | 2.40 | 1.95 |
| Nos. 156-157 (2) | 2.55 | 2.00 |
| Nos. 171-172 (2) | 2.45 | 2.00 |
| Nos. 210-211 (2) | 2.20 | 1.95 |
| Nos. 150-151 (2) | 3.60 | 2.85 |
| Nos. 15-16 (2) | 2.40 | 2.40 |
| Nos. 187-188 (2) | 2.05 | 1.60 |
| Nos. 259-260 (2) | 2.00 | 1.45 |
| Nos. 196-197 (2) | 2.05 | 1.55 |
| Nos. 274-275 (2) | 3.40 | 3.00 |
| Nos. 238-239 (2) | 2.40 | 2.00 |
| Nos. 322-323 (2) | 4.40 | 3.45 |
| Nos. 238-239 (2) | 2.45 | 2.10 |
| Set total (26) Stamps | 34.35 | 28.30 |

## Victory

Victory CD92

European victory of the Allied Nations in World War II.

### 1946, May 8

| | |
|---|---|
| Cameroun | C8 |
| Fr. Equatorial Africa | C24 |
| Fr. Guiana | C11 |
| Fr. India | C7 |

# COMMON DESIGN TYPES 35A

| | |
|---|---|
| Fr. Polynesia | C10 |
| Fr. West Africa | C4 |
| Guadeloupe | C3 |
| Indo-China | C19 |
| Madagascar | C44 |
| Martinique | C3 |
| New Caledonia | C14 |
| Reunion | C25 |
| St. Pierre & Miquelon | C8 |
| Somali Coast | C8 |
| Wallis & Futuna Isls. | C1 |

| | | |
|---|---|---|
| No. C8 (1) | 1.60 | 1.20 |
| No. C24 (1) | 1.60 | 1.25 |
| No. C11 (1) | 1.75 | 1.25 |
| No. C7 (1) | 1.00 | 4.00 |
| No. C10 (1) | 2.75 | 2.00 |
| No. C4 (1) | 1.60 | 1.20 |
| No. C3 (1) | 1.25 | 1.00 |
| No. C19 (1) | 1.00 | .55 |
| No. C44 (1) | 1.00 | .35 |
| No. C3 (1) | 1.30 | 1.00 |
| No. C14 (1) | 1.50 | 1.25 |
| No. C25 (1) | 1.10 | .90 |
| No. C8 (1) | 2.10 | 2.10 |
| No. C8 (1) | 1.75 | 1.40 |
| No. C1 (1) | 2.25 | 1.90 |
| Set total (15) Stamps | 23.55 | 21.35 |

## Chad to Rhine

Leclerc's Departure from Chad CD93

Battle at Cufra Oasis CD94

Tanks in Action, Mareth CD95

Normandy Invasion CD96

Entering Paris CD97

Liberation of Strasbourg CD98

"Chad to the Rhine" march, 1942-44, by Gen. Jacques Leclerc's column, later French 2nd Armored Division.

### 1946, June 6

| | |
|---|---|
| Cameroun | C9-C14 |
| Fr. Equatorial Africa | C25-C30 |
| Fr. Guiana | C12-C17 |
| Fr. India | C8-C13 |
| Fr. Polynesia | C11-C16 |
| Fr. West Africa | C5-C10 |
| Guadeloupe | C4-C9 |
| Indo-China | C20-C25 |
| Madagascar | C45-C50 |
| Martinique | C4-C9 |
| New Caledonia | C15-C20 |
| Reunion | C26-C31 |
| St. Pierre & Miquelon | C9-C14 |
| Somali Coast | C9-C14 |
| Wallis & Futuna Isls. | C2-C7 |

| | | |
|---|---|---|
| Nos. C9-C14 (6) | 12.05 | 9.70 |
| Nos. C25-C30 (6) | 14.70 | 10.80 |
| Nos. C12-C17 (6) | 12.65 | 10.35 |
| Nos. C8-C13 (6) | 12.80 | 15.00 |
| Nos. C11-C16 (6) | 17.55 | 13.40 |
| Nos. C5-C10 (6) | 16.05 | 11.95 |
| Nos. C4-C9 (6) | 12.00 | 9.60 |
| Nos. C20-C25 (6) | 6.40 | 6.40 |
| Nos. C45-C50 (6) | 10.30 | 8.40 |
| Nos. C4-C9 (6) | 8.85 | 7.30 |
| Nos. C15-C20 (6) | 13.40 | 11.90 |
| Nos. C26-C31 (6) | 10.25 | 6.55 |
| Nos. C9-C14 (6) | 17.30 | 14.35 |
| Nos. C9-C14 (6) | 18.10 | 12.65 |
| Nos. C2-C7 (6) | 13.75 | 10.45 |
| Set total (90) Stamps | 196.15 | 158.80 |

## UPU

French Colonials, Globe and Plane CD99

Universal Postal Union, 75th anniv.

### 1949, July 4

| | |
|---|---|
| Cameroun | C29 |
| Fr. Equatorial Africa | C34 |
| Fr. India | C17 |
| Fr. Polynesia | C20 |
| Fr. West Africa | C15 |
| Indo-China | C26 |
| Madagascar | C55 |
| New Caledonia | C24 |
| St. Pierre & Miquelon | C18 |
| Somali Coast | C18 |
| Togo | C18 |
| Wallis & Futuna Isls. | C10 |

| | | |
|---|---|---|
| No. C29 (1) | 8.00 | 4.75 |
| No. C34 (1) | 16.00 | 12.00 |
| No. C17 (1) | 11.50 | 8.75 |
| No. C20 (1) | 20.00 | 15.00 |
| No. C15 (1) | 12.00 | 8.75 |
| No. C26 (1) | 4.75 | 4.00 |
| No. C55 (1) | 4.00 | 2.75 |
| No. C24 (1) | 7.50 | 5.00 |
| No. C18 (1) | 20.00 | 12.00 |
| No. C18 (1) | 14.00 | 10.50 |
| No. C18 (1) | 8.50 | 7.00 |
| No. C10 (1) | 11.00 | 8.25 |
| Set total (12) Stamps | 137.25 | 98.75 |

## Tropical Medicine

Doctor Treating Infant — CD100

The surtax was for charitable work.

### 1950

| | |
|---|---|
| Cameroun | B29 |
| Fr. Equatorial Africa | B39 |
| Fr. India | B15 |
| Fr. Polynesia | B14 |
| Fr. West Africa | B3 |
| Madagascar | B17 |
| New Caledonia | B14 |
| St. Pierre & Miquelon | B14 |
| Somali Coast | B14 |
| Togo | B11 |

| | | |
|---|---|---|
| No. B29 (1) | 7.25 | 5.50 |
| No. B39 (1) | 7.25 | 5.50 |
| No. B15 (1) | 6.00 | 4.00 |
| No. B14 (1) | 10.50 | 8.00 |
| No. B3 (1) | 9.50 | 7.25 |
| No. B17 (1) | 5.50 | 5.50 |
| No. B14 (1) | 6.75 | 5.25 |
| No. B14 (1) | 16.00 | 15.00 |
| No. B14 (1) | 7.75 | 6.25 |
| No. B11 (1) | 5.00 | 3.50 |
| Set total (10) Stamps | 81.50 | 65.75 |

## Military Medal

Medal, Early Marine and Colonial Soldier — CD101

Centenary of the creation of the French Military Medal.

### 1952

| | |
|---|---|
| Cameroun | 322 |
| Comoro Isls. | 39 |
| Fr. Equatorial Africa | 186 |
| Fr. India | 233 |
| Fr. Polynesia | 179 |
| Fr. West Africa | 57 |
| Madagascar | 286 |
| New Caledonia | 295 |
| St. Pierre & Miquelon | 345 |
| Somali Coast | 267 |
| Togo | 327 |
| Wallis & Futuna Isls. | 149 |

| | | |
|---|---|---|
| No. 322 (1) | 7.25 | 3.25 |
| No. 39 (1) | 45.00 | 37.50 |
| No. 186 (1) | 8.00 | 5.50 |
| No. 233 (1) | 5.50 | 7.00 |
| No. 179 (1) | 13.50 | 10.00 |
| No. 57 (1) | 8.75 | 6.50 |
| No. 286 (1) | 3.75 | 2.50 |
| No. 295 (1) | 6.50 | 6.00 |
| No. 345 (1) | 16.00 | 15.00 |
| No. 267 (1) | 9.00 | 8.00 |
| No. 327 (1) | 5.50 | 4.75 |
| No. 149 (1) | 7.25 | 7.25 |
| Set total (12) Stamps | 136.00 | 113.25 |

## Liberation

Allied Landing, Victory Sign and Cross of Lorraine CD102

Liberation of France, 10th anniv.

### 1954, June 6

| | |
|---|---|
| Cameroun | C32 |
| Comoro Isls. | C4 |
| Fr. Equatorial Africa | C38 |
| Fr. India | C18 |
| Fr. Polynesia | C22 |
| Fr. West Africa | C17 |
| Madagascar | C57 |
| New Caledonia | C25 |
| St. Pierre & Miquelon | C19 |
| Somali Coast | C19 |
| Togo | C19 |
| Wallis & Futuna Isls. | C11 |

| | | |
|---|---|---|
| No. C32 (1) | 7.25 | 4.75 |
| No. C4 (1) | 32.50 | 19.00 |
| No. C38 (1) | 12.00 | 8.00 |
| No. C18 (1) | 11.00 | 8.00 |
| No. C22 (1) | 10.00 | 8.00 |
| No. C17 (1) | 12.00 | 5.50 |
| No. C57 (1) | 3.25 | 2.00 |
| No. C25 (1) | 7.50 | 5.00 |
| No. C19 (1) | 19.00 | 12.00 |
| No. C19 (1) | 10.50 | 8.50 |
| No. C19 (1) | 7.00 | 5.50 |
| No. C11 (1) | 11.00 | 8.25 |
| Set total (12) Stamps | 143.00 | 94.50 |

## FIDES

Plowmen CD103

Efforts of FIDES, the Economic and Social Development Fund for Overseas Possessions (Fonds d' Investissement pour le Developpement Economique et Social). Each stamp has a different design.

### 1956

| | |
|---|---|
| Cameroun | 326-329 |
| Comoro Isls. | 43 |
| Fr. Equatorial Africa | 180-192 |
| Fr. Polynesia | 181 |
| Fr. West Africa | 65-72 |
| Madagascar | 292-295 |
| New Caledonia | 303 |
| St. Pierre & Miquelon | 350 |
| Somali Coast | 268-269 |
| Togo | 331 |

| | | |
|---|---|---|
| Nos. 326-329 (4) | 6.90 | 3.20 |
| No. 43 (1) | 2.25 | 1.60 |
| Nos. 189-192 (4) | 3.20 | 1.65 |
| No. 181 (1) | 4.00 | 2.00 |
| Nos. 65-72 (8) | 16.00 | 6.35 |
| Nos. 292-295 (4) | 2.25 | 1.20 |
| No. 303 (1) | 1.90 | 1.10 |
| No. 350 (1) | 6.00 | 4.00 |
| Nos. 268-269 (2) | 5.35 | 3.15 |
| No. 331 (1) | 4.25 | 2.10 |
| Set total (27) Stamps | 52.10 | 26.35 |

## Flower

CD104

Each stamp shows a different flower.

### 1958-9

| | |
|---|---|
| Cameroun | 333 |
| Comoro Isls. | 45 |
| Fr. Equatorial Africa | 200-201 |
| Fr. Polynesia | 192 |
| Fr. So. & Antarctic Terr. | 11 |
| Fr. West Africa | 79-83 |
| Madagascar | 301-302 |
| New Caledonia | 304-305 |
| St. Pierre & Miquelon | 357 |
| Somali Coast | 270 |
| Togo | 348-349 |
| Wallis & Futuna Isls. | 152 |

| | | |
|---|---|---|
| No. 333 (1) | 1.60 | .80 |
| No. 45 (1) | 5.25 | 4.25 |
| Nos. 200-201 (2) | 3.60 | 1.60 |
| No. 192 (1) | 6.50 | 4.00 |
| No. 11 (1) | 8.75 | 7.50 |
| Nos. 79-83 (5) | 10.45 | 5.60 |
| Nos. 301-302 (2) | 1.60 | .60 |
| Nos. 304-305 (2) | 8.00 | 3.00 |
| No. 357 (1) | 4.50 | 2.25 |
| No. 270 (1) | 4.25 | 1.40 |
| Nos. 348-349 (2) | 1.10 | .50 |
| No. 152 (1) | 3.25 | 3.25 |
| Set total (20) Stamps | 58.85 | 34.75 |

## Human Rights

Sun, Dove and U.N. Emblem CD105

10th anniversary of the signing of the Universal Declaration of Human Rights.

### 1958

| | |
|---|---|
| Comoro Isls. | 44 |
| Fr. Equatorial Africa | 202 |
| Fr. Polynesia | 191 |
| Fr. West Africa | 85 |
| Madagascar | 300 |
| New Caledonia | 306 |
| St. Pierre & Miquelon | 356 |
| Somali Coast | 274 |
| Wallis & Futuna Isls. | 153 |

| | | |
|---|---|---|
| No. 44 (1) | 9.00 | 9.00 |
| No. 202 (1) | 2.40 | 1.25 |
| No. 191 (1) | 13.00 | 8.75 |
| No. 85 (1) | 2.40 | 2.00 |
| No. 300 (1) | .80 | .40 |
| No. 306 (1) | 2.00 | 1.50 |
| No. 356 (1) | 3.50 | 2.50 |
| No. 274 (1) | 3.50 | 2.10 |
| No. 153 (1) | 4.50 | 4.50 |
| Set total (9) Stamps | 41.10 | 32.00 |

## C.C.T.A.

CD106

Commission for Technical Cooperation in Africa south of the Sahara, 10th anniv.

### 1960

| | |
|---|---|
| Cameroun | 339 |
| Cent. Africa | 3 |
| Chad | 66 |
| Congo, P.R. | 90 |
| Dahomey | 138 |
| Gabon | 150 |
| Ivory Coast | 180 |
| Madagascar | 317 |
| Mali | 9 |
| Mauritania | 117 |
| Niger | 104 |
| Upper Volta | 89 |

| | | |
|---|---|---|
| No. 339 (1) | 1.60 | .75 |
| No. 3 (1) | 1.60 | .75 |
| No. 66 (1) | 1.75 | .50 |
| No. 90 (1) | 1.00 | 1.00 |
| No. 138 (1) | .50 | .50 |
| No. 150 (1) | 1.25 | 1.10 |
| No. 180 (1) | 1.10 | .50 |
| No. 317 (1) | .60 | .30 |
| No. 9 (1) | 1.20 | .50 |
| No. 117 (1) | .75 | .40 |
| No. 104 (1) | .85 | .45 |
| No. 89 (1) | .65 | .40 |
| Set total (12) Stamps | 12.85 | 6.90 |

## COMMON DESIGN TYPES

### Air Afrique, 1961

Modern and Ancient Africa, Map and Planes — CD107

Founding of Air Afrique (African Airlines).

**1961-62**

| | |
|---|---|
| Cameroun | C37 |
| Cent. Africa | C5 |
| Chad | C7 |
| Congo, P.R. | C5 |
| Dahomey | C17 |
| Gabon | C5 |
| Ivory Coast | C18 |
| Mauritania | C17 |
| Niger | C22 |
| Senegal | C31 |
| Upper Volta | C4 |

| | | |
|---|---|---|
| No. C37 (1) | 1.00 | .50 |
| No. C5 (1) | 1.00 | .65 |
| No. C7 (1) | 1.00 | .25 |
| No. C5 (1) | 1.75 | .90 |
| No. C17 (1) | .80 | .40 |
| No. C5 (1) | 11.00 | 6.00 |
| No. C18 (1) | 2.00 | 1.25 |
| No. C17 (1) | 2.40 | 1.25 |
| No. C22 (1) | 1.75 | .90 |
| No. C31 (1) | .80 | .30 |
| No. C4 (1) | 3.50 | 1.75 |
| Set total (11) Stamps | 27.00 | 14.15 |

### Anti-Malaria

 CD108

World Health Organization drive to eradicate malaria.

**1962, Apr. 7**

| | |
|---|---|
| Cameroun | B36 |
| Cent. Africa | B1 |
| Chad | B1 |
| Comoro Isls. | B1 |
| Congo, P.R. | B3 |
| Dahomey | B15 |
| Gabon | B4 |
| Ivory Coast | B15 |
| Madagascar | B19 |
| Mali | B1 |
| Mauritania | B16 |
| Niger | B14 |
| Senegal | B16 |
| Somali Coast | B15 |
| Upper Volta | B1 |

| | | |
|---|---|---|
| No. B36 (1) | 1.00 | .45 |
| No. B1 (1) | 1.40 | 1.40 |
| No. B1 (1) | 1.00 | .50 |
| No. B1 (1) | 3.50 | 3.50 |
| No. B3 (1) | 1.40 | 1.00 |
| No. B15 (1) | .75 | .75 |
| No. B4 (1) | 1.00 | 1.00 |
| No. B15 (1) | 1.25 | 1.25 |
| No. B19 (1) | .75 | .50 |
| No. B1 (1) | 1.25 | .60 |
| No. B16 (1) | .50 | .50 |
| No. B14 (1) | .75 | .75 |
| No. B16 (1) | 1.10 | .65 |
| No. B15 (1) | 7.00 | 7.00 |
| No. B1 (1) | .75 | .70 |
| Set total (15) Stamps | 23.40 | 20.55 |

### Abidjan Games

 CD109

Abidjan Games, Ivory Coast, Dec. 24-31, 1961. Each stamp shows a different sport.

**1962**

| | |
|---|---|
| Cent. Africa | 19-20, C6 |
| Chad | 83-84, C8 |
| Congo, P.R. | 103-104, C7 |
| Gabon | 163-164, C6 |
| Niger | 109-111 |
| Upper Volta | 103-105 |

| | | |
|---|---|---|
| Nos. 19-20,C6 (3) | 4.15 | 2.85 |
| Nos. 83-84,C8 (3) | 5.80 | 1.55 |
| Nos. 103-104,C7 (3) | 3.85 | 1.80 |
| Nos. 163-164,C6 (3) | 5.00 | 3.00 |
| Nos. 109-111 (3) | 2.60 | 1.25 |
| Nos. 103-105 (3) | 2.80 | 1.75 |
| Set total (18) Stamps | 24.20 | 12.20 |

### African and Malagasy Union

Flag of Union — CD110

First anniversary of the Union.

**1962, Sept. 8**

| | |
|---|---|
| Cameroun | 373 |
| Cent. Africa | 21 |
| Chad | 85 |
| Congo, P.R. | 105 |
| Dahomey | 155 |
| Gabon | 165 |
| Ivory Coast | 198 |
| Madagascar | 332 |
| Mauritania | 170 |
| Niger | 112 |
| Senegal | 211 |
| Upper Volta | 106 |

| | | |
|---|---|---|
| No. 373 (1) | 2.00 | .75 |
| No. 21 (1) | 1.25 | .75 |
| No. 85 (1) | 1.25 | .25 |
| No. 105 (1) | 1.50 | .50 |
| No. 155 (1) | 1.25 | .90 |
| No. 165 (1) | 1.60 | 1.25 |
| No. 198 (1) | 2.10 | .75 |
| No. 332 (1) | .80 | .80 |
| No. 170 (1) | .75 | .50 |
| No. 112 (1) | .80 | .50 |
| No. 211 (1) | .80 | .50 |
| No. 106 (1) | 1.10 | .75 |
| Set total (12) Stamps | 15.20 | 8.20 |

### Telstar

Telstar and Globe Showing Andover and Pleumeur-Bodou — CD111

First television connection of the United States and Europe through the Telstar satellite, July 11-12, 1962.

**1962-63**

| | |
|---|---|
| Andorra, French | 154 |
| Comoro Isls. | C7 |
| Fr. Polynesia | C29 |
| Fr. So. & Antarctic Terr. | C5 |
| New Caledonia | C33 |
| St. Pierre & Miquelon | C26 |
| Somali Coast | C31 |
| Wallis & Futuna Isls. | C17 |

| | | |
|---|---|---|
| No. 154 (1) | 2.00 | 1.60 |
| No. C7 (1) | 4.50 | 2.75 |
| No. C29 (1) | 11.50 | 8.00 |
| No. C5 (1) | 29.00 | 21.00 |
| No. C33 (1) | 25.00 | 18.50 |
| No. C26 (1) | 7.25 | 4.50 |
| No. C31 (1) | 1.00 | 1.00 |
| No. C17 (1) | 3.75 | 3.75 |
| Set total (8) Stamps | 84.00 | 61.10 |

### Freedom From Hunger

World Map and Wheat Emblem — CD112

U.N. Food and Agriculture Organization's "Freedom from Hunger" campaign.

**1963, Mar. 21**

| | |
|---|---|
| Cameroun | B37-B38 |
| Cent. Africa | B2 |
| Chad | B2 |
| Congo, P.R. | B4 |
| Dahomey | B16 |
| Gabon | B5 |
| Ivory Coast | B16 |
| Madagascar | B21 |
| Mauritania | B17 |
| Niger | B15 |
| Senegal | B17 |
| Upper Volta | B2 |

| | | |
|---|---|---|
| Nos. B37-B38 (2) | 2.25 | .75 |
| No. B2 (1) | 1.25 | 1.25 |
| No. B2 (1) | 1.10 | .50 |
| No. B4 (1) | 1.40 | 1.00 |
| No. B16 (1) | .80 | .80 |
| No. B5 (1) | 1.00 | 1.00 |
| No. B16 (1) | 1.50 | 1.50 |
| No. B21 (1) | .60 | .45 |
| No. B17 (1) | .60 | .60 |
| No. B15 (1) | .75 | .75 |
| No. B17 (1) | .80 | .50 |
| No. B2 (1) | .75 | .70 |
| Set total (13) Stamps | 12.80 | 9.80 |

### Red Cross Centenary

 CD113

Centenary of the International Red Cross.

**1963, Sept. 2**

| | |
|---|---|
| Comoro Isls. | 55 |
| Fr. Polynesia | 205 |
| New Caledonia | 328 |
| St. Pierre & Miquelon | 367 |
| Somali Coast | 297 |
| Wallis & Futuna Isls. | 165 |

| | | |
|---|---|---|
| No. 55 (1) | 7.50 | 6.00 |
| No. 205 (1) | 15.00 | 12.00 |
| No. 328 (1) | 8.00 | 6.75 |
| No. 367 (1) | 12.00 | 5.50 |
| No. 297 (1) | 6.25 | 6.25 |
| No. 165 (1) | 4.00 | 4.00 |
| Set total (6) Stamps | 52.75 | 40.50 |

### African Postal Union, 1963

UAMPT Emblem, Radio Masts, Plane and Mail — CD114

Establishment of the African and Malagasy Posts and Telecommunications Union.

**1963, Sept. 8**

| | |
|---|---|
| Cameroun | C47 |
| Cent. Africa | C10 |
| Chad | C9 |
| Congo, P.R. | C13 |
| Dahomey | C19 |
| Gabon | C13 |
| Ivory Coast | C25 |
| Madagascar | C75 |
| Mauritania | C22 |
| Niger | C27 |
| Rwanda | 36 |
| Senegal | C32 |
| Upper Volta | C9 |

| | | |
|---|---|---|
| No. C47 (1) | 2.25 | 1.00 |
| No. C10 (1) | 1.90 | .90 |
| No. C9 (1) | 1.80 | .60 |
| No. C13 (1) | 1.40 | .75 |
| No. C19 (1) | .75 | .25 |
| No. C13 (1) | 1.90 | .80 |
| No. C25 (1) | 2.50 | 1.50 |
| No. C75 (1) | 1.25 | .80 |
| No. C22 (1) | 1.50 | .20 |
| No. C27 (1) | 1.25 | .60 |
| No. 36 (1) | 1.10 | .75 |
| No. C32 (1) | 1.75 | .50 |
| No. C9 (1) | 1.50 | .75 |
| Set total (13) Stamps | 20.85 | 9.80 |

### Air Afrique, 1963

Symbols of Flight CD115

First anniversary of Air Afrique and inauguration of DC-8 service.

**1963, Nov. 19**

| | |
|---|---|
| Cameroun | C48 |
| Chad | C10 |
| Congo, P.R. | C14 |
| Gabon | C18 |
| Ivory Coast | C26 |
| Mauritania | C26 |
| Niger | C35 |
| Senegal | C33 |

| | | |
|---|---|---|
| No. C48 (1) | 1.25 | .40 |
| No. C10 (1) | 1.80 | .60 |
| No. C14 (1) | 1.60 | .60 |
| No. C18 (1) | 1.25 | .65 |
| No. C26 (1) | 1.00 | .50 |
| No. C26 (1) | .70 | .25 |
| No. C35 (1) | 1.00 | .55 |
| No. C33 (1) | 2.00 | .65 |
| Set total (8) Stamps | 10.60 | 4.20 |

### Europafrica

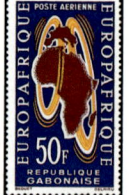

Europe and Africa Linked — CD116

Signing of an economic agreement between the European Economic Community and the African and Malagasy Union, Yaounde, Cameroun, July 20, 1963.

**1963-64**

| | |
|---|---|
| Cameroun | 402 |
| Cent. Africa | C12 |
| Chad | C11 |
| Congo, P.R. | C16 |
| Gabon | C19 |
| Ivory Coast | 217 |
| Niger | C43 |
| Upper Volta | C11 |

| | | |
|---|---|---|
| No. 402 (1) | 2.25 | .60 |
| No. C12 (1) | 2.50 | 1.75 |
| No. C11 (1) | 1.60 | .50 |
| No. C16 (1) | 1.60 | 1.00 |
| No. C19 (1) | 1.25 | .75 |
| No. 217 (1) | 1.10 | .35 |
| No. C43 (1) | .85 | .50 |
| No. C11 (1) | 1.50 | .80 |
| Set total (8) Stamps | 12.65 | 6.25 |

### Human Rights

 Scales of Justice and Globe — CD117

15th anniversary of the Universal Declaration of Human Rights.

**1963, Dec. 10**

| | |
|---|---|
| Comoro Isls. | 56 |
| Fr. Polynesia | 206 |
| New Caledonia | 329 |
| St. Pierre & Miquelon | 368 |
| Somali Coast | 300 |
| Wallis & Futuna Isls. | 166 |

| | | |
|---|---|---|
| No. 56 (1) | 7.50 | 6.00 |
| No. 205 (1) | 15.00 | 12.00 |
| No. 329 (1) | 7.00 | 6.00 |
| No. 368 (1) | 7.00 | 3.50 |
| No. 300 (1) | 8.50 | 8.50 |
| No. 166 (1) | 7.00 | 7.00 |
| Set total (6) Stamps | 52.00 | 43.00 |

### PHILATEC

Stamp Album, Champs Elysees Palace and Horses of Marly — CD118

Intl. Philatelic and Postal Techniques Exhibition, Paris, June 5-21, 1964.

**1963-64**

| | |
|---|---|
| Comoro Isls. | 60 |
| France | 1078 |
| Fr. Polynesia | 207 |
| New Caledonia | 341 |
| St. Pierre & Miquelon | 369 |
| Somali Coast | 301 |
| Wallis & Futuna Isls. | 167 |

| | | |
|---|---|---|
| No. 60 (1) | 4.00 | 3.50 |
| No. 1078 (1) | .25 | .25 |
| No. 206 (1) | 15.00 | 10.00 |

# COMMON DESIGN TYPES

| | | | |
|---|---|---|---|
| No. 341 (1) | | 6.50 | 6.50 |
| No. 369 (1) | | 11.00 | 8.00 |
| No. 301 (1) | | 7.75 | 7.75 |
| No. 167 (1) | | 3.00 | 3.00 |
| Set total (7) Stamps | | 47.50 | 39.00 |

## Cooperation

CD119

Cooperation between France and the French-speaking countries of Africa and Madagascar.

### 1964

| | |
|---|---|
| Cameroun | 409-410 |
| Cent. Africa | 39 |
| Chad | 103 |
| Congo, P.R. | 121 |
| Dahomey | 193 |
| France | 1111 |
| Gabon | 175 |
| Ivory Coast | 221 |
| Madagascar | 360 |
| Mauritania | 181 |
| Niger | 143 |
| Senegal | 236 |
| Togo | 495 |

| | | |
|---|---|---|
| Nos. 409-410 (2) | 2.50 | .50 |
| No. 39 (1) | .90 | .50 |
| No. 103 (1) | 1.00 | .25 |
| No. 121 (1) | .90 | .35 |
| No. 193 (1) | .80 | .35 |
| No. 1111 (1) | .25 | .25 |
| No. 175 (1) | .90 | .60 |
| No. 221 (1) | 1.10 | .35 |
| No. 360 (1) | .60 | .25 |
| No. 181 (1) | .60 | .35 |
| No. 143 (1) | .80 | .40 |
| No. 236 (1) | 1.60 | .85 |
| No. 495 (1) | .70 | .25 |
| Set total (14) Stamps | 12.65 | 5.25 |

## ITU

Telegraph, Syncom Satellite and ITU Emblem — CD120

Intl. Telecommunication Union, Cent.

### 1965, May 17

| | |
|---|---|
| Comoro Isls. | C14 |
| Fr. Polynesia | C33 |
| Fr. So. & Antarctic Terr. | C8 |
| New Caledonia | C40 |
| New Hebrides | 124-125 |
| St. Pierre & Miquelon | C29 |
| Somali Coast | C36 |
| Wallis & Futuna Isls. | C20 |

| | | |
|---|---|---|
| No. C14 (1) | 18.00 | 9.00 |
| No. C33 (1) | 80.00 | 52.50 |
| No. C8 (1) | 200.00 | 160.00 |
| No. C40 (1) | 10.00 | 8.00 |
| Nos. 124-125 (2) | 32.25 | 27.25 |
| No. C29 (1) | 24.00 | 11.50 |
| No. C36 (1) | 15.00 | 9.00 |
| No. C20 (1) | 16.00 | 16.00 |
| Set total (9) Stamps | 395.25 | 293.25 |

## French Satellite A-1

Diamant Rocket and Launching Installation CD121

Launching of France's first satellite, Nov. 26, 1965.

### 1965-66

| | |
|---|---|
| Comoro Isls. | C16a |
| France | 1138a |
| Reunion | 359a |
| Fr. Polynesia | C41a |
| Fr. So. & Antarctic Terr. | C10a |
| New Caledonia | C45a |
| St. Pierre & Miquelon | C31a |
| Somali Coast | C40a |
| Wallis & Futuna Isls. | C23a |

| | | |
|---|---|---|
| No. C16a (1) | 9.00 | 9.00 |
| No. 1138a (1) | .65 | .65 |
| No. 359a (1) | 3.50 | 3.00 |
| No. C41a (1) | 14.00 | 14.00 |
| No. C10a (1) | 29.00 | 24.00 |
| No. C45a (1) | 7.00 | 7.00 |
| No. C31a (1) | 14.50 | 14.50 |
| No. C40a (1) | 7.00 | 7.00 |
| No. C23a (1) | 8.50 | 8.50 |
| Set total (9) Stamps | 93.15 | 87.65 |

## French Satellite D-1

D-1 Satellite in Orbit CD122

Launching of the D-1 satellite at Hammaguir, Algeria, Feb. 17, 1966.

### 1966

| | |
|---|---|
| Comoro Isls. | C17 |
| France | 1148 |
| Fr. Polynesia | C42 |
| Fr. So. & Antarctic Terr. | C11 |
| New Caledonia | C46 |
| St. Pierre & Miquelon | C32 |
| Somali Coast | C49 |
| Wallis & Futuna Isls. | C24 |

| | | |
|---|---|---|
| No. C17 (1) | 4.00 | 4.00 |
| No. 1148 (1) | .25 | .25 |
| No. C42 (1) | 7.00 | 4.75 |
| No. C11 (1) | 57.50 | 40.00 |
| No. C46 (1) | 2.25 | 2.00 |
| No. C32 (1) | 9.00 | 6.00 |
| No. C49 (1) | 4.25 | 2.75 |
| No. C24 (1) | 3.50 | 3.50 |
| Set total (8) Stamps | 87.75 | 63.25 |

## Air Afrique, 1966

Planes and Air Afrique Emblem CD123

Introduction of DC-8F planes by Air Afrique.

### 1966

| | |
|---|---|
| Cameroun | C79 |
| Cent. Africa | C35 |
| Chad | C26 |
| Congo, P.R. | C42 |
| Dahomey | C42 |
| Gabon | C17 |
| Ivory Coast | C32 |
| Mauritania | C57 |
| Niger | C63 |
| Senegal | C47 |
| Togo | C54 |
| Upper Volta | C01 |

| | | |
|---|---|---|
| No. C79 (1) | .80 | .25 |
| No. C35 (1) | 1.00 | .50 |
| No. C26 (1) | .85 | .25 |
| No. C42 (1) | 1.00 | .25 |
| No. C42 (1) | .75 | .25 |
| No. C47 (1) | .90 | .35 |
| No. C32 (1) | 1.00 | .60 |
| No. C57 (1) | .60 | .30 |
| No. C63 (1) | .70 | .35 |
| No. C47 (1) | .80 | .30 |
| No. C54 (1) | .80 | .25 |
| No. C01 (1) | .75 | .50 |
| Set total (12) Stamps | 9.95 | 4.15 |

## African Postal Union, 1967

Telecommunications Symbols and Map of Africa — CD124

Fifth anniversary of the establishment of the African and Malagasy Union of Posts and Telecommunications, UAMPT.

### 1967

| | |
|---|---|
| Cameroun | C90 |
| Cent. Africa | C46 |
| Chad | C37 |
| Congo, P.R. | C57 |
| Dahomey | C61 |
| Gabon | C58 |
| Ivory Coast | C34 |
| Madagascar | C85 |
| Mauritania | C65 |
| Niger | C75 |
| Rwanda | C1-C3 |
| Senegal | C60 |
| Togo | C81 |
| Upper Volta | C50 |

| | | |
|---|---|---|
| No. C90 (1) | 2.40 | .65 |
| No. C46 (1) | 2.25 | .85 |
| No. C37 (1) | 2.00 | .60 |
| No. C57 (1) | 1.60 | .60 |
| No. C61 (1) | 1.75 | .95 |
| No. C58 (1) | 2.00 | .85 |
| No. C34 (1) | 3.50 | 1.50 |
| No. C85 (1) | 1.25 | .60 |
| No. C65 (1) | 1.25 | .60 |
| No. C75 (1) | 1.40 | .60 |
| Nos. C1-C3 (3) | 2.05 | 1.25 |
| No. C60 (1) | 1.75 | .50 |
| No. C81 (1) | 1.90 | .30 |
| No. C50 (1) | 1.80 | .70 |
| Set total (16) Stamps | 26.90 | 10.55 |

## Monetary Union

Gold Token of the Ashantis, 17-18th Centuries — CD125

West African Monetary Union, 5th anniv.

### 1967, Nov. 4

| | |
|---|---|
| Dahomey | 244 |
| Ivory Coast | 259 |
| Mauritania | 238 |
| Niger | 204 |
| Senegal | 294 |
| Togo | 623 |
| Upper Volta | 181 |

| | | |
|---|---|---|
| No. 244 (1) | .65 | .65 |
| No. 259 (1) | .85 | .40 |
| No. 238 (1) | .45 | .25 |
| No. 204 (1) | .55 | .25 |
| No. 294 (1) | .60 | .25 |
| No. 623 (1) | .60 | .25 |
| No. 181 (1) | .65 | .35 |
| Set total (7) Stamps | 4.35 | 2.40 |

## WHO Anniversary

Sun, Flowers and WHO Emblem CD126

World Health Organization, 20th anniv.

### 1968, May 4

| | |
|---|---|
| Afars & Issas | 317 |
| Comoro Isls. | 73 |
| Fr. Polynesia | 241-242 |
| Fr. So. & Antarctic Terr. | 31 |
| New Caledonia | 367 |
| St. Pierre & Miquelon | 377 |
| Wallis & Futuna Isls. | 169 |

| | | |
|---|---|---|
| No. 317 (1) | 3.00 | 3.00 |
| No. 73 (1) | 2.40 | 1.75 |
| Nos. 241-242 (2) | 22.00 | 12.75 |
| No. 31 (1) | 62.50 | 47.50 |
| No. 367 (1) | 4.00 | 2.25 |
| No. 377 (1) | 12.00 | 9.00 |
| No. 169 (1) | 5.75 | 5.75 |
| Set total (8) Stamps | 111.65 | 82.00 |

## Human Rights Year

Human Rights Flame — CD127

### 1968, Aug. 10

| | |
|---|---|
| Afars & Issas | 322-323 |
| Comoro Isls. | 76 |
| Fr. Polynesia | 243-244 |
| Fr. So. & Antarctic Terr. | 32 |
| New Caledonia | 369 |
| St. Pierre & Miquelon | 382 |
| Wallis & Futuna Isls. | 170 |

| | | |
|---|---|---|
| Nos. 322-323 (2) | 6.75 | 4.00 |
| No. 76 (1) | 3.25 | 3.25 |
| Nos. 243-244 (2) | 24.00 | 14.00 |
| No. 32 (1) | 55.00 | 47.50 |
| No. 369 (1) | 2.75 | 1.50 |
| No. 382 (1) | 8.00 | 5.50 |
| No. 170 (1) | 3.25 | 3.25 |
| Set total (9) Stamps | 103.00 | 79.00 |

## 2nd PHILEXAFRIQUE

CD128

Opening of PHILEXAFRIQUE, Abidjan, Feb. 14. Each stamp shows a local scene and stamp.

### 1969, Feb. 14

| | |
|---|---|
| Cameroun | C118 |
| Cent. Africa | C65 |
| Chad | C48 |
| Congo, P.R. | C77 |
| Dahomey | C94 |
| Gabon | C82 |
| Ivory Coast | C38-C40 |
| Madagascar | C92 |
| Mali | C65 |
| Mauritania | C80 |
| Niger | C104 |
| Senegal | C68 |
| Togo | C104 |
| Upper Volta | C62 |

| | | |
|---|---|---|
| No. C118 (1) | 3.25 | 1.25 |
| No. C65 (1) | 1.75 | 1.75 |
| No. C48 (1) | 2.40 | 1.00 |
| No. C77 (1) | 2.00 | 1.75 |
| No. C94 (1) | 2.25 | 2.25 |
| No. C82 (1) | 2.00 | 2.00 |
| Nos. C38-C40 (3) | 14.50 | 14.50 |
| No. C92 (1) | 1.75 | .85 |
| No. C65 (1) | 1.75 | 1.00 |
| No. C80 (1) | 1.90 | .75 |
| No. C104 (1) | 3.00 | 1.90 |
| No. C68 (1) | 2.00 | 1.40 |
| No. C104 (1) | 2.25 | .45 |
| No. C62 (1) | 4.00 | 3.25 |
| Set total (16) Stamps | 44.80 | 34.10 |

## Concorde

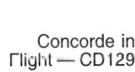

Concorde in Flight — CD129

First flight of the prototype Concorde supersonic plane at Toulouse, Mar. 1, 1969.

### 1969

| | |
|---|---|
| Afars & Issas | C56 |
| Comoro Isls. | C29 |
| France | C42 |
| Fr. Polynesia | C50 |
| Fr. So. & Antarctic Terr. | C18 |
| New Caledonia | C63 |
| St. Pierre & Miquelon | C40 |
| Wallis & Futuna Isls. | C30 |

| | | |
|---|---|---|
| No. C56 (1) | 26.00 | 16.00 |
| No. C29 (1) | 18.00 | 12.00 |
| No. C42 (1) | .75 | .35 |
| No. C50 (1) | 55.00 | 35.00 |
| No. C18 (1) | 55.00 | 37.50 |
| No. C63 (1) | 27.50 | 20.00 |
| No. C40 (1) | 32.50 | 11.00 |
| No. C30 (1) | 15.00 | 10.00 |
| Set total (8) Stamps | 229.75 | 141.85 |

## Development Bank

Bank Emblem — CD130

African Development Bank, fifth anniv.

# COMMON DESIGN TYPES

**1969**

| | |
|---|---|
| Cameroun | 499 |
| Chad | 217 |
| Congo, P.R. | 181-182 |
| Ivory Coast | 281 |
| Mali | 127-128 |
| Mauritania | 267 |
| Niger | 220 |
| Senegal | 317-318 |
| Upper Volta | 201 |

| | | |
|---|---|---|
| No. 499 (1) | .80 | .25 |
| No. 217 (1) | .90 | .25 |
| Nos. 181-182 (2) | 1.00 | .50 |
| No. 281 (1) | .70 | .40 |
| Nos. 127-128 (2) | 1.00 | .50 |
| No. 267 (1) | .60 | .25 |
| No. 220 (1) | .70 | .30 |
| Nos. 317-318 (2) | 1.55 | .50 |
| No. 201 (1) | .65 | .30 |
| Set total (12) Stamps | 7.90 | 3.25 |

### ILO

ILO Headquarters, Geneva, and Emblem — CD131

Intl. Labor Organization, 50th anniv.

**1969-70**

| | |
|---|---|
| Afars & Issas | 337 |
| Comoro Isls. | 83 |
| Fr. Polynesia | 251-252 |
| Fr. So. & Antartic Terr. | 35 |
| New Caledonia | 379 |
| St. Pierre & Miquelon | 396 |
| Wallis & Futuna Isls. | 172 |

| | | |
|---|---|---|
| No. 337 (1) | 2.75 | 2.00 |
| No. 83 (1) | 1.25 | .75 |
| Nos. 251-252 (2) | 24.00 | 12.50 |
| No. 35 (1) | 15.00 | 10.00 |
| No. 379 (1) | 2.25 | 1.10 |
| No. 396 (1) | 10.00 | 5.50 |
| No. 172 (1) | 2.75 | 2.75 |
| Set total (8) Stamps | 58.00 | 34.60 |

### ASECNA

Map of Africa, Plane and Airport — CD132

10th anniversary of the Agency for the Security of Aerial Navigation in Africa and Madagascar (ASECNA, Agence pour la Securite de la Navigation Aerienne en Afrique et a Madagascar).

**1969-70**

| | |
|---|---|
| Cameroun | 500 |
| Cent. Africa | 119 |
| Chad | 222 |
| Congo, P.R. | 197 |
| Dahomey | 269 |
| Gabon | 260 |
| Ivory Coast | 287 |
| Mali | 130 |
| Niger | 221 |
| Senegal | 321 |
| Upper Volta | 204 |

| | | |
|---|---|---|
| No. 500 (1) | 2.00 | .60 |
| No. 119 (1) | 2.00 | .80 |
| No. 222 (1) | 1.00 | .25 |
| No. 197 (1) | 2.00 | .40 |
| No. 269 (1) | .90 | .55 |
| No. 260 (1) | 1.75 | .75 |
| No. 287 (1) | .90 | .40 |
| No. 130 (1) | .90 | .40 |
| No. 221 (1) | 1.40 | .70 |
| No. 321 (1) | 1.60 | .50 |
| No. 204 (1) | 1.75 | 1.00 |
| Set total (11) Stamps | 16.20 | 6.35 |

### U.P.U. Headquarters

CD133

New Universal Postal Union headquarters, Bern, Switzerland.

**1970**

| | |
|---|---|
| Afars & Issas | 342 |
| Algeria | 443 |
| Cameroun | 503-504 |
| Cent. Africa | 125 |
| Chad | 225 |
| Comoro Isls. | 84 |
| Congo, P.R. | 216 |
| Fr. Polynesia | 261-262 |
| Fr. So. & Antarctic Terr. | 36 |
| Gabon | 258 |
| Ivory Coast | 295 |
| Madagascar | 444 |
| Mali | 134-135 |
| Mauritania | 283 |
| New Caledonia | 382 |
| Niger | 231-232 |
| St. Pierre & Miquelon | 397-398 |
| Senegal | 328-329 |
| Tunisia | 535 |
| Wallis & Futuna Isls. | 173 |

| | | |
|---|---|---|
| No. 342 (1) | 2.50 | 1.40 |
| No. 443 (1) | 1.10 | .40 |
| Nos. 503-504 (2) | 2.60 | .55 |
| No. 125 (1) | 1.75 | .70 |
| No. 225 (1) | 1.20 | .25 |
| No. 84 (1) | 5.50 | 2.00 |
| No. 216 (1) | 1.00 | .25 |
| Nos. 261-262 (2) | 20.00 | 10.00 |
| No. 36 (1) | 40.00 | 27.50 |
| No. 258 (1) | .90 | .55 |
| No. 295 (1) | 1.10 | .50 |
| No. 444 (1) | .55 | .25 |
| Nos. 134-135 (2) | 1.05 | .50 |
| No. 283 (1) | .60 | .30 |
| No. 382 (1) | 3.00 | 1.50 |
| Nos. 231-232 (2) | 1.50 | .60 |
| Nos. 397-398 (2) | 34.00 | 16.25 |
| Nos. 328-329 (2) | 1.55 | .55 |
| No. 535 (1) | .60 | .25 |
| No. 173 (1) | 3.25 | 3.25 |
| Set total (26) Stamps | 123.75 | 67.55 |

### De Gaulle

CD134

First anniversary of the death of Charles de Gaulle, (1890-1970), President of France.

**1971-72**

| | |
|---|---|
| Afars & Issas | 356-357 |
| Comoro Isls. | 104-105 |
| France | 1325a |
| Fr. Polynesia | 270-271 |
| Fr. So. & Antartic Terr. | 52-53 |
| New Caledonia | 393-394 |
| Reunion | 380a |
| St. Pierre & Miquelon | 417-418 |
| Wallis & Futuna Isls. | 177-178 |

| | | |
|---|---|---|
| Nos. 356-357 (2) | 12.50 | 7.50 |
| Nos. 104-105 (2) | 9.00 | 5.75 |
| No. 1325a (1) | 3.00 | 2.50 |
| Nos. 270-271 (2) | 51.50 | 29.50 |
| Nos. 52-53 (2) | 40.00 | 29.50 |
| Nos. 393-394 (2) | 23.00 | 11.75 |
| No. 380a (1) | 9.25 | 8.00 |
| Nos. 417-418 (2) | 56.50 | 31.00 |
| Nos. 177-178 (2) | 20.00 | 16.25 |
| Set total (16) Stamps | 224.75 | 141.75 |

### African Postal Union, 1971

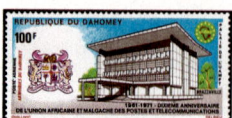

UAMPT Building, Brazzaville, Congo — CD135

10th anniversary of the establishment of the African and Malagasy Posts and Telecommunications Union, UAMPT. Each stamp has a different native design.

**1971, Nov. 13**

| | |
|---|---|
| Cameroun | C177 |
| Cent. Africa | C89 |
| Chad | C94 |
| Congo, P.R. | C136 |
| Dahomey | C146 |
| Gabon | C120 |
| Ivory Coast | C47 |
| Mauritania | C113 |
| Niger | C164 |
| Rwanda | C8 |
| Senegal | C105 |
| Togo | C166 |
| Upper Volta | C97 |

| | | |
|---|---|---|
| No. C177 (1) | 2.00 | .50 |
| No. C89 (1) | 2.25 | .85 |
| No. C94 (1) | 1.50 | .50 |
| No. C136 (1) | 1.60 | .75 |
| No. C146 (1) | 1.75 | .80 |
| No. C120 (1) | 1.75 | .70 |
| No. C47 (1) | 2.00 | 1.00 |
| No. C113 (1) | 1.10 | .65 |
| No. C164 (1) | 1.25 | .60 |
| No. C8 (1) | 2.75 | 2.50 |
| No. C105 (1) | 1.60 | .50 |
| No. C166 (1) | 1.25 | .40 |
| No. C97 (1) | 1.50 | .70 |
| Set total (13) Stamps | 22.30 | 10.45 |

### West African Monetary Union

African Couple, City, Village and Commemorative Coin — CD136

West African Monetary Union, 10th anniv.

**1972, Nov. 2**

| | |
|---|---|
| Dahomey | 300 |
| Ivory Coast | 331 |
| Mauritania | 299 |
| Niger | 258 |
| Senegal | 374 |
| Togo | 825 |
| Upper Volta | 280 |

| | | |
|---|---|---|
| No. 300 (1) | .65 | .25 |
| No. 331 (1) | 1.00 | .50 |
| No. 299 (1) | .75 | .25 |
| No. 258 (1) | .65 | .30 |
| No. 374 (1) | .50 | .30 |
| No. 825 (1) | .60 | .25 |
| No. 280 (1) | .60 | .25 |
| Set total (7) Stamps | 4.75 | 2.10 |

### African Postal Union, 1973

Telecommunications Symbols and Map of Africa — CD137

11th anniversary of the African and Malagasy Posts and Telecommunications Union (UAMPT).

**1973, Sept. 12**

| | |
|---|---|
| Cameroun | 574 |
| Cent. Africa | 194 |
| Chad | 294 |
| Congo, P.R. | 289 |
| Dahomey | 311 |
| Gabon | 320 |
| Ivory Coast | 361 |
| Madagascar | 500 |
| Mauritania | 304 |
| Niger | 287 |
| Rwanda | 540 |
| Senegal | 393 |
| Togo | 849 |
| Upper Volta | 297 |

| | | |
|---|---|---|
| No. 574 (1) | 1.75 | .40 |
| No. 194 (1) | 1.25 | .75 |
| No. 294 (1) | 1.75 | .40 |
| No. 289 (1) | 1.60 | .50 |
| No. 311 (1) | 1.25 | .55 |
| No. 320 (1) | 1.40 | .75 |
| No. 361 (1) | 2.50 | 1.00 |
| No. 500 (1) | 1.10 | .35 |
| No. 304 (1) | 1.10 | .40 |
| No. 287 (1) | .90 | .60 |
| No. 540 (1) | 3.00 | 2.00 |
| No. 393 (1) | 1.60 | .50 |
| No. 849 (1) | 1.00 | .35 |
| No. 297 (1) | 1.25 | .70 |
| Set total (14) Stamps | 21.45 | 9.25 |

### Philexafrique II — Essen

CD138

CD139

Designs: Indigenous fauna, local and German stamps. Types CD138-CD139 printed horizontally and vertically se-tenant in sheets of 10 (2x5). Label between horizontal pairs alternately commemorates Philexafrique II, Libreville, Gabon, June 1978, and 2nd International Stamp Fair, Essen, Germany, Nov. 1-5.

**1978-1979**

| | |
|---|---|
| Benin | C286a |
| Central Africa | C201a |
| Chad | C239a |
| Congo Republic | C246a |
| Djibouti | C122a |
| Gabon | C216a |
| Ivory Coast | C65a |
| Mali | C357a |
| Mauritania | C186a |
| Niger | C292a |
| Rwanda | C13a |
| Senegal | C147a |
| Togo | C364a |

| | | |
|---|---|---|
| No. C286a (1) | 9.00 | 8.50 |
| No. C201a (1) | 7.50 | 7.50 |
| No. C239a (1) | 7.50 | 4.00 |
| No. C246a (1) | 7.00 | 7.00 |
| No. C122a (1) | 6.50 | 6.50 |
| No. C216a (1) | 6.50 | 4.00 |
| No. C65a (1) | 9.00 | 9.00 |
| No. C357a (1) | 5.00 | 3.00 |
| No. C186a (1) | 5.50 | 5.00 |
| No. C292a (1) | 6.00 | 6.00 |
| No. C13a (1) | 4.00 | 4.00 |
| No. C147a (1) | 10.00 | 4.00 |
| No. C364a (1) | 3.00 | 1.50 |
| Set total (13) Stamps | 86.50 | 70.00 |

## BRITISH COMMONWEALTH OF NATIONS

The listings follow established trade practices when these issues are offered as units by dealers. The Peace issue, for example, includes only one stamp from the Indian state of Hyderabad. The U.P.U. issue includes the Egypt set. Pairs are included for those varieties issued with bilingual designs se-tenant.

### Silver Jubilee

Windsor Castle and King George V — CD301

Reign of King George V, 25th anniv.

**1935**

| | |
|---|---|
| Antigua | 77-80 |
| Ascension | 33-36 |
| Bahamas | 92-95 |
| Barbados | 186-189 |
| Basutoland | 11-14 |
| Bechuanaland Protectorate | 117-120 |
| Bermuda | 100-103 |
| British Guiana | 223-226 |
| British Honduras | 108-111 |
| Cayman Islands | 81-84 |
| Ceylon | 260-263 |
| Cyprus | 136-139 |
| Dominica | 90-93 |
| Falkland Islands | 77-80 |
| Fiji | 110-113 |
| Gambia | 125-128 |
| Gibraltar | 100-103 |
| Gilbert & Ellice Islands | 33-36 |
| Gold Coast | 108-111 |
| Grenada | 124-127 |
| Hong Kong | 147-150 |
| Jamaica | 109-112 |
| Kenya, Uganda, Tanzania | 42-45 |
| Leeward Islands | 96-99 |
| Malta | 184-187 |
| Mauritius | 204-207 |
| Montserrat | 85-88 |
| Newfoundland | 226-229 |
| Nigeria | 34-37 |
| Northern Rhodesia | 18-21 |

COMMON DESIGN TYPES 39A

Nyasaland Protectorate................47-50
St. Helena ................................111-114
St. Kitts-Nevis..............................72-75
St. Lucia ......................................91-94
St. Vincent...............................134-137
Seychelles ...............................118-121
Sierra Leone............................166-169
Solomon Islands..........................60-63
Somaliland Protectorate..............77-80
Straits Settlements ..................213-216
Swaziland ....................................20-23
Trinidad & Tobago .......................43-46
Turks & Caicos Islands ...............71-74
Virgin Islands...............................69-72

The following have different designs but are included in the omnibus set:

Great Britain ............................226-229
Offices in Morocco (Sp. Curr.).....67-70
Offices in Morocco (Br. Curr.)........226-229
Offices in Morocco (Fr. Curr.) ........422-425
Offices in Morocco (Tangier)....508-510
Australia...................................152-154
Canada.....................................211-216
Cook Islands ..............................98-100
India..........................................142-148
Nauru..........................................31-34
New Guinea.................................46-47
New Zealand ............................199-201
Niue .............................................67-69
Papua .......................................114-117
Samoa ......................................163-165
South Africa.................................68-71
Southern Rhodesia ......................33-36
South-West Africa ....................121-124

| | | |
|---|---|---|
| *Nos. 77-80 (4)* | 20.25 | *23.25* |
| *Nos. 33-36 (4)* | 58.50 | *127.50* |
| *Nos. 92-95 (4)* | 25.00 | *46.00* |
| *Nos. 186-189 (4)* | 30.00 | 50.30 |
| *Nos. 11-14 (4)* | 11.60 | *21.25* |
| *Nos. 117-120 (4)* | 15.75 | *36.00* |
| *Nos. 100-103 (4)* | 16.80 | *58.50* |
| *Nos. 223-226 (4)* | 22.35 | 35.50 |
| *Nos. 108-111 (4)* | 15.25 | *16.35* |
| *Nos. 81-84 (4)* | 21.60 | *24.50* |
| *Nos. 260-263 (4)* | 10.40 | 21.60 |
| *Nos. 136-139 (4)* | 39.75 | *34.40* |
| *Nos. 90-93 (4)* | 18.85 | 19.85 |
| *Nos. 77-80 (4)* | 55.00 | 14.75 |
| *Nos. 110-113 (4)* | 20.25 | 34.00 |
| *Nos. 125-128 (4)* | 13.05 | *25.25* |
| *Nos. 100-103 (4)* | 28.75 | 42.75 |
| *Nos. 33-36 (4)* | 36.80 | *67.00* |
| *Nos. 108-111 (4)* | 25.75 | *78.10* |
| *Nos. 124-127 (4)* | 16.70 | *40.60* |
| *Nos. 147-150 (4)* | 73.75 | 20.75 |
| *Nos. 109-112 (4)* | 24.20 | 50.50 |
| *Nos. 42-45 (4)* | 10.25 | *11.75* |
| *Nos. 96-99 (4)* | 35.75 | 49.60 |
| *Nos. 184-187 (4)* | 22.00 | 33.70 |
| *Nos. 204-207 (4)* | 44.60 | 58.25 |
| *Nos. 85-88 (4)* | 10.25 | *30.25* |
| *Nos. 226-229 (4)* | 17.50 | 12.05 |
| *Nos. 34-37 (4)* | 17.50 | *73.00* |
| *Nos. 18-21 (4)* | 17.00 | 15.00 |
| *Nos. 47-50 (4)* | 43.50 | *82.50* |
| *Nos. 111-114 (4)* | 31.15 | *36.50* |
| *Nos. 72-75 (4)* | 11.80 | *18.65* |
| *Nos. 91-94 (4)* | 16.00 | *20.80* |
| *Nos. 134-137 (4)* | 9.45 | *21.25* |
| *Nos. 118-121 (4)* | 15.75 | *40.00* |
| *Nos. 166-169 (4)* | 23.60 | *50.35* |
| *Nos. 60-63 (4)* | 29.00 | 38.00 |
| *Nos. 77-80 (4)* | 17.00 | *48.25* |
| *Nos. 213-216 (4)* | 15.00 | *25.10* |
| *Nos. 20-23 (4)* | 6.80 | 18.25 |
| *Nos. 43-46 (4)* | 18.60 | 37.50 |
| *Nos. 71-74 (4)* | 9.90 | 14.50 |
| *Nos. 69-72 (4)* | 25.00 | 55.25 |
| *Nos. 226-229 (4)* | 5.15 | *9.90* |
| *Nos. 67-70 (4)* | 13.60 | *30.70* |
| *Nos. 226-229 (4)* | 16.30 | *56.00* |
| *Nos. 422-425 (4)* | 9.35 | 3.05 |
| *Nos. 508-510 (3)* | 26.00 | *33.50* |
| *Nos. 152-154 (3)* | 49.50 | 45.35 |
| *Nos. 211-216 (6)* | 23.85 | 13.35 |
| *Nos. 98-100 (3)* | 9.65 | *12.00* |
| *Nos. 142-148 (7)* | 28.85 | 14.00 |
| *Nos. 31-34 (4)* | 12.35 | *13.15* |
| *Nos. 46-47 (2)* | 4.35 | 1.70 |
| *Nos. 199-201 (3)* | 23.00 | *28.50* |
| *Nos. 67-69 (3)* | 19.25 | *31.00* |
| *Nos. 114-117 (4)* | 9.20 | *17.50* |
| *Nos. 163-165 (3)* | 4.40 | 6.50 |
| *Nos. 68-71 (4)* | 57.50 | *153.00* |
| *Nos. 33-36 (4)* | 27.75 | *45.25* |
| *Nos. 121-124 (4)* | 13.00 | *36.10* |
| *Set total (245) Stamps* | 1,401. | 2,231. |

**Coronation**

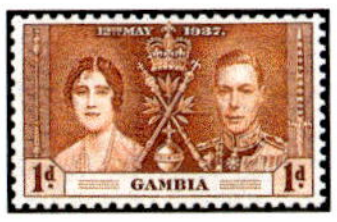

Queen Elizabeth and King George VI — CD302

**1937**

Aden .............................................13-15
Antigua ........................................81-83
Ascension......................................37-39
Bahamas ......................................97-99
Barbados ...................................190-192
Basutoland....................................15-17
Bechuanaland Protectorate......121-123
Bermuda....................................115-117
British Guiana...........................227-229
British Honduras........................112-114
Cayman Islands...........................97-99
Ceylon .......................................275-277
Cyprus .......................................140-142
Dominica......................................94-96
Falkland Islands ..........................81-83
Fiji ..............................................114-116
Gambia ......................................129-131
Gibraltar ....................................104-106
Gilbert & Ellice Islands................37-39
Gold Coast ................................112-114
Grenada.....................................128-130
Hong Kong ................................151-153
Jamaica ....................................113-115
Kenya, Uganda, Tanzania ...........60-62
Leeward Islands ........................100-102
Malta..........................................188-190
Mauritius...................................208-210
Montserrat ..................................89-91
Newfoundland...........................230-232
Nigeria ........................................50-52
Northern Rhodesia......................22-24
Nyasaland Protectorate...............51-53
St. Helena .................................115-117
St. Kitts-Nevis..............................76-78
St. Lucia ....................................107-109
St. Vincent.................................138-140
Seychelles .................................122-124
Sierra Leone..............................170-172
Solomon Islands..........................64-66
Somaliland Protectorate..............81-83
Straits Settlements ..................235-237
Swaziland ....................................24-26
Trinidad & Tobago .......................47-49
Turks & Caicos Islands ...............75-77
Virgin Islands...............................73-75

The following have different designs but are included in the omnibus set:

Great Britain ...................................234
Offices in Morocco (Sp. Curr.)..........82
Offices in Morocco (Fr. Curr.) .........439
Offices in Morocco (Tangier)...........514
Canada.............................................237
Cook Islands ............................109-111
Nauru...........................................35-38
Newfoundland...........................233-243
New Guinea..................................48-51
New Zealand ............................223-225
Niue .............................................70-72
Papua .......................................118-121
South Africa.................................74-78
Southern Rhodesia ......................38-41
South-West Africa ....................125-132

| | | |
|---|---|---|
| *Nos. 13-15 (3)* | 2.70 | *5.65* |
| *Nos. 81-83 (3)* | 1.85 | *8.00* |
| *Nos. 37-39 (3)* | 2.75 | *2.75* |
| *Nos. 97-99 (3)* | 1.05 | *3.05* |
| *Nos. 190-192 (3)* | 1.10 | 1.95 |
| *Nos. 15-17 (3)* | 1.15 | *3.00* |
| *Nos. 121-123 (3)* | .95 | 3.35 |
| *Nos. 115-117 (3)* | 1.25 | 5.00 |
| *Nos. 227-229 (3)* | 1.50 | 3.05 |
| *Nos. 112-114 (3)* | 1.20 | 2.40 |
| *Nos. 97-99 (3)* | 1.10 | 2.70 |
| *Nos. 275-277 (3)* | 8.25 | 10.35 |
| *Nos. 140-142 (3)* | 3.75 | 6.50 |
| *Nos. 94-96 (3)* | .85 | 2.40 |
| *Nos. 81-83 (3)* | 2.90 | *2.30* |
| *Nos. 114-116 (3)* | 1.35 | *5.75* |
| *Nos. 129-131 (3)* | .65 | 6.00 |
| *Nos. 104-106 (3)* | 2.25 | 6.45 |
| *Nos. 37-39 (3)* | .85 | *2.15* |
| *Nos. 112-114 (3)* | 3.10 | *10.00* |
| *Nos. 128-130 (3)* | 1.00 | .85 |
| *Nos. 151-153 (3)* | 17.00 | 17.75 |
| *Nos. 113-115 (3)* | 1.25 | 1.25 |
| *Nos. 60-62 (3)* | 1.25 | 2.35 |
| *Nos. 100-102 (3)* | 1.55 | 4.00 |
| *Nos. 188-190 (3)* | 1.25 | 1.60 |
| *Nos. 208-210 (3)* | 1.75 | 3.50 |
| *Nos. 89-91 (3)* | 1.00 | 3.35 |
| *Nos. 230-232 (3)* | 7.00 | 2.80 |
| *Nos. 50-52 (3)* | 3.25 | 8.50 |
| *Nos. 22-24 (3)* | .95 | 2.25 |
| *Nos. 51-53 (3)* | 1.05 | 1.30 |
| *Nos. 115-117 (3)* | 1.45 | 2.05 |
| *Nos. 76-78 (3)* | .95 | 2.15 |
| *Nos. 107-109 (3)* | 1.05 | 2.05 |
| *Nos. 138-140 (3)* | .80 | *4.75* |
| *Nos. 122-124 (3)* | 1.20 | *1.90* |
| *Nos. 170-172 (3)* | 1.95 | 5.65 |
| *Nos. 64-66 (3)* | .90 | 2.00 |
| *Nos. 81-83 (3)* | 1.10 | *3.50* |
| *Nos. 235-237 (3)* | 3.25 | 1.60 |
| *Nos. 24-26 (3)* | .75 | 2.70 |
| *Nos. 47-49 (3)* | 1.10 | 3.20 |
| *Nos. 75-77 (3)* | 1.25 | .95 |
| *Nos. 73-75 (3)* | 2.20 | 6.90 |
| *No. 234 (1)* | .30 | .25 |
| *No. 82 (1)* | .80 | .60 |
| *No. 439 (1)* | .50 | .25 |
| *No. 514 (1)* | 1.25 | .50 |
| *No. 237 (1)* | .35 | .25 |
| *Nos. 109-111 (3)* | .85 | .80 |
| *Nos. 35-38 (4)* | 1.25 | *5.50* |
| *Nos. 233-243 (11)* | 41.90 | 30.40 |
| *Nos. 48-51 (4)* | 1.40 | *7.90* |
| *Nos. 223-225 (3)* | 1.75 | *2.25* |
| *Nos. 70-72 (3)* | .90 | *2.05* |
| *Nos. 118-121 (4)* | 1.60 | *5.25* |
| *Nos. 74-78 (5)* | 7.60 | 9.35 |
| *Nos. 38-41 (4)* | 3.55 | 15.50 |
| *Nos. 125-132 (8)* | 5.00 | 8.40 |
| *Set total (189) Stamps* | 166.10 | 268.90 |

**Peace**

King George VI and Parliament Buildings, London — CD303

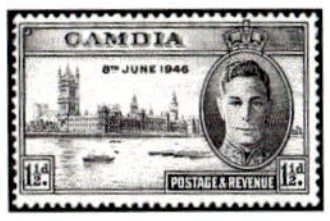

Return to peace at the close of World War II.

**1945-46**

Aden .............................................28-29
Antigua ........................................96-97
Ascension......................................50-51
Bahamas ....................................130-131
Barbados ...................................207-208
Bermuda....................................131-132
British Guiana...........................242-243
British Honduras........................127-128
Cayman Islands.........................112-113
Ceylon .......................................293-294
Cyprus .......................................156-157
Dominica....................................112-113
Falkland Islands ..........................97-98
Falkland Islands Dep.............1L9-1L10
Fiji ..............................................137-138
Gambia ......................................144-145
Gibraltar ....................................119-120
Gilbert & Ellice Islands................52-53
Gold Coast ................................128-129
Grenada.....................................143-144
Jamaica ....................................136-137
Kenya, Uganda, Tanzania ...........90-91
Leeward Islands ........................116-117
Malta..........................................206-207
Mauritius...................................223-224
Montserrat ................................104-105
Nigeria ........................................71-72
Northern Rhodesia......................46-47
Nyasaland Protectorate...............82-83
Pitcairn Islands ..............................9-10
St. Helena .................................128-129
St. Kitts-Nevis..............................91-92
St. Lucia ....................................127-128
St. Vincent.................................152-153
Seychelles .................................149-150
Sierra Leone..............................186-187
Solomon Islands..........................80-81
Somaliland Protectorate..........108-109
Trinidad & Tobago .......................62-63
Turks & Caicos Islands ...............90-91
Virgin Islands...............................88-89

The following have different designs but are included in the omnibus set:

Great Britain ............................264-265
Offices in Morocco (Tangier)....523-524
Aden
Kathiri State of Seiyun...............12-13
Qu'aiti State of Shihr and Mukalla ....................................12-13
Australia...................................200-202
Basutoland....................................29-31
Bechuanaland Protectorate......137-139
Burma .........................................66-69
Cook Islands ............................127-130
Hong Kong ................................174-175
India..........................................195-198
Hyderabad ....................................51-53
New Zealand ............................247-257
Niue .............................................90-93
Pakistan-Bahawalpur ....................O16
Samoa ......................................191-194
South Africa...............................100-102
Southern Rhodesia ......................67-70
South-West Africa ....................153-155
Swaziland ....................................38-40
Zanzibar....................................222-223

| | | |
|---|---|---|
| *Nos. 28-29 (2)* | .95 | 2.50 |
| *Nos. 96-97 (2)* | .50 | *.80* |
| *Nos. 50-51 (2)* | .80 | *2.00* |
| *Nos. 130-131 (2)* | .50 | 1.40 |
| *Nos. 207-208 (2)* | .50 | 1.10 |
| *Nos. 131-132 (2)* | .55 | .55 |
| *Nos. 242-243 (2)* | 1.05 | *1.40* |
| *Nos. 127-128 (2)* | .50 | .50 |
| *Nos. 112-113 (2)* | .80 | .80 |
| *Nos. 293-294 (2)* | .60 | *2.10* |
| *Nos. 156-157 (2)* | .90 | .70 |
| *Nos. 112-113 (2)* | .50 | .50 |
| *Nos. 97-98 (2)* | .90 | 1.35 |
| *Nos. 1L9-1L10 (2)* | 1.30 | 1.00 |
| *Nos. 137-138 (2)* | .75 | *1.75* |
| *Nos. 144-145 (2)* | .60 | .95 |
| *Nos. 119-120 (2)* | .75 | *1.00* |
| *Nos. 52-53 (2)* | .50 | *1.10* |
| *Nos. 128-129 (2)* | 1.85 | *3.75* |
| *Nos. 143-144 (2)* | .50 | *.95* |
| *Nos. 136-137 (2)* | 2.00 | *13.50* |
| *Nos. 90-91 (2)* | .65 | .85 |
| *Nos. 116-117 (2)* | .50 | 1.50 |
| *Nos. 206-207 (2)* | .65 | 2.00 |
| *Nos. 223-224 (2)* | .50 | 1.05 |
| *Nos. 104-105 (2)* | .50 | .50 |
| *Nos. 71-72 (2)* | .70 | *2.75* |
| *Nos. 46-47 (2)* | 1.25 | *2.00* |
| *Nos. 82-83 (2)* | .55 | .60 |
| *Nos. 9-10 (2)* | 1.40 | .60 |
| *Nos. 128-129 (2)* | .65 | .70 |
| *Nos. 91-92 (2)* | .50 | .50 |
| *Nos. 127-128 (2)* | .50 | .60 |
| *Nos. 152-153 (2)* | .50 | .50 |
| *Nos. 149-150 (2)* | .55 | .50 |
| *Nos. 186-187 (2)* | .50 | .50 |
| *Nos. 80-81 (2)* | .50 | 1.50 |
| *Nos. 108-109 (2)* | .70 | .50 |
| *Nos. 62-63 (2)* | .75 | 1.85 |
| *Nos. 90-91 (2)* | .50 | .50 |
| *Nos. 88-89 (2)* | .50 | .50 |
| *Nos. 264-265 (2)* | .50 | .50 |
| *Nos. 523-524 (2)* | 2.00 | 2.55 |
| *Nos. 12-13 (2)* | .50 | .90 |
| *Nos. 12-13 (2)* | .50 | *1.25* |
| *Nos. 200-202 (3)* | 1.60 | *1.25* |
| *Nos. 29-31 (3)* | 2.10 | 2.60 |
| *Nos. 137-139 (3)* | 2.05 | *4.75* |
| *Nos. 66-69 (4)* | 1.50 | 1.25 |
| *Nos. 127-130 (4)* | 2.00 | 1.85 |
| *Nos. 174-175 (2)* | 6.75 | 2.75 |
| *Nos. 195-198 (4)* | 5.60 | 5.50 |
| *Nos. 51-53 (3)* | 1.50 | 1.70 |
| *Nos. 247-257 (11)* | 3.35 | 3.65 |
| *Nos. 90-93 (4)* | 1.70 | *2.20* |
| *No. O16 (1)* | 15.00 | *10.00* |
| *Nos. 191-194 (4)* | 2.05 | 1.00 |
| *Nos. 100-102 (3)* | 1.00 | 3.25 |
| *Nos. 67-70 (4)* | 1.40 | 1.75 |
| *Nos. 153-155 (3)* | 1.85 | 3.25 |
| *Nos. 38-40 (3)* | 2.40 | *5.50* |
| *Nos. 222-223 (2)* | .65 | 1.00 |
| *Set total (151) Stamps* | 86.15 | 118.15 |

**Silver Wedding**

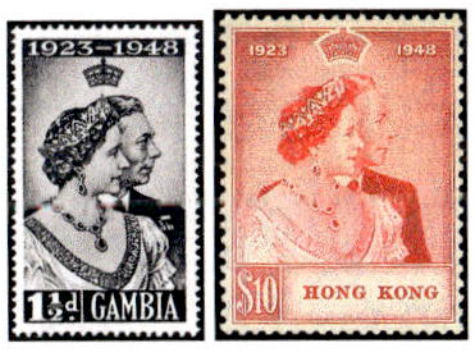

King George VI and Queen Elizabeth

CD304 CD305

**1948-49**

Aden .............................................30-31
Kathiri State of Seiyun...............14-15
Qu'aiti State of Shihr and Mukalla ....................................14-15
Antigua ........................................98-99
Ascension......................................52-53
Bahamas ....................................148-149
Barbados ...................................210-211
Basutoland....................................39-40
Bechuanaland Protectorate......147-148
Bermuda....................................133-134
British Guiana...........................244-245
British Honduras........................129-130
Cayman Islands.........................116-117
Cyprus .......................................158-159
Dominica....................................114-115
Falkland Islands ..........................99-100
Falkland Islands Dep...........1L11-1L12
Fiji ..............................................139-140
Gambia ......................................146-147
Gibraltar ....................................121-122
Gilbert & Ellice Islands................54-55
Gold Coast ................................142-143
Grenada.....................................145-146
Hong Kong ................................178-179
Jamaica ....................................138-139
Kenya, Uganda, Tanzania ...........92-93
Leeward Islands ........................118-119
Malaya
Johore ....................................128-129
Kedah .......................................55-56
Kelantan ...................................44-45
Malacca .......................................1-2
Negri Sembilan ..........................36-37

40A COMMON DESIGN TYPES

Pahang ....................................44-45
Penang .........................................1-2
Perak ......................................99-100
Perlis ............................................1-2
Selangor....................................74-75
Trengganu .................................47-48
Malta ......................................223-224
Mauritius .................................229-230
Montserrat ...............................106-107
Nigeria .......................................73-74
North Borneo...........................238-239
Northern Rhodesia .....................48-49
Nyasaland Protectorate ..............85-86
Pitcairn Islands ...........................11-12
St. Helena ...............................130-131
St. Kitts-Nevis ............................93-94
St. Lucia .................................129-130
St. Vincent ..............................154-155
Sarawak..................................174-175
Seychelles ...............................151-152
Sierra Leone............................188-189
Singapore ...................................21-22
Solomon Islands..........................82-83
Somaliland Protectorate ..........110-111
Swaziland ...................................48-49
Trinidad & Tobago ......................64-65
Turks & Caicos Islands ...............92-93
Virgin Islands..............................90-91
Zanzibar..................................224-225

The following have different designs but are included in the omnibus set:

Great Britain ............................267-268
Offices in Morocco (Sp. Curr.) ......93-94
Offices in Morocco (Tangier) ........525-526
Bahrain .......................................62-63
Kuwait.........................................82-83
Oman..........................................25-26
South Africa..................................106
South-West Africa .........................159

| | | |
|---|---|---|
| *Nos. 30-31 (2)* | 40.40 | 56.50 |
| *Nos. 14-15 (2)* | 17.85 | *16.00* |
| *Nos. 14-15 (2)* | 18.55 | *12.50* |
| *Nos. 98-99 (2)* | 13.55 | *15.75* |
| *Nos. 52-53 (2)* | 55.55 | 50.45 |
| *Nos. 148-149 (2)* | 45.25 | 40.30 |
| *Nos. 210-211 (2)* | 18.35 | 13.55 |
| *Nos. 39-40 (2)* | 52.80 | *55.25* |
| *Nos. 147-148 (2)* | 42.85 | *47.75* |
| *Nos. 133-134 (2)* | 47.75 | *55.25* |
| *Nos. 244-245 (2)* | 24.25 | *28.45* |
| *Nos. 129-130 (2)* | 25.25 | *53.20* |
| *Nos. 116-117 (2)* | 25.25 | *33.50* |
| *Nos. 158-159 (2)* | 58.50 | *78.05* |
| *Nos. 114-115 (2)* | 25.25 | *32.75* |
| *Nos. 99-100 (2)* | 112.10 | 76.10 |
| *Nos. 1L11-1L12 (2)* | 4.25 | 6.00 |
| *Nos. 139-140 (2)* | 18.20 | 11.50 |
| *Nos. 146-147 (2)* | 21.30 | 21.25 |
| *Nos. 121-122 (2)* | 61.00 | *78.00* |
| *Nos. 54-55 (2)* | 14.25 | *26.25* |
| *Nos. 142-143 (2)* | 35.25 | 48.20 |
| *Nos. 145-146 (2)* | 21.75 | 21.75 |
| *Nos. 178-179 (2)* | 329.00 | 106.75 |
| *Nos. 138-139 (2)* | 30.35 | *75.25* |
| *Nos. 92-93 (2)* | 51.00 | *68.00* |
| *Nos. 118-119 (2)* | 7.00 | 8.25 |
| *Nos. 128-129 (2)* | 29.25 | *53.25* |
| *Nos. 55-56 (2)* | 35.25 | *50.25* |
| *Nos. 44-45 (2)* | 35.75 | *62.75* |
| *Nos. 1-2 (2)* | 35.40 | *49.75* |
| *Nos. 36-37 (2)* | 28.10 | *38.20* |
| *Nos. 44-45 (2)* | 28.00 | *38.05* |
| *Nos. 1-2 (2)* | 40.50 | 37.80 |
| *Nos. 99-100 (2)* | 27.80 | *37.75* |
| *Nos. 1-2 (2)* | 33.50 | *58.00* |
| *Nos. 74-75 (2)* | 30.25 | 25.30 |
| *Nos. 47-48 (2)* | 32.75 | *61.75* |
| *Nos. 223-224 (2)* | 40.55 | 45.25 |
| *Nos. 229-230 (2)* | 19.25 | *45.25* |
| *Nos. 106-107 (2)* | 8.75 | *17.25* |
| *Nos. 73-74 (2)* | 17.85 | *22.80* |
| *Nos. 238-239 (2)* | 35.30 | *45.75* |
| *Nos. 48-49 (2)* | 100.30 | 90.25 |
| *Nos. 85-86 (2)* | 18.25 | *35.25* |
| *Nos. 11-12 (2)* | 44.50 | 54.00 |
| *Nos. 130-131 (2)* | 32.80 | *42.80* |
| *Nos. 93-94 (2)* | 13.25 | 10.50 |
| *Nos. 129-130 (2)* | 22.25 | *40.25* |
| *Nos. 154-155 (2)* | 27.75 | *30.25* |
| *Nos. 174-175 (2)* | 52.80 | *67.80* |
| *Nos. 151-152 (2)* | 16.25 | *48.25* |
| *Nos. 188-189 (2)* | 25.25 | *29.75* |
| *Nos. 21-22 (2)* | 116.00 | 45.40 |
| *Nos. 82-83 (2)* | 13.40 | 13.40 |
| *Nos. 110-111 (2)* | 8.40 | *8.75* |
| *Nos. 48-49 (2)* | 40.30 | *47.75* |
| *Nos. 64-65 (2)* | 31.80 | *50.25* |
| *Nos. 92-93 (2)* | 16.25 | *22.75* |
| *Nos. 90-91 (2)* | 16.25 | 22.25 |
| *Nos. 224-225 (2)* | 29.60 | 38.00 |
| *Nos. 267-268 (2)* | 30.40 | 25.25 |
| *Nos. 93-94 (2)* | 17.10 | 25.75 |
| *Nos. 525-526 (2)* | 22.90 | 32.75 |
| *Nos. 62-63 (2)* | 38.50 | *58.00* |
| *Nos. 82-83 (2)* | 69.50 | 45.50 |
| *Nos. 25-26 (2)* | 41.00 | *42.50* |
| *No. 106 (1)* | .80 | 1.00 |
| *No. 159 (1)* | 1.10 | .35 |
| *Set total (136) Stamps* | 2,542. | 2,754. |

## U.P.U.

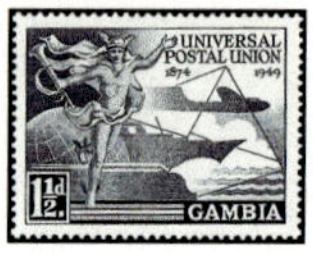

Mercury and Symbols of Communications CD306

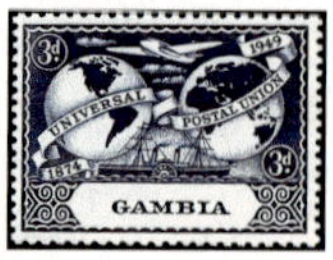

Plane, Ship and Hemispheres CD307

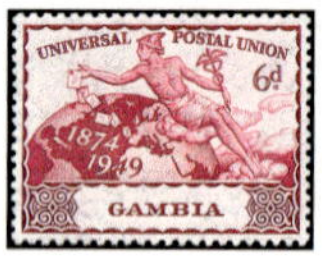

Mercury Scattering Letters over Globe — CD308

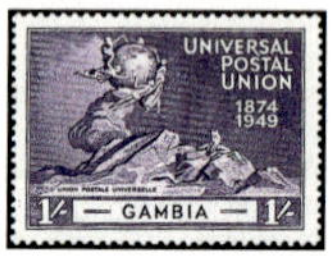

U.P.U. Monument, Bern — CD309

Universal Postal Union, 75th anniversary.

### 1949

Aden ...........................................32-35
Kathiri State of Seiyun..............16-19
Qu'aiti State of Shihr and Mukalla .....................................16-19
Antigua ...................................100-103
Ascension ...................................57-60
Bahamas .................................150-153
Barbados ................................212-215
Basutoland...................................41-44
Bechuanaland Protectorate......149-152
Bermuda .................................138-141
British Guiana..........................246-249
British Honduras......................137-140
Brunei ..........................................79-82
Cayman Islands.......................118-121
Cyprus .....................................160-163
Dominica..................................116-119
Falkland Islands ......................103-106
Falkland Islands Dep...........1L14-1L17
Fiji ............................................141-144
Gambia ....................................148-151
Gibraltar...................................123-126
Gilbert & Ellice Islands................56-59
Gold Coast ..............................144-147
Grenada...................................147-150
Hong Kong ..............................180-183
Jamaica ...................................142-145
Kenya, Uganda, Tanzania ...........94-97
Leeward Islands ......................126-129
Malaya
Johore ..................................151-154
Kedah.......................................57-60
Kelantan ...................................46-49
Malacca.....................................18-21
Negri Sembilan .........................59-62
Pahang......................................46-49
Penang......................................23-26
Perak ....................................101-104
Perlis ............................................3-6
Selangor....................................76-79
Trengganu .................................49-52
Malta .......................................225-228
Mauritius .................................231-234
Montserrat ...............................108-111
New Hebrides, British .................62-65
New Hebrides, French ................79-82
Nigeria ........................................75-78
North Borneo...........................240-243
Northern Rhodesia......................50-53
Nyasaland Protectorate...............87-90
Pitcairn Islands ............................13-16
St. Helena ...............................132-135
St. Kitts-Nevis .............................95-98
St. Lucia .................................131-134
St. Vincent ..............................170-173
Sarawak..................................176-179
Seychelles ...............................153-156
Sierra Leone............................190-193
Singapore ...................................23-26
Solomon Islands..........................84-87
Somaliland Protectorate ..........112-115
Southern Rhodesia .....................71-72
Swaziland ...................................50-53
Tonga ..........................................87-90
Trinidad & Tobago ......................66-69
Turks & Caicos Islands ...........101-104
Virgin Islands..............................92-95
Zanzibar..................................226-229

The following have different designs but are included in the omnibus set:

Great Britain ............................276-279
Offices in Morocco (Tangier) .......546-549
Australia .........................................223
Bahrain .......................................68-71
Burma ....................................116-121
Ceylon ....................................304-306
Egypt ......................................281-283
India........................................223-226
Kuwait.........................................89-92
Oman..........................................31-34
Pakistan-Bahawalpur 26-29, O25-O28
South Africa.............................109-111
South-West Africa ...................160-162

| | | |
|---|---|---|
| *Nos. 32-35 (4)* | 5.85 | *8.45* |
| *Nos. 16-19 (4)* | 2.75 | *16.00* |
| *Nos. 16-19 (4)* | 2.60 | 8.00 |
| *Nos. 100-103 (4)* | 3.60 | *7.70* |
| *Nos. 57-60 (4)* | 11.10 | 9.00 |
| *Nos. 150-153 (4)* | 5.35 | 9.30 |
| *Nos. 212-215 (4)* | 4.40 | *14.85* |
| *Nos. 41-44 (4)* | 4.75 | *10.00* |
| *Nos. 149-152 (4)* | 3.35 | *7.25* |
| *Nos. 138-141 (4)* | 4.75 | 6.15 |
| *Nos. 246-249 (4)* | 2.75 | 4.20 |
| *Nos. 137-140 (4)* | 3.30 | 6.35 |
| *Nos. 79-82 (4)* | 9.50 | 8.45 |
| *Nos. 118-121 (4)* | 3.60 | *7.25* |
| *Nos. 160-163 (4)* | 4.60 | *10.70* |
| *Nos. 116-119 (4)* | 2.30 | 5.65 |
| *Nos. 103-106 (4)* | 14.00 | 17.10 |
| *Nos. 1L14-1L17 (4)* | 14.60 | 14.50 |
| *Nos. 141-144 (4)* | 3.35 | 15.75 |
| *Nos. 148-151 (4)* | 2.75 | 7.10 |
| *Nos. 123-126 (4)* | 5.90 | *8.75* |
| *Nos. 56-59 (4)* | 4.30 | *13.00* |
| *Nos. 144-147 (4)* | 2.55 | *10.35* |
| *Nos. 147-150 (4)* | 2.15 | 3.55 |
| *Nos. 180-183 (4)* | 66.75 | 19.95 |
| *Nos. 142-145 (4)* | 2.50 | 2.45 |
| *Nos. 94-97 (4)* | 2.90 | 4.00 |
| *Nos. 126-129 (4)* | 3.05 | *9.60* |
| *Nos. 151-154 (4)* | 4.70 | 8.90 |
| *Nos. 57-60 (4)* | 4.80 | 12.00 |
| *Nos. 46-49 (4)* | 4.25 | 12.65 |
| *Nos. 18-21 (4)* | 4.25 | *17.30* |
| *Nos. 59-62 (4)* | 3.50 | 10.75 |
| *Nos. 46-49 (4)* | 3.00 | 7.25 |
| *Nos. 23-26 (4)* | 5.10 | 11.75 |
| *Nos. 101-104 (4)* | 3.65 | 10.75 |
| *Nos. 3-6 (4)* | 3.95 | 14.25 |
| *Nos. 76-79 (4)* | 4.90 | 12.30 |
| *Nos. 49-52 (4)* | 5.55 | 12.25 |
| *Nos. 225-228 (4)* | 4.50 | 4.85 |
| *Nos. 231-234 (4)* | 3.70 | 7.05 |
| *Nos. 108-111 (4)* | 3.30 | 4.35 |
| *Nos. 62-65 (4)* | 1.60 | *4.25* |
| *Nos. 79-82 (4)* | 15.40 | *22.00* |
| *Nos. 75-78 (4)* | 2.80 | *9.25* |
| *Nos. 240-243 (4)* | 7.15 | 6.50 |
| *Nos. 50-53 (4)* | 5.00 | *6.50* |
| *Nos. 87-90 (4)* | 4.55 | 6.60 |
| *Nos. 13-16 (4)* | 15.05 | 14.25 |
| *Nos. 132-135 (4)* | 4.85 | 7.10 |
| *Nos. 95-98 (4)* | 4.35 | 5.55 |
| *Nos. 131-134 (4)* | 2.55 | *3.85* |
| *Nos. 170-173 (4)* | 2.20 | *5.05* |
| *Nos. 176-179 (4)* | 13.40 | 13.35 |
| *Nos. 153-156 (4)* | 3.00 | 5.15 |
| *Nos. 190-193 (4)* | 2.90 | *9.15* |
| *Nos. 23-26 (4)* | 19.00 | 13.70 |
| *Nos. 84-87 (4)* | 4.05 | 4.90 |
| *Nos. 112-115 (4)* | 3.95 | 9.95 |
| *Nos. 71-72 (2)* | 1.95 | *2.25* |
| *Nos. 50-53 (4)* | 2.80 | 4.65 |
| *Nos. 87-90 (4)* | 3.00 | *5.25* |
| *Nos. 66-69 (4)* | 3.55 | 6.80 |
| *Nos. 101-104 (4)* | 3.05 | 8.90 |
| *Nos. 92-95 (4)* | 2.60 | 5.90 |
| *Nos. 226-229 (4)* | 4.95 | 13.50 |
| *Nos. 276-279 (4)* | 1.35 | 1.00 |
| *Nos. 546-549 (4)* | 2.60 | *16.00* |
| *No. 223 (1)* | .40 | .40 |
| *Nos. 68-71 (4)* | 4.75 | *16.50* |
| *Nos. 116-121 (6)* | 7.30 | 5.35 |
| *Nos. 304-306 (3)* | 3.35 | 4.25 |
| *Nos. 281-283 (3)* | 5.75 | 2.70 |
| *Nos. 223-226 (4)* | 27.25 | 10.50 |
| *Nos. 89-92 (4)* | 6.10 | 10.25 |
| *Nos. 31-34 (4)* | 8.00 | 17.50 |
| *Nos. 26-29,O25-O28 (8)* | 2.40 | *44.00* |
| *Nos. 109-111 (3)* | 2.00 | 2.70 |
| *Nos. 160-162 (3)* | 3.00 | 5.50 |
| *Set total (313) Stamps* | 466.45 | 742.80 |

## University

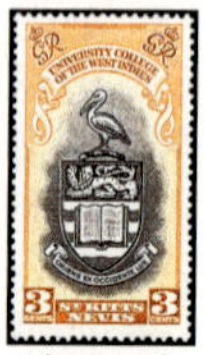

Arms of University College CD310

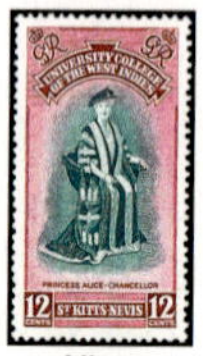

Alice, Princess of Athlone CD311

1948 opening of University College of the West Indies at Jamaica.

### 1951

Antigua ...................................104-105
Barbados ................................228-229
British Guiana..........................250-251
British Honduras......................141-142
Dominica..................................120-121
Grenada...................................164-165
Jamaica ...................................146-147
Leeward Islands ......................130-131
Montserrat ...............................112-113
St. Kitts-Nevis..........................105-106
St. Lucia .................................149-150
St. Vincent ..............................174-175
Trinidad & Tobago ......................70-71
Virgin Islands..............................96-97

| | | |
|---|---|---|
| *Nos. 104-105 (2)* | 1.35 | *3.75* |
| *Nos. 228-229 (2)* | 1.75 | 2.65 |
| *Nos. 250-251 (2)* | 1.10 | *1.25* |
| *Nos. 141-142 (2)* | 1.40 | 2.20 |
| *Nos. 120-121 (2)* | 1.40 | *1.75* |
| *Nos. 164-165 (2)* | 1.20 | *1.60* |
| *Nos. 146-147 (2)* | 1.05 | .70 |
| *Nos. 130-131 (2)* | 1.35 | 4.00 |
| *Nos. 112-113 (2)* | .85 | *2.00* |
| *Nos. 105-106 (2)* | 1.40 | 2.25 |
| *Nos. 149-150 (2)* | 1.40 | 1.50 |
| *Nos. 174-175 (2)* | 1.00 | *2.15* |
| *Nos. 70-71 (2)* | 1.00 | 4.20 |
| *Nos. 96-97 (2)* | 1.50 | *3.75* |
| *Set total (28) Stamps* | 17.75 | 33.75 |

## Coronation

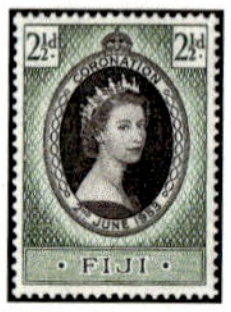

Queen Elizabeth II — CD312

### 1953

Aden ................................................47
Kathiri State of Seiyun...................28
Qu'aiti State of Shihr and Mukalla ..........................................28
Antigua ...........................................106
Ascension .........................................61
Bahamas .........................................157
Barbados .........................................234
Basutoland.........................................45
Bechuanaland Protectorate.............153
Bermuda ..........................................142
British Guiana..................................252
British Honduras..............................143
Cayman Islands...............................150
Cyprus .............................................167
Dominica..........................................141
Falkland Islands ..............................121
Falkland Islands Dependencies ....1L18
Fiji ...................................................145
Gambia ............................................152
Gibraltar...........................................131
Gilbert & Ellice Islands......................60
Gold Coast ......................................160
Grenada...........................................170
Hong Kong ......................................184
Jamaica ...........................................153
Kenya, Uganda, Tanzania ...............101
Leeward Islands ..............................132
Malaya
Johore ............................................155
Kedah...............................................82
Kelantan ...........................................71
Malacca.............................................27
Negri Sembilan .................................63
Pahang..............................................71
Penang..............................................27
Perak ..............................................126
Perlis .................................................28
Selangor..........................................101
Trengganu .........................................74
Malta ...............................................241

# COMMON DESIGN TYPES

41A

| | |
|---|---|
| Mauritius | 250 |
| Montserrat | 127 |
| New Hebrides, British | 77 |
| Nigeria | 79 |
| North Borneo | 260 |
| Northern Rhodesia | 60 |
| Nyasaland Protectorate | 96 |
| Pitcairn Islands | 19 |
| St. Helena | 139 |
| St. Kitts-Nevis | 119 |
| St. Lucia | 156 |
| St. Vincent | 185 |
| Sarawak | 196 |
| Seychelles | 172 |
| Sierra Leone | 194 |
| Singapore | 27 |
| Solomon Islands | 88 |
| Somaliland Protectorate | 127 |
| Swaziland | 54 |
| Trinidad & Tobago | 84 |
| Tristan da Cunha | 13 |
| Turks & Caicos Islands | 118 |
| Virgin Islands | 114 |

The following have different designs but are included in the omnibus set:

| | |
|---|---|
| Great Britain | 313-316 |
| Offices in Morocco (Tangier) | 579-582 |
| Australia | 259-261 |
| Bahrain | 92-95 |
| Canada | 330 |
| Ceylon | 317 |
| Cook Islands | 145-146 |
| Kuwait | 113-116 |
| New Zealand | 280-284 |
| Niue | 104-105 |
| Oman | 52-55 |
| Samoa | 214-215 |
| South Africa | 102 |
| Southern Rhodesia | 80 |
| South-West Africa | 244-248 |
| Tokelau Islands | 4 |

| | | |
|---|---|---|
| No. 47 (1) | 1.25 | 1.25 |
| No. 28 (1) | .75 | 1.50 |
| No. 28 (1) | 1.10 | .60 |
| No. 106 (1) | .40 | .75 |
| No. 61 (1) | 1.25 | 2.75 |
| No. 157 (1) | 1.40 | .75 |
| No. 234 (1) | 1.00 | .25 |
| No. 45 (1) | .50 | .60 |
| No. 153 (1) | .50 | .35 |
| No. 142 (1) | .85 | .50 |
| No. 252 (1) | .45 | .25 |
| No. 143 (1) | .60 | .40 |
| No. 150 (1) | .40 | 1.75 |
| No. 167 (1) | 2.75 | .25 |
| No. 141 (1) | .40 | .40 |
| No. 121 (1) | .90 | 1.50 |
| No. 1L18 (1) | 1.80 | 1.40 |
| No. 145 (1) | 1.00 | .60 |
| No. 152 (1) | .50 | .60 |
| No. 131 (1) | .50 | .50 |
| No. 60 (1) | .65 | 2.25 |
| No. 160 (1) | 1.00 | .25 |
| No. 170 (1) | .30 | .25 |
| No. 184 (1) | 3.00 | .30 |
| No. 153 (1) | .70 | .25 |
| No. 101 (1) | .40 | .25 |
| No. 132 (1) | 1.00 | 2.25 |
| No. 155 (1) | 1.40 | .30 |
| No. 82 (1) | 2.25 | .60 |
| No. 71 (1) | 1.60 | 1.60 |
| No. 27 (1) | 1.10 | 1.30 |
| No. 63 (1) | 1.40 | .65 |
| No. 71 (1) | 2.25 | .25 |
| No. 27 (1) | 1.75 | .30 |
| No. 126 (1) | 1.60 | .25 |
| No. 28 (1) | 1.75 | 4.00 |
| No. 101 (1) | 1.75 | .25 |
| No. 74 (1) | 1.50 | 1.00 |
| No. 241 (1) | .50 | .25 |
| No. 250 (1) | 1.10 | .25 |
| No. 127 (1) | .60 | .45 |
| No. 77 (1) | .75 | .60 |
| No. 79 (1) | .40 | .25 |
| No. 260 (1) | 1.75 | 1.00 |
| No. 60 (1) | .70 | .25 |
| No. 96 (1) | .75 | .75 |
| No. 19 (1) | 2.00 | 3.50 |
| No. 139 (1) | 1.25 | 1.25 |
| No. 119 (1) | .35 | .25 |
| No. 156 (1) | .70 | .35 |
| No. 185 (1) | .50 | .30 |
| No. 196 (1) | 1.75 | 1.75 |
| No. 172 (1) | .80 | .80 |
| No. 194 (1) | .40 | .40 |
| No. 27 (1) | 2.50 | .40 |
| No. 88 (1) | 1.00 | 1.00 |
| No. 127 (1) | .40 | .25 |
| No. 54 (1) | .30 | .25 |
| No. 84 (1) | .30 | .25 |
| No. 13 (1) | 1.00 | 1.75 |
| No. 118 (1) | .40 | 1.10 |
| No. 114 (1) | .40 | 1.00 |
| Nos. 313-316 (4) | 11.40 | 4.05 |
| Nos. 579-582 (4) | 10.90 | 5.30 |
| Nos. 259-261 (3) | 3.60 | 2.75 |
| Nos. 92-95 (4) | 15.25 | 12.75 |
| No. 330 (1) | .30 | .25 |

| | | |
|---|---|---|
| No. 317 (1) | 1.40 | .25 |
| Nos. 145-146 (2) | 2.65 | 2.65 |
| Nos. 113-116 (4) | 16.00 | 8.50 |
| Nos. 280-284 (5) | 3.30 | 4.55 |
| Nos. 104-105 (2) | 2.25 | 1.50 |
| Nos. 52-55 (4) | 14.25 | 6.50 |
| Nos. 214-215 (2) | 2.50 | .80 |
| No. 192 (1) | .45 | .30 |
| No. 80 (1) | 7.25 | 7.25 |
| Nos. 244-248 (5) | 3.00 | 2.35 |
| No. 4 (1) | 2.75 | 2.75 |
| Set total (106) Stamps | 161.55 | 114.25 |

Separate designs for each country for the visit of Queen Elizabeth II and the Duke of Edinburgh.

### Royal Visit 1953

**1953**

| | |
|---|---|
| Aden | 62 |
| Australia | 267-269 |
| Bermuda | 163 |
| Ceylon | 318 |
| Fiji | 146 |
| Gibraltar | 146 |
| Jamaica | 154 |
| Kenya, Uganda, Tanzania | 102 |
| Malta | 242 |
| New Zealand | 286-287 |

| | | |
|---|---|---|
| No. 62 (1) | .65 | 4.00 |
| Nos. 267-269 (3) | 2.75 | 2.05 |
| No. 163 (1) | .50 | .25 |
| No. 318 (1) | 1.00 | .25 |
| No. 146 (1) | .65 | .35 |
| No. 146 (1) | .50 | .30 |
| No. 154 (1) | .50 | .25 |
| No. 102 (1) | .50 | .25 |
| No. 242 (1) | .35 | .25 |
| Nos. 286-287 (2) | .60 | .50 |
| Set total (13) Stamps | 7.90 | 8.45 |

### West Indies Federation

Map of the Caribbean CD313

Federation of the West Indies, April 22, 1958.

**1958**

| | |
|---|---|
| Antigua | 122-124 |
| Barbados | 248-250 |
| Dominica | 161-163 |
| Grenada | 184-186 |
| Jamaica | 175-177 |
| Montserrat | 143-145 |
| St. Kitts-Nevis | 136-138 |
| St. Lucia | 170-172 |
| St. Vincent | 198-200 |
| Trinidad & Tobago | 86-88 |

| | | |
|---|---|---|
| Nos. 122-124 (3) | 5.80 | 3.80 |
| Nos. 248-250 (3) | 1.60 | 2.90 |
| Nos. 161-163 (3) | 1.95 | 1.85 |
| Nos. 184-186 (3) | 1.50 | 1.20 |
| Nos. 175-177 (3) | 2.65 | 3.15 |
| Nos. 143-145 (3) | 2.35 | 1.35 |
| Nos. 136-138 (3) | 3.00 | 3.10 |
| Nos. 170-172 (3) | 2.05 | 2.80 |
| Nos. 198-200 (3) | 1.50 | 1.75 |
| Nos. 86-88 (3) | 2.40 | 2.35 |
| Set total (30) Stamps | 24.80 | 24.55 |

### Freedom from Hunger

Protein Food — CD314

U.N. Food and Agricultural Organization's "Freedom from Hunger" campaign.

**1963**

| | |
|---|---|
| Aden | 65 |
| Antigua | 133 |
| Ascension | 89 |
| Bahamas | 180 |
| Basutoland | 83 |
| Bechuanaland Protectorate | 194 |
| Bermuda | 192 |
| British Guiana | 271 |
| British Honduras | 179 |
| Brunei | 100 |
| Cayman Islands | 168 |
| Dominica | 181 |
| Falkland Islands | 146 |
| Fiji | 198 |
| Gambia | 172 |
| Gibraltar | 161 |
| Gilbert & Ellice Islands | 76 |
| Grenada | 190 |
| Hong Kong | 218 |
| Malta | 291 |
| Mauritius | 270 |
| Montserrat | 150 |
| New Hebrides, British | 93 |
| North Borneo | 296 |
| Pitcairn Islands | 35 |
| St. Helena | 173 |
| St. Lucia | 179 |
| St. Vincent | 201 |
| Sarawak | 212 |
| Seychelles | 213 |
| Solomon Islands | 109 |
| Swaziland | 108 |
| Tonga | 127 |
| Tristan da Cunha | 68 |
| Turks & Caicos Islands | 138 |
| Virgin Islands | 140 |
| Zanzibar | 280 |

| | | |
|---|---|---|
| No. 65 (1) | 1.50 | 1.75 |
| No. 133 (1) | .35 | .35 |
| No. 89 (1) | 1.00 | .50 |
| No. 180 (1) | .65 | .65 |
| No. 83 (1) | .50 | .25 |
| No. 194 (1) | .50 | .50 |
| No. 192 (1) | 1.00 | .50 |
| No. 271 (1) | .45 | .25 |
| No. 179 (1) | .60 | .25 |
| No. 100 (1) | 3.25 | 2.25 |
| No. 168 (1) | .55 | .30 |
| No. 181 (1) | .30 | .30 |
| No. 146 (1) | 10.50 | 2.50 |
| No. 198 (1) | 3.50 | 2.25 |
| No. 172 (1) | .50 | .25 |
| No. 161 (1) | 4.00 | 2.25 |
| No. 76 (1) | 1.40 | .40 |
| No. 190 (1) | .30 | .25 |
| No. 218 (1) | 37.50 | 5.00 |
| No. 291 (1) | 2.00 | 2.00 |
| No. 270 (1) | .45 | .25 |
| No. 150 (1) | .55 | .35 |
| No. 93 (1) | .60 | .25 |
| No. 296 (1) | 1.90 | .75 |
| No. 35 (1) | 3.50 | 1.50 |
| No. 173 (1) | 2.25 | 1.10 |
| No. 179 (1) | .40 | .40 |
| No. 201 (1) | .90 | .50 |
| No. 212 (1) | 1.00 | 1.00 |
| No. 213 (1) | .85 | .35 |
| No. 109 (1) | 3.00 | .85 |
| No. 108 (1) | .50 | .50 |
| No. 127 (1) | .60 | .35 |
| No. 68 (1) | .75 | .35 |
| No. 138 (1) | .30 | .25 |
| No. 140 (1) | .50 | .50 |
| No. 280 (1) | 1.50 | .80 |
| Set total (37) Stamps | 90.50 | 32.80 |

### Red Cross Centenary

Red Cross and Elizabeth II — CD315

**1963**

| | |
|---|---|
| Antigua | 134-135 |
| Ascension | 90-91 |
| Bahamas | 183-184 |
| Basutoland | 84-85 |
| Bechuanaland Protectorate | 195-196 |
| Bermuda | 193-194 |
| British Guiana | 272-273 |
| British Honduras | 180-181 |
| Cayman Islands | 169-170 |
| Dominica | 182-183 |
| Falkland Islands | 147-148 |
| Fiji | 203-204 |
| Gambia | 173-174 |
| Gibraltar | 162-163 |
| Gilbert & Ellice Islands | 77-78 |
| Grenada | 191-192 |
| Hong Kong | 219-220 |
| Jamaica | 203-204 |
| Malta | 292-293 |
| Mauritius | 271-272 |
| Montserrat | 151-152 |
| New Hebrides, British | 94-95 |
| Pitcairn Islands | 36-37 |
| St. Helena | 174-175 |
| St. Kitts-Nevis | 143-144 |
| St. Lucia | 180-181 |
| St. Vincent | 202-203 |
| Seychelles | 214-215 |
| Solomon Islands | 110-111 |
| South Arabia | 1-2 |
| Swaziland | 109-110 |
| Tonga | 134-135 |
| Tristan da Cunha | 69-70 |
| Turks & Caicos Islands | 139-140 |
| Virgin Islands | 141-142 |

| | | |
|---|---|---|
| Nos. 134-135 (2) | 1.00 | 2.00 |
| Nos. 90-91 (2) | 6.75 | 3.35 |
| Nos. 183-184 (2) | 2.30 | 2.80 |
| Nos. 84-85 (2) | 1.20 | .90 |
| Nos. 195-196 (2) | .95 | .85 |
| Nos. 193-194 (2) | 3.00 | 2.80 |
| Nos. 272-273 (2) | .85 | .85 |
| Nos. 180-181 (2) | 1.00 | 2.50 |
| Nos. 169-170 (2) | 1.10 | 3.00 |
| Nos. 182-183 (2) | .70 | 1.05 |
| Nos. 147-148 (2) | 18.00 | 5.50 |
| Nos. 203-204 (2) | 3.25 | 2.80 |
| Nos. 173-174 (2) | .80 | 1.00 |
| Nos. 162-163 (2) | 6.25 | 5.40 |
| Nos. 77-78 (2) | 2.00 | 3.50 |
| Nos. 191-192 (2) | .80 | .50 |
| Nos. 219-220 (2) | 18.75 | 7.35 |
| Nos. 203-204 (2) | .75 | 1.65 |
| Nos. 292-293 (2) | 2.50 | 4.75 |
| Nos. 271-272 (2) | .85 | .50 |
| Nos. 151-152 (2) | 1.00 | .75 |
| Nos. 94-95 (2) | 1.00 | .50 |
| Nos. 36-37 (2) | 2.50 | 4.00 |
| Nos. 174-175 (2) | 1.70 | 2.30 |
| Nos. 143-144 (2) | .90 | .90 |
| Nos. 180-181 (2) | 1.25 | 1.25 |
| Nos. 202-203 (2) | .90 | .90 |
| Nos. 214-215 (2) | 1.00 | 1.50 |
| Nos. 110-111 (2) | 1.25 | 1.15 |
| Nos. 1-2 (2) | 1.25 | 1.25 |
| Nos. 109-110 (2) | 1.10 | 1.10 |
| Nos. 134-135 (2) | 1.00 | 1.25 |
| Nos. 69-70 (2) | 1.15 | .80 |
| Nos. 139-140 (2) | .55 | 1.00 |
| Nos. 141-142 (2) | .80 | 1.25 |
| Set total (70) Stamps | 90.15 | 72.70 |

### Shakespeare

Shakespeare Memorial Theatre, Stratford-on-Avon CD316

400th anniversary of the birth of William Shakespeare.

**1964**

| | |
|---|---|
| Antigua | 151 |
| Bahamas | 201 |
| Bechuanaland Protectorate | 197 |
| Cayman Islands | 171 |
| Dominica | 184 |
| Falkland Islands | 149 |
| Gambia | 192 |
| Gibraltar | 164 |
| Montserrat | 153 |
| St. Lucia | 196 |
| Turks & Caicos Islands | 141 |
| Virgin Islands | 143 |

| | | |
|---|---|---|
| No. 151 (1) | .35 | .25 |
| No. 201 (1) | .60 | .35 |
| No. 197 (1) | .35 | .35 |
| No. 171 (1) | .35 | .30 |
| No. 184 (1) | .35 | .35 |
| No. 149 (1) | 1.60 | .50 |
| No. 192 (1) | .35 | .25 |
| No. 164 (1) | .65 | .55 |
| No. 153 (1) | .35 | .25 |
| No. 196 (1) | .45 | .25 |
| No. 141 (1) | .30 | .25 |
| No. 143 (1) | .45 | .45 |
| Set total (12) Stamps | 6.15 | 4.10 |

### ITU

ITU Emblem CD317

Intl. Telecommunication Union, cent.

**1965**

| | |
|---|---|
| Antigua | 153-154 |
| Ascension | 92-93 |
| Bahamas | 219-220 |
| Barbados | 265-266 |
| Basutoland | 101-102 |
| Bechuanaland Protectorate | 202-203 |
| Bermuda | 196-197 |
| British Guiana | 293-294 |
| British Honduras | 187-188 |
| Brunei | 116-117 |
| Cayman Islands | 172-173 |
| Dominica | 185-186 |
| Falkland Islands | 154-155 |
| Fiji | 211-212 |
| Gibraltar | 167-168 |
| Gilbert & Ellice Islands | 87-88 |
| Grenada | 205-206 |
| Hong Kong | 221-222 |
| Mauritius | 291-292 |
| Montserrat | 157-158 |
| New Hebrides, British | 108-109 |

42A COMMON DESIGN TYPES

Pitcairn Islands ....52-53
St. Helena ....180-181
St. Kitts-Nevis ....163-164
St. Lucia ....197-198
St. Vincent ....224-225
Seychelles ....218-219
Solomon Islands ....126-127
Swaziland ....115-116
Tristan da Cunha ....85-86
Turks & Caicos Islands ....142-143
Virgin Islands ....159-160

| | | |
|---|---|---|
| *Nos. 153-154 (2)* | 1.45 | 1.35 |
| *Nos. 92-93 (2)* | 1.90 | 1.30 |
| *Nos. 219-220 (2)* | 1.35 | 1.50 |
| *Nos. 265-266 (2)* | 1.50 | 1.25 |
| *Nos. 101-102 (2)* | .85 | .65 |
| *Nos. 202-203 (2)* | 1.10 | .75 |
| *Nos. 196-197 (2)* | 2.15 | *2.25* |
| *Nos. 293-294 (2)* | .50 | .50 |
| *Nos. 187-188 (2)* | .75 | .75 |
| *Nos. 116-117 (2)* | 1.75 | 1.75 |
| *Nos. 172-173 (2)* | 1.00 | .85 |
| *Nos. 185-186 (2)* | .55 | .55 |
| *Nos. 154-155 (2)* | 6.75 | 3.15 |
| *Nos. 211-212 (2)* | 2.00 | 1.05 |
| *Nos. 167-168 (2)* | 9.00 | 5.95 |
| *Nos. 87-88 (2)* | .85 | .60 |
| *Nos. 205-206 (2)* | .50 | .50 |
| *Nos. 221-222 (2)* | 10.50 | 4.75 |
| *Nos. 291-292 (2)* | 1.10 | .50 |
| *Nos. 157-158 (2)* | 1.05 | 1.15 |
| *Nos. 108-109 (2)* | .65 | .50 |
| *Nos. 52-53 (2)* | 1.65 | 1.90 |
| *Nos. 180-181 (2)* | .80 | .60 |
| *Nos. 163-164 (2)* | .60 | .60 |
| *Nos. 197-198 (2)* | 1.25 | 1.25 |
| *Nos. 224-225 (2)* | .80 | .90 |
| *Nos. 218-219 (2)* | .75 | .60 |
| *Nos. 126-127 (2)* | .70 | .55 |
| *Nos. 115-116 (2)* | .70 | .70 |
| *Nos. 85-86 (2)* | 1.00 | .65 |
| *Nos. 142-143 (2)* | .50 | .50 |
| *Nos. 159-160 (2)* | .85 | .85 |
| *Set total (64) Stamps* | 56.85 | 40.70 |

### Intl. Cooperation Year

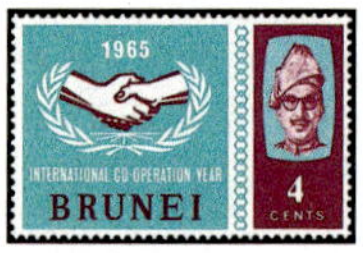


ICY Emblem
CD318

**1965**

Antigua ....155-156
Ascension ....94-95
Bahamas ....222-223
Basutoland ....103-104
Bechuanaland Protectorate ....204-205
Bermuda ....199-200
British Guiana ....295-296
British Honduras ....189-190
Brunei ....118-119
Cayman Islands ....174-175
Dominica ....187-188
Falkland Islands ....156-157
Fiji ....213-214
Gibraltar ....169-170
Gilbert & Ellice Islands ....104-105
Grenada ....207-208
Hong Kong ....223-224
Mauritius ....293-294
Montserrat ....176-177
New Hebrides, British ....110-111
New Hebrides, French ....126-127
Pitcairn Islands ....54-55
St. Helena ....182-183
St. Kitts-Nevis ....165-166
St. Lucia ....199-200
Seychelles ....220-221
Solomon Islands ....143-144
South Arabia ....17-18
Swaziland ....117-118
Tristan da Cunha ....87-88
Turks & Caicos Islands ....144-145
Virgin Islands ....161-162

| | | |
|---|---|---|
| *Nos. 155-156 (2)* | .55 | .50 |
| *Nos. 94-95 (2)* | 1.30 | 1.40 |
| *Nos. 222-223 (2)* | .65 | 1.90 |
| *Nos. 103-104 (2)* | .75 | .85 |
| *Nos. 204-205 (2)* | .85 | 1.00 |
| *Nos. 199-200 (2)* | 2.05 | 1.25 |
| *Nos. 295-296 (2)* | .55 | .50 |
| *Nos. 189-190 (2)* | .60 | .55 |
| *Nos. 118-119 (2)* | .85 | .85 |
| *Nos. 174-175 (2)* | 1.00 | .75 |
| *Nos. 187-188 (2)* | .55 | .55 |
| *Nos. 156-157 (2)* | 6.00 | 1.65 |
| *Nos. 213-214 (2)* | 1.95 | 1.25 |
| *Nos. 169-170 (2)* | 1.25 | *2.75* |
| *Nos. 104-105 (2)* | .85 | .60 |
| *Nos. 207-208 (2)* | .50 | .50 |
| *Nos. 223-224 (2)* | 11.00 | 3.50 |
| *Nos. 293-294 (2)* | .65 | .50 |
| *Nos. 176-177 (2)* | .80 | .65 |
| *Nos. 110-111 (2)* | .50 | .50 |
| *Nos. 126-127 (2)* | 12.00 | 12.00 |
| *Nos. 54-55 (2)* | 1.60 | 1.85 |
| *Nos. 182-183 (2)* | .95 | .50 |
| *Nos. 165-166 (2)* | .80 | .60 |
| *Nos. 199-200 (2)* | .55 | .55 |
| *Nos. 220-221 (2)* | .80 | .60 |
| *Nos. 143-144 (2)* | .70 | .60 |
| *Nos. 17-18 (2)* | 1.20 | .50 |
| *Nos. 117-118 (2)* | .75 | .75 |
| *Nos. 87-88 (2)* | 1.05 | .65 |
| *Nos. 144-145 (2)* | .50 | .50 |
| *Nos. 161-162 (2)* | .65 | .50 |
| *Set total (64) Stamps* | 54.75 | 41.60 |

### Churchill Memorial

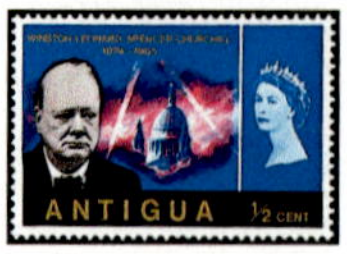


Winston Churchill and St. Paul's, London, During Air Attack — CD319

**1966**

Antigua ....157-160
Ascension ....96-99
Bahamas ....224-227
Barbados ....281-284
Basutoland ....105-108
Bechuanaland Protectorate ....206-209
Bermuda ....201-204
British Antarctic Territory ....16-19
British Honduras ....191-194
Brunei ....120-123
Cayman Islands ....176-179
Dominica ....189-192
Falkland Islands ....158-161
Fiji ....215-218
Gibraltar ....171-174
Gilbert & Ellice Islands ....106-109
Grenada ....209-212
Hong Kong ....225-228
Mauritius ....295-298
Montserrat ....178-181
New Hebrides, British ....112-115
New Hebrides, French ....128-131
Pitcairn Islands ....56-59
St. Helena ....184-187
St. Kitts-Nevis ....167-170
St. Lucia ....201-204
St. Vincent ....241-244
Seychelles ....222-225
Solomon Islands ....145-148
South Arabia ....19-22
Swaziland ....119-122
Tristan da Cunha ....89-92
Turks & Caicos Islands ....146-149
Virgin Islands ....163-166

| | | |
|---|---|---|
| *Nos. 157-160 (4)* | 3.05 | 3.05 |
| *Nos. 96-99 (4)* | 10.00 | 6.40 |
| *Nos. 224-227 (4)* | 2.30 | *3.20* |
| *Nos. 281-284 (4)* | 3.00 | 4.95 |
| *Nos. 105-108 (4)* | 2.80 | 3.25 |
| *Nos. 206-209 (4)* | 2.50 | 2.50 |
| *Nos. 201-204 (4)* | 4.00 | *4.75* |
| *Nos. 16-19 (4)* | 41.20 | 18.00 |
| *Nos. 191-194 (4)* | 2.45 | 1.30 |
| *Nos. 120-123 (4)* | 7.65 | 6.55 |
| *Nos. 176-179 (4)* | 3.10 | 3.65 |
| *Nos. 189-192 (4)* | 1.15 | 1.15 |
| *Nos. 158-161 (4)* | 12.75 | 9.55 |
| *Nos. 215-218 (4)* | 4.40 | 3.00 |
| *Nos. 171-174 (4)* | 3.05 | 5.30 |
| *Nos. 106-109 (4)* | 1.50 | 1.30 |
| *Nos. 209-212 (4)* | 1.10 | 1.10 |
| *Nos. 225-228 (4)* | 52.50 | 11.40 |
| *Nos. 295-298 (4)* | 3.70 | 3.75 |
| *Nos. 178-181 (4)* | 1.60 | 1.55 |
| *Nos. 112-115 (4)* | 2.30 | 1.00 |
| *Nos. 128-131 (4)* | 8.35 | 8.35 |
| *Nos. 56-59 (4)* | 4.45 | 6.10 |
| *Nos. 184-187 (4)* | 1.85 | 1.95 |
| *Nos. 167-170 (4)* | 1.50 | 1.70 |
| *Nos. 201-204 (4)* | 1.50 | 1.50 |
| *Nos. 241-244 (4)* | 1.50 | 1.75 |
| *Nos. 222-225 (4)* | 3.20 | 4.35 |
| *Nos. 145-148 (4)* | 1.50 | 1.60 |
| *Nos. 19-22 (4)* | 2.95 | 2.20 |
| *Nos. 119-122 (4)* | 1.70 | 2.55 |
| *Nos. 89-92 (4)* | 5.95 | 2.70 |
| *Nos. 146-149 (4)* | 1.60 | 1.75 |
| *Nos. 163-166 (4)* | 1.90 | 1.90 |
| *Set total (136) Stamps* | 204.05 | 135.10 |

### Royal Visit, 1966

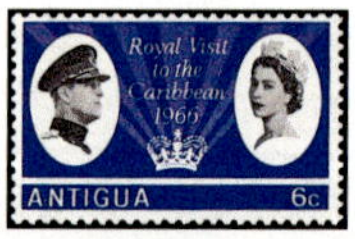


Queen Elizabeth II and Prince Philip — CD320

Caribbean visit, Feb. 4 - Mar. 6, 1966.

**1966**

Antigua ....161-162
Bahamas ....228-229
Barbados ....285-286
British Guiana ....299-300
Cayman Islands ....180-181
Dominica ....193-194
Grenada ....213-214
Montserrat ....182-183
St. Kitts-Nevis ....171-172
St. Lucia ....205-206
St. Vincent ....245-246
Turks & Caicos Islands ....150-151
Virgin Islands ....167-168

| | | |
|---|---|---|
| *Nos. 161-162 (2)* | 3.50 | 2.60 |
| *Nos. 228-229 (2)* | 3.05 | 3.05 |
| *Nos. 285-286 (2)* | 3.00 | 2.00 |
| *Nos. 299-300 (2)* | 2.35 | .85 |
| *Nos. 180-181 (2)* | 3.45 | 1.80 |
| *Nos. 193-194 (2)* | 3.00 | .60 |
| *Nos. 213-214 (2)* | .80 | .50 |
| *Nos. 182-183 (2)* | 2.00 | 1.00 |
| *Nos. 171-172 (2)* | .90 | .75 |
| *Nos. 205-206 (2)* | 1.50 | 1.35 |
| *Nos. 245-246 (2)* | 2.75 | 1.35 |
| *Nos. 150-151 (2)* | 1.00 | .50 |
| *Nos. 167-168 (2)* | 1.75 | 1.75 |
| *Set total (26) Stamps* | 29.05 | 18.10 |

### World Cup Soccer

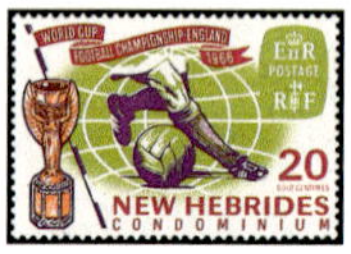


Soccer Player and Jules Rimet Cup — CD321

World Cup Soccer Championship, Wembley, England, July 11-30.

**1966**

Antigua ....163-164
Ascension ....100-101
Bahamas ....245-246
Bermuda ....205-206
Brunei ....124-125
Cayman Islands ....182-183
Dominica ....195-196
Fiji ....219-220
Gibraltar ....175-176
Gilbert & Ellice Islands ....125-126
Grenada ....230-231
New Hebrides, British ....116-117
New Hebrides, French ....132-133
Pitcairn Islands ....60-61
St. Helena ....188-189
St. Kitts-Nevis ....173-174
St. Lucia ....207-208
Seychelles ....226-227
Solomon Islands ....167-168
South Arabia ....23-24
Tristan da Cunha ....93-94

| | | |
|---|---|---|
| *Nos. 163-164 (2)* | .80 | .85 |
| *Nos. 100-101 (2)* | 2.50 | 2.00 |
| *Nos. 245-246 (2)* | .65 | .65 |
| *Nos. 205-206 (2)* | 1.75 | 1.75 |
| *Nos. 124-125 (2)* | 1.30 | 1.25 |
| *Nos. 182-183 (2)* | .75 | .65 |
| *Nos. 195-196 (2)* | 1.20 | .75 |
| *Nos. 219-220 (2)* | 1.70 | .60 |
| *Nos. 175-176 (2)* | 1.85 | 1.75 |
| *Nos. 125-126 (2)* | .70 | .60 |
| *Nos. 230-231 (2)* | .65 | *.95* |
| *Nos. 116-117 (2)* | 1.00 | 1.00 |
| *Nos. 132-133 (2)* | 7.00 | 7.00 |
| *Nos. 60-61 (2)* | 2.00 | 2.00 |
| *Nos. 188-189 (2)* | 1.25 | .60 |
| *Nos. 173-174 (2)* | .85 | .80 |
| *Nos. 207-208 (2)* | 1.15 | .90 |
| *Nos. 226-227 (2)* | .85 | .75 |
| *Nos. 167-168 (2)* | 1.10 | 1.10 |
| *Nos. 23-24 (2)* | 1.90 | .55 |
| *Nos. 93-94 (2)* | 1.25 | .80 |
| *Set total (42) Stamps* | 32.20 | 27.30 |

### WHO Headquarters

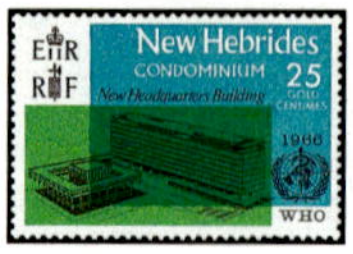


World Health Organization Headquarters, Geneva
CD322

**1966**

Antigua ....165-166
Ascension ....102-103
Bahamas ....247-248
Brunei ....126-127
Cayman Islands ....184-185
Dominica ....197-198
Fiji ....224-225
Gibraltar ....180-181
Gilbert & Ellice Islands ....127-128
Grenada ....232-233
Hong Kong ....229-230
Montserrat ....184-185
New Hebrides, British ....118-119
New Hebrides, French ....134-135
Pitcairn Islands ....62-63
St. Helena ....190-191
St. Kitts-Nevis ....177-178
St. Lucia ....209-210
St. Vincent ....247-248
Seychelles ....228-229
Solomon Islands ....169-170
South Arabia ....25-26
Tristan da Cunha ....99-100

| | | |
|---|---|---|
| *Nos. 165-166 (2)* | 1.15 | .55 |
| *Nos. 102-103 (2)* | 6.60 | 3.35 |
| *Nos. 247-248 (2)* | .80 | .80 |
| *Nos. 126-127 (2)* | 1.35 | 1.35 |
| *Nos. 184-185 (2)* | 2.25 | 1.20 |
| *Nos. 197-198 (2)* | .75 | .75 |
| *Nos. 224-225 (2)* | 4.70 | 3.30 |
| *Nos. 180-181 (2)* | 6.50 | 4.50 |
| *Nos. 127-128 (2)* | .80 | .70 |
| *Nos. 232-233 (2)* | .80 | .50 |
| *Nos. 229-230 (2)* | 11.25 | 2.30 |
| *Nos. 184-185 (2)* | 1.00 | 1.00 |
| *Nos. 118-119 (2)* | .75 | .50 |
| *Nos. 134-135 (2)* | 8.50 | 8.50 |
| *Nos. 62-63 (2)* | 5.50 | 7.00 |
| *Nos. 190-191 (2)* | 3.50 | 1.50 |
| *Nos. 177-178 (2)* | .60 | .60 |
| *Nos. 209-210 (2)* | .80 | .80 |
| *Nos. 247-248 (2)* | 1.15 | 1.05 |
| *Nos. 228-229 (2)* | 1.25 | .65 |
| *Nos. 169-170 (2)* | .95 | .80 |
| *Nos. 25-26 (2)* | 2.10 | .70 |
| *Nos. 99-100 (2)* | 1.90 | 1.25 |
| *Set total (46) Stamps* | 64.95 | 43.65 |

### UNESCO Anniversary

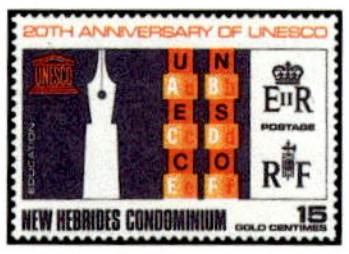


"Education"
CD323

"Science" (Wheat ears & flask enclosing globe). "Culture" (lyre & columns). 20th anniversary of the UNESCO.

**1966-67**

Antigua ....183-185
Ascension ....108-110
Bahamas ....249-251
Barbados ....287-289
Bermuda ....207-209
Brunei ....128-130
Cayman Islands ....186-188
Dominica ....199-201
Gibraltar ....183-185
Gilbert & Ellice Islands ....129-131
Grenada ....234-236
Hong Kong ....231-233
Mauritius ....299-301
Montserrat ....186-188
New Hebrides, British ....120-122
New Hebrides, French ....136-138
Pitcairn Islands ....64-66
St. Helena ....192-194
St. Kitts-Nevis ....179-181
St. Lucia ....211-213
St. Vincent ....249-251
Seychelles ....230-232
Solomon Islands ....171-173
South Arabia ....27-29
Swaziland ....123-125
Tristan da Cunha ....101-103
Turks & Caicos Islands ....155-157
Virgin Islands ....176-178

| | | |
|---|---|---|
| *Nos. 183-185 (3)* | 1.90 | *2.50* |
| *Nos. 108-110 (3)* | 11.00 | 5.80 |
| *Nos. 249-251 (3)* | 2.35 | 2.35 |
| *Nos. 287-289 (3)* | 2.35 | 2.15 |
| *Nos. 207-209 (3)* | 3.80 | *3.90* |
| *Nos. 128-130 (3)* | 4.65 | 5.40 |
| *Nos. 186-188 (3)* | 2.50 | 1.50 |
| *Nos. 199-201 (3)* | 1.60 | .75 |
| *Nos. 183-185 (3)* | 6.50 | 3.25 |
| *Nos. 129-131 (3)* | 2.50 | *2.45* |
| *Nos. 234-236 (3)* | 1.10 | 1.20 |
| *Nos. 231-233 (3)* | 49.50 | 24.00 |
| *Nos. 299-301 (3)* | 2.10 | 1.50 |
| *Nos. 186-188 (3)* | 2.40 | 2.40 |
| *Nos. 120-122 (3)* | 1.90 | 1.90 |
| *Nos. 136-138 (3)* | 7.75 | 7.75 |
| *Nos. 64-66 (3)* | 4.05 | 4.00 |
| *Nos. 192-194 (3)* | 5.25 | 3.65 |
| *Nos. 179-181 (3)* | .90 | .90 |
| *Nos. 211-213 (3)* | 1.15 | 1.15 |
| *Nos. 249-251 (3)* | 2.30 | 1.35 |
| *Nos. 230-232 (3)* | 2.40 | 2.40 |
| *Nos. 171-173 (3)* | 2.00 | 1.50 |
| *Nos. 27-29 (3)* | 5.50 | 5.50 |
| *Nos. 123-125 (3)* | 1.40 | 1.40 |
| *Nos. 101-103 (3)* | 2.00 | 1.40 |
| *Nos. 155-157 (3)* | 1.15 | 1.20 |
| *Nos. 176-178 (3)* | 1.40 | 1.30 |
| *Set total (84) Stamps* | 133.40 | 94.55 |

COMMON DESIGN TYPES 43A

### Silver Wedding, 1972

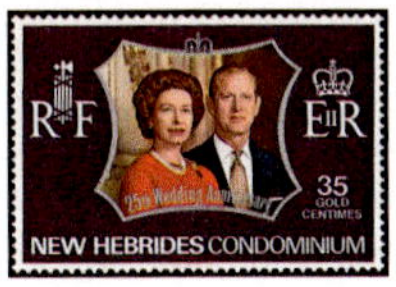


Queen Elizabeth II and Prince Philip
CD324

Designs: borders differ for each country.

**1972**

| | |
|---|---|
| Anguilla | 161-162 |
| Antigua | 295-296 |
| Ascension | 164-165 |
| Bahamas | 344-345 |
| Bermuda | 296-297 |
| British Antarctic Territory | 43-44 |
| British Honduras | 306-307 |
| British Indian Ocean Territory | 48-49 |
| Brunei | 186-187 |
| Cayman Islands | 304-305 |
| Dominica | 352-353 |
| Falkland Islands | 223-224 |
| Fiji | 328-329 |
| Gibraltar | 292-293 |
| Gilbert & Ellice Islands | 206-207 |
| Grenada | 466-467 |
| Hong Kong | 271-272 |
| Montserrat | 286-287 |
| New Hebrides, British | 169-170 |
| New Hebrides, French | 188-189 |
| Pitcairn Islands | 127-128 |
| St. Helena | 271-272 |
| St. Kitts-Nevis | 257-258 |
| St. Lucia | 328-329 |
| St.Vincent | 344-345 |
| Seychelles | 309-310 |
| Solomon Islands | 248-249 |
| South Georgia | 35-36 |
| Tristan da Cunha | 178-179 |
| Turks & Caicos Islands | 257-258 |
| Virgin Islands | 241-242 |

| | | |
|---|---|---|
| *Nos. 161-162 (2)* | 1.10 | 1.50 |
| *Nos. 295-296 (2)* | .50 | .50 |
| *Nos. 164-165 (2)* | .70 | .70 |
| *Nos. 344-345 (2)* | .60 | .60 |
| *Nos. 296-297 (2)* | .50 | .65 |
| *Nos. 43-44 (2)* | 6.50 | 5.65 |
| *Nos. 306-307 (2)* | .80 | .80 |
| *Nos. 48-49 (2)* | 2.00 | 1.00 |
| *Nos. 186-187 (2)* | .70 | .70 |
| *Nos. 304-305 (2)* | .75 | .75 |
| *Nos. 352-353 (2)* | .65 | .65 |
| *Nos. 223-224 (2)* | 1.00 | 1.15 |
| *Nos. 328-329 (2)* | .70 | .70 |
| *Nos. 292-293 (2)* | .50 | .50 |
| *Nos. 206-207 (2)* | .50 | .50 |
| *Nos. 466-467 (2)* | .70 | .70 |
| *Nos. 271-272 (2)* | 1.70 | 1.50 |
| *Nos. 286-287 (2)* | .50 | .60 |
| *Nos. 169-170 (2)* | .50 | .50 |
| *Nos. 188-189 (2)* | 1.25 | 1.25 |
| *Nos. 127-128 (2)* | .90 | .85 |
| *Nos. 271-272 (2)* | .60 | 1.20 |
| *Nos. 257-258 (2)* | .65 | .50 |
| *Nos. 328-329 (2)* | .75 | .75 |
| *Nos. 344-345 (2)* | .55 | .55 |
| *Nos. 309-310 (2)* | .90 | .90 |
| *Nos. 248-249 (2)* | .50 | .50 |
| *Nos. 35-36 (2)* | 1.40 | 1.40 |
| *Nos. 178-179 (2)* | .70 | .70 |
| *Nos. 257-258 (2)* | .50 | .50 |
| *Nos. 241-242 (2)* | .50 | .50 |
| *Set total (62) Stamps* | 30.10 | 29.15 |

### Princess Anne's Wedding

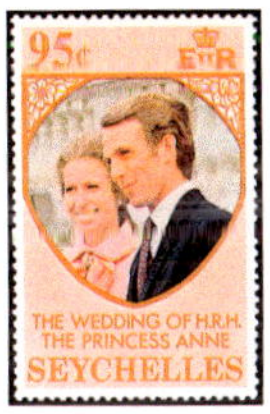


Princess Anne and Mark Phillips — CD325

Wedding of Princess Anne and Mark Phillips, Nov. 14, 1973.

**1973**

| | |
|---|---|
| Anguilla | 179-180 |
| Ascension | 177-178 |
| Belize | 325-326 |
| Bermuda | 302-303 |
| British Antarctic Territory | 60-61 |
| Cayman Islands | 320-321 |
| Falkland Islands | 225-226 |
| Gibraltar | 305-306 |
| Gilbert & Ellice Islands | 216-217 |
| Hong Kong | 289-290 |
| Montserrat | 300-301 |
| Pitcairn Islands | 135-136 |
| St. Helena | 277-278 |
| St. Kitts-Nevis | 274-275 |
| St. Lucia | 349-350 |
| St. Vincent | 358-359 |
| St. Vincent Grenadines | 1-2 |
| Seychelles | 311-312 |
| Solomon Islands | 259-260 |
| South Georgia | 37-38 |
| Tristan da Cunha | 189-190 |
| Turks & Caicos Islands | 286-287 |
| Virgin Islands | 260-261 |

| | | |
|---|---|---|
| *Nos. 179-180 (2)* | .55 | .55 |
| *Nos. 177-178 (2)* | .60 | .60 |
| *Nos. 325-326 (2)* | 1.10 | .50 |
| *Nos. 302-303 (2)* | .50 | .50 |
| *Nos. 60-61 (2)* | 1.10 | 1.10 |
| *Nos. 320-321 (2)* | .50 | .50 |
| *Nos. 225-226 (2)* | .70 | .60 |
| *Nos. 305-306 (2)* | .55 | .55 |
| *Nos. 216-217 (2)* | .50 | .50 |
| *Nos. 289-290 (2)* | 2.65 | 2.00 |
| *Nos. 300-301 (2)* | .55 | .55 |
| *Nos. 135-136 (2)* | .70 | .60 |
| *Nos. 277-278 (2)* | .50 | .50 |
| *Nos. 274-275 (2)* | .50 | .50 |
| *Nos. 349-350 (2)* | .50 | .50 |
| *Nos. 358-359 (2)* | .50 | .50 |
| *Nos. 1-2 (2)* | .50 | .50 |
| *Nos. 311-312 (2)* | .65 | .65 |
| *Nos. 259-260 (2)* | .70 | .70 |
| *Nos. 37-38 (2)* | .75 | .75 |
| *Nos. 189-190 (2)* | .50 | .50 |
| *Nos. 286-287 (2)* | .50 | .50 |
| *Nos. 260-261 (2)* | .50 | .50 |
| *Set total (46) Stamps* | 16.10 | 14.65 |

### Elizabeth II Coronation Anniv.

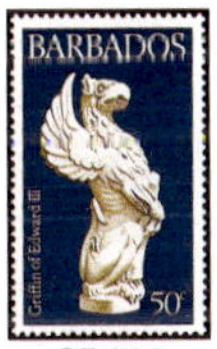


CD326

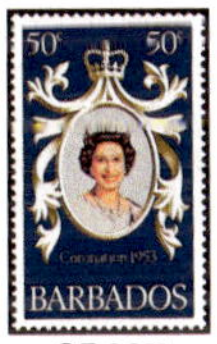


CD327

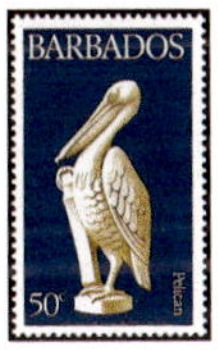


CD328

Designs: Royal and local beasts in heraldic form and simulated stonework. Portrait of Elizabeth II by Peter Grugeon. 25th anniversary of coronation of Queen Elizabeth II.

**1978**

| | |
|---|---|
| Ascension | 229 |
| Barbados | 474 |
| Belize | 397 |
| British Antarctic Territory | 71 |
| Cayman Islands | 404 |
| Christmas Island | 87 |
| Falkland Islands | 275 |
| Fiji | 384 |
| Gambia | 380 |
| Gilbert Islands | 312 |
| Mauritius | 464 |
| New Hebrides, British | 258 |
| New Hebrides, French | 278 |
| St. Helena | 317 |
| St. Kitts-Nevis | 354 |
| Samoa | 472 |
| Solomon Islands | 368 |
| South Georgia | 51 |
| Swaziland | 302 |
| Tristan da Cunha | 238 |
| Virgin Islands | 337 |

| | | |
|---|---|---|
| *No. 229 (1)* | 2.00 | 2.00 |
| *No. 474 (1)* | 1.35 | 1.35 |
| *No. 397 (1)* | 4.50 | 5.00 |
| *No. 71 (1)* | 6.00 | 6.00 |
| *No. 404 (1)* | 2.00 | 2.00 |
| *No. 87 (1)* | 3.50 | 4.00 |
| *No. 275 (1)* | 4.00 | 5.50 |
| *No. 384 (1)* | 1.75 | 1.75 |
| *No. 380 (1)* | 1.50 | 1.50 |
| *No. 312 (1)* | 1.25 | 1.25 |
| *No. 464 (1)* | 2.10 | 2.10 |
| *No. 258 (1)* | 1.75 | 1.75 |
| *No. 278 (1)* | 3.50 | 3.50 |
| *No. 317 (1)* | 1.75 | 1.75 |
| *No. 354 (1)* | 1.00 | 1.00 |
| *No. 472 (1)* | 2.10 | 2.10 |
| *No. 368 (1)* | 2.50 | 2.50 |
| *No. 51 (1)* | 3.00 | 3.00 |
| *No. 302 (1)* | 1.60 | 1.60 |
| *No. 238 (1)* | 1.50 | 1.50 |
| *No. 337 (1)* | 1.80 | 1.80 |
| *Set total (21) Stamps* | 50.45 | 52.95 |

### Queen Mother Elizabeth's 80th Birthday

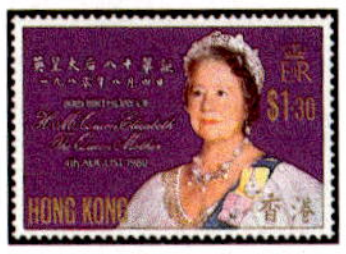


CD330

Designs: Photographs of Queen Mother Elizabeth. Falkland Islands issued in sheets of 50; others in sheets of 9.

**1980**

| | |
|---|---|
| Ascension | 261 |
| Bermuda | 401 |
| Cayman Islands | 443 |
| Falkland Islands | 305 |
| Gambia | 412 |
| Gibraltar | 393 |
| Hong Kong | 364 |
| Pitcairn Islands | 193 |
| St. Helena | 341 |
| Samoa | 532 |
| Solomon Islands | 426 |
| Tristan da Cunha | 277 |

| | | |
|---|---|---|
| *No. 261 (1)* | .40 | .40 |
| *No. 401 (1)* | .45 | .75 |
| *No. 443 (1)* | .40 | .40 |
| *No. 305 (1)* | .40 | .40 |
| *No. 412 (1)* | .40 | .50 |
| *No. 393 (1)* | .35 | .35 |
| *No. 364 (1)* | 1.10 | 1.25 |
| *No. 193 (1)* | .60 | .60 |
| *No. 341 (1)* | .50 | .50 |
| *No. 532 (1)* | .55 | .55 |
| *No. 426 (1)* | .50 | .50 |
| *No. 277 (1)* | .45 | .45 |
| *Set total (12) Stamps* | 6.10 | 6.65 |

### Royal Wedding, 1981

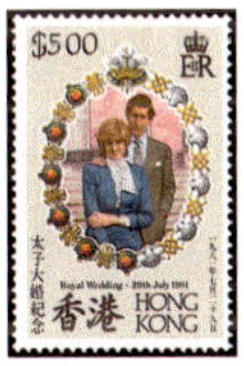


Prince Charles and Lady Diana — CD331

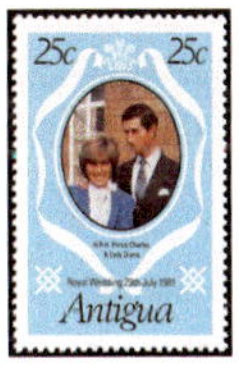


CD331a

Wedding of Charles, Prince of Wales, and Lady Diana Spencer, St. Paul's Cathedral, London, July 29, 1981.

**1981**

| | |
|---|---|
| Antigua | 623-627 |
| Ascension | 294-296 |
| Barbados | 547-549 |
| Barbuda | 497-501 |
| Bermuda | 412-414 |
| Brunei | 268-270 |
| Cayman Islands | 471-473 |
| Dominica | 701-705 |
| Falkland Islands | 324-326 |
| Falkland Islands Dep. | 1L59-1L61 |
| Fiji | 442-444 |
| Gambia | 426-428 |
| Ghana | 759-764 |
| Grenada | 1051-1055 |
| Grenada Grenadines | 440-443 |
| Hong Kong | 373-375 |
| Jamaica | 500-503 |
| Lesotho | 335-337 |
| Maldive Islands | 906-909 |
| Mauritius | 520-522 |
| Norfolk Island | 280-282 |
| Pitcairn Islands | 206-208 |
| St. Helena | 353-355 |
| St. Lucia | 543-549 |
| Samoa | 558-560 |
| Sierra Leone | 509-518 |
| Solomon Islands | 450-452 |
| Swaziland | 382-384 |
| Tristan da Cunha | 294-296 |
| Turks & Caicos Islands | 486-489 |
| Caicos Island | 8-11 |
| Uganda | 314-317 |
| Vanuatu | 308-310 |
| Virgin Islands | 406-408 |

| | | |
|---|---|---|
| *Nos. 623-627 (5)* | 6.55 | 2.55 |
| *Nos. 294-296 (3)* | 1.00 | 1.00 |
| *Nos. 547-549 (3)* | .90 | .90 |
| *Nos. 497-501 (5)* | 10.95 | 10.95 |
| *Nos. 412-414 (3)* | 2.00 | 2.00 |
| *Nos. 268-270 (3)* | 2.15 | 4.50 |
| *Nos. 471-473 (3)* | 1.20 | 1.30 |
| *Nos. 701-705 (5)* | 8.35 | 2.35 |
| *Nos. 324-326 (3)* | 1.65 | 1.70 |
| *Nos. 1L59-1L61 (3)* | 1.45 | 1.45 |
| *Nos. 442-444 (3)* | 1.35 | 1.35 |
| *Nos. 426-428 (3)* | .90 | .80 |
| *Nos. 759-764 (9)* | 6.20 | 6.20 |
| *Nos. 1051-1055 (5)* | 9.85 | 1.85 |
| *Nos. 440-443 (4)* | 2.35 | 2.35 |
| *Nos. 373-375 (3)* | 3.10 | 2.85 |
| *Nos. 500-503 (4)* | 1.45 | 1.35 |
| *Nos. 335-337 (3)* | .90 | .90 |
| *Nos. 906-909 (4)* | 1.55 | 1.55 |
| *Nos. 520-522 (3)* | 2.15 | 2.15 |
| *Nos. 280-282 (3)* | 1.75 | 1.75 |
| *Nos. 206-208 (3)* | 1.20 | 1.10 |
| *Nos. 353-355 (3)* | .85 | .85 |
| *Nos. 543-549 (5)* | 7.00 | 7.00 |
| *Nos. 558-560 (3)* | .85 | .85 |
| *Nos. 509-518 (10)* | 15.50 | 15.50 |
| *Nos. 450-452 (3)* | 1.25 | 1.25 |
| *Nos. 382-384 (3)* | 1.30 | 1.25 |
| *Nos. 294-296 (3)* | .90 | .90 |
| *Nos. 486-489 (4)* | 2.20 | 2.20 |
| *Nos. 8-11 (4)* | 5.00 | 5.00 |
| *Nos. 314-317 (4)* | 3.10 | 3.00 |
| *Nos. 308-310 (3)* | 1.15 | 1.15 |
| *Nos. 406-408 (3)* | 1.10 | 1.10 |
| *Set total (131) Stamps* | 109.15 | 92.05 |

### Princess Diana

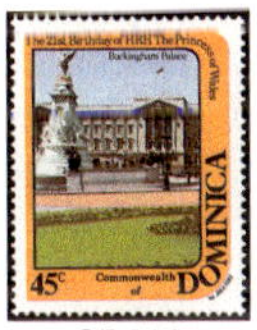


CD332

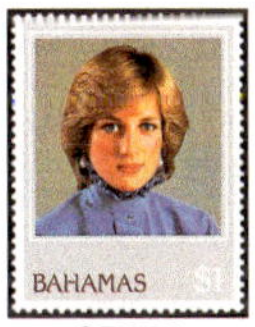


CD333

Designs: Photographs and portrait of Princess Diana, wedding or honeymoon photographs, royal residences, arms of issuing country. Portrait photograph by Clive Friend. Souvenir sheet margins show family tree, various people related to the princess. 21st birthday of Princess Diana of Wales, July 1.

**1982**

| | |
|---|---|
| Antigua | 663-666 |
| Ascension | 313-316 |
| Bahamas | 510-513 |
| Barbados | 585-588 |
| Barbuda | 544-547 |
| British Antarctic Territory | 92-95 |
| Cayman Islands | 486-489 |
| Dominica | 773-776 |
| Falkland Islands | 348-351 |
| Falkland Islands Dep. | 1L72-1L75 |
| Fiji | 470-473 |
| Gambia | 447-450 |
| Grenada | 1101A-1105 |
| Grenada Grenadines | 485-491 |
| Lesotho | 372-375 |
| Maldive Islands | 952-955 |
| Mauritius | 548-551 |
| Pitcairn Islands | 213-216 |
| St. Helena | 372-375 |
| St. Lucia | 591-594 |
| Sierra Leone | 531-534 |
| Solomon Islands | 471-474 |
| Swaziland | 406-409 |
| Tristan da Cunha | 310-313 |
| Turks and Caicos Islands | 531-534 |
| Virgin Islands | 430-433 |

| | | |
|---|---|---|
| *Nos. 663-666 (4)* | 8.25 | 7.35 |
| *Nos. 313-316 (4)* | 3.50 | 3.50 |
| *Nos. 510-513 (4)* | 6.00 | 3.85 |
| *Nos. 585-588 (4)* | 3.40 | 3.25 |
| *Nos. 544-547 (4)* | 9.75 | 7.70 |
| *Nos. 92-95 (4)* | 4.25 | 3.45 |
| *Nos. 486-489 (4)* | 4.75 | 2.70 |
| *Nos. 773-776 (4)* | 7.05 | 7.05 |
| *Nos. 348-351 (4)* | 2.95 | 2.95 |
| *Nos. 1L72-1L75 (4)* | 2.50 | 2.60 |
| *Nos. 470-473 (4)* | 3.25 | 2.95 |
| *Nos. 447-450 (4)* | 2.90 | 2.85 |
| *Nos. 1101A-1105 (7)* | 16.05 | 15.55 |
| *Nos. 485-491 (7)* | 17.65 | 17.65 |
| *Nos. 372-375 (4)* | 4.00 | 4.00 |
| *Nos. 952-955 (4)* | 5.50 | 3.90 |
| *Nos. 548-551 (4)* | 5.00 | 5.00 |
| *Nos. 213-216 (4)* | 1.90 | 1.85 |
| *Nos. 372-375 (4)* | 2.00 | 2.00 |
| *Nos. 591-594 (4)* | 8.70 | 8.70 |
| *Nos. 531-534 (4)* | 7.20 | 7.20 |
| *Nos. 471-474 (4)* | 2.90 | 2.90 |
| *Nos. 406-409 (4)* | 3.85 | 2.25 |

# COMMON DESIGN TYPES

| | | |
|---|---|---|
| Nos. 310-313 (4) | 3.65 | 1.45 |
| Nos. 486-489 (4) | 2.20 | 2.20 |
| Nos. 430-433 (4) | 3.00 | 3.00 |
| Set total (110) Stamps | 142.15 | 127.85 |

### 250th anniv. of first edition of Lloyd's List (shipping news publication) & of Lloyd's marine insurance.

CD335

Designs: First page of early edition of the list; historical ships, modern transportation or harbor scenes.

### 1984

| | |
|---|---|
| Ascension | 351-354 |
| Bahamas | 555-558 |
| Barbados | 627-630 |
| Cayes of Belize | 10-13 |
| Cayman Islands | 522-526 |
| Falkland Islands | 404-407 |
| Fiji | 509-512 |
| Gambia | 519-522 |
| Mauritius | 587-590 |
| Nauru | 280-283 |
| St. Helena | 412-415 |
| Samoa | 624-627 |
| Seychelles | 538-541 |
| Solomon Islands | 521-524 |
| Vanuatu | 368-371 |
| Virgin Islands | 466-469 |

| | | |
|---|---|---|
| Nos. 351-354 (4) | 2.90 | 2.55 |
| Nos. 555-558 (4) | 4.15 | 2.95 |
| Nos. 627-630 (4) | 6.10 | 5.15 |
| Nos. 10-13 (4) | 4.85 | 4.85 |
| Nos. 522-526 (5) | 9.30 | 8.45 |
| Nos. 404-407 (4) | 3.50 | 3.65 |
| Nos. 509-512 (4) | 5.30 | 4.90 |
| Nos. 519-522 (4) | 4.20 | 4.30 |
| Nos. 587-590 (4) | 9.40 | 9.40 |
| Nos. 280-283 (4) | 2.40 | 2.35 |
| Nos. 412-415 (4) | 2.40 | 2.40 |
| Nos. 624-627 (4) | 2.55 | 2.35 |
| Nos. 538-541 (4) | 5.00 | 5.00 |
| Nos. 521-524 (4) | 4.65 | 3.95 |
| Nos. 368-371 (4) | 1.85 | 1.85 |
| Nos. 466-469 (4) | 4.25 | 4.25 |
| Set total (65) Stamps | 72.80 | 68.35 |

### Queen Mother 85th Birthday

CD336

Designs: Photographs tracing the life of the Queen Mother, Elizabeth. The high value in each set pictures the same photograph taken of the Queen Mother holding the infant Prince Henry.

### 1985

| | |
|---|---|
| Ascension | 372-376 |
| Bahamas | 580-584 |
| Barbados | 660-664 |
| Bermuda | 469-473 |
| Falkland Islands | 420-424 |
| Falkland Islands Dep | 1L92-1L96 |
| Fiji | 531-535 |
| Hong Kong | 447-450 |
| Jamaica | 599-603 |
| Mauritius | 604-608 |
| Norfolk Island | 364-368 |
| Pitcairn Islands | 253-257 |
| St. Helena | 428-432 |
| Samoa | 649-653 |
| Seychelles | 567-571 |
| Zil Elwannyen Sesel | 101-105 |
| Solomon Islands | 543-547 |
| Swaziland | 476-480 |
| Tristan da Cunha | 372-376 |
| Vanuatu | 392-396 |

| | | |
|---|---|---|
| Nos. 372-376 (5) | 4.65 | 4.65 |
| Nos. 580-584 (5) | 7.70 | 6.45 |
| Nos. 660-664 (5) | 8.00 | 6.70 |
| Nos. 469-473 (5) | 9.40 | 9.40 |
| Nos. 420-424 (5) | 7.35 | 6.65 |
| Nos. 1L92-1L96 (5) | 8.00 | 8.00 |
| Nos. 531-535 (5) | 6.15 | 6.15 |
| Nos. 447-450 (4) | 9.50 | 8.50 |
| Nos. 599-603 (5) | 6.15 | 7.00 |
| Nos. 604-608 (5) | 11.30 | 11.30 |
| Nos. 364-368 (5) | 5.00 | 5.00 |
| Nos. 253-257 (5) | 5.30 | 5.95 |
| Nos. 428-432 (5) | 5.25 | 5.25 |
| Nos. 649-653 (5) | 8.40 | 7.55 |
| Nos. 567-571 (5) | 8.70 | 8.70 |
| Nos. 101-105 (5) | 6.60 | 6.60 |
| Nos. 543-547 (5) | 3.95 | 3.95 |
| Nos. 476-480 (5) | 7.75 | 7.25 |
| Nos. 372-376 (5) | 5.40 | 5.40 |
| Nos. 392-396 (5) | 5.25 | 5.25 |
| Set total (99) Stamps | 139.80 | 135.70 |

### Queen Elizabeth II, 60th Birthday

CD337

### 1986, April 21

| | |
|---|---|
| Ascension | 389-393 |
| Bahamas | 592-596 |
| Barbados | 675-679 |
| Bermuda | 499-503 |
| Cayman Islands | 555-559 |
| Falkland Islands | 441-445 |
| Fiji | 544-548 |
| Hong Kong | 465-469 |
| Jamaica | 620-624 |
| Kiribati | 470-474 |
| Mauritius | 629-633 |
| Papua New Guinea | 640-644 |
| Pitcairn Islands | 270-274 |
| St. Helena | 451-455 |
| Samoa | 670-674 |
| Seychelles | 592-596 |
| Zil Elwannyen Sesel | 114-118 |
| Solomon Islands | 562-566 |
| South Georgia | 101-105 |
| Swaziland | 490-494 |
| Tristan da Cunha | 388-392 |
| Vanuatu | 414-418 |
| Zambia | 343-347 |

| | | |
|---|---|---|
| Nos. 389-393 (5) | 2.80 | 3.30 |
| Nos. 592-596 (5) | 2.75 | 3.70 |
| Nos. 675-679 (5) | 3.25 | 3.10 |
| Nos. 499-503 (5) | 4.65 | 5.15 |
| Nos. 555-559 (5) | 4.55 | 5.60 |
| Nos. 441-445 (5) | 3.95 | 4.95 |
| Nos. 544-548 (5) | 3.00 | 3.00 |
| Nos. 465-469 (5) | 8.75 | 6.75 |
| Nos. 620-624 (5) | 2.75 | 2.70 |
| Nos. 470-474 (5) | 2.25 | 2.10 |
| Nos. 629-633 (5) | 3.50 | 3.50 |
| Nos. 640-644 (5) | 4.10 | 4.10 |
| Nos. 270-274 (5) | 2.80 | 2.70 |
| Nos. 451-455 (5) | 2.50 | 3.05 |
| Nos. 670-674 (5) | 2.55 | 2.55 |
| Nos. 592-596 (5) | 2.70 | 2.70 |
| Nos. 114-118 (5) | 2.15 | 2.15 |
| Nos. 562-566 (5) | 2.90 | 2.90 |
| Nos. 101-105 (5) | 3.30 | 3.65 |
| Nos. 490-494 (5) | 2.15 | 2.15 |
| Nos. 388-392 (5) | 3.00 | 3.00 |
| Nos. 414-418 (5) | 3.10 | 3.10 |
| Nos. 343-347 (5) | 1.65 | 1.60 |
| Set total (115) Stamps | 75.10 | 77.50 |

### Royal Wedding

Marriage of Prince Andrew and Sarah Ferguson — CD338

### 1986, July 23

| | |
|---|---|
| Ascension | 399-400 |
| Bahamas | 602-603 |
| Barbados | 687-688 |
| Cayman Islands | 560-561 |
| Jamaica | 629-630 |
| Pitcairn Islands | 275-276 |
| St. Helena | 460-461 |
| St. Kitts | 181-182 |
| Seychelles | 602-603 |
| Zil Elwannyen Sesel | 119-120 |
| Solomon Islands | 567-568 |
| Tristan da Cunha | 397-398 |
| Zambia | 348-349 |

| | | |
|---|---|---|
| Nos. 399-400 (2) | 1.60 | 1.60 |
| Nos. 602-603 (2) | 2.75 | 2.75 |
| Nos. 687-688 (2) | 2.00 | 1.25 |
| Nos. 560-561 (2) | 1.70 | 2.35 |
| Nos. 629-630 (2) | 1.35 | 1.35 |
| Nos. 275-276 (2) | 2.40 | 2.40 |
| Nos. 460-461 (2) | 1.05 | 1.05 |
| Nos. 181-182 (2) | 1.50 | 2.25 |
| Nos. 602-603 (2) | 2.50 | 2.50 |
| Nos. 119-120 (2) | 2.30 | 2.30 |
| Nos. 567-568 (2) | 1.00 | 1.00 |
| Nos. 397-398 (2) | 1.40 | 1.40 |
| Nos. 348-349 (2) | 1.10 | 1.30 |
| Set total (26) Stamps | 22.65 | 23.50 |

### Queen Elizabeth II, 60th Birthday

Queen Elizabeth II & Prince Philip, 1947 Wedding Portrait — CD339

Designs: Photographs tracing the life of Queen Elizabeth II.

### 1986

| | |
|---|---|
| Anguilla | 674-677 |
| Antigua | 925-928 |
| Barbuda | 783-786 |
| Dominica | 950-953 |
| Gambia | 611-614 |
| Grenada | 1371-1374 |
| Grenada Grenadines | 749-752 |
| Lesotho | 531-534 |
| Maldive Islands | 1172-1175 |
| Sierra Leone | 760-763 |
| Uganda | 495-498 |

| | | |
|---|---|---|
| Nos. 674-677 (4) | 8.00 | 8.00 |
| Nos. 925-928 (4) | 5.50 | 6.20 |
| Nos. 783-786 (4) | 23.15 | 23.15 |
| Nos. 950-953 (4) | 7.25 | 7.25 |
| Nos. 611-614 (4) | 8.25 | 7.90 |
| Nos. 1371-1374 (4) | 6.80 | 6.80 |
| Nos. 749-752 (4) | 6.75 | 6.75 |
| Nos. 531-534 (4) | 5.25 | 5.25 |
| Nos. 1172-1175 (4) | 6.25 | 6.25 |
| Nos. 760-763 (4) | 5.25 | 5.25 |
| Nos. 495-498 (4) | 8.50 | 8.50 |
| Set total (44) Stamps | 90.95 | 91.30 |

### Royal Wedding, 1986

CD340

Designs: Photographs of Prince Andrew and Sarah Ferguson during courtship, engagement and marriage.

### 1986

| | |
|---|---|
| Antigua | 939-942 |
| Barbuda | 809-812 |
| Dominica | 970-973 |
| Gambia | 635-638 |
| Grenada | 1385-1388 |
| Grenada Grenadines | 758-761 |
| Lesotho | 545-548 |
| Maldive Islands | 1181-1184 |
| Sierra Leone | 769-772 |
| Uganda | 510-513 |

| | | |
|---|---|---|
| Nos. 939-942 (4) | 7.00 | 8.75 |
| Nos. 809-812 (4) | 14.55 | 14.55 |
| Nos. 970-973 (4) | 7.25 | 7.25 |
| Nos. 635-638 (4) | 7.80 | 7.80 |
| Nos. 1385-1388 (4) | 8.30 | 8.30 |
| Nos. 758-761 (4) | 9.00 | 9.00 |
| Nos. 545-548 (4) | 7.45 | 7.45 |
| Nos. 1181-1184 (4) | 8.45 | 8.45 |
| Nos. 769-772 (4) | 5.35 | 5.35 |
| Nos. 510-513 (4) | 9.25 | 10.00 |
| Set total (40) Stamps | 84.40 | 86.90 |

### Lloyds of London, 300th Anniv.

CD341

Designs: 17th century aspects of Lloyds, representations of each country's individual connections with Lloyds and publicized disasters insured by the organization.

### 1986

| | |
|---|---|
| Ascension | 454-457 |
| Bahamas | 655-658 |
| Barbados | 731-734 |
| Bermuda | 541-544 |
| Falkland Islands | 481-484 |
| Liberia | 1101-1104 |
| Malawi | 534-537 |
| Nevis | 571-574 |
| St. Helena | 501-504 |
| St. Lucia | 923-926 |
| Seychelles | 649-652 |
| Zil Elwannyen Sesel | 146-149 |
| Solomon Islands | 627-630 |
| South Georgia | 131-134 |
| Trinidad & Tobago | 484-487 |
| Tristan da Cunha | 439-442 |
| Vanuatu | 485-488 |

| | | |
|---|---|---|
| Nos. 454-457 (4) | 5.00 | 5.00 |
| Nos. 655-658 (4) | 8.90 | 4.95 |
| Nos. 731-734 (4) | 12.50 | 8.35 |
| Nos. 541-544 (4) | 8.00 | 6.60 |
| Nos. 481-484 (4) | 5.45 | 3.85 |
| Nos. 1101-1104 (4) | 4.25 | 4.25 |
| Nos. 534-537 (4) | 11.00 | 7.85 |
| Nos. 571-574 (4) | 8.35 | 8.35 |
| Nos. 501-504 (4) | 8.70 | 7.15 |
| Nos. 923-926 (4) | 8.80 | 8.80 |
| Nos. 649-652 (4) | 12.85 | 12.85 |
| Nos. 146-149 (4) | 11.25 | 11.25 |
| Nos. 627-630 (4) | 7.00 | 4.45 |
| Nos. 131-134 (4) | 6.30 | 3.70 |
| Nos. 484-487 (4) | 10.25 | 6.35 |
| Nos. 439-442 (4) | 7.60 | 7.60 |
| Nos. 485-488 (4) | 4.85 | 4.85 |
| Set total (68) Stamps | 141.05 | 116.20 |

### Moon Landing, 20th Anniv.

CD342

Designs: Equipment, crew photographs, spacecraft, official emblems and report profiles created for the Apollo Missions. Two stamps in each set are square in format rather than like the stamp shown; see individual country listings for more information.

### 1989

| | |
|---|---|
| Ascension | 468-472 |
| Bahamas | 674-678 |
| Belize | 916-920 |
| Kiribati | 517-521 |
| Liberia | 1125-1129 |
| Nevis | 586-590 |
| St. Kitts | 248-252 |
| Samoa | 760-764 |
| Seychelles | 676-680 |
| Zil Elwannyen Sesel | 154-158 |
| Solomon Islands | 643-647 |
| Vanuatu | 507-511 |

| | | |
|---|---|---|
| Nos. 468-472 (5) | 9.40 | 8.60 |
| Nos. 674-678 (5) | 23.00 | 19.70 |
| Nos. 916-920 (5) | 29.25 | 21.60 |
| Nos. 517-521 (5) | 12.50 | 12.50 |
| Nos. 1125-1129 (5) | 8.50 | 8.50 |
| Nos. 586-590 (5) | 7.50 | 7.50 |
| Nos. 248-252 (5) | 8.00 | 8.25 |
| Nos. 760-764 (5) | 9.85 | 9.30 |
| Nos. 676-680 (5) | 16.05 | 16.05 |
| Nos. 154-158 (5) | 26.85 | 26.85 |
| Nos. 643-647 (5) | 9.00 | 6.75 |
| Nos. 507-511 (5) | 8.60 | 8.60 |
| Set total (60) Stamps | 168.50 | 154.20 |

### Queen Mother, 90th Birthday

CD343   CD344

Designs: Portraits of Queen Elizabeth, the Queen Mother. See individual country listings for more information.

### 1990

| | |
|---|---|
| Ascension | 491-492 |
| Bahamas | 698-699 |
| Barbados | 782-783 |
| British Antarctic Territory | 170-171 |
| British Indian Ocean Territory | 106-107 |

# COMMON DESIGN TYPES

## 45A

| | |
|---|---|
| Cayman Islands | 622-623 |
| Falkland Islands | 524-525 |
| Kenya | 527-528 |
| Kiribati | 555-556 |
| Liberia | 1145-1146 |
| Pitcairn Islands | 336-337 |
| St. Helena | 532-533 |
| St. Lucia | 969-970 |
| Seychelles | 710-711 |
|   Zil Elwannyen Sesel | 171-172 |
| Solomon Islands | 671-672 |
| South Georgia | 143-144 |
| Swaziland | 565-566 |
| Tristan da Cunha | 480-481 |

| | | |
|---|---|---|
| Nos. 491-492 (2) | 4.75 | 4.75 |
| Nos. 698-699 (2) | 5.25 | 5.25 |
| Nos. 782-783 (2) | 4.00 | 3.70 |
| Nos. 170-171 (2) | 6.00 | 6.00 |
| Nos. 106-107 (2) | 18.00 | 18.50 |
| Nos. 622-623 (2) | 4.00 | 5.50 |
| Nos. 524-525 (2) | 4.75 | 4.75 |
| Nos. 527-528 (2) | 6.05 | 6.05 |
| Nos. 555-556 (2) | 4.75 | 4.75 |
| Nos. 1145-1146 (2) | 3.25 | 3.25 |
| Nos. 336-337 (2) | 4.25 | 4.25 |
| Nos. 532-533 (2) | 5.25 | 5.25 |
| Nos. 969-970 (2) | 4.60 | 4.60 |
| Nos. 710-711 (2) | 6.60 | 6.60 |
| Nos. 171-172 (2) | 8.25 | 8.25 |
| Nos. 671-672 (2) | 5.00 | 5.30 |
| Nos. 143-144 (2) | 5.50 | 6.50 |
| Nos. 565-566 (2) | 4.10 | 4.10 |
| Nos. 480-481 (2) | 5.60 | 5.60 |
| Set total (38) Stamps | 109.95 | 112.95 |

### Queen Elizabeth II, 65th Birthday, and Prince Philip, 70th Birthday

 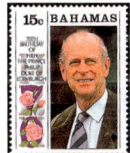

CD345     CD346

Designs: Portraits of Queen Elizabeth II and Prince Philip differ for each country. Printed in sheets of 10 + 5 labels (3 different) between. Stamps alternate, producing 5 different triptychs.

### 1991

| | |
|---|---|
| Ascension | 506a |
| Bahamas | 731a |
| Belize | 970a |
| Bermuda | 618a |
| Kiribati | 572a |
| Mauritius | 734a |
| Pitcairn Islands | 349a |
| St. Helena | 555a |
| St. Kitts | 319a |
| Samoa | 791a |
| Seychelles | 724a |
| Zil Elwannyen Sesel | 178a |
| Solomon Islands | 689a |
| South Georgia | 150a |
| Swaziland | 587a |
| Vanuatu | 541a |

| | | |
|---|---|---|
| No. 506a (1) | 3.50 | 3.75 |
| No. 731a (1) | 4.00 | 4.00 |
| No. 970a (1) | 4.25 | 4.25 |
| No. 618a (1) | 3.50 | 4.00 |
| No. 572a (1) | 4.00 | 4.00 |
| No. 734a (1) | 4.00 | 4.00 |
| No. 349a (1) | 3.25 | 3.25 |
| No. 555a (1) | 2.75 | 2.75 |
| No. 319a (1) | 3.00 | 3.00 |
| No. 791a (1) | 3.75 | 3.75 |
| No. 724a (1) | 5.00 | 5.00 |
| No. 178a (1) | 6.25 | 6.25 |
| No. 689a (1) | 3.75 | 3.75 |
| No. 150a (1) | 4.75 | 7.00 |
| No. 587a (1) | 4.00 | 4.00 |
| No. 541a (1) | 2.50 | 2.50 |
| Set total (16) Stamps | 62.25 | 65.25 |

### Royal Family Birthday, Anniversary

 CD347

Queen Elizabeth II, 65th birthday, Charles and Diana, 10th wedding anniversary: Various photographs of Queen Elizabeth II, Prince Philip, Prince Charles, Princess Diana and their sons William and Henry.

### 1991

| | |
|---|---|
| Antigua | 1446-1455 |
| Barbuda | 1229-1238 |
| Dominica | 1328-1337 |
| Gambia | 1080-1089 |
| Grenada | 2006-2015 |
| Grenada Grenadines | 1331-1340 |
| Guyana | 2440-2451 |
| Lesotho | 871-875 |
| Maldive Islands | 1533-1542 |
| Nevis | 666-675 |
| St. Vincent | 1485-1494 |
| St. Vincent Grenadines | 769-778 |
| Sierra Leone | 1387-1396 |
| Turks & Caicos Islands | 913-922 |
| Uganda | 918-927 |

| | | |
|---|---|---|
| Nos. 1446-1455 (10) | 21.70 | 20.05 |
| Nos. 1229-1238 (10) | 125.00 | 119.50 |
| Nos. 1328-1337 (10) | 30.20 | 30.20 |
| Nos. 1080-1089 (10) | 24.65 | 24.40 |
| Nos. 2006-2015 (10) | 25.45 | 22.10 |
| Nos. 1331-1340 (10) | 23.85 | 23.35 |
| Nos. 2440-2451 (12) | 21.40 | 21.15 |
| Nos. 871-875 (5) | 13.55 | 13.55 |
| Nos. 1533-1542 (10) | 28.10 | 28.10 |
| Nos. 666-675 (10) | 23.65 | 23.65 |
| Nos. 1485-1494 (10) | 26.75 | 25.90 |
| Nos. 769-778 (10) | 25.40 | 25.40 |
| Nos. 1387-1396 (10) | 26.35 | 26.35 |
| Nos. 913-922 (10) | 27.50 | 25.30 |
| Nos. 918-927 (10) | 17.65 | 17.65 |
| Set total (147) Stamps | 461.20 | 446.65 |

### Queen Elizabeth II's Accession to the Throne, 40th Anniv.

 CD348

Various photographs of Queen Elizabeth II with local Scenes.

### 1992

| | |
|---|---|
| Antigua | 1513-1518 |
| Barbuda | 1306-1311 |
| Dominica | 1414-1419 |
| Gambia | 1172-1177 |
| Grenada | 2047-2052 |
| Grenada Grenadines | 1368-1373 |
| Lesotho | 881-885 |
| Maldive Islands | 1637-1642 |
| Nevis | 702-707 |
| St. Vincent | 1582-1587 |
| St. Vincent Grenadines | 829-834 |
| Sierra Leone | 1482-1487 |
| Turks and Caicos Islands | 978-987 |
| Uganda | 990-995 |
| Virgin Islands | 742-746 |

| | | |
|---|---|---|
| Nos. 1513-1518 (6) | 15.00 | 15.10 |
| Nos. 1306-1311 (6) | 125.25 | 83.65 |
| Nos. 1414-1419 (6) | 12.50 | 12.50 |
| Nos. 1172-1177 (6) | 15.00 | 14.85 |
| Nos. 2047-2052 (6) | 15.95 | 15.95 |
| Nos. 1368-1373 (6) | 17.00 | 15.35 |
| Nos. 881-885 (5) | 11.90 | 11.90 |
| Nos. 1637-1642 (6) | 17.55 | 17.55 |
| Nos. 702-707 (6) | 13.55 | 13.55 |
| Nos. 1582-1587 (6) | 14.40 | 14.40 |
| Nos. 829-834 (6) | 19.65 | 19.65 |
| Nos. 1482-1487 (6) | 22.50 | 22.50 |
| Nos. 913-922 (10) | 27.50 | 25.30 |
| Nos. 990-995 (6) | 19.50 | 19.50 |
| Nos. 742-746 (5) | 15.50 | 15.50 |
| Set total (92) Stamps | 362.75 | 317.25 |

 CD349

### 1992

| | |
|---|---|
| Ascension | 531-535 |
| Bahamas | 744-748 |
| Bermuda | 623-627 |
| British Indian Ocean Territory | 119-123 |
| Cayman Islands | 648-652 |
| Falkland Islands | 549-553 |
| Gibraltar | 605-609 |
| Hong Kong | 619-623 |
| Kenya | 563-567 |
| Kiribati | 582-586 |
| Pitcairn Islands | 362-366 |
| St. Helena | 570-574 |
| St. Kitts | 332-336 |
| Samoa | 805-809 |
| Seychelles | 734-738 |
|   Zil Elwannyen Sesel | 183-187 |
| Solomon Islands | 708-712 |
| South Georgia | 157-161 |
| Tristan da Cunha | 508-512 |
| Vanuatu | 555-559 |
| Zambia | 561-565 |

| | | |
|---|---|---|
| Nos. 531-535 (5) | 6.10 | 6.10 |
| Nos. 744-748 (5) | 6.90 | 4.70 |
| Nos. 623-627 (5) | 7.40 | 7.55 |
| Nos. 119-123 (5) | 22.75 | 19.25 |
| Nos. 648-652 (5) | 7.60 | 6.60 |
| Nos. 549-553 (5) | 5.95 | 5.90 |
| Nos. 605-609 (5) | 5.15 | 5.50 |
| Nos. 619-623 (5) | 5.10 | 5.25 |
| Nos. 563-567 (5) | 7.80 | 7.75 |
| Nos. 582-586 (5) | 3.85 | 3.85 |
| Nos. 362-366 (5) | 5.35 | 5.35 |
| Nos. 570-574 (5) | 5.70 | 5.70 |
| Nos. 332-336 (5) | 6.60 | 5.50 |
| Nos. 805-809 (5) | 7.85 | 5.90 |
| Nos. 734-738 (5) | 10.55 | 10.55 |
| Nos. 183-187 (5) | 9.40 | 9.40 |
| Nos. 708-712 (5) | 5.00 | 5.30 |
| Nos. 157-161 (5) | 5.60 | 5.90 |
| Nos. 508-512 (5) | 8.75 | 8.30 |
| Nos. 555-559 (5) | 3.10 | 3.10 |
| Nos. 561-565 (5) | 5.20 | 5.15 |
| Set total (105) Stamps | 151.70 | 142.60 |

### Royal Air Force, 75th Anniversary

 CD350

### 1993

| | |
|---|---|
| Ascension | 557-561 |
| Bahamas | 771-775 |
| Barbados | 842-846 |
| Belize | 1003-1008 |
| Bermuda | 648-651 |
| British Indian Ocean Territory | 136-140 |
| Falkland Is. | 573-577 |
| Fiji | 687-691 |
| Montserrat | 830-834 |
| St. Kitts | 351-355 |

| | | |
|---|---|---|
| Nos. 557-561 (5) | 15.60 | 14.60 |
| Nos. 771-775 (5) | 24.65 | 21.45 |
| Nos. 842-846 (5) | 14.15 | 12.85 |
| Nos. 1003-1008 (6) | 21.15 | 16.50 |
| Nos. 648-651 (4) | 9.65 | 10.45 |
| Nos. 136-140 (5) | 16.10 | 16.10 |
| Nos. 573-577 (5) | 10.85 | 10.85 |
| Nos. 687-691 (5) | 17.75 | 17.40 |
| Nos. 830-834 (5) | 14.10 | 14.10 |
| Nos. 351-355 (5) | 22.80 | 23.55 |
| Set total (50) Stamps | 166.80 | 157.85 |

### Royal Air Force, 80th Anniv.

Design CD350 Re-inscribed

### 1998

| | |
|---|---|
| Ascension | 697-701 |
| Bahamas | 907-911 |
| British Indian Ocean Terr | 198-202 |
| Cayman Islands | 754-758 |
| Fiji | 814-818 |
| Gibraltar | 755-759 |
| Samoa | 957-961 |
| Turks & Caicos Islands | 1258-1265 |
| Tuvalu | 763-767 |
| Virgin Islands | 879-883 |

| | | |
|---|---|---|
| Nos. 697-701 (5) | 10.10 | 10.10 |
| Nos. 907-911 (5) | 13.60 | 12.65 |
| Nos. 136-140 (5) | 16.10 | 16.10 |
| Nos. 754-758 (5) | 15.25 | 15.25 |
| Nos. 814-818 (5) | 14.00 | 12.75 |
| Nos. 755-759 (5) | 9.70 | 9.70 |
| Nos. 957-961 (5) | 15.70 | 14.90 |
| Nos. 1258-1265 (2) | 27.50 | 27.50 |
| Nos. 763-767 (5) | 7.75 | 7.75 |
| Nos. 879-883 (5) | 15.00 | 15.00 |
| Set total (47) Stamps | 150.70 | 147.70 |

### End of World War II, 50th Anniv.

 CD351

 CD352

### 1995

| | |
|---|---|
| Ascension | 613-617 |
| Bahamas | 824-828 |
| Barbados | 891-895 |
| Belize | 1047-1050 |
| British Indian Ocean Territory | 163-167 |
| Cayman Islands | 704-708 |
| Falkland Islands | 634-638 |
| Fiji | 720-724 |
| Kiribati | 662-668 |
| Liberia | 1175-1179 |
| Mauritius | 803-805 |
| St. Helena | 646-654 |
| St. Kitts | 389-393 |
| St. Lucia | 1018-1022 |
| Samoa | 890-894 |
| Solomon Islands | 799-803 |
| South Georgia | 198-200 |
| Tristan da Cunha | 562-566 |

| | | |
|---|---|---|
| Nos. 613-617 (5) | 21.50 | 21.50 |
| Nos. 824-828 (5) | 22.00 | 18.70 |
| Nos. 891-895 (5) | 14.20 | 11.90 |
| Nos. 1047-1050 (4) | 8.25 | 5.90 |
| Nos. 163-167 (5) | 16.25 | 16.25 |
| Nos. 704-708 (5) | 17.65 | 13.95 |
| Nos. 634-638 (5) | 18.65 | 17.75 |
| Nos. 720-724 (5) | 17.50 | 14.50 |
| Nos. 662-668 (7) | 12.55 | 12.55 |
| Nos. 1175-1179 (5) | 15.25 | 11.15 |
| Nos. 803-805 (3) | 7.50 | 7.50 |
| Nos. 646-654 (9) | 26.10 | 26.10 |
| Nos. 389-393 (5) | 16.40 | 16.40 |
| Nos. 1018-1022 (5) | 12.25 | 10.15 |
| Nos. 890-894 (5) | 15.25 | 14.50 |
| Nos. 799-803 (5) | 14.75 | 14.75 |
| Nos. 198-200 (3) | 14.50 | 15.50 |
| Nos. 562-566 (5) | 20.10 | 20.10 |
| Set total (91) Stamps | 290.65 | 268.55 |

### UN, 50th Anniv.

 CD353

### 1995

| | |
|---|---|
| Bahamas | 839-842 |
| Barbados | 901-904 |
| Belize | 1055-1058 |
| Jamaica | 847-851 |
| Liberia | 1187-1190 |
| Mauritius | 813-816 |
| Pitcairn Islands | 436-439 |
| St. Kitts | 398-401 |
| St. Lucia | 1023-1026 |
| Samoa | 900-903 |
| Tristan da Cunha | 568-571 |
| Virgin Islands | 807-810 |

| | | |
|---|---|---|
| Nos. 839-842 (4) | 7.15 | 6.40 |
| Nos. 901-904 (4) | 7.00 | 5.75 |
| Nos. 1055-1058 (4) | 6.80 | 4.70 |
| Nos. 847-851 (5) | 5.40 | 5.45 |
| Nos. 1187-1190 (4) | 10.90 | 10.90 |
| Nos. 813-816 (4) | 4.55 | 4.55 |
| Nos. 436-439 (4) | 8.15 | 8.15 |
| Nos. 398-401 (4) | 6.15 | 7.15 |
| Nos. 1023-1026 (4) | 7.50 | 7.20 |
| Nos. 900-903 (4) | 9.35 | 8.20 |
| Nos. 568-571 (4) | 13.50 | 13.50 |
| Nos. 807-810 (4) | 7.45 | 7.45 |
| Set total (49) Stamps | 93.90 | 89.45 |

### Queen Elizabeth, 70th Birthday

 CD354

# COMMON DESIGN TYPES

## 1996

| | | |
|---|---|---|
| Ascension | | 632-635 |
| British Antarctic Territory | | 240-243 |
| British Indian Ocean Territory | | 176-180 |
| Falkland Islands | | 653-657 |
| Pitcairn Islands | | 446-449 |
| St. Helena | | 672-676 |
| Samoa | | 912-916 |
| Tokelau | | 223-227 |
| Tristan da Cunha | | 576-579 |
| Virgin Islands | | 824-828 |
| Nos. 632-635 (4) | 5.30 | 5.30 |
| Nos. 240-243 (4) | 9.45 | 8.15 |
| Nos. 176-180 (5) | 11.50 | 11.50 |
| Nos. 653-657 (5) | 13.55 | 11.20 |
| Nos. 446-449 (4) | 8.60 | 8.60 |
| Nos. 672-676 (5) | 12.45 | 12.70 |
| Nos. 912-916 (5) | 10.50 | 10.50 |
| Nos. 223-227 (5) | 10.50 | 10.50 |
| Nos. 576-579 (4) | 8.35 | 8.35 |
| Nos. 824-828 (5) | 11.30 | 11.30 |
| Set total (46) Stamps | 101.50 | 98.10 |

### Diana, Princess of Wales (1961-97)

CD355

## 1998

| | | |
|---|---|---|
| Ascension | | 696 |
| Bahamas | | 901A-902 |
| Barbados | | 950 |
| Belize | | 1091 |
| Bermuda | | 753 |
| Botswana | | 659-663 |
| British Antarctic Territory | | 258 |
| British Indian Ocean Terr. | | 197 |
| Cayman Islands | | 752A-753 |
| Falkland Islands | | 694 |
| Fiji | | 819-820 |
| Gibraltar | | 754 |
| Kiribati | | 719A-720 |
| Namibia | | 909 |
| Niue | | 706 |
| Norfolk Island | | 644-645 |
| Papua New Guinea | | 937 |
| Pitcairn Islands | | 487 |
| St. Helena | | 711 |
| St. Kitts | | 437A-438 |
| Samoa | | 955A-956 |
| Seycelles | | 802 |
| Solomon Islands | | 866-867 |
| South Georgia | | 220 |
| Tokelau | | 252B-253 |
| Tonga | | 980 |
| Niuafo'ou | | 201 |
| Tristan da Cunha | | 618 |
| Tuvalu | | 762 |
| Vanuatu | | 718A-719 |
| Virgin Islands | | 878 |
| No. 696 (1) | 5.25 | 5.25 |
| Nos. 901A-902 (2) | 5.30 | 5.30 |
| No. 950 (1) | 6.25 | 6.25 |
| No. 1091 (1) | 10.00 | 10.00 |
| No. 753 (1) | 5.00 | 5.00 |
| Nos. 659-663 (5) | 8.25 | 8.80 |
| No. 258 (1) | 5.50 | 5.50 |
| No. 197 (1) | 5.50 | 5.50 |
| Nos. 752A-753 (3) | 7.40 | 7.40 |
| No. 694 (1) | 5.00 | 5.00 |
| Nos. 819-820 (2) | 5.25 | 5.25 |
| No. 754 (1) | 4.75 | 4.75 |
| Nos. 719A-720 (2) | 4.60 | 4.60 |
| No. 909 (1) | 1.75 | 1.75 |
| No. 706 (1) | 5.50 | 5.50 |
| Nos. 644-645 (2) | 5.60 | 5.60 |
| No. 937 (1) | 6.25 | 6.25 |
| No. 487 (1) | 4.75 | 4.75 |
| No. 711 (1) | 4.25 | 4.25 |
| Nos. 437A-438 (2) | 5.15 | 5.15 |
| Nos. 955A-956 (2) | 7.00 | 7.00 |
| No. 802 (1) | 6.25 | 6.25 |
| Nos. 866-867 (2) | 5.40 | 5.40 |
| No. 220 (1) | 4.50 | 5.00 |
| Nos. 252B-253 (2) | 6.00 | 6.00 |
| No. 980 (1) | 4.00 | 4.00 |
| No. 201 (1) | 6.50 | 6.50 |
| No. 618 (1) | 5.00 | 5.00 |
| No. 762 (1) | 3.50 | 3.50 |
| Nos. 718A-719 (2) | 8.00 | 8.00 |
| No. 878 (1) | 4.50 | 4.50 |
| Set total (46) Stamps | 171.95 | 173.00 |

### Wedding of Prince Edward and Sophie Rhys-Jones

CD356

## 1999

| | | |
|---|---|---|
| Ascension | | 729-730 |
| Cayman Islands | | 775-776 |
| Falkland Islands | | 729-730 |
| Pitcairn Islands | | 505-506 |
| St. Helena | | 733-734 |
| Samoa | | 971-972 |
| Tristan da Cunha | | 636-637 |
| Virgin Islands | | 908-909 |
| Nos. 729-730 (2) | 4.50 | 4.50 |
| Nos. 775-776 (2) | 4.95 | 4.95 |
| Nos. 729-730 (2) | 14.00 | 14.00 |
| Nos. 505-506 (2) | 7.00 | 7.00 |
| Nos. 733-734 (2) | 5.00 | 5.00 |
| Nos. 971-972 (2) | 5.00 | 5.00 |
| Nos. 636-637 (2) | 7.50 | 7.50 |
| Nos. 908-909 (2) | 7.50 | 7.50 |
| Set total (16) Stamps | 55.45 | 55.45 |

### 1st Manned Moon Landing, 30th Anniv.

CD357

## 1999

| | | |
|---|---|---|
| Ascension | | 731-735 |
| Bahamas | | 942-946 |
| Barbados | | 967-971 |
| Bermuda | | 778 |
| Cayman Islands | | 777-781 |
| Fiji | | 853-857 |
| Jamaica | | 889-893 |
| Kirbati | | 746-750 |
| Nauru | | 465-469 |
| St. Kitts | | 460-464 |
| Samoa | | 973-977 |
| Solomon Islands | | 875-879 |
| Tuvalu | | 800-804 |
| Virgin Islands | | 910-914 |
| Nos. 731-735 (5) | 12.80 | 12.80 |
| Nos. 942-946 (5) | 14.10 | 14.10 |
| Nos. 967-971 (5) | 9.45 | 8.25 |
| No. 778 (1) | 9.00 | 9.00 |
| Nos. 777-781 (5) | 9.25 | 9.25 |
| Nos. 853-857 (5) | 9.25 | 8.45 |
| Nos. 889-893 (5) | 8.30 | 7.18 |
| Nos. 746-750 (5) | 8.60 | 8.60 |
| Nos. 465-469 (5) | 7.55 | 7.10 |
| Nos. 460-464 (5) | 11.35 | 11.65 |
| Nos. 973-977 (5) | 12.60 | 12.45 |
| Nos. 875-879 (5) | 7.50 | 7.50 |
| Nos. 800-804 (5) | 6.75 | 6.75 |
| Nos. 910-914 (5) | 11.75 | 11.75 |
| Set total (66) Stamps | 138.25 | 134.83 |

### Queen Mother's Century

CD358

## 1999

| | | |
|---|---|---|
| Ascension | | 736-740 |
| Bahamas | | 951-955 |
| Cayman Islands | | 782-786 |
| Falkland Islands | | 734-738 |
| Fiji | | 858-862 |
| Norfolk Island | | 688-692 |
| St. Helena | | 740-744 |
| Samoa | | 978-982 |
| Solomon Islands | | 880-884 |
| South Georgia | | 231-235 |
| Tristan da Cunha | | 638-642 |
| Tuvalu | | 805-809 |
| Nos. 736-740 (5) | 15.50 | 15.50 |
| Nos. 951-955 (5) | 13.75 | 12.65 |
| Nos. 782-786 (5) | 8.35 | 8.35 |
| Nos. 734-738 (5) | 30.00 | 28.25 |
| Nos. 858-862 (5) | 12.80 | 13.25 |
| Nos. 688-692 (5) | 9.50 | 9.50 |
| Nos. 740-744 (5) | 16.15 | 16.15 |
| Nos. 978-982 (5) | 12.50 | 12.10 |
| Nos. 880-884 (5) | 7.50 | 7.00 |
| Nos. 231-235 (5) | 29.75 | 30.00 |
| Nos. 638-642 (5) | 18.00 | 18.00 |
| Nos. 805-809 (5) | 7.00 | 7.00 |
| Set total (60) Stamps | 180.80 | 177.75 |

### Prince William, 18th Birthday

CD359

## 2000

| | | |
|---|---|---|
| Ascension | | 755-759 |
| Cayman Islands | | 797-801 |
| Falkland Islands | | 762-766 |
| Fiji | | 889-893 |
| South Georgia | | 257-261 |
| Tristan da Cunha | | 664-668 |
| Virgin Islands | | 925-929 |
| Nos. 755-759 (5) | 15.50 | 15.50 |
| Nos. 797-801 (5) | 11.15 | 10.90 |
| Nos. 762-766 (5) | 24.60 | 22.50 |
| Nos. 889-893 (5) | 12.90 | 12.90 |
| Nos. 257-261 (5) | 29.00 | 28.75 |
| Nos. 664-668 (5) | 21.50 | 21.50 |
| Nos. 925-929 (5) | 14.50 | 14.50 |
| Set total (35) Stamps | 129.15 | 126.55 |

### Reign of Queen Elizabeth II, 50th Anniv.

CD360

## 2002

| | | |
|---|---|---|
| Ascension | | 790-794 |
| Bahamas | | 1033-1037 |
| Barbados | | 1019-1023 |
| Belize | | 1152-1156 |
| Bermuda | | 822-826 |
| British Antarctic Territory | | 307-311 |
| British Indian Ocean Territory | | 239-243 |
| Cayman Islands | | 844-848 |
| Falkland Islands | | 804-808 |
| Gibraltar | | 896-900 |
| Jamaica | | 952-956 |
| Nauru | | 491-495 |
| Norfolk Island | | 758-762 |
| Papua New Guinea | | 1019-1023 |
| Pitcairn Islands | | 552 |
| St. Helena | | 788-792 |
| St. Lucia | | 1146-1150 |
| Solomon Islands | | 931-935 |
| South Georgia | | 274-278 |
| Swaziland | | 706-710 |
| Tokelau | | 302-306 |
| Tonga | | 1059 |
| Niuafo'ou | | 239 |
| Tristan da Cunha | | 706-710 |
| Virgin Islands | | 967-971 |
| Nos. 790-794 (5) | 14.10 | 14.10 |
| Nos. 1033-1037 (5) | 15.25 | 15.25 |
| Nos. 1019-1023 (5) | 12.90 | 12.90 |
| Nos. 1152-1156 (5) | 17.10 | 15.10 |
| Nos. 822-826 (5) | 18.00 | 18.00 |
| Nos. 307-311 (5) | 23.00 | 23.00 |
| Nos. 239-243 (5) | 19.40 | 19.40 |
| Nos. 844-848 (5) | 13.25 | 13.25 |
| Nos. 804-808 (5) | 23.00 | 22.00 |
| Nos. 896-900 (5) | 6.65 | 6.65 |
| Nos. 952-956 (5) | 16.65 | 16.65 |
| Nos. 491-495 (5) | 17.75 | 17.75 |
| Nos. 758-762 (5) | 15.90 | 15.90 |
| Nos. 1019-1023 (5) | 14.50 | 14.50 |
| No. 552 (1) | 8.50 | 8.50 |
| Nos. 788-792 (5) | 19.75 | 19.75 |
| Nos. 1146-1150 (5) | 12.25 | 12.25 |
| Nos. 931-935 (5) | 12.40 | 12.40 |
| Nos. 274-278 (5) | 28.00 | 28.50 |
| Nos. 706-710 (5) | 12.50 | 12.50 |
| Nos. 302-306 (5) | 14.50 | 14.50 |
| No. 1059 (1) | 8.00 | 8.00 |
| No. 239 (1) | 8.75 | 8.75 |
| Nos. 706-710 (5) | 18.50 | 18.50 |
| Nos. 967-971 (5) | 16.50 | 16.50 |
| Set total (113) Stamps | 387.10 | 384.60 |

### Queen Mother Elizabeth (1900-2002)

CD361

## 2002

| | | |
|---|---|---|
| Ascension | | 799-801 |
| Bahamas | | 1044-1046 |
| Bermuda | | 834-836 |
| British Antarctic Territory | | 312-314 |
| British Indian Ocean Territory | | 245-247 |
| Cayman Islands | | 857-861 |
| Falkland Islands | | 812-816 |
| Nauru | | 499-501 |
| Pitcairn Islands | | 561-565 |
| St. Helena | | 808-812 |
| St. Lucia | | 1155-1159 |
| Seychelles | | 830 |
| Solomon Islands | | 945-947 |
| South Georgia | | 281-285 |
| Tokelau | | 312-314 |
| Tristan da Cunha | | 715-717 |
| Virgin Islands | | 979-983 |
| Nos. 799-801 (3) | 8.85 | 8.85 |
| Nos. 1044-1046 (3) | 9.10 | 9.10 |
| Nos. 834-836 (3) | 12.25 | 12.25 |
| Nos. 312-314 (3) | 18.75 | 18.75 |
| Nos. 245-247 (3) | 17.35 | 17.35 |
| Nos. 857-861 (5) | 15.00 | 15.00 |
| Nos. 812-816 (5) | 28.50 | 28.50 |
| Nos. 499-501 (3) | 14.00 | 14.00 |
| Nos. 561-565 (5) | 15.25 | 15.25 |
| Nos. 808-812 (5) | 12.00 | 12.00 |
| Nos. 1155-1159 (5) | 12.00 | 12.00 |
| No. 830 (1) | 6.50 | 6.50 |
| Nos. 945-947 (3) | 9.25 | 9.25 |
| Nos. 281-285 (5) | 19.50 | 19.50 |
| Nos. 312-314 (3) | 11.85 | 11.85 |
| Nos. 715-717 (3) | 16.25 | 16.25 |
| Nos. 979-983 (5) | 23.50 | 23.50 |
| Set total (63) Stamps | 249.90 | 249.90 |

### Head of Queen Elizabeth II

CD362

## 2003

| | | |
|---|---|---|
| Ascension | | 822 |
| Bermuda | | 865 |
| British Antarctic Territory | | 322 |
| British Indian Ocean Territory | | 261 |
| Cayman Islands | | 878 |
| Falkland Islands | | 828 |
| St. Helena | | 820 |
| South Georgia | | 294 |
| Tristan da Cunha | | 731 |
| Virgin Islands | | 1003 |
| No. 822 (1) | 12.50 | 12.50 |
| No. 865 (1) | 50.00 | 50.00 |
| No. 322 (1) | 9.50 | 9.50 |
| No. 261 (1) | 11.00 | 11.00 |
| No. 878 (1) | 14.00 | 14.00 |
| No. 828 (1) | 9.00 | 9.00 |
| No. 820 (1) | 9.00 | 9.00 |
| No. 294 (1) | 8.50 | 8.50 |
| No. 731 (1) | 10.00 | 10.00 |
| No. 1003 (1) | 10.00 | 10.00 |
| Set total (10) Stamps | 143.50 | 143.50 |

### Coronation of Queen Elizabeth II, 50th Anniv.

CD363

## 2003

| | | |
|---|---|---|
| Ascension | | 823-825 |
| Bahamas | | 1073-1075 |
| Bermuda | | 866-868 |
| British Antarctic Territory | | 323-325 |

| British Indian Ocean Territory | 262-264 |
| --- | --- |
| Cayman Islands | 879-881 |
| Jamaica | 970-972 |
| Kiribati | 825-827 |
| Pitcairn Islands | 577-581 |
| St. Helena | 821-823 |
| St. Lucia | 1171-1173 |
| Tokelau | 320-322 |
| Tristan da Cunha | 732-734 |
| Virgin Islands | 1004-1006 |

| | | |
| --- | --- | --- |
| Nos. 823-825 (3) | 12.50 | 12.50 |
| Nos. 1073-1075 (3) | 13.00 | 13.00 |
| Nos. 866-868 (2) | 14.25 | 14.25 |
| Nos. 323-325 (3) | 23.00 | 23.00 |
| Nos. 262-264 (3) | 28.00 | 28.00 |
| Nos. 879-881 (3) | 19.25 | 19.25 |
| Nos. 970-972 (3) | 10.00 | 10.00 |
| Nos. 825-827 (3) | 13.00 | 13.00 |
| Nos. 577-581 (5) | 14.40 | 14.40 |
| Nos. 821-823 (3) | 7.25 | 7.25 |
| Nos. 1171-1173 (3) | 8.75 | 8.75 |
| Nos. 320-322 (3) | 17.25 | 17.25 |
| Nos. 732-734 (3) | 16.75 | 16.75 |
| Nos. 1004-1006 (3) | 25.00 | 25.00 |
| Set total (43) Stamps | 222.40 | 222.40 |

**Prince William, 21st Birthday**

 CD364

**2003**

| | |
| --- | --- |
| Ascension | 826 |
| British Indian Ocean Territory | 265 |
| Cayman Islands | 882-884 |
| Falkland Islands | 829 |
| South Georgia | 295 |
| Tokelau | 323 |
| Tristan da Cunha | 735 |
| Virgin Islands | 1007-1009 |

| | | |
| --- | --- | --- |
| No. 826 (1) | 7.25 | 7.25 |
| No. 265 (1) | 8.00 | 8.00 |
| Nos. 882-884 (3) | 6.95 | 6.95 |
| No. 829 (1) | 13.50 | 13.50 |
| No. 295 (1) | 8.50 | 8.50 |
| No. 323 (1) | 7.25 | 7.25 |
| No. 735 (1) | 6.00 | 6.00 |
| Nos. 1007-1009 (3) | 10.00 | 10.00 |
| Set total (12) Stamps | 67.45 | 67.45 |

# British Commonwealth of Nations

## Dominions, Colonies, Territories, Offices and Independent Members

Comprising stamps of the British Commonwealth and associated nations.

A strict observance of technicalities would bar some or all of the stamps listed under Burma, Ireland, Kuwait, Nepal, New Republic, Orange Free State, Samoa, South Africa, South-West Africa, Stellaland, Sudan, Swaziland, the two Transvaal Republics and others but these are included for the convenience of collectors.

## 1. Great Britain

Great Britain: Including England, Scotland, Wales and Northern Ireland.

## 2. The Dominions, Present and Past

### AUSTRALIA

The Commonwealth of Australia was proclaimed on Jan. 1, 1901. It consists of six former colonies as follows:

| | |
|---|---|
| New South Wales | Victoria |
| Queensland | Tasmania |
| South Australia | Western Australia |

The following islands and territories are, or have been, administered by Australia: Australian Antarctic Territory, Christmas Island, Cocos (Keeling) Islands, Nauru, New Guinea, Norfolk Island, Papua.

### CANADA

The Dominion of Canada was created by the British North America Act in 1867. The following provinces were former separate colonies and issued postage stamps:

| | |
|---|---|
| British Columbia and Vancouver Island | Newfoundland |
| New Brunswick | Nova Scotia |
| | Prince Edward Island |

### FIJI

The colony of Fiji became an independent nation with dominion status on Oct. 10, 1970.

### GHANA

This state came into existence March 6, 1957, with dominion status. It consists of the former colony of the Gold Coast and the Trusteeship Territory of Togoland. Ghana became a republic July 1, 1960.

### INDIA

The Republic of India was inaugurated on Jan. 26, 1950. It succeeded the Dominion of India which was proclaimed Aug. 15, 1947, when the former Empire of India was divided into Pakistan and the Union of India. The Republic is composed of about 40 predominantly Hindu states of three classes: governor's provinces, chief commissioner's provinces and princely states. India also has various territories, such as the Andaman and Nicobar Islands.

The old Empire of India was a federation of British India and the native states. The more important princely states were autonomous. Of the more than 700 Indian states, these 43 are familiar names to philatelists because of their postage stamps.

#### CONVENTION STATES

| | |
|---|---|
| Chamba | Jhind |
| Faridkot | Nabha |
| Gwalior | Patiala |

#### FEUDATORY STATES

| | |
|---|---|
| Alwar | Jammu and Kashmir |
| Bahawalpur | Jasdan |
| Bamra | Jhalawar |
| Barwani | Jhind (1875-76) |
| Bhopal | Kashmir |
| Bhor | Kishangarh |
| Bijawar | Kotah |
| Bundi | Las Bela |
| Bussahir | Morvi |
| Charkhari | Nandgaon |
| Cochin | Nowanuggur |
| Dhar | Orchha |
| Dungarpur | Poonch |
| Duttia | Rajasthan |
| Faridkot (1879-85) | Rajpeepla |
| Hyderabad | Sirmur |
| Idar | Soruth |
| Indore | Tonk |
| Jaipur | Travancore |
| Jammu | Wadhwan |

### NEW ZEALAND

Became a dominion on Sept. 26, 1907. The following islands and territories are, or have been, administered by New Zealand:

| | |
|---|---|
| Aitutaki | Ross Dependency |
| Cook Islands (Rarotonga) | Samoa (Western Samoa) |
| Niue | Tokelau Islands |
| Penrhyn | |

### PAKISTAN

The Republic of Pakistan was proclaimed March 23, 1956. It succeeded the Dominion which was proclaimed Aug. 15, 1947. It is made up of all or part of several Moslem provinces and various districts of the former Empire of India, including Bahawalpur and Las Bela. Pakistan withdrew from the Commonwealth in 1972.

### SOUTH AFRICA

Under the terms of the South African Act (1909) the self-governing colonies of Cape of Good Hope, Natal, Orange River Colony and Transvaal united on May 31, 1910, to form the Union of South Africa. It became an independent republic May 3, 1961.

Under the terms of the Treaty of Versailles, South-West Africa, formerly German South-West Africa, was mandated to the Union of South Africa.

### SRI LANKA (CEYLON)

The Dominion of Ceylon was proclaimed Feb. 4, 1948. The island had been a Crown Colony from 1802 until then. On May 22, 1972, Ceylon became the Republic of Sri Lanka.

## 3. Colonies, Past and Present; Controlled Territory and Independent Members of the Commonwealth

| | |
|---|---|
| Abu Dhabi | Barbuda |
| Aden | Basutoland |
| Aitutaki | Batum |
| Alderney | Bechuanaland |
| Anguilla | Bechuanaland Prot. |
| Antigua | Belize |
| Ascension | Bermuda |
| Australia | Botswana |
| Bahamas | British Antarctic Territory |
| Bahrain | British Central Africa |
| Bangladesh | British Columbia and |
| Barbados | Vancouver Island |

# BRITISH COMMONWEALTH OF NATIONS

British East Africa
British Guiana
British Honduras
British Indian Ocean Territory
British New Guinea
British Solomon Islands
British Somaliland
Brunei
Burma
Bushire
Cameroons
Canada
Cape of Good Hope
Cayman Islands
Christmas Island
Cocos (Keeling) Islands
Cook Islands
Crete,
  British Administration
Cyprus
Dominica
East Africa & Uganda
  Protectorates
Egypt
Falkland Islands
Fiji
Gambia
German East Africa
Ghana
Gibraltar
Gilbert Islands
Gilbert & Ellice Islands
Gold Coast
Grenada
Griqualand West
Guernsey
Guyana
Heligoland
Hong Kong
Indian Native States
  (see India)
Ionian Islands
Jamaica
Jersey

Jordan
Kenya
Kenya, Uganda & Tanzania
Kiribati
Kuwait
Labuan
Lagos
Leeward Islands
Lesotho
Madagascar
Malawi
Malaya
  Federated Malay States
  Johore
  Kedah
  Kelantan
  Malacca
  Negri Sembilan
  Pahang
  Penang
  Perak
  Perlis
  Selangor
  Singapore
  Sungei Ujong
  Trengganu
Malaysia
Maldive Islands
Malta
Man, Isle of
Mauritius
Mesopotamia
Montserrat
Mozambique
Muscat
Namibia
Natal
Nauru
Nevis
New Britain
New Brunswick
Newfoundland
New Guinea
New Hebrides

New Republic
New South Wales
New Zealand
Niger Coast Protectorate
Nigeria
Niue
Norfolk Island
North Borneo
Northern Nigeria
Northern Rhodesia
North West Pacific Islands
Nova Scotia
Nyasaland Protectorate
Oman
Orange River Colony
Pakistan
Palestine
Papua New Guinea
Penrhyn Island
Pitcairn Islands
Prince Edward Island
Qatar
Queensland
Rhodesia
Rhodesia & Nyasaland
Ross Dependency
Rwanda
Sabah
St. Christopher
St. Helena
St. Kitts
St. Kitts-Nevis-Anguilla
St. Lucia
St. Vincent
Samoa
Sarawak
Seychelles
Sierra Leone
Singapore
Solomon Islands
Somaliland Protectorate
South Africa
South Arabia
South Australia

South Georgia
Southern Nigeria
Southern Rhodesia
South-West Africa
Sri Lanka
Stellaland
Straits Settlements
Sudan
Swaziland
Tanganyika
Tanzania
Tasmania
Tobago
Togo
Tokelau Islands
Tonga
Transvaal
Trinidad
Trinidad and Tobago
Tristan da Cunha
Trucial States
Turks and Caicos
Turks Islands
Tuvalu
Uganda
United Arab Emirates
Vanuatu
Victoria
Virgin Islands
Western Australia
Zambia
Zanzibar
Zimbabwe
Zululand

**POST OFFICES IN FOREIGN COUNTRIES**
Africa
  East Africa Forces
  Middle East Forces
Bangkok
China
Morocco
Turkish Empire

# Make Collecting Easy with Scott Specialty Series Albums

## Scott Albums Feature:

- High quality chemically neutral paper printed on one side
- All spaces identified by Scott numbers with either illustrations or descriptions.
- All pages have matching borders
- Pages contain general postage issues, as well as complete back-of-the-book materials
- Albums supplemented annually

**For a complete list of Scott Specialty Series Pages available, visit us at www.AmosAdvantage.com or call 800-572-6885. We would be glad to help!**

# Colonies, former colonies, offices, territories controlled by parent states

## Belgium
Belgian Congo
Ruanda-Urundi

## Denmark
Danish West Indies
Faroe Islands
Greenland
Iceland

## Finland
Aland Islands

## France
### COLONIES PAST AND PRESENT, CONTROLLED TERRITORIES
Afars & Issas, Territory of
Alaouites
Alexandretta
Algeria
Alsace & Lorraine
Anjouan
Annam & Tonkin
Benin
Cambodia (Khmer)
Cameroun
Castellorizo
Chad
Cilicia
Cochin China
Comoro Islands
Dahomey
Diego Suarez
Djibouti (Somali Coast)
Fezzan
French Colonies (general issues)
French Congo
French Equatorial Africa
French Guiana
French Guinea
French India
French Morocco
French Polynesia (Oceania)
French Southern & Antarctic Territories
French Sudan
French West Africa
Gabon
Germany
Ghadames
Grand Comoro
Guadeloupe
Indo-China
Inini
Ivory Coast
Laos
Latakia
Lebanon
Madagascar
Martinique
Mauritania
Mayotte
Memel
Middle Congo
Moheli
New Caledonia
New Hebrides
Niger Territory
Nossi-Be
Obock
Reunion
Rouad, Ile
Ste.-Marie de Madagascar
St. Pierre & Miquelon
Senegal
Senegambia & Niger
Somali Coast
Syria
Tahiti
Togo
Tunisia
Ubangi-Shari
Upper Senegal & Niger
Upper Volta
Viet Nam
Wallis & Futuna Islands

### POST OFFICES IN FOREIGN COUNTRIES
China
Crete
Egypt
Turkish Empire
Zanzibar

## Germany
### EARLY STATES
Baden
Bavaria
Bergedorf
Bremen
Brunswick
Hamburg
Hanover
Lubeck
Mecklenburg-Schwerin
Mecklenburg-Strelitz
Oldenburg
Prussia
Saxony
Schleswig-Holstein
Wurttemberg

### FORMER COLONIES
Cameroun (Kamerun)
Caroline Islands
German East Africa
German New Guinea
German South-West Africa
Kiauchau
Mariana Islands
Marshall Islands
Samoa
Togo

## Italy
### EARLY STATES
Modena
Parma
Romagna
Roman States
Sardinia
Tuscany
Two Sicilies
 Naples
 Neapolitan Provinces
 Sicily

### FORMER COLONIES, CONTROLLED TERRITORIES, OCCUPATION AREAS
Aegean Islands
 Calimno (Calino)
 Caso
 Cos (Coo)
 Karki (Carchi)
 Leros (Lero)
 Lipso
 Nisiros (Nisiro)
 Patmos (Patmo)
 Piscopi
 Rodi (Rhodes)
 Scarpanto
 Simi
 Stampalia
Castellorizo
Corfu
Cyrenaica
Eritrea
Ethiopia (Abyssinia)
Fiume
Ionian Islands
 Cephalonia
 Ithaca
 Paxos
Italian East Africa
Libya
Oltre Giuba
Saseno
Somalia (Italian Somaliland)
Tripolitania

### POST OFFICES IN FOREIGN COUNTRIES
"ESTERO"*
Austria
China
 Peking
 Tientsin
Crete
Tripoli
Turkish Empire
 Constantinople
 Durazzo
 Janina
Jerusalem
Salonika
Scutari
Smyrna
Valona
*Stamps overprinted "ESTERO" were used in various parts of the world.

## Netherlands
Aruba
Caribbean Netherlands
Curacao
Netherlands Antilles (Curacao)
Netherlands Indies
Netherlands New Guinea
St. Martin
Surinam (Dutch Guiana)

## Portugal
### COLONIES PAST AND PRESENT, CONTROLLED TERRITORIES
Angola
Angra
Azores
Cape Verde
Funchal
Horta
Inhambane
Kionga
Lourenco Marques
Macao
Madeira
Mozambique
Mozambique Co.
Nyassa
Ponta Delgada
Portuguese Africa
Portuguese Congo
Portuguese Guinea
Portuguese India
Quelimane
St. Thomas & Prince Islands
Tete
Timor
Zambezia

## Russia
### ALLIED TERRITORIES AND REPUBLICS, OCCUPATION AREAS
Armenia
Aunus (Olonets)
Azerbaijan
Batum
Estonia
Far Eastern Republic
Georgia
Karelia
Latvia
Lithuania
North Ingermanland
Ostland
Russian Turkestan
Siberia
South Russia
Tannu Tuva
Transcaucasian Fed. Republics
Ukraine
Wenden (Livonia)
Western Ukraine

## Spain
### COLONIES PAST AND PRESENT, CONTROLLED TERRITORIES
Aguera, La
Cape Juby
Cuba
Elobey, Annobon & Corisco
Fernando Po
Ifni
Mariana Islands
Philippines
Puerto Rico
Rio de Oro
Rio Muni
Spanish Guinea
Spanish Morocco
Spanish Sahara
Spanish West Africa

### POST OFFICES IN FOREIGN COUNTRIES
Morocco
Tangier
Tetuan

# Dies of British colonial stamps

**DIE A:**
1. The lines in the groundwork vary in thickness and are not uniformly straight.
2. The seventh and eighth lines from the top, in the groundwork, converge where they meet the head.
3. There is a small dash in the upper part of the second jewel in the band of the crown.
4. The vertical color line in front of the throat stops at the sixth line of shading on the neck.

**DIE B:**
1. The lines in the groundwork are all thin and straight.
2. All the lines of the background are parallel.
3. There is no dash in the upper part of the second jewel in the band of the crown.
4. The vertical color line in front of the throat stops at the eighth line of shading on the neck.

**DIE I:**
1. The base of the crown is well below the level of the inner white line around the vignette.
2. The labels inscribed "POSTAGE" and "REVENUE" are cut square at the top.
3. There is a white "bud" on the outer side of the main stem of the curved ornaments in each lower corner.
4. The second (thick) line below the country name has the ends next to the crown cut diagonally.

    DIE Ia.           DIE Ib.
    1 as die II.       1 and 3 as die II.
    2 and 3 as die I.   2 as die I.

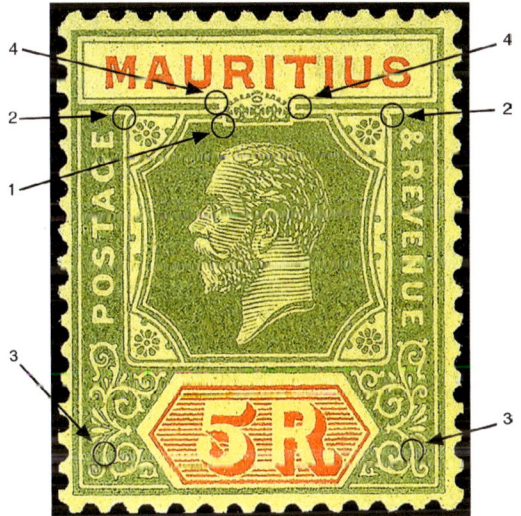

**DIE II:**
1. The base of the crown is aligned with the underside of the white line around the vignette.
2. The labels curve inward at the top inner corners.
3. The "bud" has been removed from the outer curve of the ornaments in each corner.
4. The second line below the country name has the ends next to the crown cut vertically.

# British Colonial and Crown Agents watermarks

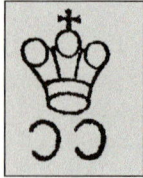
Wmk. 1
Crown and C C

Wmk. 2
Crown and C A

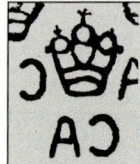
Wmk. 3
Multiple Crown
and C A

Wmk. 4
Multiple Crown
and Script C A

Wmk. 4a

Wmk. 46

Wmk. 314
St. Edward's Crown
and C A Multiple

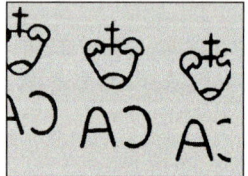
Wmk. 373

Wmk. 384

Wmk. 406

Watermarks 1 to 4, 314, 373, 384 and 406, common to many British territories, are illustrated here to avoid duplication.

The letters "CC" of Wmk. 1 identify the paper as having been made for the use of the Crown Colonies, while the letters "CA" of the others stand for "Crown Agents." Both Wmks. 1 and 2 were used on stamps printed by De La Rue & Co.

Wmk. 3 was adopted in 1904; Wmk. 4 in 1921; Wmk. 46 in 1879; Wmk. 314 in 1957; Wmk. 373 in 1974; Wmk. 384 in 1985; Wmk 406 in 2008.

In Wmk. 4a, a non-matching crown of the general St. Edwards type (bulging on both sides at top) was substituted for one of the Wmk. 4 crowns which fell off the dandy roll. The non-matching crown occurs in 1950-52 printings in a horizontal row of crowns on certain regular stamps of Johore and Seychelles, and on various postage due stamps of Barbados, Basutoland, British Guiana, Gold Coast, Grenada, Northern Rhodesia, St. Lucia, Swaziland and Trinidad and Tobago. A variation of Wmk. 4a, with the non-matching crown in a horizontal row of crown-CA-crown, occurs on regular stamps of Bahamas, St. Kitts-Nevis and Singapore.

Wmk. 314 was intentionally used sideways, starting in 1966. When a stamp was issued with Wmk. 314 both upright and sideways, the sideways varieties usually are listed also — with minor numbers. In many of the later issues, Wmk. 314 is slightly visible.

Wmk. 373 is usually only faintly visible.

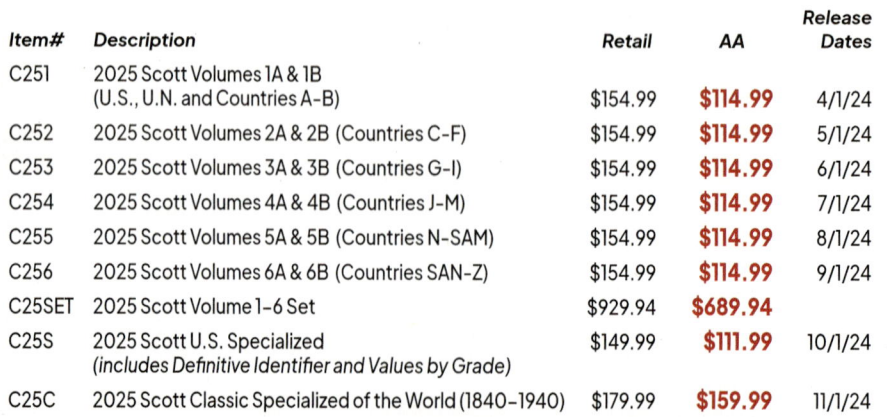

# VALUE THE WORLD

## 2025 Scott Postage Stamp Catalogues

- Two-book volumes 1–6 improve user experience
- Thousands of value changes keep pace with market fluctuations
- Hundreds of new stamp listings
- Editorial enhancements throughout include added stamp images, expanded footnotes and much more

| Item# | Description | Retail | AA | Release Dates |
|---|---|---|---|---|
| C251 | 2025 Scott Volumes 1A & 1B (U.S., U.N. and Countries A-B) | $154.99 | $114.99 | 4/1/24 |
| C252 | 2025 Scott Volumes 2A & 2B (Countries C-F) | $154.99 | $114.99 | 5/1/24 |
| C253 | 2025 Scott Volumes 3A & 3B (Countries G-I) | $154.99 | $114.99 | 6/1/24 |
| C254 | 2025 Scott Volumes 4A & 4B (Countries J-M) | $154.99 | $114.99 | 7/1/24 |
| C255 | 2025 Scott Volumes 5A & 5B (Countries N-SAM) | $154.99 | $114.99 | 8/1/24 |
| C256 | 2025 Scott Volumes 6A & 6B (Countries SAN-Z) | $154.99 | $114.99 | 9/1/24 |
| C25SET | 2025 Scott Volume 1-6 Set | $929.94 | $689.94 | |
| C25S | 2025 Scott U.S. Specialized (includes Definitive Identifier and Values by Grade) | $149.99 | $111.99 | 10/1/24 |
| C25C | 2025 Scott Classic Specialized of the World (1840-1940) | $179.99 | $159.99 | 11/1/24 |

**AmosAdvantage.com | 1-800-572-6885**

*AA prices apply to paid subscribers of Amos Media titles, or orders placed online. Prices, terms and product availability subect to change. Shipping and handling rates will apply.

# UNITED STATES

yu-ˌnī-təd ˈstāts

GOVT. — Republic
AREA — 3,615,211 sq. mi.
POP. — 331,449,520 (2020)
CAPITAL — Washington, DC

In addition to the 50 States and the District of Columbia, the Republic includes Guam, the Commonwealth of Puerto Rico, the Virgin Islands, American Samoa, Wake, Midway, and a number of small islands in the Pacific Ocean, all of which use stamps of the United States.

100 Cents = 1 Dollar

Catalogue values for unused stamps in this country are for Never Hinged items, beginning with Scott 772 in the regular postage section, Scott C19 in the air post section, Scott E17 in the special delivery section, Scott FA1 in the certified mail section, Scott O127 in officials section, Scott J88 in the postage due section, Scott RW1 in the hunting permit stamps section.

### Watermarks

Wmk. 190 — "USPS" in Single lined Capitals

Wmk. 191 — Double-lined "USPS" in Capitals

Watermark 191 has 9 letters for each horizontal row of 10 stamps. Watermark 190 has 8 to 9 letters for each horizontal row. Each watermark has 9 letters for each vertical row of 10 stamps. This results in a number of stamps in each pane showing only a small portion of 1 or more watermark letters. This is especialy true of watermark 190.

Wmk. 190Pl — PIPS, used in the Philippines
Wmk. 191Pl — PIPS, used in the Philippines
Wmk. 191C — US-C, used for Cuba
Wmk. 191R — USIR

### PROVISIONAL ISSUES BY POSTMASTERS

Values for Envelopes are for entires.

### ALEXANDRIA, VA.

A1

A2

All known examples are cut to shape.
Type I — 40 asterisks in circle.
Type II — 39 asterisks in circle.

**1846**     Typeset     *Imperf.*
1X1   A1   5c black, *buff,*
      type I                325,000.
   *a.*   5c black, *buff,* type II    625,000.

1X2   A2   5c black, *blue,*
      type I, on
      cover             1,180,000.

### ANNAPOLIS, MD.

E1

**1846**
2XU1   E1   5c carmine red,
       *white*           500,000.

Handstamped impressions of the circular design with "2" in blue or red exist on envelopes and letter sheets. Values: blue $17,500, red $30,000.
A letter sheet exists with circular design and "5" handstamped in red. Values: blue $10,000, red $12,500.
A similar circular design in blue was used as a postmark.

### BALTIMORE, MD.

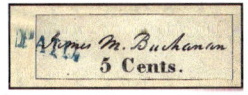
Signature of Postmaster — A1

Printed from a plate of 12 (2x6) containing nine 5c stamps and three 10c.

**1845**     Engr.     *Imperf.*
3X1   A1   5c black          6,000.
3X2   A1   10c black, on cover        80,000.
3X3   A1   5c black, *bluish*   65,000.   8,000.
3X4   A1   10c black, *bluish*        50,000.

Nos. 3X1-3X4 were printed from a plate of 12 (2x6) containing nine 5c and three 10c.

### Envelopes

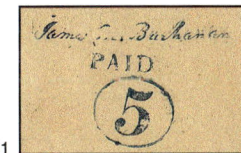
E1

The color given is that of the "PAID 5" and oval. "James M. Buchanan" is handstamped in black, blue or red. The paper is manila, buff, white, salmon or grayish.

**1845**     Handstamped
Various Papers
3XU1   E1   5c blue        4,500.
3XU2   E1   5c red        10,000.
3XU3   E1   10c blue       20,000.
3XU4   E1   10c red       20,000.

On the formerly listed "5+5" envelopes, the second "5" in oval is believed not to be part of the basic prepaid marking.

### BOSCAWEN, N. H.

A1

**1846 (?)**     Typeset     *Imperf.*
4X1   A1   5c dull blue, *yellowish,*
      on cover         85,000.

### BRATTLEBORO, VT.

Initials of Postmaster (FNP) — A1

Plate of 10 (5x2).

**1846**     *Imperf.*
Thick Softwove Paper Colored Through
5X1   A1   5c black, *buff*       7,500.

### LOCKPORT, N. Y.

A1

"Lockport, N.Y." oval and "PAID" separately handstamped in red, "5" in black ms.

**1846**     *Imperf.*
6X1   A1   5c red, *buff,* on cover     120,000.

### MILLBURY, Mass.

George Washington — A1

Printed from a woodcut, singly, on a hand press.

**1846**     *Imperf.*
7X1   A1   5c black, *bluish*
       letter paper     —   50,000.
7X2   A1   5c black, *white*
       print paper     —

No. 7X2 was printed on print paper that is substantially thicker than the letter paper on which No. 7X1 was printed.
Earliest documented use: Aug. 21, 1846.

### NEW HAVEN, CONN.

### ENVELOPES

E1

Impressed from a brass handstamp at upper right of envelope.
Signed in blue, black or magenta ms., as indicated in parentheses.

**1845**
8XU1   E1   5c red (M)      100,000.
8XU2   E1   5c red, *light bluish*
       (Bk)           75,000.
8XU3   E1   5c dull blue, *buff* (Bl)   75,000.
8XU4   E1   5c dull blue (Dl)    90,000.

Values of Nos. 8XU1-8XU4 are a guide to value. They are based on auction realizations and other sales, and take condition into consideration. All New Haven envelopes are of equal rarity (each is unique), with the exception of No. 8XU2, of which two exist. An entire of No. 8XU2 is the finest example known, and this is reflected in the value shown. The other envelopes are valued according to condition, and cut squares also are valued according to condition as much as rarity.

*Reprints were made at various times between 1871 and 1932. They can be distinguished from the originals, primarily due to differences in paper. See the Scott Specialized Catalogue of United States Stamps and Covers for more detail and values.*

### NEW YORK, N. Y.

George Washington — A1

Plate of 40 (5x8). Nos. 9X1-9X3 and varieties unused are valued without gum. Examples with original gum are extremely scarce and will command higher prices.

**9X1**   A1   5c black, signed
       ACM, connect-
       ed, *1846*      1,500.   450.
   *a.*   Signed ACM, AC connect-
       ed                1,750.   525.
   *b.*   Signed A.C.M.      4,500.   675.
   *c.*   Signed MMJr            10,000.
   *d.*   Signed RHM       13,000.   3,500.
   *e.*   Without signature   3,750.   900.

These stamps were usually initialed "ACM" in magenta ink, as a control, before being sold or passed through the mails.
*A plate of 9 (3x3) was made from which proofs were printed in black on white and deep blue papers; also in blue, green, brown and red on white bond paper. Stamps from this plate were not issued, and it is possible that it is an essay, as the design differs slightly from the issued stamps from the sheet of 40. No examples from the plate of nine are known used.*

**1847**     Engr.     *Imperf.*
Blue Wove Paper
9X2   A1   5c black, signed
       ACM connect-
       ed                6,500.   4,000.
   *a.*   Signed RHM
   *b.*   Signed ACM, AC connect-
       ed                         8,000.
   *d.*   Without signature   25,000.   7,500.

All used true blue examples carry "ACM" without periods; of the three unused examples, two lack initials.
On the only example known of No. 9X2a the "R" is illegible and does not match those of the other "RHM" signatures.
No. 9X2b is unique.

**1847**     Engr.     *Imperf.*
Gray Wove Paper
9X3   A1   5c black, signed
       ACM connect-
       ed                5,250.   3,250.
   *a.*   Signed RHM              8,500.
   *b.*   Without signature         13,000.

### PROVIDENCE, R. I.

A1 & A2

10X1   A1   5c gray black     350.   2,250.
10X2   A2   10c gray black   1,150.   16,500.
   *a.*   Se-tenant with 5c      2,000.

Plate of 12 (3x4) contains 11-5c and 1-10c.
*Reprints were made in 1898. Each stamp bears one of the following letters on the back: B O G E R T D U R B I N. Value of 5c, $65; 10c, $160; sheet, $1,250.*
*Reprint singles or sheets without back print sell for more.*

### ST. LOUIS, MO.

A1

A2

Missouri Coat of Arms — A3

Nos. 11X1-11X8 unused are valued without gum.

# UNITED STATES

## Wove Paper Colored Through

**1845, Nov.-1846**      **Imperf.**

| | | | | |
|---|---|---|---|---|
| 11X1 | A1 | 5c black, greenish | 47,500. | 8,000. |
| 11X2 | A2 | 10c black, greenish | 47,500. | 8,000. |
| 11X3 | A3 | 20c black, greenish | | 160,000. |

Printed from Plate 1 (3 varieties each of the 5c and 10c) and Plate 2 (1 variety of the 5c, 3 of the 10c, 2 of the 20c).

**1846**

| | | | | |
|---|---|---|---|---|
| 11X4 | A1 | 5c black, (III), gray lilac | — | 45,000. |
| 11X5 | A2 | 10c black, gray lilac | 50,000. | 11,500. |
| 11X6 | A3 | 20c black, gray lilac | 100,000. | 60,000. |

One variety of 5c, 3 of 10c, 2 of 20c.
No. 11X6 unused is unique. It is in the grade of fine and valued thus.

**1847**      **Pelure Paper**

| | | | | |
|---|---|---|---|---|
| 11X7 | A1 | 5c black, *bluish* | — | 11,000. |
| 11X8 | A2 | 10c black, *bluish* | 17,500. | 15,000. |
| a. | | Impression of 5c on back | | 77,500. |

Three varieties of 5c, 3 of 10c.

Values of Nos. 11X7-11X8 reflect the usual poor condition of these stamps, which were printed on fragile pelure paper. Attractive examples with minor defects sell for considerably more.

Used values are for pen-canceled stamps. No. 11X8a is unique.

---

### Please Note:

Stamps are valued in the grade of very fine unless otherwise indicated.

Values for early and valuable stamps are for examples with certificates of authenticity from acknowledged expert committees, or examples sold with the buyer having the right of certification. This applies to examples with original gum as well as examples without gum. Beware of stamps offered "as is," as the gum on some unused stamps offered with "original gum" may be fraudulent, and stamps offered as unused without gum may in some cases be altered or faintly canceled used stamps.

---

### Manuscript Cancels on Used Stamps

Manuscript (pen) cancels reduce the value of used stamps by about 50%. See the Scott U.S. Specialized Catalogue for individual valuations.

---

### GENERAL ISSUES
### All Issues from 1847 through 1894 are unwatermarked.

Benjamin Franklin — A1

**1847, July 1**    **Engr.**    **Imperf.**
**Thin Bluish Wove Paper**

| | | | | |
|---|---|---|---|---|
| 1 | A1 | 5c red brown | 6,000. | 425. |
| | | No gum | 2,100. | |
| a. | | 5c dark brown | 7,000. | 525. |
| | | No gum | 2,400. | |
| b. | | 5c orange brown | 10,000. | 675. |
| | | No gum | 3,500. | |
| c. | | 5c red orange | 25,000. | 8,500. |
| | | No gum | 9,500. | |
| d. | | 5c brown orange | — | 1,000. |
| | | No gum | 4,500. | |

George Washington — A2

| | | | | |
|---|---|---|---|---|
| 2 | A2 | 10c black | 37,500. | 850. |
| | | No gum | 15,000. | |

## REPRODUCTIONS of 1847 ISSUE

A3              A4

Actually, official imitations made from new plates of 50 subjects made by the Bureau of Engraving and Printing by order of the Post Office Department. These were not valid for postal use.

*5c.* On the originals the left side of the white shirt frill touches the oval on a level with the top of the "F" of "Five." On the reproductions it touches the oval about on a level with the top of the figure "5." On the originals, the bottom of the right leg of the "N" in "CENTS" is blunt. On the reproductions, the "N" comes to a point at the bottom.

*10c.* On the reproductions, line of coat at left points to right tip of "X" and line of coat at right points to center of "S" of CENTS. On the originals, line of coat points to "T" of TEN and between "T" and "S" of CENTS. The bottom of the right leg of the "N" of "CENTS" shows the same difference as on the 5c originals and reproductions. On the reproductions, the gap between the bottom legs of the left "X" is noticeably wider than the gap on the right "X." On the originals, the gaps are of equal width. On the reproductions, the eyes have a sleepy look, the line of the mouth is straighter, and in the curl of hair near the left cheek is a strong black dot, while the originals have only a faint one.

(See Nos. 948a and 948b for 1947 reproductions — 5c blue and 10c brown orange in larger size.)

**1875**      **Imperf.**
**Bluish paper, without gum**

| | | | | |
|---|---|---|---|---|
| 3 | A3 | 5c red brown (4779) | 1,000. | |
| 4 | A4 | 10c black (3883) | 1,300. | |

Numbers in parentheses are quantities sold.

---

Except as noted here and in footnotes for selected issues, values for 1851-57 issues are for examples that clearly show all of the illustrated type characteristics. Stamps that have weakly defined or missing type characteristics sell for less.

In Nos. 5-17, the 1¢, 3¢ and 12¢ have very small margins between the stamps. The 5¢ and 10¢ have moderate size margins. The values of these stamps take the margin size into consideration.

Values for Nos. 5A, 6b and 19b are for the less distinct positions. Best examples sell for more.

Values for No. 16 are for outer line recut at top. Other recuts sell for more.

Franklin — A5

Type I

Type Ib

ONE CENT
Type I. Has complete curved lines outside the labels with "U. S. Postage" and "One Cent." The scrolls below the lower label are turned under, forming little balls. The ornaments at top are substantially complete.
Type Ib. As type I, but balls below bottom label are not as clear. Plume-like scrolls at bottom are incomplete.

**1851-57**      **Imperf.**

| | | | | |
|---|---|---|---|---|
| 5 | A5 | 1c blue, type I (7R1E) | 115,000. | 50,000. |

Values for No. 5 are for examples with margins touching or cutting slightly into the design, or for examples with four margins and minor faults. Very few sound examples with the design untouched exist, and these sell for much more than the values shown.
Value for No. 5 unused is for a stamp with no gum. Only one example unused with original gum is recorded. It is in a multiple and is creased.

| | | | | |
|---|---|---|---|---|
| 5A | A5 | 1c blue, type 1b | 32,500. | 6,000. |
| | | No gum | 12,000. | |

Values for No. 5A are for sound examples with margins just clear to just touching the design on one or two sides. Examples with margins well clear of the design all around are scarce and will sell for more than the values shown.

A6

Type Ic

Type Ia. Same as type I at bottom, but top ornaments and outer line at top are partly cut away.
Type Ic. Same as type Ia, but bottom right plume and ball ornament incomplete. Bottom left plume is complete or nearly complete.

| | | | | |
|---|---|---|---|---|
| 6 | A6 | 1c blue, type 1a ('57) | 45,000. | 9,250. |
| | | No gum | 20,000. | |
| 6b | A6 | 1c blue, type 1c | 7,000. | 3,750. |
| | | No gum | 3,000. | |

A7

Type II — Same as Type I at top, but the little balls of the bottom scrolls and the bottoms of the lower plume ornaments are missing. The side ornaments are substantially complete.

| | | | | |
|---|---|---|---|---|
| 7 | A7 | 1c blue, type II | 1,000. | 140.00 |
| | | No gum | 375. | |

A8

Type IIIa

Type III. The top and bottom curved lines outside the labels are broken in the middle. The side ornaments are substantially complete.
Type IIIa. Similar to type III with the outer line broken at top or bottom but not both.

| | | | | |
|---|---|---|---|---|
| 8 | A8 | 1c blue, type III | 25,000. | 1,650. |
| | | No gum | 7,500. | |

Values for type III are for at least a 2mm break in each outer line. Examples of type III with wider breaks in outer lines command higher prices; those with smaller breaks sell for much less.

| | | | | |
|---|---|---|---|---|
| 8A | A8 | 1c blue, type IIIa | 6,000. | 800. |
| | | No gum | 2,250. | |

Stamps of type IIIa with bottom line broken command higher prices than those with top line broken. See note after No. 8 on width of break of outer lines.

A9

Type IV. Similar to type II, but with the curved lines outside the labels recut at top or bottom or both.

| | | | | |
|---|---|---|---|---|
| 9 | A9 | 1c blue, type IV ('52) | 725.00 | 100.00 |
| | | No gum | 260.00 | |
| a. | | Printed on both sides, reverse inverted | | 40,000. |

# The results you get are only as good as the people who produce them.

## The best results come from the best team in the business.

Scott Trepel

John Zuckerman

Corey Long

Charles Shreve

Andrew Titley

Chris Anderson

The expert team at Siegel Auction Galleries and our International division is experienced, knowledgeable, professional and dedicated.

Even more, every member is a true *philatelist* who loves stamps and covers.

To discuss the sale of your U.S. collection, call 212-753-6421.

If you have a worldwide collection, call 214-754-5991.

**The best team in the business is ready to work for you.**

## Robert A. Siegel
**ROBERT A. SIEGEL AUCTION GALLERIES, INC.**
America's premier stamp auctioneer since 1930

For buyers or sellers, Siegel Auction Galleries offers unparalleled expertise, a worldwide client base, financial reliability, intelligent marketing, and the best internet resources and search tools.

### siegelauctions.com

## UNITED STATES

### Washington — A10

All of the 3c stamps of the 1851 and 1857 issues were recut at least to the extent of the outer frame lines, sometimes the inner lines at the sides (type II stamps), and often other lines in triangles, diamond blocks, label blocks and/or top/bottom frame lines. Some of the most prominent varieties are listed below each major listing (others are described in "The 3c Stamp of U.S. 1851-57 Issue," by Carroll Chase).

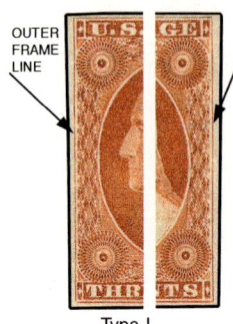

**Type I**

### THREE CENTS
Type I — There is an outer frame line on all four sides. The outer frame lines at the sides are always recut.

| 10 | A10 | 3c org brown, type I | 5,500. | 190.00 |
|---|---|---|---|---|
| | No gum | | 2,250. | |

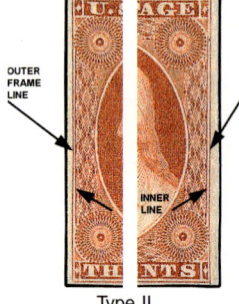

**Type II**

Type II — As type I, but with the inner lines at the sides added by recutting on the plate.

| 10A | A10 | 3c org brown, type II | 3,250. | 150.00 |
|---|---|---|---|---|
| | No gum | | 1,350. | |
| b. | Printed on both sides | | | 55,000. |

Only one example of No. 10Ab is recorded.

| 11 | A10 | 3c dull red, type I ('55) | 250.00 | 17.50 |
|---|---|---|---|---|
| | No gum | | 100.00 | |
| 11A | A10 | 3c dull red, type II ('53-'55) | 250.00 | 15.00 |
| | No gum | | 85.00 | |
| e. | Double impression | | | 30,000. |

### Thomas Jefferson — A11

### FIVE CENTS
Type I — Projections on all four sides.

| 12 | A11 | 5c red brown, type I ('56) | 30,000. | 750. |
|---|---|---|---|---|
| | No gum | | 11,000. | |

### Washington — A12

### TEN CENTS
Type I — The "shells" at the lower corners are practically complete. The outer line below the label is very nearly complete. The outer lines are broken above the middle of the top label and the "X" in each upper corner.

| 13 | A12 | 10c green, type I ('55) | 19,000. | 750. |
|---|---|---|---|---|
| | No gum | | 8,500. | |

A13

Type II — The design is complete at the top. The outer line at the bottom is broken in the middle. The shells are partly cut away, as shown.

| 14 | A13 | 10c green, type II ('55) | 5,000. | 145. |
|---|---|---|---|---|
| | No gum | | 1,800. | |

A14

Type III — The outer lines are broken above the top label and the "X" numerals. The outer line at the bottom and the shells are partly cut away, as shown, similar to type II.

| 15 | A14 | 10c green, type III ('55) | 5,000. | 145. |
|---|---|---|---|---|
| | No gum | | 1,800. | |

A15

Type IV. The outer lines have been recut at top or bottom or both.

Types I, II, III and IV have complete ornaments at the sides of the stamps and three pearls at each outer edge of the bottom panel.

| 16 | A15 | 10c green, type IV ('55) | 50,000. | 1,700. |
|---|---|---|---|---|
| | No gum | | 27,500. | |

### Washington — A16

| 17 | A16 | 12c gray black | 6,250. | 260. |
|---|---|---|---|---|
| | No gum | | 2,100. | |
| c. | Printed on both sides | | | 35,000. |

Values for 1857-61 issues are for examples that clearly show all the illustrated type characteristics. Stamps that have weakly defined or missing type characteristics sell for less.

Nos. 18-39 have small or very small margins. The values take into account the margin size. See footnotes for more specific information on selected issues.

### SAME DESIGNS AS 1851-57 ISSUES
**1857-61**      Perf. 15½

| 18 | A5 | 1c blue, type I ('61) | 2,100. | 500. |
|---|---|---|---|---|
| | No gum | | 800. | |
| | Short ornaments at either top or bottom | | | — |
| 19 | A6 | 1c blue, type Ia | 42,500. | 10,000. |
| | No gum | | 20,000. | |
| b. | blue, type Ic | | 4,250. | 4,250. |
| | No gum | | 1,750. | |
| 20 | A7 | 1c blue, type II | 850. | 275. |
| | No gum | | 375. | |
| 21 | A8 | 1c blue, type III | 17,500. | 1,350. |
| | No gum | | 6,000. | |
| a. | Horiz. pair, imperf between | | | 20,000. |
| 22 | A8 | 1c blue, type IIIa | 2,200. | 500. |
| | No gum | | 850. | |

Beware of pairs of No. 22 with faint blind perforations between that sometimes are offered as pairs imperf. between.

| 23 | A9 | 1c blue, type IV | 10,000. | 575. |
|---|---|---|---|---|
| | No gum | | 4,250. | |

### Franklin — A20

Type V — Similar to type III of 1851-57 but with side ornaments partly cut away. About one-half of all positions have side scratches. Wide breaks in top and bottom framelines.
Type Va — Stamps from Plate 5 with almost complete ornaments at right side and no side scratches. Many, but not all, stamps from Plate 5 are Type Va, the remainder being Type V.

| 24 | A20 | 1c blue, type V | 140.00 | 40.00 |
|---|---|---|---|---|
| | No gum | | 60.00 | |
| b. | Laid paper | | | 7,500. |
| 25 | A10 | 3c rose, type I | 3,000. | 190.00 |
| | No gum | | 1,050. | |
| b. | Vert. pair, imperf. horizontally | | | 25,000. |
| 25A | A10 | 3c rose, type II | 12,500. | 850. |
| | No gum | | 5,000. | |

Nos. 25 and 25A are valued in the grade of fine with perforations touching or cutting slightly on one or two sides.

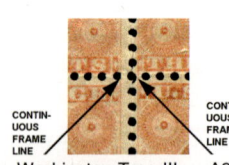

### Washington Type III — A21

Type III — There are no outer frame lines at top and bottom. The side frame lines were recut so as to be continuous from the top to the bottom of the plate. **Stamps from the top or bottom rows show the ends of the side**

frame lines and may be mistaken for Type IV.

| 26 | A21 | 3c dull red, type III | 65.00 | 10.00 |
|---|---|---|---|---|
| | No gum | | 27.50 | |
| b. | Horiz. pair, imperf. vertically | | | 14,000. |
| c. | Vert. pair, imperf. horizontally | | | 16,000. |
| d. | Horizontal pair, imperf. between | | | — |
| e. | Double impression | | | 15,000. |

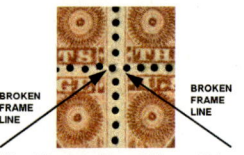

### Washington Type IV — A21a

Type IV — As type III, but the side frame lines extend only to the top and bottom of the stamp design. All Type IV stamps are from plates 10 and 11 (each of which exists in three states), and these plates produced only Type IV. The side frame lines were recut individually for each stamp, thus being broken between the stamps vertically.
**Beware of type III stamps with frame lines that stop at the top of the design (from top row of plate) or bottom of the design (from bottom row of plate). These are often mistakenly offered as No. 26A.**

| 26A | A21a | 3c dull red, type IV | 600.00 | 140.00 |
|---|---|---|---|---|
| | No gum | | 260.00 | |
| f. | Horiz. strip of 3, imperf. vert., on cover | | | 27,000. |

No. 26Af is unique.

A unique authenticated example of a No. 26A imperforate single stamp is recorded. No multiples of this variety are known.

| 27 | A11 | 5c brick red, type I ('58) | 80,000. | 1,450. |
|---|---|---|---|---|
| | No gum | | 20,000. | |
| | N.Y. Ocean Mail | | | +1,000. |
| 28 | A11 | 5c red brown, type I | 60,000. | 1,050. |
| | No gum | | 15,000. | |
| b. | Bright red brown | | 70,000. | 2,000. |
| | No gum | | 20,000. | |
| | Defective transfer (23R1) | | | 2,500. |
| 28A | A11 | 5c Indian red, type I ('58) | 160,000. | 3,750. |
| | No gum | | 40,000. | |

No. 28A unused is valued in the grade of fine. Only four examples are recorded with any amount of gum.

| 29 | A11 | 5c brown, type I ('59) | 5,500. | 325. |
|---|---|---|---|---|
| | No gum | | 1,750. | |

### Jefferson — A22

### FIVE CENTS.
Type II — The projections at top and bottom are partly cut away.

| 30 | A22 | 5c orange brown, type II ('61) | 1,200. | 1,300. |
|---|---|---|---|---|
| | No gum | | 500. | |
| 30A | A22 | 5c brown, type II ('60) | 2,250. | 375. |
| | No gum | | 850. | |
| b. | Printed on both sides | | | 35,000. |
| 31 | A12 | 10c green, type I | 35,000. | 1,200. |
| | No gum | | 11,500. | |
| 32 | A13 | 10c green, type II | 5,750. | 190. |
| | No gum | | 2,000. | |
| 33 | A14 | 10c green, type III | 5,750. | 190. |
| | No gum | | 2,000. | |
| 34 | A15 | 10c green, type IV | 50,000. | 2,300. |
| | No gum | | 20,000. | |

# UNITED STATES

Washington (Two typical examples) — A23
Example I   Example II

**TEN CENTS**
**Type V** — The side ornaments are slightly cut away. Usually only one pearl remains at each end of the lower label, but some copies show two or three pearls at the right side. At the bottom the outer line is complete and the shells nearly so. The outer lines at top are complete except over the right "X."

| | | | | |
|---|---|---|---|---|
| 35 | A23 | 10c green, type V ('59) | 210.00 | 55.00 |
| | | No gum | 95.00 | |

No. 36 outer frame lines recut on plate

**TWELVE CENTS.** Printed from two plates.
**Plate 1 (No. 36)** — Outer frame lines were recut on the plate and are complete. Very narrow spacing of stamps on the plate.

| | | | | |
|---|---|---|---|---|
| 36 | A16 | 12c black (Plate 1) | 1,700. | 325. |
| | | No gum | 600. | |
| c. | | Horizontal pair, imperf. between | | 12,500. |

Typical No. 36B, outer frame lines not recut

**Plate III (No. 36B)** — Weak outer frame lines from the die were not recut and are noticeably uneven or broken, sometimes partly missing. Somewhat wider spacing of stamps on the plate.

| | | | | |
|---|---|---|---|---|
| 36B | A16 | 12c black, plate III ('59) | 775. | 275. |
| | | No gum | 400. | |

Washington A17     Franklin A18

| | | | | |
|---|---|---|---|---|
| 37 | A17 | 24c gray lilac ('60) | 1,450. | 400. |
| a. | | 24c gray | 1,450. | 400. |
| | | No gum | 500. | |
| 38 | A18 | 30c orange ('60) | 1,900. | 500. |
| | | No gum | 700. | |

Washington — A19

| | | | | |
|---|---|---|---|---|
| 39 | A19 | 90c blue ('60) | 3,000. | 10,000. |
| | | No gum | 1,400. | |

See Die and Plate proofs in the Scott United States Specialized Catalogue for imperfs. of the 12c, 24c, 30c, 90c.
Genuine cancellations on the 90c are rare. Used examples must be accompanied by certificates of authenticity issued by recognized expertizing committees.

## REPRINTS OF 1857-60 ISSUE
### White paper, without gum.
**1875**  **Perf. 12**

| | | | |
|---|---|---|---|
| 40 | A5 | 1c bright blue | 650. |
| 41 | A10 | 3c scarlet | 3,000. |
| 42 | A22 | 5c orange brown | 1,250. |
| 43 | A12 | 10c blue green | 2,600. 13,000. |
| 44 | A16 | 12c greenish black | 3,000. |
| 45 | A17 | 24c blackish violet | 3,250. 10,000. |
| 46 | A18 | 30c yellow orange | 3,250. |
| 47 | A19 | 90c deep blue | 4,000. |

Nos. 41-46 are valued in the grade of fine.
Nos. 40-47 exist imperforate. Very infrequent sales preclude establishing a value at this time. One set of imperforate pairs is recorded and it sold for $110,000 in a 2009 auction.

### Essays-Trial Color Proofs

The paper of former Nos. 55-62 (Nos. 63E11e, 65-E15h, 67-E9e, 69-E6e, 72-E7h, Essay section, Nos. 70eTC, 71bTC, Trial Color Proof section, Scott U.S. Specialized) is thin and semitransparent. That of the postage issues is thicker and more opaque, except Nos. 62B, 70c and 70d.

Franklin — A24

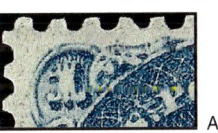

Washington — A25

Jefferson — A26

Washington — A27

A27a

Washington — A28

A28

Washington A29

Franklin A30

Washington — A31

A31

1c — There is a dash under the tip of the ornament at right of the numeral in upper left corner.
3c — Ornaments at corners end in a small ball.
5c — There is a leaflet in the foliated ornaments at each corner.
10c (A27) — A heavy curved line has been cut below the stars and an outer line added to the ornaments above them.
12c — There are corner ornaments consisting of ovals and scrolls.
90c — Parallel lines form an angle above the ribbon with "U. S. Postage"; between these lines there is a row of dashes and a point of color at the apex of the lower line.

**1861**  **Perf. 12**

| | | | | |
|---|---|---|---|---|
| 62B | A27a | 10c dark green | 8,500. | 1,800. |
| | | No gum | 3,600. | |

**1861-62**  **Perf. 12**

| | | | | |
|---|---|---|---|---|
| 63 | A24 | 1c blue | 275.00 | 45.00 |
| | | No gum | 100.00 | |
| a. | | 1c ultramarine | 2,500. | 1,900. |
| | | No gum | 1,000. | |
| b. | | 1c dark blue | 800.00 | 875.00 |
| | | No gum | 300.00 | |
| c. | | Laid paper, horiz. or vert. | 8,500. | 4,500. |
| d. | | Vertical pair, imperf. horiz. | | — |
| e. | | Printed on both sides, reverse inverted | — | 35,000. |

The editors would like to see authenticated evidence of the existence of No. 63d.
The pale milky blue shade of No. 63 is very rare.

| | | | | |
|---|---|---|---|---|
| 64 | A25 | 3c pink | 14,000. | 500.00 |
| | | No gum | 5,000. | |
| a. | | 3c pigeon blood pink | 55,000. | 4,500. |
| | | No gum | 17,500. | |
| b. | | 3c rose pink, Aug. 17, 1861 | 600.00 | 140.00 |
| | | No gum | 250.00 | |
| 65 | A25 | 3c rose | 125.00 | 3.00 |
| | | No gum | 50.00 | |
| b. | | Laid paper, horiz. or vert. | — | 1,100. |
| d. | | Vertical pair, imperf. horiz. | 12,500. | 1,500. |
| | | No gum | 5,000. | |
| e. | | Printed on both sides, reverse inverted | 40,000. | 8,250. |
| | | Printed on both sides, reverse not inverted | | 9,500. |
| f. | | Double impression | | 17,500. |

The 3c lake can be found under No. 66 in the Trial Color Proofs section of the Scott U.S. Specialized Catalogue. The imperf 3c lake under No. 66P in the same section. The imperf 3c rose can be found in the Die and Plate Proofs section of the Specialized.

| | | | | |
|---|---|---|---|---|
| 67 | A26 | 5c buff | 30,000. | 750. |
| | | No gum | 12,500. | |
| a. | | 5c brown yellow | 32,500. | 1,100. |
| | | No gum | 14,000. | |
| b. | | 5c olive yellow | | 4,850. |

Values of Nos. 67, 67a, 67b reflect the normal small margins.

| | | | | |
|---|---|---|---|---|
| 68 | A27 | 10c green | 950. | 60.00 |
| | | No gum | 375. | |
| a. | | 10c dark green | 1,350. | 90.00 |
| | | No gum | 500. | |
| b. | | Vertical pair, imperf. horiz. | | 67,500. |
| 69 | A28 | 12c black | 1,700. | 95.00 |
| | | No gum | 675. | |
| 70 | A29 | 24c red lilac ('62) | 2,900. | 300.00 |
| | | No gum | 1,100. | |
| a. | | 24c brown lilac | 3,250. | 325.00 |
| | | No gum | 1,250. | |
| b. | | 24c steel blue ('61) | 16,500. | 825.00 |
| | | No gum | 6,250. | |
| c. | | 24c violet, thin paper, Aug. 20, 1861 | 35,000. | 2,250. |
| | | reddish violet | | 3,250. |
| | | No gum | 13,500. | |
| d. | | 24c pale gray violet, thin paper | 25,000. | 3,000. |
| | | No gum | 6,000. | |

There are numerous shades of the 24c stamp in this and the following issue.
Color changelings, especially of No. 78, are frequently offered as No. 70b. Obtaining a certificate from an acknowledged expert committee is strongly advised.
Nos. 70c and 70d are on a thinner, harder and more transparent paper than Nos. 70, 70a, 70b or the latter Nos. 78, 78a, 78b and 78c.

| | | | | |
|---|---|---|---|---|
| 71 | A30 | 30c orange | 2,600. | 250. |
| | | No gum | 950. | |
| a. | | Printed on both sides | | |

Values for No. 71 are for examples with small margins, especially at sides. Large-margined examples sell for much more.

| | | | | |
|---|---|---|---|---|
| 72 | A31 | 90c blue | 3,000. | 625. |
| | | No gum | 1,200. | |
| a. | | 90c pale blue | 3,000. | 675. |
| | | No gum | 1,200. | |
| b. | | 90c dark blue | 3,750. | 950. |
| | | No gum | 1,500. | |

---

**For One of the World's Most Complete U.S. Inventories**
**www.millerstamps.com**

**BUY & SELL** U.S. Classics to the Back-of-Book
Singles, Booklets, Plate Blocks, Sheets, Ducks, Confederates, Canada, Zeppelin Stamps & Covers

**DARN!** *I should have bought my stamps from*

## MILLER'S STAMP CO.
— *A name you can trust since 1969* —
P.O. Box 1011 • Niantic, CT 06357-7011
Phone: 860-908-6200
E-mail: stamps@millerstamps.com

**Please Note:**
**Stamps are valued in the grade of very fine unless otherwise indicated.**
**Values for early and valuable stamps are for examples with certificates of authenticity from acknowledged expert committees, or examples sold with the buyer having the right of certification.**
**This applies to examples with original gum as well as examples without gum.**
**Beware of stamps offered "as is," as the gum on some unused stamps offered with "original gum" may be fraudulent, and stamps offered as unused without gum may in some cases be altered or faintly canceled used stamps.**

DESIGNS AS 1861 ISSUE

Andrew Jackson
A32

Abraham Lincoln
A33

**1861-66** ***Perf. 12***
**73** A32 2c black ('63) 350.00 75.00
No gum 150.00
*f.* Printed on both sides, reverse not inverted *25,000.*
*g.* Laid paper — *11,500.*

No. 73f unused is unique. It has perfs cut off on two sides and is valued thus.
The 3c scarlet can be found under No. 74 in the Scott U.S. Specialized Catalogue Trial Color Proofs section.

**75** A26 5c red brown ('62) 5,500. 425.
No gum 2,000.

Values for No. 75 reflect the normal small margins.

**76** A26 5c brown ('63) 1,400. 115.
No gum 550.
*a.* 5c black brown 2,250. 400.
No gum 850.
*b.* Laid paper —

Values of Nos. 76, 76a reflect the normal small margins.

**77** A33 15c black ('66) 5,000. 190.
No gum 1,900.
**78** A29 24c lilac ('62) 2,750. 400.
No gum 950.
*a.* 24c grayish lilac 2,750. 425.
No gum 950.
*b.* 24c gray 2,750. 450.
No gum 950.
*c.* 24c blackish violet *95,000.* *16,000.*
No gum *30,000.*

Only three examples are recorded of No. 78c unused with original gum. No. 78c unused with and without gum are valued in the grade of fine-very fine.

*d.* Printed on both sides, reverse inverted *22,500.*

**SAME DESIGNS AS 1861-66 ISSUES**

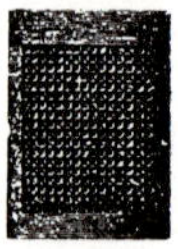
Grill

Embossed with grills of various sizes. Some authorities believe that more than one size of grill probably existed on one of the grill rolls.
A peculiarity of the United States issues from 1867 to 1870 is the grill or embossing. The object was to break the fiber of the paper so that the ink of the canceling stamp would soak in and make washing for a second using impossible. The exact date at which grilled stamps came into use is unsettled. Luff's "Postage Stamps of the United States" places the date as probably August 8, 1867.
Horizontal measurements are given first.

**GRILL WITH POINTS UP**

Grills A and C were made by a roller covered with ridges shaped like an inverted V. Pressing the ridges into the stamp paper forced the paper into the pyramidal pits between the ridges, causing irregular breaks in the paper. Grill B was made by a roller with raised bosses.

**A. GRILL COVERING THE ENTIRE STAMP**

**1867-68** ***Perf. 12***
**79** A25 3c rose 8,500. 1,300.
No gum 2,750.
*b.* Printed on both sides —

Nos. 79, 79b, are valued for fine-very fine centering but with minor perforation faults.
An essay which is often mistaken for No. 79 (#79-E15) shows the points of the grill as small squares faintly impressed in the paper, but not cutting through it.
On No. 79 the grill breaks through the paper. Examples free from defects are rare.

**80** A26 5c brown *400,000.*
*a.* 5c dark brown *400,000.*
**81** A30 30c orange *225,000.*

Four examples of Nos. 80 and 80a (two of each shade), and eight examples of No. 81 (one in the New York Public Library Miller collection and not available to collectors) are known. All are more or less faulty and/or off center. Values are for off-center examples with small perforation faults.

**B. GRILL ABOUT 18x15mm (22x18 POINTS)**

**82** A25 3c rose *900,000.*

The four known examples of No. 82 are valued in the grade of fine.
Earliest documented use: Feb. 1?, 1869 (dated cancel on off-cover stamp).

**C. GRILL ABOUT 13x16mm (16 TO 17 BY 18 TO 21 POINTS)**

The grilled area on each of four C grills in the sheet may total about 18x15mm when a normal C grill adjoins a fainter grill extending to the right or left edge of the stamp.
This is caused by a partial erasure on the grill roller when it was changed to produce C grills instead of the all-over A grill.
The imperf. can be found in the *Scott U.S. Specialized Catalogue* Die and Plate Proofs section.

**83** A25 3c rose 5,500. 1,150.
No gum 2,000.

**GRILL WITH POINTS DOWN**

The grills were produced by rollers with the surface covered, or partly covered, by pyramidal bosses. On the D, E and F grills the tips of the pyramids are vertical ridges. On the Z grill the ridges are horizontal.

**D. GRILL ABOUT 12x14mm (15 BY 18 TO 19 POINTS)**

**84** A32 2c black *16,000.* 5,250.
No gum *6,500.*

No. 84 is valued in the grade of fine.

**85** A25 3c rose *8,000.* 1,050.
No gum *2,500.*

**Z. GRILL ABOUT 11x14mm (14 TO 15 BY 17 OR 18 POINTS)**
(1c, 10c, 15c 17 rows; 2c, 3c, 12c 18 rows)

**85A** A24 1c blue *3,000,000.*

Two examples of No. 85A are currently recorded. One is contained in the New York Public Library collection, which is on long-term loan to the Smithsonian National Postal Museum.

**85B** A32 2c black 20,000. 1,100.
No gum 8,000.
**85C** A25 3c rose *25,000.* 3,750.
No gum *9,000.*
**85D** A27 10c green *750,000.*

Six examples of No. 85D are known. One is contained in the New York Public Library collection. Value is for a well-centered example with small faults.

**85E** A28 12c intense black *25,000.* 2,250.
No gum *8,500.*
**85F** A33 15c black *2,000,000.*

Two examples of No. 85F are documented, one in the grade of very good, the other extremely fine. Value is for the extremely fine example.

**E. GRILL ABOUT 11x13mm (14 BY 16 TO 18 POINTS)**

**86** A24 1c blue 3,000. 450.
No gum 1,200.
*a.* 1c dull blue 3,000. 425.
No gum 1,200.
**87** A32 2c black 1,700. 200.
No gum 650.
**88** A25 3c rose 1,050. 30.00
No gum 400.
*a.* 3c lake red 1,250. 80.00
No gum 475.
**89** A27 10c green 5,000. 350.
No gum 2,000.
**90** A28 12c black 4,750. 400.
No gum 1,900.
**91** A33 15c black 12,500. 575.
No gum 4,500.

**F. GRILL ABOUT 9x13mm (12 BY 16 TO 18 POINTS)**

**92** A24 1c blue 2,800. 450.
No gum 950.
*a.* 1c pale blue 2,300. 425.
No gum 750.
**93** A32 2c black 450. 55.00
No gum 155.
**94** A25 3c red 350. 12.50
*a.* 3c rose 350. 12.50
No gum 150.
*c.* Vertical pair, imperf. horiz. *15,000.*
*d.* Printed on both sides *9,000.* *35,000.*

The imperf. 3c can be found in the Scott U.S. Specialized Catalogue Die and Plate Proofs section.

**95** A26 5c brown 3,250. 900.
No gum 1,100.
*a.* 5c black brown 5,000. 2,400.
No gum 2,000.
Double grill —

Values of Nos. 95, 95a reflect the normal small margins.

**96** A27 10c yel grn 2,500. 275.
No gum 825.
**97** A28 12c black 2,800. 260.
No gum 1,000.
**98** A33 15c black 4,250. 275.
No gum 1,600.
**99** A29 24c gray lilac 8,500. 1,700.
No gum 3,250.
**100** A30 30c orange 12,500. 1,000.
No gum 4,500.

Values for No. 100 are for examples with small margins, especially at sides. Large-margined examples sell for much more.

**101** A31 90c blue 14,500. 2,700.
No gum 5,750.

RE-ISSUE OF 1861-66 ISSUES
Without Grill, Hard White Paper
White Crackly Gum

**1875** ***Perf. 12***
**102** A24 1c blue *750.* *1,750.*
No gum *350.*
**103** A32 2c black *3,500.* *10,500.*
No gum *1,600.*
**104** A25 3c brown red *3,750.* *13,000.*
No gum *1,700.*
**105** A26 5c brown *2,500.* *6,500.*
No gum *1,150.*
**106** A27 10c green *3,000.* *100,000.*
No gum *1,500.*
**107** A28 12c black *3,750.* *12,000.*
No gum *1,750.*
**108** A33 15c black *4,500.* *30,000.*
No gum *2,100.*
**109** A29 24c deep violet *6,000.* *17,500.*
No gum *2,750.*
**110** A30 30c brownish org *6,000.* *17,500.*
No gum *2,750.*
**111** A31 90c blue *7,000.* *225,000.*
No gum *3,500.*

These stamps can be distinguished from the 1861-66 issues by the shades and the paper which is hard and very white instead of yellowish. The gum is white and crackly.

Franklin
A34

Post Horse and Rider
A35

G. Grill measuring 9 ½x9mm
(12 by 11 to 11 ½ points)

**1869** **Hard Wove Paper** ***Perf. 12***
**112** A34 1c buff 600. 160.
No gum 225.
*b.* Without grill *32,500.*
**113** A35 2c brown 500. 90.
No gum 190.
*b.* Without grill *14,000.*
*d.* Printed on both sides *62,500.*

Locomotive
A36

Washington
A37

**114** A36 3c ultramarine 225. 30.00
No gum 90.
*a.* Without grill *13,000.* *18,000.*
Without grill, gray paper 3,750.
*e.* Printed on both sides, reverse inverted *55,000.*

Two examples recorded of No. 114a on normal paper: one with pen cancel but with original gum, 1994 Philatelic Foundation certificate; and one lifted from a cover, original gum adhering, examined, and placed back, 2011 Philatelic Foundation certificate. Also, four examples of No. 114a on gray paper: a single lifted from cover, examined, and hinged back in place, 1991 Philatelic Foundation certificate; and a strip of three on piece, mostly detached from piece, with full gum, 1978 and 2006 Philatelic Foundation certificates.
No. 114e is unique.

**115** A37 6c ultramarine 2,600. 225.
No gum 1,050.

Shield and Eagle
A38

S. S. Adriatic
A39

**116** A38 10c yellow 1,850. 110.
No gum 750.
**117** A39 12c green 1,850. 130.
No gum 725.

Landing of Columbus — A40

Type I. Picture unframed.
No. 118 has horizontal shading lines at the left and right sides of the vignette.

**118** A40 15c brn & bl, type I 9,000. 900.
No gum 3,250.
*a.* Without grill *11,500.*

A40a

No. 119 has diagonal shading lines at the left and right sides of the vignette.

**119** A40a 15c brn & bl, type II 2,600. 200.
No gum 925.
*b.* Center inverted *1,000,000.* *27,500.*
No gum *700,000.*
*c.* Center double, one inverted *80,000.*

Declaration of Independence — A41

**120** A41 24c green & violet 8,000. 675.
No gum 3,000.
*a.* Without grill *14,000.*
*b.* Center inverted *750,000.* *37,500.*

Shield, Eagle and Flags
A42

Lincoln
A43

**121** A42 30c ultra & carmine 3,750. 450.
No gum 1,400.
*a.* Without grill *10,000.*
*b.* Flags inverted *750,000.* *85,000.*
No gum *300,000.*

Seven examples of No. 121b unused are recorded. Only one has part of its original gum.

**122** A43 90c carmine & black 11,000. 2,100.
No gum 4,000.
*a.* Without grill *22,500.*

Values of varieties of Nos. 112-122 without grill are for examples with original gum.
Most examples of Nos. 119b, 120b are faulty. Values are for stamps with fine centering and only minimal faults. No. 120b unused is valued without gum, as all of the three examples available to collectors are without gum.

# Easy Online Bidding

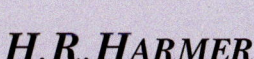
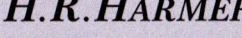
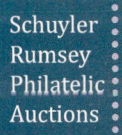

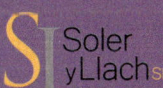

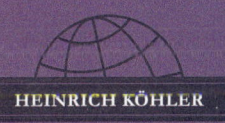

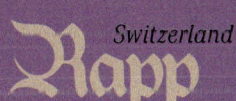

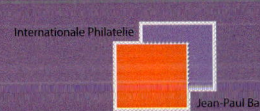

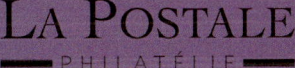

## and many more

## RE-ISSUE OF 1869 ISSUE

### Without grill, hard white paper, with white crackly gum.

The gum is almost always somewhat yellowed with age, and unused stamps with original gum are valued with such gum.

A new plate of 150 subjects was made for the 1c. The plate for the frame of the 15c was made using the same die as that used to make the type I frame for No. 118. For No. 118, the lines on each side of the vignette area were entered onto the plate itself, one position at a time. Upon close examination, each stamp position will be found to exhibit minute differences in these horizontal fringe lines.

**1875** ***Perf. 12***

| | | | |
|---|---|---|---|
| **123** A34 1c buff | | 525. | 425. |
| | No gum | 220. | |
| **124** A35 2c brown | | 600. | 750. |
| | No gum | 250. | |
| **125** A36 3c blue | | *5,000.* | *25,000.* |
| | No gum | 2,500. | |

Used value for No. 125 is for an attractive fine to very fine example with minimal faults.

| | | | |
|---|---|---|---|
| **126** A37 6c blue | | 1,900. | *3,000.* |
| | No gum | 900. | |
| **127** A38 10c yellow | | 1,600. | 1,800. |
| | No gum | 750. | |
| **128** A39 12c green | | 2,000. | *3,000.* |
| | No gum | 1,000. | |

A40b

No. 129 (type III) is similar to No. 118 (type I) but without the shading lines at each side of the vignette.

| | | | |
|---|---|---|---|
| **129** A40b 15c brn & bl, Type III | | 1,300. | 1,000. |
| | No gum | 700. | |
| *a.* | Imperf. horizontally, single | *14,000.* | *30,000.* |
| | No gum | *5,000.* | |

Two used examples of No. 129a are recorded. Both have faults and are valued thus.

| | | | |
|---|---|---|---|
| **130** A41 24c grn & violet | | 2,100. | 1,600. |
| | No gum | 1,000. | |
| **131** A42 30c ultra & car | | 2,250. | 2,750. |
| | No gum | 1,100. | |
| **132** A43 90c car & blk | | 3,750. | *6,000.* |
| | No gum | 2,000. | |

### Soft Porous Paper

**1880-82**

| | | | |
|---|---|---|---|
| **133** A34 1c buff, issued with gum | | 375. | *550.* |
| | No gum | 150. | |
| *a.* | 1c brown orange, issued without gum ('81 and '82) | 425. | *650.* |

Beware of No. 133 unused without gum offered as No. 133a. Certification is recommended for No. 133a.

## PRODUCED BY THE NATIONAL BANK NOTE COMPANY

Franklin — A44

A44

Jackson — A45

A45

Washington — A46

A46

Lincoln — A47

A47

Edwin M. Stanton — A48

A48

Jefferson — A49

A49

Henry Clay — A50

A50

Daniel Webster — A51

A51

Gen. Winfield Scott A52

Alexander Hamilton A53

Commodore O.H. Perry — A54

### H. GRILL ABOUT 10x12mm (11 TO 13 BY 14 TO 16 POINTS)

The "H" grills can be separated into early state and late state, based on the shape of the tip of the grill. Early-state grills show a point or very small vertical line at the tip of the pyramid, while late-state grills show the pyramid tips truncated and flat.

Early-state "H" grills tend to be on vertical-mesh wove paper, while later printings and all late-state grills were printed on horizontal-mesh wove paper, resulting in stamp designs being approximately ¼mm shorter than the designs printed on vertical-mesh wove paper. The late-stage "H" grills virtually all seem to have been used only after Jan. 1873.

Poor printing quality often resulted in grills that show only a few grill points or a very few rows of points. This is especially true of the "H" grills. When there are not enough grill points to clearly identify whether the grill is an "H" or an "I," it must be assumed it is the lower-valued "H" grill variety. Authentication is advised for these stamps with high catalogue values.

### White Wove Paper, Thin to Medium Thick.

**1870-71** ***Perf. 12***

| | | | |
|---|---|---|---|
| **134** A44 1c ultramarine | | 2,000. | 210.00 |
| | No gum | 700. | |
| *b.* | Pair, one without grill | | — |
| **135** A45 2c red brown | | 1,000. | 85.00 |
| | No gum | 360. | |
| **136** A46 3c green | | 575. | 35.00 |
| | No gum | 190. | |
| *c.* | Printed on both sides | | — |

The imperf. 3c can be found in the Scott U.S. Specialized Catalogue Die and Plate Proofs section.

| | | | |
|---|---|---|---|
| **137** A47 6c carmine | | 5,000. | 425. |
| | No gum | 1,750. | |
| *b.* | Pair, one without grill | | — |
| **138** A48 7c vermilion | | 4,250. | 525. |
| | No gum | 1,550. | |
| *b.* | Pair, one without grill | | — |
| **139** A49 10c brown | | 7,500. | 850. |
| | No gum | 2,700. | |
| **140** A50 12c dull violet | | *32,500.* | 4,000. |
| | No gum | *18,500.* | |
| **141** A51 15c orange | | 7,500. | 1,500. |
| | No gum | 2,500. | |
| **142** A52 24c purple | | — | 6,500. |
| **143** A53 30c black | | 20,000. | 4,000. |
| | No gum | 8,000. | |
| **144** A54 90c carmine | | 25,000. | 2,350. |
| | No gum | 10,000. | |

### I. GRILL ABOUT 8½x10mm (10 TO 11 BY 10 TO 13 POINTS)

The "I" grills can be separated into early state and late state, based on the shape of the tip of the grill. Early state grills show small tips of the pyramid, while late state grills show the pyramid tips truncated and flat.

Early state "I" grills tend to be on vertical-mesh wove paper, while later printings and all late-state grills were printed on horizontal-mesh wove paper, resulting in stamp designs being approximately ¼mm shorter than the designs printed on vertical-mesh wove paper. The late-stage "I" grills all seem to have been used only after Jan. 1873.

Values are for stamps with grills that are clearly identifiable. Poor printing quality often resulted in grills that show only a few grill points or a very few rows of points. When there are not enough grill points to clearly identify whether the grill is an "H" or an "I," it must be assumed it is the lower-valued "H" grill variety. Authentication is advised for these stamps with high catalogue values.

| | | | |
|---|---|---|---|
| **134A** A44 1c ultra | | *2,750.* | *400.00* |
| | No gum | *800.00* | |
| **135A** A45 2c red brown | | *2,000.* | *300.00* |
| | No gum | *1000.* | |
| **136A** A46 3c green | | *850.00* | *110.00* |
| *a.* | Pair, one without grill | — | |
| **137A** A47 6c carmine | | *8,500.* | *950.00* |
| **138A** A48 7c vermilion ('71) | | *6,500.* | *800.00* |
| | No gum | *2,200.* | |
| **139A** A49 10c brown | | *17,500.* | *10,000.* |
| *b.* | Strip of 3, one without grill, two with split grill | | — |

There are two unused examples of No. 139A recorded. One is fine and the other is very fine plus. The catalogue value is for the latter.

| | | | |
|---|---|---|---|
| **140A** A50 12c dull violet | | *30,000.* | — |

Two examples are recorded of No. 140A unused, and it is valued in the grade of fine.

One used example is recorded, centered to the left.

| | | | |
|---|---|---|---|
| **141A** A51 15c orange | | *16,500.* | *8,500.* |

Three singles and a block of 4 are recorded of No. 141A unused. Value for unused single is for a fine example.

| | | | |
|---|---|---|---|
| **143A** A53 30c black | | *75,000.* | |

Only one recorded example of No. 143A, which is valued in the grade of fine-very fine.

| | | | |
|---|---|---|---|
| **144A** A54 90c carmine | | — | *15,000.* |

The unused No. 144A has a vertically split grill and is unique.

### White Wove Paper Without Grill.

**1870-71** ***Perf. 12***

| | | | |
|---|---|---|---|
| **145** A44 1c ultra | | 650. | 20.00 |
| | No gum | 240. | |
| **146** A45 2c red brown | | 350. | 17.50 |
| | No gum | 150. | |
| *d.* | Double impression | *9,000.* | |
| **147** A46 3c green | | 200. | 1.80 |
| | No gum | 80. | |
| *a.* | Printed on both sides, reverse inverted | | *17,500.* |
| *b.* | Double impression | | *30,000.* |

Nos. 147a and 147b are valued in the grade of fine.

The imperf. 3c can be found in the Scott U.S. Specialized Catalogue Die and Plate Proofs section.

| | | | |
|---|---|---|---|
| **148** A47 6c carmine | | 900. | 25.00 |
| | No gum | 290. | |
| *c.* | Double paper | — | *100.00* |

No. 148b is unique.

| | | | |
|---|---|---|---|
| **149** A48 7c ver ('71) | | 900. | 100.00 |
| | No gum | 290. | |
| **150** A49 10c brown | | 2,000. | 35.00 |
| | No gum | 800. | |
| **151** A50 12c dull violet | | 2,850. | 200.00 |
| | No gum | 1,050. | |
| **152** A51 15c brt org | | 3,500. | 225.00 |
| | No gum | 1,300. | |
| *a.* | Double impression | | *9,000.* |

No. 152a is unique. It has fine centering and faults and is valued thus.

| | | | |
|---|---|---|---|
| **153** A52 24c purple | | 1,700. | 225.00 |
| | No gum | 650. | |
| *a.* | Double paper | — | — |
| **154** A53 30c black | | 7,000. | 300.00 |
| | No gum | 2,600. | |
| **155** A54 90c carmine | | 5,000. | 350.00 |
| | No gum | 1,800. | |

## PRINTED BY THE CONTINENTAL BANK NOTE COMPANY

Designs of the 1870-71 Issue with secret marks on the values from 1c to 15c, as described and illustrated:

The object of secret marks was to provide a simple and positive proof that these stamps were produced by the Continental Bank Note Company and not by their predecessors.

Almost all of the stamps of the Continental Bank Note Co. printing including the Department stamps and some of the Newspaper stamps may be found upon a paper that shows more or less the characteristics of a ribbed paper. The ribbing may be oriented either vertically or horizontally, with horizontal ribbing being far more common than vertical ribbing. Values are for the most common varieties.

Franklin — A44a

1c. In the pearl at the left of the numeral "1" there is a small crescent.

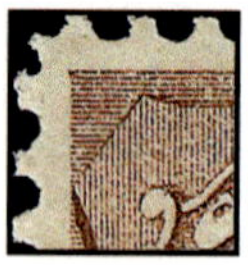
Jackson — A45a

2c. Under the scroll at the left of "U. S." there is a small diagonal line. This mark seldom shows clearly. The stamp, No. 157, can be distinguished by its color.

Washington — A46a

3c. The under part of the upper tail of the left ribbon is heavily shaded.

Lincoln — A47a

6c. The first four vertical lines of the shading in the lower part of the left ribbon have been strengthened.

Stanton — A48a

7c. Two small semi-circles are drawn around the ends of the lines that outline the ball in the lower right hand corner.

Jefferson — A49a

10c. There is a small semi-circle in the scroll at the right end of the upper label.

UNITED STATES 9

Clay — A50a

12c. The balls of the figure "2" are crescent shaped.

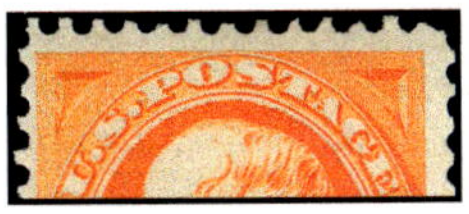

Webster — A51a

15c. In the lower part of the triangle in the upper left corner two lines have been made heavier forming a "V." This mark can be found on some of the Continental and American (1879) printings, but not all stamps show it.

Secret marks were added to the dies of the 24c, 30c and 90c but new plates were not made from them. The various printings of the 30c and 90c can be distinguished only by the shades and paper.

Experimental J. Grill about 7x9½mm exists on all values except 24c and 90c. Grill was composed of truncated pyramids and was so strongly impressed that some points often broke through the paper.

White Wove Paper, Thin to Thick
Without Grill

**1873, July (?)** ***Perf. 12***

**156** A44a 1c ultra 200. 5.75
No gum 90.
*a.* Double paper 2,000. 500.00
*e.* With grill 2,000.
*f.* Imperf., pair — 1,500.
**157** A45a 2c brown 325. 25.00
No gum 125.
*a.* Double paper 1,500. 200.00
*c.* With grill 1,850. 750.00
*d.* Double impression 16,500.

No. 157d is unique.

**158** A46a 3c green 110. 1.00
No gum 40.
*a.* Double paper 600. 100.00
*e.* With grill 550.
*h.* Horizontal pair, imperf. vert. —
*i.* Horizontal pair, imperf. between 1,300.
*j.* Double impression 7,000.
*k.* Printed on both sides 20,000.

Nos. 158j and 158k are valued in the grade of fine.

The imperf 3c, with and without grill, can be found in the Scott U.S. Specialized Catalogue Die and Plate Proofs section.

**159** A47a 6c dull pink 375. 18.00
No gum 120.
*b.* With grill 1,800.
*c.* Double paper — 900.00
**160** A48a 7c org ver 1,000. 90.00
No gum 350.
*a.* With grill 3,500.
*b.* Double paper —
**161** A49a 10c brown 800. 25.00
No gum 275.
*a.* Double paper 3,500. 900.00
*c.* With grill 3,750.
*d.* Horizontal pair, imperf. between 15,000.
**162** A50a 12c blkish vio 2,200. 150.00
No gum 775.
*a.* With grill 5,500.
**163** A51a 15c yel org 2,250. 160.00
No gum 775.
*a.* With grill 5,750.
*b.* Double paper 1,250.
**164** A52 24c purple 357,500.

The Philatelic Foundation has certified as genuine a 24c on vertically ribbed paper, and that is the unique stamp listed as No. 164. Specialists believe that only Continental used ribbed paper. It is not known for sure whether or not Continental also printed the 24c value on regular paper; if it did, specialists currently are not able to distinguish these from No. 153. The catalogue value represents a 2004 auction sale price realized.

**165** A53 30c gray black 4,000. 150.
No gum 1,300.
*a.* Double paper —
*c.* With grill 24,000.
**166** A54 90c rose car 2,100. 325.
No gum 700.

## Special Printing of the 1873 Issue

Hard, White Wove Paper
Without Gum

**1875** ***Perf. 12***

**167** A44a 1c ultramarine 13,500.
**168** A45a 2c dark brown 5,750.
**169** A46a 3c blue green 20,000. —
**170** A47a 6c dull rose 19,000.
**171** A48a 7c reddish ver 4,000.
**172** A49a 10c pale brown 18,000.
**173** A50a 12c dark violet 5,250.
**174** A51a 15c bright org 18,000.
**175** A52 24c dull purple 3,250. 22,500.
**176** A53 30c greenish blk 12,000.
**177** A54 90c vio carmine 17,000.

Although perforated, these stamps were usually cut apart with scissors. As a result, the perforations are often much mutilated and the design is frequently damaged.

These can be distinguished from the 1873 issue by the shades; also by the paper, which is very white instead of yellowish.

These and the subsequent issues listed under the heading of "Special Printings" are special printings of stamps then in current use which, together with the reprints and re-issues, were made for sale to collectors. They were available for postage except for the Officials, Newspaper and Periodical, and demonetized issues.

Only three examples of No. 175 used have been certified. They all have small faults and are valued thus.

**Yellowish Wove Paper**

**1875** ***Perf. 12***

**178** A45a 2c vermilion 325. 15.00
No gum 100.
*a.* Double paper — —
*c.* With grill 1,200. 2,750.

The imperf 2c can be found in the Scott U.S. Specialized Catalogue Die and Plate Proofs section.

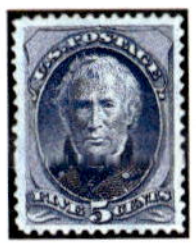

Zachary Taylor — A55

**179** A55 5c blue 700. 27.50
No gum 225.
*a.* Double paper 1,000.
*c.* With grill 9,500.

SPECIAL PRINTING OF 1875 ISSUE
Hard, White Wove Paper
Without Gum

**1875**

**180** A45a 2c carmine ver 65,000.
**181** A55 5c bright blue 460,000.

Unlike Nos. 167-177, Nos. 180-181 were seldom cut apart with scissors.

Please Note:
Stamps are valued in the grade of very fine unless otherwise indicated.
Values for early and valuable stamps are for examples with certificates of authenticity from acknowledged expert committees, or examples sold with the buyer having the right of certification.
This applies to examples with original gum as well as examples without gum.
Beware of stamps offered "as is," as the gum on some unused stamps offered with "original gum" may be fraudulent, and stamps offered as unused without gum may in some cases be altered or faintly canceled used stamps.

IMPORTANT INFORMATION
REGARDING VALUES FOR
NEVER-HINGED STAMPS

Collectors should be aware that the values given for never-hinged stamps from No. 182 on are for stamps in the grade of very fine, just as the values for all stamps in the catalogue are for very fine stamps unless indicated otherwise. The never-hinged premium as a percentage of value will be larger for stamps in extremely fine or superb grades, and the premium will be smaller for fine-very fine, fine or poor examples. This is particularly true of the issues of the late-19th and early-20th centuries.

VALUES FOR NEVER-HINGED
STAMPS
PRIOR TO SCOTT 182

This catalogue does not value pre-1879 stamps in never-hinged condition. Premiums for never-hinged condition in the classic era invariably are even larger than those premiums listed for the 1879 and later issues. Generally speaking, the earlier the stamp is listed in the catalogue, the larger will be the never-hinged premium.

For values of the most popular U.S. stamps in various conditions, including never hinged from No. 182 on, and in the grades of very good, fine, fine to very fine, very fine, very fine to extremely fine, extremely fine, extremely fine to superb, and superb, see the *Scott Stamp Values U.S. Specialized by Grade*, updated and issued each year as part of the U.S. specialized catalogue.

## PRINTED BY THE AMERICAN BANK NOTE COMPANY

SAME AS 1870-75 ISSUES
Soft Porous Paper
Varying from Thin to Thick

**1879** ***Perf. 12***

**182** A44a 1c dark ultra 200. 6.00
Never hinged 675.
No gum 80.
**183** A45a 2c vermilion 100. 5.00
Never hinged 370.
No gum 40.
*a.* Double impression — 5,500.

No. 183a is valued in the grade of fine.

**184** A46a 3c green 90. 1.00
Never hinged 325.
No gum 35.
*b.* Double impression 5,000.

No. 184b is valued in the grade of fine.

The imperf 3c can be found in the Scott U.S. Specialized Catalogue Die and Plate Proofs section.

**185** A55 5c blue 500. 16.00
Never hinged 1,600.
No gum 155.
**186** A47a 6c pink 900. 22.50
Never hinged 3,100.
No gum 275.
**187** A49 10c brn, without secret mark 3,000. 45.00
Never hinged 10,000.
No gum 1,000.
*a.* Double paper 7,500. —
**188** A49a 10c brn, with secret mark 1,800. 30.00
Never hinged 6,000.
No gum 650.
**189** A51a 15c red orange 180. 27.50
Never hinged 600.
No gum 70.
**190** A53 30c full black 850. 90.00
Never hinged 2,800.
No gum 300.
**191** A54 90c carmine 2,100. 400.00
Never hinged 7,250.
No gum 700.
*a.* Double paper —

The Continental Bank Note Co. was consolidated with the American Bank Note Co. on February 4, 1879. The American Bank Note Company used many plates of the Continental Bank Note Company to print the ordinary postage, Department and Newspaper stamps. Therefore, stamps bearing the Continental Company's imprint were not always its product.

The A. B. N. Co. also used the 30c and 90c plates of the N. B. N. Co. Some of No. 190 and all of No. 217 were from A. B. N. Co. plate 405.

Early printings of No. 188 were from Continental plates 302 and 303 which contained the normal secret mark of 1873. After these plates were re-entered by the A. B. N. Co. in 1880, pairs or multiple pieces contained combinations of normal, hairline or missing marks. The pairs or other multiples usually found contain at least one hairline mark which tended to disappear as the plate wore.

A. B. N. Co. plates 377 and 378 were made in 1881 from the National transfer roll of 1870. No. 187 from these plates has no secret mark.

The imperf. 90c can be found in the Scott U.S. Specialized Catalogue Die and Plate Proofs section.

## Special Printing of the 1879 Issue

Soft Porous Paper
Without Gum

**1880** ***Perf. 12***

**192** A44a 1c dark ultra 55,000.
**193** A45a 2c brown 15,000.
**194** A46a 3c blue green 115,000.
**195** A47a 6c dull rose 65,000.
**196** A48a 7c scarlet ver 6,500.
**197** A49a 10c deep brown 36,000.
**198** A50a 12c blkish pur 9,000.
**199** A51a 15c orange 28,500.
**200** A52 24c dark violet 8,500.
**201** A53 30c grnish blk 21,500.
**202** A54 90c dull carmine 28,500.
**203** A45a 2c scarlet ver 95,000.
**204** A55 5c deep blue 230,000.

Nos. 192 and 194 are valued in the grade of fine.

No. 197 was printed from Continental plate 302 (or 303) after plate was re-entered. Therefore, the stamp may show normal, hairline or missing secret mark.

The Post Office Department did not keep separate records of the 1875 and 1880 Special Printings of the 1873 and 1879 issues, but the total quantity sold of both is recorded. Census research indicates that numbers sold of the two sets were approximately equal.

Unlike the 1875 hard-paper Special Printings (Nos. 167-177), the 1880 soft-paper Special Printings were never cut apart with scissors.

While use of Nos. 192-204 for postage was legal, no used examples are recorded. Expertization by competent authorities would be required to establish use.

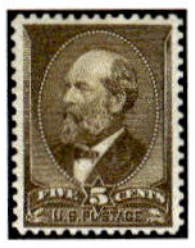

James A. Garfield — A56

**1882**

**205** A56 5c yellow brown 240. 15.00
Never hinged 775.
No gum 90.

**Special Printing**

**1882** ***Perf. 12***

**Soft porous paper, without gum**

**205C** A56 5c gray brown 47,500.

DESIGNS OF 1873 RE-ENGRAVED

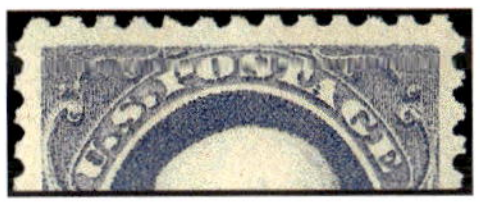

Franklin — A44b

1c — The vertical lines in the upper part of the stamp have been so deepened that the background often appears to be solid. Lines of shading have been added to the upper arabesques.

**1881-82**

**206** A44b 1c gray blue 70.00 1.00
Never hinged 225.00
No gum 25.00
*a.* Double impression —

No. 206a is a partial double impression, with "ONE 1 CENT," etc. at bottom doubled.

Earliest documented use: Oct. 11, 1881.

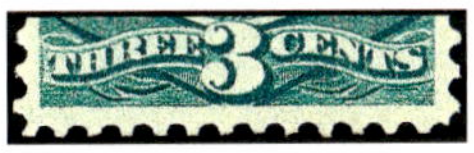

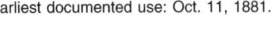

Washington — A46b

3c. The shading at the sides of the central oval appears only about one-half the previous width. A short horizontal dash has been cut about 1mm below the "TS" of "CENTS."

**207** A46b 3c blue green 80.00 .80
Never hinged 250.00
No gum 27.50
*c.* Double impression 10,000.

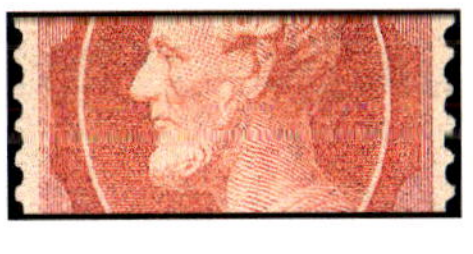

Lincoln — A47b

6c. On the original stamps four vertical lines can be counted from the edge of the panel to the outside of the stamp. On the re-engraved stamps there are but three lines in the same place.

**208** A47b 6c rose 825. 120.00
Never hinged 2,600.
No gum 250.
*a.* 6c deep brown red 600. 190.00
Never hinged 1,900.
No gum 170.

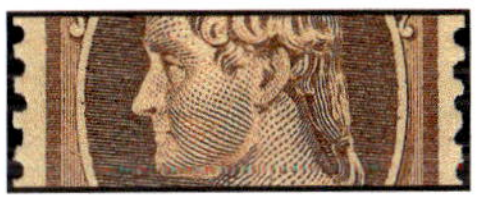

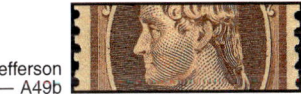

Jefferson — A49b

10c. On the original stamps there are five vertical lines between the left side of the oval and the edge of the shield. There are only four lines on the re-engraved stamps. In the lower part of the latter, also, the horizontal lines of the background have been strengthened.

**209** A49b 10c brown 175. 6.00
Never hinged 525.
No gum 65.
*b.* 10c black brown 3,000. 400.00
Never hinged 6,000.
No gum 950.
*c.* Double impression —

Specimen stamps (usually overprinted "Sample") without overprint exist in a brown shade that differs from No. 209. The unoverprinted brown specimen is cheaper than No. 209. Expertization is recommended.

10 UNITED STATES

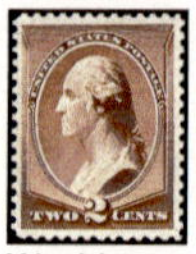

Washington A57

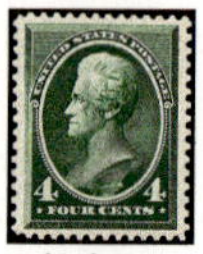

Jackson A58

Nos. 210-211 were issued to meet the reduced first class rate of 2 cents for each half ounce, and the double rate, which Congress approved Mar. 3, 1883, effective Oct. 1, 1883.

**1883, Oct. 1** ***Perf. 12***

| | | | |
|---|---|---|---|
| **210** | A57 2c red brown | 45. | .75 |
| | Never hinged | 135. | |
| | No gum | 17. | |
| **211** | A58 4c blue green | 225. | 25.00 |
| | Never hinged | 750. | |
| | No gum | 80. | |

Imperfs can be found in the Scott U.S. Specialized Catalogue Die and Plate Proofs section.

### Special Printing

**1883-85 Soft porous paper** ***Perf. 12***

| | | | |
|---|---|---|---|
| **211B** | A57 2c pale red brn, with gum ('85) | 450. | — |
| | Never hinged | 1,150. | |
| | No gum | 160. | |
| *c.* | Horizontal pair, imperf. between | *2,250.* | |
| | Never hinged | *3,250.* | |
| **211D** | A58 4c deep blue grn | *45,000.* | |

No. 211D is without gum.

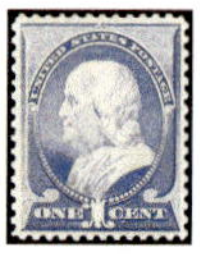

Franklin — A59

**1887** ***Perf. 12***

| | | | |
|---|---|---|---|
| **212** | A59 1c ultramarine | 90.00 | 2.50 |
| | Never hinged | 290.00 | |
| | No gum | 35.00 | |
| **213** | A57 2c green | 40.00 | .60 |
| | Never hinged | 120.00 | |
| | No gum | 15.00 | |
| *b.* | Printed on both sides | | — |

Imperf 1c, 2c can be found in the Scott U.S. Specialized Catalogue Die and Plate Proofs section.

| | | | |
|---|---|---|---|
| **214** | A46b 3c vermilion | 65.00 | 50.00 |
| | Never hinged | 190.00 | |
| | No gum | 25.00 | |
| | *Nos. 212-214 (3)* | 195.00 | 53.10 |

**1888** ***Perf. 12***

| | | | |
|---|---|---|---|
| **215** | A58 4c carmine | 180. | 30.00 |
| | Never hinged | 525. | |
| | No gum | 60. | |
| **216** | A56 5c indigo | 220. | 20.00 |
| | Never hinged | 675. | |
| | No gum | 75. | |
| **217** | A53 30c orange brn | 300. | 90.00 |
| | Never hinged | 1,075. | |
| | No gum | 90. | |
| **218** | A54 90c purple | 850. | 225.00 |
| | Never hinged | 2,750. | |
| | No gum | 250. | |
| | *Nos. 215-218 (4)* | 1,550. | 365.00 |

Imperfs can be found in the Scott U.S. Specialized Catalogue Die and Plate Proofs section.

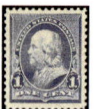

Franklin A60 Washington A61

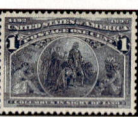

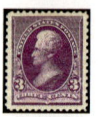

Jackson A62 Lincoln A63

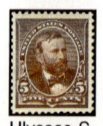

Ulysses S. Grant A64 Garfield A65

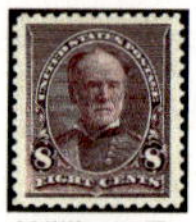

William T. Sherman A66

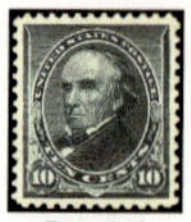

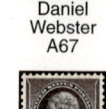

Daniel Webster A67

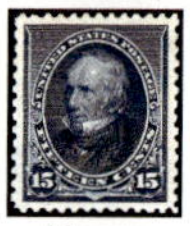

Henry Clay A68

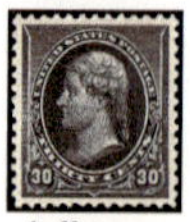

Jefferson A69

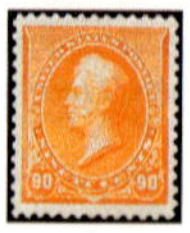

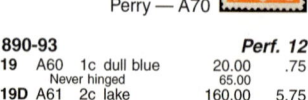

Perry — A70

**1890-93** ***Perf. 12***

| | | | |
|---|---|---|---|
| **219** | A60 1c dull blue | 20.00 | .75 |
| | Never hinged | 65.00 | |
| **219D** | A61 2c lake | 160.00 | 5.75 |
| | Never hinged | 500.00 | |

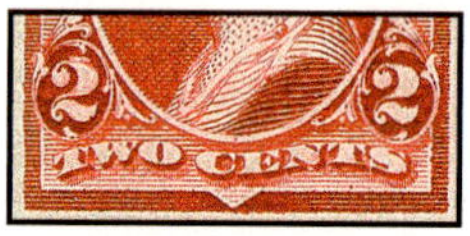

Cap only on left 2

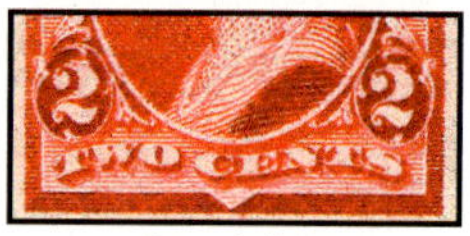

Cap on both 2s

| | | | |
|---|---|---|---|
| **220** | A61 2c carmine | 20.00 | .70 |
| | Never hinged | 60.00 | |
| *a.* | Cap on left "2" | 150.00 | 12.50 |
| | Never hinged | 450.00 | |
| *c.* | Cap on both "2's" | 650.00 | 35.00 |
| | Never hinged | 1,800. | |
| **221** | A62 3c purple | 55.00 | 9.00 |
| | Never hinged | 175.00 | |
| **222** | A63 4c dark brown | 80.00 | 4.75 |
| | Never hinged | 240.00 | |
| **223** | A64 5c chocolate | 60.00 | 4.75 |
| | Never hinged | 185.00 | |
| **224** | A65 6c brown red | 50.00 | 25.00 |
| | Never hinged | 160.00 | |
| **225** | A66 8c lilac ('93) | 45.00 | 17.00 |
| | Never hinged | 135.00 | |
| **226** | A67 10c green | 160.00 | 5.00 |
| | Never hinged | 475.00 | |
| **227** | A68 15c indigo | 180.00 | 25.00 |
| | Never hinged | 550.00 | |
| **228** | A69 30c black | 300.00 | 30.00 |
| | Never hinged | 900.00 | |
| **229** | A70 90c orange | 475.00 | 140.00 |
| | Never hinged | 1,600. | |
| | *Nos. 219-229 (12)* | 1,605. | 267.70 |

The No. 220 with "cap on right 2" variety is due to imperfect inking, not a plate defect.

Imperfs. can be found in the *Scott U.S. Specialized Catalogue* Die and Plate Proofs section.

### COLUMBIAN EXPOSITION ISSUE

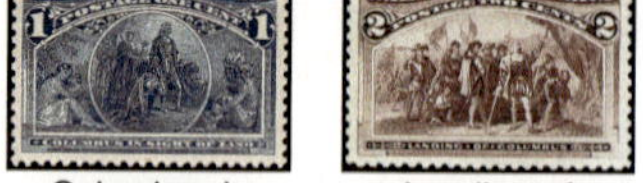

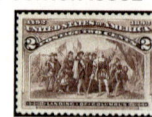

Columbus in Sight of Land — A71 Landing of Columbus — A72

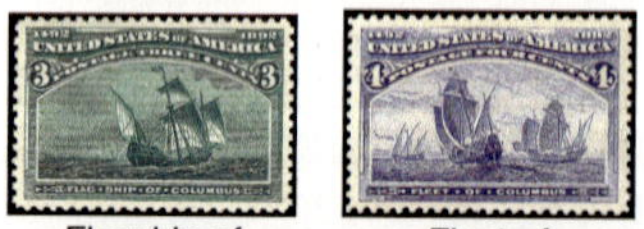

Flagship of Columbus — A73 Fleet of Columbus — A74

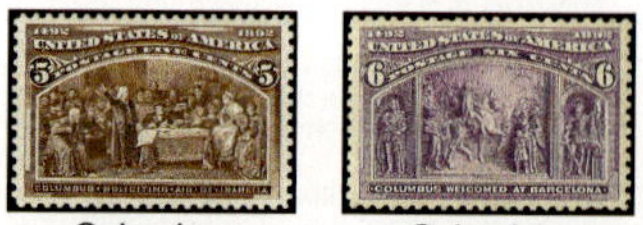

Columbus Soliciting Aid from Isabella — A75 Columbus Welcomed at Barcelona — A76

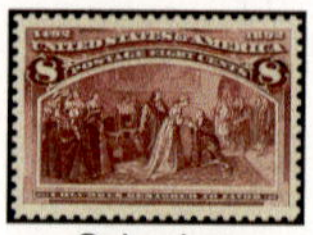

Columbus Restored to Favor — A77

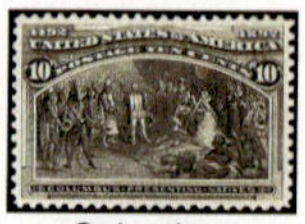

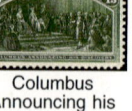

Columbus Presenting Natives — A78

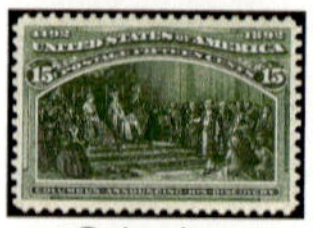

Columbus Announcing his Discovery — A79

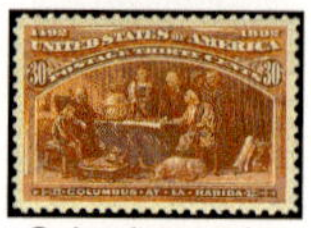

Columbus at La Rábida — A80

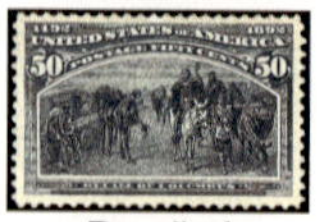

Recall of Columbus — A81

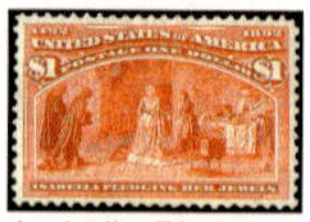

Isabella Pledging her Jewels — A82

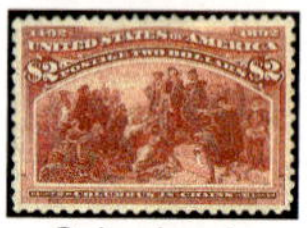

Columbus in Chains — A83

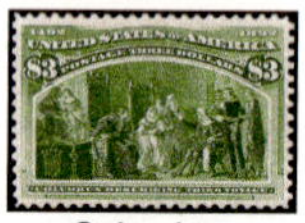

Columbus Describing his Third Voyage — A84

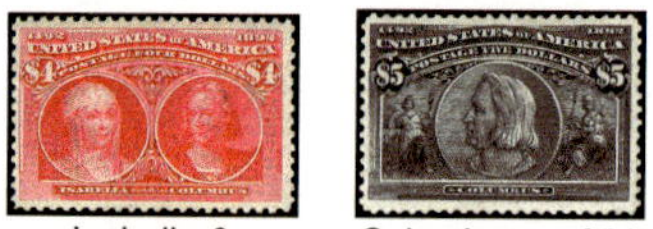

Isabella & Columbus — A85 Columbus — A86

**1893** ***Perf. 12***

| | | | |
|---|---|---|---|
| **230** | A71 1c deep blue | 14.00 | .40 |
| | Never hinged | 32.50 | |
| **231** | A72 2c brn vio | 12.50 | .30 |
| | Never hinged | 31.00 | |
| **232** | A73 3c green | 35.00 | 15.00 |
| | Never hinged | 97.50 | |
| **233** | A74 4c ultra | 55.00 | 8.00 |
| | Never hinged | 150.00 | |
| *a.* | 4c blue (error) | *18,000.* | *15,000.* |
| | Never hinged | *32,500.* | |

No. 233a exists in two shades. No. 233a used is valued with small faults, as almost all examples come thus.

| | | | |
|---|---|---|---|
| **234** | A75 5c chocolate | 55.00 | 8.50 |
| | Never hinged | 150.00 | |
| **235** | A76 6c purple | 55.00 | 22.50 |
| | Never hinged | 150.00 | |
| *a.* | 6c red violet | 65.00 | 22.50 |
| | Never hinged | 175.00 | |
| **236** | A77 8c brn pur | 50.00 | 10.00 |
| | Never hinged | 140.00 | |
| **237** | A78 10c blk brn | 95.00 | 8.00 |
| | Never hinged | 265.00 | |
| **238** | A79 15c dark green | 250.00 | 90.00 |
| | Never hinged | 700.00 | |
| **239** | A80 30c org brn | 225.00 | 90.00 |
| | Never hinged | 675.00 | |
| **240** | A81 50c slate blue | 450. | 200. |
| | Never hinged | 1,400. | |
| | No gum | 200. | |
| **241** | A82 $1 salmon | 1,000. | 525. |
| | Never hinged | 3,400. | |
| | No gum | 500. | |
| **242** | A83 $2 brown red | 1,100. | 550. |
| | Never hinged | 3,600. | |
| | No gum | 550. | |
| **243** | A84 $3 yel grn | 1,500. | 775. |
| | Never hinged | 4,750. | |
| | No gum | 750. | |
| *a.* | $3 olive green | 1,400. | 775. |
| | Never hinged | 4,350. | |
| | No gum | 700. | |
| **244** | A85 $4 crim lake | 2,100. | 975. |
| | Never hinged | 7,250. | |
| | No gum | 1,000. | |
| *a.* | $4 rose carmine | 2,000. | 975. |
| | Never hinged | 7,000. | |
| | No gum | 950. | |
| **245** | A86 $5 black | 2,500. | 1,250. |
| | Never hinged | 10,000. | |
| | No gum | 1,250. | |

World's Columbia Expo., Chicago, May 1-Oct. 30, 1893.

Nos. 230-245 are known imperf., but were not regularly issues.

See Scott U.S. Specialized Catalogue Die and Plate Proofs section for the 2c.

---

Never-Hinged Stamps

See note before No. 182 regarding premiums for never-hinged stamps.

---

### Bureau Issues

Starting in 1894, the Bureau of Engraving and Printing at Washington produced most U.S. postage stamps.

Until 1965 Bureau-printed stamps were engraved except Nos. 525-536 which were offset.

The combination of lithography and engraving (see #1253) was first used in 1964, and photogravure (see #1426) in 1971.

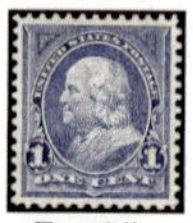

Franklin A87

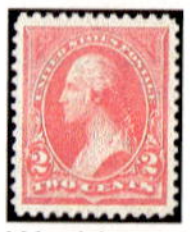

Washington A88

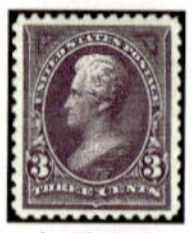

Jackson A89

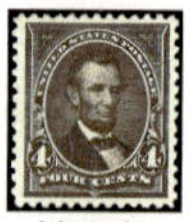

Lincoln A90

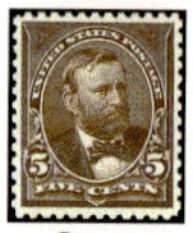

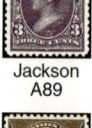

Grant A91

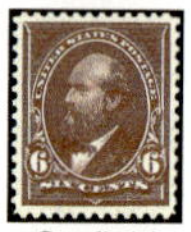

Garfield A92

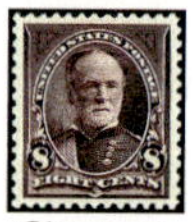

Sherman A93

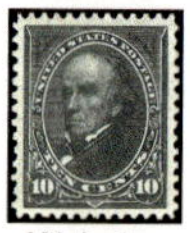

Webster A94

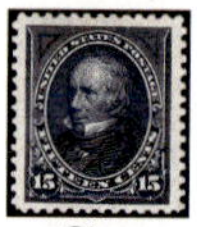

Clay A95

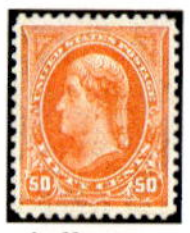

Jefferson A96

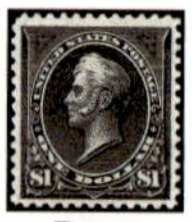

Perry A97

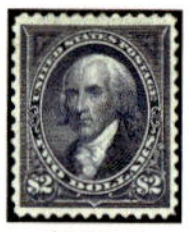

James Madison A98

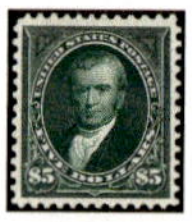

John Marshall — A99

**1894** **Unwmk.** ***Perf. 12***

| | | | |
|---|---|---|---|
| **246** | A87 1c ultramarine | 30.00 | 7.00 |
| | Never hinged | 90.00 | |
| **247** | A87 1c blue | 62.50 | 4.00 |
| | Never hinged | 180.00 | |

Triangle A (Type I)

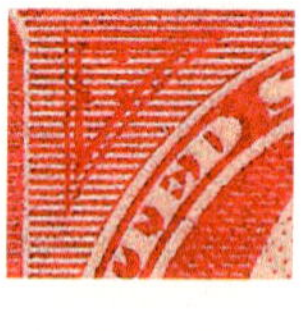

TWO CENTS

**Type I** (Triangle A). The horizontal lines of the ground work run across the triangle and are of the same thickness within it as without.

Triangle B (Type II)

**Type II** (Triangle B). The horizontal lines cross the triangle but are thinner within it than without. Other minor design differences exist,

but the change to Triangle B is a sufficient determinant.

Triangle C (Types III and IV)

**Type III** (Triangle C). The horizontal lines do not cross the double lines of the triangle. The lines within the triangle are thin, as in Type II. The rest of the design is the same as Type II, except that most of the designs had the dot in the "S" of "CENTS" removed. Stamps with this dot present are listed; some specialists refer to them as "Type IIIa" varieties.

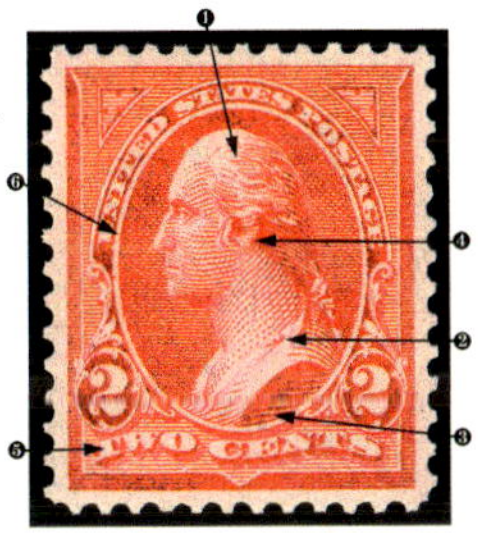

Type IV

**Type IV** (Triangle C). See No. 279B and its varieties. Type IV is from a new die with many major and minor design variations including, (1) re-cutting and lengthening of hairline, (2) shaded toga button, (3) strengthening of lines on sleeve, (4) additional dots on ear, (5) "T" of "TWO" straight at right, (6) background lines extend into white oval opposite "U" of "UNITED." Many other differences exist.

For further information concerning type IV, see also George Brett's article in the Sept. 1993 issue of the "The United States Specialist" and the 23-part article by Kenneth Diehl in the Dec. 1994 through Aug. 1997 issues of the "The United States Specialist."

| | | | | |
|---|---|---|---|---|
| **248** | A88 | 2c pink, type I | 32.50 | 10.00 |
| | | Never hinged | 97.50 | |
| *a.* | | Vert. pair, imperf horiz. | *5,500.* | |
| **249** | A88 | 2c car lake, type I | 190.00 | 7.00 |
| | | Never hinged | 550.00 | |
| *a.* | | Double impression | | — |
| **250** | A88 | 2c car, type I | 30.00 | 3.00 |
| | | Never hinged | 85.00 | |
| *a.* | | 2c rose, type I | 40.00 | 8.50 |
| | | Never hinged | 115.00 | |
| *b.* | | 2c scarlet, type I | 26.00 | 2.75 |
| | | Never hinged | 80.00 | |
| *d.* | | Horizontal pair, imperf. between | *2,000.* | |
| **251** | A88 | 2c car, type II | 425.00 | 17.50 |
| | | Never hinged | 1,250. | |
| *a.* | | 2c scarlet, type II | 400.00 | 15.00 |
| | | Never hinged | 1,175. | |
| **252** | A88 | 2c car, type III | 135.00 | 13.00 |
| | | Never hinged | 400.00 | |
| | | On cover | | 22.50 |
| *a.* | | 2c scarlet, type III | 120.00 | 15.00 |
| | | Never hinged | 360.00 | |
| *b.* | | Horiz. pair, imperf. vert. | *5,000.* | |
| *c.* | | Horiz. pair, imperf. between | *5,500.* | |

No. 252b is unique and exists only as a horizontal top plate-number strip of 3. A vertical right plate-number strip of 3 from the same plate exists containing three stamps imperforate at left and right.

| | | | | |
|---|---|---|---|---|
| **253** | A89 | 3c purple | 120.00 | 12.00 |
| | | Never hinged | 360.00 | |
| **254** | A90 | 4c dark brown | 200.00 | 11.00 |
| | | Never hinged | 600.00 | |
| **255** | A91 | 5c chocolate | 120.00 | 9.00 |
| | | Never hinged | 360.00 | |
| *c.* | | Vert. pair, imperf. horiz. | *4,000.* | |
| **256** | A92 | 6c dull brown | 160.00 | 27.50 |
| | | Never hinged | 475.00 | |
| *a.* | | Vert. pair, imperf. horiz. | *3,000.* | |
| **257** | A93 | 8c vio brn | 170.00 | 20.00 |
| | | Never hinged | 525.00 | |
| **258** | A94 | 10c dark green | 275.00 | 20.00 |
| | | Never hinged | 850.00 | |
| **259** | A95 | 15c dark blue | 275.00 | 65.00 |
| | | Never hinged | 850.00 | |
| **260** | A96 | 50c orange | 475. | 140. |
| | | Never hinged | 1,425. | |

Type I

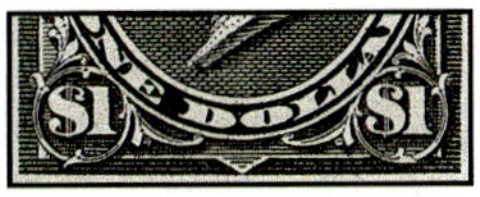

Type II

ONE DOLLAR

Type I. The circles enclosing "$1" are broken where they meet the curved line below "One Dollar."

Type II. The circles are complete.

| | | | | |
|---|---|---|---|---|
| **261** | A97 | $1 blk, type I | 1,000. | 350. |
| | | Never hinged | 3,200. | |
| | | No gum | 400. | |
| **261A** | A97 | $1 blk, type II | 2,200. | 800. |
| | | Never hinged | 6,750. | |
| | | No gum | 850. | |
| **262** | A98 | $2 bright blue | 2,750. | 1,200. |
| | | Never hinged | 9,000. | |
| | | No gum | 1,100. | |
| **263** | A99 | $5 dark green | 4,000. | 2,600. |
| | | Never hinged | 15,000. | |
| | | No gum | 2,100. | |

For imperfs. and the 2c pink, vert. pair, imperf. hoirz., see Scott U.S. Specialized Catalogue Die and plate Proofs.

### Same as 1894 Issue

### Wmk. 191 Horizontally or Vertically

**1895** *Perf. 12*

| | | | | |
|---|---|---|---|---|
| **264** | A87 | 1c blue | 6.00 | .60 |
| | | Never hinged | 17.50 | |
| **265** | A88 | 2c car, type I | 35.00 | 3.50 |
| | | Never hinged | 105.00 | |
| **266** | A88 | 2c car, type II | 40.00 | 15.00 |
| | | Never hinged | 120.00 | |
| **267** | A88 | 2c car, type III | 5.50 | .60 |
| | | Never hinged | 16.00 | |
| *a.* | | 2c pink, type III | 20.00 | 5.00 |
| | | Never hinged | 60.00 | |
| *b.* | | 2c vermilion, type III | *150.00* | *20.00* |
| *c.* | | 2c rose carmine, type III | — | — |
| | | Never hinged | *3,500.* | |

The three left vertical rows from plate 170 are type II, the balance being type III.

| | | | | |
|---|---|---|---|---|
| **268** | A89 | 3c purple | 37.50 | 2.25 |
| | | Never hinged | 115.00 | |
| **269** | A90 | 4c dark brown | 42.50 | 3.50 |
| | | Never hinged | 125.00 | |
| **270** | A91 | 5c chocolate | 35.00 | 3.50 |
| | | Never hinged | 105.00 | |
| **271** | A92 | 6c dull brown | 110.00 | 8.50 |
| | | Never hinged | 325.00 | |
| *a.* | | Wmkd. USIR | *15,000.* | *8,000.* |
| **272** | A93 | 8c violet brown | 70.00 | 2.75 |
| | | Never hinged | 210.00 | |
| *a.* | | Wmkd. USIR | *7,000.* | 950.00 |
| **273** | A94 | 10c dark green | 95.00 | 2.25 |
| | | Never hinged | 280.00 | |
| **274** | A95 | 15c dark blue | 200.00 | 17.50 |
| | | Never hinged | 600.00 | |
| **275** | A96 | 50c orange | 240. | 40.00 |
| | | Never hinged | 725. | |
| *a.* | | 50c red orange | 325. | 47.50 |
| | | Never hinged | 975. | |
| **276** | A97 | $1 black, type I | 600. | 100. |
| | | Never hinged | 1,800. | |
| | | No gum | 250. | |
| **276A** | A97 | $1 black, type II | 1,250. | 200. |
| | | Never hinged | 3,750. | |
| | | No gum | 500. | |
| **277** | A98 | $2 bright blue | 900. | 400. |
| | | Never hinged | 2,900. | |
| | | No gum | 400. | |
| *a.* | | $2 dark blue | 900. | 400. |
| | | Never hinged | 2,900. | |
| | | No gum | 400. | |
| **278** | A99 | $5 dark green | 2,000. | 600. |
| | | Never hinged | 6,250. | |
| | | No gum | 900. | |

For imperfs. and the 1c horiz. pair, imperf. vert., see Scott U.S. Specialized Catalogue Die and Plate Proofs.

For "I.R." overprints see Nos. R155, R156-R158.

No. 271a unused is valued in the grade of fine.

### Wmk. 191 Horizontally or Vertically

**1897-1903** *Perf. 12*

| | | | | |
|---|---|---|---|---|
| **279** | A87 | 1c dp grn, horiz. wmk ('98) | 9.00 | .50 |
| | | Never hinged | 25.00 | |
| *a.* | | Vert. wmk (error) | *80.00* | *7.50* |
| | | Never hinged | *240.00* | |
| **279B** | A88 | 2c red, type IV ('99) | 9.00 | .40 |
| | | Never hinged | 25.00 | |
| *c.* | | 2c rose carmine, type IV ('99) | 275.00 | 230.00 |
| | | Never hinged | 850.00 | |
| *d.* | | 2c orange red, type IV, horiz. wmk. ('00) | 11.50 | 2.00 |
| | | Never hinged | 32.50 | |
| *e.* | | 2c orange red, type IV, vert. wmk. | *80.00* | *12.50* |
| | | Never hinged | *240.00* | |
| *f.* | | 2c carmine, type IV | 10.00 | 2.00 |
| | | Never hinged | 27.50 | |
| *g.* | | 2c pink, type IV | 55.00 | 7.50 |
| | | Never hinged | 165.00 | |
| *h.* | | 2c vermilion, type IV ('99) | 12.50 | 3.00 |
| | | Never hinged | 35.00 | |
| *i.* | | 2c brown org, type IV ('99) | *400.00* | *100.00* |
| | | Never hinged | *950.00* | |
| *j.* | | Booklet pane of 6, red, type IV, horiz. wmk. ('00) | 500.00 | *3,000.* |
| | | Never hinged | 1,000. | |
| *k.* | | Booklet pane of 6, red, type IV, vertical watermark ('02) | 500.00 | — |
| | | Never hinged | 1,000. | |
| *l.* | | As No. 279B, all color missing (FO) | *500.00* | |

No. 279Bl must be collected se-tenant with a partially printed stamp.

| | | | | |
|---|---|---|---|---|
| **280** | A90 | 4c rose brn ('98) | 30.00 | 3.25 |
| | | Never hinged | 80.00 | |
| *a.* | | 4c lilac brown | 30.00 | 3.25 |
| | | Never hinged | 80.00 | |
| *b.* | | 4c orange brown | 30.00 | 3.00 |
| | | Never hinged | 80.00 | |
| **281** | A91 | 5c dk blue ('98) | 32.50 | 2.25 |
| | | Never hinged | 100.00 | |
| **282** | A92 | 6c lake ('98) | 45.00 | 6.50 |
| | | Never hinged | 140.00 | |
| *a.* | | 6c purple lake | 85.00 | 20.00 |
| | | Never hinged | 260.00 | |

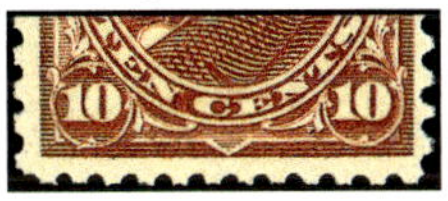

Type I. The tips of the foliate ornaments do not impinge on the white curved line below "ten cents."

| | | | | |
|---|---|---|---|---|
| **282C** | A94 | 10c brn, type I ('98) | 175.00 | 6.50 |
| | | Never hinged | 525.00 | |

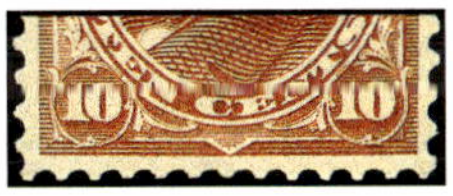

Type II. The tips of the ornaments break the curved line below the "e" of "ten" and the "t" of "cents."

| | | | | |
|---|---|---|---|---|
| **283** | A94 | 10c org brn, type II, horiz. wmk. | 150.00 | 6.00 |
| | | Never hinged | 450.00 | |
| *a.* | | Vert. wmk. ('00) | *250.00* | *15.00* |
| | | Never hinged | *775.00* | |
| **284** | A95 | 15c ol grn ('98) | 150.00 | 13.00 |
| | | Never hinged | 475.00 | |
| | | *Nos. 279-284 (8)* | 600.50 | 38.40 |

For "I.R." overprints, see Nos. R153-R155A.

### VALUES FOR VERY FINE STAMPS

**Please note: Stamps are valued in the grade of Very Fine unless otherwise indicated.**

### TRANS-MISSISSIPPI EXPOSITION ISSUE

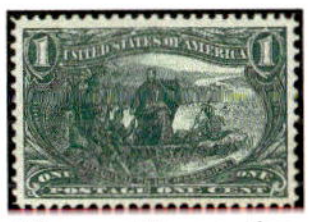

Marquette on the Mississippi A100

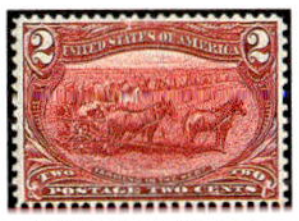

Farming in the West A101

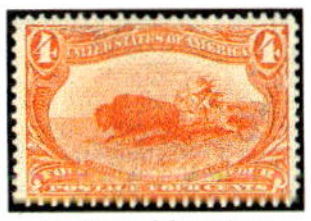

Indian Hunting Buffalo A102

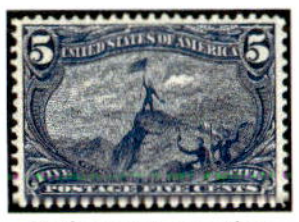

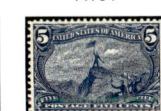

Frémont on the Rocky Mountains A103

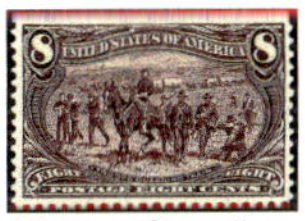

Troops Guarding Wagon Train A104

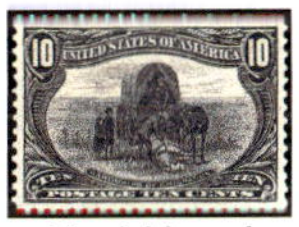

Hardships of Emigration A105

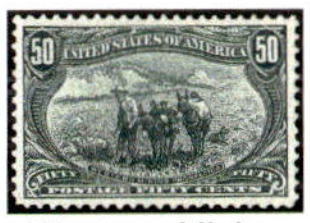

Western Mining Prospector A106

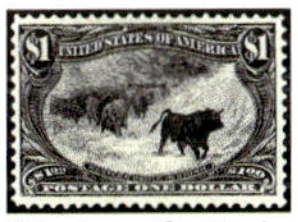

Western Cattle in Storm A107

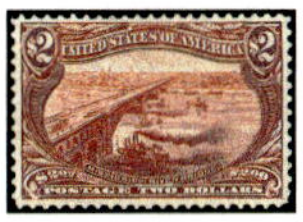

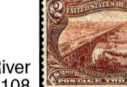

Mississippi River Bridge — A108

**1898, June 17** **Wmk. 191** *Perf. 12*

| | | | | |
|---|---|---|---|---|
| **285** | A100 | 1c dk yel grn | 27.50 | 7.00 |
| | | Never hinged | 75.00 | |
| **286** | A101 | 2c copper red | 25.00 | 2.75 |
| | | Never hinged | 72.50 | |
| **287** | A102 | 4c orange | 110.00 | 25.00 |
| | | Never hinged | 330.00 | |
| **288** | A103 | 5c dull blue | 100.00 | 25.00 |
| | | Never hinged | 300.00 | |
| **289** | A104 | 8c violet brown | 140.00 | 47.50 |
| | | Never hinged | 425.00 | |
| *a.* | | Vert. pair, imperf. horiz. | *27,500.* | |
| **290** | A105 | 10c gray vio | 140.00 | 35.00 |
| | | Never hinged | 425.00 | |
| **291** | A106 | 50c sage grn | 600.00 | 175.00 |
| | | Never hinged | 1,750. | |
| **292** | A107 | $1 black | 1,400. | 700. |
| | | Never hinged | 3,750. | |
| | | No gum | 850. | |
| **293** | A108 | $2 org brn | 2,000. | 1,000. |
| | | Never hinged | 6,000. | |
| | | No gum | 1,000. | |
| | | *Nos. 285-293 (9)* | 4,543. | 2,017. |

Trans-Mississippi Exposition, Omaha, Neb., June 1 to Nov. 1, 1898.

For "I.R" overprints see #R158A-R158B.

Never-Hinged Stamps

See note before No. 182 regarding premiums for never-hinged stamps.

### PAN-AMERICAN EXPOSITION ISSUE

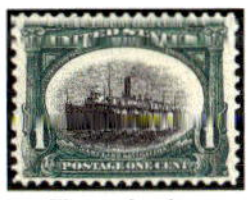

Fast Lake Navigation A109

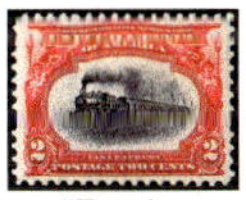

"Empire State" Express A110

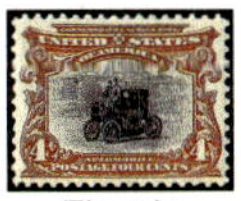

Electric Automobile A111

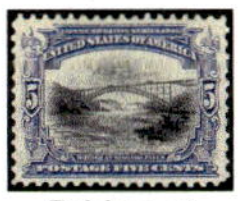

Bridge at Niagara Falls A112

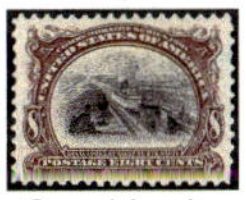

Canal Locks at Sault Ste. Marie A113

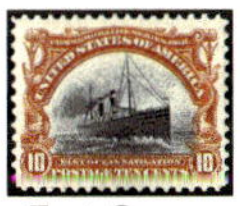

Fast Ocean Navigation A114

**1901, May 1** **Wmk. 191** *Perf. 12*

| | | | | |
|---|---|---|---|---|
| **294** | A109 | 1c grn & blk | 17.00 | 3.00 |
| | | Never hinged | 42.50 | |
| *a.* | | Center inverted | *11,500.* | *22,500.* |
| | | Never hinged | *22,500.* | |
| **295** | A110 | 2c car & blk | 16.00 | 1.00 |
| | | Never hinged | 40.00 | |
| *a.* | | Center inverted | *50,000.* | *50,000.* |
| **296** | A111 | 4c dp red brn & blk | 70.00 | 18.00 |
| | | Never hinged | 170.00 | |
| *a.* | | Center inverted | *80,000.* | — |
| **297** | A112 | 5c ultra & black | 75.00 | 17.00 |
| | | Never hinged | 180.00 | |
| **298** | A113 | 8c brn vio & blk | 90.00 | 50.00 |
| | | Never hinged | 230.00 | |
| **299** | A114 | 10c yel brn & blk | 115.00 | 30.00 |
| | | Never hinged | 325.00 | |
| | | *Nos. 294-299 (6)* | 383.00 | 119.00 |
| | | *Nos. 294-299, never hinged* | 957.50 | |

No. 296a was a special printing.

Almost all unused examples of Nos. 295a and 296a have partial or disturbed gum. Values are for examples with full original gum that is slightly disturbed.

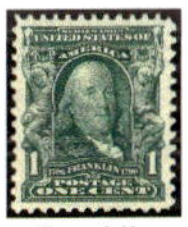

Franklin A115

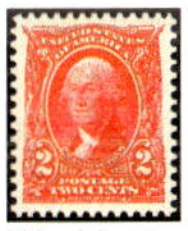

Washington A116

# 12 UNITED STATES

Jackson
A117

Lincoln
A119

Martha
Washington
A121

Benjamin
Harrison
A123

Jefferson
A125

Madison
A127

Grant
A118

Garfield
A120

Webster
A122

Clay
A124

David G.
Farragut
A126

Marshall
A128

### 1902-03    Wmk. 191    Perf. 12

| | | | | |
|---|---|---|---|---|
| 300 | A115 | 1c blue grn ('03) | 12.00 | .25 |
| | | Never hinged | 30.00 | |
| b. | | Booklet pane of 6 | 600.00 | 11,500. |
| | | Never hinged | 1,150. | |
| | | Wmk. horiz. | 2,000. | |
| 301 | A116 | 2c car ('03) | 15.00 | .50 |
| | | Never hinged | 37.50 | |
| c. | | Booklet pane of 6 | 500.00 | 6,000. |
| | | Never hinged | 950.00 | |
| 302 | A117 | 3c brt vio ('03) | 55.00 | 3.75 |
| | | Never hinged | 140.00 | |
| 303 | A118 | 4c brn ('03) | 55.00 | 2.25 |
| | | Never hinged | 140.00 | |
| 304 | A119 | 5c blue ('03) | 60.00 | 2.00 |
| | | Never hinged | 150.00 | |
| 305 | A120 | 6c claret ('03) | 60.00 | 5.50 |
| | | Never hinged | 150.00 | |
| 306 | A121 | 8c vio black | 45.00 | 3.25 |
| | | Never hinged | 110.00 | |
| 307 | A122 | 10c pale red brn ('03) | 60.00 | 3.00 |
| | | Never hinged | 150.00 | |
| 308 | A123 | 13c purple blk | 40.00 | 10.00 |
| | | Never hinged | 100.00 | |
| 309 | A124 | 15c ol grn ('03) | 185.00 | 12.50 |
| | | Never hinged | 475.00 | |
| 310 | A125 | 50c org ('03) | 425. | 35.00 |
| | | Never hinged | 1,225. | |
| 311 | A126 | $1 black ('03) | 600.00 | 90.00 |
| | | Never hinged | 1,800. | |
| | | No gum | 275.00 | |
| 312 | A127 | $2 dk bl ('03) | 825.00 | 200.00 |
| | | Never hinged | 2,500. | |
| | | No gum | 375.00 | |
| 313 | A128 | $5 dk grn ('03) | 2,250. | 750.00 |
| | | Never hinged | 10,000. | |
| | | No gum | 950.00 | |
| | | Nos. 300-313 (14) | 4,687. | 1,118. |

For listings of designs A127 and A128 with Perf. 10 see Nos. 479 and 480.

### 1906-08    Imperf.

| | | | | |
|---|---|---|---|---|
| 314 | A115 | 1c blue green | 14.00 | 17.50 |
| | | Never hinged | 30.00 | |
| 314A | A118 | 4c brn ('08) | 85,000. | 45,000. |
| | | Never hinged | 200,000. | |
| 315 | A119 | 5c blue ('08) | 350. | 1,300. |
| | | Never hinged | 600. | |

No. 314A was issued imperforate but all examples were privately perforated with large oblong perforations at the sides (Schermack type III).

Beware of examples of No. 303 with trimmed perforations and fake private perfs added.

Used examples of Nos. 314 and 315 must have contemporaneous cancels.

### COIL STAMPS

Warning! Imperforate stamps are known fraudulently perforated to resemble coil stamps and part-perforate varieties. Fully perforated stamps and booklet stamps also are known with perforations fraudulently trimmed off to resemble coil stamps.

### 1908    Perf. 12 Horizontally

| | | | | |
|---|---|---|---|---|
| 316 | A115 | 1c blue green | 150,000. | |
| 317 | A119 | 5c blue | 6,000. | — |
| | | Never hinged | 12,000. | |

### Perf. 12 Vertically

| | | | | |
|---|---|---|---|---|
| 318 | A115 | 1c blue green | 4,500. | |
| | | Never hinged | 9,500. | |

Coil stamps for use in vending and affixing machines are perforated on two sides only, either horizontally or vertically.

They were first issued in 1908, using perf. 12. This was changed to 8½ in 1910, and to 10 in 1914.

Imperforate sheets of certain denominations were sold to the vending machine companies which applied a variety of private perforations and separations.

Several values of the 1902 and later issues are found on an apparently coarse ribbed paper caused by worn blankets on the printing press and are not true paper varieties.

No. 316 is valued in the grade of fine to very fine. There are no very fine examples recorded.

All examples of Nos. 316-318 must be accompanied by certificates of authenticity issued by recognized expertizing committees.

No. 318 mint never hinged is valued in the grade of fine.

Washington — A129

The two large arrows in the illustrations highlight the two major differences of the type II stamps: closing of the thin left border line next to the laurel leaf, and strengthening of the inner frame line at the lower left corner. The small arrows point out three minor differences that are not always easily discernible: strengthening of shading lines under the ribbon just above the "T" of "TWO," a shorter shading line to the left of the "P" in "POSTAGE," and shortening of a shading line in the left side ribbon.

### Type I

### 1903, Nov. 12    Wmk. 191    Perf. 12

| | | | | |
|---|---|---|---|---|
| 319 | A129 | 2c car, type I | 6.00 | .25 |
| | | Never hinged | 15.00 | |
| a. | | 2c lake | — | |
| b. | | 2c carmine rose | 15.00 | .40 |
| | | Never hinged | 45.00 | |
| c. | | 2c scarlet | 10.00 | .30 |
| | | Never hinged | 25.00 | |
| d. | | Vert. pair, imperf. horiz., No. 319 | 7,500. | |
| | | Never hinged | 17,500. | |
| e. | | Vert. pair, imperf. between | — | |
| r. | | Vert. pair, rouletted between | 4,000. | |

During the use of No. 319, the postmaster of San Francisco discovered in his stock panes that had the perforations missing between the top two rows of stamps. To facilitate their separation, the imperf rows were roulletted, and the stamps were sold over the counter. These vertical pairs with regular perfs all around and roulletted between are No. 319r. No 319e is from a different source. One example has been authenticated, and collectors are warned that other pairs exist with faint blind perfs or indentations from the perforating machine.

| | | | | |
|---|---|---|---|---|
| g. | | Booklet pane of 6, carmine | 125.00 | 450.00 |
| | | Never hinged | 240.00 | |
| n. | | Booklet pane of 6, carmine rose | 275.00 | 700.00 |
| | | Never hinged | 500.00 | |
| p. | | Booklet pane of 6, scarlet | 185.00 | 625.00 |
| | | Never hinged | 350.00 | |

### Type II

### 1908    Wmk. 191    Perf. 12

| | | | | |
|---|---|---|---|---|
| 319F | A129 | 2c lake | 10.00 | .30 |
| | | Never hinged | 25.00 | |
| i. | | 2c carmine | 65.00 | 50.00 |
| | | Never hinged | 150.00 | |
| j. | | 2c carmine rose | 100.00 | 1.75 |
| | | Never hinged | 225.00 | |
| k. | | 2c scarlet | 70.00 | 2.00 |
| | | Never hinged | 160.00 | |
| h. | | Booklet pane of 6, carmine | 900.00 | |
| l. | | Booklet pane of 6, scarlet | — | |
| q. | | Booklet pane of 6, lake | 300.00 | 800.00 |
| | | Never hinged | 575.00 | |

### Type I

### 1906, Oct. 2    Wmk. 191    Imperf.

| | | | | |
|---|---|---|---|---|
| 320 | A129 | 2c carmine | 15.00 | 19.00 |
| | | Never hinged | 32.50 | |
| b. | | 2c scarlet | 17.50 | 15.00 |
| c. | | 2c carmine rose | 75.00 | 42.50 |
| | | Never hinged | 150.00 | |

### Type II

### 1908    Wmk. 191    Imperf.

| | | | | |
|---|---|---|---|---|
| 320A | A129 | 2c lake | 45.00 | 50.00 |
| | | Never hinged | 100.00 | |
| d. | | 2c carmine | 135.00 | |
| | | Never hinged | 200.00 | |

No. 320Ad was issued imperforate, but all examples were privately perforated with large oblong perforations at the sides (Schermack type III).

### COIL STAMPS

### 1908    Perf. 12 Horizontally

| | | | | |
|---|---|---|---|---|
| 321 | A129 | 2c car, type I, pair | 1,000,000. | 310,000. |

Four authenticated unused pairs of No. 321 are known and available to collectors. A fifth, unauthenticated pair is in the New York Public Library Miller collection, which is on long-term loan to the Smithsonian National Postal Museum. The value for an unused pair is for a fine-very fine example. Two fine pairs are recorded and one very fine pair.

There are no authenticated unused or off-cover used single stamps recorded. The used value is for a single on cover, of which two authenticated examples are known, both used from Indianapolis in 1908.

The Dec. 20, 1908, legal-size cover has not been seen in decades; the Oct. 2, 1908, cover sold in 2018 and is the cover valued.

Numerous counterfeits exist.

| | | | | |
|---|---|---|---|---|
| 322 | A129 | 2c carmine, type II | 7,000. | — |
| | | Never hinged | 15,000. | |

This Government Coil Stamp should not be confused with those of the International Vending Machine Co., which are perforated 12½.

All examples of Nos. 321-322 must be accompanied by certificates of authenticity issued by recognized expertizing committees.

### VALUES FOR VERY FINE STAMPS
**Please note:** Stamps are valued in the grade of Very Fine unless otherwise indicated.

### LOUISIANA PURCHASE EXPOSITION ISSUE

Robert R. Livingston
A130

Thomas Jefferson
A131

James Monroe
A132

William McKinley
A133

Map of Louisiana Purchase — A134

### 1904, Apr. 30    Wmk. 191    Perf. 12

| | | | | |
|---|---|---|---|---|
| 323 | A130 | 1c green | 22.50 | 4.75 |
| | | Never hinged | 60.00 | |
| 324 | A131 | 2c carmine | 22.50 | 2.00 |
| | | Never hinged | 60.00 | |
| a. | | Vertical pair, imperf. horiz. | 25,000. | |
| 325 | A132 | 3c violet | 65.00 | 27.50 |
| | | Never hinged | 170.00 | |
| 326 | A133 | 5c dark blue | 70.00 | 22.50 |
| | | Never hinged | 180.00 | |
| 327 | A134 | 10c red brown | 125.00 | 27.50 |
| | | Never hinged | 300.00 | |
| | | Nos. 323-327 (5) | 305.00 | 84.25 |
| | | Nos. 323-327, never hinged | 770.00 | |

### JAMESTOWN EXPOSITION ISSUE

Captain John Smith
A135

Founding of Jamestown
A136

Pocahontas — A137

### 1907    Wmk. 191    Perf. 12

| | | | | |
|---|---|---|---|---|
| 328 | A135 | 1c green | 30.00 | 4.50 |
| | | Never hinged | 75.00 | |
| 329 | A136 | 2c carmine | 32.50 | 4.00 |
| | | Never hinged | 85.00 | |
| a. | | 2c carmine lake | — | |
| 330 | A137 | 5c blue | 150.00 | 30.00 |
| | | Never hinged | 375.00 | |
| | | Nos. 328-330 (3) | 212.50 | 38.50 |
| | | Nos. 328-330, never hinged | 535.00 | |

Franklin
A138

Washington
A139

There are several types of some of the 2c and 3c stamps of this and succeeding issues. These types are described under the dates at which they first appeared.

Illustrations of Types I-VII of the 2c (A140) and Types I-IV of the 3c (A140) are reproduced by permission of H. L. Lindquist.

### 1908-09    Wmk. 191    Perf. 12

| | | | | |
|---|---|---|---|---|
| 331 | A138 | 1c green | 6.50 | .40 |
| | | Never hinged | 16.50 | |
| a. | | Booklet pane of 6 | 150.00 | 700.00 |
| | | Never hinged | 300.00 | |

No. 331 exists in horizontal pair, imperforate between, a variety resulting from booklet experiments. Not regularly issued. Value in the grade of fine, $3,000.

| | | | | |
|---|---|---|---|---|
| 332 | A139 | 2c carmine | 6.00 | .35 |
| | | Never hinged | 14.50 | |
| a. | | Booklet pane of 6 | 135.00 | 500.00 |
| | | Never hinged | 240.00 | |
| b. | | 2c lake | | 4,250. |

No. 332a used is valued with a contemporaneous cancel. A certificate of authenticity is advised.

No. 332b is valued in the grade of fine.

Washington — A140

TYPE I

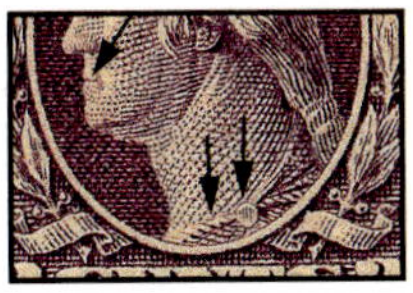

THREE CENTS

Type I. The top line of the toga rope is weak and the rope shading lines are thin. The 5th line from the left is missing. The line between the lips is thin. (For descriptions of 3c types II, III and IV, see notes and illustrations preceding Nos. 484, 529-530.)

Used on both flat plate and rotary press printings.

| | | | | |
|---|---|---|---|---|
| 333 | A140 | 3c dp vio, type I | 30.00 | 3.00 |
| | | Never hinged | 75.00 | |
| 334 | A140 | 4c org brn | 35.00 | 1.50 |
| | | Never hinged | 87.50 | |
| 335 | A140 | 5c blue | 45.00 | 2.25 |
| | | Never hinged | 110.00 | |
| 336 | A140 | 6c red orange | 62.50 | 6.00 |
| | | Never hinged | 145.00 | |
| 337 | A140 | 8c olive green | 45.00 | 2.75 |
| | | Never hinged | 105.00 | |
| 338 | A140 | 10c yellow ('09) | 70.00 | 1.80 |
| | | Never hinged | 165.00 | |
| 339 | A140 | 13c bl grn ('09) | 40.00 | 20.00 |
| | | Never hinged | 95.00 | |
| 340 | A140 | 15c pale ultra ('09) | 67.50 | 6.00 |
| | | Never hinged | 160.00 | |
| 341 | A140 | 50c violet ('09) | 275.00 | 20.00 |
| | | Never hinged | 650.00 | |
| 342 | A140 | $1 vio brn ('09) | 450.00 | 95.00 |
| | | Never hinged | 1,050. | |
| | | *Nos. 331-342 (12)* | 1,133. | 159.05 |

For listings of other perforated sheet stamps of A138, A139 and A140 see:

Nos. 357-366 Bluish paper

Nos. 374-382, 405-407 Single line wmk. Perf. 12

Nos. 423A-423C Single line wmk. Perf 12x10

Nos. 423D-423E Single line wmk. Perf 10x12

Nos. 424-430 Single line wmk. Perf. 10

Nos. 461 Single line wmk. Perf. 11

Nos. 462-469 unwmk. Perf. 10

Nos. 498-507 unwmk. Perf. 11

Nos. 519 Double line wmk. Perf. 11

Nos. 525-530 and 536 Offset printing

Nos. 538-546 Rotary press printing

***Imperf***

| | | | | |
|---|---|---|---|---|
| 343 | A138 | 1c green | 5.50 | 5.00 |
| | | Never hinged | 9.00 | |
| 344 | A139 | 2c carmine | 5.50 | 2.75 |
| | | Never hinged | 9.00 | |
| 345 | A140 | 3c dp violet, type I | 14.00 | *20.00* |
| | | Never hinged | 22.50 | |
| 346 | A140 | 4c org brn ('09) | 17.50 | *20.00* |
| | | Never hinged | 27.50 | |
| 347 | A140 | 5c blue ('09) | 30.00 | *32.50* |
| | | Never hinged | 50.00 | |
| | | *Nos. 343-347 (5)* | 72.50 | *80.25* |
| | | *Nos. 343-347, never hinged* | 118.00 | |

For listings of other imperforate stamps of designs A138, A139 and A140 see Nos. 383, 384, 408, 409 and 459 Single line wmk.

Nos. 481-485 unwmk.

Nos. 531-535 Offset printing

**The values for used coil stamps are for examples with contemporaneous cancels that can be authenticated by expertizing committees. Used coils with cancels most commonly from the 1950s exist, and these and stamps with other non-contemporaneous cancels sell for less than the values shown.**

### COIL STAMPS

**1908-10** *Perf. 12 Horizontally*

| | | | | |
|---|---|---|---|---|
| 348 | A138 | 1c green | [illegible] | [illegible] |
| | | Never hinged | 80.00 | |
| 349 | A139 | 2c carmine ('09) | 110.00 | *160.00* |
| | | Never hinged | 235.00 | |
| 350 | A140 | 4c org brn ('10) | 175.00 | *250.00* |
| | | Never hinged | 350.00 | |
| 351 | A140 | 5c blue ('09) | 175.00 | *300.00* |
| | | Never hinged | 350.00 | |
| | | *Nos. 348-351 (4)* | 505.00 | 770.00 |

**1909** *Perf. 12 Vertically*

| | | | | |
|---|---|---|---|---|
| 352 | A138 | 1c green | 110.00 | *225.00* |
| | | Never hinged | 235.00 | |
| 353 | A139 | 2c carmine | 110.00 | *220.00* |
| | | Never hinged | 220.00 | |
| 354 | A140 | 4c org brn | 250.00 | *275.00* |
| | | Never hinged | 500.00 | |
| 355 | A140 | 5c blue | 250.00 | *300.00* |
| | | Never hinged | 500.00 | |
| 356 | A140 | 10c yellow | 3,750. | *6,250.* |
| | | Never hinged | 8,500. | |

For listings of other coil stamps of designs A138, A139 and A140, see #385-396, 410-413, 441-458 (single line wmk.), #486-496 (unwatermarked).

**Beware of stamps offered as No. 356 which may be examples of No. 338 with perfs. trimmed at top and/or bottom. Beware also of plentiful fakes in the marketplace of Nos. 348-355, made by fraudulently perforating imperforate stamps or by fraudulently trimming perforations off fully perforated stamps. Authentication of all these coils is advised.**

### BLUISH PAPER

This was made with 35 percent rag stock instead of all wood pulp. The "bluish" color (actually grayish blue) goes through the paper showing clearly on the back as well as on the face.

**1909** *Perf. 12*

| | | | | |
|---|---|---|---|---|
| 357 | A138 | 1c green | 90.00 | *160.00* |
| | | Never hinged | 190.00 | |
| 358 | A139 | 2c carmine | 80.00 | *150.00* |
| | | Never hinged | 170.00 | |
| 359 | A140 | 3c dp vio, type I | 2,000. | *12,500.* |
| | | Never hinged | 4,000. | |
| 360 | A140 | 4c org brn | *27,500.* | |
| | | Never hinged | *80,000.* | |
| 361 | A140 | 5c blue | 6,500. | *20,000.* |
| | | Never hinged | *15,000.* | |

Only two examples of No. 361 used off cover (three additional on cover) are recorded. Value used is for the better of the two examples, which is well-centered but has two reattached perforations.

| | | | | |
|---|---|---|---|---|
| 362 | A140 | 6c red org | 1,300. | *12,500.* |
| | | Never hinged | 3,000. | |
| 363 | A140 | 8c olive green | *31,500.* | |
| | | Never hinged | *90,000.* | |
| 364 | A140 | 10c yellow | 1,600. | *10,000.* |
| | | Never hinged | 4,000. | |
| 365 | A140 | 13c blue green | 2,600. | *3,750.* |
| | | Never hinged | 6,000. | |
| 366 | A140 | 15c pale ultra | 1,300. | *16,000.* |
| | | Never hinged | 3,000. | |

Nos. 360 and 363 were not regularly issued.

No. 363 never hinged is valued in the grade of fine-very fine.

Used examples of Nos. 357-366 must bear contemporaneous cancels, and Nos. 359-366 used must be accompanied by certificates of authenticity issued by recognized expertizing committees.

### LINCOLN CENTENARY OF BIRTH ISSUE

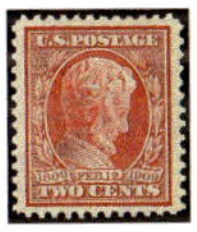

Lincoln — A141

**1909, Feb. 12** **Wmk. 191** *Perf. 12*

| | | | | |
|---|---|---|---|---|
| 367 | A141 | 2c carmine | 4.50 | 1.75 |
| | | Never hinged | 9.50 | |

***Imperf***

| | | | | |
|---|---|---|---|---|
| 368 | A141 | 2c carmine | 12.50 | 19.00 |
| | | Never hinged | 24.00 | |

**BLUISH PAPER**

***Perf. 12***

| | | | | |
|---|---|---|---|---|
| 369 | A141 | 2c carmine | 150.00 | *225.00* |
| | | Never hinged | 300.00 | |

Used examples of No. 369 must bear contemporaneous cancels. Expertizing is recommended.

### ALASKA-YUKON-PACIFIC EXPOSITION ISSUE

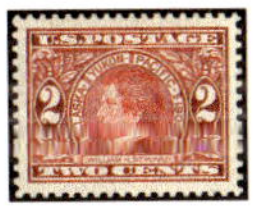

William H. Seward — A142

**1909, June 1** **Wmk. 191** *Perf. 12*

| | | | | |
|---|---|---|---|---|
| 370 | A142 | 2c carmine | 6.75 | 2.00 |
| | | Never hinged | 15.00 | |
| *a.* | | Imperf. (error), P#5209 block of 6 | | *3,500.* |

No. 370a comes from error panes found in perforated stock. Plate 5209 was used only to print the perforated Alaska-Yukon-Pacific Exposition issue. No 370a can only be collected as a plate-number stamp or multiple. Without an attached plate number 5209, the stamps from this pane cannot be differentiated from No. 371.

***Imperf***

| | | | | |
|---|---|---|---|---|
| 371 | A142 | 2c carmine | 14.00 | 21.00 |
| | | Never hinged | 30.00 | |

Seattle, Wash., June 1 to Oct. 16.

### HUDSON-FULTON CELEBRATION ISSUE

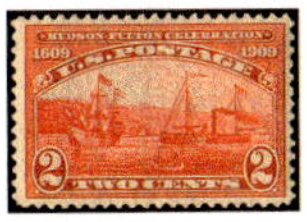

"Half Moon" and Steamship — A143

**1909, Sept. 25** **Wmk. 191** *Perf. 12*

| | | | | |
|---|---|---|---|---|
| 372 | A143 | 2c carmine | 10.00 | 4.75 |
| | | Never hinged | 21.00 | |

***Imperf***

| | | | | |
|---|---|---|---|---|
| 373 | A143 | 2c carmine | 20.00 | 27.50 |
| | | Never hinged | 40.00 | |

Tercentenary of the discovery of the Hudson River and Centenary of Robert Fulton's steamship.

### DESIGNS OF 1908-09 ISSUES

**1910-11** **Wmk. 190** *Perf. 12*

| | | | | |
|---|---|---|---|---|
| 374 | A138 | 1c green | 7.00 | .25 |
| | | Never hinged | 14.00 | |
| *a.* | | Booklet pane of 6 | 225.00 | *400.00* |
| | | Never hinged | 375.00 | |
| *b.* | | Double impression | | *300.00* |
| 375 | A139 | 2c carmine | 7.00 | .25 |
| | | Never hinged | 14.00 | |
| *a.* | | Booklet pane of 6 | 125.00 | *300.00* |
| | | Never hinged | 200.00 | |
| *b.* | | 2c lake | *825.00* | — |
| | | Never hinged | *1,000.* | |
| *c.* | | As "b," booklet pane of 6 | *10,000.* | |
| *d.* | | Double impression | *750.00* | — |
| | | Never hinged | *1,500.* | |
| 376 | A140 | 3c dp vio, type I ('11) | 20.00 | 2.00 |
| | | Never hinged | 40.00 | |
| 377 | A140 | 4c brown ('11) | 30.00 | 1.00 |
| | | Never hinged | 65.00 | |
| 378 | A140 | 5c blue ('11) | 30.00 | .75 |
| | | Never hinged | 65.00 | |
| 379 | A140 | 6c red org ('11) | 37.50 | 1.25 |
| | | Never hinged | 85.00 | |
| 380 | A140 | 8c ol grn ('11) | 90.00 | 15.00 |
| | | Never hinged | 200.00 | |
| 381 | A140 | 10c yellow ('11) | 85.00 | 6.00 |
| | | Never hinged | 200.00 | |
| 382 | A140 | 15c pale ultra ('11) | 225.00 | 20.00 |
| | | Never hinged | 500.00 | |
| | | *Nos. 374-382 (9)* | 531.50 | 46.50 |

**1910, Dec.** *Imperf.*

| | | | | |
|---|---|---|---|---|
| 383 | A138 | 1c green | 3.50 | *2.75* |
| | | Never hinged | 6.00 | |
| 384 | A139 | 2c carmine | 5.00 | 2.75 |
| | | Never hinged | 9.00 | |

**The values for used coil stamps are for examples with contemporaneous cancels that can be authenticated by expertizing committees. Used coils with cancels most commonly from the 1950s exist, and these and stamps with other non-contemporaneous cancels sell for less than the values shown.**

### COIL STAMPS

**1910, Nov. 1** *Perf. 12 Horizontally*

| | | | | |
|---|---|---|---|---|
| 385 | A138 | 1c green | 50.00 | *50.00* |
| | | Never hinged | 100.00 | |
| 386 | A139 | 2c carmine | 140.00 | 90.00 |
| | | Never hinged | 280.00 | |

**1910-11** *Perf. 12 Vertically*

| | | | | |
|---|---|---|---|---|
| 387 | A138 | 1c green | 225.00 | 140.00 |
| | | Never hinged | 450.00 | |
| 388 | A139 | 2c carmine | 1,700. | *2,250.* |
| | | Never hinged | 4,250. | |

Stamps offered as No. 388 frequently are privately perforated examples of No. 384, or examples of No. 375 with top and/or bottom perfs trimmed.

| | | | | |
|---|---|---|---|---|
| 389 | A140 | 3c dp vio, type I ('11) | *110,000.* | *9,500.* |
| | | Never hinged | *325,000.* | |

No. 389 is valued in the grade of fine.

Stamps offered as No. 389 sometimes are examples of No. 376 with top and/or bottom perfs trimmed.

Beware also of plentiful fakes in the marketplace of Nos. 385-387.

Expertization by competent authorities is recommended.


United States

At HGPI, we cater to both Novice and Advanced Collectors. With our great accurately described stamps and fair prices, we will personally help you build your United States Collection.

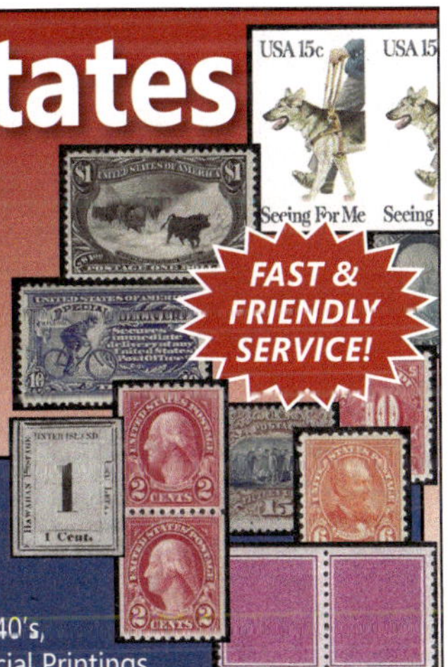

FAST & FRIENDLY SERVICE!


OUR MANY U.S. PRICE LISTS INCLUDE:

Classics, Bank Notes, Early Comms, Wash-Franks, 1920-1940's, Kans-Nebr. & Better PB's, Farley Special Printings, Modern Imperfs, Graf Zeppelins, Shanghais, Savings Stamps, Officials, Revenues, Ducks, Test Stamps, Cut Squares, Commem, Postal Cards, Errors, Confederates, U.S. Possessions, Ryukyus, Trust Territories, Die Proofs, Autographed Plate Blocks & FDC's, Photo Essays, Cachet Artwork & Plates, 20th Century Fancy Cancels

Visit our ever-growing Website with U.S. ranging from Postmaster Provisionals to Modern Imperfs.

Time Payments are Always Available

Ask about Our Monthly Purchase Plan!

See our U.S. Buy List on our Website or Call for your Free Copy! Current & Forever Postage Always Wanted!

Henry Gitner Philatelists, Inc.

P.O. Box 3077-S, Middletown, NY 10940

Tel: 845-343-5151 Fax: 845-343-0068 Toll Free: 1-800-947-8267

E-mail: hgitner@hgitner.com http://www.hgitner.com

PHILATELY - THE QUIET EXCITEMENT!

14 UNITED STATES

**1910** ***Perf. 8½ Horizontally***

390 A138 1c green 4.50 *14.00*
Never hinged 9.00
391 A139 2c carmine 45.00 *50.00*
Never hinged 90.00

**1910-13** ***Perf. 8½ Vertically***

392 A138 1c green 35.00 *50.00*
Never hinged 70.00
393 A139 2c carmine 52.50 *55.00*
Never hinged 105.00
394 A140 3c dp vio, type I ('11) 67.50 65.00
Never hinged 135.00
395 A140 4c brown ('12) 67.50 *65.00*
Never hinged 135.00
396 A140 5c blue ('13) 67.50 *65.00*
Never hinged 135.00
*Nos. 392-396 (5)* 290.00 300.00

Beware also of plentiful fakes in the marketplace of Nos. 390-393.

**PANAMA-PACIFIC EXPOSITION ISSUE**

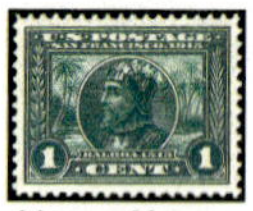


Vasco Nunez de Balboa A144

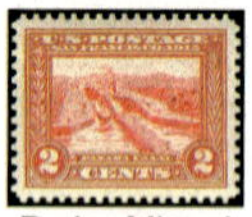


Pedro Miguel Locks, Panama Canal A145

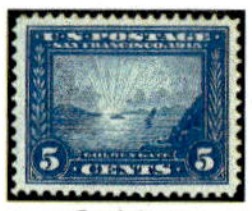


Golden Gate — A146

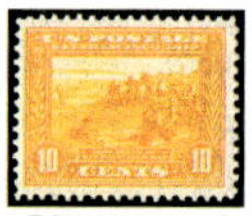

Discovery of San Francisco Bay — A147

**1913** **Wmk. 190** ***Perf. 12***

397 A144 1c green 15.00 2.00
Never hinged 35.00
398 A145 2c carmine 16.00 1.00
Never hinged 35.00
*a.* 2c carmine lake *1,600.*
Never hinged *2,500.*
*b.* 2c lake *5,250.* 3,000.
Never hinged *8,500.*
399 A146 5c blue 70.00 10.00
Never hinged 160.00
400 A147 10c orange yel 115.00 20.00
Never hinged 260.00
400A A147 10c orange 175.00 22.50
Never hinged 390.00
*Nos. 397-400A (5)* 391.00 55.50
Nos. 397-400A, never hinged 850.00

**1914-15** ***Perf. 10***

401 A144 1c green 25.00 7.00
Never hinged 60.00
402 A145 2c car ('15) 70.00 3.00
Never hinged 170.00
403 A146 5c blue ('15) 160.00 17.50
Never hinged 400.00
404 A147 10c org ('15) 675.00 70.00
Never hinged 1,700.
*Nos. 401-404 (4)* 930.00 97.50
Nos. 401-404, never hinged 2,280.

**1912-14** **Wmk. 190** ***Perf. 12***

405 A140 1c green 6.50 .25
Never hinged 15.00
*a.* Vert. pair, imperf. horiz. *2,000.* —
*b.* Booklet pane of 6 65.00 *90.00*
Never hinged 110.00
*c.* Double impression *5,500.*

TYPE I

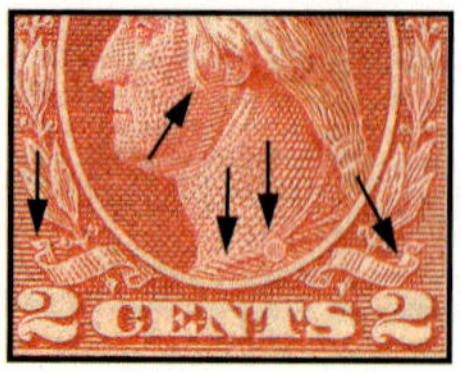


TWO CENTS
Type I. There is one shading line in the first curve of the ribbon above the left "2" and one in the second curve of the ribbon above the right "2."
The button of the toga has only a faint outline.
The top line of the toga rope, from the button to the front of the throat, is also very faint.
The shading lines of the face terminate in front of the ear with little or no joining, to form a lock of hair.
Used on both flat plate and rotary press printings.

406 A140 2c car, type I 6.50 .25
Never hinged 15.00
*a.* Booklet pane of 6 65.00 *90.00*
Never hinged 110.00
*b.* As #406, double impression *1,250.* *2,000.*
*c.* 2c lake, type I *2,000.* *6,000.*
Never hinged *4,500.*
*d.* As "c," double impression *2,750.*
407 A140 7c black ('14) 70.00 14.00
Never hinged 150.00
*Nos. 405-407 (3)* 83.00 14.50

**1912** ***Imperf.***

408 A140 1c green 1.00 1.00
Never hinged 2.00
409 A140 2c car, type I 1.20 1.20
Never hinged 2.40

**COIL STAMPS**

**1912** ***Perf. 8½ Horizontally***

410 A140 1c green 6.00 *12.50*
Never hinged 13.00
411 A140 2c carmine, type I 10.00 *17.50*
Never hinged 22.50

***Perf. 8½ Vertically***

412 A140 1c green 25.00 *40.00*
Never hinged 55.00
413 A140 2c carmine, type I 60.00 50.00
Never hinged 130.00
*Nos. 410-413 (4)* 101.00 120.00

Beware also of plentiful fakes in the marketplace of Nos. 410-413.

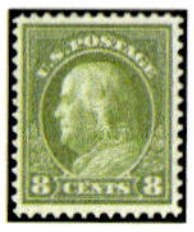


Franklin — A148

**1912-14** **Wmk. 190** ***Perf. 12***

414 A148 8c pale ol grn 45.00 2.00
Never hinged 100.00
415 A148 9c sal red ('14) 50.00 14.00
Never hinged 110.00
416 A148 10c org yel 45.00 .80
Never hinged 100.00
*a.* 10c brown yellow *1,250.* —
Never hinged *2,750.*
417 A148 12c cl brn ('14) 45.00 5.00
Never hinged 100.00
418 A148 15c gray 80.00 4.00
Never hinged 180.00
419 A148 20c ultra ('14) 190.00 17.50
Never hinged 400.00
420 A148 30c org red ('14) 115.00 17.50
Never hinged 250.00
421 A148 50c violet ('14) 350.00 27.50
Never hinged 775.00
*Nos. 414-421 (8)* 920.00 88.30

No. 421 almost always has an offset of the frame lines on the back under the gum. No. 422 does not have this offset.

**VALUES FOR VERY FINE STAMPS**
**Please note: Stamps are valued in the grade of Very Fine unless otherwise indicated.**

**1912, Feb. 12** **Wmk. 191** ***Perf. 12***

422 A148 50c violet 250.00 25.00
Never hinged 550.00
423 A148 $1 violet brown 475.00 85.00
Never hinged 1,000.

Perforated sheet stamps of type A148: #431-440 (single line wmk., perf. 10), #460 (double line wmk. perf. 10), #470-478 (unwmkd., perf. 10), #508-518 (unwmkd., perf. 11).

**1914** **Wmk. 190** ***Perf. 12x10***

423A A140 1c green *12,500.* *5,000.*
Never hinged —
423B A140 2c rose red, type I *175,000.* *15,000.*
423C A140 5c blue *17,500.*

Nos. 423A-423C formerly were Nos. 424a, 425d and 428a, respectively.
No. 423A unused is valued in the grade of fine. Values for 423A used and 423B-423C are for fine-very fine examples.

**1914** **Wmk. 190** ***Perf. 10x12***

423D A140 1c green *8,500.*
423E A140 2c rose red, type I —

Nos. 423D and 423E formerly were Nos. 424b and 425c, respectively. Only one example is recorded of No. 423E.
No. 423D is valued in the grade of fine-very fine.

**1913-15** **Wmk. 190** ***Perf. 10***

424 A140 1c grn ('14) 2.50 .25
Never hinged 5.25
*c.* Vert. pair, imperf. horiz. *3,000.* *2,500.*
Never hinged *4,500.*
*d.* Booklet pane of 6 ('13) 5.25 *7.50*
Never hinged 8.75
*f.* Vert. pair, imperf. between and with straight edge at top *13,000.*

For former Nos. 424a and 424b, see Nos. 423A and 423D.
The unique example of No. 424f is never hinged, and it is valued thus.

**Research has proven beyond doubt that all examples of the previously listed No. 424e, booklet pane of 6, imperforate and without gum, are unissued fabrications made from an ungummed press sheet on stamp paper once undoubtedly housed in the Smithsonian philatelic collection.**

425 A140 2c rose red, type I ('14) 2.50 .25
Never hinged 5.25
*e.* Booklet pane of 6 ('13) 17.50 *25.00*
Never hinged 30.00

For former Nos. 425c and 425d, see Nos. 423A and 423D.

426 A140 3c dp vio, type I ('14) 17.50 1.25
Never hinged 40.00
427 A140 4c brn ('14) 35.00 .90
Never hinged 75.00
428 A140 5c blue ('14) 32.50 .90
Never hinged 75.00

For former No. 428a, see No. 423C.

429 A140 6c red org ('14) 50.00 2.00
Never hinged 110.00
430 A140 7c black ('14) 85.00 4.75
Never hinged 190.00
431 A148 8c pale ol grn ('14) 45.00 3.00
Never hinged 100.00
*a.* Double impression —
432 A148 9c sal red ('14) 40.00 8.00
Never hinged 95.00
433 A148 10c org yel ('14) 45.00 1.00
Never hinged 100.00
*a.* 10c brown yellow —
434 A148 11c dk grn ('15) 30.00 8.00
Never hinged 75.00
435 A148 12c clar brn ('14) 30.00 5.50
Never hinged 75.00
*a.* 12c copper red 30.00 6.50
Never hinged 75.00
437 A148 15c gray ('14) 120.00 8.00
Never hinged 275.00
438 A148 20c ultra ('14) 200.00 7.00
Never hinged 450.00
439 A148 30c org red ('14) 225.00 20.00
Never hinged 500.00
440 A148 50c violet ('15) 450.00 20.00
Never hinged 1,100.
*Nos. 424-440 (16)* 1,410. 90.80

**The values for used coil stamps are for examples with contemporaneous cancels that can be authenticated by expertizing committees. Used coils with cancels most commonly from the 1950s exist, and these and stamps with other non-contemporaneous cancels sell for less than the values shown.**

**COIL STAMPS**

**1914** ***Perf. 10 Horizontally***

441 A140 1c green 1.00 *1.50*
Never hinged 2.00
442 A140 2c carmine, type I 10.00 *45.00*
Never hinged 22.50
*a.* 2c lake, type I, on cover —

**1914** ***Perf. 10 Vertically***

443 A140 1c green 30.00 *45.00*
Never hinged 65.00
444 A140 2c car, type I 50.00 40.00
Never hinged 120.00
*a.* 2c lake *2,000.*
445 A140 3c violet, type I 210.00 *250.00*
Never hinged 500.00
446 A140 4c brown 130.00 *150.00*
Never hinged 280.00
447 A140 5c blue 45.00 *110.00*
Never hinged 100.00
*Nos. 443-447 (5)* 465.00 595.00

Beware also of plentiful fakes in the marketplace of Nos. 441-447.

**ROTARY PRESS STAMPS**

The Rotary Press Stamps are printed from plates that are curved to fit around a cylinder. This curvature produces stamps that are slightly larger, either horizontally or vertically, than those printed from flat plates. Designs of stamps from flat plates measure about 18½-19mm wide by 22mm high.
When the impressions are placed sidewise on the curved plates the designs are 19½-20mm wide; when they are placed vertically the designs are 22½ to 23mm high. A line of color (not a guide line) shows where the curved plates meet or join on the press.

ROTARY PRESS COIL STAMPS
Stamp designs: 18½-19x22½mm

**1915-16** ***Perf. 10 Horizontally***

448 A140 1c green 12.50 *17.50*
Never hinged 25.00

Type II

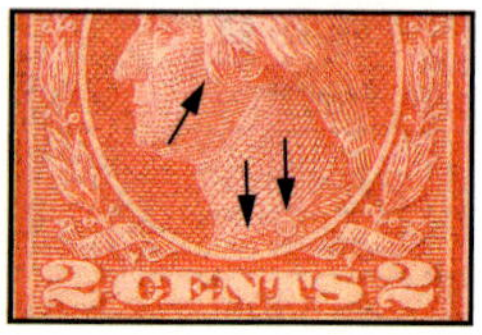


TWO CENTS
Type II. Shading lines in ribbons as on type I.
The toga button, rope and rope shading lines are heavy.
The shading lines of the face at the lock of hair end in a strong vertical curved line.
Used on rotary press printings only.

Type III

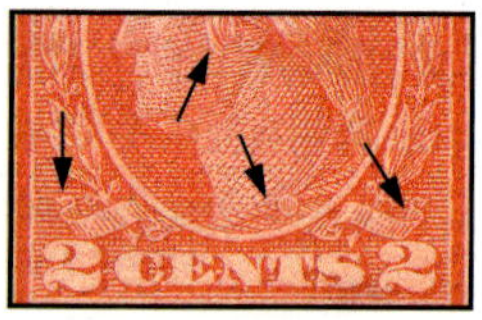


Type III. Two lines of shading in the curves of the ribbons.
Other characteristics similar to type II.
Used on rotary press printings only.

Fraudulently altered examples of type III (Nos. 455, 488, 492 and 540) have had one line of shading scraped off to make them resemble type II (Nos. 454, 487, 491 and 539).

449 A140 2c red, type I 2,500. 650.00
Never hinged 5,500.
450 A140 2c car, type III ('16) 15.00 *25.00*
Never hinged 30.00

**1914-16** ***Perf. 10 Vertically***
**Stamp designs: 19½-20x22mm**

452 A140 1c green 15.00 *17.50*
Never hinged 30.00
453 A140 2c car rose, type I 140.00 45.00
Never hinged 300.00
454 A140 2c red, type II 70.00 22.50
Never hinged 160.00
455 A140 2c car, type III 8.00 3.50
Never hinged 18.00
456 A140 3c vio, type I ('16) 250.00 170.00
Never hinged 550.00
457 A140 4c brown ('16) 32.50 30.00
Never hinged 65.00
458 A140 5c blue ('16) 35.00 30.00
Never hinged 70.00
*Nos. 452-458 (7)* 550.50 318.50

**Horizontal Coil**

**1914, June 30** ***Imperf.***

459 A140 2c car, type I 275. *1,300.*
Never hinged 400.

When the value for a used stamp is higher than the unused value, the stamp must have a contemporaneous cancel. Valuable stamps of this type should be accompanied by certificates of authenticity issued by recognized expertizing committees. The used value for No. 459 is for an example with such a certificate.
Beware of examples of No. 453 with perforations fraudulently trimmed to resemble single examples of No. 459.

FLAT PLATE PRINTINGS

**1915, Feb. 8 Wmk. 191 *Perf. 10***

460 A148 $1 violet black 650. 140.
Never hinged 1,450.

**1915, June 17 Wmk. 190 *Perf. 11***

461 A140 2c pale car red, type I 175. *375.*
Never hinged 350.

Beware of fraudulently perforated examples of No. 409 being offered as No. 461.
See note on used stamps following No. 459.

Unwatermarked

From 1916 onward all postage stamps except Nos. 519 and 832b are on unwatermarked paper.

**1916-17 Unwmk. *Perf. 10***

462 A140 1c green 7.00 .35
Never hinged 16.00
*a.* Booklet pane of 6 9.50 *12.50*
Never hinged 16.00
463 A140 2c car, type I 4.50 .40
Never hinged 10.00 .45
*a.* Booklet pane of 6 110.00 *110.00*
Never hinged 180.00

See No. 467 for P# block of 6 from plate 7942.

464 A140 3c vio, type I 65.00 17.50
Never hinged 165.00

Beware of fraudulently perforated examples of No. 483 being offered as No. 464.

465 A140 4c org brn 60.00 2.25
Never hinged 125.00
466 A140 5c blue 65.00 2.25
Never hinged 150.00
467 A140 5c car (error in plate of 2c, '17) 500.00 *3,250.*
Never hinged 800.00

No. 467 is an error caused by using a 5c transfer roll in re-entering three subjects: 7942 UL 74, 7942 UL 84, 7942 LR 18; the balance of the subjects on the plate being normal 2c entries. No. 467 imperf. is listed as No. 485. The error perf 11 on unwatermarked paper is No. 505.

468 A140 6c red orange 100.00 8.00
Never hinged 225.00
469 A140 7c black 120.00 13.00
Never hinged 270.00
470 A148 8c olive green 80.00 7.00
Never hinged 165.00
471 A148 9c salmon red 90.00 22.50
Never hinged 190.00
472 A148 10c orange yel 120.00 3.00
Never hinged 250.00
473 A148 11c dark green 50.00 22.50
Never hinged 110.00
474 A148 12c claret brn 55.00 8.00
Never hinged 120.00
*a.* 12c copper red 75.00 *15.00*
Never hinged 170.00
475 A148 15c gray 170.00 15.00
Never hinged 375.00
476 A148 20c lt ultra 240.00 17.50
Never hinged 500.00
476A A148 30c orange red 2,000.
Never hinged 4,250.

No. 476A is valued in the grade of fine.

477 A148 50c lt vio ('17) 850. 80.00
Never hinged 2,000.
478 A148 $1 violet black 600. 27.50
Never hinged 1,400.
*Nos. 462-466,468-476,477-478 (16)* 2,677. 246.75

TYPES OF 1902-03 ISSUE

**1917, Mar. 22 Unwmk. *Perf. 10***

479 A127 $2 dark blue 210.00 40.00
Never hinged 475.00
480 A128 $5 light green 170.00 37.50
Never hinged 375.00

**1916-17 *Imperf.***

481 A140 1c green 1.25 .95
Never hinged 1.80

Type Ia

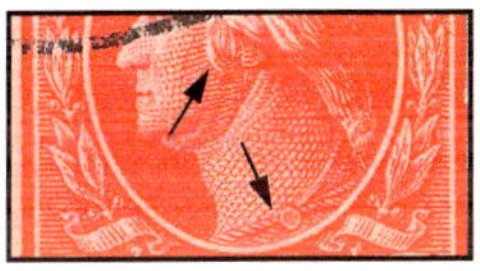

TWO CENTS

Type Ia. The design characteristics are similar to type I except that all of the lines of the design are stronger.

The toga button, toga rope and rope shading are heavy.

The latter characteristics are those of type II, which, however, occur only on impressions from rotary plates.

Used only on flat plates 10208 and 10209.

482 A140 2c car, type I 1.50 1.30
Never hinged 2.60
482A A140 2c dp rose, type Ia — *55,000.*

No. 482A was issued imperforate but all examples were privately perforated with large oblong perforations at the sides (Schermack type III).

Type II

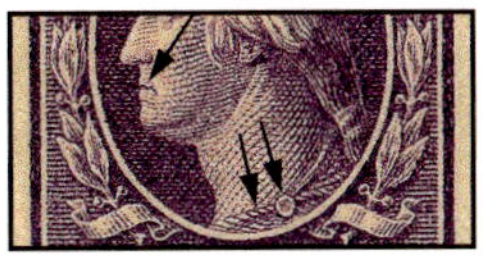

THREE CENTS

Type II. The top line of the toga rope is strong and the rope shading lines are heavy and complete.

The line between the lips is heavy.

Used on both flat plate and rotary press printings.

483 A140 3c vio, type I ('17) 12.00 10.00
Never hinged 24.00
484 A140 3c violet, type II 10.00 8.00
Never hinged 20.00
485 A140 5c car (error in plate of 2c) ('17) *10,000.*
Never hinged *14,000.*

Although No. 485 is valued as a single stamp, such examples are seldom seen in the marketplace.

No. 485 usually is seen as the center stamp in a block of 9 with 8 No. 482 (value with #485 never hinged, $22,500) or as two center stamps in a block of 12 (value with both No. 485 never hinged, $42,500).

ROTARY PRESS COIL STAMPS
(See note over No. 448)

**1916-18 *Perf. 10 Horizontally***
**Stamp designs: 18½-19x22½mm**

486 A140 1c green ('18) .85 .85
Never hinged 1.75
487 A140 2c carmine, type II 15.00 14.00
Never hinged 30.00
488 A140 2c carmine, type III 3.00 *5.00*
Never hinged 6.50
489 A140 3c vio, type I ('17) 4.50 2.25
Never hinged 10.00
*Nos. 486-489 (4)* 23.35 22.10

**1916-22 *Perf. 10 Vertically***
**Stamp designs: 19½-20x22mm**

490 A140 1c green .50 *.60*
Never hinged 1.05
491 A140 2c car, type II 2,500. 800.00
Never hinged 5,250.
492 A140 2c car, type III 9.00 1.00
Never hinged 19.00
493 A140 3c vio, type I ('17) 16.00 4.50
Never hinged 32.50
494 A140 3c vio, type II ('18) 10.00 2.50
Never hinged 21.50
495 A140 4c org brn ('17) 10.00 7.00
Never hinged 21.50
496 A140 5c blue ('19) 3.50 2.50
Never hinged 7.25
497 A148 10c org yel ('22) 17.50 17.50
Never hinged 35.00

Blind Perfs

Listings of imperforate-between varieties are for examples which show no trace of "blind perfs," traces of impressions from the perforating pins which do not cut into the paper.

Some unused stamps have had the gum removed to eliminate the impressions from the perforating pins. Unused stamps without gum and without apparent perf impressions should be carefully examined to make sure no impressions can be found.

TYPES OF 1913-15 ISSUE
FLAT PLATE PRINTINGS

**1917-19 Unwmk. *Perf. 11***

498 A140 1c green .50 .25
Never hinged 1.00
*a.* Vertical pair, imperf. horiz. 800.00
Never hinged 1,600.
*b.* Horizontal pair, imperf. between 700.00 *650.00*
Never hinged 1,500.
*c.* Vertical pair, imperf. between 700.00 —
*d.* Double impression 250.00 *3,750.*
*e.* Booklet pane of 6 2.50 *2.00*
Never hinged 4.25
*f.* Booklet pane of 30 1,050. *12,500.*
Never hinged 1,700.
*g.* Perf. 10 at top or bottom 15,000. *20,000.*
Never hinged 27,500.

No. 498g used is valued in the grade of fine.

499 A140 2c rose, type I .50 .25
Never hinged 1.00
*a.* Vertical pair, imperf. horiz., type I 3,000. *2,500.*
Never hinged 4,250.
*b.* Horiz. pair, imperf. vert., type I 550.00 *600.00*
Never hinged 1,100.
*c.* Vert. pair, imperf. btwn., type I 900.00 *300.00*
*e.* Booklet pane of 6, type I 4.00 *2.50*
Never hinged 6.75
*f.* Booklet pane of 30, type I 20,000. —
Never hinged 28,000.
*g.* Double impression, type I 200.00 *2,000.*
Never hinged 400.00
*h.* 2c lake, type I 600.00 800.00
Never hinged 1,250.
*i.* As "e," single stamp, lake *3,250.*

No. 499b is valued in the grade of fine. No 499g used is valued in the grade of fine.

500 A140 2c deep rose, type Ia 260.00 240.00
Never hinged 570.00
501 A140 3c lt vio, type I 9.00 .40
Never hinged 20.00
*b.* Booklet pane of 6, type I 75.00 *80.00*
Never hinged 125.00
*c.* Vert. pair, imper. horiz., type I 2,100.
Never hinged 3,250.
*d.* Double impression 3,750. *3,500.*
Never hinged 5,250.

No. 501d is valued in the grade of fine.

502 A140 3c dk vio, type II 12.00 .75
Never hinged 27.50
*b.* Bklt. pane of 6, type II 60.00 *75.00*
Never hinged 100.00
*c.* Vert. pair, imperf. horiz., type II 1,400. *850.00*
Never hinged 2,750.
*d.* Double impression 800.00 *1,000.*
Never hinged 1,600.
*e.* Perf. 10 at top or bottom — *30,000.*
503 A140 4c brown 8.50 .40
Never hinged 19.00
*b.* Double impression —
504 A140 5c blue 7.50 .35
Never hinged 17.00
*a.* Horizontal pair, imperf. between 20,000. —
*b.* Double impression 1,750. *1,600.*
Never hinged 3,000.
505 A140 5c rose (error in plate of 2c) 325.00 *600.00*
Never hinged 625.00
506 A140 6c red orange 11.00 .40
Never hinged 25.00
*a.* Perf. 10 at top or bottom 30,000. *8,000.*
*b.* Double impression, never hinged 2,000.

No. 506a also exists as a transitional stamp gauging partly perf 10 and partly perf 11 at top. Value thus the same as normal 506a.

No. 506b is a partial double impression. Two authenticated examples are documented.

507 A140 7c black 24.00 1.25
Never hinged 55.00
508 A148 8c olive bister 11.00 .65
Never hinged 25.00
*b.* Vertical pair, imperf. between — —
*c.* Perf. 10 at top or bottom *9,000.*
509 A148 9c salmon red 11.00 1.60
Never hinged 25.00
*a.* Perf. 10 at top or bottom *7,500.*
Never hinged 37,500.

No. 509a also exists as a transitional stamp gauging partly perf 10 and partly perf 11 at top or bottom. Value thus the same as normal 509a.

510 A148 10c org yel 15.00 .25
Never hinged 34.00
*a.* 10c brown yellow 1,400.
Never hinged 3,250.

511 A148 11c lt green 7.50 2.25
Never hinged 17.00
*a.* Perf. 10 at top or bottom 3,000. *3,250.*
Never hinged 6,000.

No. 511a also exists as a transitional stamp gauging partly perf 10 and partly perf 11 at top or bottom. Value thus the same as normal 511a.

512 A148 12c claret brown 8.50 .50
Never hinged 19.00
*a.* 12c brown carmine 8.50 .50
Never hinged 19.00
*b.* Perf. 10 at top or bottom 25,000. *15,000.*
*c.* 12c claret red 8.50 .50
Never hinged 19.00
513 A148 13c apple grn ('19) 9.50 5.50
Never hinged 21.00
514 A148 15c gray 32.50 1.40
Never hinged 75.00
*a.* Perf. 10 at bottom *10,000.*
515 A148 20c lt ultra 40.00 .45
Never hinged 85.00
*b.* Vertical pair, imperf. between 1,750. *3,250.*
*c.* Double impression 2,500.
Never hinged 5,000.
*d.* Perf. 10 at top or bottom — *11,000.*

No. 515b is valued in the grade of fine.

Beware of pairs with blind perforations inside the design of the top stamp that are offered as No. 515b.

No. 515c is a partial double impression.

516 A148 30c orange red 30.00 1.50
Never hinged 70.00
*a.* Perf. 10 at top or bottom 20,000. *15,000.*
Never hinged 37,500.
*b.* Double impression —

No. 516a used is valued in the grade of fine.

517 A148 50c red violet 50.00 .75
Never hinged 120.00
*b.* Vertical pair, imperf. between & with natural straight edge at bottom *6,000.*
*c.* Perf. 10 at top or bottom *17,000.*

No. 517b is valued in average condition and may be a unique used pair (precanceled). The editors would like to see authenticated evidence of an unused pair.

518 A148 $1 violet brown 37.50 1.50
Never hinged 95.00
*b.* $1 deep brown 2,000. *1,100.*
Never hinged 4,000.
*Nos. 498-504,506-518 (20)* 585.50 260.40

No. 518b is valued in the grade of fine to very fine.

TYPE OF 1908-09 ISSUE

This is the result of an old stock of No. 344 which was returned to the Bureau in 1917 and perforated with the then current gauge 11. Only lower left panes of No. 344 were perforated 11, and therefore only left and bottom plate blocks exist.

**1917, Oct. 10 Wmk. 191 *Perf. 11***

519 A139 2c carmine 475.00 *1,800.*
Never hinged 950.00

Beware of examples of No. 344 fraudulently perforated and offered as No. 519. Obtaining a certificate from a recognized expertizing committee is strongly recommended.

**Warning:** See note following No. 459 regarding used stamps.

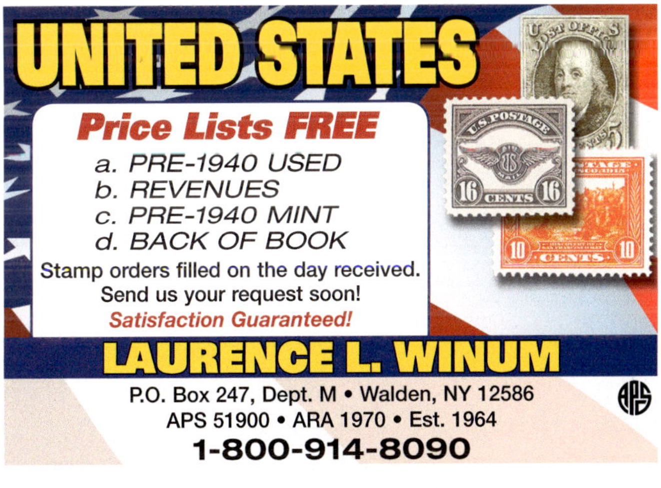
UNITED STATES
Price Lists FREE
a. PRE-1940 USED
b. REVENUES
c. PRE-1940 MINT
d. BACK OF BOOK
Stamp orders filled on the day received.
Send us your request soon!
Satisfaction Guaranteed!
LAURENCE L. WINUM
P.O. Box 247, Dept. M • Walden, NY 12586
APS 51900 • ARA 1970 • Est. 1964
1-800-914-8090

16 UNITED STATES

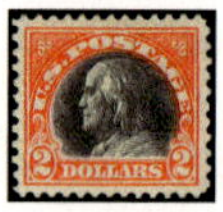

Franklin — A149

**1918, Aug. Unwmk. *Perf. 11***

523 A149 $2 org red & blk 525. 240.
Never hinged 1,175.
524 A149 $5 dp grn & blk 170. 40.
Never hinged 340.

See No. 547 for $2 carmine & black.

### TYPES OF 1917-19 ISSUE
### OFFSET PRINTING

**1918-20 Unwmk. *Perf. 11***

525 A140 1c gray green 2.50 .90
Never hinged 6.00
*a.* 1c dark green 10.00 1.75
Never hinged 25.00
*c.* Horizontal pair, imperf. between *750.00 650.00*
*d.* Double impression 40.00 *750.00*
Never hinged 90.00

No. 525c is valued in the grade of fine and with natural straight edge at right, as virtually all recorded examples come thus. No. 525d used is valued in the grade of very good.

Type IV
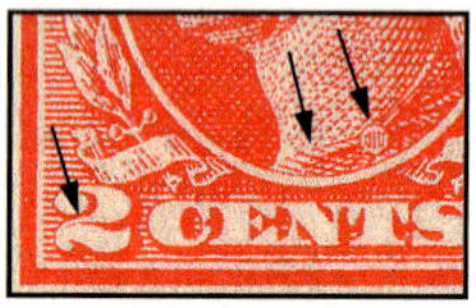

TWO CENTS

Type IV — Top line of the toga rope is broken.

The shading lines in the toga button are so arranged that the curving of the first and last form "D (reversed) ID."

The line of color in the left "2" is very thin and usually broken.

Used on offset printings only.

Type V
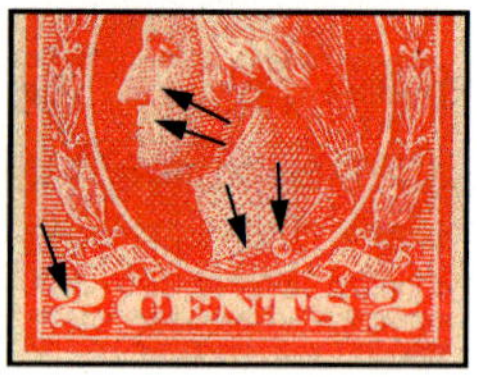

Type V — Top line of the toga is complete.

There are five vertical shading lines in the toga button.

The line of color in the left "2" is very thin and usually broken.

The shading dots on the nose are as shown on the diagram.

Used on offset printings only.

Type Va
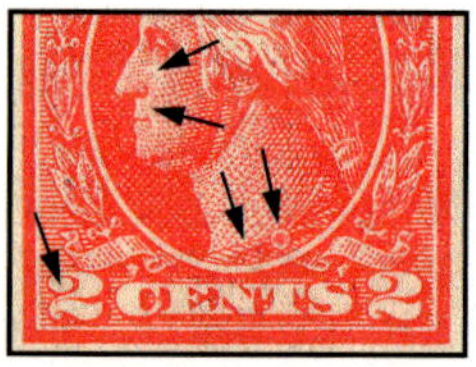

Type Va — Characteristics are the same as type V except in the shading dots of the nose. The third row of dots from the bottom has four dots instead of six. The overall height is ⅓mm shorter than the other types.

Used on offset printings only.

Type VI
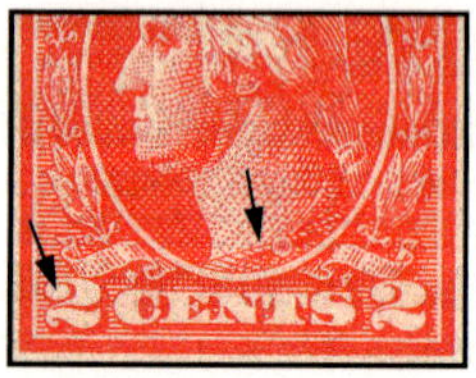

Type VI — General characteristics the same as type V except that the line of color in the left "2" is very heavy.

Used on offset printings only.

TYPE VII
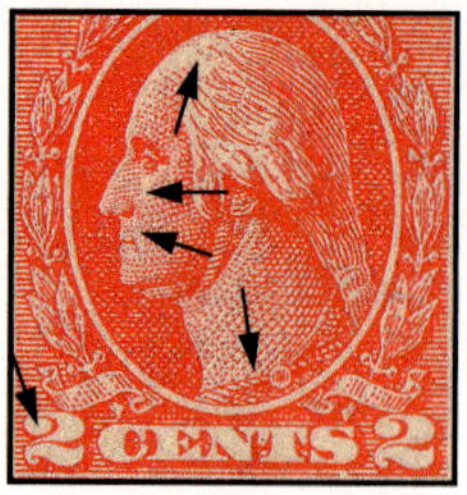

Type VII — The line of color in the left "2" is invariably continuous, clearly defined and heavier than in type V or Va but not as heavy as type VI.

An additional vertical row of dots has been added to the upper lip.

Numerous additional dots have been added to the hair on top of the head.

Used on offset printings only.

526 A140 2c car, type IV ('20) 25.00 4.00
Never hinged 57.50
527 A140 2c car, type V ('20) 18.00 1.25
Never hinged 40.00
*a.* Double impression 100.00 —
Never hinged 225.00
*b.* Vert. pair, imperf. horiz. *850.00*
Never hinged 2,000.
*c.* Horiz. pair, imperf. vert. *2,500.* —
*d.* Double impression —
528 A140 2c car, type Va ('20) 12.00 .40
Never hinged 25.00
*c.* Double impression 62.50
Never hinged 150.00
*g.* Vert. pair, imperf. between *5,500.*
528A A140 2c car, type VI ('20) 47.50 2.00
Never hinged 115.00
*d.* Double impression 200.00 *900.00*
Never hinged 450.00
*f.* Vert. pair, imperf. horiz. —
*h.* Vert. pair, imperf. between *5,000.*
528B A140 2c car, type VII ('20) 20.00 .75
Never hinged 50.00
*e.* Double impression 77.50 *400.00*

No. 528Be used is valued in the grade of very good to fine.

TYPE III
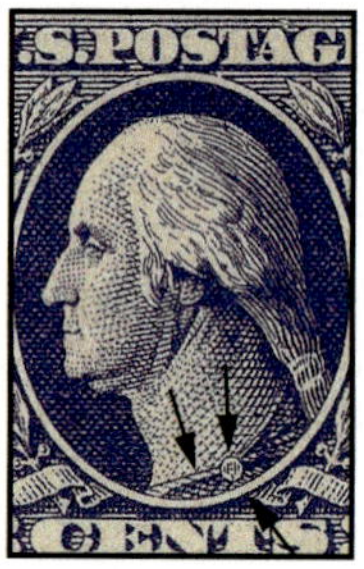

THREE CENTS

Type III — The top line of the toga rope is strong but the 5th shading line is missing as in type I.

Center shading line of the toga button consists of two dashes with a central dot.

The "P" and "O" of "POSTAGE" are separated by a line of color.

The frame line at the bottom of the vignette is complete.

Used on offset printings only.

TYPE IV
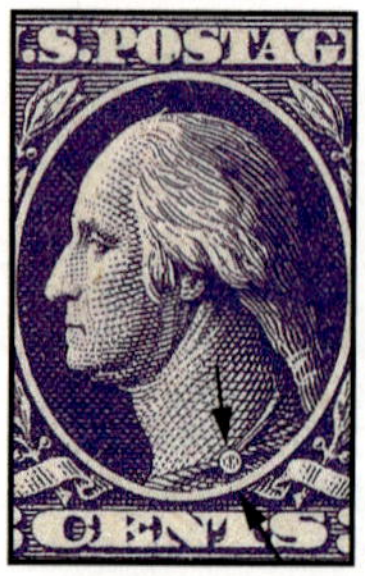

Type IV — The shading lines of the toga rope are complete.

The second and fourth shading lines in the toga button are broken in the middle and the third line is continuous with a dot in the center.

The "P" and "O" of "POSTAGE" are joined.

The frame line at the bottom of the vignette is broken.

Used on offset printings only.

529 A140 3c vio, type III 3.50 .50
Never hinged 7.75
P# block of 8, type III, plates #8370 and 8375 150.00
*a.* Double impression 50.00 *1,250.*
Never hinged 115.00
*b.* Printed on both sides *2,500.*

No. 529a used is valued in the grade of fine.

530 A140 3c pur, type IV 2.00 .30
Never hinged 4.50
*a.* Double impression 40.00 *800.00*
Never hinged 90.00
*b.* Printed on both sides *750.00*
Never hinged *1,100.*
*c.* Triple impression *1,750.* —
*Nos. 525-530 (8)* 130.50 10.10

No. 530a used is valued in the grade of fine. No. 530c unused is valued in the grade of fine.

**1918-20 *Imperf.***

531 A140 1c green ('19) 14.00 12.00
Never hinged 21.00
532 A140 2c car rose, type IV ('20) 50.00 42.50
Never hinged 80.00
533 A140 2c car, type V ('20) 135.00 *150.00*
Never hinged 200.00
534 A140 2c car, type Va ('20) 16.50 15.00
Never hinged 26.50
534A A140 2c car, type VI ('20) 52.50 40.00
Never hinged 90.00
534B A140 2c car, type VII ('20) 2,500. 1,500.
Never hinged 3,750.
535 A140 3c vio, type IV 11.00 6.00
Never hinged 18.00
*a.* Double impression 100.00 —
Never hinged 200.00
*Nos. 531-534A,535 (6)* 279.00 265.50

Beware of perforated 2c offset stamps that may have been fraudulently trimmed to resemble Nos. 532-534B.

Examples of the 2c type VII with Schermack type III vending machine perforations have been cut down at sides to simulate the rarer No. 534B imperforate. The No. 534B with Schermack type III perforations is much less expensive than the fully imperforate No. 534B listed here.

**1919, Aug. 12 *Perf. 12½***

536 A140 1c gray green 20.00 *35.00*
Never hinged 45.00
*a.* Horiz. pair, imperf. vert. *900.00*
Never hinged *1,400.*

### VICTORY ISSUE

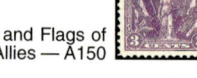

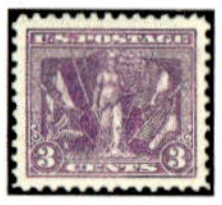
"Victory" and Flags of the Allies — A150

FLAT PLATE PRINTING

**1919, Mar. 3 Engr. *Perf. 11***

537 A150 3c violet 10.00 3.25
Never hinged 20.00
*a.* 3c deep red violet *1,300.* *1,800.*
Never hinged *2,400.*
*b.* 3c light reddish violet 150.00 50.00
Never hinged 300.00
*c.* 3c red violet 225.00 65.00
Never hinged 425.00

Victory of the Allies in World War I.
No. 537a is valued in the grade of fine.

ROTARY PRESS PRINTINGS

**1919 *Perf. 11x10***
**Stamp designs: 19½-20x22-22¼mm**

538 A140 1c green 10.00 9.00
Never hinged 23.00
*a.* Vert. pair, imperf. horiz. 60.00 *125.00*
Never hinged 125.00
539 A140 2c car rose, type II 2,800. *16,000.*
Never hinged 5,250.
540 A140 2c car rose, type III 12.00 9.50
Never hinged 27.50
*a.* Vert. pair, imperf horiz. 60.00 *140.00*
Never hinged 125.00
*b.* Horiz. pair, imperf. vert. *2,750.*
541 A140 3c vio, type II 40.00 37.50
Never hinged 100.00

The part perforate varieties of Nos. 538a and 540a were issued in sheets and may be had in blocks; similar part perforate varieties, Nos. 490 and 492, are from coils and are found only in strips.

See note over No. 448 regarding No. 539.
No. 539 is valued in the grade of fine.
No. 540b is valued in the grade of fine.

**1920, May 26 *Perf. 10x11***
**Stamp design: 19x22½-22¾mm**

542 A140 1c green 12.50 1.50
Never hinged 30.00
*a.* All color missing (EP) —

**1921 *Perf. 10***
**Stamp design: 19x22½mm**

543 A140 1c green .70 .40
Never hinged 1.75
*a.* Horizontal pair, imperf. between *4,500.*

**1922 *Perf. 11***
**Stamp design: 19x22½mm**

544 A140 1c green *22,500.* *3,500.*
Never hinged *35,000.*

No. 544 is valued in the grade of fine.

**1921**
**Stamp designs: 19½-20x22mm**

545 A140 1c green 250.00 250.00
Never hinged 600.00
546 A140 2c car rose, type III 105.00 *190.00*
Never hinged 230.00
*a.* Perf. 10 on left side *7,500.* *17,500.*

No. 546a used is valued in the grade of very good. It is unique used.

FLAT PLATE PRINTING

**1920, Nov. 1 *Perf. 11***

547 A149 $2 carmine & black 140. 40.
Never hinged 275.
*a.* $2 lake & black 200. 40.
Never hinged 425.

### PILGRIM TERCENTENARY ISSUE

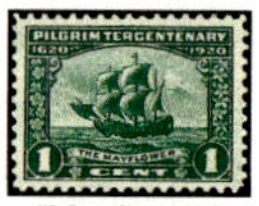
"Mayflower" A151

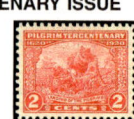

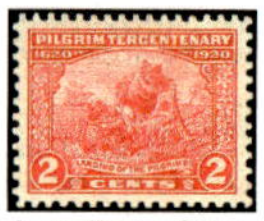
Landing of the Pilgrims A152

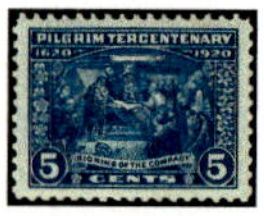
Signing of the Compact — A153

**1920, Dec. 21 *Perf. 11***

548 A151 1c green 4.00 2.00
Never hinged 10.00
549 A152 2c carmine rose 5.50 1.60
Never hinged 14.00
550 A153 5c deep blue 32.50 12.50
Never hinged 70.00
*Nos. 548-550 (3)* 42.00 16.10
Nos. 548-550, never hinged 94.00

Tercentenary of the landing of the Pilgrims at Plymouth, Mass.

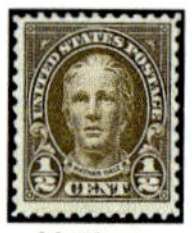
Nathan Hale A154

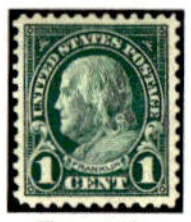
Franklin A155

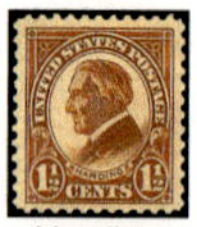
Harding A156

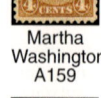

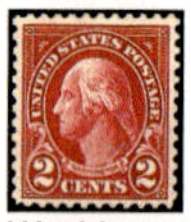
Washington A157

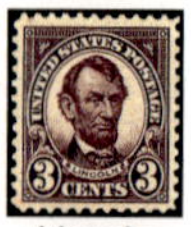
Lincoln A158

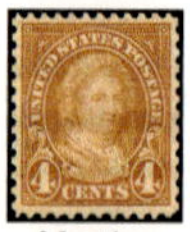
Martha Washington A159

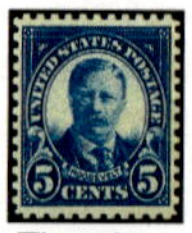
Theodore Roosevelt A160

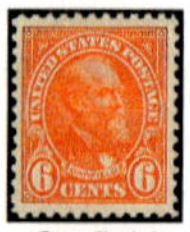
Garfield A161

UNITED STATES 17

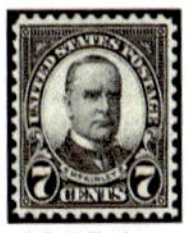
McKinley
A162

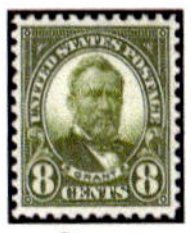
Grant
A163

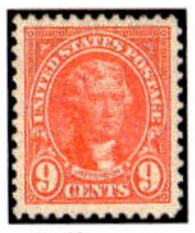
Jefferson
A164

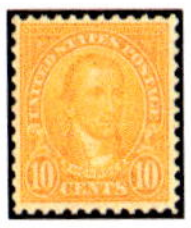
Monroe
A165

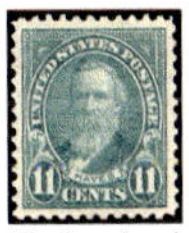
Rutherford
B. Hayes
A166

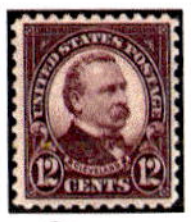
Grover
Cleveland
A167

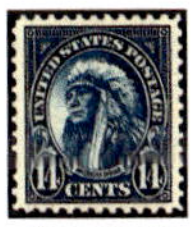
American
Indian
A168

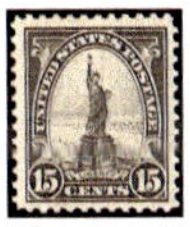
Statue of
Liberty
A169

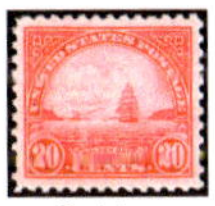
Golden
Gate
A170

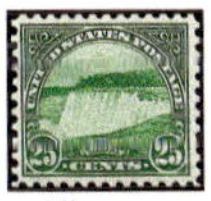
Niagara
Falls
A171

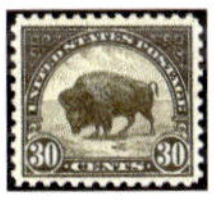
American
Buffalo
A172

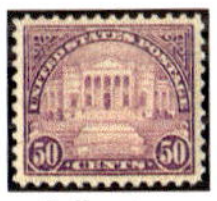
Arlington
Amphitheater
A173

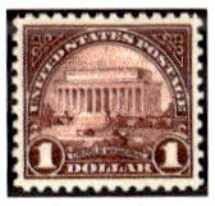
Lincoln
Memorial
A174

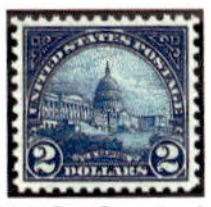
U.S. Capitol
A175

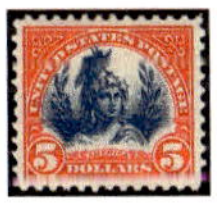
Head of Freedom Statue,
Capitol Dome — A176

FLAT PLATE PRINTINGS

**1922-25 Unwmk. *Perf. 11***

**551** A154 ½c ol brn ('25) .30 .25
Never hinged .50
**552** A155 1c dp grn ('23) 1.25 .25
Never hinged 2.75
*a.* Booklet pane of 6 7.50 4.00
Never hinged 12.50
**553** A156 1½c yel brn ('25) 2.00 .25
Never hinged 4.10
**554** A157 2c carmine ('23) 1.10 .25
Never hinged 2.50
*a.* Horiz. pair, imperf. vert. 250.00
Never hinged 475.00
*b.* Vert. pair, imperf. horiz. 6,000.
Never hinged 10,000.
*c.* Booklet pane of 6 7.00 3.00
Never hinged 12.00
*d.* Perf. 10 at top or bottom 9,000. 5,000.
Never hinged 12,000.
*e.* Imperf., pair 400.00
**555** A158 3c violet ('23) 13.00 1.20
Never hinged 27.50
**556** A159 4c yel brn ('23) 16.00 .50
Never hinged 35.00
*a.* Vert. pair, imperf. horiz. 12,500.
*b.* Perf. 10 at top or bottom 8,000. 7,000.

No. 556a is unique. It resulted from a sheet that was damaged and patched during production.

No. 556b used also exists as a transitional stamp gauging 10 at left top and 11 at right top. Value the same.

**557** A160 5c dark blue 16.00 .30
Never hinged 35.00
*a.* Imperf., pair 2,000.
Never hinged 3,500.
*b.* Horiz. pair, imperf. vert. —
*c.* Perf. 10 at top or bottom — 9,500.
**558** A161 6c red orange 30.00 1.00
Never hinged 65.00
**559** A162 7c black ('23) 7.25 .75
Never hinged 15.50
**560** A163 8c ol grn ('23) 37.50 1.00
Never hinged 80.00
**561** A164 9c rose ('23) 11.00 1.25
Never hinged 25.00
**562** A165 10c orange ('23) 13.50 .35
Never hinged 30.00
*a.* Vert. pair, imperf. horiz. 2,000.
Never hinged 3,250.
*b.* Imperf., pair 1,850.
*c.* Perf. 10 at top or bottom 25,000. 7,500.

No. 562a is valued in the grade of fine, with gum and without blue defacing lines. No. 562b is valued without gum and without blue pencil defacing lines. No. 562c is valued in the grade of fine.

**563** A166 11c greenish blue 1.25 .60
Never hinged 2.75
*a.* 11c light bluish green 1.25 .60
Never hinged 2.75
*d.* Imperf., horiz. pair 15,000.
Imperf., vert. strip of 3 20,000.

Many other intermediate shades exist for Nos. 563 and 563a, all falling within the blue or green color families.

No. 563d is known only as the two listings shown.

**564** A167 12c brn vio ('23) 4.75 .35
Never hinged 10.50
*a.* Horiz. pair, imperf. vert. 3,750.
**565** A168 14c blue ('23) 4.25 .90
Never hinged 9.50
**566** A169 15c gray 16.00 .30
Never hinged 35.00
**567** A170 20c car rose ('23) 16.00 .30
Never hinged 35.00
*a.* Horiz. pair, imperf. vert. 2,500.
Never hinged 5,000.

No. 567a is valued in the grade of fine.

**568** A171 25c yel grn 13.50 .75
Never hinged 30.00
*b.* Vert. pair, imperf. horiz. 3,500.
*c.* Perf. 10 at one side 12,000. 9,000.
Never hinged 16,000.

No. 568b is valued in the grade of fine. No. 568c used is valued in the grade of fine.

**569** A172 30c ol brn ('23) 22.50 .60
Never hinged 50.00
**570** A173 50c lilac 32.50 .40
Never hinged 70.00
**571** A174 $1 vio brn ('23) 35.00 .80
Never hinged 75.00
**572** A175 $2 dp blue ('23) 55.00 9.00
Never hinged 120.00
**573** A176 $5 car & bl ('23) 90.00 15.00
Never hinged 180.00
*a.* $5 car lake & dk bl 180.00 30.00
Never hinged 375.00
*Nos. 551-573 (23)* 439.65 36.35
*Nos. 551-573, never hinged* 940.60

No. 556a is unique. No. 554b is valued in the grade of fine. No. 562b is valued without gum and without blue pencil defacing lines. No. 568b is valued in the grade of fine.

For other listings of perforated stamps of designs A154 to A173 see:
Nos. 578 & 579, Perf. 11x10
Nos. 581-591, Perf. 10
Nos. 594-596, Perf. 11
Nos. 632-642, 653, 692-696, Perf. 11x10½
Nos. 697-701, Perf. 10½x11
This series also includes #622-623 (perf. 11), 684-687 & 720-723.

**1923-25 *Imperf.***
**Stamp design 19¼x22¼mm**

**575** A155 1c green 6.00 5.00
Never hinged 11.00
**576** A156 1½c yel brn ('25) 1.50 1.50
Never hinged 2.70

The 1½c A156 Rotary press imperforate is listed as No. 631.

**577** A157 2c carmine 1.50 1.25
Never hinged 2.70
*a.* 2c carmine lake —
*Nos. 575-577 (3)* 9.00 7.75
*Nos. 575-577, never hinged* 16.40

ROTARY PRESS PRINTINGS
(See note over No. 448)

**1923 *Perf. 11x10***
**Stamp designs: 19¾x22¼mm**

**578** A155 1c green 75.00 160.00
Never hinged 150.00
**579** A157 2c carmine 70.00 140.00
Never hinged 140.00

Nos. 578-579 were made from coil waste of Nos. 597, 599 and measure approximately 19¾x22¼mm.

**1923-26 *Perf. 10***
**Stamp designs: 19¼x22½mm**

**581** A155 1c green 10.00 .75
Never hinged 21.00
**582** A156 1½c brown ('25) 6.00 .65
Never hinged 13.00
**583** A157 2c car ('24) 3.00 .30
Never hinged 6.25
*a.* Booklet pane of 6 110.00 150.00
Never hinged 200.00
**584** A158 3c violet ('25) 27.50 3.00
Never hinged 60.00
**585** A159 4c yel brn ('25) 17.50 .65
Never hinged 37.50
**586** A160 5c blue ('25) 17.50 .40
Never hinged 37.50
*a.* Horizontal pair, imperf. vertically 7,500.

No. 586a is unique, precanceled, with average centering and small faults, and it is valued as such.

**587** A161 6c red org ('25) 9.25 .60
Never hinged 20.00
**588** A162 7c black ('26) 12.50 6.25
Never hinged 26.00
**589** A163 8c ol grn ('26) 27.50 4.50
Never hinged 57.50
**590** A164 9c rose ('26) 6.00 2.50
Never hinged 12.50
**591** A165 10c org ('25) 40.00 .50
Never hinged 85.00
*Nos. 581-591 (11)* 176.75 20.10
*Nos. 581-591, never hinged* 371.25

**Issued in sheets of 70 or 100 stamps, coil waste of Nos. 597, 599.**

**1923 *Perf. 11***
**Stamp designs approximately 19¾x22¼mm**

**594** A155 1c green 35,000. 10,500.
With gum 65,000.

The main listing for No. 594 unused is for an example without gum, both unused and used are valued with perforations just touching frameline on one side.

**595** A157 2c carmine 240.00 375.00
Never hinged 400.00
V-shaped gouge from eye down into cheek and back to hair in front of ear, plate 14731, pos.3 — —

Nos. 594-595 were made from coil waste of Nos. 597 and 599, and measure approximately 19¾x22¼mm.

**596** A155 1c green 250,000.
Precanceled 200,000.

No. 596 was made from rotary press sheet waste and measures approximately 19¼x22½mm. A majority of the examples carry the Bureau precancel "Kansas City, Mo." No. 596 is valued in the grade of fine.

**COIL STAMPS**
ROTARY PRESS

**1923-29 *Perf. 10 Vertically***
**Stamp designs approximately 19¾x22¼mm**

**597** A155 1c green .30 .25
Never hinged .60
**598** A156 1½c brown ('25) .90 .25
Never hinged 1.80

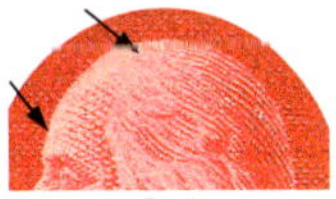
Type I

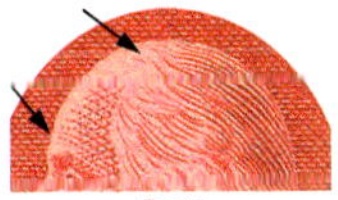
Type II

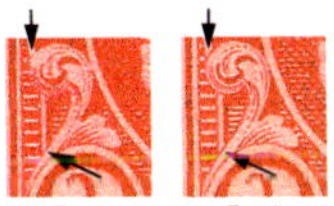
Type I Type II

TYPE I. No line outlining forehead. No heavy hair lines at top center of head. Outline of left acanthus scroll generally faint at top and toward base at left side.

TYPE II. Thin line outlining forehead. Three heavy hair lines at top center of head; two being outstanding in the white area. Outline of left acanthus scroll very strong and clearly defined at top (under left edge of lettered panel) and at lower curve (above and to left of numeral oval). This type appears only on Nos. 599A and 634A.

**599** A157 2c car, type I .35 .25
Never hinged .70
*b.* 2c carmine lake, type I, never hinged 300.00 —
**599A** A157 2c car, type II ('29) 120.00 16.00
Never hinged 240.00
**600** A158 3c violet ('24) 5.25 .25
Never hinged 10.50
**601** A159 4c yel brn 3.75 .35
Never hinged 7.50
**602** A160 5c dk blue ('24) 1.75 .25
Never hinged 3.50
**603** A165 10c orange ('24) 3.50 .25
Never hinged 7.00

The 6c design A161 coil stamp is listed as No. 723.

**1923-25 *Perf. 10 Horizontally***
**Stamp designs: 19¼x22½mm**

**604** A155 1c green ('24) .40 .25
Never hinged .80
**605** A156 1½c yel brn ('25) .40 .25
Never hinged .80
**606** A157 2c carmine .40 .25
Never hinged .80
*a.* 2c carmine lake 70.00 —
Never hinged 140.00
*Nos. 597-599,600-606 (10)* 17.00 2.60
*Nos. 597-599, 600-606, never hinged* 36.00

**HARDING MEMORIAL ISSUE**

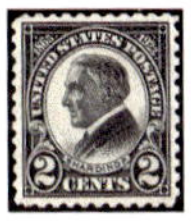
Warren G.
Harding — A177

FLAT PLATE PRINTING
**Stamp designs: 19¼x22¼mm**

**1923 *Perf. 11***

**610** A177 2c black .50 .25
Never hinged 1.00
*a.* Horiz. pair, imperf. vert. 2,000.
*b.* Imperf (error), P#14870 block of 6 20,000.

No. 610a is valued in the grade of fine.

No. 610b comes from left side error panes found in a normal pad of No. 610 stamps before No. 611 was issued. Two left side plate blocks and one top position plate block are recorded. Plate #14870 was not used to print No. 611. Loose stamps separated from the top and left plate blocks are indistinguishable from No. 611.

***Imperf***

**611** A177 2c black 4.50 4.00
Never hinged 9.00

ROTARY PRESS PRINTING
**Stamp designs: 19¼x22½mm**

***Perf. 10***

**612** A177 2c black 15.00 1.75
Never hinged 32.50

***Perf. 11***

**613** A177 2c black 35,000.

Tribute to President Warren G. Harding, who died August 2, 1923.

No. 613 was produced from rotary press sheet waste. It is valued in the grade of fine.

**HUGUENOT-WALLOON TERCENTENARY ISSUE**

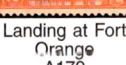

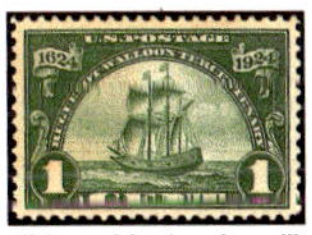
"New Netherland"
A178

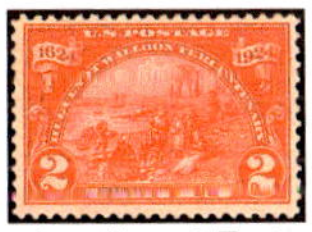
Landing at Fort
Orange
A179

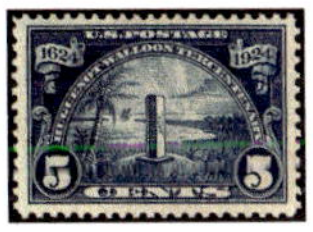
Monument to Jan
Ribault at Duvall
County,
Fla. — A180

FLAT PLATE PRINTINGS

**1924, May 1 *Perf. 11***

**614** A178 1c dark green 2.30 3.00
Never hinged 4.25
**615** A179 2c carmine rose 3.75 2.25
Never hinged 7.00
**616** A180 5c dark blue 15.00 13.00
Never hinged 27.50
*Nos. 614-616 (3)* 21.05 18.25
*Nos. 614-616, never hinged* 38.75

Tercentenary of the settling of the Walloons and in honor of the Huguenots.

**LEXINGTON-CONCORD ISSUE**

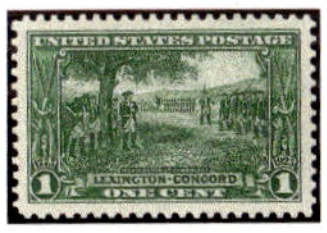
Washington at
Cambridge
A181

18　　　　　　　　　　　　　　　　　　　　　　　UNITED STATES

"Birth of Liberty,"
by Henry
Sandham — A182

The Minute Man,
by Daniel Chester
French — A183

**1925, Apr. 4**　　　　　　　　*Perf. 11*
617　A181　1c deep green　　2.00　2.50
　　　Never hinged　　　　　3.75
618　A182　2c carmine rose　3.50　4.00
　　　Never hinged　　　　　6.50
619　A183　5c dark blue　　14.00　13.00
　　　Never hinged　　　　　26.00
　　　Nos. 617-619 (3)　　19.50　19.50
　　　Nos. 617-619, never hinged　36.25

150th anniv. of the Battle of Lexington-Concord.

### NORSE-AMERICAN ISSUE

A184

Viking Ship — A185

**1925, May 18**　　　　　　　*Perf. 11*
620　A184　2c carmine & black　3.00　2.75
　　　Never hinged　　　　　6.00
621　A185　5c dark blue & black　9.00　9.00
　　　Never hinged　　　　　19.00

100th anniv. of the arrival in NY on Oct. 9, 1825, of the sloop "Restaurationen" with the first group of immigrants from Norway to the U.S.

Benjamin
Harrison
A186

Woodrow
Wilson
A187

**1925-26**　　　　　　　　　*Perf. 11*
622　A186　13c green ('26)　　9.00　.75
　　　Never hinged　　　　　19.00
623　A187　17c black　　　　9.00　.30
　　　Never hinged　　　　　19.00

### SESQUICENTENNIAL EXPOSITION ISSUE

Liberty
Bell — A188

**1926, May 10**　　　　　　　*Perf. 11*
627　A188　2c carmine rose　　2.25　.50
　　　Never hinged　　　　　4.00

150th anniv. of the Declaration of Independence, Philadelphia, June 1-Dec. 1.

### ERICSSON MEMORIAL ISSUE

Statue of John
Ericsson — A189

**1926, May 29**　　　　　　　*Perf. 11*
628　A189　5c gray lilac　　　5.00　3.25
　　　Never hinged　　　　　8.50

John Ericsson, builder of the "Monitor."

### BATTLE OF WHITE PLAINS ISSUE

Alexander Hamilton's
Battery — A190

**1926, Oct. 18**　　　　　　　*Perf. 11*
629　A190　2c carmine rose　　1.60　1.70
　　　Never hinged　　　　　2.75

Battle of White Plains, NY, 150th anniv.

### INTERNATIONAL PHILATELIC EXHIBITION ISSUE
#### Souvenir Sheet

A190a

**Condition valued:**
**Centering:** Overall centering will average very fine, but individual stamps may be better or worse.
**Perforations:** No folds along rows of perforations.
**Gum:** There may be some light gum bends but no gum creases.
**Hinging:** There may be hinge marks in the selvage and on up to two or three stamps, but no heavy hinging or hinge remnants (except in the ungummed portion of the wide selvage.
**Margins:** Top panes should have about ½ inch bottom margin and 1 inch top margin.
Bottom panes should have about ½ inch top margin and just under ¾ inch bottom margin. Both will have one wide side (usually 1 inch plus) and one narrow (½ inch) side margin. The wide margin corner will have a small diagonal notch on top panes.

**1926, Oct. 18**　　　　　　　*Perf. 11*
630　A190a　2c car rose,
　　　pane of 25　275.00　450.00
　　　Never hinged　　500.00
　a.　Single stamp (see foot-
　　　note)　　　　　10.00　—
　　　Never hinged　　14.00

Issued in panes measuring 158-160 ¼x136-146 ½mm containing 25 stamps with inscription "International Philatelic Exhibition, Oct. 16th to 23rd, 1926" in top margin.
No. 630a can be identified only when attached to the distinctive selvage as shown in illustration A190a. The four plate numbers used to print the White Plains souvenir sheets were distinct from the plate numbers used to print No. 629, and therefore all stamps in a plate block, for instance, are identifiable as No. 630a.

### VALUES FOR VERY FINE STAMPS
Please note: Stamps are valued in the grade of Very Fine unless otherwise indicated.

### TYPES OF 1922-26 ISSUE
REGULAR ISSUE
ROTARY PRESS PRINTINGS
(See note above No. 448.)

**1926, Aug. 27**　　　　　　　*Imperf.*
631　A156　1½c yellow brown　2.00　1.70
　　　Never hinged　　　　　3.00

**1926-34**　　　　　　　*Perf. 11x10½*
632　A155　1c green ('27)　　.25　.25
　　　Never hinged　　　　　.35
　a.　Booklet pane of 6　　5.00　4.00
　　　Never hinged　　　　　8.00
　b.　Vertical pair, imperf. be-
　　　tween　　　　　3,000.　3,250.
　　　Never hinged　　　　　5,500.
　c.　Horiz. pair, imperf. be-
　　　tween　　　　　　5,000.

No. 632b is valued in the grade of fine. No. 632c is valued in the grade of fine and never hinged. It is possibly unique.

633　A156　1½c yel brn ('27)　1.70　.25
　　　Never hinged　　　　　2.60
634　A157　2c car, type I　　.25　.25
　　　Never hinged　　　　　.30
　b.　2c carmine lake　180.00　500.00
　　　Never hinged　　　　　425.00
　c.　Horiz. pair, imperf. btwn.　6,000.
　d.　Booklet pane of 6, car-
　　　mine　　　　　1.50　1.50
　　　Never hinged　　　　　2.50
　e.　As "d," carmine lake　400.00　1,000.
　　　Never hinged　　　　　750.00

Shades of the carmine exist.
No. 634c is valued in the grade of fine.

634A　A157　2c car, type II
　　　　　　　　　('28)　300.00　13.50
　　　Never hinged　　　　　600.00
635　A158　3c violet ('27)　　.75　.25
　　　Never hinged　　　　　1.20
　a.　3c bright violet ('34)　.35　.25
　　　Never hinged　　　　　.45
636　A159　4c yel brn ('27)　1.90　.25
　　　Never hinged　　　　　3.00

637　A160　5c dk blue
　　　　　　　　　('27)　1.90　.25
　　　Never hinged　　　　　3.00
638　A161　6c red org
　　　　　　　　　('27)　2.00　.25
　　　Never hinged　　　　　3.20
639　A162　7c black ('27)　2.00　.25
　　　Never hinged　　　　　3.20
　a.　Vertical pair, imperf. be-
　　　tween　　　　　650.00　400.00
　　　Never hinged　　　　　1,250.
640　A163　8c yel brn ('27)　2.00　.25
　　　Never hinged　　　　　3.20
641　A164　9c rose ('27)　1.90　.25
　　　Never hinged　　　　　3.00
642　A165　10c org ('27)　3.25　.25
　　　Never hinged　　　　　5.50
　　　Nos. 632-634,635-642 (11)　17.90　2.75
　　　Nos. 632-634, 635-642
　　　never hinged　　　　　28.00

The 1½c, 2c, 4c, 5c, 6c, 8c imperf. (dry print) are printer's waste.
For ½c, 11c-50c see Nos. 653, 692-701.

### VERMONT SESQUICENTENNIAL ISSUE

Battle of Bennington, 150th anniv. and State independence.

Green Mountain
Boy — A191

#### FLAT PLATE PRINTING
**1927, Aug. 3**　　　　　　　*Perf. 11*
643　A191　2c carmine rose　1.20　.80
　　　Never hinged　　　　　2.00

### BURGOYNE CAMPAIGN ISSUE

Battles of Bennington, Oriskany, Fort Stanwix and Saratoga.

"The Surrender of
General Burgoyne
at Saratoga," by
John
Trumbull — A192

**1927, Aug. 3**　　　　　　　*Perf. 11*
644　A192　2c carmine rose　3.00　2.10
　　　Never hinged　　　　　5.25

### VALLEY FORGE ISSUE

150th anniversary of Washington's encampment at Valley Forge, Pa.

Washington at
Prayer — A193

**1928, May 26**　　　　　　　*Perf. 11*
645　A193　2c carmine rose　1.15　.50
　　　Never hinged　　　　　1.80
　a.　2c lake　　　　　　—
　　　Never hinged

### BATTLE OF MONMOUTH ISSUE

150th anniv. of the Battle of Monmouth, N.J., and "Molly Pitcher" (Mary Ludwig Hayes), the heroine of the battle.

No. 634 Overprinted

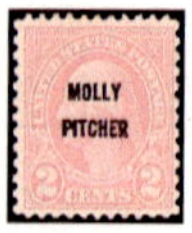

#### ROTARY PRESS PRINTING
**1928, Oct. 20**　　　　　　*Perf. 11x10½*
646　A157　2c carmine　　1.00　1.00
　　　Never hinged　　　　　1.60
　a.　"Pitcher" only　　1,000.
　b.　2c carmine lake　　　　2,500.

No. 646a is valued in the grade of fine.
Normally the overprints were placed 18mm apart vertically, but pairs exist with a space of 28mm between the overprints.

### HAWAII SESQUICENTENNIAL ISSUE

Sesquicentennial Celebration of the discovery of the Hawaiian Islands.

Nos. 634 and 637
Overprinted

#### ROTARY PRESS PRINTING
**1928, Aug. 13**　　　　　*Perf. 11x10½*
647　A157　2c carmine　　4.00　4.00
　　　Never hinged　　　　　7.25
648　A160　5c dark blue　11.00　12.50
　　　Never hinged　　　　　21.50

Nos. 647-648 were sold at post offices in Hawaii and at the Postal Agency in Washington, D.C. They were valid throughout the nation.
Normally the overprints were placed 18mm apart vertically, but pairs exist with a space of 28mm between the overprints.

### AERONAUTICS CONFERENCE ISSUE

Intl. Civil Aeronautics Conf., Washington, D.C., Dec. 12 - 14, 1928, and 25th anniv. of the 1st airplane flight by the Wright Brothers, Dec. 17, 1903.

Wright
Airplane — A194

Globe and
Airplane — A195

#### FLAT PLATE PRINTING
**1928, Dec. 12**　　　　　　　*Perf. 11*
649　A194　2c carmine rose　1.10　.80
　　　Never hinged　　　　　1.75
650　A195　5c blue　　　　4.50　3.25
　　　Never hinged　　　　　7.00

### GEORGE ROGERS CLARK ISSUE

150th anniv. of the surrender of Fort Sackville, the present site of Vincennes, Ind., to Clark.

Surrender of Fort
Sackville — A196

**1929, Feb. 25**　　　　　　　*Perf. 11*
651　A196　2c carmine & black　.70　.50
　　　Never hinged　　　　　1.15

### TYPE OF 1922-26 ISSUE
ROTARY PRESS PRINTING
**1929, May 25**　　　　　*Perf. 11x10½*
653　A154　½c olive brown　　.25　.25
　　　Never hinged　　　　　.35

### ELECTRIC LIGHT'S GOLDEN JUBILEE ISSUE

Invention of the 1st incandescent electric lamp by Thomas Alva Edison, Oct. 21, 1879, 50th anniv.

Edison's First
Lamp — A197

#### FLAT PLATE PRINTING
**1929**　　　　　　　　　　*Perf. 11*
654　A197　2c carmine rose　.65　.65
　　　Never hinged　　　　　1.10
　a.　2c lake　　　　　　—

#### ROTARY PRESS PRINTING
*Perf. 11x10½*
655　A197　2c carmine rose　.65　.25
　　　Never hinged　　　　　1.10
　　　Pair with full horiz. gutter
　　　btwn.　　　　　　—

#### ROTARY PRESS COIL STAMP
*Perf. 10 Vertically*
656　A197　2c carmine rose　10.00　1.75
　　　Never hinged　　　　　20.00

### SULLIVAN EXPEDITION ISSUE

150th anniversary of the Sullivan Expedition in New York State during the Revolutionary War.

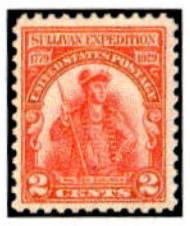

Maj. Gen. John Sullivan — A198

FLAT PLATE PRINTING

**1929, June 17** *Perf. 11*

| | | | |
|---|---|---|---|
| **657** | A198 2c carmine rose | .55 | .55 |
| | Never hinged | .95 | |
| *a.* | 2c lake | 375.00 | 250.00 |
| | Never hinged | 625.00 | |
| *b.* | Vert. pair, imperf. btwn. | *4,000.* | |

The unique No. 657b resulted from a paper foldover before perfing, and it has angled errant perfs from another row of horiz. perfs through the left side of the stamps.

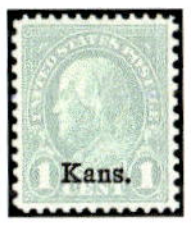

Nos. 632-634, 635-642 Overprinted

This special issue was authorized as a measure of preventing losses from post office burglaries. Approximately a year's supply was printed and issued to postmasters. The P.O. Dept. found it desirable to discontinue the State overprinted stamps after the initial supply was used.

ROTARY PRESS PRINTING

**1929, May 1** *Perf. 11x10½*

| | | | |
|---|---|---|---|
| **658** | A155 1c green | 2.50 | 2.00 |
| | Never hinged | 5.00 | |
| *a.* | Vertical pair, one without ovpt. | *300.00* | |
| | Never hinged | *500.00* | |
| **659** | A156 1½c brown | 3.25 | 2.90 |
| | Never hinged | 6.50 | |
| *a.* | Vertical pair, one without ovpt. | *475.00* | |
| **660** | A157 2c carmine | 4.00 | 1.00 |
| | Never hinged | 7.50 | |
| **661** | A158 3c violet | 17.50 | 15.00 |
| | Never hinged | 35.00 | |
| *a.* | Vertical pair, one without ovpt. | *600.00* | |
| | Never hinged | *800.00* | |
| **662** | A159 4c yellow brown | 17.50 | 9.00 |
| | Never hinged | 35.00 | |
| *a.* | Vertical pair, one without ovpt. | *500.00* | |
| **663** | A160 5c deep blue | 12.50 | 9.75 |
| | Never hinged | 25.00 | |
| **664** | A161 6c red orange | 25.00 | 18.00 |
| | Never hinged | 50.00 | |
| **665** | A162 7c black | 25.00 | 27.50 |
| | Never hinged | 50.00 | |
| **666** | A163 8c olive green | 72.50 | 65.00 |
| | Never hinged | 145.00 | |
| **667** | A164 9c light rose | 14.00 | 11.50 |
| | Never hinged | 27.50 | |
| **668** | A165 10c org yel | 22.50 | 12.50 |
| | Never hinged | 45.00 | |
| | *Nos. 658-668 (11)* | 216.25 | 174.15 |
| | *Nos. 658-668, never hinged* | 431.50 | |

See notes following No. 679.

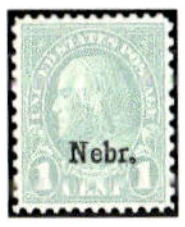

Overprinted

**1929, May 1**

| | | | |
|---|---|---|---|
| **669** | A155 1c green | 3.25 | 2.25 |
| | Never hinged | 6.50 | |
| *b.* | No period after "Nebr." (19338, 19339 UR 26, 36 and 19339 LR 26, 36) | 50.00 | |
| **670** | A156 1½c brown | 3.00 | 2.50 |
| | Never hinged | 6.00 | |
| **671** | A157 2c carmine | 3.00 | 1.30 |
| | Never hinged | 6.00 | |
| **672** | A158 3c violet | 11.00 | 12.00 |
| | Never hinged | 22.00 | |
| *a.* | Vertical pair, one without ovpt. | *500.00* | |
| **673** | A159 4c yellow brown | 17.50 | 15.00 |
| | Never hinged | 35.00 | |
| **674** | A160 5c deep blue | 15.00 | 15.00 |
| | Never hinged | 30.00 | |
| **675** | A161 6c red orange | 35.00 | 24.00 |
| | Never hinged | 70.00 | |
| **676** | A162 7c black | 22.50 | 18.00 |
| | Never hinged | 45.00 | |
| **677** | A163 8c olive green | 30.00 | 25.00 |
| | Never hinged | 60.00 | |
| **678** | A164 9c light rose | 35.00 | 27.50 |
| | Never hinged | 70.00 | |
| *a.* | Vertical pair, one without ovpt. | *800.00* | |
| **679** | A165 10c org yel | 90.00 | 22.50 |
| | Never hinged | 180.00 | |
| | *Nos. 669-679 (11)* | 265.25 | 165.05 |
| | *Nos. 669-679, never hinged* | 530.50 | |

Nos. 658-661, 669-673, 677-678 are known with the overprints on vertical pairs spaced 32mm apart instead of the normal 22mm.

**Important:** Nos. 658-679 with original gum have either one horizontal gum breaker ridge per stamp or portions of two at the extreme top and bottom of the stamps, 21mm apart. Multiple complete gum breaker ridges indicate a fake overprint. Absence of the gum breaker ridge indicates either regumming or regumming and a fake overprint.

### BATTLE OF FALLEN TIMBERS ISSUE

Memorial to Gen. Anthony Wayne and for 135th anniv. of the Battle of Fallen Timbers, Ohio.

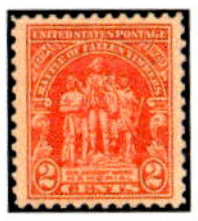

Gen. Anthony Wayne Memorial — A199

FLAT PLATE PRINTING

**1929, Sept. 14** *Perf. 11*

| | | | |
|---|---|---|---|
| **680** | A199 2c carmine rose | .65 | .65 |
| | Never hinged | 1.00 | |

### OHIO RIVER CANALIZATION ISSUE

Completion of the Ohio River Canalization Project, between Cairo, Ill. and Pittsburgh, Pa.

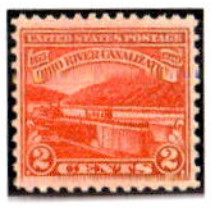

Lock No. 5, Monongahela River — A200

**1929, Oct. 19** *Perf. 11*

| | | | |
|---|---|---|---|
| **681** | A200 2c carmine rose | .55 | .55 |
| | Never hinged | .90 | |
| *a.* | 2c lake | *425.00* | — |
| | Never hinged | *650.00* | |
| *b.* | 2c carmine lake, never hinged | — | |

### MASSACHUSETTS BAY COLONY ISSUE

300th anniversary of the founding of the Massachusetts Bay Colony.

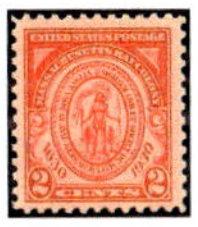

Mass. Bay Colony Seal — A201

**1930, Apr. 8** *Perf. 11*

| | | | |
|---|---|---|---|
| **682** | A201 2c carmine rose | .65 | .50 |
| | Never hinged | .95 | |

### CAROLINA-CHARLESTON ISSUE

260th anniv. of the founding of the Province of Carolina and the 250th anniv. of the city of Charleston, S.C.

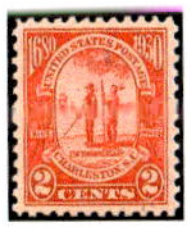

Gov. Joseph West & Chief Shadoo, a Kiowa — A202

**1930, Apr. 10** *Perf. 11*

| | | | |
|---|---|---|---|
| **683** | A202 2c carmine rose | 1.00 | 1.00 |
| | Never hinged | 1.60 | |

### TYPES OF 1922-26 ISSUE

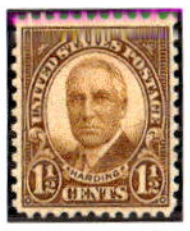

Warren G. Harding A203

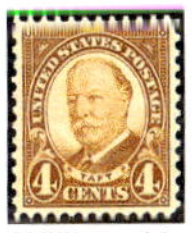

William H. Taft A204

ROTARY PRESS PRINTING

**1930** *Perf. 11x10½*

| | | | |
|---|---|---|---|
| **684** | A203 1½c brown | .50 | .25 |
| | Never hinged | .70 | |
| **685** | A204 4c brown | .80 | .25 |
| | Never hinged | 1.25 | |

ROTARY PRESS COIL STAMPS

*Perf. 10 Vertically*

| | | | |
|---|---|---|---|
| **686** | A203 1½c brown | 1.75 | .25 |
| | Never hinged | 2.60 | |
| **687** | A204 4c brown | 3.00 | .45 |
| | Never hinged | 4.50 | |

### BRADDOCK'S FIELD ISSUE

175th anniversary of the Battle of Braddock's Field, otherwise the Battle of Monongahela.

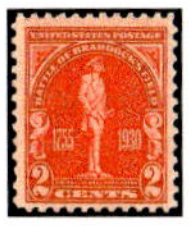

Statue of Col. George Washington — A205

FLAT PLATE PRINTING

**1930, July 9** *Perf. 11*

| | | | |
|---|---|---|---|
| **688** | A205 2c carmine rose | .85 | .85 |
| | Never hinged | 1.30 | |

### VON STEUBEN ISSUE

Baron Friedrich Wilhelm von Steuben (1730-1794), participant in the American Revolution.

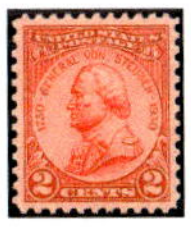

General von Steuben — A206

FLAT PLATE PRINTING

**1930, Sept. 17** *Perf. 11*

| | | | |
|---|---|---|---|
| **689** | A206 2c carmine rose | .50 | .50 |
| | Never hinged | .75 | |
| *a.* | Imperf., pair | *2,000.* | |
| | Never hinged | *3,000.* | |
| *b.* | 2c carmine lake | *950.00* | |

### PULASKI ISSUE

150th anniversary (in 1929) of the death of Gen. Casimir Pulaski, Polish patriot and hero of the American Revolutionary War.

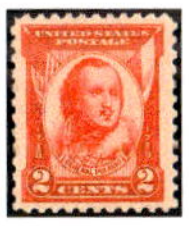

General Casimir Pulaski — A207

**1931, Jan. 16** *Perf. 11*

| | | | |
|---|---|---|---|
| **690** | A207 2c carmine rose | .30 | .25 |
| | Never hinged | .40 | |

### TYPE OF 1922-26 ISSUES

ROTARY PRESS PRINTING

**1931** *Perf. 11x10½*

| | | | |
|---|---|---|---|
| **692** | A166 11c light blue | 2.50 | .25 |
| | Never hinged | 3.75 | |
| **693** | A167 12c brown violet | 5.00 | .25 |
| | Never hinged | 8.00 | |
| **694** | A186 13c yellow green | 2.25 | .25 |
| | Never hinged | 3.50 | |
| **695** | A168 14c dark blue | 4.00 | .60 |
| | Never hinged | 6.25 | |
| **696** | A169 15c gray | 7.75 | .25 |
| | Never hinged | 12.00 | |

*Perf. 10½x11*

| | | | |
|---|---|---|---|
| **697** | A187 17c black | 4.75 | .25 |
| | Never hinged | 7.25 | |
| **698** | A170 20c carmine rose | 7.75 | .25 |
| | Never hinged | 12.50 | |
| **699** | A171 25c blue green | 8.00 | .25 |
| | Never hinged | 13.00 | |
| **700** | A172 30c brown | 12.50 | .25 |
| | Never hinged | 21.00 | |
| **701** | A173 50c lilac | 30.00 | .25 |
| | Never hinged | 50.00 | |
| | *Nos. 692-701 (10)* | 84.50 | 2.85 |
| | *Nos. 692-701, never hinged* | 137.25 | |

### RED CROSS ISSUE

50th anniversary of the founding of the American Red Cross Society.

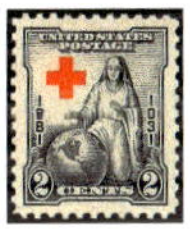

"The Greatest Mother" — A208

FLAT PLATE PRINTING

**1931, May 21** *Perf. 11*

| | | | |
|---|---|---|---|
| **702** | A208 2c black & red | .25 | .25 |
| | Never hinged | .35 | |
| *a.* | Red cross missing (FO) | *40,000.* | |

One example of No. 702a is documented; believed to be unique. Value reflects most recent sale price at auction in 1994.

### YORKTOWN ISSUE

Surrender of Cornwallis at Yorktown, 1781.

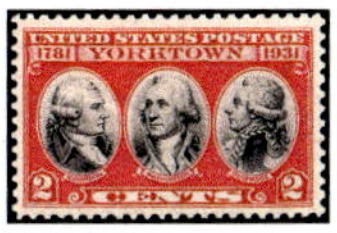

Count de Rochambeau, Washington, Count de Grasse — A209

**1931, Oct. 19** *Perf. 11*

| | | | |
|---|---|---|---|
| **703** | A209 2c car rose & blk | .35 | .25 |
| | Never hinged | .50 | |
| *a.* | 2c lake & black | 4.50 | .75 |
| | Never hinged | 6.25 | |
| *b.* | 2c dark lake & black | *500.00* | |
| | Never hinged | *950.00* | |
| *c.* | Horiz. pair, imperf. vertically | *7,000.* | |
| | Never hinged | *8,500.* | |

No. 703c is valued in the grade of fine.

### WASHINGTON BICENTENNIAL ISSUE

200th anniversary of the birth of George Washington. Various Portraits of George Washington.

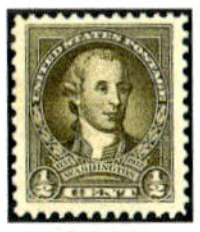

A210

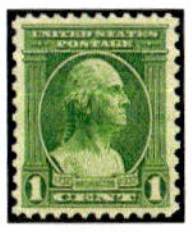

A211

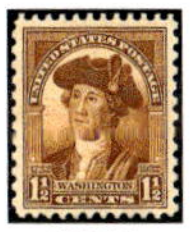

A212

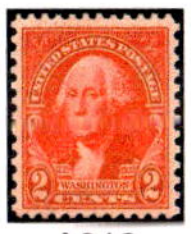

A213

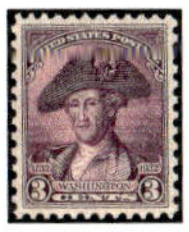

A214

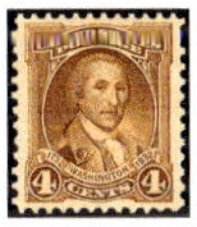

A215

Join the UNITED STATES STAMP SOCIETY

Since 1930, THE society for U.S. collectors and publishers of the *Durland Standard Plate Number Catalog* and other U.S. philatelic references. The Durland is the reference for plate number collectors with illustrations of marginal marking types and data on sheets, coils and booklet panes. Other publications include *Encyclopedia of United States Stamps and Stamp Collecting, United States Possessions: Postage Due,* and *United States Supplementary Mail.*

Sample copy of the society's journal, the *United States Specialist* is available for $2. Membership information and a complete list of publications from:

USSS, PO Box 1602
Hockessin, DE 19707-5602
www.usstamps.org

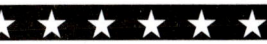

20 UNITED STATES

A216  A217

A218  A219

A220  A221

**ROTARY PRESS PRINTINGS**
**1932, Jan. 1** *Perf. 11x10½*
| | | | | |
|---|---|---|---|---|
| 704 | A210 | ½c olive brown | .25 | .25 |
| | | Never hinged | .35 | |
| 705 | A211 | 1c green | .25 | .25 |
| | | Never hinged | .35 | |
| 706 | A212 | 1½c brown | .45 | .25 |
| | | Never hinged | .60 | |
| 707 | A213 | 2c carmine rose | .30 | .25 |
| | | Never hinged | .45 | |
| 708 | A214 | 3c purple | .55 | .25 |
| | | Never hinged | .80 | |
| 709 | A215 | 4c light brown | .60 | .25 |
| | | Never hinged | .85 | |
| 710 | A216 | 5c blue | 1.40 | .25 |
| | | Never hinged | 2.25 | |
| 711 | A217 | 6c red orange | 2.75 | .25 |
| | | Never hinged | 4.50 | |
| 712 | A218 | 7c black | .60 | .25 |
| | | Never hinged | .85 | |
| 713 | A219 | 8c olive bister | 2.50 | .50 |
| | | Never hinged | 4.00 | |
| 714 | A220 | 9c pale red | 2.00 | .25 |
| | | Never hinged | 3.25 | |
| 715 | A221 | 10c orange yellow | 9.00 | .25 |
| | | Never hinged | 15.00 | |
| | | Nos. 704-715 (12) | 20.65 | 3.25 |
| | | Nos. 704-715, never hinged | 33.25 | |

### OLYMPIC WINTER GAMES ISSUE
3rd Olympic Winter Games, held at Lake Placid, N.Y., Feb. 4-13, 1932.

Skier — A222

**FLAT PLATE PRINTING**
**1932, Jan. 25** *Perf. 11*
| | | | | |
|---|---|---|---|---|
| 716 | A222 | 2c carmine rose | .35 | .25 |
| | | Never hinged | .55 | |
| a. | | 2c lake | 700.00 | |
| | | Never hinged | 1,050. | |

No. 716a should be accompanied by a certificate of authenticity issued by a recognized exertizing committee.

### ARBOR DAY ISSUE

Boy and Girl Planting Tree — A223

**ROTARY PRESS PRINTING**
**1932, Apr. 22** *Perf. 11x10½*
| | | | | |
|---|---|---|---|---|
| 717 | A223 | 2c carmine rose | .25 | .25 |
| | | Never hinged | .35 | |

60th anniv. of the 1st observance of Arbor Day in Nebr., April, 1872.
Birth centenary of Julius Sterling Morton, who conceived the plan and the name "Arbor Day," while a member of the Nebr. State Board of Agriculture.

### OLYMPIC GAMES ISSUE
Issued in honor of the 10th Olympic Games, held at Los Angeles, Calif., July 30 to Aug. 14, 1932.

Runner at Starting Mark — A224 | Myron's Discobolus — A225

**ROTARY PRESS PRINTING**
**1932, June 15** *Perf. 11x10½*
| | | | | |
|---|---|---|---|---|
| 718 | A224 | 3c purple | 1.50 | .25 |
| | | Never hinged | 2.00 | |
| 719 | A225 | 5c blue | 2.25 | .25 |
| | | Never hinged | 2.90 | |

Washington — A226

**ROTARY PRESS PRINTING**
**1932, June 16** *Perf. 11x10½*
| | | | | |
|---|---|---|---|---|
| 720 | A226 | 3c purple | .35 | .25 |
| | | Never hinged | .45 | |
| b. | | Booklet pane of 6 | 35.00 | 12.50 |
| | | Never hinged | 60.00 | |
| c. | | Vertical pair, imperf. between | 725.00 | 1,750. |
| | | Never hinged | 1,450. | |

**ROTARY PRESS COIL STAMPS**
**1932** *Perf. 10 Vertically*
| | | | | |
|---|---|---|---|---|
| 721 | A226 | 3c purple | 2.75 | .25 |
| | | Never hinged | 3.50 | |

*Perf. 10 Horizontally*
| 722 | A226 | 3c purple | 1.50 | .35 |
| | | Never hinged | 2.00 | |

Issued: #721, 6/24; #722, 10/12.

### TYPE OF 1922-26 ISSUES
**1932, Aug. 18** *Perf. 10 Vertically*
| 723 | A161 | 6c deep orange | 11.00 | .30 |
| | | Never hinged | 15.00 | |

### WILLIAM PENN ISSUE
250th anniv. of the arrival in America of Penn (1644-1718), English Quaker and founder of Pennsylvania.

William Penn — A227

**FLAT PLATE PRINTING**
**1932, Oct. 24** *Perf. 11*
| 724 | A227 | 3c purple | .45 | .25 |
| | | Never hinged | .60 | |
| a. | | Vert. pair, imperf. horiz. | — | |

### DANIEL WEBSTER ISSUE

Daniel Webster — A228

**FLAT PLATE PRINTING**
**1932, Oct. 24** *Perf. 11*
| 725 | A228 | 3c purple | .45 | .25 |
| | | Never hinged | .60 | |

Daniel Webster (1782-1852), statesman.

### GEORGIA BICENTENNIAL ISSUE
200th anniv. of the founding of the Colony of Georgia, and honoring Oglethorpe, who landed from England, Feb. 12, 1733, and personally supervised the establishing of the colony.

Gen. James Edward Oglethorpe — A229

**FLAT PLATE PRINTING**
**1933, Feb. 12** *Perf. 11*
| 726 | A229 | 3c purple | .50 | .25 |
| | | Never hinged | .65 | |

### PEACE OF 1783 ISSUE
150th anniv. of the issuance by George Washington of the official order containing the Proclamation of Peace marking officially the ending of hostilities in the War for Independence.

Washington's Headquarters, Newburgh, NY — A230

**ROTARY PRESS PRINTING**
**1933, Apr. 19** *Perf. 10½x11*
| 727 | A230 | 3c violet | .25 | .25 |
| | | Never hinged | .30 | |

See No. 752.

### CENTURY OF PROGRESS ISSUES
"Century of Progress" Intl. Exhibition, Chicago, which opened June 1, 1933, and centenary of the incorporation of Chicago as a city.

Restoration of Fort Dearborn — A231 | Federal Building at Chicago, 1933 — A232

**ROTARY PRESS PRINTING**
**1933, May 25** *Perf. 10½x11*
| 728 | A231 | 1c yellow green | .25 | .25 |
| | | Never hinged | .30 | |
| 729 | A232 | 3c purple | .25 | .25 |
| | | Never hinged | .35 | |

### AMERICAN PHILATELIC SOCIETY ISSUE
#### SOUVENIR SHEETS

Restoration of Fort Dearborn — A231a

Federal Building at Chicago, 1933 — A232a

**FLAT PLATE PRINTING**
**1933, Aug. 25** *Imperf.*
*Without Gum*
| 730 | A231a | 1c dp yel grn, pane of 25 | 20.00 | 25.00 |
| a. | | Single stamp | .70 | .50 |
| 731 | A232a | 3c pur, pane of 25 | 20.00 | 22.50 |
| a. | | Single stamp | .65 | .50 |

Issued in panes measuring 134x120mm. See Nos. 766-767.

### NATIONAL RECOVERY ACT ISSUE
Issued to direct attention to and arouse the support of the nation for the National Recovery Act.

Group of Workers — A233

**ROTARY PRESS PRINTING**
**1933, Aug. 15** *Perf. 10½x11*
| 732 | A233 | 3c purple | .25 | .25 |
| | | Never hinged | .30 | |

### BYRD ANTARCTIC ISSUE
Issued in connection with the Byrd Antarctic Expedition of 1933 and for use on letters mailed through the Little America Post Office established at the Base Camp of the Expedition in the territory of the South Pole.

World Map on van der Grinten's Projection — A234

**FLAT PLATE PRINTING**
**1933, Oct. 9** *Perf. 11*
| 733 | A234 | 3c dark blue | .50 | .50 |
| | | Never hinged | .60 | |

See Nos. 735, 753.

### KOSCIUSZKO ISSUE
Kosciuszko (1746-1817), Polish soldier and statesman served in the American Revolution, on the 150th anniv. of the granting to him of American citizenship.

Statue of Gen. Tadeusz Kosciuszko — A235

**FLAT PLATE PRINTING**
**1933, Oct. 13** *Perf. 11*
| 734 | A235 | 5c blue | .55 | .25 |
| | | Never hinged | .65 | |
| a. | | Horiz. pair, imperf. vert. | 1,750. | |
| | | Never hinged | 2,750. | |

### NATIONAL STAMP EXHIBITION ISSUE
#### SOUVENIR SHEET

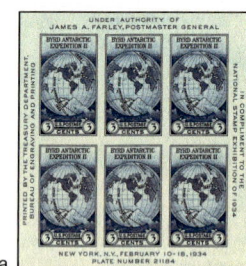
A235a

**1934, Feb. 10** *Imperf.*
*Without Gum*
| 735 | A235a | 3c dk blue, pane of 6 | 10.00 | 9.00 |
| a. | | Single stamp | 1.60 | 1.25 |

Issued in panes measuring 87x93mm. See No. 768.

### MARYLAND TERCENTENARY ISSUE
300th anniversary of the founding of Maryland.

"The Ark" and "The Dove" — A236

**FLAT PLATE PRINTING**
**1934, Mar. 23** *Perf. 11*
| 736 | A236 | 3c carmine rose | .30 | .25 |
| | | Never hinged | .40 | |
| a. | | Horizontal pair, imperf between | 4,000. | |
| b. | | 3c lake | 1,000. | |
| c. | | 3c carmine lake, never hinged | — | |

The unique No. 736a resulted from a paper foldover before perfing, and it has angled errant perfs from another column of vert. perfs through the upper-left corner of the left stamp.

### MOTHERS OF AMERICA ISSUE
Issued to commemorate Mother's Day.

Adaptation of Whistler's Portrait of his Mother — A237

**ROTARY PRESS PRINTING**
**1934, May 2** *Perf. 11x10½*
| 737 | A237 | 3c purple | .25 | .25 |
| | | Never hinged | .30 | |

# UNITED STATES

## FLAT PLATE PRINTING
*Perf. 11*

| | | | |
|---|---|---|---|
| 738 | A237 3c purple | .25 | .25 |
| | Never hinged | .30 | |

See No. 754.

### WISCONSIN TERCENTENARY ISSUE

Arrival of Jean Nicolet, French explorer, on the shores of Green Bay, 300th anniv. According to historical records, Nicolet was the 1st white man to reach the territory now comprising the State of Wisconsin.

Nicolet's Landing — A238

## FLAT PLATE PRINTING
**1934, July 7** *Perf. 11*

| | | | |
|---|---|---|---|
| 739 | A238 3c purple | .25 | .25 |
| | Never hinged | .40 | |
| a. | Vert. pair, imperf. horiz. | 575.00 | |
| | Never hinged | 1,050. | |
| b. | Horiz. pair, imperf. vert. | 1,000. | |
| | Never hinged | 1,750. | |

See No. 755.

### NATIONAL PARKS YEAR ISSUE

El Capitan, Yosemite (California) A239

Old Faithful, Yellowstone (Wyoming) A243

Grand Canyon (Arizona) — A240

Mt. Rainier and Mirror Lake (Washington) A241

Mesa Verde (Colorado) A242

Crater Lake (Oregon) — A244

Great Head, Acadia Park (Maine) A245

Great White Throne, Zion Park (Utah) A246

Great Smoky Mts. (North Carolina) A248

Mt. Rockwell (Mt. Sinopah) and Two Medicine Lake, Glacier Natl. Park (Montana) A247

## FLAT PLATE PRINTING
**1934** Unwmk. *Perf. 11*

| | | | |
|---|---|---|---|
| 740 | A239 1c green | .25 | .25 |
| | Never hinged | .40 | |
| a. | Vert. pair, imperf. horiz., with gum | 1,500. | |
| | Never hinged | 2,500. | |
| 741 | A240 2c red | .30 | .25 |
| | Never hinged | .40 | |
| a. | Vert. pair, imperf. horiz., with gum | 800.00 | |
| | Never hinged | 1,450. | |
| b. | Horiz. pair, imperf. vert., with gum | 1,000. | |
| | Never hinged | 1,750. | |
| c. | Imperf. P# 21261 block of 20 | 7,500. | |

No. 741c is a unique bottom margin plate #21261 block of 20. This plate was not used to print the imperforate Farley special printing, No. 757. Loose stamps separated from this block or from other possible imperforate No. 741 Plate #21261 blocks are indistinguishable from gummed examples of No. 757.

| | | | |
|---|---|---|---|
| 742 | A241 3c purple | .40 | .25 |
| | Never hinged | .50 | |
| a. | Vert. pair, imperf. horiz., with gum | 1,150. | |
| | Never hinged | 2,000. | |
| 743 | A242 4c brown | .50 | .40 |
| | Never hinged | .70 | |
| a. | Vert. pair, imperf. horiz., with gum | 3,750. | |
| | Never hinged | 8,500. | |
| 744 | A243 5c blue | .80 | .65 |
| | Never hinged | 1.10 | |
| a. | Horiz. pair, imperf. vert., with gum | 1,250. | |
| | Never hinged | 2,750. | |
| 745 | A244 6c dark blue | 1.20 | .85 |
| | Never hinged | 1.65 | |
| 746 | A245 7c black | .80 | .75 |
| | Never hinged | 1.10 | |
| a. | Horiz. pair, imperf. vert., with gum | 1,250. | |
| | Never hinged | 2,000. | |
| 747 | A246 8c sage green | 1.75 | 1.50 |
| | Never hinged | 2.70 | |
| 748 | A247 9c red orange | 1.60 | .65 |
| | Never hinged | 2.40 | |
| 749 | A248 10c gray black | 3.25 | 1.25 |
| | Never hinged | 5.00 | |
| | Nos. 740-749 (10) | 10.85 | 6.80 |
| | Nos. 740-749, never hinged | 15.95 | |

Beware of fakes of the part-perforate errors of Nos. 740-749, including those with gum (see "without gum" note before No. 752).

See Nos. 750-751, 750-765, 769-770, 797.

### AMERICAN PHILATELIC SOCIETY ISSUE
**SOUVENIR SHEET**

A248a

**1934, Aug. 28** *Imperf.*

| | | | |
|---|---|---|---|
| 750 | A248a 3c pur, pane of 6 | 20.00 | 27.50 |
| | Never hinged | 30.00 | |
| a. | Single stamp | 3.25 | 3.25 |
| | Never hinged | 4.00 | |

Issued in panes measuring approximately 98x93mm.
See No. 770.

### TRANS-MISSISSIPPI PHILATELIC EXPOSITION ISSUE
**SOUVENIR SHEET**

A248b

**1934, Oct. 10** *Imperf.*

| | | | |
|---|---|---|---|
| 751 | A248b 1c grn, pane of 6 | 10.00 | 12.50 |
| | Never hinged | 15.00 | |
| a. | Single stamp | 1.65 | 1.60 |
| | Never hinged | 2.25 | |

Issued in panes measuring approximately 92x99mm.
See No. 769.

### SPECIAL PRINTING
(Nos. 752-771 inclusive)

"Issued for a limited time in full sheets as printed, and in blocks thereof, to meet the requirements of collectors and others who may be interested." — From Postal Bulletin No. 16614.

Issuance of the following 20 stamps in complete sheets resulted from the protest of collectors and others at the practice of presenting, to certain governmental officials, complete sheets of unsevered panes, imperforate (except Nos. 752 and 753) and generally ungummed.

### Designs of Commemorative Issues
Without Gum

NOTE: In 1940 the P.O. Department offered to and did gum full sheets of Nos. 756-765 and 769-770 sent in by owners. No other Special Printings were accepted for gumming.

### TYPE OF PEACE ISSUE
Issued in sheets of 400
**ROTARY PRESS PRINTING**
*Perf. 10½x11*

**1935, Mar. 15** Unwmk.

| | | | |
|---|---|---|---|
| 752 | A230 3c purple | .25 | .25 |

### TYPE OF BYRD ISSUE
Issued in sheets of 200
**FLAT PLATE PRINTING**
*Perf. 11*

| | | | |
|---|---|---|---|
| 753 | A234 3c dark blue | .50 | .45 |

No. 753 is similar to No. 733. Positive identification is by blocks or pairs showing guide line between stamps. These guide lines between stamps are found only on No. 753.

### TYPE OF MOTHERS OF AMERICA ISSUE
Issued in sheets of 200
**FLAT PLATE PRINTING**
*Imperf*

| | | | |
|---|---|---|---|
| 754 | A237 3c deep purple | .60 | .60 |

### TYPE OF WISCONSIN ISSUE
Issued in sheets of 200
**FLAT PLATE PRINTING**
*Imperf*

| | | | |
|---|---|---|---|
| 755 | A238 3c deep purple | .60 | .60 |

### TYPES OF NATIONAL PARKS ISSUE
Issued in sheets of 200
**FLAT PLATE PRINTING**
*Imperf*

| | | | |
|---|---|---|---|
| 756 | A239 1c green | .25 | .25 |
| 757 | A240 2c red | .25 | .25 |
| 758 | A241 3c deep purple | .50 | .45 |
| 759 | A242 4c brown | 1.00 | .95 |
| 760 | A243 5c blue | 1.60 | 1.40 |
| 761 | A244 6c dark blue | 2.40 | 2.25 |
| 762 | A245 7c black | 1.60 | 1.40 |
| 763 | A246 8c sage green | 1.90 | 1.50 |
| 764 | A247 9c red orange | 2.00 | 1.75 |
| 765 | A248 10c gray black | 4.00 | 3.50 |
| | Nos. 756-765 (10) | 15.50 | 13.70 |
| | Nos. 756-765, with original gum, never hinged | 114.35 | |

### SOUVENIR SHEETS

**Note:** Single items from these sheets are identical with other varieties, 766 and 730, 766a and 730a, 767 and 731, 767a and 731a, 768 and 735, 768a and 735a, 769a and 756, 770a and 758.

Positive identification is by blocks or pairs showing wide gutters between stamps. These wide gutters occur only on Nos. 766-770 and measure, horizontally, 13mm on Nos. 766-767; 16mm on No. 768, and 23mm on Nos. 769-770.

### TYPE OF CENTURY OF PROGRESS ISSUE
Issued in sheets of 9 panes of 25 stamps each
**FLAT PLATE PRINTING**
*Imperf*

| | | | |
|---|---|---|---|
| 766 | A231a 1c yel grn, pane of 25 | 32.50 | 32.50 |
| a. | Single stamp | .90 | .65 |
| 767 | A232a 3c dp pur, pane of 25 | 32.50 | 32.50 |
| a. | Single stamp | .90 | .65 |

### NATIONAL EXHIBITION ISSUE TYPE OF BYRD ISSUE
Issued in sheets of 25 panes of 6 stamps each
**FLAT PLATE PRINTING**
*Imperf*

| | | | |
|---|---|---|---|
| 768 | A235a 3c dk blue, pane of 6 | 20.00 | 15.00 |
| a. | Single stamp | 2.80 | 2.40 |

### TYPES OF NATIONAL PARKS ISSUE
Issued in sheets of 20 panes of 6 stamps each
**FLAT PLATE PRINTING**
*Imperf*

| | | | |
|---|---|---|---|
| 769 | A248b 1c grn, pane of 6 | 12.50 | 11.00 |
| a. | Single stamp | 2.10 | 1.80 |
| 770 | A248a 3c dp pur, pane of 6 | 30.00 | 24.00 |
| a. | Single stamp | 3.25 | 3.10 |

### TYPE OF AIR POST SPECIAL DELIVERY
Issued in sheets of 200
**FLAT PLATE PRINTING**
*Imperf*

| | | | |
|---|---|---|---|
| 771 | APSD1 16c dark blue | 2.50 | 2.60 |

---

# QUALITY U.S. STAMPS

From #1 to Date Specializing in the Modern Varieties

Check out our new website!

## BARDO STAMPS

P.O. Box 7437 • Buffalo Grove, IL 60089
847.634.2676 • jfb7437@aol.com
www.BardoStamps.com

22     UNITED STATES

**Catalogue values for unused stamps in this section, from this point to the end, are for Never Hinged items.**

**VALUES FOR HINGED STAMPS AFTER NO. 771**
This catalogue does not value unused stamps after No. 771 in hinged condition. Hinged unused stamps from No. 772 to the present are worth considerably less than the values given for unused stamps, which are for never-hinged examples.

## CONNECTICUT TERCENTENARY ISSUE
300th anniv. of the settlement of Connecticut.

Charter Oak — A249

**ROTARY PRESS PRINTING**
*Perf. 11x10½*
1935, Apr. 26    Unwmk.
772 A249 3c rose purple    .35   .25

## CALIFORNIA PACIFIC EXPOSITION ISSUE
California Pacific Exposition at San Diego.

View of San Diego Exposition A250

1935, May 29    Unwmk.
773 A250 3c purple    .35   .25

## BOULDER DAM ISSUE
Dedication of Boulder Dam.

Boulder Dam — A251

**FLAT PLATE PRINTING**
1935, Sept. 30   Unwmk.   *Perf. 11*
774 A251 3c purple    .35   .25

## MICHIGAN CENTENARY ISSUE
Advance celebration of Michigan Statehood centenary.

Michigan State Seal — A252

**ROTARY PRESS PRINTING**
1935, Nov. 1   Unwmk.   *Perf. 11x10½*
775 A252 3c purple    .35   .25

## TEXAS CENTENNIAL ISSUE
Centennial of Texas independence.

Sam Houston, Stephen F. Austin and the Alamo — A253

1936, Mar. 2    Unwmk.
776 A253 3c purple    .35   .25

## RHODE ISLAND TERCENTENARY ISSUE
300th anniv. of the settlement of Rhode Island.

Statue of Roger Williams — A254

1936, May 4   Unwmk.   *Perf. 10½x11*
777 A254 3c purple    .35   .25

## THIRD INTERNATIONAL PHILATELIC EXHIBITION ISSUE
SOUVENIR SHEET

A254a

**FLAT PLATE PRINTING**
1936, May 9   Unwmk.   *Imperf.*
778 A254a purple, pane of 4   1.75   1.25
  a. 3c Type A249    .40   .30
  b. 3c Type A250    .40   .30
  c. 3c Type A252    .40   .30
  d. 3c Type A253    .40   .30

Issued in panes measuring 98x66mm containing four stamps, inscribed in the margins: "Printed by the Treasury Department, Bureau of Engraving and Printing, under authority of James A. Farley, Postmaster General, in compliment to the third International Philatelic Exhibition of 1936. New York, N. Y., May 9-17, 1936. Plate No. 21557."
Also used was plate 21558. Each different plate number used is inscribed in the bottom selvage of the respective souvenir sheets.

## ARKANSAS CENTENNIAL ISSUE
100th anniv. of the State of Arkansas.

Arkansas Post, Old and New State Houses — A255

**ROTARY PRESS PRINTING**
*Perf. 11x10½*
1936, June 15    Unwmk.
782 A255 3c purple    .35   .25

## OREGON TERRITORY ISSUE
Opening of the Oregon Territory, 1836, 100th anniv.

Map of Oregon Territory — A256

1936, July 14    Unwmk.
783 A256 3c purple    .35   .25

## SUSAN B. ANTHONY ISSUE
Susan Brownell Anthony (1820-1906), woman-suffrage advocate, and 16th anniv. of the ratification of the 19th Amendment which grants American women the right to vote.

Susan B. Anthony — A257

1936, Aug. 26    Unwmk.
784 A257 3c purple    .30   .25

## ARMY ISSUE
Issued in honor of the United States Army.

George Washington, Nathanael Greene and Mount Vernon — A258

Andrew Jackson, Winfield Scott and the Hermitage — A259

Generals Sherman, Grant and Sheridan — A260

Generals Robert E. Lee, "Stonewall" Jackson and Stratford Hall — A261

U.S. Military Academy, West Point — A262

1936-37    Unwmk.
785 A258 1c green    .30   .25
786 A259 2c carmine ('37)    .30   .25
787 A260 3c purple ('37)    .40   .25
788 A261 4c bl gray ('37)    .60   .25
789 A262 5c ultra ('37)    .75   .25
    Nos. 785-789 (5)    2.35   1.25

## NAVY ISSUE
Issued in honor of the United States Navy.

John Paul Jones and John Barry — A263

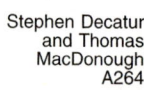
Stephen Decatur and Thomas MacDonough A264

Admirals David G. Farragut and David D. Porter — A265

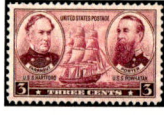
Admirals William T. Sampson, George Dewey and Winfield S. Schley — A266

Seal of U.S. Naval Academy and Naval Midshipmen A267

1936-37    Unwmk.
790 A263 1c green    .30   .25
791 A264 2c carmine ('37)    .30   .25
792 A265 3c purple ('37)    .40   .25
793 A266 4c gray ('37)    .60   .25
794 A267 5c ultra ('37)    .75   .25
    Nos. 790-794 (5)    2.35   1.25

## ORDINANCE OF 1787 SESQUICENTENNIAL ISSUE
150th anniv. of the adoption of the Ordinance of 1787 and the creation of the Northwest Territory.

Manasseh Cutler, Rufus Putnam and Map of Northwest Territory — A268

1937, July 13    Unwmk.
795 A268 3c rose purple    .30   .25

## VIRGINIA DARE ISSUE
350th anniv. of the birth of Virginia Dare, 1st child born in America of English parents (Aug. 18, 1587), and the settlement at Roanoke Island.

Virginia Dare and Parents — A269

**FLAT PLATE PRINTING**
1937, Aug. 18   Unwmk.   *Perf. 11*
796 A269 5c gray blue    .35   .25

## SOCIETY OF PHILATELIC AMERICANS ISSUE
SOUVENIR SHEET

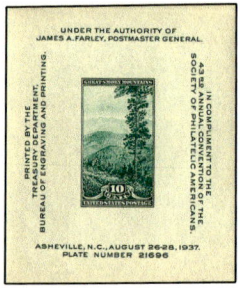
A269a

## TYPE OF NATIONAL PARKS ISSUE
1937, Aug. 26   Unwmk.   *Imperf.*
797 A269a 10c blue green    .60   .40
Issued in panes measuring 67x78mm.

## CONSTITUTION SESQUICENTENNIAL ISSUE
150th anniversary of the signing of the Constitution on September 17, 1787.

Signing of the Constitution A270

*Perf. 11x10½*
1937, Sept. 17    Unwmk.
798 A270 3c brt reddsh pur    .40   .25

## TERRITORIAL ISSUES
Hawaii

Statue of Kamehameha I, Honolulu — A271

Alaska

Landscape with Mt. McKinley — A272

Puerto Rico

La Fortaleza, San Juan — A273

# UNITED STATES

### Virgin Islands

Charlotte Amalie — A274

| 1937 | | Unwmk. | Perf. 10½x11 | |
|---|---|---|---|---|
| 799 | A271 | 3c violet | .35 | .25 |
| | | **Perf. 11x10½** | | |
| 800 | A272 | 3c violet | .40 | .25 |
| 801 | A273 | 3c bright purple | .40 | .25 |
| 802 | A274 | 3c rose violet | .40 | .25 |
| | Nos. 799-802 (4) | | 1.55 | 1.00 |

## PRESIDENTIAL ISSUE

 Benjamin Franklin A275

George Washington A276

 Martha Washington A277

John Adams A278

 Thomas Jefferson A279

James Madison A280

 White House A281

James Monroe A282

 John Q. Adams A283

Andrew Jackson A284

 Martin Van Buren A285

William H. Harrison A286

 John Tyler A287

James K. Polk A288

 Zachary Taylor A289

Millard Fillmore A290

 Franklin Pierce A291

 Abraham Lincoln A293

 Ulysses S. Grant A295

 James A. Garfield A297

 Grover Cleveland A299

 William McKinley A301

 William Howard Taft A303

 Warren G. Harding A305

 James Buchanan A292

 Andrew Johnson A294

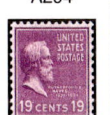 Rutherford B. Hayes A296

 Chester A. Arthur A298

 Benjamin Harrison A300

 Theodore Roosevelt A302

 Woodrow Wilson A304

 Calvin Coolidge A306

| 1938 | | | Unwmk. | |
|---|---|---|---|---|
| 803 | A275 | ½c deep orange | .30 | .25 |
| 804 | A276 | 1c green | .30 | .25 |
| b. | Booklet pane of 6 | | 2.00 | .50 |
| c. | Horiz. pair, imperf between (from booklet pane) | | — | |
| 805 | A277 | 1½c bister brown | .30 | .25 |
| b. | Horiz. pair, imperf. between | | 100.00 | 20.00 |

No. 805b unused is not precanceled. Precanceled examples are considered used and are valued in the used column. They are valued with gum; pairs without gum are worth less.

| 806 | A278 | 2c rose carmine | .30 | .25 |
| b. | Booklet pane of 6 | | 5.50 | 1.00 |
| 807 | A279 | 3c light violet | .30 | .25 |
| a. | Booklet pane of 6 | | 8.50 | 2.00 |
| b. | Horiz. pair, imperf. between | | 2,000. | |
| c. | Imperf., pair | | 3,500. | |
| d. | As "a," imperf between vert. | | 5,000. | |
| 808 | A280 | 4c brt rose pur | .75 | .25 |
| 809 | A281 | 4½c dark gray | .40 | .25 |
| 810 | A282 | 5c bright blue | .35 | .25 |
| 811 | A283 | 6c red orange | .40 | .25 |
| 812 | A284 | 7c sepia | .40 | .25 |
| 813 | A285 | 8c olive green | .40 | .25 |
| 814 | A286 | 9c rose pink | .45 | .25 |
| 815 | A287 | 10c brown red | .40 | .25 |
| 816 | A288 | 11c ultramarine | .75 | .25 |
| 817 | A289 | 12c bright mauve | 1.00 | .25 |
| 818 | A290 | 13c blue green | 1.30 | .25 |
| 819 | A291 | 14c blue | 1.00 | .25 |
| 820 | A292 | 15c blue gray | .80 | .25 |
| 821 | A293 | 16c black | 1.50 | .25 |
| 822 | A294 | 17c rose red | 1.00 | .25 |
| 823 | A295 | 18c brn car | 2.25 | .25 |
| 824 | A296 | 19c bright mauve | 1.30 | .35 |
| 825 | A297 | 20c brt bl grn | 1.20 | .25 |
| 826 | A298 | 21c dull blue | 1.30 | .25 |
| 827 | A299 | 22c vermilion | 1.20 | .40 |
| 828 | A300 | 24c gray black | 3.25 | .25 |
| 829 | A301 | 25c deep red lilac | 1.20 | .25 |
| 830 | A302 | 30c dp ultra | 3.50 | .25 |
| a. | 30c blue | | 20.00 | — |
| b. | 30c deep blue | | 375.00 | — |
| 831 | A303 | 50c mauve | 5.50 | .25 |

### FLAT PLATE PRINTING

| 1938 | | | Perf. 11 | |
|---|---|---|---|---|
| 832 | A304 | $1 pur & blk | 7.00 | .25 |
| a. | Vert. pair, imperf. horiz. | | 1,100. | |
| b. | Watermarked USIR ('51) | | 200.00 | 65.00 |
| c. | $1 red violet & black ('54) | | 6.00 | .25 |
| d. | As "c," vert. pair, imperf. horiz. | | 900.00 | |
| e. | Vert. pair, imperf. btwn. | | 7,500. | |
| f. | As "c," vert. pair, imperf. btwn. | | 10,000. | |
| g. | "c," bright magenta & black | | 70.00 | 50.00 |
| h. | As No. 832, red violet & black | | | |

No. 832c is dry printed from 400-subject flat plates on thick white paper with smooth, colorless gum.

No. 832g is the far end of the color spectrum for the No. 832c stamp, trending toward a more pinkish shade, but the shade is not pink. No. 832g is known in bright magenta and in deep bright magenta; both shades qualify as No. 832g.

No. 832h is a shade variety of the wet printing (No. 832), but the shade essentially matches the red violet normally seen on the dry printing (No. 832c).

| 833 | A305 | $2 yel grn & blk | 16.00 | 3.75 |
| 834 | A306 | $5 car & blk | 75.00 | 3.00 |
| a. | $5 red brown & black | | 3,000. | 7,000. |
| Nos. 803-834 (32) | | | 131.10 | 14.50 |

No. 834 can be chemically altered to resemble Scott 834a. No. 834a should be purchased only with competent expert certification.

### Watermarks
All stamps from No. 835 on are unwatermarked.

### CONSTITUTION RATIFICATION ISSUE

150th anniversary of the ratification of the United States Constitution.

Old Court House, Williamsburg, Va. — A307

### ROTARY PRESS PRINTING

| 1938, June 21 | | | Perf. 11x10½ | |
|---|---|---|---|---|
| 835 | A307 | 3c deep violet | .45 | .25 |

### SWEDISH-FINNISH TERCENTENARY ISSUE

Tercentenary of the founding of the Swedish and Finnish Settlement at Wilmington, Delaware.

Landing of the Swedes and Finns — A308

### FLAT PLATE PRINTING

| 1938, June 27 | | | Perf. 11 | |
|---|---|---|---|---|
| 836 | A308 | 3c brt reddsh pur | .35 | .25 |

### NORTHWEST TERRITORY SESQUICENTENNIAL

Statue Symbolizing Colonization of the West — A309

### ROTARY PRESS PRINTING

| 1938, July 15 | | | Perf. 11x10½ | |
|---|---|---|---|---|
| 837 | A309 | 3c bright rose purple | .30 | .25 |

### IOWA TERRITORY CENTENNIAL ISSUE

Old Capitol, Iowa City — A310

| 1938, Aug. 24 | | | | |
|---|---|---|---|---|
| 838 | A310 | 3c violet | .40 | .25 |

### TYPES OF 1938
### ROTARY PRESS COIL STAMPS

| 1939, Jan. 20 | | | Perf. 10 Vertically | |
|---|---|---|---|---|
| 839 | A276 | 1c green | .30 | .25 |
| 840 | A277 | 1½c bister brown | .30 | .25 |
| 841 | A278 | 2c rose carmine | .40 | .25 |
| 842 | A279 | 3c light violet | .50 | .25 |
| 843 | A280 | 4c red violet | 7.50 | .40 |
| 844 | A281 | 4½c dark gray | .70 | .40 |
| 845 | A282 | 5c bright blue | 5.00 | 2.50 |
| 846 | A283 | 6c red orange | 1.10 | .55 |
| 847 | A287 | 10c brown red | 11.00 | 1.00 |

| 1939, Jan. 27 | | | Perf. 10 Horizontally | |
|---|---|---|---|---|
| 848 | A276 | 1c green | .85 | .25 |
| 849 | A277 | 1½c bister brown | 1.25 | .30 |
| 850 | A278 | 2c rose carmine | 2.50 | .40 |
| 851 | A279 | 3c light violet | 2.50 | .40 |
| Nos. 839-851 (13) | | | 33.90 | 7.20 |

www.Philasearch.com

## GOLDEN GATE INTL. EXPOSITION, SAN FRANCISCO

"Tower of the Sun" — A311

ROTARY PRESS PRINTING
**1939, Feb. 18**    Perf. 10½x11
852   A311   3c bright purple    .30   .25

## NEW YORK WORLD'S FAIR ISSUE

Trylon and Perisphere — A312

**1939, Apr. 1**
853   A312   3c violet    .30   .25

## WASHINGTON INAUGURATION ISSUE

Sesquicentennial of the inauguration of George Washington as First President.

George Washington Taking Oath of Office — A313

FLAT PLATE PRINTING
**1939, Apr. 30**    Perf. 11
854   A313   3c bright purple    .60   .25

## BASEBALL CENTENNIAL ISSUE

Sand-lot Baseball Game — A314

ROTARY PRESS PRINTING
**1939, June 12**    Perf. 11x10½
855   A314   3c violet    1.75   .25

## PANAMA CANAL ISSUE

25th anniv. of the opening of the Panama Canal.

Theodore Roosevelt, Gen. George W. Goethals and Gaillard Cut — A315

FLAT PLATE PRINTING
**1939, Aug. 15**    Perf. 11
856   A315   3c reddish purple    .40   .25

## PRINTING TERCENTENARY ISSUE

Issued in commemoration of the 300th anniversary of printing in Colonial America. The Stephen Daye press is in the Harvard University Museum.

Stephen Daye Press — A316

ROTARY PRESS PRINTING
**1939, Sept. 25**    Perf. 10½x11
857   A316   3c violet    .30   .25

## 50th ANNIVERSARY OF STATEHOOD ISSUE

Map of North and South Dakota, Montana and Washington A317

**1939, Nov. 2**    Perf. 11x10½
858   A317   3c rose purple    .35   .25

## FAMOUS AMERICANS ISSUES
### AMERICAN AUTHORS

Washington Irving A318    James Fenimore Cooper A319

Ralph Waldo Emerson A320    Louisa May Alcott A321

Samuel L. Clemens (Mark Twain) — A322

**1940**    Perf. 10½x11
859   A318   1c bright blue green    .30   .25
860   A319   2c rose carmine    .30   .25
861   A320   3c bright purple    .30   .25
862   A321   5c ultramarine    .35   .25
863   A322   10c dark brown    1.75   1.20
    Nos. 859-863 (5)    3.00   2.20

### AMERICAN POETS

Henry W. Longfellow A323    John Greenleaf Whittier A324

James Russell Lowell A325    Walt Whitman A326

James Whitcomb Riley — A327

864   A323   1c bright blue green    .30   .25
865   A324   2c rose carmine    .30   .25
866   A325   3c bright purple    .30   .25
867   A326   5c ultramarine    .50   .25
868   A327   10c dark brown    1.75   1.25
    Nos. 864-868 (5)    3.15   2.25

### AMERICAN EDUCATORS

Horace Mann A328    Mark Hopkins A329

Charles W. Eliot A330    Frances E. Willard A331

Booker T. Washington — A332

869   A328   1c bright blue green    .30   .25
870   A329   2c rose carmine    .30   .25
871   A330   3c bright purple    .30   .25
872   A331   5c ultramarine    .50   .25
873   A332   10c dark brown    2.25   1.10
    Nos. 869-873 (5)    3.65   2.10

### AMERICAN SCIENTISTS

John James Audubon A333    Dr. Crawford W. Long A334

Luther Burbank A335    Dr. Walter Reed A336

Jane Addams — A337

874   A333   1c bright blue green    .30   .25
875   A334   2c rose carmine    .30   .25
876   A335   3c bright purple    .30   .25
877   A336   5c ultramarine    .50   .25
878   A337   10c dark brown    1.50   .85
    Nos. 874-878 (5)    2.90   1.85

### AMERICAN COMPOSERS

Stephen Collins Foster A338    John Philip Sousa A339

Victor Herbert A340    Edward MacDowell A341

Ethelbert Nevin — A342

879   A338   1c bright blue green    .30   .25
880   A339   2c rose carmine    .30   .25
881   A340   3c bright purple    .30   .25
882   A341   5c ultramarine    .50   .25
883   A342   10c dark brown    3.75   1.35
    Nos. 879-883 (5)    5.15   2.35

### AMERICAN ARTISTS

Gilbert Charles Stuart A343    James A. McNeill Whistler A344

Augustus Saint-Gaudens A345    Daniel Chester French A346

Frederic Remington — A347

884   A343   1c bright blue green    .30   .25
885   A344   2c rose carmine    .30   .25
886   A345   3c bright purple    .30   .25
887   A346   5c ultramarine    .50   .25
888   A347   10c dark brown    1.75   1.25
    Nos. 884-888 (5)    3.15   2.25

### AMERICAN INVENTORS

Eli Whitney A348    Samuel F. B. Morse A349

Cyrus Hall McCormick A350    Elias Howe A351

Alexander Graham Bell — A352

889   A348   1c brt blue grn    .30   .25
890   A349   2c rose carmine    .30   .25
891   A350   3c bright purple    .30   .25
892   A351   5c ultramarine    1.10   .25
893   A352   10c dark brown    11.00   2.00
    Nos. 889-893 (5)    13.00   3.05
    Nos. 859-893 (35)    34.00   16.05

## PONY EXPRESS, 80th ANNIV. ISSUE

Pony Express Rider — A353

**1940, Apr. 3**    Perf. 11x10½
894   A353   3c henna brown    .50   .25

## PAN AMERICAN UNION ISSUE

Founding of the Pan American Union, 50th anniv.

The Three Graces from Botticelli's "Spring" — A354

**1940, Apr. 14**    Perf. 10½x11
895   A354   3c bright rose purple    .30   .25

# UNITED STATES

## IDAHO STATEHOOD, 50th ANNIV.

Idaho Capitol, Boise — A355

**1940, July 3**      Perf. 11x10½
896 A355 3c bright mauve    .35   .25

## WYOMING STATEHOOD, 50th ANNIV.

Wyoming State Seal — A356

**1940, July 10**      Perf. 10½x11
897 A356 3c brown violet    .35   .25

## CORONADO EXPEDITION, 400th ANNIV.

"Coronado and His Captains," painted by Gerald Cassidy — A357

**1940, Sept. 7**      Perf. 11x10½
898 A357 3c bright violet    .35   .25

## NATIONAL DEFENSE ISSUE

Statue of Liberty — A358

90-millimeter Anti-aircraft Gun — A359

Torch of Enlightenment — A360

**1940, Oct. 16**
899 A358 1c bright blue green    .30   .25
   a. Vertical pair, imperf. between   600.00 —
   b. Horizontal pair, imperf. between   32.50 —
900 A359 2c rose carmine    .30   .25
   a. Horizontal pair, imperf. between   37.50 —
901 A360 3c bright mauve    .30   .25
   a. Horizontal pair, imperf. between   22.50 —
   Nos. 899-901 (3)    .90   .75

## THIRTEENTH AMENDMENT ISSUE

75th anniv. of the 13th Amendment to the Constitution abolishing slavery.

"Emancipation," Statue of Lincoln and Slave, by Thomas Ball — A361

**1940, Oct. 20**      Perf. 10½x11
902 A361 3c violet    .50   .35

## VERMONT STATEHOOD, 150th ANNIV.

Vermont Capitol, Montpelier A362

**1941, Mar. 4**      Perf. 11x10½
903 A362 3c light violet    .45   .25

## KENTUCKY STATEHOOD, 150th ANNIV.

Daniel Boone and Three Frontiersmen, from mural by Gilbert White — A363

**1942, June 1**
904 A363 3c purple    .30   .25

## WIN THE WAR ISSUE

American Eagle — A364

**1942, July 4**
905 A364 3c bright lilac    .30   .25
   b. 3c reddish purple   750.00   500.00

All examples of No. 905b are precanceled either Los Angeles, Calif., Fremont, Ohio, or St. Paul, Minn. Value is for Los Angeles, which is the more common. Value of Fremont, unused, $1,600. Value of St. Paul, used (without gum), $2,500. The stamps with St. Paul precancel are slightly less reddish than Los Angeles or Fremont, but they are in the same reddish purple/purple color family.

## CHINESE RESISTANCE ISSUE

Issued to commemorate the Chinese people's five years of resistance to Japanese aggression.

Lincoln, Sun Yat-sen & Map — A365

**1942, July 7**
906 A365 5c bright blue    4.00   .50

## ALLIED NATIONS ISSUE

Allegory of Victory — A366

**1943, Jan. 14**
907 A366 2c rose carmine    .30   .25
   **Bureau Precancels:** Denver, Baltimore.

## FOUR FREEDOMS ISSUE

A367

**1943, Feb. 12**
908 A367 1c bright blue green    .30   .25

## OVERRUN COUNTRIES ISSUE

Flag of Poland — A368

No. 909, Poland. No. 910, Czechoslovakia. No. 911, Norway. No. 912, Luxembourg. No. 913, Netherlands. No. 914, Belgium. No. 915, France. No. 916, Greece. No. 917, Yugoslavia. No. 918, Albania. No. 919, Austria. No. 920, Denmark. No. 921, Korea.

Printed by the American Bank Note Co.
**FRAMES ENGRAVED, CENTERS OFFSET LETTERPRESS ROTARY PRESS PRINTING**
Plates of 200 subjects in four panes of 50.

**1943-44**      Perf. 12
909 A368 5c blue vio, brt red & blk    .30   .25
   a. Double impression of "Poland"   200.00
   b. Double impression of black flag color and red "Poland"   —
910 A368a 5c blue vio, blue, brt red & blk    .30   .25
   a. Double impression of "Czechoslovakia"   600.00
911 A368b 5c blue vio, dk rose, dp blue & blk    .30   .25
   a. Double impression of "Norway"   225.00
912 A368c 5c blue vio, dk rose, lt blue & blk    .30   .25
   a. Double impression of "Luxembourg"   —
913 A368d 5c blue vio, dk rose, blue & blk    .30   .25
914 A368e 5c blue vio, dk rose, yel & blk    .30   .25
   a. Double impression of "Belgium"   200.00
915 A368f 5c blue vio, dp blue, dk rose & blk    .30   .25
916 A368g 5c blue vio, pale blue, grnsh blue & blk    .50   .25
917 A368h 5c blue vio, blue, dk rose & blk    .40   .25
   b. Double impression of black   250.00   200.00
918 A368i 5c blue vio, dk red & blk    .30   .25
   a. Double impression of "Albania"   800.00
919 A368j 5c blue vio, red & blk    .30   .25
   a. Double impression of "Austria"   300.00
   c. Double impression of black   —
920 A368k 5c blue vio, red & blk    .30   .25
   b. 5c blue violet, red & gray    .30   .25
921 A368m 5c blue vio, red, lt blue & gray    .30   .25
   a. Double impression of light blue (including "Korea")   —
   c. Double impression of red   — —
   Nos. 909-921 (13)   4.20   3.25

## TRANSCONTINENTAL RAILROAD ISSUE

Completion of the 1st transcontinental railroad, 75th anniv.

"Golden Spike Ceremony" Painting by John McQuarrie A369

**ENGRAVED ROTARY PRESS PRINTING**
**1944, May 10**      Perf. 11x10½
922 A369 3c violet    .30   .25

## STEAMSHIP ISSUE

1st steamship to cross the Atlantic, 125th anniv.

"Savannah" A370

**1944, May 22**
923 A370 3c violet    .30   .25

## TELEGRAPH ISSUE

1st message transmitted by telegraph, cent.

Telegraph Wires & the First Transmitted Words "What Hath God Wrought" — A371

**1944, May 24**
924 A371 3c bright purple    .30   .25

## PHILIPPINE ISSUE

Final resistance of the US and Philippine defenders on Corregidor to the Japanese invaders in 1942.

View of Corregidor A372

**1944, Sept. 27**
925 A372 3c deep violet    .30   .25

## MOTION PICTURE, 50th ANNIV.

Motion Picture Showing for the Armed Forces in South Pacific — A373

**1944, Oct. 31**
926 A373 3c deep violet    .30   .25

## FLORIDA STATEHOOD, CENTENARY

Old Florida Seal, St. Augustine Gates and State Capitol — A374

**1945, Mar. 3**
927 A374 3c bright red violet    .30   .25

## UNITED NATIONS CONFERENCE ISSUE

United Nations Conference, San Francisco, Calif.

A375

**1945, Apr. 25**
928 A375 5c ultramarine    .30   .25

## IWO JIMA (MARINES) ISSUE

Battle of Iwo Jima and honoring the achievements of the US Marines.

Marines Raising the Flag on Mt. Suribachi, Iwo Jima, from a Photograph by Joel Rosenthal — A376

**1945, July 11**      Perf. 10½x11
929 A376 3c yellow green    .30   .25

## FRANKLIN D. ROOSEVELT ISSUE

Franklin Delano Roosevelt (1882-1945).

Roosevelt and Hyde Park Home — A377

Roosevelt and "Little White House," Warm Springs, Georgia — A378

# UNITED STATES

Roosevelt and White House — A379

Roosevelt, Globe and Four Freedoms — A380

**1945-46**      Perf. 11x10½
930 A377 1c blue green .30 .25
931 A378 2c carmine rose .30 .25
932 A379 3c purple .30 .25
933 A380 5c bright blue .30 .25
     Nos. 930-933 (4) 1.20 1.00

### ARMY ISSUE
Achievements of the US Army in World War II.

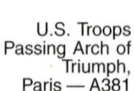
U.S. Troops Passing Arch of Triumph, Paris — A381

**1945, Sept. 28**
934 A381 3c olive .30 .25

### NAVY ISSUE
Achievements of the U.S. Navy in World War II.

U.S. Sailors — A382

**1945, Oct. 27**
935 A382 3c blue .30 .25

### COAST GUARD ISSUE
Achievements of the US Coast Guard in World War II.

Coast Guard Landing Craft and Supply Ship — A383

**1945, Nov. 10**
936 A383 3c bright blue green .30 .25

### ALFRED E. SMITH ISSUE

Alfred E. Smith — A384

**1945, Nov. 26**
937 A384 3c purple .30 .25

### TEXAS STATEHOOD, 100th ANNIV.

U.S. and Texas State Flags — A385

**1945, Dec. 29**
938 A385 3c dark blue .30 .25

### MERCHANT MARINE ISSUE
Achievements of the US Merchant Marine in World War II.

Liberty Ship Unloading Cargo — A386

**1946, Feb. 26**
939 A386 3c blue green .30 .25

### VETERANS OF WORLD WAR II ISSUE
Issued to honor all veterans of World War II.

Honorable Discharge Emblem — A387

**1946, May 9**
940 A387 3c dark violet .30 .25

### TENNESSEE STATEHOOD, 150th ANNIV.

Andrew Jackson, John Sevier & Tennessee Capitol — A388

**1946, June 1**
941 A388 3c dark violet .30 .25

### IOWA STATEHOOD, 100th ANNIV.

Iowa State Flag & Map — A389

**1946, Aug. 3**
942 A389 3c deep blue .30 .25

### SMITHSONIAN INSTITUTION ISSUE
100th anniversary of the establishment of the Smithsonian Institution, Washington, D.C.

Smithsonian Institution — A390

**1946, Aug. 10**
943 A390 3c violet brown .30 .25

### KEARNY EXPEDITION ISSUE
100th anniversary of the entry of General Stephen Watts Kearny into Santa Fe.

"Capture of Santa Fe" by Kenneth M. Chapman — A391

**1946, Oct. 16**
944 A391 3c brown violet .30 .25

### THOMAS A. EDISON ISSUE

Thomas A. Edison, Birth Centenary — A392

**1947, Feb. 11**      Perf. 10½x11
945 A392 3c bright red violet .30 .25

### JOSEPH PULITZER ISSUE

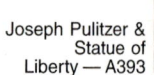
Joseph Pulitzer & Statue of Liberty — A393

**1947, Apr. 10**      Perf. 11x10½
946 A393 3c purple .30 .25

### POSTAGE STAMP CENTENARY ISSUE
Centenary of the first postage stamps issued by the United States Government

Washington & Franklin; Early and Modern Mail-carrying Vehicles — A394

**1947, May 17**
947 A394 3c deep blue .30 .25

### CENTENARY INTERNATIONAL PHILATELIC EXHIBITION ISSUE
SOUVENIR SHEET

A395

FLAT PLATE PRINTING
**1947, May 19**      Imperf.
948 A395 Pane of 2 .60 .45
   a. 5c blue, type A1 .30 .25
   b. 10c brown orange, type A2 .30 .25
Pane size varies: 96-98x66-68mm.

### DOCTORS ISSUE
Issued to honor the physicians of America.

"The Doctor," by Sir Luke Fildes — A396

ROTARY PRESS PRINTING
**1947, June 9**      Perf. 11x10½
949 A396 3c brown violet .30 .25

### UTAH ISSUE
Centenary of the settlement of Utah.

Pioneers Entering the Valley of Great Salt Lake — A397

**1947, July 24**
950 A397 3c dark violet .30 .25

### U.S. FRIGATE CONSTITUTION ISSUE
150th anniversary of the launching of the U.S. frigate Constitution ("Old Ironsides").

Naval Architect's Drawing of Frigate Constitution A398

**1947, Oct. 21**
951 A398 3c blue green .30 .25

### EVERGLADES NATIONAL PARK ISSUE
Dedication of the Everglades National Park, Florida, Dec. 6, 1947.

Great White Heron and Map of Florida — A399

**1947, Dec. 5**      Perf. 10½x11
952 A399 3c bright green .30 .25

### GEORGE WASHINGTON CARVER ISSUE
5th anniversary of the death of Dr. George Washington Carver, (1864-1943), botanist.

Dr. George Washington Carver — A400

**1948, Jan. 5**
953 A400 3c bright red violet .30 .25

### CALIFORNIA GOLD CENTENNIAL ISSUE

Sutter's Mill, Coloma, California — A401

**1948, Jan. 24**      Perf. 11x10½
954 A401 3c dark violet .30 .25

### MISSISSIPPI TERRITORY ISSUE
Mississippi Territory establishment, 150th anniv.

Map, Seal and Gov. Winthrop Sargent — A402

**1948, Apr. 7**
955 A402 3c brown violet .30 .25

### FOUR CHAPLAINS ISSUE
George L. Fox, Clark V. Poling, John P. Washington and Alexander D. Goode, the 4 chaplains who sacrificed their lives in the sinking of the S.S. Dorchester, Feb. 3, 1943.

Four Chaplains and Sinking S.S. Dorchester A403

**1948, May 28**
956 A403 3c gray black .30 .25

### WISCONSIN STATEHOOD, 100th ANNIV.

Map on Scroll & State Capitol — A404

**1948, May 29**
957 A404 3c dark violet .30 .25

### SWEDISH PIONEER ISSUE
Centenary of the coming of the Swedish pioneers to the Middle West.

Swedish Pioneer with Covered Wagon Moving Westward — A405

**1948, June 4**
958 A405 5c deep blue .30 .25

### PROGRESS OF WOMEN ISSUE
Century of progress of American Women.

Elizabeth Stanton, Carrie C. Catt & Lucretia Mott — A406

**1948, July 19**
959 A406 3c dark violet .30 .25

# UNITED STATES

### WILLIAM ALLEN WHITE ISSUE

William Allen White, Editor and Author — A407

**1948, July 31**    Perf. 10½x11
960   A407   3c bright red violet    .30   .25

### UNITED STATES-CANADA FRIENDSHIP ISSUE

Century of friendship between the US and Canada.

Niagara Railway Suspension Bridge — A408

**1948, Aug. 2**    Perf. 11x10½
961   A408   3c blue    .30   .25

### FRANCIS SCOTT KEY ISSUE

Francis Scott Key (1779-1843), Maryland lawyer and author of "The Star-Spangled Banner" (1813).

Key and American Flags of 1814 and 1948 — A409

**1948, Aug. 9**
962   A409   3c rose pink    .30   .25

### SALUTE TO YOUTH ISSUE

Issued to honor the Youth of America and to publicize "Youth Month," September, 1948.

Girl and Boy Carrying Books — A410

**1948, Aug. 11**
963   A410   3c deep blue    .30   .25

### OREGON TERRITORY ISSUE

Centenary of the establishment of Oregon Territory.

John McLoughlin, Jason Lee & Wagon on Oregon Trail — A411

**1948, Aug. 14**
964   A411   3c brown red    .30   .25

### HARLAN F. STONE ISSUE

Chief Justice Harlan Fiske Stone — A412

**1948, Aug. 25**    Perf. 10½x11
965   A412   3c bright red violet    .30   .25

### PALOMAR MOUNTAIN OBSERVATORY ISSUE

Dedication, August 30, 1948.

Observatory, Palomar Mt., Cal. — A413

**1948, Aug. 30**
966   A413   3c blue    .30   .25
   a.   Vert. pair, imperf. between    300.00

### CLARA BARTON ISSUE

Founder of the American Red Cross (1882) — A414

Designed by Charles R. Chickering.

**1948, Sept. 7**    Perf. 11x10½
967   A414   3c rose pink    .30   .25

### POULTRY INDUSTRY CENTENNIAL ISSUE

Light Brahma Rooster — A415

**1948, Sept. 9**
968   A415   3c sepia    .30   .25

### GOLD STAR MOTHERS ISSUE

Issued to honor the mothers of deceased members of the United States armed forces.

Star and Palm Frond — A416

**1948, Sept. 21**    Perf. 10½x11
969   A416   3c orange yellow    .30   .25

### FORT KEARNY ISSUE

Establishment of Fort Kearny, Neb., centenary.

Fort Kearny and Pioneer Group — A417

**1948, Sept. 22**    Perf. 11x10½
970   A417   3c violet    .30   .25

### VOLUNTEER FIREMEN ISSUE

300th anniv. of the organization of the 1st volunteer firemen in America by Peter Stuyvesant.

Peter Stuyvesant; Early and Modern Fire Engines — A418

**1948, Oct. 4**
971   A418   3c bright rose carmine    .30   .25

### INDIAN CENTENNIAL ISSUE

Centenary of the arrival in Indian Territory, later Oklahoma, of the Five Civilized Indian Tribes: Cherokee, Chickasaw, Choctaw, Muscogee and Seminole.

Map of Indian Territory & Seals of Five Tribes — A419

**1948, Oct. 15**
972   A419   3c dark brown    .30   .25

### ROUGH RIDERS ISSUE

50th anniversary of the organization of the Rough Riders of the Spanish-American War.

Statue of Capt. William O. (Bucky) O'Neill — A420

**1948, Oct. 27**
973   A420   3c violet brown    .30   .25

### JULIETTE LOW ISSUE

Low (1860-1927), founder of the Girl Scouts of America. Mrs. Low organized the 1st Girl Guides troop in 1912 at Savannah. The name was changed to Girl Scouts in 1913 and headquarters moved to New York.

Low and Girl Scout Emblem — A421

**1948, Oct. 29**
974   A421   3c blue green    .30   .25

### WILL ROGERS ISSUE

Will Rogers — A422

**1948, Nov. 4**    Perf. 10½x11
975   A422   3c bright red violet    .30   .25

Will Rogers, 1879-1935, humorist and political commentator.

### FORT BLISS CENTENNIAL ISSUE

Fort Bliss and Rocket — A423

**1948, Nov. 5**
976   A423   3c henna brown    .30   .25

### MOINA MICHAEL ISSUE

Moina Michael (1870-1944), educator who originated (1918) the Flanders Field Poppy Day idea as a memorial to the war dead.

Moina Michael and Poppy Plant — A424

**1948, Nov. 9**    Perf. 11x10½
977   A424   3c rose pink    .30   .25

### GETTYSBURG ADDRESS ISSUE

85th anniversary of Abraham Lincoln's address at Gettysburg, Pennsylvania.

Lincoln and Quotation from Gettysburg Address — A425

**1948, Nov. 19**
978   A425   3c bright blue    .30   .25

### AMERICAN TURNERS ISSUE

Formation of the American Turners Soc., cent.

Torch and American Turners' Emblem — A426

**1948, Nov. 20**    Perf. 10½x11
979   A426   3c carmine    .30   .25

### JOEL CHANDLER HARRIS ISSUE

Joel Chandler Harris — A427

**1948, Dec. 9**
980   A427   3c bright red violet    .30   .25

Harris (1848-1908), editor and author.

### MINNESOTA TERRITORY ISSUE

Establishment of Minnesota Territory, cent.

Pioneer and Red River Oxcart — A428

**1949, Mar. 3**    Perf. 11x10½
981   A428   3c blue green    .30   .25

### WASHINGTON AND LEE UNIVERSITY ISSUE

Bicentenary of Washington and Lee University.

George Washington, Robert E. Lee and University Building — A429

**1949, Apr. 12**
982   A429   3c ultramarine    .30   .25

### PUERTO RICO ELECTION ISSUE

First gubernatorial election in the Territory of Puerto Rico, Nov. 2, 1948.

Puerto Rican Farmer Holding Cogwheel and Ballot Box — A430

**1949, Apr. 27**
983   A430   3c green    .30   .25

### ANNAPOLIS TERCENTENARY ISSUE

Founding of Annapolis, Maryland, 300th anniv.

Stoddert's 1718 Map of Regions about Annapolis, Redrawn — A431

**1949, May 23**
984   A431   3c aquamarine    .30   .25

### G.A.R. ISSUE

Final encampment of the Grand Army of the Republic, Indianapolis, Aug. 28 - Sept. 1, 1949.

Union Soldier and GAR Veteran of 1949 — A432

**1949, Aug. 29**
985   A432   3c bright rose carmine    .30   .25

## UNITED STATES

### EDGAR ALLAN POE ISSUE

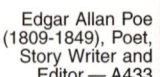

Edgar Allan Poe (1809-1849), Poet, Story Writer and Editor — A433

1949, Oct. 7     Perf. 10½x11
986   A433   3c bright red violet    .30   .25

### AMERICAN BANKERS ASSOCIATION ISSUE

75th anniv. of the formation of the Association.

Coin, Symbolizing Fields of Banking Service — A434

1950, Jan. 3     Perf. 11x10½
987   A434   3c yellow green    .30   .25

### SAMUEL GOMPERS ISSUE

Samuel Gompers (1850-1924), Labor Leader — A435

1950, Jan. 27     Perf. 10½x11
988   A435   3c bright red violet    .30   .25

### NATIONAL CAPITAL SESQUICENTENNIAL ISSUE

150th anniversary of the establishment of the National Capital, Washington, D.C.

Statue of Freedom on Capitol Dome A436

Executive Mansion A437

Supreme Court Building — A438

United States Capitol — A439

1950     Perf. 10½x11, 11x10½
989   A436   3c bright blue    .30   .25
990   A437   3c deep green    .30   .25
991   A438   3c light violet    .30   .25
992   A439   3c bright red violet    .30   .25
    Nos. 989-992 (4)    1.20   1.00

### RAILROAD ENGINEERS ISSUE

Issued to honor the Railroad Engineers of America. Stamp portrays John Luther (Casey) Jones (1864-1900), locomotive engineer killed in train wreck near Vaughn, Miss.

"Casey" Jones and Locomotives of 1900 and 1950 — A440

1950, Apr. 29     Perf. 11x10½
993   A440   3c violet brown    .30   .25

### KANSAS CITY, MISSOURI, CENTENARY ISSUE

Kansas City, Missouri, incorporation.

Kansas City Skyline, 1950 and Westport Landing, 1850 — A441

1950, June 3
994   A441   3c violet    .30   .25

### BOY SCOUTS ISSUE

Honoring the Boy Scouts of America on the occasion of the 2nd National Jamboree, Valley Forge, Pa.

Three Boys, Statue of Liberty and Scout Badge — A442

1950, June 30
995   A442   3c sepia    .30   .25

### INDIANA TERRITORY ISSUE

Establishment of Indiana Territory, 150th anniv.

Gov. William Henry Harrison & First Indiana Capitol, Vincennes A443

1950, July 4
996   A443   3c bright blue    .30   .25

### CALIFORNIA STATEHOOD ISSUE

Gold Miner, Pioneers and S.S. Oregon — A444

1950, Sept. 9
997   A444   3c yellow orange    .30   .25

### UNITED CONFEDERATE VETERANS FINAL REUNION ISSUE

Final reunion of the United Confederate Veterans, Norfolk, Virginia, May 30, 1951.

Confederate Soldier & United Confederate Veteran — A445

1951, May 30
998   A445   3c gray    .30   .25

### NEVADA CENTENNIAL ISSUE

Centenary of the settlement of Nevada.

Carson Valley, c. 1851 — A446

Designed by Charles R. Chickering.

1951, July 14
999   A446   3c light olive green    .30   .25

### LANDING OF CADILLAC ISSUE

250th anniversary of the landing of Antoine de la Mothe Cadillac at Detroit.

Detroit Skyline and Cadillac Landing — A447

1951, July 24
1000   A447   3c blue    .30   .25

### COLORADO STATEHOOD, 75th ANNIV.

Colorado Capitol and Mount of the Holy Cross — A448

1951, Aug. 1
1001   A448   3c blue violet    .30   .25

### AMERICAN CHEMICAL SOCIETY ISSUE

75th anniv. of the formation of the Society.

A.C.S. Emblem and Symbols of Chemistry A449

1951, Sept. 4
1002   A449   3c violet brown    .30   .25

### BATTLE OF BROOKLYN, 175th ANNIV.

Gen. George Washington Evacuating Army — A450

1951, Dec. 10
1003   A450   3c violet    .30   .25

### BETSY ROSS ISSUE

200th anniv. of the birth of Betsy Ross, maker of the first American flag.

Betsy Ross Showing Flag to Gen. George Washington, Robert Morris & George Ross — A451

1952, Jan. 2
1004   A451   3c carmine rose    .30   .25

### 4-H CLUB ISSUE

Farm, Club Emblem, Boy and Girl — A452

1952, Jan. 15
1005   A452   3c blue green    .30   .25

### B. & O. RAILROAD ISSUE

125th anniv. of the granting of a charter to the Baltimore and Ohio Railroad Company by the Maryland Legislature.

Charter and Three Stages of Rail Transportation A453

1952, Feb. 28
1006   A453   3c bright blue    .30   .25

### A. A. A. ISSUE

50th anniv. of the formation of the American Automobile Association.

School Girls and Safety Patrolman, Automobiles of 1902 and 1952 — A454

1952, Mar. 4
1007   A454   3c deep blue    .30   .25

### NATO ISSUE

Signing of the North Atlantic Treaty, 3rd anniv.

Torch of Liberty and Globe — A455

1952, Apr. 4
1008   A455   3c deep violet    .30   .25

### GRAND COULEE DAM ISSUE

50 years of Federal cooperation in developing the resources of rivers and streams in the West.

Spillway, Grand Coulee Dam — A456

1952, May 15
1009   A456   3c blue green    .30   .25

### LAFAYETTE ISSUE

175th anniversary of the arrival of Marquis de Lafayette in America.

Marquis de Lafayette, Flags, Cannon and Landing Party — A457

1952, June 13
1010   A457   3c bright blue    .30   .25

### MT. RUSHMORE MEMORIAL ISSUE

Dedication of the Mt. Rushmore National Memorial in the Black Hills of South Dakota, 25th anniv.

Sculptured Heads on Mt. Rushmore — A458

1952, Aug. 11     Perf. 10½x11
1011   A458   3c blue green    .30   .25

### ENGINEERING CENTENNIAL ISSUE

American Society of Civil Engineers founding.

George Washington Bridge & Covered Bridge of 1850s — A459

1952, Sept. 6     Perf. 11x10½
1012   A459   3c violet blue    .30   .25

### SERVICE WOMEN ISSUE

Women in the United States Armed Services.

Women of the Marine Corps, Army, Navy and Air Force — A460

1952, Sept. 11
1013   A460   3c deep blue    .30   .25

### GUTENBERG BIBLE ISSUE

Printing of the 1st book, the Holy Bible, from movable type, by Johann Gutenberg, 500th anniv.

Gutenberg Showing Proof to the Elector of Mainz — A461

1952, Sept. 30
1014   A461   3c violet    .30   .25

## UNITED STATES

### NEWSPAPER BOYS ISSUE

Newspaper Boy, Torch and Group of Homes — A462

**1952, Oct. 4**
1015  A462  3c violet  .30  .25

### RED CROSS ISSUE

Globe, Sun and Cross — A463

**1952, Nov. 21**
1016  A463  3c dp blue & car  .30  .25

### NATIONAL GUARD ISSUE

National Guardsman and Amphibious Landing — A464

**1953, Feb. 23**
1017  A464  3c bright blue  .30  .25

### OHIO STATEHOOD, 150th ANNIV.

Map and Ohio State Seal — A465

**1953, Mar. 2**
1018  A465  3c chocolate  .30  .25

### WASHINGTON TERRITORY ISSUE

Organization of Washington Territory, cent.

Medallion, Pioneers and Washington Scene — A466

**1953, Mar. 2**
1019  A466  3c green  .30  .25

### LOUISIANA PURCHASE, 150th ANNIV.

Monroe, Livingston and Barbé-Marbois A467

**1953, Apr. 30**
1020  A467  3c violet brown  .30  .25

### OPENING OF JAPAN CENTENNIAL ISSUE

Centenary of Commodore Matthew Calbraith Perry's negotiations with Japan, which opened her doors to foreign trade.

Commodore Perry and 1st Anchorage off Tokyo Bay — A468

**1953, July 14**
1021  A468  5c green  .30  .25

### AMERICAN BAR ASSOCIATION, 75th ANNIV.

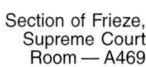
Section of Frieze, Supreme Court Room — A469

**1953, Aug. 24**
1022  A469  3c rose violet  .30  .25

### SAGAMORE HILL ISSUE

Opening of Sagamore Hill, Theodore Roosevelt's home, as a national shrine.

Home of Theodore Roosevelt — A470

**1953, Sept. 14**
1023  A470  3c yellow green  .30  .25

### FUTURE FARMERS ISSUE

25th anniversary of the organization of Future Farmers of America.

Agricultural Scene and Future Farmer — A471

**1953, Oct. 13**
1024  A471  3c deep blue  .30  .25

### TRUCKING INDUSTRY ISSUE

50th anniv. of the Trucking Industry in the US.

Truck, Farm and Distant City — A472

**1953, Oct. 27**
1025  A472  3c violet  .30  .25

### GENERAL PATTON ISSUE

Honoring Gen. George S. Patton, Jr. (1885-1945), and the armored forces of the US Army.

Gen. George S. Patton, Jr., and Tank in Action — A473

**1953, Nov. 11**
1026  A473  3c blue violet  .30  .25

### NEW YORK CITY, 300th ANNIV.

Dutch Ship in New Amsterdam Harbor — A474

**1953, Nov. 20**
1027  A474  3c bright red violet  .30  .25

### GADSDEN PURCHASE ISSUE

Centenary of James Gadsden's purchase of territory from Mexico to adjust the US-Mexico boundary.

Map and Pioneer Group — A475

**1953, Dec. 30**
1028  A475  3c copper brown  .30  .25

### COLUMBIA UNIVERSITY, 200th ANNIV.

Low Memorial Library — A476

**1954, Jan. 4**
1029  A476  3c blue  .30  .25

### Wet and Dry Printings

In 1953 the Bureau of Engraving and Printing began experiments in printing on "dry" paper (moisture content 5-10 per cent). In previous "wet" printings the paper had a moisture content of 13-35 per cent.

The new process required a thicker, stiffer paper, special types of inks and greater pressure to force the paper into the recessed plates. The "dry" printings show whiter paper, a higher sheen on the surface, feel thicker and stiffer, and the designs stand out more clearly than on the "wet" printings.

Nos. 832c and 1041 (flat plate) were the first "dry" printings to be issued of flat-plate, regular-issue stamps. No. 1063 was the first rotary-press stamp to be produced entirely by "dry" printing. Nos. QE1a, QE2a and QE3a, RF26A and RW21 (all flat plate) were the first "dry" printings of back-of-the-book issue stamps.

All postage stamps have been printed by the "dry" process since the late 1950's.

See the Scott *Specialized Catalogue of United States Stamps* for listings of the wet and dry printings and for No. 1033 on Silkote paper.

### LIBERTY ISSUE

Franklin A477

Palace of the Governors, Santa Fe — A478a 1031A

Thomas Jefferson A480

Statue of Liberty A482

The Hermitage A484

Theodore Roosevelt A486

Washington A478

Mount Vernon A479

Bunker Hill Monument, Mass. Flag, 1776 A481

Abraham Lincoln A483

James Monroe A485

Woodrow Wilson A487

A488

Statue of Liberty A489

Independence Hall — A491

Statue of Liberty — A491a

Benjamin Harrison A492

Monticello A494

Robert E. Lee A496

Susan B. Anthony A498

Alexander Hamilton — A500

The Alamo A490

John Jay A493

Paul Revere A495

John Marshall A497

Patrick Henry A499

### ROTARY PRESS PRINTING

**1954-68**   *Perf. 11x10½, 10½x11*

| | | | | |
|---|---|---|---|---|
| 1030 | A477 | ½c red org ('55) | .30 | .25 |
| 1031 | A478 | 1c dark grn | .30 | .25 |
| 1031A | A478a | 1¼c turq ('60) | .30 | .25 |
| 1032 | A479 | 1½c brn car ('56) | .30 | .25 |
| 1033 | A480 | 2c car rose | .30 | .25 |
| 1034 | A481 | 2½c gray blue ('59) | .30 | .25 |
| 1035 | A482 | 3c dp vio | .30 | .25 |
| a. | | Booklet pane of 6, June 30, 1954 | 3.50 | 1.25 |
| b. | | Horiz. pairs, imperf. btwn #1035a with foldover (two pairs recorded in two full panes) or miscut (three pairs from pane) | 5,000. | |
| e. | | Tagged ('66) | .35 | .25 |
| f. | | Imperf., pair | 3,000. | |
| g. | | Horiz. pair, imperf. between | 1,000. | |

No. 1057b measures about 19½x22mm; No. 1035f, about 18¾x22½mm.

| | | | | |
|---|---|---|---|---|
| 1036 | A483 | 4c red vio | .30 | .25 |
| b. | | Booklet pane of 6 ('58) | 2.75 | 1.25 |
| c. | | As "b," imperf. horiz. | 10,000. | |
| d. | | Horiz. pair, imperf between | 4,150. | |
| e. | | Tagged ('63) | .65 | .40 |
| 1037 | A484 | 4½c blue grn ('59) | .30 | .25 |
| 1038 | A485 | 5c dp blue | .30 | .25 |
| 1039 | A486 | 6c car ('55) | .40 | .25 |
| | | Pair with full vert. gutter btwn. | 2,750. | |
| b. | | Imperf, block of 4 (unique) | 23,000. | |
| 1040 | A487 | 7c rose car ('56) | .30 | .25 |
| a. | | dk rose car | .30 | .25 |

### FLAT PLATE PRINTING
#### Size: 22.7mm high
#### Perf. 11

| | | | | |
|---|---|---|---|---|
| 1041 | A488 | 8c dk vio blue & car | .30 | .25 |
| a. | | Double impression of carmine | 575.00 | — |

### ROTARY PRESS PRINTING
#### Size: 22.9mm high

| | | | | |
|---|---|---|---|---|
| 1041B | A488 | 8c dk vio blue & car | .40 | .25 |
| c. | | Double impression of carmine | — | |

### GIORI PRESS PRINTING
#### Redrawn design

| | | | | |
|---|---|---|---|---|
| 1042 | A489 | 8c dk vio bl & car rose ('58) | .30 | .25 |

The 8c John J. Pershing stamp, formerly No. 1042A, is now included with the regular issue of 1961-66. See No. 1214.

### ROTARY PRESS PRINTING
#### Perf. 10½x11

| | | | | |
|---|---|---|---|---|
| 1043 | A490 | 9c rose lil ('56) | .30 | .25 |
| a. | | 9c dark rose lilac | .30 | .25 |
| 1044 | A491 | 10c rose lake ('56) | .30 | .25 |
| b. | | 10c dark rose lake | .30 | .25 |
| d. | | Tagged | 2.00 | 1.00 |

### GIORI PRESS PRINTING
#### Perf. 11

| | | | | |
|---|---|---|---|---|
| 1044A | A491a | 11c car & dk vio bl ('61) | .30 | .25 |
| c. | | Tagged | 3.00 | 1.60 |

#### Perf. 11x10½, 10½x11

| | | | | |
|---|---|---|---|---|
| 1045 | A492 | 12c red ('59) | .35 | .25 |
| a. | | Tagged ('68) | .35 | .25 |
| 1046 | A493 | 15c rose lake ('58) | .60 | .25 |
| a. | | Tagged | 1.10 | .80 |
| 1047 | A494 | 20c ultra ('56) | .50 | .25 |
| | | deep bright ultra | .50 | .25 |
| 1048 | A495 | 25c grn ('58) | 1.00 | .75 |
| 1049 | A496 | 30c blk ('55) | 1.20 | .75 |
| b. | | 30c intense black | .80 | .25 |

No. 1049b is from later printings and is on a harder, whiter paper than No. 1049.

| | | | | |
|---|---|---|---|---|
| 1050 | A497 | 40c brn red ('55) | 1.75 | .25 |
| 1051 | A498 | 50c brt pur ('55) | 1.75 | .25 |
| 1052 | A499 | $1 purple ('55) | 5.00 | 1.00 |

### FLAT PLATE PRINTING
#### Perf. 11

| | | | | |
|---|---|---|---|---|
| 1053 | A500 | $5 black | 47.50 | 6.75 |
| | | Nos. 1030-1053 (27) | 65.25 | 15.00 |

### Luminescence

During 1963 quantities of certain issues (Nos. C64a, 1213b, 1213c and 1229a) were overprinted with phosphorescent coating, "tagged," for use in testing automated facing and canceling machines. Listings for tagged varieties of stamps previously issued without tagging start with Nos. 1035b and C59a.

The entire printings of Nos. 1238, 1278, 1280-1281, 1283B, 1286-1288, 1298-1305, 1323-1340, 1342-1362, 1364, and C69-C75 and all following listings, unless otherwise noted, were tagged.

Stamps tagged with zinc orthosilicate glow yellow green. Airmail stamps with calcium silicate overprint glow orange red. Both tagging overprints are activated only by shortwave ultraviolet light.

### ROTARY PRESS COIL STAMPS
#### Perf. 10 Vert., Horiz. (1¼c, 4½c)
#### 1954-80

| | | | | |
|---|---|---|---|---|
| 1054 | A478 | 1c dk grn | .60 | .25 |
| c. | | Imperf., pair | 5,000. | — |
| 1054A | A478a | 1¼c turq ('60) | .30 | .25 |
| d. | | Imperf., pair | | |

All examples of No. 1054Ad are precanceled "SEATTLE/WASH." No. 1054A with large holes exists non-precanceled as well as precanceled. The values shown are for the non-precanceled variety; precanceled stamps with large holes are quite common.

| | | | | |
|---|---|---|---|---|
| 1055 | A480 | 2c car rose | .60 | .25 |
| b. | | Tagged ('68) | .30 | .25 |
| c. | | Imperf. pair, (Bureau precanceled) | 325.00 | |
| d. | | As "b," Imperf. pair | 600.00 | |
| 1056 | A481 | 2½c gray blue ('59) | .30 | .25 |
| 1057 | A482 | 3c dp vio | .35 | .25 |
| b. | | Imperf., pair | 1,250. | 800.00 |
| d. | | Tagged ('66) | 1.00 | .50 |

No. 1057b measures about 19½x22mm; No. 1035f, about 18¾x22½mm.

| | | | | |
|---|---|---|---|---|
| 1058 | A483 | 4c red vio ('58) | .75 | .25 |
| a. | | Imperf., pair | 75.00 | 70.00 |
| 1059 | A484 | 4½c bl grn ('59) | 1.50 | 1.00 |
| 1059A | A495 | 25c grn ('65) | .50 | .30 |
| b. | | Tagged | .80 | .25 |
| d. | | Imperf., pair, tagged | 30.00 | |

Value for No. 1059Ad is for fine centering.

### NEBRASKA TERRITORY ISSUE
Establishment of the Nebraska Territory, centenary.

Mitchell Pass, Scotts Bluff & "The Sower," by Lee Lawrie — A507

#### ROTARY PRESS PRINTING
**1954, May 7**    Perf. 11x10½
1060    A507    3c violet    .30    .25

### KANSAS TERRITORY ISSUE
Establishment of the Kansas Territory, centenary.

Wheat Field and Pioneer Wagon Train — A508

**1954, May 31**
1061    A508    3c brown orange    .30    .25

### GEORGE EASTMAN ISSUE

George Eastman (1854-1932), Inventor & Philanthropist — A509

**1954, July 12**    Perf. 10½x11
1062    A509    3c violet brown    .30    .25

### LEWIS AND CLARK EXPEDITION
150th anniv. of the Lewis and Clark expedition.

Landing of Lewis and Clark — A510

**1954, July 28**    Perf. 11x10½
1063    A510    3c violet brown    .30    .25

### PENNSYLVANIA ACADEMY OF THE FINE ARTS ISSUE
150th anniversary of the founding of the Pennsylvania Academy of the Fine Arts, Philadelphia.

Charles Willson Peale in his Museum, Self-portrait — A511

**1955, Jan. 15**    Perf. 10½x11
1064    A511    3c rose brown    .30    .25

### LAND GRANT COLLEGES ISSUE
Centenary of the founding of Michigan State College and Pennsylvania State University, first of the land grant institutions.

Open Book and Symbols of Subjects Taught — A512

**1955, Feb. 12**    Perf. 11x10½
1065    A512    3c green    .30    .25

### ROTARY INTERNATIONAL, 50th ANNIV.

Torch, Globe and Rotary Emblem — A513

**1955, Feb. 23**
1066    A513    8c deep blue    .30    .25

### ARMED FORCES RESERVE ISSUE

Marine, Coast Guard, Army, Navy, & Air Force Personnel — A514

**1955, May 21**
1067    A514    3c bright red violet    .30    .25

### NEW HAMPSHIRE ISSUE
Sesquicentennial of the discovery of the "Old Man of the Mountains."

Great Stone Face — A515

**1955, June 21**    Perf. 10½x11
1068    A515    3c green    .30    .25

### SOO LOCKS ISSUE
Centenary of the opening of the Soo Locks.

Map of Great Lakes and Two Steamers — A516

**1955, June 28**    Perf. 11x10½
1069    A516    3c blue    .30    .25

### ATOMS FOR PEACE ISSUE
Issued to promote an Atoms for Peace policy.

Atomic Energy Encircling the Hemispheres A517

**1955, July 28**
1070    A517    3c deep blue    .30    .25

### FORT TICONDEROGA ISSUE
Bicentenary of Fort Ticonderoga, New York.

Map of the Fort, Ethan Allen and Artillery — A518

**1955, Sept. 18**
1071    A518    3c light brown    .30    .25

### ANDREW W. MELLON ISSUE

Andrew W. Mellon — A519

**1955, Dec. 20**    Perf. 10½x11
1072    A519    3c rose carmine    .30    .25

Mellon, U.S. Sec. of the Treasury (1921-32), financier and art collector.

### BENJAMIN FRANKLIN ISSUE
250th anniv. of the birth of Benjamin Franklin.

"Franklin Taking Electricity from the Sky," by Benjamin West — A520

**1956, Jan. 17**
1073    A520    3c bright carmine    .30    .25

### BOOKER T. WASHINGTON ISSUE
Washington (1856-1915), black educator, founder and head of Tuskegee Institute in Alabama.

Log Cabin — A521

**1956, Apr. 5**    Perf. 11x10½
1074    A521    3c deep blue    .30    .25

### FIFTH INTERNATIONAL PHILATELIC EXHIBITION ISSUES
FIPEX, New York City, Apr. 28 - May 6, 1956.

# UNITED STATES

## SOUVENIR SHEET

A522

### FLAT PLATE PRINTING
**1956, Apr. 28**     *Imperf.*
1075 A522 Pane of 2    1.20 1.50
   a.   A482 3c deep violet   .75 .60
   b.   A488 8c dark violet blue & carmine   .85 .75

No. 1075 measures 108x73mm. Nos. 1075a and 1075b measure 24x28mm.
Inscriptions printed in dark violet blue; scrolls and stars in carmine.

New York Coliseum & Columbus Monument — A523

### ROTARY PRESS PRINTING
**1956, Apr. 30**     *Perf. 11x10½*
1076 A523 3c deep violet    .30 .25

## WILDLIFE CONSERVATION ISSUE

Issued to emphasize the importance of Wildlife Conservation in America.

Wild Turkey — A524

Pronghorn Antelope — A525

King Salmon — A526

**1956**
1077 A524 3c rose lake    .30 .25
1078 A525 3c brown    .30 .25
1079 A526 3c blue green    .30 .25
  Nos. 1077-1079 (3)    .90 .75

## PURE FOOD AND DRUG LAWS, 50th ANNIV.

Harvey W. Wiley — A527

**1956, June 27**     *Perf. 10½x11*
1080 A527 3c dark blue green    .30 .25

## WHEATLAND ISSUE

President Buchanan's Home, "Wheatland," Lancaster, PA — A528

**1956, Aug. 5**
1081 A528 3c black brown    .30 .25

## LABOR DAY ISSUE

Mosaic, AFL-CIO Headquarters — A529

**1956, Sept. 3**     *Perf. 10½x11*
1082 A529 3c deep blue    .30 .25

## NASSAU HALL ISSUE

200th anniv. of Nassau Hall, Princeton University.

Nassau Hall, Princeton, NJ — A530

**1956, Sept. 22**
1083 A530 3c black, *orange*    .30 .25

## DEVILS TOWER ISSUE

Issued to commemorate the 50th anniversary of the Federal law providing for protection of American natural antiquities. Devils Tower National Monument, Wyoming, is an outstanding example.

Devils Tower — A531

**1956, Sept. 24**     *Perf. 10½x11*
1084 A531 3c violet    .30 .25

## CHILDREN'S ISSUE

Issued to promote friendship among the children of the world.

Children of the World — A532

**1956, Dec. 15**     *Perf. 11x10½*
1085 A532 3c dark blue    .30 .25

## ALEXANDER HAMILTON (1755-1804)

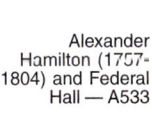 
Alexander Hamilton (1757-1804) and Federal Hall — A533

**1957, Jan. 11**
1086 A533 3c rose red    .30 .25

## POLIO ISSUE

Honoring "those who helped fight polio," and on for 20th anniv. of the Natl. Foundation for Infantile Paralysis and the March of Dimes.

Allegory — A534

**1957, Jan. 15**     *Perf. 10½x11*
1087 A534 3c red lilac    .30 .25

## COAST AND GEODETIC SURVEY ISSUE

150th anniversary of the establishment of the Coast and Geodetic Survey.

Flag of Coast and Geodetic Survey and Ships at Sea — A535

**1957, Feb. 11**     *Perf. 11x10½*
1088 A535 3c dark blue    .30 .25

## ARCHITECTS ISSUE

American Institute of Architects, centenary.

Corinthian Capital and Mushroom Type Head & Shaft — A536

**1957, Feb. 23**
1089 A536 3c red lilac    .30 .25

## STEEL INDUSTRY ISSUE

Centenary of the steel industry in America.

American Eagle and Pouring Ladle — A537

**1957, May 22**     *Perf. 10½x11*
1090 A537 3c bright ultramarine    .30 .25

## INTERNATIONAL NAVAL REVIEW ISSUE

Issued to commemorate the International Naval Review and the Jamestown Festival.

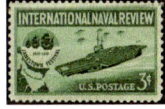
Aircraft Carrier and Jamestown Festival Emblem — A538

**1957, June 10**     *Perf. 11x10½*
1091 A538 3c blue green    .30 .25

## OKLAHOMA STATEHOOD, 50th ANNIV.

Map of Oklahoma, Arrow and Atom Diagram — A539

**1957, June 14**
1092 A539 3c dark blue    .30 .25

## SCHOOL TEACHERS ISSUE

Teacher and Pupils — A540

**1957, July 1**
1093 A540 3c rose lake    .30 .25

## FLAG ISSUE

"Old Glory" (48 Stars) — A541

### GIORI PRESS PRINTING
**1957, July 4**     *Perf. 11*
1094 A541 4c dark blue & deep carmine    .30 .25

## SHIP BUILDING ISSUE

350th anniversary of shipbuilding in America.

"Virginia of Sagadahock" and Seal of Maine — A542

### ROTARY PRESS PRINTING
**1957, Aug. 15**     *Perf. 10½x11*
1095 A542 3c deep violet    .30 .25

## CHAMPION OF LIBERTY ISSUE

Magsaysay (1907-57), Pres. of the Philippines.

Ramon Magsaysay, (1907-1957), Philippines President — A543

### GIORI PRESS PRINTING
**1957, Aug. 31**     *Perf. 11*
1096 A543 8c car, ultra & ocher    .30 .25

For other Champion of Liberty issues, see Nos. 1110-1111, 1117-1118, 1125-1126, 1136-1137, 1147-1148, 1159-1160, 1165-1166, 1168-1169, 1174-1175.

## LAFAYETTE BICENTENARY ISSUE

Marquis de Lafayette — A544

**1957, Sept. 6**     *Perf. 10½x11*
1097 A544 3c rose lake    .30 .25

## WILDLIFE CONSERVATION ISSUE

Issued to emphasize the importance of Wildlife Conservation in America.

Whooping Cranes — A545

### GIORI PRESS PRINTING
**1957, Nov. 22**     *Perf. 11*
1098 A545 3c blue, ocher & green    .30 .25

## RELIGIOUS FREEDOM ISSUE

300th anniv. of the Flushing Remonstrance.

Bible, Hat and Quill Pen — A546

### ROTARY PRESS PRINTING
**1957, Dec. 27**     *Perf. 10½x11*
1099 A546 3c black    .30 .25

## GARDENING HORTICULTURE ISSUE

Issued to honor the garden clubs of America and in connection with the centenary of the birth of Liberty Hyde Bailey, horticulturist.

# UNITED STATES

"Bountiful Earth" — A547

**1958, Mar. 15**
1100 A547 3c green .30 .25

### BRUSSELS EXHIBITION ISSUE
Issued in honor of the opening of the Universal and International Exhibition at Brussels, April 17.

U.S. Pavilion at Brussels — A551

**1958, Apr. 17** Perf. 11x10½
1104 A551 3c deep claret .30 .25

### JAMES MONROE ISSUE

James Monroe, by Gilbert Stuart — A552

**1958, Apr. 28**
1105 A552 3c purple .30 .25

### MINNESOTA STATEHOOD, 100th ANNIV.

Minnesota Lakes and Pines — A553

**1958, May 11**
1106 A553 3c green .30 .25

### GEOPHYSICAL YEAR ISSUE
International Geophysical Year, 1957-58.

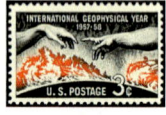
Solar Disc and Hands from Michelangelo's "Creation of Adam" — A554

GIORI PRESS PRINTING
**1958, May 31** Perf. 11
1107 A554 3c black & red orange .30 .25

### GUNSTON HALL ISSUE
Issued for the bicentenary of Gunston Hall and to honor George Mason, author of the Constitution of Virginia and the Virginia Bill of Rights.

Gunston Hall, Virginia — A555

ROTARY PRESS PRINTING
**1958, June 12** Perf. 11x10½
1108 A555 3c light green .30 .25

### MACKINAC BRIDGE ISSUE
Dedication of Mackinac Bridge, Michigan.

Mackinac Bridge — A556

**1958, June 25** Perf. 10½x11
1109 A556 3c brt greenish blue .30 .25

### CHAMPION OF LIBERTY ISSUE
Simon Bolívar, South American freedom fighter.

Simon Bolivar — A557

**1958, July 24**
1110 A557 4c olive bister .30 .25

GIORI PRESS PRINTING
Perf. 11
1111 A557 8c car, ultra & ocher .30 .25

### ATLANTIC CABLE CENTENNIAL ISSUE
Centenary of the Atlantic Cable, linking the Eastern and Western hemispheres.

Neptune, Globe and Mermaid — A558

ROTARY PRESS PRINTING
**1958, Aug. 15** Perf. 11x10½
1112 A558 4c reddish purple .30 .25

### LINCOLN SESQUICENTENNIAL ISSUE
Sesquicentennial of the birth of Abraham Lincoln. No. 1114 also for the centenary of the founding of Cooper Union, New York City. No. 1115 marks the centenary of the Lincoln-Douglas Debates.

Lincoln, by George Healy A559    Lincoln, by Gutzon Borglum A560

Abraham Lincoln and Stephen A. Douglas Debating — A561

Lincoln, by Daniel Chester French — A562

**1958-59** Perf. 10½x11
1113 A559 1c green ('59) .30 .25
1114 A560 3c dark rose ('59) .30 .25
    Perf. 11x10½
1115 A561 4c sepia .30 .25
1116 A562 4c dark blue ('59) .30 .25
    Nos. 1113-1116 (4) 1.20 1.00

### CHAMPION OF LIBERTY ISSUE
Lajos Kossuth, Hungarian freedom fighter.

Lajos Kossuth, (1802-1892) — A563

**1958, Sept. 19** Perf. 10½x11
1117 A563 4c green .30 .25

GIORI PRESS PRINTING
Perf. 11
1118 A563 8c car, ultra & ocher .30 .25

### FREEDOM OF PRESS ISSUE
Honoring Journalism and freedom of the press in connection with the 50th anniv. of the 1st School of Journalism at the University of Missouri.

Early Press and Hand Holding Quill — A564

ROTARY PRESS PRINTING
**1958, Sept. 22** Perf. 10½x11
1119 A564 4c black .30 .25

### OVERLAND MAIL ISSUE
Centenary of Overland Mail Service.

Mail Coach and Map of Southwest U.S. — A565

**1958, Oct. 10** Perf. 11x10½
1120 A565 4c crimson rose .30 .25

### NOAH WEBSTER ISSUE
Webster (1758-1843), lexicographer and author.

Noah Webster — A566

**1958, Oct. 16** Perf. 10½x11
1121 A566 4c dark carmine rose .30 .25

### FOREST CONSERVATION ISSUE
Issued to publicize forest conservation and the protection of natural resources and to honor Theodore Roosevelt, a leading forest conservationist, on the centenary of his birth.

Forest Scene — A567

GIORI PRESS PRINTING
**1958, Oct. 27** Perf. 11
1122 A567 4c green, yellow & brown .30 .25

### FORT DUQUESNE ISSUE
Bicentennial of Fort Duquesne (Fort Pitt) at future site of Pittsburgh.

Occupation of Fort Duquesne — A568

ROTARY PRESS PRINTING
**1958, Nov. 25** Perf. 11x10½
1123 A568 4c blue .30 .25

### OREGON STATEHOOD, 100th ANNIV.

Covered Wagon and Mt. Hood — A569

**1959, Feb. 14**
1124 A569 4c blue green .30 .25

### CHAMPION OF LIBERTY ISSUE
San Martin, So. American soldier and statesman.

José de San Martin — A570

**1959, Feb. 25** Perf. 10½x11
1125 A570 4c blue .30 .25
  a. Horiz. pair, imperf. between 750.00

GIORI PRESS PRINTING
Perf. 11
1126 A570 8c car, ultra & ocher .30 .25

### NATO ISSUE
North Atlantic Treaty Organization, 10th anniv.

NATO Emblem — A571

ROTARY PRESS PRINTING
**1959, Apr. 1** Perf. 10½x11
1127 A571 4c blue .30 .25

### ARCTIC EXPLORATIONS ISSUE
Conquest of the Arctic by land by Rear Admiral Robert Edwin Peary in 1909 and by sea by the submarine "Nautilus" in 1958.

North Pole, Dog Sled and "Nautilus" — A572

**1959, Apr. 6** Perf. 11x10½
1128 A572 4c brt grnsh blue .30 .25

### WORLD PEACE THROUGH WORLD TRADE ISSUE
Issued in conjunction with the 17th Congress of the International Chamber of Commerce, Washington, D.C., April 19-25.

Globe and Laurel — A573

**1959, Apr. 20**
1129 A573 8c rose lake .30 .25

### SILVER CENTENNIAL ISSUE
Discovery of silver at the Comstock Lode, Nevada.

Henry Comstock at Mount Davidson Site — A574

**1959, June 8**
1130 A574 4c black .30 .25

### ST. LAWRENCE SEAWAY ISSUE
Opening of the St. Lawrence Seaway.

Great Lakes, Maple Leaf and Eagle Emblems — A575

GIORI PRESS PRINTING
**1959, June 26** Perf. 11
1131 A575 4c red & dark blue .30 .25
  See Canada No. 387.

### 49-STAR FLAG ISSUE

U.S. Flag, 1959 — A576

# UNITED STATES

**1959, July 4**
1132 A576 4c ocher, dark blue & deep carmine .30 .25

## SOIL CONSERVATION ISSUE

Issued as a tribute to farmers and ranchers who use soil and water conservation measures.

Modern Farm — A577

**1959, Aug. 26**
1133 A577 4c blue, green & ocher .30 .25

## PETROLEUM INDUSTRY ISSUE

Centenary of the completion of the nation's first oil well at Titusville, Pa.

Oil Derrick — A578

### ROTARY PRESS PRINTING
**1959, Aug. 27** Perf. 10½x11
1134 A578 4c brown .30 .25

## DENTAL HEALTH ISSUE

Issued to publicize Dental Health and for the centenary of the American Dental Association.

Children — A579

**1959, Sept. 14** Perf. 11x10½
1135 A579 4c green .30 .25

## CHAMPION OF LIBERTY ISSUE

Ernst Reuter, Mayor of Berlin, 1948-53.

Ernst Reuter — A580

**1959, Sept. 29** Perf. 10½x11
1136 A580 4c gray .30 .25

### GIORI PRESS PRINTING
Perf. 11
1137 A580 8c car, ultra & ocher .30 .25
  a. Ocher missing (EP) 3,000.
  b. Ultramarine missing (EP) 3,750.
  c. Ocher & ultramarine missing (EP) 4,000.
  d. All colors missing (EP) 2,000.

## DR. EPHRAIM McDOWELL ISSUE

Honoring McDowell (1771-1830) on the 150th anniv. of the 1st successful ovarian operation in the US, performed at Danville, Ky., 1809.

Dr. Ephraim McDowell — A581

### ROTARY PRESS PRINTING
**1959, Dec. 3** Perf. 10½x11
1138 A581 4c rose lake .30 .25
  a. Vert. pair, imperf. btwn. 375.00
  b. Vert. pair, imperf. horiz. 200.00

## AMERICAN CREDO ISSUE

Issued to re-emphasize the ideals upon which America was founded and to honor those great Americans who wrote or uttered the credos.

Quotation from Washington's Farewell Address, 1796 — A582

Benjamin Franklin Quotation — A583

Thomas Jefferson Quotation — A584

Francis Scott Key Quotation — A585

Abraham Lincoln Quotation — A586

Patrick Henry Quotation — A587

Designed by Frank Conley.

### GIORI PRESS PRINTING
Plates of 200 subjects in four panes of 50.

**1960-61** Perf. 11
1139 A582 4c dk vio bl & car .30 .25
1140 A583 4c ol bister & grn .30 .25
1141 A584 4c gray & vermilion .30 .25
1142 A585 4c car & dark blue .30 .25
1143 A586 4c magenta & green .30 .25
1144 A587 4c green & brown .30 .25
  Nos. 1139-1144 (6) 1.80 1.50
Issued: 1/20; 3/31; 5/8; 9/14; 11/19; 1/11/61.

## BOY SCOUT JUBILEE ISSUE

50th anniv. of the Boy Scouts of America.

Boy Scout Giving Scout Sign — A588

**1960, Feb. 8**
1145 A588 4c red, dark blue & dark bister .30 .25

## OLYMPIC WINTER GAMES ISSUE

Opening of the 8th Olympic Winter Games, Squaw Valley, Feb. 18-29, 1960.

Olympic Rings and Snowflake — A589

### ROTARY PRESS PRINTING
**1960, Feb. 18** Perf. 10½x11
1146 A589 4c dull blue .30 .25

## CHAMPION OF LIBERTY ISSUE

Issued to honor Thomas G. Masaryk, founder and president of Czechoslovakia (1918-35), on the 110th anniversary of his birth.

Thomas G. Masaryk — A590

**1960, Mar. 7**
1147 A590 4c blue .30 .25
  a. Vert. pair, imperf. between 1,900.

### GIORI PRESS PRINTING
Perf. 11
1148 A590 8c car, ultra & ocher .30 .25
  a. Horiz. pair, imperf. between —

## WORLD REFUGEE YEAR ISSUE

World Refugee Year, July 1, 1959-June 30, 1960.

Refugee Family Walking Toward New Life — A591

### ROTARY PRESS PRINTING
**1960, Apr. 7** Perf. 11x10½
1149 A591 4c gray black .30 .25

## WATER CONSERVATION ISSUE

Issued to stress the importance of water conservation and to commemorate the 7th Watershed Congress, Washington, D.C.

Water, from Watershed to Consumer — A592

### GIORI PRESS PRINTING
**1960, Apr. 18** Perf. 11
1150 A592 4c dk bl, brn org & grn .30 .25
  a. Brown orange missing (EP) 2,750.

## SEATO ISSUE

South-East Asia Treaty Organization and for the SEATO Conf., Washington, D.C., May 31-June 3.

SEATO Emblem — A593

### ROTARY PRESS PRINTING
**1960, May 31** Perf. 10½x11
1151 A593 4c blue .30 .25
  a. Vertical pair, imperf. between 125.00

## AMERICAN WOMAN ISSUE

Issued to pay tribute to American women and their accomplishments in civic affairs, education, arts and industry.

Mother and Daughter — A594

**1960, June 2** Perf 11x10½
1152 A594 4c deep violet .30 .25

## 50-STAR FLAG ISSUE

U.S. Flag, 1960 — A595

### GIORI PRESS PRINTING
**1960, July 4** Perf. 11
1153 A595 4c dark blue & red .30 .25

## PONY EXPRESS CENTENNIAL ISSUE

Pony Express Rider — A596

### ROTARY PRESS PRINTING
**1960, July 19** Perf. 11x10½
1154 A596 4c sepia .30 .25

## EMPLOY THE HANDICAPPED ISSUE

Promoting the employment of the physically handicapped and publicizing the 8th World Congress of the Intl. Soc. for the Welfare of Cripples, New York City.

Man in Wheelchair Operating Drill Press — A597

**1960, Aug. 28** Perf. 10½x11
1155 A597 4c dark blue .30 .25

## WORLD FORESTRY CONGRESS ISSUE

5th World Forestry Cong., Seattle, Wash., Aug. 29-Sept. 10.

5th World Forestry Congress Seal — A598

**1960, Aug. 29**
1156 A598 4c green .30 .25

## MEXICAN INDEPENDENCE, 150th ANNIV.

A599

### GIORI PRESS PRINTING
**1960, Sept. 16** Perf. 11
1157 A599 4c green & rose red .30 .25
See Mexico No. 910.

## US-JAPAN TREATY ISSUE

Centenary of the United States-Japan Treaty of Amity and Commerce.

A600

**1960, Sept. 28**
1158 A600 4c blue & pink .30 .25

## CHAMPION OF LIBERTY ISSUE

Jan Paderewski, Polish statesman and musician.

Ignacy Jan Paderewski — A601

### ROTARY PRESS PRINTING
**1960, Oct. 8** Perf. 10½x11
1159 A601 4c blue .30 .25

### GIORI PRESS PRINTING
Perf. 11
1160 A601 8c car, ultra & ocher .30 .25

## SENATOR TAFT MEMORIAL ISSUE

Senator Robert A. Taft (1889-1953) of Ohio.

Robert A. Taft — A602

**ROTARY PRESS PRINTING**
**1960, Oct. 10**     Perf. 10½x11
1161   A602   4c dull violet     .30   .25

### WHEELS OF FREEDOM ISSUE
Issued to honor the automotive industry and in connection with the National Automobile Show, Detroit, Oct. 15-23.

Globe and Steering Wheel with Tractor, Car and Truck — A603

**1960, Oct. 15**     Perf. 11x10½
1162   A603   4c dark blue     .30   .25

### BOYS' CLUBS OF AMERICA ISSUE
Boys' Clubs of America movement, centenary.

Profile of a Boy — A604

**GIORI PRESS PRINTING**
**1960, Oct. 18**     Perf. 11
1163   A604   4c indigo, slate & rose red     .30   .25

### FIRST AUTOMATED POST OFFICE IN THE US ISSUE
Publicizing the opening of the 1st automated post office in the US at Providence, R.I.

Architect's Sketch of New Post Office, Providence, RI — A605

**1960, Oct. 20**
1164   A605   4c dark blue & carmine     .30   .25
   a.   Red missing (PS)     250.00

### CHAMPION OF LIBERTY ISSUE
Baron Karl Gustaf Emil Mannerheim (1867-1951), Marshal and President of Finland.

Baron Gustaf Emil Mannerheim — A606

**ROTARY PRESS PRINTING**
**1960, Oct. 26**     Perf. 10½x11
1165   A606   4c blue     .30   .25

**GIORI PRESS PRINTING**
Plates of 288 subjects in four panes of 72 each.
    Perf. 11
1166   A606   8c car, ultra & ocher     .30   .25

### CAMP FIRE GIRLS ISSUE
50th anniv. of the Camp Fire Girls' movement and in connection with the Golden Jubilee Convention celebration of the Camp Fire Girls.

Camp Fire Girls Emblem — A607

**GIORI PRESS PRINTING**
**1960, Nov. 1**     Perf. 11
1167   A607   4c dark blue & bright red     .30   .25

### CHAMPION OF LIBERTY ISSUE
Giuseppe Garibaldi (1807-1882), Italian patriot and freedom fighter.

Giuseppe Garibaldi (1807-1882) — A608

**ROTARY PRESS PRINTING**
**1960, Nov. 2**     Perf. 10½x11
1168   A608   4c green     .30   .25

**GIORI PRESS PRINTING**
    Perf. 11
1169   A608   8c car, ultra & ocher     .30   .25

### SENATOR GEORGE MEMORIAL ISSUE
Walter F. George (1878-1957) of Georgia.

Walter F. George (1878-1957) — A609

**ROTARY PRESS PRINTING**
**1960, Nov. 5**     Perf. 10½x11
1170   A609   4c dull violet     .30   .25

### ANDREW CARNEGIE ISSUE
Carnegie (1835-1919), industrialist & philanthropist.

Andrew Carnegie — A610

**1960, Nov. 25**
1171   A610   4c deep claret     .30   .25

### JOHN FOSTER DULLES MEMORIAL ISSUE
Dulles (1888-1959), Secretary of State (1953-59).

John Foster Dulles — A611

**1960, Dec. 6**
1172   A611   4c dull violet     .30   .25

### ECHO I — COMMUNICATIONS FOR PEACE ISSUE
World's 1st communications satellite, Echo I, placed in orbit by the Natl. Aeronautics and Space Admin., Aug. 12, 1960.

Radio Waves Connecting Echo I and Earth — A612

**1960, Dec. 15**     Perf. 11x10½
1173   A612   4c deep violet     .30   .25

### CHAMPION OF LIBERTY ISSUE
Mohandas K. Gandhi, leader in India's struggle for independence.

Mahatma Gandhi — A613

**GIORI PRESS PRINTING**
**1961, Jan. 26**     Perf. 10½x11
1174   A613   4c red orange     .30   .25

**GIORI PRESS PRINTING**
    Perf. 11
1175   A613   8c car, ultra & ocher     .30   .25

### RANGE CONSERVATION ISSUE
Issued to stress the importance of range conservation and to commemorate the meeting of the American Society of Range Management. "The Trail Boss" from a drawing by Charles M. Russell is the Society's emblem.

The Trail Boss and Modern Range — A614

**1961, Feb. 2**     Perf. 11
1176   A614   4c blue, slate & brown orange     .30   .25

### HORACE GREELEY ISSUE

Horace Greeley (1811-1872), Publisher and Editor — A615

**ROTARY PRESS PRINTING**
**1961, Feb. 3**     Perf. 10½x11
1177   A615   4c dull violet     .30   .25

### CIVIL WAR CENTENNIAL ISSUE
Centenaries of the firing on Fort Sumter (No. 1178), the Battle of Shiloh (No. 1179), the Battle of Gettysburg (No. 1180), the Battle of the Wilderness (No. 1181) and the surrender at Appomattox (No. 1182).

Sea Coast Gun of 1861 — A616

Rifleman at Shiloh, 1862 — A617

Blue and Gray at Gettysburg, 1863 — A618

Battle of the Wilderness, 1864 A619

Appomattox, 1865 A620

**1961-65**     Perf. 11x10½
1178   A616   4c light green     .30   .25
1179   A617   4c black, peach blossom     .30   .25

### GIORI PRESS PRINTING
Plates of 200 subjects in four panes of 50.
    Perf. 11
1180   A618   5c gray & blue     .30   .25
1181   A619   5c dk red & black     .30   .25
1182   A620   5c Prus. blue & blk     .30   .25
   a.   Horiz. pair, imperf. vert.     3,500.
    Nos. 1178-1182 (5)     1.50   1.25
Issued: #1178-1182, 4/12; 4/7/62; 7/1/63; 5/5/64; 4/9/65.

### KANSAS STATEHOOD, 100th ANNIV.

Sunflower, Pioneer Couple and Stockade — A621

**1961, May 10**     Perf. 11
1183   A621   4c brown, dark red & green, yellow     .30   .25

### SENATOR NORRIS ISSUE

Norris and Norris Dam, Tenn. — A622

**ROTARY PRESS PRINTING**
**1961, July 11**     Perf. 11x10½
1184   A622   4c blue green     .30   .25

### NAVAL AVIATION, 50th ANNIV.

Navy's First Plane (Curtiss A-1 of 1911) and Naval Air Wings — A623

**1961, Aug. 20**
1185   A623   4c blue     .30   .25

### WORKMEN'S COMPENSATION ISSUE
50th anniv. of the 1st successful Workmen's Compensation Law, enacted by the Wisconsin legislature.

Scales of Justice, Factory, Worker and Family — A624

**1961, Sept. 4**     Perf. 10½x11
1186   A624   4c ultramarine, grayish     .30   .25

### FREDERIC REMINGTON ISSUE
Remington (1861-1909), artist of the West. The design is from an oil painting, Amon Carter Museum of Western Art, Fort Worth, Texas.

Remington's "Smoke Signal" — A625

**GIORI PRESS PRINTING**
**1961, Oct. 4**     Perf. 11
1187   A625   4c multicolored     .30   .25

### REPUBLIC OF CHINA ISSUE
50th anniversary of the Republic of China.

# UNITED STATES

Sun Yat-sen — A626

**ROTARY PRESS PRINTING**
**1961, Oct. 10**    Perf. 10½x11
1188   A626   4c blue     .35   .25

## NAISMITH — BASKETBALL ISSUE

Honoring basketball and James Naismith (1861-1939), Canada-born director of physical education, who invented the game in 1891 at Y.M.C.A. College, Springfield, Mass.

Basketball — A627

**1961, Nov. 6**
1189   A627   4c brown     .30   .25

## NURSING ISSUE

Issued to honor the nursing profession.

Student Nurse Lighting Candle — A628

**GIORI PRESS PRINTING**
**1961, Dec. 28**    Perf. 11
1190   A628   4c bl, grn, org & blk     .30   .25

## NEW MEXICO STATEHOOD, 50th ANNIV.

Shiprock — A629

**1962, Jan. 6**
1191   A629   4c lt. blue, maroon & bister     .30   .25

## ARIZONA STATEHOOD, 50th ANNIV.

Giant Saguaro Cactus — A630

**1962, Feb. 14**
1192   A630   4c carmine, violet blue & green     .30   .25

## PROJECT MERCURY ISSUE

1st orbital flight of a US astronaut, Lt. Col. John H. Glenn, Jr., Feb. 20, 1962.

"Friendship 7" Capsule and Globe — A631

**1962, Feb. 20**
1193   A631   4c dark blue & yellow     .30   .25
Imperfs. are printers waste.

## MALARIA ERADICATION ISSUE

World Health Organization's drive to eradicate malaria.

Great Seal of U.S. and WHO Symbol — A632

**1962, Mar. 30**
1194   A632   4c blue & bister     .30   .25

## CHARLES EVANS HUGHES ISSUE

Hughes (1862-1948), Governor of New York, Chief Justice of the US.

Charles Evans Hughes — A633

**ROTARY PRESS PRINTING**
**1962, Apr. 11**    Perf. 10½x11
1195   A633   4c black, buff     .30   .25

## SEATTLE WORLD'S FAIR ISSUE

"Century 21" International Exposition, Seattle, Wash., Apr. 21-Oct. 21.

Space Needle and Monorail — A634

**GIORI PRESS PRINTING**
**1962, Apr. 25**    Perf. 11
1196   A634   4c red & dark blue     .30   .25

## LOUISIANA STATEHOOD, 150th ANNIV.

Riverboat on the Mississippi A635

**1962, Apr. 30**
1197   A635   4c blue, dark slate green & red     .30   .25

## HOMESTEAD ACT, CENTENARY

Sod Hut and Settlers — A636

**ROTARY PRESS PRINTING**
**1962, May 20**    Perf. 11x10½
1198   A636   4c slate     .30   .25

## GIRL SCOUTS ISSUE

50th anniversary of the Girl Scouts of America.

Senior Girl Scout & Flag — A637

**1962, July 24**
1199   A637   4c rose red     .30   .25

## SENATOR BRIEN McMAHON ISSUE

McMahon (1903-52) of Connecticut had a role in opening the way to peaceful uses of atomic energy through the Atomic Energy Act establishing the Atomic Energy Commission.

Brien McMahon & Atomic Diagram — A638

**1962, July 28**
1200   A638   4c purple     .30   .25

## APPRENTICESHIP ISSUE

National Apprenticeship Program and 25th anniv. of the National Apprenticeship Act.

Machinist Handing Micrometer to Apprentice A639

**1962, Aug. 31**
1201   A639   4c blk, yellow bister     .30   .25

## SAM RAYBURN ISSUE

Sam Rayburn and Capitol — A640

**GIORI PRESS PRINTING**
**1962, Sept. 16**    Perf. 11
1202   A640   4c dark blue & red brown     .30   .25

## DAG HAMMARSKJOLD ISSUE

UN Headquarters & Dag Hammarskjold, U.N. Sec. Gen., 1953-61 — A641

**1962, Oct. 23**
1203   A641   4c blk, brn & yel     .30   .25

No. 1203a can only be collected on a cover postmarked before Nov. 16, 1962 (the date the Hammarskjold Special Printing, No. 1204, was issued), or tied on dated piece (unique used pair). Covers are known machine postmarked Cuyahoga Falls, Ohio, Nov. 14, 1962, and notarized in the lower left corner by George W. Schwartz, Notary Public. Other covers are reported postmarked Oct. 26, 1962, Brooklyn, NY, Vanderveer Station. Unaddressed, uncacheted first day covers also exist, but are believed by experts to have been backdated using examples of No. 1204.
An unused pane of 50 was signed in the selvage by ten well-known philatelists attesting to its genuineness. This pane was donated to the American Philatelic Society in 1987.
An unknown number of "first day covers" exist bearing Artmaster cachets. These were contrived using examples of No. 1204.

### Hammarskjold Special Printing

**1962, Nov. 16**
1204   A641   4c black, brown & yel (yellow inverted)     .30   .25

No. 1204 was issued following discovery of No. 1203 with yellow background inverted.

## CHRISTMAS ISSUE

Wreath and Candles — A642

**1962, Nov. 1**
1205   A642   4c green & red     .30   .25

## HIGHER EDUCATION ISSUE

Higher education's role in American cultural and industrial development and the centenary celebrations of the signing of the law creating land-grant colleges and universities.

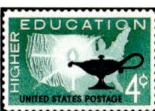
Map of U.S. and Lamp — A643

**1962, Nov. 14**
1206   A643   4c blue green & black     .30   .25

## WINSLOW HOMER ISSUE

Homer (1836-1910), painter, showing his oil, "Breezing Up," which hangs in the National Gallery, Washington, D.C.

"Breezing Up" — A644

**1962, Dec. 15**
1207   A644   4c multicolored     .30   .25
   a.   Horiz. pair, imperf. btwn. and at right     7,000.

## FLAG ISSUE

Flag over White House — A645

**1963-66**
1208   A645   5c blue & red     .30   .25
   a.   Tagged ('00)     .30   .25
   b.   Horiz. pair, imperf. between, tagged     2,250.

Beware of pairs with faint blind perfs between offered as No. 1208b.

## REGULAR ISSUE

Andrew Jackson A646

George Washington A650

John J. Pershing A651

**ROTARY PRESS PRINTING**
**1961-66**    Perf. 11x10½
1209   A646   1c green ('03)     .30   .25
   a.   Tagged ('66)     .30   .25
1213   A650   5c dk gray blue     .30   .25
   a.   Booklet pane of 5 + label     2.00   2.00
   b.   Tagged ('00)     .50   .25
   c.   As "a," tagged, ('63)     2.00   1.50
   d.   Horiz. pair, imperf. between, in #1213a with foldover or miscut     1,750.
1214   A651   8c brown ('61)     .30   .25

See Luminescence note after No. 1053.
Three different messages are found on the label in No. 1213a, and two messages on that of No. 1213c.
No. 1213d resulted from a paper foldover after perforating and before cutting into panes. Unused catalogue numbers were left vacant for additional denominations.

### COIL STAMPS
(Rotary Press)

**1962-66**    Perf. 10 Vertically
1225   A646   1c green ('63)     .40   .25
   a.   Tagged ('66)     .40   .25
1229   A650   5c dk blue gray     1.50   .25
   a.   Tagged ('63)     2.50   .25
   b.   Imperf., pair     300.00

## CAROLINA CHARTER ISSUE

Tercentenary of the Carolina Charter granting to 8 Englishmen lands extending coast-to-coast roughly along the present border of Virginia to the north and Florida to the south. Original charter on display at Raleigh.

First Page of Carolina Charter — A662

## UNITED STATES

### GIORI PRESS PRINTING
**1963, Apr. 6**     *Perf. 11*
1230   A662   5c dark carmine & brown    .30   .25

#### FOOD FOR PEACE-FREEDOM FROM HUNGER ISSUE
American "Food for Peace" program and the "Freedom from Hunger" campaign of the FAO.

Wheat — A663

**1963, June 4**
1231   A663   5c green, buff & red    .30   .25

#### WEST VIRGINIA STATEHOOD, 100th ANNIV.

Map of West Virginia & State Capitol — A664

**1963, June 20**
1232   A664   5c green, red & black    .30   .25

#### EMANCIPATION PROCLAMATION ISSUE
Centenary of Lincoln's Emancipation Proclamation freeing about 3,000,000 slaves in 10 southern states.

Severed Chain — A665

**1963, Aug. 16**
1233   A665   5c dark blue, black & red    .30   .25

#### ALLIANCE FOR PROGRESS ISSUE
2nd anniv. of the Alliance for Progress, which aims to stimulate economic growth and raise living standards in Latin America.

Alliance Emblem — A666

**1963, Aug. 17**
1234   A666   5c ultramarine & green    .30   .25

#### CORDELL HULL ISSUE
Hull (1871-1955), Secretary of State (1933-44).

Cordell Hull (1871-1955), Sec. of State (1933-44) — A667

### ROTARY PRESS PRINTING
**1963, Oct. 5**     *Perf. 10½x11*
1235   A667   5c blue green    .30   .25

#### ELEANOR ROOSEVELT ISSUE
Mrs. Franklin D. Roosevelt (1884-1962).

Mrs. Franklin D. Roosevelt (1884-1962) A668

**1963, Oct. 11**     *Perf. 11x10½*
1236   A668   5c bright purple    .30   .25

#### SCIENCE ISSUE
Honoring the sciences and in connection with the centenary of the Natl. Academy of Science.

"The Universe" — A669

### GIORI PRESS PRINTING
**1963, Oct. 14**     *Perf. 11*
1237   A669   5c Prussian blue & black    .30   .25

#### CITY MAIL DELIVERY ISSUE
Centenary of free city mail delivery.

Letter Carrier, 1863 — A670

**1963, Oct. 26**     Tagged
1238   A670   5c gray, dark blue & red    .30   .25
   b.   Dark blue missing (PS)

#### RED CROSS CENTENARY ISSUE

A671

**1963, Oct. 29**
1239   A671   5c bluish black & red    .30   .25

#### CHRISTMAS ISSUE

Natl. Christmas Tree & White House — A672

**1963, Nov. 1**
1240   A672   5c dk bl, bluish blk & red    .30   .25
   a.   Tagged    .65   .50
   b.   Horiz. pair, imperf between    4,250.
   c.   Red missing (PS)    500.00

#### JOHN JAMES AUDUBON ISSUE
Audubon (1785-1851), ornithologist and artist. The birds pictured are actually Collie's magpie jays. See No. C71.

Columbia Jays — A673

**1963, Dec. 7**
1241   A673   5c dk blue & multi    .30   .25

#### SAM HOUSTON ISSUE
Houston (1793-1863), soldier, president of Texas, US senator.

Sam Houston — A674

### ROTARY PRESS PRINTING
**1964, Jan. 10**     *Perf. 10½x11*
1242   A674   5c black    .30   .25

#### CHARLES M. RUSSELL ISSUE
Russell (1864-1926), painter. The design is from a painting, Thomas Gilcrease Institute of American History and Art, Tulsa, Okla.

"Jerked Down" — A675

### GIORI PRESS PRINTING
**1964, Mar. 19**     *Perf. 11*
1243   A675   5c multicolored    .30   .25

#### NEW YORK WORLD'S FAIR ISSUE
New York World's Fair, 1964-65.

Mall with Unisphere & "Rocket Thrower," by Donald De Lue — A676

### ROTARY PRESS PRINTING
**1964, Apr. 22**     *Perf. 11x10½*
1244   A676   5c blue green    .30   .25
   a.   All color omitted

On No. 1244a, a clear albino impression of the design is present.

#### JOHN MUIR ISSUE
Muir (1838-1914), naturalist and conservationist.

John Muir (1838-1914), naturalist and conservationist and Redwood Forest — A677

### GIORI PRESS PRINTING
**1964, Apr. 29**     *Perf. 11*
1245   A677   5c brn, grn, yel grn & ol    .30   .25

#### KENNEDY MEMORIAL ISSUE
President John Fitzgerald Kennedy, (1917-1963).

Pres. John F. Kennedy (1917-63) and Eternal Flame — A678

### ROTARY PRESS PRINTING
**1964, May 29**     *Perf. 11x10½*
1246   A678   5c blue gray    .30   .25

#### NEW JERSEY TERCENTENARY ISSUE
300th anniv. of English colonization of New Jersey. The design is from a mural by Howard Pyle in the Essex County Courthouse, Newark, N.J.

Philip Carteret Landing at Elizabethtown & Map of New Jersey — A679

**1964, June 15**     *Perf. 10½x11*
1247   A679   5c brt ultramarine    .30   .25

#### NEVADA STATEHOOD, 100th ANNIV.

Virginia City and Map of Nevada — A680

### GIORI PRESS PRINTING
**1964, July 22**     *Perf. 11*
1248   A680   5c red, yellow & blue    .30   .25

#### REGISTER AND VOTE ISSUE
Campaign to draw more voters to the polls.

Flag — A681

**1964, Aug. 1**
1249   A681   5c dark blue & red    .30   .25

#### SHAKESPEARE ISSUE
William Shakespeare (1564-1616).

William Shakespeare — A682

### ROTARY PRESS PRINTING
**1964, Aug. 14**     *Perf. 10½x11*
1250   A682   5c black brown, *tan*    .30   .25

#### DOCTORS MAYO ISSUE
Dr. William James Mayo (1861-1939) and his brother, Dr. Charles Horace Mayo (1865-1939), surgeons who founded the Mayo Foundation for Medical Education and Research in affiliation with the Univ. of Minnesota at Rochester. Heads on stamp are from a sculpture by James Earle Fraser.

Drs. William and Charles Mayo — A683

**1964, Sept. 11**
1251   A683   5c green    .30   .25

#### AMERICAN MUSIC ISSUE
50th anniv. of the founding of the American Society of Composers, Authors and Publishers (ASCAP).

Lute, Horn, Laurel, Oak and Music Score — A684

### GIORI PRESS PRINTING
**1964, Oct. 15**     *Perf. 11*
**Gray Paper with Blue Threads**
1252   A684   5c red, black & blue    .30   .25
   a.   Blue omitted    450.00
   b.   Blue missing (PS)    500.00

Beware of examples offered as No. 1252a which have traces of blue.

#### HOMEMAKERS ISSUE
Honoring American women as homemakers and for the 50th anniv. of the passage of the Smith-Lever Act. By providing economic experts under an extension service of the U.S. Dept. of Agriculture, this legislation helped to improve homelife.

Farm Scene Sampler — A685

# UNITED STATES

Engraved (Giori Press); Background Lithographed
**1964, Oct. 26**
1253 A685 5c multicolored .30 .25

## CHRISTMAS ISSUE

Holly
A686

Mistletoe
A687

Poinsettia
A688

Sprig of Conifer
A689

### GIORI PRESS PRINTING
**1964, Nov. 9**
1254 A686 5c green, car & black .30 .25
  a. Tagged .75 .50
  b. Printed on gummed side 1,850.
  c. All color missing (FO) 2,000.
1255 A687 5c car, green & black .30 .25
  a. Tagged .75 .50
1256 A688 5c car, green & black .30 .25
  a. Tagged .75 .50
1257 A689 5c black, green & car .30 .25
  a. Tagged .75 .50
  b. Block of 4, #1254-1257 1.00 1.00
  c. Block of 4, tagged 3.00 2.25

Tagged stamps issued Nov. 10.
No. 1254b resulted from a paper foldover before printing and perforating.
No. 1254c is unique and is in a block of four with the other three stamps missing parts of the designs.

## VERRAZANO-NARROWS BRIDGE ISSUE
Opening of the Verrazano-Narrows Bridge connecting Staten Island and Brooklyn.

Verrazano-Narrows Bridge and Map of NY Bay — A690

### ROTARY PRESS PRINTING
**1964, Nov. 21**    Perf. 10½x11
1258 A690 5c blue green .30 .25

## FINE ARTS ISSUE

Abstract Design by Stuart Davis — A691

### GIORI PRESS PRINTING
**1964, Dec. 2**    Perf. 11
1259 A691 5c ultra., black & dull red .30 .25

## AMATEUR RADIO ISSUE
Issued to honor the radio amateurs on the 50th anniversary of the American Radio Relay League.

Radio Waves and Dial — A692

### ROTARY PRESS PRINTING
**1964, Dec. 15**    Perf. 10½x11
1260 A692 5c red lilac .30 .25

## BATTLE OF NEW ORLEANS ISSUE
Battle of New Orleans, Chalmette Plantation, Jan. 8-18, 1815, established 150 years of peace and friendship between the US and Great Britain.

General Andrew Jackson and Sesquicentennial Medal — A693

### GIORI PRESS PRINTING
**1965, Jan. 8**    Perf. 11
1261 A693 5c deep carmine, violet blue & gray .30 .25

## PHYSICAL FITNESS-SOKOL ISSUE
Publicizing the importance of physical fitness and for the centenary of the founding of the Sokol (athletic) organization in America.

Discus Thrower — A694

**1965, Feb. 15**
1262 A694 5c maroon & black .30 .25

## CRUSADE AGAINST CANCER ISSUE
Issued to publicize the "Crusade Against Cancer" and to stress the importance of early diagnosis.

Microscope and Stethoscope — A695

**1965, Apr. 1**
1263 A695 5c black, purple & red orange .30 .25

## CHURCHILL MEMORIAL ISSUE
Sir Winston Spencer Churchill (1874-1965), British statesman and World War II leader.

Winston Churchill — A696

### ROTARY PRESS PRINTING
**1965, May 13**    Perf. 10½x11
1264 A696 5c black .30 .25

## MAGNA CARTA ISSUE
750th anniversary of the Magna Carta, the basis of English and American common law.

Procession of Barons and King John's Crown — A697

### GIORI PRESS PRINTING
**1965, June 15**    Perf. 11
1265 A697 5c black, yellow ocher & red lilac .30 .25

## INTERNATIONAL COOPERATION YEAR
ICY, 1965, and 20th anniv. of the UN.

ICY Emblem — A698

**1965, June 26**
1266 A698 5c dull blue & black .30 .25

## SALVATION ARMY ISSUE
Centenary of the founding of the Salvation Army by William Booth in London.

A699

**1965, July 2**
1267 A699 5c red, black & dark blue .30 .25

## DANTE ISSUE
Dante Alighieri (1265-1321), Italian poet.

A700

### ROTARY PRESS PRINTING
**1965, July 17**    Perf. 10½x11
1268 A700 5c maroon, tan .30 .25

## HERBERT HOOVER ISSUE
President Herbert Clark Hoover, (1874-1964).

A701

**1965, Aug. 10**
1269 A701 5c rose red .30 .25

## ROBERT FULTON ISSUE
Fulton (1765-1815), inventor of the 1st commercial steamship.

Robert Fulton & Clermont — A702

### GIORI PRESS PRINTING
**1965, Aug. 19**    Perf. 11
1270 A702 5c black & blue .30 .25

## FLORIDA SETTLEMENT ISSUE
400th anniv. of the settlement of Florida, and the 1st permanent European settlement in the continental US, St. Augustine, Fla.

Spanish Explorer, Royal Flag of Spain and Ships — A703

**1965, Aug. 28**
1271 A703 5c red, yel & blk .30 .25
  a. Yellow omitted 200.00

See Spain No. 1312.

## TRAFFIC SAFETY ISSUE
Issued to publicize traffic safety and the prevention of traffic accidents.

Traffic Signal — A704

**1965, Sept. 3**
1272 A704 5c emer, red & blk .30 .25

## JOHN SINGLETON COPLEY ISSUE
Copley (1738-1815), painter. The portrait of the artist's daughter is from the oil painting "The Copley Family," which hangs in the National Gallery of Art, Washington, D.C.

Elizabeth Clarke Copley — A705

**1965, Sept. 17**
1273 A705 5c blk, brn & olive .30 .25

## INTERNATIONAL TELECOMMUNICATION UNION, 100th ANNIV.

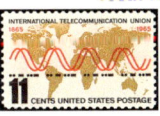
Gall Projection World Map & Radio Sine Wave — A706

**1965, Oct. 6**
1274 A706 11c blk, car & bister .35 .25

## ADLAI STEVENSON ISSUE
Adlai Ewing Stevenson (1900-65), governor of Illinois, US ambassador to the UN.

Adlai E. Stevenson — A707

LITHOGRAPHED, ENGRAVED (Giori)
**1965, Oct. 23**
1275 A707 5c pale bl, blk, car & vio bl .30 .25

## CHRISTMAS ISSUE

Angel with Trumpet — A708

### GIORI PRESS PRINTING
**1965, Nov. 2**
1276 A708 5c carmine, dark olive green & bister .30 .25
  a. Tagged .75 .25

## PROMINENT AMERICANS ISSUE

Thomas Jefferson
A710

Albert Gallatin
A711

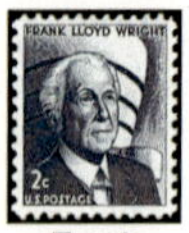

Frank Lloyd Wright & Guggenheim Museum A712

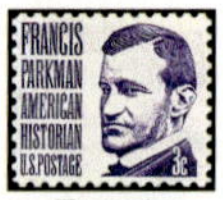

Francis Parkman A713

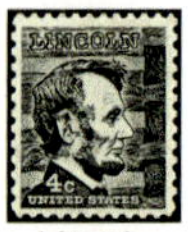

Lincoln A714

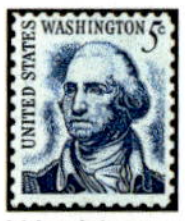

Washington A715

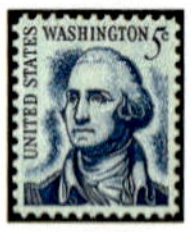

Washington (Redrawn) A715a

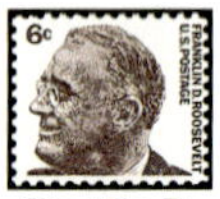

Franklin D. Roosevelt A716

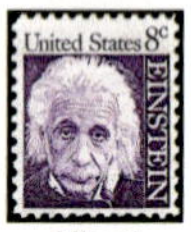

Albert Einstein A717

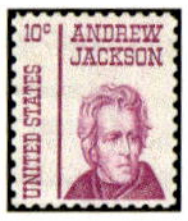

Andrew Jackson — A718

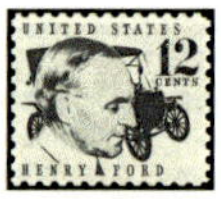

Henry Ford, 1909 Model T — A718a

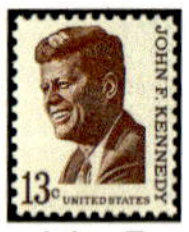

John F. Kennedy A719

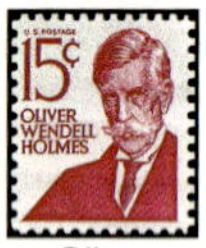

Oliver Wendell Holmes A720

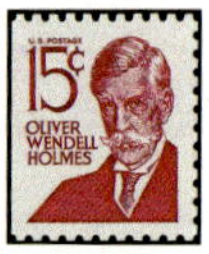

Type 3 — A720a

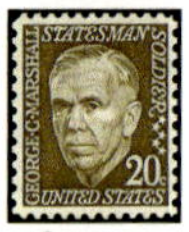

George Catlett Marshall A721

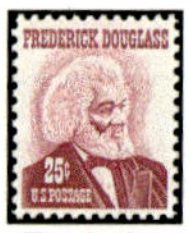

Frederick Douglass A722

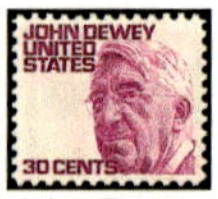

John Dewey A723

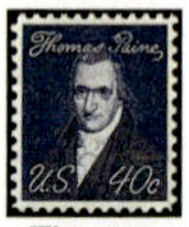

Thomas Paine A724

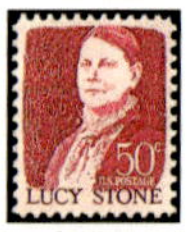

Lucy Stone A725

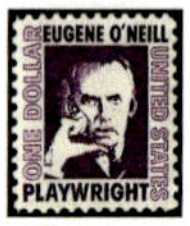

Eugene O'Neill A726

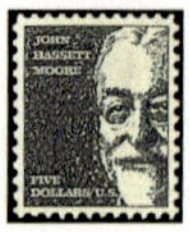

John Bassett Moore — A727

ROTARY PRESS PRINTING

**1965-78** ***Perf. 11x10½, 10½x11***

| | | | | |
|---|---|---|---|---|
| **1278** | A710 | 1c green, tagged | .30 | .25 |
| *a.* | | Booklet pane of 8 | 1.00 | .75 |
| *b.* | | Bklt. pane of 4+2 labels | .75 | .60 |
| *c.* | | Untagged (Bureau precanceled) | 6.25 | 1.25 |
| **1279** | A711 | 1¼c light green | .30 | .25 |
| **1280** | A712 | 2c dk blue gray, tagged | .30 | .25 |
| *a.* | | Bklt. pane of 5 + label | 1.25 | .80 |
| *b.* | | Untagged (Bureau precanceled) | 2.00 | .40 |
| *c.* | | Bklt. pane of 6 | 1.00 | .75 |
| **1281** | A713 | 3c violet, tagged | .30 | .25 |
| *a.* | | Untagged (Bureau precanceled) | 3.00 | .75 |
| **1282** | A714 | 4c black | .30 | .25 |
| *a.* | | Tagged | .30 | .25 |
| **1283** | A715 | 5c blue | .30 | .25 |
| *a.* | | Tagged | .30 | .25 |
| **1283B** | A715a | 5c blue, tagged | .30 | .25 |
| *d.* | | Untagged (Bureau precanceled) | 12.50 | 1.00 |

No. 1283B is redrawn; highlights, shadows softened.

| | | | | |
|---|---|---|---|---|
| **1284** | A716 | 6c gray brn | .30 | .25 |
| *a.* | | Tagged | .30 | .25 |
| *b.* | | Booklet pane of 8 | 1.50 | 1.00 |
| *c.* | | Bklt. pane of 5+ label | 1.40 | 1.00 |
| *d.* | | Horiz. pair, imperf. between | *2,250.* | |
| **1285** | A717 | 8c violet | .30 | .25 |
| *a.* | | Tagged | .30 | .25 |
| **1286** | A718 | 10c lilac, tagged | .30 | .25 |
| *b.* | | Untagged (Bureau precanceled) | 50.00 | 1.75 |
| **1286A** | 718a | 12c black, tagged | .30 | .25 |
| *c.* | | Untagged (Bureau precanceled) | 4.75 | 1.00 |
| **1287** | A719 | 13c brn, tagged | .30 | .25 |
| *a.* | | Untagged (Bureau precanceled) | 6.00 | 1.00 |
| **1288** | A720 | 15c mag, type I, tagged | .30 | .25 |
| *a.* | | Untagged (Bureau precanceled) | .75 | .75 |
| *d.* | | Type II | .55 | .25 |

Imperforates exist from printer's waste.

Values for No. 1288a are for the bars-only precancel. Also exists with city precancels, and worth more thus.

***Perf. 10 on 2 or 3 Sides***

| | | | | |
|---|---|---|---|---|
| **1288B** | A720a | 15c mag, type III | .35 | .25 |
| *c.* | | Booklet pane of 8 | 2.80 | 1.75 |
| *e.* | | As "c," vert. imperf. between | *1,000.* | |

No. 1288B issued in booklets only. All stamps have one or two straight edges. Plates made from redrawn die.

***Perf. 11x10½, 10½x11***

| | | | | |
|---|---|---|---|---|
| **1289** | A721 | 20c deep olive | .40 | .25 |
| *a.* | | Tagged | .40 | .25 |
| *b.* | | black olive | .50 | .25 |
| *c.* | | As "a," double impression | *500.00* | |
| *d.* | | As "b," tagging omitted | — | |
| **1290** | A722 | 25c rose lake | .55 | .25 |
| *a.* | | Tagged | .45 | .25 |
| *b.* | | 25c magenta | *25.00* | — |

Shades of No. 1290 rose lake exist that tend toward magenta, but are not. Competent identification is important for No. 1290b.

| | | | | |
|---|---|---|---|---|
| **1291** | A723 | 30c red lilac | .65 | .25 |
| *a.* | | Tagged | .50 | .25 |
| **1292** | A724 | 40c blue black | .80 | .25 |
| *a.* | | Tagged | .75 | .25 |
| **1293** | A725 | 50c rose mag | 1.00 | .25 |
| *a.* | | Tagged | .80 | .25 |
| **1294** | A726 | $1 dull purple | 2.25 | .25 |
| *a.* | | Tagged | 1.75 | .25 |
| *b.* | | $1 black violet | 200.00 | *350.00* |
| **1295** | A727 | $5 gray black | 10.00 | 2.25 |
| *a.* | | Tagged | 8.50 | 2.00 |
| | | *Nos. 1278-1295 (21)* | 19.90 | 7.25 |

Issued (without tagging) — 1965: 4c, 11/19.
1966: 5c, 2/22; 6c, 1/29; 8c, 3/14; $5, 12/3.
1967: 1¼c, 1/30; 20c, 10/24; 25c, 2/14; $1, 10/16.
1968: 30c, 10/21; 40c, 1/29; 50c, 8/13.
Dates for tagged: 1965: 4c, 12/1.
1966: 2c, 6/8; 5c, 2/23; 6c, 12/29; 8c, 7/6.
1967: 3c, 9/16; #1283B, 11/17; #1284b, 12/28; 10c, 3/15; 13c, 5/29.
1968: 1c, #1284c, 1/12; #1280a, 1/8; 12c, 7/30; 15c, 3/8.
1973: 20c, 25c, 30c, 40c, 50c, $1, $5, 4/3.
1978: No. 1288B, 6/14.

COIL STAMPS

***Perf. 10 Horizontally***

**1966-81** **Tagged**

| | | | | |
|---|---|---|---|---|
| **1297** | A713 | 3c violet | .30 | .25 |
| *a.* | | Imperf., pair | *22.50* | |
| *b.* | | Untagged (Bureau precanceled) | .40 | .25 |
| *c.* | | As "b," imperf. pair | 8.00 | — |
| **1298** | A716 | 6c gray brn | .30 | .25 |
| *a.* | | Imperf., pair | *1,250.* | |

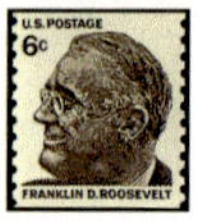

Franklin D. Roosevelt — A727a

***Perf. 10 Vertically***

| | | | | |
|---|---|---|---|---|
| **1299** | A710 | 1c green | .30 | .25 |
| *a.* | | Untagged (Bureau precanceled) | 8.00 | 1.75 |
| *b.* | | Imperf., pair | *22.50* | — |
| **1303** | A714 | 4c black | .30 | .25 |
| *a.* | | Untagged (Bureau precanceled) | 8.75 | .75 |
| *b.* | | Imperf., pair | *400.00* | |
| **1304** | A715 | 5c blue | .30 | .25 |
| *a.* | | Untagged (Bureau precanceled) | 6.50 | .65 |
| *b.* | | Imperf., pair | *110.00* | |
| *e.* | | As "a," imperf., pair | *250.00* | |
| *f.* | | Tagging omitted (not Bureau precanceled) | — | — |

No. 1304b is valued in the grade of fine.

No. 1304e is precanceled Mount Pleasant, Iowa. Also exists from Chicago, Illinois; value $1,500 for pair.

| | | | | |
|---|---|---|---|---|
| **1304C** | A715a | 5c blue | .30 | .25 |
| *d.* | | Imperf., pair | *375.00* | |
| **1305** | A727a | 6c gray brn | .30 | .25 |
| *a.* | | Imperf., pair | 55.00 | |
| *b.* | | Untagged (Bureau precanceled) | 20.00 | 1.00 |
| *m.* | | Pair, imperf. between | *250.00* | |
| **1305E** | A720 | 15c mag, type I | .30 | .25 |
| *f.* | | Untagged (Bureau precanceled) | 32.50 | — |
| *g.* | | Imperf., pair, type I | 20.00 | |
| *h.* | | Pair, imperf. between | 125.00 | |
| *i.* | | Type II | 1.50 | .25 |
| *j.* | | Imperf., pair, type II | *55.00* | |
| **1305C** | A726 | $1 dull pur | 3.25 | .40 |
| *d.* | | Imperf., pair | *900.00* | |
| | | *Nos. 1297-1305C (9)* | 5.65 | 2.40 |

Issued: 1c, 1/12/68; 3c, 11/4/75; 4c, 5/28/66; #1304, 9/8/66; 6c, #1298, 12/28/67; #1305, 2/28/68;
$1, 1/12/73; 15c, 6/14/78.

## MIGRATORY BIRD TREATY ISSUE

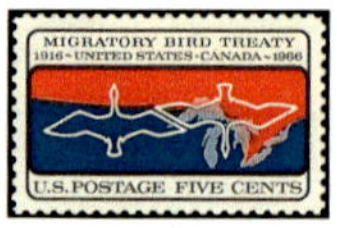

Migratory Birds over Canada-U.S. Border — A728

GIORI PRESS PRINTING

**1966, Mar. 16** ***Perf. 11***

| | | | | |
|---|---|---|---|---|
| **1306** | A728 | 5c blk, crim & dk blue | .30 | .25 |

## HUMANE TREATMENT OF ANIMALS ISSUE

Issued to promote humane treatment of all animals and for the centenary of the American Society for the Prevention of Cruelty to Animals.

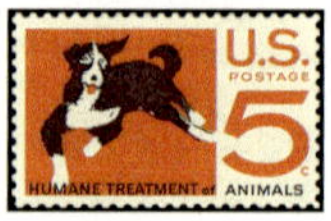

Mongrel — A729

LITHOGRAPHED, ENGRAVED (Giori)

**1966, Apr. 9**

| | | | | |
|---|---|---|---|---|
| **1307** | A729 | 5c orange brown & black | .30 | .25 |

## INDIANA STATEHOOD, 150th ANNIV.

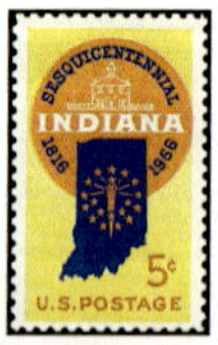

Sesquicentennial Seal — A730

GIORI PRESS PRINTING

**1966, Apr. 16**

| | | | | |
|---|---|---|---|---|
| **1308** | A730 | 5c ocher, brn & vio blue | .30 | .25 |

## AMERICAN CIRCUS ISSUE

Issued to honor the American Circus on the centenary of the birth of John Ringling.

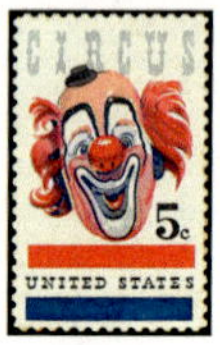

Clown — A731

**1966, May 2**

| | | | | |
|---|---|---|---|---|
| **1309** | A731 | 5c multicolored | .30 | .25 |

## SIXTH INTERNATIONAL PHILATELIC EXHIBITION ISSUES

Sixth International Philatelic Exhibition (SIPEX), Washington, D.C., May 21-30.

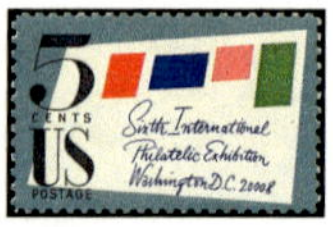

Stamped Cover — A732

LITHOGRAPHED, ENGRAVED (Giori)

**1966**

| | | | | |
|---|---|---|---|---|
| **1310** | A732 | 5c multicolored | .30 | .25 |

Souvenir Sheet

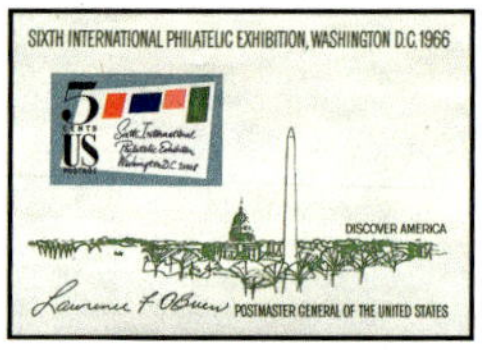


A733

***Imperf***

| | | | | |
|---|---|---|---|---|
| **1311** | A733 | 5c multicolored | .30 | .25 |

No. 1311 measures 108x74mm.

## BILL OF RIGHTS, 175th ANNIV.

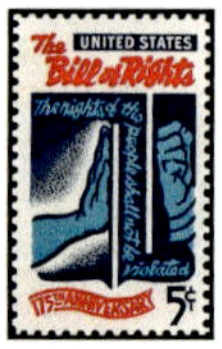

"Freedom" Checking "Tyranny" — A734

GIORI PRESS PRINTING

**1966, July 1** ***Perf. 11***

| | | | | |
|---|---|---|---|---|
| **1312** | A734 | 5c carmine, dark & light blue | .30 | .25 |

## POLISH MILLENNIUM ISSUE

Adoption of Christianity in Poland, 1000th anniv.

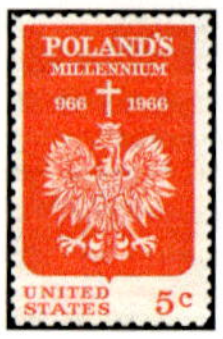

Polish Eagle and Cross — A735

ROTARY PRESS PRINTING

**1966, July 30** ***Perf. 10½x11***

| | | | | |
|---|---|---|---|---|
| **1313** | A735 | 5c red | .30 | .25 |

**Tagging Extended**

During 1966, experimental use of tagged stamps was extended to the Cincinnati Postal Region covering offices in Indiana, Kentucky and Ohio. To supply these offices about 12 percent of the following nine issues (Nos. 1314-1322) were tagged.

## NATIONAL PARK SERVICE ISSUE

50th anniv. of the Natl. Park Service of the Interior Dept. The design "Parkscape U.S.A." identifies Natl. Park Service facilities.

# UNITED STATES

National Park Service Emblem — A736

LITHOGRAPHED, ENGRAVED (Giori)
**1966, Aug. 25**    Perf. 11
1314 A736 5c yellow, black & green    .30   .25
   a.   Tagged    .35   .35

## MARINE CORPS RESERVE ISSUE

US Marine Corps Reserve founding, 50th anniv.

 A737

**1966, Aug. 29**
1315 A737 5c black, bister, red & ultra    .30   .25
   a.   Tagged    .40   .35
   b.   Black & bister (engraved) missing (EP)    16,000.

## GENERAL FEDERATION OF WOMEN'S CLUBS ISSUE

75 years of service by the General Federation of Women's Clubs

Women of 1890 and 1966 — A738

GIORI PRESS PRINTING
**1966, Sept. 12**
1316 A738 5c black, pink & blue    .30   .25
   a.   Tagged    .40   .25

## AMERICAN FOLKLORE ISSUE
### Johnny Appleseed

Issued to honor Johnny Appleseed (John Chapman 1774-1845), who wandered over 100,000 square miles planting apple trees, and who gave away and sold seedlings to Midwest pioneers.

Johnny Appleseed — A739

**1966, Sept. 24**
1317 A739 5c green, red & black    .30   .25
   a.   Tagged    .40   .25

## BEAUTIFICATION OF AMERICA ISSUE

Issued to publicize President Johnson's "Plant for a more beautiful America" campaign.

Jefferson Memorial — A740

**1966, Oct. 5**
1318 A740 5c emerald, pink & black    .30   .25
   a.   Tagged    .40   .25
   Compare with No. 4716c.

## GREAT RIVER ROAD ISSUE

Issued to publicize the 5,600-mile Great River Road connecting New Orleans with Kenora, Ontario, and following the Mississippi most of the way.

Central U.S. Map With Great River Road — A741

LITHOGRAPHED, ENGRAVED (Giori)
**1966, Oct. 21**
1319 A741 5c vermilion, yellow, blue & green    .30   .25
   a.   Tagged    .45   .25

## SAVINGS BOND-SERVICEMEN ISSUE

25th anniv. of US Savings Bonds, and honoring American servicemen.

Statue of Liberty & "Old Glory" — A742

**1966, Oct. 26**
1320 A742 5c red, dk bl, lt bl & blk    .30   .25
   a.   Tagged    .40   .25
   b.   Red, dark blue & black missing (EP)    3,750.
   c.   Dark blue (engr.) missing (EP)    5,000.

## CHRISTMAS ISSUE

Madonna and Child — A743

Modeled after "Madonna and Child with Angels," by the Flemish artist Hans Memling (c.1430-1494), Mellon Collection, National Gallery of Art, Washington, D.C.

**1966, Nov. 1**
1321 A743 5c multicolored    .30   .25
   a.   Tagged    .40   .25

## MARY CASSATT ISSUE

Cassatt (1844-1926), painter. The painting "The Boating Party" is in the Natl. Gallery of Art, Washington, D.C.

"The Boating Party" — A744

GIORI PRESS PRINTING
**1966, Nov. 17**
1322 A744 5c multicolored    .30   .25
   a.   Tagged    .40   .25

Cassatt (1844-1926), painter. The original painting is in the Natl. Gallery of Art, Washington, DC.

## NATIONAL GRANGE ISSUE

Centenary of the founding of the National Grange, American farmers' organization.

Grange Poster, 1870 — A745

**1967, Apr. 17**
1323 A745 5c org, yel, brn, grn & blk    .30   .25

### Phosphor Tagging

From No. 1323 onward, all postage issues are tagged, unless otherwise noted.

### Tagging Omitted

Inadvertent omissions of tagging occurred on Nos. 1238, 1278, 1281, 1298 and 1305. In addition many tagged issues from 1967 on exist with tagging unintentionally omitted. These errors are listed in the *Scott Specialized Catalogue of United States Stamps and Covers*.

## CANADA CENTENARY ISSUE

Centenary of Canada's emergence as a nation.

Canadian Landscape — A746

**1967, May 25**
1324 A746 5c lt bl, dp grn, ultra, olive & blk    .30   .25

## ERIE CANAL ISSUE

150th anniversary of the Erie Canal ground-breaking ceremony at Rome, N.Y. The canal links Lake Erie and New York City.

Stern of Early Canal Boat — A747

LITHOGRAPHED, ENGRAVED (Giori)
**1967, July 4**
1325 A747 5c ultra, grnsh blue, blk & crim    .30   .25

## "SEARCH FOR PEACE" — LIONS ISSUE

Issued to publicize the search for peace. "Search for Peace" was the theme of an essay contest for young men and women sponsored by Lions International on its 50th anniversary.

Peace Dove — A748

GIORI PRESS PRINTING
**1967, July 5**
Gray Paper with Blue Threads
1326 A748 5c blue, red & black    .30   .25

## HENRY DAVID THOREAU ISSUE

Henry David Thoreau (1817-1862), Writer — A749

**1967, July 12**
1327 A749 5c carmine, black & blue green    .30   .25
   b.   Carmine missing (PS)    700.00

## NEBRASKA STATEHOOD, 100th ANNIV.

Hereford Steer and Corn — A750

LITHOGRAPHED, ENGRAVED (Giori)
**1967, July 29**
1328 A750 5c dark red brown, lemon & yellow    .30   .25

## VOICE OF AMERICA ISSUE

25th anniv. of the radio branch of the United States Information Agency (USIA).

Radio Transmission Tower and Waves — A751

**1967, Aug. 1**
1329 A751 5c red, blue, black & carmine    .30   .25

## AMERICAN FOLKLORE ISSUE

Davy Crockett (1786-1836), frontiersman, hunter, and congressman from Tennessee who died at the Alamo.

Davy Crockett & Scrub Pines — A752

**1967, Aug. 17**
1330 A752 5c green, black, & yellow    .30   .25
   a.   Vertical pair, imperf. between    7,500.
   b.   Green (engr.) missing (FO)    —
   c.   Black & green (engr.) missing (FO)    —

A foldover on a pane of No. 1330 resulted in one example each of Nos. 1330b-1330c. Part of the colors appear on the back of the selvage and one freak stamp. An engraved black-and-green-only impression appears on the gummed side of one almost-complete "stamp."

## ACCOMPLISHMENTS IN SPACE ISSUE

US accomplishments in space. Printed with continuous design in horizontal rows of 5. In the left panes the astronaut stamp is 1st, 3rd and 5th, the spaceship 2nd and 4th. This arrangement is reversed in the right panes.

Space-Walking Astronaut — A753

Gemini 4 Capsule and Earth — A754

**1967, Sept. 29**
1331 A753 5c multicolored    .55   .25
1332 A754 5c multicolored    .55   .25
   b.   Pair, #1331-1332    1.25   1.25

## URBAN PLANNING ISSUE

Publicizing the importance of Urban Planning in connection with the Intl. Conf. of the American Institute of Planners, Washington, D.C., Oct. 1-6.

View of Model City — A755

**1967, Oct. 2**
1333 A755 5c dark blue, light blue & black    .30   .25

## FINNISH INDEPENDENCE, 50th ANNIV.

Finnish Coat of Arms — A756

**ENGRAVED (Giori)**
**1967, Oct. 6**
1334  A756  5c blue  .30  .25

## THOMAS EAKINS ISSUE

Eakins (1844-1916), painter and sculptor. The painting is in the Natl. Gallery of Art, Washington, D.C.

"The Biglin Brothers Racing" (Sculling on Schuylkill River, Philadelphia) A757

Printed by Photogravure & Color Co., Moonachie, N.J.

**PHOTOGRAVURE**
**1967, Nov. 2**  Perf. 12
1335  A757  5c gold & multicolored  .30  .25

## CHRISTMAS ISSUE

Madonna and Child, by Hans Memling — A758

**LITHOGRAPHED, ENGRAVED (Giori)**
**1967, Nov. 6**  Perf. 11
1336  A758  5c multicolored  .30  .25

See note on painting above No. 1321.

## MISSISSIPPI STATEHOOD, 150th ANNIV.

Magnolia — A759

**GIORI PRESS PRINTING**
**1967, Dec. 11**
1337  A759  5c brt grnsh bl, grn & red brn  .30  .25

## FLAG ISSUE

Flag and White House — A760

**1968, Jan. 24**
**Size: 19x22mm**
1338  A760  6c dk bl, red & grn  .30  .25
  k.  Vert. pair, imperf. btwn.  250.00  150.00
  s.  Red missing (FO)  —
  u.  Vert. pair, imperf horiz.  275.00
  v.  All color omitted  —
  w.  Green missing (FO)  —

No. 1338s is unique.
Beware of regumming on No. 1338u. Most examples have had the gum washed off to make it difficult or impossible to detect blind perfs. Check carefully for blind perfs. Value is for pair with original gum.
On No. 1338v, an albino impression of the engraved plate is present.

## COIL STAMP
### MULTICOLOR HUCK PRESS
**1969, May 30**  Perf. 10 Vertically
**Size: 18¼x21mm**
1338A  A760  6c dk bl, red & grn  .30  .25
  b.  Imperf., pair  350.00

### MULTICOLOR HUCK PRESS
**1970-71**  Perf. 11x10½
**Size: 18¼x21mm**
1338D  A760  6c dk bl, red & grn  .30  .25
  e.  Horiz. pair, imperf. between  115.00
1338F  A760  8c dk bl, red & slate gren ('71)  .30  .25
  i.  Imperf., vert. pair  35.00
  j.  Horiz. pair, imperf. between  45.00
  p.  Slate green omitted  350.00
  t.  Horiz. pair, imperf. vertically  —

Issued: #1338D, 8/7/70

## COIL STAMP
### MULTICOLOR HUCK PRESS
**1971, May 10**  Perf. 10 Vertically
**Size: 18¼x21mm**
1338G  A760  8c dk bl, red & slate grn  .30  .25
  h.  Imperf., pair  45.00

## ILLINOIS STATEHOOD, 150th ANNIV.

Farm House & Fields of Ripening Grain — A761

**LITHOGRAPHED, ENGRAVED (Giori)**
**1968, Feb. 12**  Perf. 11
1339  A761  6c dk blue, blue, red & ocher  .30  .25

## HEMISFAIR '68 ISSUE

HemisFair '68 exhibition, San Antonio, Texas, Apr. 6-Oct. 6, for the 250th anniv. of San Antonio.

Map of North & South America — A762

**1968, Mar. 30**
1340  A762  6c blue, rose red & white  .30  .25
  a.  White omitted  650.00

## AIRLIFT ISSUE

Eagle Holding Pennant — A763

**1968, Apr. 4**  Untagged
1341  A763  $1 sepia, dk. blue, ocher & brown red  2.00  1.25

Issued to pay for airlift of parcels from and to U.S. ports to servicemen overseas and in Alaska, Hawaii and P.R. Valid for all regular postage.
On Apr. 26, 1969, the POD ruled that henceforth No. 1341 "may be used toward paying the postage or fees for special services on airmail articles."

## "SUPPORT OUR YOUTH" — ELKS ISSUE

Support Our Youth program, and honoring the Benevolent and Protective Order of Elks, which extended its youth service program in observance of its centennial year.

Girls & Boys — A764

**1968, May 1**  Tagged
1342  A764  6c ultramarine & orange red  .30  .25

## LAW AND ORDER ISSUE

Publicizing the policeman as protector and friend and to encourage respect for law and order.

Policeman and Small Boy — A765

**GIORI PRESS PRINTING**
**1968, May 17**
1343  A765  6c chalky blue, black & red  .30  .25

## REGISTER AND VOTE ISSUE

Campaign to draw more voters to the polls. The weather vane is from an old house in the Russian Hill section of San Francisco, Cal.

Eagle Weather Vane — A766

**LITHOGRAPHED, ENGRAVED (Giori)**
**1968, June 27**
1344  A766  6c black, yellow & orange  .30  .25

## HISTORIC FLAG SERIES

Flags carried by American colonists and by citizens of the new United States. Printed se-tenant in vertical columns of 10. The flag sequence on the 2 upper panes is as listed. On the 2 lower panes the sequence is reversed with the Navy Jack in the 1st row and the Fort Moultrie flag in the 10th.

Ft. Moultrie, 1776 — A767

Ft. McHenry, 1795-1818 A768

Washington's Cruisers, 1775 — A769

Bennington, 1777 — A770

Rhode Island, 1775 — A771

First Stars and Stripes, 1777 — A772

Bunker Hill, 1775 — A773

Grand Union, 1776 — A774

Philadelphia Light Horse, 1775 — A775

First Navy Jack, 1775 — A776

**ENGR. (Giori) (#1345-1348, 1350); ENGR. & LITHO. (#1349, 1351-1354)**
**1968, July 4**
1345  A767  6c dark blue  .40  .25
1346  A768  6c dark blue & red  .40  .25
1347  A769  6c dark blue & olive green  .30  .25
1348  A770  6c dark blue & red  .30  .25
1349  A771  6c dark blue, yellow & red  .30  .25
1350  A772  6c dark blue & red  .30  .25
1351  A773  6c dark blue, olive green & red  .30  .25
1352  A774  6c dark blue & red  .30  .25
1353  A775  6c dark blue, yellow & red  .30  .25
1354  A776  6c dark blue, red & yellow  .30  .25
  a.  Strip of ten, #1345-1354  3.25  3.25
  b.  #1345b-1354b, any single, tagging omitted  65.00
  c.  As "a," imperf  4,500.

## WALT DISNEY ISSUE

Walt Disney (1901-1966), cartoonist, film producer and creator of Mickey Mouse.

Disney and Children of the World — A777

Printed by Achrovure Division of Union-Camp Corp., Englewood, N.J.

**PHOTOGRAVURE**
**1968, Sept. 11**  Perf. 12
1355  A777  6c multicolored  .40  .25
  a.  Ocher omitted ("Walt Disney," "6c," etc.)  350.00  —
  b.  Vert. pair, imperf. horiz.  575.00
  c.  Imperf., pair  425.00
  d.  Black omitted  1,000.
  e.  Horiz. pair, imperf. between  5,000.
  f.  Blue omitted  1,500.

## FATHER MARQUETTE ISSUE

Father Jacques Marquette (1637-1675), French Jesuit missionary, who together with Louis Jolliet explored the Mississippi River and its tributaries.

Father Marquette and Louis Jolliet Exploring the Mississippi A778

**LITHOGRAPHED, ENGRAVED (Giori)**
**1968, Sept. 20**  Perf. 11
1356  A778  6c black, apple green & orange brown  .30  .25

## AMERICAN FOLKLORE ISSUE

Daniel Boone (1734-1820), frontiersman and trapper.

Pennsylvania Rifle, Powder Horn, Tomahawk Pipe & Knife — A779

# UNITED STATES

**LITHOGRAPHED, ENGRAVED (Giori)**
**1968, Sept. 26**
1357 A779 6c yel, dp yel, mar & blk .30 .25

## ARKANSAS RIVER NAVIGATION ISSUE

Opening of the Arkansas River to commercial navigation.

Ship's Wheel, Power Transmission Tower & Barge — A780

**1968, Oct. 1**
1358 A780 6c bright blue, dark blue & black .30 .25

## LEIF ERIKSON ISSUE

Leif Erikson, 11th century Norse explorer, called the 1st European to set foot on the American continent, at a place he called Vinland. The statue by the American sculptor A. Stirling Calder is in Reykjavik, Iceland.

Leif Erikson, by Stirling Calder — A781

**1968, Oct. 9**
1359 A781 6c light gray brown & black brown .30 .25

The luminescent element is in the light gray brown ink of the background. The engraved parts were printed on a rotary currency press.

## CHEROKEE STRIP ISSUE

75th anniversary of the opening of the Cherokee Strip to settlers, Sept. 16, 1893.

Homesteaders Racing to Cherokee Strip — A782

**ROTARY PRESS PRINTING**
**1968, Oct. 15** Perf. 11x10½
1360 A782 6c brown .30 .25

## JOHN TRUMBULL ISSUE

Trumbull (1756-1843), painter. The stamp shows Lt. Thomas Grosvenor and his attendant Peter Salem. The painting hangs at Yale University.

Detail from "The Battle of Bunker's Hill" — A783

**LITHOGRAPHED, ENGRAVED (Giori)**
**1968, Oct. 18** Perf. 11
1361 A783 6c multicolored .30 .25
  b. Black (engr.) missing (FO) 11,000. —

## WATERFOWL CONSERVATION ISSUE

Wood Ducks — A784

**1968, Oct. 24**
1362 A784 6c blk & multi .30 .25
  a. Vertical pair, imperf. between 250.00 —
  b. Red & dark blue omitted 350.00 —
  c. Red omitted 1,750.

Dangerous fakes exist of Nos. 1362b and 1362c. Authentication by experts is required.

## CHRISTMAS ISSUE

"The Annunciation" by the 15th century Flemish painter Jan van Eyck is in the National Gallery of Art, Washington, D.C.

Gabriel, from van Eyck's Annunciation — A785

**ENGRAVED (Multicolor Huck press)**
**1968, Nov. 1**
1363 A785 6c multicolored .30 .25
  a. Untagged .30 .25
  b. Imperf., pair, tagged 140.00
  c. Light yellow omitted 60.00 —
  d. Imperf., pair, untagged 200.00

## AMERICAN INDIAN ISSUE

Honoring the American Indian and to celebrate the opening of the Natl. Portrait Gallery, Washington, D.C. Chief Joseph (Indian name, Thunder Traveling over tho Mountains), a leader of the Nez Percé, was born in eastern Oregon about 1840 and died at the Colville Reservation in Washington State in 1904.

Chief Joseph, by Cyrenius Hall — A786

**LITHOGRAPHED, ENGRAVED (Giori)**
**1968, Nov. 4**
1364 A786 6c black & multi .30 .25

## BEAUTIFICATION OF AMERICA ISSUE

Publicizing the Natural Beauty Campaign for more beautiful cities, parks, highways and streets. In the left panes Nos. 1365 and 1367 appear in 1st, 3rd and 5th place, Nos. 1366 and 1368 in 2nd and 4th place. This arrangement is reversed in the right panes.

Capitol, Azaleas and Tulips — A787

Washington Monument, Potomac River and Daffodils — A788

Poppies and Lupines along Highway — A789

Blooming Crab Apples along Street — A790

**1969, Jan. 16** Tagged
1365 A787 6c multicolored .30 .25
1366 A788 6c multicolored .30 .25
1367 A789 6c multicolored .30 .25
1368 A790 6c multicolored .30 .25
  a. Block of 4, #1365-1368 1.00 1.25

Compare with Nos. 4716a, 4716b, 4716d, 4716e.

## AMERICAN LEGION, 50th ANNIV.

Eagle from Great Seal of U.S. — A791

**1969, Mar. 15**
1369 A791 6c red, blue & black .30 .25

## AMERICAN FOLKLORE ISSUE

Grandma Moses (Anna Mary Robertson Moses, 1860-1961), primitive painter of American life.

July Fourth, by Grandma Moses — A792

**1969, May 1**
1370 A792 6c multicolored .30 .25
  a. Horizontal pair, imperf. between 140.00 —
  b. Engraved black ("6c U.S. Postage") & Prus. blue ("Grandma Moses") omitted 400.00

Beware of pairs with blind perfs. being offered as No. 1370a.
No. 1370b often comes with mottled or disturbed gum. Such stamps sell for about two-thirds as much as examples with perfect gum.

## APOLLO 8 ISSUE

Apollo 8 mission, which 1st put men into orbit around the moon, Dec. 21-27, 1968. The astronauts were: Col. Frank Borman, Capt. James Lovell and Maj. William Anders.

Moon Surface and Earth — A793

**LITHOGRAPHED, ENGRAVED (Giori)**
**1969, May 5**
1371 A793 6c black, blue & ocher .30 .25

Imperfs. exist from printer's waste.

## W.C. HANDY ISSUE

Handy (1873-1958), jazz musician and composer.

W. C. Handy (1873-1958), Jazz Musician and Composer — A794

**LITHOGRAPHED, ENGRAVED (Giori)**
**1969, May 17**
1372 A794 6c violet, deep lilac & blue .30 .25

## CALIFORNIA SETTLEMENT, 200th ANNIV.

Carmel Mission Belfry — A795

**1969, July 16**
1373 A795 6c orange, red, black & light blue .30 .25
  b. Red (engr.) missing (CM) 400.00

## JOHN WESLEY POWELL ISSUE

Powell (1834-1902), geologist who explored the Green and Colorado Rivers 1869-75, and ethnologist.

Powell Exploring Colorado River — A796

**1969, Aug. 1**
1374 A796 6c black, ocher & light blue .30 .25

## ALABAMA STATEHOOD, 150th ANNIV.

Camellia & Yellow-shafted Flicker — A797

**1969, Aug. 2**
1375 A797 6c mag, rose red, yel, dk, grn & brn .30 .25

## BOTANICAL CONGRESS ISSUE

11th Intl. Botanical Cong., Seattle, Wash., Aug. 24-Sept. 2. In left panes Nos. 1376 and 1378 appear in 1st, 3rd and 5th place; Nos. 1377 and 1379 in 2nd and 4th place. This arrangement is reversed in right panes.

Douglas Fir (Northwest) A798

Lady's-slipper (Northeast) A799

Ocotillo (Southwest) A800

Franklinia (Southeast) A801

**1969, Aug. 23**
1376 A798 6c multicolored .35 .25
1377 A799 6c multicolored .35 .25
1378 A800 6c multicolored .35 .25
1379 A801 6c multicolored .35 .25
  a. Block of 4, #1376-1379 1.40 1.75

## DARTMOUTH COLLEGE CASE ISSUE

150th anniv. of the Dartmouth College Case, which Daniel Webster argued before the Supreme Court, reasserting the sanctity of contracts.

Daniel Webster & Dartmouth Hall — A802

**ROTARY PRESS PRINTING**
**1969, Sept. 22** Perf. 10½x11
1380 A802 6c green .30 .25

## PROFESSIONAL BASEBALL, 100th ANNIV.

Batter — A803

LITHOGRAPHED, ENGRAVED (Giori)

**1969, Sept. 24** ***Perf. 11***

**1381** A803 6c yellow, red, black & green .45 .25
- *a.* Black omitted ("1869-1969, United States, 6c, Professional Baseball") *500.00*
- *c.* Double impression of black (engr.) *5,750.*

### INTERCOLLEGIATE FOOTBALL, 100th ANNIV.

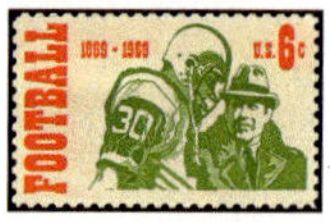

Football Player & Coach — A804

**1969, Sept. 26**

**1382** A804 6c red & green .30 .25
- *b.* Vert. pair, imperf horiz. *5,750.*
- *c.* Double impression *2,500.*

The engraved parts were printed on a rotary currency press.

No. 1382b is unique.

Two examples of No. 1382c are recorded, with the double impression on the left part of the left stamps within a lower left plate block of 4. Value given is for the plate block.

### DWIGHT D. EISENHOWER ISSUE

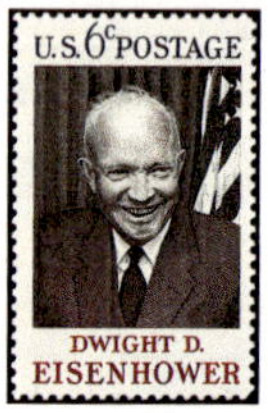

Dwight D. Eisenhower — A805

Designed by Robert J. Jones; photograph by Bernie Noble.

GIORI PRESS PRINTING

**1969, Oct. 14**

**1383** A805 6c blue, black & red .30 .25
- *b.* Blue ("U.S. 6c Postage") missing (PS) *600.00*

### CHRISTMAS ISSUE

The painting, painted about 1870 by an unknown primitive artist, is the property of the N.Y. State Historical Association, Cooperstown, N.Y.

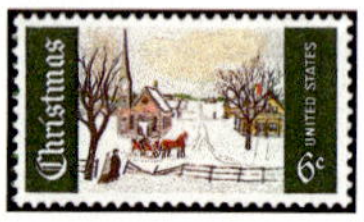

Winter Sunday in Norway, Maine — A806

ENGRAVED (Multicolor Huck)

**1969, Nov. 3** ***Perf. 11x10½***

**1384** A806 6c dark green & multicolored .30 .25
- Precancel .60 .25
- *b.* Imperf., pair *700.00*
- *c.* Light green omitted 30.00
- *d.* Light green, red & yellow omitted *600.00* —
- *e.* Yellow omitted *1,250.*
- *g.* Red & yellow omitted *2,250.*
- *h.* Light green and yellow omitted *500.00*
- *i.* Light green and red omitted —
- *j.* Vert. pair, top stamp Baltimore precancel, bottom stamp precancel missing (FO) —
- *k.* Baltimore precancel printed on gum side *175.00*
- *l.* Baltimore precancel, vert. pair, one stamp missing precancel, other stamp with precancel printed inverted on reverse (FO) *500.00*
- *m.* Inverted Baltimore precancel *225.00*
- *n.* Baltimore precancel printed inverted on reverse (FO) *150.00*
- *p.* Double impression of New Haven precancel —
- *q.* Inverted Memphis precancel *100.00*
- *t.* Inverted Atlanta precancel *500.00*

The precancel value applies to the least expensive of experimental precancels printed locally in four cities, on tagged stamps, with the names between lines 4½mm apart: in black or green, "ATLANTA, GA" and in green only "BALTIMORE, MD," "MEMPHIS, TN" and "NEW HAVEN, CT." They were sold freely to the public and could be used on any class of mail at all post offices during the experimental program and thereafter.

Most examples of No. 1384c show orange where the offset green was. Value is for this variety. Examples without orange sell for more.

On No. 1384i, almost all of the yellow is also omitted. Do not confuse with No. 1384d.

### HOPE FOR CRIPPLED ISSUE

Issued to encourage the rehabilitation of crippled children and adults and to honor the National Society for Crippled Children and Adults (Easter Seal Society) on its 50th anniversary.

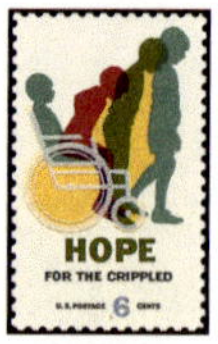

Cured Child — A807

LITHOGRAPHED, ENGRAVED (Giori)

**1969, Nov. 20** ***Perf. 11***

**1385** A807 6c multicolored .30 .25

### WILLIAM M. HARNETT ISSUE

Harnett (1848-1892), painter. The painting hangs in the Museum of Fine Arts, Boston.

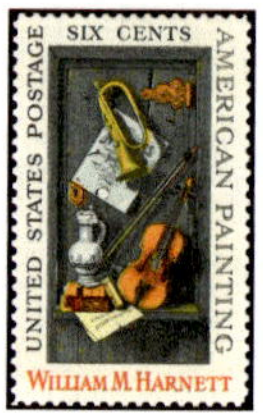

"Old Models" — A808

**1969, Dec. 3**

**1386** A808 6c multicolored .30 .25
- *a.* Red (engr.) missing (CM) —

### NATURAL HISTORY ISSUE

Centenary of the American Museum of Natural History, New York City. Nos. 1387-1388 alternate in 1st row, Nos. 1389-1390 in 2nd row. This arrangement is repeated throughout the pane.

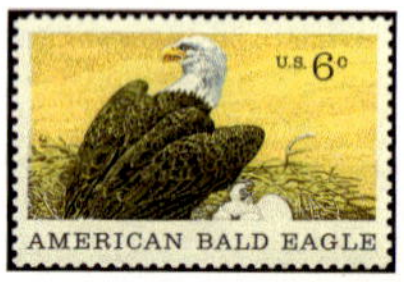

American Bald Eagle A809

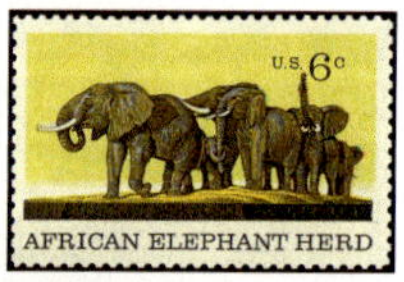

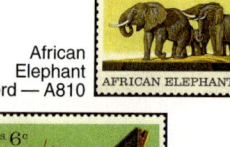

African Elephant Herd — A810

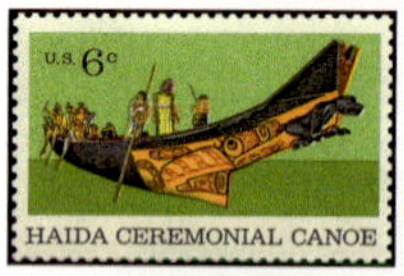

Tlingit Chief in Haida Ceremonial Canoe A811

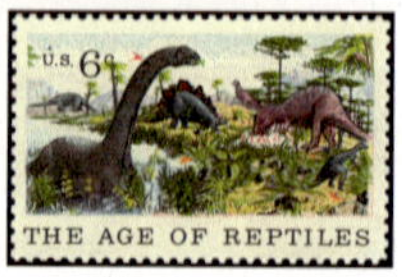

Brontosaurus, Stegosaurus & Allosaurus — A812

**1970, May 6**

**1387** A809 6c multicolored .30 .25
**1388** A810 6c multicolored .30 .25
**1389** A811 6c multicolored .30 .25
**1390** A812 6c multicolored .30 .25
- *a.* Block of 4, #1387-1390 1.00 *1.00*

### MAINE STATEHOOD, 150th ANNIV.

The painting hangs in the Metropolitan Museum of Art, New York City.

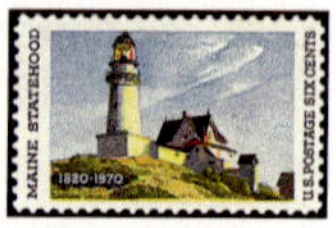

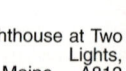

Lighthouse at Two Lights, Maine — A813

**1970, July 9** **Tagged** ***Perf. 11***

**1391** A813 6c black & multi .30 .25

### WILDLIFE CONSERVATION ISSUE

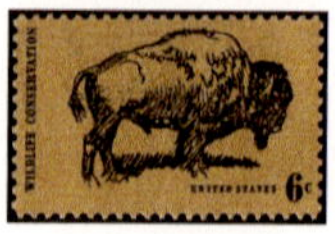

American Buffalo — A814

ROTARY PRESS PRINTING

**1970, July 20** ***Perf. 11x10½***

**1392** A814 6c black, *light brown* .30 .25

### REGULAR ISSUE
### Dwight David Eisenhower

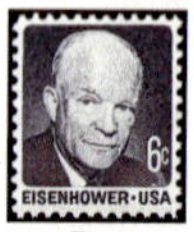

Dot between "R" and "U" A815

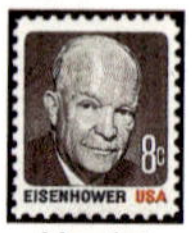

No dot between "R" and "U" — A815a

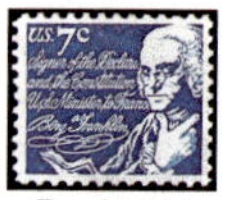

Benjamin Franklin A816

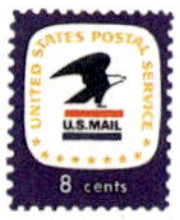

USPS Emblem A817

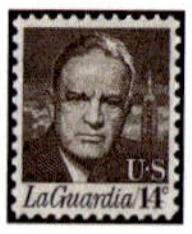

Fiorello H. LaGuardia A817a

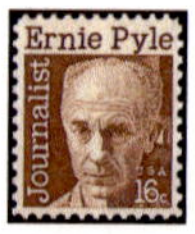

Ernest Taylor Pyle — A818

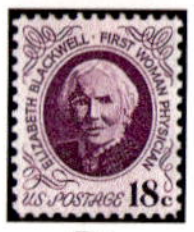

Dr. Elizabeth Blackwell A818a

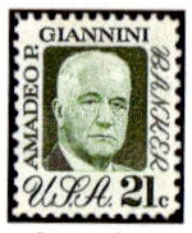

Amadeo P. Giannini A818b

ROTARY PRESS PRINTING

**1970-74**

**1393** A815 6c dk blue gray .30 .25
- *a.* Booklet pane of 8 2.00 2.00
- *b.* Booklet pane of 5 + label 1.40 1.40
- *c.* Untagged (Bureau precanceled) 12.75 3.00

***Perf. 10½x11***

**1393D** A816 7c bright blue ('73) .30 .25
- *e.* Untagged (Bureau precanceled) 4.25 1.00

GIORI PRESS PRINTING

***Perf. 11***

**1394** A815a 8c blk, red & bl gray ('71) .30 .25
- *b.* Red missing (PS) *150.00*
- *c.* Red missing (FO) *1,250.*
- *d.* Red and blue gray missing (PS) —
- *e.* Red and blue gray missing (FO or preprinting paper crease) *1,000.*
- *f.* All colors and tagging missing (FO) *1,000.*
- *g.* Printed on gum side, tagged *1,000.*

No. 1394f must be collected se-tenant with No. 1394c, 1394e, or with a partially printed No. 1394.

ROTARY PRESS PRINTING

***Perf. 11x10½ on 2 or 3 Sides***

**1395** A815 8c deep claret ('71) .30 .25
- *a.* Booklet pane of 8 2.00 2.00
- *b.* Booklet pane of 6 1.50 1.50
- *c.* Booklet pane of 4 +2 ('72) 1.65 1.10
- *d.* Booklet pane of 7 + label ('72) 1.90 1.90
- *e.* Vert. pair, imperf. between, in #1395a or 1395d with foldover *750.00*

No. 1395 was issued only in booklets.

At least 4 pairs of No. 1395e are recorded from 3 panes (one No. 1395a and two 1395d) with different foldover patterns. A pane of No. 1395d also is known with a foldover resulting in a vertical pair of stamp and label, imperf between.

PHOTOGRAVURE (Andreotti)

Plates of 400 subjects in four panes of 100.

***Perf. 11x10½***

**1396** A817 8c multi ('71) .30 .25

ROTARY PRESS PRINTING

**1397** A817a 14c gray brown ('72) .30 .25
- *a.* Untagged (Bureau precanceled) *100.00* 17.50

**1398** A818 16c brown ('72) .35 .25
- *a.* Untagged (Bureau precanceled) 22.50 5.00

**1399** A818a 18c violet ('74) .35 .25
**1400** A818b 21c green ('73) .40 .25
*Nos. 1393-1400 (9)* 2.90 2.25

Issued: 6c, 8/6/70; 7c, 10/20/72; #1394-1395, 5/10/71; #1396, 7/1/71; 14c, 4/24/72; 16c, 5/7/71; 18c, 1/23/74; 21c, 6/27/73.

COIL STAMPS

ROTARY PRESS PRINTING

**1970-71** ***Perf. 10 Vert.***

**1401** A815 6c dk blue gray .30 .25
- *a.* Untagged (Bureau precanceled) 19.50 3.00
- *b.* Imperf., pair *2,500.*

**1402** A815 8c dp claret ('71) .30 .25
- *a.* Imperf., pair 37.50
- *b.* Untagged (Bureau precanceled) 6.75 .75
- *c.* Pair, imperf. between *6,250.*

No. 1401b often found with small faults and/or without gum. Such examples sell for considerably less.

Issue dates: 6c, Aug. 6; 8c, May 10, 1971.

### EDGAR LEE MASTERS ISSUE

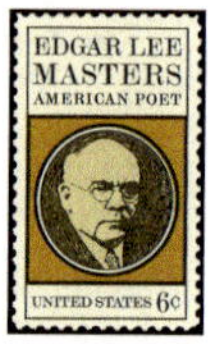

A819

LITHOGRAPHED, ENGRAVED (Giori)

**1970, Aug. 22** ***Perf. 11***

**1405** A819 6c black & olive bister .30 .25

### WOMAN SUFFRAGE ISSUE

50th anniversary of the 19th Amendment, which gave the vote to women.

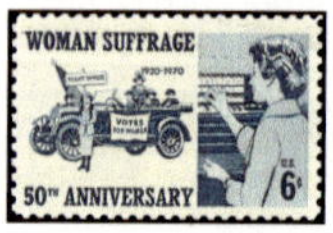

Suffragettes, 1920 & Woman Voter, 1970 — A820

GIORI PRESS PRINTING

**1970, Aug. 26**

**1406** A820 6c blue .30 .25

### SOUTH CAROLINA ISSUE

300th anniv. of the founding of Charles Town (Charleston), the 1st permanent settlement of South Carolina. Against a background of pine wood the line drawings of the design represent the economic and historic development of South Carolina: the spire of St. Philip's Church, Capitol, state flag, a ship, 17th century man and woman, a Fort Sumter cannon, barrels, cotton, tobacco and yellow jasmine.

# UNITED STATES

Symbols of South Carolina — A821

**LITHOGRAPHED, ENGRAVED (Giori)**
**1970, Sept. 12**
1407 A821 6c bister, black & red  .30  .25

## STONE MOUNTAIN MEMORIAL ISSUE

Dedication of the Stone Mountain Confederate Memorial, Georgia, May 9, 1970.

 A822

**GIORI PRESS PRINTING**
**1970, Sept. 19**
1408 A822 6c gray  .30  .25

## FORT SNELLING ISSUE

150th anniv. of Fort Snelling, Minnesota, an important outpost for the opening of the Northwest.

Fort Snelling, Keelboat & Tepees — A823

**LITHOGRAPHED, ENGRAVED (Giori)**
**1970, Oct. 17**
1409 A823 6c yellow & multi  .30  .25

## ANTI-POLLUTION ISSUE

Issued to focus attention on the problems of pollution.
In left panes Nos. 1410 and 1412 appear in 1st, 3rd and 5th place; Nos. 1411 and 1413 in 2nd and 4th place. This arrangement is reversed in right panes.

Globe and Wheat — A824

Globe and City — A825

Globe and Bluegill — A826

Globe and Seagull — A827

**PHOTOGRAVURE**
**1970, Oct. 28**  Perf. 11x10½
1410 A824 6c multicolored  .30  .25
1411 A825 6c multicolored  .30  .25
1412 A826 6c multicolored  .30  .25
1413 A827 6c multicolored  .30  .25
  a. Block of 4, #1410-1413  1.00  1.25

## CHRISTMAS ISSUE

In left panes Nos. 1415 and 1417 appear in 1st, 3rd and 5th place; Nos. 1416 and 1418 in 2nd and 4th place. This arrangement is reversed in right panes.

Nativity A828

Tin and Cast-iron Locomotive A829

Toy Horse on Wheels — A830

Mechanical Tricycle — A831

Doll Carriage — A832

**1970, Nov. 5**  Perf. 10½x11
1414 A828 6c multicolored  .30  .25
  a. Precanceled  .30  .25
  b. Black omitted  400.00
  c. As "a," blue omitted  1,100.
  d. Type II  .30  .25
  e. Type II, precanceled  .30  .25

No. 1414 has a slightly blurry impression, snowflaking in the sky and no gum breaker ridges. No. 1414d has shiny surfaced paper, sharper impression, no snowflaking and vertical and horizontal gum breaker ridges.
No. 1414a has a slightly blurry impression, snowflaking in the sky, no gum breaker ridges and the precancel is grayish black. No. 1414e has sharper impression, no snowflaking, gum breaker ridges and the precancel is intense black.

**Perf. 11x10½**
1415 A829 6c multicolored  .30  .25
  a. Precanceled  .65  .25
  b. Black omitted  1,750.
1416 A830 6c multicolored  .30  .25
  a. Precanceled  .65  .25
  b. Black omitted  1,750.
  c. Imperf. pair (#1416, 1418)  2,500.
1417 A831 6c multicolored  .30  .25
  a. Precanceled  .65  .25
  b. Black omitted  1,750.
1418 A832 6c multicolored  .30  .25
  a. Precanceled  .65  .25
  b. Block of 4, #1415-1418  1.25  1.40
  c. As "b," precanceled  3.75  3.50
  d. Black omitted  1,750.
  e. As "b," black omitted  8,000.
  f. As "b," black omitted on #1417 & 1418  4,000.
  g. P# block of 8, black omitted on #1415 & 1416  4,000.
Nos. 1415-1418 (4)  1.20  1.00

Nos. 1415-1418 and 1415a-1418a are known both without gum breaker ridges (common) and with gum breaker ridges (scarce).
The precanceled stamps, Nos. 1414a-1418a, were furnished to 68 cities. The plates include two straight (No. 1414a) or two wavy (Nos. 1415a-1418a) black lines that make up the precancellation. Unused values are for stamps with gum and used values are for stamps with an additional cancellation or without gum.

## UNITED NATIONS, 25th ANNIV.

"UN" & UN Emblem — A833

**LITHOGRAPHED, ENGRAVED (Giori)**
**1970, Nov. 20**  Perf. 11
1419 A833 6c blk, verm & ultra  .30  .25

## LANDING OF THE PILGRIMS ISSUE

350th anniv. of the landing of the Mayflower.

Mayflower & Pilgrims — A834

**1970, Nov. 21**
1420 A834 6c blk, org, yel, mag, bl & brn  .30  .25
  a. Orange & yellow omitted  425.00

## DISABLED AMERICAN VETERANS AND SERVICEMEN ISSUE

No. 1421 for the 50th anniv. of the Disabled Veterans of America Organization; No. 1422 honors the contribution of servicemen, particularly those who were prisoners of war, missing or killed in action. Nos. 1421-1422 are printed se-tenant in horizontal rows of 10.

A835  A836

**1970, Nov. 24**
1421 A835 6c dark blue, red & multicolored  .30  .25

**ENGRAVED**
1422 A836 6c dark blue, black & red  .30  .25
  a. Pair, #1421-1422  .50  .50

## AMERICAN WOOL INDUSTRY ISSUE

450th anniv. of the introduction of sheep to the North American continent and the beginning of the American wool industry.

Ewe and Lamb — A837

Plates of 200 subjects in four panes of 50.

**1971, Jan. 19**
1423 A837 6c multicolored  .30  .25
  b. Teal blue ("United States") missing (OM)  325.00

## GEN. DOUGLAS MacARTHUR ISSUE

MacArthur (1880-1964), Chief of Staff, Supreme Commander for the Allied Powers in the Pacific Area during World War II and Supreme Commander in Japan after the war.

Douglas MacArthur — A838

**GIORI PRESS PRINTING**
**1971, Jan. 26**
1424 A838 6c black, red & dark blue  .30  .25
  a. Red missing (PS)  —
  c. Blue missing (PS)  —

## BLOOD DONOR ISSUE

Salute to blood donors and spur to increased participation in the blood donor program.

Giving Blood Saves Lives — A839

**LITHOGRAPHED, ENGRAVED (Giori)**
**1971, Mar. 12**
1425 A839 6c bl, scarlet & ind  .30  .25

## MISSOURI STATEHOOD, 150th ANNIV.

The stamp design shows a Pawnee facing a hunter-trapper and a group of settlers. It is from a mural by Thomas Hart Benton in the Harry S Truman Library, Independence, Mo.

"Independence and the Opening of the West" — A840

**PHOTOGRAVURE (Andreotti)**
**1971, May 8**  Perf. 11x10½
1426 A840 8c multicolored  .30  .25

See note on Andreotti printings and their color control markings in Information for Collectors under Printing, Photogravure.

## WILDLIFE CONSERVATION ISSUE

Nos. 1427-1428 alternate in first row, Nos. 1429-1430 in second row. This arrangement repeated throughout pane.

Trout — A841

Alligator A842

Polar Bear, Cubs — A843

California Condor A844

**LITHOGRAPHED, ENGRAVED (Giori)**
**1971, June 12**  Perf. 11
1427 A841 8c multicolored  .30  .25
  a. Red omitted  1,250.
  b. Green (engr.) omitted  —
1428 A842 8c multicolored  .30  .25
1429 A843 8c multicolored  .30  .25
1430 A844 8c multicolored  .30  .25
  a. Block of 4, #1427-1430  1.00  1.00
  b. As "a," light green & dark green omitted from #1427-1428  3,250.
  c. As "a," red omitted from #1427, 1429-1430  3,000.

## ANTARCTIC TREATY ISSUE

Map of Antarctica A845

Adapted from emblem on official documents of Consultative Meetings.

## UNITED STATES

### GIORI PRESS PRINTING
**1971, June 23**

| 1431 | A845 | 8c red & dark blue | .30 | .25 |
| --- | --- | --- | --- | --- |
| b. | | Both colors missing (EP) | 500.00 | |

No. 1431b should be collected se-tenant with a normal stamp and/or a partially printed stamp.

### AMERICAN REVOLUTION BICENTENNIAL

Bicentennial Commission Emblem — A846

**LITHOGRAPHED, ENGRAVED (Giori)**
**1971, July 4**

| 1432 | A846 | 8c gray, red, blue & black | .30 | .25 |
| --- | --- | --- | --- | --- |
| a. | | Gray & black missing (EP) | 325.00 | |
| b. | | Gray ("U.S. Postage 8c") missing (EP) | 650.00 | |

### JOHN SLOAN ISSUE
John Sloan (1871-1951), painter. The painting hangs in the Phillips Gallery, Washington, D.C.

The Wake of the Ferry — A847

**1971, Aug. 2**

| 1433 | A847 | 8c multicolored | .30 | .25 |
| --- | --- | --- | --- | --- |
| b. | | Red engr. ("John Sloan" and "8") missing (CM) | 1,000. | |

### SPACE ACHIEVEMENT DECADE ISSUE
Decade of space achievements and the Apollo 15 moon exploration mission, July 26-Aug. 7. In the left panes the earth and sun stamp is 1st, 3rd and 5th, the rover 2nd and 4th. This arrangement is reversed in the right panes.

Earth, Sun, Landing Craft on Moon — A848

Lunar Rover — A849

**1971, Aug. 2**

| 1434 | A848 | 8c blk, bl, gray, yel & red | .30 | .25 |
| --- | --- | --- | --- | --- |
| 1435 | A849 | 8c blk, bl, gray, yel & red | .30 | .25 |
| b. | | Pair, #1434-1435 | .50 | .50 |
| d. | | As "b," blue & red (litho.) omitted | 1,500. | |

### EMILY DICKINSON ISSUE

Emily Elizabeth Dickinson — A850

**1971, Aug. 28**

| 1436 | A850 | 8c multi, grnsh | .30 | .25 |
| --- | --- | --- | --- | --- |
| a. | | Black & olive (engr.) omitted | 500.00 | |
| b. | | Pale rose missing (EP) | 5,000. | |
| c. | | Red omitted | — | |

### SAN JUAN ISSUE
450th anniversary of San Juan, Puerto Rico.

Sentry Box, Morro Castle, San Juan — A851

**1971, Sept. 12**

| 1437 | A851 | 8c pale brn, blk, yel, red brn & dk brn | .30 | .25 |
| --- | --- | --- | --- | --- |
| b. | | Dark brown (engr.) omitted | 1,500. | |

### VALUES FOR HINGED STAMPS AFTER NO. 771
This catalogue does not value unused stamps after No. 771 in hinged condition. Hinged unused stamps from No. 772 to the present are worth considerably less than the values given for unused stamps, which are for never-hinged examples.

### PREVENT DRUG ABUSE ISSUE
Drug Abuse Prevention Week, Oct. 3-9.

Young Woman Drug Addict — A852

**PHOTOGRAVURE (Andreotti)**
**1971, Oct. 4**     Perf. 10½x11

| 1438 | A852 | 8c blue, deep blue & black | .30 | .25 |
| --- | --- | --- | --- | --- |

### CARE ISSUE
25th anniversary of CARE, a US-Canadian Cooperative for American Relief Everywhere.

Hands Reaching for CARE — A853

**1971, Oct. 27**

| 1439 | A853 | 8c blue, blk, vio & red lilac | .30 | .25 |
| --- | --- | --- | --- | --- |
| a. | | Black omitted | 1,500. | |

### HISTORIC PRESERVATION ISSUE
Nos. 1440-1441 alternate in 1st row, Nos. 1442-1443 in 2nd row. This arrangement is repeated throughout the pane.

Decatur House, Washington, DC — A854

Whaling Ship Charles W. Morgan, Mystic, Conn. A855

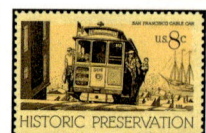
Cable Car, San Francisco A856

San Xavier del Bac Mission, Tucson, Ariz. — A857

San Xavier del Bac Mission, Tucson, Ariz. — A857

**LITHOGRAPHED, ENGRAVED (Giori)**
**1971, Oct. 29**    Tagged    Perf. 11

| 1440 | A854 | 8c blk brn & ocher, buff | .30 | .25 |
| --- | --- | --- | --- | --- |
| 1441 | A855 | 8c blk brn & ocher, buff | .30 | .25 |
| 1442 | A856 | 8c blk brn & ocher, buff | .30 | .25 |
| 1443 | A857 | 8c blk brn & ocher, buff | .30 | .25 |
| a. | | Block of 4, #1440-1443 | 1.00 | 1.00 |
| b. | | As "a," black brown omitted | 600.00 | |
| c. | | As "a," ocher omitted | 2,500. | |

### CHRISTMAS ISSUE

Adoration of the Shepherds, by Giorgione A858

Partridge in a Pear Tree, by Jamie Wyeth A859

No. 1444 after a painting by Giorgione in the National Gallery of Art, Washington D.C.

**PHOTOGRAVURE (Andreotti)**
**1971, Nov. 10**     Perf. 10½x11

| 1444 | A858 | 8c gold & multi | .30 | .25 |
| --- | --- | --- | --- | --- |
| a. | | Gold omitted | 350.00 | |
| 1445 | A859 | 8c dark green, red & multicolored | .30 | .25 |

### SIDNEY LANIER ISSUE
Lanier (1842-81), poet, musician, lawyer, educator.

Sidney Lanier (1842-1881) — A860

**GIORI PRESS PRINTING**
**1972, Feb. 3**     Perf. 11

| 1446 | A860 | 8c black, brown & light blue | .30 | .25 |
| --- | --- | --- | --- | --- |

### PEACE CORPS ISSUE

Peace Corps Poster, by David Battle — A861

**PHOTOGRAVURE (Andreotti)**
**1972, Feb. 11**     Perf. 10½x11

| 1447 | A861 | 8c dark blue, light blue & red | .30 | .25 |
| --- | --- | --- | --- | --- |

### NATIONAL PARKS CENTENNIAL ISSUE
Centenary of Yellowstone National Park, the 1st National Park, and of the entire National Park System. See No. C84.

Hulk of Ship A862    Cape Hatteras Lighthouse A863

Laughing Gulls on Driftwood A864    Laughing Gulls and Dune A865

Wolf Trap Farm, Vienna, Va. A866    Old Faithful, Yellowstone A867

Mt. McKinley, Alaska — A868

**LITHOGRAPHED, ENGRAVED (Giori)**
**1972**     Perf. 11
Plates of 400 subjects in 4 panes of 100 each

| 1448 | A862 | 2c black & multi | .30 | .25 |
| --- | --- | --- | --- | --- |
| 1449 | A863 | 2c black & multi | .30 | .25 |
| 1450 | A864 | 2c black & multi | .30 | .25 |
| 1451 | A865 | 2c black & multi | .30 | .25 |
| a. | | Block of 4, #1448-1451 | .50 | .50 |
| b. | | As "a," black (litho.) omitted | 800.00 | |
| 1452 | A866 | 6c black & multi | .30 | .25 |
| 1453 | A867 | 8c blk, bl, brn & multi | .30 | .25 |
| 1454 | A868 | 15c black & multi | .30 | .25 |
| b. | | Yellow omitted | 1,500. | |

### FAMILY PLANNING ISSUE

Family — A869

**1972, Mar. 18**

| 1455 | A869 | 8c blk & multi | .30 | .25 |
| --- | --- | --- | --- | --- |
| a. | | Yellow omitted | 300.00 | |
| c. | | Dark brown missing (FO) | 9,500. | |

### AMERICAN BICENTENNIAL ISSUE
**Colonial American Craftsmen**

In left panes Nos. 1456 and 1458 appear in 1st, 3rd and 5th place; Nos. 1457 and 1459 in 2nd and 4th place. This arrangement is reversed in right panes.

Glassmaker A870

Silversmith A871

Wigmaker — A872

UNITED STATES 45

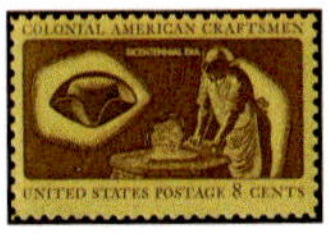


Hatter — A873

ENGRAVED

**1972, July 4** ***Perf. 11x10½***

| | | | | |
|---|---|---|---|---|
| **1456** | A870 | 8c deep brown | .30 | .25 |
| **1457** | A871 | 8c deep brown | .30 | .25 |
| **1458** | A872 | 8c deep brown | .30 | .25 |
| **1459** | A873 | 8c deep brown | .30 | .25 |
| *a.* | | Block of 4, #1456-1459 | 1.00 | 1.00 |

### OLYMPIC GAMES ISSUE

11th Winter Olympic Games, Sapporo, Japan, Feb. 3-13 and 20th Summer Olympic Games, Munich, Germany, Aug. 26-Sept. 11. See No. C85.

Bicycling and Olympic Rings — A874

Bobsledding A875

Running — A876

PHOTOGRAVURE (Andreotti)

**1972, Aug. 17** ***Perf. 11x10½***

| | | | | |
|---|---|---|---|---|
| **1460** | A874 | 6c blk, bl, red, emer & yel | .30 | .25 |
| **1461** | A875 | 8c blk, bl, red, emer & yel | .30 | .25 |
| **1462** | A876 | 15c blk, bl, red, emer & yel | .30 | .25 |
| | | *Nos. 1460-1462 (3)* | .90 | .75 |

### PARENT TEACHER ASSN., 75th ANNIV.

Blackboard A877

**1972, Sept. 15**

| | | | | |
|---|---|---|---|---|
| **1463** | A877 | 8c yellow & black | .30 | .25 |

### WILDLIFE CONSERVATION ISSUE

Nos. 1464-1465 alternate in 1st row, Nos. 1468-1469 in 2nd row. This arrangement repeated throughout pane.

Fur Seals — A878

Cardinal A879

Brown Pelican A880

Bighorn Sheep A881

LITHOGRAPHED, ENGRAVED (Giori)

**1972, Sept. 20** ***Perf. 11***

| | | | | |
|---|---|---|---|---|
| **1464** | A878 | 8c multicolored | .30 | .25 |
| **1465** | A879 | 8c multicolored | .30 | .25 |
| **1466** | A880 | 8c multicolored | .30 | .25 |
| **1467** | A881 | 8c multicolored | .30 | .25 |
| *a.* | | Block of 4, #1464-1467 | 1.00 | 1.00 |
| *b.* | | As "a," brown omitted | *2,750.* | |
| *c.* | | As "a," green & blue omitted | *2,250.* | |
| *d.* | | As "a," red & brown omitted | *2,750.* | |

### MAIL ORDER BUSINESS ISSUE

Centenary of mail order business, originated by Aaron Montgomery Ward, Chicago. Design based on Headsville, W.Va., post office in Smithsonian Institution, Washington, D.C.

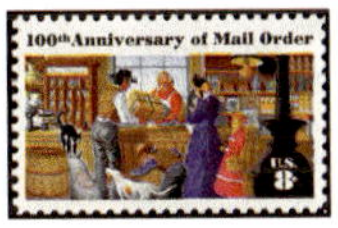

Rural Post Office Store — A882

PHOTOGRAVURE (Andreotti)

**1972, Sept, 27** ***Perf. 11x10½***

| | | | | |
|---|---|---|---|---|
| **1468** | A882 | 8c multicolored | .30 | .25 |

### OSTEOPATHIC MEDICINE ISSUE

75th anniv. of the American Osteopathic Assoc., founded by Dr. Andrew T. Still (1828-1917), who developed the principles of osteopathy in 1874.

Man's Quest for Health — A883

**1972, Oct. 9** ***Perf. 10½x11***

| | | | | |
|---|---|---|---|---|
| **1469** | A883 | 8c multicolored | .30 | .25 |

### AMERICAN FOLKLORE ISSUE

Tom Sawyer, by Norman Rockwell — A884

Designed by Bradbury Thompson.

LITHOGRAPHED, ENGRAVED (Giori)

**1972, Oct. 13** ***Perf. 11***

| | | | | |
|---|---|---|---|---|
| **1470** | A884 | 8c blk, red, yel, tan, bl & rose red | .30 | .25 |
| *a.* | | Horiz. pair, imperf. between | *6,750.* | |
| *b.* | | Red & black (engr.) omitted | *1,000.* | |
| *c.* | | Yellow & tan (litho.) omitted | *1,300.* | |
| *e.* | | Red (engr. 8c) missing (CM) | *750.* | |

### CHRISTMAS ISSUE

Angel from "Mary, Queen of Heaven" A885

Santa Claus A886

No. 1471, detail from a painting by the Master of the St. Lucy Legend in the National Gallery of Art, Washington, D.C.

PHOTOGRAVURE (Andreotti)

**1972, Nov. 9** ***Perf. 10½x11***

| | | | | |
|---|---|---|---|---|
| **1471** | A885 | 8c multicolored | .30 | .25 |
| *a.* | | Pink omitted | *100.00* | |
| *b.* | | Black omitted | *2,500.* | |
| **1472** | A886 | 8c multicolored | .30 | .25 |

### PHARMACY ISSUE

Honoring American druggists in connection with the 120th anniversary of the American Pharmaceutical Association.

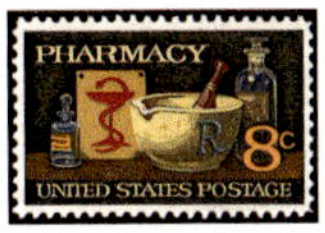

Mortar & Pestle, Bowl of Hygeia, 19th Century Medicine Bottles — A887

LITHOGRAPHED, ENGRAVED (Giori)

**1972, Nov. 10** ***Perf. 11***

| | | | | |
|---|---|---|---|---|
| **1473** | A887 | 8c black & multi | .30 | .25 |
| *a.* | | Blue & orange omitted | *600.00* | |
| *b.* | | Blue omitted | *1,250.* | |
| *c.* | | Orange omitted | *1,250.* | |
| *e.* | | Vertical pair, imperf horiz. | *2,000.* | |

### STAMP COLLECTING ISSUE

Issued to publicize stamp collecting.

U.S. No. 1 Under Magnifying Glass — A888

**1972, Nov. 17**

| | | | | |
|---|---|---|---|---|
| **1474** | A888 | 8c multicolored | .30 | .25 |
| *a.* | | Black (litho.) omitted | *325.00* | |

### LOVE ISSUE

"Love," by Robert Indiana — A889

PHOTOGRAVURE (Andreotti)

**1973, Jan. 26** ***Perf. 11x10½***

| | | | | |
|---|---|---|---|---|
| **1475** | A889 | 8c red, emer & vio blue | .30 | .25 |

### AMERICAN BICENTENNIAL ISSUE
### Communications in Colonial Times

Printer and Patriots Examining Pamphlet — A890

Posting a Broadside A891

Postrider — A892

Drummer — A893

GIORI PRESS PRINTING

**1973** ***Perf. 11***

| | | | | |
|---|---|---|---|---|
| **1476** | A890 | 8c ultra, greenish blk & red | .30 | .25 |
| *b.* | | Red missing (PS) | *300.00* | |
| **1477** | A891 | 8c blk, vermilion & ultra | .30 | .25 |

**LITHOGRAPHED, ENGRAVED (Giori)**

| | | | | |
|---|---|---|---|---|
| **1478** | A892 | 8c bl, blk, red & grn | .30 | .25 |
| *a.* | | Red missing (CM) | *1,300.* | |
| **1479** | A893 | 8c bl, blk, yel & red | .30 | .25 |
| *a.* | | Blue missing (CM) | | |
| *b.* | | Red missing (CM) | — | |
| | | *Nos. 1476-1479 (4)* | 1.20 | 1.00 |

### AMERICAN BICENTENNIAL ISSUE
### Boston Tea Party

In left panes Nos. 1480 and 1482 appear in 1st, 3rd and 5th place, Nos. 1481 and 1483 appear in 2nd and 4th place. This arrangement is reversed in right panes.

British Merchantman A894

British Three-master A895

Boats and Ship's Hull — A896

Boat and Dock — A897

**1973, July 4**

| | | | | |
|---|---|---|---|---|
| **1480** | A894 | 8c blk & multi | .30 | .25 |
| **1481** | A895 | 8c blk & multi | .30 | .25 |
| **1482** | A896 | 8c blk & multi | .30 | .25 |
| **1483** | A897 | 8c blk & multi | .30 | .25 |
| *a.* | | Block of 4, #1480-1483 | 1.00 | 1.00 |
| *b.* | | As "a," black (engraved) omitted | *1,250.* | |
| *c.* | | As "a," black (litho.) omitted | *900.00* | |
| *e.* | | As "a," dk blue omitted | *1,500.* | *750.00* |

### AMERICAN ARTS ISSUE

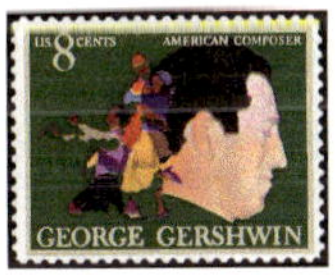

Gershwin, Sportin' Life, Porgy & Bess — A898

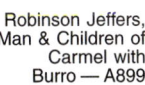

Robinson Jeffers, Man & Children of Carmel with Burro — A899

Henry Ossawa Tanner, Palette & Rainbow — A900

Willa Cather, Pioneer Family & Covered Wagon — A901

PHOTOGRAVURE (Andreotti)

**1973**

| | | | | |
|---|---|---|---|---|
| **1484** | A898 | 8c dp grn & multi | .30 | .25 |
| *a.* | | Vertical pair, imperf. horiz. | *160.00* | |
| **1485** | A899 | 8c Prus bl & multi | .30 | .25 |
| *a.* | | Vertical pair, imperf. horiz. | *160.00* | |
| **1486** | A900 | 8c yel brn & multi | .30 | .25 |
| **1487** | A901 | 8c dp brn & multi | .30 | .25 |
| *a.* | | Vertical pair, imperf. horiz. | *175.00* | |
| | | *Nos. 1484-1487 (4)* | 1.20 | 1.00 |

Honoring: No. 1484, George Gershwin (1898-1937), composer. No. 1485, Robinson Jeffers (1887-1962), poet. No. 1486, Henry Ossawa Tanner (1859-1937), black painter (portrait by Thomas Eakins). No. 1487, Willa Sibert Cather (1873-1947), novelist.

Issued: No. 1484, Feb. 28; No. 1485, Aug. 13; No. 1486, Sept. 10; No. 1487, Sept. 20.

### COPERNICUS ISSUE

Nicolaus Copernicus (1473-1543), Polish Astronomer — A902

# UNITED STATES

**LITHOGRAPHED, ENGRAVED (Giori)**
**1973, Apr. 23**
| 1488 | A902 | 8c black & orange | .30 | .25 |
|---|---|---|---|---|
| a. | | Orange omitted | 400.00 | |
| b. | | Black (engraved) omitted | 450.00 | |

The orange can be chemically removed. Expertization of No. 1488a is required.

## POSTAL SERVICE EMPLOYEES ISSUE

A tribute to US Postal Service employees. Nos. 1489-1498 are printed se-tenant in horizontal rows of 10. Emerald inscription on back, printed beneath gum in water-soluble ink, includes Postal Service emblem, "People Serving You" and a statement, differing for each of the 10 stamps, about some aspect of postal service.

Each stamp in top or bottom row has a tab with blue inscription enumerating various jobs in postal service.

Stamp Counter A903 / Mail Collection A904

Letter Facing on Conveyor Belt A905 / Parcel Post Sorting A906

Mail Canceling A907 / Manual Letter Routing A908

Electronic Letter Routing A909 / Loading Mail on Truck A910

Mailman A911

Rural Mail Delivery A912

**PHOTOGRAVURE (Andreotti)**
**1973, Apr. 30** — Perf. 10½x11
| 1489 | A903 | 8c multicolored | .30 | .25 |
|---|---|---|---|---|
| 1490 | A904 | 8c multicolored | .30 | .25 |
| 1491 | A905 | 8c multicolored | .30 | .25 |
| 1492 | A906 | 8c multicolored | .30 | .25 |
| 1493 | A907 | 8c multicolored | .30 | .25 |
| 1494 | A908 | 8c multicolored | .30 | .25 |
| 1495 | A909 | 8c multicolored | .30 | .25 |
| 1496 | A910 | 8c multicolored | .30 | .25 |
| 1497 | A911 | 8c multicolored | .30 | .25 |
| 1498 | A912 | 8c multicolored | .30 | .25 |
| a. | | Strip of 10, #1489-1498 | 2.50 | 2.50 |

## HARRY S. TRUMAN ISSUE

Harry S Truman, 33rd President (1884-1972) — A913

**GIORI PRESS PRINTING**
**1973, May 8** — Perf. 11
| 1499 | A913 | 8c carmine rose, black & blue | .30 | .25 |

## ELECTRONICS PROGRESS ISSUE

Marconi's Spark Coil and Gap — A914

Transistors and Printed Circuit Board — A915

Microphone, Speaker, Vacuum Tube, TV Camera Tube — A916

**LITHOGRAPHED, ENGRAVED (Giori)**
**1973, July 10**
| 1500 | A914 | 6c lilac & multi | .30 | .25 |
|---|---|---|---|---|
| 1501 | A915 | 8c tan & multi | .30 | .25 |
| a. | | Black (inscriptions & "U.S. 8c") omitted | 300.00 | |
| b. | | Tan (background) & lilac omitted | 600.00 | |

Many examples of No. 1501b are hinged. Value about one-half never hinged value.

| 1502 | A916 | 15c gray green & multicolored | .30 | .25 |
|---|---|---|---|---|
| a. | | Black (inscriptions & "U.S. 15c") omitted | 650.00 | |

Nos. 1500-1502 (3) .90 .75

See No. C86.

## LYNDON B. JOHNSON ISSUE

Lyndon B. Johnson (1908-1973), 36th President — A917

**PHOTOGRAVURE (Andreotti)**
**1973, Aug. 27**
| 1503 | A917 | 8c black & multi | .30 | .25 |
|---|---|---|---|---|
| a. | | Horiz. pair, imperf. vert. | 200.00 | |

## RURAL AMERICA ISSUE

Centenary of the introduction of Aberdeen Angus cattle into the US (#1504); of the Chautauqua Institution (#1505); and of the introduction of hard winter wheat into Kansas by Mennonite immigrants (#1506).

Angus and Longhorn Cattle — A918

Chautauqua Tent and Buggies — A919

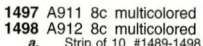
Wheat Fields and Train — A920

No. 1504 after painting by F.C. "Frank" Murphy.

**LITHOGRAPHED, ENGRAVED (Giori)**
**1973-74**
| 1504 | A918 | 8c multi | .30 | .25 |
|---|---|---|---|---|
| a. | | Green & red brown omitted | 500.00 | |
| b. | | Vert. pair, imperf. between | 5,000. | |
| d. | | Blue (engr.) missing (PS) | — | |
| 1505 | A919 | 10c multi | .30 | .25 |
| a. | | Black (litho.) omitted | 1,750. | |
| 1506 | A920 | 10c multi | .30 | .25 |
| a. | | Black and blue (engr.) omitted | 500.00 | |

Nos. 1504-1506 (3) .90 .75

## CHRISTMAS ISSUE

Small Cowper Madonna, by Raphael A921

Christmas Tree in Needlepoint A922

No. 1507 after painting in the National Gallery of Art, Washington, D.C.

**PHOTOGRAVURE (Andreotti)**
**1973, Nov. 7** — Perf. 10½x11
| 1507 | A921 | 8c multicolored | .30 | .25 |
|---|---|---|---|---|
| 1508 | A922 | 8c multicolored | .30 | .25 |
| a. | | Vertical pair, imperf. between | 225.00 | |

50-Star & 13-Star Flags A923

Jefferson Memorial & Signature A924

Mail Transport A925

Liberty Bell A926

**MULTICOLOR HUCK PRESS**
**1973-74** — Perf. 11x10½
| 1509 | A923 | 10c red & blue | .30 | .25 |
|---|---|---|---|---|
| a. | | Horizontal pair, imperf. between | 40.00 | — |
| b. | | Blue omitted | 150.00 | |
| c. | | Imperf., vert. pair | 450.00 | |
| d. | | Horiz. pair, imperf. vert. | 900.00 | |
| f. | | Vert. pair, imperf. between | | |

No. 1509 exists imperf and with red omitted from printer's waste.

**ROTARY PRESS PRINTING**
| 1510 | A924 | 10c blue | .30 | .25 |
|---|---|---|---|---|
| a. | | Untagged (Bureau precanceled) | 4.00 | 1.00 |
| b. | | Booklet pane of 5 + label | 1.65 | 1.25 |
| c. | | Booklet pane of 8 | 2.00 | 2.00 |
| d. | | Booklet pane of 6 ('74) | 5.00 | 1.75 |
| e. | | Vert. pair, imperf. horiz. | 300.00 | |
| f. | | Vert. pair, imperf. btwn., in #1510c with miscut or with foldover | 600.00 | |
| i. | | As "b," double booklet pane of 10 plus 2 horiz. pairs imperf. btwn. plus stamp and label imperf. btwn. (FO) | 1,750. | |

No. 1510f resulted from a paper foldover after perforating and before cutting into booklet panes.

**PHOTOGRAVURE (Andreotti)**
| 1511 | A925 | 10c multi | .30 | .25 |
|---|---|---|---|---|
| a. | | Yellow omitted | 40.00 | |

Beware of stamps with yellow chemically removed offered as No. 1511a.

## COIL STAMPS
### ROTARY PRESS PRINTING
**1973-74** — Perf. 10 Vert.
| 1518 | A926 | 6.3c brick red | .30 | .25 |
|---|---|---|---|---|
| a. | | Untagged (Bureau precanceled) | .35 | .25 |
| b. | | Imperf., pair | 130.00 | |
| c. | | As "a," imperf., pair | 75.00 | |

No. 1518c is precanceled Washington, DC. Columbus, Ohio and Garden City, N.Y. Values for Columbus pair $400, for Garden City pair $850.

### MULTICOLOR HUCK PRESS
| 1519 | A923 | 10c red & blue | .30 | .25 |
|---|---|---|---|---|
| a. | | Imperf., pair | 35.00 | |

Huck press printings often show parts of a joint line, but this feature is not consistent.

### ROTARY PRESS PRINTING
| 1520 | A924 | 10c blue | .30 | .25 |
|---|---|---|---|---|
| a. | | Untagged (Bureau precanceled) | 5.50 | 1.25 |
| b. | | Imperf., pair | 30.00 | |

## VETERANS OF FOREIGN WARS ISSUE

75th anniversary of Veterans of Spanish-American and Other Foreign Wars.

V.F.W. Emblem — A928

**GIORI PRESS PRINTING**
**1974, Mar. 11** — Perf. 11
| 1525 | A928 | 10c red & dark blue | .30 | .25 |
|---|---|---|---|---|
| b. | | Blue missing (PS) | 350.00 | |

## ROBERT FROST ISSUE

Robert Frost (1874-1963), Poet — A929

**1974, Mar. 26** — Perf. 10½x11
| 1526 | A929 | 10c black | .30 | .25 |

## EXPO '74 WORLD'S FAIR ISSUE

EXPO '74 World's Fair "Preserve the Environment," Spokane, Wash., May 4-Nov. 4.

"Cosmic Jumper" — A930

**PHOTOGRAVURE (Andreotti)**
**1974, Apr. 18** — Perf. 11
| 1527 | A930 | 10c multicolored | .30 | .25 |

## HORSE RACING ISSUE

Kentucky Derby, Churchill Downs, centenary.

Horses Rounding Turn — A931

**1974, May 4** — Perf. 11x10½
| 1528 | A931 | 10c yel & multi | .30 | .25 |
|---|---|---|---|---|
| a. | | Blue ("Horse Racing") omitted | 500.00 | |
| b. | | Red ("U.S. postage 10 cents") omitted | 1,750. | |

Beware of stamps offered as No. 1528b that have traces of red.

## SKYLAB ISSUE

First anniversary of the launching of Skylab I, honoring all who participated in the Skylab project.

# UNITED STATES

Skylab — A932

**LITHOGRAPHED, ENGRAVED (Giori)**
**1974, May 14**      *Perf. 11*
1529   A932   10c multicolored    .30   .25
   a.   Vert. pair, imperf. between   —
   c.   Vert. pair, imperf. horiz.   —
   d.   Double impression of magenta   —

## UNIVERSAL POSTAL UNION ISSUE

UPU cent. In the 1st row Nos. 1530-1537 are in sequence as listed. In the 2nd row Nos. 1534-1537 are followed by Nos. 1530-1533. Every row of 8 and every horizontal block of 8 contains all 8 designs. The letter writing designs are from famous works of art; some are details. The quotation on every second stamp, "Letters mingle souls," is from a letter by poet John Donne.

Michelangelo, from School of Athens — A933

Five Feminine Virtues — A934

Old Time Letter Rack — A935    Mlle. La Vergne — A936

Lady Writing Letter — A937    Inkwell and Quill — A938

Mrs. John Douglas A939    Don Antonio Noreiga A940

**PHOTOGRAVURE (Andreotti)**
**1974, June 6**
1530   A933   10c multicolored   .30   .25
1531   A934   10c multicolored   .30   .25
1532   A935   10c multicolored   .30   .25
1533   A936   10c multicolored   .30   .25
1534   A937   10c multicolored   .30   .25
1535   A938   10c multicolored   .30   .25
1536   A939   10c multicolored   .30   .25
1537   A940   10c multicolored   .30   .25
   a.   Block or strip of 8 (#1530-1537)   2.40   2.00
   b.   As "a," (block), imperf. vert.   2,500.

## MINERAL HERITAGE ISSUE

The sequence of stamps in 1st horizontal row is Nos. 1538-1541, 1538-1539. In 2nd row Nos. 1540-1541 are followed by Nos. 1538-1541.

Petrified Wood — A941
Tourmaline A942
Amethyst A943
Rhodochrosite A944

**1974, June 13**
1538   A941   10c blue & multi   .30   .25
   a.   Light blue & yellow (litho.) omitted   —
1539   A942   10c blue & multi   .30   .25
   a.   Light blue (litho.) omitted   —
   b.   Black & purple (engr.) omitted   —
1540   A943   10c blue & multi   .30   .25
   a.   Light blue & yellow (litho.) omitted   —
1541   A944   10c blue & multi   .30   .25
   a.   Block or strip of 4, #1538-1541   1.20   1.00
   b.   As "a," light blue & yellow (litho.) omitted   900.00
   c.   Light blue (litho.) omitted   —
   d.   Black & red (engr.) omitted   —
   e.   Block of 4, two right stamps being Nos. 1539b and 1541d   7,000.

No. 1541e is usually collected as a transition block of six or larger.

## KENTUCKY SETTLEMENT, 200th ANNIV.
### Fort Harrod, first settlement in Kentucky.

Fort Harrod — A945

**1974, June 15**
1542   A945   10c green & multi   .30   .25
   a.   Dull black (litho.) omitted   400.00
   b.   Green (engr. & litho.), black (engr. & litho.) & blue missing (EP)   1,750.
   c.   Green (engr.) missing (EP)   3,000.
   d.   Green (engr.) & black (litho.) missing (EP)   —
   f.   Blue (litho.) omitted   —

No. 1542f was caused by an occurrence that seems to be unique for U.S. total color omitted/missing errors. According to the BEP, oil on the printing blanket made a small area unreceptive to the blue ink. No blue at all was printed on one unique error stamp.

## AMERICAN REVOLUTION BICENTENNIAL ISSUE
### First Continental Congress

Nos. 1543-1544 alternate in 1st row, Nos. 1545-1546 in 2nd row. This arrangement is repeated throughout the pane.

Carpenters' Hall — A946

A947

A948

Independence Hall — A949

**1974, July 4**
1543   A946   10c dark blue & red   .30   .25
1544   A947   10c gray, dark blue & red   .30   .25
1545   A948   10c gray, dark blue & red   .30   .25
1546   A949   10c red & dark blue   .30   .25
   a.   Block of 4, #1543-1546   1.20   1.00

## ENERGY CONSERVATION ISSUE
Publicizing the importance of conserving all forms of energy.

A950

**LITHOGRAPHED, ENGRAVED (Giori)**
**1974, Sept. 23**
1547   A950   10c multicolored   .30   .25
   a.   Blue & orange omitted   400.00
   b.   Orange & green omitted   275.00
   c.   Green omitted   400.00

## AMERICAN FOLKLORE ISSUE
### Legend of Sleepy Hollow

The Headless Horseman in pursuit of Ichabod Crane from "Legend of Sleepy Hollow," by Washington Irving.

Legend of Sleepy Hollow — A951

**1974, Oct. 10**
1548   A951   10c dk bl, blk, org & yel   .30   .25

## RETARDED CHILDREN ISSUE

Retarded Children Can Be Helped, theme of annual convention of the National Association of Retarded Citizens.

Retarded Child — A952

### GIORI PRESS PRINTING
**1974, Oct. 12**
1549   A952   10c brown red & dark brown   .30   .25

## WARNING ABOUT SELF-ADHESIVE STAMPS

Many, though not all, self-adhesive stamps, which first appear with No. 1552, will not separate from paper or otherwise respond well to a standard warm-water soak. Consult the listings in the Scott U.S. Specialized Catalogue for information about which self-adhesives will and which will not soak. The editors strongly recommend that stamps that will not soak be collected on piece.

## CHRISTMAS ISSUE

Angel From Pérussis Altarpiece, 1480 — A953

"The Road-Winter," by Currier & Ives — A954

Designers: No. 1550, Bradbury Thompson, using detail from the Pérussis altarpiece painted by anonymous French artist, 1480, in Metropolitan Museum of Art, New York City. No. 1551, Stevan Dohanos, using Currier and Ives print from drawing by Otto Knirsch.

**PHOTOGRAVURE (Andreotti)**
**1974, Oct. 23**    *Perf. 10½x11*
1550   A953   10c multicolored   .30   .25
   *Perf. 11x10½*
1551   A954   10c multicolored   .30   .25
   a.   Buff omitted   12.50

No. 1551a is difficult to identify. Competent expertization is necessary.

Dove Weather Vane — A955

*Die Cut, Paper Backing Rouletted*
**1974, Nov. 15**    Untagged
**Self-adhesive; Inscribed "Precanceled"**
1552   A955   10c multicolored   .30   .25
   Nos. 1550-1552 (3)   .90   .75

Unused value of No. 1552 is for stamp on rouletted paper backing as issued. Used value is for stamp on piece, with or without postmark. **Most examples are becoming discolored from the adhesive. The Catalogue value is for discolored examples.**

Die cutting includes crossed slashes through dove, applied to prevent removal and re-use of the stamp. The stamp will separate into layers if soaked.

## AMERICAN ARTS ISSUE

Benjamin West (1738-1820), painter (No. 1553); Paul Laurence Dunbar (1872-1906), poet (No. 1554); David (Lewelyn) Wark Griffith (1875-1948), motion picture producer (No. 1555).

Benjamin West A956    Paul Laurence Dunbar A957

D. W. Griffith & Projector — A958

**PHOTOGRAVURE (Andreotti)**
**1975**    *Perf. 10½x11*
1553   A956   10c multicolored   .30   .25
   *Perf. 11*
1554   A957   10c multicolored   .30   .25
   a.   Imperf., pair   600.00

## LITHOGRAPHED, ENGRAVED (Giori)
*Perf. 11*

| | | | |
|---|---|---|---|
| 1555 | A958 10c brown & multicolored | .30 | .25 |
| a. | Brown (engr.) omitted | 250.00 | |
| | Nos. 1553-1555 (3) | .90 | .75 |

### SPACE ISSUES

US space accomplishments with unmanned craft. Pioneer 10 passed within 81,000 miles of Jupiter, Dec. 10, 1973. Mariner 10 explored Venus and Mercury in 1974 and Mercury again in 1975.

Pioneer 10 Passing Jupiter — A959

Mariner 10, Venus & Mercury — A960

### LITHOGRAPHED, ENGRAVED (Giori)
*1975* *Perf. 11*

| | | | |
|---|---|---|---|
| 1556 | A959 10c lt yel, dk yel, red, bl & 2 dk blues | .30 | .25 |
| a. | Red & dark yellow omitted | 750.00 | |
| b. | Dark blues (engr.) omitted | 400.00 | |
| d. | Dark yellow omitted | — | |

Imperfs. exist from printer's waste.

| | | | |
|---|---|---|---|
| 1557 | A960 10c blk, red, ultra & bister | .30 | .25 |
| a. | Red omitted | 275.00 | — |
| b. | Ultramarine & bister omitted | 1,000. | |
| d. | Red missing (PS) | 525.00 | |

### COLLECTIVE BARGAINING ISSUE

Collective Bargaining law, enacted 1935, in Wagner Act.

"Labor and Management" A961

### PHOTOGRAVURE (Andreotti)
*1975, Mar. 13*

| | | | |
|---|---|---|---|
| 1558 | A961 10c multicolored | .30 | .25 |

Imperforates exist from printer's waste.

### AMERICAN BICENTENNIAL ISSUE
*Contributors to the Cause*

Sybil Ludington, age 16, rallied militia, Apr. 26, 1777; Salem Poor, black freeman, fought in Battle of Bunker Hill; Haym Salomon, Jewish immigrant, raised money to finance Revolutionary War; Peter Francisco, Portuguese-French immigrant, joined Continental Army at 15. Emerald inscription on back, printed beneath gum in water-soluble ink, gives thumbnail sketch of portrayed contributor.

Sybil Ludington — A962

Salem Poor — A963

Haym Salomon — A964

Peter Francisco — A965

*1975, Mar. 25* *Perf. 11x10½*

| | | | |
|---|---|---|---|
| 1559 | A962 8c multicolored | .30 | .25 |
| a. | Back inscriptions omitted | 110.00 | |
| 1560 | A963 10c multicolored | .30 | .25 |
| a. | Back inscription omitted | 110.00 | |
| b. | Black missing (PS) | | |
| 1561 | A964 10c multicolored | .30 | .25 |
| a. | Back inscription omitted | 110.00 | |
| 1562 | A965 18c multicolored | .35 | .25 |
| | Nos. 1559-1562 (4) | 1.25 | 1.00 |

On No. 1560, two black plates were used. No. 1560b is missing the impression from one of those plates ("Salem Poor - U.S. Bicentennial symbol - Gallant Soldier") due to an upward shift of the horizontal perforations.

Dangerous fakes exist of No. 1561 with red apparently omitted. Professional authentication is mandatory in order to establish such a stamp as a genuine error.

### Lexington-Concord Battle, 200th Anniv.

"Birth of Liberty," by Henry Sandham — A966

*1975, Apr. 19* *Perf. 11*

| | | | |
|---|---|---|---|
| 1563 | A966 10c multicolored | .30 | .25 |
| a. | Vert. pair, imperf. horiz. | 300.00 | |

### Bunker Hill Battle, 200th Anniv.

Battle of Bunker Hill, by John Trumbull — A967

*1975, June 17*

| | | | |
|---|---|---|---|
| 1564 | A967 10c multicolored | .30 | .25 |

### Military Uniforms

Bicentenary of US Military Services. Nos. 1565-1566 alternate in one row, Nos. 1567-1568 in next row.

Soldier with Flintlock Musket, Uniform Button A968

Sailor with Grappling Hook, First Navy Jack, 1775 A969

Marine with Musket, Full-rigged Ship A970

Militiaman with Musket, Powder Horn A971

*1975, July 4*

| | | | |
|---|---|---|---|
| 1565 | A968 10c multicolored | .30 | .25 |
| 1566 | A969 10c multicolored | .30 | .25 |
| 1567 | A970 10c multicolored | .30 | .25 |
| 1568 | A971 10c multicolored | .30 | .25 |
| a. | Block of 4, #1565-1568 | 1.20 | 1.00 |

### APOLLO SOYUZ SPACE ISSUE

Apollo Soyuz space test project, Russo-American cooperation, launched July 15; link-up, July 17. Nos. in the 1st row, No. 1569 is in 1st and 3rd space, No. 1570 is 2nd space; in the 2nd row No. 1570 is in 1st and 3rd space, No. 1569 in 2nd space, etc.

Participating US and USSR crews: Thomas P. Stafford, Donald K. Slayton, Vance D. Brand, Aleksei A. Leonov, Valery N. Kubasov.

Apollo & Soyuz After Docking, Earth A972

Spacecraft Before Docking, Earth & Project Emblem — A973

*1975, July 15*

| | | | |
|---|---|---|---|
| 1569 | A972 10c multicolored | .30 | .25 |
| 1570 | A973 10c multicolored | .30 | .25 |
| a. | Pair, #1569-1570 | .60 | .50 |
| c. | As "a," vert. pair, imperf. horiz. | 800.00 | |
| d. | As "a," yellow omitted | 900.00 | |

Nos. 1569-1570 totally imperforate are printer's waste.
See Russia Nos. 4339-4340.

### INTERNATIONAL WOMEN'S YEAR ISSUE

International Women's Year 1975.

Worldwide Equality for Women — A974

*1975, Aug. 26* *Perf. 11x10½*

| | | | |
|---|---|---|---|
| 1571 | A974 10c blue, orange & dark blue | .30 | .25 |

### US POSTAL SERVICE BICENTENNIAL ISSUE

Nos. 1572-1573 alternate in 1st row, Nos. 1574-1575 in 2nd row. This arrangement is repeated throughout the pane.

Stagecoach and Trailer Truck — A975

Old and New Locomotives A976

Early Mail Plane and Jet — A977

Satellite for Transmission of Mailgrams A978

*1975, Sept. 3*

| | | | |
|---|---|---|---|
| 1572 | A975 10c multicolored | .30 | .25 |
| 1573 | A976 10c multicolored | .30 | .25 |
| 1574 | A977 10c multicolored | .30 | .25 |
| 1575 | A978 10c multicolored | .30 | .25 |
| a. | Block of 4, #1572-1575 | 1.20 | 1.00 |
| b. | As "a," red "10c" omitted, tagging omitted | — | |

### WORLD PEACE THROUGH LAW ISSUE

A prelude to 7th World Law Conference of the World Peace Through Law Center at Washington, D.C., Oct. 12-17.

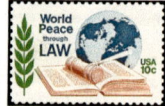
Law Book, Olive Branch and Globe — A979

### GIORI PRESS PRINTING
*1975, Sept. 29* *Perf. 11*

| | | | |
|---|---|---|---|
| 1576 | A979 10c green, Prussian blue & rose brown | .30 | .25 |
| b. | Horiz. pair, imperf vert. | 7,500. | |
| c. | All colors omitted | 725.00 | |

No. 1576c is collected in a horiz. strip as two errors se-tenant with a partially printed stamp.

### BANKING AND COMMERCE ISSUE

Banking and commerce in the U.S., and for the Centennial Convention of the American Bankers Association.

Engine Turning, Indian Head Penny & Morgan Silver Dollar — A980

Seated Liberty Quarter, $20 Gold (Double Eagle), Engine Turning — A981

### LITHOGRAPHED, ENGRAVED (Giori)
*1975, Oct. 6*

| | | | |
|---|---|---|---|
| 1577 | A980 10c multicolored | .30 | .25 |
| 1578 | A981 10c multicolored | .30 | .25 |
| a. | Pair, #1577-1578 | .60 | .50 |
| b. | As "a," brown & blue (litho) omitted | 1,100. | |
| c. | As "a," brown, blue & yellow (litho) omitted | 1,750. | |

### CHRISTMAS ISSUE

Madonna, by Domenico Ghirlandaio A982

Christmas Card, by Louis Prang, 1878 A983

### PHOTOGRAVURE (Andreotti)
*1975, Oct. 14*

| | | | |
|---|---|---|---|
| 1579 | A982 (10c) multicolored | .30 | .25 |
| a. | Imperf., pair | 75.00 | |

*Perf. 11.2*

| | | | |
|---|---|---|---|
| 1580 | A983 (10c) multicolored | .30 | .25 |
| a. | Imperf., pair | 85.00 | |
| c. | Perf. 10.9 | .30 | .25 |

*Perf. 10.5x11.3*

| | | | |
|---|---|---|---|
| 1580B | A983 (10c) multicolored | .65 | .25 |

### AMERICANA ISSUE

Inkwell and Quill A984

Speaker's Stand A985

Early Ballot Box A987

Books, Bookmark, Eyeglasses A988

Dome of Capitol A994

Contemplation of Justice A995

UNITED STATES 49

Early American Printing Press
A996

Torch
A997

Liberty Bell
A998

Eagle and Shield
A999

Fort McHenry Flag
A1001

Head, Statue of Liberty
A1002

Old North Church, Boston
A1003

Fort Nisqually
A1004

Sandy Hook Lighthouse, NJ
A1005

Morris Township School No. 2, Devils Lake, ND
A1006

Iron "Betty" Lamp, 17th-18th Cent.
A1007

Rush Lamp and Candle Holder
A1008

Kerosene Table Lamp
A1009

Railroad Conductor's Lantern, c. 1850
A1010

ROTARY PRESS PRINTING

**1975-81** ***Perf. 11¼x10½***

**Size: 18½x22½mm**

**1581** A984 1c dk bl, *grnish* .30 .25
*a.* Untagged (Bureau precanceled) 4.50 1.50
*c.* White paper, dull gum — —
**1582** A985 2c red brn, *grnsh* .30 .25
*a.* Untagged (Bureau precanceled) 4.50 1.50
*b.* Cream paper ('81) .30 .25
**1584** A987 3c olive, *grnsh* .30 .25
*a.* Untagged (Bureau precanceled), dull gum .75 .50

Values for No. 1584a are for the lines-only precancel. Also known with city precancels, and valued at $50 thus.

**1585** A988 4c rose mag, *cream* .30 .25
*a.* Untagged (Bureau precanceled) 1.00 .75

The pair with horiz. gutter between also is misperfed through the stamps horizontally. Also known with city precancels, and valued at $100 thus.

**Size: 17½x20½mm**

***Perf. 11x10½ on 3 Sides***

**1590** A994 9c slate green .45 *1.00*
From bklt. pane #1623a.

***Perf. 10x9¾ on 3 Sides***

**1590A** A994 9c slate green 12.50 12.50
From bklt. pane #1623Bc.

**Size: 18½x22½mm**

***Perf. 11¼x10½***

**1591** A994 9c sl grn, *gray* .30 .25
*a.* Untagged (Bureau precanceled) 1.75 1.00

Values for No. 1591a are for the lines-only precancel. Also known with city precancels, and valued at $32.50 thus.

**1592** A995 10c violet, *gray* .30 .25
*a.* Untagged (Bureau precanceled, Chicago) 9.50 5.00
**1593** A996 11c orange, *gray* .30 .25
**1594** A997 12c red brown, *beige* .30 .25

***Perf. 11¼x10½ on 2 or 3 Sides***

**1595** A998 13c brown .30 .25
*a.* Booklet pane of 6 2.25 1.50
*b.* Booklet pane of 7 + label 2.25 1.50
*c.* Booklet pane of 8 2.25 1.50
*d.* Booklet pane of 5 + label, *Apr. 2, 1976* 1.75 1.25
*e.* Vert. pair, imperf. btwn., in #1595c with foldover *1,500.*
*g.* Horiz. pair, imperf. btwn., in #1595d with foldover —

Nos. 1595e and 1595g resulted from paper foldovers after perforating and before cutting into panes. Beware of printer's waste consisting of complete panes with perfs around all outside edges.

PHOTOGRAVURE (Andreotti)

***Perf. 11¼ Bullseye***

**1596** A999 13c multicolored .30 .25
*a.* Imperf., pair *40.00* —
*b.* Yellow omitted *75.00*

ENGRAVED (Combination Press)

***Perf. 11x11¼***

**1597** A1001 15c gray, dk bl & red .30 .25
*b.* Gray omitted *300.00*
*c.* Vert. pair, imperf btwn and with natural straight edge at bottom *350.00*
*e.* Imperf., vert. pair *15.00*

ENGRAVED

***Perf. 11x10½ on 2 or 3 Sides***

**1598** A1001 15c gray, dk bl & red .40 .25
*a.* Booklet pane of 8 3.75 1.50

***Perf. 11¼x10½***

**1599** A1002 16c blue .35 .25
**1603** A1003 24c red, *blue* .50 .25
*b.* red, *greenish blue* .50 .25
**1604** A1004 28c brown, *blue* .55 .25
**1605** A1005 29c blue, *blue* .60 .25
**1606** A1006 30c green, *blue* .55 .25

**LITHOGRAPHED AND ENGRAVED**

***Perf. 11***

**1608** A1007 50c tan, blk & org .85 .25
*a.* Black omitted *375.00*
*b.* Vert. pair, imperf. horiz. *1,200.*

Beware of examples offered as No. 1608b that have blind perfs.

**1610** A1008 $1 tan, brn, org & yel 2.00 .25
*a.* Brown (engraved) omitted *175.00*
*b.* Tan, orange & yellow omitted *175.00*
*c.* Brown (engraved) inverted *17,000.*
**1611** A1009 $2 tan, dk grn, org & yel 3.75 .75
**1612** A1010 $5 tan, red brn, yel & org 8.50 1.75
*Nos. 1581-1612 (23)* 34.30 20.75

Nos. 1590, 1590A, 1595, 1598, 1623 and 1623b were issued only in booklets. All stamps have one or two straight edges.

Years of issue: #1591, 1595-1596, 11c, 24c, 1975. #1590, 1c-4c, 10c, 1977. #1597-1598, 16c, 28c, 29c, $2, 1978. 30c-$1, $5, 1979. 12c, 1981.

Guitar
A1011

Saxhorns
A1012

Drum
A1013

Piano
A1014

Designers: 3.1c, George Mercer. 7.7c, Susan Robb. 7.9c, Bernard Glassman. 10c, Walter Brooks. 15c, V. Jack Ruther.

COIL STAMPS
ENGRAVED

**1975-79** ***Perf. 10 Vertically***

**1613** A1011 3.1c brown ('79) .30 .25
*a.* Untagged (Bureau precanceled, lines only) .35 .35
*b.* Imperf., pair *750.00*
**1614** A1012 7.7c brown ('76) .30 .25
*a.* Untagged (Bureau precanceled) .40 .30
*b.* As "a," imperf., pair *1,250.*

No. 1614b is precanceled Washington, DC. Also exists with Marion, OH precancel; value $1,950 for pair.

**1615** A1013 7.9c carmine ('76) .30 .25
*a.* Untagged (Bureau precanceled) .40 .40
*b.* Imperf., pair *300.00*
**1615C** A1014 8.4c dark blue ('78) .30 .25
*d.* Untagged (Bureau precanceled) .50 .40
*e.* As "d," pair, imperf. between 45.00
*f.* As "d," imperf. pair, shiny gum 15.00

No. 1615Ce is precanceled with lines only. No. 1615Cf is precanceled with lines only (value shown) and also exists in pairs precanceled Newark, N.J. ($25)., Brownstown, Ind. ($900), Oklahoma City, Okla. ($1,500.) and Washington, DC ($900).

**1616** A994 9c slate green ('75) .30 .25
*a.* Imperf., pair *125.00*
*b.* Untagged (Bureau precanceled) .75 .75
*c.* As "b," imperf., pair *600.00*

Value for No. 1616b is for stamp with dull gum.

No. 1616c is precanceled Pleasantville, NY.

**1617** A995 10c violet ('77) .30 .25
*a.* Untagged (Bureau precanceled) 1.35 1.35
*b.* Imperf., pair 55.00
*c.* As "a," imperf pair *3,750.*

Values for No. 1617a and 1617b are for stamps with dull gum. These varieties with shiny gum are worth considerably more.

**1618** A998 13c brown ('75) .30 .25
*a.* Untagged (Bureau precanceled) .75 .75
*b.* Imperf., pair 22.50
*g.* Pair, imperf. between *600.00*
*h.* As "a," imperf., pair —

Value for No. 1618a is for stamp with dull gum.

**1618C** A1001 15c gray, dk bl & red ('78) .75 .25
*d.* Imperf., pair 20.00
*e.* Pair, imperf. between *100.00*
*f.* Gray omitted 30.00
**1619** A1002 16c ultra ('78) .35 .25
*a.* Huck Press Printing .50 .25
*Nos. 1613-1619 (9)* 3.20 2.25

No. 1619a (the B press printing) has a white background without bluish tinge, is a fraction of a millimeter smaller than No. 1619 (the Cottrell press printing) and has no joint lines.

See Nos. 1811, 1813, 1816.

13-Star Flag, Independence Hall — A1015

**1975-81** ***Perf. 11x10¾***

**1622** A1015 13c dk bl, red & brn red .30 .25
*a.* Horiz. pair, imperf. between 40.00
*b.* Vertical pair, imperf. *225.00*
*e.* Horiz. pair, imperf. vert. —

No. 1622 was printed on the Multicolored Huck Press. Plate markings are at top or bottom of pane.

***Perf. 11¼***

**1622C** A1015 13c dk bl, red & brn red ('81) 1.00 .25
*d.* Vertical pair, imperf 100.00

No. 1622C was printed on the Combination Press. Plate markings are at sides of pane.

Flag over Capitol — A1016

BOOKLET STAMPS

***Perf. 11x10½ on 2 or 3 Sides***

**1977, Mar. 11**

**1623** A1016 13c blue & red .30 .25
*a.* Booklet pane, 1 #1590 + 7 #1623 2.25 2.00
*d.* Pair, #1590 & #1623 .70 *1.25*

***Perf. 10x9¾ on 2 or 3 Sides***

**1623B** A1016 13c blue & red .65 .75
*c.* Booklet pane, 1 #1590A + 7 #1623B 15.00 15.00
*e.* Pair, #1590A & #1623B 14.00 14.00

COIL STAMP

**1975, Nov. 15** ***Perf. 10 Vertically***

**1625** A1016 13c dk blue, red & brown red .35 .25
*a.* Imperf., pair 20.00

**AMERICAN BICENTENNIAL ISSUE**

**The Spirit of '76**

Designed after painting by Archibald M. Willard in Abbot Hall, Marblehead, Massachusetts. Nos. 1629-1631 printed in continuous design.

Left panes contain 3 No. 1631a and one No. 1629; right panes contain one No. 1631 and 3 No. 1631a.

Drummer Boy
A1019

Old Drummer
A1020

Fifer — A1021

PHOTOGRAVURE (Andreotti)

**1976, Jan. 1** ***Perf. 11***

**1629** A1019 13c blue violet & multi .30 .25
*a.* Imperf., vert. pair
**1630** A1020 13c blue violet & multi .30 .25
**1631** A1021 13c blue violet & multi .30 .25
*a.* Strip of 3, #1629-1631 .75 .75
*b.* As "a," imperf. *600.00*
*c.* Imperf., vert. pair, #1631 *500.00*

**INTERPHIL ISSUE**

Interphil 76 International Philatelic Exhibition, Philadelphia, Pa., May 29-June 6.

"Interphil 76" — A1022

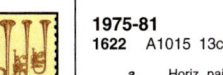

## UNITED STATES

### LITHOGRAPHED, ENGRAVED (Giori)
**1976, Jan. 17**

| | | | |
|---|---|---|---|
| 1632 | A1022 | 13c dark blue & red (engr.), ultra. & red (litho.) | .30 .25 |
| a. | | Dark blue & red (engr.) missing (CM) | — |
| c. | | Red (engr.) missing (CM) | — |

State Flags — A1023

### Photo.
**1976, Feb. 23**

| | | | |
|---|---|---|---|
| 1633 | A1023 | 13c Delaware | .30 .25 |
| 1634 | A1024 | 13c Pennsylvania | .30 .25 |
| 1635 | A1025 | 13c New Jersey | .30 .25 |
| 1636 | A1026 | 13c Georgia | .30 .25 |
| 1637 | A1027 | 13c Connecticut | .30 .25 |
| 1638 | A1028 | 13c Massachusetts | .30 .25 |
| 1639 | A1029 | 13c Maryland | .30 .25 |
| 1640 | A1030 | 13c South Carolina | .30 .25 |
| 1641 | A1031 | 13c New Hampshire | .30 .25 |
| 1642 | A1032 | 13c Virginia | .30 .25 |
| 1643 | A1033 | 13c New York | .30 .25 |
| 1644 | A1034 | 13c North Carolina | .30 .25 |
| 1645 | A1035 | 13c Rhode Island | .30 .25 |
| 1646 | A1036 | 13c Vermont | .30 .25 |
| 1647 | A1037 | 13c Kentucky | .30 .25 |
| 1648 | A1038 | 13c Tennessee | .30 .25 |
| 1649 | A1039 | 13c Ohio | .30 .25 |
| 1650 | A1040 | 13c Louisiana | .30 .25 |
| 1651 | A1041 | 13c Indiana | .30 .25 |
| 1652 | A1042 | 13c Mississippi | .30 .25 |
| 1653 | A1043 | 13c Illinois | .30 .25 |
| 1654 | A1044 | 13c Alabama | .30 .25 |
| 1655 | A1045 | 13c Maine | .30 .25 |
| 1656 | A1046 | 13c Missouri | .30 .25 |
| 1657 | A1047 | 13c Arkansas | .30 .25 |
| 1658 | A1048 | 13c Michigan | .30 .25 |
| 1659 | A1049 | 13c Florida | .30 .25 |
| 1660 | A1050 | 13c Texas | .30 .25 |
| 1661 | A1051 | 13c Iowa | .30 .25 |
| 1662 | A1052 | 13c Wisconsin | .30 .25 |
| 1663 | A1053 | 13c California | .30 .25 |
| 1664 | A1054 | 13c Minnesota | .30 .25 |
| 1665 | A1055 | 13c Oregon | .30 .25 |
| 1666 | A1056 | 13c Kansas | .30 .25 |
| 1667 | A1057 | 13c West Virginia | .30 .25 |
| 1668 | A1058 | 13c Nevada | .30 .25 |
| 1669 | A1059 | 13c Nebraska | .30 .25 |
| 1670 | A1060 | 13c Colorado | .30 .25 |
| 1671 | A1061 | 13c North Dakota | .30 .25 |
| 1672 | A1062 | 13c South Dakota | .30 .25 |
| 1673 | A1063 | 13c Montana | .30 .25 |
| 1674 | A1064 | 13c Washington | .30 .25 |
| 1675 | A1065 | 13c Idaho | .30 .25 |
| 1676 | A1066 | 13c Wyoming | .30 .25 |
| 1677 | A1067 | 13c Utah | .30 .25 |
| 1678 | A1068 | 13c Oklahoma | .30 .25 |
| 1679 | A1069 | 13c New Mexico | .30 .25 |
| 1680 | A1070 | 13c Arizona | .30 .25 |
| 1681 | A1071 | 13c Alaska | .30 .25 |
| 1682 | A1072 | 13c Hawaii | .30 .25 |
| a. | | Pane of 50 | 17.50 15.00 |

### TELEPHONE CENTENNIAL ISSUE
Centenary of first telephone call by Alexander Graham Bell, March 10, 1876.

Bell's Telephone Patent Application A1073

### ENGRAVED (Giori)
**1976, Mar. 10**

| | | | |
|---|---|---|---|
| 1683 | A1073 | 13c blk, pur & red, tan | .30 .25 |
| a. | | Black & purple missing (EP) | 450.00 |
| b. | | Red missing (EP) | — |
| c. | | All colors missing (EP) | 725.00 |

On No. 1683a, the errors have only tiny traces of red present, so are best collected as a horiz. strip of 5 with 2 or 3 error stamps. No. 1683c also must be collected as a transitional strip.

### COMMERCIAL AVIATION ISSUE
50th anniversary of first contract airmail flights: Dearborn, Mich. to Cleveland, Ohio, Feb. 15, 1926; and Pasco, Wash. to Elko, Nev., Apr. 6, 1926.

A1074

### PHOTOGRAVURE (Andreotti)
**1976, Mar. 19  Tagged  Perf. 11**

| | | | |
|---|---|---|---|
| 1684 | A1074 | 13c blue & multicolored | .30 .25 |

### CHEMISTRY ISSUE
Honoring American chemists, in conjunction with the centenary of the American Chemical Society.

A1075

### PHOTOGRAVURE (Andreotti)
**1976, Apr. 6**

| | | | |
|---|---|---|---|
| 1685 | A1075 | 13c multicolored | .30 .25 |

### AMERICAN BICENTENNIAL ISSUES
### SOUVENIR SHEETS

Designs, from Left to Right, No. 1686: a, Two British officers. b, Gen. Benjamin Lincoln. c, George Washington. d, John Trumbull, Col. Cobb, von Steuben, Lafayette, Thomas Nelson. e, Alexander Hamilton, John Laurens, Walter Stewart (all vert.).

No. 1687: a, John Adams, Roger Sherman, Robert R. Livingston. b, Jefferson, Franklin. c, Thomas Nelson, Jr., Francis Lewis, John Witherspoon, Samuel Huntington. d, John Hancock, Charles Thomson. e, George Read, John Dickinson, Edward Rutledge (a, d, vert., b, c, e, horiz.).

No. 1688: a, Boatsman. b, Washington. c, Flag bearer. d, Men in boat. e, Men on shore (a, d, horiz., b, c, e, vert.).

No. 1689: a, Two officers. b, Washington. c, Officer, black horse. d, Officer, white horse. e, Three soldiers (a, c, e, horiz., b, d, vert.).

### LITHOGRAPHED
**1976, May 29**

| | | | | |
|---|---|---|---|---|
| 1686 | A1076 | Pane of 5 | 2.75 | 2.25 |
| a.-e. | | 13c multicolored | .40 | .40 |
| f. | | "USA/13c" omitted on "b," "c" & "d," imperf, tagging omitted | — | 1,750. |
| g. | | "USA/13c" omitted on "a" & "e" | 500.00 | 300.00 |
| h. | | Imperf., tagging omitted | | 2,000. |
| i. | | "USA/13c" omitted on "b," "c" & "d" | 500.00 | |
| j. | | "USA/13c" double on "b" | — | |
| k. | | "USA/13c" omitted on "c" & "d" | 750.00 | |
| l. | | "USA/13c" omitted on "e" | 475.00 | |
| m. | | "USA/13c" omitted, imperf., tagging omitted | — | |
| n. | | As "g," imperf., tagging omitted | | 1,400. |
| o. | | "USA/13c" missing on "a" (PS) | 450.00 | |
| q. | | "USA/13c" omitted on "a" | 750.00 | |
| r. | | Imperf., tagged | — | |
| s. | | "USA/13c" missing on "b" and "d" (PS) | — | |
| 1687 | A1077 | Pane of 5 | 3.75 | 3.25 |
| a.-e. | | 18c multicolored | .50 | .50 |
| f. | | Design & marginal inscriptions omitted | 2,500. | |
| g. | | "USA/18c" omitted on "a" & "c" | 550.00 | 1,800. |
| h. | | "USA/18c" omitted on "b," "d" & "e" | 350.00 | |
| i. | | "USA/18c" omitted on "d" | 425.00 | 475.00 |
| j. | | Black omitted in design | 1,500. | |
| k. | | "USA/18c" omitted, imperf., tagging omitted | 1,250. | |
| m. | | "USA/18c" omitted on "b" & "e" | 500.00 | |
| n. | | "USA/18c" omitted on "b" & "d" | 1,000. | |
| p. | | Imperf. (tagged) | 1,000. | |
| r. | | Yellow omitted | 5,000. | |
| s. | | "USA/18c" missing on "a," "c" and "d" (PS) | — | |
| t. | | "USA/18c" missing on "a" and "d" (PS) | 300.00 | |
| u. | | "USA/18c" omitted on "a" | 5,000. | |
| 1688 | A1078 | Pane of 5 | 4.75 | 4.25 |
| a.-e. | | 24c multicolored | .65 | .65 |
| f. | | "USA/24c" omitted, imperf., tagging omitted | 1,200. | |
| g. | | "USA/24c" omitted on "d" & "e" | 400.00 | 400.00 |
| h. | | Design & marginal inscriptions omitted | 2,500. | |
| i. | | "USA/24c" omitted on "a," "b" & "c" | 400.00 | 400.00 |
| j. | | Imperf., tagging omitted | 1,250. | |
| k. | | "USA/24c" of "d" & "e" inverted | 12,500. | |
| l. | | As "i," imperf, tagging omitted | 3,250. | — |
| n. | | As No. 1688, perfs inverted and reversed | 7,500. | |
| p. | | "USA/24c" missing on "d" and "e" (CM) | — | |
| q. | | "USA/24c" omitted on "b" and "c" | — | |
| r. | | "USA/24c" omitted on "a" | 400.00 | |
| s. | | As No. 1688, imperf. | 1,250. | |
| 1689 | A1079 | Pane of 5 | 5.75 | 5.25 |
| a.-e. | | 31c multicolored | .80 | .80 |
| f. | | "USA/31c" omitted, imperf. | 1,000. | |
| g. | | "USA/31c" omitted on "a" & "c" | 375.00 | |
| h. | | "USA/31c" omitted on "b," "d" & "e" | 450.00 | — |
| i. | | "USA/31c" omitted on "e" | 375.00 | |
| j. | | Black omitted in design | 1,700. | |
| k. | | Imperf., tagging omitted | 2,000. | |
| l. | | "USA/31c" omitted on "b" & "d" | 300.00 | |
| m. | | "USA/31c" omitted on "a," "c" & "e" | 750.00 | |
| n. | | As "m," imperf., tagging omitted | — | |
| p. | | As "h," imperf., tagging omitted | 1,250. | |
| q. | | As "g," imperf., tagging omitted | 2,500. | |
| r. | | "USA/31c" omitted on "d" & "e" | 600.00 | |
| s. | | As "f," tagging omitted | 2,000. | |
| t. | | "USA/31c" omitted on "d" | 500.00 | |
| v. | | As No. 1689, perfs and tagging inverted | 10,000. | |
| w. | | "USA/31c" omitted on "a," "b," "c" and "d" (PS) | 500.00 | |
| x. | | "USA/31c" missing on "e" (CM) | — | |
| y. | | "USA/31c" omitted on "a" | 1,000. | |
| Nos. 1686-1689 (4) | | | 17.00 | |

Issued in connection with Interphil 76 International Philatelic Exhibition, Philadelphia, Pa., May 29-June 6. Size of panes: 203x152mm.

A1076 — The Surrender of Lord Cornwallis at Yorktown, From a Painting by John Trumbull

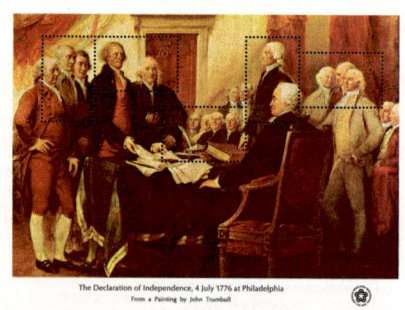

A1077 — The Declaration of Independence, 4 July 1776 at Philadelphia, From a Painting by John Trumbull

A1078 — Washington Crossing the Delaware, From a Painting by Emanuel Leutze / Eastman Johnson

A1079 — Washington Reviewing His Ragged Army at Valley Forge, From a Painting by William T. Trego

# UNITED STATES

### Benjamin Franklin

American Bicentennial: Benjamin Franklin (1706-1790), deputy postmaster general for the colonies (1753-1774) and statesman. Design based on marble bust by anonymous Italian sculptor after terra cotta bust by Jean Jacques Caffieri, 1777. Map published by R. Sayer and J. Bennett in London.

Franklin & Map of North America, 1776 — A1080

**LITHOGRAPHED, ENGRAVED (Giori)**
**1976, June 1**
1690 A1080 13c multicolored .30 .25
  a. Light blue omitted 150.00
See Canada No. 691.

### American Bicentennial Issue

A1081    A1082

A1083    A1084

Declaration of Independence, by John Trumbull
**PHOTOGRAVURE (Andreotti)**
**1976, July 4**
1691 A1081 13c multicolored .30 .25
1692 A1082 13c multicolored .30 .25
1693 A1083 13c multicolored .30 .25
1694 A1084 13c multicolored .30 .25
  a. Strip of 4, #1691-1694 1.20 1.10

### OLYMPIC GAMES ISSUE

12th Winter Olympic Games, Innsbruck, Austria, Feb. 4-15, and 21st Summer Olympic Games, Montreal, Canada, July 17-Aug. 1. Nos. 1695-1696 alternate in one row, Nos. 1697-1698 in other row.

Diving A1085    Skiing A1086

Running A1087    Skating A1088

**1976, July 16**
1695 A1085 13c multicolored .30 .25
1696 A1086 13c multicolored .30 .25
1697 A1087 13c multicolored .30 .25
1698 A1088 13c multicolored .30 .25
  a. Block of 4, #1695-1698 1.20 1.20
  b. As "a," imperf. 375.00

### CLARA MAASS ISSUE

Clara Louise Maass (1876-1901), volunteer in fight against yellow fever, birth centenary.

Clara Maass, Newark German Hospital Pin — A1089

**1976, Aug. 18**
1699 A1089 13c multicolored .30 .25
  a. Horiz. pair, imperf. vert. 350.00
  b. Dark blue missing (PS) 700.00

On No. 1699, two blue plates were used. No 1699b is missing the dark blue ("She gave her life") at bottom due to an upward shift of the horizontal perforations.

### ADOLPH S. OCHS ISSUE

Adolph S. Ochs, Publisher of the NY Times, 1896-1935 — A1090

**GIORI PRESS PRINTING**
**1976, Sept. 18**
1700 A1090 13c black & gray .30 .25

### CHRISTMAS ISSUE

Nativity, by John Singleton Copley — A1091

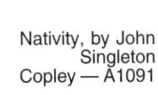

Winter Pastime, by Nathaniel Currier — A1092

**PHOTOGRAVURE (Andreotti)**
**1976, Oct. 27**
1701 A1091 13c multicolored .30 .25
  a. Imperf., pair 85.00
1702 A1092 13c multi, overall tagging .30 .25
  a. Imperf., pair 75.00

**COMBINATION PRESS**
1703 A1092 13c multicolored .30 .25
  a. Imperf., pair 75.00
  b. Vert. pair, imperf. between 275.00
  d. Red omitted 500.00
  e. Yellow omitted 675.00

No. 1702 has overall tagging. Lettering at base is black and usually ½mm below design. As a rule, no "snowflaking" in sky or pond. Pane of 50 has margins on 4 sides with slogans. Plate Nos. 37465-37478.

No. 1703 has block tagging the size of printed area. Lettering at base is gray black and usually ¾mm below design. "Snowflaking" generally in sky and pond. Plate Nos. 37617-37621 or 37634-37638.

Examples of No. 1703 are known with various amounts of red or yellow missing. Nos. 1703d-1703e are stamps with the colors totally omitted. Expertization is recommended.

### AMERICAN BICENTENNIAL ISSUE
**Washington at Princeton**

Washington's Victory over Lord Cornwallis at Princeton, N.J., bicentenary.

Washington, Nassau Hall, Hessians, 13-Star Flag — A1093

**1977, Jan. 3**
1704 A1093 13c multicolored .30 .25
  a. Horiz. pair, imperf. vert. 425.00
  b. Black (inscriptions) missing (PS) —

### SOUND RECORDING ISSUE

Centenary of the invention of the phonograph by Thomas Alva Edison and development of sophisticated recording industry.

Tin Foil Phonograph A1094

**LITHOGRAPHED, ENGRAVED (Giori)**
**1977, Mar. 23**
1705 A1094 13c black & multi .30 .25
  b. Black (engr.) and brown (engr.) missing (EP) 1,500.
  c. Black (engr.) missing (EP) 1,000.

### AMERICAN FOLK ART SERIES
**Pueblo Pottery**

Pueblo art, 1880-1920, from Museums in New Mexico, Arizona and Colorado.

Zia A1095    San Ildefonso A1096

Hopi A1097    Acoma A1098

**PHOTOGRAVURE (Andreotti)**
**1977, Apr. 13**
1706 A1095 13c multicolored .30 .25
1707 A1096 13c multicolored .30 .25
1708 A1097 13c multicolored .30 .25
1709 A1098 13c multicolored .30 .25
  a. Block or strip of 4, #1706-1709 1.20 1.00
  b. As "a," imperf. vert. 750.00

### LINDBERGH FLIGHT ISSUE

Charles A. Lindbergh's solo transatlantic flight from New York to Paris, 50th anniversary.

Spirit of St. Louis — A1099

**1977, May 20**
1710 A1099 13c multicolored .30 .25
  a. Imperf., pair 700.00

### COLORADO STATEHOOD ISSUE

Issued to honor Colorado as the "Centennial State." It achieved statehood in 1876.

Columbine & Rocky Mountains — A1100

**1977, May 21**
1711 A1100 13c multicolored .30 .25
  a. Horiz. pair, imperf. between and with natural straight edge at right 650.00
  b. Horiz. pair, imperf. vertically 500.00
  c. Perf. 11.2 .75 .25

### BUTTERFLY ISSUE

Nos. 1712-1713 alternate in 1st row, Nos. 1714-1715 in 2nd row. This arrangement is repeated throughout the pane. Butterflies represent different geographic US areas.

Swallowtail A1101

Checkerspot A1102

Dogface — A1103

Orange Tip — A1104

**1977, June 6    Tagged    Perf. 11**
1712 A1101 13c tan & multi .30 .25
1713 A1102 13c tan & multi .30 .25
1714 A1103 13c tan & multi .30 .25
1715 A1104 13c tan & multi .30 .25
  a. Block of 4, #1712-1715 1.20 1.00
  b. As "a," imperf. horiz. 9,500.

### AMERICAN BICENTENNIAL ISSUES
**Marquis de Lafayette**

200th anniversary of Lafayette's Landing on the coast of South Carolina, north of Charleston.

Marquis de Lafayette — A1105

**GIORI PRESS PRINTING**
**1977, June 13**
1716 A1105 13c blue, black & red .30 .25
  a. Red missing (PS) 300.00

### Skilled Hands for Independence

Nos. 1717-1718 alternate in 1st row, Nos. 1719-1720 in 2nd row. This arrangement is repeated throughout the pane.

Seamstress A1106

Blacksmith A1107

Wheelwright A1108

Leatherworker A1109

**1977, July 4**
1717 A1106 13c multicolored .30 .25
1718 A1107 13c multicolored .30 .25
1719 A1108 13c multicolored .30 .25
1720 A1109 13c multicolored .30 .25
  a. Block of 4, #1717-1720 1.20 1.00

### PEACE BRIDGE ISSUE

50th anniversary of the Peace Bridge, connecting Buffalo (Fort Porter), N.Y. and Fort Erie, Ontario.

52 UNITED STATES

Peace Bridge & Dove — A1110

### ENGRAVED
**1977, Aug. 4**    **Perf. 11x10½**
1721 A1110 13c blue    .30   .25

### AMERICAN BICENTENNIAL ISSUE
**Battle of Oriskany**

200th anniv. of the Battle of Oriskany, American Militia led by Brig. Gen. Nicholas Herkimer (1728-77).

Herkimer at Oriskany, by Yohn — A1111

### PHOTOGRAVURE (Andreotti)
**1977, Aug. 6**    **Perf. 11**
1722 A1111 13c multicolored    .30   .25

### ENERGY ISSUE
Conservation and development of nation's energy resources. Nos. 1723-1724 se-tenant vertically.

Energy Conservation A1112

Energy Development A1113

**1977, Oct. 20**
1723 A1112 13c multicolored    .30   .25
1724 A1113 13c multicolored    .30   .25
   a. Pair, #1723-1724    .60   .50

### ALTA CALIFORNIA ISSUE
Founding of El Pueblo de San José de Guadalupe, first civil settlement in Alta California, 200th anniversary.

Farm Houses — A1114

### LITHOGRAPHED, ENGRAVED (Giori)
**1977, Sept. 9**   **Tagged**   **Perf. 11**
1725 A1114 13c black & multi    .30   .25

### AMERICAN BICENTENNIAL ISSUE
**Articles of Confederation**

200th anniversary of drafting the Articles of Confederation, York Town, Pa.

Members of Continental Congress in Conference A1115

### ENGRAVED (Giori)
**1977, Sept. 30**
1726 A1115 13c red & brn, cream    .30   .25
   b. Red omitted    500.00
   c. Red & brown omitted    300.00

No. 1726b also has most of the brown omitted. No. 1726c must be collected as a transition multiple, certainly with No. 1726b and preferably also with No. 1726.

### TALKING PICTURES, 50th ANNIV.

Movie Projector and Phonograph A1116

### LITHOGRAPHED, ENGRAVED (Giori)
**1977, Oct. 6**
1727 A1116 13c multicolored    .30   .25
   a. Brown & black omitted    —

### AMERICAN BICENTENNIAL ISSUE
**Surrender at Saratoga**

200th anniversary of Gen. John Burgoyne's surrender at Saratoga.

Surrender of Burgoyne, by John Trumbull — A1117

### PHOTOGRAVURE (Andreotti)
**1977, Oct. 7**
1728 A1117 13c multicolored    .30   .25

### CHRISTMAS ISSUE

Washington at Valley Forge A1118

Rural Mailbox A1119

### PHOTOGRAVURE (Combination Press)
**1977, Oct. 21**
1729 A1118 13c multicolored    .30   .25
   a. Imperf., pair    50.00

See Combination Press note after No. 1703.

### PHOTOGRAVURE (Andreotti)
1730 A1119 13c multicolored    .30   .25
   a. Imperf., pair    175.00

### CARL SANDBURG ISSUE
Carl Sandburg (1878-1967), poet, biographer and collector of American folk songs, birth centenary.

Carl Sandburg, by William A. Smith, 1952 — A1120

### GIORI PRESS PRINTING
**1978, Jan. 6**
1731 A1120 13c black & brown    .30   .25
   a. Brown omitted    1,750.
   c. All colors omitted    —

No. 1731c is tagged and has a faint black tagging ghost. Authentication is advised.

### CAPTAIN COOK ISSUE
Capt. James Cook, 200th anniversary of his arrival in Hawaii, at Waimea, Kauai, Jan. 20, 1778, and of his anchorage in Cook Inlet, near Anchorage, Alaska, June 1, 1778. Nos. 1732-1733 printed in panes of 50, containing 25 each of Nos. 1732-1733 including 5 No. 1733b.

Capt. Cook, by Nathaniel Dance, 1776 A1121

"Resolution" and "Discovery," by John Webber A1122

**1978, Jan. 20**
1732 A1121 13c dark blue    .30   .25
1733 A1122 13c green    .30   .25
   a. Vert. pair, imperf. horiz.    1,000.
   b. Pair, #1732-1733    .60   .50
   c. As "b," imperf. between    4,000.

Indian Head Penny, 1877 A1123

Eagle A1124

Roses — A1126

### ENGRAVED (Giori)
**1978**
1734 A1123 13c brown & blue green, bister, Jan. 11, 1978    .30   .25
   a. Horiz. pair, imperf. vert.    175.00

### PHOTOGRAVURE (Andreotti)
1735 A1124 (15c) orange, May 22, 1978    .30   .25
   a. Imperf., pair    70.00
   b. Vert. pair, imperf. horiz.    500.00
   c. Perf. 11.2    .35   .25

### BOOKLET STAMPS
### ENGRAVED
**Perf. 11x10½ on 2 or 3 Sides**
1736 A1124 (15c) orange    .30   .25
   a. Booklet pane of 8, May 22, 1978    2.50   1.50
   c. Vert. pair, imperf. btwn., in #1736a with foldover    1,000.

**Perf. 10 on 2 or 3 Sides**
1737 A1126 15c multi    .30   .25
   a. Booklet pane of 8, July 11, 1978    2.50   2.00
   b. Imperf, pair    450.00
   c. As "a," imperf    2,250.

Robertson Windmill, Williamsburg A1127

Old Windmill, Portsmouth A1128

Cape Cod Windmill, Eastham A1129

Dutch Mill, Batavia A1130

Southwestern Windmill — A1131

### BOOKLET STAMPS
### ENGRAVED
**Perf. 11 on 2 or 3 Sides**
**1980, Feb. 7**
1738 A1127 15c sepia, yellow    .30   .25
1739 A1128 15c sepia, yellow    .30   .25
1740 A1129 15c sepia, yellow    .30   .25
1741 A1130 15c sepia, yellow    .30   .25
1742 A1131 15c sepia, yellow    .30   .25
   a. Booklet pane of 10, 2 each #1738-1742    3.50   3.00
   b. Strip of 5, #1738-1742    1.50   1.40

### COIL STAMP
**1978, May 22**    **Perf. 10 Vert.**
1743 A1124 (15c) orange    .30   .25
   a. Imperf., pair    65.00

No. 1743a is valued in the grade of fine.

### BLACK HERITAGE SERIES
Harriet Tubman (1820-1913), born a slave, helped more than 300 slaves escape to freedom.

Harriet Tubman (1820-1913), Cart Carrying Slaves — A1133

### PHOTOGRAVURE (Andreotti)
**1978, Feb. 1**    **Perf. 10½x11**
1744 A1133 13c multicolored    .30   .25

### AMERICAN FOLK ART SERIES
**Quilts**
**Basket Design**

A1134

A1135

A1136

A1137

**1978, Mar. 8**    **Perf. 11**
1745 A1134 13c multicolored    .30   .25
1746 A1135 13c multicolored    .30   .25
1747 A1136 13c multicolored    .30   .25
1748 A1137 13c multicolored    .30   .25
   a. Block of 4, #1745-1748    1.20   1.00

### AMERICAN DANCE ISSUE

Ballet — A1138

Theater A1139

Folk Dance — A1140

Modern Dance — A1141

**1978, Apr. 26**
1749 A1138 13c multicolored    .30   .25
1750 A1139 13c multicolored    .30   .25
1751 A1140 13c multicolored    .30   .25
1752 A1141 13c multicolored    .30   .25
   a. Block of 4, #1749-1752    1.20   1.00

### AMERICAN BICENTENNIAL ISSUE
French Alliance, signed in Paris, Feb. 6, 1778 and ratified by Continental Congress, May 4, 1778.

# UNITED STATES

Louis XVI and Franklin, Porcelain Sculpture by C. G. Sauvage — A1142

### GIORI PRESS PRINTING
**1978, May 4**
1753 A1142 13c blue, black & red  .30  .25
  *a.* Red missing (PS) — —

### EARLY CANCER DETECTION ISSUE
George Papanicolaou, M.D. (1883-1962), cytologist and developer of Pap Test, early cancer detection in women.

Dr. George Papanicolaou (1883-1962) — A1143

### ENGRAVED
**1978, May 18**  Perf. 10½x11
1754 A1143 13c brown  .30  .25

### PERFORMING ARTS SERIES
Jimmie Rodgers (1897-1933), the "Singing Brakeman, Father of Country Music" (No. 1755); George M. Cohan (1878-1942), actor and playwright (No. 1756).

Jimmie Rodgers and Locomotive A1144

George M. Cohan, "Yankee Doodle Dandy" and Stars A1145

### PHOTOGRAVURE (Andreotti)
**1978**  Perf. 11
1755 A1144 13c multicolored  .30  .25
1756 A1145 15c multicolored  .30  .25

### CAPEX ISSUE
CAPEX '78, Canadian International Philatelic Exhibition, Toronto, Ont., June 9-18.

Wildlife from Canadian U.S. Border — A1146

### LITHOGRAPHED, ENGRAVED (Giori)
**1978, June 10**
1757 A1146 Block of 8, multi  2.40  2.00
  *a.* 13c Cardinal  .30  .25
  *b.* 13c Mallard  .30  .25
  *c.* 13c Canada goose  .30  .25
  *d.* 13c Blue jay  .30  .25
  *e.* 13c Moose  .30  .25
  *f.* 13c Chipmunk  .30  .25
  *g.* 13c Red fox  .30  .25
  *h.* 13c Raccoon  .30  .25
  *i.* As No. 1757, yellow, green, red, brown, blue, black (litho) omitted  6,000.
  *j.* Strip of 4 (a-d), imperf. vert.  5,000.
  *k.* Strip of 4 (e-h), imperf. vert.  1,500.
  *l.* As No. 1757, "d" and "h" with black (engr.) omitted  —
  *m.* As No. 1757, "b" with blue missing (PS)  —
  *o.* Strip of 4 (e-h), all colors except black missing on "e," "f" and "g," all colors except black and brown missing on "h" (PS)  1,250.
  *p.* As No. 1757, yellow, red, brown omitted, pane of 48  —

No. 1757k is worth more when contained in the block of 8. Value is for strip only.

### PHOTOGRAPHY ISSUE
Photography's contribution to communications and understanding.

Photographic Equipment — A1147

### PHOTOGRAVURE (Andreotti)
**1978, June 26**
1758 A1147 15c multicolored  .30  .25

### VIKING MISSIONS TO MARS ISSUE
Second anniv. of landing of Viking 1 on Mars

Viking 1 Lander Scooping Up Soil on Mars — A1148

### LITHOGRAPHED, ENGRAVED (Giori)
**1978, July 20**
1759 A1148 15c multicolored  .30  .25

### WILDLIFE CONSERVATION
Nos. 1760-1761 alternate in one horizontal row. Nos. 1762-1763 in the next.

Great Gray Owl A1149

Saw-whet Owl A1150

Barred Owl A1151

Great Horned Owl A1152

**1978, Aug. 26**
1760 A1149 15c multicolored  .30  .25
1761 A1150 15c multicolored  .30  .25
1762 A1151 15c multicolored  .30  .25
1763 A1152 15c multicolored  .30  .25
  *a.* Block of 4, #1760-1763  1.25  1.25
  *c.* As "a," yellow and orange (litho.) omitted  —

Two panes of No. 1763c have been reported. On one pane, the black (engr.) is shifted to the left.

### AMERICAN TREES ISSUE

Giant Sequoia — A1153

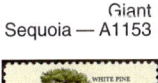

White Pine — A1154

White Oak — A1155

Gray Birch — A1156

### PHOTOGRAVURE (Andreotti)
**1978, Oct. 9**
1764 A1153 15c multicolored  .30  .25
1765 A1154 15c multicolored  .30  .25
1766 A1155 15c multicolored  .30  .25
1767 A1156 15c multicolored  .30  .25
  *a.* Block of 4, #1764-1767  1.25  1.25
  *b.* As "a," imperf. horiz.  17,500.

No. 1767b is unique.

### CHRISTMAS ISSUE

Madonna and Child with Cherubim, by Andrea della Robbia A1157

Child on Hobby-horse and Christmas Trees A1158

No. 1768, after terra cotta sculpture in National Gallery, Washington, D.C.

**1978, Oct. 18**  Perf. 11
1768 A1157 15c blue & multi  .30  .25
  *a.* Imperf., pair  70.00

Value for No. 1768a is for an uncreased pair.

1769 A1158 15c red & multi  .30  .25
  *a.* Imperf., pair  75.00
  *b.* Vert. pair, imperf. horiz.  900.00

### ROBERT F. KENNEDY ISSUE

Robert F. Kennedy (1925-68), U.S. Attorney General — A1159

### ENGRAVED
**1979, Jan. 12**
1770 A1159 15c blue  .35  .25

### BLACK HERITAGE SERIES
Dr. Martin Luther King, Jr. (1929-1968), Civil Rights leader

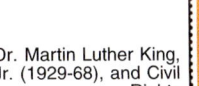

Dr. Martin Luther King, Jr. (1929-68), and Civil Rights Marchers — A1160

### PHOTOGRAVURE (Andreotti)
**1979, Jan. 13**
1771 A1160 15c multicolored  .40  .25
  *a.* Imperf., pair  750.00

### INTERNATIONAL YEAR OF THE CHILD ISSUE

Children — A1161

### ENGRAVED
**1979, Feb. 15**
1772 A1161 15c orange red  .30  .25

### LITERARY ARTS SERIES

John Steinbeck — A1162

**1979, Feb. 27**  Perf. 10½x11
1773 A1162 15c dark blue  .30  .25

### ALBERT EINSTEIN ISSUE

Albert Einstein — A1163

**1979, Mar. 4**
1774 A1163 15c chocolate  .30  .25

### AMERICAN FOLK ART SERIES
Pennsylvania Toleware, c. 1800.

Coffeepot A1164

Tea Caddy A1165

Sugar Bowl A1166

Coffeepot A1167

### PHOTOGRAVURE (Andreotti)
**1979, Apr. 19**  Perf. 11
1775 A1164 15c multicolored  .30  .25
1776 A1165 15c multicolored  .30  .25
1777 A1166 15c multicolored  .30  .25
1778 A1167 15c multicolored  .30  .25
  *a.* Block of 4, #1775-1778  1.25  1.25
  *b.* As "a," imperf. horiz.  1,500.

### AMERICAN ARCHITECTURE SERIES

Virginia Rotunda, by Thomas Jefferson A1168

Baltimore Cathedral, by Benjamin Latrobe A1169

Boston State House, by Charles Bulfinch A1170

Philadelphia Exchange, by William Strickland A1171

### ENGRAVED (Giori)
**1979, June 4**
1779 A1168 15c blk & brick red  .30  .25
1780 A1169 15c blk & brick red  .30  .25
1781 A1170 15c blk & brick red  .30  .25
1782 A1171 15c blk & brick red  .30  .25
  *a.* Block of 4, #1779-1782  1.25  1.25

# UNITED STATES

## ENDANGERED FLORA ISSUE

Persistent Trillium A1172

Hawaiian Wild Broadbean A1173

Contra Costa Wallflower A1174

Antioch Dunes Evening Primrose A1175

**PHOTOGRAVURE (Andreotti)**

**1979, June 7**
| | | | | |
|---|---|---|---|---|
| 1783 | A1172 | 15c multicolored | .30 | .25 |
| 1784 | A1173 | 15c multicolored | .30 | .25 |
| 1785 | A1174 | 15c multicolored | .30 | .25 |
| 1786 | A1175 | 15c multicolored | .30 | .25 |
| a. | | Block of 4, #1783-1786 | 1.25 | 1.25 |
| b. | | As "a," imperf. | 200.00 | |

## SEEING EYE DOGS ISSUE

1st guide dog program in the US, 50th anniv.

German Shepherd Leading Man — A1176

**PHOTOGRAVURE (Combination Press)**

**1979, June 15**
| | | | | |
|---|---|---|---|---|
| 1787 | A1176 | 15c multicolored | .30 | .25 |
| a. | | Imperf., pair | 325.00 | |
| c. | | As "a," tagging omitted | | |

## SPECIAL OLYMPICS ISSUE

Special Olympics for special children, Brockport, N.Y., Aug. 8-13.

Child Holding Winner's Medal — A1177

**PHOTOGRAVURE (Andreotti)**

**1979, Aug. 9**
| | | | | |
|---|---|---|---|---|
| 1788 | A1177 | 15c multicolored | .30 | .25 |

## JOHN PAUL JONES ISSUE

John Paul Jones (1747-1792), Naval Commander, American Revolution.

John Paul Jones, by Charles Willson Peale — A1178

**PHOTOGRAVURE (Champlain)**

**1979, Sept. 23**    **Perf. 11x12**
| | | | | |
|---|---|---|---|---|
| 1789 | A1178 | 15c multi | .30 | .25 |
| c. | | Vert. pair, imperf. horiz. | 125.00 | |

Imperforates on gummed stamp paper, including gutter pairs and blocks, are proofs from the ABNCo. archives. See No. 1789P in Proofs section of the Scott United States Specialized Catalogue.

**Perf. 11**
| | | | | |
|---|---|---|---|---|
| 1789A | A1178 | 15c multi | .55 | .25 |
| d. | | Vertical pair, imperf. horiz. | 115.00 | |

**Perf. 12**
| | | | | |
|---|---|---|---|---|
| 1789B | A1178 | 15c multi | 3,000. | 3,500. |

## OLYMPIC GAMES ISSUE

22nd Summer Olympic Games, Moscow, July 19-Aug. 3, 1980. Nos. 1791-1792 alternate in one horizontal row, Nos. 1793-1794 in next.

Javelin — A1179

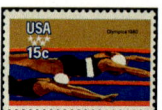
Running — A1180

Swimming A1181

Rowing — A1182

Equestrian A1183

**PHOTOGRAVURE**

**1979, Sept. 5**    **Perf. 11**
| | | | | |
|---|---|---|---|---|
| 1790 | A1179 | 10c multicolored | .30 | .25 |

**1979, Sept. 28**
| | | | | |
|---|---|---|---|---|
| 1791 | A1180 | 15c multicolored | .30 | .25 |
| 1792 | A1181 | 15c multicolored | .30 | .25 |
| 1793 | A1182 | 15c multicolored | .30 | .25 |
| 1794 | A1183 | 15c multicolored | .30 | .25 |
| a. | | Block of 4, #1791-1794 | 1.25 | 1.25 |
| b. | | As "a," imperf. | 900.00 | |

## OLYMPIC GAMES ISSUE

13th Winter Olympic Games, Lake Placid, N.Y., Feb. 12-24. Nos. 1795-1796 alternate in one horizontal row, Nos. 1797-1798 in next.

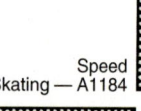
Speed Skating — A1184

Downhill Skiing — A1185

Ski Jump — A1186

Ice Hockey — A1187

**1980, Feb. 1**    **Perf. 11¼x10½**
| | | | | |
|---|---|---|---|---|
| 1795 | A1184 | 15c multicolored | .35 | .25 |
| 1796 | A1185 | 15c multicolored | .35 | .25 |
| 1797 | A1186 | 15c multicolored | .35 | .25 |
| 1798 | A1187 | 15c multicolored | .35 | .25 |
| b. | | Block of 4, #1795-1798 | 1.50 | 1.40 |

**Perf. 11**
| | | | | |
|---|---|---|---|---|
| 1795A | A1184 | 15c multicolored | 1.00 | .60 |
| 1796A | A1185 | 15c multicolored | 1.00 | .60 |
| 1797A | A1186 | 15c multicolored | 1.00 | .60 |
| 1798A | A1187 | 15c multicolored | 1.00 | .60 |
| c. | | Block of 4, #1795A-1798A | 4.00 | 3.50 |

## CHRISTMAS ISSUE

Virgin and Child, by Gerard David A1188

Santa Claus, Christmas Tree Ornament A1189

No. 1799 is designed after a painting in National Gallery of Art, Washington, D.C.

**PHOTOGRAVURE (Andreotti)**

**1979, Oct. 18**    **Perf. 11**
| | | | | |
|---|---|---|---|---|
| 1799 | A1188 | 15c multicolored | .30 | .25 |
| a. | | Imperf., pair | 70.00 | |
| b. | | Vert. pair, imperf. horiz. | 450.00 | |
| c. | | Vert. pair, imperf. between | 950.00 | |

**Perf. 11x10½**
| | | | | |
|---|---|---|---|---|
| 1800 | A1189 | 15c multicolored | .30 | .25 |
| a. | | Green & yellow omitted | 400.00 | |
| b. | | Green, yellow & tan omitted | 400.00 | |
| c. | | Vert. se-tenant pair, #1800a & 1800b | 850.00 | |

Nos. 1800a and 1800b always have the remaining colors misaligned.
Nos. 1800a, 1800b and 1800c are valued in the grade of fine.

---

**VALUES FOR HINGED STAMPS AFTER NO. 771**
This catalogue does not value unused stamps after No. 771 in hinged condition. Hinged unused stamps from No. 772 to the present are worth considerably less than the values given for unused stamps, which are for never-hinged examples.

---

## PERFORMING ARTS SERIES

Will Rogers (1879-1935), Actor and Humorist — A1190

**1979, Nov. 4**    **Tagged**    **Perf. 11**
| | | | | |
|---|---|---|---|---|
| 1801 | A1190 | 15c multicolored | .30 | .25 |
| a. | | Imperf., pair | 135.00 | |

## VIETNAM VETERANS ISSUE

A tribute to veterans of the Vietnam War.

Ribbon for Viet Nam Service Medal — A1191

**1979, Nov. 11**
| | | | | |
|---|---|---|---|---|
| 1802 | A1191 | 15c multicolored | .30 | .25 |

## PERFORMING ARTS SERIES

W.C. Fields (1880-1946), actor and comedian.

W.C. Fields (1880-1946), Actor and Comedian — A1192

**PHOTOGRAVURE**

**1980, Jan. 29**
| | | | | |
|---|---|---|---|---|
| 1803 | A1192 | 15c multicolored | .30 | — |
| a. | | Imperf., pair | | |

## BLACK HERITAGE SERIES

Benjamin Banneker (1731-1806), astronomer and mathematician.

Benjamin Banneker (1731-1806), Astronomer and Mathematician, Transverse — A1193

**1980, Feb. 15**
| | | | | |
|---|---|---|---|---|
| 1804 | A1193 | 15c multicolored | .30 | .25 |
| a. | | Horiz. pair, imperf. vert. | 275.00 | |

Imperfs, including gutter pairs and blocks, exist from printer's waste. These have been fraudulently perforated to simulate No. 1804a. Genuine examples of No. 1804a do not have colors misregistered.

## NATIONAL LETTER WRITING WEEK ISSUE

National Letter Writing Week, Feb. 24-Mar. 1. Nos. 1805-1810 are printed vertically se-tenant.

Letters Preserve Memories A1194

P.S. Write Soon A1195

Letters Lift Spirits A1196

Letters Shape Opinions A1197

**1980, Feb. 25**
| | | | | |
|---|---|---|---|---|
| 1805 | A1194 | 15c multicolored | .30 | .25 |
| 1806 | A1195 | 15c purple & multi | .30 | .25 |
| 1807 | A1194 | 15c multicolored | .30 | .25 |
| 1808 | A1195 | 15c green & multi | .30 | .25 |
| 1809 | A1197 | 15c multicolored | .30 | .25 |
| 1810 | A1195 | 15c red & multi | .30 | .25 |
| a. | | Vertical strip of 6, #1805-1810 | 1.85 | 2.00 |
| | | Nos. 1805-1810 (6) | 1.80 | 1.50 |

## AMERICANA TYPE

Weaver Violins — A1199

**COIL STAMPS**

**1980-81**    **Engr.**    **Perf. 10 Vertically**
| | | | | |
|---|---|---|---|---|
| 1811 | A984 | 1c dk blue, grnish | .30 | .25 |
| a. | | Imperf., pair | 60.00 | |
| 1813 | A1199 | 3.5c pur, yel | .30 | .25 |
| a. | | Untagged (Bureau precanceled, lines only) | .25 | .25 |
| b. | | Imperf., pair | 125.00 | |
| 1816 | A997 | 12c red brown, beige ('81) | .30 | .25 |
| a. | | Untagged (Bureau precanceled), red brown, beige | 1.25 | 1.25 |
| b. | | Imperf., pair | 135.00 | |
| c. | | As "a," brownish red, reddish beige | 1.25 | 1.25 |
| | | Nos. 1811-1816 (3) | .90 | .75 |

A1207

**PHOTOGRAVURE**

**1981, Mar. 15**    **Tagged**    **Perf. 11x10½**
| | | | | |
|---|---|---|---|---|
| 1818 | A1207 | (18c) violet | .35 | .25 |

# UNITED STATES

## BOOKLET STAMP
### ENGRAVED
*Perf. 10 on 2 or 3 Sides*

| 1819 | A1207 (18c) violet | .40 | .25 |
| a. | Booklet pane of 8 | 3.50 | 2.25 |

### COIL STAMP
*Perf. 10 Vert.*

| 1820 | A1207 (18c) violet | .40 | .25 |
| a. | Imperf., pair | 75.00 | |

## FRANCES PERKINS ISSUE

Frances Perkins (1882-1965), Secretary of Labor, 1933-1945 (first woman cabinet member).

Frances Perkins — A1208

### ENGRAVED
**1980, Apr. 10** *Perf. 10½x11*

| 1821 | A1208 15c Prussian blue | .30 | .25 |

## DOLLEY MADISON ISSUE

Dolley Madison (1768-1849), First Lady, 1809-1817.

Dolley Madison — A1209

**1980, May 20** *Perf. 11*

| 1822 | A1209 15c red brown & sepia | .30 | .25 |
| a. | Red brown missing (PS) | 575.00 | |

## EMILY BISSELL ISSUE

Emily Bissell (1861-1948), social worker; introduced Christmas seals in United States.

Emily Bissell — A1210

**1980, May 31**

| 1823 | A1210 15c black & red | .30 | .25 |
| a. | Vert. pair, imperf. horiz. | 650.00 | |
| b. | All colors missing (EP) | — | |
| c. | Red missing (FO) | — | |
| d. | Red omitted | — | |

On No. 1823d, traces of black are present.

## HELEN KELLER ISSUE

Helen Keller (1880-1968), blind and deaf writer and lecturer taught by Anne Sullivan (1867-1936).

Helen Keller and Anne Sullivan — A1211

### LITHOGRAPHED AND ENGRAVED
**1980, June 27**

| 1824 | A1211 15c multicolored | .30 | .25 |

## VETERANS ADMINISTRATION, 50th ANNIV.

Veterans Administration Emblem — A1212

## PHOTOGRAVURE
Plates of 200 subjects in four panes of 50.

**1980, July 21**

| 1825 | A1212 15c car & vio blue | .30 | .25 |
| a. | Horiz. pair, imperf. vert. | 375.00 | |

## BERNARDO DE GALVEZ ISSUE

Gen. Bernardo de Galvez (1746-1786), helped defeat British in Battle of Mobile, 1780.

Gen. Bernardo de Galvez — A1213

### LITHOGRAPHED & ENGRAVED
**1980, July 23**

| 1826 | A1213 15c multicolored | .30 | .25 |
| a. | Red, brown & blue (engr.) omitted | 550.00 | |
| b. | Light yellow, red, blue & brown (litho.) omitted | 550.00 | |

## CORAL REEFS ISSUE

Brain Coral, Beaugregory Fish A1214

Elkhorn Coral, Porkfish A1215

Chalice Coral, Moorish Idol Fish A1216

Finger Coral, Sabertooth Blenny Fish A1217

### PHOTOGRAVURE
**1980, Aug. 26**

| 1827 | A1214 15c multi | .30 | .25 |
| 1828 | A1215 15c multi | .30 | .25 |
| 1829 | A1216 15c multi | .30 | .25 |
| 1830 | A1217 15c multi | .30 | .25 |
| a. | Block of 4, #1827-1830 | 1.25 | 1.10 |
| b. | As "a," imperf. | 250.00 | |
| c. | As "a," vert. imperf. between | 1,750. | |
| d. | As "a," imperf. vert. | 2,750. | |

## ORGANIZED LABOR ISSUE

American Bald Eagle — A1218

**1980, Sept. 1**

| 1831 | A1218 15c multi | .30 | .25 |
| a. | Imperf., pair | 275.00 | |

## LITERARY ARTS SERIES

Edith Wharton (1862-1937), novelist.

Edith Wharton — A1219

### ENGRAVED
**1980, Sept. 5** *Perf. 10½x11*

| 1832 | A1219 15c purple | .30 | .25 |

## EDUCATION ISSUE

"Homage to the Square: Glow," by Josef Albers — A1220

### PHOTOGRAVURE
**1980, Sept. 12** *Perf. 11*

| 1833 | A1220 15c multi | .30 | .25 |
| a. | Horiz. pair, imperf. vert. | 150.00 | |

## AMERICAN FOLK ART SERIES
Pacific Northwest Indian Masks

Heiltsuk, Bella Bella Tribe — A1221

Chilkat Tlingit Tribe — A1222

Tlingit Tribe — A1223

Bella Coola Tribe — A1224

**1980, Sept. 25**

| 1834 | A1221 15c multi | .35 | .25 |
| 1835 | A1222 15c multi | .35 | .25 |
| 1836 | A1223 15c multi | .35 | .25 |
| 1837 | A1224 15c multi | .35 | .25 |
| a. | Block of 4, #1834-1837 | 1.50 | 1.25 |

## AMERICAN ARCHITECTURE SERIES

Smithsonian Institution, by James Renwick — A1225

Trinity Church, Boston, by Henry Hobson Richardson A1226

Pennsylvania Academy of Fine Arts, by Frank Furness — A1227

Lyndhurst, Tarrytown, NY, by Alexander Jackson Davis — A1228

### ENGRAVED (Giori)
**1980, Oct. 9**

| 1838 | A1225 15c black & red | .30 | .25 |
| a. | Red missing (PS) | — | |
| 1839 | A1226 15c black & red | .30 | .25 |
| 1840 | A1227 15c black & red | .30 | .25 |
| 1841 | A1228 15c black & red | .30 | .25 |
| a. | Block of 4, #1838-1841 | 1.25 | 1.25 |
| b. | As "a," red missing on Nos. 1838, 1839 (PS) | 400.00 | |

## CHRISTMAS ISSUE

Madonna and Child A1229

Wreath, Toys on Windowsill A1230

Design of No. 1842 after Epiphany Window, Washington Cathedral.

### PHOTOGRAVURE
**1980, Oct. 31**

| 1842 | A1229 15c multi | .30 | .25 |
| a. | Imperf., pair | 40.00 | |

### PHOTOGRAVURE (Combination Press)

| 1843 | A1230 15c multi | .30 | .25 |
| a. | Imperf., pair | 45.00 | |
| b. | Buff omitted | 22.50 | |
| c. | Vert. pair, imperf. horiz. | — | |
| d. | Horiz. pair, imperf. between | 3,250. | |

No. 1843b is difficult to identify and should have a competent certificate.

## GREAT AMERICANS ISSUE

Dorothea Dix A1231

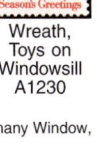

Igor Stravinsky A1232

Henry Clay A1233

Carl Schurz A1234

Pearl Buck A1235

Walter Lippmann A1236

Abraham Baldwin A1237

Henry Knox A1238

Sylvanus Thayer A1239

Richard Russell A1240

Alden Partridge A1241

Crazy Horse A1242

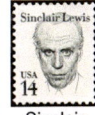

Sinclair Lewis A1243

Rachel Carson A1244

56 UNITED STATES

George Mason
A1245

Sequoyah
A1246

Ralph Bunche
A1247

Thomas H. Gallaudet
A1248

Harry S. Truman
A1249

John J. Audubon
A1250

Frank C. Laubach
A1251

Charles R. Drews MD
A1252

Robert Millikan
A1253

Grenville Clark
A1254

Lillian M. Gilbreth
A1255

Chester W. Nimitz
A1256

ENGRAVED

***Perf. 11x10½, 11 (1c, 6c-11c, 14c, No. 1862, 22c, 30c, 39c, 40c, 50c)***

**1980-85**

**1844** A1231 1c black ('83) .30 .25
*a.* Imperf., pair 250.00
*b.* Vert. pair, imperf. btwn. and with natural straight edge at bottom 1,000.
*e.* Vert. pair, imperf. horiz. 1,000.
**1845** A1232 2c brn blk ('82) .30 .25
**1846** A1233 3c ol grn ('83) .30 .25
**1847** A1234 4c violet ('83) .30 .25
**1848** A1235 5c henna brn ('83) .30 .25
**1849** A1236 6c org verm ('85) .30 .25
*a.* Vert. pair, imperf. between and with natural straight edge at bottom 750.00
**1850** A1237 7c brt car ('85) .30 .25
**1851** A1238 8c ol blk ('85) .30 .25
**1852** A1239 9c dk grn ('86) .30 .25
**1853** A1240 10c Prussian bl ('84) .30 .25
*b.* Vert. pair, imperf. between 550.00
*c.* Horiz. pair, imperf. between 1,250.
*d.* Vert. pair, imperf horiz. —

Almost all examples of No. 1853b also have a natural straight edge at bottom. At least one pair has perfs at bottom and partial perfs at top.

Completely imperforate tagged or untagged stamps are from printer's waste. Known unused and used.

**1854** A1241 11c dk blue ('85) .40 .25
**1855** A1242 13c lt maroon ('82) .40 .25
**1856** A1243 14c slate grn ('85) .30 .25
*b.* Vert. pair, imperf. horiz. 90.00
*c.* Horiz. pair, imperf. between 8.00 —
*d.* Vert. pair, imperf. between 1,250.
*e.* All color omitted —

No. 1856e comes from a partially printed pane and should be collected as a vertical strip of 10, one stamp normal, one stamp transitional and 8 stamps with color omitted.

**1857** A1244 17c green ('81) .35 .25
**1858** A1245 18c dk blue ('81) .35 .25
**1859** A1246 19c brown .45 .25
**1860** A1247 20c claret ('82) .40 .25
**1861** A1248 20c green ('83) .50 .25
**1862** A1249 20c black ('84) .40 .25
**1863** A1250 22c dk chalky bl ('85) .75 .25
*d.* Vert. pair, imperf. horiz. 1,300.
*f.* Horiz. pair, imperf. between 1,300.
*g.* Vert. pair, imperf. between —
**1864** A1251 30c ol gray ('84) .60 .25
*b.* Perf. 11.2, overall tagging 3.75 .25
**1865** A1252 35c gray ('81) .75 .25
**1866** A1253 37c blue ('82) .80 .25
**1867** A1254 39c rose lilac ('85) 1.00 .25
*a.* Vert. pair, imperf. horiz. 350.00
*b.* Vert. pair, imperf. between 1,000.
**1868** A1255 40c dk green ('84) 1.00 .25
**1869** A1256 50c brown ('85) 1.00 .25
*Nos. 1844-1869 (26)* 12.45 6.50

### EVERETT DIRKSEN (1896-1969)

Senate minority leader, 1960-1969.

A1261

ENGRAVED

**1981, Jan. 4** ***Perf. 11***

**1874** A1261 15c gray .30 .25
*a.* All color omitted 500.00

No. 1874a comes from a partially printed pane and may be collected as a vertical strip of 3 or 5 (1 or 3 stamps normal, one stamp transitional and one stamp with color omitted) or as a pair with one partially printed stamp.

### BLACK HERITAGE SERIES

Whitney Moore Young, Jr. (1921-1971), civil rights leader.

A1262

PHOTOGRAVURE

**1981, Jan. 30**

**1875** A1262 15c multi .35 .25

### FLOWER ISSUE

A1263

A1264

A1265

A1266

**1981, Apr. 23**

**1876** A1263 18c multicolored .35 .25
**1877** A1264 18c multicolored .35 .25
**1878** A1265 18c multicolored .35 .25
**1879** A1266 18c multicolored .35 .25
*a.* Block of 4, #1876-1879 1.40 1.25

### AMERICAN WILDLIFE

A1267

A1268

A1269

A1270

A1271

A1272

A1273

A1274

A1275

A1276

No. 1880, Bighorn. No. 1881, Puma. No. 1882, Harbor seal. No. 1883, American Buffalo. No. 1884, Brown bear. No. 1885, Polar bear. No. 1886, Elk (wapiti). No. 1887, Moose. No. 1888, White-tailed deer. No. 1889, Pronghorn.

ENGRAVED

**1981, May 14**

**1880** A1267 18c multicolored .50 .25
**1881** A1268 18c multicolored .50 .25
**1882** A1269 18c multicolored .50 .25
**1883** A1270 18c multicolored .50 .25
**1884** A1271 18c multicolored .50 .25
**1885** A1272 18c multicolored .50 .25
**1886** A1273 18c multicolored .50 .25
**1887** A1274 18c multicolored .50 .25
**1888** A1275 18c multicolored .50 .25
**1889** A1276 18c multicolored .50 .25
*a.* Booklet pane of 10, #1880-1889 5.00 5.00
*Nos. 1880-1889 (10)* 5.00 2.50

Nos. 1880-1889 issued in booklet only. All stamps have one or two straight edges. Imperfs are from printer's waste.

### FLAG AND ANTHEM ISSUE

A1277

A1278

A1279

A1280

ENGRAVED

**1981, Apr. 24** ***Perf. 11***

**1890** A1277 18c multicolored .35 .25
*a.* Imperf., pair 75.00
*b.* Vert. pair, imperf. horiz. 550.00
*c.* Vert. pair, imperf. between 550.00

**Coil Stamp**

***Perf. 10 Vert.***

**1891** A1278 18c multicolored .35 .25
*a.* Imperf., pair 17.50 —
*b.* Pair, imperf. between 1,750.

Beware of pairs offered as No. 1891b that have faint blind perfs.

Vertical pairs and blocks exist from printer's waste.

**Booklet Stamps**

***Perf. 11x10½ on 3 Sides***

**1892** A1279 6c dark blue & red .50 .25

***Perf. 11x10½ on 2 or 3 Sides***

**1893** A1280 18c multicolored .30 .25
*a.* Booklet pane of 8 (2 #1892, 6 #1893) 3.00 2.50
*b.* As "a," vert. imperf. between 60.00
*c.* Se-tenant pair, #1892 & #1893 .90 1.00

**Bureau Precanceled Coils**

**Starting with No. 1895b, Bureau precanceled coil stamps are valued unused as well as used. The coils issued with dull gum may be difficult to distinguish.**

**When used normally these stamps do not receive any postal markings so that used stamps with an additional postal cancellation of any kind are worth considerably less than the values shown here.**

### FLAG OVER SUPREME COURT ISSUE

A1281

**1981, Dec. 17** ***Perf. 11***

**1894** A1281 20c blk, dk bl & red .40 .25
*a.* Vert. pair, imperf. 30.00
*b.* Vert. pair, imperf. horiz. 250.00
*c.* Dark blue omitted 60.00
*d.* Black omitted 225.00

**Coil Stamp**

***Perf. 10 Vert.***

**1895** A1281 20c blk, dk bl & red .40 .25
*b.* Untagged (Bureau precanceled, lines only) .50 .50
*d.* Imperf., pair 8.00 —
*e.* Pair, imperf. between 600.00
*f.* Black omitted 45.00
*g.* Dark blue omitted 1,000.
*h.* Black field of stars instead of blue —

**BOOKLET STAMP**

***Perf. 11x10½ on 2 or 3 Sides***

**1896** A1281 20c blk, dk bl & red .40 .25
*a.* Booklet pane of 6 3.00 2.25
*b.* Booklet pane of 10, *June 1, 1982* 5.25 3.25
Scored perforations 7.50 5.00

### TRANSPORTATION ISSUE

Omnibus 1880s
A1283

Locomotive 1870s
A1284

COIL STAMPS
ENGRAVED

**1981-84** ***Perf. 10 Vert.***

**1897** A1283 1c violet ('83) .30 .25
*b.* Imperf., pair 325.00

See No. 2225.

**1897A** A1284 2c black ('82) .30 .25
*c.* Imperf., pair 45.00

See No. 2226.

Handcar 1880s — A1284a

Stagecoach 1890s — A1285

**1898** A1284a 3c dk grn ('83) .30 .25
**1898A** A1285 4c reddish brn ('82) .30 .25
*b.* Untagged (Bureau precanceled, Nonprofit Org.) .30 .25
*c.* As "b," imperf., pair 300.00
*d.* As No. 1898A, imperf. pair 400.00 —

See No. 2228.

Motorcycle 1913
A1286

Sleigh 1880s
A1287

**1899** A1286 5c gray grn ('83) .30 .25
*a.* Imperf., pair 1,000.
**1900** A1287 5.2c car ('83) .30 .25
*a.* Untagged (Bureau precanceled, lines only) .30 .25

# UNITED STATES

Bicycle 1870s A1288

Baby Buggy 1880s A1289

| 1901 | A1288 5.9c blue ('82) | .30 | .25 |
|---|---|---|---|
| a. | Untagged (Bureau precanceled, lines only) | .30 | .25 |
| b. | As "a," imperf., pair | 140.00 | |
| 1902 | A1289 7.4c brown ('84) | .30 | .25 |
| a. | Untagged (Bureau precanceled, Blk. Rt. CAR-RT SORT) | .30 | .25 |

Mail Wagon 1880s A1290

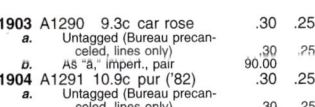

Hansom Cab 1890s A1291

| 1903 | A1290 9.3c car rose | .30 | .25 |
|---|---|---|---|
| a. | Untagged (Bureau precanceled, lines only) | .30 | .25 |
| b. | As "a," imperf., pair | 90.00 | |
| 1904 | A1291 10.9c pur ('82) | .30 | .25 |
| a. | Untagged (Bureau precanceled, lines only) | .30 | .25 |
| b. | As "a," imperf., pair | 125.00 | |

RR Caboose 1890s A1292

Electric Auto 1917 A1293

| 1905 | A1292 11c red ('84) | .30 | .25 |
|---|---|---|---|
| a. | Untagged Sept. 1991 | .25 | .25 |

Untagged stamps from plate 1 come only Bureau precanceled with lines. Untagged stamps from plate 2 come only without precancel lines.

| 1906 | A1293 17c ultra | .35 | .25 |
|---|---|---|---|
| a. | Untagged (Bureau precanceled, Presorted First Class) | .35 | .35 |
| b. | Imperf., pair | 130.00 | |
| c. | As "a," imperf., pair | 400.00 | |

Surrey 1890s A1294

Fire Pumper 1860s A1295

| 1907 | A1294 | 18c dk brn | .35 | .25 |
|---|---|---|---|---|
| a. | | Imperf., pair | 95.00 | |
| 1908 | A1295 | 20c vermilion | .35 | .25 |
| a. | | Imperf., pair | 75.00 | |
| | | Nos. 1897-1908 (14) | 4.35 | 3.50 |

A1296

**Booklet Stamp**
PHOTOGRAVURE
Perf. 10 Vert. on 1 or 2 Sides
**1983, Aug. 12**  Untagged

| 1909 | A1296 $9.35 multicolored | 19.00 | 15.00 |
|---|---|---|---|
| a. | Booklet pane of 3 | 57.50 | — |

## AMERICAN RED CROSS CENTENNIAL

A1297

Plates of 200 subjects in four panes of 50.

**1981, May 1**  Perf. 10½x11
| 1910 | A1297 18c multicolored | .35 | .25 |

## SAVINGS & LOAN SESQUICENTENNIAL

A1298

**1981, May 8**  Perf. 11
| 1911 | A1298 18c multicolored | .35 | .25 |

## SPACE ACHIEVEMENT ISSUE

A1299

A1302

A1300  A1301

A1303  A1306

A1304  A1305

Designs: A1299, Moon walk. A1300-A1301, A1304-A1305, Columbia space shuttle. A1302, Skylab. A1303, Pioneer 11. A1306, Telescope.

**1981, May 21**
| 1912 | A1299 18c multicolored | .35 | .25 |
|---|---|---|---|
| 1913 | A1300 18c multicolored | .35 | .25 |
| 1914 | A1301 18c multicolored | .35 | .25 |
| 1915 | A1302 18c multicolored | .35 | .25 |
| 1916 | A1303 18c multicolored | .35 | .25 |
| 1917 | A1304 18c multicolored | .35 | .25 |
| 1918 | A1305 18c multicolored | .35 | .25 |
| 1919 | A1306 18c multicolored | .35 | .25 |
| a. | Block of 8, #1912-1919 | 2.80 | 3.00 |
| b. | As "a," imperf. | 5,500. | |
| c. | As "a," imperf. vert. | 2,000. | |
| e. | As "a," top 4 stamps part perf, bottom 4 stamps imperf | 2,700. | |

No. 1919c is unique and has blind horiz. perfs.

## PROFESSIONAL MANAGEMENT EDUCATION CENTENARY

Joseph Wharton — A1307

**1981, June 18**
| 1920 | A1307 18c blue & black | .35 | .25 |

## PRESERVATION OF WILDLIFE HABITATS

A1308  A1309

A1310  A1311

**1981, June 26**
| 1921 | A1308 18c multicolored | .35 | .25 |
|---|---|---|---|
| 1922 | A1309 18c multicolored | .35 | .25 |
| 1923 | A1310 18c multicolored | .35 | .25 |
| 1924 | A1311 18c multicolored | .35 | .25 |
| a. | Block of 4, #1921-1924 | 1.50 | 1.25 |

## INTERNATIONAL YEAR OF THE DISABLED

Man Looking through Microscope A1312

**1981, June 29**
| 1925 | A1312 18c multicolored | .35 | .25 |
|---|---|---|---|
| a. | Vert. pair, imperf. horiz. | 1,500. | |

## EDNA ST. VINCENT MILLAY ISSUE

A1313

LITHOGRAPHED AND ENGRAVED
**1981, July 10**
| 1926 | A1313 18c multicolored | .35 | .25 |
|---|---|---|---|
| a. | Black (engr., inscriptions) omitted | 200.00 | — |

## ALCOHOLISM

A1314

ENGRAVED
**1981, Aug. 19**
| 1927 | A1314 18c blue & black | .45 | .25 |
|---|---|---|---|
| a. | Imperf., pair | 325.00 | |
| b. | Vert. pair, imperf. horiz. | 2,000. | |

## AMERICAN ARCHITECTURE SERIES

New York University Library by Sanford White — A1315

Biltmore House by Richard Morris Hunt — A1316

Palace of the Arts by Bernard Maybeck A1317

National Farmer's Bank by Louis Sullivan — A1318

**1981, Aug. 28**
| 1928 | A1315 18c black & red | .40 | .25 |
|---|---|---|---|
| 1929 | A1316 18c black & red | .40 | .25 |
| a. | Red missing (PS) | | |
| 1930 | A1317 18c black & red | .40 | .25 |
| b. | Red missing (PS) | | |
| 1931 | A1318 18c black & red | .40 | .25 |
| a. | Block of 4, #1928-1931 | 1.65 | 1.65 |

## SPORTS PERSONALITIES

Mildred Didrikson Zaharias A1319

Robert Tyre Jones A1320

**1981, Sept. 22**  Perf. 10½x11
| 1932 | A1319 18c purple | .40 | .25 |
|---|---|---|---|
| 1933 | A1320 18c green | .60 | .25 |

## FREDERIC REMINGTON

Coming Through the Rye — A1321

LITHOGRAPHED AND ENGRAVED
**1981, Oct. 9**  Perf. 11
| 1934 | A1321 18c gray, olive green & brown | .35 | .25 |
|---|---|---|---|
| a. | Vert. pair, imperf. between | 160.00 | |
| b. | Brown omitted | 190.00 | |

## JAMES HOBAN

Irish-American Architect of White House — A1322

PHOTOGRAVURE
**1981, Oct. 13**
| 1935 | A1322 18c multicolored | .35 | .25 |
|---|---|---|---|
| 1936 | A1322 20c multicolored | .35 | .25 |

See Ireland No. 504.

## AMERICAN BICENTENNIAL

Battle of Yorktown A1323

Battle of Virginia Capes — A1324

LITHOGRAPHED AND ENGRAVED
**1981, Oct. 16**
| 1937 | A1323 18c multicolored | .35 | .25 |
|---|---|---|---|
| 1938 | A1324 18c multicolored | .35 | .25 |
| a. | Pair, #1937-1938 | .90 | .75 |
| b. | As "a," black (engr., inscriptions) omitted | 275.00 | |
| d. | As "a," black (litho.) omitted | — | |

## CHRISTMAS

Madonna and Child, Botticelli A1325

Felt Bear on Sled A1326

PHOTOGRAVURE

**1981, Oct. 28**

**1939** A1325 (20c) multi .40 .25
*a.* Imperf., pair *90.00*
*b.* Vert. pair, imperf. horiz. *750.00*
**1940** A1326 (20c) multi .40 .25
*a.* Imperf., pair *175.00*
*b.* Vert. pair, imperf. horiz. *1,750.*

## JOHN HANSON

First President of Continental Congress — A1327

**1981, Nov. 5**

**1941** A1327 20c multicolored .40 .25

## DESERT PLANTS

Barrel Cactus A1328

Agave A1329

Beavertail Cactus A1330

Saguaro A1331

LITHOGRAPHED AND ENGRAVED

**1981 Dec. 11**

**1942** A1328 20c multicolored .40 .25
**1943** A1329 20c multicolored .40 .25
**1944** A1330 20c multicolored .40 .25
**1945** A1331 20c multicolored .40 .25
*a.* Block of 4, #1942-1945 1.60 1.25
*b.* As "a," deep brown (litho.) omitted *3,000.*
*c.* No. 1945 imperf., vert. pair *3,000.*
*d.* As "a," dark green & dark blue (engr.) missing (EP) *1,800.*
*e.* As "a," dark green (engr.) missing on left stamp (EP) *2,500.*

A1332

A1333

PHOTOGRAVURE

**1981, Oct. 11** ***Perf. 11x10½***

**1946** A1332 (20c) brown .40 .25
*b.* All color omitted *425.00*

No. 1946b comes from a partially printed pane with most stamps normal. It must be collected as a vertical pair or strip with normal or partially printed stamps attached.

ENGRAVED
**COIL STAMP**
***Perf. 10 Vert.***

**1947** A1332 (20c) brown .60 .25
*a.* Imperf. pair *400.00*

**BOOKLET STAMPS**
***Perf. 11 on 2 or 3 Sides***

**1948** A1333 (20c) brown .40 .25
*a.* Booklet pane of 10 4.50 3.25

A1334

BOOKLET STAMP
ENGRAVED
***Perf. 11 on 2 or 3 Sides***

**1982, Jan. 8**

**1949** A1334 20c dark blue .45 .25
*a.* Booklet pane of 10 4.75 2.50
*b.* As "a," imperf. vert. *90.00*
*c.* Type II 1.25 .25
*d.* Type II, booklet pane of 10 12.50 —

No. 1949 is 18¾mm wide and has overall tagging. No. 1949c is 18½mm wide and has block tagging.
See No. 1880.

## FRANKLIN DELANO ROOSEVELT

A1335

**1982, Jan. 30** ***Perf. 11***

**1950** A1335 20c blue .40 .25

## LOVE ISSUE

A1336

PHOTOGRAVURE

**1982, Feb. 1** ***Perf. 11¼***

**1951** A1336 20c multicolored 1.00 .25
*b.* Imperf., pair *200.00*
*c.* Blue omitted *200.00*
*d.* Yellow omitted *600.00*
*e.* Purple omitted —

No. 1951c is valued in the grade of fine.

***Perf. 11¼x10½***

**1951A** A1336 20c multicolored 1.00 .25

## GEORGE WASHINGTON

A1337

**1982, Feb. 22** ***Perf. 11***

**1952** A1337 20c multicolored .40 .25

## STATE BIRDS AND FLOWERS ISSUE

A1338

**1982, Apr. 14** ***Perf. 10½x11¼***

**1953** A1338 20c Alabama .55 .30
**1954** A1339 20c Alaska .55 .30
**1955** A1340 20c Arizona .55 .30
**1956** A1341 20c Arkansas .55 .30
**1957** A1342 20c California .55 .30
**1958** A1343 20c Colorado .55 .30
**1959** A1344 20c Connecticut .55 .30
**1960** A1345 20c Delaware .55 .30
**1961** A1346 20c Florida .55 .30
**1962** A1347 20c Georgia .55 .30
**1963** A1348 20c Hawaii .55 .30
**1964** A1349 20c Idaho .55 .30
**1965** A1350 20c Illinois .55 .30
**1966** A1351 20c Indiana .55 .30
**1967** A1352 20c Iowa .55 .30
**1968** A1353 20c Kansas .55 .30
**1969** A1354 20c Kentucky .55 .30
**1970** A1355 20c Louisiana .55 .30
**1971** A1356 20c Maine .55 .30
**1972** A1357 20c Maryland .55 .30
**1973** A1358 20c Massachusetts .55 .30
**1974** A1359 20c Michigan .55 .30
**1975** A1360 20c Minnesota .55 .30
**1976** A1361 20c Mississippi .55 .30
**1977** A1362 20c Missouri .55 .30
**1978** A1363 20c Montana .55 .30
**1979** A1364 20c Nebraska .55 .30
**1980** A1365 20c Nevada .55 .30
**1981** A1366 20c New Hampshire .55 .30
*b.* Black missing (EP) *4,000.*
**1982** A1367 20c New Jersey .55 .30
**1983** A1368 20c New Mexico .55 .30
**1984** A1369 20c New York .55 .30
**1985** A1370 20c North Carolina .55 .30
**1986** A1371 20c North Dakota .55 .30
**1987** A1372 20c Ohio .55 .30
**1988** A1373 20c Oklahoma .55 .30
**1989** A1374 20c Oregon .55 .30
**1990** A1375 20c Pennsylvania .55 .30
**1991** A1376 20c Rhode Island .55 .30
*b.* Black missing (EP) *4,000.*
**1992** A1377 20c South Carolina .55 .30
**1993** A1378 20c South Dakota .55 .30
**1994** A1379 20c Tennessee .55 .30
**1995** A1380 20c Texas .55 .30
**1996** A1381 20c Utah .55 .30
**1997** A1382 20c Vermont .55 .30
**1998** A1383 20c Virginia .55 .30
**1999** A1384 20c Washington .55 .30
**2000** A1385 20c West Virginia .55 .30
**2001** A1386 20c Wisconsin .55 .30
*b.* Black missing (EP) *4,000.*
**2002** A1387 20c Wyoming .55 .30
*b.* A1338-A1387 Pane of 50, Nos. 1953-2002 27.50 20.00
*d.* Pane of 50, imperf. *21,000.*

***Perf. 11¼x11***

**1953A** A1338 20c Alabama .60 .30
**1954A** A1339 20c Alaska .60 .30
**1955A** A1340 20c Arizona .60 .30
**1956A** A1341 20c Arkansas .60 .30
**1957A** A1342 20c California .60 .30
**1958A** A1343 20c Colorado .60 .30
**1959A** A1344 20c Connecticut .60 .30
**1960A** A1345 20c Delaware .60 .30
**1961A** A1346 20c Florida .60 .30
**1962A** A1347 20c Georgia .60 .30
**1963A** A1348 20c Hawaii .60 .30
**1964A** A1349 20c Idaho .60 .30
**1965A** A1350 20c Illinois .60 .30
**1966A** A1351 20c Indiana .60 .30
**1967A** A1352 20c Iowa .60 .30
**1968A** A1353 20c Kansas .60 .30
**1969A** A1354 20c Kentucky .60 .30
**1970A** A1355 20c Louisiana .60 .30
**1971A** A1356 20c Maine .60 .30
**1972A** A1357 20c Maryland .60 .30
**1973A** A1358 20c Massachusetts .60 .30
**1974A** A1359 20c Michigan .60 .30
**1975A** A1360 20c Minnesota .60 .30
**1976A** A1361 20c Mississippi .60 .30
**1977A** A1362 20c Missouri .60 .30
**1978A** A1363 20c Montana .60 .30
**1979A** A1364 20c Nebraska .60 .30
**1980A** A1365 20c Nevada .60 .30
**1981A** A1366 20c New Hampshire .60 .30
**1982A** A1367 20c New Jersey .60 .30
**1983A** A1368 20c New Mexico .60 .30
**1984A** A1369 20c New York .60 .30
**1985A** A1370 20c North Carolina .60 .30
**1986A** A1371 20c North Dakota .60 .30
**1987A** A1372 20c Ohio .60 .30
**1988A** A1373 20c Oklahoma .60 .30
**1989A** A1374 20c Oregon .60 .30
**1990A** A1375 20c Pennsylvania .60 .30
**1991A** A1376 20c Rhode Island .60 .30
**1992A** A1377 20c South Carolina .60 .30
**1993A** A1378 20c South Dakota .60 .30
**1994A** A1379 20c Tennessee .60 .30
**1995A** A1380 20c Texas .60 .30
**1996A** A1381 20c Utah .60 .30
**1997A** A1382 20c Vermont .60 .30
**1998A** A1383 20c Virginia .60 .30
**1999A** A1384 20c Washington .60 .30
**2000A** A1385 20c West Virginia .60 .30
**2001A** A1386 20c Wisconsin .60 .30
**2002A** A1387 20c Wyoming .60 .30
*c.* A1338-A1387 Pane of 50, Nos. 1953A-2002A 30.00 22.50

Nos. 1953-2002 are line perforated. The perforations do not meet perfectly at the corners of each stamp and extend into the narrow selvage margins of an intact pane. Nos. 1953A-2002A are comb perforated. The perforations meet perfectly at the corners of each stamp and do not extend into the narrow selvage margins of an intact pane.

## US-NETHERLANDS

200th Anniv. of Diplomatic Recognition by the Netherlands A1388

**1982, Apr. 20** ***Perf. 11***

**2003** A1388 20c multicolored .40 .25
*a.* Imperf., pair *250.00*

See Netherlands Nos. 640-641.

## LIBRARY OF CONGRESS

A1389

ENGRAVED

**1982, Apr. 21**

**2004** A1389 20c red & black .40 .25
*a.* All color missing —

No. 2004a must be collected as a right margin horiz. strip of 3, 4 or 5 with one No. 2004a, one transitional stamp and one or more normal stamps.

## CONSUMER EDUCATION

A1390

Coil Stamp

**1982, Apr. 27** ***Perf. 10 Vert.***

**2005** A1390 20c sky blue .55 .25
*a.* Imperf., pair 70.00

## KNOXVILLE WORLD'S FAIR

A1391

A1392

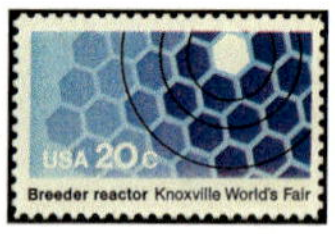


A1393

A1394

PHOTOGRAVURE

**1982, Apr. 29** ***Perf. 11***

**2006** A1391 20c multicolored .45 .25
**2007** A1392 20c multicolored .45 .25
**2008** A1393 20c multicolored .45 .25
**2009** A1394 20c multicolored .45 .25
*a.* Block of 4, #2006-2009 1.80 1.50

## HORATIO ALGER

Frontispiece from "Ragged Dick" — A1395

ENGRAVED

**1982, Apr. 30**

**2010** A1395 20c red & black, *tan* .40 .25
*a.* Red and black omitted —

The Philatelic Foundation has issued a certificate for a pane of 50 with red and black colors omitted. Recognition of this error is by the paper and by a tiny residue of red ink from the tagging roller. The engraved plates did not strike the paper.

## AGING TOGETHER

A1396

ENGRAVED

**1982, May 21**

**2011** A1396 20c brown .40 .25

# UNITED STATES

## PERFORMING ARTS SERIES

A1397

### PHOTOGRAVURE
**1982, June 8**
2012 A1397 20c multicolored .40 .25
  a. Black missing (EP)

John (1882-1942), Ethel (1879-1959), and Lionel (1878-1954) Barrymore, actors.

## DR. MARY WALKER

A1398

**1982, June 10**
2013 A1398 20c multicolored .40 .25

Dr. Mary Walker (1832-1919), 1865 recipient of Medal of Honor.

## INTERNATIONAL PEACE GARDEN

A1399

### LITHOGRAPHED AND ENGRAVED
**1982, June 30**
2014 A1399 20c multicolored .45 .25
  a. Black (engr.) omitted 200.00

## AMERICA'S LIBRARIES

A1400

### ENGRAVED
**1982, July 13**
2015 A1400 20c red & black .40 .25
  a. Vert. pair, imperf. horiz. 200.00
  c. All colors missing (EP) 175.00
  d. Imperf. pair 500.00
  e. Horz. pair, imperf. vert. —

On No. 2015c, an albino impression of the design is present.

## BLACK HERITAGE SERIES

Jackie Robinson (1919-72), baseball player.

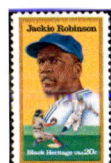
A1401

### PHOTOGRAVURE
**1982, Aug. 2**    Perf. 10½x11
2016 A1401 20c multicolored 1.00 .25

## TOURO SYNAGOGUE

A1402

### PHOTOGRAVURE AND ENGRAVED
**1982, Aug. 22**    Perf. 11
2017 A1402 20c multicolored .40 .25
  a. Imperf., pair 1,400.

## WOLF TRAP FARM PARK

A1403

### PHOTOGRAVURE
**1982, Sept. 1**
2018 A1403 20c multicolored .40 .25

## AMERICAN ARCHITECTURE SERIES

Fallingwater, Mill Run, Pa., by Frank Lloyd Wright — A1404

Illinois Institute of Technology by Ludwig Mies van der Rohe — A1405

Gropius House, Lincoln, Mass., by Walter Gropius — A1406

Dulles Airport, by Eero Saarinen A1407

### ENGRAVED
**1982, Sept. 30**
2019 A1404 20c black & brown .45 .25
  b. Red missing (PS) —
2020 A1405 20c black & brown .45 .25
  a. Red missing (PS) —
2021 A1406 20c black & brown .45 .25
2022 A1407 20c black & brown .45 .25
  a. Block of 4, #2019-2022 2.00 1.75

## FRANCIS OF ASSISI

A1408

### PHOTOGRAVURE
**1982, Oct. 7**
2023 A1408 20c multicolored .40 .25

## PONCE DE LEON

A1409

### PHOTOGRAVURE (Combination press)
**1982, Oct. 12**
2024 A1409 20c multicolored .40 .25
  a. Imperf., pair 250.00
  b. Vert. pair, imperf. between and at top 500.00

## CHRISTMAS ISSUES

A1410

A1411

A1412

A1413

A1414

A1415

### PHOTOGRAVURE
**1982, Nov. 3**
2025 A1410 13c multicolored .30 .25
  a. Imperf., pair 300.00

### PHOTOGRAVURE (Combination Press)
**1982, Oct. 28**
2026 A1411 20c multicolored .40 .25
  a. Imperf. pair 90.00
  b. Horiz. pair, imperf. vert. 900.00
  c. Vert. pair, imperf. horiz. —

### PHOTOGRAVURE
2027 A1412 20c multicolored .60 .25
2028 A1413 20c multicolored .60 .25
2029 A1414 20c multicolored .60 .25
2030 A1415 20c multicolored .60 .25
  a. Block of 4, #2027-2030 2.40 1.50
  b. As "a," imperf. 1,250.
  c. As "a," imperf. horiz. 700.00
  Nos. 2025-2030 (6) 3.10 1.50

## SCIENCE & INDUSTRY

A1416

### LITHOGRAPHED AND ENGRAVED
**1983, Jan. 19**
2031 A1416 20c multicolored .40 .25
  a. Black (engr.) omitted 750.00

## BALLOONS

A1417

A1420

A1418

A1419

### PHOTOGRAVURE
**1983, Mar. 31**    Tagged    Perf. 11
2032 A1417 20c multicolored .50 .25
2033 A1418 20c multicolored .50 .25
2034 A1419 20c multicolored .50 .25
2035 A1420 20c multicolored .50 .25
  a. Block of 4, #2032-2035 2.00 1.50
  b. As "a," imperf. 2,750.
  c. As "a," right stamp perf., otherwise imperf. 2,750.

## US-SWEDEN

A1421

### ENGRAVED
**1983, Mar. 24**
2036 A1421 20c blue, blk & red brn .40 .25
See Sweden No. 1453.

## CCC, 50TH ANNIV.

A1422

### PHOTOGRAVURE
**1983, Apr. 5**
2037 A1422 20c multicolored .40 .25
  a. Imperf., pair 1,750.
  b. Vert. pair, imperf. horiz.

## JOSEPH PRIESTLEY

A1423

**1983, Apr. 13**
2038 A1423 20c multicolored .40 .25

## VOLUNTEERISM

A1424

### ENGRAVED (Combination Press)
**1983, Apr. 20**
2039 A1424 20c red & black .40 .25
  a. Imperf., pair 225.00

## US-GERMANY

Concord, 1683 — A1425

### ENGRAVED
**1983, Apr. 29**
2040 A1425 20c brown .40 .25
See Germany No. 1397.

## BROOKLYN BRIDGE

A1426

**1983, May 17**
2041 A1426 20c blue .40 .25
  b. All color missing (EP) 90.00

On No. 2041b, an albino impression of part of the design is evident.

## TVA

A1427

### PHOTOGRAVURE AND ENGRAVED (Combination Press)
**1983, May 18**
2042 A1427 20c multicolored .40 .25

A1428

### PHOTOGRAVURE (Combination Press)
**1983, May 14**
2043 A1428 20c multicolored .40 .25

60 UNITED STATES

### BLACK HERITAGE SERIES

A1429

PHOTOGRAVURE
1983, June 9
2044 A1429 20c multicolored .50 .25
  a. Imperf., pair 300.00

### MEDAL OF HONOR

A1430

LITHOGRAPHED AND ENGRAVED
1983, June 7
2045 A1430 20c multicolored .55 .25
  a. Red omitted 150.00

### GEORGE HERMAN RUTH (1895-1948)

A1431

ENGRAVED  Perf. 10½x11
1983, July 6
2046 A1431 20c blue 1.00 .25

### LITERARY ARTS SERIES

Nathaniel Hawthorne (1804-1864), novelist.

A1432

PHOTOGRAVURE  Perf. 11
1983, July 8
2047 A1432 20c multicolored .40 .25

### 1984 SUMMER OLYMPICS

Discus — A1433

High Jump — A1434

Archery — A1435

Boxing — A1436

1983, July 28
2048 A1433 13c multicolored .35 .25
2049 A1434 13c multicolored .35 .25
2050 A1435 13c multicolored .35 .25
2051 A1436 13c multicolored .35 .25
  a. Block of 4, #2048-2051 1.50 1.25

### SIGNING OF TREATY OF PARIS

John Adams, Franklin, John Jay, David Hartley — A1437

1983, Sept. 2
2052 A1437 20c multicolored .40 .25

### CIVIL SERVICE

A1438

PHOTOGRAVURE AND ENGRAVED
1983, Sept. 9
2053 A1438 20c buff, blue & red .40 .25

### METROPOLITAN OPERA

A1439

LITHOGRAPHED AND ENGRAVED
1983, Sept. 14
2054 A1439 20c yellow & maroon .40 .25

### AMERICAN INVENTORS

A1440

A1441

A1442

A1443

LITHOGRAPHED AND ENGRAVED
1983, Sept. 21
2055 A1440 20c multicolored .50 .25
2056 A1441 20c multicolored .50 .25
2057 A1442 20c multicolored .50 .25
2058 A1443 20c multicolored .50 .25
  a. Block of 4, #2055-2058 2.00 1.50
  b. As "a," black omitted 275.00

### STREETCARS

A1444

A1445

A1446

A1447

PHOTOGRAVURE AND ENGRAVED
1983, Oct. 8
2059 A1444 20c multicolored .50 .25
2060 A1445 20c multicolored .50 .25
  a. Horiz. pair, black (engr.) missing on Nos. 2059, 2060 (EP) —
2061 A1446 20c multicolored .50 .25
  a. Vert. pair, black (engr.) missing on Nos. 2059, 2061 (EP) —
2062 A1447 20c multicolored .50 .25
  a. Block of 4, #2059-2062 2.00 1.50
  b. As "a," black (engr.) omitted 250.00
  c. As "a," black (engr.) omitted on #2059, 2061 —

### CHRISTMAS

A1448

A1449

PHOTOGRAVURE
1983, Oct. 28
2063 A1448 20c multicolored .40 .25
2064 A1449 20c multicolored .40 .25
  a. Imperf., pair 100.00

### MARTIN LUTHER (1483-1546)

Martin Luther (1483-1546), German Religious Leader — A1450

1983, Nov. 11
2065 A1450 20c multicolored .40 .25

### ALASKA STATEHOOD, 25th ANNIV.

Caribou and Alaska Pipeline — A1451

1984, Jan. 3
2066 A1451 20c multicolored .40 .25
  a. Vert. pair, imperf. horiz.

### 14th WINTER OLYMPIC GAMES

Ice Dancing A1452

Downhill Skiing A1453

Cross-country Skiing A1454

Hockey A1455

1984, Jan. 6  Perf. 10½x11
2067 A1452 20c multicolored .55 .25
2068 A1453 20c multicolored .55 .25
2069 A1454 20c multicolored .55 .25
2070 A1455 20c multicolored .55 .25
  a. Block of 4, #2067-2070 2.20 1.75

### FEDERAL DEPOSIT INSURANCE CORPORATION, 50TH ANNIV.

A1456

1984, Jan. 12  Perf. 11
2071 A1456 20c multicolored .40 .25

### LOVE

A1457

PHOTOGRAVURE AND ENGRAVED (Combination Press)
1984, Jan. 31  Perf. 11x10½
2072 A1457 20c multicolored .40 .25
  a. Horiz. pair, imperf. vert. 125.00

### BLACK HERITAGE SERIES

Carter G. Woodson (1875-1950), Historian.

A1458

PHOTOGRAVURE
1984, Feb. 1  Perf. 11
2073 A1458 20c multicolored .40 .25
  a. Horiz. pair, imperf. vert. 800.00

### SOIL & WATER CONSERVATION

A1459

1984, Feb. 6
2074 A1459 20c multicolored .40 .25

### 50TH ANNIV. OF CREDIT UNION ACT

Dollar Sign, Coin — A1460

1984, Feb. 10
2075 A1460 20c multicolored .40 .25

### ORCHIDS

A1461    A1462

A1463    A1464

# UNITED STATES

**1984, Mar. 5**

| 2076 | A1461 | 20c multicolored | .50 | .25 |
|---|---|---|---|---|
| 2077 | A1462 | 20c multicolored | .50 | .25 |
| 2078 | A1463 | 20c multicolored | .50 | .25 |
| 2079 | A1464 | 20c multicolored | .50 | .25 |
| a. | | Block of 4, #2076-2079 | 2.00 | 1.50 |

## HAWAII STATEHOOD, 25th ANNIV.

Eastern Polynesian Canoe, Golden Plover, Mauna Loa Volcano — A1465

**1984, Mar. 12**

2080  A1465  20c multicolored    .40  .25

## 50TH ANNIV., NATIONAL ARCHIVES

Abraham Lincoln, George Washington — A1466

**1984, Apr. 16**

2081  A1466  20c multicolored    .40  .25

## LOS ANGELES SUMMER OLYMPICS

Diving A1467    Long Jump A1468

Wrestling A1469    Kayak A1470

**1984, May 4**

| 2082 | A1467 | 20c multicolored | .55 | .25 |
|---|---|---|---|---|
| 2083 | A1468 | 20c multicolored | .55 | .25 |
| 2084 | A1469 | 20c multicolored | .55 | .25 |
| 2085 | A1470 | 20c multicolored | .55 | .25 |
| a. | | Block of 4, #2082-2085 | 2.40 | 1.90 |
| b. | | As "a," imperf between vertically | 9,500. | |

## LOUISIANA WORLD EXPOSITION

River Wildlife — A1471

**1984, May 11**

2086  A1471  20c multicolored    .50  .25

## HEALTH RESEARCH

Lab Equipment A1472

**1984, May 17**

2087  A1472  20c multicolored    .40  .25

## PERFORMING ARTS

A1473

### PHOTOGRAVURE AND ENGRAVED
### (Combination Press)

**1984, May 23**

2088  A1473  20c multicolored    .40  .25
   b.  Horiz. pair, imperf between    —

## JIM THORPE

A1474

### ENGRAVED

**1984, May 24**

2089  A1474  20c dark brown    .60  .25
   a.  All color omitted

On No. 2089a, an albino impression of the design is evident.

## PERFORMING ARTS

Tenor John McCormack (1884-1945) — A1475

### PHOTOGRAVURE

**1984, June 6**

2090  A1475  20c multicolored    .40  .25
See Ireland No. 594.

## ST. LAWRENCE SEAWAY, 25th ANNIV.

Aerial View of Seaway, Freighters A1476

**1984, June 26**

2091  A1476  20c multicolored    .40  .25

## WATERFOWL PRESERVATION ACT, 50th ANNIV.

"Mallards Dropping In," by Jay N. Darling — A1477

### ENGRAVED

**1984, July 2**    Perf. 11

2092  A1477  20c blue    .50  .25
   a.  Horiz. pair, imperf. vert.    275.00

## ROANOKE VOYAGES

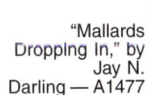

The Elizabeth — A1478

### PHOTOGRAVURE

**1984, July 13**

2093  A1478  20c multicolored    .40  .25

## LITERARY ARTS SERIES

Herman Melville (1819-1891), Author — A1479

### ENGRAVED

**1984, Aug. 1**

2094  A1479  20c sage green    .40  .25

## HORACE MOSES (1862-1947), FOUNDER OF JUNIOR ACHIEVEMENT

Junior Achievement Founder — A1480

### ENGRAVED (Combination Press)

**1984, Aug. 6**

2095  A1480  20c org & dark brn    .40  .25

## SMOKEY BEAR

Smokey Bear — A1481

### LITHOGRAPHED AND ENGRAVED

**1984, Aug. 13**

2096  A1481  20c multicolored    .40  .25
   a.  Horiz. pair, imperf. btwn.    175.00
   b.  Vert. pair, imperf. btwn.    150.00
   c.  Block of 4, imperf btwn vert. and horiz.    2,500.
   d.  Horiz. pair, imperf. vert.    450.00

## ROBERTO CLEMENTE (1934-1972)

Clemente, Puerto Rican Flag — A1482

### PHOTOGRAVURE

**1984, Aug. 17**

2097  A1482  20c multicolored    1.00  .25
   a.  Horiz. pair, imperf. vert.    1,250.

## DOGS

Beagle, Boston Terrier — A1483

Chesapeake Bay Retriever, Cocker Spaniel — A1484

Alaskan Malamute, Collie — A1485

Black & Tan Coonhound, American Foxhound A1486

**1984, Sept. 7**

| 2098 | A1483 | 20c multicolored | .50 | .25 |
|---|---|---|---|---|
| 2099 | A1484 | 20c multicolored | .50 | .25 |
| 2100 | A1485 | 20c multicolored | .50 | .25 |
| 2101 | A1486 | 20c multicolored | .50 | .25 |
| a. | | Block of 4, #2098-2101 | 2.00 | 1.90 |
| b. | | As "a," imperf horiz. | 5,500. | |

## CRIME PREVENTION

McGruff, The Crime Dog — A1487

**1984, Sept. 26**

2102  A1487  20c multicolored    .40  .25

## HISPANIC AMERICANS

A1488

**1984, Oct. 31**

2103  A1488  20c multicolored    .40  .25
   a.  Vert. pair, imperf. horiz.    1,250.

## FAMILY UNITY

A1489

### PHOTOGRAVURE AND ENGRAVED
### (Combination Press)

**1984, Oct. 1**

2104  A1489  20c multicolored    .40  .25
   a.  Horiz. pair, imperf. vert.    325.00
   c.  Vert. pair, imperf. btwn. and at bottom    —
   d.  Horiz. pair, imperf between    900.00

## ELEANOR ROOSEVELT (1884-1962)

A1490

### ENGRAVED

**1984, Oct. 11**

2105  A1490  20c deep blue    .40  .25

## NATION OF READERS

Lincoln, Son Tad — A1491

**1984, Oct. 16**

2106  A1491  20c brown & maroon    .40  .25

## CHRISTMAS

Madonna and Child by Fra Filippo Lippi A1492    Santa Claus A1493

### PHOTOGRAVURE

**1984, Oct. 30**

2107  A1492  20c multicolored    .40  .25
   a.  Imperf., pair    1,400.
2108  A1493  20c multicolored    .40  .25
   a.  Horiz. pair, imperf. vert.    750.00

No. 2108a is valued in the grade of fine.

## VIETNAM VETERANS MEMORIAL

Memorial Wall A1494

### ENGRAVED
**1984, Nov. 10**
2109 A1494 20c multicolored .50 .25

## PERFORMING ARTS

Composer Jerome Kern (1885-1945) — A1495

### PHOTOGRAVURE
**1985, Jan. 23**
2110 A1495 22c multicolored .45 .25

 A1496   A1497

### PHOTOGRAVURE
**1985, Feb. 1**  Perf. 11
2111 A1496 (22c) green .60 .25
- a. Vert. pair, imperf. 35.00
- b. Vert. pair, imperf. horiz. 750.00

### COIL STAMP
Perf. 10 Vert.
2112 A1496 (22c) green .60 .25
- a. Imperf., pair 45.00

### BOOKLET STAMP
ENGRAVED
Perf. 11 on 2 or 3 Sides
2113 A1497 (22c) green .65 .25
- a. Booklet pane of 10 6.75 3.00
- b. As "a," Horiz. imperf. btwn. 1,850.

Two examples of No. 2113b are reported, both in an unexploded booklet.

 A1498
Flag over Capitol Dome — A1499

### ENGRAVED
**1985, Mar. 29**  Perf. 11
2114 A1498 22c blue, red & black .45 .25
- a. All color missing (EP)

No. 2114a should be collected se-tenant with a normal or a partially printed stamp.

### COIL STAMP
Perf. 10 Vert.
2115 A1498 22c blue, red & black .45 .25
- c. Inscribed "T" at bottom ('87) .55 .40
- d. Black field of stars instead of blue
- f. Imperf. pair, wide block tagging 10.00
- g. Imperf., pair, narrow block tagging 10.00

### BOOKLET STAMP
Perf. 10 Horiz.
2116 A1499 22c blue, red & black .50 .25
- a. Booklet pane of 5 2.50 1.25

### BOOKLET STAMPS

Frilled Dogwinkle A1500

Reticulated Helmet A1501

---

New England Neptune A1502

Calico Scallop A1503

Lightning Whelk — A1504

### ENGRAVED
Perf. 10 on 2 or 3 Sides
**1985, Apr. 4**
2117 A1500 22c black & brown .45 .25
2118 A1501 22c black & multi .45 .25
2119 A1502 22c black & brown .45 .25
2120 A1503 22c black & violet .45 .25
2121 A1504 22c black & multi .45 .25
- a. Booklet pane of 10, 2 ea #2117-2121 4.50 3.00
- b. As "a," violet omitted on both Nos. 2120 400.00
- c. As "a," vert. imperf. between 350.00
- d. As "a," imperf.
- e. Strip of 5, Nos. 2117-2121 2.25 —

Eagle and Half Moon A1505

Type I

Type II

TYPE I: washed out, dull appearance most evident in the black of the body of the eagle, and the red in the background between the eagle's shoulder and the moon. "$10.75" appears splotchy or grainy (P# 11111).

TYPE II: brighter, more intense colors most evident in the black on the eagle's body, and red in the background. "$10.75" appears smoother, brighter, and less grainy (P# 22222).

### PHOTOGRAVURE
Perf. 10 Vert. on 1 or 2 Sides
**1985, Apr. 29**  Untagged
2122 A1505 $10.75 multi, type I 20.00 7.50
- a. Booklet pane of 3 60.00
- b. Type II, June 19, 1989 20.00 10.00
- c. As "b," booklet pane of 3 60.00

## TRANSPORTATION ISSUE

School Bus 1920s A1506

Star Route Truck 1910s A1508

Buckboard 1880s A1507

Tricycle 1880s A1509

---

Tractor 1920s A1510

Tow Truck 1920s A1512

Stutz Bearcat 1933 A1514

Pushcart 1880s A1516

Dog Sled 1920s A1518

Ambulance 1860s A1511

Oil Wagon 1890s A1513

Stanley Steamer 1909 A1515

Iceboat 1880s A1517

Bread Wagon 1880s A1519

### COIL STAMPS
ENGRAVED
**1985-89**  Tagged  Perf. 10 Vert.
2123 A1506 3.4c dk bluish green .30 .25
- a. Untagged (Bureau precancel, Nonprofit Org. CAR-RT SORT) .30 .25
2124 A1507 4.9c brn blk .30 .25
- a. Untagged (Bureau precancel, Nonprofit Org.) .30 .25
2125 A1508 5.5c dp mag ('86) .30 .25
- a. Untagged (Bureau precancel, Nonprofit Org.) .30 .25
2126 A1509 6c red brn .35 .25
- a. Untagged (Bureau precancel, Nonprofit Org.) .30 .25
- b. As "a," imperf., pair 175.00
2127 A1510 7.1c lake ('87) .30 .25
- a. Untagged (Bureau precancel) .30 .25
- c. As "a," black (precancel) omitted —

On. No. 2127c, an albino impression of the precancel is present.

2128 A1511 8.3c green .30 .25
- a. Untagged (Bureau precancel, Blk Rt CAR-RT SORT) .30 .25

On No. 2231 "Ambulance 1860s" is 18mm long; on No. 2128, 18½mm long.

2129 A1512 8.5c dk Prus grn ('87) .30 .25
- a. Untagged (Bureau precancel, Nonprofit Org.) .30 .25
2130 A1513 10.1c slate blue .55 .25
- a. Untagged (Bureau precancel "Bulk Rate Carrier Route Sort" in red) ('88) .30 .25
- b. As "a," red precancel, imperf. pair 15.00
- As "a," black precancel, imperf. pair 70.00
2131 A1514 11c dk green .30 .25
2132 A1515 12c dk bl, I .35 .25
- a. Untagged, type I (Bureau precancel, PRESORTED FIRST-CLASS), Apr. 2 .30 .25
- b. Untagged, type II (Bureau precancel, PRESORTED FIRST-CLASS) ('87) .40 .30

Type II has "Stanley Steamer 1909" ½mm shorter (17⅔mm) than No. 2132 (18mm).

2133 A1516 12.5c ol grn .35 .25
- a. Untagged (Bureau precancel, Bulk Rate) .30 .25
- b. As "a," imperf., pair 45.00

---

2134 A1517 14c sky bl, I .30 .25
- a. Imperf., pair 75.00
- b. Type II ('86) .30 .25
- c. Tagging omitted, type I 35.00

Type II design is ¼mm narrower (17¼mm) than the original stamp (17½mm) and has block tagging. No. 2134 has overall tagging.

2135 A1518 17c brt bl ('86) .75 .25
- a. Imperf., pair 300.00
2136 A1519 25c org brn ('86) .50 .25
- a. Imperf., pair 10.00
- b. Pair, imperf. between 525.00
Nos. 2123-2136 (14) 5.25 3.50

See Nos. 1897-1908, 2225-2231, 2252-2266, 2451-2468.

## BLACK HERITAGE SERIES

Mary McLeod Bethune (1875-1955), Educator — A1520

### PHOTOGRAVURE
**1985, Mar. 5**  Perf. 11
2137 A1520 22c multicolored .60 .25

## AMERICAN FOLK ART SERIES
### Duck Decoys

Broadbill A1521

Mallard — A1522

Canvasback A1523

Redhead A1524

**1985, Mar. 22**
2138 A1521 22c multicolored .90 .25
2139 A1522 22c multicolored .90 .25
2140 A1523 22c multicolored .90 .25
2141 A1524 22c multicolored .90 .25
- a. Block of 4, #2138-2141 3.60 2.75

## WINTER SPECIAL OLYMPICS

Ice Skater, Emblem, Skier — A1525

**1985, Mar. 25**
2142 A1525 22c multicolored .50 .25
- a. Vert. pair, imperf. horiz. 300.00

## LOVE

 A1526

**1985, Apr. 17**
2143 A1526 22c multicolored .45 .25
- a. Imperf., pair 800.00

# UNITED STATES

## RURAL ELECTRIFICATION ADMINISTRATION

Electrified Farm — A1527

### PHOTOGRAVURE & ENGRAVED (Combination Press)
**1985, May 11**
2144  A1527  22c multicolored   .50  .25
  a.  Vert. pair, imperf between   —

## AMERIPEX '86

U.S. No. 134 — A1528

### LITHOGRAPHED & ENGRAVED
**1985, May 25**
2145  A1528  22c multicolored   .45  .25
  a.  Red, black & blue (engr.) omitted   110.00
  b.  Red & black omitted   1,000.
  c.  Red omitted   1,000.
  d.  Black missing (PS)   450.00

## ABIGAIL ADAMS (1744-1818)

Abigail Adams (1744-1818) — A1529

### PHOTOGRAVURE
**1985, June 14**
2146  A1529  22c multicolored   .45  .25
  a.  Imperf., pair   200.00

## FREDERIC AUGUSTE BARTHOLDI (1834-1904)

Frederic Auguste Bartholdi (1834-1904), Statue of Liberty — A1530

### LITHOGRAPHED & ENGRAVED
**1985, July 18**
2147  A1530  22c multicolored   .45  .25

Examples of No. 2147 exist with most, but not all, of the engraved black omitted.

George Washington, Washington Monument A1532

Envelopes A1533

### COIL STAMPS
### PHOTOGRAVURE
**1985**   **Perf. 10 Vertically**
2149  A1532  18c multicolored   .40  .25
  a.  Untagged (Bureau precancel)   .35  .35
  b.  Imperf., pair   450.00
  c.  As "a," imperf., pair   375.00
2150  A1533  21.1c multicolored   .40  .25
  a.  Untagged (Bureau Precancel)   .40  .40
  c.  Imperf., pair

Precancellations on Nos. 2149a ("PRESORTED FIRST-CLASS") and 2150a ("ZIP+4") do not have lines.

## KOREAN WAR VETERANS

American Troops in Korea — A1535

### ENGRAVED
**1985, July 26**   **Perf. 11**
2152  A1535  22c gray green & rose red   .45  .25

## SOCIAL SECURITY ACT, 50th ANNIV.

Men, Women, Children, Corinthian Columns — A1536

### PHOTOGRAVURE
**1985, Aug. 14**
2153  A1536  22c deep & light blue   .45  .25

## WORLD WAR I VETERANS

The Battle of Marne, France, by Harvey Dunn — A1537

### ENGRAVED
**1985, Aug. 26**
2154  A1537  22c gray green & rose red   .45  .25
  a.  Red missing (PS)   300.00

## HORSES

Quarter Horse — A1538

Morgan — A1539

Saddlebred A1540

Appaloosa A1541

### PHOTOGRAVURE
**1985, Sept. 25**
2155  A1538  22c multicolored   1.10  .25
2156  A1539  22c multicolored   1.10  .25
2157  A1540  22c multicolored   1.10  .25
2158  A1541  22c multicolored   1.10  .25
  a.  Block of 4, #2155-2158   4.40  4.00

## PUBLIC EDUCATION IN AMERICA

Quill Pen, Apple, Spectacles, Penmanship Quiz — A1542

**1985, Oct. 1**
2159  A1542  22c multicolored   .45  .25

## INTERNATIONAL YOUTH YEAR

YMCA Youth Camping, Cent. — A1543

### ENGRAVED

Boy Scouts, 75th Anniv. — A1544

Big Brothers/Big Sisters Fed., 40th Anniv. — A1545

Camp Fire, Inc., 75th Anniv. — A1546

**1985, Oct. 7**
2160  A1543  22c multicolored   .70  .25
2161  A1544  22c multicolored   .70  .25
2162  A1545  22c multicolored   .70  .25
2163  A1546  22c multicolored   .70  .25
  a.  Block of 4, #2160-2163   3.00  2.25

## HELP END HUNGER

Youths and the Elderly Suffering from Malnutrition A1547

### PHOTOGRAVURE
**1985, Oct. 15**
2164  A1547  22c multicolored   .45  .25

## CHRISTMAS

Genoa Madonna, Enameled Terra-Cotta by Luca Della Robbia (1400-1482) A1548

Poinsettia Plants A1549

**1985, Oct. 30**
2165  A1548  22c multicolored   .45  .25
  a.  Imperf., pair   55.00
2166  A1549  22c multicolored   .45  .25
  a.  Imperf., pair   50.00

## ARKANSAS STATEHOOD, 150th ANNIV.

Old State House, Little Rock — A1550

**1986, Jan. 3**
2167  A1550  22c multicolored   .65  .25
  a.  Vert. pair, imperf. horiz.   500.00

## GREAT AMERICANS ISSUE

Margaret Mitchell A1551

Mary Lyon A1552

### ENGRAVED
**Perf. 11, 11½x11 (#2185), 11.2x11.1 (#2179)**
**1986-94**
2168  A1551  1c brnsh ver   .30  .25
  b.  1c red brown   .30  .30
    Pane of 100   30.00
2169  A1552  2c brt bl ('87)   .30  .25
  a.  Untagged   .40  .25

Paul Dudley White MD A1553

Father Flanagan A1554

2170  A1553  3c bright blue   .30  .25
  a.  Untagged ('94)   .30  .25
2171  A1554  4c blue violet   .30  .25
  a.  4c grayish violet, untagged   .25  .25
  b.  4c deep grayish blue, untagged   .35
  d.  All color missing (EP)   —

No. 2171d has an albino impression, and it also may be collected with a fully or partially printed stamp.

Hugo L. Black A1555

Louis Munoz Marin A1556

2172  A1555  5c dk ol grn   .30  .25
  b.  5c lt ol grn   .35  .25
2173  A1556  5c car ('90)   .30  .25
  a.  Untagged   .30  .25

Red Cloud A1557

Julia Ward Howe A1558

2175  A1557  10c lake ('87)   .30  .25
  e.  10c carmine   .80  .25
  f.  All color omitted   125.00

No. 2175f may be collected se-tenant with a partially printed stamp or longer vertical strip. Stamps not se-tenant with a partially printed stamp are identified by a light setoff on the gum side.

2176  A1558  14c crimson ('87)   .30  .25

Buffalo Bill Cody A1559

Belva Ann Lockwood A1560

2177  A1559  15c claret ('88)   1.00  .25
  d.  All color omitted   200.00

No. 2177d resulted from partially printed panes. It must be collected se-tenant with a partially printed stamp or in a longer horizontal strip showing error stamps plus partially/completely printed stamps.

2178  A1560  17c dull bl grn   .35  .25

Virginia Apgar A1561

Chester Carlson A1562

2179  A1561  20c red brn ('94)   .40  .25
  a.  20c orange brown   .75  .25
  b.  20c bright red brown   1.25  .25
2180  A1562  21c bl vio ('88)   .45  .25

Mary Cassatt A1563

Jack London A1564

2181  A1563  23c pur ('88)   .45  .25
2182  A1564  25c blue ('88)   .50  .25
  a.  Booklet pane of 10, perf. 11¼, May 3, 1988   5.00  3.75
  d.  Horiz. pair, imperf between   750.00

64 UNITED STATES

| | | |
|---|---|---|
| e. | As "a," all color omitted on right stamps | 1,250. |
| f. | As No. 2182 (sheet stamp), vert. pair, bottom stamp all color omitted | — |
| h. | As "a," all color omitted on left stamps | 1,250. |

No. 2182f may be collected se-tenant with a partially printed stamp or longer vertical strip. See Nos. 2197, 2197a.

Sitting Bull A1565

Earl Warren A1566

| 2183 | A1565 | 28c myrtle grn ('89) | .65 | .35 |
| 2184 | A1566 | 29c blue ('92) | .70 | .25 |

Thomas Jefferson A1567

Dennis Chavez A1568

| 2185 | A1567 | 29c indigo ('93) | .65 | .25 |
| 2186 | A1568 | 35c black ('91) | .75 | .25 |

Claire Chennault A1569

Harvey Cushing MD A1570

| 2187 | A1569 | 40c dk bl ('90) | .85 | .25 |
| 2188 | A1570 | 45c brt bl ('88) | 1.00 | .25 |
| a. | | 45c blue ('90) | 2.75 | .25 |

Almost all examples of No. 2188a are in the grade of fine or fine-very fine. Values are for stamps in the grade of fine-very fine.

Hubert H. Humphrey A1571

John Harvard A1572

| 2189 | A1571 | 52c pur ('91) | 1.10 | .25 |
| 2190 | A1572 | 56c scarlet | 1.20 | .25 |

H.H. 'Hap' Arnold A1573

Wendell Willkie A1574

| 2191 | A1573 | 65c dk bl ('88) | 1.30 | .25 |
| 2192 | A1574 | 75c dp mag ('92) | 1.75 | .25 |

Bernard Revel A1575

Johns Hopkins A1576

| 2193 | A1575 | $1 dk Prus grn | 3.00 | .50 |
| a. | | All color omitted | | |

No. 2193a must be collected se-tenant vertically with partially printed stamps.

| 2194 | A1576 | $1 intense dp bl ('89) | 2.25 | .50 |
| b. | | $1 dp bl ('90) | 2.50 | .50 |
| d. | | $1 dk bl ('92) | 2.50 | .50 |
| e. | | $1 blue ('93) | 2.75 | .60 |

The intense deep blue of No. 2194 is much deeper than the deep blue and dark blue of the other $1 varieties.

William Jennings Bryan A1577

Bret Harte A1578

| 2195 | A1577 | $2 brt violet | 4.50 | .50 |
| 2196 | A1578 | $5 copper red ('87) | 9.00 | 1.00 |
| | | Nos. 2168-2196 (28) | 34.25 | 8.60 |

### Booklet Stamp
**Perf. 10 on 2 or 3 Sides**

| 2197 | A1564 | 25c blue ('88) | .55 | .25 |
| a. | | Booklet pane of 6 | 3.30 | 2.50 |

Issued: No. 2182, 1/11; No. 2172, 2/27; $2, 3/19; 17c, 6/18; 1c, 6/30; 4c, 7/14; 56c, 9/3; 3c, 9/15; No. 2193, 9/23; 14c, 2/12/87; 2c, 2/28/87; 10c, 8/15/87; $5, 8/25/87; Nos. 2182a, 2197, 5/3/88; 15c, 6/6/88; 45c, 6/17/88; 21c, 10/21/88; 23c, 11/4/88; 65c, 11/5/88; No. 2194, 6/7/89; 28c, 9/14/89; No. 2173, 2/18/90; 40c, 9/6/90; Nos. 2188a, 2194b, 1990; 35c, 4/3/91; 52c, 6/3/91; No. 2173a, 1991; 75c, 2/16/92; No. 2184, 3/9/92; No. 2194d, 1992; No. 2185, 4/13/93; Nos. 2171b, 2194e, 1993; 20c, 10/24/94; Nos. 2170a, 2175e, 1994.

### UNITED STATES - SWEDEN
### STAMP COLLECTING

Handstamped Cover, No. 213, Philatelic Memorabilia A1581

Boy Examining Stamp Collection A1582

No. 836 Under Magnifying Glass, Sweden Nos. 268, 271 — A1583

1986 Presidents Miniature Sheet on First Day Cover — A1584

### BOOKLET STAMPS
### LITHOGRAPHED & ENGRAVED
**Perf. 10 Vert. on 1 or 2 Sides**
**1986, Jan. 23**

| 2198 | A1581 | 22c multicolored | .45 | .25 |
| 2199 | A1582 | 22c multicolored | .45 | .25 |
| 2200 | A1583 | 22c multicolored | .45 | .25 |
| 2201 | A1584 | 22c multicolored | .45 | .25 |
| a. | | Bklt. pane of 4, #2198-2201 | 2.00 | 1.75 |
| b. | | As "a," black omitted on Nos. 2198, 2201 | 50.00 | |
| c. | | As "a," blue (litho.) omitted on Nos. 2198-2200 | 1,500. | |
| d. | | As "a," buff (litho.) omitted | — | |

See Sweden Nos. 1585-1588.

### LOVE ISSUE

A1585

### PHOTOGRAVURE
**1986, Jan. 30** **Perf. 11**
| 2202 | A1585 | 22c multicolored | .55 | .25 |

### BLACK HERITAGE SERIES

Sojourner Truth (c. 1797-1883), Abolitionist — A1586

### PHOTOGRAVURE
**1986, Feb. 4**
| 2203 | A1586 | 22c multicolored | .55 | .25 |

### REPUBLIC OF TEXAS, 150th ANNIV.

San Jacinto, 1836, Texas State Flag and Silver Spur — A1587

**1986, Mar. 2**
| 2204 | A1587 | 22c dk bl, dk red & grayish blk | .50 | .25 |
| a. | | Horiz. pair, imperf. vert. | 600.00 | |
| b. | | Dark red omitted | 1,750. | |
| c. | | Dark blue omitted | 5,000. | |

### FISH

Muskellunge A1588

Atlantic Cod — A1589

Largemouth Bass — A1590

Bluefin Tuna — A1591

Catfish A1592

### BOOKLET STAMPS
### PHOTOGRAVURE
**Perf. 10 Horiz. on 1 or 2 Sides**
**1986, Mar. 21**

| 2205 | A1588 | 22c multicolored | .90 | .25 |
| 2206 | A1589 | 22c multicolored | .90 | .25 |
| 2207 | A1590 | 22c multicolored | .90 | .25 |
| 2208 | A1591 | 22c multicolored | .90 | .25 |
| 2209 | A1592 | 22c multicolored | .90 | .25 |
| a. | | Bklt. pane of 5, #2205-2209 | 4.50 | 2.75 |

The magenta used to print this issue is extremely fugitive. Dangerous fakes purported to be magenta omitted exist. No genuine examples are known. Panes apparently lacking red must be certified, and examples presently with certificates should be recertified.

### PUBLIC HOSPITALS

A1593

**1986, Apr. 11** **Perf. 11**
| 2210 | A1593 | 22c multicolored | .45 | .25 |
| a. | | Vert. pair, imperf. horiz. | 250.00 | |
| b. | | Horiz. pair, imperf. vert. | 800.00 | |

### PERFORMING ARTS

Edward Kennedy "Duke" Ellington (1899-1974), Jazz Composer — A1594

**1986, Apr. 29**
| 2211 | A1594 | 22c multicolored | .45 | .25 |
| a. | | Vert. pair, imperf. horiz. | 300.00 | |

### AMERIPEX '86 ISSUE
### Miniature Sheets

35 Presidents — A1599a

No. 2216: a, George Washington. b, John Adams. c, Thomas Jefferson. d, James Madison. e, James Monroe. f, John Quincy Adams. g, Andrew Jackson. h, Martin Van Buren. i, William H. Harrison.

No. 2217: a, John Tyler. b, James Knox Polk. c, Zachary Taylor. d, Millard Fillmore. e, Franklin Pierce. f, James Buchanan. g, Abraham Lincoln. h, Andrew Johnson. i, Ulysses S. Grant.

No. 2218: a, Rutherford B. Hayes. b, James A. Garfield. c, Chester A. Arthur. d, Grover Cleveland. e, Benjamin Harrison. f, William McKinley. g, Theodore Roosevelt. h, William H. Taft. i, Woodrow Wilson.

No. 2219: a, Warren G. Harding. b, Calvin Coolidge. c, Herbert Hoover. d, Franklin Delano Roosevelt. e, White House. f, Harry S. Truman. g, Dwight D. Eisenhower. h, John F. Kennedy. i, Lyndon B. Johnson.

### LITHOGRAPHED & ENGRAVED
**1986, May 22**

| 2216 | A1599a | Pane of 9 | 6.50 | 4.00 |
| a.-i. | | 22c, any single | .65 | .40 |
| j. | | Blue (engr.) omitted | 1,800. | |
| k. | | Black inscription omitted | 750.00 | |
| l. | | Imperf. | 10,500. | |
| m. | | As "k," double impression of red | 750.00 | |
| n. | | Blue omitted on b-c, e-f, i | — | |
| q. | | Double impression of red | 600.00 | |
| 2217 | A1599b | Pane of 9 | 6.50 | 4.00 |
| a.-i. | | 22c, any single | .65 | .40 |
| j. | | Black inscription omitted | 1,500. | |
| 2218 | A1599c | Pane of 9 | 6.50 | 4.00 |
| a.-i. | | 22c, any single | .65 | .40 |
| j. | | Brown (engr.) omitted | — | |
| k. | | Black inscription omitted | 1,500. | |
| 2219 | A1599d | Pane of 9 | 6.50 | 4.00 |
| a.-i. | | 22c, any single | .65 | .40 |
| j. | | Blackish blue (engr.) inscription omitted on a-b, d-e, g-h | 2,250. | |
| l. | | Blackish blue (engr.) omitted on all stamps | — | |
| | | Nos. 2216-2219 (4) | 26.00 | 16.00 |

Issued in conjunction with AMERIPEX '86 Intl. Philatelic Exhibition, Chicago, IL May 22-June 1.

### ARCTIC EXPLORERS

Elisha Kent Kane — A1600

# UNITED STATES

Adolphus W. Greely — A1601

Vilhjalmur Stefansson A1602

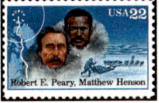
Robert E. Peary and Matthew Alexander Henson — A1603

### PHOTOGRAVURE
**1986, May 28**
| 2220 | A1600 | 22c multicolored | .65 | .25 |
|---|---|---|---|---|
| 2221 | A1601 | 22c multicolored | .65 | .25 |
| 2222 | A1602 | 22c multicolored | .65 | .25 |
| 2223 | A1603 | 22c multicolored | .65 | .25 |
| a. | | Block of 4, #2220-2223 | 2.75 | 2.25 |
| b. | | As "a," black omitted | 2,000. | |
| c. | | As "a," Nos. 2220, 2221 black omitted | 750.00 | |
| d. | | As "a," Nos. 2222, 2223 black omitted | 1,000. | |

### STATUE OF LIBERTY, 100th ANNIVERSARY

Statue of Liberty, Cent. — A1604

### ENGRAVED
**1986, July 4**
| 2224 | A1604 | 22c scar & dk bl | .45 | .25 |
|---|---|---|---|---|
| a. | | Scarlet omitted | | |

On No. 2224a, virtually all of the dark blue also is omitted, so the error stamp should be collected as part of a transition strip. See France No. 2014.

### TRANSPORTATION ISSUE
Types of 1982-85 and

A1604a — Omnibus 1880s

A1604b — Locomotive 1870s

### COIL STAMPS
### ENGRAVED
**1986-90**      *Perf. 10 Vert.*
| 2225 | A1604a | 1c violet | .30 | .25 |
|---|---|---|---|---|
| b. | | Untagged | .30 | .25 |
| c. | | Imperf., pair | 1,100. | |
| 2226 | A1604b | 2c black | .30 | .25 |
| a. | | Untagged | .00 | .25 |

### REDUCED SIZE
| 2228 | A1285 | 4c reddish brown | .30 | .25 |
|---|---|---|---|---|
| b. | | Imperf., pair | 175.00 | |

### Untagged
| 2231 | A1511 | 8.3c green (Bureau precancel) | .65 | .25 |
|---|---|---|---|---|
| | | Nos. 2225-2231 (4) | 1.55 | 1.00 |

Issued: 1c, 11/26; 2c, 3/6/87. Earliest known usage of 4c, 8/15/86; 8.3c, 8/29.
On No. 2228 "Stagecoach 1890s" is 17¾mm long, on No. 1898A, 19½mm long. On No. 2231 "Ambulance 1860s" is 18mm long, on No. 2128, 18½mm long.
No. 2226 inscribed "2 USA"; No. 1897A inscribed "USA 2c".

## AMERICAN FOLK ART SERIES
### Navajo Art

A1605

A1606

A1607

A1608

### LITHOGRAPHED & ENGRAVED
**1986, Sept. 4**      *Perf. 11*
| 2235 | A1605 | 22c multicolored | .80 | .25 |
|---|---|---|---|---|
| a. | | Black (engr.) omitted | 65.00 | |
| 2236 | A1606 | 22c multicolored | .80 | .25 |
| a. | | Black (engr.) omitted | 65.00 | |
| 2237 | A1607 | 22c multicolored | .80 | .25 |
| a. | | Black (engr.) omitted | 65.00 | |
| 2238 | A1608 | 22c multicolored | .80 | .25 |
| a. | | Black (engr.) omitted | 65.00 | |
| b. | | Block of 4, #2235-2238 | 3.25 | 2.25 |
| c. | | As "b," black (engr.) omitted | 275.00 | |

### LITERARY ARTS SERIES

T. S. Eliot (1888-1965), Poet — A1609

### ENGRAVED
**1986, Sept. 26**
| 2239 | A1609 | 22c copper red | .45 | .25 |
|---|---|---|---|---|

### AMERICAN FOLK ART SERIES
### Woodcarved Figurines

Highlander Figure A1610

Ship Figurehead A1611

Nautical Figure A1612

Cigar Store Figure A1613

### PHOTOGRAVURE
**1986, Oct. 1**
| 2240 | A1610 | 22c multicolored | .50 | .25 |
|---|---|---|---|---|
| 2241 | A1611 | 22c multicolored | .50 | .25 |
| 2242 | A1612 | 22c multicolored | .50 | .25 |
| 2243 | A1613 | 22c multicolored | .50 | .25 |
| a. | | Block of 4, #2240-2243 | 2.00 | 1.50 |
| b. | | As "a," imperf. vert. | 750.00 | |

### CHRISTMAS

Madonna, by Perugino (c. 1450-1523) A1614

Village Scene A1615

**1986, Oct. 24**
| 2244 | A1614 | 22c multicolored | .45 | .25 |
|---|---|---|---|---|
| a. | | Imperf., pair | 400.00 | |
| 2245 | A1615 | 22c multicolored | .45 | .25 |

### MICHIGAN STATEHOOD, 150th ANNIV.

White Pine — A1616

**1987, Jan. 26**
| 2246 | A1616 | 22c multicolored | .50 | .25 |
|---|---|---|---|---|

### PAN AMERICAN GAMES

Runner in Full Stride — A1617

**1987, Jan. 29**
| 2247 | A1617 | 22c multicolored | .45 | .25 |
|---|---|---|---|---|
| a. | | Silver omitted | 350.00 | |

No. 2247a is valued in the grade of fine.

### LOVE ISSUE

A1618

### PHOTOGRAVURE
**1987, Jan. 30**      *Perf. 11½x11*
| 2248 | A1618 | 22c multicolored | .45 | .25 |
|---|---|---|---|---|

### BLACK HERITAGE SERIES

Jean Baptiste Pointe du Sable (c. 1750-1818), Pioneer Trader, Founder of Chicago — A1619

**1987, Feb. 20**      *Perf. 11*
| 2249 | A1619 | 22c multicolored | .40 | .25 |
|---|---|---|---|---|

### PERFORMING ARTS SERIES

Enrico Caruso (1873-1921), Opera Tenor — A1620

### PHOTOGRAVURE
**1987, Feb. 27**
| 2250 | A1620 | 22c multicolored | .45 | .25 |
|---|---|---|---|---|
| a. | | Black omitted | 3,500. | |

### GIRL SCOUTS, 75TH ANNIVERSARY

Fourteen Achievement Badges — A1621

### LITHOGRAPHED & ENGRAVED
**1987, Mar. 12**
| 2251 | A1621 | 22c multicolored | .45 | .25 |
|---|---|---|---|---|
| a. | | All litho. colors omitted | 1,300. | |
| b. | | Red & black (engr.) omitted | 1,250. | |

All known examples of No. 2251a have been expertized and certificate must accompany purchase. The unique pane of No. 2251b has been expertized and a certificate exists for the pane of 50.

## TRANSPORTATION ISSUE

Conestoga Wagon 1800s A1622

Milk Wagon 1900s A1623

Elevator 1900s A1624

Carreta 1770s A1625

Wheel Chair 1920s A1626

Canal Boat 1880s A1627

Patrol Wagon 1880s A1628

Coal Car 1870s A1629

Tugboat 1900s A1630

Popcorn Wagon 1902 A1631

Racing Car 1911 A1632

Cable Car 1880s A1633

Fire Engine 1900s A1634

Railroad Mail Car 1920s A1635

Tandem Bicycle 1890s — A1636

### COIL STAMPS
### ENGRAVED
**1987-88**      *Perf. 10 Vert.*
| 2252 | A1622 | 3c claret ('88) | .30 | .25 |
|---|---|---|---|---|
| a. | | Untagged | .30 | .25 |
| b. | | As "a," imperf. pair | 2,100. | |
| 2253 | A1623 | 5c black | .30 | .25 |
| 2254 | A1624 | 5.3c black (Bureau precancel in red), untagged ('88) | .30 | .25 |
| 2255 | A1625 | 7.6c brown (Bureau precancel in red), untagged ('88) | .30 | .25 |
| 2256 | A1626 | 8.4c dp clar (Bureau precancel in red), untagged ('88) | .30 | .25 |
| a. | | Imperf., pair | 350.00 | |

66 UNITED STATES

| | | | | | |
|---|---|---|---|---|---|
| **2257** | A1627 | 10c | blue | .40 | .25 |
| *e.* | | | Imperf. pair | *1,000.* | |
| **2258** | A1628 | 13c | black (Bureau precancel in red), untagged ('88) | .65 | .25 |
| **2259** | A1629 | 13.2c | slate grn (Bureau precancel in red), untagged ('88) | .30 | .25 |
| *a.* | | | Imperf., pair | 75.00 | |
| **2260** | A1630 | 15c | violet ('88) | .30 | .25 |
| *c.* | | | As "a," imperf. pair | *500.00* | |
| **2261** | A1631 | 16.7c | rose (Bureau precancel in black), untagged ('88) | .30 | .30 |
| *a.* | | | Imperf., pair | *300.00* | |
| **2262** | A1632 | 17.5c | dk vio | .75 | .25 |
| *a.* | | | Untagged (Bureau precancel in red) | .65 | .30 |
| *b.* | | | Imperf., pair | *1,000.* | |
| **2263** | A1633 | 20c | blue vio ('88) | .35 | .25 |
| *a.* | | | Imperf., pair | 50.00 | |
| **2264** | A1634 | 20.5c | rose (Bureau precancel in black), untagged ('88) | .75 | .40 |
| **2265** | A1635 | 21c | olive grn (Bureau precancel in red), untagged ('88) | .50 | .40 |
| *a.* | | | Imperf., pair | 35.00 | |
| **2266** | A1636 | 24.1c | deep ultra (Bureau precancel in red), untagged ('88) | .80 | .45 |
| | | | *Nos. 2252-2266 (15)* | 6.60 | 4.30 |

5.3c, 7.6c, 8.4c, 13.2c, 16.7c, 20.5c, 21c and 24.1c only available precanceled.

See Nos. 1897-1908, 2123-2136, 2225-2231, 2451-2468.

## SPECIAL OCCASIONS

A1637

A1638

A1639

A1640

A1641

A1642

A1643

A1644

BOOKLET STAMPS
PHOTOGRAVURE

***Perf. 10 on 1, 2 or 3 Sides***

**1987, Apr. 20**

| | | | | | |
|---|---|---|---|---|---|
| **2267** | A1637 | 22c | multicolored | .75 | .25 |
| **2268** | A1638 | 22c | multicolored | .90 | .25 |
| **2269** | A1639 | 22c | multicolored | .90 | .25 |
| **2270** | A1640 | 22c | multicolored | .90 | .25 |
| **2271** | A1641 | 22c | multicolored | .90 | .25 |
| **2272** | A1642 | 22c | multicolored | .75 | .25 |
| **2273** | A1643 | 22c | multicolored | 1.50 | .25 |
| **2274** | A1644 | 22c | multicolored | .90 | .25 |
| *a.* | | | Bklt. pane of 10 (#2268-2271, 2273-2274, 2 each #2267, 2272) | 9.00 | 5.00 |
| | | | *Nos. 2267-2274 (8)* | 7.50 | 2.00 |

## UNITED WAY, 100th ANNIV.

Six Profiles — A1645

LITHOGRAPHED & ENGRAVED

**1987, Apr. 28** ***Perf. 11***

| | | | | | |
|---|---|---|---|---|---|
| **2275** | A1645 | 22c | multicolored | .45 | .25 |

A1646

A1647

A1648

Yosemite — A1649

Pheasant
A1649a

Grosbeak
A1649b

Owl — A1649c

Honeybee
A1649d

**Photo., Engr. (No. 2280). Litho. & Engr. (No. 2281)**

**1987-88** ***Perf. 11***

| | | | | | |
|---|---|---|---|---|---|
| **2276** | A1646 | 22c | multi | .45 | .25 |
| *a.* | | | Booklet pane of 20, *Nov. 30* | 9.00 | — |
| *b.* | | | As "a," vert. pair, imperf. btwn. | *1,450.* | |
| *c.* | | | As "a," miscut and inserted upside down into booklet cover, imperf between stamps and right selvage | — | |
| *d.* | | | Yellow omitted | — | |

All documented examples of No. 2276d show significant misregistration of the red ink.

| | | | | | |
|---|---|---|---|---|---|
| **2277** | A1647 | (25c) | multi ('88) | .50 | .25 |
| **2278** | A1648 | 25c | multi ('88) | .50 | .25 |
| | | | *Nos. 2276-2278 (3)* | 1.45 | .75 |

### COIL STAMPS

***Perf. 10 Vert.***

| | | | | | |
|---|---|---|---|---|---|
| **2279** | A1647 | (25c) | multi ('88) | .50 | .25 |
| *a.* | | | Imperf., pair | 60.00 | — |
| **2280** | A1649 | 25c | multi ('88) | .50 | .25 |
| *c.* | | | Imperf. pair | 10.00 | — |
| *e.* | | | Black trees | *90.00* | — |
| *f.* | | | Pair, imperf. between | *375.00* | |
| **2281** | A1649d | 25c | multi ('88) | .50 | .25 |
| *a.* | | | As No. 2281, imperf. pair | 45.00 | |
| *c.* | | | Black (litho. - "25 USA") omitted | *500.00* | |
| *d.* | | | Pair, imperf. between | *300.00* | |
| *e.* | | | Yellow (litho.) omitted | *700.00* | |
| | | | *Nos. 2279-2281 (3)* | 1.50 | .75 |

Beware of stamps with traces of the litho. black that are offered as No. 2281c.

Vertical pairs or blocks of No. 2281 and imperfs. with the engr. black missing are from printer's waste.

## BOOKLET STAMPS

PHOTOGRAVURE

***Perf. 10 on 2 or 3 Sides***

| | | | | | |
|---|---|---|---|---|---|
| **2282** | A1647 | (25c) | multi ('88) | .50 | .25 |
| *a.* | | | Booklet pane of 10 | 6.50 | 3.50 |

***Perf. 11 on 2 or 3 Sides***

| | | | | | |
|---|---|---|---|---|---|
| **2283** | A1649a | 25c | multi ('88) | .50 | .25 |
| *a.* | | | Booklet pane of 10 | 6.00 | 3.50 |
| *b.* | | | 25c multicolored, red removed from sky | 4.00 | .25 |
| *c.* | | | As "b," bklt. pane of 10 | 40.00 | — |
| *d.* | | | Vert. pair, imperf. btwn. | *275.00* | |

Imperf. panes exist from printers waste, and a large number exist. No. 2283d resulted from a foldover. Non-foldover pairs and multiples are printer's waste.

***Perf. 10 on 2 or 3 Sides***

| | | | | | |
|---|---|---|---|---|---|
| **2284** | A1649b | 25c | multi ('88) | .50 | .25 |
| **2285** | A1649c | 25c | multi ('88) | .50 | .25 |
| *b.* | | | Bklt. pane of 10, 5 each #2284-2285 | 5.00 | 3.50 |
| *d.* | | | Pair, Nos. 2284-2285 | 1.10 | .50 |
| **2285A** | A1648 | 25c | multi ('88) | .50 | .25 |
| *c.* | | | Booklet pane of 6 | 3.00 | 2.00 |
| | | | *Nos. 2282-2285A (5)* | 2.50 | 1.25 |

Issued: #2276, 5/9; #2277, 2279, 2282, 3/22; #2278, 5/6; #2280, 5/20; #2281, 9/2; #2283, 4/29; #2284-2285, 5/28; #2285A, 7/5.

## NORTH AMERICAN WILDLIFE

North American Wildlife — A1650

PHOTOGRAVURE

**1987, June 13** ***Perf. 11***

| | | | | | |
|---|---|---|---|---|---|
| **2286** | A1650 | 22c | Barn swallow | 1.00 | .50 |
| **2287** | A1651 | 22c | Monarch butterfly | 1.00 | .50 |
| **2288** | A1652 | 22c | Bighorn sheep | 1.00 | .50 |
| **2289** | A1653 | 22c | Broad-tailed hummingbird | 1.00 | .50 |
| **2290** | A1654 | 22c | Cottontail | 1.00 | .50 |
| **2291** | A1655 | 22c | Osprey | 1.00 | .50 |
| **2292** | A1656 | 22c | Mountain lion | 1.00 | .50 |
| **2293** | A1657 | 22c | Luna moth | 1.00 | .50 |
| **2294** | A1658 | 22c | Mule deer | 1.00 | .50 |
| **2295** | A1659 | 22c | Gray squirrel | 1.00 | .50 |
| **2296** | A1660 | 22c | Armadillo | 1.00 | .50 |
| **2297** | A1661 | 22c | Eastern chipmunk | 1.00 | .50 |
| **2298** | A1662 | 22c | Moose | 1.00 | .50 |
| **2299** | A1663 | 22c | Black bear | 1.00 | .50 |
| **2300** | A1664 | 22c | Tiger swallowtail | 1.00 | .50 |
| **2301** | A1665 | 22c | Bobwhite | 1.00 | .50 |
| **2302** | A1666 | 22c | Ringtail | 1.00 | .50 |
| **2303** | A1667 | 22c | Red-winged blackbird | 1.00 | .50 |
| **2304** | A1668 | 22c | American lobster | 1.00 | .50 |
| **2305** | A1669 | 22c | Black-tailed jack rabbit | 1.00 | .50 |
| **2306** | A1670 | 22c | Scarlet tanager | 1.00 | .50 |
| **2307** | A1671 | 22c | Woodchuck | 1.00 | .50 |
| **2308** | A1672 | 22c | Roseate spoonbill | 1.00 | .50 |
| **2309** | A1673 | 22c | Bald eagle | 1.00 | .50 |
| **2310** | A1674 | 22c | Alaskan brown bear | 1.00 | .50 |
| **2311** | A1675 | 22c | Iiwi | 1.00 | .50 |
| **2312** | A1676 | 22c | Badger | 1.00 | .50 |
| **2313** | A1677 | 22c | Pronghorn | 1.00 | .50 |
| **2314** | A1678 | 22c | River otter | 1.00 | .50 |
| **2315** | A1679 | 22c | Ladybug | 1.00 | .50 |
| **2316** | A1680 | 22c | Beaver | 1.00 | .50 |
| **2317** | A1681 | 22c | White-tailed deer | 1.00 | .50 |
| **2318** | A1682 | 22c | Blue jay | 1.00 | .50 |
| **2319** | A1683 | 22c | Pika | 1.00 | .50 |
| **2320** | A1684 | 22c | Bison | 1.00 | .50 |
| **2321** | A1685 | 22c | Snowy egret | 1.00 | .50 |
| **2322** | A1686 | 22c | Gray wolf | 1.00 | .50 |
| **2323** | A1687 | 22c | Mountain goat | 1.00 | .50 |
| **2324** | A1688 | 22c | Deer mouse | 1.00 | .50 |
| **2325** | A1689 | 22c | Black-tailed prairie dog | 1.00 | .50 |
| **2326** | A1690 | 22c | Box turtle | 1.00 | .50 |
| **2327** | A1691 | 22c | Wolverine | 1.00 | .50 |
| **2328** | A1692 | 22c | American elk | 1.00 | .50 |
| **2329** | A1693 | 22c | California sea lion | 1.00 | .50 |
| **2330** | A1694 | 22c | Mockingbird | 1.00 | .50 |
| **2331** | A1695 | 22c | Raccoon | 1.00 | .50 |
| **2332** | A1696 | 22c | Bobcat | 1.00 | .50 |
| **2333** | A1697 | 22c | Black-footed ferret | 1.00 | .50 |
| **2334** | A1698 | 22c | Canada goose | 1.00 | .50 |
| **2335** | A1699 | 22c | Red fox | 1.00 | .50 |
| *a.* | | | Pane of 50, #2286-2335 | 50.00 | 35.00 |
| **2286b-2335b** | | | Any single, red omitted | *2,000.* | |

## RATIFICATION OF THE CONSTITUTION BICENTENNIAL

Delaware
A1700

Pennsylvania
A1701

New Jersey
A1702

Georgia
A1703

Connecticut
A1704

Massachusetts
A1705

Maryland
A1706

South Carolina
A1707

New Hampshire
A1708

Virginia
A1709

New York
A1710

North Carolina
A1711

Rhode Island — A1712

# UNITED STATES

**LITHOGRAPHED & ENGRAVED,
PHOTOGRAVURE (#2337-2339, 2343-
2344, 2347), ENGRAVED (#2341).**

**1987-90**

| 2336 | A1700 | 22c multi | .55 | .25 |
|---|---|---|---|---|
| 2337 | A1701 | 22c multi | .55 | .25 |
| 2338 | A1702 | 22c multi | .55 | .25 |
| a. | | Black (engr.) omitted | 2,000. | |
| 2339 | A1703 | 22c multi | .55 | .25 |
| 2340 | A1704 | 22c multi | .55 | .25 |
| 2341 | A1705 | 22c dk bl & dk red | .55 | .25 |
| 2342 | A1706 | 22c multi | .55 | .25 |
| 2343 | A1707 | 25c multi | .60 | .25 |
| a. | | Strip of 3, vert. imperf btwn. | 12,500. | |
| b. | | Red missing (PS) | — | |
| 2344 | A1708 | 25c multi | .55 | .25 |
| 2345 | A1709 | 25c multi | .55 | .25 |
| 2346 | A1710 | 25c multi | .55 | .25 |
| 2347 | A1711 | 25c multi | .60 | .25 |
| 2348 | A1712 | 25c multi | .55 | .25 |
| | Nos. 2336-2348 (13) | | 7.25 | 3.25 |

No. 2343b resulted either from a shifting of all colors or from a shift of both the perforations and the cutting of the pane.

Issued: No. 2336, 7/4; No. 2337, 8/26; No. 2338, 9/11; No. 2339, 1/6/88; No. 2340, 1/9/88; No. 2341, 2/6/88; No. 2342, 2/15/88; No. 2343, 5/23/88; No. 2344, 6/21/88; No. 2345, 6/25/88; No. 2346, 7/26/88; No. 2347, 8/22/89; No. 2348, 5/29/90.

## US-MOROCCO DIPLOMATIC RELATIONS, 200th ANNIV.

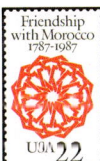

Arabesque, Dar Batha Palace, Fez — A1713

**LITHOGRAPHED & ENGRAVED**
**1987, July 17**

| 2349 | A1713 | 22c scar & blk | .50 | .25 |
|---|---|---|---|---|
| a. | | Black (engr.) omitted | 180.00 | |

See Morocco No. 642.

## LITERARY ARTS SERIES

William Cuthbert Faulkner (1897-1962), Novelist — A1714

**ENGRAVED**
**1987, Aug. 3**

| 2350 | A1714 | 22c bright green | .50 | .25 |
|---|---|---|---|---|

Used untagged imperfs exist from printer's waste.

## AMERICAN FOLK ART SERIES
### Lacemaking

A1715

A1716

A1717

A1718

**LITHOGRAPHED & ENGRAVED**
**1987, Aug. 14**

| 2351 | A1715 | 22c ultra & white | .60 | .25 |
|---|---|---|---|---|
| 2352 | A1716 | 22c ultra & white | .60 | .25 |
| 2353 | A1717 | 22c ultra & white | .60 | .25 |
| 2354 | A1718 | 22c ultra & white | .60 | .25 |
| a. | | Block of 4, #2351-2354 | 2.40 | 1.90 |
| b. | | As "a," white omitted | 350.00 | |
| c. | | Any single stamp, white omitted | 90.00 | |

## DRAFTING OF THE CONSTITUTION BICENTENNIAL
### Excerpts from the Preamble

A1719

A1720

A1721

A1722

A1723

### BOOKLET STAMPS
### PHOTOGRAVURE
**Perf. 10 Horiz. on 1 or 2 Sides**
**1987, Aug. 28**

| 2355 | A1719 | 22c multicolored | .70 | .25 |
|---|---|---|---|---|
| a. | | Grayish green (background) omitted | 400.00 | |
| 2356 | A1720 | 22c multicolored | .70 | .25 |
| a. | | Grayish green (background) omitted | 400.00 | |
| 2357 | A1721 | 22c multicolored | .70 | .25 |
| a. | | Grayish green (background) omitted | 400.00 | |
| 2358 | A1722 | 22c multicolored | .70 | .25 |
| a. | | Grayish green (background) omitted | 400.00 | |
| 2359 | A1723 | 22c multicolored | .70 | .25 |
| a. | | Bklt. pane of 5, #2355-2359 | 3.50 | 2.25 |
| b. | | Grayish green (background) omitted | 400.00 | |

## SIGNING OF THE CONSTITUTION

A1724

**LITHOGRAPHED & ENGRAVED**
**1987, Sept. 17**    **Perf. 11**

| 2360 | A1724 | 22c multicolored | .55 | .25 |
|---|---|---|---|---|
| a. | | Black (engr.) omitted | 1,000. | |

## CERTIFIED PUBLIC ACCOUNTING

A1725

**1987, Sept. 21**

| 2361 | A1725 | 22c multicolored | .60 | .25 |
|---|---|---|---|---|
| a. | | Black (engr.) omitted | 250.00 | |

## LOCOMOTIVES

Stourbridge Lion, 1829 — A1726

Best Friend of Charleston, 1830 — A1727

John Bull, 1831 — A1728

Brother Jonathan, 1832 — A1729

Gowan & Marx, 1839 — A1730

### BOOKLET STAMPS
**Perf. 10 Horiz. on 1 or 2 Sides**
**1987, Oct. 1**

| 2362 | A1726 | 22c multi | .50 | .25 |
|---|---|---|---|---|
| a. | | Red (litho.) omitted | | |
| 2363 | A1727 | 22c multi | .50 | .25 |
| a. | | Red (litho.) omitted | | |
| 2364 | A1728 | 22c multi | .50 | .25 |
| a. | | Red (litho.) omitted | | |
| 2365 | A1729 | 22c multi | .50 | .25 |
| a. | | Red omitted | 1,000. | 250.00 |
| 2366 | A1730 | 22c multi | .50 | .25 |
| a. | | Bklt. pane of 5, #2362-2366 | 2.50 | 2.00 |
| b. | | As No. 2366, black (engr.) omitted (single) | — | |
| c. | | As No. 2366, blue omitted (single) | — | |

## CHRISTMAS

Moroni Madonna A1731

Christmas Ornaments A1732

**PHOTOGRAVURE**
**1987, Oct. 23**    **Perf. 11**

| 2367 | A1731 | 22c multicolored | .45 | .25 |
|---|---|---|---|---|
| 2368 | A1732 | 22c multicolored | .45 | .25 |

## 1988 WINTER OLYMPICS, CALGARY

Skiing — A1733

**1988, Jan. 10**

| 2369 | A1733 | 22c multicolored | .50 | .25 |
|---|---|---|---|---|

## AUSTRALIA BICENTENNIAL

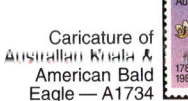

Caricature of Australian Koala & American Bald Eagle — A1734

**1988, Jan. 26**

| 2370 | A1734 | 22c multicolored | .45 | .25 |
|---|---|---|---|---|

See Australia No. 1052.

## BLACK HERITAGE SERIES

James Weldon Johnson, Author, Lyricist — A1735

**1988, Feb. 2**

| 2371 | A1735 | 22c multicolored | .50 | .25 |
|---|---|---|---|---|

## CATS

Siamese, Exotic Shorthair A1736

Abyssinian, Himalayan A1737

Maine Coon, Burmese A1738

American Shorthair, Persian — A1739

**1988, Feb. 5**

| 2372 | A1736 | 22c multicolored | .70 | .25 |
|---|---|---|---|---|
| 2373 | A1737 | 22c multicolored | .70 | .25 |
| 2374 | A1738 | 22c multicolored | .70 | .25 |
| 2375 | A1739 | 22c multicolored | .70 | .25 |
| a. | | Block of 4, #2372-2375 | 2.80 | 1.90 |

## AMERICAN SPORTS

Knute Rockne (1888-1931), Notre Dame football coach.

A1740

**LITHOGRAPHED & ENGRAVED**
**1988, Mar. 9**

| 2376 | A1740 | 22c multicolored | .50 | .25 |
|---|---|---|---|---|

## AMERICAN SPORTS

Francis Ouimet (1893-1967), 1st amateur golfer to win the US Open championship.

A1741

**PHOTOGRAVURE**
**1988, June 13**

| 2377 | A1741 | 25c multicolored | .60 | .25 |
|---|---|---|---|---|

## LOVE ISSUE (Roses)

Rose A1742

Roses A1743

**1988**

| 2378 | A1742 | 25c multi | .50 | .25 |
|---|---|---|---|---|
| a. | | Imperf., pair | 1,500. | |
| 2379 | A1743 | 45c multi | .85 | .25 |

## 1988 SUMMER OLYMPICS, SEOUL

Gymnastic Rings — A1744

**1988, Aug. 19**
2380  A1744  25c multicolored  .50  .25

## CLASSIC AUTOMOBILES

1928 Locomobile A1745

1929 Pierce-Arrow — A1746

1931 Cord — A1747

1932 Packard A1748

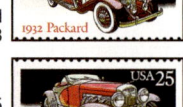
1935 Duesenberg A1749

**LITHOGRAPHED & ENGRAVED BOOKLET STAMPS**
*Perf. 10 Horiz. on 1 or 2 Sides*
**1988, Aug. 25**
2381  A1745  25c multicolored  .65  .25
2382  A1746  25c multicolored  .65  .25
2383  A1747  25c multicolored  .65  .25
2384  A1748  25c multicolored  .65  .25
2385  A1749  25c multicolored  .65  .25
  *a.*  Bklt. pane of 5, #2381-2385  3.25  2.50

## ANTARCTIC EXPLORERS

Nathaniel Palmer (1799-1877) A1750

Lt. Charles Wilkes (1798-1877) A1751

Richard E. Byrd (1888-1957) A1752

Lincoln Ellsworth (1880-1951) A1753

**PHOTOGRAVURE**
**1988, Sept. 14**  *Perf. 11*
2386  A1750  25c multicolored  .65  .25
2387  A1751  25c multicolored  .65  .25
2388  A1752  25c multicolored  .65  .25
2389  A1753  25c multicolored  .65  .25
  *a.*  Block of 4, #2386-2389  2.75  2.00
  *b.*  As "a," black omitted  600.00
  *c.*  As "a," imperf. horiz.  2,000.

## AMERICAN FOLK ART SERIES
### Carousel Animals

Deer A1754

Horse A1755

Camel A1756

Goat A1757

**LITHOGRAPHED & ENGRAVED**
**1988, Oct. 1**
2390  A1754  25c multicolored  .75  .25
2391  A1755  25c multicolored  .75  .25
2392  A1756  25c multicolored  .75  .25
2393  A1757  25c multicolored  .75  .25
  *a.*  Block of 4, #2390-2393  3.00  2.00
  *b.*  As "a," red omitted  800.00

## EXPRESS MAIL RATE

Eagle in Flight A1758

**1988, Oct. 4**
2394  A1758  $8.75 multicolored  16.00  8.00

## SPECIAL OCCASIONS

Happy Birthday — A1759

Best Wishes — A1760

Thinking of You — A1761

Love You — A1762

**BOOKLET STAMPS PHOTOGRAVURE**
*Perf. 11 on 2 or 3 Sides*
**1988, Oct. 22**
2395  A1759  25c multicolored  .50  .25
2396  A1760  25c multicolored  .50  .25
  *a.*  Bklt. pane of 6, 3 #2395 + 3 #2396 with gutter between  3.50  3.25
2397  A1761  25c multicolored  .50  .25
2398  A1762  25c multicolored  .50  .25
  *a.*  Bklt. pane of 6, 3 #2397 + 3 #2398 with gutter between  3.50  3.25
  *b.*  As "a," imperf. horiz.  2,250.
  *c.*  As "a," imperf.  —
  Nos. 2395-2398 (4)  2.00  1.00

## CHRISTMAS

Madonna and Child, by Botticelli A1763

One-horse Open Sleigh & Village Scene A1764

**LITHOGRAPHED & ENGRAVED (No. 2399), PHOTOGRAVURE (No. 2400)**
**1988, Oct. 20**  *Perf. 11½*
2399  A1763  25c multicolored  .50  .25
  *a.*  Gold omitted  25.00
2400  A1764  25c multicolored  .50  .25

## MONTANA STATEHOOD, 100th ANNIV.

C.M. Russell and Friends, by Charles M. Russell (1865-1926) A1765

**LITHOGRAPHED & ENGRAVED**
**1989, Jan. 15**  *Perf. 11*
2401  A1765  25c multicolored  .55  .25
Imperfs without gum exist from printer's waste.

## BLACK HERITAGE SERIES

Asa Philip Randolph (1889-1979), Labor & Civil Rights Leader — A1766

**PHOTOGRAVURE**
**1989, Feb. 3**
2402  A1766  25c multicolored  .50  .25

## NORTH DAKOTA STATEHOOD, 100th ANNIV.

Grain Elevator — A1767

**1989, Feb. 21**
2403  A1767  25c multicolored  .50  .25

## WASHINGTON STATEHOOD, 100th ANNIV.

Mt. Rainier — A1768

**1989, Feb. 22**
2404  A1768  25c multicolored  .50  .25

## STEAMBOATS

Experiment, 1788-1790 — A1769

Phoenix, 1809 — A1770

New Orleans, 1812 — A1771

Washington, 1816 — A1772

Walk in the Water, 1818 — A1773

**LITHOGRAPHED & ENGRAVED BOOKLET STAMPS**
*Perf. 10 Horiz. on 1 or 2 Sides*
**1989, Mar. 3**
2405  A1769  25c multicolored  .60  .25
2406  A1770  25c multicolored  .60  .25
2407  A1771  25c multicolored  .60  .25
2408  A1772  25c multicolored  .60  .25
2409  A1773  25c multicolored  .60  .25
  *a.*  Booklet pane of 5, #2405-2409  3.00  1.75

## WORLD STAMP EXPO '89
Nov. 17-Dec. 3. Washington, D.C.

No. 122 — A1774

**1989, Mar. 16**  *Perf. 11*
2410  A1774  25c grayish brn, blk & car rose  .50  .25

## PERFORMING ARTS

Arturo Toscanini (1867-1957), Conductor — A1775

**PHOTOGRAVURE**
**1989, Mar. 25**
2411  A1775  25c multicolored  .50  .25

## CONSTITUTION BICENTENNIAL SERIES

House of Representatives A1776

Senate A1777

Executive Branch A1778

Supreme Court A1779

**LITHOGRAPHED & ENGRAVED**
**1989-90**
2412  A1776  25c multi  .50  .25
2413  A1777  25c multi  .50  .25
2414  A1778  25c multi  .50  .25
2415  A1779  25c multi  .50  .25
  Nos. 2412-2415 (4)  2.00  1.00
Issued: No. 2412, 4/4; No. 2413, 4/6; No. 2414, 4/16; No. 2415, 2/2/90.

# UNITED STATES

## SOUTH DAKOTA STATEHOOD, 100th ANNIV.

Pasque Flowers, Pioneer Woman and Sod House on Grasslands A1780

### PHOTOGRAVURE
**1989, May 3**
2416 A1780 25c multicolored .60 .25
Imperfs exist from printer's waste.

## AMERICAN SPORTS

Lou Gehrig (1903-1941), New York Yankee Baseball Player — A1781

**1989, June 10**
2417 A1781 25c multicolored .60 .25

## LITERARY ARTS SERIES

Ernest Hemingway (1899-1961), Nobel Prize-winner for Literature, 1954 — A1782

**1989, July 17**
2418 A1782 25c multicolored .50 .25
   a. Vert. pair, imperf horiz. 500.00

Imperforates on gummed stamp paper, including gutter pairs and blocks, are proofs from the ABNCo. archives. See No. 2418P in Proofs section of the Scott U.S. Specialized Catalogue.

## MOON LANDING, 20TH ANNIVERSARY

Raising the Flag on Lunar Surface, July 20, 1969 — A1783

### LITHOGRAPHED & ENGRAVED
**1989, July 20**    *Perf 11x11½*
2419 A1783 $2.40 multi 4.75 2.00
   a. Black (engr.) omitted 1,350.
   b. Imperf., pair 350.00
   c. Black (litho.) omitted 1,250.

## LETTER CARRIERS

Letter Carriers — A1784

### PHOTOGRAVURE
2420 A1784 25c multicolored .50 .25

## CONSTITUTION BICENTENNIAL

Bill of Rights — A1785

### LITHOGRAPHED & ENGRAVED
**1989, Sept. 25**
2421 A1785 25c multicolored .50 .25
   a. Black (engr.) omitted 225.00

## PREHISTORIC ANIMALS

Tyrannosaurus Rex — A1786

Pteranodon A1787

Stegosaurus A1788

Brontosaurus A1789

**1989, Oct. 1**
2422 A1786 25c multicolored .70 .25
   a. Black (engr.) omitted 80.00
2423 A1787 25c multicolored .70 .25
   a. Black (engr.) omitted 80.00
2424 A1788 25c multicolored .70 .25
   a. Black (engr.) omitted 90.00
2425 A1789 25c multicolored .70 .25
   a. Black (engr.) omitted 80.00
   b. Block of 4, #2422-2425 2.80 2.00
   c. As "b," black (engr.) omitted 325.00

No. 2425c is valued in the grade of fine. Very fine blocks exist and sell for approximately $600.

## PRE-COLUMBIAN AMERICA ISSUE

Southwest Carved Figure, A. D. 1150-1350 — A1790

### PHOTOGRAVURE
**1989, Oct. 12**
2426 A1790 25c multicolored .60 .25
See No. C121.

## CHRISTMAS

Madonna and Child, by Caracci A1791

Sleigh Full of Presents A1792

### LITHOGRAPHED & ENGRAVED, PHOTOGRAVURE (#2428-2429)
**1989, Oct. 19**    *Perf. 11¼*
2427 A1791 25c multicolored .50 .25
   a. Booklet pane of 10 5.00 3.50
   b. Red (litho.) omitted 300.00
   c. As "a," imperf. —

*Perf. 11½*
2428 A1792 25c multicolored .50 .25
   a. Vert. pair, imperf. horiz. 500.00

### BOOKLET STAMP
*Perf. 11½ on 2 or 3 Sides*
2429 A1792 25c multicolored .50 .25
   a. Booklet pane of 10 5.00 3.50
   b. Vert. pair, imperf. btwn. (from miscut bklt pane) 500.00
   c. As "a," horiz. imperf. between 2,250.
   d. Red omitted —
   e. As "a," red omitted 3,250.
   f. Imperf., pair 750.00

Marked differences exist between Nos. 2428 and 2429: No. 2429 was printed in four colors, No. 2428 in five colors. The runners on the sleigh in No. 2429 are twice as thick as those on No. 2428. On No. 2429 the package at the upper left in the sleigh has a red bow, whereas the same package in No. 2428 has a red and black bow; and the ribbon on the upper right package in No. 2429 is green, whereas the same ribbon in No. 2428 is black.

Eagle and Shield — A1793

### PHOTOGRAVURE
### BOOKLET STAMP
**1989, Nov. 10**    *Die Cut*
### Self-Adhesive
2431 A1793 25c multicolored .50 .25
   a. Booklet pane of 18 10.00
   b. Vert. pair, die cutting omitted between 325.00
   c. Die cutting omitted, pair 200.00

Panes sold for $5.
Also available in strips of 18 with stamps spaced for use in affixing machines to service first day covers. Sold for $5.
No. 2431c will include part of the margins around the stamps.
Sold only in 15 test cities (Atlanta, Chicago, Cleveland, Columbus, OH, Dallas, Denver, Houston, Indianapolis, Kansas City, MO, Los Angeles, Miami, Milwaukee, Minneapolis, Phoenix, St. Louis) and through the philatelic agency.

## WORLD STAMP EXPO '89

World Stamp Expo, Washington, DC, Nov. 17-Dec. 3 — A1794

### LITHOGRAPHED & ENGRAVED
**1989, Nov. 17**    *Imperf.*
2433 A1794 Pane of 4 16.00 14.00
   a. 90c like No. 122 4.00 3.00
   b. 90c like 132TC4j 4.00 3.00
   c. 90c like 132TC4i 4.00 3.00
   d. 90c like 132TC4d 4.00 3.00
   f. Double impression of all 4 frames —

## 20th UPU CONGRESS
### Traditional Mail Delivery

Stagecoach, c. 1850 A1795

Paddlewheel Steamer A1796

Biplane A1797

Depot-hack Type Automobile A1798

**1989, Nov. 19**    *Perf. 11*
2434 A1795 25c multicolored .50 .25
2435 A1796 25c multicolored .50 .25
2436 A1797 25c multicolored .50 .25
2437 A1798 25c multicolored .50 .25
   a. Block of 4, #2434-2437 2.00 1.75
   b. As "a," dark blue (engr.) omitted 300.00

No. 2437b is valued in the grade of fine. Very fine blocks exist and sell for approximately $450.

### Souvenir Sheet
**1989, Nov. 28**    *Imperf.*
2438 Sheet of 4 5.00 3.75
   a. A1795 25c multicolored 1.25 .80
   b. A1796 25c multicolored 1.25 .80
   c. A1797 25c multicolored 1.25 .80
   d. A1798 25c multicolored 1.25 .80
   e. Dark blue & gray (engr.) omitted 4,000.

20th Universal Postal Union Congress.

## VALUES FOR HINGED STAMPS AFTER NO. 771

This catalogue does not value unused stamps after No. 771 in hinged condition. Hinged unused stamps from No. 772 to the present are worth considerably less than the values given for unused stamps, which are for never-hinged examples.

## IDAHO STATEHOOD, 100th ANNIV.

Mountain Bluebird, Sawtooth Mountains — A1799

### PHOTOGRAVURE
**1990, Jan. 6**    *Perf. 11*
2439 A1799 25c multicolored .55 .25

## LOVE

A1800

### PHOTOGRAVURE
**1990, Jan. 18**    *Perf. 12½x13*
2440 A1800 25c multi .50 .25
   a. Imperf., pair 550.00

### BOOKLET STAMP
*Perf. 11½ on 2 or 3 Sides*
2441 A1800 25c multi .50 .25
   a. Booklet pane of 10 5.00 3.50
   b. Bright pink omitted 80.00
   c. As "a," bright pink omitted 750.00

No. 2441b may be obtained from booklet panes containing both normal and color-omitted stamps.

## BLACK HERITAGE SERIES

Ida B. Wells (1862-1931), Journalist — A1801

**1990, Feb. 1**    *Perf. 11*
2442 A1801 25c multicolored .75 .25

Beach Umbrella — A1802

### BOOKLET STAMP
*Perf. 11 on 2 or 3 Sides*
**1990, Feb. 3**
2443 A1802 15c multicolored .30 .25
   a. Booklet pane of 10 3.00 2.50
   b. Blue omitted 100.00
   c. As "a," blue omitted 450.00

## WYOMING STATEHOOD, 100th ANNIV.

High Mountain Meadows, by Conrad Schwiering A1803

### LITHOGRAPHED & ENGRAVED
**1990, Feb. 23**    *Perf. 11*
2444 A1803 25c multicolored .80 .25
   a. Black (engr.) omitted 900.00

## CLASSIC FILMS

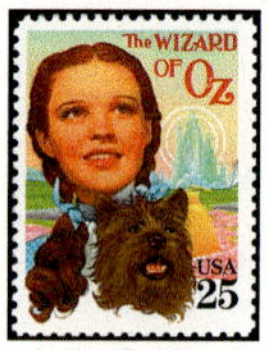

Judy Garland and Toto (The Wizard of Oz) — A1804

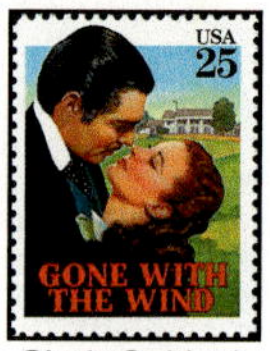

Clark Gable & Vivien Leigh (Gone With the Wind) — A1805

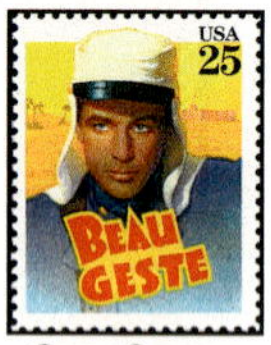

Gary Cooper (Beau Geste) A1806

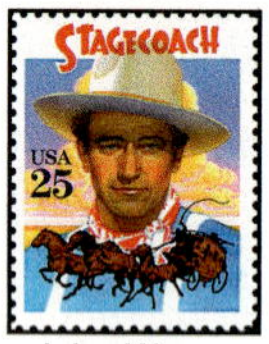

John Wayne (Stagecoach) A1807

PHOTOGRAVURE

**1990, Mar. 23**

**2445** A1804 25c multicolored 1.00 .25
**2446** A1805 25c multicolored 1.00 .25
**2447** A1806 25c multicolored 1.00 .25
**2448** A1807 25c multicolored 1.00 .25
*a.* Block of 4, #2445-2448 4.00 3.50

## LITERARY ARTS SERIES

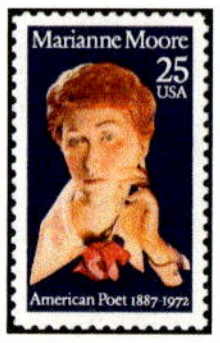

Marianne Craig Moore (1887-1972), Poet — A1808

**1990, Apr. 18**

**2449** A1808 25c multicolored .55 .25
*a.* All colors missing (EP) —

No. 2449a must be collected se-tenant with a partially printed stamp or in longer horizontal strips with a partially printed stamp and normal stamps.

## TRANSPORTATION ISSUE

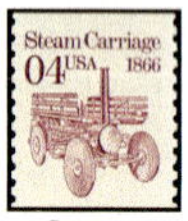

Steam Carriage 1866 A1810

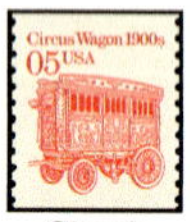

Circus Wagon 1900s A1811

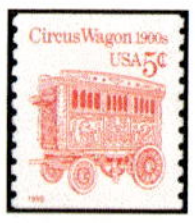

A1811a

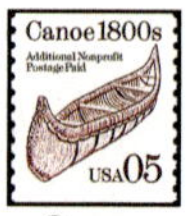

Canoe 1800s A1812

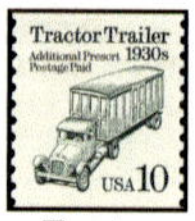

Tractor Trailer 1930s A1816

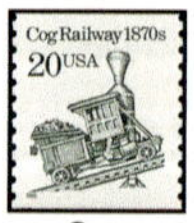

Cog Railway 1870s A1822

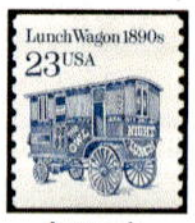

Lunch Wagon 1890s A1823

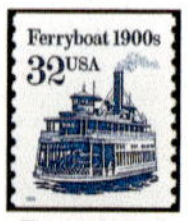

Ferryboat 1900s A1825

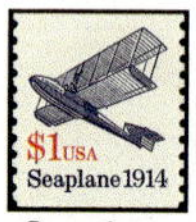

Seaplane 1914 A1827

COIL STAMPS
ENGRAVED, PHOTOGRAVURE
(#2452B, 2452D, 2454, 2458)

**1990-95** ***Perf. 9.8 Vert.***

**Untagged (Nos. 2452B, 2452D, 2453, 2454, 2457-2458)**

**Bureau Precancel in Gray (#2453-2458)**

**2451** A1810 4c claret .30 .25
*a.* Imperf., pair *450.00*
*b.* Untagged .30 .25
**2452** A1811 5c carmine .30 .25
*a.* Untagged, dull gum .30 .25
*c.* Imperf., pair *350.00*

No. 2452c is valued in the grade of fine.

**2452B** A1811 5c carmine .30 .25
**2452D** A1811a 5c carmine .30 .25
*e.* Imperf., pair *115.00*
**2453** A1812 5c brown .40 .25
*a.* Imperf., pair *150.00*
*b.* Gray omitted 1,500.
**2454** A1812 5c red .45 .25
**2457** A1816 10c green .45 .25
*a.* Imperf., pair *110.00*
*b.* All color omitted —

No. 2457b must be accompanied by a 2012 certificate of authentication confirming that stamps are from the discovery coil roll that also contained normal and partially printed stamps.

**2458** A1816 10c green .55 .25
**2463** A1822 20c green .40 .25
*a.* Imperf., pair *75.00*
**2464** A1823 23c dark blue .45 .25
*b.* Imperf., pair *100.00*
**2466** A1825 32c blue .80 .25
*a.* Imperf., pair, shiny gum *375.00*
*b.* bright blue 3.00 2.25

Some specialists refer to No. 2466b as "Bronx blue," and it is considered to be an error of color.

**2468** A1827 $1 bl & scar 2.25 .50
*a.* Imperf., pair *1,500.* *1,150.*
*Nos. 2451-2468 (12)* 6.95 3.25

Some mint pairs of No. 2468 appear to be imperf. but have faint blind perforations on the gum. Beware of examples with the gum removed.

Issued: $1, 4/20; No. 2452, 8/31; 4c, 1/25/91; 23c, 4/12/91; Nos. 2453, 2457, 5/25/91; No. 2454, 10/22/91; No. 2452B, 12/8/92; No. 2458, 5/25/94; Nos. 2452D, 3/20/95; 32c, 6/2/95; 20c, 6/9/95.

## LIGHTHOUSES

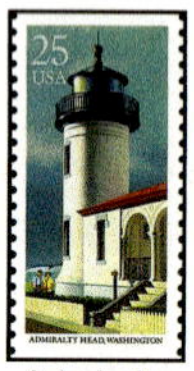

Admiralty Head, WA A1829

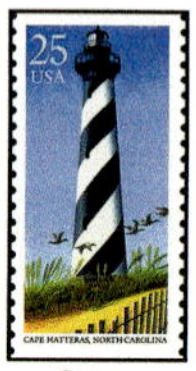

Cape Hatteras, NC A1830

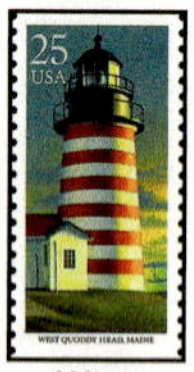

West Quoddy Head, ME A1831

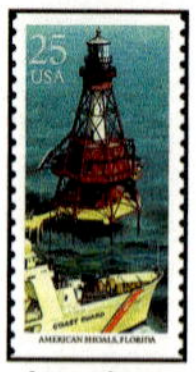

American Shoals, FL A1832

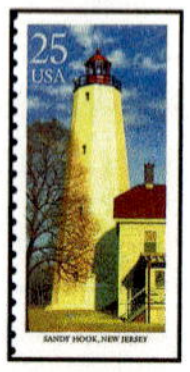

Sandy Hook, NJ — A1833

## BOOKLET STAMPS

LITHOGRAPHED & ENGRAVED

***Perf. 10 Vert. on 1 or 2 Sides***

**1990, Apr. 26**

**2470** A1829 25c multicolored 1.50 .25
**2471** A1830 25c multicolored 1.50 .25
**2472** A1831 25c multicolored 1.50 .25
**2473** A1832 25c multicolored 1.50 .25
**2474** A1833 25c multicolored 1.50 .25
*a.* Bklt. pane of 5, #2470-2474 7.50 2.00
*b.* As "a," white ("USA 25") omitted 85.00 —

Perforations on Lighthouse booklet panes separate very easily. Careful handling is required.

## FLAG

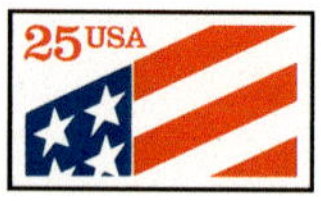

A1834

PHOTOGRAVURE

**1990, May 18 Untagged** ***Die Cut***

**Self-adhesive**

**Printed on Plastic**

**2475** A1834 25c dk red & dk bl .55 .25
*a.* Pane of 12 6.60

Sold only in panes of 12; peelable plastic backing inscribed in light ultramarine. Available for a test period of six months at 22 First National Bank automatic teller machines in Seattle.

## FLORA AND FAUNA

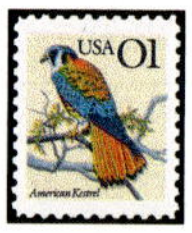

A1840

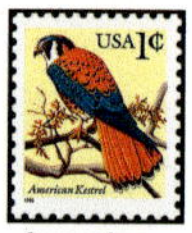

American Kestrel A1841

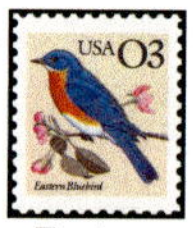

Eastern Bluebird A1842

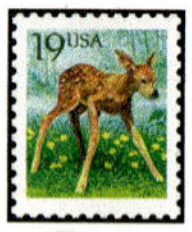

Fawn A1843

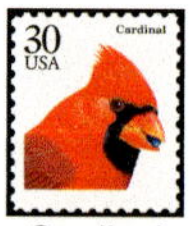

Cardinal A1844

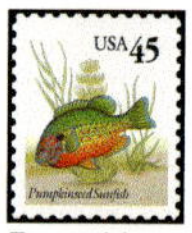

Pumpkinseed Sunfish A1845

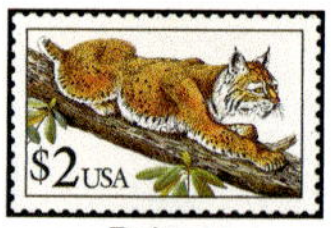

Bobcat A1846

LITHOGRAPHED

***Perf. 11, 11.2 (#2477)***

**1990-95 Untagged (1c, 3c)**

**2476** A1840 1c multi .30 .25
*a.* Quadruple impression of black inscriptions and denomination *850.00*
*b.* Quintuple impression of black inscriptions and denomination *1,500.*
**2477** A1841 1c multi .30 .25
**2478** A1842 3c multi .30 .25
*a.* Vert. pair, imperf horiz. —
*b.* Double impression of all colors except yellow *200.00*
*c.* Double impression of blue, triple impression of black —

Imperforates on gummed stamp paper, plus imperforate and perforated gutter pairs and blocks (including imperforate and perforated gutter pairs and blocks of No. 2476 se-tenant with No. 2478), are proofs from the ABNCo. archives. See Nos. 2476P and 2478P in Proofs section of the Scott U.S. Specialized Catalogue.

See Nos. 3031, 3031A, 3044. Compare design A1842 with design A2336.

PHOTOGRAVURE

**2479** A1843 19c multi .35 .25
*b.* Red omitted *250.00*
*c.* Imperf, pair *900.00*

On No. 2479b other colors are shifted.

**2480** A1844 30c multicolored, *June 22, 1991* .60 .25

LITHOGRAPHED & ENGRAVED

**2481** A1845 45c multi .90 .25
*a.* Black (engr.) omitted *150.00* —
**2482** A1846 $2 multi 3.50 1.25
*a.* Black (engr.) omitted *200.00*
*Nos. 2476-2482 (7)* 6.25 2.75

Issued: $2, 6/1; 19c, 3/11/91; No. 2476, 3c, 30c, 6/22/91; 45c, 12/2/92; No. 2477, 5/10/95.

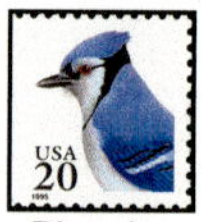

Blue Jay A1847

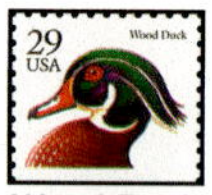

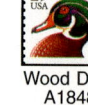

Wood Duck A1848

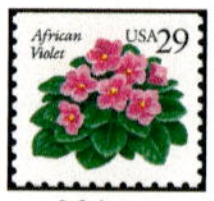

African Violets A1849

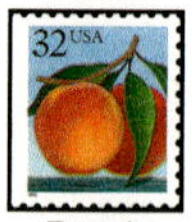

Peach A1850

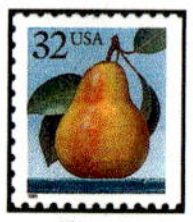

Pear A1851

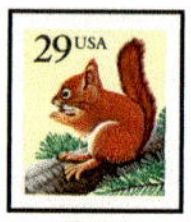

Red Squirrel A1852

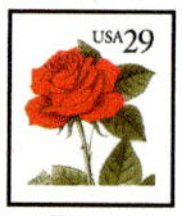

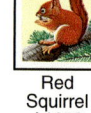

Rose A1853

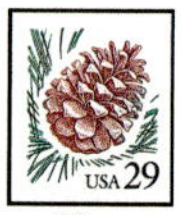

Pine Cone A1854

PHOTOGRAVURE
BOOKLET STAMPS

***Perf. 10.9x9.8 on 2 or 3 Sides***

**1991-95**

**2483** A1847 20c multi .50 .25
*a.* Booklet pane of 10 5.25 2.50
*b.* As "a," imperf —

***Perf. 10 on 2 or 3 sides***

**2484** A1848 29c blk & multi .60 .25
*a.* Booklet pane of 10 6.00 3.75
*b.* Vert. pair, imperf. horiz. *175.00*
*c.* As "b," bklt. pane of 10 *875.00*
*f.* Vert. pair, imperf between and with natural straight edge at top or bottom *175.00*
*g.* As "f," bklt. pane of 10 *875.00*

***Perf. 11 on 2 or 3 Sides***

**2485** A1848 29c red & multi .60 .25
*a.* Booklet pane of 10 6.00 4.00
*b.* Vert. pair, imperf. between *2,500.*
*c.* Imperf, pair *4,500.*
*d.* Pane of 10 with horiz. pairs, imperf. between —

No. 2485d is a pane of 10 with vertical blind perfs between stamps 4 and 5 and 9 and 10.

***Perf. 10x11 on 2 or 3 Sides***

**2486** A1849 29c multi .60 .25
*a.* Booklet pane of 10 6.00 4.00

***Perf. 11x10 on 2 or 3 Sides***

**2487** A1850 32c multi .65 .25
**2488** A1851 32c multi .65 .25
*a.* Booklet pane, 5 each #2487-2488 6.50 4.25
*b.* Pair, #2487-2488 1.30 .30

Issued: Nos. 2484-2485, 4/12; No. 2486, 10/8/93; 20c, 6/15/95; 32c, 7/8/95.

PHOTOGRAVURE, ENGRAVED
(#2491)

**1993-95** ***Die Cut***

**Self-Adhesive**

**Booklet Stamps**

**2489** A1852 29c multi .60 .25
*a.* Booklet pane of 18 11.00
*b.* As "a," die cutting omitted —
**2490** A1853 29c red, green & black .60 .25
*a.* Booklet pane of 18 11.00

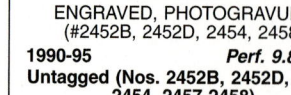

**2491** A1854 29c multi .60 .25
*a.* Booklet pane of 18 11.00
*b.* Horiz. pair, die cutting omitted between 175.00 125.00
*c.* Coil with plate # B1 — 6.00

Stamps without plate number from coil strips are indistinguishable from booklet stamps once they are removed from the backing paper.

### *Serpentine Die Cut 11.3x11.7 on 2, 3 or 4 Sides*

**2492** A1853 32c pink, green & black .65 .25
*a.* Booklet pane of 20 + label 13.00
*b.* Booklet pane of 15 + label 9.75
*c.* Horiz. pair, die cutting omitted between —
*d.* As "a," 2 stamps and parts of 7 others printed on backing liner —
*e.* Booklet pane of 14 20.00
*f.* Booklet pane of 16 20.00
*g.* Coil with plate # S111 — 5.50
*h.* Vert. pair, die cutting omitted between (from No. 2492b) 400.00
*i.* As "a," 6 pairs plus stamp and label die cutting omitted vert. btwn. (due to miscutting) 800.00
*j.* As "f," with 2 vert. pairs at bottom die cutting omitted horiz., in full bklt. #BK178D —
*k.* As "a," horiz. die cutting omitted —
*l.* As "h," with two vert. pairs at top die cutting omitted horiz., in full bklt., #BK178A —

### *Serpentine Die Cut 8.8 on 2, 3 or 4 Sides*

**2493** A1850 32c multi .65 .25
**2494** A1851 32c multi .65 .25
*a.* Booklet pane of 20, 10 each #2493-2494 + label 13.00
*b.* Pair, #2493-2494 1.30
*c.* As "b," die cutting omitted —

### COIL STAMPS
### *Serpentine Die Cut 8.8 Vert.*

**2495** A1850 32c multi 2.25 .25
**2495A** A1851 32c multi 2.25 .25
*b.* Pair, #2495-2495A 4.50

Issued: No. 2489, 6/25; No. 2490, 8/19; No. 2491, 11/5; No. 2492, 6/2/95; Nos. 2493-2495A, 7/8/95.
See Nos. 3048-3049, 3053-3054.

**Values for used self-adhesive stamps are for examples either on piece or off piece.**

## OLYMPIANS

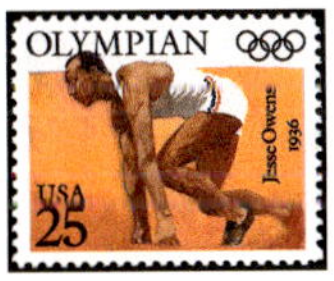

Jesse Owens, 1936 — A1855

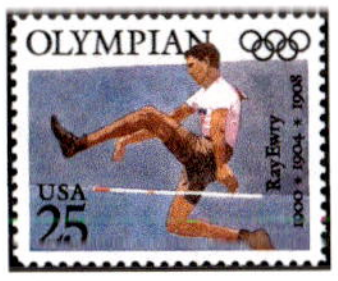

Ray Ewry, 1900-08 — A1856

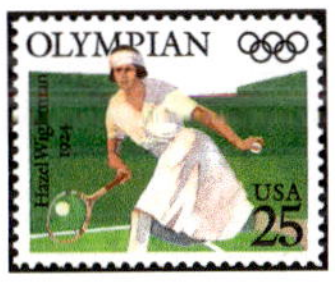

Hazel Wightman, 1924 — A1857

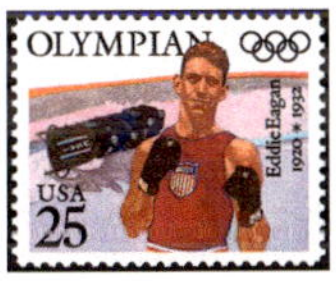

Eddie Eagan, 1920, 1932 — A1858

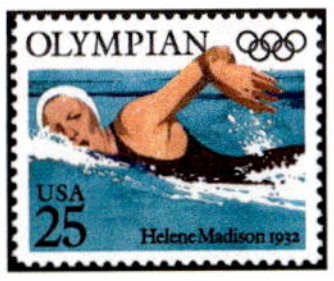

Helene Madison, 1932 — A1859

PHOTOGRAVURE

**1990, July 6** *Perf. 11*
**2496** A1855 25c multicolored .60 .25
**2497** A1856 25c multicolored .60 .25
**2498** A1857 25c multicolored .60 .25
**2499** A1858 25c multicolored .60 .25
**2500** A1859 25c multicolored .60 .25
*a.* Strip of 5, #2496-2500 3.25 2.50
*b.* As "a," blue omitted 1,750.

Imperforates on gummed stamp paper, including gutter pairs, strips and blocks, are proofs from the ABNCo. archives. See No. 2500aP in Proofs section of the Scott U.S. Specialized Catalogue.

## INDIAN HEADDRESSES

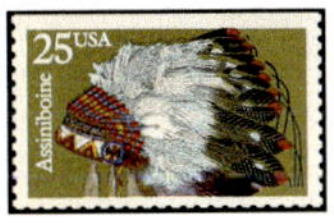

Assiniboin A1860

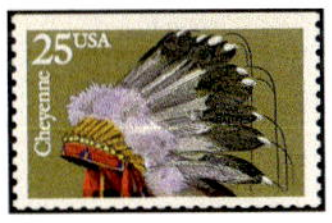

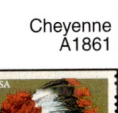

Cheyenne A1861

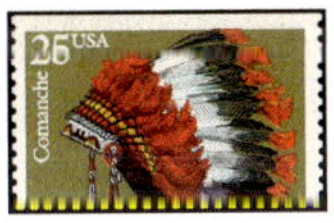

Comanche A1862

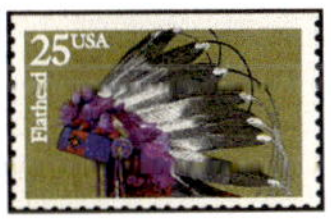

Flathead — A1863

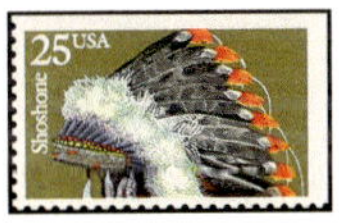

Shoshone A1864

LITHOGRAPHED & ENGRAVED
BOOKLET STAMPS
### *Perf. 11 on 2 or 3 Sides*

**1990, Aug. 17**
**2501** A1860 25c multicolored .80 .25
**2502** A1861 25c multicolored .80 .25
**2503** A1862 25c multicolored .80 .25
*a.* Black (engr.) omitted 125.00
**2504** A1863 25c multicolored .80 .25
*a.* Black (engr.) omitted 125.00 —
**2505** A1864 25c multicolored .80 .25
*a.* Bklt. pane of 10, 2 each #2501-2505 8.00 6.00
*b.* As "a," black (engr.) omitted 2,500.
*c.* Strip of 5, #2501-2505 4.00 2.50
*d.* As "a," horiz. imperf. between 2,250.

At least one of the examples of No. 2505d that have been reported is actually split at the booklet fold and is a block of 4 and a block of 6.

## MICRONESIA & MARSHALL ISLANDS

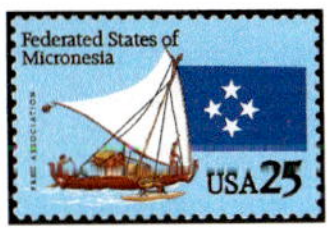

Canoe & Federated States of Micronesia Flag — A1865

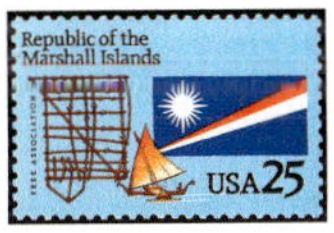

Stick Chart, Canoe & Republic of the Marshall Islands Flag — A1866

**1990, Sept. 28** *Perf. 11*
**2506** A1865 25c multicolored .50 .25
**2507** A1866 25c multicolored .50 .25
*a.* Pair, #2506-2507 1.00 .75
*b.* As "a," black (engr.) omitted 500.00

See Micronesia Nos. 124-126, Marshall Islands No. 381.

## SEA CREATURES

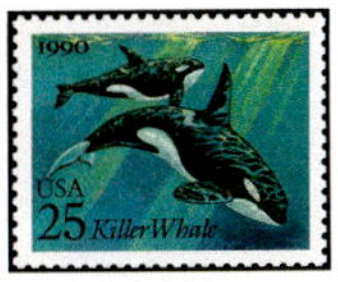

Killer Whales — A1867

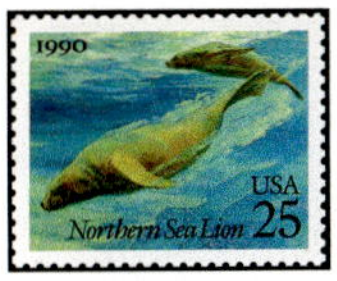

Northern Sea Lions — A1868

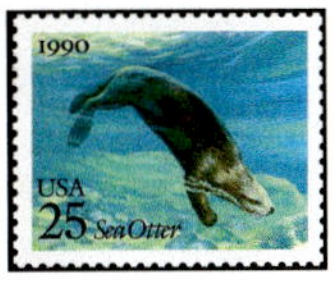

Sea Otter — A1869

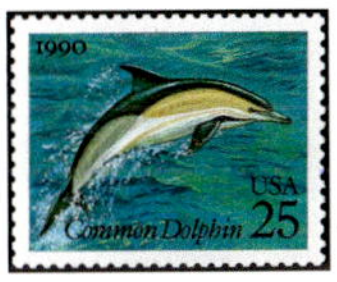

Common Dolphin — A1870

**1990, Oct. 3**
**2508** A1867 25c multicolored .55 .25
**2509** A1868 25c multicolored .55 .25
**2510** A1869 25c multicolored .55 .25
**2511** A1870 25c multicolored .55 .25
*a.* Block of 4, #2508-2511 2.25 1.90
*b.* As "a," black (engr.) omitted 250.00

See Russia Nos. 5933-5936.

## PRE-COLUMBIAN AMERICA ISSUE

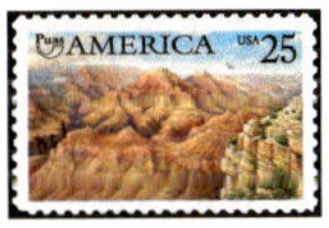

Grand Canyon — A1871

PHOTOGRAVURE

**1990, Oct. 12**
**2512** A1871 25c multicolored .55 .25

See No. C127.

## DWIGHT D. EISENHOWER, BIRTH CENTENARY

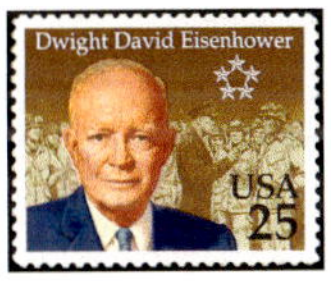

A1872

**1990, Oct. 13** **Tagged** *Perf. 11*
**2513** A1872 25c multicolored .80 .25

Imperforates on gummed stamp paper are proofs from the ABNCo. archives. See No. 2513P in Proofs section of the Scott U.S. Specialized Catalogue.

## CHRISTMAS

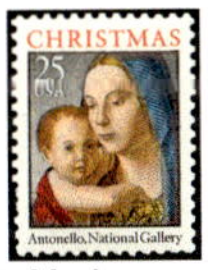

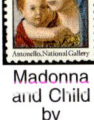

Madonna and Child by Antonello da Messina A1873

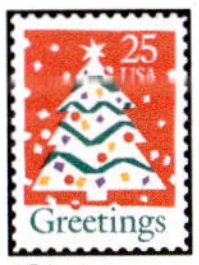

Christmas Tree A1874

LITHOGRAPHED & ENGRAVED

**1990, Oct. 18** *Perf. 11½x11½*
**2514** A1873 25c multi .50 .25
*b.* Booklet pane of 10 5.00 3.25

PHOTOGRAVURE
*Perf. 11*

**2515** A1874 25c multicolored .50 .25
*a.* Vert. pair, imperf. horiz. 500.00
*b.* All colors missing (EP) —

No. 2515b must be collected se-tenant with normal and/or partially printed stamp(s).

### BOOKLET STAMP
### *Perf. 11½x11 on 2 or 3 Sides*

**2516** A1874 25c multicolored .60 .25
*a.* Booklet pane of 10 6.00 3.25

Marked differences exist between Nos. 2515 and 2516. The background red on No. 2515 is even while that on No. 2516 is splotchy. The bands across the tree and "Greetings" are blue green on No. 2515 and yellow green on No. 2516.

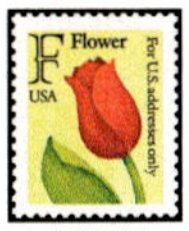

A1875

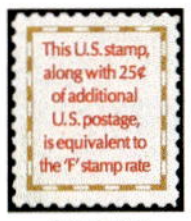

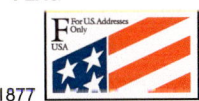

A1876

**1991, Jan. 22** *Perf. 13*
**2517** A1875 (29c) yel, blk, red & yel grn .60 .25
*a.* Imperf., pair 1,000.
*b.* Horiz. pair, imperf. vert. 1,000.

See note after No. 2518.

Gutter pairs and blocks, and cross gutter blocks, all perforated, are proofs from the ABNCo. archives. See No. 2517P in Proofs section of the Scott U.S. Specialized Catalogue.

No. 2517a is usually collected as a vertical pair, though No. 2517 can be distinguished from the other "F" stamp issues.

### COIL STAMP
### *Perf. 10 Vert.*

**2518** A1875 (29c) yel, blk, dull red & dk yel grn .60 .25
*a.* Imperf., pair 25.00

"For U.S. addresses only" is 17½mm long on No. 2517, 16½mm long on No. 2518. Design of No. 2517 measures 21½x17½mm, No. 2518, 21x18mm.

### BOOKLET STAMPS
### *Perf. 11 on 2 or 3 Sides*

**2519** A1875 (29c) yel, blk, dull red & dk grn .60 .25
*a.* Booklet pane of 10 6.50 4.50
**2520** A1875 (29c) pale yel, blk, red & brt grn 1.50 .25
*a.* Booklet pane of 10 15.00 4.50
*b.* As "a," imperf. horiz. —
*c.* Horiz. pair, imperf btwn., in error booklet pane of 12 stamps 450.00
*d.* Imperf. vert., pair —
*e.* Imperf. between (PS) —

No. 2519 has bullseye perforations that measure approximately 11.2. No. 2520 has less pronounced black lines in the leaf, which is a much brighter green than on No. 2519.

No. 2520c is from a paper foldover before perforating.

LITHOGRAPHED

**1991, Jan. 22** **Untagged** *Perf. 11*
**2521** A1876 (4c) bister & carmine .30 .25
*a.* Vert. pair, imperf. horiz. 70.00
*b.* Imperf., pair 60.00

## FLAG

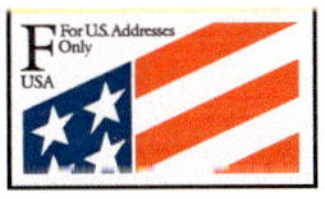

A1877

PHOTOGRAVURE

**1991, Jan. 22** **Untagged** *Die Cut*
**Self-Adhesive**
**Printed on Plastic**

**2522** A1877 (29c) blk, blue & dk red .60 .25
*a.* Pane of 12 7.25

Sold only in panes of 12; peelable plastic backing inscribed in light ultramarine. Available during a test period at First National Bank automatic teller machines in Seattle.

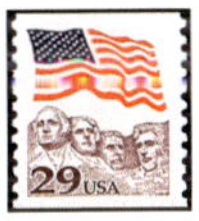

Flag Over Mt. Rushmore — A1878

COIL STAMPS
ENGRAVED

**1991, Mar. 29** **Tagged** *Perf. 10 Vert.*
**2523** A1878 29c bl, red & claret .75 .25
*b.* Imperf., pair 20.00
*c.* blue, red & brown 3.00 —

Specialists often call No. 2523c the "Toledo brown" variety.

# UNITED STATES

## PHOTOGRAVURE
**1991, July 4**
2523A A1878 29c bl, red, lt brn, med brn & dk brn .75 .25
   e. Medium brown omitted —

On No. 2523A, USA and 29 are not outlined in white and are farther from the bottom of the design.

Flower — A1879

## PHOTOGRAVURE
**1991-92**     **Perf. 11**
2524 A1879 29c dull yel, blk, red & yel grn .60 .25
See note after No. 2527.

**Perf. 13x12¾**
2524A A1879 29c dull yel, blk, red & yel grn 1.00 .25

## COIL STAMPS
**Rouletted 10 Vert.**
2525 A1879 29c pale yel, blk, red & yel grn .60 .25

**Perf. 10 Vert.**
2526 A1879 29c pale yel, blk, red & yel grn .80 .25

## BOOKLET STAMP
**Perf. 11 on 2 or 3 Sides**
2527 A1879 29c pale yel, blk, red & bright grn .60 .25
   a. Booklet pane of 10 6.00 3.50
   b. Horiz. pair, imperf. between —
   c. Horiz. pair, imperf. vert. 150.00
   d. As "a," imperf. horiz. 750.00
   e. As "a," imperf. vert. 500.00

Flower on Nos. 2524-2524A has grainy appearance, inscriptions look rougher.
Issued: Nos. 2524, 2524A, 2527, 4/5; No. 2525, 8/16; No. 2526, 3/3/92.

Flag, Olympic Rings — A1880

## BOOKLET STAMP
**Perf. 11 on 2 or 3 Sides**
**1991, Apr. 21**
2528 A1880 29c multicolored .60 .25
   a. Booklet pane of 10 6.00 3.50
   c. As "a," imperf. horiz. 2,750.
   c. Vert. pair, imperf. between, perfed at top and bottom 225.00
   d. Vert. strip of 3, top or bottom pair imperf. between —
   e. Vert. pair, imperf. horiz. 650.00
   f. As "d," two pairs in #2528a with foldover —

No. 2528c comes from misperfed booklet panes. No. 2528d resulted from paper foldovers after normal perforating and before cutting into panes. Two No. 2528d are known. No. 2528e is valued in the grade of fine.

Fishing Boat — A1881

Type I

Type II

Type I: Vertical sides of "1" are jagged. Type II stamps are created by a finer dot pattern. Vertical sides of "1" are smooth.
Nos. 2529 and 2529a have two loops of rope tying boat to piling.

## COIL STAMPS
**1991, Aug. 8**     **Perf. 9.8 Vert.**
2529 A1881 19c multi, type I .40 .25
   a. Type II ('93) .40 .25
   b. As "a," untagged ('93) 1.00 .40

Imperforates are from printer's waste.

**1994, June 25**
2529C A1881 19c multicolored .50 .25

No. 2529C has one loop of rope tying boat to piling.

Balloon — A1882

## BOOKLET STAMP
**Perf. 10 on 2 or 3 Sides**
**1991, May 17**
2530 A1882 19c multicolored .40 .25
   a. Booklet pane of 10 4.00 2.75

Flags on Parade — A1883

**1991, May 30**     **Perf. 11**
2531 A1883 29c multi .60 .25

Liberty Torch — A1884

**1991, June 25**     **Die Cut**
**Self-Adhesive**
2531A A1884 29c blk, gold & grn .60 .25
   b. Booklet pane of 18 11.00
   c. Die cutting omitted, pair 1,000.

Sold only in panes of 18; peelable paper backing inscribed in light blue. Available for consumer testing at First National Bank automatic teller machines in Seattle, WA.

## SWITZERLAND

Switzerland, 700th Anniv. — A1887

**1991, Feb. 22**     **Perf. 11**
2532 A1887 50c multi 1.00 .25
   a. Vert. pair, imperf. horiz. 1,400.

See Switzerland No. 888.
Imperfs exist from printer's waste.

## VERMONT STATEHOOD, 200th ANNIV.

A1888

**1991, Mar. 1**
2533 A1888 29c multicolored .80 .25

## SAVINGS BONDS, 50TH ANNIVERSARY

A1889

**1991, Apr. 30**     **Perf. 11**
2534 A1889 29c multicolored .60 .25

## LOVE

A1890

**1991, May 9**     **Perf. 12½x13**
2535 A1890 29c multi .60 .25
   b. Imperf., pair 1,650.

**Perf. 11**
2535A A1890 29c multi 1.00 .25

**BOOKLET STAMP (#2536)**
**Perf. 11.1x11.3 on 2 or 3 Sides**
2536 A1890 29c multi .60 .25
   a. Booklet pane of 10 3.60 3.50

"29" is closer to edge of design on No. 2536 than on No. 2535.

A1891

**Perf. 11**
2537 A1891 52c multi 1.00 .25

## LITERARY ARTS SERIES

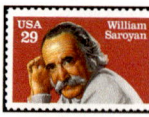

William Saroyan — A1892

**1991, May 22**     **Perf. 11**
2538 A1892 29c multicolored .60 .25
   a. All colors missing (EP) —
   b. All colors except black missing (EP) 11,000.

No. 2538a must be collected se-tenant with a partially printed stamp. On No. 2538b, only part of the black is present; it is unique.
See Russia No. 6002.

Eagle, Olympic Rings — A1893

A1894

A1895

A1896

Futuristic Space Shuttle — A1897

Space Shuttle Challenger A1898

Space Shuttle Endeavour — A1898a

**1991, Sept. 29**
2539 A1893 $1 gold & multi 2.00 .50
   a. Black omitted —

## LITHOGRAPHED & ENGRAVED
**1991, July 7**
2540 A1894 $2.90 multicolored 6.00 1.50
   a. Vert. pair, imperf. horiz. 900.00
   b. Black (engr.) omitted 750.00

Imperforates on gummed stamp paper, including gutter pairs and blocks, are proofs from the ABNCo. archives. From the same source also come imperforate progressive proofs. See No. 2540P in Proofs section of the Scott U.S. Specialized Catalogue.

**1991, June 16**     **Untagged**
2541 A1895 $9.95 multicolored 20.00 6.00
   a. Imperf., pair —

No. 2541 exists imperf plus black (engr.) omitted from printer's waste.

**1991, Aug. 31**     **Untagged**
2542 A1896 $14 multicolored 25.00 15.00
   a. Red (engr. inscriptions) omitted 750.00

No. 2542 exists imperf plus red omitted from printer's waste.

## PHOTOGRAVURE
**1993, June 3**     **Perf. 11x10¾**
2543 A1897 $2.90 multicolored 6.00 1.75

Faked examples of No. 2543, unused and used, exist with red omitted due to bleaching.

UNITED STATES 73

**1995, June 22**    Perf. 11.2
2544 A1898 $3 multicolored,
dated "1995"    5.75   1.75
   b. Dated "1996"    5.75   1.75
   c. As "b," horiz. pair, imperf
     between    1,000.
   d. As "b," imperf pair    700.00

Imperf examples of No. 2544 with "1995" date are believed to be printer's waste.

**1995, Aug. 4**    Perf. 11
2544A A1898a $10.75 multi    20.00   9.00

No. 2544A was printed on paper embedded with red fibers.
Imperf examples of No. 2544A are believed to be printer's waste.

### FISHING FLIES

Royal Wulff — A1899

Jock Scott — A1900

Apte Tarpon Fly — A1901

Lefty's Deceiver — A1902

Muddler Minnow — A1903

### PHOTOGRAVURE BOOKLET STAMPS
*Perf. 11 Horiz. on 1 or 2 Sides*

**1991, May 31**
2545 A1899 29c multicolored    1.10   .25
   a. Black omitted
   b. Horiz. pair, imperf. btwn., in
     #2549a with foldover    2,400.
2546 A1900 29c multicolored    1.10   .25
   a. Black omitted
2547 A1901 29c multicolored    1.10   .25
   a. Black omitted
2548 A1902 29c multicolored    1.10   .25
2549 A1903 29c multicolored    1.10   .25
   a. Bklt. pane of 5, #2545-2549    5.50   3.00

Horiz. pairs, imperf vert., exist from printer's waste.
No. 2545b is unique and resulted from a foldover after perfing but before cutting. Both stamps are creased.

### PERFORMING ARTS

Cole Porter (1891-1964), Composer — A1904

**1991, June 8**    Perf. 11
2550 A1904 29c multicolored    .60   .25
   a. Vert. pair, imperf. horiz.    400.00

### OPERATIONS DESERT SHIELD & DESERT STORM

S. W. Asia Service Medal — A1905

**1991, July 2**
2551 A1905 29c multicolored    .60   .25
   a. Vert. pair, imperf. horiz.    600.00

No. 2551 is 21mm wide.

### BOOKLET STAMP
*Perf. 11 Vert. on 1 or 2 Sides*
2552 A1905 29c multicolored    .60   .25
   a. Booklet pane of 5    3.00   2.25

No. 2552 is 20½mm wide. Inscriptions are shorter than on No. 2551.
No. 2552 Vert. pairs, imperf horiz., are from printer's waste.

### 1992 SUMMER OLYMPICS, BARCELONA

Pole Vault — A1907

Discus — A1908

Women's Sprints — A1909

Javelin — A1910

Women's Hurdles — A1911

**1991, July 12**    Perf. 11
2553 A1907 29c multicolored    .60   .25
2554 A1908 29c multicolored    .60   .25
2555 A1909 29c multicolored    .60   .25
2556 A1910 29c multicolored    .60   .25
2557 A1911 29c multicolored    .60   .25
   a. Strip of 5, #2553-2557    3.00   2.25

### NUMISMATICS

1858 Flying Eagle Cent, 1907 Standing Liberty Double Eagle, Series 1875 $1 Note, Series 1902 $10 National Currency Note — A1912

### LITHOGRAPHED & ENGRAVED
**1991, Aug. 13**
2558 A1912 29c multicolored    .60   .25

### WORLD WAR II

A1913

Designs and events of 1941: a, Military vehicles (Burma Road, 717-mile lifeline to China). b, Recruits (America's first peacetime draft). c, Shipments for allies (U.S. supports allies with Lend-Lease Act). d, Franklin D. Roosevelt, Winston Churchill (Atlantic Charter sets war aims of allies). e, Tank (America becomes the "arsenal of democracy.") f, Sinking of Destoyer Reuben James, Oct. 31. g, Gas mask, helmet (Civil defense mobilizes Americans at home). h, Liberty Ship, sea gull (First Liberty ship delivered December 30). i, Sinking ships (Japanese bomb Pearl Harbor, December 7). j, Congress in session (U.S. declares war on Japan, December 8). Central label is the size of 15 stamps and shows world map, extent of axis control.

### LITHOGRAPHED & ENGRAVED
**1991, Sept. 3**
2559 A1913 Block of 10    7.50   5.00
   a.-j. 29c any single    .75   .45
   k. Black (engr.) omitted    6,500.

No. 2559 has selvage at left and right and either top or bottom.

### BASKETBALL, 100TH ANNIVERSARY

Basketball, Hoop, Players' Arms — A1914

### PHOTOGRAVURE
**1991, Aug. 28**
2560 A1914 29c multicolored    .60   .25

### DISTRICT OF COLUMBIA BICENTENNIAL

Capitol Building from Pennsylvania Avenue, Circa 1903 — A1915

### LITHOGRAPHED & ENGRAVED
**1991, Sept. 7**
2561 A1915 29c multicolored    .60   .25
   a. Black (engr.) omitted    85.00

### COMEDIANS

Stan Laurel and Oliver Hardy — A1916

Edgar Bergen and Charlie McCarthy A1917

Jack Benny — A1918

Fanny Brice — A1919

Dud Abbott and Lou Costello — A1920

### BOOKLET STAMPS
*Perf. 11 on 2 or 3 Sides*
**1991, Aug. 29**
2562 A1916 29c multicolored    .80   .25
2563 A1917 29c multicolored    .80   .25
2564 A1918 29c multicolored    .80   .25
2565 A1919 29c multicolored    .80   .25
2566 A1920 29c multicolored    .80   .25
   a. Strip of 5, #2562-2566    4.00   2.25
   b. Bklt. pane of 10, 2 each #2562-2566    8.00   5.00
   c. As "b," scar & brt violet (engr.) omitted    350.00

### BLACK HERITAGE SERIES

Jan E. Matzeliger (1852-1889), Inventor — A1921

### PHOTOGRAVURE
**1991, Sept. 15**    Perf. 11
2567 A1921 29c multicolored    .60   .25
   a. Horiz. pair, imperf. vert.    600.00
   b. Vert. pair, imperf. horiz.    550.00
   c. Imperf., pair    275.00

### SPACE EXPLORATION

Mercury, Mariner 10 A1922

Venus, Mariner 2 A1923

Earth, Landsat — A1924

Moon, Lunar Orbiter — A1925

Mars, Viking Orbiter — A1926

Jupiter, Pioneer 11 A1927

Saturn, Voyager 2 A1928

Uranus, Voyager 2 A1929

Neptune, Voyager 2 A1930

Pluto — A1931

### PHOTOGRAVURE BOOKLET STAMPS
*Perf. 11 on 2 or 3 Sides*
**1991, Oct. 1**
2568 A1922 29c multicolored    .80   .25
2569 A1923 29c multicolored    .80   .25
2570 A1924 29c multicolored    .80   .25
2571 A1925 29c multicolored    .80   .25
2572 A1926 29c multicolored    .80   .25
2573 A1927 29c multicolored    .80   .25
2574 A1928 29c multicolored    .80   .25
2575 A1929 29c multicolored    .80   .25
2576 A1930 29c multicolored    .80   .25
2577 A1931 29c multicolored    .80   .25
   a. Bklt. pane of 10, #2568-2577    8.00   4.50

### CHRISTMAS

Madonna and Child by Antoniazzo Romano A1933

Santa Claus in Chimney A1934

74    UNITED STATES

Santa Checking List A1935

Santa with Present A1936

Santa at Fireplace A1937

Santa and Sleigh A1938

### LITHOGRAPHED & ENGRAVED
**1991, Oct. 17**    Perf. 11¼
| 2578 | A1933 (29c) multi | .60 | .25 |
|---|---|---|---|
| a. | Booklet pane of 10 | 6.00 | 3.25 |
| b. | Red & black (engr.) omitted | 2,250. | |

### PHOTOGRAVURE
Perf. 11
| 2579 | A1934 (29c) multi | .60 | .25 |
|---|---|---|---|
| | P# block of 4, 3#+A | 2.50 | — |
| | Zip block of 4 | 2.25 | |
| | Pane of 50 | 30.00 | |
| a. | Horiz. pair, imperf. vert. | 175.00 | |
| b. | Vert. pair, imperf. horiz. | 350.00 | |

### BOOKLET STAMPS
Size: 25x18½mm
Perf. 11 on 2 or 3 Sides
| 2580 | A1934 (29c) multi, type I | 2.00 | .25 |
|---|---|---|---|
| 2581 | A1934 (29c) multi, type II | 2.00 | .25 |
| a. | Pair #2580-2581 | 4.00 | .55 |
| b. | Bklt. pane, 2 each, #2580-2581 | 8.00 | 1.25 |
| 2582 | A1935 (29c) multi | .60 | .25 |
| a. | Bklt. pane of 4 | 2.40 | 1.25 |
| 2583 | A1936 (29c) multi | .60 | .25 |
| a. | Bklt. pane of 4 | 2.40 | 1.25 |
| 2584 | A1937 (29c) multi | .60 | .25 |
| a. | Bklt. pane of 4 | 2.40 | 1.25 |
| 2585 | A1938 (29c) multi | .60 | .25 |
| a. | Bklt. pane of 4 | 2.40 | 1.25 |
| | Nos. 2578-2585 (8) | 7.60 | 2.00 |

The far left brick from the top row of the chimney is missing from Type II, No. 2581.
Imperfs of Nos. 2581, 2583-2585 are printer's waste.

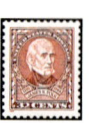
A1939

A1942

A1944

### ENGRAVED
**1994-95**    Perf. 11.2
| 2587 | A1939 32c red brown | .65 | .25 |
|---|---|---|---|

Perf. 11.5
| 2590 | A1942 $1 blue | 1.90 | .50 |
|---|---|---|---|
| 2592 | A1944 $5 slate green | 8.00 | 2.50 |

Issued: $2, 5/5; $5, 8/19; 32c, 11/2/95.

Flag — A1946

### BOOKLET STAMPS
PHOTOGRAVURE
Perf. 10 on 2 or 3 Sides
**1992, Sept. 8**
| 2593 | A1946 29c black & multi | .60 | .25 |
|---|---|---|---|
| a. | Booklet pane of 10 | 6.00 | 4.25 |
| d. | Imperf, pair | 500.00 | |

Perf. 11x10 on 2 or 3 Sides
| 2593B | A1946 29c blk & multi | 2.50 | .50 |
|---|---|---|---|
| c. | Bklt. pane of 10, shiny gum | 35.00 | 7.50 |

Perf. 11x10 on 2 or 3 Sides
**1993, Apr. 8 (?)**
| 2594 | A1946 29c red & multi | .65 | .25 |
|---|---|---|---|
| a. | Booklet pane of 10 | 6.50 | 4.25 |

Denomination is red on #2594 and black on #2593 and 2593B.

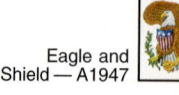
Eagle and Shield — A1947

### LITHOGRAPHED & ENGRAVED
(#2595), PHOTOGRAVURE
**1992, Sept. 25**    Die Cut
Self-Adhesive
| 2595 | A1947 29c brn & multi | .60 | .25 |
|---|---|---|---|
| a. | Bklt. pane of 17 + label | 10.50 | |
| b. | Die cutting omitted, pair | 90.00 | |
| c. | Brown omitted | 250.00 | |
| d. | As "a," die cutting omitted | 725.00 | |
| 2596 | A1947 29c bl grn & multi | .60 | .25 |
| a. | Bklt. pane of 17 + label | 10.50 | |
| 2597 | A1947 29c red & multi | .60 | .25 |
| a. | Bklt. pane of 17 + label | 10.50 | |

Plate No. and inscription reads down on No. 2595a and up on Nos. 2596a-2597a. Design is sharper and more finely detailed on Nos. 2595, 2597.
Nos. 2595a-2597a sold for $5 each.
Nos. 2595-2597 also available in strips with stamps spaced for use in affixing machines to service first day covers.

A1950

Statue of Liberty — A1951

Designed by Richard Sheaff (#2598), Tom Engeman (#2599).
Printed by Dittler Brothers, Inc. (#2599), National Label Co. for 3M (#2598).

**1994**    Die Cut
Self-Adhesive
| 2598 | A1950 29c red, cream & blue | .60 | .25 |
|---|---|---|---|
| a. | Booklet pane of 18 | 10.50 | |
| b. | Coil with P#111 | — | 5.00 |
| c. | Die cutting omitted, pair | 1,000. | |
| 2599 | A1951 29c multi | .60 | .25 |
| a. | Booklet pane of 18 | 10.50 | |
| b. | Coil with P#D1111 | — | 5.00 |

Except for Nos. 2598b and 2599b with plate numbers, coil stamps of Nos. 2595-2599 are indistinguishable from booklet stamps once they are removed from the backing paper.
See Nos. 3122-3122E.
Issued: No. 2598, 2/4; No. 2599, 6/24.

> Scott values for used self-adhesive stamps are for examples either on piece or off piece.

A1956

A1957

A1959

A1960

Flag Over White House — A1961

### COIL STAMPS
**1991-93**    Untagged    Perf. 10 Vert.
| 2602 | A1956 (10c) multi | .30 | .25 |
|---|---|---|---|
| | Imperf., pair | 3,500. | |
| 2603 | A1957 (10c) org yel & multi | .30 | .25 |
| a. | Imperf., pair | 20.00 | |
| 2604 | A1957 (10c) gold & multi | .30 | .25 |
| 2605 | A1959 23c multi | .45 | .40 |
| | Imperf., pair | | |

Vertical pairs uncut between on gummed stamp paper are proofs from the ABNCo. archives. See No. 2605P in Proofs section of the Scott U.S. Specialized Catalogue.
| 2606 | A1960 23c multi | .45 | .40 |
|---|---|---|---|

"First-Class" is 9½mm long and "23" is 6mm long on No. 2606.
| 2607 | A1960 23c multi | .45 | .40 |
|---|---|---|---|
| c. | Imperf., pair | 65.00 | |

"First-Class" is 9mm long and "23" is 6½mm long on No. 2607.
| 2608 | A1960 23c vio bl, red & blk | .80 | .40 |
|---|---|---|---|

"First-Class" is 8½mm long and "23" is 6½mm long on No. 2608.
Nos. 2602-2608 are considered precancels by the USPS.

### ENGRAVED
Tagged
| 2609 | A1961 29c blue & red | .60 | .25 |
|---|---|---|---|
| a. | Imperf., pair | 15.00 | 25.00 |
| b. | Pair, imperf. between | 60.00 | |
| c. | Indigo blue & red | 22.50 | — |
| | Nos. 2602-2609 (8) | 3.65 | 2.60 |

Beware of pairs with blind perfs sometimes offered as No. 2609b.
Issued: No. 2605, 9/27; No. 2602, 12/31; 29c, 4/23/92; No. 2606, 7/21/92; No. 2607, 10/9/92; Nos. 2603-2604, 5/29/93; No. 2608, 5/14/93.
See Nos. 2907, 3270-3271.

### WINTER OLYMPICS

Hockey — A1963

Figure Skating — A1964

Speed Skating — A1965

Skiing — A1966

Bobsledding A1967

### PHOTOGRAVURE
**1992, Jan. 11**    Perf. 11
| 2611 | A1963 29c multicolored | .60 | .25 |
|---|---|---|---|
| 2612 | A1964 29c multicolored | .60 | .25 |
| 2613 | A1965 29c multicolored | .60 | .25 |
| 2614 | A1966 29c multicolored | .60 | .25 |
| 2615 | A1967 29c multicolored | .60 | .25 |
| a. | Strip of 5, #2611-2615 | 3.00 | 2.50 |

### WORLD COLUMBIAN STAMP EXPO

Portion of Vignette of No. 129 — A1968

### LITHOGRAPHED & ENGRAVED
**1992, Jan. 24**
| 2616 | A1968 29c multicolored | .60 | .25 |
|---|---|---|---|

### BLACK HERITAGE SERIES

W.E.B. Du Bois (1868-1963), Civil Rights Leader — A1969

**1992, Jan. 31**
| 2617 | A1969 29c multicolored | .60 | .25 |
|---|---|---|---|

### LOVE

A1970

### PHOTOGRAVURE
**1992, Feb. 6**
| 2618 | A1970 29c multicolored | .60 | .25 |
|---|---|---|---|
| a. | Horiz. pair, imperf. vert. | 300.00 | |
| b. | As "a," green omitted on right stamp | 1,250. | |

### OLYMPIC BASEBALL

A1971

**1992, Apr. 3**    Tagged    Perf. 11
| 2619 | A1971 29c multicolored | .60 | .25 |
|---|---|---|---|

### VOYAGES OF COLUMBUS

Seeking Queen Isabella's Support — A1972

Crossing the Atlantic — A1973

Approaching Land — A1974

Coming Ashore — A1975

### LITHOGRAPHED & ENGRAVED
**1992, Apr. 24**
| 2620 | A1972 29c multicolored | .65 | .25 |
|---|---|---|---|
| 2621 | A1973 29c multicolored | .65 | .25 |
| 2622 | A1974 29c multicolored | .65 | .25 |
| 2623 | A1975 29c multicolored | .65 | .25 |
| a. | Block of 4, #2620-2623 | 2.60 | 2.00 |

See Italy Nos. 1877-1880.

### Souvenir Sheets

A1976

# UNITED STATES

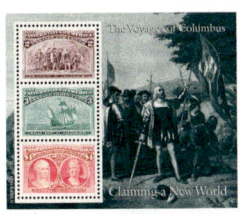
A1977

A1978

A1979

A1980

A1981

| 1992, May 22 | | | Perf. 10½ | |
|---|---|---|---|---|
| Tagged (15c-$5), Untagged | | | | |
| 2624 | A1976 | Pane of 3 | 2.35 | 1.50 |
| a. | A71 1c deep blue | | .30 | .25 |
| b. | A74 4c ultramarine | | .30 | .25 |
| c. | A82 $1 salmon | | 1.75 | 1.00 |
| 2625 | A1977 | Pane of 3 | 7.50 | 5.00 |
| a. | A72 2c brown violet | | .30 | .25 |
| b. | A73 3c green | | .30 | .25 |
| c. | A85 $4 crimson lake | | 7.00 | 4.00 |
| 2626 | A1978 | Pane of 3 | 1.80 | 1.25 |
| a. | A75 5c chocolate | | .30 | .25 |
| b. | A80 30c orange brown | | .60 | .30 |
| c. | A81 50c slate blue | | .90 | .50 |
| 2627 | A1979 | Pane of 3 | 6.10 | 3.75 |
| a. | A76 6c purple | | .30 | .25 |
| b. | A77 8c magenta | | .30 | .25 |
| c. | A84 $3 yellow green | | 5.50 | 3.00 |
| 2628 | A1980 | Pane of 3 | 4.30 | 3.00 |
| a. | A78 10c black brown | | .30 | .25 |
| b. | A79 15c dark green | | .30 | .25 |
| c. | A83 $2 brown red | | 3.50 | 2.00 |
| 2629 | A1981 | $5 Pane of 1 | 8.75 | 6.00 |
| a. | A86 $5 black, single stamp | | 8.50 | 5.00 |
| Nos. 2624-2629 (6) | | | 30.80 | 20.50 |

See Italy Nos. 1883-1888, Portugal Nos. 1918-1923 and Spain Nos. 2677-2682.

Imperforate souvenir sheets on gummed stamp paper, singly or in pairs and blocks, are proofs from the ABNCo. archives. Additionally, one imperforate essay, with the background of No. 2622 combined with the stamps of No. 2620, is recorded. See Nos. 2624P-2629P in Proofs section of the Scott U.S. Specialized Catalogue.

## NEW YORK STOCK EXCHANGE BICENTENNIAL

A1982

| 1992, May 17 | | | Perf. 11 |
|---|---|---|---|
| 2630 | A1982 29c green, red & black | .60 | .25 |
| a. | Black missing (EP) | 4,000. | |
| b. | Black missing (CM) | 4,000. | |
| c. | Center (black engr.) inverted | 17,000. | |
| d. | Se-tenant pair, #2630b and #2630c | 22,500. | |

No. 2630a resulted from extraneous paper that blocked the black from appearing on the stamp paper. It is from a unique pane that contained four color-missing errors plus a fifth stamp missing half the black center.

No. 2630a must be collected se-tenant with a normal stamp or with a stamp with half of black engraving missing, or se-tenant with a normal stamp and an additional 2630a.

No. 2630b may be collected alone or se-tenant with No. 2630c.

Two panes, each containing 28 No. 2630c and 12 No. 2630b, have been documented.

## SPACE ACCOMPLISHMENTS

 Cosmonaut, U.S. Space Shuttle A1983

 Astronaut, Russian Space Station A1984

 Sputnik, Vostok, Apollo Command & Lunar Modules A1985

 Soyuz, Mercury and Gemini Spacecraft A1986

### PHOTOGRAVURE

| 1992, May 29 | | | |
|---|---|---|---|
| 2631 | A1983 29c multicolored | .60 | .25 |
| 2632 | A1984 29c multicolored | .60 | .25 |
| 2633 | A1985 29c multicolored | .60 | .25 |
| 2634 | A1986 29c multicolored | .60 | .25 |
| a. | Block of 4, #2631-2634 | 2.40 | 2.00 |
| b. | As "a," yellow omitted | 4,750. | |

The yellow color in Nos. 2631-2634 is easily removed by exposure to sunlight. Expertization of No. 2634b is essential.

See Russia Nos. 6080-6083.

## ALASKA HIGHWAY, 50th ANNIVERSARY

A1987

### LITHOGRAPHED & ENGRAVED

| 1992, May 30 | | | |
|---|---|---|---|
| 2635 | A1987 29c multicolored | .60 | .25 |
| a. | Black (engr.) omitted | 575.00 | — |

Almost half the recorded No. 2635a errors are poorly centered. These sell for approximately $400.

## KENTUCKY STATEHOOD BICENTENNIAL

A1988

### PHOTOGRAVURE

| 1992, June 1 | | | |
|---|---|---|---|
| 2636 | A1988 29c multicolored | .60 | .25 |
| a. | Dark blue missing (EP) | — | |
| b. | Dark blue and red missing (EP) | — | |
| c. | All colors missing (EP) | — | |

Nos. 2636a-2636c must be collected se-tenant with normal stamps.

## SUMMER OLYMPICS

Soccer — A1989

Gymnastics A1990

Volleyball A1991

Boxing — A1992

Swimming A1993

| 1992, June 11 | | | |
|---|---|---|---|
| 2637 | A1989 29c multicolored | .60 | .25 |
| 2638 | A1990 29c multicolored | .60 | .25 |
| 2639 | A1991 29c multicolored | .60 | .25 |
| 2640 | A1992 29c multicolored | .60 | .25 |
| 2641 | A1993 29c multicolored | .60 | .25 |
| a. | Strip of 5, #2637-2641 | 3.00 | 2.50 |

## HUMMINGBIRDS

 Ruby-throated A1994

 Broad-billed A1995

 Costa's A1996

 Rufous A1997

Calliope — A1998

## BOOKLET STAMPS
### Perf. 11 Vert. on 1 or 2 Sides

| 1992, June 15 | | | |
|---|---|---|---|
| 2642 | A1994 29c multicolored | .60 | .25 |
| 2643 | A1995 29c multicolored | .60 | .25 |
| 2644 | A1996 29c multicolored | .60 | .25 |
| 2645 | A1997 29c multicolored | .60 | .25 |
| 2646 | A1998 29c multicolored | .60 | .25 |
| a. | Bklt. pane of 5, #2642-2646 | 3.00 | 2.50 |

Imperforate singles, booklet panes and pane multiples or varieties on gummed stamp paper are proofs from the ABNCo. archives. From the same source also come imperforate progressive proofs. See No. 2646aP in Proofs section of the Scott U.S. Specialized Catalogue.

## WILDFLOWERS

A1999

### LITHOGRAPHED

| 1992, July 24 | | | Perf. 11 | |
|---|---|---|---|---|
| 2647 | A1999 | 20c Indian paintbrush | .60 | .60 |
| 2648 | A2000 | 29c Fragrant water lily | .60 | .60 |
| 2649 | A2001 | 29c Meadow beauty | .60 | .60 |
| 2650 | A2002 | 29c Jack-in-the-pulpit | .60 | .60 |
| 2651 | A2003 | 29c California poppy | .60 | .60 |
| 2652 | A2004 | 29c Large-flowered trillium | .60 | .60 |
| 2653 | A2005 | 29c Tickseed | .60 | .60 |
| 2654 | A2006 | 29c Shooting star | .60 | .60 |
| 2655 | A2007 | 29c Stream violet | .60 | .60 |
| 2656 | A2008 | 29c Bluets | .60 | .60 |
| 2657 | A2009 | 29c Herb Robert | .60 | .60 |
| 2658 | A2010 | 29c Marsh marigold | .60 | .60 |
| 2659 | A2011 | 29c Sweet white violet | .60 | .60 |
| 2660 | A2012 | 29c Claret cup cactus | .60 | .60 |
| 2661 | A2013 | 29c White mountain avens | .60 | .60 |
| 2662 | A2014 | 29c Sessile bellwort | .60 | .60 |
| 2663 | A2015 | 29c Blue flag | .60 | .60 |
| 2664 | A2016 | 29c Harlequin lupine | .60 | .60 |
| 2665 | A2017 | 29c Twinflower | .60 | .60 |
| 2666 | A2018 | 29c Common sunflower | .60 | .60 |
| 2667 | A2019 | 29c Sego lily | .60 | .60 |
| 2668 | A2020 | 29c Virginia bluebells | .60 | .60 |
| 2669 | A2021 | 29c Ohi'a lehua | .60 | .60 |
| 2670 | A2022 | 29c Rosebud orchid | .60 | .60 |
| 2671 | A2023 | 29c Showy evening primrose | .60 | .60 |
| 2672 | A2024 | 29c Fringed gentian | .60 | .60 |
| 2673 | A2025 | 29c Yellow lady's slipper | .60 | .60 |
| 2674 | A2026 | 29c Passionflower | .60 | .60 |
| 2675 | A2027 | 29c Bunchberry | .60 | .60 |
| 2676 | A2028 | 29c Pasqueflower | .60 | .60 |
| 2677 | A2029 | 29c Round-lobed hepatica | .60 | .60 |
| 2678 | A2030 | 29c Wild columbine | .60 | .60 |
| 2679 | A2031 | 29c Fireweed | .60 | .60 |
| 2680 | A2032 | 29c Indian pond lily | .60 | .60 |
| 2681 | A2033 | 29c Turk's cap lily | .60 | .60 |
| 2682 | A2034 | 29c Dutchman's breeches | .60 | .60 |
| 2683 | A2035 | 29c Trumpet honeysuckle | .60 | .60 |
| 2684 | A2036 | 29c Jacob's ladder | .60 | .60 |
| 2685 | A2037 | 29c Plains prickly pear | .60 | .60 |
| 2686 | A2038 | 29c Moss campion | .60 | .60 |
| 2687 | A2039 | 29c Bearberry | .60 | .60 |
| 2688 | A2040 | 29c Mexican hat | .60 | .60 |
| 2689 | A2041 | 29c Harebell | .60 | .60 |
| 2690 | A2042 | 29c Desert five spot | .60 | .60 |
| 2691 | A2043 | 29c Smooth Solomon's seal | .60 | .60 |
| 2692 | A2044 | 29c Red maids | .60 | .60 |
| 2693 | A2045 | 29c Yellow skunk cabbage | .60 | .60 |
| 2694 | A2046 | 29c Rue anemone | .60 | .60 |
| 2695 | A2047 | 29c Standing cypress | .60 | .60 |
| 2696 | A2048 | 29c Wild flax | .60 | .60 |
| a. | A1999-A2048 Pane of 50, #2647-2696 | | 30.00 | |

## WORLD WAR II

A2049

No. 2697 — Events of 1942: a, B-25's take off to raid Tokyo, Apr. 18. b, Ration coupons (Food and other commodities rationed). c, Divebomber and deck crewman (US wins Battle of the Coral Sea, May). d, Prisoners of war (Corregidor falls to Japanese, May 6). e, Dutch Harbor buildings on fire (Japan invades Aleutian Islands, June). f, Headphones, coded message (Allies decipher secret enemy codes). g, Yorktown lost, U.S. wins at Midway. h, Woman with drill (Millions of women join war effort). i, Marines land on Guadalcanal, Aug. 7. j, Tank in desert (Allies land in North Africa, Nov.).

Central label is the size of 15 stamps and shows world map, extent of axis control.

### LITHOGRAPHED & ENGRAVED
1992, Aug. 17
2697  A2049  Block of 10        7.50   5.00
 a.-j.        29c any single     .75    .30
 k.           Red (litho.) omitted  4,000.

No. 2697 has selvage at left and right and either top or bottom.

## LITERARY ARTS SERIES

A2050

### PHOTOGRAVURE
1992, Aug. 22
2698  A2050  29c multicolored   .60   .25

Dorothy Parker (1893-1967), author.

## THEODORE VON KARMAN

A2051

1992, Aug. 31
2699  A2051  29c multicolored   .60   .25

Von Karman (1881-1963), rocket scientist.

## MINERALS

Azurite A2052

Copper A2053

Variscite A2054

Wulfenite A2055

### LITHOGRAPHED & ENGRAVED
1992, Sept. 17
2700  A2052  29c multicolored   .60   .25
2701  A2053  29c multicolored   .60   .25
2702  A2054  29c multicolored   .60   .25
2703  A2055  29c multicolored   .60   .25
 a.   Block or strip of 4, #2700-2703        2.40  2.00
 b.   As "a," silver (litho.) omitted   6,000.
 d.   As "a," silver omitted on two stamps   900.00

## JUAN RODRIGUEZ CABRILLO

Cabrillo, Ship, Map of San Diego Bay Area — A2056

1992, Sept. 28
2704  A2056  29c multicolored   .60   .25
 a.   Black (engr.) omitted     2,000.

## WILD ANIMALS

Giraffe — A2057

Giant Panda — A2058

Flamingo — A2059

King Penguins A2060

White Bengal Tiger — A2061

### PHOTOGRAVURE
### BOOKLET STAMPS
**Perf. 11 Horiz. on 1 or 2 Sides**
1992, Oct. 1
2705  A2057  29c multicolored   .65   .25
2706  A2058  29c multicolored   .65   .25
2707  A2059  29c multicolored   .65   .25
2708  A2060  29c multicolored   .65   .25
2709  A2061  29c multicolored   .65   .25
 a.   Booklet pane of 5, #2705-2709        3.25  2.25
 b.   As "a," imperf.           2,000.

## CHRISTMAS

Madonna and Child, by Giovanni Bellini — A2062

Horse and Rider A2063

Fire Pumper A2064

Train Engine A2065

Riverboat A2066

### LITHOGRAPHED & ENGRAVED
1992                         Perf. 11¼
2710  A2062  29c multicolored   .60   .25
 a.   Booklet pane of 10       6.00  3.50

### LITHOGRAPHED
**Perf. 11¼x11**
2711  A2063  29c multicolored   .75   .25
2712  A2064  29c multicolored   .75   .25
2713  A2065  29c multicolored   .75   .25
2714  A2066  29c multicolored   .75   .25
 a.   Block of 4, #2711-2714   3.00  1.10

### Booklet Stamps
### PHOTOGRAVURE
**Perf. 11 on 2 or 3 Sides**
2715  A2063  29c multicolored   .90   .25
2716  A2064  29c multicolored   .90   .25
2717  A2065  29c multicolored   .90   .25
2718  A2066  29c multicolored   .90   .25
 a.   Booklet pane of 4, #2715-2718      3.60  1.25

Imperforates and part-perforates on gummed stamp paper are proofs from the ABNCo. archives. From the same source come imperforates with Toys only and imperforates without denominations. See No. 2718aP in Proofs section of the Scott U.S. Specialized Catalogue.

### Self-Adhesive
*Die Cut*
2719  A2065  29c multicolored   .65   .25
 a.   Booklet pane of 18      12.00

"Greetings" is 27mm long on Nos. 2711-2714, 25mm long on Nos. 2715-2718 and 21½mm long on No. 2719. Nos. 2715-2719 differ in color from Nos. 2711-2714.
Issued: #2710-2718, 10/22; #2719, 10/28.

## CHINESE NEW YEAR

Year of the Rooster — A2067

### LITHOGRAPHED & ENGRAVED
1992, Dec. 30                Perf. 11
2720  A2067  29c multicolored   .60   .25

See Nos. 3895j, 3997j.

## AMERICAN MUSIC SERIES

Elvis Presley — A2068

Oklahoma! A2069

Hank Williams — A2070

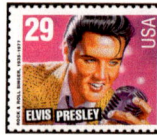

Elvis Presley — A2071

Bill Haley — A2072

Clyde McPhatter A2073

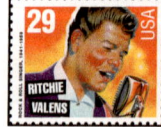

Ritchie Valens — A2074

Otis Redding — A2075

Buddy Holly — A2076

Dinah Washington A2077

### PHOTOGRAVURE
1993                         Perf. 11
2721  A2068  29c multicolored   .60   .25
 a.   Imperf, pair             —
**Perf. 10**
2722  A2069  29c multicolored   .60   .25
2723  A2070  29c multicolored   .75   .25
**Perf. 11.2x11.5**
2723A A2070  29c multicolored  12.00 10.00
1993, June 16                **Perf. 10**
2724  A2071  29c multicolored   .70   .25
2725  A2072  29c multicolored   .70   .25
2726  A2073  29c multicolored   .70   .25
2727  A2074  29c multicolored   .70   .25
2728  A2075  29c multicolored   .70   .25
2729  A2076  29c multicolored   .70   .25
2730  A2077  29c multicolored   .70   .25
 a.   Vert. strip of 7, #2724-2730       5.50  3.00

### Booklet Stamps
**Perf. 11 Horiz. on 1 or 2 Sides**
2731  A2071  29c multicolored   .65   .25
2732  A2072  29c multicolored   .65   .25
2733  A2073  29c multicolored   .65   .25
2734  A2074  29c multicolored   .65   .25
2735  A2075  29c multicolored   .65   .25
2736  A2076  29c multicolored   .65   .25
2737  A2077  29c multicolored   .65   .25
 a.   Booklet pane, 2 #2731, 1 each #2732-2737   5.25  2.25
 b.   Booklet pane, #2731, 2735-2737 + tab      2.60  1.50

Nos. 2731-2737 have smaller design sizes, brighter colors and shorter inscriptions than Nos. 2724-2730, as well as framelines around the designs and other subtle design differences.

No. 2737b without tab is indistinguishable from broken No. 2737a.

Imperforates of both No. 2737a and 2737b on gummed stamp paper are proofs from the ABNCo. archives. Perforated booklet pane multiples and varieties also exist from the same source. See Nos. 2737aP-2737bP in Proofs section of the Scott U.S. Specialized Catalogue.

See Nos. 2769, 2771, 2775 and designs A2112-A2117.

## SPACE FANTASY

A2086

A2087

A2088

A2089

# UNITED STATES

A2090

## BOOKLET STAMPS

**1993, Jan. 25**      **Perf. 11 Vert.**

| 2741 | A2086 | 29c multicolored | .60 | .25 |
| 2742 | A2087 | 29c multicolored | .60 | .25 |
| 2743 | A2088 | 29c multicolored | .60 | .25 |
| 2744 | A2089 | 29c multicolored | .60 | .25 |
| 2745 | A2090 | 29c multicolored | .60 | .25 |
| a. | | Booklet pane of 5, #2741-2745 | 3.00 | 2.25 |

## BLACK HERITAGE SERIES

Percy Lavon Julian (1899-1975), Chemist — A2091

### LITHOGRAPHED & ENGRAVED
**1993, Jan. 29**      **Perf. 11**

| 2746 | A2091 | 29c multicolored | .60 | .25 |

## OREGON TRAIL

A2092

**1993, Feb. 12**

| 2747 | A2092 | 29c multicolored | .60 | .25 |
| b. | | Blue omitted | 650.00 | |

## WORLD UNIVERSITY GAMES

A2093

### PHOTOGRAVURE
**1993, Feb. 25**

| 2748 | A2093 | 29c multicolored | .60 | .25 |

## GRACE KELLY (1929-1982)

Actress, Princess of Monaco — A2094

### ENGRAVED
**1993, Mar. 24**

| 2749 | A2094 | 29c deep ultra | .75 | .25 |

See Monaco No. 1851.

## CIRCUS

Clown A2095     Ringmaster A2096

Trapeze Artist A2097     Elephant A2098

### LITHOGRAPHED
**1993, Apr. 6**

| 2750 | A2095 | 29c multicolored | .60 | .25 |
| 2751 | A2096 | 29c multicolored | .60 | .25 |
| 2752 | A2097 | 29c multicolored | .60 | .25 |
| 2753 | A2098 | 29c multicolored | .60 | .25 |
| a. | | Block of 4, #2750-2753 | 2.40 | 1.75 |

## CHEROKEE STRIP LAND RUN, CENTENNIAL

A2099

### LITHOGRAPHED & ENGRAVED
**1993, Apr. 17**

| 2754 | A2099 | 29c multicolored | .60 | .25 |

Imperforates on gummed stamp paper, including gutter pairs and blocks, are proofs from the ABNCo. archives. From the same source also come perforated gutter pairs and blocks, plus imperforates missing the red text and black denomination and "USA." An approved die proof also is recorded. See No. 2754P in Proofs section of the Scott U.S. Specialized Catalogue.

## DEAN ACHESON (1893-1971)

Secretary of State — A2100

### ENGRAVED
**1993, Apr. 21**

| 2755 | A2100 | 29c greenish gray | .60 | .25 |

## SPORTING HORSES

Steeplechase A2101

Thoroughbred Racing — A2102

Harness Racing — A2103

Polo — A2104

### LITHOGRAPHED & ENGRAVED
**1993, May 1**      **Perf. 11x11½**

| 2756 | A2101 | 29c multicolored | .60 | .25 |
| 2757 | A2102 | 29c multicolored | .60 | .25 |
| 2758 | A2103 | 29c multicolored | .60 | .25 |
| 2759 | A2104 | 29c multicolored | .60 | .25 |
| a. | | Block of 4, #2756-2759 | 2.40 | 2.00 |
| b. | | As "a," black (engr.) omitted | 500.00 | |

## GARDEN FLOWERS

Hyacinth A2105

Daffodil A2106

Tulip A2107

Iris A2108

Lilac — A2109

### LITHOGRAPHED & ENGRAVED
### BOOKLET STAMPS
**1993, May 15**      **Perf. 11 Vert.**

| 2760 | A2105 | 29c multicolored | .60 | .25 |
| 2761 | A2106 | 29c multicolored | .60 | .25 |
| 2762 | A2107 | 29c multicolored | .60 | .25 |
| 2763 | A2108 | 29c multicolored | .60 | .25 |
| 2764 | A2109 | 29c multicolored | .60 | .25 |
| a. | | Booklet pane of 5, #2760-2764 | 3.00 | 2.25 |
| b. | | As "a," black (engr.) omitted | 135.00 | |
| c. | | As "a," imperf. | 700.00 | |

## WORLD WAR II

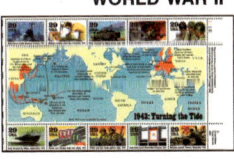

A2110

Designs and events of 1943: a, Destroyers (Allied forces battle German U-boats). b, Military medics treat the wounded. c, Amphibious landing craft on beach (Sicily attacked by Allied forces, July). d, B-24s hit Ploesti refineries, August. e, V-mail delivers letters from home. f, PT boat (Italy invaded by Allies, Sept.). g, Nos. WS7, WS8, savings bonds, (Bonds and stamps help war effort). h, "Willie and Joe" keep spirits high. i, Banner in window (Gold Stars mark World War II losses). j, Marines assault Tarawa, Nov.

Central label is the size of 15 stamps and shows world map with extent of Axis control and Allied operations.

**1993, May 31**      **Perf. 11**

| 2765 | A2110 | Block of 10 | 7.50 | 5.00 |
| a.-j. | | 29c any single | .75 | .40 |

No. 2765 has selvage at left and right and either top or bottom.

## JOE LOUIS (1914-1981)

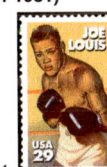

A2111

### LITHOGRAPHED & ENGRAVED
**1993, June 22**

| 2766 | A2111 | 29c multicolored | .60 | .25 |

## AMERICAN MUSIC SERIES
### Oklahoma! Type and

Show Boat — A2112

Porgy & Bess — A2113

My Fair Lady — A2114

### BOOKLET STAMPS
### PHOTOGRAVURE
**Perf. 11 Horiz. on 1 or 2 Sides**
**1993, July 14**

| 2767 | A2112 | 29c multicolored | .60 | .25 |
| 2768 | A2113 | 29c multicolored | .60 | .25 |
| 2769 | A2069 | 29c multicolored | .60 | .25 |
| 2770 | A2114 | 29c multicolored | .60 | .25 |
| a. | | Booklet pane of 4, #2767-2770 | 2.75 | 2.25 |

No. 2769 has smaller design size, brighter colors and shorter inscription than No. 2722, as well as a frameline around the design and other subtle design differences.

Imperforate booklet panes, singly or in multiples, on gummed stamp paper are proofs from the ABNCo. archives. From the same source come imperforate progressive proofs, plus imperforate proofs/essays showing slightly altered designs. See No. 2770aP in Proofs section of the Scott U.S. Specialized Catalogue.

## AMERICAN MUSIC SERIES
### Hank Williams Type and

Patsy Cline — A2115

The Carter Family — A2116

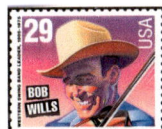

Bob Wills — A2117

### PHOTOGRAVURE
**1993, Sept. 25**      **Perf. 10**

| 2771 | A2070 | 29c multicolored | .75 | .25 |
| 2772 | A2115 | 29c multicolored | .75 | .25 |
| 2773 | A2116 | 29c multicolored | .75 | .25 |
| 2774 | A2117 | 29c multicolored | .75 | .25 |
| a. | | Block or horiz. strip of 4, #2771-2774 | 3.00 | 1.75 |

### Booklet Stamps
**Perf. 11 Horiz. on one or two sides**
**With Black Frameline**

| 2775 | A2070 | 29c multicolored | .60 | .25 |
| 2776 | A2116 | 29c multicolored | .60 | .25 |
| 2777 | A2115 | 29c multicolored | .60 | .25 |
| 2778 | A2117 | 29c multicolored | .60 | .25 |
| a. | | Booklet pane of 4, #2775-2778 | 2.50 | 2.00 |

Inscription at left measures 27½mm on No. 2723, 27mm on No. 2771 and 22mm on No. 2775. No. 2723 shows only two tuning keys on guitar, while No. 2771 shows these two and parts of two others.

Imperforate booklet panes on gummed stamp paper, singly or in multiples, are proofs from the ABNCo. archives. From the same source come panes perfed horiz. but uncut vertically, plus imperforate progressive proofs and other die proof varieties. See No. 2778aP in Proofs section in the Scott U.S. Specialized Catalogue.

## NATIONAL POSTAL MUSEUM

Independence Hall, Benjamin Franklin, Printing Press, Colonial Post Rider — A2118

Pony Express Rider, Civil War Soldier, Concord Stagecoach — A2119

78 UNITED STATES

JN-4H Biplane, Charles Lindbergh, Railway Mail Car, 1931 Model A Ford Mail Truck — A2120

California Gold Rush Miner's Letter, Nos. 39, 295, C3a, C13, Barcode & Circular Date Stamp — A2121

LITHOGRAPHED AND ENGRAVED

**1993, July 30 Tagged *Perf. 11***

**2779** A2118 29c multicolored .60 .25
**2780** A2119 29c multicolored .60 .25
**2781** A2120 29c multicolored .60 .25
**2782** A2121 29c multicolored .60 .25
*a.* Block or strip of 4, #2779-2782 2.40 2.00
*b.* As "a," engr. maroon (USA/29) and black ("My dear...") omitted 2,500.
*c.* As "a," imperf 2,500.

### AMERICAN SIGN LANGUAGE

A2122

A2123

PHOTOGRAVURE

**1993, Sept. 20 *Perf. 11½***

**2783** A2122 29c multicolored .60 .25
**2784** A2123 29c multicolored .60 .25
*a.* Pair, #2783-2784 1.20 .75

### CLASSIC BOOKS

A2124

A2125

A2126

A2127

Designs: No. 2785, Rebecca of Sunnybrook Farm, by Kate Douglas Wiggin. No. 2786, Little House on the Prairie, by Laura Ingalls Wilder. No. 2787, The Adventures of Huckleberry Finn, by Mark Twain. No. 2788, Little Women, by Louisa May Alcott.

LITHOGRAPHED & ENGRAVED

**1993, Oct. 23 *Perf. 11***

**2785** A2124 29c multicolored .60 .25
**2786** A2125 29c multicolored .60 .25
**2787** A2126 29c multicolored .60 .25
**2788** A2127 29c multicolored .60 .25
*a.* Block or horiz. strip of 4, #2785-2788 2.40 2.00

Imperforates on gummed stamp paper, including gutter pairs and blocks, are proofs from the ABNCo. archives. See No. 2788aP in Proofs section of the Scott U.S. Specialized Catalogue.

### CHRISTMAS

Madonna and Child in a Landscape, by Giovanni Battista Cima — A2128

Jack-in-the-Box A2129

Red-Nosed Reindeer A2130

Snowman A2131

Toy Soldier Blowing Horn A2132

**1993, Oct. 21**

**2789** A2128 29c multicolored .60 .25

**Booklet Stamp**

**Size: 18x25mm**

***Perf. 11½x11 on 2 or 3 Sides***

**2790** A2128 29c multicolored .60 .25
*a.* Booklet pane of 4 2.40 1.75
*b.* Imperf., pair —
*c.* As "a," imperf —

Nos. 2789-2790 have numerous design differences.

**1993 *Perf. 11½***

PHOTOGRAVURE

**2791** A2129 29c multicolored .60 .25
**2792** A2130 29c multicolored .60 .25
**2793** A2131 29c multicolored .60 .25
**2794** A2132 29c multicolored .60 .25
*a.* Block or strip of 4, #2791-2794 2.40 2.00

**Booklet Stamps**

**Size: 18x21mm**

***Perf. 11x10 on 2 or 3 Sides***

**2795** A2132 29c multicolored .85 .25
**2796** A2131 29c multicolored .85 .25
**2797** A2130 29c multicolored .85 .25
**2798** A2129 29c multicolored .85 .25
*a.* Booklet pane, 3 each #2795-2796, 2 each #2797-2798 8.50 4.00
*b.* Booklet pane, 3 each #2797-2798, 2 each #2795-2796 8.50 4.00
*c.* Block of 4, #2795-2798 3.40 1.75

**Self-Adhesive**

**Size: 19½x26½mm**

***Die Cut***

**2799** A2131 29c multicolored .75 .25
*a.* Coil with plate # V1111111 — 6.00
*b.* Horiz. coil strip of 4, #2799-2802 3.00
**2800** A2132 29c multicolored .75 .25
**2801** A2129 29c multicolored .75 .25
**2802** A2130 29c multicolored .75 .25
*a.* Booklet pane, 3 each #2799-2802 9.00
*b.* Block of 4, #2799-2802 3.00

Except for No. 2799a with plate number, coil stamps are indistinguishable from booklet stamps once they are removed from the backing paper.

**Size: 17x20mm**

**2803** A2131 29c multicolored .60 .25
*a.* Booklet pane of 18 11.00

Snowman on Nos. 2793, 2799 has three buttons and seven snowflakes beneath nose (placement differs on both stamps). No. 2796 has two buttons and five snowflakes beneath nose. No. 2803 has two orange buttons and four snowflakes beneath nose.

Issued: #2791-2798, 10/21; #2799-2803, 10/28.

### MARIANA ISLANDS

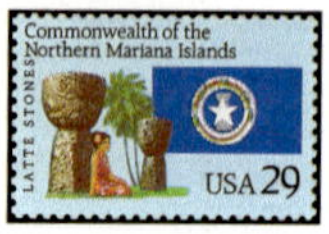


A2133

LITHOGRAPHED AND ENGRAVED

**1993, Nov. 4 *Perf. 11***

**2804** A2133 29c multicolored .60 .25

### COLUMBUS' LANDING IN PUERTO RICO, 500th ANNIVERSARY

A2134

PHOTOGRAVURE

**1993, Nov. 19 *Perf. 11.2***

**2805** A2134 29c multicolored .60 .25

### AIDS AWARENESS

A2135

**1993, Dec. 1**

**2806** A2135 29c black & red .60 .25
*a.* Perf. 11 vert. on 1 or 2 sides, from bklt. pane .70 .25
*b.* As "a," booklet pane of 5 3.50 2.00

### WINTER OLYMPICS

Slalom A2136

Luge A2137

Ice Dancing A2138

Cross-Country Skiing A2139

Ice Hockey — A2140

LITHOGRAPHED

**1994, Jan. 6**

**2807** A2136 29c multicolored .60 .25
**2808** A2137 29c multicolored .60 .25
**2809** A2138 29c multicolored .60 .25
**2810** A2139 29c multicolored .60 .25
**2811** A2140 29c multicolored .60 .25
*a.* Strip of 5, #2807-2811 3.00 2.50

### EDWARD R. MURROW, JOURNALIST (1908-65)

A2141

ENGRAVED

**1994, Jan. 21**

**2812** A2141 29c brown .60 .25

### LOVE

A2142

A2143

A2144

Booklet Stamps

LITHOGRAPHED & ENGRAVED

**1994 *Die Cut***

**Self-adhesive**

**2813** A2142 29c multicolored .60 .25
*a.* Booklet pane of 18 11.00
*b.* Coil with plate # B1 — 5.00

Except for No. 2813b with plate number, coil stamps are indistinguishable from booklet stamps once they are removed from the backing paper.

PHOTOGRAVURE

***Perf. 10.9x11.1 on 2 or 3 sides***

**2814** A2143 29c multicolored .60 .25
*a.* Booklet pane of 10 6.00 3.50
*b.* Imperf, pair —
*d.* As "a," imperf. —

Horiz. pairs, imperf between, are printer's waste.

No. 2814 was issued in booklets only.

LITHOGRAPHED & ENGRAVED

***Perf. 11.1***

**2814C** A2143 29c multicolored .70 .25

Size of No. 2814C is 20x28mm. No. 2814 is 18x24½mm.

PHOTOGRAVURE & ENGRAVED

***Perf. 11.2***

**2815** A2144 52c multicolored 1.00 .25

Issued: No. 2813, Jan. 27; Nos. 2814-2815, Feb. 14; No. 2814C, June 11.

### BLACK HERITAGE SERIES

Dr. Allison Davis (1902-83), Social Anthropologist, Educator — A2145

ENGRAVED

**1994, Feb. 1 *Perf. 11.2***

**2816** A2145 29c red brown & brown .60 .25

### CHINESE NEW YEAR

Year of the Dog — A2146

PHOTOGRAVURE

**1994, Feb. 5**

**2817** A2146 29c multicolored .80 .25

See Nos. 3895k, 3997k.

### BUFFALO SOLDIERS

A2147

LITHOGRAPHED & ENGRAVED

**1994, Apr. 22 *Perf. 11.5x11.2***

**2818** A2147 29c multicolored .60 .25
*a.* Double impression (second impression light) of red brown (engr. inscriptions) —

### SILENT SCREEN STARS

Rudolph Valentino (1895-1926) A2148

Clara Bow (1905-65) A2149

# UNITED STATES

Charlie Chaplin (1889-1977) A2150

John Gilbert (1895-1936) A2152

Harold Lloyd (1894-1971) A2154

Theda Bara (1885-1955) A2156

Lon Chaney (1883-1930) A2151

Zasu Pitts (1898-1963) A2153

Keystone Cops A2155

Buster Keaton (1895-1966) A2157

**1994, Apr. 27**    Perf. 11.2
| | | | |
|---|---|---|---|
| 2819 | A2148 | 29c red, blk & brt vio | 1.10 .30 |
| 2820 | A2149 | 29c red, blk & brt vio | 1.10 .30 |
| 2821 | A2150 | 29c red, blk & brt vio | 1.10 .30 |
| 2822 | A2151 | 29c red, blk & brt vio | 1.10 .30 |
| 2823 | A2152 | 29c red, blk & brt vio | 1.10 .30 |
| 2824 | A2153 | 29c red, blk & brt vio | 1.10 .30 |
| 2825 | A2154 | 29c red, blk & brt vio | 1.10 .30 |
| 2826 | A2155 | 29c red, blk & brt vio | 1.10 .30 |
| 2827 | A2156 | 29c red, blk & brt vio | 1.10 .30 |
| 2828 | A2157 | 29c red, blk & brt vio | 1.10 .30 |
| a. | Block of 10, #2819-2828 | | 11.00 5.00 |
| b. | As "a," black (litho.) omitted | | — |
| c. | As "a," blk, red & brt vio (litho.) omitted | | — |

## GARDEN FLOWERS

Lily A2158

Gladiola A2160

Zinnia A2159

Marigold A2161

Rose — A2162

**1994, Apr. 28**    Perf. 10.9 Vert.
**Booklet Stamps**
| | | | |
|---|---|---|---|
| 2829 | A2158 | 29c multicolored | .60 .25 |
| 2830 | A2159 | 29c multicolored | .60 .25 |
| 2831 | A2160 | 29c multicolored | .60 .25 |
| 2832 | A2161 | 29c multicolored | .60 .25 |
| 2833 | A2162 | 29c multicolored | .60 .25 |
| a. | Booklet pane of 5, #2829-2833 | | 3.00 2.25 |
| b. | As "a," imperf | | 200.00 |
| c. | As "a," black (engr.) omitted | | 125.00 |

## 1994 WORLD CUP SOCCER CHAMPIONSHIPS

A2163

A2163a

A2164

A2165

Design: 40c, Soccer player, diff.

**PHOTOGRAVURE**
**1994, May 26**    Perf. 11.1
| | | | |
|---|---|---|---|
| 2834 | A2163 | 29c multicolored | .60 .25 |
| 2835 | A2163a | 40c multicolored | .80 .25 |
| 2836 | A2164 | 50c multicolored | 1.00 .25 |
| | Nos. 2834-2836 (3) | | 2.40 .75 |

**Souvenir Sheet of 3**
| | | | |
|---|---|---|---|
| 2837 | A2165 | #a.-#c. | 4.50 3.00 |

No. 2837c has a portion of the yellow map in the LR corner.

## WORLD WAR II

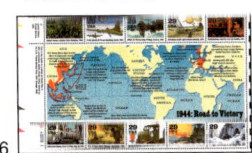
A2166

Designs and events of 1944: a, Allied forces retake New Guinea. b, P-51s escort B-17s on bombing raids. c, Troops running from landing craft (Allies in Normandy, D-Day, June 6). d, Airborne units spearhead attacks. e, Officer at periscope (Submarines shorten war in Pacific). f, Parade (Allies free Rome, June 4; Paris, Aug. 25).
g, Soldier firing flamethrower (US troops clear Saipan bunkers). h, Red Ball Express speeds vital supplies. i, Battleship firing main battery (Battle for Leyte Gulf, Oct. 23-26). j, Soldiers in snow (Bastogne and Battle of the Bulge, Dec.).
Central label is size of 15 stamps and shows world map with extent of Axis control and Allied operations.
Illustration reduced.

**LITHOGRAPHED & ENGRAVED**
**1994, June 6**    Perf. 10.9
| | | | |
|---|---|---|---|
| 2838 | A2166 | Block of 10 | 17.00 10.00 |
| a.-j. | 29c any single | | 1.70 .50 |

No. 2838 has selvage at left and right and either top or bottom.

## NORMAN ROCKWELL

A2167

A2168

**1994, July 1**    Perf. 10.9x11.1
| | | | |
|---|---|---|---|
| 2839 | A2167 | 29c multicolored | .60 .25 |

**Souvenir Sheet**
**LITHOGRAPHED**
| | | | |
|---|---|---|---|
| 2840 | A2168 | Sheet of 4 | 4.50 2.75 |
| a. | 50c Freedom From Want | | 1.10 .65 |
| b. | 50c Freedom From Fear | | 1.10 .65 |
| c. | 50c Freedom of Speech | | 1.10 .65 |
| d. | 50c Freedom of Worship | | 1.10 .65 |

## Moon Landing, 25th Anniv.

A2169

A2170

**Miniature Sheet**
**1994, July 20**    Perf. 11.2x11.1
| | | | |
|---|---|---|---|
| 2841 | A2169 | 29c Sheet of 12 | 10.50 |
| a. | Single stamp | | .85 .60 |

**LITHOGRAPHED & ENGRAVED**
Perf. 10.7x11.1
| | | | |
|---|---|---|---|
| 2842 | A2170 | $9.95 multicolored | 20.00 16.00 |

## LOCOMOTIVES

Hudson's General — A2171

McQueen's Jupiter — A2172

Eddy's No. 242 — A2173

Ely's No. 10 — A2174

Buchanan's No. 999 — A2175

**PHOTOGRAVURE**
**1994, July 28**    Perf. 11 Horiz.
**Booklet Stamps**
| | | | |
|---|---|---|---|
| 2843 | A2171 | 29c multicolored | .75 .25 |
| 2844 | A2172 | 29c multicolored | .75 .25 |
| 2845 | A2173 | 29c multicolored | .75 .25 |
| 2846 | A2174 | 29c multicolored | .75 .25 |
| 2847 | A2175 | 29c multicolored | .75 .25 |
| a. | Booklet pane of 5, #2843-2847 | | 3.75 2.00 |
| b. | As "a," imperf. | | 2,500. |

## GEORGE MEANY, LABOR LEADER (1894-1980)

A2176

**ENGRAVED**
**1994, Aug. 16**    Perf. 11.1x11
| | | | |
|---|---|---|---|
| 2848 | A2176 | 29c blue | .60 .25 |

## AMERICAN MUSIC SERIES
### Popular Singers

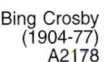
Al Jolson (1886-1950) A2177

Bing Crosby (1904-77) A2178

Ethel Waters (1896-1977) A2179

Nat "King" Cole (1919-65) A2180

Ethel Merman (1908-84) A2181

### Jazz Singers

Bessie Smith (1894-1937) A2182

Muddy Waters (1915-83) A2183

Billie Holiday (1915-59) A2184

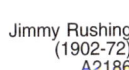
Robert Johnson (1911-38) A2185

Jimmy Rushing (1902-72) A2186

"Ma" Rainey (1886-1939) A2187

Mildred Bailey (1907-51) A2188

79

80 UNITED STATES

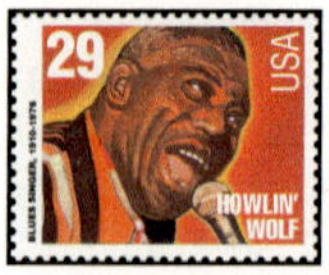

Howlin' Wolf (1910-76) A2189

PHOTOGRAVURE

**1994, Sept. 1** ***Perf. 10.1x10.2***

| | | | |
|---|---|---|---|
| 2849 A2177 29c multicolored | .85 | .25 |
| 2850 A2178 29c multicolored | .85 | .25 |
| 2851 A2179 29c multicolored | .85 | .25 |
| 2852 A2180 29c multicolored | .85 | .25 |
| 2853 A2181 29c multicolored | .85 | .25 |
| *a.* Vert. strip of 5, #2849-2853 | 4.25 | 2.00 |
| *b.* Pane of 20, imperf | *10,000.* | |

**1994, Sept. 17** ***Perf. 11x10.8***

LITHOGRAPHED

| | | |
|---|---|---|
| 2854 A2182 29c multicolored | 1.50 | .25 |
| 2855 A2183 29c multicolored | 1.50 | .25 |
| 2856 A2184 29c multicolored | 1.50 | .25 |
| 2857 A2185 29c multicolored | 1.50 | .25 |
| 2858 A2186 29c multicolored | 1.50 | .25 |
| 2859 A2187 29c multicolored | 1.50 | .25 |
| 2860 A2188 29c multicolored | 1.50 | .25 |
| 2861 A2189 29c multicolored | 1.50 | .25 |
| *a.* Block of 10, #2854-2861 +2 additional stamps | 15.00 | 4.50 |

**LITERARY ARTS SERIES**

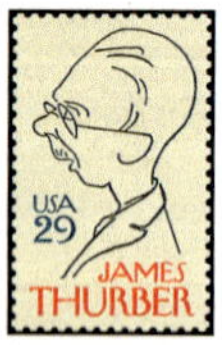

James Thurber (1894-1961) — A2190

LITHOGRAPHED & ENGRAVED

**1994, Sept. 10** ***Perf. 11***

| | | |
|---|---|---|
| 2862 A2190 29c multicolored | .60 | .25 |

**WONDERS OF THE SEA**

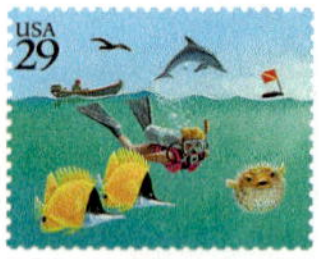

Diver, Motorboat A2191

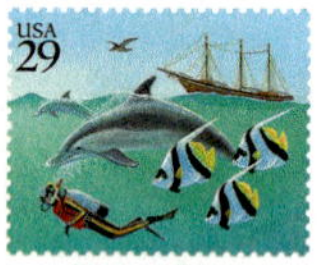

Diver, Ship A2192

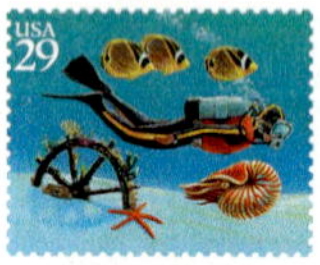

Diver, Ship's Wheel — A2193

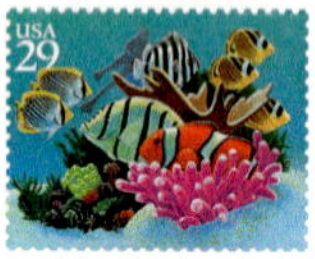

Diver, Coral — A2194

LITHOGRAPHED

**1994, Oct. 3** ***Perf. 11x10.9***

| | | |
|---|---|---|
| 2863 A2191 29c multicolored | .75 | .25 |
| 2864 A2192 29c multicolored | .75 | .25 |
| 2865 A2193 29c multicolored | .75 | .25 |
| 2866 A2194 29c multicolored | .75 | .25 |
| *a.* Block of 4, #2863-2866 | 3.00 | 1.50 |
| *b.* As "a," imperf | *350.00* | |

**CRANES**

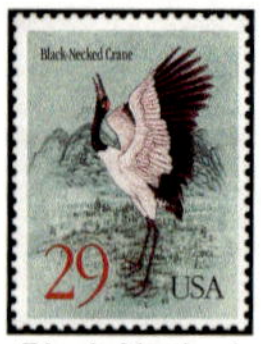

Black-Necked A2195

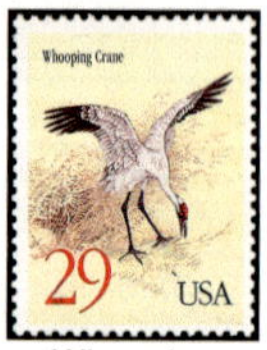

Whooping A2196

LITHOGRAPHED & ENGRAVED

**1994, Oct. 9** ***Perf. 10.8x11***

| | | |
|---|---|---|
| 2867 A2195 29c multicolored | .70 | .25 |
| 2868 A2196 29c multicolored | .70 | .25 |
| *a.* Pair, #2867-2868 | 1.40 | .75 |
| *b.* As "a," black & magenta (engr.) omitted | *1,250.* | |
| *c.* As "a," double impression of engr. black (Birds' names and "USA") & magenta ("29") | *3,000.* | |
| *d.* As "a," double impression of engr. black ("USA") & magenta ("29") | *3,000.* | |

See People's Republic of China Nos. 2528-2529.

**LEGENDS OF THE WEST**

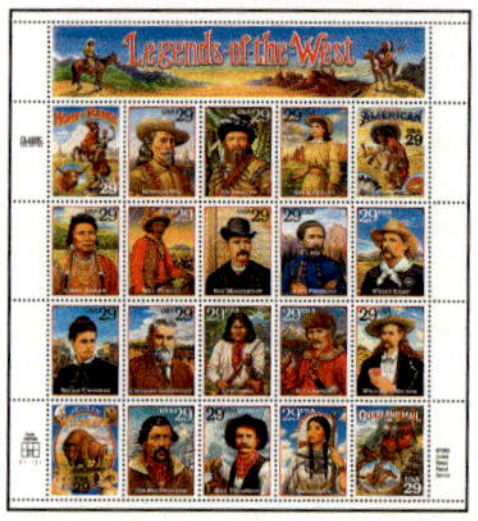

A2197

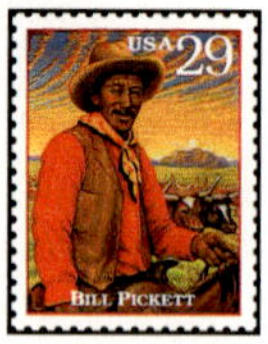

g. Bill Pickett (1870-1932) (Revised)

Designs: a, Home on the Range. b, Buffalo Bill Cody (1846-1917). c, Jim Bridger (1804-81). d, Annie Oakley (1860-1926). e, Native American Culture. f, Chief Joseph (c. 1840-1904). h, Bat Masterson (1853-1921). i, John C. Fremont (1813-90). j, Wyatt Earp (1848-1929). k, Nellie Cashman (c. 1849-1925). l, Charles Goodnight (1826-1929). m, Geronimo (1823-1909). n, Kit Carson (1809-68). o, Wild Bill Hickok (1837-76). p, Western Wildlife. q, Jim Beckwourth (c. 1798-1866). r, Bill Tilghman (1854-1924). s, Sacagawea (c. 1787-1812). t, Overland Mail.

PHOTOGRAVURE

**1994, Oct. 18** ***Perf. 10.1x10***

| | | |
|---|---|---|
| 2869 A2197 Pane of 20 | 15.00 | 10.00 |
| *a.-t.* 29c any single | .75 | .50 |
| *u.* As No. 2869, a.-e. imperf. f.-j. part perf. | — | |

**LEGENDS OF THE WEST (Recalled)**

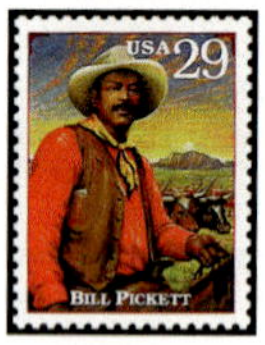

g. Bill Pickett (Recalled)

Nos. 2870b-2870d, 2870f-2870o, 2870q-2870s have a frameline around the vignette that is half the width of the frameline on similar stamps in No. 2869. Other design differences may exist.

**1994**

| | | |
|---|---|---|
| 2870 A2197 29c Pane of 20 | 125.00 | — |

150,000 panes of No. 2870 were made available through a drawing. Panes were delivered in an envelope. Value is for pane without envelope. Panes with envelopes sell for somewhat more.

**CHRISTMAS**

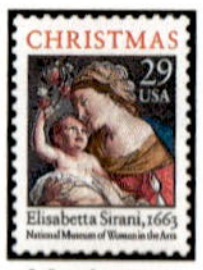

Madonna and Child, by Elisabetta Sirani A2200

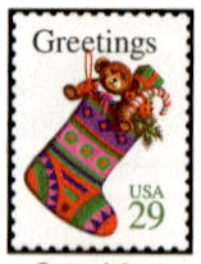

Stocking A2201

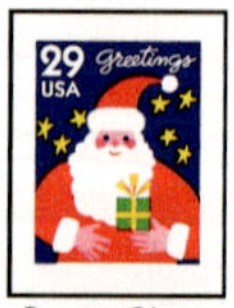

Santa Claus A2202

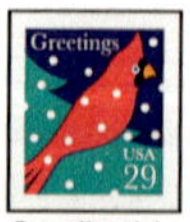

Cardinal in Snow A2203

LITHOGRAPHED & ENGRAVED

**1994, Oct. 20** ***Perf. 11¼***

| | | |
|---|---|---|
| 2871 A2200 29c multi | .60 | .25 |

**BOOKLET STAMP**

***Perf. 9¾x11***

| | | |
|---|---|---|
| 2871A A2200 29c multi | .60 | .25 |
| *b.* Booklet pane of 10 | 6.25 | 3.50 |
| *c.* Imperf, pair | *350.00* | |
| *d.* As "b," imperf | — | |

LITHOGRAPHED

***Perf. 11¼***

| | | |
|---|---|---|
| 2872 A2201 29c multi | .60 | .25 |
| *a.* Booklet pane of 20 | 12.50 | 6.00 |
| *b.* Imperf., pair | — | |
| *c.* Vert. pair, imperf. horiz. | — | |
| *d.* Quadruple impression of black, triple impression of blue, double impressions of red and yellow, green normal | *900.00* | |
| *e.* Vert. pair, imperf. between | *125.00* | |
| *f.* As "a," imperf. | — | |

PHOTOGRAVURE

**BOOKLET STAMPS**

**Self-Adhesive**

***Die Cut***

| | | |
|---|---|---|
| 2873 A2202 29c multi | .70 | .25 |
| *a.* Booklet pane of 12 | 8.50 | |
| *b.* Coil with plate #V1111 | — | 5.75 |

Except for No. 2873b with plate number, coil stamps are indistinguishable from booklet stamps once they are removed from the backing paper.

| | | |
|---|---|---|
| 2874 A2203 29c multi | .60 | .25 |
| *a.* Booklet pane of 18 | 11.00 | |

**BUREAU OF ENGRAVING & PRINTING**

Souvenir Sheet

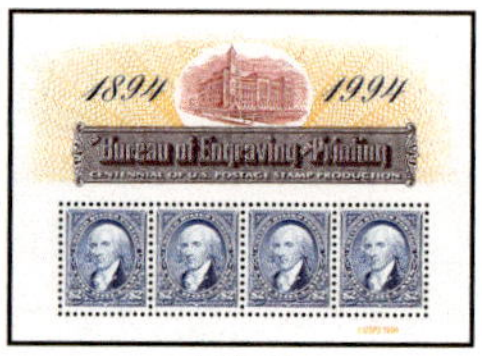

A2204

LITHOGRAPHED & ENGRAVED

**1994, Nov. 3** ***Perf. 11***

| | | |
|---|---|---|
| 2875 A2204 $2 Pane of 4 | 16.00 | 13.50 |
| *a.* Single stamp | 4.00 | 2.00 |
| *b.* Pane of 4 with double impression of the brown lettering panel | *1,000.* | — |

The double impression is clear, but may be seen best in the scrolls at lower right.

**CHINESE NEW YEAR**

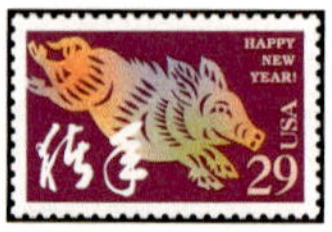

Year of the Boar — A2205

PHOTOGRAVURE

**1994, Dec. 30** ***Perf. 11.2x11.1***

| | | |
|---|---|---|
| 2876 A2205 29c multicolored | .70 | .25 |

See Nos. 3895l, 3997l.

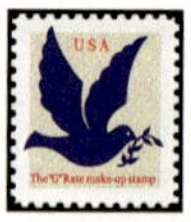

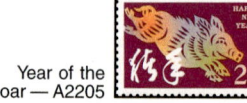

A2206

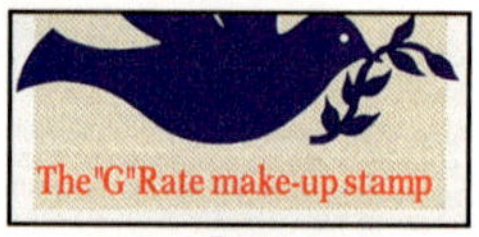

Type I

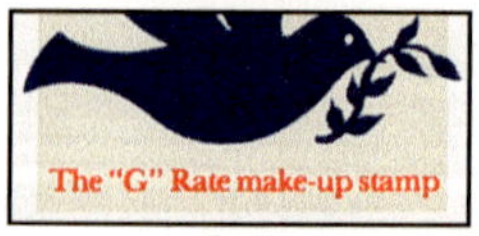

Type II

Inscriptions on No. 2877 are in a thin typeface. Those on No. 2878 are in heavy, bold type.

LITHOGRAPHED

***Perf. 11x10.8***

**1994, Dec. 13** **Untagged**

| | | |
|---|---|---|
| 2877 A2206 (3c) tan, brt bl & red, type I | .30 | .25 |
| *a.* Imperf., pair | *115.00* | |
| *b.* Double impression of red | *175.00* | |

No. 2877 imperf and with blue omitted is known from printer's waste.

***Perf. 10.8x10.9***

**Untagged**

| | | |
|---|---|---|
| 2878 A2206 (3c) tan, dk bl & red, type II | .30 | .25 |

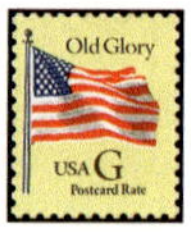

A2207

PHOTOGRAVURE

***Perf. 11.2x11.1***

| | | |
|---|---|---|
| 2879 A2207 (20c) black "G," yel & multi | .40 | .25 |
| *a.* Imperf., pair | — | |

***Perf. 11x10.9***

| | | |
|---|---|---|
| 2880 A2207 (32c) red "G," yel & multi | .75 | .25 |

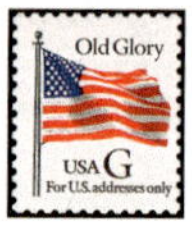

A2208

***Perf. 11.2x11.1***

| | | |
|---|---|---|
| 2881 A2208 (32c) black "G" & multi | 1.25 | .25 |
| *a.* Booklet pane of 10 | 12.50 | 5.00 |

***Perf. 11x10.9***

| | | |
|---|---|---|
| 2882 A2208 (32c) red "G" & multi | .60 | .25 |

Distance on #2882 from bottom of red G to top of flag immediately above is 13¾mm.

**BOOKLET STAMPS**

***Perf. 10x9.9 on 2 or 3 Sides***

| | | |
|---|---|---|
| 2883 A2208 (32c) black "G" & multi | .65 | .25 |
| *a.* Booklet pane of 10 | 6.50 | 3.75 |

***Perf. 10.9 on 2 or 3 Sides***

| | | |
|---|---|---|
| 2884 A2208 (32c) blue "G" & multi | .65 | .25 |
| *a.* Booklet pane of 10 | 6.50 | 3.75 |
| *b.* As "a," imperf | *4,500.* | |
| *c.* Horiz. pair, imperf. btwn. due to miscut | — | |
| *d.* Horiz. pair, imperf. vert. | — | |

***Perf. 11x10.9 on 2 or 3 Sides***

| | | |
|---|---|---|
| 2885 A2208 (32c) red "G" & multi | .90 | .25 |
| *a.* Booklet pane of 10 | 9.00 | 4.50 |
| *b.* Horiz. pair, imperf vert. | *750.00* | |
| *c.* Horiz. pair, imperf. btwn., in #2885a with foldover | — | |

Distance on #2885 from bottom of red G to top of flag immediately above is 13½mm. See note below #2882.

No. 2885c resulted from a paper foldover after perforating and before cutting into panes.

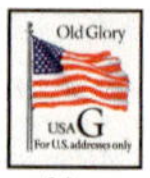

No. 2886

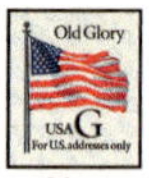

No. 2887

***Die Cut***

***Self-Adhesive***

| | | |
|---|---|---|
| 2886 A2208 (32c) gray, bl, lt bl, red & blk | .70 | .25 |
| *a.* Booklet pane of 18 | 12.50 | |
| *b.* Coil with plate # V11111 | — | 9.50 |

No. 2886 is printed on prephosphored paper that is opaque, thicker and brighter than that of No. 2887 and has only a small number of blue shading dots in the white stripes immediately below the flag's blue field.

Except for No. 2886b with plate number, coil stamps are indistinguishable from booklet stamps once they are removed from the backing paper.

| | | |
|---|---|---|
| 2887 A2208 (32c) black, blue & red | .70 | .25 |
| *a.* Booklet pane of 18 | 12.50 | |

No. 2887 has noticeable blue shading in the white stripes immediately below the blue field and has overall tagging. The paper is translucent, thinner and duller than No. 2886.

# UNITED STATES

A2209

## COIL STAMPS
### Perf. 9.8 Vert.

| 2888 | A2209 | (25c) black "G" | .75 | .50 |
| 2889 | A2208 | (32c) black "G" | 1.50 | .25 |
| a. | | Imperf., pair | 250.00 | |
| 2890 | A2208 | (32c) blue "G" | .65 | .25 |
| 2891 | A2208 | (32c) red "G" | .85 | .25 |

### Rouletted 9.8 Vert.

| 2892 | A2208 | (32c) red "G" | .75 | .25 |

A2210

## PHOTOGRAVURE
**1995 Untagged**  Perf. 9.8 Vert.

| 2893 | A2210 | (5c) green & multi | .50 | .25 |

Flag Over Porch — A2212

**1995, May 19**  Perf. 10.4

| 2897 | A2212 | 32c multicolored | .75 | .25 |
| a. | | Imperf., vert. pair | 55.00 | |

See Nos. 2913-2916, 2920-2921, 3133.

Butte — A2217

## COIL STAMPS
**1995-97**  Perf. 9.8 Vert.
**Untagged (Nos. 2902-2912B)**
**Self-Adhesive (#2902B)**

| 2902 | A2217 | (5c) yel, red & bl | .30 | .25 |
| a. | | Imperf., pair | 350.00 | |

### Serpentine Die Cut 11.5 Vert.
**Untagged**

| 2902B | A2217 | (5c) yel, red & bl ('96) | .35 | .25 |

### Perf. 9.8 Vert.

Mountain — A2218

### Self-Adhesive (#2904A-2904B)
**Untagged**

| 2903 | A2218 | (5c) purple & multi ('96) | .30 | .25 |

Letters of inscription "USA NONPROFIT ORG." outlined in purple on No. 2903. No. 2903 has purple "1996" at left bottom.

**Untagged**

| 2904 | A2218 | (5c) blue & multi ('96) | .30 | .25 |
| c. | | Imperf., pair | 250.00 | |

Letters of inscription have no outline on No. 2904. No. 2904 has blue "1996" at bottom left.

### Serpentine Die Cut 11.2 Vert.
**Untagged**

| 2904A | A2218 | (5c) purple & multi ('96) | .40 | .25 |

### Serpentine Die Cut 9.8 Vert.
**Untagged**

| 2904B | A2218 | (5c) purple & multi ('97) | .25 | .25 |

Letters of inscription outlined in purple on No. 2904B, not outlined on No. 2904A. No. 2904A has large purple "1996" at bottom left. No. 2904B has small purple "1997" at bottom left.

Auto — A2220

### Self-Adhesive (#2906-2907)
**Perf. 9.8 Vert.**
**Untagged**

| 2905 | A2220 | (10c) blk, red brn & brn, small "1995" date | .30 | .25 |
| a. | | Medium "1995" date | .35 | .25 |
| b. | | Large "1995" date ('96) | .60 | .25 |
| c. | | As "b," brown omitted, P#S33 single | 400.00 | |

Date on 2905 is approximately 1.9mm long, on No. 2905a 2mm long, and on No. 2905b 2.1mm long.

### Serpentine Die Cut 11.5 Vert.
**Untagged**

| 2906 | A2220 | (10c) blk, brn & red brn ('96) | .50 | .25 |

**Untagged**

| 2907 | A1957 | (10c) gold & multi ('96) | .75 | .25 |

Auto Tail Fin — A2223

### Self-Adhesive (#2910)
**Perf. 9.8 Vert.**
**Untagged**

| 2908 | A2223 | (15c) dk org yel & multi | .30 | .30 |

No. 2908 has "1995" in blue and has dark, bold colors, heavy shading lines and heavily shaded chrome.

**Untagged**

| 2909 | A2223 | (15c) buff & multi | .30 | .30 |

No. 2909 has "1995" in black and has shinier chrome, more subdued colors and finer details than No. 2908.

### Serpentine Die Cut 11.5 Vert.
**Untagged**

| 2910 | A2223 | (15c) buff & multi ('96) | .30 | .30 |

Juke Box — A2225

### Perf. 9.8 Vert.
**Untagged**

| 2911 | A2225 | (25c) dk red, dk yel grn & multi | .50 | .50 |
| a. | | Imperf. pair | 400.00 | |

No. 2911 has dark, saturated colors and dark blue lines in the music selection board. See No. 3132.

**Untagged**

| 2912 | A2225 | (25c) brt org red, brt yel grn & multi | .50 | .50 |

No. 2912 has bright colors, less shading and light blue lines in the music selection board.

### Serpentine Die Cut 11.5 Vert.
**Untagged**
**Self-Adhesive**

| 2912A | A2225 | (25c) brt org red, brt yel grn & multi ('96) | .50 | .50 |

### Serpentine Die Cut 9.8 Vert.
**Untagged**

| 2912B | A2225 | (25c) dk red, dk yel grn & multi ('97) | .75 | .50 |

### Perf. 9.8 Vert.

| 2913 | A2212 | 32c bl, tan, brn, red & lt bl | .65 | .25 |
| a. | | Imperf., pair | 30.00 | |

No. 2913 has pronounced light blue shading in the flag and red "1995" at left bottom. See No. 3133.

| 2914 | A2212 | 32c bl, yel brn, red & gray | .80 | .25 |

No. 2914 has pale gray shading in the flag and blue "1995" at left bottom.

### Serpentine Die Cut 8.7 Vert.
**Self-Adhesive (#2915-2915D)**

| 2915 | A2212 | 32c multi | 1.25 | .30 |

No. 2915 has blue "1995" at bottom left.

### Serpentine Die Cut 9.8 Vert.

| 2915A | A2212 | 32c dk bl, tan, brn, red & lt bl ('96) | .65 | .25 |
| h. | | Die cutting omitted, pair | 32.50 | |
| i. | | Tan omitted | 30.00 | |
| j. | | Double die cutting | 30.00 | |

No. 2915A has red "1996" at left bottom. Sky on No. 3133 shows color gradation at LR, not on No. 2915A.
On No. 2915Ai all other colors except brown are severely shifted.
On No. 2915Aj, the second die cutting is a different gauge than the normal 9.8.

Examples of a self-adhesive Flag Over Porch coil stamp resembling Scott 2915C with a "1995" year date are test stamps and listed in that section of this catalog.

### Serpentine Die Cut 11.5 Vert.

| 2915B | A2212 | 32c dk bl, tan, brn, red & lt bl ('96) | 1.00 | .90 |

### Serpentine Die Cut 10.9 Vert.

| 2915C | A2212 | 32c dk bl, tan, brn, red & lt bl | | |

Flag Over Field — A2230

### Self-Adhesive (#2919-2921)
**Die Cut**

| 2919 | A2230 | 32c multi | .65 | .25 |
| a. | | Booklet pane of 18 | 12.00 | |
| b. | | Vert. pair, die cutting omitted btwn. | — | |

### Serpentine Die Cut 8.7 on 2, 3 or 4 Adjacent Sides

| 2920 | A2212 | 32c multi, dated blue "1995" | .65 | .25 |
| a. | | Booklet pane of 20+label | 13.00 | |
| b. | | Small date | 4.00 | .35 |
| c. | | As "b," booklet pane of 20+label | 80.00 | |
| f. | | As No. 2920, pane of 15+label | 9.75 | |
| g. | | As "a," partial pane of 10, 3 stamps and parts of 7 stamps printed on backing liner | | |
| h. | | As No. 2920, booklet pane of 15 | 47.50 | |
| i. | | As No. 2920, die cutting omitted, pair | — | |
| j. | | Dark blue omitted (from No. 2920a) | 2,100. | |
| k. | | Vert. pair, die cutting missing btwn., three examples in No. 2920a with shift in die cutting (PS) | — | |

Date on No. 2920 is nearly twice as large as date on No. 2920b. No. 2920f comes in various configurations.

No. 2920h is a pane of 16 with one stamp removed. The missing stamp is the lower right stamp in the pane or (more rarely) the upper left stamp. No. 2920h cannot be made from No. 2920f, a pane of 15 + label. The label is located in the sixth or seventh row of the pane and is die cut. If the label is removed, an impression of the die cutting appears on the backing paper.

### Serpentine Die Cut 11.3 on 3 sides

| 2920D | A2212 | 32c multi, dated blue "1996" ('96) | .80 | .25 |
| e. | | Booklet pane of 10 | 8.00 | |
| f. | | As "e," die cutting omitted | | |

### Serpentine Die Cut 9.8 on 2 or 3 Adjacent Sides

| 2921 | A2212 | 32c dk bl, tan, brn, red & lt bl, dated red "1996" ('96) | .90 | .25 |
| a. | | Booklet pane of 10, dated red "1996" | 9.00 | |
| b. | | As No. 2921, dated red "1997," Jan. 24, 1997 | 1.20 | .25 |
| c. | | As "a," dated red "1997" | 12.00 | |
| d. | | Booklet pane of 5 + label, dated red "1997," Jan. 24, 1997 | 8.00 | |
| e. | | As "a," die cutting omitted | 200.00 | |

Issued: #2902, 2905, 3/10/95; #2908-2909, 2911-2912, 2919, 3/17/95; #2915, 2920, 4/18/95; #2897, 2913-2914, 2916, 5/19/95; #2920D, 1/20/96; #2904A, 2012B, 2015D, 2921b-2921d, 1/24/97; #2903-2904, 3/16/96; #2915A, 5/21/97; #2907, 2921, 5/21/96; #2902B, 2904A, 2906, 2910, 2912A, 2915B, 6/15/96; #2915C, 5/21/96.

See Nos. 3132-3133.

**Scott values for used self-adhesive stamps are for examples either on piece or off piece.**

## GREAT AMERICANS ISSUE

Milton S. Hershey
A2248

Cal Farley
A2249

Henry R. Luce
A2250

Lila and DeWitt Wallace
A2251

Ruth Benedict
A2253

Alice Hamilton, MD
A2255

Justin S. Morrill
A2256

Mary Breckinridge
A2257

Alice Paul — A2258

82 UNITED STATES

**ENGRAVED**

**1995-99**

**Self-Adhesive (#2941-2942)**

**Perf. 11.2, Serpentine Die Cut 11.7x11.5 (#2941-2942)**

| | | | | |
|---|---|---|---|---|
| 2933 | A2248 | 32c brown | .75 | .25 |
| 2934 | A2249 | 32c green ('96) | .75 | .25 |
| 2935 | A2250 | 32c lake ('98) | .65 | .35 |
| 2936 | A2251 | 32c gray blue ('98) | .65 | .35 |
| a. | | 32c light blue | 2.00 | .50 |
| 2938 | A2253 | 46c carmine | .90 | .25 |
| 2940 | A2255 | 55c green | 1.15 | .25 |
| a. | | Imperf., pair | | |
| 2941 | A2256 | 55c black ('99) | 1.10 | .25 |
| 2942 | A2257 | 77c blue ('98) | 1.50 | .40 |
| 2943 | A2258 | 78c bright violet | 1.60 | .25 |
| a. | | 78c dull violet | 1.60 | |
| b. | | 78c pale violet | 3.00 | .30 |
| | Nos. 2933-2943 (9) | | 9.05 | 2.65 |

The pale violet ink on No. 2943b luminesces bright pink under long-wave ultraviolet light.

**LOVE**

A2263

Cherub from Sistine Madonna, by Raphael — A2264

**LITHOGRAPHED & ENGRAVED**

**1995, Feb. 1**   Perf. 11.2

| 2948 | A2263 | (32c) multi | .65 | .25 |

**Self-Adhesive**
**Die Cut**

| 2949 | A2264 | (32c) multi | .65 | .25 |
| a. | | Booklet pane of 20 + label | 13.00 | |
| b. | | Red (engr.) omitted | 100.00 | |
| c. | | As "a," red (engr.) omitted | 2,000. | |
| d. | | Red (engr.) missing (CM) | | |

No. 2949d must be collected se-tenant with a normal stamp. The error comes from the top row of three stamps of the booklet pane of 20 plus label.

See Nos. 2957-2960, 3030.

**FLORIDA STATEHOOD**

A2265

**LITHOGRAPHED**

**1995, Mar. 3**   Perf. 11.1

| 2950 | A2265 | 32c multicolored | .65 | .25 |

**EARTH DAY**

Earth Clean-Up A2266

Solar Energy — A2267

Tree Planting — A2268

Beach Clean-Up A2269

**1995, Apr. 20**   Perf. 11.1x11

| 2951 | A2266 | 32c multicolored | .65 | .25 |
| 2952 | A2267 | 32c multicolored | .65 | .25 |
| 2953 | A2268 | 32c multicolored | .65 | .25 |
| 2954 | A2269 | 32c multicolored | .65 | .25 |
| a. | | Block of 4, #2951-2954 | 2.60 | 1.75 |

**RICHARD M. NIXON**
**37th President (1913-94)**

Richard M. Nixon, 37th President (1913-94) — A2270

**LITHOGRAPHED & ENGRAVED**

**1995, Apr. 26**   Perf. 11.2

| 2955 | A2270 | 32c multicolored | .65 | .25 |
| a. | | Red (engr.) missing (CM) | 800.00 | |

No. 2955 is known with red (engr. "Richard Nixon") inverted, and with red engr. omitted but only half the Nixon portrait present, both from printer's waste. No. 2955a shows a complete Nixon portrait.

**BLACK HERITAGE SERIES**

Bessie Coleman, Aviator — A2271

**ENGRAVED**

**1995, Apr. 27**

| 2956 | A2271 | 32c red & black | .85 | .25 |

**LOVE**

A2272

A2273

A2274

**LITHOGRAPHED & ENGRAVED**

**1995, May 12**

| 2957 | A2272 | 32c multicolored | .65 | .25 |
| | | Compare with No. 3030. | | |
| 2958 | A2273 | 55c multicolored | 1.10 | .25 |

**BOOKLET STAMPS**
**Perf. 9.8x10.8**

| 2959 | A2272 | 32c multicolored | .65 | .25 |
| a. | | Booklet pane of 10 | 6.50 | 3.25 |
| b. | | Imperf, pair | 100.00 | |
| c. | | As "a," imperf. | 500.00 | |

**Self-Adhesive**
**Die Cut**

| 2960 | A2274 | 55c multicolored | 1.10 | .25 |
| a. | | Booklet pane of 20 + label | 22.50 | |

See Nos. 2948-2949, 3030.

**RECREATIONAL SPORTS**

Volleyball A2275

Softball — A2276

Bowling — A2277

Tennis — A2278

Golf — A2279

**LITHOGRAPHED**

**1995, May 20**

| 2961 | A2275 | 32c multicolored | .65 | .25 |
| 2962 | A2276 | 32c multicolored | .65 | .25 |
| 2963 | A2277 | 32c multicolored | .65 | .25 |
| 2964 | A2278 | 32c multicolored | .65 | .25 |
| 2965 | A2279 | 32c multicolored | .65 | .25 |
| a. | | Vert. strip of 5, #2961-2965 | 3.25 | 2.00 |
| b. | | As "a," imperf | 1,750. | |
| c. | | As "a," yellow omitted | 1,400. | |
| d. | | As "a," yellow, blue & magenta omitted | 1,600. | |

**PRISONERS OF WAR & MISSING IN ACTION**

A2280

**1995, May 29**

| 2966 | A2280 | 32c multicolored | .65 | .25 |

**LEGENDS OF HOLLYWOOD**

Marilyn Monroe (1926-62) — A2281

**PHOTOGRAVURE**

**1995, June 1**   Perf. 11.1

| 2967 | A2281 | 32c multicolored | .80 | .25 |
| a. | | Imperf., pair | 225.00 | |

Perforations in corner of each stamp are star-shaped.

**TEXAS STATEHOOD**

A2282

**LITHOGRAPHED**

**1995, June 16**   Perf. 11.2

| 2968 | A2282 | 32c multicolored | .70 | .25 |

**GREAT LAKES LIGHTHOUSES**

Split Rock, Lake Superior A2283

St. Joseph, Lake Michigan A2284

Spectacle Reef, Lake Huron A2285

Marblehead, Lake Erie A2286

Thirty Mile Point, Lake Ontario — A2287

**PHOTOGRAVURE**
**BOOKLET STAMPS**

**1995, June 17**   Perf. 11.2 Vert.

| 2969 | A2283 | 32c multicolored | .90 | .30 |
| 2970 | A2284 | 32c multicolored | .90 | .30 |
| 2971 | A2285 | 32c multicolored | .90 | .30 |
| 2972 | A2286 | 32c multicolored | .90 | .30 |
| 2973 | A2287 | 32c multicolored | .90 | .30 |
| a. | | Booklet pane of 5, #2969-2973 | 4.50 | 2.50 |
| b. | | As "a," two vert. pairs imperf. horiz. of #2972 and 2973, in pane of 7+ stamps in cplt. bklt. #BK230 (due to foldover) | — | |

**U.N., 50th ANNIV.**

A2288

**ENGRAVED**

**1995, June 26**   Perf. 11.2

| 2974 | A2288 | 32c blue | .65 | .25 |

**CIVIL WAR**

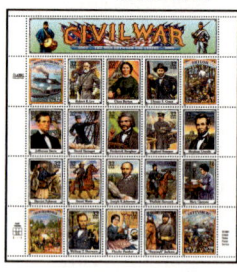

A2289

Designs: a, Monitor and Virginia. b, Robert E. Lee. c, Clara Barton. d, Ulysses S. Grant. e, Battle of Shiloh. f, Jefferson Davis. g, David Farragut. h, Frederick Douglass. i, Raphael Semmes. j, Abraham Lincoln. k, Harriet Tubman. l, Stand Watie. m, Joseph E. Johnston. n, Winfield Hancock. o, Mary Chesnut. p, Battle of Chancellorsville. q, William T. Sherman. r, Phoebe Pember. s, "Stonewall" Jackson. t, Battle of Gettysburg.

**PHOTOGRAVURE**

**1995, June 29**   Perf. 10.1

| 2975 | A2289 | Pane of 20 | 32.50 | 17.50 |
| a.-t. | | 32c any single | 1.50 | .60 |
| u. | | As No. 2975, a.-e. imperf, f.-j. part perf, others perf | 800.00 | |
| v. | | As No. 2975, k.-t. imperf, f.-j. part perf, others perf | 1,250. | |
| w. | | As No. 2975, imperf | 800.00 | |
| x. | | Block of 9 (f.-h., k.-m., p.-r.) k.-l. & p.-q. imperf. vert. | 800.00 | |
| y. | | As No. 2975, a.-b. perf, c., f.-h. part perf, others imperf | 800.00 | |
| z. | | As No. 2975, o. and t. imperf, j., n. & s. part perf, others perf | — | |
| aa. | | As No. 2975, c.-e. imperf, b., g.-j. part perf, others perf | 500.00 | |

**AMERICAN FOLK ART SERIES**
**Carousel Horses**

A2290

A2291

UNITED STATES 83

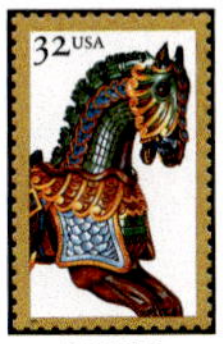

A2292

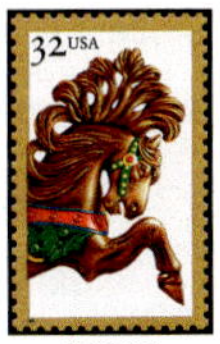

A2293

LITHOGRAPHED

**1995, July 21** *Perf. 11*

**2976** A2290 32c multicolored .65 .25
**2977** A2291 32c multicolored .65 .25
**2978** A2292 32c multicolored .65 .25
**2979** A2293 32c multicolored .65 .25
*a.* Block or strip of 4, #2976-2979 2.60 2.00

## WOMAN SUFFRAGE

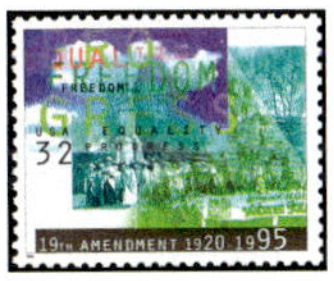


A2294

LITHOGRAPHED & ENGRAVED

**1995, Aug. 26** *Perf. 11.1x11*

**2980** A2294 32c multicolored .65 .25
*a.* Black (engr.) omitted *275.00*
*b.* Imperf., pair *750.00*
*c.* Vert. pair, imperf between and at bottom *500.00*

No. 2980a is valued in the grade of fine. Very fine examples exist and sell for much more.

## WORLD WAR II

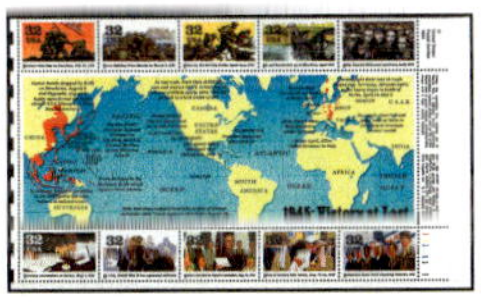

A2295

Designs and events of 1945: a, Marines raise flag on Iwo Jima. b, Fierce fighting frees Manila by March 3, 1945. c, Soldiers advancing (Okinawa, the last big battle). d, Destroyed bridge (US and Soviets link up at Elbe River). e, Allies liberate Holocaust survivors. f, Germany surrenders at Reims. g, Refugees (By 1945, World War II has uprooted millions). h, Truman announces Japan's surrender. i, Sailor kissing nurse (News of victory hits home). j, Hometowns honor their returning veterans.

Central label is size of 15 stamps and shows world map with extent of Axis control and Allied operations.

**1995, Sept. 2** *Perf. 11.1*

**2981** A2295 Block of 10 15.00 7.50
*a.-j.* 32c any single 1.50 .50

No. 2981 has selvage at left and right and either top or bottom.

## AMERICAN MUSIC SERIES

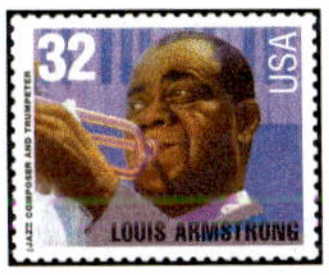


Louis Armstrong A2296

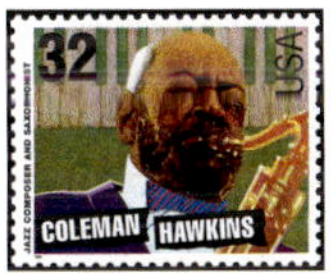


Coleman Hawkins — A2297

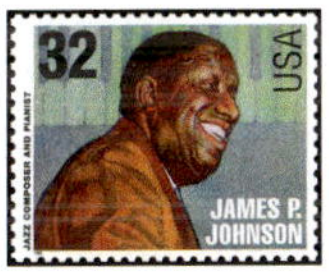


James P. Johnson — A2298

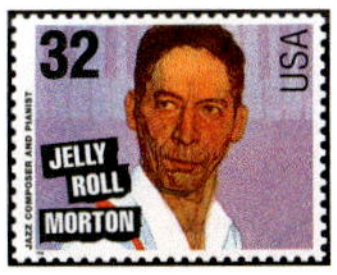


Jelly Roll Morton — A2299

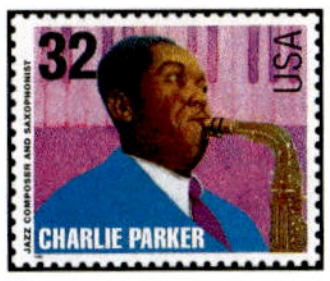


Charlie Parker — A2300

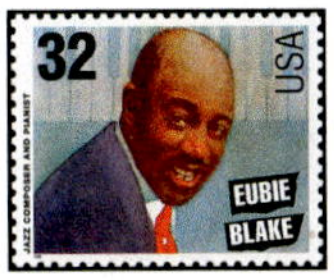


Eubie Blake — A2301

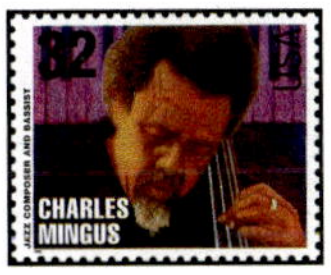


Charles Mingus — A2302

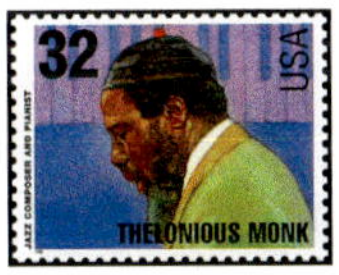


Thelonious Monk — A2303

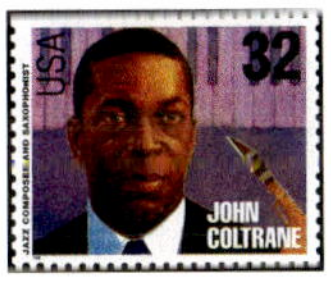


John Coltrane — A2304

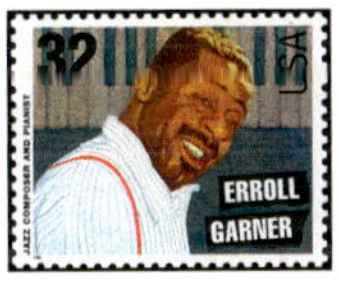


Erroll Garner — A2305

LITHOGRAPHED

Plates of 120 in six panes of 20

**1995** *Perf. 11.1x11*

**2982** A2296 32c white denomination .90 .25
*a.* Imperf, pair —
**2983** A2297 32c multicolored 2.25 .30
**2984** A2296 32c black denomination 2.25 .30
**2985** A2298 32c multicolored 2.25 .30
**2986** A2299 32c multicolored 2.25 .30
**2987** A2300 32c multicolored 2.25 .30
**2988** A2301 32c multicolored 2.25 .30
**2989** A2302 32c multicolored 2.25 .30
**2990** A2303 32c multicolored 2.25 .30
**2991** A2304 32c multicolored 2.25 .30
**2992** A2305 32c multicolored 2.25 .30
*a.* Vert. block of 10, #2983-2992 23.00 7.50
*b.* Pane of 20, dark blue (inscriptions) omitted —
*c.* Imperf pair of Nos. 2991-2992 *5,000.*

An imperf. block of Nos. 2983-2992 is believed to be printer's waste.

## GARDEN FLOWERS

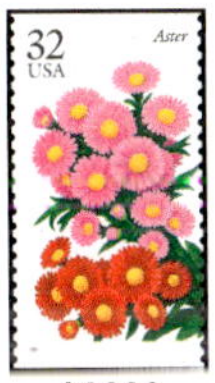


A2306

A2307

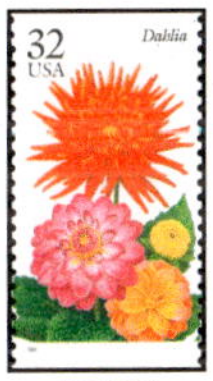


A2308

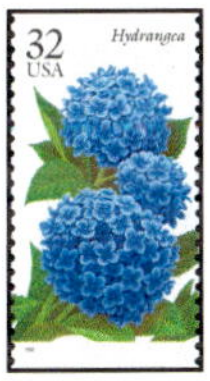


A2309

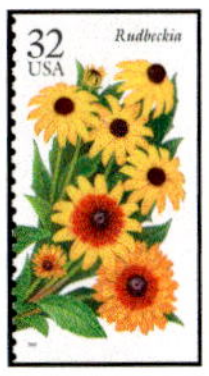


A2310

LITHOGRAPHED & ENGRAVED
BOOKLET STAMPS

**1995, Sept. 19** *Perf. 10.9 Vert.*

**2993** A2306 32c multi .65 .25
**2994** A2307 32c multi .65 .25
**2995** A2308 32c multi .65 .25
**2996** A2309 32c multi .65 .25
**2997** A2310 32c multi .65 .25
*a.* Booklet pane of 5, #2993-2997 3.25 2.25
*b.* As "a," imperf *2,250.*
*c.* As "a," black (engr.) omitted —

## EDDIE RICKENBACKER (1890-1973), AVIATOR

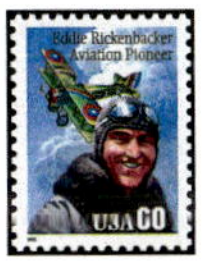


A2311

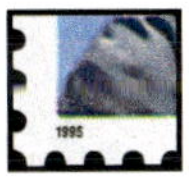

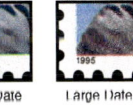

Small Date

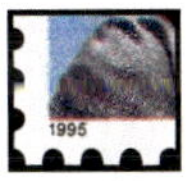

Large Date

PHOTOGRAVURE

**1995, Sept. 25** *Perf. 11¼*

**2998** A2311 60c multi, small "1995" year date 1.40 .50
*a.* Large "1995" date, Oct. [illegible] [illegible] .50

Date on No. 2998 is 1mm long, on No. 2998a 1½mm long.

## REPUBLIC OF PALAU

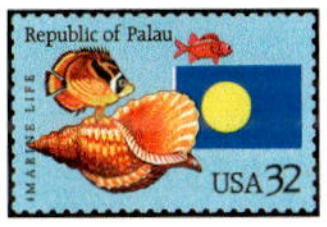


A2312

LITHOGRAPHED

**1995, Sept. 29** *Perf. 11.1*

**2999** A2312 32c multicolored .65 .25

See Palau Nos. 377-378.

## COMIC STRIPS

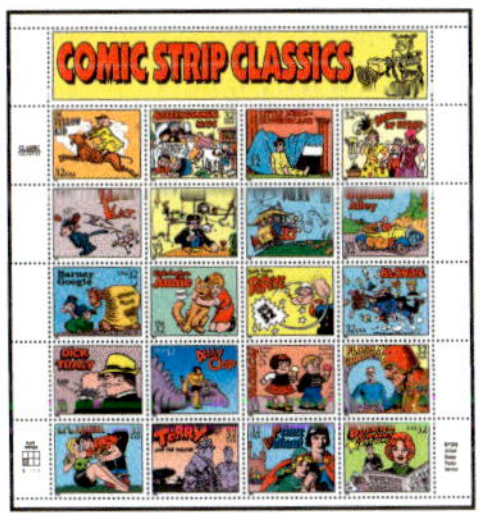


A2313

Designs: a, The Yellow Kid. b, Katzenjammer Kids. c, Little Nemo in Slumberland. d, Bringing Up Father. e, Krazy Kat. f, Rube Goldberg's Inventions. g, Toonerville Folks. h, Gasoline Alley. i, Barney Google. j, Little Orphan Annie. k, Popeye. l, Blondie. m, Dick Tracy. n, Alley Oop. o, Nancy. p, Flash Gordon. q, Li'l Abner. r, Terry and the Pirates. s, Prince Valiant. t, Brenda Starr, Reporter.

PHOTOGRAVURE

**1995, Oct. 1** *Perf. 10.1*

**3000** A2313 Pane of 20 13.00 10.00
*a.-t.* 32c any single .65 .50
*u.* As No. 3000, a.-h. imperf., i.-l. part perf *3,250.*
*v.* As No. 3000, m.-t. imperf., i.-l. part perf *3,250.*
*w.* As No. 3000, a.-l. imperf.,m.-t. imperf vert. *3,250.*
*x.* As No. 3000, imperf *4,250.*

## U.S. NAVAL ACADEMY, 150th ANNIVERSARY

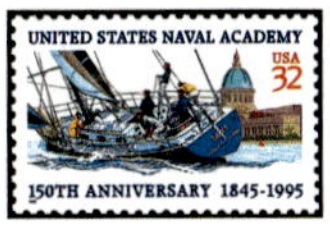


A2314

LITHOGRAPHED

**1995, Oct. 10** *Perf. 10.9*

**3001** A2314 32c multicolored .65 .25

## LITERARY ARTS SERIES

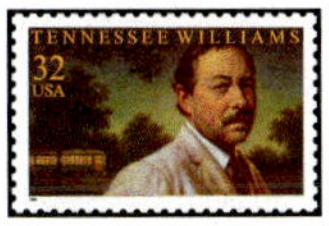


Tennessee Williams (1911-83) A2315

**1995, Oct. 13** *Perf. 11.1*

**3002** A2315 32c multicolored .65 .25

## CHRISTMAS

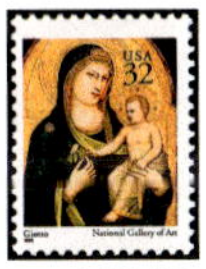


Madonna and Child — A2316

LITHOGRAPHED & ENGRAVED

**1995** *Perf. 11.2*

**3003** A2316 32c multi .65 .25
*c.* Black (engr., denomination) omitted *200.00* —

BOOKLET STAMP

*Perf. 9.8x10.9*

**3003A** A2316 32c multi .65 .25
*b.* Booklet pane of 10 6.50 4.00

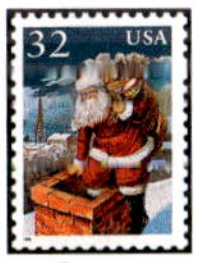


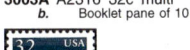

Santa Claus Entering Chimney A2317

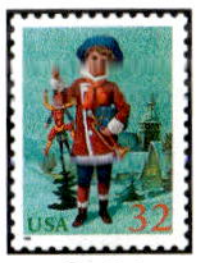


Child Holding Jumping Jack A2318

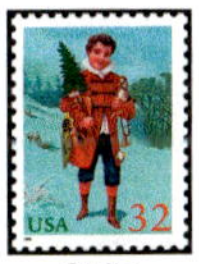


Child Holding Tree A2319

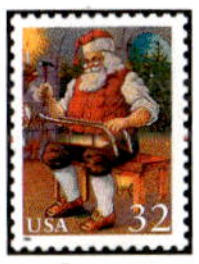


Santa Claus Working on Sled A2320

LITHOGRAPHED

*Perf. 11.25*

**3004** A2317 32c multi .70 .25
**3005** A2318 32c multi .70 .25
**3006** A2319 32c multi .70 .25
**3007** A2320 32c multi .70 .25
*a.* Block or strip of 4, #3004-3007 2.80 1.25
*b.* Booklet pane of 10, 3 each #3004-3005, 2 each #3006-3007 8.00 4.00
*c.* Booklet pane of 10, 2 each #3004-3005, 3 each #3006-3007 8.00 4.00
*d.* As "a," imperf *325.00*
*e.* As "b," miscut and inserted upside down into booklet cover, with full bottom selvage —

PHOTOGRAVURE

**Self-Adhesive Stamps**

***Serpentine Die Cut 11.25 on 2, 3 or 4 sides***

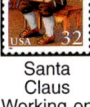

**3008** A2320 32c multi .95 .25
**3009** A2318 32c multi .95 .25
**3010** A2317 32c multi .95 .25
**3011** A2319 32c multi .95 .25
*a.* Booklet pane of 20, 5 each #3008-3011 + label 19.00
*b.* Strip of 4, #3008-3011 3.80

84 UNITED STATES

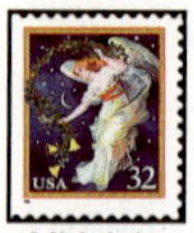

Midnight Angel A2321

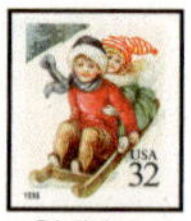

Children Sledding A2322

**LITHOGRAPHED**

***Serpentine Die Cut 11.3x11.6 on 2, 3 or 4 sides***

**3012** A2321 32c multi .65 .25
- *a.* Booklet pane of 20 + label 13.00
- *b.* Vert. pair, die cutting omitted between —
- *c.* Booklet pane of 15 + label, *1996* 12.00
- *d.* Booklet pane of 15 *30.00*

No. 3012a comes either with no die cutting in the label (1995 printing) or with the die cutting from the 1996 printing.

No. 3012d is a pane of 16 with one stamp removed. The missing stamp can be from either row 1, 2, 3, 7 or 8 of the pane. No. 3012d cannot be made from No. 3012c, a pane of 15 + label. The label is die cut. If the label is removed, an impression of the die cutting appears on the backing paper.

**PHOTOGRAVURE**

***Die Cut***

**3013** A2322 32c multi .65 .25
- *a.* Booklet pane of 18 12.00

**Self-Adhesive Coil Stamps**

***Serpentine Die Cut 11.2 Vert.***

**3014** A2320 32c multi 3.00 .30
**3015** A2318 32c multi 3.00 .30
**3016** A2317 32c multi 3.00 .30
**3017** A2319 32c multi 3.00 .30
- *a.* Strip of 4, #3014-3017 12.00

**LITHOGRAPHED**

***Serpentine Die Cut 11.6 Vert.***

**3018** A2321 32c multi 1.10 .30

Nos. 3005-3006 have "USA" printed in green. It is red on the self-adhesive stamps.

Issued: #3003-3003A, 3012-3013, 3018, 10/19; #3004-3011, 3014-3017, 9/30.

**ANTIQUE AUTOMOBILES**

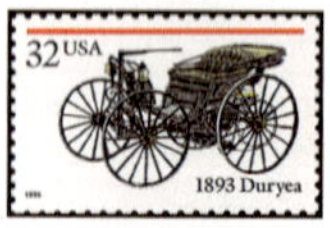

1893 Duryea — A2323

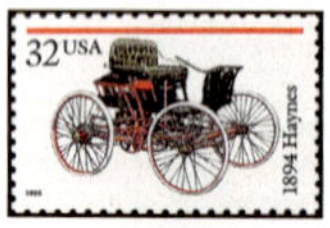

1894 Haynes — A2324

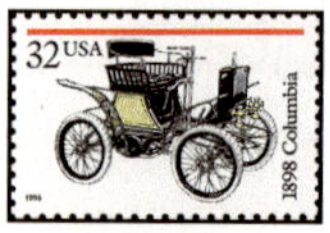

1898 Columbia A2325

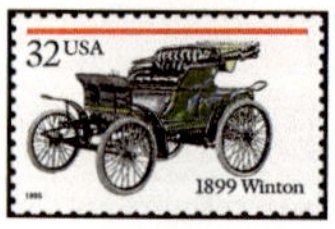

1899 Winton — A2326

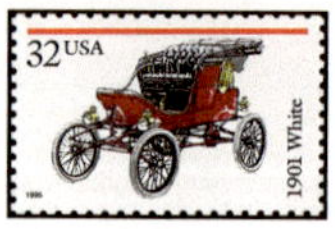

1901 White — A2327

PHOTOGRAVURE

**1995, Nov. 3** ***Perf. 10.1x11.1***

**3019** A2323 32c multicolored .90 .25
**3020** A2324 32c multicolored .90 .25
**3021** A2325 32c multicolored .90 .25
**3022** A2326 32c multicolored .90 .25
**3023** A2327 32c multicolored .90 .25
- *a.* Vert. or horiz. strip of 5, #3019-3023 4.50 2.00

Vert. and horiz. strips are all in different order.

**UTAH STATEHOOD CENTENARY**

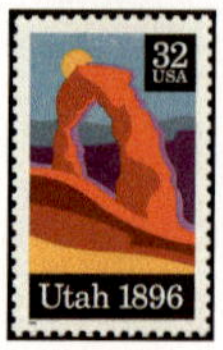

Delicate Arch, Arches Natl. Park — A2328

LITHOGRAPHED

**1996, Jan. 4** ***Perf. 11.1***

**3024** A2328 32c multicolored .75 .25

**GARDEN FLOWERS**

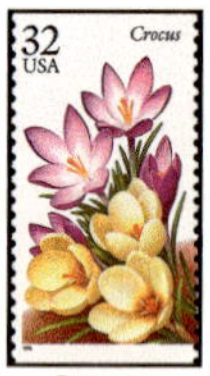

Crocus A2329

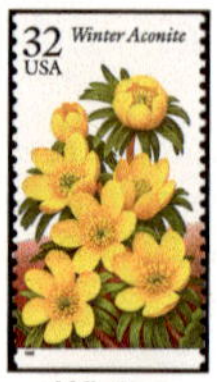

Winter Aconite A2330

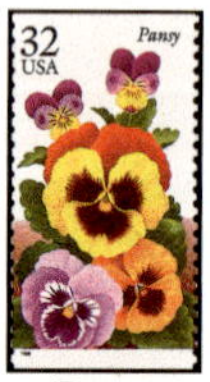

Pansy A2331

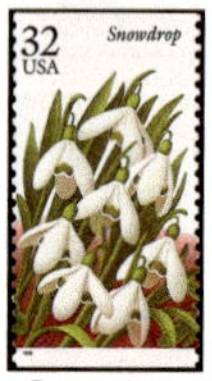

Snowdrop A2332

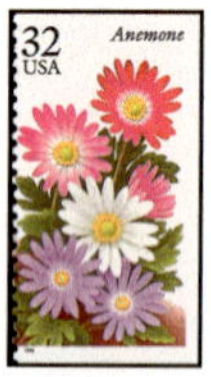

Anemone — A2333

LITHOGRAPHED & ENGRAVED
BOOKLET STAMPS

**1996, Jan. 19** ***Perf. 10.9 Vert.***

**3025** A2329 32c multi .65 .25
**3026** A2330 32c multi .65 .25
**3027** A2331 32c multi .65 .25
**3028** A2332 32c multi .65 .25
**3029** A2333 32c multi .65 .25
- *a.* Booklet pane of 5, #3025-3029 3.25 2.50
- *b.* As "a," imperf. —

**LOVE**

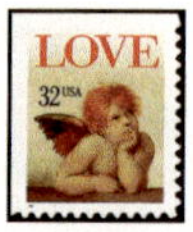

Cherub from Sistine Madonna, by Raphael — A2334

BOOKLET STAMP

***Serpentine Die Cut 11.3x11.7***

**1996, Jan. 20**

**Self-Adhesive**

**3030** A2334 32c multicolored .65 .25
- *a.* Booklet pane of 20 + label 13.00
- *b.* Booklet pane of 15 + label 9.75
- *c.* Red (engr. "Love") omitted *75.00*
- *d.* Red (engr. "Love") missing (CM) —
- *e.* Double impression of red (engr. "Love") *450.00*
- *f.* Die cutting omitted, pair *225.00*
- *g.* As "a," stamps 1-5 double impression of red (engr. "LOVE") *1,000.*
- *h.* As "a," red (engr. "LOVE") omitted *1,000.*
- *i.* As "a," die cutting omitted —
- *j.* As "e," two examples in booklet pane of 20 (No. 3030a) *1,000.*
- *k.* As "d," three examples in booklet pane of 20 (No. 3030a) *310.00*

No. 3030d must be collected se-tenant with a stamp bearing the red engraving.

See Nos. 2948-2949, 2957-2960.

**FLORA AND FAUNA SERIES**

Kestrel, Blue Jay and Rose Types of 1993-95 and

***Serpentine Die Cut 10½***

**1996-2002** **Untagged**

**Self-Adhesive (#3031, 3031A)**

**3031** A1841 1c multicolored .30 .25
- *c.* Die cutting omitted, pair —

***Serpentine Die Cut 11¼***

**Untagged**

**3031A** A1841 1c multicolored .30 .25
- *b.* Die cutting omitted, pane of 50 *325.00*

No. 3031A has blue inscription and year. See No. 2477.

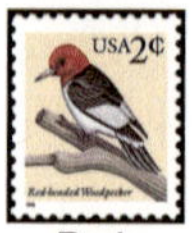

Red-headed Woodpecker A2335

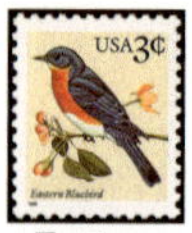

Eastern Bluebird A2336

Sheets of 400 in four panes of 100

***Perf. 11***

**Untagged**

**3032** A2335 2c multicolored .30 .25
**3033** A2336 3c multicolored .30 .25

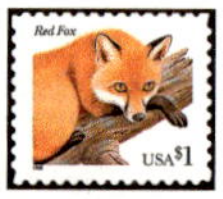

Red Fox — A2339

***Serpentine Die Cut 11½x11¼***

**Self-Adhesive**

**3036** A2339 $1 multicolored *10.00* *.50*
- *a.* Serpentine die cut 11¾x11 ('02) *11.00* *.50*

---

Beginning with Nos. 3036 and 3036a, hidden 3-D images can be seen on some stamps when they are viewed with a special "Stamp Decoder" lens sold by the USPS. See the *Scott Specialized Catalogue of U.S. Stamps and Covers* for descriptions of these images. Stamps with 3-D images are 3036-3036a, 3167, 3168-3172, 3178, 3206, 3230-3234, 3238-3242, 3261-3262, 3321-3324, 3472-3473, 3647-3648, 3651, 3771, 3787-3791, 3808-3811, 3838 and 3862.

---

**COIL STAMPS**

**Untagged**

***Perf. 9¾ Vert.***

**3044** A1841 1c multicolored, small date .30 .25
- *a.* Large date .30 .25

Date on No. 3044 is 1mm long, on No. 3044a 1.5mm long.

**Untagged**

**3045** A2335 2c multicolored .30 .25

Issued: #3032, 2/2/96; #3033, 4/3/96; #3044, 1/20/96; #3036, 8/14/98; #3045, 6/22/99; #3031, 11/19/99; #3031A, 10/00.

**BOOKLET STAMPS**

PHOTOGRAVURE

***Serpentine Die Cut 10.4x10.8 on 3 Sides***

**Tagged**

**Self-Adhesive**

**3048** A1847 20c multi .40 .25
- *a.* Booklet pane of 10 4.00
- *b.* Booklet pane of 4 70.00
- *c.* Booklet pane of 6 100.00

Nos. 3048b-3048c are from the vending machine booklet No. BK237 that has a glue strip at the top edge of the top pane, the peelable strip removed and the rouletting line 2mm lower than on No. 3048a on some booklets, when the panes are compared with bottoms aligned. Vending booklets with plate #S2222 always have gauge 8½ rouletting on booklet covers. Convertible booklets (No. 3048a) with plate #S2222 always have gauge 12½ rouletting on booklet covers. Vending booklets with plate #S1111 can have either 8½ or 12½ gauge rouletting on booklet cover, and it may be impossible to tell a vending booklet with 12½ gauge rouletting and plate #S1111 from a convertible booklet with peelable strip removed.

***Serpentine Die Cut 11.3x11.7 on 2, 3 or 4 Sides***

**3049** A1853 32c yel, org, grn & blk .65 .25
- *a.* Booklet pane of 20 + label 13.00
- *b.* Booklet pane of 4 2.60
- *c.* Booklet pane of 5 + label 3.50
- *d.* Booklet pane of 6 4.00

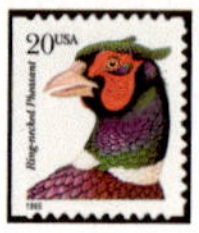

Ring-necked Pheasant — A2350

***Serpentine Die Cut 11.2 on 3 Sides***

**3050** A2350 20c multi .65 .25
- *a.* Booklet pane of 10, all stamps upright 6.50
- *b.* Serpentine die cut 11 3.25 .25
- *c.* As "b," booklet pane of 10, all stamps upright 35.00

***Serpentine Die Cut 10½x11 on 3 Sides***

**3051** A2350 20c multi 1.25 .25

***Serpentine Die Cut 10.6x10.4 on 3 Sides***

**3051A** A2350 20c multicolored 7.00 .50
- *b.* Booklet pane of 5, 4 #3051, 1 #3051A turned sideways at top 10.00
- *c.* Booklet pane of 5, 4 #3051, 1 #3051A turned sideways at bottom 10.00

No. 3051 represents the eight upright stamps on the booklet panes Nos. 3051Ab and 3051Ac. The two stamps turned sideways on those panes are No. 3051A.

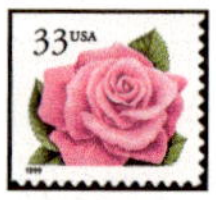

Coral Pink Rose — A2351

***Serpentine Die Cut 11½x11¼ on 2, 3 or 4 Sides***

**3052** A2351 33c multi .90 .25
- *a.* Booklet pane of 4 3.60
- *b.* Booklet pane of 5 + label 4.50
- *c.* Booklet pane of 6 5.50
- *d.* Booklet pane of 20 + label 17.50
- *j.* Die cutting omitted, pair —
- *k.* As "d," die cutting omitted *5,500.*

***Serpentine Die Cut 10¾x10½ on 2 or 3 sides***

**3052E** A2351 33c multi .75 .25
- *f.* Booklet pane of 20 15.00
- *g.* Black ("33 USA," etc.) omitted 350.00
- *h.* As "f," all 12 stamps on one side with black omitted —
- *i.* Horiz. pair, die cutting missing between due to miscutting of the pane —
- *j.* As "f," vert. die cutting missing between due to miscutting of the pane —

No. 3052Ef is a double-sided booklet pane with 12 stamps on one side and 8 stamps plus label on the other side.

**COIL STAMPS**

***Serpentine Die Cut 11½ Vert.***

**3053** A1847 20c multi .50 .25
- *a.* Die cutting omitted, pair *2,100.*

**Yellow Rose, Ring-necked Pheasant Types of 1996-98**

LITHOGRAPHED

**Self-Adhesive**

**3054** A1858 32c yel, mag, blk & grn .65 .25
- *a.* Die cutting omitted, pair *85.00*
- *b.* Black, yellow & green omitted —
- *c.* Black, yellow & green omitted, die cutting omitted, pair —
- *d.* Black omitted *250.00*
- *e.* Black omitted, die cutting omitted, pair *550.00*
- *f.* All colors omitted, die cutting omitted —
- *g.* Pair, die cutting omitted, containing one stamp each of "c" and "e" —

Nos. 3054b and 3054d also are miscut and with shifted die cuttings.

No. 3054f must be collected se-tenant with a partially printed stamp(s).

**3055** A2350 20c multi .40 .25
- *a.* Die cutting omitted, pair *125.00*

No. 3055a exists miscut. It is more common in this form and is valued thus.

Issued: #3048, 3053, 8/2/96; #3049, 10/24/96; #3054, 8/1/97; #3050, 3055, 7/31/98; #3051, 7/99; #3052, 8/13/99; #3052E, 4/7/00.

# UNITED STATES

## BLACK HERITAGE SERIES

Ernest E. Just (1883-1941), Marine Biologist — A2358

### LITHOGRAPHED
**1996, Feb. 1**     *Perf. 11.1*
3058   A2358   32c gray & black    .65   .25

## SMITHSONIAN INSTITUTION, 150TH ANNIVERSARY

A2359

**1996, Feb. 7**
3059   A2359   32c multicolored    .65   .25

## CHINESE NEW YEAR

Year of the Rat — A2360

### PHOTOGRAVURE
**1996, Feb. 8**
3060   A2360   32c multicolored    .90   .25
   a.   Imperf., pair    325.00

See Nos. 3895a, 3997a.

## PIONEERS OF COMMUNICATION

Eadweard Muybridge A2361

Ottmar Mergenthaler A2362

Frederic E. Ives — A2363

William Dickson — A2364

### LITHOGRAPHED
**1996, Feb. 22**     *Perf. 11.1x11*
3061   A2361   32c multicolored    .65   .25
3062   A2362   32c multicolored    .65   .25
3063   A2363   32c multicolored    .65   .25
3064   A2364   32c multicolored    .65   .25
   a.   Block or strip of 4, #3061-3064    2.60   2.00

Muybridge (1830-1904), Photographer; Mergenthaler (1854-99), Inventor of Linotype; Ives (1856-1937), Developer of Halftone Process; Dickson (1860-1935), Co-developer of Kinetoscope.

## FULBRIGHT SCHOLARSHIPS, 50th ANNIVERSARY

A2365

### LITHOGRAPHED & ENGRAVED
**1996, Feb. 28**     *Perf. 11.1*
3065   A2365   32c multicolored    .75   .25

## JACQUELINE COCHRAN (1910-80), PILOT

A2366

**1996, Mar. 9**
3066   A2366   50c multicolored    1.00   .40
   a.   Black (engr.) omitted    45.00

## MARATHON

A2367

### LITHOGRAPHED
**1996, Apr. 11**
3067   A2367   32c multicolored    .65   .25

## 1996 SUMMER OLYMPIC GAMES

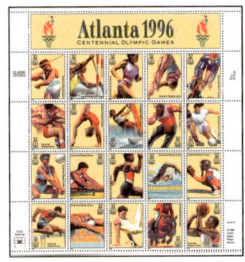

A2368

Designs: a, Decathlon (javelin). b, Men's canoeing. c, Women's running. d, Women's diving. e, Men's cycling. f, Freestyle wrestling. g, Women's gymnastics. h, Women's sailboarding. i, Men's shot put. j, Women's soccer. k, Beach volleyball. l, Men's rowing. m, Men's sprints. n, Women's swimming. o, Women's softball. p, Men's hurdles. q, Men's swimming. r, Men's gymnastics (pommel horse). s, Equestrian. t, Men's basketball.

### PHOTOGRAVURE
**1996, May 2**     *Perf. 10.1*
3068   A2368   Pane of 20    14.00   10.00
   a.-t.   32c any single    .70   .50
   u.   As No. 3068, imperf    350.00
   v.   As No. 3068, back inscriptions omitted on a., f., k. & p., incorrect back inscriptions on others    —
   w.   As No. 3068, e. imperf, d., i.-j. part perf, all others perf    750.00

## GEORGIA O'KEEFFE (1887-1986)

A2369

### PHOTOGRAVURE
**1996, May 23**     *Perf. 11.6x11.4*
3069   A2369   32c multicolored    .85   .25
   a.   Imperf., pair    110.00

## TENNESSEE STATEHOOD BICENTENNIAL

A2370

**1996, May 31**     *Perf. 11.1*
3070   A2370   32c multicolored    .65   .25
   a.   Imperf., pair    —

One pane of 3070 containing 3069a is known. Some stamps on that pane have blind horizontal perforations.

### Booklet Stamp
### Self-Adhesive
### *Serpentine Die Cut 9.9x10.8*
3071   A2370   32c multicolored    .65   .30
   a.   Booklet pane of 20, #S11111    13.00
   b.   Horiz. pair, die cutting omitted btwn.    300.00
   c.   Die cutting omitted, pair    —
   d.   Horiz. pair, die cutting omitted vert.    —

## AMERICAN INDIAN DANCES

A2371            A2372

A2373            A2374

A2375

### LITHOGRAPHED
**1996, June 7**     *Perf. 11.1*
3072   A2371   32c Fancy    1.20   .25
3073   A2372   32c Butterfly    1.20   .25
3074   A2373   32c Traditional    1.20   .25
3075   A2374   32c Raven    1.20   .25
3076   A2375   32c Hoop    1.20   .25
   a.   Strip of 5, #3072-3076    6.00   2.50

## PREHISTORIC ANIMALS

A2376

A2377

A2378

A2379

**1996, June 8**     *Perf. 11.1x11*
3077   A2376   32c Eohippus    .65   .25
3078   A2377   32c Woolly Mammoth    .65   .25
3079   A2378   32c Mastodon    .65   .25
3080   A2379   32c Saber-tooth Cat    .65   .25
   a.   Block or strip of 4, #3077-3080    2.60   2.00

## BREAST CANCER AWARENESS

A2380

**1996, June 15**     *Perf. 11.1*
3081   A2380   32c multicolored    .65   .25

## LEGENDS OF HOLLYWOOD

A2381

### PHOTOGRAVURE
**1996, June 24**
3082   A2381   32c multicolored    .65   .25
   a.   Imperf., pair    100.00
   b.   As "a," red (USA 32c) missing (CM) and tan (JAMES DEAN) omitted    —
   c.   As "a," tan (JAMES DEAN) omitted    —
   d.   As "a," top stamp red missing (CM) and tan (JAMES DEAN) omitted, bottom stamp tan omitted    —
   e.   As No. 3082 pane of 20, right two columns perf, left three columns imperf    1,750.

Perforations in corner of each stamp are star shaped. No. 3082 was also available on the first day of issue in at least 127 Warner Bros. Studio stores.

Nos. 3082b-3082d come from the same error pane. The top row is No. 3082b; rows 2-4 are No. 3082c. No. 3082d is a vertical pair with one stamp from No. 3082b at top and one stamp from No. 3082c at bottom.

## FOLK HEROES

A2382            A2383

    (PECOS BILL)

A2384            A2385

### LITHOGRAPHED
**1996, July 11**     *Perf. 11.1x11*
3083   A2382   32c multicolored    .65   .25
3084   A2383   32c multicolored    .65   .25
3085   A2384   32c multicolored    .65   .25
3086   A2385   32c multicolored    .65   .25
   a.   Block or strip of 4, #3083-3086    2.60   2.00

## CENTENNIAL OLYMPIC GAMES

Myron's Discobolus — A2386

### ENGRAVED
**1996, July 19**    *Tagged*     *Perf. 11.1*
3087   A2386   32c brown    .75   .25

Sheet margin of the pane of 20 is lithographed.

86 UNITED STATES

## IOWA STATEHOOD, 150TH ANNIVERSARY

Young Corn, by Grant Wood — A2387

**LITHOGRAPHED**
**1996, Aug. 1**
3088  A2387  32c multicolored  .80  .25

**BOOKLET STAMP**
**Self-Adhesive**
*Serpentine Die Cut 11.6x11.4*
3089  A2387  32c multicolored  .65  .30
   a.  Booklet pane of 20  13.00

## RURAL FREE DELIVERY, CENT.

 A2388

**LITHOGRAPHED & ENGRAVED**
**1996, Aug. 7**  *Perf. 11.2x11*
3090  A2388  32c multicolored  .80  .25

## RIVERBOATS

Robt. E. Lee — A2389

Sylvan Dell — A2390

Far West — A2391

Rebecca Everingham A2392

Bailey Gatzert — A2393

**PHOTOGRAVURE**
*Serpentine Die Cut 11x11.1*
**1996, Aug. 22**
**Self-Adhesive**
3091  A2389  32c multicolored  .65  .40
3092  A2390  32c multicolored  .65  .40
3093  A2391  32c multicolored  .65  .40
3094  A2392  32c multicolored  .65  .40
3095  A2393  32c multicolored  .65  .40
   a.  Vert. strip of 5, #3091-3095  3.25
   b.  Strip of 5, #3091-3095, with special die cutting, die cut 11 ¼  35.00  35.00

The serpentine die cutting runs through the peelable backing to which Nos. 3091-3095 are affixed. No. 3095a exists with stamps in different sequences.
On the long side of each stamp in No. 3095b, the die cutting is missing 3 "perforations" between the stamps, one near each end and one in the middle. This allows a complete strip to be removed from the backing paper for use on a first day cover.

## AMERICAN MUSIC SERIES
### Big Band Leaders

Count Basie — A2394

Tommy & Jimmy Dorsey — A2395

Glenn Miller — A2396

Benny Goodman A2397

### Songwriters

Harold Arlen — A2398

Johnny Mercer — A2399

Dorothy Fields — A2400

Hoagy Carmichael A2401

**LITHOGRAPHED**
**1996, Sept. 11**  *Perf. 11.1x11*
3096  A2394  32c multicolored  .75  .25
3097  A2395  32c multicolored  .75  .25
3098  A2396  32c multicolored  .75  .25
3099  A2397  32c multicolored  .75  .25
   a.  Block or strip of 4, #3096-3099  3.00  2.00
3100  A2398  32c multicolored  .75  .25
3101  A2399  32c multicolored  .75  .25
3102  A2400  32c multicolored  .75  .25
3103  A2401  32c multicolored  .75  .25
   a.  Block or strip of 4, #3100-3103  3.00  2.00

## LITERARY ARTS SERIES

F. Scott Fitzgerald (1896-1940) A2402

**PHOTOGRAVURE**
**1996, Sept. 27**  *Perf. 11.1*
3104  A2402  23c multicolored  .55  .25

## ENDANGERED SPECIES

A2403

Designs: a, Black-footed ferret. b, Thick-billed parrot. c, Hawaiian monk seal. d, American crocodile. e, Ocelot. f, Schaus swallowtail butterfly. g, Wyoming toad. h, Brown pelican. i, California condor. j, Gila trout. k, San Francisco garter snake. l, Woodland caribou. m, Florida panther. n, Piping plover. o, Florida manatee.

**LITHOGRAPHED**
**1996, Oct. 2**  *Perf. 11.1x11*
3105  A2403  Pane of 15  12.00  8.00
   a.-o.  32c any single  .80  .50
See Mexico No. 1995.

## COMPUTER TECHNOLOGY

A2404

**LITHOGRAPHED & ENGRAVED**
**1996, Oct. 8**  *Perf. 10.9x11.1*
3106  A2404  32c multicolored  .65  .25

## CHRISTMAS

Madonna and Child from Adoration of the Shepherds, by Paolo de Matteis — A2405

Family at Fireplace A2406

Decorating Tree A2407

Dreaming of Santa Claus A2408

Holiday Shopping A2409

**LITHOGRAPHED & ENGRAVED**
**1996**  *Perf. 11.1x11.2*
3107  A2405  32c multicolored  .65  .25
   a.  Black (engr.) omitted at bottom  600.00

On No. 3107a, an albino impression of the lettering at bottom is present, but there is no trace of black ink.
No. 3107b is missing the black lettering at bottom due to a small upward shift of the horizontal perforations. This lettering is the only engraved black on the stamp.

**LITHOGRAPHED**
*Perf. 11.3*
3108  A2406  32c multicolored  .65  .25
3109  A2407  32c multicolored  .65  .25
3110  A2408  32c multicolored  .65  .25
3111  A2409  32c multicolored  .65  .25
   a.  Block or strip of 4, #3108-3111  2.60  1.75
   b.  Strip of 4, #3110-3111, 3108-3109, with #3109 imperf., #3108 imperf. at right  500.00
   c.  Strip of 4, #3108-3111, with #3111 imperf, #3110 imperf at right  1,000.

**BOOKLET STAMPS**
**Self-Adhesive**
**LITHOGRAPHED & ENGRAVED**
*Serpentine Die Cut 10 on 2, 3 or 4 Sides*
3112  A2405  32c multicolored  .75  .25
   a.  Booklet pane of 20 + label  15.00
   b.  Die cutting omitted, pair  40.00
   c.  As "a," die cutting omitted  400.00
   d.  As "a," top seven stamps with black (engr.) missing (PS)  —

No. 3112d is missing the black lettering at bottom due to a small upward shift of the horizontal perforations. This lettering is the only engraved black on the stamp.

**LITHOGRAPHED**
*Serpentine Die Cut 11.8x11.5 on 2, 3 or 4 Sides*
3113  A2406  32c multicolored  .65  .25
3114  A2407  32c multicolored  .65  .25
3115  A2408  32c multicolored  .65  .25
3116  A2409  32c multicolored  .65  .25
   a.  Booklet pane of 20, 5 ea #3113-3116  13.00
   b.  Strip of 4, #3113-3116  2.60
   c.  As "a," die cutting omitted  1,250.
   d.  As "b," die cutting omitted  500.00
   e.  Block of 6, die cutting omitted  700.00

Skaters — A2410

**PHOTOGRAVURE**
*Die Cut*
3117  A2410  32c multicolored  .65  .25
   a.  Booklet pane of 18  12.00

Issued: #3108-3111, 3113-3117, 10/8; #3107, 3112, 11/1.

## HANUKKAH

A2411

*Serpentine Die Cut 11.1*
**1996, Oct. 22**
**Self-Adhesive**
3118  A2411  32c multicolored  .65  .25

See Nos. 3352, 3547, 3672, Israel No. 1289. For booklet see No. BK258.

## CYCLING
### Souvenir Sheet

A2412

**1996, Nov. 1**  *Perf. 11x11.1*
3119  A2412  Sheet of 2  2.75  2.00
   a.  50c orange & multi  1.30  1.00
   b.  50c blue green & multi  1.30  1.00

No. 3119 exists overprinted in gold and in silver for the Tour of China '96. This overprint is a private production. Value, set of 2 sheets $12.50.

## CHINESE NEW YEAR

Year of the Ox — A2413

**1997, Jan. 5**  *Perf. 11.2*
3120  A2413  32c multicolored  .80  .25

See Nos. 3895b, 3997b.

## BLACK HERITAGE SERIES

Brig. Gen. Benjamin O. Davis, Sr. (1880-1970) — A2414

**LITHOGRAPHED**
*Serpentine Die Cut 11.4*
**1997, Jan. 28**
**Self-Adhesive**
3121  A2414  32c multicolored  .70  .25

# UNITED STATES

### Statue of Liberty Type of 1994
#### PHOTOGRAVURE
##### Serpentine Die Cut 11 on 2, 3 or 4 Sides
**1997, Feb. 1**
**Self-Adhesive**

| 3122 | A1951 | 32c red, lt bl, dk bl & yel | .70 | .25 |
| a. | | Booklet pane of 20 + label | 14.00 | |
| b. | | Booklet pane of 4 | 2.80 | |
| c. | | Booklet pane of 5 + label | 3.75 | |
| d. | | Booklet pane of 6 | 4.25 | |
| h. | | As "a," die cutting omitted | — | |

##### Serpentine Die Cut 11.5x11.8 on 2, 3 or 4 Sides
**1997**
**Self-Adhesive**

| 3122E | A1951 | 32c red, lt bl, dk bl & yel | 1.25 | .25 |
| f. | | Booklet pane of 20 + label | 25.00 | |
| g. | | Booklet pane of 6 | 7.50 | |

### LOVE

A2415

Swans — A2416

#### LITHOGRAPHED
##### Serpentine Die Cut 11.8x11.6 on 2, 3 or 4 Sides
**1997, Feb. 4**
**Self-Adhesive**

| 3123 | A2415 | 32c multicolored | .65 | .25 |
| a. | | Booklet pane of 20 + label | 13.00 | |
| b. | | Die cutting omitted, pair | 100.00 | |
| c. | | As "a," die cutting omitted | 675.00 | |
| d. | | As "a," black omitted | — | |

##### Serpentine Die Cut 11.6x11.8 on 2, 3 or 4 Sides

| 3124 | A2416 | 55c multicolored | 1.10 | .25 |
| a. | | Booklet pane of 20 + label | 22.00 | |

### HELPING CHILDREN LEARN

A2417

#### PHOTOGRAVURE
##### Serpentine Die Cut 11.6x11.7
**1997, Feb. 18**
**Self-Adhesive**

| 3125 | A2417 | 32c multicolored | .65 | .25 |

### MERIAN BOTANICAL PRINTS

Citron, Moth, Larvae, Pupa, Beetle A2418

Flowering Pineapple, Cockroaches A2419

No. 3128 (r), No. 3129 (l), No. 3128a below

##### Serpentine Die Cut 10.9x10.2 on 2, 3 or 4 Sides
**1997, Mar. 3**
**Self-Adhesive**

| 3126 | A2418 | 32c multicolored | .65 | .25 |
| 3127 | A2419 | 32c multicolored | .65 | .25 |
| a. | | Booklet pane, 10 ea #3126-3127 + label | 13.00 | |
| b. | | Pair, #3126-3127 | 1.30 | |
| c. | | Vert. pair, die cutting omitted between | 350.00 | |

##### Size: 18.5x24mm
##### Serpentine Die Cut 11.2x10.8 on 2 or 3 Sides

| 3128 | A2418 | 32c multicolored | 1.00 | .25 |
| a. | | See footnote | 2.50 | .25 |
| b. | | Booklet pane, 2 ea #3128-3129, 1 #3128a | 6.50 | |
| 3129 | A2419 | 32c multicolored | 1.00 | .25 |
| a. | | See footnote | 4.50 | .35 |
| b. | | Booklet pane, 2 ea #3128-3129, 1 #3129a | 8.50 | |
| c. | | Pair, #3128-3129 | 2.00 | |

Nos. 3128a-3129a are placed sideways on the pane and are serpentine die cut 11.2 on top and bottom, 10.8 on left side. One of the two No. 3128a per pane has a straight edge at left. The right side is 11.2 broken by a sloping die cut where the stamp meets the vertical die cutting of the two stamps above it. See illustration above.

### PACIFIC 97

Sailing Ship A2420

Stagecoach — A2421

#### ENGRAVED
**1997, Mar. 13**   **Tagged**   **Perf. 11.2**

| 3130 | A2420 | 32c blue | .65 | .30 |
| 3131 | A2421 | 32c red | .65 | .30 |
| a. | | Pair, #3130-3131 | 1.30 | .75 |

Juke Box — A2225a

#### PHOTOGRAVURE
#### COIL STAMPS
**1997, Mar. 14**   **Untagged**   **Imperf.**
**Self-Adhesive**

| 3132 | A2225a | (25c) brt org red, brt yel grn & multi | 1.50 | .50 |

**Tagged**
**Serpentine Die Cut 9.9 Vert.**

| 3133 | A2212 | 32c dk bl, tan, brn, red & lt bl | 2.50 | .25 |

Nos. 3132-3133 were issued without backing paper. No. 3132 has simulated perforations ending in black bars at the top and bottom edges of the stamp. Sky on No. 3133 shows color gradation at LR not on Nos. 2915A or 2915D, and it has blue "1996" at left bottom.

See Nos. 2897, 2913-2916, 2920-2921.

### LITERARY ARTS SERIES

Thornton Wilder (1897-1975) A2422

#### LITHOGRAPHED
**1997, Apr. 17**   **Perf. 11.1**

| 3134 | A2422 | 32c multicolored | .65 | .25 |

### RAOUL WALLENBERG (1912-47)
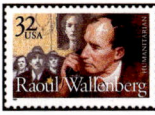
Wallenberg and Jewish Refugees A2423

**1997, Apr. 24**

| 3135 | A2423 | 32c multicolored | .65 | .25 |

### DINOSAURS
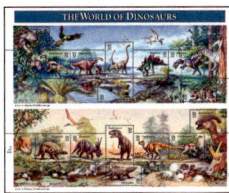
A2424

Designs: a, Ceratosaurus. b, Camptosaurus. c, Camarasaurus. d, Brachiosaurus. e, Goniopholis. f, Stegosaurus. g, Allosaurus. h, Opisthias. i, Edmontonia. j, Einiosaurus. k, Daspletosaurus. l, Palaeosaniwa. m, Corythosaurus. n, Ornithomimus. o, Parasaurolophus.

**1997, May 1**   **Perf. 11x11.1**

| 3136 | A2424 | Sheet of 15 | 10.00 | 8.00 |
| a.-o. | | 32c any single | .65 | .50 |
| p. | | As No. 3136, bottom 7 stamps imperf. | 2,500. | |
| q. | | As No. 3136, top 8 stamps imperf | 2,500. | |
| r. | | As No. 3136, all colors and tagging missing (EP) | — | |

No. 3136r resulted from double sheeting in the sheet-fed press. It is properly gummed and perforated.

No. 3136 completely imperf. is believed to be printer's waste.

### BUGS BUNNY

A2425

#### PHOTOGRAVURE
**1997, May 22**   **Serpentine Die Cut 11**
**Self-Adhesive**

| 3137 | | Pane of 10 #3137a | 6.75 | |
| a. | A2425 | 32c single | .65 | .25 |
| b. | | Pane of 9 #3137a | 6.00 | |
| c. | | Pane of 1 #3137a | .65 | |

Die cutting on #3137 does not extend through the backing paper.

| 3138 | | Pane of 10, #3138c, 9 #3138a | 130.00 | |
| a. | A2425 | 32c single | 2.75 | |
| b. | | Pane of 9 #3138a | 20.00 | |
| c. | | Pane of 1, no die cutting | 100.00 | |

Die cutting on No. 3138b extends through the backing paper.

An untagged promotional piece similar to No. 3137c exists on the same backing paper as the pane, with the same design image, but without Bugs' signature and the single stamp. Replacing the stamp is an enlarged "32 / USA" in the same style as used on the stamp. This promotional piece was not valid for postage.

### PACIFIC 97

Franklin A2426

Washington A2427

#### LITHOGRAPHED & ENGRAVED
**1997**   **Perf. 10.5x10.4**

| 3139 | | Pane of 12 | 12.00 | 9.00 |
| a. | A2426 | 50c single | 1.00 | .50 |
| 3140 | | Pane of 12 | 14.50 | 11.00 |
| a. | A2427 | 60c single | 1.20 | .60 |

Selvage on Nos. 3139-3140 is lithographed.
Issued: No. 3139, 5/29; No. 3140, 5/30.

### MARSHALL PLAN, 50TH ANNIV.

Gen. George C. Marshall, Map of Europe — A2428

**1997, June 4**   **Perf. 11.1**

| 3141 | A2428 | 32c multicolored | .65 | .25 |

### CLASSIC AMERICAN AIRCRAFT

A2429

Designs: a, Mustang. b, Model B. c, Cub. d, Vega. e, Alpha. f, B-10. g, Corsair. h, Stratojet. i, GeeBee. j, Staggerwing. k, Flying Fortress. l, Stearman. m, Constellation, n, Lightning. o, Peashooter. p, Tri-Motor, q, DC-3. r, 314 Clipper. s, Jenny. t, Wildcat.

#### PHOTOGRAVURE
**1997, July 19**   **Perf. 10.1**

| 3142 | A2429 | Pane of 20 | 13.00 | 10.00 |
| a.-t. | | 32c any single | .65 | .65 |

### FOOTBALL COACHES

Bear Bryant — A2430

Pop Warner — A2431

Vince Lombardi A2432

George Halas — A2433

#### LITHOGRAPHED
**1997**   **Perf. 11.2**

| 3143 | A2430 | 32c multicolored | .65 | .25 |
| 3144 | A2431 | 32c multicolored | .65 | .25 |
| 3145 | A2432 | 32c multicolored | .65 | .25 |
| 3146 | A2433 | 32c multicolored | .65 | .25 |
| a. | | Block or strip of 4, #3143-3146 | 2.60 | 1.50 |

##### With Red Bar Above Coach's Name
**Perf. 11**

| 3147 | A2433 | 32c multicolored | .65 | .45 |
| 3148 | A2430 | 32c multicolored | .65 | .45 |
| 3149 | A2431 | 32c multicolored | .65 | .45 |
| 3150 | A2433 | 32c multicolored | .65 | .45 |

Issued: #3143-3146, 7/25; #3147, 8/5; #3148, 8/7; #3149, 8/8; #3150, 8/16.

### AMERICAN DOLLS
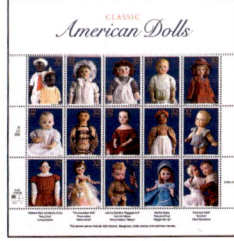
A2434

Designs: a, "Alabama Baby," and doll by Martha Chase. b, "Columbian Doll." c, Johnny Gruelle's "Raggedy Ann." d, Doll by Martha Chase. e, "American Child." f, "Baby Coos." g, Plains Indian. h, Doll by Izannah Walker. i, "Babyland Rag." j, "Scootles." k, Doll by Ludwig Greiner. l, "Betsy McCall." m, Percy Crosby's "Skippy." n, "Maggie Mix-up." o, Dolls by Albert Schoenhut.

| 1997, July 28 | | Perf. 10.9x11.1 | |
|---|---|---|---|
| 3151 A2434 | Pane of 15 | 13.50 | — |
| a.-o. | 32c any single | .90 | .60 |

### LEGENDS OF HOLLYWOOD
Humphrey Bogart (1899-1957).

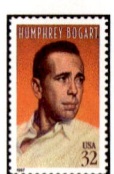 A2435

### PHOTOGRAVURE

| 1997, July 31 | | Perf. 11.1 | |
|---|---|---|---|
| 3152 A2435 | 32c multicolored | .85 | .25 |

Perforations in corner of each stamp are star-shaped.

### "THE STARS AND STRIPES FOREVER!"

 A2436

| 1997, Aug. 21 | | | |
|---|---|---|---|
| 3153 A2436 | 32c multicolored | .65 | .25 |

### AMERICAN MUSIC SERIES
Opera Singers

 Lily Pons — A2437

 Richard Tucker — A2438

 Lawrence Tibbett — A2439

 Rosa Ponselle — A2440

### LITHOGRAPHED

| 1997, Sept. 10 | | Perf. 11 | |
|---|---|---|---|
| 3154 A2437 | 32c multicolored | .75 | .25 |
| 3155 A2438 | 32c multicolored | .75 | .25 |
| 3156 A2439 | 32c multicolored | .75 | .25 |
| 3157 A2440 | 32c multicolored | .75 | .25 |
| a. | Block or strip of 4, #3154-3157 | 3.00 | 2.00 |

### AMERICAN MUSIC SERIES
Classical Composers & Conductors

 Leopold Stokowski A2441

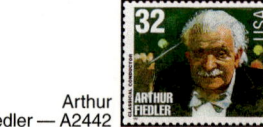 Arthur Fiedler — A2442

 George Szell — A2443

 Eugene Ormandy A2444

 Samuel Barber — A2445

 Ferde Grofé — A2446

 Charles Ives — A2447

 Louis Moreau Gottschalk A2448

### LITHOGRAPHED

| 1997, Sept. 12 | | Perf. 11 | |
|---|---|---|---|
| 3158 A2441 | 32c multicolored | 1.50 | .25 |
| 3159 A2442 | 32c multicolored | 1.50 | .25 |
| 3160 A2443 | 32c multicolored | 1.50 | .25 |
| 3161 A2444 | 32c multicolored | 1.50 | .25 |
| 3162 A2445 | 32c multicolored | 1.50 | .25 |
| 3163 A2446 | 32c multicolored | 1.50 | .25 |
| 3164 A2447 | 32c multicolored | 1.50 | .25 |
| 3165 A2448 | 32c multicolored | 1.50 | .25 |
| a. | Block of 8, #3158-3165 | 12.00 | 4.00 |

### PADRE FÉLIX VARELA (1788-1853)

 A2449

| 1997, Sept. 15 | | Perf. 11.2 | |
|---|---|---|---|
| 3166 A2449 | 32c purple | .65 | .25 |

### DEPARTMENT OF THE AIR FORCE, 50TH ANNIV.

Thunderbirds Aerial Demonstration Squadron — A2450

| 1997, Sept. 18 | | Perf. 11.2x11.1 | |
|---|---|---|---|
| 3167 A2450 | 32c multicolored | .65 | .25 |

### CLASSIC MOVIE MONSTERS

 A2451

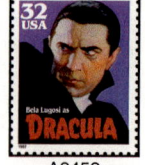 A2452

 A2453

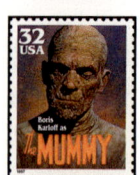 A2454

 A2455

### PHOTOGRAVURE

| 1997, Sept. 30 | | Perf. 10.2 | |
|---|---|---|---|
| 3168 A2451 | 32c multicolored | .75 | .25 |
| 3169 A2452 | 32c multicolored | .75 | .25 |
| 3170 A2453 | 32c multicolored | .75 | .25 |
| 3171 A2454 | 32c multicolored | .75 | .25 |
| 3172 A2455 | 32c multicolored | .75 | .25 |
| a. | Strip of 5, #3168-3172 | 3.75 | 2.25 |

### FIRST SUPERSONIC FLIGHT, 50TH ANNIV.

 A2456

### LITHOGRAPHED
**Serpentine Die Cut 11.4**
1997, Oct. 14
Self-Adhesive

| 3173 A2456 | 32c multicolored | .65 | .25 |

### WOMEN IN MILITARY SERVICE

 A2457

| 1997, Oct. 18 | | Perf. 11.1 | |
|---|---|---|---|
| 3174 A2457 | 32c multicolored | .65 | .25 |

### KWANZAA

 A2458

### PHOTOGRAVURE
**1997, Oct. 22  Serpentine Die Cut 11**
Self-Adhesive

| 3175 A2458 | 32c multicolored | .65 | .25 |

See Nos. 3368, 3548, 3673.

### CHRISTMAS

 Madonna and Child A2459

 Holly A2460

### LITHOGRAPHED
**Serpentine Die Cut 9.9 on 2, 3 or 4 Sides**
1997

**Booklet Stamps**
Self-Adhesive

| 3176 A2459 | 32c multicolored | .65 | .25 |
| a. | Booklet pane of 20 + label | 13.00 | |

**Serpentine Die Cut 11.2x11.6 on 2, 3 or 4 Sides**

| 3177 A2460 | 32c multicolored | .65 | .25 |
| a. | Booklet pane of 20 + label | 13.00 | |
| b. | Booklet pane of 4 | 2.60 | |
| c. | Booklet pane of 5 + label | 3.25 | |
| d. | Booklet pane of 6 | 3.90 | |

Madonna and Child, by Sano di Pietro. Issued: No. 3176, 10/27; No. 3177, 10/30.

### MARS PATHFINDER
Souvenir Sheet

Mars Rover Sojourner — A2461

### PHOTOGRAVURE

| 1997, Dec. 10  Tagged | Perf. 11x11.1 | |
|---|---|---|
| 3178 A2461 | $3 multicolored | 6.00 4.00 |
| a. | $3, single stamp | 5.50 3.00 |
| b. | Single souvenir sheet from sheet of 18 | 7.50 — |
| c. | As No. 3178, imperf. | |

The perforations at the bottom of the stamp contain the letters "USA." Vertical rouletting extends from the vertical perforations of the stamp to the bottom of the souvenir sheet.

Sheet of 18 has vertical perforations separating the three columns of souvenir sheets. These were cut away when No. 3178 was produced. Thus, the souvenir sheet from the sheet of 18 is wider and has vertical perforations on one or two sides.

### CHINESE NEW YEAR

Year of the Tiger — A2462

| 1998, Jan. 5 | | Perf. 11.2 | |
|---|---|---|---|
| 3179 A2462 | 32c multicolored | .80 | .25 |

See Nos. 3895c, 3997c.

### ALPINE SKIING

 A2463

### LITHOGRAPHED

| 1998, Jan. 22 | | Perf. 11.2 | |
|---|---|---|---|
| 3180 A2463 | 32c multicolored | .75 | .25 |

### BLACK HERITAGE SERIES

 A2464

**Serpentine Die Cut 11.6x11.3**
1998, Jan. 28
Self-Adhesive

| 3181 A2464 | 32c sepia & black | .70 | .25 |

# UNITED STATES

## CELEBRATE THE CENTURY

1900s
A2465

**No. 3182:** a, Model T Ford. b, Theodore Roosevelt. c, Motion picture "The Great Train Robbery," 1903. d, Crayola Crayons introduced, 1903. e, St. Louis World's Fair, 1904. f, Design used on Hunt's Remedy stamp (#RS56), Pure Food & Drug Act, 1906. g, Wright Brothers first flight, Kitty Hawk, 1903. h, Boxing match shown in painting "Stag at Sharkey's," by George Bellows of the Ash Can School. i, Immigrants arrive. j, John Muir, preservationist. k, "Teddy" Bear created. l, W.E.B. Du Bois, social activist. m, Gibson Girl. n, First baseball World Series, 1903. o, Robie House, Chicago, designed by Frank Lloyd Wright.

1910s
A2466

**No. 3183:** a, Charlie Chaplin as the Little Tramp. b, Federal Reserve System created, 1913. c, George Washington Carver. d, Avant-garde art introduced at Armory Show, 1913. e, First transcontinental telephone line, 1914. f, Panama Canal opens, 1914. g, Jim Thorpe wins decathlon at Stockholm Olympics, 1912. h, Grand Canyon National Park, 1919. i, U.S. enters World War I. j, Boy Scouts started in 1910, Girl Scouts formed in 1912. k, Woodrow Wilson. l, First crossword puzzle published, 1913. m, Jack Dempsey wins heavyweight title, 1919. n, Construction toys. o, Child labor reform.

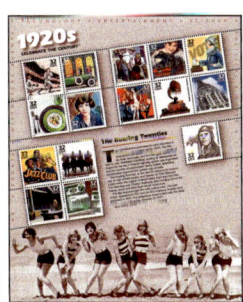
1920s
A2467

**No. 3184:** a, Babe Ruth. b, The Gatsby style. c, Prohibition enforced. d, Electric toy trains. e, 19th Amendment (woman voting). f, Emily Post's Etiquette. g, Margaret Mead, anthropologist. h, Flappers do the Charleston. i, Radio entertains America. j, Art Deco style (Chrysler Building). k, Jazz flourishes. l, Four Horsemen of Notre Dame. m, Lindbergh flies the Atlantic. n, American realism (Automat, by Edward Hopper). o, Stock Market crash, 1929.

1930s
A2468

**No. 3185:** a, Franklin D. Roosevelt. b, The Empire State Building. c, 1st Issue of Life Magazine, 1936. d, Eleanor Roosevelt. e, FDR's New Deal. f, Superman arrives, 1938. g, Household conveniences. h, "Snow White and the Seven Dwarfs," 1937. i, "Gone with the Wind," 1936. j, Jesse Owens. k, Streamline design. l, Golden Gate Bridge. m, America survives the Depression. n, Bobby Jones wins golf Grand Slam, 1938. o, The Monopoly Game.

1940s
A2469

**No. 3186:** a, World War II. b, Antibiotics save lives. c, Jackie Robinson. d, Harry S Truman. e, Women support war effort. f, TV entertains America. g, Jitterbug sweeps nation. h, Jackson Pollock, Abstract Expressionism. i, GI Bill, 1944. j, Big Band Sound. k, Intl. style of architecture (UN Headquarters). l, Postwar baby boom. m, Slinky, 1945. n, "A Streecar Named Desire," 1947. o, Orson Welles' "Citizen Kane."

1950s
A2470

**No. 3187:** a, Polio vaccine developed. b, Teen fashions. c, The "Shot Heard 'Round the World." d, US launches satellites. e, Korean War. f, Desegregating public schools. g, Tail fins, chrome. h, Dr. Seuss' "The Cat in the Hat." i, Drive-in movies. j, World Series rivals. k, Rocky Marciano, undefeated boxer. l, "I Love Lucy." m, Rock 'n Roll. n, Stock car racing. o, Movies go 3-D.

1960s
A2471

**No. 3188:** a, Martin Luther King, Jr., "I Have a Dream." b, Woodstock. c, Man walks on the moon. d, Green Bay Packers. e, Star Trek. f, The Peace Corps. g, Viet Nam War. h, Ford Mustang. i, Barbie Doll. j, Integrated circuit. k, Lasers. l, Super Bowl I. m, Peace symbol. n, Roger Maris, 61 in '61. o, The Beatles "Yellow Submarine."

1970s
A2472

**No. 3189:** a, Earth Day celebrated. b, "All in the Family" television series. c, "Sesame Street" television series character, Big Bird. d, Disco music. e, Pittsburgh Steelers win four Super Bowls. f, US Celebrates 200th birthday. g, Secretariat wins Triple Crown. h, VCRs transform entertainment. i, Pioneer 10. j, Women's rights movement. k, 1970s fashions. l, "Monday Night Football." m, Smiley face buttons. n, Jumbo jets. o, Medical imaging.

1980s
A2473

**No. 3190:** a, Space shuttle program. b, "Cats" Broadway show. c, San Francisco 49ers. d, Hostages in Iran come home. e, Figure skating. f, Cable TV. g, Vietnam Veterans Memorial. h, Compact discs. i, Cabbage Patch Kids. j, "The Cosby Show" television series. k, Fall of the Berlin Wall. l, Video games. m, "E.T. The Extra-Terrestrial" movie. n, Personal computers. o, Hip-hop culture.

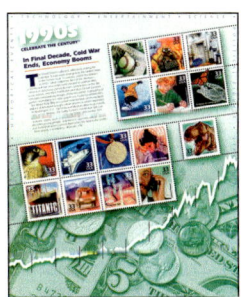
1990s
A2474

**No. 3191:** a, New baseball records. b, Gulf War. c, "Seinfeld" television series. d, Extreme sports. e, Improving education. f, Computer art and graphics. g, Recovering species. h, Return to space. i, Special Olympics. j, Virtual reality. k, Movie "Jurassic Park." l, Movie "Titanic." m, Sport utility vehicles. n, World Wide Web. o, Cellular phones.

### LITHOGRAPHED, ENGRAVED
(#3182m, 3183f, 3184m, 3185h, 3186k, 3187a, 3188c, 3189h)

| | | 1998-2000 | | Perf. 11½ | |
|---|---|---|---|---|---|
| 3182 | A2465 | Pane of 15 | | 10.00 | 8.50 |
| a.-o. | | 32c any single | | .75 | .65 |
| p. | | Engr. red (No. 3182m, Gibson girl) omitted, in pane of 15 | | 3,000. | |
| 3183 | A2466 | Pane of 15 | | 10.00 | 8.50 |
| a.-o. | | 32c any single | | .75 | .65 |
| p. | | Nos. 3183g, 3183 l-3183o imperf, in pane of 15 | | 7,000. | |
| 3184 | A2467 | Pane of 15 | | 12.50 | 8.50 |
| a.-o. | | 32c any single | | .80 | .65 |
| 3185 | A2468 | Pane of 15 | | 12.50 | 8.50 |
| a.-o. | | 32c any single | | .80 | .65 |
| 3186 | A2469 | Pane of 15 | | 13.00 | 8.50 |
| a.-o. | | 33c any single | | .85 | .65 |
| 3187 | A2470 | Pane of 15 | | 13.00 | 8.50 |
| a.-o. | | 33c any single | | .85 | .65 |
| 3188 | A2471 | Pane of 15 | | 13.00 | 8.50 |
| a.-o. | | 33c any single | | .85 | .65 |
| 3189 | A2472 | Pane of 15 | | 13.00 | 8.50 |
| a.-o. | | 33c any single | | .85 | .65 |
| 3190 | A2473 | Pane of 15 | | 13.00 | 8.50 |
| a.-o. | | 33c any single | | .85 | .65 |
| 3191 | A2474 | Pane of 15 | | 13.00 | 8.50 |
| a.-o. | | 33c any single | | .85 | .65 |
| | | Nos. 3182-3191 (10) | | 123.00 | 85.00 |

Issued: #3182-3183, 2/3; #3184, 5/28; #3185, 9/10; #3186, 2/18/99; #3187, 5/26/99; #3188, 9/17/99; #3189, 11/18/99; #3190, 1/12/00; #3191, 5/2/00.

### "REMEMBER THE MAINE"

A2475

### LITHOGRAPHED & ENGRAVED
**1998, Feb. 15**    Perf. 11.2x11
3192   A2475   32c red & black   .70   .25

### FLOWERING TREES

Southern Magnolia
A2476

Blue Paloverde
A2477

Yellow Poplar
A2478

Prairie Crab Apple
A2479

Pacific Dogwood — A2480

### LITHOGRAPHED
**1998, Mar. 19**    Die Cut Perf 11.3
**Self-Adhesive**

| 3193 | A2476 | 32c multicolored | 2.00 | .40 |
|---|---|---|---|---|
| 3194 | A2477 | 32c multicolored | 2.00 | .40 |
| 3195 | A2478 | 32c multicolored | 2.00 | .40 |
| 3196 | A2479 | 32c multicolored | 2.00 | .40 |
| 3197 | A2480 | 32c multicolored | 2.00 | .40 |
| a. | | Strip of 5, #3193-3197 | 10.00 | — |
| b. | | As "a," die cutting omitted | | |

### ALEXANDER CALDER (1898-1976), SCULPTOR

Black Cascade, 13 Verticals, 1959 — A2481

Untitled, 1965 — A2482

Roaring Stallion, 1928 — A2483

Portrait of a Young Man, c. 1945 — A2484

# UNITED STATES

Un Effet du Japonais, 1945 — A2485

### PHOTOGRAVURE
**1998, Mar. 25**  **Perf. 10.2**
| | | | | |
|---|---|---|---|---|
| 3198 | A2481 | 32c multicolored | .65 | .25 |
| 3199 | A2482 | 32c multicolored | .65 | .25 |
| 3200 | A2483 | 32c multicolored | .65 | .25 |
| 3201 | A2484 | 32c multicolored | .65 | .25 |
| 3202 | A2485 | 32c multicolored | .65 | .25 |
| a. | | Strip of 5, #3198-3202 | 3.25 | 2.25 |

### CINCO DE MAYO

A2486

*Serpentine Die Cut 11.7x10.9*
**1998, Apr. 16**  **Self-Adhesive**
3203  A2486  32c multicolored  .65  .25
  See Mexico No. 2066. For 33c version, see No. 3309.

### SYLVESTER & TWEETY

A2487

*Serpentine Die Cut 11.1*
**1998, Apr. 27**  **Self-Adhesive**
| 3204 | | Pane of 10 #3204a | 6.75 | |
| a. | | A2487 32c single | .65 | .25 |
| b. | | Pane of 9 #3204a | 6.00 | |
| c. | | Pane of 1 #3204a | .65 | |

Die cutting on No. 3204b does not extend through the backing paper.

| 3205 | | Pane of 10, #3205c, 9 #3205a | 11.00 | |
| a. | | A2487 32c single | .90 | |
| b. | | Pane of 9 #3205a | 7.00 | |
| c. | | Pane of 1, no die cutting | 3.00 | |

Die cutting on #3205a extends through the backing paper.

### WISCONSIN STATEHOOD

A2488

*Serpentine Die Cut 10.8x10.9*
**1998, May 29**  **Self-Adhesive**
3206  A2488  32c multicolored  .65  .30

Wetlands
A2489

Diner
A2490

### COIL STAMPS
**1998**  **Untagged**  **Perf. 10 Vert.**
3207  A2489  (5c) multicolored  .30  .25

*Serpentine Die Cut 9.8 Vert.*
**Self-adhesive**
**Untagged**
| 3207A | A2489 | (5c) multicolored, small date | .30 | .25 |
| b. | | Large date | .30 | .25 |

Date on No. 3207A is approximately 1.4mm long, on No. 3207Ab approx. 1.6mm long.

*Perf. 10 Vert.*
**Untagged**
3208  A2490  (25c) multicolored  .50  .50

*Serpentine Die Cut 9.8 Vert.*
**Self-Adhesive**
**Untagged**
3208A  A2490  (25c) multicolored  .50  .50
  Issued: #3207-3208, 6/5; #3208A, 9/30; #3207A, 12/14.

### 1898 TRANS-MISSISSIPPI STAMPS, CENT.

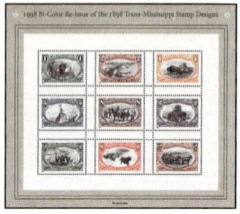
A2491

### LITHOGRAPHED & ENGRAVED
**1998, June 18**  **Perf. 12x12.4**
| 3209 | A2491 | Pane of 9 | 9.50 | 7.00 |
| a. | A100 | 1c green & black | .30 | .25 |
| b. | A108 | 2c red brown & black | .30 | .25 |
| c. | A102 | 4c orange & black | .30 | .25 |
| d. | A103 | 5c blue & black | .30 | .25 |
| e. | A104 | 8c dark lilac & black | .30 | .25 |
| f. | A105 | 10c purple & black | .30 | .25 |
| g. | A106 | 50c green & black | 1.25 | .60 |
| h. | A107 | $1 red & black | 2.50 | 1.25 |
| i. | A101 | $2 red brown & black | 4.25 | 2.50 |

Vignettes on Nos. 3209b and 3209i are reversed in comparison to the original issue.

| 3210 | A107 | $1 Pane of 9 | | |
| | | #3209h | 22.50 | — |

### BERLIN AIRLIFT, 50th ANNIV.

A2492

### PHOTOGRAVURE
**1998, June 26**  **Perf. 11.2**
3211  A2492  32c multicolored  .65  .25

### AMERICAN MUSIC SERIES
### Folk Singers

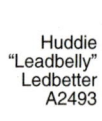
Huddie "Leadbelly" Ledbetter A2493

Woody Guthrie — A2494

Sonny Terry — A2495

Josh White — A2496

**1998, June 26**  **Perf. 10.1x10.2**
| 3212 | A2493 | 32c multicolored | .90 | .25 |
| 3213 | A2494 | 32c multicolored | .90 | .25 |
| 3214 | A2495 | 32c multicolored | .90 | .25 |
| 3215 | A2496 | 32c multicolored | .90 | .25 |
| a. | | Block or strip of 4, #3212-3215 | 3.60 | 2.00 |

### AMERICAN MUSIC SERIES
### Gospel Singers

Mahalia Jackson — A2497

Roberta Martin — A2498

Clara Ward — A2499

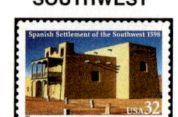
Sister Rosetta Tharpe — A2500

**1998, July 15**  **Perf. 10.1x10.3**
| 3216 | A2497 | 32c multicolored | 1.00 | .25 |
| 3217 | A2498 | 32c multicolored | 1.00 | .25 |
| 3218 | A2499 | 32c multicolored | 1.00 | .25 |
| 3219 | A2500 | 32c multicolored | 1.00 | .25 |
| a. | | Block or strip of 4, #3216-3219 | 4.00 | 2.00 |

### SPANISH SETTLEMENT OF THE SOUTHWEST

La Mision de San Miguel de San Gabriel, Española, NM — A2501

### LITHOGRAPHED
**1998, July 11**  **Perf. 11.2**
3220  A2501  32c multicolored  .65  .25

### LITERARY ARTS SERIES

Stephen Vincent Benét — A2502

**1998, July 22**  **Perf. 11.2**
3221  A2502  32c multicolored  .65  .25

### TROPICAL BIRDS

Antillean Euphonia — A2503

Green-throated Carib — A2504

Crested Honeycreeper A2505

Cardinal Honeyeater A2506

**1998, July 29**
| 3222 | A2503 | 32c multicolored | .65 | .25 |
| 3223 | A2504 | 32c multicolored | .65 | .25 |
| 3224 | A2505 | 32c multicolored | .65 | .25 |
| 3225 | A2506 | 32c multicolored | .65 | .25 |
| a. | | Block or strip of 4, #3222-3225 | 2.60 | 2.00 |

### LEGENDS OF HOLLYWOOD

A2507

### PHOTOGRAVURE
**1998, Aug. 3**  **Perf. 11.1**
3226  A2507  32c multicolored  .75  .25
  Perforations in corner of each stamp are star-shaped.

### ORGAN & TISSUE DONATION

A2508

*Serpentine Die Cut 11.7*
**1998, Aug. 5**  **Self-Adhesive**
3227  A2508  32c multicolored  .65  .25

### MODERN BICYCLE

A2509

Small Date

Large Date

### COIL STAMP
*Serpentine Die Cut 9.8 Vert.*
**1998, Aug. 14**  **Untagged**
**Self-Adhesive (#3228)**
| 3228 | A2509 | (10c) multicolored, small "1998" year date | .30 | .25 |
| a. | | Large date | .35 | .25 |

Date on No. 3228a is approximately 1 ½mm; on No. 3228 approximately 1mm.

**Untagged**
**Perf. 9.9 Vert.**
3229  A2509  (10c) multicolored  .30  .25
Date on No. 3229 is approximately 2mm wide.

### BRIGHT EYES

Dog — A2510

Fish — A2511

UNITED STATES 91

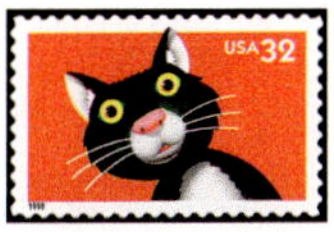
Cat — A2512

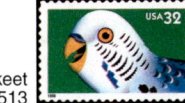

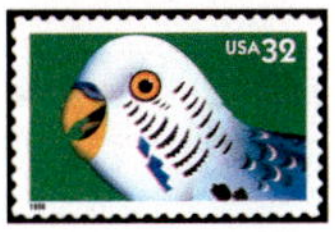
Parakeet A2513

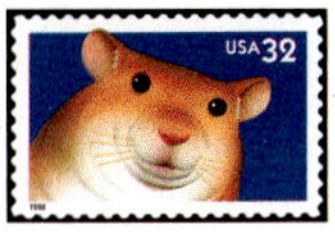
Hamster — A2514

*Serpentine Die Cut 9.9*

**1998, Aug. 20**

**Self-Adhesive**

| | | | | |
|---|---|---|---|---|
| **3230** | A2510 | 32c multicolored | .75 | .40 |
| **3231** | A2511 | 32c multicolored | .75 | .40 |
| **3232** | A2512 | 32c multicolored | .75 | .40 |
| **3233** | A2513 | 32c multicolored | .75 | .40 |
| **3234** | A2514 | 32c multicolored | .75 | .40 |
| *a.* | | Strip of 5, #3230-3234 | 3.75 | |

## KLONDIKE GOLD RUSH, CENTENNIAL

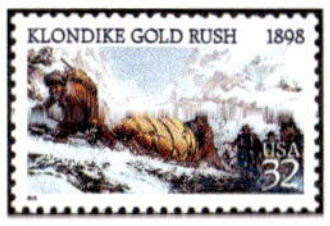

A2515

LITHOGRAPHED

**1998, Aug. 21** *Perf. 11.1*

| | | | | |
|---|---|---|---|---|
| **3235** | A2515 | 32c multicolored | .65 | .25 |

## AMERICAN ART

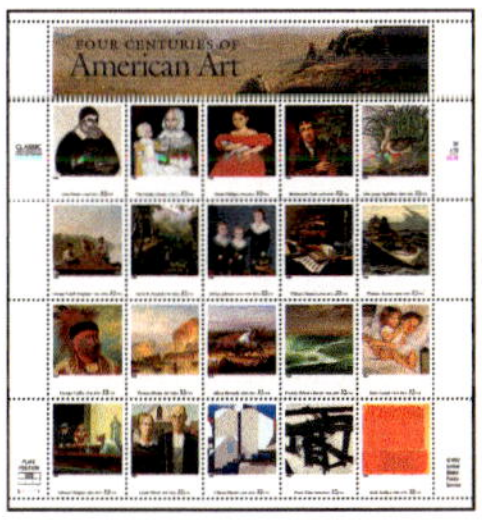

A2516

Paintings: a, "Portrait of Richard Mather," by John Foster. b, "Mrs. Elizabeth Freake and Baby Mary," by The Freake Limner. c, "Girl in Red Dress with Cat and Dog," by Ammi Phillips. d, "Rubens Peale with a Geranium," by Rembrandt Peale. e, "Long-billed Curlew, Numenius Longrostris," by John James Audubon. f, "Boatmen on the Missouri," by George Caleb Bingham. g, "Kindred Sprits," by Asher B. Durand. h, "The Westwood Children," by Joshua Johnson. i, "Music and Literature," by William Harnett. j, "The Fog Warning," by Winslow Homer. k, "The White Cloud, Head Chief of the Iowas," by George Catlin. l, "Cliffs of Green River," by Thomas Moran. m, "The Last of the Buffalo," by Alfred Bierstadt. n, "Niagara," by Frederic Edwin Church. o, "Breakfast in Bed," by Mary Cassatt. p, "Nighthawks," by Edward Hopper. q, "American Gothic," by Grant Wood. r, "Two Against the White," by Charles Sheeler. s, "Mahoning," by Franz Kline. t, "No. 12," by Mark Rothko.

PHOTOGRAVURE

**1998, Aug. 27** *Perf. 10.2*

| | | | | |
|---|---|---|---|---|
| **3236** | A2516 | Pane of 20 | 18.00 | 10.00 |
| *a.-t.* | | 32c any single | .90 | .60 |

## AMERICAN BALLET

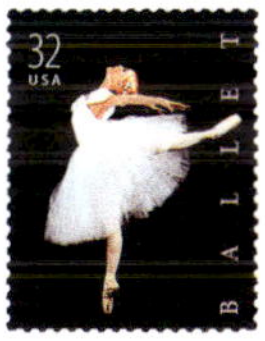

A2517

LITHOGRAPHED

**1998, Sept. 16** *Perf. 10.9x11.1*

| | | | | |
|---|---|---|---|---|
| **3237** | A2517 | 32c multicolored | .65 | .25 |

## SPACE DISCOVERY

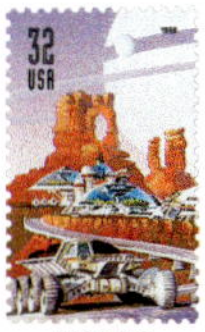
A2518

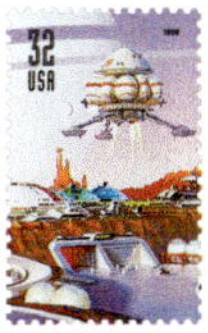
A2519

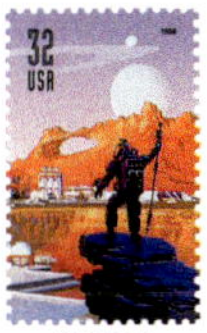
A2520

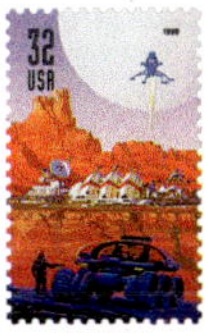
A2521

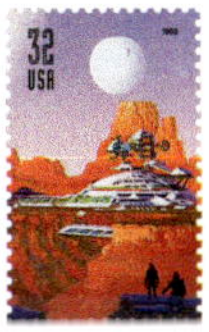
A2522

PHOTOGRAVURE

**1998, Oct. 1** *Perf. 11.1*

| | | | | |
|---|---|---|---|---|
| **3238** | A2518 | 32c multicolored | .65 | .25 |
| **3239** | A2519 | 32c multicolored | .65 | .25 |
| **3240** | A2520 | 32c multicolored | .65 | .25 |
| **3241** | A2521 | 32c multicolored | .65 | .25 |
| **3242** | A2522 | 32c multicolored | .65 | .25 |
| *a.* | | Strip of 5, #3238-3242 | 3.25 | 2.25 |

## GIVING AND SHARING

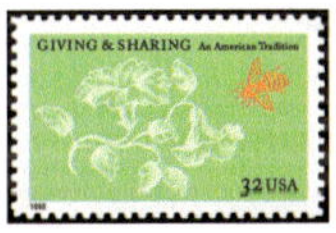

A2523

PHOTOGRAVURE

*Serpentine Die Cut 11.1*

**1998, Oct. 7**

**Self-Adhesive**

| | | | | |
|---|---|---|---|---|
| **3243** | A2523 | 32c multicolored | .65 | .25 |

## CHRISTMAS

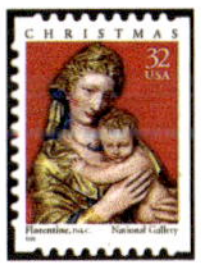

Madonna and Child, Florence, 15th Cent. — A2524

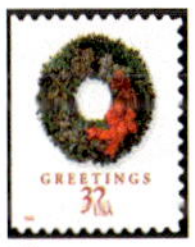

Evergreen A2525

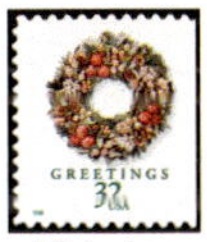

Victorian A2526

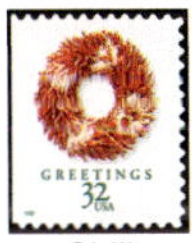

Chili Pepper A2527

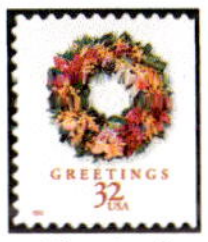

Tropical A2528

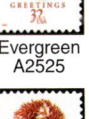

LITHOGRAPHED

*Serpentine Die Cut 10.1x9.9 on 2, 3 or 4 Sides*

**1998, Oct. 15**

**Self-Adhesive**

**Booklet Stamps**

| | | | | |
|---|---|---|---|---|
| **3244** | A2524 | 32c multicolored | .65 | .25 |
| *a.* | | Booklet pane of 20 + label | 13.00 | |
| *b.* | | Die cutting omitted, pair | — | |

**Size: 22x25mm**

*Serpentine Die Cut 11.3x11.7 on 2 or 3 Sides*

| | | | | |
|---|---|---|---|---|
| **3245** | A2525 | 32c multicolored | 3.25 | .25 |
| **3246** | A2526 | 32c multicolored | 3.25 | .25 |
| **3247** | A2527 | 32c multicolored | 3.25 | .25 |
| **3248** | A2528 | 32c multicolored | 3.75 | .25 |
| *a.* | | Booklet pane of 4, #3245-3248 | 13.00 | |
| *b.* | | Booklet pane of 5, #3245-3246, 3248, 2 #3247 + label | 16.25 | |
| *c.* | | Booklet pane of 6, #3247-3248, 2 each #3245-3246 | 19.50 | |
| *d.* | | As "a," die cutting omitted | — | |
| *e.* | | As "b," die cutting omitted | — | |
| *f.* | | As "c," die cutting omitted | — | |
| *g.* | | Block of 4, #3245-3248 | 13.00 | |

**Size: 23x30mm**

*Serpentine Die Cut 11.4x11.5 on 2, 3, or 4 Sides*

| | | | | |
|---|---|---|---|---|
| **3249** | A2525 | 32c multicolored | 1.35 | .25 |
| *a.* | | Serp. die cut 11.7x11.6 on 2, 3, or 4 sides | 1.75 | .25 |
| **3250** | A2526 | 32c multicolored | 1.35 | .25 |
| *a.* | | Serp. die cut 11.7x11.6 on 3 or 4 sides | 1.75 | .25 |
| **3251** | A2527 | 32c multicolored | 1.35 | .25 |
| *a.* | | Serp. die cut 11.7x11.6 on 3 or 4 sides | 1.75 | .25 |
| **3252** | A2528 | 32c multi + label | 1.35 | .25 |
| *a.* | | Serp. die cut 11.7x11.6 on 2, 3, or 4 sides | 1.75 | .25 |
| *b.* | | Block or strip of 4, #3249-3252 | 5.40 | |
| *c.* | | Booklet pane of 20, 5 each #3249-3252 + label | 30.00 | |
| *d.* | | Block or strip of 4, #3249a-3252a | 7.00 | |
| *e.* | | Booklet pane of 20, 5 each #3249a-3252a + label | 35.00 | |
| *f.* | | Block or strip of 4, #3249-3252, red ("Greetings 32 USA" and "1998") omitted on #3249, 3252 | 625.00 | |
| *g.* | | Block or strip of 4, #3249-3252, red ("Greetings 32 USA" and "1998") omitted on #3249, 3252; green (same) omitted on #3250, 3251 | — | |
| *h.* | | As "b," die cutting omitted | — | |
| *i.* | | As "c," die cutting omitted | 4,500. | |

Dedicated printing plates were used to print the red and green denominations, salutations and dates. Red and green appearing in the wreaths come from other plates and, therefore, are not part of the color omissions.

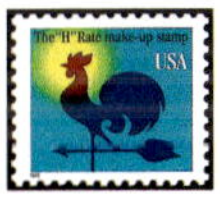

Weather Vane — A2529

LITHOGRAPHED

**1998** **Untagged** *Perf. 11.2*

| | | | | |
|---|---|---|---|---|
| **3257** | A2529 | (1c) multi | .30 | .25 |
| *a.* | | Black omitted | 125.00 | |
| *b.* | | Horiz. pair, imperf. vert. and at top | — | |

**Untagged**

| | | | | |
|---|---|---|---|---|
| **3258** | A2529 | (1c) multi | .30 | .25 |
| *a.* | | Black missing (PS) | — | |

No. 3257 is 18mm high, has thin letters, white USA, and black 1998. No. 3258 is 17mm high, has thick letters, pale blue USA and blue 1998.

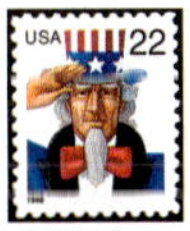

Uncle Sam A2530

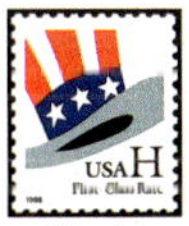

Uncle Sam's Hat A2531

PHOTOGRAVURE

*Serpentine Die Cut 10.8*

**Self-Adhesive (#3259, 3261-3263, 3265-3269)**

| | | | | |
|---|---|---|---|---|
| **3259** | A2530 | 22c multi | .45 | .25 |
| *a.* | | Die cut 10.8x10.5 | 2.50 | .25 |
| *b.* | | Vert. pair, No. 3259 + 3259a | 3.50 | |

See No. 3353.

*Perf. 11.2*

| | | | | |
|---|---|---|---|---|
| **3260** | A2531 | (33c) multi | .65 | .25 |

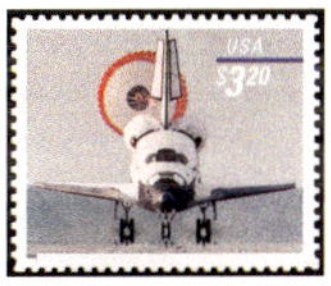

Space Shuttle Landing — A2532

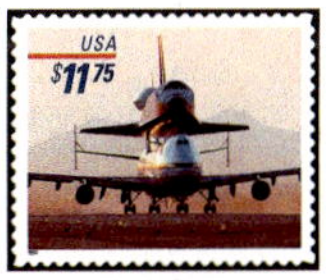

Piggyback Space Shuttle — A2533

LITHOGRAPHED

Sheets of 120 in six panes of 20 (#3261-3262)

*Serpentine Die Cut 11.5*

| | | | | |
|---|---|---|---|---|
| **3261** | A2532 | $3.20 multi | 6.00 | 1.50 |
| **3262** | A2533 | $11.75 multi | 22.50 | 10.00 |

Hidden 3-D images (ENTERPRISE/COLUMBIA/CHALLENGER/ATLANTIS/ENDEAVOR/DISCOVERY) can be seen on Nos. 3261 and 3262 when viewed with a special "Stamp Decoder" lens sold by the USPS.

## COIL STAMPS

PHOTOGRAVURE

*Serpentine Die Cut 9.9 Vert.*

| | | | | |
|---|---|---|---|---|
| **3263** | A2530 | 22c multi | .45 | .25 |
| *a.* | | Die cutting omitted, pair | *450.00* | |

See No. 3353.

*Perf. 9.8 Vert.*

| | | | | |
|---|---|---|---|---|
| **3264** | A2531 | (33c) multi | .65 | .25 |
| *a.* | | Imperf, pair | *325.00* | |

*Serpentine Die Cut 9.9 Vert.*

| | | | | |
|---|---|---|---|---|
| **3265** | A2531 | (33c) multi | .80 | .25 |
| *a.* | | Die cutting omitted, pair | 65.00 | — |
| *b.* | | Red omitted | *300.00* | |
| *c.* | | Black omitted | *1,400.* | |
| *d.* | | Black omitted, die cutting omitted, pair | *700.00* | |
| *e.* | | Red omitted, die cutting omitted, pair | *650.00* | |
| *f.* | | Blue omitted | — | |

Unused examples of No. 3265 are on backing paper the same size as the stamps. Corners of the stamp are 90 degree angles.

On No. 3265b, the blue and gray colors are shifted down and to the right.

On No. 3265f, the red is misregistered to right by 10½ stamps and gray by 3mm.

*Serpentine Die Cut 9.9 Vert.*

| | | | | |
|---|---|---|---|---|
| **3266** | A2531 | (33c) multi | 2.25 | .25 |

Unused examples of No. 3266 are on backing paper larger than the stamps, and the stamps are spaced approximately 2mm. apart. Corners of stamps are rounded.

## BOOKLET STAMPS

*Serpentine Die Cut 9.9 on 2 or 3 Sides*

| | | | | |
|---|---|---|---|---|
| **3267** | A2531 | (33c) multi | .75 | .25 |
| *a.* | | Booklet pane of 10 | 7.50 | |

*Serpentine Die Cut 11¼ on 3 Sides (#3268, 3268a)*

*or 11 on 2, 3 or 4 sides (#3268b, 3268c)*

| | | | | |
|---|---|---|---|---|
| **3268** | A2531 | (33c) multi | .75 | .25 |
| *a.* | | Booklet pane of 10 | 7.50 | |
| *b.* | | Serpentine die cut 11 | .75 | .25 |
| *c.* | | As "b," booklet pane of 20 + label | 15.00 | |

*Die Cut 8 on 2, 3 or 4 Sides*

| | | | | |
|---|---|---|---|---|
| **3269** | A2531 | (33c) multi | .65 | .25 |
| *a.* | | Booklet pane of 18 | 12.00 | |

Issued: No. 3262, 11/19, others, 11/9.

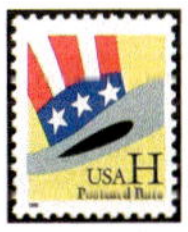


Unused and used examples of an "H" nondenominated stamp inscribed "Postcard Rate" exist in the marketplace. There is no evidence that these stamps were ever officially issued. Values: unused $2,400, used $1,750.

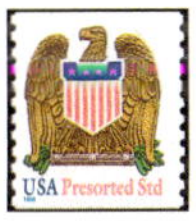

A2534

PHOTOGRAVURE

COIL STAMPS

*Perf. 9.8 Vert.*

**1998, Dec. 14** **Untagged**

| | | | | |
|---|---|---|---|---|
| **3270** | A2534 | (10c) multi, small date | .30 | .25 |
| *a.* | | Large date | .75 | .25 |

**Self-Adhesive**

**Untagged**

*Serpentine Die Cut 9.9 Vert.*

| | | | | |
|---|---|---|---|---|
| **3271** | A2534 | (10c) multi, small date | .30 | .25 |
| *a.* | | Large date | 1.00 | .25 |

Dates on Nos. 3270a and 3271a are approximately 1¾mm; on Nos. 3270-3271 approximately 1¼mm.

92 UNITED STATES

Compare to Nos. 2602-2604, 2907.

Scott values for used self-adhesive stamps are for examples either on piece or off piece.

## CHINESE NEW YEAR

Year of the Rabbit — A2535

**1999, Jan. 5**   **Perf. 11.2**
3272   A2535   33c multicolored   .80   .25
See Nos. 3895d, 3997d.

## BLACK HERITAGE SERIES

Malcolm X — A2536

**LITHOGRAPHED**
**Serpentine Die Cut 11.4**
**1999, Jan. 20**
**Self-Adhesive**
3273   A2536   33c multicolored   1.00   .25

## VICTORIAN LOVE

A2537    A2538

**PHOTOGRAVURE**
**1999, Jan. 28**   **Die Cut**
**Booklet Stamp**
**Self-Adhesive**
3274   A2537   33c multicolored   .65   .25
   a.   Booklet pane of 20   13.00
   b.   Die cutting omitted, pair   100.00
   c.   As "a," die cutting omitted   800.00
3275   A2538   55c multicolored   1.10   .35

## HOSPICE CARE

A2539

**LITHOGRAPHED**
**Serpentine Die Cut 11.4**
**1999, Feb. 9**
3276   A2539   33c multicolored   .65   .25
   a.   Horiz. pair, vert. die cutting omitted   650.00

Flag & City — A2540

**PHOTOGRAVURE**
**1999, Feb. 25**   **Perf. 11.2**
**Self-Adhesive (#3278, 3278F, 3279, 3281-3282)**
3277   A2540   33c multi   .70   .25
No. 3277 has red date.

**Serpentine Die Cut 11 on 2, 3 or 4 Sides**
3278   A2540   33c multi   .65   .25
   a.   Booklet pane of 4   2.60
   b.   Booklet pane of 5 + label   3.25
   c.   Booklet pane of 6   3.90
   d.   Booklet pane of 10   13.00
   e.   Booklet pane of 20 + label   17.00
   h.   As "e," die cutting omitted   —

   i.   Serpentine die cut 11¼   .90   .25
   j.   As "i," booklet pane of 10   9.00
No. 3278 has black date.

**BOOKLET STAMPS**
**Serpentine Die Cut 11½x11¾ on 2, 3 or 4 Sides**
3278F   A2540b   33c multi   1.40   .25
   g.   Booklet pane of 20 + label   28.00
No. 3278F has black date.

**Serpentine Die Cut 9.8 on 2 or 3 Sides**
3279   A2540   33c multi   .85   .25
   a.   Booklet pane of 10   8.50
No. 3279 has red date.

**COIL STAMPS**
**Perf. 9.9 Vert.**
3280   A2540   33c multi, small "1999" year date   .65   .25
   a.   Large date   2.00   .25
   b.   As No. 3280, imperf pair   125.00   150.00

**Serpentine Die Cut 9.8 Vert.**
Two types of No. 3281: Type I, Long vertical feature at left and right of tallest building consists of 3 separate lines; Type II, Same features consist of solid color.
3281   A2540   33c multi, type I, large "1999" year date   .65   .25
   a.   As No. 3281, die cutting omitted, pair   30.00
   b.   Light blue and yellow omitted   275.00
   c.   Small date, type II   .65   .25
   d.   Small date, type I   5.00   .30
   e.   As "c," die cutting omitted, pair   —

Corners are square on No. 3281. Unused examples are on backing paper the same size as the stamps, and the stamps are adjoining. Date on Nos. 3280a and 3281 is approximately 1¾mm; on Nos. 3280, 3281c and 3281d approximately 1¼mm.

3282   A2540   33c multi   .65   .25
Corners are rounded on #3282. Unused examples are on backing paper larger than the stamps, and the stamps are spaced approximately 2mm. apart.

Flag & Chalkboard — A2541

Printed by Avery Dennison.

**PHOTOGRAVURE**
**Serpentine Die Cut 7.9 on 2, 3 or 4 Sides**
**1999, Mar. 13**
**Self-Adhesive**
**BOOKLET STAMP**
3283   A2541   33c multicolored   .65   .25
   a.   Booklet pane of 18   12.00
   b.   Die cutting omitted, pair   —

## IRISH IMMIGRATION

A2542

**LITHOGRAPHED**
**1999, Feb. 26**   **Perf. 11.2**
3286   A2542   33c multicolored   .65   .25
See Ireland No. 1168.

## PERFORMING ARTS SERIES
Alfred Lunt (1892-1977), Lynn Fontanne (1887-1983), Actors

A2543

**LITHOGRAPHED**
**1999, Mar. 2**   **Perf. 11.2**
3287   A2543   33c multicolored   .65   .25

## ARCTIC ANIMALS

A2544    A2545

A2546    A2547

A2548

**LITHOGRAPHED**
**1999, Mar. 12**   **Perf. 11**
3288   A2544   33c Arctic Hare   .85   .25
3289   A2545   33c Arctic Fox   .85   .25
3290   A2546   33c Snowy Owl   .85   .25
3291   A2547   33c Polar Bear   .85   .25
3292   A2548   33c Gray Wolf   .85   .25
   a.   Strip of 5, #3288-3292   4.25

## SONORAN DESERT

A2549

Designs: a, Cactus wren, brittlebush, teddy bear cholla. b, Desert tortoise. c, White-winged dove, prickly pear. d, Gambel quail. e, Saguaro cactus. f, Desert mule deer. g, Desert cottontail, hedgehog cactus. h, Gila monster. i, Western diamondback rattlesnake, cactus mouse. j, Gila woodpecker.

**LITHOGRAPHED**
**Serpentine Die Cut Perf 11.2**
**1999, Apr. 6**
**Self-Adhesive**
3293   A2549   Pane of 10   8.00
   a.-j.   33c any single   .80   .50

## BERRIES

Blueberries    Raspberries
A2550    A2551

Strawberries    Blackberries
A2552    A2553

**PHOTOGRAVURE**
**Serpentine Die Cut 11¼x11½ on 2, 3 or 4 Sides (Nos. 3294-3297), or 2 or 3 sides (Nos. 3294a-3297a)**
**1999, Apr. 10**
**Self-Adhesive**
3294   A2550   33c multicolored   .85   .25
   a.   Dated "2000"   1.25   .25
3295   A2551   33c multicolored   .85   .25
   a.   Dated "2000"   1.25   .25
3296   A2552   33c multicolored   .85   .25
   a.   Dated "2000"   1.25   .25
3297   A2553   33c multicolored   .85   .25
   a.   Dated "2000"   1.25   .25
   b.   Booklet pane of 20, 5 each #3294-3297 + label   17.50

   c.   Block or strip of 4, #3294-3297   3.50
   d.   Booklet pane of 20, 5 #3297e + label   25.00
   e.   Block of 4, #3294a-3297a   5.00

No. 3297d is a double-sided booklet pane, with 12 stamps on one side and eight stamps plus label on the other side.

**Serpentine Die Cut 9½x10 on 2 or 3 Sides**
3298   A2550   33c multicolored   1.00   .25
3299   A2552   33c multicolored   1.00   .25
3300   A2551   33c multicolored   1.00   .25
3301   A2553   33c multicolored   1.00   .25
   a.   Booklet pane of 4, #3298-3301   4.00
   b.   Booklet pane of 5, #3298, 3299, 3301, 2 #3300 + label   5.00
   c.   Booklet pane of 6, #3300, 3301, 2 #3298, 3299   6.00
   d.   Block of 4, #3298-3301   4.00

**COIL STAMPS**
**Serpentine Die Cut 8.5 Vert.**
3302   A2550   33c multicolored   2.25   .25
3303   A2551   33c multicolored   2.25   .25
3304   A2553   33c multicolored   2.25   .25
3305   A2552   33c multicolored   2.25   .25
   a.   Strip of 4, #3302-3305   9.00

See Nos. 3404-3407.

## DAFFY DUCK

A2554

**PHOTOGRAVURE**
**Serpentine Die Cut 11.1**
**1999, Apr. 16**
**Self-Adhesive**
3306   Pane of 10 #3306a   6.75
   a.   A2554 33c single   .65   .25
   b.   Pane of 9 #3306a   6.00
   c.   Pane of 1 #3306a   .65

Die cutting on #3306b does not extend through the backing paper.

3307   Pane of 10, #3307c, 9 #3307a   13.00
   a.   A2554 33c single   1.10
   b.   Pane of 9 #3307a   10.00
   c.   Pane of 1, no die cutting   2.75
   d.   As "a," vert. pair, die cutting omitted btwn. pos. 6 and 9 (unique)   4,250.

Die cutting on #3307b extends through the backing paper.

## LITERARY ARTS SERIES

Ayn Rand (1905-82) — A2555

**LITHOGRAPHED**
**1999, Apr. 22**   **Perf. 11.2**
3308   A2555   33c multicolored   .65   .25

**Cinco De Mayo Type of 1998**
**LITHOGRAPHED**
**Serpentine Die Cut 11.6x11.3**
**1999, Apr. 27**
**Self-Adhesive**
3309   A2486   33c multicolored   .70   .25

## TROPICAL FLOWERS

Bird of Paradise — A2556

Royal Poinciana A2557

# UNITED STATES

Gloriosa Lily — A2558

Chinese Hibiscus — A2559

**PHOTOGRAVURE**
**BOOKLET STAMPS**
*Serpentine Die Cut 10.9 on 2 or 1 Sides*
**1999, May 1**
**Self-Adhesive**

| | | | | |
|---|---|---|---|---|
| 3310 | A2556 | 33c multicolored | .65 | .30 |
| 3311 | A2557 | 33c multicolored | .65 | .30 |
| 3312 | A2558 | 33c multicolored | .65 | .30 |
| 3313 | A2559 | 33c multicolored | .65 | .30 |
| a. | Block of 4, #3310-3313 | | 2.60 | |
| b. | Booklet pane, 5 each #3313a | | 13.00 | |

No. 3313b is a double-sided booklet pane with 12 stamps on one side and 8 stamps plus label on the other side.

**JOHN (1699-1777) & WILLIAM (1739-1823) BARTRAM, BOTANISTS**

A2560

**LITHOGRAPHED**
*Serpentine Die Cut 11½*
**1999, May 18**
**Self-Adhesive**

| | | | | |
|---|---|---|---|---|
| 3314 | A2560 | 33c multicolored | .65 | .25 |

**PROSTATE CANCER AWARENESS**

A2561

**PHOTOGRAVURE**
**1999, May 28** *Serpentine Die Cut 11*
**Self-Adhesive**

| | | | | |
|---|---|---|---|---|
| 3315 | A2561 | 33c multicolored | .65 | .25 |

**CALIFORNIA GOLD RUSH, 150TH ANNIV.**

A2562

**LITHOGRAPHED**
**1999, June 18** *Perf. 11¼*

| | | | | |
|---|---|---|---|---|
| 3316 | A2562 | 33c multicolored | .65 | .25 |

**AQUARIUM FISH**

A2563

A2564

Reef Fish — A2566

A2565

Designs: No. 3317, Yellow fish, red fish, cleaner shrimp. No. 3318, Fish, thermometer. No. 3319, Red fish, blue & yellow fish. No. 3320, Fish, heater/aerator.

**LITHOGRAPHED**
*Serpentine Die Cut 11½*
**1999, June 24**
**Self-Adhesive**

| | | | | |
|---|---|---|---|---|
| 3317 | A2563 | 33c multicolored | .65 | .30 |
| 3318 | A2564 | 33c multicolored | .65 | .30 |
| 3319 | A2565 | 33c multicolored | .65 | .30 |
| 3320 | A2566 | 33c multicolored | .65 | .30 |
| b. | Strip of 4, #3317-3320 | | 2.60 | |

**EXTREME SPORTS**

A2567

A2568

A2569 A2570

**PHOTOGRAVURE**
*Serpentine Die Cut 11*
**1999, June 25**
**Self-Adhesive**

| | | | | |
|---|---|---|---|---|
| 3321 | A2567 | 33c multicolored | .75 | .30 |
| 3322 | A2568 | 33c multicolored | .75 | .30 |
| 3323 | A2569 | 33c multicolored | .75 | .30 |
| 3324 | A2570 | 33c multicolored | .75 | .30 |
| a. | Block or strip of 4, #3321-3324 | | 3.00 | |

**AMERICAN GLASS**

Free-Blown Glass A2571

Mold-Blown Glass A2572

Pressed Glass A2573

Art Glass A2574

**LITHOGRAPHED**
**1999, June 29** *Perf. 11*

| | | | | |
|---|---|---|---|---|
| 3325 | A2571 | 33c multicolored | 1.90 | .25 |
| 3326 | A2572 | 33c multicolored | 1.90 | .25 |
| 3327 | A2573 | 33c multicolored | 1.90 | .25 |
| 3328 | A2574 | 33c multicolored | 1.90 | .25 |
| a. | Strip or block of 4, #3325-3328 | | 7.75 | 3.00 |

**LEGENDS OF HOLLYWOOD**

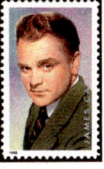
James Cagney (1899-1986) — A2575

**PHOTOGRAVURE**
**1999, July 22** *Perf. 11*

| | | | | |
|---|---|---|---|---|
| 3329 | A2575 | 33c multicolored | .80 | .25 |

Perforations in corner of each stamp are star-shaped.

**GEN. WILLIAM "BILLY" L. MITCHELL (1879-1936), AVIATION PIONEER**

A2576

*Serpentine Die Cut 9¾x10*
**1999, July 30**
**Self-Adhesive**

| | | | | |
|---|---|---|---|---|
| 3330 | A2576 | 55c multicolored | 1.10 | .30 |

**HONORING THOSE WHO SERVED**

A2577

*Serpentine Die Cut 11*
**1999, Aug. 16**
**Self-Adhesive**

| | | | | |
|---|---|---|---|---|
| 3331 | A2577 | 33c black, blue & red | .65 | .25 |

**UNIVERSAL POSTAL UNION**

A2578

**LITHOGRAPHED**
**1999, Aug. 25** *Perf. 11*

| | | | | |
|---|---|---|---|---|
| 3332 | A2578 | 45c multicolored | 1.00 | .45 |

**FAMOUS TRAINS**

Daylight — A2579

Congressional A2580

20th Century Limited — A2581

Hiawatha A2582

Super Chief — A2583

**1999, Aug. 26**

| | | | | |
|---|---|---|---|---|
| 3333 | A2579 | 33c multicolored | .75 | .25 |
| 3334 | A2580 | 33c multicolored | .75 | .25 |
| 3335 | A2581 | 33c multicolored | .75 | .25 |
| 3336 | A2582 | 33c multicolored | .75 | .25 |
| 3337 | A2583 | 33c multicolored | .75 | .25 |
| a. | Strip of 5, #3333-3337 | | 3.75 | — |

Stamps in No. 3337a are arranged in four different orders.

**FREDERICK LAW OLMSTED (1822-1903), LANDSCAPE ARCHITECT**

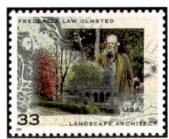
A2584

**1999, Sept. 12**

| | | | | |
|---|---|---|---|---|
| 3338 | A2584 | 33c multicolored | .65 | .25 |

**AMERICAN MUSIC SERIES**
**Hollywood Composers**

Max Steiner (1888-1971) A2585

Dimitri Tiomkin (1894-1975) A2586

Bernard Herrmann (1911-75) A2587

Franz Waxman (1906-67) A2588

Alfred Newman (1907-70) A2589

Erich Wolfgang Korngold (1897-1957) A2590

**1999, Sept. 16** *Perf. 11*

| | | | | |
|---|---|---|---|---|
| 3339 | A2585 | 33c multicolored | 1.40 | .25 |
| 3340 | A2586 | 33c multicolored | 1.40 | .25 |
| 3341 | A2587 | 33c multicolored | 1.40 | .25 |
| 3342 | A2588 | 33c multicolored | 1.40 | .25 |
| 3343 | A2589 | 33c multicolored | 1.40 | .25 |
| 3344 | A2590 | 33c multicolored | 1.40 | .25 |
| a. | Block of 6, #3339-3344 | | 8.50 | 4.50 |

**AMERICAN MUSIC SERIES**
**Broadway Songwriters**

Ira (1896-1983) & George (1898-1937) Gershwin A2591

Alan Jay Lerner (1918-86) & Frederick Loewe (1901-88) A2592

# UNITED STATES

Lorenz Hart (1895-1943) A2593

Richard Rodgers (1902-79) & Oscar Hammerstein II (1895-1960) A2594

Meredith Willson (1902-84) A2595

Frank Loesser (1910-69) A2596

**1999, Sept. 21**

| 3345 | A2591 | 33c multicolored | 1.25 | .25 |
|---|---|---|---|---|
| 3346 | A2592 | 33c multicolored | 1.25 | .25 |
| 3347 | A2593 | 33c multicolored | 1.25 | .25 |
| 3348 | A2594 | 33c multicolored | 1.25 | .25 |
| 3349 | A2595 | 33c multicolored | 1.25 | .25 |
| 3350 | A2596 | 33c multicolored | 1.25 | .25 |
| a. | | Block of 6, #3345-3350 | 7.50 | 4.50 |

## INSECTS & SPIDERS

A2597

Designs: a, Black widow. b, Elderberry longhorn. c, Lady beetle. d, Yellow garden spider. e, Dogbane beetle. f, Flower fly. g, Assassin bug. h, Ebony jewelwing. i, Velvet ant. j, Monarch caterpillar. k, Monarch butterfly. l, Eastern Hercules beetle. m, Bombardier beetle. n, Dung beetle. o, Spotted water beetle. p, True katydid. q, Spinybacked spider. r, Periodical cicada. s, Scorpionfly. t, Jumping spider.

**1999, Oct. 1**     *Perf. 11*

| 3351 | A2597 | Pane of 20 | 14.00 | 10.00 |
|---|---|---|---|---|
| a.-t. | | 33c any single | .70 | .50 |

### Hanukkah Type of 1996
PHOTOGRAVURE

**1999, Oct. 8**     *Serpentine Die Cut 11*
**Self-Adhesive**

| 3352 | A2411 | 33c multicolored | .65 | .25 |
|---|---|---|---|---|

See Nos. 3352, 3547, 3672, Israel No. 1289.

### Uncle Sam Type of 1998
COIL STAMP

**1999, Oct. 8**     *Perf. 9¾ Vert.*

| 3353 | A2530 | 22c multicolored | .45 | .25 |
|---|---|---|---|---|

See Nos. 3259, 3263.

### NATO, 50TH ANNIV.

A2598

LITHOGRAPHED

**1999, Oct. 13**     *Perf. 11¼*

| 3354 | A2598 | 33c multicolored | .65 | .25 |
|---|---|---|---|---|

## CHRISTMAS

Madonna and Child, by Bartolomeo Vivarini — A2599

*Serpentine Die Cut 11¼ on 2 or 3 sides*

**1999, Oct. 20**
**Booklet Stamp**
**Self-Adhesive**

| 3355 | A2599 | 33c multicolored | .90 | .25 |
|---|---|---|---|---|
| a. | | Booklet pane of 20 | 18.00 | |

Deer — A2600

*Serpentine Die Cut 11¼*

| 3356 | A2600 | 33c gold & red | 2.25 | .25 |
|---|---|---|---|---|
| 3357 | A2260 | 33c gold & blue | 2.25 | .25 |
| 3358 | A2260 | 33c gold & purple | 2.25 | .25 |
| 3359 | A2260 | 33c gold & green | 2.25 | .25 |
| a. | | Block or strip of 4, #3356-3359 | 9.00 | |

**Booklet Stamps**
*Serpentine Die Cut 11¼ on 2, 3 or 4 sides*

| 3360 | A2260 | 33c gold & red | 1.10 | .25 |
|---|---|---|---|---|
| 3361 | A2260 | 33c gold & blue | 1.10 | .25 |
| 3362 | A2260 | 33c gold & purple | 1.10 | .25 |
| 3363 | A2600 | 33c gold & green | 1.10 | .25 |
| a. | | Booklet pane of 20, 5 each #3360-3363 | 22.50 | |
| b. | | Block or strip of 4, #3360-3363 | 4.40 | |
| c. | | As "b," die cutting omitted | 100.00 | |
| d. | | As "a," die cutting omitted | 500.00 | |

Size: 21x19mm
*Serpentine Die Cut 11½x11¼ on 2 or 3 sides*

| 3364 | A2260 | 33c gold & red | 1.35 | .25 |
|---|---|---|---|---|
| 3365 | A2260 | 33c gold & blue | 1.35 | .25 |
| 3366 | A2260 | 33c gold & purple | 1.35 | .25 |
| 3367 | A2260 | 33c gold & green | 1.35 | .25 |
| a. | | Booklet pane of 4, #3364-3367 | 5.50 | |
| b. | | Booklet pane of 5, #3364, 3366, 3367, 2 #3365 + label | 7.00 | |
| c. | | Booklet pane of 6, #3365, 3367, 2 each #3364 & 3366 | 8.00 | |
| d. | | Block of 4, #3364-3367 | 5.50 | |

The frame on Nos. 3356-3359 is narrow and the space between it and the hoof is a hairline. The frame on Nos. 3360-3363 is much thicker, and the space between it and the hoof is wider.

### Kwanzaa Type of 1997
PHOTOGRAVURE

**1999, Oct. 29**     *Serpentine Die Cut 11*
**Self-Adhesive**

| 3368 | A2458 | 33c multicolored | .65 | .25 |
|---|---|---|---|---|

See Nos. 3175, 3548, 3673.

## YEAR 2000

Baby New Year — A2601

LITHOGRAPHED
*Serpentine Die Cut 11¼*

**1999, Dec. 27**
**Self-Adhesive**

| 3369 | A2601 | 33c multicolored | .65 | .25 |
|---|---|---|---|---|

## CHINESE NEW YEAR

Year of the Dragon — A2602

**2000, Jan. 6**     *Perf. 11¼*

| 3370 | A2602 | 33c multicolored | .80 | .25 |
|---|---|---|---|---|

See Nos. 3895e, 3997e.

## BLACK HERITAGE SERIES

Patricia Roberts Harris — A2603

*Serpentine Die Cut 11½x11¼*

**2000, Jan. 27**
**Self-Adhesive**

| 3371 | A2603 | 33c indigo | .65 | .25 |
|---|---|---|---|---|

## SUBMARINES

S Class — A2604

Los Angeles Class — A2605

Ohio Class — A2606

USS Holland — A2607

Gato Class A2608

**2000, Mar. 27**     *Perf. 11*

| 3372 | A2605 | 33c multi, with microprinted "USPS" at base of sail | .75 | .25 |
|---|---|---|---|---|

**BOOKLET STAMPS**

| 3373 | A2604 | 22c multicolored | .75 | .75 |
|---|---|---|---|---|
| 3374 | A2605 | 33c multi, no microprinting | 1.00 | 1.00 |
| 3375 | A2606 | 55c multicolored | 1.50 | 1.25 |
| 3376 | A2607 | 60c multicolored | 1.75 | 1.50 |
| 3377 | A2608 | $3.20 multicolored | 10.00 | 5.00 |
| a. | | Booklet pane of 5, #3373-3377 | 15.00 | |

No. 3377a was issued with two types of text in the selvage.

## PACIFIC COAST RAIN FOREST

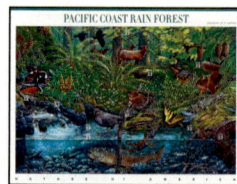

A2609

Designs: a, Harlequin duck. b, Dwarf oregongrape, snail-eating ground beetle. c, American dipper, horiz. d, Cutthroat trout, horiz. e, Roosevelt elk. f, Winter wren. g, Pacific giant salamander, Rough-skinned newt. h, Western tiger swallowtail, horiz. i, Douglas squirrel, foliose lichen. j, Foliose lichen, banana slug.

*Serpentine Die Cut 11¼x11½, 11½ (horiz. stamps)*

**2000, Mar. 29**
**Self-Adhesive**

| 3378 | A2609 | Pane of 10 | 10.00 | |
|---|---|---|---|---|
| a.-j. | | 33c any single | 1.00 | .50 |

## LOUISE NEVELSON (1899-1988), SCULPTOR

Silent Music I — A2610

Royal Tide I — A2611

Black Chord A2612

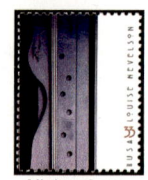

Nightsphere-Light A2613

Dawn's Wedding Chapel I — A2614

**2000, Apr. 6**     *Perf. 11x11¼*

| 3379 | A2610 | 33c multicolored | .65 | .25 |
|---|---|---|---|---|
| 3380 | A2611 | 33c multicolored | .65 | .25 |
| 3381 | A2612 | 33c multicolored | .65 | .25 |
| 3382 | A2613 | 33c multicolored | .65 | .25 |
| 3383 | A2614 | 33c multicolored | .65 | .25 |
| a. | | Strip of 5, #3379-3383 | 3.25 | — |

## HUBBLE SPACE TELESCOPE IMAGES

Eagle Nebula A2615

Ring Nebula A2616

Lagoon Nebula A2617

Egg Nebula A2618

Galaxy NGC 1316 — A2619

PHOTOGRAVURE

**2000, Apr. 10**     *Perf. 11*

| 3384 | A2615 | 33c multicolored | .65 | .25 |
|---|---|---|---|---|
| 3385 | A2616 | 33c multicolored | .65 | .25 |
| 3386 | A2617 | 33c multicolored | .65 | .25 |
| 3387 | A2618 | 33c multicolored | .65 | .25 |
| 3388 | A2619 | 33c multicolored | .65 | .25 |
| a. | | Strip of 5, #3384-3388 | 3.25 | 2.00 |
| b. | | As "a," imperf | 700.00 | |

## AMERICAN SAMOA

Samoan Double Canoe — A2620

# UNITED STATES

### LITHOGRAPHED
**2000, Apr. 17**
3389 A2620 33c multicolored .85 .25

### LIBRARY OF CONGRESS

A2621

**2000, Apr. 24**
3390 A2621 33c multicolored .65 .25

### ROAD RUNNER & WILE E. COYOTE

A2622

*Serpentine Die Cut 11*
**2000, Apr. 26**
**Self-Adhesive**
3391 Pane of 10 #3391a 10.00
 a. A2622 33c single .85 .25
 b. Pane of 9 #3391a 8.00
 c. Pane of 1 #3391a 1.50
 d. All die cutting omitted, pane of 10 2,250.

Die cutting on #3391b does not extend through the backing paper.

3392 Pane of 10, #3392c, 9 #3392a 30.00
 a. A2622 33c single 2.75
 b. Pane of 9 #3392a 25.00
 c. Pane of 1, no die cutting 5.00

Die cutting on #3392a extends through the backing paper. Used examples of No. 3392a are identical to those of No. 3391a.

Nos. 3391b-3391c and 3392b-3392c are separated by a vertical line of microperforations.

### DISTINGUISHED SOLDIERS

A2623

A2624

A2625

A2626

Designs: No. 3393, Maj. Gen. John L. Hines. No. 3394, Gen. Omar N. Bradley. No. 3395, Sgt. Alvin C. York. No. 3396, Second Lt. Audie L. Murphy.

**2000, May 3** **Perf. 11**
3393 A2623 33c multicolored .70 .25
3394 A2624 33c multicolored .70 .25
3395 A2625 33c multicolored .70 .25
3396 A2626 33c multicolored .70 .25
 a. Block or strip of 4, #3393-3396 2.80 1.50

### SUMMER SPORTS

Runners — A2627

**2000, May 5**
3397 A2627 33c multicolored .65 .25

### ADOPTION

Stick Figures — A2628

*Serpentine Die Cut 11½*
**2000, May 10**
**Self-Adhesive**
3398 A2628 33c multicolored .65 .25
 a. Die cutting omitted, pair 2,500.

See note after No. 1549.

### YOUTH TEAM SPORTS

A2629   A2630
A2631   A2632

**2000, May 27** **Perf. 11**
3399 A2629 33c Basketball .70 .25
3400 A2630 33c Football .70 .25
3401 A2631 33c Soccer .70 .25
3402 A2632 33c Baseball .70 .25
 a. Block or strip of 4, #3399-3402 2.80 1.75

### THE STARS AND STRIPES

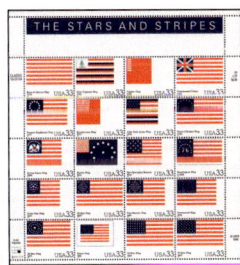
A2633

Designs: a, Sons of Liberty Flag, 1775. b, New England Flag, 1775. c, Forster Flag, 1775. d, Continental Colors, 1776. e, Francis Hopkinson Flag, 1777. f, Brandywine Flag, 1777. g, John Paul Jones Flag, 1779. h, Pierre L'Enfant Flag, 1783. i, Indian Peace Flag, 1803. j, Easton Flag, 1814. k, Star-Spangled Banner, 1814. l, Bennington Flag, c. 1820. m, Great Star Flag, 1837. n, 29-Star Flag, 1847. o, Fort Sumter Flag, 1861. p, Centennial Flag, 1876. q, 38-Star Flag, 1877. r, Peace Flag, 1891. s, 48-Star Flag, 1912. t, 50-Star Flag, 1960.

**2000, June 14** **Perf. 10½x11**
3403 A2633 Pane of 20 15.00 11.00
 a.-t. 33c any single .75 .50

### BERRIES

Blueberries A2634

Strawberries A2635

Blackberries A2636

Raspberries A2637

See designs A2550-A2553.

### PHOTOGRAVURE COIL STAMPS
*Serpentine Die Cut 8½ Horiz.*
**2000, June 16** **Tagged**
**Self-Adhesive**
3404 A2634 33c multicolored 3.50 .25
3405 A2635 33c multicolored 3.50 .25
3406 A2636 33c multicolored 3.50 .25
3407 A2637 33c multicolored 3.50 .25
 a. Strip of 4, #3404-3407 15.00

Nos. 3404-3407 are linerless coils issued without backing paper. The adhesive is strong and can remove the ink from stamps in the roll.

### LEGENDS OF BASEBALL

A2638

Designs: a, Jackie Robinson. b, Eddie Collins. c, Christy Mathewson. d, Ty Cobb. e, George Sisler. f, Rogers Hornsby. g, Mickey Cochrane. h, Babe Ruth. i, Walter Johnson. j, Roberto Clemente. k, Lefty Grove. l, Tris Speaker. m, Cy Young. n, Jimmie Foxx. o, Pie Traynor. p, Satchel Paige. q, Honus Wagner. r, Josh Gibson. s, Dizzy Dean. t, Lou Gehrig.

### LITHOGRAPHED
*Serpentine Die Cut 11¼*
**2000, July 6**
**Self-Adhesive**
3408 A2638 Pane of 20 15.00
 a.-t. 33c any single .75 .50

### SPACE
**Souvenir Sheets**

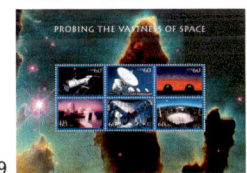
A2639

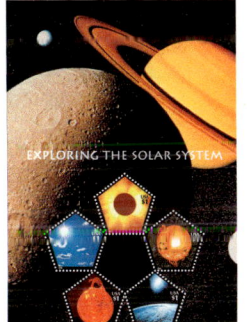
A2640

A2641

A2642

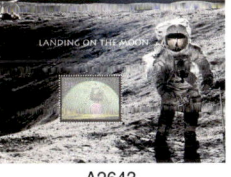
A2643

Designs: No. 3409: a, Hubble Space Telescope. b, Radio Interferometer very large array, New Mexico. c, Optical and infrared telescopes, Keck Observatory, Hawaii. d, Optical telescopes, Cerro Tololo Observatory, Chile. e, Optical telescope, Mount Wilson Observatory, California. f, Radio telescope, Arecibo Observatory, Puerto Rico.
No. 3410: a, Sun and corona. b, Cross-section of sun. c, Sun and earth. d, Sun and solar flare. e, Sun and clouds.
No. 3411: a, Space Shuttle and Space Station. b, Astronauts working in space.

### PHOTOGRAVURE
**2000** **Perf. 10½x11**
3409 A2639 Sheet of 6 15.00 7.00
 a.-f. 60c any single 2.25 1.00

**Perf. 10¾**
3410 A2640 Sheet of 5 + label 17.50 10.00
 a.-e. $1 any single 3.00 1.75
 f. As No. 3410, imperf 2,000.
 g. As No. 3410, with hologram from No. 3411b applied 1,500.

**Untagged**
**Photogravure with Hologram Affixed**
**Perf. 10½, 10¾ (#3412)**
3411 A2641 Sheet of 2 22.50 10.00
 a.-b. $3.20 any single 10.00 4.00
 c. Hologram omitted on right stamp —
3412 A2642 multicolored 40.00 17.50
 a. $11.75 single 35.00 15.00
 b. Hologram omitted —
 c. Hologram omitted on No. 3412 in uncut sheet of 5 panes —
3413 A2643 multicolored 40.00 17.50
 a. $11.75 single 35.00 15.00
 b. Double hologram 3,500.
 c. Double hologram on No. 3413 in uncut sheet of 5 panes —
 d. Hologram omitted on No. 3413 in uncut sheet of 5 panes —
 Nos. 3409-3413 (5) 135.00 62.00

Issued: No. 3409, 7/10; No. 3410, 7/11; No. 3411, 7/9; No. 3412, 7/7; No. 3413, 7/8.

The holograms on Nos. 3411-3413 scratch easily. Values are for examples with minimal scratches. Examples without scratches are worth more.

**Warning:** Soaking in water may affect holographic images.

## STAMPIN' THE FUTURE CHILDREN'S STAMP DESIGN CONTEST WINNERS

by Zachary Canter — A2644

by Sarah Lipsey — A2645

by Morgan Hill — A2646

by Ashley Young — A2647

**LITHOGRAPHED**
*Serpentine Die Cut 11¼*
**2000, July 13**
**Self-Adhesive**

| | | | | |
|---|---|---|---|---|
| 3414 | A2644 | 33c multicolored | .65 | .30 |
| 3415 | A2645 | 33c multicolored | .65 | .30 |
| 3416 | A2646 | 33c multicolored | .65 | .30 |
| 3417 | A2647 | 33c multicolored | .65 | .30 |
| a. | | Horiz. strip of 4, #3414-3417 | 2.60 | |

## DISTINGUISHED AMERICANS

Gen. Joseph W. Stilwell A2650

Wilma Rudolph (1940-94), Athlete A2652

Sen. Claude Pepper A2656

Sen. Margaret Chase Smith (1897-1995) A2657

James A. Michener (1907-97), Author — A2657a

Dr. Jonas Salk (1914-95), Polio Vaccine Pioneer A2658

Harriet Beecher Stowe (1811-96), Author A2660

Sen. Hattie Caraway (1878-1950) — A2661

Edward Trudeau (1848-1915), Phthisiologist — A2661b

Mary Lasker (1900-94), Philanthropist — A2661c

Edna Ferber (1887-1968), Writer A2662

Edna Ferber (With Curving Shoulder) A2663

Dr. Albert Sabin (1906-93), Polio Vaccine Pioneer — A2664

**LITHOGRAPHED & ENGRAVED, LITHOGRAPHED (#3427A, 3432A, 3432B)**

*Perf. 11 (#3420, 3426), Serpentine Die Cut 11¼x10¾ (#3422, 3430, 3432B), 11¼x11 (#3427A, 3428, 3432A, 3435), 11 (#3427, 3431), 11½x11 (#3432), 11x11¾ (#3433), 11¼ (#3434)*

**2000-09**
**Self-Adhesive (All Except #3420, 3426)**

| | | | | |
|---|---|---|---|---|
| 3420 | A2650 | 10c red & blk | .30 | .25 |
| a. | | Imperf, pair | 300.00 | |
| 3422 | A2652 | 23c red & blk | .45 | .25 |
| a. | | Imperf, pair | 600.00 | |
| 3426 | A2656 | 33c red & blk | .65 | .25 |
| 3427 | A2657 | 58c red & blk | 1.25 | .25 |
| b. | | Black (engr.) omitted | 200.00 | |
| 3427A | A2657a | 59c multi | 1.30 | |
| c. | | Blue, magenta and yellow omitted | 1,500. | |
| d. | | Blue and yellow omitted | — | |

On No. 3427Ad, traces of magenta, where it would not normally appear, are present.

| | | | | |
|---|---|---|---|---|
| 3428 | A2658 | 63c red & blk | 1.25 | .25 |
| a. | | Black (litho.) omitted | 275.00 | |
| 3430 | A2660 | 75c red & blk | 1.50 | .25 |
| 3431 | A2661 | 76c red & blk | 1.50 | .25 |
| 3432 | A2661 | 76c red & blk | 4.00 | 2.00 |
| 3432A | A2661b | 76c multi | 2.00 | .25 |
| 3432B | A2661c | 78c multi | 1.60 | .25 |
| 3433 | A2662 | 83c red & blk | 1.70 | .30 |
| 3434 | A2663 | 83c red & blk | 1.60 | .30 |
| 3435 | A2664 | 87c red & blk | 1.75 | .30 |

**LITHOGRAPHED**
**BOOKLET STAMP**
*Serpentine Die Cut 11¼x10¾ on 3 Sides*
**Self-Adhesive**

| | | | | |
|---|---|---|---|---|
| 3436 | A2652 | 23c red & blk | .45 | .25 |
| a. | | Booklet pane of 4 | 1.80 | |
| b. | | Booklet pane of 6 | 2.70 | |
| c. | | As "a" & "b" in cplt booklet of 10 (No. BK279A), die cutting omitted and peel strip intact, P#P44 | — | |
| d. | | Booklet pane of 10 | 4.50 | |
| e. | | As "d," die cutting omitted | — | |

The backing on No. 3436b has a different product number (672900) than that found on the lower portion of No. 3436d (673000).

Issued: 10c, 8/24; 33c, 9/7; No. 3432, 2/21/01; No. 3433, 7/29/02; No. 3434, Aug. 2003; 23c, 7/14/04; 63c, 87c, 3/2/06; 58c, 75c, 6/13/07; 59c, No. 3432A, 5/12/08; No. 3432B, 5/15/09.

## CALIFORNIA STATEHOOD, 150TH ANNIV.

Big Sur and Iceplant — A2668

**PHOTOGRAVURE**
**2000, Sept. 8** *Serpentine Die Cut 11*
**Self-Adhesive**

| | | | | |
|---|---|---|---|---|
| 3438 | A2668 | 33c multicolored | 1.00 | .25 |

## DEEP SEA CREATURES

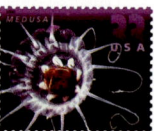
Fanfin Anglerfish A2669

Sea Cucumber A2670

Fangtooth A2671

Amphipod A2672

Medusa — A2673

**2000, Oct. 2** **Tagged** *Perf. 10x10¼*

| | | | | |
|---|---|---|---|---|
| 3439 | A2669 | 33c multicolored | .75 | .25 |
| 3440 | A2670 | 33c multicolored | .75 | .25 |
| 3441 | A2671 | 33c multicolored | .75 | .25 |
| 3442 | A2672 | 33c multicolored | .75 | .25 |
| 3443 | A2673 | 33c multicolored | .75 | .25 |
| a. | | Vert. strip of 5, #3439-3443 | 3.75 | 2.00 |

## LITERARY ARTS SERIES

Thomas Wolfe (1900-38), Novelist — A2674

**LITHOGRAPHED**
**2000, Oct. 3** *Perf. 11*

| | | | | |
|---|---|---|---|---|
| 3444 | A2674 | 33c multicolored | .65 | .25 |

## WHITE HOUSE, 200TH ANNIV.

A2675

*Serpentine Die Cut 11¼*
**2000, Oct. 18**
**Self-Adhesive**

| | | | | |
|---|---|---|---|---|
| 3445 | A2675 | 33c multicolored | 1.00 | .25 |

## LEGENDS OF HOLLYWOOD

Edward G. Robinson (1893-1973), Actor — A2676

**PHOTOGRAVURE**
**2000, Oct. 24** *Perf. 11*

| | | | | |
|---|---|---|---|---|
| 3446 | A2676 | 33c multicolored | 1.60 | .25 |

Perforations in corner of each stamp are star-shaped.

New York Public Library Lion — A2677

**PHOTOGRAVURE**
**COIL STAMP**
*Serpentine Die Cut 11½ Vert.*
**2000, Nov. 9** **Untagged**
**Self-Adhesive**

| | | | | |
|---|---|---|---|---|
| 3447 | A2677 | (10c) multi, "2000" year date | .30 | .25 |
| a. | | "2003" year date | .30 | .25 |

See No. 3769.

Flag Over Farm — A2678

**LITHOGRAPHED (#3448-3449), PHOTOGRAVURE (#3450)**
**2000, Dec. 15** *Perf. 11¼*

| | | | | |
|---|---|---|---|---|
| 3448 | A2678 | (34c) multicolored | 1.00 | .25 |

**Self-Adhesive**
*Serpentine Die Cut 11¼*

| | | | | |
|---|---|---|---|---|
| 3449 | A2678 | (34c) multicolored | 1.00 | .25 |

**Booklet Stamp**
**Self-Adhesive**
*Serpentine Die Cut 8 on 2, 3 or 4 Sides*

| | | | | |
|---|---|---|---|---|
| 3450 | A2678 | (34c) multicolored | .85 | .25 |
| a. | | Booklet pane of 18 | 16.00 | |
| b. | | Die cutting omitted, pair | — | |

A2679

**PHOTOGRAVURE**
*Serpentine Die Cut 11 on 2, 3 or 4 Sides*
**2000, Dec. 15**
**Self-Adhesive**
**Booklet Stamp**

| | | | | |
|---|---|---|---|---|
| 3451 | A2679 | (34c) multicolored | 1.10 | .25 |
| a. | | Booklet pane of 20 | 22.00 | |
| b. | | Booklet pane of 4 | 4.40 | |
| c. | | Booklet pane of 6 | 6.60 | |
| d. | | As "a," die cutting omitted | — | |

Statue of Liberty — A2680

**Coil Stamps**
*Perf. 9¾ Vert.*

| | | | | |
|---|---|---|---|---|
| 3452 | A2680 | (34c) multicolored | 1.10 | .25 |

*Serpentine Die Cut 10 Vert.*
**Self-Adhesive**

| | | | | |
|---|---|---|---|---|
| 3453 | A2680 | (34c) multi, small date | .70 | .25 |
| a. | | Die cutting omitted, pair | 300.00 | |
| b. | | Large date | .75 | .25 |

The date on No. 3453 is 1.4mm long, on No. 3453b 1.55mm long and darker in color.

A2681

A2682

A2683

Flowers — A2684

UNITED STATES 97

PHOTOGRAVURE

***Serpentine Die Cut 10½x10¾ on 2 or 3 Sides***

**2000, Dec. 15**

**Booklet Stamps**

**Self-Adhesive**

**3454** A2681 (34c) purple & multi 1.10 .25
**3455** A2682 (34c) tan & multi 1.10 .25
**3456** A2683 (34c) green & multi 1.10 .25
**3457** A2684 (34c) red & multi 1.10 .25
*a.* Block of 4, #3454-3457 4.40
*b.* Booklet pane of 4, #3454-3457 4.40
*c.* Booklet pane of 6, #3456, 3457, 2 each #3454-3455 7.00
*d.* Booklet pane of 6, #3454, 3455, 2 each #3456-3457 7.00
*e.* Booklet pane of 20, 5 each #3454-3457 + label 22.50

No. 3457e is a double-sided booklet pane, with 12 stamps on one side and eight stamps plus label on the other side.

***Serpentine Die Cut 11½x11¾ on 2 or 3 Sides***

**3458** A2681 (34c) purple & multi 5.00 .25
**3459** A2682 (34c) tan & multi 5.00 .25
**3460** A2683 (34c) green & multi 5.00 .25
**3461** A2684 (34c) red & multi 5.00 .25
*a.* Block of 4, #3458-3461 20.00
*b.* Booklet pane of 20, 2 each #3461a, 3 each #3457a 55.00
*c.* Booklet pane of 20, 2 each #3457a, 3 each #3461a 90.00

Nos. 3461b and 3461c are double-sided booklet panes, with 12 stamps on one side and eight stamps plus label on the other side.

**Coil Stamps**

***Serpentine Die Cut 8½ Vert.***

**3462** A2683 (34c) green & multi 4.50 .25
**3463** A2684 (34c) red & multi 4.50 .25
**3464** A2682 (34c) tan & multi 4.50 .25
**3465** A2681 (34c) purple & multi 4.50 .25
*a.* Strip of 4, #3462-3465 20.00

Lettering on No. 3462 has black outline not found on No. 3456. Zeroes of "2000" are rounder on Nos. 3454-3457 than on Nos. 3462-3465.

Statue of Liberty — A2685

***Serpentine Die Cut 9¾ Vert.***

**2001, Jan. 7**

**Coil Stamp**

**Self-Adhesive**

**3466** A2685 34c multi .70 .25

George Washington A2686

American Buffalo A2687

Designed by Carl Herrman (#3467, 3468), Richard Sheaff (#3468A).

Printed by Sterling Sommer for Ashton-Potter (USA) Ltd. (#3467), Avery Dennison (#3468), Banknote Corporation of America (#3468A).

Sheets of 400 in four panes of 100 (#3467), Sheets of 200 in 10 panes of 20 (#3468), Sheets of 120 in six panes of 20 (#3468A)

**Self-Adhesive (#3468-3468A)**

**2001** ***Perf. 11¼x11***

**3467** A2687 21c multi .50 .25

***Serpentine Die Cut 11***

**3468** A2687 21c multi .50 .25

**Litho.**

***Serpentine Die Cut 11¼x11¾***

**3468A** A2686 23c green .50 .25

Flag Over Farm — A2688

**Photo.**

***Perf. 11¼***

**3469** A2688 34c multi .75 .25

***Serpentine Die Cut 11¼***

**3470** A2688 34c multi 1.00 .25

Eagle — A2696

***Serpentine Die Cut 10¾***

**3471** A2696 55c multi 1.10 .25
**3471A** A2696 57c multi 1.10 .25

Capitol Dome A2697

Washington Monument A2698

***Serpentine Die Cut 11¼x11½***

**Litho.**

**Self-Adhesive (#3473)**

**3472** A2697 $3.50 multi 7.00 2.00
*a.* Die cutting omitted, pair *500.00*
**3473** A2698 $12.25 multi 22.50 10.00

**COIL STAMPS**

**Self-Adhesive (#3475-3475A, 3477-3481)**

**Photo.**

***Serpentine Die Cut 8½ Vert.***

**3475** A2687 21c multi .50 .25
**3475A** A2686 23c green .75 .25

Compare No. 3475A ("2001" date at lower left) with No. 3617 ("2002" date at lower left).

***Perf. 9¾ Vert.***

**3476** A2685 34c multi .90 .25

***Serpentine Die Cut 9¾ Vert.***

**3477** A2685 34c multi .80 .25
*a.* Die cutting omitted, pair *65.00*

No. 3477 has right angle corners and backing paper as high as the stamp. No. 3466 has rounded corners and is on backing paper larger than the stamp.

A2690

A2691

A2692

Flowers — A2693

***Serpentine Die Cut 8½ Vert.***

**3478** A2690 34c green & multi 1.50 .25
**3479** A2691 34c red & multi 1.50 .25
**3480** A2692 34c tan & multi 1.50 .25
**3481** A2693 34c purple & multi 1.50 .25
*a.* Strip of 4, #3478-3481 6.00

**BOOKLET STAMPS**

**Litho.**

**Self-Adhesive**

***Serpentine Die Cut 11¼x11 on 3 Sides***

**3482** A2686 20c dk car .55 .25
*a.* Booklet pane of 10 5.50
*b.* Booklet pane of 4 2.20
*c.* Booklet pane of 6 3.30

***Serpentine Die Cut 10½x11 on 3 Sides***

**3483** A2686 20c dk car 5.50 1.25
*a.* Booklet pane of 4, 2 #3482 at L, 2 #3483 at R 12.50
*b.* Booklet pane of 6, 3 #3482 at L, 3 #3483 at R 20.00
*c.* Booklet pane of 10, 5 #3482 at L, 5 #3483 at R 30.00
*d.* Booklet pane of 4, 2 #3483 at L, 2 #3482 at R 12.50
*e.* Booklet pane of 6, 3 #3483 at L, 3 #3482 at R 20.00
*f.* Booklet pane of 10, 5 #3483 at L, 5 #3482 at R 30.00
*g.* Pair, #3482 at L, #3483 at R 6.00
*h.* Pair, #3483 at L, #3482 at R 6.00

***Serpentine Die Cut 11¼ on 3 Sides***

**3484** A2687 21c multi .60 .25
*b.* Booklet pane of 4 2.40
*c.* Booklet pane of 6 3.60
*d.* Booklet pane of 10 6.00

***Serpentine Die Cut 10½x11¼***

**3484A** A2687 21c multi 5.50 1.50
*e.* Booklet pane of 4, 2 #3484 at L, 2 #3484A at R 12.50
*f.* Booklet pane of 6, 3 #3484 at L, 3 #3484A at R 20.00
*g.* Booklet pane of 10, 5 #3484 at L, 5 #3484A at R 30.00
*h.* Booklet pane of 4, 2 #3484A at L, 2 #3484 at R 12.50
*i.* Booklet pane of 6, 3 #3484A at L, 3 #3484 at R 20.00
*j.* Booklet pane of 10, 5 #3484A at L, 5 #3484 at R 30.00
*k.* Pair, #3484 at L, #3484A at R 6.00
*l.* Pair, #3484A at L, #3484 at R 6.00

Statue of Liberty — A2689

**Photo.**

***Serpentine Die Cut 11 on 2, 3 or 4 Sides***

**3485** A2689 34c multi .70 .25
*a.* Booklet pane of 10 7.00
*b.* Booklet pane of 20 14.00
*c.* Booklet pane of 4 2.80
*d.* Booklet pane of 6 4.50
*e.* Die cutting omitted, pair (from No. 3485b) —
*f.* As "e," booklet pane of 20 —

***Serpentine Die Cut 10½x10¾ on 2 or 3 Sides***

**3487** A2693 34c purple & multi .85 .25
**3488** A2692 34c tan & multi .85 .25
**3489** A2690 34c green & multi .85 .25
**3490** A2691 34c red & multi .85 .25
*a.* Block of 4, #3487-3490 3.50
*b.* Booklet pane of 4, #3487-3490 3.50
*c.* Booklet pane of 6, #3489-3490, 2 each #3487-3488 5.00
*d.* Booklet pane of 6, #3487-3488, 2 each #3489-3490 5.00
*e.* Booklet pane of 20, 5 each #3490a + label 20.00

No. 3490e is a double-sided booklet pane, with 12 stamps on one side and eight stamps plus label on the other side.

Apple A2694

Orange A2695

**Litho.**

***Serpentine Die Cut 11¼ on 2, 3 or 4 Sides***

**3491** A2694 34c multi .70 .25
**3492** A2695 34c multi .70 .25
*a.* Pair, #3491-3492 1.40
*b.* Booklet pane, 10 each #3491-3492 14.00
*c.* As "a," black ("34 USA") omitted —
*d.* As "a," die cutting omitted *1,100.*
*e.* As "b," die cutting omitted *5,500.*
*f.* As "b," right four stamps yellow omitted *3,500.*

***Serpentine Die Cut 11½x10¾ on 2 or 3 Sides***

**3493** A2694 34c multi 1.05 .25
**3494** A2695 34c multi 1.05 .25
*a.* Pair, #3493-3494 2.10
*b.* Booklet pane, 2 each #3493-3494 4.20
*c.* Booklet pane, 3 each #3493-3494, #3493 at UL 6.30
*d.* Booklet pane, 3 each #3493-3494, #3494 at UL 6.30

***Serpentine Die Cut 8 on 2, 3, or 4 Sides***

**3495** A2688b34c multi 1.10 .25
*a.* Booklet pane of 18 18.00

Issued: Nos. 3472-3473, 1/29; Nos. 3469, 3476-3481, 3485, 3487-3490, 2/7; Nos. 3468, 3471, 3475, 3482, 3483, 2/22; Nos. 3470, 3491-3492, 3/6; Nos. 3493-3494, May; Nos. 3467, 3468A, 3471A, 3475A, 3483, 3484A, 9/20; No. 3495, 12/17.

See Nos. 3616-3619.

**LOVE**

Rose, Apr. 20, 1763 Love Letter by John Adams A2699

Rose, Apr. 20, 1763 Love Letter by John Adams A2700

Rose, Aug. 11, 1763 Love Letter by Abigail Smith (Abigail Adams in 1764) — A2701

LITHOGRAPHED

***Serpentine Die Cut 11¼ on 2, 3 or 4 Sides***

**2001**

**Self-Adhesive**

**Booklet Stamps (Nos. 3496-3498)**

**3496** A2699 (34c) multi 1.10 .25
*a.* Booklet pane of 20 22.00
*b.* Vert. pair, die cutting omitted between —

***Serpentine Die Cut 11¼ on 2, 3 or 4 Sides***

**3497** A2700 34c multi .90 .25
*a.* Booklet pane of 20 18.00
*b.* Vertical pair, die cutting omitted between —

**Size: 18x21mm**

***Serpentine Die Cut 11½x10¾ on 2 or 3 Sides***

**3498** A2700 34c multi .85 .25
*a.* Booklet pane of 4 3.50
*b.* Booklet pane of 6 5.10

***Serpentine Die Cut 11¼***

**3499** A2701 55c multi 1.10 .25

Issued: No. 3496, 1/19; others, 2/14.

See No. 3551.

**CHINESE NEW YEAR**

Year of the Snake — A2702

**2001, Jan. 20** ***Perf. 11¼***

**3500** A2702 34c multicolored .75 .25

See Nos. 3895f, 3997f.

**BLACK HERITAGE SERIES**

Roy Wilkins (1901-81), Civil Rights Leader — A2703

***Serpentine Die Cut 11½x11¼***

**2001, Jan. 24**

**Self-Adhesive**

**3501** A2703 34c blue .70 .25

## UNITED STATES

### AMERICAN ILLUSTRATORS

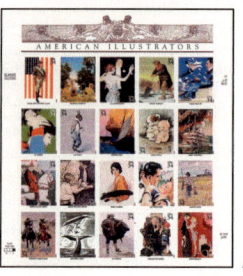 A2704

No. 3502: a, Marine Corps poster "First in the Fight, Always Faithful," by James Montgomery Flagg. b, "Interlude (The Lute Players)," by Maxfield Parrish. c, Advertisement for Arrow Collars and Shirts, by J. C. Leyendecker. d, Advertisement for Carrier Corp. Refrigeration, by Robert Fawcett. e, Advertisement for Luxite Hosiery, by Coles Phillips. f, Illustration for correspondence school lesson, by Al Parker. g, "Br'er Rabbit," by A. B. Frost. h, "An Attack on a Galleon," by Howard Pyle. i, Kewpie and Kewpie Doodle Dog, by Rose O'Neill. j, Illustration for cover of True Magazine, by Dean Cornwell. k, "Galahad's Departure," by Edwin Austin Abbey. l, "The First Lesson," by Jessie Willcox Smith. m, Illustration for cover of McCall's Magazine, by Neysa McMein. n, "Back Home For Keeps," by Jon Whitcomb. o, "Something for Supper," by Harvey Dunn. p, "A Dash for the Timber," by Frederic Remington. q, Illustration for "Moby Dick," by Rockwell Kent. r, "Captain Bill Bones," by N. C. Wyeth. s, Illustration for cover of The Saturday Evening Post, by Norman Rockwell. t, "The Girl He Left Behind," by John Held, Jr.

**PHOTOGRAVURE**
*Serpentine Die Cut 11¼*
**2001, Feb. 1**  Self-Adhesive
3502  A2704  Pane of 20  19.00
a.-t.  34c any single  .90  .60

### DIABETES AWARENESS

 A2705

**LITHOGRAPHED**
*Serpentine Die Cut 11¼x11½*
**2001, Mar. 16**  Self-Adhesive
3503  A2705  34c multicolored  .65  .25

### NOBEL PRIZE CENTENARY

 Alfred Nobel and Obverse of Medals — A2706

**LITHOGRAPHED & ENGRAVED**
**2001, Mar. 22**  Perf. 11
3504  A2706  34c multicolored  .70  .25
a.  Imperf, pair  500.00
See Sweden No. 2415.

### PAN-AMERICAN EXPOSITION INVERT STAMPS, CENT.

A2707

No. 3505: Reproductions (dated 2001) of: a, #294a. b, #295a. c, #296a. d, Commemorative "cinderella" stamp depicting a buffalo.

**LITHOGRAPHED (#3505d), ENGRAVED (others)**
*Perf. 12 (#3505d), 12½x12 (others)*
**2001, Mar. 29**
*Tagged (#3505d), Untagged (others)*
3505  A2707  Pane of 7, #3505a-3505c, 4 #3505d  10.00  7.00
a.  A109 1c green & black  .75  .25
b.  A110 2c carmine & black  .75  .25
c.  A111 4c deep red brown & black  .75  .25
d.  80c red & blue  1.90  .35
e.  As #3505, all colors except black (vignettes) missing on a.-c. (CM)  15,000.

On No. 3505e, the green, carmine and deep red brown frames appear 4mm above Nos. 3505a-3505c on the pane.

### GREAT PLAINS PRAIRIE

A2708

No. 3506 — Wildlife and flowers: a, Pronghorns, Canada geese. b, Burrowing owls, American buffalos. c, American buffalo, Black-tailed prairie dogs, wild alfalfa, horiz. d, Black-tailed prairie dog, American buffalos,. e, Painted lady butterfly, American buffalo, prairie coneflowers, prairie wild roses, horiz. f, Western meadowlark, camel cricket, prairie coneflowers, prairie wild roses. g, Badger, harvester ants. h, Eastern short-horned lizard, plains pocket gopher. i, Plains spadefoot, dung beetle, prairie wild roses, horiz. j, Two-striped grasshopper, Ord's kangaroo rat.

**LITHOGRAPHED**
*Serpentine Die Cut 10*
**2001, Apr. 19**  Self-Adhesive
3506  A2708  Pane of 10  10.00
a.-j.  34c Any single  1.00  .50

### PEANUTS COMIC STRIP

Snoopy — A2709

*Serpentine Die Cut 11¼x11½*
**2001, May 17**  Self-Adhesive
3507  A2709  34c multicolored  .80  .25

### HONORING VETERANS

 A2710

**2001, May 23**  Self-Adhesive
3508  A2710  34c multicolored  .80  .25

### FRIDA KAHLO (1907-54), PAINTER

Self-portrait — A2711

**2001, June 21**  Perf. 11¼
3509  A2711  34c multicolored  .70  .25

### LEGENDARY PLAYING FIELDS

 Ebbets Field — A2712

 Tiger Stadium A2713

Crosley Field — A2714

 Yankee Stadium A2715

Polo Grounds A2716

 Forbes Field — A2717

Fenway Park — A2718

 Comiskey Park — A2719

 Shibe Park — A2720

 Wrigley Field — A2721

**PHOTOGRAVURE**
*Serpentine Die Cut 11¼x11½*
**2001, June 27**  Self-Adhesive
3510  A2712  34c multicolored  .90  .60
3511  A2713  34c multicolored  .90  .60
3512  A2714  34c multicolored  .90  .60
3513  A2715  34c multicolored  .90  .60
3514  A2716  34c multicolored  .90  .60
3515  A2717  34c multicolored  .90  .60
3516  A2718  34c multicolored  .90  .60
3517  A2719  34c multicolored  .90  .60
3518  A2720  34c multicolored  .90  .60
3519  A2721  34c multicolored  .90  .60
a.  Block of 10, #3510-3519  9.00

### ATLAS STATUE, NEW YORK CITY

 A2722

**COIL STAMP**
*Serpentine Die Cut 8½ Vert.*
**2001, June 29**  Untagged
Self-Adhesive
3520  A2722  (10c) multicolored  .30  .25

No. 3520 is dated 2001. See No. 3770.
No. 3520 is known with extremely faint tagging, most likely from contamination in the paper-making process.

### LEONARD BERNSTEIN (1918-90), CONDUCTOR

 A2723

**LITHOGRAPHED**
**2001, July 10**  Perf. 11¼
3521  A2723  34c multicolored  .70  .25

### WOODY WAGON

 A2724

**PHOTOGRAVURE COIL STAMP**
*Serpentine Die Cut 11½ Vert.*
**2001, Aug. 3**  Untagged
Self-Adhesive
3522  A2724  (15c) multicolored  .30  .25

### LEGENDS OF HOLLYWOOD

 Lucille Ball (1911-89) — A2725

**LITHOGRAPHED**
**2001, Aug. 6**  *Serpentine Die Cut 11*
Self-Adhesive
3523  A2725  34c multicolored  1.00  .25
a.  Die cutting omitted, pair  700.00

### AMERICAN TREASURES SERIES
**Amish Quilts**

 Diamond in the Square, c. 1920 — A2726

 Lone Star, c. 1920 — A2727

 Sunshine and Shadow, c. 1910 A2728

 Double Ninepatch Variation A2729

UNITED STATES 99

***Serpentine Die Cut 11¼x11½***
**2001, Aug. 9**
**Self-Adhesive**

| 3524 | A2726 | 34c multicolored | .70 | .30 |
|---|---|---|---|---|
| 3525 | A2727 | 34c multicolored | .70 | .30 |
| 3526 | A2728 | 34c multicolored | .70 | .30 |
| 3527 | A2729 | 34c multicolored | .70 | .30 |
| a. | Block or strip of 4, #3524-3527 | | 2.80 | |

## CARNIVOROUS PLANTS

Venus Flytrap A2730

Yellow Trumpet A2731

Cobra Lily A2732

English Sundew A2733

**PHOTOGRAVURE**
***Serpentine Die Cut 11½***
**2001, Aug. 23**
**Self-Adhesive**

| 3528 | A2730 | 34c multicolored | .70 | .25 |
|---|---|---|---|---|
| 3529 | A2731 | 34c multicolored | .70 | .25 |
| 3530 | A2732 | 34c multicolored | .70 | .25 |
| 3531 | A2733 | 34c multicolored | .70 | .25 |
| a. | Block or strip of 4, #3528-3531 | | 2.80 | |

## EID

"Eid Mubarak" — A2734

***Serpentine Die Cut 11¼***
**2001, Sept. 1**
**Self-Adhesive**

| 3532 | A2734 | 34c multicolored | .70 | .25 |

See Nos. 3674, 4117, 4202, 4351, 4416.

## ENRICO FERMI (1901-54), PHYSICIST

A2735

**LITHOGRAPHED**
**2001, Sept. 29**  **Perf. 11**

| 3533 | A2735 | 34c multicolored | .70 | .25 |

## THAT'S ALL FOLKS!

Porky Pig at Mailbox — A2736

**PHOTOGRAVURE**
**2001, Oct. 1**  ***Serpentine Die Cut 11***
**Self-Adhesive**

| 3534 | | Pane of 10 #3534a | 7.00 | |
|---|---|---|---|---|
| a. | A2736 34c single | | .70 | .25 |
| b. | Pane of 9 #3534a | | 6.25 | |
| c. | Pane of 1 #3534a | | .70 | |

Die cutting on No. 3534b does not extend through the backing paper.

| 3535 | | Pane of 10, #3535c, 9 #3535a | 50.00 | |
|---|---|---|---|---|
| a. | A2736 34c single | | 2.75 | |
| b. | Pane of 9 #3535a | | 25.00 | |
| c. | Pane of 1, no die cutting | | 25.00 | |

Die cutting on No. 3535a extends through backing paper.
Nos. 3534b-3534c and 3535b-3535c are separated by a vertical line of microperforations.

## CHRISTMAS

Virgin and Child, by Lorenzo Costa — A2737

***Serpentine Die Cut 11½ on 2, 3 or 4 Sides***
**2001, Oct. 10**
**Self-Adhesive**
**Booklet Stamps #3536, 3537a-3540a, 3537b, 3538b, 3539b, 3540e, 3541-3544)**

| 3536 | A2737 | 34c multicolored | .75 | .25 |
|---|---|---|---|---|
| a. | Booklet pane of 20 | | 15.00 | |

A2738

A2739

A2740

19th Century Chromolithographs of Santa Claus — A2741

***Serpentine Die Cut 10¾x11***
**Black Inscriptions**

| 3537 | A2738 | 34c multi, large date | .70 | .25 |
|---|---|---|---|---|
| a. | Small date (from booklet pane) | | .90 | .25 |
| b. | Large date (from booklet pane) | | 2.00 | .25 |
| 3538 | A2739 | 34c multi, large date | .70 | .25 |
| a. | Small date (from booklet pane) | | .90 | .25 |
| b. | Large date (from booklet pane) | | 2.00 | .25 |
| 3539 | A2740 | 34c multi, large date | .70 | .25 |
| a. | Small date (from booklet pane) | | .90 | .25 |
| b. | Large date (from booklet pane) | | 2.00 | .25 |
| 3540 | A2741 | 34c multi, large date | .70 | .25 |
| a. | Small date (from booklet pane) | | .90 | .25 |
| b. | Block or strip of 4, #3537-3540 | | 2.80 | |
| c. | Block of 4, small date, #3537a-3540a | | 3.60 | |
| d. | Booklet pane of 20, 5 #3540c + label | | 18.00 | |
| e. | Large date (from booklet pane) | | 2.00 | |
| f. | Block of 4, large date, #3537b-3539b, 3540e | | 8.00 | |
| g. | Booklet pane of 20, 5 #3540f + label | | 40.00 | |

Nos. 3540d and 3540g are double-sided booklet panes, with 12 stamps on one side and eight stamps plus label on the other side.
Numerals "3" and "4" are distinctly separate on Nos. 3537-3540, and touching or separated by a slight hairline on the booklet pane stamps.
Designs of booklet stamps Nos. 3537a-3539a and 3537b-3539b are slightly taller than Nos. 3537-3539. Nos. 3540a and 3540e measure the same as No. 3540.

***Serpentine Die Cut 11 on 2 or 3 Sides***
**Size: 21x18½mm**
**Green and Red Inscriptions**

| 3541 | A2738 | 34c multicolored | .90 | .25 |
|---|---|---|---|---|
| 3542 | A2739 | 34c multicolored | .90 | .25 |
| 3543 | A2740 | 34c multicolored | .90 | .25 |
| 3544 | A2741 | 34c multicolored | .90 | .25 |
| a. | Block of 4, #3541-3544 | | 3.60 | |
| b. | Booklet pane of 4, #3541-3544 | | 3.60 | |

| c. | Booklet pane of 6, #3543-3544, 2 #3541-3542 | | 5.40 | |
|---|---|---|---|---|
| d. | Booklet pane of 6, #3541-3542, 2 #3543-3544 | | 5.40 | |
| | Nos. 3536-3544 (9) | | 7.15 | 2.25 |

## JAMES MADISON (1751-1836)

Madison and His Home, Montpelier A2742

**LITHOGRAPHED & ENGRAVED**
**2001, Oct. 18**  **Perf. 11x11¼**

| 3545 | A2742 | 34c green & black | .70 | .25 |

## THANKSGIVING

Cornucopia — A2743

**LITHOGRAPHED**
***Serpentine Die Cut 11¼***
**2001, Oct. 19**
**Self-Adhesive**

| 3546 | A2743 | 34c multicolored | .70 | .25 |

**Hanukkah Type of 1996**
**PHOTOGRAVURE**
**2001, Oct. 21**  ***Serpentine Die Cut 11***
**Self-Adhesive**

| 3547 | A2411 | 34c multicolored | .70 | .25 |

**Kwanzaa Type of 1997**
**2001, Oct. 21**
**Self-Adhesive**

| 3548 | A2458 | 34c multicolored | .70 | .25 |

## UNITED WE STAND

A2744

**LITHOGRAPHED**
**BOOKLET STAMPS**
***Serpentine Die Cut 11¼ on 2, 3, or 4 Sides***
**2001, Oct. 24**
**Self-Adhesive**

| 3549 | A2744 | 34c multicolored | .75 | .25 |
|---|---|---|---|---|
| a. | Booklet pane of 20 | | 15.00 | |

**PHOTOGRAVURE**
***Serpentine Die Cut 10½x10¾ on 2 or 3 Sides***
**2002, Jan.**
**Self-Adhesive**

| 3549B | A2744 | 34c multicolored | .85 | .25 |
|---|---|---|---|---|
| c. | Booklet pane of 4 | | 3.40 | |
| d. | Booklet pane of 6 | | 5.10 | |
| e. | Booklet pane of 20 | | 18.00 | |

No. 3549Be is a double-sided booklet pane, with 12 stamps on one side and eight stamps plus label on the other side.
"First day covers" of No. 3549B are dated Oct. 24, 2001.

## COIL STAMPS Self-Adhesive

***Serpentine Die Cut 9¾ Vert.***
**2001, Oct. 24**

| 3550 | A2744 | 34c multicolored | 1.25 | .25 |
|---|---|---|---|---|
| 3550A | A2744 | 34c multicolored | 1.75 | .25 |

No. 3550 has right angle corners and backing paper as high as the stamp. No. 3550A has rounded corners, the backing paper larger than the stamp, and the stamps are spaced approximately 2mm apart.

**Love Letters Type of 2001**
**LITHOGRAPHED**
***Serpentine Die Cut 11¼***
**2001, Nov. 19**
**Self-Adhesive**

| 3551 | A2701 | 57c multicolored | 1.20 | .25 |

## WINTER OLYMPICS

Ski Jumping — A2745

Snowboarding A2746

Ice Hockey — A2747

Figure Skating — A2748

**PHOTOGRAVURE**
***Serpentine Die Cut 11½x10¾***
**2002, Jan. 8**
**Self-Adhesive**

| 3552 | A2745 | 34c multicolored | .70 | .35 |
|---|---|---|---|---|
| 3553 | A2746 | 34c multicolored | .70 | .35 |
| 3554 | A2747 | 34c multicolored | .70 | .35 |
| 3555 | A2748 | 34c multicolored | .70 | .35 |
| a. | Block or strip of 4, #3552-3555 | | 2.80 | |
| b. | Die cutting inverted, pane of 20 | | 100.00 | |
| c. | Die cutting omitted, block of 4 | | 825.00 | |

## MENTORING A CHILD

Child and Adult — A2749

***Serpentine Die Cut 11x10¾***
**2002, Jan. 10**
**Self-Adhesive**

| 3556 | A2749 | 34c multicolored | .70 | .25 |

## BLACK HERITAGE SERIES

Langston Hughes (1902-67), Writer — A2750

**LITHOGRAPHED**
***Serpentine Die Cut 10¼x10½***
**2002, Feb. 1**
**Self-Adhesive**

| 3557 | A2750 | 34c multicolored | .70 | .25 |
|---|---|---|---|---|
| a. | Die cutting omitted, pair | | 725.00 | |

Beware of pairs/panes with extremely faint die cutting offered as imperf. errors.

## HAPPY BIRTHDAY

A2751

**PHOTOGRAVURE**
**2002, Feb. 8**  ***Serpentine Die Cut 11***

| 3558 | A2751 | 34c multicolored | .75 | .25 |

See Nos. 3695, 4079.

## CHINESE NEW YEAR

Year of the Horse — A2752

LITHOGRAPHED

***Serpentine Die Cut 10½x10¼***

**2002, Feb. 11**

**Self-Adhesive**

**3559** A2752 34c multicolored .75 .25
*a.* Horiz. pair, vert. die cutting omitted *5,000.*

See Nos. 3895g, 3997g.

## U.S. MILITARY ACADEMY, BICENT.

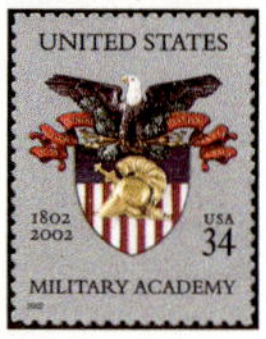


Military Academy Coat of Arms — A2753

PHOTOGRAVURE

***Serpentine Die Cut 10½x11***

**2002, Mar. 16**

**Self-Adhesive**

**3560** A2753 34c multicolored .75 .25

## GREETINGS FROM AMERICA

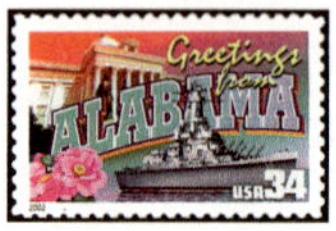


Alabama A2754

***Serpentine Die Cut 10¾***

**2002, Apr. 4**

**Self-Adhesive**

| | | | | | |
|---|---|---|---|---|---|
| **3561** | A2754 | 34c | Alabama | .70 | .60 |
| **3562** | A2755 | 34c | Alaska | .70 | .60 |
| **3563** | A2756 | 34c | Arizona | .70 | .60 |
| **3564** | A2757 | 34c | Arkansas | .70 | .60 |
| **3565** | A2758 | 34c | California | .70 | .60 |
| **3566** | A2759 | 34c | Colorado | .70 | .60 |
| **3567** | A2760 | 34c | Connecticut | .70 | .60 |
| **3568** | A2761 | 34c | Delaware | .70 | .60 |
| **3569** | A2762 | 34c | Florida | .70 | .60 |
| **3570** | A2763 | 34c | Georgia | .70 | .60 |
| **3571** | A2764 | 34c | Hawaii | .70 | .60 |
| **3572** | A2765 | 34c | Idaho | .70 | .60 |
| **3573** | A2766 | 34c | Illinois | .70 | .60 |
| **3574** | A2767 | 34c | Indiana | .70 | .60 |
| **3575** | A2768 | 34c | Iowa | .70 | .60 |
| **3576** | A2769 | 34c | Kansas | .70 | .60 |
| **3577** | A2770 | 34c | Kentucky | .70 | .60 |
| **3578** | A2771 | 34c | Louisiana | .70 | .60 |
| **3579** | A2772 | 34c | Maine | .70 | .60 |
| **3580** | A2773 | 34c | Maryland | .70 | .60 |
| **3581** | A2774 | 34c | Massachusetts | .70 | .60 |
| **3582** | A2775 | 34c | Michigan | .70 | .60 |
| **3583** | A2776 | 34c | Minnesota | .70 | .60 |
| **3584** | A2777 | 34c | Mississippi | .70 | .60 |
| **3585** | A2778 | 34c | Missouri | .70 | .60 |
| **3586** | A2779 | 34c | Montana | .70 | .60 |
| **3587** | A2780 | 34c | Nebraska | .70 | .60 |
| **3588** | A2781 | 34c | Nevada | .70 | .60 |
| **3589** | A2782 | 34c | New Hampshire | .70 | .60 |
| **3590** | A2783 | 34c | New Jersey | .70 | .60 |
| **3591** | A2784 | 34c | New Mexico | .70 | .60 |
| **3592** | A2785 | 34c | New York | .70 | .60 |
| **3593** | A2786 | 34c | North Carolina | .70 | .60 |
| **3594** | A2787 | 34c | North Dakota | .70 | .60 |
| **3595** | A2788 | 34c | Ohio | .70 | .60 |
| **3596** | A2789 | 34c | Oklahoma | .70 | .60 |
| **3597** | A2790 | 34c | Oregon | .70 | .60 |
| **3598** | A2791 | 34c | Pennsylvania | .70 | .60 |
| **3599** | A2792 | 34c | Rhode Island | .70 | .60 |
| **3600** | A2793 | 34c | South Carolina | .70 | .60 |
| **3601** | A2794 | 34c | South Dakota | .70 | .60 |
| **3602** | A2795 | 34c | Tennessee | .70 | .60 |
| **3603** | A2796 | 34c | Texas | .70 | .60 |
| **3604** | A2797 | 34c | Utah | .70 | .60 |
| **3605** | A2798 | 34c | Vermont | .70 | .60 |
| **3606** | A2799 | 34c | Virginia | .70 | .60 |
| **3607** | A2800 | 34c | Washington | .70 | .60 |
| **3608** | A2801 | 34c | West Virginia | .70 | .60 |
| **3609** | A2802 | 34c | Wisconsin | .70 | .60 |
| **3610** | A2803 | 34c | Wyoming | .70 | .60 |
| *a.* | | | Pane of 50, #3561-3610 | 35.00 | |

See Nos. 3696-3745.

## LONGLEAF PINE FOREST

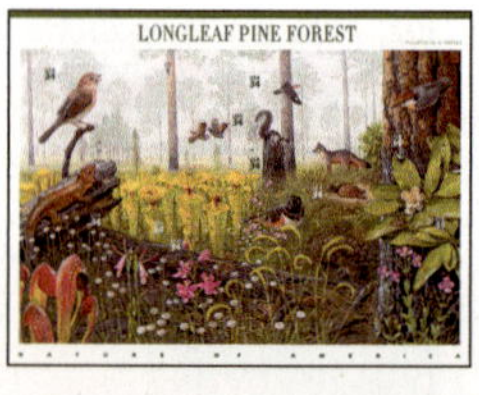


A2804

No. 3611 — Wildlife and flowers: a, Bachman's sparrow. b, Northern bobwhite, yellow pitcher plants. c, Fox squirrel, red-bellied woodpecker. d, Brown-headed nuthatch. e, Broadhead skink, yellow pitcher plants, pipeworts. f, Eastern towhee, yellow pitcher plants, Savannah meadow beauties, toothache grass. g, Gray fox, gopher tortoise, horiz. h, Blind click beetle, sweetbay, pine woods treefrog. i, Rosebud orchid, pipeworts, southern toad, yellow pitcher plants. j, Grass-pink orchid, yellow-sided skimmer, pipeworts, yellow pitcher plants, horiz.

***Serpentine Die Cut 10½x10¾, 10¾x10½***

**2002, Apr. 26**

**Self-Adhesive**

**3611** A2804 Pane of 10 19.00
*a.-j.* 34c Any single 1.90 .50
*k.* As No. 3611, die cutting omitted *2,500.*

## AMERICAN DESIGN SERIES

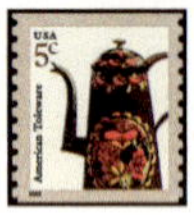


Toleware Coffeepot — A2805

PHOTOGRAVURE

COIL STAMP

***Perf. 9¾ Vert.***

**2002, May 31** **Untagged**

**3612** A2805 5c multicolored .30 .25
*a.* Imperf, pair 450.00

No. 3612a is valued with disturbed gum. It is also known without gum and is valued only slightly less thus.

See Nos. 3756-3756A.

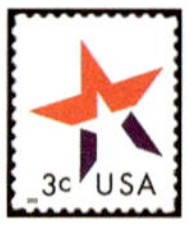


Star — A2806

LITHOGRAPHED

***Serpentine Die Cut 11***

**2002, June 7** **Untagged**

**Self-Adhesive (#3613-3614)**

**Year at Lower Left**

**3613** A2806 3c red, blue & black .30 .25
*a.* Die cutting omitted, pair —

PHOTOGRAVURE

***Serpentine Die Cut 10***

**Year at Lower Right**

**Untagged**

**3614** A2806 3c red, blue & black .30 .25

**Coil Stamp**

***Perf. 9¾ Vert.***

**Year at Lower Left**

**Untagged**

**3615** A2806 3c red, blue & black .30 .25

**Washington Type of 2001**

LITHOGRAPHED, PHOTOGRAVURE (#3617)

**2002, June 7** ***Perf. 11¼***

**3616** A2686 23c green .50 .25

**Self-Adhesive**

**Coil Stamp**

***Serpentine Die Cut 8½ Vert.***

**3617** A2686 23c gray green .45 .25
*a.* Die cutting omitted, pair 500.00

Compare No. 3617 ("2002" date at lower left) with No. 3475A ("2001" date at lower left).

LITHOGRAPHED

**Booklet Stamps**

***Serpentine Die Cut 11¼x11 on 3 Sides***

**3618** A2686 23c green .50 .25
*a.* Booklet pane of 4 2.00
*b.* Booklet pane of 6 3.00
*c.* Booklet pane of 10 5.00
*d.* Nos. 3619c and 3619d, in bklt. of 10 (#BK289A), imperf. vert. btwn. on both panes *1,100.*

***Serpentine Die Cut 10½x11 on 3 Sides***

**3619** A2686 23c green 4.50 1.75
*a.* Booklet pane of 4, 2 #3619 at L, 2 #3618 at R 10.00
*b.* Booklet pane of 6, 3 #3619 at L, 3 #3618 at R 15.00
*c.* Booklet pane of 4, 2 #3618 at L, 2 #3619 at R 10.00
*d.* Booklet pane of 6, 3 #3618 at L, 3 #3619 at R 15.00
*e.* Booklet pane of 10, 5 #3619 at L, 5#3618 at R 27.50
*f.* Booklet pane of 10, 5 #3618 at L, 5 #3619 at R 27.50
*g.* Pair, #3619 at L, #3618 at R 5.00
*h.* Pair, #3618 at L, #3619 at R 5.00

See Nos. 3468A, 3475A, 3482-3483, 3819.

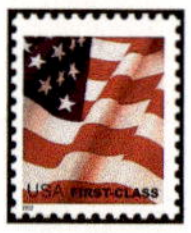


Flag — A2807

LITHOGRAPHED

**2002, June 7** ***Perf. 11¼x11***

**3620** A2807 (37c) multicolored 1.10 .25

LITHOGRAPHED, PHOTOGRAVURE (#3622)

**Self-Adhesive**

***Serpentine Die Cut 11¼x11***

**3621** A2807 (37c) multicolored 1.10 .25

**Coil Stamp**

***Serpentine Die Cut 10 Vert.***

**3622** A2807 (37c) multicolored 1.10 .25
*a.* Die cutting omitted, pair *650.00*
*b.* Yellow omitted —

**Booklet Stamps**

***Serpentine Die Cut 11¼ on 2, 3 or 4 Sides***

**3623** A2807 (37c) multicolored 1.10 .25
*a.* Booklet pane of 20 22.00

No. 3623 has "USPS" microprinted in the top red stripe of the flag.

***Serpentine Die Cut 10½x10¾ on 2 or 3 Sides***

**3624** A2807 (37c) multicolored 1.10 .25
*a.* Booklet pane of 4 4.40
*b.* Booklet pane of 6 6.60
*c.* Booklet pane of 20 22.00

No. 3624 does not have a microprinted "USPS."

***Serpentine Die Cut 8 on 2, 3 or 4 Sides***

**3825** A2807e(37c) multicolored 1.10 .25
*a.* Booklet pane of 18 19.00

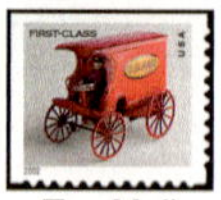


Toy Mail Wagon A2808

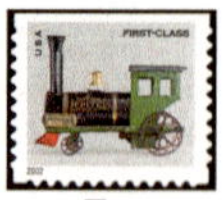


Toy Locomotive A2809

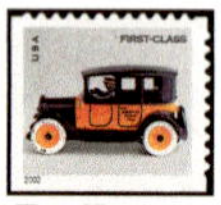


Toy Taxicab A2810

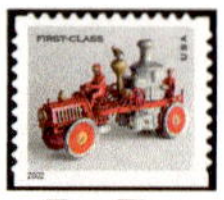


Toy Fire Pumper A2811

PHOTOGRAVURE

***Serpentine Die Cut 11 on 2, 3 or 4 Sides***

**2002, June 7**

**Booklet Stamps**

**Self-Adhesive**

**3626** A2808 (37c) multicolored 1.10 .25
**3627** A2809 (37c) multicolored 1.10 .25
**3628** A2810 (37c) multicolored 1.10 .25
**3629** A2811 (37c) multicolored 1.10 .25
*a.* Block or strip of 4, #3626-3629 4.40
*b.* Booklet pane of 4, #3626-3629 4.40
*c.* Booklet pane of 6, #3627, 3629, 2 each #3626, 3628 6.60
*d.* Booklet pane of 6, #3626, 3628, 2 each #3627, 3629 6.60
*e.* Booklet pane of 20, 5 each #3626-3629 22.00

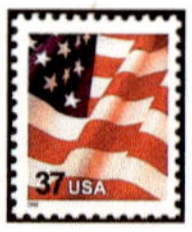


Flag — A2812

LITHOGRAPHED

**2002-05** ***Perf. 11¼***

**3629F** A2812 37c multi .90 .25
*g.* Imperf, pair *100.00*

No. 3629F has microprinted "USA" in top red stripe of flag.

***Serpentine Die Cut 11¼x11***

**Self-Adhesive (#3630, 3632-3637)**

**3630** A2812 37c multi .90 .25

No. 3630 has microprinted "USA" in top red stripe of flag.

**COIL STAMPS**

***Perf. 9¾ Vert.***

**3631** A2812 37c multi .75 .25

***Serpentine Die Cut 9¾ Vert.***

**3632** A2812 37c multi .75 .25
*b.* Die cutting omitted, pair 55.00 55.00

***Serpentine Die Cut 10¼ Vert.***

**3632A** A2812 37c multi .75 .25
*f.* Die cutting omitted, pair *250.00*
*g.* Vert. pair, horiz. die-cut slits omitted *1,250.*

No. 3632A lacks points of stars at margin at left top, and was printed in "logs" of adjacent coil rolls that are connected at the top or bottom, wherein each roll could be separated from an adjacent roll as needed.

No. 3632 has "2002" date at left bottom. No. 3632A has "2003" date at left bottom.

***Serpentine Die Cut 11¾ Vert.***

**3632C** A2812 37c multi 1.50 .25

No. 3632C is the only 37c Flag coil stamp with a "2004" date at left bottom.

LITHOGRAPHED, PHOTOGRAVURE (#3633)

***Serpentine Die Cut 8½ Vert.***

**3633** A2812 37c multi .75 .25
**3633A** A2812 37c multi 2.25 .25

No. 3633A has right angle corners and backing paper as high as the stamp, and is dated "2003." No. 3633 is dated "2002," has rounded corners, the backing paper larger than the stamp, and the stamps are spaced approximately 2mm apart.

***Serpentine Die Cut 9½ Vert.***

**3633B** A2812 37c multi 9.00 .25

No. 3633B has microprinted "USA" in top red stripe of flag, and has "2005" date at bottom left.

LITHOGRAPHED, PHOTOGRAVURE (#3634, 3636, 3636D)

**Booklet Stamps**

***Serpentine Die Cut 11.1 on 3 Sides (#3634)***

**3634** A2812 37c multi, large "2002" year date .75 .25
*a.* Booklet pane of 10 7.50
*b.* Small "2003" date, die cut 11 .75 .25
*c.* Booklet pane, 4 #3634b 3.00
*d.* Booklet pane, 6 #3634b 4.50
*e.* As #3634, die cut 11.3 1.00 .25
*f.* As "e," booklet pane of 10 10.00

***Serpentine Die Cut 11.3 on 2, 3 or 4 Sides***

**3635** A2812 37c multi .75 .25
*a.* Booklet pane of 20 15.00
*b.* Black omitted *3,000.*

No. 3635 has "USPS" microprinted in the top red flag stripe and has a small "2002" year date.

***Serpentine Die Cut 10½x10¾ on 2 or 3 Sides***

**3636** A2812 37c multi .75 .25
*a.* Booklet pane of 4 3.00
*b.* Booklet pane of 6 4.50
*c.* Booklet pane of 20 15.00
*f.* As "c," 11 stamps and part of 12th stamp on reverse printed on backing liner, the 8 stamps on front side die cutting omitted 1,700.

No. 3636c is a double-sided booklet pane, with 12 stamps on one side and eight stamps plus label on the other side.

***Serpentine Die Cut 11¼x11 on 2 or 3 Sides***

**3636D** A2812 37c multi 1.25 .25
*e.* Booklet pane of 20 25.00

No. 3636D lacks points of stars at margin at UL. No. 3636D is the only 37c Flag booklet stamp with a "2004" date at left bottom. No. 3636De is a double-sided booklet pane with 12 stamps on one side and eight stamps plus label on the other side.

LITHOGRAPHED

***Serpentine Die Cut 8 on 2, 3 or 4 Sides***

**3637** A2812 37c multi .75 .25
*a.* Booklet pane of 18 13.50

Issued: Nos. 3630-3632, 3633, 3634, 3635-3636, 6/7; No. 3637, 2/4/03; No. 3633A, Apr. 2003; No. 3632A, 8/7/03; No. 3634b, 10/23/03; No. 3629F, 11/24/03; No. 3636D, July 2004; No. 3632C, 2004; No. 3633B, 6/7/05.

# UNITED STATES

Toy Locomotive A2813

Toy Mail Wagon A2814

Toy Fire Pumper A2815

Toy Taxicab A2816

### PHOTOGRAVURE
*Serpentine Die Cut 8½ Horiz.*
**2002-03**
**Self-Adhesive**
**Coil Stamps**

| 3638 | A2813 | 37c multi | 1.50 | .25 |
|---|---|---|---|---|
| 3639 | A2814 | 37c multi | 1.50 | .25 |
| 3640 | A2815 | 37c multi | 1.50 | .25 |
| 3641 | A2816 | 37c multi | 1.50 | .25 |
| a. | | Strip of 4, #3638-3641 | 6.00 | |

*Serpentine Die Cut 11 on 2, 3 or 4 Sides*
**Booklet Stamps**

| 3642 | A2814 | 37c multi, "2002" year date | .75 | .25 |
|---|---|---|---|---|
| a. | | Serpentine die cut 11x11¼ on 2 or 3 sides, dated "2003" | .75 | .25 |
| 3643 | A2813 | 37c multi, "2002" year date | .75 | .25 |
| a. | | Serpentine die cut 11x11¼ on 2 or 3 sides, dated "2003" | .75 | .25 |
| 3644 | A2816 | 37c multi, "2002" year date | .75 | .25 |
| a. | | Serpentine die cut 11x11¼ on 2 or 3 sides, dated "2003" | .75 | .25 |
| 3645 | A2815 | 37c multi, "2002" year date | .75 | .25 |
| a. | | Block or strip of 4, #3642-3645 | 3.00 | |
| b. | | Booklet pane of 4, #3642-3645 | 3.00 | |
| c. | | Booklet pane of 6, #3643, 3645, 2 each #3642, 3644 | 4.50 | |
| d. | | Booklet pane of 6, #3642, 3644, 2 each #3643, 3645 | 4.50 | |
| e. | | Booklet pane of 20, 5 each #3642-3645 | 15.00 | |
| f. | | Serpentine die cut 11x11¼ on 2 or 3 sides, dated "2003" | .75 | .25 |
| g. | | Block of 4, #3642a, 3643a, 3644a, 3645f | 3.00 | |
| h. | | Booklet pane of 20, 5 #3645g | 15.00 | |

No. 3645h is a double-sided booklet with 12 stamps on one side and 8 stamps plus label (booklet cover) on the other side. Nos. 3642a, 3643a, 3644a and 3645f have slightly narrower designs than Nos. 3642-3645.

Issued: Nos. 3638-3645, 7/26; Nos. 3642a, 3643a, 3644a, 3645f, 9/3/03.

Coverlet Eagle — A2817

### LITHOGRAPHED
*Serpentine Die Cut 11x11¼*
**2002, July 12**
**Self-Adhesive**

| 3646 | A2817 | 60c multicolored | 1.25 | .25 |
|---|---|---|---|---|

Jefferson Memorial A2818  — Capitol Dome A2819

*Serpentine Die Cut 11¼ (#3647, 3648), 11x10¾ (#3647A)*
**2002-03** **Tagged**
**Self-Adhesive**

| 3647 | A2818 | $3.85 multi | 7.50 | 2.00 |
|---|---|---|---|---|
| 3647A | A2818 | $3.85 multi | 9.00 | 2.00 |
| 3648 | A2819 | $13.65 multi | 27.50 | 10.00 |

No. 3647 is dated 2002, and No. 3647A is dated 2003.

## MASTERS OF AMERICAN PHOTOGRAPHY

A2820

No. 3649: a, Portrait of Daniel Webster, by Albert Sands Southworth and Josiah Johnson Hawes. b, Gen. Ulysses S. Grant and Officers, by Timothy H. O'Sullivan. c, "Cape Horn, Columbia River," by Carleton E. Watkins. d, "Blessed Art Thou Among Women," by Gertrude Käsebier. e, "Looking for Lost Luggage, Ellis Island," by Lewis W. Hine. f, "The Octopus," by Alvin Langdon Coburn. g, "Lotus, Mount Kisco, New York," by Edward Steichen. h, "Hands and Thimble," by Alfred Stieglitz. i, "Rayograph," by Man Ray. j, "Two Shells," by Edward Weston. k, "My Corsage," by James VanDerZee. l, "Ditched, Stalled, and Stranded, San Joaquin Valley, California," by Dorothea Lange. m, "Washroom and Dining Area of Floyd Burroughs' Home, Hale County, Alabama," by Walker Evans. n, "Frontline Soldier with Canteen, Saipan," by W. Eugene Smith. o, "Steeple," by Paul Strand. p, "Sand Dunes, Sunrise," by Ansel Adams. q, "Age and Its Symbols," by Imogen Cunningham. r, New York cityscape, by André Kertész. s, Photograph of pedestrians, by Garry Winogrand. t, "Bristol, Vermont," by Minor White.

### PHOTOGRAVURE
*Serpentine Die Cut 10½x10¾*
**2002, June 13**
**Self-Adhesive**

| 3649 | A2820 | Pane of 20 | 22.50 | |
|---|---|---|---|---|
| a.-t. | | 37c Any single | 1.00 | .50 |
| u. | | As No. 3649, die cutting omitted | — | |

## AMERICAN TREASURES SERIES

Scarlet and Louisiana Tanagers, by John James Audubon — A2821

*Serpentine Die Cut 10¾*
**2002, June 27**
**Self-Adhesive**

| 3650 | A2821 | 37c multicolored | 1.00 | .25 |
|---|---|---|---|---|

## HARRY HOUDINI (1874-1926), MAGICIAN

A2822

### LITHOGRAPHED
*Serpentine Die Cut 11¼*
**2002, July 3**
**Self-Adhesive**

| 3651 | A2822 | 37c multicolored | .75 | .25 |
|---|---|---|---|---|

## ANDY WARHOL (1928-87), ARTIST

Self-Portrait — A2823

### PHOTOGRAVURE
*Serpentine Die Cut 10½x10¾*
**2002, Aug. 9**
**Self-Adhesive**

| 3652 | A2823 | 37c multicolored | .75 | .25 |
|---|---|---|---|---|

## TEDDY BEARS, CENTENNIAL

Bruin Bear, c. 1907 — A2824

"Stick" Bear, 1920s — A2825

Gund Bear, c. 1948 — A2826

Ideal Bear, c. 1905 — A2827

*Serpentine Die Cut 10½*
**2002, Aug. 15**
**Self-Adhesive**

| 3653 | A2824 | 37c multicolored | 1.00 | .30 |
|---|---|---|---|---|
| 3654 | A2825 | 37c multicolored | 1.00 | .30 |
| 3655 | A2826 | 37c multicolored | 1.00 | .30 |
| 3656 | A2827 | 37c multicolored | 1.00 | .30 |
| a. | | Block or vert. strip of 4, #3653-3656 | 4.00 | |

## LOVE

A2828

A2829

### LITHOGRAPHED (#3657), PHOTOGRAVURE
*Serpentine Die Cut 11 on 2, 3 or 4 Sides*
**2002, Aug. 16**
**Booklet Stamp (#3657)**
**Self-Adhesive**

| 3657 | A2828 | 37c multicolored | .75 | .25 |
|---|---|---|---|---|
| a. | | Booklet pane of 20 | 15.00 | |
| b. | | As "a," silver ("Love 37 USA") missing on top five stamps (CM) | 750.00 | |
| c. | | Strip of 5, silver ("Love 37 USA") omitted on one stamp | 1,000. | |

*Serpentine Die Cut 11*

| 3658 | A2829 | 60c multicolored | 1.25 | .25 |
|---|---|---|---|---|

Beware of examples of No. 3658 with gold ink fraudulently removed.

## LITERARY ARTS

Ogden Nash (1902-71), Poet — A2830

### PHOTOGRAVURE
*Serpentine Die Cut 11*
**2002, Aug. 19**
**Self-Adhesive**

| 3659 | A2830 | 37c multicolored | .75 | .25 |
|---|---|---|---|---|

## DUKE KAHANAMOKU (1890-1968), "FATHER OF SURFING" AND OLYMPIC SWIMMER

Kahanamoku and Surfers at Waikiki Beach — A2831

### PHOTOGRAVURE
*Serpentine Die Cut 11½x11¾*
**2002, Aug. 24**
**Self-Adhesive**

| 3660 | A2831 | 37c multicolored | .75 | .25 |
|---|---|---|---|---|

## AMERICAN BATS

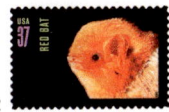
Red Bat — A2832

Leaf-nosed Bat — A2833

Pallid Bat — A2834

Spotted Bat — A2835

*Serpentine Die Cut 10¾*
**2002, Sept. 13**
**Self-Adhesive**

| 3661 | A2832 | 37c multicolored | .75 | .30 |
|---|---|---|---|---|
| 3662 | A2833 | 37c multicolored | .75 | .30 |
| 3663 | A2834 | 37c multicolored | .75 | .30 |
| 3664 | A2835 | 37c multicolored | .75 | .30 |
| a. | | Block or strip of 4, #3661-3664 | 3.00 | |

## WOMEN IN JOURNALISM

Nellie Bly (1864-1922) A2836

Ida M. Tarbell (1857-1944) A2837

Ethel L. Payne (1911-91) A2838

Marguerite Higgins (1920-66) A2839

*Serpentine Die Cut 11x10½*
**2002, Sept. 14**
**Self-Adhesive**

| 3665 | A2836 | 37c multicolored | 1.25 | .35 |
|---|---|---|---|---|
| 3666 | A2837 | 37c multicolored | 1.25 | .35 |
| 3667 | A2838 | 37c multicolored | 1.25 | .35 |
| 3668 | A2839 | 37c multicolored | 1.25 | .35 |
| a. | | Block or horiz. strip of 4, #3665-3668 | 5.00 | |

## IRVING BERLIN (1888-1989), COMPOSER

Berlin and Score of "God Bless America" — A2840

*Serpentine Die Cut 11*
**2002, Sept. 15**
**Self-Adhesive**

| 3669 | A2840 | 37c multicolored | .75 | .25 |
|---|---|---|---|---|

## UNITED STATES

### NEUTER AND SPAY

Kitten — A2841

Puppy — A2842

**Serpentine Die Cut 10¾x10½**
**2002, Sept. 20**
**Self-Adhesive**

| 3670 | A2841 | 37c multicolored | 1.00 | .25 |
|------|-------|------------------|------|-----|
| 3671 | A2842 | 37c multicolored | 1.00 | .25 |
| a. | Horiz. or vert. pair, #3670-3671 | | 2.00 | |

**Hanukkah Type of 1996**
**2002, Oct. 10  Serpentine Die Cut 11**
**Self-Adhesive**

| 3672 | A2411 | 37c multicolored | .75 | .25 |

**Kwanzaa Type of 1997**
**2002, Oct. 10  Serpentine Die Cut 11**
**Self-Adhesive**

| 3673 | A2458 | 37c multicolored | .75 | .25 |

**Eid Type of 2001**
**2002, Oct. 10  Serpentine Die Cut 11**
**Self-Adhesive**

| 3674 | A2734 | 37c multicolored | .75 | .25 |

### CHRISTMAS

Madonna and Child, by Jan Gossaert — A2843

**LITHOGRAPHED**
**Serpentine Die Cut 11x11¼ on 2, 3 or 4 Sides**
**2002, Oct. 10**
**Self-Adhesive**
**Booklet Stamp**
**Design size: 19x27mm**

| 3675 | A2843 | 37c multicolored | .75 | .25 |
| a. | Booklet pane of 20 | 15.00 | | |

Compare to No. 3820, which measures 19½x28mm.
See No. 3820.

### CHRISTMAS

Snowman with Red and Green Plaid Scarf A2844

Snowman with Blue Plaid Scarf A2845

Snowman with Pipe A2846

Snowman with Top Hat A2847

**PHOTOGRAVURE**
**Serpentine Die Cut 11**
**2002, Oct. 28**    **Tagged**
**Self-Adhesive**

| 3676 | A2844 | 37c multicolored | .90 | .25 |
| 3677 | A2845 | 37c multicolored | .90 | .25 |
| 3678 | A2846 | 37c multicolored | .90 | .25 |
| 3679 | A2847 | 37c multicolored | .90 | .25 |
| a. | Block or vert. strip of 4, #3676-3679 | | 3.75 | |

Snowman with Blue Plaid Scarf A2848

Snowman with Top Hat A2850

Snowman with Pipe A2849

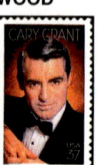
Snowman with Red and Green Plaid Scarf A2851

**COIL STAMPS**
**Serpentine Die Cut 8½ Vert.**

| 3680 | A2848 | 37c multicolored | 3.25 | .25 |
| 3681 | A2849 | 37c multicolored | 3.25 | .25 |
| 3682 | A2850 | 37c multicolored | 3.25 | .25 |
| 3683 | A2851 | 37c multicolored | 3.25 | .25 |
| a. | Strip of 4, #3680-3683 | | 13.00 | |

**BOOKLET STAMPS**
**Serpentine Die Cut 10¾x11 on 2 or 3 Sides**

| 3684 | A2844 | 37c multicolored | 1.25 | .25 |
| 3685 | A2845 | 37c multicolored | 1.25 | .25 |
| 3686 | A2846 | 37c multicolored | 1.25 | .25 |
| 3687 | A2847 | 37c multicolored | 1.25 | .25 |
| a. | Block of 4, #3684-3687 | | 5.00 | |
| b. | Booklet pane of 20, 5 #3687a + label | | 25.00 | |

No. 3687b is a double-sided booklet pane with 12 stamps on one side and eighter stamps plus label on the other side.
Colors of Nos. 3684-3687 are deeper and designs are slightly smaller than those found on Nos. 3676-3679.

**Serpentine Die Cut 11 on 2 or 3 Sides**

| 3688 | A2851 | 37c multicolored | 1.15 | .25 |
| 3689 | A2848 | 37c multicolored | 1.15 | .25 |
| 3690 | A2849 | 37c multicolored | 1.15 | .25 |
| 3691 | A2850 | 37c multicolored | 1.15 | .25 |
| a. | Block of 4, #3688-3691 | | 4.60 | |
| b. | Booklet pane of 4, #3688-3691 | | 4.60 | |
| c. | Booklet pane of 6, #3690-3691, 2 each #3688-3689 | | 7.00 | |
| d. | Booklet pane of 6, #3688-3689, 2 each #3690-3691 | | 7.00 | |
| | Nos. 3676-3691 (16) | 26.20 | 4.00 | |

### LEGENDS OF HOLLYWOOD

Cary Grant (1904-86), Actor — A2852

**Serpentine Die Cut 10¾**
**2002, Oct. 15**
**Self-Adhesive**

| 3692 | A2852 | 37c multicolored | 1.25 | .25 |

Sea Coast — A2853

**PHOTOGRAVURE COIL STAMP**
**Serpentine Die Cut 8½ Vert.**
**2002, Oct. 21**
**Self-Adhesive**

| 3693 | A2853 | (5c) multicolored | .30 | .25 |

See Nos. 3775, 3785, 3864, 3874-3875, 4348.

### HAWAIIAN MISSIONARY STAMPS

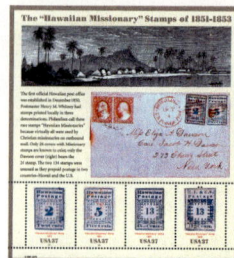
A2854

No. 3694: a, 2c stamp of 1851 (Hawaii Scott 1). b, 5c stamp of 1851 (Hawaii Scott 2) c, 13c stamp of 1851 (Hawaii Scott 3). d, 13c stamp of 1852 (Hawaii Scott 4).

**LITHOGRAPHED**
**2002, Oct. 24  Tagged  Perf. 11**

| 3694 | A2854 | Pane of 4 | 5.00 | 2.50 |
| a.-d. | 37c Any single | 1.25 | .50 |

**Happy Birthday Type of 2002**
**PHOTOGRAVURE**
**2002, Oct. 25  Serpentine Die Cut 11**
**Self-Adhesive**

| 3695 | A2751 | 37c multicolored | .75 | .25 |

### GREETINGS FROM AMERICA TYPE OF 2002

**Serpentine Die Cut 10¾**
**2002, Oct. 25**
**Self-Adhesive**

| 3696 | A2754 | 37c Alabama | .75 | .60 |
| 3697 | A2755 | 37c Alaska | .75 | .60 |
| 3698 | A2756 | 37c Arizona | .75 | .60 |
| 3699 | A2757 | 37c Arkansas | .75 | .60 |
| 3700 | A2758 | 37c California | .75 | .60 |
| 3701 | A2759 | 37c Colorado | .75 | .60 |
| 3702 | A2760 | 37c Connecticut | .75 | .60 |
| 3703 | A2761 | 37c Delaware | .75 | .60 |
| 3704 | A2762 | 37c Florida | .75 | .60 |
| 3705 | A2763 | 37c Georgia | .75 | .60 |
| 3706 | A2764 | 37c Hawaii | .75 | .60 |
| 3707 | A2765 | 37c Idaho | .75 | .60 |
| 3708 | A2766 | 37c Illinois | .75 | .60 |
| 3709 | A2767 | 37c Indiana | .75 | .60 |
| 3710 | A2768 | 37c Iowa | .75 | .60 |
| 3711 | A2769 | 37c Kansas | .75 | .60 |
| 3712 | A2770 | 37c Kentucky | .75 | .60 |
| 3713 | A2771 | 37c Louisiana | .75 | .60 |
| 3714 | A2772 | 37c Maine | .75 | .60 |
| 3715 | A2773 | 37c Maryland | .75 | .60 |
| 3716 | A2774 | 37c Massachusetts | .75 | .60 |
| 3717 | A2775 | 37c Michigan | .75 | .60 |
| 3718 | A2776 | 37c Minnesota | .75 | .60 |
| 3719 | A2777 | 37c Mississippi | .75 | .60 |
| 3720 | A2778 | 37c Missouri | .75 | .60 |
| 3721 | A2779 | 37c Montana | .75 | .60 |
| 3722 | A2780 | 37c Nebraska | .75 | .60 |
| 3723 | A2781 | 37c Nevada | .75 | .60 |
| 3724 | A2782 | 37c New Hampshire | .75 | .60 |
| 3725 | A2783 | 37c New Jersey | .75 | .60 |
| 3726 | A2784 | 37c New Mexico | .75 | .60 |
| 3727 | A2785 | 37c New York | .75 | .60 |
| 3728 | A2786 | 37c North Carolina | .75 | .60 |
| 3729 | A2787 | 37c North Dakota | .75 | .60 |
| 3730 | A2788 | 37c Ohio | .75 | .60 |
| 3731 | A2789 | 37c Oklahoma | .75 | .60 |
| 3732 | A2790 | 37c Oregon | .75 | .60 |
| 3733 | A2791 | 37c Pennsylvania | .75 | .60 |
| 3734 | A2792 | 37c Rhode Island | .75 | .60 |
| 3735 | A2793 | 37c South Carolina | .75 | .60 |
| 3736 | A2794 | 37c South Dakota | .75 | .60 |
| 3737 | A2795 | 37c Tennessee | .75 | .60 |
| 3738 | A2796 | 37c Texas | .75 | .60 |
| 3739 | A2797 | 37c Utah | .75 | .60 |
| 3740 | A2798 | 37c Vermont | .75 | .60 |
| 3741 | A2799 | 37c Virginia | .75 | .60 |
| 3742 | A2800 | 37c Washington | .75 | .60 |
| 3743 | A2801 | 37c West Virginia | .75 | .60 |
| 3744 | A2802 | 37c Wisconsin | .75 | .60 |
| 3745 | A2803 | 37c Wyoming | .75 | .60 |
| a. | Pane of 50, #3696-3745 | 37.50 | | |

See Nos. 3561-3610.

### BLACK HERITAGE SERIES

Thurgood Marshall (1908-93), Supreme Court Justice — A2855

**LITHOGRAPHED**
**Serpentine Die Cut 11½**
**2003, Jan. 7**
**Self-Adhesive**

| 3746 | A2855 | 37c black & gray | .75 | .25 |

### CHINESE NEW YEAR

Year of the Ram — A2856

**Serpentine Die Cut 11½**
**2003, Jan. 15**
**Self-Adhesive**

| 3747 | A2856 | 37c multicolored | .75 | .25 |

See Nos. 3895h, 3997h.

### LITERARY ARTS

Zora Neale Hurston (1891-1960), Writer — A2857

**PHOTOGRAVURE**
**Serpentine Die Cut 10¾**
**2003, Jan. 24**
**Self-Adhesive**

| 3748 | A2857 | 37c multicolored | .90 | .25 |

### AMERICAN DESIGN SERIES

Toleware Coffeepot Type of 2002 and

Tiffany Lamp A2866

Navajo Necklace A2858

**LITHOGRAPHED, PHOTOGRAVURE**
**(#3750, 3751)**
**Self-Adhesive (#3749-3757)**
**2003-14  Serpentine Die Cut 11¼x11**

| 3749 | A2866 | 1c multi | .30 | .25 |
| 3749A | A2866 | 1c multi | .30 | .25 |

No. 3749A has "USPS" microprinted on a white field high on the lamp stand, just below the shade and is dated "2008." No. 3749 has "USPS" microprinted lower on the lamp stand and not on a white field and is dated "2007."

**Serpentine Die Cut 11**

| 3750 | A2858 | 2c multi | .30 | .25 |

A reprinting of No. 3750 shows the borders in a much brighter deep turquoise blue shade.

**Serpentine Die Cut 11¼x11½**

| 3751 | A2858 | 2c multi | 1.00 | .25 |

**Serpentine Die Cut 11¼x11**
**With "USPS" Microprinting**

| 3752 | A2858 | 2c multi | .30 | .25 |

**Serpentine Die Cut 11¼x10¾**

| 3753 | A2858 | 2c multi | .30 | .25 |

Silver Coffeepot — A2868

**LITHOGRAPHED**
**Serpentine Die Cut 11¼x11**

| 3754 | A2868 | 3c multi | .30 | .25 |

Microprinted "USPS" on No. 3752 is found on top silver appendage next to and below the middle turquoise stone on the right side of the necklace. Microprinting on No. 3753 is found on the top silver appendage next to and below the lower turquoise stone on the left side of the necklace. Nos. 3751 and 3752 are dated "2006." No. 3753 is dated "2007."

Chippendale Chair — A2859

LITHOGRAPHED
***Serpentine Die Cut 10¾x10¼***

**3755** A2859 4c multi .30 .25

LITHOGRAPHED, PHOTOGRAVURE
(#3756)
***Serpentine Die Cut 11¼x11¾***

**3756** A2805 5c multi .30 .25

***Serpentine Die Cut 11¼x10¾***

**3756A** A2805 5c multi .30 .25
*b.* Die cutting omitted, pair 400.00

No. 3756A has microprinting on the lower part of the coffeepot handle and is dated "2007." No. 3756 has no microprinting and is dated "2004." Existence of No. 3756A was reported in Aug. 2008.

No. 3756A is known printed with non-reactive cream-colored background ink and also with luminescent cream-colored ink that glows orange under both shortwave and longwave ultraviolet light.

American Clock — A2860

LITHOGRAPHED

**3757** A2860 10c multi .30 .25
*a.* Die cutting omitted, pair —

PHOTOGRAVURE
***Perf. 9¾ Vert.***
**COIL STAMPS**

**3758** A2866 1c multi .30 .25
**3758A** A2866 1c multi .30 .25
**3758B** A2858 2c multi .30 .25
**3759** A2868 3c multi .30 .25
**3761** A2859 4c multi, dated "2007" at LL .30 .25
**3761A** A2859 4c multi, dated "2013" at UL .30 .25

On plate number singles, the plate number is at the lower right on No. 3761 and centered at bottom on No. 3761A.

LITHOGRAPHED, PHOTOGRAVURE
(#3762)

**3762** A2860 10c multi .30 .25
**3763** A2860 10c multi .30 .25

No. 3763 is dated "2008," has a microprinted "USPS" as the middle "I" in "VIII," and has a network of beige dots on clock face. No. 3762 is dated "2006," lacks microprinting, and has network of gray dots on clock face.

Issued: No. 3757, 1/24; No. 3758, 3/1; No. 3755, 3/5/04; No. 3756, 6/25/04; No. 3750, 8/20/04; No. 3759, 9/16/05; Nos. 3751-3752, 12/8/05; No. 3762, 8/4/06; Nos. 3749, 3754, 3/16/07; No. 3753, 5/12/07; No. 3761, 7/19/07; No. 3740A, 3/7/08; No. 3758A, 6/7/08; No. 3758B, 2/12/11; No. 3763, 7/15/08; No. 3756A, Aug. 2008.

This is an ongoing set. Numbers may change.

See No. 3612.

**AMERICAN CULTURE SERIES**

Wisdom, Rockefeller Center, New York City — A2875

LITHOGRAPHED
***Serpentine Die Cut 11¼x11***
**2003, Feb. 28**
**Self-Adhesive**

**3766** A2875 $1 multicolored 2.00 .40
*a.* Dated "2008" 2.00 .40

**New York Public Library Lion Type of 2000**
PHOTOGRAVURE
COIL STAMP
***Perf. 9¾ Vert.***
**2003, Feb. 4** **Untagged**

**3769** A2677 (10c) multicolored .30 .25

**Atlas Statue Type of 2001**
PHOTOGRAVURE
***Serpentine Die Cut 11 Vert.***
**2003, Oct.** **Untagged**
**Coil Stamp**
**Self-Adhesive**

**3770** A2722 (10c) multicolored .30 .25

No. 3770 is dated 2003.

See No. 3520.

**SPECIAL OLYMPICS**

Athlete with Medal — A2879

***Serpentine Die Cut 11***
**2003, Feb. 13**
**Self-Adhesive**

**3771** A2879 80c multicolored 1.60 .35

**AMERICAN FILMMAKING: BEHIND THE SCENES**

A2880

No. 3772: a, Screenwriting (segment of script from *Gone With the Wind*). b, Directing (John Cassavetes). c, Costume design (Edith Head). d, Music (Max Steiner working on score). e, Makeup (Jack Pierce working on Boris Karloff's makeup for *Frankenstein*). f, Art direction (Perry Ferguson working on sketch for *Citizen Kane*). g, Cinematography (Paul Hill, assistant cameraman for *Nagana*). h, Film editing (J. Watson Webb editing *The Razor's Edge*). i, Special effects (Mark Siegel working on model for *E.T. The Extra-Terrestrial*). j, Sound (Gary Summers works on control panel).

***Serpentine Die Cut 11 Horiz.***
**2003, Feb. 25**
**Self-Adhesive**

**3772** A2880 Pane of 10 12.00
*a.-j.* 37c Any single 1.20 .50

**OHIO STATEHOOD BICENTENNIAL**

Aerial View of Farm Near Marietta — A2881

LITHOGRAPHED
***Serpentine Die Cut 11¾x11½***
**2003, Mar. 1**
**Self-Adhesive**

**3773** A2881 37c multicolored .75 .25

**PELICAN ISLAND NATIONAL WILDLIFE REFUGE, CENT.**

Brown Pelican — A2882

***Serpentine Die Cut 12x11½***
**2003, Mar. 14**
**Self-Adhesive**

**3774** A2882 37c multicolored .75 .25

**Sea Coast Type of 2002**
PHOTOGRAVURE
COIL STAMP
***Perf. 9¾ Vert.***
**2003, Mar. 19** **Untagged**

**3775** A2853 (5c) multicolored .30 .25

See No. 3864. No. 3775 has "2003" year date in blue, dots that run together in surf area, and a distinct small orange cloud. No. 3864 has "2004" year date in black, rows of distinctly separated dots in surf area, and the small orange cloud is indistinct.

See Nos. 3693, 3785, 3864, 3874-3875, 4348.

**OLD GLORY**

Uncle Sam on Bicycle with Liberty Flag, 20th Cent. A2883

1888 Presidential Campaign Badge A2884

1893 Silk Bookmark A2885

Modern Hand Fan A2886

Carving of Woman with Flag and Sword, 19th Cent. — A2887

LITHOGRAPHED
BOOKLET STAMPS
***Serpentine Die Cut 10x9¾***
**2003, Apr. 3**
**Self-Adhesive**

**3776** A2883 37c multicolored .75 .50
**3777** A2884 37c multicolored .75 .50
**3778** A2885 37c multicolored .75 .50
**3779** A2886 37c multicolored .75 .50
**3780** A2887 37c multicolored .75 .50
*a.* Horiz. strip of 5, #3776-3780 3.75
*b.* Booklet pane, 2 #3780a 7.50

Nos. 3776-3780 were issued in booklets containing two No. 3780b, each with a different backing.

**CESAR E. CHAVEZ (1927-93), LABOR ORGANIZER**

A2888

***Serpentine Die Cut 11¾x11½***
**2003, Apr. 23**
**Self-Adhesive**

**3781** A2888 37c multicolored .75 .25

**LOUISIANA PURCHASE, BICENTENNIAL**

English Translation of Treaty, Map of U.S., Treaty Signers — A2889

PHOTOGRAVURE
***Serpentine Die Cut 10¾***
**2003, Apr. 30**
**Self-Adhesive**

**3782** A2889 37c multicolored .95 .40

**FIRST FLIGHT OF WRIGHT BROTHERS, CENT.**

Orville Wright Piloting 1903 Wright Flyer — A2890

**2003, May 22** ***Serpentine Die Cut 11***
**Self-Adhesive**

**3783** Pane of 10 9.00
*a.* A2890 37c single .90 .40
*b.* Pane of 9 #3783a 8.00
*c.* Pane of 1 #3783a .90

**PURPLE HEART**

A2891

LITHOGRAPHED
**2003** ***Serpentine Die Cut 11¼x10¾***
**Self-Adhesive**

**3784** A2891 37c multi .75 .25
*b.* Printed on back of backing paper —
*d.* Die cutting omitted, pair —

***Serpentine Die Cut 10¾x10¼***

**3784A** A2891 37c multi .75 .25
*e.* Die cutting omitted, pair 150.00

See Nos. 4032, 4164, 4263-4264, 4390.

**Sea Coast Type of 2002**
**COIL STAMP**
PHOTOGRAVURE
***Serpentine Die Cut 9½x10***
**2003, June** **Untagged**
**Self-Adhesive**

**3785** A2853 (5c) multicolored .30 .25
*a.* Serp. die cut 9¼x10 .30 .25

On No. 3785, the stamps are spaced on backing paper that is taller than the stamps.

One printing of No. 3785 has more of a scarlet shade in the sky than do other examples of Nos. 3785 and 3785a. Nos. 3785 and 3785a have black "2003" year date.

See Nos. 3693, 3775, 3864, 3874-3875, 4348.

**LEGENDS OF HOLLYWOOD**

Audrey Hepburn (1929-93), Actress — A2892

***Serpentine Die Cut 10¾***
**2003, June 11**
**Self-Adhesive**

**3786** A2892 37c multicolored 1.25 1.00

**SOUTHEASTERN LIGHTHOUSES**

Old Cape Henry, Virginia A2893

Cape Lookout, North Carolina A2894

Morris Island, South Carolina A2895

Tybee Island, Georgia A2896

# UNITED STATES

Hillsboro Inlet, Florida — A2897

### Serpentine Die Cut 10¾
**2003, June 13**
**Self-Adhesive**

| 3787 | A2893 | 37c multicolored | 1.10 | .30 |
|---|---|---|---|---|
| 3788 | A2894 | 37c multicolored | 1.10 | .30 |
| a. | | Bottom of "USA" even with top of upper half-diamond of lighthouse (pos. 2) | 4.00 | 2.50 |
| 3789 | A2895 | 37c multicolored | 1.10 | .30 |
| 3790 | A2896 | 37c multicolored | 1.10 | .30 |
| 3791 | A2897 | 37c multicolored | 1.10 | .30 |
| a. | | Strip of 5, #3787-3791 | | 5.50 |
| b. | | Strip of 5, #3787, 3788a, 3789-3791 | | 9.50 |

Eagle in Gold on Colored Background A2898

Colored Eagle on Gold Background A2899

### COIL STAMPS
**Dated "2003"**

### Serpentine Die Cut 11¾ Vert.
**2003, June 26** — Untagged
**Self-Adhesive**

| 3792 | A2898 | (25c) gray & gold | .50 | .25 |
|---|---|---|---|---|
| 3793 | A2899 | (25c) gold & red | .50 | .25 |
| 3794 | A2898 | (25c) dull blue & gold | .50 | .25 |
| 3795 | A2899 | (25c) gold & Prussian blue | .50 | .25 |
| 3796 | A2898 | (25c) green & gold | .50 | .25 |
| 3797 | A2899 | (25c) gold & gray | .50 | .25 |
| 3798 | A2898 | (25c) Prussian blue & gold | .50 | .25 |
| 3799 | A2899 | (25c) gold & dull blue | .50 | .25 |
| 3800 | A2898 | (25c) red & gold | .50 | .25 |
| 3801 | A2899 | (25c) gold & green | .50 | .25 |
| b. | | Strip of 10, #3792-3801 | | 5.00 |

**Dated "2005"**

### Serpentine Die Cut 11½ Vert.
**2005, Aug. 5** — Untagged

| 3792d | A2898 | (25c) gray & gold | .50 | .25 |
|---|---|---|---|---|
| 3793d | A2899 | (25c) gold & red | .50 | .25 |
| 3794d | A2898 | (25c) dull blue & gold | .50 | .25 |
| 3795d | A2899 | (25c) gold & Prussian blue | .50 | .25 |
| 3796d | A2898 | (25c) green & gold | .50 | .25 |
| 3797d | A2899 | (25c) gold & gray | .50 | .25 |
| 3798d | A2898 | (25c) Prussian blue & gold | .50 | .25 |
| 3799d | A2899 | (25c) gold & dull blue | .50 | .25 |
| 3800d | A2898 | (25c) red & gold | .50 | .25 |
| 3801d | A2899 | (25c) gold & green | .50 | .25 |
| e. | | Strip of 10, #3792d-3801d | | 5.00 |

See Nos. 3844-3853.

### ARCTIC TUNDRA

A2900

No. 3802 — Wildlife and vegetation: a, Gyrfalcon. b, Gray wolf, vert. c, Common raven, vert. d, Musk oxen and caribou, vert. e, Grizzly bears, caribou. f, Caribou, willow ptarmigans. g, Arctic ground squirrel, vert. h, Willow ptarmigan, bearberry. i, Arctic grayling. j, Singing vole, thin-legged wolf spider, lingonberry, Labrador tea.

### LITHOGRAPHED
### Serpentine Die Cut 10¾x10½, 10½x10¾
**2003, July 2**
**Self-Adhesive**

| 3802 | A2900 | Pane of 10 | | 8.50 |
|---|---|---|---|---|
| a.-j. | | 37c Any single | .85 | .50 |

### KOREAN WAR VETERANS MEMORIAL

Memorial in Snow — A2901

### Serpentine Die Cut 11½x11¾
**2003, July 27**
**Self-Adhesive**

| 3803 | A2901 | 37c multicolored | .75 | .25 |

### MARY CASSATT PAINTINGS

Young Mother, 1888 A2902

Children Playing on the Beach, 1884 A2903

On a Balcony, 1878-79 A2904

Child in a Straw Hat, c. 1886 A2905

### PHOTOGRAVURE
### Serpentine Die Cut 10¾ on 2 or 3 Sides
**2003, Aug. 7**
**Self-Adhesive**
**Booklet Stamps**

| 3804 | A2902 | 37c multicolored | .75 | .30 |
|---|---|---|---|---|
| 3805 | A2903 | 37c multicolored | .75 | .30 |
| 3806 | A2904 | 37c multicolored | .75 | .30 |
| 3807 | A2905 | 37c multicolored | .75 | .30 |
| a. | | Block of 4, #3804-3807 | | 3.00 |
| b. | | Booklet pane of 20, 5 #3807a | | 15.00 |

No. 3807b is a double-sided booklet with 12 stamps on one side and 8 stamps plus label (booklet cover) on the other side.

### EARLY FOOTBALL HEROES

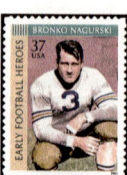

Bronko Nagurski (1908-90) A2906

Ernie Nevers (1903-76) A2907

Walter Camp (1859-1925) A2908

Red Grange (1903-91) A2909

### Serpentine Die Cut 11½x11¾
**2003, Aug. 8**
**Self-Adhesive**

| 3808 | A2906 | 37c multicolored | .75 | .35 |
|---|---|---|---|---|
| 3809 | A2907 | 37c multicolored | .75 | .35 |
| 3810 | A2908 | 37c multicolored | .75 | .35 |
| 3811 | A2909 | 37c multicolored | .75 | .35 |
| a. | | Block or strip of 4, #3808-3811 | | 3.00 |

### ROY ACUFF

Acuff (1903-92), Country Music Artist, and Fiddle — A2910

### Serpentine Die Cut 11
**2003, Sept. 13**
**Self-Adhesive**

| 3812 | A2910 | 37c multicolored | .75 | .25 |

### DISTRICT OF COLUMBIA

Map, National Mall, Row Houses and Cherry Blossoms A2911

**2003, Sept. 23**
**Self-Adhesive**

| 3813 | A2911 | 37c multicolored | .80 | .25 |

### REPTILES AND AMPHIBIANS

Scarlet Kingsnake A2912

Blue-Spotted Salamander A2913

Reticulate Collared Lizard — A2914

Ornate Chorus Frog — A2915

Ornate Box Turtle — A2916

**2003, Oct. 7**
**Self-Adhesive**

| 3814 | A2912 | 37c multicolored | .80 | .40 |
|---|---|---|---|---|
| 3815 | A2913 | 37c multicolored | .80 | .40 |
| 3816 | A2914 | 37c multicolored | .80 | .40 |
| 3817 | A2915 | 37c multicolored | .80 | .40 |
| 3818 | A2916 | 37c multicolored | .80 | .40 |
| a. | | Vert. strip of 5, #3814-3818 | | 4.00 |

### Washington Type of 2002
### PHOTOGRAVURE
**2003, Oct.** — Serpentine Die Cut 11
**Self-Adhesive**

| 3819 | A2686 | 23c gray green | 2.00 | .25 |

### Christmas Type of 2002
### LITHOGRAPHED
### Serpentine Die Cut 11¼ on 2 or 3 Sides
**2003, Oct. 23**
**Self-Adhesive**
**Booklet Stamp**
**Size: 19½x28mm**

| 3820 | A2843 | 37c multicolored | .75 | .25 |
|---|---|---|---|---|
| a. | | Booklet pane of 20 | | 15.00 |
| b. | | Die cutting omitted, pair | — | |

See No. 3675.

No. 3820a is a double-sided booklet with 12 stamps on one side and 8 stamps plus label (booklet cover) on the other side.

Compare to No. 3675, which measures 19x27mm.

### CHRISTMAS

Reindeer with Pan Pipes A2917

Santa Claus with Drum A2918

Santa Claus with Trumpet A2919

Reindeer with Horn A2920

Reindeer with Pan Pipes A2921

Santa Claus with Drum A2922

Santa Claus with Trumpet A2923

Reindeer with Horn A2924

### PHOTOGRAVURE
### Serpentine Die Cut 11¾x11
**2003, Oct. 23**
**Self-Adhesive**

| 3821 | A2917 | 37c multicolored | 1.00 | .25 |
|---|---|---|---|---|
| 3822 | A2918 | 37c multicolored | 1.00 | .25 |
| 3823 | A2919 | 37c multicolored | 1.00 | .25 |
| 3824 | A2920 | 37c multicolored | 1.00 | .25 |
| a. | | Block or strip of 4, #3821-3824 | | 4.00 |
| b. | | Booklet pane of 20, 5 each #3821-3824 | | 20.00 |

No. 3824b is a double-sided booklet with 12 stamps on one side and 8 stamps plus label (booklet cover) on the other side.

### BOOKLET STAMPS
### Serpentine Die Cut 10½x10¾ on 2 or 3 Sides

| 3825 | A2921 | 37c multicolored | 1.00 | .25 |
|---|---|---|---|---|
| 3826 | A2922 | 37c multicolored | 1.00 | .25 |
| 3827 | A2923 | 37c multicolored | 1.00 | .25 |
| 3828 | A2924 | 37c multicolored | 1.00 | .25 |
| a. | | Block of 4, #3825-3828 | | 4.00 |
| b. | | Booklet pane of 4, #3825-3828 | | 4.00 |
| c. | | Booklet pane of 6, #3827-3828, 2 each #3825-3826 | | 6.00 |
| d. | | Booklet pane of 6, #3825-3826, 2 each #3827-3828 | | 6.00 |

Snowy Egret — A2925

# UNITED STATES

## COIL STAMPS
### PHOTOGRAVURE
*Serpentine Die Cut 8½ Vert.*

2003-04                  Tagged
**Self-Adhesive**
3829   A2925   37c multi      .75   .25
    b.   Black omitted

### LITHOGRAPHED
*Serpentine Die Cut 9½ Vert.*
3829A   A2925   37c multi     .85   .25

*Serpentine Die Cut 11½x11 on 2, 3 or 4 Sides*
### Booklet Stamps
### PHOTOGRAVURE
3830   A2925   37c multi      .75   .25
    a.   Booklet pane of 20   15.00
    b.   As "a," die cutting omitted   250.00

**With "USPS" Microprinted on Bird's Breast**
**Litho.**
3830D   A2925   37c multi     5.00   .25
    e.   Booklet pane of 20   100.00
    f.   Die cutting omitted, pair   150.00
    g.   As "e," die cutting omitted   1,200.

Issued: No. 3829, 10/24; No. 3830, 1/30/04; No. 3829A, Mar. 2004; No. 3830D, 2004.
Nos 3829, 3829A, 3830 and 3830D all have "2003" year dates even though some were issued in 2004.

## PACIFIC CORAL REEF

Pacific Coral Reef — A2926

No. 3831 — Marine life: a, Emperor angelfish, blue coral, mound coral, vert. b, Humphead wrasse, Moorish idol. c, Dumphead parrotfish, vert. d, Black spotted puffer, threadfin butterflyfish, staghorn coral. e, Hawksbill turtle, palette surgeonfish. f, Pink anemonefish, magnificent sea anemone, vert. g, Snowflake moray eel, Spanish dancer. h, Lionfish, vert. i, Triton's trumpet. j, Oriental sweetlips, bluestreak cleaner wrasse, mushroom coral, vert.

### PHOTOGRAVURE
*Serpentine Die Cut 10¾*
2004, Jan. 2
**Self-Adhesive**
3831   A2926   Pane of 10    9.00
    a.-j.   37c Any single    .90   .40

## CHINESE NEW YEAR

Year of the Monkey — A2927

*Serpentine Die Cut 10¾*
2004, Jan. 13
**Self-Adhesive**
3832   A2927   37c multicolored   .75   .25
    a.   Yellow omitted

See Nos. 3895i, 3997i.

## LOVE

Candy Hearts — A2928

### BOOKLET STAMP
*Serpentine Die Cut 10¾ on 2, 3 or 4 Sides*
2004, Jan. 14
**Self-Adhesive**
3833   A2928   37c multicolored   .75   .25
    a.   Booklet pane of 20   15.00

## BLACK HERITAGE SERIES

Paul Robeson (1898-1976), Actor, Singer, Athlete and Activist — A2929

### PHOTOGRAVURE
*Serpentine Die Cut 10¾*
2004, Jan. 20
**Self-Adhesive**
3834   A2929   37c multicolored   .85   .25

## THEODOR SEUSS GEISEL (DR. SEUSS)

Dr. Seuss (1904-91), Children's Book Writer, and Book Characters A2930

### PHOTOGRAVURE
*Serpentine Die Cut 10¾x10½*
2004, Mar. 2
**Self-Adhesive**
3835   A2930   37c multicolored   .85   .25
    a.   Die cutting omitted, pair   1,400.

## FLOWERS

White Lilacs and Pink Roses A2931     Five Varieties of Pink Roses A2932

### LITHOGRAPHED (#3836), PHOTOGRAVURE BOOKLET STAMP (#3836)
*Serpentine Die Cut 10¾ on 2, 3 or 4 Sides*
2004, Mar. 4
**Self-Adhesive**
3836   A2931   37c multicolored   .75   .25
    a.   Booklet pane of 20   15.00

*Serpentine Die Cut 11½x11*
3837   A2932   60c multicolored   2.00   .25

## UNITED STATES AIR FORCE ACADEMY, 50TH ANNIV.

Cadet Chapel — A2933

### PHOTOGRAVURE
*Serpentine Die Cut 10¾*
2004, Apr. 1
**Self-Adhesive**
3838   A2933   37c multicolored   .75   .25

## HENRY MANCINI

Henry Mancini (1924-94), Composer, and Pink Panther — A2934

2004, Apr. 13
**Self-Adhesive**
3839   A2934   37c multicolored   .75   .25

## AMERICAN CHOREOGRAPHERS

Martha Graham (1893-1991) A2935

Alvin Ailey (1931-89), and Dancers — A2936

Agnes de Mille (1909-93), and Dancers — A2937

George Balanchine (1904-83), and Dancers — A2938

### LITHOGRAPHED
2004, May 4
**Self-Adhesive**
3840   A2935   37c multicolored   .75   .35
3841   A2936   37c multicolored   .75   .35
3842   A2937   37c multicolored   .75   .35
3843   A2938   37c multicolored   .75   .35
    a.   Horiz. strip of 4, #3840-3843   3.00
    b.   Strip of 4, die cutting omitted   300.00
    c.   Pane of 20 misprinted and miscut to show 5 #3843 and half of 5 #3842 at left, lower center plate position diagram at center, and 10 blank stamps at right.

### Eagle Types of 2003
### PHOTOGRAVURE
### COIL STAMPS
*Perf. 9¾ Vert.*
2004, May 12         Untagged
3844   A2898   (25c) gray & gold   1.25   .25
3845   A2899   (25c) gold & green   1.25   .25
3846   A2898   (25c) red & gold   1.25   .25
3847   A2899   (25c) gold & dull blue   1.25   .25
3848   A2898   (25c) Prussian blue & gold   1.25   .25
3849   A2899   (25c) gold & gray   1.25   .50
3850   A2898   (25c) green & gold   1.25   .25
3851   A2899   (25c) gold & Prussian blue   1.25   .25
3852   A2898   (25c) dull blue & gold   1.25   .25
3853   A2899   (25c) gold & red   1.25   .25
    a.   Strip of 10, #3844-3853   12.50

## LEWIS & CLARK EXPEDITION, BICENTENNIAL

Meriwether Lewis (1774-1809) and William Clark (1770-1838) On Hill — A2939

Lewis — A2940

Clark — A2941

### LITHOGRAPHED & ENGRAVED
*Serpentine Die Cut 10¾*
2004, May 14
**Self-Adhesive**
3854   A2939   37c green & multi   1.10   .25
### Booklet Stamps
*Serpentine Die Cut 10½x10¾*
3855   A2940   37c blue & multi   .90   .45
3856   A2941   37c red & multi   .90   .45
    a.   Horiz. or vert. pair, #3855-3856   1.80
    b.   Booklet pane, 5 each #3855-3856   9.00

Nos. 3855-3856 were issued in booklets containing two No. 3856b, each with a different backing. The booklets sold for $8.95.

## ISAMU NOGUCHI (1904-88), SCULPTOR

  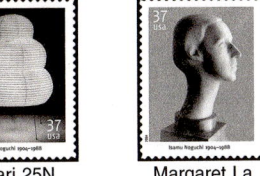

Akari 25N A2942     Margaret La Farge Osborn A2943

Black Sun — A2944     Mother and Child — A2945

Figure (Detail) — A2946

### LITHOGRAPHED
*Serpentine Die Cut 10½x10¾*
2004, May 18
**Self-Adhesive**
3857   A2942   37c black   .90   .40
3858   A2943   37c black   .90   .40
3859   A2944   37c black   .90   .40
3860   A2945   37c black   .90   .40
3861   A2946   37c black   .90   .40
    a.   Horiz. strip of 5, #3857-3861   4.50

## NATIONAL WORLD WAR II MEMORIAL

A2947

*Serpentine Die Cut 10¾*
2004, May 29
**Self-Adhesive**
3862   A2947   37c multicolored   .75   .25

Scott values for used self-adhesive stamps are for examples either on piece or off piece.

## OLYMPIC GAMES, ATHENS, GREECE

Stylized Runner — A2948

2004, June 9
**Self-Adhesive**
3863   A2948   37c multicolored   .75   .25

### Sea Coast Type of 2002
### PHOTOGRAVURE
### COIL STAMP
*Perf. 9¾ Vert.*
2004, June 11        Untagged
3864   A2853   (5c) multicolored   .30   .25

No. 3864 has "2004" year date in black, rows of distinctly separated dots in surf area, and the small orange cloud is indistinct.
No. 3775 has "2003" year date in blue, dots that run together in surf area, and a distinct small orange cloud.
See Nos. 3693, 3775, 3785, 3874-3875, 4348.

## THE ART OF DISNEY: FRIENDSHIP

Goofy, Mickey Mouse, Donald Duck
A2949

Bambi, Thumper
A2950

Mufasa, Simba
A2951

Jiminy Cricket, Pinocchio
A2952

### LITHOGRAPHED
*Serpentine Die Cut 10½x10¾*
**2004, June 23**
**Self-Adhesive**

| | | | | |
|---|---|---|---|---|
| 3865 | A2949 | 37c multicolored | 1.00 | .30 |
| 3866 | A2950 | 37c multicolored | 1.00 | .30 |
| 3867 | A2951 | 37c multicolored | 1.00 | .30 |
| 3868 | A2952 | 37c multicolored | 1.00 | .30 |
| a. | Block or vert. strip of 4, #3865-3868 | | 4.00 | |

## U.S.S. CONSTELLATION

A2953

### ENGRAVED
*Serpentine Die Cut 10½*
**2004, June 30**
**Self-Adhesive**

3869 A2953 37c brown .75 .25

## R. BUCKMINSTER FULLER (1895-1983), ENGINEER

*Time* Magazine Cover Depicting Fuller, by Boris Artzybasheff — A2954

### LITHOGRAPHED
*Serpentine Die Cut 10½x10¾*
**2004, July 12**
**Self-Adhesive**

3870 A2954 37c multicolored .75 .25

## LITERARY ARTS

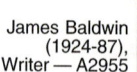
James Baldwin (1924-87), Writer — A2955

*Serpentine Die Cut 10¾*
**2004, July 23**
**Self-Adhesive**

3871 A2955 37c multicolored .75 .25
a. Die cutting omitted, pair 750.00

## AMERICAN TREASURES SERIES

Giant Magnolias on a Blue Velvet Cloth, by Martin Johnson Heade — A2956

### PHOTOGRAVURE BOOKLET STAMP
*Serpentine Die Cut 10¾ on 2 or 3 Sides*
**2004, Aug. 12**
**Self-Adhesive**

3872 A2956 37c multicolored .70 .25
a. Booklet pane of 20 15.00
b. Die cutting omitted, pair, in #3872a with foldover

No. 3872a is a double-sided booklet pane with 12 stamps on one side and eight stamps plus label on the other side.

## ART OF THE AMERICAN INDIAN

A2957

No. 3878: a, Mimbres bowl. b, Kutenai parfleche. c, Tlingit sculptures. d, Ho-Chunk bag. e, Seminole doll. f, Mississippian effigy. g, Acoma pot. h, Navajo weaving. i, Seneca carving. j, Luiseño basket.

*Serpentine Die Cut 10¾x11*
**2004, Aug. 21**
**Self-Adhesive**

3873 A2957 Pane of 10 25.00
a.-j. 37c Any single 2.50 .40

### Sea Coast Type of 2002
### LITHOGRAPHED COIL STAMPS
*Serpentine Die Cut 10 Vert.*
**2004-05**  **Untagged**
**Self-Adhesive**

3874 A2853 (5c) multi, large "2003" year date .30 .25
a. Small "2003" year date ('05) .30 .25

*Serpentine Die Cut 11½ Vert.*
**Untagged**

3875 A2853 (5c) multi, "2004" year date .30 .25

On Nos. 3874, 3874a and 3875, the stamps are spaced on backing paper that is taller than the stamps.
See Nos. 3693, 3775, 3785, 3864, 4348.

## LEGENDS OF HOLLYWOOD

John Wayne (1907-79), Actor — A2958

*Serpentine Die Cut 10¾*
**2004, Sept. 9**
**Self-Adhesive**

3876 A2958 37c multicolored .85 .25

## SICKLE CELL DISEASE AWARENESS

Mother and Child — A2959

*Serpentine Die Cut 11*
**2004, Sept. 29**
**Self-Adhesive**

3877 A2959 37c multicolored .75 .25

## CLOUDSCAPES

A2960

No. 3878 — Clouds: a, Cirrus radiatus. b, Cirrostratus fibratus. c, Cirrocumulus undulatus. d, Cumulonimbus mammatus. e, Cumulonimbus incus. f, Altocumulus stratiformis. g, Altostratus translucidus. h, Altocumulus undulatus. i, Altocumulus castellanus. j, Altocumulus lenticularis. k, Stratocumulus undulatus. l, Stratus opacus. m, Cumulus humilis. n, Cumulus congestus. o, Cumulonimbus with tornado.

**2004, Oct. 4**
**Self-Adhesive**

3878 A2960 Pane of 15 15.00
a.-o. 37c Any single 1.00 .50

## CHRISTMAS

Madonna and Child, by Lorenzo Monaco — A2961

### LITHOGRAPHED BOOKLET STAMP
*Serpentine Die Cut 10¾x11 on 2 or 3 Sides*
**2004, Oct. 14**
**Self-Adhesive**

3879 A2961 37c multicolored .75 .25
a. Booklet pane of 20 15.00
b. As "a," die cutting omitted —

No. 3879a is a double-sided booklet pane with 12 stamps on one side and eight stamps plus label that serves as a booklet cover on the other side.

## HANUKKAH

Dreidel — A2962

*Serpentine Die Cut 10¾*
**2004, Oct. 15**
**Self-Adhesive**

3880 A2962 37c multicolored .75 .25
a. Die cuts applied to wrong sides of stamp (hyphen-hole die cuts and wavy line on face, die cut 10¾ on reverse) —

See Nos. 4118, 4219, 4372.

## KWANZAA

People in Robes — A2963

*Serpentine Die Cut 10¾*
**2004, Oct. 16**
**Self-Adhesive**

3881 A2963 37c multicolored .75 .25
See Nos. 4119, 4220, 4373.

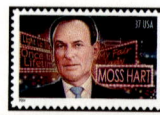
Moss Hart (1904-61), Playwright A2964

### PHOTOGRAVURE
**2004, Oct. 25** *Serpentine Die Cut 11*
**Self-Adhesive**

3882 A2964 37c multicolored .75 .25

## CHRISTMAS

Purple Santa Ornament A2965

Green Santa Ornament A2966

Blue Santa Ornament A2967

Red Santa Ornament A2968

*Serpentine Die Cut 11½x11*
**2004, Nov. 16**
**Self-Adhesive**

| | | | | |
|---|---|---|---|---|
| 3883 | A2965 | 37c purple & multi | 1.00 | .25 |
| 3884 | A2966 | 37c green & multi | 1.00 | .25 |
| 3885 | A2967 | 37c blue & multi | 1.00 | .25 |
| 3886 | A2968 | 37c red & multi | 1.00 | .25 |
| a. | Block or strip of 4, #3883-3886 | | 4.00 | |
| b. | Booklet pane of 20, 5 #3886a blocks | | 20.00 | |

Purple Santa Ornament A2969

Green Santa Ornament A2970

Blue Santa Ornament A2971

Red Santa Ornament A2972

**Booklet Stamps**
*Serpentine Die Cut 10½x10¾ on 2 or 3 Sides*

| | | | | |
|---|---|---|---|---|
| 3887 | A2969 | 37c purple & multi | .90 | .25 |
| 3888 | A2970 | 37c green & multi | .90 | .25 |
| 3889 | A2971 | 37c blue & multi | .90 | .25 |
| 3890 | A2972 | 37c red & multi | .90 | .25 |
| a. | Block of 4, #3887-3890 | | 3.60 | |
| b. | Booklet pane of 4, #3887-3890 | | 3.60 | |
| c. | Booklet pane of 6, #3889-3890, 2 each #3887-3888 | | 5.50 | |
| d. | Booklet pane of 6, #3887-3888, 2 each #3889-3890 | | 5.50 | |

*Serpentine Die Cut 8 on 2, 3 or 4 Sides*

| | | | | |
|---|---|---|---|---|
| 3891 | A2970 | 37c green & multi | 2.00 | .25 |
| 3892 | A2969 | 37c purple & multi | 2.00 | .25 |
| 3893 | A2972 | 37c red & multi | 2.00 | .25 |
| 3894 | A2971 | 37c blue & multi | 2.00 | .25 |
| a. | Block of 4, #3891-3894 | | 8.00 | |
| b. | Booklet pane of 18, 6 each #3891, 3893, 3 each # 3892, 3894 | | 36.00 | |
| | Nos. 3883-3894 (12) | | 15.60 | 3.00 |

No. 3886b is a double-sided booklet with 12 stamps on one side and 8 stamps plus label that serves as a booklet cover on the other side.

The design of No. 3894b shows ornaments in a wooden box. The pattern of the wooden box dividers creates three types of each design. Rows 1 and 4 are Type 1, with a top horizontal strip of frame extending from edge to edge while the bottom strip of frame stops at the design's width. Rows 2 and 5 are Type 2, with both top and bottom strips of frame stopping at the design's width. Rows 3 and 6 are Type 3, with the top strip of frame stopping at design's width while the bottom strip of frame extends from edge to edge. Each variety is equally common.

UNITED STATES

### Chinese New Year Types of 1992-2004
#### PHOTOGRAVURE
*Serpentine Die Cut 10¾*

**2005, Jan. 6**
**Self-Adhesive**

| 3895 | Double sided pane of 24, 2 each #a-l | 18.00 | |
|---|---|---|---|
| a. | A2360 37c Rat | .75 | .40 |
| b. | A2413 37c Ox | .75 | .40 |
| c. | A2462 37c Tiger | .75 | .40 |
| d. | A2535 37c Rabbit | .75 | .40 |
| e. | A2602 37c Dragon | .75 | .40 |
| f. | A2702 37c Snake | .75 | .40 |
| g. | A2752 37c Horse | .75 | .40 |
| h. | A2856 37c Ram | .75 | .40 |
| i. | A2927 37c Monkey | .75 | .40 |
| j. | A2067 37c Rooster | .75 | .40 |
| k. | A2146 37c Dog | .75 | .40 |
| l. | A2205 37c Boar | .75 | .40 |
| m. | As No. 3895, die cutting missing on "a", "b", and "c" on reverse side (PS) | | 900.00 |

No. 3895h has "2005" year date and is photogravure while No. 3747 has "2003" year date and is lithographed.
Stamps are on the right side of the front and on the left side of the reverse.
See Nos. 2720, 2817, 2876, 3060, 3120, 3179, 3272, 3370, 3500, 3559, 3747, 3832, 3997.

### BLACK HERITAGE SERIES

Marian Anderson (1897-1993), Singer — A2973

**2005, Jan. 27**
**Self-Adhesive**

| 3896 | A2973 37c multicolored | .85 | .25 |

### RONALD REAGAN

Ronald Reagan (1911-2004), 40th President — A2974

**2005, Feb. 9**
**Self-Adhesive**

| 3897 | A2974 37c multicolored | .75 | .25 |

See No. 4078.

### LOVE

Hand and Flower Bouquet — A2975

**BOOKLET STAMP**
*Serpentine Die Cut 10¾x11 on 2, 3 or 4 Sides*

**2005, Feb. 18**
**Self-Adhesive**

| 3898 | A2975 37c multicolored | .75 | .25 |
| a. | Booklet pane of 20 | 15.00 | |

### NORTHEAST DECIDUOUS FOREST

*Serpentine Die Cut 10¾*
**2005, Mar. 3**
**Self-Adhesive**

| 3899 | A2976 Pane of 10 | 8.50 | |
| a.-j. | 37c Any single | .85 | .40 |

### SPRING FLOWERS

Hyacinth A2977    Daffodil A2978

Tulip A2979    Iris A2980

#### LITHOGRAPHED BOOKLET STAMPS
*Serpentine Die Cut 10¾ on 2 or 3 Sides*

**2005, Mar. 15**
**Self-Adhesive**

| 3900 | A2977 37c multicolored | .85 | .30 |
| 3901 | A2978 37c multicolored | .85 | .30 |
| 3902 | A2979 37c multicolored | .85 | .30 |
| 3903 | A2980 37c multicolored | .85 | .30 |
| a. | Block of 4, #3900-3903 | 3.40 | |
| b. | Booklet pane of 20, 5 each #3900-3903 | 17.00 | |
| c. | As "b," die cutting omitted on side with 8 stamps | | |

No. 3903b is a double-sided booklet with 12 stamps on one side and 8 stamps plus label (booklet cover) on the other side.

### LITERARY ARTS

Robert Penn Warren (1905-89), Writer — A2981

#### PHOTOGRAVURE
*Serpentine Die Cut 10¾*
**2005, Apr. 22**
**Self-Adhesive**

| 3904 | A2981 37c multicolored | .75 | .25 |

### EDGAR Y. "YIP" HARBURG

Harburg (1896-1981), Lyricist — A2982

#### LITHOGRAPHED
**2005, Apr. 28**
**Self-Adhesive**

| 3905 | A2982 37c multicolored | .75 | .25 |

### AMERICAN SCIENTISTS

Barbara McClintock (1902-92), Geneticist A2983

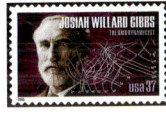

Josiah Willard Gibbs (1839-1903), Thermodynamicist A2984

John von Neumann (1903-57), Mathematician A2985

Richard Feynman (1918-88), Physicist A2986

**2005, May 4**
**Self-Adhesive**

| 3906 | A2983 37c multicolored | 1.00 | .35 |
| 3907 | A2984 37c multicolored | 1.00 | .35 |
| 3908 | A2985 37c multicolored | 1.00 | .35 |
| a. | Vert. pair, die cutting omitted, #3906 & 3908 | — | |
| 3909 | A2986 37c multicolored | 1.00 | .35 |
| a. | Block or horiz. strip of 4, #3906-3909 | 4.00 | |
| b. | All colors omitted, tagging omitted, pane of 20 | — | |
| c. | As "a," printing on back of stamps omitted | — | |
| d. | Vert. pair, die cutting omitted, #3907 & 3909 | — | |

On No. 3909b, the printing on the back of the pane and all die cutting is normal.

### MODERN AMERICAN ARCHITECTURE

A2987

No. 3910 — Buildings: a, Guggenheim Museum, New York. b, Chrysler Building, New York. c, Vanna Venturi House, Philadelphia. d, TWA Terminal, New York. e, Walt Disney Concert Hall, Los Angeles. f, 860-880 Lake Shore Drive, Chicago. g, National Gallery of Art, Washington, DC. h, Glass House, New Canaan, CT. i, Yale Art and Architecture Building, New Haven, CT. j, High Museum of Art, Atlanta. k, Exeter Academy Library, Exeter, NH. l, Hancock Center, Chicago.

*Serpentine Die Cut 10¾x11*
**2005, May 19**
**Self-Adhesive**

| 3910 | A2987 Pane of 12 | 11.00 | |
| a.-l. | 37c Any single | .90 | .50 |
| m. | As No. 3910, orange yellow omitted | 400.00 | |

### LEGENDS OF HOLLYWOOD

Henry Fonda (1905-82), Actor — A2988

Sheets of 180 in nine panes of 20
*Serpentine Die Cut 11x10¾*
**2005, May 20**
**Self-Adhesive**

| 3911 | A2988 37c multicolored | .90 | .25 |

### THE ART OF DISNEY: CELEBRATION

Pluto, Mickey Mouse A2989    Mad Hatter, Alice A2990

Flounder, Ariel A2991    Snow White, Dopey A2992

*Serpentine Die Cut 10½x10¾*
**2005, June 30**
**Self-Adhesive**

| 3912 | A2989 37c multi | .85 | .30 |
| 3913 | A2990 37c multi | .85 | .30 |
| 3914 | A2991 37c multi | .85 | .30 |

| 3915 | A2992 37c multi | .85 | .30 |
| a. | Block or vert. strip of 4, #3912-3915 | 3.40 | |
| b. | Die cutting omitted, pane of 20 | 5,500. | 1,400. |
| c. | Printed on backing paper, pane of 20 | | |

On the unique used pane of No. 3915b, the outer selvage was removed by cutting.

### ADVANCES IN AVIATION

Boeing 247 — A2993

Consolidated PBY Catalina — A2994

Grumman F6F Hellcat — A2995

Republic P-47 Thunderbolt A2996

Engineering and Research Corporation Ercoupe 415 — A2997

Lockheed P-80 Shooting Star — A2998

Consolidated B-24 Liberator A2999

Boeing B-29 Superfortress A3000

Beechcraft 35 Bonanza A3001

Northrop YB-49 Flying Wing — A3002

*Serpentine Die Cut 10¾x10½*
**2005, July 29**
**Self-Adhesive**

| 3916 | A2993 37c multicolored | .80 | .40 |
| 3917 | A2994 37c multicolored | .80 | .40 |
| 3918 | A2995 37c multicolored | .80 | .40 |
| 3919 | A2996 37c multicolored | .80 | .40 |
| 3920 | A2997 37c multicolored | .80 | .40 |
| 3921 | A2998 37c multicolored | .80 | .40 |
| 3922 | A2999 37c multicolored | .80 | .40 |
| 3923 | A3000 37c multicolored | .80 | .40 |
| 3924 | A3001 37c multicolored | .80 | .40 |
| 3925 | A3002 37c multicolored | .80 | .40 |
| a. | Block of 10, #3916-3925 | 8.00 | |

## RIO GRANDE BLANKETS

 A3003

 A3004

 A3005

 A3006

### LITHOGRAPHED
### BOOKLET STAMPS
*Serpentine Die Cut 10¾ on 2 or 3 Sides*

**2005, July 30**
**Self-Adhesive**

| | | | | |
|---|---|---|---|---|
| 3926 | A3003 | 37c multicolored | .75 | .30 |
| 3927 | A3004 | 37c multicolored | .75 | .30 |
| 3928 | A3005 | 37c multicolored | .75 | .30 |
| 3929 | A3006 | 37c multicolored | .75 | .30 |
| a. | | Block of 4, #3926-3929 | 3.00 | |
| b. | | Booklet pane, 5 each #3926-3929 | 15.00 | |

No. 3929b is a double-sided booklet with 12 stamps on one side and 8 stamps plus label (booklet cover) on the other side.

## PRESIDENTIAL LIBRARIES ACT, 50th ANNIV.

Presidential Seal — A3007

*Serpentine Die Cut 10¾*
**2005, Aug. 4**
**Self-Adhesive**

| | | | | |
|---|---|---|---|---|
| 3930 | A3007 | 37c multicolored | .80 | .25 |

## SPORTY CARS OF THE 1950S

1953 Studebaker Starliner — A3008

1954 Kaiser Darrin — A3009

1953 Chevrolet Corvette — A3010

1952 Nash Healey — A3011

1955 Ford Thunderbird — A3012

### BOOKLET STAMPS
*Serpentine Die Cut 10¾ on 2 or 3 Sides*

**2005, Aug. 20**    Tagged
**Self-Adhesive**

| | | | | |
|---|---|---|---|---|
| 3931 | A3008 | 37c multicolored | 2.00 | .40 |
| 3932 | A3009 | 37c multicolored | 2.00 | .40 |
| 3933 | A3010 | 37c multicolored | 2.00 | .40 |
| 3934 | A3011 | 37c multicolored | 2.00 | .40 |
| 3935 | A3012 | 37c multicolored | 2.00 | .40 |
| a. | | Vert. strip of 5, #3931-3935 | 10.00 | |
| b. | | Booklet pane, 4 each #3931-3935 | 40.00 | |

Stamps in No. 3935a are not adjacent, as rows of selvage are between stamps one and two, and between stamps three and four.

No. 3935b is a double-sided booklet pane with 12 stamps on one side (2 each #3931, 3933, 3935, and 3 each #3932, 3934) and eight stamps (1 each #3932, 3934, and 2 each #3931, 3933, 3935) plus label on the other side.

## ARTHUR ASHE

Arthur Ashe (1943-93), Tennis Player — A3013

*Serpentine Die Cut 10¾*
**2005, Aug. 27**
**Self-Adhesive**

| | | | | |
|---|---|---|---|---|
| 3936 | A3013 | 37c multicolored | .75 | .25 |

## TO FORM A MORE PERFECT UNION

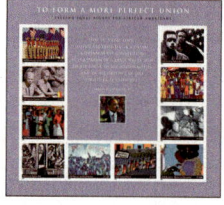
A3014

No. 3937 — Inscriptions and artwork: a, 1948 Executive Order 9981 (Training for War, by William H. Johnson). b, 1965 Voting Rights Act (Youths on the Selma March, 1965, photograph by Bruce Davidson). c, 1960 Lunch Counter Sit-ins (National Civil Rights Museum exhibits, by StudioEIS). d, 1957 Little Rock Nine (America Cares, by George Hunt). e, 1955 Montgomery Bus Boycott (Walking, by Charles Alston). f, 1961 Freedom Riders (Freedom Riders, by May Stevens). g, 1964 Civil Rights Act (Dixie Café, by Jacob Lawrence). h, 1963 March on Washington (March on Washington, by Alma Thomas). i, 1965 Selma March (Selma March, by Bernice Sims). j, 1954 Brown v. Board of Education (The Lamp, by Romare Bearden).

*Serpentine Die Cut 10¾x10½*
**2005, Aug. 30**
**Self-Adhesive**

| | | | | |
|---|---|---|---|---|
| 3937 | A3014 | Pane of 10 | 11.00 | |
| a.-j. | | 37c Any single | 1.10 | .40 |

## CHILD HEALTH

Child and Doctor — A3015

### PHOTOGRAVURE
*Serpentine Die Cut 10½x11*
**2005, Sept. 7**
**Self-Adhesive**

| | | | | |
|---|---|---|---|---|
| 3938 | A3015 | 37c multicolored | .75 | .25 |

## LET'S DANCE

Merengue A3016

Salsa A3017

Cha Cha Cha A3018

Mambo A3019

*Serpentine Die Cut 10¾*
**2005, Sept. 17**
**Self-Adhesive**

| | | | | |
|---|---|---|---|---|
| 3939 | A3016 | 37c multicolored | 1.00 | .35 |
| 3940 | A3017 | 37c multicolored | 1.00 | .35 |
| 3941 | A3018 | 37c multicolored | 1.00 | .35 |
| 3942 | A3019 | 37c multicolored | 1.00 | .35 |
| a. | | Vert. strip of 4, #3939-3942 | 4.00 | |

Stamps in the vertical strip are not adjacent as rows of selvage are between the stamps. The backing paper of stamps from the 2nd and 4th columns have Spanish inscriptions, while the other columns have English inscriptions.

## GRETA GARBO

Garbo (1905-90), Actress — A3020

### ENGRAVED
**2005, Sept. 23**
**Self-Adhesive**

| | | | | |
|---|---|---|---|---|
| 3943 | A3020 | 37c black | .75 | .25 |

See Sweden No. 2517.

## JIM HENSON AND THE MUPPETS

A3021

No. 3944: a, Kermit the Frog. b, Fozzie Bear. c, Sam the Eagle and flag. d, Miss Piggy. e, Statler and Waldorf. f, The Swedish Chef and fruit. g, Animal. h, Dr. Bunsen Honeydew and Beaker. i, Rowlf the Dog. j, The Great Gonzo and Camilla the Chicken. k, Jim Henson.

Nos. 3944a-3944j are 30x30mm; No. 3944k, 28x37mm.

### PHOTOGRAVURE
*Serpentine Die Cut 10½, 10½x10¾ (#3944k)*
**2005, Sept. 28**
**Self-Adhesive**

| | | | | |
|---|---|---|---|---|
| 3944 | A3021 | Pane of 11 | 9.00 | |
| a.-k. | | 37c Any single | .80 | .50 |

## CONSTELLATIONS

Leo A3022

Orion A3023

Lyra A3024

Pegasus A3025

### LITHOGRAPHED
*Serpentine Die Cut 10¾*
**2005, Oct. 3**
**Self-Adhesive**

| | | | | |
|---|---|---|---|---|
| 3945 | A3022 | 37c multicolored | .85 | .35 |
| 3946 | A3023 | 37c multicolored | .85 | .35 |
| 3947 | A3024 | 37c multicolored | .85 | .35 |
| 3948 | A3025 | 37c multicolored | .85 | .35 |
| a. | | Block or vert. strip of 4, #3945-3948 | 3.40 | |
| b. | | As "a," die cutting omitted | 750.00 | |

## CHRISTMAS COOKIES

Santa Claus A3026

Snowmen A3027

Angel A3028

Elves A3029

### LITHOGRAPHED
*Serpentine Die Cut 10¾x11*
**2005, Oct. 20**
**Self-Adhesive**
*Design Size: 19x26mm*

| | | | | |
|---|---|---|---|---|
| 3949 | A3026 | 37c multicolored | .85 | .25 |
| 3950 | A3027 | 37c multicolored | .85 | .25 |
| 3951 | A3028 | 37c multicolored | .85 | .25 |
| 3952 | A3029 | 37c multicolored | .85 | .25 |
| a. | | Block or vert. strip of 4, #3949-3952 | 3.50 | |

### Booklet Stamps
*Serpentine Die Cut 10¾x11 on 2 or 3 Sides*
*Design Size: 19½x27mm*

| | | | | |
|---|---|---|---|---|
| 3953 | A3026 | 37c multicolored | 1.00 | .25 |
| 3954 | A3027 | 37c multicolored | 1.00 | .25 |
| 3955 | A3028 | 37c multicolored | 1.00 | .25 |
| 3956 | A3029 | 37c multicolored | 1.00 | .25 |
| a. | | Block of 4, #3953-3956 | 4.00 | |
| b. | | Booklet pane of 20, 5 #3956a | 20.00 | |

Santa Claus A3030

Snowmen A3031

Angel A3032

Elves A3033

*Serpentine Die Cut 10½x10¾*

| | | | | |
|---|---|---|---|---|
| 3957 | A3030 | 37c multicolored | 1.10 | .25 |
| 3958 | A3031 | 37c multicolored | 1.10 | .25 |
| 3959 | A3032 | 37c multicolored | 1.10 | .25 |
| 3960 | A3033 | 37c multicolored | 1.10 | .25 |
| a. | | Block of 4, #3957-3960 | 4.50 | |
| b. | | Booklet pane of 4, #3957-3960 | 4.50 | |
| c. | | Booklet pane of 6, #3959-3960, 2 each #3957-3958 | 7.00 | |
| d. | | Booklet pane of 6, #3957-3958, 2 each #3959-3960 | 7.00 | |

No. 3956b is a double-sided booklet pane with 12 stamps on one side and eight stamps plus label that serves as a booklet cover on the other side. Nos. 3949-3952 have a small "2005" year date, while Nos. 3953-3956 have a large year date. Other design differences caused by different cropping of the images can

UNITED STATES 109

be found, with Nos. 3953-3956 showing slightly more design features on one or more sides.

### DISTINGUISHED MARINES

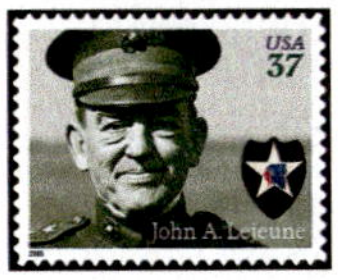
Lt. Gen. John A. Lejeune (1867-1942), 2nd Infantry Division Insignia — A3034

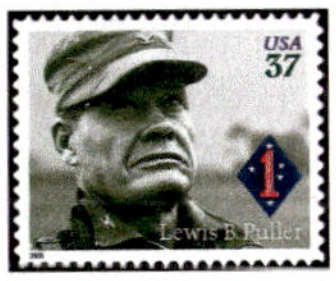
Lt. Gen. Lewis B. Puller (1898-1971), 1st Marine Division Insignia — A3035

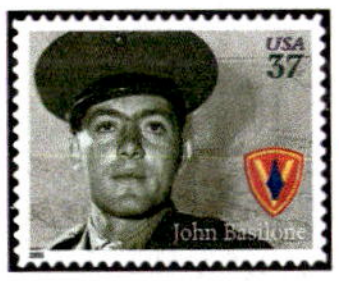
Sgt. John Basilone (1916-45), 5th Marine Division Insignia — A3036

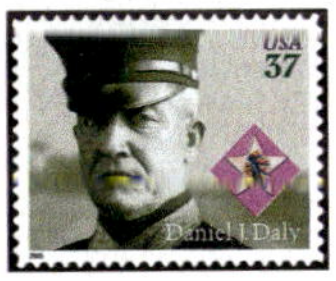
Sgt. Major Daniel J. Daly (1873-1937), 73rd Machine Gun Company, 6th Marine Regiment Insignia — A3037

LITHOGRAPHED

*Serpentine Die Cut 11x10½*

**2005, Nov. 10**

**Self-Adhesive**

**3961** A3034 37c multicolored 1.00 .35
**3962** A3035 37c multicolored 1.00 .35
**3963** A3036 37c multicolored 1.00 .35
**3964** A3037 37c multicolored 1.00 .35
*a.* Block or horiz. strip of 4, #3961-3964 4.00

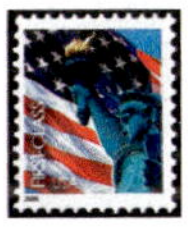
Flag and Statue of Liberty — A3038

LITHOGRAPHED

**2005, Dec. 8** *Perf. 11¼*

**3965** A3038 (39c) multicolored 1.10 .25

**Self-Adhesive (#3966, 3968-3975)**

*Serpentine Die Cut 11¼x10¾*

**3966** A3038 (39c) multicolored 1.10 .25
*a.* Booklet pane of 20 22.00
*b.* As "a," die cutting omitted 3,100.

LITHOGRAPHED (#3970), PHOTOGRAVURE

**COIL STAMPS**

*Perf. 9¾ Vert.*

**3967** A3038 (39c) multicolored 1.10 .25

*Serpentine Die Cut 8½ Vert.*

**3968** A3038 (39c) multicolored 1.10 .25

*Serpentine Die Cut 10¼ Vert.*

**3969** A3038 (39c) multicolored 1.50 .25

*Serpentine Die Cut 9½ Vert.*

**3970** A3038 (39c) multicolored 3.50 .25

LITHOGRAPHED (#3974), PHOTOGRAVURE

**BOOKLET STAMPS**

*Serpentine Die Cut 11¼x10¾ on 2 or 3 Sides*

**3972** A3038 (39c) multicolored 1.10 .25
*a.* Booklet pane of 20 22.00

*Serpentine Die Cut 10½x10¾ on 2 or 3 Sides*

**3973** A3038 (39c) multicolored 1.10 .25
*a.* Booklet pane of 20 22.00

On both Nos. 3972 and 3973, the sky immediately above the date is bright blue and extends from the left side to beyond the "6" in the date, the left arm of the star at the upper left barely touches the frame line and is without the "USPS" microprinting. They are distinguishable by the die cutting. Nos. 3872a and 3973a are double-sided booklet panes with 12 stamps on one side and eight stamps plus label that serves as a booklet cover on the other side.

No. 3973 was not available until January 2006.

*Serpentine Die Cut 11¼x10¾ on 2 or 3 Sides*

**3974** A3038 (39c) multicolored 1.10 .25
*a.* Booklet pane of 4 4.40
*b.* Booklet pane of 6 6.60

*Serpentine Die Cut 8 on 2, 3 or 4 Sides*

**3975** A3038 (39c) multicolored 1.10 .25
*a.* Booklet pane of 18 20.00
*Nos. 3965-3975 (10)* 13.80 2.50

Nos. 3965-3975 are dated "2006."

On No. 3966, the sky immediately above the date is bright blue and extends from the left side to beyond the "6" in the date, the left arm of the star at upper left is clear of the top frame, and "USPS" is microprinted on the top red flag stripe.

On No. 3974, the sky immediately above the date is dark blue and extends from the left side to the second "0" in the date, the left arm of the star at upper left touches the top frame, and lacks the microprinting found on No. 3966.

Nos. 3965 and 3970 also have "USPS" microprinted on the top red flag stripe.

Nos. 3966a and 3972a are double-sided booklet panes with 12 stamps on one side and eight stamps plus label that serves as a booklet cover on the other side. On No. 3966a, the stamps on one side are upside-down with relation to the stamps on the other side. On No. 3972a the stamps are all aligned the same on both sides.

### LOVE

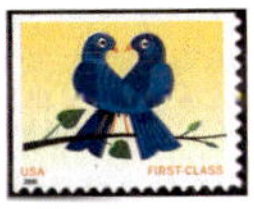
Birds — A3039

PHOTOGRAVURE

*Serpentine Die Cut 11 on 2, 3, or 4 Sides*

**2006, Jan. 3**

**BOOKLET STAMP**

**Self-Adhesive**

**3976** A3039 (39c) multicolored 1.10 .25
*a.* Booklet pane of 20 22.00

See No. 4029.

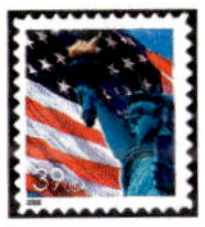
Flag and Statue of Liberty — A3040

LITHOGRAPHED

**2006** *Serpentine Die Cut 11¼x10¾*

**Self-Adhesive (#3978, 3980-3985)**

**3978** A3040 39c multi .85 .25
*a.* Booklet pane of 10 8.50
*b.* Booklet pane of 20 17.00
*c.* As "b," die cutting omitted on side with 8 stamps —

No. 3978 has "USPS" microprinted on top red flag stripe.

No. 3978b is a double-sided booklet with 12 stamps on one side and 8 stamps plus label (booklet cover) on the other side.

LITHOGRAPHED (#3981), PHOTOGRAVURE (#3979-3980, 3982-3983)

**COIL STAMPS**

*Perf. 9¾ Vert.*

**3979** A3040 39c multi 1.00 .25

*Serpentine Die Cut 11 Vert.*

**3980** A3040b 39c multi .80 .25

No. 3980 has rounded corners and lacks microprinting. Unused examples are on backing paper taller than the stamp, and the stamps are spaced approximately 3mm apart.

*Serpentine Die Cut 9½ Vert.*

**3981** A3040 39c multi 1.40 .25
*a.* Die cutting omitted, pair 150.00

No. 3981 has "USPS" microprinted on top red flag stripe.

*Serpentine Die Cut 10¼ Vert.*

**3982** A3040 39c multi 1.25 .25
*a.* Vert. pair, unslit between 500.00

*Serpentine Die Cut 8½ Vert.*

**3983** A3040 39c multi .80 .25

PHOTOGRAVURE

**BOOKLET STAMP**

*Serpentine Die Cut 11¼x10¾ on 2 or 3 Sides*

**3985** A3040 39c multi .80 .25
*a.* Booklet pane of 20 16.00
*b.* Serpentine die cut 11.1 on 2 or 3 sides .80 .25
*c.* Booklet pane of 4 #3985b 3.20
*d.* Booklet pane of 6 #3985b 4.80

Nos. 3983 and 3985 lack the microprinting found on Nos. 3978 and 3981. No. 3982 was not made available until June, despite the official first day of issue. No. 3983 was not made available until July and No. 3985 was not made available until August, despite the official first day of issue. No. 3985a is a double-sided booklet with 12 stamps on one side and 8 stamps plus label (booklet cover) on the other side.

Issued: No. 3980, 1/9; No. 3979, 3/8; Nos. 3978, 3981, 3982, 3985, 4/8.

### CHILDREN'S BOOK ANIMALS

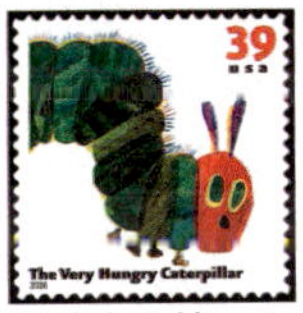
The Very Hungry Caterpillar, from *The Very Hungry Caterpillar,* by Eric Carle — A3041

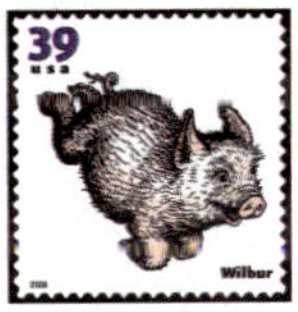
Wilbur, from *Charlotte's Web,* by E. B. White — A3042

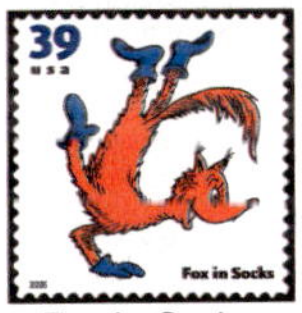
Fox in Socks, from *Fox in Socks,* by Dr. Seuss A3043

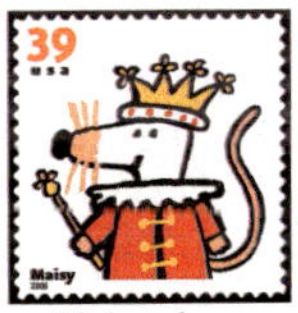
Maisy, from *Maisy's ABC,* by Lucy Cousins A3044

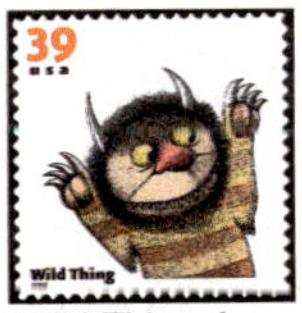
Wild Thing, from *Where the Wild Things Are,* by Maurice Sendak — A3045

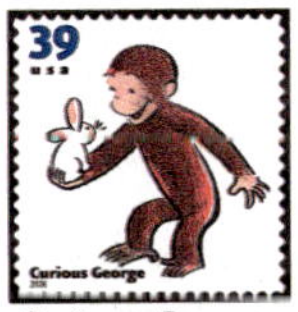
Curious George, from *Curious George,* by Margaret and H. A. Rey — A3046

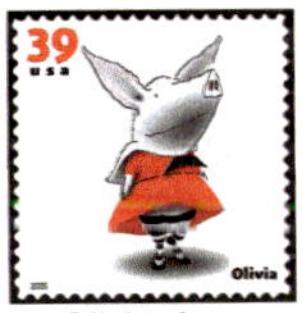
Olivia, from *Olivia,* by Ian Falconer A3047

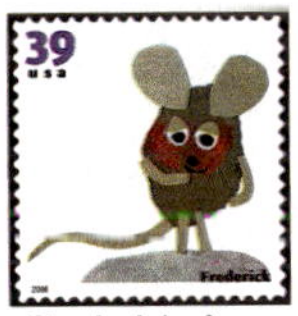
Frederick, from *Frederick,* by Leo Lionni A3048

PHOTOGRAVURE

*Serpentine Die Cut 10¾*

**2006, Jan. 10**

**Self-Adhesive**

**3987** A3041 39c multicolored .80 .40
**3988** A3042 39c multicolored .80 .40
**3989** A3043 39c multicolored .80 .40
**3990** A3044 39c multicolored .80 .40
**3991** A3045 39c multicolored .80 .40
**3992** A3046 39c multicolored .80 .40
**3993** A3047 39c multicolored .80 .40
**3994** A3048 39c multicolored .80 .40
*a.* Block of 8, #3987-3994 6.50

See Great Britain Nos. 2340-2341.

### 2006 WINTER OLYMPICS, TURIN, ITALY

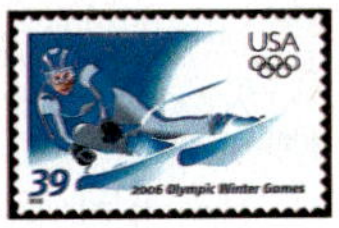
Skier — A3049

LITHOGRAPHED

**2006, Jan. 11**

**Self-Adhesive**

**3995** A3049 39c multicolored .80 .25

### BLACK HERITAGE SERIES

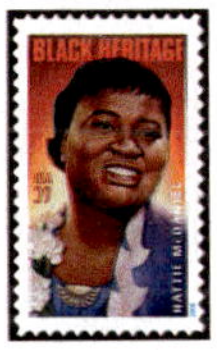
Hattie McDaniel (1895-1952), Actress — A3050

**2006, Jan. 25**

**Self-Adhesive**

**3996** A3050 39c multicolored .80 .25

### Chinese New Year Types of 1992-2004

**2006, Jan. 29**

**Self-Adhesive**

**3997** Pane of 12 12.00
*a.* A2360 39c Rat 1.00 .50
*b.* A2413 39c Ox 1.00 .50
*c.* A2462 39c Tiger 1.00 .50
*d.* A2535 39c Rabbit 1.00 .50
*e.* A2602 39c Dragon 1.00 .50
*f.* A2702 39c Snake 1.00 .50
*g.* A2752 39c Horse 1.00 .50
*h.* A2856 39c Ram 1.00 .50
*i.* A2927 39c Monkey 1.00 .50
*j.* A2067 39c Rooster 1.00 .50
*k.* A2146 39c Dog 1.00 .50
*l.* A2205 39c Boar 1.00 .50

See Nos. 2720, 2817, 2876, 3060, 3120, 3179, 3272, 3370, 3500, 3559, 3747, 3832, 3895.

### WEDDING DOVES

Dove Facing Left A3051

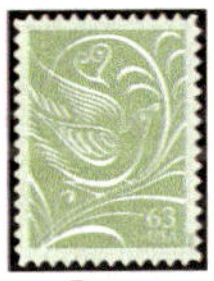
Dove Facing Right A3052

BOOKLET STAMPS

*Serpentine Die Cut 10¾x11 on 2, 3 or 4 Sides*

**2006, Mar. 1**

**Self-Adhesive**

**3998** A3051 39c pale lilac .80 .25
*a.* Booklet pane of 20 16.00
*b.* As "a," die cutting omitted

*Serpentine Die Cut 10¾x11*

**3999** A3052 63c pale yellow green 1.40 .50
*a.* Booklet pane, 20 each #3998-3999 45.00
*b.* Horiz. pair, #3998-3999 with vertical gutter between 2.25 1.50

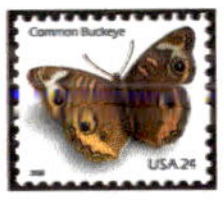
Common Buckeye Butterfly — A3053

LITHOGRAPHED (#4000), PHOTOGRAVURE (#4001-4002)

**2006, Mar. 8** *Perf. 11¼*

**4000** A3053 24c multicolored .50 .25

**Self-Adhesive**

*Serpentine Die Cut 11*

**4001** A3053 24c multicolored .55 .25
*a.* Serpentine die cut 10¾x11¼ on 3 sides (from booklet panes) .50 .25
*b.* Booklet pane of 10 #4001a 5.00
*c.* Booklet pane of 4 #4001a 2.00
*d.* Booklet pane of 6 #4001a 3.00

No. 4001b is a convertible booklet that was sold flat. It has a self-adhesive panel that covers the rouletting on the inside of the booklet cover. Nos. 4001c and 4001d are component panes of a vending machine booklet, which was sold pre-folded and sealed, and which does not have the self-adhesive panel covering the rouletting on the inside of the booklet cover.

### COIL STAMP

***Serpentine Die Cut 8½ Horiz.***

**4002** A3053 24c multicolored .50 .25

### CROPS OF THE AMERICAS

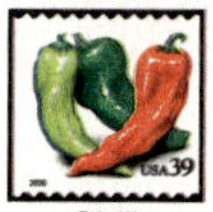

Chili Peppers A3054

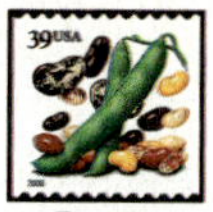

Beans A3055

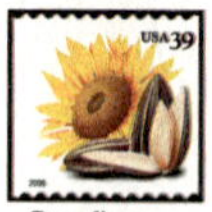

Sunflower and Seeds A3056

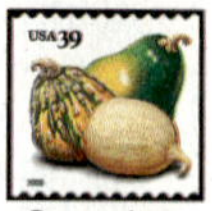

Squashes A3057

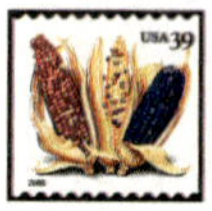

Corn — A3058

PHOTOGRAVURE

***Serpentine Die Cut 10¼ Horiz.***

**2006, Mar. 16**

**Self-Adhesive**

**Coil Stamps**

| | | | | |
|---|---|---|---|---|
| **4003** | A3054 | 39c multicolored | 2.40 | .35 |
| **4004** | A3055 | 39c multicolored | 2.40 | .35 |
| **4005** | A3056 | 39c multicolored | 2.40 | .35 |
| **4006** | A3057 | 39c multicolored | 2.40 | .35 |
| **4007** | A3058 | 39c multicolored | 2.40 | .35 |
| *a.* | | Strip of 5, #4003-4007 | 12.00 | |

**Booklet Stamps**

***Serpentine Die Cut 10¾x10½ on 2 or 3 Sides***

| | | | | |
|---|---|---|---|---|
| **4008** | A3058 | 39c multicolored | 1.25 | .35 |
| **4009** | A3057 | 39c multicolored | 1.25 | .35 |
| **4010** | A3056 | 39c multicolored | 1.25 | .35 |
| **4011** | A3055 | 39c multicolored | 1.25 | .35 |
| **4012** | A3054 | 39c multicolored | 1.25 | .35 |
| *a.* | | Horiz. strip of 5, #4008-4012 | 6.25 | |
| *b.* | | Booklet pane, 4 each #4008-4012 | 25.00 | |

LITHOGRAPHED

***Serpentine Die Cut 10¾x11¼ on 2 or 3 Sides***

| | | | | |
|---|---|---|---|---|
| **4013** | A3054 | 39c multicolored | 1.50 | .35 |
| **4014** | A3058 | 39c multicolored | 1.50 | .35 |
| **4015** | A3057 | 39c multicolored | 1.50 | .35 |
| **4016** | A3056 | 39c multicolored | 1.50 | .35 |
| *a.* | | Booklet pane of 4, #4013-4016 | 6.00 | |
| **4017** | A3055 | 39c multicolored | 1.50 | .35 |
| *a.* | | Horiz. strip of 5, #4013-4017 | 7.50 | |
| *b.* | | Booklet pane of 4, #4013-4015, 4017 | 6.00 | |
| *c.* | | Booklet pane of 6, #4013-4016, 2 #4017 | 9.00 | |
| *d.* | | Booklet pane of 6, #4013-4015, 4017, 2 #4016 | 9.00 | |

Stamps in Nos. 4012a and 4017a are not adjacent, as one or two rows of selvage is between stamps (or a blank space where selvage was removed by the manufacturer).

No. 4012b is a double-sided booklet with 12 stamps on one side and 8 stamps plus label (booklet cover) on the other side.

"USA" is at right of "39" on No. 4004, at left of "39" on Nos. 4011, 4017. Top of "USA" is aligned with top of "39" on No. 4013, with bottom of "39" on Nos. 4003, 4012.

### X-PLANES

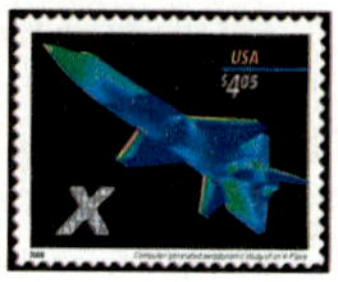

A3059

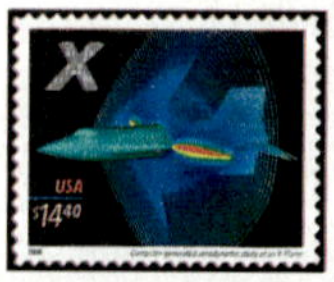

A3060

LITHOGRAPHED WITH HOLOGRAM AFFIXED

***Serpentine Die Cut 10¾x10½***

**2006, Mar. 17 Self-Adhesive**

| | | | | |
|---|---|---|---|---|
| **4018** | A3059 | $4.05 multi | 8.00 | 5.00 |
| *a.* | | Silver foil ("X") omitted | — | |
| **4019** | A3060 | $14.40 multi | 27.50 | 15.00 |

Beware of Nos. 4018 and 4019 with "X" hologram chemically removed. Certification is strongly recommended.

### SUGAR RAY ROBINSON (1921-89), BOXER

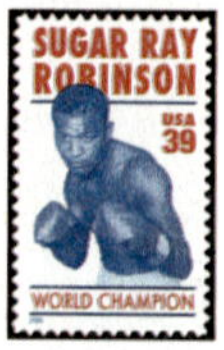

A3061

PHOTOGRAVURE

**2006, Apr. 7** ***Serpentine Die Cut 11***

**Self-Adhesive**

**4020** A3061 39c red & blue .80 .25

### BENJAMIN FRANKLIN (1706-90)

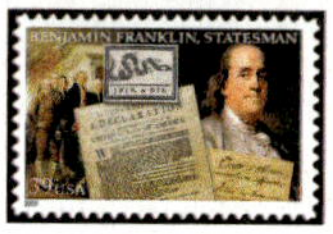

Statesman A3062

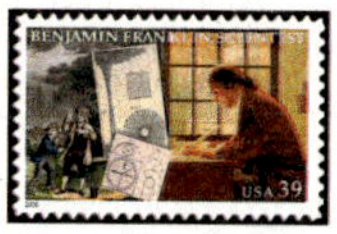

Scientist — A3063

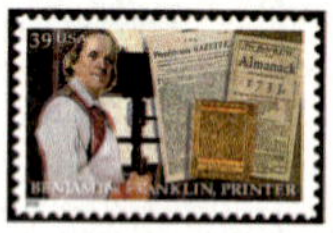

Printer — A3064

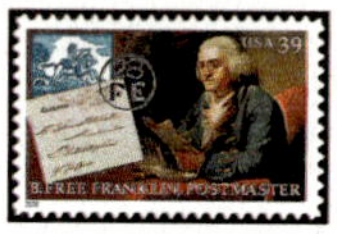

Postmaster A3065

**2006, Apr. 7**

| | | | | |
|---|---|---|---|---|
| **4021** | A3062 | 39c multicolored | 1.25 | .35 |
| **4022** | A3063 | 39c multicolored | 1.25 | .35 |
| **4023** | A3064 | 39c multicolored | 1.25 | .35 |
| **4024** | A3065 | 39c multicolored | 1.25 | .35 |
| *a.* | | Block or horiz. strip of 4 | 5.00 | |

### THE ART OF DISNEY: ROMANCE

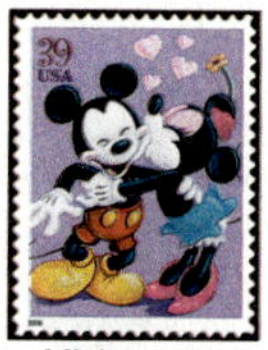

Mickey and Minnie Mouse A3066

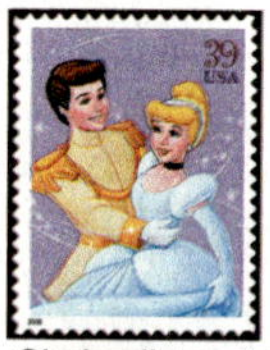

Cinderella and Prince Charming A3067

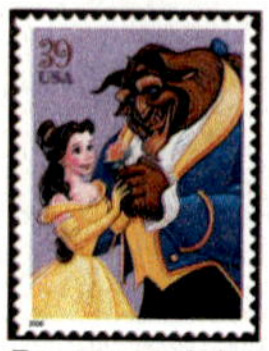

Beauty and the Beast A3068

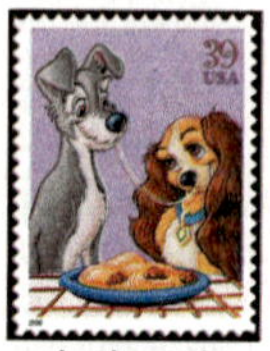

Lady and Tramp A3069

LITHOGRAPHED

***Serpentine Die Cut 10½x10¾***

**2006, Apr. 21**

**Self-Adhesive**

| | | | | |
|---|---|---|---|---|
| **4025** | A3066 | 39c multicolored | .80 | .30 |
| **4026** | A3067 | 39c multicolored | .80 | .30 |
| **4027** | A3068 | 39c multicolored | .80 | .30 |
| **4028** | A3069 | 39c multicolored | .80 | .30 |
| *a.* | | Block or vert. strip of 4, #4025-4028 | 3.20 | |

### LOVE

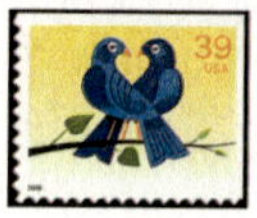

Birds — A3070

PHOTOGRAVURE

***Serpentine Die Cut 11 on 2, 3 or 4 Sides***

**2006, May 1**

**Self-Adhesive**

**Booklet Stamp**

| | | | | |
|---|---|---|---|---|
| **4029** | A3070 | 39c multicolored | .95 | .25 |
| *a.* | | Booklet pane of 20 | 19.00 | |

See No. 3976.

### LITERARY ARTS

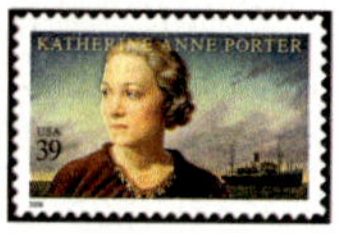

Katherine Anne Porter (1890-1980), Author — A3071

LITHOGRAPHED

***Serpentine Die Cut 10¾***

**2006, May 15**

**Self-Adhesive**

**4030** A3071 39c multicolored .80 .25

### AMBER ALERT

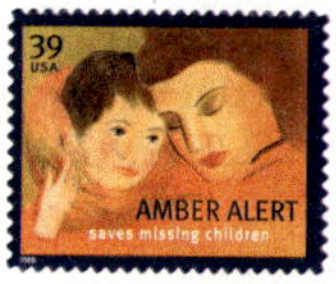

Mother and Child — A3072

PHOTOGRAVURE

***Serpentine Die Cut 10¾***

**2006, May 25**

**Self-Adhesive**

**4031** A3072 39c multicolored .80 .25

**Purple Heart Type of 2003**

LITHOGRAPHED

***Serpentine Die Cut 11¼x11***

**2006, May 26**

**Self-Adhesive**

| | | | | |
|---|---|---|---|---|
| **4032** | A2891 | 39c multicolored | .80 | .25 |
| *a.* | | Die cutting omitted, pair | — | |

See Nos. 3784-3784A, 4164, 4263-4264, 4390.

### WONDERS OF AMERICA

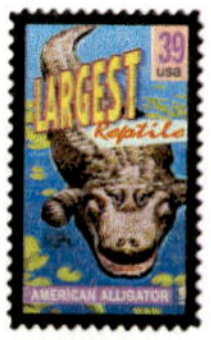

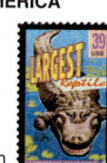

American Alligator — A3073

Designs: No. 4033, American alligator, largest reptile. No. 4034, Moloka'i, highest sea cliffs. No. 4035, Saguaro, tallest cactus. No. 4036, Bering Glacier, largest glacier. No. 4037, Great Sand Dunes, tallest dunes. No. 4038, Chesapeake Bay, largest estuary. No. 4039, Cliff Palace, largest cliff dwelling. No. 4040, Crater Lake, deepest lake. No. 4041, American bison, largest land mammal. No. 4042, Off the Florida Keys, longest reef. No. 4043, Pacific Crest Trail, longest hiking trail. No. 4044, Gateway Arch, tallest man-made monument. No. 4045, Appalachians, oldest mountains. No. 4046, American lotus, largest flower. No. 4047, Lake Superior, largest lake. No. 4048, Pronghorn, fastest land animal. No. 4049, Bristlecone pines, oldest trees. No. 4050, Yosemite Falls, tallest waterfall. No. 4051, Great Basin, largest desert. No. 4052, Verrazano-Narrows Bridge, longest span. No. 4053, Mount Washington, windiest place. No. 4054, Grand Canyon, largest canyon. No. 4055, American bullfrog, largest frog. No. 4056, Oroville Dam, tallest dam. No. 4057, Peregrine falcon, fastest bird. No. 4058, Mississippi River Delta, largest delta. No. 4059, Steamboat, tallest geyser. No. 4060, Rainbow Bridge, largest natural bridge. No. 4061, White sturgeon, largest freshwater fish. No. 4062, Rocky Mountains, longest mountain chain. No. 4063, Coast redwoods, tallest trees. No. 4064, American beaver, largest rodent. No. 4065, Mississippi-Missouri, longest river system. No. 4066, Mount Wai'ale'ale, rainiest spot. No. 4067, Kilauea, most active volcano. No. 4068, Mammoth Cave, longest cave. No. 4069, Blue whale, loudest animal. No. 4070, Death Valley, hottest spot. No. 4071, Cornish-Windsor Bridge, longest covered bridge. No. 4072, Quaking aspen, largest plant.

PHOTOGRAVURE

***Serpentine Die Cut 10¾***

**2006, May 27**

**Self-Adhesive**

| | | | | |
|---|---|---|---|---|
| **4033** | A3073 | 39c multicolored | .80 | .60 |
| **4034** | A3074 | 39c multicolored | .80 | .60 |
| **4035** | A3075 | 39c multicolored | .80 | .60 |
| **4036** | A3076 | 39c multicolored | .80 | .60 |
| **4037** | A3077 | 39c multicolored | .80 | .60 |
| **4038** | A3078 | 39c multicolored | .80 | .60 |
| **4039** | A3079 | 39c multicolored | .80 | .60 |
| **4040** | A3080 | 39c multicolored | .80 | .60 |
| **4041** | A3081 | 39c multicolored | .80 | .60 |
| **4042** | A3082 | 39c multicolored | .80 | .60 |
| **4043** | A3083 | 39c multicolored | .80 | .60 |
| **4044** | A3084 | 39c multicolored | .80 | .60 |
| **4045** | A3085 | 39c multicolored | .80 | .60 |
| **4046** | A3086 | 39c multicolored | .80 | .60 |
| **4047** | A3087 | 39c multicolored | .80 | .60 |
| **4048** | A3088 | 39c multicolored | .80 | .60 |
| **4049** | A3089 | 39c multicolored | .80 | .60 |
| **4050** | A3090 | 39c multicolored | .80 | .60 |
| **4051** | A3091 | 39c multicolored | .80 | .60 |
| **4052** | A3092 | 39c multicolored | .80 | .60 |
| **4053** | A3093 | 39c multicolored | .80 | .60 |
| **4054** | A3094 | 39c multicolored | .80 | .60 |
| **4055** | A3095 | 39c multicolored | .80 | .60 |
| **4056** | A3096 | 39c multicolored | .80 | .60 |
| **4057** | A3097 | 39c multicolored | .80 | .60 |
| **4058** | A3098 | 39c multicolored | .80 | .60 |
| **4059** | A3099 | 39c multicolored | .80 | .60 |
| **4060** | A3100 | 39c multicolored | .80 | .60 |
| **4061** | A3101 | 39c multicolored | .80 | .60 |
| **4062** | A3102 | 39c multicolored | .80 | .60 |
| **4063** | A3103 | 39c multicolored | .80 | .60 |
| **4064** | A3104 | 39c multicolored | .80 | .60 |
| **4065** | A3105 | 39c multicolored | .80 | .60 |
| **4066** | A3106 | 39c multicolored | .80 | .60 |
| **4067** | A3107 | 39c multicolored | .80 | .60 |
| **4068** | A3108 | 39c multicolored | .80 | .60 |
| **4069** | A3109 | 39c multicolored | .80 | .60 |
| **4070** | A3110 | 39c multicolored | .80 | .60 |
| **4071** | A3111 | 39c multicolored | .80 | .60 |
| **4072** | A3112 | 39c multicolored | .80 | .60 |
| *a.* | | Pane of 40, #4033-4072 | 32.00 | |

### EXPLORATION OF EAST COAST BY SAMUEL DE CHAMPLAIN, 400TH ANNIV.

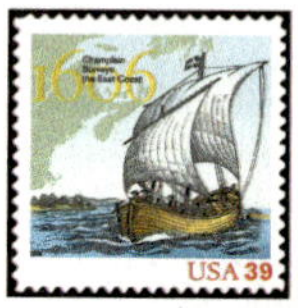

Ship and Map — A3113

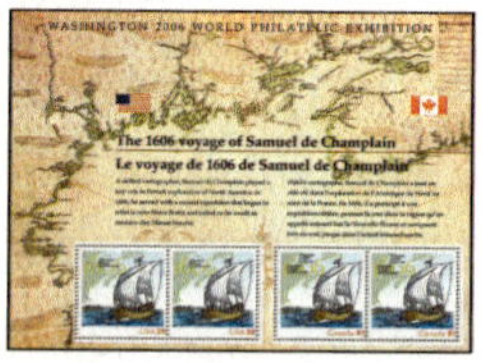

A3114

LITHOGRAPHED & ENGRAVED

***Serpentine Die Cut 10¾***

**2006, May 28**

**Self-Adhesive (#4073)**

**4073** A3113 39c multicolored .85 .25

**Souvenir Sheet**

***Perf. 11***

| | | | | |
|---|---|---|---|---|
| **4074** | A3114 | Pane of 4, 2 each #4074a, Canada #2156a | 8.50 | 8.50 |
| *a.* | | A3113 39c multicolored | 2.00 | .25 |

Washington 2006 World Philatelic Exhibition (#4074). Canada No. 2156, which was sold only by Canada Post, has a bar code in the lower left margin of the pane. No. 4074, which was sold only by the United States Postal Service for $1.75, lacks this bar code.

UNITED STATES 111

## WASHINGTON 2006 WORLD PHILATELIC EXHIBITION
Souvenir Sheet

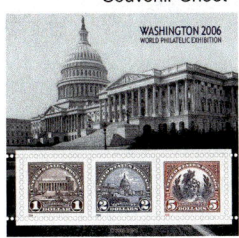
A3115

### LITHOGRAPHED (MARGIN) & ENGRAVED
2006, May 29     Perf. 10¾x10½
| 4075 | A3115 | Pane of 3 | 16.00 | 6.00 |
|---|---|---|---|---|
| a. | A174 $1 violet brown | | 2.00 | .50 |
| b. | A175 $2 deep blue | | 4.00 | 1.00 |
| c. | A176 $5 carmine & blue | | 10.00 | 2.50 |

## DISTINGUISHED AMERICAN DIPLOMATS
Souvenir Sheet

A3116

No. 4076: a, Robert D. Murphy (1894-1978). b, Frances E. Willis (1899-1983). c, Hiram Bingham IV (1903-88). d, Philip C. Habib (1920-92). e, Charles E. Bohlen (1904-74). f, Clifton R. Wharton, Sr. (1899-1990).

### PHOTOGRAVURE
*Serpentine Die Cut 10¾*
2006, May 29
**Self-Adhesive**
| 4076 | A3116 | Pane of 6 | 6.00 | |
|---|---|---|---|---|
| a.-f. | | 39c any single | 1.00 | .40 |

## LEGENDS OF HOLLYWOOD

Judy Garland (1922-69), Actress — A3117

### LITHOGRAPHED
2006, June 10
**Self-Adhesive**
| 4077 | A3117 | 39c multicolored | 1.00 | .25 |
|---|---|---|---|---|
| a. | Pair, die cutting omitted | | 750.00 | |

### Ronald Reagan Type of 2005
PHOTOGRAVURE
2006, June 14
**Self-Adhesive**
| 4078 | A2974 | 39c multicolored | .90 | .25 |

See No. 3897.

### Happy Birthday Type of 2002
*Serpentine Die Cut 11*
2006, June 23
**Self-Adhesive**
| 4079 | A2761 | 39c multicolored | .90 | .25 |

See Nos. 3558, 3695.

## BASEBALL SLUGGERS

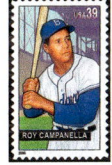
Roy Campanella (1921-93)
A3118

Hank Greenberg (1911-86)
A3119

Mel Ott (1909-58)
A3120

Mickey Mantle (1931-95)
A3121

*Serpentine Die Cut 10¾*
2006, July 15
**Self-Adhesive**
| 4080 | A3118 | 39c multicolored | .80 | .30 |
|---|---|---|---|---|
| 4081 | A3119 | 39c multicolored | .80 | .30 |
| 4082 | A3120 | 39c multicolored | .80 | .30 |
| 4083 | A3121 | 39c multicolored | .80 | .30 |
| a. | Block or vert. strip of 4, #4080-4083 | | 3.20 | |

## DC COMICS SUPERHEROES

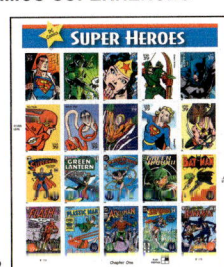
A3122

No. 4084: a, Superman. b, Green Lantern. c, Wonder Woman. d, Green Arrow. e, Batman. f, The Flash. g, Plastic Man. h, Aquaman. i, Supergirl. j, Hawkman. k, Cover of *Superman #11*. l, Cover of *Green Lantern #4*. m, Cover of *Wonder Woman #22 (Second Series)*. n, Cover of *Green Arrow #15*. o, Cover of *Batman #1*. p, Cover of *The Flash #111*. q, Cover of *Plastic Man #4*. r, Cover of *Aquaman #5 (of 5)*. s, Cover of *The Daring New Adventures of Supergirl #1*. t, Cover of *The Brave and the Bold Presents Hawkman #36*.

*Serpentine Die Cut 10½x10¾*
2006, July 20
**Self-Adhesive**
| 4084 | A3122 | Pane of 20 | 16.00 | |
|---|---|---|---|---|
| a.-t. | | 39c Any single | .80 | .50 |
| u. | As No. 4084, all inscriptions omitted on reverse | | 2,000. | |

## MOTORCYCLES

1940 Indian Four — A3123

1918 Cleveland
A3124

Generic "Chopper," c. 1970 — A3125

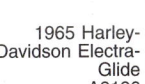

1965 Harley-Davidson Electra-Glide
A3126

*Serpentine Die Cut 10¾x10½*
2006, Aug. 7
**Self-Adhesive**
| 4085 | A3123 | 39c multicolored | 1.00 | .35 |
|---|---|---|---|---|
| 4086 | A3124 | 39c multicolored | 1.00 | .35 |
| 4087 | A3125 | 39c multicolored | 1.00 | .35 |
| 4088 | A3126 | 39c multicolored | 1.00 | .35 |
| a. | Block or horiz. strip of 4, #4085-4088 | | 4.00 | |

## AMERICAN TREASURES SERIES
Quilts of Gee's Bend, Alabama

Housetop Variation, by Mary Lee Bendolph
A3127

Pig in a Pen Medallion, by Minnie Sue Coleman
A3128

Nine Patch, by Ruth P. Mosely
A3129

Housetop Four Block Half Log Cabin Variation, by Lottie Mooney
A3130

Roman Stripes Variation, by Loretta Pettway
A3131

Chinese Coins Variation, by Arlonzia Pettway
A3132

Blocks and Strips, by Annie Mae Young
A3133

Medallion, by Loretta Pettway
A3134

Bars and String-pieced Columns, by Jessie T. Pettway
A3135

Medallion With Checkerboard Center, by Patty Ann Williams
A3136

### BOOKLET STAMPS
*Serpentine Die Cut 10¾ on 2 or 3 Sides*
2006, Aug. 24
**Self-Adhesive**
| 4089 | A3127 | 39c multicolored | 1.10 | .40 |
|---|---|---|---|---|
| 4090 | A3128 | 39c multicolored | 1.10 | .40 |
| 4091 | A3129 | 39c multicolored | 1.10 | .40 |
| 4092 | A3130 | 39c multicolored | 1.10 | .40 |
| 4093 | A3131 | 39c multicolored | 1.10 | .40 |
| 4094 | A3132 | 39c multicolored | 1.10 | .40 |
| 4095 | A3133 | 39c multicolored | 1.10 | .40 |
| 4096 | A3134 | 39c multicolored | 1.10 | .40 |
| 4097 | A3135 | 39c multicolored | 1.10 | .40 |
| 4098 | A3136 | 39c multicolored | 1.10 | .40 |
| a. | Block of 10, #4089-4098 | | 11.00 | |
| b. | Booklet pane of 20, 2 each #4089-4098 | | 22.50 | |

No. 4098b is a double-sided booklet pane with 12 stamps on one side (1 each #4090-4093, 4095-4098, and 2 each #4089, 4094) and eight stamps (1 each #4090-4093, 4095-4098) plus label (booklet cover) on the other side.

## SOUTHERN FLORIDA WETLAND

A3137

No. 4099 — Wildlife: a, Snail kite. b, Wood storks. c, Florida panther. d, Bald eagle, horiz. e, American crocodile, horiz. f, Roseate spoonbills, horiz. g, Everglades mink. h, Cape Sable seaside sparrow, horiz. i, American alligator, horiz. j, White ibis.

*Serpentine Die Cut 10¾*
2006, Oct. 4
**Self-Adhesive**
| 4099 | A3137 | Pane of 10 | 9.00 | |
|---|---|---|---|---|
| a.-j. | | 39c any single | .90 | .40 |

## CHRISTMAS

Madonna and Child with Bird, by Ignacio Chacón
A3138

Snowflake
A3139

Snowflake
A3140

Snowflake
A3141

Snowflake — A3142

### LITHOGRAPHED
*Serpentine Die Cut 10¾x11 on 2 or 3 Sides*
2006
**Self-Adhesive**
**Booklet Stamps (#4100, 4105-4116)**
| 4100 | A3138 | 39c multi | .80 | .25 |
|---|---|---|---|---|
| a. | Booklet pane of 20 | | 16.00 | |

**Base of Denomination Higher Than Year Date**
*Serpentine Die Cut 11¼x11*
| 4101 | A3139 | 39c multi | .90 | .25 |
|---|---|---|---|---|
| 4102 | A3140 | 39c multi | .90 | .25 |
| 4103 | A3141 | 39c multi | .90 | .25 |
| 4104 | A3142 | 39c multi | .90 | .25 |
| a. | Block or vert. strip of 4, #4101-4104 | | 3.60 | |

**Base of Denominations Even With Year Date**
*Serpentine Die Cut 11¼x11½ on 2 or 3 Sides*
| 4105 | A3139 | 39c multi | .90 | .25 |
|---|---|---|---|---|
| a. | Red missing (PS) | | | |
| 4106 | A3140a | 39c multi | .90 | .25 |
| a. | Red missing (PS) | | — | |
| 4107 | A3141 | 39c multi | .90 | .25 |
| 4108 | A3142 | 39c multi | .90 | .25 |
| a. | Block of 4, #4105-4108 | | 3.60 | |
| b. | Booklet pane of 20, 5 #4108a | | 18.00 | |
| c. | As "a," red ("USA") and green ("39") omitted | | | |

*Serpentine Die Cut 11¼x10¾ on 2 or 3 Sides*
| 4109 | A3139 | 39c multi | 1.00 | .25 |
|---|---|---|---|---|
| 4110 | A3140 | 39c multi | 1.00 | .25 |
| 4111 | A3141 | 39c multi | 1.00 | .25 |
| 4112 | A3142 | 39c multi | 1.00 | .25 |
| a. | Block of 4, #4109-4112 | | 4.00 | |
| b. | Booklet pane of 4, #4109-4112 | | 4.00 | |
| c. | Booklet pane of 6, #4111-4112, 2 each #4109-4110 | | 6.00 | |
| d. | Booklet pane of 6, #4109-4110, 2 each #4111-4112 | | 6.00 | |

## UNITED STATES

### Serpentine Die Cut 8 on 2, 3 or 4 Sides
#### PHOTOGRAVURE
| | | | | |
|---|---|---|---|---|
| 4113 | A3139 | 39c multi | 1.50 | .35 |
| a. | | Red and green missing (PS) | | |
| 4114 | A3141 | 39c multi | 1.50 | .35 |
| 4115 | A3140 | 39c multi | 1.50 | .35 |
| 4116 | A3142 | 39c multi | 1.50 | .35 |
| a. | | Block or strip of 4, #4113-4116 | 6.00 | |
| b. | | Booklet pane of 18, 4 each #4114, 4116, 5 each #4113, 4115 | 27.00 | |
| | | Nos. 4100-4116 (17) | 18.00 | 4.65 |

No. 4108b is a double-sided booklet pane with 12 stamps on one side and eight stamps plus label that serves as a booklet cover on the other side. Snowflakes on Nos. 4101-4104 are slightly smaller than those on Nos. 4105-4116.

Issued: No. 4100, 10/17, Nos. 4101-4116, 10/5.

### Eid Type of 2001
#### PHOTOGRAVURE
**2006, Oct. 6** *Serpentine Die Cut 11*
**Self-Adhesive**
| 4117 | A2734 | 39c multicolored | .80 | .25 |
|---|---|---|---|---|

See Nos. 3532, 3674, 4202, 4351, 4416.

### Hanukkah Type of 2004
#### LITHOGRAPHED
*Serpentine Die Cut 10¾x11*
**2006, Oct. 6**
**Self-Adhesive**
| 4118 | A2962 | 39c multicolored | .80 | .25 |
|---|---|---|---|---|
| a. | | Die cutting omitted, pane of 20 | — | |

See Nos. 3880, 4219, 4372.

### Kwanzaa Type of 2004
*Serpentine Die Cut 11x10¾*
**2006, Oct. 6**
**Self-Adhesive**
| 4119 | A2963 | 39c multicolored | .80 | .25 |
|---|---|---|---|---|

See Nos. 3881, 4220, 4373.

### BLACK HERITAGE SERIES

Ella Fitzgerald (1917-96), Singer — A3143

*Serpentine Die Cut 11*
**2007, Jan. 10**
**Self-Adhesive**
| 4120 | A3143 | 39c multicolored | .80 | .25 |
|---|---|---|---|---|

### OKLAHOMA STATEHOOD, 100TH ANNIV.

Cimarron River — A3144

**2007, Jan. 11**
**Self-Adhesive**
| 4121 | A3144 | 39c multicolored | .80 | .25 |
|---|---|---|---|---|

### LOVE

Hershey's Kiss — A3145

#### PHOTOGRAVURE
*Serpentine Die Cut 10¾x11 on 2, 3 or 4 Sides*
**2007, Jan. 13**
#### BOOKLET STAMP
**Self-Adhesive**
| 4122 | A3145 | 39c multicolored | .80 | .25 |
|---|---|---|---|---|
| a. | | Booklet pane of 20 | 16.00 | |

### INTERNATIONAL POLAR YEAR
**Souvenir Sheet**

A3146

No. 4123: a, Aurora borealis. b, Aurora australis.

#### LITHOGRAPHED
*Serpentine Die Cut 10¾*
**2007, Feb. 21**
**Self-Adhesive**
| 4123 | A3146 | Pane of 2 | 4.00 | |
|---|---|---|---|---|
| a.-b. | | 84c Either single | 2.00 | .50 |

### LITERARY ARTS

Henry Wadsworth Longfellow (1807-82), Poet — A3147

**2007, Mar. 15**
**Self-Adhesive**
| 4124 | A3147 | 39c multicolored | .80 | .25 |
|---|---|---|---|---|

Beginning with No. 4125, the United States Postal Service began issuing "Forever" stamps that satisfy the domestic 1-ounce first-class letter rate and the 1-ounce international letter rate regardless of future rate increases. The denomination in parentheses in the catalogue listing represents the face value at the time of issue. The face value increases to the new letter rate whenever rates change.

### "FOREVER" STAMP

Liberty Bell — A3148

Large Microprinting (#4125, 4128)    Small Microprinting (#4126)

Medium Microprinting (#4127)

#### PHOTOGRAVURE
*Serpentine Die Cut 11¼x10¾ on 2 or 3 Sides*
**2007-09**
#### Booklet Stamps
**Self-Adhesive**
**Large Microprinting, Bell 16mm Wide**
| 4125 | A3148 | (41c) multi, dated "2007," Apr. 12 | 1.40 | .25 |
|---|---|---|---|---|
| a. | | Booklet pane of 20 | 28.00 | |
| b. | | (42c) Dated "2008" | 1.40 | .25 |
| c. | | Booklet pane of 20 #4125b | 28.00 | |
| d. | | As "c," copper ("FOREVER") omitted | 1,000. | |
| e. | | As "c," copper ("FOREVER") omitted on side with 12 stamps, copper splatters on side with 8 stamps | — | |
| f. | | (44c) Dated "2009" ('09) | 1.40 | .25 |
| g. | | Booklet pane of 20 #4125f | 28.00 | |
| h. | | As No. 4125, copper ("FOREVER") omitted | — | |
| i. | | As No. 4125, die cutting missing, horiz. pair (PS) | — | |
| j. | | As "b," copper ("FOREVER") omitted | — | |

#### LITHOGRAPHED
**Small Microprinting, Bell 16mm Wide**
| 4126 | A3148 | (41c) multi, dated "2007" | 1.40 | .25 |
|---|---|---|---|---|
| a. | | Booklet pane of 20 | 28.00 | |
| b. | | (42c) Dated "2008" ('08) | 1.40 | .25 |
| c. | | Booklet pane of 20 #4126b | 28.00 | |
| d. | | (44c) Dated "2009" in copper ('09) | 1.40 | .25 |
| e. | | Booklet pane of 20 #4126d | 28.00 | |
| f. | | As "b," copper ("FOREVER") omitted | 1,400. | |
| g. | | As "c," die cutting omitted | — | |

**Medium Microprinting, Bell 15mm Wide**
| 4127 | A3148 | (41c) multi, dated "2007" ('07) | 1.40 | .25 |
|---|---|---|---|---|
| a. | | Booklet pane of 20 | 28.00 | |
| b. | | Booklet pane of 4 | 5.60 | |
| c. | | Booklet pane of 6 | 8.40 | |
| d. | | (42c) Dated "2008" ('08) | 1.40 | .25 |
| e. | | As "d," booklet pane of 20 | 28.00 | |
| f. | | (42c) Dated "2008," date in smaller type ('08) | 1.40 | .25 |
| g. | | As "f," booklet pane of 4 | 5.60 | |
| h. | | As "f," booklet pane of 6 | 8.40 | |
| i. | | (44c) Dated "2009" in copper ('09) | 1.40 | .25 |
| j. | | As "i," booklet pane of 20 | 28.00 | |
| k. | | As "i," die cutting omitted, pair | 300.00 | |
| l. | | As No. 4127, copper ("FOREVER") and "USA FIRST-CLASS" missing (PS) | — | |
| m. | | As "e," die cutting omitted | 600.00 | |

#### PHOTOGRAVURE
**Large Microprinting, Bell 16mm Wide**
*Serpentine Die Cut 8 on 2, 3 or 4 Sides*
| 4128 | A3148 | (41c) multi, dated "2007" | 1.40 | .25 |
|---|---|---|---|---|
| a. | | Booklet pane of 18 | 25.20 | |
| b. | | (42c) Dated "2009" ('09) | 1.40 | .25 |
| c. | | As "b," booklet pane of 18 | 25.20 | |
| | | Nos. 4125-4128 (4) | 5.60 | 1.00 |

Nos. 4125-4128 were sold for 41c on the day of issue and will be valid for the one ounce first class postage rate after any new rates go into effect. As of May 12, 2008, any "Forever" stamp (Nos. 4125-4128 and 4127d) in stock was sold for 42c. As of May 15, 2009, all "Forever" stamps in stock were sold for 44c, etc.

Nos. 4125a, 4125c, 4126a, 4126c, 4127a, 4127e and 4127j are double-sided booklet panes, with 12 stamps on one side and eight stamps plus a label that serves as a booklet cover on the other side.

Nos. 4127b and 4127c exist with rouletting on backing paper of either gauge 9½ or 13.

See No. 4437.

Flag — A3149

#### LITHOGRAPHED
**2007, Apr. 12**    *Perf. 11¼*
| 4129 | A3149 | (41c) multicolored | .90 | .40 |
|---|---|---|---|---|

**Self-Adhesive**
*Serpentine Die Cut 11¼x10¾*
| 4130 | A3149 | (41c) multicolored | 1.10 | .25 |
|---|---|---|---|---|

#### COIL STAMPS
*Perf. 9¾ Vert.*
| 4131 | A3149 | (41c) multicolored | 1.10 | .40 |
|---|---|---|---|---|

**Self-Adhesive (#4132-4135)**
**With Perpendicular Corners**
*Serpentine Die Cut 9½ Vert.*
| 4132 | A3149 | (41c) multicolored | 1.20 | .25 |
|---|---|---|---|---|

*Serpentine Die Cut 11 Vert.*
| 4133 | A3149 | (41c) multicolored | 1.20 | .25 |
|---|---|---|---|---|
| a. | | Die cutting omitted, pair | 500.00 | |

*Serpentine Die Cut 8½ Vert.*
#### PHOTOGRAVURE
| 4134 | A3149 | (41c) multicolored, overall tagging | 1.10 | .25 |
|---|---|---|---|---|

**With Rounded Corners**
*Serpentine Die Cut 11 Vert.*
| 4135 | A3149 | (41c) multicolored | 1.25 | .75 |
|---|---|---|---|---|
| | | Nos. 4129-4135 (7) | 7.85 | 2.55 |

Nos. 4132-4134 are on backing paper as high as the stamp. No. 4135 is on backing paper that is larger than the stamp.

### SETTLEMENT OF JAMESTOWN, 400TH ANNIV.

Ships Susan Constant, Godspeed and Discovery — A3150

#### LITHOGRAPHED
*Serpentine Die Cut 10½x10½x10¾*
**2007, May 11**
**Self-Adhesive**
| 4136 | A3150 | 41c multicolored | 1.10 | .25 |
|---|---|---|---|---|

### WILDLIFE

Bighorn Sheep A3151    Florida Panther A3152

#### LITHOGRAPHED, PHOTOGRAVURE
(#4138, 4142)
**2007**    *Perf. 11¼x11*
| 4137 | A3152 | 26c multi | .60 | .25 |
|---|---|---|---|---|

**Self-Adhesive**
*Serpentine Die Cut 11*
| 4138 | A3151 | 17c multi | .35 | .25 |
|---|---|---|---|---|

*Serpentine Die Cut 11¼x11*
| 4139 | A3152 | 26c multi | .55 | .25 |
|---|---|---|---|---|

#### Coil Stamps
*Serpentine Die Cut 11 Vert.*
| 4140 | A3151 | 17c multi | .35 | .25 |
|---|---|---|---|---|
| 4141 | A3152 | 26c multi | .75 | .25 |
| a. | | Die cutting omitted, pair | 350.00 | |

#### Booklet Stamp
*Serpentine Die Cut 11¼x11 on 3 Sides*
| 4142 | A3152 | 26c multi | .55 | .25 |
|---|---|---|---|---|
| a. | | Booklet pane of 10 | 5.50 | |

Nos. 4137 and 4139 have microprinted "USPS" to the left and above the lower left whisker. No. 4140 has microprinted "USPS" on right horn. No. 4141 has microprinted "USPS" along the right edge of the stamp just above the panther. Nos. 4138 and 4142 lack microprinting.

Issued: Nos. 4137, 4139, 4141, 4142, 5/12; No. 4138, 5/14; No. 4140, 5/21.

### PREMIERE OF MOVIE "STAR WARS," 30TH ANNIVERSARY

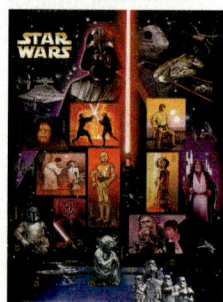

A3153

No. 4143: a, Darth Vader (40x53mm). b, Millennium Falcon (47x25mm). c, Emperor Palpatine (41x26mm). d, Anakin Skywalker and Obi-Wan Kenobi (41x33mm). e, Luke Skywalker (31x41mm). f, Princess Leia and R2-D2 (41x33mm). g, C-3PO (21x65mm). h, Queen Padmé Amidala (26x48mm). i, Obi-Wan Kenobi (31x48mm). j, Boba Fett (32x40mm). k, Darth Maul (26x41mm). l, Chewbacca and Han Solo (48x31mm). m, X-wing Starfighter (41x26mm). n, Yoda (31x48mm). o, Stormtroopers (41x31mm).

#### LITHOGRAPHED
**2007, May 25**    *Serpentine Die Cut 11*
**Self-Adhesive**
| 4143 | A3153 | Pane of 15 | 15.00 | |
|---|---|---|---|---|
| a.-o. | | 41c Any single | 1.00 | .50 |

UNITED STATES 113

## PRESIDENTIAL AIRCRAFT

Air Force One — A3154

Marine One — A3155

LITHOGRAPHED & ENGRAVED (#4144), LITHOGRAPHED (#4145)

***Serpentine Die Cut 10¾***

**2007, June 13**

**Self-Adhesive**

| | | | | |
|---|---|---|---|---|
| **4144** | A3154 | $4.60 multi | 9.25 | 5.00 |
| *a.* | | Black (engr.) omitted | *200.00* | |
| **4145** | A3155 | $16.25 multi | 30.00 | 16.00 |

## PACIFIC LIGHTHOUSES

Diamond Head Lighthouse, Hawaii A3156

Five Finger Lighthouse, Alaska A3157

Grays Harbor Lighthouse, Washington A3158

Umpqua River Lighthouse, Oregon A3159

St. George Reef Lighthouse, California — A3160

PHOTOGRAVURE

***Serpentine Die Cut 11***

**2007, June 21**

**Self-Adhesive**

| | | | | |
|---|---|---|---|---|
| **4146** | A3156 | 41c multicolored | 1.20 | .40 |
| **4147** | A3157 | 41c multicolored | 1.20 | .40 |
| **4148** | A3158 | 41c multicolored | 1.20 | .40 |
| **4149** | A3159 | 41c multicolored | 1.20 | .40 |
| **4150** | A3160 | 41c multicolored | 1.20 | .40 |
| *a.* | | Horiz. strip of 5, #4146-4150 | 6.00 | |

## WEDDING HEARTS

Heart With Lilac Background A3161

Heart With Pink Background A3162

LITHOGRAPHED (#4151), PHOTOGRAVURE (#4152) BOOKLET STAMP (#4151)

***Serpentine Die Cut 10¾ on 2, 3 or 4 Sides***

**2007, June 27**

**Self-Adhesive**

| | | | | |
|---|---|---|---|---|
| **4151** | A3161 | 41c multicolored | 1.00 | .25 |
| *a.* | | Booklet pane of 20 | 20.00 | |

***Serpentine Die Cut 10¾x11***

| | | | | |
|---|---|---|---|---|
| **4152** | A3162 | 58c multicolored | 1.25 | .25 |

## POLLINATION

Purple Nightshade, Morrison's Bumblebee A3163

Hummingbird Trumpet, Calliope Hummingbird A3164

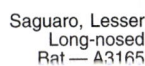

Saguaro, Lesser Long-nosed Bat — A3165

Prairie Ironweed, Southern Dogface Butterfly — A3166

No. 4153: Type I, Tip of bird wing is directly under center of "U" in "USA," straight edge at left. Type II, Tip of bird wing is directly under the right line of the "U" in "USA," straight edge at right.

No. 4154: Type I, Tip of bird wing is even with the top of denomination, straight edge at right. Type II, Tip of bird wing is well above denomination, straight edge at left.

No. 4155: Type I, Top of "USA" is even with the lower portion of the nearest unopened green saguaro flower bud, straight edge at left. Type II, Top of "USA" is even with the point where the flower and unopened green saguaro bud meet, straight edge at right.

No. 4156: Type I, Bottom of denomination is even with top point of the white triangle found between the bottom of the purple flower and the green leaf below it, straight edge at right. Type II, Bottom of denomination is even with the lower point of the white triangle found between the bottom of the purple flower and the green leaf below it, straight edge at left.

LITHOGRAPHED

***Serpentine Die Cut 11 on 2, 3 or 4 Sides***

**2007, June 29** **Tagged**

**Self-Adhesive**

**Booklet Stamps**

| | | | | |
|---|---|---|---|---|
| **4153** | A3163 | 41c multi, Type I | .85 | .30 |
| *a.* | | Type II | .85 | .30 |
| **4154** | A3164 | 41c multi, Type I | .85 | .30 |
| *a.* | | Type II | .85 | .30 |
| **4155** | A3165 | 41c multi, Type I | .85 | .30 |
| *a.* | | Type II | .85 | .30 |
| **4156** | A3166 | 41c multi, Type I | .85 | .30 |
| *a.* | | Type II | .85 | .30 |
| *b.* | | Block of 4, #4153-4156 | 3.40 | |
| *c.* | | Block of 4, #4153a-4156a | 3.40 | |
| *d.* | | Booklet pane of 20, 3 each #4153-4156, 2 each #4153a-4156a | 17.00 | |

No. 4156d is a double-sided booklet with 12 stamps (2 each #4153-4156, 1 each #4153a-4156a) on one side and 8 stamps plus label (booklet cover) on the other side.

Patriotic Banner — A3167

PHOTOGRAVURE (#4157), LITHOGRAPHED (#4158)

***Serpentine Die Cut 11 Vert.***

**2007, July 4** **Untagged**

**Coil Stamps**

**Self-Adhesive**

| | | | | |
|---|---|---|---|---|
| **4157** | A3167 | (10c) red, gold & blue | .30 | .25 |

***Serpentine Die Cut 11¾ Vert.***

| | | | | |
|---|---|---|---|---|
| **4158** | A3167 | (10c) red, gold & blue | .30 | .25 |

See No. 4385.

## MARVEL COMICS SUPERHEROES

A3168

No. 4159: a, Spider-man. b, The Hulk. c, Sub-Mariner. d, The Thing. e, Captain America. f, Silver Surfer. g, Spider-Woman. h, Iron Man. i, Elektra. j, Wolverine. k, Cover of *The Amazing Spider-Man #1*. l, Cover of *The Incredible Hulk #1*. m, Cover of *Sub-Mariner #1*. n, Cover of *The Fantastic Four #3*. o, Cover of *Captain America #100*. p, Cover of *The Silver Surfer #1*. q, Cover of *Marvel Spotlight on The Spider-Woman #32*. r, Cover of *Iron Man #1*. s, Cover of *Daredevil #176 Featuring Elektra*. t, Cover of *The X-Men #1*.

PHOTOGRAVURE

***Serpentine Die Cut 10½x10¾***

**2007, July 26**

**Self-Adhesive**

| | | | | |
|---|---|---|---|---|
| **4159** | A3168 | Pane of 20 | 20.00 | |
| *a.-t.* | | 41c Any single | 1.00 | .50 |

## VINTAGE MAHOGANY SPEEDBOATS

1915 Hutchinson A3169

1954 Chris-Craft A3170

1939 Hacker-Craft A3171

1931 Gar Wood A3172

LITHOGRAPHED

***Serpentine Die Cut 10½***

**2007, Aug. 4**

**Self-Adhesive**

| | | | | |
|---|---|---|---|---|
| **4160** | A3169 | 41c multicolored | .85 | .35 |
| **4161** | A3170 | 41c multicolored | .85 | .35 |
| **4162** | A3171 | 41c multicolored | .85 | .35 |
| **4163** | A3172 | 41c multicolored | .85 | .35 |
| *a.* | | Horiz. strip of 4, #4160-4163 | 3.40 | |

**Purple Heart Type of 2003**

LITHOGRAPHED

***Serpentine Die Cut 11¼x10¾***

**2007, Aug. 7**

**Self-Adhesive**

| | | | | |
|---|---|---|---|---|
| **4164** | A2891 | 41c multicolored | .85 | .25 |

See Nos. 3784-3784A, 4032, 4263-4264, 4390.

## AMERICAN TREASURES SERIES

Magnolia and Irises, Stained Glass by Louis Comfort Tiffany — A3173

BOOKLET STAMP

***Serpentine Die Cut 10¾ on 2 or 3 Sides***

**2007, Aug. 9**

**Self-Adhesive**

| | | | | |
|---|---|---|---|---|
| **4165** | A3173 | 41c multicolored | .85 | .25 |
| *a.* | | Booklet pane of 20 | 17.00 | |

No. 4165a is a double-sided booklet pane with 12 stamps on one side and eight stamps plus label (booklet cover) on the other side.

## FLOWERS

Iris A3174

Dahlia A3175

Magnolia A3176

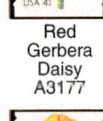

Red Gerbera Daisy A3177

Coneflower A3178

Tulip A3179

Water Lily A3180

Poppy A3181

Chrysanthemum A3182

Orange Gerbera Daisy A3183

LITHOGRAPHED

***Serpentine Die Cut 9½ Vert.***

**2007, Aug. 10**

**COIL STAMPS**

**Self-Adhesive**

| | | | | |
|---|---|---|---|---|
| **4166** | A3174 | 41c multicolored | 2.00 | .35 |
| **4167** | A3175 | 41c multicolored | 2.00 | .35 |
| **4168** | A3176 | 41c multicolored | 2.00 | .35 |
| **4169** | A3177 | 41c multicolored | 2.00 | .35 |
| **4170** | A3178 | 41c multicolored | 2.00 | .35 |
| **4171** | A3179 | 41c multicolored | 2.00 | .35 |
| **4172** | A3180 | 41c multicolored | 2.00 | .35 |
| **4173** | A3181 | 41c multicolored | 2.00 | .35 |
| **4174** | A3182 | 41c multicolored | 2.00 | .35 |
| **4175** | A3183 | 41c multicolored | 2.00 | .35 |
| *a.* | | Strip of 10, #4166-4175 | 20.00 | |

PHOTOGRAVURE

**BOOKLET STAMPS**

***Serpentine Die Cut 11¼x11½ on 2 or 3 Sides***

| | | | | |
|---|---|---|---|---|
| **4176** | A3182 | 41c multicolored | 1.25 | .35 |
| **4177** | A3183 | 41c multicolored | 1.25 | .35 |
| **4178** | A3174 | 41c multicolored | 1.25 | .35 |
| **4179** | A3175 | 41c multicolored | 1.25 | .35 |
| **4180** | A3176 | 41c multicolored | 1.25 | .35 |
| **4181** | A3177 | 41c multicolored | 1.25 | .35 |
| **4182** | A3180 | 41c multicolored | 1.25 | .35 |
| **4183** | A3181 | 41c multicolored | 1.25 | .35 |
| **4184** | A3178 | 41c multicolored | 1.25 | .35 |
| **4185** | A3179 | 41c multicolored | 1.25 | .35 |
| *a.* | | Booklet pane of 20, 2 each #4176-4185 | 25.00 | |
| *b.* | | As "a," die cutting missing on Nos. 4178 & 4183 on side with 8 stamps (PS) | *1,000.* | |

No. 4185a is a double-sided booklet pane with 12 stamps on one side (2 each #4176-4177, 1 each #4178-4185) and eight stamps (#4178-4185) plus label (booklet cover) on the other side.

Flag — A3184

**LITHOGRAPHED**
*Serpentine Die Cut 9½ Vert.*
2007, Aug. 15
**COIL STAMPS**
**Self-Adhesive**
**With "USPS" Microprinted on Right Side of Flagpole**
**With Perpendicular Corners**
4186  A3184  41c multicolored    1.20   .25
**With "USPS" Microprinted on Left Side of Flagpole**
*Serpentine Die Cut 11 Vert.*
4187  A3184  41c multicolored    1.20   .25
**PHOTOGRAVURE**
**Without "USPS" Microprinting on Flagpole**
*Serpentine Die Cut 8½ Vert.*
4188  A3184  41c multicolored     .85   .25
*Serpentine Die Cut 11 Vert.*
**With Rounded Corners**
4189  A3184  41c multicolored     .85   .25

No. 4188 is on backing paper as high as the stamp. No. 4189 is on backing paper that is larger than the stamp.

**LITHOGRAPHED**
**BOOKLET STAMPS**
*Serpentine Die Cut 11¼x10¾ on 3 Sides*
**With "USPS" Microprinted on Right Side of Flagpole**
4190  A3184  41c multicolored     .85   .25
   a. Booklet pane of 10         8.50
**With "USPS" Microprinted on Left Side of Flagpole**
*Serpentine Die Cut 11¼x10¾ on 2 or 3 Sides*
4191  A3184  41c multicolored     .85   .25
   a. Booklet pane of 20       17.00

The microprinting on Nos. 4190 and 4191 is under the ball of the flagpole. The flagpole is light gray on No. 4190 and dark gray on No. 4191. No. 4191a is a double-sided booklet with 12 stamps on one side of the peelable backing and 8 stamps plus label (booklet cover) on the other side.

### THE ART OF DISNEY: MAGIC

Mickey Mouse
A3185

Peter Pan and Tinker Bell
A3186

Dumbo and Timothy Mouse
A3187

Aladdin and Genie
A3188

**PHOTOGRAVURE**
*Serpentine Die Cut 10½x10¾*
2007, Aug. 16
**Self-Adhesive**
4192  A3185  41c multicolored     .85   .30
4193  A3186  41c multicolored     .85   .30
4194  A3187  41c multicolored     .85   .30
4195  A3188  41c multicolored    1.00   .30
   a. Block or strip of 4, #4192-4195    4.00

### CELEBRATE

A3189

**LITHOGRAPHED**
*Serpentine Die Cut 10¾*
2007, Aug. 17
**Self-Adhesive**
4196  A3189  41c multicolored     .85   .25
See Nos. 4335, 4407.

### LEGENDS OF HOLLYWOOD

James Stewart (1908-97), Actor — A3190

2007, Aug. 17
**Self-Adhesive**
4197  A3190  41c multicolored    1.00   .25

### ALPINE TUNDRA

A3191

No. 4198 — Wildlife: a, Elk. b, Golden eagle, horiz. c, Yellow-bellied marmot. d, American pika. e, Bighorn sheep. f, Magdalena alpine butterfly. g, White-tailed ptarmigan. h, Rocky Mountain parnassian butterfly. i, Melissa arctic butterfly, horiz. j, Brown-capped rosy-finch, horiz.

**PHOTOGRAVURE**
2007, Aug. 28
**Self-Adhesive**
4198  A3191  Pane of 10            8.50
   a.-j.    41c any single        .85   .40

### GERALD R. FORD

Gerald R. Ford (1913-2006), 38th President — A3192

**LITHOGRAPHED**
*Serpentine Die Cut 11*
2007, Aug. 31
**Self-Adhesive**
4199  A3192  41c multicolored     .85   .25

### JURY DUTY

Twelve Jurors — A3193

*Serpentine Die Cut 10½*
2007, Sept. 12
**Self-Adhesive**
4200  A3193  41c multicolored     .85   .25

### MENDEZ v. WESTMINSTER, 60th ANNIV.

A3194

**LITHOGRAPHED**
*Serpentine Die Cut 11*
2007, Sept. 14
**Self-Adhesive**
4201  A3194  41c multicolored     .85   .25

**Eid Type of 2001**
**PHOTOGRAVURE**
*Serpentine Die Cut 11*
2007, Sept. 28
**Self-Adhesive**
4202  A2734  41c multicolored     .90   .25
See Nos. 3532, 3674, 4117, 4351, 4416.

### AURORAS

Aurora Borealis — A3195

Aurora Australis — A3196

**LITHOGRAPHED**
*Serpentine Die Cut 10¾*
2007, Oct. 1
**Self-Adhesive**
4203  A3195  41c multicolored    1.25   .30
4204  A3196  41c multicolored    1.25   .30
   a. Horiz. or vert. pair, #4203-4204    2.50

### YODA

A3197

*Serpentine Die Cut 10½x10¾*
2007, Oct. 25
**Self-Adhesive**
4205  A3197  41c multicolored    1.00   .25

### CHRISTMAS

Madonna of the Carnation, by Bernardino Luini — A3198

**LITHOGRAPHED**
*Serpentine Die Cut 10¾x11 on 2 or 3 Sides*
2007, Oct. 25
**Self-Adhesive**
**Booklet Stamps (#4206, 4210b, 4211-4218)**
4206  A3198  41c multicolored     .85   .25
   a. Booklet pane of 20       17.00

No. 4206a is a double-sided booklet pane with 12 stamps on one side and eight stamps plus label that serves as a booklet cover on the other side.

Knit Reindeer
A3199

Knit Christmas Tree
A3200

Knit Snowman
A3201

Knit Bear
A3202

*Serpentine Die Cut 10¾ on 2, 3 or 4 Sides*
4207  A3199  41c multicolored     .85   .25
4208  A3200  41c multicolored     .85   .25
4209  A3201  41c multicolored     .85   .25
4210  A3202  41c multicolored, overall tagging    .85   .25
   b. Block or vert. strip of 4, #4207-4210    3.40
   d. Booklet pane of 20      17.00

No. 4210d is a double-sided booklet pane with 12 stamps on one side and eight stamps plus label that serves as a booklet cover on the other side.

Knit Reindeer
A3203

Knit Christmas Tree
A3204

Knit Snowman
A3205

Knit Bear
A3206

*Serpentine Die Cut 11¼x11 on 2 or 3 Sides*
4211  A3203  41c multicolored    1.25   .25
4212  A3204  41c multicolored    1.25   .25
4213  A3205  41c multicolored    1.25   .25
4214  A3206  41c multicolored    1.25   .25
   a. Block of 4, #4211-4214    5.00
   b. Booklet pane of 4, #4211-4214    5.00
   c. Booklet pane of 6, #4213-4214, 2 each #4211-4212    7.50
   d. Booklet pane of 6, #4211-4212, 2 each #4213-4214    7.50

**PHOTOGRAVURE**
*Serpentine Die Cut 8 on 2, 3 or 4 Sides*
4215  A3203  41c multicolored    1.50   .25
4216  A3204  41c multicolored    1.50   .25
4217  A3205  41c multicolored    1.50   .25
4218  A3206  41c multicolored    1.50   .25
   a. Block or strip of 4, #4215-4218    6.00
   b. Booklet pane of 18, 4 each #4215, 4218, 5 each #4216, 4217   27.00
Nos. 4206-4218 (13)    15.25   3.25

**Hanukkah Type of 2004**
**LITHOGRAPHED**
*Serpentine Die Cut 10¾x11*
2007, Oct. 26
**Self-Adhesive**
4219  A2962  41c multicolored     .85   .25
See Nos. 3880, 4118, 4372.

**Kwanzaa Type of 2004**
**LITHOGRAPHED**
*Serpentine Die Cut 11x10¾*
2007, Oct. 26
**Self-Adhesive**
4220  A2963  41c multicolored     .85   .25
See Nos. 3881, 4119, 4373.

### CHINESE NEW YEAR

Year of the Rat — A3207

**PHOTOGRAVURE**
*Serpentine Die Cut 10¾*
2008, Jan. 9   **Self-Adhesive**
4221  A3207  41c multicolored     .85   .25

UNITED STATES 115

## BLACK HERITAGE SERIES

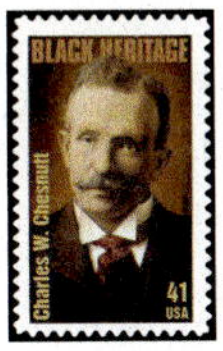


Charles W. Chesnutt (1858-1932), Writer — A3208

***Serpentine Die Cut 11***

**2008, Jan. 31 Self-Adhesive**

4222 A3208 41c multicolored .85 .25

## LITERARY ARTS SERIES

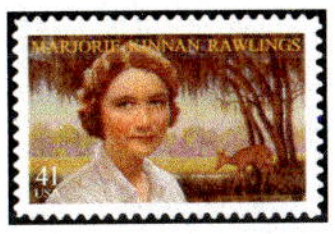


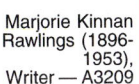

Marjorie Kinnan Rawlings (1896-1953), Writer — A3209

***Serpentine Die Cut 11***

**2008, Feb. 21**

**Self-Adhesive**

4223 A3209 41c multicolored .85 .25

## AMERICAN SCIENTISTS

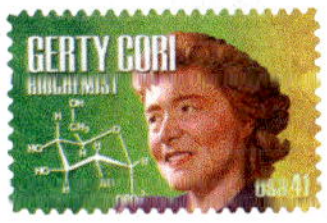


Gerty Cori (1896-1957), Biochemist A3210

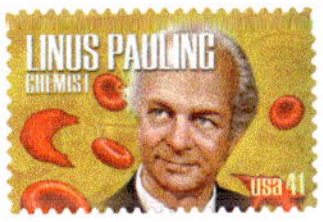


Linus Pauling (1901-94), Structural Chemist — A3211

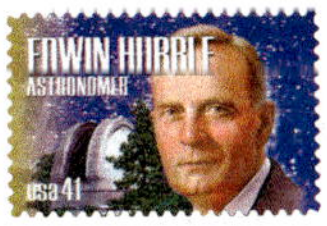


Edwin Hubble (1889-1953), Astronomer A3212

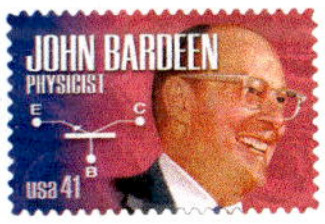


John Bardeen (1908-91), Theoretical Physicist — A3213

**2008, Mar. 6**

**Self-Adhesive**

4224 A3210 41c multicolored 1.00 .35
4225 A3211 41c multicolored 1.00 .35
4226 A3212 41c multicolored 1.00 .35
4227 A3213 41c multicolored 1.00 .35
a. Horiz. strip of 4, #4224-4227 4.00

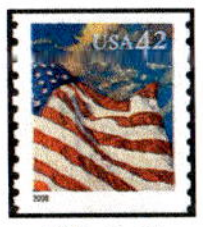


Flag at Dusk A3214

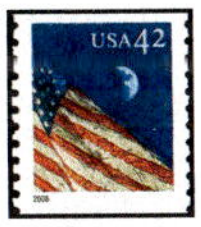


Flag at Night A3215

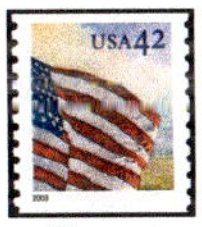


Flag at Dawn A3216

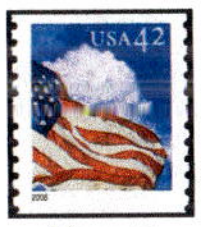


Flag at Midday A3217

PHOTOGRAVURE

**2008, Apr. 18 *Perf. 9¾ Vert.***

**COIL STAMPS**

4228 A3214 42c multicolored 2.50 .40
4229 A3215 42c multicolored 2.50 .40
4230 A3216 42c multicolored 2.50 .40
4231 A3217 42c multicolored 2.50 .40
a. Horiz. strip of 4, #4228-4231 10.00 1.60

**Self-Adhesive**

**With Perpendicular Corners**

***Serpentine Die Cut 9½ Vert.***

4232 A3214 42c multicolored 2.25 .25
4233 A3215 42c multicolored 2.25 .25
4234 A3216 42c multicolored 2.25 .25
4235 A3217 42c multicolored 2.25 .25
a. Horiz. strip of 4, #4232-4235 9.00

***Serpentine Die Cut 11 Vert.***

4236 A3214 42c multicolored 2.50 .25
4237 A3215 42c multicolored 2.50 .25
4238 A3216 42c multicolored 2.50 .25
4239 A3217 42c multicolored 2.50 .25
a. Horiz. strip of 4, #4236-4239 10.00

***Serpentine Die Cut 8½ Vert.***

4240 A3214 42c multicolored 2.00 .25
4241 A3215 42c multicolored 2.00 .25
4242 A3216 42c multicolored 2.00 .25
4243 A3217 42c multicolored 2.00 .25
a. Horiz. strip of 4, #4240-4243 8.00

***Serpentine Die Cut 11 Vert.***

**With Rounded Corners**

4244 A3214 42c multicolored 1.25 .30
4245 A3215 42c multicolored 1.25 .30
4246 A3216 42c multicolored 1.25 .30
4247 A3217 42c multicolored 1.25 .30
a. Horiz. strip of 4, #4244-4247 6.00
*Nos. 4228-4247 (20)* 42.00 5.80

Nos. 4232-4243 are on backing paper as high as the stamp. Nos. 4244-4247 are on backing paper that is larger than the stamp. Nos. 4232-4235 have "USPS" microprinted on the right side of a white flag stripe. Nos. 4236-4239 have "USPS" micorprinted on red flag stripes. On Nos. 4244-4247, the paper, vignette size and "2008" year date are slightly larger than those features on Nos. 4236-4239.

## AMERICAN JOURNALISTS

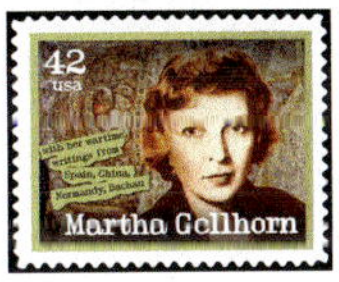


Martha Gellhorn (1908-98) A3218

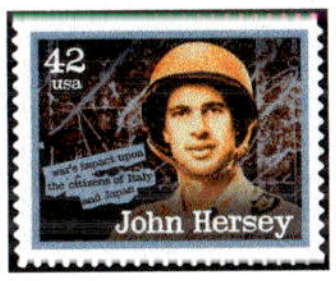


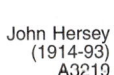

John Hersey (1914-93) A3219

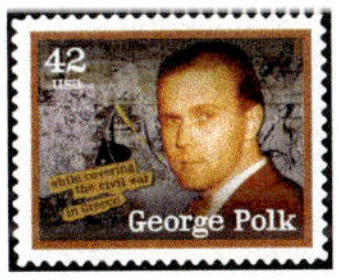


George Polk (1913-48) A3220

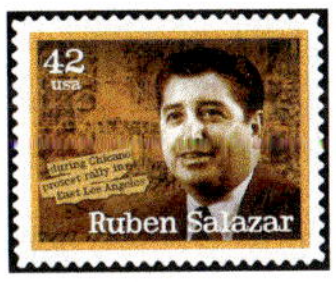


Ruben Salazar (1928-70) A3221

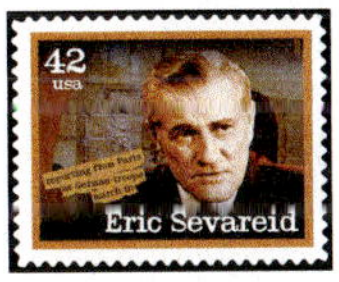


Eric Sevareid (1912-92) A3222

LITHOGRAPHED

***Serpentine Die Cut 10¾x10½***

**2008, Apr. 22**

**Self-Adhesive**

4248 A3218 42c multicolored 1.40 .40
4249 A3219 42c multicolored 1.40 .40
4250 A3220 42c multicolored 1.40 .40
4251 A3221 42c multicolored 1.40 .40
4252 A3222 42c multicolored 1.40 .40
a. Vert. strip of 5, #4248-4252 7.00

## TROPICAL FRUIT

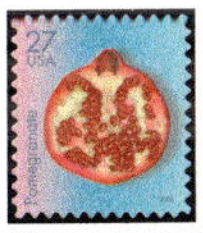


Pomegranate A3223

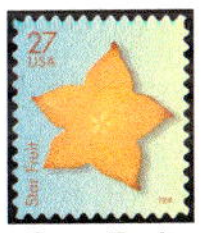


Star Fruit A3224

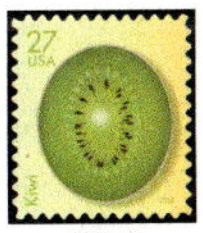


Kiwi A3225

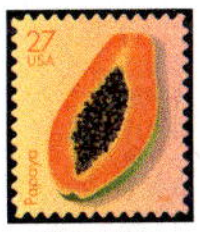


Papaya A3226

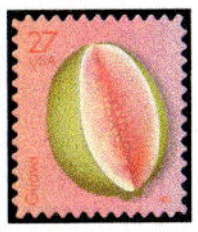


Guava — A3227

LITHOGRAPHED

***Serpentine Die Cut 11¼x10¾***

**2008, Apr. 25**

**Self-Adhesive**

4253 A3223 27c multicolored 1.25 .25
4254 A3224 27c multicolored 1.25 .25
4255 A3225 27c multicolored 1.25 .25
4256 A3226 27c multicolored 1.25 .25
4257 A3227 27c multicolored 1.25 .25
a. Horiz. strip of 5, #4253-4257 6.25

PHOTOGRAVURE

**COIL STAMPS**

***Serpentine Die Cut 8½ Vert.***

4258 A3226 27c multicolored 2.00 .25
4259 A3227 27c multicolored 2.00 .25
4260 A3223 27c multicolored 2.00 .25
4261 A3224 27c multicolored 2.00 .25
4262 A3225 multicolored 2.00 .25
a. Strip of 5, #4258-4262 10.00
b. As No. 4262, light green ("27 USA," "Kiwi" and year date) omitted —
*Nos. 4253-4262 (10)* 16.25 2.50

**Purple Heart Type of 2003**

LITHOGRAPHED

**2008, Apr. 30 *Perf. 11¼***

4263 A2891 42c multicolored .90 .25

**Self-Adhesive**

***Serpentine Die Cut 11¼x10¾***

4264 A2891 42c multicolored .85 .25

See Nos. 4032, 4164, 4390.

## FRANK SINATRA

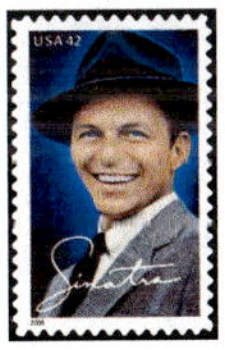


Frank Sinatra (1915-98), Singer and Actor — A3228

***Serpentine Die Cut 10¾***

**2008, May 13**

**Self-Adhesive**

4265 A3228 42c multicolored .85 .25

## MINNESOTA STATEHOOD, 150th ANNIV.

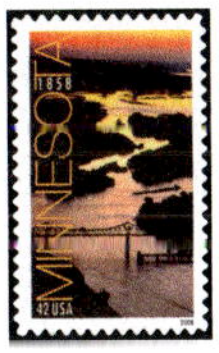


Bridge Over Mississippi River Near Winona — A3229

***Serpentine Die Cut 10¾***

**2008, May 17**

**Self-Adhesive**

4266 A3229 42c multicolored .85 .25

## WILDLIFE

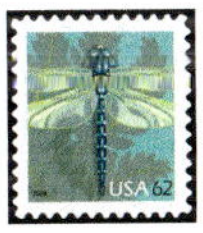


Dragonfly — A3230

LITHOGRAPHED

***Serpentine Die Cut 11¼x11***

**2008, May 19**

**Self-Adhesive**

4267 A3230 62c multicolored 2.50 .25

## AMERICAN LANDMARKS

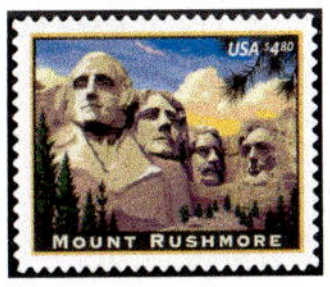


Mount Rushmore A3231

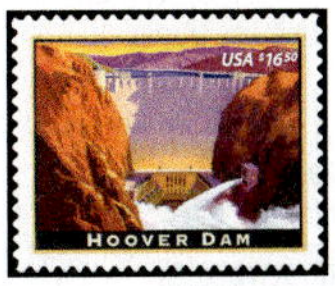


Hoover Dam — A3232

**2008 *Serpentine Die Cut 10¾x10½***

**Self-Adhesive**

4268 A3231 $4.80 multi 12.00 5.00
4269 A3232 $16.50 multi 35.00 17.00

Issued: $4.80, 6/6; $16.50, 6/20.

## LOVE

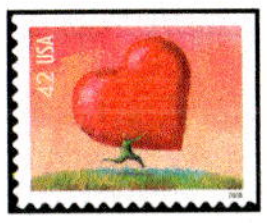


Man Carrying Heart — A3233

PHOTOGRAVURE

***Serpentine Die Cut 10¾ on 2, 3, or 4 Sides***

**2008, June 10**

**Booklet Stamp**

**Self-Adhesive**

4270 A3233 42c multicolored .95 .25
a. Booklet pane of 20 19.00

## WEDDING HEARTS

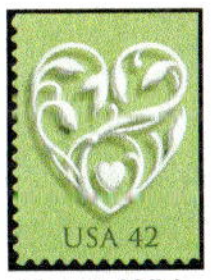


Heart With Light Green Background A3234

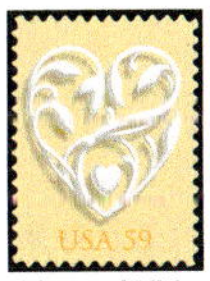


Heart With Buff Background A3235

LITHOGRAPHED (#4271), PHOTOGRAVURE (#4272) BOOKLET STAMP (#4271)

***Serpentine Die Cut 10¾ on 2, 3 or 4 Sides***

**2008, June 10**

**Self-Adhesive**

4271 A3234 42c multicolored .90 .25
a. Booklet pane of 20 18.00

***Serpentine Die Cut 10¾***

4272 A3235 59c multicolored 1.25 .25

## FLAGS OF OUR NATION

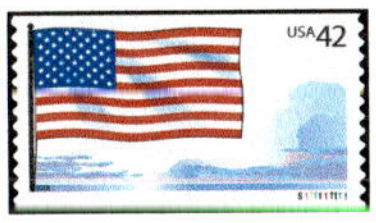


American Flag and Clouds A3236

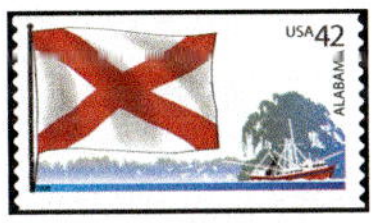


Alabama Flag and Shrimp Boat — A3237

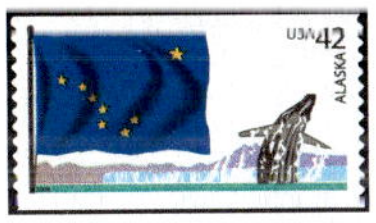


Alaska Flag and Humpback Whale A3238

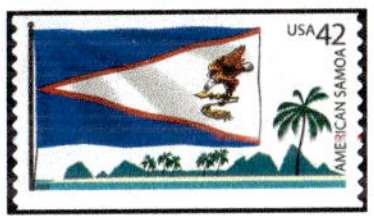


American Samoa Flag and Island Peaks and Trees — A3239

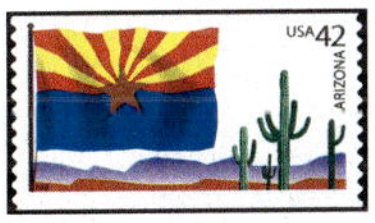


Arizona Flag and Saguaro Cacti — A3240

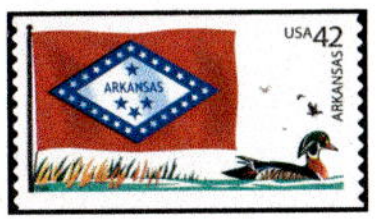


Arkansas Flag and Wood Duck — A3241

116 UNITED STATES

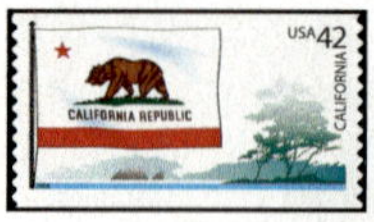
California Flag and Coast — A3242

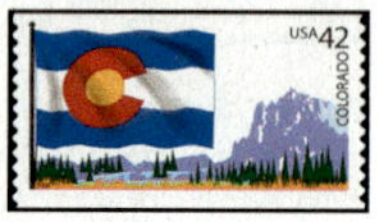
Colorado Flag and Mountain A3243

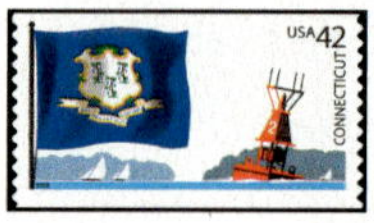
Connecticut Flag, Sailboats and Buoy — A3244

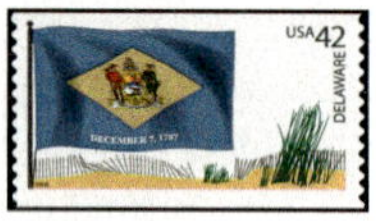
Delaware Flag and Beach A3245

PHOTOGRAVURE

***Serpentine Die Cut 11 Vert.***

**2008, June 14**

**Self-Adhesive**

**Coil Stamps**

| | | | | | |
|---|---|---|---|---|---|
| **4273** | A3236 | 42c | multicolored | 1.00 | .30 |
| **4274** | A3237 | 42c | multicolored | 1.00 | .30 |
| **4275** | A3238 | 42c | multicolored | 1.00 | .30 |
| **4276** | A3239 | 42c | multicolored | 1.00 | .30 |
| **4277** | A3240 | 42c | multicolored | 1.00 | .30 |
| *a.* | Strip of 5, #4273-4277 | | | 5.00 | |
| **4278** | A3241 | 42c | multicolored | 1.00 | .30 |
| **4279** | A3242 | 42c | multicolored | 1.00 | .30 |
| **4280** | A3243 | 42c | multicolored | 1.00 | .30 |
| **4281** | A3244 | 42c | multicolored | 1.00 | .30 |
| **4282** | A3245 | 42c | multicolored | 1.00 | .30 |
| *a.* | Strip of 5, #4278-4282 | | | 5.00 | |
| *b.* | P # set of 10, #4277a + 4282a | | | 10.00 | |

No. 4273 always has a plate number. No. 4282b may be collected as one continuous strip, but the item will not fit in any standard album.

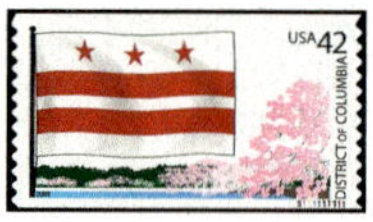
District of Columbia Flag and Cherry Tree — A3246

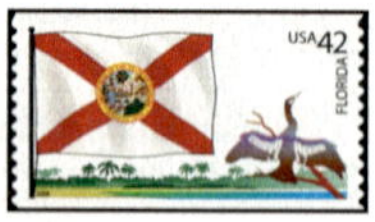
Florida Flag and Anhinga A3247

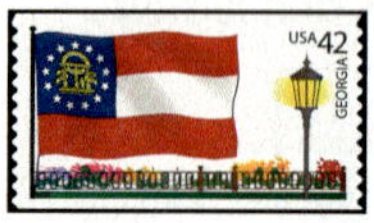
Georgia Flag, Fence and Lamppost A3248

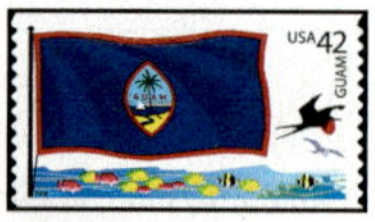
Guam Flag, Fish and Tropicbird A3249

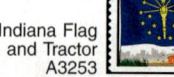

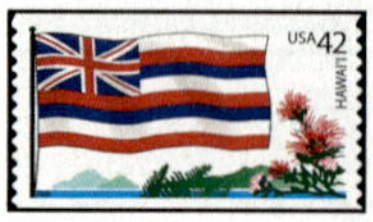
Hawaii Flag and Ohia Lehua Flowers A3250

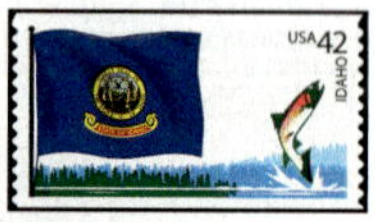
Idaho Flag and Rainbow Trout — A3251

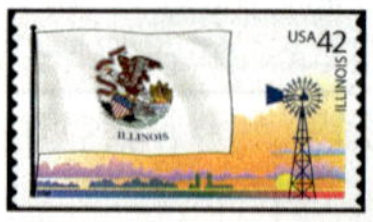
Illinois Flag and Windmill A3252

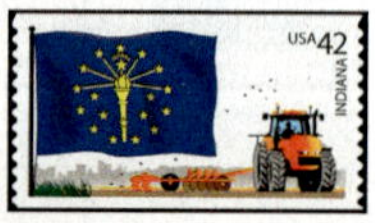
Indiana Flag and Tractor A3253

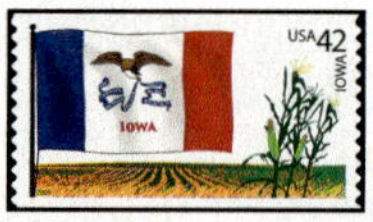
Iowa Flag, Farm Field and Cornstalks A3254

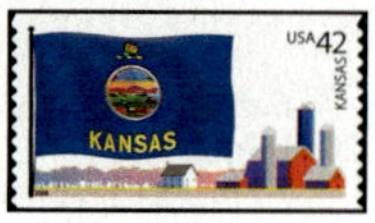
Kansas Flag and Farm Buildings A3255

**2008, Sept. 2**

**Self-Adhesive**

**Coil Stamps**

| | | | | | |
|---|---|---|---|---|---|
| **4283** | A3246 | 42c | multicolored | 1.00 | .30 |
| **4284** | A3247 | 42c | multicolored | 1.00 | .30 |
| **4285** | A3248 | 42c | multicolored | 1.00 | .30 |
| **4286** | A3249 | 42c | multicolored | 1.00 | .30 |
| **4287** | A3250 | 42c | multicolored | 1.00 | .30 |
| *a.* | Strip of 5, #4283-4287 | | | 5.00 | |
| **4288** | A3251 | 42c | multicolored | 1.00 | .30 |
| **4289** | A3252 | 42c | multicolored | 1.00 | .30 |
| **4290** | A3253 | 42c | multicolored | 1.00 | .30 |
| **4291** | A3254 | 42c | multicolored | 1.00 | .30 |
| **4292** | A3255 | 42c | multicolored | 1.00 | .30 |
| *a.* | Strip of 5, #4288-4292 | | | 5.00 | |
| *b.* | P # set of 10, #4287a + 4192a | | | 10.00 | |

No. 4283 always has a plate number. No. 4292b may be collected as one continuous strip, but the item will not fit in any standard album.

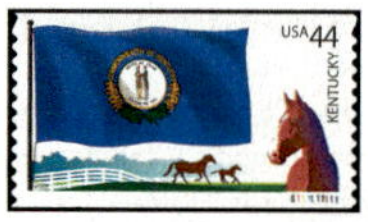
Kentucky Flag, Fence and Horses A3256

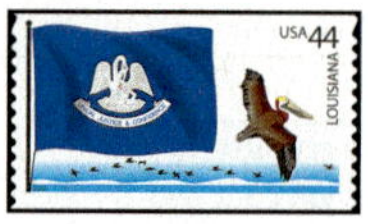
Louisiana Flag and Brown Pelicans A3257

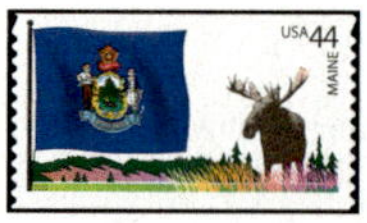
Maine Flag and Moose A3258

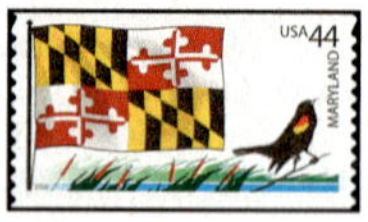
Maryland Flag and Red-winged Blackbird A3259

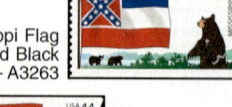

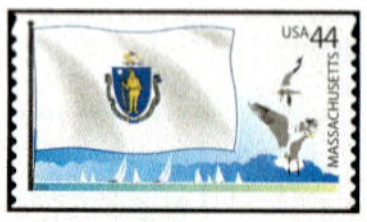
Massachusetts Flag, Sea Birds and Sailboats A3260

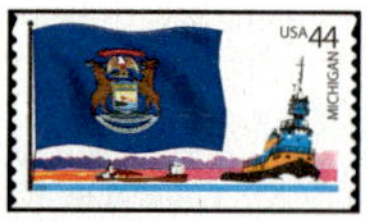
Michigan Flag and Great Lakes Ships — A3261

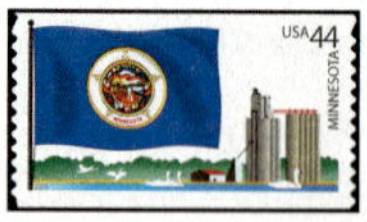
Minnesota Flag, Swans and Grain Elevator A3262

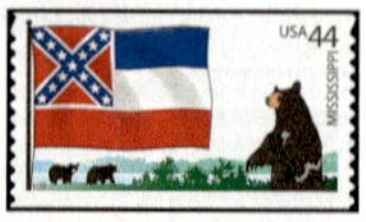
Mississippi Flag and Black Bears — A3263

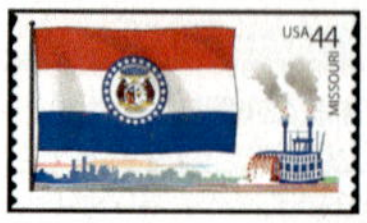
Missouri Flag and Paddle Wheeler A3264

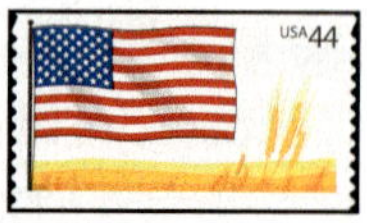
American Flag and Wheat A3265

**2009, Aug. 6**

**Self-Adhesive**

**Coil Stamps**

| | | | | | |
|---|---|---|---|---|---|
| **4293** | A3256 | 44c | multicolored | 1.00 | .30 |
| **4294** | A3257 | 44c | multicolored | 1.00 | .30 |
| **4295** | A3258 | 44c | multicolored | 1.00 | .30 |
| **4296** | A3259 | 44c | multicolored | 1.00 | .30 |
| **4297** | A3260 | 44c | multicolored | 1.00 | .30 |
| *a.* | Strip of 5, #4293-4297 | | | 5.00 | |
| **4298** | A3261 | 44c | multicolored | 1.00 | .30 |
| **4299** | A3262 | 44c | multicolored | 1.00 | .30 |
| **4300** | A3263 | 44c | multicolored | 1.00 | .30 |
| **4301** | A3264 | 44c | multicolored | 1.00 | .30 |
| **4302** | A3265 | 44c | multicolored | 1.00 | .30 |
| *a.* | Strip of 5, #4298-4302 | | | 5.00 | |
| *b.* | P # set of 10, #4297a + 4302a | | | 10.00 | |

No. 4293 always has a plate number. No. 4302b may be collected as one continuous strip, but the item will not fit in any standard album.

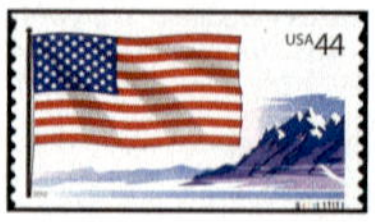
American Flag and Mountains A3266

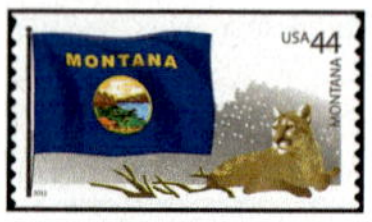
Montana Flag and Mountain Lion — A3267

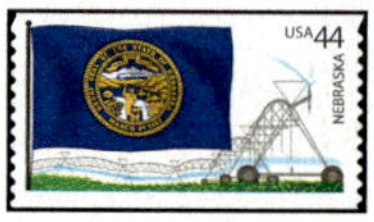
Nebraska Flag and Central-pivot Irrigation System A3268

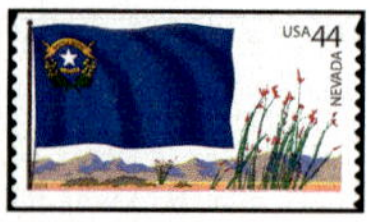
Nevada Flag, Mountains and Ocotillos A3269

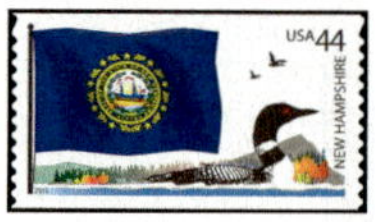
New Hampshire Flag and Loon — A3270

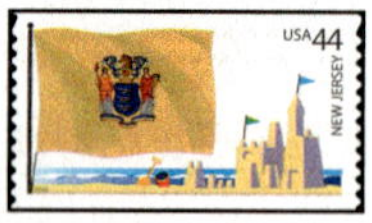
New Jersey Flag and Sand Castle A3271

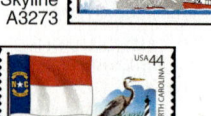

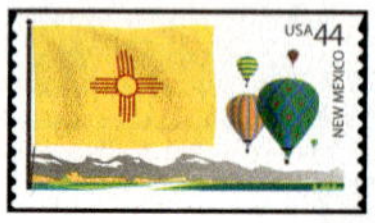
New Mexico Flag, Mountains and Hot Air Balloons A3272

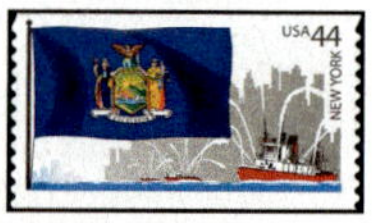
New York Flag, Fireboats and City Skyline A3273

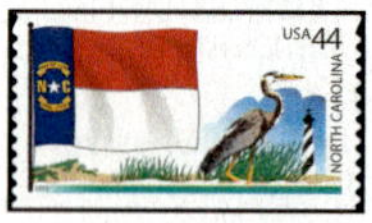
North Carolina Flag, Great Blue Heron and Cape Hatteras Lighthouse A3274

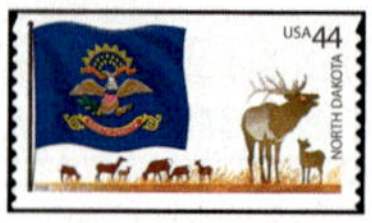
North Dakota Flag and Elk — A3275

**2010, Apr. 16**

**Self-Adhesive**

**Coil Stamps**

| | | | | | |
|---|---|---|---|---|---|
| **4303** | A3266 | 44c | multicolored | 1.00 | .30 |
| **4304** | A3267 | 44c | multicolored | 1.00 | .30 |
| **4305** | A3268 | 44c | multicolored | 1.00 | .30 |
| **4306** | A3269 | 44c | multicolored | 1.00 | .30 |
| **4307** | A3270 | 44c | multicolored | 1.00 | .30 |
| *a.* | Strip of 5, #4303-4307 | | | 5.00 | |
| **4308** | A3271 | 44c | multicolored | 1.00 | .30 |
| **4309** | A3272 | 44c | multicolored | 1.00 | .30 |
| **4310** | A3273 | 44c | multicolored | 1.00 | .30 |
| **4311** | A3274 | 44c | multicolored | 1.00 | .30 |
| **4312** | A3275 | 44c | multicolored | 1.00 | .30 |
| *a.* | Strip of 5, #4308-4312 | | | 5.00 | |
| *b.* | P # set of 10, #4307a + 4312a | | | 10.00 | |

No. 4303 always has a plate number. No. 4312b may be collected as one continuous strip, but the item will not fit in any standard album.

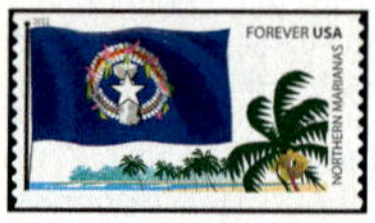
Northern Marianas Flag, Beach and Palm Trees — A3276

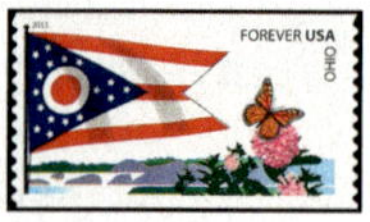
Ohio Flag, Butterfly, Milkweed Flowers and River — A3277

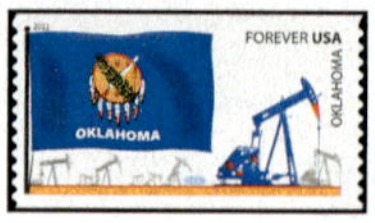
Oklahoma Flag and Oil Pumps A3278

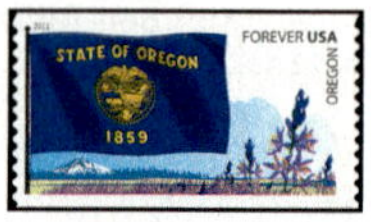
Oregon Flag, Mount Hood and Camas Lilies — A3279

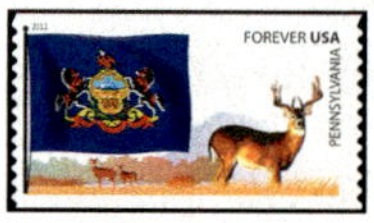
Pennsylvania Flag and White-tailed Deer — A3280

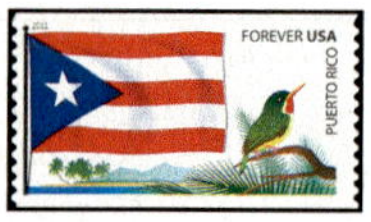
Puerto Rico Flag and Puerto Rican Tody Bird — A3281

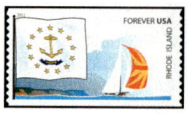

Rhode Island Flag and Sailboat A3282

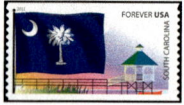

South Carolina Flag, Marsh and Gazebo A3283

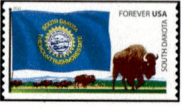

South Dakota Flag and Bison — A3284

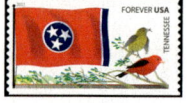

Tennessee Flag and Scarlet Tanagers A3285

PHOTOGRAVURE

***Serpentine Die Cut 11 Vert.***

**2011, Aug. 11**

**Self-Adhesive**

**Coil Stamps**

| | | | | | |
|---|---|---|---|---|---|
| **4313** | A3276 | (44c) | multicolored | 1.50 | .30 |
| **4314** | A3277 | (44c) | multicolored | 1.50 | .30 |
| **4315** | A3278 | (44c) | multicolored | 1.50 | .30 |
| **4316** | A3279 | (44c) | multicolored | 1.50 | .30 |
| **4317** | A3280 | (44c) | multicolored | 1.50 | .30 |
| *a.* | Strip of 5, #4313-4317 | | | 7.50 | |
| **4318** | A3281 | (44c) | multicolored | 1.50 | .30 |
| **4319** | A3282 | (44c) | multicolored | 1.50 | .30 |
| **4320** | A3283 | (44c) | multicolored | 1.50 | .30 |
| **4321** | A3284 | (44c) | multicolored | 1.50 | .30 |
| **4322** | A3285 | (44c) | multicolored | 1.50 | .30 |
| *a.* | Strip of 5, #4318-4322 | | | 7.50 | |
| *b.* | P# set of 10, #4317a + 4322a | | | 15.00 | |

Alternating examples of the five examples of No. 4313 in the roll have a plate number. No. 4322b may be collected as one continuous strip, but the item will not fit in any standard album.

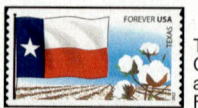

Texas Flag, Cotton Plant and Field — A3286

# UNITED STATES

Utah Flag, Cactus and Rock — A3287

Vermont Flag and Owls — A3288

Virgin Islands Flag, Sailfish and Boat — A3289

Virginia Flag and Replicas of Ships that Carried Settlers to Jamestown A3290

Washington Flag and Evergreen Forest — A3291

West Virginia Flag and Wild Turkeys A3292

Wisconsin Flag and Dairy Cows — A3293

Wyoming Flag and Bighorn Sheep A3294

American Flag and Fruited Plain — A3295

**PHOTOGRAVURE**
*Serpentine Die Cut 11 Vert.*
**2012, Aug. 16**
**Self-Adhesive**
**Coil Stamps**

| 4323 | A3286 | (45c) multicolored | 3.00 | .30 |
|---|---|---|---|---|
| 4324 | A3287 | (45c) multicolored | 3.00 | .30 |
| 4325 | A3288 | (45c) multicolored | 3.00 | .30 |
| 4326 | A3289 | (45c) multicolored | 3.00 | .30 |
| 4327 | A3290 | (45c) multicolored | 3.00 | .30 |
| a. | | Strip of 5, #4323-4327 | 15.00 | |
| 4328 | A3291 | (45c) multicolored | 3.00 | .30 |
| 4329 | A3292 | (45c) multicolored | 3.00 | .30 |
| 4330 | A3293 | (45c) multicolored | 3.00 | .30 |
| 4331 | A3294 | (45c) multicolored | 3.00 | .30 |
| 4332 | A3295 | (45c) multicolored | 3.00 | .30 |
| a | | Strip of 5, #4328-4332 | 15.00 | |
| b. | | P# set of 10, #4327a + 4332a | 30.00 | |

Alternating examples of the five examples of No. 4323 in the roll have a plate number. No. 4332b may be collected as one continuous strip, but the item will not fit in any standard album.

**CHARLES (1907-78) AND RAY (1912-88) EAMES, DESIGNERS**

A3296

No. 4333: a, Christmas card depicting Charles and Ray Eames. b, "Crosspatch" fabric design. c, Stacking chairs. d, Case Study House #8, Pacific Palisades, CA. e, Wire-base table. f, Lounge chair and ottoman. g, Hang-it-all. h, La Chaise. i, Scene from film, "Tops." j, Wire mesh chair. k, Cover of May 1943 edition of *California Arts & Architecture* Magazine. l, House of Cards. m, Molded plywood sculpture. n, Eames Storage Unit. o, Aluminum group chair. p, Molded plywood chair.

**PHOTOGRAVURE**
*Serpentine Die Cut 10¾x10½*
**2008, June 17**
**Self-Adhesive**

| 4333 | A3296 | Pane of 16 + label | 18.00 | |
|---|---|---|---|---|
| a.-p. | | 42c Any single | 1.10 | .50 |

**SUMMER OLYMPIC GAMES, BEIJING, CHINA**

Gymnast A3297

**LITHOGRAPHED**
*Serpentine Die Cut 10¾*
**2008, June 19**
**Self-Adhesive**

| 4334 | A3297 | 42c multicolored | .85 | .25 |
|---|---|---|---|---|

**Celebrate Type of 2007**
*Serpentine Die Cut 10¾*
**2008, July 10**
**Self-Adhesive**

| 4335 | A3189 | 42c multicolored | .85 | .25 |
|---|---|---|---|---|

**VINTAGE BLACK CINEMA**

Poster for "Black and Tan" A3298

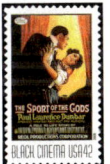
Poster for "The Sport of the Gods" A3299

Poster for "Prinsesse Tam-Tam" A3300

Poster for "Caldonia" A3301

Poster for "Hallelujah" — A3302

*Serpentine Die Cut 10¾*
**2008, July 16**     Tagged
**Self-Adhesive**

| 4336 | A3298 | 42c multicolored | .95 | .45 |
|---|---|---|---|---|
| 4337 | A3299 | 42c multicolored | .95 | .45 |
| 4338 | A3300 | 42c multicolored | .95 | .45 |
| 4339 | A3301 | 42c multicolored | .95 | .45 |
| 4340 | A3302 | 42c multicolored | .95 | .45 |
| a. | | Horiz. strip of 5, #4336-4340 | 4.75 | |

**"TAKE ME OUT TO THE BALLGAME," CENT.**

Baseball Players and First Six Notes of Song — A3303

**PHOTOGRAVURE**
*Serpentine Die Cut 11*
**2008, July 16**
**Self-Adhesive**

| 4341 | A3303 | 42c multicolored | .85 | .25 |
|---|---|---|---|---|

**THE ART OF DISNEY: IMAGINATION**

Pongo and Pup — A3304

Steamboat Willie — A3305

Princess Aurora, Flora, Fauna and Merryweather A3306

Mowgli and Baloo A3307

*Serpentine Die Cut 10½x10¾*
**2008, Aug. 7**
**Self-Adhesive**

| 4342 | A3304 | 42c multicolored | .85 | .30 |
|---|---|---|---|---|
| 4343 | A3305 | 42c multicolored | .85 | .30 |
| 4344 | A3306 | 42c multicolored | .85 | .30 |
| 4345 | A3307 | 42c multicolored | .85 | .30 |
| a. | | Block or strip of 4, #4342-4345 | 3.40 | |

**AMERICAN TREASURES SERIES**

Valley of the Yosemite, by Albert Bierstadt A3308

**LITHOGRAPHED BOOKLET STAMP**
*Serpentine Die Cut 11 on 2 or 3 Sides*
**2008, Aug. 14**
**Self-Adhesive**

| 4346 | A3308 | 42c multicolored | .85 | .25 |
|---|---|---|---|---|
| a. | | Booklet pane of 20 | 17.00 | |

No. 4346a is a double-sided booklet pane with 12 stamps on one side and eight stamps plus label (booklet cover) on the other side.

Sunflower — A3309

**BOOKLET STAMP**
*Serpentine Die Cut 11¼x10¾ on 2 or 3 Sides*
**2008, Aug. 15**
**Self-Adhesive**

| 4347 | A3309 | 42c multicolored | .85 | .25 |
|---|---|---|---|---|
| a. | | Booklet pane of 20 | 17.00 | |

No. 4347a is a double-sided booklet pane with 12 stamps on one side and eight stamps plus label (booklet cover) on the other side.

**Sea Coast Type of 2002**
**LITHOGRAPHED COIL STAMP**
*Perf. 9¾ Vert.*
**2008, Sept. 5**     Untagged

| 4348 | A2853 | (5c) multicolored | .30 | .25 |
|---|---|---|---|---|

No. 4348 has "2008" year date in black, and microprinted "USPS" at the end of the purple rock to the right of the crashing wave.

See Nos. 3693, 3775, 3785, 3864, 3874-3875.

**LATIN JAZZ**

Musicians A3310

**PHOTOGRAVURE**
*Serpentine Die Cut 11x10¾*
**2008, Sept. 8**
**Self-Adhesive**

| 4349 | A3310 | 42c multicolored | .85 | .25 |
|---|---|---|---|---|

**LEGENDS OF HOLLYWOOD**

Bette Davis (1908-89), Actress — A3311

**LITHOGRAPHED**
*Serpentine Die Cut 10¾*
**2008, Sept. 18**
**Self-Adhesive**

| 4350 | A3311 | 42c multicolored | 1.00 | .25 |
|---|---|---|---|---|

**Eid Type of 2001**
**PHOTOGRAVURE**
*Serpentine Die Cut 11*
**2008, Sept. 23**
**Self-Adhesive**

| 4351 | A2734 | 42c multicolored | .85 | .25 |
|---|---|---|---|---|

**GREAT LAKES DUNES**

A3312

No. 4352 — Wildlife: a, Vesper sparrow. b, Red fox, vert. c, Piping plover. d, Eastern hog-nose snake. e, Common mergansers. f, Spotted sandpiper, vert. g, Tiger beetle, vert. h, White-footed mouse, vert. i, Piping plover nestlings. j, Red admiral butterfly, vert.

*Serpentine Die Cut 10¾*
**2008, Oct. 2**
**Self-Adhesive**

| 4352 | A3312 | Pane of 10 | 10.00 | |
|---|---|---|---|---|
| a.-j. | | 42c Any single | 1.00 | .40 |

**AUTOMOBILES OF THE 1950s**

1959 Cadillac Eldorado A3313

1957 Studebaker Golden Hawk — A3314

1957 Pontiac Safari — A3315

1957 Lincoln Premiere A3316

1957 Chrysler 300C — A3317

118 UNITED STATES

LITHOGRAPHED

**2008, Oct. 3**

**Self-Adhesive**

**4353** A3313 42c multicolored .85 .45
**4354** A3314 42c multicolored .85 .45
**4355** A3315 42c multicolored .85 .45
**4356** A3316 42c multicolored .85 .45
**4357** A3317 42c multicolored .85 .45
*a.* Vert. strip of 5, #4353-4357 4.25

**ALZHEIMER'S DISEASE AWARENESS**

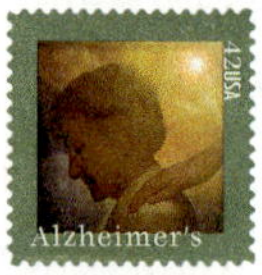


A3318

PHOTOGRAVURE

***Serpentine Die Cut 10¾***

**2008, Oct. 17**

**Self-Adhesive**

**4358** A3318 42c multicolored .85 .25

**CHRISTMAS**

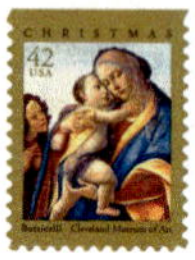

Virgin and Child with the Young John the Baptist, by Sandro Botticelli A3319

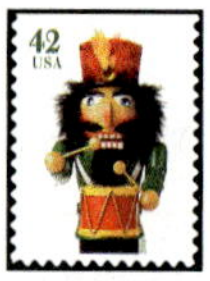

Drummer Nutcracker A3320

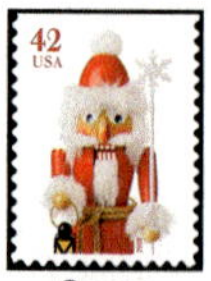

Santa Claus Nutcracker A3321

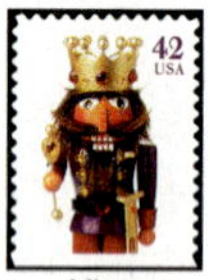

King Nutcracker A3322

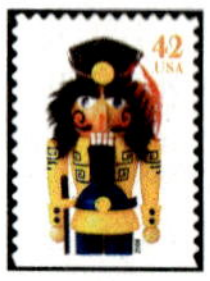

Soldier Nutcracker — A3323

LITHOGRAPHED

***Serpentine Die Cut 10¾x11 on 2 or 3 Sides***

**2008, Oct. 23**

**Self-Adhesive**

**Booklet Stamps**

**4359** A3319 42c multicolored .85 .25
*a.* Booklet pane of 20 17.00
*b.* Die cutting omitted, pair —
**4360** A3320 42c multicolored 1.00 .25
**4361** A3321 42c multicolored 1.00 .25
**4362** A3322 42c multicolored 1.00 .25
**4363** A3323 42c multicolored 1.00 .25
*a.* Block of 4, #4360-4363 4.00
*b.* Booklet pane of 20, 5 each #4360-4363 20.00

No. 4359a is a double-sided booklet pane with 12 stamps on one side and eight stamps plus label that serves as a booklet cover on the other side. No. 4363b is a double-sided booklet pane with 12 stamps on one side (3 each of Nos. 4360-4363) and eight stamps (2 each of Nos. 4360-4363) plus label that serves as a booklet cover on the other side.

Drummer Nutcracker A3324

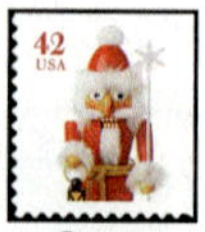

Santa Claus Nutcracker A3325

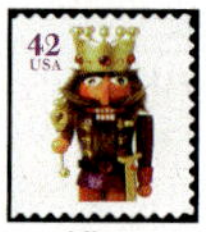

King Nutcracker A3326

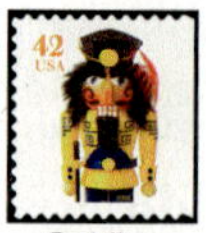

Soldier Nutcracker A3327

***Serpentine Die Cut 11¼x11 on 2 or 3 Sides***

**4364** A3324 42c multicolored 1.25 .25
**4365** A3325 42c multicolored 1.25 .25
**4366** A3326 42c multicolored 1.25 .25
**4367** A3327 42c multicolored 1.25 .25
*a.* Block of 4, #4364-4367 5.00
*b.* Booklet pane of 4, #4364-4367 5.00
*c.* Booklet pane of 6, #4366-4367, 2 each #4364-4365 7.50
*d.* Booklet pane of 6, #4364-4365, 2 each #4366-4367 7.50

***Serpentine Die Cut 8 on 2, 3 or 4 Sides***

PHOTOGRAVURE

**4368** A3324 42c multicolored 1.25 .25
**4369** A3325 42c multicolored 1.25 .25
**4370** A3326 42c multicolored 1.25 .25
**4371** A3327 42c multicolored 1.25 .25
*a.* Block or strip of 4, #4368-4371 5.00
*b.* Booklet pane of 18, 5 each #4368-4369, 4 each #4370-4371 22.50
*Nos. 4359-4371 (13)* 14.85 3.25

**Hanukkah Type of 2004**

LITHOGRAPHED

***Serpentine Die Cut 10¾x11***

**2008, Oct. 24**

**Self-Adhesive**

**4372** A2962 42c multicolored .85 .25

**Kwanzaa Type of 2004**

***Serpentine Die Cut 11x10¾***

**2008, Oct. 24**

**Self-Adhesive**

**4373** A2963 42c multicolored .85 .25

**ALASKA STATEHOOD, 50TH ANNIV.**

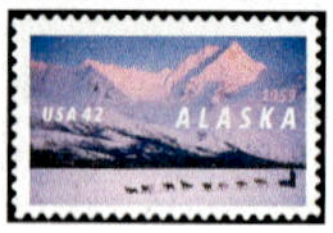


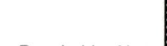

Dogsledder Near Rainy Pass — A3328

***Serpentine Die Cut 10¾***

**2009, Jan. 3**

**Self-Adhesive**

**4374** A3328 42c multicolored .85 .25

**CHINESE NEW YEAR**

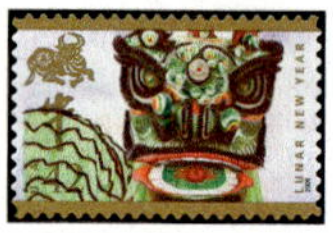


Year of the Ox — A3329

**2009, Jan. 8**

**Self-Adhesive**

**4375** A3329 42c multicolored .85 .25

**OREGON STATEHOOD, 150TH ANNIV.**

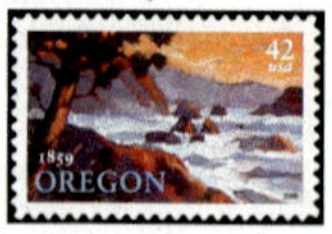


Pacific Coast of Oregon — A3330

**2009, Jan. 14**

**Self-Adhesive**

**4376** A3330 42c multicolored .85 .25

**EDGAR ALLAN POE**

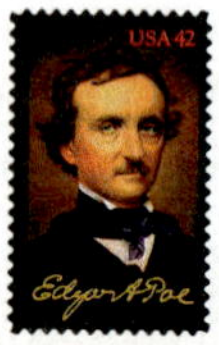

Edgar Allan Poe (1809-49), Writer — A3331

PHOTOGRAVURE

**2009, Jan. 16**

**Self-Adhesive**

**4377** A3331 42c multicolored .90 .25

**AMERICAN LANDMARKS**

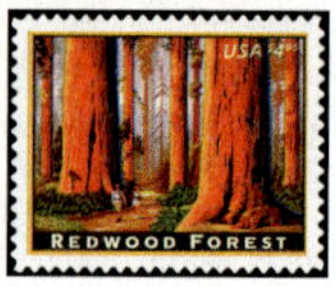


Redwood Forest — A3332

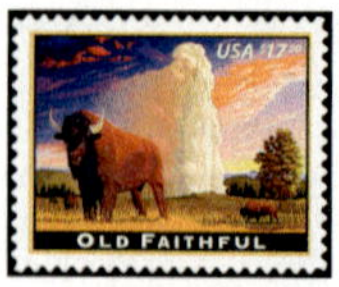


Old Faithful — A3333

LITHOGRAPHED

***Serpentine Die Cut 10¾x10½***

**2009, Jan. 16**

**Self-Adhesive**

**4378** A3332 $4.95 multi 11.00 5.00
**4379** A3333 $17.50 multi 40.00 20.00

**ABRAHAM LINCOLN (1809-65), 16TH PRESIDENT**

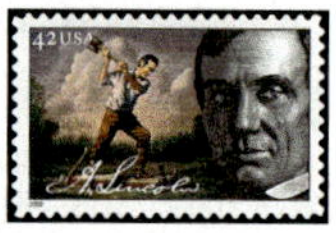

Lincoln as Rail-splitter A3334

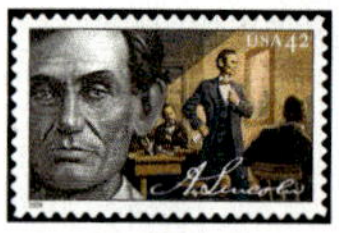

Lincoln as Lawyer — A3335

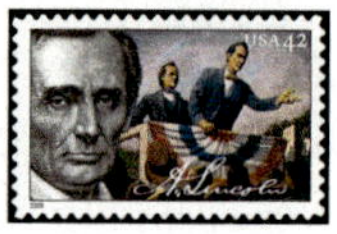

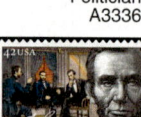

Lincoln as Politician A3336

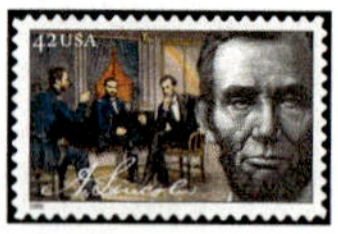

Lincoln as President A3337

***Serpentine Die Cut 10¾***

**2009, Feb. 9**

**Self-Adhesive**

**4380** A3334 42c multicolored 1.50 .35
**4381** A3335 42c multicolored 1.50 .35
**4382** A3336 42c multicolored 1.50 .35
**4383** A3337 42c multicolored 1.50 .35
*a.* Horiz. strip of 4, #4380-4383 6.00

**CIVIL RIGHTS PIONEERS**

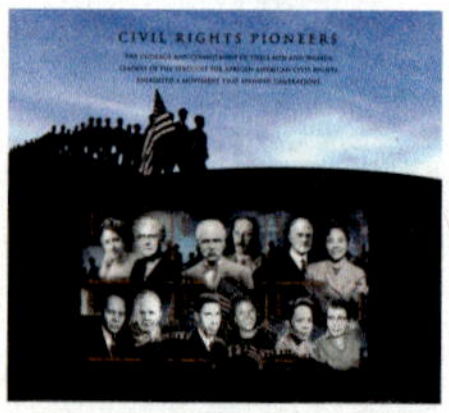


A3338

No. 4384: a, Mary Church Terrell (1863-1954), writer, Mary White Ovington (1865-1951), journalist. b, J. R. Clifford (1848-1933), attorney, Joel Elias Spingarn (1875-1939), educator. c, Oswald Garrison Villard (1872-1949), co-founder of National Association for the Advancement of Colored People (NAACP), Daisy Gatson Bates (1914-99), mentor of black Little Rock Central High School students. d, Charles Hamilton Houston (1895-1950), lawyer, Walter White (1893-1955), chief secretary of NAACP. e, Medgar Evers (1925-63), assassinated Mississippi NAACP field secretary, Fannie Lou Hamer (1917-77), voting rights activist. f, Ella Baker (1903-86), activist, Ruby Hurley (1909-80), NAACP Southeast Regional Director.

PHOTOGRAVURE

**2009, Feb. 21**

**Self-Adhesive**

**4384** A3338 Pane of 6 9.00
*a.-f.* 42c Any single 1.50 .40

**Patriotic Banner Type of 2007**

LITHOGRAPHED

COIL STAMP

***Perf. 9¾ Vert.***

**2009, Feb. 24** **Untagged**

**4385** A3167 (10c) multicolored .30 .25

See Nos. 4157-4158.

**LITERARY ARTS**

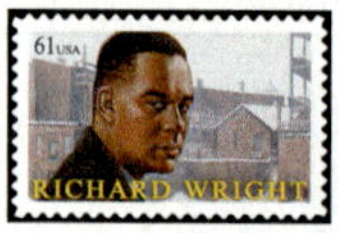


Richard Wright (1908-60), Author — A3339

***Serpentine Die Cut 10¾***

**2009, Apr. 9**

**Self-Adhesive**

**4386** A3339 61c multicolored 1.25 .25

**WILDLIFE**

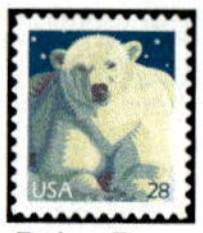

Polar Bear A3340

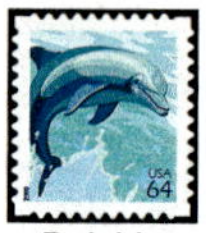

Dolphin A3341

LITHOGRAPHED (#4387), PHOTOGRAVURE

**2009** ***Serpentine Die Cut 11¼x11***

**Self-Adhesive**

**4387** A3340 28c multi .75 .25
*a.* Die cutting omitted, pane of 20 *7,250.*

***Serpentine Die Cut 11***

**4388** A3341 64c multi 1.40 .25

**COIL STAMP**

***Serpentine Die Cut 8½ Vert.***

**4389** A3340 28c multi .60 .25

Issued: Nos. 4387, 4389, 4/16; No. 4388, 6/12.

**Purple Heart Type of 2003**

LITHOGRAPHED

***Serpentine Die Cut 11¼x10¾***

**2009, Apr. 28**

**Self-Adhesive**

**4390** A2891 44c multicolored .90 .25

See Nos. 3784-3784A, 4032, 4164, 4263-4264.

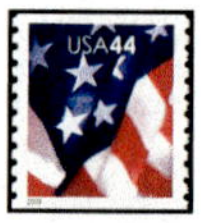

Flag — A3342

LITHOGRAPHED

**2009** ***Perf. 9¾ Vert.***

**COIL STAMPS**

**4391** A3342 44c multi 1.00 1.00

**Self-Adhesive**

***Serpentine Die Cut 11 Vert.***

**With Pointed Corners**

**4392** A3342 44c multi 2.00 .25
*a.* Die cutting omitted, pair *350.00*

***Serpentine Die Cut 9½ Vert.***

**4393** A3342 44c multi 1.50 .25

***Serpentine Die Cut 8½ Vert.***

PHOTOGRAVURE

**4394** A3342 44c multi 1.50 .25

***Serpentine Die Cut 11 Vert.***

**With Rounded Corners**

**4395** A3342 44c multi 1.25 .25

**BOOKLET STAMP**

***Serpentine Die Cut 11¼x10¾ on 3 Sides***

**4396** A3342 44c multi .90 .25
*a.* Booklet pane of 10 9.00

Nos. 4392-4394 are on backing paper as high as the stamp. No. 4395 is on backing paper that is taller than the stamp. No. 4393

# UNITED STATES

has microprinted "USPS" on white stripe below the blue field.
Issued: Nos. 4391, 4395, 5/1; Nos. 4392-4394, 5/8, No. 4396, 6/5.

## WEDDINGS

Wedding Rings
A3343

Wedding Cake
A3344

**LITHOGRAPHED, PHOTOGRAVURE (#4398)**
*Serpentine Die Cut 10¾*
**2009, May 1**
**Self-Adhesive**

| 4397 | A3343 | 44c multicolored | .90 | .25 |
| 4398 | A3344 | 61c multicolored | 1.40 | .25 |

See Nos. 4521, 4602, 4735, 4867, 5000.

## THE SIMPSONS TELEVISION SHOW, 20TH ANNIV.

Homer Simpson
A3345

Marge Simpson
A3346

Bart Simpson
A3347

Lisa Simpson
A3348

Maggie Simpson — A3349

**LITHOGRAPHED BOOKLET STAMPS**
*Serpentine Die Cut 10¾ on 2, 3 or 4 Sides*
**2009, May 7**
**Self-Adhesive**

| 4399 | A3345 | 44c multicolored | 1.15 | .40 |
| 4400 | A3346 | 44c multicolored | 1.15 | .40 |
| 4401 | A3347 | 44c multicolored | 1.15 | .40 |
| 4402 | A3348 | 44c multicolored | 1.15 | .40 |
| 4403 | A3349 | 44c multicolored | 1.15 | .40 |
| a. | | Horiz. strip of 5, #4399-4403 | 5.75 | |
| b. | | Booklet pane of 20, 4 each #4399-4403 | 23.00 | |

## LOVE

King of Hearts
A3350

Queen of Hearts
A3351

**PHOTOGRAVURE BOOKLET STAMPS**
*Serpentine Die Cut 10¾ on 2, 3 or 4 Sides*
**2009, May 8**
**Self-Adhesive**

| 4404 | A3350 | 44c multicolored | 1.15 | .25 |
| 4405 | A3351 | 44c multicolored | 1.15 | .25 |
| a. | | Horiz. or vert. pair, #4404-4405 | 2.30 | |
| b. | | Booklet pane of 20, 10 each #4404-4405 | 23.00 | |

## BOB HOPE

Bob Hope (1903-2003), Actor, Comedian — A3352

**LITHOGRAPHED**
*Serpentine Die Cut 10¾*
**2009, May 29**
**Self-Adhesive**

| 4406 | A3352 | 44c multicolored | 1.00 | .25 |

**Celebrate Type of 2007**
**2009, June 10**
**Self-Adhesive**

| 4407 | A3189 | 44c multicolored | .90 | .25 |
| a. | | Die cutting omitted, pair | 175.00 | |

See Nos. 4196, 4335.

## BLACK HERITAGE

Anna Julia Cooper (c. 1858-1964), Educator — A3353

**2009, June 11**
**Self-Adhesive**

| 4408 | A3353 | 44c multicolored | .90 | .25 |

## GULF COAST LIGHTHOUSES

Matagorda Island Lighthouse, Texas
A3354

Sabine Pass Lighthouse, Louisiana
A3355

Biloxi Lighthouse, Mississippi
A3356

Sand Island Lighthouse, Alabama
A3357

Fort Jefferson Lighthouse, Florida — A3358

*Serpentine Die Cut 11x10¾*
**2009, July 23**
**Self-Adhesive**

| 4409 | A3354 | 44c multicolored | .90 | .40 |
| 4410 | A3355 | 44c multicolored | .90 | .40 |
| 4411 | A3356 | 44c multicolored | .90 | .40 |
| 4412 | A3357 | 44c multicolored | .90 | .40 |
| 4413 | A3358 | 44c multicolored | .90 | .40 |
| a. | | Horiz. strip of 5, #4409-4413 | 4.50 | |

## EARLY TV MEMORIES

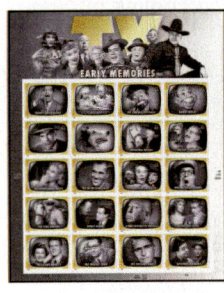
A3359

No. 4414: a, Milton Berle in "Texaco Star Theater." b, Lucille Ball and Vivian Vance in "I Love Lucy." c, Red Skelton in "The Red Skelton Show." d, Marionette Howdy Doody in "Howdy Doody." e, Jack Webb in "Dragnet." f, Lassie in "Lassie." g, William Boyd and horse, Topper, in "Hopalong Cassidy." h, Groucho Marx in "You Bet Your Life." i, Dinah Shore in "The Dinah Shore Show." j, Ed Sullivan in "The Ed Sullivan Show." k, Fran Allison and puppets, Kukla and Ollie in "Kukla, Fran and Ollie." l, Phil Silvers in "The Phil Silvers Show." m, Clayton Moore and horse, Silver, in "The Lone Ranger." n, Raymond Burr and William Talman in "Perry Mason." o, Alfred Hitchcock in "Alfred Hitchcock Presents." p, George Burns and Gracie Allen in "Burns and Allen." q, Ozzie and Harriet Nelson in "Ozzie and Harriet." r, Steve Allen in "The Tonight Show." s, Rod Serling in "The Twilight Zone." t, Jackie Gleason and Art Carney in "The Honeymooners."

*Serpentine Die Cut 10¾x10½*
**2009, Aug. 11**
**Self-Adhesive**

| 4414 | A3359 | Pane of 20 | 20.00 | |
| a.-t. | | 44c Any single | 1.00 | .50 |

## HAWAII STATEHOOD, 50TH ANNIV.

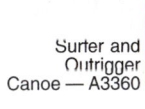
Surfer and Outrigger Canoe — A3360

**PHOTOGRAVURE**
*Serpentine Die Cut 11*
**2009, Aug. 21**
**Self-Adhesive**

| 4415 | A3360 | 44c multicolored | 1.25 | .25 |

**Eid Type of 2001**
**PHOTOGRAVURE**
**2009, Sept. 3**
**Self-Adhesive**

| 4416 | A2734 | 44c multicolored | .90 | .25 |

See Nos. 3532, 3674, 4117, 4202, 4351.

## THANKSGIVING DAY PARADE

Crowd, Street Sign, Bear Balloon — A3361

Drum Major, Musicians A3362

Musicians, Balloon, Horse — A3363

Cowboy, Turkey Balloon, Crowd, Television Cameraman A3364

*Serpentine Die Cut 11x10¾*
**2009, Sept. 9**
**Self-Adhesive**

| 4417 | A3361 | 44c multicolored | .90 | .35 |
| 4418 | A3362 | 44c multicolored | .90 | .35 |
| 4419 | A3363 | 44c multicolored | .90 | .35 |
| 4420 | A3364 | 44c multicolored | .90 | .35 |
| a. | | Horiz. strip of 4, #4417-4420 | 3.60 | |

## LEGENDS OF HOLLYWOOD

Gary Cooper (1901-61), Actor — A3365

*Serpentine Die Cut 11*
**2009, Sept. 10**
**Self-Adhesive**

| 4421 | A3365 | 44c multicolored | 1.00 | .25 |

## SUPREME COURT JUSTICES
Souvenir Sheet

A3366

No. 4422: a, Felix Frankfurter (1882-1965). b, William J. Brennan, Jr. (1906-97). c, Louis D. Brandeis (1856-1941). d, Joseph Story (1779-1845).

**LITHOGRAPHED**
*Serpentine Die Cut 11x10½*
**2009, Sept. 22**
**Self-Adhesive**

| 4422 | A3366 | Pane of 4 | 4.00 | |
| a.-d. | | 44c Any single | 1.00 | .30 |

## KELP FOREST

A3367

Wildlife: a, Brown pelican. b, Western gull, southern sea otters, red sea urchin. c, Harbor seal. d, Lion's mane nudibranch, vert. e, Yellowtail rockfish, white-spotted rose anemone. f, Vermilion rockfish. g, Copper rockfish. h, Pacific rock crab, jeweled top snail. i, Northern kelp crab, vert. j, Treefish, Monterey turban snail, brooding sea anemones.

**PHOTOGRAVURE**
*Serpentine Die Cut 10¾*
**2009, Oct. 1**
**Self-Adhesive**

| 4423 | A3367 | Pane of 10 | 14.00 | |
| a.-j. | | 44c Any single | 1.40 | .40 |

## CHRISTMAS

Madonna and Sleeping Child, by Sassoferrato (Giovanni Battista Salvi)
A3368

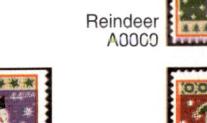
Reindeer
A3369

Snowman
A3370

Gingerbread Man
A3371

Toy Soldier
A3372

Reindeer
A3373

120 UNITED STATES

Snowman
A3374

Gingerbread Man
A3375

Toy Soldier — A3376

### LITHOGRAPHED, PHOTOGRAVURE
(#4429-4432)
*Serpentine Die Cut 10¾x11 on 2 or 3 Sides*
2009
**Self-Adhesive**
**Booklet Stamps**

| | | | | |
|---|---|---|---|---|
| 4424 | A3368 | 44c multicolored | .90 | .25 |
| a. | | Booklet pane of 20 | 18.00 | |
| 4425 | A3369 | 44c multicolored | 1.10 | .25 |
| 4426 | A3370 | 44c multicolored | 1.10 | .25 |
| 4427 | A3371 | 44c multicolored | 1.10 | .25 |
| 4428 | A3372 | 44c multicolored | 1.10 | .25 |
| a. | | Block of 4, #4425-4428 | 4.40 | |
| b. | | Booklet pane of 20, 5 each #4425-4428 | 22.00 | |
| c. | | As "b," die cutting omitted on side with 12 stamps | — | |
| d. | | As "b," die cutting omitted on side with 8 stamps | — | |
| e. | | As "a," die cutting omitted | 375.00 | |

*Serpentine Die Cut 8 on 2, 3 or 4 Sides*

| | | | | |
|---|---|---|---|---|
| 4429 | A3373 | 44c multicolored | 1.25 | .25 |
| 4430 | A3374 | 44c multicolored | 1.25 | .25 |
| 4431 | A3375 | 44c multicolored | 1.25 | .25 |
| 4432 | A3376 | 44c multicolored | 1.25 | .25 |
| a. | | Block or strip of 4, #4429-4432 | 5.00 | |
| b. | | Booklet pane of 18, 5 each #4429, 4431, 4 each #4430, 4432 | 22.50 | |
| | | Nos. 4424-4432 (9) | 10.30 | 2.35 |

No. 4424a is a double-sided booklet pane with 12 stamps on one side and eight stamps plus label that serves as a booklet cover on the other side. No. 4428b is a double-sided booklet pane with 12 stamps on one side (3 each of Nos. 4425-4428) and eight stamps (2 each of Nos. 4425-4428) plus label that serves as a booklet cover on the other side.

### HANUKKAH

Menorah — A3377

**LITHOGRAPHED**
*Serpentine Die Cut 10¾x11*
2009, Oct. 9
**Self-Adhesive**

| | | | | |
|---|---|---|---|---|
| 4433 | A3377 | 44c multicolored | .90 | .25 |

### KWANZAA

Family — A3378

2009, Oct. 9
**Self-Adhesive**

| | | | | |
|---|---|---|---|---|
| 4434 | A3378 | 44c multicolored | .90 | .25 |

### CHINESE NEW YEAR

Year of the Tiger — A3379

**PHOTOGRAVURE**
*Serpentine Die Cut 11*
2010, Jan. 14 Tagged
**Self-Adhesive**

| | | | | |
|---|---|---|---|---|
| 4435 | A3379 | 44c multicolored | 1.10 | .25 |

### 2010 WINTER OLYMPICS, VANCOUVER

Snowboarder — A3380

**PHOTOGRAVURE**
*Serpentine Die Cut 11*
2010, Jan. 22 Tagged
**Self-Adhesive**

| | | | | |
|---|---|---|---|---|
| 4436 | A3380 | 44c multicolored | .90 | .25 |

**"Forever" Liberty Bell Type of 2007**
*Serpentine Die Cut 11¼x10¾ on 2, 3 or 4 Sides*
2010, Feb. 3 Self-Adhesive Litho.
**Booklet Stamp**
**Medium Microprinting, Bell 16mm Wide**
**Dated "2009" in Copper**

| | | | | |
|---|---|---|---|---|
| 4437 | A3148 | (44c) multicolored | 1.40 | .25 |
| a. | | Booklet pane of 18 | 25.20 | |

On No. 4437, the "2009" date is smaller than that on No. 4127i, which has a 15mm wide bell. The bell on No. 4437 is also 17mm tall while No. 4127i is 16mm tall. The microprinted "Forever" is on a dotted background on No. 4437 and on a white background on No. 4127i.

See also Nos. 4125, 4128c.

### AMERICAN LANDMARKS

Mackinac Bridge, Michigan
A3381

Bixby Creek Bridge, California
A3382

**PHOTOGRAVURE**
*Serpentine Die Cut 10¾x10½*
2010, Feb. 3 Tagged
**Self-Adhesive**

| | | | | |
|---|---|---|---|---|
| 4438 | A3381 | $4.90 multi | 11.00 | 5.00 |
| 4439 | A3382 | $18.30 multi | 45.00 | 18.00 |

### DISTINGUISHED SAILORS

Admiral William S. Sims (1858-1936), Emblem of USS W.S. Sims — A3383

Admiral Arleigh A. Burke (1901-96), Emblem of USS Arleigh Burke — A3384

Lieutenant Commander John McCloy (1876-1945), Emblem of USS McCloy — A3385

Petty Officer 3rd Class Doris Miller (1919-43), Emblem of USS Miller — A3386

**PHOTOGRAVURE**
*Serpentine Die Cut 10¾x10½*
2010, Feb. 4 Tagged
**Self-Adhesive**

| | | | | |
|---|---|---|---|---|
| 4440 | A3383 | 44c multicolored | .90 | .40 |
| 4441 | A3384 | 44c multicolored | .90 | .40 |
| 4442 | A3385 | 44c multicolored | .90 | .40 |
| 4443 | A3386 | 44c multicolored | .90 | .40 |
| a. | | Block or horiz. strip of 4, #4440-4443 | 3.60 | |

### ABSTRACT EXPRESSIONISTS

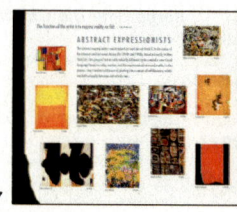
A3387

No. 4444: a, The Golden Wall, by Hans Hofmann (30x30mm). b, Asheville, by Willem de Kooning (38x38mm). c, Orange and Yellow, by Mark Rothko (35x49mm). d, Convergence, by Jackson Pollock (63x43mm). e, The Liver Is the Cock's Comb, by Arshile Gorky (39x32mm). f, 1948-C, by Clyfford Still (35x49mm). g, Elegy to the Spanish Republic No. 34, by Robert Motherwell (54x49mm). h, La Grande Vallée 0, by Joan Mitchell (35x49mm). i, Romanesque Façade, by Adolph Gottlieb (35x49mm). j, Achilles, by Barnett Newman (35x49mm).

**LITHOGRAPHED**
*Serpentine Die Cut 10¾x11, 10¾ (#4444a, 4444b, 4444e), 11x10¾ (#4444d)*
2010, Mar. 11 Tagged
**Self-Adhesive**

| | | | | |
|---|---|---|---|---|
| 4444 | A3387 | Pane of 10 | 12.50 | |
| a.-j. | | 44c Any single | 1.25 | .40 |

### BILL MAULDIN (1921-2003), CARTOONIST

A3388

**LITHOGRAPHED**
*Serpentine Die Cut 10¾*
2010, Mar. 31 Tagged
**Self-Adhesive**

| | | | | |
|---|---|---|---|---|
| 4445 | A3388 | 44c multicolored | .90 | .25 |

### COWBOYS OF THE SILVER SCREEN

Roy Rogers (1911-98)
A3389

Tom Mix (1880-1940)
A3390

William S. Hart (1864-1946)
A3391

Gene Autry (1907-98)
A3392

**LITHOGRAPHED**
*Serpentine Die Cut 10½x10¾*
2010, Apr. 17
**Self-Adhesive**

| | | | | |
|---|---|---|---|---|
| 4446 | A3389 | 44c multicolored | 1.25 | .35 |
| 4447 | A3390 | 44c multicolored | 1.25 | .35 |
| 4448 | A3391 | 44c multicolored | 1.25 | .35 |
| 4449 | A3392 | 44c multicolored | 1.25 | .35 |
| a. | | Block or strip of 4, #4446-4449 | 5.00 | |

### LOVE

Pansies in a Basket — A3393

**PHOTOGRAVURE**
*Serpentine Die Cut 10¾*
2010, Apr. 22
**Self-Adhesive**

| | | | | |
|---|---|---|---|---|
| 4450 | A3393 | 44c multicolored | .90 | .25 |

### ANIMAL RESCUE

Wire-haired Jack Russell Terrier
A3394

Maltese
A3395

Calico
A3396

Yellow Labrador Retriever
A3397

Golden Retriever
A3398

Gray, White and Tan Cat
A3399

Black, White and Tan Cat
A3400

Australian Shepherd
A3401

Boston Terrier
A3402

Orange Tabby
A3403

**LITHOGRAPHED**
*Serpentine Die Cut 10¾*
2010, Apr. 30
**Self-Adhesive**

| | | | | |
|---|---|---|---|---|
| 4451 | A3394 | 44c multicolored | 1.50 | .40 |
| 4452 | A3395 | 44c multicolored | 1.50 | .40 |
| 4453 | A3396 | 44c multicolored | 1.50 | .40 |
| 4454 | A3397 | 44c multicolored | 1.50 | .40 |
| 4455 | A3398 | 44c multicolored | 1.50 | .40 |
| 4456 | A3399 | 44c multicolored | 1.50 | .40 |
| 4457 | A3400 | 44c multicolored | 1.50 | .40 |
| 4458 | A3401 | 44c multicolored | 1.50 | .40 |
| 4459 | A3402 | 44c multicolored | 1.50 | .40 |
| 4460 | A3403 | 44c multicolored | 1.50 | .40 |
| a. | | Block of 10, #4451-4460 | 15.00 | |

### LEGENDS OF HOLLYWOOD

Katharine Hepburn (1907-2003), Actress — A3404

**PHOTOGRAVURE**
*Serpentine Die Cut 10¾*
2010, May 12
**Self-Adhesive**

| | | | | |
|---|---|---|---|---|
| 4461 | A3404 | 44c black | 1.00 | .25 |

UNITED STATES

### MONARCH BUTTERFLY

A3405

**PHOTOGRAVURE**
*Serpentine Die Cut 10½*
2010, May 17
**Self-Adhesive**

4462 A3405 64c multicolored 1.50 .25

### KATE SMITH

Kate Smith (1907-86), Singer — A3406

**PHOTOGRAVURE**
2010, May 27 *Serpentine Die Cut 11*
**Self-Adhesive**

4463 A3406 44c multicolored .90 .25

### BLACK HERITAGE

Oscar Micheaux (1884-1951), Film Director — A3407

*Serpentine Die Cut 11*
2010, June 22
**Self-Adhesive**

4464 A3407 44c multicolored .90 .25

### NEGRO LEAGUES BASEBALL

 Play at the Plate — A3408

Andrew "Rube" Foster (1879-1930), Founder of Negro National League — A3409

**PHOTOGRAVURE**
*Serpentine Die Cut 11*
2010, July 15
**Self-Adhesive**

| 4465 | A3408 | 44c multicolored | .90 | .30 |
| 4466 | A3409 | 44c multicolored | .90 | .30 |
| a. | Horiz. pair, #4465-4466 | | 1.80 | |

### SUNDAY FUNNIES

 Beetle Bailey A3410

 Calvin and Hobbes A3411

 Archie A3412

 Garfield A3413

 Dennis the Menace — A3414

**LITHOGRAPHED**
*Serpentine Die Cut 10½x10¾*
2010, July 16
**Self-Adhesive**

| 4467 | A3410 | 44c multicolored | 1.00 | .30 |
| 4468 | A3411 | 44c multicolored | 1.00 | .30 |
| 4469 | A3412 | 44c multicolored | 1.00 | .30 |
| 4470 | A3413 | 44c multicolored | 1.00 | .30 |
| 4471 | A3414 | 44c multicolored | 1.00 | .30 |
| a. | Horiz. strip of 5, #4467-4471 | | 5.00 | |

### BOY SCOUTS OF AMERICA, CENTENNIAL

Boy Scouts — A3415

**PHOTOGRAVURE**
*Serpentine Die Cut 11*
2010, July 27
**Self-Adhesive**

4472 A3415 44c multicolored .90 .25

 Boys in a Pasture, by Winslow Homer (1836-1910) A3416

*Serpentine Die Cut 10¾*
2010, Aug. 12
**Self-Adhesive**

4473 A3416 44c multicolored 1.00 .25

### HAWAIIAN RAIN FOREST

A3417

No. 4474: a, Hawaii 'amakihi, Hawaii 'elepaio, ohi'a lehua. b, 'Akepa, 'ope'ape'a vert. c, 'I'iwi, haha. d, 'Oma'o, kanawao, 'ohelo kau la'au, vert. e, 'Oha, vert. f, Pulelehua butterfly, kolea lau nui, 'ilihia. g, Koele Mountain damselfly, 'akala, vert. h, 'Apapane, Hawaiian mint, vert. i, Jewel orchid, vert. j, Happyface spider, 'ala'ala wai nui, vert.

**LITHOGRAPHED**
*Serpentine Die Cut 10¾*
2010, Sept. 1
**Self-Adhesive**

| 4474 | A3417 | Pane of 10 | 10.00 | |
| a.-j. | 44c Any single | | 1.00 | .40 |

### MOTHER TERESA

Mother Teresa (1910-97), Humanitarian, 1979 Nobel Peace Laureate — A3418

**PHOTOGRAVURE**
2010, Sept. 5 *Serpentine Die Cut 11*
**Self-Adhesive**

4475 A3418 44c multicolored .90 .25

### LITERARY ARTS

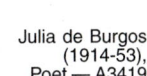
Julia de Burgos (1914-53), Poet — A3419

**PHOTOGRAVURE**
*Serpentine Die Cut 11*
2010, Sept. 14
**Self-Adhesive**

4476 A3419 44c multicolored .90 .25

### CHRISTMAS

Angel with Lute, Detail of Fresco by Melozzo da Forli — A3420

**PHOTOGRAVURE (#4477), LITHOGRAPHED**
*Serpentine Die Cut 10¾*
2010, Oct. 21 Tagged
**Self-Adhesive**

4477 A3420 44c multi 1.00 .25

 Ponderosa Pine A3421

 Eastern Red Cedar A3422

 Balsam Fir A3423

 Blue Spruce A3424

**Booklet Stamps**
*Serpentine Die Cut 11 on 2 or 3 Sides*

| 4478 | A3421 | (44c) multi | 2.50 | .25 |
| 4479 | A3422 | (44c) multi | 2.50 | .25 |
| 4480 | A3423 | (44c) multi | 2.50 | .25 |
| 4481 | A3424 | (44c) multi | 2.50 | .25 |
| a. | Block of 4, #4478-4481 | | 10.00 | |
| b. | Booklet pane of 20, 5 each #4478-4481 | | 50.00 | |
| c. | As "a," die cutting omitted | | — | 500.00 |
| d. | As "b," die cutting omitted on side with 12 stamps | | | 400.00 |
| e. | As "b," die cutting omitted on side with 8 stamps | | | 450.00 |
| f. | As "b," die cutting omitted on side with 12 stamps, die cutting omitted on bottom 4 stamps on side with 8 stamps | | | 950.00 |

 Ponderosa Pine A3425

 Eastern Red Cedar A3426

 Balsam Fir A3427

 Blue Spruce A3428

*Serpentine Die Cut 11¼x10¾ on 2, 3 or 4 Sides*

| 4482 | A3425 | (44c) multi | 2.50 | .25 |
| 4483 | A3426 | (44c) multi | 2.50 | .25 |
| 4484 | A3427 | (44c) multi | 2.50 | .25 |
| 4485 | A3428 | (44c) multi | 2.50 | .25 |
| a. | Block or strip of 4, #4482-4485 | | 10.00 | |

| b. | Booklet pane of 18, 5 each #4482, 4484, 4 each #4483, 4485 | | 45.00 | |
| | Nos. 4477-4485 (9) | | 21.00 | 2.25 |

No. 4481b is a double-sided booklet pane with 12 stamps on one side (3 each of Nos. 4478-4481) and eight stamps (2 each of Nos. 4478-4481) plus label that serves as a booklet cover on the other side.

 Statue of Liberty A3429

 Flag A3430

**LITHOGRAPHED (#4486-4489)**
*Serpentine Die Cut 9½ Vert.*
2010, Dec. 1
**COIL STAMPS**
**Self-Adhesive**

| 4486 | A3429 | (44c) multicolored | 1.50 | .25 |
| 4487 | A3430 | (44c) multicolored | 1.50 | .25 |
| a. | Pair, #4486-4487 | | 3.00 | |

*Serpentine Die Cut 11 Vert.*

| 4488 | A3429 | (44c) multicolored | 1.50 | .25 |
| a. | Vert. pair, horiz. unslit btwn. | | | |
| 4489 | A3430 | (44c) multicolored | 1.50 | .25 |
| a. | Pair, #4488-4489 | | 3.00 | |
| b. | Block of 4 (one pair each from two different coil rolls), horiz. unslit btwn. | | 900.00 | |

*Serpentine Die Cut 8½ Vert.*

| 4490 | A3429 | (44c) multicolored | 1.50 | .25 |
| 4491 | A3430 | (44c) multicolored | 1.50 | .25 |
| a. | Pair, #4490-4491 | | 3.00 | |
| | Nos. 4486-4491 (6) | | 9.00 | 1.50 |

Microprinting reads "4evR" on Nos. 4486-4487, "4evr" on Nos. 4488-4489, and "4EVR" on Nos. 4490-4491. The microprinting is found above the Statue of Liberty's hair, and at the bottom of the lowest red stripe of the flag.
See Nos. 4518-4519, 4559-4564.

### CHINESE NEW YEAR

Year of the Rabbit — A3431

**PHOTOGRAVURE**
*Serpentine Die Cut 11*
2011, Jan. 22
**Self-Adhesive**

4492 A3431 (44c) multicolored 1.40 .25

### KANSAS STATEHOOD, 150TH ANNIV.

Windmill and Wind Turbines — A3432

**LITHOGRAPHED**
*Serpentine Die Cut 11*
2011, Jan. 27
**Self-Adhesive**

4493 A3432 (44c) multicolored 1.40 .25

### PRES. RONALD REAGAN (1911-2004)

Pres. Ronald Reagan — A3433

**PHOTOGRAVURE**
*Serpentine Die Cut 10½*
2011, Feb. 10
**Self-Adhesive**

4494 A3433 (44c) multicolored 1.40 .25

 Art Deco Bird — A3434

## UNITED STATES

**LITHOGRAPHED**
*Serpentine Die Cut 10 Vert.*
2011, Feb. 11    Untagged
**COIL STAMP**
Self-Adhesive
4495   A3434   (5c) multicolored   .30   .25

Quill and Inkwell — A3435

**LITHOGRAPHED**
*Serpentine Die Cut 11¾ Vert.*
2011, Feb. 14
**COIL STAMP**
Self-Adhesive
4496   A3435   44c multicolored   .95   .25

**LATIN MUSIC LEGENDS**

Tito Puente (1923-2000) A3436

Carmen Miranda (1909-55) A3437

Selena (1971-95) A3438

Carlos Gardel (1890-1935) A3439

Celia Cruz (1925-2003) — A3440

**PHOTOGRAVURE**
*Serpentine Die Cut 10¾*
2011, Mar. 16
Self-Adhesive
4497   A3436   (44c) multicolored   1.40   .40
4498   A3437   (44c) multicolored   1.40   .40
4499   A3438   (44c) multicolored   1.40   .40
4500   A3439   (44c) multicolored   1.40   .40
4501   A3440   (44c) multicolored   1.40   .40
   a.   Horiz. strip of 5, #4497-4501   7.00

**CELEBRATE**

A3441

**PHOTOGRAVURE**
*Serpentine Die Cut 11x11½*
2011, Mar. 25
Self-Adhesive
4502   A3441   (44c) multicolored   1.40   .25
Compare with type A3855.
Counterfeits exist of No. 4502. See the Postal Counterfeits section of this catalog.

**JAZZ**

Musicians — A3442

**PHOTOGRAVURE**
*Serpentine Die Cut 10¾*
2011, Mar. 26
Self-Adhesive
4503   A3442   (44c) multicolored   1.40   .25

**Statue of Liberty and Flag Types of 2010 and**

George Washington — A3443

**LITHOGRAPHED (#4504, 4518-4519)**
2011    *Serpentine Die Cut 11¼x10¾*
Self-Adhesive
4504   A3443   20c multicolored   .40   .25

Oregano A3444

Flax A3445

Foxglove A3446

Lavender A3447

Sage A3448

Oveta Culp Hobby (1905-95), First Health, Education and Welfare Department Secretary A3449

**PHOTOGRAVURE (#4505-4510)**
*Serpentine Die Cut 11*
4505   A3444   29c multicolored   1.50   .25
4506   A3445   29c multicolored   1.50   .25
4507   A3446   29c multicolored   1.50   .25
4508   A3447   29c multicolored   1.50   .25
4509   A3448   29c multicolored   1.50   .25
   a.   Horiz. strip of 5, #4505-4509   7.50
4510   A3449   84c multicolored   1.75   .35

New River Gorge Bridge, West Virginia — A3450

**LITHOGRAPHED (#4511)**
*Serpentine Die Cut 10¾x10½*
4511   A3450   $4.95 multicolored   10.00   5.00
   Nos. 4504-4511 (7)   17.90   6.50

**LITHOGRAPHED (#4512)**
**Coil Stamps**
*Serpentine Die Cut 9½ Vert.*
4512   A3443   20c multicolored   .40   .25
No. 4512a is recorded only on a single cover bearing a strip of 9 and three strips of 10. The editors would welcome reports of unused examples.

**LITHOGRAPHED (#4512)**
*Serpentine Die Cut 8½ Vert.*
4513   A3446   29c multicolored   2.00   .25
4514   A3447   29c multicolored   2.00   .25
4515   A3448   29c multicolored   2.00   .25
4516   A3444   29c multicolored   2.00   .25
4517   A3445   29c multicolored   2.00   .25
   a.   Horiz. strip of 5, #4513-4517   10.00
   Nos. 4512-4517 (6)   10.40   1.50

**LITHOGRAPHED (#4518-4519)**
**Booklet Stamps**
**Thin Paper**
*Serpentine Die Cut 11¼x10¾ on 2, 3, or 4 Sides*
4518   A3429   (44c) multicolored   1.40   .25
4519   A3430   (44c) multicolored   1.40   .25
   a.   Pair, #4518-4519   2.80
   b.   Booklet pane of 18, 9 each #4518-4519   25.20

Issued: Nos. 4504, 4511, 4512, 4/11; Nos. 4505-4509, 4513-4517, 4/7; No. 4510, 4/15; Nos. 4518-4519, 4/8.

**Wedding Cake Type of 2009 With "USA" in Serifed Type and**

Wedding Roses — A3450i

**LITHOGRAPHED (#4520), PHOTOGRAVURE (#4521)**
2011    *Serpentine Die Cut 11*
Self-Adhesive
4520   A3450i   (44c) multicolored   5.00   .25
   a.   Die cutting omitted, pair   250.00
4521   A3344   64c multicolored   2.50   .25

**CIVIL WAR SESQUICENTENNIAL**

Battle of Fort Sumter A3451

First Battle of Bull Run A3452

**LITHOGRAPHED**
*Serpentine Die Cut 11*
2011, Apr. 12
Self-Adhesive
4522   A3451   (44c) multicolored   1.40   .30
4523   A3452   (44c) multicolored   1.40   .30
   a.   Pair, #4522-4523   2.80

**GO GREEN**

A3453

No. 4524 — Messages: a, Buy local produce, reuse bags. b, Fix water leaks. c, Share rides. d, Turn off lights not in use. e, Choose to walk. f, Go Green, reduce our environmental footprint step by step. g, Compost. h, Let nature do the work. i, Recycle more. j, Ride a bike. k, Plant trees. l, Insulate the home. m, Use public transportation. n, Use efficient light bulbs. o, Adjust the thermostat. p, Maintain tire pressure.

**PHOTOGRAVURE**
*Serpentine Die Cut 10¾*
2011, Apr. 14
Self-Adhesive
4524   A3453   Pane of 16   22.40
   a.-p.   (44c) Any single   1.40   .50

**HELEN HAYES**

Helen Hayes (1900-93), Actress — A3454

*Serpentine Die Cut 11*
2011, Apr. 25    Tagged
Self-Adhesive
4525   A3454   (44c) multicolored   1.40   .25

**LEGENDS OF HOLLYWOOD**

Gregory Peck (1916-2003), Actor — A3455

*Serpentine Die Cut 10¾*
2011, Apr. 28
Self-Adhesive
4526   A3455   (44c) black   1.40   .25

**SPACE FIRSTS**

Alan B. Shepard, Jr. (1923-98), First American in Space — A3456

Messenger, First Spacecraft to Orbit Mercury — A3457

**LITHOGRAPHED**
2011, May 4    *Serpentine Die Cut 11*
Self-Adhesive
4527   A3456   (44c) multicolored   1.40   .30
4528   A3457   (44c) multicolored   1.40   .30
   a.   Horiz. pair, #4527-4528   2.80

Purple Heart and Ribbon — A3458

*Serpentine Die Cut 11¼x10¾*
2011, May 5
Self-Adhesive
4529   A3458   (44c) multicolored   1.40   .25

**INDIANAPOLIS 500, CENT.**

Ray Harroun Driving Marmon Wasp — A3459

**LITHOGRAPHED**
*Serpentine Die Cut 10¾*
2011, May 20
Self-Adhesive
4530   A3459   (44c) multicolored   1.40   .25

**GARDEN OF LOVE**

Pink Flower A3460

Red Flower A3461

Blue Flowers A3462

Butterfly A3463

# UNITED STATES

Green Vine Leaves
A3464

Blue Flower
A3465

Doves
A3466

Orange Red Flowers
A3467

Strawberry
A3468

Yellow Orange Flowers
A3469

Designed by Derry Noyes. Printed by Avery Dennison.

**PHOTOGRAVURE**
*Serpentine Die Cut 10¾*
**2011, May 23**
**Self-Adhesive**

| 4531 | A3460 | (44c) multicolored | 2.00 | .40 |
|---|---|---|---|---|
| 4532 | A3461 | (44c) multicolored | 2.00 | .40 |
| 4533 | A3462 | (44c) multicolored | 2.00 | .40 |
| 4534 | A3463 | (44c) multicolored | 2.00 | .40 |
| 4535 | A3464 | (44c) multicolored | 2.00 | .40 |
| 4536 | A3465 | (44c) multicolored | 2.00 | .40 |
| 4537 | A3466 | (44c) multicolored | 2.00 | .40 |
| 4538 | A3467 | (44c) multicolored | 2.00 | .40 |
| 4539 | A3468 | (44c) multicolored | 2.00 | .40 |
| 4540 | A3469 | (44c) multicolored | 2.00 | .40 |
| a. | Block of 10, #4531-4540 | | 20.00 | |
| | Nos. 4531-4540 (10) | | 20.00 | 4.00 |

The two blocks of 10 on the pane are separated by a gutter.

## AMERICAN SCIENTISTS

Melvin Calvin (1911-97), Chemist — A3470

Asa Gray (1810-88), Botanist — A3471

Maria Goeppert Mayer (1906-72), Physicist
A3472

Severo Ochoa (1905-93), Biochemist
A3473

**LITHOGRAPHED**
*Serpentine Die Cut 11*
**2011, June 16**
**Self-Adhesive**

| 4541 | A3470 | (44c) multicolored | 1.40 | .50 |
|---|---|---|---|---|
| 4542 | A3471 | (44c) multicolored | 1.40 | .50 |
| 4543 | A3472 | (44c) multicolored | 1.40 | .50 |
| 4544 | A3473 | (44c) multicolored | 1.40 | .50 |
| a. | Horiz. strip of 4, #4541-4544 | | 5.60 | |
| b. | Horiz. strip of 4, die cutting missing on backing paper (from misaligned die-cutting mat) | | 375.00 | |

## LITERARY ARTS

Mark Twain (Samuel L. Clemens) (1835-1910), Writer — A3474

**PHOTOGRAVURE**
*Serpentine Die Cut 11*
**2011, June 25**
**Self-Adhesive**

| 4545 | A3474 | (44c) multicolored | 1.40 | .25 |
|---|---|---|---|---|

## PIONEERS OF AMERICAN INDUSTRIAL DESIGN

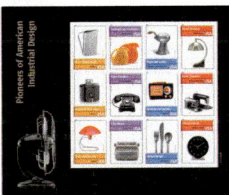
A3475

No. 4546: a, "Normandie" pitcher, designed by Peter Müller-Munk (1904-67). b, Fiesta dinnerware, designed by Frederick Hurten Rhead (1880-1942). c, Streamlined pencil sharpener, designed by Raymond Loewy (1893-1986). d, Table lamp, designed by Donald Deskey (1894-1989). e, Kodak "Baby Brownie" camera, designed by Walter Dorwin Teague (1883-1960). f, Model 302 Bell telephone, designed by Henry Dreyfuss (1904-72). g, Emerson "Patriot" radio, designed by Norman Bel Geddes (1893-1958). h, Streamlined sewing machines, designed by Dave Chapman (1909-78). i, "Anywhere" lamp, designed by Greta von Nessen (1900-74). j, IBM "Selectric" typewriter, designed by Eliot Noyes (1910-77). k, "Highlight/Pinch" flatware, designed by Russel Wright (1904-76). l, Herman Miller electric clock, designed by Gilbert Rohde (1894-1944).

**PHOTOGRAVURE**
*Serpentine Die Cut 10¾*
**2011, June 29**
**Self-Adhesive**

| 4546 | A3475 | Pane of 12 | 16.80 | |
|---|---|---|---|---|
| a.-l. | | (44c) Any single | 1.40 | .50 |

## OWNEY, THE POSTAL DOG

Owney, His Medals and Tags — A3476

**PHOTOGRAVURE**
*Serpentine Die Cut 11*
**2011, July 27**
**Self-Adhesive**

| 4547 | A3476 | (44c) multicolored | 1.50 | .25 |
|---|---|---|---|---|

## U.S. MERCHANT MARINE

Clipper Ship — A3477

Auxiliary Steamship
A3478

Liberty Ship — A3479

Container Ship — A3480

**PHOTOGRAVURE**
*Serpentine Die Cut 11*
**2011, July 28**
**Self-Adhesive**

| 4548 | A3477 | (44c) multicolored | 1.40 | .35 |
|---|---|---|---|---|
| 4549 | A3478 | (44c) multicolored | 1.40 | .35 |
| 4550 | A3479 | (44c) multicolored | 1.40 | .35 |
| 4551 | A3480 | (44c) multicolored | 1.40 | .35 |
| a. | Block or horiz. strip of 4, #4548-4551 | | 5.60 | |

## EID

"Eid Mubarak" — A3481

**PHOTOGRAVURE**
*Serpentine Die Cut 11¼*
**2011, Aug. 12**
**Self-Adhesive**

| 4552 | A3481 | (44c) mar, gray & gold | 1.40 | .25 |
|---|---|---|---|---|

## CHARACTERS FROM DISNEY-PIXAR FILMS
*Send a Hello*

Lightning McQueen and Mater from *Cars*
A3482

Remy the Rat and Linguini from *Ratatouille*
A3483

Buzz Lightyear and Aliens from *Toy Story* — A3484

Carl Fredricksen and Dug the Dog from *Up* — A3485

WALL-E from *WALL-E* — A3486

**PHOTOGRAVURE**
*Serpentine Die Cut 10½*
**2011, Aug. 19**
**Self-Adhesive**

| 4553 | A3482 | (44c) multicolored | 1.40 | .40 |
|---|---|---|---|---|
| 4554 | A3483 | (44c) multicolored | 1.40 | .40 |
| 4555 | A3484 | (44c) multicolored | 1.40 | .40 |
| 4556 | A3485 | (44c) multicolored | 1.40 | .40 |
| 4557 | A3486 | (44c) multicolored | 1.40 | .40 |
| a. | Horiz. strip of 5, #4553-4557 | | 7.00 | |

Adjacent horizontal or vertical stamps will have selvage between the stamps.

## AMERICAN TREASURES SERIES

The Long Leg, by Edward Hopper (1882-1967)
A3487

**PHOTOGRAVURE**
*Serpentine Die Cut 11*
**2011, Aug. 24**
**Self-Adhesive**

| 4558 | A3487 | (44c) multicolored | 1.40 | .25 |
|---|---|---|---|---|

## Statue of Liberty and Flag Types of 2010
**LITHOGRAPHED (#4559-4562), PHOTOGRAVURE**
*Serpentine Die Cut 11¼x11 on 2 or 3 Sides*
**2011, Sept. 14**
**BOOKLET STAMPS**
**Self-Adhesive**

| 4559 | A3429 | (44c) multicolored | 1.50 | .25 |
|---|---|---|---|---|
| 4560 | A3430 | (44c) multicolored | 1.50 | .25 |
| a. | Pair, #4559-4560 | | 3.00 | |
| b. | Booklet pane of 20, 10 each #4559-4560 | | 30.00 | |
| 4561 | A3429 | (44c) multicolored | 1.50 | .25 |
| 4562 | A3430 | (44c) multicolored | 1.50 | .25 |
| a. | Pair, #4561-4562 | | 3.00 | |
| b. | Booklet pane of 20, 10 each #4561-4562 | | 30.00 | |

*Serpentine Die Cut 11¼x11½ on 2 or 3 Sides*

| 4563 | A3429 | (44c) multicolored | 1.50 | .25 |
|---|---|---|---|---|
| 4564 | A3430 | (44c) multicolored | 1.50 | .25 |
| a. | Pair, #4563-4564 | | 3.00 | |
| b. | Booklet pane of 20, 10 each #4563-4564 | | 30.00 | |
| | Nos. 4559-4564 (6) | | 9.00 | 1.50 |

Microprinting reads "4evR" on Nos. 4559-4560, "4evr" on Nos. 4561-4562, and "4EVR" on Nos. 4563-4564. The microprinting is found above the Statue of Liberty's hair, and at the bottom of the lowest red stripe of the flag. Nos. 4560b, 4562b and 4564b are double-sided booklet panes with 12 stamps one one side (6 each of types A3429-A3430) and 8 stamps (4 each of types A3429-A3430) on the other side. The paper used on Nos. 4561-4562 is thicker than that used on Nos. 4518-4519.

## BLACK HERITAGE

Barbara Jordan (1936-96), Congresswoman
A3488

**LITHOGRAPHED**
*Serpentine Die Cut 10¾*
**2011, Sept. 16**
**Self-Adhesive**

| 4565 | A3488 | (44c) multicolored | 1.40 | .25 |
|---|---|---|---|---|

## ART OF ROMARE BEARDEN (1911-88)

Conjunction
A3489

Odysseus: Poseidon, The Sea God - Enemy of Odysseus
A3490

Prevalence of Ritual: Conjur Woman
A3491

Falling Star
A3492

**PHOTOGRAVURE**
*Serpentine Die Cut 10¾*
**2011, Sept. 28**
**Self-Adhesive**

| 4566 | A3489 | (44c) multicolored | 1.40 | .40 |
|---|---|---|---|---|
| 4567 | A3490 | (44c) multicolored | 1.40 | .40 |
| 4568 | A3491 | (44c) multicolored | 1.40 | .40 |
| 4569 | A3492 | (44c) multicolored | 1.40 | .40 |
| a. | Horiz. strip of 4, #4566-4569 | | 5.60 | |

## CHRISTMAS

Madonna of the Candelabra, by Raphael — A3493

124 UNITED STATES

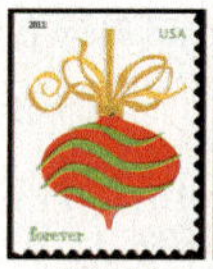 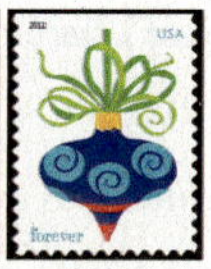

A3494 A3495

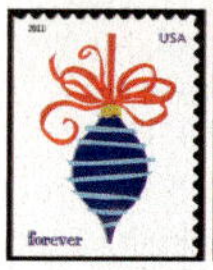 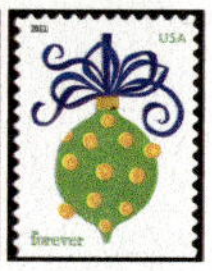

A3496 A3497

LITHOGRAPHED

***Serpentine Die Cut 10¾x 11 on 2 or 3 Sides***

**2011, Oct. 13**

**Booklet Stamps**
**Self-Adhesive**

**4570** A3493 (44c) multicolored 1.40 .25
*a.* Booklet pane of 20 28.00

**With "USPS" Microprinted on Collar of Ornament**

**4571** A3494 (44c) multicolored 1.50 .25
**4572** A3495 (44c) multicolored 1.50 .25
**4573** A3496 (44c) multicolored 1.50 .25
**4574** A3497 (44c) multicolored 1.50 .25
*a.* Block of 4, #4571-4574 6.00
*b.* Booklet pane of 20, 5 each #4571-4574 30.00

**Microprinted "USPS" in Places Other Than Collar of Ornament**

**4575** A3494 (44c) multicolored 1.50 .25
**4576** A3495 (44c) multicolored 1.50 .25
**4577** A3496 (44c) multicolored 1.50 .25
**4578** A3497 (44c) multicolored 1.50 .25
*a.* Block of 4, #4575-4578 6.00
*b.* Booklet pane of 20, 5 each #4575-4578 30.00

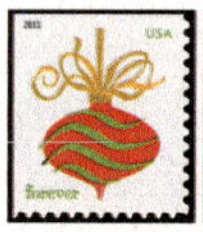 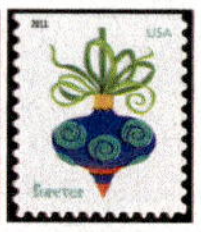

A3498 A3499

 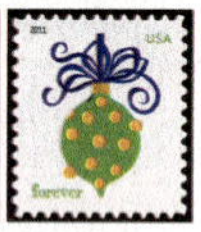

Ornaments
A3500 A3501

***Serpentine Die Cut 11¼x11 on 2, 3 or 4 Sides***

**4579** A3498 (44c) multicolored 2.00 .25
**4580** A3499 (44c) multicolored 2.00 .25
**4581** A3500 (44c) multicolored 2.00 .25
**4582** A3501 (44c) multicolored 2.00 .25
*a.* Block or strip of 4, #4579-4582 8.00
*b.* Booklet pane of 18, 5 each #4579, 4582, 4 each #4580-4581 36.00
*Nos. 4570-4582 (13)* 21.40 3.25

The microprinted "USPS" is to the left of the third stripe on Nos. 4575 and 4579, on the left side of the bottom ribbon of the ribbon cluster above the ornament collar on Nos. 4576 and 4578, below the bottom stripe near the bottom tip on No. 4577, on the vertical ribbon on No. 4580, on a curved ribbon above the collar on No. 4581, and on the left side of the ornament, below the collar, on No. 4582.

No. 4570a is a double-sided booklet with 12 stamps on one side and eight stamps plus a label that serves as a booklet cover on the other side. Nos. 4574b and 4578b are double sided booklets with 12 stamps (3 each of types A3494-A3497) on one side and eight stamps (2 each of types A3494-A3497) plus a label that serves as a booklet cover on the other side.

**HANUKKAH**

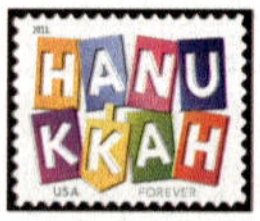

A3502

***Serpentine Die Cut 11x10¾***

**2011, Oct. 14**

**Self-Adhesive**

**4583** A3502 (44c) multicolored 1.40 .25

**KWANZAA**

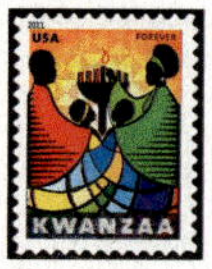

Family — A3503

***Serpentine Die Cut 10¾x11***

**2011, Oct. 14**

**Self-Adhesive**

**4584** A3503 (44c) multicolored 1.40 .25

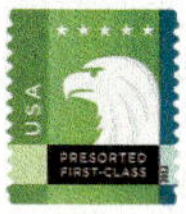

Eagle — A3504

PHOTOGRAVURE

***Serpentine Die Cut 11 Vert.***

**2012, Jan. 3**

**Coil Stamps**
**Self-Adhesive**
**Color Behind "USA"**

**4585** A3504 (25c) green .50 .25
**4586** A3504 (25c) blue green .50 .25
**4587** A3504 (25c) blue .50 .25
**4588** A3504 (25c) red violet .50 .25
**4589** A3504 (25c) brown orange .50 .25
**4590** A3504 (25c) yellow orange .50 .25
*a.* Strip of 6, #4585-4590 3.00

**NEW MEXICO STATEHOOD CENTENNIAL**

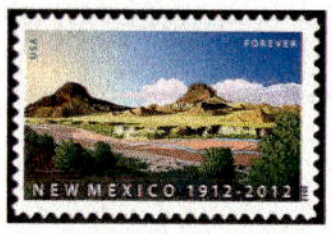

Sanctuary II, Painting by Doug West — A3505

PHOTOGRAVURE

**2012, Jan. 6** ***Serpentine Die Cut 11***

**Self-Adhesive**

**4591** A3505 (44c) multicolored 1.40 .25

**ALOHA SHIRTS**

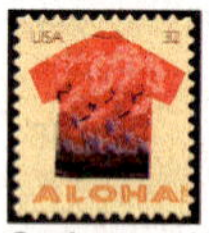 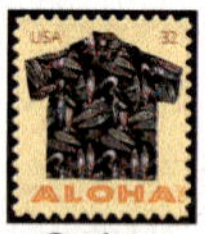

Surfers and Palm Trees A3506 — Surfers A3507

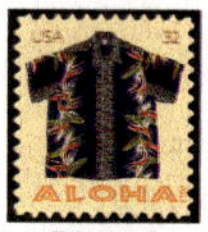 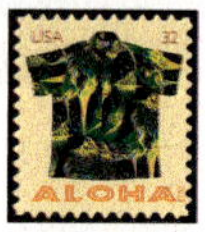

Bird of Paradise Flowers A3508 — Kilauea Volcano A3509

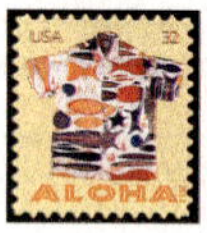

Fossil Fish, Shells and Starfish — A3510

PHOTOGRAVURE

***Serpentine Die Cut 11***

**2012, Jan. 19**

**Self-Adhesive**

**4592** A3506 32c multicolored 2.00 .30
**4593** A3507 32c multicolored 2.00 .30
**4594** A3508 32c multicolored 2.00 .30
**4595** A3509 32c multicolored 2.00 .30
**4596** A3510 32c multicolored 2.00 .30
*a.* Horiz. strip of 5, #4592-4596 10.00

LITHOGRAPHED

**Coil Stamps**

***Serpentine Die Cut 11 Vert.***

**4597** A3510 32c multicolored 2.00 .30
**4598** A3506 32c multicolored 2.00 .30
**4599** A3507 32c multicolored 2.00 .30
**4600** A3508 32c multicolored 2.00 .30
**4601** A3509 32c multicolored 2.00 .30
*a.* Strip of 5, #4597-4601 10.00
*b.* As "a," die cutting omitted 125.00
*Nos. 4592-4601 (10)* 20.00 3.00

On Nos. 4592-4596, the top of the shirt collars are all higher than the cross line of the "A" in "USA," and on Nos. 4597-4601, they are even with or slightly below the cross line.

See Nos. 4682-4686.

**Wedding Cake Type of 2009**

LITHOGRAPHED

***Serpentine Die Cut 10¾***

**2012, Jan. 20**

**Self-Adhesive**

**4602** A3344 65c multicolored 2.50 .25

See Nos. 4398, 4521, 4735, 4867, 5000.

**BALTIMORE CHECKERSPOT BUTTERFLY**

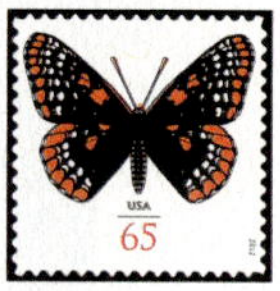

A3511

PHOTOGRAVURE

***Serpentine Die Cut 10¾***

**2012, Jan. 20**

**Self-Adhesive**

**4603** A3511 65c multicolored 1.50 .25

**DOGS AT WORK**

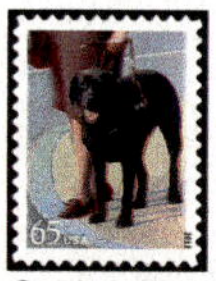 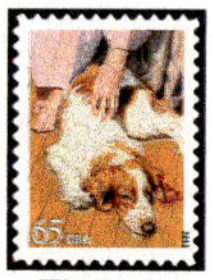

Seeing Eye Dog A3512 — Therapy Dog A3513

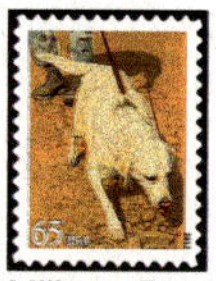 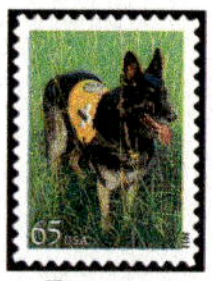

Military Dog A3514 — Rescue Dog A3515

PHOTOGRAVURE

***Serpentine Die Cut 10¾***

**2012, Jan. 20**

**Self-Adhesive**

**4604** A3512 65c multicolored 1.30 .30
**4605** A3513 65c multicolored 1.30 .30
**4606** A3514 65c multicolored 1.30 .30
**4607** A3515 65c multicolored 1.30 .30
*a.* Block or vert. strip of 4, #4604-4607 5.20

**BIRDS OF PREY**

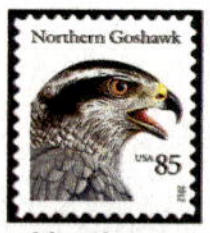 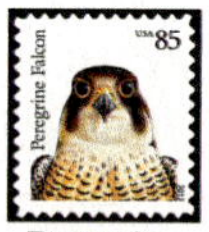

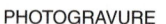

Northern Goshawk A3516 — Peregrine Falcon A3517

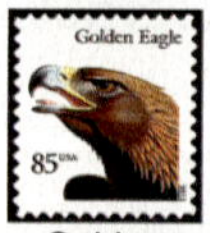 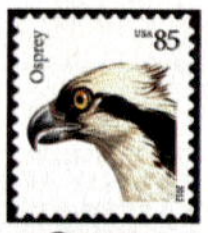

Golden Eagle A3518 — Osprey A3519

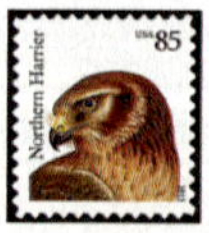

Northern Harrier — A3520

LITHOGRAPHED

***Serpentine Die Cut 11¼x10¾***

**2012, Jan. 20**

**Self-Adhesive**

**4608** A3516 85c multicolored 1.75 .35
**4609** A3517 85c multicolored 1.75 .35
**4610** A3518 85c multicolored 1.75 .35
**4611** A3519 85c multicolored 1.75 .35
**4612** A3520 85c multicolored 1.75 .35
*a.* Horiz. strip of 5, #4608-4612 8.75

**WEATHER VANES**

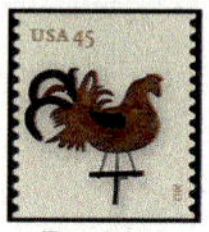 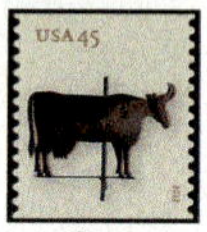

Rooster With Perch A3521 — Cow A3522

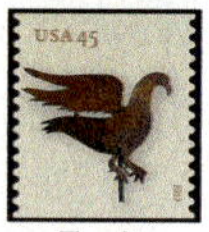 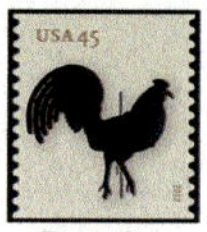

Eagle A3523 — Rooster Without Perch A3524

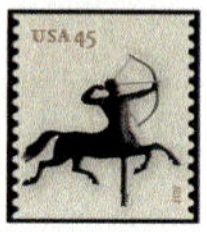

Centaur — A3525

LITHOGRAPHED

***Serpentine Die Cut 11¾ Vert.***

**2012, Jan. 20**

**Coil Stamps**
**Self-Adhesive**

**4613** A3521 45c multicolored 1.50 .30
**4614** A3522 45c multicolored 1.50 .30
**4615** A3523 45c multicolored 1.50 .30
**4616** A3524 45c multicolored 1.50 .30
**4617** A3525 45c multicolored 1.50 .30
*a.* Strip of 5, #4613-4617 7.50

**BONSAI**

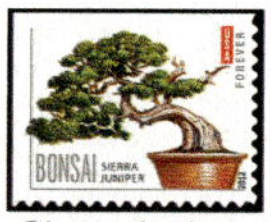 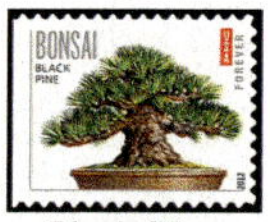

Sierra Juniper A3526 — Black Pine A3527

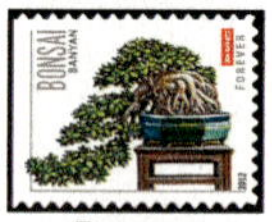 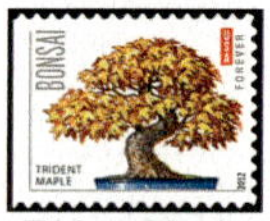

Banyan A3528 — Trident Maple A3529

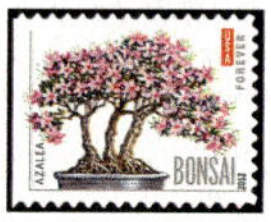

Azalea — A3530

LITHOGRAPHED

***Serpentine Die Cut 11x10¾ on 2 or 3 Sides***

**2012, Jan. 23**

**Booklet Stamps**
**Self-Adhesive**

**4618** A3526 (45c) multicolored 2.00 .40
**4619** A3527 (45c) multicolored 2.00 .40
**4620** A3528 (45c) multicolored 2.00 .40
**4621** A3529 (45c) multicolored 2.00 .40
**4622** A3530 (45c) multicolored 2.00 .40
*a.* Vert. strip of 5, #4618-4622 10.00
*b.* Booklet pane of 20, 4 each #4618-4622 40.00

Stamps in No. 4622a are not adjacent, as rows of selvage are between stamps two and three, and between stamps four and five.

No. 4622b is a double-sided booklet with 12 stamps on one side (3 each #4618, 4621, 2 each #4619, 4620, 4622) and eight stamps (#4618, 4621, 2 each #4619, 4620, 4622) plus label that serves as a booklet cover on the other side.

**CHINESE NEW YEAR**

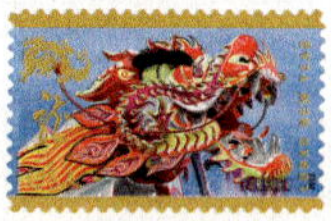

Year of the Dragon — A3531

# UNITED STATES

### PHOTOGRAVURE
*Serpentine Die Cut 11x10¾*
2012, Jan. 23
**Self-Adhesive**

| 4623 | A3531 | (45c) multicolored | 1.40 | .25 |

### BLACK HERITAGE

John H. Johnson (1918-2005), Magazine Publisher — A3532

### LITHOGRAPHED
*Serpentine Die Cut 10¾*
2012, Jan. 31
**Self-Adhesive**

| 4624 | A3532 | (45c) multicolored | 1.40 | .25 |

### HEART HEALTH

Tree, Man, Sun and Apple — A3533

### PHOTOGRAVURE
2012, Feb. 9 *Serpentine Die Cut 11*
**Self-Adhesive**

| 4625 | A3533 | (45c) multicolored | 1.40 | .25 |

### LOVE

Ribbons — A3534

### LITHOGRAPHED
*Serpentine Die Cut 10¾*
2012, Feb. 14
**Self-Adhesive**

| 4626 | A3534 | (45c) red | 1.40 | .25 |
| a. | Die cutting omitted, pair | | 200.00 | |

Postal Service officials declared on Feb. 2 that No. 4626 could be sold in post offices as of that date to make the stamp available to customers before St. Valentine's Day, but the first day ceremony for the stamp was held Feb. 14 in Colorado Springs, CO. Official first day covers have that date and city.

### ARIZONA STATEHOOD CENTENNIAL

Cathedral Rock — A3535

### PHOTOGRAVURE
*Serpentine Die Cut 11*
2012, Feb. 14
**Self-Adhesive**

| 4627 | A3535 | (45c) multicolored | 1.40 | .25 |

### DANNY THOMAS

Thomas (1912-91), Comedian, and St. Jude's Children's Research Hospital, Memphis
A3536

### LITHOGRAPHED
*Serpentine Die Cut 10¾x10½*
2012, Feb. 16
**Self-Adhesive**

| 4628 | A3536 | (45c) multicolored | 1.40 | .25 |

Flag and "Equality" A3537

Flag and "Freedom" A3539

Flag and "Justice" A3538

Flag and "Liberty" A3540

### PHOTOGRAVURE
*Serpentine Die Cut 8½ Vert.*
2012, Feb. 22
**Coil Stamps**
**Self-Adhesive**

| 4629 | A3537 | (45c) multicolored | 1.50 | .25 |
| 4630 | A3538 | (45c) multicolored | 1.50 | .25 |
| 4631 | A3539 | (45c) multicolored | 1.50 | .25 |
| 4632 | A3540 | (45c) multicolored | 1.50 | .25 |
| a. | Strip of 4, #4629-4632 | | 6.00 | |

### LITHOGRAPHED (#4633-4648)
*Serpentine Die Cut 9½ Vert.*

| 4633 | A3537 | (45c) multicolored | 1.40 | .25 |
| 4634 | A3538 | (45c) multicolored | 1.40 | .25 |
| 4635 | A3539 | (45c) multicolored | 1.40 | .25 |
| 4636 | A3540 | (45c) multicolored | 1.40 | .25 |
| b. | Strip of 4, #4633-4636 | | 5.60 | |

*Serpentine Die Cut 11 Vert.*

| 4637 | A3537 | (45c) multicolored | 1.50 | .25 |
| 4638 | A3538 | (45c) multicolored | 1.50 | .25 |
| 4639 | A3539 | (45c) multicolored | 1.50 | .25 |
| 4640 | A3540 | (45c) multicolored | 1.50 | .25 |
| a. | Strip of 4, #4637-4640 | | 6.00 | |
| b. | As "a," die cutting omitted | | 450.00 | |
| | Nos. 4629-4640 (12) | | 17.60 | 3.00 |

**Booklet Stamps**
**Colored Dots in Stars**
**18½mm From Lower Left to Lower Right Corners of Flag**
*Serpentine Die Cut 11¼x10¾ on 2 or 3 Sides*

| 4641 | A3539 | (45c) multicolored | 1.40 | .25 |
| 4642 | A3540 | (45c) multicolored | 1.40 | .25 |
| 4643 | A3537 | (45c) multicolored | 1.40 | .25 |
| 4644 | A3538 | (45c) multicolored | 1.40 | .25 |
| b. | Block of 4, #4641-4644 | | 5.60 | |
| c. | Booklet pane of 20, 5 each #4641-4644 | | 28.00 | |

**Dark Dots Only in Stars**
**19mm from Lower Left to Lower Right Corners of Flag**

| 4645 | A3539 | (45c) multicolored | 1.50 | .25 |
| 4646 | A3540 | (45c) multicolored | 1.50 | .25 |
| 4647 | A3537 | (45c) multicolored | 1.50 | .25 |
| 4648 | A3538 | (45c) multicolored | 1.50 | .25 |
| a. | Block of 4, #4645-4648 | | 6.00 | |
| b. | Booklet pane of 20, 5 each #4645-4648 | | 30.00 | |
| | Nos. 4641-4648 (8) | | 11.60 | 2.00 |

On Nos. 4641-4644, the blue canton of the flag is made up of blue and red inks. The paper is tagged over each block of 4, with no tagging on the paper between the blocks. The tagging is a dull yellow green under ultraviolet light. The words are slightly longer than those on Nos. 4645-4648.

On Nos. 4645-4648, the blue canton is made up of blue and dull blue inks. The paper is prephosphored with the tagging appearing bright yellow green under ultraviolet light. The words are slightly shorter than those on Nos. 4641-4644.

No. 4644b is a double-sided booklet with 12 stamps on one side (3 each #4641-4644) and eight stamps (2 each #4641-4644) plus label that serves as a booklet cover on the other side.

No. 4648b is a double-sided booklet with 12 stamps on one side (3 each #4645-4648) and eight stamps (2 each #4645-4648) plus label that serves as a booklet cover on the other side.

See Nos. 4673-4676.

### AMERICAN LANDMARKS ISSUE

Sunshine Skyway Bridge, Florida — A3541

Carmel Mission, Carmel, CA — A3542

### LITHOGRAPHED
*Serpentine Die Cut 10¾x10½*
2012, Feb. 28
**Self-Adhesive**

| 4649 | A3541 | $5.15 multi | 11.00 | 5.75 |
| 4650 | A3542 | $18.95 multi | 42.50 | 19.00 |

### CHERRY BLOSSOM CENTENNIAL

Cherry Blossoms and Washington Monument A3543

Cherry Blossoms and Jefferson Memorial A3544

### LITHOGRAPHED
*Serpentine Die Cut 10¾*
2012, Mar. 24
**Tagged**
**Self-Adhesive**

| 4651 | A3543 | (45c) multicolored | 1.40 | .25 |
| 4652 | A3544 | (45c) multicolored | 1.40 | .25 |
| a. | Horiz. pair #4651-4652 | | 2.80 | |

See Japan No. 3413.

### AMERICAN TREASURES SERIES

Flowers, by William H. Johnson (1901-70) — A3545

### PHOTOGRAVURE
*Serpentine Die Cut 10¾*
2012, Apr. 11
**Tagged**
**Self-Adhesive**

| 4653 | A3545 | (45c) multicolored | 1.40 | .35 |

### TWENTIETH CENTURY POETS

Joseph Brodsky (1940-96)
A3546

Gwendolyn Brooks (1917-2000)
A3547

William Carlos Williams (1883-1963)
A3548

Robert Hayden (1913-80)
A3549

Sylvia Plath (1932-63)
A3550

Elizabeth Bishop (1911-79)
A3551

Wallace Stevens (1879-1955)
A3552

Denise Levertov (1923-97)
A3553

E. E. Cummings (1894-1962)
A3554

Theodore Roethke (1908-63)
A3555

### LITHOGRAPHED
Sheets of 160 in eight panes of 20
*Serpentine Die Cut 10¾x11*
2012, Apr. 21
**Tagged**
**Self-Adhesive**

| 4654 | A3546 | (45c) multicolored | 2.50 | .50 |
| 4655 | A3547 | (45c) multicolored | 2.50 | .50 |
| 4656 | A3548 | (45c) multicolored | 2.50 | .50 |
| 4657 | A3549 | (45c) multicolored | 2.50 | .50 |
| 4658 | A3550 | (45c) multicolored | 2.50 | .50 |
| 4659 | A3551 | (45c) multicolored | 2.50 | .50 |
| 4660 | A3552 | (45c) multicolored | 2.50 | .50 |
| 4661 | A3553 | (45c) multicolored | 2.50 | .50 |
| 4662 | A3554 | (45c) multicolored | 2.50 | .50 |
| 4663 | A3555 | (45c) multicolored | 2.50 | .50 |
| a. | Block of 10, #4654-4663 | | 25.00 | |
| | Nos. 4654-4663 (10) | | 25.00 | 5.00 |

### CIVIL WAR SESQUICENTENNIAL

Battle of New Orleans A3556

Battle of Antietam A3557

### LITHOGRAPHED
*Serpentine Die Cut 11*
2012, Apr. 24
**Tagged**
**Self-Adhesive**

| 4664 | A3556 | (45c) multicolored | 1.40 | .30 |
| 4665 | A3557 | (45c) multicolored | 1.40 | .30 |
| a. | Pair, #4664-4665 | | 2.80 | |

### DISTINGUISHED AMERICANS

José Ferrer (1912-92), Actor — A3558

### LITHOGRAPHED
*Serpentine Die Cut 10¾x11*
2012, Apr. 20
**Tagged**
**Self-Adhesive**

| 4666 | A3558 | (45c) multicolored | 1.40 | .25 |

### LOUISIANA STATEHOOD BICENTENNIAL

Sunset Over Flat Lake — A3559

## PHOTOGRAVURE
*Serpentine Die Cut 11*

2012, Apr. 30        Tagged
**Self-Adhesive**

| 4667 | A3559 | (45c) multicolored | 1.40 | .25 |

### GREAT FILM DIRECTORS

John Ford (1894-1973), Scene From *The Searchers,* Starring John Wayne — A3560

Frank Capra (1897-1991), Scene From *It Happened One Night,* Starring Clark Gable and Claudette Colbert — A3561

Billy Wilder (1906-2002), Scene From *Some Like It Hot,* Starring Marilyn Monroe — A3562

John Huston (1906-87), Scene From *The Maltese Falcon,* Starring Humphrey Bogart — A3563

## PHOTOGRAVURE
*Serpentine Die Cut 10¾*

2012, May 23
**Self-Adhesive**

| 4668 | A3560 | (45c) multicolored | 1.40 | .40 |
| 4669 | A3561 | (45c) multicolored | 1.40 | .40 |
| 4670 | A3562 | (45c) multicolored | 1.40 | .40 |
| 4671 | A3563 | (45c) multicolored | 1.40 | .40 |
| a. | | Block or horiz. strip of 4, #4668-4671 | 5.60 | |

### WILDLIFE

 Bobcat — A3564

## LITHOGRAPHED
*Serpentine Die Cut 10 Vert.*

2012, June 1
**Coil Stamp**
**Self-Adhesive**

| 4672 | A3564 | 1c multicolored | .30 | .25 |
| a. | | Dated "2015" | .30 | .25 |

Issued: No. 4672a, 2/21/15. Microprinting is on bobcat's ear on No. 4672 and on the bobcat's leg on No. 4672a.
See No. 4802.

### Flags Type of 2012
## PHOTOGRAVURE
*Serpentine Die Cut 11¼x10¾ on 3 Sides*

2012, June 1        Tagged
**Booklet Stamps**
**Self-Adhesive**
**Colored Dots in Stars**
**19¼mm From Lower Left to Lower Right Corners of Flag**

| 4673 | A3539 | (45c) multicolored | 1.40 | .25 |
| 4674 | A3540 | (45c) multicolored | 1.40 | .25 |
| 4675 | A3537 | (45c) multicolored | 1.40 | .25 |
| 4676 | A3538 | (45c) multicolored | 1.40 | .25 |
| a. | | Block of 4, #4673-4676 | 5.60 | |
| b. | | Booklet pane of 10, 3 each #4673-4674, 2 each #4675-4676 | 14.00 | |

Nos. 4673 and No. 4675 have straight edge on left side only. No. 4674 and 4676 have straight edge on right side only. Nos. 4641-4648 each have a straight edge at top or bottom. The letters in the "USPS" microprinting on Nos. 4673-4676, found at the right side of the bottom white flag stripe, are printed in a distinct curve, with the tops of the middle letters, "SP," being below the tops of the outside letters, "U" and "S," and the letters can be difficult to distinguish against the shading on the stripe. The letters in the microprinting on Nos. 4641-4648, found in the same place on the stamp, are printed in a straight line, and are printed boldly, making them easily distinguishable from the shading. The lettering on Nos. 4673-4767 has a fuzzier, less distinct appearance under magnification than the lettering on Nos. 4641-4648, which is most evident in the year "2012."

### CHARACTERS FROM DISNEY-PIXAR FILMS
Mail a Smile

Flik and Dot From *A Bug's Life* A3565

Bob Parr and Dashiell Parr From *The Incredibles* A3566

Nemo and Squirt From *Finding Nemo* — A3567

Jessie, Woody and Bullseye From *Toy Story 2* — A3568

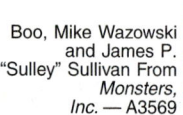

Boo, Mike Wazowski and James P. "Sulley" Sullivan From *Monsters, Inc.* — A3569

## PHOTOGRAVURE
*Serpentine Die Cut 10½*

2012, June 1
**Self-Adhesive**

| 4677 | A3565 | (45c) multicolored | 1.40 | .40 |
| 4678 | A3566 | (45c) multicolored | 1.40 | .40 |
| 4679 | A3567 | (45c) multicolored | 1.40 | .40 |
| 4680 | A3568 | (45c) multicolored | 1.40 | .40 |
| 4681 | A3569 | (45c) multicolored | 1.40 | .40 |
| a. | | Horiz. strip of 5, #4677-4681 | 7.00 | |

Adjacent horizontal or vertical stamps will have selvage between the stamps.

### Aloha Shirts Type of 2012
## LITHOGRAPHED
**Tagged**
*Serpentine Die Cut 11¼x10¾ on 3 Sides*

2012, June 2
**Booklet Stamps**
**Self-Adhesive**

| 4682 | A3506 | 32c multicolored | 8.50 | .30 |
| 4683 | A3508 | 32c multicolored | 8.50 | .30 |
| 4684 | A3510 | 32c multicolored | 8.50 | .30 |
| 4685 | A3507 | 32c multicolored | 8.50 | .30 |
| 4686 | A3509 | 32c multicolored | 8.50 | .30 |
| a. | | Vert. strip of 5, #4682-4686 | 42.50 | |
| b. | | Booklet pane of 10, 2 each #4682-4686 | 85.00 | |

Stamps in No. 4686a are not adjacent, as a row of selvage is between stamps two and three.
See Nos. 4592-4601.

### BICYCLING

Child on Bicycle with Training Wheels — A3570

Commuter on Bicycle with Panniers A3571

Road Racer — A3572

BMX Rider — A3573

## LITHOGRAPHED
*Serpentine Die Cut 10¾*

2012, June 7
**Self-Adhesive**

| 4687 | A3570 | (45c) multicolored | 1.40 | .35 |
| 4688 | A3571 | (45c) multicolored | 1.40 | .35 |
| 4689 | A3572 | (45c) multicolored | 1.40 | .35 |
| 4690 | A3573 | (45c) multicolored | 1.40 | .35 |
| a. | | Horiz. strip of 4, #4687-4690 | 5.60 | |

### GIRL SCOUTS OF AMERICA, CENT.

 Girl Scouts — A3574

## LITHOGRAPHED
*Serpentine Die Cut 10¾*

2012, June 9
**Self-Adhesive**

| 4691 | A3574 | (45c) multicolored | 1.40 | .25 |
| a. | | Die cutting omitted, pair | — | |

### MUSICIANS

 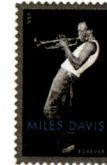

Edith Piaf (1915-63), Singer A3575

Miles Davis (1926-91), Jazz Trumpet Player A3576

## PHOTOGRAVURE
*Serpentine Die Cut 10¾x11*

2012, June 12
**Self-Adhesive**

| 4692 | A3575 | (45c) multicolored | 1.40 | .30 |
| 4693 | A3576 | (45c) multicolored | 1.40 | .30 |
| a. | | Pair, #4692-4693 | 2.80 | |

See France Nos. 4256-4257.

**Imperforate Uncut Press Sheets** Beginning with Nos. 4694-4697, the United States Postal Service made available for sale imperforate uncut press sheets of selected commemorative and definitive issues. These sheets, along with their corresponding multiples, are described and valued in footnotes following each issue in the Scott *Specialized Catalogue of United States Stamps and Covers.* For descriptions and illustrations of typical press-sheet multiples, see the note after No. 2868 in the Scott U.S. Specialized catalogue.

### MAJOR LEAGUE BASEBALL ALL-STARS

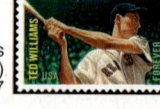

Ted Williams (1918-2002) A3577

Larry Doby (1923-2003) A3578

Willie Stargell (1940-2001) A3579

Joe DiMaggio (1914-99) A3580

## PHOTOGRAVURE
*Serpentine Die Cut 10¾x11*

2012, July 20
**Self-Adhesive**

| 4694 | A3577 | (45c) multicolored | 1.40 | .30 |
| a. | | Imperforate | 2.50 | |
| 4695 | A3578 | (45c) multicolored | 1.40 | .30 |
| a. | | Imperforate | 2.50 | |
| 4696 | A3579 | (45c) multicolored | 1.40 | .30 |
| a. | | Imperforate | 2.50 | |
| 4697 | A3580 | (45c) multicolored | 1.40 | .30 |
| a. | | Imperforate | 2.50 | |
| b. | | Horiz. strip or block of 4, #4694-4697 | 5.60 | |
| c. | | Imperf. horiz. strip or block of 4, #4694a-4697a | 14.00 | |

Panes containing 20 of the same stamp were issued on July 21 in Boston, MA (for No. 4694), Cleveland, OH (for No. 4695), Pittsburgh, PA (for No. 4696) and New York, NY (for No. 4697).

### INNOVATIVE CHOREOGRAPHERS

Isadora Duncan (1877-1927) A3581

José Limón (1908-72) A3582

Katherine Dunham (1909-2006) A3583

Bob Fosse (1927-87) A3584

## LITHOGRAPHED
*Serpentine Die Cut 10¾x11*

2012, July 28
**Self-Adhesive**

| 4698 | A3581 | (45c) multicolored | 1.40 | .35 |
| 4699 | A3582 | (45c) multicolored | 1.40 | .35 |
| 4700 | A3583 | (45c) multicolored | 1.40 | .35 |
| 4701 | A3584 | (45c) multicolored | 1.40 | .35 |
| a. | | Vert. strip of 4, #4698-4701 | 5.40 | |

### EDGAR RICE BURROUGHS

Edgar Rice Burroughs (1875-1950), Writer, and Tarzan — A3585

## LITHOGRAPHED
*Serpentine Die Cut 10¾*

2012, Aug. 17
**Self-Adhesive**

| 4702 | A3585 | (45c) multicolored | 1.40 | .25 |

# UNITED STATES

## WAR OF 1812 BICENTENNIAL

Painting of U.S.S. Constitution, by Michele Felice Corné — A3586

**PHOTOGRAVURE**
*Serpentine Die Cut 10¾x10½*
**2012, Aug. 18**
**Self-Adhesive**

| 4703 | A3586 | (45c) multicolored | 1.75 | .25 |
|---|---|---|---|---|
| a. | | Imperforate | 2.75 | |

### Purple Heart and Ribbon

Purple Heart and Ribbon — A3587

**PHOTOGRAVURE**
**2012, Sept. 4** *Serpentine Die Cut 11*
**Self-Adhesive**

| 4704 | A3587 | (45c) multicolored | 1.40 | .25 |
|---|---|---|---|---|
| a. | | Imperforate | 2.50 | — |
| b. | | Dated "2014" | 1.40 | .25 |

Compare with Type A3458.

## LITERARY ARTS

O. Henry (William S. Porter) (1862-1910), New York City Buildings and Elevated Trains — A3588

**PHOTOGRAVURE**
*Serpentine Die Cut 11*
**2012, Sept. 11**
**Self-Adhesive**

| 4705 | A3588 | (45c) multicolored | 1.40 | .25 |

### Flags Type of 2012
**LITHOGRAPHED**
*Serpentine Die Cut 11¼x10¾ on 2, 3 or 4 Sides*
**2012, Sept. 22**
**Booklet Stamps**
**Self-Adhesive**
**Colored Dots in Stars**
**18½mm From Lower Left to Lower Right Corners of Flag**
**Thin Paper**

| 4706 | A3539 | (45c) multicolored | 1.40 | .25 |
|---|---|---|---|---|
| 4707 | A3540 | (45c) multicolored | 1.40 | .25 |
| 4708 | A3537 | (45c) multicolored | 1.40 | .25 |
| 4709 | A3538 | (45c) multicolored | 1.40 | .25 |
| a. | | Block or strip of 4, #4706-4709 | 5.60 | |
| b. | | Booklet pane of 18, 5 each #4706-4707, 4 each #4708-4709 | 25.20 | |
| | | Nos. 4706-4709 (4) | 5.60 | 1.00 |

The overall-tagged paper used for Nos. 4706-4709 is glossier than that used on Nos. 4641-4644. The blue canton of the flag on Nos. 4706-4709 is made up of blue and red inks, similar to Nos. 4641-4644.

## EARTHSCAPES

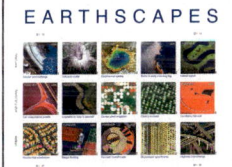

A3589

No. 4710: a, Glacier and icebergs. b, Volcanic crater. c, Geothermal spring. d, Butte in early morning fog. e, Inland marsh. f, Salt evaporation ponds. g, Log rafts on way to sawmill. h, Center-pivot irrigation. i, Cherry orchard. j, Cranberry harvest. k, Residential subdivision. l, Barge fleeting. m, Railroad roundhouse. n, Skyscraper apartments. o, Highway interchange.

**LITHOGRAPHED**
*Serpentine Die Cut 10¾*
**2012, Oct. 1**
**Self-Adhesive**

| 4710 | A3589 | Pane of 15 | 33.00 | |
|---|---|---|---|---|
| a.-o. | | (45c) Any single | 1.65 | .50 |
| p. | | Imperforate pane of 15 | 75.00 | |

## CHRISTMAS

Holy Family and Donkey A3590

Reindeer in Flight, Moon A3591

Santa Claus and Sleigh A3592

Reindeer Over Roof A3593

Snow-covered Buildings — A3594

**LITHOGRAPHED**
*Serpentine Die Cut 11 on 2 or 3 Sides*
**2012**
**Booklet Stamps**
**Self-Adhesive**

| 4711 | A3590 | (45c) multi | 1.40 | .25 |
|---|---|---|---|---|
| a. | | Booklet pane of 20 | 28.00 | |
| b. | | Imperforate | 1.75 | — |
| c. | | Imperforate booklet pane of 20 | 35.00 | |

*Serpentine Die Cut 11x10¾ on 2 or 3 sides*

| 4712 | A3591 | (45c) multi | 1.50 | .25 |
|---|---|---|---|---|
| 4713 | A3592 | (45c) multi | 1.50 | .25 |
| 4714 | A3593 | (45c) multi | 1.50 | .25 |
| 4715 | A3594 | (45c) multi | 1.50 | .25 |
| a. | | Block of 4, #4712-4715 | 6.00 | |
| b. | | Booklet pane of 20, 5 each #4712-4715 | 30.00 | |
| c. | | Imperforate block of 4 | 8.00 | |
| d. | | Imperforate booklet pane of 20 | 40.00 | |
| | | Nos. 4711-4715 (5) | 7.40 | 1.25 |

Issued: No. 4711, Oct. 10, Nos. 4712-4715, Oct. 13.
No. 4711a is a double-sided booklet with 12 stamps on one side and eight stamps plus a label that serves as a booklet cover on the other side. No. 4715b is a double-sided booklet with 12 stamps on one side (3 each of Nos. 4712-4715) and eight stamps (2 each of Nos. 4712-4715) plus a label that serves as a booklet cover on the other side.
See No. 4813.

## LADY BIRD JOHNSON

A3595

No. 4716: a, Blooming crab apples lining avenue (Plant for more Beautiful Streets). b, Washington Monument, Potomac River and daffodils (Plant for more Beautiful Parks). c, Jefferson Memorial, Tidal Basin and cherry blossoms (Plant for a more Beautiful America). d, Poppies and lupines along highway (Plant for more Beautiful Highways). e, Capitol, azaleas and tulips (Plant for more Beautiful Cities). f, Lady Bird Johnson (1912-2007), First Lady, vert.

**LITHOGRAPHED**
*Serpentine Die Cut 10¾*
**2012, Nov. 30**
**Self-Adhesive**

| 4716 | A3595 | Pane of 6 | 9.00 | |
|---|---|---|---|---|
| a.-f. | | (45c) Any single | 1.50 | .40 |
| g. | | Imperforate pane of 6 | 25.00 | |

## WAVES OF COLOR

A3596

A3597

A3598

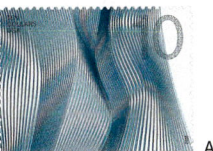

A3599

**LITHOGRAPHED & ENGRAVED**
*Serpentine Die Cut 11, 10¾ (#4719)*
**2012, Dec. 1**
**Self-Adhesive**

| 4717 | A3596 | $1 multi | 4.50 | .50 |
|---|---|---|---|---|
| 4718 | A3597 | $2 multi | 1.60 | 1.25 |
| 4719 | A3598 | $5 multi | 8.75 | 2.50 |
| 4720 | A3599 | $10 multi | 17.50 | 9.00 |
| | | Nos. 4717-4720 (4) | 35.25 | 13.25 |

Adjacent horizontal or vertical stamps have selvage between the stamps. Plate blocks have sheet margins on the top or bottom and both sides.

## EMANCIPATION PROCLAMATION, 150th ANNIV.

A3600

**PHOTOGRAVURE**
**2013, Jan. 1** *Serpentine Die Cut 11*
**Self-Adhesive**

| 4721 | A3600 | (45c) multicolored | 1.40 | .25 |
|---|---|---|---|---|
| a. | | Imperforate | 2.00 | — |

## KALEIDOSCOPE FLOWERS

A3601

A3602

A3603

A3604

**LITHOGRAPHED**
*Serpentine Die Cut 11 Vert.*
**2013, Jan. 14**
**Coil Stamps**
**Self-Adhesive**
**Color of Large Outer Leaves**

| 4722 | A3601 | 46c yellow orange | 1.25 | .25 |
|---|---|---|---|---|
| 4723 | A3602 | 46c yellow green | 1.25 | .25 |
| 4724 | A3603 | 46c red violet | 1.25 | .25 |
| 4725 | A3604 | 46c red | 1.25 | .25 |
| a. | | Strip of 4, #4722-4725 | 5.00 | |
| | | Nos. 4722-4725 (4) | 5.00 | 1.00 |

## CHINESE NEW YEAR

Year of the Snake — A3605

**PHOTOGRAVURE**
*Serpentine Die Cut 11*
**2013, Jan. 16**
**Self-Adhesive**

| 4726 | A3605 | (45c) multicolored | 1.40 | .25 |
|---|---|---|---|---|
| a. | | Imperforate | 2.00 | — |

## APPLES

Northern Spy Apple A3606

Golden Delicious Apple A3607

Granny Smith Apple A3608

Baldwin Apple A3609

**LITHOGRAPHED**
*Serpentine Die Cut 11¼x10¾*
**2013, Jan. 17**
**Self-Adhesive**

| 4727 | A3606 | 33c multicolored | 1.25 | .25 |
|---|---|---|---|---|
| 4728 | A3607 | 33c multicolored | 1.25 | .25 |
| 4729 | A3608 | 33c multicolored | 1.25 | .25 |
| 4730 | A3609 | 33c multicolored | 1.25 | .25 |
| a. | | Block or strip of 4, #4727-4730 | 5.00 | |
| b. | | Imperforate block or strip of 4 | 6.50 | — |

**Coil Stamps**
*Serpentine Die Cut 11 Vert.*

| 4731 | A3609 | 33c multicolored | 1.50 | .25 |
|---|---|---|---|---|
| 4732 | A3606 | 33c multicolored | 1.50 | .25 |
| 4733 | A3607 | 33c multicolored | 1.50 | .25 |
| 4734 | A3608 | 33c multicolored | 1.50 | .25 |
| a. | | Strip of 4, #4731-4734 | 6.00 | |
| | | Nos. 4727-4734 (8) | 11.00 | 2.00 |

### Wedding Cake Type of 2009
**LITHOGRAPHED**
*Serpentine Die Cut 10¾*
**2013, Jan. 18**
**Self-Adhesive**

| 4735 | A3344 | 66c multicolored | 1.75 | .25 |
|---|---|---|---|---|
| a. | | Imperforate | 3.50 | — |

See Nos. 4398, 4521, 4602, 4867, 5000.

## SPICEBUSH SWALLOWTAIL BUTTERFLY

A3610

**PHOTOGRAVURE**
*Serpentine Die Cut 10¾*
**2013, Jan. 23**
**Self-Adhesive**

| 4736 | A3610 | 66c multicolored | 1.40 | .25 |
|---|---|---|---|---|
| a. | | Imperforate | 3.00 | — |

## TUFTED PUFFINS

A3611

128 UNITED STATES

LITHOGRAPHED
***Serpentine Die Cut 11¼x10¾***
**2013, Jan. 23**
**"2013" in Orange Red Solid Color in "Tufted Puffins" and "86"**
**Self-Adhesive**

**4737** A3611 86c multicolored 1.80 .35
*b.* Imperforate 4.00 —

**"2013" in Black With Dots in "Tufted Puffins" and "86"**

**4737A** A3611 86c multi 5.00 .35

**AMERICAN LANDMARKS ISSUE**

Arlington Green Bridge, Vermont — A3612

Grand Central Terminal, New York City — A3613

PHOTOGRAVURE
**2013** ***Serpentine Die Cut 10¾x10½***
**Self-Adhesive**

**4738** A3612 $5.60 multi 11.00 6.25
**4739** A3613 $19.95 multi 40.00 21.00

Earth — A3614

PHOTOGRAVURE
**2013, Jan. 28** ***Serpentine Die Cut***
**Self-Adhesive**

**4740** A3614 ($1.10) multi 3.25 .50
*a.* Imperforate 5.00

Unused values are for stamps with surrounding selvage. Adjacent stamps are separated by rouletting.

**LOVE**

Envelope With Wax Seal — A3615

PHOTOGRAVURE
***Serpentine Die Cut 10¾***
**2013, Jan. 30**
**Self-Adhesive**

**4741** A3615 (46c) multicolored 1.40 .25
*a.* Imperforate 2.00 —

**ROSA PARKS**

Parks (1913-2005), Civil Rights Pioneer — A3616

PHOTOGRAVURE
***Serpentine Die Cut 10¾***
**2013, Feb. 4**
**Self-Adhesive**

**4742** A3616 (46c) multicolored 1.40 .25
*a.* Imperforate 2.00 —

**MUSCLE CARS**

1969 Dodge Charger Daytona — A3617

1966 Pontiac GTO — A3618

1967 Ford Mustang Shelby GT 500 — A3619

1970 Chevrolet Chevelle SS — A3620

1970 Plymouth Hemi Barracuda A3621

PHOTOGRAVURE
***Serpentine Die Cut 10¾***
**2013, Feb. 22** **Tagged**
**Self-Adhesive**

**4743** A3617 (46c) multicolored 1.40 .30
**4744** A3618 (46c) multicolored 1.40 .30
**4745** A3619 (46c) multicolored 1.40 .30
**4746** A3620 (46c) multicolored 1.40 .30
**4747** A3621 (46c) multicolored 1.40 .30
*a.* Vert. strip of 5, #4743-4747 7.00
Vert. P# block of 10, 5# + V 14.00
Horiz. P# block of 8, 2 sets of 5# + V 11.20
*b.* Imperforate vert. strip of 5 10.00 —
*Nos. 4743-4747 (5)* 7.00 1.50

**MODERN ART IN AMERICA**

A3622

No. 4748: a, I Saw the Figure 5 in Gold, by Charles Demuth (37x51mm). b, Sunset, Maine Coast, by John Marin (43x43mm). c, House and Street, by Stuart Davis (51x41mm). d, Painting, Number 5, by Marsden Hartley (37x51mm). e, Black Mesa Landscape, New Mexico/Out Back of Marie's II, by Georgia O'Keeffe (51x41mm). f, Noire et Blanche, by Man Ray (43x41mm). g, The Prodigal Son, by Aaron Douglas (34x51mm). h, American Landscape, by Charles Sheeler (43x41mm). i, Brooklyn Bridge, by Joseph Stella (38x47mm). j, Razor, by Gerald Murphy (43x43mm). k, Nude Descending a Staircase, No. 2, by Marcel Duchamp (34x58mm). l, Fog Horns, by Arthur Dove (43x37mm).

PHOTOGRAVURE
***Serpentine Die Cut 10½***
**2013, Mar. 7**
**Self-Adhesive**

**4748** A3622 Pane of 12 16.80
*a.-l.* (46c) Any single 1.40 .50
*m.* Imperforate pane of 12 70.00

Armory Show, cent.

Patriotic Star — A3623

LITHOGRAPHED
***Serpentine Die Cut 10¾ Vert.***
**2013, Mar. 19**
**Coil Stamp**
**Self-Adhesive**

**4749** A3623 46c multicolored 1.25 .25

**LA FLORIDA**

A3624 A3625

A3626 A3627

PHOTOGRAVURE
***Serpentine Die Cut 10½***
**2013, Apr. 3**
**Self-Adhesive**

**4750** A3624 (46c) multicolored 1.40 .25
**4751** A3625 (46c) multicolored 1.40 .25
**4752** A3626 (46c) multicolored 1.40 .25
**4753** A3627 (46c) multicolored 1.40 .25
*a.* Block of 4, #4750-4753 5.60
*b.* Imperforate block of 4 10.00 —
*Nos. 4750-4753 (4)* 5.60 1.00

Naming of Florida, 500th anniv.

**VINTAGE SEED PACKETS**

Phlox A3628

Calendula A3629

Digitalis A3630

Linum A3631

Alyssum A3632

Zinnias A3633

Pinks A3634

Cosmos A3635

Aster A3636

Primrose A3637

PHOTOGRAVURE
***Serpentine Die Cut 10¾ on 2 or 3 Sides***
**2013, Apr. 5**
**Booklet Stamps**
**Self-Adhesive**

**4754** A3628 (46c) multicolored 2.50 .25
**4755** A3629 (46c) multicolored 2.50 .25
**4756** A3630 (46c) multicolored 2.50 .25
**4757** A3631 (46c) multicolored 2.50 .25
**4758** A3632 (46c) multicolored 2.50 .25
**4759** A3633 (46c) multicolored 2.50 .25
**4760** A3634 (46c) multicolored 2.50 .25
**4761** A3635 (46c) multicolored 2.50 .25
**4762** A3636 (46c) multicolored 2.50 .25
**4763** A3637 (46c) multicolored 2.50 .25
*a.* Block of 10, #4754-4763 25.00
*b.* Booklet pane of 20, 2 each #4754-4763 50.00
*Nos. 4754-4763 (10)* 25.00 2.50

No. 4763b is a double-sided booklet pane with 12 stamps on one side (2 each #4754, 4759, 1 each #4755-4758, 4760-4763), and eight stamps (1 each #4755-4758, 4760-4763) plus label (booklet cover) on the other side.

**WEDDING FLOWERS**

Flowers A3638

Flowers and "Yes I Do" A3639

LITHOGRAPHED
***Serpentine Die Cut 10¾***
**2013, Apr. 11**
**Self-Adhesive**

**4764** A3638 (46c) multicolored 1.40 .25
*a.* Dated "2014" 1.40 .25
*b.* Imperforate 2.50 —
**4765** A3639 66c multicolored 1.40 .30
*a.* Imperforate 3.00 —

Flag in Autumn A3640

Flag in Winter A3641

Flag in Spring A3642

Flag in Summer A3643

PHOTOGRAVURE
**2013** ***Serpentine Die Cut 8½ Vert.***
**Coil Stamps**
**Self-Adhesive**

**4766** A3640 (46c) multicolored 2.25 .25
**4767** A3641 (46c) multicolored 2.25 .25
**4768** A3642 (46c) multicolored 2.25 .25
**4769** A3643 (46c) multicolored 2.25 .25
*a.* Strip of 4, #4766-4769 9.00

LITHOGRAPHED (#4770-4785)
***Serpentine Die Cut 9½ Vert.***

**4770** A3640 (46c) multicolored 2.25 .25
**4771** A3641 (46c) multicolored 2.25 .25
**4772** A3642 (46c) multicolored 2.25 .25
**4773** A3643 (46c) multicolored 2.25 .25
*a.* Strip of 4, #4770-4773 9.00

***Serpentine Die Cut 11 Vert.***

**4774** A3641 (46c) multicolored 3.00 .25
**4775** A3642 (46c) multicolored 3.00 .25
**4776** A3643 (46c) multicolored 3.00 .25
**4777** A3640 (46c) multicolored 3.00 .25
*a.* Strip of 4, #4774-4777 12.00
*b.* Block of 28 (4x7), #4774-4777, with no horiz. slits —
*Nos. 4766-4777 (12)* 30.00 3.00

**Booklet Stamps**
**With Microprinted "USPS" at Lower Left Corner of Flag**
***Serpentine Die Cut 11¼x10¾ on 2 or 3 Sides***

**4778** A3642 (46c) multicolored 1.40 .25
**4779** A3643 (46c) multicolored 1.40 .25
**4780** A3640 (46c) multicolored 1.40 .25
**4781** A3641 (46c) multicolored 1.40 .25
*a.* Block of 4, #4778-4781 5.60
*b.* Booklet pane of 20, 5 each #4778-4781 28.00

**With Microprinted "USPS" Near Top of Pole or at Lower Left Corner Near Rope (#4783, 4783b)**
**Pre-phosphored Paper**

**4782** A3642 (46c) multicolored 1.40 .25
*b.* As #4782, dated "2014" 1.40 .25
**4783** A3643 (46c) multicolored 1.40 .25
*b.* As #4783, dated "2014" 1.40 .25
**4784** A3640 (46c) multicolored 1.40 .25
*b.* As #4784, dated "2014" 1.40 .25
*c.* Tagging omitted —
**4785** A3641 (46c) multicolored 1.40 .25
*b.* As #4785, dated "2014" 1.40 .25
*c.* Block of 4, #4782-4785 5.60
*d.* Booklet pane of 20, 5 each #4782-4785 28.00
*f.* Booklet pane of 10, 3 each #4782a, 4783a, 2 each #4784a, 4785a 14.00

# UNITED STATES

g. Block of 4, #4782b, 4783b, 4784b, 4785b     5.60
h. Booklet pane of 20, 5 each #4782b, 4783b, 4784b, 4785b     28.00
i. As "h," die cutting omitted on side with 8 stamps and 3 pairs on side with 12 stamps     1,800.
Nos. 4778-4785 (8)     11.20   2.00

Issued: Nos. 4766-4777, 5/3; Nos. 4778-4785, 5/17. No. 4781b is a double-sided booklet with 12 stamps on one side (3 each #4778-4781) and eight stamps (2 each #4778-4781) plus label that serves as a booklet cover on the other side.

No. 4785c is a double-sided booklet with 12 stamps on one side (3 each #4782-4785) and eight stamps (2 each #4782-4785) plus label that serves as a booklet cover on the other side.

A microprinted "USPS" is found on tree trunk to the left of the "F" in "Forever" on No. 4766, on tree trunk near lower left corner of flag on No. 4767, on white flag stripe at lower right on No. 4768, and on the top of the flagpole below the ball on No. 4769. Nos. 4770-4773 are microprinted "USPS" in the same places as on Nos. 4778-4781. Nos. 4774-4777 are microprinted "USPS" in the same places as on Nos. 4782-4785.

No. 4785e comprises stamps printed on paper with overall tagging. For detailed listings, see the *Scott Specialized Catalogue of United States Stamps and Covers.*

See Nos. 4796-4799.

Issued: Nos. 4702b, 4700b, 4704b, 4705b, 3/17/14. Nos. 4782b, 4783b, 4784b and 4785b each sold for 49c on day of issue.

## MUSIC ICONS

Lydia Mendoza (1916-2007), Tejano Music Recording Artist — A3644

### PHOTOGRAVURE
*Serpentine Die Cut 10¾*
**2013, May 15**
**Self-Adhesive**

4786   A3644   (46c) multicolored   1.40   .25
a.   Imperforate   1.75   —

Adjacent horizontal or vertical stamps have selvage between the stamps.

## CIVIL WAR SESQUICENTENNIAL

Battle of Vicksburg A3645

Battle of Gettysburg A3646

### LITHOGRAPHED
**2013, May 23**   *Serpentine Die Cut 11*
**Self-Adhesive**

4787   A3645   (46c) multicolored   1.40   .30
4788   A3646   (46c) multicolored   1.40   .30
a.   Pair, #4787-4788   2.00
b.   Imperforate pair, #4787-4788   5.50   —

## MUSIC ICONS

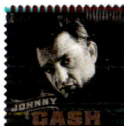

Johnny Cash (1932-2003), Country Music Recording Artist — A3647

### PHOTOGRAVURE
*Serpentine Die Cut 10¾*
**2013, June 5**
**Self-Adhesive**

4789   A3647   (46c) multicolored   1.40   .25
a.   Imperforate   1.75   —

## WEST VIRGINIA STATEHOOD, 150th ANNIV.

Hills in Monongahela National Forest — A3648

### PHOTOGRAVURE
*Serpentine Die Cut 11*
**2013, June 20**
**Self-Adhesive**

4790   A3648   (46c) multicolored   1.40   .25
a.   Imperforate   1.75   —

## NEW ENGLAND COASTAL LIGHTHOUSES

Portland Head Lighthouse, Maine A3649

Portsmouth Harbor Lighthouse, New Hampshire A3650

Boston Harbor Lighthouse, Massachusetts A3651

Point Judith Lighthouse, Rhode Island A3652

New London Harbor Lighthouse, Connecticut — A3653

Original

"FOREVER" and "USA" 1mm higher than original

### LITHOGRAPHED
*Serpentine Die Cut 11x10¾*
**2013, July 13**
**Self-Adhesive**

4791   A3649   (46c) multicolored   1.40   .40
a.   "FOREVER" and "USA" 1mm higher than normal (pos. 1)   2.00   1.00
b.   Horiz. strip of 5, #4791a, 4792-4795   7.20
4792   A3650   (46c) multicolored   1.40   .40
4793   A3651   (46c) multicolored   1.40   .40
4794   A3652   (46c) multicolored   1.40   .40
4795   A3653   (46c) multicolored   1.40   .40
a.   Horiz. strip of 5, #4791-4795   7.00
b.   Imperforate horiz. strip of 5   11.00   —
c.   Imperforate horiz. strip of 5, pos. 1 as No. 4791a   13.00   —
Nos. 4791-4795 (5)   7.00   2.00

## Flag Types of 2013
### PHOTOGRAVURE
*Serpentine Die Cut 11¼x11½ on 2 or 3 Sides*
**2013, Aug. 8**
**Booklet Stamps**
**Self-Adhesive**

4796   A3642   (46c) multicolored   1.50   .25
4797   A3643   (46c) multicolored   1.50   .25
4798   A3640   (46c) multicolored   1.50   .25
4799   A3641   (46c) multicolored   1.50   .25
a.   Block of 4, #4796-4799   6.00
b.   Booklet pane of 20, 5 each #4796-4799   30.00
Nos. 4796-4799 (4)   6.00   1.00

No. 4799b is a double-sided booklet with 12 stamps on one side (3 each #4796-4799) and eight stamps (2 each #4796-4799) plus label that serves as a booklet cover on the other side. Nos. 4796-4799 are microprinted "USPS" in the same places as Nos. 4766-4769.

## EID

"Eid Mubarak" — A3654

### LITHOGRAPHED
**2013, Aug. 8**   *Serpentine Die Cut 11*
**Self-Adhesive**

4800   A3654   (46c) dk grn, gray & gold   1.40   .25
a.   Imperforate   2.00   —

## BUILDING A NATION

Airplane Mechanic, Photograph by Lewis Hine — A3655

Derrick Man on Empire State Building, Photograph by Lewis Hine — A3656

Millinery Apprentice, Photograph by Lewis Hine — A3657

Man on Hoisting Ball on Empire State Building, Photograph by Lewis Hine — A3658

Linotype Operator, Photograph by Lewis Hine — A3659

Welder on Empire State Building, Photograph by Lewis Hine — A3660

Coal Miner, by Anonymous Photographer A3661

Riveters on Empire State Building, Photograph by Lewis Hine A3662

Powerhouse Mechanic, Photograph by Lewis Hine — A3663

Railroad Track Walker, Photograph by Lewis Hine — A3664

Textile Worker, Photograph by Lewis Hine — A3665

Man Guiding Beam on Empire State Building, Photograph by Lewis Hine — A3666

### PHOTOGRAVURE
*Serpentine Die Cut 10½x10¾*
**2013, Aug. 8**
**Self-Adhesive**

4801   Pane of 12   16.80
a.   A3655   (46c) black & gray   1.40   .50
b.   A3656   (46c) black & gray   1.40   .50
c.   A3657   (46c) black & gray   1.40   .50
d.   A3658   (46c) black & gray   1.40   .50
e.   A3659   (46c) black & gray   1.40   .50
f.   A3660   (46c) black & gray   1.40   .50
g.   A3661   (46c) black & gray   1.40   .50
h.   A3662   (46c) black & gray   1.40   .50
i.   A3663   (46c) black & gray   1.40   .50
j.   A3664   (46c) black & gray   1.40   .50
k.   A3665   (46c) black & gray   1.40   .50
l.   A3666   (46c) black & gray   1.40   .50
m.   Imperforate pane of 12   70.00

No. 4801 was printed with five different sheet margins depicting coal miner from No. 4801g, man on hoisting ball on Empire State Building, man measuring bearings in large gearwheel, man on cable at Empire State Building, and woman welder. Value is for sheet with any margin.

## Bobcat Type of 2012
### LITHOGRAPHED
**2013, Aug. 9**   **Perf. 9¾ Vert.**
**Coil Stamp**

4802   A3564   1c multicolored   .30   .25
See No. 4672.

## BLACK HERITAGE

Althea Gibson (1927-2003), Tennis Player — A3667

### PHOTOGRAVURE
*Serpentine Die Cut 11*
**2013, Aug. 23**
**Self-Adhesive**

4803   A3667   (46c) multicolored   1.40   .25
a.   Imperforate   1.75   —

130 UNITED STATES

## MARCH ON WASHINGTON, 50th ANNIV.

Marchers and Washington Monument — A3668

PHOTOGRAVURE

***Serpentine Die Cut 10¾***

**2013, Aug. 23**

**Self-Adhesive**

**4804** A3668 (46c) multicolored 1.40 .25
*a.* Imperforate 1.75 —

## WAR OF 1812 BICENTENNIAL

Painting of Battle of Lake Erie, by William Henry Powell — A3669

LITHOGRAPHED

***Serpentine Die Cut 10¾***

**2013, Sept. 10**

**Self-Adhesive**

**4805** A3669 (46c) multicolored 1.40 .25
*a.* Imperforate 1.75 —

## INVERTED JENNY

Miniature Sheet

A3670

LITHOGRAPHED & ENGRAVED

***Serpentine Die Cut 10½x11¼***

**2013, Sept. 22**

**Self-Adhesive**

**4806** A3670 multicolored 24.00
*a.* $2 Single stamp 4.00 1.25
*b.* Imperforate pane of 6 72.50 —
*c.* As "b," single stamp 12.00 —
*d.* Pane of 6, airplane right-side up *60,000.*
*e.* As "d," single stamp *13,500.*

No. 4806, along with a piece of white cardboard backing, was placed in a sealed envelope. The envelope, along with a piece of gray cardboard backing, was inside a sealed plastic outerwrap. One hundred panes were produced that contain the airplane right-side up. These panes were included in the same envelope and outerwrap and were distributed randomly. No returns or refunds were offered for any opened packages. Values for No. 4806 are for panes removed from the envelope.

A book containing an unused and a first-day canceled example of No. 4806, along with items that are termed "proofs" and "die wipes" sold for $200.

## MUSIC ICONS

Ray Charles (1930-2004), Recording Artist — A3671

LITHOGRAPHED

***Serpentine Die Cut 10½***

**2013, Sept. 23**

**Self-Adhesive**

**4807** A3671 (46c) multicolored 1.40 .25
*a.* Imperforate 1.75 —

Adjacent horizontal or vertical stamps have selvage between the stamps.

## SNOWFLAKES

A3672

A3673

A3674

A3675

A3676

PHOTOGRAVURE

***Serpentine Die Cut 11 Vert.***

**2013, Oct. 1**

**Coil Stamps**

**Self-Adhesive**

**4808** A3672 (10c) lt bl & multi .30 .25
**4809** A3673 (10c) pale bl & multi .30 .25
**4810** A3674 (10c) lt bl & multi .30 .25
**4811** A3675 (10c) pale bl & multi .30 .25
**4812** A3676 (10c) lil & multi .30 .25
*a.* Strip of 5, #4808-4812 1.25
*Nos. 4808-4812 (5)* 1.50 1.25

### Holy Family and Donkey Type of 2012 Dated "2013" and

Wreath A3677

Virgin and Child, by Jan Gossaert A3678

Poinsettia A3679

Gingerbread House With Red Door A3680

Gingerbread House With Blue Door A3681

Gingerbread House With Green Door A3682

Gingerbread House With Orange Door A3683

Poinsettia A3684

LITHOGRAPHED, PHOTOGRAVURE (#4821)

**2013** ***Serpentine Die Cut 11***

**Self-Adhesive**

**4813** A3590 (46c) multicolored 1.40 .25
*a.* Imperforate 1.75 —

***Serpentine Die Cut***

**4814** A3677 ($1.10) multicolored 3.25 .50
*a.* Imperforate 4.00 —

**Booklet Stamps**

***Serpentine Die Cut 11 on 2 or 3 Sides***

**4815** A3678 (46c) multicolored 1.40 .25
*a.* Booklet pane of 20 28.00
*b.* Imperforate 1.75 —
*c.* Imperforate booklet pane of 20 35.00
**4816** A3679 (46c) multicolored 1.40 .25
*a.* Booklet pane of 20 28.00
*b.* Dated "2014" 1.40 .25
*c.* As #4816a, dated "2014" 28.00
*d.* Imperforate, dated "2013" 1.75 —
*e.* Imperforate booklet pane of 20 35.00
**4817** A3680 (46c) multicolored 1.40 .25
**4818** A3681 (46c) multicolored 1.40 .25
**4819** A3682 (46c) multicolored 1.40 .25
**4820** A3683 (46c) multicolored 1.40 .25
*b.* Block of 4, #4817-4820 5.60
*c.* Booklet pane of 20, 5 each #4817-4820 28.00
*f.* Imperforate block of 4 8.00 —
*g.* Imperforate booklet pane of 20 40.00

***Serpentine Die Cut 8 on 2, 3 or 4 Sides***

**4821** A3684 (46c) multicolored 1.40 .25
*a.* Booklet pane of 18 25.20
*Nos. 4815-4821 (7)* 9.80 1.75

Issued: Nos. 4813, 4815, 10/11; No. 4814, 10/24; Nos. 4816, 4821, 10/10; Nos. 4817-4820, 11/6.

## MEDALS OF HONOR

Navy Medal of Honor A3685

Army Medal of Honor A3686

LITHOGRAPHED

***Serpentine Die Cut 11***

**2013, Nov. 11**

**Self-Adhesive**

**4822** A3685 (46c) multicolored 1.40 .30
*a.* Dated "2014" 1.40 .30
*b.* Dated "2015" 1.40 .30
**4823** A3686 (46c) multicolored 1.40 .30
*a.* Dated "2014" 1.40 .30
*b.* Dated "2015" 1.40 .30
*c.* Pair, #4822-4823 2.80
*d.* Pair, #4822a-4823a 2.80
*e.* Pair, 4822b-4823b 2.80
Dated "2015," P# block of 4, 6#+S 5.60
Dated "2015," folio of 20 28.00
*f.* Imperf. pair, #4822-4823 4.50 —
*g.* Imperf. pair, #4822a-4823a 4.50 —

Issued: Nos. 4822a, 4823a, 7/26/14. Nos. 4822a, 4822b, 4823a and 4823b sold for 49c on day of issue. Folios containing Nos. 4822a and 4823a have different images of Medal of Honor recipients, product numbers (on folio margins) and text on the paper backing than that found on the folios with Nos. 4822 and 4823. Nos. 4822b and 4823b were in a folio with No. 4988.

## HANUKKAH

Menorah — A3687

LITHOGRAPHED

***Serpentine Die Cut 11***

**2013, Nov. 19**

**Self-Adhesive**

**4824** A3687 (46c) multicolored 1.40 .25
*a.* Imperforate 1.75 —

Postal Service officials declared on Nov. 8 that No. 4824 could be sold in post offices on Nov. 9, but the first day ceremony was held on Nov. 19 in New York, NY. Official first day covers have that date and city.

## SCENES FROM HARRY POTTER MOVIES

Harry Potter A3688

Harry Potter and Ron Weasley A3689

Harry Potter, Ron Weasley, Hermione Granger A3690

Hermione Granger A3691

Harry Potter and Fawkes the Phoenix A3692

Hedwig the Owl A3693

Dobby the House Elf — A3694

Harry Potter and Buckbeak the Hippogriff — A3695

Headmaster Albus Dumbledore A3696

Professor Severus Snape A3697

Rubeus Hagrid A3698

Professor Minerva McGonagall A3699

Harry Potter, Ron Weasley, Hermione Granger A3700

Luna Lovegood A3701

Fred and George Weasley A3702

Ginny Weasley A3703

UNITED STATES 131

Draco Malfoy A3704

Harry Potter A3705

Lord Voldemort A3706

Bellatrix Lestrange A3707

LITHOGRAPHED

***Serpentine Die Cut 11***

**2013, Nov. 19**

**Booklet Stamps**

**Self-Adhesive**

**4825** A3688 (46c) multicolored 2.00 .30
**4826** A3689 (46c) multicolored 2.00 .30
**4827** A3690 (46c) multicolored 2.00 .30
**4828** A3691 (46c) multicolored 2.00 .30
*a.* Booklet pane of 4, #4825-4828, + central label 8.00
*b.* Imperf. booklet pane of 4 12.50 —
**4829** A3692 (46c) multicolored 2.00 .30
**4830** A3693 (46c) multicolored 2.00 .30
**4831** A3694 (46c) multicolored 2.00 .30
**4832** A3695 (46c) multicolored 2.00 .30
*a.* Booklet pane of 4, #4829-4832, + central label 8.00
*b.* Imperf. booklet pane of 4 12.50 —
**4833** A3696 (46c) multicolored 2.00 .30
**4834** A3697 (46c) multicolored 2.00 .30
**4835** A3698 (46c) multicolored 2.00 .30
**4836** A3699 (46c) multicolored 2.00 .30
*a.* Booklet pane of 4, #4833-4836, + central label 8.00
*b.* Imperf. booklet pane of 4 12.50 —
**4837** A3700 (46c) multicolored 2.00 .30
**4838** A3701 (46c) multicolored 2.00 .30
**4839** A3702 (46c) multicolored 2.00 .30
**4840** A3703 (46c) multicolored 2.00 .30
*a.* Booklet pane of 4, #4837-4840, + central label 8.00
*b.* Imperf. booklet pane of 4 12.50 —
**4841** A3704 (46c) multicolored 2.00 .30
**4842** A3705 (46c) multicolored 2.00 .30
**4843** A3706 (46c) multicolored 2.00 .30
**4844** A3707 (46c) multicolored 2.00 .30
*a.* Booklet pane of 4, #4841-4844, + central label 8.00
*b.* Imperf. booklet pane of 4 12.50 —
*Nos. 4825-4844 (20)* 40.00 6.00

**KWANZAA**

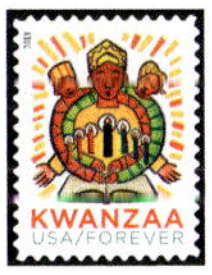


People, Candles and Book — A3708

LITHOGRAPHED

***Serpentine Die Cut 11***

**2013, Nov. 26**

**Self-Adhesive**

**4845** A3708 (46c) multicolored 1.40 .25
*a.* Imperforate 1.75 —

**CHINESE NEW YEAR**

Year of the Horse — A3709

PHOTOGRAVURE

***Serpentine Die Cut 11***

**2014, Jan. 15**

**Self-Adhesive**

**4846** A3709 (46c) multicolored 1.40 .25
*a.* Imperforate 2.00 —

**LOVE**

Heart — A3710

PHOTOGRAVURE

***Serpentine Die Cut 10¾***

**2014, Jan. 21**

**Self-Adhesive**

**4847** A3710 (46c) multicolored 1.40 .25
*a.* Imperforate 2.00 —

**FERNS**

Fortune's Holly Fern A3711

Soft Shield Fern A3712

Autumn Fern A3713

Goldie's Wood Fern A3714

Painted Fern — A3715

PHOTOGRAVURE

***Serpentine Die Cut 11 Vert.***

**2014, Jan. 27**

**Coil Stamps**

**Self-Adhesive**

**4848** A3711 49c multicolored 1.50 .25
**4849** A3712 49c multicolored 1.50 .25
**4850** A3713 49c multicolored 1.50 .25
**4851** A3714 49c multicolored 1.50 .25
**4852** A3715 49c multicolored 1.50 .25
*a.* Strip of 5, #4848-4852 7.50
*Nos. 4848-4852 (5)* 7.50 1.25

Fort McHenry Flag and Fireworks — A3716

PHOTOGRAVURE

***Serpentine Die Cut 8½ Vert.***

**2014, Jan. 28**

**Coil Stamps**

**Self-Adhesive**

**4853** A3716 (49c) multicolored 1.40 .25
Pair 2.80

LITHOGRAPHED (#4854-4855)

***Serpentine Die Cut 9½ Vert.***

**4854** A3716 (49c) multicolored 1.40 .25
Pair 2.00
*a.* Die cutting omitted, pair 150.00

**Booklet Stamp**

***Serpentine Die Cut 11¼x10¾ on 2 or 3 Sides***

**4855** A3716 (49c) multicolored 1.40 .25
*a.* Booklet pane of 20 28.00

No. 4855a is a double-sided booklet with 12 stamps on one side and eight stamps plus a label that serves as the booklet cover on the other side.

Nos. 4854 and 4855 each have a microprinted "USPS" on the right side of the lowest white stripe of the flag.

See Nos. 4868-4871.

**BLACK HERITAGE**

Shirley Chisholm (1924-2005), Congresswoman A3717

PHOTOGRAVURE

***Serpentine Die Cut 11***

**2014, Jan. 31**

**Self-Adhesive**

**4856** A3717 (49c) multicolored 1.40 .25
*a.* Imperforate 2.00 —

**WILDLIFE ISSUE**

Hummingbird — A3718

LITHOGRAPHED

***Serpentine Die Cut 11¼x10¾***

**2014, Feb. 7**

**Self-Adhesive**

**4857** A3718 34c multicolored .70 .25

**Coil Stamp**

***Serpentine Die Cut 9½ Vert.***

**4858** A3718 34c multicolored .70 .25
*a.* Overall tagging .70 .25
*b.* As "a," die cutting omitted, pair —

**GREAT SPANGLED FRITILLARY BUTTERFLY**

A3719

PHOTOGRAVURE

***Serpentine Die Cut 10¾***

**2014, Feb. 10**

**Self-Adhesive**

**4859** A3719 70c multicolored 1.50 .25
*a.* Imperforate 3.25 —

Statue of Abraham Lincoln in Lincoln Memorial — A3720

PHOTOGRAVURE

***Serpentine Die Cut 11***

**2014, Feb. 12**

**Self-Adhesive**

**4860** A3720 21c multicolored .45 .25
*a.* Imperforate 1.25 —

**Coil Stamp**

***Serpentine Die Cut 8½ Vert.***

**4861** A3720 21c multicolored .45 .25

**WINTER FLOWERS**

Amaryllis A3721

Cyclamen A3722

Paperwhite A3723

Christmas Cactus A3724

LITHOGRAPHED

***Serpentine Die Cut 11 on 2 or 3 Sides***

**2014, Feb. 14**

**Booklet Stamps**

**Self-Adhesive**

**4862** A3721 (49c) multicolored 1.50 .30
**4863** A3722 (49c) multicolored 1.50 .30
**4864** A3723 (49c) multicolored 1.50 .30
**4865** A3724 (49c) multicolored 1.50 .30
*a.* Block of 4, #4862-4865 6.00
*b.* Booklet pane of 20, 5 each #4862-4865 30.00
*c.* Imperforate block of 4 7.00 —
*d.* Imperforate booklet pane of 20 35.00
*Nos. 4862-4865 (4)* 6.00 1.20

No. 4865b is a double-sided booklet pane with 12 stamps on one side (3 each #4862-4865), and eight stamps (2 each #4862-4865) plus label (booklet cover) on the other side.

**LITERARY ARTS**

Ralph Ellison (1913-94), Buildings in Harlem — A3725

PHOTOGRAVURE

***Serpentine Die Cut 11***

**2014, Feb. 18**

**Self-Adhesive**

**4866** A3725 91c multicolored 1.90 .45
*a.* Imperforate 4.00 —

**Wedding Cake Type of 2009**

LITHOGRAPHED

***Serpentine Die Cut 10¾***

**2014, Feb. 22**

**Self-Adhesive**

**4867** A3344 70c multicolored 2.00 .25

See Nos. 4398, 4521, 4602, 4735, 5000.

**Fort McHenry Flag and Fireworks Type of 2014**

LITHOGRAPHED

**Coil Stamp Self-Adhesive With "USPS" Microprinted in Fireworks Above Flagpole**

***Serpentine Die Cut 11 Vert.***

**2014, Mar. 3**

**4868** A3716 (49c) multicolored 1.40 .25
*a.* Vert. strip of 3 (one single each from three different coil rolls), horiz. unslit between 60.00
*b.* Pair, die cutting omitted —

PHOTOGRAVURE (#4869), LITHOGRAPHED (#4870-4871)

**Booklet Stamps Without Microprinted "USPS"**

***Serpentine Die Cut 11¼x11½ on 2 or 3 Sides***

**4869** A3716 (49c) multicolored 1.40 .25
*a.* Booklet pane of 20 28.00

**With "USPS" Microprinted in Fireworks Above Flagpole**

***Serpentine Die Cut 11¼x10¾ on 2 or 3 Sides***

**4870** A3716 (49c) multicolored 1.40 .25
*a.* Booklet pane of 20 28.00

The actual design images on Nos. 4855, 4869 and 4870 differ slightly in size. This is easiest seen by measuring the height of the flagpole: No. 4855 is 13mm, No. 4869 is 14mm, and No. 4870 is 12mm.

**Thin Paper**

***Serpentine Die Cut 11¼x11 on 2, 3 or 4 Sides***

**4871** A3716 (49c) multicolored 1.40 .25
*a.* Booklet pane of 18 28.00

Nos. 4869a and 4870a are double-sided booklets with 12 stamps on one side and eight stamps plus a label that serves as the booklet cover on the other side.

**AMERICAN LANDMARKS ISSUE**

Verrazano-Narrows Bridge, New York — A3726

USS Arizona Memorial, Hawaii — A3727

LITHOGRAPHED

**2014** ***Serpentine Die Cut 10¾x10½***

**Self-Adhesive**

**4872** A3726 $5.60 multi 11.00 6.25
**4873** A3727 $19.99 multi 40.00 21.00
*a.* Imperforate 55.00 —

Issued: $5.60, 3/4; $19.99, 3/13.

# 132 UNITED STATES

## FERNS

Fortune's Holly Fern A3728

Soft Shield Fern A3729

Autumn Fern A3730

Goldie's Wood Fern A3731

Painted Fern — A3732

**PHOTOGRAVURE**
*Serpentine Die Cut 11 Vert.*
2014, Mar. 6      **Coil Stamps**
                  **Self-Adhesive**

| 4874 | A3728 | (49c) multicolored | 2.00 | .25 |
| 4875 | A3729 | (49c) multicolored | 2.00 | .25 |
| 4876 | A3730 | (49c) multicolored | 2.00 | .25 |
| 4877 | A3731 | (49c) multicolored | 2.00 | .25 |
| 4878 | A3732 | (49c) multicolored | 2.00 | .25 |
| a.   | Strip of 5, #4874-4878 |    | 10.00 | |
|      | Nos. 4874-4878 (5) |        | 10.00 | 1.25 |

## DISTINGUISHED AMERICANS

C. Alfred "Chief" Anderson (1907-96), Aviator — A3733

**LITHOGRAPHED**
*Serpentine Die Cut 10¾x11*
2014, Mar. 13     **Self-Adhesive**

| 4879 | A3733 | 70c multicolored | 1.40 | .30 |
| a.   | Imperforate |        | 3.00 | — |

## MUSIC ICONS

Jimi Hendrix (1942-70), Rock Guitarist — A3734

**PHOTOGRAVURE**
2014, Mar. 13     Tagged
                  **Self-Adhesive**

| 4880 | A3734 | (49c) multicolored | 1.40 | .25 |
| a.   | Imperforate |        | 1.75 | — |

Adjacent horizontal or vertical stamps have selvage between the stamps. Any stamp on the pane is rotated 90 degrees with respect to any adjacent stamp, so that any block of four has stamps oriented in each of the four directions. See No. 4765.

### Flowers and "Yes I Do" Type of 2013

**LITHOGRAPHED**
*Serpentine Die Cut 10¾*
2014, Mar. 21     **Self-Adhesive**

| 4881 | A3639 | 70c multicolored | 1.40 | .30 |
|      | See Nos. 4765, 5001. |

## SONGBIRDS

Western Meadowlark A3735

Mountain Bluebird A3736

Western Tanager A3737

Painted Bunting A3738

Baltimore Oriole A3739

Evening Grosbeak A3740

Scarlet Tanager A3741

Rose-breasted Grosbeak A3742

American Goldfinch A3743

White-throated Sparrow A3744

**LITHOGRAPHED**
*Serpentine Die Cut 10¾ on 2 or 3 Sides*
2014, Apr. 5      **Booklet Stamps**
                  **Self-Adhesive**

| 4882 | A3735 | (49c) multicolored | 1.50 | .40 |
| 4883 | A3736 | (49c) multicolored | 1.50 | .40 |
| 4884 | A3737 | (49c) multicolored | 1.50 | .40 |
| 4885 | A3738 | (49c) multicolored | 1.50 | .40 |
| 4886 | A3739 | (49c) multicolored | 1.50 | .40 |
| 4887 | A3740 | (49c) multicolored | 1.50 | .40 |
| 4888 | A3741 | (49c) multicolored | 1.50 | .40 |
| 4889 | A3742 | (49c) multicolored | 1.50 | .40 |
| 4890 | A3743 | (49c) multicolored | 1.50 | .40 |
| 4891 | A3744 | (49c) multicolored | 1.50 | .40 |
| a.   | Block of 10, #4882-4891 | | 15.00 | |
| b.   | Booklet pane of 20, 2 each #4882-4891 | | 30.00 | |
| c.   | Imperforate block of 10 | | 20.00 | |
| d.   | Imperforate booklet pane of 20 | | 40.00 | |
|      | Nos. 4882-4891 (10) | | 15.00 | 4.00 |

No. 4891b is a double-sided booklet pane with 12 stamps on one side (Nos. 4883-4886, 4888-4891, 2 each Nos. 4882, 4887) and eight stamps (Nos. 4883-4886, 4888-4891) plus label (booklet cover) on the other side.

## LEGENDS OF HOLLYWOOD

Charlton Heston (1923-2008), Actor — A3745

**LITHOGRAPHED**
*Serpentine Die Cut 11*
2014, Apr. 11     **Self-Adhesive**

| 4892 | A3745 | (49c) multicolored | 1.40 | .25 |
| a.   | Imperforate |        | 1.75 | — |

Map of Sea Surface Temperatures A3746

**LITHOGRAPHED**
2014, Apr. 22     *Serpentine Die Cut*
                  **Self-Adhesive**

| 4893 | A3746 | ($1.15) multi | 3.25 | .50 |
| a.   | Imperforate |        | 3.50 | — |

Unused values are for stamps with surrounding selvage. Adjacent stamps are separated by rouletting.

## FLAGS

Flag With 5 Full and 3 Partial Stars A3747

Flag With 3 Full Stars A3748

Flag With 4 Full and 2 Partial Stars A3749

Flag With 2 Full and 2 Partial Stars A3750

**PHOTOGRAVURE**
*Serpentine Die Cut 11 Vert.*
2014, Apr. 25     **Coil Stamps**
                  **Self-Adhesive**

| 4894 | A3747 | (49c) blue & red | 1.40 | .25 |
| 4895 | A3748 | (49c) blue & red | 1.40 | .25 |
| 4896 | A3749 | (49c) blue & red | 1.40 | .25 |
| 4897 | A3750 | (49c) blue & red | 1.40 | .25 |
| a.   | Strip of 4, #4894-4897 | | 5.60 | |
|      | Nos. 4894-4897 (4) | | 5.60 | 1.00 |

## CIRCUS POSTERS

Barnum and Bailey Circus Poster With Clown A3751

Sells-Floto Circus Poster — A3752

Ringling Bros. Barnum and Bailey Circus Poster With Dainty Miss Leitzel A3753

Al G. Barnes Wild Animal Circus Poster — A3754

Ringling Bros. Shows Poster With Hillary Long A3755

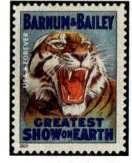
Barnum and Bailey Circus Poster With Tiger — A3756

Ringling Bros. Barnum and Bailey Circus Poster With Elephant A3757

Carl Hagenbeck-Wallace Circus Poster — A3758

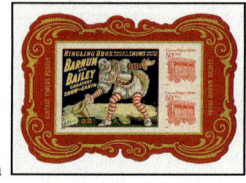
A3758a

**LITHOGRAPHED, ENGRAVED (50c), SHEET MARGIN (#4905b)**
**LITHOGRAPHED WITH FOIL APPLICATION**
*Serpentine Die Cut 11*
2014, May 5       **Self-Adhesive**

| 4898 | A3751 | (49c) multicolored | 1.40 | .45 |
| 4899 | A3752 | (49c) multicolored | 1.40 | .45 |
| 4900 | A3753 | (49c) multicolored | 1.40 | .45 |
| 4901 | A3754 | (49c) multicolored | 1.40 | .45 |
| 4902 | A3755 | (49c) multicolored | 1.40 | .45 |
| 4903 | A3756 | (49c) multicolored | 1.40 | .45 |
| 4904 | A3757 | (49c) multicolored | 1.40 | .45 |
| 4905 | A3758 | (49c) multicolored | 1.40 | .45 |
| a.   | Block of 8, #4898-4905 | | 11.20 | |
| b.   | Imperforate block of 8 | | 16.00 | — |
| c.   | A3758a Imperforate souvenir sheet of 3, #4905d, 2 #4905c | | 9.00 | — |
| d.   | A1811 50c red, imperforate | | 2.25 | — |
| e.   | $1 multicolored (57x48mm stamp similar to #4898), imperforate | | 4.50 | — |
| f.   | As "c," gold omitted in sheet margin | | — | — |
|      | Nos. 4898-4905 (8) | | 11.20 | 3.60 |

No. 4905c was printed only in press sheets containing 12 souvenir sheets. No. 4905c has die cutting around the souvenir sheet margin, but values for unused examples are for souvenir sheets having the white press sheet margin surrounding the die cutting. Examples of No. 4905c with serpentine die cutting around the three stamps were sold only with the USPS 2014 Stamp Yearbook, which sold for $64.95. The souvenir sheets sold with the yearbook are punched out from the press sheets and lack the white press sheet margin.

UNITED STATES 133

### HARVEY MILK

Harvey Milk (1930-78), Homosexual Rights Advocate and Politician — A3759

**LITHOGRAPHED**
Sheets of 240 in 12 panes of 20
*Serpentine Die Cut 10¾*
**2014, May 22**
**Self-Adhesive**

| 4906 | A3759 | (49c) multicolored | 1.40 | .25 |
| a. | | Imperforate | 1.75 | |

### NEVADA STATEHOOD, 150th ANNIV.

Fire Canyon — A3760

**LITHOGRAPHED**
*Serpentine Die Cut 10¾*
**2014, May 29**
**Self-Adhesive**

| 4907 | A3760 | (49c) multicolored | 1.40 | .25 |
| a. | | Imperforate | 1.75 | |

### HOT RODS

Rear of 1932 Ford "Deuce" Roadster A3761

Front of 1932 Ford "Deuce" Roadster A3762

**PHOTOGRAVURE**
*Serpentine Die Cut 11¾x11¼ on 2 or 3 Sides*
**2014, June 6**
**Booklet Stamps**
**Self-Adhesive**

| 4908 | A3761 | (49c) multicolored | 1.40 | .25 |
| 4909 | A3762 | (49c) multicolored | 1.40 | .25 |
| a. | | Pair, #4908-4909 | 2.80 | |
| b. | | Booklet pane of 20, 10 each #4908-4909 | 28.00 | |
| c. | | Imperforate pair | 4.00 | |
| d. | | Imperforate booklet pane of 20 | 40.00 | |

No. 4909b is a double-sided booklet pane with 12 stamps on one side (6 each Nos. 4908-4909) and eight stamps (4 each Nos. 4908-4909) plus label (booklet cover) on the other side.

### CIVIL WAR SESQUICENTENNIAL

Battle of Petersburg A3763

Battle of Mobile Bay A3764

**LITHOGRAPHED**
*Serpentine Die Cut 11*
**2014, July 30**
**Self-Adhesive**

| 4910 | A3763 | (49c) multicolored | 1.40 | .35 |
| 4911 | A3764 | (49c) multicolored | 1.40 | .35 |
| a. | | Pair, #4910-4911 | 2.80 | |
| b. | | Imperforate pair | 5.00 | |

### FARMERS MARKETS

Breads A3765

Fruits and Vegetables A3766

Flowers A3767

Plants A3768

**LITHOGRAPHED**
*Serpentine Die Cut 10¾*
**2014, Aug. 7**
**Self-Adhesive**

| 4912 | A3765 | (49c) multicolored | 1.40 | .30 |
| 4913 | A3766 | (49c) multicolored | 1.40 | .30 |
| 4914 | A3767 | (49c) multicolored | 1.40 | .30 |
| 4915 | A3768 | (49c) multicolored | 1.40 | .30 |
| a. | | Horiz. strip of 4, #4912-4915 | 5.00 | |
| b. | | Imperf. horiz. strip of 4 | 9.00 | |
| | | Nos. 4912-4915 (4) | 5.60 | 1.20 |

### MUSIC ICONS

Janis Joplin (1943-70), Rock Singer — A3769

**LITHOGRAPHED**
*Serpentine Die Cut 10½*
**2014, Aug. 8**
**Self-Adhesive**

| 4916 | A3769 | (49c) multicolored | 1.30 | .25 |
| a. | | Imperforate | 1.75 | |

### HUDSON RIVER SCHOOL PAINTINGS

*Grand Canyon*, by Thomas Moran (1837-1926) A3770

*Summer Afternoon*, by Asher B. Durand (1796-1886) A3771

*Sunset*, by Frederic Edwin Church (1826-1900) A3772

*Distant View of Niagara Falls*, by Thomas Cole (1801-48) A3773

**PHOTOGRAVURE**
*Serpentine Die Cut 10¾ on 2 or 3 Sides*
**2014, Aug. 21**
**Booklet Stamps**
**Self-Adhesive**

| 4917 | A3770 | (49c) multicolored | 1.50 | .30 |
| 4918 | A3771 | (49c) multicolored | 1.50 | .30 |
| 4919 | A3772 | (49c) multicolored | 1.50 | .30 |
| 4920 | A3773 | (49c) multicolored | 1.50 | .30 |
| a. | | Block of 4, #4917-4920 | 6.00 | |
| b. | | Booklet pane of 20, 5 each #4917-4920 | 30.00 | |
| c. | | Imperforate block of 4 | 8.00 | |
| d. | | Imperforate booklet pane of 20 | 40.00 | |
| | | Nos. 4917-4920 (4) | 6.00 | 1.20 |

No. 4920b is a double-sided booklet pane with 12 stamps on one side (3 each #4917-4920), and eight stamps (2 each #4917-4920) plus label (booklet cover) on the other side.

### WAR OF 1812 BICENTENNIAL

Bombardment of Fort McHenry A3774

**PHOTOGRAVURE**
*Serpentine Die Cut 10¾x10½*
**2014, Sept. 13**
**Self-Adhesive**

| 4921 | A3774 | (49c) multicolored | 1.40 | .25 |
| | | Pane of 20 | 28.00 | |
| a. | | Imperforate | 1.75 | |

### CELEBRITY CHEFS

Edna Lewis (1916-2006) A3775

Felipe Rojas-Lombardi (1946-91) A3776

Joyce Chen (1917-94) A3777

James Beard (1903-85) A3778

Julia Child (1912-2004) — A3779

**LITHOGRAPHED**
*Serpentine Die Cut 11x10¾*
**2014, Sept. 26**
**Self-Adhesive**

| 4922 | A3775 | (49c) multicolored | 1.40 | .45 |
| 4923 | A3776 | (10c) multicolored | 1.40 | .45 |
| 4924 | A3777 | (49c) multicolored | 1.40 | .45 |
| 4925 | A3778 | (49c) multicolored | 1.40 | .45 |
| 4926 | A3779 | (49c) multicolored | 1.40 | .45 |
| a. | | Horiz. strip of 5, #4922-4926 | 7.00 | |
| b. | | Imperf. horiz. strip of 5 | 8.00 | |
| | | Nos. 4922-4926 (5) | 7.00 | 2.25 |

The gray shading of the inner curve of the dinner plate shown in the margin of the pane continues into the white frames surrounding some of the stamps in the pane's outer rows and columns.

### AMERICAN LANDMARKS ISSUE

Glade Creek Grist Mill, West Virginia — A3780

**LITHOGRAPHED**
*Serpentine Die Cut 10¾x10½*
**2014, Sept. 29**
**Self-Adhesive**

| 4927 | A3780 | $5.75 multi | 11.50 | 6.50 |
| a. | | Imperforate | 15.00 | |

### BATMAN

Bat Signal A3781

Bat Signal A3782

Bat Signal A3783

Bat Signal A3784

Batman A3785

Batman and Bat Signal A3786

Batman and Rope A3787

Batman A3788

**LITHOGRAPHED**
**2014, Oct. 9**   *Serpentine Die Cut*
**Self-Adhesive**

| 4928 | A3781 | (49c) multicolored | 3.00 | .40 |
| 4929 | A3782 | (49c) multicolored | 3.00 | .40 |
| 4930 | A3783 | (49c) multicolored | 3.00 | .40 |
| 4931 | A3784 | (49c) multicolored | 3.00 | .40 |

*Serpentine Die Cut 11x10¾*

| 4932 | A3785 | (49c) multicolored | 1.40 | .40 |
| 4933 | A3786 | (49c) multicolored | 1.40 | .40 |
| 4934 | A3787 | (49c) multicolored | 1.40 | .40 |
| 4935 | A3788 | (49c) multicolored | 1.40 | .40 |
| a. | | Vert. block of 8, #4928-4935 | 17.60 | |
| b. | | Imperf. vert. block of 8 | 20.00 | |
| | | Nos. 4928-4935 (8) | 17.60 | 3.20 |

Silver Bells Wreath — A3789

**LITHOGRAPHED**
**2014, Oct. 23**   *Serpentine Die Cut*
**Self-Adhesive**

| 4936 | A3789 | ($1.15) multicolored | 3.25 | .50 |
| a. | | Imperforate | 4.00 | |

Unused values are for stamps with surrounding selvage. Adjacent stamps are separated by rouletting.

### WINTER FUN

Skaters A3790

Child Making Snowman A3791

Cardinal A3792

Child Making Snow Angel A3793

134 UNITED STATES

PHOTOGRAVURE

***Serpentine Die Cut 10¾x11 on 2 or 3 Sides***

**2014, Oct. 23**

**Booklet Stamps Self-Adhesive**

| | | | | | |
|---|---|---|---|---|---|
| **4937** | A3790 | (49c) | multicolored | 1.40 | .30 |
| **4938** | A3791 | (49c) | multicolored | 1.40 | .30 |
| **4939** | A3792 | (49c) | multicolored | 1.40 | .30 |
| **4940** | A3793 | (49c) | multicolored | 1.40 | .30 |
| *a.* | Block of 4, #4937-4940 | | | 5.60 | |
| *b.* | Booklet pane of 20, 5 each #4937-4940 | | | 28.00 | |
| *c.* | Imperforate block of 4 | | | 7.00 | — |
| *d.* | Imperf. booklet pane of 20 | | | 35.00 | |

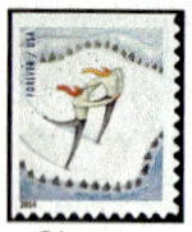
Skaters A3794

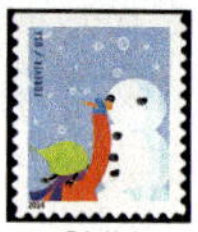
Child Making Snowman A3795

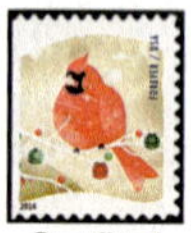
Cardinal A3796

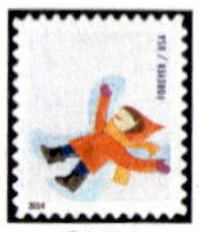
Child Making Snow Angel A3797

LITHOGRAPHED

***Serpentine Die Cut 11¼x11 on 2, 3 or 4 Sides***

**Thin Paper**

| | | | | | |
|---|---|---|---|---|---|
| **4941** | A3794 | (49c) | multicolored | 5.00 | .30 |
| **4942** | A3795 | (49c) | multicolored | 5.00 | .30 |
| **4943** | A3796 | (49c) | multicolored | 5.00 | .30 |
| **4944** | A3797 | (49c) | multicolored | 5.00 | .30 |
| *a.* | Block or strip of 4, #4941-4944 | | | 20.00 | |
| *b.* | Booklet pane of 18, 5 each #4941-4942, 4 each #4943-4944 | | | 90.00 | |
| | *Nos. 4937-4944 (8)* | | | 25.60 | 2.40 |

**CHRISTMAS**

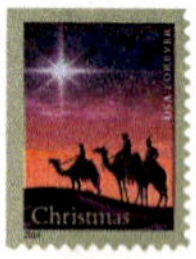
Magi A3798

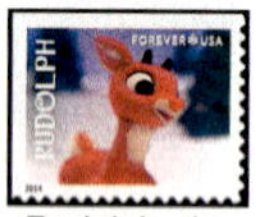
Rudolph, the Red-Nosed Reindeer A3799

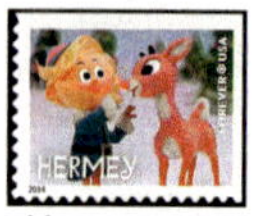
Hermey and Rudolph A3800

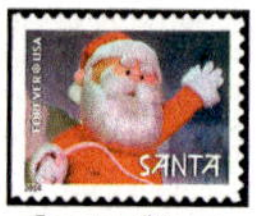
Santa Claus A3801

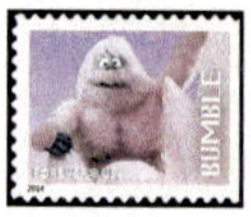
Bumble — A3802

LITHOGRAPHED (#4945), PHOTOGRAVURE

***Serpentine Die Cut 10¾x11 on 2 or 3 Sides***

**2014**

**Booklet Stamps Self-Adhesive**

| | | | | | |
|---|---|---|---|---|---|
| **4945** | A3798 | (49c) | multi | 1.40 | .25 |
| *a.* | Booklet pane of 20 | | | 28.00 | |
| *b.* | Imperforate | | | 1.75 | — |
| *c.* | Imperf. booklet pane of 20 | | | 35.00 | |

***Serpentine Die Cut 11x10¾ on 2 or 3 sides***

| | | | | | |
|---|---|---|---|---|---|
| **4946** | A3799 | (49c) | multi | 1.40 | .30 |
| **4947** | A3800 | (49c) | multi | 1.40 | .30 |
| **4948** | A3801 | (49c) | multi | 1.40 | .30 |
| **4949** | A3802 | (49c) | multi | 1.40 | .30 |
| *a.* | Block of 4, #4946-4949 | | | 5.60 | |
| *b.* | Booklet pane of 20, 5 each #4946-4949 | | | 28.00 | |
| *c.* | Imperf. block of 4 | | | 7.50 | — |
| *d.* | Imperf. booklet pane of 20 | | | 37.50 | |
| | *Nos. 4945-4949 (5)* | | | 7.00 | 1.45 |

Issued: No. 4945, 11/19; Nos. 4946-4949, 11/6.

Premiere of *Rudolph, the Red-Nosed Reindeer* animated television show, 50th anniv.

No. 4945a is a double-sided booklet with 12 stamps on one side and eight stamps plus a label that serves as a booklet cover on the other side. No. 4949b is a double-sided booklet with 12 stamps on one side (3 each of Nos. 4946-4949) and eight stamps (2 each of Nos. 4946-4949) plus a label that serves as a booklet cover on the other side.

**WILT CHAMBERLAIN (1936-99), BASKETBALL PLAYER**

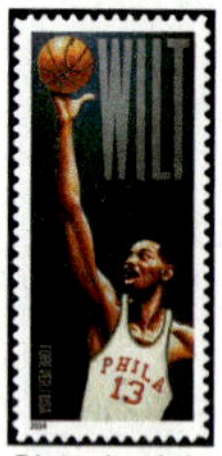

Chamberlain in Philadelphia Warriors Uniform A3803

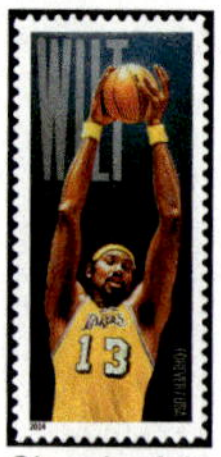

Chamberlain in Los Angeles Lakers Uniform A3804

LITHOGRAPHED

***Serpentine Die Cut 11x10¾***

**2014, Dec. 5**

**Self-Adhesive**

| | | | | | |
|---|---|---|---|---|---|
| **4950** | A3803 | (49c) | multicolored | 1.40 | .25 |
| **4951** | A3804 | (49c) | multicolored | 1.40 | .25 |
| *a.* | Pair, #4950-4951 | | | 2.80 | |
| *b.* | Imperforate pair | | | 3.50 | — |

**WAR OF 1812 BICENTENNIAL**

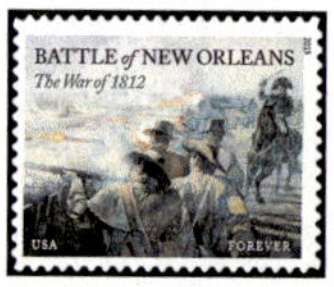

Battle of New Orleans — A3805

PHOTOGRAVURE

***Serpentine Die Cut 10¾x10½***

**2015, Jan. 8**

**Self-Adhesive**

| | | | | | |
|---|---|---|---|---|---|
| **4952** | A3805 | (49c) | multicolored | 1.40 | .25 |
| *a.* | Imperforate | | | 1.75 | — |

**PATRIOTIC WAVES**

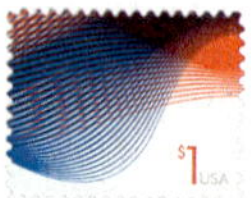
A3806

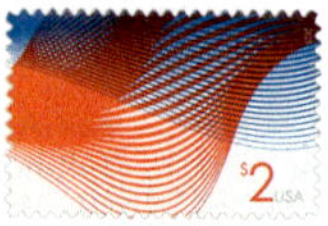
A3807

LITHOGRAPHED

***Serpentine Die Cut 11***

**2015** **Tagged**

**Self-Adhesive**

| | | | | | |
|---|---|---|---|---|---|
| **4953** | A3806 | $1 | multicolored | 2.00 | .50 |
| *a.* | Imperforate | | | 3.00 | — |
| **4954** | A3807 | $2 | multicolored | 4.00 | 1.00 |
| *a.* | Imperforate | | | 5.00 | — |

**LOVE**

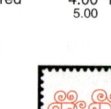

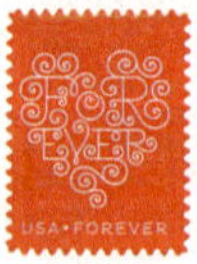
A3808

A3809

LITHOGRAPHED

***Serpentine Die Cut 11***

**2015, Jan. 22** **Tagged**

**Self-Adhesive**

| | | | | | |
|---|---|---|---|---|---|
| **4955** | A3808 | (49c) | red | 1.40 | .25 |
| **4956** | A3809 | (49c) | red & gray | 1.40 | .25 |
| *a.* | Pair, #4955-4956 | | | 2.80 | |
| *b.* | Imperforate pair | | | 3.50 | — |

**CHINESE NEW YEAR**

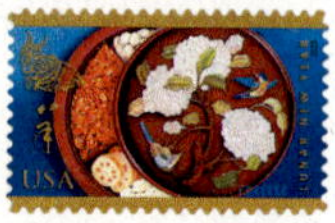
Year of the Ram — A3810

LITHOGRAPHED

**2015, Feb. 7** ***Serpentine Die Cut 11***

**Self-Adhesive**

| | | | | | |
|---|---|---|---|---|---|
| **4957** | A3810 | (49c) | multicolored | 1.40 | .25 |
| *a.* | Imperforate | | | 1.75 | — |

**BLACK HERITAGE**

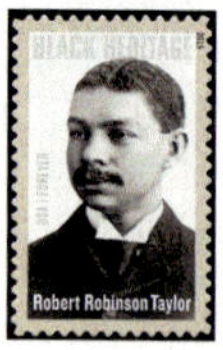

Robert Robinson Taylor (1868-1942), Architect — A3811

LITHOGRAPHED

***Serpentine Die Cut 11***

**2015, Feb. 12**

**Self-Adhesive**

| | | | | | |
|---|---|---|---|---|---|
| **4958** | A3811 | (49c) | multicolored | 1.40 | .25 |
| *a.* | Imperforate | | | 2.25 | — |

**FLOWERS**

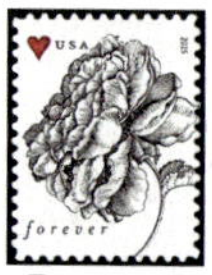
Rose and Heart A3812

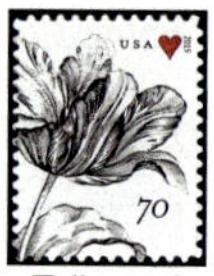
Tulip and Heart A3813

ENGRAVED

***Serpentine Die Cut 10¾x 11***

**2015, Feb. 14**

**Self-Adhesive**

| | | | | | |
|---|---|---|---|---|---|
| **4959** | A3812 | (49c) | red & black | 5.00 | .25 |
| *a.* | Imperforate | | | 1.75 | — |
| **4960** | A3813 | 70c | black & red | 3.00 | .30 |
| *a.* | Imperforate | | | 2.50 | — |

See No. 5002.

**FLAGS**

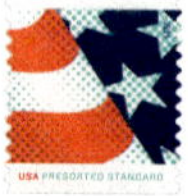
Stripes at Left, Stars at Right A3814

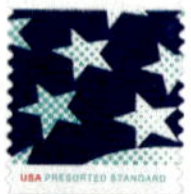
Stars and White Stripe A3815

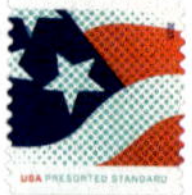
Stars at Left, Stripes at Right — A3816

LITHOGRAPHED

***Serpentine Die Cut 11 Vert.***

**2015, Feb. 27**

**Coil Stamps Self-Adhesive**

| | | | | | |
|---|---|---|---|---|---|
| **4961** | A3814 | (10c) | multicolored | .30 | .25 |
| **4962** | A3815 | (10c) | multicolored | .30 | .25 |
| **4963** | A3816 | (10c) | multicolored | .30 | .25 |
| *a.* | Strip of 3, #4961-4963 | | | .75 | |
| | *Nos. 4961-4963 (3)* | | | .90 | .75 |

**WATER LILIES**

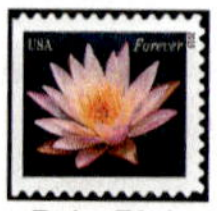
Pale Pink Water Lily A3817

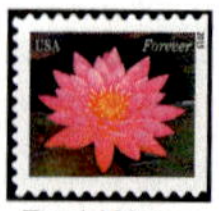
Red Water Lily A3818

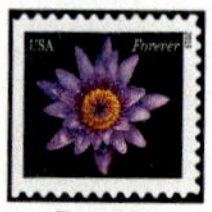
Purple Water Lily A3819

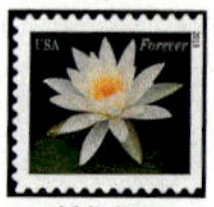
White Water Lily A3820

LITHOGRAPHED

***Serpentine Die Cut 11x11¼ on 2 or 3 Sides***

**2015, Mar. 20**

**Booklet Stamps Self-Adhesive**

| | | | | | |
|---|---|---|---|---|---|
| **4964** | A3817 | (49c) | multicolored | 1.50 | .25 |
| **4965** | A3818 | (49c) | multicolored | 1.50 | .25 |
| **4966** | A3819 | (49c) | multicolored | 1.50 | .25 |
| **4967** | A3820 | (49c) | multicolored | 1.50 | .25 |
| *a.* | Block of 4, #4964-4967 | | | 6.00 | |
| *b.* | Booklet pane of 20, 5 each #4964-4967 | | | 30.00 | |
| *c.* | Imperf. block of 4 | | | 7.00 | — |
| *d.* | Imperf. booklet pane of 20 | | | 35.00 | |
| | *Nos. 4964-4967 (4)* | | | 6.00 | 1.00 |

No. 4967b is a double-sided booklet pane with 12 stamps on one side (3 each Nos. 4964-4967) and eight stamps (2 each Nos. 4964-4967) plus label (booklet cover) on the other side.

**ART BY MARTIN RAMIREZ (1895-1963)**

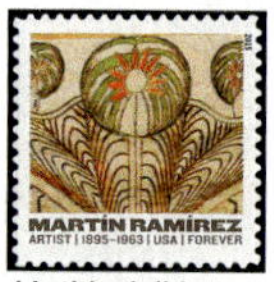

Untitled (Horse and Rider With Trees), 1954 A3821

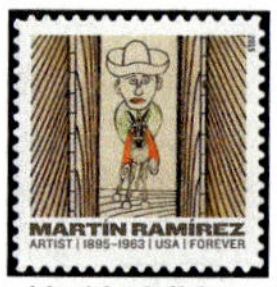

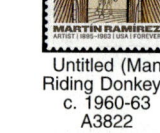

Untitled (Man Riding Donkey), c. 1960-63 A3822

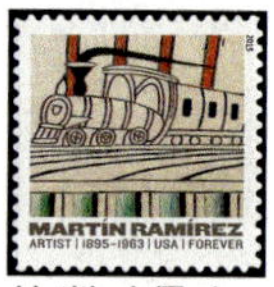

Untitled (Trains on Inclined Tracks), c. 1960-63 A3823

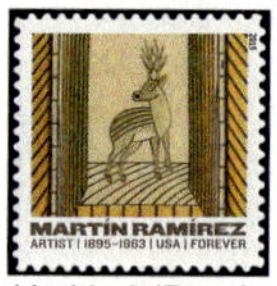

Untitled (Deer), c. 1960-63 A3824

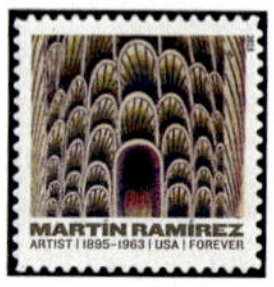

Untitled (Tunnel with Cars and Buses), 1954 — A3825

LITHOGRAPHED

***Serpentine Die Cut 10¾***

**2015, Mar. 26**

**Self-Adhesive**

| | | | | | |
|---|---|---|---|---|---|
| **4968** | A3821 | (49c) | multicolored | 1.40 | .40 |
| **4969** | A3822 | (49c) | multicolored | 1.40 | .40 |
| **4970** | A3823 | (49c) | multicolored | 1.40 | .40 |
| **4971** | A3824 | (49c) | multicolored | 1.40 | .40 |
| **4972** | A3825 | (49c) | multicolored | 1.40 | .40 |
| *a.* | Vert. strip of 5, #4968-4972 | | | 7.00 | |
| *b.* | Imperf. vert. strip of 5 | | | 7.50 | — |

**Ferns Type of 2014**

LITHOGRAPHED

***Serpentine Die Cut 11 Vert.***

**2015, Mar. 27**

**Coil Stamps Self-Adhesive With Microprinted "USPS" Dated "2014"**

| | | | | | |
|---|---|---|---|---|---|
| **4973** | A3729 | (49c) | multicolored | 1.40 | .25 |
| *a.* | Dated "2015" | | | 1.40 | .25 |
| **4974** | A3730 | (49c) | multicolored | 1.40 | .25 |
| *a.* | Dated "2015" | | | 1.40 | .25 |
| **4975** | A3731 | (49c) | multicolored | 1.40 | .25 |
| *a.* | Dated "2015" | | | 1.40 | .25 |
| **4976** | A3732 | (49c) | multicolored | 1.40 | .25 |
| *a.* | Dated "2015" | | | 1.40 | .25 |
| **4977** | A3728 | (49c) | multicolored | 1.40 | .25 |
| *a.* | Dated "2015" | | | 1.40 | .25 |
| *b.* | Strip of 5, #4973-4977 | | | 7.00 | |
| *c.* | Strip of 5, #4973a-4977a | | | 7.00 | |
| | *Nos. 4973-4977 (5)* | | | 7.00 | 1.25 |

Nos. 4973a-4977a are from coil rolls containing 3,000 stamps. Nos. 4973-4977 are from coil rolls containing 10,000 stamps. Microprinted "USPS" is near the end of the upper left fern branch on No. 4973 and near the base of the fern's stem on Nos. 4974-

# UNITED STATES

4977. Nos. 4973a-4977a have same microprinting locations as Nos. 4973-4977. Nos. 4874-4878 lack microprinted "USPS."

## FROM ME TO YOU

A3826

**LITHOGRAPHED**
Sheets of 120 in six panes of 20
**2015, Apr. 1    Serpentine Die Cut 11**
**Self-Adhesive**

| 4978 | A3826 | (49c) | multicolored | 1.40 | .25 |
|---|---|---|---|---|---|
| a. | Imperforate | | | 2.00 | — |

## MAYA ANGELOU (1928-2014), WRITER

Angelou and Quotation
A3827

**LITHOGRAPHED**
**2015, Apr. 7    Serpentine Die Cut 11**
**Self-Adhesive**

| 4979 | A3827 | (10c) | multicolored | 1.40 | .25 |
|---|---|---|---|---|---|
| a. | Imperforate | | | 1.75 | — |

The quotation on the stamp is not Angelou's but is similar to a quote by Joan Walsh Anglund.

## CIVIL WAR SESQUICENTENNIAL

Battle of Five Forks
A3828

Surrender at Appomattox Court House — A3829

**LITHOGRAPHED**
Double-sided sheets of 72 in six panes of 12 (60 on one side, 12 on other side)
**2015, Apr. 9    Serpentine Die Cut 11**
**Self-Adhesive**

| 4980 | A3828 | (49c) | multicolored | 1.40 | .30 |
|---|---|---|---|---|---|
| 4981 | A3829 | (49c) | multicolored | 1.40 | .30 |
| a. | Pair, #4980-4981 | | | 2.80 | |
| b. | Imperforate pair | | | 27.50 | — |

## GIFTS OF FRIENDSHIP

Lincoln Memorial and Cherry Blossoms
A3830

U.S. Capitol and Dogwood Blossoms
A3831

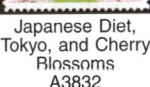
Japanese Diet, Tokyo, and Cherry Blossoms
A3832

Clock Tower, Tokyo, and Dogwood Blossoms
A3833

**LITHOGRAPHED**
Sheets of 72 in six panes of 12
**Serpentine Die Cut 11**
**2015, Apr. 10**
**Self-Adhesive**

| 4982 | A3830 | (49c) | multicolored | 1.40 | .30 |
|---|---|---|---|---|---|
| 4983 | A3831 | (49c) | multicolored | 1.40 | .30 |
| a. | Horiz. pair, #4982-4983 | | | 2.80 | |
| b. | Imperforate pair | | | 4.50 | — |
| 4984 | A3832 | (49c) | multicolored | 5.00 | .30 |
| 4985 | A3833 | (49c) | multicolored | 5.00 | .30 |
| a. | Horiz. pair, #4984-4985 | | | 10.00 | |
| b. | Imperforate pair | | | 12.50 | — |
| | Nos. 4982-4985 (4) | | | 12.80 | 1.20 |

See Japan No. 3814.

## SPECIAL OLYMPICS WORLD GAMES

Emblem — A3834

**LITHOGRAPHED**
**Serpentine Die Cut 10¾**
**2015, May 9**
**Self-Adhesive**

| 4986 | A3834 | (49c) | multicolored | 1.40 | .25 |
|---|---|---|---|---|---|
| a. | Imperforate | | | 1.75 | — |

## HELP FIND MISSING CHILDREN

Forget-me-nots
A3835

**LITHOGRAPHED**
**Serpentine Die Cut 10¾**
**2015, May 18**
**Self-Adhesive**

| 4987 | A3835 | (49c) | multicolored | 1.40 | .25 |
|---|---|---|---|---|---|
| a. | Imperforate | | | 1.75 | — |

## MEDAL OF HONOR

Air Force Medal of Honor — A3836

**LITHOGRAPHED**
**2015, May 25    Serpentine Die Cut 11**
**Self-Adhesive**

| 4988 | A3836 | (49c) | multicolored | 1.40 | .25 |
|---|---|---|---|---|---|
| a. | Horiz. strip of 3, #4822c, 4823b, 4988 | | | 4.20 | |
| b. | Imperforate strip of 3 | | | 6.00 | — |

## WILDLIFE ISSUE

Emperor Penguins — A3837

**LITHOGRAPHED**
**Serpentine Die Cut 11¼x11**
**2015, June 1**
**Self-Adhesive**

| 4989 | A3837 | (22c) | multicolored | .50 | .25 |
|---|---|---|---|---|---|
| a. | Imperforate | | | 1.00 | — |

**Coil Stamp**
**Serpentine Die Cut 11 Vert.**

| 4990 | A3837 | (22c) | multicolored | .50 | .25 |
|---|---|---|---|---|---|

## COASTAL BIRDS

Red Knot
A3838

King Eider
A3839

Spoonbill
A3840

Frigatebird
A3841

**LITHOGRAPHED**
**Serpentine Die Cut 11¼x11**
**2015, June 1**
**Self-Adhesive**

| 4991 | A3838 | (35c) | multicolored | 1.10 | .25 |
|---|---|---|---|---|---|
| 4992 | A3839 | (35c) | multicolored | 1.10 | .25 |
| 4993 | A3840 | (35c) | multicolored | 1.10 | .25 |
| 4994 | A3841 | (35c) | multicolored | 1.10 | .25 |
| a. | Block or vert. strip of 4, #4991-4994 | | | 4.40 | |
| b. | Imperforate block or vert. strip of 4 | | | 4.50 | — |

**Coil Stamps**
**Serpentine Die Cut 9½ Vert.**

| 4995 | A3840 | (35c) | multicolored | 1.10 | .25 |
|---|---|---|---|---|---|
| 4996 | A3841 | (35c) | multicolored | 1.10 | .25 |
| 4997 | A3838 | (35c) | multicolored | 1.10 | .25 |
| 4998 | A3839 | (35c) | multicolored | 1.10 | .25 |
| a. | Horiz. strip of 4, #4995-4998 | | | 4.40 | |

## EASTERN TIGER SWALLOWTAIL BUTTERFLY

A3842

**LITHOGRAPHED**
**Serpentine Die Cut 10½**
**2015, June 1**
**Self-Adhesive**

| 4999 | A3842 | (71c) | multicolored | 2.25 | .25 |
|---|---|---|---|---|---|
| a. | Imperforate | | | 2.50 | — |

Wedding Cake — A3843

**LITHOGRAPHED**
**Serpentine Die Cut 10¾**
**2015, June 1**
**Self-Adhesive**

| 5000 | A3843 | (71c) | multicolored | 5.00 | .25 |
|---|---|---|---|---|---|

Flowers and "Yes, I Do" — A3844

**LITHOGRAPHED**
**Serpentine Die Cut 10¾**
**2015, June 1    Tagged**
**Self-Adhesive**

| 5001 | A3844 | (71c) | multicolored | 5.00 | .25 |
|---|---|---|---|---|---|

See Nos. 4765, 4881.

Tulip and Heart — A3845

**ENGRAVED**
**2015, June 1    Serpentine Die Cut 11**
**Self-Adhesive**

| 5002 | A3845 | (71c) | black & red | 6.00 | .25 |
|---|---|---|---|---|---|

See No. 4960.

## LITERARY ARTS

Flannery O'Connor (1925-64), Novelist — A3846

**LITHOGRAPHED**
**Serpentine Die Cut 10¾**
**2015, June 5**
**Self-Adhesive**

| 5003 | A3846 | (93c) | multicolored | 2.40 | .30 |
|---|---|---|---|---|---|
| a. | Imperforate | | | 2.50 | — |

## SUMMER HARVEST

Watermelon
A3847

Sweet Corn
A3848

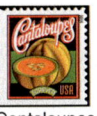
Cantaloupes
A3849

Tomatoes
A3850

**LITHOGRAPHED**
**Serpentine Die Cut 11¼x10¾ on 2 or 3 Sides**
**2015, July 11**
**Booklet Stamps**
**Self-Adhesive**

| 5004 | A3847 | (10c) | multicolored | 1.50 | .30 |
|---|---|---|---|---|---|
| 5005 | A3848 | (49c) | multicolored | 1.50 | .30 |
| 5006 | A3849 | (49c) | multicolored | 1.50 | .30 |
| 5007 | A3850 | (49c) | multicolored | 1.50 | .30 |
| a. | Block of 4, #5004-5007 | | | 6.00 | |
| b. | Booklet pane of 20, 5 each #5004-5007 | | | 30.00 | |
| c. | As "a," imperforate | | | 7.00 | |
| d. | As "b," imperforate | | | 35.00 | |
| | Nos. 5004-5007 (4) | | | 6.00 | 1.20 |

No. 5007b is a double-sided booklet pane with 12 stamps on one side (3 each #5004-5007), and eight stamps (2 each #5004-5007) plus label (booklet cover) on the other side.

## COAST GUARD

MH-65 Dolphin Helicopter and Cutter Eagle — A3851

**LITHOGRAPHED**
**Serpentine Die Cut 10¾**
**2015, Aug. 4    Tagged**
**Self-Adhesive**

| 5008 | A3851 | (49c) | multicolored | 1.40 | .25 |
|---|---|---|---|---|---|
| a. | Imperforate | | | 1.75 | — |

## MUSIC ICONS

Elvis Presley (1935-77), Singer — A3852

**LITHOGRAPHED**
**Serpentine Die Cut 10½**
**2015, Aug. 12**
**Self-Adhesive**

| 5009 | A3852 | (49c) | multicolored | 1.40 | .25 |
|---|---|---|---|---|---|
| a. | Imperforate | | | 1.75 | — |

## 2016 WORLD STAMP SHOW, NEW YORK CITY

Star — A3853

**LITHOGRAPHED**
**Serpentine Die Cut 11**
**2015, Aug. 20**
**Self-Adhesive**

| 5010 | A3853 | (49c) | red | 1.40 | .25 |
|---|---|---|---|---|---|
| 5011 | A3853 | (49c) | blue | 1.40 | .25 |
| a. | Pair, #5010-5011 | | | 2.80 | |
| b. | As "a," imperforate | | | 4.00 | — |

### LEGENDS OF HOLLYWOOD

Ingrid Bergman (1915-82), Actress — A3854

LITHOGRAPHED
***Serpentine Die Cut 11***
**2015, Aug. 20**
**Self-Adhesive**

**5012** A3854 (49c) multicolored 1.50 .25
*a.* Imperforate 1.75 —

See Sweden Nos. 2756-2758.

**Eagle Type of 2012**
LITHOGRAPHED
***Serpentine Die Cut 10¼ Vert.***
**2015, Sept. 2**
**Coil Stamps**
**Self-Adhesive**
**Color Behind "USA"**

**5013** A3504 (25c) green .50 .25
**5014** A3504 (25c) blue green .50 .25
**5015** A3504 (25c) blue .50 .25
**5016** A3504 (25c) red violet .50 .25
**5017** A3504 (25c) orange .50 .25
**5018** A3504 (25c) yellow orange .50 .25
*a.* Strip of 6, #5013-5018 3.00
*Nos. 5013-5018 (6)* 3.00 1.50

See Nos. 4585-4590.

### CELEBRATE

A3855

LITHOGRAPHED
***Serpentine Die Cut 10¾***
**2015, Sept. 9**
**Self-Adhesive**

**5019** A3855 (49c) multicolored 1.40 .25

Compare with type A3441.
Counterfeits exist of No. 5019. See the Postal Counterfeits section of this catalog.

### PAUL NEWMAN (1925-2008), ACTOR AND PHILANTHROPIST

A3856

LITHOGRAPHED
***Serpentine Die Cut 10¾***
**2015, Sept. 18**
**Self-Adhesive**

**5020** A3856 (49c) multicolored 1.40 .25
*a.* Imperforate 1.75 —

### CHRISTMAS

Charlie Brown Carrying Christmas Tree A3857

Charlie Brown, Pigpen and Dirty Snowman A3858

Snoopy, Lucy, Violet, Sally and Schroeder Skating A3859

Characters, Dog House and Christmas Tree A3860

Linus and Christmas Tree A3861

Charlie Brown Looking in Mailbox A3862

Charlie Brown and Linus Behind Brick Wall — A3863

Charlie Brown, Linus and Christmas Tree — A3864

Charlie Brown Screaming, Snoopy Decorating Dog House A3865

Charlie Brown Hanging Ornament on Christmas Tree A3866

LITHOGRAPHED
***Serpentine Die Cut 10¾ on 2 or 3 Sides***
**2015, Oct. 1**
**Booklet Stamps**
**Self-Adhesive**

**5021** A3857 (49c) multicolored 2.50 .40
**5022** A3858 (49c) multicolored 2.50 .40
**5023** A3859 (49c) multicolored 2.50 .40
**5024** A3860 (49c) multicolored 2.50 .40
**5025** A3861 (49c) multicolored 2.50 .40
**5026** A3862 (49c) multicolored 2.50 .40
**5027** A3863 (49c) multicolored 2.50 .40
**5028** A3864 (49c) multicolored 2.50 .40
**5029** A3865 (49c) multicolored 2.50 .40
**5030** A3866 (49c) multicolored 2.50 .40
*a.* Block of 10, #5021-5030 25.00
*b.* Booklet pane of 20, 2 each #5021-5030 50.00
*c.* As "a," imperforate 17.50 —
*d.* As "b," imperforate 35.00
*Nos. 5021-5030 (10)* 25.00 4.00

Premiere of *A Charlie Brown Christmas* animated television show, 50th anniv.

No. 5030b is a double-sided booklet pane with 12 stamps on one side (Nos. 5023-5030, 2 each Nos. 5021-5022) and eight stamps (Nos. 5023-5030) plus label (booklet cover) on the other side.

### GEOMETRIC SNOWFLAKES

A3867

A3868

A3869

A3870

LITHOGRAPHED
***Serpentine Die Cut 11¼x10¾ on 2 or 3 Sides***
**2015, Oct. 23**
**Booklet Stamps**
**Self-Adhesive**
**Snowflake Colors**

**5031** A3867 (49c) purple & lilac 1.40 .30
**5032** A3868 (49c) dark blue & blue 1.40 .30
**5033** A3869 (49c) dark green & green 1.40 .30
**5034** A3870 (49c) crimson & pink 1.40 .30
*a.* Block of 4, #5031-5034 5.60
*b.* Booklet pane of 20, 5 each #5031-5034 28.00
*c.* As "a," imperforate 7.00 —
*d.* As "b," imperforate 35.00
*Nos. 5031-5034 (4)* 5.60 1.20

No. 5034b is a double-sided booklet pane with 12 stamps on one side (3 each Nos. 5031-5034), and eight stamps (2 each Nos. 5031-5034) plus label (booklet cover) on the other side.

**Purple Heart and Ribbon Type of 2012**
LITHOGRAPHED
**2015, Oct.** ***Serpentine Die Cut 11***
**Self-Adhesive**
**With "USPS" Microprinted At Left of Ribbon**

**5035** A3587 (49c) multicolored 1.40 .25

See Nos. 4529, 4704.

### LOVE

Quilled Paper Heart — A3871

LITHOGRAPHED
***Serpentine Die Cut 10¾***
**2016, Jan. 12**
**Self-Adhesive**

**5036** A3871 (49c) multicolored 1.40 .25
*a.* Imperforate 1.75 —
*b.* Die cutting omitted, P#B11111 block of 4 *100.00*

No. 5036b was printed from P#B11111 only and may also be collected in plate blocks of 6, half panes of 10 and full panes of 20. Pairs or other multiples without P#B11111 selvage attached cannot be distinguished from No. 5036a, which was printed only from P#S11111.

### FRUIT

Albemarle Pippin Apples A3872

Pinot Noir Grapes A3873

Red Pears — A3874

LITHOGRAPHED
***Serpentine Die Cut 10 Vert.***
**2016** **Self-Adhesive**
**Coil Stamps**

**5037** A3872 1c multicolored .30 .25
**5038** A3873 5c multicolored .30 .25

***Serpentine Die Cut 10¾ Vert.***

**5039** A3874 10c multicolored .30 .25

See Nos. 5177-5178 for sheet versions of Nos. 5038-5039, also see No. 5201, 5256.

### AMERICAN LANDMARKS ISSUE

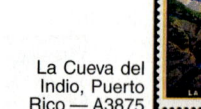

La Cueva del Indio, Puerto Rico — A3875

Columbia River Gorge — A3876

LITHOGRAPHED
***Serpentine Die Cut 10¾x10½***
**2016, Jan. 17**
**Self-Adhesive**

**5040** A3875 $6.45 multi 20.00 7.50
*a.* Imperforate 17.50 —
**5041** A3876 $22.95 multi *85.00* 24.00
*a.* Imperforate *200.00* —

### BOTANICAL ART

Corn Lilies A3877

Tulips A3878

Tulips A3879

Dahlias A3880

Stocks A3881

Roses A3882

Japanese Irises A3883

Tulips A3884

Petunias A3885

Jonquils A3886

LITHOGRAPHED
***Serpentine Die Cut 10¾ on 2 or 3 Sides***
**2016, Jan. 29**
**Booklet Stamps**
**Self-Adhesive**

**5042** A3877 (49c) multicolored 2.50 .40
**5043** A3878 (49c) multicolored 2.50 .40
**5044** A3879 (49c) multicolored 2.50 .40
**5045** A3880 (49c) multicolored 2.50 .40
**5046** A3881 (49c) multicolored 2.50 .40
**5047** A3882 (49c) multicolored 2.50 .40
**5048** A3883 (49c) multicolored 2.50 .40
**5049** A3884 (49c) multicolored 2.50 .40
**5050** A3885 (49c) multicolored 2.50 .40
**5051** A3886 (49c) multicolored 2.50 .40
*a.* Block of 10, #5042-5051 25.00
*b.* Booklet pane of 10, #5042-5051 25.00
*c.* Booklet pane of 20, 2 each #5042-5051 50.00
*d.* Imperforate block of 10 125.00 —
*e.* Imperforate booklet pane of 20 225.00
*f.* As "c," horiz. die cutting missing between all stamps front and reverse —
*Nos. 5042-5051 (10)* 25.00 4.00

No. 5051c is a double-sided booklet pane with 12 stamps on one side (Nos. 5042-5049, 2 each Nos. 5050-5051) and eight stamps (Nos. 5042-5049) plus label (booklet cover) on the other side.

No. 5051f resulted from a misregistration of the die cutting/pane cutting and the printed web. The horizontal rows are reversed from their normal positions, and horizontal die cutting appears at the top and bottom of the pane.

Flag — A3887

# UNITED STATES

**LITHOGRAPHED**
*Serpentine Die Cut 11 Vert.*
2016, Jan. 29
**Coil Stamps**
**Self-Adhesive**
**Microprinted "USPS" To Right of Pole Under Flag**

| 5052 | A3887 | (49c) multicolored | 1.40 | .25 |
| a. | Die cutting omitted, pair | | 200.00 | |
| b. | As "a," grayish blue (inscription and date) omitted | | 200.00 | |

*Serpentine Die Cut 9½ Vert.*
**Microprinted "USPS" on Second White Flag Stripe**

| 5053 | A3887 | (49c) multicolored | 1.40 | .25 |

**Booklet Stamps**
**Microprinted "USPS" To Right of Pole Under Flag**
*Serpentine Die Cut 11¼x10¾ on 2 or 3 Sides*

| 5054 | A3887 | (49c) multicolored | 1.40 | .25 |
| a. | Booklet pane of 10 | | 14.00 | |
| b. | Booklet pane of 20 | | 28.00 | |
| c. | As "b," horiz. die cutting omitted on side with 12 stamps | | — | |

**Microprinted "USPS" on Second White Flag Stripe**

| 5055 | A3887 | (49c) multicolored | 1.40 | .25 |
| a. | Booklet pane of 20 | | 28.00 | |

Nos. 5054b and 5055a are double-sided booklets with 12 stamps on one side and eight stamps plus a label that serves as the booklet cover on the other side.

## BLACK HERITAGE

Richard Allen (1760-1831), Founder of African Methodist Episcopal Church — A3888

**LITHOGRAPHED**
*Serpentine Die Cut 10¾*
2016, Feb. 2
**Self-Adhesive**

| 5056 | A3888 | (49c) multicolored | 1.40 | .25 |
| a. | Imperforate | | 3.00 | |

## CHINESE NEW YEAR

Year of the Monkey — A3889

**LITHOGRAPHED**
*Serpentine Die Cut 10¾*
2016, Feb. 5
**Self-Adhesive**

| 5057 | A3889 | (49c) multicolored | 1.40 | .25 |
| a. | Imperforate | | 1.75 | |

Moon — A3890

**LITHOGRAPHED**
2016, Feb. 22  *Serpentine Die Cut*
**Self-Adhesive**

| 5058 | A3890 | ($1.20) multicolored | 3.25 | .50 |

Unused values are for stamps with surrounding selvage. Adjacent stamps are separated by rouletting.

## MUSIC ICONS

Sarah Vaughan (1924-90), Singer — A3891

**LITHOGRAPHED**
*Serpentine Die Cut 10½*
2016, Mar. 29
**Self-Adhesive**

| 5059 | A3891 | (49c) multicolored | 1.40 | .25 |

## LEGENDS OF HOLLYWOOD

Shirley Temple (1928-2014), Actress and Diplomat — A3892

**LITHOGRAPHED**
*Serpentine Die Cut 10¾*
2016, Apr. 18
**Self-Adhesive**

| 5060 | A3892 | (47c) multicolored | 2.00 | .25 |

"USA" and Star — A3893

**LITHOGRAPHED**
*Serpentine Die Cut 10 Vert.*
2016, Apr. 28
**COIL STAMP**
**Self-Adhesive**

| 5061 | A3893 | (5c) multicolored | .30 | .25 |

See No. 5172.

## 2016 WORLD STAMP SHOW, NEW YORK CITY

Star — A3894

**ENGRAVED**
*Serpentine Die Cut 10¾*
2016, May 28
**Self-Adhesive**

| 5062 | A3894 | (47c) blue | 1.40 | .25 |
| 5063 | A3894 | (47c) red | 1.40 | .25 |
| a. | Pair, #5062-5063 | | 2.80 | |

## REPEAL OF THE STAMP ACT, 250TH ANNIV.

Man Posting of Notice of Repeal on Tree — A3895

**LITHOGRAPHED**
*Serpentine Die Cut 10¾*
2016, May 29
**Self-Adhesive**

| 5064 | A3895 | (47c) multicolored | 1.40 | .25 |

## SERVICE CROSS MEDALS

Distinguished Service Cross A3896    Navy Cross A3897

Air Force Cross A3898    Coast Guard Cross A3899

**LITHOGRAPHED**
*Serpentine Die Cut 10¾*
2016, May 30
**Self-Adhesive**

| 5065 | A3896 | (47c) multicolored | 1.40 | .30 |
| 5066 | A3897 | (47c) multicolored | 1.40 | .30 |
| 5067 | A3898 | (47c) multicolored | 1.40 | .30 |
| 5068 | A3899 | (47c) multicolored | 1.40 | .30 |
| a. | Block or horiz. strip of 4, #5065-5068 | | 5.60 | |
| | Nos. 5065-5068 (4) | | 5.60 | 1.20 |

## VIEWS OF OUR PLANETS

Mercury A3900    Venus A3901

Earth — A3902    Mars — A3903

Jupiter A3904     Saturn A3905

Uranus A3906    Neptune A3907

**LITHOGRAPHED**
*Serpentine Die Cut 10½*
2016, May 31
**Self-Adhesive**

| 5069 | A3900 | (47c) multicolored | 2.00 | .40 |
| 5070 | A3901 | (47c) multicolored | 2.00 | .40 |
| 5071 | A3902 | (47c) multicolored | 2.00 | .40 |
| 5072 | A3903 | (47c) multicolored | 2.00 | .40 |
| 5073 | A3904 | (47c) multicolored | 2.00 | .40 |
| 5074 | A3905 | (47c) multicolored | 2.00 | .40 |
| 5075 | A3906 | (47c) multicolored | 2.00 | .40 |
| 5076 | A3907 | (47c) multicolored | 2.00 | .40 |
| a. | Block of 8, #5069-5076 | | 16.00 | |
| | Nos. 5069-5076 (8) | | 16.00 | 3.20 |

## PLUTO EXPLORED

Pluto A3908    New Horizons Probe A3909

**LITHOGRAPHED**
*Serpentine Die Cut 10½*
2016, May 31
**Self-Adhesive**

| 5077 | A3908 | (47c) multicolored | 1.40 | .25 |
| 5078 | A3909 | (47c) multicolored | 1.40 | .25 |
| a. | Pair, #5077-5078 | | 2.80 | |

## CLASSICS FOREVER

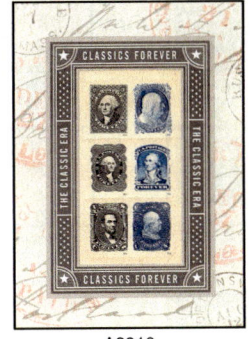

A3910

No. 5079: a, George Washington (redrawn type A16). b, Benjamin Franklin (redrawn type A5). c, Washington (redrawn type A17). d, Washington (redrawn type A19). e, Abraham Lincoln (redrawn type A33). f, Franklin (redrawn type A24).

**LITHOGRAPHED & ENGRAVED**
*Serpentine Die Cut 10¾*
2016, June 1
**Self-Adhesive**

| 5079 | A3910 | Pane of 6 | 8.40 | |
| a. | (47c) tan & black | 1.40 | .40 |
| b. | (47c) tan & blue | 1.40 | .40 |
| c. | (47c) tan & black | 1.40 | .40 |
| d. | (47c) tan & blue | 1.40 | .40 |
| e. | (47c) tan & blue | 1.40 | .40 |
| f. | (47c) tan & blue | 1.40 | .40 |

## NATIONAL PARK SERVICE, CENT.

A3911

No. 5080: a, Iceberg in Glacier Bay National Park and Preserve, Alaska (48x31mm). b, Mount Rainier National Park (48x31mm). c, *Scenery in the Grand Tetons*, painting by Albert Bierstadt, at Marsh-Billings-Rockefeller National Historic Park, Vermont (24x31mm). d, Bass Harbor Head Lighthouse, Acadia National Park, Maine (48x31mm). e, *The Grand Canyon of Arizona*, painting by Thomas Moran, at Grand Canyon National Park, Arizona (48x31mm). f, Horses at Assateague Island National Seashore, Virginia and Maryland (48x31mm). g, Ship *Balclutha*, at San Francisco Maritime National Historic Park, California (24x31mm). h, Stone arch at Arches National Park, Utah (24x31mm). i, Aerial view of Theodore Roosevelt National Park, North Dakota (24x31mm). j, Water lily at Kenilworth Park and Aquatic Gardens, Washington, D.C. (24x31mm). k, Administration Building at Frijoles Canyon, drawing by Helmuth Naumer, Sr., at Bandelier National Monument, New Mexico (48x31mm). l, Everglades National Park, Florida (48x31mm). m, Rainbow at Haleakala National Park, Hawaii (48x31mm). n, Bison at Yellowstone National Park, Idaho, Montana and Wyoming (48x31mm). o, Carlsbad Caverns National Park, New Mexico (48x31mm). p, Heron at Gulf Islands National Seashore, Florida and Mississippi (24x31mm).

**LITHOGRAPHED**
*Serpentine Die Cut 10½x10¾*
2016, June 2
**Self-Adhesive**

| 5080 | A3911 | Pane of 16 + label | 22.40 | |
| a.-p. | (47c) Any single | | 1.40 | .50 |

## COLORFUL CELEBRATIONS

Bird and Flowers A3912     Birds and Flowers A3913

138 UNITED STATES

Flowers A3914 Flowers A3915

Flowers A3916 Flowers A3917

Birds and Flower A3918 Bird and Flower A3919

Flowers A3920 Birds and Flower A3921

LITHOGRAPHED

***Serpentine Die Cut 11 on 2 or 3 Sides***

**2016, June 3**

**Booklet Stamps Self-Adhesive**

| | | | | | |
|---|---|---|---|---|---|
| **5081** | A3912 (47c) | lt blue | | 2.00 | .40 |
| **5082** | A3913 (47c) | orange | | 2.00 | .40 |
| **5083** | A3914 (47c) | violet | | 2.00 | .40 |
| **5084** | A3915 (47c) | magneta | | 2.00 | .40 |
| **5085** | A3916 (47c) | lt blue | | 2.00 | .40 |
| **5086** | A3917 (47c) | orange | | 2.00 | .40 |
| **5087** | A3918 (47c) | violet | | 2.00 | .40 |
| **5088** | A3919 (47c) | magneta | | 2.00 | .40 |
| **5089** | A3920 (47c) | magneta | | 2.00 | .40 |
| **5090** | A3921 (47c) | violet | | 2.00 | .40 |
| *a.* | Block of 10, #5081-5090 | | | 20.00 | |
| *b.* | Booklet pane of 20, 2 each #5081-5090 | | | 40.00 | |
| | *Nos. 5081-5090 (10)* | | | 20.00 | 4.00 |

No. 5090b is a double-sided booklet pane with 12 stamps on one side (Nos. 5083-5090, 2 each Nos. 5081-5082) and eight stamps (Nos. 5083-5090) plus label (booklet cover) on the other side.

**INDIANA STATEHOOD, 200th ANNIV.**

Corn Field Near Milford — A3922

LITHOGRAPHED

***Serpentine Die Cut 10¾***

**2016, June 7**

**Self-Adhesive**

**5091** A3922 (47c) multicolored 1.40 .25

**EID**

"Eidukum Mubarak" — A3923

LITHOGRAPHED

***Serpentine Die Cut 11***

**2016, June 10**

**Self-Adhesive**

**5092** A3923 (47c) multicolored 1.40 .25

**SODA FOUNTAIN FAVORITES**

Ice Cream Cone A3924 Egg Cream A3925

Banana Split A3926

Root Beer Float A3927

Hot Fudge Sundae — A3928

No. 5095 No. 5095a

LITHOGRAPHED

***Serpentine Die Cut 10¾***

**2016, June 30**

**Booklet Stamps Self-Adhesive**

| | | | | |
|---|---|---|---|---|
| **5093** | A3924 (47c) multicolored | | 1.50 | .40 |
| **5094** | A3925 (47c) multicolored | | 1.50 | .40 |
| **5095** | A3926 (47c) multicolored (long sloping die cut at bottom) | | 1.50 | .40 |
| *a.* | Long sloping die cut at top | | 1.50 | .40 |
| **5096** | A3927 (47c) multicolored | | 1.50 | .40 |
| **5097** | A3928 (47c) multicolored | | 1.50 | .40 |
| *a.* | Horiz. strip of 5, #5093-5097 | | 7.50 | |
| *b.* | Horiz. strip of 5, #5093-5094, 5095a, 5096-5097 | | 7.50 | |
| *c.* | Booklet pane of 20, 4 each #5093-5094, 5096-5097, 2 each #5095, 5095a | | 30.00 | |
| | *Nos. 5093-5097 (5)* | | 7.50 | 2.00 |

**STAR QUILTS**

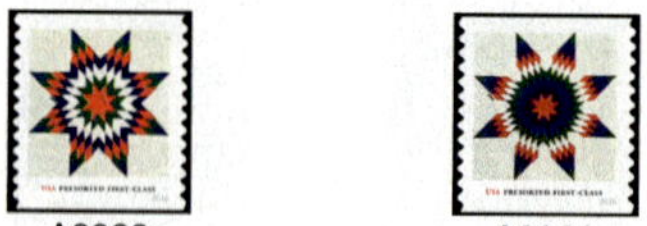

A3929 A3930

LITHOGRAPHED

***Serpentine Die Cut 11 Vert.***

**2016, July 6**

**Coil Stamps Self-Adhesive**

| | | | |
|---|---|---|---|
| **5098** | A3929 (25c) multicolored | .50 | .25 |
| **5099** | A3930 (25c) multicolored | .50 | .25 |
| *a.* | Pair, #5098-5099 | 1.00 | |

**JAIME ESCALANTE**

Jaime Escalante (1930-2010), High School Calculus Teacher — A3931

LITHOGRAPHED

***Serpentine Die Cut 10¾***

**2016, July 13**

**Self-Adhesive**

**5100** A3931 (47c) multicolored 1.40 .25

Adjacent horizontal or vertical stamps have selvage between the stamps.

**PICKUP TRUCKS**

1938 International Harvester D-2 A3932 1953 Chevrolet A3933

1948 Ford F-1 A3934 1965 Ford F-100 A3935

LITHOGRAPHED

***Serpentine Die Cut 11 on 2 or 3 Sides***

**2016, July 15**

**Booklet Stamps Self-Adhesive**

| | | | |
|---|---|---|---|
| **5101** | A3932 (47c) multicolored | 1.40 | .30 |
| **5102** | A3933 (47c) multicolored | 1.40 | .30 |
| **5103** | A3934 (47c) multicolored | 1.40 | .30 |
| **5104** | A3935 (47c) multicolored | 1.40 | .30 |
| *a.* | Block of 4, #5101-5104 | 5.60 | |
| *b.* | Booklet pane of 20, 5 each #5101-5104 | 28.00 | |
| | *Nos. 5101-5104 (4)* | 5.60 | 1.20 |

No. 5104b is a double-sided booklet pane with 12 stamps on one side (3 each Nos. 5101-5104) and eight stamps (2 each Nos. 5101-5104) plus label (booklet cover) on the other side.

**LITERARY ARTS**

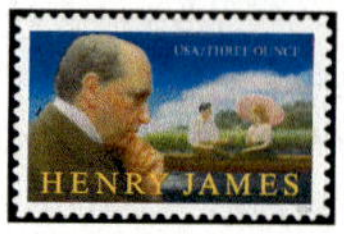


Henry James (1843-1916), Novelist — A3936

LITHOGRAPHED

***Serpentine Die Cut 11***

**2016, July 31**

**Self-Adhesive**

**5105** A3936 (89c) multicolored 2.40 .30

**PETS**

Puppy A3937 Betta Fish A3938

Iguana A3939 Hamster A3940

Goldfish A3941 Kitten A3942

Rabbit A3943 Tortoise A3944

Guinea Pig A3945 Parrot A3946

Corn Snake A3947 Mouse A3948

Hermit Crab A3949 Chinchilla A3950

Gerbil A3951 Gecko A3952

Cat A3953 Horse A3954

Parakeets A3955 Dog A3956

LITHOGRAPHED

***Serpentine Die Cut 11 on 2 or 3 Sides***

**2016, Aug. 2**

**Booklet Stamps Self-Adhesive**

| | | | |
|---|---|---|---|
| **5106** | A3937 (47c) multicolored | 1.50 | .50 |
| **5107** | A3938 (47c) multicolored | 1.50 | .50 |
| **5108** | A3939 (47c) multicolored | 1.50 | .50 |
| **5109** | A3940 (47c) multicolored | 1.50 | .50 |
| **5110** | A3941 (47c) multicolored | 1.50 | .50 |
| **5111** | A3942 (47c) multicolored | 1.50 | .50 |
| **5112** | A3943 (47c) multicolored | 1.50 | .50 |
| **5113** | A3944 (47c) multicolored | 1.50 | .50 |
| **5114** | A3945 (47c) multicolored | 1.50 | .50 |
| **5115** | A3946 (47c) multicolored | 1.50 | .50 |
| **5116** | A3947 (47c) multicolored | 1.50 | .50 |
| **5117** | A3948 (47c) multicolored | 1.50 | .50 |
| **5118** | A3949 (47c) multicolored | 1.50 | .50 |
| **5119** | A3950 (47c) multicolored | 1.50 | .50 |
| **5120** | A3951 (47c) multicolored | 1.50 | .50 |
| **5121** | A3952 (47c) multicolored | 1.50 | .50 |
| **5122** | A3953 (47c) multicolored | 1.50 | .50 |
| **5123** | A3954 (47c) multicolored | 1.50 | .50 |
| **5124** | A3955 (47c) multicolored | 1.50 | .50 |
| **5125** | A3956 (47c) multicolored | 1.50 | .50 |
| *a.* | Booklet pane of 20, #5106-5125 | 30.00 | |
| | *Nos. 5106-5125 (20)* | 30.00 | 10.00 |

No. 5125a is a double-sided booklet pane with 12 stamps on one side (Nos. 5106-5117) and eight stamps (Nos. 5118-5125) plus label (booklet cover) on the other side.

**SONGBIRDS IN SNOW**

Golden-crowned Kinglets A3957 Cedar Waxwing A3958

Northern Cardinal A3959 Red-breasted Nuthatches A3960

LITHOGRAPHED

***Serpentine Die Cut 10¾ on 2 or 3 Sides***

**2016, Aug. 4**

**Booklet Stamps Self-Adhesive**

| | | | |
|---|---|---|---|
| **5126** | A3957 (47c) multicolored | 1.50 | .30 |
| **5127** | A3958 (47c) multicolored | 1.50 | .30 |
| **5128** | A3959 (47c) multicolored | 1.50 | .30 |
| **5129** | A3960 (47c) multicolored | 1.50 | .30 |
| *a.* | Block of 4, #5126-5129 | 6.00 | |
| *b.* | Booklet pane of 20, 5 each #5126-5129 | 30.00 | |
| | *Nos. 5126-5129 (4)* | 6.00 | 1.20 |

No. 5129b is a double-sided booklet pane with 12 stamps on one side (3 each Nos.

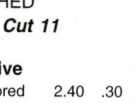

UNITED STATES 139

5126-5129) and eight stamps (2 each Nos. 5126-5129) plus label (booklet cover) on the other side.

## PATRIOTIC SPIRAL

Stars — A3961

**LITHOGRAPHED**
*Serpentine Die Cut 10 Vert.*
**2016, Aug. 19**
**Coil Stamp**
**Self-Adhesive**
5130 A3961 (47c) multicolored 1.40 .25

**Booklet Stamp**
*Serpentine Die Cut 11 on 2 or 3 Sides*
5131 A3961 (47c) multicolored 1.40 .25
a. Booklet pane of 10 14.00

## STAR TREK TELEVISION SHOW, 50TH ANNIV

Starship Enterprise and Starfleet Insignia
A3962

Crewman in Transporter
A3963

Starship Enterprise and Planet
A3964

Starship Enterprise, Planet, Vulcan Hand Salute
A3965

**LITHOGRAPHED**
**2016, Sept. 2** *Serpentine Die Cut 11*
**Self-Adhesive**
5132 A3962 (47c) multicolored 1.40 .30
5133 A3963 (47c) multicolored 1.40 .30
5134 A3964 (47c) multicolored 1.40 .30
5135 A3965 (47c) multicolored 1.40 .30
a. Block or vert. strip of 4, #5132-5135 5.60
Nos. 5132-5135 (4) 5.60 1.20

## EASTERN TAILED-BLUE BUTTERFLY

A3966

**LITHOGRAPHED**
*Serpentine Die Cut 10½*
**2016, Sept. 24**
**Self-Adhesive**
5136 A3966 (68c) multicolored 4.00 .35

## JACK-O'-LANTERNS

Four Teeth
A3967

Five Teeth
A3968

Three Teeth
A3969

Nine Teeth
A3970

**LITHOGRAPHED**
*Serpentine Die Cut 11x10¾ on 2 or 3 Sides*
**2016, Sept. 29**
**Booklet Stamps**
**Self-Adhesive**
5137 A3967 (47c) multicolored 1.40 .30
5138 A3968 (47c) multicolored 1.40 .30
5139 A3969 (47c) multicolored 1.40 .30
5140 A3970 (47c) multicolored 1.40 .30
a. Block of 4, #5137-5140 5.60
b. Booklet pane of 20, 5 each #5137-5140 28.00
Nos. 5137-5140 (4) 5.60 1.20

No. 5140b is a double-sided booklet pane with 12 stamps on one side (3 each Nos. 5137-5140) and eight stamps (2 each Nos. 5137-5140) plus label (booklet cover) on the other side.

## KWANZAA

Woman, Fruits and Vegetables — A3971

**LITHOGRAPHED**
**2016, Oct. 1** *Serpentine Die Cut 11*
**Self-Adhesive**
5141 A3971 (47c) multicolored 1.40 .25

## DIWALI

Diya — A3972

**LITHOGRAPHED**
**2016, Oct. 5** *Serpentine Die Cut 11*
**Self-Adhesive**
5142 A3972 (47c) multicolored 1.40 .25

## CHRISTMAS

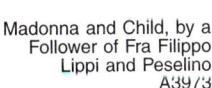

Madonna and Child, by a Follower of Fra Filippo Lippi and Peseleino
A3973

Nativity
A3974

Candle in Window
A3975

Wreath in Window
A3976

Star in Window
A3977

Christmas Tree in Window
A3978

**LITHOGRAPHED**
*Serpentine Die Cut 10¾x11 on 2 or 3 Sides*
**2016**
**Booklet Stamps**
**Self-Adhesive**
5143 A3973 (47c) multicolored 1.40 .25
a. Booklet pane of 20 28.00
5144 A3974 (47c) multicolored 1.40 .25
a. Booklet pane of 20 28.00
5145 A3975 (47c) multicolored 1.40 .25
5146 A3976 (47c) multicolored 1.40 .25
5147 A3977 (47c) multicolored 1.40 .25
5148 A3978 (47c) multicolored 1.40 .25
a. Block of 4, #5145-5148 5.60
b. Booklet pane of 20, 5 each #5145-5148 28.00
Nos. 5143-5148 (6) 8.40 1.50

Issued: No. 5143, 10/18; No. 5144, 11/3; Nos. 5145-5148, 10/6. Nos. 5143a and 5144a are double-sided booklet panes with 12 stamps on one side and eight stamps plus label (booklet cover) on the other side. No. 5148b is a double-sided booklet pane with 12 stamps on one side (3 each Nos. 5145-5148) and eight stamps (2 each Nos. 5145-5148) plus label (booklet cover) on the other side.

## WONDER WOMAN, 75TH ANNIVERSARY

Modern Age Wonder Woman
A3979

Bronze Age Wonder Woman
A3980

Silver Age Wonder Woman
A3981

Golden Age Wonder Woman
A3982

**LITHOGRAPHED**
**2016, Oct. 7** *Serpentine Die Cut 11*
**Self-Adhesive**
5149 A3979 (47c) multicolored 1.50 .30
5150 A3980 (47c) multicolored 1.50 .30
5151 A3981 (47c) multicolored 1.50 .30
5152 A3982 (47c) multicolored 1.50 .30
a. Vert. strip of 4 #5149-5152 6.00
Nos. 5149-5152 (4) 6.00 1.20

## HANUKKAH

Menorah — A3983

**LITHOGRAPHED**
**2016, Nov. 1** *Serpentine Die Cut 11*
**Self-Adhesive**
5153 A3983 (47c) multicolored 1.40 .25

## CHINESE NEW YEAR

Year of the Rooster — A3984

**LITHOGRAPHED**
*Serpentine Die Cut 10¾*
**2017, Jan. 5**
**Self-Adhesive**
5154 A3984 (47c) multicolored 1.40 .25

## LOVE

Airplane and Skywriting — A3985

**LITHOGRAPHED**
*Serpentine Die Cut 11x10¾*
**2017, Jan. 7**
**Self-Adhesive**
5155 A3985 (47c) light blue 1.40 .25

## AMERICAN LANDMARKS ISSUE

Lili'uokalani Gardens, Hilo, Hawaii — A3986

Gateway Arch, St. Louis, Missouri — A3987

**LITHOGRAPHED**
*Serpentine Die Cut 10¾x10½*
**2017, Jan. 22**
**Self-Adhesive**
5156 A3986 $6.65 multi 17.50 7.75
5157 A3987 $20.75 multi 75.00 25.00

Flag — A3988

**LITHOGRAPHED**
*Serpentine Die Cut 11 Vert.*
**2017, Jan. 27**
**Coil Stamps**
**Self-Adhesive**
**Microprinted "USPS" On Right End of Fourth Red Stripe**
5158 A3988 (49c) multicolored 1.40 .25
a. Die cutting omitted, pair —
b. Vert. pair, unslit between —

*Serpentine Die Cut 9½ Vert.*
**Microprinted "USPS" On Right End of Second White Flag Stripe**
5159 A3988 (49c) multicolored 1.40 .25

**Booklet Stamps**
**Microprinted "USPS" On Right End of Fourth Red Stripe**
*Serpentine Die Cut 11¼x10¾ on 2 or 3 Sides*
5160 A3988 (49c) multicolored 1.40 .25
a. Booklet pane of 10 14.00
b. Booklet pane of 20 28.00

**Microprinted "USPS" On Right End of Second White Flag Stripe**
5161 A3988c (49c) multicolored 1.40 .25
a. Booklet pane of 20 28.00

**Microprinted "USPS" on Left End of Second White Flag Stripe Near Blue Field**
**Thin Paper**
*Serpentine Die Cut 11¼x10¾ on 2, 3 or 4 Sides*
5162 A3988 (49c) multicolored 2.75 .25
a. Booklet pane of 18 50.00
Nos. 5160-5162 (3) 5.55 .75

Nos. 5160b and 5161a are double-sided booklets with 12 stamps on one side and eight stamps plus a label that serves as the booklet cover on the other side.

## SHELLS

Queen Conch
A3989

Pacific Calico Scallop
A3990

Alphabet Cone
A3991

Zebra Nerite
A3992

LITHOGRAPHED

***Serpentine Die Cut 11¼x10¾***

**2017, Jan. 28**

**Self-Adhesive**

| | | | | |
|---|---|---|---|---|
| **5163** | A3989 (34c) multicolored | 1.10 | .25 |
| **5164** | A3990 (34c) multicolored | 1.10 | .25 |
| **5165** | A3991 (34c) multicolored | 1.10 | .25 |
| **5166** | A3992 (34c) multicolored | 1.10 | .25 |
| *a.* | Horiz. or vert. strip of 4, #5163-5166 | 4.40 | |
| | *Nos. 5163-5166 (4)* | 4.40 | 1.00 |

**Coil Stamps**

***Serpentine Die Cut 9¾ Vert.***

| | | | |
|---|---|---|---|
| **5167** | A3991 (34c) multicolored | 1.10 | .25 |
| **5168** | A3992 (34c) multicolored | 1.10 | .25 |
| **5169** | A3989 (34c) multicolored | 1.10 | .25 |
| **5170** | A3990 (34c) multicolored | 1.10 | .25 |
| *a.* | Horiz. strip of 4, #5167-5170 | 4.40 | |
| | *Nos. 5167-5170 (4)* | 4.40 | 1.00 |

**BLACK HERITAGE**

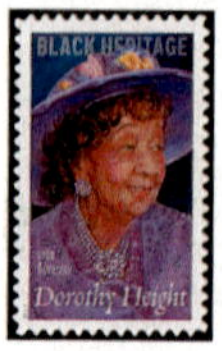

Dorothy Height (1912-2010), President of National Council of Negro Women — A3993

LITHOGRAPHED

**2017, Feb. 1** ***Serpentine Die Cut 11***

**Self-Adhesive**

**5171** A3993 (49c) multicolored 1.40 .25

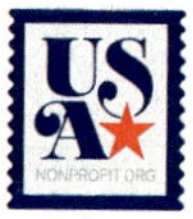

"USA" and Star With Blue Frame — A3994

LITHOGRAPHED

***Serpentine Die Cut 10 Vert.***

**2017, Feb. 10**

**COIL STAMP**

**Self-Adhesive**

| | | | |
|---|---|---|---|
| **5172** | A3994 (5c) multicolored | .30 | .25 |
| *a.* | Red omitted | | — |

The discovery example of No. 5172a is on piece, uncanceled.

**OSCAR DE LA RENTA**

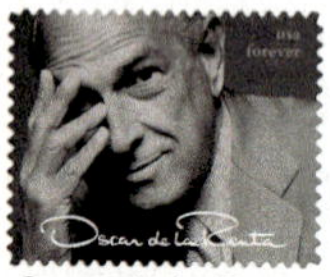

Oscar de la Renta (1932-2014), Fashion Designer — A3995

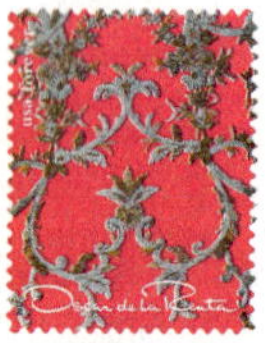

A3996

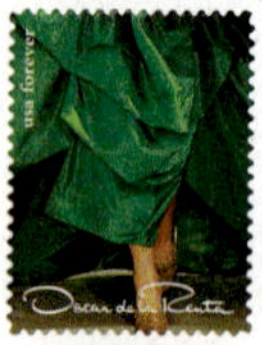

A3997

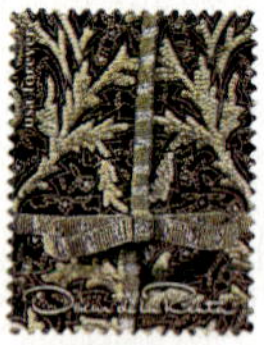

A3998

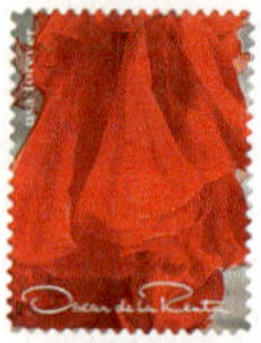

A3999

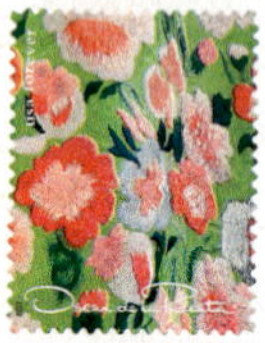

A4000

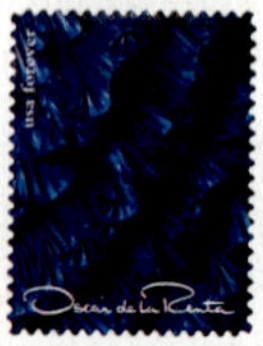

A4001

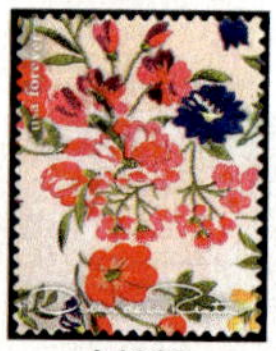

A4002

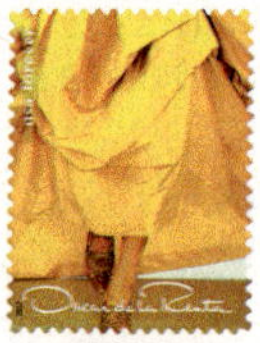

A4003

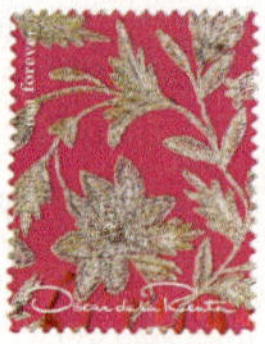

A4004

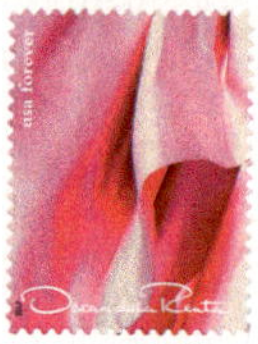

A4005

LITHOGRAPHED

***Serpentine Die Cut 11x10¾ (No. 5173a), 10¾x11***

**2017, Feb. 16**

**Self-Adhesive**

| | | | |
|---|---|---|---|
| **5173** | Pane of 11 | 19.25 | |
| *a.* | A3995 (49c) multicolored | 1.75 | .50 |
| *b.* | A3996 (49c) multicolored | 1.75 | .50 |
| *c.* | A3997 (49c) multicolored | 1.75 | .50 |
| *d.* | A3998 (49c) multicolored | 1.75 | .50 |
| *e.* | A3999 (49c) multicolored | 1.75 | .50 |
| *f.* | A4000 (49c) multicolored | 1.75 | .50 |
| *g.* | A4001 (49c) multicolored | 1.75 | .50 |
| *h.* | A4002 (49c) multicolored | 1.75 | .50 |
| *i.* | A4003 (49c) multicolored | 1.75 | .50 |
| *j.* | A4004 (49c) multicolored | 1.75 | .50 |
| *k.* | A4005 (49c) multicolored | 1.75 | .50 |

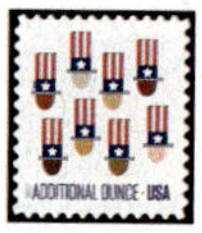

People Wearing Uncle Sam Hats — A4006

LITHOGRAPHED

***Serpentine Die Cut 11¼x11***

**2017, Feb. 18**

**Self-Adhesive**

**5174** A4006 (21c) multicolored .50 .25

See No. 5341.

**PRES. JOHN F. KENNEDY (1917-63)**

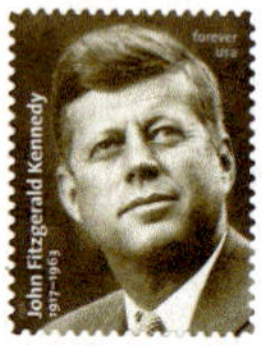

Pres. John F. Kennedy — A4007

LITHOGRAPHED

***Serpentine Die Cut 10¾***

**2017, Feb. 20**

**Self-Adhesive**

**5175** A4007 (49c) brown 1.40 .25

**Fruits Type of 2016**

Designs: 5c, Pinot Noir Grapes. 10c, Red Pears.

LITHOGRAPHED

**2017** ***Serpentine Die Cut 11¼x11***

**Self-Adhesive**

**5177** A3873 5c multicolored .30 .25

See Nos. 5038, 5039.

**5178** A3874 10c multicolored .30 .25

Issued: 5c, 2/24; 10c, 3/23.

See Nos. 5038-5039, 5201, 5256.

**NEBRASKA STATEHOOD, 150th ANNIV.**

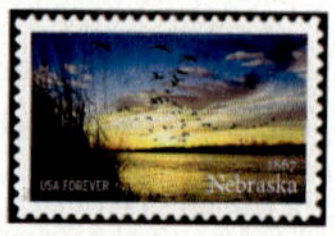

Sandhill Cranes Flying Over Platte River — A4008

LITHOGRAPHED

***Serpentine Die Cut 10¾***

**2017, Mar. 1**

**Self-Adhesive**

**5179** A4008 (49c) multicolored 1.40 .25

**WORKS PROGRESS ADMINISTRATION (WORK PROJECTS ADMINISTRATION) POSTERS**

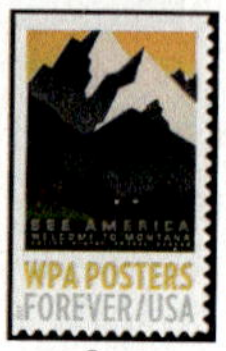

See America Welcome to Montana Poster A4009

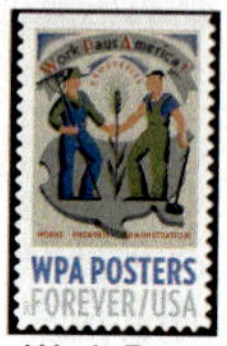

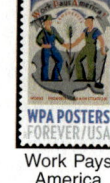

Work Pays America Poster A4010

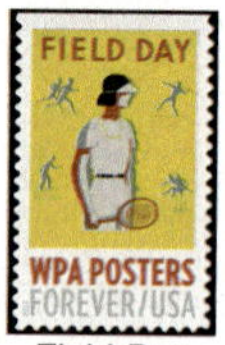

Field Day Poster A4011

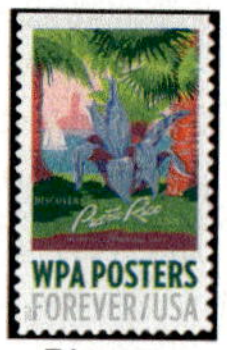

Discover Puerto Rico Poster A4012

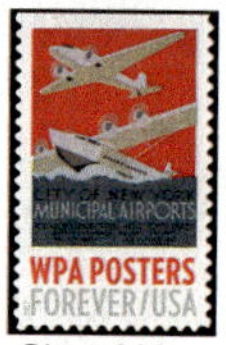

City of New York Municipal Airports Poster A4013

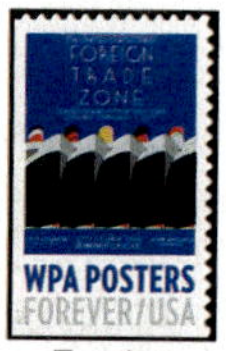

Foreign Trade Zone Poster A4014

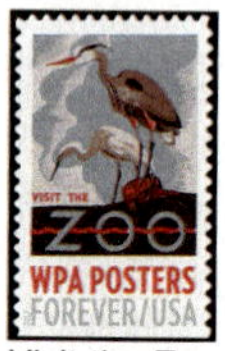

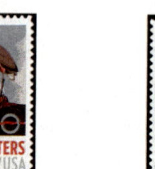

Visit the Zoo Poster A4015

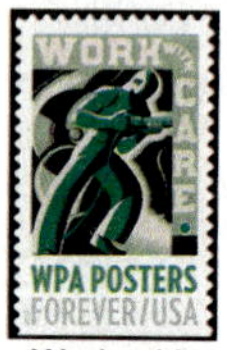

Work with Care Poster A4016

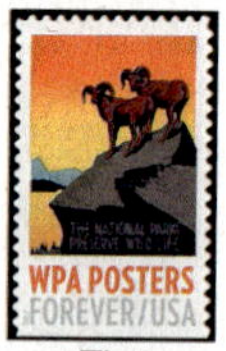

The National Parks Preserve Wild Life Poster A4017

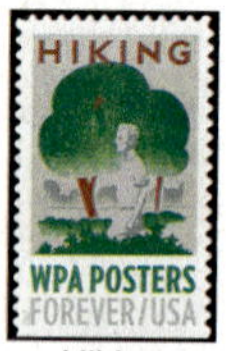

Hiking Poster A4018

LITHOGRAPHED

***Serpentine Die Cut 11 on 2 or 3 Sides***

**2017, Mar. 7**

**Booklet Stamps**

**Self-Adhesive**

| | | | |
|---|---|---|---|
| **5180** | A4009 (49c) multicolored | 1.50 | .40 |
| **5181** | A4010 (49c) multicolored | 1.50 | .40 |
| **5182** | A4011 (49c) multicolored | 1.50 | .40 |
| **5183** | A4012 (49c) multicolored | 1.50 | .40 |
| **5184** | A4013 (49c) multicolored | 1.50 | .40 |
| **5185** | A4014 (49c) multicolored | 1.50 | .40 |
| **5186** | A4015 (49c) multicolored | 1.50 | .40 |
| **5187** | A4016 (49c) multicolored | 1.50 | .40 |
| **5188** | A4017 (49c) multicolored | 1.50 | .40 |
| **5189** | A4018 (49c) multicolored | 1.50 | .40 |
| *a.* | Block of 10, #5180-5189 | 15.00 | |
| *b.* | Booklet pane of 20, 2 each #5180-5189 | 30.00 | |
| | *Nos. 5180-5189 (10)* | 15.00 | 4.00 |

No. 5189b is a double-sided booklet pane with 12 stamps on one side (Nos. 5181-5184, 5186-5189, 2 each Nos. 5180, 5185) and eight stamps (Nos. 5181-5184, 5186-5189) plus label (booklet cover) on the other side.

**MISSISSIPPI STATEHOOD, 200th ANNIV.**

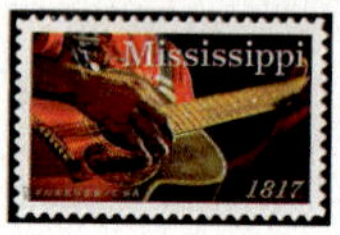

Guitarist — A4019

LITHOGRAPHED

***Serpentine Die Cut 10¾***

**2017, Mar. 31**

**Self-Adhesive**

**5190** A4019 (49c) multicolored 1.40 .25

**DISTINGUISHED AMERICANS**

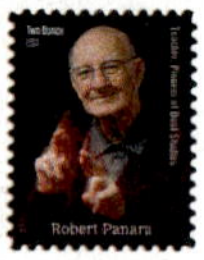

Robert Panara (1920-2014), Educator of the Deaf — A4020

LITHOGRAPHED

***Serpentine Die Cut 10¾***

**2017, Apr. 11** **Tagged**

**Self-Adhesive**

**5191** A4020 (70c) multicolored 1.90 .25

Adjacent horizontal or vertical stamps have selvage between the stamps.

**DELICIOSO (LATIN AMERICAN DISHES)**

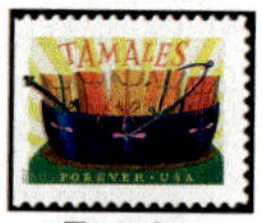

Tamales A4021

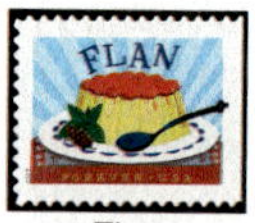

Flan A4022

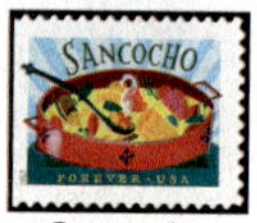

Sancocho A4023

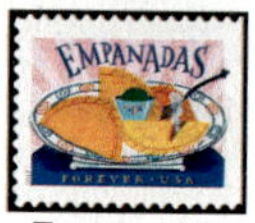

Empanadas A4024

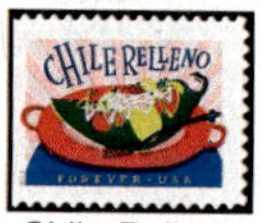

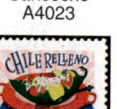

Chile Relleno A4025

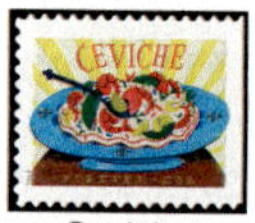

Ceviche A4026

LITHOGRAPHED

***Serpentine Die Cut 11 on 2 or 3 Sides***

**2017, Apr. 20** **Tagged**

**Booklet Stamps**

**Self-Adhesive**

| | | | |
|---|---|---|---|
| **5192** | A4021 (49c) multicolored | 1.40 | .40 |
| **5193** | A4022 (49c) multicolored | 1.40 | .40 |
| **5194** | A4023 (49c) multicolored | 1.40 | .40 |
| **5195** | A4024 (49c) multicolored | 1.40 | .40 |
| **5196** | A4025 (49c) multicolored | 1.40 | .40 |
| **5197** | A4026 (49c) multicolored | 1.40 | .40 |
| *a.* | Block of 6, #5192-5197 | 8.40 | |
| *b.* | Booklet pane of 20, 4 each #5192-5193, 3 each #5194-5197 | 28.00 | |
| | *Nos. 5192-5197 (6)* | 8.40 | 2.40 |

No. 5197b is a double-sided booklet pane with 12 stamps on one side (2 each Nos. 5192-5197) and eight stamps (Nos. 5194-5197, 2 each Nos. 5192-5193) plus label (booklet cover) on the other side.

Echeveria — A4027

# UNITED STATES

## LITHOGRAPHED
*Serpentine Die Cut*
**2017, Apr. 28**    Tagged
**Self-Adhesive**

| 5198 | A4027 | ($1.15) multicolored | 3.25 | .50 |

Unused values are for stamps with surrounding selvage. Adjacent stamps are separated by rouletting.
Counterfeits exist of No. 5198. See the Postal Counterfeits section of this catalog.

## CELEBRATION FLOWERS

Boutonniere
A4028

Corsage
A4029

## LITHOGRAPHED
*Serpentine Die Cut 10¾*
**2017, May 2**    Tagged
**Self-Adhesive**

| 5199 | A4028 | (49c) multicolored | 1.30 | .25 |
| 5200 | A4029 | (70c) multicolored | 1.90 | .25 |

## FRUIT

Strawberries — A4030

## LITHOGRAPHED
*Serpentine Die Cut 10 Vert.*
**2017, May 5**
**Coil Stamps**
**Self-Adhesive**

| 5201 | A4030 | 3c multicolored | .30 | .25 |

## HENRY DAVID THOREAU

Henry David Thoreau (1817-62), Writer, and Sumac Leaves — A4031

## LITHOGRAPHED
*Serpentine Die Cut 10¾*
**2017, May 23**
**Self-Adhesive**

| 5202 | A4031 | (49c) multicolored | 1.40 | .25 |

## SPORTS BALLS

Football
A4032

Volleyball
A4033

Soccer Ball — A4034

Golf Ball — A4035

Baseball
A4036

Basketball
A4037

Tennis Ball
A4038

Kickball
A4039

## LITHOGRAPHED & TYPOGRAPHED
*Serpentine Die Cut*
**2017, June 14**
**Self-Adhesive**

| 5203 | A4032 | (49c) multicolored | 1.40 | .40 |
| 5204 | A4033 | (49c) multicolored | 1.40 | .40 |
| 5205 | A4034 | (49c) multicolored | 1.40 | .40 |
| 5206 | A4035 | (49c) multicolored | 1.40 | .40 |
| 5207 | A4036 | (49c) multicolored | 1.40 | .40 |
| 5208 | A4037 | (49c) multicolored | 1.40 | .40 |
| 5209 | A4038 | (49c) multicolored | 1.40 | .40 |
| 5210 | A4039 | (49c) multicolored | 1.40 | .40 |
| a. | Block of 8, #5203-5210 | | 11.20 | |
| | Nos. 5203-5210 (8) | | 11.20 | 3.20 |

The typographed printing imitates the texture of the ball.

## AUGUST 21, 2017, TOTAL SOLAR ECLIPSE

Total Solar Eclipse — A4040

## LITHOGRAPHED
*Serpentine Die Cut 10½*
**2017, June 20**
**Self-Adhesive**

| 5211 | A4040 | (49c) multicolored | 1.40 | .25 |

The moon is covered with a circle of thermochromic ink, which when warmed, allows the moon and the corona of the sun around the moon to be seen.

## PAINTINGS BY ANDREW WYETH (1917-2009)

Wind from the Sea, 1947 — A4041

Big Room, 1988 — A4042

Christina's World, 1948 — A4043

Alvaro and Christina, 1968 — A4044

Frostbitten, 1962 — A4045

Sailor's Valentine, 1985 — A4046

Soaring, 1942-50 — A4047

North Light, 1984 — A4048

Spring Fed, 1967 — A4049

The Carry, 2003 — A4050

Young Bull, 1960 — A4051

My Studio, 1974 — A4052

## LITHOGRAPHED
*Serpentine Die Cut 10¾x10½*
**2017, July 12**
**Self-Adhesive**

| 5212 | | Pane of 12 | 19.80 | |
| a. | A4041 | (49c) multicolored | 1.65 | .50 |
| b. | A4042 | (49c) multicolored | 1.65 | .50 |
| c. | A4043 | (49c) multicolored | 1.65 | .50 |
| d. | A4044 | (49c) multicolored | 1.65 | .50 |
| e. | A4045 | (49c) multicolored | 1.65 | .50 |
| f. | A4046 | (49c) multicolored | 1.65 | .50 |
| g. | A4047 | (49c) multicolored | 1.65 | .50 |
| h. | A4048 | (49c) multicolored | 1.65 | .50 |
| i. | A4049 | (49c) multicolored | 1.65 | .50 |
| j. | A4050 | (49c) multicolored | 1.65 | .50 |
| k. | A4051 | (49c) multicolored | 1.65 | .50 |
| l. | A4052 | (49c) multicolored | 1.65 | .50 |

## DISNEY VILLAINS

The Queen from *Snow White and the Seven Dwarfs*
A4053

Honest John from *Pinocchio*
A4054

Lady Tremaine from *Cinderella*
A4055

Queen of Hearts from *Alice in Wonderland*
A4056

Captain Hook from *Peter Pan*
A4057

Maleficent from *Sleeping Beauty*
A4058

Cruella De Vil from *One Hundred and One Dalmatians*
A4059

Ursula from *The Little Mermaid*
A4060

Gaston from *Beauty and the Beast* — A4061

Scar from *The Lion King* — A4062

## LITHOGRAPHED
*Serpentine Die Cut 10½x10¾*
**2017, July 15**
**Self-Adhesive**

| 5213 | A4053 | (49c) multicolored | 1.40 | .40 |
| 5214 | A4054 | (49c) multicolored | 1.40 | .40 |
| 5215 | A4055 | (49c) multicolored | 1.40 | .40 |
| 5216 | A4056 | (49c) multicolored | 1.40 | .40 |
| 5217 | A4057 | (49c) multicolored | 1.40 | .40 |
| 5218 | A4058 | (49c) multicolored | 1.40 | .40 |
| 5219 | A4059 | (49c) multicolored | 1.40 | .40 |
| 5220 | A4060 | (49c) multicolored | 1.40 | .40 |
| 5221 | A4061 | (49c) multicolored | 1.40 | .40 |
| 5222 | A4062 | (49c) multicolored | 1.40 | .40 |
| a. | Block of 10, #5213-5222 | | 14.00 | |
| | Nos. 5213-5222 (10) | | 14.00 | 4.00 |

## SHARKS

Mako Shark — A4063

Whale Shark — A4064

Thresher Shark — A4065

Hammerhead Shark — A4066

Great White Shark — A4067

## LITHOGRAPHED
*Serpentine Die Cut 10¾*
**2017, July 26**
**Self-Adhesive**

| 5223 | A4063 | (49c) multicolored | 1.50 | .40 |
| 5224 | A4064 | (49c) multicolored | 1.50 | .40 |
| 5225 | A4065 | (49c) multicolored | 1.50 | .40 |
| 5226 | A4066 | (49c) multicolored | 1.50 | .40 |

142      UNITED STATES

| 5227 | A4067 | (49c) multicolored | 1.50 | .40 |
|---|---|---|---|---|
| a. | Vert. strip of 5, #5223-5227 | | 7.50 | |
| | Nos. 5223-5227 (5) | | 7.50 | 2.00 |

### PROTECT POLLINATORS

Monarch Butterfly on Purple Coneflower A4068

Western Honeybee on Golden Ragwort A4069

Monarch Butterfly on Red Zinnia — A4070

Western Honeybee on Purple New England Aster — A4071

Monarch Butterfly on Goldenrod A4072

**LITHOGRAPHED**
*Serpentine Die Cut 10¾*
**2017, Aug. 3**
**Self-Adhesive**

| 5228 | A4068 | (49c) multicolored | 1.50 | .40 |
|---|---|---|---|---|
| 5229 | A4069 | (49c) multicolored | 1.50 | .40 |
| 5230 | A4070 | (49c) multicolored | 1.50 | .40 |
| 5231 | A4071 | (49c) multicolored | 1.50 | .40 |
| 5232 | A4072 | (49c) multicolored | 1.50 | .40 |
| a. | Vert. strip of 5, #5228-5232 | | 7.50 | |
| | Nos. 5228-5232 (5) | | 7.50 | 2.00 |

### FLOWERS FROM THE GARDEN

Red Camellias and Yellow Forsythia in Yellow Pitcher A4073

White Peonies and Pink Tree Peonies in Clear Vase A4074

Blue Hydrangeas in Blue Pot A4075

Assorted Flowers in White Vase A4076

Red Camellias and Yellow Forsythia in Yellow Pitcher A4077

Assorted Flowers in White Vase A4078

White Peonies and Pink Tree Peonies in Clear Vase A4079

Blue Hydrangeas in Blue Pot A4080

**LITHOGRAPHED**
*Serpentine Die Cut 10¾ Vert.*
**2017, Aug. 16**
**Coil Stamps**
**Self-Adhesive**

| 5233 | A4073 | (49c) multicolored | 1.40 | .30 |
|---|---|---|---|---|
| 5234 | A4074 | (49c) multicolored | 1.40 | .30 |
| 5235 | A4075 | (49c) multicolored | 1.40 | .30 |
| 5236 | A4076 | (49c) multicolored | 1.40 | .30 |
| a. | Strip of 4, #5233-5236 | | 5.60 | |
| | Nos. 5233-5236 (4) | | 5.60 | 1.20 |

**Booklet Stamps**
*Serpentine Die Cut 11 on 2 or 3 Sides*

| 5237 | A4077 | (49c) multicolored | 1.40 | .30 |
|---|---|---|---|---|
| 5238 | A4078 | (49c) multicolored | 1.40 | .30 |
| 5239 | A4079 | (49c) multicolored | 1.40 | .30 |
| 5240 | A4080 | (49c) multicolored | 1.40 | .30 |
| a. | Block of 4, #5237-5240 | | 5.60 | |
| b. | Booklet pane of 20, 5 each #5237-5240 | | 28.00 | |
| | Nos. 5237-5240 (4) | | 5.60 | 1.20 |

No. 5240b is a double-sided booklet pane with 12 stamps on one side (3 each Nos. 5237-5240) and eight stamps (2 each Nos. 5237-5240) plus label (booklet cover) on the other side.

### FATHER THEODORE ("TED") HESBURGH

Hesburgh (1917-2015), President of University of Notre Dame — A4081

**LITHOGRAPHED**
*Serpentine Die Cut 11*
**2017, Sept. 1**      **Tagged**
**Self-Adhesive**

| 5241 | A4081 | (49c) multicolored | 1.40 | .25 |
|---|---|---|---|---|

**Coil Stamp**
*Serpentine Die Cut 9½ Horiz.*

| 5242 | A4081 | (49c) multicolored | 1.50 | .25 |
|---|---|---|---|---|

### "THE SNOWY DAY," BY EZRA JACK KEATS

Peter Making Snowball A4082

Peter Sliding Down Mountain of Snow A4083

Peter Making Snow Angel A4084

Peter Leaving Footprints in Snow A4085

**LITHOGRAPHED**
*Serpentine Die Cut 10¾ on 2 or 3 Sides*
**2017, Oct. 4**
**Booklet Stamps**
**Self-Adhesive**

| 5243 | A4082 | (49c) multicolored | 1.40 | .30 |
|---|---|---|---|---|
| 5244 | A4083 | (49c) multicolored | 1.40 | .30 |
| 5245 | A4084 | (49c) multicolored | 1.40 | .30 |
| 5246 | A4085 | (49c) multicolored | 1.40 | .30 |
| a. | Block of 4, #5243-5246 | | 5.60 | |
| b. | Booklet pane of 20, 5 each #5243-5246 | | 28.00 | |
| | Nos. 5243-5246 (4) | | 5.60 | 1.20 |

No. 5246b is a double-sided booklet pane with 12 stamps on one side (3 each Nos. 5243-5246), and eight stamps (2 each Nos. 5243-5246) plus label (booklet cover) on the other side.

### CHRISTMAS CAROLS

Christmas Lights, Cookies, and Line From "Deck the Halls" A4086

Star of Bethlehem, Lamb, and Line From "Silent Night" A4087

Snowflakes, Horse, and Line From "Jingle Bells" A4088

Child, Santa Claus, and Line From "Jolly Old St. Nicholas" A4089

**LITHOGRAPHED**
*Serpentine Die Cut 10¾ on 2 or 3 Sides*
**2017, Oct. 5**
**Booklet Stamps**
**Self-Adhesive**

| 5247 | A4086 | (49c) multicolored | 1.40 | .30 |
|---|---|---|---|---|
| 5248 | A4087 | (49c) multicolored | 1.40 | .30 |
| 5249 | A4088 | (49c) multicolored | 1.40 | .30 |
| 5250 | A4089 | (49c) multicolored | 1.40 | .30 |
| a. | Block of 4, #5247-5250 | | 5.60 | |
| b. | Booklet pane of 20, 5 each #5247-5250 | | 28.00 | |
| | Nos. 5247-5250 (4) | | 5.60 | 1.20 |

No. 5250b is a double-sided booklet pane with 12 stamps on one side (3 each Nos. 5247-5250), and eight stamps (2 each Nos. 5247-5250) plus label (booklet cover) on the other side.

### NATIONAL MUSEUM OF AFRICAN AMERICAN HISTORY AND CULTURE

Museum Building, Washington, D.C. — A4090

**LITHOGRAPHED**
*Serpentine Die Cut 10¾x10½*
**2017, Oct. 13**      **Tagged**
**Self-Adhesive**

| 5251 | A4090 | (49c) multicolored | 1.40 | .25 |
|---|---|---|---|---|

### HISTORY OF ICE HOCKEY

Player Wearing Helmet and Protective Gear A4091

Player Wearing Hat and Scarf A4092

**LITHOGRAPHED**
**2017, Oct. 20** *Serpentine Die Cut 11*
**Self-Adhesive**

| 5252 | A4091 | (49c) multicolored | 1.40 | .25 |
|---|---|---|---|---|
| a. | As No. 5252, matte-finish stamp | | 1.40 | .25 |
| 5253 | A4092 | (49c) multicolored | 1.40 | .25 |
| a. | As No. 5253, matte-finish stamp | | 1.40 | .25 |
| b. | Vert. pair, #5252-5253 | | 2.80 | |
| c. | Souvenir sheet of 2, #5252a-5253a | | 2.80 | |

On Nos. 5253b and 5253c, stamps are printed tete-beche. Stamps from No. 5253b have a glossier finish than those on No. 5253c. Adjacent horizontal stamps have selvage between them.
See Canada Nos. 3039-3041.

### CHINESE NEW YEAR

Year of the Dog — A4093

**LITHOGRAPHED**
*Serpentine Die Cut 10¾*
**2018, Jan. 11**
**Self-Adhesive**

| 5254 | A4093 | (49c) multicolored | 1.40 | .25 |
|---|---|---|---|---|

### LOVE

Flowers — A4094

**LITHOGRAPHED**
*Serpentine Die Cut 11x10¾*
**2018, Jan. 18**
**Self-Adhesive**

| 5255 | A4094 | (49c) multicolored | 1.40 | .25 |
|---|---|---|---|---|

### FRUIT

Meyer Lemons — A4095

**LITHOGRAPHED**
*Serpentine Die Cut 10¾ Vert.*
**2018, Jan. 19**
**Coil Stamp**
**Self-Adhesive**

| 5256 | A4095 | 2c multicolored | .30 | .25 |
|---|---|---|---|---|

### AMERICAN LANDMARKS ISSUE

Byodo-In Temple, Kaneohe, Hawaii — A4096

Sleeping Bear Dunes, Michigan A4097

**LITHOGRAPHED**
*Serpentine Die Cut 10¾x10½*
**2018, Jan. 21**
**Self-Adhesive**

| 5257 | A4096 | $6.70 multi | 17.50 | 7.75 |
|---|---|---|---|---|
| 5258 | A4097 | $24.70 multi | 75.00 | 25.00 |

### BLACK HERITAGE

Lena Horne (1917-2010), Singer — A4098

# UNITED STATES

**LITHOGRAPHED**
*Serpentine Die Cut 10¾*
**2018, Jan. 30**
**Self-Adhesive**
5259 A4098 (50c) multicolored 1.40 .25

Flag — A4099

**LITHOGRAPHED**
*Serpentine Die Cut 9½ Vert.*
**2018, Feb. 9**
**Coil Stamps**
**Self-Adhesive**
Microprinted "USPS" at Left of Flag Fold on Fourth White Stripe
5260 A4099 (50c) multicolored 1.40 .25
*Serpentine Die Cut 11 Vert.*
Microprinted "USPS" at Right of Flag Fold on Fifth White Stripe
5261 A4099 (50c) multicolored 1.40 .25
**Booklet Stamps Microprinted "USPS" at Left of Flag Fold on Fourth Red Stripe**
*Serpentine Die Cut 11¼x10¾ on 2 or 3 Sides*
5262 A4099 (50c) multicolored 1.40 .25
a. Booklet pane of 20 28.00
Microprinted "USPS" at Right of Flag Fold on Fifth White Stripe
5263 A4099 (50c) multicolored 1.40 .25
a. Booklet pane of 20 28.00

Nos. 5262a and 5263a are double-sided booklets with 12 stamps on one side and eight stamps plus a label that serves as the booklet cover on the other side.

## BIOLUMINESCENT LIFE

Octopus — A4100

Jellyfish — A4101

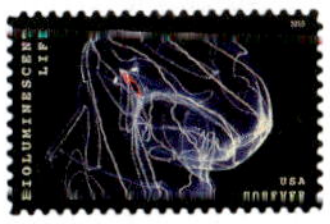

Comb Jelly — A4102

Mushrooms A4103

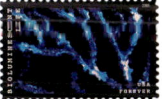
Firefly — A4104

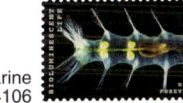
Bamboo Coral — A4105

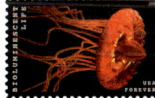
Marine Worm — A4106

Crown Jellyfish — A4107

Marine Worm — A4108

Sea Pen — A4109

**LITHOGRAPHED**
*Serpentine Die Cut 11*
**2018, Feb. 22**
**Self-Adhesive**
5264 A4100 (50c) multicolored 1.50 .40
5265 A4101 (50c) multicolored 1.50 .40
5266 A4102 (50c) multicolored 1.50 .40
5267 A4103 (50c) multicolored 1.50 .40
5268 A4104 (50c) multicolored 1.50 .40
5269 A4105 (50c) multicolored 1.50 .40
5270 A4106 (50c) multicolored 1.50 .40
5271 A4107 (50c) multicolored 1.50 .40
5272 A4108 (50c) multicolored 1.50 .40
5273 A4109 (50c) multicolored 1.50 .40
a. Block of 10, #5264-5273 15.00
Nos. 5264-5273 (10) 15.00 4.00

## ILLINOIS STATEHOOD, 200TH ANNIV.

Map of Illinois and Sun Rays — A4110

**LITHOGRAPHED**
**2018, Mar. 5** *Serpentine Die Cut 11*
**Self-Adhesive**
5274 A4110 (50c) multicolored 1.40 .25

## MISTER ROGERS

Fred Rogers (1928-2003), Host of Children's Television Show, *Mister Rogers*, and Puppet, King Friday XIII — A4111

**LITHOGRAPHED**
*Serpentine Die Cut 11*
**2018, Mar. 23**
**Self-Adhesive**
5275 A4111 (50c) multicolored 1.40 .25

## SCIENCE, TECHNOLOGY, ENGINEERING AND MATHEMATICS (STEM) EDUCATION

Head and Symbols of Science Education A4112

Head and Symbols of Technology Education A4113

Head and Symbols of Engineering Education A4114

Head and Symbols of Mathematics Education A4115

**LITHOGRAPHED**
**2018, Apr. 6** *Serpentine Die Cut 11*
**Self-Adhesive**
5276 A4112 (50c) multicolored 1.40 .30
5277 A4113 (50c) multicolored 1.40 .30
5278 A4114 (50c) multicolored 1.40 .30
5279 A4115 (50c) multicolored 1.40 .30
a. Vert. strip of 4, #5276-5279 5.60
Nos. 5276-5279 (4) 5.60 1.20

Peace Rose — A4116

**LITHOGRAPHED**
*Serpentine Die Cut 11¼x10¾ on 2 or 3 Sides*
**2018, Apr. 21**
**Booklet Stamp**
**Self-Adhesive**
5280 A4116 (50c) multicolored 1.40 .25
a. Booklet pane of 20 28.00

No. 5280a is a double-sided booklet with 12 stamps on one side and eight stamps plus a label that serves as the booklet cover on the other side.
See note after No. 1549.

## AIR MAIL, CENT.

Curtiss JN-4H "Jenny" Biplane — A4117

**ENGRAVED**
**2018** *Serpentine Die Cut 10¾*
**Self-Adhesive**
5281 A4117 (50c) blue 1.40 .25
5282 A4117 (50c) carmine lake 1.40 .25
Issued: No. 5281, 5/1. No. 5282, 8/11.

## SALLY RIDE

Sally Ride (1951-2012), First American Woman in Space, and Space Shuttle Launch — A4118

**LITHOGRAPHED**
*Serpentine Die Cut 10½x10¾*
**2018, May 23**
**Self-Adhesive**
5283 A4118 (50c) multicolored 1.40 .25

## FLAG ACT OF 1818, BICENT.

20-Star Flag — A4119

**LITHOGRAPHED**
*Serpentine Die Cut 10¾*
**2018, June 9**
**Self-Adhesive**
5284 A4119 (50c) multicolored 1.40 .25

## FROZEN TREATS

A4120

A4121

A4122

A4123

A4124

A4126

A4128

A4125

A4127

A4129

**LITHOGRAPHED**
*Serpentine Die Cut 11¼x10¾ on 2 or 3 Sides*
**2018, June 20**
**Booklet Stamps**
**Self-Adhesive**
5285 A4120 (50c) multicolored 1.40 .40
5286 A4121 (50c) multicolored 1.40 .40
5287 A4122 (50c) multicolored 1.40 .40
5288 A4123 (50c) multicolored 1.40 .40
5289 A4124 (50c) multicolored 1.40 .40
5290 A4125 (50c) multicolored 1.40 .40
5291 A4126 (50c) multicolored 1.40 .40
5292 A4127 (50c) multicolored 1.40 .40
5293 A4128 (50c) multicolored 1.40 .40
5294 A4129 (50c) multicolored 1.40 .40
a. Block of 10, #5285-5294 14.00
b. Booklet pane of 20, 2 each #5285-5294 28.00
Nos. 5285-5294 (10) 14.00 4.00

Nos. 5294b has a scratch-and-sniff coating with a fruity aroma, and is a double-sided booklet with 12 stamps on one side (Nos. 5286-5289, 5291-5294, 2 each Nos 5285, 5290), and eight stamps (Nos. 5286-5289, 5291-5294) plus a label that serves as the booklet cover on the other side.

## STATUE OF FREEDOM

Head of Statue of Freedom on U.S. Capitol Dome — A4130

**LITHOGRAPHED & ENGRAVED**
*Serpentine Die Cut 10¾x10½*
**2018, June 27**
**Self-Adhesive**
5295 A4130 $1 emer, reddsh pink & blk 2.00 .50
5296 A4130 $2 indigo, reddsh pink & blk 4.00 1.00
5297 A4130 $5 blk red, reddsh pink & blk 10.00 2.50
Nos. 5295-5297 (3) 16.00 4.00

Optically-variable ink was used for the numerals in the denominations.

## O BEAUTIFUL

Death Valley National Park, California and Nevada A4131

Three Fingers Mountain, Washington A4132

Double Rainbow Over Field, Kansas A4133

Great Smoky Mountains National Park, North Carolina and Tennessee A4134

# UNITED STATES

Field of Wheat, Wisconsin
A4135

Plowed Wheat Fields, Palouse Hills, Washington
A4136

Grasslands Wildlife Management Area, Merced County, California
A4137

Field of Wheat, Montana
A4138

Yosemite National Park, California
A4139

Crater Lake National Park, Oregon
A4140

Monument Valley Navajo Tribal Park, Arizona and Utah
A4141

Maroon Bells, Colorado
A4142

Sunrise Near Orinda, California
A4143

Pigeon Point, Near Pescadero, California
A4144

Edna Valley, San Luis Obispo County, California
A4145

Livermore, California
A4146

Napali Coast State Wilderness Park, Hawaii
A4147

Lone Ranch Beach, Oregon
A4148

Canaveral National Seashore, Florida
A4149

Bailey Island, Maine
A4150

### LITHOGRAPHED
*Serpentine Die Cut 10½*
**2018, July 4**
**Self-Adhesive**

| 5298 | | Pane of 20 | 35.00 | |
|---|---|---|---|---|
| a. | A4131 | (50c) multicolored | 1.75 | .50 |
| b. | A4132 | (50c) multicolored | 1.75 | .50 |
| c. | A4133 | (50c) multicolored | 1.75 | .50 |
| d. | A4134 | (50c) multicolored | 1.75 | .50 |
| e. | A4135 | (50c) multicolored | 1.75 | .50 |
| f. | A4136 | (50c) multicolored | 1.75 | .50 |
| g. | A4137 | (50c) multicolored | 1.75 | .50 |
| h. | A4138 | (50c) multicolored | 1.75 | .50 |
| i. | A4139 | (50c) multicolored | 1.75 | .50 |
| j. | A4140 | (50c) multicolored | 1.75 | .50 |
| k. | A4141 | (50c) multicolored | 1.75 | .50 |
| l. | A4142 | (50c) multicolored | 1.75 | .50 |
| m. | A4143 | (50c) multicolored | 1.75 | .50 |
| n. | A4144 | (50c) multicolored | 1.75 | .50 |
| o. | A4145 | (50c) multicolored | 1.75 | .50 |
| p. | A4146 | (50c) multicolored | 1.75 | .50 |
| q. | A4147 | (50c) multicolored | 1.75 | .50 |
| r. | A4148 | (50c) multicolored | 1.75 | .50 |
| s. | A4149 | (50c) multicolored | 1.75 | .50 |
| t. | A4150 | (50c) multicolored | 1.75 | .50 |

### SCOOBY-DOO

Cartoon Character Scooby-Doo Watering Plant — A4151

### LITHOGRAPHED
*Serpentine Die Cut 10¾x10½*
**2018, July 14**
**Self-Adhesive**

| 5299 | A4151 | (50c) multicolored | 1.40 | .25 |
|---|---|---|---|---|

### WORLD WAR I, CENT.

Member of American Expeditionary Force Holding Flag — A4152

### LITHOGRAPHED
*Serpentine Die Cut 10¾*
**2018, July 27**
**Self-Adhesive**

| 5300 | A4152 | (50c) multicolored | 1.40 | .25 |
|---|---|---|---|---|

### THE ART OF MAGIC

Rabbit in Hat — A4153

Fortune Teller and Crystal Ball — A4154

Levitating Woman and Hoop — A4155

Empty Bird Cage — A4156

Bird Emerging From Flower — A4157

### LITHOGRAPHED (Nos. 5301-5305), TYPOGRAPHED WITH LENTICULAR LENS AFFIXED (No. 5306)
*Serpentine Die Cut 10½x10¾*
**2018, Aug. 7**
**Self-Adhesive**

| 5301 | A4153 | (50c) multicolored | 1.40 | .40 |
|---|---|---|---|---|
| 5302 | A4154 | (50c) multicolored | 1.40 | .40 |
| 5303 | A4155 | (50c) multicolored | 1.40 | .40 |
| 5304 | A4156 | (50c) multicolored | 1.40 | .40 |
| 5305 | A4157 | (50c) multicolored | 1.40 | .40 |
| a. | | Horiz. strip of 5, #5301-5305 | 7.00 | |
| | | Nos. 5301-5305 (5) | 7.00 | 2.00 |

**Souvenir Sheet**

| 5306 | A4153 | Sheet of 3 #5306a | 4.20 | |
|---|---|---|---|---|
| a. | | (50c) Single stamp | 1.40 | .40 |
| b. | | As No. 5306, die cutting omitted | 800.00 | |

The printing method used on No. 5306a makes the rabbit in the vignette appear and disappear when the stamp is tilted.

### DRAGONS

Green Dragon and Castle
A4158

Purple Dragon and Castle
A4159

Black Dragon and Ship
A4160

Orange Dragon and Pagoda
A4161

### LITHOGRAPHED WITH FOIL APPLICATION
*Serpentine Die Cut 10¾*
**2018, Aug. 9**
**Self-Adhesive**

| 5307 | A4158 | (50c) multicolored | 1.40 | .30 |
|---|---|---|---|---|
| 5308 | A4159 | (50c) multicolored | 1.40 | .30 |
| 5309 | A4160 | (50c) multicolored | 1.40 | .30 |
| 5310 | A4161 | (50c) multicolored | 1.40 | .30 |
| a. | | Strip or block of 4, #5307-5310 | 5.60 | |
| b. | | Horiz. strip of 4, #5307-5310, with die cutting missing (PS) | 400.00 | |
| | | Nos. 5307-5310 (4) | 5.60 | 1.20 |

Poinsettia — A4162

### LITHOGRAPHED
**2018, Aug. 26** *Serpentine Die Cut*
**Self-Adhesive**

| 5311 | A4162 | ($1.15) multicolored | 3.25 | .50 |
|---|---|---|---|---|

Unused values are for stamps with surrounding selvage. Adjacent stamps are separated by rouletting.

### MUSIC ICONS

John Lennon (1940-80), Rock Musician — A4163

### LITHOGRAPHED
*Serpentine Die Cut 10¾*
**2018, Sept. 7**
**Self-Adhesive**
**Color of Shoulders**

| 5312 | A4163 | (50c) red | 1.40 | .30 |
|---|---|---|---|---|
| 5313 | A4163 | (50c) red lilac | 1.40 | .30 |
| 5314 | A4163 | (50c) dark violet | 1.40 | .30 |
| 5315 | A4163 | (50c) blue | 1.40 | .30 |
| a. | | Vert. strip of 4, #5312-5315 | 5.60 | |
| b. | | As "a," die cutting omitted | — | |
| | | Nos. 5312-5315 (4) | 5.60 | 1.20 |

Adjacent horizontal or vertical stamps have selvage between the stamps.

### FIRST RESPONDERS

Firefighter, Paramedic, and Law Enforcement Officer — A4164

### LITHOGRAPHED
*Serpentine Die Cut 11*
**2018, Sept. 13**
**Self-Adhesive**

| 5316 | A4164 | (50c) multicolored | 1.40 | .30 |
|---|---|---|---|---|

### BIRDS IN WINTER

Black-capped Chickadee
A4165

Northern Cardinal
A4166

Red-bellied Woodpecker
A4167

Blue Jay
A4168

### LITHOGRAPHED
*Serpentine Die Cut 10¾ on 2 or 3 Sides*
**2018, Sept. 22**
**Booklet Stamps**
**Self-Adhesive**

| 5317 | A4165 | (50c) multicolored | 1.40 | .30 |
|---|---|---|---|---|
| 5318 | A4166 | (50c) multicolored | 1.40 | .30 |
| 5319 | A4167 | (50c) multicolored | 1.40 | .30 |
| 5320 | A4168 | (50c) multicolored | 1.40 | .30 |
| a. | | Block of 4, #5317-5320 | 5.60 | |
| b. | | Booklet pane of 20, 5 each #5317-5320 | 28.00 | |
| | | Nos. 5317-5320 (4) | 5.60 | 1.20 |

No. 5320b is a double-sided booklet pane with 12 stamps on one side (3 each Nos. 5317-5320), and eight stamps (2 each Nos. 5317-5320) plus label (booklet cover) on the other side.

### HOT WHEELS TOY CARS, 50TH ANNIV.

Purple Passion — A4169

Rocket-Bye-Baby A4170

# UNITED STATES

145

 Rigor Motor — A4171

 Rodger Dodger — A4172

 Mach Speeder — A4173

 Twin Mill — A4174

 Bone Shaker — A4175

 HW40 — A4176

 Deora II — A4177

 Sharkruiser A4178

**LITHOGRAPHED**
*Serpentine Die Cut 10¾*
2018, Sept. 29
**Self-Adhesive**

| 5321 | A4169 | (50c) multicolored | 1.40 | .40 |
|---|---|---|---|---|
| 5322 | A4170 | (50c) multicolored | 1.40 | .40 |
| 5323 | A4171 | (50c) multicolored | 1.40 | .40 |
| 5324 | A4172 | (50c) multicolored | 1.40 | .40 |
| 5325 | A4173 | (50c) multicolored | 1.40 | .40 |
| 5326 | A4174 | (50c) multicolored | 1.40 | .40 |
| 5327 | A4175 | (50c) multicolored | 1.40 | .40 |
| 5328 | A4176 | (50c) multicolored | 1.40 | .40 |
| 5329 | A4177 | (50c) multicolored | 1.40 | .40 |
| 5330 | A4178 | (50c) multicolored | 1.40 | .40 |
| | | Nos. 5321-5330 (10) | 14.00 | 4.00 |

## CHRISTMAS

 Madonna and Child, by Bachiacca A4179

 Head of Santa Claus, by Haddon Sundblom A4180

 Santa Claus and Wreath, by Sundblom A4181  / Santa Claus and Book, by Sundblom A4182

 Santa Claus and Card, by Sundblom — A4183

 Santa Claus and Book, by Sundblom — A4184

**LITHOGRAPHED**
*Serpentine Die Cut 10¾x11 on 2 or 3 Sides*
2018
**Booklet Stamps**
**Self-Adhesive**

| 5331 | A4179 | (50c) multicolored | 1.40 | .25 |
|---|---|---|---|---|
| a. | | Booklet pane of 20 | 28.00 | |
| 5332 | A4180 | (50c) multicolored | 1.40 | .30 |
| 5333 | A4181 | (50c) multicolored | 1.40 | .30 |
| 5334 | A4182 | (50c) multicolored | 1.40 | .30 |
| 5335 | A4183 | (50c) multicolored | 1.40 | .30 |
| a. | | Block of 4, #5332-5335 | 5.60 | |
| b. | | Booklet pane of 20, 5 each #5332-5335 | 28.00 | |
| c. | | As "a," die cutting omitted | | |
| | | Nos. 5331-5335 (5) | 7.00 | 1.45 |

**Souvenir Sheet**
*Serpentine Die Cut 10¾*

| 5336 | A4184 | (50c) multicolored | 1.40 | .30 |
|---|---|---|---|---|
| a. | | Single stamp | 1.40 | .30 |

Issued: No. 5331, 10/3; Nos. 5332-5336, 10/11.

No. 5331a is a double-sided booklet panes with 12 stamps on one side and eight stamps plus label (booklet cover) on the other side. No. 5335b is a double-sided booklet pane with 12 stamps on one side (3 each Nos. 5332-5335) and eight stamps (2 each Nos. 5332-5335) plus label (booklet cover) on the other side.

The three examples of No. 5335c are from a booklet pane missing the stamps on the 8-stamp side.

## KWANZAA

 Family and Kinara — A4185

**LITHOGRAPHED**
*Serpentine Die Cut 10¾*
2018, Oct. 10
**Self-Adhesive**

| 5337 | A4185 | (50c) multicolored | 1.40 | .25 |

## HANUKKAH

 Menorah — A4186

**LITHOGRAPHED**
*Serpentine Die Cut 10¾*
2018, Oct. 16
**Self-Adhesive**

| 5338 | A4186 | (50c) multicolored | 1.40 | .25 |

See Israel No. 2200.

## LOVE

 Hearts — A4187

**LITHOGRAPHED**
*Serpentine Die Cut 10¾x11*
2019, Jan. 10
**Self-Adhesive**

| 5339 | A4187 | (50c) multicolored | 1.40 | .25 |

## CHINESE NEW YEAR

 Year of the Boar — A4188

**LITHOGRAPHED**
*Serpentine Die Cut 10¾*
2019, Jan. 17
**Self-Adhesive**

| 5340 | A4188 | (50c) multicolored | 1.40 | .25 |

**People Wearing Uncle Sam Hats Type of 2017**
**LITHOGRAPHED**
*Serpentine Die Cut 11 Vert.*
2019, Jan. 27 Tagged
**Coil Stamp**
**Self-Adhesive**

| 5341 | A4006 | (15c) multicolored | .50 | .25 |

See No. 5174.

 Flag — A4189

**LITHOGRAPHED**
*Serpentine Die Cut 9½ Horiz.*
2019, Jan. 27
**Coil Stamps**
**Self-Adhesive**
**Microprinted "USPS" at Lower Flag Grommet**

| 5342 | A4189 | (55c) multicolored | 1.40 | .25 |

*Serpentine Die Cut 11 Horiz.*
**Microprinted "USPS" to Right of Sixth Red Flag Stripe**

| 5343 | A4189 | (55c) multicolored | 1.40 | .25 |
| a. | | Die cutting omitted, pair | | |

Used example of No. 5343 is single stamp on cover.

**Booklet Stamps**
**Microprinted "USPS" at Upper Left Corner of Flag**
*Serpentine Die Cut 10¾x11¼ on 2 or 3 Sides*

| 5344 | A4189 | (55c) multicolored | 1.40 | .25 |
| a. | | Booklet pane of 20 | 28.00 | |

**Microprinted "USPS" to Right of Sixth Red Flag Stripe**

| 5345 | A4189 | (55c) multicolored | 1.40 | .25 |
| a. | | Booklet pane of 20 | 28.00 | |

Nos. 5344a and 5345a are double-sided booklets with 12 stamps on one side and eight stamps plus a label that serves as the booklet cover on the other side.

## CALIFORNIA DOGFACE BUTTERFLY

 A4190

**LITHOGRAPHED**
*Serpentine Die Cut 10½*
2019, Jan. 27
**Self-Adhesive**

| 5346 | A4190 | (70c) multicolored | 2.25 | .25 |

## AMERICAN LANDMARKS ISSUE

 Joshua Tree — A4191

 Bethesda Fountain, Central Park, New York City — A4192

**LITHOGRAPHED**
*Serpentine Die Cut 10¾x10½*
2019, Jan. 27
**Self-Adhesive**

| 5347 | A4191 | $7.35 multi | 20.00 | 7.50 |
| 5348 | A4192 | $25.50 multi | 125.00 | 25.00 |

## BLACK HERITAGE

 Gregory Hines (1946-2003), Tap Dancer — A4193

**LITHOGRAPHED**
*Serpentine Die Cut 10¾*
2019, Jan. 28
**Self-Adhesive**

| 5349 | A4193 | (55c) multicolored | 1.40 | .25 |

## CACTUS FLOWERS

 Opuntia Engelmannii A4194

Rebutia Minuscula A4195

 Echinocereus Dasyacanthus A4196

Echinocereus Poselgeri A4197

 Echinocereus Coccineus A4198

Pelecyphora Aselliformis A4199

 Parodia Microsperma A4200

Echinocactus Horizonthalonius A4201

 Thelocactus Heterochromus A4202

 Parodia Scopa A4203

**LITHOGRAPHED**
*Serpentine Die Cut 11 on 2 or 3 Sides*
2019, Feb. 15
**Booklet Stamps**
**Self-Adhesive**

| 5350 | A4194 | (55c) multicolored | 2.50 | .40 |
| 5351 | A4195 | (55c) multicolored | 2.50 | .40 |
| 5352 | A4196 | (55c) multicolored | 2.50 | .40 |
| 5353 | A4197 | (55c) multicolored | 2.50 | .40 |
| 5354 | A4198 | (55c) multicolored | 2.50 | .40 |
| 5355 | A4199 | (55c) multicolored | 2.50 | .40 |
| 5356 | A4200 | (55c) multicolored | 2.50 | .40 |
| 5357 | A4201 | (55c) multicolored | 2.50 | .40 |
| 5358 | A4202 | (55c) multicolored | 2.50 | .40 |
| 5359 | A4203 | (55c) multicolored | 2.50 | .40 |
| a. | | Block of 10, #5350-5359 | 25.00 | |
| b. | | Booklet pane of 20, 2 each #5350-5359 | 50.00 | |
| | | Nos. 5350-5359 (10) | 25.00 | 4.00 |

No. 5359b is a double-sided booklet pane with 12 stamps on one side (Nos. 5352-5359, 2 each Nos. 5350-5351), and eight stamps (Nos. 5352-5359) plus label (booklet cover) on the other side.

146 UNITED STATES

### ALABAMA STATEHOOD, BICENT.

Pulpit Rock, Cheaha State Park — A4204

**LITHOGRAPHED**
*Serpentine Die Cut 11x10¾*
2019, Feb. 23    Self-Adhesive
5360  A4204  (55c) multicolored   1.40   .25

Star Ribbon — A4205

**LITHOGRAPHED**
*Serpentine Die Cut 11¼x10¾*
2019, Mar. 22    Self-Adhesive
5361  A4205  (55c) multicolored   1.40   .25
Coil Stamp
*Serpentine Die Cut 10¾ Vert.*
5362  A4205  (55c) multicolored   1.40   .25

### CORAL REEFS

Elkhorn Coral and French Angelfish A4206

Brain Coral and Spotted Moray Eel A4207

Pillar Coral, Coney Grouper and Neon Gobies A4208

Staghorn Coral and Blue-striped Grunts A4209

**LITHOGRAPHED**
*Serpentine Die Cut 11¼x10¾*
2019, Mar. 29    Self-Adhesive
5363  A4206  (35c) multicolored   1.10   .25
5364  A4207  (35c) multicolored   1.10   .25
5365  A4208  (35c) multicolored   1.10   .25
5366  A4209  (35c) multicolored   1.10   .25
  a.  Horiz. or vert. strip of 4, #5363-5366   4.40
  Nos. 5363-5366 (4)   4.40   1.00
Coil Stamps
*Serpentine Die Cut 9½ Vert.*
5367  A4208  (35c) multicolored   1.10   .25
  a.  Aqua ("POSTCARD") color omitted   —
5368  A4209  (35c) multicolored   1.10   .25
  a.  Aqua ("POSTCARD") color omitted   —
5369  A4206  (35c) multicolored   1.10   .25
  a.  Aqua ("POSTCARD") color omitted   —
5370  A4207  (35c) multicolored   1.10   .25
  a.  Aqua ("POSTCARD") color omitted   —
  b.  Horiz. strip of 4, #5367-5370   4.40
  Nos. 5367-5370 (4)   4.40   1.00

### MUSIC ICONS

Marvin Gaye (1939-84), Singer — A4210

**LITHOGRAPHED**
*Serpentine Die Cut 10½*
2019, Apr. 2    Self-Adhesive
5371  A4210  (55c) multicolored   1.40   .25

### POST OFFICE MURALS

Piggott, Arkansas Mural *Air Mail*, by Daniel Rhodes A4211

Florence, Colorado Mural, *Antelope*, by Olive Rush A4212

Rockville, Maryland Mural, *Sugarloaf Mountain*, by Judson Smith A4213

Anadarko, Oklahoma Mural, *Kiowas Moving Camp*, by Stephen Mopope, James Auchiah, and Spencer Asah A4214

Deming, New Mexico Mural, *Mountains and Yucca*, by Kenneth Miller Adams A4215

**LITHOGRAPHED**
*Serpentine Die Cut 11½x11*
2019, Apr. 10    Self-Adhesive
5372  A4211  (55c) multicolored   1.40   .40
5373  A4212  (55c) multicolored   1.40   .40
5374  A4213  (55c) multicolored   1.40   .40
5375  A4214  (55c) multicolored   1.40   .40
5376  A4215  (55c) multicolored   1.40   .40
  a.  Vert. strip of 5, #5372-5376   7.00
  Nos. 5372-5376 (5)   7.00   2.00

### MAUREEN CONNOLLY BRINKER

Maureen "Little Mo" Connolly Brinker (1934-69), Tennis Player — A4216

**LITHOGRAPHED**
*Serpentine Die Cut 10¾*
2019, Apr. 23    Self-Adhesive
5377  A4216  (55c) multicolored   1.40   .25

### TRANSCONTINENTAL RAILROAD, 150TH ANNIV.

Jupiter Locomotive A4217

Golden Spike A4218

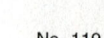
No. 119 Locomotive A4219

**LITHOGRAPHED WITH FOIL APPLICATION**
*Serpentine Die Cut 10¾x10½*
2019, May 10    Self-Adhesive
5378  A4217  (55c) multicolored   1.40   .30
5379  A4218  (55c) multicolored   1.40   .30
5380  A4219  (55c) multicolored   1.40   .30
  a.  Horiz. strip of 3, #5378-5380   4.20
  Nos. 5378-5380 (3)   4.20   .90

### WILD AND SCENIC RIVERS

A4220

No. 5381: a, Merced River. b, Owyhee River. c, Koyukuk River. d, Niobrara River. e, Snake River. f, Flathead River. g, Missouri River. h, Skagit River. i, Deschutes River. j, Tlikakila River. k, Ontonagon River. l, Clarion River.

**LITHOGRAPHED**
*Serpentine Die Cut 10¾x10½*
2019, May 21    Self-Adhesive
5381  A4220  Pane of 12   16.80
  a.-l.  (55c) Any single   1.40   .50

### ART OF ELLSWORTH KELLY (1923-2015)

Yellow White, 1961 — A4221

Colors for a Large Wall, 1951 — A4222

Blue Red Rocker, 1963 — A4223

Spectrum I, 1953 — A4224

South Ferry, 1956 — A4225

Blue Green, 1962 — A4226

 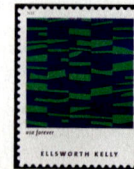
Orange Red Relief (for Delphine Seyrig), 1990 — A4227

Meschers, 1951 — A4228

Red Blue, 1964 — A4229

Gaza, 1956 — A4230

**LITHOGRAPHED**
*Serpentine Die Cut 10½x10¾*
2019, May 31    Self-Adhesive
5382  A4221  (55c) multicolored   1.40   .40
5383  A4222  (55c) multicolored   1.40   .40
5384  A4223  (55c) multicolored   1.40   .40
5385  A4224  (55c) multicolored   1.40   .40
5386  A4225  (55c) multicolored   1.40   .40
5387  A4226  (55c) multicolored   1.40   .40
5388  A4227  (55c) multicolored   1.40   .40
5389  A4228  (55c) multicolored   1.40   .40
5390  A4229  (55c) multicolored   1.40   .40
5391  A4230  (55c) multicolored   1.40   .40
  a.  Block of 10, #5382-5391   14.00
  Nos. 5382-5391 (10)   14.00   4.00

### COMMISSIONING OF U.S.S. MISSOURI, 75th ANNIV.

U.S.S. Missouri — A4231

**LITHOGRAPHED**
*Serpentine Die Cut 10¾*
2019, June 11    Tagged    Self-Adhesive
5392  A4231  (55c) multicolored   1.40   .25
  a.  Die cutting omitted, pair

### GEORGE HERBERT WALKER BUSH

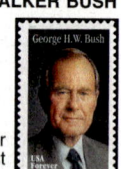
George Herbert Walker Bush (1924-2018), 41st President — A4232

**LITHOGRAPHED**
*Serpentine Die Cut 10¾*
2019, June 12    Tagged    Self-Adhesive
5393  A4232  (55c) multicolored   1.40   .25
  a.  Die cutting omitted, pair   500.00

### SESAME STREET CHILDREN'S TELEVISION SHOW, 50th ANNIV.

Muppet Characters — A4233

No. 5394: a, Big Bird. b, Ernie. c, Bert. d, Cookie Monster. e, Rosita. f, The Count. g, Oscar the Grouch. h, Abby Cadabby. i, Herry Monster. j, Julia. k, Guy Smiley. l, Snuffleupagus. m, Elmo. n, Telly. o, Grover. p, Zoe.

**LITHOGRAPHED**
*Serpentine Die Cut 10¾*
2019, June 22    Tagged    Self-Adhesive
5394  A4233  Pane of 16   22.40
  a.-p.  (55c) Any single   1.40   .50

## UNITED STATES

### FROGS

Pacific Tree Frog — A4234

Northern Leopard Frog — A4235

American Green Tree Frog — A4236

Squirrel Tree Frog — A4237

**LITHOGRAPHED**
*Serpentine Die Cut 11x10¾ on 2 or 3 Sides*

2019, July 9     Tagged
**Booklet Stamps**
**Self-Adhesive**

| | | | | |
|---|---|---|---|---|
| 5395 | A4234 | (55c) multicolored | 1.40 | .30 |
| 5396 | A4235 | (55c) multicolored | 1.40 | .30 |
| 5397 | A4236 | (55c) multicolored | 1.40 | .30 |
| 5398 | A4237 | (55c) multicolored | 1.40 | .30 |
| a. | Block of 4, #5395-5398 | | 5.60 | |
| b. | Booklet pane of 20, 5 each #5395-5398 | | 28.00 | |
| | Nos. 5395-5398 (4) | | 5.60 | 1.20 |

### FIRST MOON LANDING, 50TH ANNIV.

Astronaut Edwin E. "Buzz" Aldrin, Jr. on Moon A4238

Moon with Landing Site Highlighted A4239

**LITHOGRAPHED**
*Serpentine Die Cut 10¾*

2019, July 19
**Self-Adhesive**

| | | | | |
|---|---|---|---|---|
| 5399 | A4238 | (55c) multicolored | 1.40 | .25 |
| 5400 | A4239 | (55c) multicolored | 1.40 | .25 |
| a. | Pair, #5399-5400 | | 2.80 | |

Adjacent horizontal or vertical stamps have selvage between the stamps.

### STATE AND COUNTY FAIRS

Farmers Unloading Large Fruits and Vegetables A4240

Girl and Farm Animals A4241

Parents and Children A4242

Child Buying Candy Apple A4243

**LITHOGRAPHED**
*Serpentine Die Cut 10½x10¾*

2019, July 25
**Self-Adhesive**

| | | | | |
|---|---|---|---|---|
| 5401 | A4240 | (55c) multicolored | 1.40 | .30 |
| 5402 | A4241 | (55c) multicolored | 1.40 | .30 |
| 5403 | A4242 | (55c) multicolored | 1.40 | .30 |
| 5404 | A4243 | (55c) multicolored | 1.40 | .30 |
| a. | Horiz. strip of 4, #5401-5404 | | 5.60 | |
| | Nos. 5401-5404 (4) | | 5.60 | 1.20 |

Adjacent vertical stamps have selvage between the stamps.

### MILITARY WORKING DOGS

German Shepherd A4244

Labrador Retriever A4245

Belgian Malinois A4246

Dutch Shepherd A4247

**LITHOGRAPHED**
*Serpentine Die Cut 10¾x10½ (Nos. 5405, 5408), 10½x10¾ (Nos. 5406-5407)*

2019, Aug. 1
**Booklet Stamps**
**Self-Adhesive**

| | | | | |
|---|---|---|---|---|
| 5405 | A4244 | (55c) multicolored | 1.40 | .30 |
| 5406 | A4245 | (55c) multicolored | 1.40 | .30 |
| 5407 | A4246 | (55c) multicolored | 1.40 | .30 |
| 5408 | A4247 | (55c) multicolored | 1.40 | .30 |
| a. | Block of 4, #5405-5408 | | 5.60 | |
| b. | Booklet pane of 20, 5 each #5405-5408 | | 28.00 | |
| | Nos. 5405-5408 (4) | | 5.60 | 1.20 |

Adjacent horizontal and vertical stamps have selvage between the stamps. No. 5408b is a double-sided booklet pane with 12 stamps on one side (3 each Nos. 5405-5408), and eight stamps (2 each Nos. 5405-5408) plus label (booklet cover) on the other side.

### WOODSTOCK MUSIC FESTIVAL, 50TH ANNIV.

Dove — A4248

**TYPOGRAPHED**
*Serpentine Die Cut 10¾*

2019, Aug. 8
**Self-Adhesive**

| | | | | |
|---|---|---|---|---|
| 5409 | A4248 | (55c) multicolored | 1.40 | .25 |

### TYRANNOSAURUS REX

Juvenile Tyrannosaurus Rex, Egg, and Insect — A4249

Adult Tyrannosaurus Rex — A4250

Young Adult Tyrannosaurus Rex and Juvenile Triceratops A4251

Juvenile Tyrannosaurus Rex Chasing Mammal — A4252

**TYPOGRAPHED WITH LENTICULAR LENS AFFIXED**
*Serpentine Die Cut 10¾x10½*

2019, Aug. 29
**Self-Adhesive**

| | | | | |
|---|---|---|---|---|
| 5410 | A4249 | (55c) multicolored | 1.40 | .30 |
| 5411 | A4250 | (55c) multicolored | 1.40 | .30 |
| 5412 | A4251 | (55c) multicolored | 1.40 | .30 |
| 5413 | A4252 | (55c) multicolored | 1.40 | .30 |
| a. | Block of 4, #5410-5413 | | 5.60 | |
| | Nos. 5410-5413 (4) | | 5.60 | 1.20 |

Adjacent stamps have selvage between them. Only Nos. 5411 and 5412 show movement in the design when viewed from different positions.

### LITERARY ARTS

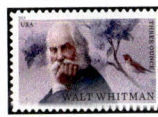
Walt Whitman (1819-92), Poet — A4253

**LITHOGRAPHED**
*Serpentine Die Cut 10¾*

2019, Sept. 12
**Self-Adhesive**

| | | | | |
|---|---|---|---|---|
| 5414 | A4253 | (85c) multicolored | 2.40 | .30 |

### WINTER BERRIES

Winterberry A4254

Juniper Berry A4255

Beautyberry A4256

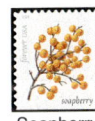
Soapberry A4257

**LITHOGRAPHED**
*Serpentine Die Cut 11¼x10¾ on 2 or 3 Sides*

2019, Sept. 17
**Booklet Stamps**
**Self-Adhesive**

| | | | | |
|---|---|---|---|---|
| 5415 | A4254 | (55c) multicolored | 1.40 | .30 |
| 5416 | A4255 | (55c) multicolored | 1.40 | .30 |
| 5417 | A4256 | (55c) multicolored | 1.40 | .30 |
| 5418 | A4257 | (55c) multicolored | 1.40 | .30 |
| a. | Block of 4, #5415-5418 | | 5.60 | |
| b. | Booklet pane of 20, 5 each #5415-5418 | | 28.00 | |
| | Nos. 5415-5418 (4) | | 5.60 | 1.20 |

No. 5398b is a double-sided booklet pane with 12 stamps on one side (3 each Nos. 5395-5398), and eight stamps (2 each Nos. 5395-5398) plus label (booklet cover) on the other side.

Purple Heart and Ribbon With Frame — A4258

**LITHOGRAPHED**
*Serpentine Die Cut 11¼x10¾*

2019, Oct. 4
**Self-Adhesive**

| | | | | |
|---|---|---|---|---|
| 5419 | A4258 | (55c) multicolored | 1.40 | .25 |

### SPOOKY SILHOUETTES

Cat and Raven A4259

Ghosts A4260

Spider and Web A4261

Bats A4262

**TYPOGRAPHED WITH FOIL APPLICATION**
*Serpentine Die Cut 10¾*

2019, Oct. 11
**Self-Adhesive**
**Color of Foil**

| | | | | |
|---|---|---|---|---|
| 5420 | A4259 | (55c) silver | 1.40 | .30 |
| 5421 | A4260 | (55c) orange | 1.40 | .30 |
| 5422 | A4261 | (55c) red | 1.40 | .30 |
| 5423 | A4262 | (55c) violet | 1.40 | .30 |
| a. | Block of 4, #5420-5423 | | 5.60 | |
| | Nos. 5420-5423 (4) | | 5.60 | 1.20 |

### CHRISTMAS WREATHS

Aspidistra Leaf Wreath A4263

Wreath Made of Gilded Pine Cones and Magnolia Pods A4264

Wreath Made of Gilded Hydrangea, Eucalyptus, Nandina and Ribbon A4265

Wreath Made of Woodland Bush Ivy and Red Winterberry A4266

**LITHOGRAPHED**
*Serpentine Die Cut 11¼x10¾ on 2 or 3 Sides*

2019, Oct. 25
**Booklet Stamps**
**Self-Adhesive**

| | | | | |
|---|---|---|---|---|
| 5424 | A4263 | (55c) multicolored | 1.40 | .30 |
| 5425 | A4264 | (55c) multicolored | 1.40 | .30 |
| 5426 | A4265 | (55c) multicolored | 1.40 | .30 |
| 5427 | A4266 | (55c) multicolored | 1.40 | .30 |
| a. | Block of 4, #5424-5427 | | 5.60 | |
| b. | Booklet pane of 20, 5 each #5424-5427 | | 28.00 | |
| | Nos. 5424-5427 (4) | | 5.60 | 1.20 |

No. 5398b is a double-sided booklet pane with 12 stamps on one side (3 each Nos. 5395-5398), and eight stamps (2 each Nos. 5395-5398) plus label (booklet cover) on the other side.

### CHINESE NEW YEAR

Year of the Rat — A4267

**LITHOGRAPHED WITH FOIL APPLICATION**
*Serpentine Die Cut 10¾*

2020, Jan. 11
**Self-Adhesive**

| | | | | |
|---|---|---|---|---|
| 5428 | A4267 | (55c) multicolored | 1.40 | .25 |

## AMERICAN LANDMARKS ISSUE

Big Bend National Park, Texas — A4268

Grand Island Ice Caves, Michigan A4269

LITHOGRAPHED

***Serpentine Die Cut 10¾x10½***

**2020, Jan. 18**

**Self-Adhesive**

**5429** A4268 $7.75 multi 15.50 7.75
**5430** A4269 $26.35 multi 53.00 26.50

## LOVE

Hearts — A4270

LITHOGRAPHED

***Serpentine Die Cut 10¾***

**2020, Jan. 23**

**Self-Adhesive**

**5431** A4270 (55c) multicolored 1.40 .25

## BLACK HERITAGE

Gwen Ifill (1955-2016), Television Newscaster — A4271

LITHOGRAPHED

***Serpentine Die Cut 10¾***

**2020, Jan. 30**

**Self-Adhesive**

**5432** A4271 (55c) multicolored 1.40 .25

Star and Stripes — A4272

LITHOGRAPHED

***Serpentine Die Cut 10¾ Vert.***

**2020, Feb. 3**

**COIL STAMP**

**Self-Adhesive**

**5433** A4272 (10c) multicolored .30 .25

## CELEBRATE

A4273

LITHOGRAPHED WITH FOIL APPLICATION

***Serpentine Die Cut 10¾***

**2020, Feb. 14**

**Self-Adhesive**

**5434** A4273 (55c) multicolored 1.40 .25
*a.* Die cutting omitted, pair —

## WILD ORCHIDS

Platanthera Grandiflora A4274

Cyrtopodium Polyphyllum A4275

Calopogon Tuberosus A4276

Spiranthes Odorata A4277

Triphora Trianthophoros A4278

Cypripedium Californicum A4279

Hexalectris Spicata A4280

Cypripedium Reginae A4281

Platanthera Leucophaea A4282

Triphora Trianthophoros A4283

Triphora Trianthophoros A4284

Cypripedium Californicum A4285

Hexalectris Spicata A4286

Cypripedium Reginae A4287

Spiranthes Odorata A4288

Platanthera Leucophaea A4289

Triphora Trianthophoros A4290

Platanthera Grandiflora A4291

Cyrtopodium Polyphyllum A4292

Calopogon Tuberosus A4293

LITHOGRAPHED

***Serpentine Die Cut 10¾ Vert.***

**2020, Feb. 21**

**Coil Stamps**

**Self-Adhesive**

**5435** A4274 (55c) multicolored 1.40 .40
**5436** A4275 (55c) multicolored 1.40 .40
**5437** A4276 (55c) multicolored 1.40 .40
**5438** A4277 (55c) multicolored 1.40 .40
**5439** A4278 (55c) multicolored 1.40 .40
**5440** A4279 (55c) multicolored 1.40 .40
**5441** A4280 (55c) multicolored 1.40 .40
**5442** A4281 (55c) multicolored 1.40 .40
**5443** A4282 (55c) multicolored 1.40 .40
**5444** A4283 (55c) multicolored 1.40 .40
*a.* Horiz. strip of 10, #5435-5444 14.00
*Nos. 5435-5444 (10)* 14.00 4.00

**Booklet Stamps**

***Serpentine Die Cut 10¾x11 on 2 or 3 Sides***

**5445** A4284 (55c) multicolored 1.40 .40
**5446** A4285 (55c) multicolored 1.40 .40
**5447** A4286 (55c) multicolored 1.40 .40
**5448** A4287 (55c) multicolored 1.40 .40
**5449** A4288 (55c) multicolored 1.40 .40
**5450** A4289 (55c) multicolored 1.40 .40
**5451** A4290 (55c) multicolored 1.40 .40
**5452** A4291 (55c) multicolored 1.40 .40
**5453** A4292 (55c) multicolored 1.40 .40
**5454** A4293 (55c) multicolored 1.40 .40
*a.* Block of 10, #5445-5454 14.00
*b.* Booklet pane of 20, 2 each #5445-5454 28.00
*Nos. 5445-5454 (10)* 14.00 4.00

Nos. 5454b is a double-sided booklet with 12 stamps on one side (Nos. 5446-5449, 5451-5454, 2 each Nos 5445, 5450), and eight stamps (Nos. 5446-5449, 5451-5454) plus a label that serves as the booklet cover on the other side.

## ARNOLD PALMER

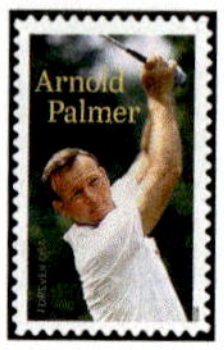


Arnold Palmer (1929-2016), Professional Golfer — A4294

LITHOGRAPHED

***Serpentine Die Cut 10¾***

**2020, Mar. 4**

**Self-Adhesive**

**5455** A4294 (55c) multicolored 1.40 .25

## MAINE STATEHOOD BICENTENARY

*Sea at Ogunquit,* by Edward Hopper (1882-1967) A4295

LITHOGRAPHED

***Serpentine Die Cut 10¾***

**2020, Mar. 15**

**Self-Adhesive**

**5456** A4295 (55c) multicolored 1.40 .25

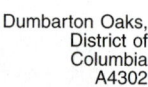

Boutonniere A4296

Corsage A4297

LITHOGRAPHED

***Serpentine Die Cut 10¾x11***

**2020, Apr. 2**

**Self-Adhesive**

**5457** A4296 (55c) multicolored 1.40 .25
**5458** A4297 (70c) multicolored 1.90 .25

## EARTH DAY, 50th ANNIV.

Stylized Globe — A4298

LITHOGRAPHED

***Serpentine Die Cut 11x10¾ on 2 or 3 Sides***

**2020, Apr. 18**

**Booklet Stamp**

**Self-Adhesive**

**5459** A4298 (55c) multicolored 1.40 .25
*a.* Booklet pane of 20 28.00

No. 5459a is a double-sided booklet with 12 stamps on one side and eight stamps plus a label that serves as the booklet cover on the other side.

Chrysanthemum A4299

LITHOGRAPHED

Sheets of 90 in nine panes of 10

***Serpentine Die Cut***

**2020, Apr. 24** **Tagged**

**Self-Adhesive**

**5460** A4299 ($1.20) multicolored 3.25 .50

Unused values are for stamps with surrounding selvage. Adjacent stamps are separated by rouletting.

## AMERICAN GARDENS

Brooklyn Botanic Garden, New York — A4300

Stan Hywet Hall and Gardens, Ohio — A4301

Dumbarton Oaks, District of Columbia A4302

Coastal Maine Botanical Gardens, Maine — A4303

Chicago Botanic Garden, Illinois — A4304

Winterthur Garden, Delaware A4305

Biltmore Estate Gardens, North Carolina — A4306

Alfred B. Maclay Gardens State Park, Florida — A4307

The Huntington Botanical Gardens, California A4308

Norfolk Botanical Garden, Virginia — A4309

UNITED STATES 149

LITHOGRAPHED

***Serpentine Die Cut 10¾x10½***

**2020, May 13**

**Self-Adhesive**

| | | | | | |
|---|---|---|---|---|---|
| **5461** | A4300 | (55c) | multicolored | 1.40 | .40 |
| **5462** | A4301 | (55c) | multicolored | 1.40 | .40 |
| **5463** | A4302 | (55c) | multicolored | 1.40 | .40 |
| **5464** | A4303 | (55c) | multicolored | 1.40 | .40 |
| **5465** | A4304 | (55c) | multicolored | 1.40 | .40 |
| **5466** | A4305 | (55c) | multicolored | 1.40 | .40 |
| **5467** | A4306 | (55c) | multicolored | 1.40 | .40 |
| **5468** | A4307 | (55c) | multicolored | 1.40 | .40 |
| **5469** | A4308 | (55c) | multicolored | 1.40 | .40 |
| **5470** | A4309 | (55c) | multicolored | 1.40 | .40 |
| *a.* | Block of 10, #5461-5470 | | | 14.00 | |
| | *Nos. 5461-5470 (10)* | | | 14.00 | 4.00 |

Die cut uncut press sheets of Nos. 5461-5470 were made available for sale. Values: cross gutter block of 10, $18; pairs with gutters between, $4.25 each. See note after No. 4693.

See note after No. 1549.

Counterfeits exist of Nos. 5461-5470. See the Postal Counterfeits section of this catalog.

**VOICES OF THE HARLEM RENAISSANCE**

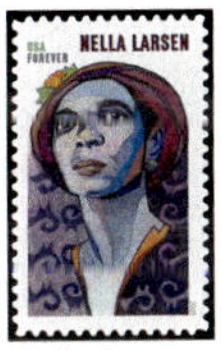

Nella Larsen (1891-1964), Novelist A4310

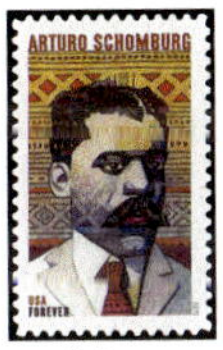

Arturo Schomburg (1874-1938), Historian A4311

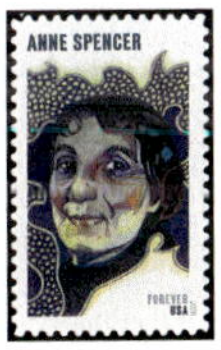

Anne Spencer (1882-1975), Poet A4312

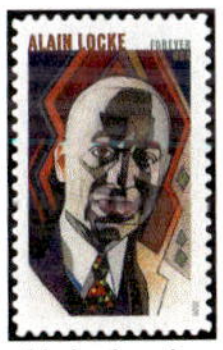

Alain Locke (1885-1954), Writer A4313

LITHOGRAPHED

***Serpentine Die Cut 10¾***

**2020, May 21**

**Self-Adhesive**

| | | | | | |
|---|---|---|---|---|---|
| **5471** | A4310 | (55c) | multicolored | 1.40 | .30 |
| **5472** | A4311 | (55c) | multicolored | 1.40 | .30 |
| **5473** | A4312 | (55c) | multicolored | 1.40 | .30 |
| **5474** | A4313 | (55c) | multicolored | 1.40 | .30 |
| *a.* | Horiz. or vert. strip of 4, #5471-5474 | | | 5.60 | |
| | *Nos. 5471-5474 (4)* | | | 5.60 | 1.20 |

Die cut uncut press sheets of Nos. 5471-5474 were made available for sale. Values: cross gutter block of 8, $16; pairs with gutters between, $4.25 each. See note after No. 4693.

See note after No. 1549.

**ENJOY THE GREAT OUTDOORS**

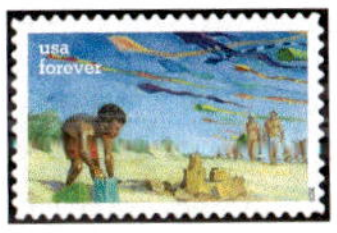

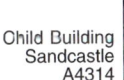

Child Building Sandcastle A4314

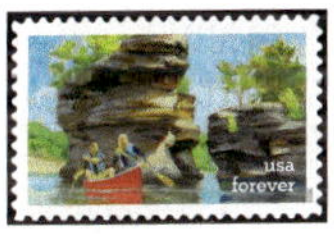

Canoeing A4315

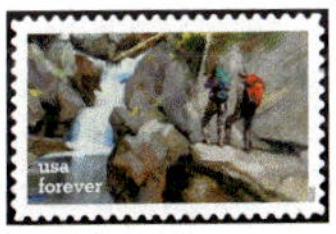

Hiking — A4316

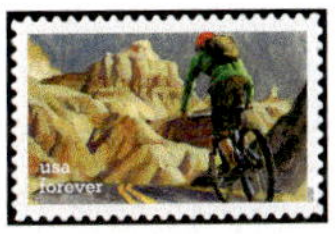

Bicycling A4317

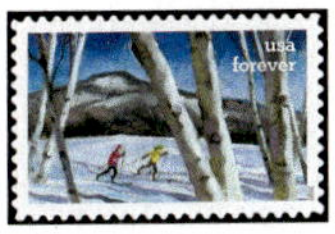

Cross-country Skiing — A4318

LITHOGRAPHED

***Serpentine Die Cut 10¾***

**2020, June 13**

**Self-Adhesive**

| | | | | | |
|---|---|---|---|---|---|
| **5475** | A4314 | (55c) | multicolored | 1.40 | .40 |
| **5476** | A4315 | (55c) | multicolored | 1.40 | .40 |
| **5477** | A4316 | (55c) | multicolored | 1.40 | .40 |
| **5478** | A4317 | (55c) | multicolored | 1.40 | .40 |
| **5479** | A4318 | (55c) | multicolored | 1.40 | .40 |
| *a.* | Vert. strip of 5, #5475-5479 | | | 7.00 | |
| | *Nos. 5475-5479 (5)* | | | 7.00 | 2.00 |

**HIP HOP**

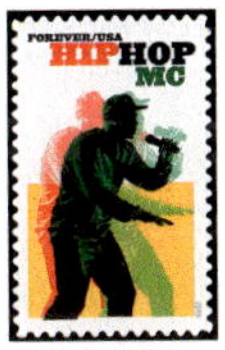

MC With Microphone Rapping A4319

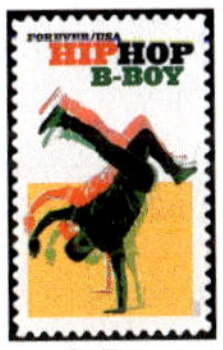

B-Boy Dancing A4320

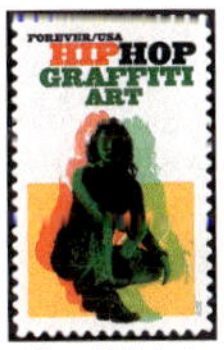

Graffiti Art A4321

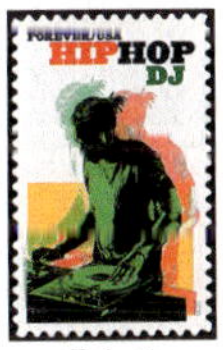

DJ at Turntable A4322

LITHOGRAPHED

***Serpentine Die Cut 10¾***

**2020, July 1**

**Self-Adhesive**

| | | | | | |
|---|---|---|---|---|---|
| **5480** | A4319 | (55c) | multicolored | 1.40 | .30 |
| **5481** | A4320 | (55c) | multicolored | 1.40 | .30 |
| **5482** | A4321 | (55c) | multicolored | 1.40 | .30 |
| **5483** | A4322 | (55c) | multicolored | 1.40 | .30 |
| *a.* | Block or vert. strip of 4, #5480-5483 | | | 5.60 | |
| | *Nos. 5480-5483 (4)* | | | 5.60 | 1.20 |

**FRUITS AND VEGETABLES**

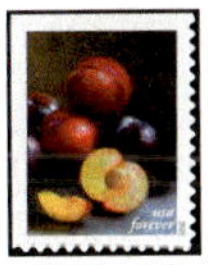

Red and Black Plums A4323

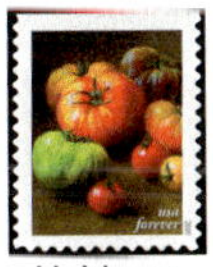

Heirloom and Cherry Tomatoes A4324

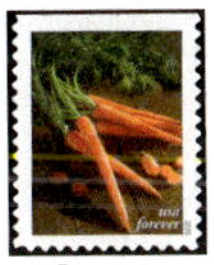

Carrots A4325

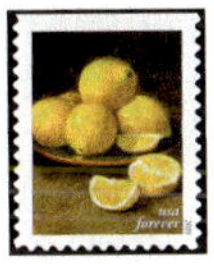

Lemons A4326

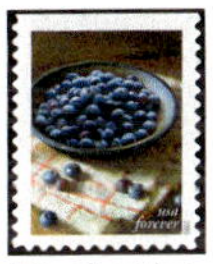

Blueberries A4327

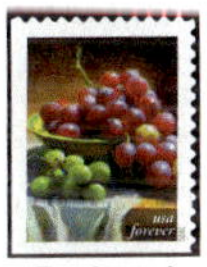

Red and Green Grapes A4328

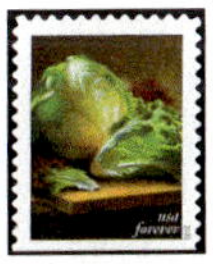

Lettuce A4329

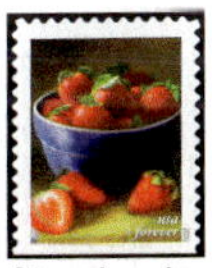

Strawberries A4330

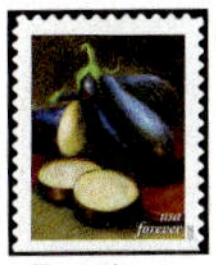

Eggplants A4331

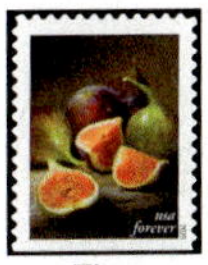

Figs A4332

LITHOGRAPHED

***Serpentine Die Cut 10¾x11 on 2 or 3 Sides***

**2020, July 17**

**Booklet Stamps**

**Self-Adhesive**

| | | | | | |
|---|---|---|---|---|---|
| **5484** | A4323 | (55c) | multicolored | 1.40 | .40 |
| **5485** | A4324 | (55c) | multicolored | 1.40 | .40 |
| **5486** | A4325 | (55c) | multicolored | 1.40 | .40 |
| **5487** | A4326 | (55c) | multicolored | 1.40 | .40 |
| **5488** | A4327 | (55c) | multicolored | 1.40 | .40 |
| **5489** | A4328 | (55c) | multicolored | 1.40 | .40 |
| **5490** | A4329 | (55c) | multicolored | 1.40 | .40 |
| **5491** | A4330 | (55c) | multicolored | 1.40 | .40 |
| **5492** | A4331 | (55c) | multicolored | 1.40 | .40 |
| **5493** | A4332 | (55c) | multicolored | 1.40 | .40 |
| *a.* | Block of 10, #5484-5493 | | | 14.00 | |
| *b.* | Booklet pane of 20, 2 each #5484-5493 | | | 28.00 | |
| | *Nos. 5484-5493 (10)* | | | 14.00 | 4.00 |

Nos. 5493b is a double-sided booklet pane with 12 stamps on one side (Nos. 5485-5488, 5490-5493, 2 each Nos. 5484, 5489) and eight stamps (Nos. 5485-5488, 5490-5493) plus label (booklet cover) on the other side.

**BUGS BUNNY, 80th ANNIV.**

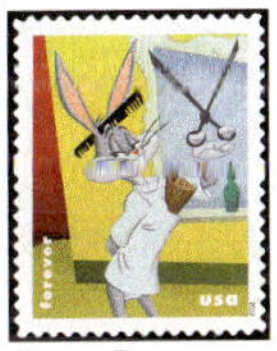

Bugs Bunny as Barber, From *Rabbit of Seville,* 1950 — A4333

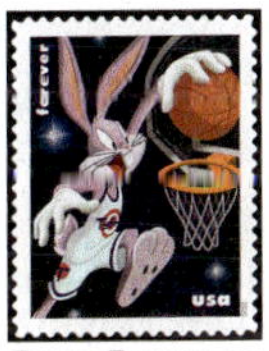

Bugs Bunny as Basketball Player, From *Space Jam,* 1996 — A4334

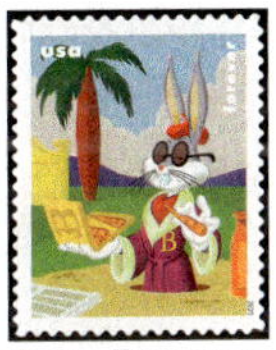

Bugs Bunny as Hollywood Celebrity, From *A Hare Grows in Manhattan,* 1947 — A4335

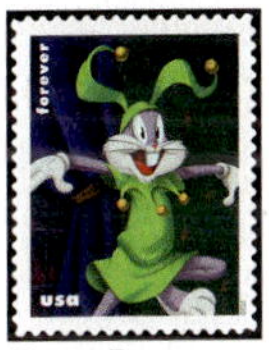

Bugs Bunny as Court Jester, From *Knighty Knight Bugs,* 1958 — A4336

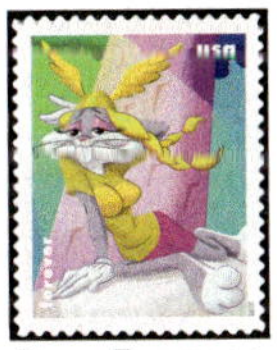

Bugs Bunny as Brunhilde, From *What's Opera, Doc?,* 1957 — A4337

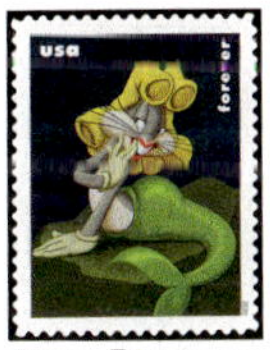

Bugs Bunny as Mermaid, From *Hare Ribbin',* 1944 — A4338

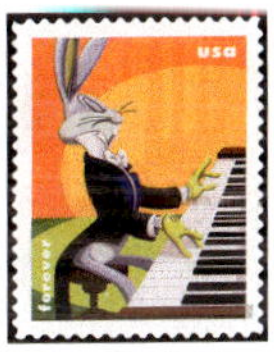

Bugs Bunny as Piano Player, From *Rhapsody Rabbit,* 1946 — A4339

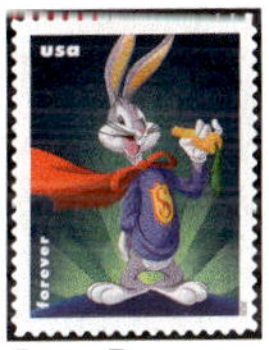

Bugs Bunny as Super-Rabbit, From *Super Rabbit,* 1943 — A4340

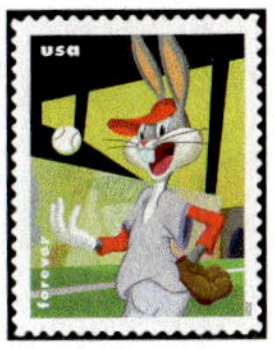

Bugs Bunny as Baseball Player, From *Baseball Bugs,* 1946 A4341

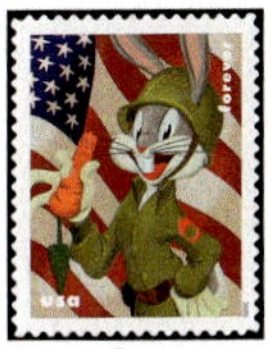

Bugs Bunny as Soldier, From World War II Poster A4342

LITHOGRAPHED

***Serpentine Die Cut 10½x10¾***

**2020, July 27**

**Self-Adhesive**

| | | | | | |
|---|---|---|---|---|---|
| **5494** | A4333 | (55c) | multicolored | 1.40 | .40 |
| **5495** | A4334 | (55c) | multicolored | 1.40 | .40 |
| **5496** | A4335 | (55c) | multicolored | 1.40 | .40 |
| **5497** | A4336 | (55c) | multicolored | 1.40 | .40 |
| **5498** | A4337 | (55c) | multicolored | 1.40 | .40 |
| **5499** | A4338 | (55c) | multicolored | 1.40 | .40 |
| **5500** | A4339 | (55c) | multicolored | 1.40 | .40 |
| **5501** | A4340 | (55c) | multicolored | 1.40 | .40 |
| **5502** | A4341 | (55c) | multicolored | 1.40 | .40 |
| **5503** | A4342 | (55c) | multicolored | 1.40 | .40 |
| *a.* | Block of 10, #5494-5503 | | | 14.00 | |
| | *Nos. 5494-5503 (10)* | | | 14.00 | 4.00 |

**WIRE SCULPTURES BY RUTH ASAWA (1926-2013)**

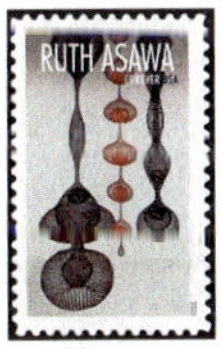

Three Untitled Sculptures From 1958, 1978 and 1959 A4343

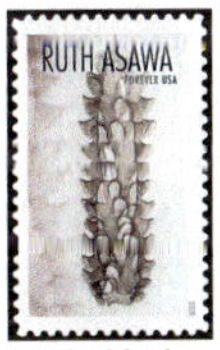

Untitled Sculpture From 1959 A4344

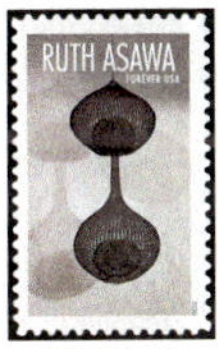

Untitled Sculpture From 1958 A4345

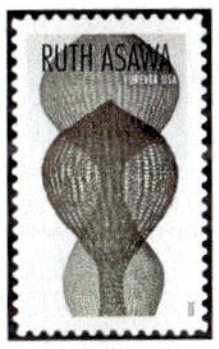

Untitled Sculpture From 1955 A4346

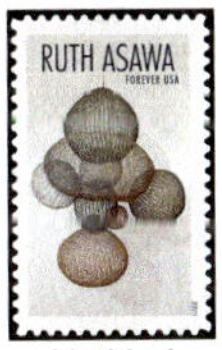

Untitled Sculpture From 1955 A4347

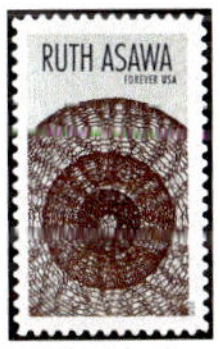

Untitled Sculpture From 1980 A4348

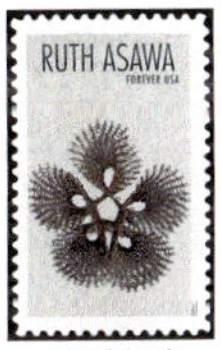

Untitled Sculpture From 1978 A4349

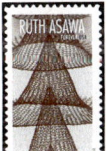

Untitled Sculpture From 1952 A4350

150 UNITED STATES

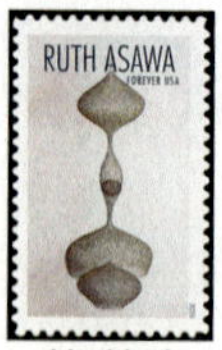

Untitled Sculpture From 1954
A4351

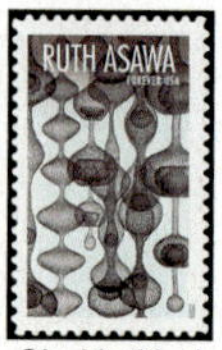

Six Untitled Sculptures From Various Years
A4352

LITHOGRAPHED

***Serpentine Die Cut 10¾***

**2020, Aug. 13**

**Self-Adhesive**

| | | | | |
|---|---|---|---|---|
| **5504** | A4343 | (55c) multicolored | 1.40 | .40 |
| **5505** | A4344 | (55c) multicolored | 1.40 | .40 |
| **5506** | A4345 | (55c) multicolored | 1.40 | .40 |
| **5507** | A4346 | (55c) multicolored | 1.40 | .40 |
| **5508** | A4347 | (55c) multicolored | 1.40 | .40 |
| **5509** | A4348 | (55c) multicolored | 1.40 | .40 |
| **5510** | A4349 | (55c) multicolored | 1.40 | .40 |
| **5511** | A4350 | (55c) multicolored | 1.40 | .40 |
| **5512** | A4351 | (55c) multicolored | 1.40 | .40 |
| **5513** | A4352 | (55c) multicolored | 1.40 | .40 |
| *a.* | | Block of 10, #5504-5513 | 14.00 | |

**INNOVATION**

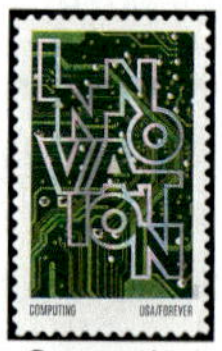

Computing
A4353

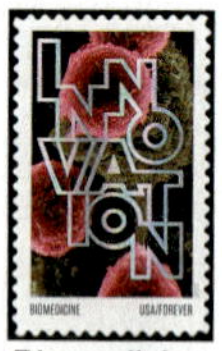

Biomedicine
A4354

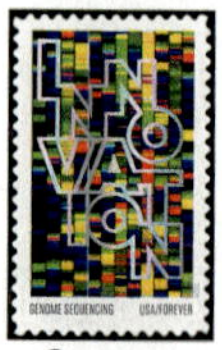

Genome Sequencing
A4355

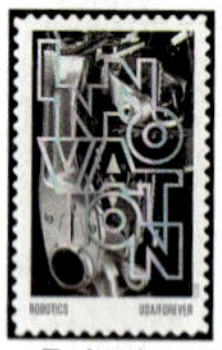

Robotics
A4356

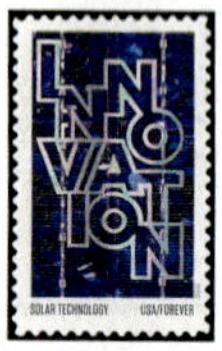

Solar Technology — A4357

LITHOGRAPHED WITH FOIL APPLICATION

Sheets of 120 in six panes of 20

***Serpentine Die Cut 10¾***

**2020, Aug. 20**

**Self-Adhesive**

| | | | | |
|---|---|---|---|---|
| **5514** | A4353 | (55c) multicolored | 1.40 | .40 |
| **5515** | A4354 | (55c) multicolored | 1.40 | .40 |
| **5516** | A4355 | (55c) multicolored | 1.40 | .40 |
| **5517** | A4356 | (55c) multicolored | 1.40 | .40 |
| **5518** | A4357 | (55c) multicolored | 1.40 | .40 |
| *a.* | | Horiz. strip of 5, #5514-5518 | 7.00 | |
| | | *Nos. 5514-5518 (5)* | 7.00 | 2.00 |

**THANK YOU**

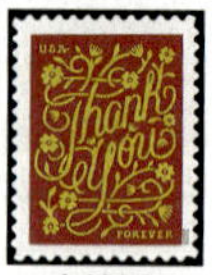

A4358

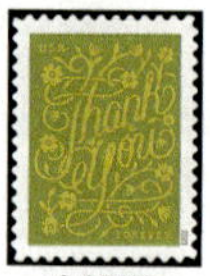

A4359

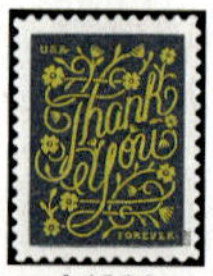

A4360

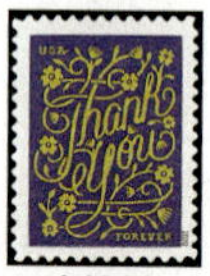

A4361

TYPOGRAPHED WITH FOIL APPLICATION

***Serpentine Die Cut 10¾***

**2020, Aug. 21**

**Self-Adhesive**

| | | | | |
|---|---|---|---|---|
| **5519** | A4358 | (55c) rose brown & gold | 1.40 | .40 |
| **5520** | A4359 | (55c) olive & gold | 1.40 | .40 |
| **5521** | A4360 | (55c) slate blue & gold | 1.40 | .40 |
| **5522** | A4361 | (55c) violet & gold | 1.40 | .40 |
| *a.* | | Block of 4, #5519-5522 | 5.60 | |
| | | *Nos. 5519-5522 (4)* | 5.60 | 1.60 |

**WOMAN SUFFRAGE CENTENARY**

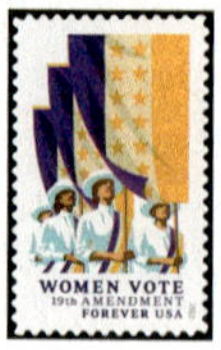

Suffragists Marching for Passage of 19th Amendment — A4362

LITHOGRAPHED

***Serpentine Die Cut 10¾***

**2020, Aug. 22**

**Self-Adhesive**

**5523** A4362 (55c) multicolored 1.40 .25

**MAYFLOWER IN PLYMOUTH HARBOR, 400th ANNIV.**

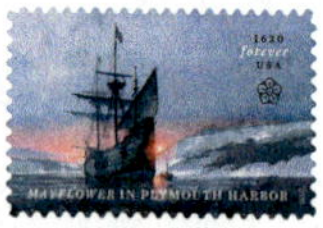

The Mayflower in Plymouth Harbor and Mayflower
A4363

LITHOGRAPHED & ENGRAVED

***Serpentine Die Cut 10¾***

**2020, Sept. 17**

**Self-Adhesive**

**5524** A4363 (55c) multicolored 1.40 .25

A pane of No. 5524, imperforate panes of single-color progressive proofs in cyan, magenta, yellow, and lithographed black, a commemorative book, and a numbered certificate were produced in a quantity of 2,500 and sold as a unit for $59.95.

**CHRISTMAS**

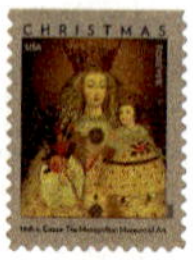

Our Lady of Guápulo, by Unknown 18th Century Peruvian Artist
A4364

Ornament
A4365

Christmas Tree
A4366

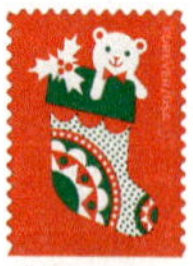

Christmas Stocking
A4367

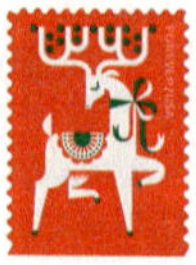

Reindeer — A4368

LITHOGRAPHED

***Serpentine Die Cut 10¾ on 2 or 3 Sides***

**2020**

**Booklet Stamps**

**Self-Adhesive**

| | | | | |
|---|---|---|---|---|
| **5525** | A4364 | (55c) multicolored | 1.40 | .25 |
| *a.* | | Booklet pane of 20 | 28.00 | |
| **5526** | A4365 | (55c) multicolored | 1.40 | .30 |
| **5527** | A4366 | (55c) multicolored | 1.40 | .30 |
| **5528** | A4367 | (55c) multicolored | 1.40 | .30 |
| **5529** | A4368 | (55c) multicolored | 1.40 | .30 |
| *a.* | | Block of 4, #5526-5529 | 5.60 | |
| *b.* | | Booklet pane of 20, 5 each #5526-5529 | 28.00 | |
| | | *Nos. 5525-5529 (5)* | 7.00 | 1.45 |

Issued: No. 5525, 10/20; Nos. 5526-5529, 9/24.

No. 5525a is a double-sided booklet pane with 12 stamps on one side, and eight stamps plus label (booklet cover) on the other side.

No. 5529b is a double-sided booklet pane with 12 stamps on one side (3 each Nos. 5526-5529), and eight stamps (2 each Nos. 5526-55290) plus label (booklet cover) on the other side.

**HANUKKAH**

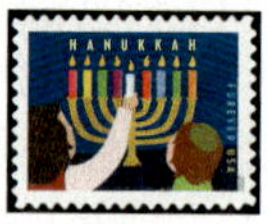

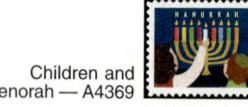

Children and Menorah — A4369

LITHOGRAPHED

***Serpentine Die Cut 10¾***

**2020, Oct. 6**

**Self-Adhesive**

**5530** A4369 (55c) multicolored 1.40 .25

**KWANZAA**

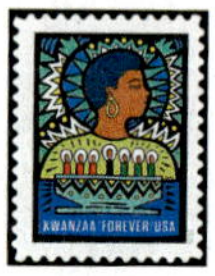

Woman and Kinara — A4370

LITHOGRAPHED

***Serpentine Die Cut 10¾***

**2020, Oct. 13**

**Self-Adhesive**

**5531** A4370 (55c) multicolored 1.40 .25

**WINTER SCENES**

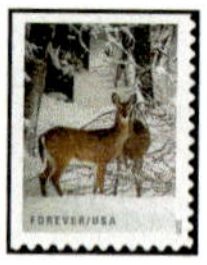

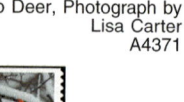

Two Deer, Photograph by Lisa Carter
A4371

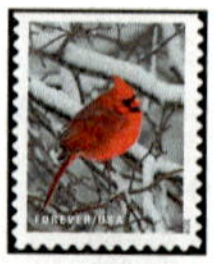

Cardinal, Photograph by Gerald A. DeBoer
A4372

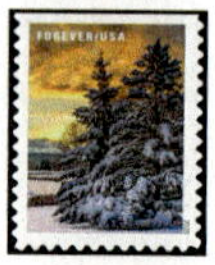

Snowy Morning at Sunrise, Photograph by Lisa Lacasse
A4373

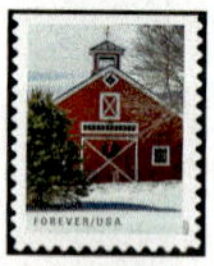

Red Barn with Wreath, Photograph by Lisa Lacasse
A4374

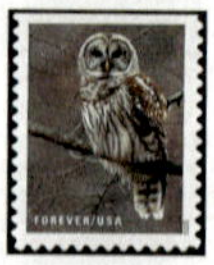

Barred Owl, Photograph by Malachi Ives
A4375

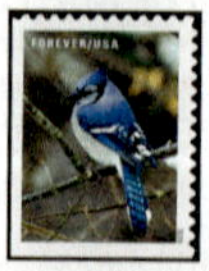

Blue Jay, Photograph by Edgar Lee Espe
A4376

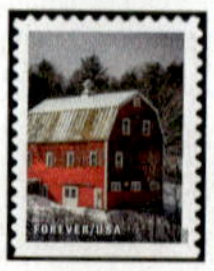

Mackenzie Barn, Woodstock, Vermont, Photograph by Lisa Lacasse
A4377

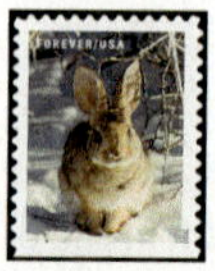

Rabbit, Photograph by Melani Wright
A4378

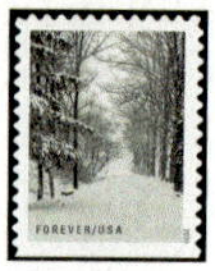

After the Snowfall, Photograph by Lisa Lacasse
A4379

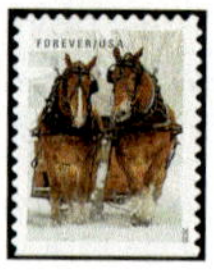

Mike and Burt, the Belgian Draft Horses, Photograph by Lisa Lacasse
A4380

LITHOGRAPHED

***Serpentine Die Cut 10¾ on 2 or 3 Sides***

**2020, Oct. 16**

**Booklet Stamps**

**Self-Adhesive**

| | | | | |
|---|---|---|---|---|
| **5532** | A4371 | (55c) multicolored | 1.40 | .40 |
| **5533** | A4372 | (55c) multicolored | 1.40 | .40 |
| **5534** | A4373 | (55c) multicolored | 1.40 | .40 |
| **5535** | A4374 | (55c) multicolored | 1.40 | .40 |
| **5536** | A4375 | (55c) multicolored | 1.40 | .40 |
| **5537** | A4376 | (55c) multicolored | 1.40 | .40 |
| **5538** | A4377 | (55c) multicolored | 1.40 | .40 |
| **5539** | A4378 | (55c) multicolored | 1.40 | .40 |
| **5540** | A4379 | (55c) multicolored | 1.40 | .40 |
| **5541** | A4380 | (55c) multicolored | 1.40 | .40 |
| *a.* | | Block of 10, #5532-5541 | 14.00 | |
| *b.* | | Booklet pane of 20, 2 each #5532-5541 | 28.00 | |
| | | *Nos. 5532-5541 (10)* | 14.00 | 4.00 |

Nos. 5541b is a double-sided booklet with 12 stamps on one side (Nos. 5533-5536, 5538-5541, 2 each Nos 5532, 5537), and eight stamps (Nos. 5533-5536, 5538-5541) plus a label that serves as the booklet cover on the other side.

**DRUG FREE USA**

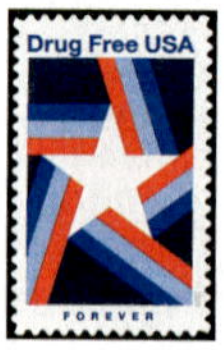

Star and Stripes — A4381

LITHOGRAPHED

***Serpentine Die Cut 10¾***

**2020, Oct. 27**

**Self-Adhesive**

**5542** A4381 (55c) multicolored 1.40 .25

**LOVE**

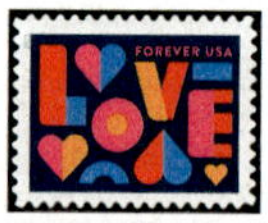

A4382

LITHOGRAPHED

***Serpentine Die Cut 11***

**2021, Jan. 14**

**Self-Adhesive**

| | | | | |
|---|---|---|---|---|
| **5543** | A4382 | (55c) multicolored | 1.40 | .25 |
| *a.* | | Imperforate | 1.50 | — |

**BRUSH RABBIT**

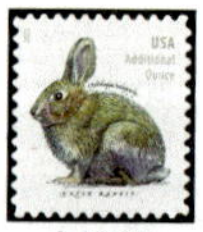

A4383

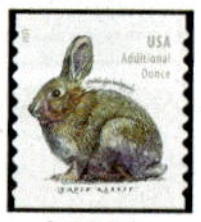

A4383a

LITHOGRAPHED

***Serpentine Die Cut 11¼x11***

**2021, Jan. 24**

**Self-Adhesive**

**5544** A4383 (20c) multicolored .50 .25

**Coil Stamp**

***Serpentine Die Cut 9½ Vert.***

**5545** A4383 (20c) multicolored .50 .25

# UNITED STATES

## BARNS

Round Barn
A4384

Barn With Gambrel Roof, Windmill
A4385

Forebay Barn
A4386

Snow-covered Western Barn
A4387

**LITHOGRAPHED**
*Serpentine Die Cut 11x11¼*
**2021, Jan. 24**
**Self-Adhesive**

| 5546 | A4384 | (36c) multicolored | 1.10 | .30 |
|---|---|---|---|---|
| 5547 | A4385 | (36c) multicolored | 1.10 | .30 |
| 5548 | A4386 | (36c) multicolored | 1.10 | .30 |
| 5549 | A4387 | (36c) multicolored | 1.10 | .30 |
| a. | Block or horiz. strip of 4, #5546-5549 | | 4.40 | |
| | Nos. 5546-5549 (4) | | 4.40 | 1.20 |

Counterfeits exist of Nos. 5546-5549. See the Postal Counterfeits section of this catalog.

**Coil Stamps**
*Serpentine Die Cut 11 Horiz.*

| 5550 | A4385 | (36c) multicolored | 1.10 | .30 |
|---|---|---|---|---|
| 5551 | A4387 | (36c) multicolored | 1.10 | .30 |
| 5552 | A4386 | (36c) multicolored | 1.10 | .30 |
| 5553 | A4384 | (36c) multicolored | 1.10 | .30 |
| a. | Vert. strip of 4, #5550-5553 | | 4.40 | |

## AMERICAN LANDMARKS ISSUE

Castillo de San Marcos, St. Augustine, Florida — A4388

**LITHOGRAPHED**
*Serpentine Die Cut 10¾x10½*
**2021, Jan. 24**
**Self-Adhesive**

| 5554 | A4388 | $7.95 multi | 16.00 | 8.00 |
|---|---|---|---|---|

## BLACK HERITAGE

August Wilson (1945-2005), Playwright — A4389

**LITHOGRAPHED**
*Serpentine Die Cut 11*
**2021, Jan. 28**
**Self-Adhesive**

| 5555 | A4389 | (55c) multicolored | 1.40 | .25 |
|---|---|---|---|---|
| a. | Imperforate | | 2.00 | |

## CHINESE NEW YEAR

Year of the Ox — A4390

**LITHOGRAPHED & TYPOGRAPHED WITH FOIL APPLICATION**
**2021, Feb. 2** *Serpentine Die Cut 11*
**Self-Adhesive**

| 5556 | A4390 | (55c) multi | 1.40 | .25 |
|---|---|---|---|---|
| a. | Imperforate | | 3.00 | |

## CHIEN-SHIUNG WU

Dr. Chien-Shiung Wu (1912-97), Nuclear Physicist — A4391

**LITHOGRAPHED**
*Serpentine Die Cut 11*
**2021, Feb. 11**
**Self-Adhesive**

| 5557 | A4391 | (55c) multicolored | 1.40 | .25 |
|---|---|---|---|---|
| a. | Imperforate | | 6.00 | — |

## GARDEN BEAUTY

Pink Flowering Dogwood
A4392

Orange and Yellow Tulip
A4393

Allium
A4394

Pink Moth Orchid with Mottled Petals
A4395

Magenta Dahlia
A4396

Yellow Moth Orchid with Pink Center
A4397

Pink and White Sacred Lotus
A4398

White Asiatic Lily
A4399

Rose Pink and White Tulip
A4400

Pink American Lotus
A4401

**LITHOGRAPHED**
*Serpentine Die Cut 11 on 2 or 3 Sides*
**2021, Feb. 23**
**Booklet Stamps**
**Self-Adhesive**

| 5558 | A4392 | (55c) multicolored | 1.40 | .40 |
|---|---|---|---|---|
| 5559 | A4393 | (55c) multicolored | 1.40 | .40 |
| 5560 | A4394 | (55c) multicolored | 1.40 | .40 |
| 5561 | A4395 | (55c) multicolored | 1.40 | .40 |
| 5562 | A4396 | (55c) multicolored | 1.40 | .40 |
| 5563 | A4397 | (55c) multicolored | 1.40 | .40 |
| 5564 | A4398 | (55c) multicolored | 1.40 | .40 |
| 5565 | A4399 | (55c) multicolored | 1.40 | .40 |
| 5566 | A4400 | (55c) multicolored | 1.40 | .40 |
| 5567 | A4401 | (55c) multicolored | 1.40 | .40 |
| a. | Block of 10, #5558-5567 | | 14.00 | |
| b. | Booklet pane of 20, 2 each #5558-5567 | | 28.00 | |
| | Nos. 5558-5567 (10) | | 14.00 | 4.00 |

No. 5567b is a double-sided booklet pane with 12 stamps on one side (Nos. 5560-5567, 2 each Nos. 5558-5559), and eight stamps (Nos. 5560-5567) plus label (booklet cover) on the other side.

## COLORADO HAIRSTREAK BUTTERFLY

A4402

**LITHOGRAPHED**
*Serpentine Die Cut 10½*
**2021, Mar. 9**
**Self-Adhesive**

| 5568 | A4402 | (75c) multicolored | 2.40 | .25 |
|---|---|---|---|---|

## ESPRESSO DRINKS

Caffe Latte
A4403

Espresso
A4404

Caffe Mocha
A4405

Cappuccino
A4406

**LITHOGRAPHED**
*Serpentine Die Cut 11¼x10¾ on 2 or 3 Sides*
**2021, Apr. 9**
**Booklet Stamps**
**Self-Adhesive**

| 5569 | A4403 | (55c) multicolored | 1.40 | .30 |
|---|---|---|---|---|
| 5570 | A4404 | (55c) multicolored | 1.40 | .30 |
| 5571 | A4405 | (55c) multicolored | 1.40 | .30 |
| 5572 | A4406 | (55c) multicolored | 1.40 | .30 |
| a. | Block of 4, #5569-5572 | | 5.60 | |
| b. | Booklet pane of 20, 5 each #5569-5572 | | 28.00 | |
| | Nos. 5569-5572 (4) | | 5.60 | 1.20 |

No. 5398b is a double-sided booklet pane with 12 stamps on one side (3 each Nos. 5395-5398), and eight stamps (2 each Nos. 5395-5398) plus label (booklet cover) on the other side.

## STAR WARS MOVIE DROIDS

IG-11
A4407

R2-D2
A4408

K-2SO
A4409

D-O
A4410

L3-37
A4411

BB-8
A4412

C-3PO
A4413

Gonk Droid
A4414

2-1B Droid
A4415

Chopper
A4416

**LITHOGRAPHED & TYPOGRAPHED**
*Serpentine Die Cut 10¾*
**2021, May 4**
**Self-Adhesive**

| 5573 | A4407 | (55c) multicolored | 1.40 | .40 |
|---|---|---|---|---|
| a. | Imperforate | | 6.00 | — |
| 5574 | A4408 | (55c) multicolored | 1.40 | .40 |
| a. | Imperforate | | 6.00 | — |
| 5575 | A4409 | (55c) multicolored | 1.40 | .40 |
| a. | Imperforate | | 6.00 | — |
| 5576 | A4410 | (55c) multicolored | 1.40 | .40 |
| a. | Imperforate | | 6.00 | — |
| 5577 | A4411 | (55c) multicolored | 1.40 | .40 |
| a. | Imperforate | | 6.00 | — |
| 5578 | A4412 | (55c) multicolored | 1.40 | .40 |
| a. | Imperforate | | 6.00 | — |
| 5579 | A4413 | (55c) multicolored | 1.40 | .40 |
| a. | Imperforate | | 6.00 | — |
| 5580 | A4414 | (55c) multicolored | 1.40 | .40 |
| a. | Imperforate | | 6.00 | — |
| 5581 | A4415 | (55c) multicolored | 1.40 | .40 |
| a. | Imperforate | | 6.00 | — |
| 5582 | A4416 | (55c) multicolored | 1.40 | .40 |
| a. | Imperforate | | 6.00 | — |
| b. | Block of 10, #5573-5582 | | 14.00 | |
| c. | Imperforate block of 10, #5573a-5582a | | 60.00 | |
| | Nos. 5573-5582 (10) | | 14.00 | 4.00 |

## HERITAGE BREEDS

Mulefoot Hog
A4417

Wyandotte Chicken
A4418

Milking Devon Cow
A4419

Narragansett Turkey
A4420

American Mammoth Jackstock Donkey
A4421

Cotton Patch Goose
A4422

152 UNITED STATES

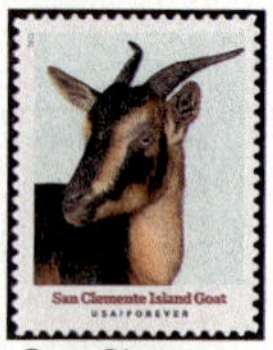
San Clemente Island Goat — A4423

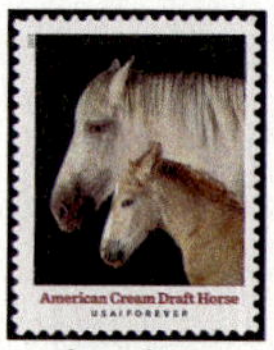
American Cream Draft Horse — A4424

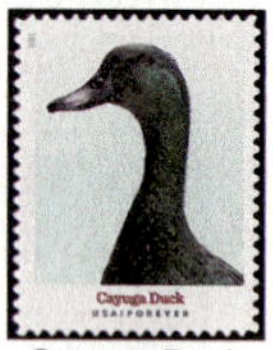
Cayuga Duck A4425

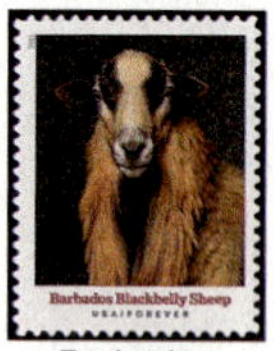
Barbados Blackbelly Sheep A4426

LITHOGRAPHED & TYPOGRAPHED

***Serpentine Die Cut 10½x10¾***

**2021, May 17**

**Self-Adhesive**

| | | | | | |
|---|---|---|---|---|---|
| **5583** | A4417 | (55c) | multicolored | 1.40 | .40 |
| *a.* | | | Imperforate | 6.00 | — |
| **5584** | A4418 | (55c) | multicolored | 1.40 | .40 |
| *a.* | | | Imperforate | 6.00 | — |
| **5585** | A4419 | (55c) | multicolored | 1.40 | .40 |
| *a.* | | | Imperforate | 6.00 | — |
| **5586** | A4420 | (55c) | multicolored | 1.40 | .40 |
| *a.* | | | Imperforate | 6.00 | — |
| **5587** | A4421 | (55c) | multicolored | 1.40 | .40 |
| *a.* | | | Imperforate | 6.00 | — |
| **5588** | A4422 | (55c) | multicolored | 1.40 | .40 |
| *a.* | | | Imperforate | 6.00 | — |
| **5589** | A4423 | (55c) | multicolored | 1.40 | .40 |
| *a.* | | | Imperforate | 6.00 | — |
| **5590** | A4424 | (55c) | multicolored | 1.40 | .40 |
| *a.* | | | Imperforate | 6.00 | — |
| **5591** | A4425 | (55c) | multicolored | 1.40 | .40 |
| *a.* | | | Imperforate | 6.00 | — |
| **5592** | A4426 | (55c) | multicolored | 1.40 | .40 |
| *a.* | | | Imperforate | 6.00 | — |
| *b.* | | | Block of 10, #5583-5592 | 14.00 | |
| *c.* | | | Imperforate block of 10, #5583a-5592a | 60.00 | |
| | | | *Nos. 5583-5592 (10)* | 14.00 | 4.00 |

**GO FOR BROKE**

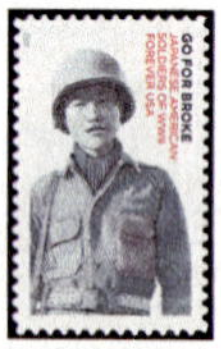
Japanese-American Soldier of World War II — A4427

LITHOGRAPHED & ENGRAVED

***Serpentine Die Cut 10¾***

**2021, June 3**

**Self-Adhesive**

| | | | | | |
|---|---|---|---|---|---|
| **5593** | A4427 | (55c) | blue & red | 1.40 | .25 |
| *a.* | | | Imperforate | 2.00 | — |

**PAINTINGS BY EMILIO SANCHEZ (1921-99)**

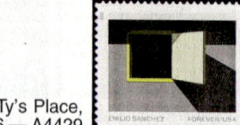

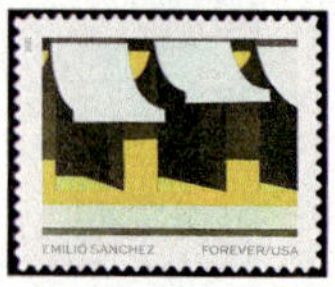
Los Toldos, 1973 — A4428

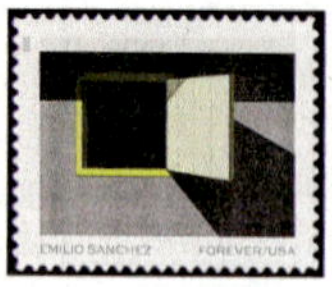
Ty's Place, 1976 — A4429

En el Souk, 1972 — A4430

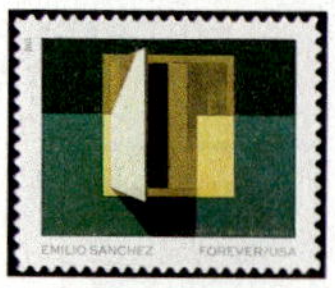
Untitled (Ventanita Entreabierta), 1981 — A4431

LITHOGRAPHED

***Serpentine Die Cut 10¾***

**2021, June 10**

**Self-Adhesive**

| | | | | | |
|---|---|---|---|---|---|
| **5594** | A4428 | (55c) | multicolored | 1.40 | .30 |
| *a.* | | | Imperforate | 2.00 | — |
| **5595** | A4429 | (55c) | multicolored | 1.40 | .30 |
| *a.* | | | Imperforate | 2.00 | — |
| **5596** | A4430 | (55c) | multicolored | 1.40 | .30 |
| *a.* | | | Imperforate | 2.00 | — |
| **5597** | A4431 | (55c) | multicolored | 1.40 | .30 |
| *a.* | | | Imperforate | 2.00 | — |
| *b.* | | | Horiz. or vert. strip of 4, #5594-5597 | 5.60 | |
| *c.* | | | Imperforate horiz. or vert. strip of 4, #5594a-5597a | 8.00 | |
| | | | *Nos. 5594-5597 (4)* | 5.60 | 1.20 |

**SUN SCIENCE**

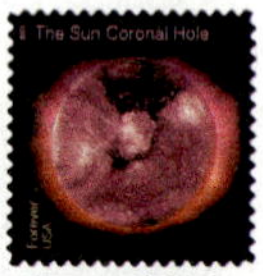
Coronal Hole A4432

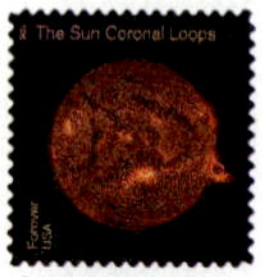
Coronal Loops A4433

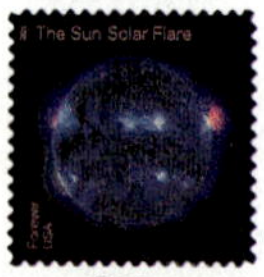
Solar Flare — A4434

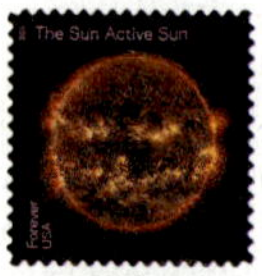
Active Sun — A4435

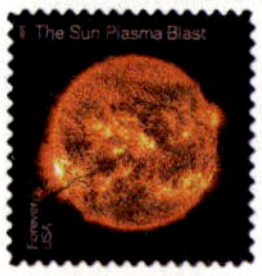
Plasma Blast A4436

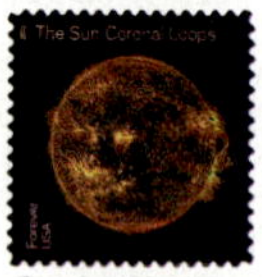
Coronal Loops A4437

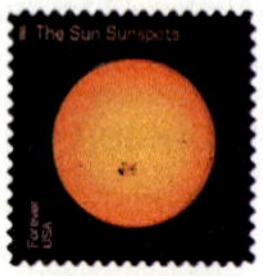
Sunspots A4438

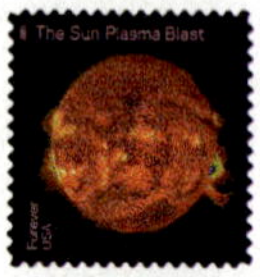
Plasma Blast A4439

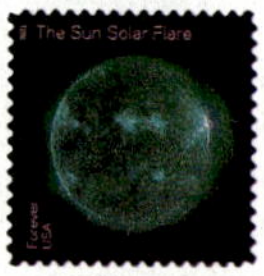
Solar Flare — A4440

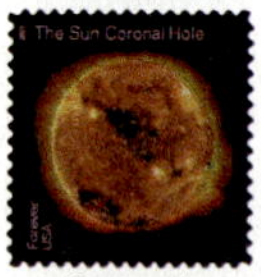
Coronal Hole — A4441

TYPOGRAPHED WITH FOIL APPLICATION

***Serpentine Die Cut 10¾x10½***

**2021, June 18**

**Self-Adhesive**

| | | | | | |
|---|---|---|---|---|---|
| **5598** | A4432 | (55c) | multicolored | 1.40 | .40 |
| *a.* | | | Imperforate | 5.00 | — |
| **5599** | A4433 | (55c) | multicolored | 1.40 | .40 |
| *a.* | | | Imperforate | 5.00 | — |
| **5600** | A4434 | (55c) | multicolored | 1.40 | .40 |
| *a.* | | | Imperforate | 5.00 | — |
| **5601** | A4435 | (55c) | multicolored | 1.40 | .40 |
| *a.* | | | Imperforate | 5.00 | — |
| **5602** | A4436 | (55c) | multicolored | 1.40 | .40 |
| *a.* | | | Imperforate | 5.00 | — |
| **5603** | A4437 | (55c) | multicolored | 1.40 | .40 |
| *a.* | | | Imperforate | 5.00 | — |
| **5604** | A4438 | (55c) | multicolored | 1.40 | .40 |
| *a.* | | | Imperforate | 5.00 | — |
| **5605** | A4439 | (55c) | multicolored | 1.40 | .40 |
| *a.* | | | Imperforate | 5.00 | — |
| **5606** | A4440 | (55c) | multicolored | 1.40 | .40 |
| *a.* | | | Imperforate | 5.00 | — |
| **5607** | A4441 | (55c) | multicolored | 1.40 | .40 |
| *a.* | | | Imperforate | 5.00 | — |
| *b.* | | | Block of 10, #5598-5607 | 14.00 | |
| *c.* | | | Imperforate block of 10, #5598a-5607a | 50.00 | |
| | | | *Nos. 5598-5607 (10)* | 14.00 | 4.00 |

**YOGI BERRA**

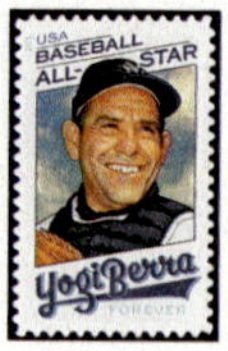
Lawrence Peter "Yogi" Berra (1925-2015), Baseball Player — A4442

LITHOGRAPHED & TYPOGRAPHED

***Serpentine Die Cut 10¾***

**2021, June 24**

**Self-Adhesive**

| | | | | | |
|---|---|---|---|---|---|
| **5608** | A4442 | (55c) | multicolored | 1.40 | .25 |
| *a.* | | | Imperforate | 2.00 | — |

**TAP DANCE**

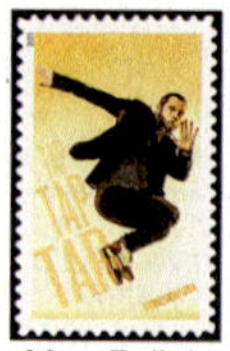
Max Pollak A4443

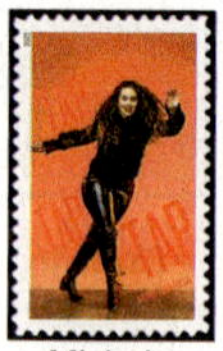
Michela Marino Lerman A4444

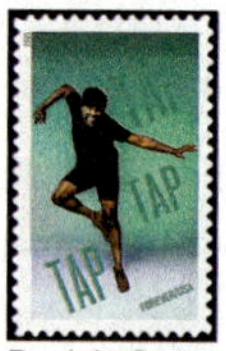
Derick Grant A4445

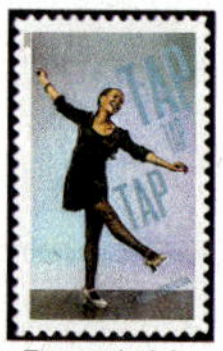
Dormeshia Sumbry-Edwards A4446

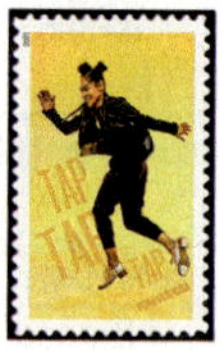
Ayodele Casel — A4447

LITHOGRAPHED

***Serpentine Die Cut 11***

**2021, July 10**

**Color of "TAP"**

**Self-Adhesive**

| | | | | | |
|---|---|---|---|---|---|
| **5609** | A4443 | (55c) | buff | 1.40 | .40 |
| *a.* | | | Imperforate | 3.00 | — |
| **5610** | A4444 | (55c) | rose | 1.40 | .40 |
| *a.* | | | Imperforate | 3.00 | — |
| **5611** | A4445 | (55c) | greenish blue | 1.40 | .40 |
| *a.* | | | Imperforate | 3.00 | — |
| **5612** | A4446 | (55c) | light blue | 1.40 | .40 |
| *a.* | | | Imperforate | 3.00 | — |
| **5613** | A4447 | (55c) | bister | 1.40 | .40 |
| *a.* | | | Imperforate | 3.00 | — |
| *b.* | | | Horiz. strip of 5, #5609-5613 | 7.00 | |
| *c.* | | | Imperforate strip of 5, #5609a-5613a | 15.00 | |
| | | | P# block of 10, 2 sets of 4# + P | 14.00 | |
| | | | *Nos. 5609-5613 (5)* | 7.00 | 2.00 |

**MYSTERY MESSAGE**

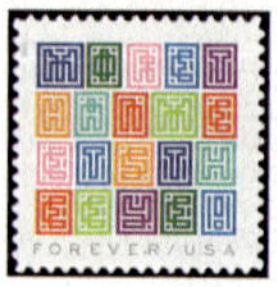
"More Than Meets The Eye" — A4448

LITHOGRAPHED & TYPOGRAPHED

***Serpentine Die Cut 10½***

**2021, July 14**

**Self-Adhesive**

| | | | | | |
|---|---|---|---|---|---|
| **5614** | A4448 | (55c) | multicolored | 1.40 | .25 |
| *a.* | | | Imperforate | 1.50 | — |

**WESTERN WEAR**

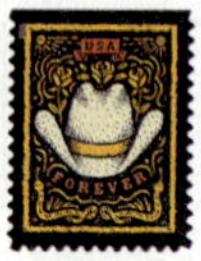
Cowboy Hat, Snakes and Roses A4449

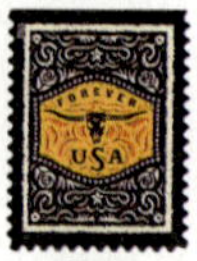
Belt Buckle, Roses, Stars and Spurs A4450

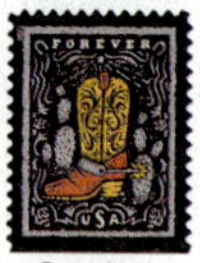
Cowboy Boot With Spur, Roses, Cacti and Star A4451

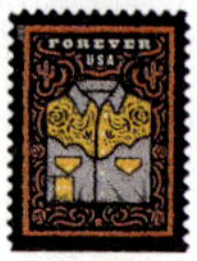
Western Shirt, Roses, Cacti and Star A4452

LITHOGRAPHED

***Serpentine Die Cut 10¾ on 2 or 3 Sides***

**2021, July 23**

**Booklet Stamps**

**Self-Adhesive**

| | | | | | |
|---|---|---|---|---|---|
| **5615** | A4449 | (55c) | multicolored | 1.40 | .30 |
| **5616** | A4450 | (55c) | multicolored | 1.40 | .30 |
| **5617** | A4451 | (55c) | multicolored | 1.40 | .30 |
| **5618** | A4452 | (55c) | multicolored | 1.40 | .30 |
| *a.* | | | Block of 4, #5615-5618 | 5.40 | |
| *b.* | | | Booklet pane of 20, 5 each #5615-5618 | 28.00 | |
| | | | *Nos. 5615-5618 (4)* | 5.60 | 1.20 |

No. 5618b is a double-sided booklet pane with 12 stamps on one side (3 each Nos. 5615-5618), and eight stamps (2 each Nos. 5615-5618) plus label (booklet cover) on the other side.

**LITERARY ARTS**

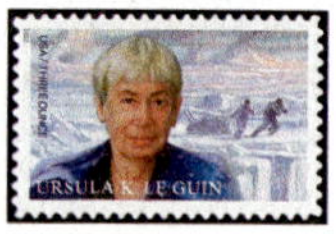
Ursula K. Le Guin (1929-2018), Science Fiction Novelist — A4453

LITHOGRAPHED

***Serpentine Die Cut 10¾***

**2021, July 27**

**Self-Adhesive**

| | | | | | |
|---|---|---|---|---|---|
| **5619** | A4453 | (95c) | multicolored | 2.40 | .30 |

**RAVEN STORY**

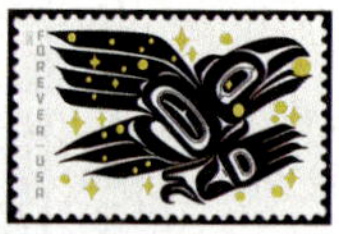
Mythological Raven from Stories of Indigenous People of the Northern Northwest Coast — A4454

TYPOGRAPHED WITH FOIL APPLICATION

***Serpentine Die Cut 10¾***

**2021, July 30**

**Self-Adhesive**

| | | | | | |
|---|---|---|---|---|---|
| **5620** | A4454 | (55c) | multicolored | 1.40 | .25 |
| *a.* | | | Imperforate | *20.00* | — |

**MID-ATLANTIC LIGHTHOUSES**

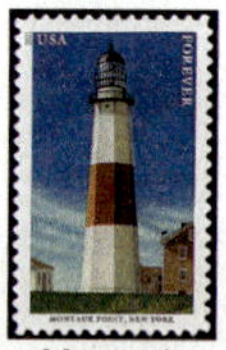
Montauk Point Lighthouse, New York A4455

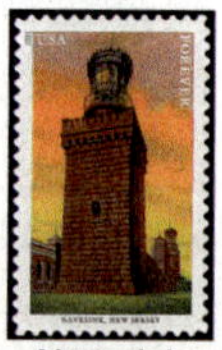
Navesink Twin Lighthouses, New Jersey A4456

UNITED STATES 153

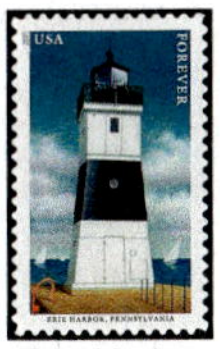
Erie Harbor Lighthouse, Pennsylvania A4457

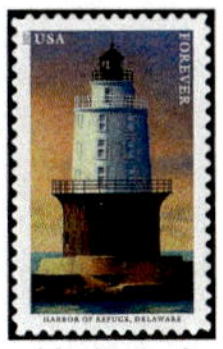
Harbor of Refuge Lighthouse, Delaware A4458

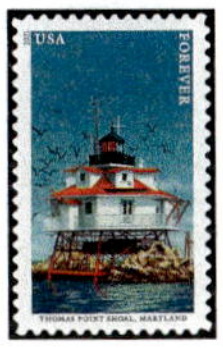
Thomas Point Shoal Lighthouse, Maryland — A4459

LITHOGRAPHED

***Serpentine Die Cut 10¾***

**2021, Aug. 6**

**Self-Adhesive**

| | | | |
|---|---|---|---|
| **5621** A4455 (55c) multicolored | 1.40 | .40 |
| *a.* Imperforate | 1.50 | — |
| **5622** A4456 (55c) multicolored | 1.40 | .40 |
| *a.* Imperforate | 1.50 | — |
| **5623** A4457 (55c) multicolored | 1.40 | .40 |
| *a.* Imperforate | 1.50 | — |
| **5624** A4458 (55c) multicolored | 1.40 | .40 |
| *a.* Imperforate | 1.50 | — |
| **5625** A4459 (55c) multicolored | 1.40 | .40 |
| *a.* Imperforate | 1.50 | — |
| *b.* Horiz. strip of 5, #5621-5625 | 7.00 | |
| *c.* Imperforate strip of 5, #5621a-5625a | 7.50 | |
| *Nos. 5621-5625 (5)* | 7.00 | 2.00 |

**MISSOURI STATEHOOD BICENTENARY**

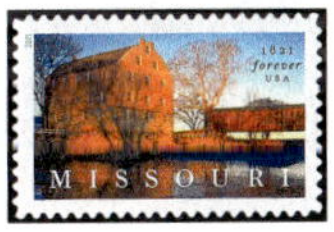
Bollinger Mill and Burfordville Covered Bridge — A4460

LITHOGRAPHED

***Serpentine Die Cut 10¾***

**2021, Aug. 10**

**Self-Adhesive**

| | | |
|---|---|---|
| **5626** A4460 (55c) multicolored | 1.40 | .25 |
| *a.* Imperforate | 1.50 | — |

**BACKYARD GAMES**

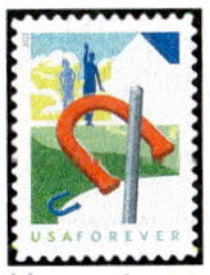
Horseshoes A4461

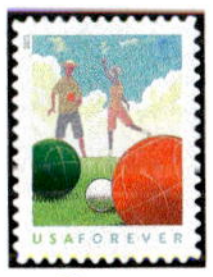
Bocce A4462

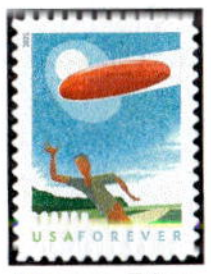
Flying Disc A4463

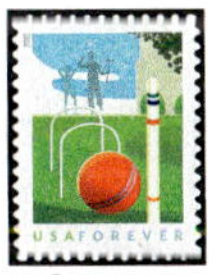
Croquet A4464

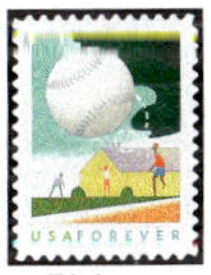
Pick-up Baseball Variation A4465

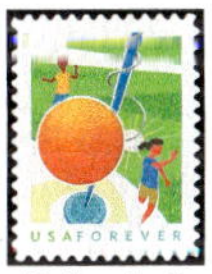
Tetherball A4466

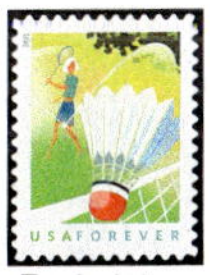
Badminton A4467

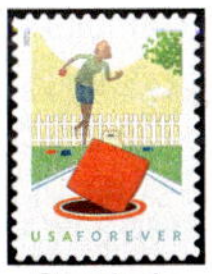
Cornhole A4468

LITHOGRAPHED

***Serpentine Die Cut 10¾***

**2021, Aug. 12**

**Self-Adhesive**

| | | |
|---|---|---|
| **5627** A4461 (55c) multicolored | 1.40 | .40 |
| *a.* Imperforate | 2.00 | — |
| **5628** A4462 (55c) multicolored | 1.40 | .40 |
| *a.* Imperforate | 2.00 | — |
| **5629** A4463 (55c) multicolored | 1.40 | .40 |
| *a.* Imperforate | 2.00 | — |
| **5630** A4464 (55c) multicolored | 1.40 | .40 |
| *a.* Imperforate | 2.00 | — |
| **5631** A4465 (55c) multicolored | 1.40 | .40 |
| *a.* Imperforate | 2.00 | — |
| **5632** A4466 (55c) multicolored | 1.40 | .40 |
| *a.* Imperforate | 2.00 | — |
| **5633** A4467 (55c) multicolored | 1.40 | .40 |
| *a.* Imperforate | 2.00 | — |
| **5634** A4468 (55c) multicolored | 1.40 | .40 |
| *a.* Imperforate | 2.00 | — |
| *b.* Block of 8, #5627-5634 | 11.20 | |
| *c.* Imperforate block of 8, #5627a-5634a | 16.00 | |
| *Nos. 5627-5634 (8)* | 11.20 | 3.20 |

**HAPPY BIRTHDAY**

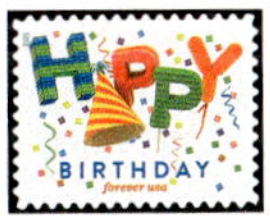
Birthday Hat, Confetti and Streamers — A4469

LITHOGRAPHED

**2021, Sept. 9** ***Serpentine Die Cut 11***

**Self-Adhesive**

| | | |
|---|---|---|
| **5635** A4469 (58c) multicolored | 1.40 | .25 |

**MESSAGE MONSTERS**

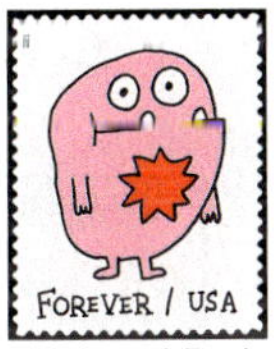
Pink and Red Monster A4470

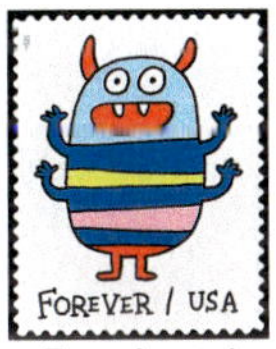
Four-Armed Monster A4471

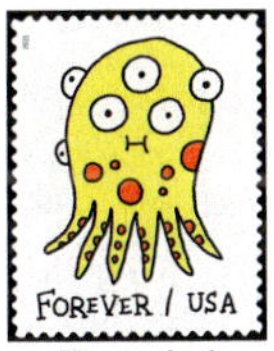
Tentacled Monster A4472

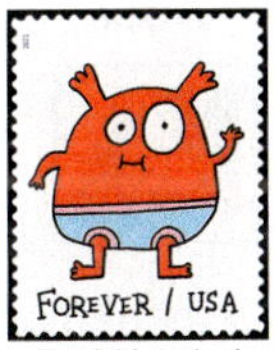
Red-Headed Monster A4473

LITHOGRAPHED

***Serpentine Die Cut 10½x10¾***

**2021, Sept. 24**

**Self-Adhesive**

| | | |
|---|---|---|
| **5636** A4470 (58c) multicolored | 1.40 | .30 |
| *a.* Imperforate | 2.00 | — |
| **5637** A4471 (58c) multicolored | 1.40 | .30 |
| *a.* Imperforate | 2.00 | — |
| **5638** A4472 (58c) multicolored | 1.40 | .30 |
| *a.* Imperforate | 2.00 | — |
| **5639** A4473 (58c) multicolored | 1.40 | .30 |
| *a.* Imperforate | 2.00 | — |
| *b.* Horiz. or vert. strip of 4, #5636-5639 | 5.60 | |
| *c.* Imperforate strip of 4 #5636a-5639a | 8.00 | |
| *Nos. 5636-5639 (4)* | 5.60 | 1.20 |

**DAY OF THE DEAD**

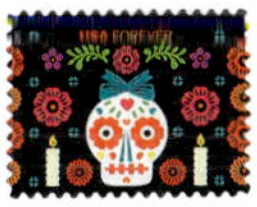
Girl's Skull With Bow — A4474

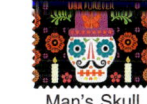

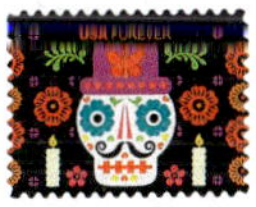
Man's Skull With Hat — A4475

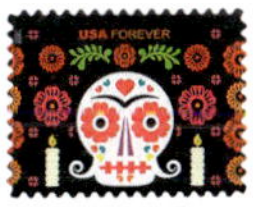
Woman's Skull With Curled Hair — A4476

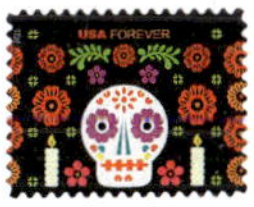
Boy's Skull — A4477

LITHOGRAPHED

***Serpentine Die Cut 11***

**2021, Sept. 30**

**Self-Adhesive**

| | | |
|---|---|---|
| **5640** A4474 (58c) multicolored | 1.40 | .30 |
| *a.* Imperforate | 1.75 | — |
| **5641** A4475 (58c) multicolored | 1.40 | .30 |
| *a.* Imperforate | 1.75 | — |
| **5642** A4476 (58c) multicolored | 1.40 | .30 |
| *a.* Imperforate | 1.75 | — |
| **5643** A4477 (58c) multicolored | 1.40 | .30 |
| *a.* Imperforate | 1.75 | — |
| *b.* Horiz. strip of 4, #5640-5643 | 5.60 | |
| *c.* Imperforate strip of 4, #5640a-5643a | 7.00 | |
| *Nos. 5640-5643 (4)* | 5.60 | 1.20 |

**CHRISTMAS**

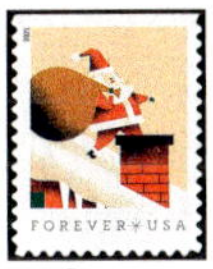
Santa Claus on Roof A4478

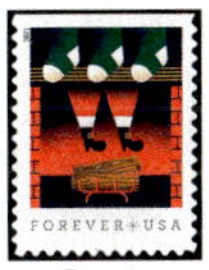
Santa Claus in Fireplace A4479

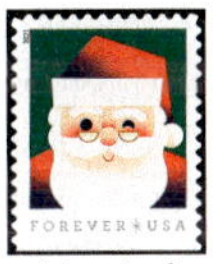
Head of Santa Claus A4480

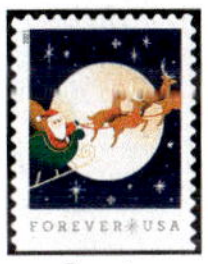
Santa Claus, Sleigh and Reindeer in Flight A4481

LITHOGRAPHED

***Serpentine Die Cut 10¾x11 on 2 or 3 Sides***

**2021, Oct. 7**

**Booklet Stamps**

**Self-Adhesive**

| | | |
|---|---|---|
| **5644** A4478 (58c) multicolored | 1.40 | .30 |
| **5645** A4479 (58c) multicolored | 1.40 | .30 |
| **5646** A4480 (58c) multicolored | 1.40 | .30 |
| **5647** A4481 (58c) multicolored | 1.40 | .30 |
| *a.* Block of 4, #5644-5647 | 5.60 | |
| *b.* Booklet pane of 20, 5 each #5644-5647 | 28.00 | |
| *Nos. 5644-5647 (4)* | 5.60 | 1.20 |

No. 5618b is a double-sided booklet pane with 12 stamps on one side (3 each Nos. 5615-5618), and eight stamps (2 each Nos. 5615-5618) plus label (booklet cover) on the other side.

**OTTERS IN SNOW**

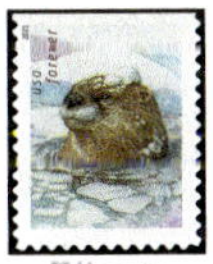
Otter in Water A4482

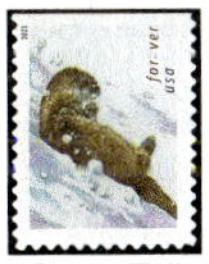
Otter, Tail at Right A4483

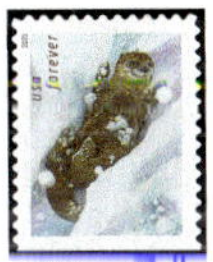
Otter, Tail at Left A4484

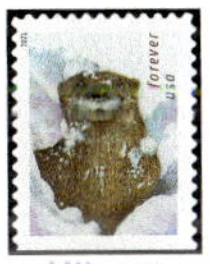
Otter in Snow A4485

LITHOGRAPHED

***Serpentine Die Cut 10¾x11 on 2 or 3 Sides***

**2021, Oct. 12**

**Booklet Stamps**

**Self-Adhesive**

| | | |
|---|---|---|
| **5648** A4482 (58c) multicolored | 1.40 | .30 |
| **5649** A4483 (58c) multicolored | 1.40 | .30 |
| **5650** A4484 (58c) multicolored | 1.40 | .30 |
| **5651** A4485 (58c) multicolored | 1.40 | .30 |
| *a.* Block of 4, #5648-5651 | 5.40 | |
| *b.* Booklet pane of 20, 5 each #5648-5651 | 28.00 | |
| *Nos. 5648-5651 (4)* | 5.60 | 1.20 |

No. 5618b is a double-sided booklet pane with 12 stamps on one side (3 each Nos. 5615-5618), and eight stamps (2 each Nos. 5615-5618) plus label (booklet cover) on the other side.

**FRUIT**

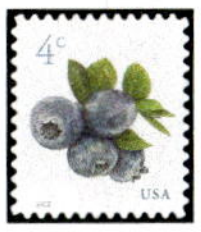
Blueberries — A4486

LITHOGRAPHED

***Serpentine Die Cut 11¼x11***

**2022, Jan. 9**

**Self-Adhesive**

| | | |
|---|---|---|
| **5652** A4486 4c multicolored | .30 | .25 |

**Coil Stamp**

***Serpentine Die Cut 10¾ Vert.***

| | | |
|---|---|---|
| **5653** A4486 4c multicolored | .30 | .25 |

See note after No. 1549.

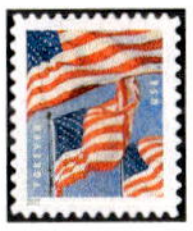
Flags — A4487

LITHOGRAPHED

***Serpentine Die Cut 11¼x11***

**2022, Jan. 9**

**Self-Adhesive**

**Microprinted "USPS" Above Lower Connector on Flagpole at Left**

| | | |
|---|---|---|
| **5654** A4487 (58c) multicolored | 1.40 | .25 |

**Coil Stamps**

**Stamps Not Adjacent on Coil Roll Backing Paper Taller Than Stamp**

***Serpentine Die Cut 10¾ Vert.***

| | | |
|---|---|---|
| **5655** A4487 (58c) multicolored | 1.40 | .25 |

***Serpentine Die Cut 11 Vert.***

**Stamps Adjacent on Coil Roll Backing Paper Same Height as Stamp**

| | | |
|---|---|---|
| **5656** A4487 (58c) multicolored | 1.40 | .25 |

**Microprinted "USPS" Above Lowest Blue Flag Field**

***Serpentine Die Cut 9½ Vert.***

| | | |
|---|---|---|
| **5657** A4487 (58c) multicolored | 1.40 | .25 |
| *Nos. 5655-5657 (3)* | 4.20 | .75 |

**Booklet Stamps**

**Microprinted "USPS" Above Lower Connector on Flagpole at Left**

***Serpentine Die Cut 11¼x10¾ on 2 or 3 Sides***

| | | |
|---|---|---|
| **5658** A4487 (58c) multicolored | 1.40 | .25 |
| *a.* Booklet pane of 20 | 28.00 | |

**Microprinted "USPS" Above Lowest Blue Flag Field**

| | | |
|---|---|---|
| **5659** A4487 (58c) multicolored | 1.40 | .25 |
| *a.* Booklet pane of 20 | 28.00 | |

Nos. 5262a and 5263a are double-sided booklets with 12 stamps on one side and eight stamps plus a label that serves as the booklet cover on the other side.

**LOVE**

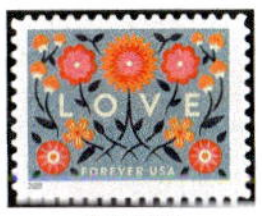
A4488

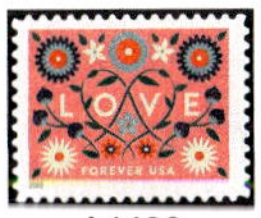
A4489

LITHOGRAPHED

***Serpentine Die Cut 11***

**2022, Jan. 14**

**Self-Adhesive**

**Background Color**

| | | |
|---|---|---|
| **5660** A4488 (58c) blue gray | 1.40 | .25 |
| *a.* Imperforate | 1.50 | — |
| **5661** A4489 (58c) pink | 1.40 | .25 |
| *a.* Imperforate | 1.50 | — |
| *b.* Horiz. or vert. pair, #5660-5661 | 2.80 | |
| *c.* Imperforate horiz. or vert. pair, #5660a-5661a | 3.00 | |

**CHINESE NEW YEAR**

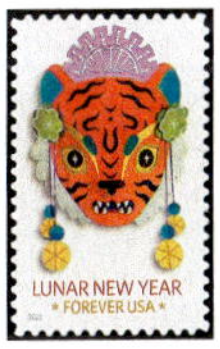
Year of the Tiger — A4490

## 154 UNITED STATES

**LITHOGRAPHED & TYPOGRAPHED WITH FOIL APPLICATION**
*Serpentine Die Cut 11*
2022, Jan. 20
Self-Adhesive
5662 A4490 (58c) multi 1.40 .25
  a. Imperforate 1.50 —

### BLACK HERITAGE

Edmonia Lewis (c. 1844-1907), Sculptor — A4491

**LITHOGRAPHED**
*Serpentine Die Cut 10¾*
2022, Jan. 26
Self-Adhesive
5663 A4491 (58c) multicolored 1.40 .25
  a. Imperforate 1.50 —

### BUTTERFLY GARDEN FLOWERS

 Cosmos A4492
 Scabiosas A4493

**LITHOGRAPHED**
*Serpentine Die Cut 10¾ Vert.*
2022, Feb. 1
Coil Stamps
Self-Adhesive
5664 A4492 (5c) multicolored .30 .25
5665 A4493 (5c) multicolored .30 .25
  a. Pair, #5664-5665 .30

### AMERICAN LANDMARKS ISSUE

 Monument Valley, Utah — A4494

 Palace of Fine Arts, San Francisco, California A4495

**LITHOGRAPHED**
*Serpentine Die Cut 10¾x10½*
2022, Feb. 14
Self-Adhesive
5666 A4494 $8.95 multi 18.00 8.00
5667 A4495 $26.95 multi 55.00 27.50

### TITLE IX CIVIL RIGHTS LAW, 50TH ANNIV.

 Runner A4496
 Swimmer A4497
 Gymnast A4498
 Soccer Player A4499

**LITHOGRAPHED**
*Serpentine Die Cut 10¾*
2022, Mar. 3
Self-Adhesive
5668 A4496 (58c) multicolored 1.40 .30
  a. Imperforate 1.50
5669 A4497 (58c) multicolored 1.40 .30
  a. Imperforate 1.50
5670 A4498 (58c) multicolored 1.40 .30
  a. Imperforate 1.50
5671 A4499 (58c) multicolored 1.40 .30
  a. Imperforate 1.50
  b. Block or vert. strip of 4, #5668-5671 5.60
  c. Imperforate block or vert. strip of 4 #5668a-5671a 6.00
Nos. 5668-5671 (4) 5.60 1.20

### MOUNTAIN FLORA

 Wood Lily A4500
 Alpine Buttercup A4501
 Woods' Rose A4502
 Pasqueflower A4503
 Pasqueflower A4504
 Wood Lily A4505
 Alpine Buttercup A4506
 Woods' Rose A4507

**LITHOGRAPHED**
*Serpentine Die Cut 10 Vert.*
2022, Mar. 14
Coil Stamps
Self-Adhesive
5672 A4500 (58c) multicolored 1.40 .30
5673 A4501 (58c) multicolored 1.40 .30
5674 A4502 (58c) multicolored 1.40 .30
5675 A4503 (58c) multicolored 1.40 .30
  a. Horiz. strip of 4, #5672-5675 5.60
Nos. 5672-5675 (4) 5.60 1.20

**Booklet Stamps**
*Serpentine Die Cut 10¾x11 on 2 or 3 Sides*
5676 A4504 (58c) multicolored 1.40 .30
5677 A4505 (58c) multicolored 1.40 .30
5678 A4506 (58c) multicolored 1.40 .30
5679 A4507 (58c) multicolored 1.40 .30
  a. Block of 4, #5676-5679 5.60
  b. Booklet pane of 20, 5 each #5676-5679 28.00
Nos. 5676-5679 (4) 5.60 1.20

Nos. 5679b is a double-sided booklet with 12 stamps on one side (3 each Nos 5676-5679), and eight stamps (2 each Nos. 5676-5679) plus a label that serves as the booklet cover on the other side.

 African Daisy — A4508

**LITHOGRAPHED**
2022, Mar. 14 *Serpentine Die Cut*
Self-Adhesive
5680 A4508 ($1.30) multicolored 3.25 .60
Unused values are for stamps with surrounding selvage. Adjacent stamps are separated by rouletting.

 Tulips A4509
 Sunflower Bouquet A4510

**LITHOGRAPHED**
*Serpentine Die Cut 11x10¾*
2022, Mar. 24
Self-Adhesive
5681 A4509 (58c) multicolored 1.40 .25
  a. Die cutting omitted, pair
*Serpentine Die Cut 10¾x11*
5682 A4510 (78c) multicolored 1.90 .25

### SHEL SILVERSTEIN (1930-99), CHILDREN'S BOOK WRITER

Boy Catching Apple, Illustration From *The Giving Tree*, by Silverstein — A4511

**LITHOGRAPHED**
2022, Apr. 8 *Serpentine Die Cut 11*
Self-Adhesive
5683 A4511 (58c) multicolored 1.40 .25
  a. Imperforate 1.40

### FLAGS ON BARNS

 Flag on Red Barn Near Well A4512
 Flag on White Barn in Winter A4513
 Flag on White Barn With Gambrel Roof A4514
Flag on Barn Near Windmill A4515

**LITHOGRAPHED**
*Serpentine Die Cut 10½ Vert.*
2022, Apr. 14
Coil Stamps
Self-Adhesive
5684 A4512 (10c) multicolored .30 .25
5685 A4513 (10c) multicolored .30 .25
5686 A4514 (10c) multicolored .30 .25
5687 A4515 (10c) multicolored .30 .25
  a. Strip of 4, #5684-5687 1.20
Nos. 5684-5687 (4) 1.20 1.00

### PAINTINGS BY GEORGE MORRISON (1919-2000)

 Sun and River, 1949 — A4516
 Phenomena Against the Crimson: Lake Superior Landscape, 1985 — A4517

 Lake Superior Landscape, 1981 — A4518
 Spirit Path, New Day, Red Rock Variation: Lake Superior Landscape, 1990 — A4519

 Untitled, 1995 — A4520

**LITHOGRAPHED**
*Serpentine Die Cut 10¾*
2022, Apr. 22
Self-Adhesive
5688 A4516 (58c) multicolored 1.40 .40
  a. Imperforate 1.50
5689 A4517 (58c) multicolored 1.40 .40
  a. Imperforate 1.50
5690 A4518 (58c) multicolored 1.40 .40
  a. Imperforate 1.50
5691 A4519 (58c) multicolored 1.40 .40
  a. Imperforate 1.50
5692 A4520 (58c) multicolored 1.40 .40
  a. Imperforate 1.50
  b. Vert. strip of 5, #5688-5692 7.00
  c. Imperforate strip of 5, #5688a-5692a 7.50
Nos. 5688-5692 (5) 7.00 2.00

### EUGENIE CLARK (1922-2015), ICHTHYOLOGIST

 Clark and Lemon Shark — A4521

**LITHOGRAPHED**
*Serpentine Die Cut 10¾*
2022, May 4
Self-Adhesive
5693 A4521 (58c) multicolored 1.40 .25
  a. Imperforate 1.50

### WOMEN'S ROWING

 Women Wearing Red Shirts, No Oar Splash — A4522

 Women Wearing Red Shirts, Oar Splash at Lower Left — A4523

 Women Wearing Blue Shirts, Oar Splash at Center — A4524

 Women Wearing Blue Shirts, No Oar Splash — A4525

**LITHOGRAPHED**
*Serpentine Die Cut 10¾*
2022, May 13
Self-Adhesive
5694 A4522 (58c) multicolored 1.40 .30
  a. Imperforate 1.50
5695 A4523 (58c) multicolored 1.40 .30
  a. Imperforate 1.50
  b. Horiz. pair, #5694-5695 2.80
  c. Imperforate horiz. pair, #5694a-5695a 3.00
5696 A4524 (58c) multicolored 1.40 .30
  a. Imperforate 1.50
5697 A4525 (58c) multicolored 1.40 .30
  a. Imperforate 1.50
  b. Horiz. pair, #5696-5697 2.80
  c. Imperforate horiz. pair, #5696a-5697a 3.00
Nos. 5694-5697 (4) 5.60 1.20

UNITED STATES 155

## MIGHTY MISSISSIPPI

Views of the Mississippi River from States Along its Route — A4526

No. 5698 — Photographs of: a, Headwaters of the Mississippi River, Lake Itasca, Minnesota. b, Great River Road, Wisconsin. c, Steamboat *American Queen*, Iowa. d, Sailboat and limestone cliff, Illinois. e, Gateway Arch and St. Louis skyline, Missouri. f, Mississippi River from Fort Jefferson Hill Park, Wickliffe, Kentucky. g, Curved levee and farmland, Arkansas. h, Towboat pushing barges near Memphis, Tennessee. i, Crescent City Connection Bridges, New Orleans, Louisiana. j, Cypress trees in bayou, Mississippi.

**LITHOGRAPHED**
*Serpentine Die Cut 10¾*
2022, May 23
**Self-Adhesive**

| 5698 | A4526 | Pane of 10 | 14.00 | |
|------|-------|------------|-------|-----|
| a.-j. | | (58c) Any single | 1.40 | .50 |
| k. | | As #5698, imperforate | 1.50 | — |
| l. | | As #5698a, imperforate | 1.50 | — |
| m. | | As #5698b, imperforate | 1.50 | — |
| n. | | As #5698c, imperforate | 1.50 | — |
| o. | | As #5698d, imperforate | 1.50 | — |
| p. | | As #5698e, imperforate | 1.50 | — |
| q. | | As #5698f, imperforate | 1.50 | — |
| r. | | As #5698g, imperforate | 1.50 | — |
| s. | | As #5698h, imperforate | 1.50 | — |
| t. | | As #5698i, imperforate | 1.50 | — |
| u. | | As #5698j, imperforate | 1.50 | — |

## DISTINGUISHED AMERICANS

Katherine Graham (1917-2001), Publisher of the *Washington Post* — A4527

**LITHOGRAPHED**
*Serpentine Die Cut 10¾*
2022, June 14
**Self-Adhesive**

| 5699 | A4527 | (78c) multicolored | 1.90 | .25 |

Adjacent horizontal or vertical stamps have selvage between the stamps.

## FLORAL GEOMETRY

A4528

A4529

**LITHOGRAPHED WITH FOIL APPLICATION**
*Serpentine Die Cut 10¾*
2022, June 20
**Self-Adhesive**

| 5700 | A4528 | $2 multicolored | 4.00 | 1.00 |
| 5701 | A4529 | $5 multicolored | 10.00 | 2.50 |

Adjacent horizontal or vertical stamps have selvage between the stamps.

## NANCY REAGAN (1921-2016), ACTRESS AND FIRST LADY

A4530

**LITHOGRAPHED**
2022, July 6   *Serpentine Die Cut 11*
**Self-Adhesive**

| 5702 | A4530 | (58c) multicolored | 1.40 | .25 |
| a. | | Imperforate | 1.50 | — |

## MARIACHI

Guitarist and Moon A4531

Violinist and Sun A4533

Guitarist and Sun A4532

Bass Guitarist and Sun A4534

Trumpet Player and Sun — A4535

**LITHOGRAPHED**
*Serpentine Die Cut 10¾*
2022, July 15

| 5703 | A4531 | (60c) multicolored | 1.40 | .40 |
| a. | | Imperforate | 1.50 | — |
| 5704 | A4532 | (60c) multicolored | 1.40 | .40 |
| a. | | Imperforate | 1.50 | — |
| 5705 | A4533 | (60c) multicolored | 1.40 | .40 |
| a. | | Imperforate | 1.50 | — |
| 5706 | A4534 | (60c) multicolored | 1.40 | .40 |
| a. | | Imperforate | 1.50 | — |
| 5707 | A4535 | (60c) multicolored | 1.40 | .40 |
| a. | | Imperforate | 1.50 | — |
| b. | | Horiz. strip of 5, #5703-5707 | 7.00 | |
| c. | | Imperforate strip of 5, #5703a-5707a | 7.50 | |

Nos. 5703-5707 (5)   7.00  2.00

## MUSIC ICONS

Pete Seeger (1919-2014), Folk Singer — A4536

**LITHOGRAPHED**
*Serpentine Die Cut 10½*
2022, July 21
**Self-Adhesive**

| 5708 | A4536 | (60c) multicolored | 1.40 | .25 |
| a. | | Imperforate | 1.50 | — |

## BUZZ LIGHTYEAR

Head in Profile A4537

Running A4539

Standing With Legs Visible A4538

Standing, Feet Not Visible A4540

**LITHOGRAPHED**
2022, Aug. 3   *Serpentine Die Cut 11*

| 5709 | A4537 | (60c) multicolored | 1.40 | .30 |
| a. | | Imperforate | 1.50 | — |
| 5710 | A4538 | (60c) multicolored | 1.40 | .30 |
| a. | | Imperforate | 1.50 | — |
| 5711 | A4539 | (60c) multicolored | 1.40 | .30 |
| a. | | Imperforate | 1.50 | — |
| 5712 | A4540 | (60c) multicolored | 1.40 | .30 |
| a. | | Imperforate | 1.50 | — |
| b. | | Vert. or horiz. strip of 4, #5709-5712 | 5.60 | |
| c. | | Imperforate vert. or horiz. strip of 4, #5709a-5712a | 6.00 | |

Nos. 5709-5712 (4)   5.60  1.20

## NATIONAL MARINE SANCTUARIES

A4541

No. 5713: a, Balloon fish, Florida Keys National Marine Sanctuary (26x26mm). b, Red-footed boobies, Papahanaumokuakea Marine National Monument (20x41mm). c, Humpback whale, Stellwagen Bank National Marine Sanctuary (41x26mm). d, Sea stacks, Olympic Coast National Marine Sanctuary (41x41mm). e, Mallows Bay-Potomac River Marine Sanctuary at sunset (26x41mm). f, Farallon Islands, Greater Farallones National Marine Sanctuary (41x26mm). g, Elkhorn coral, Florida Keys National Marine Sanctuary (26x41mm). h, Hawaiian monk seal, Hawaiian Islands Humpback Whale National Marine Sanctuary (41x26mm). i, Queen angelfish, Flower Garden Banks National Marine Sanctuary (41x26mm). j, Sea otter, Monterey Bay National Marine Sanctuary (26x41mm). k, Young rockfish exploring reef, Cordell Bank National Marine Sanctuary (41x26mm). l, Atlantic sea nettle, Gray's Reef National Marine Sanctuary (26x41mm). m, Sea lions, Channel Islands National Marine Sanctuary (41x41mm). n, Sand tiger shark, Monitor National Marine Sanctuary (41x26mm). o, Corals and fish, Rose Atoll, National Marine Sanctuary of American Samoa (26x41mm). p, Ice on shoreline, Thunder Bay National Marine Sanctuary (26x26mm).

**LITHOGRAPHED**
2022, Aug. 5   *Serpentine Die Cut 11*
**Self-Adhesive**

| 5713 | A4541 | Pane of 16 + 2 labels | 22.40 | |
| a.-p. | | (60c) Any single | 1.40 | .50 |
| q. | | As #5713, imperforate | 24.00 | — |
| r. | | As #5713a, imperforate | 1.50 | — |
| s. | | As #5713b, imperforate | 1.50 | — |
| t. | | As #5713c, imperforate | 1.50 | — |
| u. | | As #5713d, imperforate | 1.50 | — |
| v. | | As #5713e, imperforate | 1.50 | — |
| w. | | As #5713f, imperforate | 1.50 | — |
| x. | | As #5713g, imperforate | 1.50 | — |
| y. | | As #5713h, imperforate | 1.50 | — |
| z. | | As #5713i, imperforate | 1.50 | — |
| aa. | | As #5713j, imperforate | 1.50 | — |
| ab. | | As #5713k, imperforate | 1.50 | — |
| ac. | | As #5713l, imperforate | 1.50 | — |
| ad. | | As #5713m, imperforate | 1.50 | — |
| ae. | | As #5713n, imperforate | 1.50 | — |
| af. | | As #5713o, imperforate | 1.50 | — |
| ag. | | As #5713p, imperforate | 1.50 | — |

## ELEPHANTS

Adult Elephant and Calf — A4542

**LITHOGRAPHED**
*Serpentine Die Cut 11 on 2 or 3 Sides*
2022, Aug. 12
**Booklet Stamp**
**Self-Adhesive**

| 5714 | A4542 | (60c) multicolored | 1.40 | .25 |
| a. | | Booklet pane of 20 | 28.00 | |

No. 5459a is a double-sided booklet with 12 stamps on one side and eight stamps plus a label that serves as the booklet cover on the other side.

## PONY CARS

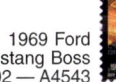

1969 Ford Mustang Boss 302 — A4543

1970 Dodge Challenger R/T — A4544

1969 Chevrolet Camaro Z/28 — A4545

1967 Mercury Cougar XR-7 GT — A4546

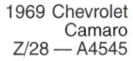

1969 AMC Javelin SST — A4547

**LITHOGRAPHED**
*Serpentine Die Cut 10¾*
2022, Aug. 25
**Self-Adhesive**

| 5715 | A4543 | (60c) multicolored | 1.40 | .40 |
| a. | | Imperforate | 1.50 | — |
| 5716 | A4544 | (60c) multicolored | 1.40 | .40 |
| a. | | Imperforate | 1.50 | — |
| 5717 | A4545 | (60c) multicolored | 1.40 | .40 |
| a. | | Imperforate | 1.50 | — |
| 5718 | A4546 | (60c) multicolored | 1.40 | .40 |
| a. | | Imperforate | 1.50 | — |
| 5719 | A4547 | (60c) multicolored | 1.40 | .40 |
| a. | | Imperforate | 1.50 | — |
| b. | | Vert. strip of 5, #5715-5719 | 7.00 | |
| c. | | Imperforate strip of 5, #5715a-5719a | 7.50 | |

Nos. 5715-5719 (5)   7.00  2.00

## JAMES WEBB SPACE TELESCOPE

James Webb Space Telescope A4548

**LITHOGRAPHED**
2022, Sept. 8   *Serpentine Die Cut 11*
**Self-Adhesive**

| 5720 | A4548 | (60c) multicolored | 1.40 | .25 |
| a. | | Imperforate | 1.50 | .25 |

Adjacent horizontal or vertical stamps have selvage between the stamps.

## CHRISTMAS

Virgin and Child, by the Master of the Scandicci Lamentation A4549

Elf and Teddy Bear A4550

Elf Tying Ribbon A4551

Elf With Toy Car A4552

Elf With Rocket — A4553

**LITHOGRAPHED**
*Serpentine Die Cut 11 on 2 or 3 Sides*
**2022**
**Booklet Stamps**
**Self-Adhesive**

| | | | | |
|---|---|---|---|---|
| 5721 | A4549 | (60c) multicolored | 1.40 | .25 |
| a. | Booklet pane of 20 | | 28.00 | |
| 5722 | A4550 | (60c) multicolored | 1.40 | .30 |
| 5723 | A4551 | (60c) multicolored | 1.40 | .30 |
| 5724 | A4552 | (60c) multicolored | 1.40 | .30 |
| 5725 | A4553 | (60c) multicolored | 1.40 | .30 |
| a. | Block of 4, #5722-5725 | | 5.60 | |
| b. | Booklet pane of 20, 5 each #5722-5725 | | 28.00 | |
| c. | As, "a," horiz. imperforate-between (PS) | | — | |
| d. | As, "b," horiz. imperforate-between on 12-stamp side | | — | |
| | Nos. 5721-5725 (5) | | 7.00 | 1.45 |

Issued: No. 5721, 9/22; Nos. 5722-5725, 9/15.

No. 5721a is a double-sided booklet pane with 12 stamps on one side, and eight stamps plus label (booklet cover) on the other side.

No. 5725b is a double-sided booklet pane with 12 stamps on one side (3 each Nos. 5722-5725), and eight stamps (2 each Nos. 5722-5725) plus label (booklet cover) on the other side.

### CHARACTERS FROM PEANUTS COMIC STRIP, BY CHARLES M. SCHULZ (1922-2000)

Charlie Brown A4554

Lucy A4555

Franklin A4556

Sally A4557

Pigpen A4558

Linus A4559

Snoopy and Woodstock A4560

Schroeder A4561

Peppermint Patty A4562

Marcie A4563

**LITHOGRAPHED**
*Serpentine Die Cut 11*
**2022, Sept. 30**
**Self-Adhesive**

| | | | | |
|---|---|---|---|---|
| 5726 | | Pane of 20, 2 each #5726a-5726j, + central label | 28.00 | |
| a. | A4554 | (60c) multicolored | 1.40 | .40 |
| b. | A4555 | (60c) multicolored | 1.40 | .40 |
| c. | A4556 | (60c) multicolored | 1.40 | .40 |
| d. | A4557 | (60c) multicolored | 1.40 | .40 |
| e. | A4558 | (60c) multicolored | 1.40 | .40 |
| f. | A4559 | (60c) multicolored | 1.40 | .40 |
| g. | A4560 | (60c) multicolored | 1.40 | .40 |
| h. | A4561 | (60c) multicolored | 1.40 | .40 |
| i. | A4562 | (60c) multicolored | 1.40 | .40 |
| j. | A4563 | (60c) multicolored | 1.40 | .40 |
| k. | | Imperforate sheet of 20, 2 each #5726l-5726u, + central label | 30.00 | — |
| l. | A4554 | (60c) Imperforate | 1.50 | — |
| m. | A4555 | (60c) Imperforate | 1.50 | — |
| n. | A4556 | (60c) Imperforate | 1.50 | — |
| o. | A4557 | (60c) Imperforate | 1.50 | — |
| p. | A4558 | (60c) Imperforate | 1.50 | — |
| q. | A4559 | (60c) Imperforate | 1.50 | — |
| r. | A4560 | (60c) Imperforate | 1.50 | — |
| s. | A4561 | (60c) Imperforate | 1.50 | — |
| t. | A4562 | (60c) Imperforate | 1.50 | — |
| u. | A4563 | (60c) Imperforate | 1.50 | — |

### SNOWY BEAUTY

Camellia A4564

Winter Aconite A4565

Crocuses A4566

Hellebore A4567

Winterberry A4568

Pansies A4569

Plum Blossoms A4570

Grape Hyacinths A4571

Daffodils A4572

Ranunculus A4573

**LITHOGRAPHED**
*Serpentine Die Cut 11 on 2 or 3 Sides*
**2022, Oct. 11**
**Booklet Stamps**
**Self-Adhesive**

| | | | | |
|---|---|---|---|---|
| 5727 | A4564 | (60c) multicolored | 1.40 | .40 |
| 5728 | A4565 | (60c) multicolored | 1.40 | .40 |
| 5729 | A4566 | (60c) multicolored | 1.40 | .40 |
| 5730 | A4567 | (60c) multicolored | 1.40 | .40 |
| 5731 | A4568 | (60c) multicolored | 1.40 | .40 |
| 5732 | A4569 | (60c) multicolored | 1.40 | .40 |
| 5733 | A4570 | (60c) multicolored | 1.40 | .40 |
| 5734 | A4571 | (60c) multicolored | 1.40 | .40 |
| 5735 | A4572 | (60c) multicolored | 1.40 | .40 |
| 5736 | A4573 | (60c) multicolored | 1.40 | .40 |
| a. | Block of 10, #5727-5736 | | 14.00 | |
| b. | Booklet pane of 20, 2 each #5727-5736 | | 28.00 | |
| | Nos. 5727-5736 (10) | | 14.00 | 4.00 |

No. 5736b is a double-sided booklet pane with 12 stamps on one side (Nos. 5729-5736, 2 each Nos. 5727-5728), and eight stamps (Nos. 5729-5736) plus label (booklet cover) on the other side.

### KWANZAA

Girl, Boy and Kinara — A4574

**LITHOGRAPHED**
*Serpentine Die Cut 10¾x11*
**2022, Oct. 13**
**Self-Adhesive**

| | | | | |
|---|---|---|---|---|
| 5737 | A4574 | (60c) multicolored | 1.40 | .25 |

### WOMEN CRYPTOLOGISTS OF WORLD WAR II

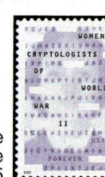
Woman and Japanese Purple Code Characters — A4575

**LITHOGRAPHED**
*Serpentine Die Cut 10¾*
**2022, Oct. 18**
**Self-Adhesive**

| | | | | |
|---|---|---|---|---|
| 5738 | A4575 | (60c) multicolored | 1.40 | .25 |
| a. | Imperforate | | 1.50 | — |

### HANUKKAH

Menorah — A4576

**LITHOGRAPHED**
**2022, Oct. 20** *Serpentine Die Cut 11*
**Self-Adhesive**

| | | | | |
|---|---|---|---|---|
| 5739 | A4576 | (60c) multicolored | 1.40 | .25 |

### SCHOOL BUS AND SCHOOL

A4577

A4578

**LITHOGRAPHED**
**2023, Jan. 5** *Serpentine Die Cut 11*
**Self-Adhesive**

| | | | | |
|---|---|---|---|---|
| 5740 | A4577 | (24c) multicolored | .50 | .25 |

**Coil Stamp**
*Serpentine Die Cut 11 Horiz.*

| | | | | |
|---|---|---|---|---|
| 5741 | A4578 | (24c) multicolored | .50 | .25 |

### RED FOX

A4579           A4579a

**LITHOGRAPHED**
*Serpentine Die Cut 11¼x11*
**2023, Jan. 5**
**Self-Adhesive**

| | | | | |
|---|---|---|---|---|
| 5742 | A4579 | 40c multicolored | .80 | .25 |

**Coil Stamp**
*Serpentine Die Cut 11 Vert.*

| | | | | |
|---|---|---|---|---|
| 5743 | A4579a | 40c multicolored | .80 | .25 |
| | Pair | | 1.60 | |
| | P# strip of 5, #B11111 | | 7.25 | |
| | P# single, #B11111 | | — | 2.00 |

See note after No. 1549.
Counterfeits exist of No. 5743. See the Postal Counterfeits section of this catalog.

### CHINESE NEW YEAR

Year of the Rabbit — A4580

**LITHOGRAPHED & TYPOGRAPHED WITH FOIL APPLICATION**
*Serpentine Die Cut 11*
**2023, Jan. 12**
**Self-Adhesive**

| | | | | |
|---|---|---|---|---|
| 5744 | A4580 | (60c) multi | 1.40 | .25 |
| a. | Imperforate | | 1.50 | |

### LOVE

Kitten and Heart A4581

Puppy and Heart A4582

**LITHOGRAPHED**
*Serpentine Die Cut 11*
**2023, Jan. 19**
**Self-Adhesive**

| | | | | |
|---|---|---|---|---|
| 5745 | A4581 | (60c) multicolored | 1.40 | .25 |
| a. | Imperforate | | 1.50 | — |
| 5746 | A4582 | (60c) multicolored | 1.40 | .25 |
| a. | Imperforate | | 1.50 | — |
| b. | Horiz. or vert. pair, #5745-5746 | | 2.80 | |
| c. | Imperforate horiz. or vert. pair, #5745a-5746a | | 3.00 | |

### SAILBOATS

Two Sailboats A4583

One Sailboat A4584

**LITHOGRAPHED**
*Serpentine Die Cut 11¼x11*
**2023, Jan. 22**
**Self-Adhesive**

| | | | | |
|---|---|---|---|---|
| 5747 | A4583 | (48c) multicolored | 1.10 | .25 |
| 5748 | A4584 | (48c) multicolored | 1.10 | .25 |
| a. | Horiz. or vert. pair, #5747-5748 | | 2.20 | |

**Coil Stamps**
*Serpentine Die Cut 9½ Vert.*

| | | | | |
|---|---|---|---|---|
| 5749 | A4584 | (48c) multicolored | 1.10 | .25 |
| 4550 | A4583 | (48c) multicolored | 1.10 | .25 |
| a. | Pair, #5749-5750 | | 2.20 | |

### AMERICAN LANDMARKS ISSUE

Florida Everglades A4585

Great Smoky Mountains, Tennessee and North Carolina — A4586

UNITED STATES 157

LITHOGRAPHED

***Serpentine Die Cut 11x10¾***

**2023, Jan. 22**

**Self-Adhesive**

| | | | | | |
|---|---|---|---|---|---|
| **5751** | A4585 | $9.65 | multi | 19.50 | 9.75 |
| **5752** | A4586 | $28.75 | multi | 57.50 | 29.00 |

**BLACK HERITAGE**

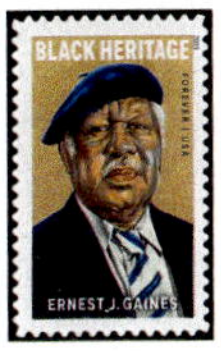


Ernest J. Gaines (1933-2019), Writer — A4587

LITHOGRAPHED

***Serpentine Die Cut 11***

**2023, Jan. 23**

**Self-Adhesive**

| | | | | | |
|---|---|---|---|---|---|
| **5753** | A4587 | (63c) | multicolored | 1.40 | .25 |
| *a.* | | | Imperforate | 1.50 | — |

**WOMEN'S SOCCER**

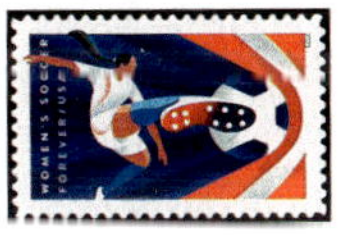

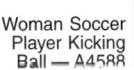

Woman Soccer Player Kicking Ball — A4588

LITHOGRAPHED

***Serpentine Die Cut 11***

**2023, Feb. 16**

**Self-Adhesive**

| | | | | | |
|---|---|---|---|---|---|
| **5754** | A4588 | (63c) | multicolored | 1.40 | .25 |
| *a.* | | | Imperforate | 1.50 | — |

**FLORAL GEOMETRY**

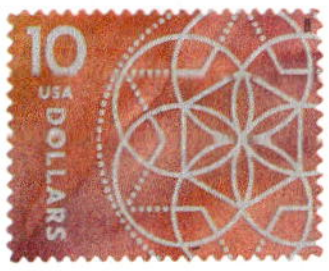


A4589

LITHOGRAPHED WITH FOIL APPLICATION

***Serpentine Die Cut 10¾***

**2023, Feb. 24**

**Self-Adhesive**

| | | | | | |
|---|---|---|---|---|---|
| **5755** | A4589 | $10 | multicolored | 20.00 | 5.00 |

Adjacent horizontal or vertical stamps have selvage between the stamps.

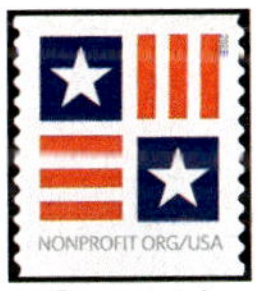


Stars and Bars — A4590

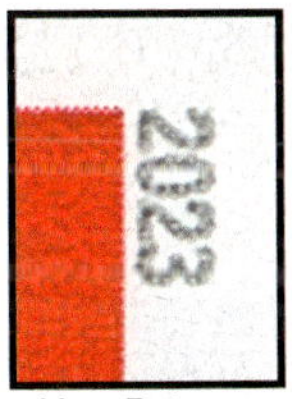


Year Date on No. 5756

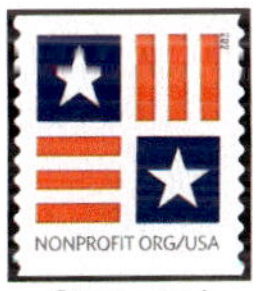


Stars and Bars —A4590a

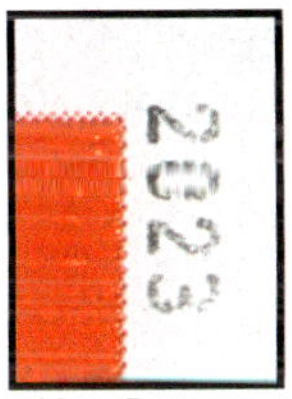


Year Date on No. 5756A

Height of "2023": Approximately 1¾mm, with numerals close together.

Size from left side of left blue square to right side of right blue square, from top of left blue square to bottom of right blue square, from left side of left red bars to right side of right red bars, and from top of right red bars to bottom of left red bars: approximately 17½mm.

PHOTOGRAVURE

**2023** ***Serpentine Die Cut 10¾ Vert.***

**COIL STAMP**

**Self-Adhesive**

| | | | | | |
|---|---|---|---|---|---|
| **5756** | A4590 | (5c) | multicolored | .30 | .25 |
| **5756A** | A4590a | (5c) | multicolored | .30 | .25 |

Height of "2023": Approximately 2¼mm with numerals farther apart than on No. 5756.

Size from left side of left blue square to right side of right blue square, from top of left blue square to bottom of right blue square, from left side of left red bars to right side of right red bars, and from top of right red bars to bottom of left red bars: approximately 18mm.

**TONI MORRISON**

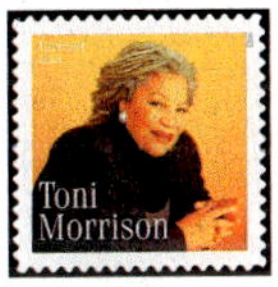


Toni Morrison (1931-2019), Writer — A4591

LITHOGRAPHED

***Serpentine Die Cut 10¾***

**2023, Mar. 7**

**Self-Adhesive**

| | | | | | |
|---|---|---|---|---|---|
| **5757** | A4591 | (63c) | multicolored | 1.40 | .25 |
| *a.* | | | Imperforate | 1.50 | — |

**HISTORIC RAILROAD STATIONS**

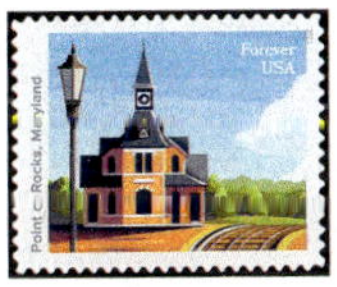


Point of Rocks Station, Maryland A4592

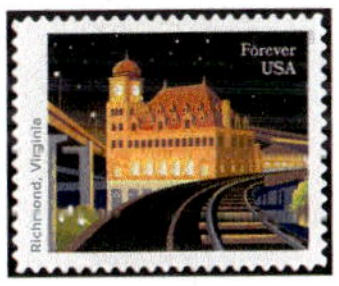


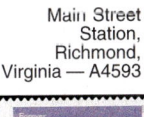

Main Street Station, Richmond, Virginia — A4593

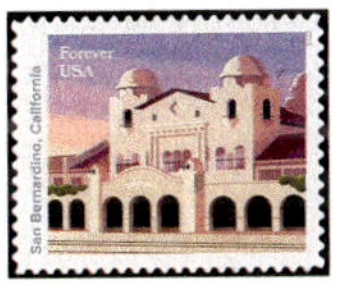


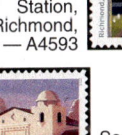

Santa Fe Station, San Bernardino, California A4594

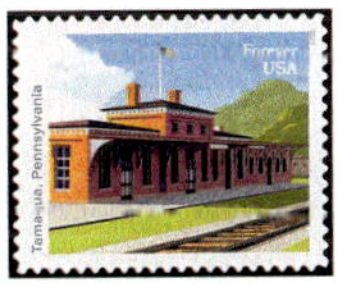


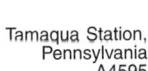

Tamaqua Station, Pennsylvania A4595

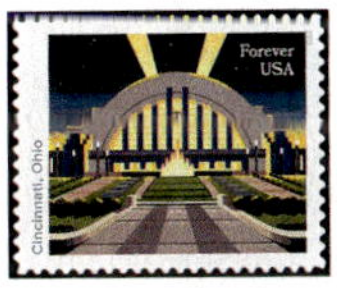


Union Terminal, Cincinnati, Ohio — A4596

LITHOGRAPHED & TYPOGRAPHED

***Serpentine Die Cut 10¾***

**2023, Mar. 9**

**Self-Adhesive**

| | | | | | |
|---|---|---|---|---|---|
| **5758** | A4592 | (63c) | multicolored | 1.40 | .40 |
| *a.* | | | Imperforate | 1.50 | — |
| **5759** | A4593 | (63c) | multicolored | 1.40 | .40 |
| *a.* | | | Imperforate | 1.50 | — |
| **5760** | A4594 | (63c) | multicolored | 1.40 | .40 |
| *a.* | | | Imperforate | 1.50 | — |
| **5761** | A4595 | (63c) | multicolored | 1.40 | .40 |
| *a.* | | | Imperforate | 1.50 | — |
| **5762** | A4596 | (63c) | multicolored | 1.40 | .40 |
| *a.* | | | Imperforate | 1.50 | — |
| *b.* | | | Vert. strip of 5, #5758-5762 | 7.00 | |
| *c.* | | | Imperforate vert. strip of 5, #5758a-5762a | 7.50 | |
| | | | *Nos. 5758-5762 (5)* | 7.00 | 2.00 |

**ART OF THE SKATEBOARD**

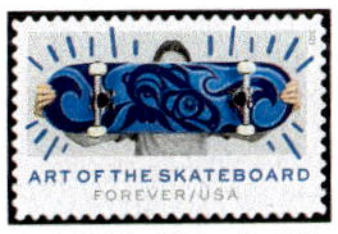


Skateboard With Tlingit Athabascan Salmon Design by Crystal Worl — A4597

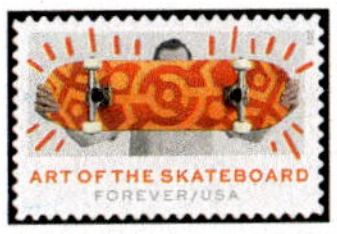


Skateboard With Abstract Design by William James Taylor — A4598

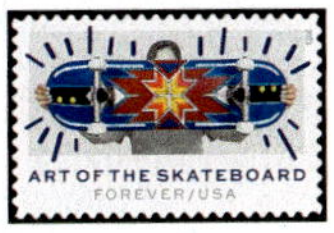


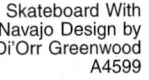

Skateboard With Navajo Design by Di'Orr Greenwood A4599

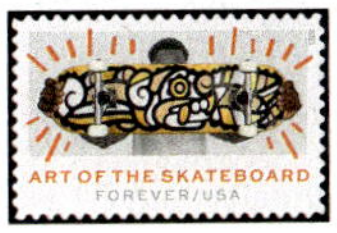


Skateboard With Jaguar Design by MasPaz (Frederico Frum) — A4600

LITHOGRAPHED

***Serpentine Die Cut 11***

**2023, Mar. 24**

**Self-Adhesive**

| | | | | | |
|---|---|---|---|---|---|
| **5763** | A4597 | (63c) | multicolored | 1.40 | .30 |
| *a.* | | | Imperforate | 1.50 | — |
| **5764** | A4598 | (63c) | multicolored | 1.40 | .30 |
| *a.* | | | Imperforate | 1.50 | — |
| **5765** | A4599 | (63c) | multicolored | 1.40 | .30 |
| *a.* | | | Imperforate | 1.50 | — |
| **5766** | A4600 | (63c) | multicolored | 1.40 | .30 |
| *a.* | | | Imperforate | 1.50 | — |
| *b.* | | | Horiz. or vert. strip of 4, #5763-5766 | 5.60 | |
| *c.* | | | Imperforate horiz. or vert. strip of 4, #5763a-5766a | 6.00 | |
| | | | *Nos. 5763-5766 (4)* | 5.60 | 1.20 |

**TULIP BLOSSOMS**

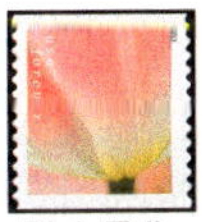

Pink Tulip with Yellowish Base A4601

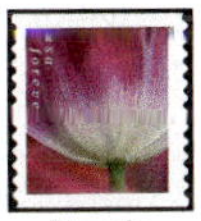

Purple Tulip with White Base A4602

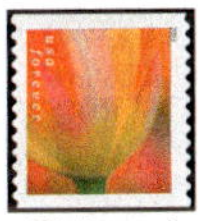

Pink and Orange Tulip A4603

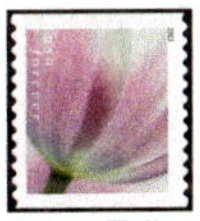

Lilac Tulip A4604

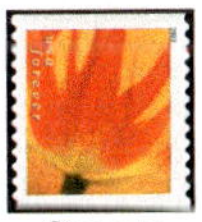

Orange and Red Tulip A4605

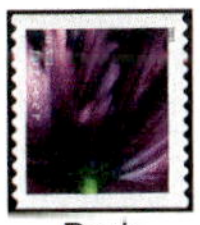

Dark Purple Tulip A4606

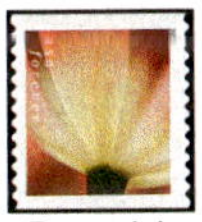

Brownish Tulip with White Base A4607

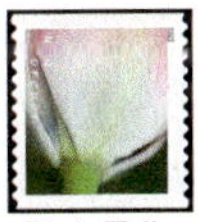

Pink Tulip with White Base A4608

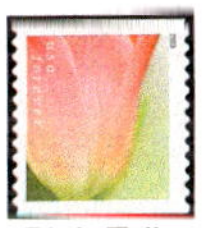

Pink Tulip and Yellowish Background A4609

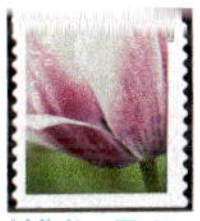

White Tulip with Purplish Base A4610

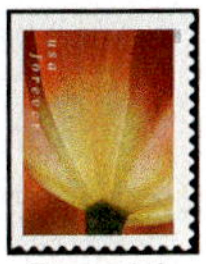

Brownish Tulip with White Base A4611

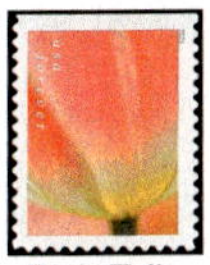

Pink Tulip with Yellowish Base A4612

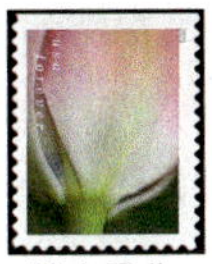

Pink Tulip with White Base A4613

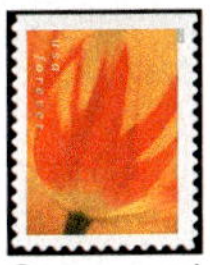

Orange and Red Tulip A4614

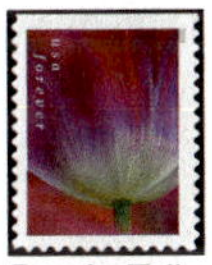

Purple Tulip with White Base A4615

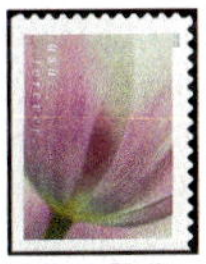

Lilac Tulip A4616

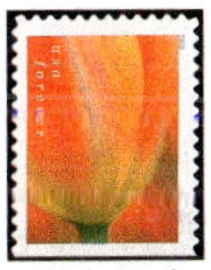

Pink and Orange Tulip A4617

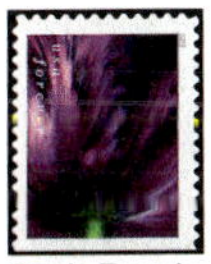

Dark Purple Tulip A4618

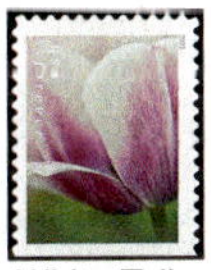

White Tulip with Purplish Base A4619

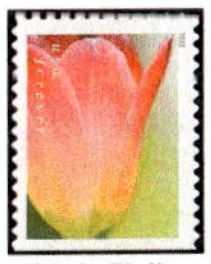

Pink Tulip and Yellowish Background A4620

LITHOGRAPHED

***Serpentine Die Cut 10¾ Vert.***

**2023, Apr. 5**

**Coil Stamps**

**Self-Adhesive**

| | | | | | |
|---|---|---|---|---|---|
| **5767** | A4601 | (63c) | multicolored | 1.40 | .40 |
| **5768** | A4602 | (63c) | multicolored | 1.40 | .40 |
| **5769** | A4603 | (63c) | multicolored | 1.40 | .40 |
| **5770** | A4604 | (63c) | multicolored | 1.40 | .40 |
| **5771** | A4605 | (63c) | multicolored | 1.40 | .40 |
| **5772** | A4606 | (63c) | multicolored | 1.40 | .40 |
| **5773** | A4607 | (63c) | multicolored | 1.40 | .40 |
| **5774** | A4608 | (63c) | multicolored | 1.40 | .40 |
| **5775** | A4609 | (63c) | multicolored | 1.40 | .40 |
| **5776** | A4610 | (63c) | multicolored | 1.40 | .40 |
| *a.* | | | Horiz. strip of 10, #5767-5776 | 14.00 | |
| | | | *Nos. 5767-5776 (10)* | 14.00 | 4.00 |

**Booklet Stamps**

***Serpentine Die Cut 10¾x11 on 2 or 3 Sides***

| | | | | | |
|---|---|---|---|---|---|
| **5777** | A4611 | (63c) | multicolored | 1.40 | .40 |
| **5778** | A4612 | (63c) | multicolored | 1.40 | .40 |
| **5779** | A4613 | (63c) | multicolored | 1.40 | .40 |
| **5780** | A4614 | (63c) | multicolored | 1.40 | .40 |
| **5781** | A4615 | (63c) | multicolored | 1.40 | .40 |
| **5782** | A4616 | (63c) | multicolored | 1.40 | .40 |
| **5783** | A4617 | (63c) | multicolored | 1.40 | .40 |
| **5784** | A4618 | (63c) | multicolored | 1.40 | .40 |
| **5785** | A4619 | (63c) | multicolored | 1.40 | .40 |
| **5786** | A4620 | (63c) | multicolored | 1.40 | .40 |
| *a.* | | | Block of 10, #5777-5786 | 14.00 | |
| *b.* | | | Booklet pane of 20, 2 each #5777-5786 | 28.00 | |
| | | | *Nos. 5777-5786 (10)* | 14.00 | 4.00 |

Nos. 5786b is a double-sided booklet with 12 stamps on one side (Nos. 5778-5781, 5783-5786, 2 each Nos 5777, 5782), and eight stamps (Nos. 5778-5781, 5783-5786) plus a label that serves as the booklet cover on the other side.

158 UNITED STATES

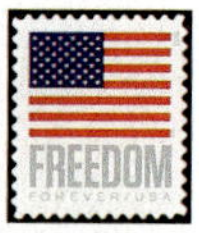


Flag and "Freedom" — A4621

LITHOGRAPHED

***Serpentine Die Cut 11¼x10¾***

**2023, Apr. 10**

**With Microprinted "USPS" At Right of Lowest Flag Stripe**
**Self-Adhesive**

5787 A4621 (63c) multicolored 1.40 .25

**COIL STAMPS**

***Serpentine Die Cut 9½ Vert.***

**With Microprinted "USPS" Below Lower Left Corner of Flag Field Stamps Adjacent on Coil Roll**

5788 A4621 (63c) multicolored 1.40 .25
*a.* Die cutting omitted, pair —

***Serpentine Die Cut 10¾ Vert.***

**With Microprinted "USPS" At Right of Lowest Flag Stripe Stamps on Roll Not Adjacent On Backing Paper Larger Than the Stamp**

5789 A4621 (63c) multicolored 1.40 .25
5789A A4621 (63c) multicolored 1.40 .25
*b.* Die cutting omitted, pair 10.00
*Nos. 5788-5789A (3)* 4.20 .75

**BOOKLET STAMPS**

***Serpentine Die Cut 11¼x10¾ on 2 or 3 Sides***

**With Microprinted "USPS" Below Lower Left Corner of Flag Field**

5790 A4621 (63c) multicolored 1.40 .25
*a.* Booklet pane of 20 28.00

**With Microprinted "USPS" At Right of Lowest Flag Stripe**

5791 A4621 (63c) multicolored 1.40 .25
*a.* Booklet pane of 20 28.00

Nos. 5790a and 5791a are double-sided booklets with 12 stamps on one side and eight stamps plus a label that serves as the booklet cover on the other side.

## PAINTINGS BY ROY LICHTENSTEIN (1923-97)

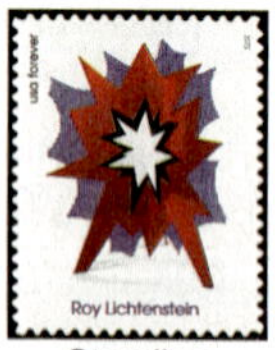


Standing Explosion (Red), 1965 — A4622

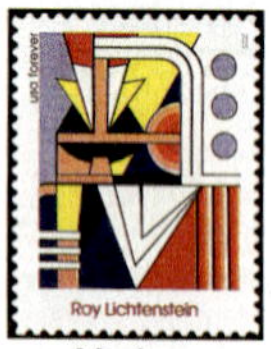


Modern Painting I, 1966 — A4623

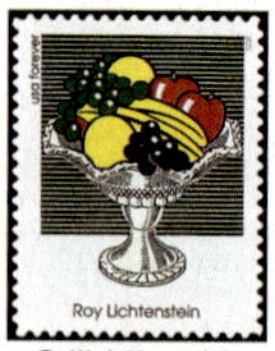


Still Life with Crystal Bowl, 1972 — A4624

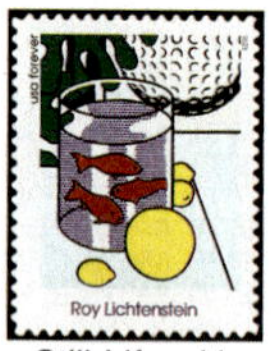


Still Life with Goldfish, 1972 — A4625

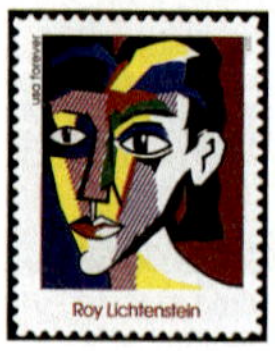


Portrait of a Woman, 1979 — A4626

LITHOGRAPHED & TYPOGRAPHED

***Serpentine Die Cut 10½x10¾***

**2023, Apr. 24**

**Self-Adhesive**

5792 A4622 (63c) multicolored 1.40 .40
*a.* Imperforate 1.50 —
5793 A4623 (63c) multicolored 1.40 .40
*a.* Imperforate 1.50 —
5794 A4624 (63c) multicolored 1.40 .40
*a.* Imperforate 1.50 —
5795 A4625 (63c) multicolored 1.40 .40
*a.* Imperforate 1.50 —
5796 A4626 (63c) multicolored 1.40 .40
*a.* Imperforate 1.50 —
*b.* Horiz. strip of 5, #5792-5796 7.00
*c.* Imperforate horiz. strip of 5, #5792a-5796a 7.50
*Nos. 5792-5796 (5)* 7.00 2.00

## TOMIE DEPAOLA (1934-2020), AUTHOR OF CHILDREN'S BOOKS

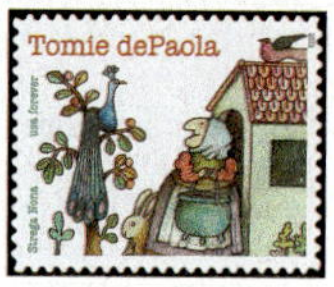


Cover Illustration of *Strega Nona* — A4627

LITHOGRAPHED

***Serpentine Die Cut 10¾x10½***

**2023, May 5**

**Self-Adhesive**

5797 A4627 (63c) multicolored 1.40 .25
*a.* Imperforate 1.50 —

## CHIEF STANDING BEAR

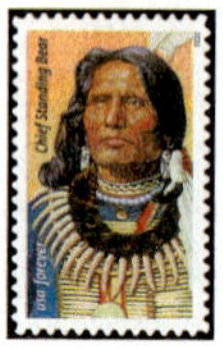

Standing Bear (c. 1829-1908), Ponca Chief — A4628

LITHOGRAPHED

**2023, May 12 *Serpentine Die Cut 11***

**Self-Adhesive**

5798 A4628 (63c) multicolored 1.40 .25
*a.* Imperforate 1.50 —

## ENDANGERED SPECIES

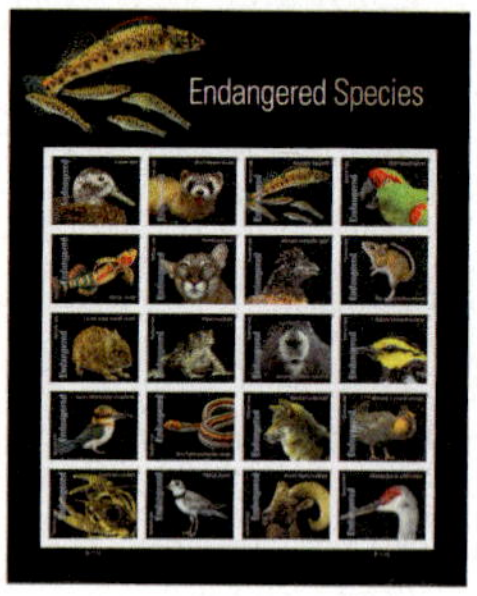


A4629

No. 5799: a, Laysan teal. b, Black-footed ferret. c, Roanoake logperch. d, Thick-billed parrot. e, Candy darter. f, Florida panther. g, Masked bobwhite quail. h, Key Largo cotton mouse. i, Lower Keys marsh rabbit. j, Wyoming toad. k, Vancouver Island marmot. l, Golden-cheeked warbler. m, Guam Micronesian kingfisher. n, San Francisco garter snake. o, Mexican gray wolf. p, Attwater's prairie chicken. q, Nashville crayfish. r, Piping plover. s, Desert bighorn sheep. t, Mississippi sandhill crane.

LITHOGRAPHED & TYPOGRAPHED

***Serpentine Die Cut 10¾***

**2023, May 19**

**Self-Adhesive**

5799 A4629 Pane of 20 28.00
*a.-t.* (63c) Any single 1.40 .50
*u.* As #5799, imperforate 28.00 —
*v.* As #5799a, imperforate 1.50 —
*w.* As #5799b, imperforate 1.50 —
*x.* As #5799c, imperforate 1.50 —
*y.* As #5799d, imperforate 1.50 —
*z.* As #5799e, imperforate 1.50 —
*aa.* As #5799f, imperforate 1.50 —
*ab.* As #5799g, imperforate 1.50 —
*ac.* As #5799h, imperforate 1.50 —
*ad.* As #5799i, imperforate 1.50 —
*ae.* As #5799j, imperforate 1.50 —
*af.* As #5799k, imperforate 1.50 —
*ag.* As #5799l, imperforate 1.50 —
*ah.* As #5799m, imperforate 1.50 —
*ai.* As #5799n, imperforate 1.50 —
*aj.* As #5799o, imperforate 1.50 —
*ak.* As #5799p, imperforate 1.50 —
*al.* As #5799q, imperforate 1.50 —
*am.* As #5799r, imperforate 1.50 —
*an.* As #5799s, imperforate 1.50 —
*ao.* As #5799t, imperforate 1.50 —

A pane of No. 5799, an imperforate pane without tagging and the back printing, an imperforate pane without the special coating over the animals, an imperforate pane without the shiny coating over the "Endangered" inscription, an imperforate pane with black and white inks, imperforate panes of single-color progressive proofs in cyan, magenta, yellow, and black, glassine interleaving, a commemorative book, and a numbered certificate were produced in a quantity of 4,000 and sold as a unit for $59.95.

## WATERFALLS

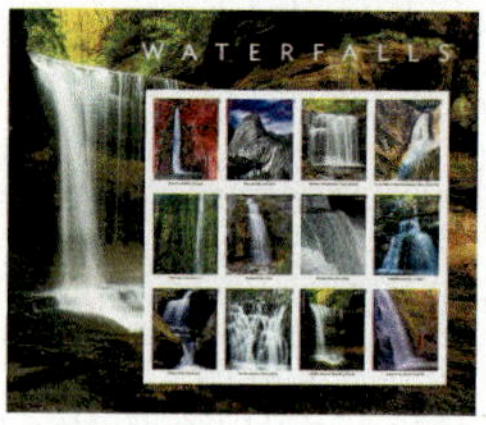


A4630

No. 5800: a, Deer Creek Falls, Arizona. b, Nevada Fall, California. c, Harrison Wright Falls, Pennsylvania. d, Lower Falls of the Yellowstone River, Wyoming. e, Waimoku Falls, Hawaii. f, Stewart Falls, Utah. g, Niagara Falls, New York. h, Dark Hollow Falls, Virginia. i, Grotto Falls, Tennessee. j, Sunbeam Falls, Washington. k, LaSalle Canyon Waterfall, Illinois. l, Upper Falls, North Carolina.

LITHOGRAPHED

***Serpentine Die Cut 10½x10¾***

**2023, June 13**

**Self-Adhesive**

5800 A4630 Pane of 12 16.80
*a.-l.* (63c) Any single 1.40 .50
*m.* As #5800, imperforate 18.00 —
*n.* As #5800a, imperforate 1.50 —
*o.* As #5800b, imperforate 1.50 —
*p.* As #5800c, imperforate 1.50 —
*q.* As #5800d, imperforate 1.50 —
*r.* As #5800e, imperforate 1.50 —
*s.* As #5800f, imperforate 1.50 —
*t.* As #5800g, imperforate 1.50 —
*u.* As #5800h, imperforate 1.50 —
*v.* As #5800i, imperforate 1.50 —
*w.* As #5800j, imperforate 1.50 —
*x.* As #5800k, imperforate 1.50 —
*y.* As #5800l, imperforate 1.50 —

## JOHN LEWIS

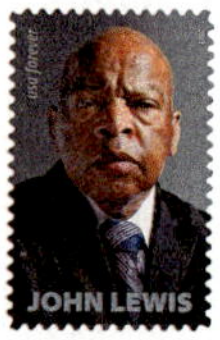


John Lewis (1940-2020), Civil Rights Leader and Congressman — A4631

LITHOGRAPHED

***Serpentine Die Cut 11***

**2023, July 21**

**Self-Adhesive**

5801 A4631 (66c) multicolored 1.40 .25
*a.* Imperforate 1.50 —

Adjacent horizontal or vertical stamps have selvage between the stamps.

## LIFE MAGNIFIED

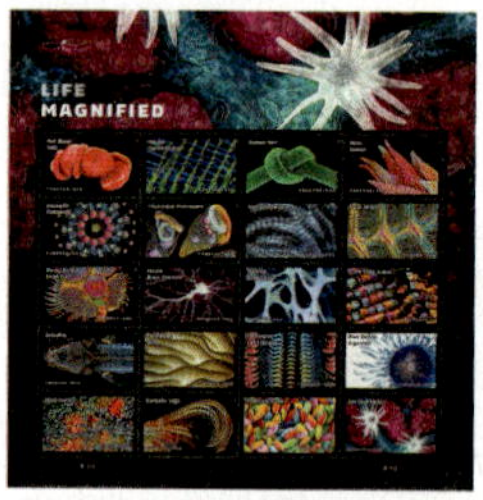


A4632

No. 5802 — Magnified images of: a, Red blood cells. b, Macaw parrot feather. c, Human hair. d, Moss leaves. e, Arranged diatoms. f, Freshwater protozoans. g, Acorn barnacle. h, Moth antenna. i, Diving beetle front foot. j, Mouse brain neurons. k, Starling bone tissue. l, Moth wing scales. m, Zebrafish. n, Mushroom gills. o, Freshwater snail tongue. p, Blue button organism. q, Mold spores. r, Barnacle legs. s, Flame lily pollen. t, Oak leaf surface.

LITHOGRAPHED & TYPOGRAPHED

***Serpentine Die Cut 10¾***

**2023, Aug. 10**

**Self-Adhesive**

5802 A4632 Pane of 20 28.00
*a.-t.* (66c) Any single 1.40 .50
*u.* As #5802, imperforate 30.00 —
*v.* As #5802a, imperforate 1.50 —
*w.* As #5802b, imperforate 1.50 —
*x.* As #5802c, imperforate 1.50 —
*y.* As #5802d, imperforate 1.50 —
*z.* As #5802e, imperforate 1.50 —
*aa.* As #5802f, imperforate 1.50 —
*ab.* As #5802g, imperforate 1.50 —
*ac.* As #5802h, imperforate 1.50 —
*ad.* As #5802i, imperforate 1.50 —
*ae.* As #5802j, imperforate 1.50 —
*af.* As #5802k, imperforate 1.50 —
*ag.* As #5802l, imperforate 1.50 —
*ah.* As #5802m, imperforate 1.50 —
*ai.* As #5802n, imperforate 1.50 —
*aj.* As #5802o, imperforate 1.50 —
*ak.* As #5802p, imperforate 1.50 —
*al.* As #5802q, imperforate 1.50 —
*am.* As #5802r, imperforate 1.50 —
*an.* As #5802s, imperforate 1.50 —
*ao.* As #5802t, imperforate 1.50 —

Die cut and imperforate uncut press sheets of No. 5802 were made available for sale. Values: panes with gutters between, $60.

See note after No. 4693. See note after No. 1549.

## THINKING OF YOU

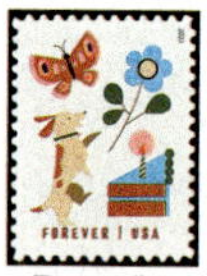

Butterfly, Flower, Dog, Slice of Birthday Cake A4633

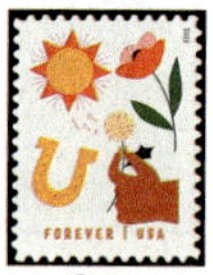

Sun, Flower, Horseshoe, Hand Holding Dandelion A4634

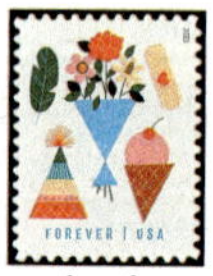

Leaf, Flower Bouquet, Bandage, Birthday Party Hat, Ice Cream Cone A4635

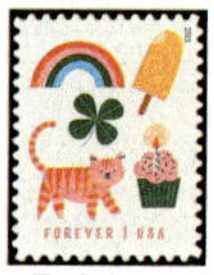

Rainbow, Ice Cream Bar, Four-leaf Clover, Cat, Cupcake and Candle A4636

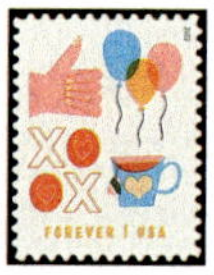

Hand with Raised Thumb, Party Balloons, "XOOX," Cup of Tea — A4637

LITHOGRAPHED & TYPOGRAPHED

***Serpentine Die Cut 10¾***

**2023, Aug. 11**

**Self-Adhesive**

5803 A4633 (66c) multicolored 1.40 .40
*a.* Imperforate 1.50 —
5804 A4634 (66c) multicolored 1.40 .40
*a.* Imperforate 1.50 —
5805 A4635 (66c) multicolored 1.40 .40
*a.* Imperforate 1.50 —
5806 A4636 (66c) multicolored 1.40 .40
*a.* Imperforate 1.50 —
5807 A4637 (66c) multicolored 1.40 .40
*a.* Imperforate 1.50 —
*b.* Horiz. strip of 5, #5803-5807 7.00
*c.* Imperforate horiz. strip of 5, #5803a-5807a 7.50
*Nos. 5803-5807 (5)* 7.00 2.00

## BRIDGES

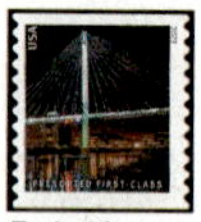

Bob Kerrey Pedestrian Bridge, Omaha, Nebraska to Council Bluffs, Iowa A4638

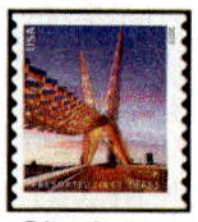

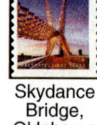

Skydance Bridge, Oklahoma City, Oklahoma A4639

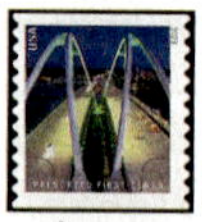

Iowa-Illinois Memorial Bridge, Bettendorf, Iowa to Moline, Illinois A4640

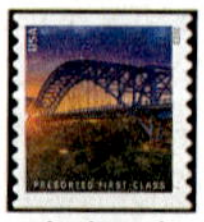

Arrigoni Bridge, Middletown, Connecticut to Portland, Connecticut A4641

# UNITED STATES

Designed by Ethel Kessler. Printed by Ashton-Potter (USA) Ltd.

**LITHOGRAPHED**
*Serpentine Die Cut 10 Vert.*
2023, Aug. 24                      Tagged
**Coil Stamps**
**Self-Adhesive**

| 5808 | A4638 | (25c) multicolored | .50 | .30 |
|---|---|---|---|---|
| 5809 | A4639 | (25c) multicolored | .50 | .30 |
| 5810 | A4640 | (25c) multicolored | .50 | .30 |
| 5811 | A4641 | (25c) multicolored | .50 | .30 |
| a. | | Horiz. strip of 7, #5808, 2 each #5809-5811, #P1111 | 2.00 | |
| | | P# strip of 9, 2 each #5808-5810, 3 #5811, #P1111 | 4.75 | |
| | | P# single (#5811), #P1111 | 5.50 | 2.50 |
| Nos. 5808-5811 (4) | | | 2.00 | 1.20 |

See note after No. 1549.

## PIÑATAS

Donkey Piñata Facing Left A4642

Star Piñata With Purple Background A4643

Star Piñata With Green Background A4644

Donkey Piñata Facing Right A4645

**LITHOGRAPHED**
*Serpentine Die Cut 11 on 2 or 3 Sides*
2023, Sept. 8
**Booklet Stamps**
**Self-Adhesive**

| 5812 | A4642 | (66c) multicolored | 1.40 | .30 |
|---|---|---|---|---|
| 5813 | A4643 | (66c) multicolored | 1.40 | .30 |
| 5814 | A4644 | (66c) multicolored | 1.40 | .30 |
| 5815 | A4645 | (66c) multicolored | 1.40 | .30 |
| a. | | Block of 4, #5812-5815 | 5.60 | |
| b. | | Booklet pane of 20, 5 each #5812-5815 | 28.00 | |
| Nos. 5812-5815 (4) | | | 5.60 | 1.20 |

No. 5618b is a double-sided booklet pane with 12 stamps on one side (3 each Nos. 5615-5618), and eight stamps (2 each Nos. 5615-5618) plus label (booklet cover) on the other side.

## CHRISTMAS

Snowman in Snow Globe A4646

Santa Claus in Snow Globe A4647

Reindeer in Snow Globe A4648

Christmas Tree in Snow Globe A4649

**LITHOGRAPHED**
*Serpentine Die Cut 11 on 2 or 3 Sides*
2023, Sept. 19
**Booklet Stamps**
**Self-Adhesive**

| 5816 | A4646 | (66c) multicolored | 1.40 | .30 |
|---|---|---|---|---|
| 5817 | A4647 | (66c) multicolored | 1.40 | .30 |
| 5818 | A4648 | (66c) multicolored | 1.40 | .30 |
| 5819 | A4649 | (66c) multicolored | 1.40 | .30 |
| a. | | Block of 4, #5816-5819 | 5.60 | |
| b. | | Booklet pane of 20, 5 each #5816-5819 | 28.00 | |
| Nos. 5816-5819 (4) | | | 5.60 | 1.20 |

No. 5618b is a double-sided booklet pane with 12 stamps on one side (3 each Nos. 5615-5618), and eight stamps (2 each Nos. 5615-5618) plus label (booklet cover) on the other side.

## RETURN TO EARTH FROM ASTEROID BENNU OF OSIRIS-REx PROBE

OSIRIS-REx Capsule Returning to Earth — A4650

**LITHOGRAPHED**
*Serpentine Die Cut 11*
2023, Sept. 22
**Self-Adhesive**

| 5820 | A4650 | (66c) multicolored | 1.40 | .25 |
|---|---|---|---|---|
| a. | | Imperforate | 1.40 | |

## RUTH BADER GINSBURG

Ruth Bader Ginsburg (1933-2020), Supreme Court Associate Justice — A4651

**LITHOGRAPHED**
2023, Oct. 2    *Serpentine Die Cut 11*
**Self-Adhesive**

| 5821 | A4651 | (66c) multicolored | 1.40 | .25 |
|---|---|---|---|---|
| a. | | Imperforate | 1.40 | |

## WINTER WOODLAND ANIMALS

Deer A4652

Rabbit A4653

Owl A4654

Fox A4655

**LITHOGRAPHED**
*Serpentine Die Cut 11 on 2 or 3 Sides*
2023, Oct. 10
**Booklet Stamps**
**Self-Adhesive**

| 5822 | A4652 | (66c) multicolored | 1.40 | .30 |
|---|---|---|---|---|
| 5823 | A4653 | (66c) multicolored | 1.40 | .30 |
| 5824 | A4654 | (66c) multicolored | 1.40 | .30 |
| 5825 | A4655 | (66c) multicolored | 1.40 | .30 |
| a. | | Block of 4, #5822-5825 | 5.60 | |
| b. | | Booklet pane of 20, 5 each #5822-5825 | 28.00 | |
| Nos. 5822-5825 (4) | | | 5.60 | 1.20 |

No. 5825b is a double-sided booklet pane with 12 stamps on one side (3 each Nos. 5822-5825), and eight stamps (2 each Nos. 5822-5825) plus label (booklet cover) on the other side.

## LOVE

Bird Carrying Envelope — A4656

**LITHOGRAPHED**
*Serpentine Die Cut 10¾*
2024, Jan. 12
**Self-Adhesive**

| 5826 | A4656 | (66c) multicolored | 1.40 | .25 |
|---|---|---|---|---|
| a. | | Imperforate | 1.40 | |

## STELLAR FORMATIONS ISSUE

Pillars of Creation — A4657

Cosmic Cliffs — A4658

**LITHOGRAPHED**
*Serpentine Die Cut 10¾*
2024, Jan. 22
**Self-Adhesive**

| 5827 | A4657 | $9.85 multi | 20.00 | 10.00 |
|---|---|---|---|---|
| 5828 | A4658 | $30.45 multi | 60.00 | 30.00 |

## CHINESE NEW YEAR

Year of the Dragon — A4659

**LITHOGRAPHED & TYPOGRAPHED WITH FOIL APPLICATION**
*Serpentine Die Cut 11*
2024, Jan. 25
**Self-Adhesive**

| 5829 | A4659 | (68c) multi | 1.40 | .25 |
|---|---|---|---|---|
| a. | | Imperforate | 1.40 | |

## BLACK HERITAGE

Constance Baker Motley (1921-2005), Federal Judge and Politician — A4660

**LITHOGRAPHED**
*Serpentine Die Cut 11*
2024, Jan. 31
**Self-Adhesive**

| 5830 | A4660 | (68c) multicolored | 1.40 | .25 |
|---|---|---|---|---|
| a. | | Imperforate | 1.40 | |

**WALTER KASELL STAMPS**

Quality United States Stamps

Classics, U.S. Possessions & Plate Blocks

175 Richdale Ave., Cambridge, MA 02140 • (617) 694-9360
Email: wbkasell@yahoo.com

**SUBJECT INDEX OF REGULAR, COMMEMORATIVE & AIR POST ISSUES**


**A Charlie Brown Christmas ... 5021-5030**
A Streetcar Named Desire ... 3186n
Abbey, Edwin Austin ... 3502k
Abbott, Bud ... 2566
Abby Cadabby ... 5394h
Abstract Expressionists ... 4444
Acadia National Park ... 746, 762, 5080d, C138
Accounting, Certified Public ... 2361
Acheson, Dean ... 2755
Acoma Pot ... 1709, 3873g
Acorn Barnacle ... 5802g
Acuff, Roy ... 3812
Adams, Abigail ... 2146
Adams, Ansel ... 3649p
Adams, John ... 806, 841, 850, 2216b
Adams, John Q. ... 811, 846, 2216f
Addams, Jane ... 878
Admiralty Head Lighthouse, WA ... 2470
Adoption ... 3398
Adriatic, S.S. ... 117, 128
Advances in Aviation ... 3916-3925
Adventures of Huckleberry Finn ... 2787
African Daisy ... 5680
African Elephant Herd ... 1388
African Violet ... 2486
Agave ... 1943
Aging Together ... 2011
AIDS Awareness ... 2806
Ailey, Alvin ... 3841
Aircraft, Classic American ... 3142
Air Force Cross ... 5067
Air Force Medal of Honor ... 4988
Air Force One ... 4144
Air Force, U.S. ... C49, 3167
Air Mail, 50th Anniversary ... C74
Air Mail, 100th Anniversary ... 5281-5282
Air Service Emblem ... C5
Airborne Attack Units ... 2838d
Airlift $ ... 11341
Alabama Flag ... 1654, 4274
Alabama Statehood ... 1375, 5360
Alamo, The ... 1043
Alaska Flag ... 1681, 4275
Alaska Highway ... 2635
Alaska Purchase ... C70
Alaska Statehood ... 2066, 4374, C53
Alaska Territory ... 800
Alaska-Yukon Pacific Exposition ... 370, 371
Alaskan Brown Bear ... 2310
Alaskan Malamute ... 2100
Albania, Flag ... 918
Alcoholism ... 1927
Alcott, Louisa May ... 862
Aleutian Islands, Japanese Invasion of ... 2697e
Alexandria, Virginia ... C40
Alfred Hitchcock Presents ... 4414o
Alger, Horatio ... 2010
All in the Family ... 3189b
Allen, Richard ... 5056
Alley Oop ... 3000n
Alliance for Progress ... 1234
Allied Nations ... 907
Alligator ... 1428
Allosaurus ... 3136g
Aloha Shirts ... 4592-4601, 4682-4686
Alpha Airplane ... 3142e
Alphabet Cone ... 5165, 5167
Alpine Buttercup ... 5673, 5678
Alpine Skiing ... 3180
Alpine Tundra ... 4198
Alta California ... 1725
Altocumulus Castellanus ... 3878i
Altocumulus Lenticularis ... 3878j
Altocumulus Stratiformis ... 3878f
Altocumulus Undulatus ... 3878h
Altostratus Translucidus ... 3878g
Alyssum ... 4758
Alzheimer's Disease Awareness ... 4358, B6
Amateur Radio ... 1260
Amber Alert ... 4031
Ambulance ... 2128, 2231
AMC Javelin SST ... 5719
American Alligator ... 4033
American Arts ... 1484-1487, 1553-1555, 3236
American Automobile Association ... 1007
American Bald Eagle ... 1387, 2309
American Bankers Association ... 987
American Bar Association ... 1022
American Beaver ... 4064
American Bicentennial ... 1456-1459, 1476-1479, 1480-1483, 1543-1546, 1559-1568, 1629-1631, 1686-1694, 1704, 1716-1720, 1722, 1726, 1728, 1753, 1789, 1937-1938, 2052
American Buffalo ... 569, 700, 1392, 1883, 2320, 3467, 3468, 3475, 3484, 3484A, 4041
American Bullfrog ... 4055
American Chemical Society ... 1002, 1685
American Clock ... 3757, 3762, 3763
American Cream Draft Horse ... 5590
American Crocodile ... 3105d
American Design Issue ... 3612, 3749, 3749A, 3750-3756, 3756A, 3757-3758, 3758A. 3758B, 3759, 3761-3763
American Elk ... 2328
American Folklore ... 1317, 1330, 1357, 1370, 1470, 1548
American Foxhound ... 2101
American Gardens ... 5461-5470
American Goldfinch ... 4890
American Illustrators ... 3502
American Indian ... 565, 695, 1364
American Indian Dances ... 3072-3076
American Institute of Architects ... 1089
American Kestrel ... 2476-2477, 3031-3031A, 3044
American Legion ... 1369
American Lobster ... 2304
American Lotus ... 4046
American Mammoth Jackstock Donkey ... 5587
American Music ... 1252, 2721-2737, 2767-2778, 2849-2861, 2982-2992, 3096-3103, 3154-3165, 3212-3219, 3339-3350
American Philatelic Society ... 750
American Realism (art) ... 3184n
American Red Cross ... 1910
American Revolution Bicentennial. 1432
American Samoa ... 3389
American Samoa Flag ... 4276
American Shoals Lighthouse, FL ... 2473
American Treasures ... 3524-3527, 3650, 3804-3807, 3872, 3926-3929, 4089-4098, 4165, 4346, 4473, 4653
American Woman ... 1152
Americana Issue ... 1581-1585, 1590, 1590A, 1591-1599, 1603-1606, 1608, 1610-1615, 1615C, 1616-1618, 1618C, 1619
AMERIPEX '86 ... 2145, 2216-2219
Amethyst ... 1540
Amish Horse and Buggy ... C150
Amphipod ... 3442
Anadarko, Oklahoma Post Office Mural ... 5375
Anderson, C. Alfred "Chief" ... 4879
Anderson, Marian ... 3896
Anemone ... 3029
Angelou, Maya ... 4979
Angus Cattle ... 1504
Animal (Muppet) ... 3944g
Animal Rescue ... 4451-4460
Annapolis Tercentenary ... 984
Antarctic Treaty ... 1431, C130
Anthony, Susan B. ... 784, 1051
Antibiotics ... 3186b
Antietam, Battle of ... 4665
Antillean Euphonia ... 3222
Antioch Dunes Evening Primrose ... 1786
Anti-aircraft Gun ... 900
Anti-Pollution ... 1410-1413
Apgar, Virginia ... 2179
Apollo ... 81371
Apollo-Soyuz Space Project ... 1569-1570
Appalachians ... 4045
Appaloosa Horse ... 2158
Apple ... 3491, 3493, 4727-4734, 5037
Appleseed, Johnny ... 1317
Appomattox Surrender ... 1182, 4981
Apprenticeship ... 1201
Apte Tarpon Fly ... 2547
Aquaman ... 4084h, 4084r
Arbor Day ... 717
Arches National Park ... 5080h
Archie ... 4469
Architecture, American ... 1779-1782, 1838-1841, 1928-1931, 2019-2022, 3910
Arctic Animals ... 3288-3292
Arctic Explorations ... 1128
Arctic Fox ... 3289
Arctic Hare ... 3288
Arctic Tundra ... 3802
Arizona Flag ... 1680, 4277
Arizona Statehood ... 1192, 4627
Arkansas Flag ... 1657, 4278
Arkansas River Navigation ... 1358
Arkansas Statehood ... 782, 2167
Arlen, Harold ... 3100
Arlington Amphitheater ... 570, 701
Arlington Green Bridge ... 4738
Armadillo ... 2296
Armed Forces Reserve ... 1067
Armory Show ... 3183d
Armstrong, Edwin ... 2056
Armstrong, Louis ... 2982, 2984
Army ... 785-789, 934
Army, Continental ... 1565
Army Medal of Honor ... 4823
Arnold, H.H. "Hap" ... 2191
Arranged Diatoms ... 5802e
Arrigoni Bridge ... 5811
Arsenal of Democracy ... 2559e
Art Deco Bird ... 4495
Art Deco Style ... 3184j
Art Direction ... 3772f
Art of the American Indian ... 3873
Art of Magic, The ... 5301-5306
Art of the Skateboard ... 5763-5766
Arthur, Chester A. ... 826, 2218c
Articles of Confederation ... 1726
Artists ... 884-888
Asawa, Ruth, Wire Sculptures by ... 5504-5513
Ash Can School ... 3182h
Ashe, Arthur ... 3936
Assateague Island National Seashore ... 5080f
Assassin Bug ... 3351g
Assiniboin Headdress ... 2501
Aster ... 2993, 4762
Atlantic Cable Centenary ... 1112
Atlas Statue ... 3520, 3770
Atomic Energy Act ... 1200
Atoms for Peace ... 1070
Audubon, John J. ... 874, 1241, 1863, 3236e, 3650, C71
Aurora Australis ... 4123b, 4204
Aurora Borealis ... 4123a. 4203
Australia Bicentennial ... 2370
Austria, Flag ... 919
Authors ... 859-863
Automated Post Office ... 1164
Automobile, Electric ... 296
Automobiles ... 2381-2385, 2905-2906, 3019-3023, 4353-4357
Automobile Tail Fin ... 2908-2910
Autry, Gene ... 4449
Autumn Fern ... 4850, 4876, 4974
Auxiliary Steamship (Merchant Marine) ... 4549
Azalea Bonsai ... 4622
Azurite ... 2700

**B-10 Airplane ... 3142f**
B-24 Liberator ... 3922
B-29 Superfortress ... 3923
Baby Boom ... 3186l
Baby Buggy ... 1902
Backyard Games ... 5627-5634
Badger ... 2312
Badminton ... 5633
Bailey Gatzert Riverboat ... 3095
Bailey, Mildred ... 2860
Baker, Ella ... 4384f
Balanchine, George ... 3843
Balboa, Vasco Nunez de ... 397, 401
Bald Eagle ... 1387, 2309
Baldwin, Abraham ... 1850
Baldwin, James ... 3871
Ball, Lucille ... 3523
Ballet ... 1749, 3237
Balloons ... 2032-2035, 2530, C54
Ballot Box ... 1584
Balls, Sports ... 5203-5210
Baltimore Cathedral ... 1780
Baltimore Checkerspot Butterfly ... 4592-4601
Baltimore & Ohio Railroad ... 1006
Baltimore Oriole ... 4886
Banana Split ... 5095
Bandelier National Monument ... 5080k
Bankers Association, American ... 987
Banking and Commerce ... 1577-1578
Banneker, Benjamin ... 1804
Banyan Bonsai ... 4620
Bara, Theda ... 2827
Barbados Blackbelly Sheep ... 5592
Barber, Samuel ... 3162
Barbie Doll ... 3188i
Bardeen, John ... 4227
Barge Fleeting ... 4710l
Barnacle Legs ... 5802r
Barney Google ... 3000i
Barn Swallow ... 2286
Barns ... 5546-5553, 5684-5687
Barred Owl ... 1762
Barrel Cactus ... 1942
Barry, John ... 790
Barrymore, John, Ethel & Lionel ... 2012
Bartholdi, Frederic Auguste ... 2147
Barton, Clara ... 967, 2975c
Bartram, John & William ... 3314
Baseball ... 855, 1381, 2619, 3186c, 3187c, 3187j, 3402, 3408, 5207, 5631
Baseball Stadiums ... 3510-3519
Basie, Count ... 3096
Basilone, Sgt. John ... 3963
Basketball ... 1189, 2560, 3399, 5208
Bass, Largemouth ... 2207
Bastogne & Battle of the Bulge ... 2838j
Bat Signal ... 4928-4931
Bates, Daisy Gaston ... 4384c
Batman ... 4084e, 4084o, 4932-4935
Bats ... 3661-3664, 5423
BB-8 ... 5578
Beach Umbrella ... 2443
Beacon on Rocky Mountains ... C11
Beagle ... 2098
Beaker and Dr. Bunsen Honeydew ... 3944h
Beans ... 4004, 4011, 4017
Bearberry ... 2687
Beard, James ... 4925
Bearden, Romare ... 4566-4569
Beau Geste ... 2447
Beautification of America ... 1318, 1365-1368, 4716a, 4716b, 4716c, 4716d, 4716e
Beautyberry ... 5417
Beaver ... 2316, 4064
Beavertail Cactus ... 1944
Beckwourth, Jim ... 2869q, 2870
Beechcraft 35 Bonanza ... 3924
Beetle Bailey ... 4467
Bel Geddes, Norman ... 4546g
Belgian Malinois ... 5407
Belgium, Flag ... 914
Bell, Alexander Graham ... 893
Benedict, Ruth ... 2938
Benet, Stephen Vincent ... 3221
Benny, Jack ... 2564
Bergen, Edgar ... 2563
Bergman, Ingrid ... 5012
Bering Glacier ... 4036
Bering Land Bridge ... C131
Berlin Airlift ... 3211
Berlin, Irving ... 3669
Bernstein, Leonard ... 3521
Berra, Lawrence "Yogi" ... 5608
Bert ... 5394c
Best Friend of Charleston Locomotive ... 2363
Best Wishes ... 2271, 2396
Bethesda Fountain ... 5348
Bethune, Mary McLeod ... 2137
Betta Fish ... 5107
Bicentennial Celebrations ... 3189f
Bicycle ... 1901, 3119, 3228-3229, 4687-4690
Bierstadt, Albert ... 3236m, 4346
Big Bend National Park ... 5429
Big Bird5 ... 394a
Big Brothers/Big Sisters ... 2162
Bighorn Sheep ... 1467, 1880, 1949, 2288, 4138, 4140
Biglin Brothers ... 1335
Bill of Rights ... 1312, 2421
Biloxi Lighthouse, MS ... 4411

SUBJECT INDEX OF REGULAR, COMMEMORATIVE & AIR POST ISSUES 161


Biltmore Estate Gardens .............. 5467
Biltmore House ............................ 1929
Bingham, George Caleb .............. 3236f
Bingham IV, Hiram ...................... 4076c
Bioluminescent Life ............. 5264-5273
Biomedicine ................................. 5515
Biplane ............................ 2436, 2438c
Big Band Sound .......................... 3186j
Bird of Paradise Flower ................ 3310
Birds and Flowers, State ...... 1953-2002
Birds, Coastal ...................... 4991-4998
Birds in Winter .. 5126-5129, 5317-5320
Birds of Prey ........................ 4608-4612
Birds, Tropical ...................... 3222-3225
Birth of Liberty ............................... 618
Bishop, Elizabeth ........................... 4659
Bison ...............(See American Buffalo)
Bissell, Emily ................................. 1823
Bixby Creek Bridge ...................... 4439
Black and Tan (movie) .................. 4336
Black and Tan Coonhound ............ 2101
Black Bear .................................... 2299
Black Heritage .......... 1744, 1771, 1804, 1875, 2016, 2044, 2073, 2137, 2203, 2249, 2371, 2402, 2442, 2567, 2617, 2746, 2816, 2956, 3058, 3121, 3181, 3273, 3371, 3501, 3557, 3746, 3834, 3896, 3996, 4120, 4222, 4408, 4464, 4565, 4624, 4803, 4856, 4958, 5056, 5171, 5259, 5349, 5432, 5555, 5663, 5753
"Black Jack" ........................................ 73
Black, Hugo L. ............................... 2172
Black Pine Bonsai ......................... 4619
Black Widow ................................ 3351a
Black-capped Chickadee .............. 5317
Black-footed Ferret ........... 2333, 3105a
Black-necked Crane ...................... 2867
Black-tailed Jack Rabbit ............... 2305
Black-tailed Prairie Dog ................. 2325
Blackberries ..... 3297, 3301, 3304, 3406
Blacksmith .................................... 1718
Blackwell, Elizabeth ....................... 1399
Blair, Montgomery ........................... C66
Blake, Eubie .................................. 2988
Blondie ........................................ 3000l
Blood Donor .................................. 1425
Blue Button Organism ................ 5802p
Blue Flag ....................................... 2663
Blue Jay ........ 1757d, 2318, 2483, 3048, 3053, 5320
Blue Paloverde .............................. 3194
Blue Whale .................................... 4069
Blueberries ..... 3294, 3298, 3302, 3404, 5488, 5652-5653
Bluebird, Eastern ................ 2478, 3033
Bluebird, Mountain ......................... 4883
Bluets ............................................ 2656
Blue-spotted Salamander ............. 3815
Bly, Nellie ....................................... 3665
BMX Biking .................................... 3322
Bob Kerrey Pedestrian Bridge ....... 5808
Bobcat ............ 2332, 2482, 4672, 4802
Bobwhite ........................................ 2301
Bocce ............................................. 5628
Boeing 247 Airplane ...................... 3916
Bogart, Humphrey .......................... 3152
Bohlen, Charles E. ...................... 4076e
Bolivar, Simon ....................... 1110-1111
Bombardier Beetle ...................... 3351m
Bone Shaker .................................. 5327
Bonsai .................................. 4618-4622
Books, Bookmark, and Eyeglasses ................................... 1585
Boone, Daniel ................................ 1357
Boston Harbor Lighthouse, MA ..... 4793
Boston State House ...................... 1781
Boston Tea Party ................. 1480-1483
Boston Terrier ................................ 2098
Botanical Art ......................... 5042-5051
Botanical Prints by M. S. Merian ................................ 3126-3129
Botanical Congress ............. 1376-1379
Boulder (Hoover) Dam ........... 774, 4269
Boutonniere ......................... 5199, 5457
Bow, Clara ..................................... 2820
Bowling .......................................... 2963
Box Turtle ...................................... 2326
Boy Scouts ...... 995, 1145, 2161, 3183j, 4472
Boys' Clubs of America ................ 1163
Brachiosaurus ............................ 3136d
Braddock's Field ............................. 688
Bradley, Gen. Omar N. ................. 3394
Brain Coral ................. 1827, 5364, 5370
Brandeis, Louis D. ...................... 4422c
Bread Wagon ................................. 2136
Breast Cancer Awareness ....3081, B1, B5
Breckinridge, Mary ........................ 2942
Breeder Reactor ............................ 2008
Brenda Starr ................................ 3000t
Brennan, William J., Jr. .............. 4422b
Brice, Fanny .................................. 2565
Bridge at Niagara Falls .................... 297
Bridge, Mississippi River ................. 293
Bridger, Jim ...................... 2869c, 2870
Bridges ................................ 5808-5811
Bringing Up Father ..................... 3000d
Brinker, Maureen Connolly ............ 5377
Bristlecone Pines ........................... 4049
Broad-billed Hummingbird ............ 2643
Broad-tailed Hummingbird ............ 2289
Broadbill Decoy ............................. 2138
Brodsky, Joseph ............................ 4654
Brontosaurus ................................. 2425
Brooklyn Botanic Garden .............. 5461
Brooklyn Bridge ............................. 2041
Brooklyn, Battle of ......................... 1003
Brooks, Gwendolyn ....................... 4655
Brother Jonathan Locomotive ....... 2365
Brown Bear .................................... 1884
Brown Pelican .................. 1466, 3105h
Brown v. Board of Education ........ 3937j
Brush Rabbit ........................ 5544-5545
Brussels International Exhibition ... 1104
Bryan, William Jennings ................ 2195
Bryant, Bear ...................... 3143, 3148
Bryce Canyon National Park ......... C139
Buchanan, James ............... 820, 2217f
Buchanan's No. 999 ...................... 2847
Buck, Pearl ..................................... 1848
Buckboard ..................................... 2124
Buffalo ..............(See American Buffalo)
Buffalo Soldiers ............................. 2818
Bugs Bunny ...... 3137-3138, 5494-5503
Building a Nation ........................... 4801
Bull Run, First Battle of ................. 4523
Bunchberry .................................... 2675
Bunche, Ralph ............................... 1860
Bunker Hill Monument ......... 1034, 1056
Bunker Hill, Battle of ...................... 1564
Burbank, Luther ............................... 876
Bureau of Engraving and Printing ........................................ 2875
Burgos, Julia de ............................. 4476
Burgoyne, Surrender of ... 644, 1728, 2590
Burke, Admiral Arleigh A. ............ 4441
Burma Road ................................ 2559a
Burns and Allen .......................... 4414p
Burroughs, Edgar Rice ................. 4702
Bush, George Herbert Walker ....... 5393
Butte ...................... 2902, 2902B, 4710d
Butterflies ................ 1712-1715, 3105f, 4000-4002, 4462, 4603, 4736, 4859, 4999, 5136, 5508
Butterfly Garden Flowers ...... 5664-5665
Buzz Lightyear ...................... 5709-5712
Byodo-In Temple ........................... 5257
Byrd Antarctic ................. 733, 753, 768
Byrd, Richard E. ........................... 2388

**C-3PO .......................................... 5579**
Cabbage Patch Kids ................... 3190i
Cable Car ........................... 1442, 2263
Cable TV ..................................... 3190f
Caboose ........................................ 1905
Cabrillo, Juan Rodriguez ............... 2704
Cacti ..................................... 1942-1945
Cactus Flowers .................... 5350-5359
Cadabby, Abby .......................... 5394h
Cadillac Eldorado .......................... 4353
Cadillac, Landing of ....................... 1000
Caffe Latte ..................................... 5569
Caffe Mocha .................................. 5571
Cagney, James ............................. 3329
Calder, Alexander ............... 3198-3202
Caldonia (movie) ............................ 4339
Calendula ...................................... 4755
Calico Scallop Shell ...................... 2120
California Condor ............... 1430, 3105i
California Dogface Butterfly .......... 5346
California Flag .................... 1663, 4279
California Gold ................................. 954
California Gold Rush ..................... 3316
California Poppy ............................ 2651
California Sea Lion ........................ 2329
California Settlement ..................... 1373
California Statehood ............. 997, 3438
California-Pacific Exposition ........... 773
Calliope Hummingbird ................... 2646
Calvin and Hobbes ........................ 4468
Calvin, Melvin ................................ 4541
Camarasaurus ............................ 3136c
Camellia ......................................... 1877
Camilla the Chicken and The Great Gonzo ........................ 3944j
Camp, Walter ................................. 3810
Camp Fire Girls .............................. 1167
Camp Fire, Inc. .............................. 2163
Campanella, Roy ........................... 4080
Camptosaurus ............................ 3136b
Canada Centenary ........................ 1324
Canada Goose ................. 1757c, 2334
Canada-U.S. Friendship .................. 961
Canal Boat ..................................... 2257
Canal Locks at Sault Ste. Marie ...... 298
Cancer .............................. 1263, 1754
Canoe ............................... 2453, 2454
Canoeing ....................................... 5476
Cantaloupes .................................. 5006
Canvasback Decoy ....................... 2140
Cape Hatteras Lighthouse, NC ..... 2471
Cape Hatteras National Seashore ............................ 1448-1451
Cape Lookout Lighthouse, NC ...... 3788
CAPEX '78 ..................................... 1757
Cappucino ..................................... 5572
Capra, Frank ................................. 4669
Captain America ............. 4159e, 4159o
Captain Hook from "Peter Pan" .... 5217
Caraway, Hattie ................. 3431, 3432
Cardinal ... 1465, 1757a, 2480, 5128, 5318
Cardinal Honeyeater ..................... 3225
CARE ............................................. 1439
Caribou, Woodland ...................... 3105l
Carlsbad Caverns National Park .... 5080o
Carlson, Chester ............................ 2180
Carmel Mission .............................. 4650
Carmichael, Hoagy ........................ 3103
Carnegie, Andrew .......................... 1171
Carnivorous Plants .............. 3528-3531
Carolina Charter ............................ 1230
Carolina-Charleston ......................... 683
Carousel Animals ................ 2390-2393, 2976-2979
Carpenter's Hall ............................ 1543
Carreta .......................................... 2255
Carrots .......................................... 5486
Carson, Kit ...................... 2869n, 2870
Carson, Rachel .............................. 1857
Carter Family ...................... 2773, 2777
Caruso, Enrico ............................... 2250
Carved Figures .................. 2426, C121
Carver, George Washington .... 953, 3183c
Cash, Johnny ................................. 4789
Cashman, Nellie ................ 2869k, 2870
Cassatt, Mary ........ 1322, 2181, 3236o, 3804-3807
Castillod de San Marcos ............... 5554
Cat and Raven ............................... 5420
Catfish ........................................... 2209
Cather, Willa .................................. 1487
Catlin, George ............................. 3236k
Cats ....... 2372-2375, 3232, 4452, 4453, 4456, 4457, 4460, 5122
"Cats" Broadway Show .............. 3190b
Catt, Carrie Chapman ...................... 959
Cattle ............................................. 1504
Cayuga Duck ................................. 5591
Cedar Waxwing ............................. 5127
Celebrate ....... 4196, 4335, 4407, 4502, 5019, 5434
Celebrate the Century .......... 3182-3191
Celebrity Chefs .................... 4922-4926
Cellular Phones ........................... 3191o
Center-pivot Irrigation ................. 4710h
Century of Progress ... 728-731, 766-767
Ceratosaurus ............................. 3136a
Certified Public Accounting ........... 2361
Ceviche ......................................... 5197
Cha Cha Cha ................................. 3941
Chalice Coral ................................. 1829
Chamberlain, Wilt ................ 4950-4951
Champions of Liberty ................... 1096, 1110-1111, 1117-1118, 1125-1126, 1136-1137, 1147-1148, 1159-1160, 1165-1166, 1168-1169, 1174-1175
Champlain, East Coast Explorations of Samuel de .... 4073-4074
Chancellorsville, Battle of ........... 2975p
Chaney, Lon ...................... 2822, 3168
Chaney, Lon, Jr. ............................ 3172
Chanute, Octave .................. C93-C94
Chaplains, Four ............................... 956
Chaplin, Charlie ................ 2821, 3183a
Chapman, Dave .......................... 4546h
Charles, Ray .................................. 4807
Charles W. Morgan Ship ............... 1441
Chautauqua ................................... 1505
Chavez, Cesar E. .......................... 3781
Chavez, Dennis ............................. 2186
Checkerspot Butterfly ................... 1713
Chemical Society, American .......... 1002
Chemistry ...................................... 1685
Chen, Joyce ................................... 4924
Chennault, Claire ........................... 2187
Cherokee Strip ..................... 1360, 2754
Cherry Blossom Centennial ... 4651-4652
Cherry Orchard ............................ 4710i
Chesapeake Bay ........................... 4038
Chesapeake Bay Retriever ........... 2099
Chesnut, Mary ............................ 2975o
Chesnutt, Charles W. .................... 4222
Chevrolet Camaro Z/28 ................ 5717
Chevrolet Chevelle SS .................. 4746
Chevrolet Corvette ........................ 3933
Chevrolet truck .............................. 5102
Cheyenne Headdress .................... 2502
Chicago Botanic Garden ............... 5465
Chief Joseph .................................. 1364
Child Building Sandcastle ............. 5475
Child Health ................................... 3938
Child, Julia ..................................... 4926
Child Labor Reform .................... 3183o
Children's Friendship ..................... 1085
Children's Stick Drawing ............... 2104
Chile Relleno ................................. 5196
Chili Peppers ............ 4003, 4012, 4013
China Clipper ....................... C20-C22
Chinchilla ....................................... 5119
Chinese Hibiscus ........................... 3313
Chinese New Year ............. 2720, 2817, 2876, 3060, 3120, 3179, 3272, 3370, 3500, 3559, 3747, 3832, 3895, 3997, 4221, 4375, 4435, 4492, 4623, 4726, 4846, 4957, 5057, 5154, 5254, 5340, 5428, 5556, 5662, 5744
Chinese Resistance ......................... 906
Chipmunk ........................ 1757f, 2297
Chippendale Chair ... 3755, 3761, 3761A
Chisholm, Shirley ........................... 4856
Chopper Droid ............................... 5582
Chopper Motorcycle ...................... 4087
Choreographers ................... 4698-4701
Christmas ........ 1205, 1240, 1254-1257, 1276, 1321, 1336, 1363, 1384, 1414-1418, 1444-1445, 1471-1472, 1507-1508, 1550-1552, 1579-1580B, 1701-1703, 1729-1730, 1768-1769, 1799-1800, 1842-1843, 1939-1940, 2025-2030, 2063-2064, 2107-2108, 2165-2166, 2244-2245, 2367-2368, 2399-2400, 2427-2429, 2514-2516, 2578-2585, 2710-2719, 2789-2803, 2871-2874, 3003-3018, 3107-3117, 3176-3177, 3244-3252, 3355-3367, 3536-3544, 3675-3691, 3820-3828, 3879, 3883-3894, 3949-3960, 4100-4116, 4206-4218, 4359-4371, 4424-4432, 4477-4485, 4570-4582, 4711-4715, 4813-4821, 4945-4949, 5021-5030, 5143-5148, 5247-5250, 5331-5336, 5424-5427, 5525-5529, 5644-5647, 5721-5725, 5816-5819
Chrysanthemum ................. 2994, 5460
Chrysler Building ........................ 3910b
Chrysler 300C ................................ 4357
Church, Frederick ............. 3236n, 4919
Churchill, Winston S. ........ 1264, 2559d
CIA Invert .................................... 1610c
Cinematography ......................... 3772g
Cincinnati, OH Union Terminal ...... 5762
Cinco de Mayo ................... 3203, 3309
CIPEX .............................................. 948
Circus, American ........ 1309, 2750-2753
Circus Posters ..................... 4898-4905
Circus Wagon ...... 2452, 2452B, 2452D, 4905c
Cirrocumulus Undulatus .............. 3878c
Cirrostratus Fibratus .................... 3878b
Cirrus Radiatus ........................... 3878a
Citizen Kane ............................... 3186o

162 SUBJECT INDEX OF REGULAR, COMMEMORATIVE & AIR POST ISSUES

City Mail Delivery.......... 1238
Civil Defense.......... 2559g
Civil Rights Act of 1964.......... 3937g
Civil Rights Pioneers.......... 4384
Civil Service.......... 2053
Civil War.......... 1178-1182, 2975, 4522-4523, 4664-4665, 4787-4788, 4910-4911, 4980-4981
Civilian Conservation Corps.......... 2037
Claret Cup Cactus.......... 2660
Clarion River.......... 5381l
Clark, Eugenie.......... 5693
Clark, George Rogers.......... 651
Clark, Grenville.......... 1867
Clark, William.......... 3854, 3856
Classics Forever.......... 5079
Clay, Henry..... 140, 151, 162, 173, 198, 227, 259, 274, 284, 309, 1846
Clemens, Samuel L. .......... 863, 4545
Clemente, Roberto.......... 2097, 3408j
Cleveland, Grover...564, 693, 827, 2218d
Cleveland Motorcycle.......... 4086
Cliff Palace.......... 4039
Clifford, J. R. .......... 4384b
Cline, Patsy.......... 2772, 2777
Clipper Ship (Merchant Marine).......... 4548
Cloudscapes.......... 3878
Coal Car.......... 2259
Coast and Geodetic Survey.......... 1088
Coast Guard.......... 936, 5008
Coast Guard Cross.......... 5068
Coast Redwoods.......... 4063
Coastal Maine Botanical Gardens.... 5464
Cobb, Ty.......... 3408d
Cobra Lily.......... 3530
Coburn, Alvin Langdon.......... 3649f
Cochran, Jacqueline.......... 3066
Cochrane, Mickey.......... 3408g
Cocker Spaniel.......... 2099
Cod, Atlantic.......... 2206
Code Deciphering.......... 2697f
Cody, Buffalo Bill..... 2177, 2869b, 2870
Cog Railroad.......... 2463
Cohan, George M. .......... 1756
Cole, Nat "King".......... 2852
Cole, Thomas.......... 4920
Coleman, Bessie.......... 2956
Collective Bargaining.......... 1558
Collie.......... 2100
Collins, Eddie.......... 3408b
Colonial Communications.... 1476-1479
Colonial Craftsmen.......... 1456-1459
Colorado Flag.......... 1670, 4280
Colorado Hairstreak Butterfly.......... 5568
Colorado Statehood.......... 1001, 1711
Colorful Celebrations.......... 5081-5090
Coltrane, John.......... 2991
Columbia River Gorge.......... 5041
Columbia University.......... 1029
Columbian Exposition.......... 230-245, 2624-2629
Columbus' Discovery.......... 2426, 2512, 2620-2623, 2805, C121, C127, C131
Comanche Headdress.......... 2503
Comedians.......... 2562-2566
Comic Strips.......... 3000, 4467-4471
Comiskey Park.......... 3517
Commerce.......... 1578
Commercial Aviation.......... 1684
Common Buckeye Butterfly.... 4000-4002
Common Sunflower.......... 2666
Commonwealth of the Northern Mariana Islands.......... 2804
Communications for Peace.......... 1173
Compact Discs.......... 3190h
Compact, Signing of the.......... 550
Composers.......... 879-883, 3100-3103
Computer Art and Graphics.......... 3191f
Computer Technology.......... 3106
Computing.......... 5514
Comstock, Henry.......... 1130
Condor, California.......... 1430, 3105i
Conestoga Wagon.......... 2252
Confederate Veterans, United.......... 998
Confederation, Articles of.......... 1726
Congratulations.......... 2267
Congressional.......... 3334
Connecticut Flag.......... 1637, 4281
Connecticut Statehood.......... 2340
Connecticut Tercentenary.......... 772
Connolly, Maureen.......... 5377
Constellation Airplane.......... 3142m
Constellations.......... 3945-3948
Constitution Bicentennial..... 2412-2414
Constitution Drafting.......... 2355-2359
Constitution Ratification...835, 2336-2348
Constitution Signing.......... 798, 2360
Constitution, U.S. Frigate.......... 951, 4703
Construction Toys.......... 3182n
Consumer Education.......... 2005
Container Ship (Merchant Marine).... 4548
Contemplation of Justice.... 1592, 1617
Continental Army.......... 1565
Continental Marines.......... 1567
Continental Navy.......... 1566
Contra Costa Wallflower.......... 1785
Contributors to the Cause.... 1559-1562
Cook, Capt. James.......... 1732-1733
Cookie Monster.......... 5394d
Coolidge, Calvin.......... 834, 2219b
Cooper, Anna Julia.......... 4408
Cooper, Gary.......... 2447, 4421
Cooper, James Fenimore.......... 860
Copernicus, Nicolaus.......... 1488
Copley, John Singleton.......... 1273
Copper.......... 2701
Coral Pink Rose.......... 3052
Coral Reefs.......... 1827-1830, 5363-5370
Coral Sea, Battle of.......... 2697c
Cord (automobile).......... 2383
Cori, Gerty.......... 4224
Corn.......... 4007, 4008, 4014, 5005
Corn Snake.......... 5116
Cornhole.......... 5634
Cornish-Windsor Covered Bridge.... 4070
Cornwell, Dean.......... 3502j
Coronado Expedition.......... 898
Corregidor.......... 925, 2697d
Corsair Airplane.......... 3142g
Corsage.......... 5200, 5458
Corythosaurus.......... 3136m
"Cosby Show, The".......... 3190j
Cosmos.......... 4761
Costello, Lou.......... 2566
Costume Design.......... 3772c
Cotton Patch Goose.......... 5588
Cottontail.......... 2290
Count, The.......... 5394f
Cowboys of the Silver Screen... 4446-4449
CPA.......... 2361
Cranberry Harvest.......... 4710j
Cranes.......... 1097, 2867-2868
Crater Lake.......... 745, 761, 4040
Crayola Crayons.......... 3182d
Crazy Horse.......... 1855
Credit Union Act.......... 2075
Credo.......... 1139-1144
Crested Honeycreeper.......... 3224
Crime, Take a Bite out of.......... 2102
Crippled, Hope for.......... 1385
Crockett, Davy.......... 1330
Crocodile, American.......... 3105d
Crocus.......... 3025
Croquet.......... 5630
Crosby, Bing.......... 2850
Crosley Field.......... 3512
Cross-country Skiing.......... 5479
Crossword Puzzle, First.......... 3183l
Cruella De Vil from "One Hundred and One Dalmatians".......... 5219
Cruz, Celia.......... 4501
Cub Airplane.......... 3142c
Cueva del Indio, La.......... 5040
Cummings, E. E. .......... 4662
Cumulonimbus Incus.......... 3878e
Cumulonimbus Mammatus.......... 3878d
Cumulonimbus with Tornado.......... 3878o
Cumulus Congestus.......... 3878n
Cumulus Humilis.......... 3878m
Cunningham, Imogen.......... 3649q
Curious George.......... 3992
Curtiss Jenny.......... C1-C3, 3142s
Curtiss, Glenn.......... C100
Cushing, Harvey.......... 2188
Cycling.......... 3119, 5478
Czechoslovakia, Flag.......... 910

**D-O.......... 5576**
Daffodil.......... 2761, 3901
Daffy Duck.......... 3306-3307
Dahlia.......... 1878, 2995
Daly, Sgt. Major Daniel J. .......... 3964
Dance, American.......... 1749-1752
Dances, American Indian..... 3072-3076
Dante.......... 1268
Dare, Virginia.......... 796
Daredevil Comic Book.......... 4159s
Dark Hollow Falls, VA.......... 5800h
Dartmouth College Case.......... 1380
Daspletosaurus.......... 3136k
Davis, Dr. Allison.......... 2816
Davis, Benjamin O. .......... 3121
Davis, Bette.......... 4350
Davis, Jefferson.......... 2975f
Davis, Miles.......... 4693
Davis, Stuart.......... 1259, 4748c
Day of the Dead.......... 5640-5643
Daylight.......... 3333
DC Comics Superheroes.......... 4084
DC-3 Airplane.......... 3142q
DC-4 Skymaster.......... C32-C33, C37, C39, C41
D-Day.......... 2838c
De Burgos, Julia.......... 4476
De Haviland Biplane.......... C6
De la Renta, Oscar.......... 5173
De Mille, Agnes.......... 3842
Dean, Dizzy.......... 3408s
Dean, James.......... 3082
Death Valley.......... 4070
Decatur House.......... 1440
Decatur, Stephen.......... 791
Declaration of Independence.......... 120, 130, 627,1545, 1691-1695
Declaration of War on Japan.......... 2559j
Deep Sea Creatures.......... 3439-3443
Deer Creek Falls, AZ.......... 5800a
Deer.......... 5822
Deer (Fawn).......... 2479
Deer Mouse.......... 2324
Defense, National.......... 899-901
Delaware Flag.......... 1633, 4282
Delaware Statehood.......... 2336
Delta Wing.......... C77
Deming New Mexico Post Office Mural.......... 5376
Dempsey, Jack.......... 3183m
Demuth, Charles.......... 4748a
Denmark, Flag.......... 920
Dennis the Menace.......... 4471
Dental Health.......... 1135
Deora II.......... 5329
DePaola, Tomie.......... 5797
Depression.......... 3185m
Deschutes River.......... 5381i
Desegregating Public Schools.......... 3187f
Desert Fire Spot.......... 2690
Desert Plants.......... 1942-1945
Desert Shield/Desert Storm.... 2551-2552
Deskey, Donald.......... 4546d
Destroyer Reuben James.......... 2559f
Devils Tower.......... 1084
Dewey, George.......... 793
Dewey, John.......... 1291
Diabetes Awareness.......... 3503
Diamond Head Lighthouse, HI.......... 4146
Dickinson, Emily.......... 1436
Dickson, William.......... 3064
Dick Tracy.......... 3000m
Digitalis.......... 4756
DiMaggio, Joe.......... 4697
Dinah Shore Show, The.......... 4414i
Diner.......... 3208, 3208A
Dinosaurs.......... 2422-2425, 3136
Diplomats, Distinguished American...4076
Directing.......... 3772b
Dirksen, Everett.......... 1874
Disabled, Intl. Year of the.......... 1925
Disabled Veterans.......... 1421
Disco Music.......... 3189d
Disney, Walt.......... 1355
Disney Characters.......... 3865-3868, 3912-3915, 4025-4028, 4192-4195, 4342-4345, 5213-5222
Disney-Pixar Films Characters.......... 4553-4557, 4677-4681
Distinguished Americans Issue.... 3420, 3422, 3426-3427, 3427A, 3428, 3430-3432, 3432A, 3432B, 3433-3436, 4510, 4666, 4879, 5191, 5699
Distinguished Service Cross.......... 5065
District of Columbia.......... 2561, 3813
District of Columbia Flag.......... 4283
Diving Beetle Front Foot.......... 5802i
Diwali.......... 5142
Dix, Dorothea.......... 1844
Doby, Larry.......... 4695
Dr. Seuss' "The Cat in the Hat"... 3187h
Doctors.......... 949
Dodge Challenger R/T.......... 5716
Dodge Charger Daytona.......... 4743
Dogbane Beetle.......... 3351e
Dogface Butterfly.......... 1714
Dog Sled.......... 2135
Dogs.......... 2098-2101, 3230, 4451, 4454, 4455, 4458, 4459, 5125
Dogs at Work.......... 4604-4607
Dogs, Military Working.......... 5405-5408
Dolls.......... 3151
Dolphin.......... 2511, 4388
Dome of Capitol.......... 1590-1591, 1616, 1809, 3472
Dorsey, Tommy & Jimmy.......... 3097
Douglas, Aaron.......... 4748g
Douglass, Frederick.......... 1290, 2975h
Dove, Arthur.......... 4748l
Dracula.......... 3169
Dragnet.......... 4414e
Dragonfly.......... 4267
Dragons.......... 5307-5310
Drew, Charles R. .......... 1865
Dreyfuss, Henry.......... 4546f
Drive-In Movies.......... 3187i
Drug Abuse, Prevent.......... 1438
Drug Free USA.......... 5542
Drum.......... 1615
Du Bois, W.E.B. .......... 2617, 3182l
Du Sable, Jean Baptiste Pointe..... 2249
Duchamp, Marcel.......... 4748k
Duck Decoys.......... 2138-2141
Duck, Wood.......... 2484-2485
Duesenberg.......... 2385
Dulles Airport.......... 2022
Dulles, John Foster.......... 1172
Dumbarton Oaks.......... 5463
Dunbar, Paul Laurence.......... 1554
Duncan, Isadora.......... 4698
Dung Beetle.......... 3351n
Dunham, Katherine.......... 4700
Dunn, Harvey.......... 3502o
Durand, Asher B. .......... 3236g, 4918
Dutch Shepherd.......... 5408
Dutchman's Breeches.......... 2682

**"E. T. The Extra-Terrestrial"..... 3190m**
Eagan, Eddie.......... 2499
Eagle..... 1735-1736, 1743, 1818-1820, 1909, 1946-1948, 2111-2113, 2122, 2309, 2394, 2540, 2541, 2542, 2598, 3471-3471A, 3646, 4585-4590, 5013-5018, C48, C50, C67
Eagle and Shield... 116, 127, 771, 1596, 2431, 2595-2597, 2602-2604, 2907, 3270-3271, 3792-3801, 3844-3853, CE1-CE2
Eagle Holding Shield, etc. ...121, 131, C23
Eagle Nebula.......... 3384
Eakins, Thomas.......... 1335
Eames, Charles and Ray.......... 4333
Earhart, Amelia.......... C68
Early Football Heroes.......... 3808-3811
Early TV Memories.......... 4414
Earp, Wyatt.......... 2869j, 2870
Earth..... 2277, 2279, 2282, 2570, 4740, 5071
Earth Day.......... 2951-2954, 3189a, 5459
Earthscapes.......... 4710
Eastern Bluebird.......... 2478, 3033
Eastern Chipmunk.......... 2297
Eastern Hercules Beetle.......... 3351l
Eastern Tailed-Blue Butterfly.......... 5136
Eastern Tiger Swallowtail Butterfly... 4999
Eastman, George.......... 1062
Ebbets Field.......... 3510
Ebony Jewelwing.......... 3351h
Echeveria.......... 5198
Echo I.......... 1173
Ed Sullivan Show, The.......... 4414j
Eddy's No. 242.......... 2845
Edison, Thomas A. .......... 654-656, 945
Edmontonia.......... 3136i
Education.......... 1833
Educators.......... 869-873
Egg Cream.......... 5094
Egg Nebula.......... 3387
Eggplants.......... 5492
Eid.......... 3532, 3674, 4117, 4202, 4351, 4416, 4552, 4800, 5092
Einiosaurus.......... 3136j
Einstein, Albert.......... 1285, 1774
Eisenhower, Dwight D. .......... 1383, 1393-1395, 1401-1402, 2219g, 2513

SUBJECT INDEX OF REGULAR, COMMEMORATIVE & AIR POST ISSUES 163

Elderberry Longhorn....................3351b
Electric Auto..........................296, 1906
Electric Light.............................654-656
Electric Toy Trains.........................3184d
Electronics..................1500-1502, C86
Elektra ............................41591, 4159s
Elephants.............................................5714
Elevator ............................................2254
Eliot, Charles W. ..................................871
Eliot, T.S. .........................................2239
Elk.......................................................1886
Elkhorn Coral............1828, 5363, 5369
Elks, B.P.O. .......................................1342
Ellington, "Duke" ...............................2211
Ellison, Ralph.....................................4866
Ellsworth, Lincoln ..............................2389
Elmo ...............................................5394m
Ely's No. .........................................102846
Emancipation Proclamation....1233, 4721
Emerson, Ralph Waldo..........................861
Emigration, Hardships of.......................290
Empanadas .......................................5195
Emperor Penguins...............4989-4990
Empire State Building.....................3185b
Empire State Express............................295
Endangered Flora.................1783-1786
Endangered Species ...........3105, 5799
Energy .............1723-1724, 2006-2009
Energy Conservation .........................1547
Engineering Education ......................5278
Engineers, American Society of
Civil...................................................1012
English Sundew.................................3531
Enjoy the Great Outdoors.....5475-5479
Envelopes..........................................2150
Eohippus ..........................................3077
Ercoupe 415 .....................................3920
Ericsson, John, Statue of .....................628
Erie Canal ..........................................1325
Erie Harbor Lighthouse, PA..............5623
Erikson, Leif......................................1359
Ernie ..............................................5394b
Escalante, Jaime ...............................5100
Espresso...........................................5570
Etiquette ...........................................3184
Evans, Walker................................3649m
Evening Grosbeak .............................4887
Everglades, Florida............................5751
Everglades National Park .....952, 5080l
Evers, Medgar ...............................4384e
Ewry, Ray..........................................2497
Executive Branch of Gov't.................2414
Executive Order 9981......................3937a
Exeter Academy Library .................3910k
Experiment Steamboat......................2405
Explorer II Balloon ............................2035
Explorers .........2024, 2093, 2220-2223,
2386-2389
EXPO '74 ..........................................1527

**F6F Hellcat ................................... 3918**
Fairbanks, Douglas............................2088
Fairs, State and County........5401-5404
Fall of the Berlin Wall......................3190k
Fallen Timbers, Battle of......................680
Fallingwater ......................................2019
Family Planning .................................1455
Family Unity......................................2104
Famous Americans...................859-893
Fanfin Anglerfish ...............................3439
Fangtooth .........................................3441
Fantastic Four, The........................4159n
Far West Riverboat ...........................3093
Farley, Carl.......................................2934
Farmers Markets ..................4912-4915
Farming in the West.............................286
Farnsworth, Philo T. ..........................2058
Farragut, David G. ......311, 792, 2975g
Fashions, 1970s ..............................3189k
Faulkner, William...............................2350
Fawcett, Robert...............................3502d
Fawn.................................................2479
Federal Deposit Insurance Corp. .....2071
Federal Reserve System ..................3183b
Federated States of Micronesia ....2506
Fenway Park.....................................3516
Ferber, Edna .........................3433, 3434
Fermi, Enrico ....................................3533
Ferns ..............4848-4852, 4874-4878,
4973-4977
Ferrer, Jose.......................................4666
Ferret, Black-footed ..........2333, 3105a
Ferryboat ..........................................2466
Feynman, Richard .............................3909
Fiedler, Arthur ...................................3159
Fields, Dorothy ..................................3102
Fields, W.C. ......................................1803
Figs...................................................5493
Figure Skating ................................3190e
Fillmore, Millard .................818, 2217d
Film Directors ......................4668-4671
Film Editing....................................3772h
Filmmaking .......................................3772
Films......................................2445-2448
Fine Arts ...........................................1259
Finger Coral ......................................1830
Finnish Independence .......................1334
FIPEX................................................1075
Fire Engine........................................2264
Fire Pumper ......................................1908
Fireweed ...........................................2679
First Continental Congress...1543-1546
First Moon Landing .............5399-5400
First Responders ...............................5316
Fish.........2205-2209, 2863-2866 3231,
3317-3320
Fishing Boat .........................2529, 2529C
Fishing Flies..........................2545-2549
Fitzgerald, Ella...................................4120
Fitzgerald, F. Scott.............................3104
Five Finger Lighthouse, AK ..............4147
Five Forks, Battle of ..........................4980
Flag Act of 1818 ................................5284
Flag, Foreign.............................909-921
Flag, Fort McHenry....1346, 1597-1598,
1618, 1618C, 4853-4855, 4868-4871
Flag, U.S. .......1094, 1132, 1153, 1208,
1338-1338G, 1345-1354, 1509, 1519,
1597, 1618C, 1622-1623B, 1625,
1890-1891, 1893-1896, 2114-2116,
2276, 2278, 2280, 2285A, 2475, 2522,
2523, 2523A, 2528, 2531, 2593-2594,
2605-2609, 2879-2893, 2897, 2913-
2916, 2919-2921, 3133, 3277-3282,
3283, 3403, 3448-3450, 3469-3470,
3495, 3549-3550A, 3620-3625,
3629F-3637, 3965-3970, 3972-3975,
3978-3983, 3985, 4129-4135, 4186-
4191, 4228-4247, 4273, 4302, 4303,
4332, 4391-4396, 4487, 4489, 4491,
4519, 4560, 4562, 4564, 4629-4648,
4673-4676, 4706-4709, 4766-4785,
4796-4799, 4894-4897, 4961-4963,
5052-5055, 5158-5162, 5260-5263,
5342-5345, 5654-5659, 5684-5687,
5787-5791
Flagg, James Montgomery..........3502a
Flags of Our Nation ..............4273-4332
Flags on Barns ......................5684-5687
Flags, 50 States....................1633-1682
Flags, Historic.......................1345-1354
Flame Lily Pollen ............................5802s
Flamingo ...........................................2707
Flan...................................................5193
Flanagan, Father Edward Joseph...2171
Flappers.........................................3184h
Flash, The ..........................4084f, 4084p
Flash Gordon .................................3000p
Flathead Headdress ...........................2504
Flathead River ................................5381f
Flax.........................................4506, 4517
Flight of Wright Brothers, First ......3783
Floral Geometry..........5700-5701, 5755
Florence, Colorado Post
Office Mural .....................................5373
Florida Everglades.............................5751
Florida Flag..............................1059, 4204
Florida Manatee..............................3105o
Florida, Naming of, 500th
Anniv. ..................................4750-4753
Florida Panther......3105m, 4137, 4139,
4141, 4142
Florida Settlement .............................1271
Florida Statehood.....................927, 2950
Flower Fly .......................................3351f
Flowers............1876-1879, 2076-2079,
2517-2520, 2524-2527, 2647-2696,
2760-2764, 2829-2833, 2993-2997,
3025-3029, 3310-3313, 3454-3465,
3478-3481, 3487-3490, 3836-3837,
4166-4185, 4722-4725, 4750-4753,
4754-4763, 4764-4765, 4862-4865,
4881, 5001, 5233-5240, 5664-5665,
5672-5679, 5680, 5681-5682, 5727-
5736
Flowers and Birds, State......1953-2002
Flushing Remonstrance.....................1099
Flying Disc ........................................5629
Flying Fortress Airplane..............3142k
Folk Art, American..............1706-1709,
1745-1748, 1775-1778, 1834-1837,
2138-2141, 2240-2243, 2351-2354,
2390-2393
Fonda, Henry ....................................3911
Fontanne, Lynn & Lunt, Alfred.......3287
Food for Peace ..................................1231
Football......................3400, 5203
Football, Intercollegiate .....................1382
For Defense ..............................899-901
Forbes Field.......................................3515
Ford, Gerald R. .................................4199
Ford, John ........................................4668
Ford, Henry.....................................1286A
Ford F-1 truck...................................5103
Ford F-100 truck................................5104
Ford Mustang .................................3188h
Ford Mustang Boss 302 ...................5715
Ford Mustang Shelby GT .................4745
Ford Roadster Hot Rods ......4908-4909
Ford Thunderbird...............................3935
Forest Conservation ..........................1122
Forestry Congress, 5th World........1156
Forget-me-nots .................................4987
Fort Bliss ............................................976
Fort Duquesne...................................1123
Fort Jefferson Lighthouse, FL .......4413
Fort Kearny .........................................970
Fort McHenry, Bombardment of....4921
Fort Nisqually ....................................1604
Fort Orange, Landing at ......................615
Fort Snelling .....................................1409
Fort Sumter ........................1178, 4522
Fort Ticonderoga ...............................1071
Fortune's Holly Fern ..4848, 4874, 4977
Fosse, Bob ........................................4701
Fossil Fuels.......................................2009
Foster, John...................................3236a
Foster, Rube .....................................4466
Foster, Stephen Collins .......................879
Four Freedoms ....................................908
Four-H Clubs .....................................1005
Four Horseman of Notre Dame ....3184l
Fox....................................................5825
Fox, Red...1757g, 2335, 3036, 5742-5743
Fox in Socks......................................3989
Foxglove ...............................4507, 4513
Foxx, Jimmie .................................3408n
Fozzie Bear....................................3944b
Fragrant Water Lily ...........................2648
France, Flag.........................................915
Francis of Assisi ................................2023
Francisco, Peter ................................1562
Frankenstein......................................3170
Frankfurter, Felix..............................4422a
Franklin, Benjamin.......1, 3, 5-5A, 6-8A,
9, 18-24, 38, 40, 46, 63, 71, 81, 85,
85A, 86, 92, 100, 102, 110, 112, 123,
133 134, 145, 156, 167, 182, 192,
206, 212, 219, 246-247, 264, 279, 300,
314, 316, 318, 331, 343, 348, 352, 357,
374, 383, 385, 387, 390, 392, 414-423,
431-440, 460, 470-478, 497, 508-518,
523-524, 547, 552, 575, 578, 581,
594, 596-597, 604, 632, 658, 669, 803,
1030, 1073, 1393D, 1690, 3139, 4021-
4024, 5079b, 5079f
Frederick...........................................3994
Freedom from Hunger .......................1231
Freedom of the Press ........................1119
Freedom Riders ...............................3937f
Fremont, John C. ...............2869i, 2870
Fremont on the Rocky Mountains ...288
French Alliance .................................1753
French Revolution .............................C120
French, Daniel Chester........................887
Freshwater Protozoans ..................5802f
Freshwater Snail Tongue ...............5802o
Frigatebird ...........................4994, 4996
Frilled Dogwinkle Shell .....................2117
Fringed Gentian ................................2672
Frogs ....................................5395-5398
From Me to You ................................4978
Frost, A. B. ...................................3502g
Frost, Robert .....................................1526
Frozen Treats.......................5285-5294
Fruit...5037-5039, 5177-5178, 5201, 5256
Fruit Berries......3294-3305, 3404-3407
Fruit, Tropical........................4253-4262
Fruits and Vegetables...........5484-5493
Fulbright Scholarships.......................3065
Fuller, R. Buckminster .......................3870
Fulton, Robert....................................1270
Fur Seal ............................................1464
Future Farmers ..................................1024
Futuristic Mail Delivery ........C122-C126

**Gable, Clark & Leigh, Vivien ....... 2446**
Gadsden Purchase.............................1028
Gaines, Ernest J. ...............................5753
Galaxy NGC1316...............................3388
Gallatin, Albert ..................................1279
Gallaudet, Thomas H. ........................1861
Galvez, Gen. Bernardo de .................1826
Games, Backyard .................5627-5634
Gandhi, Mahatma.................1174-1175
Garbo, Greta......................................3943
Gardel, Carlos....................................4500
Garden Beauty ......................5558-5567
Garden of Love......................4531-4540
Gardening-Horticulture......................1100
Garfield (comic strip) ........................4470
Garfield, James A. .......205, 205C, 216,
224, 256, 271, 282, 305, 558, 587, 638,
664, 675, 723, 825, 2218b
Garibaldi, Giuseppe.............1168-1169
Garland, Judy .......................2445, 4077
Garner, Erroll.....................................2992
Gasoline Alley ................................3000h
Gaston from "Beauty and the
Beast" ..............................................5221
Gateway Arch .......................4044, 5157
Gato Class Submarine .......................3377
Gatsby Style...................................3184b
Gaye, Marvin .....................................5371
Gecko ...............................................5121
Gee's Bend, Alabama Quilts...4089-4098
Geebee Airplane..............................3142i
Gehrig, Lou.........................2417, 3408t
Geisel, Theodor Seuss .......................3835
Gellhorn, Martha...............................4248
Genome Sequencing..........................5516
George, Walter F. ..............................1170
Georgia Bicentennial ...........................726
Georgia Flag .........................1636, 4285
Georgia Statehood ............................2339
Geothermal Spring ..........................4710c
Gerbil................................................5120
German Immigration.........................2040
German Shepherd ..............................5405
Geronimo..............................2869m, 2870
Gershwin, George.................1484, 3345
Gershwin, Ira .....................................3345
Get Well ............................................2268
Gettysburg Address ............................978
Gettysburg, Battle of...1180, 2975t, 4788
Ghosts ..............................................5421
GI Bill...............................................3186i
Giannini, Amadeo P. .........................1400
Giant Panda.......................................2706
Giant Sequoia....................................1764
Gibbs, Josiah Willard.........................3907
Gibson, Althea ...................................4803
Gibson Girl....................................3182m
Gibson, Josh ..................................3408r
Gifts of Friendship ................4982-4985
Gila Trout .......................................3105j
Gilbert, John ......................................2823
Gilbreth, Lillian M. ............................1868
Ginsburg, Ruth Bader.........................5821
Giraffe...............................................2705
Girl Scouts...... 974, 1199, 2251, 3182k,
4691
Giving & Sharing...............................3243
Glacier and Icebergs .......................4710a
Glacier Bay National Park and
Preserve .......................................5080a
Glacier National Park.....748, 764, C149
Glade Creek Grist Mill .......................4927
Gladiola ............................................2831
Glass, American ....................3325-3328
Glass House ...................................3910h
Gloriosa Lily......................................3312
Go For Broke .....................................5593
Go Green ..........................................4524
Goddard, Robert H. ............................C69
Gold Star Banner.............................2765i
Gold Star Mothers ...............................969
Golden-crowned Kinglets...................5126
Golden Eagle .....................................4610
Golden Gate ....399, 403, 567, 698, 3185l
Golden Gate Exposition .......................852
Golden Spike......................................5379

164 SUBJECT INDEX OF REGULAR, COMMEMORATIVE & AIR POST ISSUES


Goldfish ........................................ 5110
Goldie's Wood Fern... 4851, 4877, 4975
Golf ................................................ 2965
Golf Ball ........................................ 5206
Gompers, Samuel ............................ 988
Gone With the Wind .......... 2446, 3185i
Goniopholis ................................ 3136e
Gonk Droid .................................... 5580
Goodman, Benny ........................... 3099
Goodnight, Charles ........... 2869l, 2870
Gorky, Arshile ............................. 4444e
Gottlieb, Adolph ........................... 4444i
Gottschalk, Louis Moreau ............ 3165
Gowan & Marx Locomotive............ 2366
Graf Zeppelin................. C13-C15, C18
Graham, Katherine ........................ 5699
Graham, Martha ............................ 3840
Grand Army of the Republic........... 985
Grand Canyon ... 741, 757 2512, 3183h, 4054, 5080e, C135
Grand Central Terminal................. 4739
Grand Coulee Dam........................ 1009
Grand Island Ice Caves ................. 5430
Grand Teton National Park ...........C147
Grange........................................... 1323
Grange, Red ................................. 3811
Grant, Cary ................................... 3692
Grant, U.S. ..... 223, 255, 270, 281, 303, 314A, 560, 589, 640, 666, 677, 787, 823, 2217i, 2975d
Grapes....................... 5038, 5177, 5489
Gray, Asa ...................................... 4542
Gray Birch...................................... 1767
Gray Squirrel.................................. 2295
Gray Wolf ............................ 2322, 3292
Grays Harbor Lighthouse, WA....... 4148
Great Americans Issue ........ 1844-1869, 2168-2173, 2175-2197, 2933-2936, 2938, 2940-2943
Great Basin................................... 4051
Great Gonzo and Camilla the Chicken ...................................... 3944j
Great Gray Owl.............................. 1760
Great Horned Owl ......................... 1763
Great Lakes Dunes........................ 4352
Great Plains Prairie........................ 3506
Great River Road........................... 1319
Great Sand Dunes ......................... 4037
Great Smoky Mountains................ 5752
Great Smoky Mountains National Park ......................749, 765, 797, C140
Great Spangled Fritillary Butterfly . 4859
Great Train Robbery, The............ 3182c
Great White Shark ........................ 5227
Greece, Flag ................................... 916
Greeley, Horace ............................ 1177
Greely, Adolphus W. ..................... 2221
Green Arrow ................... 4084d, 4084n
Green Bay Packers...................... 3188d
Green Lantern.................. 4084b, 4084l
Green-throated Carib .................... 3223
Greenberg, Hank ........................... 4081
Greene, Nathanael........................... 785
Greetings From America......3561-3610, 3696-3745
Griffith, D.W. ................................ 1555
Grofe, Ferde .................................. 3163
Gropius House.............................. 2021
Grosbeak....................................... 2284
Grosbeak, Evening ........................ 4887
Grosbeak, Rose-breasted ............ 4889
Grotto Falls, TN5 .......................... 800i
Grove, Lefty ................................ 3408k
Grover.......................................... 5394o
Guadalcanal, Battle of................. 2697i
Guam Flag..................................... 4286
Guava ................................ 4257, 4259
Guggenheim Museum ................ 3910a
Guinea Pig .................................... 5114
Guitar............................................ 1613
Gulf Islands National Seashore ... 5080p
Gulf War....................................... 3191b
Gunston Hall.................................. 1108
Gutenberg Bible ............................ 1014
Guthrie, Woody.............................. 3213
Guy Smiley ................................. 5394k

**Habib, Philip C. ........................ 4076d**
Hagatna Bay, Guam .....................C143
Haida Canoe.................................. 1389
Halas, George....................... 3146, 3150
Hale, Nathan........................... 551, 653
Haleakala National Park ............ 5080m
Haley, Bill.............................. 2725, 2732
Half Moon and Steamship........372-373
Hallelujah (movie) ......................... 4340
Hamer, Fannie Lou ..................... 4384e
Hamilton, Alexander....... 143, 154, 165, 176, 190, 201, 217, 1053, 1086
Hamilton, Alice ............................. 2940
Hammarskjold, Dag.............1203-1204
Hammerhead Shark ...................... 5226
Hammerstein II, Oscar & Rodgers, Richard ......................................... 3348
Hamster............................. 3234, 5109
Hancock Center, Chicago ........... 3910l
Hancock, Winfield ...................... 2975n
Handcar......................................... 1898
Handicapped................................. 1155
Handy, W.C. ................................. 1372
Hansom Cab ................................. 1904
Hanson, John ................................ 1941
Hanukkah ....... 3118, 3352, 3547, 3672, 3880, 4118, 4219, 4372, 4433, 4583, 4824, 5153, 5338, 5530, 5739
Happy Birthday......... 2272, 2395, 3558, 3695, 4079, 5635
Happy New Year....... 2720, 2817, 2876, 3060, 3120, 3179, 3272, 3369, 3370, 3500, 3559, 3747, 3832, 3895, 3997, 4221, 4375, 4435, 4492, 4623
Harbor of Refuge Lighthouse, DE.....5624
Harbor Seal .................................. 1882
Harburg, Edgar Y. "Yip" ................ 3905
Harding, Warren G. ........ 553, 576, 582, 598, 605, 610-613, 631, 633, 659, 670, 684, 686, 833, 2219a
Hardy, Oliver................................. 2562
Harebell ........................................ 2689
Harlem Renaissance............5471-5474
Harlequin Lupine .......................... 2664
Harley-Davidson Electra-Glide Motorcycle.................................. 4088
Harnett, William M. ............ 1386, 3236i
Harris, Joel Chandler....................... 980
Harris, Patricia Roberts ................ 3371
Harrison, Benjamin......... 308, 622, 694, 828, 1045, 2218e
Harrison, William H. ..... 814, 996, 2216i
Harrison Wright Falls, PA............ 5800c
Harry Potter Movie Characters..........................4825-4844
Hart, Lorenz.................................. 3347
Hart, Moss..................................... 3882
Hart, William S. ............................ 4448
Harte, Bret..................................... 2196
Hartley, Marsden ......................... 4748d
Harvard, John ................................ 2190
Hawaii..............................................C46
Hawaii Flag......................... 1682, 4287
Hawaii Sesquicentennial ..........647-648
Hawaii Statehood........2080, 4415, C55
Hawaii Territory............................... 799
Hawaiian Missionary Stamps ........ 3694
Hawaiian Monk Seal.................... 3105c
Hawaiian Rain Forest.................... 4474
Hawaiian Wild Broadbean ............ 1784
Hawes, Josiah Johnson & Southworth, Albert Sands .......... 3649a
Hawkins, Coleman ........................ 2983
Hawkman ......................... 4084j, 4084t
Hawthorne, Nathaniel.................... 2047
Hayden, Robert ............................. 4657
Hayes, Helen ................................ 4525
Hayes, Rutherford B. ..... 563, 692, 824, 2218a
Head of Freedom Statue, Capitol Dome .................... 573, 4075c
Heade, Martin Johnson ................ 3872
Healing Post-Traumatic Stress Disorder...........................................B7
Health Research ........................... 2087
Heart Health .................................. 4625
Height, Dorothy ............................ 5171
Held, John, Jr. ............................ 3502t
Help Find Missing Children .......... 4987
Helping Children Learn................. 3125
Hemingway, Ernest M. ................ 2418
HemisFair '68 ................................ 1340
Hendrix, Jimi ................................. 4880
Henry, O. ...................................... 4705
Henry, Patrick................................ 1052
Henson, Jim ................................ 3944k
Henson, Matthew, & Peary, Robert E. ..................................... 2223
Hepburn, Audrey ........................... 3786
Hepburn, Katharine ...................... 4461
Herb Robert................................... 2657
Herbert, Victor ................................. 881
Heritage Animal Breeds........5583-5592
Herkimer at Oriskany .................... 1722
Hermit Crab................................... 5118
Hermitage, The........... 786, 1037, 1059
Heroes of 2001 ..................................B2
Herrmann, Bernard........................ 3341
Herry Monster.............................. 5394i
Hersey, John.................................. 4249
Hershey, Milton.............................. 2933
Hesburgh, Father Ted..........5241-5242
Heston, Charlton ........................... 4892
Hiawatha....................................... 3336
Hickok, Wild Bill................ 2869o, 2870
Higgins, Marguerite ...................... 3668
High Museum of Art .................... 3910j
Higher Education........................... 1206
Highway Interchange.................. 4710o
Hiking ........................................... 5477
Hillsboro Inlet Lighthouse, FL........ 3791
Hine, Lewis W. .......................... 3649e
Hines, Gregory.............................. 5349
Hines, Maj. Gen. John L. ............. 3393
Hip-hop Culture........3190o, 5480-5483
Hispanic Americans....................... 2103
Historic Preservation ...........1440-1443
History of Ice Hockey ..........5252-5253
Hitchcock, Alfred .......................... 3226
Ho-Chunk Bag............................ 3873d
Hoban, James .....................1935-1936
Hobby, Oveta Culp ....................... 4510
Hofmann, Hans .......................... 4444a
Holiday, Billie ................................ 2856
Holly, Buddy ....................... 2729, 2736
Holmes, Oliver Wendell ....1288, 1288B, 1305E
Home on the Range .......... 2869a, 2870
Homemakers ................................ 1253
Homer, Winslow ....... 1207, 3236j, 4473
Homestead Act.............................. 1198
Honest John from "Pinocchio"...... 5214
Honeybee ...................................... 2281
Honeydew, Dr. Bunsen, and Beaker ....................................... 3944h
Honeymooners, The.................... 4414t
Honoring Those Who Served ........ 3331
Honoring U.S. Servicemen........... 1422
Honoring Veterans........................ 3508
Hoover (Boulder) Dam.......... 774, 4269
Hoover, Herbert C. ............ 1269, 2219c
Hopalong Cassidy...................... 4414g
Hope, Bob ..................................... 4406
Hopi Pottery .................................. 1708
Hopkins, Johns.............................. 2194
Hopkins, Mark ................................. 870
Hopper, Edward................ 3236p, 4558
Horne, Lena................................... 5259
Hornsby, Rogers.......................... 3408f
Horse Racing................................. 1528
Horses .... 2155-2158, 2756-2759, 5123
Horseshoes ................................... 5627
Horticulture.................................... 1100
Hospice Care................................. 3276
Hospitals ....................................... 2210
Hostages in Iran Return.............. 3190d
Hot Fudge Sundae ........................ 5097
Hot Rods ............................4908-4909
Hot Wheels Toy Cars...........5321-5330
Houdini, Harry ............................... 3651
Household Conveniences ........... 3185g
House of Representatives, U.S. ... 2412
Houston, Charles Hamilton ......... 4384d
Houston, Sam......................... 776, 1242
Hovercraft.......................C123, C126b
Howdy Doody............................ 4414d
Howe, Elias...................................... 892
Howe, Julia Ward .......................... 2176
Howlin' Wolf................................... 2861
Hubble, Edwin ............................... 4226
Hubble Space Telescope.....3384-3388, 3409a
Hudson-Fulton Celebration......372-373
Hudson River School Paintings............................4917-4920
Hudson's General.......................... 2843
Hughes, Charles Evans ................. 1195
Hughes, Langston ......................... 3557
Huguenot-Walloon Tercentenary ...........................614-616
Hulk, The Incredible.......... 4159b, 4159l
Hull, Cordell .................................. 1235
Human Hair ................................ 5802c
Humane Treatment of Animals ...... 1307
Hummingbirds.... 2642-2646, 4857-4858
Humphrey, Hubert ......................... 2189
Hunger, Help End .......................... 2164
Huntington Botanical Gardens ...... 5469
Hurley, Ruby ............................... 4384f
Hurston, Zora Neale ...................... 3748
Huston, John ................................. 4671
HW40............................................. 5328
Hyacinth ............................. 2760, 3900
Hydrangea..................................... 2996

**I Love Lucy ..................... 3187l, 4414b**
Ice Cream Cone............................. 5093
Ice Hockey, History of .........5252-5253
Iceboat .......................................... 2134
Idaho Flag............................ 1675, 4288
Idaho Statehood.................... 896, 2439
Ifill, Gwen ...................................... 5432
IG-11 ............................................. 5572
Iguana............................................ 5108
Iiwi ................................................ 2311
Illinois Flag.......................... 1653, 4289
Illinois Institute of Technology ....... 2020
Illinois Statehood................. 1339, 5274
Immigrants Arrive ........................ 3182i
Improving Education .................. 3191e
Independence Hall ... 1044, 1546, 1622, 1622C, 1625
Independence Spirit, Rise of... 1476-1479
Independence, Skilled Hands for ........................................1717-1720
Indian Centenary ............................ 972
Indian Headdresses.............2501-2505
Indian Head Penny ....................... 1734
Indian Hunting Buffalo.................... 287
Indian Masks, Pacific Northwest ...........................1834-1837
Indian Motorcycle.......................... 4085
Indian Paintbrush .......................... 2647
Indian Pond Lily............................. 2680
Indiana Flag......................... 1651, 4290
Indiana Statehood .............. 1308, 5091
Indiana Territory.............................. 996
Indianapolis ........................... 5004530
Industrial Design, Pioneers of American ...................................... 4546
Inkwell and Quill ........ 1581, 1811, 4496
Inland Marsh.............................. 4710e
Innovation............................5514-5518
Insects & Spiders .......................... 3351
Integrated circuit ......................... 3188j
Int'l Aeronautics Conference....649-650
International Cooperation Year...... 1266
International Geophysical Year...... 1107
International Harvester D-2 truck .. 5101
International Peace Garden........... 2014
International Philatelic Exhibition ... 630, 778, 1075-1076, 1310-1311, 1632, 1757, 2145, 2216-2219
International Polar Year ................ 4123
Int'l Telecommunications Union .... 1274
International Women's Year.......... 1571
International Year of the Child ....... 1772
Int'l Year of the Disabled .............. 1925
International Youth Year........2160-2163
Interphil '76.................................... 1632
Intrepid Balloon ............................ 2032
Inventors............. 889-893, 2055-2058
Inverted Jenny.......................C3a, 4806
Iowa Flag ............................ 1661, 4291
Iowa Statehood ...........942, 3088-3089
Iowa Territory .................................. 838
Iowa-Illinois Memorial Bridge........ 5810
Iris ....................................... 2763, 3903
Irish Immigration........................... 3286
Iron "Betty" Lamp.......................... 1608
Iron Man ............................ 4159h, 4159r
Irving, Washington.......................... 859
Italy, Invasion of........................ 2765f
Ives, Charles ................................. 3164
Ives, Frederic E. ........................... 3063
Iwo Jima ......................................... 929

**Jack-in-the-pulpit ....................... 2650**
Jack-O'-Lanterns ................5137-5140
Jackson, Andrew..................73, 84-85, 85B, 87, 93, 103, 135, 146, 157, 168, 178, 180, 183, 193, 203, 211, 211D, 215, 221, 253, 268, 302, 786, 812, 941, 1209, 1225, 1286, 2216g, 2592
Jackson, Mahalia........................... 3216

SUBJECT INDEX OF REGULAR, COMMEMORATIVE & AIR POST ISSUES 165


Jackson, "Stonewall" .......... 788, 2975s
Jacob's Ladder .......... 2684
James, Henry .......... 5105
James Webb Space Telescope .......... 5720
Jamestown Exposition .......... 328-330
Jamestown Festival .......... 1091
Jamestown, Founding of .......... 329, 4136
Japan .......... 1021, 1158
Japanese Diet .......... 4984
Jay, John .......... 1046
Jazz .......... 4503
Jazz Flourishes .......... 3184k
Jeffers, Robinson .......... 1485
Jefferson Memorial .......... 1510, 1520, 3647-3647A, 4652
Jefferson, Thomas .......... 12, 27-30A, 42, 67, 75-76, 80, 95, 105, 139, 150, 161, 172, 187-188, 197, 209, 228, 260, 275, 310, 324, 561, 590, 641, 667, 678, 807, 842, 851, 1033, 1055, 1278, 1299, 2185, 2216c
Jenny Airplane .......... C1-C3, 3142s
Jenny Invert .......... C3a, 4806
Jet Airliner Silhouette .......... C51-C52, C60-C61, C78, C82
Jitterbug .......... 3186g
Jock Scott .......... 2546
John Bull Locomotive .......... 2364
John Henry .......... 3085
Johnson, Andrew .......... 822, 2217h
Johnson, James P. .......... 2985
Johnson, James Weldon .......... 2371
Johnson, John H. .......... 4624
Johnson, Joshua .......... 3236h
Johnson, Lady Bird .......... 4716f
Johnson, Lyndon B. .......... 1503, 2219i
Johnson, Robert .......... 2857
Johnson, Walter .......... 3408i
Johnson, William H. .......... 4653
Johnston, Joseph E. .......... 2975m
Jolson, Al .......... 2849
Jones, Casey .......... 993
Jones, John Paul .......... 790, 1789-1789B
Jones, Robert Tyre (Bobby) .......... 1933, 3185n
Joplin, Janis .......... 4916
Joplin, Scott .......... 2044
Jordan, Barbara .......... 4565
Joseph, Chief .......... 1364, 2869f, 2870
Joshua Tree .......... 5347
Journalists, American .......... 4248-4252
Juke Box .......... 2911-2912B, 3132
Julia .......... 5394j
Julian, Percy Lavon .......... 2746
Jumbo Jets .......... 3189n
Jumping Spider .......... 3351t
Juniper Berry .......... 5416
Jupiter .......... 2573, 5073
Jupiter Balloon .......... C54
Jupiter Locomotive .......... 5378
Jurassic Park .......... 3191k
Jury Duty .......... 4200
Just, Ernest E. .......... 3058

**K-250 .......... 5575**
Kahanamoku, Duke .......... 3660
Kahlo, Frida .......... 3509
Kaiser Darrin .......... 3932
Kaleidoscope Flowers .......... 4722-4725
Kane, Elisha Kent .......... 2220
Kansas City, Missouri .......... 994
Kansas Flag .......... 1666, 4292
Kansas Hard Winter Wheat .......... 1506
Kansas Statehood .......... 1183, 4493
Kansas Territory .......... 1061
Karloff, Boris .......... 3170, 3171
Karman, Theodore von .......... 2699
Kasebier, Gertrude .......... 3649d
Katzenjammer Kids .......... 3000b
Kearny Expedition .......... 944
Keaton, Buster .......... 2828
Keep in Touch .......... 2274
Keller, Helen, & Anne Sullivan .......... 1824
Kelly, Ellsworth .......... 5382-5391
Kelly, Grace .......... 2749
Kelp Forest .......... 4423
Kenilwoth Park and Aquatic Gardens .......... 5080j
Kennedy, John F. ... 1246, 1287, 2219h, 5175
Kennedy, Robert F. .......... 1770
Kent, Rockwell .......... 3502q
Kentucky Flag .......... 1647, 4293
Kentucky Settlement .......... 1542
Kentucky Statehood .......... 904, 2636
Kermit the Frog .......... 3944a
Kern, Jerome .......... 2110
Kerosene Table Lamp .......... 1611
Kertesz, Andre .......... 3649r
Kestrel, American .......... 2476-2477, 3031, 3044
Key, Francis Scott .......... 962
Keystone Cops .......... 2826
Kickball .......... 5210
Kilauea Volcano .......... 4067
Killer Whale .......... 2508
King, Jr., Dr. Martin Luther .......... 1771, 3188a
King Eider .......... 4992, 4998
King Penguins .......... 2708
Kinglets, Golden-crowned .......... 5126
Kitten .......... 3670, 5111
Kitten and Puppy .......... 2025
Kiwi .......... 4255, 4262
Kline, Franz .......... 3236s
Klondike Gold Rush .......... 3235
Knox, Henry .......... 1851
Knoxville World's Fair .......... 2006-2009
Kooning, Willem de .......... 4444b
Korea, Flag .......... 921
Korean War .......... 3187e
Korean War Veterans Memorial .......... 3803
Kosciuszko, Gen. Tadeusz .......... 734
Kossuth, Lajos .......... 1117-1118
Koyukuk River .......... 5381c
Krazy Kat .......... 3000e
Kukla, Fran and Ollie .......... 4414k
Kutenai Parfleche .......... 3873b
Kwanzaa .......... 3175, 3368, 3548, 3673, 3881, 4119, 4220, 4373, 4434, 4584, 4845, 5141, 5337, 5531, 5737

**L3-37 .......... 5577**
La Florida .......... 4750-4753
Labor Day .......... 1082
Labrador Retriever .......... 5406
Lacemaking .......... 2351-2354
Lady Tremaine from "Cinderella" ... 5215
Ladybeetle, Ladybug .......... 2315, 3351c
Lafayette, Marquis de ... 1010, 1097, 1716
Lagoon Nebula .......... 3386
LaGuardia, Fiorello H. .......... 1397
Lake Erie, Battle of .......... 4805
Lake Shore Drive Buildings, Chicago .......... 3910f
Lake Superior .......... 4047
Lancaster County, Pennsylvania ... C150
Land-Grant Colleges .......... 1065, 1206
Landing of Columbus .......... 118-119, 129
Lange, Dorothea .......... 3649l
Langley, Samuel P. .......... C118
Lanier, Sidney .......... 1446
Large-flowered Trillium .......... 2652
Larsen, Nella .......... 5471
LaSalle Canyon Waterfall, IL .......... 5800k
Lasers .......... 3188k
Lasker, Mary .......... 3432B
Lassie .......... 4414f
Latin American Dishes .......... 5192-5197
Latin Jazz .......... 4349
Latin Music Legends .......... 4497-4501
Laubach, Frank C. .......... 1864
Laurel, Stanley .......... 2562
Lavender .......... 4508, 4514
Law and Order .......... 1343
Le Guin, Ursula K. .......... 5619
Leadbelly (Huddie Ledbetter) .......... 3212
Leatherworker .......... 1720
Lee, Jason .......... 964
Lee, Robert E. .......... 788, 1049, 2975b
Lefty's Deceiver .......... 2548
Legend of Sleepy Hollow .......... 1548
Legends of Baseball .......... 3408
Legends of Hollywood .......... 2967, 3082, 3152, 3226, 3329, 3446, 3523, 3692, 3786, 3876, 3911, 4077, 4197, 4350, 4421, 4461, 4526, 4892, 5012, 5060
Legends of the West .......... 2869-2870
Leigh, Vivien & Gable, Clark .......... 2446
Lejeune, Lt. Gen. John A. .......... 3961
Lemons .......... 5256, 5487
Lend Lease .......... 2559c
Lennon, John .......... 5312-5315
Leo Constellation .......... 3945
Leon, Ponce de .......... 2024
Lerner, Alan Jay & Loewe, Frederick .......... 3346
Letter Carriers .......... 2420
Letters Lift Spirits .......... 1807
Letters Mingle Souls .......... 1530, 1532, 1534, 1536
Letters Preserve Memories .......... 1805
Letters Shape Opinions .......... 1809
Lettuce .......... 5490
Levertov, Denise .......... 4661
Lewis and Clark Expedition .......... 1063, 3854-3856
Lewis, Edmonia .......... 5663
Lewis, Edna .......... 4922
Lewis, John .......... 5801
Lewis, Meriwether .......... 3854, 3855
Lewis, Sinclair .......... 1856
Lexington-Concord .......... 617-619, 1563
Leyendecker, J. C. .......... 3502c
Leyte Gulf, Battle of .......... 2838i
Liberation of Rome and Paris .......... 2838f
Liberty Bell .......... 627, 1518, 1595, 1618, 4125-4128, 4437, C57, C62
Liberty Issue .......... 1030-1031, 1031A, 1032-1041, 1041B, 1042, 1042A, 1043-1044, 1044A, 1045-1054, 1054A, 1055-1059, 1059A
Liberty Ships .......... 2559h, 4550
Libraries, America's .......... 2015
Library of Congress .......... 2004, 3390
Lichtenstein, Roy .......... 5792-5796
Life Magazine .......... 3185c
Life Magnified .......... 5802
Lighthouses .......... 1605, 2470-2474, 2969-2973, 3787-3791, 4146-4150, 4409-4413, 4791-4795, 5621-5625
Lightning Airplane .......... 3142n
Lightning Whelk Shell .......... 2121
Lightyear, Buzz .......... 5709-5712
Li'l Abner .......... 3000q
Lilac .......... 2764
Lili'uokalani Gardens .......... 5156
Lily .......... 1879, 2829
Limner, The Freake .......... 3236b
Limon, Jose .......... 4699
Lincoln Memorial .......... 571, 4075a, 4982
Lincoln, Abraham .......... 77, 85F, 91, 98, 108, 122, 132, 137, 148, 159, 170, 186, 195, 208, 222, 254, 269, 280, 304, 315, 317, 367-369, 555, 584, 600, 635, 661, 672, 821, 906, 978, 1036, 1058, 1113-1116, 1282, 1303, 2217g, 2433, 2975j, 4380-4383, 4860-4861, 5079e, C59
Lincoln-Douglas Debates .......... 1115
Lincoln Premiere .......... 4356
Lindbergh Flight .......... 1710, 3184m, C10
Linum .......... 4757
Lion, New York Public Library .......... 3447, 3769
Lions International .......... 1326
Lippmann, Walter .......... 1849
Literary Arts .......... 1773, 1832, 2047, 2094, 2239, 2350, 2418, 2449, 2538, 2698, 2862, 3002, 3104, 3134, 3221, 3308, 3444, 3659, 3748, 3871, 3904, 4030, 4124, 4223, 4386, 4476, 4545, 4705, 4866, 5003, 5105, 5414, 5619
Little House on the Prairie .......... 2786
Little Mo .......... 5377
Little Nemo in Slumberland .......... 3000c
Little Orphan Annie .......... 3000j
Little Rock Nine .......... 3937d
Little Women .......... 2788
Livingston, Robert R. .......... 323
Lloyd, Harold .......... 2825
Locke, Alain .......... 5474
Lockwood, Belva Ann .......... 2178
Locomobile .......... 2381
Locomotive .......... 114, 125, 1897A, 2226, 2362-2366, 2843-2847
Loesser, Frank .......... 3350
Loewe, Frederick & Lerner, Alan Jay .......... 3346
Loewy, Raymond .......... 4546c
Log Rafts .......... 4710g
Lombardi, Vince .......... 3145, 3147
London, Jack .......... 2182, 2197
Lone Ranger, The .......... 4414m
Long, Dr. Crawford W. .......... 875
Longfellow, Henry W. .......... 864, 4124
Longleaf Pine Forest .......... 3611
Los Angeles Class Submarine .......... 3372, 3374
Louis, Joe .......... 2766
Louisiana Flag .......... 1650, 4294
Louisiana Purchase .......... 1020, 3782
Louisiana Purchase Exposition ... 323-327
Louisiana Purchase, Map of .......... 327
Louisiana Statehood .......... 1197, 4667
Louisiana World Exposition .......... 2086
Love .......... 1475, 1951-1951A, 2072, 2143, 2202, 2248, 2378-2379, 2398, 2440-2441, 2535-2535A, 2536-2537, 2618, 2813-2815, 2948-2949, 2957-2960, 3030, 3123-3124, 3274-3275, 3496-3499, 3551, 3657-3658, 3833, 3898, 3976, 4029, 4122, 4270, 4404-4405, 4450, 4531-4540, 4626, 4741, 4847, 4955-4956, 5036, 5155, 5255, 5339, 5431, 5542, 5660-5661, 5745-5746
Love You, Dad .......... 2270
Love You, Mother .......... 2273
Low, Juliette Gordon .......... 974
Lowell, James Russell .......... 866
Lower Fallsof the Yellowstone River, WY .......... 5800d
Luce, Henry R. .......... 2935
Ludington, Sybil .......... 1559
Lugosi, Bela .......... 3169
Luiseno Basket .......... 3873j
Luna Moth .......... 2293
Lunch Counter Sit-ins .......... 3937c
Lunch Wagon .......... 2464
Lunt, Alfred & Fontanne, Lynn .......... 3287
Luther, Martin .......... 2065
Luxembourg, Flag .......... 912
Lyndhurst .......... 1841
Lyon, Mary .......... 2169
Lyra Constellation .......... 3947

**Maass, Clara .......... 1699**
MacArthur, Gen. Douglas .......... 1424
Macaw Parrot Feather .......... 5802b
MacDonough, Thomas .......... 791
MacDowell, Edward .......... 882
Mach Speeder .......... 5325
Mackinac Bridge .......... 1109, 4438
Maclay Gardens State Park .......... 5468
Madison, Dolley .......... 1822
Madison, Helene .......... 2500
Madison, James .......... 262, 277, 312, 479, 808, 843, 2216d, 2875a, 3545
Magic, The Art of .......... 5301-5306
Magna Carta .......... 1265
Magsaysay, Ramon .......... 1096
Mail Automobile .......... 2437, 2438d
Mail Order Business .......... 1468
Mail Transport - ZIP Code .......... 1511
Mail Wagon .......... 1903
Maine Flag .......... 1655, 4295
Maine Statehood .......... 1391, 5456
Maisy .......... 3990
Makeup .......... 3772e
Mako Shark .......... 5223
Malaria .......... 1194
Malcolm X .......... 3273
Maleficent from "Sleeping Beauty" ... 5218
Mallard .......... 1757b
Mallard Decoy .......... 2139
Mambo .......... 3942
Mammoth Cave .......... 4068
Mammoth, Woolly .......... 3078
Manatee, Florida .......... 3105o
Mancini, Henry .......... 3839
Mann, Horace .......... 869
Mannerheim, Baron Gustaf Emil .......... 1165-1166
Mantle, Mickey .......... 4083
Map of Sea Surface Temperatures ... 4893
Map, U.S. .......... C7-C9
Marathon .......... 3067
Marblehead Lighthouse .......... 2972
March on Washington .......... 3937h, 4804
Marciano, Rocky .......... 3187k
Mariachi .......... 5703-5707
Mariana Islands .......... 2804
Marigold .......... 2832
Marin, John .......... 4748b
Marin, Luis, Munoz .......... 2173
Marine Corps Reserve .......... 1315
Marine One .......... 4145
Mariner 10 .......... 1557
Marines .......... 3961-3964
Marines, Continental .......... 1567
Marines, World War II .......... 929
Maris, Roger .......... 3188n
Marquette on the Mississippi .......... 285
Marquette, Jacques .......... 1356
Mars .......... 2572, 5072

166 SUBJECT INDEX OF REGULAR, COMMEMORATIVE & AIR POST ISSUES


Mars Pathfinder and Sojourner ..... 3178
Marsh-Billings-Rockefeller National Historic Park ..... 5080c
Marsh Marigold ..... 2658
Marshall, George C. ..... 1289
Marshall Islands ..... 2507
Marshall, John ..... 263, 278, 313, 480, 1050, 2415
Marshall Plan ..... 3141
Marshall, Thurgood3746
Martin, Roberta ..... 3217
Marvel Comics Superheroes ..... 4159
Maryland Flag ..... 1639, 4296
Maryland Statehood ..... 2342
Maryland Tercentenary ..... 736
Masaryk, Thomas G. ..... 1147-1148
Mason, George ..... 1858
Massachusetts Bay Colony ..... 682
Massachusetts Flag ..... 1638, 4297
Massachusetts Statehood ..... 2341
Masters, Edgar Lee ..... 1405
Masters of American Photography ..... 3649
Masterson, Bat ..... 2869h, 2870
Mastodon ..... 3079
Matagorda Island Lighthouse, TX... 4409
Mathematics Education ..... 5279
Mathewson, Christy ..... 3408c
Mauldin, Bill ..... 4445
Mayer, Maria Goeppert ..... 4543
Mayflower ..... 548, 5524
Matzeliger, Jan ..... 2567
Mayo, Drs. William and Charles ..... 1251
Mazzei, Philip ..... C98-C98A
McClintock, Barbara ..... 3906
McCloy, Lt. Commander John ..... 4442
McCormack, John ..... 2090
McCormick, Cyrus Hall ..... 891
McDaniel, Hattie ..... 3996
McDowell, Dr. Ephraim ..... 1138
McKinley, William.... 326, 559, 588, 639, 665, 676, 829, 2218f
McLoughlin, John ..... 964
McMahon, Brien ..... 1200
McMein, Neysa ..... 3502m
McPhatter, Clyde ..... 2726, 2733
McQueen's Jupiter ..... 2844
Mead, Margaret ..... 3184g
Meadow Beauty ..... 2649
Meany, George ..... 2848
Medal of Honor... 2045, 4822-4823, 4988
Medical Imaging ..... 3189o
Medusa ..... 3443
Mellon, Andrew W. ..... 1072
Melville, Herman ..... 2094
Mendez v. Westminster ..... 4201
Mendoza, Lydia ..... 4786
Mentoring a Child ..... 3556
Merced River ..... 5381a
Mercer, Johnny ..... 3101
Merchant Marine ..... 939, 4548-4551
Mercury ..... 2568, 5069
Mercury Cougar XR-7 GT ..... 5718
Merengue3939
Mergenthaler, Ottmar ..... 3062
Merman, Ethel ..... 2853
Mesa Verde ..... 743, 759
Message Monsters ..... 5636-5639
Messenger Spacecraft ..... 4528
Metropolitan Opera ..... 2054
Mexican Hat ..... 2688
Mexican Independence ..... 1157
Michael, Moina ..... 977
Micheaux, Oscar ..... 4464
Michener, James A. ..... 3427A
Michigan Centenary ..... 775
Michigan Flag ..... 1658, 4298
Michigan State College ..... 1065
Michigan Statehood ..... 2246
Micronesia, Federated States of ... 2506
Midway, Battle of ..... 2697g
Migratory Bird Treaty ..... 1306
Mighty Casey ..... 3083
Mighty Mississippi ..... 5698
Military Dog ..... 4606
Military Medics ..... 2765b
Military Services Bicentenary ... 1565-1568
Military Uniforms ..... 1565-1568
Military Working Dogs ..... 5405-5408
Militia, American ..... 1568
Milk, Harvey ..... 4906
Milk Wagon ..... 2253
Milking Devon Cow ..... 5585
Millay, Edna St. Vincent ..... 1926
Miller, Doris ..... 4443
Miller, Glenn ..... 3098
Millikan, Robert ..... 1866
Mimbres Bowl ..... 3873a
Minerals ..... 1538-1541, 2700-2703
Mingus, Charles ..... 2989
Mining Prospector ..... 291
Minnesota Flag ..... 1664, 4299
Minnesota Statehood ..... 1106, 4266
Minnesota Territory ..... 981
Minute Man, The ..... 619
Miranda, Carmen ..... 4498
Miss Piggy ..... 3944d
Mississippi Flag ..... 1652, 4300
Mississippi River ..... 5698
Mississippi River Delta ..... 4058
Mississippi Statehood ..... 1337, 5190
Mississippi Territory ..... 955
Mississippi-Missouri River System ... 4065
Mississippian Effigy ..... 3873f
Missouri Flag ..... 1656, 4301
Missouri River ..... 5381g
Missouri Statehood ..... 1426, 5626
Mister Rogers ..... 5275
Mitchell, Joan ..... 4444h
Mitchell, Margaret ..... 2168
Mitchell, Gen. William "Billy" L. ..... 3330
Mix, Tom ..... 4447
Mobile, Battle of ..... 1826
Mobile Bay, Battle of ..... 4910
Mockingbird ..... 2330
Model B Airplane ..... 3142b
Model T Ford ..... 3182a
Modern Art ..... 4748
Mold Spores ..... 5802q
Moloka'i ..... 4034
Monarch Butterfly.... 2287, 3351k, 4462
Monarch Caterpillar ..... 3351j
Monday Night Football ..... 3189 l
Monitor and Virginia, Battle of ..... 2975a
Monk, Thelonious ..... 2990
Monmouth, Battle of ..... 646
Monopoly Game ..... 3185o
Monroe, James ... 325, 562, 591, 603, 642, 668, 679, 810, 845, 1038, 1105, 2216e
Monroe, Marilyn ..... 2967
Monsters, Message ..... 5636-5639
Montana Flag ..... 1673, 4304
Montana Statehood ..... 858, 2401
Montauk Point Lighthouse, NY ..... 5621
Montgomery, Ala. Bus Boycott ... 3937e
Monticello ..... 1047
Monument Valley ..... 5666
Moon ..... 2571, 5058
Moon Landing ..... 2419, 2841-2842, 3188c, 3413, C76
Moon Rover ..... 1435, C124, C126c
Moore, John Bassett ..... 1295
Moore, Marianne ..... 2449
Moose ..... 1757e, 1887, 2298
Moran, Thomas ..... 3236l, 4917
More than Meets the Eye ..... 5614
Morgan Horse ..... 2156
Morocco-U.S. Diplomatic Relations ..... 2349
Morrill, Justin S. ..... 2941
Morris Island Lighthouse, SC ..... 3789
Morris Township School, ND ..... 1606
Morrison, George ..... 5688-5692
Morrison, Toni ..... 5757
Morse, Samuel F.B. ..... 890
Morton, Jelly Roll ..... 2986
Moses, (Grandma) Anna Mary Robertson ..... 1370
Moses, Horace ..... 2095
Moss Campion ..... 2686
Moss Leaves ..... 5802d
Moth Antenna ..... 5802h
Moth Wing Scales ..... 5802l
Mother Teresa ..... 4475
Mothers of America ..... 737-738, 754
Motherwell, Robert ..... 4444g
Motion Pictures ..... 926
Motorcycle ..... 1899, 4085-4088
Mott, Lucretia ..... 959
Mount McKinley ..... 1454, C137
Mount Rainier National Park... 742, 758, 770, 5080b
Mount Rushmore.... 1011, 2523, 2523A, 4268, C88
Mount Vernon ..... 785, 1032
Mount Wai'ale'ale ..... 4066
Mount Washington ..... 4053
Mountain ..... 2903-2904B
Mountain Bluebird ..... 4883
Mountain Flora ..... 5672-5679
Mountain Goat ..... 2323
Mountain Lion ..... 2292
Mouse ..... 5117
Mouse Brain Neurons ..... 5802j
Movies Go 3-D ..... 3187o
Muddler Minnow ..... 2549
Muir, John ..... 1245, 3182j
Mule Deer ..... 2294
Mulefoot Hog ..... 5583
Muller-Munk, Peter ..... 4546a
Mummy, The ..... 3171
Munoz Marin, Luis ..... 2173
Muppets ..... 3944a-3944j
Murphy, Second Lt. Audie L. ..... 3396
Murphy, Gerald ..... 4748j
Murphy, Robert D. ..... 4076a
Murrow, Edward R. ..... 2812
Muscle Cars ..... 4743-4747
Mushroom Gills ..... 5802n
Music (films) ..... 3772d
Music Icons ..... 4786, 4789, 4807, 4880, 4916, 5009, 5059, 5312-5315, 5371, 5708
Muskellunge ..... 2205
Mustang Airplane ..... 3142a
Muybridge, Eadweard ..... 3061
My Fair Lady ..... 2770
Mystery Message ..... 5614

**Nagurski, Bronko ..... 3808**
Naismith-Basketball ..... 1189
Nancy ..... 3000o
Narragansett Turkey ..... 5586
Nash Healey ..... 3934
Nash, Ogden ..... 3659
Nassau Hall ..... 1083
Nation of Readers ..... 2106
National Academy of Science ..... 1237
National Archives ..... 2081
National Capital Sesquicentennial ..... 989-992
National Gallery of Art ..... 3910g
National Grange ..... 1323
National Guard ..... 1017
National Letter Writing Week 1805-1810
National Marine Sanctuaries ..... 5713
National Museum of African American History and Culture ..... 5251
National Park Service ..... 1314, 5080
National Parks ..... 740-749, 756-765, 769-770, 1448-1454, C84
National Postal Museum ..... 2779-2782
National Recovery Administration ... 732
National Stamp Exhibition ..... 735
National World War II Memorial ..... 3862
Native American Culture.... 2869e, 2870
NATO ..... 1008, 1127, 3354
Natural History Museum ..... 1387-1390
Navajo Blankets ..... 2235-2238
Navajo Necklace ..... 3750-3753, 3758B
Navajo Weaving ..... 3873h
Naval Aviation ..... 1185
Naval Review ..... 1091
Navesink Twin Lighthouses, NJ ..... 5622
Navigation, Lake ..... 294
Navigation, Ocean ..... 299
Navy, Continental ..... 1566
Navy Cross ..... 5066
Navy Medal of Honor ..... 4822
Navy, U.S. ..... 790-794, 935
Nebraska Flag ..... 1669, 4305
Nebraska Statehood ..... 1328, 5179
Nebraska Territory ..... 1060
Negro Leagues Baseball ..... 4465-4466
Neptune ..... 2576, 5076
Netherlands ..... 2003
Netherlands, Flag ..... 913
Neumann, John von ..... 3908
Neuter and Spay ..... 3670-3671
Nevada Fall, CA ..... 5800b
Nevada Flag ..... 1668, 4306
Nevada Settlement ..... 999
Nevada Statehood ..... 1248, 4907
Nevelson, Louise ..... 3379-3383
Nevers, Ernie ..... 3809
Nevin, Ethelbert ..... 883
New Baseball Records ..... 3191a
New Deal ..... 3185e
New England Neptune Shell ..... 2119
New Guinea, Allied Recapture of....2838a
New Hampshire ..... 1068
New Hampshire Flag ..... 1641, 4307
New Hampshire Statehood ..... 2344
New Horizons Probe ..... 5078
New Jersey Flag ..... 1635, 4308
New Jersey Statehood ..... 2338
New Jersey Tercentenary ..... 1247
New London Harbor Lighthouse, CT ..... 4795
New Mexico Flag ..... 1679, 4309
New Mexico Statehood ..... 1191, 4591
New Netherland ..... 614
New Orleans, 1815 Battle of...1261, 4952
New Orleans, 1862 Battle of ..... 4664
New Orleans Steamboat ..... 2407
New River Gorge Bridge ..... 4511
New Sweden Settlement ..... C117
New York City ..... 1027, C38
New York Coliseum ..... 1076
New York Flag ..... 1643, 4310
New York Skyline & Statue of Liberty ..... C35
New York Statehood ..... 2346
New York Stock Exchange ..... 2630
New York University Library ..... 1928
New York World's Fair ..... 853, 1244
Newburgh, New York ..... 727
Newman, Alfred ..... 3343
Newman, Barnett ..... 4444j
Newman, Paul ..... 5020
Newspaper Boys ..... 1015
Niagara Falls, NY ..... 568, 699, 5800g, C133
Nimitz, Chester M. ..... 1869
Nine-Mile Prairie ..... C136
Nineteenth Amendment ..... 3184e
Niobrara River ..... 5381d
Nixon, Richard ..... 2955
No. 119 Locomotive ..... 5380
Nobel Prize ..... 3504
Noguchi, Isamu ..... 3857-3861
Non-Denominated ..... 1735-1736, 1743, 1818-1820, 1946-1948, 2111-2113, 2277, 2279, 2282, 2517-2522, 2602-2604, 2877-2893, 2902, 2902B, 2903-2904, 2904A, 2904B, 2905-2912, 2912A, 2912B, 2948-2949, 3207, 3207A, 3208, 3208A, 3228-3229, 3257-3258, 3260, 3264-3271, 3447-3465, 3496, 3520, 3522
Norfolk Botanical Garden ..... 5470
Norris, George W. ..... 1184
Norse-American ..... 620, 621
North African Invasion ..... 2697j
North Carolina Flag ..... 1644, 4311
North Carolina Statehood ..... 2347
North Dakota Flag ..... 1671, 4312
North Dakota Statehood ..... 858, 2403
Northeast Deciduous Forest ..... 3899
Northern Goshawk ..... 4608
Northern Harrier ..... 4612
Northern Mariana Islands, Commonwealth of the ..... 2804
Northern Marianas Flag ..... 4313
Northwest Ordinance ..... 795
Northwest Territory ..... 837
Norway, Flag ..... 911
Noyes, Eliot ..... 4546j
NRA ..... 732
Numismatics ..... 2558
Nursing ..... 1190
Nuthatches, Red-breasted ..... 5129

**O Beautiful ..... 5298**
Oak Leaf Surface ..... 5802t
Oakley, Annie ..... 2869d, 2870
Ocelot ..... 3105e
Ochoa, Severo ..... 4544
Ochs, Adolph S. ..... 1700
O'Connor, Flannery ..... 5003
Off the Florida Keys, Reef ..... 4042
Oglethorpe, Gen. James Edward ..... 726
Ohi'a Lehua ..... 2669
Ohio Class Submarine ..... 3375
Ohio Flag ..... 1649, 4314
Ohio River Canalization ..... 681
Ohio Statehood ..... 1018, 3773
Oil Wagon ..... 2130
O'Keeffe, Georgia ..... 3069, 4748e
Okefenokee Swamp ..... C142
Oklahoma! (musical) ..... 2722, 2769
Oklahoma Flag ..... 1678, 4315

SUBJECT INDEX OF REGULAR, COMMEMORATIVE & AIR POST ISSUES 167


Oklahoma Statehood .......... 1092, 4121
Old Cape Henry Lighthouse, VA.... 3787
Old Faithful, Yellowstone........ 744, 760, 1453, 4379
Old Glory ............................. 3776-3780
Old North Church, Boston............ 1603
Olivia.............................................. 3993
Olmsted, Frederick Law ............... 3338
Olympics ...............716, 718-719, 1146, 1460-1462, 1695-1698, 1790-1798, 1795A-1798A, 2048-2051, 2067-2070, 2082-2085, 2369, 2380, 2528, 2496-2500, 2539-2542, 2553-2557, 2611-2615, 2619, 2637-2641, 2807-2811, 3068, 3087, 3552-3555, 3863, 3995, 4334, 4436, C85, C97, C101-C112
Omnibus ............................ 1897, 2225
O'Neill, Eugene.................1294, 1305C
O'Neill, Rose........................... 3502i
Ontonagon River ....................... 5381k
Opisthias ................................... 3136h
Orange............................... 3492, 3494
Orange-tip Butterfly...................... 1715
Orchids ................................2076-2079
Orchids, Wild ........................5435-5444
Oregano............................. 4505, 4516
Oregon Flag......................... 1665, 4316
Oregon Statehood......... 1124, 4376
Oregon Territory....................... 783, 964
Oregon Trail2 ................................. 747
Organ & Tissue Donation.............. 3227
Organized Labor............................ 1831
Orion Constellation....................... 3946
Oriskany, Battle of ......................... 1722
Ormandy, Eugene.......................... 3161
Ornate Box Turtle .......................... 3818
Ornate Chorus Frog....................... 3817
Ornithomimus ............................. 3136n
Oroville Dam.................................. 4056
Oscar the Grouch ....................... 5394g
OSIRIS-REx Probe ........................ 5820
Osprey ............................. 2291, 4611
Osteopathic Medicine .................. 1469
O'Sullivan, Timothy H. ............... 3649b
Ott, Mel......................................... 4082
Otters in Snow........................5648-5651
Ouimet, Francis ............................ 2377
Overland Mail ........... 1120, 2869t, 2870
Overrun Countries ....................909-921
Ovington, Mary White.................. 4384a
Owatonna, Minnesota Bank.......... 1931
Owens, Jesse .................... 2496, 3185j
Owl .........1760-1763, 2285, 3290, 5824
Owney, the Postal Dog.................. 4547
Owyhee River ............................. 5381b
Ozzie and Harriet........................ 4414q

**P-47 Thunderbolt......................... 3919**
P-51s Escorting B-17s ................ 2838b
P-80 Shooting Star......................... 3921
Pacific Calico Scallop.......... 5164, 5170
Pacific Calypso Orchid ................. 2079
Pacific Coast Rain Forest.............. 3378
Pacific Coral Reef ......................... 3831
Pacific Crest Trail........................... 4043
Pacific Dogwood ........................... 3197
Pacific .......... 973130-3131, 3139-3140
Packard ........................................ 2384
Paderewski, Ignacy Jan........1159-1160
Paige, Satchel ............................ 3408p
Paine, Thomas............................... 1292
Painted Bunting............................. 4885
Painted Fern ............. 4852, 4878, 4976
Palace of Fine Arts, San Francisco............................ 1930, 5667
Palace of the Governors, Santa Fe ........................1031A, 1054A
Palaeosaniwa ............................... 3136l
Palau............................................. 2999
Palmer, Arnold .............................. 5455
Palmer, Nathaniel.......................... 2386
Palomar Observatory....................... 966
Pan American Games...........2247, C56
Pan American Union................895, C34
Pan-American Exposition.........294-299
Pan-American Exposition, Cent. ... 3505
Panama Canal ..................... 856, 3183f
Panama Canal, Pedro Miguel Locks........................................ 398, 402
Panama-Pacific Exposition ......397-404
Panara, Robert .............................. 5191
Pansy............................................ 3027
Panther, Florida ..... 3105m, 4137, 4139, 4141, 4142
Papanicolaou, Dr. George ............. 1754
Papaya ................................ 4256, 4258
Parakeets ............................ 3233, 5124
Parasaurolophus ......................... 3136o
Parent Teacher Association........... 1463
Parker, Al .................................... 3502f
Parker, Charlie .............................. 2987
Parker, Dorothy............................. 2698
Parkman, Francis................ 1281, 1297
Parks, Rosa .................................. 4742
Parrish, Maxfield......................... 3502b
Parrot ............................................ 5115
Parrot, Thick-Billed..................... 3105b
Partridge, Alden............................ 1854
Pasqueflower............ 2676, 5675, 5676
Passionflower ................................ 2674
Patriotic Banner..........4157-4158, 4385
Patriotic Spiral .......................5130-5131
Patriotic Star................................. 4749
Patriotic Waves....................4953-4954
Patrol Wagon ................................ 2258
Patton, Gen. George S., Jr. .......... 1026
Paul, Alice..................................... 2943
Paul Bunyan ................................. 3084
Pauling, Linus ............................... 4225
Payne, Ethel L. ............................. 3667
PBY Catalina ................................ 3916
Peace Bridge ................................ 1721
Peace Corps...................... 1447, 3188f
Peace of 1783 ........................ 727, 752
Peace Rose ................................... 5280
Peace Symbol ............................ 3188m
Peacetime Draft ......................... 2559b
Peach ....................... 2487, 2493, 2495
Peale, Rembrandt ....................... 3236d
Peanuts Comic Strip Characters.....3507, 5021-5030, 5726
Pear .....2488, 2494, 2495A, 5039, 5178
Pearl Harbor ................................ 2559i
Peary, Robert E., & Matthew Henson ......................................... 2223
Peashooter Airplane.................... 3142o
Peck, Gregory............................... 4526
Pecos Bill...................................... 3086
Pegasus Constellation.................. 3948
Pelican Island National Wildlife Refuge .......................................... 3774
Pember, Phoebe.......................... 2975r
Penguins, Emperor..............4989-4990
Penn, William.................................. 724
Pennsylvania Academy ....... 1064, 1840
Pennsylvania Flag............... 1634, 4317
Pennsylvania State University....... 1065
Pennsylvania Statehood............... 2337
Pennsylvania Toleware ... 1775-1778, 3612
Pepper, Claude............................. 3426
Peppers, Chili ........... 4003, 4012, 4013
Peregrine Falcon ................ 4057, 4609
Performing Arts .........1755-1756, 1801, 1803, 2012, 2088, 2090, 2110, 2211, 2250, 2411, 2550
Periodical Cicada ........................ 3351r
Perkins, Frances............................ 1821
Perry, Commodore Matthew C. .... 1021
Perry, Commodore O.H. ........ 144, 155, 166, 177, 191, 202, 218, 229, 261-261A, 276-276A
Perry Mason .............................. 4414n
Pershing, Gen. John J. ................ 1214
Persistent Trillium ......................... 1783
Personal Computers.................... 3190n
Petersburg, Battle of .................... 4910
Petrified Wood .............................. 1538
Petroleum Industry ........................ 1134
Pets ..................................... 5106-5125
Phantom of the Opera, The........... 3168
Pharmacy ..................................... 1473
Pheasant ........2283, 3050-3051A, 3055
Phil Silvers Show, The ................. 4414l
Philadelphia Exchange .................. 1782
Phillips, Ammi ............................ 3236c
Phillips, Coles ............................. 3502e
Phlox ............................................ 4754
Phoenix Steamboat....................... 2406
Photography........................ 1758, 3649
Physical Fitness............................ 2043
Physical Fitness-Sokol .................. 1262
Piaf, Edith ..................................... 4692
Piano ......................................... 1615C
Pickett, Bill........................ 2869g, 2870
Pickup Trucks ........................5101-5104
Pierce, Franklin ..................... 819, 2217e
Pierce-Arrow.................................. 2382
Piggott, Arkansas Post Office Mural ........................................... 5372
Pika............................................... 2319
Pilgrim Tercentenary.................548-550
Pilgrims, Landing of the......... 549, 1420
Pillar Coral .......................... 5365, 5367
Pinatas.................................5812-5815
Pine Cone ........................... 1257, 2491
Pinks ............................................ 4760
Pioneer 10 ......................... 1556, 3189i
Pioneers of American Industrial Design .......................................... 4546
Piper, William ..................... C129, C132
Piping Plover ............................. 3105n
Pitcher, Molly ................................. 646
Pitts, Zasu ..................................... 2824
Pittsburgh Steelers ..................... 3189e
Plains Prickly Pear......................... 2685
Plan for Better Cities ..................... 1333
Plane and Globes ...................C89-C90
Plastic Man..................... 4084g, 4084q
Plath, Sylvia.................................. 4658
Pledge of Allegiance.........2594, 2594B
Ploesti Refineries, Bombing of.... 2765d
Plover, Piping .............................. 3105n
Plums............................................ 5484
Pluto ................................. 2577, 5077
Plymouth Hemi Barracuda ........... 4747
Pocahontas ..................................... 330
Poe, Edgar Allan..................... 986, 4377
Poets .................. 864-868, 4654-4663
Point Judith Lighthouse, RI ........... 4794
Point of Rocks Station, MD........... 5758
Poinsettia...................................... 5311
Poland, Flag ................................... 909
Polar Bear....... 1429, 1885, 3291, 4387, 4389
Polio ................................. 1087, 3187a
Polish Millennium ......................... 1313
Polk, George................................. 4250
Polk, James K. ......... 816, 2217b, 2587
Pollination...........................4153-4156
Pollock, Jackson ............ 3186h, 4444d
Polo Grounds ................................ 3514
Pomegranate...................... 4253, 4260
Pons, Lily....................................... 3154
Ponselle, Rosa.............................. 3157
Pontiac GTO ................................. 4744
Pontiac Safari ............................... 4355
Pony Cars ...........................5715-5719
Pony Express........................ 894, 1154
Poor, Salem .................................. 1560
Popcorn Wagon............................. 2261
Popeye ........................................ 3000k
Poppy, Memorial ............................ 977
Porgy & Bess ................................ 2768
Porky Pig ............................3534-3535
Porter, Cole................................... 2550
Porter, David D. .............................. 792
Porter, Katherine Anne ................. 4030
Portland Head Lighthouse, ME ..... 4791
Portsmouth Harbor Lighthouse, NH............................. 4792
Post Horse & Rider................. 113, 124
Post, Emily.................................. 3182f
Post Office Murals...............5372-5375
Post, Wiley..............................C95-C96
Postal Service Bicentenary....1572-1575
Postal Service Emblem ................. 1396
Postal Service Employees....1489-1498
Post-Traumatic Stress Disorder ........B7
Poultry Industry .............................. 968
POW/MIA...................................... 2966
Powell, John Wesley...................... 1374
Powered Flight ......................3783, C47
PrairieCrab Apple ......................... 3196
Preserve Wetlands........................ 2092
Presidential Issue ..... 803-834, 839-851
Presidential Libraries .................... 3930
Presidents of the United States ...............................2216-2219
Presley, Elvis.... 2721, 2724, 2731, 5009
Priestley, Joseph .......................... 2038
Primrose ....................................... 4763
Prince Valiant.............................. 3000s
Prinsesse Tam-Tam (movie).......... 4338
Printing ........................................... 857
Printing Press, Early American ...... 1593
Prisoners of War/Missing in Action ............................... 1422, 2966
Professional Management............ 1920
Prohibition Enforced.................... 3184c
Project Mercury ............................ 1193
Prominent Americans Issue .... 1278-1283, 1283B, 1284-1286, 1286A, 1287-1288, 1288B, 1289-1295, 1297-1299, 1303, 1304, 1304C, 1305, 1305E, 1305C, 1393, 1393D, 1394-1402
Pronghorn................. 1889, 2313, 4048
Propeller and Radiator....................C4
Prostate Cancer Awareness.......... 3315
Protect Pollinators ................5228-5232
P.S. Write Soon.......... 1806, 1808, 1810
PTA .............................................. 1463
Pteranodon................................... 2423
PTSD, Healing ..................................B7
Public Education ........................... 2159
Pueblo Pottery......................1706-1709
Puente, Tito .................................. 4497
Puerto Rico Elections ..................... 983
Puerto Rico Flag........................... 4318
Puerto Rico Territory....................... 801
Puffins, Tufted ....................4737-4737A
Pulaski, Gen. Casimir ..................... 690
Pulitzer, Joseph ............................. 946
Puller, Lt. Gen. Lewis B. ............... 3962
Puma ............................................ 1881
Pumpkinseed Sunfish.................... 2481
Puppy ................................ 3671, 5106
Puppy and Kitten........................... 2025
Pure Food and Drug Act.............. 3182f
Purple Heart ...........3784-3784A, 4032, 4164, 4263-4264, 4390, 4529, 4704, 5035, 5419
Purple Passion ............................. 5321
Pushcart ....................................... 2133
Pyle, Ernie T. ................................ 1398
Pyle, Howard .............................. 3502h

**Quaking Aspen ........................... 4072**
Quarter Horse............................... 2155
Queen Conch ...................... 5163, 5169
Queen from "Snow White and the Seven Dwarves" ..................... 5213
Queen of Hearts from "Alice in Wonderland"................................ 5216
Quill and Inkwell ........................... 4496
Quilts ............... 1745-1748, 3524-3527, 4089-4098, 5098-5099
Quimby, Harriet ...........................C128

**R2-D2........................................... 5574**
Rabbit.....3272, 5112, 5544-5545, 5823
Raccoon ........................... 1757h, 2331
Racing Car.................................... 2262
Radio Entertains America............ 3184i
Railroad Conductor's Lantern ....... 1612
Railroad Engineers ......................... 993
Railroad Mail Car.......................... 2265
Railroad Roundhouse................ 4710m
Railroad Stations, Historic.... 5758-5762
Railroad, Transcontinental ............. 922, 5378-5380
Rainbow Bridge ............................ 4060
Rainey, Ma.................................... 2859
Ramirez, Martin ...................4968-4972
Rand, Ayn ..................................... 3308
Randolph, Asa Philip .................... 2402
Range Conservation ..................... 1176
Raspberries ..... 3295, 3300, 3303, 3407
Ration Coupons.......................... 2697b
Raven and Cat .............................. 5420
Raven Story .................................. 5620
Rawlings, Marjorie Kinnan............ 4223
Ray, Man......................... 3649i, 4748f
Rayburn, Sam ............................... 1202
Readers, Nation of......................... 2106
Reagan, Nancy ............................. 5702
Reagan, Ronald............ 3897, 4078, 4494
Rebecca Everingham Riverboat.... 3094
Rebecca of Sunnybrook Farm....... 2785
Recognizing Deafness................... 2783
Recovering Species.................... 3191g
Red Ball Express ........................ 2838h
Red Blood Cells.......................... 5802a
Red Cloud ..................................... 2175
Red Cross ... 702, 967, 1016, 1239, 1910
Red Fox...1757g, 2335, 3036, 5742-5743
Red Knot ............................ 4991, 4997
Red Maid ...................................... 2692
Red Skelton Show, The ............. 4414c
Red-breasted Nuthatches ............. 5129
Red-bellied Woodpecker............... 5319
Red-headed Woodpecker ... 3032, 3045

Red-winged Blackbird 2303
Redding, Otis 2728, 2735
Redhead Decoy 2141
Redwood Forest 4378
Reed, Dr. Walter 877
Register and Vote 1249, 1344
Religious Freedom 1099
Remember The Maine 3192
Remington, Frederic... 888, 1187, 1934, 3502p
Repeal of the Stamp Act 5064
Reptiles, Age of 1390
Reptiles and Amphibians 3814-3818
Rescue Dog 4607
Residential Subdivision 4710k
Restaurationen, sloop 620
Retarded Children 1549
Reticulate Collared Lizard 3816
Reticulated Helmet Shell 2118
Return to Space 3191h
Reuter, Ernst 1136-1137
Revel, Bernard 2193
Revere, Paul 1048, 1059A
Rhead, Frederick Hurten 4546b
Rhode Island Flag 1645, 4319
Rhode Island Statehood 2348
Rhode Island Tercentenary 777
Rhodochrosite 1541
Ribault, Jan, Monument to 616
Richmond, VA Main Street Station 5759
Rickenbacker, Eddie 2998
Ride, Sally 5283
Rigor Motor 5323
Riley, James Whitcomb 868
Ring Nebula 3385
Ringtail 2302
Rio Grande C134
Rio Grande Blankets 3926-3929
Rise of Spirit of Independence 1476-1479
River Otter 2314
Riverboats 3091-3095
Rivers 5381
Road Runner & Wile E. Coyote 3391-3392
Roanoke Voyages 2093
Robeson, Paul 3834
Robie House 3182o
Robinson, Edward G. 3446
Robinson, Jackie... 2016, 3186c, 3408a
Robinson, Sugar Ray 4020
Robotics 5517
Robt. E. Lee Riverboat 3091
Rocket-Bye-Baby 5322
Rockne, Knute 2376
Rock 'n Roll 3187m
Rockville, Maryland Post Office Mural 5374
Rockwell, Norman 2839-2840, 3502s
Rocky Mountains 4062
Rodger Dodger 5324
Rodgers, Jimmie 1755
Rodgers, Richard & Hammerstein II, Oscar 3348
Roethke, Theodore 4663
Rogers, Fred 5275
Rogers, Roy 4446
Rogers, Will 975, 1801
Rohde, Gilbert 4546l
Rojas-Lombardi, Felipe 4923
Roosevelt, Eleanor 1236, 2105, 3185d
Roosevelt, Franklin D. 930-933, 1284, 1298, 1305, 1950, 2219d, 2559d, 3185a
Roosevelt, Theodore 557, 586, 602, 637, 663, 674, 830, 1039, 2218g, 3182b
Root Beer Float 5096
Roseate Spoonbill 2308
Rosebud Orchid 2670
Rose-breasted Grosbeak 4889
Roses 1737, 1876, 2378-2379, 2490, 2492, 2833, 3049, 3052E, 3054, 4520, 4959, 5280
Rosita 5394e
Ross, Betsy 1004
Rotary International 1066
Rothko, Mark 3236t, 4444c
Rough Riders 973
Round-lobed Hepatica 2677
Rowlf the Dog 3944i
Royal Poinciana 3311
Royal Wulff 2545
Rube Goldberg 3000f
Ruby-throated Hummingbird 2642
Rudbeckia 2997
Rudolph, Wilma 3422, 3436
Rue Anemone 2694
Rufous Hummingbird 2645
Rural America 1504-1506
Rural Electrification Administration 2144
Rural Free Delivery 3090
Rush Lamp and Candle Holder 1610
Rushing, Jimmy 2858
Russell, Charles M. 1243
Russell, Richard 1853
Ruth, Babe 2046, 3184a, 3408h

**S Class Submarine 3373**
Saber-tooth Cat 3080
Sabin, Dr. Albert 3435
Sabine Pass Lighthouse, LA 4410
Sacagawea 2869s, 2870
Saddlebred Horse 2157
Sagamore Hil l1023
Sage 4509, 4515
Saguaro 1945, 4035
Sailboats 5747-5750
Saint-Gaudens, Augustus 886
St. George Reef Lighthouse, CA 4150
St. John, VI C145
St. Joseph Lighthouse 2970
St. Lawrence Seaway 1131, 2091
St. Louis World's Fair 3182e
Saipan, Battle of 2838g
Salazar, Ruben 4251
Salk, Dr. Jonas 3428
Salomon, Haym 1561
Salsa 3940
Salt Evaporation Ponds 4710f
Salvation Army 1267
Sam the Eagle 3944c
Sampson, Adm. William T. 793
San Bernardino, CA Santa Fe Station 5760
San Clemente Island Goat 5589
San Francisco Bay, Discovery of 400-400A, 404
San Francisco Garter Snake 3105k
San Francisco Maritime National Historic Park 5080g
San Francisco-Oakland Bay Bridge C36
San Francisco 49ers 3190c
San Ildefonso Pottery 1707
San Juan 1437
San Martin, Jose de 1125-1126
San Xavier del Bac Mission 1443
Sanchez, Emilio, Paintings by 5594-5597
Sancocho 5194
Sand Island Lighthouse, AL 4412
Sandburg, Carl 1731
Sandy Hook Lighthouse, NJ 1605
Saratoga, Surrender at 1728, 2590
Saroyan, William 2538
Satellite Launched 3187d
Saturn 2574, 5074
Save Our Air, Cities, Soil, Water 1410-1413
Save Vanishing Species B4
Savings & Loan 1911
Savings Bonds, 50th Anniv. 2534
Savings Bonds-Servicemen 1320
Saw-whet Owl 1761
Sawyer, Tom 1470
Saxhorns 1614
Scar from "The Lion King" 5222
Scarlet Kingsnake 3814
Scarlet Tanager 2306, 4888
Scenic American Landscapes Issue C133-C148
Schaus Swallowtail Butterfly 3105f
Schley, Adm. Winfield S. 794
Schomburg, Arturo 5472
School Bus 2123
School Bus and School 5740-5741
Schurz, Carl 1847
Science Education 5276
Science & Industry 2031
Science, National Academy of 1237
Scientists 874-878, 4224-4227, 4541-4544
Scooby-Doo 5299
Scorpionfly 3351s
Scott, Blanche Stuart C99
Scott, Gen. Winfield 142, 153, 164, 175, 200, 786
Scouting 4472
Screenwriting 3772a
Scuba Diving 2863-2866
Sea Coast 3693, 3775, 3785, 3864, 3874-3875, 4348
Sea Creatures 2508-2511
Sea Cucumber 3440
Sea Lions, Northern 2509
Sea Otter 2510
Sea Shells 2117-2121, 5163-5170
Seal, Hawaiin Monk 3105c
Seamstress 1717
Seaplane 2468
Search for Peace 1326
Seashells 2117-2121
SEATO 1151
Seattle World's Fair 1196
Secretariat 3189g
Seeger, Pete 5708
Seeing Eye Dogs 1787, 4604
Sego Lily 2667
Seinfeld 3191c
Selena 4499
Selma, Ala. March 3937i
Seminole Doll 3873e
Semmes, Raphael 2975i
Senate, U.S. 2413
Seneca Carving 3873i
Sequoyah 1859
Serra, Father Junipero C116
Service Women 1013
Servicemen 1422
Servicemen-Savings Bonds 1320
Sesame Street 3189c, 5394
Sesquicentennial Exposition 627
Sessile Bellwort 2662
Sevareid, Eric 4252
Sevier, John 941
Seward, William H. 370-371
Shakespeare, William 1250
Sharkruiser 5330
Sharks 5223-5227
Sheeler, Charles 3236r, 4748h
Shepard, Alan B., Jr. 4527
Sheridan, Philip H. 787
Sherman, William T. 225, 257, 272, 787, 2975a
Shibe Park 3518
Shiloh, Battle of 1179, 2975e
Shipbuilding 1095
Shooting Star 2654
Shoshone Headdress 2505
"Shot Heard 'Round the World" 3187c
Show Boat 2767
Showy Evening Primrose 2671
Sicily, Invasion of 2765c
Sickle Cell Disease Awareness 3877
Sierra Juniper Bonsai 4618
Sign Language 2783-2784
Sikorsky, Igor C119
Silhouettes, Sppoky 5420-5423
Silver Bells Wreath 4936
Silver Centennial 1130
Silver Coffeepot 3754, 3759
Silver Surfer 4159f, 4159p
Silverstein, Shel 5683
Simpsons, The 4399-4403
Sims, Admiral William S. 4440
Sinatra, Frank 4265
SIPEX 1310-1311
Sisler, George 3408e
Sister Rosetta 3219
Sitting Bull 2183
Skagit River 5381h
Skateboarding 3321
Skateboards 5763-5766
Skating, Inline 3324
Skiing 3180
Skilled Hands for Independence 1717-1720
Skydance Bridge 5809
Skylab 1529
Skyscraper Apartments 4710n
Sleeping Bear Dunes 5258
Sleepy Hollow 1548
Sleigh 1900
Slinky 3186m
Sloan, John 1433
Smiley Face 3189m
Smiley, Guy 5394k
Smith, Alfred E. 937
Smith, Bessie 2854
Smith, Capt. John 328
Smith, Jessie Willcox 3502l
Smith, Kate 4463
Smith, Margaret Chase 3427
Smith, W. Eugene 3649n
Smithsonian Institution 943, 1838, 3059
Smokey the Bear 2096
Smooth Soloman's Seal 2691
Snake River 5381e
Snake, San Francisco Garter 3105k
Snowboarding 3323
Snowdrop 3028
Snowflakes 4808-4812, 5031-5034
Snow White & the Seven Dwarfs 3185h
Snowy Beauty 5727-5736
Snowy Day, The 5243-5246
Snowy Egret 2321, 3829-3830D
Snowy Owl 3290
Snuffleupagus 5394l
Soapberry 5418
Soccer Ball 5205
Soccer, Women's 5754
Soccer, Youth 3401
Social Security Act 2153
Society of Philatelic Americans 797
Soda Fountain Favorites 5080a
Soft Shield Fern 4849, 4875, 4973
Softball 2962
Soil Conservation 1133
Soil and Water Conservation 2074
Sokol-Physical Fitness 1262
Solar Energy 2006
Solar Technology 5518
Songbirds 4882-4891, 5126-5129
Sonoran Desert 3293
Soo Locks 1069
Sound (film) 3772j
Sound Recording 1705
Sousa, John Philip 880
South Carolina Flag 1640, 4320
South Carolina Statehood 2343
South Carolina Tercentenary 1407
South Dakota Flag 1672, 4321
South Dakota Statehood 858, 2416
Southern Florida Wetland 4099
Southern Magnolia 3193
Southwest Carved Figure 2426
Southworth, Albert Sands & Hawes, Josiah Johnson 3649a
Space Accomplishments 1331-1332, 1529, 1556-1557, 1569-1570, 1759, 1912-1919, 2568-2577, 2631-2634, 3409-3413
Space Achievement Decade 1434-1435
Space Discovery 3238-3242
Spacecraft C122, C126a
Space Fantasy 2543, 2741-2745
Space Shuttle 1913-1914, 1917-1918, 2544-2544A, 3261-3262, 3190a, 3411a, C125, C126d
Spanish-American War 3192
Spanish Settlement In Southwest 3220
Speaker, Tris 3408l
Speaker's Stand 1582
Special Effects 3772i
Special Occasions 2267-2274, 2395-2398
Special Olympics 1788, 2142, 3191i, 3771
Special Olympics World Games 4986
Spectacle Reef Lighthouse 2971
Speedboats, Mahogany 4160-4163
Spencer, Anne 5473
Sperry, Lawrence and Elmer C114
Spicebush Swallowtail Butterfly 4736
Spider and Web 5422
Spider-man 4159a, 4159k
Spider-woman 4159g, 4159q
Spingarn, Joel Elias 4384b
Spinybacked Spider 3351q
Spirit of '76 1629-1631
Spirit of St. Louis C10
Split Rock Lighthouse 2969
Spooky Silhouettes 5420-5423
Spoonbill 4993, 4995
Sport of the Gods, The (movie) 4337
Sport Utility Vehicles 3191m
Sports, Extreme 3321-3324, 3191d
Spotted Water Beetle 3351o
Spreading Pogonia Orchid 2078

SUBJECT INDEX OF REGULAR, COMMEMORATIVE & AIR POST ISSUES 169


Squashes.................. 4006, 4009, 4015
Squirrel ........................................ 2489
Stagecoach...1898A, 2228, 2434, 2438a
Stagecoach (film).......................... 2448
Staggerwing Airplane .................. 3142j
Staghorn Coral ................... 5366, 5368
Stamp Act, Repeal of ................... 5064
Stamp Centenary .......................... 947
Stamp Collecting........1474, 2198-2201
Stampin' the Future.............3414-3417
Stan Hywet Hall and Gardens ....... 5462
Standing Bear, Chief..................... 5798
Standing Cypress ......................... 2695
Stanley Steamer ........................... 2132
Stanton, Edwin M. ......... 138, 149, 160, 171, 196
Stanton, Elizabeth ......................... 959
Star.............................3613-3615, 4749
Star and Stripes............................ 5433
Star Fruit............................ 4254, 4261
Star Quilts.............................5098-5099
Star Ribbon .........................5361-5362
Star Route Truck.......................... 2125
Star Trek ..................3188e, 5132-5135
Star Wars...................4143, 5573-5582
Stargell, Willie ............................... 4696
Starling Bone Tissue .................. 5802k
Stars ........................................C72-C73
Stars and Bars............................. 5756
Stars and "6" ................................ 1892
"Stars and Stripes Forever"........... 3153
State and County Fairs.........5401-5404
State Birds and Flowers ......1953-2002, 1953A-2002A
State Flags ...........................1633-1682
Statehood: North Dakota, South Dakota, Montana, Washington....... 858
Statler and Waldorf...................... 3944e
Statue of Freedom........989, 5295-5297
Statue of Liberty... 566, 696, 899, 1035, 1041-1042, 1044A, 1057, 1075, 1594, 1599, 1619, 1816, 2147, 2224, 2599, 3122, 3122E, 3451-3453, 3466, 3476-3477, 3485, 3965-3970, 3972-3975, 3978-3983, 3985, C58, C63, C80, C87
Statue of Liberty & New York Skyline............................................C35
Statue of Liberty Replica, Las Vegas, NV ......... 4486, 4488, 4490, 4518, 4559, 4561, 4563
Steam Carriage............................. 2451
Steamboat Geyser......................... 4059
Steamboats ....2405-2409, 2435, 2438b
Steamship Savannah....................... 923
Stearman Airplane....................... 3142l
Steel Industry ............................... 1090
Stefansson, Vilhjalmur.................. 2222
Stegosaurus ....................... 2424, 3136f
Steichen, Edward ........................ 3649g
Steinbeck, John............................ 1773
Steiner, Max.................................. 3339
Steinmetz, Charles ........................ 2055
Stella, Joseph.............................. 4748i
Steuben, Baron Friedrich von.......... 689
Stevens, Wallace .......................... 4660
Stevenson, Adlai E. ...................... 1275
Stewart Falls, UT ......................... 5800f
Stewart, James.............................. 4197
Stieglitz, Alfred ........................... 3649h
Still, Clyfford ................................ 4444f
Stilwell, Gen. Joseph W. ............... 3420
Stock Car Racing ......................... 3187n
Stock Market Crash..................... 3184o
Stokowski, Leopold....................... 3158
Stone Mountain Memorial ............ 1408
Stone, Harlan Fiske ........................ 965
Stone, Lucy .................................. 1293
Stop Family Violence.........................B3
Story, Joseph ............................... 4422d
Stourbridge Lion Locomotive........ 2362
Stowe, Harriet Beecher ................. 3430
Strand, Paul................................. 3649o
Stratford Hall .................................. 788
Stratocumulus Undulatus............ 3878k
Stratojet Airplane......................... 3142h
Stratus Opacus ............................ 3878l
Stravinsky, Igor............................. 1845
Strawberries ... 3296, 3299, 3305, 3405, 5201, 5491
Streamline Design ....................... 3185k
Stream Violet ................................ 2655
Streetcars .............................2059-2062
Stuart, Gilbert Charles ..................... 884
Studebaker Golden Hawk ............. 4354
Studebaker Starliner...................... 3931
Stutz Bearcat................................. 2131
Stuyvesant, Peter ............................ 971
Sub-mariner.................... 4159c, 4159m
Submarines ..........................3372-3377
Submarines in Pacific................. 2838e
Sullivan, Anne, and Helen Keller ............................................. 1824
Sullivan, Maj. Gen. John................. 657
Summer Harvest..................5004-5007
Summer Sports ............................ 3397
Sun ............................................... 3410
Sun Science .........................5598-5607
Sun Yat-sen ........................ 906, 1188
Sunbeam Falls, WA ..................... 5800j
Sunday Funnies...................4467-4471
Sunflower ............................ 4347, 5682
Sunflower and Seeds... 4005, 4010, 4016
Sunshine Skyway Bridge.............. 4649
Super Bowl I ................................ 3188l
Super Chief................................... 3337
Supergirl ..............................4084i, 4084s
Superman............ 3185f, 4084a, 4084k
Supersonic Flight.......................... 3173
Supreme Court Bicentennial ......... 2415
Supreme Court Building.................. 991
Supreme Court Justices................. 4422
Surrender of Burgoyne at Saratoga........................................ 2590
Surrender of Cornwallis at Yorktown....................................... 1686
Surrey ........................................... 1907
Swallowtail Butterfly....................... 1712
Sweden-U.S. Treaty ...................... 2036
Swedish Chef, The ...................... 3944f
Swedish Pioneers........................... 958
Swedish-Finnish Tercentenary ........ 836
Sweet White Violet ...................... 2659
Switzerland, 700th Anniv. ............. 2532
Sylvan Dell Riverboat ................... 3092
Sylvester the Cat .................3204-3205
Synthetic Fuels ............................. 2007
Szell, George ................................ 3160

**2-1B Droid ................................... 5581**
Taft, Robert A. .............................. 1161
Taft, William H. .... 685, 687, 831, 2218h
Tail Fins & Chrome...................... 3187g
Take Me Out to the Ballgame........ 4341
Talking Pictures ............................ 1727
Tamales ........................................ 5192
Tamaqua, PA Station .................... 5761
Tandem Bicycle ............................ 2266
Tanner, Henry Ossawa.................. 1486
Tap Dance ...........................5609-5613
Tarawa, Invasion of...................... 2765j
Tarbell, Ida M. ............................. 3666
Taylor, Robert Robinson ............... 4958
Taylor, Zachary ....... 179, 181, 185, 204, 817, 2217c
Teachers ....................................... 1093
Teague, Walter Dorwin................ 4546e
Technology Education .................. 5277
Teddy Bear Centennial .........3653-3656
Teddy Bear Created.................... 3182k
Teen Fashions............................. 3187b
Telegraph Centenary ....................... 924
Telephone Centenary.................... 1683
Telescopes.................................... 3409
Television .................................. 3186f
Telly............................................ 5394n
Temple, Shirley ............................. 5060
Tennessee Flag.................. 1648, 4322
Tennessee Statehood...941, 3070-3071
Tennessee Valley Authority........... 2042
Tennis .......................................... 2964
Tennis Ball ................................... 5209
Terrell, Mary Church ................... 4384a
Terry and the Pirates.................. 3000r
Terry, Sonny................................. 3214
Tesla, Nikola ................................ 2057
Tetherball ..................................... 5632
Texaco Star Theater ................... 4414a
Texas Flag.......................... 1660, 4323
Texas Independence ...................... 776
Texas Republic ............................. 2204
Texas Statehood.................. 938, 2968
Thank You..................2269, 5519-5522
Thanksgiving ................................ 3546
Thanksgiving Day Parade.....4417-4420
Tharpe, Sister Rosetta.................. 3219
That's All Folks ....................3534-3535
Thayer, Sylvanus........................... 1852
Theodore Roosevelt National Park....5080i
Therapy Dog................................. 4605
Thick-billed Parrot ...................... 3105b
Thinking of You..........2397, 5803-5807
Thing, The....................... 4159d, 4159n
Third International Philatelic Exhibition......................................... 778
Thirteen-Mile Woods, NH .............C144
Thirteenth Amendment................... 902
35 Bonanza Airplane .................... 3924
Thirty Mile Point Lighthouse.......... 2973
Thomas, Danny ............................ 4628
Thomas Point Shoal Lighthouse, MD ......................... 5625
Thoreau, Henry David......... 1327, 5202
Thorpe, Jim ..................... 2089, 3183g
314 Clipper Airplane................... 3142r
Thresher Shark ............................. 5225
Thurber, James............................. 2862
Tibbett, Lawrence.......................... 3156
Tickseed ....................................... 2653
Tiffany Lamp....3749, 3749A, 3758, 3758A
Tiffany, Louis Comfort .................. 4165
Tiger Stadium ............................... 3511
Tiger Swallowtail .......................... 2300
Tilghman, Bill.................... 2869r, 2870
Tiomkin, Dimitri............................. 3340
Titanic ......................................... 3191l
Title IX Civil Rights Law........5668-5671
Tlikakila River............................. 5381j
Tlingit Sculptures........................ 3873c
To Form a More Perfect Union ...... 3937
Toad, Wyoming........................... 3105g
Tokyo Clock Tower ...................... 4985
Tokyo Raid ................................. 2697a
Toleware....1775-1778, 3612, 3756, 3756A
Tom Sawyer .................................. 1470
Tomatoes ............................. 5007, 5485
Tonight Show, The....................... 4414r
Toonerville Folks ........................ 3000g
Torch...............901, 1594, 1816, 2531A
Tortoise ........................................ 5113
Toscanini, Arturo........................... 2411
Total Solar Eclipse ........................ 5211
Tourmaline .................................... 1539
Touro Synagogue .......................... 2017
Tow Truck ..................................... 2129
Toys, Antique.... 3626-3629, 3638-3645
Tractor ......................................... 2127
Tractor Trailer...................... 2457, 2458
Traditional Mail Delivery........2434-2438
Traffic Safety................................. 1272
Trains ..................................3333-3337
Transcontinental Telephone Line........................................... 3183e
Transcontinental Railroad.............. 922, 5378-5380
Trans-Mississippi Exposition....285-293
Trans-Mississippi Philatelic Exposition....................................... 751
Trans-Mississippi Stamps, Cent. .........................................3209-3210
Transpacific Airmail .......................C115
Transportation Coil Issue ... 1897, 1897A, 1898, 1898A, 1899-1909, 2123-2136, 2225, 2226, 2228, 2231, 2252-2266, 2451-2452, 2452B, 2452D, 2453-2454, 2457-2458, 2463-2464, 2466, 2468
Transport Plane .....................C25-C31
Traynor, Pie................................ 3408o
Treaty of Paris.............................. 2052
Trees, American ... 1764-1767, 3193-3197
Tricycle ......................................... 2126
Trident Maple Bonsai.................... 4621
Tri-Motor Airplane....................... 3142p
Trinity Church, Boston.................. 1839
Troops Guarding Train ..................... 289
Trout ................................ 1427, 3105j
Trucking Industry ......................... 1025
Trudeau, Edward ....................... 3432A
True Katydid .............................. 3351p
Truman, Harry S....... 1499, 1862, 2219f, 3186d
Trumbull, John .............................. 1361
Trumpet Honeysuckle................... 2683
Trunk Bay, St. John, VI .................C145
Truth, Sojourner............................ 2203
Tubman, Harriet................ 1744, 2975k
Tucker, Richard ............................ 3155
Tufted Puffins ....................4737-4737A
Tugboat ........................................ 2260
Tulip ....... 2517-2520, 2524-2527, 2762, 3902, 4960, 5002, 5681, 5767-5786
Tuna, Bluefin ................................ 2208
Turk's Cap Lily ............................. 2681
Turners, American Society of .......... 979
TWA Terminal, New York ............ 3910d
Twain, Mark ........................... 863, 4545
20th Century Limited .................... 3335
Tweety Bird........................3204-3205
Twilight Zone, The ...................... 4414s
Twin Mill ....................................... 5326
Twinflower.................................... 2665
247 Airplane ................................. 3916
Tybee Island Lighthouse, GA......... 3790
Tyler, John.................... 815, 847, 2217a
Tyrannosaurus Rex.....2422, 5410-5413

**U-boat Battles.............................. 2765a**
Umbrella ....................................... 2443
Umpqua River Lighthouse, OR...... 4149
Uncle Sam................ 3259, 3263, 3353
Uncle Sam's Hat........3260, 3264-3269, 5174, 5341
United Confederate Veterans .......... 998
United Nations.................... 1419, 2974
United Nations Conference ............. 928
United Nations Secretariat .......... 3186k
U.S. Air Force Academy ................ 3838
U.S. Capitol ... 572, 992, 1590-1591, 1616, 1623, 1623B, 1809, 2114-2116, 3472, 3648, 4075b, 4983, C64-C65
U.S. Military Academy........... 789, 3560
U.S.-Canada Friendship.................. 961
U.S.-Canada Peace Bridge ........... 1721
U.S.-Japan Treaty......................... 1158
U.S.-Morocco Diplomatic Relations........................................ 2349
U.S. Naval Academy ............ 794, 3001
U.S.-Netherlands Diplomatic Relations........................................ 2003
U.S.-Sweden Treaty...................... 2036
United Way ................................... 2275
United We Stand ................3549-3550A
Universal Postal Congress ..2434-2438, C122-C126
Universal Postal Union ........1530-1537, 3332, C42-C44
Upper Falls, NC .......................... 5800l
Uranus ................................ 2575, 5075
Urban Planning ............................. 1333
Ursula from "The Little Mermaid" ... 5220
"USA" and Jet .......................... C75, C81
"USA" and Star....................... 5061, 5172
USPS Emblem.............................. 1396
USPS Emblem & Olympic Rings ... 2539
USS Arizona Memorial ................. 4873
USS Constellation ........................ 3869
USS Constitution................... 951, 4703
USS Holland ................................. 3376
USS Missouri................................ 5392
Utah Flag ............................. 1677, 4324
Utah Settlement .............................. 950
Utah Statehood ............................ 3024

**Valens, Ritchie .................. 2727, 2734**
Valentino, Rudolph ........................ 2819
Valley Forge ........................... 645, 1729
Van Buren, Martin............... 813, 2216h
VanDerZee, James ..................... 3649k
Vanna Venturi House ................. 3910c
Varela, Felix .................................. 3166
Variscite ....................................... 2702
Vaughan, Sarah ............................ 5059
VCRs ......................................... 3189h
Vega Airplane............................. 3142d
Velvet Ant ................................... 3351i
Venus................................... 2569, 5070
Venus Flytrap ............................... 3528
Vermont Flag ........................ 1646, 4325
Vermont Sesquicentennial ............... 643
Vermont Statehood ............... 903, 2533
Verrazano-Narrows Bridge .......... 1258, 4052, 4872
Verville, Alfred V. ..........................C113
Very Hungry Caterpillar, The.......... 3987
Veterans....................................... 3508
Veterans Administration ................ 1825
Veterans of Foreign Wars ............. 1525
Veterans, Korean War................... 2152
Veterans, Viet Nam War................ 1802
Veterans, World War I .................. 2154
Veterans, World War I .................. 1940
Vicksburg, Battle of ....................... 4787

| Entry | Number(s) |
|---|---|
| Victory | 537 |
| Video Games | 3190 l |
| Viet Nam Veterans' Memorial | 2109, 3190g |
| Viet Nam War | 3188g |
| Viking Missions to Mars | 1759 |
| Viking Ship | 621 |
| Villard, Oswald Garrison | 4384b |
| Vintage Black Cinema | 4336-4340 |
| Vintage Seed Packets | 4754-4763 |
| Violins | 1813 |
| Virgin Islands Flag | 4326 |
| Virgin Islands Territory | 802 |
| Virginia Bluebells | 2668 |
| Virginia Capes, Battle of | 1938 |
| Virginia Flag | 1642, 4327 |
| Virginia Rotunda | 1779 |
| Virginia Statehood | 2345 |
| Virtual Reality | 3191j |
| V-mail | 2765e |
| Voice of America | 1329 |
| Volcanic Crater | 4710b |
| Volleyball | 2961, 5204 |
| Volunteer, Lend a Hand | 2039 |
| Volunteer Firemen | 971 |
| Von Karman, Theodore | 2699 |
| Von Nessen, Greta | 4546i |
| Von Neumann, John | 3908 |
| Voting Rights Act of 1965 | 3937b |
| Voyages of Columbus | 2620-2629 |
| Voyageurs National Park | C148 |
| Wagner, Honus | 3408q |
| Waimoku Falls, HI | 5800e |
| Walk in the Water Steamboat | 2409 |
| Walker, C. J. | 3181 |
| Walker, Dr. Mary E. | 2013 |
| Wallace, Lila and DeWitt | 2936 |
| Wallenberg, Raoul | 3135 |
| Walt Disney Concert Hall | 3910e |
| War of 1812 | 4703, 4805, 4921, 4952 |
| War Savings Bonds & Stamps | 2765g |
| Ward, Clara | 3218 |
| Warhol, Andy | 3652 |
| Warner, Pop | 3144, 3149 |
| Warren, Earl | 2184 |
| Warren, Robert Penn | 3904 |
| Washington and Lee University | 982 |
| Washington at Cambridge | 617 |
| Washington Crossing the Delaware | 1688 |
| Washington Flag | 1674, 4328 |
| Washington Mounument | 2149, 3473, 4651 |
| Washington Reviewing Army at Valley Forge | 1689 |
| Washington Statehood | 858, 2404 |
| Washington Steamboat | 2408 |
| Washington Territory | 1019 |
| Washington 2006 World Philatelic Exhibition | 4075 |
| Washington, Booker T. | 873, 1074 |
| Washington, D.C. | 989-992, 2561 |
| Washington, Dinah | 2730, 2737 |
| Washington, George | 2, 4, 10-11A, 13-17, 25-26A, 31-37, 39, 41, 43-45, 47, 62B, 64-66, 68-70, 72, 74, 78-79, 82-83, 85, 85C-85E, 88-90, 94, 96-97, 99, 101, 104, 106-107, 109, 111, 115, 126, 136, 147, 158, 169, 184, 194, 207, 210-211, 211B, 213-214, 219D, 220, 248-252, 265-267, 279B, 301, 319-322, 332-342, 344-347, 349-351, 353-356, 358-366, 375-382, 384, 386, 388-389, 391, 393-396, 405-413, 423A-423E, 424-430, 441-450, 452-459, 461-469, 481-496, 498-507, 519, 525-536, 538-546, 554, 577, 579, 583, 595, 599-599A, 606, 634-634A, 660, 671, 704-715, 720-722, 785, 804, 839, 848, 854, 947-948, 1003, 1031, 1054, 1213, 1229, 1283, 1283B, 1304, 1304C, 1686, 1688-1689, 1704, 1729, 1952, 2149, 2216a, 2592, 3140, 3468A, 3475, 3482-3483, 3616-3619, 3819, 4504, 4512, 5079a, 5079c, 5079d |
| Washington, Martha | 306, 556, 585, 601, 636, 662, 673, 805, 840, 849 |
| Water Conservation | 1150 |
| Water Lilies | 4964-4967 |
| Waterfalls | 5800 |
| Waterfowl Conservation | 1362 |
| Waterfowl Preservation Act | 2092 |
| Watermelon | 5004 |
| Waters, Ethel | 2851 |
| Waters, Muddy | 2855 |
| Watie, Stand | 2975l |
| Watkins, Carleton E. | 3649c |
| Waves of Color | 4717-4720 |
| Waxman, Franz | 3342 |
| Waxwing, Cedar | 5127 |
| Wayne, Gen. Anthony | 680 |
| Wayne, John | 2448, 3876 |
| Weather Vane | 3257-3258, 4613-4617 |
| Webb Space Telescope | 5720 |
| Webster, Daniel | 141, 152, 163, 174, 189, 199, 226, 258, 273, 282C, 283, 307, 725, 1380 |
| Webster, Noah | 1121 |
| Wedding Cake | 4398, 4521, 4602, 4735, 4867, 5000 |
| Wedding Doves | 3998-3999 |
| Wedding Flowers | 4764-4765 |
| Wedding Hearts | 4151-4152, 4271-4272 |
| Wedding Rings | 4397 |
| Wedding Roses | 4520 |
| Wells, Ida B. | 2442 |
| West, Benjamin | 1553 |
| Western Cattle in Storm | 292 |
| Western Meadowlark | 4882 |
| Western Tanager | 4884 |
| Western Wear | 5615-5618 |
| Western Wildlife | 2869p, 2870 |
| West Point | 789, 3560 |
| West Quoddy Head Lighthouse, ME | 2472 |
| West Virginia Flag | 1667, 4329 |
| West Virginia Statehood | 1232, 4790 |
| Weston, Edward | 3649j |
| Wetlands | 3207-3207A |
| Whale Shark | 5224 |
| Wharton, Sr., Clifton R. | 4076f |
| Wharton, Edith | 1832 |
| Wharton, Joseph | 1920 |
| Wheat Fields | 1506 |
| Wheatland | 1081 |
| Wheel Chair | 2256 |
| Wheels of Freedom | 1162 |
| Wheelwright | 1719 |
| Whistler, James A. McNeil | l885 |
| Whitcomb, Jon | 3502n |
| White Bengal Tiger | 2709 |
| White House | 809, 844, 1338, 1338D, 1338A, 1338F, 1338G, 2219e, 2609, 3445 |
| White Mountain Avens | 2661 |
| White Oak | 1766 |
| White Pine | 1765 |
| White Plains, Battle of | 629-630 |
| White Sturgeon | 4061 |
| White, Josh | 3215 |
| White, Minor | 3649t |
| White, Paul Dudley | 2170 |
| White, Walter | 4384d |
| White, William Allen | 960 |
| White-tailed Deer | 1888, 2317 |
| White-throated Sparrow | 4891 |
| Whitman, Walt | 867, 5414 |
| Whitney, Eli | 889 |
| Whittier, John Greenleaf | 865 |
| Whooping Crane | 1098, 2868 |
| Wilbur | 3988 |
| Wildcat Airplane | 3142t |
| Wild Columbine | 2678 |
| Wild Flax | 2696 |
| Wild Animals | 2705-2709 |
| Wild Orchids | 5435-5444 |
| Wild Pink Orchid | 2076 |
| Wild Thing | 3991 |
| Wilder, Billy | 4670 |
| Wilder, Thornton | 3134 |
| Wilderness, Battle of the | 1181 |
| Wildlife | 1921-1924, 2286-2335 |
| Wildlife Conservation | 1077-1079, 1098, 1392, 1427-1430, 1464-1467, 1760-1763 |
| Wile E. Coyote & Road Runner | 3391-3392 |
| Wiley, Harvey W. | 1080 |
| Wilkes, Lt. Charles | 2387 |
| Wilkins, Roy | 3501 |
| Willard, Frances E. | 872 |
| Williams, Hank | 2723-2723A, 2771, 2775 |
| Williams, Ted | 4694 |
| Williams, Tennessee | 3002 |
| Williams, William Carlos | 4656 |
| Willie and Joe | 2765h |
| Willis, Frances E. | 4076b |
| Willkie, Wendell | 2192 |
| Wills, Bob | 2774, 2778 |
| Willson, Meredith | 3349 |
| Wilson, August | 5555 |
| Wilson, Woodrow | 623, 697, 832, 1040, 2218i |
| Win the War | 905 |
| Windmills | 1738-1742 |
| Winged Airmail Envelope | C79-C83 |
| Winged Globe | C12, C16-C17, C19, C24 |
| Winogrand, Garry | 3649r |
| Winter Aconite | 3026 |
| Winter Fun | 4937-4944 |
| Winter Scenes | 5532-5541 |
| Winter Woodland Animals | 5822-5825 |
| Winterberry | 5415 |
| Winterthur Garden | 5466 |
| Wisconsin Flag | 1662, 4330 |
| Wisconsin Statehood | 957, 3206 |
| Wisconsin Tercentenary | 739, 755 |
| Wisdom Statue | 3766 |
| Wizard of Oz, The | 2445 |
| Wolf Trap Farm Park | 1452, 2018 |
| Wolfe, Thomas | 3444 |
| Wolfman, The | 3172 |
| Wolverine | 2327 |
| Wolverine (comic book character) | 4159j |
| Woman Suffrage | 1406, 2980, 3184e, 5523 |
| Women | 1152 |
| Women, Armed Services | 1013, 3174 |
| Women Cryptologists of World War II | 5738 |
| Women in Journalism | 3665-3668 |
| Women in War Effort | 2697h, 3186e |
| Women, Progress of | 959 |
| Womens' Clubs | 1316 |
| Women's Rights Movement | 3189j |
| Women's Rowing | 5694-5697 |
| Women's Soccer | 5754 |
| Wonder Woman | 4084c, 4084m, 5149-5152 |
| Wonders of America | 4033-4072 |
| Wonders of the Sea | 2863-2866 |
| Wood Carvings | 2240-2243 |
| Woodchuck | 2307 |
| Wood Duck | 2484-2485 |
| Wood, Grant | 3236q |
| Wood Lily | 5672, 5675 |
| Woodland Caribou | 3105l |
| Woodpecker, Red-bellied | 5319 |
| Woodpecker, Red-headed | 3032 |
| Woods' Rose | 5674, 5679 |
| Woodson, Carter G. | 2073 |
| Woodstock Music Festival | 3188b, 5409 |
| Woody Wagon | 3522 |
| Wool Industry | 1423 |
| Woolly Mammoth | 3078 |
| Workman's Compensation | 1186 |
| Works Progress Administration Posters | 5180-5189 |
| World Columbian Stamp Expo | 2616 |
| World Cup Soccer Championships | 2834-2837 |
| World Peace Through Law | 1576 |
| World Peace Through World Trade | 1129 |
| World Refugee Year | 1149 |
| World Series | 3182g, 3187j |
| World Stamp Expo '89 | 2410, 2433 |
| World Stamp Show 2016 | 5010-5011, 5062-5063 |
| World's Fair | 853, 1196, 1244, 2006-2009, 2086, 3182e |
| World University Games | 2748 |
| World War I, Cent. | 5300 |
| World War I, U.S. Involvement | 3183i |
| World War II | 2559, 2697, 2765, 2838, 2981, 3186a |
| World War II Memorial | 3862 |
| World Wide Web | 3191n |
| WPA Posters | 5180-5189 |
| Wright Brothers | 649, C45, C47, C91-C92, 3182g, 3783 |
| Wright, Frank Lloyd | 1280 |
| Wright, Richard | 4386 |
| Wright, Russel | 4546k |
| Wrigley Field | 3519 |
| Wu, Chien-shiung | 5557 |
| Wulfenite | 2703 |
| Wyandotte Chicken | 5584 |
| Wyeth, Andrew | 5212 |
| Wyeth, N. C. | 3502r |
| Wyoming Flag | 1676, 4331 |
| Wyoming Statehood | 897, 2444 |
| Wyoming Toad | 3105g |
| X-Men | 4159t |
| X-Planes | 4018-4019 |
| Yale Art and Architecture Building | 3910i |
| Yankee Stadium | 3513 |
| YB-49 Flying Wing | 3925 |
| Year 2000 | 3369 |
| Yellow Garden Spider | 3351d |
| Yellow Kid | 3000a |
| Yellow Lady's Slipper | 2077, 2673 |
| Yellow Poplar | 3195 |
| Yellow Skunk Cabbage | 2693 |
| Yellow Submarine, The Beatles | 3188o |
| Yellow Trumpet | 3529 |
| Yellowstone National Park | 744, 760, 1453, 5080n |
| YMCA Youth Camping | 2160 |
| Yoda | 4143n, 4205 |
| York, Sgt. Alvin C. | 3395 |
| Yorktown, Battle of | 1937 |
| Yorktown, Surrender of | 703 |
| Yorktown, Sinking of the | 2697g |
| Yosemite Falls | 4050 |
| Yosemite National Park | 740, 756, 769, 2280, C141 |
| You Bet Your Life | 4414h |
| Young, Cy | 3408m |
| Young, Whitney Moore | 1875 |
| Youth Month | 963 |
| Youth, Support Our | 1342 |
| Youth Team Sports | 3399-3402 |
| Yugoslavia, Flag | 917 |
| Zaharias, Mildred Didrikson | 1932 |
| Zebra Nerite | 5166, 5168 |
| Zebrafish | 5802m |
| Zeppelin, Gra | fC13-C15, C18 |
| Zia Pottery | 1706 |
| Zinnia | 2830, 4759 |
| Zion National Park | 747, 763, C146 |
| ZIP Code | 1511 |
| Zoe | 5394p |

# UNITED STATES

## SEMI-POSTAL STAMPS

### BREAST CANCER RESEARCH

SP1

**PHOTOGRAVURE**
*Serpentine Die Cut 11*
1998, July 29
**Self-Adhesive**
B1 SP1 (32c+8c) multicolored  1.00  .25

### HEROES OF 2001

Firemen Atop World Trade Center Rubble — SP2

**LITHOGRAPHED**
*Serpentine Die Cut 11¼*
2002, June 7
**Self-Adhesive**
B2 SP2 (34c+11c) multicolored  .80  .35

### STOP FAMILY VIOLENCE

SP3

**PHOTOGRAVURE**
2003, Oct. 8  *Serpentine Die Cut 11*
**Self-Adhesive**
B3 SP3 (37c+8c) multicolored  .80  .45

### SAVE VANISHING SPECIES

Amur Tiger Cub — SP4

**PHOTOGRAVURE**
*Serpentine Die Cut 10¾*
2011, Sept. 20
**Self-Adhesive**
B4 SP4 (44c+11c) multicolored  1.40  .50

The 11c surtax was for the Multinational Species Conservation Funds of the U.S. Fish and Wildlife Service.

**Breast Cancer Awareness Type of 1998**
**LITHOGRAPHED**
*Design Size: 20x35mm*
*Serpentine Die Cut 11x10¾*
2014, Sept. 30
**Dated 2014**
**Self-Adhesive**
B5 SP1 (49c+11c) multicolored  1.40  .50
a. Imperforate (from uncut press sheet)  2.25  —
b. Imperf. pair (error, see footnote)

Imperforates from imperforate uncut press sheets (No. B5a) do not have die cutting on either the front or the reverse. On the imperforate error (No. B5b), there is die cutting on the reverse.

### ALZHEIMER'S DISEASE AWARENESS

SP5

**LITHOGRAPHED**
*Serpentine Die Cut 10½x10¾*
2017, Nov. 30
**Self-Adhesive**
B6 SP5 (49c+11c) multicolored  1.40  .60

The 11c surtax was for the National Institutes of Health.

### HEALING POST-TRAUMATIC STRESS DISORDER

Plant Sprout and Fallen Leaves — SP6

**LITHOGRAPHED**
*Serpentine Die Cut 10¾*
2019, Dec. 2  **Tagged**
**Self-Adhesive**
B7 SP6 (55c+10c) multicolored  1.40  .60

The 10c surtax was for the National Center for Post-traumatic Stress Disorder of the Department of Veterans Affairs to assist in treatment of those impacted by post-traumatic stress disorder.

## AIR POST

Curtiss Jenny — AP1

**FLAT PLATE PRINTINGS**
| 1918 | Unwmk. | Engr. | Perf. 11 |
|---|---|---|---|
| C1 | AP1 6c orange | | 55. 30. |
| | Never hinged | | 110. |
| C2 | AP1 16c green | | 60. 35. |
| | Never hinged | | 120. |
| C3 | AP1 24c car rose & blue | | 65. 35. |
| | Never hinged | | 130. |
| a. | Center inverted | | 450,000. |
| | Never hinged | | 950,000. |
| | Nos. C1-C3 (3) | | 180.00 100.00 |
| | Nos. C1-C3, never hinged | | 360.00 |

Wooden Propeller and Radiator AP2

Emblem of Air Service AP3

De Havilland Biplane — AP4

**1923**
| C4 | AP2 8c dark green | 17.50 | 15.00 |
|---|---|---|---|
| | Never hinged | 35.00 | |
| C5 | AP3 16c dark blue | 60.00 | 30.00 |
| | Never hinged | 120.00 | |
| C6 | AP4 24c carmine | 65.00 | 30.00 |
| | Never hinged | 130.00 | |
| | Nos. C4-C6 (3) | 142.50 | 75.00 |
| | Nos. C4-C6, never hinged | 285.00 | |

Map of U.S. and Two Mail Planes AP5

**1926-27**
| C7 | AP5 10c dark blue | 2.25 | .35 |
|---|---|---|---|
| | Never hinged | 4.00 | |
| C8 | AP5 15c olive brown | 2.50 | 2.50 |
| | Never hinged | 4.75 | |
| C9 | AP5 20c yellow green | 6.50 | 2.00 |
| | Never hinged | 12.50 | |
| | Nos. C7-C9 (3) | 11.25 | 4.85 |
| | Nos. C7-C9, never hinged | 21.25 | |

Lindbergh's Airplane "Spirit of St. Louis" — AP6

**1927, June 18**
| C10 | AP6 10c dark blue | 7.00 | 2.50 |
|---|---|---|---|
| | Never hinged | 12.50 | |
| a. | Booklet pane of 3 | 70.00 | 65.00 |
| | Never hinged | 115.00 | |
| b. | Double impression | 350.00 | 16,500. |

Singles from No. C10a are imperf. at sides or imperf. at sides and bottom. Only one example is recorded of No. C10b.

Beacon on Rocky Mountains — AP7

**1928, July 25**
| C11 | AP7 5c carmine and blue | 5.50 | .85 |
|---|---|---|---|
| | Never hinged | 10.00 | |
| a. | Vert. pair, imperf. between | 7,000. | |

No. C11a is unique. It is torn and valued thus.

Winged Globe — AP8

**1930, Feb. 10**
*Stamp design: 46½x19mm*
| C12 | AP8 5c violet | 9.50 | .50 |
|---|---|---|---|
| | Never hinged | 17.50 | |
| a. | Horiz. pair, imperf. between | 4,500. | |

See Nos. C16-C17, C19.

### GRAF ZEPPELIN ISSUE

Zeppelin over Atlantic Ocean AP9

Zeppelin between Continents AP10

Zeppelin Passing Globe AP11

**1930, Apr. 19**
| C13 | AP9 65c green | 180. | 160. |
|---|---|---|---|
| | Never hinged | 250. | |
| C14 | AP10 $1.30 brown | 375. | 360. |
| | Never hinged | 575. | |
| C15 | AP11 $2.60 blue | 525. | 550. |
| | Never hinged | 850. | |
| | Nos. C13-C15 (3) | 1,080. | 1,070. |
| | Nos. C13-C15, never hinged | 1,075. | |

**ROTARY PRESS PRINTING**
**1931-32**  *Perf. 10½x11*
*Stamp design: 47½x19mm*
| C16 | AP8 5c violet | 4.75 | .60 |
|---|---|---|---|
| | Never hinged | 8.50 | |
| C17 | AP8 8c olive bister ('32) | 2.25 | .40 |
| | Never hinged | 3.75 | |

### CENTURY OF PROGRESS ISSUE

Airship "Graf Zeppelin" AP12

**FLAT PLATE PRINTING**
**1933, Oct. 2**  *Perf. 11*
| C18 | AP12 50c green | 45.00 | 47.50 |
|---|---|---|---|
| | Never hinged | 75.00 | |

Catalogue values for unused stamps in this section, from this point to the end, are for Never Hinged items.

**Type of 1930 Issue**
**ROTARY PRESS PRINTING**
**1934, June 30**  *Perf. 10½x11*
| C19 | AP8 6c dull orange | 3.50 | .25 |

### TRANSPACIFIC ISSUES

The "China Clipper" over the Pacific — AP13

**FLAT PLATE PRINTING**
**1935, Nov. 22**  *Perf. 11*
| C20 | AP13 25c blue | 1.40 | 1.00 |

The "China Clipper" over the Pacific — AP14

**1937, Feb. 15**
| C21 | AP14 20c green | 10.00 | 1.75 |
|---|---|---|---|
| C22 | AP14 50c carmine | 10.00 | 5.00 |

Eagle Holding Shield, Olive Branch and Arrows — AP15

**1938, May 14**
| C23 | AP15 6c dark blue & carmine | .70 | .25 |
|---|---|---|---|
| a. | Vert. pair, imperf. horiz. | 300.00 | 300.00 |
| b. | Horiz. pair, imperf. vert. | 12,500. | |
| c. | 6c ultra & car | 350.00 | 2,000. |
| | On cover | | 2,250. |

### TRANSATLANTIC ISSUE

Winged Globe AP16

**1939, May 16**
| C24 | AP16 30c dull blue | 11.00 | 1.50 |

Twin-Motored Transport Plane — AP17

**ROTARY PRESS PRINTING**
**1941-44**  *Perf. 11x10½*
| C25 | AP17 6c carmine | .30 | .25 |
|---|---|---|---|
| a. | Booklet pane of 3 | 3.50 | 1.50 |
| b. | Horiz. pair, imperf. between | 2,250. | |

Singles from No. C25a are imperf. at sides or at sides and bottom.
Value of No. C25b is for pair without blue crayon P. O. rejection mark on front. Very fine pairs with crayon mark sell for about $1,500.

| C26 | AP17 8c olive green | .30 | .25 |
|---|---|---|---|
| a. | All color omitted | | |

No. C26a has an albino impression and exists as a pair of stamps within a double-paper spliced strip of six stamps.

| C27 | AP17 10c violet | 1.10 | .25 |
|---|---|---|---|
| C28 | AP17 15c brown carmine | 2.10 | .35 |
| C29 | AP17 20c bright green | 2.10 | .30 |
| C30 | AP17 30c blue | 2.10 | .35 |
| C31 | AP17 50c orange | 11.00 | 3.25 |
| | Nos. C25-C31 (7) | 19.00 | 5.00 |

DC-4 Skymaster AP18

**1946, Sept. 25**  *Perf. 11x10½*
| C32 | AP18 5c carmine | .30 | .25 |

# UNITED STATES

DC-4 Skymaster — AP19

**1947, Mar. 26**    Perf. 10½x11
C33   AP19   5c carmine    .30   .25

Pan American Union Building, Washington, DC — AP20

Statue of Liberty & New York Skyline — AP21

Plane over San Francisco-Oakland Bay Bridge — AP22

**1947**    Perf. 11x10½
C34   AP20   10c black    .35   .25
   a.   Dry printing    .40   .25
C35   AP21   15c bright blue green    .50   .25
   a.   Horiz. pair, imperf. between    1,500.
   b.   Dry printing    .55   .25
C36   AP22   25c blue    .90   .25
   a.   Dry printing    1.20   .25
   Nos. C34-C36 (3)    1.75   .75

See note on wet and dry printings following No. 1029.

No. C35a is valued in the grade of fine.

### Type of 1947
**ROTARY PRESS COIL STAMP**
**1948, Jan. 15**    Perf. 10 Horizontally
C37   AP19   5c carmine    1.00   .80

### NEW YORK CITY ISSUE

Map of Five Boroughs, Circular Band & Planes — AP23

50th anniv. of the consolidation of the five boroughs of New York City.

**ROTARY PRESS PRINTING**
**1948, July 31**    Perf. 11x10½
C38   AP23   5c bright carmine    .30   .25

### Type of 1947
**1949**    Perf. 10½x11
C39   AP19   6c carmine    .30   .25
   a.   Booklet pane of 6    12.00   5.00
   b.   Dry printing    .50   .25
   c.   As "a," dry printing    25.00   —

See note on wet and dry printings following No. 1029.

### ALEXANDRIA BICENTENNIAL ISSUE

Home of John Carlyle, Alexandria Seal & Gadsby's Tavern — AP24

200th anniv. of the founding of Alexandria, Va.

**1949, May 11**    Perf. 11x10½
C40   AP24   6c carmine    .30   .25

### Type of 1947
**ROTARY PRESS COIL STAMP**
**1949, Aug. 25**    Perf. 10 Horizontally
C41   AP19   6c carmine    3.00   .30

### UNIVERSAL POSTAL UNION ISSUE

Post Office Department Building — AP25

Globe & Doves Carrying Messages AP26

Boeing Stratocruiser & Globe — AP27

**ROTARY PRESS PRINTING**
**1949**    Perf. 11x10½
C42   AP25   10c violet    .30   .25
C43   AP26   15c ultramarine    .40   .25
C44   AP27   25c rose carmine    .60   .40
   Nos. C42-C44 (3)    1.30   .90

### WRIGHT BROTHERS ISSUE

Wilbur & Orville Wright and their Plane — AP28

**1949, Dec. 17**
C45   AP28   6c magenta    .30   .25

Diamond Head, Honolulu, Hawaii — AP29

**1952, Mar. 26**
C46   AP29   80c bright red violet    3.75   1.25

### POWERED FLIGHT, 50th ANNIV.

First Plane and Modern Plane — AP30

**1953, May 29**
C47   AP30   6c carmine    .30   .25

Eagle in Flight — AP31

Issued primarily for use on domestic post cards.

**1954, Sept. 3**
C48   AP31   4c bright blue    .30   .25

### AIR FORCE, 50th ANNIV.

B-52 Stratofortress and F-104 Starfighters AP32

**1957, Aug. 1**
C49   AP32   6c ultra & blue    .30   .25

### Type of 1954
**1958, July 31**
C50   AP31   5c red    .30   .25

Silhouette of Jet Airliner — AP33

**1958, July 31**    Perf. 10½x11
C51   AP33   7c blue    .30   .25
   a.   Booklet pane of 6    6.50   5.00
   b.   Vert. pair, imperf. between (from booklet pane)    4,000.

No. C51b resulted from a paper foldover after perforating and before cutting into panes. Two or three pairs are believed to exist.

**ROTARY PRESS COIL STAMP**
**Perf. 10 Horizontally**
C52   AP33   7c blue    2.00   .25

### ALASKA STATEHOOD ISSUE

Big Dipper, North Star & Map of Alaska — AP34

**ROTARY PRESS PRINTING**
**1959, Jan. 3**    Perf. 11x10½
C53   AP34   7c dark blue    .30   .25

### BALLOON JUPITER ISSUE

Balloon & Crowd — AP35

Centenary of the carrying of mail by the balloon Jupiter from Lafayette to Crawfordsville, Ind.

**GIORI PRESS PRINTING**
**1959, Aug. 17**    Perf. 11
C54   AP35   7c dark blue & red    .30   .25

### HAWAII STATEHOOD ISSUE

Alii Warrior, Map of Hawaii & Star of Statehood AP36

**ROTARY PRESS PRINTING**
**1959, Aug. 21**    Perf. 11x10½
C55   AP36   7c rose red    .30   .25

### PAN AMERICAN GAMES ISSUE

Runner Holding Torch — AP37

3rd Pan American Games, Chicago, Aug. 27-Sept. 7, 1959.

**GIORI PRESS PRINTING**
**1959, Aug. 27**    Perf. 11
C56   AP37   10c red, white & blue    .30   .25

Liberty Bell — AP38

Statue of Liberty — AP39

Abraham Lincoln — AP40

**1959-66**
C57   AP38   10c black & green ('60)    1.00   .70
C58   AP39   15c black & orange    .35   .25
C59   AP40   25c black & maroon ('60)    .50   .25
   a.   Tagged ('66)    .60   .30
   Nos. C57-C59 (3)    1.85   1.20

Airmail stamps starting with No. C69 are tagged unless otherwise noted.

### Type of 1958
**ROTARY PRESS PRINTING**
**1960, Aug. 12**    Perf. 10½x11
C60   AP33   7c carmine    .30   .25
   a.   Booklet pane of 6    7.00   6.00
   b.   Vert. pair, imperf between (from booklet pane)    5,500.

No. C60b resulted from a paper foldover after perforating and before cutting into panes. Two pairs are known.

### Type of 1958
**ROTARY PRESS COIL STAMP**
**1960, Oct. 22**    Perf. 10 Horizontally
C61   AP33   7c carmine    4.00   .25

### Type of 1959-60 and

Statue of Liberty — AP41

**GIORI PRESS PRINTING**
**1961-67**    Perf. 11
C62   AP38   13c black & red    .40   .25
   a.   Tagged ('67)    .75   .50
C63   AP41   15c black & orange    .30   .25
   a.   Tagged ('67)    .35   .25
   b.   As "a," horiz. pair, imperf. vert.    15,000.
   c.   As "a," horiz. pair, imperf between and at left    2,750.
   d.   All color omitted    100.00

On No. C63d, there is a clear albino plate impression.

Jet Airliner Over Capitol — AP42

**ROTARY PRESS PRINTING**
**1962, Dec. 5**    Perf. 10½x11
C64   AP42   8c carmine    .30   .25
   a.   Tagged ('63)    .25   .25
   b.   Booklet pane of 5 + label    6.00   3.00
   c.   As "b," tagged ('64)    1.75   .75

Nos. C64a and C64c were made by overprinting Nos. C64 and C64b with phosphorescent ink. No. C64a was first issued at Dayton, Ohio, for experiments in high speed mail sorting. The tagging is visible in shortwave ultraviolet light.

**COIL STAMP; ROTARY PRESS**
**Perf. 10 Horizontally**
C65   AP42   8c carmine    .40   .25
   a.   Tagged ('64)    .35   .25

### MONTGOMERY BLAIR ISSUE

Montgomery Blair — AP43

Montgomery Blair (1813-83), Postmaster General (1861-64), who called the 1st Intl. Postal Conf., Paris, 1863, forerunner of the UPU.

**GIORI PRESS PRINTING**
**1963, May 3**    Perf. 11
C66   AP43   15c dull red, dark brown & blue    .55   .50

Bald Eagle — AP44

Issued primarily for use on domestic post cards.

**ROTARY PRESS PRINTING**
**1963, July 12**    Perf. 11x10½
C67   AP44   6c red    .30   .25
   a.   Tagged ('67)    4.00   3.00

# UNITED STATES

## AMELIA EARHART ISSUE

Amelia Earhart & Lockheed Electra — AP45

### GIORI PRESS PRINTING
**1963, July 24**    *Perf. 11*
C68 AP45 8c carmine & maroon   .30   .25

## ROBERT H. GODDARD ISSUE

Robert H. Goddard, Atlas Rocket & Launching Tower, Cape Kennedy — AP46

**1964, Oct. 5**
C69 AP46 8c blue, red & bister   .35   .25

### Luminescence
Air Post stamps issued after mid-1964 are tagged.

## ALASKA PURCHASE ISSUE

Tlingit Totem, Southern Alaska — AP47

**1967, Mar. 30**
C70 AP47 8c brown   .30   .25

"Columbia Jays," by Audubon — AP48

**1967, Apr. 26**
C71 AP48 20c multicolored   .75   .25
See note over No. 1241.

50-Star Runway — AP49

### ROTARY PRESS PRINTING
**1968, Jan. 5**    *Perf. 11x10½*
C72 AP49 10c carmine   .30   .25
   b. Booklet pane of 8   2.25   2.00
   c. Booklet pane of 5 + label   3.50   1.25
   d. Vert. pair, imperf. btwn., in #C72b with foldover   5,000.

No. C72d resulted from a paper foldover after perforating and before cutting into panes. Two pairs are recorded from different panes.

### ROTARY PRESS COIL STAMP
*Perf. 10 Vertically*
C73 AP49 10c carmine   .30   .25
   a. Imperf., pair   400.00

The $1 Airlift stamp is listed as No. 1341.

## 50th ANNIVERSARY OF AIR MAIL ISSUE

Curtiss Jenny — AP50

50th anniv. of regularly scheduled air mail service.

### LITHOGRAPHED, ENGRAVED (GIORI)
**1968, May 15**    *Perf. 11*
C74 AP50 10c blue, black & red   .30   .25

USA and Jet — AP51

**1968, Nov. 22**
C75 AP51 20c red, blue & black   .35   .25
See No. C81.

## MOON LANDING ISSUE

First Man on the Moon AP52

**1969, Sept. 9**
C76 AP52 10c multicolored   .30   .25
   a. Rose red (litho.) omitted   550.00

On No. C76a, the lithographed rose red is missing from the entire vignette-the dots on top of the yellow areas as well as the flag shoulder patch.

Silhouette of Delta Wing Plane AP53

Silhouette of Jet Airliner AP54

Winged Airmail Envelope AP55

Statue of Liberty AP56

### ROTARY PRESS PRINTING
**1971-73**    *Perf. 10½x11*
C77 AP53 9c red   .30   .25

No. C77 issued primarily for use on domestic post cards.

*Perf. 11x10½*
C78 AP54 11c carmine   .30   .25
   a. Booklet pane of 4 + 2 labels   1.25   1.00
   b. Untagged (Bureau precanceled)   .85   .85
C79 AP55 13c carmine ('73)   .30   .25
   a. Booklet pane of 5 + label ('73)   1.50   1.00
   b. Untagged (Bureau precanceled)   .85   .85
   c. Green instead of red tagging (single from booklet pane)

No. C78b Bureau precanceled "WASHINGTON D.C." (or "DC" - more valuable thus), No. C79b "WASHINGTON DC" only; both for use of Congressmen, but available to any permit holder.

### GIORI PRESS PRINTING
*Perf. 11*
C80 AP56 17c bluish black, red, & dark green   .35   .25

### "USA" & Jet Type of 1968
### LITHOGRAPHED, ENGRAVED (GIORI)
C81 AP51 21c red, blue & black   .40   .25
   b. Black (engr.) missing (FO)   2,750.

The two recorded examples of No. C81b are in a single full pane. Catalogue value is for both errors.

### COIL STAMPS
### ROTARY PRESS PRINTING
**1971-73**    *Perf. 10 Vertically*
C82 AP54 11c carmine   .30   .25
   a. Imperf., pair   160.00
C83 AP55 13c carmine ('73)   .30   .25
   a. Imperf., pair   60.00

## NATIONAL PARKS CENTENNIAL ISSUE
### City of Refuge, Hawaii

Kii Statue & Temple, City of Refuge, Hawaii — AP57

### LITHOGRAPHED, ENGRAVED (GIORI)
**1972, May 3**    *Perf. 11*
C84 AP57 11c orange & multicolored   .30   .25
   a. Blue & green (litho.) omitted   400.00   900.00

## OLYMPIC GAMES ISSUE

Skiing & Olympic Rings — AP58

11th Winter Olympic Games, Sapporo, Japan, Feb. 3-13, and 20th Summer Olympic Games, Munich, Germany, Aug. 26-Sept. 11.

### PHOTOGRAVURE (Andreotti)
**1972, Aug. 17**    *Perf. 11x10½*
C85 AP58 11c black, blue, red, emerald & yellow   .30   .25

## ELECTRONICS PROGRESS ISSUE

De Forest Audions — AP59

### LITHOGRAPHED, ENGRAVED (GIORI)
**1973, July 10**    *Perf. 11*
C86 AP59 11c multicolored   .30   .25
   a. Vermilion & olive (litho.) omitted   500.00
   c. Olive omitted   700.00

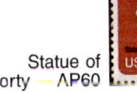

Statue of Liberty — AP60

Mt. Rushmore National Memorial — AP61

### GIORI PRESS PRINTING
**1974**
C87 AP60 18c carmine, black & ultramarine   .35   .30
C88 AP61 26c ultramarine, black & carmine   .60   .25

Plane & Globes — AP62

Plane, Globes & Flag — AP63

**1976, Jan. 2**
C89 AP62 25c red, blue & black   .50   .25
C90 AP63 31c red, blue & black   .60   .25
   b. All colors omitted

On No. C90b, there is a colorless embossed image and a tagging ghost plane visible under UV light.

## WRIGHT BROTHERS ISSUE

Orville and Wilbur Wright, Flyer A AP64

Wright Brothers, Flyer A and Shed AP65

### LITHOGRAPHED, ENGRAVED (GIORI)
**1978, Sept. 23**
C91 AP64 31c ultra & multi   .65   .30
C92 AP65 31c ultra & multi   .65   .30
   a. Vert. pair, #C91-C92   1.30   1.20
   b. As "a," ultra & black (engr.) omitted   475.00
   c. As "a," black (engr.) omitted   1,750.
   d. As "a," black, yellow, magenta, blue & brown (litho.) omitted   1,100.

## OCTAVE CHANUTE ISSUE

Chanute & Biplane Hangglider AP66

Biplane Hanggliders & Chanute AP67

**1979, Mar. 29**
C93 AP66 21c blue & multi   .70   .35
C94 AP67 21c blue & multi   .70   .35
   a. Vert. pair, #C93-C94   1.40   1.20
   b. As "a," ultra & black (engr.) omitted   4,000.

## WILEY POST ISSUE

Wiley Post & "Winnie Mae" AP68

NR-105 W, Post in Pressurized Suit, Portrait AP69

**1979, Nov. 20**
C95 AP68 25c blue & multi   .90   .45
C96 AP69 25c blue & multi   .90   .45
   a. Vert. pair, #C95-C96   1.80   1.50

## OLYMPIC GAMES ISSUE

High Jump — AP70

### PHOTOGRAVURE
**1979, Nov. 1**
C97 AP70 31c multicolored   .70   .30

## PHILIP MAZZEI (1730-1816)

Philip Mazzei (1730-1816), Italian-born Political Writer — AP71

**1980, Oct. 13**
C98 AP71 40c multicolored   .80   .25
   b. Imperf., pair   2,250.

**1982**    *Perf. 10½x11¼*
C98A AP71 40c multicolored   5.00   1.50
   c. Horiz. pair, imperf. vert.   3,250.

# UNITED STATES

## BLANCHE STUART SCOTT

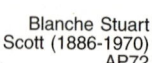 

Blanche Stuart
Scott (1886-1970)
AP72

**1980, Dec. 30**     **Perf. 11**
C99   AP72 28c multicolored    .60   .25
   *a.*   Imperf., pair    1,850.

## GLENN CURTISS

Glenn Curtiss
(1878-1930)
AP73

**1980, Dec. 30**
C100   AP73 35c multicolored    .65   .25
   *a.*   Light blue (background)
     omitted    2,000.

## SUMMER OLYMPICS 1984

Women's
Gymnastics
AP74

Hurdles
AP75

Women's
Basketball
AP76

Soccer
AP77

**1983, June 17**
C101   AP74 28c multicolored   1.00   .30
C102   AP75 28c multicolored   1.00   .30
C103   AP76 28c multicolored   1.00   .30
C104   AP77 28c multicolored   1.00   .30
   *a.*   Block of 4, #C101-C104   4.25   2.50
   *b.*   As "a," imperf. vert.   5,000.

Shot Put — AP78

Men's
Gymnastics
AP79

Women's
Swimming
AP80

Weight
Lifting — AP81

**1983, Apr. 8**     **Perf. 11.2 Bullseye**
C105   AP78 40c multicolored   .90   .40
C106   AP79 40c multicolored   .90   .40
C107   AP80 40c multicolored   .90   .40
C108   AP81 40c multicolored   .90   .40
   *b.*   Block of 4, #C105-C108   4.25   3.00
   *d.*   Block of 4, imperf.   600.00

Women's
Fencing — AP82

Cycling — AP83

Women's
Volleyball — AP84

Pole
Vaulting — AP85

**1983, Nov. 4**     **Perf. 11**
C109   AP82 35c multicolored   .90   .55
C110   AP83 35c multicolored   .90   .55
C111   AP84 35c multicolored   .90   .55
C112   AP85 35c multicolored   .90   .55
   *a.*   Block of 4, #C109-C112   4.00   3.25

## AVIATION PIONEERS

Alfred V.
Verville — AP86

Lawrence & Elmer
Sperry — AP87

**1985, Feb. 13**   **Tagged**   **Perf. 11**
C113   AP86 33c multicolored   .65   .25
   *a.*   Imperf., pair    500.00
C114   AP87 39c multicolored   .80   .25
   *a.*   Imperf., pair    1,250.

## TRANSPACIFIC AIRMAIL
## 50th Anniversary

Transpacific
Airmail — AP88

**1985, Feb. 15**
C115   AP88 44c multicolored   .85   .25
   *a.*   Imperf., pair    550.00

## FR. JUNIPERO SERRA (1713-1784)
## California Missionary

Outline Map of
Southern
California, Portrait,
San Gabriel
Mission — AP89

**1985, Aug. 22**
C116   AP89 44c multicolored   1.00   .35
   *a.*   Imperf., pair    850.00

## SETTLING OF NEW SWEDEN, 350th ANNIV.

Settling of New
Sweden, 350th
Anniv. — AP90

### LITHOGRAPHED AND ENGRAVED

**1988, Mar. 29**
C117   AP90 44c multicolored   1.00   .25
See Sweden No. 1672 and Finland No. 768.

## SAMUEL P. LANGLEY (1834-1906)

Langley and
Unmanned
Aerodrome
No. 5 — AP91

**1988, May 14**
C118   AP91 45c multicolored   1.00   .25

## IGOR SIKORSKY (1889-1972)

Sikorsky and
VS300 Helicopter,
1939 — AP92

### PHOTOGRAVURE AND ENGRAVED

**1988, June 23**
C119   AP92 36c multicolored   .70   .25
   *a.*   Red, dk blue & black (en-
     graved) omitted    750.00

Beware of examples with traces of engraved red offered as "red omitted" varieties.

## FRENCH REVOLUTION BICENTENNIAL

Liberty,
Equality and
Fraternity
AP93

### LITHOGRAPHED AND ENGRAVED

**1989, July 14**     **Perf. 11½x11**
C120   AP93 45c multicolored   .95   .25
See France Nos. 2143-2145a.

## PRE-COLUMBIAN AMERICA ISSUE

UPAE Emblem & *Key
Marco Cat* — AP94

### PHOTOGRAVURE

**1989, Oct. 12**     **Perf. 11**
C121   AP94 45c multicolored   .90   .25

## 20th UPU CONGRESS
## Futuristic Mail Delivery

Spacecraft — AP95

Air-suspended
Hover
Car — AP96

Moon
Rover — AP97

Space
Shuttle — AP98

### LITHOGRAPHED & ENGRAVED

**1989, Nov. 27**
C122   AP95 45c multicolored   1.00   .50
C123   AP96 45c multicolored   1.00   .50
C124   AP97 45c multicolored   1.00   .50
C125   AP98 45c multicolored   1.00   .50
   *a.*   Block of 4, #C122-C125   4.00   3.00
   *b.*   As "a," light blue (engr.)
     omitted    475.00
   *c.*   As "a," tagging omitted    —

### Souvenir Sheet
### LITHOGRAPHED & ENGRAVED

**1989, Nov. 24**     **Imperf.**
C126   Sheet of 4   5.00   4.00
   *a.*   AP95 45c multicolored   1.25   .50
   *b.*   AP96 45c multicolored   1.25   .50
   *c.*   AP97 45c multicolored   1.25   .50
   *d.*   AP98 45c multicolored   1.25   .50

## PRE-COLUMBIAN AMERICA ISSUE

Tropical
Coast — AP99

### PHOTOGRAVURE

**1990, Oct. 12**     **Perf. 11**
C127   AP99 45c multicolored   .90   .25

## HARRIET QUIMBY, 1ST AMERICAN WOMAN PILOT

Harriet Quimby,
Bleriot
Aircraft — AP100

**1991, Apr. 27**
C128   AP100 50c multicolored   1.00   .25
   *a.*   Vert. pair, imperf. horiz.   800.00
   *b.*   Perf. 11.2 bullseye,
     prephosphored uncoated
     paper ('93)   1.25   .25

## WILLIAM T. PIPER, AIRCRAFT MANUFACTURER

William T. Piper,
Piper
Cub — AP101

**1991, May 17**
C129   AP101 40c multicolored,
     shiny gum   .80   .25

Blue sky is plainly visible all the way across stamp above Piper's head.
See No. C132.

## ANTARCTIC TREATY, 30TH ANNIVERSARY

Antarctic Treaty,
30th
Anniv. — AP102

**1991, June 21**
C130   AP102 50c multicolored   1.00   .35

## PRE-COLUMBIAN AMERICA ISSUE

First Americans
Crossed Over
From
Asia — AP103

**1991, Oct. 12**
C131   AP103 50c multicolored   1.00   .35

### Piper Type of 1991
**1993**     **Perf. 11.2 Bullseye**
C132   AP101 40c multicolored,
     low gloss gum   3.50   .65

Piper's hair touches top edge of design. No selvage inscriptions.

"All LC (Letters and Cards) mail receives First-Class Mail service in the United States, is dispatched by the fastest transportation available, and travels by airmail or priority service in the destination country. All LC mail should be marked 'AIRMAIL' or 'PAR AVION.'" (U.S. Postal Service, Pub. 51).

No. C133 listed below was issued to meet the LC rate to Canada and Mexico and is inscribed with the silhouette of a jet plane next to the denomination indicating the need for airmail service. This is unlike No. 2998, which met the LC rate to other countries, but contained no indication that it was intended for that use.

Future issues that meet a specific international airmail rate and contain the airplane silhouette will be treated by Scott as Air Post stamps. Stamps similar to No. 2998 will be listed in the Postage section.

UNITED STATES 175

## SCENIC AMERICAN LANDSCAPES

Niagara Falls — AP104

**1999, May 12** *Serpentine Die Cut 11*
**Self-Adhesive**
C133 AP104 48c multicolored 1.00 .25

Rio Grande — AP105

**1999, July 30**
**Self-Adhesive**
C134 AP105 40c multicolored .80 .60

Grand Canyon — AP106

**LITHOGRAPHED**
*Serpentine Die Cut 11¼x11½*
**2000, Jan. 20**
**Self-Adhesive**
C135 AP106 60c multi 1.25 .25
  a. Die cutting omitted, pair 1,150.
  b. Vert. pair, die cutting omitted horiz. —
  c. Horiz. pair, die cutting omitted between —
  d. Horiz. pair, die cutting omitted vert. —

Nine-Mile Prairie, Nebraska AP107

**LITHOGRAPHED**
**2001, Mar. 6**
**Self-Adhesive**
C136 AP107 70c multi 1.40 .30

Mt. McKinley AP108

**PHOTOGRAVURE**
*Serpentine Die Cut 11*
**2001, Apr. 17**
**Self-Adhesive**
C137 AP108 80c multi 1.60 .35

Acadia National Park — AP109

**LITHOGRAPHED**
*Serpentine Die Cut 11.25x11.5*
**2001-05**
**Self-Adhesive**
C138 AP109 60c multi 1.25 .25
  a. Serpentine die cut 11½x11¾ 1.25 .25
  b. As "a," with "2005" year date 1.25 .25
  c. As "b," printed on back of backing paper, pane of 20 3,500.

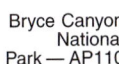

Bryce Canyon National Park — AP110

Great Smoky Mountains National Park — AP111

## LITHOGRAPHED
*Serpentine Die Cut 10¾*
**2006, Feb. 24**
**Self-Adhesive**
C139 AP110 63c multicolored 1.25 .25
  a. Die cutting omitted, pair 450.00
C140 AP111 75c multicolored 1.50 .35
  a. Die cutting omitted, pair 500.00

Yosemite National Park — AP112

**PHOTOGRAVURE**
*Serpentine Die Cut 11*
C141 AP112 84c multicolored 1.75 .35
Nos. C139-C141 (3) 4.50 .95

Okefenokee Swamp, Georgia and Florida — AP113

Hagatña Bay, Guam — AP114

**LITHOGRAPHED (#C142), PHOTOGRAVURE (#C143)**
*Serpentine Die Cut 10¾*
**2007, June 1**
**Self-Adhesive**
C142 AP113 69c multicolored 1.40 .30
*Serpentine Die Cut 11*
C143 AP114 90c multicolored 1.80 .40

13-Mile Woods, New Hampshire AP115

Trunk Bay, St. John, Virgin Islands — AP116

**LITHOGRAPHED (#C144), PHOTOGRAVURE (#C145)**
*Serpentine Die Cut 10¾*
**2008, May 16**
**Self-Adhesive**
C144 AP115 72c multicolored 1.50 .30
*Serpentine Die Cut 11*
C145 AP116 94c multicolored 1.90 .45

AP117

AP118

**LITHOGRAPHED, PHOTOGRAVURE (#C147)**
*Serpentine Die Cut 10¾*
**2009, June 28**
**Self-Adhesive**
C146 AP117 79c multicolored 2.00 .35
*Serpentine Die Cut 11*
C147 AP118 98c multicolored 2.00 .45

Voyageurs National Park, Minnesota AP119

## LITHOGRAPHED
*Serpentine Die Cut 10¾*
**2011, Apr. 11**
**Self-Adhesive**
C148 AP119 80c multicolored 2.50 .25
See note after No. 1549.

Glacier National Park, Montana — AP120

Amish Horse and Buggy on Road, Lancaster County, Pennsylvania — AP121

**LITHOGRAPHED**
**2012** *Serpentine Die Cut 10¾*
**Self-Adhesive**
C149 AP120 85c multicolored 3.25 .35
C150 AP121 $1.05 multicolored 2.75 .45
  a. Die cutting omitted on front, pair 500.00
  b. Silver (airplane silhouette) missing (PS)
Issued: 85c, 1/19; $1.05, 1/20.

## AIR POST SPECIAL DELIVERY STAMPS

To provide for the payment of both the postage and the special delivery fee in one stamp.

Great Seal of United States — APSD1

**1934, Aug. 30 Unwmk. Perf. 11**
CE1 APSD1 16c dark blue .70 .80
  Never hinged .90
For imperforate variety see No. 771.

Great Seal of United States — APSD2

**1936, Feb. 10**
CE2 APSD2 16c red & blue .45 .35
  Never hinged .65
  a. Horiz. pair, imperf. vert. 4,250.
  Never hinged 5,250.

## SPECIAL DELIVERY STAMPS

When affixed to any letter or article of mailable matter, secured immediate delivery, between 7 A. M. and midnight, at any post office.

Messenger Running — SD1

**Flat Plate Printing**
**1885 Unwmk. Perf. 12**
E1 SD1 10c blue 600.00 80.00
  Never hinged 1,300.

Messenger Running — SD2

**1888, Sept. 6**
E2 SD2 10c blue 500.00 45.00
  Never hinged 1,150.

## COLUMBIAN EXPOSITION ISSUE

Though not issued expressly for the Exposition, No. E3 is considered to be part of that issue.

**1893, Jan. 24**
E3 SD2 10c orange 300.00 50.00
  Never hinged 650.

Messenger Running — SD3

**1894, Oct. 10 Line under "TEN CENTS"**
E4 SD3 10c blue 900.00 110.00
  Never hinged 2,000.

No. E5a

**1895, Aug. 16 Wmk. 191**
E5 SD3 10c blue 210.00 12.50
  Never hinged 475.00
  a. Dots in curved frame above messenger (Pl. 882) 400.00 50.00
  Never hinged 800.00

Messenger on Bicycle — SD4

**1902, Dec. 9**
E6 SD4 10c ultramarine 240.00 10.00
  Never hinged 500.00
  a. 10c blue 300.00 12.50
  Never hinged 750.00

Helmet of Mercury and Olive Branch — SD5

**1908, Dec. 12**
E7 SD5 10c green 65.00 50.00
  Never hinged 140.00

**1911, Jan. Wmk. 190 Perf. 12**
E8 SD4 10c ultramarine 120.00 10.00
  Never hinged 250.00
  b. 10c violet blue 160.00 14.00
  Never hinged 350.00

**1914, Sept. Perf. 10**
E9 SD4 10c ultramarine 190.00 12.00
  Never hinged 425.00
  a. 10c blue 260.00 15.00
  Never hinged 575.00

**1916, Oct. 19 Unwmk. Perf. 10**
E10 SD4 10c pale ultramarine 350.00 50.00
  Never hinged 750.00
  a. 10c blue 400.00 55.00
  Never hinged 800.00

**1917, May 2 Perf. 11**
E11 SD4 10c ultramarine 20.00 .75
  Never hinged 45.00
  b. 10c gray violet 33.00 0.00
  Never hinged 75.00
  c. 10c blue 100.00 5.00
  Never hinged 210.00
  d. Perf. 10 at left —

Postman and Motorcycle SD6

**1922, July 12**
E12 SD6 10c gray violet 45.00 3.00
  Never hinged 95.00
  a. 10c deep ultramarine 55.00 3.50
  Never hinged 130.00

Post Office Truck — SD7

**1925**

| | | | |
|---|---|---|---|
| **E13** | SD6 15c deep orange | 40.00 | 3.75 |
| | Never hinged | 75.00 | |
| **E14** | SD7 20c black | 2.00 | 1.00 |
| | Never hinged | 4.00 | |
| | *Nos. E12-E14 (3)* | 87.00 | 7.75 |

**Motorcycle Type of 1922**

ROTARY PRESS PRINTING

**1927-31** ***Perf. 11x10½***

| | | | |
|---|---|---|---|
| **E15** | SD6 10c gray violet | 1.25 | .25 |
| | Never hinged | 2.00 | |
| | On cover | | .50 |
| *a.* | 10c red lilac | .80 | .25 |
| | Never hinged | 1.40 | |
| *b.* | 10c gray lilac | .90 | .25 |
| | Never hinged | 1.60 | |
| *c.* | Horiz. pair, imperf. btwn., red lilac shade | *350.00* | |
| | Never hinged | *575.00* | |
| **E16** | SD6 15c orange ('31) | .60 | .25 |
| | Never hinged | .90 | |

**Catalogue values for unused stamps in this section, from this point to the end, are for Never Hinged items.**

**1944-51**

| | | | |
|---|---|---|---|
| **E17** | SD6 13c blue | .60 | .25 |
| **E18** | SD6 17c orange yellow | 3.50 | 2.50 |
| **E19** | SD7 20c black ('51) | 1.20 | .25 |

Special Delivery Letter, Hand to Hand — SD8

**1954, Oct. 13** ***Perf. 11x10½***

| | | | |
|---|---|---|---|
| **E20** | SD8 20c deep blue | .40 | .25 |

**1957, Sept. 3**

| | | | |
|---|---|---|---|
| **E21** | SD8 30c lake | .50 | .25 |

Arrows — SD9

GIORI PRESS PRINTING

**1969, Nov. 21** ***Perf. 11***

| | | | |
|---|---|---|---|
| **E22** | SD9 45c red & blue | 1.20 | .25 |

**1971, May 10**

| | | | |
|---|---|---|---|
| **E23** | SD9 60c blue & red | 1.25 | .25 |

From 1885 to the present, special delivery stamps have not been and are not valid for the payment of postage of any description, nor for registry fees.

## REGISTRATION STAMP

Issued for the prepayment of registry fees; not usable for postage.

Eagle — RS1

**1911, Dec. 1** **Wmk. 190** ***Perf. 12***

| | | | |
|---|---|---|---|
| **F1** | RS1 10c ultramarine | 75.00 | 15.00 |
| | Never hinged | 160.00 | |

## CERTIFIED MAIL STAMP

For use on first-class mail for which no indemnity value is claimed, but for which proof of mailing and proof of delivery are available at less cost than registered mail.

**Catalogue value for the unused stamp in this section is for a Never Hinged item.**

Letter Carrier — CM1

ROTARY PRESS PRINTING

**1955, June 6** **Unwmk.** ***Perf. 10½x11***

| | | | |
|---|---|---|---|
| **FA1** | CM1 15c red | .75 | .50 |

## POSTAGE DUE STAMPS

For affixing, by a postal clerk to any piece of mailable matter, to denote the amount to be collected from the addressee because of insufficient prepayment of postage.

D1

**Printed by the American Bank Note Co.**

Plates of 200 subjects in two panes of 100 each.

**1879** **Unwmk.** **Engr.** ***Perf. 12***

| | | | |
|---|---|---|---|
| **J1** | D1 1c brown | 100.00 | 14.00 |
| | Never hinged | 270.00 | |
| **J2** | D1 2c brown | 450.00 | 25.00 |
| | Never hinged | 1,050. | |
| **J3** | D1 3c brown | 100.00 | 6.00 |
| | Never hinged | 280.00 | |
| **J4** | D1 5c brown | 800.00 | 70.00 |
| | Never hinged | 1,950. | |
| **J5** | D1 10c brown | 950.00 | 70.00 |
| | Never hinged | *2,500.* | |
| *a.* | Imperf., pair | *2,500.* | |
| **J6** | D1 30c brown | 425.00 | 65.00 |
| | Never hinged | 900.00 | |
| **J7** | D1 50c brown | 625.00 | 90.00 |
| | Never hinged | 1,600. | |
| | *Nos. J1-J7 (7)* | 3,450. | 340.00 |

Special Printing

| | | | |
|---|---|---|---|
| **J8** | D1 1c deep brown | *16,000.* | |
| | Never hinged | — | |
| | No gum | *6,500.* | |
| **J9** | D1 2c deep brown | *15,000.* | |
| | No gum | *6,000.* | |
| **J10** | D1 3c deep brown | *20,000.* | |
| | No gum | *8,500.* | |
| **J11** | D1 5c deep brown | *14,000.* | |
| | No gum | *5,250.* | |
| **J12** | D1 10c deep brown | *6,750.* | |
| | No gum | *2,900.* | |
| **J13** | D1 30c deep brown | *7,250.* | |
| | No gum | *3,000.* | |
| **J14** | D1 50c deep brown | *7,500.* | |
| | No gum | *3,000.* | |

**1884**

| | | | |
|---|---|---|---|
| **J15** | D1 1c red brown | 70.00 | 7.00 |
| | Never hinged | 200.00 | |
| **J16** | D1 2c red brown | 80.00 | 6.00 |
| | Never hinged | 225.00 | |
| **J17** | D1 3c red brown | 1,050. | 350.00 |
| | Never hinged | 2,500. | |
| **J18** | D1 5c red brown | 550.00 | 50.00 |
| | Never hinged | 1,300. | |
| **J19** | D1 10c red brown | 550.00 | 35.00 |
| | Never hinged | 1,300. | |
| **J20** | D1 30c red brown | 225.00 | 70.00 |
| | Never hinged | 550.00 | |
| **J21** | D1 50c red brown | 1,900. | 250.00 |
| | Never hinged | 4,000. | |
| | *Nos. J15-J21 (7)* | 4,425. | 768.00 |

**1891**

| | | | |
|---|---|---|---|
| **J22** | D1 1c bright claret | 30.00 | 2.00 |
| | Never hinged | 85.00 | |
| **J23** | D1 2c bright claret | 32.50 | 2.00 |
| | Never hinged | 90.00 | |
| **J24** | D1 3c bright claret | 67.50 | 16.00 |
| | Never hinged | 180.00 | |
| **J25** | D1 5c bright claret | 100.00 | 16.00 |
| | Never hinged | 290.00 | |
| **J26** | D1 10c bright claret | 165.00 | 30.00 |
| | Never hinged | 500.00 | |
| **J27** | D1 30c bright claret | 575.00 | 225.00 |
| | Never hinged | 1,700. | |
| **J28** | D1 50c bright claret | 650.00 | 225.00 |
| | Never hinged | 1,750. | |
| | *Nos. J22-J28 (7)* | 1,620. | 516.00 |

Nos. J22-J28 fluoresce orange under longwave ultraviolet light. Nos. J15-J21 do not.

See Die and Plate Proofs in the Scott U.S. Specialized catalog for imperfs. on stamp paper.

**The color on Nos. J29-J44 will run when immersed in water. Extreme caution is advised.**

D2

**Printed by the Bureau of Engraving and Printing.**

**1894**

| | | | |
|---|---|---|---|
| **J29** | D2 1c vermilion | 2,400. | 750. |
| | Never hinged | *6,000.* | |
| **J30** | D2 2c vermilion | 800. | 350. |
| | Never hinged | 1,900. | |

**1894-95**

| | | | |
|---|---|---|---|
| **J31** | D2 1c deep claret | 72.50 | 12.00 |
| | Never hinged | 260.00 | |
| *b.* | Vertical pair, imperf. horiz. | — | |
| **J32** | D2 2c deep claret | 62.50 | 10.00 |
| | Never hinged | 240.00 | |
| **J33** | D2 3c deep claret ('95) | 200.00 | 50.00 |
| | Never hinged | 575.00 | |
| **J34** | D2 5c deep claret ('95) | 300.00 | 55.00 |
| | Never hinged | 850.00 | |
| **J35** | D2 10c deep claret | 350.00 | 40.00 |
| | Never hinged | 1,000. | |
| **J36** | D2 30c deep claret ('95) | 550.00 | 250.00 |
| | Never hinged | 1,250. | |
| *a.* | 30c carmine | 675.00 | 275.00 |
| | Never hinged | 1,600. | |
| *b.* | 30c pale rose | 475.00 | 200.00 |
| | Never hinged | 1,150. | |
| **J37** | D2 50c deep claret ('95) | 1,800. | 800.00 |
| | Never hinged | 4,250. | |
| *a.* | 50c pale rose | 1,600. | 725.00 |
| | Never hinged | 3,750. | |
| | *Nos. J31-J37 (7)* | 3,335. | 1,217. |

Shades are numerous in the 1894 and later issues.

See Die and Plate Proofs in the Scott U.S. Specialized catalog for imperfs. on stamp paper.

**1895-97** **Wmk. 191**

| | | | |
|---|---|---|---|
| **J38** | D2 1c deep claret | 13.50 | 1.00 |
| | Never hinged | 40.00 | |
| **J39** | D2 2c deep claret | 13.50 | 1.00 |
| | Never hinged | 40.00 | |
| **J40** | D2 3c deep claret | 100.00 | 5.00 |
| | Never hinged | 225.00 | |
| **J41** | D2 5c deep claret | 110.00 | 5.00 |
| | Never hinged | 280.00 | |
| **J42** | D2 10c deep claret | 110.00 | 7.50 |
| | Never hinged | 280.00 | |
| **J43** | D2 30c deep claret ('97) | 600.00 | 80.00 |
| | Never hinged | 1,500. | |
| **J44** | D2 50c deep claret ('96) | 375.00 | 60.00 |
| | Never hinged | 925.00 | |
| | *Nos. J38-J44 (7)* | 1,322. | 159.50 |

**1910-12** **Wmk. 190**

| | | | |
|---|---|---|---|
| **J45** | D2 1c deep claret | 40.00 | 5.00 |
| | Never hinged | 115.00 | |
| *a.* | 1c rose carmine | 35.00 | 5.00 |
| | Never hinged | 105.00 | |
| **J46** | D2 2c deep claret | 40.00 | 2.00 |
| | Never hinged | 115.00 | |
| *a.* | 2c rose carmine | 35.00 | 2.00 |
| | Never hinged | 105.00 | |
| **J47** | D2 3c deep claret | 625.00 | 60.00 |
| | Never hinged | 1,600. | |
| **J48** | D2 5c deep claret | 120.00 | 12.00 |
| | Never hinged | 275.00 | |
| *a.* | 5c rose carmine | 120.00 | 12.00 |
| | Never hinged | 275.00 | |
| **J49** | D2 10c deep claret | 125.00 | 20.00 |
| | Never hinged | 280.00 | |
| *a.* | 10c rose carmine | 125.00 | 20.00 |
| | Never hinged | 280.00 | |
| **J50** | D2 50c deep claret ('12) | 1,100. | 200.00 |
| | Never hinged | 2,900. | |
| *a.* | 50c rose carmine | 1,150. | 190.00 |
| | Never hinged | *3,000.* | |
| | *Nos. J45-J50 (6)* | 2,050. | 299.00 |

**1914** ***Perf. 10***

| | | | |
|---|---|---|---|
| **J52** | D2 1c carmine lake | 80.00 | 15.00 |
| | Never hinged | 220.00 | |
| *a.* | 1c dull rose | 85.00 | 15.00 |
| | Never hinged | 230.00 | |
| **J53** | D2 2c carmine lake | 62.50 | 1.00 |
| | Never hinged | 170.00 | |
| *a.* | 2c dull rose | 67.50 | 2.00 |
| | Never hinged | 180.00 | |
| *b.* | 2c vermilion | 67.50 | 2.00 |
| | Never hinged | 180.00 | |
| **J54** | D2 3c carmine lake | 1,050. | 75.00 |
| | Never hinged | 3,000. | |
| *a.* | 3c dull rose | 1,000. | 75.00 |
| | Never hinged | 2,900. | |
| **J55** | D2 5c carmine lake | 50.00 | 6.00 |
| | Never hinged | 140.00 | |
| *a.* | 5c dull rose | 45.00 | 4.00 |
| | Never hinged | 130.00 | |
| **J56** | D2 10c carmine lake | 75.00 | 4.00 |
| | Never hinged | 200.00 | |
| *a.* | 10c dull rose | 80.00 | 5.00 |
| | Never hinged | 210.00 | |
| **J57** | D2 30c carmine lake | 225.00 | 55.00 |
| | Never hinged | 525.00 | |
| **J58** | D2 50c carmine lake | *11,500.* | 1,700. |
| | Never hinged | *22,000.* | |
| | *Nos. J52-J58 (7)* | 13,043. | 1,856. |

No. J58 unused is valued in the grade of fine to very fine.

**1916** **Unwmk.** ***Perf. 10***

| | | | |
|---|---|---|---|
| **J59** | D2 1c rose | 4,000. | 750.00 |
| | Never hinged | 9,000. | |
| **J60** | D2 2c rose | 250.00 | 75.00 |
| | Never hinged | 625.00 | |

**1917** ***Perf. 11***

| | | | |
|---|---|---|---|
| **J61** | D2 1c carmine rose | 2.75 | .25 |
| | Never hinged | 9.00 | |
| *a.* | 1c rose red | 2.75 | .25 |
| | Never hinged | 9.00 | |
| *b.* | 1c deep claret | 2.75 | .25 |
| | Never hinged | 9.00 | |
| **J62** | D2 2c carmine rose | 2.75 | .25 |
| | Never hinged | 9.00 | |
| *a.* | 2c rose red | 2.75 | .25 |
| | Never hinged | 9.00 | |
| *b.* | 2c deep claret | 2.75 | .25 |
| | Never hinged | 9.00 | |
| **J63** | D2 3c carmine rose | 13.50 | .80 |
| | Never hinged | 35.00 | |
| *a.* | 3c rose red | 13.50 | .80 |
| | Never hinged | 35.00 | |
| *b.* | 3c deep claret | 13.50 | .80 |
| | Never hinged | 35.00 | |
| **J64** | D2 5c carmine | 11.00 | .80 |
| | Never hinged | 32.50 | |
| *a.* | 5c rose red | 11.00 | .80 |
| | Never hinged | 32.50 | |
| *b.* | 5c deep claret | 11.00 | .80 |
| | Never hinged | 32.50 | |
| **J65** | D2 10c carmine rose | 22.50 | 1.00 |
| | Never hinged | 65.00 | |
| *a.* | 10c rose red | 22.50 | 1.00 |
| | Never hinged | 65.00 | |
| *b.* | 10c deep claret | 22.50 | 1.00 |
| | Never hinged | 65.00 | |
| **J66** | D2 30c carmine rose | 80.00 | 2.00 |
| | Never hinged | 220.00 | |
| *a.* | 30c deep claret | 80.00 | 2.00 |
| | Never hinged | 220.00 | |
| *b.* | As "a," perf 10 at top, precanceled | | *21,000.* |

No. J66b is valued with small faults and fine centering, as the two recorded examples are in this condition and grade.

| | | | |
|---|---|---|---|
| **J67** | D2 50c carmine rose | 140.00 | 1.00 |
| | Never hinged | 325.00 | |
| *a.* | 50c rose red | 140.00 | 1.00 |
| | Never hinged | 325.00 | |
| *b.* | 50c deep claret | 140.00 | 1.00 |
| | Never hinged | 325.00 | |
| | *Nos. J61-J67 (7)* | 272.50 | 6.10 |
| | *Nos. J61-J67, never hinged* | 695.50 | |

WALTER KASELL STAMPS

**Quality United States Stamps**

**Classics, U.S. Possessions & Plate Blocks**

175 Richdale Ave., Cambridge, MA 02140 • (617) 694-9360
Email: wbkasell@yahoo.com

**1925**

**J68** D2 ½c dull red 1.00 .25
Never hinged 1.75

D3

D4

**1930** ***Perf. 11***

**J69** D3 ½c carmine 4.25 1.90
Never hinged 9.50
**J70** D3 1c carmine 2.75 .35
Never hinged 6.25
**J71** D3 2c carmine 3.75 .35
Never hinged 8.50
**J72** D3 3c carmine 20.00 2.75
Never hinged 47.50
**J73** D3 5c carmine 18.00 5.00
Never hinged 42.50
**J74** D3 10c carmine 42.50 2.00
Never hinged 95.00
**J75** D3 30c carmine 125.00 4.00
Never hinged 275.00
**J76** D3 50c carmine 175.00 2.00
Never hinged 375.00
**J77** D4 $1 carmine 32.50 .35
Never hinged 65.00
*a.* $1 scarlet 27.50 .35
Never hinged 55.00
**J78** D4 $5 dull carmine 37.50 .35
Never hinged 85.00
*a.* scarlet 32.50 .35
Never hinged 70.00

**Type of 1930-31 Issue**
**Rotary Press Printing**

**1931** ***Perf. 11x10½***

**J79** D3 ½c dull carmine 1.40 .25
Never hinged 2.00
*a.* ½c scarlet .90 .25
Never hinged 1.30
P# block of 4 20.00 —
**J80** D3 1c dull carmine .45 .25
Never hinged .60
*a.* scarlet .25 .25
Never hinged .30
**J81** D3 2c dull carmine .45 .25
Never hinged .60
*a.* scarlet .25 .25
Never hinged .30
**J82** D3 3c dull carmine .45 .25
Never hinged .60
*a.* scarlet .30 .25
Never hinged .45
**J83** D3 5c dull carmine .90 .25
Never hinged 1.40
*a.* scarlet .50 .25
Never hinged .75
**J84** D3 10c dull carmine 1.90 .25
Never hinged 3.00
*a.* scarlet 1.25 .25
Never hinged 1.90
**J85** D3 30c dull carmine 14.00 .25
Never hinged 22.50
*a.* 30c scarlet 7.50 .25
Never hinged 11.50
P# block of 4 35.00 —
**J86** D3 50c dull carmine 14.00 .25
Never hinged 22.50
*a.* 50c scarlet 9.00 .25
Never hinged 15.00
P# block of 4 52.50 —

**Design measures 22½x19mm**

**1956** ***Perf. 10½x11***

**J87** D4 $1 scarlet 30.00 .25
Never hinged 52.50
*Nos. J79-J87 (9)* 63.55 2.25
*Nos. J79-J87, never hinged* 99.45

For listings of other color shades and printing varieties see the *Scott Specialized Catalogue of United States Stamps and Covers.*

**Catalogue values for unused stamps in this section, from this point to the end, are for Never Hinged items.**

D5

Denominations added in black by rubber plates in an operation similar to precanceling.

**Rotary Press Printing**
***Perf. 11x10½***

**1959, June 19** **Unwmk.**

**Denomination in Black**

**J88** D5 ½c carmine rose 1.50 1.10
**J89** D5 1c carmine rose .25 .25
*a.* Denomination omitted 150.00
*b.* Pair, one without "1 CENT" 350.00
**J90** D5 2c carmine rose .25 .25
**J91** D5 3c carmine rose .25 .25
*a.* Pair, one without "3 CENTS" 550.00
**J92** D5 4c carmine rose .25 .25
**J93** D5 5c carmine rose .25 .25
*a.* Pair, one without "5 CENTS" 1,500.
**J94** D5 6c carmine rose .25 .25
*a.* Pair, one without "6 CENTS" 700.00
**J95** D5 7c carmine rose .25 .25
**J96** D5 8c carmine rose .25 .25
*a.* Pair, one without "8 CENTS" 750.00
**J97** D5 10c carmine rose .25 .25
**J98** D5 30c carmine rose .70 .25
**J99** D5 50c carmine rose 1.10 .25

**Straight Numeral Outlined in Black**

**J100** D5 $1 carmine rose 2.00 .25
**J101** D5 $5 carmine rose 9.00 .25
*Nos. J88-J101 (14)* 16.55 4.35

**All single stamps with denomination omitted are catalogued as No. J89a.**

**1978-85** **Denomination in Black**

**J102** D5 11c carmine rose .25 .25
**J103** D5 13c carmine rose .25 .25
**J104** D5 17c carmine rose ('85) .40 .35

## UNITED STATES OFFICES IN CHINA

Issued for sale by the postal agency at Shanghai, at their surcharged value in local currency. Valid to the amount of their original values for the prepayment of postage on mail dispatched from the U.S. postal agency at Shanghai to addresses in the U.S.

Nos. 498-499, 502-504, 506-510, 512, 514-518 Surcharged

**1919** **Unwmk.** ***Perf. 11***

**K1** A140 2c on 1c green 22.50 *70.00*
Never hinged 67.50
**K2** A140 4c on 2c rose, type I 22.50 *70.00*
Never hinged 67.50
**K3** A140 6c on 3c vio, type II 55.00 *140.00*
Never hinged 140.00
**K4** A140 8c on 4c brown 55.00 *140.00*
Never hinged 140.00
**K5** A140 10c on 5c blue 60.00 *140.00*
Never hinged 160.00
**K6** A140 12c on 6c red org 80.00 *210.00*
Never hinged 210.00
**K7** A140 14c on 7c black 82.50 *210.00*
Never hinged 215.00
**K8** A148 16c on 8c ol bis 65.00 *160.00*
Never hinged 170.00
*a.* 16c on 8c ol grn 55.00 *140.00*
Never hinged 150.00
**K9** A148 18c on 9c sal red 60.00 *175.00*
Never hinged 150.00
**K10** A148 20c on 10c org yel 55.00 *140.00*
Never hinged 140.00
**K11** A148 24c on 12c brn car 75.00 *160.00*
Never hinged 190.00
*a.* 24c on 12c cl brn 110.00 *240.00*
Never hinged 275.00
**K12** A148 30c on 15c gray 82.50 *230.00*
Never hinged 200.00
**K13** A148 40c on 20c deep ultra 120.00 *325.00*
Never hinged 300.00
**K14** A148 60c on 30c org red 110.00 *275.00*
Never hinged 280.00
**K15** A148 $1 on 50c lt vio 550.00 *1,000.*
Never hinged 1,200.
**K16** A148 $2 on $1 vio brn 425.00 *750.00*
Never hinged 925.00
*a.* Double surcharge 10,500. *11,500.*
Never hinged 17,500.
*Nos. K1-K16 (16)* 1,920. *4,195.*

Fake surcharges exist, but most are rather crudely made.

Nos. 498 and 528B Surcharged

**1922, July 3**

**K17** A140 2c on 1c green 100.00 *225.00*
Never hinged 225.00
**K18** A140 4c on 2c car, type VII 100.00 *225.00*
Never hinged 225.00
*a.* "SHANGHAI" omitted 7,500.
*b.* "CHINA" only 16,000.

## OFFICIAL STAMPS

The franking privilege having been abolished, as of July 1, 1873, these stamps were provided for each of the departments of Government for the prepayment of postage on official matter.

Penalty franks were first authorized in 1877, and their expanded use after 1879 reduced the need for official stamps, the use of which was finally abolished on July 5, 1884.

Designs, except Post Office, resemble those illustrated but are not identical. Each bears the name of Department. Portraits are as follows: 1c, Franklin; 2c, Jackson; 3c, Washington; 6c, Lincoln; 7c, Stanton; 10c, Jefferson; 12c, Clay; 15c, Webster; 24c, Scott; 30c, Hamilton; 90c, Perry.

**Special printings overprinted "SPECIMEN" follow No. O120.**

**Printed by the Continental Bank Note Co.**

O1

**Thin Hard Paper**
**AGRICULTURE**

**1873** **Engr.** **Unwmk.** ***Perf. 12***

**O1** O1 1c yellow 300.00 *200.00*
Never hinged 1,000.
No gum 170.00
**O2** O1 2c yellow 275.00 100.00
Never hinged 575.00
No gum 130.00
**O3** O1 3c yellow 225.00 17.50
Never hinged 450.00
No gum 105.00
**O4** O1 6c yellow 275.00 60.00
Never hinged 575.00
No gum 130.00
**O5** O1 10c yellow 525.00 200.00
Never hinged 1,150.
No gum 240.00
**O6** O1 12c yellow 450.00 260.00
Never hinged 1,000.
No gum 250.00
**O7** O1 15c yellow 425.00 230.00
Never hinged 950.00
No gum 225.00
**O8** O1 24c yellow 425.00 250.00
Never hinged 950.00
No gum 225.00
**O9** O1 30c yellow 550.00 280.00
Never hinged 1,200.
No gum 275.00
*Nos. O1-O9 (9)* 3,450. 1,598.

**EXECUTIVE**

Franklin—O2

**1873**

**O10** O2 1c carmine 900.00 550.00
Never hinged 3,500.
No gum 450.00
**O11** O2 2c carmine 575.00 260.00
Never hinged 1,400.
No gum 260.00
**O12** O2 3c carmine 700.00 225.00
Never hinged 1,600.
No gum 325.00
*a.* 3c violet rose 1,100. 275.00
Never hinged 2,500.
No gum 500.00
On cover —
**O13** O2 6c carmine 900.00 600.00
Never hinged —
No gum 425.00
**O14** O2 10c carmine 1,200. 1,000.
Never hinged 2,500.
No gum 600.00
*Nos. O10-O14 (5)* 4,275. 2,635.

**INTERIOR**

O3

**1873**

**O15** O3 1c vermilion 75.00 10.00
Never hinged 170.00
No gum 35.00
**O16** O3 2c vermilion 70.00 12.00
Never hinged 160.00
No gum 30.00
**O17** O3 3c vermilion 80.00 6.00
Never hinged 175.00
No gum 40.00
**O18** O3 6c vermilion 70.00 10.00
Never hinged 160.00
No gum 30.00
**O19** O3 10c vermilion 70.00 20.00
Never hinged 160.00
No gum 30.00
**O20** O3 12c vermilion 90.00 12.00
Never hinged 200.00
No gum 45.00
**O21** O3 15c vermilion 200.00 25.00
Never hinged 450.00
No gum 90.00
**O22** O3 24c vermilion 180.00 20.00
Never hinged 400.00
No gum 85.00
*a.* Double impression —
**O23** O3 30c vermilion 290.00 20.00
Never hinged 625.00
No gum 130.00
**O24** O3 90c vermilion 325.00 50.00
Never hinged 700.00
No gum 140.00
*Nos. O15-O24 (10)* 1,450. 185.00

**JUSTICE**

O4

**1873**

**O25** O4 1c purple 250.00 100.00
Never hinged 550.00
No gum 120.00
**O26** O4 2c purple 310.00 110.00
Never hinged 700.00
No gum 135.00
**O27** O4 3c purple 300.00 35.00
Never hinged 700.00
No gum 125.00
**O28** O4 6c purple 310.00 45.00
Never hinged 700.00
No gum 135.00
**O29** O4 10c purple 310.00 100.00
Never hinged 1,250.
No gum 135.00
**O30** O4 12c purple 260.00 75.00
Never hinged 1,500.
No gum 125.00
**O31** O4 15c purple 500.00 200.00
Never hinged 1,300.
No gum 240.00
**O32** O4 24c purple 1,250. 425.00
Never hinged 4,250.
No gum 600.00
**O33** O4 30c purple 1,300. 350.00
Never hinged —
No gum 625.00
**O34** O4 90c purple 1,900. 900.00
Never hinged 4,000.
No gum 900.00
*Nos. O25-O34 (10)* 6,690. 2,340.

**NAVY**

O5

**1873**

**O35** O5 1c ultramarine 160.00 50.00
Never hinged 350.00
No gum 75.00
*a.* 1c dull blue 200.00 50.00
Never hinged 400.00
No gum 87.50
**O36** O5 2c ultramarine 160.00 25.00
Never hinged 350.00
No gum 75.00
*a.* 2c dull blue 200.00 25.00
Never hinged 400.00
No gum 87.50
**O37** O5 3c ultramarine 170.00 15.00
Never hinged 1,750.
No gum 80.00
*a.* 3c dull blue 225.00 15.00
Never hinged 450.00
No gum 100.00
**O38** O5 6c ultramarine 150.00 25.00
Never hinged 450.00
No gum 70.00
*a.* 6c dull blue 175.00 25.00
Never hinged 385.00
No gum 82.50
**O39** O5 7c ultramarine 700.00 230.00
Never hinged 1,600.
No gum 325.00
*a.* 7c dull blue 750.00 230.00
Never hinged 1,600.
No gum 325.00
**O40** O5 10c ultramarine 210.00 45.00
Never hinged 1,000.
No gum 95.00
*a.* 10c dull blue 225.00 45.00
Never hinged 1,000.
No gum 110.00
**O41** O5 12c ultramarine 240.00 45.00
Never hinged 900.00
No gum 115.00
**O42** O5 15c ultramarine 425.00 80.00
Never hinged —
No gum 200.00
**O43** O5 24c ultramarine 425.00 85.00
Never hinged 1,750.
No gum 200.00

178 UNITED STATES

a. 24c dull blue 425.00 80.00
Never hinged *1,350.*
No gum 200.00
**O44** O5 30c ultramarine 350.00 50.00
Never hinged *3,000.*
No gum 160.00
**O45** O5 90c ultramarine 1,050. 375.00
Never hinged *6,000.*
No gum 500.00
a. Double impression *20,000.*
*Nos. O35-O45 (11)* 4,040. 1,025.

### POST OFFICE

Stamps of the Post Office Department are often on paper with a gray surface. This is essentially a wiping problem, caused by an over-milled carbon black pigment that released acid and etched the plates. There is no premium for stamps on paper with a gray surface.

O6

**1873**
**O47** O6 1c black 25.00 12.00
Never hinged 60.00
No gum 12.00
**O48** O6 2c black 30.00 10.00
Never hinged 75.00
No gum 14.00
**O49** O6 3c black 10.00 2.00
Never hinged 25.00
No gum 4.50
a. Printed on both sides *7,500.*
b. Double paper — —
**O50** O6 6c black 30.00 8.00
Never hinged 75.00
No gum 14.00
a. Diagonal half used as 3c on cover *5,000.*
b. Double impression *3,000.*
**O51** O6 10c black 140.00 55.00
Never hinged 325.00
No gum 65.00
**O52** O6 12c black 120.00 12.00
Never hinged 275.00
No gum 55.00
**O53** O6 15c black 140.00 20.00
Never hinged 325.00
No gum 65.00
**O54** O6 24c black 225.00 25.00
Never hinged 500.00
No gum 105.00
a. Double paper — —
**O55** O6 30c black 250.00 25.00
Never hinged 550.00
No gum 110.00
**O56** O6 90c black 260.00 25.00
Never hinged 575.00
No gum 120.00
a. Double paper — —
*Nos. O47-O56 (10)* 1,230. 194.00

### STATE

Franklin — O7

Seward — O8

**1873**
**O57** O7 1c dark green 260.00 75.00
Never hinged 575.00
No gum 125.00
**O58** O7 2c dark green 310.00 100.00
Never hinged —
No gum 150.00
**O59** O7 3c dark green 220.00 25.00
Never hinged 500.00
No gum 105.00
b. Double paper — —
**O60** O7 6c dark green 250.00 30.00
Never hinged 550.00
No gum 120.00
**O61** O7 7c dark green 290.00 65.00
Never hinged 650.00
No gum 140.00
**O62** O7 10c dark green 250.00 55.00
Never hinged 575.00
No gum 120.00
**O63** O7 12c dark green 310.00 125.00
Never hinged 700.00
No gum 150.00
**O64** O7 15c dark green 350.00 90.00
Never hinged 775.00
No gum 170.00
**O65** O7 24c dark green 550.00 230.00
Never hinged *1,200.*
No gum 275.00
**O66** O7 30c dark green 525.00 180.00
Never hinged *1,150.*
No gum 260.00
**O67** O7 90c dark green 1,100. 325.00
Never hinged *2,400.*
No gum 525.00
**O68** O8 $2 green & black 1,800. 3,000.
Never hinged *3,750.*
No gum 850.00
**O69** O8 $5 green & black 8,000. *13,000.*
Never hinged —
No gum 3,750.
**O70** O8 $10 green & black 4,500. *12,500.*
Never hinged 10,500.
No gum 2,500.

Nos. O68-O70 used are valued with neat handstamp cancels. Examples with black smudge or similar nondescript cancels sell for much less.

**O71** O8 $20 green & black 5,000. 5,500.
Never hinged 11,500.
No gum 2,500.

No. O71 used is valued with a blue or red handstamp favor cancel. Nos. O68-O71 with pen cancels sell for approximately 25-40% of the values shown.

### TREASURY

O9

**1873**
**O72** O9 1c brown 120.00 10.00
Never hinged 250.00
No gum 55.00
**O73** O9 2c brown 125.00 8.00
Never hinged 275.00
No gum 57.50
**O74** O9 3c brown 110.00 2.00
Never hinged 230.00
No gum 50.00
a. Double impression *5,000.*
b. Double paper —
**O75** O9 6c brown 120.00 4.00
Never hinged 250.00
No gum 55.00
**O76** O9 7c brown 250.00 35.00
Never hinged 550.00
No gum 120.00
**O77** O9 10c brown 240.00 12.00
Never hinged 525.00
No gum 110.00
a. Double paper — —
**O78** O9 12c brown 350.00 10.00
Never hinged 750.00
No gum 160.00
**O79** O9 15c brown 300.00 12.00
Never hinged 650.00
No gum 140.00
**O80** O9 24c brown 725.00 100.00
Never hinged —
No gum 325.00
**O81** O9 30c brown 400.00 12.00
Never hinged —
No gum 180.00
**O82** O9 90c brown 500.00 17.50
Never hinged *1,000.*
No gum 225.00
a. Double paper — —
*Nos. O72-O82 (11)* 3,240. 222.50

### WAR

O10

**1873**
**O83** O10 1c rose 240.00 15.00
Never hinged *850.00*
No gum 115.00
**O84** O10 2c rose 260.00 15.00
Never hinged 1,200.0
No gum 125.00
**O85** O10 3c rose 275.00 5.00
Never hinged 650.00
No gum 135.00
**O86** O10 6c rose 675.00 12.50
Never hinged 1,450.
No gum 325.00

Examples of Nos. O114-O117 which bear Continental Bank Note Co. imprints are often mistaken for/offered as Nos. O83-O86. If there are doubts, expert opinions should be requested.

**O87** O10 7c rose 175.00 90.00
Never hinged 600.00
No gum 90.00
**O88** O10 10c rose 140.00 25.00
Never hinged 375.00
No gum 65.00
**O89** O10 12c rose 275.00 12.00
Never hinged 700.00
No gum 130.00
**O90** O10 15c rose 85.00 15.00
Never hinged 260.00
No gum 40.00
**O91** O10 24c rose 85.00 12.00
Never hinged 190.00
No gum 40.00
**O92** O10 30c rose 130.00 12.00
Never hinged 375.00
No gum 65.00
**O93** O10 90c rose 225.00 60.00
Never hinged 800.00
No gum 110.00
*Nos. O83-O93 (11)* 2,565. 273.50

### Printed by the American Bank Note Co.

**1879**
**Soft Porous Paper**

### AGRICULTURE

**O94** O1 1c yel, no gum 6,000.
**O95** O1 3c yellow 550.00 150.00
Never hinged 1,250.
No gum 260.00

### INTERIOR

**O96** O3 1c vermilion 300.00 *400.00*
Never hinged 550.00
No gum 150.00
**O97** O3 2c vermilion 10.00 3.00
Never hinged 17.50
No gum 4.50
**O98** O3 3c vermilion 10.00 3.00
Never hinged 22.50
No gum 4.50
**O99** O3 6c vermilion 10.00 *12.50*
Never hinged 17.50
No gum 4.50
**O100** O3 10c vermilion 110.00 75.00
Never hinged 250.00
No gum 55.00
**O101** O3 12c vermilion 230.00 115.00
Never hinged 525.00
No gum 115.00
**O102** O3 15c pale vermilion 400.00 500.00
Never hinged 900.00
No gum 200.00
**O103** O3 24c pale vermilion 4,500. *6,250.*
Never hinged 10,000.
No gum 2,200.
*Nos. O96-O103 (8)* 5,570. 7,359.

### JUSTICE

**O106** O4 3c bluish pur 250.00 125.00
Never hinged 575.00
No gum 120.00
**O107** O4 6c bluish pur 475.00 300.00
Never hinged 1,050.
No gum 250.00

### POST OFFICE

**O108** O6 3c black 30.00 10.00
Never hinged 70.00
No gum 14.00

### TREASURY

**O109** O9 3c brown 80.00 10.00
Never hinged 175.00
No gum 35.00
**O110** O9 6c brown 200.00 50.00
Never hinged 450.00
No gum 90.00
**O111** O9 10c brown 275.00 80.00
Never hinged 650.00
No gum 130.00
**O112** O9 30c brown *2,750.* 550.00
Never hinged —
No gum 1,200.
**O113** O9 90c brown *11,000.* 750.00
Never hinged —
No gum 5,000.
*Nos. O109-O113 (5)* 14,305. 1,440.

### WAR

**O114** O10 1c rose red 7.50 4.00
Never hinged 15.00
No gum 3.50
**O115** O10 2c rose red 15.00 4.00
Never hinged 30.00
No gum 7.00
**O116** O10 3c rose red 10.00 2.00
Never hinged 20.00
No gum 3.25
a. Imperf., pair *5,000.*
b. Double impression *7,500.*
**O117** O10 6c rose red 12.50 3.00
Never hinged 25.00
No gum 6.00
**O118** O10 10c rose red 75.00 50.00
Never hinged 150.00
No gum 35.00
**O119** O10 12c rose red 70.00 14.00
Never hinged 140.00
No gum 35.00
**O120** O10 30c rose red 225.00 100.00
Never hinged 500.00
No gum 110.00
*Nos. O114-O120 (7)* 415.00 177.00

### SPECIAL PRINTINGS

Special printings of Official stamps were made in 1875 at the time the other Reprints, Re-issues and Special Printings were printed. They are ungummed.

Although perforated, these stamps were sometimes (but not always) cut apart with scissors. As a result the perforations may be mutilated and the design damaged. Values are for very fine stamps with intact perforations.

All values exist imperforate.

### Printed by the Continental Bank Note Co.
### Similar to Type D, without period, 11mm long
### AGRICULTURE

Overprinted in Block Letters

**Thin, hard white paper**
**Carmine Overprint**

**1875** *Perf. 12*
**O1S** D 1c yellow 32.50
a. "Sepcimen" error *2,500.*
b. Horiz. ribbed paper 37.50
c. As "b," small dotted "i" in "Specimen" 575.00
**O2S** D 2c yellow 55.00
a. "Sepcimen" error *3,000.*
**O3S** D 3c yellow 400.00
a. "Sepcimen" error *19,000.*
**O4S** D 6c yellow 400.00
a. "Sepcimen" error *22,500.*
**O5S** D 10c yellow 400.00
P# strip of 5, Impt. —
a. "Sepcimen" error *19,000.*
**O6S** D 12c yellow 400.00
a. "Sepcimen" error *15,000.*
**O7S** D 15c yellow 400.00
a. "Sepcimen" error *12,500.*
**O8S** D 24c yellow 400.00
a. "Sepcimen" error *12,500.*
**O9S** D 30c yellow 400.00
a. "Sepcimen" error *13,500.*
*Nos. O1S-O9S (9)* 2,888.

### EXECUTIVE
**Blue Overprint**

**O10S** D 1c carmine 32.50
a. Horiz. ribbed paper 40.00
b. As "a," small dotted "i" in "Specimen" 500.00
**O11S** D 2c carmine 55.00
**O12S** D 3c carmine 67.50
**O13S** D 6c carmine 67.50
**O14S** D 10c carmine 67.50
*Nos. O10S-O14S (5)* 290.00

### INTERIOR
**Blue Overprint**

**O15S** D 1c vermilion 60.00
**O16S** D 2c vermilion 140.00
a. "Sepcimen" error —

The existence of a genuine example of No. O16Sa has been questioned by specialists. The editors would like to see authenticated evidence of the existence of the single reported example.

**O17S** D 3c vermilion *2,500.*
**O18S** D 6c vermilion *2,500.*
**O19S** D 10c vermilion *2,500.*
**O20S** D 12c vermilion *2,500.*
**O21S** D 15c vermilion *2,500.*
**O22S** D 24c vermilion *2,500.*
**O23S** D 30c vermilion *2,500.*
**O24S** D 90c vermilion *2,500.*
*Nos. O15S-O24S (10)* *20,200.*

### JUSTICE
**Blue Overprint**

**O25S** D 1c purple 32.50
a. "Sepcimen" error *2,500.*
b. Horiz. ribbed paper 35.00
c. As "b," small dotted "i" in "Specimen" 500.00
**O26S** D 2c purple 55.00
a. "Sepcimen" error *3,500.*
**O27S** D 3c purple 1,250.
a. "Sepcimen" error *11,000.*
**O28S** D 6c purple 1,250.
**O29S** D 10c purple 1,250.
a. "Sepcimen" error *21,000.*
**O30S** D 12c purple 1,250.
a. "Sepcimen" error *19,000.*
**O31S** D 15c purple 1,250.
a. "Sepcimen" error *25,000.*
**O32S** D 24c purple 1,250.
a. "Sepcimen" error *20,000.*
**O33S** D 30c purple 1,250.
a. "Sepcimen" error *47,000.*
**O34S** D 90c purple 1,250.
*Nos. O25S-O34S (10)* 10,088.

### NAVY
**Carmine Overprint**

**O35S** D 1c ultramarine 35.00
a. "Sepcimen" error *2,750.*
b. Double "Specimen" overprint *1,900.*
**O36S** D 2c ultramarine 75.00
a. "Sepcimen" error *4,500.*
**O37S** D 3c ultramarine 1,750.
**O38S** D 6c ultramarine 1,750.
**O39S** D 7c ultramarine 550.00
a. "Sepcimen" error *18,500.*
**O40S** D 10c ultramarine 1,750.
a. "Sepcimen" error *47,000.*
**O41S** D 12c ultramarine 1,750.
a. "Sepcimen" error *21,000.*
**O42S** D 15c ultramarine 1,750.
a. "Sepcimen" error *16,000.*
**O43S** D 24c ultramarine 1,750.
a. "Sepcimen" error *47,000.*

UNITED STATES

179

| O44S | D | 30c ultramarine | 1,750. |
|---|---|---|---|
| a. | | "Specimen" error | 53,000. |
| O45S | D | 90c ultramarine | 1,750. |
| Nos. O35S-O45S (11) | | | 14,660. |

### POST OFFICE
#### Carmine Overprint

| O47S | D | 1c black | 45.00 |
|---|---|---|---|
| a. | | "Specimen" error | 3,250. |
| b. | | Inverted overprint | 2,500. |
| O48S | D | 2c black | 325.00 |
| a. | | "Specimen" error | 19,500. |
| O49S | D | 3c black | 1,600. |
| a. | | "Specimen" error | 37,500. |
| O50S | D | 6c black | 1,600. |
| O51S | D | 10c black | 1,000. |
| a. | | "Specimen" error | 47,000. |
| O52S | D | 12c black | 1,600. |
| O53S | D | 15c black | 1,600. |
| a. | | "Specimen" error | 26,000. |
| O54S | D | 24c black | 1,600. |
| a. | | "Specimen" error | 22,000. |
| O55S | D | 30c black | 1,600. |
| O56S | D | 90c black | 1,600. |
| a. | | "Specimen" error | 25,000. |
| Nos. O47S-O56S (10) | | | 12,570. |

### STATE
#### Carmine Overprint

| O57S | D | 1c bluish green | 32.50 |
|---|---|---|---|
| a. | | "Specimen" error | 2,500. |
| b. | | Horiz. ribbed paper | 35.00 |
| c. | | As "b," small dotted "i" in "Specimen" | 650.00 |
| d. | | Double "Specimen" overprint | 3,850. |
| O58S | D | 2c bluish green | 90.00 |
| a. | | "Specimen" error | 2,500. |
| O59S | D | 3c bluish green | 140.00 |
| a. | | "Specimen" error | 7,000. |
| O60S | D | 6c bluish green | 350.00 |
| a. | | "Specimen" error | 12,500. |
| O61S | D | 7c bluish green | 175.00 |
| a. | | "Specimen" error | 9,000. |
| O62S | D | 10c bluish green | 550.00 |
| a. | | "Specimen" error | 27,500. |
| O63S | D | 12c bluish green | 550.00 |
| a. | | "Specimen" error | 17,500. |
| O64S | D | 15c bluish green | 600.00 |
| O65S | D | 24c bluish green | 600.00 |
| a. | | "Specimen" error | 25,000. |
| O66S | D | 30c bluish green | 600.00 |
| a. | | "Specimen" error | 27,500. |
| O67S | D | 90c bluish green | 600.00 |
| a. | | "Specimen" error | 27,500. |
| O68S | D | $2 green & blk | 6,500. |
| O69S | D | $5 green & blk | 55,000. |
| O70S | D | $10 green & blk | 100,000. |
| O71S | D | $20 green & blk | 145,000. |
| Nos. O57S-O67S (11) | | | 4,288. |

### TREASURY
#### Blue Overprint

| O72S | D | 1c dark brown | 80.00 |
|---|---|---|---|
| O73S | D | 2c dark brown | 450.00 |
| O74S | D | 3c dark brown | 1,600. |
| O75S | D | 6c dark brown | 1,600. |
| O76S | D | 7c dark brown | 950.00 |
| O77S | D | 10c dark brown | 1,600. |
| O78S | D | 12c dark brown | 1,600. |
| O79S | D | 15c dark brown | 1,600. |
| O80S | D | 24c dark brown | 1,600. |
| O81S | D | 30c dark brown | 1,600. |
| O82S | D | 90c dark brown | 1,650. |
| Nos. O72S-O82S (11) | | | 14,330. |

### WAR
#### Blue Overprint

| O83S | D | 1c deep rose | 35.00 |
|---|---|---|---|
| a. | | "Specimen" error | 3,000. |
| O84S | D | 2c deep rose | 125.00 |
| a. | | "Specimen" error | 3,500. |
| O85S | D | 3c deep rose | 1,400. |
| a. | | "Specimen" error | 25,000. |
| O86S | D | 6c deep rose | 1,400. |
| a. | | "Specimen" error | 32,000. |
| O87S | D | 7c deep rose | 425.00 |
| a. | | "Specimen" error | 20,000. |
| O88S | D | 10c deep rose | 1,400. |
| a. | | "Specimen" error | 27,500. |
| O89S | D | 12c deep rose | 1,400. |
| a. | | "Specimen" error | 32,000. |
| O90S | D | 15c deep rose | 1,400. |
| a. | | "Specimen" error | 30,000. |
| O91S | D | 24c deep rose | 1,400. |
| a. | | "Specimen" error | 30,000. |
| O92S | D | 30c deep rose | 1,400. |
| a. | | "Specimen" error | 25,000. |
| O93S | D | 90c deep rose | 1,400. |
| a. | | "Specimen" error | 30,000. |
| Nos. O83S-O93S (11) | | | 11,785. |

### EXECUTIVE
Printed by the American Bank Note Co.
Soft Porous Paper

**1881**     **Blue Overprint**

| O10xS | D | 1c violet rose | 95.00 |
|---|---|---|---|

### NAVY
#### Carmine Overprint

| O35xS | D | 1c gray blue | 100.00 |
|---|---|---|---|
| a. | | Double overprint | 1,200. |

### STATE

| O57xS | D | 1c yellow green | 180.00 |
|---|---|---|---|

### OFFICIAL POSTAL SAVINGS MAIL

These stamps were used to prepay postage on official correspondence of the Postal Savings Division of the POD. Discontinued Sept. 23, 1914.

 O11

**Printed by the Bureau of Engraving & Printing**

**1910-11**    **Engr.**    **Wmk. 191**

| O121 | O11 | 2c black | 17.50 | 2.00 |
|---|---|---|---|---|
| | | Never hinged | 40.00 | |
| O122 | O11 | 50c dark green | 175.00 | 60.00 |
| | | Never hinged | 425.00 | |
| O123 | O11 | $1 ultramarine | 200.00 | 15.00 |
| | | Never hinged | 450.00 | |

   **Wmk. 190**

| O124 | O11 | 1c dark violet | 12.50 | 2.00 |
|---|---|---|---|---|
| | | Never hinged | 27.50 | |
| O125 | O11 | 2c black | 65.00 | 7.00 |
| | | Never hinged | 150.00 | |
| O126 | O11 | 10c carmine | 20.00 | 2.00 |
| | | Never hinged | 50.00 | |
| Nos. O121-O126 (6) | | | 490.00 | 88.00 |

**Catalogue values for unused stamps in this section, from this point to the end, are for Never Hinged items.**

**Catalogue values for used stamps are for regularly used examples, not for examples removed from first day covers.**

**From No. O127 onward, all official stamps are tagged unless noted**

### OFFICIAL MAIL

 O12

**Engraved Unwmk.**

**1983, Jan. 12-1985**    **Perf. 11**

| O127 | O12 | 1c red, blue & black | .25 | .25 |
|---|---|---|---|---|
| O128 | O12 | 4c red, blue & black | .25 | .25 |
| O129 | O12 | 13c red, blue & black | .50 | 15.00 |
| O129A | O12 | 14c red, blue & black | .45 | .50 |
| O130 | O12 | 17c red, blue & black | .55 | .40 |
| O132 | O12 | $1 red, blue & black | 2.25 | 1.00 |
| O133 | O12 | $5 red, blue & black | 9.50 | 20.00 |
| Nos. O127-O133 (7) | | | 13.75 | 37.40 |

No. O129A does not have a "c" after the "14."

**COIL STAMPS**    **Perf. 10 Vert.**

| O135 | O12 | 20c red, blue & black | 1.75 | 2.00 |
|---|---|---|---|---|
| a. | | Imperf., pair | 750.00 | |
| O136 | O12 | 22c red, blue & blk ('85) | 1.00 | £.00 |
| b. | | Imperf, pair | 1,750. | |

**Inscribed: Postal Card Rate D**

**1985, Feb. 4**    **Perf. 11**

| O138 | O12 | (14c) red, blue & black | 5.00 | 15.00 |
|---|---|---|---|---|

Frame line completely around blue design — O13

Inscribed: No. O139, Domestic Letter Rate D; No. O140, Domestic Mail E.

**COIL STAMPS**    **Litho., Engr. (#O139)**

**1985-88**    **Perf. 10 Vert.**

| O138A | O13 | 15c red, blue & blk | .50 | .50 |
|---|---|---|---|---|
| O138B | O13 | 20c red, blue & blk | .50 | .30 |
| O139 | O12 | (22c) red, blue & blk | 5.25 | 20.00 |
| O140 | O13 | (25c) red, blue & blk | .75 | 2.00 |
| O141 | O13 | 25c red, blue & blk | .65 | .50 |
| a. | | Imperf., pair | 700.00 | |
| Nos. O138A-O141 (5) | | | 7.65 | 23.30 |

Issue dates: 1985; E, Mar. 22, 1988; 15c, June 11; 20c, May 19; 25c, June 11.
See Nos. O143, O145-O151, O153-O156.

**Plates of 400 in four panes of 100.**

**1989, July 5**    **Litho.**    **Perf. 11**

| O143 | O13 | 1c red, blue & black | .25 | .25 |
|---|---|---|---|---|

On No. O143, the denomination is shown as "1". See No. O154.

**Type of 1985**

 O14

**Type of 1985 and**

**COIL STAMPS**

**1991**    **Litho.**    **Perf. 10 Vert.**

| O144 | O14 | (29c) red, blue & blk | .80 | .50 |
|---|---|---|---|---|
| O145 | O13 | 29c red, blue & blk | .70 | .30 |

**Plates of 400 in four panes of 100.**

**1991-93**    **Litho.**    **Perf. 11**

| O146 | O13 | 4c red, blue & blk | .25 | .30 |
|---|---|---|---|---|
| O146A | O13 | 10c red, blue & blk | .30 | .30 |
| O147 | O13 | 19c red, blue & blk | .40 | .50 |
| O148 | O13 | 23c red, blue & blk | .50 | .30 |

   **Perf. 11¼**

| O151 | O13 | $1 red, blue & blk | 5.00 | .75 |
|---|---|---|---|---|
| Nos. O146-O151 (5) | | | 6.45 | 2.15 |

Nos. O146A, O151 have a line of microscopic printing below eagle.
See No. O156 for 23c with microscopic text below eagle.
Imperfs of No. O148 are printer's waste.
Issued: No. O146, 4/6; Nos. O147-O148, 5/24; 10c, 10/19/93; No. O151, 9/1993.

**COIL STAMPS**

Inscribed: No. O152, For U.S. addresses only G.

   **Perf. 9.8 Vert.**

| O152 | O14 | (32c) red, blue & blk | .65 | .50 |
|---|---|---|---|---|
| O153 | O13 | 32c red, blue & blk | 1.50 | .50 |

Nos. O146A, O151, O153 have a line of microscopic text below the eagle.

**1995, May 9**    **Untagged**    **Perf. 11.2**

| O154 | O13 | 1c red, blue & black | .25 | .50 |
|---|---|---|---|---|

Denomination on No. O154 has a cent sign. See No. O143.

| O155 | O13 | 20c red, blue & black | .55 | .50 |
|---|---|---|---|---|
| O156 | O13 | 23c red, blue & black | .60 | .50 |

**COIL STAMP**

**1999, Oct. 8**    **Perf. 9¾ Vert.**

| O157 | O13 | 33c red, blue & black | 2.25 | — |
|---|---|---|---|---|

**Type of 1985 COIL STAMP**

**2001, Feb. 27**    **Perf. 9¾ Vert.**

| O158 | O13 | 34c red, blue & black | 2.25 | .50 |
|---|---|---|---|---|

Nos. O154-O158 have a line of microscopic text below the eagle.

**Type of 1985 COIL STAMP**

**2002, Aug. 2**    **Photo.**    **Perf. 10 Vert.**

| O159 | O13 | 37c red, blue & black | .75 | .50 |
|---|---|---|---|---|

**Type of 1985 COIL STAMP**

**2006, Mar. 8**    **Perf. 10 Vert.**

| O160 | O13 | 39c red, blue & black | 1.00 | 1.00 |
|---|---|---|---|---|

**Type of 1988**

**2006, Sept. 29**    **Litho.**    **Perf. 11¼**

| O161 | O13 | $1 red, blue & black | 5.00 | 1.25 |
|---|---|---|---|---|

No. O161 has a solid blue background. No. O151 has a background of crosshatched lines.

**Type of 1985 COIL STAMP**

**2007, June 25**    **Perf. 9¾**

| O162 | O13 | 41c red, blue & black | 1.00 | 1.00 |
|---|---|---|---|---|

Nos. O159-O162 have solid blue backgrounds. Nos. O138A-O158 have a background of crosshatched lines.

**Type of 1985**
*Serpentine Die Cut 11½x10¾*

**2009, Feb. 24**    **Untagged**
**Self-Adhesive**

| O163 | O13 | 1c red, blue & black | .25 | .40 |
|---|---|---|---|---|

### NEWSPAPER STAMPS

For the prepayment of postage on bulk shipments of newspapers and periodicals. From 1875 on, the stamps were affixed to pages of receipt books, sometimes canceled and retained by the post office. Discontinued on July 1, 1898.

Virtually all used stamps of Nos. PR1-PR4 are canceled by blue brush strokes. All are rare. Most used stamps of Nos. PR9-PR32, PR57-PR79 and PR81-PR89 are pen canceled (or uncanceled), with some of Nos. PR9-PR32 also known canceled by a thick blue brush stroke.

Handstamp cancellations on any of these issues are rare and sell for much more than catalogue values which are for pen-canceled examples.

Used values for Nos. PR90-PR125 are for stamps with handstamp cancellations.

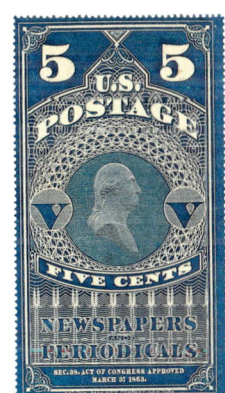

Washington — N1

Franklin
N2

180 UNITED STATES

Lincoln
N3

Values for Nos. PR1-PR8 are for examples with perforations on all four sides. Examples with natural straight edges sell for somewhat less. Some panes were fully perforated, while others have natural straight edges either at top or bottom affecting five stamps in the pane of ten.

**Printed by the National Bank Note Co.**
**Thin hard paper, without gum**
**Size of design: 51x95mm**

**Typographed and Embossed**
**1865 Unwmk.** *Perf. 12*
**Colored Border**

| | | | | |
|---|---|---|---|---|
| **PR1** | N1 | 5c dark blue | 750.00 | *1,750.* |
| *a.* | | 5c light blue | 1,350. | *3,750.* |
| **PR2** | N2 | 10c blue green | 300.00 | *2,000.* |
| *a.* | | 10c green | 300.00 | *2,000.* |
| *b.* | | Pelure paper | 400.00 | *1,750.* |
| **PR3** | N3 | 25c orange red | 400.00 | *2,250.* |
| *a.* | | 25c carmine red | 475.00 | *2,250.* |
| *b.* | | Pelure paper | 500.00 | |

Nos. PR1-PR3 used are valued with faults.

**White Border**
**Yellowish paper**

| | | | | |
|---|---|---|---|---|
| **PR4** | N1 | 5c light blue | 900.00 | *4,000.* |
| *a.* | | 5c dark blue | 900.00 | — |
| *b.* | | Pelure paper | 975.00 | — |
| | | *Nos. PR1-PR4 (4)* | 2,350. | |

No. PR4 used is valued with faults.

**REPRINTS of 1865 ISSUE**
**Printed by the Continental Bank Note Co. using the original National Bank Note Co. plates**

**1875**
**Hard white paper, without gum**
**5c White Border, 10c and 25c Colored Border**

| | | | |
|---|---|---|---|
| **PR5** | N1 | 5c dull blue | 225.00 |
| *a.* | | Printed on both sides | *5,750.* |
| **PR6** | N2 | 10c dark bluish green | 250.00 |
| *a.* | | Printed on both sides | *4,250.* |
| **PR7** | N3 | 25c dark carmine | 300.00 |
| | | *Nos. PR5-PR7 (3)* | 775.00 |

The 5c has white border, 10c and 25c have colored borders.

Many fakes exist of Nos. PR1-PR7, some of high quality. Certification is highly recommended.

The Continental Bank Note Co. made another special printing from new plates, which did not have the colored border. These exist imperforate and perforated, but they were not regularly issued. Value, imperf. set $2,500.

**Printed by the American Bank Note Co.**
**Soft porous paper, without gum**

**1881 White Border**

| | | | |
|---|---|---|---|
| **PR8** | N1 | 5c dark blue | 750. |

Statue of Freedom — N4

"Justice"
N5

Ceres
N6

"Victory"
N7

Clio
N8

Minerva
N9

Vesta
N10

"Peace"
N11

"Commerce"
N12

Hebe
N13

Indian Maiden
N14

Values for used examples of Nos. PR9-PR113 are for fine-very fine examples for denominations to $3, and fine for denominations of $5 or higher. Used examples of some Scott numbers might not exist without faults.

**Printed by the Continental Bank Note Co.**
**Size of design: 24x35mm**

**1875, Jan. 1** **Engr.**

| | | | | |
|---|---|---|---|---|
| **PR9** | N4 | 2c black | 350.00 | 45.00 |
| | | No gum | 140.00 | |
| **PR10** | N4 | 3c black | 350.00 | 50.00 |
| | | No gum | 140.00 | |
| **PR11** | N4 | 4c black | 350.00 | 45.00 |
| | | No gum | 140.00 | |
| **PR12** | N4 | 6c black | 350.00 | 50.00 |
| | | No gum | 140.00 | |
| **PR13** | N4 | 8c black | 350.00 | 75.00 |
| | | No gum | 140.00 | |
| **PR14** | N4 | 9c black | 600.00 | 140.00 |
| | | No gum | 225.00 | |
| **PR15** | N4 | 10c black | 375.00 | 67.50 |
| | | No gum | 135.00 | |
| **PR16** | N5 | 12c rose | 800.00 | 110.00 |
| | | No gum | 325.00 | |
| **PR17** | N5 | 24c rose | 1,000. | 175.00 |
| | | No gum | 400.00 | |
| **PR18** | N5 | 36c rose | 1,000. | 200.00 |
| | | No gum | 400.00 | |
| **PR19** | N5 | 48c rose | 1,250. | 500.00 |
| | | No gum | 450.00 | |
| **PR20** | N5 | 60c rose | 1,500. | 125.00 |
| | | No gum | 550.00 | |
| **PR21** | N5 | 72c rose | 1,500. | 450.00 |
| | | No gum | 550.00 | |
| **PR22** | N5 | 84c rose | 1,850. | 450.00 |
| | | No gum | 650.00 | |
| **PR23** | N5 | 96c rose | *2,250.* | 300.00 |
| | | No gum | 875.00 | |
| **PR24** | N6 | $1.92 dk brn | *2,250.* | 300.00 |
| | | No gum | 825.00 | |
| **PR25** | N7 | $3 ver | 2,500. | 600.00 |
| | | No gum | 975.00 | |
| **PR26** | N8 | $6 ultra | *4,250.* | 650.00 |
| | | No gum | 1,700. | |
| **PR27** | N9 | $9 yel org | 4,500. | *2,400.* |
| | | No gum | 1,750. | |
| **PR28** | N10 | $12 bl grn | 4,750. | *1,250.* |
| | | No gum | 1,850. | |
| **PR29** | N11 | $24 dk gray vio | 4,750. | *1,400.* |
| | | No gum | 1,850. | |
| **PR30** | N12 | $36 brn rose | *5,500.* | *1,600.* |
| | | No gum | 2,250. | |
| **PR31** | N13 | $48 red brn | *7,500.* | *1,800.* |
| | | No gum | 2,750. | |
| **PR32** | N14 | $60 violet | *7,000.* | *2,000.* |
| | | No gum | 2,600. | |

**SPECIAL PRINTING of 1875 ISSUE**
**Printed by the Continental Bank Note Co.**
**Hard white paper, without gum**

**1875**

| | | | |
|---|---|---|---|
| **PR33** | N4 | 2c gray black | 700.00 |
| *a.* | | Horiz. ribbed paper | 500.00 |
| **PR34** | N4 | 3c gray black | 700.00 |
| *a.* | | Horiz. ribbed paper | 550.00 |
| **PR35** | N4 | 4c gray black | 700.00 |
| | | Horiz. ribbed paper | 1,000. |
| **PR36** | N4 | 6c gray black | 1,000. |
| **PR37** | N4 | 8c gray black | 1,100. |
| **PR38** | N4 | 9c gray black | 1,200. |
| **PR39** | N4 | 10c gray black | 1,500. |
| **PR40** | N5 | 12c pale rose | 1,600. |
| **PR41** | N5 | 24c pale rose | 2,250. |
| **PR42** | N5 | 36c pale rose | 3,000. |
| **PR43** | N5 | 48c pale rose | 4,000. |
| **PR44** | N5 | 60c pale rose | 4,750. |
| **PR45** | N5 | 72c pale rose | 4,500. |
| **PR46** | N5 | 84c pale rose | 5,750. |
| **PR47** | N5 | 96c pale rose | *10,000.* |
| **PR48** | N6 | $1.92 dk brn | *20,000.* |
| **PR49** | N7 | $3 vermilion | *42,500.* |
| **PR50** | N8 | $6 ultra | *70,000.* |
| **PR51** | N9 | $9 yellow org | *350,000.* |
| **PR52** | N10 | $12 blue green | *225,000.* |
| **PR53** | N11 | $24 dk gray vio | *500,000.* |
| **PR54** | N12 | $36 brn rose | *400,000.* |
| **PR55** | N13 | $48 red brown | — |
| **PR56** | N14 | $60 violet | — |

Nos. PR50 and PR52 are valued in the grade of fine.

Although four examples of No. PR51 were sold, only one is currently documented.

No. PR54 is valued in the grade of fine. Although two stamps were sold, only one is currently documented.

All values of this issue, Nos. PR33 to PR56, exist imperforate but were not regularly issued thus. Value, set $100,000.

**Printed by the American Bank Note Co.**
**Soft porous paper**

**1879**

| | | | | |
|---|---|---|---|---|
| **PR57** | N4 | 2c black | 75.00 | 17.50 |
| | | No gum | 30.00 | |
| **PR58** | N4 | 3c black | 85.00 | 22.50 |
| | | No gum | 35.00 | |
| **PR59** | N4 | 4c black | 85.00 | 22.50 |
| | | No gum | 35.00 | |
| *a.* | | Double paper | — | |
| **PR60** | N4 | 6c black | 125.00 | 40.00 |
| | | No gum | 50.00 | |
| **PR61** | N4 | 8c black | 135.00 | 40.00 |
| | | No gum | 55.00 | |
| **PR62** | N4 | 10c black | 135.00 | 40.00 |
| | | No gum | 55.00 | |
| **PR63** | N5 | 12c red | 500.00 | 140.00 |
| | | No gum | 210.00 | |
| **PR64** | N5 | 24c red | 500.00 | 140.00 |
| | | No gum | 210.00 | |
| **PR65** | N5 | 36c red | 1,000. | 375.00 |
| | | No gum | 475.00 | |
| **PR66** | N5 | 48c red | 1,000. | 350.00 |
| | | No gum | 450.00 | |
| **PR67** | N5 | 60c red | 1,250. | 325.00 |
| | | No gum | 550.00 | |
| *a.* | | Imperf., pair | *5,500.* | |
| **PR68** | N5 | 72c red | 1,500. | 475.00 |
| | | No gum | 700.00 | |
| **PR69** | N5 | 84c red | 1,250. | 400.00 |
| | | No gum | 575.00 | |
| **PR70** | N5 | 96c red | 1,500. | 325.00 |
| | | No gum | 700.00 | |
| **PR71** | N6 | $1.92 pale brn | 550.00 | 200.00 |
| | | No gum | 225.00 | |
| **PR72** | N7 | $3 red ver | 625.00 | 230.00 |
| | | No gum | 250.00 | |
| **PR73** | N8 | $6 blue | 1,050. | 350.00 |
| | | No gum | 400.00 | |
| **PR74** | N9 | $9 orange | 800.00 | 260.00 |
| | | No gum | 325.00 | |
| **PR75** | N10 | $12 yel grn | 850.00 | 260.00 |
| | | No gum | 325.00 | |
| **PR76** | N11 | $24 dk vio | 800.00 | 350.00 |
| | | No gum | 300.00 | |
| **PR77** | N12 | $36 Indian red | 850.00 | 400.00 |
| | | No gum | 350.00 | |
| **PR78** | N13 | $48 yel brn | 900.00 | 525.00 |
| | | No gum | 350.00 | |
| **PR79** | N14 | $60 purple | 850.00 | 450.00 |
| | | No gum | 350.00 | |
| | | *Nos. PR57-PR70 (14)* | 9,140. | 2,713. |

**SPECIAL PRINTING of 1879 ISSUE**
Printed by the American Bank Note Co.
**Without gum**

**1883**

| | | | |
|---|---|---|---|
| **PR80** | N4 | 2c intense black | 1,750. |

**REGULAR ISSUE**
**With gum**

**1885**

| | | | | |
|---|---|---|---|---|
| **PR81** | N4 | 1c black, *July 1, 1885* | 95.00 | 14.00 |
| | | Never hinged | 225.00 | |
| | | No gum | 42.50 | |
| **PR82** | N5 | 12c carmine | 200.00 | 35.00 |
| | | Never hinged | 450.00 | |
| | | No gum | 85.00 | |
| **PR83** | N5 | 24c carmine | 225.00 | 35.00 |
| | | Never hinged | 500.00 | |
| | | No gum | 95.00 | |
| **PR84** | N5 | 36c carmine | 350.00 | 65.00 |
| | | Never hinged | 800.00 | |
| | | No gum | 145.00 | |
| **PR85** | N5 | 48c carmine | 425.00 | 85.00 |
| | | Never hinged | 975.00 | |
| | | No gum | 180.00 | |
| **PR86** | N5 | 60c carmine | 600.00 | 120.00 |
| | | No gum | 260.00 | |
| **PR87** | N5 | 72c carmine | 600.00 | 130.00 |
| | | No gum | 260.00 | |
| **PR88** | N5 | 84c carmine | 900.00 | 290.00 |
| | | No gum | 350.00 | |
| **PR89** | N5 | 96c carmine | 750.00 | 225.00 |
| | | Never hinged | 2,250. | |
| | | No gum | 300.00 | |
| | | *Nos. PR81-PR89 (9)* | 4,145. | 999.00 |

See the Scott U.S. Specialized Catalogue Die and Plate Proof section for imperforates.

**Printed by the Bureau of Engraving and Printing**

**1894**
**Soft wove paper, with pale, whitish gum**

| | | | | |
|---|---|---|---|---|
| **PR90** | N4 | 1c intense blk | 400.00 | *5,000.* |
| | | Never hinged | 900.00 | |
| | | No gum | 160.00 | |
| **PR91** | N4 | 2c intense blk | 450.00 | — |
| | | Never hinged | 1,075. | |
| | | No gum | 190.00 | |
| **PR92** | N4 | 4c intense blk | 550.00 | *13,500.* |
| | | Never hinged | 1,275. | |
| | | No gum | 210.00 | |
| **PR93** | N4 | 6c intense blk | 4,500. | |
| | | Never hinged | *11,500.* | |
| | | No gum | 1,900. | |
| **PR94** | N4 | 10c intense blk | 1,400. | — |
| | | Never hinged | *2,750.* | |
| | | No gum | 550.00 | |
| **PR95** | N5 | 12c pink | 2,400. | *4,500.* |
| | | Never hinged | *3,500.* | |
| | | No gum | 1,100. | |
| **PR96** | N5 | 24c pink | 3,750. | *8,000.* |
| | | Never hinged | *8,500.* | |
| | | No gum | 1,850. | |
| **PR97** | N5 | 36c pink | *45,000.* | |
| **PR98** | N5 | 60c pink | *35,000.* | *15,000.* |
| **PR99** | N5 | 96c pink | *45,000.* | *52,500.* |
| **PR100** | N7 | $3 scarlet | *50,000.* | |
| **PR101** | N8 | $6 pale blue | *50,000.* | *41,250.* |
| | | No gum | *25,000.* | |

Nos. PR90, PR95-PR98 used are valued with fine centering and small faults.

No. PR97 unused is valued in the grade of very good to fine. No. PR98 unused is valued in the grade of fine. Nos. PR99-101 unused are valued in the grade of fine-very fine.

Statue of Freedom
N15

"Justice"
N16

"Victory"
N17

Clio
N18

UNITED STATES 181

Vesta
N19

"Peace"
N20

"Commerce"
N21

Indian
Maiden
N22

**Size of designs: 1c-50c, 21x34mm; $2-$100, 24x35mm**

**1895, Feb. 1**

| | | | | |
|---|---|---|---|---|
| **PR102** | N15 | 1c black | 230.00 | *125.00* |
| | | Never hinged | 500.00 | |
| | | No gum | 90.00 | |
| **PR103** | N15 | 2c black | 230.00 | *125.00* |
| | | Never hinged | 500.00 | |
| | | No gum | 90.00 | |
| **PR104** | N15 | 5c black | 300.00 | *300.00* |
| | | Never hinged | 650.00 | |
| | | No gum | 125.00 | |
| **PR105** | N15 | 10c black | 600.00 | *600.00* |
| | | Never hinged | 1,300. | |
| | | No gum | 240.00 | |
| **PR106** | N16 | 25c car | 750.00 | *650.00* |
| | | Never hinged | 1,650. | |
| | | No gum | 300.00 | |
| **PR107** | N16 | 50c car | *2,750.* | *2,000.* |
| | | Never hinged | *6,250.* | |
| | | No gum | *875.00* | |
| **PR108** | N17 | $2 scarlet | 2,250. | *1,100.* |
| | | Never hinged | *5,000.* | |
| | | No gum | 850.00 | |
| **PR109** | N18 | $5 ultra | 2,250. | *1,750.* |
| | | No gum | 850.00 | |
| **PR110** | N19 | $10 green | 2,500. | *2,000.* |
| | | No gum | 900.00 | |
| **PR111** | N20 | $20 slate | 3,250. | *2,500.* |
| | | No gum | 1,200. | |
| **PR112** | N21 | $50 dull rose | 2,750. | *950.00* |
| | | Never hinged | *6,250.* | |
| | | No gum | 1,050. | |
| **PR113** | N22 | $100 purple | 3,500. | *6,500.* |
| | | No gum | 1,400. | |
| | | *Nos. PR102-PR113 (12)* | 21,360. | 18,600. |

**1895-97 Wmk. 191**

| | | | | |
|---|---|---|---|---|
| **PR114** | N15 | 1c black | 8.00 | *25.00* |
| | | Never hinged | 20.00 | |
| | | No gum | 2.75 | |
| **PR115** | N15 | 2c black | 8.00 | *25.00* |
| | | Never hinged | 20.00 | |
| | | No gum | 2.75 | |
| **PR116** | N15 | 5c black | 13.00 | *40.00* |
| | | Never hinged | 27.50 | |
| | | No gum | 4.25 | |
| **PR117** | N15 | 10c black | 13.00 | *25.00* |
| | | Never hinged | 27.50 | |
| | | No gum | 4.25 | |
| **PR118** | N16 | 25c carmine | 20.00 | *65.00* |
| | | Never hinged | 45.00 | |
| | | No gum | 7.00 | |
| **PR119** | N16 | 50c carmine | 25.00 | *75.00* |
| | | Never hinged | 55.00 | |
| | | No gum | 8.50 | |
| **PR120** | N17 | $2 scarlet | 30.00 | *110.00* |
| | | Never hinged | 73.00 | |
| | | No gum | 10.00 | |
| **PR121** | N18 | $5 dark bl | 40.00 | *175.00* |
| | | Never hinged | 100.00 | |
| | | No gum | 13.50 | |
| *a.* | | $5 light blue | 200.00 | *500.00* |
| | | Never hinged | 500.00 | |
| | | No gum | 67.50 | |
| **PR122** | N19 | $10 green | 42.50 | *175.00* |
| | | Never hinged | 105.00 | |
| | | No gum | 14.00 | |
| **PR123** | N20 | $20 slate | 45.00 | *200.00* |
| | | Never hinged | 110.00 | |
| | | No gum | 15.00 | |
| **PR124** | N21 | $50 dull rose | 75.00 | *400.00* |
| | | Never hinged | 170.00 | |
| | | No gum | 27.50 | |
| **PR125** | N22 | $100 purple | 65.00 | *300.00* |
| | | Never hinged | 150.00 | |
| | | No gum | 22.50 | |
| | | *Nos. PR114-PR125 (12)* | 384.50 | *1,615.* |
| | | *Nos. PR114-PR125, never hinged* | 905.00 | |

*In 1899 the Government sold 26,989 sets of these stamps, but, as the stock of high values was not sufficient to make up the required number, an additional printing was made of the $5, $10, $20, $50 and $100. These are virtually indistinguishable from earlier printings.*

For overprints, see Nos. R159-R160.

## PARCEL POST STAMPS

Issued for the prepayment of postage on parcel post packages only.

Post Office Clerk — PP1

City Carrier — PP2

Railway Postal Clerk — PP3

Rural Carrier — PP4

Mail Train — PP5

Steamship and Mail Tender — PP6

Automobile Service — PP7

Airplane Carrying Mail — PP8

Manufacturing PP9

Dairying PP10

Harvesting PP11

Fruit Growing PP12

**1913 Wmk. 190 Engr. *Perf. 12***

| | | | | |
|---|---|---|---|---|
| **Q1** | PP1 | 1c carmine rose | 4.25 | 1.60 |
| | | Never hinged | 12.00 | |
| **Q2** | PP2 | 2c carmine rose | 5.00 | 1.25 |
| | | Never hinged | 12.50 | |
| *a.* | | 2c lake | *3,750.* | |
| *b.* | | 2c carmine lake | *350.00* | |

No. Q2a is valued in the grade of fine-very fine.

| | | | | |
|---|---|---|---|---|
| **Q3** | PP3 | 3c carmine | 9.00 | 6.00 |
| | | Never hinged | 24.00 | |
| **Q4** | PP4 | 4c carmine rose | 27.50 | 3.00 |
| | | Never hinged | 77.50 | |
| **Q5** | PP5 | 5c carmine rose | 22.50 | 2.25 |
| | | Never hinged | 62.50 | |
| **Q6** | PP6 | 10c carmine rose | 40.00 | 3.00 |
| | | Never hinged | 90.00 | |
| **Q7** | PP7 | 15c carmine rose | 60.00 | 13.50 |
| | | Never hinged | 170.00 | |
| **Q8** | PP8 | 20c carmine rose | 110.00 | 25.00 |
| | | Never hinged | 260.00 | |
| **Q9** | PP9 | 25c carmine rose | 52.50 | 8.00 |
| | | Never hinged | 145.00 | |
| **Q10** | PP10 | 50c carmine rose | 210.00 | 45.00 |
| | | Never hinged | 525.00 | |
| **Q11** | PP11 | 75c carmine rose | 85.00 | 35.00 |
| | | Never hinged | 190.00 | |
| **Q12** | PP12 | $1 carmine rose | 260.00 | 40.00 |
| | | Never hinged | 625.00 | |
| | | *Nos. Q1-Q12 (12)* | 885.75 | 183.60 |
| | | Nos. Q1-Q12, never hinged | 2,273. | |

## PARCEL POST POSTAGE DUE STAMPS

For affixing by a postal clerk to any parcel post package, to denote the amount to be collected from the addressee because of insufficient prepayment of postage.

PPD1

**1913 Wmk. 190 Engr. *Perf. 12***

| | | | | |
|---|---|---|---|---|
| **JQ1** | PPD1 | 1c dark green | 8.00 | 4.00 |
| | | Never hinged | 22.50 | |
| **JQ2** | PPD1 | 2c dark green | 60.00 | 16.00 |
| | | Never hinged | 160.00 | |
| **JQ3** | PPD1 | 5c dark green | 9.00 | 4.50 |
| | | Never hinged | 24.00 | |
| **JQ4** | PPD1 | 10c dark green | 110.00 | 40.00 |
| | | Never hinged | 290.00 | |
| **JQ5** | PPD1 | 25c dark green | 70.00 | 4.50 |
| | | Never hinged | 185.00 | |
| | | *Nos. JQ1-JQ5 (5)* | 257.00 | 69.00 |
| | | Nos. JQ1-JQ5, never hinged | 642.50 | |

## SPECIAL HANDLING STAMPS

For use on fourth-class mail to secure the same expeditious handling accorded to first-class mail matter.

PP13

**1925-28 Engr. Unwmk. *Perf. 11***

| | | | | |
|---|---|---|---|---|
| **QE1** | PP13 | 10c **yellow green**, wet printing, *1928* | 3.00 | 1.50 |
| | | Never hinged | 5.25 | |
| **QE2** | PP13 | 15c **yellow green**, wet printing, *1928* | 3.25 | 1.50 |
| | | Never hinged | 5.75 | |
| **QE3** | PP13 | 20c **yellow green**, wet printing, *1928* | 4.75 | 2.50 |
| | | Never hinged | 8.75 | |
| **QE4** | PP13 | 25c dp grn ('25) | 20.00 | 4.00 |
| | | Never hinged | 37.50 | |
| *a.* | | yel grn ('28) | 16.50 | *22.50* |
| | | Never hinged | 30.00 | |
| | | *Nos. QE1-QE4 (4)* | 31.00 | 9.50 |
| | | Nos. QE1-QE4, never hinged | 57.25 | |

## COMPUTER VENDED POSTAGE

CVP1

CVP2

**1989, Aug. 23 Tagged *Guillotined***
**Self-Adhesive**

**Washington, DC, Machine 82**
**Date Other Than First Day**

| | | | | |
|---|---|---|---|---|
| **CVP1** | CVP1 | 25c First Class | 6.00 | — |
| *a.* | | First day dated, serial Nos. 12501-15500 | 5.00 | — |
| *b.* | | First day dated, serial Nos. 00001-12500 | 5.00 | — |
| *c.* | | First day dated, over No. 27500 | — | — |
| **CVP2** | CVP1 | $1 Third Class | — | — |
| *a.* | | First day dated, serial Nos. 24501-27500 | — | — |
| *b.* | | First day dated, over No. 27500 | — | — |
| **CVP3** | CVP2 | $1.69 Parcel Post | — | — |
| *a.* | | First day dated, serial Nos. 21501-24500 | — | — |
| *b.* | | First day dated, over No. 27500 | — | — |
| **CVP4** | CVP1 | $2.40 Priority Mail | — | — |
| *a.* | | First day dated, serial Nos. 18501-21500 | — | — |
| *b.* | | Priority Mail ($2.74), with bar code (CVP2) | *100.00* | |
| *c.* | | First day dated, over No. 27500 | — | — |
| **CVP5** | CVP1 | $8.75 Express Mail | — | — |
| *a.* | | First day dated, serial Nos. 15501-18500 | — | — |
| *b.* | | First day dated, over No. 27500 | — | — |

**Washington, DC, Machine 83**
**Date Other Than First Day**

| | | | | |
|---|---|---|---|---|
| **CVP6** | CVP1 | 25c First Class | 6.00 | — |
| *a.* | | First day dated, serial Nos. 12501-15500 | 5.00 | — |
| *b.* | | First day dated, serial Nos. 00001-12500 | 5.00 | — |
| *c.* | | First day dated, over No. 27500 | — | — |
| **CVP7** | CVP1 | $1 Third Class | — | — |
| *a.* | | First day dated, serial Nos. 24501-27500 | — | — |
| *b.* | | First day dated, over No. 27500 | — | — |
| **CVP8** | CVP2 | $1.69 Parcel Post | 15.00 | — |
| *a.* | | First day dated, serial Nos. 21501-24500 | — | — |
| *b.* | | First day dated, over No. 27500 | — | — |
| **CVP9** | CVP1 | $2.40 Priority Mail | — | — |
| *a.* | | First day dated, serial Nos. 18501-21500 | — | — |
| *b.* | | First day dated, over No. 27500 | — | — |

A Priority Mail $3.25 value also exists unused. A Priority Mail stamp exists on cover with error date 11/17/90 exists, and an unused stamp with error date 11/18/90 exists.

| | | | | |
|---|---|---|---|---|
| *c.* | | Priority Mail ($2.74), with bar code (CVP2) | *100.00* | |

Error date 11/18/90 exists.

| | | | | |
|---|---|---|---|---|
| **CVP10** | CVP1 | $8.75 Express Mail | — | — |
| *a.* | | First day dated, serial Nos. 15501-18500 | — | — |
| *b.* | | First day dated, over No. 27500 | — | — |

Error date 11/17/90 exists.

**1989, Sept. 1**

**Kensington, MD, Machine 82**
**Date Other Than First Day**

| | | | | |
|---|---|---|---|---|
| **CVP11** | CVP1 | 25c First Class | 6.00 | — |
| *a.* | | First day dated, serial Nos. 12501-15500 | 5.00 | — |
| *b.* | | First day dated, serial Nos. 00001-12500 | 5.00 | — |
| *c.* | | First day dated, over No. 27500 | — | — |
| **CVP12** | CVP1 | $1 Third Class | — | — |
| *a.* | | First day dated, serial Nos. 24501-27500 | — | — |
| *b.* | | First day dated, over No. 27500 | — | — |
| **CVP13** | CVP2 | $1.69 Parcel Post | — | — |
| *a.* | | First day dated, serial Nos. 21501-24500 | — | — |
| *b.* | | First day dated, over No. 27500 | — | — |
| **CVP14** | CVP1 | $2.40 Priority Mail | — | — |
| *a.* | | First day dated, serial Nos. 18501-21500 | — | — |
| *b.* | | First day dated, over No. 27500 | — | — |
| *c.* | | Priority Mail ($2.74), with bar code (CVP2) | *100.00* | |
| **CVP15** | CVP1 | $8.75 Express Mail | — | — |
| *a.* | | First day dated, serial Nos. 15501-18500 | — | — |
| *b.* | | First day dated, over No. 27500 | — | — |

**Kensington, MD, Machine 83**
**Date Other Than First Day**

| | | | | |
|---|---|---|---|---|
| **CVP16** | CVP1 | 25c First Class | 6.00 | — |
| *a.* | | First day dated, serial Nos. 12501-15500 | 5.00 | — |
| *b.* | | First day dated, serial Nos. 00001-12500 | 5.00 | — |
| *c.* | | First day dated, over No. 27500 | — | — |
| **CVP17** | CVP1 | $1 Third Class | — | — |
| *a.* | | First day dated, serial Nos. 24501-27500 | — | — |
| *b.* | | First day dated, over No. 27500 | — | — |
| **CVP18** | CVP2 | $1.69 Parcel Post | — | *12.50* |
| *a.* | | First day dated, serial Nos. 21501-24500 | — | — |
| *b.* | | First day dated, over No. 27500 | — | — |
| **CVP19** | CVP1 | $2.40 Priority Mail | — | — |
| *a.* | | First day dated, serial Nos. 18501-21500 | — | — |
| *b.* | | First day dated, over No. 27500 | — | — |
| *c.* | | Priority Mail ($2.74), with bar code (CVP2) | 100.00 | |
| **CVP20** | CVP1 | $8.75 Express Mail | — | — |
| *a.* | | First day dated, serial Nos. 15501-18500 | — | — |
| *b.* | | First day dated, over No. 27500 | — | — |

**1989, Nov.**

**Washington, DC, Machine 11**

| | | | | |
|---|---|---|---|---|
| **CVP21** | CVP1 | 25c First Class | *150.00* | |
| *a.* | | First Class, with bar code (CVP2) | | — |

Stamps in CVP1 design with $1.10 denominations exist (certified first class) dated

182    UNITED STATES

11/20/89. Value, unused, $650. A 45c denomination exists unused (dated 11/22/89) on cover to Europe and on Certificate of Mailing.

| | | | |
|---|---|---|---|
| CVP22 | CVP1 | $1 Third Class | 500.00 |
| CVP23 | CVP2 | $1.69 Parcel Post | 500.00 |
| CVP24 | CVP1 | $2.40 Priority Mail | 500.00 |
| a. | | Priority Mail ($2.74), with bar code (CVP2) | — |
| CVP25 | CVP1 | $8.75 Express Mail | 500.00 |

### Washington, DC, Machine 12
| | | | |
|---|---|---|---|
| CVP26 | CVP1 | 25c First Class | 200.00 |

No. CVP26, dated 12/13/89 is known on cover. $1.10 Certified First Class stamps dated 11/20/89 exist on covers.

| | | | |
|---|---|---|---|
| CVP27 | CVP1 | $1 Third Class | 600.00 |

A $1.40 Third Class stamp of type CVP2, dated Dec. 1 is known on a Dec. 2 cover.

| | | | |
|---|---|---|---|
| CVP28 | CVP2 | $1.65 Parcel Post | 600.00 |
| CVP29 | CVP1 | $2.40 Priority Mail | 600.00 |
| a. | | Priority Mail ($2.74), with bar code (CVP2) | — |
| CVP30 | CVP1 | $8.75 Express Mail | 600.00 |

An $8.50 Express Mail stamp, dated Dec. 2, exists on cover.

CVP3 — Type I     CVP3 — Type II

**1992, Aug. 20   Engr.   Perf. 10 Horiz.**
**Coil Stamp**

| | | | | |
|---|---|---|---|---|
| CVP31 | CVP3 | 29c red & blue, type I | .75 | .25 |
| c. | | 32c Type II ('94) | 1.25 | .40 |

No. CVP31 was available in all denominations from 1c to $99.99.
The listing is for the first class rate. Other denominations, se-tenant combinations, or "errors" are not listed.
Type II denomination has large sans-serif numerals preceded by an asterisk measuring 2mm across. No. CVP31 has small numerals with serifs preceded by an asterisk 1½mm across.

CVP4

**1994, Feb. 19   Photo.   Perf. 9.9 Vert.**

| | | | | |
|---|---|---|---|---|
| CVP32 | CVP4 | 29c dark red & dark blue | .75 | .35 |

No. CVP32 was available in all denominations from 19c to $99.99.
The listing is for the first class rate at time of issue. Other denominations, se-tenant combinations, or "errors" will not be listed.

**1996, Jan. 26**

| | | | | |
|---|---|---|---|---|
| CVP33 | CVP4 | 32c brt red & blue, "1996" below design | .75 | .25 |

Letters in "USA" on No. CVP33 are thicker than on No. CVP32. Numerous other design differences exist in the moire pattern and in the bunting. No. CVP33 has "1996" in the lower left corner; No. CVP32 has no date.
For No. CVP33, the 32c value has been listed because it was the first class rate in effect at the time the stamp was issued.

CVP5

**1999, June   Tagged   Die Cut**
**Self-Adhesive**

| | | | |
|---|---|---|---|
| CVP34 | CVP5 | 33c black | 50.00 |
| a. | | "Priority Mail" under encryption at LL | — |
| b. | | "Express Mail" under encryption at LL | — |

No. CVP34 was available from 15 NCR Automated Postal Center machines located in central Florida. Machines could produce values in any denomination required. The backing paper is taller and wider than the stamp.
Sales of No. CVP34 were discontinued in 2000 or 2001.

CVP6

**1999, May 7   Tagged   Die Cut**
**Self-Adhesive**
**Size: 77½x39mm**
**Microprinting Above Red Orange Line**

| | | | |
|---|---|---|---|
| CVP35 | CVP6 | 33c blk & red org, control numbers only at LL, round corners | 20.00 |
| a. | | "Priority Mail" at LL, square corners | 150.00 |
| b. | | "Priority Mail AS" and text string at LL, square corners | 150.00 |

**No Microprinting Above Red Orange Line**

| | | | |
|---|---|---|---|
| CVP36 | CVP6 | 33c blk & red org, control numbers only at LL, round corners | 9.00 |
| a. | | "Priority Mail" at LL, square corners | 125.00 |
| b. | | "Priority Mail AS" and text string at LL, square corners | 125.00 |

**Size: 73½x42mm**

| | | | |
|---|---|---|---|
| CVP37 | CVP6 | 33c blk & pink, control numbers only at LL | 3.75 |
| a. | | "Priority Mail" at LL | 5.00 |
| b. | | "Priority Mail AS" and text string at LL | 5.00 |

Nos. CVP35-CVP37 were available from 18 IBM Neopost machines located in central Florida, and at least one machine in the Washington, DC area (Merrifield, VA Automated Postal Center). The backing paper is taller than the stamp. Any denomination could be printed up to $99.99.

Simplypostage.com — CVP8

**Serpentine Die Cut 8 at Right**
**2001   Self-Adhesive**
**Eagle and Stars Background**

| | | | |
|---|---|---|---|
| CVP39 | CVP8 | 34c blk, blue & org, 2001 | — |
| CVP40 | CVP8 | 34c blk, blue & org, with control number at UL, 2001 | — |

**Flag Background**

| | | | |
|---|---|---|---|
| CVP41 | CVP8 | 34c blk, blue & org, with control number at UL, 2001 | 50.00 |
| CVP42 | CVP8 | 34c blk, blue & org, with control number at LL, 2001 | 50.00  20.00 |

**Large Flag Design**

The item shown was produced by Neopost. It was found that the large flag image hampered the barcode from being scanned. It is believed no examples were actually sold to the public. Five panes of four are believed to exist. Value, pane of 4, $300.

Neopostage.com
CVP9

**Serpentine Die Cut 8¾ at Right**
**2002, June   Self-Adhesive**

| | | | |
|---|---|---|---|
| CVP43 | CVP9 | 21c blk, blue & org | 15.00 |
| a. | | Booklet pane of 10 | 200.00 |
| CVP44 | CVP9 | 23c blk, blue & org | 10.00 |
| a. | | Booklet pane of 10 | 120.00 |
| CVP45 | CVP9 | 34c blk, blue & org | 20.00 |
| a. | | Booklet pane of 10 | 250.00 |
| CVP46 | CVP9 | 37c blk, blue & org | 12.50 |
| a. | | Booklet pane of 10 | 150.00 |
| CVP47 | CVP9 | 50c blk, blue & org | 15.00 |
| a. | | Booklet pane of 10 | 180.00 |
| CVP47B | CVP9 | 57c blk, blue & org | — |
| a. | | Booklet pane of 10 | — |
| CVP48 | CVP9 | 60c blk, blue & org | 14.00 |
| a. | | Booklet pane of 10 | 160.00 |
| CVP49 | CVP9 | 70c blk, blue & org | 16.00 |
| a. | | Booklet pane of 10 | 200.00 |
| CVP50 | CVP9 | 80c blk, blue & org | 18.00 |
| a. | | Booklet pane of 10 | 200.00 |
| CVP51 | CVP9 | $3.50 blk, blue & org | 60.00 |
| a. | | Booklet pane of 1 | — |
| b. | | Booklet pane of 2 | — |
| c. | | Booklet pane of 5 | — |
| d. | | Booklet pane of 10 | 700.00 |
| CVP52 | CVP9 | $3.85 blk, blue & org | 55.00 |
| a. | | Booklet pane of 1 | — |
| b. | | Booklet pane of 2 | — |
| c. | | Booklet pane of 5 | — |
| d. | | Booklet pane of 10 | 600.00 |
| CVP52E | CVP9 | $12.45 blk, blue & org | — |
| a. | | Booklet pane of 1 | — |
| CVP53 | CVP9 | $13.65 blk, blue & org | — |
| a. | | Booklet pane of 1 | — |
| b. | | Booklet pane of 2 | — |
| c. | | Booklet pane of 5 | — |
| d. | | Booklet pane of 10 | — |

Nos. CVP43-CVP53 were printed only with the stated values.
Denominations of 34c, 57c, $3.50 and perhaps others exist with an ICNOVA kiosk location designation. These were produced during pre-issue testing at a location not publicly accessible and are not considered to be valid postage. Stamps from the ICNOVA location have much smaller 2-D bar code squares. The denominations listed above come from other publicly accessible kiosk locations from June 20, 2002, forward. Official sales of these stamps began on June 20, 2002, or later for some denominations.
The 21c, 34c, 57c, $3.50 and $12.45 denominations were only sold from June 21 to June 29, 2002. They are all scarce, and some are rare. The 37c, $3.85 and $13.65 denominations were not sold until June 30, 2002, when the rate change took effect.
While the name on Nos. CVP39-CVP42 reads simplypostage.com and the name on Nos. CVP43-CVP53 reads neopostage.com, both were products of Neopost.
Issued:  Nos. CVP43-CVP49, CVP51-CVP53, 6/2002; No. CVP50, 7/2002.
Earliest documented use: Nos. CVP43, CVP47, CVP51-CVP52, not known used; Nos. CVP44, CVP46, CVP48-CVP49, CVP53, 6/30; No. CVP45, 6/21; No. CVP50, 7/3.

CVP10

IBM Pitney Bowes CVP11

**2004, Apr. 14                    Die Cut**
**Self-Adhesive**

| | | | |
|---|---|---|---|
| CVP54 | CVP10 | 37c black & pink | 5.00 |
| a. | | "First Class Mail" under encryption at LL | 2.50 |
| b. | | "Priority Mail" under encryption at LL | 2.50 |
| c. | | "Parcel Post" under encryption at LL | 2.50 |
| d. | | "International" under encryption at LL | 2.50 |
| CVP55 | CVP11 | 37c black, "US Postage" under encryption at LL | 5.00 |
| a. | | "First Class Mail" under encryption at LL | 2.50 |
| b. | | "Priority Mail" under encryption at LL | 2.50 |
| c. | | "Parcel Post" under encryption at LL | 2.50 |
| d. | | "International" under encryption at LL | 2.50 |

Nos. CVP54-CVP55 could be printed in any denomination up to $99.99. Catalogue values for Nos. CVP54-CVP54d and CVP55 are for stamps with low denominations. Stamps with denominations appropriate to the service described are valued correspondingly higher.

CVP12

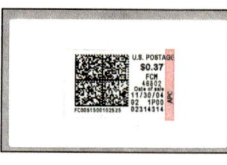

IBM Pitney Bowes CVP13

**2004, Nov. 19                    Die Cut**
**Self-Adhesive**
**Serial Number Under Encryption**
**APC**

| | | | | |
|---|---|---|---|---|
| CVP56 | CVP12 | 37c black | 2.50 | .45 |
| CVP57 | CVP13 | 37c black & pink | 1.25 | .45 |

Nos. CVP56-CVP57 could be printed in any denomination. No. CVP56 could be printed with three different rate inscriptions under the denomination. No. CVP57 could be printed with 18 different rate inscriptions and/or service indicators under the denomination, and at least 27 different rate inscriptions and or/service indicators under the denomination on stamps with a four-digit code after the zip code.

**Blank Under Denomination**
**"IM" and Numbers Under Encryption**

| | | | | |
|---|---|---|---|---|
| CVP58 | CVP13 | 60c black & pink | 3.00 | .50 |
| CVP59 | CVP13 | 80c black & pink | 3.75 | .50 |

**"PM" and Numbers Under Encryption**

| | | | | |
|---|---|---|---|---|
| CVP60 | CVP13 | $3.85 black & pink | 15.00 | .50 |

**"EM" and Numbers Under Encryption**

| | | | | |
|---|---|---|---|---|
| CVP61 | CVP13 | $13.65 black & pink | 42.50 | 1.00 |

**"IB" and Numbers Under Encryption**

**CVP62** CVP13 $1 black & pink 4.00 .25

Nos. CVP58-CVP61 could only be printed in denominations listed. No. CVP62 could be printed in any denomination above 99c. As of May 12, 2008, it was possible to create stamps with "IB" and numbers under encryption in any denomination. The computer software was later changed to once again only permit stamps of certain denominations to be created with "IB" and numbers under the encryption.

**IBM Pitney Bowes Type of 2004**

**2006 Self-Adhesive *Die Cut***

**Blank Under Denomination**

**"IM" and Numbers Under Encryption**

**CVP63** CVP13 48c black & pink 1.50 .40
**CVP64** CVP13 63c black & pink 1.75 .50
**CVP65** CVP13 84c black & pink 2.25 .50

**"PM" and Numbers Under Encryption**

**CVP66** CVP13 $4.05 black & pink 11.00 .50
**CVP66A** CVP13 $8.10 black & pink 30.00 1.00

**"EM" and Numbers Under Encryption**

**CVP67** CVP13 $14.40 black & pink 32.50 1.00

Nos. CVP63-CVP67 could only be printed in denominations listed.

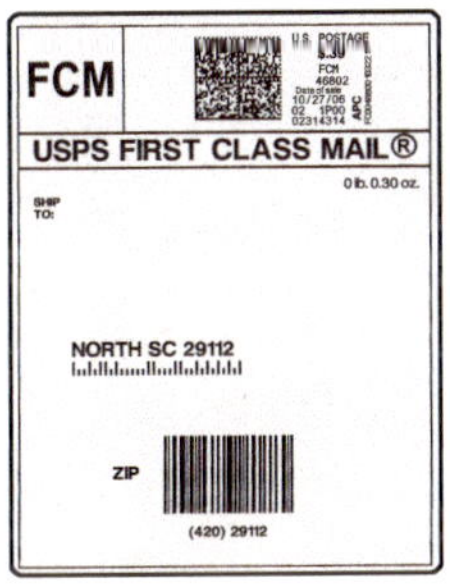


IBM Pitney Bowes CVP14

**2006 Self-Adhesive *Die Cut***

**No Inscription Under Encryption**

**Serial Number to Right of "APC"**

**"Ship To:" Above Destination City**

**CVP69** CVP14 39c black 2.25 .25

Nos. CVP69 could be printed in any denomination, with 14 different rate inscriptions and/or service indicators under the denomination on stamps having "Ship To:" at the left and no code below the weight, and at least 29 different rate inscriptions and/or service indicators under the denomination on stamps having a four-digit code at the right that is even with the words "Ship To:" and below the weight.

**IBM Pitney Bowes Type of 2004**

**2006(?)-07 Self-Adhesive *Die Cut***

**Blank Under Denomination**

**"IB" and Numbers Under Encryption**

**CVP70** CVP13 39c black & pink 1.00 .50
**CVP71** CVP13 41c black & pink 1.75 .50
**CVP72** CVP13 69c black & pink 2.50 .70

**"IM" and Numbers Under Encryption**

**CVP73** CVP13 61c black & pink 2.25 .50
**CVP74** CVP13 90c black & pink 3.50 .95

Nos. CVP70-CVP74 could only be printed in the denominations listed.

Nos. CVP71-CVP74 issued May, 2007. No. CVP70 was issued before the May rate change. As of May 12, 2008, it was possible to create stamps with "IB" and numbers under encryption in any denomination. The computer software was later changed to once again only permit stamps of certain denominations to be created with "IB" and numbers under the encryption. No. CVP70 was available for sale from Nov. 2006 to May 13, 2007. Nos. CVP71-CVP72 were available for sale from May 14, 2007 to May 11, 2008.

Pitney Bowes With Eagle at Right CVP15

**2006, Dec. Self-Adhesive *Die Cut***

**CVP75** CVP15 41c blk & pink, no inscription below sold date — —
- *a.* "Mailed From Zip Code ..." on bottom line 35.00 —
- *b.* "Postcard" on bottom line 15.00 —
- *c.* "First-Class Mail" on bottom line 15.00 —
- *d.* "First-Class Mail Intl" on bottom line 15.00 —
- *e.* "Priority" on bottom line 15.00 —
- *f.* "Priority Envelope" on bottom line 15.00 —
- *g.* "Priority Box" on bottom line 15.00 —
- *h.* "Express Mail" on bottom line 30.00 —
- *i.* "Express Envelope" on bottom line 30.00 —
- *j.* "Parcel Post" on bottom line — —
- *k.* "Priority Tube" on bottom line — —
- *l.* "First Class" on bottom line 15.00 —

No. CVP75 was put into service at large companies and universities in Dec. 2006, with the majority of the machines not being available to the general public. Information about this stamp was not made available until 2007. Other rates and inscriptions might be available.

Nos. CVP75a could be printed in any denomination. Nos. CVP75b-CVP75f could be printed only in pre-programmed denominations based on the current rates for the service, or in any denominations at or above the minimum rates for the service. Values are for stamps with low denominations. A stamp with "Priority - Irregular Shape" on the bottom line has been reported to exist but has not been seen by the editors. Inscriptions generated by the software may vary from machine to machine depending on when the software was installed.

Two distinctly different colors of phosphor stripes on labels used in Mail & Go machines are known, with many Mail & Go adhesives appearing in both versions.

Private sector operators of Pitney Bowes "Mail & Go" machines are not bound to use only label paper supplied by Pitney Bowes. Competing label paper producers make and sell labels in the formats required for the machines that dispense Nos. CVP75 and CVP84. Thus, Nos. CVP75 and CVP84 without the Pitney Bowes logo on the reverse are not errors.

**IBM Pitney Bowes Type of 2004**

**2008, May Self-Adhesive *Die Cut***

**Blank Under Denomination**

**"IM" and Numbers Under Encryption**

**CVP76** CVP13 94c black & pink 3.00 .60
**CVP77** CVP13 $1.20 black & pink 3.75 1.25

Nos. CVP76-CVP77 could only be printed in the denominations listed.

IBM CVP16

***Die Cut With Rounded Corners***

**2008, June 4 Self-Adhesive**

**CVP78** CVP16 42c black & pink 4.25 —
- *a.* Without "date of sale" inscription, *2009* — —

***Die Cut With Perpendicular Corners***

**CVP79** CVP16 42c black & pink 4.25 —
- *a.* Without "date of sale" inscription, *2009* — —

Nos. CVP78-CVP79 were made available during a pilot study to evaluate a new IBM kiosk at Schaumburg, IL. No. CVP78 could be printed in any denomination from 1c to $25. Each kiosk transaction was limited to $100. Individual panes with 6, 7, 8, 9 or 10 stamps could be purchased as long as the total face value of the pane did not exceed $100. The pane of 10 exists with the vertical pink tagging stripe along the left side of the stamps. The pane of 10 could only be bought with stamps denominated from 1c to $10. Stamps denominated from $10.01 to $16.66 could only be purchased in panes containing fewer than 10 stamps. Stamps denominated from $16.67 to $25 could only be purchased as a single stamp.

**IBM Pitney Bowes Type of 2004**

**2009 Self-Adhesive *Die Cut***

**Blank Under Denomination**

**"IM" and Numbers Under Encryption**

**CVP80** CVP13 98c black & pink 2.00 .60
**CVP81** CVP13 $1.24 black & pink 2.50 1.25

Nos. CVP80-CVP81 could only be printed in denominations listed.

IBM (Statue of Liberty) CVP17

Illustration reduced.

***Die Cut With Rounded Corners***

**2009, June 5 Self-Adhesive**

**CVP82** CVP17 44c black & pink 7.50 —
- *a.* Without "date of sale" inscription, *2009* — —

***Die Cut With Perpendicular Corners***

**CVP83** CVP17 44c black & pink 7.50 —
- *a.* Without "date of sale" inscription, *2009* — —

No. CVP82 could be printed in any denomination from 1c to $25. Nos. CVP82-CVP83 were made available during a pilot study to evaluate a new IBM kiosk at Schaumburg, IL. The machine study at Schaumburg was scheduled to end on July 31, 2009. No. CVP82 was created for purchases of one to five individual stamps or any extra stamps beyond multiples of 10 ending in numerals 1 to 5.

INVERTS

Labels used to produce stamps in the dimensions of many items of CVP54 and similar later issues in this format were packaged in a fanfolded strip two labels wide and packaged in boxes that are stored in the machines from which the labels are fed to printers as purchases occur. Nothing prevents the labels from being fed in reverse, which results in inverted paper "errors." Such "inverts" (with phosphor stripe appearing on the opposite edge of the stamp than the intended edge) can be deliberately produced, and therefore are not listed.

SERVICE-INSCRIBED STAMPS

Listings of small label stamps from CVP84 reveal that various service-related abbreviations appear under the denominations of some stamps. From CVP84 onward (including the FOLD HERE varieties), all denominated stamps may be purchased that include service-specific indicators under the denominations (e.g., EXPRESS for a clearly identifiable service as well as abbreviations that are less clear such as EM HFPU FRB). When a machine asks a mailer if any postage is already affixed to an item, the mailer can indicate that all postage but one cent or more is affixed. A customer stating that almost all required postage is already affixed will result in the stamp vending machine dispensing a stamp with a service-specific indicator that has a face value as low as one cent. For this reason, listings no longer include small format vended stamps with service-specific indicators beyond No. CVP84, because the stamps can be produced to show any face value, use not being restricted to the class indicated, and all types may be used on any mail matter.

Flag — CVP18

***Serpentine Die Cut 13¼x12½***

**2011, Oct. 18 Self-Adhesive**

**CVP84** CVP18 44c multi, date sold only on bottom line — —
- *a.* Date sold and "Postcard" on bottom line — —
- *b.* Date sold and "First-Class" on bottom line — —

No. CVP84 was issued in panes of 10. It was made available at Mail & Go postal stations in Super Target stores in the Dallas, TX area. Panes could be printed in any denomination from 29c to $9.99. Serpentine die cut 9 examples of No. CVP84 with dates earlier than Oct. 18 were produced at Pitney Bowes facilities. This serpentine die cut 9 sticker stock is not known to have been sent out for use in machines that were available for use by the general public. No. CVP84 was made available in 2013 with dozens of images other than the flag shown. These optional images are for various holidays and events, as well as social causes, such as support for breast cancer, education and recycling. One image, for bridal showers, has been made available in two different types.

Pitney Bowes With Eagle at Left — CVP18a

Pitney Bowes Without Eagle — CVP18b

***Die Cut With Perpendicular Corners***

**2011, Oct. 18 Self-Adhesive**

**CVP84C** CVP18a 46c black & pink, no inscription below sold date 5.00 —
- *d.* CVP18b 46c With eagle emblem omitted — —
- *e.* "Mailed From Zip Code ..." on bottom line — —
- *f.* "Postcard" on bottom line 7.50 —
- *g.* "First-Class Mail" on bottom line 5.00 —
- *h.* "First-Class Mail Intl" on bottom line — —
- *i.* "Priority Mail" on bottom line — —
- *j.* "Priority Envelope" on bottom line — —
- *k.* "Priority Box" on bottom line — —
- *l.* "Priority Tube" on bottom line — —
- *m.* "Priority - Irregular Shape" on bottom line — —
- *n.* "Express Mail" on bottom line — —

No. CVP84C was made available at Mail & Go postal stations in Super Target stores in the Dallas, TX area, and presumably could be printed in any denomination.

In 2013, twelve Mail & Go machines vending No. CVP84C and the holiday and social cause designs noted under No. CVP84 were installed and operated at thirteen Rite Aid drug stores in central California along the Highway 1 corridor. The machines were installed by the LePages Company (a USPS-licensed manufacturer and wholesaler of USPS-brand mailing supplies). They were placed under the jurisdiction of the Oakland, CA region of the USPS throughout most of 2014-15. Postmasters in the towns supported the machines officially with Priority Mail containers, postal labels and daily mail collection. The locations were listed by the USPS in its online Internet database of self-service post office locations. The machines appear to have been removed between Oct. 2015 and Jan. 2016.

The stamps vended by these machines were officially approved by the USPS and are no different than stamps sold from the same models of machines installed at colleges and universities across the nation. Locations of about 40 other privately supported Mail & Go machines have been recorded. These other machines are installed and operated by Pitney Bowes employees who manage mail rooms the company operates under contracts. At those locations, the mail room staff takes the daily mail to the local post officce, and there is no USPS logistical support.

The USPS regulations classify Mail & Go machines as "third party kiosks." No. CVP84Cd is an error that Pitney Bowes technicians could not explain. It appeared for a short time on a machine in Illinois and at the U.S. Department of Defense Medical HQ facility mailroom in Annandale, Va., and other unidentified locations.

184 UNITED STATES

Thermal prints generated by vending machines with too little electrically generated heat tend to fade very quickly.

APC With Vertical Coding at Right of Date CVP19

***Die Cut With Rounded Corners***

**2012, Apr. 12 Self-Adhesive**

**CVP85** CVP19 black & pink 1.50 —

*a.* Die cut with perpendicular corners, colored bar at left, "Fold Here" at center, 100x38mm — —

No. CVP85 has "APC" reading upwards at right. No. CVP78 has "IBM" reading upwards at right. No. CVP85 was available during a nationwide test of machines, and could be printed in any denomination from 1c to $99.99.

No. CVP85a was produced on label stock normally used for No. CVP87 when machines ran out of label stock to produce orders for Nos. CVP85, CVP85B, and varieties of CVP86.

APC With Vertical Coding At Left of Date — CVP19a

***Die Cut With Rounded Corners***

**2012 Self-Adhesive**

**CVP85B** CVP19a black & pink 2.00 —

*c.* Die cut with perpendicular corners, colored bar at left, "FOLD HERE" at center, 100x38mm 2.00 —

No. CVP85Bc was produced on label stock normally used for No. CVP87 when machines ran out of stock to produce orders for Nos. CVP85, CVP85B, and varieties of CVP86.

APC Variable Vignette Stamp CVP20

***Die Cut With Rounded Corners***

**2012, Apr. 12 Self-Adhesive**

**CVP86** CVP20 (45c) black & pink 2.50 —

*a.* Die cut with perpendicular corners, colored bar at left, "Fold Here" at center, 100x38mm 3.00 —

No. CVP86 was available during a nationwide test of machines, and could be printed only as "Forever" stamps. The vignette portion of the stamp at left could be chosen from a gallery of six images (Mr. Zip, Heart, Flowers, Flag, Eagle, and Balloons and "Celebrate!", which is depicted). Values are for any vignette, or for any other vignette that may be programmed into the machine at a later date. Each vignette design could be purchased in a quantities ranging from 1 stamp to 100 stamps, but because a $1 minimum purchase was required, at least three examples of the first stamp chosen had to be purchased. A maximum of ten stamps could be printed on a sheet. Sales of stamps that are not in multiples of 10 were printed in strips, smaller-sized sheets containing an even number of stamps, or in sheets having one label inscribed "This Block Is Not Valid Postage" when the sheet contained an odd number of stamps.

No. CVP86a was produced on wide-label stock normally used for No. CVP87 when the small-label printer was defective or the machine had run out of small-label stock.

Examples of No. CVP86 without a printed image at left are the result of machines having their image-printing capability shut off so preprinted label stock for producing No. CVP88 could be substituted for the blank label stock used for Nos. CVP85 and CVP86. See footnote under No. CVP88 for information about examples of No. CVP86 with date of purchase inscriptions to right of "Forever."

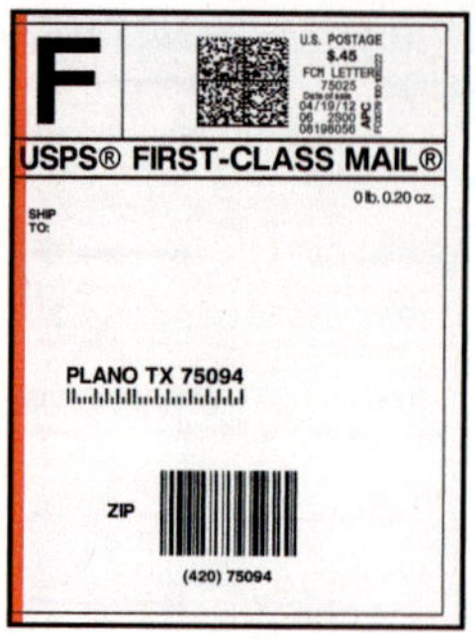

APC With Vertical Coding to Right of Date CVP21

***Die Cut With Perpendicular Corners***

**2012, Apr. 12 Self-Adhesive**

**CVP87** CVP21 black & pink — —

No. CVP87 was available during a nationwide test of machines, and could be printed in any denomination from 1c to $99.99. Stamps can be inscribed with a variety of different service inscriptions.

APC With Vertical Coding to Left of Date — CVP21a

***Die Cut With Perpendicular Corners***

**2012 Self-Adhesive**

**CVP87A** CVP21a black & pink — —

Labels of type CVP21a with postage indicia inscribed FCM LETTER below the denomination have only a bar code and the Zip code of the destination at the bottom third rather than a USPS TRACKING NUMBER. Labels for which a Certified Mail fee has been paid have a CERTIFIED MAIL bar code. Express Mail labels have POSTAL USE ONLY form at the bottom.

On Nov. 7, 2013, the USPS had distributed and had begun requiring the use of "signalling label" stock with a clear phosphor stripe. The clear stripe appears positioned vertically along the left margin of the labels. Labels with pink stripes along the right margin continued to be used until stocks were exhausted or labels with pre-printed vignettes were issued for use in some machines on Apr. 1, 2014 (CVP90-CVP91).

APC With Vertical Coding at Left of Date And Clear Phosphor Stripe Along Left Margin — CVP21b

***Die Cut With Rounded Corners***

**2013, Nov. 7 Self-Adhesive**

**CVP87B** CVP21b black 5.00 —

*c.* Die cut with perpendicular corners, colored bar at left, "Fold Here" at center, 100x38mm 8.50 —

The Scheduled Delivery and Expected Delivery inscriptions, date and times seen on Nos. CVP89B and CVP89C replaced "THIS BLOCK IS NOT VALID FOR POSTAGE" on labels normally found adjacent to Nos, CVP87B and CVP92A when sold for other than Priority Mail.

Mailbox CVP22

***Die Cut With Rounded Corners***

**2012, Oct. 31 Self-Adhesive**

**CVP88** CVP22 (45c) multicolored 3.50 —

The mailbox vignette is preprinted on No. CVP88. This preprinted stock was placed in machines in November 2012 and was to be removed from machines on December 31, 2012. The earliest known date of sale is Nov. 10, 2012.

Examples of No. CVP88 with the mailbox design covered by images used for Nos. CVP85 and CVP86 were the result of machines having their blank label stock replaced with the pre-printed label stock while the machine's image-printing capability was not shut off to accommodate the preprinted stock.

On No. CVP88, the number of the month and last two digits of the year in which the stamp was purchased, separated by an asterisk, appear to the right of "Forever." If the operator of the machine programmed it to sell No. CVP88 but failed to turn off the vignettes available as No. CVP86 and did not load the preprinted Christmas Mailbox label stock, the resulting vended product would be No. CVP86 with the month and year appearing to the right of "FOREVER."

Labels inscribed "This Block Is Not Valid For Postage" differ from similar labels created with No. CVP86. Various sizes of "Void" overprints on these labels exist.

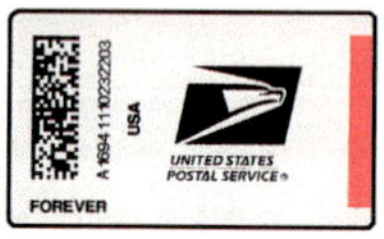

USPS Emblem — CVP22a

***Die Cut With Rounded Corners***

**2013, Oct. 31 Self-Adhesive**

**CVP88A** CVP22a (46c) black & pink 3.00 —

*b.* Die cut with perpendicular corners, colored bar at left, "Fold Here" at center, 100x38mm 7.50 —

This design was first placed in a few machines in the Washington, DC and Merrifield, VA area on Oct. 31, 2013. Stamps vended with encoded dates prior to Nov. 7, 2013 were test stamps. On Nov. 6, 2013, the USPS declared the test to be successful and the image was released for general use as a fall-back design.

No. CVP88Ab was produced on wide-label stock normally used to produce No. CVP87 when the small-label printer was either defective or machines ran out of stock to produce orders for No. CVP88A. The earliest known sale date of No. CVP88Ab is Nov. 2, 2013.

Examples of CVP88A lacking the eagle vignette could be made if the machine had blank label stock in the feeder but was set to print on pre-printed labels such as No. CVP89. When the machine has pre-printed labels (starting with No. CVP89) in the feeder and is set to print on blank labels, the Eagle vignette will print on top of the preprinted image.

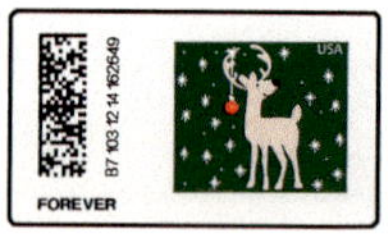

Reindeer CVP23

***Die Cut With Rounded Corners***

**2013, Nov. 7 Self-Adhesive**

**CVP89** CVP23 (46c) multicolored 3.00 2.00

The reindeer vignette is preprinted on No. CVP89. The issue date is the earliest documented sale date.

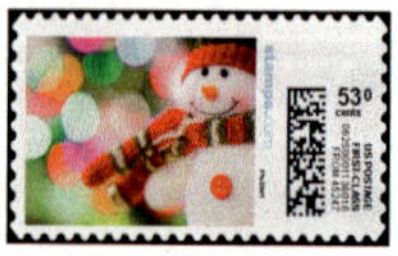

USPS Emblem With Clear Phosphor Stripe Along Left Margin — CVP23a

***Die Cut With Rounded Corners***

**2014, Jan. 8 Self-Adhesive**

**CVP89A** CVP23a (46c) black 3.00 —

*d.* (50c) Vertical serial number with no leading letter, *2018* 2.50 —

Examples of CVP89A lacking the eagle vignette could be made if the machine had blank label stock in the feeder but was set to print on pre-printed labels such as No. CVP89. When the machine has pre-printed labels (starting with No. CVP89) in the feeder and is set to print on blank labels, the Eagle vignette will print on top of the preprinted image. Examples known include 2018-generation stamps with serial number with no leading letter.

APC With Scheduled Delivery — CVP23b

***Die Cut With Perpendicular Corners***

**2014, Jan. Self-Adhesive**

**CVP89B** CVP23b black & pink — —

No. CVP89B is generated when the mailer answers a machine-system prompt with a "no" answer when asked if the full-length label (Type CVP21) will fit on the mailer's item. This is vended only when pre-printed labels are installed in the machine or the small-label printer is defective.

For selected mail service the USPS doesn't track, the field to the right of "FOLD HERE" remains blank (in effect creating No. CVP87Bc).

APC With Expected Delivery — CVP23c

***Die Cut With Perpendicular Corners***

**2014, Jan. Self-Adhesive**

**CVP89C** CVP23c black & pink — —

See note after No. CVP89B.

Spiderman CVP24

***Die Cut With Rounded Corners***

**2014, Apr. 1 Self-Adhesive**

**CVP90** CVP24 (49c) multicolored 3.00 1.25

The Spiderman vignette is preprinted on No. CVP90.

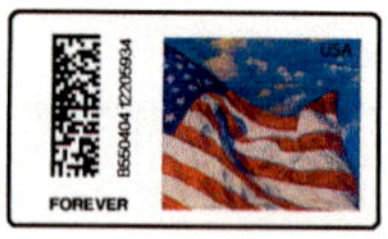

Flag — CVP25

***Die Cut With Rounded Corners***

**2014, Apr. 1 Self-Adhesive**

**CVP91** CVP25 (49c) multicolored 3.00 1.25

*a.* "FOREVER" (only) missing — —

*b.* (50c) With vertical serial number with no leading letter, *2018* 3.00 1.50

The flag vignette is preprinted on No. CVP91.

Examples of No. CVP91b exist with the USPS Eagle emblem (see illustration at design CVP23a) printed on top of the preprinted flag design label; value, $5. It is theoretically possible that blank labels without a preprinted flag or other preprinted design could be inserted in the new machine, and (likely) be printed without the operator having turned on the thermal-printed USPS logo that machines can produce on-site, leaving an indicia and value printed on a stamp without any pictorial element. Such varieties are products of local operator error that has occurred on all issues from No. CVP88 in 2013 and can be manufactured through illicit cooperation of postal officials.

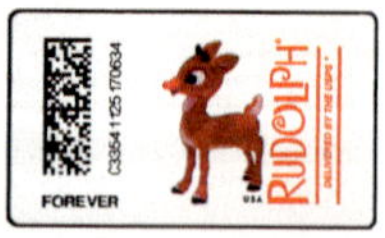

Rudolph, the Red-Nosed Reindeer CVP26

***Die Cut With Rounded Corners***

**2014, Nov. 6 Self-Adhesive**

**CVP92** CVP26 (49c) multicolored 4.00 1.75

The Rudolph vignette is preprinted on No. CVP92.

# UNITED STATES

From Nov. 14, 2014, Automated Postal Centers (APC) vending machines were renamed by the USPS to be Self Service Kiosks (SSK), and the machines were changed to issue stamps inscribed "SSK" rather than "APC."

 SSK With Vertical Coding at Left of Date — CVP27

### Die Cut With Rounded Corners
**2014, Nov. 14**    **Self-Adhesive**
CVP93   CVP27   black & pink
a.   Black, with vertical transparent stripe at left   1.00 —

No. CVP93 was available at machines that had not yet retired the pink-striped labels.
It was not intended by the USPS that indicia inscribed with SSK would be printed on pink-striped labels. The design was shifted to appear farther to the right, to insure the bar code would remain uncompromised and at a safe distance from the clear phosphor stripe on the newer labels. Almost all examples of this issue will have SSK appearing within the pink stripe.
Value of No. CVP93a is for 49c denomination, current at the time. Other denominations pro-rata.

SSK With Vertical Coding to Left of Date CVP28

### Die Cut With Perpendicular Corners
**2014, Nov. 14**    **Self-Adhesive**
CVP94   CVP28   black & pink   2.50
a.   Indicia at upper right with no leading letter, various service level indicators, 2018   2.50

Like No. CVP87A, No. CVP94 exists in other denominations inscribed with various mail service inscriptions or with blackened square in place of letters such as "F," above.

SSK With Blank Area at Right of "Fold Here" CVP29

### Die Cut With Perpendicular Corners
**2014, Nov. 14**    **Self-Adhesive**
CVP95   CVP29   black & pink   5.00
a.   black, vertical serial number with no leading letter, clear phosphor stripe, 2018   5.00

See note below No. CVP89B.

SSK With "Expected Delivery" at Right of "Fold Here" — CVP30

### Die Cut With Perpendicular Corners
**2014, Nov. 14**    **Self-Adhesive**
CVP96   CVP30   black & pink
a.   black, vertical serial number with no leading letter, various service level indicators, clear phosphor stripe, 2018   3.00

See note below No. CVP89B.

SSK With "Scheduled Delivery" at Right of "Fold Here" — CVP31

### Die Cut With Perpendicular Corners
**2014, Nov. 14**    **Self-Adhesive**
CVP97   CVP31   black & pink
a.   black, vertical serial number with no leading letter, various service level indicators, clear phosphor stripe, 2018   3.00 —

See note below No. CVP89B.

Charlie Brown Looking in Mailbox CVP32

### Die Cut With Rounded Corners
**2015, Oct. 20**    **Self-Adhesive**
CVP98   CVP32   (49c) multicolored   4.00   1.00

The Charlie Brown vignette is preprinted on No. CVP98. Issue date is earliest recorded sale date. Post offices were authorized to place the labels in machines at the close of business on Oct. 20, which many did prior to the SSK system-wide date change that occurs daily prior to midnight.

mPOS CVP33

### Die Cut With Rounded Corners
**2015**    **Self-Adhesive**
CVP99   CVP33   black

No. CVP99 is generated by a mobile hand-held point-of-sale vending machine with integrated thermal postage printer and embedded credit/debit card acceptance processor. Possible denominations are limited to the postage prices applicable to each available pre-printed type of Priority and Express Mail flat rate envelopes and packages (rate determined by scanning the bar code on the package the customer needs). While this indicia is intended to be affixed to mail matter at the time it is presented, postage can be generated and sold in quantities to take away for later use. Labels are generated from vertical coils with blank labels.

Wreath in Window CVP34

### Die Cut With Rounded Corners
**2016, Oct. 27**    **Self-Adhesive**
CVP100   CVP34   (47c) multi   3.00   1.00

The wreath in window vignette is preprinted on No. CVP100. Issue date is earliest recorded sale date.

Christmas Cookies CVP35

### Die Cut With Rounded Corners
**2017, Oct. 17**    **Self-Adhesive**
CVP101   CVP35   (49c) multi   3.00   1.00
a.   On 2018-generation stamp with serial number with no leading letter

The Christmas cookies vignette is preprinted on No. CVP101. Issue date is earliest recorded sale date.

Flag — CVP36

### Die Cut With Rounded Corners
**2018, Aug. 23**    **Self-Adhesive**
CVP108   CVP36   (50c) multi   3.00   1.00

The flag vignette is preprinted on No. CVP108. Issue date is earliest recorded sale date.

Santa Claus CVP37

### Die Cut With Rounded Corners
**2018, Oct. 21**    **Self-Adhesive**
CVP109   CVP37   (50c) multi   2.50   1.00

The Santa Claus vignette is preprinted on No. CVP109. Issue date is earliest recorded sale date.

Christmas Stocking CVP38

### Die Cut With Rounded Corners
**2020, Nov. 16**    **Self-Adhesive**
CVP110   CVP38   (55c) multi   2.50   1.00

The Christmas stocking vignette is preprinted on No. CVP110.

Santa Claus, Sleigh and Reindeer in Flight CVP39

### Die Cut With Rounded Corners
**2021, Nov.**    **Self-Adhesive**
CVP111   CVP39   (58c) multi   2.50   1.00

The Santa Claus vignette is preprinted on No. CVP111.

Elf Tying Ribbon CVP40

### Die Cut With Rounded Corners
**2022, Nov.**    **Self-Adhesive**
CVP112   CVP40   (60c) multi   2.50   1.00

The elf vignette is preprinted on No. CVP112.

Snowman CVP41

### Die Cut With Rounded Corners
**2023, Nov. 13**    **Self-Adhesive**
CVP113   CVP41   (66c) multi   2.50   1.00

The snowman vignette is preprinted on No. CVP113.

## PERSONAL COMPUTER POSTAGE

Personal computer postage, approved by the US Postal Service, was created by subscribing to Stamps.com, an Internet website. Customers ordered self-adhesive labels showing vignettes, but lacking any franking value. The franking value indicia of the stamps could be printed at the customer's convenience at any computer with an Internet connection, using the customer's access codes. Any postage printed would be charged against the customer's account.

### Neopost

CVPA1

**2000**    *Serpentine Die Cut 8*
**Self-Adhesive**
1CVP1   CVPA1   33c black, yellow & pink   — —

### Stamps.com

Flag and Star — CVPA1a

*Serpentine Die Cut 5¾ at Left*
**2002, July**
"Stamps.com" in Lower Case Letters
**Identification Code Below Zip Code**
**No Mail Class Inscribed**
1CVP2   CVPA1a   37c black, blue & orange   7.00   3.00
**Identification Code Above Zip Code**
**Inscribed "US Postage" only**
1CVP2A   CVPA1a   37c black, blue & orange   4.00   3.00
a.   "First Class" below "US Postage"   2.75   2.00
b.   "Priority" below "US Postage"   8.25   2.50
c.   "Express" below "US Postage"   25.00   5.00
d.   "Media Mail" below "US Postage"   7.75   2.50
e.   "Parcel Post" below "US Postage"   7.75   2.50
f.   "Bound Printed Matter" below "US Postage"   7.75   2.50
g.   "BPM" below "US Postage"   7.75   2.50

See Nos. 1CVP9, 1CVP21.

No. 1CVP2 apparently could be printed in denominations up to and including 37c. The 37c denomination comes with "FIRST-CLASS" between the Zip code and the identification code.
Later versions of the Stamps.com software allow any denomination to be printed, as well as additional or different mail-class inscriptions, on any basic stamp except for No. 1CVP2.
Values for Nos. 1CVP2A and 1CVP3-1CVP42 are for items appropriate to the service described. Stamps with denominations far lower than those appropriate to the service are valued correspondingly lower.
The software changes allow Nos. 1CVP2A and 1CVP3-1CVP37 to be printed with the mail-class inscriptions described for Nos. 1CVP38f-1CVP38p.
Later software changes allow Nos. 1CVP2A, 1CVP3-1CVP42 and 1CVP51-1CVP58 to be printed with mail-class inscriptions "Library Mail," "Intl. First Class," "Intl Priority," "Intl Express," and "M-Bag" with any denomination.

# UNITED STATES

Love — CVPA2

## 2002  Serpentine Die Cut 5¾ at Left

**1CVP3** CVPA2 37c black, blue & orange  4.00  4.00
- a. "First Class" below "US Postage"  2.75  2.00
- b. "Priority" below "US Postage"  8.25  2.50
- c. "Express" below "US Postage"  25.00  5.00
- d. "Media Mail" below "US Postage"  7.75  2.50
- e. "Parcel Post" below "US Postage"  7.75  2.50
- f. "Bound Printed Matter" below "US Postage"  7.75  2.50
- g. "BPM" below "US Postage"  7.75  2.50

Statue of Liberty and Flag — CVPA3    Liberty Bell and Flag — CVPA4

Eagle and Flag — CVPA5    George Washington and Flag — CVPA6

Capitol Building and Flag — CVPA7

### Serpentine Die Cut 5¾ at Left
**2003, June**

**1CVP4** CVPA3 37c black, blue & orange  3.50  2.00
- a. "First Class" below "US Postage"  3.25  2.00
- b. "Priority" below "US Postage"  8.00  1.00
- c. "Express" below "US Postage"  25.00  3.00
- d. "Media Mail" below "US Postage"  7.50  1.00
- e. "Parcel Post" below "US Postage"  7.50  1.00
- f. "Bound Printed Matter" below "US Postage"  7.50  1.00
- g. "BPM" below "US Postage"  7.50  1.00

**1CVP5** CVPA4 37c black, blue & orange  3.50  2.00
- a. "First Class" below "US Postage"  3.25  2.00
- b. "Priority" below "US Postage"  8.00  1.00
- c. "Express" below "US Postage"  25.00  3.00
- d. "Media Mail" below "US Postage"  7.50  1.00
- e. "Parcel Post" below "US Postage"  7.50  1.00
- f. "Bound Printed Matter" below "US Postage"  7.50  1.00
- g. "BPM" below "US Postage"  7.50  1.00

**1CVP6** CVPA5 37c black, blue & orange  3.50  2.00
- a. "First Class" below "US Postage"  3.25  2.00
- b. "Priority" below "US Postage"  8.00  1.00
- c. "Express" below "US Postage"  25.00  3.00
- d. "Media Mail" below "US Postage"  7.50  1.00
- e. "Parcel Post" below "US Postage"  7.50  1.00
- f. "Bound Printed Matter" below "US Postage"  7.50  1.00
- g. "BPM" below "US Postage"  7.50  1.00

**1CVP7** CVPA6 37c black, blue & orange  3.50  2.00
- a. "First Class" below "US Postage"  3.25  .25
- b. "Priority" below "US Postage"  8.00  1.00
- c. "Express" below "US Postage"  25.00  3.00
- d. "Media Mail" below "US Postage"  7.50  1.00
- e. "Parcel Post" below "US Postage"  7.50  1.00
- f. "Bound Printed Matter" below "US Postage"  7.50  1.00
- g. "BPM" below "US Postage"  7.50  1.00

**1CVP8** CVPA7 37c black, blue & orange  3.50  2.00
- a. "First Class" below "US Postage"  3.25  .45
- b. "Priority" below "US Postage"  8.00  1.00
- c. "Express" below "US Postage"  25.00  3.00
- d. "Media Mail" below "US Postage"  7.50  1.00
- e. "Parcel Post" below "US Postage"  7.50  1.00
- f. "Bound Printed Matter" below "US Postage"  7.50  1.00
- g. "BPM" below "US Postage"  7.50  1.00
- h. Strip of 5, #1CVP4-1CVP8  17.50

### Flag and Star Type of 2002 Redrawn With "Stamps.com" in Upper Case Letters
### Serpentine Die Cut 5¾ at Left
**2003, June**
### Identification Code Above Zip Code

**1CVP9** CVPA1a 37c black, blue & orange, "US Postage" only  3.00  1.50
- a. "First Class" below "US Postage"  2.00  .45
- b. "Priority" below "US Postage"  8.00  1.00
- c. "Express" below "US Postage"  25.00  3.00
- d. "Media Mail" below "US Postage"  7.50  1.00
- e. "Parcel Post" below "US Postage"  7.50  1.00
- f. "Bound Printed Matter" below "US Postage"  7.50  1.00
- g. "BPM" below "US Postage"  7.50  1.00

Snowman CVPA8    Snowflakes CVPA9

Holly CVPA10    Dove CVPA11

Gingerbread Man and Candy — CVPA12

### Serpentine Die Cut 4½ at Left
**2003, Dec.**

**1CVP10** CVPA8 37c black, blue & orange  3.00  1.50
- a. "First Class" below "US Postage"  2.00  1.00
- b. "Priority" below "US Postage"  8.00  1.00
- c. "Express" below "US Postage"  25.00  3.00
- d. "Media Mail" below "US Postage"  7.50  1.00
- e. "Parcel Post" below "US Postage"  7.50  1.00
- f. "Bound Printed Matter" below "US Postage"  7.50  1.00
- g. "BPM" below "US Postage"  7.50  1.00

**1CVP11** CVPA9 37c black, blue & orange  3.00  1.50
- a. "First Class" below "US Postage"  2.00  1.00
- b. "Priority" below "US Postage"  8.00  1.00
- c. "Express" below "US Postage"  25.00  3.00
- d. "Media Mail" below "US Postage"  7.50  1.00
- e. "Parcel Post" below "US Postage"  7.50  1.00
- f. "Bound Printed Matter" below "US Postage"  7.50  1.00
- g. "BPM" below "US Postage"  7.50  1.00

**1CVP12** CVPA10 37c black, blue & orange  3.00  1.50
- a. "First Class" below "US Postage"  2.00  1.00
- b. "Priority" below "US Postage"  8.00  1.00
- c. "Express" below "US Postage"  25.00  3.00
- d. "Media Mail" below "US Postage"  7.50  1.00
- e. "Parcel Post" below "US Postage"  7.50  1.00
- f. "Bound Printed Matter" below "US Postage"  7.50  1.00
- g. "BPM" below "US Postage"  7.50  1.00

**1CVP13** CVPA11 37c black, blue & orange  3.00  1.50
- a. "First Class" below "US Postage"  2.00  1.00
- b. "Priority" below "US Postage"  8.00  1.00
- c. "Express" below "US Postage"  25.00  3.00
- d. "Media Mail" below "US Postage"  7.50  1.00
- e. "Parcel Post" below "US Postage"  7.50  1.00
- f. "Bound Printed Matter" below "US Postage"  7.50  1.00
- g. "BPM" below "US Postage"  7.50  1.00

**1CVP14** CVPA12 37c black, blue & orange  3.00  1.50
- a. "First Class" below "US Postage"  2.00  1.00
- b. "Priority" below "US Postage"  8.00  1.00
- c. "Express" below "US Postage"  25.00  3.00
- d. "Media Mail" below "US Postage"  7.50  1.00
- e. "Parcel Post" below "US Postage"  7.50  1.00
- f. "Bound Printed Matter" below "US Postage"  7.50  1.00
- g. "BPM" below "US Postage"  7.50  1.00
- h. Strip of 5, #1CVP10-1CVP14  12.50

Mailbox — CVPA13

### Serpentine Die Cut 6½ at Left
**2004, Mar.**

**1CVP15** CVPA13 37c black, blue & orange  25.00  15.00
- a. "First Class" below "US Postage"  25.00  15.00
- b. "Priority" below "US Postage"  —  —
- c. "Express" below "US Postage"  
- d. "Media Mail" below "US Postage"  
- e. "Parcel Post" below "US Postage"  
- f. "Bound Printed Matter" below "US Postage"  
- g. "BPM" below "US Postage"  

Blank sheets of No. 1CVP15 were sent free of charge to those who responded to special Stamps.com promotions which offered a fixed amount of free postage as an enticement to new subscribers. The franking portion of the stamps could only be applied after subscribing.

George Washington CVPA14    Thomas Jefferson CVPA15

Abraham Lincoln CVPA16    Theodore Roosevelt CVPA17

John F. Kennedy — CVPA18

### Serpentine Die Cut 6½ at Left
**2004, Apr.**

**1CVP16** CVPA14 37c black, blue & orange  2.00  1.00
- a. "First Class" below "US Postage"  1.10  .75
- b. "Priority" below "US Postage"  5.00  2.50
- c. "Express" below "US Postage"  20.00  5.00
- d. "Media Mail" below "US Postage"  5.00  2.50
- e. "Parcel Post" below "US Postage"  5.00  2.50
- f. "Bound Printed Matter" below "US Postage"  5.00  2.50
- g. "BPM" below "US Postage"  5.00  2.50

**1CVP17** CVPA15 37c black, blue & orange  2.00  1.00
- a. "First Class" below "US Postage"  1.10  .75
- b. "Priority" below "US Postage"  5.00  2.50
- c. "Express" below "US Postage"  20.00  5.00
- d. "Media Mail" below "US Postage"  5.00  2.50
- e. "Parcel Post" below "US Postage"  5.00  2.50
- f. "Bound Printed Matter" below "US Postage"  5.00  2.50
- g. "BPM" below "US Postage"  5.00  2.50

**1CVP18** CVPA16 37c black, blue & orange  2.00  1.00
- a. "First Class" below "US Postage"  1.10  .75
- b. "Priority" below "US Postage"  5.00  2.50
- c. "Express" below "US Postage"  20.00  5.00
- d. "Media Mail" below "US Postage"  5.00  2.50
- e. "Parcel Post" below "US Postage"  5.00  2.50
- f. "Bound Printed Matter" below "US Postage"  5.00  2.50
- g. "BPM" below "US Postage"  5.00  2.50

**1CVP19** CVPA17 37c black, blue & orange  2.00  1.00
- a. "First Class" below "US Postage"  1.10  .75
- b. "Priority" below "US Postage"  5.00  2.50
- c. "Express" below "US Postage"  20.00  5.00
- d. "Media Mail" below "US Postage"  5.00  2.50
- e. "Parcel Post" below "US Postage"  5.00  2.50
- f. "Bound Printed Matter" below "US Postage"  5.00  2.50
- g. "BPM" below "US Postage"  5.00  2.50

**1CVP20** CVPA18 37c black, blue & orange  2.00  1.00
- a. "First Class" below "US Postage"  1.10  .75
- b. "Priority" below "US Postage"  5.00  2.50
- c. "Express" below "US Postage"  20.00  5.00
- d. "Media Mail" below "US Postage"  5.00  2.50
- e. "Parcel Post" below "US Postage"  5.00  2.50
- f. "Bound Printed Matter" below "US Postage"  5.00  2.50
- g. "BPM" below "US Postage"  5.00  2.50
- h. Horiz. strip of 5, #1CVP16-1CVP20  10.00

# UNITED STATES

**Flag and Star Type of 2002 Redrawn With Orange Stars and Text at Left**
*Serpentine Die Cut 6½ at Left*
2004, Apr.
"Stamps.com" in Upper Case Letters
Identification Code Above Zip Code

| | | | | |
|---|---|---|---|---|
| 1CVP21 | CVPA1a 37c black, blue & orange | | 2.00 | 1.00 |
| a. | "First Class" below "US Postage" | | 1.35 | .75 |
| b. | "Priority" below "US Postage" | | 6.00 | 2.50 |
| c. | "Express" below "US Postage" | | 22.50 | 5.00 |
| d. | "Media Mail" below "US Postage" | | 6.00 | 2.50 |
| e. | "Parcel Post" below "US Postage" | | 6.00 | 2.50 |
| f. | "Bound Printed Matter" below "US Postage" | | 6.00 | 2.50 |
| g. | "BPM" below "US Postage" | | 6.00 | 2.50 |

Bicycling CVPA19
Running CVPA20
Swimming CVPA21
Boxing CVPA22
Equestrian CVPA23
Basketball CVPA24
Judo CVPA25
Soccer CVPA26
Gymnastics CVPA27
Tennis CVPA28

*Serpentine Die Cut 6½ at Left*
2004, Apr.

| | | | | |
|---|---|---|---|---|
| 1CVP22 | CVPA19 37c black, blue & orange | | 3.00 | 2.00 |
| a. | "First Class" below "US Postage" | | 2.50 | 1.50 |
| b. | "Priority" below "US Postage" | | 8.00 | 1.00 |
| c. | "Express" below "US Postage" | | 25.00 | 3.00 |
| d. | "Media Mail" below "US Postage" | | 7.50 | 1.00 |
| e. | "Parcel Post" below "US Postage" | | 7.50 | 1.00 |
| f. | "Bound Printed Matter" below "US Postage" | | 7.50 | 1.00 |
| g. | "BPM" below "US Postage" | | 7.50 | 1.00 |

| | | | | |
|---|---|---|---|---|
| 1CVP23 | CVPA20 37c black, blue & orange | | 3.00 | 2.00 |
| a. | "First Class" below "US Postage" | | 2.50 | 1.50 |
| b. | "Priority" below "US Postage" | | 8.00 | 1.00 |
| c. | "Express" below "US Postage" | | 25.00 | 3.00 |
| d. | "Media Mail" below "US Postage" | | 7.50 | 1.00 |
| e. | "Parcel Post" below "US Postage" | | 7.50 | 1.00 |
| f. | "Bound Printed Matter" below "US Postage" | | 7.50 | 1.00 |
| g. | "BPM" below "US Postage" | | 7.50 | 1.00 |

| | | | | |
|---|---|---|---|---|
| 1CVP24 | CVPA21 37c black, blue & orange | | 3.00 | 2.00 |
| a. | "First Class" below "US Postage" | | 2.50 | 1.50 |
| b. | "Priority" below "US Postage" | | 8.00 | 1.00 |
| c. | "Express" below "US Postage" | | 25.00 | 3.00 |
| d. | "Media Mail" below "US Postage" | | 7.50 | 1.00 |
| e. | "Parcel Post" below "US Postage" | | 7.50 | 1.00 |
| f. | "Bound Printed Matter" below "US Postage" | | 7.50 | 1.00 |
| g. | "BPM" below "US Postage" | | 7.50 | 1.00 |

| | | | | |
|---|---|---|---|---|
| 1CVP25 | CVPA22 37c black, blue & orange | | 3.00 | 2.00 |
| a. | "First Class" below "US Postage" | | 2.50 | 1.50 |
| b. | "Priority" below "US Postage" | | 8.00 | 1.00 |
| c. | "Express" below "US Postage" | | 25.00 | 3.00 |
| d. | "Media Mail" below "US Postage" | | 7.50 | 1.00 |
| e. | "Parcel Post" below "US Postage" | | 7.50 | 1.00 |
| f. | "Bound Printed Matter" below "US Postage" | | 7.50 | 1.00 |
| g. | "BPM" below "US Postage" | | 7.50 | 1.00 |

| | | | | |
|---|---|---|---|---|
| 1CVP26 | CVPA23 37c black, blue & orange | | 3.00 | 2.00 |
| a. | "First Class" below "US Postage" | | 2.50 | 1.50 |
| b. | "Priority" below "US Postage" | | 8.00 | 1.00 |
| c. | "Express" below "US Postage" | | 25.00 | 3.00 |
| d. | "Media Mail" below "US Postage" | | 7.50 | 1.00 |
| e. | "Parcel Post" below "US Postage" | | 7.50 | 1.00 |
| f. | "Bound Printed Matter" below "US Postage" | | 7.50 | 1.00 |
| g. | "BPM" below "US Postage" | | 7.50 | 1.00 |
| h. | Horiz. strip of 5, #1CVP22-1CVP26 | | 15.00 | |

| | | | | |
|---|---|---|---|---|
| 1CVP27 | CVPA24 37c black, blue & orange | | 3.00 | 2.00 |
| a. | "First Class" below "US Postage" | | 2.50 | 1.50 |
| b. | "Priority" below "US Postage" | | 8.00 | 1.00 |
| c. | "Express" below "US Postage" | | 25.00 | 3.00 |
| d. | "Media Mail" below "US Postage" | | 7.50 | 1.00 |
| e. | "Parcel Post" below "US Postage" | | 7.50 | 1.00 |
| f. | "Bound Printed Matter" below "US Postage" | | 7.50 | 1.00 |
| g. | "BPM" below "US Postage" | | 7.50 | 1.00 |

| | | | | |
|---|---|---|---|---|
| 1CVP28 | CVPA25 37c black, blue & orange | | 3.00 | 2.00 |
| a. | "First Class" below "US Postage" | | 2.50 | 1.50 |
| b. | "Priority" below "US Postage" | | 8.00 | 1.00 |
| c. | "Express" below "US Postage" | | 25.00 | 3.00 |
| d. | "Media Mail" below "US Postage" | | 7.50 | 1.00 |
| e. | "Parcel Post" below "US Postage" | | 7.50 | 1.00 |
| f. | "Bound Printed Matter" below "US Postage" | | 7.50 | 1.00 |
| g. | "BPM" below "US Postage" | | 7.50 | 1.00 |

| | | | | |
|---|---|---|---|---|
| 1CVP29 | CVPA26 37c black, blue & orange | | 3.00 | 2.00 |
| a. | "First Class" below "US Postage" | | 2.50 | 1.50 |
| b. | "Priority" below "US Postage" | | 8.00 | 1.00 |
| c. | "Express" below "US Postage" | | 25.00 | 3.00 |
| d. | "Media Mail" below "US Postage" | | 7.50 | 1.00 |
| e. | "Parcel Post" below "US Postage" | | 7.50 | 1.00 |
| f. | "Bound Printed Matter" below "US Postage" | | 7.50 | 1.00 |
| g. | "BPM" below "US Postage" | | 7.50 | 1.00 |

| | | | | |
|---|---|---|---|---|
| 1CVP30 | CVPA27 37c black, blue & orange | | 3.00 | 2.00 |
| a. | "First Class" below "US Postage" | | 2.50 | 1.50 |
| b. | "Priority" below "US Postage" | | 8.00 | 1.00 |
| c. | "Express" below "US Postage" | | 25.00 | 3.00 |
| d. | "Media Mail" below "US Postage" | | 7.50 | 1.00 |
| e. | "Parcel Post" below "US Postage" | | 7.50 | 1.00 |
| f. | "Bound Printed Matter" below "US Postage" | | 7.50 | 1.00 |
| g. | "BPM" below "US Postage" | | 7.50 | 1.00 |

| | | | | |
|---|---|---|---|---|
| 1CVP31 | CVPA28 37c black, blue & orange | | 3.00 | 2.00 |
| a. | "First Class" below "US Postage" | | 2.50 | 1.50 |
| b. | "Priority" below "US Postage" | | 8.00 | 1.00 |
| c. | "Express" below "US Postage" | | 25.00 | 3.00 |
| d. | "Media Mail" below "US Postage" | | 7.50 | 1.00 |
| e. | "Parcel Post" below "US Postage" | | 7.50 | 1.00 |
| f. | "Bound Printed Matter" below "US Postage" | | 7.50 | 1.00 |
| g. | "BPM" below "US Postage" | | 7.50 | 1.00 |
| h. | Horiz. strip of 5, #1CVP27-1CVP31 | | 15.00 | |

The item pictured above was produced by Stamps.com for a special promotional mailing of its own and was not made available unused to customers.

Leaning Tower of Pisa CVPA29
Sphinx and Pyramids CVPA30
Sydney Opera House CVPA31
Mayan Pyramid CVPA32
Asian Temple CVPA33

*Serpentine Die Cut 6½ at Left*
2004, July

| | | | | |
|---|---|---|---|---|
| 1CVP32 | CVPA29 37c black, blue & orange | | 3.00 | 2.00 |
| a. | "First Class" below "US Postage" | | 2.30 | 1.50 |
| b. | "Priority" below "US Postage" | | 8.00 | 1.00 |
| c. | "Express" below "US Postage" | | 25.00 | 3.00 |
| d. | "Media Mail" below "US Postage" | | 7.50 | 1.00 |
| e. | "Parcel Post" below "US Postage" | | 7.50 | 1.00 |
| f. | "Bound Printed Matter" below "US Postage" | | 7.50 | 1.00 |
| g. | "BPM" below "US Postage" | | 7.50 | 1.00 |

| | | | | |
|---|---|---|---|---|
| 1CVP33 | CVPA30 37c black, blue & orange | | 3.00 | 2.00 |
| a. | "First Class" below "US Postage" | | 2.30 | 1.50 |
| b. | "Priority" below "US Postage" | | 8.00 | 1.00 |
| c. | "Express" below "US Postage" | | 25.00 | 3.00 |
| d. | "Media Mail" below "US Postage" | | 7.50 | 1.00 |
| e. | "Parcel Post" below "US Postage" | | 7.50 | 1.00 |
| f. | "Bound Printed Matter" below "US Postage" | | 7.50 | 1.00 |
| g. | "BPM" below "US Postage" | | 7.50 | 1.00 |

| | | | | |
|---|---|---|---|---|
| 1CVP34 | CVPA31 37c black, blue & orange | | 3.00 | 2.00 |
| a. | "First Class" below "US Postage" | | 2.30 | 1.50 |
| b. | "Priority" below "US Postage" | | 8.00 | 1.00 |
| c. | "Express" below "US Postage" | | 25.00 | 3.00 |
| d. | "Media Mail" below "US Postage" | | 7.50 | 1.00 |
| e. | "Parcel Post" below "US Postage" | | 7.50 | 1.00 |
| f. | "Bound Printed Matter" below "US Postage" | | 7.50 | 1.00 |
| g. | "BPM" below "US Postage" | | 7.50 | 1.00 |

| | | | | |
|---|---|---|---|---|
| 1CVP35 | CVPA32 37c black, blue & orange | | 3.00 | 2.00 |
| a. | "First Class" below "US Postage" | | 2.30 | 1.50 |
| b. | "Priority" below "US Postage" | | 8.00 | 1.00 |
| c. | "Express" below "US Postage" | | 25.00 | 3.00 |
| d. | "Media Mail" below "US Postage" | | 7.50 | 1.00 |
| e. | "Parcel Post" below "US Postage" | | 7.50 | 1.00 |
| f. | "Bound Printed Matter" below "US Postage" | | 7.50 | 1.00 |
| g. | "BPM" below "US Postage" | | 7.50 | 1.00 |

| | | | | |
|---|---|---|---|---|
| 1CVP36 | CVPA33 37c black, blue & orange | | 3.00 | 2.00 |
| a. | "First Class" below "US Postage" | | 2.30 | 1.50 |
| b. | "Priority" below "US Postage" | | 8.00 | 1.00 |
| c. | "Express" below "US Postage" | | 25.00 | 3.00 |
| d. | "Media Mail" below "US Postage" | | 7.50 | 1.00 |
| e. | "Parcel Post" below "US Postage" | | 7.50 | 1.00 |
| f. | "Bound Printed Matter" below "US Postage" | | 7.50 | 1.00 |
| g. | "BPM" below "US Postage" | | 7.50 | 1.00 |
| h. | Strip of 5, #1CVP32-1CVP36 | | 15.00 | |

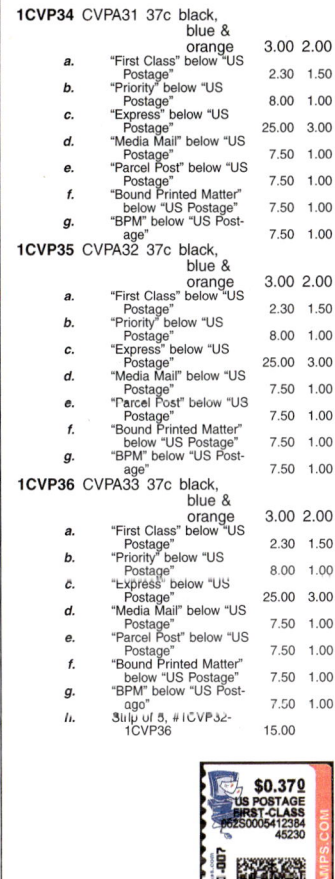

Computer and Letters — CVPA34

*Serpentine Die Cut 6½ at Left*
2005, Mar.

| | | | | |
|---|---|---|---|---|
| 1CVP37 | CVPA34 37c black, blue & orange | | 25.00 | 15.00 |
| a. | "First Class" below "US Postage" | | 25.00 | 15.00 |
| b. | "Priority" below "US Postage" | | — | |
| c. | "Express" below "US Postage" | | — | |
| d. | "Media Mail" below "US Postage" | | — | |
| e. | "Parcel Post" below "US Postage" | | — | |
| f. | "Bound Printed Matter" below "US Postage" | | — | |
| g. | "BPM" below "US Postage" | | — | |

Blank sheets of No. 1CVP37 were sent free of charge to those who responded to special Stamps.com promotions which offered a fixed amount of free postage as an enticement to new subscribers. The franking portion of the stamps could only be applied after subscribing.

Logo — CVPA35

2005, Aug. *Die Cut Perf. 6½ at Left*

| | | | | |
|---|---|---|---|---|
| 1CVP38 | CVPA35 37c black, blue & orange | | 1.00 | .45 |
| a. | "Priority" below "US Postage" | | 8.00 | 1.00 |
| b. | "Express" below "US Postage" | | 25.00 | 3.00 |
| c. | "Media Mail" below "US Postage" | | 7.50 | 1.00 |
| d. | "Parcel Post" below "US Postage" | | 7.50 | 1.00 |
| e. | "BPM" below "US Postage" | | 7.50 | 1.00 |
| f. | "Aerogramme" below "US Postage" | | 1.40 | 1.00 |
| g. | "Intl Air Letter" below "US Postage" | | 1.25 | 1.00 |
| h. | "Intl Eco Letter" (Economy Letter Mail) below "US Postage" | | 5.50 | 1.00 |
| i. | "GXG" (Global Express Guaranteed) below "US Postage" | | 50.00 | 6.00 |

188 UNITED STATES

| | | | |
|---|---|---|---|
| *j.* | "EMS" (Global Express Mail) below "US Postage" | 32.50 | 4.00 |
| *k.* | "GPM" (Global Priority Mail) below "US Postage" | 8.00 | 1.00 |
| *l.* | "Intl Air Parcel" (Air Parcel Post) below "US Postage" | 26.00 | 3.00 |
| *m.* | "Intl Eco Parcel" (Economy Parcel Post) below "US Postage" | 32.50 | 4.00 |
| *n.* | "M-Bag (Air)" below "US Postage" | 35.00 | 5.00 |
| *o.* | "M-Bag (Economy)" below "US Postage" | 18.00 | 3.00 |
| *p.* | "Mat for Blind" below "US Postage" | 1.25 | — |
| *q.* | "Library Mail" | 5.00 | 1.00 |

Values for lettered varieties on Nos. 1CVP38 are based on the prices set as the minimum values for each service classification in the software available at the time the stamps were issued. In mid-December 2005, the software was changed to allow for a 1c minimum value for any of these lettered varieties.

In 2006, No. 1CVP38 was made available on a coil roll. Value, $1.40.

Snowman CVPA36

Candy Cane CVPA37

Dove CVPA38

Stylized Christmas Tree and Window CVPA39

**2005, Nov.** ***Die Cut Perf. 6 at Right***

| | | | |
|---|---|---|---|
| **1CVP39** | CVPA36 37c multi | 1.60 | 1.00 |
| *a.* | "Priority" below "US Postage" | 8.00 | 1.00 |
| *b.* | "Express" below "US Postage" | 25.00 | 3.00 |
| *c.* | "Media Mail" below "US Postage" | 7.50 | 1.00 |
| *d.* | "Parcel Post" below "US Postage" | 7.50 | 1.00 |
| *e.* | "BPM" below "US Postage" | 7.50 | 1.00 |
| *f.* | "Aerogramme" below "US Postage" | 1.40 | 1.00 |
| *g.* | "Intl Air Letter" below "US Postage" | 1.25 | 1.00 |
| *h.* | "Intl Eco Letter" (Economy Letter Mail) below "US Postage" | 5.50 | 1.00 |
| *i.* | "GXG" (Global Express Guaranteed) below "US Postage" | 50.00 | 6.00 |
| *j.* | "EMS" (Global Express Mail) below "US Postage" | 32.50 | 4.00 |
| *k.* | "GPM" (Global Priority Mail) below "US Postage" | 8.00 | 1.00 |
| *l.* | "Intl Air Parcel" (Air Parcel Post) below "US Postage" | 26.00 | 3.00 |
| *m.* | "Intl Eco Parcel" (Economy Parcel Post) below "US Postage" | 32.50 | 4.00 |
| *n.* | "M-Bag (Air)" below "US Postage" | 35.00 | 5.00 |
| *o.* | "M-Bag (Economy)" below "US Postage" | 18.00 | 3.00 |
| *p.* | "Mat for Blind" below "US Postage" | .25 | — |
| **1CVP40** | CVPA37 37c multi | 1.60 | 1.00 |
| *a.* | "Priority" below "US Postage" | 8.00 | 1.00 |
| *b.* | "Express" below "US Postage" | 25.00 | 3.00 |
| *c.* | "Media Mail" below "US Postage" | 7.50 | 1.00 |
| *d.* | "Parcel Post" below "US Postage" | 7.50 | 1.00 |
| *e.* | "BPM" below "US Postage" | 7.50 | 1.00 |
| *f.* | "Aerogramme" below "US Postage" | 1.40 | 1.00 |
| *g.* | "Intl Air Letter" below "US Postage" | 1.25 | 1.00 |
| *h.* | "Intl Eco Letter" (Economy Letter Mail) below "US Postage" | 5.50 | 1.00 |
| *i.* | "GXG" (Global Express Guaranteed) below "US Postage" | 50.00 | 6.00 |
| *j.* | "EMS" (Global Express Mail) below "US Postage" | 32.50 | 4.00 |
| *k.* | "GPM" (Global Priority Mail) below "US Postage" | 8.00 | 1.00 |
| *l.* | "Intl Air Parcel" (Air Parcel Post) below "US Postage" | 26.00 | 3.00 |
| *m.* | "Intl Eco Parcel" (Economy Parcel Post) below "US Postage" | 32.50 | 4.00 |
| *n.* | "M-Bag (Air)" below "US Postage" | 35.00 | 5.00 |
| *o.* | "M-Bag (Economy)" below "US Postage" | 18.00 | 3.00 |
| *p.* | "Mat for Blind" below "US Postage" | .45 | — |
| **1CVP41** | CVPA38 37c multi | 1.60 | 1.00 |
| *a.* | "Priority" below "US Postage" | 8.00 | 1.00 |
| *b.* | "Express" below "US Postage" | 25.00 | 3.00 |
| *c.* | "Media Mail" below "US Postage" | 7.50 | 1.00 |
| *d.* | "Parcel Post" below "US Postage" | 7.50 | 1.00 |
| *e.* | "BPM" below "US Postage" | 7.50 | 1.00 |
| *f.* | "Aerogramme" below "US Postage" | 1.40 | 1.00 |
| *g.* | "Intl Air Letter" below "US Postage" | 1.25 | 1.00 |
| *h.* | "Intl Eco Letter" (Economy Letter Mail) below "US Postage" | 5.50 | 1.00 |
| *i.* | "GXG" (Global Express Guaranteed) below "US Postage" | 50.00 | 6.00 |
| *j.* | "EMS" (Global Express Mail) below "US Postage" | 32.50 | 4.00 |
| *k.* | "GPM" (Global Priority Mail) below "US Postage" | 8.00 | 1.00 |
| *l.* | "Intl Air Parcel" (Air Parcel Post) below "US Postage" | 26.00 | 3.00 |
| *m.* | "Intl Eco Parcel" (Economy Parcel Post) below "US Postage" | 32.50 | 4.00 |
| *n.* | "M-Bag (Air)" below "US Postage" | 35.00 | 5.00 |
| *o.* | "M-Bag (Economy)" below "US Postage" | 18.00 | 3.00 |
| *p.* | "Mat for Blind" below "US Postage" | .45 | — |
| **1CVP42** | CVPA39 37c multi | 1.60 | 1.00 |
| *a.* | "Priority" below "US Postage" | 8.00 | 1.00 |
| *b.* | "Express" below "US Postage" | 25.00 | 3.00 |
| *c.* | "Media Mail" below "US Postage" | 7.50 | 1.00 |
| *d.* | "Parcel Post" below "US Postage" | 7.50 | 1.00 |
| *e.* | "BPM" below "US Postage" | 7.50 | 1.00 |
| *f.* | "Aerogramme" below "US Postage" | 1.40 | 1.00 |
| *g.* | "Intl Air Letter" below "US Postage" | 1.25 | 1.00 |
| *h.* | "Intl Eco Letter" (Economy Letter Mail) below "US Postage" | 5.50 | 1.00 |
| *i.* | "GXG" (Global Express Guaranteed) below "US Postage" | 50.00 | 6.00 |
| *j.* | "EMS" (Global Express Mail) below "US Postage" | 32.50 | 4.00 |
| *k.* | "GPM" (Global Priority Mail) below "US Postage" | 8.00 | 1.00 |
| *l.* | "Intl Air Parcel" (Air Parcel Post) below "US Postage" | 26.00 | 3.00 |
| *m.* | "Intl Eco Parcel" (Economy Parcel Post) below "US Postage" | 32.50 | 4.00 |
| *n.* | "M-Bag (Air)" below "US Postage" | 35.00 | 5.00 |
| *o.* | "M-Bag (Economy)" below "US Postage" | 18.00 | 3.00 |
| *p.* | "Mat for Blind" below "US Postage" | .45 | — |
| *q.* | Vert. strip, 2 each #1CVP39-1CVP42 | 6.00 | |

Values for lettered varieties on Nos. 1CVP39-1CVP42 are based on the prices set as the minimum values for each service classification in the software available at the time the stamps were issued. In mid-December 2005, the software was changed to allow for a 1c minimum value for any of these lettered varieties.

### Endicia.com

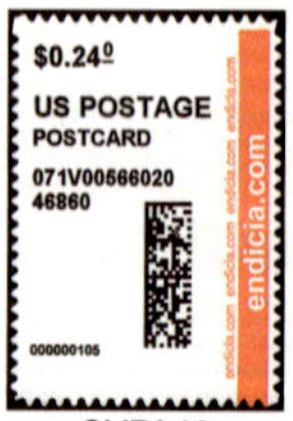

CVPA40

CVPA41

**2005-06** ***Serpentine Die Cut 10¼***

| | | | |
|---|---|---|---|
| **1CVP43** | CVPA40 24c black & bright rose | 10.00 | 4.00 |
| *a.* | 39c "First Class" under "US Postage" | 2.00 | .50 |
| *b.* | 63c "Intl. Mail" under "US Postage" | 3.25 | 2.50 |
| *c.* | $4.05 "Priority Mail" under "US Postage" | 12.00 | 2.50 |

### Coil Stamps

***Serpentine Die Cut 10½x10¼ on 2 Sides***

| | | | |
|---|---|---|---|
| **1CVP44** | CVPA41 24c black & pink | 11.00 | 4.00 |
| *a.* | 39c "First Class" under "US Postage" | 2.25 | .50 |
| *b.* | 63c "Intl. Mail" under "US Postage" | 3.50 | 2.50 |
| *c.* | $4.05 "Priority Mail" under "US Postage" | 12.50 | 2.50 |

Issued: Nos. 1CVP43, Nov. 2005; Nos. 1CVP44, Jan. 2006.

Originally, face values of 2c, 52c, 63c, 87c, $1.11, $1.35, $1.59, $1.83, $2.07, $2.31, $2.55, $2.79, $3.03, and $3.27 could also be printed on stamps with the "First class" inscription. Additionally, an 84c face value could be printed on stamps with the "Intl. Mail" inscription, and a $8.10 face value could be printed on stamps with the "Priority Mail" inscription. Values for Nos. 1CVP43-1CVP44 are for stamps with the listed face values and mail-class inscription. Values for stamps with lower or higher face values are correspondingly lower or higher.

In 2007, software changes permitted Nos. 1CVP43 and 1CVP44 to be printed with mail class inscriptions "Media Mail," "BPM," "Parcel Post," "Library Mail," and "Express Mail," as well as any face value for any mail-class inscription.

Nos. 1CVP43 and 1CVP44 printed after the software changes are inscribed "First Class" under "US Postage" and sell for considerably less than the values shown. Stamps printed before the software changes are inscribed "Postcard" under "US Postage," as shown in the illustrations.

### Stamps.com

Flag and Mount Rushmore CVPA42

Flag and Eagle CVPA43

Flag and Statue of Liberty CVPA44

Flag and Liberty Bell CVPA45

**2006, Mar.** ***Die Cut Perf. 6 at Right***

| | | | |
|---|---|---|---|
| **1CVP51** | CVPA42 39c multi | 1.25 | 1.00 |
| **1CVP52** | CVPA43 39c multi | 1.25 | 1.00 |
| **1CVP53** | CVPA44 39c multi | 1.25 | 1.00 |
| **1CVP54** | CVPA45 39c multi | 1.25 | 1.00 |
| *a.* | Vert. strip of 8, 2 each #1CVP51-1CVP54 | 8.00 | |

Other service incriptions with any possible face value can be printed on Nos. 1CVP51-1CVP54.

### Stamps.com

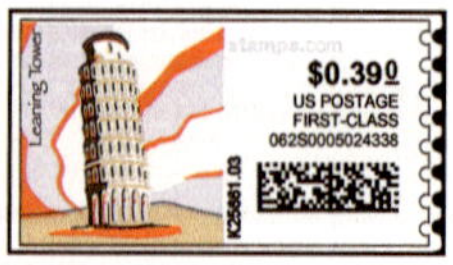

Leaning Tower of Pisa CVPA46

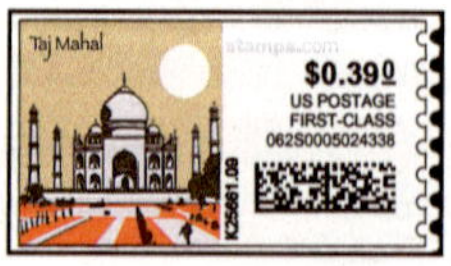

Taj Mahal CVPA47

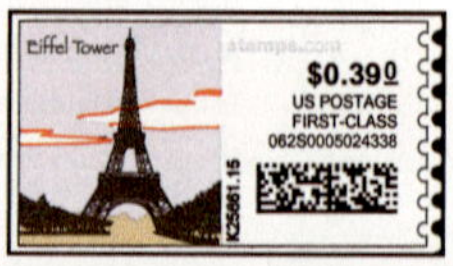

Eiffel Tower CVPA48

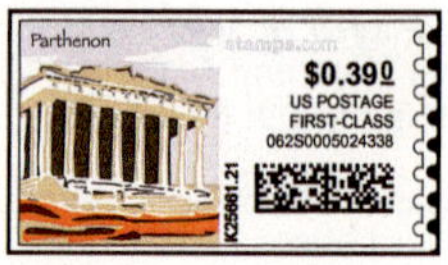

Parthenon CVPA49

**2006** ***Die Cut Perf 6 at Right***

| | | | |
|---|---|---|---|
| **1CVP55** | CVPA46 39c multi | 1.25 | 1.00 |
| **1CVP56** | CVPA47 39c multi | 1.25 | 1.00 |
| **1CVP57** | CVPA48 39c multi | 1.25 | 1.00 |
| **1CVP58** | CVPA49 39c multi | 1.25 | 1.00 |
| *a.* | Vert. strip, 2 each #1CVP55-1CVP58 | 8.00 | |

With the introduction of the new software in December 2005, any stamp could have any denomination 1c and above, and any service classification.

### Pitney Bowes Stamp Expressions

CVPA50

**2006** ***Die Cut Perf. 6 Horiz.***

**Inscribed "pitneybowes.com/se" at Right**

| | | | |
|---|---|---|---|
| **1CVP59** | CVPA50 39c black + label | 1.35 | .80 |

The stamp and label are separated by vertical roulettes. Users could create their own label images on the Pitney Bowes Stamp Expressions website (which required approval of the image from Pitney Bowes before it could be used), or download various pre-approved label images from the website into their personal computers. Stamps could be printed without label images. Stamps were printed on rolls of tagged thermal paper from a device that could be operated without a direct connection to the personal computer. See No. 1CVT1.

### Stamps.com

CVPA51

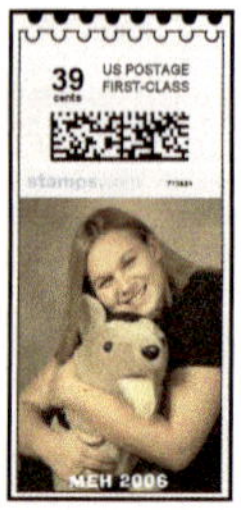

Personalizable Images — CVPA52

**2006, Sept.** ***Die Cut Perf. 6 at Right***

| | | | |
|---|---|---|---|
| **1CVP60** | CVPA51 39c multi | 1.50 | .95 |
| *a.* | Numerals in denomination 2½mm high, thicker text | 1.50 | .95 |

***Perf. Die Cut Perf. 6 at Top***

| | | | |
|---|---|---|---|
| **1CVP61** | CVPA52 39c multi | 1.50 | .95 |
| *a.* | Numerals in denomination 2½mm high, thicker text | 1.50 | .95 |

Users could requisition sheets of Nos. 1CVP60 and 1CVP61 with images of their choice from Stamps.com at $4.99 per sheet of 24. Priority and Express service classifications could also be printed on Nos. 1CVP60-1CVP61 with any denomination. Stamps exist with slightly larger die cutting (60x30mm and 30x60mm) in both squared and rounded corners. The denomination type shown on Nos. 1CVP60-1CVP61 can be placed on label types CVPA36-CVPA39, CVPA42-CVPA49, CVPA53-CVPA60 and any later stamps.com labels of this size.

Numerals in denomination are 3mm tall on Nos. 1CVP60-1CVP61. Serial numbers on Nos. 1CPVP60-1CVP61 lack periods and have small bank-check style numerals.

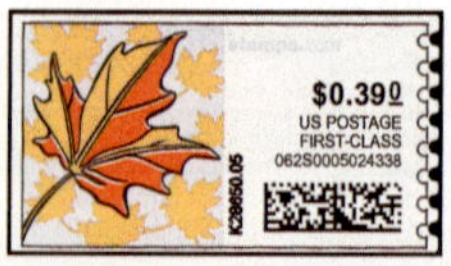

Autumn Leaves CVPA53

UNITED STATES 189

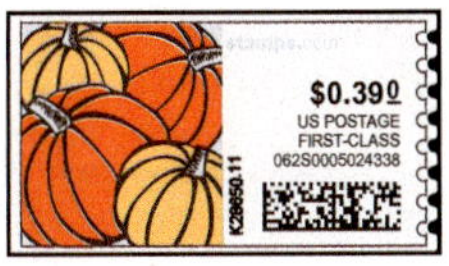
Pumpkins CVPA54

Basket of Apples, Sheaf of Wheat, Falling Leaves and Pumpkins CVPA55

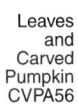

Leaves and Carved Pumpkin CVPA56

**2006** ***Die Cut Perf. 6 at Right***

**1CVP62** CVPA53 39c multi 1.25 1.00
**1CVP63** CVPA54 39c multi 1.25 1.00
**1CVP64** CVPA55 39c multi 1.25 1.00
**1CVP65** CVPA56 39c multi 1.25 1.00
*a.* Vert. strip, 2 each #1CVP62-1CVP65 10.00

See note after No. 1CVP58.

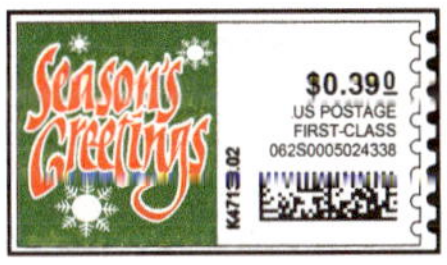
"Season's Greetings" CVPA57

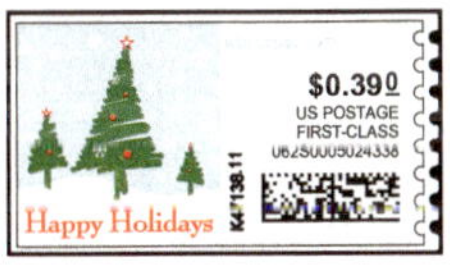
Christmas Trees CVPA58

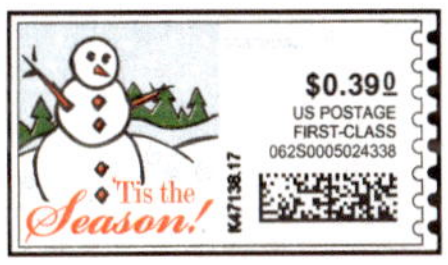
Snowman CVPA59

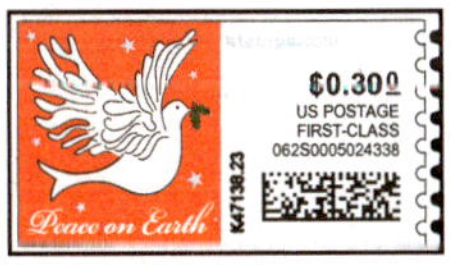
Dove CVPA60

**2006** ***Die Cut Perf. 6 at Right***

**1CVP66** CVPA57 39c multi 1.25 .45
**1CVP67** CVPA58 39c multi 1.25 .45
**1CVP68** CVPA59 39c multi 1.25 .45
**1CVP69** CVPA60 39c multi 1.25 .45
*a.* Vert. strip, 2 each #1CVP66-1CVP69 10.00

See note after No. 1CVP58.

Flag CVPA61

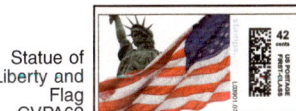

Statue of Liberty and Flag CVPA62

Bald Eagle and Flag CVPA63

Flag Painted on Building CVPA64

**2008** ***Die Cut Perf. 5½ at Right***

**Serial Number With Period, Large Letters and Numerals**

**1CVP70** CVPA61 42c multi 1.25 1.00
**1CVP71** CVPA62 42c multi 1.25 1.00
**1CVP72** CVPA63 42c multi 1.25 1.00
**1CVP73** CVPA64 42c multi 1.25 1.00

On Nos. 1CVP70-1CVP105, and perhaps on other stamps, placement of the stamp serial number and the stamps.com logo might differ on various printings of the label stock. Descriptive text outside the frame might also vary or not be present on these various printings.

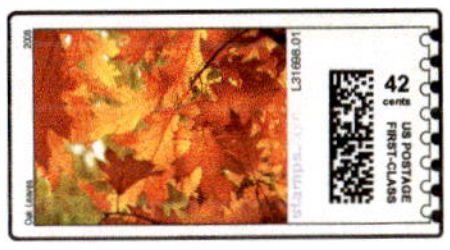
Autumn CVPA65

Designs: No. 1CVP74, Oak leaves. No. 1CVP75, Pumpkin patch. No. 1CVP76, Autumn reflection. No. 1CVP77, Pumpkins and gourds.

**2008**

**Serial Number With Period, Large Letters and Numerals**

**1CVP74** CVPA65 42c multi 2.00 1.00
**1CVP75** CVPA65 42c multi 2.00 1.00
**1CVP76** CVPA65 42c multi 2.00 1.00
**1CVP77** CVPA65 42c multi 2.00 1.00

Flowers CVPA66

Designs: No. 1CVP78, Sunflowers. No. 1CVP79, Daisies. No. 1CVP80, Sunflower sky. No. 1CVP81, Treasure flowers.

**2008**

**Serial Number With Period, Large Letters and Numerals**

**1CVP78** CVPA66 42c multi 1.25 1.00
**1CVP79** CVPA66 42c multi 1.25 1.00
**1CVP80** CVPA66 42c multi 1.25 1.00
**1CVP81** CVPA66 42c multi 1.25 1.00

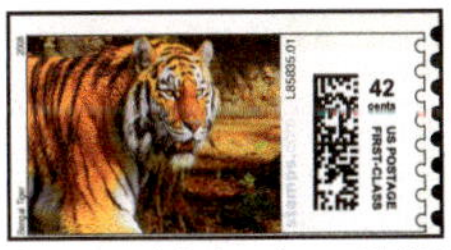
Endangered Animals CVPA67

Designs: No. 1CVP82, Bengal tiger. No. 1CVP83, Hawksbill turtle. No. 1CVP84, Panda. No. 1CVP85, African rhino.

**2008**

**Serial Number With Period, Large Letters and Numerals**

**1CVP82** CVPA67 42c multi 2.00 1.00
**1CVP83** CVPA67 42c multi 2.00 1.00
**1CVP84** CVPA67 42c multi 2.00 1.00
**1CVP85** CVPA67 42c multi 2.00 1.00

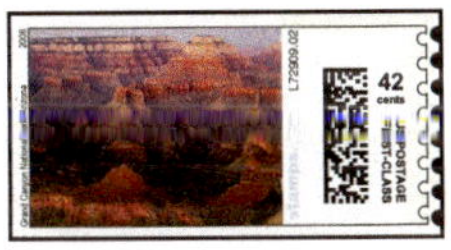
Parks CVPA68

Designs: No. 1CVP86, Grand Canyon National Park, Arizona. No. 1CVP87, Yosemite National Park, California. No. 1CVP88, Niagara Falls. No. 1CVP89, Arches National Park, Utah.

**2008**

**Serial Number With Period, Large Letters and Numerals**

**1CVP86** CVPA68 42c multi 1.25 1.00
**1CVP87** CVPA68 42c multi 1.25 1.00
**1CVP88** CVPA68 42c multi 1.25 1.00
**1CVP89** CVPA68 42c multi 1.25 1.00

City Skylines CVPA69

Designs: No. 1CVP90, New York City. No. 1CVP91, St. Louis. No. 1CVP92, Chicago. No. 1CVP93, San Francisco.

**2008**

**Serial Number With Period, Large Letters and Numerals**

**1CVP90** CVPA69 42c multi 2.00 1.00
**1CVP91** CVPA69 42c multi 2.00 1.00
**1CVP92** CVPA69 42c multi 2.00 1.00
**1CVP93** CVPA69 42c multi 2.00 1.00

Presidential Memorials — CVPA70

Designs: No. 1CVP94, Washington Monument. No. 1CVP95, Lincoln Memorial. No. 1CVP96, Jefferson Memorial. No. 1CVP97, Mount Rushmore.

**2008**

**Serial Number With Period, Large Letters and Numerals**

**1CVP94** CVPA70 42c multi 1.25 1.00
**1CVP95** CVPA70 42c multi 1.25 1.00
**1CVP96** CVPA70 42c multi 1.25 1.00
**1CVP97** CVPA70 42c multi 1.25 1.00

Christmas CVPA71

Designs: No. 1CVP98, Ornament, "Happy Holidays." No. 1CVP99, Gingerbread men, "Season's Greetings." No. 1CVP100, Snowflake, "Happy Holidays." No. 1CVP101, Christmas tree, "Season's Greetings."

**2008**

**Serial Number With Period, Large Letters and Numerals**

**Without Year or Text at Left**

**1CVP98** CVPA71 42c multi 2.00 1.00
**1CVP99** CVPA71 42c multi 2.00 1.00
**1CVP100** CVPA71 42c multi 2.00 1.00
**1CVP101** CVPA71 42c multi 2.00 1.00

Love CVPA72

"Love" and: No. 1CVP102, Rose. No. 1CVP103, Small hearts. No. 1CVP104, Large heart. No. 1CVP105, Hearts on curtain.

**2009**

**Serial Number With Period, Large Letters and Numerals**

**Without Year or Text at Left**

**1CVP102** CVPA72 42c multi 1.25 1.00
**1CVP103** CVPA72 42c multi 1.25 1.00
**1CVP104** CVPA72 42c multi 1.25 1.00
**1CVP105** CVPA72 42c multi 1.25 1.00

Wavy Lines — CVPA73

**2009** ***Die Cut Perf 6½ at Right***

**1CVP106** CVPA73 44c multi 1.25 .45

White Label — CVPA73a

Clear Label — CVPA73b

**2020?** ***Die Cut Perf 6½ at Right***

**1CVP106A** CVPA73a 53c multi 1.25 .45
**1CVP106B** CVPA73b 53c multi 1.25 .45

**Endicia.com**

Globe — CVPA74

Globe — CVPA74a

**2009** ***Serpentine Die Cut 10¼x10½***

**1CVP107** CVPA74 44c org & blk 1.25 .45
**1CVP107A** CVPA74a 45c org & blk — —

Software allowed for six other inscriptions below "US Postage" (Priority Mail, Media Mail, Parcel Post, Library Mail, Express Mail and Intl Mail) and any face value for any mail-class inscription.

No. 1CVP107 with space between denomination and "US POSTAGE". No. 1CVP107A with no space between denomination and "US POSTAGE".

**Stamps.com**

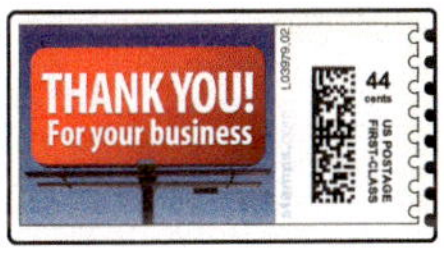
Thank You For Your Business CVPA75

Text: No. 1CVP108, On billboard. No. 1CVP109, And building. No. 1CVP110, On red background. No. 1CVP111, And two people shaking hands.

**2009** ***Die Cut Perf. 5½ at Right***

**Serial Number With Period, Large Letters and Numerals**

**Without Year or Text at Left**

**1CVP108** CVPA75 44c multi 1.25 1.00
**1CVP109** CVPA75 44c multi 1.25 1.00
**1CVP110** CVPA75 44c multi 1.25 1.00
**1CVP111** CVPA75 44c multi 1.25 1.00

We're Moving CVPA76

Text: No. 1CVP112, Stack of three boxes, green background. No. 1CVP113, Eleven boxes, orange background. No. 1CVP114, Four boxes, green background. No. 1CVP115, Four boxes, red background.

**2009**

**Serial Number With Period, Large Letters and Numerals**

**Without Year or Text at Left**

**1CVP112** CVPA76 44c multi 1.25 1.00
**1CVP113** CVPA76 44c multi 1.25 1.00
**1CVP114** CVPA76 44c multi 1.25 1.00
**1CVP115** CVPA76 44c multi 1.25 1.00

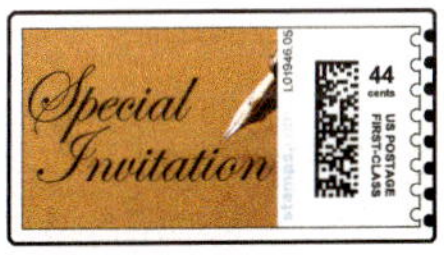
Special Invitation CVPA77

Text: No. 1CVP116, And pen nib. No. 1CVP117, And circled "15" on calendar. No.

1CVP118, On card on envelope. No. 1CVP119, On wax seal.

**2009**
**Serial Number With Period, Large Letters and Numerals**
**Without Year or Text at Left**

| | | | | |
|---|---|---|---|---|
| 1CVP116 | CVPA77 | 44c multi | 1.25 | 1.00 |
| 1CVP117 | CVPA77 | 44c multi | 1.25 | 1.00 |
| 1CVP118 | CVPA77 | 44c multi | 1.25 | 1.00 |
| 1CVP119 | CVPA77 | 44c multi | 1.25 | 1.00 |

US Flag CVPA78

Flag: No. 1CVP120, On flagpole. No. 1CVP121, Behind Statue of Liberty. No. 1CVP122, Behind bald eagle. No. 1CVP123, On United States map.

**2009**
**Serial Number With Period, Large Letters and Numerals**
**Without Year or Text at Left**

| | | | | |
|---|---|---|---|---|
| 1CVP120 | CVPA78 | 44c multi | 2.00 | 1.00 |
| 1CVP121 | CVPA78 | 44c multi | 2.00 | 1.00 |
| 1CVP122 | CVPA78 | 44c multi | 2.00 | 1.00 |
| 1CVP123 | CVPA78 | 44c multi | 2.00 | 1.00 |

Patriotic Symbols CVPA79

Designs: No. 1CVP124, Statue of Liberty. No. 1CVP125, Flag. No. 1CVP126, Bald eagle.

**2010** *Die Cut Perf. 5½ Vert.*

| | | | | |
|---|---|---|---|---|
| 1CVP124 | CVPA79 | 44c multi | 1.25 | 1.00 |
| 1CVP125 | CVPA79 | 44c multi | 1.25 | 1.00 |
| 1CVP126 | CVPA79 | 44c multi | 1.25 | 1.00 |

Jewish Symbols CVPA80

Designs: No. 1CVP127, Menorah. No. 1CVP125, Dreidel. No. 1CVP126, Star of David.

**2010** *Die Cut Perf. 5½ Vert.*

| | | | | |
|---|---|---|---|---|
| 1CVP127 | CVPA80 | 44c multi | 1.25 | 1.00 |
| 1CVP128 | CVPA80 | 44c multi | 1.25 | 1.00 |
| 1CVP129 | CVPA80 | 44c multi | 1.25 | 1.00 |

Christmas CVPA81

Designs: No. 1CVP130, Christmas stocking. No. 1CVP131, Christmas tree. No. 1CVP132, Santa Claus.

**2010** *Die Cut Perf. 5½ Vert.*

| | | | | |
|---|---|---|---|---|
| 1CVP130 | CVPA81 | 44c multi | 1.25 | 1.00 |
| 1CVP131 | CVPA81 | 44c multi | 1.25 | 1.00 |
| 1CVP132 | CVPA81 | 44c multi | 1.25 | 1.00 |

Valentine's Day — CVPA82

Designs: No. 1CVP133, Hearts. No. 1CVP134, Rose. No. 1CVP135, Candy hearts.

**2011** *Die Cut Perf. 5½ Vert.*

| | | | | |
|---|---|---|---|---|
| 1CVP133 | CVPA82 | 44c multi | 2.00 | 1.00 |
| 1CVP134 | CVPA82 | 44c multi | 2.00 | 1.00 |
| 1CVP135 | CVPA82 | 44c multi | 2.00 | 1.00 |

Christian Symbols CVPA83

Designs: No. 1CVP136, Cross. No. 1CVP137, Fish. No. 1CVP138, Rosary beads.

**2011** *Die Cut Perf. 5½ Vert.*

| | | | | |
|---|---|---|---|---|
| 1CVP136 | CVPA83 | 44c multi | 1.25 | 1.00 |
| 1CVP137 | CVPA83 | 44c multi | 1.25 | 1.00 |
| 1CVP138 | CVPA83 | 44c multi | 1.25 | 1.00 |

Thank You — CVPA84

**2020** *Die Cut Perf. 5½ at Right*

| | | | | |
|---|---|---|---|---|
| 1CVP139 | CVPA84 | 53c multi | 2.00 | 1.00 |

Star Spangled Banner — CVPA85

**2021** *Die Cut Perf. 5½ at Right*

| | | | | |
|---|---|---|---|---|
| 1CVP140 | CVPA85 | 53c multi | 2.00 | 1.00 |

Flowers CVPA86

Designs: No. 1CVP141, "sunflower sky." No. 1CVP142, "treasure flowers." No. 1CVP143, "spring honey bee." No. 1CVP144, "summer flower." No. 1CVP145, "spring blossoms." No. 1CVP146, "dandelion wishes." No. 1CVP147, "pink cosmos."

**2021** *Die Cut Perf. 5½ at Right*

| | | | | |
|---|---|---|---|---|
| 1CVP141 | CVPA86 | 53c multi | 2.00 | 1.00 |
| 1CVP142 | CVPA86 | 53c multi | 2.00 | 1.00 |
| 1CVP143 | CVPA86 | 53c multi | 2.00 | 1.00 |
| 1CVP144 | CVPA86 | 53c multi | 2.00 | 1.00 |
| 1CVP145 | CVPA86 | 53c multi | 2.00 | 1.00 |
| 1CVP146 | CVPA86 | 53c multi | 2.00 | 1.00 |
| 1CVP147 | CVPA86 | 53c multi | 2.00 | 1.00 |

Cherry Blossoms — CVPA87

Designs: No. 1CVP148, Jefferson Memorial with cherry blossoms. No. 1CVP149, cherry trees.

**2022** *Die Cut Perf. 5½ at Right*

| | | | | |
|---|---|---|---|---|
| 1CVP148 | CVPA87 | 53c multi | 2.00 | 1.00 |
| 1CVP149 | CVPA87 | 53c multi | 2.00 | 1.00 |

Fall CVPA88

Designs: No. 1CVP150, "fall river." No. 1CVP151, pumpkins.

**2022** *Die Cut Perf. 5½ at Right*

| | | | | |
|---|---|---|---|---|
| 1CVP150 | CVPA88 | 53c multi | 2.00 | 1.00 |
| 1CVP151 | CVPA88 | 53c multi | 2.00 | 1.00 |

Winter CVPA89

Designs: No. 1CVP152, "snowman hugs." No. 1CVP153, "holiday treats." No. 1CVP154, "warm wishes" hot cocoa. No. 1CVP155, "frosty hot cocoa." No. 1CVP156, "let it snow!" No. 1CVP157, snowflake ornaments.

**2022** *Die Cut Perf. 5½ at Right*

| | | | | |
|---|---|---|---|---|
| 1CVP152 | CVPA89 | 53c multi | 2.00 | 1.00 |
| 1CVP153 | CVPA89 | 53c multi | 2.00 | 1.00 |
| 1CVP154 | CVPA89 | 53c multi | 2.00 | 1.00 |
| | On cover | | | 2.50 |
| 1CVP155 | CVPA89 | 53c multi | 2.00 | 1.00 |
| 1CVP156 | CVPA89 | 53c multi | 2.00 | 1.00 |
| 1CVP157 | CVPA89 | 53c multi | 2.00 | 1.00 |

Dog With Sunglasses — CVPA90

**2022** *Die Cut Perf. 5½ at Right*

| | | | | |
|---|---|---|---|---|
| 1CVP158 | CVPA90 | 53c multi | 2.00 | 1.00 |

Hawksbill Turtle CVPA91

**2022** *Die Cut Perf. 5½ at Right*

| | | | | |
|---|---|---|---|---|
| 1CVP159 | CVPA91 | 53c multi | 2.00 | 1.00 |

### OFFICAL STAMPS PRINTED TO ORDER

1CVPO1

1CVPO2

**2002-06** *Serpentine Die Cut 10.6*
**Self-Adhesive**

1CVPO1  1CVPO1  37c blk, red & bluish gray  —  —

No denomination below vignette.

1CVPO2  1CVPO2  37c blk, red & blue  —  —

Denomination below vignette.

1CVPO3  1CVPO2  39c blk, red & blue  —  —

Denomination below vignette.

1CVPO5  1CVPO2  $4.05 blk, red & blue  —  —

Denomination below vignette.

Endicia filled federal agency orders for stamps to be limited for use by government officials. Nos. 1CVPO1 and 1CVPO2 were printed in sheets of 10. 39c and 41c denominations are thought to exist.

### NON-PERSONALIZABLE POSTAGE

**Stamps.com**

These stamps, approved by the USPS, were non-personalizable stamps that could be purchased directly from private manufacturers, which shipped them to the customer. Other non-personalizable stamps have been created by a variety of companies, all sold at excessive amounts over face value as "collectibles". Such items are not listed here. Most items created that sold for excessive amounts over face value have vignettes that are licensed images, usually depicting sport team emblems or other sports-related themes, or celebrities.

Personalized postage stamps, first available in 2004, created by a variety of different companies, and heretofore listed with Scott numbers having a "2CVP" prefix, are no longer listed. Personalized stamps, though valid for postage, are not sold at any U.S. Postal Service post office. They are available only by on-line ordering through the company's website. Stamps are only available from the companies in full panes of 20. Each pane is sold at a significant premium above the stated face value to cover the costs of personalization, shipping and handling.

In recent years, there has been a steadily increasing number of private companies, either directly licensed by the USPS or created as spinoff companies of these licensees, creating distinctly different personalized stamps. None of the companies has issued fewer than seven stamps for each rate change, with one issuing as many as 42 different stamps. Because mailing rates set by the USPS are expected to change yearly, the collective output of distinctly different, rate-based stamps from these various companies likely will increase. There are no restrictions in place to prevent more firms from bringing personalized stamps to the marketplace, or to keep stamp producers from offering even more customer options. Some personalized stamps do not differ in any appreciable manner from some of the non-personalizable stamps sold as collectibles and not listed here.

CVPC1

CVPC2

**2007, May** *Die Cut*
**Self-Adhesive**

| | | | | |
|---|---|---|---|---|
| 3CVP1 | CVPC1 | 2c black & gray green | 1.00 | 1.00 |
| a. | Inscribed "US Postag" | | | |

*Die Cut Perf. 5¼ at Right*

| | | | | |
|---|---|---|---|---|
| 3CVP2 | CVPC2 | 2c multicolored | 1.00 | 1.00 |
| a. | Tagged | | 2.00 | 2.00 |

**2008** ***Die Cut***

### Self-Adhesive

**3CVP3** CVPC1 1c black & gray 1.00 1.00

No. 3CVP1 was printed in sheets of 40 stamps. Stamps with serial numbers ending in "06" are No. 3CVP1a. Sheets were sold for face value plus a shipping charge and were obtainable through the stamps.com website.

No. 3CVP2 was printed in sheets of 20. Full sheets were given free of charge to first-time stamps.com customers, but the full sheets were available for sale to other customers at face value plus a shipping charge through the stamps.com website.

### Stamps.com Type of 2007

**2019** ***Die Cut***

### Self-Adhesive

**3CVP4** CVPC1 5c black & gray 1.00 1.00

No. 3CVP4 was printed in sheets of 40 stamps that were sold for face value plus a shipping charge and were obtainable through the stamps.com website.

---

## CARRIERS' STAMPS

## GENERAL ISSUE CARRIER STAMPS

Issued by the U.S. Government to facilitate payment of fees for delivering and collecting letters.

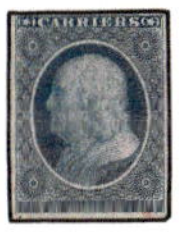

Franklin — OC1

**1851** **Engr.** **Unwmk.** ***Imperf.***

**LO1** OC1 (1c) dull blue, *rose* *7,000.* *8,000.*

### U.S.P.O. Despatch

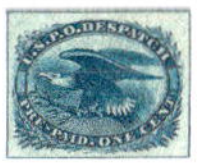

Eagle — OC2

**1851**

**LO2** OC2 1c blue (shades) 50.00 *80.00*

**1875** ***Imperf.***

**LO3** OC1 (1c) blue, *rose* 60.

***Perf. 12***

**LO4** OC1 (1c) blue *16,000.*

No. LO4 is valued in the grade of average to fine.

### Eagle Reprints

***Imperf.***

**LO5** OC2 1c blue 25.

***Perf. 12***

**LO6** OC2 1c blue 175.

Reprints of the Franklin Carrier are printed in dark blue, instead of the dull blue or deep blue of the originals. Two reprintings of 10,000 each were made in 1875 on the same rose paper as the originals. A third reprinting of 5,000 in 1881 is on soft wove paper.

The first two reprintings of 10,000 each of the Eagle carrier are on hard white paper, ungummed and sometimes perforated. A third reprinting of 10,000 stamps in 1881 is on soft wove paper. Originals are on yellowish paper with brown gum.

No. LO6 is valued with the perfs cutting slightly into the design.

## CITY CARRIER DEPARTMENT STAMPS

Issued by officials or employees of the U.S. Government for the purpose of securing or indicating payment of carriers' fees.

All are imperforate.

### Baltimore, Md.

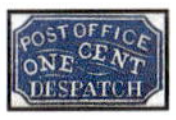

C1

**1850-55** **Typo.**

### Settings of 10 (2x5) varieties

**1LB1** C1 1c red, *bluish* 180. 160.
**1LB2** C1 1c blue, *bluish* 200. 150.
*a.* Bluish laid paper — —

**1LB3** C1 1c blue 160. 100.
*a.* Laid paper 200. 150.
*b.* Block of 14 containing three tete-beche gutter pairs (unique) *6,250.*
**1LB4** C1 1c green — 1,000.
**1LB5** C1 1c red 2,250. 1,750.

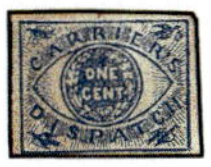

C2

**1856** **Typo.**

**1LB6** C2 1c blue (shades) 130. 90.
**1LB7** C2 1c red (shades) 130. 90.

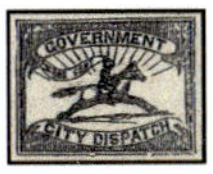

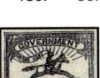

C3

The sheet consisted of at least four panes of 10 placed horizontally, the two center panes tete beche. This makes possible five horizontal tete beche gutter pairs.

### Plate of 10 (2x5); 10 Varieties

**1857**

**1LB8** C3 1c black (shades) 65. 50.
*a.* "SENT" 100. 75.
*b.* Short rays 100. 75.
**1LB9** C3 1c red 100. 90.
*a.* "SENT" 140. 110.
*b.* Short rays 140. 110.
*c.* As "b," double impression *800.*

### Boston, Mass.

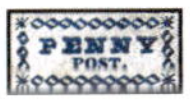

C6

### Several Varieties

**1849-50** **Pelure Paper** **Typeset**

**3LB1** C6 1c blue 375. 180.
*a.* Wrong ornament at left *400.*

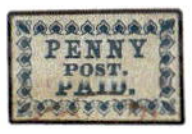

C7

### Several Varieties

**1851**

### Wove Paper Colored Through

**3LB2** C7 1c blue (shades), *slate* 190. 160.

### Charleston, S. C.

### Honour's City Express

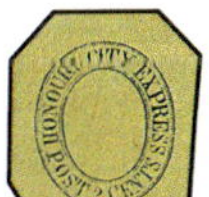

C8

**1849** **Typo.**

### Wove Paper Colored Through

**4LB1** C8 2c blk, *brn rose* *10,000.*
Cut to shape *4,000.* *4,000.*
**4LB2** C8 2c blk, *yel,* cut to shape —

No. 4LB1 unused is a unique uncanceled stamp on piece. The used cut-to-shape stamp is also unique. In addition two covers exist bearing No. 4LB1.

No. 4LB2 unused (uncanceled) off cover is unique; three known on cover.

See the Scott U.S. Specialized Catalogue.

**4LB2A** C8 2c blk, *bl gray,* on cover, cut to shape —

No. 4LB2A is unique.

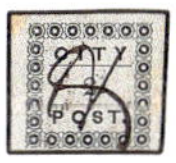

C10

**1854** **Wove Paper** **Typeset**

**4LB3** C10 2c black *1,500.*

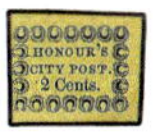

C11

### Several Varieties

**1849-50**

### Wove Paper Colored Through

**4LB5** C11 2c black, *bluish,* pelure *750.* *500.*
*a.* "Ceuts" *5,750.*
**4LB7** C11 2c black, *yellow* *750.* *1,000.*
*a.* "Ccnts," ms. tied on cover *14,500.*

No. 4LB5a is unique. It is without gum and is valued thus. No. 4LB7a also is unique.

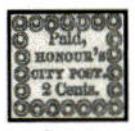

C13

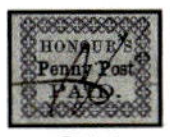

C14

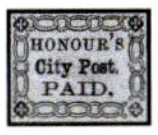

C15

### Several varieties of each type

**1851-58**

### Wove Paper Colored Through

**4LB8** C13 2c black, *bluish* 350. 175.
*a.* Period after "PAID" 500. 250.
*b.* "Cens" 700. *900.*
*c.* "Conours" and "Bents" —

The No. 4LB8 with No. 2 combination cover is unique. It is a cover front only and is valued thus.

No. 4LB8a on cover with 5c No. 1 is unique.

**4LB9** C13 2c black, *bluish,* pelure *850.* *950.*
**4LB10** C13 2c black, *pink,* pelure, on cover *7,000.*
**4LB11** C14 (2c) black, *bluish* — *375.*
**4LB12** C14 (2c) black, *bluish,* pelure — —
**4LB13** C15 (2c) black, *bluish* ('58) 750. 400.
*a.* Comma after "PAID" *1,100.*
*b.* No period after "Post" *1,400.*

### Kingman's City Post

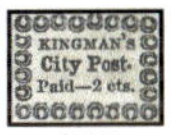

C16

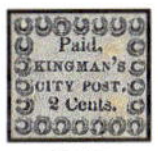

C17

### Several varieties of each

### Wove Paper Colored Through

**1851(?)-58(?)**

**4LB14** C16 2c black, *bluish* *1,400.* *900.*
*a.* "Kingman's" erased *5,000.*
**4LB15** C17 2c black, *bluish* *800.* *800.*
*a.* "Kingman's" erased, on cover with 3c #11, tied by pen cancel (unique) *4,500.*

### Martin's City Post

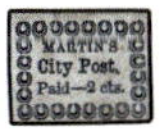

C18

### Several Varieties

**1858** **Typeset**

### Wove Paper Colored Through

**4LB16** C18 2c black, *bluish* *8,000.*

### Beckman's City Post

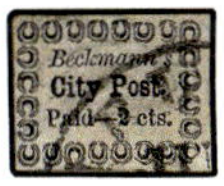

C19

**1860**

**4LB17** C19 2c black, on cover —

No. 4LB17 is unique.

### Steinmeyer's City Post

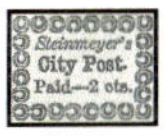

C19a

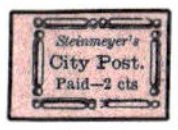

C20

### Several varieties of Type C19

### Type C20 printed from plate of 10 (2x5) varieties

**1859** **Typeset**

### Wove Paper Colored Through

**4LB18** C19a 2c black, *bluish* *21,000.*
**4LB19** C20 2c black, *bluish* *4,500.* —
**4LB20** C20 2c black, *pink* *225.* —
**4LB21** C20 2c black, *yellow* 225.

### Cincinnati, Ohio
### Williams' City Post

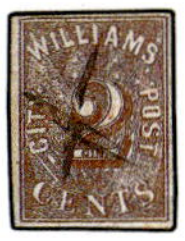

C20a

**1854** **Wove Paper** **Litho.**

**9LB1** C20a 2c brown — *4,000.*

### Cleveland, Ohio
### Bishop's City Post

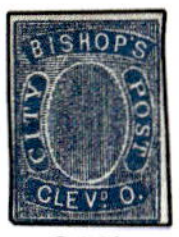

C20b

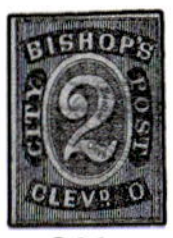

C20c

**1854** **Wove Paper** **Litho.**

**10LB1** C20b blue *5,000.* *4,000.*

### Vertically Laid Paper

**10LB2** C20c 2c black, *bluish* *4,000.* *6,000.*

No. 10LB2 unused is unique. It is cut in at bottom and without gum, and is valued thus.

### Louisville, Ky.
### Wharton's U.S.P.O. Despatch

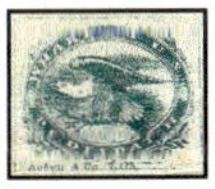

C21

**1857** **Lithographed**

**5LB1** C21 (2c) bluish green (shades) 125.

### Brown & McGill's U. S. P. O. Despatch

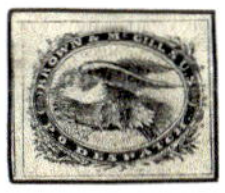

C22

**1858, Nov.-1860** **Lithographed**

**5LB2** C22 (2c) blue (shades) 250. *750.*

**1858, Feb.-Aug.**

**5LB3** C22 (2c) black *4,500.* *15,000.*
On cover, not tied, with 3c #26 *17,500.*

The value for No. 5LB3 used refers to the finer of the two known used (canceled) examples; it is extremely fine and on a piece with a 3c #26.

### New York, N. Y.
### United States City Despatch Post

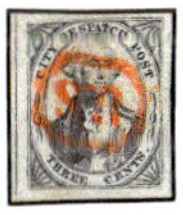

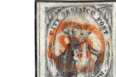

C23

### Wove Paper Colored Through

**1842** **Engr.**

**6LB1** C23 3c black, *grayish* *2,000.*

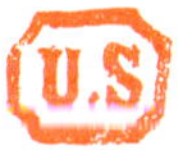


Used examples are Carriers' stamps only when canceled with the regular government cancellation "U.S." in octagonal frame (see illustration), "U.S.CITY DESPATCH POST," or New York circular postmark.

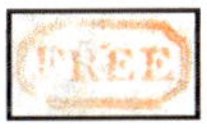


When canceled "FREE" in frame they were used as local stamps. See No. 40L1 in the Scott Specialized Catalogue of United States Stamps.

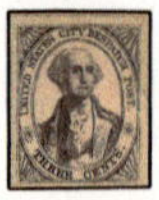

C24

### Wove Paper (unsurfaced) Colored Through

**1842-45**

| | | | | |
|---|---|---|---|---|
| **6LB2** | C24 | 3c black, *rosy buff* | *5,000.* | |
| **6LB3** | C24 | 3c black, *light blue* | *1,500.* | 750. |
| **6LB4** | C24 | 3c black, *green* | *11,500.* | |
| *a.* | | 3c black, *apple green* | | — |

Some authorities consider No. 6LB2 to be an essay, and No. 6LB4 a color changeling. No. 6LB2 unused is valued without gum.

### Glazed Paper, Surface Colored

| | | | | |
|---|---|---|---|---|
| **6LB5** | C24 | 3c black, *blue green* (shades) | 200. | 175. |
| *a.* | | Double impression | | *1,500.* |
| | | On cover | | 4,500. |
| *b.* | | 3c black, *blue* | 650. | *300.* |
| *c.* | | As "b," double impression | | *1,000.* |
| *d.* | | 3c black, *green* | *1,250.* | *750.* |
| | | black, *apple green* | | *2,000.* |
| | | Pair | | *2,750.* |
| *e.* | | As "d," double impression | — | |
| **6LB6** | C24 | 3c black, *pink*, on cover front | | *14,500.* |

No. 6LB6 is unique.

No. 6LB5 Surcharged in Red

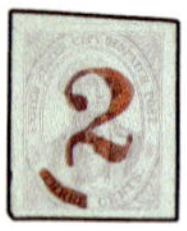

**1846**

| | | | | |
|---|---|---|---|---|
| **6LB7** | C24 | 2c on 3c black, *bluish grn*, on cover | | *14,000.* |
| | | On cover, not tied, with certificate | | *70,000.* |

The City Despatch 2c red is listed in the Scott U.S. Specialized Catalogue as a Local stamp.

### U.S. MAIL

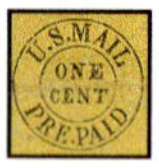

C27

**1849** **Typo.**

### Wove Paper, Colored Through

| | | | | |
|---|---|---|---|---|
| **6LB9** | C27 | 1c black, *rose* | 100. | 100. |

**1849-50** **Glazed Surface Paper**

| | | | | |
|---|---|---|---|---|
| **6LB10** | C27 | 1c black, *yellow* | 100. | 100. |
| **6LB11** | C27 | 1c black, *buff* | 100. | 100. |
| *a.* | | Pair, one stamp sideways | | *2,850.* |

### Philadelphia, Pa.

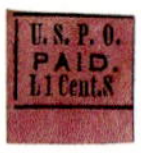

C28

### Several Varieties

### Thick Wove Paper Colored Through

**1849-50** **Typeset**

| | | | | |
|---|---|---|---|---|
| **7LB1** | C28 | 1c black, *rose* (with "L P") | 450. | |
| **7LB2** | C28 | 1c black, *rose* (with "S") | *3,000.* | |
| **7LB3** | C28 | 1c black, *rose* (with "H") | 275. | |
| **7LB4** | C28 | 1c black, *rose* (with "L S") | 400. | *500.* |
| **7LB5** | C28 | 1c black, *rose* (with "J J") | | *7,500.* |

The used No. 7LB5 also is unique and is an uncanceled stamp on a cover front.

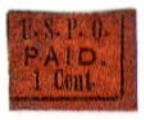

C29

### Several Varieties

| | | | | |
|---|---|---|---|---|
| **7LB6** | C29 | 1c black, *rose* | 300. | 250. |
| **7LB7** | C29 | 1c black, *blue*, glazed | *1,000.* | |
| **7LB8** | C29 | 1c blk, *ver*, glazed | *700.* | |
| **7LB9** | C29 | 1c blk, *yel*, glazed | *2,750.* | *2,250.* |

Cancellations on Nos. 7LB1-7LB9: Normally these stamps were left uncanceled on the letter, but occasionally were accidentally tied by the Philadelphia town postmark which was normally struck in blue ink.

A 1c black on buff (unglazed) of type C29 is believed to be a color changeling.

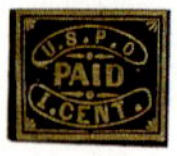

C30

### Settings of 25 (5x5) varieties (Five basic types)

**1850-52** **Litho.**

| | | | | |
|---|---|---|---|---|
| **7LB11** | C30 | 1c gold, *black*, glazed | 175. | 110. |
| **7LB12** | C30 | 1c blue | 400. | 300. |
| **7LB13** | C30 | 1c black | *750.* | *550.* |

25 varieties of C30.

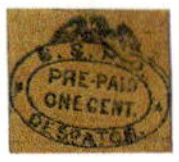

C31

### Handstamped

| | | | | |
|---|---|---|---|---|
| **7LB14** | C31 | 1c blue, *buff* | 3,250. | |

**1855(?)**

| | | | | |
|---|---|---|---|---|
| **7LB16** | C31 | 1c black | | *5,000.* |

C32

**1856(?)** **Handstamped**

| | | | | |
|---|---|---|---|---|
| **7LB18** | C32 | 1c black | *1,250.* | *2,000.* |

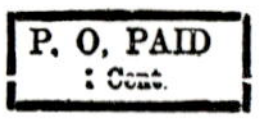

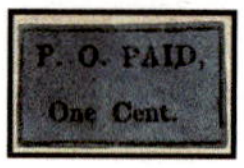

Labels of these designs are believed by most specialists not to be carrier stamps. Those seen are uncanceled, either off cover or affixed to stampless covers of the early 1850s. Some students believe they should be given carrier status.

### St. Louis, Mo.

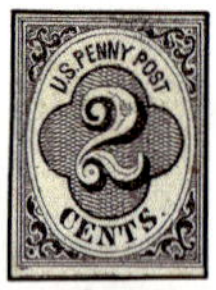

C36

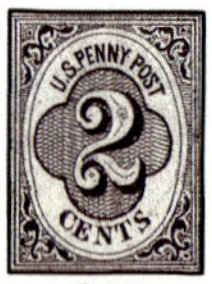

C37

Illustrations enlarged to show details of the two types (note upper corners especially). Sizes of actual designs are 17 1/2x22mm.

**1849** **White Wove Paper** **Litho.**

### Two Types

| | | | | |
|---|---|---|---|---|
| **8LB1** | C36 | 2c black | *7,000.* | *3,000.* |
| **8LB2** | C37 | 2c black | *6,000.* | — |

Cancellation on Nos. 8LB1-8LB2: Black town.

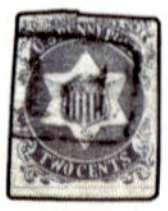

C38

**1857** **Litho.**

| | | | | |
|---|---|---|---|---|
| **8LB3** | C38 | 2c blue | | *22,500.* |

The used example off cover is unique. Five covers are recorded.

Cancellations on No. 8LB3: Black boxed "1ct," "Paid" in arc, black pen.

## STAMPED ENVELOPES & WRAPPERS

### VALUES

Unless otherwise noted, values are for cut squares in a grade of very fine.

Very fine cut squares will have the design well centered within moderately large margins. Precanceled cut squares must include the entire precancellation.

Values for unused entires are for those without printed or manuscript address. Values for letter sheets are for folded entires. Unfolded examples sell for more. A "full corner" includes back and side flaps and commands a premium.

Entire envelopes and wrappers are listed in the Scott U.S. Specialized Catalogue.

Wrappers are listed with envelopes of corresponding designs, and indicated by prefix letter "W" instead of "U."

An ALBINO impression is where two or more envelope blanks are fed into the printing press. The one adjacent to the printing die receives the color and the embossing, while the others are embossed only. Albinos are printing errors and are sometimes worth more than normal, inked impressions. Because of the nature of the printing process, many albinos were produced, and most collectors will not pay much, or any, premium for most of them. Albinos of earlier issues, canceled while current, are scarce.

The papers of these issues vary greatly in texture, and in color from yellowish to bluish white and from amber to dark buff.

"+" Some authorities claim that Nos. U37, U48, U49, U110, U124, U125, U130, U133A, U137A, U137B, U137C, W138, U145, U162, U178A, U185, U220, U285, U286, U298, U299, UO3, UO32, UO38, UO45 and UO45A (each with "+" before number) were not regularly issued and are not known to have been used.

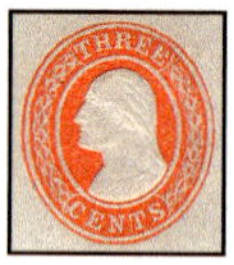

U1

"THREE" in short label with curved ends; 13mm wide at top. Twelve varieties.

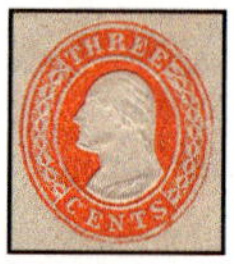

Washington — U2

"THREE" in short label with straight ends; 15½mm wide at top. Three varieties.

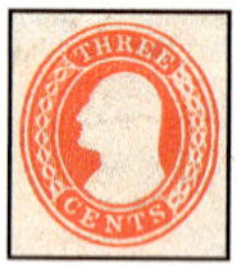

U3

"THREE" in short label with octagonal ends. Two varieties.

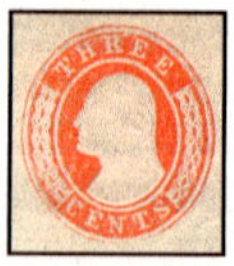

U4

"THREE" in wide label with straight ends; 20mm wide at top.

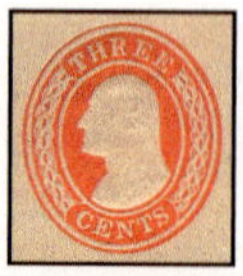

U5

"THREE" in medium wide label with curved ends; 14½mm wide at top. Ten varieties. A sub-variety shows curved lines at either end of label omitted; both T's have longer cross stroke; R is smaller (20 varieties).

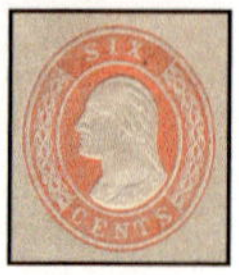

Four varieties.

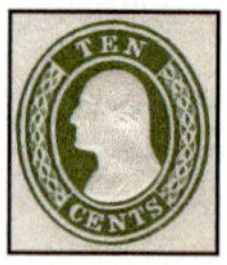

"TEN" in short label; 15½mm wide at top.

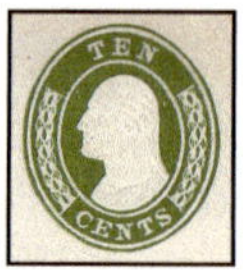

U8

"TEN" in wide label; 20mm wide at top.

**1853-55**

### On Diagonally Laid Paper (Early printings of No. U1 on Horizontally Laid Paper)

| | | | | |
|---|---|---|---|---|
| **U1** | U1 | 3c red | 350.00 | 35.00 |
| **U2** | U1 | 3c red, *buff* | 90.00 | 30.00 |
| **U3** | U2 | 3c red | 950.00 | 50.00 |
| **U4** | U2 | 3c red, *buff* | 425.00 | 45.00 |
| **U17** | U8 | 10c green ('55) | 375.00 | 140.00 |
| *a.* | | 10c pale green | 275.00 | 125.00 |
| **U18** | U8 | 10c green, *buff* ('55) | 375.00 | 100.00 |
| *a.* | | 10c pale green, *buff* | 325.00 | 100.00 |

Earliest documented uses: No. U1, July 6, 1853; No. U2, July 12, 1853 (Nesbitt seal); No. U3, July 7, 1853 (Nesbitt seal); No. U4, July 7, 1853 (flap missing); No. U5, Feb. 18, 1854; No. U6, Feb. 24, 1854; No. U7, Oct. 6, 1853; No. U8, Nov. 9, 1853; No. U9, May 30, 1854; No. U10, Mar. 24, 1854; No. U11, Mar. 25, 1855; No. U12, Feb. 22, 1855; No. U13, Nov. 29, 1853; No. U14, Nov. 10, 1853; No. U15, Oct. 15, 1856; No. U16, May 15, 1857 (cut square), June 15, 1857 (entire); No. U16a, Dec. 19, 1856 (cut square), June 4, 1857 (entire); No. U17, no dates documented; No. U17a, Nov. 14, 1855; No. U18, June 1, 1855; No. U18a, Sept. 4, 1855.

Nos. U9, U10, U11, U12, U13, U14, U17, and U18 have been reprinted on white and buff papers, wove or vertically laid, and are not known entire. The originals are on diagonally laid paper. Value, set of 8 reprints on laid, $225. Reprints on wove sell for more.

The first printings of Nos. U1, U2, U3, U4 and U7 have G.F. Nesbitt crests printed on the envelope flaps. These sell for a premium. Such examples of Nos. U1-U4 with 1853 year-dated cancels sell for a very large premium.

No. U1 with watermark having a space between lines and on horizontally laid paper sells for a substantial premium.

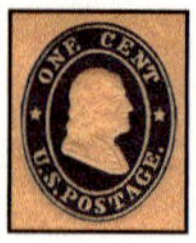

U9

Period after "POSTAGE." (Eleven varieties.)

Franklin, Period after "POSTAGE." — U10

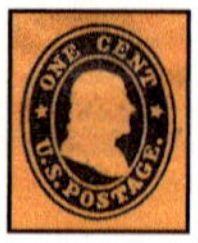

Bust touches inner frame-line at front and back.

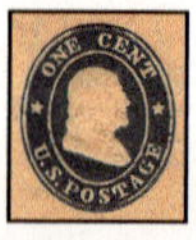

No period after "POSTAGE" — U11

No period after "POSTAGE." (Two varieties.)

# UNITED STATES

Washington — U12

Nine varieties of type U12.

Envelopes are on diagonally laid paper.

Wrappers on vertically or horizontally laid paper, or on unwatermarked wove paper (Nos. U21A, W22, W25)

**1860-61**

| | | | | |
|---|---|---|---|---|
| W18B | U9 | 1c blue ('61) | | 4,125. |
| U19 | U9 | 1c blue, buff | 35.00 | 12.50 |
| W20 | U9 | 1c bl, buff ('61) | 65.00 | 50.00 |
| W21 | U9 | 1c bl, man ('61) | 55.00 | 45.00 |
| U21A | U9 | 1c bl, org | 950.00 | 325.00 |
| W22 | U9 | 1c bl, org ('61) | 3,000. | |
| U23 | U10 | 1c bl, org | 500.00 | 350.00 |
| U24 | U11 | 1c bl, amb | 350.00 | 110.00 |
| W25 | U11 | 1c bl, man ('61) | 6,750. | 1,500. |
| W25A | U11 | 3c bl, man ('61) | | 1,650. |
| U26 | U12 | 3c red | 25.00 | 17.50 |
| U27 | U12 | 3c red, buff | 22.50 | 12.50 |
| U28 | U12+U9 | 3c +1c red & bl | 250.00 | 225.00 |
| U29 | U12+U9 | 3c +1c red & bl, buff | 250.00 | 250.00 |
| U30 | U12 | 6c red | 1,800. | 1,500. |
| U31 | U12 | 6c red, buff | 3,500. | 1,450. |
| U32 | U12 | 10c green | 1,250. | 450.00 |
| U33 | U12 | 10c green, buff | 1,250. | 400.00 |

Nos. U26, U27, U30 to U33 have been reprinted on the same vertically laid paper as the reprints of the 1853-55 issue, and are not known entire. Value, Nos. U26-U27, $75 each; Nos. U30-U33, $75 each.

U13

U14

Washington — U16

U15

Envelopes are on diagonally laid paper.

U36 and U45 come on vertically or horizontally laid paper.

**1861**

| | | | | |
|---|---|---|---|---|
| U34 | U13 | 3c pink | 27.50 | 5.00 |
| U35 | U13 | 3c pink, buff | 32.50 | 6.00 |
| U36 | U13 | 3c pink, blue (Letter Sheet) | 60.00 | 60.00 |
| +U37 | U13 | 3c pink, orange | 2,750. | |
| U38 | U14 | 6c pink | 100.00 | 80.00 |
| U39 | U14 | 6c pink, buff | 60.00 | 60.00 |
| U40 | U15 | 10c yellow green | 40.00 | 30.00 |
| a. | | 10c blue green | 40.00 | 30.00 |
| U41 | U15 | 10c yel grn, buff | 40.00 | 30.00 |
| a. | | 10c blue green, buff | 40.00 | 30.00 |
| U42 | U16 | 12c red & brn, buff | 180.00 | 180.00 |
| a. | | 12c lake & brown, buff | 2,500. | |
| U43 | U16 | 20c red & bl, buff | 250.00 | 225.00 |
| U44 | U16 | 24c red & grn, buff | 225.00 | 210.00 |
| a. | | 24c lake & green, salmon | 275.00 | 225.00 |
| U45 | U16 | 40c blk & red, buff | 325.00 | 400.00 |

Nos. U38 and U39 have been reprinted on the same papers as the reprints of the 1853-55 issue, and are not known entire. Value, set of 2 reprints, $60.

Jackson — U17

"U.S. POSTAGE" above. Downstroke and tail of "2" unite near the point (seven varieties).

Jackson — U18

"U.S. POSTAGE" above. The downstroke and tail of the "2" touch but do not merge.

Jackson — U19

"U.S. POST" above. Stamp 24-25mm wide (Sixteen varieties).

Jackson — U20

"U.S. POST" above. Stamp 25½-20¼mm wide. (Twenty-five varieties.)

Envelopes are on diagonally laid paper. Wrappers on vertically or horizontally laid paper.

Envelopes are on diagonally laid paper.

Wrappers on vertically or horizontally laid paper.

**1863-64**

| | | | | |
|---|---|---|---|---|
| U46 | U17 | 2c black, buff | 50.00 | 24.00 |
| W47 | U17 | 2c black, dark manila | 75.00 | 65.00 |
| +U48 | U18 | 2c black, buff | 2,250. | |
| +U49 | U18 | 2c black, orange | 1,750. | |
| U50 | U19 | 2c black, buff ('64) | 17.50 | 11.00 |
| W51 | U19 | 2c black, buff ('64) | 425.00 | 275.00 |
| U52 | U19 | 2c black, orange ('64) | 20.00 | 11.00 |
| W53 | U19 | 2c black, dark manila ('64) | 42.50 | 40.00 |
| U54 | U20 | 2c black, buff ('64) | 17.50 | 9.50 |
| W55 | U20 | 2c black, buff ('64) | 95.00 | 65.00 |
| U56 | U20 | 2c black, orange ('64) | 17.50 | 10.00 |
| W57 | U20 | 2c black, light manila ('64) | 22.50 | 14.00 |

Washington — U21

79 varieties for Nos. U58-U61; 2 varieties for Nos. U63-U65.

Washington — U22

**1864-65**

| | | | | |
|---|---|---|---|---|
| U58 | U21 | 3c pink | 8.00 | 1.60 |
| U59 | U21 | 3c pink, buff | 7.50 | 1.25 |
| U60 | U21 | 3c brown ('65) | 60.00 | 40.00 |
| U61 | U21 | 3c brown, buff ('65) | 50.00 | 30.00 |
| U62 | U21 | 6c pink | 75.00 | 29.00 |
| U63 | U21 | 6c pink, buff | 35.00 | 27.50 |
| U64 | U21 | 6c purple ('65) | 50.00 | 26.00 |
| U65 | U21 | 6c purple, buff ('65) | 40.00 | 20.00 |
| U66 | U22 | 9c lemon, buff | 375.00 | 250.00 |
| U67 | U22 | 9c orange, buff ('65) | 125.00 | 90.00 |
| a. | | 9c orange yellow, buff | 150.00 | 90.00 |
| U68 | U22 | 12c brown, buff ('65) | 275.00 | 275.00 |
| U69 | U22 | 12c red brown, buff ('65) | 125.00 | 55.00 |
| U70 | U22 | 18c red, buff ('65) | 70.00 | 95.00 |
| U71 | U22 | 24c blue, buff ('65) | 70.00 | 95.00 |
| U72 | U22 | 30c green, buff ('65) | 80.00 | 80.00 |
| a. | | 30c yellow green, buff | 75.00 | 75.00 |
| U73 | U22 | 40c rose, buff ('65) | 80.00 | 250.00 |

**Printed by George H. Reay, Brooklyn, N. Y.**

The engravings in this issue are finely executed.

Franklin — U23

Bust points to the end of the "N" of "ONE."

Jackson — U24

Bust narrow at back. Small, thick figures of value.

Washington — U25

Queue projects below bust.

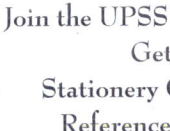

Lincoln — U26

Neck very long at the back.

Stanton — U27

Bust pointed at the back; figures "7" are normal.

Jefferson — U28

Queue forms straight line with the bust.

Clay — U29

Ear partly concealed by hair, mouth large, chin prominent.

Webster — U30

Has side whiskers.

Scott — U31

Straggling locks of hair at top of head; ornaments around the inner oval end in squares.

Hamilton — U32

Back of bust very narrow, chin almost straight, labels containing figures of value are exactly parallel.

Perry — U33

Front of bust very narrow and pointed; inner lines of shields project very slightly beyond the oval.

---

**UNITED POSTAL STATIONERY SOCIETY**

$5 or $500?
Join the UPSS to find out!
Get
Stationery Catalogs
Reference books
Bimonthly journal
Auctions

404 Sundown Road, Knoxville, TN 37934
www.upss.org

## 194 UNITED STATES

**1870-71**

| | | | | |
|---|---|---|---|---|
| U74 | U23 | 1c blue | 32.50 | 30.00 |
| a. | | 1c ultramarine | 60.00 | 35.00 |
| U75 | U23 | 1c blue, amber | 25.00 | 27.50 |
| a. | | 1c ultramarine, amber | 55.00 | 30.00 |
| U76 | U23 | 1c blue, orange | 17.00 | 15.00 |
| W77 | U23 | 1c blue, manila | 35.00 | 35.00 |
| U78 | U24 | 2c brown | 35.00 | 16.00 |
| U79 | U24 | 2c brown, amber | 14.00 | 10.00 |
| U80 | U24 | 2c brown, orange | 8.00 | 6.50 |
| W81 | U24 | 2c brown, manila | 25.00 | 20.00 |
| U82 | U25 | 3c green | 7.00 | 1.00 |
| a. | | 3c brown (error), entire | 6,750. | |
| U83 | U25 | 3c green, amber | 6.00 | 2.00 |
| U84 | U25 | 3c green, cream | 8.00 | 4.50 |
| U85 | U26 | 6c dark red | 17.50 | 16.00 |
| a. | | 6c vermilion | 17.50 | 16.00 |
| U86 | U26 | 6c dark red, amber | 30.00 | 20.00 |
| a. | | 6c vermilion, amber | 30.00 | 20.00 |
| U87 | U26 | 6c dark red, cream | 30.00 | 25.00 |
| a. | | 6c vermilion, cream | 25.00 | 20.00 |
| U88 | U27 | 7c vermilion, amber ('71) | 55.00 | 175.00 |
| U89 | U28 | 10c olive black | 650.00 | 900.00 |
| U90 | U28 | 10c olive black, amber | 625.00 | 800.00 |
| U91 | U28 | 10c brown | 82.50 | 70.00 |
| U92 | U28 | 10c brown, amber | 85.00 | 52.50 |
| a. | | 10c dark brown, amber | 85.00 | 75.00 |
| U93 | U29 | 12c plum | 100.00 | 82.50 |
| U94 | U29 | 12c plum, amber | 110.00 | 100.00 |
| U95 | U29 | 12c plum, cream | 225.00 | 200.00 |
| U96 | U30 | 15c red orange | 75.00 | 75.00 |
| a. | | 15c orange | | 75.00 |
| U97 | U30 | 15c red orange, amber | 160.00 | 275.00 |
| a. | | 15c orange, amber | 170.00 | |
| U98 | U30 | 15c red orange, cream | 325.00 | 375.00 |
| a. | | 15c orange, cream | 325.00 | |
| U99 | U31 | 24c purple | 110.00 | 125.00 |
| U100 | U31 | 24c purple, amber | 180.00 | 300.00 |
| U101 | U31 | 24c purple, cream | 225.00 | 450.00 |
| U102 | U32 | 30c black | 60.00 | 120.00 |
| U103 | U32 | 30c black, amber | 180.00 | 450.00 |
| U104 | U32 | 30c black, cream | 150.00 | 450.00 |
| U105 | U33 | 90c carmine | 125.00 | 300.00 |
| U106 | U33 | 90c carmine, amber | 350.00 | 900.00 |
| U107 | U33 | 90c carmine, cream | 175.00 | 2,250. |

**Printed by Plimpton Manufacturing Co.**

The profiles in this issue are inferior to the fine engraving of the Reay issue.

U34

Bust forms an angle at the back near the frame. Lettering poorly executed. Distinct circle in "O" of "Postage."

U35

Lower part of bust points to the end of the "E" in "ONE." Head inclined downward.

U36

Bust narrow at back. Thin numerals. Head of "P" narrow. Bust broad at front, ending in sharp corners.

U37

Bust broad. Figures of value in long ovals.

U38

Similar to U37 but the figure "2" at the left touches the oval.

U39

Similar to U37 but the "O" of "TWO" has the center netted instead of plain and the "G" of "POSTAGE" and the "C" of "CENTS" have diagonal crossline.

U40

Bust broad: numerals in ovals short and thick.

U41

Similar to U40 but the ovals containing the numerals are much heavier. A diagonal line runs from the upper part of the "U" to the white frame-line.

U42

Similar to U40 but the middle stroke of "N" in "CENTS" is as thin as the vertical strokes.

U43

Bottom of bust cut almost semi-circularly.

U44

Thin lettering, long thin figures of value.

U45

Thick lettering, well-formed figures of value, queue does not project below bust.

U46

Top of head egg-shaped; knot of queue well marked and projects triangularly.

Taylor — U47

Die 1 - Figures of value with thick, curved tops

Die 2 - Figures of value with long, thin tops

U48

Neck short at back.

U49

Figures of value turned up at the ends.

U50

Very large head.

U51

Knot of queue stands out prominently.

U52

Ear prominent, chin receding.

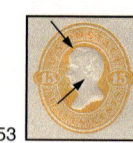
U53

No side whiskers, forelock projects above head.

U54

Hair does not project; ornaments around the inner oval end in points.

U55

Back of bust rather broad, chin slopes considerably; labels containing figures of value are not exactly parallel.

U56

Front of bust sloping; inner lines of shields project considerably into the inner oval.

**1874-86 — Design U34**

| | | | |
|---|---|---|---|
| U108 | 1c dark blue | 175.00 | 60.00 |
| a. | 1c light blue | 175.00 | 60.00 |
| U109 | 1c dk bl, amb | 150.00 | 75.00 |
| +U110 | 1c dk blue, cr | 1,000. | |
| U111 | 1c dk blue, org | 15.00 | 15.00 |
| a. | dk blue, org | 12.50 | 12.50 |
| W112 | 1c dk blue, man | 62.50 | 40.00 |

**Design U35**

| | | | |
|---|---|---|---|
| U113 | 1c light blue | 2.25 | 1.00 |
| a. | 1c dark blue | 6.50 | 6.50 |
| U114 | 1c lt blue, amb | 3.25 | 3.25 |
| a. | dk blue, amb | 17.50 | 10.00 |
| U115 | 1c blue, cr | 4.25 | 4.25 |
| a. | dk blue, cr | 17.50 | 8.50 |
| U116 | 1c lt blue, org | .75 | .40 |
| a. | dk blue, org | 4.00 | 2.50 |
| U117 | 1c lt bl, bl ('80) | 6.50 | 5.00 |
| U118 | 1c lt bl, fawn ('79) | 7.00 | 5.00 |
| U119 | 1c lt bl, man ('86) | 8.00 | 3.25 |
| W120 | 1c lt bl, man | 1.25 | 1.10 |
| a. | dk bl, man | 8.00 | 7.00 |
| U121 | 1c lt bl, amb man | 17.50 | 10.00 |

**Design U36**

| | | | |
|---|---|---|---|
| U122 | 2c brown | 140.00 | 65.00 |
| U123 | 2c brown, amb | 67.50 | 40.00 |
| +U124 | 2c brn, crm | 1,000. | |
| +U125 | 2c brn, org | 18,000. | |
| W126 | 2c brn, man | 125.00 | 85.00 |
| W127 | 2c ver, man | 2,250. | 500.00 |

**Design U37**

| | | | |
|---|---|---|---|
| U128 | 2c brown | 60.00 | 35.00 |
| U129 | 2c brn, amb | 80.00 | 45.00 |
| +U130 | 2c brn, cr | 35,000. | |
| W131 | 2c brn, man | 17.50 | 15.00 |

**Design U38**

| | | | |
|---|---|---|---|
| U132 | 2c brown | 70.00 | 27.50 |
| U133 | 2c brn, amb | 325.00 | 70.00 |
| +U133A | 2c brn, cr | 70,000. | |

**Design U39**

| | | | |
|---|---|---|---|
| U134 | 2c brown | 800.00 | 160.00 |
| U135 | 2c brn, amb | 425.00 | 150.00 |
| U136 | 2c brn, org | 50.00 | 27.50 |
| W137 | 2c brn, man | 75.00 | 40.00 |
| +U137A | 2c ver | 32,500. | |
| +U137B | 2c ver, amb | 30,000. | |
| +U137C | 2c ver, org | 70,000. | |
| +W138 | 2c ver, man | 25,000. | |

**Design U40**

| | | | |
|---|---|---|---|
| U139 | 2c brn ('75) | 57.50 | 37.50 |
| U140 | 2c brn, amb ('75) | 85.00 | 62.50 |
| +U140A | 2c reddish brn, org ('75) | 17,500. | |
| W141 | 2c brn, man ('75) | 32.50 | 25.00 |
| U142 | 2c ver ('75) | 8.00 | 5.00 |
| a. | 2c pink | 8.00 | 5.00 |
| U143 | 2c ver, amb ('75) | 9.00 | 5.00 |
| U144 | 2c ver, cr ('75) | 17.50 | 7.00 |
| +U145 | 2c ver, org ('75) | 35,000. | |
| U146 | 2c ver, bl ('80) | 110.00 | 40.00 |
| U147 | 2c ver, fawn ('75) | 7.00 | 5.00 |
| W148 | 2c ver, man ('75) | 4.00 | 3.50 |

**Design U41**

| | | | |
|---|---|---|---|
| U149 | 2c ver ('78) | 45.00 | 25.00 |
| a. | 2c pink | 52.50 | 27.00 |
| U150 | 2c ver, amb ('78) | 45.00 | 15.00 |
| U151 | 2c ver, bl ('80) | 10.00 | 8.00 |
| a. | 2c pink, blue | 11.00 | 8.00 |
| U152 | 2c ver, fawn ('78) | 10.00 | 4.00 |

**Design U42**

| | | | |
|---|---|---|---|
| U153 | 2c ver ('76) | 75.00 | 30.00 |
| U154 | 2c ver, amb ('76) | 300.00 | 90.00 |
| W155 | 2c ver, man ('76) | 20.00 | 10.00 |

**Design U43**

| | | | |
|---|---|---|---|
| U156 | 2c ver ('81) | 1,250. | 175.00 |
| U157 | 2c ver, amb ('81) | 42,500. | 27,500. |
| W158 | 2c ver, man ('81) | 90.00 | 55.00 |

UNITED STATES 195

### Design U44

**U159** 3c green 35.00 10.00
**U160** 3c grn, *amb* 35.00 10.00
**U161** 3c grn, *cr* 35.00 12.00
**+U162** 3c grn, *bl* *50,000.*

### Design U45

**U163** 3c green 1.40 .30
**U164** 3c grn, *amb* 1.50 .70
**U165** 3c grn, *cr* 8.50 6.50
**U166** 3c grn, *bl* 7.50 6.00
**U167** 3c grn, *fawn* ('75) 4.75 3.50

### Design U46

**U168** 3c grn ('81) 1,000. 80.00
**U169** 3c grn, *amb* 450.00 140.00
**U170** 3c grn, *bl* ('81) *11,500.* *2,750.*
**U171** 3c grn, *fawn* ('81) *40,000.* *2,750.*

### Design U47

**U172** 5c bl, die I ('75) 10.00 10.00
**U173** 5c bl, die I, *amb* ('75) 12.50 11.00
**U174** 5c bl, die I, *cr* ('75) 95.00 45.00
**U175** 5c bl, die I, *bl* ('75) 22.50 17.50
**U176** 5c bl, die I, *fawn* ('75) 150.00 65.00
**U177** 5c bl, die 2 ('75) 11.00 9.00
**U178** 5c bl, die 2, *amb* ('75) 8.00 8.00
**+U178A** 5c bl, die 2, *cr* ('76) *10,000.*
**U179** 5c bl, die 2, *bl* ('75) 20.00 12.50
**U180** 5c bl, die 2, *fawn* ('75) 125.00 50.00

### Design U48

**U181** 6c red 8.00 6.50
*a.* 6c vermilion 8.00 6.50
**U182** 6c red, *amber* 12.50 6.50
*a.* 6c ver, *amb* 12.50 6.50
**U183** 6c red, *cream* 50.00 17.50
*a.* 6c ver, *cr* 45.00 15.00
**U184** 6c red, *fawn* ('75) 17.50 12.50

### Design U49

**+U185** 7c vermilion *1,200.*
**U186** 7c ver, *amb* 125.00 75.00

### Design U50

**U187** 10c brown 40.00 20.00
**U188** 10c brn, *amb* 75.00 35.00

### Design U51

**U189** 10c choc ('75) 6.00 4.00
*a.* 10c bister brown 7.00 5.00
*b.* 10c yellow ocher *3,000.*
**U190** 10c choc, *amb* ('75) 7.00 6.00
*a.* 10c bis brn, *amb* 7.00 6.00
*b.* 10c yel ocher, *amb* *3,000.*
**U191** 10c brn, *oriental buff* ('86) 12.50 0.75
**U192** 10c brn, *bl* ('86) 12.50 8.00
*a.* 10c gray blk, *bl* 12.50 7.50
*b.* 10c red brn, *bl* 12.50 7.50
**U193** 10c brn, *man* ('86) 12.50 10.00
*a.* 10c red brn, *man* 12.50 10.00
**U194** 10c brn, *amb man* ('86) 17.50 9.00
*a.* 10c red brn, *amb man* 17.50 9.00

### Design U52

**U195** 12c plum 250.00 100.00
**U196** 12c plum, *amb* 200.00 160.00
**U197** 12c plum, *cr* 450.00 130.00

### Design U53

**U198** 15c orange 50.00 35.00
**U199** 15c org, *amb* 140.00 130.00
**U200** 15c org, *cr* 550.00 300.00

### Design U54

**U201** 24c purple 175.00 150.00
**U202** 24c pur, *amb* 180.00 100.00
**U203** 24c pur, *cr* 375.00 100.00

### Design U55

**U204** 30c black 55.00 25.00
**U205** 30c blk, *amb* 70.00 60.00
**U206** 30c blk, *cr* ('75) 300.00 325.00
**U207** 30c blk, *oriental buff* ('81) 90.00 80.00
**U208** 30c blk, *bl* ('81) 90.00 80.00
**U209** 30c blk, *man* ('81) 80.00 70.00
**U210** 30c blk, *amb man* ('86) 190.00 100.00

### Design U56

**U211** 90c car ('75) 80.00 75.00
**U212** 90c car, *amb* ('75) 175.00 250.00
**U213** 90c car, *cr* ('75) 1,000.
**U214** 90c car, *oriental buff* ('86) 140.00 250.00
**U215** 90c car, *bl* ('86) 160.00 250.00
**U216** 90c car, *man* ('86) 120.00 225.00
**U217** 90c car, *amb man* ('86) 140.00 *200.00*

Note: No. U206 has watermark #2; No. U207 watermark #6 or #7. No U213 has watermark #2; No. U214 watermark #7. These envelopes cannot be positively identified except by the watermark.

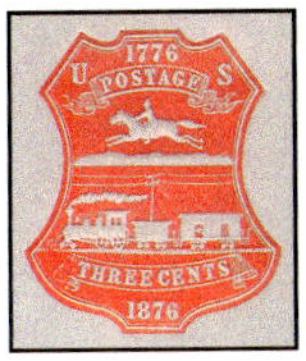

Single line under "POSTAGE" — U57

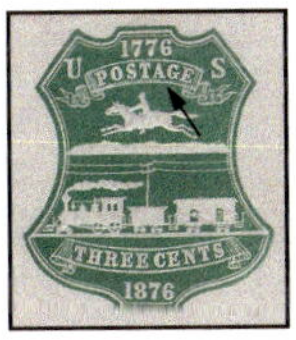

Double line under "POSTAGE" — U58

**1876**

**U218** U57 3c red 30.00 25.00
**U219** U57 3c green 30.00 17.50
**+U220** U58 3c red *27,500.*
**U221** U58 3c green 30.00 25.00

Cent. of the U.S., and the World's Fair at Philadelphia.

Used examples of Nos. U218-U221 with exposition cancels and/or typed addresses sell for a premium.

See No. U582.

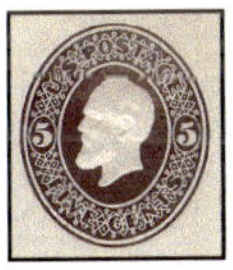

Garfield — U59

**1882-86**

**U222** U59 5c brown 5.00 3.00
**U223** U59 5c brn, *amb* 5.25 3.50
**+U224** U59 5c brn, *oriental buff* ('86) 130.00
**+U225** U59 5c brn, *bl* 75.00
**U226** U59 5c brn, *fawn* 300.00

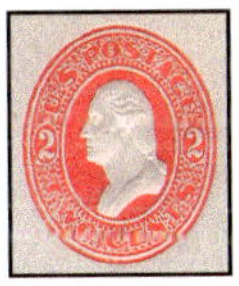

Washington — U60

**1883, October**

**U227** U60 2c red 5.50 2.25
*a.* 2c brown (error), entire *2,000.*
**U228** U60 2c red, *amb* 6.50 2.75
**U229** U60 2c red, *blue* 8.00 5.00
**U230** U60 2c red, *fawn* 9.00 5.25

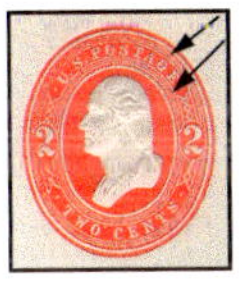

Wavy lines fine and clear — U61

**1883, November**

**Four Wavy Lines in Oval**

**U231** U61 2c red 5.00 2.50
**U232** U61 2c red, *amb* 6.00 3.75
**U233** U61 2c red, *blue* 10.00 7.50
**U234** U61 2c red, *fawn* 7.50 4.75
**W235** U61 2c red, *man* 18.00 6.25

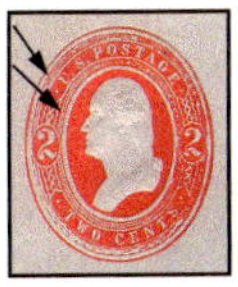

Wavy lines thick and blurred — U62

Retouched die.

**1884, June**

**U236** U62 2c red 15.00 4.00
**U237** U62 2c red, *amber* 20.00 10.00
**U238** U62 2c red, *blue* 29.00 12.00
**U239** U62 2c red, *fawn* 20.00 11.00

See Nos. U260-W269.

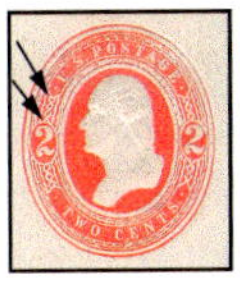

3 ½ links over left "2" — U63

**U240** U63 2c red 90.00 45.00
**U241** U63 2c red, *amb* 550.00 300.00
**U242** U63 2c red, *fawn* *25,000.*

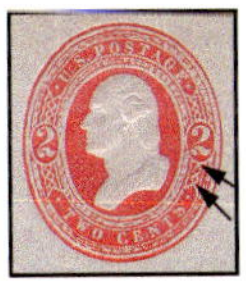

2 links below right "2" — U64

**U243** U64 2c red 110.00 75.00
**U244** U64 2c red, *amb* 250.00 100.00
**U245** U64 2c red, *blue* 275.00 125.00
**U246** U64 2c red, *fawn* 275.00 175.00

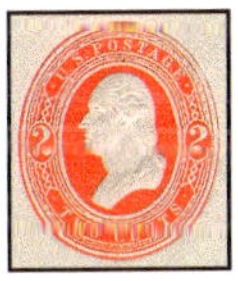

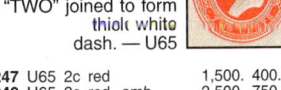

Round "O" in "TWO." White lines above "WO" of "TWO" joined to form thick white dash. — U65

**U247** U65 2c red 1,500. 400.00
**U248** U65 2c red, *amb* 2,500. 750.00
**U249** U65 2c red, *fawn* 750. 500.00

See Nos. U270-U276.

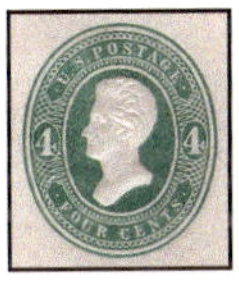

Jackson — U66

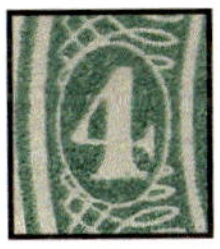

Die 1 - Numeral at left is 2 ¾ mm wide

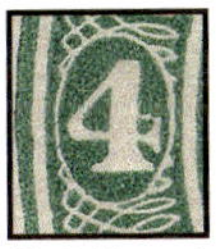

Die 2 Numeral at left is 3 ¼ mm wide

**1883-86**

**U250** U66 4c green, die 1 4.00 3.50
**U251** U66 4c grn, die 1, *amb* 5.00 3.50
**U252** U66 4c grn, die 1, *oriental buff* ('86) 13.00 9.00
**U253** U66 4c green, die 1, *blue* ('86) 11.00 6.50
**U254** U66 4c grn, die 1, *man* ('86) 10.00 7.50
**U255** U66 4c grn, die 1, *amb man* ('86) 22.50 10.00
**U256** U66 4c green, die 2 8.00 5.00
**U257** U66 4c grn, die 2, *amb* 12.50 7.00
**U258** U66 4c grn, die 2, *man* ('86) 12.50 7.50
**U259** U66 4c grn, die 2, *amb man* ('86) 12.50 7.50

**1884, May**

**U260** U61 2c brown 17.50 5.75
**U261** U61 2c brown, *amber* 17.50 6.50
**U262** U61 2c brown, *blue* 17.50 10.00
**U263** U61 2c brown, *fawn* 15.00 9.25
**W264** U61 2c brown, *manila* 15.00 11.50

**1884, June**

**Retouched Die**

**U265** U62 2c brown 15.00 6.50
**U266** U62 2c brn, *amb* 60.00 40.00
**U267** U62 2c brown, *blue* 22.50 9.00
**U268** U62 2c brown, *fawn* 15.00 11.00
**W269** U62 2c brn, *man* 25.00 15.00

**2 Links Below Right "2"**

**U270** U64 2c brown 115.00 50.00
**U271** U64 2c brn, *amb* 425.00 125.00
**U272** U64 2c brown, *fawn* *7,000.* *2,000.*

**Round "O" in "Two"**

**U273** U65 2c brown 225.00 100.00
**U274** U65 2c brn, *amb* 225.00 100.00
**U275** U65 2c brown, *blue* *10,000.*
**U276** U65 2c brown, *fawn* 700.00 750.00

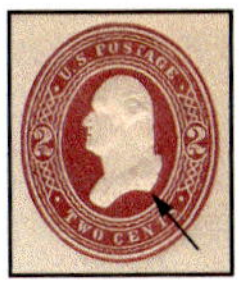

U67

Extremity of bust below the queue forms a point.

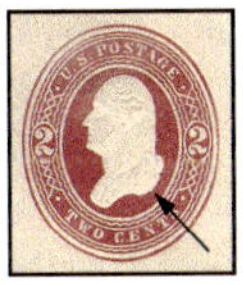

Washington — U68

Extremity of bust is rounded.

Similar to U61
Two wavy lines in oval

**1884-86**

**U277** U67 2c brown .50 .25
*a.* 2c brown lake, die 1 22.50 21.00
**U278** U67 2c brn, *amb* .65 .50
*a.* 2c brown lake, *amber* 35.00 25.00
**U279** U67 2c brn, *oriental buff* ('86) 6.00 2.10
**U280** U67 2c brown, *blue* 3.00 2.10
**U281** U67 2c brown, *fawn* 3.75 2.40
**U282** U67 2c brn, *man* ('86) 12.00 4.00
**W283** U67 2c brn, *man* 8.00 5.00
**U284** U67 2c brn, *amb man* ('86) 7.00 5.75
**+U285** U67 2c red 600.00
**+U286** U67 2c red, *blue* 225.00
**W287** U67 2c red, *manila* 150.00
**U288** U68 2c brown 325.00 50.00
**U289** U68 2c brn, *amb* 20.00 13.00
**U290** U68 2c brown, *blue* 850.00 325.00
**U291** U68 2c brown, *fawn* 25.00 25.00
**W292** U68 2c brn, *man* 30.00 19.00

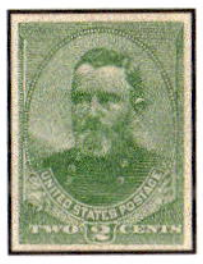

Gen. U.S. Grant — US1

**Letter Sheet, 160x271mm**

**1886** **Creamy White Paper**

**U293** US1 2c green, entire 30.00 20.00

See the Scott U.S. Specialized Catalogue for perforation and inscription varieties.

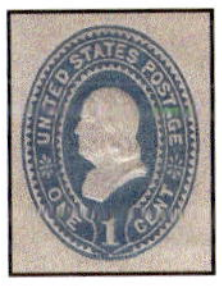

Franklin — U69

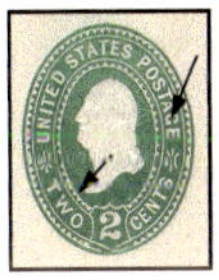

Washington — U70

Bust points between third and fourth notches of inner oval "G" of "POSTAGE" has no bar.

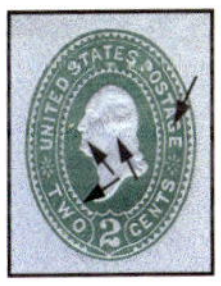

U71

Bust points between second and third notches of inner oval; "G" of "POSTAGE" has a bar; ear is indicated by one heavy line; one vertical line at corner of mouth.

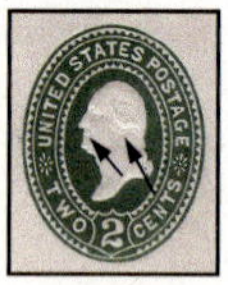

U72

Frame same as U71; upper part of head more rounded; ear indicated by two curved lines with two locks of hair in front; two vertical lines at corner of mouth.

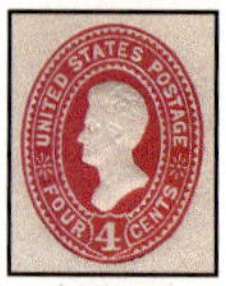

Jackson U73

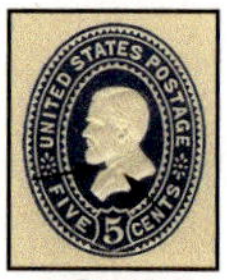

Grant U74

There is a space between the beard and the collar of the coat. A button is on the collar.

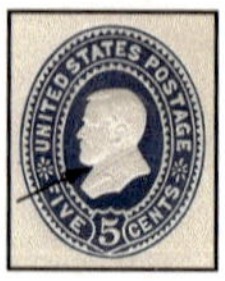

U75

The collar touches the beard and there is no button.

**1887-94** **Design U69**

| | | | |
|---|---|---|---|
| **U294** | 1c blue | .55 | .25 |
| **U295** | 1c dk bl ('94) | 6.50 | 2.50 |
| **U296** | 1c bl, *amb* | 3.25 | 1.25 |
| **U297** | 1c dk bl, *amb* ('94) | 40.00 | 22.50 |
| **+U298** | 1c bl, *oriental buff* | 7,000. | — |
| **+U299** | 1c bl, *bl* | 10,000. | |
| **U300** | 1c bl, *man* | .65 | .35 |
| **W301** | 1c bl, *man* | .45 | .30 |
| **U302** | 1c dk bl, *man* ('94) | 27.50 | 12.50 |
| **W303** | 1c DK bl, *man* ('94) | 12.50 | 10.00 |
| **U304** | 1c bl, *amb man* | 12.50 | 5.00 |

**Design U70**

| | | | |
|---|---|---|---|
| **U305** | 2c green | 15.00 | 10.00 |
| **U306** | 2c grn, *amb* | 40.00 | 17.50 |
| **U307** | 2c grn, *oriental buff* | 80.00 | 40.00 |
| **U308** | 2c grn, *bl* | 12,500. | 4,250. |
| **U309** | 2c grn, *man* | 10,000. | 1,000. |
| **U310** | 2c grn, *amb man* | 28,000. | 4,000. |

**Design U71**

| | | | |
|---|---|---|---|
| **U311** | 2c green | .30 | .25 |
| | *a.* 2c dark green ('94) | .45 | .30 |
| | *b.* Double impression, entire | 375.00 | |
| **U312** | 2c grn, *amb* | .40 | .25 |
| | *a.* Double impression | 90.00 | |
| | *b.* 2c dk grn, *amb* ('94) | .55 | .35 |
| **U313** | 2c grn, *oriental buff* | .55 | .25 |
| | *a.* 2c dk grn, *oriental buff* ('94) | 2.00 | 1.00 |
| | *b.* Double impression | 150.00 | |
| **U314** | 2c grn, *bl* | .60 | .30 |
| | *a.* 2c dk grn, *bl* ('94) | .80 | .40 |
| **U315** | 2c grn, *man* | 2.00 | .50 |
| | *a.* 2c dk grn, *man* ('94) | 2.75 | .75 |
| **W316** | 2c grn, *man* | 3.50 | 2.50 |
| **U317** | 2c grn, *amb man* | 2.50 | 1.90 |
| | *a.* 2c dk grn, *amb man* ('94) | 3.50 | 3.00 |

**Design U72**

| | | | |
|---|---|---|---|
| **U318** | 2c green | 110.00 | 12.50 |
| **U319** | 2c grn, *amb* | 160.00 | 27.50 |
| **U320** | 2c grn, *oriental buff* | 125.00 | 40.00 |
| **U321** | 2c grn, *bl* | 150.00 | 70.00 |
| **U322** | 2c grn, *man* | 225.00 | 70.00 |
| **U323** | 2c grn, *amb man* | 400.00 | 100.00 |

**Design U73**

| | | | |
|---|---|---|---|
| **U324** | 4c carmine | 3.25 | 2.00 |
| | *a.* 4c lake | 3.50 | 2.00 |
| | *b.* 4c scarlet ('94) | 3.50 | 2.00 |
| **U325** | 4c car, *amb* | 3.50 | 3.50 |
| | *a.* 4c lake, *amber* | 3.50 | 3.50 |
| | *b.* 4c scarlet, *amber* ('94) | 4.00 | 3.75 |
| **U326** | 4c car, *oriental buff* | 6.00 | 3.50 |
| | *a.* 4c lake, *oriental buff* | 7.00 | 3.50 |
| **U327** | 4c car, *bl* | 5.50 | 4.00 |
| | *a.* 4c lake, *blue* | 6.00 | 4.00 |
| **U328** | 4c car, *man* | 8.00 | 7.00 |
| | *a.* 4c lake, *manila* | 8.00 | 6.00 |
| | *b.* 4c pink, *manila* | 15.00 | 10.00 |
| **U329** | 4c car, *amb man* | 6.00 | 3.25 |
| | *a.* 4c lake, *amb man* | 6.00 | 3.25 |
| | *b.* 4c pink, *amb man* | 15.00 | 10.00 |

**Design U74**

| | | | |
|---|---|---|---|
| **U330** | 5c blue | 3.75 | 4.00 |
| **U331** | 5c bl, *amb* | 6.00 | 2.50 |
| | *a.* Double impression, entire | — | |
| **U332** | 5c bl, *oriental buff* | 6.50 | 4.00 |
| **U333** | 5c blue, *blue* | 7.00 | 6.00 |

**Design U75**

| | | | |
|---|---|---|---|
| **U334** | 5c blue ('94) | 20.00 | 12.50 |
| **U335** | 5c bl, *amb* ('94) | 11.00 | 7.50 |

**Design U55**

| | | | |
|---|---|---|---|
| **U336** | 30c red brn | 40.00 | 45.00 |
| | *a.* 30c yellow brown | 40.00 | 45.00 |
| | *b.* 30c chocolate | 40.00 | 45.00 |
| **U337** | 30c red brn, *amb* | 40.00 | 45.00 |
| | *a.* 30c yel brn, *amb* | 40.00 | 45.00 |
| | *b.* 30c choc, *amb* | 40.00 | 45.00 |
| **U338** | 30c red brn, *oriental buff* | 40.00 | 45.00 |
| | *a.* 30c yel brn, *oriental buff* | 40.00 | 45.00 |
| **U339** | 30c red brn, *bl* | 40.00 | 45.00 |
| | *a.* 30c yel brn, *bl* | 40.00 | 45.00 |
| **U340** | 30c red brn, *man* | 40.00 | 45.00 |
| | *a.* 30c brown, *manila* | 40.00 | 45.00 |
| **U341** | 30c red brn, *amb man* | 40.00 | 45.00 |
| | *a.* 30c yel brn, *amb man* | 40.00 | 45.00 |

**Design U56**

| | | | |
|---|---|---|---|
| **U342** | 90c purple | 55.00 | 85.00 |
| **U343** | 90c pur, *amb* | 70.00 | 85.00 |
| **U344** | 90c pur, *oriental buff* | 75.00 | 85.00 |
| **U345** | 90c pur, *bl* | 75.00 | 85.00 |
| **U346** | 90c pur, *man* | 80.00 | 85.00 |
| **U347** | 90c pur, *amb man* | 80.00 | 85.00 |

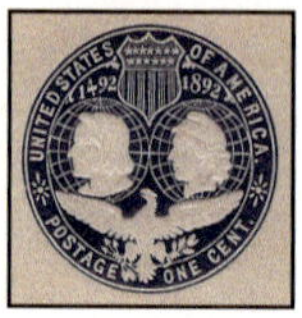

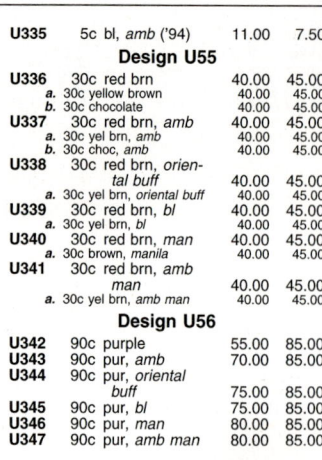

Columbus and Liberty — U76

**1893**

| | | | |
|---|---|---|---|
| **U348** | U76 1c deep blue | 2.00 | 1.25 |
| **U349** | U76 2c violet | 1.50 | .50 |
| | *a.* 2c dark slate (error) | *1,500.* | |
| **U350** | U76 5c chocolate | 6.50 | 7.00 |
| | *a.* 5c slate brown (error) | *700.00* | *1,400.* |
| **U351** | U76 10c slate brown | 25.00 | 27.50 |
| | *Nos. U348-U351 (4)* | 35.00 | 36.25 |

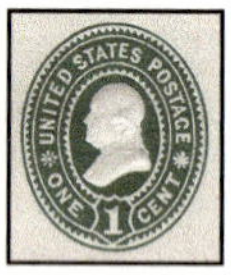

Franklin — U77

Bust points to fourth notch of inner circle.

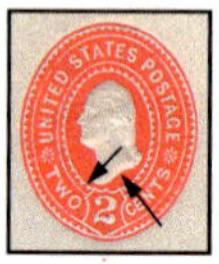

Washington — U78

Bust points to first notch of inner oval and is only slightly concave below.

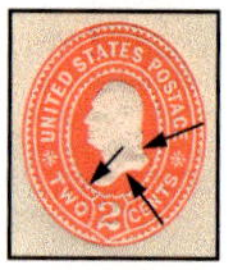

U79

Bust points to middle of second notch of inner oval and is quite hollow below. Queue has ribbon around it.

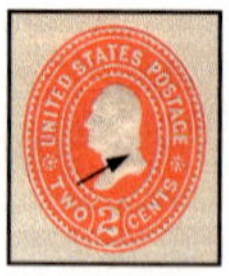

U80

Same as die 2, but hair flowing. No ribbon on queue.

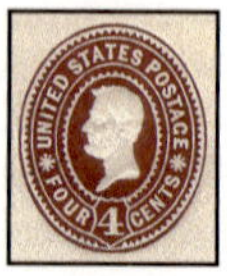

Lincoln — U81

Bust pointed but not draped.

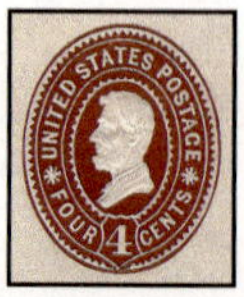

U82

Bust broad and draped.

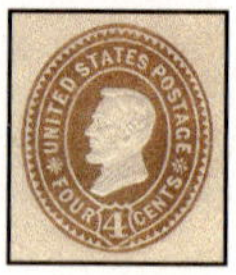

U83

Head larger, inner oval has no notches.

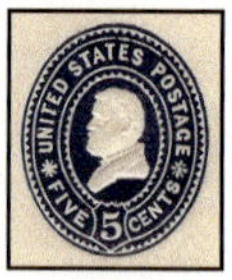

Grant — U84

Similar to design of 1887-95 but smaller.

**1899**

| | | | |
|---|---|---|---|
| **U352** | U77 1c green | 2.75 | .25 |
| **U353** | U77 1c green, *amber* | 5.00 | 1.50 |
| **U354** | U77 1c green, *oriental buff* | 10.00 | 2.75 |
| **U355** | U77 1c green, *blue* | 10.00 | 7.50 |
| **U356** | U77 1c green, *manila* | 2.50 | .95 |
| **W357** | U77 1c green, *manila* | 2.75 | 1.10 |
| **U358** | U78 2c carmine | 3.00 | 1.75 |
| **U359** | U78 2c car, *amb* | 15.00 | 12.50 |
| **U360** | U78 2c carmine, *oriental buff* | 17.50 | 11.00 |
| **U361** | U78 2c carmine, *blue* | 55.00 | 35.00 |
| **U362** | U79 2c carmine | .35 | .25 |
| | *a.* 2c dark lake | 30.00 | 30.00 |
| **U363** | U79 2c car, *amb* | 1.75 | .25 |
| **U364** | U79 2c carmine, *oriental buff* | 1.20 | .25 |
| **U365** | U79 2c carmine, *blue* | 1.50 | .55 |
| **W366** | U79 2c car, *man* | 9.00 | 3.25 |
| **U367** | U80 2c carmine | 5.00 | 2.75 |
| **U368** | U80 2c car, *amb* | 8.00 | 6.50 |
| **U369** | U80 2c carmine, *oriental buff* | 17.50 | 12.50 |
| **U370** | U80 2c carmine, *blue* | 11.00 | 10.00 |
| **U371** | U81 4c brown | 15.00 | 12.50 |
| **U372** | U81 4c brown, *amber* | 15.00 | 12.50 |
| **U373** | U82 4c brown | *6,500.* | 1,000. |
| **U374** | U83 4c brown | 10.00 | 8.00 |
| **U375** | U83 4c brown, *amber* | 60.00 | 25.00 |
| **W376** | U83 4c brown, *manila* | 12.50 | 12.50 |
| **U377** | U84 5c blue | 9.00 | 9.00 |
| **U378** | U84 5c blue, *amber* | 10.00 | 10.00 |

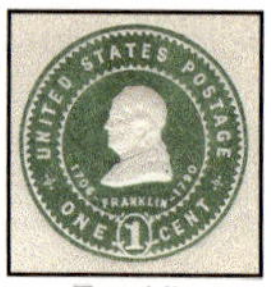

Franklin U85

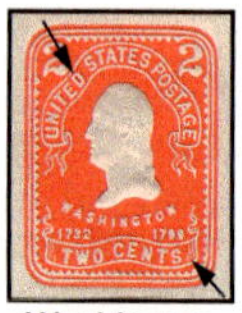

Washington U86

"D" of "UNITED" contains vertical line at right that parallels the left vertical line. One short and two long vertical lines at the right of "CENTS."

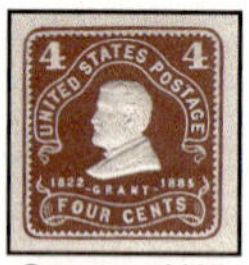

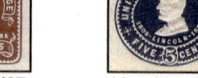

Grant — U87

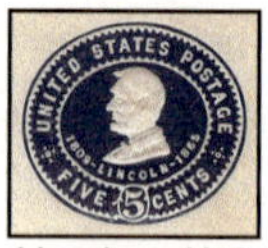

Lincoln — U88

**1903**

| | | | |
|---|---|---|---|
| **U379** | U85 1c green | .75 | .25 |
| **U380** | U85 1c green, *amber* | 10.00 | 2.00 |
| **U381** | U85 1c green, *oriental buff* | 12.50 | 2.50 |
| **U382** | U85 1c green, *blue* | 15.00 | 2.50 |
| **U383** | U85 1c green, *manila* | 3.50 | .90 |
| **W384** | U85 1c green, *manila* | 2.50 | .40 |
| | *a.* Double impression, entire letter sheet | *275.00* | |
| **U385** | U86 2c carmine | .40 | .25 |
| | *a.* 2c pink | 2.00 | 1.50 |
| | *b.* 2c red | 2.00 | 1.50 |
| **U386** | U86 2c carmine, *amber* | 2.00 | .50 |
| | *a.* 2c pink, *amber* | 5.50 | 3.00 |
| | *b.* 2c red, *amber* | 12.50 | 7.00 |
| **U387** | U86 2c carmine, *oriental buff* | 2.00 | .30 |
| | *a.* 2c pink, *oriental buff* | 3.50 | 2.00 |
| | *b.* 2c red, *oriental buff* | 4.00 | 2.25 |
| **U388** | U86 2c carmine, *blue* | 1.75 | .50 |
| | *a.* 2c pink, *blue* | 17.50 | 14.00 |
| | *b.* 2c red, *blue* | 17.50 | 14.00 |
| **W389** | U86 2c carmine, *manila* | 15.00 | 9.00 |
| **U390** | U87 4c choc | 17.50 | 11.00 |
| **U391** | U87 4c choc, *amber* | 17.50 | 11.00 |
| **W392** | U87 4c choc, *manila* | 20.00 | 12.50 |
| **U393** | U88 5c blue | 15.00 | 11.00 |
| **U394** | U88 5c blue, *amber* | 15.00 | 11.00 |

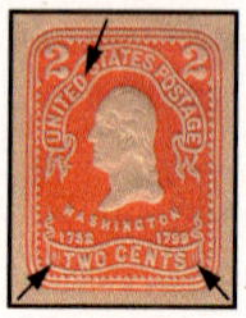

U89

Re-cut die — "D" of "UNITED" is well rounded at right. The three lines at the right of "CENTS" and at the left of "TWO" are usually all short; the lettering is heavier and the ends of the ribbons slightly changed.

**1904** **Re-cut Die**

| | | | |
|---|---|---|---|
| **U395** | U89 2c carmine | .75 | .25 |
| | *a.* 2c pink | 5.00 | 2.50 |
| **U396** | U89 2c carmine, *amber* | 7.50 | 1.00 |
| | *a.* 2c pink, *amber* | 8.50 | 3.00 |
| **U397** | U89 2c carmine, *oriental buff* | 5.00 | 1.10 |
| | *a.* 2c pink, *oriental buff* | 6.50 | 2.75 |
| **U398** | U89 2c carmine, *blue* | 3.75 | .90 |
| | *a.* 2c pink, *blue* | 5.00 | 2.50 |
| **W399** | U89 2c carmine, *manila* | 12.50 | 8.00 |
| | *a.* 2c pink, *manila* | 25.00 | 17.50 |
| | *b.* Double impression, entire | *375.00* | |

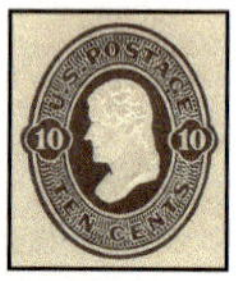

Franklin — U90

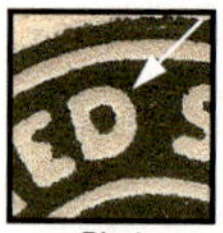

Die 1

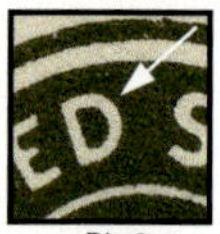

Die 2

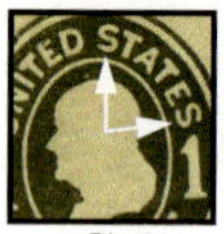

Die 3

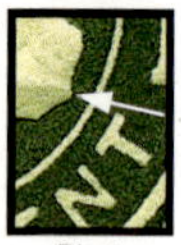

Die 4

Die 1 — Wide "D" in "UNITED."
Die 2 — Narrow "D" in "UNITED."
Die 3 — Wide "S-S" in "STATES" (1910).
Die 4 — Sharp angle at back of bust, "N" and "E" of "ONE" are parallel (1912).

**1907-16** **Die 1**

| | | | |
|---|---|---|---|
| **U400** | U90 1c green | .35 | .25 |
| | *a.* Die 2 | .85 | .25 |
| | *b.* Die 3 | .85 | .55 |
| | *c.* Die 4 | .85 | .25 |
| **U401** | U90 1c green, *amber* | 2.00 | .40 |
| | *a.* Die 2 | 2.50 | 1.00 |
| | *b.* Die 3 | 3.25 | 3.00 |
| | *c.* Die 4 | 2.00 | 1.00 |
| **U402** | U90 1c green, *oriental buff* | 9.00 | .75 |
| | *a.* Die 2 | 12.50 | 1.50 |
| | *b.* Die 3 | 14.00 | 1.50 |
| | *c.* Die 4 | 3.50 | .75 |
| **U403** | U90 1c green, *blue* | 9.00 | .75 |
| | *a.* Die 2 | 12.50 | 3.00 |
| | *b.* Die 3 | 11.50 | 3.00 |
| | *c.* Die 4 | .75 | .65 |
| **U404** | U90 1c green, *manila* | 2.00 | 1.90 |
| | *a.* Die 3 | 4.50 | 3.00 |
| **W405** | U90 1c green, *manila* | .65 | .25 |
| | *a.* Die 2 | 60.00 | 25.00 |
| | *b.* Die 3 | 11.00 | 4.00 |

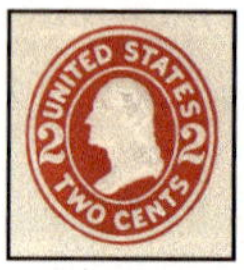

Washington — U91 — brown red

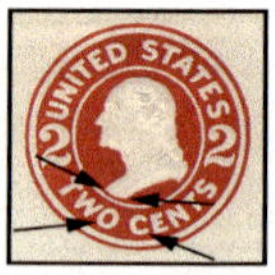

Die 1, Washington — U91 — carmine

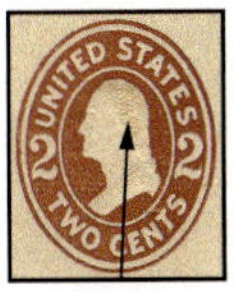
Die 2

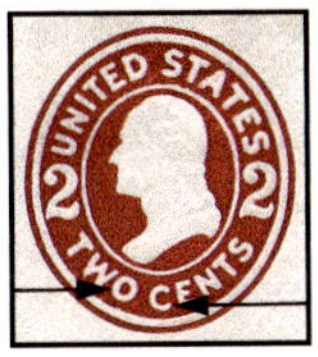
Die 3

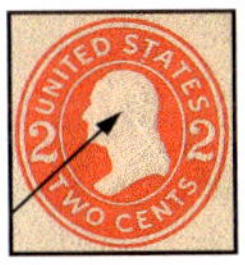
Die 4

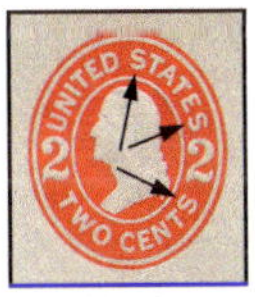
Die 5

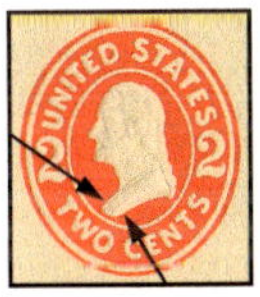
Die 6

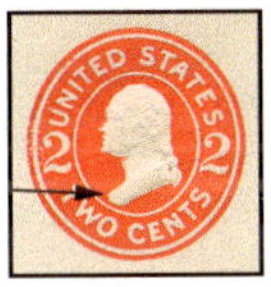
Die 7

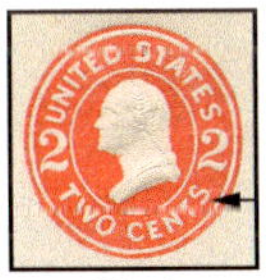
Die 8

Die 1 — Oval "O" in "TWO" and "C" in "CENTS." Front of bust broad.
Die 2 — Similar to 1 but hair re-cut in two distinct locks at top of head.
Die 3 — Round "O" in "TWO" and "C" in "CENTS," coarse lettering.
Die 4 — Similar to 3 but lettering fine and clear, hair lines clearly embossed. Inner oval thin and clear.
Die 5 — All "S's" wide (1910).
Die 6 — Similar to 1 but front of bust narrow (1913).
Die 7 — Similar to 6 but upper corner of front of bust cut away (1916).
Die 8 — Similar to 7 but lower stroke of "S" in "CENTS" is a straight line. Hair as in Die 2 (1916).

**Die 1**

| | | | |
|---|---|---|---|
| **U406** | U91 2c brown red | .90 | .25 |
| *a.* | Die 2 | 40.00 | 7.00 |
| *b.* | Die 3 | .80 | .25 |
| **U407** | U91 2c brown red, *amber* | 6.50 | 2.00 |
| *a.* | Die 2 | 350.00 | 65.00 |
| *b.* | Die 3 | 4.50 | 1.25 |
| **U408** | U91 2c brown red, *oriental buff* | 8.75 | 1.50 |
| *a.* | Die 2 | 275.00 | 125.00 |
| *b.* | Die 3 | 7.50 | 2.50 |
| **U409** | U91 2c brn red, *blue* | 5.75 | 2.00 |
| *a.* | Die 2 | 375.00 | 200.00 |
| *b.* | Die 3 | 5.75 | 1.75 |
| **W410** | U91 2c brn red, *man* | 35.00 | 35.00 |
| **U411** | U91 2c carmine | .35 | .25 |
| *a.* | Die 2 | .75 | .25 |
| *b.* | Die 3 | .75 | .25 |
| *c.* | Die 4 | .65 | .25 |
| *d.* | Die 5 | .65 | .30 |
| *e.* | Die 6 | .60 | .25 |
| *f.* | Die 7 | 3.00 | 3.00 |
| *g.* | Die 8 | 37.50 | 25.00 |
| *h.* | #U411 with added impression of #U400, entire | 475.00 | |
| *i.* | #U411 with added impression of #U416a, entire | 475.00 | |
| *k.* | As No. U411, double impression, entire | 175.00 | |
| **U412** | U91 2c carmine, *amb* | .50 | .25 |
| *a.* | Die 2 | 1.00 | .25 |
| *b.* | Die 3 | 2.25 | 2.00 |
| *c.* | Die 4 | .55 | .25 |
| *d.* | Die 5 | .90 | .35 |
| *e.* | Die 6 | .70 | .25 |
| *f.* | Die 7 | 35.00 | 25.00 |
| **U413** | U91 2c car, *oriental buff* | .55 | .25 |
| *a.* | Die 2 | 2.00 | .45 |
| *b.* | Die 3 | 9.00 | 3.00 |
| *c.* | Die 4 | .55 | 1.00 |
| *d.* | Die 5 | 3.50 | 1.25 |
| *e.* | Die 6 | 1.00 | .70 |
| *f.* | Die 7 | 100.00 | 45.00 |
| *g.* | Die 8 | 25.00 | 17.50 |
| **U414** | U91 2c carmine, *blue* | .55 | .25 |
| *a.* | Die 2 | 1.00 | 1.00 |
| *b.* | Die 3 | 2.75 | 2.00 |
| *c.* | Die 4 | .50 | .50 |
| *d.* | Die 5 | 1.00 | .45 |
| *e.* | Die 6 | .65 | .30 |
| *f.* | Die 7 | 37.50 | 25.00 |
| *g.* | Die 8 | 37.50 | 25.00 |
| **W415** | U91 2c car, *manila* | 5.00 | 2.00 |
| *a.* | Die 2 | 5.50 | 1.25 |
| *b.* | Die 5 | 5.50 | 2.50 |
| *c.* | Die 7 | 120.00 | 97.50 |

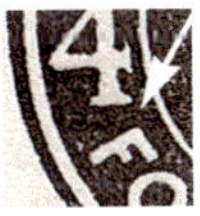
U90 4c Die 1

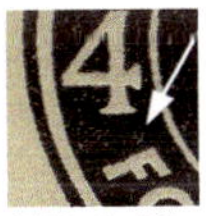
U90 4c Die 2

Die 1 — "F" close to (1mm) left "4."
Die 2 — "F" far from (1¾mm) left "4."

| | | | |
|---|---|---|---|
| **U416** | U90 4c black, die 2, laid paper | 2.00 | 1.50 |
| *a.* | Die 1 | 1.50 | 2.00 |
| **U417** | U90 4c black, *amb*, die 2 | 7.50 | 2.50 |
| *a.* | Die 1 | .75 | 2.00 |

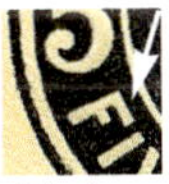
Die 1 — Tall "F" in "FIVE"

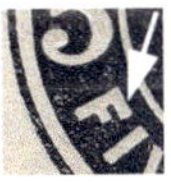
Die 2 — Short "F" in "FIVE"

| | | | |
|---|---|---|---|
| **U418** | U91 5c Die 2 | 1.50 | 1.50 |
| *a.* | Die 1 | 7.00 | 2.25 |
| *b.* | 5c blue, *buff*, die 2 (error) | 3,250. | |
| *c.* | 5c blue, *blue*, die 2 (error) | 3,000. | |
| *d.* | As "c," die 1 (error), entire | 6,250. | |
| **U419** | U91 5c blue, *amber*, die 2, laid paper | 1.00 | .75 |
| *a.* | Die 1 | 15.00 | 12.00 |

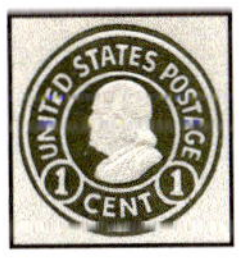
Franklin — U92

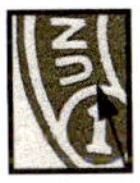
Die 1

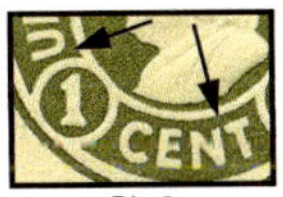
Die 2

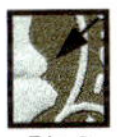
Die 3

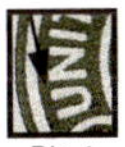
Die 4

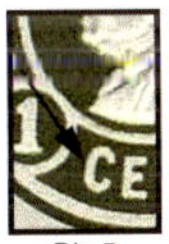
Die 5

(The 1c and 4c dies are the same except for figures of value.)
Die 1 — UNITED nearer inner circle than outer circle.
Die 2 — Large U, large NT closely spaced.
Die 3 — Knob of hair at back of neck. Large NT widely spaced.
Die 4 — UNITED nearer outer circle than inner circle.
Die 5 — Narrow oval C, (also O and G).

**1915-32** **Die 1**

| | | | |
|---|---|---|---|
| **U420** | U92 1c green ('17) | .25 | .25 |
| *a.* | Die 2 | 100.00 | 55.00 |
| *b.* | Die 3 | .35 | .25 |
| *c.* | Die 4 | .55 | .40 |
| *d.* | Die 5 | .45 | .35 |
| **U421** | U92 1c grn, *amber* ('17) | .55 | .30 |
| *a.* | Die 2 | 400.00 | 175.00 |
| *b.* | Die 3 | 1.40 | .65 |
| *c.* | Die 4 | 1.90 | .85 |
| *d.* | Die 5 | 1.10 | .55 |
| **U422** | U92 1c grn, *oriental buff* ('17) | 2.40 | .90 |
| *a.* | Die 4 | 5.50 | 1.25 |
| **U423** | U92 1c grn, *bl* ('17) | .50 | .35 |
| *a.* | Die 3 | .80 | .45 |
| *b.* | Die 4 | 1.40 | .65 |
| *c.* | Die 5 | .85 | .35 |
| **U424** | U92 1c grn, *manila* (unglazed) ('16) | 6.50 | 4.00 |
| **W425** | U92 1c grn, *manila* (unglazed) ('16) | .30 | .25 |
| *a.* | Die 3 | 175.00 | 125.00 |
| **U426** | U92 1c grn, *brown* (glazed) ('20) | 45.00 | 16.00 |
| **W427** | U92 1c grn, *brown* (glazed) ('20) | 65.00 | 35.00 |
| *a.* | Printed on unglazed side | *400.00* | |
| | Entire | *750.00* | |
| *b.* | Unglazed on both sides | | *150.00* |
| **U428** | U92 1c grn, *brown* (unglazed) ('20) | 12.50 | 7.50 |
| **W428A** | U92 1c grn, *brown* (unglazed) ('20) | | *3,000.* |

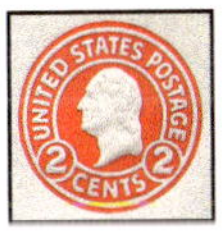
Washington — U93

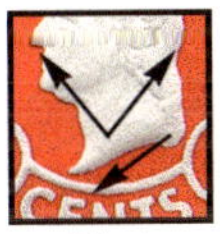
Die 1

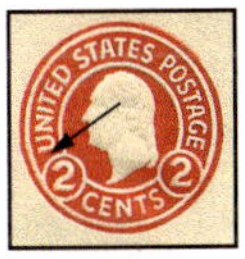
Die 2

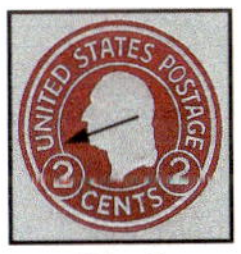
Die 3

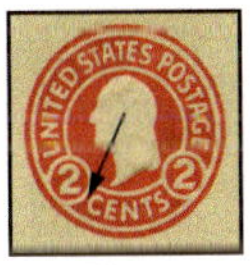
Die 4

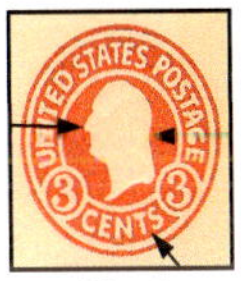
Die 5

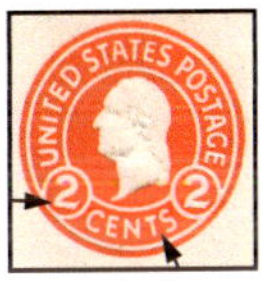
Die 6

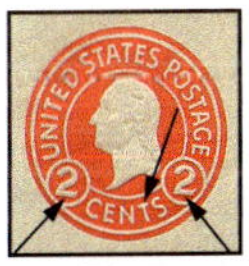
Die 7

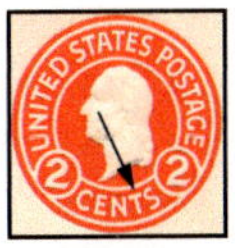
Die 8

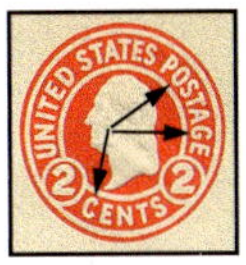
Die 9

(The 1½c, 2c, 3c, 5c, and 6c dies are the same except for figures of value.)
Die 1 — Letters broad. Numerals vertical. Large head (9¼mm). from tip of nose to back of neck. E closer to inner circle than N of cents.
Die 2 — Similar to 1; but U far from left circle.
Die 3 — Similar to 2; but all inner circles very thin (Rejected die).
Die 4 — Large head as in Die 1. C of CENTS close to circle. Baseline of right numeral "2" slants downward to right. Left numeral "2" is larger.
Die 5 — Small head (8¾mm) from tip of nose to back of neck. T and S of CENTS close at bottom.
Die 6 — Similar to 5; but T and S of CENTS far apart at bottom. Left numeral slopes to right.
Die 7 — Large head. Both numerals slope to right. Clean cut lettering. All letters T have short top strokes.
Die 8 — Similar to 7; but all letters T have long top strokes.
Die 9 — Narrow oval C (also O and G).

**1915-32** **Die 1**

| | | | |
|---|---|---|---|
| **U429** | U93 2c carmine | .25 | .25 |
| *a.* | Die 2 | 15.00 | 7.00 |
| *b.* | Die 3 | 40.00 | 50.00 |
| *c.* | Die 4 | 25.00 | 15.00 |
| *d.* | Die 5 | .55 | .35 |
| *e.* | Die 6 | .65 | .30 |
| *f.* | Die 7 | .70 | .25 |
| *g.* | Die 8 | .50 | .25 |
| *h.* | Die 9 | .50 | .25 |
| *i.* | 2c green (error), die 1, entire | *12,500.* | |
| *j.* | #U429 with added impression of #U420 | 600.00 | |
| *k.* | #U429 with added impression of #U416a, entire | *3,500.* | |
| *l.* | #U429 with added impression of #U400, entire | 950.00 | |
| *m.* | #U429, double impression, entire | 1,500. | |
| *n.* | As "f," double impression, entire | *750.00* | |
| *o.* | As "e," triple impression | — | |
| *p.* | As "m," second impression on side flap, entire | | *250.00* |
| **U430** | U93 2c car, *amber* ('16) | .30 | .25 |
| *a.* | Die 2 | 20.00 | 12.50 |
| *b.* | Die 4 | 50.00 | 25.00 |
| *c.* | Die 5 | 1.60 | .35 |
| *d.* | Die 6 | 1.25 | .40 |
| *e.* | Die 7 | .75 | .35 |
| *f.* | Die 8 | .70 | .30 |
| *g.* | Die 9 | .65 | .25 |
| *h.* | As No. U430, with added impression of 4c black (#U416a), entire | *600.00* | |
| *i.* | As "g," with added impression of 2c car. die 1 on side flap, entire | — | |
| **U431** | U93 2c car, *oriental buff* ('16) | 2.25 | .65 |
| *a.* | Die 2 | 180.00 | 75.00 |
| *b.* | Die 4 | 75.00 | 60.00 |
| *c.* | Die 5 | 3.50 | 2.00 |
| *d.* | Die 6 | 3.50 | 2.00 |
| *e.* | Die 7 | 3.50 | 2.00 |
| **U432** | U93 2c car, *blue* ('16) | .30 | .25 |
| *b.* | Die 2 | 35.00 | 25.00 |
| *c.* | Die 3 | 130.00 | 90.00 |
| *d.* | Die 4 | 60.00 | 50.00 |
| *e.* | Die 5 | 1.10 | .30 |
| *f.* | Die 6 | 1.10 | .40 |
| *g.* | Die 7 | .85 | .35 |
| *h.* | Die 8 | .65 | .25 |
| *i.* | Die 9 | 1.00 | .30 |
| *j.* | 2c purple (error), die 9 | — | |
| *k.* | Double impression | 650.00 | |
| **U432A** | U93 2c car, *manila*, die 7, entire | *50,000.* | |
| **W433** | U93 2c car, *manila*, ('16) | .25 | .25 |
| **W434** | U93 2c car, *brn* (glazed) ('20) | 70.00 | 45.00 |
| **W435** | U93 2c car, *brn* (unglazed) ('20) | 90.00 | 60.00 |

198 UNITED STATES

| | | | |
|---|---|---|---|
| U436 | U93 3c purple ('32) | .30 | .25 |
| a. | 3c dark violet, die 1 ('17) | .60 | .25 |
| b. | 3c dark violet, die 5 ('17) | 1.75 | .75 |
| c. | 3c dark violet, die 6 ('17) | 2.10 | 1.40 |
| d. | 3c dark violet, die 7 ('17) | 1.50 | .95 |
| e. | 3c purple, die 7 ('32) | .70 | .30 |
| f. | 3c purple, die 9 ('32) | .45 | .25 |
| g. | 3c carmine (error), die 1 | 35.00 | 35.00 |
| h. | 3c carmine (error), die 5 | 27.50 | — |
| i. | #U436 with added impression of #U420, entire | 900.00 | |
| j. | #U436 with added impression of #U429, entire | 900.00 | 950.00 |
| k. | As "f," double impression, preprinted, entire | 600.00 | |
| U437 | U93 3c purple, amb ('32) | .35 | .25 |
| a. | 3c dk vio, die 1 ('17) | 5.50 | 1.25 |
| b. | 3c dk vio, die 5 ('17) | 8.50 | 2.50 |
| c. | 3c dk vio, die 6 ('17) | 8.50 | 2.50 |
| d. | 3c dk vio, die 7 ('17) | 8.50 | 2.25 |
| e. | 3c pur, die 7 ('32) | .75 | .25 |
| f. | 3c pur, die 9 ('32) | .55 | .25 |
| g. | 3c carmine (error), die 5 | 375.00 | 400.00 |
| h. | 3c black (error), die 1 | 190.00 | — |
| U438 | U93 3c dk vio, oriental buff ('17) | 22.50 | 5.50 |
| a. | Die 5 | 22.50 | 5.50 |
| b. | Die 6 | 30.00 | 8.00 |
| c. | Die 7 | 30.00 | 10.00 |
| U439 | U93 3c purple, bl ('32) | .35 | .25 |
| a. | 3c dark violet, die 1 ('17) | 7.00 | 2.00 |
| b. | 3c dark violet, die 5 ('17) | 7.50 | 6.00 |
| c. | 3c dark violet, die 6 ('17) | 7.50 | 6.00 |
| d. | 3c dark violet, die 7 ('17) | 10.00 | 6.00 |
| e. | 3c purple, die 7 ('32) | .75 | .25 |
| f. | 3c purple, die 9 ('32) | .60 | .25 |
| g. | 3c carmine (error), die 5 | 225.00 | 300.00 |
| U440 | U92 4c black ('18) | 1.75 | .60 |
| a. | With added impression of 2c carmine (#U429), die 1, entire | 450.00 | |
| U441 | U92 4c black, amb ('18) | 3.00 | .85 |
| a. | 4c black, amb, with added impression of 2c car (#U429), die 1 | 175.00 | |
| U442 | U92 4c blk, bl ('21) | 3.25 | .85 |
| U443 | U93 5c blue ('18) | 3.25 | 2.75 |
| U444 | U93 5c blue, amber ('18) | 4.00 | 1.60 |
| U445 | U93 5c bl, blue ('21) | 3.25 | 3.25 |

For 1½c and 6c see Nos. U481-W485, U529-U531.

**Double or triple surcharge listings of 1920-25 are for examples with surcharge directly or partly upon the stamp.**

**Surcharged on 1874-1920 Envelopes indicated by Numbers in Parentheses**

Type 1

**1920-21   Surcharged in Black**

| | | | |
|---|---|---|---|
| U446 | U93 2c on 3c dark vio (U436a, die 1) | 11.00 | 10.00 |
| a. | On No. U436b (die 5) | 11.00 | 10.00 |
| b. | As U446, double surcharge | 140.00 | |

**Surcharged**

Type 2

**Rose Surcharge**

| | | | |
|---|---|---|---|
| U447 | U93 2c on 3c dark vio (U436a, die 1) | 8.00 | 7.50 |
| b. | On No. U436c (die 6) | 10.00 | 8.50 |

**Black Surcharge**

| | | | |
|---|---|---|---|
| U447A | U92 2c on 1c green (U420, die 1) Entire | 2,250. | |
| U447C | U93 2c on 2c carmine (U429, die 1) | — | |
| U447D | U93 2c on 2c car, amb (U430, die 1) | 12,000. | |
| U448 | U93 2c on 3c dark vio (U436a, die 1) | 2.75 | 2.00 |
| a. | On No. U436b (die 5) | 2.75 | 2.00 |
| b. | On No. U436c (die 6) | 3.50 | 2.00 |
| c. | On No. U436d (die 7) | 2.75 | 2.00 |
| U449 | U93 2c on 3c dk vio, amb (U437a, die 1) | 6.50 | 6.00 |
| a. | On No. U437b (die 5) | 13.00 | 7.50 |
| b. | On No. U437c (die 6) | 9.50 | 6.00 |
| c. | On No. U437d (die 7) | 8.50 | 6.50 |
| U450 | U93 2c on 3c dk vio, oriental buff (U438, die 1) | 12.50 | 15.00 |
| a. | On No. U438a (die 5) | 15.00 | 15.00 |
| b. | On No. U438b (die 6) | 15.00 | 15.00 |
| c. | On No. U438c (die 7) | 130.00 | 90.00 |
| U451 | U93 2c on 3c dk vio, blue (U439a, die 1) | 11.00 | 10.50 |
| b. | On No. U439b (die 5) | 11.00 | 10.50 |
| c. | On No. U439c (die 6) | 11.00 | 10.50 |
| d. | On No. U439d (die 7) | 22.50 | 22.50 |

**Surcharged**

Type 3

**Bars 2mm apart, 25 to 26mm in length from outer edges of end bars**

| | | | |
|---|---|---|---|
| U451A | U90 2c on 1c green (U400, die 1) | 25,000. | |
| U452 | U92 2c on 1c green (U420, die 1) | 1,750. | |
| a. | On No. U420b (die 3) | 2,750. | |
| b. | As No. U452, double surcharge | 3,750. | |
| U453 | U91 2c on 2c car (U411b, die 3) | 3,500. | |
| a. | On No. U411 (die 1) | 3,250. | |
| U453B | U91 2c on 2c car, bl (U414e, die 6) | 1,250. | 750.00 |
| U453C | U91 2c on 2c car, oriental buff (U413e, die 6) | 1,400. | 750.00 |
| d. | On No. U413 (die 1) | 1,400. | |
| U454 | U93 2c on 2c car (U429e, die 6) | 125.00 | |
| a. | On No. U429 (die 1) | 300.00 | |
| b. | On No. U429d (die 5) | 500.00 | |
| c. | On No. U429f (die 7) | 125.00 | |
| U455 | U93 2c on 2c car, amb (U430, die 1) | 1,250. | |
| a. | On No. U430d (die 6) | 1,500. | |
| b. | On No. U430e (die 7) | 1,500. | |
| U456 | U93 2c on 2c car, oriental buff (U431a, die 2) | 225.00 | |
| a. | On No. U431c (die 5) | 225.00 | |
| b. | On No. U431e (die 7) | 800.00 | |
| c. | As No. U456, double surcharge | 700.00 | |
| U457 | U93 2c on 2c car, bl (U432f, die 6) | 500.00 | |
| a. | On No. U432e (die 5) | 275.00 | |
| b. | On No. U432g (die 7) | 650.00 | |
| U458 | U93 2c on 3c dark vio (U436a, die 1) | .50 | .35 |
| a. | On No. U436b (die 5) | .50 | .40 |
| b. | On No. U436c (die 6) | .50 | .35 |
| c. | On No. U436d (die 7) | .50 | .35 |
| d. | As U458, double surcharge | 25.00 | 7.50 |
| e. | As U458, triple surcharge | 90.00 | |
| f. | As U458, dbl. surch., 1 in magenta | 90.00 | |
| g. | As U458, dbl. surch., types 2 & 3 | 140.00 | |
| h. | As "a," double surcharge | 27.50 | 15.00 |
| i. | As "a," triple surcharge | 110.00 | |
| j. | As "a," double surch., both magenta | 110.00 | |
| k. | As "b," double surcharge | 25.00 | 8.00 |
| l. | As "c," double surcharge | 25.00 | 8.00 |
| m. | As "c," triple surcharge | 110.00 | |
| n. | Double impression of indicia, single surcharge, entire | 450.00 | |
| U459 | U93 2c on 3c dk vio, amb (U437c, die 6) | 3.00 | 1.00 |
| a. | On No. U437 (die 1) | 4.00 | 1.00 |
| b. | On No. U437b (die 5) | 4.00 | 1.00 |
| c. | On No. U437d (die 7) | 3.00 | 1.00 |
| d. | As U459, double surcharge | 35.00 | |
| e. | As "a," double surcharge | 35.00 | |
| f. | As "b," double surcharge | 35.00 | |
| g. | As "b," double surcharge, types 2 & 3 | 125.00 | |
| h. | As "c," double surcharge | 35.00 | |
| U460 | U93 2c on 3c dk vio, oriental buff (U438a, die 5) | 3.50 | 2.00 |
| a. | On No. U438 (die 1) | 3.50 | 2.00 |
| b. | On No. U438b (die 6) | 4.00 | 2.00 |
| c. | As #U460, double surcharge | 20.00 | |
| d. | As "a," double surcharge | 20.00 | |
| e. | As "b," double surcharge | 20.00 | |
| f. | As "b," triple surcharge | 150.00 | |
| U461 | U93 2c on 3c dk vio, bl (U439a, die 1) | 6.00 | 1.00 |
| a. | On No. U439b (die 5) | 6.00 | 1.00 |
| b. | On No. U439c (die 6) | 6.00 | 2.50 |
| c. | On No. U439d (die 7) | 12.50 | 7.50 |
| d. | As #U461, double surcharge | 17.50 | |
| e. | As "a," double surcharge | 17.50 | |
| f. | As "b," double surcharge | 17.50 | |
| g. | As "c," double surcharge | 17.50 | |
| U462 | U87 2c on 4c choc (U390) | 475.00 | 260.00 |
| U463 | U87 2c on 4c choc, amb (U391) | 750.00 | 350.00 |
| U463A | U90 2c on 4c black (U416, die 2) | 800.00 | 400.00 |
| U464 | U93 2c on 5c blue (U443) | 850.00 | |

**Surcharged**

Type 4

**Bars 1 mm apart, 21 to 23 mm in length from outer edges of end bars**

| | | | |
|---|---|---|---|
| U465 | U92 2c on 1c green (U420, die 1) | 900.00 | |
| a. | On No. U420b (die 3) | 1,100. | |
| U466 | U91 2c on 2c car (U411e, die 6), entire | 22,500. | |
| U466A | U93 2c on 2c carmine (U429, die 1) | 700.00 | |
| c. | On No. U429d (die 5) | 900.00 | |
| d. | On No. U429e (die 6) | 900.00 | |
| e. | On No. U429f (die 7) | 750.00 | |
| U466B | U93 2c on 2c car, amb (U430) | 15,000. | |
| U466C | U93 2c on 2c car, oriental buff (U431), entire | 15,000. | |
| U466D | U25 2c on 3c green, die 2 (U82) | 9,500. | |
| U467 | U45 2c on 3c green, die 2 (U163) | 325.00 | |
| U468 | U93 2c on 3c dark vio (U436a, die 1) | .70 | .45 |
| a. | On No. U436b (die 5) | .70 | .50 |
| b. | On No. U436c (die 6) | .70 | .50 |
| c. | On No. U436d (die 7) | .70 | .50 |
| d. | As #U468, double surcharge | 20.00 | |
| e. | As #U468, triple surcharge | 90.00 | |
| f. | As #U468, dbl. surch., types 2 & 4 | 125.00 | |
| g. | As "a," double surcharge | 20.00 | |
| h. | As "b," double surcharge | 20.00 | |
| i. | As "c," double surcharge | 20.00 | |
| j. | As "c," triple surcharge | 100.00 | |
| k. | As "c," inverted surcharge | 75.00 | |
| l. | 2c on 3c carmine (error), (U436h) | 600.00 | |
| m. | As "U468, triple surcharge, one inverted, entire | 700.00 | |
| U469 | U93 2c on 3c dk vio, amb (U437a, die 1) | 3.75 | 2.25 |
| a. | On No. U437b (die 5) | 3.75 | 2.25 |
| b. | On No. U437c (die 6) | 3.75 | 2.25 |
| c. | On No. U437d (die 7) | 3.75 | 2.25 |
| d. | As #U469, double surcharge | 30.00 | |
| e. | As "a," double surcharge | 30.00 | |
| f. | As "a," double surcharge, types 2 & 4 | 100.00 | |
| g. | As "b," double surcharge | 30.00 | |
| h. | As "c," double surcharge | 30.00 | |
| U470 | U93 2c on 3c dk vio, oriental buff (U438, die 1) | 6.00 | 2.50 |
| a. | On No. U438a (die 5) | 6.00 | 2.50 |
| b. | On No. U438b (die 6) | 6.00 | 2.50 |
| c. | On No. U438c (die 7) | 42.50 | 32.50 |
| d. | As U470, double surcharge | 25.00 | |
| e. | As #U470, double surch., types 2 & 4 | 80.00 | |
| f. | As "a," double surcharge | 25.00 | |
| g. | As "b," double surcharge | 25.00 | |
| U471 | U93 2c on 3c dk vio, bl (U439a, die 1) | 6.00 | 1.75 |
| a. | On No. U439b (die 5) | 7.00 | 1.75 |
| b. | On No. U439c (die 6) | 7.00 | 1.75 |
| c. | On No. U439d (die 7) | 10.00 | 10.00 |
| d. | As #U471, double surcharge | 25.00 | |
| e. | As #U471, double surch., types 2 & 4 | 160.00 | |
| f. | As "a," double surcharge | 25.00 | |
| g. | As "b," double surcharge | 25.00 | |
| U471A | U83 2c on 4c brown, (U374), entire | 500.00 | |
| U472 | U87 2c on 4c choc (U390) | 11.00 | 11.00 |
| a. | Double surcharge | 150.00 | |
| U473 | U87 2c on 4c choc, amb (U391) | 17.00 | 10.00 |

**Surcharged**

**Double Surcharge, Type 4 and 1c as above**

| | | | |
|---|---|---|---|
| U474 | U93 2c on 1c on 3c dark violet (U436a, die 1) | 175.00 | 500.00 |
| a. | On No. U436b (die 5) | 200.00 | |
| b. | On No. U436d (die 7) | 850.00 | |
| U475 | U93 2c on 1c on 3c dk vio, amb (U437a, die 1) | 150.00 | |

**Surcharged**

Type 5

| | | | |
|---|---|---|---|
| U476 | U93 2c on 3c dk vio, amb (U437a, die 1) | 200.00 | |
| a. | On No. U437c (die 6) | 700.00 | |
| b. | As #U476, double surcharge | — | |

**Surcharged**

Type 6

| | | | |
|---|---|---|---|
| U477 | U93 2c on 3c dark vio (U436a, die 1) | 120.00 | |
| a. | On No. U436b (die 5) | 250.00 | |
| b. | On No. U436c (die 6) | 250.00 | |
| c. | On No. U436d (die 7) | 250.00 | |
| U478 | U93 2c on 3c dk vio, amb (U437a, die 1) | 250.00 | |

Handstamped Surcharge in Black or Violet — Type 7

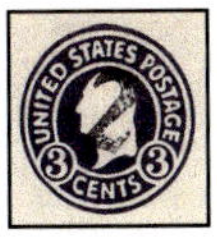

**U479** U93 2c on 3c dark violet (Bk) (U436a, die 1) 240.00 —
*a.* On No. U436b (die 5) 625.00
*b.* On No. U436d (die 7) 425.00
**U480** U93 2c on 3c dark violet (V) (U436d, die 7) *4,250.*
*a.* Double overprint —

Expertization by competent authorities is required for Nos. U476-U480.

### Type of 1916-32 Issue

**1925-34** **Die 1**

**U481** U93 1½c brown .25 .25
*a.* Die 8 .70 .25
*b.* 1½c purple, die 1 (error) ('34) 55.00
**U482** U93 1½c brown, *amber* .90 .40
*a.* Die 8 1.75 .75
**U483** U93 1½c brown, *bl* 1.60 .95
*a.* Die 8 2.40 1.25
**U484** U93 1½c brown, *manila* 5.00 3.00
**W485** U93 1½c brown, *manila* .85 .25
*a.* With added impression of #W433 120.00 —

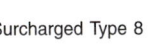

Surcharged Type 8

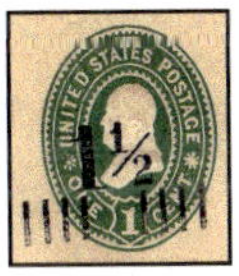

**1925** **On Envelopes of 1887**

**U486** U71 1½c on 2c grn (U311) 500.00
**U487** U71 1½c on 2c green, *amb* (U312) 650.00
**U488** U77 1½c on 1c green (U352) 500.00
**U489** U77 1½c on 1c grn, *amb* (U353) 110.00 60.
**U490** U90 1½c on 1c green (U400, die 1) 6.25 3.50
*a.* On No. U400a (die 2) 15.00 9.00
*b.* On No. U400b (die 3) 35.00 17.50
*c.* On No. U400c (die 4) 9.00 2.50
**U491** U90 1½c on 1c grn, *amb* (U401c, die 4) 7.00 3.00
*a.* On No. U401 (die 1) 12.50 3.50
*b.* On No. U401a (die 2) 110.00 70.00
*c.* On No. U401b (die 3) 60.00 50.00
**U492** U90 1½c on 1c grn, *oriental buff* (U402a, die 2) 500.00 150.00
*a.* On No. U402c (die 4) 700.00 250.00
**U493** U90 1½c on 1c grn, *bl* (U403c, die 4) 100.00 65.00
*a.* On No. U403a (die 2) 100.00 67.50
**U494** U90 1½c on 1c grn, *man* (U404, die 1) 250.00 100.00
*a.* On No. U404a (die 3) 700.00
**U495** U92 1½c on 1c green (U420, die 1) .80 .25
*a.* On No. U420a (die 2) 80.00 52.50
*b.* On No. U420b (die 3) 2.10 .70
*c.* On No. U420c (die 4) 2.10 .85
*d.* As #U495, double surcharge 10.00 3.00
*e.* As "b," double surcharge 10.00 3.00
*f.* As "c," double surcharge 10.00 3.00
**U496** U92 1½c on 1c grn, *amb* (U421, die 1) 15.00 12.50
*a.* On No. U421b (die 3) 725.00
*b.* On No. U421c (die 4) 15.00 12.50
**U497** U92 1½c on 1c grn, *oriental buff* (U422, die 1) 3.75 1.90
*a.* On No. U422b (die 4) 67.50
**U498** U92 1½c on 1c grn, *bl* (U423c, die 4) 1.40 .75
*a.* On No. U423 (die 1) 2.40 1.50
*b.* On No. U423b (die 3) 1.75 1.50
**U499** U92 1½c on 1c grn, *man* (U424) 8.00 6.00
**U500** U92 1½c on 1c grn, *brn* (unglazed) (U428) 60.00 30.00
**U501** U92 1½c on 1c grn, *brn* (glazed) (U426) 65.00 30.00
**U502** U93 1½c on 2c car (U429, die 1) 200.00 —
*a.* On No. U429d (die 5) 250.00
*b.* On No. U429f (die 7) 250.00
*c.* On No. U429e (die 6) 325.00
*d.* On No. U429g (die 8) 450.00
**U503** U93 1½c on 2c car, *oriental buff* (U431c, die 5) 200.00 —
*a.* Double surcharge —
*b.* Double surcharge, one inverted *700.00*
**U504** U93 1½c on 2c car, *bl* (U432, die 1) 300.00 —
*a.* On No. U432g (die 7) 300.00
*b.* As "a," double surcharge, entire *350.00*
*c.* On No. U432f (die 6), entire *400.00*
**U505** U93 1½c on 1½c brn (U481, die 1) 300.00
*a.* On No. U481a (die 8) 400.00
*b.* As No. U505, double surcharge, entire *2,000.*
**U506** U93 1½c on 1½c brn, *bl* (U483a, die 8) 200.00
*a.* On No. U483 (die 1) 300.00

The paper of No. U500 is not glazed and appears to be the same as that used for the wrappers of 1920.

Surcharged Type 9

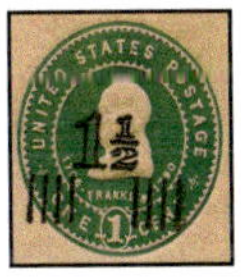

### Black Surcharge

**U507** U69 1½c on 1c blue (U294) 1,750.
**U507B** U69 1½c on 1c blue, *manila* (U300) 2,750.
**U508** U77 1½c on 1c grn, *amb* (U353) 55.00
**U508A** U85 1½c on 1c grn (U379) 2,750.
**U509** U85 1½c on 1c grn, *amb* (U380) 12.50 10.00
*a.* Double surcharge 75.00
**U509B** U85 1½c on 1c green, *oriental buff* (U381) 40.00 40.00
**U510** U90 1½c on 1c green (U400, die 1) 2.75 1.25
*b.* On No. U400a (die 2) 9.00 4.00
*c.* On No. U400b (die 3) 37.50 8.00
*d.* On No. U400c (die 4) 3.50 1.25
*e.* As No. U510, double surcharge 25.00
**U511** U90 1½c on 1c grn, *amb* (U401, die 1) 200.00 100.00
**U512** U90 1½c on 1c grn, *oriental buff* (U402, die 1) 7.00 4.00
*a.* On No. U402c (die 4) 21.00 14.00
**U513** U90 1½c on 1c grn, *bl* (U403, die 1) 6.00 4.00
*a.* On No. U403c (die 4) 6.00 4.00
**U514** U90 1½c on 1c grn, *man* (U404, die 1) 30.00 9.00
*a.* On No. U404a (die 3) 77.50 40.00
**U515** U92 1½c on 1c green (U420, die 1) .40 .25
*a.* On No. U420a (die 2) 15.00 15.00
*b.* On No. U420b (die 3) .40 .25
*c.* On No. U420c (die 4) .40 .25
*d.* As #U515, double surcharge 10.00
*e.* As #U515, inverted surcharge 15.00
*f.* As #U515, triple surcharge 15.00
*g.* As #U515, dbl. surch., one invtd., entire —
*h.* As "b," double surcharge 10.00
*i.* As "b," inverted surcharge 15.00
*j.* As "b," triple surcharge 25.00
*k.* As "c," double surcharge 10.00
*l.* As "c," inverted surcharge 15.00
**U516** U92 1½c on 1c grn, *amb* (U421c, die 4) 50.00 27.50
*a.* On No. U421 (die 1) 55.00 32.50
**U517** U92 1½c on 1c grn, *oriental buff* (U422, die 1) 6.25 1.25
*a.* On No. U422a (die 4) 7.25 1.50
**U518** U92 1½c on 1c grn, *bl* (U423b, die 4) 5.00 1.50
*a.* On No. U423 (die 1) 8.25 4.50
*b.* On No. U423a (die 3) 27.50 7.50
*c.* As "a," double surcharge 30.00
**U519** U92 1½c on 1c grn, *man* (U424, die 1) 25.00 12.00
*a.* Double surcharge 100.00
**U520** U93 1½c on 2c car (U429, die 1) 300.00 —
*a.* On No. U429d (die 5) 275.00
*b.* On No. U429e (die 6) 275.00
*c.* On No. U429f (die 7) 275.00
**U520D** U93 1½c on 2c car, *amber* (U430c, die 5), entire —
**U520E** U92 1½c on 4c black (U440, die 1), entire —

### Magenta Surcharge

**U521** U92 1½c on 1c grn (U420b, die 3) 4.25 3.50
*a.* Double surcharge 75.00

### Sesquicentennial Exposition Issue

150th anniversary of the Declaration of Independence.

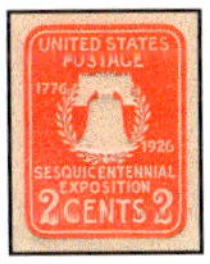

Liberty Bell — U94

Die 1. The center bar of "E" of "postage" is shorter than top bar.
Die 2. The center bar of "E" of "postage" is of same length as top bar.

**1926, July 27**

**U522** U94 2c carmine, die 1 1.00 .50
*a.* Die 2 5.50 3.75

### Washington Bicentennial Issue

200th anniversary of the birth of George Washington.

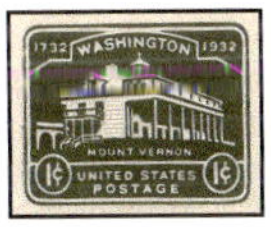

Mount Vernon — U95

2c Die 1 — "S" of "Postage" normal.
2c Die 2 — "S" of "Postage" raised.

**1932**

**U523** U95 1c olive green 1.00 .80
**U524** U95 1½c chocolate 2.00 1.50
**U525** U95 2c car, die 1 .40 .25
*a.* 2c carmine, die 2 60.00 20.00
*b.* 2c carmine, *blue*, die 1 (error) entire *30,000.*
**U526** U95 3c violet 1.75 .35
**U527** U95 4c black 15.00 17.50
**U528** U95 5c dark blue 3.50 3.50
*Nos. U523-U528 (6)* 23.65 23.90

### Type of 1916-32 Issue

**1932, Aug. 18**

**U529** U93 6c orange, die 7 6.00 4.00
**U530** U93 6c orange, *amber*, die 7 10.00 10.00
**U531** U93 6c orange, *blue*, die 7 10.00 10.00

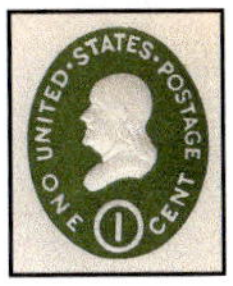

Franklin — U96

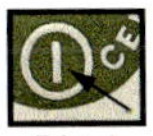

Die 1

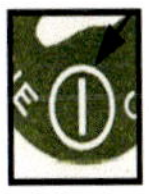

Die 2

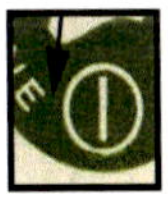

Die 3

Die 1 — Short (3½mm) and thick "l" in thick circle.
Die 2 — Tall (4½mm) and thin "1" in thin circle; upper and lower bars of E in ONE long and 1mm from circle.
Die 3 — As in Die 2, but E normal and 1½mm from circle.

**1950**

**U532** U90 1c green, die 1 5.00 1.75
*a.* Die 2 6.50 3.00
*b.* Die 3 6.50 3.00
Precanceled, die 3 1.25

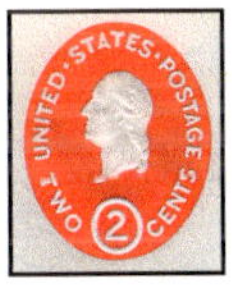

Washington — U97

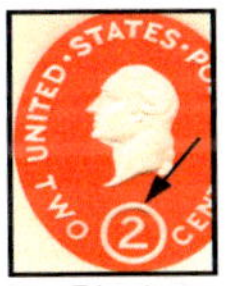

Die 1

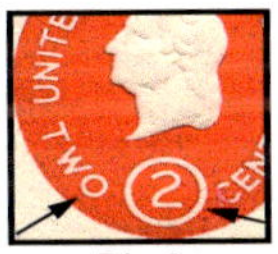

Die 2

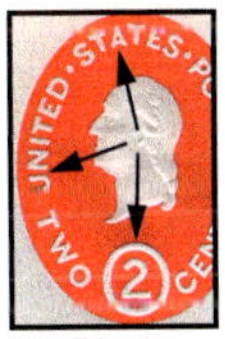

Die 3

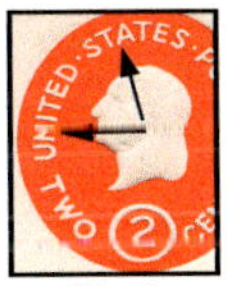

Die 4

Die 1 — Thick "2" in thick circle; toe of "2" is acute angle.
Die 2 — Thin "2" in thin circle; toe of "2" is almost right angle; line through left stand of "N" in UNITED and stand of "E" in POSTAGE goes considerably below tip of chin; "N" of UNITED is tall; "O" of TWO is high.
Die 3 — Figure "2" as in Die 2. Short UN in UNITED thin crossbar in A of STATES.
Die 4 — Tall UN in UNITED; thick crossbar in A of STATES; otherwise like Die 3.

**U533** U97 2c carmine, die 3 .70 .25
*a.* Die 1 .80 .30
*b.* Die 2 1.40 .85
*c.* Die 4 1.30 .60

Die 1

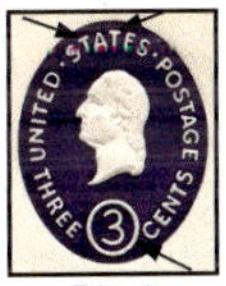

Die 2

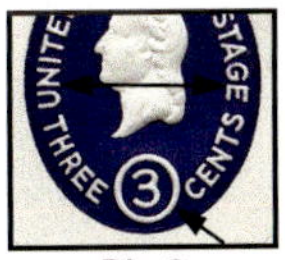

Die 3

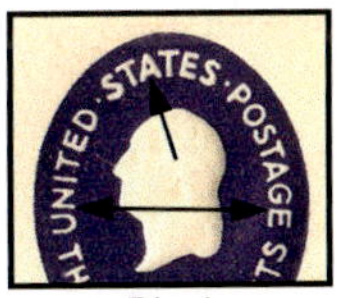

Die 4

# UNITED STATES

Die 5

Die 1 — Thick and tall (4½mm) "3" in thick circle; long top bars and short stems in T's of STATES.
Die 2 — Thin and tall (4½mm) "3" in medium circle; short top bars and long stems in T's of STATES.
Die 3 — Thin and short (4mm) "3" in thin circle; lettering wider than Dies 1 and 2; line from left stand of N to stand of E is distinctly below tip of chin.
Die 4 — Figure and letters as in Die 3. Line hits tip of chin; short N in UNITED and thin crossbar in A of STATES.
Die 5 — Figure, letter and chin line as in Die 4; but tall N in UNITED and thick crossbar in A of STATES.

| U534 | U97 3c dark violet, die 4 | .35 | .25 |
|---|---|---|---|
| a. | Die 1 | 1.90 | .70 |
| b. | Die 2 | .75 | .50 |
| c. | Die 3 | .55 | .25 |
| d. | Die 5 | .75 | .45 |
| e. | As "c," double impression | 300.00 | |

Washington — U98

**1952**
U535 U98 1½c brown ..... 4.50 3.50
Precanceled ..... 1.25

Die 1

Die 2

Die 3

Die 1 — Head high in oval (2mm below T of STATES). Circle near (1mm) bottom of colored oval.
Die 2 — Head low in oval (3mm). Circle 1½mm from edge of oval. Right leg of A in POSTAGE shorter than left. Short leg on P.
Die 3 — Head centered in oval (2½mm). Circle as in Die 2. Legs of A of POSTAGE about equal. Long leg on P.

**1958**
| U536 | U96 4c red violet, die 1 | .75 | .25 |
|---|---|---|---|
| a. | Die 2 | .90 | .25 |
| b. | Die 3 | .90 | .25 |

**Nos. U429, U429f, U429h, U533, U533a-U533c Surcharged in Red at Left of Stamp**

**1958**
| U537 | U93 2c + 2c carmine, die 1 | 3.25 | 1.50 |
|---|---|---|---|
| a. | Die 7 | 10.00 | 7.00 |
| b. | Die 9 | 4.75 | 5.00 |
| U538 | U97 2c + 2c carmine, die 1 | .70 | .80 |
| a. | Die 2 | .90 | 1.00 |
| b. | Die 3 | .70 | .70 |
| c. | Die 4 | .70 | 1.00 |

**Nos. U436a, U436e-U436f, U534, U534b-U534d Surcharged in Green at Left of Stamp**

| U539 | U93 3c + 1c purple, die 1 | 12.50 | 9.00 |
|---|---|---|---|
| a. | Die 7 | 11.00 | 7.50 |
| b. | Die 9 | 17.50 | 15.00 |
| U540 | U97 3c + 1c dark violet, die 3 | .40 | 1.00 |
| a. | Die 2, entire | 3,500. | |
| b. | Die 4 | .65 | 1.00 |
| c. | Die 5 | .70 | 1.00 |

Benjamin Franklin — U99

George Washington — U100

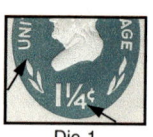
Die 1    Die 2

**Dies of 1¼c**
Die 1 — The "4" is 3mm high. Upper leaf in left cluster is 2mm from "U."
Die 2 — The "4" is 3½mm high. Leaf clusters are larger. Upper leaf at left is 1mm from "U."

**1960**
| U541 | U99 1¼c turquoise, die 1 | .65 | .50 |
|---|---|---|---|
| | Die 1, precanceled | | .25 |
| a. | Die 2, precanceled | | 1.25 |
| U542 | U100 2½c dull blue | .80 | .50 |
| | Precanceled | | .25 |

**Precanceled cut squares**
Precanceled envelopes do not normally receive another cancellation. Since the lack of a cancellation makes it impossible to distinguish between cut squares from used and unused envelopes, they are valued here as used only.

**Pony Express Centennial Issue**

Pony Express Rider — U101

Envelope White Outside, Blue Inside.

**1960**
U543 U101 4c brown ..... .55 .30

Die 1

Die 2

Die 3

Die 1 — Center bar of E of POSTAGE is above the middle. Center bar of E of STATES slants slightly upward. Nose sharper, more pointed. No offset ink specks inside envelope on back of die impression.
Die 2 — Center bar of E of POSTAGE in middle. P of POSTAGE has short stem. Ink specks on back of die impression.
Die 3 — FI of FIVE closer than Die 1 or 2. Second T of STATES seems taller than ES. Ink specks on back of die impression.

**1962**
| U544 | U102 5c dark blue, die 2 | .80 | .25 |
|---|---|---|---|
| a. | Die 1 | .80 | .25 |
| b. | Die 3 | .85 | .35 |
| c. | Die 2 with albino impression of 4c (#U536) | 50.00 | |
| d. | Die 3 with albino impression of 4c (#U536), entire | 125.00 | |
| e. | Die 3 on complete impression of 4c (#U536), cut square | 125.00 | |

**No. U536 Surcharged in Green at left of Stamp**

Two types of surcharge:
Type I — "U.S. POSTAGE" 18½mm high. Serifs on cross of T both diagonal. Two lines of shading in C of CENT.
Type II — "U.S. POSTAGE" 17½mm high. Right serif on cross of T is vertical. Three shading lines in C.

**1962**
| U545 | U96 4c + 1c red vio, die 1, type I | 1.25 | 1.10 |
|---|---|---|---|
| a. | Type II | 1.25 | 1.10 |

**Values for used envelopes are for examples used within the period of issue. Envelopes used much later sell at substantially reduced prices.**

**New York World's Fair Issue**
Issued to publicize the New York World's Fair, 1964-65.

Globe with Satellite Orbit — U103

**1964**
U546 U103 5c maroon ..... .55 .40

Liberty Bell U104

Old Ironsides U105

Eagle U106    Head of Statue of Liberty U107

**1965-69**
| U547 | U104 1¼c brown | .50 |
|---|---|---|
| U548 | U104 1⁴⁄₁₀c brown ('68) | .50 |
| U548A | U104 1⁴⁄₁₀c orange ('69) | .50 |
| b. | 1⁴⁄₁₀c brown (error), entire | 5,000. |
| U549 | U105 4c bright blue | .90 .25 |
| U550 | U106 5c bright purple | .75 .25 |
| a. | Bar tagged ('67) | 3.00 1.00 |

**Tagged**
| U551 | U107 6c lt green ('68) | .70 .25 |
|---|---|---|
| a. | 6c dark gray green, entire | 200.00 |

**Nos. U549-U550 Surcharged in Red or Green at Left of Stamp**

**1968, Feb. 5**
| U552 | U105 4c + 2c bright blue (R) | 3.25 2.00 |
|---|---|---|
| U553 | U106 5c + 1c bright purple (G) | 3.00 2.75 |
| a. | Tagged | 3.00 2.75 |
| b. | With 2c surcharge type "b" (error) | 400.00 |

**Tagged**
Envelopes from No. U554 onward are tagged, except for bulk-rate and non-profit envelopes, which are untagged. The tagging element is in the ink through No. 608 unless otherwise noted. From No. 611 on, envelopes have bar or block tagging unless otherwise noted.

**Herman Melville Issue**
Issued to honor Herman Melville (1819-1891), writer, and the whaling industry.

Moby Dick — U108

**1970, Mar. 7**
U554 U108 6c blue ..... .50 .25

**Youth Conference Issue**
Issued to publicize the White House Conference on Youth, Estes Park, Colo., Apr. 18-22.

Youth Conference Emblem — U109

**1971, Feb. 24**
U555 U109 6c light blue ..... .70 1.00

**Liberty Bell Type of 1965 and**

Eagle — U110

**1971**
| U556 | U104 1⁷⁄₁₀c deep lilac, untagged | .35 |
|---|---|---|
| U557 | U110 8c ultramarine | .40 .25 |

UNITED STATES 201

### Nos. U551 and U555 Surcharged in Green at Left of Stamp

**1971, May 16**
U561 U107 6c + (2c) light green .90 1.25
  *a.* Inverted surcharge, entire 275.00
U562 U109 6c + (2c) light blue 2.00 2.50
  *a.* Inverted surcharge printed on reverse, entire —

### Bowling Issue

Issued as a salute to bowling and in connection with the 7th World Tournament of the International Bowling Federation, Milwaukee, Wis.

Bowling Ball and Pin — U111

**1971, Aug. 21**
U563 U111 8c rose red .60 .25

### Aging Conference Issue

White House Conference on Aging, Washington, D.C., Nov. 28-Dec. 2, 1971.

Conference Symbol — U112

**1971, Nov. 15**
U564 U112 8c light blue .50 .25

### International Transportation Exhibition Issue

U.S. International Transportation Exhibition, Dulles International Airport, Washington, D.C., May 27-June 4.

Transportation Exhibition Emblem — U113

**1972, May 2**
U565 U113 8c ultramarine & rose red .50 .25

### No. U557 Surcharged in Ultramarine at Left of Stamp

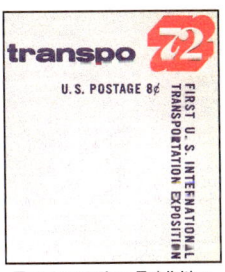

**1973, Dec. 1**
U566 U110 8c + 2c brt. ultra .40 1.25

Liberty Bell — U114

**1973, Dec. 5**
U567 U114 10c emerald .40 .25

"Volunteer Yourself" — U115

**1974, Aug. 23** Untagged
U568 U115 1 9/10c blue green .25

### Tennis Centenary Issue

Centenary of tennis in the United States.

Tennis Racquet — U116

**1974, Aug. 31** Block Tagged
U569 U116 10c yellow, brt. blue & light green .55 .25

### Bicentennial Era Issue

The Seafaring Tradition — Compass Rose — U118

The American Homemaker — Quilt Pattern — U119

The American Farmer — Sheaf of Wheat — U120

The American Doctor — U121

The American Craftsman — Tools, c. 1750 — U122

Designs (in brown on left side of envelope): 10c, Norwegian sloop Restaurationen. No. U572, Spinning wheel. No. U573, Plow. No. U574, Colonial era medical instruments and bottle. No. U575, Shaker rocking chair.

**1975-76** Embossed
**Light Brown Diagonally Laid Paper**
U571 U118 10c brown & blue .30 .25
  *a.* Brown ("10c/USA," etc.) omitted, entire 125.00

U572 U119 13c brn & blue grn .35 .25
  *a.* Brown ("13c/USA," etc.) omitted, entire 125.00
U573 U120 13c brn & brt grn .35 .25
  *a.* Brown ("13c/USA," etc.) omitted, entire 100.00
U574 U121 13c brn & org .35 .25
  *a.* Brown ("13c/USA," etc.) omitted, entire 100.00
U575 U122 13c brn & car .35 .25
  *a.* Brown ("13c/USA," etc.) omitted, entire 100.00
Nos. U571-U575 (5) 1.70 1.25

Liberty Tree, Boston, 1646 — U123

**1975, Nov. 8** Embossed
U576 U123 13c orange brown .30 .25

Star and Pinweel — U124

U125

U126

Eagle — U127

"Uncle Sam" — U128

**1976-78** Embossed
U577 U124 2c red, untagged .25
U578 U125 2.1c grn, untagged .25
U579 U126 2.7c grn, untagged .25
U580 U127 (15c) orange .40 .25
U581 U128 15c red, ink tagged .40 .25
  *a.* Bar tagged 7.00 7.00

For No. U581 with surcharge, see No. U586b.

### Bicentennial Issue

Centennial Envelope, 1876 — U129

**1976, Oct. 15** Embossed
U582 U129 13c emerald .35 .25

### Golf Issue

Golf Club in Motion and Golf Ball U130

**Photogravure and Embossed**
**1977, Apr. 7**
U583 U130 13c blk, blue & yel grn .65 .25
  *a.* Black omitted, entire 650.00
  *b.* Black & blue omitted, entire 700.00
  *c.* Black, blue & yellow green omitted, entire 700.00
On No. U583c, the embossing is present.

### Energy Issue

Conservation and development of national resources.

Energy Conservation U131

Energy Development U132

**1977, Oct. 20** Photo.
**Bar Tagged**
U584 U131 13c blk, red & yel .45 .25
  *a.* Red, yellow & tagging omitted, entire 250.00
  *b.* Yellow & tagging omitted, entire 200.00
  *c.* Black omitted, entire 135.00
  *d.* Black & red omitted, entire 300.00
U585 U132 13c blk, red & yel .45 .25

Olive Branch and Star — U133

**1978, July 28** Embossed
**Black Surcharge**
U586 U133 15c on 16c blue .40 .25
  *a.* Surcharge omitted, entire 225.00 1,000.
  *b.* Surcharge on No. U581, entire 260.00
  *c.* As "a," with surcharge printed on envelope flap 175.00 —
  *d.* Surcharge inverted (in lower left corner), entire 200.00 —

### Auto Racing Issue

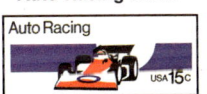

Indianapolis 500 Racing Car — U134

**1978, Sept. 2** Embossed
U587 U134 15c red, blue & black .45 .25
  *a.* Black omitted, entire 100.00
  *b.* Black & blue omitted, entire 170.00
  *c.* Red & tagging omitted, entire 100.00
  *d.* Red, blue & tagging omitted, entire 170.00
  *e.* Tagging bar inverted at LL, entire 100.00
  *f.* Tagging bar on reverse, entire

### No. U576 Surcharged

**1978, Nov. 28** Embossed
U588 U123 15c on 13c org brn .40 .25
  *a.* Surcharge inverted (in lower left corner), entire 450.00

U135

**1979, May 18** Embossed Untagged
U589 U135 3.1c ultramarine .35

Weaver Violins — U136

**1980, June 23** Untagged
U590 U136 3.5c purple .35
  *a.* 3.5c violet, tagged (in ink), error of color and tagging using ink intended for No. U592, entire 300.00 500.00

202 UNITED STATES

**1982, Feb. 17** Untagged
U591 U137 5.9c brown .35

Eagle — U138
**1981, Mar. 15**
U592 U138 (18c) violet .45 .25

Star — U139
**1981, Apr. 2**
U593 U139 18c dark blue .45 .25

Eagle — U140
**1981, Oct. 11**
U594 U140 (20c) brown .45 .25

**Veterinary Medicine Issue**

Seal of Veterinarians U141

Design at left side of envelope shows 5 animals and bird in brown, "Veterinary Medicine" in gray.

**1979, July 24**
U595 U141 15c brown & gray .50 .25
a. Gray omitted, entire 375.00
b. Brown omitted, entire 375.00
c. Gray & brown omitted, tagging omitted, entire 325.00

On No. U595c, the embossing of the seal is present.

**Olympic Games Issue**
22nd Olympic Games, Moscow, July 19–Aug. 3, 1980.

U142

Design (multicolored on left side of envelope) shows two soccer players with ball.

**1979, Dec. 10**
U596 U142 15c red, grn & blk .60 .25
a. Red & green omitted, tagging omitted, entire 200.00
b. Black omitted, tagging omitted, entire 200.00
c. Black & green omitted, entire 200.00
d. Red omitted, tagging omitted, entire 325.00
e. All colors omitted 250.00
f. Tagging omitted, entire 125.00
g. Black omitted, tagged, entire —

No. U596c exists with a portion of the green present in the Olympics 1980 design at the lower left corner of the envelope.
On No. U596e, the blind embossing of "USA 15c" remains.

Highwheeler Bicycle U143
Design (blue on left side of envelope) shows racing bicycle.
**1980, May 16**
U597 U143 15c blue & rose claret .40 .25
a. Blue ("15c USA") omitted, entire 80.00

Racing Yacht — U144
**1980, Sept. 15**
U598 U144 15c blue & red .40 .25

Italian Honeybee and Orange Blossoms U145
Bee and petals colorless embossed.
**Photogravure and Embossed**
**1980, Oct. 10**
U599 U145 15c brn, grn & yel .35 .25
a. Brown ("USA 15c") omitted, entire 80.00
b. Green omitted, entire 80.00

No. U599b also has almost all of the brown color missing.

U146
Hand and braille colorless embossed.
**1981, Aug. 13** Embossed
U600 U146 18c blue & red .45 .25
a. Blue omitted, entire 80.00
b. Red omitted, entire 210.00

Capitol Dome — U147
**1981, Nov. 13**
U601 U147 20c dp mag, ink tagged .45 .25
a. Bar tagged 4.50 1.50

U148
**1982, June 15**
U602 U148 20c dk blue, blk & mag .45 .25
a. Dark blue omitted, entire 125.00
b. Dark blue & magenta omitted, entire 225.00
c. All colors omitted, entire 300.00

On No. 602c, the colorless embossed impression of the Great Seal is present.

U149

**1982, Aug. 6**
U603 U149 20c purple & black .75 .25
a. Black omitted, entire 80.00
b. Purple omitted, entire 80.00

U150
**1983, Mar. 21** Untagged
U604 U150 5.2c orange .90

U151
**1983, Aug. 3**
U605 U151 20c red, blue & black .45 .25
a. Red omitted, entire 260.00
b. Blue omitted, entire 260.00
c. Red & black omitted, entire 125.00
d. Blue & black omitted, entire 125.00
e. Black omitted, entire 230.00

U152
Design shows storefronts at lower left. Stamp and design continue on back of envelope.
**1984, May 7** Photo.
U606 U152 20c multi .50 .25

U153
**1985, Feb. 1** Embossed
U607 U153 (22c) deep green .55 .30

American Buffalo — U154
**1985, Feb. 25**
U608 U154 22c vio brn, ink tagged .55 .25
a. Untagged, 3 blue precancel lines, unwmk'd ('86) .25
b. Bar tagged 2.00 1.00

Frigate U.S.S. Constitution, "Old Ironsides" — U155
**1985, May 3** Untagged
U609 U155 6c green blue .35

Mayflower — U156
**1986, Dec. 4** Untagged
Precanceled
U610 U156 8.5c black & gray .65

Stars — U157
**1988, Mar. 26** Typo. & Embossed
U611 U157 25c dark red & deep blue .60 .25
a. Dark red (25) omitted, tagging omitted 50.00 —
c. Dark red (25) omitted, tagging not omitted 60.00

Sea Gulls, Frigate USS Constellation — U158
**1988, Apr. 12** Untagged
Precanceled
U612 U158 8.4c blk & brt blue .65
a. Black omitted, entire 175.00

Snowflake U159
"Holiday Greetings!" inscribed in lower left.
**1988, Sept. 8** Typo.
U613 U159 25c dark red & green 1.25 20.00

Stars and "*Philatelic Mail*" Continuous in Dark Red Below Vignette U160

"Philatelic Mail" and asterisks in dark red below vignette; continuous across envelope face and partly on reverse.

**1989, Mar. 10**
U614 U160 25c dark red & deep blue .50 .25
b. Red omitted, entire 125.00

"USA" and Stars — U161
**1989, July 10** Unwmk.
U615 U161 25c dark red & deep blue .50 .25
a. Dark red omitted, entire 425.00

Lined with a blue design to provide security for enclosures.

Love — U162
**Litho. & Typo.**
**1989, Sept. 22** Unwmk.
U616 U162 25c dk red & brt blue .50 .75
a. Dark red and bright blue omitted, entire 150.00
b. Bright blue omitted, entire 150.00

No. U616 has light blue lines printed diagonally over the entire surface of the envelope.

UNITED STATES 203

Shuttle Docking at Space Station U163

**1989, Dec. 3   Typo.   Unwmk.**
**Die Cut**
U617  U163 25c ultramarine   .90   .60
a. Ultramarine omitted, entire   400.00

A hologram, visible through the die cut window to the right of "USA 25," is affixed to the inside of the envelope.
See Nos. U625, U639.

Vince Lombardi Trophy, Football Players U164

**1990, Sept. 9   Unwmk.   Die Cut**
U618  U164 25c vermilion   .90   .60

A hologram, visible through the die cut window to the right of "USA 25," is affixed to the inside of the envelope.

Star — U165

**Typo. & Embossed**
**1991, Jan. 24   Wmk.**
U619  U165 29c ultra & rose   .60   .30
a. Ultramarine omitted, entire   300.00
b. Rose omitted, tagged, entire   250.00
c. Rose omitted, tagging omitted, entire   275.00

See No. U623.

Birds — U166

Stamp and design continue on back of envelope.

**1991, May 3   Typo.   Wmk.**
**Untagged, Precanceled**
U620  U166 11.1c blue & red   —   .90
a. Blue omitted, entire

Love U167

**1991, May 9   Litho.   Unwmk.**
U621  U167 29c lt blue, pur & brt rose   .60   .60
a. Bright rose omitted, entire   80.00
b. Purple omitted, entire   400.00

Magazine Industry, 250th Anniv. — U168

**Photo. & Typo.**
**1991, Oct. 7   Unwmk.**
U622  U168 29c multicolored   .70  1.00

The photogravure vignette, visible through the die cut window to the right of "USA 29," is affixed to the inside of the envelope.

Star — U169

Stamp and design continue on back of envelope.

**1991, July 20   Typo.   Unwmk.**
U623  U169 29c ultra & rose   .60   .30
a. Ultra omitted, entire   275.00
b. Rose omitted, entire   135.00

Lined with a blue design to provide security for enclosures.

Country Geese — U170

**1991, Nov. 8   Litho. & Typo.   Wmk.**
U624  U170 29c blue gray & yel   .60   .60

**Space Shuttle Type of 1989**
**Unwmk.**
**1992, Jan. 21   Typo.   Die Cut**
U625  U163 29c yellow green   .80   .50

A hologram, visible through the die cut window to the right of "USA 29," is affixed to the inside of the envelope.

U171

**Typo. & Litho.**
**1992, Apr. 10   Die Cut**
U626  U171 29c multicolored   .60  1.00

The lithographed vignette, visible through the die cut window to the right of "USA 29," is affixed to the inside of the envelope.

Hillebrandia — U172

**1992, Apr. 22**
U627  U172 29c multicolored   .65  1.00

The lithographed vignette, visible through the die cut window to the right of "29 USA," is affixed to the inside of the envelope.

U173

**Typo. & Embossed**
**1992, May 19   Precanceled**
**Untagged**
U628  U173 19.8c red & blue   .40

U174

**1992, July 22   Typo.**
U629  U174 29c red & blue   .60   .30

U175

**1993, Oct. 2   Typo. & Litho.   Die Cut**
U630  U175 29c multicolored   1.10  1.10

The lithographed vignette, visible through the die cut window to the right of "USA 29," is affixed to the inside of the envelope.

U176

**Typo. & Embossed**
**1994, Sept. 17**
U631  U176 29c brn & blk   .70  1.25
a. Black ("29/USA") omitted, entire   175.00

Liberty Bell — U177

**1995, Jan. 3   Typo. & Embossed**
U632  U177 32c grnsh blue & blue   .65   .30
a. Greenish blue omitted   120.00
b. Blue ("USA 32") omitted   90.00
c. All colors omitted, entire   125.00

A colorless embossed design is present on No. U632c.
See No. U638.

U178

Design sizes: 49x38mm (#U633), 53x44mm (U634). Stamp and design continue on back of envelope.

**1995   Typo.**
U633  U178 (32c) blue & red   1.25  2.00
U634  U178 (32c) blue & red   1.25  2.00
a. Red & tagging omitted, entire   275.00
b. Blue omitted, entire   275.00

Originally, Nos. U633-U634 were only available through the Philatelic Fulfillment Center after their announcement 1/12/95.

U179

Stamp and design continue on back of envelope.

**1995, Mar. 10**
**Precanceled, Untagged**
U635  U179 (5c) grn & red brn   .40

Graphic Eagle U180

**1995, Mar. 10**
**Precanceled, Untagged**
U636  U180 (10c) dk car & blue   1.50

Spiral Heart — U181

**1995, May 12**
U637  U181 32c red, light blue   .65   .30
a. Red omitted, entire   175.00

**Liberty Bell Type of 1995**
**1995, May 16**
U638  U177 32c greenish blue & blue   .70   .30
a. Greenish blue omitted, entire   175.00

**Space Shuttle Type of 1989**
**1995, Sept. 22   Die Cut**
U639  U163 32c carmine rose   .75   .35

A hologram, visible through the die cut window to the right of "USA 32," is affixed to the inside of the envelope.

U182

**Typo. & Litho.**
**1996, Apr. 20   Die Cut**
U640  U182 32c multicolored   .70   .30

The lithographed vignette, visible through the die cut window to the right of "USA 32c," is affixed to the inside of the envelope.

U183

**1996, May 2**
U641  U183 32c multicolored   .70   .30
a. Blue & red omitted, entire   260.00
b. Blue & gold omitted, entire   260.00
c. Red omitted, entire   260.00
d. Black & red omitted, entire   260.00
e. Blue omitted, entire   260.00

U184

U184a

**1999, Jan. 11   Typo. & Embossed**
U642  U184 33c yellow, blue & red, tagging bar to left of design   1.00   .30
a. Tagging bar to right of design   7.50  3.00
b. As "a," blue omitted, entire   175.00
c. As "a," yellow omitted, entire   175.00
d. As "a," yellow and blue omitted, entire   175.00
e. As "a," blue and red omitted, entire   175.00
f. As "a," all colors omitted, entire   175.00
g. As No. U642, red omitted, entire   450.00
h. As No. U642, yellow and red omitted, entire   175.00
i. As No. U642, blue and red omitted, entire   —
j. Tagging omitted

On No. U642f, the distinctive tagging bar is present. Expertization is required.

## 204 UNITED STATES

**1999, Jan. 11**    Typo.
U643 U184a 33c blue & red   1.00   .30
  a. Tagging bar to right of design   10.00   5.00

U185

**1999, Jan. 28**    Litho.
U644 U185 33c violet   .65   .30
  a. Tagging bar to right of design   .65   .30

Lincoln — U186

**1999, June 5**    Typo. & Litho.
U645 U186 33c blue & black   .65   .30

Eagle — U187

**2001, Jan. 7**    Typo.
U646 U187 34c blue gray & gray   .70   .30
  a. Blue gray omitted   175.00
Many color shades known.

Lovebirds U188

**2001, Feb. 14**    Litho.
U647 U188 34c rose & dull violet   .70   .30

Community Colleges, Cent. U189

**2001, Feb. 20**    Typo.
U648 U189 34c dk blue & org brn   .70   .30

Ribbon Star — U190

**2002, June 7**
U649 U190 37c red, blue & gray   .75   .35
  a. Gray omitted, entire   75.00
  b. Blue and gray omitted, entire   175.00

All No. U649 were printed on recycled paper. It was also produced using a different blue-gray recycled paper starting in 2002.

**Type of 1995 Inscribed "USA / Presorted / Standard"**
**2002, Aug. 8**    Untagged
      Precanceled
U650 U180 (10c) dk car & blue   .25

Nurturing Love — U191

**2003, Jan. 25**
U651 U191 37c ol grn & yel org   .80   .35

**Jefferson Memorial Type**
**2003, Dec. 29**
U652 A2818 $3.85 multicolored   12.50   6.25
On No. U652, the stamp indicia is printed on the flap of the envelope.

**Disney Type of 2004**
**2004, June 23**   Letter Sheet   Litho.
U653 A2949 37c multicolored   2.50   2.25
U654 A2950 37c multicolored   2.50   2.25
U655 A2951 37c multicolored   2.50   2.25
  a. All color missing on reverse, entire   —
U656 A2952 37c multicolored   2.50   2.25
  a. Booklet of 12 letter sheets, 3 each #U653-U656   30.00
No. U656a sold for $14.95.

**White Lilacs and Pink Roses Type of 2004**
**2005, Mar. 3**   Letter Sheet
U657 A2931 37c multicolored   3.00   2.50
No. U657 was sold in pads of 12 for $14.95.

Computer-generated Study of an X-Plane — U192

**2006, Jan. 5**    Typo.
U658 U192 $4.05 multicolored   10.00   9.00

Benjamin Franklin — U193

**2006, Jan. 9**
U659 U193 39c blue green & black   .80   .40
  a. All color omitted, entire
  b. Tagging omitted, entire   37.50
On No. 659a, the tagging bar and the blue green printing on the reverse are present.

Air Force One — U194

**2007, May 6**
U660 U194 $4.60 multicolored   12.50   10.00

Marine One — U195

**2007, May 6**
U661 U195 $16.25 multicolored   35.00   20.00

Horses U196

**2007, May 12**
U662 U196 41c reddish brown & black   .85   .40

Elk — U197

**2008, May 2**
U663 U197 42c green & black, tagging bar 20mm tall   .85   .40
  a. Tagging bar 26mm tall   .85   .40
  b. As No. U663, litho., tagging bar 19mm tall   .85   .40

No. U663 was printed by National Envelope for Ashton-Potter (USA) Ltd. No. U663a was printed by Westvaco.

No. U663b was printed by Ashton-Potter (USA) Ltd. The lithographed impressions of No. U663b are slightly sharper (some tree branches are slightly thinner and more distinct) than the typographed impressions on Nos. U663 and U663a, but because of the nature of the design are nonetheless difficult to distinguish without measuring the tagging bar.

Mount Rushmore U198

**2008, May 12**
U664 U198 $4.80 multicolored   12.50   10.00

**Sunflower Type of 2008 Letter Sheet**
**2008, Aug. 15**    Litho.
U665 A3309 42c multicolored   4.00   3.00
No. U665 was sold in packs of 10 for $14.95.

**Redwood Forest Type of 2009**
**2009, Jan. 16**    Typo.
U666 A3332 $4.95 multicolored   10.00   7.50

U199

**2009-11**    Litho.
U667 U199 (44c) multicolored   .90   .90
  a. As #U667, typographed   .90   .45
  b. As #U667, dated "2011," "FOREVER" multicolored (with color dots)   .90   .90
  c. As #U667b, "FOREVER" in brown (solid color)   .90   .90

Issued: No. U667, 5/11; No. U667a, 8/16; Nos. U667b, U667c, 1/3/11.

No. U667 had a franking value of 44c on the day of issue and will be valid for the one ounce first class postage rate after any new rates go into effect.

The typographed version (No. U667a) can be distinguished from No. U667 by the position of the recycle logo on the back. On the litho. version it is to the right of the recycle text; on the typo. version it is to the left of the text.

U200

**2009, May 11**
U668 U200 44c multicolored   .90   .45
  a. As #U668, typographed   .90   .45
  b. As No. U668, triple impression of black, entire

On No. U668a, the screened blue dots cover the entire area between the "S" and the "C" on No. U668, but appear more random on No. U668a. The pattern of blue dots running towards the shoulder under the head and neck of the horse is long and distinct on No. U668, but barely noticeable, with only a few dots showing, on No. U668a.

See second paragraph of No. U667 footnote, which also applies to Nos. U668 and U668a.

**Gulf Coast Lighthouses Type of 2009**
**2009, July 23**    Litho.
U669 A3354 44c multicolored   3.75   3.00
U670 A3355 44c multicolored   3.75   3.00
U671 A3356 44c multicolored   3.75   3.00
U672 A3357 44c multicolored   3.75   3.00
U673 A3358 44c multicolored   3.75   3.00
Nos. U669-U673 (5)   18.75   15.00
Pack of ten, containing two of each letter sheet, sold for $15.95.

Mackinac Bridge — U201

**2010, Jan. 4**    Typo.   Unwmk.
U674 U201 $4.90 multicolored   12.50   10.00
No. U674 was sold only in packs of 5.

New River Gorge Bridge, West Virginia — U202

**2011, Jan. 3**    Typo.   Unwmk.
U675 U202 $4.95 multicolored   12.50   10.00
No. U675 was sold only in packs of 5.

Sunshine Skyway Bridge, Florida — U203

**2012, Jan. 3**    Typo.   Unwmk.
U676 U203 $5.15 multicolored   12.50   10.00
No. U676 was sold only in packs of 5.

Purple Martin U204

**2012, Jan. 23**    Litho.   Unwmk.
**Design Size: 48x33mm**
U677 U204 (45c) multicolored   1.50   .50
**Design Size: 50x35mm**
U678 U204 (45c) multicolored   1.50   .50

No. U677 was from No. 6¾ size envelopes only. No. U678 was from No. 9 and No. 10 size envelopes.

No. U678 was reprinted in June 2012 without the 'Cradle to Cradle' recycling logo on the back.

**Arlington Green Bridge Type of 2013**
**2013, Jan. 25**    Typo.   Unwmk.
U679 A3612 $5.60 multicolored   11.00   8.00
No. U679 was sold only in packs of 5.

Bank Swallows — U205

**2013, Mar. 1**    Litho.   Unwmk.
**Design Size: 38x35mm**
U680 U205 (46c) multicolored   1.50   .50
**Design Size: 41x38mm**
U681 U205 (46c) multicolored   1.50   .50

No. U680 is from No. 6¾ size envelopes only. No. U681 is from No. 9 and No. 10 size envelopes.

UNITED STATES 205

Eagle, Shield and Flags — U206

**2013, Aug. 9     Litho.     Unwmk.**
U682  U206  (46c) multicolored    .95    .50
  a.  Double impression of magenta, entire    —
  b.  Triple impression of light blue, entire    —
  c.  Blurry microprinting Entire    4.00    5.00

**Verrazano-Narrows Bridge Type of 2014**

**2014, Mar. 4     Typo.     Unwmk.**
U683  A3726  $5.60 multicolored    12.50    8.00
  No. U683 was sold only in packs of 5, 10 or 25.

Poinsettia U207    Snowflake U208

Snowflake U209    Cardinal U210

Child Making Snowman — U211

**2014, Oct. 1     Litho.     Unwmk.**
U684  U207  (49c) multicolored    2.50    1.50
U685  U208  (49c) multicolored    2.50    1.50
U686  U209  (49c) multicolored    2.50    1.50
U687  U210  (49c) multicolored    2.50    1.50
U688  U211  (49c) multicolored    2.50    1.50
  Nos. U684-U688 (5)    12.50    7.50

Packs of 10 No. U684 and 10 self-adhesive stickers sold for $9.95. Packs containing 5 each of Nos. U685 and U686 and 10 self-adhesive stickers sold for $9.95. Packs containing 5 each of Nos. U687 and U688 and 10 self-adhesive stickers sold for $9.95. Nos. U684-U688 were available only as No. 10 size envelopes.

**Glade Creek Grist Mill Type of 2014**

**2015, Jan. 12     Typo.     Unwmk.**
U689  A3700  $5.75 multicolored    11.50    8.25
  No. U689 was sold only in packs of 5.

Red Water Lily — U212    White Water Lily — U213

**2015, Apr. 17     Litho.     Unwmk.**
U690  U212  (49c) multicolored    2.50    1.75
U691  U213  (49c) multicolored    2.50    1.75

Nos. U690 and U691 were only sold in packets of 10 containing five of each envelope and 10 stickers for $9.95. Nos. U690 and U691 were only available in #10 size with self-adhesive flap.

Forget-me-nots U214

**2015, May 18     Litho.     Unwmk.**
U692  U214  (49c) multicolored    2.50    1.75

No. U692 was sold only in packets of 10 + 10 stickers for $9.95. It was only available in #10 size with self-adhesive flap.

**La Cueva del Indio Type of 2016**

**2016, Jan. 17     Typo.     Unwmk.**
U693  A3875  $6.45 multicolored    13.00    9.50
  No. U693 was sold only in packs of 5.

Northern Cardinal — U215

Designed by Derry Noyes.

**2016, Nov. 3     Litho.     Unwmk.**
U694  U215  (47c) multicolored    1.75    1.75

No. U694 was sold only in packets of 12 + 12 stickers for $9.95. It was only available in #10 size with self-adhesive flap. Packets of No. U694 were sold in post offices in Ohio and Puerto Rico (and perhaps elsewhere) in late December, prior to the acknowledgement of the existence of the envelope by USPS Stamp Fulfillment Services. The packets were not offered for sale by USPS Stamp Fulfillment Services until Jan. 4, 2017. In late January, the packet was made available for direct order on the USPS Stamp Fulfillment Services website, which then noted that the day of issue was Jan. 8, 2017, even though the packets could be ordered on Jan. 4. The official first day of issue was announced as Nov. 3, 2016 in the Feb. 16, 2017 Postal Bulletin, but no indication was given that any first day cancels would be made available for this issue. The earliest documented use is postmarked Jan. 3, 2017.

**Lili'uokalani Gardens Type of 2017**

**2017, Jan. 22     Typo.     Unwmk.**
U695  A3986  $6.65 multicolored    13.50    9.75
  No. U695 was sold only in packs of 5.

Barn Swallows U216

**2017, Mar. 3     Litho.     Unwmk.**
U696  U216  (10c) multicolored    1.25    .50

**Byodo-In Temple Type of 2018**

**2018, Jan. 21     Typo.     Unwmk.**
U697  A4096  $6.70 multicolored    13.50    9.75
  No. U697 was sold only in packs of 5.

**Joshua Tree Type of 2019**

**2019, Jan. 27     Typo.     Unwmk.**
U698  A4191  $7.35 multicolored    15.00    10.00
  No. U698 was sold only in packs of 5 or 10.

**Big Bend National Park Type of 2020**

Designed by Greg Breeding.

**2020, Jan. 18     Typo.     Unwmk.**
U699  A4268  $7.75 multicolored    15.50    10.50
  No. U699 was sold only in packs of 5 or 10.

Flag and Stars — U217

**2020, June 15     Litho.     Unwmk.**
U700  U217  (55c) multicolored    1.40    .50

**Castillo de San Marcos Type of 2021**

**2021, Jan. 24     Typo.     Unwmk.**
U701  A4388  $7.95 multicolored    16.00    11.00
  No. U701 was sold only in packs of 5, 10 or 25.

Northern Cardinal U218

**Litho. & Typo.**

**2023, July 9     Unwmk.**
U702  U218  (66c) multicolored    1.75    .60

## AIR POST STAMPED ENVELOPES & AIR LETTER SHEETS

UC1

5c — Vertical rudder is not semi circular but slopes down to the left. The tail of the plane projects into the G of POSTAGE.

UC2

Die 2 (5c and 8c): Vertical rudder is semicircular. The tail of the plane touches but does not project into the G of POSTAGE.
Die 2 (6c) — Same as UC2 except three types of numeral.
  2a — The numeral "6" is 6½mm wide.
  2b — The numeral "6" is 6mm wide.
  2c — The numeral "6" is 5½mm wide.
Die 3 (6c): Vertical rudder leans forward. S closer to O than to T of POSTAGE. E of POSTAGE has short center bar. Border types b and d, also without border.

**1929-44**
UC1  UC1  5c blue    3.00    2.00
  a.  Orange and blue border, type b    375.00    450.00
UC2  UC2  5c blue, die 2    9.00    5.00
UC3  UC2  6c orange, die 2a ('34)    1.25    .40
  a.  With added impression of 3c purple (#U436a), entire without border    4,000.
  b.  Double impression of indicium, entire, with bicolored border    —
UC4  UC2  6c orange, die 2b ('42)    3.00    2.00
  Entire, without border    4.50    2.50
UC5  UC2  6c orange, die 2c ('44)    .70    .30
UC6  UC2  6c orange, die 3 ('42)    1.00    .35
  a.  6c orange, blue, die 3 (error) Entire, without border    15,000.
  b.  Double impression, entire    400.00    10,000.
UC7  UC2  8c olive green, die 2 ('32)    10.00    3.50

**Surcharged in Black on Envelopes Indicated by Number in Parenthesis**

**1945**
UC8  U93  6c on 2c carmine (U429, die 1)    1.25    .65
  a.  On U429f, die 7    2.25    1.50
  b.  On U429g, die 8    1.90    1.10
  c.  On U429h, die 9    8.00    7.50
  d.  6c on 1c green (error) (U420)    1,750.
  e.  6c on 3c dk violet (error) (U436a)    2,000.
  f.  6c on 3c dk violet (error), amber (U437a)    3,000.
  g.  6c on 3c violet (error) (U526)    3,000.
UC9  U95  6c on 2c carmine (U525)    40.00    35.00

**Surcharged in Black**

Surcharged on 6c orange air post envelopes without borders.

**1946**
UC10  UC2  5c on 6c orange, die 2a    2.75    1.50
  a.  Double surcharge    75.00
UC11  UC2  5c on 6c orange, die 2b    8.00    5.50
UC12  UC2  5c on 6c orange, die 2c    .75    .50
  a.  Double surcharge    75.00    900.00
UC13  UC2  5c on 6c orange, die 3    .70    .60
  a.  Double surcharge    75.00    50.00
  c.  Double surcharge, one on reverse    —
UC13B  U93  5c on 6c (UC8a), on tire    —

The 6c borderless envelopes and the revalued envelopes were issued primarily for use to and from members of the armed forces. The 5c rate came into effect Oct. 1, 1946.

DC-4 Skymaster — UC3

Die 1 — The end of the wing at the right is a smooth curve. The juncture of the front end of the plane and the engine forms an acute angle. The first T of STATES and the E's of UNITED STATES lean to the left.
Die 2 — The end of the wing at the right is a straight line. The juncture of the front end of the plane and the engine is wide open. The first T of STATES and the E's of UNITED STATES lean to the right.

**1946**
UC14  UC3  5c carmine, die 1    .75    .25
UC15  UC3  5c carmine, die 2    .75    .25
  See Nos. UC18, UC26.

DC-4 Skymaster — UC4

**1947-55     Typo.**
**Letter Sheets for Foreign Postage**
UC16  UC4  10c brt red, pale bl, entire    8.50    7.00
  e.  Blue omitted, entire    400.00
  f.  Overlay omitted front & back, entire    100.00
  g.  Overlay omitted from front only, entire    500.00
  a.  "Air Letter" on face, 4-line inscription on back ('51), entire    17.50    10.00
  b.  As "a," 10c chocolate, pale bl, entire    450.00
  c.  "Air Letter" and "Aerogramme" on face, 4-line inscription on back ('53), entire    45.00    12.50
  d.  As "c," 2 line inscription on back ('55), entire    9.00    8.00

**Postage Stamp Centenary Issue**

Centenary of the first postage stamps issued by the United States Government.

Washington & Franklin, Early and Modern Mail-carrying Vehicles — UC5

Two dies: Rotary, design measures 22¼mm high; and flat bed press, design 21¾mm high.

**Embossed, Rotary Press Printing**
**1947, May 21**
**For Domestic Postage**
UC17  UC5  5c carmine (rotary)    .50    .30
  a.  Flat plate printing    .50    .30

### Type of 1946

Type I: 6's lean to right.
Type II: 6's upright.

**1950, Sept. 22**
UC18 UC3 6c carmine, type I .75 .25
   *a.* Type II .90 .25
   Several other types differ slightly from the two listed.

### Nos. UC14, UC15, UC18 Surcharged in Red Left of Stamp

**1951**
UC19 UC3 6c on 5c carmine,
    die 1 .85 1.50
   *a.* Surcharge inverted at lower left, entire —
UC20 UC3 6c on 5c carmine,
    die 2 .85 1.50
   *a.* 6c on 6c carmine (error) entire 1,500.
   *b.* Double surcharge 975.00 —
   To qualify as No. UC20b, both surcharges must be to the left of the indicia.

### Nos. UC14-UC15 Surcharged in Red at Left of Stamp

**1952**
UC21 UC3 6c on 5c carmine,
    die 1 25.00 20.00
   *a.* Double surcharge, entire 600.00
UC22 UC3 6c on 5c carmine,
    die 2 3.75 2.50
   *a.* Double surcharge 250.00
   *b.* Triple surcharge, entire 275.00
   To qualify as Nos. UC22a or UC22b, all surcharges must be to the left of the indicia.

### No. UC17 Surcharged in Red

UC23 UC5 6c on 5c carmine 850.
The 6c on 4c black (No. U440) is believed to be a favor printing.

### Fifth International Philatelic Exhibition Issue

FIPEX, the Fifth International Philatelic Exhibition, New York, N.Y., Apr. 28-May 6, 1956.

 Eagle in Flight — UC6

**1956, May 2**
UC25 UC6 6c red .75 .50
Two types exist, differing slightly in the clouds at top.

### Skymaster Type of 1946

**1958, July 31**
UC26 UC3 7c blue .65 .50

### Nos. UC3-UC5, UC18 and UC25 Surcharged in Green at Left of Stamp

**1958**
UC27 UC2 6c + 1c orange,
    die 2a 250.00 300.00
UC28 UC2 6c + 1c orange,
    die 2b 65.00 80.00
UC29 UC2 6c + 1c orange,
    die 2c 30.00 55.00
UC30 UC3 6c + 1c carmine,
    type I 1.00 .50
   *a.* Type II 1.00 .50
UC31 UC6 6c + 1c red 1.00 .50

Jet Airliner — UC7

Type I: Back inscription in 3 lines.
Type II: Back inscription in 2 lines.

### Letter Sheet for Foreign Postage
**Typographed, Without Embossing**
**1958-59**
UC32 UC7 10c blue & red,
    *blue,* entire 6.00 5.00
   *a.* Type I ('58), entire 10.00 5.00
   *b.* Red omitted, II, entire 475.00
   *c.* Blue omitted, II, entire 400.00
   *d.* Red omitted, I, entire 700.00

 Silhouette of Jet Airliner — UC8

**1958, Nov. 21** Embossed
UC33 UC8 7c blue .60 .25

**1960, Aug. 18**
UC34 UC8 7c carmine .60 .25

 Jet Plane and Globe — UC9

### Letter Sheet for Foreign Postage
**Typographed, Without Embossing**
**1961, June 16**
UC35 UC9 11c red & blue,
    *blue,* entire 3.00 3.50
   *a.* Red omitted, entire 475.00
   *b.* Blue omitted, entire 475.00

 UC10

**1962, Nov. 17** Embossed
UC36 UC10 8c red .55 .25

UC11

**1965-67**
UC37 UC11 8c red .45 .25
   *a.* Tagged 3.50 .30
No. UC37a has a 8x24mm panel at left of stamp that glows orange red under ultraviolet light.

 Pres. John F. Kennedy and Jet Plane — UC12

### Letter Sheets for Foreign Postage
**Typographed, Without Embossing**
**1965, May 29**
UC38 UC12 11c red & dark
    blue, *blue,* entire 3.75 4.00

**1967, May 29**
UC39 UC12 13c red & dark
    blue, *blue,* entire 3.25 4.00
   *a.* Red omitted, entire 400.00
   *b.* Dark blue omitted, entire 400.00

 UC13

**1968, Jan. 8** Tagged Embossed
UC40 UC13 10c red .50 .25

### No. UC37 Surcharged in Red at Left of Stamp

**1968, Feb. 5**
UC41 UC11 8c + 2c red .65 .25

### Tagging

Envelopes and Letter Sheets from No. UC42 onward are tagged unless otherwise noted.

### Human Rights Year Issue

Issued for International Human Rights Year, and to commemorate the 20th anniversary of the United Nations' Declaration of Human Rights.

Globes and Flock of Birds UC14

### Letter Sheet for Foreign Postage
**1968, Dec. 3** Photo.
UC42 UC14 13c gray, brown,
    orange & black, *blue,* entire 8.00 7.50
   *a.* Orange omitted, entire 800.00
   *b.* Brown omitted, entire 375.00
   *c.* Black omitted, entire 700.00
   *d.* Gray and black omitted, entire —
   *e.* Tagging omitted, entire 150.00
No. UC42 has a luminescent panel ⅜x1 inch on the right globe. The panel glows orange red under ultraviolet light.

Birds in Flight and "usa" UC16

**1971, May 6** Embossed (Plane)
UC43 UC15 11c red & blue .50 1.75

### Letter Sheet for Foreign Postage
**1971** Photo.
UC44 UC16 15c gray, red,
    white & blue, *blue,* entire 1.50 7.50
   *a.* "AEROGRAMME" added to inscription, entire 1.50 7.50
   *b.* As #UC44, red omitted, entire 300.00
   *c.* As "a", red omitted, entire 500.00
Folding instructions (2 steps) in capitals on No. C44; (4 steps) in upper and lower case on No. UC44a.
On Nos. UC44-UC44a the white rhomboid background of "USA postage 15c" is luminescent. No. UC44 is inscribed: "VIA AIR MAIL-PAR AVION". "postage 15c" is in gray. See No. UC46.

### No. UC40 Surcharged in Green at Left of Stamp

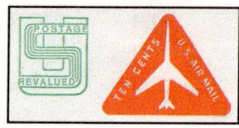

**1971, June 28** Embossed
UC45 UC13 10c + (1c) red 1.50 .75

### HOT AIR BALLOONING CHAMPIONSHIPS ISSUE

Hot Air Ballooning World Championships, Albuquerque, N.M., Feb. 10-17, 1973.

### "usa" Type of 1971

Design: Three balloons and cloud at left in address section; no birds beside stamp. Inscribed "INTERNATIONAL HOT AIR BALLOONING." "postage 15c" in blue.

### Letter Sheet for Foreign Postage
**1973, Feb. 10**
UC46 UC16 15c red, white &
    blue, *blue,* entire 1.00 7.50
Folding instructions as on No. UC44a. See notes after No. UC44.

 Bird in Flight — UC17

**1973, Dec. 1** Luminescent Ink
UC47 UC17 13c rose red .30 .25

Beginning with No. UC48, all listings are letter sheets for foreign postage.

 UC18

**1974, Jan. 4** Photo.
UC48 UC18 18c red & blue,
    *blue,* entire 1.00 6.00
   *a.* Red omitted, entire 200.00

### 25TH ANNIVERSARY OF NATO ISSUE

UC19

Design: "NATO" and NATO emblem at left in address section.

**1974, Apr. 4**
UC49 UC19 18c red & blue,
    *blue,* entire 1.00 6.00
   Die cutting reversed, entire 100.00

 UC20

**1976, Jan. 16**
UC50 UC20 22c red & blue, *blue,*
    entire 1.00 6.00
   *a.* Red color missing due to foldover and die cutting —

UC21

**1978, Nov. 3**
UC51 UC21 22c blue, *blue,* entire 1.00 3.00

# UNITED STATES

### 22nd OLYMPIC GAMES, MOSCOW, JULY 19-AUG. 3, 1980.

 UC22

Design (multicolored in bottom left corner) shows discus thrower.

**1979, Dec. 5**
UC52  UC22  22c red, black & green, *bluish,* entire    1.50  6.00

 UC23

Design (brown on No. UC53, green and brown on No. UC54): lower left, Statue of Liberty. Inscribed "Tour the United States." Folding area shows tourist attractions.

**1980, Dec. 29**
UC53  UC23  30c blue, red & brown, *blue,* entire    .85  6.00
a. Red (30) omitted, entire    70.00

**1981, Sept. 21**
UC54  UC23  30c multi, *blue,* entire    .65  6.00

 UC24

Design: "Made in USA . . . world's best buys!" on flap, ship, tractor in lower left. Reverse folding area shows chemicals, jet silhouette, wheat, typewriter and computer tape disks.

**1982, Sept. 16**
UC55  UC24  30c multi, *blue,* entire    .80  6.00

### WORLD COMMUNICATIONS YEAR

World Map Showing Locations of Satellite Tracking Stations — UC25

Design: Reverse folding area shows satellite, tracking station.

**1983, Jan. 7**
UC56  UC25  30c multi, *blue,* entire    .90  8.00

### 1984 OLYMPICS

 UC26

Indicia in black, multicolor design of woman equestrian at lower left with montage of competitive events on reverse folding area.

**1983, Oct. 14**
UC57  UC26  30c black & multi, *light blue,* entire    .85  8.00

### WEATHER SATELLITES, 25TH ANNIV.

 UC27

Design: Landsat orbiting the earth at lower left with three Landsat photographs on reverse folding area. Inscribed: "Landsat views the Earth."

**1985, Feb. 14**
UC58  UC27  36c multi, *blue,* entire    1.25  12.50

### NATIONAL TOURISM WEEK

 Urban Skyline — UC28

Design: Inscribed "Celebrate America" at lower left and "Travel. . . the perfect freedom" on folding area. Skier, Indian chief, cowboy, jazz trumpeter and pilgrims on reverse folding area.

**1985, May 21**
UC59  UC28  36c multi, *blue,* entire    1.25  12.50
a. Black omitted, entire    600.00

### MARK TWAIN AND HALLEY'S COMET

Comet Tail Viewed from Space — UC29

Design: Portrait of Twain at lower left and inscribed "I came in with Halley's Comet in 1835. It is coming again next year, and I expect to go out with it. It will be the greatest disappointment of my life if I don't go out with Halley's Comet." "1835 . Mark Twain . 1910 . Halley's Comet . 1985" and Twain, Huckleberry Finn, steamboat and comet on reverse folding areas.

**1985, Dec. 4**
UC60  UC29  36c multi, entire    2.00  12.50

 UC30

**1988, May 9**    Litho.
UC61  UC30  39c multi, entire    1.25  12.50
a. Tagging bar to left of design ('89)    1.25  1.50

On No. UC61, the tagging bar is between "USA" and "39."

### MONTGOMERY BLAIR, POSTMASTER GENERAL 1861-64

Montgomery Blair and Pres. Lincoln — UC31

Design: Mail bags and "Free city delivery," "Railway mail service" and "Money order system" at lower left. Globe, locomotive, bust of Blair, UPU emblem and "The Paris conference of 1863, initiated by Postmaster General Blair, led, in 1874, to the founding of the Universal Postal Union" contained on reverse folding area.

**1989, Nov. 20**
UC62  UC31  39c multicolored, entire    1.40  16.00
a. Double impression    —
b. Triple impression    —
c. Quadruple impression    —

 UC32

**1991, May 17**
UC63  UC32  45c gray, red & blue, *blue,* entire    1.40  16.00
a. White paper, entire    1.00  16.00

Thaddeus Lowe (1832-1913), Balloonist — UC33

**1995, Sept. 23**
UC64  UC33  50c multicolored, *blue,* entire    1.50  20.00

Voyageurs Natl. Park, Minnesota UC34

**1999, May 15**
UC65  UC34  60c multicolored, *blue,* entire    1.75  12.50

No. UC65 used is often found with additional postage affixed.

---

### OFFICIAL STAMPED ENVELOPES

By the Act of Congress, January 31, 1873, the franking privilege of officials was abolished as of July 1, 1873 and the Postmaster General was authorized to prepare official envelopes. At the same time official stamps were prepared for all Departments. Department envelopes became obsolete July 5, 1884. After that, government offices began to use franked envelopes of varied design. These indicate no denomination and lie beyond the scope of this Catalogue.

### Post Office Department

"2" 9mm high — UO1

"3" 9mm high — UO2

"6" 9½mm high — UO3

**1873**
UO1  UO1  2c black, *lemon*    25.00  10.00
UO2  UO2  3c black, *lemon*    12.50  6.50
+UO3  UO2  3c black    17,500.
UO4  UO3  6c black, *lemon*    25.00  17.50

"2" 9¼mm high — UO4

"3" 9¼mm high — UO5

"6" 10½mm high — UO6

**1874-79**
UO5  UO4  2c black, *lemon*    8.00  4.25
UO6  UO4  2c black    120.00  37.50
UO7  UO5  3c black, *lemon*    2.75  .75
UO8  UO5  3c black    1,750.  1,200.
UO9  UO5  3c black, *amber*    120.00  37.50
UO10  UO5  3c black, *blue*    —
UO11  UO5  3c blue, *blue* ('75)    20,000.
UO12  UO6  6c black, *lemon*    12.50  6.50
UO13  UO6  6c black    1,250.  1,750.

Fakes exist of Nos. UO3, UO8 and UO13.

### Postal Service

UO7

**1877**
UO14  UO7  black    6.00  4.50
UO15  UO7  black, *amber*    125.00  42.50
UO16  UO7  blue, *amber*    125.00  40.00
UO17  UO7  blue, *blue*    7.50  6.75

### War Department

Franklin — UO8

Bust points to the end of "N" of "ONE".

Jackson — UO9

Bust narrow at the back.

Washington — UO10

Queue projects below the bust.

Lincoln — UO11

Neck very long at the back.

Jefferson — UO12

208                                    UNITED STATES

Queue forms straight line with bust.

Clay — UO13

Ear partly concealed by hair, mouth large, chin prominent.

Webster — UO14

Has side whiskers.

Scott           Hamilton
UO15            UO16

Back of bust very narrow; chin almost straight; the labels containing the letters "U S" are exactly parallel.

### Reay Issue
**1873**

| | | | | |
|---|---|---|---|---|
| UO18 | UO8 | 1c dk red | 350.00 | 200.00 |
| WO18A | UO8 | 1c dk red, man, entire | | — |
| UO19 | UO9 | 2c dk red | 1,000. | |
| UO20 | UO10 | 3c dk red | 12.50 | 30.00 |
| UO21 | UO10 | 3c dk red, amb | 27,500. | |
| UO22 | UO10 | 3c dk red, cr | 500.00 | 250.00 |
| UO23 | UO11 | 6c dk red | 250.00 | 100.00 |
| UO24 | UO11 | 6c dk red, cr | 4,000. | 425.00 |
| UO25 | UO12 | 10c dk red | 7,500. | |
| UO26 | UO13 | 12c dk red | 90.00 | |
| UO27 | UO14 | 15c dk red | 125.00 | 55.00 |
| UO28 | UO15 | 24c dk red | 100.00 | 40.00 |
| UO29 | UO16 | 30c dk red | 250.00 | 150.00 |
| UO30 | UO8 | 1c ver | 200.00 | |
| WO31 | UO8 | 1c ver, man | 17.50 | 14.00 |
| +UO32 | UO9 | 2c ver | 400.00 | |
| WO33 | UO9 | 2c ver, man | 250.00 | |
| UO34 | UO10 | 3c ver | 75.00 | 40.00 |
| UO35 | UO10 | 3c ver, amb | 85.00 | 40.00 |
| UO36 | UO10 | 3c ver, cr | 12.50 | 12.50 |
| UO37 | UO11 | 6c ver | 75.00 | |
| +UO38 | UO11 | 6c ver, cr | 400.00 | |
| UO39 | UO12 | 10c ver | 300.00 | |
| UO40 | UO13 | 12c ver | 130.00 | |
| UO41 | UO14 | 15c ver | 200.00 | |
| UO42 | UO15 | 24c ver | 300.00 | |
| UO43 | UO16 | 30c ver | 250.00 | |

UO17

Bottom serif on "S" is thick and short; bust at bottom below hair forms a sharp point.

UO18

Bottom serif on "S" is thick and short; front part of bust is rounded.

UO19

Bottom serif on "S" is short; queue does not project below bust.

UO20

Neck very short at the back.

UO21

Knot of queue stands out prominently.

UO22

UO23

Ear prominent, chin receding. No "dot" uner "T" of "Dept."

Has no side whiskers; forelock projects above head.

UO24

Back of bust rather broad; chin slopes considerably; the label containing letters "U S" are not exactly parallel.

### Plimpton Issue
**1875**

| | | | | |
|---|---|---|---|---|
| UO44 | UO17 | 1c red | 175.00 | 85.00 |
| +UO45 | UO17 | 1c red, amb | 600.00 | |
| +UO45A | UO17 | 1c red, org | 24,000. | |
| WO46 | UO17 | 1c red, man | 4.50 | 2.75 |
| UO47 | UO18 | 2c red | 90.00 | — |
| UO48 | UO18 | 2c red, amber | 12.50 | 17.50 |
| UO49 | UO18 | 2c red, orange | 12.50 | 17.50 |
| WO50 | UO18 | 2c red, manila | 90.00 | 40.00 |
| UO51 | UO19 | 3c red | 11.00 | 10.00 |
| UO52 | UO19 | 3c red, amber | 12.50 | 10.00 |
| UO53 | UO19 | 3c red, cream | 5.00 | 3.75 |
| UO54 | UO19 | 3c red, blue | 3.00 | 2.00 |
| UO55 | UO19 | 3c red, fawn | 6.00 | 5.00 |
| UO56 | UO20 | 6c red | 45.00 | 30.00 |
| UO57 | UO20 | 6c red, amber | 65.00 | 40.00 |
| UO58 | UO20 | 6c red, cream | 175.00 | 85.00 |
| UO59 | UO21 | 10c red | 180.00 | 80.00 |
| UO60 | UO21 | 10c red, amber | 650.00 | |
| UO61 | UO22 | 12c red | 25.00 | 25.00 |
| UO62 | UO22 | 12c red, amber | 400.00 | |
| UO63 | UO22 | 12c red, cream | 450.00 | |
| UO64 | UO23 | 15c red | 200.00 | 125.00 |
| UO65 | UO23 | 15c red, amber | 650.00 | |
| UO66 | UO23 | 15c red, cream | 525.00 | |
| UO67 | UO24 | 30c red | 150.00 | 140.00 |
| UO68 | UO24 | 30c red, amber | 550.00 | |
| UO69 | UO24 | 30c red, cream | 675.00 | |

## POSTAL SAVINGS ENVELOPES

UO25

**1911**

| | | | | |
|---|---|---|---|---|
| UO70 | UO25 | 1c green | 75.00 | 25.00 |
| UO71 | UO25 | 1c green, oriental buff | 175.00 | 85.00 |
| UO72 | UO25 | 2c carmine | 12.50 | 4.00 |
| a. | | 2c carmine, manila (error) | 1,200. | 1,000. |

### Used Values
Catalogue values for regularly used entires. Those with first-day cancels generally sell for much less.

### Tagged
Envelopes from No. UO73 onward are tagged unless otherwise noted.

### OFFICIAL MAIL

UO26

**1983, Jan. 12**  Typo. & Embossed
UO73  UO26  20c blue, entire  1.00  10.00

UO27

**1985, Feb. 26**  Typo. & Embossed
UO74  UO27  22c blue, entire  .90  5.00

UO28

**1987, Mar. 2**  Typo.
UO75  UO28  22c blue, entire  1.50  25.00
Used exclusively to mail U.S. Savings Bonds.

UO29

**1988, Mar. 22**
UO76  UO29  (25c) black & blue, entire  1.25  15.00
Used exclusively to mail U.S. Savings Bonds.

UO30

UO31

**1988, Apr. 11**  Typo. & Embossed
UO77  UO30  25c black & blue, entire  .85  6.00
a.  Denomination & lettering as on No. UO78, entire  5.00  6.00

Nos. UO77 and UO77a used to mail U.S. Savings Bonds and also occasionally used by the director of admissions at the U.S. Air Force Academy and by Air Force recruiting stations for intra-agency correspondence.

Typo.
UO78  UO31  25c black & blue, entire  1.00  35.00
a.  Denomination & lettering as on No. UO77, entire  1.00  35.00

Used to mail U.S. Savings Bonds. Also used by the Department of Agriculture.

### Used Values
Postally used examples of Nos. UO79-UO94 seldom appear in the marketplace and thus cannot be valued with as much certainty as the editors would like. They must show evidence of postal usage. Clear cancels are valued even higher. The editors would like to have records of sales of examples of these used envelopes. If a value exists, it is based on a known transaction(s) or consultation with experts.

**1990, Mar. 17**
Stars and "E Pluribus Unum" illegible. "Official" is 13mm, "USA" is 16mm long.
UO79  UO31  45c black & blue, entire  1.25  80.00
UO80  UO31  65c black & blue, entire  1.75  100.00
Used exclusively to mail U.S. passports.

UO32

Stars and "E Pluribus Unum" clear and sharply printed. "Official" is 14½mm, "USA" is 17mm long.

**1990, Aug. 10**  Litho.
UO81  UO32  45c black & blue, entire  1.25  100.00
UO82  UO32  65c black & blue, entire  1.75  160.00
Used exclusively to mail U.S. passports.

UO33

**1991, Jan. 22**  Typo.  Wmk.
UO83  UO33  (29c) black & blue, entire  1.00  20.00
Used exclusively to mail U.S. Savings Bonds.

UO34

**Litho. & Embossed**
**1991, Apr. 6**  Wmk.
UO84  UO34  29c black & blue, entire  .70  5.00
a.  Unwatermarked paper, entire  7.50  4.00

No. UO84a has a "recycled" imprint under the flap.

UO35

**1991, Apr. 17**  Wmk.
UO85  UO35  29c black & blue, entire  .70  20.00
Used exclusively to mail U.S. Savings Bonds.

Consular Service, Bicent. — UO36

**1992, July 10 Litho. Unwmk.**

**UO86** UO36 52c blue & red, entire 6.00 *20.00*
*a.* 52c blue & red, *blue-white*, entire 1.50 *20.00*

**UO87** UO36 75c blue & red, entire 11.00 *30.00*
*a.* 75c blue & red, *blue-white*, entire 2.50 *30.00*

Used exclusively to mail U.S. passports. Available only in 4⅜ inch x 8⅞ inch size with self-adhesive flap.

UO37

**1995-99 Typo. & Embossed**

**UO88** UO37 32c blue & red, entire .90 *7.00*

**UO89** UO37 33c blue & red, entire .90 *8.00*

**Type of 1995**

**2001, Feb. 27**

**UO90** UO37 34c blue & red, entire 1.00 *10.00*

**Type of 1995**

**2002, Aug. 2**

**UO91** UO37 37c blue & red, type I, entire 1.00 *15.00*
*a.* Type II, entire 1.00 *35.00*

Type I has 29x28mm blue panel, top of "USA" even with the bottom of the eagle's neck and is made with "100% recycled paper" as noted on reverse. Type II has a 27½x27½mm blue panel, top of "USA" even with the highest arrow, and has no mention of "100% recycled paper" on reverse.

**Type of 1995**

**2006, Jan. 9**

**UO92** UO37 39c blue & red, entire 2.00 *12.50*

**Type of 1995**

**2007, May 12**

**UO93** UO37 41c blue & red, entire 2.00 *25.00*

**Type of 1995**

**2008, June 20 Typo.**

**UO94** UO37 42c blue & red, entire 2.00 *25.00*

## REVENUE STAMPS

Nos. R1-R102 were used to pay taxes on documents and proprietary articles including playing cards. Until Dec. 25, 1862, the law stated that a revenue stamp could be used only for payment of the tax upon the particular instrument or article specified on its face. After that date stamps, except the Proprietary, could be used indiscriminately.

Values quoted are for pen-canceled stamps. Stamps with handstamped cancellations sell at higher prices. Stamps canceled with cuts, punches or holes sell for less. See the Scott U.S. Specialized Catalogue.

**General Issue**

**First Issue**

Head of Washington in Oval. Various Frames as Illustrated.

Nos. R1b to R42b, part perforate, occur perforated sometimes at sides only and sometimes at top and bottom only. The higher values, part perforate, are perforated at sides only. Imperforate and part perforate revenues often bring much more in pairs or blocks than as single stamps. Part perforate revenues with an asterisk (*) after the value exist imperforate horizontally or vertically.

The experimental silk paper is a variety of the old paper and has only a very few minute fragments of fiber.

Some of the stamps were in use eight years and were printed several times. Many color variations occurred, particularly when unstable pigments were used and the color was intended to be purple or violet, such as the 4c Proprietary, 30c and $2.50 stamps. Before 1868 dull colors predominate on these and the early red stamps. In later printings of the 4c Proprietary, 30c and $2.50 stamps, red predominates in the mixture, and on the dollar values the red is brighter. The early $1.90 stamp is dull purple, imperf. or perforated. In a later printing, perforated only, the purple is darker.

R1

George Washington — R2

**Old Paper**

**1862-71 Engr. Perf. 12**

**R1** R1 1c Express, red
*a.* Imperf. 125.00
*b.* Part perf. 75.00*
*c.* Perf. 1.50
*d.* As No. R1c, silk paper *450.00*
*e.* As No. R1c, vertical pair, imperf. between *200.00*

**R2** R1 1c Playing Cards, red
*a.* Imperf. 4,500.
*b.* Part perf. 2,500.
*c.* Perf. 250.00

**R3** R1 1c Proprietary, red
*a.* Imperf. 1,800.
*b.* Part perf. 350.00*
*c.* Perf. .50
*d.* As No. R3c, silk paper 100.00

**R4** R1 1c Telegraph, red
*a.* Imperf. 1,000.
*c.* Perf. 20.00

**R5** R2 2c Bank Check, blue
*a.* Imperf. 1.50
*b.* Part perf. 5.50*
*c.* Perf. .50
*e.* As No. R5c, Double impression *1,500.*
*f.* As No. R5c, pair imperf between 500.00

**R6** R2 2c Bank Check, orange
*b.* Part perf. 60.00*
*c.* Perf. .45
*d.* As No. R6c, silk paper 275.00
*e.* As No. R6c, orange, *green* 1,000.

**R7** R2 2c Certificate, blue
*a.* Imperf. 20.00
*c.* Perf. 32.50

**R8** R2 2c Certificate, orange
*c.* Perf. 50.00

**R9** R2 2c Express, blue
*a.* Imperf. 15.00
*b.* Part perf. 35.00*
*c.* Perf. .40

**R10** R2 2c Express, orange
*b.* Part perf. *3,250.*
*c.* Perf. 14.00
*d.* As No. R10c, silk paper 500.00

**R11** R2 2c Playing Cards, blue
*a.* Imperf. *1,750.*
*b.* Part perf. 825.00
*c.* Perf. 4.50

**R12** R2 2c Playing Cards, org
*c.* Perf. 55.00

**R13** R2 2c Proprietary, blue
*a.* Imperf. 2,000.
*b.* Part perf. 250.
*c.* Perf. .40
*d.* As No. R13c, silk paper 350.00
Double transfer (T13a) 500.00
*e.* ultramarine 400.00

**R14** R2 2c Proprietary, orange
*c.* Perf. 70.00

**R15** R2 2c U.S. Internal Revenue, orange ('64)
*c.* Perf. .25
*d.* As No. R15c, silk paper 1.00
*e.* As No. R15c, orange, *green* *2,500.*

R3

**R16** R3 3c Foreign Exchange, green
*b.* Part perf. 1,750.*
*c.* Perf. 5.00
*d.* As No. R16c, silk paper 300.00

**R17** R3 3c Playing Cards, green ('63)
*a.* Imperf. *27,500.*
*c.* Perf. 200.00

**R18** R3 3c Proprietary, green
*b.* Part perf. 1,250.
*c.* Perf. 9.00
*d.* As No. R18c, silk paper 350.00
*e.* As No. R18c, double impression *1,750.*
*f.* As No. R18c, printed on both sides *4,000.*

**R19** R3 3c Telegraph, green
*a.* Imperf. 100.00
*b.* Part perf. 30.00
*c.* Perf. 3.00

**R20** R3 4c Inland Exchange, brown ('63)
*c.* Perf. 2.25
*d.* As No. R20c, silk paper 225.00

**R21** R3 4c Playing Cards, slate ('63)
*c.* Perf. 700.00

**R22** R3 4c Proprietary, purple
*a.* Imperf. —
*b.* Part perf. 500.00
*c.* Perf. 8.50
*d.* As No. R22c, silk paper 250.00

There are shade and color variations of Nos. R21-R22.

**R23** R3 5c Agreement, red
*c.* Perf. .50
*d.* As No. R23c, silk paper 4.50

**R24** R3 5c Certificate, red
*a.* Imperf. 4.00
*b.* Part perf. 15.00
*c.* Perf. .50
*d.* As No. R24c, silk paper 1.10
*f.* As No. R24d, impression of No. R3 on back *3,000.*

**R25** R3 5c Express, red
*a.* Imperf. 8.00
*b.* Part perf. 8.00*
*c.* Perf. .40

**R26** R3 5c Foreign Exchange, red
*b.* Part perf. *2,600.*
*c.* Perf. .50
*d.* As No. R26c, silk paper 850.00

**R27** R3 5c Inland Exchange, red
*a.* Imperf. 10.00
*b.* Part perf. 6.75
*c.* Perf. .60
*d.* As No. R27c, silk paper 17.50
*e.* As No. R27c, double impression *3,500.*

**R28** R3 5c Playing Cards, red ('63)
*c.* Perf. 40.00
*e.* Double impression *2,000.*

**R29** R3 5c Proprietary, red ('64)
*c.* Perf. 30.00
*d.* As No. R29c, silk paper 400.00

**R30** R3 6c Inland Exchange, orange ('63)
*b.* Part perf. (imperf. vert.), on document —
*c.* Perf. 2.25
*d.* As No. R30c, silk paper 350.00

**R31** R3 6c Proprietary, orange ('71)
*c.* Perf. *1,800.*

Nearly all examples of No. R31 are faulty or repaired and poorly centered. The catalogue value is for a fine centered stamp with minor faults which do not detract from its appearance.

**R32** R3 10c Bill of Lading, blue
*a.* Imperf. 90.00
*b.* Part perf. 600.00*
*c.* Perf. 1.75

**R33** R3 10c Certificate, blue
*a.* Imperf. 400.00
*b.* Part perf. 850.00*
*c.* Perf. .35
*d.* As No. R33c, silk paper 6.00

**R34** R3 10c Contract, blue
*b.* Part perf. 700.00*
*be.* As No. R34b, ultramarine 1,000.
*c.* Perf. .50
*ce.* As No. R34c, ultramarine 1.00
*d.* As No. R34c, silk paper 4.25

**R35** R3 10c Foreign Exchange, blue
*c.* Perf. 14.00
*d.* As No. R35c, silk paper —
*e.* As No. R35c, ultramarine 20.00

**R36** R3 10c Inland Exchange, blue
*a.* Imperf. 500.00
*b.* Part perf. 4.50*
*c.* Perf. .30
*d.* As No. R36c, silk paper 125.00

**R37** R3 10c Power of Attorney, blue
*a.* Imperf. 1,000.
*b.* Part perf. 30.00
*c.* Perf. 1.00

**R38** R3 10c Proprietary, blue ('64)
*c.* Perf. 19.00

**R39** R3 15c Foreign Exchange, brown ('63)
*c.* Perf. 35.00
*e.* Double impression *1,750.*

**R40** R3 15c Inland Exchange, brown
*a.* Imperf. 45.00
*b.* Part perf. 14.00
*c.* Perf. 2.00
*e.* As No. R40b, double impression *2,250.*
*f.* As No. R40c, double impression *1,250.*

**R41** R3 20c Foreign Exchange, red
*a.* Imperf. 100.00
*c.* Perf. 80.00
*d.* As No. R41c, silk paper 650.00

**R42** R3 20c Inland Exchange, red
*a.* Imperf. 17.00
*b.* Part perf. 22.50
*c.* Perf. .45
*d.* As No. R42c, silk paper —

R4

R5

**R43** R4 25c Bond, red
*a.* Imperf. 300.00
*b.* Part perf. 6.75
*c.* Perf. 3.75

**R44** R4 25c Certificate, red
*a.* Imperf. 11.00
*b.* Part perf. 6.75*
*c.* Perf. .50
*d.* As No. R44c, silk paper 2.75
*e.* As No. R44c, printed on both sides *3,500.*
*f.* As No. R44c, impression of No. R48 on back *6,000.*

**R45** R4 25c Entry of Goods, red
*a.* Imperf. 22.50
*b.* Part perf. 500.00*
*c.* Perf. 1.50
*d.* As No. R45c, silk paper 200.00

**R46** R4 25c Insurance, red
*a.* Imperf. 12.50
*b.* Part perf. 19.00
*c.* Perf. .30
*d.* As No. R46c, silk paper 7.00
*e.* As No. R46c, double impression *1,000.*

**R47** R4 25c Life Insurance, red
*a.* Imperf. 50.00
*b.* Part perf. 1,250.
*c.* Perf. 11.00

**R48** R4 25c Power of Attorney, red
*a.* Imperf. 10.00
*b.* Part perf. 45.00
*c.* Perf. 1.00
*d.* As No. R48c, silk paper *1,750.*

**R49** R4 25c Protest, red
*a.* Imperf. 35.00
*b.* Part perf. 1,000.
*c.* Perf. 10.00

**R50** R4 25c Warehouse Receipt, red
*a.* Imperf. 55.00
*b.* Part perf. 1,300.
*c.* Perf. 45.00

**R51** R4 30c Foreign Exchange, lilac
*a.* Imperf. 200.00
*b.* Part perf. *11,000.*
*c.* Perf. 60.00
*d.* As No. R51c, silk paper *675.00*

**R52** R4 30c Inland Exchange, lilac
*a.* Imperf. 75.00
*b.* Part perf. 90.00
*c.* Perf. 8.50
*d.* As No. R52c, silk paper *1,750.*

**R53** R4 40c Inland Exchange, brown
*a.* Imperf. *2,500.*
*b.* Part perf. 9.00
*c.* Perf. 8.00
*d.* As No. R53c, silk paper 550.00
*f.* As No. R53c, double impression *2,000.*

**R54** R5 50c Conveyance, blue
*a.* Imperf. 20.00
*b.* Part perf. 3.50
*c.* Perf. .35
*ce.* As No. R54c, ultramarine .50
*d.* As No. R54c, silk paper, blue 3.00
*de.* As No. R54d, ultramarine —

**R55** R5 50c Entry of Goods, blue
*b.* Part perf. 17.50
*c.* Perf. .00
*d.* As No. R55c, silk paper 200.00

**R56** R5 50c Foreign Exchange, blue
*a.* Imperf. 75.00
*b.* Part perf. 125.00*
*c.* Perf. 7.50
*e.* As No. R56c, double impression *1,000.*

**R57** R5 50c Leases, blue
*a.* Imperf. 35.00
*b.* Part perf. 250.00
*c.* Perf. 10.00

**R58** R5 50c Life Insurance, blue
*a.* Imperf. 45.00
*b.* Part perf. 200.00
*c.* Perf. 1.75
*e.* As No. R58c, double impression *1,100.*

**R59** R5 50c Mortgage, blue
*a.* Imperf. 22.50
*b.* Part perf. 5.00
*c.* Perf. .70
*d.* As No. R59c, silk paper —
*e.* As No. R59a, double impression —
*f.* As No. R59c, double impression —

**R60** R5 50c Original Process, blue
*a.* Imperf. 5.50
*b.* Part perf. *5,000.*
*c.* Perf. 1.00
*d.* As No. R60c, silk paper 7.50

**R61** R5 50c Passage Ticket, blue
*a.* Imperf. 140.00
*b.* Part perf. 750.00*
*c.* Perf. 2.25

**R62** R5 50c Probate of Will, blue
*a.* Imperf. 55.00
*b.* Part perf. 250.00
*c.* Perf. 22.50

210 UNITED STATES

**R63** R5 50c Surety Bond, blue 400.00
*a.* Imperf. 400.00
*b.* Part perf. 2.75
*c.* Perf. .30
*e.* As No. R63c, ultramarine .75

**R64** R5 60c Inland Exchange, orange
*a.* Imperf. 120.00
*b.* Part perf. 90.00
*c.* Perf. 9.00
*d.* As No. R64c, silk paper 100.00

**R65** R5 70c Foreign Exchange, green
*a.* Imperf. 750.00
*b.* Part perf. 200.00
*c.* Perf. 14.00
*d.* As No. R65c, silk paper 75.00

R6

R7

**R66** R6 $1 Conveyance, red
*a.* Imperf. 27.50
*b.* Part perf. *4,500.*
*c.* Perf. 27.50
*d.* As No. R66c, silk paper 225.00

**R67** R6 $1 Entry of Goods, red
*a.* Imperf. 50.00
*c.* Perf. 2.75
*d.* As No. R67c, silk paper 200.00

**R68** R6 $1 Foreign Exchange, red
*a.* Imperf. 125.00
*c.* Perf. .75
*d.* As No. R68c, silk paper 175.00

**R69** R6 $1 Inland Exchange, red
*a.* Imperf. 17.00
*b.* Part perf. *8,000.**
*c.* Perf. .70
*d.* As No. R69c, silk paper 6.00
*e.* As No. R69c, horiz. pair, imperf. vert. —

No. R69e is an error from a pane of stamps that was intended to be issued fully perforated. It can be differentiated from No. R69b by the color, paper and date of cancel. Expertization is strongly recommended and some specialists doubt the existence of No. R69b.

**R70** R6 $1 Lease, red
*a.* Imperf. 50.00
*c.* Perf. 4.50

**R71** R6 $1 Life Insurance, red
*a.* Imperf. 300.00
*c.* Perf. 10.00
*d.* As No. R71c, silk paper *1,000.*

**R72** R6 $1 Manifest, red
*a.* Imperf. 47.50
*c.* Perf. 40.00

**R73** R6 $1 Mortgage, red
*a.* Imperf. 27.50
*c.* Perf. 300.00

**R74** R6 $1 Passage Ticket, red
*a.* Imperf. 350.00
*c.* Perf. 350.00

**R75** R6 $1 Power of Attorney, red
*a.* Imperf. 100.00
*c.* Perf. 2.75

**R76** R6 $1 Probate of Will, red
*a.* Imperf. 100.00
*c.* Perf. 55.00

**R77** R7 $1.30 Foreign Exchange, orange ('63)
*a.* Imperf. *11,000.*
*c.* Perf. 120.00

**R78** R7 $1.50 Inland Exchange, blue
*a.* Imperf. 32.50
*c.* Perf. 7.00

**R79** R7 $1.60 Foreign Exchange, green ('63)
*a.* Imperf. 1,400.
*c.* Perf. 180.00

**R80** R7 $1.90 Foreign Exchange, purple ('63)
*a.* Imperf. *12,500.*
*c.* Perf. 200.00
*d.* As No. R80c, silk paper 650.00

R8

**R81** R8 $2 Conveyance, red
*a.* Imperf. 250.00
*b.* Part perf. 5,500.
*c.* Perf. 4.00
*d.* As No. R81c, silk paper 40.00

**R82** R8 $2 Mortgage, red
*a.* Imperf. 200.00
*c.* Perf. 7.00
*d.* As No. R82c, silk paper 60.00

**R83** R8 $2 Probate of Will, red ('63)
*a.* Imperf. *5,500.*
*c.* Perf. 90.00

**R84** R8 $2.50 Inland Exchange, purple ('63)
*a.* Imperf. *10,000.*
*c.* Perf. 22.50
*d.* As No. R84c, silk paper 40.00
*e.* As No. R84c, double impression *2,000.*

There are many shade and color variations of Nos. R84c and R84d.

**R85** R8 $3 Charter Party, green
*a.* Imperf. 250.00
*c.* Perf. 11.00
*d.* As No. R85c, silk paper 175.00
*e.* As No. R85c, printed on both sides *7,000.*
*g.* As No. R85c, impression of No. RS208 on back *17,000.*

**R86** R8 $3 Manifest, green
*a.* Imperf. 250.00
*c.* Perf. 55.00

**R87** R8 $3.50 Inland Exchange, blue ('63)
*a.* Imperf. *8,500.*
*c.* Perf. 70.00
*e.* As No. R87c, printed on both sides *4,000.*

The $3.50 has stars in upper corners.

R9

R10

**R88** R9 $5 Charter Party, red
*a.* Imperf. 350.00
*c.* Perf. 10.00
*d.* As No. R88c, silk paper 170.00

**R89** R9 $5 Conveyance, red
*a.* Imperf. 50.00
*c.* Perf. 11.00
*d.* As No. R89c, silk paper 160.00

**R90** R9 $5 Manifest, red
*a.* Imperf. 250.00
*c.* Perf. 120.00

**R91** R9 $5 Mortgage, red
*a.* Imperf. 200.00
*c.* Perf. 25.00

**R92** R9 $5 Probate of Will, red
*a.* Imperf. 750.00
*c.* Perf. 27.50

**R93** R9 $10 Charter Party, green
*a.* Imperf. 900.00
*c.* Perf. 37.50

**R94** R9 $10 Conveyance, green
*a.* Imperf. 175.00
*c.* Perf. 77.50

**R95** R9 $10 Mortgage, green
*a.* Imperf. 800.00
*c.* Perf. 40.00

**R96** R9 $10 Probate of Will, green
*a.* Imperf. *3,500.*
*c.* Perf. 45.00

**R97** R10 $15 Mortgage, blue
*a.* Imperf. 4,500.
*c.* Perf. 300.00
*e.* As No. R97c, ultramarine 500.00
*f.* As No. R97c, milky blue 525.00

**R98** R10 $20 Conveyance, orange
*a.* Imperf. 150.00
*c.* Perf. 110.00
*d.* As No. R98c, silk paper 175.00

**R99** R10 $20 Probate of Will, orange
*a.* Imperf. 2,500.
*c.* Perf. 3,000.

**R100** R10 $25 Mortgage, red ('63)
*a.* Imperf. 3,250.
*c.* Perf. 250.00
*d.* As No. R100c, silk paper 300.00
*e.* As No. R100c, horiz. pair, imperf. between *6,000.*

**R101** R10 $50 U.S. Internal Revenue, green ('63)
*a.* Imperf. 325.00
*c.* Perf. 210.00

R11

**R102** R11 $200 U.S. Int. Rev., green & red ('64)
*a.* Imperf. 2,500.
*c.* Perf. 650.00

### DOCUMENTARY STAMPS
### Second Issue

After release of the First Issue revenue stamps, the Bureau of Internal Revenue received many reports of fraudulent cleaning and re-use. The Bureau ordered a Second Issue with new designs and colors, using a patented "chameleon" paper which is usually violet or pinkish, with silk fibers.

While designs are different from those of the first issue, stamp sizes and make up of the plates are the same as for corresponding denominations.

R12

R12a

**George Washington**
Various Frames and Numeral Arrangements

**1871** ***Perf. 12***

**R103** R12 1c blue & black 100.00
Cut cancel 40.00
*a.* Inverted center *2,000.*
Cut cancel *750.00*

**R104** R12 2c blue & black 2.75
Cut cancel .30
*a.* Inverted center *2,500.*
Cut cancel *3,500.*

**R105** R12a 3c blue & black 85.00
Cut cancel 30.00

**R106** R12a 4c blue & black 160.00
Cut cancel 65.00

**R107** R12a 5c blue & black 2.00
Cut cancel .50
*a.* Inverted center *2,000.*
Cut cancel *2,500.*

**R108** R12a 6c blue & black 300.00
Cut cancel 100.00

**R109** R12a 10c blue & black 1.50
Cut cancel .30
*a.* Inverted center *2,500.*
Cut cancel *1,250.*
*b.* Double impression of center —

No. R109a is valued in the grade of fine.

**R110** R12a 15c blue & black 100.00
Cut cancel 35.00

**R111** R12a 20c blue & black 10.00
Cut cancel 4.00
*a.* Inverted center *5,000.*

No. R111a is valued in the grade of fine and with small faults, as almost all examples have faults.

R13

R13a

**R112** R13 25c blue & black 1.50
Cut cancel .30
*a.* Inverted center *13,000.*
Cut cancel *6,500.*
*b.* Imperf. —

**R113** R13 30c blue & black 175.00
Cut cancel 70.00

**R114** R13 40c blue & black 150.00
Cut cancel 50.00

**R115** R13a 50c blue & black 1.40
Cut cancel .35
*a.* Inverted center 400.00
Cut cancel 500.00
Punch cancel 250.00

**R116** R13a 60c blue & black 250.00
Cut cancel 80.00

**R117** R13a 70c blue & black 100.00
Cut cancel 35.00
*a.* Inverted center *4,000.*
Cut cancel *1,750.*

R13b

**R118** R13b $1 blue & black 10.00
Cut cancel 2.25
*a.* Inverted center *6,000.*
Cut cancel *1,500.*
Punch cancel *1,150.*

**R119** R13b $1.30 blue & black 650.00
Cut cancel 175.00

**R120** R13b $1.50 blue & black 22.50
Cut cancel 9.00

**R121** R13b $1.60 blue & black 650.00
Cut cancel 325.00

**R122** R13b $1.90 blue & black 400.00
Cut cancel 150.00

R13c

**R123** R13c $2 blue & black 25.00
Cut cancel 10.00

**R124** R13c $2.50 blue & black 60.00
Cut cancel 30.00

**R125** R13c $3 blue & black 75.00
Cut cancel 35.00

**R126** R13c $3.50 blue & black 450.00
Cut cancel 250.00

R13d

**R127** R13d $5 blue & black 40.00
Cut cancel 15.00
*a.* Inverted center *3,750.*
Cut cancel *1,500.*
Punch cancel *1,100.*

**R128** R13d $10 blue & black 260.00
Cut cancel 90.00

R13e

**R129** R13e $20 blue & black 800.00
Cut cancel 275.00

**R130** R13e $25 blue & black 750.00
Cut cancel 275.00

**R131** R13e $50 blue & black 900.00
Cut cancel 325.00

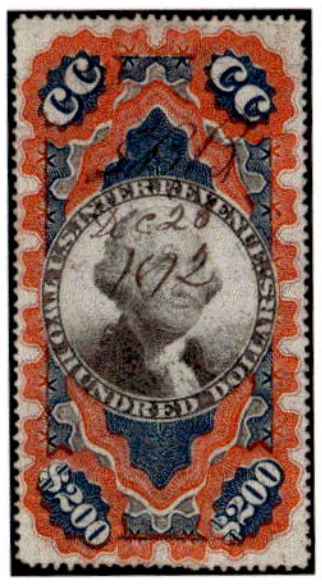
R13f

R132 R13f $200 red, blue & black 8,500.
Cut cancel 3,500.

Printed in sheets of one.

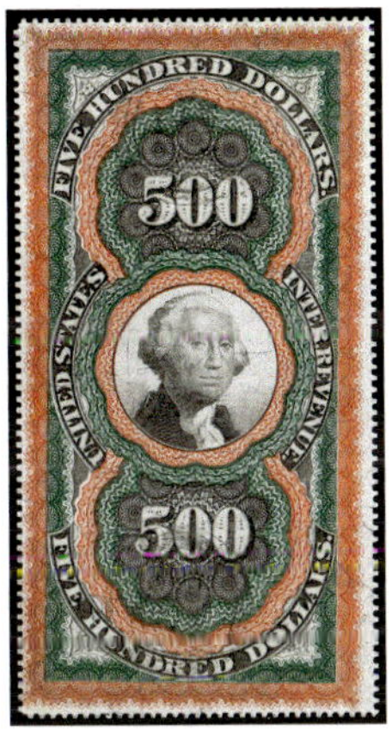
R13g

R133 R13g $500 red org, grn & blk 17,500.
Cut cancel 8,500.

Printed in sheets of one.

Value for No. R133 is for a very fine appearing example with a light circular cut cancel or with minor flaws.

**Inverted Centers:** Fraudulently produced inverted centers exist, some excellently made.

---

Confusion resulting from the fact that all 1c through $50 denominations of the Second Issue were uniform in color, caused the ordering of a new printing with values in distinctive colors.

Plates used were those of the preceding issue.

---

### Third Issue

Various Frames and Numeral Arrangements.

Violet "Chameleon" Paper with Silk Fibers.

**1871-72** ***Perf. 12***

R134 R12 1c claret & black ('72) 65.00
Cut cancel 30.00
R135 R12 2c orange & black .40
Cut cancel .25
*a.* 2c vermilion & black (error) 900.00
*b.* Inverted center 425.00
Cut cancel 300.00
*c.* Imperf., pair —
*d.* As No. R135, double impression of frame 2,500.
*e.* As No. R135, frame printed on both sides 1,800.
*f.* As No. R135, double impression of center 150.00
R136 R12a 4c brown & black ('72) 110.00
Cut cancel 45.00
R137 R12a 5c orange & black .35
Cut cancel .25
*a.* Inverted center 6,500.
Cut cancel 3,750.

No. R137a is valued in the grade of fine.

R138 R12a 6c orange & black ('72) 150.00
Cut cancel 50.00
R139 R12a 15c brown & black ('72) 30.00
Cut cancel 10.00
*a.* Inverted center 16,000.
Cut cancel 9,000.
R140 R13 30c orange & black ('72) 50.00
Cut cancel 15.00
*a.* Inverted center 3,500.
Cut cancel 1,750.
R141 R13 40c brown & black ('72) 110.00
Cut cancel 35.00
R142 R13a 60c orange & black ('72) 140.00
Cut cancel 55.00
R143 R13a 70c green & black ('72) 90.00
Cut cancel 30.00
R144 R13b $1 green & black ('72) 3.00
Cut cancel .80
*a.* Inverted center 12,500.
Cut cancel 10,000.

No. R144a is valued in the grade of fine.

R145 R13c $2 vermilion & black ('72) 65.00
Cut cancel 25.00
R146 R13c $2.50 claret & black ('72) 125.00
Cut cancel 35.00
*a.* Inverted center 25,000.
Cut cancel 17,000.
R147 R13c $3 green & black ('72) 125.00
Cut cancel 35.00
R148 R13d $5 vermilion & black ('72) 50.00
Cut cancel 20.00
R149 R13d $10 green & black ('72) 400.00
Cut cancel 85.00
R150 R13e $20 orange & black ('72) 900.00
Cut cancel 350.00
*a.* $20 vermilion & black (error) 1,250.
Cut cancel 700.00

See note on Inverted Centers after No. R133.

**1874** ***Perf. 12***

R151 R12 2c orange & black, *green* .25
Cut cancel .25
*a.* Inverted center 800.00
Cut cancel 375.00

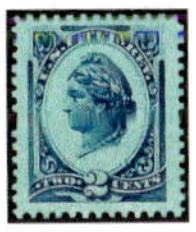
Liberty — R14

**1875-78** ***Perf. 12***

R152 R14 2c blue, *blue*
*a.* silk paper 3.00 .45
*b.* Wmk. 191R ('78) 2.00 .35
*c.* Wmk. 191R, rouletted 6 150.00 32.50
*d.* As "a," vert. pair, imperf. horiz. 525.00
*e.* As "b," imperf., pair 350.00
*f.* As "b," vert. pair, imperf. horiz. 350.00

The watermarked paper came into use in 1878. The rouletted stamps probably were introduced in 1881.

### Nos. 279, 267a, 267, 279Bg, 279B, 272-274 Overprinted in Red or Blue

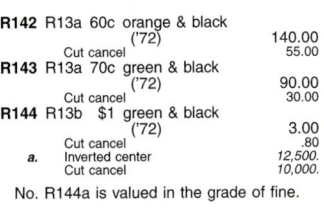

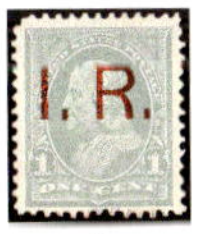
a

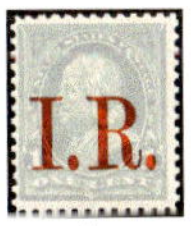
b

**1898** **Wmk. 191** ***Perf. 12***

For Nos. R153-R160, values in the first column are for unused examples, values in the second column are for used.

R153 A87(a) 1c deep grn (R) 5.00 2.75
R154 A87(b) 1c green (R) .35 .35
*a.* Overprint inverted 45.00 30.00
*b.* Overprint on back instead of face, inverted 4,000.
*c.* Pair, one without overprint 10,000.
R155 A88(b) 2c pink, III (Bl) .30 .25
*b.* 2c **carmine,** type III (Bl) .35 .25
*c.* As No. R155, overprint inverted 10.00 7.50
*d.* Vertical pair, one without overprint 1,750.
*e.* Horiz. pair, one without overprint —
*f.* As No. R155, overprint on back instead of face, inverted 350.00
*i.* Double ovt., one split 850.00
R155A A88(b) 2c pink, IV (Bl) .25 .25
*g.* 2c **carmine,** type IV (Bl) .25 .25
*h.* As No. R155A, overprint inverted 2.75 2.00

### Handstamped Type "b" or Type "c" in Magenta

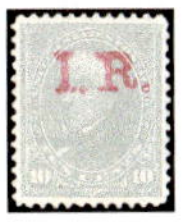
c

R156 A93(b) 8c violet brown 5,250.
R157 A94(b) 10c dark green 4,000.
*a.* As No. R157, handstamped type "c" — —
R158 A95(b) 15c dark blue 6,250.

Nos. R156-R158 were emergency provisionals, privately prepared, not officially issued.

### Privately Prepared Provisionals

No. 285 Overprinted in Red

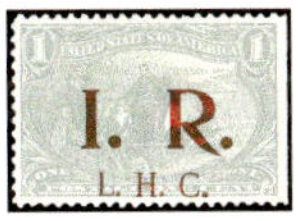

**1898** **Wmk. 191** ***Perf. 12***

R158A A100 1c dark yellow green 15,000. 12,500.

No. R158A is valued in sound condition and in the grade of fine to very fine. Most examples have faults, and such examples sell for less.

No. 285 Ovptd. "I.R./P.I.D. & Son" in Red

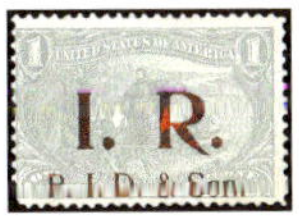

R158B A100 1c dark yellow green 25,000. 30,000.

No. R158B is valued with small faults as each of the four recorded examples have faults.

Nos. R158A-R158B were overprinted with federal government permission by the Purvis Printing Co. upon order of Capt. L. H. Chapman of the Chapman Steamboat Line. Both the Chapman Line and P. I. Daprix & Son operated freight-carrying steamboats on the Erie Canal. The Chapman Line touched at Syracuse, Utica, Little Falls and Fort Plain; the Daprix boat ran between Utica and Rome. Overprintings of 250 of each stamp were made.

Dr. Kilmer & Co. provisional overprints and St. Louis provisional proprietary stamps are listed under "Private Die Medicine Stamps" in the Scott U.S. Specialized Catalogue.

Newspaper Stamp No. PR121 Srchd. Vertically in Red

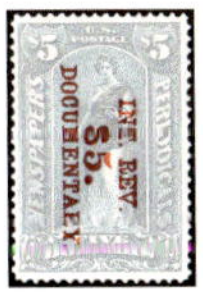

**1898** ***Perf. 12***

R159 N18 $5 dark blue, surcharge reading down 550.00 325.00
R160 N18 $5 dark blue, surcharge reading up 150.00 140.00

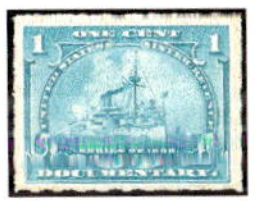
Battleship — R15

### Inscribed: "Series of 1898" and "Documentary."

There are 2 styles of rouletting for the 1898 proprietary and documentary stamps, an ordinary roulette 5½ and one where small rectangles of the paper are cut out, called hyphen hole perf. 7.

**1898** **Wmk. 191R** ***Rouletted 5½***

R161 R15 ½c orange 5.00 25.00
R162 R15 ½c dark gray .30 .25
*a.* Vert. pair, imperf. horiz. 125.00
R163 R15 1c pale blue .25 .25
*a.* Vert. pair, imperf. horiz. 8.00
*b.* Imperf., pair 600.00
R164 R15 2c car rose .30 .30
*a.* Vert. pair, imperf. horiz. 125.00
*b.* Imperf., pair 400.00
*c.* Horiz. pair, imperf. vert. 375.00
R165 R15 3c dark blue 3.50 .35
R166 R15 4c pale rose 2.50 .35
*a.* Vert. pair, imperf. horiz. 250.00
R167 R15 5c lilac .65 .35
*a.* Pair, imperf. horiz. or vert. 350.00 175.00
*b.* Horiz. pair, imperf. btwn. 650.00
R168 R15 10c dark brown 2.00 .25
*a.* Vert. pair, imperf. horiz. 40.00 35.00
*b.* Horiz. pair, imperf. vert. —
R169 R15 25c pur brown 7.50 .50
R170 R15 40c blue lilac 125.00 1.50
Cut cancellation .35
R171 R15 50c slate violet 35.00 .25
*a.* Imperf., pair 650.00
*b.* Horiz. pair, imperf. btwn. 750.00
R172 R15 80c bister 125.00 .50
Cut cancellation .25

No. R167b may not be genuine.

### *Hyphen Hole Perf. 7*

*R163p* 1c .30 .25
*R164p* 2c .35 .25
*R165p* 3c 40.00 1.40
*R166p* 4c 17.50 1.60
*R167p* 5c 17.50 .35
*R168p* 10c 10.00 .25
*R169p* 25c 20.00 .50
*R170p* 40c 210.00 35.00
Cut cancellation 12.50
*R171p* 50c 75.00 1.00
*b.* Horiz. pair, imperf. btwn. — 250.00
*R172p* 80c 250.00 60.00
Cut cancellation 20.00

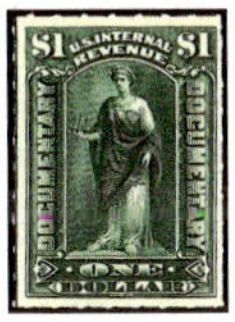
Commerce — R16

**1898** ***Rouletted 5½***

R173 R16 $1 dark green 45.00 .25
*a.* Vert. pair, imperf. horiz. 800.00
*b.* Horiz. pair, imperf. vert. — 325.00
*p.* Hyphen hole perf. 7 50.00 2.00
Cut cancel .75
R174 R16 $3 dark brown 80.00 1.25
Cut cancellation .30
*a.* Horiz. pair, imperf. vert. 500.00
*p.* Hyphen hole perf. 7 125.00 3.50
Cut cancellation .40
R175 R16 $5 orange red 125.00 2.00
Cut cancellation .30
R176 R16 $10 black 225.00 3.50
Cut cancellation .65
*a.* Horiz. pair, imperf. vert. —
R177 R16 $30 red 850.00 175.00
Cut cancellation 47.50
R178 R16 $50 gray brown 500.00 7.00
Cut cancellation 2.50

See Nos. R182-R183.

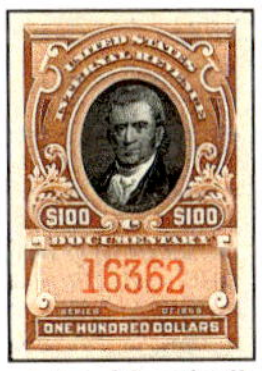
John Marshall R17

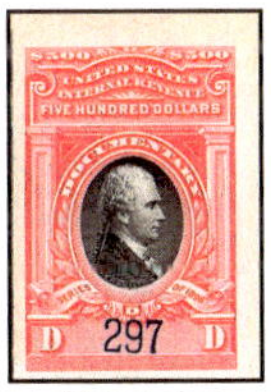
Alexander Hamilton R18

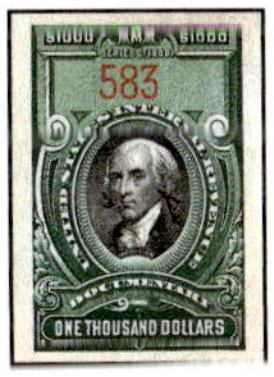
James Madison — R19

**1899** ***Imperf.***

### Without Gum

R179 R17 $100 yel brn & blk 500.00 40.00
Cut cancel 22.50
R180 R18 $500 car lake & blk 2,500. 1,000.
Cut cancel 350.00
R181 R19 $1000 grn & blk 1,750. 350.00
Cut cancel 150.00

**1900** ***Hyphen-hole perf. 7***

### Allegorical Figure of Commerce

R182 R16 $1 carmine 75.00 .55
Cut cancel .30
R183 R16 $3 lake (fugitive ink) 400.00 60.00
Cut cancel 10.00

**Warning:** The ink on No. R183 will run in water.

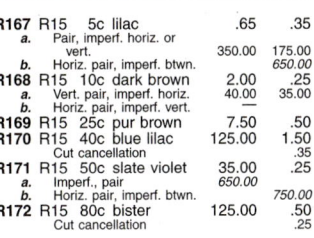

212 UNITED STATES

a

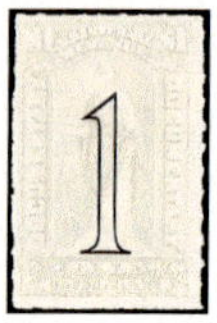

### Surcharged type "a"

| 1900 | | | | |
|---|---|---|---|---|
| R184 | R16 | $1 gray | 60.00 | .40 |
| | | Cut cancel | | .30 |
| | | *a.* Horiz. pair, imperf. vert | — | |
| | | *b.* Surcharge omitted | 140.00 | |
| | | As "b," cut cancel | | 82.50 |
| R185 | R16 | $2 gray | 60.00 | .40 |
| | | Cut cancel | | .25 |
| R186 | R16 | $3 gray | 250.00 | 15.00 |
| | | Cut cancel | | 6.00 |
| R187 | R16 | $5 gray | 130.00 | 11.00 |
| | | Cut cancel | | 1.60 |
| R188 | R16 | $10 gray | 350.00 | 25.00 |
| | | Cut cancel | | 4.50 |
| R189 | R16 | $50 gray | 2,750. | 575.00 |
| | | Cut cancel | | 140.00 |

b

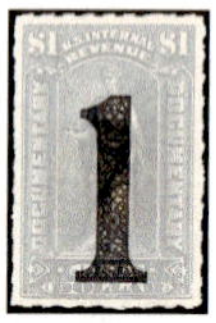

### Surcharged type "b"

Warning: If Nos. R190-R194 are soaked, the center part of the surcharged numeral may wash off. Before the surcharging, a square of soluble varnish was applied to the middle of some stamps.

| 1902 | | | | |
|---|---|---|---|---|
| R190 | R16 | $1 green | 80.00 | 3.50 |
| | | Cut cancel | | .30 |
| | | *a.* Inverted surcharge | | 190.00 |
| R191 | R16 | $2 green | 80.00 | 2.50 |
| | | Cut cancel | | .45 |
| | | *a.* Surcharged as No. R185 | 150.00 | 90.00 |
| | | *b.* Surcharged as No. R185, in violet | 2,000. | — |
| | | *c.* As "a," double surcharge | 150.00 | |
| | | *d.* As "a," triple surcharge | 2,500. | |
| | | *e.* Pair, Nos. R191c and R191d | 5,000. | |
| R192 | R16 | $5 green | 325.00 | 42.50 |
| | | Cut cancel | | 5.00 |
| | | *a.* Surcharge omitted | 400.00 | |
| | | *b.* Pair, one without surcharge | 700.00 | |
| R193 | R16 | $10 green | 525.00 | 225.00 |
| | | Cut cancel | | 80.00 |
| R194 | R16 | $50 green | 3,000. | 1,250. |
| | | Cut cancel | | 500.00 |

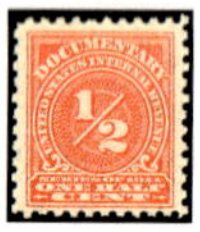

R20

### Inscribed "Series of 1914"

**Offset Printing**

**1914 Wmk. 190 *Perf. 10***

| | | | | |
|---|---|---|---|---|
| R195 | R20 | ½c rose | 16.00 | 5.00 |
| R196 | R20 | 1c rose | 3.50 | .30 |
| R197 | R20 | 2c rose | 5.00 | .30 |
| R198 | R20 | 3c rose | 125.00 | 40.00 |
| R199 | R20 | 4c rose | 35.00 | 2.50 |
| R200 | R20 | 5c rose | 12.00 | .40 |
| R201 | R20 | 10c rose | 10.00 | .25 |
| R202 | R20 | 25c rose | 60.00 | .60 |
| R203 | R20 | 40c rose | 40.00 | 3.00 |
| R204 | R20 | 50c rose | 15.00 | .35 |
| R205 | R20 | 80c rose | 250.00 | 17.00 |
| | | *Nos. R195-R205 (11)* | 571.50 | 69.70 |

**Wmk. 191R**

| | | | | |
|---|---|---|---|---|
| R206 | R20 | ½c rose | 1.60 | .50 |
| R207 | R20 | 1c rose | .25 | .25 |
| R208 | R20 | 2c rose | .30 | .25 |
| R209 | R20 | 3c rose | 1.50 | .25 |
| R210 | R20 | 4c rose | 4.50 | .50 |
| R211 | R20 | 5c rose | 2.00 | .35 |
| R212 | R20 | 10c rose | .80 | .25 |
| R213 | R20 | 25c rose | 10.00 | 1.50 |
| R214 | R20 | 40c rose | 175.00 | 15.00 |
| | | Cut cancel | | .50 |
| R215 | R20 | 50c rose | 35.00 | .40 |
| | | Cut cancel | | .25 |
| R216 | R20 | 80c rose | 250.00 | 35.00 |
| | | Cut cancel | | 1.25 |
| | | *Nos. R206-R216 (11)* | 480.95 | 54.25 |

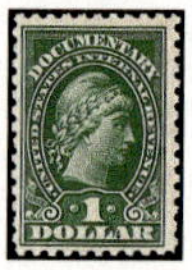

Liberty — R21

### Inscribed "Series 1914"

**Engr.**

| | | | | |
|---|---|---|---|---|
| R217 | R21 | $1 green | 125.00 | .55 |
| | | Cut cancel | | .25 |
| | | *a.* $1 yellow green | 110.00 | .25 |
| R218 | R21 | $2 carmine | 200.00 | 1.00 |
| | | Cut cancel | | .25 |
| R219 | R21 | $3 purple | 250.00 | 5.00 |
| | | Cut cancel | | .80 |
| R220 | R21 | $5 blue | 175.00 | 4.50 |
| | | Cut cancel | | .65 |
| R221 | R21 | $10 yel org | 475.00 | 7.50 |
| | | Cut cancel | | 1.10 |
| R222 | R21 | $30 vermilion | 1,250. | 21.00 |
| | | Cut cancel | | 2.25 |
| R223 | R21 | $50 violet | 2,000. | 1,250. |
| | | Cut cancel | | 600.00 |

See Nos. R240-R245, R257-R259, R276-R281.

Portrait Types of 1899 Inscribed "Series of 1915" (#R224), or "Series of 1914"

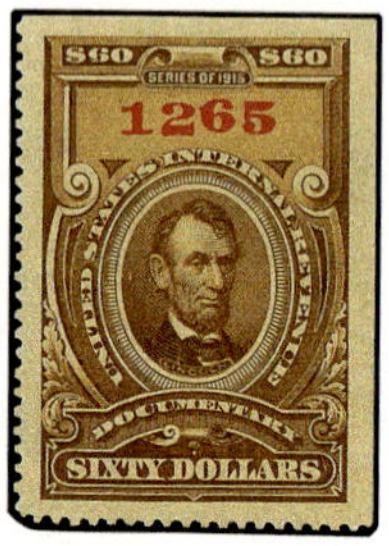

**1914-15 Without Gum *Perf. 12***

| | | | | |
|---|---|---|---|---|
| R224 | R19 | $60 brown *(Lincoln)* | 350.00 | 150.00 |
| | | Cut cancel | | 70.00 |
| R225 | R17 | $100 green *(Washington)* | 110.00 | 45.00 |
| | | Cut cancel | | 16.00 |
| R226 | R18 | $500 blue *(Hamilton)* | 13,000. | 650.00 |
| | | Cut cancel | | 275.00 |
| R227 | R19 | $1000 orange *(Madison)* | — | 750.00 |
| | | Cut cancel | | 325.00 |

The stamps of types R17, R18 and R19 in this and subsequent issues were issued in vertical strips of 4 which are imperforate at the top, bottom and right side; therefore, single stamps are always imperforate on one or two sides.

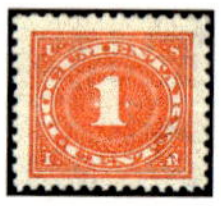

R22

**Offset Printing**

**1917 Wmk. 191R *Perf. 11***

| | | | | |
|---|---|---|---|---|
| R228 | R22 | 1c carmine rose | .35 | .25 |
| R229 | R22 | 2c carmine rose | .25 | .25 |
| R230 | R22 | 3c carmine rose | 1.75 | .40 |
| R231 | R22 | 4c carmine rose | .75 | .25 |
| R232 | R22 | 5c carmine rose | .30 | .25 |
| R233 | R22 | 8c carmine rose | 3.00 | .35 |
| R234 | R22 | 10c carmine rose | .40 | .25 |
| R235 | R22 | 20c carmine rose | .75 | .25 |
| R236 | R22 | 25c carmine rose | 1.75 | .25 |
| R237 | R22 | 40c carmine rose | 2.25 | .50 |
| R238 | R22 | 50c carmine rose | 2.50 | .25 |
| R239 | R22 | 80c carmine rose | 9.00 | .35 |
| | | *Nos. R228-R239 (12)* | 23.05 | 3.60 |

### Liberty Type of 1914 without "Series 1914"

**1917-33 Engr.**

| | | | | |
|---|---|---|---|---|
| R240 | R21 | $1 yellow green | 17.50 | .30 |
| | | *a.* $1 green | 12.50 | .25 |
| R241 | R21 | $2 rose | 30.00 | .25 |
| R242 | R21 | $3 violet | 110.00 | 1.50 |
| | | Cut cancel | | .30 |
| R243 | R21 | $4 yellow brown ('33) | 75.00 | 2.00 |
| | | Cut cancel | | .30 |
| R244 | R21 | $5 dark blue | 50.00 | .35 |
| | | Cut cancel | | .25 |
| R245 | R21 | $10 orange | 110.00 | 1.40 |
| | | Cut cancel | | .30 |

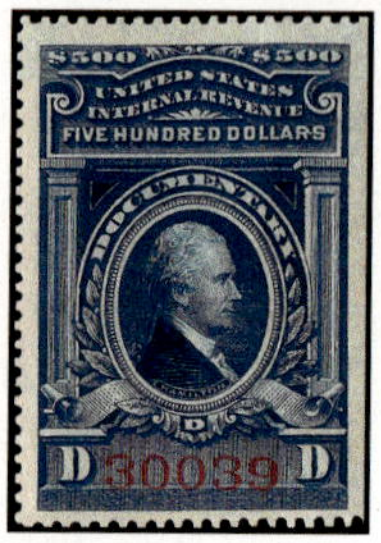

Portrait Types of 1899 without "Series of" and Date

Portraits: $30, Grant. $60, Lincoln. $100, Washington. $500, Hamilton. $1,000, Madison.

**1917 Without Gum *Perf. 12***

| | | | | |
|---|---|---|---|---|
| R246 | R17 | $30 dp org, green numerals | 75.00 | 13.00 |
| | | Cut cancel | | 2.25 |
| | | *a.* As "b," imperf. pair | | 1,000. |
| | | *b.* Numerals in blue | 150.00 | 3.50 |
| | | Cut cancel | | 1.50 |
| R247 | R19 | $60 brown | 90.00 | 8.00 |
| | | Cut cancel | | .85 |
| R248 | R17 | $100 green | 65.00 | 2.00 |
| | | Cut cancel | | .50 |
| R249 | R18 | $500 blue, red numerals | 350.00 | 50.00 |
| | | Cut cancel | | 15.00 |
| | | *a.* Numerals in orange | 425.00 | 65.00 |
| | | Cut cancel | | 20.00 |
| R250 | R19 | $1000 orange | 200.00 | 20.00 |
| | | Cut cancel | | 7.50 |
| | | *a.* Imperf., pair | | 2,000. |

See note after No. R227.

**1928-29 Offset Printing *Perf. 10***

| | | | | |
|---|---|---|---|---|
| R251 | R22 | 1c carmine rose | 2.10 | 1.60 |
| R252 | R22 | 2c carmine rose | .60 | .30 |
| R253 | R22 | 4c carmine rose | 7.00 | 4.00 |
| R254 | R22 | 5c carmine rose | 1.75 | .55 |
| R255 | R22 | 10c carmine rose | 2.75 | 1.25 |
| R256 | R22 | 20c carmine rose | 6.00 | 4.50 |

**Engr.**

| | | | | |
|---|---|---|---|---|
| R257 | R21 | $1 green | 200.00 | 45.00 |
| | | Cut cancel | | 5.00 |
| R258 | R21 | $2 rose | 90.00 | 5.00 |
| R259 | R21 | $10 orange | 325.00 | 75.00 |
| | | Cut cancel | | 30.00 |

**1929 Offset Printing *Perf. 11x10***

| | | | | |
|---|---|---|---|---|
| R260 | R22 | 2c carmine rose ('30) | 3.00 | 2.75 |
| R261 | R22 | 5c carmine rose ('30) | 2.00 | 1.90 |
| R262 | R22 | 10c carmine rose | 9.25 | 6.75 |
| R263 | R22 | 20c carmine rose | 15.00 | 8.25 |

Used values for Nos. R264-R734 are for stamps which are neither cut nor perforated with initials. Examples with cut cancellations or perforated initials are valued in the Scott U. S. Specialized Catalogue.

### Types of 1917-33 Overprinted in Black

SERIES 1940

**Offset Printing**

**1940 Wmk. 191R *Perf. 11***

| | | | | |
|---|---|---|---|---|
| R264 | R22 | 1c rose pink | 3.75 | 2.40 |
| R265 | R22 | 2c rose pink | 5.00 | 2.25 |
| R266 | R22 | 3c rose pink | 11.00 | 5.00 |
| R267 | R22 | 4c rose pink | 5.00 | .80 |
| R268 | R22 | 5c rose pink | 5.00 | 1.25 |
| R269 | R22 | 8c rose pink | 22.50 | 17.00 |
| R270 | R22 | 10c rose pink | 2.50 | .65 |
| R271 | R22 | 20c rose pink | 3.25 | .80 |
| R272 | R22 | 25c rose pink | 8.00 | 1.50 |
| R273 | R22 | 40c rose pink | 6.75 | .90 |
| R274 | R22 | 50c rose pink | 11.00 | .55 |
| R275 | R22 | 80c rose pink | 14.00 | 1.75 |

**Engr.**

| | | | | |
|---|---|---|---|---|
| R276 | R21 | $1 green | 80.00 | 1.25 |
| R277 | R21 | $2 rose | 80.00 | 2.00 |
| R278 | R21 | $3 violet | 115.00 | 37.50 |
| | | *b.* Vert. pair, imperf. horiz. | | 750.00 |

Only one example of No. R278b is recorded. It is thinned and is valued thus.

| | | | | |
|---|---|---|---|---|
| R279 | R21 | $4 yellow brown | 210.00 | 35.00 |
| R280 | R21 | $5 dark blue | 100.00 | 20.00 |
| R281 | R21 | $10 orange | 275.00 | 50.00 |

### Types of 1917 Handstamped "Series 1940" like R264-R281

**1940 Wmk. 191R *Perf. 12***

**Without Gum**

| | | | | |
|---|---|---|---|---|
| R282 | R17 | $30 vermilion (B) | | 1,250. |
| | | *a.* With black 2-line handstamp in larger type | | 25,000. |
| R283 | R19 | $60 brown (B, G) | | 2,400. |
| | | *a.* As #R282a, cut cancel | | 12,500. |
| R284 | R17 | $100 green (B) | | 4,500. |
| R285 | R18 | $500 blue (V) | | 3,000. |
| | | *a.* As #R282a | 4,500. | 4,000. |
| R286 | R19 | $1000 orange (B, G) | | 1,250. |
| | | *b.* Double overprint, cut cancel | | — |

### Types of 1917 Handstamped with black 2-line "Series 1941" in larger type.

| 1941 | | | | |
|---|---|---|---|---|
| R287 | R17 | $30 vermilion | | 35,000. |
| R287A | R19 | $60 brown | | 35,000. |

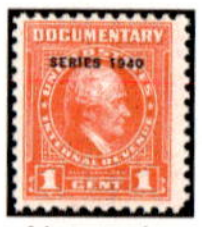

Alexander Hamilton R23

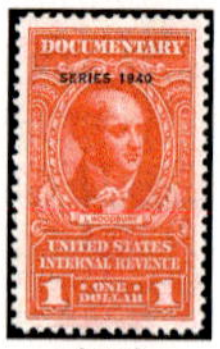

Levi Woodbury R24

Overprinted in Black SERIES 1940

Various Portraits: 2c, Oliver Wolcott, Jr. 3c, Samuel Dexter. 4c, Albert Gallatin. 5c. G. W. Campbell. 8c, Alexander Dallas. 10c, William H. Crawford. 20c, Richard Rush. 25c, S. D. Ingham. 40c. Louis McLane. 50c, William J. Duane. 80c, Roger B. Taney. $2, Thomas Ewing. $3, Walter Forward. $4, J. C. Spencer. $5, G. M. Bibb. $10, R. J. Walker. $20, William M. Meredith.

**1940 Engr. Wmk. 191R *Perf. 11***

| | | | | |
|---|---|---|---|---|
| R288 | R23 | 1c carmine | 5.75 | 4.50 |
| | | *a.* Imperf, pair, without gum | 200.00 | |
| R289 | R23 | 2c carmine | 8.50 | 4.00 |
| | | *a.* Imperf, pair, without gum | 200.00 | |
| R290 | R23 | 3c carmine | 30.00 | 12.00 |
| | | *a.* Imperf, pair, without gum | 200.00 | |
| R291 | R23 | 4c carmine | 62.50 | 27.50 |
| | | *a.* Imperf, pair, without gum | 200.00 | |
| R292 | R23 | 5c carmine | 4.75 | .80 |
| | | *a.* Imperf, pair, without gum | 200.00 | |
| R293 | R23 | 8c carmine | 85.00 | 60.00 |
| | | *a.* Imperf, pair, without gum | 200.00 | |
| R294 | R23 | 10c carmine | 4.25 | .60 |
| | | *a.* Imperf, pair, without gum | 200.00 | |
| R295 | R23 | 20c carmine | 5.50 | 4.25 |
| | | *a.* Imperf, pair, without gum | 200.00 | |
| R296 | R23 | 25c carmine | 5.00 | .75 |
| | | *a.* Imperf, pair, without gum | 200.00 | |
| R297 | R23 | 40c carmine | 75.00 | 30.00 |
| | | *a.* Imperf, pair, without gum | 200.00 | |
| R298 | R23 | 50c carmine | 8.00 | .60 |
| | | *a.* Imperf, pair, without gum | 200.00 | |
| R299 | R23 | 80c carmine | 200.00 | 110.00 |
| | | *a.* Imperf, pair, without gum | 400.00 | |
| R300 | R24 | $1 carmine | 50.00 | .60 |
| | | *a.* Imperf, pair, without gum | 250.00 | |
| R301 | R24 | $2 carmine | 100.00 | .90 |
| | | *a.* Imperf, pair, without gum | — | |
| R302 | R24 | $3 carmine | 230.00 | 95.00 |
| | | *a.* Imperf, pair, without gum | 1,400. | |
| R303 | R24 | $4 carmine | 175.00 | 50.00 |
| | | *a.* Imperf, pair, without gum | — | |
| R304 | R24 | $5 carmine | 100.00 | 3.00 |
| | | *a.* Imperf, pair, without gum | — | |
| R305 | R24 | $10 carmine | 175.00 | 10.00 |
| R305A | R24 | $20 carmine | 3,000. | 1,750. |
| | | *b.* Imperf, pair, without gum | 700.00 | |

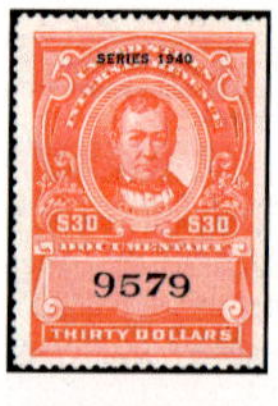

Thomas Corwin — R25

Various Frames and Portraits: $50, James Guthrie. $60, Howell Cobb. $100, P. F. Thomas. $500, J. A. Dix, $1,000, S. P. Chase.

UNITED STATES 213

### *Perf. 12*
### *Without Gum*

| | | | | |
|---|---|---|---|---|
| **R306** | R25 | $30 car | 450.00 | 75.00 |
| **R306A** | R25 | $50 car | — | *8,500.* |
| **R307** | R25 | $60 car | 550.00 | 100.00 |
| *a.* | | Vert. pair, imperf. btwn. | *2,750.* | *1,500.* |
| **R308** | R25 | $100 car | 450.00 | 100.00 |
| **R309** | R25 | $500 car | — | 5,000. |
| **R310** | R25 | $1000 car | — | |

The $30 to $1,000 denominations in this and following similar issues, and the $2,500, $5,000 and $10,000 stamps of 1952-58 have straight edges on one or two sides. They were issued without gum through No. R723.

Editors would like to see a used uncut example of No. R310.

### Nos. R288-R310 Overprinted

SERIES 1941

| 1941 | | Wmk. 191R | | *Perf. 11* |
|---|---|---|---|---|
| **R311** | R23 | 1c carmine | 5.00 | 2.75 |
| **R312** | R23 | 2c carmine | 5.25 | 1.10 |
| **R313** | R23 | 3c carmine | 10.00 | 4.25 |
| **R314** | R23 | 4c carmine | 7.50 | 1.75 |
| **R315** | R23 | 5c carmine | 1.50 | .40 |
| **R316** | R23 | 8c carmine | 21.00 | 8.50 |
| **R317** | R23 | 10c carmine | 2.00 | .35 |
| **R318** | R23 | 20c carmine | 4.75 | .65 |
| **R319** | R23 | 25c carmine | 2.40 | .65 |
| **R320** | R23 | 40c carmine | 16.00 | 3.25 |
| **R321** | R23 | 50c carmine | 3.50 | .30 |
| **R322** | R23 | 80c carmine | 65.00 | 12.00 |
| **R323** | R24 | $1 carmine | 15.00 | .30 |
| **R324** | R24 | $2 carmine | 20.00 | .50 |
| **R325** | R24 | $3 carmine | 32.50 | 3.50 |
| **R326** | R24 | $4 carmine | 47.50 | 27.50 |
| **R327** | R24 | $5 carmine | 60.00 | 1.10 |
| **R328** | R24 | $10 carmine | 100.00 | 6.00 |
| **R329** | R24 | $20 carmine | 850.00 | 500.00 |

### *Perf. 12*
### *Without Gum*

| | | | | |
|---|---|---|---|---|
| **R330** | R25 | $30 car | 325.00 | 55.00 |
| **R331** | R25 | $50 car | 1,500. | 1,000. |
| **R332** | R25 | $60 car | 325.00 | 87.50 |
| **R333** | R25 | $100 car | 175.00 | 37.50 |
| **R334** | R25 | $500 car | — | 375.00 |
| **R335** | R25 | $1000 car | 1,500. | 225.00 |

### Nos. R288-R310 Overprinted

SERIES 1942

| 1942 | | Wmk. 191R | | *Perf. 11* |
|---|---|---|---|---|
| **R336** | R23 | 1c carmine | 2.00 | .60 |
| **R337** | R23 | 2c carmine | 2.00 | .60 |
| **R338** | R23 | 3c carmine | 2.00 | .80 |
| **R339** | R23 | 4c carmine | 3.00 | 1.10 |
| **R340** | R23 | 5c carmine | .60 | .35 |
| **R341** | R23 | 8c carmine | 9.50 | 4.75 |
| **R342** | R23 | 10c carmine | 1.75 | .35 |
| **R343** | R23 | 20c carmine | 4.50 | .60 |
| **R344** | R23 | 25c carmine | 3.00 | .55 |
| **R345** | R23 | 40c carmine | 6.50 | 1.75 |
| **R346** | R23 | 50c carmine | 4.00 | .35 |
| **R347** | R23 | 80c carmine | 27.50 | 13.00 |
| **R348** | R24 | $1 carmine | 12.50 | .25 |
| **R349** | R24 | $2 carmine | 15.00 | .30 |
| **R350** | R24 | $3 carmine | 27.50 | 3.25 |
| **R351** | R24 | $4 carmine | 35.00 | 7.50 |
| **R352** | R24 | $5 carmine | 37.50 | 1.50 |
| **R353** | R24 | $10 carmine | 85.00 | 3.75 |
| **R354** | R24 | $20 carmine | 300.00 | 45.00 |
| *a.* | | Imperf., perf. initials | | — |

### *Perf. 12*
### *Without Gum*

| | | | | |
|---|---|---|---|---|
| **R355** | R25 | $30 carmine | 150.00 | 42.50 |
| **R356** | R25 | $50 carmine | 2,250. | 1,400. |
| **R357** | R25 | $60 carmine | *5,000.* | 1,500. |
| **R358** | R25 | $100 carmine | 375.00 | 175.00 |
| **R359** | R25 | $500 carmine | *2,000.* | 275.00 |
| **R360** | R25 | $1000 carmine | 6,500. | 175.00 |

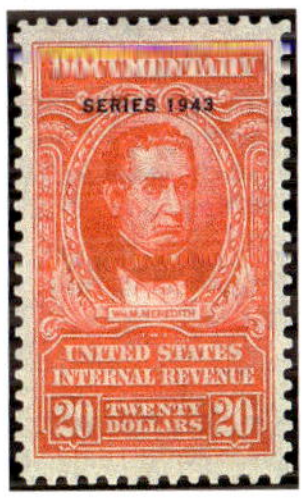


Nos. R288-R310 Overprinted

| 1943 | | Wmk. 191R | | *Perf. 11* |
|---|---|---|---|---|
| **R361** | R23 | 1c carmine | .80 | .65 |
| **R362** | R23 | 2c carmine | .65 | .55 |
| **R363** | R23 | 3c carmine | 3.75 | 3.50 |
| **R364** | R23 | 4c carmine | 1.60 | 1.50 |
| **R365** | R23 | 5c carmine | .70 | .45 |
| **R366** | R23 | 8c carmine | 6.00 | 4.00 |
| **R367** | R23 | 10c carmine | .85 | .30 |
| **R368** | R23 | 20c carmine | 2.50 | .80 |
| **R369** | R23 | 25c carmine | 2.75 | .50 |
| **R370** | R23 | 40c carmine | 7.50 | 4.00 |
| **R371** | R23 | 50c carmine | 2.00 | .30 |
| **R372** | R23 | 80c carmine | 27.50 | 8.00 |
| **R373** | R24 | $1 carmine | 9.00 | .35 |
| **R374** | R24 | $2 carmine | 18.00 | .35 |
| **R375** | R24 | $3 carmine | 30.00 | 3.00 |
| **R376** | R24 | $4 carmine | 55.00 | 10.00 |
| **R377** | R24 | $5 carmine | 52.50 | .75 |
| **R378** | R24 | $10 carmine | 85.00 | 5.00 |
| **R379** | R24 | $20 carmine | 350.00 | 60.00 |

### *Perf. 12*
### *Without Gum*

| | | | | |
|---|---|---|---|---|
| **R380** | R25 | $30 carmine | 275.00 | 25.00 |
| **R381** | R25 | $50 carmine | 300.00 | 75.00 |
| **R382** | R25 | $60 carmine | 450.00 | 125.00 |
| **R383** | R25 | $100 carmine | 65.00 | 22.50 |
| **R384** | R25 | $500 carmine | *800.00* | 325.00 |
| **R385** | R25 | $1000 carmine | *800.00* | 200.00 |

Nos. R288-R310 Overprinted

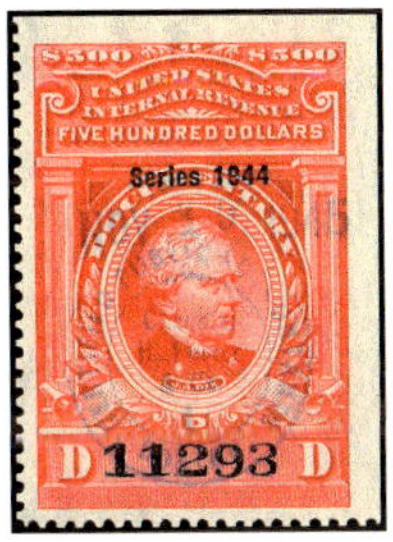


| 1944 | | Wmk. 191R | | *Perf. 11* |
|---|---|---|---|---|
| **R386** | R23 | 1c carmine | .50 | .45 |
| **R387** | R23 | 2c carmine | .65 | .55 |
| **R388** | R23 | 3c carmine | .65 | .40 |
| **R389** | R23 | 4c carmine | .75 | .65 |
| **R390** | R23 | 5c carmine | .40 | .25 |
| **R391** | R23 | 8c carmine | 2.25 | 1.75 |
| **R392** | R23 | 10c carmine | .50 | .25 |
| **R393** | R23 | 20c carmine | 1.10 | .35 |
| **R394** | R23 | 25c carmine | 2.00 | .30 |
| **R395** | R23 | 40c carmine | 3.75 | .80 |
| **R396** | R23 | 50c carmine | 4.00 | .35 |
| **R397** | R23 | 80c carmine | 21.00 | 5.50 |
| **R398** | R24 | $1 carmine | 10.00 | .30 |
| **R399** | R24 | $2 carmine | 15.00 | .45 |
| **R400** | R24 | $3 carmine | 25.00 | 2.40 |
| **R401** | R24 | $4 carmine | 32.50 | 11.50 |
| **R402** | R24 | $5 carmine | 32.50 | .50 |
| **R403** | R24 | $10 carmine | 65.00 | 1.60 |
| **R404** | R24 | $20 carmine | 275.00 | 19.00 |

### *Perf. 12*
### *Without Gum*

| | | | | |
|---|---|---|---|---|
| **R405** | R25 | $30 carmine | 130.00 | 35.00 |
| **R406** | R25 | $50 carmine | 60.00 | 22.50 |
| **R407** | R25 | $60 carmine | 450.00 | 75.00 |
| **R408** | R25 | $100 carmine | 85.00 | 12.50 |
| **R409** | R25 | $500 carmine | — | *3,250.* |
| **R410** | R25 | $1000 carmine | *4,000.* | 500.00 |

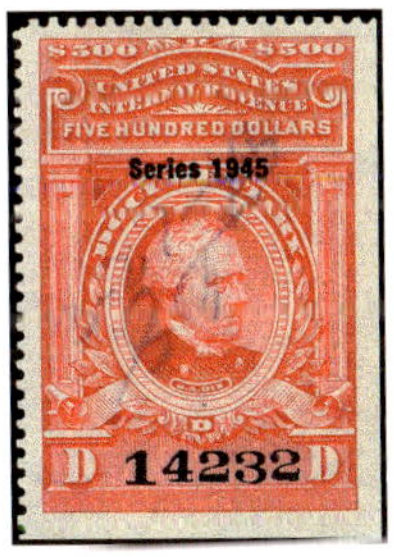


Nos. R288-R310 Overprinted

| 1945 | | Wmk. 191R | | *Perf. 11* |
|---|---|---|---|---|
| **R411** | R23 | 1c carmine | .40 | .30 |
| **R412** | R23 | 2c carmine | .40 | .30 |
| **R413** | R23 | 3c carmine | .75 | .50 |
| **R414** | R23 | 4c carmine | .45 | .35 |
| **R415** | R23 | 5c carmine | .45 | .30 |
| **R416** | R23 | 8c carmine | 6.25 | 2.75 |
| **R417** | R23 | 10c carmine | 1.25 | .25 |
| **R418** | R23 | 20c carmine | 8.00 | 1.50 |
| **R419** | R23 | 25c carmine | 1.75 | .30 |
| **R420** | R23 | 40c carmine | 9.00 | 1.25 |
| **R421** | R23 | 50c carmine | 4.00 | .25 |
| **R422** | R23 | 80c carmine | 26.00 | 14.00 |
| **R423** | R24 | $1 carmine | 13.50 | .30 |
| **R424** | R24 | $2 carmine | 13.50 | .40 |
| **R425** | R24 | $3 carmine | 27.50 | 3.00 |
| **R426** | R24 | $4 carmine | 35.00 | 4.25 |
| **R427** | R24 | $5 carmine | 35.00 | .50 |
| **R428** | R24 | $10 carmine | 65.00 | 2.50 |
| **R429** | R24 | $20 carmine | 400.00 | 16.00 |

### *Perf. 12*
### *Without Gum*

| | | | | |
|---|---|---|---|---|
| **R430** | R25 | $30 carmine | 300.00 | 40.00 |
| **R431** | R25 | $50 carmine | 260.00 | 45.00 |
| **R432** | R25 | $60 carmine | 525.00 | 80.00 |
| **R433** | R25 | $100 carmine | 65.00 | 20.00 |
| **R434** | R25 | $500 carmine | 900.00 | 325.00 |
| **R435** | R25 | $1000 carmine | 600.00 | 125.00 |

### Nos. R288-R310 Overprinted

Series 1946

| 1946 | | Wmk. 191R | | *Perf. 11* |
|---|---|---|---|---|
| **R436** | R23 | 1c carmine | .30 | .30 |
| **R437** | R23 | 2c carmine | .45 | .35 |
| **R438** | R23 | 3c carmine | .55 | .40 |
| **R439** | R23 | 4c carmine | .80 | .65 |
| **R440** | R23 | 5c carmine | .45 | .30 |
| **R441** | R23 | 8c carmine | 2.50 | 2.00 |
| **R442** | R23 | 10c carmine | 1.10 | .30 |
| **R443** | R23 | 20c carmine | 1.75 | .50 |
| **R444** | R23 | 25c carmine | 6.00 | .35 |
| **R445** | R23 | 40c carmine | 4.50 | .85 |
| **R446** | R23 | 50c carmine | 6.00 | .30 |
| **R447** | R23 | 80c carmine | 17.50 | 5.00 |
| **R448** | R24 | $1 carmine | 16.00 | .30 |
| **R449** | R24 | $2 carmine | 19.00 | .30 |
| **R450** | R24 | $3 carmine | 27.50 | 5.00 |
| **R451** | R24 | $4 carmine | 60.00 | 20.00 |
| **R452** | R24 | $5 carmine | 40.00 | .50 |
| **R453** | R24 | $10 carmine | 72.50 | 1.75 |
| **R454** | R24 | $20 carmine | 300.00 | 16.00 |

### *Perf. 12*
### *Without Gum*

| | | | | |
|---|---|---|---|---|
| **R455** | R25 | $30 carmine | 85.00 | 17.50 |
| **R456** | R25 | $50 carmine | 75.00 | 12.50 |
| **R457** | R25 | $60 carmine | 130.00 | 22.50 |
| **R458** | R25 | $100 carmine | 110.00 | 12.50 |
| **R459** | R25 | $500 carmine | *1,750.* | 150.00 |
| **R460** | R25 | $1000 carmine | *750.00* | 160.00 |

### Nos. R288-R310 Overprinted

Series 1947

| 1947 | | Wmk. 191R | | *Perf. 11* |
|---|---|---|---|---|
| **R461** | R23 | 1c carmine | .85 | .55 |
| **R462** | R23 | 2c carmine | .75 | .55 |
| **R463** | R23 | 3c carmine | .85 | .55 |
| **R464** | R23 | 4c carmine | .90 | .75 |
| **R465** | R23 | 5c carmine | .55 | .40 |
| **R466** | R23 | 8c carmine | 1.75 | .80 |
| **R467** | R23 | 10c carmine | 1.40 | .30 |
| **R468** | R23 | 20c carmine | 2.25 | .55 |
| **R469** | R23 | 25c carmine | 3.00 | .70 |
| **R470** | R23 | 40c carmine | 5.50 | 1.10 |
| **R471** | R23 | 50c carmine | 3.75 | .40 |
| **R472** | R23 | 80c carmine | 12.00 | 8.00 |
| **R473** | R24 | $1 carmine | 8.25 | .35 |
| **R474** | R24 | $2 carmine | 14.00 | .65 |
| **R475** | R24 | $3 carmine | 17.50 | 6.00 |
| **R476** | R24 | $4 carmine | 19.00 | 5.00 |
| **R477** | R24 | $5 carmine | 27.50 | .60 |
| **R478** | R24 | $10 carmine | 67.50 | 3.00 |
| **R479** | R24 | $20 carmine | 110.00 | 14.00 |

### *Perf. 12*
### *Without Gum*

| | | | | |
|---|---|---|---|---|
| **R480** | R25 | $30 carmine | 210.00 | 27.50 |
| **R481** | R25 | $50 carmine | 175.00 | 17.50 |
| **R482** | R25 | $60 carmine | 300.00 | 60.00 |
| **R483** | R25 | $100 carmine | 100.00 | 15.00 |
| **R484** | R25 | $500 carmine | *900.00* | 250.00 |
| **R485** | R25 | $1000 carmine | *850.00* | 100.00 |

Nos. R288-R310 Overprinted

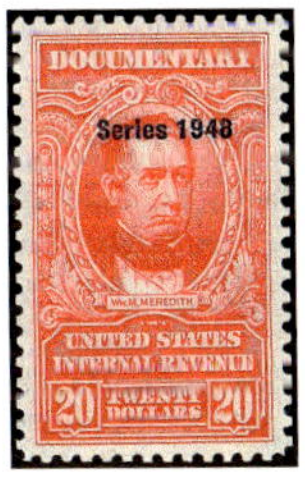


| 1948 | | Wmk. 191R | | *Perf. 11* |
|---|---|---|---|---|
| **R486** | R23 | 1c carmine | .35 | .30 |
| **R487** | R23 | 2c carmine | .50 | .45 |
| **R488** | R23 | 3c carmine | .60 | .40 |
| **R489** | R23 | 4c carmine | .55 | .40 |
| **R490** | R23 | 5c carmine | .50 | .25 |
| **R491** | R23 | 8c carmine | 1.00 | .50 |
| **R492** | R23 | 10c carmine | 1.00 | .25 |
| **R493** | R23 | 20c carmine | 2.50 | .40 |
| **R494** | R23 | 25c carmine | 2.25 | .30 |
| **R495** | R23 | 40c carmine | 7.00 | 1.75 |
| **R496** | R23 | 50c carmine | 2.50 | .30 |
| **R497** | R23 | 80c carmine | 12.00 | 8.00 |
| **R498** | R24 | $1 carmine | 10.50 | .30 |
| **R499** | R24 | $2 carmine | 18.00 | .40 |
| **R500** | R24 | $3 carmine | 24.00 | 3.50 |
| **R501** | R24 | $4 carmine | 35.00 | 4.00 |
| **R502** | R24 | $5 carmine | 30.00 | .50 |
| **R503** | R24 | $10 carmine | 70.00 | 1.50 |
| *a.* | | Pair, one dated "1946" | | |
| **R504** | R24 | $20 carmine | 400.00 | 18.00 |

### *Perf. 12*
### *Without Gum*

| | | | | |
|---|---|---|---|---|
| **R505** | R25 | $30 carmine | 165.00 | 35.00 |
| **R506** | R25 | $50 carmine | 210.00 | 27.50 |
| *a.* | | Vert. pair, imperf. btwn. | *2,500.* | |
| **R507** | R25 | $60 carmine | 350.00 | 75.00 |
| *a.* | | Vert. pair, imperf. btwn. | *4,250.* | |
| **R508** | R25 | $100 carmine | 175.00 | 20.00 |
| *a.* | | Vert. pair, imperf. btwn. | | *2,000.* |

No. R508a is known as four used singles, all four positions from a single pane of four, clearly imperf. horiz. before being separated.

| | | | | |
|---|---|---|---|---|
| **R509** | R25 | $500 carmine | 1,500. | 200.00 |
| **R510** | R25 | $1000 carmine | 550.00 | 125.00 |

### Nos. R288-R310 Overprinted

Series 1949

| 1949 | | Wmk. 191R | | *Perf. 11* |
|---|---|---|---|---|
| **R511** | R23 | 1c carmine | .40 | .35 |
| **R512** | R23 | 2c carmine | .75 | .45 |
| **R513** | R23 | 3c carmine | .60 | .50 |
| **R514** | R23 | 4c carmine | .80 | .60 |
| **R515** | R23 | 5c carmine | .55 | .30 |
| **R516** | R23 | 8c carmine | 1.00 | .70 |
| **R517** | R23 | 10c carmine | .60 | .35 |
| **R518** | R23 | 20c carmine | 1.75 | .75 |
| **R519** | R23 | 25c carmine | 2.25 | .85 |
| **R520** | R23 | 40c carmine | 6.50 | 2.75 |
| **R521** | R23 | 50c carmine | 5.00 | .40 |
| **R522** | R23 | 80c carmine | 15.00 | 7.50 |
| **R523** | R24 | $1 carmine | 13.50 | .85 |
| **R524** | R24 | $2 carmine | 17.00 | 2.50 |
| **R525** | R24 | $3 carmine | 27.50 | 8.00 |
| **R526** | R24 | $4 carmine | 30.00 | 8.00 |
| **R527** | R24 | $5 carmine | 32.50 | 4.25 |
| **R528** | R24 | $10 carmine | 72.50 | 5.25 |
| **R529** | R24 | $20 carmine | 150.00 | 15.00 |

### *Perf. 12*
### *Without Gum*

| | | | | |
|---|---|---|---|---|
| **R530** | R25 | $30 carmine | 230.00 | 35.00 |
| **R531** | R25 | $50 carmine | 250.00 | 60.00 |
| **R532** | R25 | $60 carmine | 475.00 | 70.00 |
| **R533** | R25 | $100 carmine | 125.00 | 21.00 |
| **R534** | R25 | $500 carmine | *1,250.* | 260.00 |
| **R535** | R25 | $1000 carmine | *1,000.* | 160.00 |

### Nos. R288-R310 Overprinted

Series 1950

| 1950 | | Wmk. 191R | | *Perf. 11* |
|---|---|---|---|---|
| **R536** | R23 | 1c carmine | .40 | .25 |
| **R537** | R23 | 2c carmine | .40 | .35 |
| **R538** | R23 | 3c carmine | .50 | .40 |
| **R539** | R23 | 4c carmine | .70 | .50 |
| **R540** | R23 | 5c carmine | .45 | .35 |
| **R541** | R23 | 8c carmine | 1.75 | .80 |
| **R542** | R23 | 10c carmine | .80 | .30 |
| **R543** | R23 | 20c carmine | 1.40 | .45 |
| **R544** | R23 | 25c carmine | 2.00 | .45 |
| **R545** | R23 | 40c carmine | 6.00 | 2.10 |
| **R546** | R23 | 50c carmine | 8.00 | .35 |
| **R547** | R23 | 80c carmine | 15.00 | 8.50 |
| **R548** | R24 | $1 carmine | 15.00 | .40 |
| **R549** | R24 | $2 carmine | 17.50 | 2.75 |
| **R550** | R24 | $3 carmine | 20.00 | 6.00 |
| **R551** | R24 | $4 carmine | 27.50 | 7.50 |
| **R552** | R24 | $5 carmine | 35.00 | 1.00 |
| **R553** | R24 | $10 carmine | 70.00 | 10.00 |
| **R554** | R24 | $20 carmine | 150.00 | 15.00 |

### *Perf. 12*
### *Without Gum*

| | | | | |
|---|---|---|---|---|
| **R555** | R25 | $30 carmine | 175.00 | 70.00 |
| **R556** | R25 | $50 carmine | 150.00 | 22.50 |
| *a.* | | Vert. pair, imperf. horiz. | | — |
| **R557** | R25 | $60 carmine | 300.00 | 75.00 |
| **R558** | R25 | $100 carmine | 120.00 | 22.50 |
| **R559** | R25 | $500 carmine | *1,250.* | 125.00 |
| **R560** | R25 | $1000 carmine | *900.00* | 65.00 |

### Nos. R288-R310 Overprinted

Series 1951

| 1951 | | Wmk. 191R | | *Perf. 11* |
|---|---|---|---|---|
| **R561** | R23 | 1c carmine | .30 | .25 |
| **R562** | R23 | 2c carmine | .30 | .35 |
| **R563** | R23 | 3c carmine | .30 | .35 |
| **R564** | R23 | 4c carmine | .30 | .35 |
| **R565** | R23 | 5c carmine | .30 | .35 |
| **R566** | R23 | 8c carmine | 1.25 | .45 |
| **R567** | R23 | 10c carmine | .30 | .35 |
| **R568** | R23 | 20c carmine | .30 | .55 |
| **R569** | R23 | 25c carmine | .30 | .50 |
| **R570** | R23 | 40c carmine | 3.75 | 1.60 |
| **R571** | R23 | 50c carmine | 3.00 | .60 |
| **R572** | R23 | 80c carmine | 10.00 | 3.25 |
| **R573** | R24 | $1 carmine | 16.00 | .30 |
| **R574** | R24 | $2 carmine | 21.00 | .55 |
| **R575** | R24 | $3 carmine | 16.00 | 4.00 |
| **R576** | R24 | $4 carmine | 20.00 | 12.50 |
| **R577** | R24 | $5 carmine | 10.00 | .70 |
| **R578** | R24 | $10 carmine | 18.00 | 2.50 |
| **R579** | R24 | $20 carmine | 55.00 | 16.00 |

### *Perf. 12*
### *Without Gum*

| | | | | |
|---|---|---|---|---|
| R580 | R25 | $30 carmine | 175.00 | 25.00 |
| a. | | Imperf., pair | 2,500. | 2,000. |
| R581 | R25 | $50 carmine | 350.00 | 45.00 |
| R582 | R25 | $60 carmine | 450.00 | 75.00 |
| R583 | R25 | $100 carmine | 110.00 | 25.00 |
| R584 | R25 | $500 carmine | 900.00 | 175.00 |
| R585 | R25 | $1000 carmine | 750.00 | 150.00 |

No. R583 is known imperf horizontally. It exists as a reconstructed used vertical strip of 4 that was separated into single stamps.

## Documentary Stamps and Types of 1940 Overprinted in Black

Series 1952

Designs: 55c, $1.10, $1.65, $2.20, $2.75, $3.30, L. J. Gage; $2500, William Windom; $5000, C. J. Folger; $10,000, W. Q. Gresham.

**1952 Wmk. 191R *Perf. 11***

| | | | | |
|---|---|---|---|---|
| R586 | R23 | 1c carmine | .35 | .30 |
| R587 | R23 | 2c carmine | .50 | .35 |
| R588 | R23 | 3c carmine | .40 | .35 |
| R589 | R23 | 4c carmine | .45 | .30 |
| R590 | R23 | 5c carmine | .35 | .30 |
| R591 | R23 | 8c carmine | .90 | .60 |
| R592 | R23 | 10c carmine | .50 | .30 |
| R593 | R23 | 20c carmine | 1.25 | .40 |
| R594 | R23 | 25c carmine | 2.50 | .45 |
| R595 | R23 | 40c carmine | 6.00 | 1.75 |
| R596 | R23 | 50c carmine | 3.50 | .30 |
| R597 | R23 | 55c carmine | .60 | 15.00 |
| R598 | R23 | 80c carmine | 19.00 | 4.00 |
| R599 | R24 | $1 carmine | 7.00 | 1.50 |
| R600 | R24 | $1.10 carmine | 25.00 | 30.00 |
| R601 | R24 | $1.65 carmine | 175.00 | 62.50 |
| R602 | R24 | $2 carmine | 17.00 | .90 |
| R603 | R24 | $2.20 carmine | 160.00 | 70.00 |
| R604 | R24 | $2.75 carmine | 190.00 | 70.00 |
| R605 | R24 | $3 carmine | 32.50 | 6.00 |
| a. | | Horiz. pair, imperf. btwn. | 1,300. | |
| R606 | R24 | $3.30 carmine | 225.00 | 90.00 |
| R607 | R24 | $4 carmine | 37.50 | 6.00 |
| R608 | R24 | $5 carmine | 32.50 | 1.25 |
| R609 | R24 | $10 carmine | 60.00 | 1.25 |
| R610 | R24 | $20 carmine | 92.50 | 16.00 |

### *Perf. 12*
### *Without Gum*

| | | | | |
|---|---|---|---|---|
| R611 | R25 | $30 carmine | 110.00 | 27.50 |
| R612 | R25 | $50 carmine | 110.00 | 35.00 |
| R613 | R25 | $60 carmine | 750.00 | 70.00 |
| R614 | R25 | $100 carmine | 125.00 | 10.00 |
| R615 | R25 | $500 carmine | 750.00 | 160.00 |
| R616 | R25 | $1000 carmine | 400.00 | 75.00 |
| R617 | R25 | $2500 carmine | 1,250. | 275.00 |
| R618 | R25 | $5000 carmine | — | 5,000. |
| R619 | R25 | $10,000 carmine | 1,750. | 1,400. |

## Documentary Stamps and Types of 1940 Overprinted in Black

Series 1953

**1953 Wmk. 191R *Perf. 11***

| | | | | |
|---|---|---|---|---|
| R620 | R23 | 1c carmine | .40 | .35 |
| R621 | R23 | 2c carmine | .40 | .30 |
| R622 | R23 | 3c carmine | .45 | .35 |
| R623 | R23 | 4c carmine | .60 | .45 |
| R624 | R23 | 5c carmine | .50 | .30 |
| a. | | Vert. pair, imperf. horiz. | | 1,150. |
| R625 | R23 | 8c carmine | 1.10 | .85 |
| R626 | R23 | 10c carmine | .65 | .35 |
| R627 | R23 | 20c carmine | 1.50 | .50 |
| R628 | R23 | 25c carmine | 1.75 | .65 |
| R629 | R23 | 40c carmine | 2.50 | .90 |
| R630 | R23 | 50c carmine | 3.00 | .35 |
| R631 | R23 | 55c carmine | 7.00 | 2.00 |
| a. | | Horiz. pair, imperf. vert. | 550.00 | |
| R632 | R23 | 80c carmine | 10.00 | 2.10 |
| R633 | R24 | $1 carmine | 5.25 | .35 |
| R634 | R24 | $1.10 carmine | 12.00 | 2.50 |
| a. | | Horiz. pair, imperf. vert. | 700.00 | |
| b. | | Imperf. pair | 850.00 | |
| R635 | R24 | $1.65 carmine | 12.00 | 4.50 |
| R636 | R24 | $2 carmine | 9.00 | .75 |
| R637 | R24 | $2.20 carmine | 20.00 | 6.00 |
| R638 | R24 | $2.75 carmine | 1.75 | 7.00 |
| R639 | R24 | $3 carmine | 17.00 | 4.00 |
| R640 | R24 | $3.30 carmine | 50.00 | 17.50 |
| R641 | R24 | $4 carmine | 40.00 | 15.00 |
| R642 | R24 | $5 carmine | 27.50 | 1.25 |
| R643 | R24 | $10 carmine | 60.00 | 2.25 |
| R644 | R24 | $20 carmine | 140.00 | 22.50 |

### *Perf. 12*
### *Without Gum*

| | | | | |
|---|---|---|---|---|
| R645 | R25 | $30 car | 210.00 | 40.00 |
| R646 | R25 | $50 car | 210.00 | 50.00 |
| R647 | R25 | $60 car | 1,000. | 425.00 |
| R648 | R25 | $100 car | 70.00 | 15.00 |
| R649 | R25 | $500 car | 3,500. | 175.00 |
| R650 | R25 | $1000 car | 800.00 | 80.00 |
| R651 | R25 | $2500 car | 2,000. | 1,750. |
| R652 | R25 | $5000 car | — | 7,500. |
| R653 | R25 | $10,000 car | — | 4,250. |

In 1955, the BEP began printing flat plate documentary stamps Nos. R654-R681 using the dry-printing method. This method used paper with a 5-10% moisture content versus the 15-35% moisture content for the wet printing. The dry-printed stamps from the same plates are .25-.75mm larger than the wet-printed examples. Four sub-varieties are known: (1) wet printing with ridged yellow gum, (2) wet printing with smooth yellow gum, (3) dry printing with smooth yellow gum, and (4) dry printing with smooth white gum.

## Types of 1940
Without Overprint

**1954 Wmk. 191R *Perf. 11***

| | | | | |
|---|---|---|---|---|
| R654 | R23 | 1c carmine | .25 | .25 |
| a. | | Horiz. pair, imperf. vert. | 1,500. | |
| R655 | R23 | 2c carmine | .25 | .30 |
| R656 | R23 | 3c carmine | .25 | .30 |
| R657 | R23 | 4c carmine | .25 | .30 |
| R658 | R23 | 5c carmine | .25 | .25 |
| a. | | Vert. pair, imperf. horiz. | — | |
| R659 | R23 | 8c carmine | .25 | .25 |
| R660 | R23 | 10c carmine | .25 | .25 |
| R661 | R23 | 20c carmine | .30 | .40 |
| R662 | R23 | 25c carmine | .35 | .45 |
| R663 | R23 | 40c carmine | .75 | .60 |
| R664 | R23 | 50c carmine | 1.00 | .25 |
| a. | | Horiz. pair, imperf. vert. | 900.00 | |
| R665 | R23 | 55c carmine | .90 | 1.25 |
| R666 | R23 | 80c carmine | 1.50 | 1.90 |
| R667 | R24 | $1 carmine | .90 | .35 |
| R668 | R24 | $1.10 carmine | 2.00 | 2.50 |
| R669 | R24 | $1.65 carmine | 25.00 | 25.00 |
| R670 | R24 | $2 carmine | 1.00 | .45 |
| R671 | R24 | $2.20 carmine | 2.25 | 3.75 |
| R672 | R24 | $2.75 carmine | 25.00 | 55.00 |
| R673 | R24 | $3 carmine | 2.00 | 2.00 |
| R674 | R24 | $3.30 carmine | 3.50 | 5.00 |
| R675 | R24 | $4 carmine | 2.75 | 4.00 |
| R676 | R24 | $5 carmine | 3.25 | .50 |
| R677 | R24 | $10 carmine | 5.00 | 1.50 |
| R678 | R24 | $20 carmine | 10.00 | 6.50 |

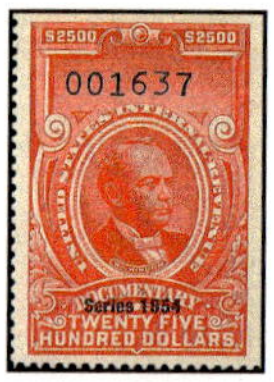


Documentary Stamps & Type of 1940 Ovptd. in Black

**1954 Wmk. 191R *Perf. 12***
**Without Gum**

| | | | | |
|---|---|---|---|---|
| R679 | R25 | $30 carmine | 40.00 | 17.50 |
| a. | | Booklet pane of 4 | 160.00 | |
| R680 | R25 | $50 carmine | 40.00 | 29.00 |
| a. | | Booklet pane of 4 | 160.00 | |
| R681 | R25 | $60 carmine | 40.00 | 30.00 |
| a. | | Booklet pane of 4 | 160.00 | |
| R682 | R25 | $100 carmine | 40.00 | 7.50 |
| a. | | Booklet pane of 4 | 160.00 | |
| R683 | R25 | $500 carmine | 110.00 | 87.50 |
| a. | | Booklet pane of 4 | 440.00 | |
| R684 | R25 | $1000 carmine | 125.00 | 90.00 |
| a. | | Booklet pane of 4 | 500.00 | |
| R685 | R25 | $2500 carmine | 200.00 | 350.00 |
| a. | | Booklet pane of 4 | 800.00 | |
| R686 | R25 | $5000 carmine | 1,750. | 2,750. |
| a. | | Booklet pane of 4 | 7,000. | |
| R687 | R25 | $10,000 carmine | 1,000. | 2,250. |
| a. | | Booklet pane of 4 | 7,000. | |

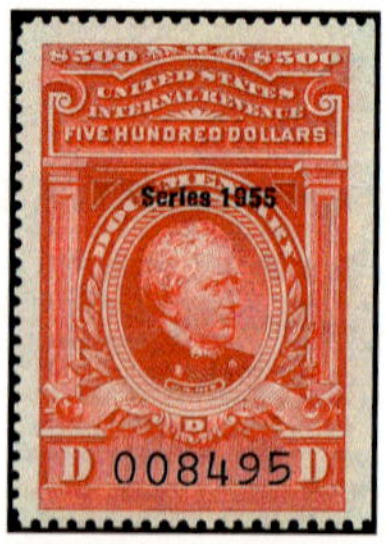


Documentary Stamps and Type of 1940 Overprinted in Black

**1955 Wmk. 191R *Perf. 12***
**Without Gum**

| | | | | |
|---|---|---|---|---|
| R688 | R25 | $30 carmine | 125.00 | 17.50 |
| R689 | R25 | $50 carmine | 150.00 | 30.00 |
| R690 | R25 | $60 carmine | 250.00 | 45.00 |
| R691 | R25 | $100 carmine | 190.00 | 20.00 |
| R692 | R25 | $500 carmine | 1,250. | 200.00 |
| R693 | R25 | $1000 carmine | 1,800. | 80.00 |
| R694 | R25 | $2500 carmine | 1,250. | 275.00 |
| R695 | R25 | $5000 carmine | 4,000. | 2,000. |
| R696 | R25 | $10,000 carmine | — | 1,250. |

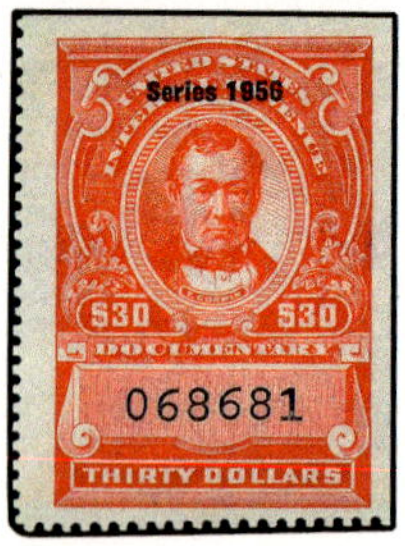


Documentary Stamps and Type of 1940 Overprinted

**1956 Wmk. 191R *Perf. 12***
**Without Gum**

| | | | | |
|---|---|---|---|---|
| R697 | R25 | $30 carmine | 210.00 | 20.00 |
| R698 | R25 | $50 carmine | 350.00 | 27.50 |
| R699 | R25 | $60 carmine | 300.00 | 60.00 |
| R700 | R25 | $100 carmine | 150.00 | 15.00 |
| R701 | R25 | $500 carmine | 1,500. | 150.00 |
| R702 | R25 | $1000 carmine | 1,750. | 100.00 |
| R703 | R25 | $2500 carmine | — | 750.00 |
| R704 | R25 | $5000 carmine | — | 2,000. |
| R705 | R25 | $10,000 carmine | — | 750.00 |

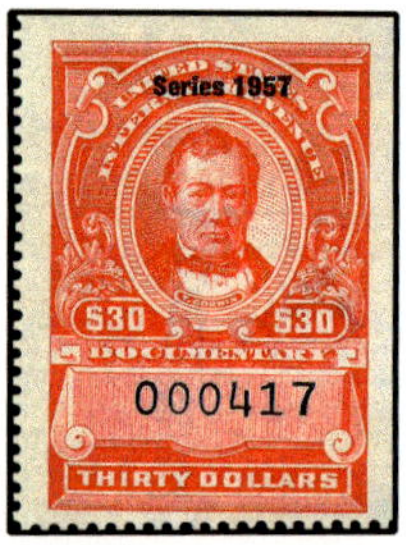


Documentary Stamps and Type of 1940 Overprinted

**1957 Wmk. 191R *Perf. 12***
**Without Gum**

| | | | | |
|---|---|---|---|---|
| R706 | R25 | $30 carmine | 375.00 | 60.00 |
| R707 | R25 | $50 carmine | 190.00 | 47.50 |
| R708 | R25 | $60 carmine | 1,500. | 400.00 |
| R709 | R25 | $100 carmine | 160.00 | 20.00 |
| R710 | R25 | $500 carmine | 900.00 | 200.00 |
| R711 | R25 | $1000 carmine | 4,000. | 100.00 |
| R712 | R25 | $2500 carmine | — | 1,200. |
| R713 | R25 | $5000 carmine | 4,250. | 1,800. |
| R714 | R25 | $10,000 carmine | — | 650.00 |

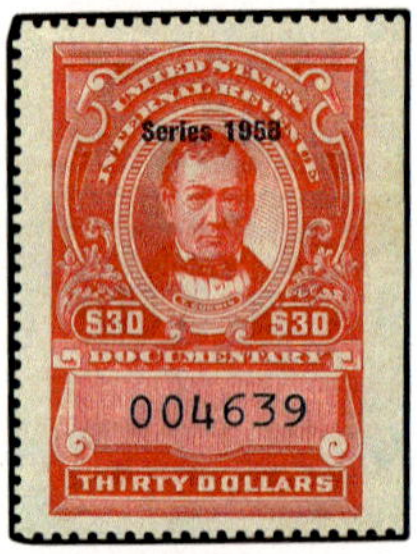


Documentary Stamps and Type of 1940 Overprinted in Black

**1958 Wmk. 191R *Perf. 12***
**Without Gum**

| | | | | |
|---|---|---|---|---|
| R715 | R25 | $30 carmine | 160.00 | 27.50 |
| R716 | R25 | $50 carmine | 210.00 | 35.00 |
| R717 | R25 | $60 carmine | 250.00 | 42.50 |
| R718 | R25 | $100 carmine | 260.00 | 15.00 |
| R719 | R25 | $500 carmine | 750.00 | 125.00 |
| R720 | R25 | $1000 carmine | 2,750. | 90.00 |
| R721 | R25 | $2500 carmine | — | 1,500. |
| R722 | R25 | $5000 carmine | — | 4,250. |
| R723 | R25 | $10,000 carmine | — | 2,750. |

## Documentary Stamps and Type of 1940 Without Overprint

**1958 Wmk. 191R *Perf. 12***
**With Gum**

| | | | | |
|---|---|---|---|---|
| R724 | R25 | $30 carmine | 7.00 | 7.00 |
| a. | | Booklet pane of 4 | 28.00 | |
| b. | | Vert. pair, imperf. horiz. | 3,000. | |
| R725 | R25 | $50 carmine | 10.00 | 7.00 |
| a. | | Booklet pane of 4 | 40.00 | |
| b. | | Vert. pair, imperf. horiz. | | 3,500. |
| R726 | R25 | $60 carmine | 12.00 | 21.00 |
| a. | | Booklet pane of 4 | 48.00 | |
| R727 | R25 | $100 carmine | 10.00 | 4.75 |
| a. | | Booklet pane of 4 | 40.00 | |
| R728 | R25 | $500 carmine | 12.00 | 26.00 |
| a. | | Booklet pane of 4 | 48.00 | |
| R729 | R25 | $1000 carmine | 12.00 | 21.00 |
| a. | | Booklet pane of 4 | 48.00 | |
| b. | | Vert. pair, imperf. horiz. | | 1,750. |
| c. | | Vert. pair, imperf. btwn. | 1,500. | |
| R730 | R25 | $2500 carmine | 100.00 | 175.00 |
| a. | | Booklet pane of 4 | 400.00 | |
| R731 | R25 | $5000 carmine | 150.00 | 175.00 |
| a. | | Booklet pane of 4 | 600.00 | |
| R732 | R25 | $10,000 carmine | 150.00 | 140.00 |
| a. | | Booklet pane of 4 | 600.00 | |

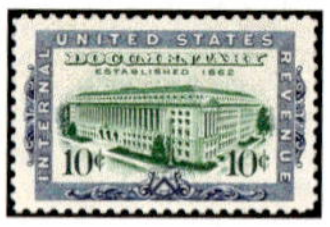


Internal Revenue Building, Washington, DC — R26

Centenary of the Internal Revenue Service.

### Giori Press Printing

**1962, July 2 Unwmk. *Perf. 11***

| | | | | |
|---|---|---|---|---|
| R733 | R26 | 10c violet blue & bright green | 1.00 | .40 |
| | | Never hinged | 1.25 | |

**1963**

### "Established 1862" Removed

| | | | | |
|---|---|---|---|---|
| R734 | R26 | 10c violet blue & bright green | 3.00 | .70 |
| | | Never hinged | 5.00 | |

Documentary revenue stamps were no longer required after Dec. 31, 1967.

## PROPRIETARY STAMPS

Stamps for use on proprietary articles were included in the first general issue of 1862-71. They are Nos. R3, R13-R14, R18, R22, R29, R31, R38.

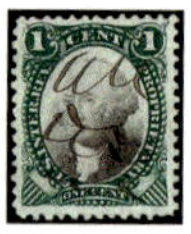

Washington — RB1

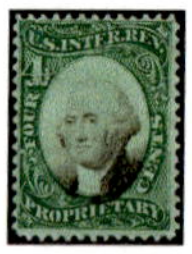

RB1a

Various Frame Designs

**1871-74 Engr. *Perf. 12***

| | | | |
|---|---|---|---|
| RB1 | RB1 | 1c grn & blk | |
| a. | | Violet paper ('71) | 8.00 |
| b. | | Green paper ('74) | 14.00 |
| c. | | As "a," Imperf. | 80.00 |
| d. | | As "a," Inverted center | 5,250. |
| RB2 | RB1 | 2c grn & blk | |
| a. | | Violet paper ('71) | 8.75 |
| b. | | Green paper ('74) | 30.00 |
| c. | | As "a," Invtd. center | 40,000. |
| d. | | As "b," Invtd. center | 8,000. |
| e. | | As "b," vert. half used as 1c on document | — |

Only three examples recorded of the inverted center on violet paper, No. RB2c. Value is for example with very good to fine centering and very small faults.

RB2d is valued with fine centering and small faults.

| | | | |
|---|---|---|---|
| RB3 | RB1a | 3c grn & blk | |
| a. | | Violet paper ('71) | 32.50 |
| b. | | Green paper ('74) | 67.50 |
| c. | | As "a," privately perforated, sewing machine perfs | 800.00 |
| d. | | As "a," inverted center | 14,000. |

No. RB3d is valued with small faults because all of the 8 recorded examples have faults.

| | | | |
|---|---|---|---|
| RB4 | RB1a | 4c grn & blk | |
| a. | | Violet paper ('71) | 16.00 |
| b. | | Green paper ('74) | 25.00 |
| c. | | As "a," inverted center | 15,000. |
| d. | | As "b," vert. half used as 2c on document | — |

No. RB4c is valued with small faults as all seven of the recorded examples have faults.

UNITED STATES 215

| | | | | |
|---|---|---|---|---|
| **RB5** | RB1a | 5c grn & blk | | |
| *a.* | Violet paper ('71) | | 175.00 | |
| *b.* | Green paper ('74) | | 250.00 | |
| *c.* | As "a," inverted center | | *155,000.* | |

No. RB5c is unique. Value represents price realized in 2000 auction sale.

| | | | | |
|---|---|---|---|---|
| **RB6** | RB1a | 6c grn & blk | | |
| *a.* | Violet paper ('71) | | 57.50 | |
| *b.* | Green paper ('74) | | 140.00 | |
| **RB7** | RB1a | 10c grn & blk ('73) | | |
| *a.* | Violet paper ('71) | | 300.00 | |
| *b.* | Green paper ('74) | | 65.00 | |

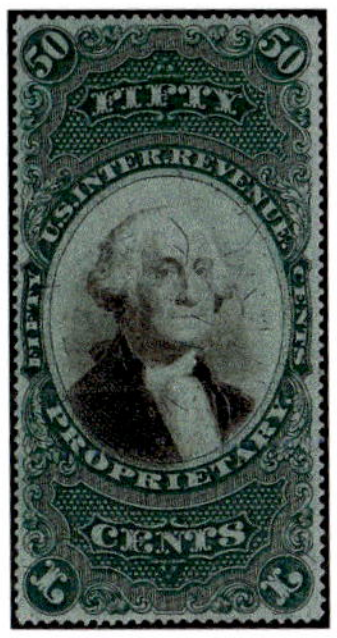
RB1b

| | | | | |
|---|---|---|---|---|
| **RB8** | RB1b | 50c grn & blk ('73) | | |
| *a.* | Violet paper ('71) | | 1,000. | |
| *b.* | Green paper ('74) | | 850.00 | |
| **RB9** | RB1b | $1 grn & blk ('73) | | |
| *a.* | Violet paper ('71) | | *3,500.* | |
| *b.* | Green paper ('74) | | *12,500.* | |

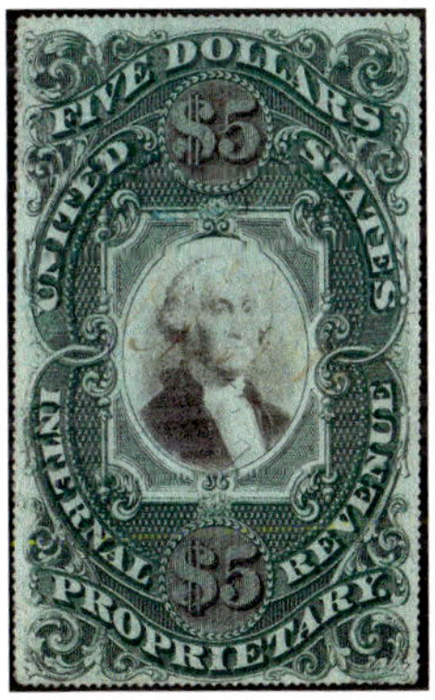
RB1c

| | | | | |
|---|---|---|---|---|
| **RB10** | RB1c | $5 grn & blk ('73) | | |
| *a.* | Violet paper ('71) | | *11,000.* | |
| *b.* | Green paper ('74) | | *75,000.* | |

No. RB10b is valued with small faults.

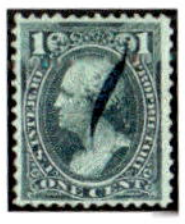
Washington RB2

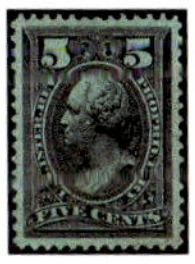
RB2a

Various Frame Designs
Green Paper

**1875-81** *Perf. 12*

**Unmwkd. (Silk Paper), Wmk. 191R**

| | | | | |
|---|---|---|---|---|
| **RB11** | RB2 | 1c green | | |
| *a.* | Silk paper | | | 2.25 |
| *b.* | Wmk 191R | | | .50 |
| *c.* | Rouletted 6 | | | 200.00 |
| *d.* | As No. RB11b, vert. pair, imperf btwn. | | | *400.00* |
| **RB12** | RB2 | 2c brown | | |
| *a.* | Silk paper | | | 3.25 |
| *b.* | Wmk 191R | | | 2.00 |
| *c.* | Rouletted 6 | | | 225.00 |
| **RB13** | RB2a | 3c orange | | |
| *a.* | Silk paper | | | 14.00 |
| *b.* | Wmk 191R | | | 4.00 |
| *c.* | Rouletted 6 | | | 160.00 |
| *d.* | As No. RB13c, horiz. pair, imperf. between | | | *2,500.* |
| *e.* | As No. RB13c, vert. pair, imperf. between | | | *2,500.* |
| *f.* | Privately perforated, sewing machine perfs | | | — |
| **RB14** | RB2a | 4c red brown | | |
| *a.* | Silk paper | | | 10.00 |
| *b.* | Wmk 191R | | | 9.00 |
| *c.* | Rouletted 6 | | | *22,000.* |
| **RB15** | RB2a | 4c red | | |
| *b.* | Wmk 191R | | | 6.00 |
| *c.* | Rouletted 6 | | | 450.00 |
| **RB16** | RB2a | 5c black | | |
| *a.* | Silk paper | | | 200.00 |
| *b.* | Wmk 191R | | | 125.00 |
| *c.* | Rouletted 6 | | | *1,850.* |
| **RB17** | RB2a | 6c violet blue | | |
| *a.* | Silk paper | | | 35.00 |
| *b.* | Wmk 191R | | | 25.00 |
| *c.* | Rouletted 6 | | | *1,100.* |
| | Pair | | | — |
| **RB18** | RB2a | 6c violet | | |
| *b.* | Wmk 191R | | | 35.00 |
| *c.* | Rouletted 6 | | | *2,500.* |
| **RB19** | RB2a | 10c blue ('81) | | |
| *b.* | Wmk 191R | | | 400.00 |

Many fraudulent roulettes exist.

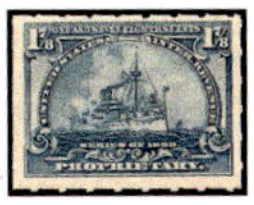
Battleship — RB3

Inscribed "Series of 1898." and "Proprietary."

See note on rouletting preceding No. R161.

*Rouletted 5½*

**1898** **Wmk. 191R** **Engr.**

| | | | | |
|---|---|---|---|---|
| **RB20** | RB3 | ⅛c yel grn | .25 | .25 |
| *a.* | Vert. pair, imperf. horiz. | | — | |
| *b.* | Vert. pair, imperf. btwn. | | *1,100.* | |
| **RB21** | RB3 | ¼c brown | .25 | .25 |
| *a.* | ¼c red brown | | .25 | .25 |
| *b.* | ¼c yellow brown | | .25 | .25 |
| *c.* | ¼c orange brown | | .25 | .25 |
| *d.* | ¼c bister | | .25 | .25 |
| *e.* | Vert. pair, imperf. horiz. | | — | — |
| *f.* | Printed on both sides | | — | |
| **RB22** | RB3 | ⅜c dp org | .30 | .30 |
| *a.* | Horiz. pair, imperf. vert. | | 12.50 | |
| *b.* | Vert. pair, imperf. horiz. | | — | |
| **RB23** | RB3 | ⅝c deep ultra | .25 | .25 |
| *a.* | Vert. pair, imperf. horiz. | | 85.00 | — |
| *b.* | Horiz. pair, imperf. btwn. | | *450.00* | *400.00* |
| **RB24** | RB3 | 1c dark green | 2.25 | .50 |
| *a.* | Vert. pair, imperf. horiz. | | *600.00* | |
| **RB25** | RB3 | 1¼c violet | .35 | .25 |
| *a.* | 1¼c brown violet | | .25 | .25 |
| *b.* | Vert. pair, imperf. btwn. | | — | |
| **RB26** | RB3 | 1⅞c dull blue | 15.00 | 2.00 |
| **RB27** | RB3 | 2c violet brown | 1.40 | .35 |
| *a.* | Horiz. pair, imperf. vert. | | 60.00 | |
| **RB28** | RB3 | 2½c lake | 5.00 | .35 |
| *a.* | Vert. pair, imperf. horiz. | | 400.00 | |
| **RB29** | RB3 | 3¾c olive gray | 42.50 | 15.00 |
| **RB30** | RB3 | 4c purple | 16.00 | 1.50 |
| **RB31** | RB3 | 5c brn org | 15.00 | 1.50 |
| *a.* | Vert. pair, imperf. horiz. | | — | *400.00* |
| *b.* | Horiz. pair, imperf. vert. | | — | *750.00* |
| | *Nos. RB20-RB31 (12)* | | 98.55 | 22.50 |

***Hyphen Hole Perf. 7***

| | | | |
|---|---|---|---|
| *RB20p* | ⅛c | .30 | .25 |
| *RB21p* | ¼c | .25 | .25 |
| *b.* | ¼c yellow brown | .25 | .25 |
| *c.* | ¼c orange brown | .25 | .25 |
| *d.* | ¼c bister | .25 | .25 |
| *RB22p* | ⅜c | .50 | .35 |
| *RB23p* | ⅝c | .30 | .25 |
| *RB24p* | 1c | 30.00 | 15.00 |
| *RB25p* | 1¼c | .30 | .30 |
| *a.* | 1¼c brown violet | .25 | .25 |
| *RB26p* | 1⅞c | 40.00 | 9.00 |
| *RB27p* | 2c | 10.00 | 1.00 |
| *RB28p* | 2½c | 7.50 | .40 |
| *RB29p* | 3¾c | 100.00 | 27.50 |
| *RB30p* | 4c | 70.00 | 22.50 |
| *RB31p* | 5c | 85.00 | 25.00 |

See note before No. R161.

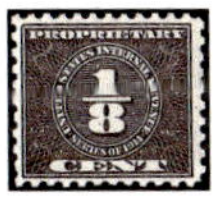
RB4

**Inscribed "Series of 1914"**

**Offset Printing**

**1914** **Wmk. 190** ***Perf. 10***

| | | | | |
|---|---|---|---|---|
| **RB32** | RB4 | ⅛c black | .25 | .35 |
| **RB33** | RB4 | ¼c black | 4.00 | 1.50 |
| **RB34** | RB4 | ⅜c black | .35 | .35 |
| **RB35** | RB4 | ⅝c black | 10.00 | 0.00 |
| **RB36** | RB4 | 1¼c black | 7.50 | 1.75 |
| **RB37** | RB4 | 1⅞c black | 80.00 | 22.50 |
| **RB38** | RB4 | 2½c black | 19.00 | 3.50 |
| **RB39** | RB4 | 3⅛c black | 230.00 | 67.50 |
| **RB40** | RB4 | 3¾c black | 75.00 | 27.50 |
| **RB41** | RB4 | 4c black | 110.00 | 45.00 |
| **RB42** | RB4 | 4⅜c black | *3,000.* | — |
| **RB43** | RB4 | 5c black | 200.00 | 110.00 |
| | *Nos. RB32-RB41,RB43 (11)* | | 736.10 | 282.95 |

**Wmk. 191R**

| | | | | |
|---|---|---|---|---|
| **RB44** | RB4 | ⅛c black | .35 | .30 |
| **RB45** | RB4 | ¼c black | .25 | .25 |
| **RB46** | RB4 | ⅜c black | .75 | .45 |
| **RB47** | RB4 | ½c black | 4.25 | 3.75 |
| **RB48** | RB4 | ⅝c black | .30 | .25 |
| **RB49** | RB4 | 1c black | 5.50 | 5.50 |
| **RB50** | RB4 | 1¼c black | .65 | .40 |
| **RB51** | RB4 | 1½c black | 4.25 | 3.00 |
| **RB52** | RB4 | 1⅞c black | 1.35 | .90 |
| **RB53** | RB4 | 2c black | 7.50 | 6.00 |
| **RB54** | RB4 | 2½c black | 2.00 | 1.40 |
| **RB55** | RB4 | 3c black | 6.00 | 4.00 |
| **RB56** | RB4 | 3⅛c black | 10.00 | 5.00 |
| **RB57** | RB4 | 3¾c black | 22.50 | 11.00 |
| **RB58** | RB4 | 4c black | .50 | .30 |
| **RB59** | RB4 | 4⅜c black | 22.50 | 11.00 |
| **RB60** | RB4 | 5c black | 6.00 | 3.75 |
| **RB61** | RB4 | 6c black | 90.00 | 52.50 |
| **RB62** | RB4 | 8c black | 30.00 | 16.00 |
| **RB63** | RB4 | 10c black | 20.00 | 11.00 |
| **RB64** | RB4 | 20c black | 40.00 | 24.00 |
| | *Nos. RB44-RB64 (21)* | | 274.65 | 160.75 |

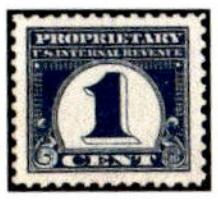
RB5

**1919** **Offset Printing** ***Perf. 11***

| | | | | |
|---|---|---|---|---|
| **RB65** | RB5 | 1c dark blue | .25 | .25 |
| **RB66** | RB5 | 2c dark blue | .35 | .25 |
| **RB67** | RB5 | 3c dark blue | 1.50 | .75 |
| **RB68** | RB5 | 4c dark blue | 2.25 | .75 |
| **RB69** | RB5 | 5c dark blue | 3.00 | 1.25 |
| **RB70** | RB5 | 8c dark blue | 27.50 | 20.00 |
| **RB71** | RB5 | 10c dark blue | 12.50 | 5.00 |
| **RB72** | RB5 | 20c dark blue | 20.00 | 7.50 |
| **RB73** | RB5 | 40c dark blue | 75.00 | 25.00 |
| | *Nos. RB65-RB73 (9)* | | 142.35 | 60.75 |

## FUTURE DELIVERY STAMPS

Issued to facilitate the collection of a tax upon each sale, agreement of sale or agreement to sell any products or merchandise at any exchange or board of trade, or other similar place for future delivery.

**Documentary Stamps of 1917 Overprinted in Black or Red**

Documentary Stamps Nos. R228-R250 Overprinted in Black or Red

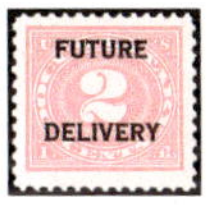


**Offset Printing**

**1918-34** **Wmk. 191R** ***Perf. 11***

**Overprint Horizontal (Lines 8mm apart)**

**Left Value — Unused With Gum**

**Right Value — Used**

| | | | | |
|---|---|---|---|---|
| **RC1** | R22 | 2c carmine rose | 10.00 | .25 |
| **RC2** | R22 | 3c carmine rose ('34) | 47.50 | 37.50 |
| | Cut cancel | | | 20.00 |
| **RC3** | R22 | 4c carmine rose | 25.00 | .25 |
| *b.* | Double impression of stamp | | | 10.00 |
| **RC3A** | R22 | 5c carmine rose ('33) | 100.00 | 7.50 |
| **RC4** | R22 | 10c carmine rose | 30.00 | .35 |
| *a.* | Double overprint | | — | 5.25 |
| *b.* | "FUTURE" omitted | | — | *500.00* |
| *c.* | "DELIVERY FUTURE" | | | 37.50 |
| **RC5** | R22 | 20c carmine rose | 50.00 | .25 |
| *a.* | Double overprint | | | 21.00 |
| **RC6** | R22 | 25c carmine rose | 100.00 | .60 |
| | Cut cancel | | | .30 |
| **RC7** | R22 | 40c carmine rose | 125.00 | 1.25 |
| | Cut cancel | | | .35 |
| **RC8** | R22 | 50c carmine rose | 35.00 | .35 |
| *a.* | "DELIVERY" omitted | | — | *110.00* |
| **RC9** | R22 | 80c carmine rose | 250.00 | 15.00 |
| | Cut cancel | | | 4.00 |
| *a.* | Double overprint | | | 37.50 |

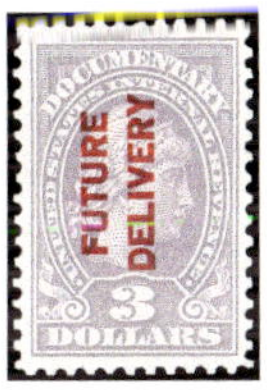


**Engr.**

**Overprint Vertical, Reading Up (Lines 2mm apart)**

| | | | | |
|---|---|---|---|---|
| **RC10** | R21 | $1 green (R) | 75.00 | .35 |
| | Cut cancel | | | .25 |
| *a.* | Overprint reading down | | | *450.00* |
| *b.* | Black overprint | | | — |
| | Cut cancel | | | 125.00 |
| **RC11** | R21 | $2 rose | 110.00 | .45 |
| | Cut cancel | | | .25 |
| **RC12** | R21 | $3 violet (R) | 310.00 | 3.50 |
| | Cut cancel | | | .30 |
| *a.* | Overprint reading down | | — | 52.50 |
| **RC13** | R21 | $5 dark blue (R) | 175.00 | .60 |
| | Cut cancel | | | .25 |
| **RC14** | R21 | $10 orange | 210.00 | 1.35 |
| | Cut cancel | | | .30 |
| *a.* | "DELIVERY FUTURE" | | | *110.00* |
| **RC15** | R21 | $20 olive bister | 550.00 | 9.00 |
| | Cut cancel | | | .80 |

**Overprint Horizontal (Lines 11½mm apart)**

***Perf. 12***

**Without Gum**

| | | | | |
|---|---|---|---|---|
| **RC16** | R17 | $30 vermilion, green numerals | 175.00 | 5.50 |
| | Cut cancel | | | 1.75 |
| *a.* | Numerals in blue | | 190.00 | 4.75 |
| | Cut cancel | | | 2.00 |
| *b.* | Imperf., blue numerals | | | *175.00* |
| **RC17** | R19 | $50 olive green (Cleveland) | 150.00 | 3.00 |
| | Cut cancel | | | .90 |
| *a.* | $50 olive bister | | 150.00 | 2.75 |
| | Cut cancel | | | .25 |
| **RC18** | R19 | $60 brown | 190.00 | 9.00 |
| | Cut cancel | | | 1.20 |
| *a.* | Vert. pair, imperf. horiz. | | | *950.00* |
| **RC19** | R17 | $100 yellow green ('34) | 300.00 | 37.50 |
| | Cut cancel | | | 9.00 |
| **RC20** | R18 | $500 blue, red numerals (R) | 375.00 | 25.00 |
| | Cut cancel | | | 9.00 |
| *a.* | Numerals in orange | | *750.00* | 70.00 |
| | Cut cancel | | | 20.00 |
| **RC21** | R19 | $1000orange | 300.00 | 7.50 |
| | Cut cancel | | | 2.00 |
| *a.* | Vert. pair, imperf. horiz. | | | *1,350.* |

See note after No. R227.

**1923-24** **Offset Printing** ***Perf. 11***

**Overprint Horizontal (Lines 2mm apart)**

| | | | | |
|---|---|---|---|---|
| **RC22** | R22 | 1c carmine rose | 1.25 | .25 |
| **RC23** | R22 | 80c carmine rose | 250.00 | 3.50 |
| | Cut cancel | | | .70 |

Documentary Stamps of 1917 Overprinted in Black or Red

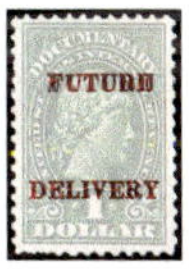


**1925-34** **Engr.**

| | | | | |
|---|---|---|---|---|
| **RC25** | R21 | $1 green (R) | 125.00 | 2.00 |
| | Cut cancel | | | .45 |
| **RC26** | R21 | $10 orange (Bk) ('34) | 300.00 | 29.00 |
| | Cut cancel | | | 18.00 |

**Overprint Type I**

**1928-29** **Offset Printing** ***Perf. 10***

| | | | | |
|---|---|---|---|---|
| **RC27** | R22 | 10c carmine rose | | *5,000.* |
| **RC28** | R22 | 20c carmine rose | | *5,000.* |

## STOCK TRANSFER STAMPS

Issued to facilitate the collection of a tax on all sales or agreements to sell, or memoranda of sales or delivery of, or transfers of legal title to shares or certificates of stock.

Documentary Stamps Nos. R228-R259 Overprinted in Black or Red

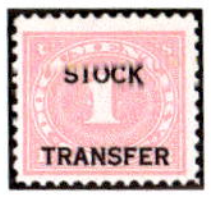


**Offset Printing**

**1918-22** **Wmk. 191R** ***Perf. 11***

**Overprint Horizontal (Lines 8mm apart)**

| | | | | |
|---|---|---|---|---|
| **RD1** | R22 | 1c carmine rose | 1.00 | .25 |
| *a.* | Double overprint | | — | — |
| **RD2** | R22 | 2c carmine rose | .25 | .25 |
| *a.* | Double overprint | | — | 15.00 |
| | Double overprint, cut cancel | | | 7.50 |
| **RD3** | R22 | 4c carmine rose | .25 | .25 |
| *a.* | Double overprint | | — | 4.25 |
| | Double overprint, cut cancel | | | 2.10 |
| *b.* | "STOCK" omitted | | | 10.50 |
| *d.* | Ovpt. lines 10mm apart | | — | |
| **RD4** | R22 | 5c carmine rose | .30 | .25 |
| **RD5** | R22 | 10c carmine rose | .30 | .25 |
| *a.* | Double overprint | | — | 5.25 |
| | Double overprint, cut cancel | | | 2.75 |
| *b.* | "STOCK" omitted | | | — |

216 UNITED STATES

RD6 R22 20c carmine rose .55 .25
a. Double overprint 6.25
b. "STOCK" double —
RD7 R22 25c carmine rose 2.25 .30
Cut cancel .25
RD8 R22 40c carmine rose ('22) 2.25 .25
RD9 R22 50c carmine rose .80 .25
a. Double overprint —
RD10 R22 80c carmine rose 10.00 .45
Cut cancel .25

### Engr.
### Overprint Vertical, Reading Up (Lines 2mm apart)

RD11 R21 $1 green (R) 250.00 40.00
Cut cancel 10.00
a. Overprint reading down 375.00 60.00
Overprint reading down, cut cancel 20.00
RD12 R21 $1 green (Bk) 3.00 .30
a. Pair, one without overprint — 180.00
b. Overprinted on back instead of face, inverted — 150.00
c. Overprint reading down — 7.50
d. $1 yellow green 3.00 .25
RD13 R21 $2 rose 3.00 .25
a. Overprint reading down 11.50
Overprint reading down, cut cancel 1.50
b. Vert. pair, imperf. horiz. 800.00
RD14 R21 $3 violet (R) 35.00 6.00
Cut cancel .30
RD15 R21 $4 yellow brown 15.00 .30
Cut cancel .25
RD16 R21 $5 dark blue (R) 10.00 .30
Cut cancel .25
a. Overprint reading down 42.50 1.35
Overprint reading down, cut cancel .25
RD17 R21 $10 orange 37.50 .45
Cut cancel .25
RD18 R21 $20 olive bister ('21) 150.00 18.00
Cut cancel 4.50
a. Overprint reading down —

### Overprint Horizontal (Lines 11½mm apart)

**1918 Without Gum Perf. 12**

RD19 R17 $30 ver, grn numerals 65.00 6.50
Cut cancel 2.25
a. Numerals in blue 200.00 75.00
RD20 R19 $50 ol grn, Cleveland 160.00 70.00
Cut cancel 27.50
RD21 R19 $60 brown 350.00 30.00
Cut cancel 12.00
RD22 R17 $100 green 65.00 7.50
Cut cancel 3.00
RD23 R18 $500 blue (R) 750.00 160.00
Cut cancel 75.00
a. Numerals in orange 175.00
RD24 R19 $1,000 orange, dark blue numerals 600.00 110.00
Cut cancel 35.00
a. Numerals in light blue —

See note after No. R227.

**1928 Offset Printing Perf. 10**

### Overprint Horizontal (Lines 8mm apart)

RD25 R22 2c carmine rose 5.50 .30
RD26 R22 4c carmine rose 5.50 .30
RD27 R22 10c carmine rose 5.50 .30
a. Inverted overprint 1,400.
b. Ovpt. lines 9½mm apart —
RD28 R22 20c carmine rose 6.50 .35
RD29 R22 50c carmine rose 10.00 .50

### Engr.
### Overprint Vertical, Reading Up (Lines 2mm apart)

RD30 R21 $1 green 75.00 .35
a. $1 yellow green 75.00 .50
RD31 R21 $2 carmine rose 70.00 .35
a. Pair, one without overprint 225.00 190.00
RD32 R21 $10 orange 75.00 .50

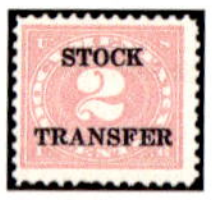

Overprinted Horiz. in Black

**1920 Offset Printing Perf. 11**

RD33 R22 2c carmine rose 12.50 1.00
RD34 R22 10c carmine rose 3.00 .35
b. Inverted overprint 2,250. 1,250.
RD35 R22 20c carmine rose 5.75 .25
a. Horiz. pair, one without overprint 950.00
d. Inverted overprint (perf. initials) —
RD36 R22 50c carmine rose 5.00 .30

### Engr.

RD37 R21 $1 green 110.00 17.50
RD38 R21 $2 rose 125.00 17.50

### Offset Printing
### Perf. 10

RD39 R22 2c carmine rose 13.00 1.10
RD40 R22 10c carmine rose 5.25 .55
RD41 R22 20c carmine rose 6.00 .25

Used values for Nos. RD42-RD372 are for stamps which are neither cut nor perforated with initials. Stamps with cut cancellations or perforated initials are valued in the Scott U.S. Specialized Catalogue.

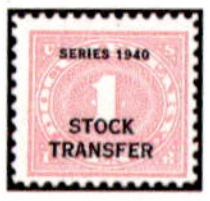

Documentary Stamps of 1917-33 Overprinted in Black

**1940 Perf. 11**

RD42 R22 1c rose pink 4.50 .65
a. "Series 1940" inverted (pos. 31LR) 1,000. 600.00

No. RD42a always comes with a natural straight edge at left.

RD43 R22 2c rose pink 6.00 .65
RD45 R22 4c rose pink 7.50 .35
RD46 R22 5c rose pink 8.00 .25
RD48 R22 10c rose pink 14.00 .35
RD49 R22 20c rose pink 17.00 .35
RD50 R22 25c rose pink 17.00 1.10
RD51 R22 40c rose pink 11.00 1.00
RD52 R22 50c rose pink 12.50 .35
RD53 R22 80c rose pink 280.00 110.00

### Engr.

RD54 R21 $1 green 60.00 .60
RD55 R21 $2 rose 65.00 1.00
RD56 R21 $3 violet 350.00 18.00
RD57 R21 $4 yellow brown 140.00 1.60
RD58 R21 $5 dark blue 115.00 2.00
RD59 R21 $10 orange 325.00 10.00
RD60 R21 $20 olive bister 600.00 150.00

### Nos. RD19-RD24 Handstamped in Blue "Series 1940"

**1940 Perf. 12**

### Without Gum

RD61 R17 $30 ver 2,000. 1,500.
RD62 R19 $50 ol grn 2,500. 2,500.
a. Double ovpt., perf. initial 1,400.
RD63 R19 $60 brown 5,500. 3,000.
RD64 R17 $100 green 5,000. 850.00
RD65 R18 $500 blue 4,250.
RD66 R19 $1,000 orange
Cut cancel 5,000.

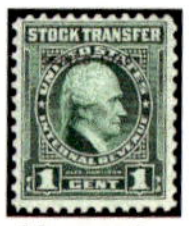

Alexander Hamilton ST1

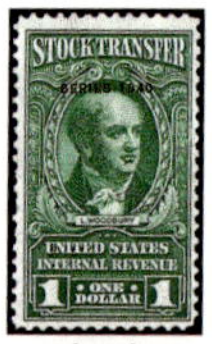

Levi Woodbury ST2

Overprinted in Black SERIES 1940

Same Portraits as Nos. R288-R310.

**1940 Engr. Perf. 11**

RD67 ST1 1c brt grn 17.50 3.25
a. Imperf, pair, without gum 200.00
RD68 ST1 2c brt grn 10.00 1.75
a. Imperf, pair, without gum 200.00
RD70 ST1 4c brt grn 19.00 4.50
a. Imperf, pair, without gum 200.00
RD71 ST1 5c brt grn 12.00 1.75
a. Imperf, pair, without gum 200.00
b. Without overprint, cut cancel 850.00
RD73 ST1 10c brt grn 16.00 2.10
a. Imperf, pair, without gum 200.00
RD74 ST1 20c brt grn 19.00 2.40
a. Imperf, pair, without gum 200.00
RD75 ST1 25c brt grn 60.00 10.50
a. Imperf, pair, without gum 200.00
RD76 ST1 40c brt grn 125.00 50.00
a. Imperf, pair, without gum 200.00
RD77 ST1 50c brt grn 16.00 2.10
a. Imperf, pair, without gum 200.00
RD78 ST1 80c brt grn 180.00 75.00
a. Imperf, pair, without gum 200.00
RD79 ST2 $1 brt grn 75.00 4.25
a. Without overprint, perf. initial 750.00
RD80 ST2 $2 brt grn 75.00 12.00
a. Imperf, pair, without gum 200.00
RD81 ST2 $3 brt grn 110.00 15.00
a. Imperf, pair, without gum 200.00
RD82 ST2 $4 brt grn 1,000. 300.00
a. Imperf, pair, without gum 200.00
RD83 ST2 $5 brt grn 110.00 16.00
a. Imperf, pair, without gum 200.00
RD84 ST2 $10 brt grn 250.00 60.00
a. Imperf, pair, without gum 200.00
RD85 ST2 $20 brt grn 1,250. 125.00
a. Imperf, pair, without gum 200.00

Nos. RD67-RD85 exist imperforate, without overprint. Value, set of pairs, $750.

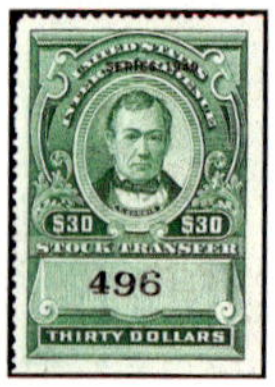

Thomas Corwin — ST3

### Overprinted "SERIES 1940"

Various frames and portraits as Nos. R306-R310.

### Perf. 12
### Without Gum

RD86 ST3 $30 brt grn 6,000. 200.00
RD87 ST3 $50 brt grn 3,250. 900.00
RD88 ST3 $60 brt grn 5,000. 2,250.
RD89 ST3 $100 brt grn 3,000. 450.00
RD90 ST3 $500 brt grn —
RD91 ST3 $1,000 brt grn 4,000.

Nos. RD86-RD91 exist as unfinished imperforates with complete receipt tabs, without overprints or serial numbers. Known in singles, pairs (Nos. RD86-RD88 and Nos. RD90-RD91, value $300 per pair; No. RD89, value $150 per pair), panes of four with plate number, uncut sheets of four panes (with two plate numbers), cross gutter blocks of eight, and blocks of four with vertical gutter between and plate number.

RD89 exists without serial number and perforated on all four sides.

### Stock Transfer Stamps and Type of 1940 Overprinted in Black

Nos. RD67-RD91 Overprinted SERIES 1941 Instead:

**1941 Perf. 11**

RD92 ST1 1c brt grn .80 .55
RD93 ST1 2c brt grn .60 .30
RD95 ST1 4c brt grn .65 .25
RD96 ST1 5c brt grn .60 .25
RD98 ST1 10c brt grn 1.10 .25
RD99 ST1 20c brt grn 2.40 .30
RD100 ST1 25c brt grn 2.40 .45
RD101 ST1 40c brt grn 3.75 .75
RD102 ST1 50c brt grn 5.00 .35
RD103 ST1 80c brt grn 35.00 10.00
RD104 ST2 $1 brt grn 25.00 .25
RD105 ST2 $2 brt grn 27.50 .30
RD106 ST2 $3 brt grn 40.00 1.50
RD107 ST2 $4 brt grn 65.00 8.50
RD108 ST2 $5 brt grn 65.00 .65
RD109 ST2 $10 brt grn 140.00 5.50
RD110 ST2 $20 brt grn 500.00 110.00

### Perf. 12
### Without Gum

RD111 ST3 $30 brt grn 2,250. 500.00
RD112 ST3 $50 brt grn 1,250. 750.00
RD113 ST3 $60 brt grn 2,500. 1,000.
RD114 ST3 $100 brt grn 650.00 210.00
RD115 ST3 $500 brt grn 4,000. 3,500.
RD116 ST3 $1,000 brt grn — 4,000.

### Stock Transfer Stamps and Type of 1940 Overprinted in Black

Nos. RD67-RD91 overprinted SERIES 1942 instead:

**1942 Perf. 11**

RD117 ST1 1c brt grn .75 .30
RD118 ST1 2c brt grn .65 .35
RD119 ST1 4c brt grn 3.50 1.10
RD120 ST1 5c brt grn .70 .25
a. Overprint inverted 1,000.
RD121 ST1 10c brt grn 2.25 .25
RD122 ST1 20c brt grn 2.75 .25
RD123 ST1 25c brt grn 2.50 .25
RD124 ST1 40c brt grn 5.75 .40
RD125 ST1 50c brt grn 6.50 .25
RD126 ST1 80c brt grn 30.00 6.00
RD127 ST2 $1 brt grn 27.50 .40
RD128 ST2 $2 brt grn 45.00 .40
RD129 ST2 $3 brt grn 50.00 1.10
RD130 ST2 $4 brt grn 65.00 24.00
RD131 ST2 $5 brt grn 60.00 .40
a. Double overprint, perf. initial 2,500.
RD132 ST2 $10 brt grn 125.00 9.50
RD133 ST2 $20 brt grn 350.00 65.00

### Perf. 12
### Without Gum

RD134 ST3 $30 brt grn 900.00 250.00
RD135 ST3 $50 brt grn 950.00 400.00
RD136 ST3 $60 brt grn 2,500. 350.00
RD137 ST3 $100 brt grn 900.00 110.00
RD138 ST3 $500 brt grn 15,000.
RD139 ST3 $1,000 brt grn — 2,750.

### Stock Transfer Stamps and Type of 1940 Overprinted in Black

Nos. RD67-RD91 overprinted SERIES 1943 instead

**1943 Perf. 11**

RD140 ST1 1c brt grn .55 .30
RD141 ST1 2c brt grn .60 .40
RD142 ST1 4c brt grn 2.10 .25
RD143 ST1 5c brt grn .60 .25
RD144 ST1 10c brt grn 1.50 .25
RD145 ST1 20c brt grn 2.25 .25
RD146 ST1 25c brt grn 6.75 .35
RD147 ST1 40c brt grn 6.25 .30
RD148 ST1 50c brt grn 5.75 .30
RD149 ST1 80c brt grn 35.00 7.50
RD150 ST2 $1 brt grn 27.50 .25
RD151 ST2 $2 brt grn 30.00 .50
RD152 ST2 $3 brt grn 35.00 2.50
RD153 ST2 $4 brt grn 85.00 30.00
RD154 ST2 $5 brt grn 90.00 .60
RD155 ST2 $10 brt grn 140.00 7.50
RD156 ST2 $20 brt grn 450.00 90.00

### Perf. 12
### Without Gum

RD157 ST3 $30 brt grn 2,500. 750.00
RD158 ST3 $50 brt grn 2,500. 450.00
RD159 ST3 $60 brt grn 4,000. 2,750.
RD160 ST3 $100 brt grn 300.00 90.00
RD161 ST3 $500 brt grn — 2,250.
RD162 ST3 $1,000 brt grn 2,500. 2,000.

### Stock Transfer Stamps and Type of 1940 Overprinted in Black

Series 1944

**1944 Perf. 11**

RD163 ST1 1c brt grn .90 .75
RD164 ST1 2c brt grn .70 .25
RD165 ST1 4c brt grn .70 .35
RD166 ST1 5c brt grn .65 .25
RD167 ST1 10c brt grn 1.00 .30
RD168 ST1 20c brt grn 2.25 .25
RD169 ST1 25c brt grn 3.25 .90
RD170 ST1 40c brt grn 17.50 8.00
RD171 ST1 50c brt grn 5.50 .30
RD172 ST1 80c brt grn 17.50 6.25
RD173 ST2 $1 brt grn 17.50 .50

UNITED STATES 217

| | | | | | |
|---|---|---|---|---|---|
| RD174 | ST2 | $2 | brt grn | 60.00 | .75 |
| RD175 | ST2 | $3 | brt grn | 55.00 | 2.00 |
| RD176 | ST2 | $4 | brt grn | 95.00 | 17.50 |
| RD177 | ST2 | $5 | brt grn | 65.00 | 3.50 |
| RD178 | ST2 | $10 | brt grn | 150.00 | 7.25 |
| RD179 | ST2 | $20 | brt grn | 425.00 | 25.00 |

***Perf. 12***

**Without Gum**

Designs: $2,500, William Windom. $5,000, C. J. Folger. $10,000, W. Q. Gresham.

| | | | | | |
|---|---|---|---|---|---|
| RD180 | ST3 | $30 | brt grn | 1,000. | 125.00 |
| RD181 | ST3 | $50 | brt grn | 1,000. | 150.00 |
| RD182 | ST3 | $60 | brt grn | *4,750.* | 750.00 |
| RD183 | ST3 | $100 | brt grn | 3,250. | 100.00 |
| RD184 | ST3 | $500 | brt grn | *2,500.* | *2,250.* |
| RD185 | ST3 | $1,000 | brt grn | *3,000.* | 2,500. |
| RD185A | ST3 | $2,500 | brt grn | | — |
| RD185B | ST3 | $5,000 | brt grn | | *65,000.* |
| RD185C | ST3 | $10,000 | brt grn, cut cancel | | *45,000.* |
| | | | Perf. initial | | *35,000.* |

**Stock Transfer Stamps and Type of 1940 Overprinted in Black**

**Series 1945**

**1945** ***Perf. 11***

| | | | | | |
|---|---|---|---|---|---|
| RD186 | ST1 | 1c | brt grn | .45 | .25 |
| RD187 | ST1 | 2c | brt grn | .45 | .35 |
| RD188 | ST1 | 4c | brt grn | .50 | .35 |
| RD189 | ST1 | 5c | brt grn | .45 | .25 |
| RD190 | ST1 | 10c | brt grn | 1.25 | .35 |
| RD191 | ST1 | 20c | brt grn | 2.25 | .45 |
| RD192 | ST1 | 25c | brt grn | 3.50 | .40 |
| RD193 | ST1 | 40c | brt grn | 5.00 | .25 |
| RD194 | ST1 | 50c | brt grn | 11.00 | .45 |
| RD195 | ST1 | 80c | brt grn | 17.50 | 4.75 |
| RD196 | ST2 | $1 | brt grn | 20.00 | .30 |
| RD197 | ST2 | $2 | brt grn | 37.50 | .90 |
| RD198 | ST2 | $3 | brt grn | 65.00 | 1.75 |
| RD199 | ST2 | $4 | brt grn | 65.00 | 4.25 |
| RD200 | ST2 | $5 | brt grn | 40.00 | 1.00 |
| RD201 | ST2 | $10 | brt grn | 95.00 | 12.00 |
| RD202 | ST2 | $20 | brt grn | 375.00 | 25.00 |

***Perf. 12***

**Without Gum**

| | | | | | |
|---|---|---|---|---|---|
| RD203 | ST3 | $30 | brt grn | 375.00 | 90.00 |
| RD204 | ST3 | $50 | brt grn | 350.00 | 70.00 |
| RD205 | ST3 | $60 | brt grn | 1,750. | 500.00 |
| RD206 | ST3 | $100 | brt grn | 750.00 | 75.00 |
| RD207 | ST3 | $500 | brt grn | — | 1,400. |
| RD208 | ST3 | $1,000 | brt grn | *3,250.* | 2,250. |
| RD208A | ST3 | $2,500 | brt grn, perf. initial | | *20,000.* |
| RD208B | ST3 | $5,000 | brt grn, cut cancel | | *45,000.* |
| RD208C | ST3 | $10,000 | brt grn, cut cancel | | *45,000.* |

**Stock Transfer Stamps and Type of 1940 Overprinted in Black**

**Series 1946**

**1946** ***Perf. 11***

| | | | | | |
|---|---|---|---|---|---|
| RD209 | ST1 | 1c | brt grn | .50 | .35 |
| *a.* | | | Pair, one dated "1945" | *850.00* | |
| RD210 | ST1 | 2c | brt grn | .50 | .25 |
| RD211 | ST1 | 4c | brt grn | .50 | .25 |
| RD212 | ST1 | 5c | brt grn | .55 | .25 |
| RD213 | ST1 | 10c | brt grn | 1.25 | .25 |
| RD214 | ST1 | 20c | brt grn | 2.50 | .30 |
| RD215 | ST1 | 25c | brt grn | 3.00 | .40 |
| RD216 | ST1 | 40c | brt grn | 6.50 | 1.25 |
| RD217 | ST1 | 50c | brt grn | 6.75 | .25 |
| RD218 | ST1 | 80c | brt grn | 24.00 | 9.50 |
| RD219 | ST2 | $1 | brt grn | 17.50 | .00 |
| RD220 | ST2 | $2 | brt grn | 19.00 | 1.00 |
| RD221 | ST2 | $3 | brt grn | 35.00 | 2.25 |
| RD222 | ST2 | $4 | brt grn | 35.00 | 9.00 |
| RD223 | ST2 | $5 | brt grn | 60.00 | 2.25 |
| RD224 | ST2 | $10 | brt grn | 100.00 | 4.25 |
| RD225 | ST2 | $20 | brt grn | 550.00 | 75.00 |

***Perf. 12***

***Without Gum***

| | | | | | |
|---|---|---|---|---|---|
| RD226 | ST3 | $30 | brt grn | 425.00 | 62.50 |
| RD227 | ST3 | $50 | brt grn | 550.00 | 75.00 |
| RD228 | ST3 | $60 | brt grn | 1,250. | 250.00 |
| RD229 | ST3 | $100 | brt grn | 300.00 | 90.00 |
| RD230 | ST3 | $500 | brt grn | *2,500.* | 350.00 |
| RD231 | ST3 | $1,000 | brt grn | 2,000. | 300.00 |
| RD232 | ST3 | $2,500 | brt grn | | *25,000.* |
| RD233 | ST3 | $5,000 | brt grn, cut cancel | | *17,500.* |
| RD234 | ST3 | $10,000 | brt grn, cut cancel | | *22,500.* |

**Stock Transfer Stamps and Type of 1940 Overprinted in Black**

**Series 1947**

**1947** ***Perf. 11***

| | | | | | |
|---|---|---|---|---|---|
| RD235 | ST1 | 1c | bright green | 2.75 | .90 |
| RD236 | ST1 | 2c | bright green | 2.75 | .90 |
| RD237 | ST1 | 4c | bright green | 2.00 | .70 |
| RD238 | ST1 | 5c | bright green | 2.00 | .60 |
| RD239 | ST1 | 10c | bright green | 2.00 | .90 |
| RD240 | ST1 | 20c | bright green | 3.75 | .90 |
| RD241 | ST1 | 25c | bright green | 6.00 | .90 |
| RD242 | ST1 | 40c | bright green | 6.00 | 1.40 |
| RD243 | ST1 | 50c | bright green | 7.50 | .35 |
| RD244 | ST1 | 80c | bright green | 32.50 | 14.00 |
| RD245 | ST2 | $1 | bright green | 25.00 | 1.00 |
| RD246 | ST2 | $2 | bright green | 35.00 | 1.25 |
| RD247 | ST2 | $3 | bright green | 50.00 | 2.50 |
| RD248 | ST2 | $4 | bright green | 70.00 | 9.50 |
| RD249 | ST2 | $5 | bright green | 50.00 | 3.25 |
| RD250 | ST2 | $10 | bright green | 225.00 | 11.00 |
| RD251 | ST2 | $20 | bright green | 300.00 | 50.00 |

***Perf. 12***

***Without Gum***

| | | | | | |
|---|---|---|---|---|---|
| RD252 | ST3 | $30 | brt grn | 2,000. | 85.00 |
| RD253 | ST3 | $50 | brt grn | 1,500. | 325.00 |
| RD254 | ST3 | $60 | brt grn | 2,750. | 250.00 |
| RD255 | ST3 | $100 | brt grn | 210.00 | 70.00 |
| RD256 | ST3 | $500 | brt grn | 2,500. | 850.00 |
| RD257 | ST3 | $1,000 | brt grn | 2,750. | 140.00 |
| RD258 | ST3 | $2,500 | brt grn | *3,000.* | |
| | | | Cut cancel | | 400.00 |
| RD259 | ST3 | $5,000 | brt grn | 2,500. | |
| | | | Cut cancel | | 600.00 |
| RD260 | ST3 | $10,000 | brt grn | — | |
| | | | Cut cancel | | 75.00 |
| *a.* | | | Vert. pair, imperf. horiz., cut cancel | | — |

**Stock Transfer Stamps and Type of 1940 Overprinted in Black**

**Series 1948**

**1948** ***Perf. 11***

| | | | | | |
|---|---|---|---|---|---|
| RD261 | ST1 | 1c | bright green | .45 | .35 |
| RD262 | ST1 | 2c | bright green | .45 | .35 |
| RD263 | ST1 | 4c | bright green | .80 | .45 |
| RD264 | ST1 | 5c | bright green | .45 | .25 |
| RD265 | ST1 | 10c | bright green | .55 | .35 |
| RD266 | ST1 | 20c | bright green | 1.60 | .40 |
| RD267 | ST1 | 25c | bright green | 1.90 | .55 |
| RD268 | ST1 | 40c | bright green | 5.00 | 1.00 |
| RD269 | ST1 | 50c | bright green | 7.00 | .45 |
| RD270 | ST1 | 80c | bright green | 30.00 | 9.50 |
| RD271 | ST2 | $1 | bright green | 17.50 | .50 |
| RD272 | ST2 | $2 | bright green | 35.00 | 1.00 |
| RD273 | ST2 | $3 | bright green | 60.00 | 10.00 |
| RD274 | ST2 | $4 | bright green | 70.00 | 20.00 |
| RD275 | ST2 | $5 | bright green | 80.00 | 5.00 |
| RD276 | ST2 | $10 | bright green | 90.00 | 7.25 |
| RD277 | ST2 | $20 | bright green | 400.00 | 30.00 |

***Perf. 12***

**Without Gum**

| | | | | | |
|---|---|---|---|---|---|
| RD278 | ST3 | $30 | brt grn | 425.00 | 100.00 |
| RD279 | ST3 | $50 | brt grn | 500.00 | 95.00 |
| RD280 | ST3 | $60 | brt grn | 2,000. | 350.00 |
| RD281 | ST3 | $100 | brt grn | 225.00 | 30.00 |
| RD282 | ST3 | $500 | brt grn | 2,500. | 375.00 |
| RD283 | ST3 | $1,000 | brt grn | 2,500. | 125.00 |
| RD284 | ST3 | $2,500 | brt grn | 2,500. | 1,750. |
| RD285 | ST3 | $5,000 | brt grn | 2,500. | 1,750. |
| RD286 | ST3 | $10,000 | brt grn | | |

**Stock Transfer Stamps and Type of 1940 Overprinted in Black**

**Series 1949**

**1949** ***Perf. 11***

| | | | | | |
|---|---|---|---|---|---|
| RD287 | ST1 | 1c | bright green | 2.25 | .70 |
| RD288 | ST1 | 2c | bright green | 2.25 | .75 |
| RD289 | ST1 | 4c | bright green | 2.50 | .75 |
| RD290 | ST1 | 5c | bright green | 3.00 | .75 |
| RD291 | ST1 | 10c | bright green | 7.50 | 1.00 |
| RD292 | ST1 | 20c | bright green | 12.00 | 1.00 |
| RD293 | ST1 | 25c | bright green | 13.00 | 1.25 |
| RD294 | ST1 | 40c | bright green | 30.00 | 3.25 |
| RD295 | ST1 | 50c | bright green | 35.00 | .45 |
| RD296 | ST1 | 80c | bright green | 45.00 | 10.00 |
| RD297 | ST2 | $1 | bright green | 32.50 | 1.00 |
| RD298 | ST2 | $2 | bright green | 60.00 | 1.75 |
| RD299 | ST2 | $3 | bright green | 110.00 | 10.00 |
| RD300 | ST2 | $4 | bright green | 110.00 | 20.00 |
| RD301 | ST2 | $5 | bright green | 85.00 | 3.00 |
| RD302 | ST2 | $10 | bright green | 150.00 | 12.50 |
| RD303 | ST2 | $20 | bright green | 325.00 | 22.50 |

***Perf. 12***

**Without Gum**

| | | | | | |
|---|---|---|---|---|---|
| RD304 | ST3 | $30 | brt grn | 3,000. | 150.00 |
| RD305 | ST3 | $50 | brt grn | 2,250. | 300.00 |
| RD306 | ST3 | $60 | brt grn | 2,500. | 400.00 |
| RD307 | ST3 | $100 | brt grn | 300.00 | 70.00 |
| RD308 | ST3 | $500 | brt grn | *1,500.* | 300.00 |
| RD309 | ST3 | $1,000 | brt grn | *1,500.* | 85.00 |
| RD310 | ST3 | $2,500 | brt grn | | |
| RD311 | ST3 | $5,000 | brt grn | | |
| RD312 | ST3 | $10,000 | brt grn | | 475.00 |
| *a.* | | | Pair, one without ovpt., cut cancel | | *8,000.* |

No. RD312a is unique.

**Stock Transfer Stamps and Type of 1940 Overprinted in Black**

**Series 1950**

**1950** ***Perf. 11***

| | | | | | |
|---|---|---|---|---|---|
| RD313 | ST1 | 1c | bright green | .80 | .40 |
| RD314 | ST1 | 2c | bright green | .70 | .35 |
| RD315 | ST1 | 4c | bright green | .65 | .40 |
| RD316 | ST1 | 5c | bright green | .75 | .25 |
| RD317 | ST1 | 10c | bright green | 3.25 | .30 |
| RD318 | ST1 | 20c | bright green | 5.00 | .80 |
| RD319 | ST1 | 25c | bright green | 10.00 | 1.00 |
| RD320 | ST1 | 40c | bright green | 15.00 | 1.50 |
| RD321 | ST1 | 50c | bright green | 19.00 | .50 |
| RD322 | ST1 | 80c | bright green | 27.50 | 7.25 |
| RD323 | ST2 | $1 | bright green | 27.50 | .55 |
| RD324 | ST2 | $2 | bright green | 40.00 | 1.25 |
| RD325 | ST2 | $3 | bright green | 70.00 | 8.50 |
| RD326 | ST2 | $4 | bright green | 85.00 | 20.00 |
| RD327 | ST2 | $5 | bright green | 70.00 | 3.25 |
| RD328 | ST2 | $10 | bright green | 210.00 | 12.50 |
| RD329 | ST2 | $20 | bright green | 300.00 | 60.00 |

***Perf. 12***

**Without Gum**

| | | | | | |
|---|---|---|---|---|---|
| RD330 | ST3 | $30 | brt grn | 750.00 | 250.00 |
| RD331 | ST3 | $50 | brt grn | 800.00 | 225.00 |
| RD332 | ST3 | $60 | brt grn | 1,000. | 250.00 |
| RD333 | ST3 | $100 | brt grn | 200.00 | 55.00 |
| *a.* | | | Vert. pair, imperf. btwn. | 2,000. | *1,750.* |
| RD334 | ST3 | $500 | brt grn | — | 350.00 |
| RD335 | ST3 | $1,000 | brt grn | 350.00 | 85.00 |
| RD336 | ST3 | $2,500 | brt grn | 5,500. | 2,500. |
| RD337 | ST3 | $5,000 | brt grn | 5,500. | 2,500. |
| RD338 | ST3 | $10,000 | brt grn | 5,500. | 1,500. |

**Stock Transfer Stamps and Type of 1940 Overprinted in Black**

**Series 1951**

**1951** ***Perf. 11***

| | | | | | |
|---|---|---|---|---|---|
| RD339 | ST1 | 1c | bright green | 3.00 | .75 |
| RD340 | ST1 | 2c | bright green | 2.50 | .50 |
| RD341 | ST1 | 4c | bright green | 3.00 | .75 |
| RD342 | ST1 | 5c | bright green | 2.25 | .55 |
| RD343 | ST1 | 10c | bright green | 3.00 | .35 |
| RD344 | ST1 | 20c | bright green | 10.00 | 1.25 |
| RD345 | ST1 | 25c | bright green | 12.00 | 1.50 |
| RD346 | ST1 | 40c | bright green | 50.00 | 12.50 |
| RD347 | ST1 | 50c | bright green | 20.00 | 1.50 |
| RD348 | ST1 | 80c | bright green | 40.00 | 14.00 |
| RD349 | ST2 | $1 | bright green | 40.00 | 1.25 |
| RD350 | ST2 | $2 | bright green | 55.00 | 1.75 |
| RD351 | ST2 | $3 | bright green | 70.00 | 14.00 |
| RD352 | ST2 | $4 | bright green | 350.00 | 25.00 |
| RD353 | ST2 | $5 | bright green | 90.00 | 4.00 |
| RD354 | ST2 | $10 | bright green | 170.00 | 11.00 |
| RD355 | ST2 | $20 | bright green | 400.00 | 35.00 |

***Perf. 12***

**Without Gum**

| | | | | | |
|---|---|---|---|---|---|
| RD356 | ST3 | $30 | brt grn | *2,500.* | 200.00 |
| RD357 | ST3 | $50 | brt grn | *2,500.* | 250.00 |
| RD358 | ST3 | $60 | brt grn | *2,500.* | *1,600.* |
| RD359 | ST3 | $100 | brt grn | 325.00 | 100.00 |
| RD360 | ST3 | $500 | brt grn | *2,500.* | 550.00 |
| RD361 | ST3 | $1,000 | brt grn | 400.00 | 125.00 |
| RD362 | ST3 | $2,500 | brt grn | | *4,250.* |
| RD363 | ST3 | $5,000 | brt grn | — | *3,250.* |
| RD364 | ST3 | $10,000 | brt grn | *2,000.* | 250.00 |

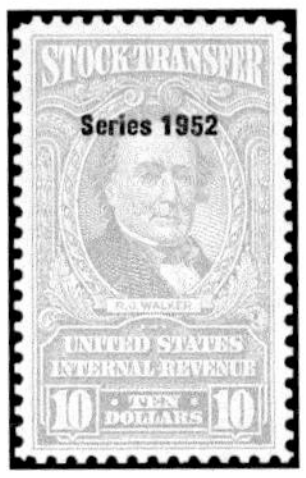


Stock Transfer Stamps and Type of 1940 Overprinted in Black

**1952** ***Perf. 11***

| | | | | | |
|---|---|---|---|---|---|
| RD365 | ST1 | 1c | brt grn | 42.50 | 27.50 |
| RD366 | ST1 | 10c | brt grn | 45.00 | 27.50 |
| RD367 | ST1 | 20c | brt grn | 400.00 | — |
| RD368 | ST1 | 25c | brt grn | 550.00 | — |
| RD369 | ST1 | 40c | brt grn | 140.00 | 55.00 |
| RD370 | ST2 | $4 | brt grn | *1,500.* | 1,250. |
| RD371 | ST2 | $10 | brt grn | *3,500.* | — |
| RD372 | ST2 | $20 | brt grn | *6,000.* | — |

Stock Transfer Stamps were discontinued in 1952.

**Catalogue values for all unused stamps in this section are for stamps with never-hinged original gum. Minor natural gum skips and bends are normal on Nos. RW1-RW20. No-gum stamps are without signature or other cancel.**

## HUNTING PERMIT STAMPS

**Catalogue values for all unused stamps in this section are for stamps with never-hinged original gum. Hinged examples from No. RW13 to present usually sell for 40%-60% of the values of never-hinged examples. Minor natural gum skips and bends are normal on Nos. RW1-RW20. No-gum stamps are without signature or other cancel.**

**Nos. RW1-RW12 were issued in panes of 28, of which 10 stamps have a straight edge on one or two sides. Such examples sell for 20%-30% less than the values shown.**

**Department of Agriculture**

Various Designs Inscribed "U. S. Department of Agriculture"

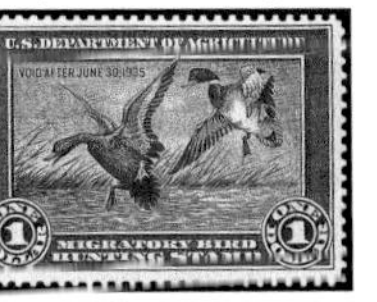


Mallards Alighting — HP1

Engraved: Flat Plate Printing

**1934** **Unwmk.** ***Perf. 11***

**Inscribed "Void after June 30, 1935"**

| | | | | |
|---|---|---|---|---|
| RW1 | HP1 | $1 blue | 775. | 175. |
| | | Hinged | 300. | |
| | | No gum | 175. | |

Used value is for stamp with handstamp or manuscript cancel.

It is almost certain that examples of No. RW1 offered as imperforate vertical pairs or as vertical pairs imperforate horizontally are from printer's waste. Additionally, it is almost certain that all imperforate vertical pairs are pairs imperforate horizontally that have had the vertical perforations trimmed off. No horizontal imperforate pairs are known. All recorded pairs are vertical, with narrow side margins. Most examples exist without gum and with faults. Some pairs have gum on the front (which in some cases appears to have been removed).

The stamps imperforate horizontally are recorded as a unique vertical block of eight, with the other recorded varieties being the manufactured imperforate vertical pairs.

# UNITED STATES

Canvasbacks Taking to Flight — HP2

**1935**
**Inscribed "Void after June 30, 1936"**
RW2  HP2  $1 rose lake          700.   160.
           deep rose lake         —
           Hinged                375.
           No gum                175.

Canada Geese in Flight — HP3

**1936**
**Inscribed "Void after June 30, 1937"**
RW3  HP3  $1 brown black        325.   100.
           Hinged                150.
           No gum                 90.

Scaup Ducks Taking to Flight — HP4

**1937**
**Inscribed "Void after June 30, 1938"**
RW4  HP4  $1 light green        300.    65.
           Hinged                140.
           No gum                 85.

Pintail Drake and Hen Alighting HP5

**1938**
**Inscribed "Void after June 30, 1939"**
RW5  HP5  $1 light violet       425.    75.
           Hinged                200.
           No gum                 85.

**Department of the Interior**
Various Designs Inscribed
"U. S. Department of the Interior"

Green-Winged Teal — HP6

**1939**
**Inscribed "Void after June 30, 1940"**
RW6  HP6  $1 chocolate          250.    50.
           Hinged                115.
           No gum                 60.

Black Mallards HP7

**1940**
**Inscribed "Void after June 30, 1941"**
RW7  HP7  $1 sepia              250.    50.
           Hinged                115.
           No gum                 60.

**1941**
**Inscribed "Void after June 30, 1942"**
RW8  HP8  $1 brown carmine      225.    50.
           Hinged                 95.
           No gum                 45.

**1942**
**Inscribed "Void after June 30, 1943"**
RW9  HP9  $1 violet brown       225.    45.
           Hinged                 95.
           No gum                 45.

**1943**
**Inscribed "Void After June 30, 1944"**
RW10 HP10 $1 deep rose          120.    35.
           Hinged                 55.
           No gum                 35.

**1944**
**Inscribed "Void after June 30, 1945"**
RW11 HP11 $1 red orange         125.    35.
           Hinged                 45.
           No gum                 35.

**1945**
**Inscribed "Void after June 30, 1946"**
RW12 HP12 $1 black              100.    25.
           Hinged                 45.
           No gum                 35.

**1946**
**Inscribed "Void after June 30, 1947"**
RW13 HP13 $1 red brown           50.  12.50
           No gum                 15.00

The previously listed No. RW13a in a bright rose pink shade has been determined to be a chemically induced changeling.

**1947**
**Inscribed "Void after June 30, 1948"**
RW14 HP14 $1 black               55.  15.00
           No gum                 18.00

**1948**
**Inscribed "Void after June 30, 1949"**
RW15 HP15 $1 bright blue         60.  12.00
           No gum                 15.00

Goldeneye Ducks — HP16

**1949**
**Inscribed "Void after June 30, 1950"**
RW16 HP16 $2 bright green        70.  15.00
           No gum                 20.00

**1950**
**Inscribed "Void after June 30, 1951"**
RW17 HP17 $2 violet              90.  15.00
           No gum                 20.00

**1951**
**Inscribed "Void after June 30, 1952"**
RW18 HP18 $2 gray black          90.  15.00
           No gum                 20.00

**1952**
**Inscribed "Void after June 30, 1953"**
RW19 HP19 $2 dp ultra            90.  15.00
           No gum                 20.00

**1953**
**Inscribed "Void after June 30, 1954"**
RW20 HP20 $2 dp rose brn         90.  15.00
           No gum                 20.00

No. RW21 and following issues are printed on dry, pregummed paper and the back inscription is printed on top of the gum, except for the self-adhesive stamp issues starting in 1998.

**1954**
**Inscribed "Void after June 30, 1955"**
RW21 HP21 $2 black               85.  15.00
           No gum                 20.00

**1955**
**Inscribed "Void after June 30, 1956"**
RW22 HP22 $2 dark blue           85.  12.50
           No gum                 20.00
  a.  Back inscription inverted  1,500.  4,500.

**1956**
**Inscribed "Void after June 30, 1957"**
RW23 HP23 $2 black               85.  12.50
           No gum                 20.00

**1957**
**Inscribed "Void after June 30, 1958"**
RW24 HP24 $2 emerald             85.  12.50
           No gum                 20.00
  a.  Back inscription inverted   4,500.

**1958**
**Inscribed "Void after June 30, 1959"**
RW25 HP25 $2 black               85.00 12.50
           No gum                 20.00
  a.  Back inscription inverted   —

Labrador Retriever Carrying Mallard Drake — HP26

Giori Press Printing

**1959**
**Inscribed "Void after June 30, 1960"**
RW26 HP26 $3 multi              130.00  12.50
           No gum                 45.00
  a.  Back inscription inverted  7,500.  6,500.

Redhead Ducks — HP27

**1960**
**Inscribed "Void after June 30, 1961"**
RW27 HP27 $3 multi               95.00  12.50
           No gum                 30.00

**1961**
**Inscribed "Void after June 30, 1962"**
RW28 HP28 $3 multicolored        95.00  12.50
           No gum                 30.00

Pintail Drakes — HP29

**1962**
**Inscribed "Void after June 30, 1963"**
RW29 HP29 $3 multicolored       110.00  12.50
           No gum                 35.00
  a.  Back inscription omitted   4,250.

**1963**
**Inscribed "Void after June 30, 1964"**
RW30 HP30 $3 multicolored       100.00  12.50
           No gum                 35.00

**1964**
**Inscribed "Void after June 30, 1965"**
RW31 HP31 $3 multicolored       100.00  12.50
           No gum                 35.00

**1965**
**Inscribed "Void after June 30, 1966"**
RW32 HP32 $3 multicolored       100.00  12.50
           No gum                 40.00

Whistling Swans — HP33

**1966**
**Inscribed "Void after June 30, 1967"**
RW33 HP33 $3 multi              100.00  12.50
           No gum                 40.00

**1967**
**Inscribed "Void after June 30, 1968"**
RW34 HP34 $3 multicolored       100.00  12.50
           No gum                 40.00

**1968**
**Inscribed "Void after June 30, 1969"**
RW35 HP35 $3 multicolored        65.00  12.50
           No gum                 20.00
  a.  Back inscription omitted   3,750.

White-winged Scoters — HP36

**1969**
**Inscribed "Void after June 30, 1970"**
RW36 HP36 $3 multi               65.00   8.00
           No gum                 20.00

**1970**  Engraved & Lithographed
**Inscribed "Void after June 30, 1971"**
RW37 HP37 $3 multi               65.00   8.00
           No gum                 20.00

**1971**
**Inscribed "Void after June 30, 1972"**
RW38 HP38 $3 multi               42.50   8.00
           No gum                 15.00

**1972**
**Inscribed "Void after June 30, 1973"**
RW39 HP39 $5 multi               30.00   6.00
           No gum                  8.00

**1973**
**Inscribed "Void after June 30, 1974"**
RW40 HP40 $5 multi               18.00   6.00
           No gum                  7.00

**1974**
**Inscribed "Void after June 30, 1975"**
RW41 HP41 $5 multi               18.00   5.00
           No gum                  6.00
  a.  Back inscription missing, but printed vertically on face of stamp and selvage, from foldover   4,750.

**1975**
**Inscribed "Void after June 30, 1976"**
RW42 HP42 $5 multi               15.00   5.00
           No gum                  7.00

**1976**  Engr.
**Inscribed "Void after June 30, 1977"**
RW43 HP43 $5 grn & blk           12.50   5.00
           No gum                  7.00

**1977**  Litho. & Engr.
**Inscribed "Void after June 30, 1978"**
RW44 HP44 $5 multi               10.00   5.00
           No gum                  7.00

Hooded Merganser — HP45

**1978**
**Inscribed "Void after June 30, 1979"**
RW45 HP45 $5 multicolored        10.00   5.00
           No gum                  7.00

**1979**
**Inscribed "Void after June 30, 1980"**
RW46 HP46 $7.50 multi            12.50   6.00
           No gum                  8.00

**1980**
**Inscribed "Void after June 30, 1981"**
RW47 HP47 $7.50 multi            12.50   6.00
           No gum                  8.00

**1981**
**Inscribed "Void after June 30, 1982"**
RW48 HP48 $7.50 multi            12.50   6.00
           No gum                  8.00

**1982**
**Inscribed "Void after June 30, 1983"**
RW49 HP49 $7.50 multi            15.00   7.00
           No gum                  9.00
  a.  Orange and violet omitted   10,000.

A certificate from a recognized expertization committee is required for No. RW49a.

**1983**
**Inscribed "Void after June 30, 1984"**
RW50 HP50 $7.50 multi            15.00   7.00
           No gum                  7.00

UNITED STATES 219

**1984**
**Inscribed "Void after June 30, 1985"**
**RW51** HP51 $7.50 multi 12.50 7.00
No gum 7.00

**1985**
**Inscribed "Void after June 30, 1986"**
**RW52** HP52 $7.50 multi 15.00 8.00
No gum 7.00
*a.* Light blue (litho.) omitted *12,500.*

The omitted color on No. RW52a coincides with a double paper splice affecting the top row of five stamps from the sheet and top ⅓ of stamps in the second row. There is also a color changeling of the brownish red ducks and their reflections in the water to yellow and yellow orange, respectively, on the error stamps. This error currently exists as three vertical strips of 6 (top stamp the error) and a plate number block of 12 (2x6, top two stamps the error).

**1986**
**Inscribed "Void after June 30, 1987"**
**RW53** HP53 $7.50 multi 15.00 8.00
No gum 9.00
*a.* Black omitted *600.00*

**1987** ***Perf. 11½x11***
**Inscribed "Void after June 30, 1988"**
**RW54** HP54 $10 multi 17.50 8.00
No gum 8.00

**1988**
**Inscribed "Void after June 30, 1989"**
**RW55** HP55 $10 multicolored 17.50 8.00
No gum 8.00

**1989**
**Inscribed "Void after June 30, 1990"**
**RW56** HP56 $12.50 multi 21.50 8.00
No gum 9.00

**1990**
**Inscribed "Void after June 30, 1991"**
**RW57** HP57 $12.50 multi 20.00 8.00
No gum 9.00
*a.* Back inscription omitted *200.00*

The back inscription is normally on top of the gum so beware of examples with gum removed offered as No. RW57a. Full original gum must be intact on No. RW57a. Used examples of No. RW57a cannot exist.

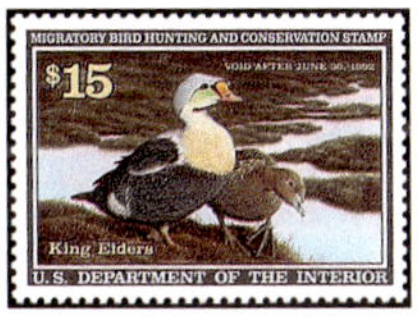

King Eiders — HP58

**1991**
**Inscribed "Void after June 30, 1992"**
**RW58** HP58 $15 multi 30.00 8.00
No gum 15.00
*a.* Black (engr.) omitted *20,000.*

**1992**
**Inscribed "Void after June 30, 1993"**
**RW59** HP59 $15 multi 30.00 10.00
No gum 15.00

**1993**
**Inscribed "Void after June 30, 1994"**
**RW60** HP60 $15 multi 27.50 9.00
No gum 15.00
*a.* Black (engr.) omitted *750.00* *1,500.*

**1994** ***Perf. 11¼x11***
**Inscribed "Void after June 30, 1995"**
**RW61** HP61 $15 multi 27.50 10.00
No gum 15.00

**1995**
**Inscribed "Void after June 30, 1996"**
**RW62** HP62 $15 multi 32.50 12.00
No gum 15.00

**1996**
**Inscribed "Void after June 30, 1997"**
**RW63** HP63 $15 multi 32.50 12.00
No gum 12.50

**1997**
**Inscribed "Void after June 30, 1998"**
**RW64** HP64 $15 multi 27.50 12.00
No gum 15.00

**1998** ***Perf. 11¼***
**Inscribed "Void after June 30, 1999"**
**RW65** HP65 $15 multi 45.00 22.50
No gum 22.50

**Self-Adhesive**
***Die Cut Perf. 10***
**RW65A** HP65 $15 multi 30.00 15.00
No gum 15.00

Nos. RW65 and later issues were sold in panes of 30 (RW65 and RW66) or 20 (RW67 and later issues), with four plate numbers per pane. The self-adhesives starting with No. RW65A were sold in panes of 1. The self-adhesives are valued unused as complete panes and used as single stamps.

**1999** ***Perf. 11¼***
**Inscribed "Void after June 30, 2000"**
**RW66** HP66 $15 multi 40.00 20.00
No gum 22.50

**Self-Adhesive**
***Die Cut Perf. 10***
**RW66A** HP66 $15 multi 30.00 12.00
No gum 15.00

**2000** ***Perf. 11¼***
**Inscribed "Void after June 30, 2001"**
**RW67** HP67 $15 multi 35.00 15.00
No gum 17.50

**Self-Adhesive**
***Die Cut Perf. 10***
**RW67A** HP67 $15 multi 30.00 14.00
No gum 17.50

**2001** ***Perf. 11¼***
**Inscribed "Void after June 30, 2002"**
**RW68** HP68 $15 multi 35.00 18.00
No gum 17.50

**Self-Adhesive**
***Die Cut Perf. 10***
**RW68A** HP68 $15 multi 30.00 14.00
No gum 15.00

**2002** ***Perf. 11¼***
**Inscribed "Void after June 30, 2003"**
**RW69** HP69 $15 multi 35.00 16.00
No gum 17.50

**Self-Adhesive**
***Serpentine Die Cut 11x10¾***
**RW69A** HP69 $15 multi 30.00 12.00
No gum 15.00

**2003** ***Perf. 11***
**Inscribed "Void after June 30, 2004"**
**RW70** HP70 $15 multi 35.00 16.00
No gum 17.50
*b.* Imperf, pair *5,000.*
*c.* Back inscription omitted *4,750.*

**Self-Adhesive**
***Serpentine Die Cut 11x10¾***
**RW70A** HP70 $15 multi 30.00 12.00
No gum 15.00

**2004** ***Perf. 11***
**Inscribed "Void after June 30, 2005"**
**RW71** HP71 $15 multicolored 35.00 16.00
No gum 17.00

**Self-Adhesive**
***Serpentine Die Cut 11x10¾***
**RW71A** HP71 $15 multicolored 30.00 12.00
No gum 15.00

**2005** **Litho. & Engr.** ***Perf. 11***
**Inscribed "Void after June 30, 2006"**
**RW72** HP72 $15 multi, type I 30.00 16.00
No gum 16.00
*b.* Souvenir sheet of 1 *1,950.*
*c.* Type II 30.00 16.00
No gum 16.00
*d.* As "b," without artist's signature (error) *3,250.*

There are two types of RW72: type I has no frame lines; type II has gray frame lines at top, right and bottom edges of design. No. RW72c, the type II stamp, is any stamp from the right two panes of the sheet of four panes. No. RW72, the Type I stamp, is any stamp from the left two panes.

No. RW72b sold for $20. 1,000 No. RW72b were issued. Approximately 750 were signed by the artist in black, value $1,950 as shown. Approximately 150 were signed in blue ink, value $2,500. Approximately 100 were signed in gold ink, value $3,000. Most examples of No. RW72b are in the grade of F-VF. Catalogue values are for Very Fine examples.

The Duck Stamp Office never announced the existence of No. RW72b to the public through a press release or a website announcement during the time the sheet was on sale, apparently because it was not clear beforehand that the souvenir sheet could be produced successfully and on time. No. RW72b sold out before a public announcement of the item's existence could be made.

**Self-Adhesive**
**Litho. & Debossed**
***Serpentine Die Cut 11x10¾***
**RW72A** HP72 $15 multi 27.50 11.00
No gum 15.00

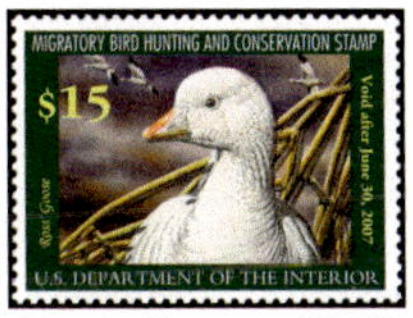

Ross's Goose — HP73

**2006** **Litho. & Engr.** ***Perf. 11***
**Inscribed "Void after June 30, 2007"**
**RW73** HP73 $15 multi 25.00 11.00
No gum 15.00
*b.* Souvenir sheet of 1 95.00 —
*c.* As "b," without artist's signature (error) *2,500.*

No. RW73b sold for $25. All examples of No. RW73b have a black signature of the artist on a designated line in the sheet margin. Ten thousand were issued.

The sheet margin has a line designated for the signature of the engraver, Piotr Naszarkowski, but no sheets were sold with his signature. Naszarkowski signed approximately 2,500 sheets during three days at the Washington 2006 World Philatelic Exhibition, and he signed another 2,500 or more after the conclusion of the exhibition. Value $150.

An example of No. RW73c is known with the engraver↔s signature.

**Self-Adhesive**
***Serpentine Die Cut 11x10¾***
**RW73A** HP73 $15 multi 25.00 11.00
No gum 15.00

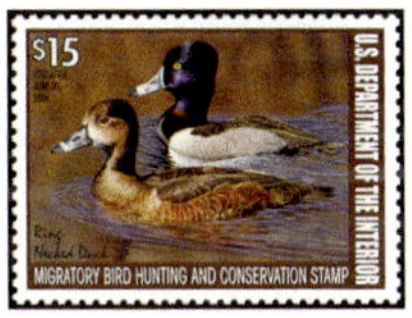

Ring-necked Ducks — HP74

**2007** **Litho.** ***Perf. 11***
**Inscribed "Void after June 30, 2008"**
**RW74** HP74 $15 multi 35.00 11.00
No gum 16.00
*b.* Souvenir sheet of 1 140.00
*c.* As "b", without artist's signature (error) *2,750.*

No. RW74b sold for $25 plus a shipping fee. The artist signed No. RW74b on a designated line in the sheet margin. Ten thousand were issued. There is no back inscription on No. RW74b.

**Self-Adhesive**
***Serpentine Die Cut 11x10¾***
**RW74A** HP74 $15 multi 27.50 11.00
No gum 15.00

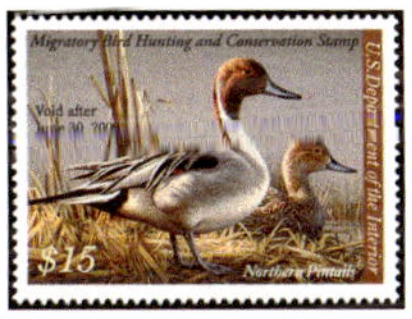

Northern Pintails — HP75

**2008** **Litho.** ***Perf. 13¼***
**Inscribed "Void after June 30, 2009"**
**RW75** HP75 $15 multi 35.00 11.00
No gum 16.00
*b.* Souvenir sheet of 1 70.00 —
*c.* As "b," without artist's signature (error) *500.00*

**Self-Adhesive**
***Serpentine Die Cut 10¾***
**RW75A** HP75 $15 multi 35.00 11.00
No gum 25.00

**2009** **Litho.** ***Perf. 13¼***
**Inscribed "Void after June 30, 2010"**
**RW76** HP76 $15 multi 30.00 11.00
No gum 16.00
*b.* Souvenir sheet of 1 60.00
*c.* As "b," without artist's signature (error) *400.00*

No. RW76b sold for $30 plus a shipping fee. The artist signed No. RW76b on a designated line in the sheet margin. Ten thousand were prepared.

**Self-Adhesive**
***Serpentine Die Cut 11x10¾***
**RW76A** HP76 $15 multi 30.00 11.00
No gum 20.00

**2010** **Litho.** ***Perf. 11¼x11***
**Inscribed "Void after June 30, 2011"**
**RW77** HP77 $15 multi 30.00 11.00
No gum 16.00
*b.* Souvenir sheet of 1, perf. 13¼ 55.00
*c.* As "b," without artist's signature (error) *200.00*

No. RW77b was sold for $30 plus a shipping fee. The artist signed No. RW77b on a designated line in the sheet margin. Ten thousand were prepared. There is no back inscription on No. RW77b, and the stamp on the sheet is tagged.

**Self-Adhesive**
***Serpentine Die Cut 11x10¾***
**RW77A** HP77 $15 multi 30.00 11.00
No gum 20.00

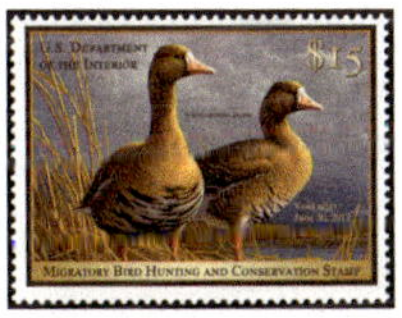

White-fronted Geese — HP78

QUACK! QUACK!
U.S. Fish & Wildlife Service
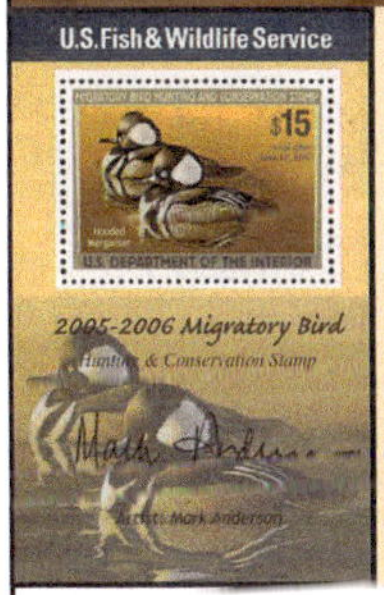

RW72B
ONLY 1000 PRINTED.
Only 1000 complete collections can exist. Do you have one?
Call for current pricing & availability
FEDERAL DUCKS - OVER 20 GRADES OFFERED IN USED, UNUSED, MINT + GRADED DUCKS
Complete sets starting at $495.00
FEDERAL DUCK PLATE BLOCKS
STATE DUCK STAMPS
NON-PICTORIAL WATERFOWL
INDIAN RESERVATION STAMPS
DUCK FIRST DAY COVERS
LARGE DUCK PRINT INVENTORY
NEW ISSUE SERVICE AVAILABLE
COMPREHENSIVE ILLUSTRATED PRICELIST AVAILABLE
MICHAEL JAFFE STAMPS INC.
(in business since 1975)
PO BOX 61484 VANCOUVER WA 98666
Phone: 360-695-6161 Fax: 360-695-1616
Toll Free: 800-782-6770
Email: mjaffe@brookmanstamps.com
www.duckstamps.com
NSDA, ARA
SRS, DU

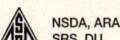

| 2011 | Litho. | Perf. 13¼ |
|---|---|---|

Inscribed "Void after June 30, 2012"

| RW78 | HP78 $15 multi | 37.50 11.00 |
|---|---|---|
| | No gum | 16.00 |
| b. | Souvenir sheet of 1 | 60.00 |
| c. | As "b," without artist's signature (error) | 175.00 |

No. RW78b was sold for $25 plus a shipping fee. The artist signed No. RW78b on a designated line in the sheet margin. Ten thousand were prepared.

### Self-Adhesive
*Serpentine Die Cut 11x10¾*

| RW78A | HP78 $15 multi | 40.00 11.00 |
|---|---|---|
| | No gum | 20.00 |

Wood Duck — HP79

| 2012 | Litho. | Perf. 13¼ |
|---|---|---|

Inscribed "Void after June 30, 2013"

| RW79 | HP79 $15 multi | 37.50 11.00 |
|---|---|---|
| | No gum | 16.00 |
| b. | Souvenir sheet of 1 | 60.00 |
| c. | As "b," without artist's signature (error) | 1,750. |

No. RW79b was sold for $25 plus a shipping fee. The artist signed No. RW79b on a designated line in the sheet margin. There is a back inscription on No. RW79b. Five thousand were prepared.

One No. RW79b was signed in red ink as a "surprise" for a random buyer. This was not authorized.

### Self-Adhesive
*Serpentine Die Cut 11x10¾*

| RW79A | HP79 $15 multi | 40.00 11.00 |
|---|---|---|
| | No gum | 20.00 |

Common Goldeneye — HP80

| 2013 | Litho. | Perf. 13¼ |
|---|---|---|

Inscribed "Void after June 30, 2014"

| RW80 | HP80 $15 multi | 37.50 11.00 |
|---|---|---|
| | No gum | 16.00 |
| b. | Souvenir sheet of 1 | 80.00 |
| c. | As "b," without artist's signature (error) | 1,250. |

No. RW80b was sold for $25 plus a shipping fee. The artist signed No. RW80b on a designated line in the sheet margin. There is a back inscription on No. RW80b. Five thousand were prepared.

### Self-Adhesive
*Serpentine Die Cut 11x10¾*

| RW80A | HP80 $15 multi | 35.00 11.00 |
|---|---|---|
| | No gum | 20.00 |

Canvasbacks — HP81

| 2014 | Litho. | Perf. 13¼ |
|---|---|---|

Inscribed "Void after June 30, 2015"

| RW81 | HP81 $15 multi | 40.00 11.00 |
|---|---|---|
| | No gum | 16.00 |

### Self-Adhesive
*Serpentine Die Cut 11x10¾*

| RW81A | HP81 $15 multi | 40.00 12.50 |
|---|---|---|
| | No gum | 20.00 |

Ruddy Ducks — HP82

| 2015 | Litho. | Perf. 13¼ |
|---|---|---|

Inscribed "Void after June 30, 2016"

| RW82 | HP82 $25 multi | 55.00 12.00 |
|---|---|---|
| | No gum | 25.00 |

### Self-Adhesive
*Serpentine Die Cut 11x10¾*

| RW82A | HP82 $25 multi | 55.00 12.50 |
|---|---|---|
| | No gum | 32.50 |

Trumpeter Swans — HP83

| 2016 | Litho. | Perf. 13¼ |
|---|---|---|

Inscribed "Void after June 30, 2017"

| RW83 | HP83 $25 multi | 90.00 15.00 |
|---|---|---|
| | No gum | 40.00 |

### Self-Adhesive
*Serpentine Die Cut 11x10¾*

| RW83A | HP83 $25 multi | 65.00 12.50 |
|---|---|---|
| | No gum | 32.50 |

Canada Geese — HP84

| 2017 | Litho. | Perf. 13¼ |
|---|---|---|

Inscribed "Void after June 30, 2018"

| RW84 | HP84 $25 multi | 45.00 12.50 |
|---|---|---|
| | No gum | 25.00 |

### Self-Adhesive
*Serpentine Die Cut 11x10¾*

| RW84A | HP84 $25 multi | 40.00 12.50 |
|---|---|---|
| | No gum | 32.50 |

Mallards — HP85

*Serpentine Die Cut 11x10¾*

| 2018 | | Litho. |
|---|---|---|

Inscribed "Void after June 30, 2019"
### Self-Adhesive

| RW85 | HP85 $25 multi | 55.00 12.50 |
|---|---|---|
| | No gum | 25.00 |
| b. | Souvenir sheet of 4 | 200.00 |

### Sheet of 1

| RW85A | HP85 $25 multi | 50.00 12.50 |
|---|---|---|
| | No gum | 32.50 |

Inscriptions on the backing paper differ for Nos. RW85, RW85A, and RW85b. Once removed from the backing paper, used examples are considered to be No. RW85.

Wood Duck and Decoy — HP86

*Serpentine Die Cut 11x10¾*

| 2019 | | Litho. |
|---|---|---|

Inscribed "Void after June 30, 2020"
### Self-Adhesive

| RW86 | HP86 $25 multi | 45.00 12.50 |
|---|---|---|
| | No gum | 25.00 |

### Sheet of 1

| RW86A | HP86 $25 multi | 45.00 12.50 |
|---|---|---|
| | No gum | 32.50 |

Inscriptions on the backing paper differ for Nos. RW86 and RW86A. Once removed from the backing paper, used examples are considered to be No. RW86.

Black-bellied Whistling Ducks — HP87

*Serpentine Die Cut 11x10¾*

| 2020 | | Litho. |
|---|---|---|

Inscribed "Void after June 30, 2021"
### Self-Adhesive

| RW87 | HP87 $25 multi | 37.50 12.50 |
|---|---|---|
| | No gum | 25.00 |

### Sheet of 1

| RW87A | HP87 $25 multi | 37.50 12.50 |
|---|---|---|
| | No gum | 32.50 |

Inscriptions on the backing paper differ for Nos. RW87 and RW87A. Once removed from the backing paper, used examples are considered to be No. RW87.

Lesser Scaup — HP88

*Serpentine Die Cut 11x10¾*

| 2021 | | Litho. |
|---|---|---|

Inscribed "Void after June 30, 2022"
### Self-Adhesive

| RW88 | HP88 $25 multi | 37.50 12.50 |
|---|---|---|
| | No gum | 25.00 |

### Sheet of 1

| RW88A | HP88 $25 multi | 37.50 12.50 |
|---|---|---|

Inscriptions on the backing paper differ for Nos. RW88 and RW88A. Once removed from the backing paper, used examples are considered to be No. RW88.

Redheads — HP89

Printed by Banknote Corporation of America.

*Serpentine Die Cut 11x10¾*
### Litho., Engr. & Embossed

| 2022 | | Tagged |
|---|---|---|

Inscribed "Void after June 30, 2023"
### Self-Adhesive

| RW89 | HP89 $25 multi | 37.50 12.50 |
|---|---|---|
| | No gum | 25.00 |
| | P# block of 4 | 160.00 |

### Sheet of 1

| RW89A | HP89 $25 multi | 37.50 12.50 |
|---|---|---|

Inscriptions on the backing paper differ for Nos. RW89 and RW89A. Once removed from the backing paper, used examples are considered to be No. RW89.

Tundra Swans — HP90

Printed by Ashton-Potter (USA) Ltd.

*Serpentine Die Cut 11x10¾*

| 2023 | Litho. | Tagged |
|---|---|---|

Inscribed "Void after June 30, 2024"
### Self-Adhesive

| RW90 | HP90 $25 multi | 37.50 12.50 |
|---|---|---|
| | No gum | 25.00 |
| | P# block of 4 | 160.00 |

### Sheet of 1

| RW90A | HP90 $25 multi | 37.50 12.50 |
|---|---|---|

Inscriptions on the backing paper differ for Nos. RW90 and RW90A. Once removed from the backing paper, used examples are considered to be No. RW90.

# CONFEDERATE STATES OF AMERICA

### 3¢ 1861 POSTMASTERS' PROVISIONALS

With the secession of South Carolina from the Union on Dec. 20, 1860, a new era began in U.S. history as well as its postal history. Other Southern states quickly followed South Carolina's lead, which in turn led to the formation of the provisional government of the Confederate States of America on Feb. 4, 1861.

President Jefferson Davis' cabinet was completed Mar. 6, 1861, with the acceptance of the position of Postmaster General by John H. Reagan of Texas. The provisional government had already passed regulations that required payment for postage in cash and that effectively carried over the U.S. 3c rate until the new Confederate Post Office Department took over control of the system.

Soon after entering on his duties, Reagan directed the postmasters in the Confederate States and in the newly seceded states to "continue the performance of their duties as such, and render all accounts and pay all moneys (sic) to the order of the Government of the U.S. as they have heretofore done, until the Government of the Confederate States shall be prepared to assume control of its postal affairs."

As coinage was becoming scarce, postal patrons began having problems buying individual stamps or paying for letters individually, especially as stamp stocks started to run short in certain areas. Even though the U.S. Post Office Department was technically in control of the postal system and southern postmasters were operating under Federal authority, the U.S.P.O. was hesitant in re-supplying seceded states with additional stamps and stamped envelopes.

The U.S. government had made the issuance of postmasters' provisionals illegal many years before, but the southern postmasters had to do what they felt was necessary to allow patrons to pay for postage and make the system work. Therefore, a few postmasters took it upon themselves to issue provisional stamps in the 3c rate then in effect.

Interestingly, these were stamps and envelopes that the U.S. government did not recognize as legal, but they did do postal duty unchallenged in the Confederate States. Yet the proceeds were to be remitted to the U.S. government in Washington! Six authenticated postmasters' provisionals in the 3c rate have been recorded.

On May 13, 1861, Postmaster General Reagan issued his proclamation "assuming control and direction of postal service within the limits of the Confederate States of America on and after the first day of June," with new postage rates and regulations.

The Federal government suspended operations in the Confederate States (except for western Virginia and the seceding state of Tennessee) by a proclamation issued by Postmaster General Montgomery Blair on May 27, 1861, effective from May 31, 1861, and June 10 for western and middle Tennessee.

As Tennessee did not join the Confederacy until July 2, 1861, the unissued 3c Nashville provisional was produced in a state that was in the process of seceding, while the other provisionals were used in the Confederacy before the June 1 assumption of control of postal service by the Confederate States of America.

Illustrations are reduced in size.
XU numbers are envelope entires.

### DARLINGTON C.H., S. C.

 E1

**Handstamped Envelope**
8AXU1  E1  3c black  3,500.

One example of No. 8AXU1 is recorded, used under a pair of C.S.A. No. 7. To be a provisional, the 3c marking must be unused or used under Confederate stamps.

### FORT VALLEY, GA.

 E1    E2

**Handstamped Envelope**
7AXU1  E1  3c black  —

### HILLSBORO, N.C.

A1

**Handstamped Adhesive**
1AX1  A1  3c bluish black, on cover  11,500.

No. 1AX1 is unique. This is the same handstamp as used for No. 39X1. 3c usage is determined from the May 27, 1861 circular date stamp.

### JACKSON, MISS.

E1

**Handstamped Envelope**
2AXU1  E1  3c black  3,000.

See Nos. 43XU1-43XU4.
No. 2AXU1 is unique. It is on a southern patriotic cover.

### MADISON COURT HOUSE, FLA.

 A1    "CNETS"

**Typeset Adhesive**
3AX1  A1  3c gold  20,000.
 a.  "CNETS"  22,500.

No. 3AX1a is unique.
See No. 137XU1.

### NASHVILLE, TENN.

A1

**Typeset Adhesive (5 varieties)**
4AX1  A1  3c carmine  300.

For more than 150 years, it has been believed that No. 4AX1 was prepared by Postmaster McNish with the U.S. rate, but it was not issued. Recent research and historical evidence indicate that this "stamp" most likely is a fantasy rather than a genuine stamp.
See Nos. 61X2-61XU2.

### SELMA, ALA.

E1

**Handstamped Envelope**
5AXU1  E1  3c black  1,950.

See Nos. 77XU1-77XU3.

### TUSCUMBIA, ALA.

E1

**Handstamped Envelope, impression at upper right**
6AXU1  E1  3c dull red, buff  30,000.

Dangerous forgeries exist of No. 6AXU1.
See Nos. 84XU1-84XU3.

For later additions, listed out of numerical sequence, see:
#7AXU1, Fort Valley, Ga.
#8AXU1, Darlington, C.H., S.C.

## POSTMASTERS' PROVISIONAL ISSUES

These stamps and envelopes were issued by individual postmasters generally between June 1, 1861, when the use of U.S. stamps stopped in the Confederacy, and Oct. 16, 1861, when the 1st Confederate Government stamps were issued.

They were occasionally issued at later periods, especially in Texas, when regular issues of Government stamps were unavailable.

Canceling stamps of the post offices were often used to produce envelopes, some of which were supplied in advance by private citizens.

These envelopes and other stationery therefore may be found in a wide variety of papers, colors, sizes & shapes, including patriotic and semi-official types.

It is often difficult to determine whether the impression made by the canceling stamp indicates provisional usage or merely postage paid at the time the letter was deposited in the post office. Occasionally the same mark was used for both purposes.

The *press-printed* provisional envelopes are in a different category. They were produced in quantity, using envelopes procured in advance by the postmaster, such as those of Charleston, Lynchburg, Memphis, etc.

The press-printed envelopes are listed and valued on all known papers.

The handstamped provisional envelopes are listed and valued according to type and variety of handstamp, but not according to paper. Many exist on such a variety of papers that they defy accurate, complete listing.

The value of a handstamped provisional envelope is determined *primarily* by the clarity of the markings and its overall condition and attractiveness, rather than type of paper.

*All handstamped provisional envelopes, when used, should also show the postmark of the town of issue.*

Most handstamps are impressed at top right, although they exist from some towns in other positions.

Illustrations in this section are reduced in size.

**XU numbers are envelope entires.**

### ABERDEEN, MISS.

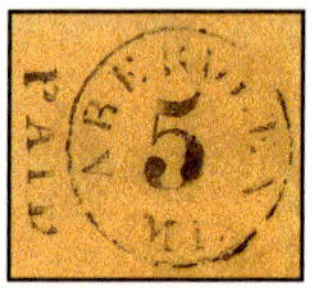
E1

**Handstamped Envelopes**

| | | | |
|---|---|---|---|
| **1XU1** | E1 | 5c black | *5,500.* |
| *a.* | | 10c (ms.) on 5c black | *9,000.* |

No. 1XU1a is unique.

### ABINGDON, VA.

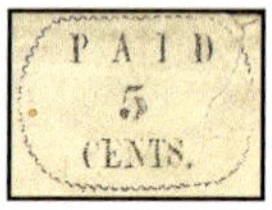
E1

**Handstamped Envelopes**

| | | | | |
|---|---|---|---|---|
| **2XU1** | E1 | 2c black | | *12,500.* |
| *a.* | | 5c (ms.) on 2c black | | *15,000.* |
| **2XU2** | E1 | 5c black | | *1,500.* |
| **2XU3** | E1 | 10c black | *2,200.* | *3,500.* |

No. 2XU1 is unique. No. 2XU3 unused and used are each unique.

### ALBANY, GA.

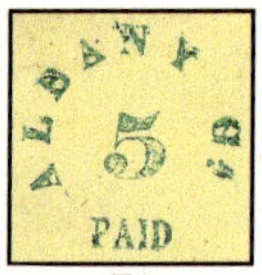
E1

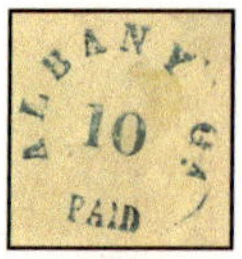
E2

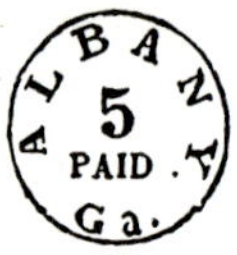
E3

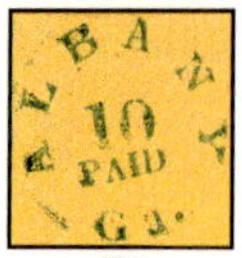
E4

**Handstamped Envelopes**

| | | | |
|---|---|---|---|
| **3XU1** | E1 | 5c greenish blue | 600. |
| **3XU2** | E2 | 10c greenish blue | *1,750.* |
| *a.* | | 10c on 5c greenish blue | *3,500.* |
| **3XU5** | E3 | 5c greenish blue | — |
| **3XU6** | E4 | 10c greenish blue | *3,500.* |

Only one example each recorded of Nos. 3XU2, 3XU2a and 3XU6. No. 3XU2 is a cover front only and is valued as such. No. 3XU2a is the unique Confederate example of one provisional marking revaluing another.

The existence of No. 3XU5 is in question. The editors would like to see an authenticated example of this marking.

### ANDERSON COURT HOUSE, S.C.

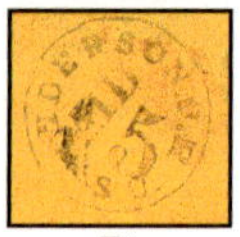
E1

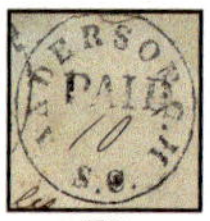
E2

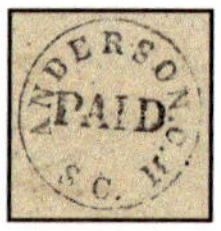
E3

**Handstamped Envelopes**

| | | | | |
|---|---|---|---|---|
| **4XU1** | E1 | 5c black | 1,000. | *2,750.* |
| **4XU2** | E2 | 10c (ms.) black | | *2,500.* |
| **4XU3** | E3 | (2c) black, denomination omitted (circular rate) | *600.* | *3,000.* |

### ATHENS, GA

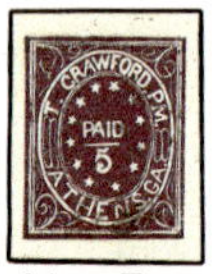
A1 — Type I

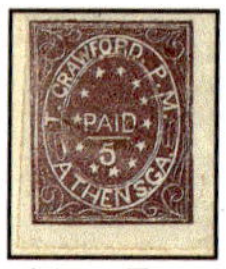
A1 — Type II

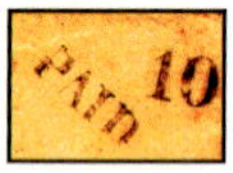
E1

**Typographed Adhesives (from woodcuts of two types)**

Pairs, both horizontal and vertical, always show one of each type.

| | | | | |
|---|---|---|---|---|
| **5X1** | A1 | 5c purple (shades) | 1,000. | 1,400. |
| *a.* | | Tete beche pair (vertical) | | *7,500.* |
| **5X2** | A1 | 5c red, type II | 5,750. | 3,000. |

The colorless ornaments in the four corners of No. 5X2 were recut making them wider than those in No. 5X1.

Dangerous fakes exist of Nos. 5X1 and 5X2. Certificates of authenticity from recognized committees are strongly recommended.

No. 5X2 is unique.

**Handstamped Envelopes**

| | | | |
|---|---|---|---|
| **5XU1** | E1 | 10c black, on patriotic cover | *2,500.* |

The markings on No. 5XU1 are the same as those used on stampless envelopes. On the unique listed example of No. 5XU1, there is a handwritten note on the inside of the flap: 'Andrew had these envelopes stamped & I am obliged to use them or loose the postage.' Two or more similar covers from the same correspondence are known, but without the note under the flap. While these also may be provisional use, it cannot be proven, and these covers are considered handstamp paid covers.

### ATLANTA, GA.

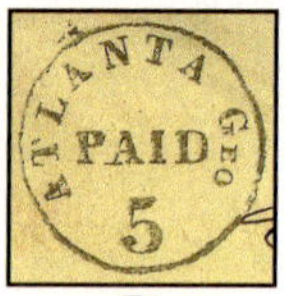
E1

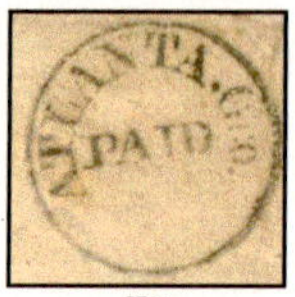
E2

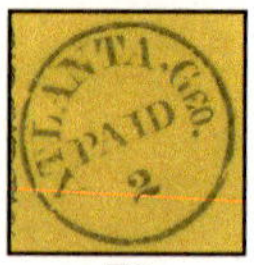
E3

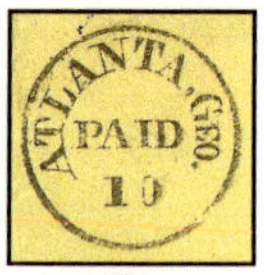
E4

**Handstamped Envelopes**

| | | | | |
|---|---|---|---|---|
| **6XU1** | E1 | 5c red | | *3,500.* |
| **6XU2** | E1 | 5c black | 160. | 450. |
| *a.* | | 10c on 5c black | | *2,500.* |
| **6XU4** | E3 | 2c black | | *2,750.* |
| **6XU5** | E3 | 5c black | | 1,000. |
| *a.* | | 10c on 5c black | | *1,750.* |
| **6XU6** | E4 | 10c black | | 550. |

Only one example recorded of No. 6XU1.

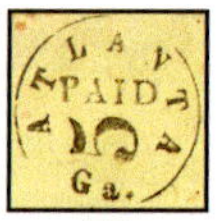
E3

**Handstamped Envelopes**

| | | | |
|---|---|---|---|
| **6XU8** | E3 | 5c black | 3,500. |
| **6XU9** | E3 | 10c black ("10" upright) | 3,000. |

Only one example recorded of No. 6XU8.

### AUSTIN, MISS.

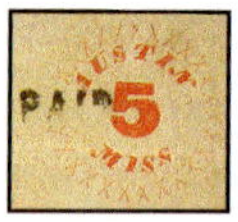
E1

**Press-printed Envelope (typeset)**

| | | | |
|---|---|---|---|
| **8XU1** | E1 | 5c red, *amber* | *75,000.* |

One example recorded.

### AUSTIN, TEX.

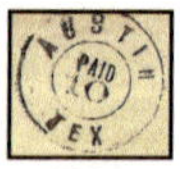
E1a

**Handstamped Adhesive**

| | | | |
|---|---|---|---|
| **9X1** | E1a | 10c black, *white* or *buff* | — |

**Handstamped Envelope**

| | | | |
|---|---|---|---|
| **9XU1** | E1a | 10c black | 2,500. |

### AUTAUGAVILLE, ALA.

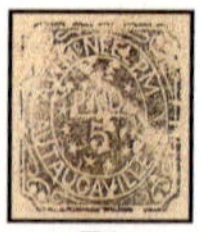
E1

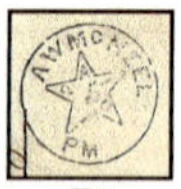
E2

**Handstamped Envelopes**

| | | | |
|---|---|---|---|
| **10XU1** | E1 | 5c black | *20,000.* |
| **10XU2** | E2 | 5c black | *20,000.* |

No. 10XU2 is unique.

### BALCONY FALLS, VA.

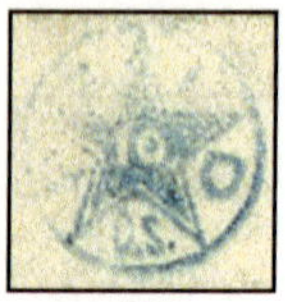
E1

**Handstamped Envelope**

| | | | |
|---|---|---|---|
| **122XU1** | E1 | 10c blue | *2,000.* |

The use of No. 122XU1 as a provisional marking is in question. The editors would like to see authenticated evidence of its use as a provisional.

### BARNWELL COURT HOUSE, S. C.

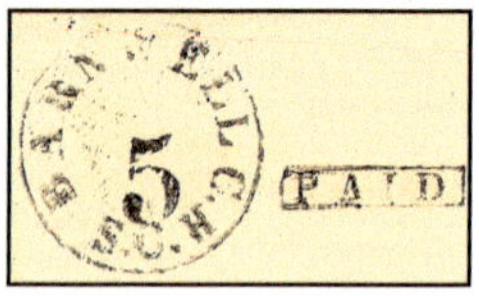
E1

**Handstamped Envelope**

| | | | |
|---|---|---|---|
| **123XU1** | E1 | 5c black | *3,000.* |

These are two separate handstamps.

All recorded uses are on addressed covers without postmarks.

### BATON ROUGE, LA.

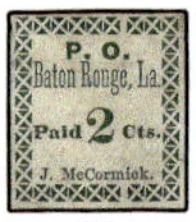
A1

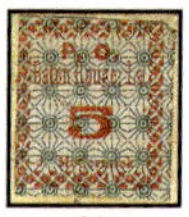
A2

**Typeset Adhesives**

Ten varieties of each

| | | | | |
|---|---|---|---|---|
| **11X1** | A1 | 2c green | *8,250.* | *5,000.* |
| *a.* | | "McCcrmick" | *35,000.* | *35,000.* |
| **11X2** | A2 | 5c **green & carmine** | 1,500. | 1,300. |
| *a.* | | "McCcrmick" | *10,000.* | *3,500.* |

Only one example each is recorded of No. 11X1a unused, used and on cover.

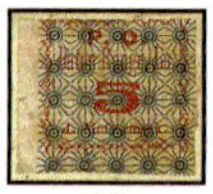
A3

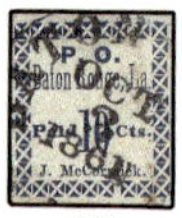
A4

Ten varieties of each

| | | | | |
|---|---|---|---|---|
| **11X3** | A3 | 5c green & carmine | *10,000.* | *4,000.* |
| *a.* | | "McCcrmick" | | *32,500.* |
| **11X4** | A4 | 10c blue | | *50,000.* |

### BEAUFORT, S. C.

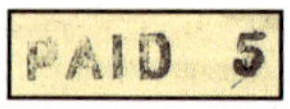
E1

**Handstamped Envelope**

| | | | | |
|---|---|---|---|---|
| **150XU1** | E1 | 5c black | — | *3,500.* |

To be the No. 150XU1 provisional, the cover must be unused, used under a Confederate stamp, or used from another town. Two examples are recorded.

### BEAUMONT, TEX.

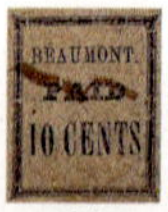
A1

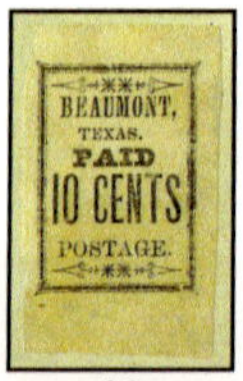
A2

# CONFEDERATE STATES OF AMERICA

## Typeset Adhesives
Several varieties of each
| | | | |
|---|---|---|---|
| 12X1 | A1 | 10c black, *yellow* | 65,000. |
| 12X2 | A1 | 10c black, *pink* | 40,000. |
| 12X3 | A2 | 10c black, *yellow*, on cover | 250,000. |

One example recorded of No. 12X3. Value represents auction realization in 2019.

## BLUFFTON, S. C.

E1

### Handstamped Envelope
| | | | |
|---|---|---|---|
| 124XU1 | E1 | 5c black | 4,750. |

Only one example recorded of No. 124XU1.

## BRIDGEVILLE, ALA.

A1

### Handstamped Adhesive in black within red pen-ruled squares
| | | | |
|---|---|---|---|
| 13X1 | A1 | 5c black & red, pair on cover | 10,000. |

The pair on cover with pen cancels is the unique example of No. 13X1.

## CAMDEN, S. C.

E1      E2

### Handstamped Envelopes
| | | | |
|---|---|---|---|
| 125XU1 | E1 | 5c black | 2,500. |
| 125XU2 | E2 | 10c black | 750. |

No. 125XU2 unused was privately carried and is addressed but has no postal markings. No. 125XU2 is indistinguishable from a handstamp paid cover when used.

## CANTON, MISS.

E1

"P" in star is initial of Postmaster William Priestly.

### Handstamped Envelopes
| | | | |
|---|---|---|---|
| 14XU1 | E1 | 5c black | 2,000. |
| a. | | 10c (ms.) on 5c black | 4,500. |

## CAROLINA CITY, N. C.

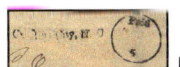
E1

### Handstamped Envelope
| | | | |
|---|---|---|---|
| 118XU1 | E1 | 5c black | 5,000. |

## CARTERSVILLE, GA.

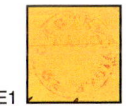
E1

### Handstamped Envelope
| | | | |
|---|---|---|---|
| 126XU1 | E1 | (5c) red | 1,500. |

## CHAPEL HILL, N. C.

E1

### Handstamped Envelope
| | | | |
|---|---|---|---|
| 15XU1 | E1 | 5c black | 6,500. |

## CHARLESTON, S. C.

A1           E1

E2

### Lithographed Adhesive
| | | | | |
|---|---|---|---|---|
| 16X1 | A1 | 5c blue | 1,400. | 800. |

Values are for stamps showing parts of the outer frame lines on at least 3 sides. The vast majority of this stamp small faults and are valued thus. Completely sound examples are scarce and sell for more.

### Press-printed Envelopes
(typographed from woodcut)
| | | | | |
|---|---|---|---|---|
| 16XU1 | E1 | 5c blue | 1,500. | 1,500. |
| 16XU2 | E1 | 5c blue, *amber* | 1,250. | 2,000. |
| 16XU3 | E1 | 5c blue, *orange* | 1,250. | 2,000. |
| 16XU4 | E1 | 5c blue, *buff* | 1,250. | 1,250. |
| 16XU5 | E1 | 5c blue, *blue* | 1,250. | 2,000. |
| 16XU6 | E2 | 10c blue, *orange* | | 55,000. |

The No. 16XU6 used entire is unique; value based on 2022 auction sale.
Beware of fakes of the E1 design.

### Handstamped Cut Square
| | | | |
|---|---|---|---|
| 16XU7 | E2 | 10c black | 2,000. |

There is only one example of No. 16XU7. It is a cutout, not an entire. It may not have been mailed from Charleston, and it may not have paid postage.

## CHARLOTTE, N. C.

E1

### Handstamped Envelope
| | | | |
|---|---|---|---|
| 146XU1 | E1 | 5c blue, "5" in circle and straight line "PAID" | 2,500. |

These markings were also used on stampless covers and are recognized as provisionals only when postally unused or when a general issue is postally used over them.

## CHARLOTTESVILLE, VA.

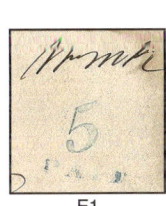 
E1             E2

### Handstamped Envelopes, Manuscript Initials "WmMK"
| | | | |
|---|---|---|---|
| 127XU1 | E1 | 5c blue | 2,250. |
| 127XU2 | E2 | 10c blue | 2,250. |

The control initials appear at the upper right on the front of the envelope. Only one example each is recorded of Nos. 127XU1 and 127XU2.

## CHATTANOOGA, TENN.

E1        E2

### Handstamped Envelopes
| | | | |
|---|---|---|---|
| 17XU2 | E1 | 5c black | 1,900. |
| 17XU3 | E2 | 5c on 2c black | 5,000. |

No. 17XU3 is unique.

## CHRISTIANSBURG, VA.

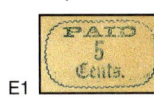
E1

### Handstamped Envelopes
Impressed at top right
| | | | |
|---|---|---|---|
| 99XU1 | E1 | 5c black | 2,250. |
| 99XU2 | E1 | 5c blue | 1,750. |
| 99XU4 | E1 | 5c green on U.S. envelope No. U27 | 4,250. |
| 99XU5 | E1 | 10c blue | 3,500. |

The absence of 5c and 10c handstamped paid markings from this town suggests that Nos. 99XU1-99XU5 were used as both provisional and handstamped paid markings. Nos. 99XU4 and 99XU5 are each unique.

## COLAPARCHEE, GA.

E1        Control

### Handstamped Envelope
| | | | |
|---|---|---|---|
| 119XU1 | E1 | 5c black | 3,500. |

There are only two recorded examples of No. 119XU1, and both are used from Savannah with a general issue stamp. The control appears on the front of the envelope.

## COLUMBIA, S. C.

Oval         Circular
Control      Control

E1

E2

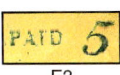 
E3        E4

E5        E6

E7        E8

### Handstamped Envelopes
| | | | | |
|---|---|---|---|---|
| 18XU1 | E1 | 5c blue | 550. | 1,500. |
| a. | | 10c on 5c blue | | 3,500. |
| 18XU4 | E2 | 5c blue, oval control on front | | 2,500. |
| a. | | Oval control on back | | 1,100. |
| 18XU7 | E3 | 5c blue, oval control on back | | 1,000. |
| 18XU8 | E4 | 5c blue oval control on back | | 1,000. |
| a. | | Circular control on back | | 2,000. |
| 18XU9 | E4 | 10c blue oval control on back | | 1,250. |
| 18XU10 | E5 | 10c blue oval control on back | | 1,500. |
| 18XU11 | E6 | 5c blue oval control on front | | 2,500. |
| 18XU12 | E6 | 10c blue oval control on back | | 1,250. |
| 18XU13 | E7 | 5c blue oval control on back | | 1,000. |
| a. | | Circular control on back | | 2,000. |
| 18XU14 | E8 | 5c blue oval control on back | | 1,000. |
| a. | | No control (unused) | | — |

## COLUMBIA, TENN.

E1

### Handstamped Envelope
| | | | |
|---|---|---|---|
| 113XU1 | E1 | 5c red | 6,000. |

One example recorded.

## COLUMBUS, GA.

E1

### Handstamped Envelopes
| | | | |
|---|---|---|---|
| 19XU1 | E1 | 5c blue | 900. |
| 19XU2 | E1 | 10c red | 3,250. |

## COURTLAND, ALA.

E1

### Handstamped Envelopes (from woodcut)
| | | | |
|---|---|---|---|
| 103XU1 | E1 | 5c red | 32,500. |

One example recorded.

## CUTHBERT, GA

E1

### Handstamped Envelope
| | | | |
|---|---|---|---|
| 95XU1 | E1 | 10c black | 1,000. |

The unique example of No. 95XU1 was used by having a C.S.A. 10c #12c placed over it.

## DALTON, GA

E1

### Handstamped Envelopes
| | | | |
|---|---|---|---|
| 20XU1 | E1 | 5c black | 850. |
| a. | | Denomination omitted (5c rate) | 900. |

## CONFEDERATE STATES OF AMERICA

**b.** 10c (ms.) on 5c black    1,500.
**c.** 20c (ms.) on 5c black
**20XU2** E1 10c black    1,100.

---

### DANVILLE, VA.

A1

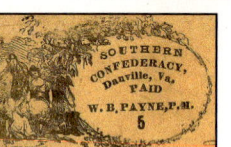

Design measures 60x37mm — E1

E2

E3

E4    E5

E6

**Typeset Adhesive**
**Wove Paper**
**21X1** A1 5c red    6,000.
   Two varieties known.

**Laid Paper**
**21X2** A1 5c red    10,000.
   No. 21X2 is unique.

**Press-printed Envelopes (typographed)**
Two types: "SOUTHERN" in straight or curved line
Impressed (usually) at top left
**21XU1** E1 5c black    5,000.
**21XU2** E1 5c black, *light yellowish*    5,000.
**21XU3** E1 5c black, *dark buff*    5,000.
   Unissued 10c envelopes (type E1, in red) are known. All recorded examples are envelopes that show evidence of added stamps being torn off.
   Dangerous forgeries exist of No. 21XU1.

**Handstamped Envelopes**
**21XU3A** E2 5c black (ms "WBP" initials)    1,000.
**21XU3B** E3 5c black (ms "WPB" initials)    8,500.
**21XU4** E4 10c black    2,500.
**21XU6** E5 10c black    2,750.
**21XU7** E6 10c black (ms "WBP" initials)    —
   Types E4 and E5 both exist on one cover. On No. 21XU3B, the "PAID 5 Cents" handstamp is to the left, and the "PAID" and ms. "5" are toward the right. It is unique.

---

### DEMOPOLIS, ALA.

E1

---

### Handstamped Envelopes, Signature in ms.
**22XU1** E1 5c black ("Jno. T. Hall")    3,000.
**22XU2** E1 5c black ("J. T. Hall")    3,000.
**22XU3** E1 5c (ms.) black ("J. T. Hall")    2,500.

---

### EATONTON, GA.

E1

E2

**Handstamped Envelopes**
**23XU1** E1 5c black    3,000.
   **a.** 10 (ms) on 5c black    —
**23XU2** E2 5c + 5c black    5,500.

---

### EMORY, VA.

A1

**Handstamped Adhesives ("PAID" and "5" in circle on selvage of U.S. 1c 1857 issue)**
**Perf. 15 on three sides**
**24X1** A1 5c blue, on cover, tied    27,500.
   On cover, not tied    22,500.
   Also known with "5" above "PAID."

E1

E2

**Handstamped Envelopes**
**24XU1** E1 5c blue    4,000.
**24XU2** E2 10c black    5,000.
   One example each recorded of Nos. 24XU1 and 24XU2.

---

### FINCASTLE, VA.

E1

**Press-printed Envelope (typeset) Impressed at top right**
**104XU1** E1 10c black    20,000.
   One example recorded of No. 104XU1.

---

### FORSYTH, GA.

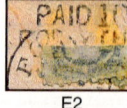
E1    E2

**Handstamped Envelope**
**120XU1** E1 10c black    2,000.
**120XU2** E2 10c black    4,500.
   Only one example each recorded of Nos. 120XU1 and 120XU2.

---

### FORT VALLEY, GA.

E1    E2

**Handstamped Envelope**
**148XU1** E1 5c on 3c black    3,250.
   Black circle control on front of envelope. Unique.

---

### FRANKLIN, N. C.

E1    E2

**Press-printed Envelope (typeset) (No. 25XU1)**
**Impressed at top right**
**25XU1** E1 5c blue, *buff*    45,000.
**25XU2** E2 5c black, large "5" woodcut in 31mm circular town mark    2,500.
   The one known No. 25XU1 envelope shows black circular Franklin postmark with manuscript date.

---

### FRAZIERSVILLE, S. C.

E1

**Handstamped Envelope, "5" manuscript**
**128XU1** E1 5c black    5,000.
   Only one example recorded of No. 128XU1.

---

### FREDERICKSBURG, VA.

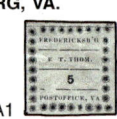
A1

Sheets of 20, two panes of 10 varieties each

**Typeset Adhesives**
**Thin bluish paper**
**26X1** A1 5c blue, *bluish*    1,200.    2,000.
**26X2** A1 10c red (shades), *bluish*    2,250.

---

### GAINESVILLE, ALA.

 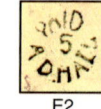
E1    E2

E3

**Handstamped Envelopes**
**27XU1** E1 5c black    3,000.
**27XU2** E2 5c black    5,000.
**27XU3** E3 10c ("01") black    12,000.

---

### GALVESTON, TEX.

E1

**Handstamped Envelopes**
**98XU1** E1 5c black    500.    1,500.
**98XU2** E1 10c black    2,500.

E2

E3

**Handstamped Envelopes**
**98XU3** E2 10c black    550.    2,750.
**98XU4** E2 20c black    3,500.
**98XU5** E3 5c black    4,500.

---

### GASTON, N. C.

E1

**Handstamped Envelope**
**129XU1** E1 5c black    6,000.
   Only one example recorded of No. 129XU1.

---

### GEORGETOWN, S. C.

E1    Control

E2

**Handstamped Envelopes**
**28XU1** E1 5c black    900.
**28XU2** E2 5c black, separate "5" and straightline "PAID" handstamps, control on reverse    —    1,750.

---

### GOLIAD, TEX.

A1    A2

**Typeset Adhesives**
**29X1** A1 5c black    16,500.
**29X2** A1 5c black, *gray*    11,500.
**29X3** A1 5c black, *rose*    12,000.
**29X4** A1 10c black    —    25,000.
**29X5** A1 10c black, *rose*    12,000.
   Type A1 stamps are signed "Clarke-P.M." vertically in black or red.
**29X6** A2 5c black, *gray*    22,500.
   **a.** "GOILAD"    12,000.
**29X7** A2 10c black, *bluish gray*    12,000.
   **a.** "GOILAD"    15,000.
**29X8** A2 5c black, *dark blue*, on cover    18,000.
**29X9** A2 10c black, *dark blue*    27,500.

# CONFEDERATE STATES OF AMERICA

## GONZALES, TEX.

Colman & Law were booksellers when John B. Law (of the firm) was appointed Postmaster. The firm used a small lithographed label on drugs and on the front or inside of books they sold.

 A1

### Lithographed Adhesives on colored glazed paper

| | | | |
|---|---|---|---|
| 30X1 | A1 | (5c) gold, *dark blue*, pair on cover, 1861 | 15,000. |
| 30X2 | A1 | (10c) gold, *garnet*, on cover, 1864 | 35,000. |
| 30X3 | A1 | (10c) gold, *black*, on cover, 1865 | 35,000. |

No. 30X1 must bear double-circle town cancel as validating control. The control was applied to the labels in the sheet before their sale as stamps. When used, the stamps bear an additional Gonzales double-circle postmark.

## GREENSBORO, ALA.

 E1     E2

 E3

### Handstamped Envelopes

| | | | |
|---|---|---|---|
| 31XU1 | E1 | 5c black | 3,250. |
| 31XU2 | E1 | 10c black | 3,750. |
| 31XU3 | E2 | 10c black | 6,000. |
| 31XU4 | E3 | 10c on 5c black | 3,000. |

## GREENSBORO, N. C.

 E1

### Handstamped Envelope

| | | | |
|---|---|---|---|
| 32XU1 | E1 | 10c red | 1,250. |
| a. | | Rerated to due 10 by "Due 10" handstamp on provisional handstamp | 2,000. |

## GREENVILLE, ALA.

 A1     A2

### Typeset Adhesives
On pinkish surface-colored glazed paper.

| | | | |
|---|---|---|---|
| 33X1 | A1 | 5c blue & red | 35,000. |
| 33X2 | A2 | 10c red & blue, on cover | 35,000. |

Two used examples each are known of Nos. 33X1-33X2, and all are on covers. Covers bear a postmark but it was not used to cancel the stamps.

The former No. 33X1a has been identified as a fake.

## GREENVILLE, TENN.

 E1

| | | | |
|---|---|---|---|
| 144XU1 | E1 | 5c black | 5,000. |

Only one example of No. 144XU1 is recorded.

## GREENVILLE COURT HOUSE, S. C.

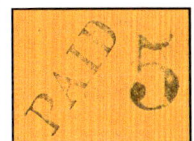 E1

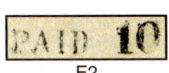 E2     Control A

 Control B     Control C

### Handstamped Envelopes (Several types)

| | | | |
|---|---|---|---|
| 34XU1 | E1 | 5c black | 1,750. |
| 34XU2 | E2 | 10c black | 1,750. |
| a. | | 20c (ms.) on 10c black | 3,000. |

Envelopes must bear one of three different postmark controls on the back. When the control postmark is dated, the date must be the same or prior to the date of the postmark on the front of the envelope.

## GREENWOOD DEPOT, VA.

 A1

### "PAID" Handstamped Adhesive ("PAID" with value and signature in ms.)
Laid Paper

| | | | |
|---|---|---|---|
| 35X1 | A1 | 10c black, *gray blue*, on cover | 22,500. |

## GRIFFIN, GA.

 E1

### Handstamped Envelopes

| | | | |
|---|---|---|---|
| 102XU1 | E1 | 5c black | 2,000. |
| 102XU2 | E1 | 10c black | 5,000. |

No. 102XU2 is on a large piece of an envelope with July 25 postmark at left. It is unique.

## GROVE HILL, ALA.

 A1

### Handstamped Adhesive (from woodcut)

| | | | |
|---|---|---|---|
| 36X1 | A1 | 5c black | 125,000. |

Two examples are recorded. One is on cover tied by the postmark. The other is canceled by magenta pen on a cover front. Value is for the complete cover.

## HALLETTSVILLE, TEX.

 A1

### Handstamped Adhesive Ruled Letter Paper

| | | | |
|---|---|---|---|
| 37X1 | A1 | 10c black, *gray blue*, on cover | 10,000. |

One example known.

## HAMBURGH, S. C.

 E1

### Handstamped Envelope

| | | | |
|---|---|---|---|
| 112XU1 | E1 | 5c black | 7,000. |

## HARRISBURGH (Harrisburg), TEX.

 E1    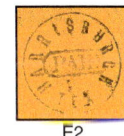 E2

### Handstamped Envelope

| | | | |
|---|---|---|---|
| 130XU1 | E1 | 5c black | 5,500. |
| 130XU2 | E2 | 10c black | — |

The unused 5c entire is the only example recorded of No. 130XU1.

## HELENA, TEX.

 A1

### Typeset Adhesives
Several varieties

| | | | |
|---|---|---|---|
| 38X1 | A1 | 5c black, *buff* | 20,000. 20,000. |
| 38X2 | A1 | 10c black, *gray* | 20,000. |

On 10c "Helena" is in upper and lower case italics.

Used examples are valued with small faults or repairs, as all recorded have faults.

## HILLSBORO, N. C.

   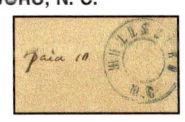

A1

### Handstamped Adhesive

| | | | |
|---|---|---|---|
| 39X1 | A1 | 5c black, on cover | 10,000. |

See 3c 1861 Postmaster's Provisional No. 1AX1.

No. 39X1 is unique.

### Ms./Handstamped Envelope

| | | | |
|---|---|---|---|
| 39XU1 | E1 | 10c "paid 10" in manuscript with undated blue town cancel as control on face | 2,250. |

No. 39XU1 is unique.

## HOLLANDALE, TEX.

 E1

### Handstamped Envelope

| | | | |
|---|---|---|---|
| 132XU1 | E1 | 5c black | — |

No. 123XU1 is unique.

## HOUSTON, TEX.

 E1     No. 40XU1a

### Handstamped Envelopes

| | | | |
|---|---|---|---|
| 40XU1 | E1 | 5c red | 800. |
| a. | | 10c (ms.) on 5c red | 6,500. |
| 40XU2 | E1 | 10c red | 1,750. |
| 40XU3 | E1 | 10c black | 6,750. |
| 40XU4 | E1 | 5c +10c red | 2,500. |
| 40XU5 | E1 | 10c +10c red | 2,500. |

Nos. 40XU2-40XU5 show "TEX" instead of "TXS."

## HUNTSVILLE, TEX.

 E1    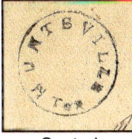 Control

 E2

 E3

### Handstamped Envelope

| | | | |
|---|---|---|---|
| 92XU1 | E1 | 5c black | 5,000. |
| 92XU2 | E2 | 5c black | — |
| 92XU3 | E3 | 10c black | — |

## INDEPENDENCE, TEX.

 A1     A2

### Handstamped Adhesives

| | | | |
|---|---|---|---|
| 41X1 | A1 | 10c black, *buff*, on cover, uncanceled, cut to shape | 70,000. |
| 41X2 | A1 | 10c black, *dull rose*, on cover | — |

### With small "10" and "Pd" in manuscript

| | | | |
|---|---|---|---|
| 41X3 | A2 | 10c black, *buff*, on cover, uncanceled, cut to shape | 20,000. |

No. 41X1 is unique.

225

# CONFEDERATE STATES OF AMERICA

All known examples of Nos. 41X1-41X3 are uncanceled on covers with black "INDEPENDANCE TEX." (sic) postmark. The existence of No. 41X2 has been questioned by specialists. The editors would like to see authenticated evidence of the existence of this item.

## ISABELLA, GA.

 E1

### Handstamped Envelope, Manuscript "5"

133XU1  E1  5c black  5,000.

Only one example recorded of No. 133XU1.

## IUKA, MISS.

 E1

### Handstamped Envelope

42XU1  E1  5c black  1,750.

## JACKSON, MISS.

 E1

### Handstamped Envelopes
Two types of numeral

43XU1  E1  5c black  900.
  a.  10c on 5c black  2,750.
  b.  5c on 3c black  1,500.
43XU2  E1  10c black  2,000.
  a.  5c on 10c black  3,750.
43XU4  E1  10c on 5c blue  2,750.

The 5c also exists on a lettersheet. See 3c 1861 Postmaster's Provisional No. 2AXU1.

## JACKSONVILLE, ALA.

 E1

### Handstamped Envelope

110XU1  E1  5c black  —  3,000.

## JACKSONVILLE, FLA.

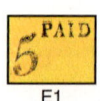 E1     Control

### Handstamped Envelope

134XU1  E1  5c black  4,000.

Undated double circle postmark control on reverse. No. 134XU1 is unique.

## JETERSVILLE, VA.

 A1

### Handstamped Adhesive ("5" with ms. "AHA." initials)
Laid Paper

44X1  A1  5c black, vertical pair on cover, uncanceled  16,000.

## JONESBORO, TENN.

 E1

### Handstamped Envelopes

45XU1  E1  5c black  6,000.
45XU2  E1  5c dark blue  5,000.

## KINGSTON, GA.

 E1     E2

 E3

 E4

### Typeset Envelopes
(design types E1-E2, E4 are handstamps; typeset design E3 probably impressed by hand but possibly press printed)

46XU1  E1  5c black  3,000.
46XU2  E2  5c black  9,500.
  a.  Without "CS" at sides of "5"  3,500.
46XU4  E3  5c black  12,500.
46XU5  E4  5c black  2,000.

There is only one recorded example of No. 46XU4.

## KNOXVILLE, TENN.

 A1

### Typographed Adhesives (stereotype from woodcut)
Grayish Laid Paper

47X1  A1  5c brick red  1,750.  1,500.
47X2  A1  5c carmine  2,750.  2,250.
47X3  A1  10c green, on cover  70,000.

The #47X3 cover is unique. Value is based on 1997 auction sale.

 E1     E2

### Press-printed Envelopes (typographed)

47XU1  E1  5c blue  3,000.
47XU2  E1  5c blue, orange  5,000.
47XU3  E1  10c red (cut to shape)  7,000.
47XU4  E1  10c red, orange (cut to shape)  6,000.

Only one example each recorded of Nos. 47XU3 and 47XU4. Dangerous fakes exist of Nos. 47XU1 and 47XU2.

### Handstamped Envelopes

47XU5  E2  5c black  1,400.
  a.  10c on 5c black  3,500.

Type E2 exists with "5" above or below "PAID."

## LA GRANGE, TEX.

 E1

### Handstamped Envelopes

48XU1  E1  5c black  —  4,000.
48XU2  E1  10c black  4,000.

## LAKE CITY, FLA.

  E1     Control Type A

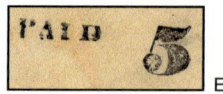 Control Type B

### Handstamped Envelope

96XU1  E1  10c black  4,000.

Envelopes have black circle control mark, or printed name of E. R. Ives, postmaster, on back.

## LAURENS COURT HOUSE, S. C.

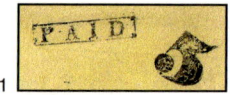 E1

 E2

 Control

### Handstamped Envelopes

116XU1  E1  5c black  2,000.
116XU2  E2  5c black  2,000.

Envelopes have a 25mm undated control mark on reverse. No. 116XU1 is unique.

## LENOIR, N. C.

 A1     A2

 E1

### Handstamped Adhesive (from woodcut)
White wove paper with cross-ruled orange lines

49X1  A1  5c blue & orange  7,250.  6,750.

### Handstamped Envelopes

49XU1  A1  5c blue  4,000.
49XU2  A2  10c (5c+5c) blue  25,000.
49XU3  E1  5c blue  4,500.
49XU4  E1  5c black  4,500.

No. 49XU2 is unique.

## LEXINGTON, MISS.

 E1

### Handstamped Envelopes

50XU1  E1  5c black  3,750.
50XU2  E1  10c black  5,000.

Only one example is recorded of No. 50XU2.

## LEXINGTON, VA.

 E1

### Handstamped Envelopes

135XU1  E1  5c blue  350.
135XU2  E1  10c blue  350.

Nos. 135XU1-135XU2 by themselves are indistinguishable from stampless covers when used.

## LIBERTY, VA. (and Salem, Va.)

 A1

### Typeset Adhesive (probably impressed by hand)
Laid Paper

74X1  A1  5c black, on cover, uncanceled  25,000.

Two known on covers with Liberty, Va. postmark; one cover known with the nearby Salem, Va. office postmark.

## LIMESTONE SPRINGS, S. C.

 A1

### Handstamped Adhesive

121X1  A1  5c black, light blue, on cover  10,000.
121X2  A1  5c black, white, two on cover  32,500.

Stamps are cut round or rectangular. Covers are not postmarked. The No. 121X2 cover bears the only two recorded examples of this stamp.

## LIVINGSTON, ALA.

 A1

### Lithographed Adhesive

51X1  A1  5c blue  10,000.

## LYNCHBURG, VA.

 A1     E1

# CONFEDERATE STATES OF AMERICA

### Typographed Adhesive (stereotype from woodcut)
52X1  A1  5c blue (shades)  1,800.  1,500.

### Press-printed Envelopes (typographed)
Impressed at top right or left
52XU1  E1  5c black  700.00  3,000.
52XU2  E1  5c black, amber  3,000.
52XU3  E1  5c black, buff  3,000.
52XU4  E1  5c black, brown  3,000.

---

## MACON, GA.

 A1   A2

 A3   A4

### Typeset Adhesives
Several varieties of type A1, 10 of A2, 5 of A3

#### Wove Paper
53X1  A1  5c black, *light blue green* (shades)  1,250. 1,000.

Warning: Dangerous forgeries exist of the normal variety and the Comma after "OFFICE" variety. Certificates of authenticity from recognized committees are strongly recommended.

53X3  A2  5c black, *yellow*  2,500. 1,250.
53X4  A3  5c black, *yellow* (shades)  3,000. 3,000.
 a.  Vertical tête bêche pair, on cover  60,000.
53X5  A4  2c black, *gray green*  —

#### Laid Paper
53X6  A2  5c black, *yellow*  6,000. 6,000.
53X7  A3  5c black, *yellow*  6,000.
53X8  A1  5c black, *light blue green*  1,750. 2,250.

No. 53X4a is unique.

 E1

### Handstamped Envelope
Two types: "PAID" over "5," "5" over "PAID"
53XU1  E1  5c black  250.  650.

Values are for "PAID" over "5" variety. "5" over "PAID" is much scarcer.

---

## MADISON, GA.

 E1

### Handstamped Envelope
136XU1  E1  5c red  600.

No. 136XU1 is indistinguishable from a handstamp paid cover when used.

---

## MADISON COURT HOUSE, FLA.

 E1

### Typeset Envelope
137XU1  E1  5c black, *yellow*  35,000.

No. 137XU1 is unique.
See 3c 1861 Postmaster's Provisional No. 3AX1.

---

## MARIETTA, GA.

 E1 Control

 E2

### Handstamped Envelopes
54XU1  E1  5c black  500.
 a.  10c on 5c black  1,750.

### With Double Circle Control
54XU3  E1  10c black
54XU4  E2  5c black  2,000.

The existence of No. 54XU3 has been questioned by specialists. The editors would like to see authenticated evidence that verifies this listing.

---

## MARION, VA.

 A1

### Adhesives with Typeset frame and Handstamped numeral in center
55X1  A1  5c black  6,500.
55X2  A1  10c black  10,000. 10,000.
55X2A  A1  10c 10c black, *bluish*, tied on cover  15,000.
55X3  A1  5c black, *bluish*, laid paper
55X4  A1  5c black, *bluish*, tied on cover  6,000.

The 2c, 3c, 15c and 20c are believed to be bogus items printed later using the original typeset frame.

---

## MARS BLUFF, S. C.

 E1

145XU1  E1  5c black  2,000.

The No. 145XU1 marking is a provisional only when unused, used from another town or used under a general issue.

---

## MEMPHIS, TENN.

 A1   56X1a Partial Print

 A2

### Typographed Adhesives (stereotyped from woodcut)
56X1  A1  2c blue (shades)  100. 1,250.
 a.  Partial print  250.
56X2  A2  5c red (shades)  150.  250.
 a.  Tête bêche pair  1,500.
 b.  Pair, one sideways  2,500.
 c.  Pelure paper  —

### Press-printed Envelopes (typographed)
56XU1  A2  5c red (shades)  3,000.
56XU2  A2  5c red, *amber*  3,000.
56XU3  A2  5c red, *orange*  2,500.
56XU4  A2  5c red, *cream*  5,750.

Only one example of No. 56XU4 is recorded. It is on a cover on which a C.S.A. No. 11 is affixed over the provisional to pay the postage.

---

## MICANOPY, FLA.

 E1

### Handstamped Envelope
105XU1  E1  5c black  11,500.

Two examples are recorded.

---

## MILLEDGEVILLE, GA.

 E1

 E2

 E3

### Handstamped Envelopes
Two types of No. 57XU5: Type I, tall, thin "1" and "0" of "10"; Type II, short, fat "1" and "0" of "10."
57XU1  E1  5c black  800.
 a.  Wide spacing between "I" and "D" of "PAID"  900.
 b.  10c on 5c black  1,250.
57XU2  E1  5c blue  800.
57XU4  E2  10c black  375. 1,200.
 a.  Wide spacing between "I" and "D" of "PAID"  1,200.
57XU5  E3  10c black, type I  450.  950.
 a.  Type II  1,500.

On No. 57XU4, the "PAID/10" virtually always falls outside the Milledgeville control marking (as in illustration E1).
The existence of No. 57XU2 as a provisional has been questioned by specialists. The editors would like to see authenticated evidence of provisional use of this marking.

---

## MILTON, N. C.

 E1

### Handstamped Envelope, "5" Manuscript
138XU1  E1  5c black  3,750.

---

## MOBILE, ALA.

 A1

### Lithographed Adhesives
58X1  A1  2c black  2,250. 1,200.
58X2  A1  5c blue  350.  450.

---

## MONTGOMERY, ALA.

 E1  E1a

### Handstamped Envelopes
59XU1  E1  5c red  950.
 a.  10c on 5c red  2,750.
59XU2  E1  5c blue  400. 1,000.
59XU3  E1a  10c red  950.
59XU4  E1a  10c blue  1,250.
59XU5  E1a  10c black  850.

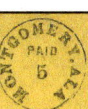 E2   E3

59XU7  E2  2c red  2,500.
59XU7A  E2  2c blue  3,500.
59XU8  E2  5c black  2,000.
59XU9  E3  10c black  2,000.
59XU10  E3  10c red  1,750.

The existence of No. 59XU10 is in question. The editors would like to see an authenticated example of this marking.

---

## MOUNT LEBANON, LA.

 A1

### Woodcut Adhesive (mirror image of design)
60X1  A1  5c red brown, on cover  235,000.

One example known. Value represents sale price at 2009 auction.

---

## MOUNT PLEASANT, N. C.

 E1

### Handstamped Envelope
151XU1  E1  10c blue  3,500.

One example of No. 151XU1 is recorded, posted in January 1866 and covered by a U.S. 3¢ stamp subsequently removed to reveal the provisional.

---

## NASHVILLE, TENN.

 A2  E1

### Typographed Adhesives (stereotyped from woodcut)
Gray Blue Ribbed Paper
61X2  A2  5c carmine (shades)  1,000.  800.
 a.  Vertical tête bêche pair  4,000.
61X3  A2  5c brick red (shades)  900.  850.
 a.  Vertical tête bêche pair  3,000.
61X4  A2  5c gray (shades)  1,250. 1,500.
61X5  A2  5c violet brown (shades)  1,250.  750.
 a.  Vertical tête bêche pair  5,000. 7,500.
61X6  A2  10c green  — 3,750.

### Handstamped Envelopes
61XU1  E1  5c blue  900.
61XU2  E1  10c on 5c blue  2,750.

See 3c Postmaster's Provisional No. 4AX1.

---

## NEW ORLEANS, LA.

 A1   A2

### Typographed Adhesives (stereotyped from woodcut)
62X1  A1  2c blue  225.  800.
 a.  Printed on both sides, on cover  10,500.

228 CONFEDERATE STATES OF AMERICA

| 62X2 | A1 | 2c red (shades) | 190. | 1,000. |
|---|---|---|---|---|
| 62X3 | A2 | 5c brown, white | 300. | 275. |
| | a. | Printed on both sides | | 3,750. |
| | b. | 5c ocher | 700. | 625. |
| 62X4 | A2 | 5c red brn, bluish | 325. | 200. |
| | a. | Printed on both sides | | 3,000. |
| 62X5 | A2 | 5c yel brn, off-white | 160. | 240. |
| 62X6 | A2 | 5c red (shades) | 18,500. | 15,000. |
| 62X7 | A2 | 5c red (shades), bluish | | 16,500. |

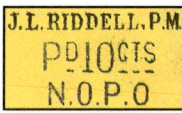
E1

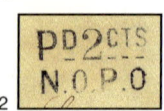
E2

**Handstamped Envelopes**
62XU1  E1  5c black    4,500.
62XU2  E1  10c black   11,500.

**"J. L. RIDDELL, P. M." omitted**
62XU3  E2  2c black    8,500.

Some authorities question the use of No. 62XU3 as a provisional.

### NEW SMYRNA, FLA.

A1

**Handstamped Adhesive**
On white paper with blue ruled lines
63X1  A1  10c ("O1") on 5c black    75,000.

One example known. It is uncanceled on a postmarked patriotic cover.

### NORFOLK, VA.

E1   E2

Manuscript Signature

**Handstamped Envelopes**
Ms Signature on Back
139XU1  E1  5c blue    1,000.  1,750.
139XU2  E2  10c blue           1,750.

### OAKWAY, S. C.

A1

**Handstamped Adhesive (from woodcut)**
115X1  A1  5c black, on cover    60,000.

Two used examples of No. 115X1 are recorded, both on cover. Value represents 2012 auction realization for the cover on which the stamp is tied by manuscript "Paid."

### OXFORD, N. C.

E1

**Handstamped Envelope**
152XU1  E1  10c black    3,500.

One example of No. 152XU1 is recorded, covered by a C.S.A. 10¢ No. 12 that paid the postage.

### PATTERSON, N. C.

E1          E2

Control

**Handstamped Envelopes**
149XU1  E1  5c black    750.
149XU2  E2  10c black   2,500.

Nos. 149XU1 and 149XU2 must have an undated postmark on the cover as a control.

### PENSACOLA, FLA.

E1

**Handstamped Envelopes**
106XU1  E1  5c black    4,500.
    a.  10c (ms.) on 5c black    4,750.

### PETERSBURG, VA.

A1

**Typeset Adhesive**
Ten varieties
65X1  A1  5c red (shades)    2,250.  500.

### PITTSYLVANIA COURT HOUSE, VA.

A1

**Typeset Adhesives**
66X1  A1  5c dull red, wove paper    6,500.  9,000.
66X2  A1  5c dull red, laid paper    5,500.

### PLAINS OF DURA, GA.

E1

**Handstamped Envelopes, Ms. Initials**
140XU1  E1  5c black    —
140XU2  E1  10c black   5,000.

No. 140XU2 is unique.

### PLEASANT SHADE, VA.

A1

**Typeset Adhesive**
Five varieties
67X1  A1  5c blue    6,000.  15,000.

### PLUM CREEK, TEX.

E1

**Manuscript Adhesive**
141X1  E1  10c black, blue, on cover    6,500.

The stamps have ruled lines with the value "10" in manuscript. Size and shape vary.

### PORT GIBSON, MISS.

E1

Manuscript Signature

**Handstamped Envelope, Ms Signature**
142XU1  E1  5c black    —

### PORT LAVACA, TEX.

A1

**Typeset Adhesive**
107X1  A1  10c black, on cover    27,000.

One example known. It is uncanceled on a postmarked cover.

### RALEIGH, N. C.

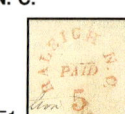
E1

**Handstamped Envelopes**
68XU1  E1  5c red    500.
68XU2  E1  5c blue   5,000.

### RHEATOWN, TENN.

A1

**Typeset Adhesive**
Three varieties
69X1  A1  5c red    6,000.  6,500.

### RICHMOND, TEX.

E1

**Handstamped Envelopes or Letter Sheets**
70XU1  E1  5c red    2,250.
    a.  10c on 5c red    11,750.
70XU2  E1  10c red    2,000.
    a.  15c (ms.) on 10c red    5,000.

### RINGGOLD, GA.

E1

**Handstamped Envelope**
71XU1  E1  5c blue black    8,500.

### RUTHERFORDTON, N. C.

A1

**Handstamped Adhesive, Ms. "Paid 5cts"**
72X1  A1  5c black, cut round, on cover (uncanceled)    60,000.

No. 72X1 is unique.

### SALEM, N. C.

"Paid 5" in Ms. — E1     "Paid 5" Handstamped — E2

**Handstamped Envelopes**
73XU1  E1  5c black    1,500.
73XU2  E1  10c black   3,500.
73XU3  E2  5c black    2,250.
    a.  10c on 5c black    2,800.

Reprints exist on various papers. They either lack the "Paid" and value or have them counterfeited.

Salem, Va.
See No. 74X1 under Liberty, Va.

### SALISBURY, N. C.

E1

**Press-printed Envelope (typeset)**
Impressed at top left
75XU1  E1  5c black, greenish    15,000.

One example known. Part of the envelope was torn away (now repaired), leaving part of design missing.

### SAN ANTONIO, TEX.

E1          E2

Control

## CONFEDERATE STATES OF AMERICA

### Handstamped Envelopes

| 76XU1 | E1 | 10c black | 500. | 2,000. |
|---|---|---|---|---|
| 76XU1A | E2 | 5c black | | 13,000. |
| 76XU2 | E1 | 10c black | | 2,500. |

Black circle control mark is on front or back. One example of No. 76XU1A is recorded.

### SAVANNAH, GA.

E1

Control

E2

### Handstamped Envelopes

| 101XU1 | E1 | 5c black | 450. |
|---|---|---|---|
| a. | | 10c on 5c black | 1,500. |
| 101XU2 | E2 | 5c black | 600. |
| a. | | 20c on 5c black | 2,000. |
| 101XU3 | E1 | 10c black | 750. |
| 101XU4 | E2 | 10c black | 750. |

Envelopes must have octagonal control mark. One example is known of No.101XU2a.

### SELMA, ALA.

E1

### Handstamped Envelopes; Signature in Ms.

| 77XU1 | E1 | 5c black | 1,250. |
|---|---|---|---|
| a. | | 10c on 5c black | 3,000. |
| 77XU2 | E1 | 10c black | 2,500. |

Signature is that of Postmaster William H. Eagar.
See 3c 1861 Postmaster's Provisional No. 5AX1.

### SPARTA, GA.

E1

### Handstamped Envelopes

| 93XU1 | E1 | 5c red | — | 2,250. |
|---|---|---|---|---|
| 93XU2 | E1 | 10c red | | 5,000. |

Only one example recorded of No. 93XU2.

### SPARTANBURG, S. C.

A1

A2

### Handstamped Adhesives
(on ruled or plain wove paper)

| 78X1 | A1 | 5c black, cut to shape | — |
|---|---|---|---|
| a. | | "Paid" instead of denomination, revalued to 5c with "PAID" and "5" in small circle handstamps, on cover | 6,000. |

| 78X2 | A2 | 5c black, bluish, on cover | 9,000. |
|---|---|---|---|
| 78X3 | A2 | 5c black, brown, on cover | 12,500. |

Most examples of Nos. 78X1-78X3 are cut round. Cut square examples in sound condition are worth much more.
No. 78X1a is unique. Also, only one example of No. 78X2 is recorded; part of the stamp is missing, and the cover is valued thus.

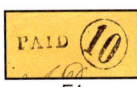
E1

Control

### Handstamped Envelopes

| 78XU1 | E1 | 10c black (control on reverse) | 4,500. |
|---|---|---|---|

### STATESVILLE, N. C.

E1

### Handstamped Envelopes

| 79XU1 | E1 | 5c black | 1,500. |
|---|---|---|---|
| a. | | 10c on 5c black, handstamped "10" | 3,000. |
| b. | | 10c on 5c black, manuscript "10" | 2,500. |

There are four identifiable varieties of No. 79XU1.
Unused examples of No. 79XU1 are reprints.

### SUMTER, S. C.

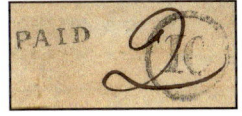
E1

### Handstamped Envelopes

| 80XU1 | E1 | 5c black | 500. |
|---|---|---|---|
| a. | | 10c on 5c black | 900. |
| 80XU2 | E1 | 10c black | 500. |
| a. | | 2c (ms.) on 10c black | 1,100. |

Used examples of Nos. 80XU1-80XU2 are indistinguishable from handstamped "Paid" covers.

### TALBOTTON, GA.

E1

### Handstamped Envelopes

| 94XU1 | E1 | 5c black | 900. |
|---|---|---|---|
| a. | | 10c on 5c black | 2,000. |
| 94XU2 | E1 | 10c black | 1,250. |

### TALLADEGA, ALA.

E1

### Handstamped Envelopes

| 143XU1 | E1 | 5c black | 1,500. | — |
|---|---|---|---|---|
| 143XU2 | E1 | 10c black | 1,500. | — |

These same markings were used on handstamped "Paid" covers.

### TELLICO PLAINS, TENN.

A1

### Typeset Adhesives
Laid Paper

| 81X1 | A1 | 5c red | 2,000. | 10,000. |
|---|---|---|---|---|
| 81X2 | A1 | 10c red | 3,750. | |

### THOMASVILLE, GA.

E1

Control

### Handstamped Envelopes

| 82XU1 | E1 | 5c black | 750. |
|---|---|---|---|

On No. 82XU1, the control is on the reverse of the cover. The dated control is known with five different dates, including June 1, June 13, June 21, and August 23. The patriotic envelope is unique.

E2

| 82XU2 | E2 | 5c black | 1,400. |
|---|---|---|---|

### TULLAHOMA, TENN.

E1

Control

### Handstamped Envelope

| 111XU1 | E1 | 10c black | 5,000. |
|---|---|---|---|

The control appears either on the front or the back of the envelope.

### TUSCALOOSA, ALA.

E1

### Handstamped Envelopes

| 83XU1 | E1 | 5c black | 250. |
|---|---|---|---|
| 83XU2 | E1 | 10c black | 250. |

Used examples of Nos. 83XU1-83XU2 are indistinguishable from handstamped "Paid" covers.

### TUSCUMBIA, ALA.

E1

### Handstamped Envelopes

| 84XU1 | E1 | 5c black | 2,750. |
|---|---|---|---|
| 84XU2 | E1 | 5c red | 5,000. |
| 84XU3 | E1 | 10c black | 5,250. |

See 3c 1861 Postmaster's Provisional No. 6AXU1.

### UNIONTOWN, ALA.

A1

### Typeset Adhesives
(settings of 4 (2x2), 4 varieties of each value)
Laid Paper

| 86X1 | A1 | 2c dark blue, gray blue, on cover | | 45,000. |
|---|---|---|---|---|
| 86X2 | A1 | 2c dark blue, sheet of 4 | 30,000. | |
| 86X3 | A1 | 5c green, gray blue | 4,000. | 3,250. |
| 86X4 | A1 | 5c green | 4,000. | 3,250. |
| 86X5 | A1 | 10c red, gray blue | | 10,000. |

Two examples known of No. 86X1, both on cover (drop letters), one uncanceled and one pen canceled.
The only recorded examples of No. 86X2 are in a unique sheet of 4.
The item listed as No. 86X5 used is an uncanceled stamp on a large piece with part of addressee's name in manuscript. The value for the stamp on cover is for the cover with the stamp pen canceled.

### UNIONVILLE, S. C.

A1

### Handstamped Adhesive
"PAID" and "5" applied separately
Paper with Blue Ruled Lines

| 87X1 | A1 | 5c black, grayish | 3,500. |
|---|---|---|---|

### VALDOSTA, GA.

E1

Control

E2

### Handstamped Envelopes

| 100XU1 | E1 | 10c black | 9,000. |
|---|---|---|---|
| 100XU2 | E2 | 5c +5c black | — |

The black circle control must appear on front of the No. 100XU2 envelope and on the back of the No. 100XU1 envelope.
There is one recorded cover each of Nos. 100XU1-100XU2.

### VICTORIA, TEX.

A1

A2

### Typeset Adhesives
Surface colored paper

| 88X1 | A1 | 5c red brown, green | 17,500. |
|---|---|---|---|
| 88X2 | A1 | 10c red brown, green | 22,500. |
| 88X3 | A2 | 10c red brown, green, pelure paper | 30,000. | 30,000. |

### WALTERBOROUGH, S. C.

E1

### Handstamped Envelopes

| 108XU1 | E1 | 10c black, buff | — |
|---|---|---|---|
| 108XU2 | E1 | 10c carmine | 3,500. |

The existence of No. 108XU1 is in question. The editors would like to see authenticated evidence of its existence.

## WARRENTON, GA.

E1

### Handstamped Envelopes
89XU1 E1 5c black 1,500.
   *a.* 10c (ms.) on 5c black 900.

Fakes of the Warrenton provisional marking based on the illustration shown are known on addressed but postally unused covers.

## WASHINGTON, GA.

E1

### Handstamped Envelope
117XU1 E1 10c black 2,000.

Envelopes must have black circle postmark control on the back. Examples with the undated control on the front are not considered provisional unless a dated postmark is also present.

## WEATHERFORD, TEX.

E1

### Handstamped Envelopes
(woodcut with "PAID" inserted in type)
109XU1 E1 5c black 2,000.
109XU2 E1 5c +5c black 11,000.

One example is known of No. 109XU2.

## WILKESBORO, N. C.

E1

### Handstamped Envelope
147XU1 E1 5c black, revalued to 10c 3,500.

No. 147XU1 is unique.

## WILLISTON, S.C.

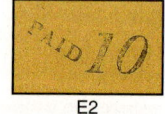
E1

### Handstamped Envelopes
153XU1 E1 10c brown 1,250.

No. 153XU1 is unique. Value is based on 2020 auction sale. This cover must be either unused (as the one recorded example is) or covered by a C.S.A. stamp.

## WINNSBOROUGH, S. C.

E1         E2

Control

### Handstamped Envelopes
97XU1 E1 5c black 1,500.
97XU2 E2 10c black 1,000. 2,000.

Envelopes must have black circle control on front or back.

## WYTHEVILLE, VA.

E1        Control

E1

### Handstamped Envelope
114XU1 E1 5c black 900.
114XU2 E2 5c black 2,250.

For later additions, listed out of numerical sequence, see:
#74X1, Liberty, Va.
#92XU1, Huntsville, Tex.
#92XU2, Huntsville, Tex.
#92XU3, Huntsville, Tex.
#93XU1, Sparta, Ga.
#94XU1, Talbotton, Ga.
#95XU1, Cuthbert, GA
#96XU1, Lake City, Fla.
#97XU1, Winnsborough, S.C.
#98XU1, Galveston, Tex.
#99XU1, Christianburg, Va.
#100XU1, Valdosta, Ga.
#101XU1, Savannah, Ga.
#102XU1, Griffin, Ga.
#103XU1, Courtland, Ala.
#104XU1, Fincastle, Va.
#105XU1, Micanopy, Fla.
#106XU1, Pensacola, Fla.
#107X1, Port Lavaca, Tex.
#108XU1, Walterborough, S.C.
#109XU1, Weatherford, Tex.
#110XU1, Jacksonville, Ala.
#111XU1, Tullahoma, Tenn.
#112XU1, Hamburgh, S.C.
#113XU1, Columbia, Tenn.
#114XU1, Wytheville, Va.
#115X1, Oakway, S.C.
#116XU1, Laurens Court House, S.C.
#117XU1, Washington, Ga.
#118XU1, Carolina City, N.C.
#119XU1, Colaparchee, Ga.
#120XU1, Forsyth, Ga.
#121XU1, Limestone Springs, S.C.
#122XU1, Balcony Falls, Va.
#123XU1, Barnwell Court House, S.C.
#124XU1, Bluffton, S.C.
#125XU1, Camden, S.C.
#126XU1, Cartersville, Ga.
#127XU1, Charlottesville, Va.
#128XU1, Fraziersville, S.C.
#129XU1, Gaston, N.C.
#130XU1, Harrisburgh, Tex.
#132XU1, Hollandale, Tex.
#133XU1, Isabella, Ga.
#134XU1, Jacksonville, Fla.
#135XU1, Lexington, Va.
#136XU1, Madison, Ga.
#137XU1, Madison Court House, Fla.
#138XU1, Milton, N.C.
#139XU1, Norfolk, Va.
#140XU1, Plains of Dura, Ga.
#141X1, Plum Creek, Tex.
#142XU1, Port Gibson, Miss.
#143XU1, Talladega, Ala.
#144XU1, Greenville, Tenn.
#145XU1, Mars Bluff, S.C.
#146XU1, Charlotte, N.C.
#147XU1, Wilkesboro, N.C.
#148XU1, Fort Valley, Ga.
#149XU1, Patterson, N.C.
#150XU1, Beaufort, S.C.
#151XU1, Mount Pleasant, N.C.
#152XU1, Oxford, N.C.
#153XU1, Williston, S.C.

## GENERAL ISSUES

Due to its tendency to damage the paper and color of the stamps, the gum on most (but not all) Confederate States stamps is removed. Except for the De La Rue-printed Nos. 6 and 14, which are valued both with original gum and without gum, unused values for all Confederate States stamps are for stamps without gum. Stamps with original gum sell for about the same prices, if the gum has not deteriorated and damaged the paper or stamp color.

**Jefferson Davis — A1**

| | | | | |
|---|---|---|---|---|
| **1861** | | **Unwmk.** | **Litho.** | ***Imperf.*** |
| | | **Soft Porous Paper** | | |
| 1 | A1 | 5c green (shades) | 300. | 175. |
| *a.* | | 5c light green | 275. | 175. |
| *b.* | | 5c dark green | 375. | 250. |
| *c.* | | 5c olive green | 425. | 250. |

**Thomas Jefferson — A2**

**1861-62**
| | | | | |
|---|---|---|---|---|
| 2 | A2 | 10c blue | 275. | 180. |
| *a.* | | 10c light blue | 300. | 200. |
| *b.* | | 10c dark blue | 700. | 300. |
| *c.* | | 10c indigo | 5,000. | 7,500. |
| *d.* | | Printed on both sides | | 1,750. |
| *e.* | | light milky blue | 1,250. | 325. |

Specialists have questioned the existence of No. 2bd, the Hoyer & Ludwig printed on both sides. The editors would like to see authenticated evidence of its existence.

The earliest printings of No. 2 were made by Hoyer & Ludwig, the later ones by J. T. Paterson & Co.

Stamps of the later printings usually have a small colored dash below the lowest point of the upper left spandrel.

**Andrew Jackson — A3**

**1862**
| | | | | |
|---|---|---|---|---|
| 3 | A3 | 2c green | 1,000. | 750. |
| *a.* | | 2c bright yellow green | 2,000. | |
| 4 | A1 | 5c blue | 225. | 125. |
| *a.* | | 5c dark blue | 275. | 175. |
| *b.* | | 5c light milky blue | 350. | 200. |
| 5 | A2 | 10c rose (shades) | 2,400. | 400. |
| *a.* | | 10c carmine | 3,750. | 1,900. |

**Jefferson Davis — A4**

**Typo.**
| | | | | |
|---|---|---|---|---|
| 6 | A4 | 5c light blue | 20. | 30. |
| | | No gum | 10. | |
| 7 | A4 | 5c blue (De La Rue thin paper) | 22. | 22. |
| *a.* | | 5c deep blue | 28. | 35. |
| *b.* | | Printed on both sides | 2,500. | 1,400. |

No. 6 has fine, clear impression. No. 7 has coarser impression and the color is duller and often blurred.

Both 2c and 10c stamps, types A4 and A10, were privately printed in various colors.

**Andrew Jackson — A5**

**1863**         **Engr.**
| | | | | |
|---|---|---|---|---|
| 8 | A5 | 2c brown red | 75. | 350. |
| *a.* | | 2c pale red | 90. | 450. |

A6

**Thick or Thin Paper**
| | | | | |
|---|---|---|---|---|
| 9 | A6 | 10c blue | 950. | 500. |
| *a.* | | 10c milky blue (first printing) | 1,050. | 550. |
| *b.* | | 10c gray blue | 1,050. | 600. |

**Jefferson Davis — A6a**

| | | | | |
|---|---|---|---|---|
| 10 | A6a | 10c blue (with dividing lines) | 5,500. | 2,500. |
| *a.* | | 10c milky blue | 5,500. | 2,500. |
| *b.* | | 10c greenish blue | 6,000. | 2,500. |
| *c.* | | 10c dark blue | 6,000. | 2,500. |

Values of Nos. 10, 10a, 10b and 10c are for examples showing parts of lines on at least three sides. Used stamps showing 4 complete lines sell for approximately 3 to 4 times the values given. Unused stamps showing 4 complete lines are exceedingly rare (only two recorded), and the one sound example is valued at $35,000.

A7

There are many slight differences between A7 and A8, the most noticeable being the additional line outside the ornaments at the four corners of A8.

**1863-64**
| | | | | |
|---|---|---|---|---|
| 11 | A7 | 10c blue | 18. | 20. |
| *a.* | | 10c milky blue | 55. | 60. |
| *b.* | | 10c dark blue | 25. | 30. |
| *c.* | | 10c greenish blue | 30. | 50. |
| *d.* | | 10c green | 100. | 80. |
| *e.* | | Officially perforated 12½ (Archer & Daly printing) | 450. | 350. |

A8

| | | | | |
|---|---|---|---|---|
| 12 | A8 | 10c blue | 22. | 25. |
| *a.* | | 10c milky blue | 55. | 60. |
| *b.* | | 10c light blue | 21. | 22. |
| *c.* | | 10c greenish blue | 40. | 50. |
| *d.* | | 10c dark blue | 24. | 25. |
| *e.* | | 10c green | 150. | 140. |
| *f.* | | Officially perforated 12½ (Archer & Daly printing) | 450. | 375. |

The paper of Nos. 11 and 12 varies from thin hard to thick soft.

**George Washington — A9**

**1863**
| | | | | |
|---|---|---|---|---|
| 13 | A9 | 20c green | 45. | 400. |
| *a.* | | 20c yellow green | 80. | 450. |
| *b.* | | 20c dark green | 65. | 500. |
| *c.* | | 20c bluish green | 100. | — |
| *d.* | | Diagonal half used as 10c on cover | | 1,400. |
| *e.* | | Horizontal half used as 10c on cover | | 2,500. |

**John C. Calhoun — A10**

CONFEDERATE STATES OF AMERICA — CANAL ZONE 231

**1862** **Typo.**

| | | | | |
|---|---|---|---|---|
| 14 | A10 | 1c orange | 110. | |
| | | No gum | 60. | |
| *a.* | | 1c deep orange | 145. | |
| | | No gum | 85. | |

No. 14 was never put in use.

## CANAL ZONE

kə-'nal 'zōn

LOCATION — A strip of land 10 miles wide, extending through the Republic of Panama, between the Atlantic and Pacific Oceans.

GOVT. — From 1904-79 a U.S. Government Reservation; from 1979-99 under joint control of the Republic of Panama and the U.S.

AREA — 552.8 sq. mi.

POP. — 41,800 (est. 1976)

The Canal Zone, site of the Panama Canal, was leased in perpetuity to the U.S. for a cash payment of $10,000,000 and a yearly rental. Treaties between the two countries provided for joint jurisdiction by the U.S. and Panama, 1979-1999, with Panama handling postal service. At the end of 1999, the canal, in its entirety, reverted to Panama.

100 Centavos = 1 Peso
100 Centesimos = 1 Balboa
100 Cents = 1 Dollar

**Catalogue values for unused stamps in this country are for Never Hinged items, beginning with Scott 118 in the regular post age section and Scott C6 in the air post section.**

### Watermarks

Wmk. 190 — "USPS" in Single-lined Capitals

Wmk. 191 — Double-lined "USPS" in Capitals

Panama Nos. 72, 72a-72c, 78-79 Handstmped in Violet to Violet-Blue

On the 2c "PANAMA" is normally 13mm long. On the 5c and 10c it measures about 15mm.

On the 2c, "PANAMA" reads up on the upper half of the sheet and down on the lower half. On the 5c and 10c, "PANAMA" reads up at left and down at right on each stamp.

On the 2c only, varieties exist with inverted "V" for "A," accent on "A," inverted "N," etc., in "PANAMA."

**Unwmk.**

**1904, June 24** **Engr.** ***Perf. 12***

| | | | | |
|---|---|---|---|---|
| 1 | A3 | 2c rose, both "PANAMA" reading up or down | 650. | 400. |
| *a.* | | "CANAL ZONE" inverted | *1,000.* | 850. |
| *b.* | | "CANAL ZONE" double | *4,250.* | 2,000. |
| *c.* | | "CANAL ZONE" double, both inverted | *20,000.* | |
| *d.* | | "PANAMA" reading down and up | 750. | 650. |
| *e.* | | As "d," "CANAL ZONE" invtd. | *9,000.* | *9,000.* |
| *f.* | | Vert. pair, "PANAMA" reading up on top 2c, down on other | *2,100.* | *2,100.* |
| *g.* | | As "f," "CANAL ZONE" inverted | *20,000.* | |
| 2 | A3 | 5c blue | 300. | 190. |
| *a.* | | "CANAL ZONE" inverted | 775. | 600. |
| *b.* | | "CANAL ZONE" double | 2,250. | 1,500. |
| *c.* | | Pair, one without "CANAL ZONE" overprint | *5,000.* | *5,000.* |
| *d.* | | "CANAL ZONE" overprint diagonal, reading down to right | 800. | 700. |
| 3 | A3 | 10c yellow | 400. | 210. |
| *a.* | | "CANAL ZONE" inverted | 775. | 600. |
| *b.* | | "CANAL ZONE" double | | *14,000.* |
| *c.* | | Pair, one without "CANAL ZONE" overprint | *6,000.* | *5,000.* |
| | | *Nos. 1-3 (3)* | 1,350. | 800.00 |

Cancellations consist of town and/or bars in magenta or black, or a mixture of both colors.

Nos. 1-3 were withdrawn July 17, 1904.

Forgeries of the "Canal Zone" overprint and cancellations are numerous.

United States Nos. 300, 319, 304, 306 & 307 Ovptd. in Black

**1904, July 18** **Wmk. 191**

| | | | | |
|---|---|---|---|---|
| 4 | A115 | 1c blue green | 35.00 | 22.50 |
| 5 | A129 | 2c carmine | 25.00 | 25.00 |
| *a.* | | 2c scarlet | 32.50 | 30.00 |
| 6 | A119 | 5c blue | 85.00 | 60.00 |
| 7 | A121 | 8c violet black | 130.00 | 85.00 |
| 8 | A122 | 10c pale red brown | 120.00 | 80.00 |
| | | *Nos. 4-8 (5)* | 395.00 | 272.50 |

Beware of fake overprints.

### Stamps of Panama Overprinted in Black

12ovpt

CANAL
ZONE
Regular Type

CANAL
ZONE
Antique Type

**1904-06** **Unwmk.**

| | | | | |
|---|---|---|---|---|
| 9 | A5 | 1c green | 2.50 | 2.00 |
| *a.* | | "CANAL" in antique type | 90.00 | 90.00 |
| *b.* | | "ZONE" in antique type | 60.00 | 60.00 |
| *c.* | | Inverted overprint | *7,500.* | *6,000.* |
| *d.* | | Double overprint | *2,750.* | *2,000.* |
| 10 | A5 | 2c rose | 4.00 | 2.50 |
| *a.* | | Inverted overprint | 225.00 | 275.00 |
| *b.* | | "L" of "CANAL" sideways | *2,000.* | *2,250.* |

### "PANAMA" (15mm long) reading up at left, down at right

### Overprint "CANAL ZONE" in Black, "PANAMA" and Bar in Red

| | | | | |
|---|---|---|---|---|
| 11 | A3 | 2c rose | 6.50 | 1.50 |
| *a.* | | "ZONE" in antique type | 175.00 | 175.00 |
| *b.* | | "PANAMA" overprint inverted, bar at bottom | 600.00 | *675.00* |
| 12 | A3 | 5c blue | 7.50 | 2.75 |
| *a.* | | "CANAL" in antique type | 75.00 | 65.00 |
| *b.* | | "ZONE" in antique type | 75.00 | 65.00 |
| *c.* | | "CANAL ZONE" double | 800.00 | 800.00 |
| *d.* | | "PANAMA" double | 1,100. | 1,000. |
| *e.* | | "PANAMA" inverted, bar at bottom | 1,000. | 1,250. |
| *f.* | | "PANAAM" at right | *950.00* | *850.00* |
| 13 | A3 | 10c yellow | 17.00 | 12.00 |
| *a.* | | "CANAL" in antique type | 180.00 | 180.00 |
| *b.* | | "ZONE" in antique type | 175.00 | 160.00 |
| *c.* | | "PANAMA" ovpt. double | 650.00 | 650.00 |
| *d.* | | "PANAMA" overprint in red brown | 27.50 | 22.50 |
| | | *Nos. 11-13 (3)* | 31.00 | 19.25 |

### With Added Surcharge in Red

a

| | | | | |
|---|---|---|---|---|
| 14 | A3 | 8c on 50c bister brown | 25.00 | 25.00 |
| *a.* | | "ZONE" in antique type | 1,150. | 1,150. |
| *b.* | | "CANAL ZONE" inverted | 450.00 | 425.00 |
| *c.* | | "PANAMA" overprint in rose brown | 35.00 | 35.00 |
| *d.* | | As "c," "CANAL" in antique type | *1,750.* | *850.00* |
| *e.* | | As "c," "ZONE" in antique type | *1,750.* | |
| *f.* | | As "c," "8 cts" double | *1,100.* | |
| *g.* | | As "c," "8" omitted | *4,500.* | |
| *h.* | | As "c," "cts 8" | — | |

Nos. 11-14 are overprinted or surcharged on Panama Nos. 77, 77e, 78, 78c, 78d, 78f, 78g, 78h, 79 79c, 79e, 79g and 81 respectively.

On No. 14 with original gum, the gum is almost always disturbed. Unused stamps are valued thus.

### Panama No. 74a, 74b Overprinted "CANAL ZONE" in Regular Type in Black and Surcharged

### Type "a" in Red

### Both "PANAMA" (13mm long) Reading Up

| | | | | |
|---|---|---|---|---|
| 15 | A3(a) | 8c on 50c bister brown | 2,000. | *4,750.* |
| *a.* | | "PANAMA" reading down and up | *6,000.* | — |

On No. 15 with original gum, the gum is almost always disturbed. Unused stamps are valued thus.

Panama Nos. 19 and 21 Surcharged in Black

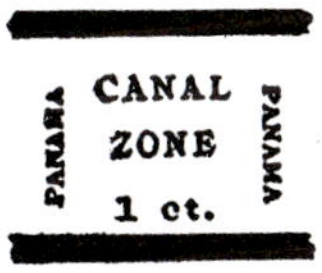


a

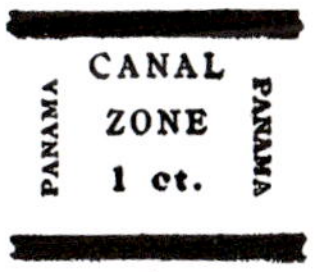


b

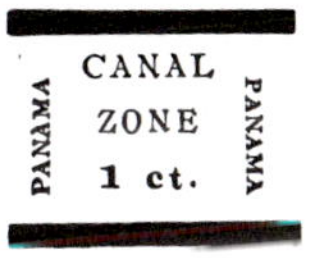


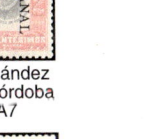

c

d

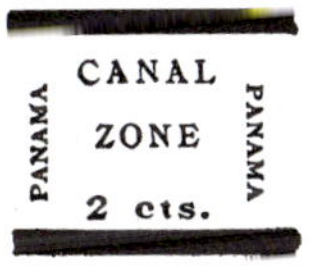


e

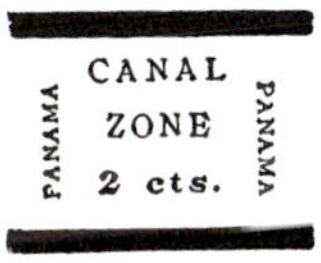


f

There were three printings of each denomination, differing principally in the relative position of the various parts of the surcharges. Varieties occur with inverted "V" for the final "A" in "PANAMA," "CA" spaced, "ZO" spaced, "2c" spaced, accents in various positions, and with bars shifted so that two bars appear on top or bottom of the stamp (either with or without the corresponding bar on top or bottom) and sometimes with only one bar at top or bottom.

**1906**

| | | | | |
|---|---|---|---|---|
| 16 | A4 | 1c on 20c violet, type a | 1.90 | 1.60 |
| *a.* | | Type b | 1.90 | 1.60 |
| *b.* | | Type c | 1.90 | 1.50 |
| *c.* | | As No. 16, double surcharge | | *2,000.* |
| 17 | A4 | 2c on 1p lake, type d | 2.25 | 2.25 |
| *a.* | | Type e | 2.25 | 2.25 |
| *b.* | | Type f | 20.00 | 20.00 |

### Panama Nos. 74, 74a and 74b Overprinted "CANAL ZONE" in Regular Type in Black and Surcharged in Red

b

c

**1905-06**

### Both "PANAMA" Reading Up

| | | | | |
|---|---|---|---|---|
| 18 | A3(b) | 8c on 50c bister brown | 45.00 | 45.00 |
| *a.* | | "ZONE" in antique type | 200.00 | 180.00 |
| *b.* | | "PANAMA" reading down and up | 160.00 | 150.00 |
| 19 | A3(c) | 8c on 50c bister brown | 45.00 | 37.50 |
| *a.* | | "CANAL" in antique type | 210.00 | 180.00 |
| *b.* | | "ZONE" in antique type | 210.00 | 180.00 |
| *c.* | | "8 cts" double | *1,100.* | *1,100.* |
| *d.* | | "PANAMA" reading down and up | 110.00 | 90.00 |

On Nos. 18-19 with original gum, the gum is usually disturbed. Unused stamps are valued thus.

### Panama No. 81 Overprinted "CANAL ZONE" in Regular Type in Black and Surcharged in Red Type "c" plus Period

### "PANAMA" reading up and down

| | | | | |
|---|---|---|---|---|
| 20 | A3(c) | 8c on 50c bister brown | 35.00 | 37.50 |
| *a.* | | "CANAL" antique type | 200.00 | 180.00 |
| *b.* | | "ZONE" in antique type | 200.00 | 180.00 |
| *c.* | | "8 cts" omitted | 800.00 | 800.00 |
| *d.* | | "8 cts" double | *1,500.* | |
| *e.* | | "cts 8" | — | |

Nos. 14 and 18-20 exist without CANAL ZONE overprint but were not regularly issued and are considered printer's waste. Forgeries of the overprint varieties of Nos. 9-15 and 18-20 are known.

On No. 20 with original gum, the gum is usually disturbed. Unused stamps are valued thus.

Francisco Hernandez de Cordoba A5

Vasco Nunez de Balboa A6

Fernández de Córdoba A7

Justo Arosemena A8

Manuel J. Hurtado A9

Jose de Obaldia A10

### Stamps of Panama Overprinted in Black

**1906-07** ***Perf. 12***

### Overprint Reading Up

| | | | | |
|---|---|---|---|---|
| 21 | A5 | 2c red & black | 25.00 | 25.00 |
| *a.* | | "CANAL" only | *4,000.* | |

### Overprint Reading Down

| | | | | |
|---|---|---|---|---|
| 22 | A6 | 1c green & black | 2.00 | .90 |
| *a.* | | Horiz. pair, imperf. btwn. | 1,100. | 1,100. |
| *b.* | | Vert. pair, imperf. btwn. | *2,000.* | *2,000.* |
| *c.* | | Vert. pair, imperf. horiz. | *2,250.* | *1,750.* |
| *d.* | | Inverted overprint reading up | 550.00 | 550.00 |
| *e.* | | Double overprint | 275.00 | 275.00 |
| *f.* | | Double overprint, one inverted | 1,750. | 1,600. |
| *g.* | | Invtd. center, ovpt. reading up | *3,500.* | *4,500.* |
| *h.* | | Horiz. pair, imperf vert. | *5,000.* | |
| 23 | A7 | 2c red & black | 3.00 | 1.00 |
| *a.* | | Horizontal pair, imperf. between | 2,000. | 2,000. |
| *b.* | | Vertical pair, one without overprint | 2,500. | 2,500. |
| *c.* | | Double overprint | 600.00 | 700.00 |
| *d.* | | Double overprint, one diagonal | 800.00 | 800.00 |
| *e.* | | Double overprint, one diagonal, in pair with normal | 2,500. | |
| *f.* | | 2c carmine red & black | 5.00 | 2.75 |
| *g.* | | As "f," inverted center and overprint reading up | | *14,000.* |
| *h.* | | As "d," one "ZONE CANAL" | *4,000.* | |
| *i.* | | "CANAL" double | *6,500.* | |
| 24 | A8 | 5c ultramarine & black | 5.75 | 2.00 |
| *a.* | | Double overprint | 500.00 | 400.00 |
| *d.* | | "CANAL" only | *7,000.* | |
| *e.* | | "ZONE CANAL" | *5,000.* | |
| 25 | A9 | 8c purple & black | 20.00 | 8.00 |
| *a.* | | Horizontal pair, imperf. between and at left margin | *1,600.* | *4,000.* |
| 26 | A10 | 10c violet & black | 20.00 | 7.00 |
| *a.* | | Dbl. ovpt., one reading up | *5,000.* | |
| *b.* | | Overprint reading up | *5,500.* | |
| | | *Nos. 22-26 (5)* | 50.75 | 18.90 |

Nos. 22-25 occur with "CA" of "CANAL" spaced ½mm further apart on position No. 50 of the setting.

The used pair of No. 25a is unique.

Cordoba
A11

Arosemena
A12

Hurtado
A13

Jose de Obaldia
A14

**1909**

**Overprint Reading Down**

**27** A11 2c vermilion & black 12.00 5.00
*a.* Horizontal pair, one without overprint *2,500.*
*b.* Vert. pair, one without ovpt. *3,250.*
*c.* Vert. pair, one without "ZONE" —
**28** A12 5c deep blue & black 40.00 12.50
**29** A13 8c violet & black 37.50 14.00
**30** A14 10c violet & black 40.00 14.00
*a.* Horizontal pair, one without overprint *4,000.*
*b.* Vertical pair, one without overprint *4,000.*
*c.* Horizontal pair, one with "ZONE" omitted *4,000.*
*Nos. 27-30 (4)* 129.50 45.50

Nos. 27-30 occur with "CA" spaced (position 50).

Do not confuse No. 27 with Nos. 39d or 53a. On No. 30a, the stamp with "ZONE" omitted is also missing most of "CANAL."

For designs A11-A14 with overprints reading up, see Nos. 32-35, 39-41, 47-48, 53-54, 56-57.

**Black Overprint Reading Up**

Vasco Nunez de Balboa — A15

Type I

Type I Overprint: "C" with serifs both top and bottom. "L," "Z" and "E" with slanting serifs.

Compare Type I overprint with Types II to V illustrated before Nos. 38, 46, 52 and 55.

**1909-10**

**31** A15 1c dark green & black 4.25 1.25
*a.* Inverted center and overprint reading down *22,500.*
*c.* Bklt. pane of 6, handmade, perf. margins *500.00*
**32** A11 2c vermilion & black 4.50 1.25
*a.* Vert. pair, imperf. horiz. 1,000. 1,000.
*c.* Bklt. pane of 6, handmade, perf. margins *800.00*
*d.* Double overprint (I) *6,000.*
**33** A12 5c deep blue & black 17.00 3.50
*a.* Double overprint 375.00 375.00
**34** A13 8c violet & black 11.00 5.00
*a.* Vertical pair, one without overprint *1,750.*
**35** A14 10c violet & black 47.50 20.00
*Nos. 31-35 (5)* 84.25 31.00

No. 32d is unique and has small faults. See Nos. 38, 46, 52, 55.

A16

A17

**Black Surcharge**

**1911, Jan. 14**

**36** A16 10c on 13c gray 6.00 2.00
*a.* "10 cts" inverted 325.00 325.00
*b.* "10 cts" omitted 300.00

Many used stamps offered as No. 36b are merely No. 36 from which the surcharge has been chemically removed.

**1914, Jan. 6**

**37** A17 10c gray 47.50 11.00

**Black Overprint Reading Up**

Type II: "C" with serif at top only. "L" and "E" with vertical serifs. "O" tilts to left

**1912-16**

**38** A15 1c green & black 10.00 3.00
*a.* Vertical pair, one without overprint 1,750. 1,750.
*b.* Booklet pane of 6, imperf. margins 575.00
*c.* Booklet pane of 6, handmade, perf. margins *1,000.*
*d.* Horizontal booklet pair, right stamp without "ZONE" *1,000.*
**39** A11 2c vermilion & black 8.00 1.10
*a.* Horiz. pair, right stamp without overprint *1,250.*
*b.* Horiz. pair, left stamp without overprint *1,500.*
*c.* Booklet pane of 6, imperf. margins 550.00
*d.* Overprint reading down 200.00
*e.* As "d," inverted center 600.00 *750.00*
*f.* As "e," booklet pane of 6, handmade, perf. margins *8,000.*
*g.* As "c," handmade, perf. margins 900.00 800.00
*h.* As No. 39, "CANAL" only (1) *2,500.*
**40** A12 5c deep blue & black 20.00 2.50
*a.* With Cordoba portrait of 2c *12,500.*
**41** A14 10c violet & black 60.00 7.50
*Nos. 38-41 (4)* 98.00 14.10

Map of Panama Canal — A18

Balboa Takes Possession of the Pacific Ocean — A19

Gatun Locks — A20

Culebra Cut — A21

**1915, Mar. 1**

**Blue Overprint, Type II**

**42** A18 1c dark green & black 8.75 6.50
**43** A19 2c carmine & black 12.00 4.25
**44** A20 5c blue & black 10.00 5.75
**45** A21 10c orange & black 19.00 11.00
*Nos. 42-45 (4)* 49.75 27.50

**Black Overprint Reading Up**

Type III Overprint: Similar to Type I but letters appear thinner, particularly the lower bar of "L," "Z" and "E." Impressions are often light, rough and irregular, and not centered.

**1915-20**

**46** A15 1c green & black 175.00 125.00
*a.* Overprint reading down 375.00
*b.* Double overprint 225.00
*c.* "ZONE" double *6,500.*
*d.* Double overprint, one reads "ZONE CANAL" 2,000.
**47** A11 2c orange vermilion & black 2,750. 60.00
**48** A12 5c deep blue & black 425.00 130.00
*Nos. 46-48 (3)* 3,350. 315.00

Spacing between words of overprint on Nos. 46-48 is 9¼mm; spacing varieties are not known. This should not be confused with a fairly common 9¼mm spacing of the 2c value of type I, nor with an uncommon 9¼mm spacing variety of the 5c of type I.

S.S. "Panama" in Culebra Cut — A22

S.S. "Panama" in Culebra Cut — A23

S.S. "Cristobal" in Gatun Locks — A24

**1917, Jan. 23**

**Blue Overprint, Type II**

**49** A22 12c purple & black 17.50 5.25
**50** A23 15c bright blue & black 50.00 17.50
**51** A24 24c yellow brown & black 35.00 13.00
*Nos. 49-51 (3)* 102.50 35.75

**Black Overprint Reading Up**

Type IV: "C" thick at bottom, "E" with center bar same length as top and bottom bars

**1918-20**

**52** A15 1c green & black 32.50 10.00
*a.* Overprint reading down 175.00 —
*b.* Booklet pane of 6 600.00
*c.* Booklet pane of 6, left vertical row of 3 without overprint *7,500.*
*d.* Booklet pane of 6, right vertical row of 3 with double overprint *7,500.*
*e.* Horiz. bklt. pair, left stamp without overprint *3,000.*
*f.* Horiz. bklt. pair, right stamp with double overprint *3,000.*
*g.* Double overprint, booklet single 3,000.
*h.* "CANAL" omitted —
**53** A11 2c vermilion & black 110.00 6.00
*a.* Overprint reading down 150.00 150.00
*b.* Horiz. pair, right stamp without ovpt. (from misregistered overprints) 2,000.
*c.* Booklet pane of 6 1,050.
*d.* Booklet pane of 6, left vertical row of 3 without overprint *15,000.*
*e.* Horiz. bklt. pair, left stamp without overprint *3,000.*
*f.* Horiz. sheet pair, left stamp without overprint (2) *1,750.*
**54** A12 5c deep blue & black 150.00 32.50
*Nos. 52-54 (3)* 292.50 48.50

No. 53e used is unique and is on cover.

**Black Overprint Reading Up**

Type V: Smaller block type 1¾mm high. "A" with flat top

**1920-21**

**55** A15 1c light green & black 22.50 3.25
*a.* Overprint reading down 300.00 225.00
*b.* Horiz. pair, right stamp without ovpt. *1,750.*
*c.* Horiz. pair, left stamp without ovpt. 1,100.
*d.* "ZONE" only *4,000.* —
*e.* Booklet pane of 6 *2,250.*
*f.* As No. 55, "CANAL" double *1,750.*
*g.* Vert. pair, one without overprint (2) 3,000.
*h.* Vert. pair,one "ZONE" only, one without overprint (1) *4,000.*
**56** A11 2c orange vermilion & black 8.50 1.75
*a.* Double overprint 500.00
*b.* Double overprint, one reading down 600.00
*c.* Horiz. pair, right stamp without overprint 1,400.
*d.* Horiz. pair, left stamp without overprint 1,000.
*e.* Vertical pair, one without overprint 1,500.
*f.* "ZONE" double 900.00
*g.* Booklet pane of 6 900.00
*h.* As No. 56, "CANAL" double 800.00
**57** A12 5c deep blue & black 300.00 45.00
*a.* Horiz. pair, right stamp without overprint *2,000.*
*b.* Horiz. pair, left stamp without overprint *2,000.*
*Nos. 55-57 (3)* 331.00 50.00

Drydock at Balboa — A25

Ship in Pedro Miguel Locks — A26

**1920, Sept.**

**Black Overprint Type V**

**58** A25 50c orange & black 250.00 160.00
**59** A26 1b dark violet & black 175.00 50.00

Jose Vallarino
A27

The "Land Gate"
A28

Bolivar's Tribute — A29

Municipal Building in 1821 and 1921 — A30

Statue of Balboa
A31

Tomas Herrera
A32

Jose de Fabrega — A33

**Type V overprint in black, reading up, on all values except the 5c which is overprinted with larger type in red**

**1921, Nov. 13**

**60** A27 1c green 3.75 1.50
*a.* "CANAL" double *1,900.*
*b.* Booklet pane of 6 *900.00*
**61** A28 2c carmine 2.75 1.00
*a.* Overprint reading down 200.00 *225.00*
*b.* Double overprint 900.00
*c.* Vertical pair, one without overprint *3,500.*
*d.* "CANAL" double *1,900.*
*e.* "ZONE" only (1) *4,000.*
*f.* Booklet pane of 6 *2,000.*
**62** A29 5c blue (R) 10.00 3.00
*a.* Overprint reading down (R) 65.00
**63** A30 10c violet 18.00 7.50
*a.* Overprint, reading down 90.00
**64** A31 15c light blue 47.50 17.50
**65** A32 24c black brown 67.50 22.50
**66** A33 50c black 145.00 85.00
*Nos. 60-66 (7)* 294.50 138.00

Experts question the status of the 5c with a small type V overprint in red or black.

**Type III overprint in black, reading up**

**1924, Jan. 28**

**67** A27 1c green 500. 200.
*a.* "ZONE CANAL" reading down 800.
*b.* "ZONE" only, reading down *1,900.*
*c.* Se-tenant pair, #67a and 67b *2,750.*

Coat of Arms — A34

**1924, Feb.**

**68** A34 1c dark green 10.00 4.50
**69** A34 2c carmine 7.00 2.75

The 5c to lb values were prepared but never issued. See listing in the Scott U.S. specialized catalogue.

### United States Nos. 551-554, 557, 562, 564-566, 569, 570 and 571 Overprinted in Red (No. 70) or Black (all others)

Type A: Letters "A" with Flat Tops

### Type A

Letters "A" with Flat Tops

**1924-25 Unwmk. *Perf. 11***

**70** A154 ½c olive brown .25 .70
Never hinged .40
**71** A155 1c deep green 1.40 1.00
Never hinged 2.50
*a.* Inverted overprint 500.00 500.00
*b.* "ZONE" inverted 350.00 325.00
*c.* "CANAL" only 1,150.
*d.* "ZONE CANAL" 400.00
*e.* Booklet pane of 6 80.00 —
*f.* Se-tenant pair, #71c and 71d 1,750.
**72** A156 1½c yellow brown 2.00 1.70
Never hinged 3.25
**73** A157 2c carmine 6.75 1.70
Never hinged 10.50
*a.* Booklet pane of 6 175.00
**74** A160 5c dark blue 16.00 7.00
Never hinged 25.00
**75** A165 10c orange 40.00 20.00
Never hinged 65.00
**76** A167 12c brown violet 32.50 30.00
Never hinged 62.50
*a.* "ZONE" inverted 3,750. 3,000.
**77** A168 14c dark blue 27.50 22.50
Never hinged 45.00
**78** A169 15c gray 45.00 37.50
Never hinged 70.00
**79** A172 30c olive brown 32.50 20.00
Never hinged 52.50
**80** A173 50c lilac 75.00 45.00
Never hinged 150.00
**81** A174 $1 violet brown 225.00 95.00
Never hinged 400.00
*Nos. 70-81 (12)* 503.90 282.10

Normal spacing between words of the overprint is 9¼mm. Minor spacing variations are known.

All examples of Nos. 71b and 76a have a natural straight edge at right.

Type B: Letters "A" with Sharp Pointed Tops

### Type B

**1925-28**

**84** A157 2c carmine 27.50 8.00
Never hinged 45.00
*a.* "CANAL" only 2,250.
*b.* "ZONE CANAL" 425.00
*c.* Horizontal pair, one without overprint 3,500.
*d.* Booklet pane of 6 175.00
*e.* Se-tenant pair, #84a and 84b 3,000.
**85** A158 3c violet 3.75 3.00
Never hinged 6.00
*a.* "ZONE ZONE" 550.00 550.00
**86** A160 5c dark blue 3.50 2.75
Never hinged 6.00
*a.* "ZONE ZONE" (LR18) 1,000.
*b.* "CANAL" inverted (LR7) 950.00
*c.* Inverted overprint 500.00
*d.* Horizontal pair, one without overprint 3,250.
*e.* Overprinted "ZONE CANAL" 350.00
*f.* "ZONE" only 2,000.
*g.* Vertical pair, one without overprint, other overprint inverted 2,000.
*h.* "CANAL" only 2,000.
*i.* Se-tenant pair, #86e and 86f 2,500.
**87** A165 10c orange 35.00 12.00
Never hinged 52.50
*a.* "ZONE ZONE" (LR18) 3,000.
*b.* "ZONE" only (1) 4,000.
**88** A167 12c brown violet 20.00 12.50
Never hinged 34.00
*a.* "ZONE ZONE" (LR18) 5,000.
**89** A168 14c dark blue 27.50 15.00
Never hinged 45.00
**90** A169 15c gray 7.50 4.50
Never hinged 12.00
*a.* "ZONE ZONE" (LR18) 5,500.
**91** A187 17c black 4.50 2.75
Never hinged 7.50
*a.* "ZONE" only 1,000.
*b.* "CANAL" only (11) 1,900.
*c.* "ZONE CANAL" 275.00
*d.* Se-tenant pair, #91a and 91c 1,400.
**92** A170 20c carmine rose 7.25 3.25
Never hinged 12.00
*a.* "CANAL" inverted (UR48) 6,500.
*b.* "ZONE" inverted (LL76) 4,750.
*c.* "ZONE CANAL" (LL91) 4,750.
**93** A172 30c olive brown 5.75 3.75
Never hinged 9.00
**94** A173 50c lilac 230.00 165.00
Never hinged 400.00
**95** A174 $1 violet brown 120.00 55.00
Never hinged 250.00
*Nos. 84-95 (12)* 492.25 287.50

Overprint Type B on U.S. No. 627

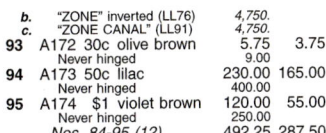

**1926**

**96** A188 2c carmine rose 4.50 3.75
Never hinged 7.00

On this stamp there is a space of 5mm instead of 9mm between the two words of the overprint.

Overprint Type B in Black on U.S. Nos. 583, 584, 591

**1926-27 *Perf. 10***

**97** A157 2c carmine 45.00 11.00
Never hinged 75.00
*a.* Pair, one without overprint 2,250.
*b.* Booklet pane of 6 500.00
*c.* "CANAL" only 2,000.
*d.* "ZONE" only 2,750.
**98** A158 3c violet 7.50 4.25
Never hinged 11.00
**99** A165 10c orange 18.00 7.50
Never hinged 27.50
*Nos. 97-99 (3)* 70.50 22.75

No. 97d is valued in the grade of fine. Very fine examples are not known.

Overprint Type B in Black on U.S. Nos. 632, 634 (Type I), 635, 637, 642

**1927-31 *Perf. 11x10½***

**100** A155 1c green 1.75 1.40
Never hinged 2.60
*a.* Vertical pair, one without overprint 3,250.
**101** A157 2c carmine 1.75 1.00
Never hinged 2.50
*a.* Booklet pane of 6 200.00
**102** A158 3c violet 4.25 2.75
Never hinged 6.25
*a.* Booklet pane of 6, handmade, perf. margins 6,500.
**103** A160 5c blue 25.00 10.00
Never hinged 45.00
**104** A165 10c orange 17.50 10.00
Never hinged 26.00
*Nos. 100-104 (5)* 50.25 25.15

**Wet and Dry Printings**

Canal Zone stamps printed by both the "wet" and "dry" process are Nos. 105, 100-109, 111-114, 117, 138-140, C21-C24, C26, J25, J27. Starting with Nos. 147 and C27, the Bureau of Engraving and Printing used the "dry" method exclusively. Late dry printings of Nos. 105, 108, 112-114, 117, 138 and 152 also exist with dull gum.

See note on Wet and Dry Printings following U.S. No. 1029.

Maj. Gen. William Crawford Gorgas A35

Maj. Gen. George Washington Goethals A36

Gaillard Cut A37

Maj. Gen. Harry Foote Hodges A38

Lt. Col. David DuB. Gaillard A39

Maj. Gen. William L. Sibert A40

Jackson Smith A41

Rear Adm. Harry H. Rousseau A42

Col. Sydney B. Williamson A43

J.C.S. Blackburn A44

**1928-40 *Perf. 11***

**105** A35 1c green .25 .25
Never hinged .25
**106** A36 2c carmine .25 .25
Never hinged .30
*a.* Booklet pane of 6 15.00 20.00
Never hinged 22.50
**107** A37 5c blue 1.00 .40
Never hinged 1.30
**108** A38 10c orange .25 .25
Never hinged .25
**109** A39 12c brown violet .75 .60
Never hinged 1.00
**110** A40 14c blue .85 .85
Never hinged 1.20
**111** A41 15c gray black .40 .35
Never hinged .55
**112** A42 20c dark brown .60 .25
Never hinged .80
**113** A43 30c black .80 .70
Never hinged 1.10
**114** A44 50c rose lilac 1.50 .65
Never hinged 2.00
*Nos. 105-114 (10)* 6.65 4.55

For surcharges and overprints, see Nos. J21-J24, O1-O8.
Coils are listed as Nos. 160-161.

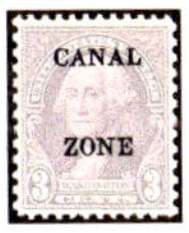

United States Nos. 720 and 695 Overprinted type B

**1933, Jan. 14 *Perf. 11x10½***

**115** A226 3c deep violet 2.75 .25
Never hinged 4.00
*b.* "CANAL" only 2,600.
*c.* Booklet pane of 6, handmade, perf. margins 80.00 —
*d.* Vertical pair, one without overprint —
**116** A168 14c dark blue 4.50 3.50
Never hinged 7.00
*a.* "ZONE CANAL" 1,500.

Gen. George Washington Goethals — A45

20th anniversary of the opening of the Panama Canal.

**1934 *Perf. 11***

**117** A45 3c red violet .25 .25
Never hinged .30
*a.* Booklet pane of 6 12.50 32.50
*b.* As "a," handmade, perf. margins 160.00 —

Coil is listed as No. 153.

**Catalogue values for unused stamps in this section, from this point to the end, are for Never Hinged items.**

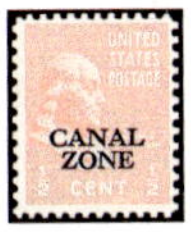

United States Nos. 803 and 805 Overprinted in Black

**1939, Sept. 1 *Perf. 11x10½***

**118** A275 ½c red orange .25 .25
**119** A277 1½c bister brown .25 .25

### Panama Canal Anniversary Issue

Balboa-Before A46

Balboa-After A47

Gaillard Cut-Before — A48

Gaillard Cut-After A49

Bas Obispo-Before A50

Bas Obispo-After A51

Gatun Locks-Before A52

Gatun Locks-After — A53

Canal Channel-Before A54

Canal Channel-After A55

Gamboa- Before A56

Gamboa-After A57

Pedro Miguel Locks-Before A58

Pedro Miguel Locks-After — A59

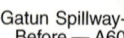

Gatun Spillway-Before — A60

Gatun Spillway-After A61

25th anniversary of the opening of the Panama Canal.

**1939, Aug. 15**

| | | | | |
|---|---|---|---|---|
| 120 | A46 | 1c yellow green | .60 | .30 |
| 121 | A47 | 2c rose carmine | .70 | .35 |
| 122 | A48 | 3c purple | .70 | .25 |
| 123 | A49 | 5c dark blue | 2.00 | 1.25 |
| 124 | A50 | 6c red orange | 4.50 | 3.00 |
| 125 | A51 | 7c black | 4.75 | 3.00 |
| 126 | A52 | 8c green | 7.00 | 3.25 |
| 127 | A53 | 10c ultramarine | 5.50 | 5.00 |
| 128 | A54 | 11c blue green | 11.00 | 8.00 |
| 129 | A55 | 12c brown carmine | 11.00 | 7.50 |
| 130 | A56 | 14c dark violet | 11.00 | 7.00 |
| 131 | A57 | 15c olive green | 14.00 | 5.75 |
| 132 | A58 | 18c rose pink | 15.00 | 8.50 |
| 133 | A59 | 20c brown | 17.50 | 7.00 |
| 134 | A60 | 25c orange | 27.50 | 15.00 |
| 135 | A61 | 50c violet brown | 30.00 | 6.00 |
| | | *Nos. 120-135 (16)* | 162.75 | 81.15 |

Maj. Gen. George W. Davis A62

Gov. Charles E. Magoon A63

Theodore Roosevelt A64

John F. Stevens A65

John F. Wallace — A66

**1946-49**

**Size: 19x22mm**

| | | | | |
|---|---|---|---|---|
| 136 | A62 | ½c bright red | .40 | .25 |
| 137 | A63 | 1½c chocolate | .40 | .25 |
| 138 | A64 | 2c light rose carmine | .25 | .25 |
| 139 | A65 | 5c dark blue | .35 | .25 |
| 140 | A66 | 25c green | .85 | .55 |
| | | *Nos. 136-140 (5)* | 2.25 | 1.55 |

See Nos. 155, 162, 164. For overprint, see No. O9.

Map of Biological Area and Coati-Mundi A67

25th anniversary of the establishment of the Canal Zone Biological Area on Barro Colorado Island.

**1948, Apr. 17**

| | | | | |
|---|---|---|---|---|
| 141 | A67 | 10c black | 1.75 | 1.00 |

"Forty-niners" Arriving at Chagres A68

Journey by "Bungo" to Las Cruces A69

Las Cruces Trail to Panama A70

Departure for San Francisco A71

Centenary of the California Gold Rush.

**1949, June 1**

| | | | | |
|---|---|---|---|---|
| 142 | A68 | 3c blue | .65 | .25 |
| 143 | A69 | 6c violet | .65 | .30 |
| 144 | A70 | 12c bright blue green | 1.75 | .90 |
| 145 | A71 | 18c deep red lilac | 2.00 | 1.50 |
| | | *Nos. 142-145 (4)* | 5.05 | 2.95 |

Workers in Culebra Cut — A72

Contribution of West Indian laborers in the construction of the Panama Canal.

**1951, Aug. 15**

| | | | | |
|---|---|---|---|---|
| 146 | A72 | 10c carmine | 3.50 | 1.50 |

Centenary of the completion of the Panama Railroad and the first transcontinental railroad trip in the Americas.

Early Railroad Scene — A73

**1955, Jan. 28**

| | | | | |
|---|---|---|---|---|
| 147 | A73 | 3c violet | 1.00 | .60 |

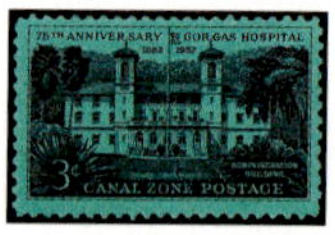

Gorgas Hospital and Ancon Hill — A74

75th anniversary of Gorgas Hospital.

**1957, Nov. 17**

| | | | | |
|---|---|---|---|---|
| 148 | A74 | 3c black, *dull blue grn* | .45 | .35 |

S.S. Ancon — A75

**1958, Aug. 30**

| | | | | |
|---|---|---|---|---|
| 149 | A75 | 4c greenish blue | .40 | .30 |

Roosevelt Medal and Map — A76

Centenary of the birth of Theodore Roosevelt (1858-1919).

**1958, Nov. 15**

| | | | | |
|---|---|---|---|---|
| 150 | A76 | 4c brown | .60 | .30 |

Boy Scout Badge — A77

50th anniversary of the Boy Scouts of America.

**1960, Feb. 8 Giori Press Printing**

| | | | | |
|---|---|---|---|---|
| 151 | A77 | 4c dark blue, red & bister | .55 | .40 |

Administration Building — A78

**1960, Nov. 1**

| | | | | |
|---|---|---|---|---|
| 152 | A78 | 4c rose lilac | .25 | .25 |

**Types of 1934, 1960 and 1946 Coil Stamps**

**1960-62 Unwmk. *Perf. 10 Vertically***

| | | | | |
|---|---|---|---|---|
| 153 | A45 | 3c deep violet | .25 | .25 |
| | | ***Perf. 10 Horizontally*** | | |
| 154 | A78 | 4c dull rose lilac | .25 | .25 |
| | | ***Perf. 10 Vertically*** | | |
| 155 | A65 | 5c deep blue | .25 | .25 |
| | | *Nos. 153-155 (3)* | .75 | .75 |

Girl Scout Badge and Camp at Gatun Lake — A79

50th anniversary of the Girl Scouts.

**Giori Press Printing**

**1962, Mar. 12 *Perf. 11***

| | | | | |
|---|---|---|---|---|
| 156 | A79 | 4c blue, dark green & bister | .40 | .30 |

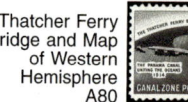

Thatcher Ferry Bridge and Map of Western Hemisphere A80

Opening of the Thatcher Ferry Bridge, spanning the Panama Canal.

**Giori Press Printing**

**1962, Oct. 12**

| | | | | |
|---|---|---|---|---|
| 157 | A80 | 4c black & silver | .35 | .25 |
| a. | | Silver (bridge) omitted *(50)* | *8,000.* | |
| | | Hinged | *6,000.* | |

Goethals Memorial, Balboa A81

Fort San Lorenzo A82

**1968-71 Giori Press Printing**

| | | | | |
|---|---|---|---|---|
| 158 | A81 | 6c green & ultra. | .30 | .30 |
| 159 | A82 | 8c slate green, blue, dark brown & ocher | .35 | .25 |

**Types of 1928, 1932 and 1948 Coil Stamps**

**1975, Feb. 14 *Perf. 10 Vertically***

| | | | | |
|---|---|---|---|---|
| 160 | A35 | 1c green | .25 | .25 |
| 161 | A38 | 10c orange | .70 | .40 |
| 162 | A66 | 25c yellow green | 2.75 | 2.75 |
| | | *Nos. 160-162 (3)* | 3.70 | 3.40 |

Dredge Cascadas — A83

**Giori Press Printing**

**1976, Feb. 23**

| | | | | |
|---|---|---|---|---|
| 163 | A83 | 13c multicolored | .35 | .25 |
| a. | | Booklet pane of 4 | 3.00 | — |

No. 163a exists with and without staple holes in selvage tab.

**Stevens Type of 1946**

**1977 *Perf. 11x10½***

**Size: 19x22½mm**

| | | | | |
|---|---|---|---|---|
| 164 | A65 | 5c deep blue | .60 | .85 |
| a. | | Tagged, dull gum | *12.00* | 15.00 |

No. 164 exists with both shiny gum and dull gum. Stamps with dull gum exist with and without tagging.

No. 164a exists even though there was no equipment in the Canal Zone to detect tagging.

Value for No. 164a on cover is for covers postmarked prior to Sept. 30, 1979.

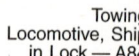

Towing Locomotive, Ship in Lock — A84

**1978, Oct. 25 *Perf. 11***

| | | | | |
|---|---|---|---|---|
| 165 | A84 | 15c dp grn & bl grn | .35 | .25 |

## AIR POST STAMPS

Nos. 105-106 Surcharged in Dark Blue

Type I - Flag of "Five" pointing up

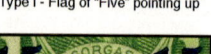

Type II - Flag of "5" curved

**1929-31 Engr. Unwmk. *Perf. 11***

| | | | | |
|---|---|---|---|---|
| C1 | A35 | 15c on 1c green, type I | 7.50 | 4.75 |
| | | Never hinged | 11.50 | |
| C2 | A35 | 15c on 1c yellow green, type II | 60.00 | 47.50 |
| | | Never hinged | 120.00 | |
| C3 | A36 | 25c on 2c carmine | 3.50 | 2.00 |
| | | Never hinged | 5.25 | |
| | | *Nos. C1-C3 (3)* | 71.00 | 54.25 |

Nos. 114 and 106 Surcharged

**1929, Dec. 31**

| | | | | |
|---|---|---|---|---|
| C4 | A44 | 10c on 50c lilac | 8.00 | 5.75 |
| | | Never hinged | 12.00 | |
| C5 | A36 | 20c on 2c carmine | 4.50 | 1.25 |
| | | Never hinged | 7.50 | |
| a. | | Dropped "2" in surcharge | 85.00 | 60.00 |

**Catalogue values for unused stamps in this section, from this point to the end, are for Never Hinged items.**

Gaillard Cut — AP1

**1931-49**

| | | | | |
|---|---|---|---|---|
| C6 | AP1 | 4c red violet | .75 | .65 |
| C7 | AP1 | 5c yellow green | .60 | .30 |
| C8 | AP1 | 6c yellow brown | .75 | .35 |
| C9 | AP1 | 10c orange | 1.00 | .35 |
| C10 | AP1 | 15c blue | 1.25 | .30 |
| C11 | AP1 | 20c red violet | 2.00 | .25 |
| C12 | AP1 | 30c rose lake | 7.50 | 1.50 |
| C13 | AP1 | 40c yellow | 3.50 | 1.10 |
| C14 | AP1 | $1 black | 10.00 | 1.60 |
| | | *Nos. C6-C14 (9)* | 27.35 | 6.40 |

For overprints, see Nos. CO1-CO14.

Douglas Plane over Sosa Hill — AP2

Planes and Map of Central America — AP3

Pan American Clipper and Scene near Fort Amador — AP4

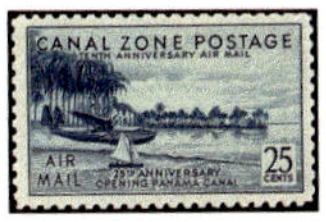
Pan American Clipper at Cristobal Harbor — AP5

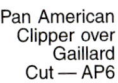

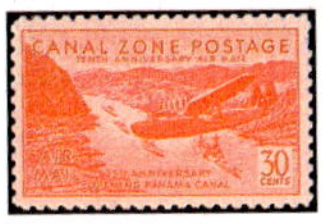
Pan American Clipper over Gaillard Cut — AP6

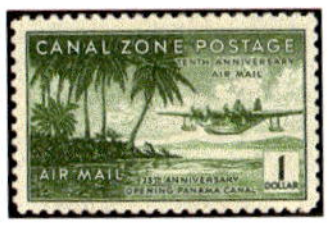
Pan American Clipper Landing — AP7

10th anniversary of Air Mail service and the 25th anniversary of the opening of the Panama Canal.

**1939, July 15**

| | | | | |
|---|---|---|---|---|
| **C15** AP2 | 5c greenish black | 3.75 | 2.25 |
| **C16** AP3 | 10c dull violet | 3.50 | 3.00 |
| **C17** AP4 | 15c light brown | 5.00 | 1.00 |
| **C18** AP5 | 25c blue | 17.50 | 8.00 |
| **C19** AP6 | 30c rose carmine | 17.50 | 6.00 |
| **C20** AP7 | $1 green | 45.00 | 27.50 |
| | *Nos. C15-C20 (6)* | 92.25 | 47.75 |

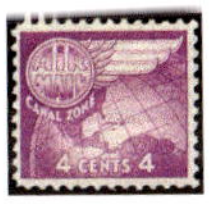
Globe and Wing — AP8

**1951, July 16**

| | | | |
|---|---|---|---|
| **C21** AP8 | 4c lt red violet | .75 | .35 |
| **C22** AP8 | 6c lt brown | .50 | .25 |
| **C23** AP8 | 10c lt red orange | .90 | .35 |
| **C24** AP8 | 21c lt blue | 8.00 | 4.00 |
| **C25** AP8 | 31c cerise | 9.50 | 3.75 |
| *a.* | Horiz. pair, imperf. vert. | 1,000. | — |
| **C26** AP8 | 80c lt gray black | 6.00 | 1.50 |
| | *Nos. C21-C26 (6)* | 25.65 | 10.20 |

**Flat Plate Printing**

**1958, Aug. 16 Unwmk. *Perf. 11***

| | | | |
|---|---|---|---|
| **C27** AP8 | 5c yellow green | 1.00 | .60 |
| **C28** AP8 | 7c olive | 1.00 | .45 |
| **C29** AP8 | 15c brown violet | 4.50 | 2.75 |
| **C30** AP8 | 25c orange yellow | 12.50 | 2.75 |
| **C31** AP8 | 35c dark blue | 9.00 | 2.75 |
| | *Nos. C27-C31 (5)* | 28.00 | 9.30 |
| | *Nos. C21-C31 (11)* | 53.65 | 19.50 |

See No. C34.

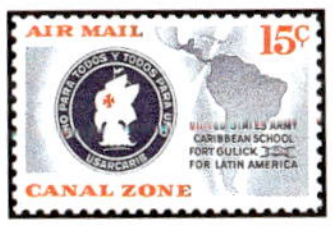
Emblem of U.S. Army Caribbean School — AP9

US Army Caribbean School for Latin America at Fort Gulick.

**1961, Nov. 21**

| | | | |
|---|---|---|---|
| **C32** AP9 | 15c red & blue | 1.60 | .75 |

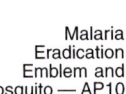

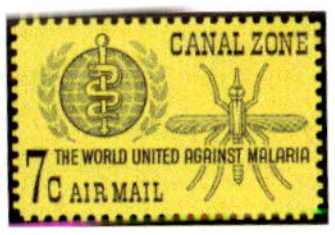
Malaria Eradication Emblem and Mosquito — AP10

World Health Organization drive to eradicate malaria.

**1962, Sept. 24**

| | | | |
|---|---|---|---|
| **C33** AP10 | 7c yellow & black | .50 | .40 |

**Globe-Wing Type of 1951**

**1963, Jan. 7 *Perf. 10½x11***

| | | | |
|---|---|---|---|
| **C34** AP8 | 8c carmine | .75 | .30 |

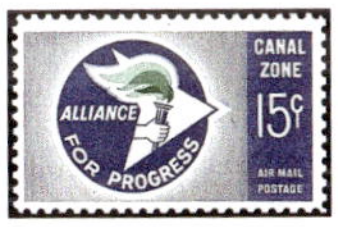
Alliance Emblem — AP11

2nd anniv. of the Alliance for Progress, which aims to stimulate economic growth and raise living standards in Latin America.

**1963, Aug. 17 *Perf. 11***

| | | | |
|---|---|---|---|
| **C35** AP11 | 15c gray, grn & dk ultra | 1.50 | .85 |

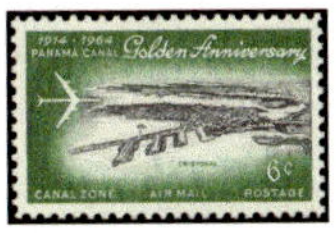
Jet over Canal Zone Views — AP12

50th anniversary of the opening of the Panama Canal.

Designs: 6c, Cristobal. 8c, Gatun Locks. 15c, Madden Dam. 20c, Gaillard Cut. 30c, Miraflores Locks. 80c, Balboa.

**1964, Aug. 15**

| | | | |
|---|---|---|---|
| **C36** AP12 | 6c green & black | .60 | .35 |
| **C37** AP12 | 8c rose red & black | .60 | .35 |
| **C38** AP12 | 15c blue & black | 1.25 | .75 |
| **C39** AP12 | 20c rose lilac & black | 1.60 | 1.00 |
| **C40** AP12 | 30c reddish brown & black | 2.75 | 2.25 |
| **C41** AP12 | 80c olive bister & black | 4.75 | 3.00 |
| | *Nos. C36-C41 (6)* | 11.55 | 7.70 |

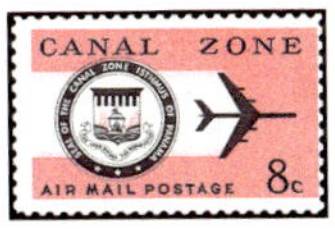
Seal and Jet Plane — AP13

**1965, July 15**

| | | | |
|---|---|---|---|
| **C42** AP13 | 6c green & black | .50 | .30 |
| **C43** AP13 | 8c rose red & black | .45 | .25 |
| **C44** AP13 | 15c blue & black | .75 | .25 |
| **C45** AP13 | 20c lilac & black | .80 | .30 |
| **C46** AP13 | 30c redsh brn & blk | 1.10 | .30 |
| | On cover, single franking, to Australasia, Asia or sub-Sahara Africa | | 25.00 |
| **C47** AP13 | 80c bister & black | 2.50 | .75 |
| | *Nos. C42-C47 (6)* | 6.10 | 2.15 |

**1968-76**

| | | | |
|---|---|---|---|
| **C48** AP13 | 10c dull orange & black | .35 | .25 |
| *a.* | Booklet pane of 4 | 4.25 | — |
| **C49** AP13 | 11c olive & black | .35 | .25 |
| *a.* | Booklet pane of 4 | 3.50 | — |
| **C50** AP13 | 13c emerald & black | .85 | .25 |
| *a.* | Booklet pane of 4 | 6.00 | — |
| **C51** AP13 | 22c vio & blk | 1.10 | *2.00* |
| **C52** AP13 | 25c pale yellow & black | .80 | .70 |
| **C53** AP13 | 35c salmon & black | 1.25 | *2.00* |
| | *Nos. C48-C53 (6)* | 4.70 | *5.45* |

## AIR POST OFFICIAL STAMPS

Beginning in March 1915, stamps for use on official mail were identified by a large "P" perforated through each stamp. These were replaced by overprinted issues in 1941. The use of official stamps was discontinued December 31, 1951. During their currency, they were not for sale in mint condition and were sold to the public only when canceled with a parcel post rotary canceler reading "Balboa Heights, Canal Zone" between two wavy lines.

After having been withdrawn from use, mint stamps (except Nos. CO8-CO12 and O3, O8) were made available to the public at face value for three months beginning Jan. 2, 1952. **Values for used examples of Nos. CO1-CO7, CO14, O1-O2, O4-O9, are for canceled-to-order stamps with original gum, postally used stamps being worth more.**

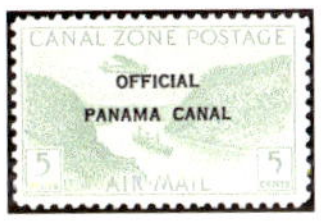
Nos. C7, C9-C14 Overprinted in Black

Two types of overprint

**Type I — "PANAMA CANAL" 19-20mm long**

**1941-42 Unwmk. *Perf. 11***

| | | | |
|---|---|---|---|
| **CO1** AP1 | 5c yellow green | 6.50 | 1.50 |
| **CO2** AP1 | 10c orange | 8.50 | 1.75 |
| **CO3** AP1 | 15c blue | 11.00 | 1.75 |
| **CO4** AP1 | 20c red violet | 13.00 | 4.00 |
| **CO5** AP1 | 30c rose lake | 17.50 | 5.00 |
| **CO6** AP1 | 40c yellow | 17.50 | 7.50 |
| **CO7** AP1 | $1 black | 20.00 | 10.00 |
| | *Nos. CO1-CO7 (7)* | 94.00 | 31.50 |

Overprint varieties occur on Nos. CO1-CO7 and CO14: "O" of "OFFICIAL" over "N" of "PANAMA" (entire third row). "O" of "OFFICIAL" broken at top (position 31). "O" of "OFFICIAL" over second "A" of "PANAMA" (position 45). First "F" of "OFFICIAL" over second "A" of "PANAMA" (position 50).

**Type II — "PANAMA CANAL" 17mm long**

**1941, Sept. 22**

| | | | |
|---|---|---|---|
| **CO8** AP1 | 5c yellow green | — | 150.00 |
| **CO9** AP1 | 10c orange | *1,100.* | 260.00 |
| **CO10** AP1 | 20c red violet | — | 160.00 |
| **CO11** AP1 | 30c rose lake | *900.* | 60.00 |
| **CO12** AP1 | 40c yellow | — | 170.00 |
| | *Nos. CO8-CO12 (5)* | | 800.00 |

**Type I — "PANAMA CANAL" 19-20mm long**

**1947, Nov.**

| | | | |
|---|---|---|---|
| **CO14** AP1 | 6c yellow brown | 13.00 | 5.50 |
| *a.* | Inverted overprint *(50)* | | *2,000.* |

## POSTAGE DUE STAMPS

Prior to 1914, many of the postal issues were handstamped "Postage Due" and used as postage due stamps.

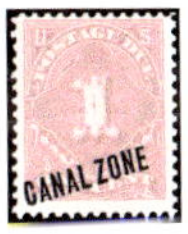
Postage Due Stamps of the U.S. Nos. J45a, J46a and J49a Overprinted in Black

**1914, Mar. Wmk. 190 *Perf. 12***

| | | | |
|---|---|---|---|
| **J1** D2 | 1c rose carmine | 85.00 | 15.00 |
| **J2** D2 | 2c rose carmine | 250.00 | 42.50 |
| **J3** D2 | 10c rose carmine | 900.00 | 40.00 |
| | *Nos. J1-J3 (3)* | 1,235. | 97.50 |

**Blue Overprint, Type II, on Postage Due Stamps of Panama**

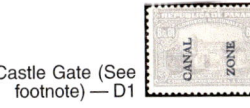

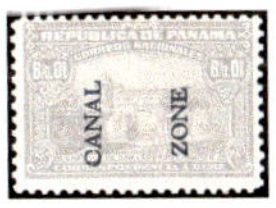
Castle Gate (See footnote) — D1

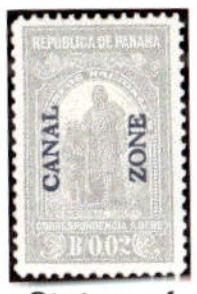
Statue of Columbus D2

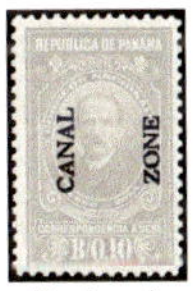
Pedro J. Sosa D3

**1915, Mar. Unwmk.**

| | | | |
|---|---|---|---|
| **J4** D1 | 1c olive brown | 11.00 | 5.00 |
| **J5** D2 | 2c olive brown | 225.00 | 17.50 |
| **J6** D3 | 10c olive brown | 50.00 | 10.00 |
| | *Nos. J4-J6 (3)* | 286.00 | 32.50 |

Type D1 was intended to show a gate of San Lorenzo Castle, Chagres, and is so labeled. By error the stamp actually shows the main gate of San Geronimo Castle, Portobelo.

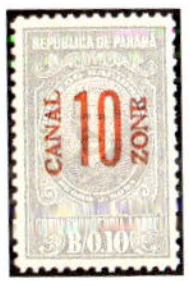
Surcharged in Red

**1915, Nov.**

| | | | |
|---|---|---|---|
| **J7** D1 | 1c on 1c olive brown | 110.00 | 14.00 |
| **J8** D2 | 2c on 2c olive brown | 22.50 | 7.50 |
| **J9** D3 | 10c on 10c olive brown | 22.50 | 5.00 |
| | *Nos. J7-J9 (3)* | 155.00 | 26.50 |

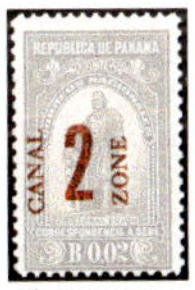
Columbus Statue D4

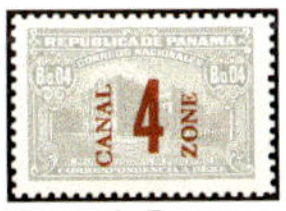
Capitol, Panama City D5

**1919, Dec.**

**Surcharged in Carmine by Panama Canal Press, Mount Hope, C. Z.**

**"Canal Zone" Type III**

| | | | |
|---|---|---|---|
| **J10** D4 | 2c on 2c olive brown | 40.00 | 12.50 |
| **J11** D5 | 4c on 4c olive brown | 45.00 | 15.00 |
| *a.* | "ZONE" omitted | *9,250.* | |
| *b.* | "4" omitted | *8,500.* | |

**Blue Overprint, Type V, on Postage Due Stamp of Panama**

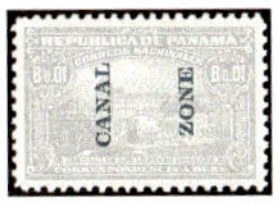

**1922**

| | | | |
|---|---|---|---|
| **J11C** D1 | 1c dark olive brown | — | 5.00 |
| *d.* | "CANAL ZONE" reading down | 200.00 | |

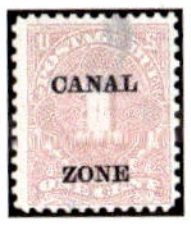
United States Postage Due Stamps Nos. J61, J62b and J65b Overprinted

**Type A**

**Letters "A" with Flat Tops**

**1924, July 1 *Perf. 11***

| | | | |
|---|---|---|---|
| **J12** D2 | 1c carmine rose | 110.00 | 27.50 |
| **J13** D2 | 2c deep claret | 55.00 | 15.00 |
| **J14** D2 | 10c deep claret | 250.00 | 50.00 |
| | *Nos. J12-J14 (3)* | 415.00 | 92.50 |

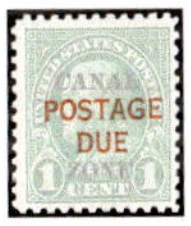
U.S. Postage Stamps Nos. 552, 554 and 562 Overprinted Type A and additional Overprint in Red or Blue

**1925, Feb.**

| | | | |
|---|---|---|---|
| **J15** A155 | 1c deep green (R) | 90.00 | 15.00 |
| **J16** A157 | 2c carmine (Bl) | 22.50 | 7.00 |
| **J17** A165 | 10c orange (R) | 55.00 | 11.00 |
| *a.* | "POSTAGE DUE" double | 800.00 | |
| *b.* | "E" of "POSTAGE" omitted | 750.00 | |
| *c.* | As "b," "POSTAGE DUE" double | *3,250.* | |
| | *Nos. J15-J17 (3)* | 167.50 | 33.00 |

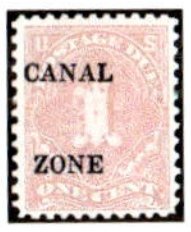
On U.S. Postage Due Stamps Nos. J61, J62, J65, J65a

**Overprinted Type B**

**Letters "A" with Sharp Pointed Tops**

**1925, June 24**

| | | | |
|---|---|---|---|
| **J18** D2 | 1c carmine rose | 8.00 | 2.75 |
| *a.* | "ZONE ZONE" (LR18) | 1,500. | |
| **J19** D2 | 2c carmine rose | 15.00 | 2.75 |
| *a.* | "ZONE ZONE" (LR18) | 1,500. | |
| **J20** D2 | 10c carmine rose | 150.00 | 20.00 |
| *a.* | Vert. pair, one without ovpt. | *3,000.* | |
| *b.* | 10c rose red | *250.00* | 150.00 |
| *c.* | As "b," double overprint | *450.00* | — |
| | *Nos. J18-J20 (3)* | 173.00 | 25.50 |

**Regular Issue of 1928-29 Surcharged**

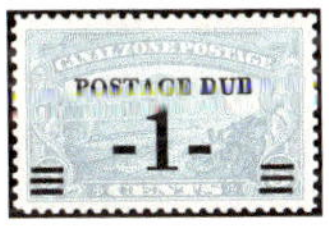

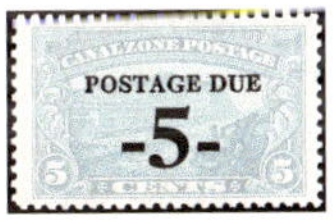

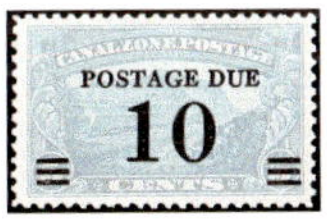

**1929-30**

| | | | | |
|---|---|---|---|---|
| J21 | A37 | 1c on 5c blue | 4.00 | 1.75 |
| | | Never hinged | 8.00 | |
| a. | | "POSTAGE DUE" missing | *5,500.* | |
| J22 | A37 | 2c on 5c blue | 7.50 | 2.50 |
| | | Never hinged | 15.00 | |
| J23 | A37 | 5c on 5c blue | 7.50 | 2.75 |
| | | Never hinged | 15.00 | |
| J24 | A37 | 10c on 5c blue | 7.50 | 2.75 |
| | | Never hinged | 15.00 | |
| | | *Nos. J21-J24 (4)* | 26.50 | 9.75 |

On No. J23 the three short horizontal bars in the lower corners of the surcharge are omitted.

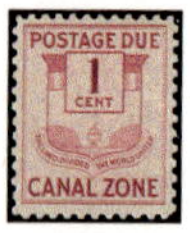
Canal Zone Seal — D6

**1932-41**

| | | | | |
|---|---|---|---|---|
| J25 | D6 | 1c claret | .25 | .25 |
| | | Never hinged | .30 | |
| J26 | D6 | 2c claret | .25 | .25 |
| | | Never hinged | .30 | |
| J27 | D6 | 5c claret | .35 | .25 |
| | | Never hinged | .50 | |
| J28 | D6 | 10c claret | 2.00 | 1.50 |
| | | Never hinged | 3.00 | |
| J29 | D6 | 15c claret | 1.50 | 1.00 |
| | | Never hinged | 2.50 | |
| | | *Nos. J25-J29 (5)* | 4.35 | 3.25 |

## OFFICIAL STAMPS

See note at beginning of Air Post Official Stamps

**Regular Issues of 1928-34 Overprinted in Black**

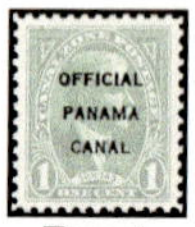
Type 1

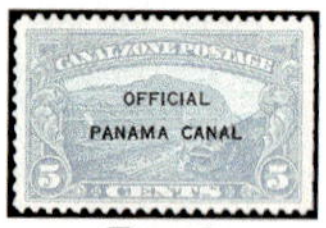
Type 2

Type 1 — "PANAMA" 10mm long
Type 1a — "PANAMA" 9mm long
Type 2 — "PANAMA CANAL" 19-20mm long

**Unwmk.**

**1941, Mar. 31 Engr. *Perf. 11***

| | | | | |
|---|---|---|---|---|
| O1 | A35 | 1c yellow green, type 1 | 2.00 | .40 |
| O2 | A45 | 3c deep violet, type 1 | 3.75 | .75 |
| O3 | A37 | 5c blue, type 2 | *1,000.* | 25.00 |
| O4 | A38 | 10c orange, type 1 | 7.50 | 1.90 |
| O5 | A41 | 15c gray black, type 1 | 15.00 | 2.25 |
| O6 | A42 | 20c olive brown, type 1 | 17.50 | 2.75 |
| O7 | A44 | 50c lilac, type 1 | 42.50 | 5.50 |
| O8 | A44 | 50c rose lilac, type 1a | | 550.00 |
| | | *Nos. O1-O2,O4-O7 (6)* | 88.25 | 13.55 |

**No. 139 Overprinted in Black**

**1947, Feb.**

| | | | | |
|---|---|---|---|---|
| O9 | A65 | 5c deep blue, type 1 | 12.50 | 3.75 |

# CUBA

'kyü-bə

LOCATION — The largest island of the West Indies; south of Florida.
GOVT. — socialist; under US military governor 1899-1902 and US provisional governor 1906-1909.
AREA — 44,206 sq. mi.
POP. — 9,710,000 (1981)
CAPITAL — Havana

Formerly a Spanish possession, Cuba's attempts to gain freedom led to US intervention in 1898. Under Treaty of Paris of that year, Spain relinquished the island to US trust. In 1902, a republic was established and Cuban Congress took over government from US military authorities.

100 Cents = 1 Dollar

**Watermark**

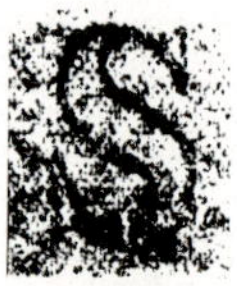
Wmk. 191 — Double-lined "USPS" in Capitals

The basic stamps used for overprinting at Puerto Principe are normally poorly centered. Values for Nos. 176-220 are for stamps with fine centering, as typically found. Furthermore, values are for stamps accompanied by certificates issued by competent experts. Convincing fakes and counterfeits are plentiful.

Values for Nos. 221-J4 are for very fine examples.

**Issued under Administration of the United States**

**Puerto Principe Issue**

Issues of Cuba of 1898 and 1896 Surcharged

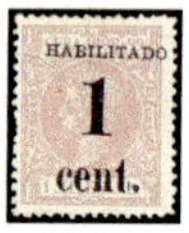
a

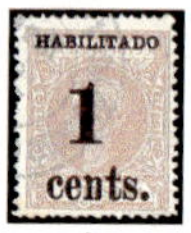
b

**Black Surcharge on Nos. 156-158, 160**

Types a, c, d, e, f, g and h are 17½mm high, the others are 19½mm high.

**1898-99**

| | | | | |
|---|---|---|---|---|
| 176 | A19 (a) | 1c on 1m org brn | 100.00 | 60.00 |
| 177 | A19 (b) | 1c on 1m org brn | 600.00 | 115.00 |
| a. | | Broken figure "1" | *3,000.* | 275.00 |
| b. | | Inverted surcharge | | *500.00* |
| d. | | As "a," inverted | | *1,500.* |

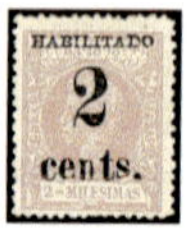
c

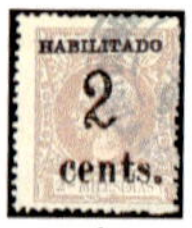
d

| | | | | |
|---|---|---|---|---|
| 178 | A19 (c) | 2c on 2m org brn | 65.00 | 62.50 |
| a. | | Inverted surcharge | 500.00 | 100.00 |
| 179 | A19 (d) | 2c on 2m org brn | 82.50 | 77.50 |
| a. | | Inverted surcharge | — | *500.00* |

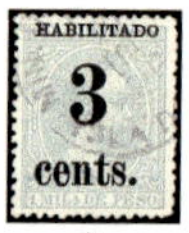
k

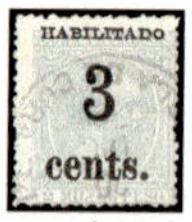
l

| | | | | |
|---|---|---|---|---|
| 179B | A19 (k) | 3c on 1m org brn | 300. | 175. |
| c. | | Double surcharge | — | *3,000.* |

An unused example is known with "cents" omitted.

| | | | | |
|---|---|---|---|---|
| 179D | A19 (l) | 3c on 1m org brn | *1,350.* | *675.00* |

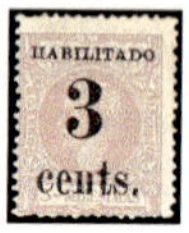
e

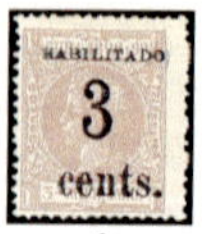
f

| | | | | |
|---|---|---|---|---|
| 179F | A19 (e) | 3c on 2m org brn | | *1,500.* |

Value is for examples with minor faults.

| | | | | |
|---|---|---|---|---|
| 179G | A19 (f) | 3c on 2m org brn | — | *2,000.* |

Value is for examples with minor faults.

| | | | | |
|---|---|---|---|---|
| 180 | A19 (e) | 3c on 3m org brn | 150. | *100.* |
| a. | | Inverted surcharge | | 375. |
| 181 | A19 (f) | 3c on 3m org brn | 600. | 400. |
| a. | | Inverted surcharge | | *750.* |

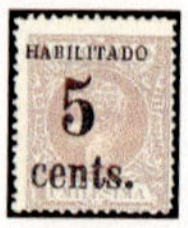
g

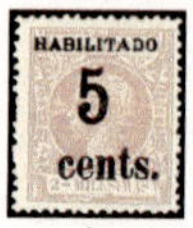
h

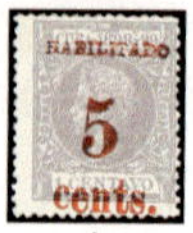
i

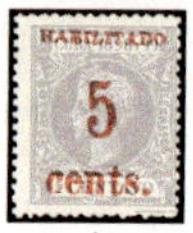
j

| | | | | |
|---|---|---|---|---|
| 182 | A19 (g) | 5c on 1m org brn | 1,000. | 165. |
| a. | | Inverted surcharge | — | *1,000.* |
| 183 | A19 (h) | 5c on 1m org brn | *1,500.* | *1,000.* |
| a. | | Inverted surcharge | — | *1,500.* |
| 184 | A19 (g) | 5c on 2m org brn | 1,000. | 275. |
| 185 | A19 (h) | 5c on 2m org brn | 1,500. | 600. |
| 186 | A19 (g) | 5c on 3m org brn | 1,500. | 350. |
| a. | | Inverted surcharge | 1,200. | 700. |
| 187 | A19 (h) | 5c on 3m org brn | — | 1,000. |
| a. | | Inverted surcharge | — | *1,000.* |
| 188 | A19 (g) | 5c on 5m org brn | 145. | 230. |
| a. | | Inverted surcharge | — | 750. |
| b. | | Double surcharge | — | — |
| 189 | A19 (h) | 5c on 5m org brn | 3,000. | 425. |
| a. | | Inverted surcharge | *3,000.* | *900.* |
| b. | | Double surcharge | — | — |

The 2nd printing of Nos. 188-189 has shiny ink. Values are for the 1st printing.

| | | | | |
|---|---|---|---|---|
| 189C | A19 (i) | 5c on 5m org brn | | *7,500.* |

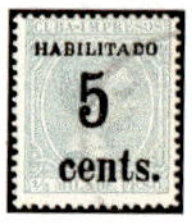
No. 191

**Black Surcharge on No. P25**

| | | | | |
|---|---|---|---|---|
| 190 | N2 (g) | 5c on ½m bl grn | 375. | 115. |
| a. | | Inverted surcharge | 1,000. | 210. |
| b. | | Pair, one without surcharge | | 500. |

Value for 190b is for pair with unsurcharged stamp at right. Also exists with unsurcharged stamp at left.

| | | | | |
|---|---|---|---|---|
| 191 | N2 (h) | 5c on ½m bl grn | 1,000. | 275. |
| a. | | Inverted surcharge | | *1,000.* |
| 192 | N2 (i) | 5c on ½m bl grn | 3,000. | 100. |
| a. | | Dbl. surch., one diagonal | *3,500.* | — |
| 193 | N2 (j) | 5c on ½m bl grn | 900. | 500. |

**Red Surcharge on No. 161**

| | | | | |
|---|---|---|---|---|
| 196 | A19 (k) | 3c on 1c blk vio | 150. | 125. |
| a. | | Inverted surcharge | | 500. |
| 197 | A19 (l) | 3c on 1c blk vio | 250. | 200. |
| a. | | Inverted surcharge | | *1,500.* |
| 198 | A19 (i) | 5c on 1c blk vio | 92.50 | 72.50 |
| a. | | Inverted surcharge | | 500. |
| b. | | Surcharge vert. reading up | | — |
| c. | | Double surcharge | *600.* | *2,750.* |
| d. | | Double invtd. surch. | | — |

Value for No. 198b is for surcharge reading up. One example is known with surcharge reading down.

| | | | | |
|---|---|---|---|---|
| 199 | A19 (j) | 5c on 1c blk vio | 150. | 115. |
| a. | | Inverted surcharge | | *3,000.* |
| b. | | Vertical surcharge | — | — |
| c. | | Double surcharge | *3,000.* | *3,000.* |

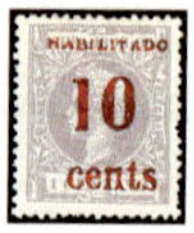
m

| | | | | |
|---|---|---|---|---|
| 200 | A19 (m) | 10c on 1c blk vio | 62.50 | *92.50* |
| a. | | Broken figure "1" | 160.00 | *225.00* |

**Black Surcharge on Nos. P26-P30**

| | | | | |
|---|---|---|---|---|
| 201 | N2 (k) | 3c on 1m bl grn | 350. | 350. |
| a. | | Inverted surcharge | | 450. |
| b. | | "EENTS" | 600. | 450. |
| c. | | As "b", inverted | | 850. |
| 202 | N2 (l) | 3c on 1m bl grn | 1,000. | 400. |
| a. | | Inverted surcharge | | 850. |
| 203 | N2 (k) | 3c on 2m bl grn | 1,650. | 400. |
| a. | | "EENTS" | 1,650. | 500. |
| b. | | Inverted surcharge | | 1,500. |
| c. | | As "a," inverted | | *2,750.* |
| 204 | N2 (l) | 3c on 2m bl grn | 2,750. | 600. |
| a. | | Inverted surcharge | | *1,500.* |
| 205 | N2 (k) | 3c on 3m bl grn | 900. | 400. |
| a. | | Inverted surcharge | | 750. |
| b. | | "EENTS" | 1,250. | 450. |
| c. | | As "b," inverted | | *2,750.* |
| 206 | N2 (l) | 3c on 3m bl grn | 1,500. | 550. |
| a. | | Inverted surcharge | | *1,000.* |
| 211 | N2 (i) | 5c on 1m bl grn | | 1,800. |
| a. | | "EENTS" | — | 3,000. |
| 212 | N2 (j) | 5c on 1m bl grn | — | 2,250. |
| 213 | N2 (i) | 5c on 2m bl grn | 3,000. | 1,800. |
| a. | | "EENTS" | 3,000. | 3,000. |
| 214 | N2 (j) | 5c on 2m bl grn | 3,250. | 1,750. |
| 215 | N2 (i) | 5c on 3m bl grn | | 550. |
| a. | | "EENTS" | | 1,000. |
| 216 | N2 (j) | 5c on 3m bl grn | 3,000. | 1,000. |
| 217 | N2 (i) | 5c on 4m bl grn | *3,000.* | 900. |
| a. | | "EENTS" | *3,000.* | 1,500. |
| b. | | Inverted surcharge | | *2,000.* |
| c. | | As "a," inverted | | *3,000.* |
| 218 | N2 (j) | 5c on 4m bl grn | 3,000. | *1,500.* |
| a. | | Inverted surcharge | | *2,000.* |
| 219 | N2 (i) | 5c on 8m bl grn | *2,500.* | 1,250. |
| a. | | Inverted surcharge | | 1,500. |
| b. | | "EENTS" | 3,000. | 2,750. |
| c. | | As "b," inverted | | 2,500. |
| 220 | N2 (j) | 5c on 8m bl grn | | 2,000. |
| a. | | Inverted surcharge | | 2,500. |

Beware of forgeries of the Puerto Principe issue. Obtaining expert opinions is recommended.

United States Stamps Nos. 279, 267, 267b, 279Bf, 279Bh, 268, 281, 282C and 283 Surcharged in Black

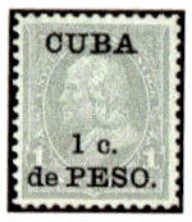

**1899 Wmk. 191 *Perf. 12***

| | | | | |
|---|---|---|---|---|
| 221 | A87 | 1c on 1c yel grn | 4.50 | .40 |
| | | Never hinged | 11.50 | |
| 222 | A88 | 2c on 2c reddish car, III | 10.00 | .75 |
| | | Never hinged | 25.00 | |
| b. | | 2c on 2c vermilion, type III | 10.00 | .75 |
| 222A | A88 | 2c on 2c reddish car, IV | 6.00 | .40 |
| | | Never hinged | 15.00 | |
| c. | | 2c on 2c vermilion, IV | 6.00 | .40 |
| d. | | As No. 222A, inverted surcharge | *5,500.* | *4,000.* |
| 223 | A88 | 2½c on 2c reddish car, III | 6.00 | .80 |
| | | Never hinged | 15.00 | |
| b. | | 2½c on 2c vermilion, III | 6.00 | .80 |
| 223A | A88 | 2½c on 2c reddish car, IV | 3.50 | .50 |
| | | Never hinged | 8.75 | |
| c. | | 2½c on 2c vermilion, IV | 3.50 | .50 |
| 224 | A89 | 3c on 3c purple | 12.00 | 1.75 |
| | | Never hinged | 30.00 | |
| a. | | Period between "B" and "A" | 40.00 | 35.00 |
| 225 | A91 | 5c on 5c blue | 12.50 | 2.00 |
| | | Never hinged | 30.00 | |
| 226 | A94 | 10c on 10c brn, I | 25.00 | 6.00 |
| | | Never hinged | 70.00 | |
| b. | | "CUBA" omitted | *7,000.* | *4,000.* |
| 226A | A94 | 10c on 10c brn, II | *6,000.* | |
| | | *Nos. 221-226 (8)* | 79.50 | 12.60 |

The 2½c was sold and used as a 2c stamp. Excellent counterfeits of this and the preceding issue exist, especially inverted and double surcharges.

**Issues of the Republic under US Military Rule**

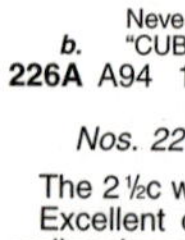
Statue of Columbus A20

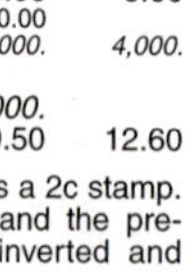
Royal Palms A21

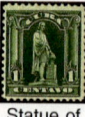

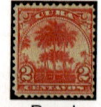

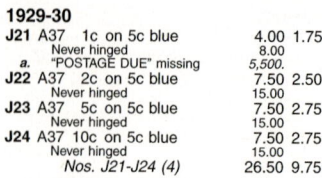

# CUBA — DANISH WEST INDIES AND UNITED STATES VIRGIN ISLANDS

"Cuba" A22

Ocean Liner A23

Cane Field — A24

### 1899    Wmk. US-C (191C)    Perf. 12
| | | | | |
|---|---|---|---|---|
| 227 | A20 | 1c yellow green | 3.50 | .25 |
| | | Never hinged | 8.75 | |
| 228 | A21 | 2c carmine | 3.50 | .25 |
| | | Never hinged | 8.75 | |
| a. | | scarlet | 3.50 | .25 |
| b. | | Booklet pane of 6 | 5,500. | |
| 229 | A22 | 3c purple | 3.50 | .30 |
| | | Never hinged | 8.75 | |
| 230 | A23 | 5c blue | 4.50 | .30 |
| | | Never hinged | 11.00 | |
| 231 | A24 | 10c brown | 11.00 | .80 |
| | | Never hinged | 27.50 | |
| | | Nos. 227-231 (5) | 26.00 | 1.90 |

No. 228b was issued by the Republic. See Nos. 233-237 in Scott Standard Catalogue Vol 2. For surcharge see No. 232.

## SPECIAL DELIVERY STAMPS

### Issued under Administration of the United States

US No. E5 Surcharged in Red

### 1899    Wmk. 191    Perf. 12
| | | | | |
|---|---|---|---|---|
| E1 | SD3 | 10c blue | 130. | 100. |
| | | Never hinged | 300. | |
| a. | | No period after "CUBA" | 575. | 400. |

### Issue of the Republic under US Military Rule

Special Delivery Messenger — SD2

### Printed by the US Bureau of Engraving and Printing

### 1899    Wmk. US-C (191C)
### Inscribed: "Immediata"
| | | | | |
|---|---|---|---|---|
| E2 | SD2 | 10c orange | 52.50 | 15.00 |
| | | Never hinged | 120.00 | |

## POSTAGE DUE STAMPS

### Issued under Administration of the United States

Postage Due Stamps of the United States Nos. J38, J39, J41 and J42 Srchd in Black Like Nos. 221-226A

### 1899    Wmk. 191    Perf. 12
| | | | | |
|---|---|---|---|---|
| J1 | D2 | 1c dp claret | 45.00 | 5.25 |
| | | Never hinged | 110.00 | |
| J2 | D2 | 2c dp claret | 45.00 | 5.25 |
| | | Never hinged | 110.00 | |
| a. | | Inverted surcharge | | 4,000. |
| J3 | D2 | 5c dp claret | 42.50 | 5.25 |
| | | Never hinged | 105.00 | |
| J4 | D2 | 10c dp claret | 25.00 | 2.50 |
| | | Never hinged | 60.00 | |
| | | Nos. J1-J4 (4) | 157.50 | 18.25 |

## DANISH WEST INDIES AND UNITED STATES VIRGIN ISLANDS

ˈdā-nish ˈwest ˈin-dēs

**LOCATION** — Group of islands in the West Indies, lying east of Puerto Rico
**GOVT.** — Danish colony
**AREA** — 132 sq. mi.
**POP.** — 27,086 (1911)
**CAPITAL** — Charlotte Amalie

The US bought these islands in 1917 and they became the US Virgin Islands, using US stamps and currency.

100 Cents = 1 Dollar
100 Bit = 1 Franc (1905)

Wmk. 111 — Small Crown

Wmk. 112 — Crown

Wmk. 113 Crown

Wmk. 114 — Multiple Crosses

Coat of Arms — A1

### Yellowish Paper
### Yellow Wavy-line Burelage, UL to LR

### 1856    Typo.    Wmk. 111    Imperf.
| | | | | |
|---|---|---|---|---|
| 1 | A1 | 3c dark carmine, brown gum | 210. | 235. |
| a. | | 3c dark carmine, yellow gum | 350. | 375. |
| b. | | 3c carmine, white gum | 3,750. | 3,750. |

No. 228b was issued by the Republic. The brown and yellow gums were applied locally.
*Reprint: 1981, carmine, back-printed across two stamps ("Reprint by Dansk Post og Telegrafmuseum 1978"), value, pair, $10.*

### White Paper

### 1866
### Yellow Wavy-line Burelage UR to LL
| | | | | |
|---|---|---|---|---|
| 2 | A1 | 3c rose | 42.50 | 50. |

*No. 2 reprints, unwatermarked. 1930, carmine, value $100. 1942, rose carmine, back-printed across each row ("Nytryk 1942 G. A. Hagemann Danmark og Dansk Vestindiens Frimaerker Bind 2"), value $50.*

### 1872     Perf. 12½
| | | | | |
|---|---|---|---|---|
| 3 | A1 | 3c rose | 130. | 320. |

### 1873    Without Burelage
| | | | | |
|---|---|---|---|---|
| 4 | A1 | 4c dull blue | 325. | 700. |
| a. | | Imperf., pair | 775. | |
| b. | | Horiz. pair, imperf. vert. | 575. | |

*The 1930 reprint of No. 4 is ultramarine, unwatermarked and imperf., value $100. The 1942 4c reprint is blue, unwatermarked, imperf. and has printing on back (see note below No. 2), value $60.*

A2

Normal Frame     Inverted Frame

The arabesques in the corners have a main stem and a branch. When the frame is in normal position, in the upper left corner the branch leaves the main stem half way between two little leaflets. In the lower right corner the branch starts at the foot of the second leaflet. When the frame is inverted the corner designs are, of course, transposed.
Values for inverted frames, covers and blocks are for the cheapest variety.

### White Wove Paper
### Varying from Thin to Thick
### 1874-79    Wmk. 112    Perf. 14x13½
| | | | | |
|---|---|---|---|---|
| 5 | A2 | 1c green & brown red | 35.00 | 32.50 |
| a. | | 1c green & rose lilac, thin paper | 160.00 | 190.00 |
| b. | | 1c green & red violet, medium paper | 50.00 | 65.00 |
| c. | | 1c green & claret, thick paper | 32.50 | 26.00 |
| e. | | As "c," inverted frame | 40.00 | 26.00 |
| f. | | As "a," inverted frame | 900.00 | 1,900. |

No. 5 exists with a surcharge similar to the surcharge on No. 15, with 10 CENTS value and 1895 date. This stamp is an essay.

| | | | | |
|---|---|---|---|---|
| 6 | A2 | 3c blue & carmine | 35.00 | 18.00 |
| a. | | 3c light blue & rose carmine, thin paper | 45.00 | 35.00 |
| b. | | 3c deep blue & dark carmine, medium paper | 45.00 | 25.00 |
| c. | | 3c greenish blue & lake, thick paper | 29.00 | 18.00 |
| d. | | Imperf., pair | 325.00 | — |
| e. | | Inverted frame, thick paper | 45.00 | 35.00 |
| f. | | As "a," inverted frame | 800.00 | 1,200. |
| 7 | A2 | 4c brown & dull blue | 23.00 | 22.50 |
| b. | | 4c brown & ultramarine, thin paper | 290.00 | 250.00 |
| c. | | Diagonal half used as 2c on cover | | 103.00 |
| d. | | As "b," inverted frame | 1,450. | 2,400. |
| 8 | A2 | 5c grn & gray ('76) | 45.00 | 29.00 |
| a. | | 5c yellow green & dark gray, thin paper | 85.00 | 45.00 |
| b. | | Inverted frame, thick paper | 37.50 | 26.00 |
| 9 | A2 | 7c lilac & orange | 40.00 | 135.00 |
| a. | | 7c lilac & yellow | 120.00 | 130.00 |
| b. | | Inverted frame | 65.00 | 220.00 |
| 10 | A2 | 10c blue & brn ('76) | 57.50 | 34.00 |
| b. | | 10c dark blue & black brown, thin paper | 85.00 | 47.50 |
| c. | | Period between "t" & "s" of "cents" | 72.50 | 47.50 |
| d. | | Inverted frame | 26.00 | 27.50 |
| 11 | A2 | 12c red lil & yel grn ('77) | 60.00 | 170.00 |
| a. | | 12c lilac & deep green | 230.00 | 240.00 |
| 12 | A2 | 14c lilac & green | 1,050. | 1,750. |
| a. | | Inverted frame | 4,000. | 4,800. |
| 13 | A2 | 50c vio, thin paper ('79) | 260.00 | 390.00 |
| a. | | 50c gray violet, thick paper | 310.00 | 525.00 |
| | | Nos. 5-13 (9) | 1,606. | 2,581. |

The central element in the fan-shaped scrollwork at the outside of the lower left corner of Nos. 5a and 7b looks like an elongated diamond.
See Nos. 16-20. For surcharges see Nos. 14-15, 23-28, 40.

### No. 9 Surcharged in Black

a

### 1887
| | | | | |
|---|---|---|---|---|
| 14 | A2 (a) | 1c on 7c lilac & orange | 140.00 | 275.00 |
| b. | | 1c on 7c lilac & yellow | 190.00 | 300.00 |
| d. | | Inverted frame | 175.00 | 525.00 |

### No. 13 Surcharged in Black

b

### 1895
| | | | | |
|---|---|---|---|---|
| 15 | A2 (b) | 10c on 50c violet, thin paper | 45.00 | 72.50 |

The "b" surcharge also exists on No. 5, with "10" found in two sizes. These are essays.

### Type of 1874-79

### 1896-1901     Perf. 13
| | | | | |
|---|---|---|---|---|
| 16 | A2 | 1c grn & red vio, inverted frame ('98) | 26.00 | 36.50 |
| a. | | Normal frame | 590.00 | 735.00 |
| 17 | A2 | 3c blue & lake, inverted frame ('98) | 15.50 | 17.00 |
| a. | | Normal frame | 400.00 | 600.00 |
| 18 | A2 | 4c bister & dull blue ('01) | 21.50 | 13.50 |
| a. | | Diagonal half used as 2c on cover | | 67.50 |
| b. | | Inverted frame | 85.00 | 110.00 |
| c. | | As "b," diagonal half used as 2c on cover | | 425.00 |
| 19 | A2 | 5c green & gray, inverted frame | 47.50 | 42.50 |
| a. | | Normal frame | 1,375. | 1,700. |
| 20 | A2 | 10c blue & brn ('01) | 110.00 | 145.00 |
| a. | | Inverted frame | 1,550. | 2,925. |
| b. | | Period between "t" and "s" of "cents" | 155.00 | 180.00 |
| | | Nos. 16-20 (5) | 220.50 | 254.50 |

Arms — A5

### 1900
| | | | | |
|---|---|---|---|---|
| 21 | A5 | 1c light green | 2.60 | 2.25 |
| 22 | A5 | 5c light blue | 17.00 | 25.00 |

See Nos. 29-30. For surcharges see Nos. 41-42.

### Nos. 6, 17, 20 Surcharged

c

### Surcharge "c" in Black
### 1902     Perf. 14x13½
| | | | | |
|---|---|---|---|---|
| 23 | A2 | 2c on 3c blue & carmine, inverted frame | 1,075. | 1,450. |
| a. | | "2" in date with straight tail | 1,200. | 1,600. |
| b. | | Normal frame | | |

### Perf. 13
| | | | | |
|---|---|---|---|---|
| 24 | A2 | 2c on 3c blue & lake, inverted frame | 11.50 | 32.00 |
| a. | | "2" in date with straight tail | 30.00 | 50.00 |
| b. | | Dated "1001" | 1,000. | 1,000. |
| c. | | Normal frame | 320.00 | 825.00 |
| d. | | Dark green surcharge | 3,000. | — |
| e. | | As "d" & "a" | — | — |
| f. | | As "d" & "c" | | |

The overprint on No. 24b exists in two types: with "1901" measuring 2.5 mm or 2.2 mm high.
Only one example of No. 24f can exist.

| | | | | |
|---|---|---|---|---|
| 25 | A2 | 8c on 10c blue & brown | 26.00 | 55.00 |
| a. | | "2" with straight tail | 35.00 | 65.00 |
| b. | | On No. 20b | 55.00 | 85.00 |
| c. | | Inverted frame | 300.00 | 675.00 |

d

### Surcharge "d" in Black
### 1902     Perf. 13
| | | | | |
|---|---|---|---|---|
| 27 | A2 | 2c on 3c blue & lake, inverted frame | 15.75 | 63.00 |
| a. | | Normal frame | 415.00 | 720.00 |
| 28 | A2 | 8c on 10c blue & brown | 14.00 | 15.00 |
| a | | On No. 20b | 26.00 | 32.00 |
| b. | | Inverted frame | 415.00 | 675.00 |
| | | Nos. 23-28 (5) | 1,142. | 1,615. |

### 1903     Wmk. 113
| | | | | |
|---|---|---|---|---|
| 29 | A5 | 2c carmine | 9.50 | 25.00 |
| 30 | A5 | 8c brown | 36.00 | 62.00 |

King Christian IX — A8

St. Thomas Harbor — A9

### 1905    Typo.    Perf. 13
| | | | | |
|---|---|---|---|---|
| 31 | A8 | 5b green | 4.75 | 3.00 |
| 32 | A8 | 10b red | 4.75 | 3.00 |
| 33 | A8 | 20b green & blue | 9.50 | 8.00 |
| 34 | A8 | 25b ultramarine | 9.50 | 8.00 |
| 35 | A8 | 40b red & gray | 9.50 | 7.00 |
| 36 | A8 | 50b yellow & gray | 14.00 | 11.00 |

### Perf. 12
### Wmk. Two Crowns (113)
### Frame Typographed, Center Engraved
| | | | | |
|---|---|---|---|---|
| 37 | A9 | 1fr green & blue | 17.50 | 50.00 |
| 38 | A9 | 2fr orange red & brown | 32.50 | 67.50 |
| 39 | A9 | 5fr yellow & brown | 85.00 | 315.00 |
| | | Nos. 31-39 (9) | 187.00 | 472.50 |

Favor cancels exist on Nos. 37-39. Value 25% less.

237

Nos. 18, 22 and 30 Surcharged in Black

**1905 Wmk. 112**

| | | | |
|---|---|---|---|
| **40** | A2 5b on 4c bister & dull blue | 17.50 | *70.00* |
| *a.* | Inverted frame | 110.00 | *190.00* |
| **41** | A5 5b on 5c light blue | 13.00 | *64.00* |
| | **Wmk. 113** | | |
| **42** | A5 5b on 8c brown | 13.00 | *75.00* |
| | *Nos. 40-42 (3)* | 43.50 | 209.00 |

Favor cancels exist on Nos. 40-42. Value 25% less.

Frederik VIII — A10

**Frame Typographed, Center Engraved**

**1908**

| | | | |
|---|---|---|---|
| **43** | A10 5b green | 2.75 | 1.90 |
| **44** | A10 10b red | 2.75 | 1.90 |
| **45** | A10 15b violet & brown | 5.00 | *5.75* |
| **46** | A10 20b green & blue | 32.50 | 27.50 |
| **47** | A10 25b blue & dark blue | 2.25 | *2.50* |
| **48** | A10 30b claret & slate | 67.50 | *60.00* |
| **49** | A10 40b vermilion & gray | 8.00 | *11.50* |
| **50** | A10 50b yellow & brown | 8.50 | *10.00* |
| | *Nos. 43-50 (8)* | 129.25 | 121.05 |

Christian X — A11

**1915 Wmk. 114 *Perf. 14x14½***

| | | | |
|---|---|---|---|
| **51** | A11 5b yellow green | 5.25 | *6.25* |
| **52** | A11 10b red | 5.25 | *110.00* |
| **53** | A11 15b lilac & red brown | 5.25 | *110.00* |
| **54** | A11 20b green & blue | 5.25 | *110.00* |
| **55** | A11 25b blue & dark blue | 5.25 | *16.00* |
| **56** | A11 30b claret & black | 5.25 | *200.00* |
| **57** | A11 40b orange & black | 5.25 | *200.00* |
| **58** | A11 50b yellow & brown | 5.25 | *200.00* |
| | *Nos. 51-58 (8)* | 42.00 | *952.25* |

Forged and favor cancellations exist.

## POSTAGE DUE STAMPS

Royal Cipher, "Christian 9 Rex" — D1

**1902 Litho. Unwmk. *Perf. 11½***

| | | | |
|---|---|---|---|
| **J1** | D1 1c dark blue | 8.25 | *45.00* |
| **J2** | D1 4c dark blue | 20.00 | *45.00* |
| **J3** | D1 6c dark blue | 40.00 | *87.50* |
| **J4** | D1 10c dark blue | 40.00 | *87.50* |
| | *Nos. J1-J4 (4)* | 108.25 | *265.00* |

There are five types of each value. On the 4c they may be distinguished by differences in the figure "4"; on the other values differences are minute.

Used values of Nos. J1-J8 are for canceled stamps. Uncanceled stamps without gum have probably been used. Value 60% of unused.

Excellent counterfeits of Nos. J1-J4 exist.

Numeral of value — D2

**1905-13 *Perf. 13***

| | | | |
|---|---|---|---|
| **J5** | D2 5b red & gray | 6.50 | *8.00* |
| **J6** | D2 20b red & gray | 11.50 | *14.50* |
| **J7** | D2 30b red & gray | 9.50 | *14.50* |
| **J8** | D2 50b red & gray | 9.00 | *36.00* |
| *a.* | Perf. 14x14½ ('13) | 75.00 | *290.00* |
| *b.* | Perf. 11½ | 475.00 | |
| | *Nos. J5-J8 (4)* | 36.50 | *73.00* |

All values of this issue are known imperforate, but were not regularly issued.

Used values of Nos. J5-J8 are for canceled stamps. Uncanceled examples without gum have probably been used. Value 60% of unused.

No. J8b is valued in the grade of fine.

Counterfeits of Nos. J5-J8 exist.

Danish West Indies stamps were replaced by those of the U.S. in 1917, after the U.S. bought the islands.

# GUAM

ˈgwäm

LOCATION — One of the Mariana Islands in the Pacific Ocean, about 1450 miles east of the Philippines
GOVT. — United States Possession
AREA — 206 sq. mi.
POP. — 9,000 (est. 1899)
CAPITAL — Agaña

Formerly a Spanish possession, Guam was ceded to the United States in 1898 following the Spanish-American War. Stamps overprinted "Guam" were superseded by the regular postage stamps of the United States in 1901.

100 Cents = 1 Dollar

United States Nos. 279, 279B, 279Bc, 268, 280a, 281, 282, 272, 282C, 283, 284, 275, 275a, 276 and 276A Overprinted

**1899 Wmk. 191 *Perf. 12***

**Black Overprint**

| | | | |
|---|---|---|---|
| **1** | A87 1c deep green | 20.00 | *25.00* |
| | Never hinged | 40.00 | |

A bogus inverted overprint exists.

| | | | |
|---|---|---|---|
| **2** | A88 2c red, type IV | 17.50 | *25.00* |
| | Never hinged | 35.00 | |
| *a.* | rose carmine, type IV | 30.00 | 30.00 |
| | Never hinged | 60.00 | |
| **3** | A89 3c purple | 140.00 | *175.00* |
| | Never hinged | 275.00 | |
| **4** | A90 4c lilac brown | 125.00 | *175.00* |
| | Never hinged | 250.00 | |
| **5** | A91 5c blue | 32.50 | *45.00* |
| | Never hinged | 65.00 | |
| **6** | A92 6c lake | 125.00 | *190.00* |
| | Never hinged | 250.00 | |
| **7** | A93 8c violet brown | 125.00 | *160.00* |
| | Never hinged | 275.00 | |
| **8** | A94 10c brown, type I | 45.00 | *55.00* |
| | Never hinged | 90.00 | |
| **9** | A94 10c brown, type II | *2,750.* | — |
| | Never hinged | *5,500.* | |
| **10** | A95 15c olive green | 150.00 | 140.00 |
| | Never hinged | 300.00 | |
| **11** | A96 50c orange | 350.00 | *400.00* |
| | Never hinged | 700.00 | |
| *a.* | 50c red orange | 550.00 | — |
| | Never hinged | 1,100. | |
| | **Red Overprint** | | |
| **12** | A97 $1 black, type I | 350.00 | *400.00* |
| | Never hinged | 700.00 | |
| **13** | A97 $1 black, type II | *3,750.* | |
| | Never hinged | — | |
| | *Nos. 1-8,10-12 (11)* | 1,480. | *1,790.* |

Counterfeits of the overprint exist.
No. 13 exists only in the special printing.

## SPECIAL DELIVERY STAMP

United States No. E5 Overprinted in Red

**1899 Wmk. 191 *Perf. 12***

| | | | |
|---|---|---|---|
| **E1** | SD3 10c blue | 150. | *200.00* |
| | Never hinged | 275. | |
| *a.* | Dots in curved frame above messenger (Plate 882) | 200. | |
| | Never hinged | 400. | |

Counterfeits of the overprint exist.

The special stamps for Guam were replaced by the regular issues of the United States.

Guam Guard Mail stamps of 1930 are listed in the Scott U.S. specialized catalogue.

# HAWAII

hə-ˈwä-yē

LOCATION — Group of 20 islands in the Pacific Ocean, about 2,000 miles southwest of San Francisco.
GOVT. — Former Kingdom and Republic
AREA — 6,435 sq. mi.
POP. — 150,000 (est. 1899)
CAPITAL — Honolulu

Until 1893 an independent kingdom, from 1893 to 1898 a republic, the Hawaiian Islands were annexed to the US in 1898. The Territory of Hawaii achieved statehood in 1959.

100 Cents = 1 Dollar

Values for Nos. 1-4 are for examples with minor damage that has been skillfully repaired.

**Values of Hawaii stamps vary considerably according to condition. For Nos. 1-4, values are for examples with minor damage that has been skillfully repaired.**

A1

A2

A3

**1851-52 Unwmk. Typeset *Imperf.***

**Pelure Paper**

| | | | |
|---|---|---|---|
| **1** | A1 2c blue | *625,000.* | *250,000.* |
| **2** | A1 5c blue | *55,000.* | *45,000.* |
| **3** | A2 13c blue | *37,000.* | *32,500.* |
| **4** | A3 13c blue | *52,500.* | *42,500.* |

Nos. 1-4 are known as the "Missionaries."

Two varieties of each. Nos. 1-4, off cover, are almost invariably damaged.

No. 1 unused is unique.

**Values for Nos. 5-82 are for very fine examples. Extremely fine to superb stamps sell at much higher prices, and inferior or poor stamps sell at reduced prices, depending on the condition of the individual example.**

King Kamehameha III

A4

A5

Printed in Sheets of 20 (4x5)

**1853 Engr.**

**Thick White Wove Paper**

| | | | |
|---|---|---|---|
| **5** | A4 5c blue | 1,900. | 1,900. |
| *a.* | Line through "Honolulu" (Pos. 2) | *3,000.* | *3,000.* |
| **6** | A5 13c dark red | 900. | *1,700.* |

See Nos. 8-11.

A6

**1857**

| | | | |
|---|---|---|---|
| **7** | A6 5c on 13c dark red | *7,000.* | *10,000.* |

Beware of fake manuscript surcharges. Expertization is strongly recommended.

**1857 Thin White Wove Paper**

| | | | |
|---|---|---|---|
| **8** | A4 5c blue | 700. | *750.* |
| *a.* | Line through "Honolulu" (Pos. 2) | *1,350.* | *1,350.* |
| *b.* | Double impression | *4,250.* | *4,750.* |

**1861 Thin Bluish Wove Paper**

| | | | |
|---|---|---|---|
| **9** | A4 5c blue | 400. | 400. |
| *a.* | Line through "Honolulu" (Pos. 2) | *950.* | *1,000.* |

**RE-ISSUE**

**1868 Ordinary White Wove Paper**

| | | | |
|---|---|---|---|
| **10** | A4 5c blue | 27.50 | |
| *a.* | Line through "Honolulu" (Pos. 2) | 80. | |
| **11** | A5 13c dull rose | 325. | |

Remainders of Nos. 10 and 11 were overprinted "SPECIMEN." See Nos. 10S-11Sb in the Scott U.S. Specialized Catalogue.

Nos. 10 and 11 were never placed in use but stamps (both with and without overprint) were sold at face value at the Honolulu post office.

**REPRINTS (Official Imitations)**

Original

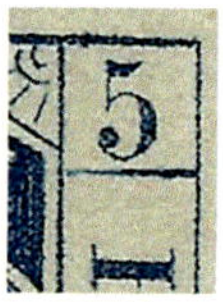

Reprint

Original

Reprint

*5c — Originals have two small dots near the left side of the square in the upper right corner. These dots are missing in the reprints.*

*13c — The bottom of the 3 of 13 in the upper left corner is flattened in the originals and rounded in the reprints. The "t" of "Cts" on the left side is as tall as the "C" in the reprints, but shorter in the originals.*

**1889**

| | | |
|---|---|---|
| **10R** | A4 5c blue | 65. |
| **11R** | A5 13c orange red | 300. |

On August 19, 1892, the remaining supply of reprints was overprinted in black "REPRINT." The reprints (both with and without overprint) were sold at face value. See the Scott U.S. Specialized Catalogue.

**Values for the Numeral stamps, Nos. 12-26, are for examples with four reasonably large margins. Unused values are for stamps without gum.**

A7

A8

A9

**1859-62** **Typeset**

12 A7 1c light blue, *bluish white* 15,000. 15,000.

a. "1 Ce" omitted 22,500.

b. "nt" omitted — —

No. 12a is unique.

13 A7 2c light blue, *bluish white* 6,250. 5,000.

a. 2c dark blue, *grayish white* 6,750. 5,000.

b. Comma after "Cents" — 6,750.

c. No period after "LETA" — —

14 A7 2c black, *greenish blue* ('62) 8,000. 6,000.

a. "2-Cents." —

**1859-63**

15 A7 1c black, *grayish* ('63) 650. 2,750.

a. Tête bêche pair 9,000.

b. "NTER" —

c. Period omitted after "Postage" 850.

d. 1c black, *bluish gray* 850.

16 A7 2c black, *grayish* 1,000. 850.

a. "2" at top of rectangle 3,750. 3,750.

b. Printed on both sides — 21,000.

c. "NTER" 3,250. 6,500.

d. 2c black, *grayish white* 1,000. 850.

e. Period omitted after "Cents" —

f. Overlapping impressions — —

g. "TAGE" —

17 A7 2c dark blue, *bluish* ('63) 12,000. 8,750.

a. "ISL" — —

18 A7 2c black, *blue gray* ('63) 3,250. 6,000.

**1864-65**

19 A7 1c black 625. 10,000.

20 A7 2c black 775. 1,500.

21 A8 5c blue, *blue* ('65) 900. 700.

a. Tête bêche pair 10,500.

b. 5c bluish black, *grayish white* 11,000. 3,750.

No. 21b unused is unique. No. 21b used is also unique but defective.

22 A9 5c blue, *blue* ('65) 575. 900.

a. Tête bêche pair 18,000.

b. 5c blue, *grayish white* —

c. Overlapping impressions —

**1864** **Laid Paper**

23 A7 1c black 300. 2,500.

a. "HA" instead of "HAWAIIAN" 3,500.

b. Tête bêche pair 6,000.

c. Tête bêche pair, Nos. 23, 23a 18,000.

24 A7 2c black 350. 1,050.

a. "NTER" 3,250.

b. "S" of "POSTAGE" omitted 1,500.

c. Tête bêche pair 7,000.

A10

**1865** **Wove Paper**

25 A10 1c dark blue 350.

a. Double impression —

b. With inverted impression of No. 21 on face 18,500.

26 A10 2c dark blue 350.

Nos. 12 to 26 were typeset and were printed in settings of ten, each stamp differing from the others.

King Kamehameha IV — A11

**1861-63** **Litho.**

**Horizontally Laid Paper**

27 A11 2c pale rose 350. 350.

a. 2c carmine rose ('63) 3,000. 2,850.

**Vertically Laid Paper**

28 A11 2c pale rose 325. 325.

a. 2c carmine rose ('63) 400. 450.

**RE-ISSUE**

**1869** **Engr.** **Thin Wove Paper**

29 A11 2c red 45.00 —

No. 29 was not issued for postal purposes although canceled examples are known. It was sold only at the Honolulu post office, at first without overprint and later with overprint "CANCELLED." See No. 29S in the Scott U.S. Specialized Catalogue.

See Nos. 50-51 and note following No. 51.

Princess Victoria Kamamalu — A12

King Kamehameha IV — A13

King Kamehameha V — A14

King Kamehameha V — A15

Mataio Kekuanaoa — A16

**1864-86** **Engr.** ***Perf. 12***

**Wove Paper**

30 A12 1c purple ('86) 11.00 8.00

Never hinged 25.00

a. 1c mauve ('71) 60.00 20.00

Never hinged 95.00

b. 1c violet ('78) 20.00 10.00

Never hinged 45.00

31 A13 2c rose vermilion 65.00 12.50

Never hinged 150.00

a. 2c vermilion ('86) 55.00 17.50

Never hinged 130.00

b. Half used as 1c on cover with #32 7,500.

32 A14 5c blue ('66) 175.00 30.00

Never hinged 375.00

33 A15 6c yellow green ('71) 45.00 10.00

Never hinged 100.00

a. 6c bluish green ('78) 35.00 10.00

Never hinged 85.00

b. As "a," horiz. pair, imperf. 2,250.

34 A16 18c dull rose ('71) 100.00 45.00

Never hinged 220.00

*Nos. 30-34 (5)* 396.00 105.50

Set, never hinged 860.00

No. 32 has traces of rectangular frame lines surrounding the design. Nos. 39 and 52C have no such frame lines.

For overprints see Nos. 53, 58-60, 65, 66C, 71.

King David Kalakaua A17

Prince William Pitt Leleiohoku A18

**1875**

35 A17 2c brown 9.00 3.00

Never hinged 22.00

36 A18 12c black 75.00 32.50

Never hinged 165.00

See Nos. 38, 43, 46. For overprints see Nos. 55, 62-63, 66, 69.

Princess Likelike A19

King David Kalakaua A20

Queen Kapiolani — A21

Statue of King Kamehameha I — A22

King William Lunalilo A23

Queen Emma Kaleleonalani A24

**1882**

37 A19 1c blue 11.00 6.00

Never hinged 27.50

38 A17 2c lilac rose 125.00 47.50

Never hinged 275.00

39 A14 5c ultramarine 15.00 3.00

Never hinged 35.00

a. Vert. pair, imperf. horiz. 5,000. 6,000.

40 A20 10c black 50.00 25.00

Never hinged 115.00

41 A21 15c red brown 70.00 27.50

Never hinged 150.00

*Nos. 37-41 (5)* 271.00 109.00

Set, never hinged 602.50

**1883-86**

42 A19 1c green 3.00 2.00

Never hinged 7.00

43 A17 2c rose ('86) 5.00 1.00

Never hinged 11.00

a. 2c dull red 65.00 22.50

Never hinged 140.00

44 A20 10c red brown ('84) 40.00 12.00

Never hinged 90.00

45 A20 10c vermilion 45.00 14.00

Never hinged 100.00

46 A18 12c red lilac 90.00 40.00

Never hinged 225.00

47 A22 25c dark violet 160.00 65.00

Never hinged 350.00

48 A23 50c red 200.00 95.00

Never hinged 425.00

49 A24 $1 rose red 325.00 275.00

Never hinged 675.00 8,000.

Maltese cross cancellation 150.00

*Nos. 42-49 (8)* 868.00 504.00

Set, never hinged 1,833.

Other fiscal cancellations exist on No. 49.

Nos. 48-49 are valued used with postal cancels. Canceled-to-order cancels exist and are worth less.

**REPRODUCTION and REPRINT**

Yellowish Wove Paper

**1886-89** **Engr.** ***Imperf.***

50 A11 2c orange vermilion 170.00

Never hinged 275.00

51 A11 2c carmine ('89) 35.00

Never hinged 60.00

In 1885, the Postmaster General wished to have on sale complete sets of Hawaii's portrait stamps, but was unable to find either the stone from which Nos. 27 and 28 were printed, or the plate from which No. 29 was printed. He therefore sent an example of No. 29 to the American Bank Note Company, with an order to engrave a new plate like it and print 10,000 stamps therefrom, of which 5000 were overprinted "SPECIMEN" in blue.

The original No. 29 was printed in sheets of fifteen (5x3), but the plate of these "Official Imitations" was made up of fifty stamps (10x5). Later, in 1887, the original die for No. 29 was discovered, and, after retouching, a new plate was made and 37,500 stamps were printed (No. 51). These, like the originals, were printed in sheets of fifteen. They were delivered during 1889 and 1890. In 1892, all remaining unsold in the Post Office were overprinted "Reprint".

No. 29 is red in color, and printed on very thin white wove paper. No. 50 is orange vermilion in color, on medium, white to buff paper. In No. 50 the vertical line on the left side of the portrait touches the horizontal line over the label "Elua Keneta", while in the other two varieties, Nos. 29 and 51, it does not touch the horizontal line by half a millimeter. In No. 51 there are three parallel lines on the left side of the King's nose, while in No. 29 and No. 50 there are no such lines. No. 51 is carmine in color and printed on thick, yellowish to buff, wove paper.

It is claimed that both Nos. 50 and 51 were available for postage, although not made to fill a postal requirement. They exist with favor cancellation. No. 51 also is known postally used. See Nos. 50S-51S in the Scott U.S. specialized catalogue.

Queen Liliuokalani — A25

**1890-91** ***Perf. 12***

52 A25 2c dull violet ('91) 15.00 1.50

Never hinged 25.00

a. Vert. pair, imperf. horiz. 3,750.

52C A14 5c deep indigo 125.00 150.00

Never hinged 280.00

Stamps of 1864-91 Overprinted in Red

Three categories of double overprints:

I. Both overprints heavy.

II. One overprint heavy, one of moderate strength.

III. One overprint heavy, one of light or weak strength.

**1893 Overprinted in Red**

53 A12 1c violet 9.00 13.00
Never hinged 20.00
a. "189" instead of "1893" 600.00 —
b. No period after "GOVT" *275.00 275.00*
f. Double overprint (III) *600.00*
54 A19 1c blue 9.00 *15.00*
Never hinged 21.00
b. No period after "GOVT" *140.00 150.00*
e. Double overprint (II) *1,500.*
f. Double overprint (III) *400.00*
55 A19 1c green 2.00 *3.00*
Never hinged 4.00
d. Double overprint (I) *650.00 650.00*
f. Double overprint (III) *250.00 250.00*
g. Pair, one without ovpt. *10,000.*
56 A17 2c brown 12.50 *20.00*
Never hinged 27.50
b. No period after "GOVT" *325.00* —
57 A25 2c dull violet 2.00 1.50
Never hinged 3.00
a. "18 3" instead of "1893" *900.00 900.00*
d. Double overprint (I) *1,300. 1,000.*
f. Double overprint (III) *190.00 190.00*
g. Inverted overprint *4,000. 4,750.*
58 A14 5c deep indigo 15.00 *30.00*
Never hinged 32.00
b. No period after "GOVT" *275.00 275.00*
f. Double overprint (III) *1,250. 675.00*
59 A14 5c ultramarine 7.00 3.00
Never hinged 15.00
d. Double overprint (I) *6,500.*
e. Double overprint (II) *3,750. 3,750.*
f. Double overprint (III) *600.00*
g. Inverted overprint *1,500. 1,500.*
60 A15 6c green 17.50 *25.00*
Never hinged 40.00
e. Double overprint (II) *1,100.*
61 A20 10c black 14.00 *20.00*
Never hinged 30.00
e. Double overprint (II) *1,000. 900.00*
f. Double overprint (III) *225.00*
61B A20 10c red brown *15,000. 29,000.*
Never hinged *25,000.*
62 A18 12c black 14.00 *20.00*
Never hinged 30.00
d. Double overprint (I) *1,500.*
e. Double overprint (II) *1,100.*
f. Double overprint (III) —
63 A18 12c red lilac 175.00 *250.00*
Never hinged 400.00
64 A22 25c dark violet 35.00 *45.00*
Never hinged 70.00
b. No period after "GOVT" *350.00 350.00*
Never hinged *600.00*
f. Double overprint (III) *1,250.*
*Nos. 53-61,62-64 (12)* 312.00 *445.50*
Nos. 53-61, 62-64 never hinged 692.75

Virtually all known examples of No. 61B are cut in at the top.

Overprinted in Black

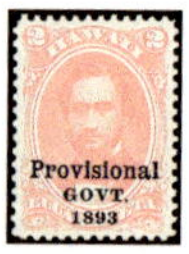

65 A13 2c vermilion 85.00 *90.00*
Never hinged 200.00
b. No period after "GOVT" *300.00 300.00*
66 A17 2c rose 2.50 *2.50*
Never hinged 3.75
b. No period after "GOVT" 70.00 70.00
d. Double overprint (I) *4,000.*
e. Double overprint (II) *2,750.*
f. Double overprint (III) *300.00*
66C A15 6c green *15,000. 29,000.*
67 A20 10c vermilion 22.50 *30.00*
Never hinged 45.00
f. Double overprint (III) *1,250.*
68 A20 10c red brown 12.00 *13.00*
Never hinged 24.00
f. Double overprint (III) *4,000.*
69 A18 12c red lilac 350.00 *500.00*
Never hinged 575.00
70 A21 15c red brown 27.50 *35.00*
Never hinged 55.00
e. Double overprint (II) *2,000.*
71 A16 18c dull rose 40.00 40.00
Never hinged 80.00
a. "18 3" instead of "1893" *525.00 525.00*
b. No period after "GOVT" *350.00 350.00*
d. Double overprint (I) *650.00*
f. Double overprint (III) *275.00* —
g. Pair, one without ovpt. *3,500.*
h. As "b," double overprint (II) *1,750.*
72 A23 50c red 90.00 *120.00*
Never hinged 180.00
b. No period after "GOVT" *500.00 500.00*
Never hinged *775.00*
f. Double overprint (III) *1,000.*

73 A24 $1 rose red 160.00 *190.00*
Never hinged 325.00
b. No period after "GOVT" *525.00* 500.00
*Nos. 65-66,67-73 (9)* 789.50 *1,021.*
Nos. 65-66, 67-73 never hinged 1,485.

Coat of Arms A26

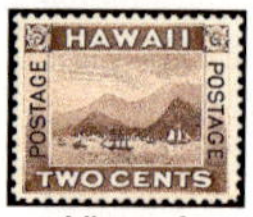

View of Honolulu A27

Statue of Kamehameha I — A28

Stars and Palms A29

S. S. "Arawa" A30

Pres. Sanford Ballard Dole — A31

**1894**

74 A26 1c yellow 2.00 1.50
Never hinged 4.00
75 A27 2c brown 2.00 .60
Never hinged 4.00
76 A28 5c rose lake 5.00 2.00
Never hinged 11.00
77 A29 10c yellow green 8.00 5.00
Never hinged 18.00
78 A30 12c blue 17.50 *20.00*
Never hinged 37.50
79 A31 25c deep blue 22.50 17.50
Never hinged 47.50
*Nos. 74-79 (6)* 57.00 *46.60*
Set, never hinged 122.50

Numerous double transfers exist on Nos. 75 and 81.

"CENTS" Added — A32

**1899**

80 A26 1c dark green 2.00 1.50
Never hinged 4.50
81 A27 2c rose 1.50 1.00
Never hinged 3.50
a. 2c salmon 1.50 1.50
Never hinged 3.50
b. Vert. pair, imperf. horiz. *4,250.*
82 A32 5c blue 8.00 4.00
Never hinged 20.00
*Nos. 80-82 (3)* 11.50 6.50
Set, never hinged 28.00

**OFFICIAL STAMPS**

Lorrin Andrews Thurston — O1

**1896 Engr. Unwmk. *Perf. 12***

O1 O1 2c green 45.00 20.00
Never hinged 90.00
O2 O1 5c black brown 45.00 20.00
Never hinged 90.00
O3 O1 6c deep ultramarine 45.00 20.00
Never hinged 90.00
O4 O1 10c bright rose 45.00 20.00
Never hinged 90.00
O5 O1 12c orange 55.00 22.50
Never hinged 110.00
O6 O1 25c gray violet 65.00 22.50
Never hinged 130.00
*Nos. O1-O6 (6)* 300.00 125.00
Set, never hinged 600.00

Used values for Nos. O1-O6 are for stamps canceled-to-order "FOREIGN OFFICE/HONOLULU H.I." in double circle without date. Values of postally used stamps: Nos. O1-O2, O4, $50 each; No. O3, $125; No. O5, $160; No. O6, $200.

The stamps of Hawaii were replaced by those of the United States.

# PHILIPPINES

ˌfi-lə-ˈpēnz

LOCATION — Group of 7,100 islands and islets in the Malay Archipelago, north of Borneo, in the North Pacific Ocean
GOVT. — US Admin., 1898-1946
AREA — 115,748 sq. mi.
POP. — 16,971,100 (est. 1941)
CAPITAL — Quezon City

The islands were ceded to the US by Spain in 1898. On Nov. 15, 1935, they were given their independence, subject to a transition period which ended July 4, 1946. On that date the Commonwealth became the "Republic of the Philippines."

100 Cents = 1 Dollar (1899)
100 CENTAVOS = 1 PESO (1906)

Wmk. 191PI — Double-lined PIPS

Wmk. 190PI — Single-lined PIPS

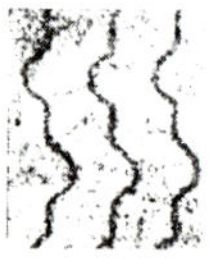

Wmk. 257 — Curved Wavy Lines

**Issued under U.S. Administration**

Regular Issues of the United States Overprinted in Black

**1899-1901 Unwmk. *Perf. 12***
**On U.S. Stamp No. 260**

212 A96 50c orange 300. 225.
Never hinged 775.

**On U.S. Stamps Nos. 279, 279B, 279Bd, 279Bj, 279Bf, 279Bc, 268, 281, 282C, 283, 284, 275, 275a**

Regular Issues of the United States Overprinted in Black

**Wmk. Double-lined USPS (191)**

213 A87 1c yellow green 3.50 .60
Never hinged 10.00
a. Inverted overprint *77,500.*
214 A88 2c red, type IV 1.75 .60
Never hinged 4.25
a. 2c orange red, type IV, ('01) 1.75 .60
Never hinged 4.25
b. Bklt. pane of 6, red, type IV ('00) 200.00 *300.00*
Never hinged 450.00
c. 2c reddish carmine, type IV 2.50 1.00
Never hinged 6.00
d. 2c rose carmine, type IV 3.00 1.10
Never hinged 7.25
215 A89 3c purple 9.00 1.25
Never hinged 21.50
216 A91 5c blue 9.00 1.00
Never hinged 21.50
a. Inverted overprint *6,500.*

No. 216a is valued in the grade of fine.

217 A94 10c brown, type I 35.00 4.00
Never hinged 80.00
217A A94 10c org brn, type II 110.00 27.50
Never hinged 275.00

No. 217A was overprinted on U.S. No. 283a, vertical watermark. The watermark on No. 217 is horizontal.

218 A95 15c olive green 40.00 8.00
Never hinged 95.00
219 A96 50c orange 125.00 37.50
Never hinged 300.00
a. 50c red orange 250.00 55.00
Never hinged 600.00
*Nos. 213-219 (8)* 333.25 80.45

**Regular Issue**

U.S. Stamps Nos. 280b, 282 and 272 Overprinted in Black

**1901, Aug. 30**

220 A90 4c orange brown 35.00 5.00
Never hinged 80.00
221 A92 6c lake 40.00 7.00
Never hinged 95.00
222 A93 8c purple brown 40.00 7.50
Never hinged 95.00
*Nos. 220-222 (3)* 115.00 19.50

**Same Overprint in Red On U.S. Stamps Nos. 276, 276A, 277a and 278**

223 A97 $1 black, type I 300.00 200.00
Never hinged 1,000.
223A A97 $1 black, type II 1,500. 750.00
Never hinged 5,000.
224 A98 $2 dark blue 350.00 325.00
Never hinged 1,150.
225 A99 $5 dark green 500.00 *900.00*
Never hinged 1,600.

U.S. Stamps Nos. 300-310 and Shades Overprinted in Black

**Regular Issue**

**1903-04**

226 A115 1c blue green 7.00 .40
Never hinged 15.50
227 A116 2c carmine 9.00 1.10
Never hinged 20.00
228 A117 3c bright violet 67.50 12.50
Never hinged 150.00
229 A118 4c brown 80.00 22.50
Never hinged 175.00
a. 4c orange brown 80.00 20.00
Never hinged 175.00
230 A119 5c blue 17.50 1.00
Never hinged 40.00
231 A120 6c brnsh lake 85.00 22.50
Never hinged 190.00
232 A121 8c violet black 50.00 15.00
Never hinged 125.00
233 A122 10c pale red brn 35.00 2.25
Never hinged 80.00
a. 10c red brown 35.00 3.00
Never hinged 80.00
b. Pair, one without overprint *1,500.*
234 A123 13c purple black 35.00 17.50
Never hinged 80.00
a. 13c brown violet 35.00 17.50
Never hinged 80.00
235 A124 15c olive green 60.00 15.00
Never hinged 135.00
236 A125 50c orange 125.00 35.00
Never hinged 275.00
*Nos. 226-236 (11)* 571.00 144.75
Set, never hinged 1,285.

**Same Overprint in Red On U.S. Stamps Nos. 311, 312 and 313**

237 A126 $1 black 300.00 200.00
Never hinged 800.00
238 A127 $2 dark blue 550.00 *800.00*
Never hinged 1,500.
239 A128 $5 dark green 800.00 *2,750.*
Never hinged 2,000.

**Same Overprint in Black On U.S. Stamp Nos. 319 and 319c**

240 A129 2c carmine 8.00 2.25
Never hinged 17.50
a. Booklet pane of 6 *1,500.*
b. 2c scarlet 8.00 2.75
Never hinged 19.00
c. As "b," booklet pane of 6 —

José Rizal A40

Arms of City of Manila A41

Designs: 4c, McKinley. 6c, Ferdinand Magellan. 8c, Miguel Lopez de Legaspi. 10c, Gen. Henry W. Lawton. 12c, Lincoln. 16c, Adm. William T. Sampson. 20c, Washington. 26c, Francisco Carriedo. 30c, Franklin. 2p-10p, Arms of City of Manila.

PHILIPPINES 241

**Wmk. Double-lined PIPS (191PI)**

**1906, Sept. 8** *Perf. 12*

241 A40 2c deep green .40 .25
Never hinged 1.00
a. 2c yellow green ('10) .60 .25
Never hinged 1.50
b. Booklet pane of 6 *750.00 800.00*
Never hinged *1,500.*
242 A40 4c carmine .50 .25
Never hinged 1.25
a. 4c carmine lake ('10) 1.00 .25
Never hinged 2.50
b. Booklet pane of 6 *650.00 700.00*
Never hinged *1,250.*
243 A40 6c violet 2.50 .25
Never hinged 6.25
244 A40 8c brown 4.50 .90
Never hinged 11.00
245 A40 10c blue 3.50 .30
Never hinged 8.75
a. 10c dark blue 3.50 .30
Never hinged 8.75
246 A40 12c brown lake 9.00 2.50
Never hinged 22.50
247 A40 16c violet black 6.00 .35
Never hinged 15.00
248 A40 20c org brn 7.00 .35
Never hinged 17.50
249 A40 26c vio brn 11.00 3.00
Never hinged 27.50
250 A40 30c olive green 6.50 1.75
Never hinged 16.00
251 A41 1p orange 55.00 17.50
Never hinged 130.00
252 A41 2p black 50.00 1.75
Never hinged 130.00
253 A41 4p dark blue 160.00 20.00
Never hinged 375.00
254 A41 10p dark green 225.00 80.00
Never hinged 575.00
*Nos. 241-254 (14)* 540.90 129.15
Set, never hinged 1,316.

**1909-13** **Change of Colors**

255 A40 12c red orange 11.00 3.00
Never hinged 27.50
256 A40 16c olive green 6.00 .75
Never hinged 15.00
257 A40 20c yellow 9.00 1.25
Never hinged 22.50
258 A40 26c blue green 3.50 1.25
Never hinged 8.75
259 A40 30c ultramarine 13.00 3.50
Never hinged 32.50
260 A41 1p pale violet 45.00 5.00
Never hinged 110.00
260A A41 2p vio brn ('13) 100.00 12.00
Never hinged 250.00
*Nos. 255-260A (7)* 187.50 26.75
Set, never hinged 466.25

**Wmk. Single-lined PIPS (190PI)**

**1911**

261 A40 2c green .75 .25
Never hinged 1.80
a. Booklet pane of 6 *800.00 900.00*
Never hinged *1,400.*
262 A40 4c carmine lake 3.00 .25
Never hinged 6.75
a. 4c carmine — —
b. Booklet pane of 6 *600.00 700.00*
Never hinged *1,100.*
263 A40 6c deep violet 3.00 .25
Never hinged 6.75
264 A40 8c brown 9.50 .50
Never hinged 21.50
265 A40 10c blue 4.00 .25
Never hinged 9.00
266 A40 12c orange 4.00 .45
Never hinged 9.00
267 A40 16c olive green 4.50 .40
Never hinged 10.00
a. 16c pale olive green 4.50 .50
Never hinged 10.00
268 A40 20c yellow 3.50 .25
Never hinged 7.75
a. 20c orange 4.00 .30
Never hinged 9.00
269 A40 26c blue green 6.00 .30
Never hinged 13.50
270 A40 30c ultramarine 6.00 .50
Never hinged 13.50
271 A41 1p pale violet 27.50 .60
Never hinged 62.50
272 A41 2p violet brown 45.00 1.00
Never hinged 100.00
273 A41 4p deep blue 550.00 110.00
Never hinged 1,100.
274 A41 10p deep green 200.00 30.00
Never hinged 400.00
*Nos. 261-274 (14)* 866.75 145.00
Set, never hinged 1,862.

**1914**

275 A40 30c gray 12.00 .50
Never hinged 27.50

**1914** *Perf. 10*

276 A40 2c green 3.00 .25
Never hinged 7.00
a. Booklet pane of 6 *600.00 800.00*
Never hinged *1,250.*
277 A40 4c carmine 4.00 .30
Never hinged 9.00
a. Booklet pane of 6 *600.00*
Never hinged *1,300.*
278 A40 6c light violet 45.00 9.50
Never hinged 100.00
a. 6c deep violet 50.00 6.25
Never hinged 110.00
279 A40 8c brown 55.00 10.50
Never hinged 125.00
280 A40 10c dark blue 30.00 .25
Never hinged 67.50
281 A40 16c olive green 100.00 5.00
Never hinged 225.00
282 A40 20c orange 40.00 1.00
Never hinged 85.00
283 A40 30c gray 60.00 4.50
Never hinged 130.00
284 A41 1p pale violet 150.00 3.75
Never hinged 350.00
*Nos. 276-284 (9)* 487.00 35.05
Set, never hinged 1,020.

**Wmk. Single-lined PIPS (190PI)**

**1918** *Perf. 11*

285 A40 2c green 21.00 4.25
Never hinged 40.00
a. Booklet pane of 6 *600.00 800.00*
Never hinged *1,100.*
286 A40 4c carmine 26.00 6.00
Never hinged 55.00
a. Booklet pane of 6 *1,350. 2,000.*
287 A40 6c deep violet 40.00 6.00
Never hinged 90.00
287A A40 8c light brown 220.00 25.00
Never hinged 400.00
288 A40 10c dark blue 60.00 3.00
Never hinged 140.00
289 A40 16c olive green 110.00 10.00
Never hinged 250.00
289A A40 20c orange 175.00 12.00
Never hinged 400.00
289C A40 30c gray 95.00 18.00
Never hinged 215.00
289D A41 1p pale violet 100.00 25.00
Never hinged 225.00
*Nos. 285-289D (9)* 847.00 109.25
Set, never hinged 1,815.

**1917** **Unwmk.** *Perf. 11*

290 A40 2c yellow green .25 .25
Never hinged .55
Never hinged 140.00
a. 2c dark green .30 .25
Never hinged .65
b. Vert. pair, imperf. horiz. *2,750.*
c. Horiz. pair, imperf. between *1,500.* —
d. Vertical pair, imperf. btwn. *1,750. 1,000.*
e. Booklet pane of 6 27.50 *30.00*
Never hinged 60.00
291 A40 4c carmine .30 .25
Never hinged .65
a. 4c light rose .30 .25
Never hinged .65
b. Booklet pane of 6 20.00 *22.50*
Never hinged 35.00
292 A40 6c deep violet .35 .25
Never hinged .70
a. 6c lilac .40 .25
Never hinged .80
b. 6c red violet .40 .25
Never hinged .70
c. Booklet pane of 6 *550.00 800.00*
Never hinged *900.00*
293 A40 8c yellow brown .30 .25
Never hinged .50
a. 8c orange brown .30 .25
Never hinged .50
294 A40 10c deep blue .30 .25
Never hinged .65
295 A40 12c red orange .35 .25
Never hinged .75
296 A40 16c light olive green 65.00 .25
Never hinged 130.00
a. 16c olive bister 65.00 .50
Never hinged 130.00
297 A40 20c orange yellow .35 .25
Never hinged .75
298 A40 26c green .50 .45
Never hinged 1.10
a. 26c blue green .60 .25
Never hinged 1.35
299 A40 30c gray .55 .25
Never hinged 1.35
300 A41 1p pale violet 40.00 2.00
Never hinged 90.00
a. 1p red lilac 40.00 2.50
Never hinged 90.00
b. 1p pale rose lilac 40.00 1.10
Never hinged 90.00
301 A41 2p violet brown 35.00 1.00
Never hinged 77.50
302 A41 4p blue 32.50 .50
Never hinged 72.50
a. 4p dark blue 35.00 .55
Never hinged 77.50
*Nos. 290-302 (13)* 175.75 6.20
Set, never hinged 377.00

**1923-26**

Design: 16c, Adm. George Dewey.

303 A40 16c olive bister 1.00 .25
Never hinged 2.25
a. 16c olive green 1.25 .25
Never hinged 2.75
304 A41 10p dp grn ('26) 50.00 20.00
Never hinged 110.00

Legislative Palace — A42

**1926, Dec. 20** *Perf. 12*

319 A42 2c green & black .50 .25
Never hinged 1.25
a. Horiz. pair, imperf. between *275.00* —
b. Vert. pair, imperf. between *375.00*
320 A42 4c car & blk .55 .40
Never hinged 1.20
a. Horiz. pair, imperf. between *350.00* —
b. Vert. pair, imperf. between *400.00*
321 A42 16c ol grn & blk 1.00 .65
Never hinged 2.25
a. Horiz. pair, imperf. between *250.00* —
b. Vert. pair, imperf. between *425.00* —
c. Double impression of center *675.00*
322 A42 18c lt brn & blk 1.10 .50
Never hinged 2.50
a. Double impression of center *850.00*
b. Vertical pair, imperf. between *475.00*
323 A42 20c orange & black 2.00 1.00
Never hinged 4.50
a. 20c orange & brown *600.00* —
b. As No. 323, imperf., pair *575.00 575.00*
c. As "a," imperf., pair *1,750.* —
d. Vert. pair, imperf. between *500.00*
324 A42 24c gray & black 1.00 .55
Never hinged 2.25
a. Vert. pair, imperf. between *500.00*
325 A42 1p rose lil & blk 47.50 50.00
Never hinged 70.00
a. Vert. pair, imperf. between *500.00*
*Nos. 319-325 (7)* 53.65 53.35
Set, never hinged 83.95

Opening of the Legislative Palace.
No. 322a is valued in the grade of fine.
For overprints, see Nos. O1-O4.

**Rizal Type of 1906**
**Coil Stamp**

**1928** *Perf. 11 Vertically*

326 A40 2c green 7.50 *12.50*
Never hinged 19.00

**Types of 1906-1923**

**1925-31** *Imperf.*

340 A40 2c yel green ('31) .50 .50
Never hinged .90
a. 2c green ('25) .80 .75
Never hinged 1.80
341 A40 4c car rose ('31) .50 *1.00*
Never hinged 1.00
a. 4c carmine ('25) 1.20 1.00
Never hinged 2.75
342 A40 6c violet ('31) 3.00 3.75
Never hinged 5.00
a. 6c deep violet ('25) 12.00 8.00
Never hinged 26.00
343 A40 8c brown ('31) 2.00 *5.00*
Never hinged 4.00
a. 8c yellow brown ('25) 13.00 8.00
Never hinged 26.00
344 A40 10c blue ('31) 5.00 *7.50*
Never hinged 12.00
a. 10c deep blue ('25) 45.00 20.00
Never hinged 100.00
345 A40 12c dp orange ('31) 8.00 10.00
Never hinged 15.00
a. 12c red orange ('25) 60.00 35.00
Never hinged 135.00
346 A40 16c olive green 6.00 7.50
Never hinged 11.00
a. 16c bister green ('25) 42.50 18.00
Never hinged 100.00
347 A40 20c dp yel org ('31) 5.00 *7.50*
Never hinged 11.00
a. 20c yellow orange ('25) 45.00 20.00
Never hinged 100.00
348 A40 26c green ('31) 6.00 *9.00*
Never hinged 11.00
a. 26c blue green ('25) 45.00 25.00
Never hinged 110.00
349 A40 30c light gray ('31) 8.00 10.00
Never hinged 16.00
a. 30c gray ('25) 45.00 25.00
Never hinged 110.00
350 A41 1p light violet ('31) 10.00 *15.00*
Never hinged 20.00
a. 1p violet ('25) 200.00 100.00
Never hinged 425.00
351 A41 2p brn vio ('31) 30.00 *45.00*
Never hinged 80.00
a. 2p violet brown ('25) 400.00 400.00
Never hinged 675.00
352 A41 4p blue ('31) 80.00 90.00
Never hinged 150.00
a. 4p deep blue ('25) 2,200. 1,100.
Never hinged 3,500.
353 A41 10p green ('31) 175.00 *225.00*
Never hinged 300.00
a. 10p deep green ('25) 2,750. *2,950.*
Never hinged 4,250.
*Nos. 340-353 (14)* 339.00 436.75
Set, never hinged 636.90
*Nos. 340a-353a (14)* 5,860. 4,711.

Nos. 340a-353a were the original post office issue. These were reprinted twice in 1931 for sale to collectors (Nos. 340-353).

Mount Mayon, Luzon — A43

Post Office, Manila — A44

Pier No. 7, Manila Bay A45

(See footnote) A46

Rice Planting — A47

Rice Terraces — A48

Baguio Zigzag — A49

**1932, May 3** *Perf. 11*

354 A43 2c yellow green .75 .30
Never hinged 1.25
355 A44 4c rose carmine .75 .30
Never hinged 1.25
356 A45 12c orange .90 .75
Never hinged 1.30
357 A46 18c red orange 45.00 15.00
Never hinged 72.50
358 A47 20c yellow 1.00 .75
Never hinged 1.60
359 A48 24c deep violet 1.60 1.00
Never hinged 2.75
360 A49 32c olive brown 1.60 1.00
Never hinged 2.75
*Nos. 354-360 (7)* 51.60 19.10
Set, never hinged 83.40

The 18c vignette was intended to show Pagsanjan Falls in Laguna, central Luzon, and is so labeled. Through error the stamp pictures Vernal Falls in Yosemite National Park, California.

For overprints see #C29-C35, C47-C51, C63.

Nos. 302, 302a Surcharged in Orange or Red

**1932**

**368** A41 1p on 4p blue (O) 6.00 1.00
Never hinged 9.75
*a.* 1p on 4p dark blue (O) 6.00 1.00
Never hinged 9.25
P# block of 10, Impt. 140.00
Never hinged 175.00
**369** A41 2p on 4p dark blue (R) 9.00 1.50
Never hinged 15.00
P# block of 10, Impt. 160.00
Never hinged 200.00
*a.* 2p on 4p blue (R) 9.00 1.00
Never hinged 15.00

### Far Eastern Championship

Issued in commemoration of the Tenth Far Eastern Championship Games.

Baseball Players — A50

Tennis Player — A51

Basketball Players — A52

**1934, Apr. 14** ***Perf. 11½***

**380** A50 2c yellow brown 1.50 .80
Never hinged 2.25
**381** A51 6c ultramarine .25 .25
Never hinged .30
*a.* Vertical pair, imperf. between *700.00*
Never hinged *1,100.*
**382** A52 16c violet brown .50 .50
Never hinged .75
*a.* Vert. pair, imperf. horiz. *950.00*
Never hinged *1,500.*
*Nos. 380-382 (3)* 2.25 1.55
Set, never hinged 3.30

José Rizal A53

Woman and Carabao A54

La Filipina A55

Pearl Fishing A56

Fort Santiago — A57

Salt Spring — A58

Magellan's Landing, 1521 A59

"Juan de la Cruz" A60

Rice Terraces — A61

"Blood Compact," 1565 — A62

Barasoain Church, Malolos — A63

Battle of Manila Bay, 1898 — A64

Montalban Gorge A65

George Washington A66

**1935, Feb. 15** ***Perf. 11***

**383** A53 2c rose .25 .25
Never hinged .25
**384** A54 4c yellow green .25 .25
Never hinged .25
**385** A55 6c dark brown .25 .25
Never hinged .35
**386** A56 8c violet .25 .25
Never hinged .35
**387** A57 10c rose carmine .30 .25
Never hinged .45
**388** A58 12c black .35 .25
Never hinged .50
**389** A59 16c dark blue .35 .25
Never hinged .55
**390** A60 20c light olive green .35 .25
Never hinged .45
**391** A61 26c indigo .40 .40
Never hinged .60
**392** A62 30c orange red .40 .40
Never hinged .60
**393** A63 1p red org & blk 2.00 1.25
Never hinged 3.00
**394** A64 2p bis brn & blk 12.00 2.00
Never hinged 16.00
**395** A65 4p blue & black 12.00 4.00
Never hinged 16.00
**396** A66 5p green & black 25.00 5.00
Never hinged 50.00
*Nos. 383-396 (14)* 54.15 15.05
Set, never hinged 74.45

For overprints & surcharges see Nos. 411-424, 433-446, 449, 463-466, 468, 472-474, 478-484, 485-494, C52-C53, O15-O36, O38, O40-O43, N2-N9, N28, NO2-NO6.

### Issues of the Commonwealth

Issued to commemorate the inauguration of the Philippine Commonwealth, Nov. 15, 1935.

The Temples of Human Progress A67

**1935, Nov. 15**

**397** A67 2c carmine rose .25 .25
Never hinged .35
**398** A67 6c deep violet .25 .25
Never hinged .35
**399** A67 16c blue .25 .25
Never hinged .40
**400** A67 36c yellow green .40 .30
Never hinged .65
**401** A67 50c brown .70 .55
Never hinged 1.00
*Nos. 397-401 (5)* 1.85 1.60
Set, never hinged 2.75

### Jose Rizal Issue

75th anniversary of the birth of Jose Rizal (1861-1896), national hero of the Filipinos.

Jose Rizal — A68

**1936, June 19** ***Perf. 12***

**402** A68 2c yellow brown .25 .25
Never hinged .25
**403** A68 6c slate blue .25 .25
Never hinged .25
*a.* Imperf. vertically, pair *1,000.*
Never hinged *1,500.*
**404** A68 36c red brown .50 *.70*
Never hinged .75
*Nos. 402-404 (3)* 1.00 1.20
Set, never hinged 1.25

### Commonwealth Anniversary Issue

Issued in commemoration of the first anniversary of the Commonwealth.

President Manuel L. Quezon — A69

**1936, Nov. 15** ***Perf. 11***

**408** A69 2c orange brown .25 .25
Never hinged .30
**409** A69 6c yellow green .25 .25
Never hinged .30
**410** A69 12c ultramarine .25 .25
Never hinged .30
*Nos. 408-410 (3)* .75 .75
Set, never hinged .90

### Stamps of 1935 Overprinted in Black

a

b

**1936-37**

**411** A53(a) 2c rose .25 .25
Never hinged .25
*a.* Bklt. pane of 6 ('37) 2.50 2.00
Never hinged 4.00
*b.* Hyphen omitted 125.00 100.00
**412** A54(b) 4c yel grn ('37) .45 *4.00*
Never hinged .70
P# block of 6 35.00
Never hinged 45.00
**413** A55(a) 6c dark brown .25 .25
Never hinged .25
**414** A56(b) 8c violet ('37) .25 .25
Never hinged .35
**415** A57(b) 10c rose carmine .25 .25
Never hinged .25
*a.* "COMMONWEALT" 20.00 —
Never hinged 30.00
**416** A58(b) 12c black ('37) .25 .25
Never hinged .30
**417** A59(b) 16c dark blue .25 .25
Never hinged .40
**418** A60(a) 20c lt ol grn ('37) .90 .40
Never hinged 1.50
**419** A61(b) 26c indigo ('37) .80 .35
Never hinged 1.40
**420** A62(b) 30c orange red .45 .25
Never hinged .75
**421** A63(b) 1p red org & blk .90 .25
Never hinged 1.50
**422** A64(b) 2p bis brn & blk ('37) 12.50 4.00
Never hinged 21.00
**423** A65(b) 4p bl & blk ('37) 45.00 8.00
Never hinged 72.50
**424** A66(b) 5p grn & blk ('37) 12.50 *25.00*
Never hinged 21.00
*Nos. 411-424 (14)* 75.00 43.75
Set, never hinged 122.15

### Eucharistic Congress Issue

Issued to commemorate the 33rd International Eucharistic Congress held at Manila, Feb. 3-7, 1937.

Map of Philippines — A70

**1937, Feb. 3**

**425** A70 2c yellow green .25 .25
Never hinged .25
**426** A70 6c light brown .25 .25
Never hinged .25
**427** A70 12c sapphire .25 .25
Never hinged .25
**428** A70 20c deep orange .30 .25
Never hinged .50
**429** A70 36c deep violet .55 .40
Never hinged .80
**430** A70 50c carmine .70 .35
Never hinged 1.10
*Nos. 425-430 (6)* 2.30 1.75
Set, never hinged 3.15

Arms of Manila — A71

**1937, Aug. 27**

**431** A71 10p gray 5.00 2.00
Never hinged 7.25
P# block of 6 [illegible]
Never hinged 85.00
**432** A71 20p henna brown 4.00 1.40
Never hinged 6.50

### Stamps of 1935 Overprinted in Black

a

b

**1938-40**

**433** A53(a) 2c rose ('39) .25 .25
Never hinged .25
P# block of 6 8.00
Never hinged 10.00
*a.* Booklet pane of 6 3.50 3.50
Never hinged 5.50
*b.* As "a," lower left-hand stamp overprinted "WEALTH COMMON-" *2,000.*
Never hinged *3,250.*
*c.* Hyphen omitted 100.00 50.00
**434** A54(b) 4c yel grn ('40) 3.00 *30.00*
Never hinged 4.75
P# block of 6 35.00
Never hinged 45.00
**435** A55(a) 6c dk brn ('39) .25 .25
Never hinged .40
*a.* 6c golden brown .25 .25
Never hinged .40
P# block of 6 5.50
Never hinged 7.00
**436** A56(b) 8c violet ('39) .25 *1.75*
Never hinged .25
P# block of 6 8.00
Never hinged 10.00
*a.* "COMMONWEALT" (LR 31) 90.00
Never hinged 140.00
**437** A57(b) 10c rose car ('39) .25 .25
Never hinged .25
P# block of 6 8.00
Never hinged 10.00
*a.* "COMMONWEALT" (LR 31) 65.00 —
Never hinged 100.00
**438** A58(b) 12c black ('40) .25 *1.00*
Never hinged .25
P# block of 6 8.00
Never hinged 10.00
**439** A59(b) 16c dark blue .25 .25
Never hinged .25
P# block of 6 16.00
Never hinged 20.00
**440** A60(a) 20c lt ol grn ('39) .25 .25
Never hinged .25
P# block of 6 12.00
Never hinged 15.00
**441** A61(b) 26c indigo ('40) 1.00 *2.50*
Never hinged 1.50
P# block of 6 16.00
Never hinged 20.00
**442** A62(b) 30c org red ('39) 3.00 .70
Never hinged 5.00
P# block of 6 22.50
Never hinged 35.00
**443** A63(b) 1p red org & blk .60 .25
Never hinged 1.00
**444** A64(b) 2p bis brn & blk ('39) 10.00 1.00
Never hinged 15.00
P# block of 4 87.50
Never hinged 110.00
**445** A65(b) 4p bl & blk ('40) 150.00 250.00
Never hinged 325.00
**446** A66(b) 5p grn & blk ('40) 20.00 8.00
Never hinged 35.00
P# block of 4 200.00
Never hinged 250.00
*Nos. 433-446 (14)* 189.35 *296.45*
Set, never hinged 414.15

Overprint "b" measures 18½x1¾mm.
No. 433b occurs in booklet pane, No. 433a, position 5; all examples are straight-edged, left and bottom.

### First Foreign Trade Week Issue
### Nos. 384, 298a and 432 Surcharged in Red, Violet or Black

a

b

c

**1939, July 5**

**449** A54(a) 2c on 4c yel grn (R) .25 .25
Never hinged .35

**450** A40(b) 6c on 26c blue grn (V) .25 .50
Never hinged .35
*a.* 6c on 26c green 3.00 1.00
Never hinged 5.00
**451** A71(c) 50c on 20p henna brn (Bk) 1.25 1.00
Never hinged 2.00 5.00
*Nos. 449-451 (3)* 1.75 1.75
Set, never hinged 2.70

**Commonwealth 4th Anniversary Issue (#452-460)**

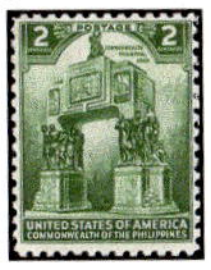

Triumphal Arch — A72

**1939, Nov. 15**

**452** A72 2c yellow green .25 .25
Never hinged .25
**453** A72 6c carmine .25 .25
Never hinged .25
**454** A72 12c bright blue .25 .25
Never hinged .25
*Nos. 452-454 (3)* .75 .75
Set, never hinged .75

For overprints see Nos. 469, 476.

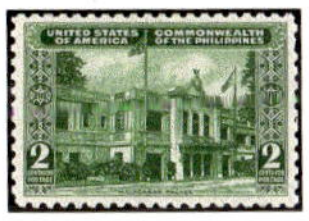

Malacañan Palace — A73

**1939, Nov. 15**

**455** A73 2c green .25 .25
Never hinged .25
**456** A73 6c orange .25 .25
Never hinged .25
**457** A73 12c carmine .25 .25
Never hinged .25
*Nos. 455-457 (3)* .75 .75
Set, never hinged .75

For overprint, see No. 470.

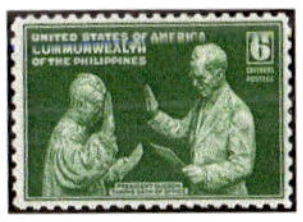

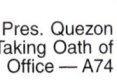

Pres. Quezon Taking Oath of Office — A74

**1940, Feb. 8**

**458** A74 2c dark orange .25 .25
Never hinged .25
**459** A74 6c dark green .25 .25
Never hinged .25
**460** A74 12c purple .25 .25
Never hinged .30
*Nos. 458-460 (3)* .75 .75
Set, never hinged .80

For overprints, see Nos. 471, 477.

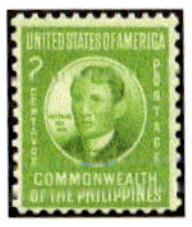

José Rizal — A75

ROTARY PRESS PRINTING

**1941, Apr. 14** *Perf. 11x10½*

**Size: 19x22½mm**

**461** A75 2c apple green .25 .50
Never hinged .25

FLAT PLATE PRINTING

**1941, Nov. 14** *Perf. 11*

**Size: 18¾x22¼mm**

**462** A75 2c pale apple green 1.00 —
Never hinged 1.25
*a.* Booklet pane of 6 6.00 —
Never hinged 7.50

No. 461 was issued only in sheets. No. 462 was issued only in booklet panes on Nov. 14, 1941, just before the war, and only a few used stamps and covers exist. All examples have one or two straight edges. Mint booklets reappeared after the war. In August 1942, the booklet pane was reprinted in a darker shade (apple green). However, the apple green panes were available only to U.S. collectors during the war years, so no war-period used stamps from the Philippines exist. Value of apple green booklet pane, never hinged, $6.

For type A75 overprinted, see Nos. 464, O37, O39, N1 and NO1.

Philippine Stamps of 1935-41, Handstamped in Violet

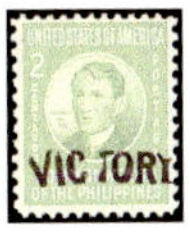

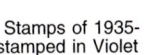

**1944** *Perf. 11, 11x10½*

**463** A53 2c rose (On 411) *1,250. 650.00*
*a.* Booklet pane of 6 *12,500.*
**463B** A53 2c rose (On 433) *2,000. 1,750.*
**464** A75 2c apple grn (On 461) 12.50 10.00
Never hinged 22.50
*a.* Pair, one without ovpt. — —
**465** A54 4c yel grn (On 384) 47.50 *50.00*
Never hinged 80.00
**466** A55 6c dk brn (On 385) *3,250. 2,000.*
**467** A69 6c yel grn (On 409) 300.00 *150.00*
Never hinged *525.00*
**468** A55 6c dk brn (On 413) *4,000. 825.00*
**469** A72 6c car (On 453) *350.00 125.00*
**470** A73 6c org (On 456) *1,750. 725.00*
**471** A74 6c dk grn (On 459) *500.00 225.00*
**472** A56 8c vio (On 436) 17.50 *30.00*
Never hinged 30.00
**473** A57 10c car rose (On 415) *350.00 150.00*
**474** A57 10c car rose (On 437) *275.00 200.00*
Never hinged *475.00*
**475** A69 12c ultra (On 410) *1,100. 400.00*
**476** A72 12c brt bl (On 454) *7,000. 2,500.*
**477** A74 12c pur (On 460) *500.00 275.00*
**478** A59 16c dk bl (On 389) *3,000.* —
**479** A59 16c dk bl (On 417) *1,500. 1,000.*
**480** A59 16c dk bl (On 439) *500.00 200.00*
**481** A60 20c lt ol grn (On 440) 140.00 35.00
Never hinged 230.00
**482** A62 30c org red (On 420) *450.00 1,500.*
**483** A62 30c org red (On 442) *800.00 375.00*
**484** A63 1p red org & blk (On 443) *6,250. 4,500.*

Nos. 463-484 are valued in the grade of fine to very fine.

No. 463 comes only from the booklet pane. All examples have one or two straight edges.

**Types of 1935-37 Overprinted**

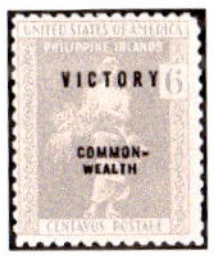

a

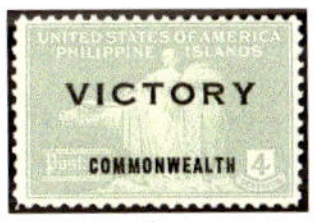

b

Nos. 431-432 Overprinted in Black — c

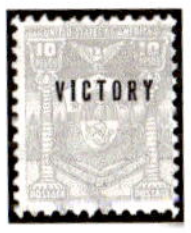

**1945** *Perf. 11*

**485** A53(a) 2c rose .25 .25
Never hinged .25
**486** A54(b) 4c yellow green .25 .25
Never hinged .25
**487** A55(a) 6c golden brown .25 .25
Never hinged .25
**488** A56(b) 8c violet .25 .25
Never hinged .25
**489** A57(b) 10c rose carmine .25 .25
Never hinged .25
**490** A58(b) 12c black .25 .25
Never hinged .25
**491** A59(b) 16c dark blue .25 .25
Never hinged .30
**492** A60(a) 20c lt olive green .30 .25
Never hinged .40
**493** A62(b) 30c orange red .50 .35
Never hinged .75
**494** A63(b) 1p red org & blk 1.10 .25
Never hinged 1.60
**495** A71(c) 10p gray 55.00 13.50
Never hinged 90.00
**496** A71(c) 20p henna brown 50.00 15.00
Never hinged 75.00
*Nos. 485-496 (12)* 108.65 31.10
Set, never hinged 169.55

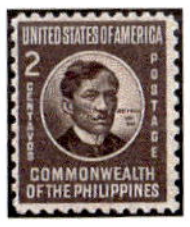

José Rizal — A76

**1946, May 28** *Perf. 11x10½*

**497** A76 2c sepia .25 .25
Never hinged .25

For overprints see Nos. 503, O44.

**Catalogue values for unused stamps in this section, from this point to the end of the section, are for Never Hinged items.**

Later issues, released by the Philippine Republic on July 4, 1946, and thereafter, are listed in Scott's Standard Postage Stamp Catalogue, Vol. 5A.

**AIR POST STAMPS**

**Madrid-Manila Flight Issue**

Issued to commemorate the flight of Spanish aviators Gallarza and Loriga from Madrid to Manila.

Regular Issue of 1917-26 Overprinted In Red or Violet

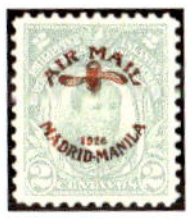

Designs: Nos. C7-C8, Adm. William T. Sampson. No. C9, Adm. George Dewey.

**1926, May 13** **Unwmk.** ***Perf. 11***

**C1** A40 2c green (R) 20.00 25.00
Never hinged 45.00
**C2** A40 4c carmine (V) 30.00 35.00
Never hinged 55.00
*a.* Inverted overprint *2,600.* —
**C3** A40 6c lilac (R) 60.00 90.00
Never hinged 125.00
**C4** A40 8c org brn (V) 60.00 85.00
Never hinged 125.00
**C5** A40 10c deep blue (R) 80.00 85.00
Never hinged 140.00
**C6** A40 12c red org (V) 70.00 95.00
Never hinged 150.00
**C7** A40 16c lt ol grn (V) *2,800. 3,250.*
**C8** A40 16c ol bister (R) *5,000. 5,000.*
**C9** A40 16c ol grn (V) 90.00 125.00
Never hinged 160.00
**C10** A40 20c org ye (V) 90.00 125.00
Never hinged 160.00
**C11** A40 26c blue grn (V) 90.00 125.00
Never hinged 160.00
**C12** A40 30c gray (V) 90.00 125.00
Never hinged 160.00
**C13** A41 2p vio brn (R) 500.00 600.00
Never hinged 1,100.
**C14** A41 4p dk blue (R) 800.00 900.00
Never hinged 1,300.
**C15** A41 10p dp grn (V) 1,000. 1,350.

**Same Overprint on No. 269**

**Wmk. Single-lined PIPS (190)**

***Perf. 12***

**C16** A40 26c blue grn (V) *5,000.*

**Same Overprint on No. 284**

***Perf. 10***

**C17** A41 1p pale violet (V) [illegible] 250.00
Never hinged 450.00

**London-Orient Flight Issue**

Issued Nov. 9, 1928, to celebrate the arrival of a British squadron of hydroplanes.

Regular Issue of 1917-25 Overprinted in Red

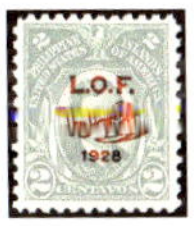

**1928, Nov. 9** ***Perf. 11***

**C18** A40 2c green 1.00 1.00
Never hinged 2.00
**C19** A40 4c carmine 1.25 1.50
Never hinged 2.00
**C20** A40 6c violet 5.00 3.00
Never hinged 10.00
**C21** A40 8c orange brown 5.00 3.00
Never hinged 10.00
**C22** A40 10c deep blue 5.00 3.00
Never hinged 10.00
**C23** A40 12c red orange 8.00 4.00
Never hinged 12.00
**C24** A40 16c ol grn (No. 303a) 8.00 4.00
Never hinged 12.00
**C25** A40 20c orange yellow 8.00 4.00
Never hinged 12.00
**C26** A40 26c blue green 20.00 8.00
Never hinged 35.00
**C27** A40 30c gray 20.00 8.00
Never hinged 35.00

**Same Overprint on No. 271**

**Wmk. Single-lined PIPS (190)**

***Perf. 12***

**C28** A41 1p pale violet 55.00 30.00
Never hinged 90.00
*Nos. C18-C28 (11)* 136.25 69.50
Set, never hinged 230.00

**Von Gronau Issue**

Commemorating the visit of Capt. Wolfgang von Gronau's airplane on its round-the-world flight.

Nos. 354-360 Overprinted

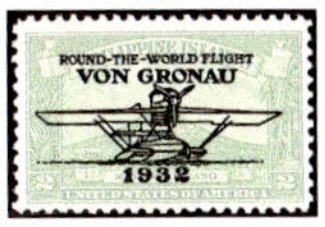


**1932, Sept. 27** **Unwmk.** ***Perf. 11***

**C29** A43 2c yellow green .90 .60
Never hinged 1.40
**C30** A44 4c rose carmine .90 .40
Never hinged 1.40
**C31** A45 12c orange 1.25 .65
Never hinged 2.00
**C32** A46 18c red orange 5.00 5.00
Never hinged 8.00
**C33** A47 20c yellow 3.50 3.50
Never hinged 5.75
**C34** A48 24c deep violet 3.50 4.00
Never hinged 5.75
**C35** A49 32c olive brown 3.50 3.00
Never hinged 5.75
*Nos. C29-C35 (7)* 18.55 17.15
Set, never hinged 31.55

**Rein Issue**

Commemorating the flight from Madrid to Manila of the Spanish aviator Fernando Rein y Loring

Regular Issue of 1917-25 Overprinted

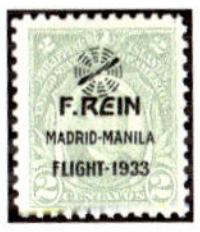


**1933, Apr. 11**

**C36** A40 2c green .75 .45
Never hinged 1.10
**C37** A40 4c carmine .90 .45
Never hinged 1.40
**C38** A40 6c deep violet 1.10 .80
Never hinged 1.75
**C39** A40 8c orange brown 3.75 2.00
Never hinged 5.75
P# block of 10, Impt. 120.00
Never hinged 150.00
**C40** A40 10c dark blue 3.75 2.25
Never hinged 5.75
P# block of 10, Impt. 120.00
Never hinged 150.00
**C41** A40 12c orange 3.75 2.00
Never hinged 5.75
P# block of 10, Impt. 120.00
Never hinged 150.00
**C42** A40 16c olive green 3.50 2.00
Never hinged 5.25
P# block of 6 160.00
Never hinged 200.00
**C43** A40 20c yellow 3.75 2.00
Never hinged 5.75
P# block of 10, Impt. 160.00
Never hinged 200.00
**C44** A40 26c green 3.75 2.75
Never hinged 5.75
*a.* 26c blue green 4.00 2.00
Never hinged 6.00
**C45** A40 30c gray 4.00 3.00
Never hinged 6.00
*Nos. C36-C45 (10)* 29.00 17.70
Set, never hinged 44.25

No. 290a Overprinted

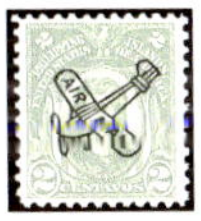

Printed by the Philippine Bureau.

**1933, May 26**

**C46** A40 2c green .65 .40
Never hinged 1.00
P# block of 6 12.00
Never hinged 15.00

Regular Issue of 1932 Overprinted

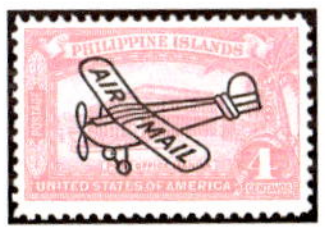

**C47** A44 4c rose carmine .30 .25
Never hinged .45
P# block of 6 16.00
Never hinged 20.00
**C48** A45 12c orange .60 .25
Never hinged .90
P# block of 6 20.00
Never hinged 25.00

**C49** A47 20c yellow .60 .25
Never hinged .90
P# block of 6 20.00
Never hinged 25.00
**C50** A48 24c deep violet .65 .25
Never hinged 1.00
P# block of 6 24.00
Never hinged 30.00
**C51** A49 32c olive brown .85 .35
Never hinged 1.40
*Nos. C46-C51 (6)* 3.65 1.75
Set, never hinged 5.65

### Transpacific Issue

Issued to commemorate the China Clipper flight from Manila to San Francisco, Dec. 2-5, 1935.

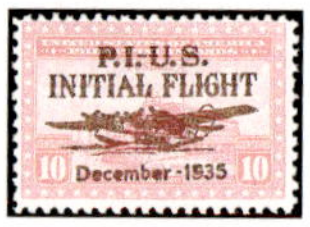


Nos. 387, 392 Overprinted in Gold

**1935, Dec. 2**
**C52** A57 10c rose carmine .40 .25
Never hinged .60
**C53** A62 30c orange red .60 .35
Never hinged .90

### Manila-Madrid Flight Issue

Issued to commemorate the Manila-Madrid flight by aviators Antonio Arnaiz and Juan Calvo.

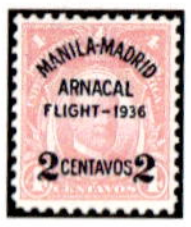


Regular Issue of 1917-25 Surcharged in Various Colors

**1936, Sept. 6**
**C54** A40 2c on 4c carmine (Bl) .25 .25
Never hinged .25
**C55** A40 6c on 12c red org (V) .25 .25
Never hinged .30
**C56** A40 16c on 26c blue grn (Bk) .25 .25
Never hinged .40
*a.* 16c on 26c green 2.00 .70
Never hinged 3.00
*Nos. C54-C56 (3)* .75 .75
Set, never hinged .95

### Air Mail Exhibition Issue

Issued to commemorate the first Air Mail Exhibition, held Feb. 17-19, 1939.

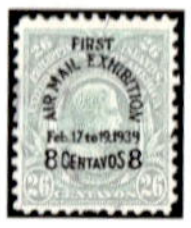

Regular Issue of 1917-37 Surcharged in Black or Red

**1939, Feb. 17**
**C57** A40 8c on 26c blue grn (Bk) 2.00 2.00
Never hinged 4.00
*a.* 8c on 26c green (Bk) 10.00 4.00
Never hinged 16.00
**C58** A71 1p on 10p gray (R) 8.00 4.00
Never hinged 12.00

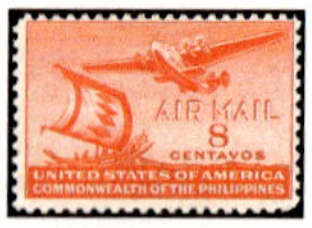


Moro Vinta and Clipper — AP1

**1941, June 30**
**C59** AP1 8c carmine 2.00 .60
Never hinged 2.75
**C60** AP1 20c ultramarine 3.00 .50
Never hinged 4.00
**C61** AP1 60c blue green 3.00 1.00
Never hinged 4.00
**C62** AP1 1p sepia .70 .50
Never hinged 1.00
*Nos. C59-C62 (4)* 8.70 2.60
Set, never hinged 11.75

For overprint see No. NO7. For surcharges see Nos. N10-N11, N35-N36.

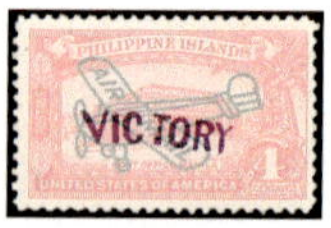


No. C47 Hstmpd. in Violet

**1944, Dec. 3**
**C63** A44 4c rose carmine *3,750. 2,750.*

## SPECIAL DELIVERY STAMPS

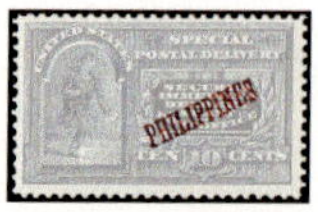


United States No. E5 Overprinted in Red

**Wmk. Double-lined USPS (191)**
**1901, Oct. 15** *Perf. 12*
**E1** SD3 10c dark blue 100. 80.
Never hinged 185.
*a.* Dots in curved frame above messenger (Pl. 882) *175. 160.*

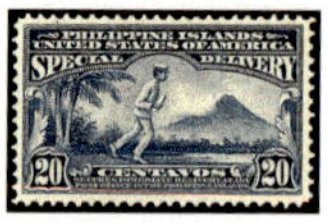


Special Delivery Messenger SD2

**Wmk. Double-lined PIPS (191PI)**
**1906, Sept. 8**
**E2** SD2 20c deep ultra 45.00 8.00
Never hinged 90.00
*b.* 20c pale ultramarine 35.00 8.00
Never hinged 70.00

See Nos. E3-E6. For overprints see Nos. E7-E10, EO1.

## SPECIAL PRINTING

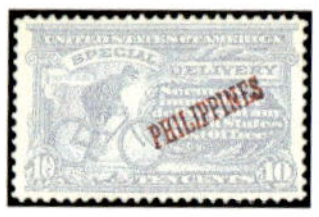


U.S. No. E6 Overprinted in Red

**Wmk. Double-lined USPS (191)**
**1907**
**E2A** SD4 10c ultramarine *3,250.*

**Wmk. Single-lined PIPS (190PI)**
**1911, Apr.**
**E3** SD2 20c deep ultra 22.00 1.75
Never hinged 42.00

**1916** *Perf. 10*
**E4** SD2 20c deep ultra 175.00 150.00
Never hinged 275.00

**1919** **Unwmk.** *Perf. 11*
**E5** SD2 20c ultramarine .60 .25
Never hinged .90
*a.* 20c pale blue .75 .25
Never hinged 1.00
*b.* 20c dull violet .60 .25
Never hinged .90

### Type of 1906 Issue

**1925-31** *Imperf.*
**E6** SD2 20c dull violet ('31) 27.50 *75.00*
Never hinged 40.00
*a.* 20c violet blue ('25) 50.00 —
Never hinged 80.00

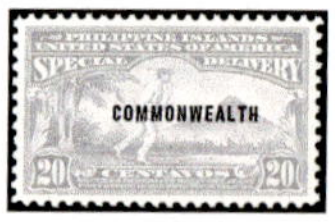


Type of 1919 Overprinted in Black

**1939, Apr. 27** *Perf. 11*
**E7** SD2 20c blue violet .25 .25
Never hinged .40

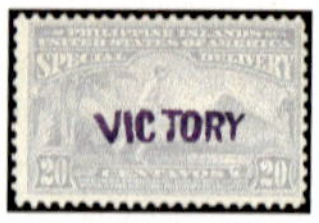


Nos. E5b and E7, Hstmpd. in Violet

**1944**
**E8** SD2 20c dull violet (On E5b) *1,400. 550.00*
On cover —
Block of 4 *6,000.*
**E9** SD2 20c blue violet (On E7) *550.00 250.00*

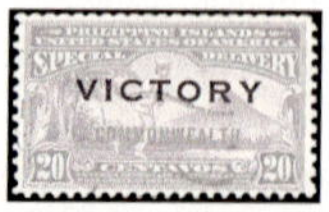


Type SD2 Overprinted

**1945, May 1**
**E10** SD2 20c blue violet .70 .55
Never hinged 1.10
*a.* "IC" close together 3.25 2.75
Never hinged 4.75

## SPECIAL DELIVERY OFFICIAL STAMP

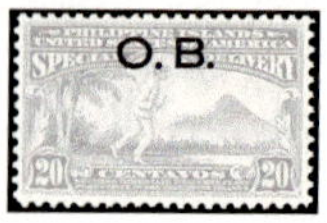


Type of 1906 Issue Overprinted

**1931** **Unwmk.** *Perf. 11*
**EO1** SD2 20c dull violet 3.00 *75.00*
Never hinged 4.50
P# block of 6 150.00
Never hinged 190.00
*a.* No period after "B" 50.00 *250.00*
Never hinged 75.00
*b.* Double overprint —

It is strongly recommended that expert opinion be acquired for Nos. EO1 and EO1a used.

## POSTAGE DUE STAMPS

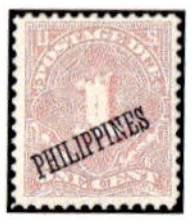


U.S. Nos. J38-J44 Overprinted in Black

**Wmk. Double-lined USPS (191)**
**1899, Aug. 16** *Perf. 12*
**J1** D2 1c deep claret 7.50 2.50
Never hinged 15.00
**J2** D2 2c deep claret 7.50 2.50
Never hinged 15.00
**J3** D2 5c deep claret 15.00 2.50
Never hinged 30.00
**J4** D2 10c deep claret 19.00 5.50
Never hinged 37.50
**J5** D2 50c deep claret 250.00 100.00
Never hinged 425.00

No. J1 was used to pay regular postage Sept. 5-19, 1902.

**1901, Aug. 31**
**J6** D2 3c deep claret 17.50 7.00
Never hinged 35.00
**J7** D2 30c deep claret 250.00 110.00
Never hinged 415.00
*Nos. J1-J7 (7)* 566.50 230.00
Set, never hinged 882.50

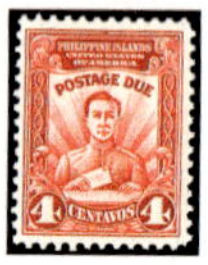


Post Office Clerk — D3

**1928, Aug. 21** **Unwmk.** *Perf. 11*
**J8** D3 4c brown red .25 .25
Never hinged .25
P# block of 6 14.00
Never hinged 17.50
**J9** D3 6c brown red .30 .75
Never hinged .45
P# block of 6 14.00
Never hinged 17.50
**J10** D3 8c brown red .25 .75
Never hinged .35
P# block of 6 14.00
Never hinged 17.50
**J11** D3 10c brown red .30 .75
Never hinged .45
P# block of 6 14.00
Never hinged 17.50
**J12** D3 12c brown red .25 .75
Never hinged .35
P# block of 6 14.00
Never hinged 17.50
**J13** D3 16c brown red .30 .75
Never hinged .45
P# block of 6 14.00
Never hinged 17.50
**J14** D3 20c brown red .30 .75
Never hinged .45
P# block of 6 14.00
Never hinged 17.50
*Nos. J8-J14 (7)* 1.95 4.75
Set, never hinged 2.75

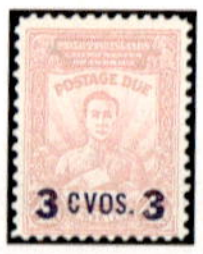


No. J8 Surcharged in Blue

**1937, July 29** **Unwmk.** *Perf. 11*
**J15** D3 3c on 4c brown red .25 .25
Never hinged .35

See note after No. NJ1.

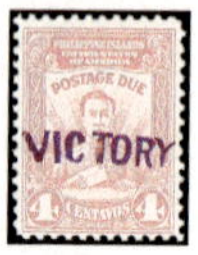


Nos. J8 to J14 Handstamped in Violet

**1944, Dec. 3**
**J16** D3 4c brown red *150.00* —
**J17** D3 6c brown red *100.00* —
**J18** D3 8c brown red *110.00 350.00*
**J19** D3 10c brown red *100.00* —
**J20** D3 12c brown red *100.00* —
**J21** D3 16c brown red *100.00* 350.00
*a.* Pair, one without ovpt. —
**J22** D3 20c brown red *110.00* —
*Nos. J16-J22 (7)* *770.00*

## OFFICIAL STAMPS

### Official Handstamped Overprints

"Officers purchasing stamps for government business may, if they so desire, surcharge them with the letters O.B. either in writing with black ink or by rubber stamps but in such a manner as not to obliterate the stamp that postmasters will be unable to determine whether the stamps have been previously used." C.M. Cotterman, Director of Posts, December 26, 1905.

Beginning January 1, 1906, all branches of the Insular Government used postage stamps to prepay postage instead of franking them as before. Some officials used manuscript, some utilized the typewriting machines but by far the larger number provided themselves with rubber stamps. The majority of these read "O.B." but other forms were: "OFFICIAL BUSINESS" or "OFFICIAL MAIL" in two lines, with variations on many of these.

These "O.B." overprints are known on U.S. 1899-1901 stamps; on 1903-06 stamps in red and blue; on 1906 stamps in red, blue, black, yellow and green.

"O.B." overprints were also made on the centavo and peso stamps of the Philippines, per order of May 25, 1907.

Beginning in 1926 the Bureau of Posts issued press-printed official stamps, but many government offices continued to handstamp ordinary postage stamps "O.B." The press-printed "O.B." overprints are listed below.

During the Japanese occupation period 1942-45, the same system of handstamped official overprints prevailed, but the handstamp usually consisted of "K.P.", initials of the Tagalog words, "Kagamitang Pampamahalaan" (Official Business), and the two Japanese characters used in the printed overprint on Nos. NO1 to NO4.

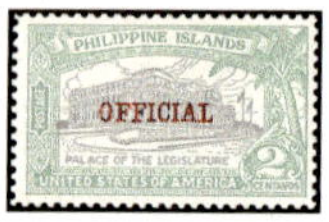


Regular Issue of 1926 Ovptd. in Red

**1926, Dec. 20** **Unwmk.** *Perf. 12*
**O1** A42 2c green & black 3.00 1.00
Never hinged 4.50
**O2** A42 4c car & blk 3.00 1.25
Never hinged 4.50
*a.* Vertical pair, imperf. between 550.00
**O3** A42 18c lt brn & blk 8.00 4.00
Never hinged 12.00
**O4** A42 20c org & blk 7.75 1.75
Never hinged 11.50
*Nos. O1-O4 (4)* 21.75 8.00
Set, never hinged 32.50

Opening of the Legislative Palace.

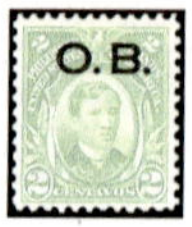


Regular Issue of 1917-26 Overprinted by the U.S. Bureau of Engraving and Printing

**1931** *Perf. 11*
**O5** A40 2c green .40 .25
Never hinged .65
P# block of 6 20.00
Never hinged 25.00
*a.* No period after "B" 17.50 17.50
Never hinged 27.50
*b.* No period after "O" 40.00 30.00
**O6** A40 4c carmine .45 .25
Never hinged .70
P# block of 6 20.00
Never hinged 25.00
*a.* No period after "B" 40.00 20.00
Never hinged 60.00

O7 A40 6c deep violet .75 .25
Never hinged 1.25
P# block of 10, Impt. 40.00
Never hinged 50.00
O8 A40 8c yellow brown .75 .25
Never hinged 1.25
P# block of 6 32.00
Never hinged 40.00
P# block of 10, Impt. 40.00
Never hinged 50.00
O9 A40 10c deep blue 1.20 .25
Never hinged 1.90
P# block of 10, Impt. 32.00
Never hinged 40.00
O10 A40 12c red orange 2.00 .25
Never hinged 3.00
P# block of 6 65.00
Never hinged 80.00
P# block of 10, Impt. 80.00
Never hinged 95.00
*a.* No period after "B" 80.00 80.00
Never hinged 120.00
O11 A40 16c lt ol grn 1.00 .25
Never hinged 1.50
P# block of 6 24.00
Never hinged 30.00
*a.* 16c olive bister 2.00 .25
Never hinged 3.00
P# block of 6 20.00
Never hinged 25.00
O12 A40 20c orange yellow 1.25 .25
Never hinged 1.90
P# block of 10, Impt. 75.00
Never hinged 95.00
*a.* No period after "B" 80.00 80.00
Never hinged 120.00
O13 A40 26c green 2.00 1.00
Never hinged 3.25
P# block of 6 120.00
Never hinged 150.00
*a.* 26c blue green 2.50 1.50
Never hinged 4.00
P# block of 6 130.00
Never hinged 165.00
O14 A40 30c gray 2.00 .25
Never hinged 3.25
P# block of 10, Impt. 80.00
Never hinged 100.00
*Nos. O5-O14 (10)* 11.80 3.25
Set, never hinged 18.65

Many collectors prefer to collect the plate blocks of 6 of Nos. O5-O6, O8, O10-O11a and O14 as blocks of 10 so they fit aesthetically with the other plate blocks of 10 with imprints.

Overprinted on Nos. 383-392

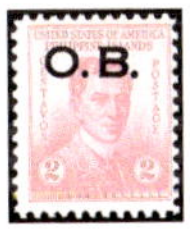

**1935**

O15 A53 2c rose .25 .25
Never hinged .30
P# block of 6 4.75
Never hinged 6.00
*a.* No period after "B" 15.00 10.00
Never hinged 22.50
*b.* No period after "O" — —
O16 A54 4c yellow green .25 .25
Never hinged .30
P# block of 6 4.00
Never hinged 5.00
*a.* No period after "B" 15.00 *40.00*
Never hinged 22.50
O17 A55 6c dark brown .25 .25
Never hinged .40
P# block of 6 8.00
Never hinged 10.00
*a.* No period after "B" 35.00 35.00
Never hinged 52.50
O18 A56 8c violet .30 .25
Never hinged .45
P# block of 6 9.50
Never hinged 12.00
O19 A57 10c rose carmine .30 .25
Never hinged .45
P# block of 6 8.00
Never hinged 10.00
O20 A58 12c black .75 .25
Never hinged 1.10
P# block of 6 8.00
Never hinged 10.00
O21 A59 16c dark blue .55 .25
Never hinged .85
P# block of 6 8.00
Never hinged 10.00
O22 A60 20c light olive green .60 .25
Never hinged .90
P# block of 6 12.00
Never hinged 15.00
O23 A61 26c indigo .90 .25
Never hinged 1.50
P# block of 6 20.00
Never hinged 25.00
O24 A62 30c orange red .80 .25
Never hinged 1.20
P# block of 6 20.00
Never hinged 25.00
*Nos. O15-O24 (10)* 4.95 2.50
Set, never hinged 7.40

Nos. 411 and 418 with Additional Overprint in Black

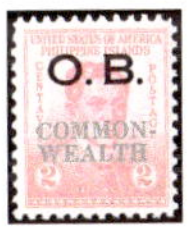

**1937-38**

O25 A53 2c rose .25 .25
Never hinged .30
*a.* No period after "B" 25.00 25.00
Never hinged 45.00
*b.* Period after "B" raised (UL 4) 150.00

O26 A60 20c lt ol grn ('38) .70 .50
Never hinged 1.10
P# block of 6 20.00
Never hinged 25.00

## Regular Issue of 1935 Overprinted In Black

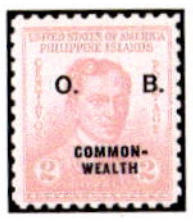
a

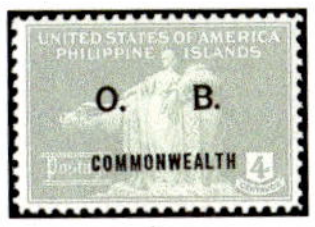
b

**1938-40**

O27 A53(a) 2c rose .25 .25
Never hinged .30
P# block of 6 4.75
Never hinged 6.00
*a.* Hyphen omitted 10.00 10.00
Never hinged 15.00
*b.* No period after "B" 20.00 *30.00*
Never hinged 30.00
O28 A54(b) 4c yellow green .75 1.00
Never hinged 1.10
P# block of 6 24.00
Never hinged 30.00
O29 A55(a) 6c dark brown .30 .25
Never hinged .45
P# block of 6 12.00
Never hinged 15.00
O30 A56(b) 8c violet .75 .85
Never hinged 1.10
P# block of 6 9.50
Never hinged 12.00
O31 A57(b) 10c rose carmine .25 .25
Never hinged .30
P# block of 6 16.00
Never hinged 20.00
*a.* No period after "O" 50.00 40.00
Never hinged 75.00
O32 A58(b) 12c black .30 .25
Never hinged .45
P# block of 6 12.00
Never hinged 15.00
O33 A59(b) 16c dark blue .30 .25
Never hinged .45
P# block of 6 16.00
Never hinged 20.00
O34 A60(a) 20c lt ol grn ('40) .55 .85
Never hinged .85
P# block of 6 16.00
Never hinged 20.00
O35 A61(b) 26c indigo 1.50 *2.00*
Never hinged 2.25
P# block of 6 12.00
Never hinged 15.00
O36 A62(b) 30c orange red .75 .85
Never hinged 1.10
P# block of 6 16.00
Never hinged 20.00
*Nos. O27-O36 (10)* 5.70 6.80
Set, never hinged 8.25

No. 461 Overprinted in Black — c

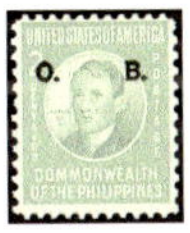

**1941, Apr. 14** ***Perf. 11x10½***

O37 A75(c) 2c apple green .25 *.40*
Never hinged .30

Official Stamps Handstamped in Violet

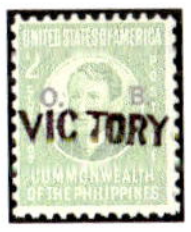

**1944** ***Perf. 11, 11x10½***

O38 A53 2c rose (On O27) *375.00* *200.00*
Never hinged *750.00*
O39 A75 2c apple grn (On O37) 15.00 *20.00*
Never hinged 20.00
O40 A54 4c yel grn (On O16) 45.00 *30.00*
Never hinged 80.00
O40A A55 6c dk brn (On O29) *8,000.* —
O41 A57 10c rose car (On O31) *500.00*
*a.* No period after "O" *4,000.*
O42 A60 20c lt ol grn (On O22) *8,000.*
O43 A60 20c lt ol grn (On O26) *1,750.*

## No. 497 Overprinted Type "c" in Black

**1946, June 19** ***Perf. 11x10½***

O44 A76 2c sepia .25 .25
Never hinged .25
*a.* Vertical pair, bottom stamp without ovpt. —

## OCCUPATION STAMPS

## Issued Under Japanese Occupation

No. 461 Overprinted in Black

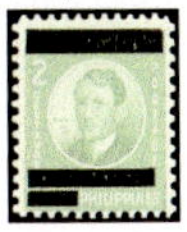

No. 438 Overprinted in Black

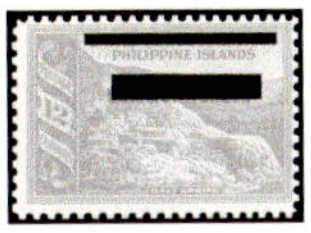

No. 439 Overprinted in Black

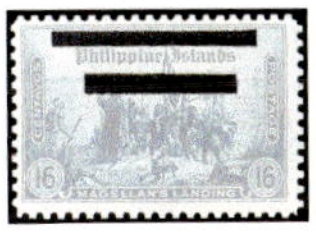

**1942-43 Unwmk.** ***Perf. 11x10½, 11***

N1 A75 2c apple green .25 *1.00*
Never hinged .30
*a.* Pair, one without overprint —
N2 A58 12c black ('43) .25 *2.00*
Never hinged .40
P# block of 6 12.00
Never hinged 15.00
N3 A59 16c dark blue 5.00 3.75
Never hinged 7.50
P# block of 6 37.50
Never hinged 55.00
*Nos. N1-N3 (3)* 5.50 6.75
Set, never hinged 8.20

## Nos. 435a, 435, 442, 443, and 423 Surcharged in Black

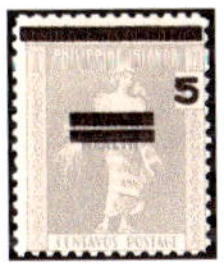
a

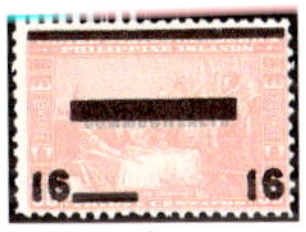
b

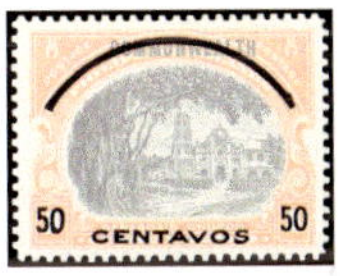
c

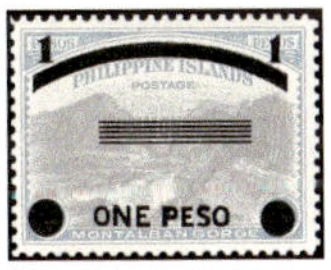
d

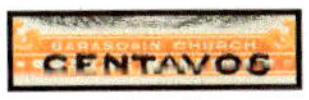
Type I

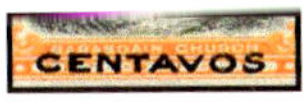
Type II

Two types of 50c surcharge
Type I: Center of "A" is a triangle.
Type II: Center of "A" is a pin hole.

**1942-43** ***Perf. 11***

N4 A55(a) 5(c) on 6c golden brown .25 *.75*
Never hinged .35
*a.* Top bar shorter and thinner .25 *1.00*
Never hinged .35
P# block of 6 50.00
Never hinged 60.00
*b.* 5(c) on 6c dark brown .25 *.85*
Never hinged .35
*c.* As "b," top bar shorter and thinner .25 *1.00*
Never hinged .35
*d.* Double surcharge, on cover —
N5 A62(b) 16(c) on 30c org red ('43) .25 *.60*
Never hinged .45
N6 A63(c) 50c on 1p red org & blk ('43) .75 *1.25*
Never hinged 1.10
P# block of 4, 2 P# 16.00
Never hinged 20.00
*a.* Double surcharge *300.00*
*b.* Type I surcharge 100.00 90.00
Never hinged 125.00
P# block of 4 500.00
Never hinged 600.00

N7 A65(d) 1p on 4p bl & blk ('43) 100.00 *150.00*
Never hinged 155.00
*Nos. N4-N7 (4)* 101.25 152.60
Set, never hinged 156.90

On Nos. N4 and N4b, the top bar measures 1½x22½mm. On Nos. N4a and N4c, the top bar measures 1x21mm and the "5" is smaller and thinner.

The used value for No. N7 is for postal cancellation. Used stamps exist with first day cancellations. They are worth somewhat less.

## No. 384 Surcharged in Black

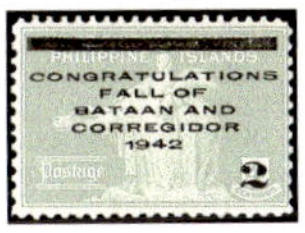

**1942, May 18**

N8 A54 2(c) on 4c yellow green 4.00 5.00
Never hinged 8.75

Issued to commemorate Japan's capture of Bataan and Corregidor. The American-Filipino forces finally surrendered May 7, 1942. No. N8 exists with "R" for "B" in BATAAN.

## No. 384 Surcharged in Black

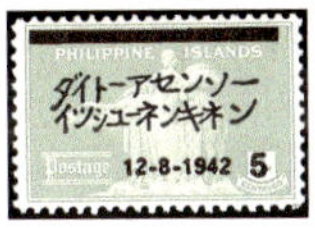

**1942, Dec. 8**

N9 A54 5(c) on 4c yellow green .50 *1.00*
Never hinged .75

1st anniversary of the "Greater East Asia War."

## Nos. C59 and C62 Surcharged in Black

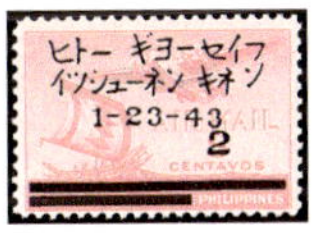

**1943, Jan. 23**

N10 AP1 2(c) on 8c carmine .25 *1.00*
Never hinged .35
P# block of 6 20.00
Never hinged 25.00
N11 AP1 5c on 1p sepia .50 *1.50*
Never hinged .75

1st anniv. of the Philippine Executive Commission.

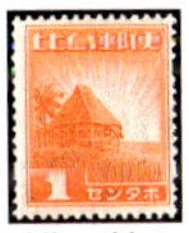
Nipa Hut
OS1

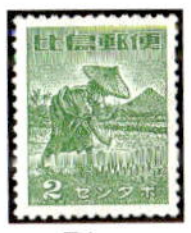
Rice Planting
OS2

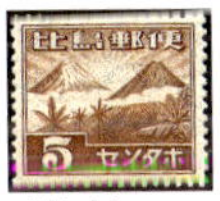
Mt. Mayon and Mt. Fuji
OS3

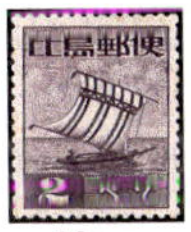
Moro Vinta
OS4

The "c" currency is indicated by four Japanese characters, "p" currency by two.

## Engraved; Typographed (2c, 6c, 25c)

**1943-44 Wmk. 257** ***Perf. 13***

N12 OS1 1c dp orange .25 .40
Never hinged .30
Margin block of 6, inscription 2.40
Never hinged 3.00
N13 OS2 2c brt green .25 .40
Never hinged .30
Margin block of 6, inscription 2.40
Never hinged 3.00
N14 OS1 4c slate green .25 .40
Never hinged .30
Margin block of 6, inscription 2.40
Never hinged 3.00

**N15** OS3 5c orange brown .25 .40
Never hinged .30
Margin block of 6, inscription 2.40
Never hinged 3.00
**N16** OS2 6c red .25 .60
Never hinged .30
Margin block of 6, inscription 2.40
Never hinged 3.00
**N17** OS3 10c blue green .25 .40
Never hinged .30
Margin block of 6, inscription 2.40
Never hinged 3.00
**N18** OS4 12c steel blue 1.00 1.50
Never hinged 1.50
Margin block of 6, inscription 11.00
Never hinged 14.00
**N19** OS4 16c dk brown .25 .40
Never hinged .30
Margin block of 6, inscription 2.40
Never hinged 3.00
**N20** OS1 20c rose violet 1.25 1.75
Never hinged 1.90
Margin block of 6, inscription 15.00
Never hinged 19.00
**N21** OS3 21c violet .25 .40
Never hinged .35
Margin block of 6, inscription 2.40
Never hinged 3.00
**N22** OS2 25c pale brown .25 .40
Never hinged .35
Margin block of 6, inscription 2.40
Never hinged 3.00
**N23** OS3 1p dp carmine .75 1.25
Never hinged 1.15
Margin block of 6, inscription 9.50
Never hinged 12.00
**N24** OS4 2p dull violet 6.50 6.50
Never hinged 10.00
**N25** OS4 5p dark olive 16.00 18.00
Never hinged 25.00
*Nos. N12-N25 (14)* 27.75 32.80
Set, never hinged 42.00

Issued: Nos. N13, N15, 4/1; Nos. N12, N14, N23, 6/7; Nos. N16-N19, 7/14; Nos. N20-N22, 8/16; No. N24, 9/16; No. N25, 4/1/44.

For surcharges see Nos. NB5-NB7.

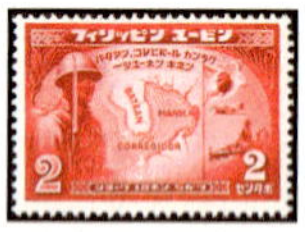

OS5

**1943, May 7 Photo. Unwmk.**

**N26** OS5 2c carmine red .25 *.75*
Never hinged .30
Margin block of 6, inscription 4.00
Never hinged 5.00
**N27** OS5 5c bright green .25 *1.00*
Never hinged .35
Margin block of 6, inscription 6.50
Never hinged 8.00

1st anniversary of the fall of Bataan and Corregidor.

No. 440 Surcharged in Black

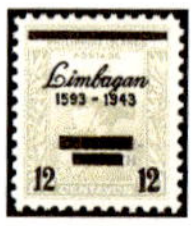


**1943, June 20 Engr. *Perf. 11***

**N28** A60 12(c) on 20c light olive green .25 *.75*
Never hinged .35
*a.* Double surcharge —

350th anniversary of the printing press in the Philippines. "Limbagan" is Tagalog for "printing press."

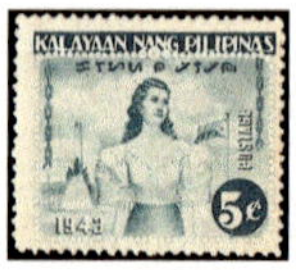

Rizal Monument, Filipina and Philippine Flag — OS6

**1943, Oct. 14 Photo. *Perf. 12***

**N29** OS6 5c light blue .25 *.90*
Never hinged .30
*a.* Imperf. .25 *.90*
**N30** OS6 12c orange .25 *.90*
Never hinged .30
*a.* Imperf. .25 *.90*
**N31** OS6 17c rose pink .25 *.90*
Never hinged .30
*a.* Imperf. .25 *.90*
*Nos. N29-N31 (3)* .75 *2.70*
Set, never hinged .90

"Independence of the Philippines." Japan granted "independence" Oct. 14, 1943, when the puppet republic was founded.

The imperforate stamps were issued without gum.

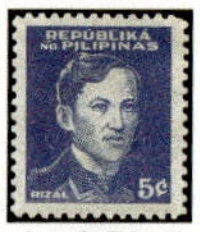

José Rizal
OS7

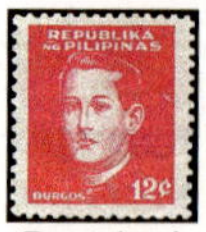

Rev. José Burgos
OS8

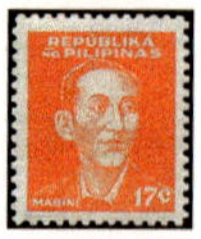

Apolinario Mabini — OS9

**1944, Feb. 17 Litho.**

**N32** OS7 5c blue .25 *1.00*
Never hinged .30
*a.* Imperf. .25 *2.00*
Never hinged .35
**N33** OS8 12c carmine .25 *1.00*
Never hinged .30
*a.* Imperf. .25 *2.00*
Never hinged .35
**N34** OS9 17c deep orange .25 *1.00*
Never hinged .30
*a.* Imperf. .25 *2.00*
Never hinged .35
*Nos. N32-N34 (3)* .75 *3.00*
Set, never hinged .90

See No. NB8.

Nos. C60 and C61 Surcharged in Black

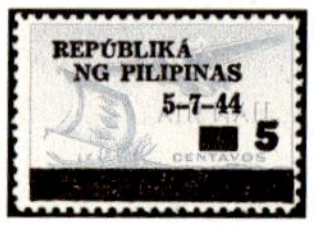


**1944, May 7 *Perf. 11***

**N35** AP1 5(c) on 20c ultra .50 1.00
Never hinged .75
P# block of 6 32.50
Never hinged 40.00
**N36** AP1 12(c) on 60c blue green 1.75 1.75
Never hinged 2.50
P# block of 6 42.50
Never hinged 52.50

2nd anniversary of the fall of Bataan and Corregidor.

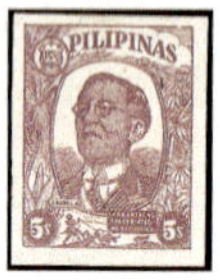

OS10

**1945, Jan. 12 Litho. *Imperf.***
**Without Gum**

**N37** OS10 5c dull violet brown .25 *.50*
Never hinged .30
**N38** OS10 7c blue green .25 *.50*
Never hinged .30
**N39** OS10 20c chalky blue .25 *.50*
Never hinged .30
*Nos. N37-N39 (3)* .75 *1.50*
Set, never hinged .90

Issued belatedly on Jan. 12, 1945, to commemorate the first anniversary of the puppet Philippine Republic, Oct. 14, 1944. "S" stands for "sentimos."

---

## OCCUPATION SEMI-POSTAL STAMPS

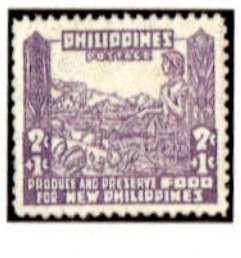

Woman, Farming and Cannery — OSP1

**Unwmk.**
**1942, Nov. 12 Litho. *Perf. 12***

**NB1** OSP1 2c + 1c pale violet .25 *.60*
Never hinged .30
**NB2** OSP1 5c + 1c brt grn .25 *1.00*
Never hinged .30
**NB3** OSP1 16c + 2c orange 25.00 *32.50*
Never hinged 42.00
*Nos. NB1-NB3 (3)* 25.50 34.10
Set, never hinged 42.60

Issued to promote the campaign to produce and conserve food. The surtax aided the Red Cross.

Souvenir Sheet

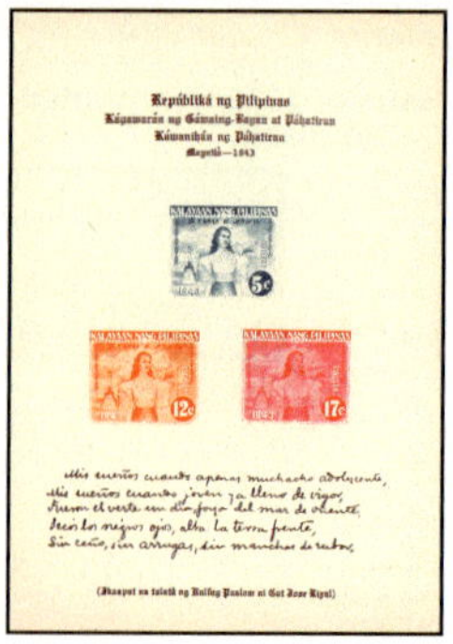

OSP2

**1943, Oct. 14 Without Gum *Imperf.***

**NB4** OSP2 Sheet of 3 60.00 *17.50*

"Independence of the Philippines."

No. NB4 contains one each of Nos. N29a-N31a. Marginal inscription is from Rizal's "Last Farewell." Sold for 2.50p.

The value of No. NB4 used is for a sheet from a first day cover. Commercially used sheets are extremely scarce and worth much more.

Nos. N18, N20 and N21 Surcharged in Black

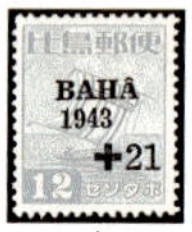


**1943, Dec. 8 Wmk. 257 *Perf. 13***

**NB5** OS4 12c + 21c steel blue .25 *1.50*
Never hinged .30
Margin block of 6, inscription 4.00
Never hinged 5.00
**NB6** OS1 20c + 36c rose violet .25 *1.50*
Never hinged .30
Margin block of 6, inscription 4.00
Never hinged 5.00
**NB7** OS3 21c + 40c violet .25 *2.00*
Never hinged .30
Margin block of 6, inscription 4.75
Never hinged 6.00
*Nos. NB5-NB7 (3)* .75 *5.00*
Set, never hinged .90

The surtax was for the benefit of victims of a Luzon flood. "Baha" is Tagalog for "flood."

Souvenir Sheet

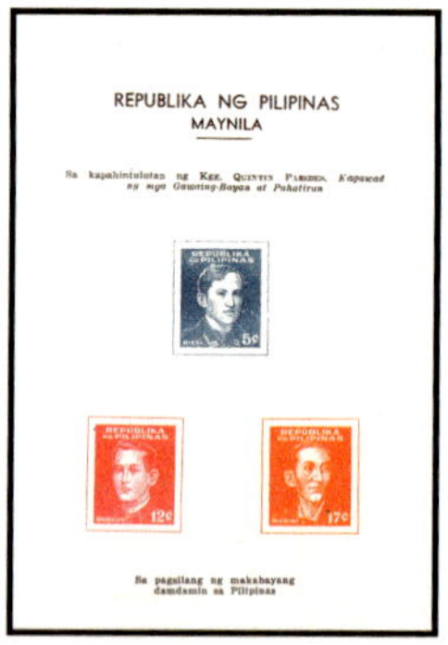


OSP3

**Unwmk.**
**1944, Feb. 9 Litho. *Imperf.***
**Without Gum**

**NB8** OSP3 Sheet of 3 6.50 3.50

No. NB8 contains 1 each of Nos. N32a-N34a.

Sheet sold for 1p, surtax going to a fund for the care of heroes' monuments.

The value for No. NB8 used is for a stamp from a first day cover. Commercially used examples are worth much more.

---

## OCCUPATION POSTAGE DUE STAMP

No. J15 Overprinted in Blue

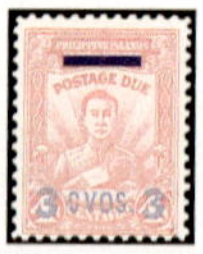

**1942, Oct. 14 Unwmk. *Perf. 11***

**NJ1** D3 3c on 4c brown red 25.00 *35.00*
Never hinged 37.50

On examples of No. J15, two lines were drawn in India ink with a ruling pen across "United States of America" by employees of the Short Paid Section of the Manila Post Office to make a provisional 3c postage due stamp which was used from Sept. 1, 1942 (when the letter rate was raised from 2c to 5c) until Oct. 14 when No. NJ1 went on sale. Value on cover, $175.

Bottom plate blocks of 6 of No. NJ1 are much scarcer than the right side plate blocks. Value $325 hinged, $450 never hinged.

---

## OCCUPATION OFFICIAL STAMPS

Nos. 461, 413, 435, 435a and 442 Ovptd. or Srchd. in Black with Bars and

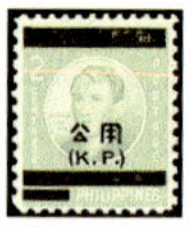


**1943-44 Unwmk. *Perf. 11x10½, 11***

**NO1** A75 2c apple green .25 *.75*
Never hinged .30
*a.* Double overprint 400.00
Never hinged 600.00
**NO2** A55 5(c) on 6c dk brn (On No. 413) ('44) 40.00 *45.00*
Never hinged 55.00
**NO3** A55 5(c) on 6c golden brn (On No. 435a) .25 *.90*
Never hinged .35
P# block of 6 14.00
Never hinged 17.50
*a.* Narrower spacing between bars .25 *.90*
Never hinged .35
*b.* 5(c) on 6c dark brown (On No. 435) .25 *.90*
Never hinged .35
*c.* As "b," narrower spacing between bars .25 *.90*
Never hinged .35
*d.* Double overprint —
**NO4** A62 16(c) on 30c org red .30 *1.25*
Never hinged .45
P# block of 6 20.00
Never hinged 25.00
*a.* Wider spacing between bars .30 *1.25*
Never hinged .45
*Nos. NO1-NO4 (4)* 40.80 47.90
Set, never hinged 56.10

On Nos. NO3 and NO3b the bar deleting "United States of America" is 9¾ to 10mm above the bar deleting "Common." On Nos. NO3a and NO3c, the spacing is 8 to 8½mm.

On No. NO4, the center bar is 19mm long, 3½mm below the top bar and 6mm above the Japanese characters. On No. NO4a, the center bar is 20½mm long, 9mm below the top bar and 1mm above the Japanese characters.

"K.P." stands for Kagamitang Pampamahalaan, "Official Business" in Tagalog.

Nos. 435 & 435a Surcharged in Black

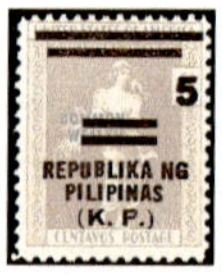


**1944, Aug. 28 *Perf. 11***

**NO5** A55 (5c) on 6c gldn brn .30 *.40*
Never hinged .45
P# block of 6 20.00
Never hinged 25.00
*a.* 5(c) on 6c dark brown .30 *.40*
Never hinged .45
P# block of 6 20.00
Never hinged 25.00

**Nos. O34 and C62 Overprinted in Black**

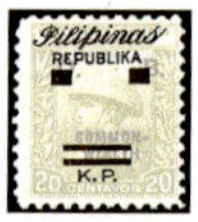

a

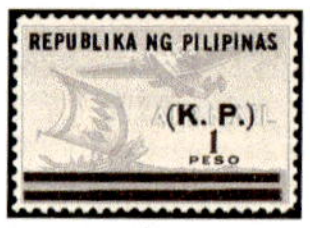


b

**NO6** A60(a) 20c light olive green .40 *.50*
Never hinged .60
P# block of 6 12.00
Never hinged 15.00
**NO7** AP1(b) 1p sepia .90 *1.00*
Never hinged 1.45
P# block of 6 20.00
Never hinged 25.00
*Nos. NO5-NO7 (3)* 1.60 1.90
Set, never hinged 2.05

## PUERTO RICO

ˌpwer-tə-ˈrē-ˌkō

(Porto Rico)

LOCATION — Large island in the West Indies, east of Hispaniola
GOVT. — Former Spanish possession
AREA — 3,435 sq. mi.
POP. — 953,243 (1899)
CAPITAL — San Juan

The island was ceded to the US by the Treaty of 1898.

Spanish issues of 1855-73 used in both Puerto Rico and Cuba are listed as Cuba Nos. 1-4, 9-14, 18-21, 32-34, 35A-37, 39-41, 43-45, 47-49, 51-53, 55-57.

Spanish issues of 1873-1898 for Puerto Rico only are listed in Vol. 4 of this Catalogue.

100 Cents = 1 Dollar (1898)

### Issued under U.S. Administration
### LOCAL ISSUES
### Ponce Issue

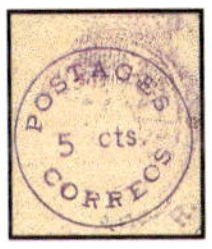
A11

**Handstamped**

**1898** **Unwmk.** ***Imperf.***

| | | | |
|---|---|---|---|
| **200** | A11 5c violet | | — |

No. 200 is a violet handstamp and control mark used on envelopes. Some examples have no control mark. There are three types of circular markings known, and two control marks. Uses on 2¢ U.S. stamps on cover were strictly as a cancellation, not as local postage. Because genuine usage is extremely difficult to authenticate with certainty, certification by competent authorities is essential.

### Coamo Issue

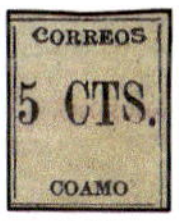
A12

**Typeset, setting of 10**

**1898, Aug.**

| | | | |
|---|---|---|---|
| **201** | A12 5c black | 700. | *1,250.* |

See the Scott U.S. Specialized Catalogue for more detailed listings.

The stamps bear the control mark "F. Santiago" in violet. About 500 were issued.

Dangerous forgeries exist.

### Regular Issue

United States Nos. 279, 279Bf, 281, 272 and 282C Overprinted in Black at 36 degree angle

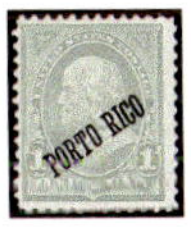

**1899** **Wmk. 191** ***Perf. 12***

| | | | |
|---|---|---|---|
| **210** | A87 1c yellow green | 6.00 | 1.40 |
| | Never hinged | 10.00 | |
| *a.* | Overprint at 25 degree angle | 8.00 | 2.25 |
| | Never hinged | 17.50 | |
| **211** | A88 2c redsh car, type IV | 5.00 | 1.25 |
| | Never hinged | 11.00 | |
| *a.* | Overprint at 25 degree angle, *Mar. 15* | 6.50 | 2.25 |
| | Never hinged | 14.00 | |
| **212** | A91 5c blue | 12.50 | 2.50 |
| | Never hinged | 27.50 | |
| **213** | A93 8c violet brown | 40.00 | 17.50 |
| | Never hinged | 90.00 | |
| *a.* | Overprint at 25 degree angle | 45.00 | 19.00 |
| | Never hinged | 100.00 | |
| *c.* | "PORTO RIC" | 150.00 | 110.00 |
| **214** | A94 10c brown, type I | 22.50 | 6.00 |
| | Never hinged | 50.00 | |
| | *Nos. 210-214 (5)* | 86.00 | 28.65 |

Misspellings of the overprint on Nos. 210-214 (PORTO RICU, PORTU RICO, FORTO RICO) are actually broken letters.

United States Nos. 279 and 279B Overprinted Diagonally in Black

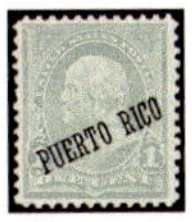

**1900**

| | | | |
|---|---|---|---|
| **215** | A87 1c yellow green | 7.50 | 1.40 |
| | Never hinged | 17.50 | |
| **216** | A88 2c red, type IV | 5.50 | 2.00 |
| | Never hinged | 12.50 | |
| *b.* | Inverted overprint | | *12,500.* |

### POSTAGE DUE STAMPS

United States Nos. J38, J39 and J42 Overprinted in Black at 36 degree angle

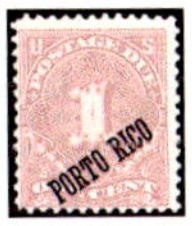

**1899** **Wmk. 191** ***Perf. 12***

| | | | |
|---|---|---|---|
| **J1** | D2 1c deep claret | 22.50 | 5.50 |
| | Never hinged | 50.00 | |
| *a.* | Overprint at 25 degree angle | 22.50 | 7.50 |
| | Never hinged | 50.00 | |
| **J2** | D2 2c deep claret | 20.00 | 6.00 |
| | Never hinged | 45.00 | |
| *a.* | Overprint at 25 degree angle | 20.00 | 7.00 |
| | Never hinged | 45.00 | |
| **J3** | D2 10c deep claret | 180.00 | 55.00 |
| | Never hinged | 375.00 | |
| *a.* | Overprint at 25 degree angle | 160.00 | 75.00 |
| | Never hinged | 330.00 | |
| | *Nos. J1-J3 (3)* | 222.50 | 66.50 |

Stamps of Puerto Rico were replaced by those of the United States.

## RYUKYU ISLANDS

rē-ˈyü-ˌkyü ˈī-lənds

LOCATION — Chain of 63 islands between Japan and Formosa, separating the East China Sea from the Pacific Ocean.
GOVT. — Semi-autonomous under United States administration.
AREA — 848 sq. mi.
POP. — 945,465 (1970)
CAPITAL — Naha, Okinawa

The Ryukyus were part of Japan until American forces occupied them in 1945. The islands reverted to Japan May 15, 1972.

Before the general issue of 1948, a number of provisional stamps were used. These included a mimeographed-handstamped adhesive for Kume Island, and various current stamps of Japan handstamped with chops by the postmasters of Okinawa, Amami, Miyako and Yaeyama. Although authorized by American authorities, these provisionals were local in nature, so are omitted in the listings that follow. They are listed in the *Scott United States Specialized Catalogue.*

100 Sen = 1 Yen
100 Cents = 1 Dollar (1958)

Catalogue values for unused stamps in this country are for Never Hinged items.

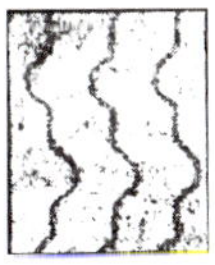
Wmk. 257

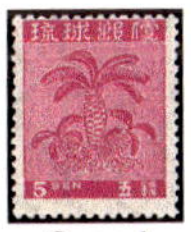
Cycad A1

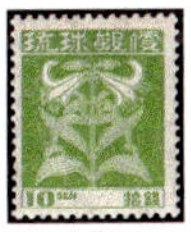
Lily A2

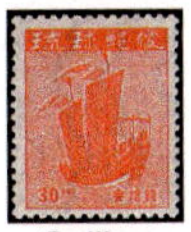
Sailing Ship A3

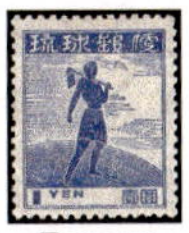
Farmer A4

**1948-49** **Typo.** **Wmk. 257** ***Perf. 13***

**Second Printing, July 18, 1949**

| | | | |
|---|---|---|---|
| **1** | A1 5s magenta | 2.00 | 2.00 |
| **2** | A2 10s yellow green | 5.00 | 5.00 |
| **3** | A1 20s yellow green | 3.00 | 3.00 |
| **4** | A3 30s vermilion | 1.25 | 1.25 |
| **5** | A2 40s magenta | 1.25 | 1.25 |
| **6** | A3 50s ultramarine | 5.00 | *4.00* |
| **7** | A4 1y ultramarine | 5.00 | 5.00 |
| | *Nos. 1-7 (7)* | 22.50 | 21.50 |

**First Printing, July 1, 1948**

| | | | |
|---|---|---|---|
| **1a** | A1 5s magenta | 3.00 | *3.50* |
| **2a** | A2 10s yellow green | 2.00 | *2.00* |
| **3a** | A1 20s yellow green | 2.00 | *2.00* |
| **4a** | A3 30s vermilion | 4.00 | *3.50* |
| **5a** | A2 40s magenta | 50.00 | 50.00 |
| **6a** | A3 50s ultramarine | 4.00 | 4.00 |
| **7a** | A4 1y ultramarine | 400.00 | 325.00 |
| | *Nos. 1a-7a (7)* | 465.00 | 390.00 |

First printing: thick yellow gum, dull colors, rough perforations, grayish paper. Second printing: white gum, sharp colors, clean-cut and rough perforations, white paper. Third printing (Sept. 28, 1950): 5s to 50s denominations, white gum, clean-cut perforations, cream paper (same values as second printings).

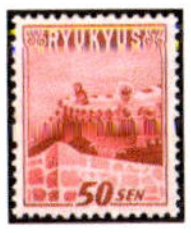
Tile Rooftop and Shishi — A5

Designs: 50s, Tile rooftop and Shisa. 1y, Ryukyuan girl. 2y, Main hall of Shuri Castle. 3y, Female dragonhead statue. 4y, Two women. 5y, Sea shells.

***Perf. 13x13¼***

**1950, Jan. 21** **Photo.** **Unwmk.**

**Off-white Paper**

| | | | |
|---|---|---|---|
| **8** | A5 50s dark carmine rose | .25 | .25 |
| *a.* | White paper, third printing, *Sept. 6, 1958* | .50 | .50 |
| *b.* | "White Sky" variety (pos. 76) | 3.50 | 3.50 |
| **9** | A5 1y deep blue | 3.25 | 3.00 |
| **10** | A5 2y rose violet | 9.00 | 6.00 |
| **11** | A5 3y carmine rose | 22.50 | 11.00 |
| **12** | A5 4y greenish gray | 11.00 | 11.00 |
| **13** | A5 5y blue green | 6.50 | 6.00 |
| | *Nos. 8-13 (6)* | 52.50 | 37.25 |

The original first two printings (No. 8) were printed on off-white paper with yellowish gum and a 5-character imprint in the sheet margin. The first printing is a deep carmine red or dark red, and the second printing a dark carmine rose. The first printing was issued Jan. 21, 1950; the second printing received in Naha Sept. 22, 1950, and the third printing (No. 8a) Sept. 6, 1958. Quantities: first printing: 300,000; second printing: 3,000,000; and third printing: 300,000. The first printing unused is much scarcer than the second printing because most of the first printing was used as postage.

No. 8a has colorless gum and an 8-character imprint in the sheet margin. The color is a deep red.

For No. 8b, a defect in position 76 of the plates used resulted in the sky above the roof being predominantly white in the second printing, whereas in the first printing the 'white sky' is not as pronounced. The master negative and plate were reworked for the third printing, so position 76 in this printing does not have the "white sky" variety.

For surcharges see Nos. 16-17.

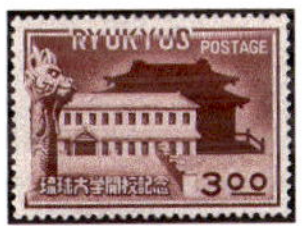
Ryukyu University and Female Dragonhead Statue — A6

**1951, Feb. 12** ***Perf. 13½x13¼***

| | | | |
|---|---|---|---|
| **14** | A6 3y red brown | 45.00 | 25.00 |

Opening of Ryukyu University, Feb. 12.

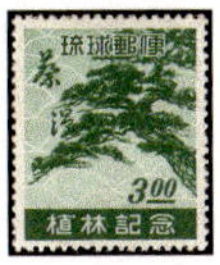
Ryukyuan Pine Tree — A7

**1951, Feb. 19** ***Perf. 13¼***

| | | | |
|---|---|---|---|
| **15** | A7 3y dark green | 40.00 | 22.50 |

Reforestation Week, Feb. 18-24.

**No. 8 surcharged in Black**

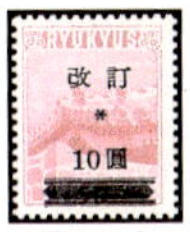
Type I

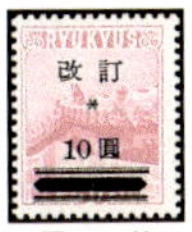
Type II

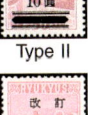

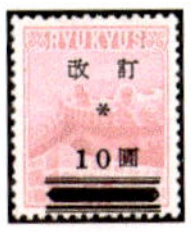
Type III

There are three types of 10y surcharge:

Type I: narrow-spaced rules, "10" normal spacing, "Kai Tei" characters in 9-point type. First printing, Jan. 1, 1952.

Type II: wide-spaced rules, "10" normal spacing, "Kai Tei" characters in 9-point type. Second printing, June 5, 1952.

Type III: rules and "10" both wide-spaced, "Kai Tei" characters in 8-point type. Third printing, Dec. 8, 1952.

Both eight and nine point type were used in overprinting Nos. 16-17. In the varieties listed below, the first number indicates the size of the "Kai" character, and the second number is the size of the "Tei" character.

**1952** ***Perf. 13½x13***

| | | | |
|---|---|---|---|
| **16** | A5 10y on 50s dark carmine rose (II) | 8.00 | 8.00 |
| *c.* | 8/8 point Kai Tei | 8.00 | 8.00 |
| *d.* | 9/8 point Kai Tei | 80.00 | 80.00 |
| *f.* | Surcharge transposed | 1,700. | — |
| *g.* | Legend of surcharge only (no obliteration bars) | 1,200. | |
| *h.* | Wrong font for "0" (pos. 59) | 150.00 | 150.00 |
| *i.* | Wrong font for "Yen" symbol (pos. 69) | 150.00 | 150.00 |
| *j.* | Surcharge on "white sky" variety (No. 8b) (pos. 76) | 150.00 | 150.00 |

On No. 16e, the entire obliteration-bars portion of the surcharge normally under the 10 Yen must be visible at the top of the stamp. Ten examples of No. 16e exist (pos. 91-100) with the full obliteration bars also in the bottom selvage.

Forgeries to defraud the Postal Agency of revenue are known, used only, at the Gusikawa Post Office. Two types. Value, $500 each.

| | | | |
|---|---|---|---|
| **16A** | A5 10y on 50s dark carmine rose (I) | 30.00 | 30.00 |
| *a.* | 8/8 point Kai Tei | 30.00 | 30.00 |
| *b.* | Bottom two bars inverted (pos. 17) | 150.00 | 150.00 |
| *c.* | Wrong font for "0" (pos. 73) | 250.00 | 250.00 |
| *d.* | Surcharge on "white sky" variety (No. 8b) (pos. 76) | 250.00 | 250.00 |
| *e.* | Wide spaced obliterating bars (pos. 72) | 150.00 | 150.00 |
| *f.* | Wide spaced bottom obliterating bars (pos. 86, 95) | 80.00 | 80.00 |
| **16B** | A5 10y on 50s dark carmine rose (III) | 45.00 | 35.00 |
| *a.* | Wrong font for "Yen" symbol (pos. 25, 35, 65) | 200.00 | 200.00 |
| *b.* | Wrong font for "Tei" (pos. 26) | 350.00 | 350.00 |
| *c.* | Asterisk missing (pos. 54) | — | — |
| *d.* | "Kai Tei" 1.25mm above asterisk (pos. 54) | 350.00 | 350.00 |
| *e.* | "Kai" omitted (pos. 71) | — | |
| *f.* | Narrow spaced "10" (pos. 98) | 350.00 | 350.00 |
| *g.* | Surcharge on "white sky" variety (No. 8b) | 350.00 | 350.00 |
| *h.* | Extra wide spaced "10" (pos. 60) | 200.00 | 200.00 |
| *i.* | Asterisk within 2.0mm of "Kai Tei" (pos. 87) | 200.00 | 200.00 |

The Kai Tei of the third printing measures the same as the 8-point type in the earlier printings but has differing characteristics. The Top curved line of the Kai is shorter and the lower curved line is also much shorter.

# RYUKYU ISLANDS

No. 10 surcharged 100y in black

17  A5  100y on 2y rose violet, Kai Tei characters in 9/9-point type, June 16, 1952      2,000.   1,400.
  a. 8/8 point Kai Tei           2,000.   1,400.
  b. 9/8 point Kai Tei           3,250.   3,250.
  c. Center "0" in wrong font, stamp with 9/9 Kai Tei (pos. 42)   4,000.   4,000.
  d. Center "0" in wrong font, stamp with 8/8 Kai Tei (pos. 67, 86)   3,500.   3,500.
  e. Center "0" in wrong font, stamp with 9/8 Kai Tei (pos. 53)   5,000.   5,000.
  f. Wrong font for last "0" (pos. 59)   5,000.   5,000.
  g. Wrong font for "yen" symbol (pos. 69)   5,000.   5,000.
  h. "Tei" in wrong font (pos. 9)   4,000.   4,000.

Varieties of shifted and damaged surcharge characters exist, most notably a damaged ("clipped") Kai (pos. 26, 85).
The "Tei" on No. 17h is the character used on Nos. 16 and 16A.
See note after 16B to differentiate between 8-point and 9-point characters.
Surcharge forgeries are known. Authentication by competant experts is recommended.

Dove, Bean Sprout and Map — A8

**1952, Apr. 1**                    **Perf. 13¼**
18  A8  3y deep plum              80.00   40.00
Establishment of the Government of the Ryukyu Islands (GRI), April 1, 1952.

Madanbashi Bridge — A9

Designs: 2y, Main Hall, Shuri Castle. 3y, Shureimon Gate. 6y, Stone Gate, Sogen-ji Temple, Naha. 10y, Benzaiten-do Temple. 30y, Sonohyan Utaki (altar) at Shuri Castle. 50y, Tamaudun (royal mausoleum). Shuri. 100y, Stone Bridge, Hojo Pond, Enkaku Temple.

**1952-53**                         **Perf. 13x13¼**
19  A9   1y red                       .30     .30
20  A9   2y green                     .40     .40
21  A9   3y aquamarine                .50     .50
22  A9   6y blue                     2.00    2.00
23  A9   10y crimson rose            2.50    1.00
24  A9   30y olive green             9.00    7.50
  a. 30y light olive green, 1958   50.00
25  A9   50y rose violet           12.50    9.00
26  A9   100y claret               15.00    5.00
      Nos. 19-26 (8)               42.20   25.70

Issued: 1y, 2y and 3y, 11/20/52. Others, 1/20/53.

Reception at Shuri Castle — A10

Perry and American Fleet in Naha Port — A11

**1953, May 26**                    **Perf. 13x13¼**
27  A10  3y deep magenta           12.00    6.50
28  A11  6y chalky blue             1.25    1.50
Centenary of the arrival of Commodore Matthew Calbraith Perry at Naha, Okinawa.

Chofu Ota and Pencil-shaped Matrix — A12

**1953, Oct. 1**                    **Perf. 13¼x13**
29  A12  4y orange brown          11.00    5.00
Third Newspaper Week, Oct. 1-7.

Shigo Toma and Pen — A13

**1954, Oct. 1**
30  A13  4y blue                  10.00    7.50
Fourth Newspaper Week, Oct. 1-7.

Ryukyu Pottery — A14

Designs: 4y, Dachibin (sake or water flask). 15y, Tsuikin lacquerware tray. 20y, Kajimayaa pattern on Kijoka-bashofu textile.

**1954-55**   **Photo.**           **Perf. 13x13¼**
31  A14  4y brown                   .90     .50
32  A14  15y vermilion             3.50    3.50
33  A14  20y yellow orange         2.25    2.25
      Nos. 31-33 (3)                6.65    6.25
For surcharges see Nos. C19, C21, C23.

Noguni Shrine and Sweet Potato Plant — A15

**1955, Nov. 26**                   **Perf. 13¼**
34  A15  4y blue                  10.00    7.00
350th anniv. of the introduction of the sweet potato to the Ryukyu Islands.

Stylized Trees — A16

**1956, Feb. 18**                   **Perf. 13**
35  A16  4y blue green            10.00    6.00
Arbor Week, Feb. 18-24.

Yanaji (Willow) Dance — A17

8y, Munjuru (Straw Hat) Dance. 14y, Nido Tichiuchi Dance.

**1956, May 1**                     **Perf. 13x13¼**
36  A17  5y rose lilac             1.00     .60
37  A17  8y dk vio blue            2.00    2.00
38  A17  14y reddish brown         2.50    2.50
      Nos. 36-38 (3)                5.50    5.10
For surcharges see Nos. C20, C22.

Telephone A18

**1956, June 8**
39  A18  4y violet blue           12.50    8.00
Establishment of dial telephone system.

Garland of Pine, Bamboo and Plum — A19

**1956, Dec. 1**                    **Perf. 13¼**
40  A19  2y multicolored           1.60    1.60
New Year, 1957.

Map of Okinawa and Pencil Rocket — A20

**1957, Oct. 1**   **Photo.**       **Perf. 13**
41  A20  4y deep violet blue       1.00    1.00
Seventh Newspaper Week, Oct. 1-7.

Phoenix — A21

**1957, Dec. 1**                    **Perf. 13x13¼**
42  A21  2y multicolored            .25     .25
New Year, 1958.

Ryukyu Stamps A22

**1958, July 1**                    **Perf. 13½**
43  A22  4y multicolored            .80     .80
10th anniv. of 1st Ryukyu stamps.

Yen Symbol and Dollar Sign — A23

***Perf. 10.3, 10.8, 11.1 & Compound***
**1958, Sept. 16**                  **Typo.**
**Without Gum**
44  A23  ½c orange                  .80     .80
  a. Imperf., pair                1,500.
  b. Horiz. pair, imperf. between   225.00
  c. Vert. pair, imperf. between    575.00
  d. Vert. strip of 4, imperf. between   800.00
45  A23  1c yellow green           1.25    1.25
  a. Horiz. pair, imperf. between   200.00
  b. Vert. pair, imperf. between    150.00
  c. Vert. strip of 3, imperf. between   650.00
  d. Vert. strip of 4, imperf. between   800.00
  e. Block of 4, imperf. btwn. vert. & horiz.   10,000.
46  A23  2c gray blue              2.00    2.00
  a. Horiz. pair, imperf. between   200.00
  b. Vert. pair, imperf. between   2,200.
  c. Horiz. strip of 3, imperf. between   450.00
  d. Horiz. strip of 4, imperf. between   700.00
47  A23  3c deep carmine           1.50    1.50
  a. Horiz. pair, imperf. between   200.00
  b. Vert. pair, imperf. between    150.00
  c. Vert. strip of 3, imperf. between   400.00
  d. Vert. strip of 4, imperf. between   750.00
  e. Block of 4, imperf. btwn. vert. & horiz.   10,000.
48  A23  4c lt blue grn            2.00    2.00
  a. Horiz. pair, imperf. between   400.00
  b. Vert. pair, imperf. between    175.00
49  A23  5c orange brown           4.00    3.75
  a. Horiz. pair, imperf. between   200.00
  b. Vert. pair, imperf. between    850.00
50  A23  10c aquamarine            5.25    4.75
  a. Horiz. pair, imperf. between   200.00
  b. Vert. pair, imperf. between    150.00
  c. Vert. strip of 3, imperf. between   750.00
51  A23  25c bright violet blue    7.50    6.00
  a. Gummed paper, perf. 10.3 ('61)   15.00   15.00
  b. Horiz. pair, imperf. between  2,200.
  c. Vert. pair, imperf. between   5,000.
  d. Vert. strip of 3, imperf. between   900.00
52  A23  50c gray                 15.00   10.00
  a. Gummed paper, perf. 10.3 ('61)   15.00   15.00
  b. Horiz. pair, imperf. between  1,750.
53  A23  $1 reddish purple        11.00    5.50
  a. Horiz. pair, imperf. between   450.00
  b. Vert. pair, imperf. between   2,250.
      Nos. 44-53 (10)              50.30   37.55

Printed locally. Perforation, paper and shade varieties exist. Nos. 51a and 52a are on off-white paper and perf 10.3.

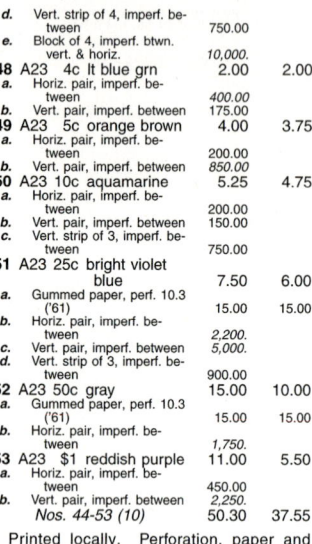
Gate of Courtesy A24

**1958, Oct. 15**  **Photo.**  **Perf. 13x13¼**
54  A24  3c multicolored           1.25    1.25
Restoration of Shureimon, Gate of Courtesy, on road leading to Shuri City.
Imitations of this stamp were distributed in 1972 to discourage speculation in Ryukyuan stamps. The imitations were printed without gum and have a lengthy message in light blue printed on the back. A second type exists, with printed black perforations and three Japanese characters on the back ("Mozo Hin" — imitation) in black. Value, sheet of 10 $15.

Lion Dance — A25

**1958, Dec. 10**                   **Perf. 13¼x13**
55  A25  1½c multicolored           .30     .30
New Year, 1959.

Trees and Mountains — A26

**1959, Apr. 30**                   **Perf. 13¼**
56  A26  3c blue, yellow green, green & red   .70   .60
"Make the Ryukyus Green" movement.

Yonaguni Moth — A27

**1959, July 23**  **Photo.**       **Perf. 13x13¼**
57  A27  3c multicolored           1.20    1.00
Meeting of the Japanese Biological Education Society in Okinawa.

Hibiscus — A28

琉球郵便
Inscribed

Designs: 3c, Fish (Moorish idol). 8c, Sea shell (Phalium bandatum). 13c, Butterfly (Kallinia inachus eucerca), denomination at left, butterfly going up. 17c, Jellyfish (Dactylometra pacifera Goette).

**1959, Aug. 10** *Perf. 12¾x13*

**58** A28 ½c multicolored .30 .25
**59** A28 3c multicolored .75 .40
**60** A28 8c light ultramarine, black & ocher 10.00 5.50
**61** A28 13c light blue, gray & orange 1.75 1.75
**62** A28 17c dp ultra, org red & yel 20.00 9.00
*Nos. 58-62 (5)* 32.80 16.90

Four-character inscription measures 10x2mm on ½c; 12x3mm on 3c, 8c; 8½x2mm on 13c, 17c. See Nos. 76-80.

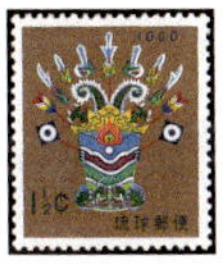
Toy (Yakaji) — A29

**1959, Dec. 1** *Perf. 13x13¼*

**63** A29 1½c gold & multi .55 .40

New Year, 1960.

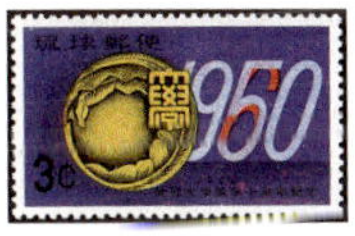
University Badge — A30

**1960, May 22** **Photo.**

**64** A30 3c multicolored .95 .75

10th anniv. opening of Ryukyu University.

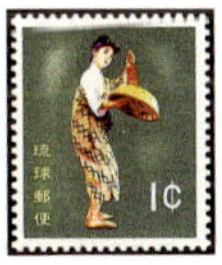
Straw Hat Folk Dancer — A31

Designs: 2½c, Nufwabushi. 5c, Hatumabushi. 10c, Hanafu.

**1960, Nov. 1** **Photo.** *Perf. 13¼*
**Dark Gray Background**

**65** A31 1c yel, red & vio 2.00 .80
**66** A31 2½c crim, blue & yel 3.00 1.00
**67** A31 5c dk blue, yel & red 1.00 .50
**68** A31 10c dk blue, yel & red 1.00 .70
*Nos. 65-68 (4)* 7.00 3.00

See Nos. 81-87, 220.

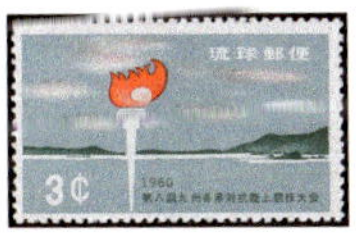
Torch and Nago Bay — A32

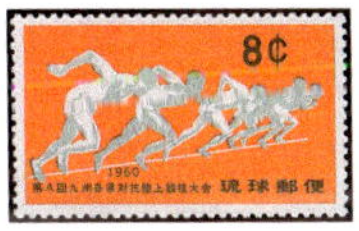
Runners at Starting Line — A33

**1960, Nov. 8** **Litho.** *Perf. 13x13¼*

**72** A32 3c lt blue, dp bluish grn & ver 5.00 3.00
**73** A33 8c org & dp bluish grn 1.00 .75

8th Kyushu Inter-Prefectural Athletic Meet, Nago, Northern Okinawa, Nov. 6-7.

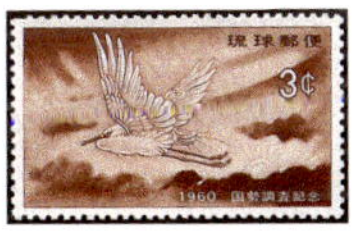
Little Egret and Rising Sun — A34

**1960, Dec. 1** **Photo.**

**74** A34 3c reddish brown 5.00 3.50

National census.

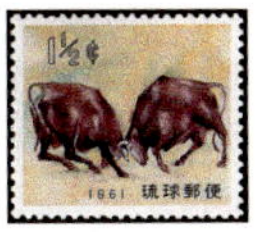
Okinawa Bull Fight — A35

**1960, Dec. 10**

**75** A35 1½c bister, dark blue & red brown 1.50 1.50

New Year, 1961.

**Type of 1959 With Japanese Inscription Redrawn**

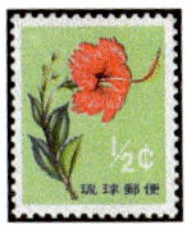
A28a

**1960-61** **Photo.**

**76** A28a ½c multicolored .60 .45
**77** A28a 3c multicolored 1.00 .35
**78** A28a 8c lt ultra, blk & ocher 1.25 .80
**79** A28a 13c lt blue & multi 1.50 .90
**80** A28a 17c dp ultra, brn rose & yel 12.50 6.00
*Nos. 76-80 (5)* 16.85 8.50

Size of Japanese inscription on Nos. 78-80 is 10½x1½mm. On No.79 the denomination is at right, butterfly going down.

Issued: Nos. 78-80, 7/1/60; No. 77, 8/23/61; No. 76, 10/61.

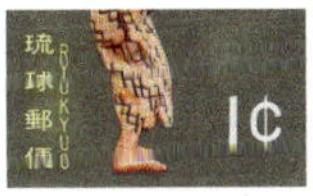
Dancer Type of 1960 with "RYUKYUS" Added in English

Designs: 20c, Shudun. 25c, Haodori. 50c, Nubui Kuduchi. $1, Koteibushi.

**1961-64** *Perf. 13¼*

**81** A31 1c multicolored .25 .25
**82** A31 2½c multicolored .25 .25
**83** A31 5c multicolored .25 .25
**84** A31 10c multicolored .45 .40
**84A** A31 20c multicolored 3.00 1.40
**85** A31 25c multicolored 1.00 .90
**86** A31 50c multicolored 2.50 1.40
**87** A31 $1 multicolored 5.50 .25
*Nos. 81-87 (8)* 13.20 5.10

Issued: Nos. 86-87, 9/1/61; No. 81, 12/5/61; No. 85, 2/1/62; Nos. 82-84, 6/20/62; No. 84A, 1/20/64.

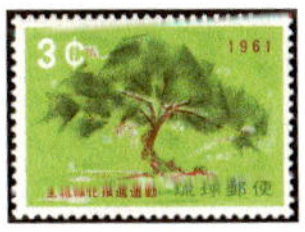
Pine Tree — A36

**1961, May 1** **Litho.**

**88** A36 3c yel grn & red 1.75 1.25

"Make the Ryukyus Green" movement.

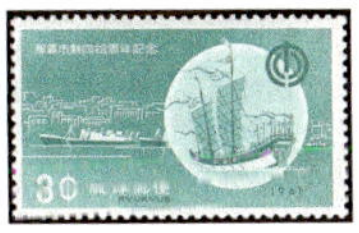
Naha, Steamer and Sailboat — A37

**1961, May 20** **Photo.**

**89** A37 3c aquamarine 2.25 1.50

40th anniv. of Naha.

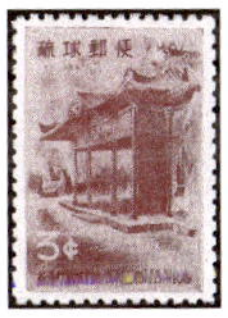
White Silver Temple — A38

*Perf. 10¾, 10¾x10¼*

**1961, Oct. 1** **Typo.** **Unwmk.**

**90** A38 3c red brown 2.50 2.00
*a.* Horiz. pair, imperf. between 1,000.
*b.* Vert. pair, imperf. between 700.00

Merger of townships Takamine, Kanegushiku and Miwa with Itoman.

A 3-cent stamp to commemorate the merger of two cities, Shimoji-cho and Hirara-shi of Miyako Island, was scheduled to be issued on Oct. 30, 1961. However, the merger was called off and the stamp was never issued. It features a white chaplet on Kiyako linen on a blue background.

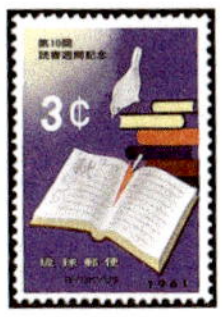
Books and Bird — A39

**1961, Nov. 12** **Litho.** *Perf. 13¼*

**91** A39 3c multicolored 1.10 .90

Book Week, 10th anniversary.

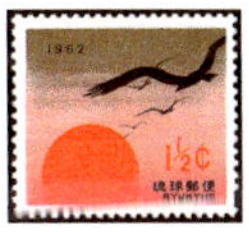
Rising Sun and Eagles — A40

**1961, Dec. 10** **Photo.**

**92** A40 1½c gold, ver & blk 2.00 2.00

New Year, 1962.

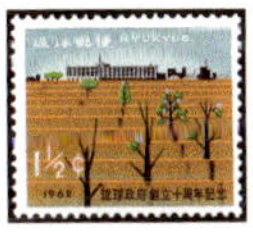
Symbolic Steps, Trees and Government Building — A41

Design: 3c, Government Building.

**1962, Apr. 1** *Perf. 13½*

**93** A41 1½c multicolored .60 .60
**94** A41 3c brt grn, red & gray .80 .80

10th anniv. of the Government of the Ryukyu Islands (GRI).

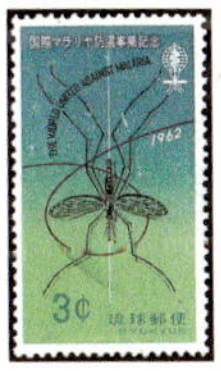
Anopheles Hyrcanus Sinensis — A42

Design: 8c, Malaria eradication emblem and Shurei gate.

**1962, Apr. 7** *Perf. 13½x13*

**95** A42 3c multicolored .60 .60
**96** A42 8c multicolored .90 .75

World Health Organization drive to eradicate malaria.

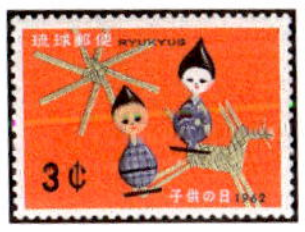
Dolls and Toys — A43

**1962, May 5** *Perf. 13x13¼*

**97** A43 3c red, black, blue & buff 1.10 1.00

Children's Day, 1962.

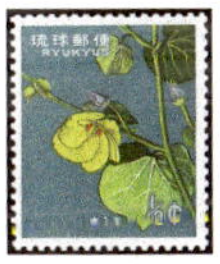
Linden or Sea Hibiscus — A44

Flowers: 3c, Deigo tree (Erythrina variegata var. orientealis). 8c, Iju (Schima liukiuensis Nakal). 13c, Touch-me-not (Impatiens balsamina). 17c, Shell flower (Alpinia speciosa).

**1962, June 1** **Photo.** *Perf. 13¼*

**98** A44 ½c multicolored .35 .25
**99** A44 3c multicolored .30 .25
**100** A44 8c multicolored .55 .45
**101** A44 13c multicolored .75 .60
**102** A44 17c multicolored 1.25 .80
*Nos. 98-102 (5)* 3.20 2.35

See Nos. 107 and 114 for 1½c and 15c flower stamps. For surcharge see No. 190.

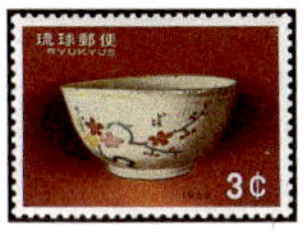
Akae (Earthenware) A45

**1962, July 5**

**103** A45 3c multicolored 3.50 2.50

Philatelic Week, July 5-12.

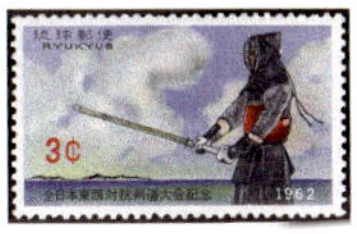
Japanese Fencing (Kendo) — A46

**1962, July 25** *Perf. 13¼x13*

**104** A46 3c multicolored 3.50 2.50

All-Japan Kendo Meeting in Okinawa, July 24-25, 1962.

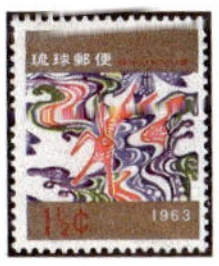
Rabbit Playing near Water, Bingata Cloth Design — A47

**1962, Dec. 10** *Perf. 13¼*

**105** A47 1½c gold & multi 1.00 .80

New Year, 1963.

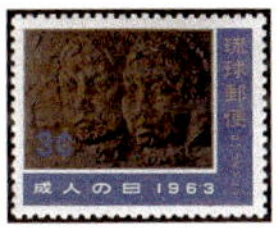
Young Man and Woman, Stone Relief — A48

**1963, Jan. 15** **Photo.**

**106** A48 3c gold, black & blue .90 .80

Adult Day.

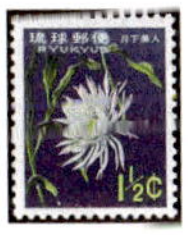
Gooseneck Cactus (Epiphyllum strictum) — A49

**1963, Apr. 5** *Perf. 13x13¼*

**107** A49 1½c dark blue green, yellow & pink .25 .25

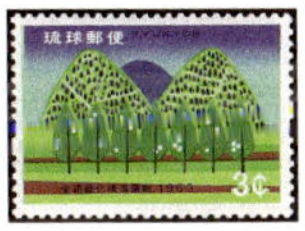
Trees and Wooded Hills — A50

**1963, Mar. 25** *Perf. 13¼*

**108** A50 3c ultra, grn & red brn 1.00 .80

"Make the Ryukyus Green" movement.

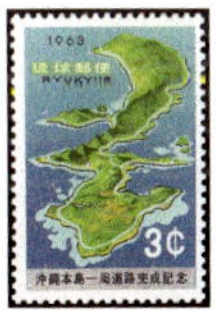
Map of Okinawa — A51

**1963, Apr. 30**

**109** A51 3c multicolored 1.25 1.00

Opening of the Round Road on Okinawa.

# RYUKYU ISLANDS

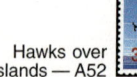

Hawks over Islands — A52

**1963, May 10**     Photo.
110 A52   3c multicolored    1.10   .95
Bird Day, May 10.

Shioya Bridge — A53

**1963, June 5**
111 A53   3c multicolored    1.10   .95
Opening of Shioya Bridge over Shioya Bay.

Tsuikin-wan Lacquerware Bowl — A54

**1963, July 1**     Perf. 13¼
112 A54   3c multicolored    2.75   2.50
Philatelic Week.

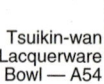

Map of Far East and JCI Emblem — A55

**1963, Sept. 16**     Photo.
113 A55   3c multicolored    .70   .70
Meeting of the International Junior Chamber of Commerce (JCI), Naha, Okinawa, Sept. 16-19.

Hamaomoto (Crinum asiaticum var. japonica) — A56

**1963, Oct. 15**     Perf. 13x13¼
114 A56   15c multicolored    1.25   .80

Site of Nakagusuku Castle — A57

**1963, Nov. 1**     Perf. 13¼
115 A57   3c multicolored    .60   .60
Protection of national cultural treasures.

Flame — A58

**1963, Dec. 10**
116 A58   3c red, dark blue & yellow    .65   .60
15th anniv. of the Universal Declaration of Human Rights.

Dragon — A59

**1963, Dec. 10**     Photo.
117 A59   1½c multicolored    .55   .50
New Year, 1964.

Carnation — A60

**1964, May 10**     Perf. 13¼
118 A60   3c blue, yel, blk & car    .40   .35
Mothers Day.

Pineapples and Sugar Cane — A61

**1964, June 1**
119 A61   3c multicolored    .40   .35
Agricultural census.

Minsah Obi (Sash Woven of Kapok) — A62

**1964, July 1**     Perf. 13¼
120 A62   3c deep blue, magenta & ocher    .50   .50
   a.   3c deep blue, deep carmine & ocher    .65   .65
Philatelic Week.

Girl Scout and Emblem — A63

**1964, Aug. 31**     Photo.
121 A63   3c multicolored    .45   .40
10th anniv. of Ryukyuan Girl Scouts.

Shuri Relay Station A64

Parabolic Antenna and Map A65

**1964, Sept. 1**     Unwmk.
**Black Overprint**
122 A64   3c deep green    .65   .65
   a.   Figure "1" inverted    30.00   30.00
   b.   Overprint inverted    1,500.
   c.   Overprint missing    3,500.
   d.   Overprint inverted and figure "1" inverted    5,000.
123 A65   8c ultramarine    1.25   1.25
   a.   Overprint missing    3,500.
Opening of the Ryukyu Islands-Japan microwave system carrying telephone and telegraph messages. The overprints indicate the system was not actually opened until 1964. Many of the stamps with overprint errors listed above are damaged. The values listed here are for stamps in very fine condition.

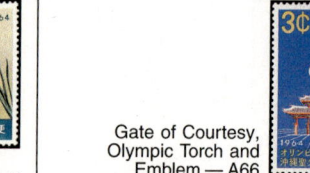

Gate of Courtesy, Olympic Torch and Emblem — A66

**1964, Sept. 7**     Photo.     Perf. 13¼
124 A66   3c ultra, yel & red    .30   .25
Relaying the Olympic torch on Okinawa en route to Tokyo.

"Naihanchi," Karate Stance — A67

"Makiwara," Strengthening Hands and Feet — A68

"Kumite," Simulated Combat — A69

**1964-65**     Photo.
125 A67   3c dull clar, yel & blk    .50   .45
126 A68   3c yel & multi    .40   .40
127 A69   3c gray, red & blk    .40   .40
   Nos. 125-127 (3)    1.30   1.25
Karate, Ryukyuan self-defense sport. Issued: No. 125, 10/5/64; No. 126, 2/5/65; No. 127, 6/5/65.

Miyara Dunchí — A70

**1964, Nov. 1**
128 A70   3c multicolored    .30   .25
Protection of national cultural treasures. Miyara Dunchi was built as a residence by Pei-chin Miyara Touen in 1819.

Snake and Iris (Bingata) — A71

**1964, Dec. 10**     Photo.
129 A71   1½c multicolored    .30   .25
New Year, 1965.

Boy Scouts — A72

**1965, Feb. 6**     Perf. 13¼
130 A72   3c light blue & multi    .45   .40
10th anniv. of Ryukyuan Boy Scouts.

Main Stadium, Onoyama — A73

**1965, July 1**     Perf. 13x13¼
131 A73   3c multicolored    .25   .25
Inauguration of the main stadium of the Onoyama athletic facilities.

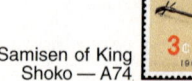

Samisen of King Shoko — A74

**1965, July 1**     Photo.     Perf. 13¼
132 A74   3c buff & multi    .45   .40
Philatelic Week.

Kin Power Plant — A75

**1965, July 1**
133 A75   3c green & multi    .25   .25
Completion of Kin power plant.

ICY Emblem, Ryukyu Map — A76

**1965, Aug. 24**     Photo.
134 A76   3c multicolored    .25   .25
20th anniv. of the UN and International Cooperation Year, 1964-65.

Naha City Hall — A77

**1965, Sept. 18**
135 A77   3c blue & multi    .35   .25
Completion of Naha City Hall.

Chinese Box Turtle (Cyclemys flavomarginata) A78

Turtles: No. 137, Hawksbill turtle (Eretochelys imbricata bissa) (denomination at top, country name at bottom). No. 138, Asian terrapin (Geoemyda japonica) (denomination and country name at top).

**1965-66**     Photo.     Perf. 13¼
136 A78   3c golden brown & multi    .30   .30
137 A78   3c multi    .30   .30
138 A78   3c multicolored    .30   .30
   Nos. 136-138 (3)    .90   .90
Issued: No. 136, 10/20/65; No. 137, 1/20/66; No. 138, 4/20/66.

Horse (Bingata) — A79

**1965, Dec. 10**     Photo.
139 A79   1½c multicolored    .25   .25
   a.   Gold omitted    2,000.   2,000.
New Year, 1966.
There are 92 unused and 2 used examples of No. 139a known.

# RYUKYU ISLANDS

Noguchi's Okinawa Woodpecker (Dendrocopus noguchii) A80

Sika Deer (Cervus nippon var. keramae) A81

Design: No. 142, Dugong (Dugong dugong).

**1966**  Photo.
140 A80 3c blue green & multi .25 .25
141 A81 3c bl, red, blk, brn & grn .25 .25
142 A81 3c bl, yel grn, blk & red .25 .25
  Nos. 140-142 (3) .75 .75

Nature Conservation. Issued No. 140, 2/15; No. 141, 3/15; No. 142, 4/20.

Ryukyu Bungalow Swallow (Hirundo tahitica) — A82

**1966, May 10**  Photo.  Perf. 13¼
143 A82 3c sky blue, black & brown .25 .25

4th Bird Week, May 10-16.

Lilies and Ruins — A83

**1966, June 23**  Perf. 13
144 A83 3c multicolored .25 .25

Memorial Day, end of the Battle of Okinawa, June 23, 1945.

University of the Ryukyus — A84

**1966, July 1**
145 A84 3c multicolored .25 .25

Transfer of the University of the Ryukyus from U.S. authority to the Ryukyu Government.

Chinkin Ukuhan Lacquerware, 18th Century — A85

**1966, Aug. 1**  Perf. 13¼
146 A85 3c gray & multicolored .25 .25

Philatelic Week.

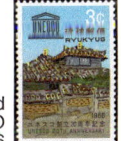

Tile-Roofed House and UNESCO Emblem — A86

**1966, Sept. 20**  Photo.
147 A86 3c multicolored .25 .25

20th anniv. of UNESCO.

Government Museum and Dragon Statue — A87

**1966, Oct. 6**
148 A87 3c multicolored .25 .25

Completion of the GRI (Government of the Ryukyu Islands) Museum, Shuri.

Tomb of Nakasone-Toyomiya Genga, Ruler of Miyako — A88

**1966, Nov. 1**  Photo.
149 A88 3c multicolored .25 .25

Protection of national cultural treasures.

Ram in Iris Wreath (Bingata) — A89

**1966, Dec. 10**  Photo.  Perf. 13¼
150 A89 1½c dark blue & multi .25 .25

New Year, 1967.

Clown Fish (Amphiprion frenatus) — A90

Fish: No. 152, Young boxfish (Ostracion cubicus) (white numeral at lower left). No. 153, Forceps fish (Forcipiger longirostris) (pale buff numeral at lower right). No. 154, Spotted triggerfish (Balistoides conspicillum) (orange numeral at upper right). No. 155, Saddleback butterflyfish (Chaetodon ephippium) (carmine numeral, lower left).

**1966-67**
151 A90 3c orange red & multi .25 .25
152 A90 3c org yel & multi .25 .25
153 A90 3c multicolored .40 .25
154 A90 3c multicolored .35 .25
155 A90 3c multicolored .30 .25
  Nos. 151-155 (5) 1.55 1.25

Issued No. 151, 12/20/66; No. 152, 1/10/67; No. 153, 4/10/67; No. 154, 5/25/67; No. 155, 6/10/67.

A 3-cent stamp to commemorate Japanese-American-Ryukyuan Joint Arbor Day was scheduled for release on March 16, 1967. However, it was not released. The stamp in light blue and white features American and Japanese flags joined by a shield containing a tree.

Tsuboya Urn — A91

**1967, Apr. 20**
156 A91 3c yellow & multicolored .25 .25

Philatelic Week.

Episcopal Miter (Mitra mitra) — A92

Seashells: No. 158, Venus comb murex (Murex pecten). No. 159, Chiragra spider (Lambis chiragra). No. 160, Green turban (Turbo marmoratus). No. 161, Bubble conch (Euprotomus bulla).

**1967-68**  Photo.  Perf. 13¼
157 A92 3c light green & multi .25 .25
158 A92 3c grnsh bl & multi .25 .25
159 A92 3c brt grn & multi .25 .25
160 A92 3c light blue & multi .30 .25
161 A92 3c bright blue & multi .60 .25
  Nos. 157-161 (5) 1.65 1.50

Issued: No. 157, 6/20/67; No. 159, 1/18/68; No. 160, 2/20/68; No. 161, 6/5/68; No. 158, 8/30/68.

Red-tiled Roofs and ITY Emblem — A93

**1967, Sept. 11**  Photo.
162 A93 3c multicolored .25 .25

International Tourist Year.

Mobile TB Clinic — A94

**1967, Oct. 13**  Photo.
163 A94 3c lilac & multicolored .25 .25

15th anniv. of the Anti-Tuberculosis Society.

Hojo Bridge, Enkaku Temple, 1498 — A95

**1967, Nov. 1**
164 A95 3c blue green & multi .25 .25

Protection of national cultural treasures.

Monkey (Bingata) — A96

**1967, Dec. 11**  Photo.  Perf. 13¼
165 A96 1½c silver & multi .25 .25

New Year, 1968.

TV Tower and Map — A97

**1967, Dec. 22**
166 A97 3c multicolored .25 .25

Opening of Miyako and Yaeyama television stations.

Dr. Kijin Nakachi and Helper — A98

**1968, Mar. 15**  Photo.
167 A98 3c multicolored .30 .25

120th anniv. of the first vaccination in the Ryukyu Islands, by Dr. Kijin Nakachi.

Pill Box (Inro) — A99

**1968, Apr. 18**
168 A99 3c gray & multicolored .45 .45

Philatelic Week.

Young Man, Library, Book and Map of Ryukyu Islands — A100

**1968, May 13**
169 A100 3c multicolored .30 .25

10th International Library Week.

Mailmen's Uniforms and Stamp of 1948 — A101

**1968, July 1**  Photo.  Perf. 13¼
170 A101 3c multicolored .30 .25

First Ryukyuan postage stamps, 20th anniv.

Main Gate, Enkaku Temple — A102

**1968, July 15**  Photo. & Engr.
171 A102 3c multicolored .30 .25

Restoration of the main gate Enkaku Temple, built 1492-1495, destroyed during World War II.

Old Man's Dance — A103

**1968, Sept. 15**  Photo.
172 A103 3c gold & multicolored .30 .25

Old People's Day.

Mictyris Longicarpus — A104

Crabs: No. 174, Uca dubia stimpson. No. 175, Baptozius vinosus. No. 176, Cardisoma carnifex. No. 177, Ocypode ceratophthalma pallas.

**1968-69**  Photo.  Perf. 13¼
173 A104 3c blue, ocher & black .30 .25
174 A104 3c lt bl grn & multi .35 .25
175 A104 3c light green & multi .35 .30
176 A104 3c light ultra & multi .45 .40
177 A104 3c gray blue & multi .45 .40
  Nos. 173-177 (5) 1.90 1.65

Issued: No. 173, 10/10/68; No. 174, 2/5/69; No. 175, 3/5/69; No. 176, 5/15/69; No. 177, 6/2/69.

Saraswati Pavilion (Benzaitan-do Temple) — A105

**1968, Nov. 1**  Photo.
178 A105 3c multicolored .30 .25

Restoration of the Sarawati Pavilion (in front of Enkaku Temple), destroyed during World War II.

# RYUKYU ISLANDS

Tennis Player — A106

**1968, Nov. 23**    Photo.
179   A106   3c green & multi    .40   .35
35th All-Japan East-West Men's Soft-ball Tennis Tournament, Naha City, Nov. 23-24.

Cock and Iris (Bingata) — A107

**1968, Dec. 10**
180   A107   1½c orange & multi    .25   .25
New Year, 1969.

Boxer — A108

**1969, Jan. 3**
181   A108   3c gray & multi    .40   .30
20th All-Japan Amateur Boxing Championships held at the University of the Ryukyus, Jan. 3-5.

Ink Slab Screen — A109

**1969, Apr. 17**   Photo.   Perf. 13¼x13
182   A109   3c salmon, indigo & red    .40   .35
Philatelic Week.

Box Antennas and Map of Radio Link — A110

**1969, July 1**    Photo.
183   A110   3c multicolored    .30   .25
Opening of the UHF (radio) circuit system between Okinawa and the outlying Miyako-Yaeyama Islands.

Gate of Courtesy and Emblems — A111

**1969, Aug. 1**    Photo.
184   A111   3c Prussian blue, gold & vermilion    .30   .25
22nd All-Japan Formative Education Study Conf., Naha, Aug. 1-3.

Tug of War Festival — A112

Hari Boat Race — A113

Izaiho Ceremony, Kudaka Island — A114

Mortar Drum Dance (Ushideiku) A115

Sea God Dance (Ungami) A116

**1969-70**   Photo.   Perf. 13¼x13
185   A112   3c multicolored   .30   .25
186   A113   3c multicolored   .35   .30
187   A114   3c multicolored   .35   .30
188   A115   3c multicolored   .50   .45
189   A116   3c multicolored   .50   .45
Nos. 185-189 (5)   2.00   1.75
Folklore. Issued, No. 185, 8/1/69; No. 186, 9/5/69; No. 187, 10/3/69; No. 188, 1/20/70; No. 189, 2/27/70.

No. 99 Surcharged

**1969, Oct. 15**   Photo.   Perf. 13¼
190   A44   ½c on 3c multicolored   1.00   1.00
   a.   "½c" only surcharge   950.00
No. 190a are right margin stamps from a pane with a leftward misregistration of the surcharging plate.

Nakamura-ke Farm House, Built 1713-51 — A117

**1969, Nov. 1**   Photo.   Perf. 13¼x13
191   A117   3c multicolored   .25   .25
Protection of national cultural treasures.

Statue of Kyuzo Toyama, Maps of Hawaiian and Ryukyu Islands — A118

**1969, Dec. 5**   Photo.   Perf. 13¼
192   A118   3c light ultra & multi   .50   .50
   a.   Without overprint   3,000.
   b.   Wide-spaced bars   700.00   500.00
70th anniv. of Ryukyu-Hawaii emigration led by Kyuzo Toyama.
The overprint "1969" at lower left and bars across "1970" at upper right was applied before No. 192 was issued.

Dog and Flowers (Bingata) — A119

**1969, Dec. 10**    Perf. 13¼x13
193   A119   1½c pink & multi   .25   .25
New Year, 1970.

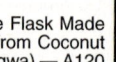

Sake Flask Made from Coconut (Yashi-gwa) — A120

**1970, Apr. 15**   Photo.   Perf. 13¼
194   A120   3c multicolored   .25   .25
Philatelic Week, 1970.

"The Bell" (Shushin Kaneiri) A121

Child and Kidnapper (Chunusudu) A122

Robe of Feathers (Mekarushi) A123

Vengeance of Two Young Sons (Nidotichiuchi) A124

The Virgin and the Dragon (Kokonomaki) A125

**1970**   Photo.   Perf. 13¼
195   A121   3c dull blue & multi   .60   .40
   a.   Souvenir sheet of 4   4.00   4.00
196   A122   3c light blue & multi   .60   .40
   a.   Souvenir sheet of 4   4.00   4.00
197   A123   3c bluish grn & multi   .60   .40
   a.   Souvenir sheet of 4   4.00   4.00
198   A124   3c dull bl grn & multi   .60   .40
   a.   Souvenir sheet of 4   4.00   4.00
199   A125   3c multicolored   .60   .40
   a.   Souvenir sheet of 4   4.00   4.00
Nos. 195-199 (5)   3.00   2.00
Nos. 195a-199a (5)   20.00   20.00
Classic Opera. Issued No. 195, 4/28; No. 196, 5/29; No. 197, 6/30; No. 198, 7/30; No. 199, 8/25.

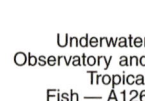

Underwater Observatory and Tropical Fish — A126

**1970, May 22**
200   A126   3c blue green & multi   .30   .25
Completion of the underwater observatory of Busena-Misaki, Nago.

Noboru Jahana (1865-1908), Politician — A127

Portraits: No. 202, Saion Gushichan Bunjaku (1682-1761), statesman. No. 203, Choho Giwan (1823-1876), regent and poet.

**1970-71**    Engr.
201   A127   3c rose claret   .50   .45
202   A127   3c dull blue green   .75   .65
203   A127   3c black   .50   .45
Nos. 201-203 (3)   1.75   1.55
Issued: No. 201, 9/25.70; No. 202, 12/22/70; No. 203, 1/22/71.

Map of Okinawa and People — A128

**1970, Oct. 1**    Photo.
204   A128   3c red & multicolored   .25   .25
Oct. 1, 1970 census.

Great Cycad of Une — A129

**1970, Nov. 2**   Photo.   Perf. 13¼
205   A129   3c gold & multicolored   .25   .25
Protection of national treasures.

Japanese Flag, Diet and Map of Ryukyus — A130

**1970, Nov. 15**    Photo.
206   A130   3c ultra & multi   .80   .75
Citizen's participation in national administration to Japanese law of Apr. 24, 1970.

Wild Boar and Cherry Blossoms (Bingata) — A131

**1970, Dec. 10**    Perf. 13¼x13
207   A131   1½c multicolored   .25   .25
New Year, 1971.

Low Hand Loom (Jibata) A132

Farmer Wearing Palm Bark Raincoat (Shurunnui) and Kuba Leaf Hat (Kubagasa) A133

Fisherman's Wooden Box (Yutui) and Scoop (Umifujo) — A134

Designs: No. 209, Woman running a filature (reel). No. 211, Woman hulling rice with cylindrical "Shiri-ushi."

**1971**   Photo.   Perf. 13¼
208   A132   3c light blue & multi   .30   .25
209   A132   3c pale grn & multi   .30   .25
210   A133   3c pale blue & multi   .35   .30
211   A132   3c yellow & multi   .40   .35
212   A134   3c gray & multi   .35   .30
Nos. 208-212 (5)   1.70   1.45
Issued: No. 208, 2/16; No. 209, 3/16; No. 210, 4/30; No. 211, 5/20; No. 212, 6/15.

Water Carrier (Taku) — A135

**1971, Apr. 15**    Photo.
213   A135   3c blue grn & multi   .35   .30
Philatelic Week.

Old and New Naha, and City Emblem — A136

**1971, May 20**    Perf. 13¼x13
214   A136   3c ultra & multi   .25   .25
50th anniv. of Naha as a municipality.

# RYUKYU ISLANDS

Madder (Sandanka) — A137

Design: 3c, Ogocho (Caesalpinia pulcherrima).

**1971**         **Photo.**         **Perf. 13¼**
215  A137  2c gray blue & multi   .25   .25
216  A137  3c gray grn & multi    .25   .25

Issued No. 216, 5/10; No. 215, 9/30.

View from Mabuni Hill — A138

Mt. Arashi from Haneji Sea — A139

Yabuchi Island from Yakena Port — A140

**1971-72**
217  A138  3c green & multi       .25   .25
218  A139  3c blue & multi        .25   .25
219  A140  4c multicolored        .25   .25
Nos. 217-219 (3)                  .75   .75

Government parks. Issued: No. 217, 7/30/71; No. 218, 8/30/71; No. 219, 1/20/72.

For the 4-cent unissued "stamp" picturing Iriomote Park, originally planned for issue in 1971 but never released, see the note after No. RQ8 in the Scott U.S. Specialized catalogue.

Dancer (Nu-fwa-bushi) — A141

**1971, Nov. 1**   **Photo.**   **Perf. 13¼**
220  A141  4c Prussian blue & multicolored   .25   .25

Deva King (Misshaku Kongo), Torin-ji Temple — A142

**1971, Dec. 1**
221  A142  4c dp blue & multi    .25   .25

Protection of national cultural treasures.

Rat and Chrysanthemums A143

**1971, Dec. 10**   **Perf. 13¼x13**
222  A143  2c brown orange & multi   .25   .25

New Year, 1972.

Student Nurse — A144

**1971, Dec. 24**   **Perf. 13¼**
223  A144  4c dp mauve & multi   .25   .25

Nurses' training, 25th anniversary.

Birds on Seashore A145

Sun over Islands A147

Coral Reef — A146

**1972**        **Photo.**
224  A145  5c brt blue & multi   .40   .35
225  A146  5c multi              .40   .35
226  A147  5c ocher & multi      .40   .35
Nos. 224-226 (3)                1.20  1.05

Issued: No. 226, 3/21; No. 225, 3/30; No. 224, 4/14.

Dove, US and Japanese Flags — A148

**1972, Apr. 17**   **Photo.**
227  A148  5c bright blue & multi   .80   .80

Ratification of Ryukyu Islands Reversion Agreement.

Antique Sake Container (Yushibin) — A149

**1972, Apr. 20**
228  A149  5c ultra & multi   .60   .60

Philatelic Week.

Ryukyu stamps were replaced by those of Japan after May 15, 1972.

---

## AIR POST STAMPS

Catalogue values for all unused stamps in this section are for Never Hinged items.

Dove and Map of Ryukyus — AP1

**Perf. 13x13¼**
**1950, Feb. 15**   **Photo.**   **Unwmk.**
C1  AP1  8y bright blue     110.00  40.00
C2  AP1  12y lt green        17.50  17.50
C3  AP1  16y rose carmine     9.00   9.00
Nos. C1-C3 (3)              136.50  66.50

Heavenly Maiden — AP2

**1951-54**   **Perf. 13¼x13**
C4  AP2  13y chalky blue    2.00   2.00
C5  AP2  18y green          3.00   3.00
C6  AP2  30y cerise         4.50   1.50
C7  AP2  40y purple         6.50   6.50
C8  AP2  50y orange red     7.50   7.50
Nos. C4-C8 (5)             23.50  20.50

Issued: Nos. C4-C6, 10/1/51; Nos. C7-C8, 8/16/54.

Heavenly Maiden Playing Flute — AP3

**1957, Aug. 1**   **Engr.**   **Perf. 13x13¼**
C9   AP3  15y deep blue green    7.50   4.00
C10  AP3  20y scarlet            9.00   7.00
C11  AP3  35y yellow green      10.00   8.00
  a.   35y light yellow green, 1958   125.00
C12  AP3  45y reddish brown     14.00  10.00
C13  AP3  60y gray & blk        16.00  12.00
Nos. C9-C13 (5)                 56.50  41.00

On one printing of No. C10, position 49 shows an added spur on the right side of the second character from the left. Value unused, $175.

Surcharged in Scarlet, Light Ultramarine & Carmine Red

**1959, Dec. 20**   **Engr.**
C14  AP3  9c on 15y blue green (S)   2.50   2.00
  a.   Inverted surcharge        800.00
  b.   Pair, one without surcharge   25,000.
C15  AP3  14c on 20y scarlet (L.U.)   3.00   3.25
C16  AP3  19c on 35y yellow green (CR)   7.00   6.00
C17  AP3  27c on 45y reddish brown (L.U.)   12.50   6.00
C18  AP3  35c on 60y gray (CR)   11.00   9.00
Nos. C14-C18 (5)                36.00  26.25

No. C15 is found with the variety described below No. C13. Value unused, $125.

**Nos. 31-33, 36 and 38 Surcharged in Black, Brown, Red, Blue or Green**

**1960, Aug. 3**   **Photo.**
C19  A14  9c on 4y brown    2.50   1.00
  a.   Surcharge inverted and transposed   12,500.  12,500.
  b.   Inverted surcharge (legend only)   10,000.
  c.   Surcharge transposed    800.00
  d.   Legend of surcharge only   3,500.
  e.   Vert. pair, one without surcharge   11,000.

Nos. C19c and C19d are from a single sheet of 100 with surcharge shifted downward. Ten examples of No. C19c exist with "9c" also in bottom selvage. No. C19d is from the top row of the sheet.

No. C19e is unique, pos. 100, caused by paper foldover.

C20  A17  14c on 5y rose lilac (Br)   3.00   3.00
C21  A14  19c on 15y vermilion (R)   2.50   3.00
C22  A17  27c on 14y reddish brown (Bl)   7.00   2.50
C23  A14  35c on 20y yellow orange (G)   5.00   5.00
Nos. C19-C23 (5)                20.00  14.50

Wind God — AP4

Designs: 9c, Heavenly Maiden (as on AP2). 14c, Heavenly Maiden (as on AP3). 27c, Wind God at right. 35c, Heavenly Maiden over treetops.

**1961, Sept. 21**   **Perf. 13¼**
C24  AP4  9c multicolored    .30   .25
C25  AP4  14c multicolored   .60   .75
C26  AP4  19c multicolored   .70   .85
C27  AP4  27c multicolored  3.00   .60
C28  AP4  35c multicolored  2.00  1.25
Nos. C24-C28 (5)            6.60  3.70

Jet over Gate of Courtesy AP5

Jet Plane AP6

**1963, Aug. 28**   **Perf. 13x13¼**
C29  AP5  5½c multicolored   .25   .25
C30  AP6  7c multicolored    .30   .30

---

## SPECIAL DELIVERY STAMP

Catalogue value for the unused stamp in this section is for a Never Hinged item.

Sea Horse and Map of Ryukyus — SD1

**Perf. 13¼**
**1950, Feb. 15**   **Unwmk.**   **Photo.**
E1  SD1  5y bright blue    25.00  17.50

# UNITED NATIONS, OFFICES IN NEW YORK

yu-ˌnī-təd 'nā-shənz

United Nations stamps are used on UN official mail sent from UN Headquarters in New York City, the UN European Office in Geneva, Switzerland, or from the Donaupark Vienna International Center or Atomic Energy Agency in Vienna, Austria to points throughout the world. They may be used on private correspondence sent through the UN post offices and are valid only at the individual UN post offices.

The UN stamps issued for use in Geneva and Vienna are listed in separate sections. Geneva issues were denominated in centimes and francs and Vienna issues in schillings (now cents and euros) and are valid only in Geneva or Vienna. The UN stamps issued for use in New York, denominated in cents and dollars, are valid only in New York.

Letters bearing Nos. 170-174 provide an exception as they were carried by the Canadian postal system.

See Switzerland Nos. 7O1-7O39 in Volume 6 of the Scott *Standard Postage Stamp Catalogue* for stamps issued by the Swiss Government for official use of the UN European Office and other UN affiliated organizations. See France official stamp listings for stamps issued by the French Government for official use of UNESCO.

Catalogue values for all unused stamps in this section are for Never Hinged items. Values for used UN stamps are for postally used stamps with contemporaneous cancels. Used stamps soaked off of first day covers sell for less.

Stamps are inscribed in English, French, or Spanish or are multilingual.

Wmk. 309 — Wavy Lines

Peoples of the World A1

UN Headquarters Building A2

"Peace, Justice, Security" A3

UN Flag A4

UN Children's Fund — A5

World Unity — A6

*Perf. 13x12½, 12½x13*

| 1951 | | Engr. and Photo. | Unwmk. | |
|---|---|---|---|---|
| 1 | A1 | 1c magenta | .25 | .25 |
| 2 | A2 | 1½c blue green | .25 | .25 |
| 3 | A3 | 2c purple | .25 | .25 |
| 4 | A4 | 3c magenta & blue | .25 | .25 |
| 5 | A5 | 5c blue | .25 | .25 |
| 6 | A1 | 10c chocolate | .25 | .25 |
| 7 | A4 | 15c violet & blue | .25 | .25 |
| 8 | A6 | 20c dark brown | .30 | .25 |
| 9 | A4 | 25c olive gray & blue | .35 | .25 |
| 10 | A2 | 50c indigo | 3.00 | 1.50 |
| 11 | A3 | $1 red | 1.25 | .90 |
| | | Nos. 1-11 (11) | 6.65 | 4.65 |

Veteran's War Memorial Building, San Francisco — A7

7th anniversary of the signing of the United Nations Charter.

| 1952, Oct. 24 | | | *Perf. 12* | |
|---|---|---|---|---|
| 12 | A7 | 5c blue | .50 | .35 |

Globe and Encircled Flame — A8

4th anniversary of the adoption of the Universal Declaration of Human Rights.

| 1952, Dec. 10 | | | *Perf. 13½x14* | |
|---|---|---|---|---|
| 13 | A8 | 3c deep green | .45 | .35 |
| 14 | A8 | 5c blue | .55 | .40 |

Refugee Family — A9

Issued to publicize "Protection for Refugees."

| 1953, Apr. 24 | | | *Perf. 12½x13* | |
|---|---|---|---|---|
| 15 | A9 | 3c dark red brown & rose brown | .25 | .25 |
| 16 | A9 | 5c indigo & blue | .45 | .40 |

Envelope, UN Emblem and Map — A10

Issued to honor the UPU.

| 1953, June 12 | | | *Perf. 13* | |
|---|---|---|---|---|
| 17 | A10 | 3c black brown | .40 | .40 |
| 18 | A10 | 5c dark blue | 1.25 | 1.00 |

Gearwheels and UN Emblem — A11

UN activities in the field of technical assistance.

| 1953, Oct. 24 | | | *Perf. 13x12½* | |
|---|---|---|---|---|
| 19 | A11 | 3c dark gray | .25 | .25 |
| 20 | A11 | 5c dark green | .40 | .45 |

Hands Reaching Toward Flame — A12

Human Rights Day.

| 1953, Dec. 10 | | | *Perf. 12½x13* | |
|---|---|---|---|---|
| 21 | A12 | 3c bright blue | .30 | .30 |
| 22 | A12 | 5c rose red | 1.00 | 1.00 |

Ear of Wheat — A13

Issued to honor the FAO.

| 1954, Feb. 11 | | | *Perf. 12½x13* | |
|---|---|---|---|---|
| 23 | A13 | 3c dark green & yellow | .30 | .25 |
| 24 | A13 | 8c indigo & yellow | .75 | .50 |

UN Emblem and Anvil — A14

Issued to honor the ILO.

| 1954, May 10 | | | *Perf. 12½x13* | |
|---|---|---|---|---|
| 25 | A14 | 3c brown | .25 | .25 |
| 26 | A14 | 8c magenta | 1.00 | .85 |

UN European Office, Geneva — A15

Issued on the occasion of UN Day.

| 1954, Oct. 25 | | | *Perf. 14* | |
|---|---|---|---|---|
| 27 | A15 | 3c dark blue violet | 1.25 | 1.00 |
| 28 | A15 | 8c red | .35 | .30 |

Mother and Child — A16

Human Rights Day.

| 1954, Dec. 10 | | | *Perf. 14* | |
|---|---|---|---|---|
| 29 | A16 | 3c red orange | 3.50 | 2.50 |
| 30 | A16 | 8c olive green | .75 | .35 |

Symbol of Flight — A17

International Civil Aviation Organization.

| 1955, Feb. 9 | | | *Perf. 13½x14* | |
|---|---|---|---|---|
| 31 | A17 | 3c blue | 1.00 | .75 |
| 32 | A17 | 8c rose carmine | .60 | .50 |

UNESCO Emblem — A18

Issued to honor the UN Educational, Scientific and Cultural Organization.

| 1955, May 11 | | | *Perf. 13½x14* | |
|---|---|---|---|---|
| 33 | A18 | 3c lilac rose | .35 | .30 |
| 34 | A18 | 8c light blue | .30 | .30 |

UN Charter — A19

10th anniversary of the United Nations.

| 1955, Oct. 24 | | | *Perf. 13½x14* | |
|---|---|---|---|---|
| 35 | A19 | 3c deep plum | .90 | .55 |
| 36 | A19 | 4c dull green | .50 | .35 |
| 37 | A19 | 8c bluish black | .35 | .25 |
| | | Nos. 35-37 (3) | 1.75 | 1.15 |

**Souvenir Sheet**

| 1955, Oct. 24 | | Wmk. 309 | *Imperf.* | |
|---|---|---|---|---|
| 38 | A19 | Sheet of 3 | 50.00 | 18.00 |
| | a. | 3c deep plum | 7.00 | 3.00 |
| | b. | 4c dull green | 7.00 | 3.00 |
| | c. | 8c bluish black | 7.00 | 3.00 |
| | d. | As No. 38, corrected plates (see footnote) | 55.00 | 27.50 |

Two printings were made of the sheet: No. 38 (200,000) and No. 38d (50,000). No. 38 may be distinguished by the broken lines in the background shading on the 8c. It leaves a small white spot below the left leg of the "n" of "Unies." On No. 38d, the broken line was retouched, eliminating the white spot. The 4c was also retouched.

Nos. 38 and 38d used are valued with first day of issue cancels. Postally used examples are worth substantially more.

Hand Holding Torch — A20

Issued in honor of Human Rights Day.

| 1955, Dec. 9 | | Unwmk. | *Perf. 14x13½* | |
|---|---|---|---|---|
| 39 | A20 | 3c ultramarine | .30 | .30 |
| 40 | A20 | 8c green | .40 | .30 |

Symbols of Telecommunication — A21

Honoring the International Telecommunication Union.

| 1956, Feb. 17 | | | *Perf. 14* | |
|---|---|---|---|---|
| 41 | A21 | 3c turquoise blue | .25 | .25 |
| 42 | A21 | 8c deep carmine | .30 | .30 |

Globe & Caduceus — A22

Issued in honor of the World Health Organization.

| 1956, Apr. 6 | | | *Perf. 14* | |
|---|---|---|---|---|
| 43 | A22 | 3c bright greenish blue | .25 | .25 |
| 44 | A22 | 8c golden brown | .25 | .25 |

General Assembly — A23

Issued to commemorate UN Day.

| 1956, Oct. 24 | | | *Perf. 14* | |
|---|---|---|---|---|
| 45 | A23 | 3c dark blue | .25 | .25 |
| 46 | A23 | 8c gray olive | .25 | .25 |

Flame and Globe — A24

Issued to publicize Human Rights Day.

## UNITED NATIONS, OFFICES IN NEW YORK

**1956, Dec. 10**    *Perf. 14*
47 A24 3c plum    .25   .25
48 A24 8c dark blue    .25   .25

Weather Balloon — A25

Issued to honor the World Meterological Organization.

**1957, Jan. 28**    *Perf. 14*
49 A25 3c violet blue    .25   .25
50 A25 8c dark carmine rose    .25   .25

Badge of UN Emergency Force — A26

Issued in honor of the UN Emergency Force.

**1957, Apr. 8**    *Perf 14x12½*
51 A26 3c light blue    .25   .25
52 A26 8c rose carmine    .25   .25

**Nos. 51-52 Re-engraved**

**1957, Apr.-May**    *Perf. 14x12½*
53 A26 3c blue    .25   .25
54 A26 8c rose carmine    .35   .25

On Nos. 53-54 the background within and around the circles is shaded lightly, giving a halo effect. The lettering is more distinct with a line around each letter.

UN Emblem and Globe — A27

Issued to honor the Security Council.

**1957, Oct. 24**    *Perf. 12½x13*
55 A27 3c orange brown    .25   .25
56 A27 8c dark blue green    .25   .25

Flaming Torch — A28

Issued in honor of Human Rights Day.

**1957, Dec. 10**    *Perf. 14*
57 A28 3c red brown    .25   .25
58 A28 8c black    .25   .25

Atom & UN Emblem — A29

Issued in honor of the International Atomic Energy Agency.

**1958, Feb. 10**    *Perf. 12*
59 A29 3c olive    .25   .25
60 A29 8c blue    .25   .25

Central Hall, Westminster — A30

Central Hall, Westminster, London, was the site of the first session of the United Nations General Assembly, 1946.

**1958, Apr. 14**    *Perf. 12*
61 A30 3c blue    .25   .25
62 A30 8c rose claret    .25   .25

UN Seal — A31

Engraved and printed by Bradbury, Wilkinson & Co., Ltd., England. Panes of 50. Designed by Herbert M. Sanborn.

**1958, Oct. 24**    *Perf. 13½x14*
63 A31 4c red orange    .25   .25

**1958, June 2**    *Perf. 13x14*
64 A31 8c bright blue    .25   .25

Issue dates: 4c, Oct. 24; 8c, June 2.

Gearwheels — A32

Issued to honor the Economic and Social Council.

**1958, Oct. 24**    *Unwmk.*    *Perf. 12*
65 A32 4c blue green    .25   .25
66 A32 8c vermilion    .25   .25

Hands Upholding Globe — A33

Human Rights Day and to commemorate the 10th anniversary of the signing of the Universal Declaration of Human Rights.

**1958, Dec. 10**    *Unwmk.*    *Perf. 12*
67 A33 4c yellow green    .25   .25
68 A33 8c red brown    .25   .25

New York City Building, Flushing Meadows — A34

Site of many General Assembly meetings, 1946-50.

**1959, Mar. 30**    *Unwmk.*    *Perf. 12*
69 A34 4c light lilac rose    .25   .25
70 A34 8c aquamarine    .25   .25

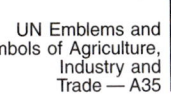

UN Emblems and Symbols of Agriculture, Industry and Trade — A35

Issued to honor the Economic Commission for Europe.

**1959, May 18**    *Unwmk.*    *Perf. 12*
71 A35 4c blue    .25   .25
72 A35 8c red orange    .25   .25

Figure Adapted from Rodin's "Age of Bronze" — A36

Issued to honor the Trusteeship Council.

**1959, Oct. 23**    *Unwmk.*    *Perf. 12*
73 A36 4c bright red    .25   .25
74 A36 8c dark olive green    .25   .25

World Refugee Year Emblem — A37

World Refugee Year, July 1, 1959-June 30, 1960.

**1959, Dec. 10**    *Unwmk.*    *Perf. 12*
75 A37 4c ol brn & red    .25   .25
76 A37 8c ol brn & brt grnsh blue    .25   .25

Chaillot Palace, Paris — A38

Chaillot Palace in Paris was the site of General Assembly meetings in 1948 and 1951.

**1960, Feb. 29**    *Unwmk.*    *Perf. 14*
77 A38 4c rose lilac & blue    .25   .25
78 A38 8c dull green & brown    .25   .25

Map of Far East and Steel Beam — A39

Honoring the Economic Commission for Asia and the Far East (ECAFE).

*Perf. 13x13½*
**1960, Apr. 11**    *Photo.*    *Unwmk.*
79 A39 4c dp clar, blue grn & dull yel    .25   .25
80 A39 8c ol grn, blue & rose    .25   .25

Tree, FAO and UN Emblems — A40

Fifth World Forestry Congress, Seattle, Washington, Aug. 29-Sept. 10.

*Perf. 13½*
**1960, Aug. 29**    *Photo.*    *Unwmk.*
81 A40 4c dk blue, grn & org    .25   .25
82 A40 8c yel grn, blk & org    .25   .25

UN Headquarters and Preamble to UN Charter — A41

Issued to commemorate the 15th anniversary of the United Nations.

**1960, Oct. 24**    *Unwmk.*    *Perf. 11*
83 A41 4c blue    .25   .25
84 A41 8c gray    .25   .25

**Souvenir Sheet**
*Imperf*
85    Sheet of 2    1.25   1.25
    a. A41 4c blue    .55   .55
    b. A41 8c gray    .55   .55

Block and Tackle — A42

Honoring the International Bank for Reconstruction and Development.

*Perf. 13½x13*
**1960, Dec. 9**    *Photo.*    *Unwmk.*
86 A42 4c multicolored    .25   .25
87 A42 8c multicolored    .25   .25

Scales of Justice — A43

Issued to honor the International Court of Justice.

*Perf. 13½x13*
**1961, Feb. 13**    *Photo.*    *Unwmk.*
88 A43 4c yel, org brn & blk    .25   .25
89 A43 8c yel, grn & blk    .25   .25

Seal of International Monetary Fund — A44

Issued to honor the International Monetary Fund.

*Perf. 13x13½*
**1961, Apr. 17**    *Photo.*    *Unwmk.*
90 A44 4c bright bluish green    .25   .25
91 A44 7c terra cotta & yellow    .25   .25

All UN Stamps by The William Henry Stamp Company

All United Nations Stamps. All for sale. All the time.

www.AllUNStamps.com

• Mint • Used • MI4's • FDC's • Sheets
Souvenir Cards • Stationery • Year Sets

Send for FREE U.N. PRICE LIST of Mint and Used...
P.O. Box 150010, Kew Gardens, NY 11415-0010
Telephone/Fax: (347) 829-3400 • E-Mail: wmhenry@msn.com

# UNITED NATIONS, OFFICES IN NEW YORK

Abstract Group of Flags — A45

**Perf. 11½**
**1961, June 5    Photo.    Unwmk.**
92  A45  30c multicolored    .45  .30
See UN Offices in Geneva No. 10.

Cogwheel and Map of Latin America — A46

Issued to honor the Economic Commission for Latin America.

**Perf. 13½**
**1961, Sept. 18    Photo.    Unwmk.**
93  A46  4c blue, red & citron    .25  .25
94  A46  11c grn, lilac & org ver    .25  .25

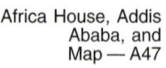
Africa House, Addis Ababa, and Map — A47

Issued to honor the Economic Commission for Africa.

**Perf. 11½**
**1961, Oct. 24    Photo.    Unwmk.**
95  A47  4c ultramarine, orange, yellow & brown    .25  .25
96  A47  11c emerald, orange, yellow & brown    .25  .25

Mother Bird Feeding Young and UNICEF Seal — A48

15th anniversary of the United Nations Children's Fund.

**Perf. 11½**
**1961, Dec. 4    Photo.    Unwmk.**
97  A48  3c brown, gold, orange & yellow    .25  .25
98  A48  4c brown, gold, blue & emerald    .25  .25
99  A48  13c deep green, gold, purple & pink    .25  .25
Nos. 97-99 (3)    .75  .75

Family and Symbolic Buildings — A49

UN program for housing and urban development.

**Perf. 14½x14**
**1962, Feb. 28    Photo.    Unwmk.**
Central design multicolored
100  A49  4c bright blue    .25  .25
  a.    Black omitted    200.00
  b.    Yellow omitted    —
  c.    Brown omitted    —
101  A49  7c orange brown    .25  .25
  a.    Red omitted    —
  b.    Black omitted    —
  c.    Gold omitted    —

"The World Against Malaria" — A50

Issued in honor of the WHO and to call attention to the international campaign to eradicate malaria from the world.

**Perf. 14x14½**
**1962, Mar. 30    Photo.    Unwmk.**
Word frame in gray
102  A50  4c orange, yellow, brown, green & black    .25  .25
103  A50  11c green, yellow, brown & indigo    .25  .25

"Peace" A51

UN Flag A52

Hands Combining "UN" and Globe — A53

UN Emblem over Globe — A54

**Photo.; Engr. (5c)**
**Perf. 14x14½**
**1962, May 25**
104  A51  1c vermilion, blue, black & gray    .25  .25
105  A52  3c light green, Prussian blue, yellow & gray    .25  .25

**Perf. 12**
106  A53  5c dark carmine rose    .25  .25

**Perf. 12½**
107  A54  11c dark & light blue & gold    .25  .25
Nos. 104-107 (4)    1.00  1.00
See #167 and UN Offices in Geneva #2, 6. Compare A51 with A76.

Flag at Half-mast and UN Headquarters — A55

Issued on the 1st anniversary of the death of Dag Hammarskjold, Secretary General of the United Nations 1953-61, in memory of those who died in the service of the United Nations.

**Perf. 11½**
**1962, Sept. 17    Photo.    Unwmk.**
108  A55  5c black, light blue & blue    .25  .25
109  A55  15c black, gray olive & blue    .25  .25

World Map Showing Congo — A56

Issued to commemorate the United Nations Operation in the Congo.

**Perf. 11½**
**1962, Oct. 24    Photo.    Unwmk.**
110  A56  4c olive, orange, black & yellow    .25  .25
111  A56  11c blue green, orange, black & yellow    .25  .25

Globe in Universe and Palm Frond — A57

Issued to honor the Committee on Peaceful Uses of Outer Space.

**Perf. 14x13½**
**1962, Dec. 3    Engr.    Unwmk.**
112  A57  4c violet blue    .25  .25
113  A57  11c rose claret    .25  .25

Development Decade Emblem — A58

UN Development Decade and UN Conference on the Application of Science and Technology for the Benefit of the Less Developed Areas, Geneva, Feb. 4-20.

**Perf. 11½**
**1963, Feb. 4    Photo.    Unwmk.**
114  A58  5c pale green, maroon, dark blue & Prussian blue    .25  .25
115  A58  11c yellow, maroon, dark blue & Prussian blue    .25  .25

Stalks of Wheat — A59

Issued for the "Freedom from Hunger" campaign of the Food and Agriculture Organization.

**Perf. 11½**
**1963, Mar. 22    Photo.    Unwmk.**
116  A59  5c vermilion, green & yellow    .25  .25
117  A59  11c vermilion, deep claret & yellow    .25  .25

Bridge over Map of New Guinea — A60

1st anniversary of the United Nations Temporary Executive Authority (UNTEA) in West New Guinea (West Irian).

**Perf. 11½**
**1963, Oct. 1    Photo.    Unwmk.**
118  A60  25c blue, green & gray    .50  .40

General Assembly Building, New York — A61

Since October 1955 all sessions of the General Assembly have been held in the General Assembly Hall, UN Headquarters, NY.

**Unwmk.**
**1963, Nov. 4    Photo.    Perf. 13**
119  A61  5c violet blue, blue, yellow green & red    .25  .25
120  A61  11c green, yellow green, blue, yellow & red    .25  .25

Flame — A62

15th anniversary of the signing of the Universal Declaration of Human Rights.

**Unwmk.**
**1963, Dec. 10    Photo.    Perf. 13**
121  A62  5c green, gold, red & yellow    .25  .25
122  A62  11c carmine, gold, blue & yellow    .25  .25

Ships at Sea and IMCO Emblem — A63

Issued to honor the Intergovernmental Maritime Consultative Organization.

**Perf. 11½**
**1964, Jan. 13    Photo.    Unwmk.**
123  A63  5c blue, olive, ocher & yellow    .25  .25
124  A63  11c dark blue, dark green, emerald & yellow    .25  .25

Map of the World A64

UN Emblem A65

Three Men United Before Globe — A66

Stylized Globe and Weather Vane — A67

**1964-71    Photo.    Unwmk.    Perf. 14**
125  A64  2c light & dark blue, orange & yellow green    .25  .25
  a.    Perf. 13x13½    .25  .25

**Perf. 11½**
126  A65  7c dark blue, orange brown & black    .25  .25
127  A66  10c blue green, olive green & black    .25  .25
128  A67  50c multicolored    .55  .45
Nos. 125-128 (4)    1.30  1.20
Issued: 2c, 7c, May 29; 50c, Mar. 6.
See UN Offices in Geneva Nos. 3, 12.

Arrows Showing Global Flow of Trade — A68

Issued to commemorate the UN Conference on Trade and Development, Geneva, Mar. 23-June 15.

**Unwmk.**
**1964, June 15    Photo.    Perf. 13**
129  A68  5c black, red & yellow    .25  .25
130  A68  11c black, olive & yellow    .25  .25

Poppy Capsule and Hands — A69

Honoring international efforts and achievements in the control of narcotics.

**Unwmk.**
**1964, Sept. 21    Engr.    Perf. 12**
131  A69  5c rose red & black    .25  .25
132  A69  11c emerald & black    .25  .25

Padlocked Atomic Blast — A70

Signing of the nuclear test ban treaty pledging an end to nuclear explosions in the atmosphere, outer space and under water.

**Litho. and Engr.**
**Perf. 11x11½**
**1964, Oct. 23    Unwmk.**
133  A70  5c dark red & dark brown    .25  .25

"Education for Progress" — A71

# UNITED NATIONS, OFFICES IN NEW YORK

Issued to publicize the UNESCO world campaign for universal literacy and for free compulsory primary education.

**Perf. 12½**

**1964, Dec. 7   Photo.   Unwmk.**

| 134 | A71 | 4c orange, red, bister, green & blue | .25 | .25 |
| 135 | A71 | 5c bister, red, dark & light blue | .25 | .25 |
| 136 | A71 | 11c green, light blue, black & rose | .25 | .25 |
|  |  | Nos. 134-136 (3) | .75 | .75 |

Progress Chart, Key & Globe — A72

Issued to publicize the Special Fund program to speed economic growth and social advancement in low-income countries.

**Perf. 13½x13**

**1965, Jan. 25   Photo.   Unwmk.**

| 137 | A72 | 5c dull blue, dark blue, yellow & red | .25 | .25 |
| 138 | A72 | 11c yellow green, dark blue, yellow & red | .25 | .25 |
| a. |  | Black omitted (UN emblem on key) | — |  |

Leaves & View of Cyprus — A73

Issued to honor the United Nations Peace-keeping Force on Cyprus.

**Perf. 11½**

**1965, Mar. 4   Photo.   Unwmk.**

| 139 | A73 | 5c orange, olive & black | .25 | .25 |
| 140 | A73 | 11c yellow green, blue green & black | .25 | .25 |

"From Semaphore to Satellite" — A74

Centenary of the International Telecommunication Union.

**Perf. 11½**

**1965, May 17   Photo.   Unwmk.**

| 141 | A74 | 5c aquamarine, orange, blue & purple | .25 | .25 |
| 142 | A74 | 11c light violet, red orange, bister & bright green | .25 | .25 |

ICY Emblem — A75

20th anniversary of the United Nations and International Cooperation Year.

**Perf. 14x13½**

**1965, June 26   Engr.   Unwmk.**

| 143 | A75 | 5c dark blue | .25 | .25 |
| 144 | A75 | 15c lilac rose | .25 | .25 |

**Souvenir Sheet**

| 145 | A75 | Sheet of two | .35 | .35 |

"Peace" A76

Opening Words, UN Charter A77

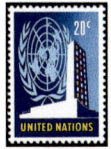

UN Headquarters, Emblem A78

UN Emblem A79

UN Emblem — A80

**Perf. 13½x13**

**1965-66   Photo.   Unwmk.**

| 146 | A76 | 1c vermilion, blue, black & gray | .25 | .25 |

**Perf. 14**

| 147 | A77 | 15c olive bister, dull yellow, black & deep claret | .25 | .25 |

**Perf. 12**

| 148 | A78 | 20c dark blue, blue, red & yellow | .25 | .25 |
| a. |  | Yellow omitted |  |  |

**Litho. and Embossed**
**Perf. 14**

| 149 | A79 | 25c light & dark blue | .30 | .25 |
| a. |  | 25c light & dark blue, new dk blue plate/cylinder (see footnote) | .30 | .25 |
| b. |  | As "a," tagged | 10.00 | 10.00 |

**Photo.**
**Perf. 11½**

| 150 | A80 | $1 aquamarine & sapphire | 1.60 | 1.60 |
|  |  | Nos. 146-150 (5) | 2.65 | 2.60 |

Issued: 1c, No. 149, 9/20/65; No. 149a, 11/5/65; 15c, 20c, 10/25/65; $1, 3/25/66.
On No. 149, the dark blue "halo" of the U.N. emblem is large, overlapping the "25c." On No. 149a, a new dark blue plate/cylinder was used, making the "halo" of the U.N. emblem smaller.
See UN Offices in Geneva Nos. 5, 9, 11.

Fields & People — A81

Design: 11c, French inscription.
Issued to emphasize the importance of the world's population growth and its problems and to call attention to population trends and development.

**Unwmk.**

**1965, Nov. 29   Photo.   Perf. 12**

| 151 | A81 | 4c multicolored | .25 | .25 |
| 152 | A81 | 5c multicolored | .25 | .25 |
| 153 | A81 | 11c multicolored | .25 | .25 |
|  |  | Nos. 151-153 (3) | .75 | .75 |

Globe & Flags of UN Members — A82

Design: 11c, French inscription.
Issued to honor the World Federation of United Nations Associations.

**Perf. 11½**

**1966, Jan. 31   Photo.   Unwmk.**

| 154 | A82 | 5c multicolored | .25 | .25 |
| 155 | A82 | 15c multicolored | .25 | .25 |

WHO Headquarters, Geneva — A83

Design: 11c, French inscription.
Issued to commemorate the opening of the World Health Organization Headquarters, Geneva.

UN Headquarters — A83 (?)

**1966, May 26   Photo.   Perf. 12½x12**
**Granite Paper**

| 156 | A83 | 5c lt & dk blue, orange, green & bister | .25 | .25 |
| 157 | A83 | 11c orange, lt & dk blue, green & bister | .25 | .25 |

Coffee — A84

Design: 11c, Spanish inscription.
Issued to commemorate the International Coffee Agreement of 1962.

**1966, Sept. 19   Photo.   Perf. 13½x13**

| 158 | A84 | 5c orange, lt blue, green, red & dk brown | .25 | .25 |
| 159 | A84 | 11c lt blue, yellow, green, red & dk brown | .25 | .25 |

UN Observer — A85

Issued to honor the Peace Keeping United Nation Observers.
Printed by Courvoisier, S.A. Panes of 50.
Designed by Ole G. Hamann.

**1966, Oct. 24   Photo.   Perf. 11½**
**Granite Paper**

| 160 | A85 | 15c steel blue, orange, black & green | .25 | .25 |

Children of Various Races — A86

20th anniversary of the United Nations Children's Fund (UNICEF).

**1966, Nov. 28   Litho.   Perf. 13x13½**

| 161 | A86 | 4c pink & multi | .25 | .25 |
| 162 | A86 | 5c pale green & multi | .25 | .25 |
| a. |  | Yellow omitted |  |  |
| 163 | A86 | 11c light ultramarine & multi | .25 | .25 |
| b. |  | Dark blue omitted |  |  |
|  |  | Nos. 161-163 (3) | .75 | .75 |

Hand Rolling up Sleeve & Chart Showing Progress — A87

Design: 11c, French inscription.
United Nations Development Program.

**1967, Jan. 23   Photo.   Perf. 12½**

| 164 | A87 | 5c green, yellow, purple & orange | .25 | .25 |
| 165 | A87 | 11c blue, chocolate, light green & orange | .25 | .25 |

**Type of 1962 and**

UN Headquarters, New York & World Map — A88

**1967   Photo.   Perf. 11½**

| 166 | A88 | 1½c ultramarine, black, orange & ocher | .25 | .25 |

**Size: 33x23mm**

| 167 | A53 | 5c red brown, brown & orange yellow | .25 | .25 |

Issue dates: 1½c, Mar. 17; 5c, Jan. 23.
See UN Offices in Geneva No. 1.

Fireworks — A89

Design: 11c, French inscription.
Issued to honor all nations which gained independence since 1945.

**1967, Mar. 17   Photo.   Perf. 14x14½**

| 168 | A89 | 5c dark blue & multi | .25 | .25 |
| 169 | A89 | 11c brown lake & multi | .25 | .25 |

"Peace" A90     UN Pavilion, EXPO '67 A91

EXPO '67, International Exhibition, Montreal, Apr. 28-Oct. 27, 1967.

**Engr. & Litho.**

**1967, Apr. 28        Perf. 11**

| 170 | A90 | 4c red & red brown | .25 | .25 |
| 171 | A90 | 5c blue & red brown | .25 | .25 |

**Litho.**

| 172 | A91 | 8c multicolored | .25 | .25 |

**Engr. and Litho.**

| 173 | A90 | 10c green & red brown | .25 | .25 |
| 174 | A90 | 15c dark brown & red brown | .25 | .25 |
|  |  | Nos. 170-174 (5) | 1.25 | 1.25 |

Nos. 170-174 were issued in Canadian dollars.

Luggage Tags and UN Emblem — A92

Issued to publicize International Tourist Year, 1967.

**1967, June 19   Litho.   Perf. 14**

| 175 | A92 | 5c reddish brown & multi | .25 | .25 |
| 176 | A92 | 15c ultramarine & multi | .25 | .25 |

Quotation from Isaiah 2:4 — A93

Design: 13c, French inscription.
Issued to publicize the UN General Assembly's resolutions on general and complete disarmament and for suspension of nuclear and thermonuclear tests.

**1967, Oct. 24   Photo.   Perf. 14**

| 177 | A93 | 6c ultramarine, yellow, gray & brown | .25 | .25 |
| 178 | A93 | 13c magenta, yellow, gray & brown | .25 | .25 |

**Art at UN Issue**
**Miniature Sheet**

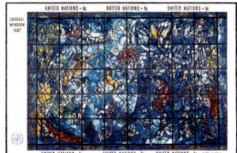

Memorial Window A94

"The Kiss of Peace" — A95

# UNITED NATIONS, OFFICES IN NEW YORK

**1967, Nov. 17  Litho.  Rouletted 9**
179  A94  6c Sheet of 6, #a.-f.  .40  .40
**Perf. 13x13½**
180  A95  6c multicolored  .25  .25

No. 179 contains six 6c stamps, each rouletted on 3 sides, imperf. on fourth side. Size: 124x80mm. On Nos. 179a-179c, "United Nations 6c" appears at top; on Nos. 179d-179f, at bottom. No. 179f includes name "Marc Chagall."

Globe and Major UN Organs — A96

Design: 13c, French inscription.
Issued to honor the United Nations Secretariat.

**1968, Jan. 16  Photo.  Perf. 11½**
181  A96  6c multicolored  .25  .25
182  A96  13c multicolored  .25  .25

### Art at UN Issue

Statue by Henrik Starcke — A97

**1968, Mar. 1  Photo.  Perf. 11½**
183  A97  6c blue & multi  .25  .25
184  A97  75c rose lake & multi  1.10  .90

The 6c is part of the "Art at the UN" series. The 75c belongs to the regular definitive series. The teakwood Starcke statue, which stands in the Trusteeship Council Chamber, represents mankind's search for freedom and happiness.
See UN Offices in Geneva No. 13.

Factories and Chart — A98

Design: 13c, French inscription ("ONUDI," etc.).
Issued to publicize the UN Industrial Development Organization.

**1968, Apr. 18  Litho.  Perf. 12**
185  A98  6c greenish blue, lt greenish blue, black & dull claret  .25  .25
186  A98  13c dull red brown, light red brown, black & ultra  .25  .25

UN Headquarters — A99

**1968, May 31  Litho.  Perf. 12x13½**
187  A99  6c green, blue, black & gray  .25  .25

Radarscope and Globes — A100

Design: 20c, French inscription.
Issued to publicize World Weather Watch, a new weather system directed by the World Meteorological Organization.

**1968, Sept. 19  Photo.  Perf. 13x13½**
188  A100  6c green, black, ocher & blue  .25  .25
189  A100  20c lilac, black, ocher, red & blue  .30  .25

Human Rights Flame — A101

Design: 13c, French inscription.
Issued for International Human Rights Year, 1968.

**Photo.; Foil Embossed**
**1968, Nov. 22  Perf. 12½**
190  A101  6c bright blue, deep ultra & gold  .25  .25
191  A101  13c rose red, dark red & gold  .25  .25

Books and UN Emblem — A102

Design: 13c, French inscription in center, denomination panel at bottom.
United Nations Institute for Training and Research (UNITAR).

**1969, Feb. 10  Litho.  Perf. 13½**
192  A102  6c yellow green & multi  .25  .25
193  A102  13c bluish lilac & multi  .25  .25

UN Building, Santiago, Chile — A103

Design: 15c, Spanish inscription.
The UN Building in Santiago, Chile, is the seat of the UN Economic Commission for Latin America and of the Latin American Institute for Economic and Social Planning.

**1969, Mar. 14  Litho.  Perf. 14**
194  A103  6c light blue, violet blue & light green  .25  .25
195  A103  15c pink, cream & red brown  .25  .25

"UN" and UN Emblem — A104

**1969, Mar. 14  Photo.  Perf. 13½**
196  A104  13c bright blue, black & gold  .25  .25

See UN Offices in Geneva No. 7.

UN Emblem and Scales of Justice — A105

Design: 13c, French inscription.
20th anniversary session of the UN International Law Commission.

**Granite Paper**
**1969, Apr. 21  Photo.  Perf. 11½**
197  A105  6c bright green, ultra & gold  .25  .25
198  A105  13c crimson, lilac & gold  .25  .25

Allegory of Labor, Emblems of UN and ILO — A106

Design: 20c, French inscription.
Issued to publicize "Labor and Development" and to commemorate the 50th anniversary of the International Labor Organization.

**1969, June 5  Photo.  Perf. 13**
199  A106  6c blue, deep blue, yellow & gold  .25  .25
200  A106  20c orange vermilion, magenta, yellow & gold  .25  .25

### Art at UN Issue

Ostrich, Tunisian Mosaic, 3rd Century — A107

Design: 13c, Pheasant; French inscription.

**1969, Nov. 21  Photo.  Perf. 14**
201  A107  6c blue & multi  .25  .25
202  A107  13c red & multi  .25  .25

### Art at UN Issue

Peace Bell, Gift of Japanese — A108

Design: 25c, French inscription.
The Peace Bell was a gift of the people of Japan in 1954, cast from donated coins and metals. It is housed in a Japanese cypress structure at UN Headquarters, New York.

**1970, Mar. 13  Photo.  Perf. 13½x13**
203  A108  6c violet blue & multi  .25  .25
204  A108  25c claret & multi  .30  .25

Mekong River, Power Lines and Map of Delta — A109

Design: 13c, French inscription.
Issued to publicize the Lower Mekong Basin Development project under UN auspices.

**1970, Mar. 13  Perf. 14**
205  A109  6c dark blue & multi  .25  .25
206  A109  13c deep plum & multi  .25  .25

"Fight Cancer" — A110

Design: 13c, French inscription.
Issued to publicize the fight against cancer in connection with the 10th International Cancer Congress of the International Union Against Cancer, Houston, Texas, May 22-29.

**1970, May 22  Litho.  Perf. 14**
207  A110  6c blue & black  .25  .25
208  A110  13c olive & black  .25  .25

UN Emblem and Olive Branch A111   UN Emblem A112

Design: 13c, French inscription.
25th anniv. of the UN. First day covers were postmarked at UN Headquarters, NY, and at San Francisco.

**1970, June 26  Photo.  Perf. 11½**
209  A111  6c red, gold, dark & light blue  .25  .25
210  A111  13c dark blue, gold, green & red  .25  .25
**Perf. 12½**
211  A112  25c dark blue, gold & light blue  .35  .25
Nos. 209-211 (3)  .85  .75

### Souvenir Sheet
*Imperf*
212    Sheet of 3  .80  .80
a.  A111 6c red, gold & multicolored  .25  .25
b.  A111 13c violet blue, gold & multi  .25  .25
c.  A112 25c violet blue, gold & light blue  .30  .30

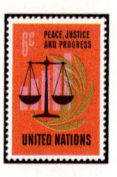

Scales, Olive Branch, Progress Symbol — A113

Design: 13c, French inscription.
Issued to publicize "Peace, Justice and Progress" in connection with the 25th anniversary of the United Nations.

**1970, Nov. 20  Photo.  Perf. 13½**
213  A113  6c gold & multi  .25  .25
214  A113  13c silver & multi  .25  .25

Sea Bed, Fish, Underwater Research — A114

Issued to publicize peaceful uses of the sea bed.

**Photo. & Engr.**
**1971, Jan. 25  Perf. 13**
215  A114  6c blue & multi  .25  .25
See UN Offices in Geneva No. 15.

Refugees, Sculpture by Kaare K. Nygaard — A115

International support for refugees.

**1971, Mar. 2  Litho.  Perf. 13x12½**
216  A115  6c brown, ocher & black  .25  .25
217  A115  13c ultramarine, greenish blue & black  .25  .25
See UN Offices in Geneva No. 16.

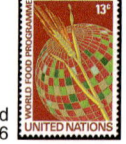

Wheat and Globe — A116

Publicizing the UN World Food Program.

**1971, Apr. 13  Photo.  Perf. 14**
218  A116  13c red & multicolored  .25  .25
See UN Offices in Geneva No. 17.

UPU Headquarters, Bern — A117

Opening of new Universal Postal Union Headquarters, Bern.

**1971, May 28  Photo.  Perf. 11½**
219  A117  20c brown orange & multi  .30  .25
See UN Offices in Geneva No. 18.

"Eliminate Racial Discrimination" — A118

# UNITED NATIONS, OFFICES IN NEW YORK

International Year Against Racial Discrimination.

**1971, Sept. 21   Photo.   Perf. 13½**
220 A118   8c yellow green & multi   .25   .25
221 A119   13c blue & multi   .25   .25
See UN Offices in Geneva Nos. 19-20.

UN Headquarters, New York — A120

UN Emblem and Symbolic Flags — A121

**1971, Oct. 22   Photo.   Perf. 13½**
222 A120   8c violet blue & multi   .25   .25
**Perf. 13**
223 A121   60c ultra & multi   .80   .80

Maia by Pablo Picasso — A122

To publicize the UN International School.

**1971, Nov. 19   Photo.   Perf. 11½**
224 A122   8c olive & multi   .25   .25
225 A122   21c ultra & multi   .25   .25

Letter Changing Hands — A123

**1972, Jan. 5   Litho.   Perf. 14**
226 A123   95c carmine & multi   1.30   1.10

"No More Nuclear Weapons" A124

To promote non-proliferation of nuclear weapons.

**1972, Feb. 14   Photo.   Perf. 13½x14**
227 A124   8c dull rose, black, blue & gray   .25   .25
See UN Offices in Geneva No. 23.

Proportions of Man (c. 1509), by Leonardo da Vinci — A125

World Health Day, Apr. 7.

**Litho. & Engr.**
**1972, Apr. 7   Perf. 13x13½**
228 A125   15c black & multi   .25   .25
See UN Offices in Geneva No. 24.

"Human Environment" — A126

UN Conf. on Human Environment, Stockholm, June 5-16, 1972.

**Litho. & Embossed**
**1972, June 5   Perf. 12½x14**
229 A126   8c red, buff, green & blue   .25   .25
230 A126   15c blue green, buff, green & blue   .25   .25
See UN Offices in Geneva Nos. 25-26.

"Europe" and UN Emblem — A127

Economic Commission for Europe, 25th anniversary.

**1972, Sept. 11   Litho.   Perf. 13x13½**
231 A127   21c yellow brown & multi   .30   .30
See UN Offices in Geneva No. 27.

**Art at UN Issue**

The Five Continents, by José Maria Sert — A128

**1972, Nov. 17   Photo.   Perf. 12x12½**
232 A128   8c gold, brown & golden brown   .25   .25
233 A128   15c gold, blue green & brown   .25   .25
See UN Offices in Geneva Nos. 28-29.

Olive Branch and Broken Sword — A129

Disarmament Decade, 1970-79.

**1973, Mar. 9   Litho.   Perf. 13½x13**
234 A129   8c blue & multi   .25   .25
235 A129   15c lilac rose & multi   .25   .25
See UN Offices in Geneva Nos. 30-31.

Poppy Capsule and Skull — A130

Fight against drug abuse.

**1973, Apr. 13   Photo.   Perf. 13½**
236 A130   8c deep orange & multi   .25   .25
237 A130   15c pink & multi   .25   .25
See UN Offices in Geneva No. 32.

Honeycomb — A131

5th anniversary of the United Nations Volunteer Program.

**1973, May 25   Photo.   Perf. 14**
238 A131   8c olive bister & multi   .25   .25
239 A131   21c gray blue & multi   .30   .30
See UN Offices in Geneva No. 33.

Map of Africa with Namibia — A132

To publicize Namibia (South-West Africa) for which the UN General Assembly ended the mandate of South Africa and established the UN Council for Namibia to administer the territory until independence.

**1973, Oct. 1   Photo.   Perf. 14**
240 A132   8c emerald & multi   .25   .25
241 A132   15c bright rose & multi   .25   .25
See UN Offices in Geneva No. 34.

UN Emblem, Human Rights Flame — A133

25th anniversary of the adoption and proclamation of the Universal Declaration of Human Rights.

**1973, Nov. 16   Photo.   Perf. 13½**
242 A133   8c deep carmine & multi   .25   .25
243 A133   21c blue green & multi   .25   .25
See UN Offices in Geneva Nos. 35-36.

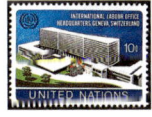
ILO Headquarters, Geneva — A134

New Headquarters of International Labor Organization.

**1974, Jan. 11   Photo.   Perf. 14**
244 A134   10c ultra & multi   .25   .25
245 A134   21c blue green & multi   .30   .25
See UN Offices in Geneva Nos. 37-38.

Post Horn Encircling Globe — A135

Centenary of Universal Postal Union.

**1974, Mar. 22   Litho.   Perf. 12½**
246 A135   10c gold & multi   .25   .25
See UN Offices in Geneva Nos. 39-40.

**Art at UN Issue**

Peace Mural, by Candido Portinari — A136

The mural, a gift of Brazil, is in the Delegates' Lobby, General Assembly Building.

**1974, May 6   Photo.   Perf. 14**
247 A136   10c gold & multi   .25   .25
248 A136   18c ultra & multi   .35   .30
See UN Offices in Geneva Nos. 41-42.

Dove & UN Emblem — A137

UN Headquarters A138

Globe, UN Emblem, Flags A139

**1974, June 10   Photo.   Perf. 14**
249 A137   2c dark & light blue   .25   .25
250 A138   10c multicolored   .25   .25
251 A139   18c multicolored   .25   .25
Nos. 249-251 (3)   .75   .75

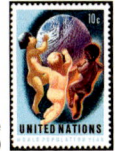
Children of the World — A140

World Population Year.

**1974, Oct. 18   Photo.   Perf. 14**
252 A140   10c light blue & multi   .25   .25
253 A140   18c lilac & multi   .35   .25
See UN Offices in Geneva Nos. 43-44.

Law of the Sea — A141

Declaration of UN General Assembly that the sea bed is common heritage of mankind, reserved for peaceful purposes.

**1974, Nov. 22   Photo.   Perf. 14**
254 A141   10c green & multi   .25   .25
255 A141   26c orange red & multi   .35   .30
See UN Offices in Geneva No. 45.

Satellite and Globe — A142

Peaceful uses (meteorology, industry, fishing, communications) of outer space.

**1975, Mar. 14   Litho.   Perf. 13**
256 A142   10c multicolored   .25   .25
257 A142   26c multicolored   .35   .30
See UN Offices in Geneva Nos. 46-47.

Equality Between Men and Women — A143

International Women's Year.

**1975, May 9   Litho.   Perf. 15**
258 A143   10c multicolored   .25   .25
259 A143   18c multicolored   .35   .30
See UN Offices in Geneva Nos. 48-49.

UN Flag and "XXX" — A144

30th anniversary of the United Nations.

**1975, June 26   Litho.   Perf. 13**
260 A144   10c olive bister & multi   .25   .25
261 A144   26c purple & multi   .40   .35

**Souvenir Sheet**
**Imperf**
262   Sheet of 2   .60   .50
  a.   A144 10c olive bister & multicolored   .25   .25
  b.   A144 26c purple & multicolored   .35   .25
See Offices in Geneva Nos. 50-52.

## UNITED NATIONS, OFFICES IN NEW YORK

Hand Reaching up over Map of Africa & Namibia — A145

"Namibia-United Nations direct responsibility." See note after No. 241.

| 1975, Sept. 22 | Photo. | Perf. 13½ |
|---|---|---|
| 263 A145 10c multicolored | .25 | .25 |
| 264 A145 18c multicolored | .30 | .30 |

See UN Offices in Geneva Nos. 53-54.

Wild Rose Growing from Barbed Wire — A146

United Nations Peace-keeping Operations.

| 1975, Nov. 21 | Engr. | Perf. 12½ |
|---|---|---|
| 265 A146 13c ultramarine | .25 | .25 |
| 266 A146 26c rose carmine | .40 | .40 |

See UN Offices in Geneva Nos. 55-56.

Symbolic Flags Forming Dove A147

UN Emblem A149

People of All Races A148

UN Flag A150

Dove and Rainbow — A151

| 1976 | Litho. | Perf. 13x13½, 13½x13 |
|---|---|---|
| 267 A147 3c multicolored | .25 | .25 |
| 268 A148 4c multicolored | .25 | .25 |

Photo. Perf. 14

| 269 A149 9c multicolored | .25 | .25 |

Litho. Perf. 13x13½

| 270 A150 30c blue, emerald & black | .35 | .35 |
| 271 A151 50c yellow green & multi | .65 | .65 |
| Nos. 267-271 (5) | 1.75 | 1.75 |

Issue dates: 3c, 4c, 30c, 50c, Jan. 6; 9c, Nov. 19.

See UN Offices in Vienna No. 8.

Interlocking Bands — A152

World Federation of United Nations Associations.

| 1976, Mar. 12 | Photo. | Perf. 14 |
|---|---|---|
| 272 A152 13c car & multi | .25 | .25 |
| 273 A152 26c blk & multi | .35 | .30 |

See UN Offices in Geneva No. 57.

Cargo, Globe and Graph — A153

UN Conference on Trade and Development (UNCTAD), Nairobi, Kenya, May 1976.

| 1976, Apr. 23 | Photo. | Perf. 11½ |
|---|---|---|
| 274 A153 13c deep magenta & multi | .25 | .25 |
| 275 A153 31c dull blue & multi | .40 | .30 |

See UN Offices in Geneva No. 58.

Houses Around Globe — A154

Habitat, UN Conference on Human Settlements, Vancouver, Canada, May 31-June 11.

| 1976, May 28 | Photo. | Perf. 14 |
|---|---|---|
| 276 A154 13c red brown & multi | .25 | .25 |
| 277 A154 25c green & multi | .40 | .30 |

See UN Offices in Geneva Nos. 59-60.

Magnifying Glass, Sheet of Stamps, UN Emblem — A155

United Nations Postal Administration, 25th anniversary.

| 1976, Oct. 8 | Photo. | Perf. 11½ |
|---|---|---|
| 278 A155 13c blue & multi | .25 | .25 |
| 279 A155 31c green & multi | 1.00 | 1.00 |

See UN Offices in Geneva Nos. 61-62.

Grain — A156

World Food Council.

| 1976, Nov. 19 | Litho. | Perf. 14½ |
|---|---|---|
| 280 A156 13c multicolored | .25 | .25 |

See UN Offices in Geneva No. 63.

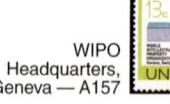

WIPO Headquarters, Geneva — A157

World Intellectual Property Organization (WIPO).

| 1977, Mar. 11 | Photo. | Perf. 14 |
|---|---|---|
| 281 A157 13c citron & multi | .25 | .25 |
| 282 A157 31c bright green & multi | .45 | .35 |

See UN Offices in Geneva No. 64.

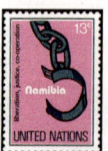

Drops of Water Falling into Funnel — A158

UN Water Conference, Mar del Plata, Argentina, Mar. 14-25.

| 1977, Apr. 22 | Photo. | Perf. 13½x13 |
|---|---|---|
| 283 A158 13c yellow & multi | .25 | .25 |
| 284 A158 25c salmon & multi | .40 | .35 |

See UN Offices in Geneva Nos. 65-66.

Burning Fuse Severed — A159

UN Security Council.

| 1977, May 27 | Photo. | Perf. 14 |
|---|---|---|
| 285 A159 13c purple & multi | .25 | .25 |
| 286 A159 31c dark blue & multi | .45 | .30 |

See UN Offices in Geneva Nos. 67-68.

"Combat Racism" — A160

Fight against racial discrimination.

| 1977, Sept. 19 | Litho. | Perf. 13½x13 |
|---|---|---|
| 287 A160 13c black & yellow | .25 | .25 |
| 288 A160 25c black & vermilion | .40 | .30 |

See UN Offices in Geneva Nos. 69-70.

Atom, Grain, Fruit and Factory — A161

Peaceful uses of atomic energy.

| 1977, Nov. 18 | Photo. | Perf. 14 |
|---|---|---|
| 289 A161 13c yellow bister & multi | .25 | .25 |
| 290 A161 18c dull green & multi | .30 | .25 |

See UN Offices in Geneva Nos. 71-72.

Opening Words of UN Charter — A162    "Live Together in Peace" — A163

People of the World — A164

| 1978, Jan. 27 | Litho. | Perf. 14½ |
|---|---|---|
| 291 A162 1c gold, brown & red | .25 | .25 |
| 292 A163 25c multicolored | .35 | .30 |
| 293 A164 $1 multicolored | 1.25 | 1.25 |
| Nos. 291-293 (3) | 1.85 | 1.80 |

See UN Offices in Geneva No. 73.

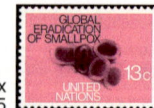

Smallpox Virus — A165

Global eradication of smallpox.

| 1978, Mar. 31 | Photo. | Perf. 12x11½ |
|---|---|---|
| 294 A165 13c rose & black | .25 | .25 |
| 295 A165 31c blue & black | .40 | .40 |

See UN Offices in Geneva Nos. 74-75.

Liberation, justice and cooperation for Namibia.

| 1978, May 5 | Photo. | Perf. 12 |
|---|---|---|
| 296 A166 13c multicolored | .25 | .25 |
| 297 A166 18c multicolored | .30 | .25 |

See UN Offices in Geneva No. 76.

Multicolored Bands and Clouds — A167

International Civil Aviation Organization for "Safety in the Air."

| 1978, June 12 | Photo. | Perf. 14 |
|---|---|---|
| 298 A167 13c multicolored | .25 | .25 |
| 299 A167 25c multicolored | .35 | .30 |

See UN Offices in Geneva Nos. 77-78.

General Assembly — A168

| 1978, Sept. 15 | Photo. | Perf. 13½ |
|---|---|---|
| 300 A168 13c multicolored | .25 | .25 |
| 301 A168 18c multicolored | .35 | .30 |

See UN Offices in Geneva Nos. 79-80.

Hemispheres as Cogwheels — A169

Technical Cooperation Among Developing Countries Conference, Buenos Aires, Argentina, Sept. 1978.

| 1978, Nov. 17 | Photo. | Perf. 14 |
|---|---|---|
| 302 A169 13c multicolored | .25 | .25 |
| 303 A169 31c multicolored | .50 | .40 |

See UN Offices in Geneva No. 81.

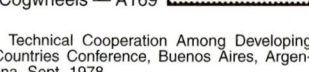

Hand Holding Olive Branch A170     Tree of Various Races A171

Globe, Dove with Olive Branch A172

Birds and Globe A173

| 1979, Jan. 19 | Photo. | Perf. 14 |
|---|---|---|
| 304 A170 5c multicolored | .25 | .25 |
| 305 A171 14c multicolored | .25 | .25 |
| 306 A172 15c multicolored | .25 | .25 |
| 307 A173 20c multicolored | .30 | .25 |
| Nos. 304-307 (4) | 1.05 | 1.00 |

UNDRO Against Fire and Water — A174

Office of the UN Disaster Relief Coordinator (UNDRO).

**1979, Mar. 9 Photo. *Perf. 14***
**308** A174 15c multicolored .25 .25
**309** A174 20c multicolored .35 .30

See UN Offices in Geneva Nos. 82-83.

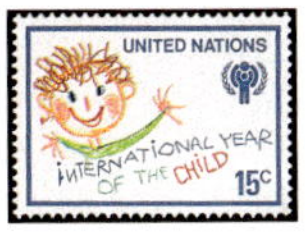


Child and ICY Emblem — A175

International Year of the Child.

**1979, May 4 Photo. *Perf. 14***
**310** A175 15c multicolored .25 .25
**311** A175 31c multicolored .35 .35

See UN Offices in Geneva Nos. 84-85.

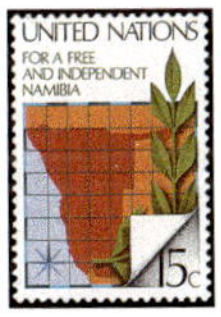


Map of Namibia, Olive Branch — A176

For a free and independent Namibia.

**1979, Oct. 5 Litho. *Perf. 13½***
**312** A176 15c multicolored .25 .25
**313** A176 31c multicolored .50 .35

See UN Offices in Geneva No. 86.

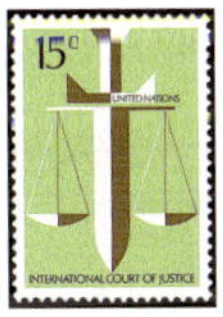


Scales and Sword of Justice — A177

International Court of Justice, The Hague, Netherlands.

**1979, Nov. 9 Litho. *Perf. 13x13½***
**314** A177 15c multicolored .25 .25
**315** A177 20c multicolored .30 .35

See UN Offices in Geneva Nos. 87-88.

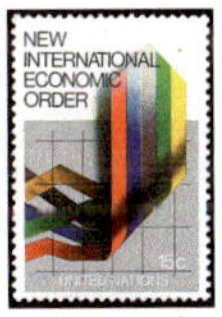


Graph of Economic Trends A178

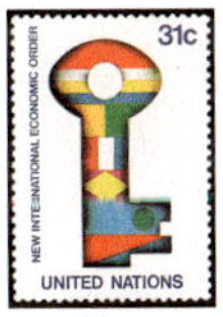


Key A179

New International Economic Order.

**1980, Jan. 11 Litho. *Perf. 15x14½***
**316** A178 15c multicolored .25 .25
**317** A179 31c multicolored .45 .35

See UN Offices in Geneva No. 89; Vienna No. 7.

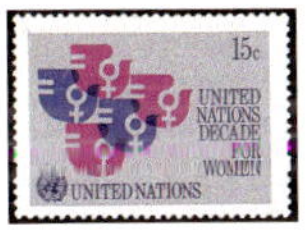


Women's Year Emblems — A180

United Nations Decade for Women.

**1980, Mar. 7 Litho. *Perf. 14½x15***
**318** A180 15c multicolored .25 .25
**319** A180 20c multicolored .30 .25

See UN Offices in Geneva Nos. 90-91; Vienna Nos. 9-10.

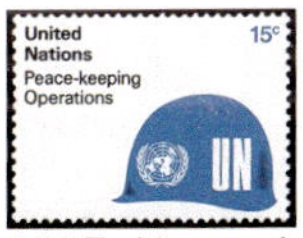


UN Emblem and "UN" on Helmet — A181

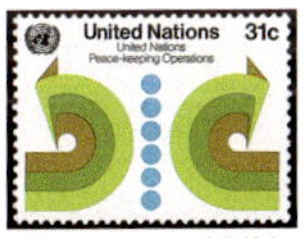


Arrows and UN Emblem — A182

United Nations Peace-keeping Operations.

**1980, May 16 Litho. *Perf. 14x13***
**320** A181 15c blue & black .25 .25
**321** A182 31c multicolored .40 .40

See UN Offices in Geneva No. 92; Vienna No. 11.

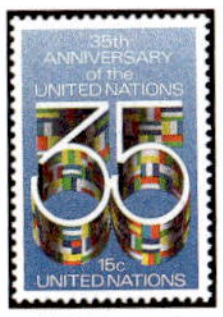


"35" and Flags A183

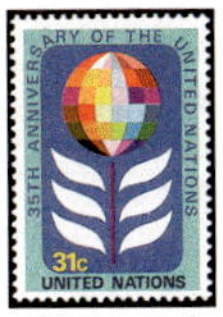


Globe and Laurel A184

35th Anniversary of the United Nations.

**1980, June 26 Litho. *Perf. 13x13½***
**322** A183 15c multicolored .25 .25
**323** A184 31c multicolored .40 .35

**Souvenir Sheet**

***Imperf***

**324** Sheet of 2 .65 .65
*a.* A183 15c multicolored .25 .25
*b.* A184 31c multicolored .40 .40

See UN Offices in Geneva Nos. 93-95; Vienna Nos. 12-14.

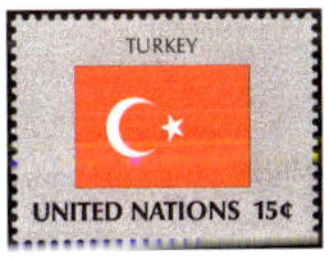


Flag of Turkey — A185

**1980, Sept. 26 Litho. *Perf. 12***

**Granite Paper**

**325** A185 15c shown .25 .25
**326** A185 15c Luxembourg .25 .25
**327** A185 15c Fiji .25 .25
**328** A185 15c Viet Nam .25 .25
*a.* Se-tenant block of 4, #325-328 1.00 1.00
**329** A185 15c Guinea .25 .25
**330** A185 15c Surinam .25 .25
**331** A185 15c Bangladesh .25 .25
**332** A185 15c Mali .25 .25
*a.* Se-tenant block of 4, #329-332 1.00 1.00
**333** A185 15c Yugoslavia .25 .25
**334** A185 15c France .25 .25
**335** A185 15c Venezuela .25 .25
**336** A185 15c El Salvador .25 .25
*a.* Se-tenant block of 4, #333-336 1.00 1.00
**337** A185 15c Madagascar .25 .25
**338** A185 15c Cameroon .25 .25
**339** A185 15c Rwanda .25 .25
**340** A185 15c Hungary .25 .25
*a.* Se-tenant block of 4, #337-340 1.00 1.00
*Nos. 325-340 (16)* 4.00 4.00

Issued in 4 panes of 16. Each pane contains 4 blocks of 4 (Nos. 325-328, 329-332, 333-336, 337-340). A se-tenant block of 4 designs centers each pane.

See Nos. 350-365, 374-389, 399-414, 425-440, 450-465, 477-492, 499-514, 528-543, 554-569, 690-697, 719-726, 744-751, 795-802, 921-924, 1063-1066, 1083-1086.

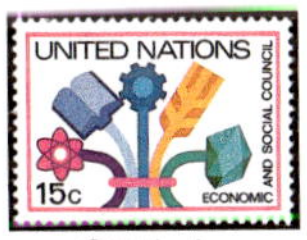


Symbolic Flowers — A186

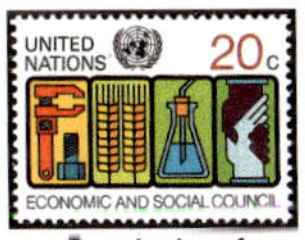


Symbols of Progress — A187

**1980, Nov. 21 Litho. *Perf. 13½x13***
**341** A186 15c multicolored .25 .25
**342** A187 20c multicolored .40 .35

See UN Offices in Geneva, Nos. 96-97; Vienna Nos. 15-16.

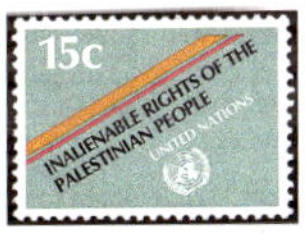


Inalienable Rights of the Palestinian People — A188

**1981, Jan. 30 Photo. *Perf. 12x11½***
**343** A188 15c multicolored .30 .25

See UN Offices in Geneva No. 98; Vienna No. 17.

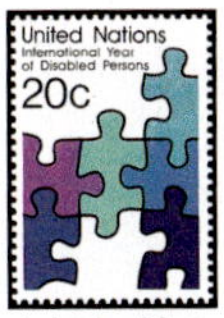


Interlocking Puzzle Pieces A189

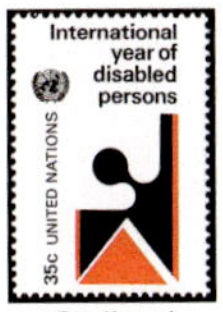


Stylized Person A190

International Year of the Disabled.

**1981, Mar. 6 Photo. *Perf. 14***
**344** A189 20c multicolored .25 .25
**345** A190 35c black & orange .40 .45

See UN Offices in Geneva Nos. 99-100; Vienna Nos. 18-19.

**Art at UN Issue**

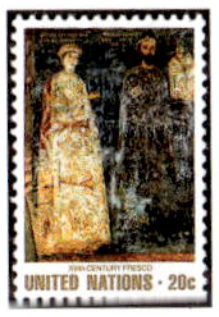


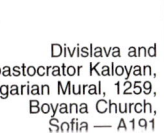

Divislava and Sebastocrator Kaloyan, Bulgarian Mural, 1259, Boyana Church, Sofia — A191

**1981, Apr. 15 Photo. *Perf. 11½***

**Granite Paper**

**346** A191 20c multicolored .25 .25
**347** A191 31c multicolored .40 .45

See UN Offices in Geneva No. 101; Vienna No. 20.

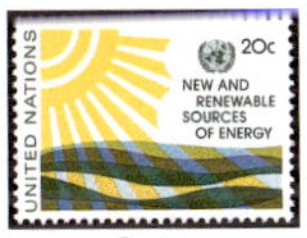


Solar Energy — A192

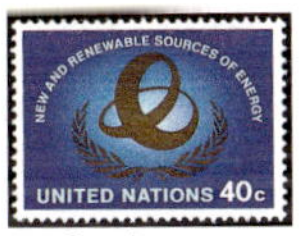


Conference Emblem — A193

Conference on New and Renewable Sources of Energy, Nairobi, Aug. 10-21.

**1981, May 29 Litho. *Perf. 13***
**348** A192 20c multicolored .25 .25
**349** A193 40c multicolored .50 .50

See UN Offices in Geneva No. 102; Vienna No. 21.

**Flag Type of 1980**

**1981, Sept. 25 Litho.**

**Granite Paper**

**350** A185 20c Djibouti .25 .25
**351** A185 20c Sri Lanka .25 .25
**352** A185 20c Bolivia .25 .25
**353** A185 20c Equatorial Guinea .25 .25
*a.* Se-tenant block of 4, #350-353 1.00 1.00
**354** A185 20c Malta .25 .25
**355** A185 20c Czechoslovakia .25 .25
**356** A185 20c Thailand .25 .25
**357** A185 20c Trinidad & Tobago .25 .25
*a.* Se-tenant block of 4, #354-357 1.00 1.00
**358** A185 20c Ukrainian SSR .25 .25
**359** A185 20c Kuwait .25 .25
**360** A185 20c Sudan .25 .25
**361** A185 20c Egypt .25 .25
*a.* Se-tenant block of 4, #358-361 1.00 1.00
**362** A185 20c US .25 .25
**363** A185 20c Singapore .25 .25
**364** A185 20c Panama .25 .25
**365** A185 20c Costa Rica .25 .25
*a.* Se-tenant block of 4, #362-365 1.00 1.00
*Nos. 350-365 (16)* 4.00 4.00

See note after No. 340.

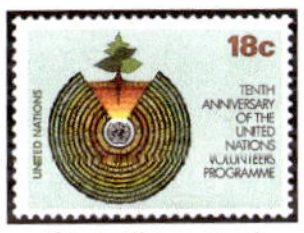


Seedling and Tree Cross Section — A194

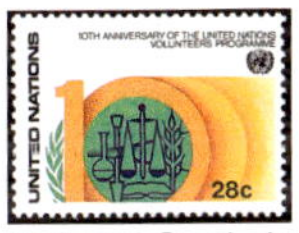


"10" and Symbols of Progress — A195

United Nations Volunteers Program, 10th anniv.

**1981, Nov. 13 Litho.**
**366** A194 18c multicolored .25 .25
**367** A195 28c multicolored .55 .55

See UN Offices in Geneva Nos. 103-104; Vienna Nos. 22-23.

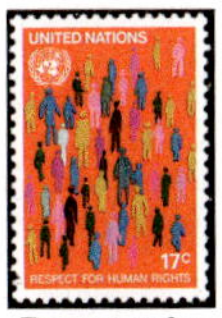


Respect for Human Rights A196

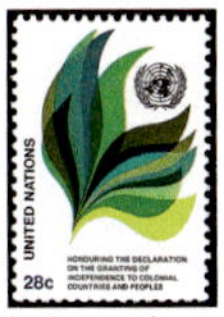


Independence of Colonial Countries and People A197

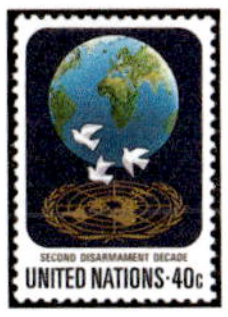


Second Disarmament Decade — A198

**1982, Jan. 22 *Perf. 11½x12***
**368** A196 17c multicolored .25 .25
**369** A197 28c multicolored .45 .40
**370** A198 40c multicolored .75 .70
*Nos. 368-370 (3)* 1.45 1.35

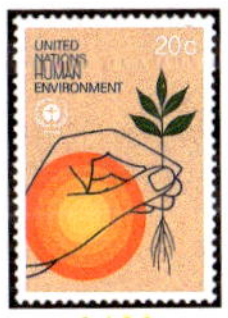


A199

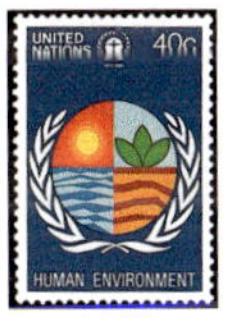


A200

10th Anniversary of United Nations Environment Program.

**1982, Mar. 19 Litho. *Perf. 13½x13***
**371** A199 20c multicolored .25 .25
**372** A200 40c multicolored .65 .65

See UN Offices in Geneva Nos. 107-108; Vienna Nos. 25-26.

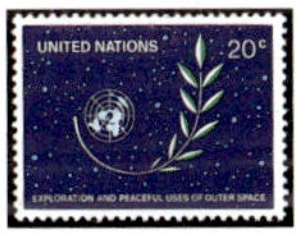


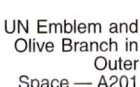

UN Emblem and Olive Branch in Outer Space — A201

Exploration and Peaceful Uses of Outer Space.

**1982, June 11 Litho. *Perf. 13x13½***
**373** A201 20c multicolored .45 .45

See UN Offices in Geneva Nos. 109-110; Vienna No. 27.

**Flag Type of 1980**

**1982, Sept. 24 Litho. *Perf. 12***

**Granite Paper**

**374** A185 20c Austria .25 .25
**375** A185 20c Malaysia .25 .25
**376** A185 20c Seychelles .25 .25
**377** A185 20c Ireland .25 .25
*a.* Se-tenant block of 4, #374-377 1.50 1.50
**378** A185 20c Mozambique .25 .25
**379** A185 20c Albania .25 .25
**380** A185 20c Dominica .25 .25
**381** A185 20c Solomon Islnads .25 .25
*a.* Se-tenant block of 4, #378-381 1.50 1.50
**382** A185 20c Philippines .25 .25
**383** A185 20c Swaziland .25 .25
**384** A185 20c Nicaragua .25 .25
**385** A185 20c Burma .25 .25
*a.* Se-tenant block of 4, #382-385 1.50 1.50
**386** A185 20c Cape Verde .25 .25
**387** A185 20c Guyana .25 .25
**388** A185 20c Belgium .25 .25
**389** A185 20c Nigeria .25 .25
*a.* Se-tenant block of 4, #386-389 1.50 1.50
*Nos. 374-389 (16)* 4.00 4.00

See note after No. 340.

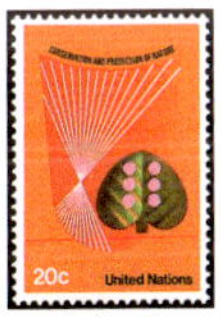


Conservation and Protection of Nature — A202

**1982, Nov. 19 Photo. *Perf. 14***
**390** A202 20c Leaf .30 .30
**391** A202 28c Butterfly .55 .50

See UN Offices in Geneva Nos. 111-112; Vienna Nos. 28-29.

# UNITED NATIONS, OFFICES IN NEW YORK

A203    World Communications Year — A204

World Communications Year.

**1983, Jan. 28   Litho.   Perf. 13**
392 A203 20c multicolored .25 .25
393 A204 40c multicolored .65 .65

See UN Offices in Geneva No. 113; Vienna No. 30.

A205   Safety at Sea — A206

Safety at Sea.

**1983, Mar. 18   Litho.   Perf. 14½**
394 A205 20c multicolored .25 .25
395 A206 37c multicolored .60 .55

See UN Offices in Geneva Nos. 114-115; Vienna Nos. 31-32.

World Food Program — A207

**1983, Apr. 22   Engr.   Perf. 13½**
396 A207 20c rose lake .35 .35

See UN Offices in Geneva No. 116; Vienna Nos. 33-34.

A208

Trade and Development — A209

UN Conference on Trade and Development.

**1983, June 6   Litho.   Perf. 14**
397 A208 20c multicolored .25 .35
398 A209 28c multicolored .70 .65

See UN Offices in Geneva Nos. 117-118; Vienna Nos. 35-36.

### Flag Type of 1980

**1983, Sept. 23   Photo.   Perf. 12**
### Granite Paper
399 A185 20c Great Britain .25 .25
400 A185 20c Barbados .25 .25
401 A185 20c Nepal .25 .25
402 A185 20c Israel .25 .25
  a. Se-tenant block of 4, #399-402 1.50 1.50
403 A185 20c Malawi .25 .25
404 A185 20c Byelorussian SSR .25 .25
405 A185 20c Jamaica .25 .25
406 A185 20c Kenya .25 .25
  a. Se-tenant block of 4, #403-406 1.50 1.80
407 A185 20c People's Republic of China .25 .25
408 A185 20c Peru .25 .25
409 A185 20c Bulgaria .25 .25
410 A185 20c Canada .25 .25
  a. Se-tenant block of 4, #407-410 1.50 1.80
411 A185 20c Somalia .25 .25
412 A185 20c Senegal .25 .25
413 A185 20c Brazil .25 .25
414 A185 20c Sweden .25 .25
  a. Se-tenant block of 4, #411-414 1.50 1.80
  Nos. 399-414 (16) 4.00 4.00

See note after No. 340.

A210   35th Anniv. of the Universal Declaration of Human Rights — A211

35th Anniversary of the Universal Declaration of Human Rights.

**Photo. & Engr.**
**1983, Dec. 9   Perf. 13½**
415 A210 20c multicolored .30 .25
416 A211 40c multicolored .70 .65

See UN Offices in Geneva Nos. 119-120; Vienna Nos. 37-38.

Intl. Population Conference — A212

**1984, Feb. 3   Litho.   Perf. 14**
417 A212 20c multicolored .25 .25
418 A212 40c multicolored .65 .65

See UN Offices in Geneva No. 121; Vienna No. 39.

Tractor Plowing — A213

Rice Paddy — A214

World Food Day, Oct. 16.

**1984, Mar. 15   Litho.   Perf. 14½**
419 A213 20c multicolored .30 .30
420 A214 40c multicolored .60 .60

See UN Offices in Geneva Nos. 122-123; Vienna Nos. 40-41.

Grand Canyon — A215   Ancient City of Polonnaruwa, Sri Lanka — A216

World Heritage.

**1984, Apr. 18   Litho.   Perf. 14**
421 A215 20c multicolored .25 .25
422 A216 50c multicolored .75 .75

See Nos. 601-602, UN Offices in Geneva Nos. 124-125, 211-212; Vienna Nos. 42-43, 125-126.

A217   A218

Future for Refugees.

**1984, May 29   Photo.   Perf. 11½**
423 A217 20c multicolored .30 .30
424 A218 50c multicolored .90 .90

See UN Offices in Geneva Nos. 126-127; Vienna Nos. 44-45.

### Flag Type of 1980

**1984, Sept. 21   Photo.   Perf. 12**
### Granite Paper
425 A185 20c Burundi .25 .25
426 A185 20c Pakistan .25 .25
427 A185 20c Benin .25 .25
428 A185 20c Italy .25 .25
  a. Se-tenant block of 4, #425-428 1.80 1.80
429 A185 20c Tanzania .25 .25
430 A185 20c United Arab Emirates .25 .25
431 A185 20c Ecuador .25 .25
432 A185 20c Bahamas .25 .25
  a. Se-tenant block of 4, #429-432 1.80 1.80
433 A185 20c Poland .25 .25
434 A185 20c Papua New Guinea .25 .25
435 A185 20c Uruguay .25 .25
436 A185 20c Chile .25 .25
  a. Se-tenant block of 4, #433-436 1.80 1.80
437 A185 20c Paraguay .25 .25
438 A185 20c Bhutan .25 .25
439 A185 20c Central African Republic .25 .25
440 A185 20c Australia .25 .25
  a. Se-tenant block of 4, #437-440 1.80 1.80
  Nos. 425-440 (16) 4.00 4.00

See note after No. 340.

Intl. Youth Year — A219

**1984, Nov. 15   Litho.   Perf. 13½**
441 A219 20c multicolored .35 .35
442 A219 35c multicolored .85 .85

See UN Offices in Geneva No. 128; Vienna Nos. 46-47.

ILO Turin Center — A220

Printed by the Government Printing Bureau, Japan. Panes of 50. Engraved by Mamoru Iwakuni and Hiroshi Ozaki, Japan.

**1985, Feb. 1   Engr.   Perf. 13½**
443 A220 23c blue .45 .45

See UN Offices in Geneva Nos. 129-130; Vienna No. 48.

UN University A221

50c, Farmer plowing, discussion group.

**1985, Mar. 15   Photo.   Perf. 11½**
444 A221 50c multi .95 .95

See UN Offices in Geneva Nos. 131-132; Vienna No. 49.

Peoples of the World — A222   Painting UN Emblem — A223

**1985, May 10   Litho.   Perf. 14**
445 A222 22c multicolored .30 .30
446 A223 $3 multicolored 3.75 1.50

See UN Offices in Geneva Nos. 133-134; Vienna Nos. 50-51.

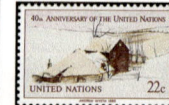

The Corner — A224

---

Alvaro Raking Hay — A225

UN 40th anniversary. Oil paintings (details) by American artist Andrew Wyeth (b. 1917).

**Perf. 12 x 11½**
**1985, June 26   Photo.**
447 A224 22c multicolored .35 .35
448 A225 45c multicolored 1.00 1.00

### Souvenir Sheet
*Imperf*
449   Sheet of 2   1.10 1.30
  a. A224 22c multicolored .40 .50
  b. A225 45c multicolored .70 .80

See UN Offices in Geneva Nos. 135-137; Vienna Nos. 52-54.

### Flag Type of 1980

**1985, Sept. 20   Photo.   Perf. 12**
### Granite Paper
450 A185 22c Grenada .30 .30
451 A185 22c Federal Republic of Germany .30 .30
452 A185 22c Saudi Arabia .30 .30
453 A185 22c Mexico .30 .30
  a. Se-tenant block of 4, #450-453 2.75 3.00
454 A185 22c Uganda .30 .30
455 A185 22c St. Thomas & Prince .30 .30
456 A185 22c USSR .30 .30
457 A185 22c India .30 .30
  a. Se-tenant block of 4, #454-457 2.75 3.00
458 A185 22c Liberia .30 .30
459 A185 22c Mauritius .30 .30
460 A185 22c Chad .30 .30
461 A185 22c Dominican Republic .30 .30
  a. Se-tenant block of 4, #458-461 2.75 3.00
462 A185 22c Sultanate of Oman .30 .30
463 A185 22c Ghana .30 .30
464 A185 22c Sierra Leone .30 .30
465 A185 22c Finland .30 .30
  a. Se-tenant block of 4, #462-465 2.75 3.00
  Nos. 450-465 (16) 4.80 4.80

See note after 340.

A226

UNICEF Child Survival Campaign.

**Photo. & Engr.**
**1985, Nov. 22   Perf. 13½**
466 A226 22c Asian Toddler .30 .30
467 A226 33c Breastfeeding .65 .65

See UN Offices in Geneva Nos. 138-139; Vienna Nos. 55-56.

A227

Africa in Crisis, campaign against hunger.

**1986, Jan. 31   Photo.   Perf. 11½x12**
468 A227 22c multicolored .40 .40

See UN Offices in Geneva No. 140; Vienna No. 57.

Water Resources — A228

**1986, Mar. 14   Photo.   Perf. 13½**
469 A228 22c Dam .50 .50
470 A228 22c Irrigation .50 .50
471 A228 22c Hygiene .50 .50
472 A228 22c Well .50 .50
  a. Block of 4, #469-472 2.00 2.00

UN Development Program. No. 472a has continuous design. See UN Offices in Geneva Nos. 141-144; Vienna Nos. 58-61.

## UNITED NATIONS, OFFICES IN NEW YORK

Human Rights Stamp of 1954 — A229

Stamp collecting: 44c, Engraver.

**1986, May 22    Engr.    Perf. 12½**
473  A229  22c dk vio & brt blue   .25   .25
474  A229  44c brn & emer grn      .75   .75

See UN Offices in Geneva Nos. 146-147; Vienna Nos. 62-63.

 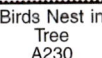

Birds Nest in Tree — A230
Peace in Seven Languages — A231 

**Photo. & Embossed**
**1986, June 20    Perf. 13½**
475  A230  22c multicolored     .50   .50
476  A231  33c multicolored    1.25  1.25

International Peace Year.
See UN Offices in Geneva Nos. 148-149; Vienna Nos. 64-65.

**Flag Type of 1980**
**1986, Sept. 19    Photo.    Perf. 12**
**Granite Paper**
477  A185  22c New Zealand     .30  .30
478  A185  22c Lao PDR         .30  .30
479  A185  22c Burkina Faso    .30  .30
480  A185  22c Gambia          .30  .30
  a.   Se-tenant block of 4, #477-480  2.75  3.00
481  A185  22c Maldives        .30  .30
482  A185  22c Ethiopia        .30  .30
483  A185  22c Jordan          .30  .30
484  A185  22c Zambia          .30  .30
  a.   Se-tenant block of 4, #481-484  2.75  3.00
485  A185  22c Iceland         .30  .30
486  A185  22c Antigua & Barbuda  .30  .30
487  A185  22c Angola          .30  .30
488  A185  22c Botswana        .30  .30
  a.   Se-tenant block of 4, #485-488  2.75  3.00
489  A185  22c Romania         .30  .30
490  A185  22c Togo            .30  .30
491  A185  22c Mauritania      .30  .30
492  A185  22c Colombia        .30  .30
  a.   Se-tenant block of 4, #489-492  2.75  3.00
     Nos. 477-492 (16)        4.80  4.80

See note after No. 340.

**Souvenir Sheet**

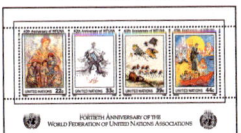

World Federation of UN Associations, 40th Anniv. — A232

22c, Mother Earth, by Edna Hibel, U.S. 33c, Watercolor by Salvador Dali (b. 1904), Spain. 39c, New Dawn, by Dong Kingman, U.S. 44c, Watercolor by Chaim Gross, U.S.

**1986, Nov. 14    Litho.    Perf. 13x13½**
493  A232  Sheet of 4         2.50  2.50
  a.   22c multicolored        .30   .40
  b.   33c multicolored        .40   .40
  c.   39c multicolored        .60   .50
  d.   44c multicolored        .90   .75

See UN Offices in Geneva No. 150; Vienna No. 66.

Trygve Halvdan Lie (1896-1968), 1st Secretary-General A233

**Photo. & Engr.**
**1987, Jan. 30    Perf. 13½**
494  A233  20c multicolored    .75   .75

See Offices in Geneva No. 151; Vienna No. 67.

Intl. Year of Shelter for the Homeless A234

22c, Surveying and blueprinting. 44c, Cutting lumber.

**Perf. 13½x12½**
**1987, Mar. 13    Litho.**
495  A234  22c multicolored    .35   .35
496  A234  44c multicolored    .90   .90

See Offices in Geneva Nos. 154-155; Vienna Nos. 68-69.

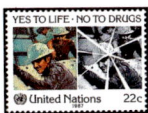

Fight Drug Abuse — A235

22c, Construction. 33c, Education.

**1987, June 12    Litho.    Perf. 14½x15**
497  A235  22c multicolored    .45   .45
498  A235  33c multicolored    .90   .90

See Offices in Geneva Nos. 156-157; Vienna Nos. 70-71.

**Flag Type of 1980**
**1987, Sept. 18    Photo.    Perf. 12**
**Granite Paper**
499  A185  22c Comoros         .30  .35
500  A185  22c Yemen PDR       .30  .35
501  A185  22c Mongolia        .30  .35
502  A185  22c Vanuatu         .30  .35
  a.   Se-tenant block of 4, #499-502  3.25  3.25
503  A185  22c Japan           .30  .35
504  A185  22c Gabon           .30  .35
505  A185  22c Zimbabwe        .30  .35
506  A185  22c Iraq            .30  .35
  a.   Se-tenant block of 4, #503-506  3.25  3.25
507  A185  22c Argentina       .30  .35
508  A185  22c Congo           .30  .35
509  A185  22c Niger           .30  .35
510  A185  22c St. Lucia       .30  .35
  a.   Se-tenant block of 4, #507-510  3.25  3.25
511  A185  22c Bahrain         .30  .35
512  A185  22c Haiti           .30  .35
513  A185  22c Afghanistan     .30  .35
514  A185  22c Greece          .30  .35
  a.   Se-tenant block of 4, #511-514  3.25  3.25
     Nos. 499-514 (16)         4.80  5.60

See note after No. 340.

UN Day — A236

Multinational people in various occupations.

**1987, Oct. 23    Litho.    Perf. 14½x15**
515  A236  22c multicolored    .35   .35
516  A236  39c multicolored    .55   .55

See Offices in Geneva Nos. 158-159; Vienna Nos. 74-75.

Immunize Every Child — A237

22c, Measles. 44c, Tetanus.

**1987, Nov. 20    Litho.    Perf. 15x14½**
517  A237  22c multicolored    .75   .75
518  A237  44c multicolored   1.50  1.50

See Offices in Geneva Nos. 160-161; Vienna Nos. 76-77.

Intl. Fund for Agricultural Development (IFAD) — A238

22c, Fishing. 33c, Farming.

**1988, Jan. 29    Litho.    Perf. 13½**
519  A238  22c multicolored    .35   .35
520  A238  33c multicolored    .75   .75

See Offices in Geneva Nos. 162-163; Vienna Nos. 78-79.

A239

**1988, Jan. 29    Photo.    Perf. 13½x14**
521  A239  3c multicolored     .25   .25

Survival of the Forests — A240

Tropical rain forest: 25c, Treetops. 44c, Ground vegetation and tree trunks. Printed se-tenant in a continuous design.

**1988, Mar. 18    Litho.    Perf. 14x15**
522  A240  25c multicolored    .75   .75
523  A240  44c multicolored   1.00  1.00
  a.   Pair, #522-523          2.00  3.00

See Offices in Geneva Nos. 165-166; Vienna Nos. 80-81.

Intl. Volunteer Day — A241

25c, Eduraton. 50c, Vocational training, horiz.

**Perf. 13x14, 14x13**
**1988, May 6    Litho.**
524  A241  25c multicolored    .45   .45
525  A241  50c multicolored    .95   .95

See Offices in Geneva Nos. 167-168; Vienna Nos. 82-83.

Health in Sports — A242

25c, Cycling, vert. 35c, Marathon.

**Perf. 13½x13, 13x13½**
**1988, June 17    Litho.**
526  A242  25c multicolored    .45   .45
527  A242  38c multicolored   1.00  1.00

See Offices in Geneva Nos. 169-170; Vienna Nos. 84-85.

**Flag Type of 1980**
**1988, Sept. 15    Photo.    Perf. 12**
**Granite Paper**
528  A185  25c Spain           .45  .45
529  A185  25c St. Vincent & Grenadines  .45  .45
530  A185  25c Ivory Coast     .45  .45
531  A185  25c Lebanon         .45  .45
  a.   Se-tenant block of 4, #528-531  3.00  3.00
532  A185  25c Yemen (Arab Republic)  .45  .45
533  A185  25c Cuba            .45  .45
534  A185  25c Denmark         .45  .45
535  A185  25c Libya           .45  .45
  a.   Se-tenant block of 4, #532-535  3.00  3.00
536  A185  25c Qatar           .45  .45
537  A185  25c Zaire           .45  .45
538  A185  25c Norway          .45  .45
539  A185  25c German Democratic Republic  .45  .45
  a.   Se-tenant block of 4, #536-539  3.00  3.00
540  A185  25c Iran            .45  .45
541  A185  25c Tunisia         .45  .45
542  A185  25c Samoa           .45  .45
543  A185  25c Belize          .45  .45
  a.   Se-tenant block of 4, #540-543  3.00  3.00
     Nos. 528-543 (16)         7.20  7.20

See note after No. 340.

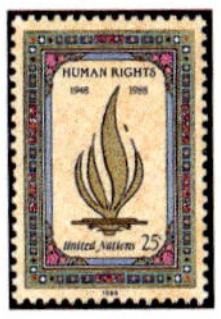

A243

**Photo. & Engr.**
**1988, Dec. 9    Perf. 11x11½**
544  A243  25c multicolored    .45   .45

**Souvenir Sheet**
545  A243  $1 multicolored    1.00  1.00

Universal Declaration of Human Rights, 40th anniv.

See Offices in Geneva Nos. 171-172; Vienna Nos. 86-87.

A244

**1989, Jan. 27    Litho.    Perf. 13x14**
546  A244  25c Energy and nature  .60  .60
547  A244  45c Agriculture    1.10  1.10

World Bank. See Offices in Geneva Nos. 173-174; Vienna Nos. 88-89.

UN Peace-Keeping Force, 1988 Nobel Peace Prize Winner — A245

UN Peace-Keeping Force, awarded 1988 Nobel Peace Prize.

**1989, Mar. 17    Litho.    Perf. 14x13½**
548  A245  25c multicolored    .45   .45

See Offices in Geneva No. 175; Vienna No. 90.

Aerial Photograph of New York Headquarters — A246

**1989, Mar. 17    Litho.    Perf. 14½x14**
549  A246  45c multicolored    .65   .65

World Weather Watch, 25th Anniv. (in 1988) — A247

Satellite photographs: 25c, Storm system off the U.S. east coast. 36c, Typhoon Abby in the north-west Pacific.

**1989, Apr. 21    Litho.    Perf. 13x14**
550  A247  25c multicolored    .50   .50
551  A247  36c multicolored   1.10  1.10

See Offices in Geneva Nos. 176-177; Vienna Nos. 91-92.

A248    A249

## UNITED NATIONS, OFFICES IN NEW YORK

**Photo. & Engr., Photo. (90c)**
**1989, Aug. 23**    *Perf. 14*
| 552 | A248 | 25c multicolored | 1.25 | 1.25 |
| 553 | A249 | 90c multicolored | 2.50 | 2.50 |

See Offices in Geneva Nos. 178-179; Vienna Nos. 93-94.

### Flag Type of 1980
**1989, Sept. 22**    **Photo.**    *Perf. 12*
**Granite Paper**
| 554 | A185 | 25c Indonesia | .60 | .55 |
| 555 | A185 | 25c Lesotho | .60 | .55 |
| 556 | A185 | 25c Guatemala | .60 | .55 |
| 557 | A185 | 25c Netherlands | .60 | .55 |
| a. | | Se-tenant block of 4, #554-557 | 4.00 | 4.00 |
| 558 | A185 | 25c South Africa | .60 | .55 |
| 559 | A185 | 25c Portugal | .60 | .55 |
| 560 | A185 | 25c Morocco | .60 | .55 |
| 561 | A185 | 25c Syrian Arab Republic | .60 | .55 |
| a. | | Se-tenant block of 4, #558-561 | 4.00 | 4.00 |
| 562 | A185 | 25c Honduras | .60 | .55 |
| 563 | A185 | 25c Kampuchea | .60 | .55 |
| 564 | A185 | 25c Guinea-Bissau | .60 | .55 |
| 565 | A185 | 25c Cyprus | .60 | .55 |
| a. | | Se-tenant block of 4, #562-565 | 4.00 | 4.00 |
| 566 | A185 | 25c Algeria | .60 | .55 |
| 567 | A185 | 25c Brunei | .60 | .55 |
| 568 | A185 | 25c St. Kitts and Nevis | .60 | .55 |
| 569 | A185 | 25c United Nations | .60 | .55 |
| a. | | Se-tenant block of 4, #566-569 | 4.00 | 4.00 |
| | | Nos. 554-569 (16) | 9.60 | 8.80 |

See note after No. 340.

Declaration of Human Rights, 40th Anniv. (in 1988) — A250

Paintings: 25c, The Table of Universal Brotherhood, by Jose Clemente Orozco. 45c, Study for Composition II, by Vassily Kandinsky.

**1989, Nov. 17**    **Litho.**    *Perf. 13½*
| 570 | A250 | 25c multicolored | .35 | .35 |
| 571 | A250 | 45c multicolored | .80 | .80 |

Panes of 12+12 se-tenant labels containing Articles 1 (25c) or 2 (45c) inscribed in English, French or German.

See Nos. 582-583, 599-600, 616-617, 627-628; Offices in Geneva Nos. 180-181, 193-194, 209-210, 224-225, 234-235; Vienna Nos. 95-96, 108-109, 123-124, 139-140, 150-151.

Intl. Trade Center — A251

**1990, Feb. 2**    **Litho.**    *Perf. 14½x15*
| 572 | A251 | 25c multicolored | 1.00 | 1.00 |

See Offices in Geneva No. 182; Vienna No. 97.

Fight AIDS Worldwide A252

40c, Shadow over crowd.

*Perf. 13½x12½*
**1990, Mar. 16**    **Litho.**
| 573 | A252 | 25c multicolored | .35 | .35 |
| 574 | A252 | 40c multicolored | 1.15 | 1.15 |

See Offices in Geneva Nos. 184-185, Vienna Nos. 99-100.

Medicinal Plants — A253

25c, Catharanthus roseus. 90c, Panax quinquefolium.

**1990, May 4**    **Photo.**    *Perf. 11½*
**Granite Paper**
| 575 | A253 | 25c multi | .45 | .45 |
| 576 | A253 | 90c multi | 1.40 | 1.40 |

See Offices in Geneva Nos. 186-187, Vienna Nos. 101-102.

United Nations, 45th Anniv. — A254

45c, "45," emblem.

**1990, June 26**    **Litho.**    *Perf. 14½x13*
| 577 | A254 | 25c multicolored | .50 | .50 |
| 578 | A254 | 45c multicolored | 1.90 | 1.90 |

**Souvenir Sheet**
| 579 | | Sheet of 2, #577-578 | 3.50 | 3.50 |

See Offices in Geneva Nos. 188-190; Vienna Nos. 103-105.

Crime Prevention — A255

**1990, Sept. 13**    **Photo.**    *Perf. 14*
| 580 | A255 | 25c Crimes of youth | .65 | .65 |
| 581 | A255 | 36c Organized crime | 1.25 | 1.25 |

See Offices in Geneva Nos. 191-192; Vienna Nos. 106-107.

### Human Rights Type of 1989

25c, Fragment from the sarcophagus of Plotinus, c. 270 A.D. 45c, Combined Chambers of the High Court of Appeal by Charles Paul Renouard.

**1990, Nov. 16**    **Litho.**    *Perf. 13½*
| 582 | A250 | 25c black, gray & tan | .35 | .35 |
| 583 | A250 | 45c black & brown | .65 | .65 |

See Offices in Geneva Nos. 193-194; Vienna Nos. 108-109.

Economic Commission for Europe — A256

**1991, Mar. 15**    **Litho.**    *Perf. 14*
| 584 | A256 | 30c Two storks | .85 | .85 |
| 585 | A256 | 30c Woodpecker, ibex | .85 | .85 |
| 586 | A256 | 30c Capercaille, plover | .85 | .85 |
| 587 | A256 | 30c Falcon, marmot | .85 | .85 |
| a. | | Block of 4, #584-587 | 3.75 | 3.75 |

See Offices in Geneva Nos. 195-198; Vienna Nos. 110-113.

Namibian Independence A257

**1991, May 10**    **Litho.**    *Perf. 14*
| 588 | A257 | 30c Dunes, Namib Desert | .50 | .50 |
| 589 | A257 | 50c Savanna | 1.10 | 1.00 |

See Offices in Geneva Nos. 199-200; Vienna Nos. 114-115.

A258

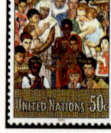

The Golden Rule by Norman Rockwell — A259

UN Headquarters, New York — A260

**1991**    **Litho.**    *Perf. 13½*
| 590 | A258 | 30c multi | .60 | .60 |

**Photo.**
*Perf. 12x11½*
| 591 | A259 | 50c multi | 1.00 | 1.00 |

**Engr.**
| 592 | A260 | $2 dark blue | 2.75 | 2.75 |

Rights of the Child — A261

**1991, June 14**    **Litho.**    *Perf. 14½*
| 593 | A261 | 30c Children, globe | 1.00 | 1.00 |
| 594 | A261 | 70c House, rainbow | 2.00 | 2.00 |

See Offices in Geneva Nos. 203-204; Vienna Nos. 117-118.

Banning of Chemical Weapons A262

90c, Hand holding back chemical drums.

**1991, Sept. 11**    **Litho.**    *Perf. 13½*
| 595 | A262 | 30c multicolored | .75 | .75 |
| 596 | A262 | 90c multicolored | 2.25 | 2.25 |

See Offices in Geneva Nos. 205-206; Vienna Nos. 119-120.

UN Postal Administration, 40th Anniv. — A263

**1991, Oct. 24**    **Litho.**    *Perf. 14x15*
| 597 | A263 | 30c No. 1 | .65 | .65 |
| 598 | A263 | 40c No. 3 | .85 | .85 |

See Offices in Geneva Nos. 207-208; Vienna Nos. 121-122.

### Human Rights Type of 1989

30c, The Last of England, by Ford Madox Brown. 40c, The Emigration to the East, by Tito Salas.

**1991, Nov. 20**    **Litho.**    *Perf. 13½*
| 599 | A250 | 30c multicolored | .35 | .35 |
| 600 | A250 | 50c multicolored | .80 | 1.00 |

See Offices in Geneva Nos. 209-210; Vienna Nos. 123-124.

### World Heritage Type of 1984

30c, Uluru Natl. Park, Australia. 50c, The Great Wall of China.

**1992, Jan. 24**    **Litho.**    *Perf. 13*
**Size: 35x28mm**
| 601 | A215 | 30c multicolored | .55 | .55 |
| 602 | A215 | 50c multicolored | .90 | .90 |

See Offices in Geneva Nos. 211-212; Vienna Nos. 125-126.

Clean Oceans — A264

**1992, Mar. 13**    **Litho.**    *Perf. 14*
| 603 | A264 | 29c Ocean surface | .45 | .50 |
| 604 | A264 | 29c Ocean bottom | .45 | .50 |
| a. | | Pair, #603-604 | .90 | 1.10 |

See Offices in Geneva Nos. 214-215; Vienna Nos. 127-128.

Earth Summit — A265

No. 605, Globe at LR. No. 606, Globe at LL. No. 607, Globe at UR. No. 608, Globe at UL.

**1992, May 22**    **Photo.**    *Perf. 11½*
| 605 | A265 | 29c multicolored | .65 | .65 |
| 606 | A265 | 29c multicolored | .65 | .65 |
| 607 | A265 | 29c multicolored | .65 | .65 |
| 608 | A265 | 29c multicolored | .65 | .65 |
| a. | | Block of 4, #605-608 | 4.00 | 3.50 |

See Offices in Geneva Nos. 216-219, Vienna Nos. 129-132.

Mission to Planet Earth A266

No. 609, Satellites over city, sailboats, fishing boat. No. 610, Satellite over coast, passenger liner, dolphins, whale, volcano.

**1992, Sept. 4**    **Photo.**    *Rouletted 8*
**Granite Paper**
| 609 | | 29c multicolored | 1.50 | 1.50 |
| 610 | | 29c multicolored | 1.50 | 1.50 |
| a. | A266 | Pair, #609-610 | 3.00 | 3.00 |

See Offices in Geneva Nos. 220-221; Vienna Nos. 133-134.

Science and Technology for Development A267

50c, Animal, man drinking.

**1992, Oct. 2**    **Litho.**    *Perf. 14*
| 611 | A267 | 29c multicolored | .40 | .40 |
| 612 | A267 | 50c multicolored | .70 | .70 |

UN University Building, Tokyo — A268

UN Headquarters A269

40c, UN University Building, Tokyo, diff.

*Perf. 14, 13½x13 (29c)*
**1992, Oct. 2**    **Litho.**
| 613 | A268 | 4c multicolored | .25 | .25 |
| 614 | A269 | 29c multicolored | .50 | .50 |
| 615 | A268 | 40c multicolored | .65 | .65 |
| | | Nos. 613-615 (3) | 1.40 | 1.40 |

### Human Rights Type of 1989

29c, Lady Writing a Letter with her Maid, by Vermeer. 50c, The Meeting, by Ester Almqvist.

**1992, Nov. 20**    **Litho.**    *Perf. 13½*
| 616 | A250 | 29c multicolored | .40 | .40 |
| 617 | A250 | 50c multicolored | .60 | .60 |

See Offices in Geneva Nos. 224-225; Vienna Nos. 139-140.

Aging With Dignity — A270

29c, Elderly couple, family. 52c, Old man, physician, woman holding fruit basket.

# UNITED NATIONS, OFFICES IN NEW YORK

**1993, Feb. 5**    Litho.    *Perf. 13*
618 A270 29c multicolored    .45 .45
619 A270 52c multicolored    1.00 1.00
See Offices in Geneva Nos. 226-227; Vienna Nos. 141-142.

**Endangered Species — A271**

No. 620, Hairy-nosed wombat. No. 621, Whooping crane. No. 622, Giant clam. No. 623, Giant sable antelope.

**1993, Mar. 2**    Litho.    *Perf. 13x12½*
620 A271 29c multicolored    .45 .45
621 A271 29c multicolored    .45 .45
622 A271 29c multicolored    .45 .45
623 A271 29c multicolored    .45 .45
  a. Block of 4, #620-623    2.00 2.00

See Nos. 639-642, 657-660, 674-677, 700-703, 730-733, 757-760, 773-776; Offices in Geneva Nos. 228-231, 246-249, 264-267, 280-283, 298-301, 318-321, 336-339, 352-355; Vienna Nos. 143-146, 162-165, 180-183, 196-199, 214-217, 235-238, 253-256, 269-272.

**Healthy Environment A272**

29c, Personal. 50c, Family.

**1993, May 7**    Litho.    *Perf. 15x14½*
624 A272 29c Man    .50 .50
625 A272 50c Family    .90 .90
See Offices in Geneva Nos. 232-233; Vienna Nos. 147-148.

**A273**

**1993, May 7**    Litho.    *Perf. 15x14*
626 A273 5c multicolored    .25 .25

**Human Rights Type of 1989**

29c, Shucking Corn, by Thomas Hart Benton. 35c, The Library, by Jacob Lawrence.

**1993, June 11**    Litho.    *Perf. 13½*
627 A250 29c multicolored    .40 .40
628 A250 35c multicolored    .45 .45
See Offices in Geneva Nos. 234-235; Vienna Nos. 150-151.

**Intl. Peace Day — A274**

Denomination at: #629, UL #630, UR. #631, LL. #632, LR.

**Rouletted 12½**
**1993, Sept. 21**    Litho. & Engr.
629 A274 29c blue & multi    .75 .75
630 A274 29c blue & multi    .75 .75
631 A274 29c blue & multi    .75 .75
632 A274 29c blue & multi    .75 .75
  a. Block of 4, #629-632    4.00 4.00
See Offices in Geneva Nos. 236-239; Vienna Nos. 152-155.

**Environment-Climate A275**

No. 633, Chameleon. No. 634, Palm trees, top of funnel cloud. No. 635, Bottom of funnel cloud, deer, antelope. No. 636, Bird of paradise.

**1993, Oct. 29**    Litho.    *Perf. 14½*
633 A275 29c multicolored    .75 .75
634 A275 29c multicolored    .75 .75
635 A275 29c multicolored    .75 .75
636 A275 29c multicolored    .75 .75
  a. Strip of 4, #633-636    4.00 4.00
See Offices in Geneva Nos. 240-243; Vienna Nos. 156-159.

**Intl. Year of the Family — A276**

29c, Mother holding child, two children, woman. 45c, People tending crops.

**1994, Feb. 4**    Litho.    *Perf. 13.1*
637 A276 29c green & multi    .70 .70
638 A276 45c blue & multi    .90 .90
See Offices in Geneva Nos. 244-245; Vienna Nos. 160-161.

**Endangered Species Type of 1993**

No. 639, Chimpanzee. No. 640, St. Lucia Amazon. No. 641, American crocodile. No. 642, Dama gazelle.

**1994, Mar. 18**    Litho.    *Perf. 12.7*
639 A271 29c multicolored    .45 .45
640 A271 29c multicolored    .45 .45
641 A271 29c multicolored    .45 .45
642 A271 29c multicolored    .45 .45
  a. Block of 4, #639-642    2.00 2.00
See Offices in Geneva Nos. 246-249; Vienna Nos. 162-165.

**Protection for Refugees — A277**

**1994, Apr. 29**    Litho.    *Perf. 14.3x14.8*
643 A277 50c multicolored    .90 .90
See Offices in Geneva No. 250; Vienna No. 166.

**Dove of Peace — A278**

**Sleeping Child, by Stanislaw Wyspianski A279**

**Mourning Owl, by Vanessa Isitt A280**

**1994, Apr. 29**    Litho.    *Perf. 12.9*
644 A278 10c multicolored    .25 .25
645 A279 19c multicolored    .50 .50

**Engr.**
**Perf. 13.1**
646 A280 $1 red brown    1.50 1.50
  Nos. 644-646 (3)    2.05 2.05

**Intl. Decade for Natural Disaster Reduction — A281**

Earth seen from space, outline map of: #647, North America. #648, Eurasia. #649, South America, #650, Australia and South Asia.

**1994, May 27**    Litho.    *Perf. 13.9x14.2*
647 A281 29c multicolored    1.75 1.75
648 A281 29c multicolored    1.75 1.75
649 A281 29c multicolored    1.75 1.75
650 A281 29c multicolored    1.75 1.75
  a. Block of 4, #647-650    7.50 7.50
See Offices in Geneva Nos. 251-254; Vienna Nos. 170-173.

**Population and Development A282**

29c, Children playing. 52c, Family with house, car, other possessions.

**1994, Sept. 1**    Litho.    *Perf. 13.2x13.6*
651 A282 29c multicolored    .40 .40
652 A282 52c multicolored    .80 .80
See Offices in Geneva Nos. 258-259; Vienna Nos. 174-175.

**UNCTAD, 30th Anniv. — A283**

**1994, Oct. 28**
653 A283 29c multicolored    .40 .40
654 A283 50c multi, diff.    .80 .80
See Offices in Geneva Nos. 260-261; Vienna Nos. 176-177.

**UN, 50th Anniv. — A284**

**Litho. & Engr.**
**1995, Jan. 1**    *Perf. 13.4*
655 A284 32c multicolored    .90 .90
See Offices in Geneva No. 262; Vienna No. 178.

**Social Summit, Copenhagen — A285**

656 A285 50c multicolored    1.00 1.00
See Offices in Geneva No. 263; Vienna No. 179.

**Endangered Species Type of 1993**

No. 657, Giant armadillo. No. 658, American bald eagle. No. 659, Fijian/Tongan banded iguana. No. 660, Giant panda.

**1995, Mar. 24**    Litho.    *Perf. 13x12½*
657 A271 32c multicolored    .40 .40
658 A271 32c multicolored    .40 .40
659 A271 32c multicolored    .40 .40
660 A271 32c multicolored    .40 .40
  a. Block of 4, 657-660    2.25 2.25
See Offices in Geneva Nos. 264-267; Vienna Nos. 180-183.

**Intl. Youth Year, 10th Anniv. — A286**

32c, Seated child. 55c, Children cycling.

**1995, May 26**    Litho.    *Perf. 14.4x14.7*
661 A286 32c multicolored    .55 .55
662 A286 55c multicolored    .95 .95
See Offices in Geneva Nos. 268-269; Vienna Nos. 184-185.

**UN, 50th Anniv. — A287**

32c, Hand with pen signing UN Charter, flags. 50c, Veterans' War Memorial, Opera House, San Francisco.

**Perf. 13.3x13.6**
**1995, June 26**    Engr.
663 A287 32c black    .55 .55
664 A287 50c maroon    1.00 1.00

**Souvenir Sheet**
**Litho. & Engr.**
**Imperf**
665    Sheet of 2, #663-664    3.00 3.00
  a. A287 32c black    1.25 1.25
  b. A287 50c maroon    1.50 1.50
No. 665 exists with gold China 1996 overprint. Value $20.
See Offices in Geneva Nos. 270-272; Vienna Nos. 186-188.

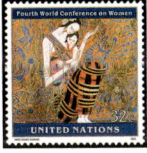

**4th World Conference on Women, Beijing — A288**

32c, Mother and child. 40c, Seated woman, cranes flying above.

**1995, Sept. 5**    Photo.    *Perf. 12*
666 A288 32c multicolored    .50 .50
**Size: 28x50mm**
667 A288 40c multicolored    .85 .85
See Offices in Geneva Nos. 273-274; Vienna Nos. 189-190.

**UN Headquarters A289**

**1995, Sept. 5**    Litho.    *Perf. 15*
668 A289 20c multicolored    .35 .35

**Miniature Sheet**

**United Nations, 50th Anniv. — A290**

**1995, Oct. 24**    Litho.    *Perf. 14*
669 A290 Sheet of 12    4.75 4.75
  a.-l. 32c any single    .40 .40
670    Souvenir booklet    5.50
  a. A290 32c Booklet pane of 3, vert. strip of 3 from UL of sheet    1.35 1.35
  b. A290 32c Booklet pane of 3, vert. strip of 3 from UR of sheet    1.35 1.35
  c. A290 32c Booklet pane of 3, vert. strip of 3 from LL of sheet    1.35 1.35
  d. A290 32c Booklet pane of 3, vert. strip of 3 from LR of sheet    1.35 1.35
See Offices in Geneva Nos. 275-276; Vienna Nos. 191-192.

# UNITED NATIONS, OFFICES IN NEW YORK

WFUNA, 50th Anniv. — A291

**1996, Feb. 2 Litho. Perf. 13x13½**
671 A291 32c multicolored .50 .50
See Offices in Geneva No. 277; Vienna No. 193.

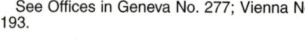

Mural, by Fernand Leger — A292

**1996, Feb. 2 Litho. Perf. 14½x15**
672 A292 32c multicolored .45 .45
673 A292 60c multi, diff. .95 .95

**Endangered Species Type of 1993**
No. 674, Masdevallia veitchiana. No. 675, Saguaro cactus. No. 676, West Australian pitcher plant. No. 677, Encephalartos horridus.

**1996, Mar. 14 Litho. Perf. 12½**
674 A271 32c multicolored .45 .45
675 A271 32c multicolored .45 .45
676 A271 32c multicolored .45 .45
677 A271 32c multicolored .45 .45
 a. Block of 4, #674-677 2.25 2.25
See Offices in Geneva Nos. 280-283; Vienna Nos. 196-199.

City Summit (Habitat II) — A293

No. 678, Deer. No. 679, Man, child, dog sitting on hill, overlooking town. No. 680, People walking in park, city skyline. No. 681, Tropical park, Polynesian woman, boy. No. 682, Polynesian village, orchids, bird.

**1996, June 3 Litho. Perf. 14x13½**
678 A293 32c multicolored .80 .80
679 A293 32c multicolored .80 .80
680 A293 32c multicolored .80 .80
681 A293 32c multicolored .80 .80
682 A293 32c multicolored .80 .80
 a. Strip of 5, #678-682 7.00 7.00
See Offices in Geneva Nos. 284-288; Vienna Nos. 200-204.

Sport and the Environment — A294

32c, Men's basketball. 50c, Women's volleyball, horiz.

**Perf. 14x14½, 14½x14**
**1996, July 19 Litho.**
683 A294 32c multicolored .65 .65
684 A294 50c multicolored 1.40 1.40

**Souvenir Sheet**
685 A294 Sheet of 2, #683-684 2.50 2.50
See Offices in Geneva Nos. 289-291; Vienna Nos. 205-207.
1996 Summer Olympic Games, Atlanta, GA.

Plea for Peace — A295

32c, Doves. 60c, Stylized dove.

**1996, Sept. 17 Litho. Perf. 14½x15**
686 A295 32c multicolored .50 .50
687 A295 60c multicolored .90 .90
See Offices in Geneva Nos. 292-293; Vienna Nos. 208-209.

UNICEF, 50th Anniv. — A296

Fairy Tales: 32c, Yeh-Shen, China. 60c, The Ugly Duckling, by Hans Christian Andersen.

**1996, Nov. 20 Litho. Perf. 14½x15**
688 A296 32c multicolored .45 .45
689 A296 60c multicolored 1.00 1.00
See Offices in Geneva Nos. 294-295; Vienna Nos. 210-211.

**Flag Type of 1980**
**1997, Feb. 12 Photo. Perf. 12**
**Granite Paper**
690 A185 32c Tadjikistan .75 1.00
691 A185 32c Georgia .75 1.00
692 A185 32c Armenia .75 1.00
693 A185 32c Namibia .75 1.00
 a. Block of 4, #690-693 10.00 13.00
694 A185 32c Liechtenstein .75 1.00
695 A185 32c Republic of Korea .75 1.00
696 A185 32c Kazakhstan .75 1.00
697 A185 32c Latvia .75 1.00
 a. Block of 4, #694-697 10.00 13.00
See note after No. 340.

Cherry Blossoms, UN Headquarters A297

Peace Rose A298

**1997, Feb. 12 Litho. Perf. 14½**
698 A297 8c multicolored .25 .25
699 A298 55c multicolored .90 .90

**Endangered Species Type of 1993**
No. 700, African elephant. No. 701, Major Mitchell's cockatoo. No. 702, Black-footed ferret. No. 703, Cougar.

**1997, Mar. 13 Litho. Perf. 12½**
700 A271 32c multicolored .40 .40
701 A271 32c multicolored .40 .40
702 A271 32c multicolored .40 .40
703 A271 32c multicolored .40 .40
 a. Block of 4, #700-703 2.25 2.25
See Offices in Geneva Nos. 298-301; Vienna Nos. 214-217.

Earth Summit, 5th Anniv. — A299

No. 704, Sailboat. No. 705, Three sailboats. No. 706, Two people watching sailboat, sun. No. 707, Person, sailboat.
$1, Combined design similar to Nos. 704-707.

**1997, May 30 Photo. Perf. 11.5**
**Granite Paper**
704 A299 32c multicolored .90 .90
705 A299 32c multicolored .90 .90
706 A299 32c multicolored .90 .90
707 A299 32c multicolored .90 .90
 a. Block of 4, #704-707 5.00 5.00

**Souvenir Sheet**
708 A299 $1 multicolored 3.25 3.25
 a. Ovptd. in sheet margin 17.50 17.50
See Offices in Geneva Nos. 302-306; Vienna Nos. 218-222.
No. 708 contains one 60x43mm stamp. Overprint in sheet margin of No. 708a reads "PACIFIC 97 / World Philatelic Exhibition / San Francisco, California / 29 May - 8 June 1997".

Transportation — A300

Ships: No. 709, Clipper ship. No. 710, Paddle steamer. No. 711, Ocean liner. No. 712, Hovercraft. No. 713, Hydrofoil.

**1997, Aug. 29 Litho. Perf. 14x14½**
709 A300 32c multicolored .65 .65
710 A300 32c multicolored .65 .65
711 A300 32c multicolored .65 .65
712 A300 32c multicolored .65 .65
713 A300 32c multicolored .65 .65
 a. Strip of 5, #709-713 4.25 4.25
See Offices in Geneva Nos. 307-311; Vienna Nos. 223-227.
No. 713a has continuous design.

Philately — A301

32c, No. 473. 50c, No. 474.

**1997, Oct. 14 Litho. Perf. 13½x14**
714 A301 32c multicolored .60 .60
715 A301 50c multicolored 1.50 1.50
See Offices in Geneva Nos. 312-313; Vienna Nos. 228-229.

World Heritage Convention, 25th Anniv. — A302

Terracotta warriors of Xian: 32c, Single warrior. 60c, Massed warriors. No. 718a, like No. 716. No. 718b, like #717. No. 718c, like Geneva #314. No. 718d, like Geneva #315. No. 718e, like Vienna #230. No. 718f, like Vienna #231.

**1997, Nov. 19 Litho. Perf. 13½**
716 A302 32c multicolored .75 .75
717 A302 60c multicolored 1.25 1.25
718 Souvenir booklet 8.50
 a.-f. A302 8c any single .35 .35
 g. Booklet pane of 4 #718a 1.40 1.40
 h. Booklet pane of 4 #718b 1.40 1.40
 i. Booklet pane of 4 #718c 1.40 1.40
 j. Booklet pane of 4 #718d 1.40 1.40
 k. Booklet pane of 4 #718e 1.40 1.40
 l. Booklet pane of 4 #718f 1.40 1.40
See Offices in Geneva Nos. 314-316; Vienna Nos. 230-232.

**Flag Type of 1980**
Printed by Helio Courvoisier, S.A., Switzerland. Designed by Oliver Corwin, and Robert Stein, US. Each pane contains 4 blocks of 4 (Nos. 719-722, 723-726). A se-tenant block of 4 designs centers each pane.

**1998, Feb. 13 Photo. Perf. 12**
**Granite Paper**
719 A185 32c Micronesia .80 .80
720 A185 32c Slovakia .80 .80
721 A185 32c Deocratic People's Republic of Korea .80 .80
722 A185 32c Azerbaijan .80 .80
 a. Block of 4, #719-722 12.50 12.50
723 A185 32c Uzbekistan .80 .80
724 A185 32c Monaco .80 .80
725 A185 32c Czech Republic .80 .80
726 A185 32c Estonia .80 .80
 a. Block of 4, #723-726 12.50 12.50
 Nos. 719-726 (8) 6.40 6.40

A303   A304

A305

**Perf. 14½x15, 15x14½**
**1998, Feb. 13 Litho.**
727 A303 1c multicolored .25 .25
728 A304 2c multicolored .25 .25
729 A305 21c multicolored .40 .40
 Nos. 727-729 (3) .90 .90

**Endangered Species Type of 1993**
No. 730, Lesser galago. No. 731, Hawaiian goose. No. 732, Golden birdwing. No. 733, Sun bear.

**1998, Mar. 13 Litho. Perf. 12½**
730 A271 32c multicolored .45 .45
731 A271 32c multicolored .45 .45
732 A271 32c multicolored .45 .45
733 A271 32c multicolored .45 .45
 a. Block of 4, #730-733 2.25 2.25
See Offices in Geneva Nos. 318-321; Vienna Nos. 235-238.

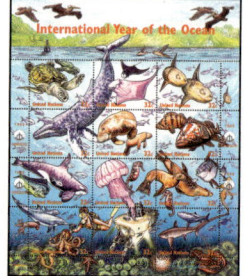

Intl. Year of the Ocean A306

**1998, May 20 Litho. Perf. 13x13½**
734 A306 Sheet of 12 9.00 9.00
 a.-l. 32c any single .75 .75
See Offices in Geneva No. 322; Vienna No. 239.

Rain Forests — A307

**1998, June 19 Litho. Perf. 13x13½**
735 A307 32c Jaguar .50 .50

**Souvenir Sheet**
736 A307 $2 like #735 3.00 3.00
See Offices in Geneva Nos. 323-324; Vienna Nos. 240-241.

U.N. Peacekeeping Forces, 50th Anniv. — A308

33c, Commander with binoculars. 40c, Two soldiers on vehicle.

**1998, Sept. 15 Photo. Perf. 12**
737 A308 33c multicolored .50 .50
738 A308 40c multicolored .75 .75
See Offices in Geneva Nos. 325-326; Vienna Nos. 242-243.

Universal Declaration of Human Rights, 50th Anniv. — A309

Stylized people: 32c, Carrying flag. 55c, Carrying pens.

UNITED NATIONS, OFFICES IN NEW YORK 267

**Litho. & Photo.**

**1998, Oct. 27** *Perf. 13*

| | | | | |
|---|---|---|---|---|
| **739** | A309 | 32c multicolored | .45 | .45 |
| **740** | A309 | 55c multicolored | .90 | .90 |

See Offices in Geneva Nos. 327-328; Vienna Nos. 244-245.

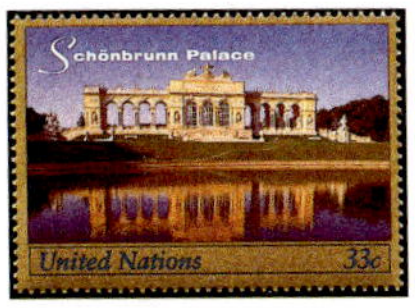

Schönnbrun Palace, Vienna — A310

33c, #743f, The Gloriette. 60c, #743b, Wall painting on fabric (detail), by Johann Wenzl Bergl, vert. No. 743a, Blue porcelain vase, vert. No. 743c, Porcelain stove, vert. No. 743d, Palace. No. 743e, Great Palm House (conservatory).

**1998, Dec. 4** **Litho.** *Perf. 14*

| | | | | |
|---|---|---|---|---|
| **741** | A310 | 33c multicolored | .55 | .55 |
| **742** | A310 | 60c multicolored | 1.25 | 1.00 |

**Souvenir Booklet**

| | | | | |
|---|---|---|---|---|
| **743** | | Booklet | 19.50 | |
| *a.-c.* | A310 | 11c any single | .35 | .35 |
| *d.-f.* | A310 | 15c any single | 1.40 | 1.40 |
| *g.* | | Booklet pane of 4 #743d | 5.50 | 5.50 |
| *h.* | | Booklet pane of 3 #743a | 1.00 | 1.00 |
| *i.* | | Booklet pane of 3 #743b | 1.00 | 1.00 |
| *j.* | | Booklet pane of 3 #743c | 1.00 | 1.00 |
| *k.* | | Booklet pane of 4 #743e | 5.50 | 5.50 |
| *l.* | | Booklet pane of 4 #743f | 5.50 | 5.50 |

See Offices in Geneva Nos. 329-331; Vienna Nos. 246-248.

**Flag Type of 1980**

**1999, Feb. 5** **Photo.** *Perf. 12*

| | | | | |
|---|---|---|---|---|
| **744** | A185 | 33c Lithuania | .75 | .75 |
| **745** | A185 | 33c San Marino | .75 | .75 |
| **746** | A185 | 33c Turkmenistan | .75 | .75 |
| **747** | A185 | 33c Marshall Islands | .75 | .75 |
| *a.* | | Block of 4, #744-747 | 8.00 | 8.00 |
| **748** | A185 | 33c Moldova | .75 | .75 |
| **749** | A185 | 33c Kyrgyzstan | .75 | .75 |
| **750** | A185 | 33c Bosnia & Herzegovina | .75 | .75 |
| **751** | A185 | 33c Eritrea | .75 | .75 |
| *a.* | | Block of 4, #748-751 | 8.00 | 8.00 |
| | | *Nos. 744-751 (8)* | 6.00 | 6.00 |

See note after No. 340.

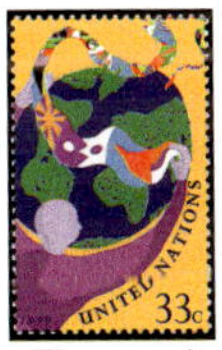

Flags and Globe A311

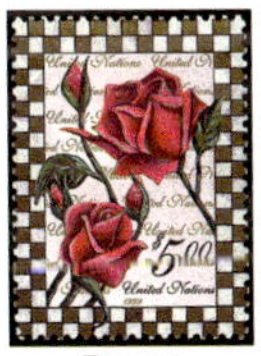

Roses A312

**1999, Feb. 5** **Litho.** *Perf. 14x13½*

| | | | | |
|---|---|---|---|---|
| **752** | A311 | 33c multicolored | .50 | .50 |

**Photo.**

**Granite Paper**

*Perf. 11½x12*

| | | | | |
|---|---|---|---|---|
| **753** | A312 | $5 multicolored | 6.00 | 6.00 |

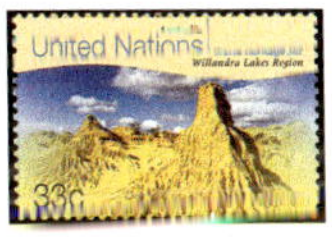

World Heritage Sites, Australia — A313

33c, #756f, Willandra Lakes region. 60c, #756b, Wet tropics of Queensland. No. 756a, Tasmanian wilderness. No. 756c, Great Barrier Reef. No. 756d, Uluru-Kata Tjuta Natl. Park. No. 756e, Kakadu Natl. Park.

**1999, Mar. 19** **Litho.** *Perf. 13*

| | | | | |
|---|---|---|---|---|
| **754** | A313 | 33c multicolored | .60 | .60 |
| **755** | A313 | 60c multicolored | 1.25 | 1.25 |

**Souvenir Booklet**

| | | | | |
|---|---|---|---|---|
| **756** | | Booklet | 35.00 | |
| *a.-c.* | A313 | 5c any single | .70 | .70 |
| *d.-f.* | A313 | 15c any single | 1.50 | 1.50 |
| *g.* | | Booklet pane of 4, #756a | 2.80 | 2.80 |
| *h.* | | Booklet pane of 4, #756d | 6.00 | 6.00 |
| *i.* | | Booklet pane of 4, #756b | 2.80 | 2.80 |
| *j.* | | Booklet pane of 4, #756e | 6.00 | 6.00 |
| *k.* | | Booklet pane of 4, #756c | 2.80 | 2.80 |
| *l.* | | Booklet pane of 4, #756f | 6.00 | 6.00 |

See Offices in Geneva Nos. 333-335; Vienna Nos. 250-252.

**Endangered Species Type of 1993**

No. 757, Tiger. No. 758, Secretary bird. No. 759, Green tree python. No. 760, Long-tailed chinchilla.

**1999, Apr. 22** **Litho.** *Perf. 12½*

| | | | | |
|---|---|---|---|---|
| **757** | A271 | 33c multicolored | .60 | .60 |
| **758** | A271 | 33c multicolored | .60 | .60 |
| **759** | A271 | 33c multicolored | .60 | .60 |
| **760** | A271 | 33c multicolored | .60 | .60 |
| *a.* | | Block of 4, #757-760 | 3.00 | 3.00 |

See Offices in Geneva Nos. 336-339; Vienna Nos. 253-256.

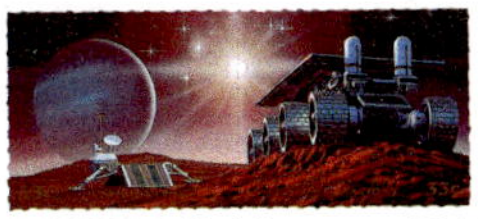

UNISPACE III, Vienna — A314

No. 761, Probe on planet's surface. No. 762, Planetary rover. No. 763, Composite of #761-762.

**1999, July 7** **Photo.** *Rouletted 8*

| | | | | |
|---|---|---|---|---|
| **761** | A314 | 33c multicolored | .50 | .50 |
| **762** | A314 | 33c multicolored | .50 | .50 |
| *a.* | | Pair, #761-762 | 1.75 | 1.75 |

**Souvenir Sheet**

*Perf. 14½*

| | | | | |
|---|---|---|---|---|
| **763** | A314 | $2 multicolored | 4.00 | 4.00 |
| *a.* | | Ovptd. in sheet margin | 15.00 | 15.00 |

No. 763a was issued 7/7/00 and is overprinted in violet blue "WORLD STAMP EXPO 2000 / ANAHEIM, CALIFORNIA / U.S.A./ 7-16 JULY 2000."

See Offices in Geneva Nos. 340-342; Vienna Nos. 257-259.

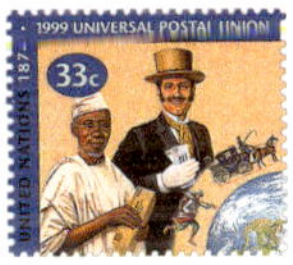

UPU, 125th Anniv. — A315

Various people, 19th century methods of mail transportation, denomination at: No. 764, UL. No. 765, UR. No. 766, LL. No. 767, LR.

**1999, Aug. 23** **Photo.** *Perf. 11¾*

| | | | | |
|---|---|---|---|---|
| **764** | A315 | 33c multicolored | .45 | .45 |
| **765** | A315 | 33c multicolored | .45 | .45 |
| **766** | A315 | 33c multicolored | .45 | .45 |
| **767** | A315 | 33c multicolored | .45 | .45 |
| *a.* | | Block of 4, #764-767 | 2.50 | 2.50 |

See Offices in Geneva Nos. 343-346; Vienna Nos. 260-263.

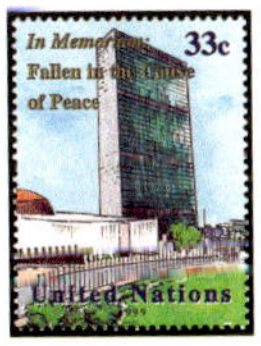

In Memoriam — A316

Designs: 33c, $1, UN Headquarters. Size of $1 stamp: 34x63mm.

**1999, Sept. 21** **Litho.** *Perf. 14½x14*

| | | | | |
|---|---|---|---|---|
| **768** | A316 | 33c multicolored | .80 | .80 |

**Souvenir Sheet**

*Perf. 14*

| | | | | |
|---|---|---|---|---|
| **769** | A316 | $1 multicolored | 2.00 | 2.00 |

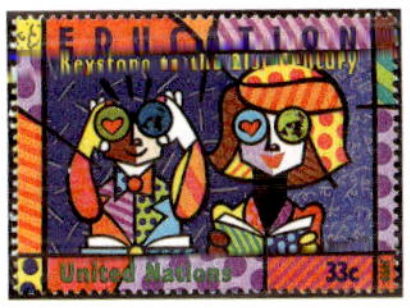

Education, Keystone to the 21st Century A317

*Perf. 13½x13¾*

**1999, Nov. 18** **Litho.**

| | | | | |
|---|---|---|---|---|
| **770** | A317 | 33c Two readers | .50 | .50 |
| **771** | A317 | 60c Heart | 1.00 | 1.00 |

See Offices in Geneva Nos. 349-350, Vienna Nos. 266-267.

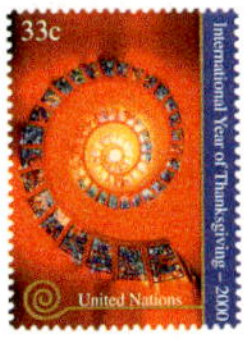

International Year of Thanksgiving — A318

**2000, Jan. 1** **Litho.** *Perf. 13¼x13½*

| | | | | |
|---|---|---|---|---|
| **772** | A318 | 33c multicolored | .50 | .50 |

On No. 772 parts of the design were applied by a thermographic process producing a shiny, raised effect. See Offices in Geneva No. 351, Vienna No. 268.

**Endangered Species Type of 1993**

No. 773, Brown bear. No. 774, Black-bellied bustard. No. 775, Chinese crocodile lizard. No. 776, Pygmy chimpanzee.

**2000, Apr. 6** **Litho.** *Perf. 12¾x12½*

| | | | | |
|---|---|---|---|---|
| **773** | A271 | 33c multicolored | .50 | .50 |
| **774** | A271 | 33c multicolored | .50 | .50 |
| **775** | A271 | 33c multicolored | .50 | .50 |
| **776** | A271 | 33c multicolored | .50 | .50 |
| *a.* | | Block of 4, #773-776 | 2.50 | 2.50 |

See Offices in Geneva Nos. 352-355; Vienna Nos. 269-272.

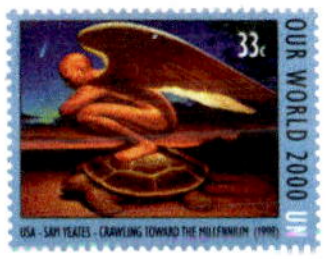

Our World 2000 — A319

Winning artwork in Millennium painting competition: 33c, Crawling Toward the Millennium, by Sam Yeates, US. 60c, Crossing, by Masakazu Takahata, Japan, vert.

*Perf. 13x13½, 13½x13*

**2000, May 30** **Litho.**

| | | | | |
|---|---|---|---|---|
| **777** | A319 | 33c multicolored | .60 | .60 |
| **778** | A319 | 60c multicolored | 1.00 | 1.00 |

See Offices in Geneva No. 356-357, Vienna No. 273-274.

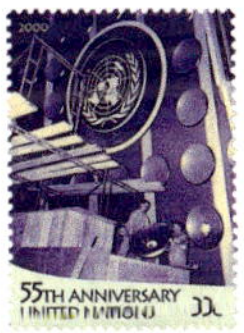

UN, 55th Anniv. — A320

33c, Workmen removing decorative discs in General Assembly Hall, 1956. 55c, UN Building in 1951.

**2000, July 7** **Litho.** *Perf. 13¼x13*

| | | | | |
|---|---|---|---|---|
| **779** | A320 | 33c multicolored | .55 | .55 |
| **780** | A320 | 55c multicolored | .95 | .95 |

**Souvenir Sheet**

| | | | | |
|---|---|---|---|---|
| **781** | A320 | Sheet of 2, #779-780 | 3.00 | 3.00 |

See Offices in Geneva No. 358-360, Vienna No. 275-277.

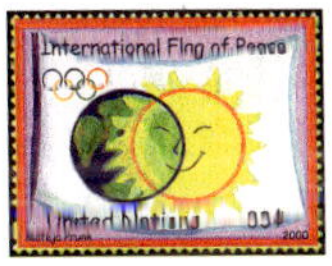

International Flag of Peace — A321

**2000, Sept. 15** **Litho.** *Perf. 14½x14*

| | | | | |
|---|---|---|---|---|
| **782** | A321 | 33c multicolored | .65 | .65 |

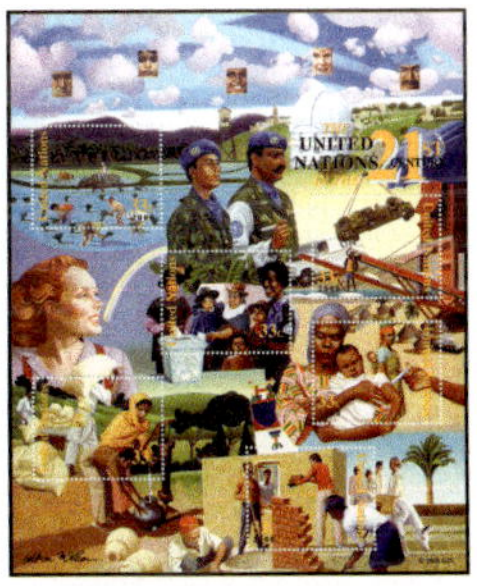

The UN in the 21st Century A322

No. 783: a, Farmers, animals in rice paddy. b, Vehicle chassis being lifted. c, People voting. d, Baby receiving inoculation. e, Woman, man at pump. f, Mason, construction workers.

**2000, Sept. 15** **Litho.** *Perf. 14*

| | | | | |
|---|---|---|---|---|
| **783** | A322 | Sheet of 6 | 7.50 | 7.50 |
| *a.-f.* | | 33c any single | 1.25 | 1.25 |

See Offices in Geneva No. 361; Vienna No. 278.

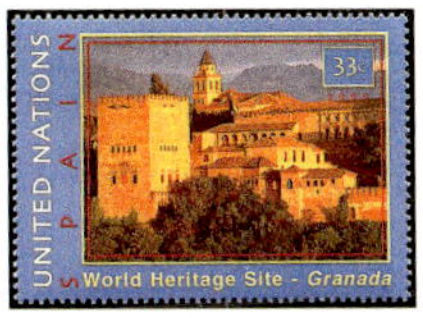

World Heritage Sites, Spain A323

Nos. 784, 786a, Alhambra, Generalife and Albayzin, Granada. Nos. 785, 786d, Amphitheater of Mérida. #786b, Walled Town of Cuenca. #786c, Aqueduct of Segovia. #786e, Toledo. #786f, Güell Park, Barcelona.

**2000, Oct. 6** **Litho.** *Perf. 14¾x14½*

| | | | | |
|---|---|---|---|---|
| **784** | A323 | 33c multicolored | .55 | .55 |
| **785** | A323 | 60c multicolored | 1.10 | 1.10 |

**Souvenir Booklet**

| | | | | |
|---|---|---|---|---|
| **786** | | Booklet | 15.00 | |
| *a.-c.* | A323 | 5c any single | .45 | .45 |
| *d.-f.* | A323 | 15c any single | .80 | .80 |
| *g.* | | Booklet pane of 4, #786a | 1.80 | 1.80 |
| *h.* | | Booklet pane of 4, #786d | 3.20 | 3.20 |
| *i.* | | Booklet pane of 4, #786b | 1.80 | 1.80 |
| *j.* | | Booklet pane of 4, #786e | 3.20 | 3.20 |
| *k.* | | Booklet pane of 4, #786c | 1.80 | 1.80 |
| *l.* | | Booklet pane of 4, #786f | 3.20 | 3.20 |

See Offices in Geneva Nos. 362-364, Vienna Nos. 279-281.

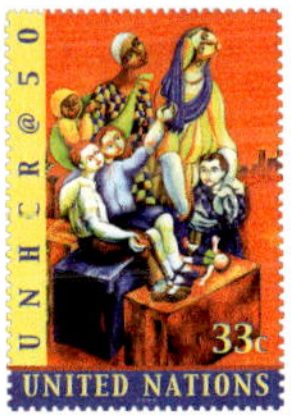

Respect for Refugees — A324

**2000, Nov. 9** **Litho.** *Perf. 13¼x12¾*

| | | | | |
|---|---|---|---|---|
| **787** | A324 | 33c multicolored | .75 | .75 |

**Souvenir Sheet**

| | | | | |
|---|---|---|---|---|
| **788** | A324 | $1 multicolored | 2.00 | 2.00 |

See Offices in Geneva Nos. 365-366, Vienna Nos. 282-283.

**Endangered Species Type of 1993**

No. 789, Common spotted cuscus. No. 790, Resplendent quetzal. No. 791, Gila monster. No. 792, Guereza.

**2001, Feb. 1** **Litho.** *Perf. 12¾x12½*

| | | | | |
|---|---|---|---|---|
| **789** | A271 | 34c multicolored | .60 | .60 |
| **790** | A271 | 34c multicolored | .60 | .60 |
| **791** | A271 | 34c multicolored | .60 | .60 |
| **792** | A271 | 34c multicolored | .60 | .60 |
| *a.* | | Block of 4, #789-792 | 3.00 | 3.00 |

See Offices in Geneva Nos. 367-370; Vienna Nos. 284-287.

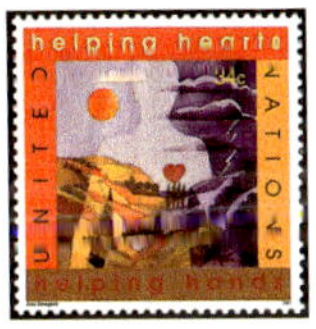

Intl. Volunteers Year — A325

Paintings by: 34c, Jose Zaragoza, Brazil. 80c, John Terry, Australia.

**2001, Mar. 29** **Litho.** *Perf. 13¼*

| | | | | |
|---|---|---|---|---|
| **793** | A325 | 34c multicolored | .65 | .65 |
| **794** | A325 | 80c multicolored | 1.60 | 1.60 |

See Offices in Geneva Nos. 371-372; Vienna Nos. 288-289.

**Flag Type of 1980**

Printed by Helio Courvoisier, Switzerland. Designed by Ole Hamann. Issued in panes of 16; each contains 4 blocks of 4 (Nos. 795-798, 799-802). A se-tenant block of 4 designs centers each pane.

268 UNITED NATIONS, OFFICES IN NEW YORK

**2001, May 25 Photo. *Perf. 12***

**Granite Paper**

**795** A185 34c Slovenia 1.25 1.25
**796** A185 34c Palau 1.25 1.25
**797** A185 34c Tonga 1.25 1.25
**798** A185 34c Croatia 1.25 1.25
*a.* Block of 4, #795-798 15.00 15.00
**799** A185 34c Former Yugoslav Republic of Macedonia 1.25 1.25
**800** A185 34c Kiribati 1.25 1.25
**801** A185 34c Andorra 1.25 1.25
**802** A185 34c Nauru 1.25 1.25
*a.* Block of 4, #799-802 15.00 15.00
*Nos. 795-802 (8)* 10.00 10.00

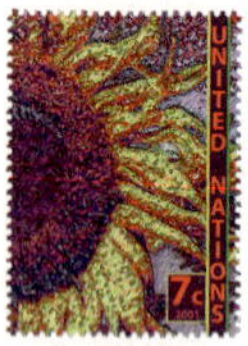

Sunflower
A326

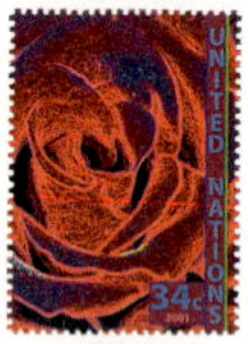

Rose
A327

**2001, May 25 Litho. *Perf. 13¼x13¾***

**803** A326 7c multicolored .25 .25
**804** A327 34c multicolored .60 .60

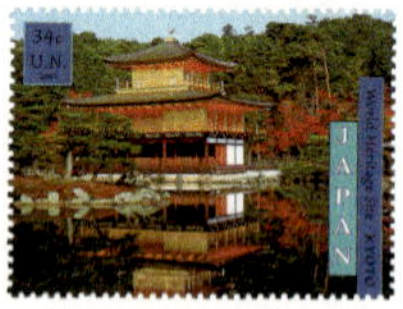

World Heritage Sites, Japan
A328

34c, #807a, Kyoto. 70c, #807d, Shirakawa-Go and Gokayama. #807b, Nara. #807c, Himeji-Jo. #807e, Itsukushima Shinto Shrine. #807f, Nikko.

**2001, Aug. 1 Litho. *Perf. 12¾x13¼***

**805** A328 34c multicolored .60 .60
**806** A328 70c multicolored 1.25 1.25

**Souvenir Booklet**

**807** Booklet 14.00
*a.-c.* A328 5c any single .40 .40
*d.-f.* A328 20c any single .75 .75
*g.* Booklet pane of 4, #807a 1.60 1.60
*h.* Booklet pane of 4, #807d 3.00 3.00
*i.* Booklet pane of 4, #807b 1.60 1.60
*j.* Booklet pane of 4, #807e 3.00 3.00
*k.* Booklet pane of 4, #807c 1.60 1.60
*l.* Booklet pane of 4, #807f 3.00 3.00

See Offices in Geneva Nos. 373-375, Vienna Nos. 290-292.

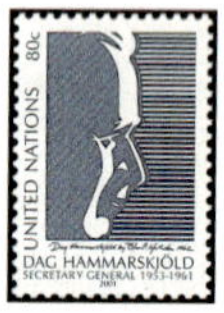

Dag Hammarskjöld (1905-61), UN Secretary General — A329

**2001, Sept. 18 Engr. *Perf. 11x11¼***

**808** A329 80c blue 1.50 1.50

See Offices in Geneva No. 376, Vienna No. 293.

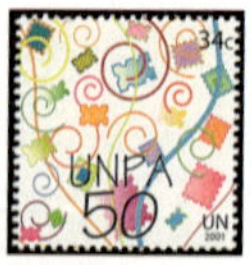

A330

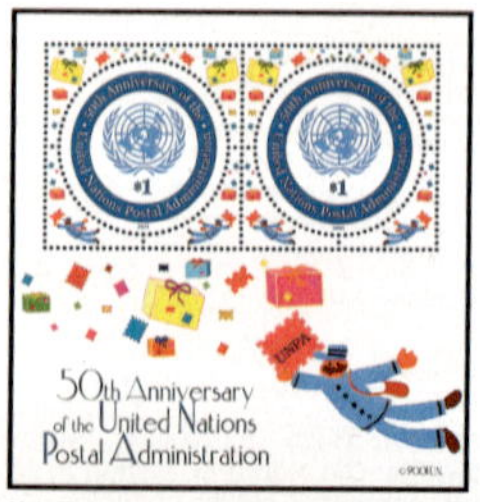

UN Postal Administration, 50th Anniv. — A331

**2001, Oct. 18 Litho. *Perf. 13½***

**809** A330 34c Stamps, streamers .55 .55
**810** A330 80c Stamps, gifts 1.50 1.50

**Souvenir Sheet**

**811** A331 Sheet of 2 #811a 8.00 8.00
*a.* $1 blue & light blue, 38mm diameter 4.00 4.00

See Offices in Geneva Nos. 377-379, Vienna Nos. 294-296.

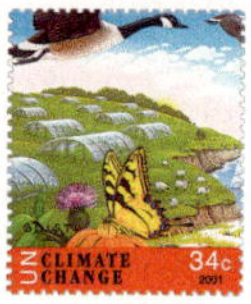

Climate Change — A332

No. 812, Canada geese, greenhouses, butterfly, thistle. No. 813, Canada geese, iceberg, penguins, tomato plant. No. 814, Palm tree, solar collector. No. 815, Hand planting ginkgo cutting.

**2001, Nov. 16 Litho. *Perf. 13¼***

**812** A332 34c multicolored 1.00 1.00
**813** A332 34c multicolored 1.00 1.00
**814** A332 34c multicolored 1.00 1.00
**815** A332 34c multicolored 1.00 1.00
*a.* Horiz. strip, #812-815 4.50 4.50

See Offices in Geneva Nos. 380-383, Vienna Nos. 297-300.

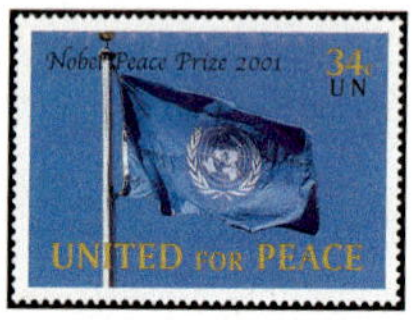

Awarding of Nobel Peace Prize to Secretary General Kofi Annan and UN — A333

**2001, Dec. 10 Litho. *Perf. 13¼***

**816** A333 34c multicolored .70 .70

See Offices in Geneva Nos. 384, Vienna Nos. 301.

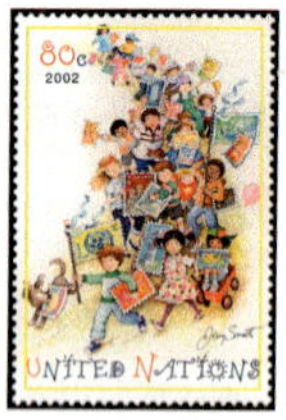

Children and Stamps — A334

**2002, Mar. 1 Litho. *Perf. 13¾***

**817** A334 80c multicolored 1.40 1.40

**Endangered Species Type of 1993**

No. 818, Hoffmann's two-toed sloth. No. 819, Bighorn sheep. No. 820, Cheetah. No. 821, San Esteban Island chuckwalla.

**2002, Apr. 4 Litho. *Perf. 12¾x12½***

**818** A271 34c multicolored .80 .80
**819** A271 34c multicolored .80 .80
**820** A271 34c multicolored .80 .80
**821** A271 34c multicolored .80 .80
*a.* Block of 4, #818-821 3.25 3.25

See Offices in Geneva Nos. 386-389; Vienna 308-311.

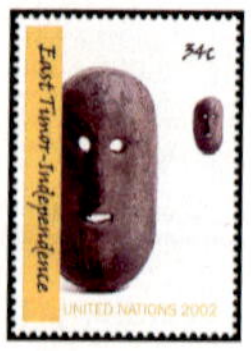

Independence of East Timor — A335

34c, Wooden ritual mask. 57c, Decorative door panel.

**2002, May 20 Litho. *Perf. 14x14½***

**822** A335 34c multicolored .70 .70
**823** A335 57c multicolored 1.20 1.20

See Offices in Geneva Nos. 390-391; Vienna Nos. 312-313.

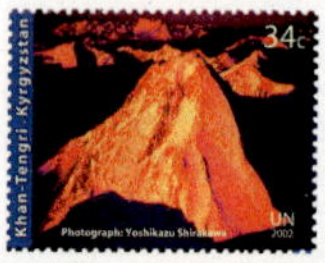

Intl. Year of Mountains
A336

No. 824, Khan Tengri, Kyrgyzstan. No. 825, Mt. Kilimanjaro, Tanzania. No. 826, Mt. Foraker, US. No. 827, Paine Grande, Chile.

**2002, May 24 Litho. *Perf. 13x13¼***

**824** A336 34c multicolored .75 .75
**825** A336 34c multicolored .75 .75
**826** A336 80c multicolored 1.25 1.50
**827** A336 80c multicolored 1.25 1.50
*a.* Vert. strip or block of four, #824-827 5.00 5.00

See Offices in Geneva Nos. 392-395; Vienna Nos. 314-317.

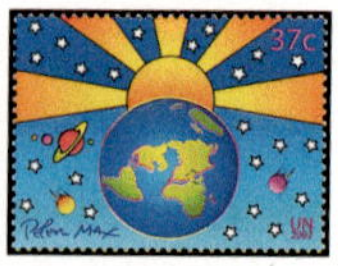

World Summit on Sustainable Development, Johannesburg
A337

No. 828, Sun, Earth, planets, stars. No. 829, Three women. No. 830, Sailboat. No. 831, Three faceless people.

**2002, June 27 Litho. *Perf. 14½x14***

**828** A337 37c multicolored .75 .75
**829** A337 37c multicolored .75 .75
**830** A337 60c multicolored 1.25 1.25
**831** A337 60c multicolored 1.25 1.25
*a.* Vert. strip or block of four, #828-831 5.00 10.00

See Offices in Geneva Nos. 396-399; Vienna Nos. 318-321.

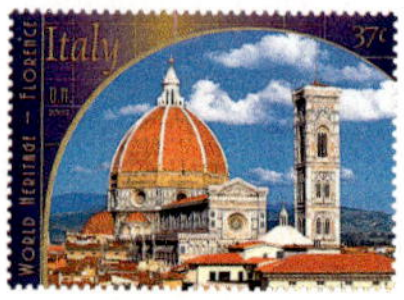

World Heritage Sites, Italy — A338

37c, #834d, Florence. 70c, #834a, Amalfi Coast. #834b, Aeolian Islands. #834c, Rome. #834e, Pisa. #834f, Pompeii.

***Perf. 13½x13¼***

**2002, Aug. 30 Litho.**

**832** A338 37c multicolored .70 .70
**833** A338 70c multicolored 1.40 1.40

**Souvenir Booklet**

**834** Booklet 16.00
*a.-c.* A338 5c any single .40 .40
*d.-f.* A338 15c any single .90 .90
*g.* Booklet pane of 4, #834d 3.60 3.60
*h.* Booklet pane of 4, #834a 1.60 1.60
*i.* Booklet pane of 4, #834e 3.60 3.60
*j.* Booklet pane of 4, #834b 1.60 1.60
*k.* Booklet pane of 4, #834f 3.60 3.60
*l.* Booklet pane of 4, #834c 1.60 1.60

See Offices in Geneva Nos. 400-402, Vienna Nos. 322-324.
See Italy Nos. 2506-2507.

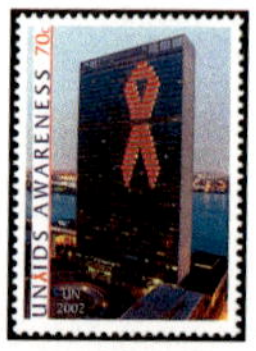

AIDS Awareness — A339

**2002, Oct. 24 Litho. *Perf. 13½***

**835** A339 70c multicolored 1.50 1.50

See No. B1, Offices in Geneva Nos. 403, B1, Vienna Nos. 325, B1.

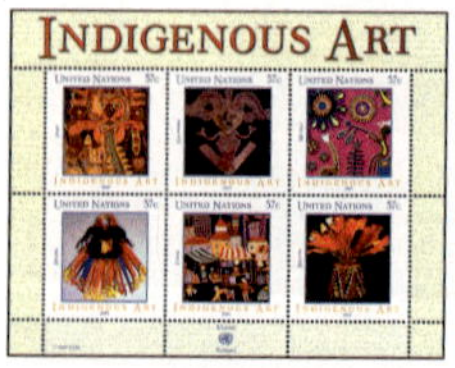

Indigenous Art
A340

No. 836: a, Detail of Paracas textile, Peru. b, Sinu culture anthropo-zoomorphic pendant, Colombia. c, Hicholi Indian embroidery, Mexico. d, Rigpaktsa back ornament, Brazil. e, Wool crafts, Chile. f, Huari feathered woven hat, Bolivia.

**2003, Jan. 31 Litho. *Perf. 14¼***

**836** A340 Sheet of 6 8.50 8.50
*a.-f.* 37c Any single 1.40 1.40

See Offies in Geneva No. 405; Vienna No. 326.

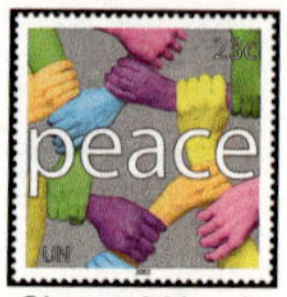

Clasped Hands
A341

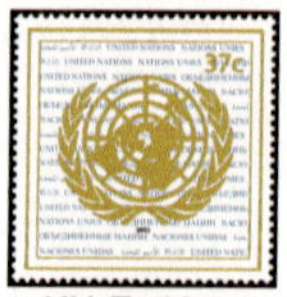

UN Emblem
A342

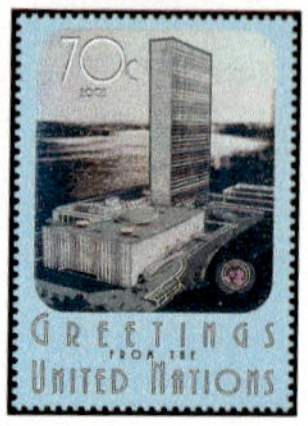

UN Headquarters
A343

**2003, Mar. 28 Litho. *Perf. 14¼***

**837** A341 23c multicolored .40 .40

**Litho. with Foil Application**

**838** A342 37c gold & multicolored .60 .60

**Litho. with Hologram**

***Perf. 13¼x12¾***

**839** A343 70c multicolored 1.40 1.40

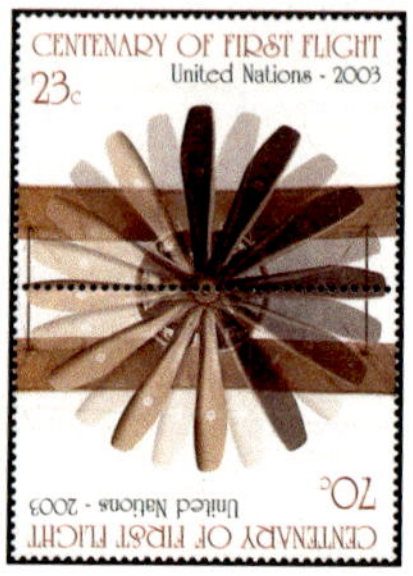

Powered Flight, Cent.
A344

***Perf. 13½x13¾***

**2003, Mar. 28 Litho.**

**840** 23c multicolored 1.00 1.00
**841** 70c multicolored 1.75 1.75
*a.* A344 Tete beche pair, #840-841 3.00 3.00

**Endangered Species Type of 1993**

No. 842, Great hornbill. No. 843, Scarlet ibis. No. 844, Knob-billed goose. No. 845, White-faced whistling duck.

**2003, Apr. 3 Litho. *Perf. 12¾x12½***

**842** A271 37c multicolored .80 .80
**843** A271 37c multicolored .80 .80
**844** A271 37c multicolored .80 .80
**845** A271 37c multicolored .80 .80
*a.* Block of 4, #842-845 3.25 3.25

See Offices in Geneva Nos. 407-410; Vienna 329-332.

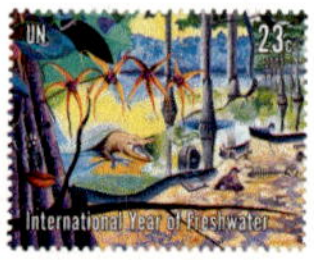

Intl. Year of Freshwater — A345

***Perf. 14¼x14½***

**2003, June 20 Litho.**

**846** A345 23c Wildlife, garbage 1.50 1.50
**847** A345 37c Trees, canoe 2.00 2.00
*a.* Horiz. pair, #846-847 7.50 7.50

See Offices in Geneva, Nos. 411-412; Vienna Nos. 333-334.

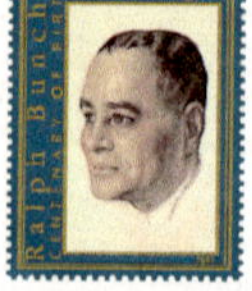

Ralph Bunche (1903-71), Diplomat — A346

**Litho. With Foil Application**

**2003, Aug. 7 *Perf. 13½x14***

**848** A346 37c blue & multi .80 .80

See Offices in Geneva No. 413; Vienna No. 336.

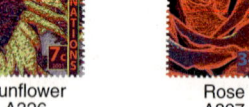

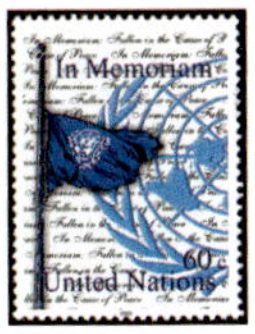

In Memoriam of Victims of Aug. 19 Bombing of UN Complex in Baghdad, Iraq — A347

**2003, Oct. 24 Litho. *Perf. 13¼x13***

**849** A347 60c multicolored 1.25 1.25

See Offices in Geneva No. 414, Vienna No. 337.

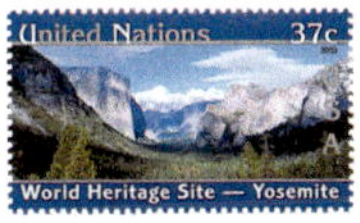

World Heritage Sites, United States — A348

37c, #852a, Yosemite National Park. 60c, #852d, Hawaii Volcanoes National Park. #852b, Great Smoky Mountains National Park. #852c, Olympic National Park. #852e, Everglades National Park. #852f, Yellowstone National Park.

**2003, Oct. 24 Litho. *Perf. 14½x14¼***

**850** A348 37c multicolored .90 .90
**851** A348 60c multicolored 1.50 1.50

**Souvenir Booklet**

**852** Booklet 15.00
*a.-c.* A348 10c any single .35 .35
*d.-f.* A348 20c any single .70 .70
*g.* Booklet pane of 4 #852a 1.40 1.40
*h.* Booklet pane of 4 #852d 2.80 2.80
*i.* Booklet pane of 4 #852b 1.40 1.40
*j.* Booklet pane of 4 #852e 2.80 2.80
*k.* Booklet pane of 4 #852c 1.40 1.40
*l.* Booklet pane of 4 #852f 2.80 2.80

See Offices in Geneva Nos. 415-417, Vienna Nos. 338-340.

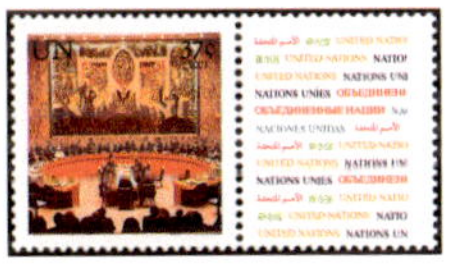

UN Security Council A349

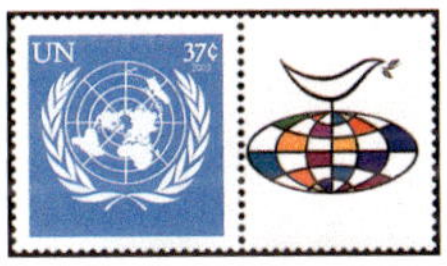

UN Emblem A350

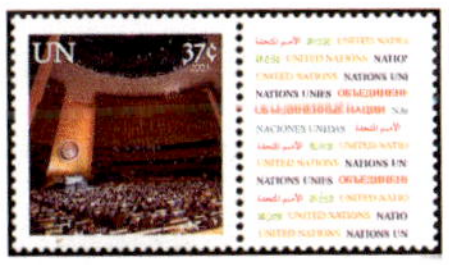

UN General Assembly A351

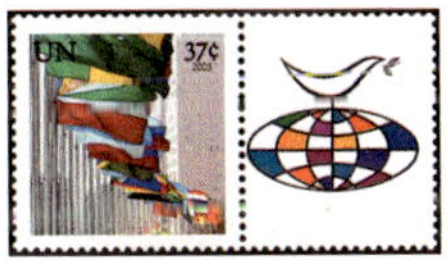

Flags A352

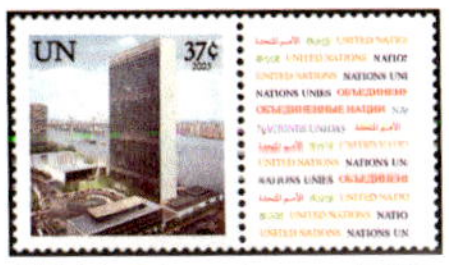

UN Headquarters — A353

**2003, Nov. 26 Litho. *Perf. 13¼***

**853** A349 37c multi + label 10.00 10.00
**854** A350 37c multi + label 10.00 10.00
**855** A351 37c multi + label 10.00 10.00
**856** A352 37c multi + label 10.00 10.00
**857** A353 37c multi + label 10.00 10.00
*a.* Vert. strip of 5, #853-857, + 5 labels 50.00 50.00

The full sheet sold for $14.95 with or without personalized labels. The personalization of labels was available only at UN Headquarters, and not through mail order.

One thousand full sheets with sheet margins inscribed "Hong Kong Stamp Expo" were sold only at that venue. Value $135. Also exists with sheet margins inscribed "Essen." Value $125.

A sheet containing two strips of five stamps similar to Nos. 853-857 but dated "2005" and ten labels sold for $4.95. These sheets were only available canceled. Value $100. An imperforate error of this sheet is known.

**Endangered Species Type of 1993**

No. 858, American black bear. No. 859, Musk deer. No. 860, Golden snub-nosed monkey. No. 861, Wild yak.

**2004, Jan. 29 Litho. *Perf. 12¾x12½***

**858** A271 37c multicolored .90 .90
**859** A271 37c multicolored .90 .90
**860** A271 37c multicolored .90 .90
**861** A271 37c multicolored .90 .90
*a.* Block of 4, #858-861 4.00 4.00

See Offices in Geneva Nos. 418-421; Vienna Nos. 342-345.

**Indigenous Art Type of 2003**

No. 862: a, Viking wood carving depicting Saga of Sigurd Favnesbane, Norway. b, Stele, Italy. c, Detail of matador's suit, Spain. d, Amphora, Greece. e, Bronze figurine of bull, Czech Republic. f, Detail of lacquer box illustration depicting scene from "On the Seashore," by Alexander Pushkin, Russia.

**2004, Mar. 4 Litho. *Perf. 13¼***

**862** A340 Sheet of 6 6.00 6.00
*a.-f.* 37c Any single 1.00 1.00

See Offices in Geneva No. 422; Vienna No. 346.

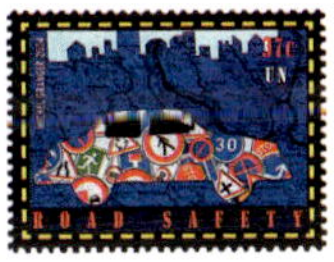

Road Safety — A354

Road map art with: 37c, Automobile with road signs, city skyline. 70c, Automobile, hand, vert.

***Perf. 13x13¼, 13¼x13***

**2004, Apr. 7 Litho.**

**863** A354 37c multicolored .85 .85
**864** A354 70c multicolored 1.40 1.40

See Offices in Geneva Nos. 423-424, Vienna Nos. 347-348.

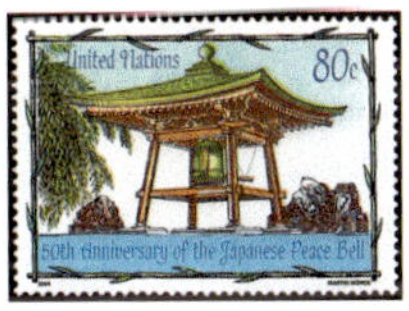

Japanese Peace Bell, 50th Anniv. A355

**Litho. & Engr.**

**2004, June 3 *Perf. 13¼x13***

**865** A355 80c multicolored 1.25 1.25

See Offices in Geneva No. 425; Vienna No. 349.

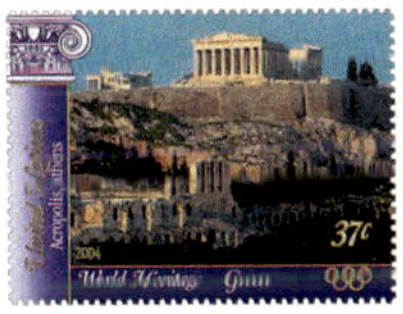

World Heritage Sites, Greece A356

No. 866, Acropolis, Athens. Nos. 867, 868e, Delos. No. 868a, Delphi. No. 868b, Pythagoreion and Heraion of Samos. No. 868c, Olympia. No. 868d, Mycenae and Tiryns.

**2004, Aug. 12 Litho. *Perf. 14x13¼***

**866** A356 37c multicolored .70 .70
*a.* Booklet pane of 4 3.00 —
**867** A356 60c multicolored 1.10 1.10

**Souvenir Booklet**

**868** Booklet, #866a, 868f-868j 15.00
*a.-d.* A356 23c any single .55 .55
*e.* A356 37c multi .90 .90
*f.* Booklet pane of 4 #868a 2.20 2.20
*g.* Booklet pane of 4 #868b 2.20 2.20
*h.* Booklet pane of 4 #868c 2.20 2.20
*i.* Booklet pane of 4 #868d 2.20 2.20
*j.* Booklet pane of 4 #868e 3.60 3.60

See Offices in Geneva Nos. 426-428, Vienna Nos. 350-352. No. 868 sold for $7.20.

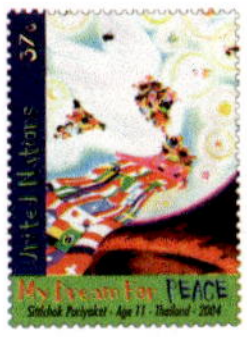

My Dream for Peace — A357

Winning designs of Lions Club International children's global peace poster contest by: 37c, Sittichok Pariyaket, Thailand. 80c, Bayan Fais Abu Bial, Israel.

**2004, Sept. 21 Litho. *Perf. 14***

**869** A357 37c multicolored .60 .60
**870** A357 80c multicolored 1.40 1.40

See Offices in Geneva Nos. 429-430, Vienna Nos. 353-354.

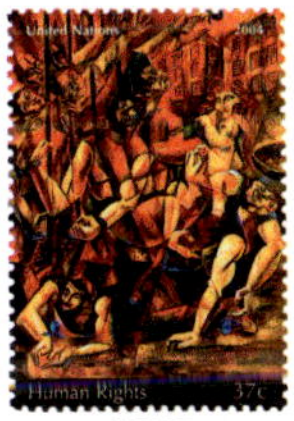

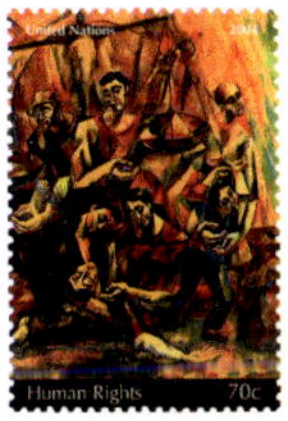

A358 Human Rights — A359

**2004, Oct. 14 Litho. *Perf. 11¼***

**871** A358 37c multicolored .75 .75
**872** A359 70c multicolored 1.40 1.40

See Offices in Geneva Nos. 431-432, Vienna Nos. 355-356.

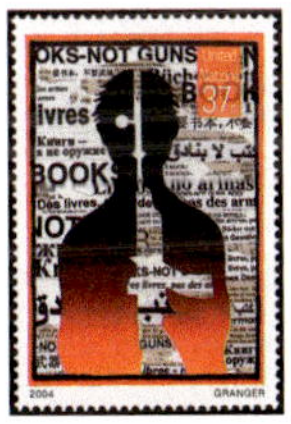

Disarmament A360

**2004, Oct. 15 Litho. *Perf. 13¾***

**873** A360 37c multicolored .80 .80

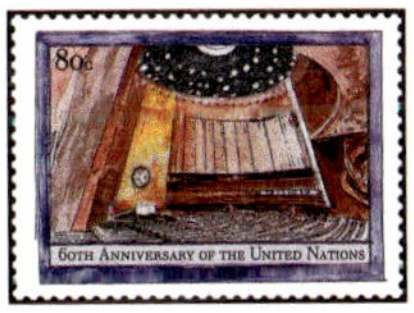

United Nations, 60th Anniv. A361

**Litho. & Engr.**

**2005, Feb. 4 *Perf. 11x11¼***

**874** A361 80c multicolored 1.50 1.50

**Souvenir Sheet**

**Litho.**

***Imperf***

**875** A361 $1 multicolored 12.50 12.50

See Offices in Geneva Nos. 434-435; Vienna Nos. 357-358.

**Endangered Species Type of 1993**

Designs: No. 876, Blue orchid. No. 877, Swan orchid. No. 878, Christmas orchid. No. 879, Aerangis modesta.

**2005, Mar. 3 Litho. *Perf. 12¾x12½***

**876** A271 37c multicolored 1.10 1.10
**877** A271 37c multicolored 1.10 1.10
**878** A271 37c multicolored 1.10 1.10
**879** A271 37c multicolored 1.10 1.10
*a.* Block of 4, #876-879 4.50 4.50

See Offices in Geneva Nos. 436-439; Vienna Nos. 360-363.

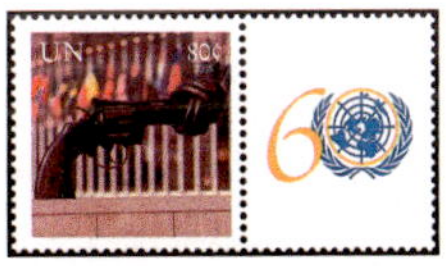

Non-Violence, Sculpture by Carl Fredrik Reuterswärd, New York — A362

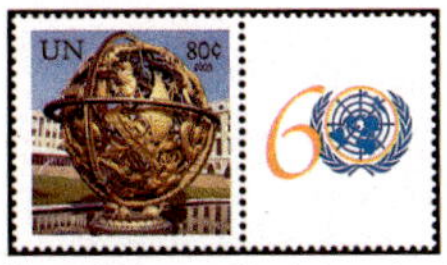

Armillary Sphere, Sculpture by Paul Manship, Geneva A363

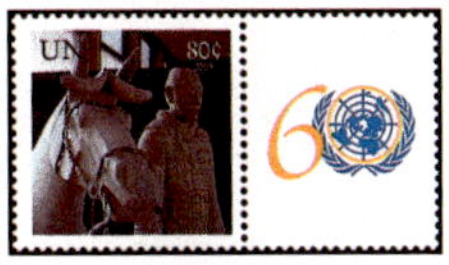

Terra Cotta Warriors, Vienna A364

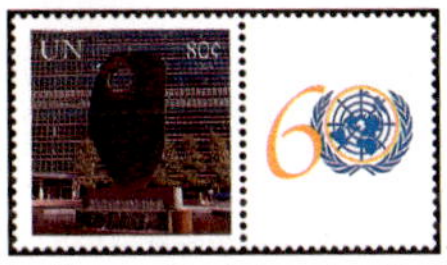

Single Form, Sculpture by Barbara Hepworth, New York A365

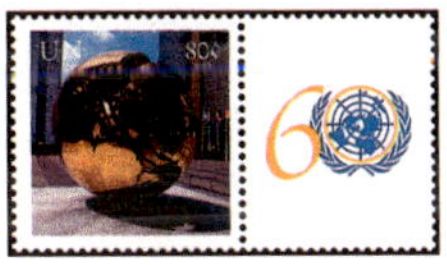

Sphere Within a Sphere, Sculpture by Arnaldo Pomodoro, New York A366

**2005, Mar. 3 Litho. *Perf. 13¼***

**880** A362 80c multi + label *35.00 35.00*
**881** A363 80c multi + label *35.00 35.00*
**882** A364 80c multi + label *35.00 35.00*
**883** A365 80c multi + label *35.00 35.00*
**884** A366 80c multi + label *35.00 35.00*
*a.* Vert. strip of 5, #880-884, + 5 labels *175.00 175.00*
*b.* Sheet of 10, both #884 37c (error) *3,250.*
*c.* Vert. strip of 5, #884 37c (error) *1,450.*

The full sheet sold for $14.95 with or without personalized labels. The personalization of labels was available only at UN Headquarters, and not through mail order.

The full sheet exists with sheet margins and labels commemorating the Riccione 2005 Philatelic Exhibition. This sheet went on sale 8/20/05 and was also sold for $14.95. Value $175.

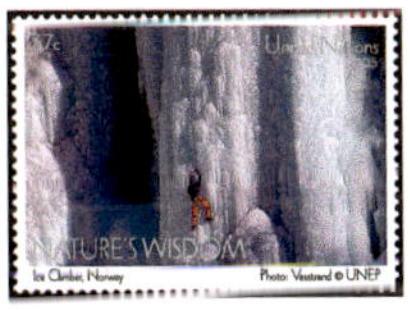

Nature's Wisdom A367

37c, Ice climber, Norway. 80c, Egret, Japan.

**2005, Apr. 21 Litho. *Perf. 13½x13¼***

**885** A367 37c multicolored .65 .65
**886** A367 80c multicolored 1.50 1.50

See Offices in Geneva Nos. 440-441, Vienna Nos. 364-365.

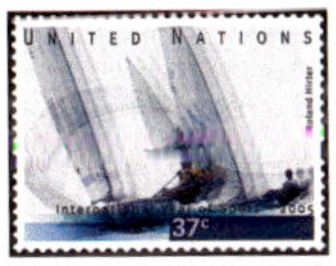

Intl. Year of Sport — A368

**2005, June 3 Litho. *Perf. 13x13¼***

**887** A368 37c Sailing .65 .65
**888** A368 70c Running 1.25 1.25

See Offices in Geneva Nos. 442-443; Vienna Nos. 366-367.

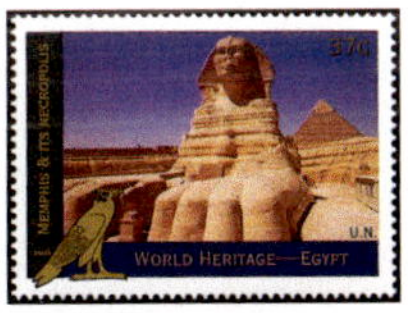

World Heritage Sites, Egypt A369

Nos. 889, 891a, Memphis and its Necropolis. Nos. 890, 891d, Ancient Thebes. No. 891b,

270 UNITED NATIONS, OFFICES IN NEW YORK

Philae. No. 891c, Abu Mena. No. 891e, Islamic Cairo. No. 891f, St. Catherine area.

**2005, Aug. 4 Litho. *Perf. 14x13¼***

| | | | |
|---|---|---|---|
| **889** | A369 37c multicolored | .60 | .60 |
| **890** | A369 80c multicolored | 1.40 | 1.40 |

### Souvenir Booklet

| | | | |
|---|---|---|---|
| **891** | Booklet, #891g-891l | 15.00 | |
| *a.-c.* | A369 23c any single | .50 | .50 |
| *d.-f.* | A369 37c any single | .75 | .75 |
| *g.* | Booklet pane of 4 #891a | 2.00 | 2.00 |
| *h.* | Booklet pane of 4 #891b | 2.00 | 2.00 |
| *i.* | Booklet pane of 4 #891c | 2.00 | 2.00 |
| *j.* | Booklet pane of 4 #891d | 3.00 | 3.00 |
| *k.* | Booklet pane of 4 #891e | 3.00 | 3.00 |
| *l.* | Booklet pane of 4 #891f | 3.00 | 3.00 |

See Offices in Geneva Nos. 444-446, Vienna Nos. 368-370.

### My Dream for Peace Type of 2004

Winning designs of Lions Club International children's global peace poster contest by: 37c, Vittoria Sansebastiano, Italy. 80c, Jordan Harris, US.

**2005, Sept. 21 Litho. *Perf. 14***

| | | | |
|---|---|---|---|
| **892** | A357 37c multicolored | .60 | .60 |
| **893** | A357 80c multicolored | 1.40 | 1.40 |

See Offices in Geneva Nos. 447-448, Vienna Nos. 371-372.

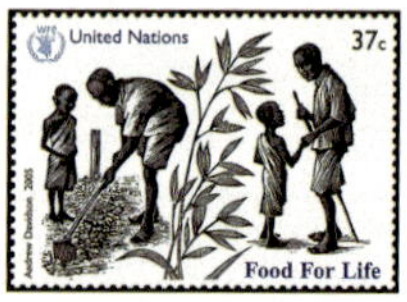

Food for Life — A370

37c, Oats, children and adults. 80c, Wheat, mothers breastfeeding babies.

**2005, Oct. 20 Litho. *Perf. 13¾***

| | | | |
|---|---|---|---|
| **894** | A370 37c multicolored | .60 | .60 |
| **895** | A370 80c multicolored | 1.40 | 1.40 |

See Offices in Geneva Nos. 449-450; Vienna Nos. 373-374.

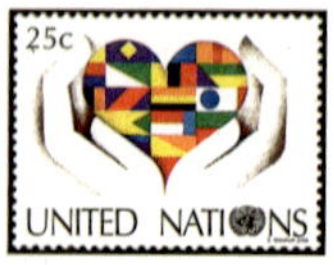

Stylized Flags in Heart and Hands — A371

**2006, Feb. 3 Litho. *Perf. 13x13¼***

| | | | |
|---|---|---|---|
| **896** | A371 25c multicolored | .75 | .75 |

### Indigenous Art Type of 2003

No. 897 — Musical instruments: a, Drum, Ivory Coast. b, Drum, Tunisia. c, Stringed instruments, Morocco. d, Drums, Sudan. e, Instruments, Cameroun. f, Harp, Congo.

**2006, Feb. 3 Litho. *Perf. 13¼***

| | | | |
|---|---|---|---|
| **897** | A340 Sheet of 6 | 10.00 | 10.00 |
| *a.-f.* | 37c Any single | 1.50 | 1.50 |

See Offices in Geneva No. 452; Vienna No. 375.

### UN Symbols Type of 2003

**2006, Mar. 6 Litho. *Perf. 13¼***

| | | | |
|---|---|---|---|
| **898** | A349 39c multi + label | 5.00 | 5.00 |
| **899** | A350 39c multi + label | 5.00 | 5.00 |
| **900** | A351 39c multi + label | 5.00 | 5.00 |
| **901** | A352 39c multi + label | 5.00 | 5.00 |
| **902** | A353 39c multi + label | 5.00 | 5.00 |
| *a.* | Vert. strip of 5, #898-902, + 5 labels | 25.00 | 25.00 |

The full sheet sold for $14.95 with or without personalized labels. The personalization of labels was available only at UN Headquarters, and not through mail order.

### Sculpture Type of 2005

**2006, Mar. 6 Litho. *Perf. 13¼***

| | | | |
|---|---|---|---|
| **903** | A362 84c multi + label | 12.00 | 12.00 |
| *a.* | Perf. 14½x14 + label | 16.00 | 16.00 |
| **904** | A363 84c multi + label | 12.00 | 12.00 |
| *a.* | Perf. 14½x14 + label | 16.00 | 16.00 |
| **905** | A364 84c multi + label | 12.00 | 12.00 |
| *a.* | Perf. 14½x14 + label | 16.00 | 16.00 |
| **906** | A365 84c multi + label | 12.00 | 12.00 |
| *a.* | Perf. 14½x14 + label | 16.00 | 16.00 |
| **907** | A366 84c multi + label | 12.00 | 12.00 |
| *a.* | Perf. 14½x14 + label | 16.00 | 16.00 |
| *b.* | Vert. strip of 5, #903-907, + 5 labels | *60.00* | *60.00* |
| *c.* | Vert. strip of 5, #903a-907a, + 5 labels | *80.00* | *80.00* |

The full sheet sold for $14.95 with or without personalized labels. The personalization of labels was available only at UN Headquarters, and not through mail order.

Nos. 903a-907a issued 9/21/06. Nos. 903a-907a were from sheet for 2006 Berlin Stamp Show. The year "2006" is slightly smaller on Nos. 903a-907a than on Nos. 903-907.

Full sheets with different margins were sold at the Washington 2006 World Philatelic Exhibition, where the labels could be personalized. These are worth slightly more than the generic No. 907b sheet.

### Endangered Species Type of 1993

No. 908, Golden mantella. No. 909, Panther chameleon. No. 910, Peruvian rainbow boa. No. 911, Dyeing poison frog.

***Perf. 12¾x12½***

**2006, Mar. 16 Litho.**

| | | | |
|---|---|---|---|
| **908** | A271 39c multicolored | .90 | .90 |
| **909** | A271 39c multicolored | .90 | .90 |
| **910** | A271 39c multicolored | .90 | .90 |
| **911** | A271 39c multicolored | .90 | .90 |
| *a.* | Block of 4, #908-911 | 4.00 | 4.00 |

See Offices in Geneva Nos. 453-456; Vienna Nos. 376-379.

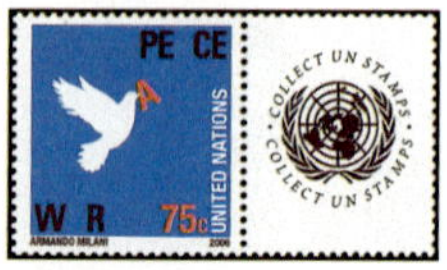

Dove Between War and Peace A372

**2006, Apr. 10 Litho. *Perf. 13¼***

| | | | |
|---|---|---|---|
| **912** | A372 75c multi + label | 3.75 | 3.75 |

The full sheet sold for $14.95 with or without personalized labels. The personalization of labels was available only at UN Headquarters, and not through mail order.

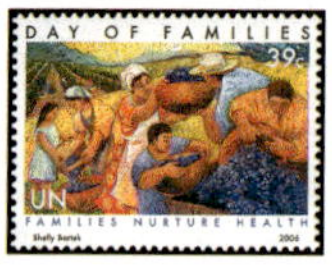

Intl. Day of Families — A373

39c, Family harvesting grapes. 84c, Children playing with toy sailboats.

**2006, May 27 Litho. *Perf. 14x13½***

| | | | |
|---|---|---|---|
| **913** | A373 39c multicolored | .70 | .70 |
| **914** | A373 84c multicolored | 1.50 | 1.50 |

See Offices in Geneva Nos. 457-458; Vienna Nos. 380-381.

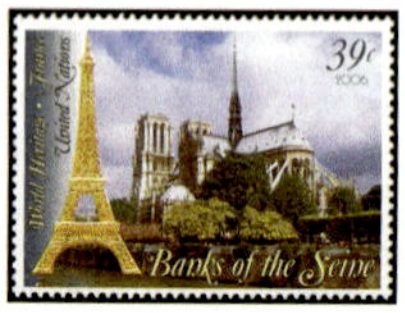

World Heritage Sites, France A374

Eiffel Tower and: Nos. 915, 917a, Banks of the Seine. Nos. 916, 917d, Roman Aqueduct. No. 917b, Provins. No. 917c, Carcassonne. No. 917e, Mont Saint-Michel. No. 917f, Chateau de Chambord.

### Litho. & Embossed with Foil Application

**2006, June 17 *Perf. 13½x13¼***

| | | | |
|---|---|---|---|
| **915** | A374 39c multicolored | .75 | .75 |
| **916** | A374 84c multicolored | 1.75 | 1.75 |

### Souvenir Booklet

| | | | |
|---|---|---|---|
| **917** | Booklet, #917g-917l | 16.00 | |
| *a.-c.* | A374 24c any single | .50 | .50 |
| *d.-f.* | A374 39c any single | .80 | .80 |
| *g.* | Booklet pane of 4 #917a | 2.00 | 2.00 |
| *h.* | Booklet pane of 4 #917b | 2.00 | 2.00 |
| *i.* | Booklet pane of 4 #917c | 2.00 | 2.00 |
| *j.* | Booklet pane of 4 #917d | 3.25 | 3.25 |
| *k.* | Booklet pane of 4 #917e | 3.25 | 3.25 |
| *l.* | Booklet pane of 4 #917f | 3.25 | 3.25 |

See Offices in Geneva Nos. 459-461, Vienna Nos. 382-384.

### My Dream for Peace Type of 2004

Winning designs of Lions Club International children's global peace poster contest by: 39c, Cheuk Tat Li, Hong Kong. 84c, Kosshapan Paitoon, Thailand.

**2006, Sept. 21 Litho. *Perf. 13½x13***

| | | | |
|---|---|---|---|
| **918** | A357 39c multicolored | .80 | .80 |
| **919** | A357 84c multicolored | 1.75 | 1.75 |

See Offices in Geneva Nos. 462-463; Vienna Nos. 385-386.

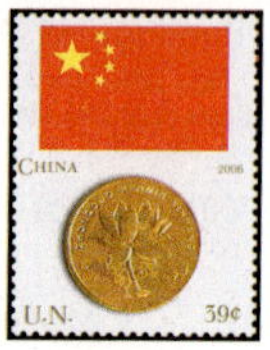

Flags and Coins — A375

No. 920 — Flag of: a, People's Republic of China, 1 yuan coin. b, Australia, 1 dollar coin. c, Ghana, 50 cedi coin. d, Israel, 10 agorot coin. e, Russia, 1 ruble coin. f, Mexico, 10 peso coin. g, Japan, 10 yen coin. h, Cambodia, 200 riel coin.

**2006, Oct. 5 Litho. *Perf. 13¼x13***

| | | | |
|---|---|---|---|
| **920** | Sheet of 8 | 7.00 | 7.00 |
| *a.-h.* | A375 39c Any single | .75 | .75 |

A column of rouletting in the middle of the sheet separates it into two parts. See Nos. 930, 953, 998, 1022, 1039, 1078, 1103; Offices in Geneva Nos. 464, 469, 484, 512, 532, 546, 576, 594; Vienna Nos. 387, 392, 421, 459, 483, 507, 539, 558.

### Flag Type of 1980

**2007, Feb. 2 Litho. *Perf. 14***

| | | | |
|---|---|---|---|
| **921** | A185 39c Tuvalu | 1.10 | 1.10 |
| **922** | A185 39c Switzerland | 1.10 | 1.10 |
| **923** | A185 39c Timor-Leste | 1.10 | 1.10 |
| **924** | A185 39c Montenegro | 1.10 | 1.10 |
| *a.* | Block of 4, #921-924 | 12.50 | 12.50 |
| | *Nos. 921-924 (4)* | *4.40* | *4.40* |

### Endangered Species Type of 1993

No. 925, Drill. No. 926, Common squirrel monkey. No. 927, Ring-tailed lemur. No. 928, Collared mangabey.

***Perf. 12¾x12½***

**2007, Mar. 15 Litho.**

| | | | |
|---|---|---|---|
| **925** | A271 39c multicolored | .85 | .85 |
| **926** | A271 39c multicolored | .85 | .85 |
| **927** | A271 39c multicolored | .85 | *.85* |
| **928** | A271 39c multicolored | .85 | .85 |
| *a.* | Block of 4, #925-928 | 3.50 | 3.50 |

See Offices in Geneva Nos. 465-468; Vienna Nos. 388-391.

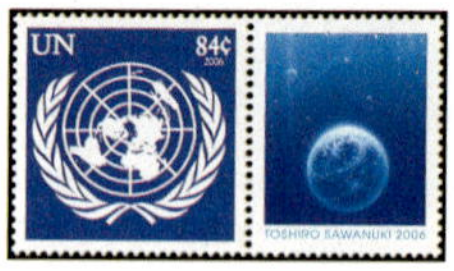

UN Emblem A376

**2007, Feb. 5 Litho. *Perf. 14½x14***

| | | | |
|---|---|---|---|
| **929** | A376 84c dk blue + label | *17.50* | *5.00* |

The full sheet sold for $14.95. The sheet has two each of five different labels that could not be personalized. The sheet was distributed to members of the Japanese mission on Sept. 21, 2006, but it was not sold to the public until 2007. The sheet's availability to the public was not announced through press releases or on the UNPA website prior to the day of issue or afterward. It was sent to standing order customers in May 2007.

Compare with Type A377.

### Flags and Coins Type of 2006

No. 930 — Flag of: a, Brazil, 50 centavo coin. b, Thailand, 1 baht coin. c, Viet Nam, 5,000 dong coin. d, Ecuador, 10 centavo coin. e, India, 5 rupee coin. f, South Africa, 5 cent coin. g, Barbados, 25 cent coin. h, Republic of Korea, 500 won coin.

**2007, May 3 Litho. *Perf. 13¼x13***

| | | | |
|---|---|---|---|
| **930** | Sheet of 8 | 8.00 | 8.00 |
| *a.-h.* | A375 39c Any single | .75 | .75 |

A column of rouletting in the middle of the sheet separates it into two parts. See Offices in Geneva No. 469; Vienna No. 392.

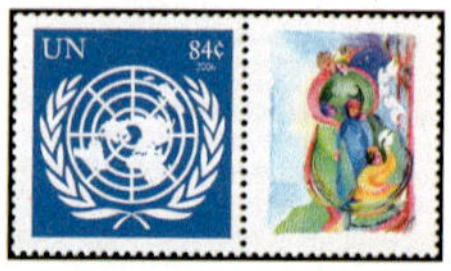

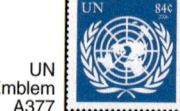

UN Emblem A377

**2007, June 1 Litho. *Perf. 13¼***

| | | | |
|---|---|---|---|
| **931** | A377 84c blue + label | *4.50* | *4.50* |

The full sheet sold for $14.95. The sheet has two each of five different labels that could not be personalized.

Compare with Type A376.

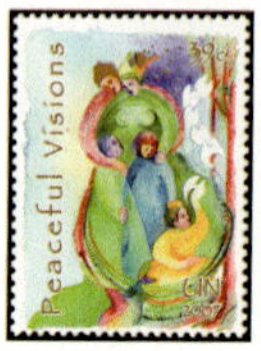

Peaceful Visions — A378

39c, "Nest." 84c, "Sisters Weave the Olive Branch."

**2007, June 1 Litho. *Perf. 13x12½***

| | | | |
|---|---|---|---|
| **932** | A378 39c multicolored | .90 | .90 |
| **933** | A378 84c multicolored | 1.80 | 1.80 |

See Offices in Geneva Nos. 470-471; Vienna Nos. 398-399.

### UN Symbols Type of 2003

**2007, May 14 Litho. *Perf. 13¼***

| | | | |
|---|---|---|---|
| **934** | A349 41c multi + label | 3.25 | 3.25 |
| **935** | A350 41c multi + label | 3.25 | 3.25 |
| **936** | A351 41c multi + label | 3.25 | 3.25 |
| **937** | A352 41c multi + label | 3.25 | 3.25 |
| **938** | A353 41c multi + label | 3.25 | 3.25 |
| *a.* | Vert. strip of 5, #934-938, + 5 labels | 17.00 | 17.00 |

The full sheet sold for $14.95 with or without personalized labels. The personalization of labels was available only at UN Headquarters, and not through mail order.

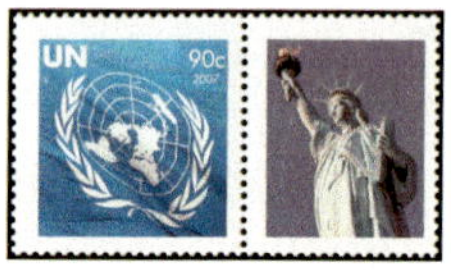

UN Flag A379

**2007, May 14 Litho. *Perf. 13¼***

| | | | |
|---|---|---|---|
| **939** | A379 90c blue + label | *5.00* | *6.00* |

The full sheet sold for $14.95. The sheet has two each of five different labels that could not be personalized.

A second printing of No. 939 has the "U" and "N" more closely spaced, and it has different labels and different pane borders. Value about the same.

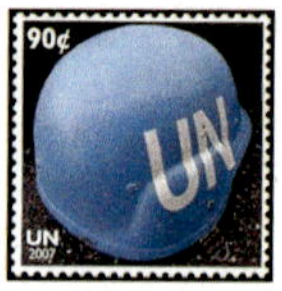

Helmet of UN Peacekeeper — A380

**2007, Aug. 9 Litho. *Perf. 12½x13¼***

| | | | |
|---|---|---|---|
| **940** | A380 90c multicolored | 1.90 | 1.90 |

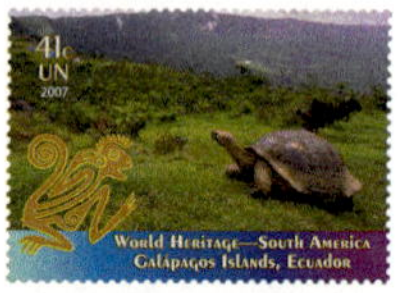

World Heritage Sites, South America A381

No. 941, Galapagos Islands, Ecuador. Nos. 942, 943a, Rapa Nui, Chile. No. 943b, Cueva de las Manos, Argentina. No. 943c, Machu Picchu, Peru. No. 943d, Tiwanaku, Bolivia. No. 943e, Iguaçu National Park, Brazil.

**2007, Aug. 9 Litho. *Perf. 13¼x13***

| | | | |
|---|---|---|---|
| **941** | A381 41c multicolored | .85 | .85 |
| *a.* | Booklet pane of 4 | 3.40 | — |
| **942** | A381 90c multicolored | 1.90 | 1.90 |

### Souvenir Booklet

| | | | |
|---|---|---|---|
| **943** | Booklet, #941a, 943f-943j | 17.00 | |
| *a.-c.* | A381 26c Any single | .60 | .60 |
| *d.-e.* | A381 41c Either single | 1.00 | 1.00 |
| *f.* | Booklet pane of 4 #943a | 2.40 | 2.40 |
| *g.* | Booklet pane of 4 #943b | 2.40 | 2.40 |
| *h.* | Booklet pane of 4 #943c | 2.40 | 2.40 |
| *i.* | Booklet pane of 4 #943d | 4.00 | 4.00 |
| *j.* | Booklet pane of 4 #943e | 4.00 | 4.00 |

See Offices in Geneva Nos. 472-474, Vienna Nos. 400-402. No. 943 sold for $8.50.

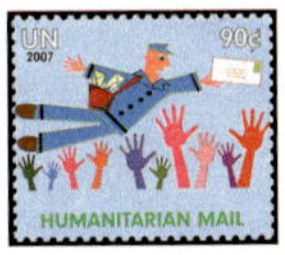

Humanitarian Mail — A382

**2007, Sept. 6 Litho. *Perf. 12½x13¼***

**944** A382 90c multicolored 1.90 1.90

See Offices in Geneva No. 475, Vienna No. 403, Switzerland No. 9O21.

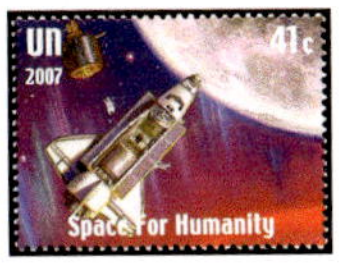

Space for Humanity — A383

41c, Space Shuttle. 90c, Astronauts spacewalking. $1, International Space Station.

**2007, Oct. 25 Litho. *Perf. 13½x14***

**945** A383 41c multicolored .85 .85
**946** A383 90c multicolored 1.90 1.90

**Souvenir Sheet**

**947** A383 $1 multicolored 2.50 2.50
*a.* With World Space Week emblem in margin 3.00 3.00

See Offices in Geneva Nos. 476-478, Vienna Nos. 409-411.

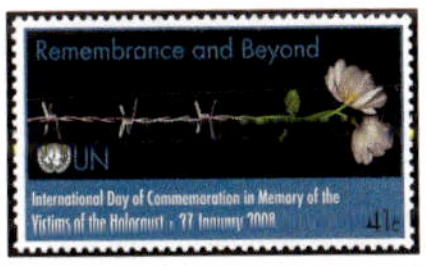

Intl. Holocaust Remembrance Day — A384

**2008, Jan. 27 Litho. *Perf. 13***

**948** A384 41c multicolored .85 .85

See Offices in Geneva No. 479, Vienna No. 412, Israel No. 1715.

**Endangered Species Type of 1993**

No. 949, South African fur seal. No. 950, Orange cup coral. No. 951, Longsnout seahorse. No. 952, Gray whale.

**2008, Mar. 6 Litho. *Perf. 12¾x12½***

**949** A271 41c multicolored 1.00 1.00
**950** A271 41c multicolored 1.00 1.00
**941** A271 41c multicolored 1.00 1.00
**952** A271 41c multicolored 1.00 1.00
*a.* Block of 4, #949-952 4.50 4.50

See Offices in Geneva Nos. 480-483; Vienna Nos. 417-420.

**Flags and Coins Type of 2006**

No. 953 — Flag of: a, United Kingdom, 2 pound coin. b, Singapore, 5 dollar coin. c, Colombia, 500 peso coin. d, Sri Lanka, 10 rupee coin. e, Philippines, 1 peso coin. f, Indonesia, 500 rupiah coin. g, United Arab Emirates, 1 dirham coin. h, Libya, 50 dinar coin.

**2008, May 8 Litho. *Perf. 13¼x13***

**953** Sheet of 8 7.00 7.00
*a.-h.* A375 41c Any single .85 .85

A column of rouletting in the middle of the sheet separates it into two parts. See Offices in Geneva No. 484; Vienna No. 421.

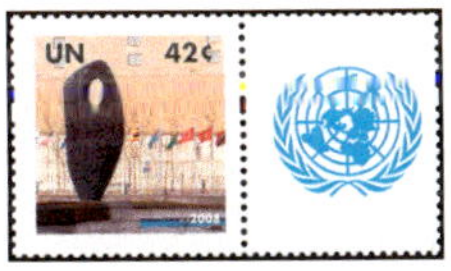

Sculpture and Flags A385

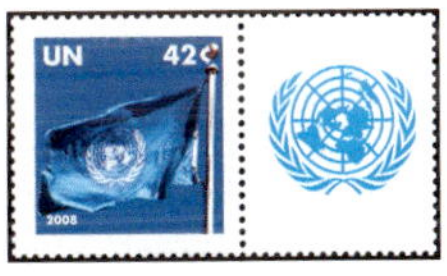

UN Flag A386

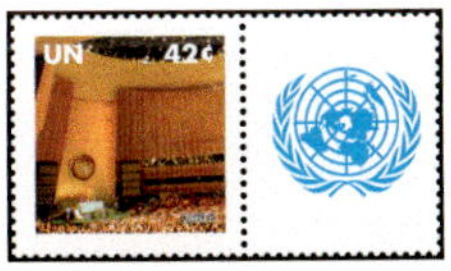

UN General Assembly A387

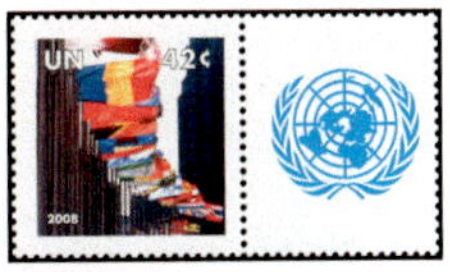

Flags A388

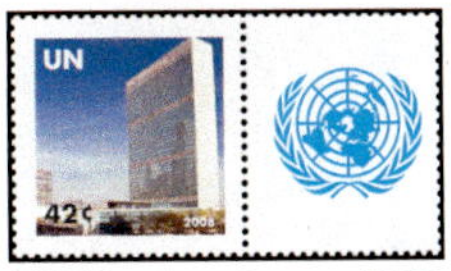

UN Headquarters — A389

**2008, May 12 Litho. *Perf. 13¼***

**954** A385 42c multi + label *3.50* 3.50
**955** A386 42c multi + label *3.50* 3.50
**956** A387 42c multi + label *3.50* 3.50
**957** A388 42c multi + label *3.50* 3.50
**958** A389 42c multi + label *3.50* 3.50
*a.* Vert. strip of 5, #954-958, + 5 labels *17.50* *17.50*

The full sheet sold for $14.95 with or without personalized labels. The personalization of labels was available only at UN Headquarters, and not through mail order.

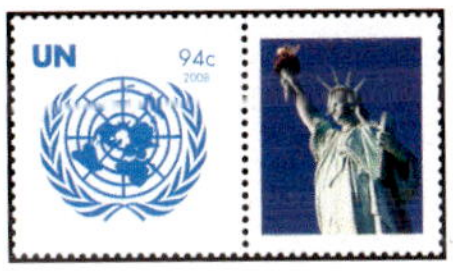

UN Emblem A390

**2008, May 12 Litho. *Perf. 13¼***

**959** A390 94c blue + label *4.50* *4.50*

The full sheet sold for $14.95 with or without labels that could be personalized. There are five non-personalized labels. The personalization of labels was available only at UN Headquarters, and not through mail order.

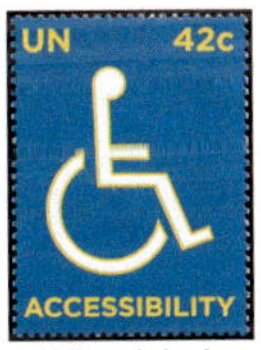

Wheelchair Accessibility Symbol A391

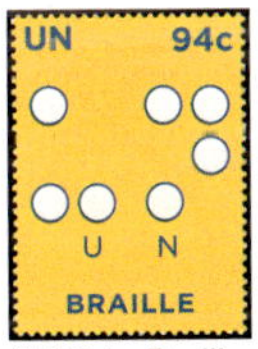

"UN" in Braille A392

**Litho. & Embossed**

**2008, June 6 *Perf. 14x13¼***

**960** A391 42c blue & yellow .85 .85
**961** A392 94c yellow & blue 1.90 1.90

Convention on the Rights of Persons with Disabilities. See Offices in Geneva Nos. 485-486, Vienna Nos. 427-428.

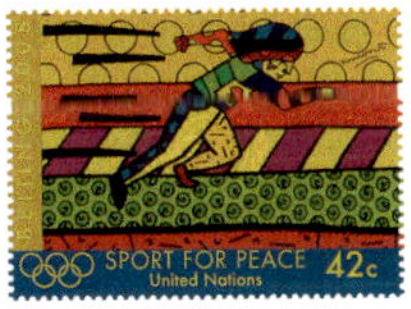

Sport for Peace A393

42c, $1.25, Sprinter. 94c, Hurdler.

**2008, Aug. 8 Litho. *Perf. 14½***

**962** A393 42c multicolored .85 .85
**963** A393 94c multicolored 1.90 1.90

**Souvenir Sheet**

***Perf. 12¾x13¼***

**964** A393 $1.25 multicolored 6.00 6.00

2008 Summer Olympics, Beijing. See Offices in Geneva Nos. 487-489, Vienna Nos. 429-431.

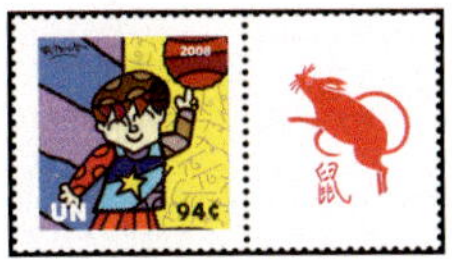

Sport for Peace A394

**2008, Aug. 8 Litho. *Perf. 13¼***

**965** A394 94c multi + label *3.75* *3.75*

2008 Summer Olympics, Beijing. The full pane sold for $14.95 with or without personalized labels. There are two non-personalized labels. The personalization of labels was available only at UN Headquarters, and not through mail order.

No. 965 is often collected as a single stamp with the two different labels attached; value thus $6.50.

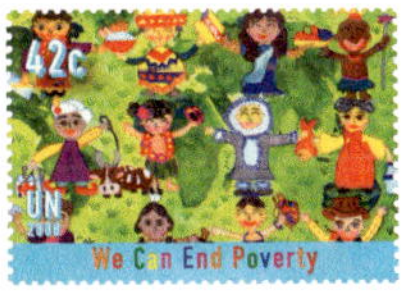

"We Can End Poverty" A395

Winning designs in children's art contest by: 42c, Grace Tsang, Hong Kong. 94c, Bryan Jevoncia, Indonesia, vert.

***Perf. 12¾x12½***

**2008, Sept. 18 Litho.**

**966** A395 42c multicolored .85 .85

***Perf. 12½x12¾***

**967** A395 94c multicolored 1.90 1.90

See Offices in Geneva Nos. 490-491, Vienna Nos. 432-433.

**Climate Change Types of Geneva and Vienna and**

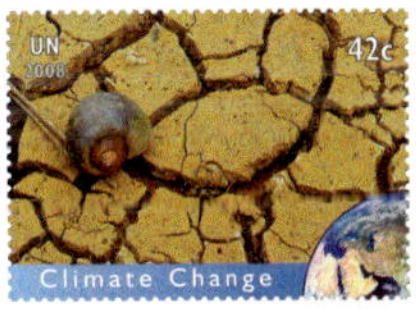

A396

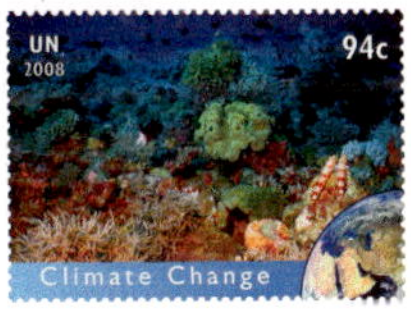

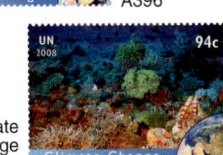

Climate Change A397

No. 968 — Parched ground and snail shell with quarter of Earth in: a, LR. b, LL. c, UR. d, UL.

No. 969 — Coral reef with quarter of Earth in: a, LR. b, LL. c, UR. d, UL.

No. 970: a, Like #969a. b, Like #969b. c, Like #969c. d, Like #969d. e, Like Geneva #400a. f, Like Geneva #493b. g, Like Geneva #493c. h, Like Geneva #493d. i, Like Vienna #434a. j, Like Vienna #434b. k, Like Vienna #434c. l, Like Vienna #434d. m, Like Geneva #492a. n, Like Geneva #492b. o, Like Geneva #492c. p, Like Geneva #492d. q, Like Vienna #435a. r, Like Vienna #435b. s, Like Vienna #435c. t, Like Vienna #435d.

All stamps have blue panels inscribed "Climate Change."

**2008, Oct. 23 Litho. *Perf. 13¼x13***

**968** Sheet of 4 4.75 4.75
*a.-d.* A396 42c Any single 1.10 1.10
*e.* Booklet pane of 4, #968a-968d 8.00 8.00
**969** Sheet of 4 10.00 10.00
*a.-d.* A397 94c Any single 2.50 2.50

**Souvenir Booklet**

**970** Booklet, #968e, 970u-970y 20.00
*a.-d.* A397 27c Any single .75 .75
*e.-h.* G77 27c Any single .75 .75
*i.-l.* V72 27c Any single .75 .75
*m.-p.* G76 42c Any single 1.00 1.00
*q.-t.* V73 42c Any single 1.00 1.00
*u.* Booklet pane of 4, #970a-970d 3.00 3.00
*v.* Booklet pane of 4, #970e-970h 3.00 3.00
*w.* Booklet pane of 4, #970i-970l 3.00 3.00
*x.* Booklet pane of 4, #970m-970p 4.00 4.00
*y.* Booklet pane of 4, #970q-970t 4.00 4.00

No. 970 sold for $9. See Offices in Geneva Nos. 492-494, Vienna Nos. 434-436.

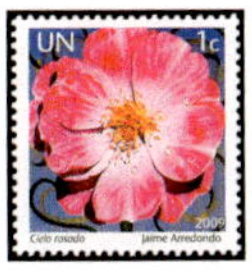

A398

Designs: 1c, Cielo rosado. 9c, Rosa de sangre. 10c, Espíritu de mujer.

**2009, Feb. 6 Litho. *Perf. 13¼***

**971** A398 1c multicolored .30 .30
**972** A398 9c multicolored .30 .30
**973** A398 10c multicolored .30 .30
*Nos. 971-973 (3)* .90 .90

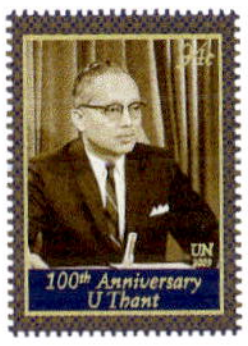

A399

**Litho. With Foil Application**

**2009, Feb. 6 *Perf. 14x13½***

**974** A399 94c purple & multi 2.00 2.00

See Offices in Geneva No. 495, Vienna No. 437.

**Endangered Species Type of 1993**

No. 975, Emperor dragonfly. No. 976, Southern wood ant. No. 977, Rosalia longicorn. No. 978, Apollo butterfly.

**2009, Apr. 16 Litho. *Perf. 12¾x12½***

**975** A271 42c multicolored 1.25 1.25
**976** A271 42c multicolored 1.25 1.25
**977** A271 42c multicolored 1.25 1.25
**978** A271 42c multicolored 1.25 1.25
*a.* Block of 4, #975-978 5.50 5.50
*b.* Pane of 16, imperf. *5,000.*

See Offices in Geneva Nos. 496-499; Vienna Nos. 438-441.

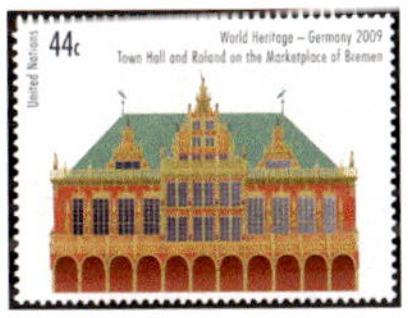

A400

Nos. 979, 981a, Town Hall and Roland on the Marketplace, Bremen. Nos. 980, 981d, Aachen Cathedral. No. 981b, Wartburg Castle. No. 981c, Palaces and Parks of Potsdam and Berlin. No. 981e, Luther Memorials in Eisleben and Wittenberg. No. 981f, Monastic Island of Reichenau.

**2009, May 7 Litho. *Perf. 14x13½***

**979** A400 44c multicolored .90 .90
**980** A400 98c multicolored 2.00 2.00

**Souvenir Booklet**

**981** Booklet, #981g-981l 20.00
*a.-c.* A400 27c any single .60 .60
*d.-f.* A400 42c any single 1.00 1.00
*g.* Booklet pane of 4 #981a 2.40 2.40
*h.* Booklet pane of 4 #981b 2.40 2.40
*i.* Booklet pane of 4 #981c 2.40 2.40
*j.* Booklet pane of 4 #981d 4.00 4.00
*k.* Booklet pane of 4 #981e 4.00 4.00
*l.* Booklet pane of 4 #981f 4.00 4.00

See Offices in Geneva Nos. 500-502, Vienna Nos. 442-444.

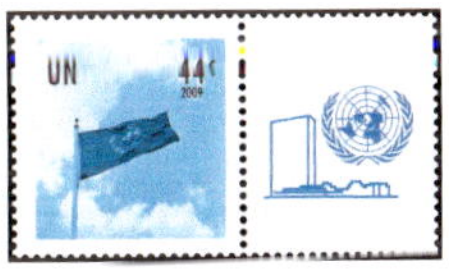

UN Flag A401

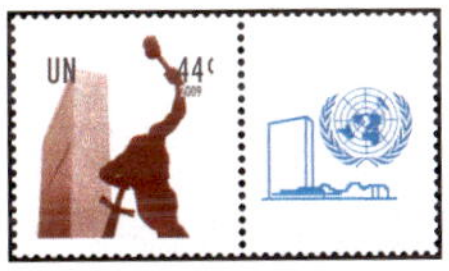

Let Us Beat Swords Into Plowshares, Sculpture by Evgeny Vuchetich — A402

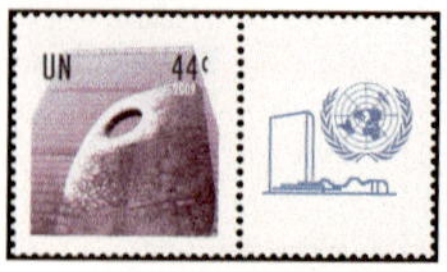

Single Form, Sculpture by Barbara Hepworth A403

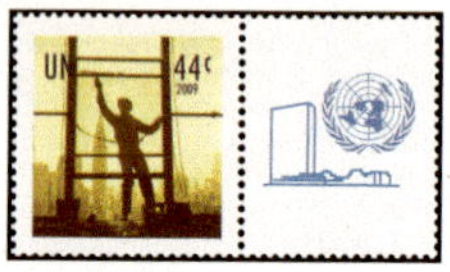

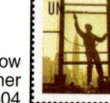

Window Cleaner A404

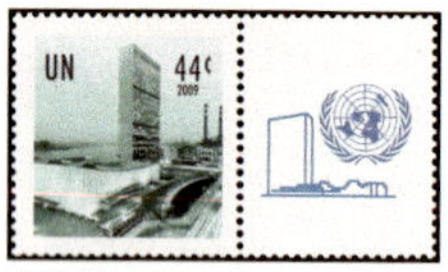

UN Headquarters — A405

**2009, June 5** ***Perf. 13¼***

**982** A401 44c multi + label 2.00 2.00
*a.* Perf. 11¼x11 + label 10.00 10.00
*b.* Perf. 14¼x14½ + label 1.80 1.80
**983** A402 44c multi + label 2.00 2.00
*a.* Perf. 11¼x11 + label 10.00 10.00
*b.* Perf. 14¼x14½ + label 1.80 1.80
**984** A403 44c multi + label 2.00 2.00
*a.* Perf. 11¼x11 + label 10.00 10.00
*b.* Perf. 14¼x14½ + label 1.80 1.80
**985** A404 44c multi + label 2.00 2.00
*a.* Perf. 11¼x11 + label 10.00 10.00
*b.* Perf. 14¼x14½ + label 1.80 1.80
**986** A405 44c multi + label 2.00 2.00
*a.* Perf. 11¼x11 + label 10.00 10.00
*b.* Perf. 14¼x14½ + label 1.80 1.80
*c.* Vert. strip of 5, #982-986, + 5 labels 10.00 10.00
*d.* Vert. strip of 5, #982a-986a, + 5 labels 50.00 50.00
*e.* Vert. strip of 5, #982b-986b, + 5 labels 9.00 7.50

The full sheets sold for $14.95 with or without personalized labels. The personalization of labels was available only at UN Headquarters, and not through mail order. The sheet of No. 986d has "ver. 2" in the lower right selvage. The sheet of No. 986e has "Ver. 3" in the lower right selvage.

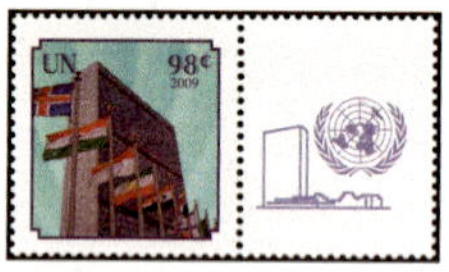

Flags and UN Headquarters — A406

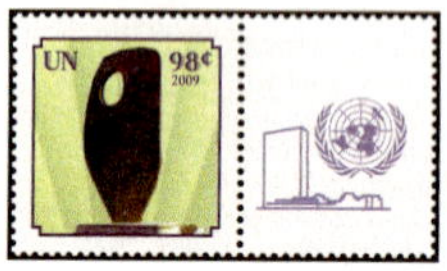

Single Form, Sculpture by Barbara Hepworth A407

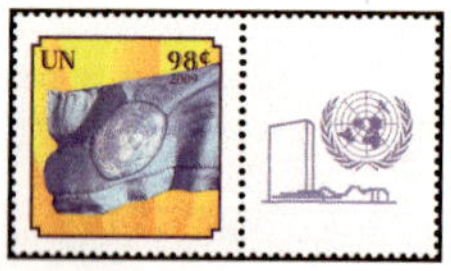

UN Flag A408

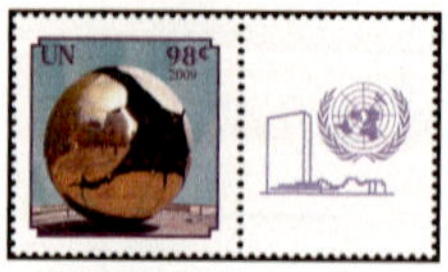

Sphere Within a Sphere, Sculpture by Arnaldo Pomodoro A409

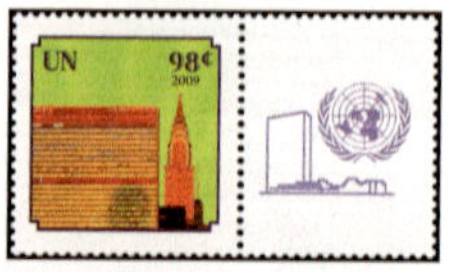

UN Headquarters and Chrysler Building — A410

**2009, June 5**

**987** A406 98c multi + label 4.00 4.00
*a.* Perf. 11¼x11 + label 9.00 9.00
*b.* Perf. 14¼x14½ + label 3.50 3.50
**988** A407 98c multi + label 4.00 4.00
*a.* Perf. 11¼x11 + label 9.00 9.00
*b.* Perf. 14¼x14½ + label 3.50 3.50
**989** A408 98c multi + label 4.00 4.00
*a.* Perf. 11¼x11 + label 9.00 9.00
*b.* Perf. 14¼x14½ + label 3.50 3.50
**990** A409 98c multi + label 4.00 4.00
*a.* Perf. 11¼x11 + label 9.00 9.00
*b.* Perf. 14¼x14½ + label 3.50 3.50
**991** A410 98c multi + label 4.00 4.00
*a.* Perf. 11¼x11 + label 9.00 9.00
*b.* Perf. 14¼x14½ + label 3.50 3.50
*c.* Vert. strip of 5, #987-991, + 5 labels 20.00 20.00
*d.* Vert. strip of 5, #987a-991a, + 5 labels 45.00 45.00
*e.* Vert. strip of 5, #987b-991b, + 5 labels 17.50 17.50

The full sheets sold for $14.95 with or without personalized labels. The personalization of labels was available only at UN Headquarters, and not through mail order. The sheet of No. 991d has "ver. 2" in the lower right selvage. The sheet of No. 991e has "VER. 3" in the lower right selvage.

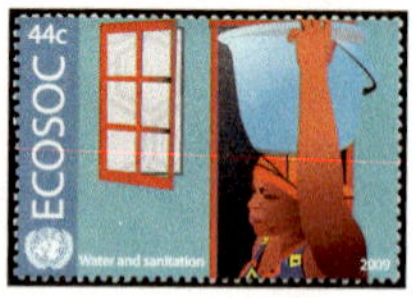


Economic and Social Council A411

Designs: 44c, Water and sanitation. 98c, Traditional medicines.

**2009, Aug. 6** ***Perf. 12¾x12½***

**992** A411 44c multicolored 2.00 .90
**993** A411 98c multicolored 5.00 2.00

See Offices in Geneva Nos. 503-504, Vienna Nos. 450-451.

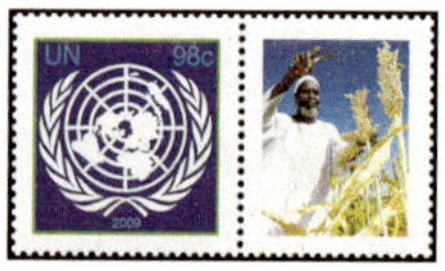

UN Emblem A412

**2009, Sept. 22** ***Perf. 13¼***

**994** A412 98c multi + label 5.50 5.50
*a.* Perf. 11¼x11 + label 5.00 5.00

The full sheets sold for $14.95 with or without personalized labels. There are five different non-personalized labels. The personalization of labels was available only at UN Headquarters, and not through mail order. The sheet of No. 994a has "ver. 2" in the lower right selvage.

Miniature Sheet

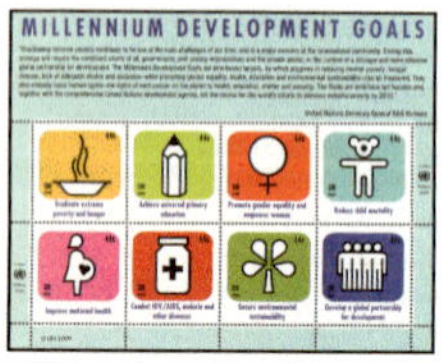


Millennium Development Goals — A413

No. 995: a, Bowl of hot food. b, Pencil. c, Female symbol. d, Teddy bear. e, Pregnant woman, heart. f, Medicine bottle. g, Stylized tree. h, Conjoined people.

**2009, Sept. 25**

**995** A413 Sheet of 8 8.50 8.50
*a.-h.* 44c Any single 1.20 1.20

See Offies in Geneva No. 505; Vienna No. 457.

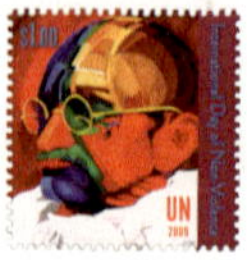

Mohandas K. Gandhi — A414

**2009, Oct. 2**

**996** A414 $1 multicolored 2.25 2.25

Miniature Sheet

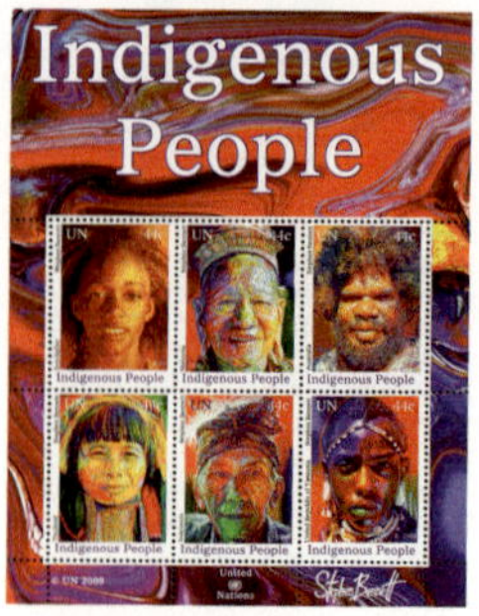


Indigenous People — A415

No. 997 — Portraits of person from: a, Seychelles. b, Malaysia. c, Australia. d, Thailand. e, Indonesia. f, Tanzania.

**2009, Oct. 8** ***Perf. 12½***

**997** A415 Sheet of 6 7.00 7.00
*a.-f.* 44c Any single 1.15 1.15

See Offices in Geneva No. 511, Vienna No. 458.

### Flags and Coins Type of 2006

No. 998 — Flag of: a, Bahamas, 10 cent coin. b, Jamaica, 20 dollar coin. c, Honduras, 50 centavo coin. d, Kuwait, 100 fils coin. e, Panama, 1 cuarto de Balboa coin. f, Guatemala, 50 centavo coin. g, St. Lucia, 1 cent coin. h, Yemen, 20 rial coin.

**2010, Feb. 5 Litho.** ***Perf. 13¼x13***

**998** Sheet of 8 9.75 9.75
*a.-h.* A375 44c Any single 1.20 1.20

A column of rouletting in the middle of the sheet separates it into two parts. See Offices in Geneva No. 512; Vienna No. 459.

### Endangered Species Type of 1993

No. 999, Monkey puzzle tree. No. 1000, Quiver tree. No. 1001, Bristlecone pine tree. No. 1002, Scarlet ball cactus.

**2010, Apr. 15 Litho.** ***Perf. 12¾x12½***

**999** A271 44c multicolored 1.25 1.25
**1000** A271 44c multicolored 1.25 1.25
**1001** A271 44c multicolored 1.25 1.25
**1002** A271 44c multicolored 1.25 1.25
*a.* Block of 4, #999-1002 5.50 5.50

See Offices in Geneva Nos. 513-516; Vienna Nos. 465-468.

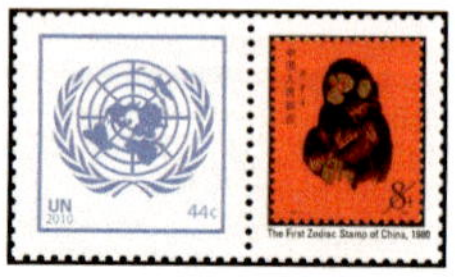

The stamp pictured above was printed in limited quantities and sold for far more than face value. The label attached to the stamp could not be personalized. Value for stamp and label, $3. A similar stamp dated "2011" with a different label attached exists.

### One Planet, One Ocean Types of Geneva and Vienna and

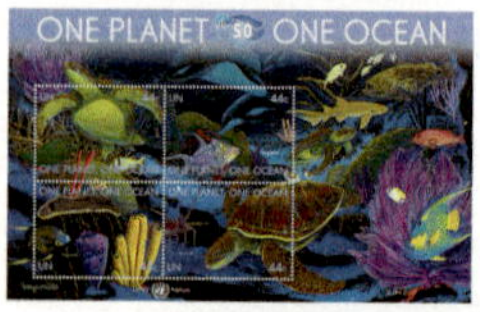


A416

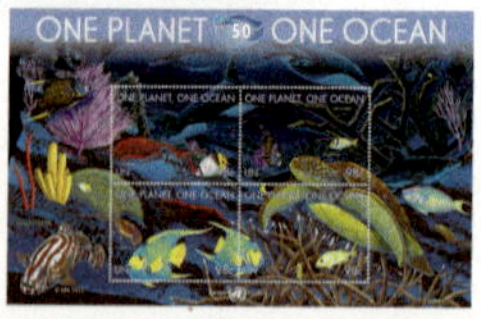


One Planet, One Ocean A417

No. 1003: a, Turtle at top, eel at left, fish at LR. b, Fish at LL, turtle's flipper at bottom. c, Fish at left, yellow sponge at LR, Lobster at right. d, Lobster at left, turtle at right.

No. 1004: a, Octopus at left, fish at LR. b, Fish at left and right, turtle's head at bottom. c, Lobster at left. fish at LL and LR. d, Fish at LL and LR, turtle's body at UR.

No. 1005: a, Like #1003a. b, Like #1003b, c, Like #1003c, d, Like #1003d. e, Like Vienna #471a. f, Like Vienna #471b. g, Like Vienna #471c, h, Like Vienna #471d. i, Like Geneva #519a. j, Like Geneva #519b, k, Like Geneva #519c. l, Like Geneva #519d. m, Like #1004a. n, Like #1004b. o, Like #1004c, p, Like #1004d. q, Like Vienna #472a. r, Like Vienna #472b. s, Like Vienna #472c. t, Like Vienna #472d. u, Like Geneva #520a. v, Like Geneva #520b. w, Like Geneva #520c. x, Like Geneva #520d.

**2010, May 6 Litho.** ***Perf. 14x13¼***

**1003** A416 Sheet of 4 3.60 3.60
*a.-d.* 44c Any single .90 .90
**1004** A417 Sheet of 4 8.00 8.00
*a.-d.* 98c Any single 2.00 2.00

**Souvenir Booklet**

***Perf. 13¼x13***

**1005** Booklet, #1005y-1005z, 1005aa-1005ad 18.00
*a.-d.* A416 28c any single .60 .60
*e.-h.* V91 28c any single .60 .60
*i.-l.* G85 28c any single .60 .60
*m.-p.* A417 44c any single .90 .90
*q.-t.* V92 44c any single .90 .90
*u.-x.* G86 44c any single .90 .90
*y.* Booklet pane of 4 #1005a-1005d 2.40 2.40
*z.* Booklet pane of 4 #1005e-1005h 2.40 2.40
*aa.* Booklet pane of 4 #1005i-1005l 2.40 2.40
*ab.* Booklet pane of 4 #1005m-1005p 3.60 3.60
*ac.* Booklet pane of 4 #1005q-1005t 3.60 3.60
*ad.* Booklet pane of 4 #1005u-1005x 3.60 3.60

Intl. Oceanographic Commission, 50th anniv. See Offices in Geneva Nos. 519-521, Vienna Nos. 471-473.

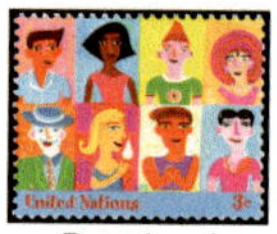

People of Different Cultures A418

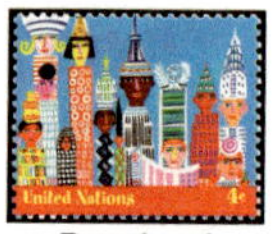

People of Different Cultures as New York Buildings A419

**2010, June 4 Litho.** ***Perf. 13***

**1006** A418 3c multicolored .25 .25
**1007** A419 4c multicolored .25 .25

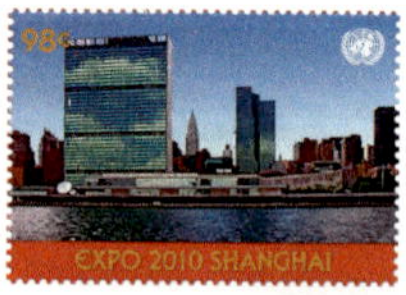


UN Headquarters and New York Skyline A420

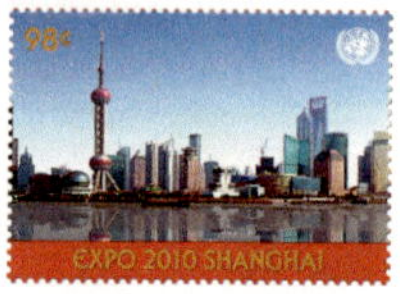


Shanghai Skyline A421

**2010, June 4 Litho.** ***Perf. 13¼***

**1008** A420 98c multicolored 3.00 3.00
**1009** A421 98c multicolored 3.00 3.00
*a.* Horiz. pair, #1008-1009 6.00 6.00

Expo 2010, Shanghai. Nos. 1008-1009 were sold only in full panes for $14.95.

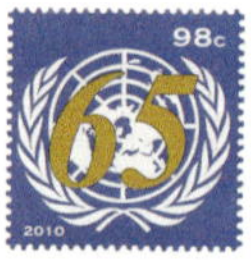

United Nations, 65th Anniv. — A422

**Litho. With Foil Application**

**2010, June 28** ***Perf. 13¼***

**1010** A422 98c light blue & gold 2.25 2.25

**Souvenir Sheet**

**1011** Sheet of 2 #1011a 5.00 5.00
*a.* A422 98c dark blue & gold 2.50 2.50

See Offices in Geneva No. 522, Vienna No. 474.

# UNITED NATIONS, OFFICES IN NEW YORK

 A423

 A424

 A425

A426

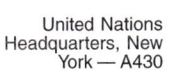 

United Nations Sea Transport — A427

**2010, Sept. 2    Litho.    Perf. 13¼x13**
| 1012 | A423 | 44c multicolored | .90 | .90 |
| 1013 | A424 | 44c multicolored | .90 | .90 |
| 1014 | A425 | 44c multicolored | .90 | .90 |
| 1015 | A426 | 44c multicolored | .90 | .90 |
| 1016 | A427 | 44c multicolored | .90 | .90 |
| a. | Horiz. strip of 5, #1012-1016 | | 5.00 | 5.00 |

See Offices in Geneva Nos. 523-527; Vienna Nos. 475-479.

Intl. Year of Biodiversity — A428

Drawings from Art Forms from Nature, by Ernst Heinrich: 15c, Hummingbird. $1.50, Liverwort.

**2010, Oct. 18    Litho.    Perf. 13**
| 1017 | A428 | 15c multicolored | .30 | .30 |
| 1018 | A428 | $1.50 multicolored | 3.00 | 3.00 |

See Offices in Geneva Nos. 517-518; Vienna Nos. 469-470.

Miniature Sheet

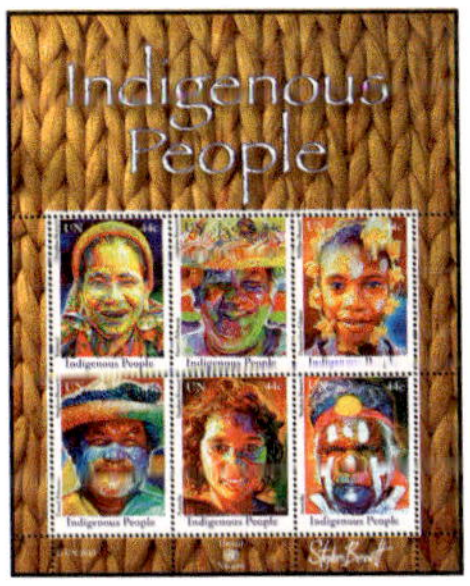

Indigenous People — A429

No. 1019 — Portraits of person from: a, Thailand. b, French Polynesia (woman, denomination in black). c, Papua New Guinea. d, French Polynesia (man, denomination in white). e, Australia (child). f, Australia (old man with headband).

**2010, Oct. 21    Litho.    Perf. 13**
| 1019 | A429 | Sheet of 6 | 6.00 | 6.00 |
| a.-f. | 44c Any single | | 1.00 | 1.00 |

See Offices in Geneva No. 529; Vienna No. 480.

United Nations Headquarters, New York — A430

United Nations Headquarters: 11c, Aerial view. $5, Ground-level view.

**2011, Feb. 4    Litho.    Perf. 13**
| 1020 | A430 | 11c multicolored | .25 | .25 |
| 1021 | A430 | $5 multicolored | 9.00 | 9.00 |

See Offices in Geneva Nos. 530-531; Vienna Nos. 481-482.

### Flags and Coins Type of 2006

No. 1022 — Flag of: a, Mauritius, 1 rupee coin. b, Guyana, 10 dollar coin. c, Timor, 5 cent coin. d, Iceland, 100 krónur coin. e, Chile, 1 peso coin. f, Norway, 20 kroner coin. g, Fiji, 50 cent coin. h, Comoro Islands, 100 franc coin.

**2011, Mar. 3    Litho.    Perf. 13¼x13**
| 1022 | | Sheet of 8 | 9.00 | 8.75 |
| a.-h. | A375 44c Any single | | 1.10 | 1.10 |

A column of roulettling in the middle of the sheet separates it into two parts. See Offices in Geneva No. 532; Vienna No. 483.

  UN Emblem A431

**2011, Apr. 7    Litho.    Perf. 14¾**
| 1023 | A431 | 98c blue + label | 4.00 | 4.00 |

Printed in sheets of 10 + 10 different labels which are not personalizable. The full sheet sold for $14.95.

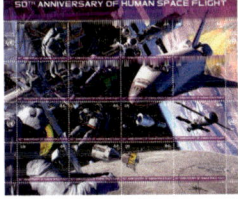

Human Space Flight, 50th Anniv. A432

No. 1024: Various parts of outer space scene.
No. 1025: a, Cosmonaut and rocket. b, Astronaut on ladder of Lunar Module.

**2011, Apr. 12    Litho.    Perf. 13x13¼**
| 1024 | A432 | Sheet of 16 | 16.00 | 16.00 |
| a.-p. | 44c any single | | 1.00 | 1.00 |

### Souvenir Sheet
| 1025 | A432 | Sheet of 2 | 15.00 | 15.00 |
| a. | 44c multi | | 4.50 | 4.50 |
| b. | 98c multi | | 11.50 | 11.50 |

See Offices in Geneva Nos. 533-534; Vienna Nos. 484-485. No. 1024 contains two 40x48mm stamps that were printed as part of a larger sheet of six stamps, Vienna No. 485c, which was broken up into its component two-stamp souvenir sheets, and also sold as one unit. Value $75, complete unit.

UNESCO World Heritage Sites in Nordic Countries A433

Designs: 44c, Surtsey Volcanic Island, Iceland. 98c, Drottningholm Castle, Sweden.

**2011, May 5    Litho.    Perf. 14x13½**
| 1026 | A433 | 44c multicolored | .90 | .90 |
| 1027 | A433 | 98c multicolored | 2.00 | 2.00 |

See Offices in Geneva Nos. 535-536; Vienna Nos. 496-497.

AIDS Ribbon — A434

**2011, June 3    Litho.    Die Cut**
**Self-Adhesive**
| 1028 | A434 | 44c red & blue | 1.75 | 1.75 |

See Offices in Geneva No. 537; Vienna No. 498.

Economic and Social Council (ECOSOC) A435

**2011, July 1    Litho.    Perf. 14¼**
| 1029 | A435 | 44c multicolored | 1.50 | 1.50 |
| 1030 | A435 | 98c multicolored | 3.50 | 3.50 |

See Offices in Geneva Nos. 538-539; Vienna Nos. 499-500.

### Endangered Species Type of 1993

Designs: No. 1031, Bali starling. No. 1032, California condor. No. 1033, Japanese crane. No. 1034, Black-fronted piping-guan.

**2011, Sept. 7    Perf. 12¾x12½**
| 1031 | A271 | 44c multicolored | 1.10 | 1.10 |
| 1032 | A271 | 44c multicolored | 1.10 | 1.10 |
| 1033 | A271 | 44c multicolored | 1.10 | 1.10 |
| 1034 | A271 | 44c multicolored | 1.10 | 1.10 |
| a. | Block of 4, #1031-1034 | | 5.00 | 5.00 |

See Offices in Geneva Nos. 540-543; Vienna Nos. 501-504.

Intl. Year of Forests — A436

Designs: 44c, Tree with wildlife, man with mask. 98c, Tree roots.

### Litho. With Foil Application
**2011, Oct. 13    Perf. 12½**
| 1035 | | 44c multicolored | 1.25 | 1.25 |
| 1036 | | 98c multicolored | 2.50 | 2.50 |
| a. | A436 Vert. pair, #1035-1036 | | 3.75 | 3.75 |

See Offices in Geneva Nos. 544-545; Vienna Nos. 505-506.

UN Emblem A437

**2012, Jan. 23    Litho.    Perf. 14¾**
| 1037 | A437 | $1.05 blue + label | 2.75 | 2.75 |
| | | Sheet of 10 + 10 labels | 27.50 | — |

The full sheet sold for $14.95. The generic label exists as shown, and with dragon in yellow against red background. Labels could be personalized. The personalization of labels was available only at UN Headquarters, and not through mail order.

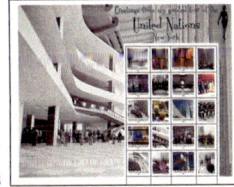

A438

No. 1038: a, Desk in lobby. b, Sculpture of Jesus holding lamb. c, Stained-glass window. d, Meeting room. e, Guided tour. f, Flags in front of United Nations buildings. g, United Nations Peacekeepers helmet in showcase. h, Gift shop. i, View of curved floors above lobby. j, Street signs.

**2012, Jan. 23    Litho.    Perf. 14¾**
| 1038 | A438 | Sheet of 10 | 30.00 | 30.00 |
| a.-j. | $1.05 Any single + label | | 3.00 | 3.00 |

The full sheet sold for $14.95. The generic labels are shown. Labels could be personalized. The personalization of labels was available only at UN Headquarters, and not through mail order.

### Flags and Coins Type of 2006

No. 1039 — Flag of: a, Nepal, 1 rupee coin. b, Bahrain, 100 fils coin. c, Paraguay, 1000 guarani coin. d, Ethiopia, 25 cent coin. e, Peru, 1 sol coin. f, Solomon Islands, 20 cent coin. g, Dominican Republic, 1 peso coin. h, Canada, 1 dollar coin.

**2012, Feb. 3    Litho.    Perf. 13¼x13**
| 1039 | | Sheet of 8 | 7.25 | 7.25 |
| a.-h. | A375 45c Any single | | .90 | .90 |

A column of roulettling in the middle of the sheet separates it into two parts. See Offices in Geneva No. 546; Vienna No. 507.

 A439

Autism Awareness — A440

Drawings by autistic people: No. 1040, An Abstract Garden II, by Trent Altman, U.S. No. 1041, Crazy Love, by Hannah Kandel, U.S.

**2012, Apr. 2    Litho.    Perf. 14x13½**
| 1040 | A439 | $1.05 multicolored | 2.10 | 2.10 |
| 1041 | A440 | $1.05 multicolored | 2.10 | 2.10 |
| a. | Pair, #1040-1041 | | 4.20 | 4.20 |

See Offices in Geneva Nos. 547-548; Vienna Nos. 508-509.

### Endangered Species Type of 1993

Designs: No. 1042, Giant panda. No. 1043, Short-horned chameleon. No. 1044, Oncilla. No. 1045, Cotton-headed tamarin.

**2012, Apr. 10    Litho.    Perf. 12¾x12½**
| 1042 | A271 | 45c multicolored | 1.10 | 1.10 |
| 1043 | A271 | 45c multicolored | 1.10 | 1.10 |
| 1044 | A271 | 45c multicolored | 1.10 | 1.10 |
| 1045 | A271 | 45c multicolored | 1.10 | 1.10 |
| a. | Block of 4, #1042-1045 | | 5.00 | 5.00 |

See Offices in Geneva Nos. 549-552; Vienna Nos. 511-514.

Tinker Bell A441

Tinker Bell A442

**2012, June 1    Litho.    Perf. 14¾**
| 1046 | A441 | $1.05 multi + label | 3.00 | 3.00 |
| 1047 | A442 | $1.05 multi + label | 3.00 | 3.00 |
| a. | Vert. pair, #1046-1047, + 2 labels | | 6.00 | 6.00 |
| | Sheet of 10, 5 each #1046-1047, + 10 labels | | 30.00 | 30.00 |

The full sheet sold for $14.95. The generic labels are shown. Labels could be personalized. The personalization of labels was available only at UN Headquarters, and not through mail order.

# UNITED NATIONS, OFFICES IN NEW YORK

Rio + 20 Conference on Sustainable Development, Rio de Janeiro — A443

**2012, June 1   Litho.   Perf. 13x13¼**
1048  A443  $1.05 multicolored   2.10  2.10

See Offices in Geneva No. 553; Vienna No. 515.

Sport for Peace A444

2012 Paralympics events: 45c, Goalball. $1.05, Sitting volleyball.

**Litho. With Foil Application**
**2012, Aug. 17   Perf. 14½**
1049  A444   45c multicolored   .90  .90
1050  A444  $1.05 multicolored  2.10 2.10
 a.   Souvenir sheet of 1        3.50 3.50

See Offices in Geneva Nos. 554-555; Vienna Nos. 516-517.

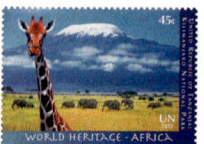

UNESCO World Heritage Sites in Africa — A445

Designs: 45c, Kilamanjaro National Park, Tanzania. $1.05, Old Towns of Djenné, Mali.

**2012, Sept. 5   Litho.   Perf. 13¼**
1051  A445   45c multicolored   .90  .90
1052  A445  $1.05 multicolored  2.10 2.10

See Offices in Geneva Nos. 556-557; Vienna Nos. 518-519.

**Miniature Sheet**

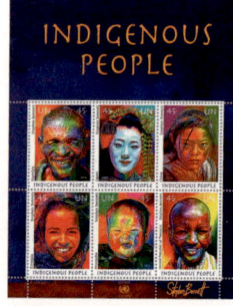

Indigenous People — A446

No. 1053 — Portrait of person from: a, Namibia. b, Japan. c, China. d, Ethiopia. e, Mongolia. f, Tanzania.

**2012, Oct. 11   Litho.   Perf. 13¼x13**
1053  A446  Sheet of 6         5.50 5.50
 a.-f.  45c Any single          .90  .90

See Offices in Geneva No. 558; Vienna No. 520.

UN Emblem A447

**2013, Jan. 28   Litho.   Perf. 14¾**
1054  A447  $1.10 multi + label  4.00 4.00
       Sheet of 10 + 10 labels  40.00

The full sheet sold for $14.95. The generic label exists as shown, and with snake against red background. Labels could be personalized. The personalization of labels was available only at UN Headquarters, and not through mail order.

A448

No. 1055: a, Flags in front of Secretariat Building, brown panel at right. b, Aerial view of headquarters and East River, yellow orange panel at left. c, Secretariat Building and wall of General Assembly building, yellow orange panel at left. d, Headquarters and East River, brown panel at right. e, General Asembly and Secretariat Buildings, flags at right, brown panel at right. f, Sculpture and fountain at night, yellow orange panel at left. g, Secretariat Building and cherry blossoms, yellow orange panel at left. h, Secretariat Building, trees without leaves, flags at left, brown panel at right. i, Aerial view of headquarters at night, brown panel at right. j, Headquarters, yellow panel at left.

**2013, Jan. 28   Litho.   Perf. 14¾**
1055  A448  Sheet of 10       30.00 30.00
 a.-j.  $1.10 Any single + label  3.00 3.00

The full sheet sold for $14.95. The generic labels are shown. Labels could be personalized. The personalization of labels was available only at UN Headquarters, and not through mail order.

World Radio Day — A449

Designs: 46c, Radio antenna. $1.10, Audrey Hepburn at microphone.

**2013, Feb. 13   Litho.   Perf. 13¼x13**
1056  A449   46c multicolored   .95  .95
1057  A449  $1.10 multicolored  2.25 2.25

See Offices in Geneva Nos. 559-560; Vienna Nos. 521-522.

Circle of People A450    United Nations Headquarters A451

**2013, Mar. 5   Litho.   Perf. 14x13½**
1058  A450  $1.10 multicolored  2.25 2.25

**Perf. 13½x14**
1059  A451   $3 multicolored    6.00 6.00

See Offices in Geneva Nos. 561-562; Vienna Nos. 523-524.

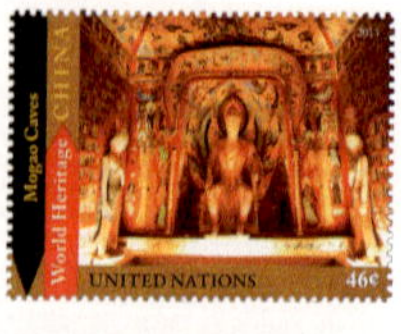

World Heritage Sites, China A452

Designs: Nos. 1060, 1062a, Mogao Caves. No. 1061, 1062d, Imperial Palace, Beijing. No. 1062b, Potala Palace, Lhasa. No. 1062c, Great Wall of China. No. 1062e, Mount Huangshan. No. 1062f, Mausoleum of the First Qing Emperor.

**2013, Apr. 11   Litho.   Perf. 14x13½**
1060  A452   46c multicolored   .95  .95
1061  A452  $1.10 multicolored  2.25 2.25

**Souvenir Booklet**
1062   Booklet, #1062g-
        1062l                  20.00
 a.-c.  A452 33c any single     .70  .70
 d.-f.  A452 46c any single     .95  .95
 g.   Booklet pane of 4 #1062a  2.80
 h.   Booklet pane of 4 #1062b  2.80  —
 i.   Booklet pane of 4 #1062c  2.80  —
 j.   Booklet pane of 4 #1062d  3.80  —
 k.   Booklet pane of 4 #1062e  3.80  —
 l.   Booklet pane of 4 #1062f  3.80  —

See Offices in Geneva Nos. 563-565, Vienna Nos. 525-527.

## Flag Type of 1980

Printed by Lowe Martin Group, Canada. Designed by Rorie Katz, US. Issued in panes of 16; each pane contains 4 blocks of 4. A se-tenant block of 4 designs centers each pane.

**2013, May 2   Litho.   Perf. 13**
1063  A185  $1.10 Myanmar            2.25 2.25
1064  A185  $1.10 Russian Fed-
             eration                 2.25 2.25
1065  A185  $1.10 South Sudan        2.25 2.25
1066  A185  $1.10 Cape Verde         2.25 2.25
 a.   Block of 4, #1063-1066         15.00 12.00
      Nos. 1063-1066 (4)             9.00  9.00

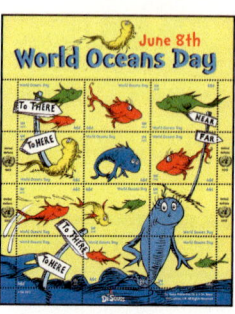

World Oceans Day A453

No. 1067 — Fish from *One Fish, Two Fish, Red Fish, Blue Fish*, by Dr. Seuss: a, Green fish, red fish, sign. b, Red fish facing right. c, Green fish facing left, sign. d, Yellow fish, sign. e, Blue fish. f, Red fish facing left, sign. g, Red fish facing right, water droplets, tail of yellow and red fish, sign. h, Yellow and red fish, green fish, side of blue fish. i, Head of blue fish, sign post. j, Sign and wave. k, Sign, red fish, side and tail of blue fish, wave. l, Side of blue fish, green fish, wave.

**2013, May 31   Litho.   Perf. 13**
1067  A453  Sheet of 12        11.50 11.50
 a.-l.  46c any single          .95  .95

See Offices in Geneva No. 566; Vienna No. 528.

Nebulae — A454

Designs: No. 1068, V838 Mon. No. 1069, WR 25, Tr16-244. 46c, 30 Doradus.

**2013, Aug. 9   Litho.   Perf. 13¼**
1068  A454  $1.10 multicolored  2.25 2.25
1069  A454  $1.10 multicolored  2.25 2.25
 a.   Pair, #1068-1069          4.50 4.50

**Souvenir Sheet**
1070  A454   46c multicolored   2.50 2.50

No. 1070 contains one 44x44mm stamp. See Offices in Geneva Nos. 567-569; Vienna Nos. 529-531.

World Humanitarian Day — A455

No. 1071 — "The World Needs More" in speech balloon in: a, Somali (Uduunku. . .). b, Thai. c, Arabic (people in background). d, Portuguese (O Mundo. . .). e, Russian. f, Korean. g, Swahili (Mahitaji. . .). h, Chinese. i, Urdu (aerial view of village in background). j, English.

**2013, Aug. 19   Litho.   Perf. 14¾**
1071  A455  Sheet of 10       30.00 30.00
 a.-j.  $1.10 Any single + label  3.00 3.00

The full sheet sold for $14.95. The generic labels are shown. Labels could be personalized. The personalization of labels was available only at UN Headquarters, and not through mail order.

Works of Disabled Artists — A456

Designs: 46c, Self-portrait II by Chuck Close, U.S. $1.10, Tears and Laughter, by Josephine King, United Kingdom.

**2013, Sept. 20   Litho.   Perf. 13¼x13**
1072  A456   46c multicolored   .95  .95
1073  A456  $1.10 multicolored  2.25 2.25

See Offices in Geneva Nos. 570-571; Vienna Nos. 532-533.

## Endangered Species Type of 1993

Designs: No. 1074, Asian tapir. No. 1075, Mongoose lemur. No. 1076, Flat-headed cat. No. 1077, Aye-aye.

**2013, Oct. 10   Litho.   Perf. 12¾x12½**
1074  A271  $1.10 multicolored  2.50 2.50
1075  A271  $1.10 multicolored  2.50 2.50
1076  A271  $1.10 multicolored  2.50 2.50
1077  A271  $1.10 multicolored  2.50 2.50
 a.   Block of 4, #1074-1077   11.00 11.00

See Offices in Geneva Nos. 572-575; Vienna Nos. 534-537.

## Flags and Coins Type of 2006

No. 1078 — Flag of: a, Montenegro, 20 cent coin. b, Grenada, 5 cent coin. c, United States, 25 cent coin. d, Gabon, 100 franc coin. e, Palau, 1 cent coin. f, Niger, 100 franc coin. g, Saint Kitts and Nevis, 5 cent coin. h, Venezuela, 1 bolivar coin.

**2013, Nov. 6   Litho.   Perf. 13¼x13**
1078        Sheet of 8           7.75 7.75
 a.-h.  A375 46c Any single       .95  .95

A column of rouletting in the middle of the sheet separates it into two parts. See Offices in Geneva No. 576; Vienna No. 539.

UN Emblem A457

**2014, Jan. 28   Litho.   Perf. 14¾**
1079  A457  $1.15 multi + label  3.00 3.00

A458

No. 1080: a, The Golden Rule, mosaic by Norman Rockwell, dark green panel at right. b, Renovated Delegate's Lounge, yellow green panel at left. c, Renovated ECOSOC Chamber, red brown panel at left. d, Dag Hammarskjold Library, dark blue panel at right. e, Helmet of United Nations Peacekeeper and United Nations Flag, dark blue panel at right. f, United Nations Headquarters, dark green panel at left. g, Renovated Security Council Chamber, yellow green panel at left. h, Flags of member nations, red brown panel at right. i, Mankind's Struggle for Lasting Peace, by José Vela-Zanetti, dark blue panel at right. j, Relational Painting No. 90, by Fritz Glarner, yellow green panel at left.

**2014, Jan. 28   Litho.   Perf. 14¾**
1080  A458  Sheet of 10       30.00 30.00
 a.-j.  $1.15 Any single + label  3.00 3.00

The full sheet sold for $14.95. The generic labels are shown. Labels could be personalized. The personalization of labels was available only at UN Headquarters, and not through mail order.

International Day of Happiness — A459

Designs: 47c, Woman smiling, photograph by Mario Castello, "Happy." $1.15, People kissing on beach, photograph by Henryk T. Kaiser, "Feliz."

**2014, Mar. 17 Litho. *Perf. 13¼x13***

| | | | | | |
|---|---|---|---|---|---|
| **1081** | A459 | 47c multicolored | .95 | .95 |
| **1082** | A459 | $1.15 multicolored | 2.40 | 2.40 |

See Offices in Geneva Nos. 577-578; Vienna Nos. 540-541.

### Flag Type of 1980

Printed by Lowe Martin Group, Canada. Designed by Rorie Katz, U.S. Issued in panes of 16; each pane contains 4 blocks of 4. A se-tenant block of 4 designs centers each pane.

**2014, Mar. 27 Litho. *Perf. 13x13¼***

| | | | | |
|---|---|---|---|---|
| **1083** A185 | $1.15 Afghanistan | 3.50 | 3.00 |
| **1084** A185 | $1.15 Serbia | 3.50 | 3.00 |
| **1085** A185 | $1.15 Cambodia | 3.50 | 3.00 |
| **1086** A185 | $1.15 Democratic Republic of the Congo | 3.50 | 3.00 |
| *a.* | Block of 4, #1083-1086 | 16.00 | 15.00 |
| | *Nos. 1083-1086 (4)* | 14.00 | 12.00 |

Miniature Sheet

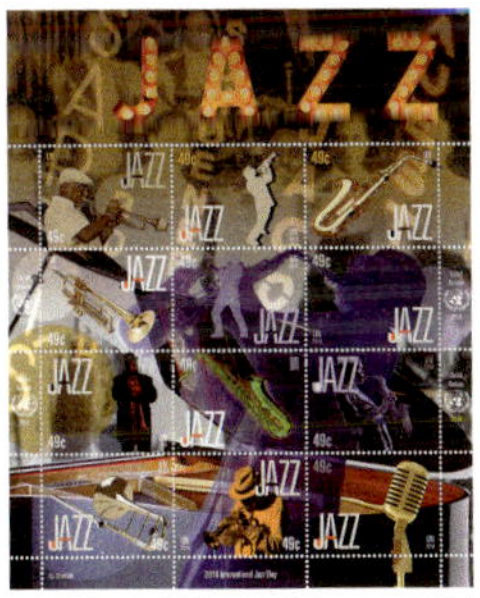


International Year of Jazz — A460

No. 1087: a, Trumpeter with cap and mute in trumpet. b, Silhouette of trumpeter in tan. c, Saxophone. d, Trumpet. e, Silhouette of trumpeter in lilac. f, Saxophonist wearing hat. g, Man with hat holding trombone. h, Green saxophone. i, Saxophonist without hat. j, Trombone. k, Trumpeter wearing hat. l, Microphone.

**2014, Apr. 30 Litho. *Perf. 13x13¼***

| | | | |
|---|---|---|---|
| **1087** A460 | Sheet of 12 | 12.00 | 12.00 |
| | First day cover | | 15.00 |
| *a.-l.* | 49c Any single | 1.00 | 1.00 |

See Offices in Geneva No. 579; Vienna No. 542.

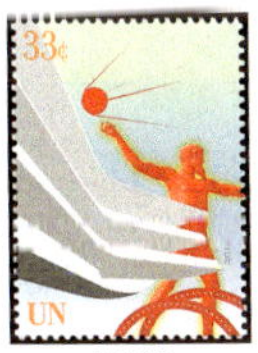


A461

A462

Printed by Lowe-Martin Group, Canada. Panes of 20. Designed by Sergio Baradat, U.S.

**2014, June 6 Litho. *Perf. 13¼x13***

| | | | |
|---|---|---|---|
| **1088** A461 | 33c multicolored | .70 | .70 |
| **1089** A462 | $2 multicolored | 4.00 | 4.00 |

See Offices in Geneva Nos. 580-581; Vienna Nos. 544-545.

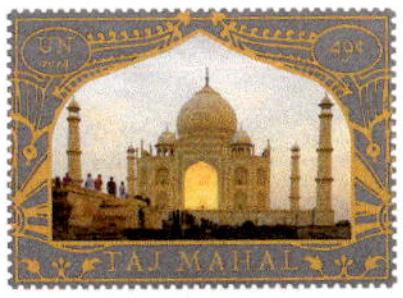


Taj Mahal and Tourists A463

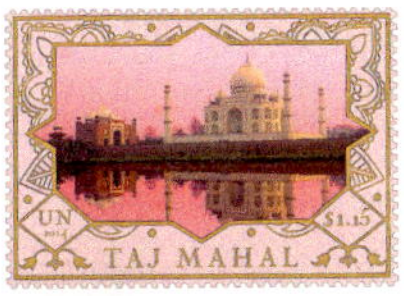


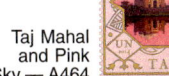

Taj Mahal and Pink Sky — A464

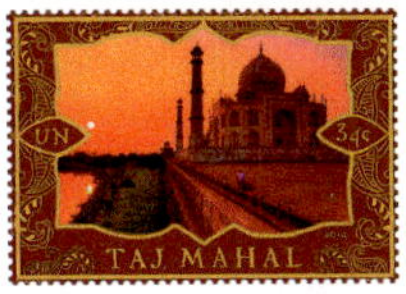


Taj Mahal and Sun — A465

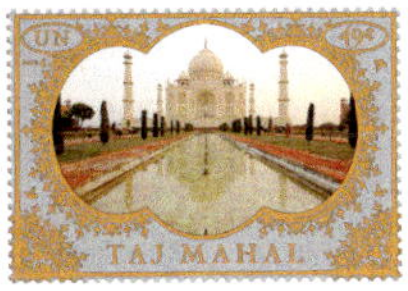


Taj Mahal and Reflecting Pool — A466

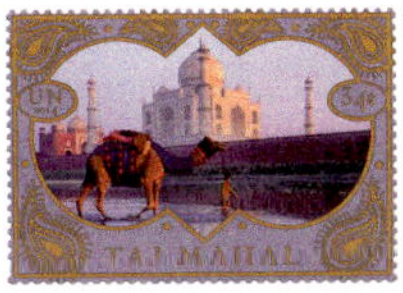


Taj Mahal and Camel A467

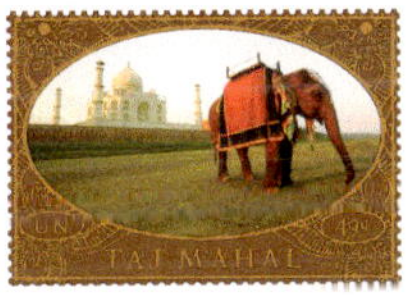


Taj Mahal and Elephant A468

**2014, July 16 Engr. *Perf. 13¼x13***

| | | | |
|---|---|---|---|
| **1090** A463 | 49c multicolored | 1.00 | 1.00 |
| **1091** A464 | $1.15 multicolored | 2.40 | 2.40 |

#### Souvenir Booklet

| | | | |
|---|---|---|---|
| **1092** | Booklet, #1092g-1092l | 20.50 | |
| *a.* | A463 34c multi | .70 | .70 |
| *b.* | A465 34c multi | .70 | .70 |
| *c.* | A466 34c multi | .70 | .70 |
| *d.* | A464 49c multi | 1.00 | 1.00 |
| *e.* | A467 49c multi | 1.00 | 1.00 |
| *f.* | A468 49c multi | 1.00 | 1.00 |
| *g.* | Booklet pane of 4 #1092a | 2.80 | — |
| *h.* | Booklet pane of 4 #1092b | 2.80 | — |
| *i.* | Booklet pane of 4 #1092c | 2.80 | — |
| *j.* | Booklet pane of 4 #1092d | 4.00 | — |
| *k.* | Booklet pane of 4 #1092e | 4.00 | — |
| *l.* | Booklet pane of 4 #1092f | 4.00 | — |

See Offices in Geneva Nos. 582-584, Vienna Nos. 546-548.

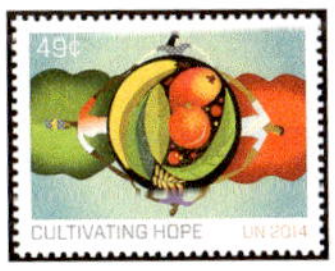


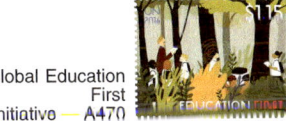

International Year of Family Farming — A469

**2014, Aug. 21 Litho. *Perf. 13x13¼***

| | | | |
|---|---|---|---|
| **1093** A469 | 49c multicolored | 1.00 | 1.00 |
| **1094** A469 | $1.15 multicolored | 2.40 | 2.40 |

See Offices in Geneva Nos. 585-586; Vienna Nos. 549-550.

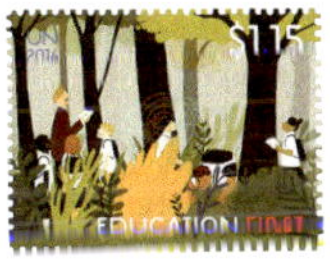


Global Education First Initiative — A470

Designs: $1.15, Teacher and students in forest. $1.50, Chemistry teacher and student.

**2014, Sept. 18 Litho. *Perf. 13x13¼***

| | | | |
|---|---|---|---|
| **1095** A470 | $1.15 multicolored | 2.40 | 2.40 |

#### Souvenir Sheet
***Perf. 12½***

| | | | |
|---|---|---|---|
| **1096** A470 | $1.50 multicolored | 6.00 | 5.00 |

No. 1096 contains one 32x32mm stamp. See Offices in Geneva Nos. 588-589; Vienna Nos. 551-552.

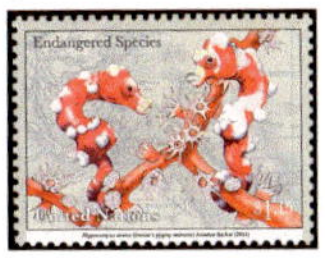


Endangered Species — A471

Maps and: No. 1097, Denise's pygmy seahorses. No. 1098, Whale shark. No. 1099, Scalloped hammerhead shark. No. 1100, Asian arowana.

**2014, Oct. 23 Litho. *Perf. 12¾x12½***

| | | | |
|---|---|---|---|
| **1097** A471 | $1.15 multicolored | 2.40 | 2.40 |
| **1098** A471 | $1.15 multicolored | 2.40 | 2.40 |
| **1099** A471 | $1.15 multicolored | 2.40 | 2.40 |
| **1100** A471 | $1.15 multicolored | 2.40 | 2.40 |
| *a.* | Block of 4, #1097-1100 | 9.75 | 9.75 |

See Offices in Geneva Nos. 590-593; Vienna Nos. 553-556.

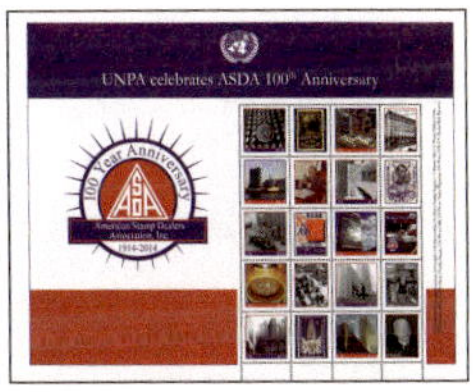


A472

No. 1101: a, United Nations emblem in gray, bottom panel in blue. b, Aerial view of United Nations Headquarters, bottom panel in red, year date at left. c, View of United Nations Headquarters from across East River, bottom panel in red, year date at right. d, Interior balconies, bottom panel in blue. e, Crowd in lobby, bottom panel in blue. f, Sun reflecting off United Nations Building, street lights, bottom panel in red. g, United Nations emblem in brown, bottom panel in red. h, Woman and two men near General Assembly Building, bottom panel in blue. i, United Nations Building, flags, trees without leaves, bottom panel in blue. j, General Assembly and United Nations Buildings, bottom panel in red.

**2014, Oct. 23 Litho. *Perf. 14¾***

| | | | |
|---|---|---|---|
| **1101** A472 | Sheet of 10 | *32.50* | *32.50* |
| *a.-j.* | $1.15 Any single + label | *3.00* | *3.00* |

The full sheet sold for $14.95. The generic labels are shown. Labels could be personalized. The personalization of labels was available only at UN Headquarters, and not through mail order.

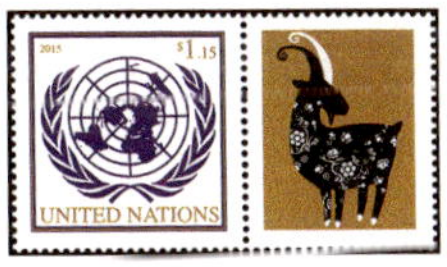


UN Emblem A473

**2015, Jan. 23 Litho. *Perf. 14¾***

| | | | |
|---|---|---|---|
| **1102** A473 | $1.15 multi + label | *3.00* | *3.00* |
| | Sheet of 10 + 10 labels | *30.00* | — |

The full sheet sold for $14.95. The generic label exists as shown, with ram on deep bister background. Labels could be personalized. The personalization of labels was available only at UN Headquarters, and not through mail order.

### Flags and Coins Type of 2006

No. 1103 — Flag of: a, Kiribati, 10 cent coin. b, Tonga, 2 seniti coin. c, Costa Rica, 10 centimos coin. d, Bhutan, 25 chetrum coin. e, Zimbabwe, 5 dollar coin. f, Angola, 1 kwanza coin. g, Congo Democratic Republic, 1 franc coin. h, Liberia, 25 cent coin.

**2015, Feb. 6 Litho. *Perf. 13¼x13***

| | | | |
|---|---|---|---|
| **1103** | Sheet of 8 | 8.00 | 8.00 |
| *a.-h.* | A375 49c Any single | 1.00 | 1.00 |

A column of rouletting in the middle of the sheet separates it into two parts. See Offices in Geneva No. 594; Vienna No. 558.

Miniature Sheets

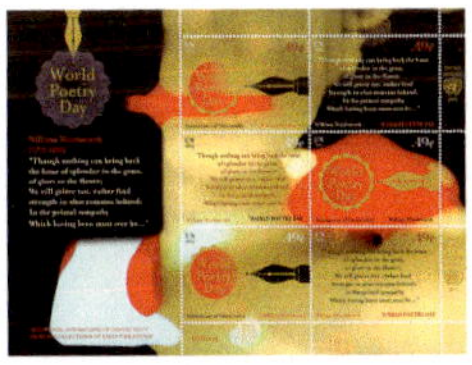


A474

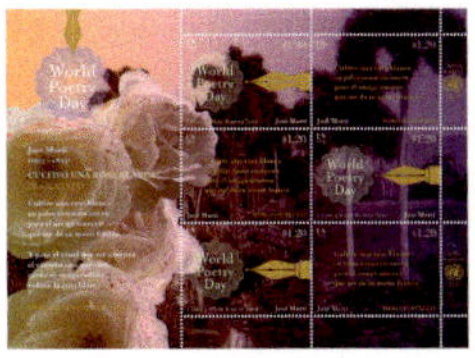


World Poetry Day A475

No. 1104: a, Black pen, denomination in red brown. b, William Wordsworth quotation in white, denomination in red. c, Wordsworth quotation in red brown, denomination in white. d, Gold pen, denomination in white. e, Black pen, denomination in white. f, Wordsworth quotation in black, denomination in red brown.

No. 1105: a, Gold pen, denomination in white, tree top and rose in background. b, José Martí quotation, denomination in lilac, tree tops in background. c, Martí quotation, denomination in white, tree top and rose in background. d, Gold pen, denomination in lilac, tree trunks and tree top in background. e, Gold pen, denomination in lilac, tree trunks and rose in background. f, Martí quotation, denomination in lilac, tree trunks in background.

***Perf. 14½x14¼***
**2015, Mar. 20 Litho.**

| | | | |
|---|---|---|---|
| **1104** A474 | Sheet of 6 | 6.00 | 6.00 |
| *a.-f.* | 49c Any single | 1.00 | 1.00 |
| **1105** A475 | Sheet of 6 | 14.50 | 14.50 |
| *a.-f.* | $1.20 Any single | 2.40 | 2.40 |

See Offices in Geneva Nos. 595-596; Vienna Nos. 559-560.

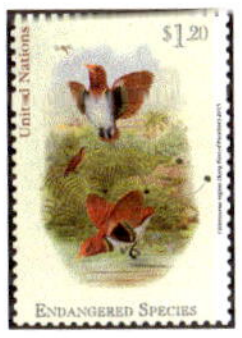


Endangered Species — A476

Designs: No. 1106, King bird-of-paradise. No. 1107, Blue bird-of-paradise. No. 1108, Princess Stephanie's bird-of-paradise. No. 1109, Carola's parotia.

**2015, Apr. 16 Litho. *Perf. 12½x12¾***

| | | | |
|---|---|---|---|
| **1106** A476 | $1.20 multicolored | 2.40 | 2.40 |
| **1107** A476 | $1.20 multicolored | 2.40 | 2.40 |
| **1108** A476 | $1.20 multicolored | 2.40 | 2.40 |
| **1109** A476 | $1.20 multicolored | 2.40 | 2.40 |
| *a.* | Block of 4, #1106-1109 | 9.75 | 9.75 |
| | *Nos. 1106-1109 (4)* | 9.60 | 9.60 |

See Offices in Geneva Nos. 597-600; Vienna Nos. 561-564.

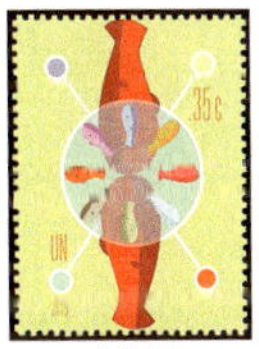


A477

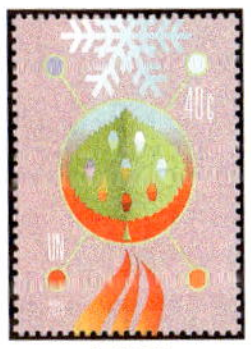


A478

**2015, May 7 Litho. *Perf. 13¼x13***

| | | | |
|---|---|---|---|
| **1110** A477 | 35c multicolored | .70 | .70 |
| **1111** A478 | 40c multicolored | .80 | .80 |

See Offices in Vienna Nos. 565-566.

Miniature Sheet

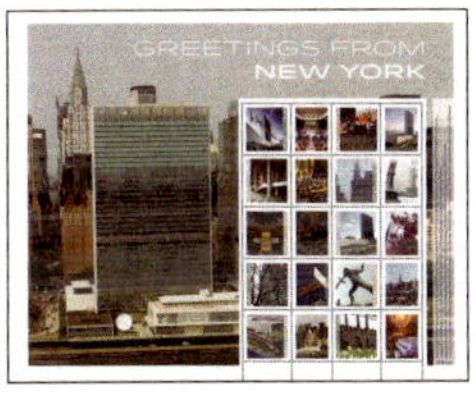


A479

No. 1112: a, United Nations Headquarters and flags, panel at right. b, Flags, panel at left. c, Stairway and pillars, panel at left. d, Reflection of buildings in windows, panel at right. e, Circular meeting room, panel at right. f, United Nations Headquarters, panel at left. g, Trees and United Nations Building, panel at left. h, Let Us Beat Swords Into Plowshares statue, panel at right. i, General Assembly Building, flags and street, panel at right. j, Arrival sculpture, panel at left.

## UNITED NATIONS, OFFICES IN NEW YORK

**2015, May 7** Litho. Perf. 14¾
1112  A479  Sheet of 10  30.00  30.00
a.-j.  $1.20 Any single + label  3.00  3.00

The full sheet sold for $14.95. The generic labels are shown. Labels could be personalized. The personalization of labels was available only at UN Headquarters, and not through mail order.

World Heritage Sites, Southeast Asia — A480

Designs: Nos. 1113, 1115a, Luang Prabang, Laos. Nos. 1114, 1115d, Borobudur Temple, Indonesia. No. 1115b, Angkor Wat, Cambodia. No. 1115c, Ayutthaya, Thailand. No. 1115e, Cordillera, Philippines. No. 1115f, Hué Monuments, Viet Nam.

**2015, June 5** Litho. Perf. 14x13½
1113  A480  49c multicolored  1.00  1.00
1114  A480  $1.20 multicolored  2.40  2.40

**Souvenir Booklet**
1115  Booklet,  #1115g-1115l  20.50
a.-c.  A480 35c any single  .70  .70
d.-f.  A480 49c any single  1.00  1.00
g.  Booklet pane of 4 #1115a  2.80  —
h.  Booklet pane of 4 #1115b  2.80  —
i.  Booklet pane of 4 #1115c  2.80  —
j.  Booklet pane of 4 #1115d  4.00  —
k.  Booklet pane of 4 #1115e  4.00  —
l.  Booklet pane of 4 #1115f  4.00  —

See Offices in Geneva Nos. 601-603; Vienna Nos. 567-569.

End Violence Against Children A481

Designs: 49c, Armed violence reduction. $1.20, Sexual violence against children.

Perf. 14½x14¼
**2015, Aug. 20**  Litho.
1116  A481  49c multicolored  1.00  1.00
1117  A481  $1.20 multicolored  2.40  2.40

See Offices in Geneva Nos. 604-605; Vienna Nos. 570-571.

United Nations, 70th Anniv. A482

Designed by Sergio Baradat, U.S.

**2015, Sept. 25** Litho. Perf. 14¾
1118  A482  $1.20 multi + label  3.00  3.00
Sheet of 10 + 10 labels  30.00  —

The full sheet sold for $14.95. The generic label exists as shown, depicting Pope Francis. Labels could be personalized. The personalization of labels was available only at UN Headquarters, and not through mail order. On Sept. 27, No. 1118 was issued in a sheet of 10 + 10 labels depicting Chinese characters. See Vienna No. 577.

General Assembly Hall — A483

Visitors Lobby — A484

Security Council — A485

Woodrow Wilson Reading Room of Dag Hammarskjöld Library — A486

General Assembly Hall — A487

Printed by Cartor Security Printing, France. Panes of 6. Designed by Rorie Katz, U.S.

**2015, Oct. 25** Litho. Perf. 13¾
1119  A483  49c multicolored  1.00  1.00
1120  A484  49c multicolored  1.00  1.00
a.  Pair, #1119-1120  2.00  2.00
1121  A485  $1.20 multicolored  2.40  2.40
1122  A486  $1.20 multicolored  2.40  2.40
a.  Pair, #1121-1122  4.80  4.80
Nos. 1119-1122 (4)  6.80  6.80

**Souvenir Sheet**
Perf. 13½
1123  A487  $1.20 multicolored  4.00  4.00

United Nations, 70th anniv. See Offices in Geneva Nos. 607-611; Vienna Nos. 572-576.

United Nations Educational, Scientific and Cultural Organization (UNESCO), 70th Anniv. — A488

**2015, Nov. 5** Litho. Perf. 14¾
1124  A488  $1.20 multi + label  3.50  3.50
Sheet of 10 + 10 labels  35.00  —

The full sheet sold for $14.95. Ten different generic labels, one of which is shown, are on the sheet. Labels could be personalized. The personalization of labels was available only at UN Headquarters, and not through mail order.

21st United Nations Climate Change Conference, Paris — A489

**2015, Nov. 24** Litho. Perf. 13¼
1125  A489  $1.20 multicolored  2.40  2.40

Values are for stamps with surrounding selvage. See Offices in Geneva No. 612; Vienna No. 578.

UN Emblem A490

**2016, Jan. 8** Litho. Perf. 14¾
1126  A490  $1.20 multicolored + label  3.00  3.00
Sheet of 10 + 10 labels  30.00  —

The full sheet sold for $14.95. The generic label, with monkey on red background, is shown. A sheet of 10 No. 1126 + 10 labels depicting M. S. Subbulaskshmi was issued on Oct. 2, 2016. Labels could be personalized. The personalization of labels was available only at UN Headquarters, and not through mail order. See Nos. 1231, 1263.

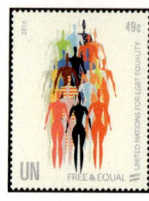

Free and Equal — A491

Designs: 49c, Group of stylized people. $1.20, Woman with butterfly wings.

**2016, Feb. 5** Litho. Perf. 13½x13¼
1127  A491  49c multicolored  1.00  1.00
1128  A491  $1.20 multicolored  2.40  2.40

See Offices in Geneva Nos. 613-614; Vienna Nos. 579-580.

HeForShe Movement — A492

Designs: 49c, Man, green background. $1.20, Woman, yellow background.

**2016, Mar. 8** Litho. Perf. 12½x13
1129  A492  49c multicolored  1.00  1.00
1130  A492  $1.20 multicolored  2.40  2.40

See Offices in Geneva Nos. 615-616; Vienna Nos. 581-582.

**Miniature Sheet**

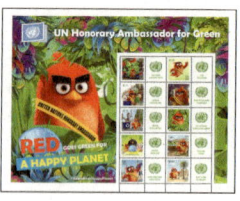

Angry Birds A493

No. 1131: a, Red, the Pigs, double-decker bus. b, Red with wing extended. c, Red and five Hatchlings. d, Red, New York City skyscrapers. e, Red, Eiffel Tower, recycling container. f, Red in jungle. g, Earth, Hatchlings, Chuck, Red, Bomb, Stella and Matilda. h, Red turning faucet, Pigs in tub. i, Red drinking from squirt bottle, Lower Manhattan skyline. j, Red with shovel, Pyramids.

**2016, Apr. 22** Litho. Perf. 14¾
1131  A493  Sheet of 10  30.00  30.00
a.-j.  $1.15 Any single + label  3.00  3.00

The full sheet sold for $14.95. The generic labels are shown. Labels could be personalized. The personalization of labels was available only at UN Headquarters, and not through mail order.

**Miniature Sheets**

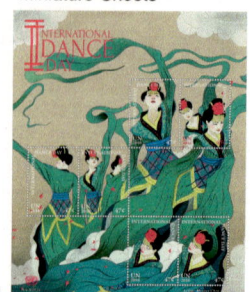

A494

International Dance Day — A495

No. 1132 — Illustration of Chinese dancers by Marcos Chin: a, Woman with arm extended upward. b, Two women, denomination in magenta. c, Woman facing left with arm extended outward. d, Two women, denomination in white. e, Woman with closed eyes. f, Woman with closed eyes with two pale yellow lines touching flower.

No. 1133 — Illustration of Thai dancers by Chin: a, Back of dancer's head, hand of another dancer. b, Dancer wearing mask, leg and arm of other dancers. c, Dancer with costume with blue shoulders, dancer with arm extended. d, Dancer with arm extended, leg and arm of other dancers. e, Two dancers with green and yellow costumes. f, Dancer with green and yellow costume.

**2016, Apr. 29** Litho. Perf. 13¼x13
1132  A494  Sheet of 6  5.75  5.75
a.-f.  47c Any single  .95  .95
1133  A495  Sheet of 6  14.50  14.50
a.-f.  $1.15 Any single  2.40  2.40
g.  As #1133, with "Thailand 2018 / World Stamp Exhibition / 28 Nov. - 3 Dec." overprinted in sheet margin  65.00  65.00

Issued: No. 1133g, 11/28/18. See Offices in Geneva Nos. 617-618; Vienna Nos. 583-584.

International Day of United Nations Peacekeepers — A496

Designs: 47c, Peacekeeper saluting. $1.15, Man disabling landmine.

**Litho. With Foil Application**
**2016, May 29** Perf. 13¼x13
1134  A496  47c multicolored  .95  .95
1135  A496  $1.15 multicolored  2.40  2.40

See Offices in Geneva Nos. 619-620; Vienna Nos. 586-587.

**Miniature Sheet**

United Nations Postal Administration, 65th Anniv. — A497

No. 1136 — Old United Nations stamps: a, New York #1. b, New York #127. c, Vienna #86. d, New York #415. e, New York #301. f, New York #548. g, New York #474. h, Vienna #100. i, New York #476. j, Vienna #122.

**2016, May 30** Litho. Perf. 14¾
1136  A497  Sheet of 10  30.00  30.00
a.-j.  $1.15 Any single + label  3.00  3.00

The full sheet sold for $14.95. The generic labels are shown. Labels could be personalized. The personalization of labels was available only at UN Headquarters, and not through mail order.

Sport for Peace A498

Olympic rings and: No. 1137, Shot put, high jump. No. 1138, Runner, javelin. No. 1139, Dove facing left. No. 1140, Dove facing right.

**2016, July 22 Litho. *Perf. 14¼***

**1137** A498 47c multicolored .95 .95
**1138** A498 47c multicolored .95 .95
*a.* Pair, #1137-1138 1.90 1.90
**1139** A498 $1.15 multicolored 2.40 2.40
**1140** A498 $1.15 multicolored 2.40 2.40
*a.* Pair, #1139-1140 4.80 4.80
*Nos. 1137-1140 (4)* 6.70 6.70

See Offices in Geneva Nos. 621-624; Vienna Nos. 588-591.

Souvenir Sheet

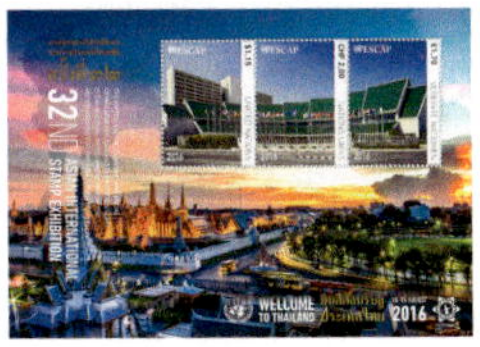

United Nations Economic and Social Commission for Asia and the Pacific Building, Bangkok — A499

No. 1141: a, Left third of building, b, Center third of building, c, Right third of building.

**2016, Aug. 10 Litho. *Perf. 13¼x13***

**1141** A499 Sheet of 3 21.00 21.00
*a.* $1.15 multi 4.00 4.00
*b.* 2fr multi 9.00 9.00
*c.* €1.70 multi 8.00 8.00

32nd Asian International Stamp Exhibition. No. 1141 sold for $6.

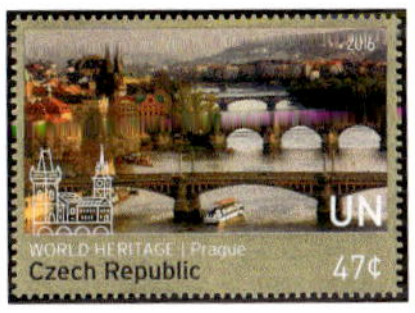

World Heritage Sites, Czech Republic A500

Designs: Nos. 1142, 1144a, Historic Center of Prague. Nos. 1143, 1144d, Holy Trinity Column, Olomouc. No. 1144b, Gardens and Castle at Kromeríz. No. 1144c, Historic Town Center of Kutná Hora. No. 1144e, Lednice-Valtice Cultural Landscape. No. 1144f, Historic Center of Cesky Krumlov.

**2016, Sept. 8 Litho. *Perf. 14¼***

**1142** A500 47c multicolored .95 .95
**1143** A500 $1.15 multicolored 2.40 2.40

**Souvenir Booklet**

**1144** Booklet, #1144g-1144l 20.00
*a.-c.* A500 34c any single .70 .70
*d.-f.* A500 47c any single .95 .95
*g.* Booklet pane of 4 #1144a 2.80 —
*h.* Booklet pane of 4 #1144b 2.80 —
*i.* Booklet pane of 4 #1144c 2.80 —
*j.* Booklet pane of 4 #1144d 3.80 —
*k.* Booklet pane of 4 #1144e 3.80 —
*l.* Booklet pane of 4 #1144f 3.80 —

See Offices in Geneva Nos. 625-627; Vienna Nos. 592-594, Czech Republic Nos. 3683-3684.

Miniature Sheet

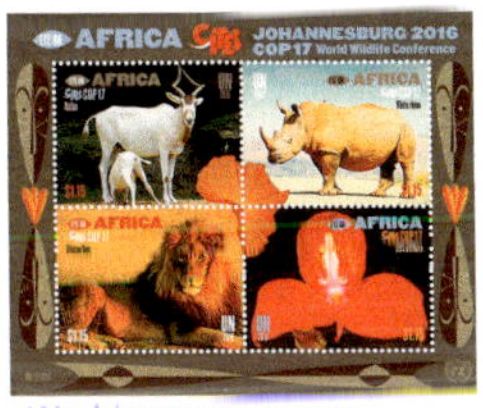

World Wildlife Conference, Johannesburg — A501

No. 1145 — Part of map of Africa and: a, Addax. b, White rhinoceros. c, African lion. d, Disa uniflora.

**2016, Sept. 24 Litho. *Perf. 13x13½***

**1145** A501 Sheet of 4 9.75 9.75
*a.-d.* $1.15 Any single 2.40 2.40

See Offices in Geneva No. 628; Vienna No. 596.

Miniature Sheet

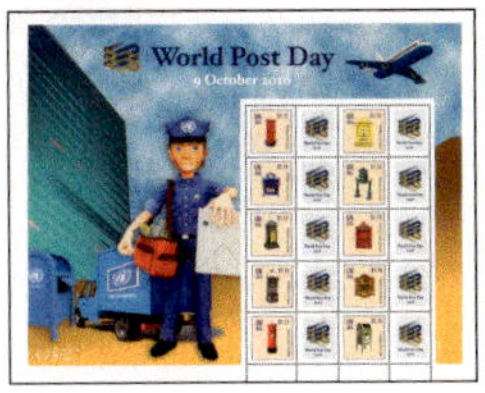

World Post Day A502

No. 1146 — Mail box from: a, Japan. b, Spain. c, Germany. d, Brazil. e, China. f, Denmark. g, India. h, Austria. i, England. j, United States.

**2016, Oct. 6 Litho. *Perf. 14¾***

**1146** A502 Sheet of 10 *30.00 30.00*
*a.-j.* $1.15 Any single + label *3.00 3.00*

The full sheet sold for $14.95. The generic labels are shown. Labels could be personalized. The personalization of labels was available only at UN Headquarters, and not through mail order.

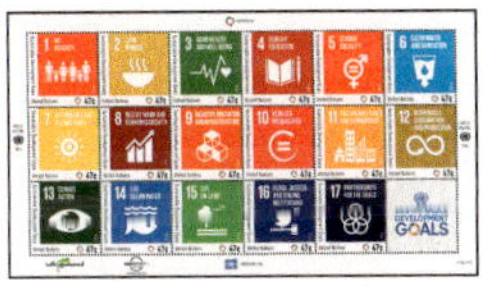

Sustainable Development Goals — A503

No. 1147 — Inscription: a, 1 No poverty. b, 2 Zero hunger. c, 3 Good health and well-being. d, 4 Quality education. e, 5 Gender equality. f, 6 Clean water and sanitation. g, 7 Affordable and clean energy. h, 8 Decent work and economic growth. i, 9 Industry, innovation and infrastructure. j, 10 Reduced inequalities. k, 11 Sustainable cities and communities. l, 12 Responsible consumption and production. m, 13 Climate action. n, 14 Life below water. o, 15 Life on land. p, 16 Peace, justice and strong institutions. q, 17 Partnerships for the goals.

**2016, Oct. 24 Litho. *Perf. 13¼***

**1147** A503 Sheet of 17 + label 17.00 17.00
*a.-q.* 47c Any single 1.00 1.00

See Offices in Geneva No. 629; Vienna No. 597.

Souvenir Sheet

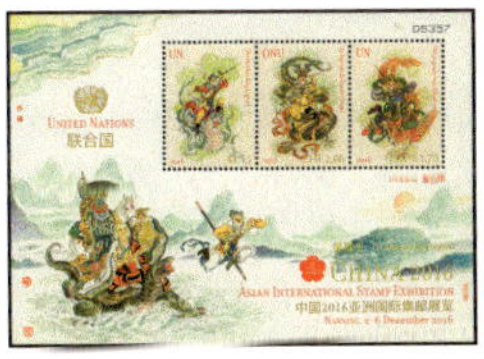

Monkey King From Chinese Novel *Journey to the West* A504

No. 1148 — Various depictions of Monkey King with inscriptions in: a, English. b, French. c, German.

**Litho. With Foil Application**

**2016, Dec. 2 *Perf. 12***

**1148** A504 Sheet of 3 24.50 20.00
*a.* $1.15 multi 5.50 4.00
*b.* 2fr multi 8.50 7.00
*c.* €1.70 multi 8.25 6.75

33rd Asian International Stamp Exhibition, Nanning, People's Republic of China. No. 1148 sold for $6.

**United Nations Emblem Type of 2014 Dated "2017" In Purple**

**2017, Jan. 13 Litho. *Perf. 14¾***

**1149** A457 $1.15 multi + label *3.00 3.00*
Sheet of 10 + 10 labels *30.00* —

The full sheet sold for $14.95. The generic label exists as shown, with rooster on red background. Labels could be personalized. The personalization of labels was available only at UN Headquarters, and not through mail order.

**Flag Type of 1980**

Printed by Lowe Martin Company, Inc., Canada. Designed by Sergio Baradat, U.S. Issued in panes of 16; each pane contains 4 blocks of 4. A se-tenant block of 4 designs centers each pane.

**2017, Feb. 3 Litho. *Perf. 13x13¼***

**1150** A185 $1.15 Albania 2.50 2.40
**1151** A185 $1.15 Benin 2.50 2.40
**1152** A185 $1.15 Bulgaria 2.50 2.40
**1153** A185 $1.15 Comoros 2.50 2.40
*a.* Block of 4, #1150-1153 12.50 12.00
**1154** A185 $1.15 Congo Republic 2.50 2.40
**1155** A185 $1.15 Ethiopia 2.50 2.40
**1156** A185 $1.15 Georgia 2.50 2.40
**1157** A185 $1.15 Iraq 2.50 2.40
*a.* Block of 4, #1154-1157 12.50 12.00
*Nos. 1150-1157 (8)* 20.00 19.20

Miniature Sheet

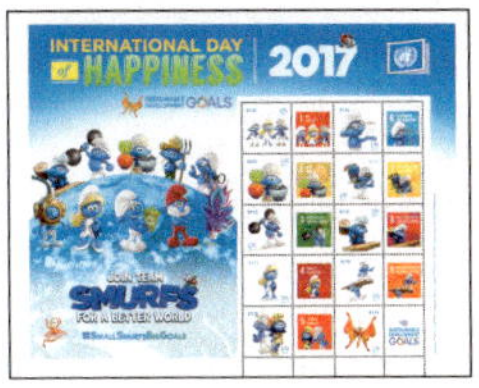

A505

No. 1158: a, Three Smurfs. b, Smurf holding glass of water. c, Smurf holding fruit. d, Smurf with backpack with solar panels. e, Smurf lifting dumbbell. f, Smurf carrying mallet. g, Smurf holding book. h, Two Smurfs with ladder. i, Male and female Smurfs. j, Butterfly.

**2017, Mar. 20 Litho. *Perf. 14¾***

**1158** A505 Sheet of 10 *30.00 30.00*
*a.-j.* $1.15 Any single + label *3.00 3.00*

The full sheet sold for $14.95. The generic labels are shown. Labels could be personalized. The personalization of labels was available only at UN Headquarters, and not through mail order.

Miniature Sheets

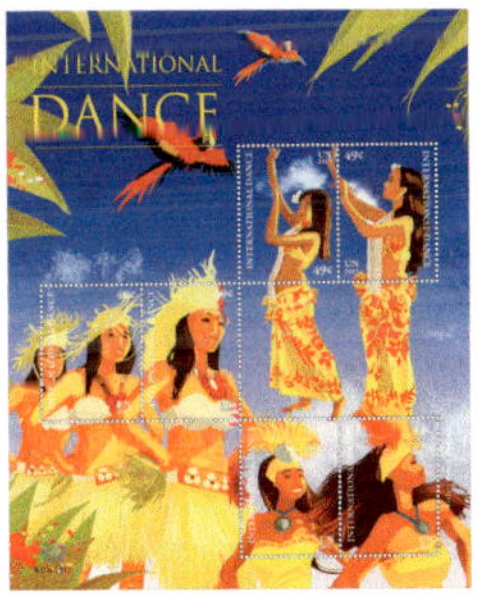

A506

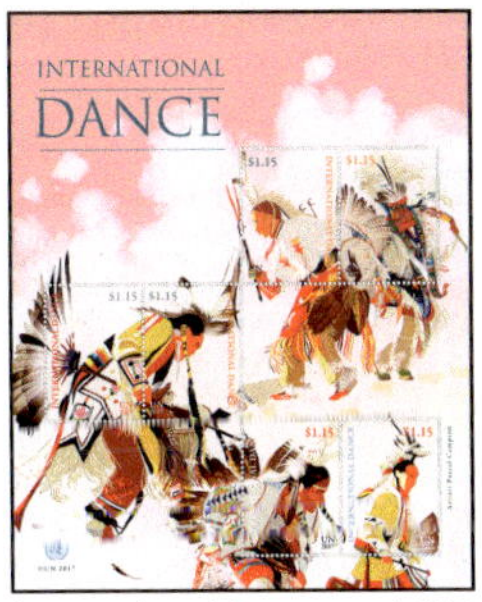

International Dance — A507

No. 1159 — Illustration of Polynesian dancers by Pascal Campion: a, Woman with arms raised, denomination at LR. b, Woman with arms raised, denomination at UL. c, Two women wearing head coverings, red necklace, denomination at UR. d, One woman wearing head covering and red necklace, denomination at UR. e, Woman with feathered headdress, green necklace, hair of another woman at right, denomination at UR. f, Woman wearing feathered headdress and green necklace, denomination at UR.

No. 1160 — Illustration of Native American tribal dancers by Campion: a, Dancer facing right, denomination in blue at UL. b, Dancer, denomination in orange at UL. c, Back of dancer, denomination in gray lilac at UR. d, Dancer looking downward, denomination in gray lilac at UL. e, Dancer with headband over eyebrows, denomination in orange red at UR, "International Dance" in white. f, Dancer, denomination in orange red at UR, "International Dance" in light blue.

**2017, Mar. 23 Litho. *Perf. 13¼x13***

**1159** A506 Sheet of 6 6.00 6.00
*a.-f.* 49c Any single 1.00 1.00
**1160** A507 Sheet of 6 14.50 14.50
*a.-f.* $1.15 Any single 2.40 2.40

See Offices in Geneva Nos. 630-631; Vienna Nos. 599-600.

Souvenir Sheet

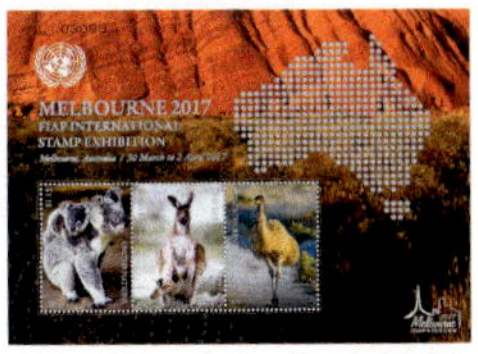

Australian Animals — A508

No. 1161: a, Koalas. b, Kangaroos. c, Emu.

**Litho. With Foil Application**

**2017, Mar. 30 *Perf. 13¼x13***

**1161** A508 Sheet of 3 12.00 12.00
*a.* $1.15 multi 4.00 4.00
*b.* 2fr multi 4.00 4.00
*c.* €1.70 multi 4.00 4.00

2017 FIAP International Stamp Exhibition, Melbourne, Australia. No. 1161 sold for $6.

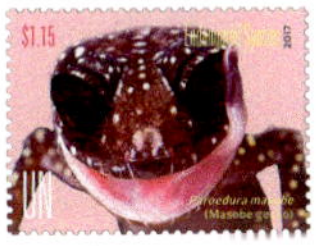

Endangered Species — A509

Designs: No. 1162, Masobe gecko. No. 1163, Thresher shark. No. 1164, Clarion angelfish. No. 1165, Blaine's fishhook cactus.

**2017, May 11 Litho. *Perf. 12¾x12½***

**1162** A509 $1.15 multicolored 2.40 2.40
**1163** A509 $1.15 multicolored 2.40 2.40
**1164** A509 $1.15 multicolored 2.40 2.40
**1165** A509 $1.15 multicolored 2.40 2.40
*a.* Block of 4, #1162-1165 9.75 9.75
*Nos. 1162-1165 (4)* 9.60 9.60

See Offices in Geneva Nos. 632-635; Vienna Nos. 601-604.

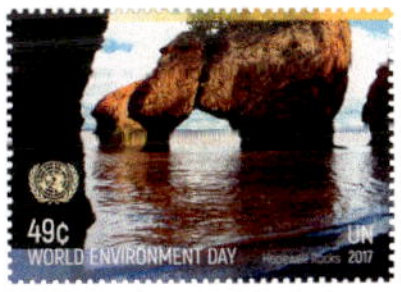

World Environment Day — A510

Designs: 49c, Hopewell Rocks, New Brunswick, Canada. $1.15, Polar bear, Baffin Island, Nunavut, Canada.

**2017, June 5 Litho. *Perf. 13¼***

**1166** A510 49c multicolored 1.00 1.00
**1167** A510 $1.15 multicolored 2.40 2.40

See Offices in Geneva Nos. 636-637; Vienna Nos. 605-606.

Miniature Sheet

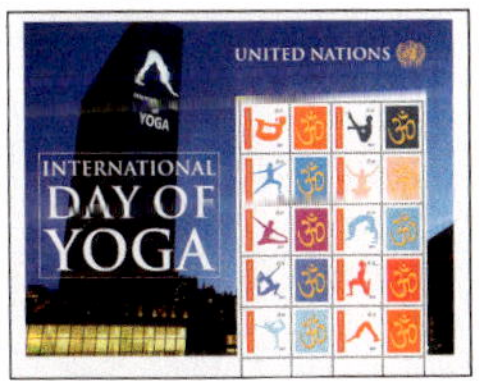

International Day of Yoga — A511

No. 1168: a, Orange woman on stomach holding her legs. b, Dark blue man siting with legs raised. c, Blue woman with arms extended. d, Beige man sitting with legs crossed and arms raised. e, Purple man with arms extended leaning backward to touch toes. f, Light blue woman bent backward with feet and hands on ground. g, Blue violet woman bent backward to touch raised leg. h, Red woman on one knee. i, Pale blue woman with arms extended touching raised leg. j, Orange man bent over with hands on ground.

**2017, June 21 Litho. *Perf. 14¾***

**1168** A511 Sheet of 10 *30.00 30.00*
*a.-j.* $1.15 Any single + label *3.00 3.00*

The full sheet sold for $14.95. The generic labels are shown. Labels could be personalized. The personalization of labels was available only at UN Headquarters, and not through mail order.

# UNITED NATIONS, OFFICES IN NEW YORK

World Heritage Sites Along the Silk Roads
A512

Designs: Nos. 1169, 1171a, Longmen Grottoes, People's Republic of China. Nos. 1170, 1171d, Sulaiman-Too Sacred Mountain, Kyrgyzstan. No. 1171b, Historic Center of Bukhara, Uzbekistan. No. 1171c, Tabriz Historic Bazaar Complex, Iran. No. 1171e, Kunya-Urgench, Turkmenistan. No. 1171f, Safranbolu, Turkey.

| 2017, Aug. 3 | Litho. | Perf. 14¼ | | |
|---|---|---|---|---|
| 1169 | A512 | 49c multicolored | 1.00 | 1.00 |
| 1170 | A512 | $1.15 multicolored | 2.40 | 2.40 |

### Souvenir Booklet

| 1171 | Booklet, #1115g-1115l | | 22.50 | |
|---|---|---|---|---|
| a.-c. | A512 34c any single | | .75 | .75 |
| d.-f. | A512 49c any single | | 1.10 | 1.10 |
| g. | Booklet pane of 4 #1171a | | 3.00 | — |
| h. | Booklet pane of 4 #1171b | | 3.00 | — |
| i. | Booklet pane of 4 #1171c | | 3.00 | — |
| j. | Booklet pane of 4 #1171d | | 4.50 | — |
| k. | Booklet pane of 4 #1171e | | 4.50 | — |
| l. | Booklet pane of 4 #1171f | | 4.50 | — |

Complete booklet sold for $11. See Offices in Geneva Nos. 638-640; Vienna Nos. 607-609.

Doves A513

Moths A514

Doves A515

Printed by Johann Enschedé and Sons, the Netherlands. Panes of 20. Designed by Stranger and Stranger, U.S.

| 2017, Sept. 21 | Litho. | Perf. 14x14¼ | | |
|---|---|---|---|---|
| 1172 | A513 | 49c multicolored | 1.00 | 1.00 |
| 1173 | A514 | $1.15 multicolored | 2.40 | 2.40 |

### Souvenir Sheet
Perf. 14¼x13¾

| 1174 | A515 | $1.15 multicolored | 2.40 | 2.40 |

International Day of Peace. See Offices in Geneva Nos. 641-643; Vienna Nos. 611-613.

World Food Day — A516

Designs: 49c, Vegetables. $1.15, Bowls of food, jar of oil.

| 2017, Oct. 16 | Litho. | Perf. 13¼x14 | | |
|---|---|---|---|---|
| 1175 | A516 | 49c multicolored | 1.00 | 1.00 |
| 1176 | A516 | $1.15 multicolored | 2.40 | 2.40 |

See Offices in Geneva Nos. 644-645; Vienna Nos. 614-615.

### Souvenir Sheet

Universal Declaration of Human Rights — A517

No. 1177 — Text of Universal Declaration of Human Rights in: a, English. b, French. c, German.

### Litho. With Foil Application
2017, Oct. 27    Perf. 14x13¼

| 1177 | A517 | Sheet of 3 | 12.00 | 12.00 |
|---|---|---|---|---|
| a. | | $1.15 multi | 4.00 | 4.00 |
| b. | | 2fr multi | 4.00 | 4.00 |
| c. | | €1.70 multi | 4.00 | 4.00 |

United Nations Expo 2017, Bellefonte, Pennsylvania. No. 1177 sold for $6.

### Souvenir Sheet

Landmarks in Paris — A518

No. 1178: a, Fame of Louis XVI, statue by Antoine Coysevox. b, Fontaines de la Concorde. c, Gargoyle on Notre Dame Cathedral.

| 2017, Nov. 9 | Litho. | Perf. 13¼x14 | | |
|---|---|---|---|---|
| 1178 | A518 | Sheet of 3 | 12.00 | 12.00 |
| a. | | $1.15 multi | 4.00 | 4.00 |
| b. | | 2fr multi | 4.00 | 4.00 |
| c. | | €1.70 multi | 4.00 | 4.00 |

Autumn Philatelic Show, Paris. No. 1178 sold for $6.

### Flag Type of 1980

Printed by Lowe Martin Group, Canada. Designed by Rorie Katz, U.S. Issued in panes of 16; each pane contains 4 blocks of 4. A se-tenant block of 4 designs centers each pane.

| 2018, Jan. 12 | Litho. | Perf. 13x13¼ | | |
|---|---|---|---|---|
| 1179 | A185 | $1.15 Lesotho | 2.40 | 2.40 |
| 1180 | A185 | $1.15 Libya | 2.40 | 2.40 |
| 1181 | A185 | $1.15 Mozambique | 2.40 | 2.40 |
| 1182 | A185 | $1.15 Romania | 2.40 | 2.40 |
| a. | | Block of 4, #1179-1182 | 12.00 | 12.00 |
| 1183 | A185 | $1.15 Rwanda | 2.40 | 2.40 |
| 1184 | A185 | $1.15 Seychelles | 2.40 | 2.40 |
| 1185 | A185 | $1.15 South Africa | 2.40 | 2.40 |
| 1186 | A185 | $1.15 Ukraine | 2.40 | 2.40 |
| a. | | Block of 4, #1183-1186 | 12.00 | 12.00 |
| | | Nos. 1179-1186 (8) | 19.20 | 19.20 |

### United Nations Emblem Type of 2014 Dated "2018" In Purple

| 2018, Feb. 2 | Litho. | Perf. 14¾ | | |
|---|---|---|---|---|
| 1187 | A457 | $1.15 multi + label | 3.00 | 3.00 |
| | | Sheet of 10 + 10 labels | 30.00 | — |

The full sheet sold for $14.95. The generic label depicts a dog. Labels could be personalized. The personalization of labels was available only at UN Headquarters, and not through mail order.

Endangered Species — A519

Designs: No. 1188, Red-crested turaco. No. 1189, Andean hairy armadillo. No. 1190, Lurestan newt. No. 1191, Goldenseal.

| 2018, Mar. 2 | Litho. | Perf. 12¾x12½ | | |
|---|---|---|---|---|
| 1188 | A519 | $1.15 multicolored | 2.40 | 2.40 |
| 1189 | A519 | $1.15 multicolored | 2.40 | 2.40 |
| 1190 | A519 | $1.15 multicolored | 2.40 | 2.40 |
| 1191 | A519 | $1.15 multicolored | 2.40 | 2.40 |
| a. | | Block of 4, #1188-1191 | 9.75 | 9.75 |
| | | Nos. 1188-1191 (4) | 9.60 | 9.60 |

See Offices in Geneva Nos. 646-649; Vienna Nos. 616-619.

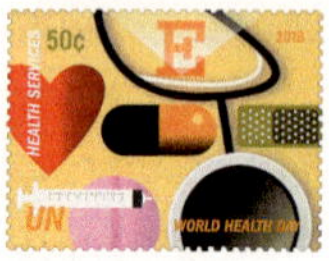

World Health Day — A520

Designs: 50c, Heart, pill, bandage, letter from eye chart, syringe and stethoscope. $1.15, Head with gears, heart, clock, stylized people, circle with arrows.

| 2018, Apr. 6 | Litho. | Perf. 13x13¼ | | |
|---|---|---|---|---|
| 1192 | A520 | 50c multicolored | 1.00 | 1.00 |
| 1193 | A520 | $1.15 multicolored | 2.40 | 2.40 |

See Offices in Geneva Nos. 650-651; Vienna Nos. 620-621.

Universal Declaration of Human Rights, 70th Anniv. A521

| 2018, May 3 | Litho. | Perf. 13¼ | | |
|---|---|---|---|---|
| 1194 | A521 | $2.50 multicolored | 5.00 | 5.00 |

United Nations Headquarters A522

| 2018, May 29 | Litho. | Perf. 13¼ | | |
|---|---|---|---|---|
| 1195 | A522 | 65c multicolored | 1.40 | 1.40 |

UNISPACE + 50 Conferences A523

Designs: 50c, Milky Way Galaxy. No. 1197, International Space Station and Space Shuttle Endeavour.
No. 1198, Astronaut Scott Kelly during spacewalk.

| 2018, June 20 | Litho. | Perf. 14x14¼ | | |
|---|---|---|---|---|
| 1196 | A523 | 50c multicolored | 1.00 | 1.00 |
| 1197 | A523 | $1.15 multicolored | 2.40 | 2.40 |

### Souvenir Sheet
Perf. 13¾

| 1198 | A523 | $1.15 multicolored | 3.00 | 3.00 |

No. 1198 contains one 45x45mm stamp. See Offices in Geneva Nos. 653-655; Vienna Nos. 623-625.

World Heritage Sites in the United Kingdom A524

Designs: Nos. 1199, 1201a, Giant's Causeway. Nos. 1200, 1201d, Palace of Westminster. No. 1201b, Stonehenge. No. 1201c, Conwy Castle. No. 1201e, Edinburgh. No. 1201f, Maritime Greenwich.

| 2018, Aug. 15 | Litho. | Perf. 14¼ | | |
|---|---|---|---|---|
| 1199 | A524 | 50c multicolored | 1.00 | 1.00 |
| 1200 | A524 | $1.15 multicolored | 2.40 | 2.40 |

### Souvenir Booklet

| 1201 | Booklet, #1115g-1115l | | 22.50 | |
|---|---|---|---|---|
| a.-c. | A524 35c any single | | .75 | .75 |
| d.-f. | A524 50c any single | | 1.10 | 1.10 |
| g. | Booklet pane of 4 #1201a | | 3.00 | — |
| h. | Booklet pane of 4 #1201b | | 3.00 | — |
| i. | Booklet pane of 4 #1201c | | 3.00 | — |
| j. | Booklet pane of 4 #1201d | | 4.50 | — |
| k. | Booklet pane of 4 #1201e | | 4.50 | — |
| l. | Booklet pane of 4 #1201f | | 4.50 | — |

Complete booklet sold for $11. See Offices in Geneva Nos. 657-659; Vienna Nos. 626-628.

### Miniature Sheet

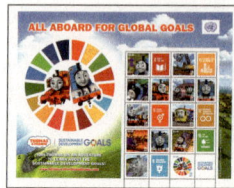

Thomas the Tank Engine A525

No. 1202: a, Thomas and four people. b, Reg lifting bicycle. c, Thomas, conductor holding potted plant. d, Ashima and Thomas. e, Thomas and Nia. f, Passenger car, children and tuba. g, Thomas and giraffe. h, Monkeys on Thomas. i, Water splashing on grimy Thomas. j, Nia, Thomas and ring of colors.

| 2018, Sept. 12 | Litho. | Perf. 14¾ | | |
|---|---|---|---|---|
| 1202 | A525 | Sheet of 10 | 30.00 | 30.00 |
| a.-j. | | $1.15 Any single + label | 3.00 | 3.00 |

The full sheet sold for $14.95. The generic labels are shown. Labels could be personalized. The personalization of labels was available only at UN Headquarters, and not through mail order.

### Souvenir Sheet

Characters From Cantonese Opera
Hua Mulan — A526

No. 1203: a, Baozhen. b, Guanyu. c, Mulan.

| 2018, Sept. 21 | Litho. | Perf. 13¼x13 | | |
|---|---|---|---|---|
| 1203 | A526 | Sheet of 3 | 13.00 | 13.00 |
| a. | | $1.15 multi | 4.25 | 4.25 |
| b. | | 2fr multi | 4.25 | 4.25 |
| c. | | €1.80 multi | 4.25 | 4.25 |

Macao 2018 Asian International Stamp Exhibition. The vignettes are laser cut. No. 1203 sold for $6.30.

### Miniature Sheet

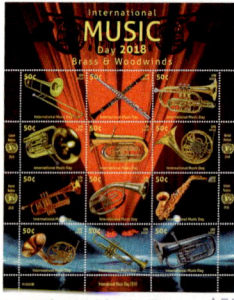

International Music Day — A527

No. 1204: a, Trombone. b, Flute and clarinet. c, Cornet. d, Tuba, bell at right. e, Tuba, bell at left, red in background. f, French horn, red in background. g, Trumpet, bell at UR. h, Baritone horn. i, Saxophone. j, French horn, blue in background. k, Trumpet, bell at LR. l, Tuba, bell at left, blue in background.

| 2018, Oct. 1 | Litho. | Perf. 14x13¼ | | |
|---|---|---|---|---|
| 1204 | A527 | Sheet of 12 | 12.00 | 12.00 |
| a.-l. | | 50c Any single | 1.00 | 1.00 |

See Offices in Geneva No. 660; Vienna No. 629.

Non-Violence, Sculpture by Carl Fredrik Reuterswärd — A528

Printed by Johann Enschedé Stamps BV, the Netherlands. Panes of 50. Designed by Martin Mörck, Norway.

| 2018, Oct. 2 | Litho. | Perf. 13¼x14 | | |
|---|---|---|---|---|
| 1205 | A528 | 1c multicolored | .25 | .25 |

See Offices in Vienna Nos. 630-631.

# UNITED NATIONS, OFFICES IN NEW YORK

Diwali Candles A529

Diwali Candles A530

**2018, Oct. 19   Litho.   Perf. 14¾**
| | | | | |
|---|---|---|---|---|
| 1206 | A529 | $1.15 multi + label | 3.00 | 3.00 |
| 1207 | A530 | $1.15 multi + label | 3.00 | 3.00 |
| a. | | Vert. pair, #1206-1207, + 2 labels | 6.00 | 6.00 |
| | | Sheet of 10, 5 each #1206-1207, + 10 labels | 30.00 | 30.00 |

The full sheet sold for $14.95. The generic labels are shown. Labels could be personalized. The personalization of labels was available only at UN Headquarters, and not through mail order.

### Souvenir Sheet

Arena di Verona A531

No. 1208: a, Left side of Arena. b, Central portion of Arena with four upper-tier arches. c, Right side of Arena.

**2018, Nov. 23   Litho.   Perf. 13¼x13**
| | | | | |
|---|---|---|---|---|
| 1208 | A531 | Sheet of 3 | 13.00 | 13.00 |
| a. | | $1.15 multi | 4.25 | 4.25 |
| b. | | 2fr multi | 4.25 | 4.25 |
| c. | | €1.80 multi | 4.25 | 4.25 |

Veronafil 2018 Stamp Exhibition, Verona, Italy. No. 1208 sold for $6.30.

### United Nations Emblem Type of 2014 Dated "2019" in Purple

**2019, Jan. 11   Litho.   Perf. 14¾**
| | | | | |
|---|---|---|---|---|
| 1209 | A457 | $1.15 multi + label | 3.00 | 3.00 |
| | | Sheet of 10 + 10 labels | 30.00 | — |

The full sheet sold for $14.95. The generic label depicts a pig. Labels could be personalized. The personalization of labels was available only at UN Headquarters, and not through mail order.

### Miniature Sheet

World Languages — A532

No. 1210 — Word bubbles with word for "Hello" in: a, Chinese and Portuguese (Olá). b, Swahili (Habari) and Persian. c, Italian (Ciao). d, Bengali. e, English. f, Thai and Czech or Slovak (Ahoj).

**2019, Feb. 21   Litho.   Perf. 13¼x13**
| | | | | |
|---|---|---|---|---|
| 1210 | A532 | Sheet of 6 | 8.00 | 6.75 |
| a.-f. | | 55c Any single | 1.30 | 1.30 |

See Offices in Geneva No. 661; Vienna No. 632.

Stop Sexual Exploitation and Abuse — A533

Printed by Lowe-Martin Group, Canada. Panes of 20. Designed by Chris Gash, U.S.

**2019, Mar. 15   Litho.   Perf. 13¼x13**
| | | | | |
|---|---|---|---|---|
| 1211 | A533 | 85c multicolored | 1.75 | 1.75 |

Endangered Species — A534

Designs: No. 1212, Hawksbill turtle. No. 1213, Queen conch. No. 1214, Mushroom coral. No. 1215, Humpback whale.

**2019, Apr. 26   Litho.   Perf. 12¾x12½**
| | | | | |
|---|---|---|---|---|
| 1212 | A534 | $1.15 multicolored | 2.40 | 2.40 |
| 1213 | A534 | $1.15 multicolored | 2.40 | 2.40 |
| 1214 | A534 | $1.15 multicolored | 2.40 | 2.40 |
| 1215 | A534 | $1.15 multicolored | 2.40 | 2.40 |
| a. | | Block of 4, #1212-1215 | 9.75 | 9.75 |

See Offices in Geneva Nos. 663-666; Vienna Nos. 634-637.

### Souvenir Sheet

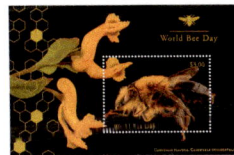

Diphaglossine Bee and Corydalis Flavula — A535

### Litho. With Foil Application

**2019, May 20   Perf. 13**
| | | | | |
|---|---|---|---|---|
| 1216 | A535 | $0 multicolored | 7.50 | 7.50 |

World Bee Day. See Offices in Geneva No. 667; Vienna No. 638.

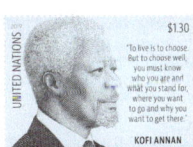

Kofi Annan (1938-2018), Seventh United Nations Secretary-General — A536

**2019, May 31   Litho.   Perf. 14x14¼**
| | | | | |
|---|---|---|---|---|
| 1217 | A536 | $1.30 gray blue & black | 2.60 | 2.60 |

### Souvenir Sheet

Pandas A537

No. 1218: a, Qiqia. b, Qigi and Diandian. c, Diandian.

**2019, June 11   Litho.   Perf. 13½x13**
| | | | | |
|---|---|---|---|---|
| 1218 | A537 | Sheet of 3 | 13.00 | 13.00 |
| a. | | $1.15 multi | 4.25 | 4.25 |
| b. | | 2fr multi | 4.25 | 4.25 |
| c. | | €1.80 multi | 4.25 | 4.25 |

China 2019 World Stamp Exhibition, Wuhan, People's Republic of China. On July 31, 2019, a sheet containing Nos. 1218a-1218c with a different sheet margin was issued for Singpex 2019 International Stamp Exhibition, with a printing quantity of 21,000 sheets. No. 1218 and the sheet issued in July each sold for $6.30. Value, $15.

A538    A539

A540    A541

The ILO Centenary

International Labor Organization, Cent. — A542

**2019, June 28   Litho.   Perf. 13½x14**
| | | | | |
|---|---|---|---|---|
| 1219 | A538 | 55c multicolored | 1.10 | 1.10 |
| 1220 | A539 | 55c multicolored | 1.10 | 1.10 |
| 1221 | A540 | 55c multicolored | 1.10 | 1.10 |
| 1222 | A541 | 55c multicolored | 1.10 | 1.10 |
| 1223 | A542 | 55c multicolored | 1.10 | 1.10 |
| a. | | Horiz. strip of 5, #1219-1223 | 5.50 | 5.50 |
| | | Nos. 1219-1223 (5) | 5.50 | 5.50 |

See Offices in Geneva Nos. 668-672; Vienna Nos. 639-643.

Climate Change A543

Designs: 55c, Mountain. No. 1225, Fish. No. 1226, Polar bear.

**2019, Sept. 23   Litho.   Perf. 14¼**
| | | | | |
|---|---|---|---|---|
| 1224 | A543 | 55c multicolored | 1.10 | 1.10 |
| 1225 | A543 | $1.15 multicolored | 2.40 | 2.40 |

### Souvenir Sheet

**Perf.**
| | | | | |
|---|---|---|---|---|
| 1226 | A543 | $1.15 multicolored | 2.40 | 2.40 |

2019 United Nations Climate Change Conference, Madrid. No. 1226 contains one 47mm diameter stamp. See Offices in Geneva Nos. 673-675; Vienna Nos. 649-651.

Mohandas K. Gandhi (1869-1948), Indian Nationalist Leader A544

Printed by Johann Enschedé Stamps BV, the Netherlands. Panes of 20. Designed by Rorie Katz, U.S.

**2019, Oct. 2   Litho.   Perf. 14¼**
| | | | | |
|---|---|---|---|---|
| 1227 | A544 | $2.75 pink & black | 5.50 | 5.50 |

World Heritage Sites in Cuba — A545

Designs: Nos. 1228, 1230a, Morro Castle. Nos. 1229, 1230d, Vinales Valley. No. 1230b, Trinidad. No. 1230c, Camagüey. No. 1230e, Cienfuegos. No. 1230f, San Pedro de la Rosa Castle.

### Litho. With Foil Application

**2019, Oct. 24   Perf. 14¼**
| | | | | |
|---|---|---|---|---|
| 1228 | A545 | 55c multicolored | 1.10 | 1.10 |
| 1229 | A545 | $1.15 multicolored | 2.40 | 2.40 |

### Souvenir Booklet

| | | | | |
|---|---|---|---|---|
| 1230 | | Booklet, #1115g-1115l | 24.00 | |
| a.-c. | A545 | 35c Any single | .75 | .75 |
| d.-f. | A545 | 55c Any single | 1.25 | 1.25 |
| g. | | Booklet pane of 4 #1230a | 3.00 | — |
| h. | | Booklet pane of 4 #1230b | 3.00 | — |
| i. | | Booklet pane of 4 #1230c | 3.00 | — |
| j. | | Booklet pane of 4 #1230d | 5.00 | — |
| k. | | Booklet pane of 4 #1230e | 5.00 | — |
| l. | | Booklet pane of 4 #1230f | 5.00 | — |

Complete booklet sold for $12. See Offices in Geneva Nos. 677-679; Vienna Nos. 652-654.

### United Nations Emblem Type of 2016 Dated "2020" in Purple

**2020, Jan. 10   Litho.   Perf. 14¾**
| | | | | |
|---|---|---|---|---|
| 1231 | A490 | $1.20 multi + label | 3.00 | 3.00 |
| | | Sheet of 10 + 10 labels | 30.00 | — |

The full sheet sold for $14.95. The generic label has a rat on red background. The personalization of labels was available only at UN Headquarters, and not through mail order.

Endangered Species — A546

Designs: No. 1232, Great hammerhead shark. No. 1233, Egyptian vulture. No. 1234, Andean flamingo. No. 1235, Argali sheep.

**Perf. 12¾x12½**

**2020, Feb. 17   Litho.**
| | | | | |
|---|---|---|---|---|
| 1232 | A546 | $1.20 multicolored | 2.40 | 2.40 |
| 1233 | A546 | $1.20 multicolored | 2.40 | 2.40 |
| 1234 | A546 | $1.20 multicolored | 2.40 | 2.40 |
| 1235 | A546 | $1.20 multicolored | 2.40 | 2.40 |
| a. | | Block of 4, #1232-1235 | 9.75 | 9.75 |

See Offices in Geneva Nos. 680-683; Vienna Nos. 655-658.

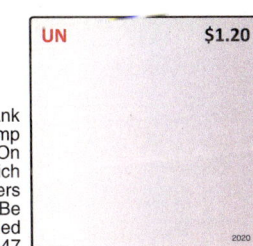

Blank Stamp On Which Stickers Can Be Applied A547

Designs: No. 1212, Hawksbill turtle. No. 1213, Queen conch. No. 1214, Mushroom coral. No. 1215, Humpback whale.

**2020, Mar. 19   Litho.   Die Cut Self-Adhesive**
| | | | | |
|---|---|---|---|---|
| 1236 | A547 | $1.20 multi with rounded corners | 2.40 | 2.40 |
| a. | | With perpendicular corners and black frame line | 2.40 | 2.40 |
| b. | | Booklet pane of 6 #1236a | 14.50 | |

No. 1236 was issued as a souvenir sheet having two different sheet margins, each with different stickers. No. 1236a was issued in a booklet containing six panes of one stamp, with each pane having different margins and stickers. Each booklet pane contained one sticker depicting Hello Kitty, a color wheel with Hello Kitty at the center, one of six different Sustainable Development Goal emblems, along with a variety of other stickers. The two souvenir sheets had the same sheet margin and stickers found on two of the panes of No. 1236b. No. 1236b was sold folded, without any means of separation between the individual panes.

### Miniature Sheet

Act Now Climate Action Campaign — A548

No. 1237: a, Man in shower. b, Hand on light switch. c, Bicyclist. d, Electric plug and socket. e, Knife, fork, vegetables. f, Hand, container and recycling arrow. g, Produce stand. h, Clothing on clothes hanger. i, Man placing bottle in recycling bin. j, Man carrying reusable shopping bag.

**2020, Mar. 27 Litho. *Perf. 14¾***

**1237** A548 Sheet of 10 + 10 labels *30.00 30.00*
*a.-j.* $1.20 Any single + label *3.00 3.00*

The full sheet sold for $14.95. The generic labels are shown. Labels could be personalized. The personalization of labels was available only at UN Headquarters, and not through mail order.

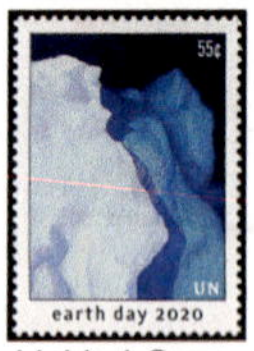

Linblad Cove, Antarctica, Drawing by Zaria Forman A549

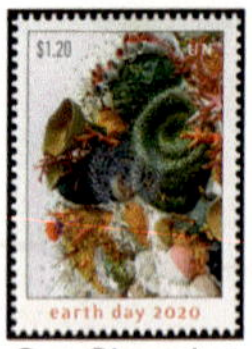

Our Changing Seas IV, Glazed Stoneware and Porcelain Item by Courtney Mattison A550

**2020, Apr. 22 Litho. *Perf. 13¼***

**1238** A549 55c multicolored 1.10 1.10
**1239** A550 $1.20 multicolored 2.40 2.40

Earth Day, 50th anniv. Because of the COVID-19 pandemic, Nos. 1238-1239 were not available for sale on day of issue stated on the first-day covers as they had not yet been printed and delivered. See Offices in Geneva Nos. 685-686; Vienna Nos. 660-661.

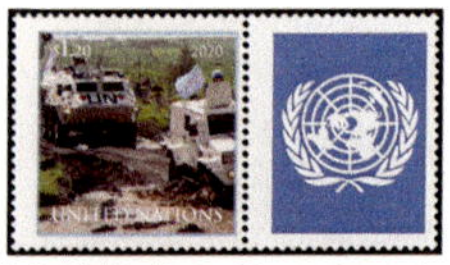
United Nations Peacekeeping Vehicles — A551

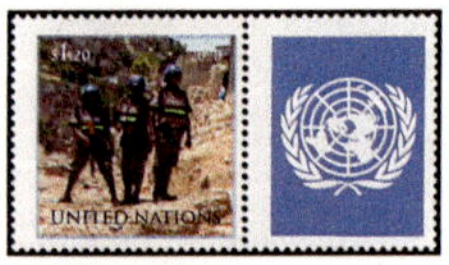
United Nations Peacekeepers — A552

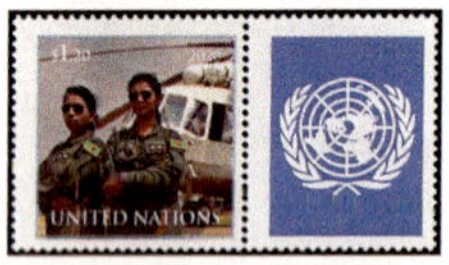
Two Female United Nations Peacekeepers and Helicopter — A553

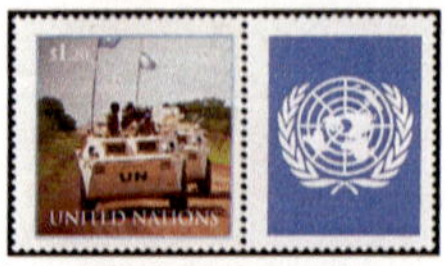
United Nations Peacekeeping Vehicles — A554

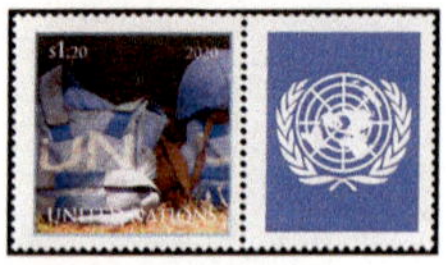
Helmet and Knapsacks of United Nations Peacekeepers — A555

**2020, May 29 Litho. *Perf. 14¾***

**1240** A551 $1.20 multi + label *3.00 3.00*
**1241** A552 $1.20 multi + label *3.00 3.00*
**1242** A553 $1.20 multi + label *3.00 3.00*
**1243** A554 $1.20 multi + label *3.00 3.00*
**1244** A555 $1.20 multi + label *3.00 3.00*
*a.* Vert. strip of 5, #1240-1244, + 5 labels *15.00 15.00*

International Day of United Nations Peacekeepers. The full sheet sold for $14.95. The generic labels are shown. Labels could be personalized. The personalization of labels was available only at UN Headquarters, and not through mail order.

**Flag Type of 1980**

**2020, Aug. 20 Litho. *Perf. 14x13¼***

**1245** A185 $1.20 Bahrain 2.40 2.40
**1246** A185 $1.20 Belarus 2.40 2.40
**1247** A185 $1.20 Brazil 2.40 2.40
**1248** A185 $1.20 Cyprus 2.40 2.40
*a.* Block of 4, #1245-1248 9.60 9.60
**1249** A185 $1.20 Dominica 2.40 2.40
**1250** A185 $1.20 Mauritania 2.40 2.40
**1251** A185 $1.20 Mongolia 2.40 2.40
**1252** A185 $1.20 Paraguay 2.40 2.40
*a.* Block of 4, #1249-1252 9.60 9.60
*Nos. 1245-1252 (8)* 19.20 19.20

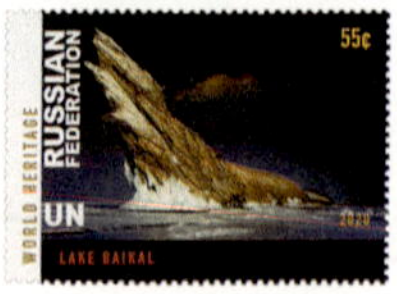

World Heritage Sites in Russia A556

Designs: Nos. 1253, 1255a, Lake Baikal. Nos. 1254, 1255d, Kremlin and Red Square, Moscow. No. 1255b, Kazan Kremlin. No. 1255c, Novodevichy Convent. No. 1255e, Saint Petersburg. No. 1255f, Kizhi Pogost.

***Perf. 14½x14¼***

**2020, Sept. 11 Litho.**

**1253** A556 55c multicolored 1.10 1.10
**1254** A556 $1.20 multicolored 2.40 2.40

**Souvenir Booklet**

**1255** Booklet, #1115g-1115l 24.00
*a.-c.* A556 35c any single .75 .75
*d.-f.* A556 55c any single 1.25 1.25
*g.* Booklet pane of 4 #1255a 3.00 —
*h.* Booklet pane of 4 #1255b 3.00 —
*i.* Booklet pane of 4 #1255c 3.00 —
*j.* Booklet pane of 4 #1255d 5.00 —
*k.* Booklet pane of 4 #1255e 5.00 —
*l.* Booklet pane of 4 #1255f 5.00 —

Complete booklet sold for $12. See Offices in Geneva Nos. 688-690; Vienna Nos. 663-665.

Souvenir Sheet

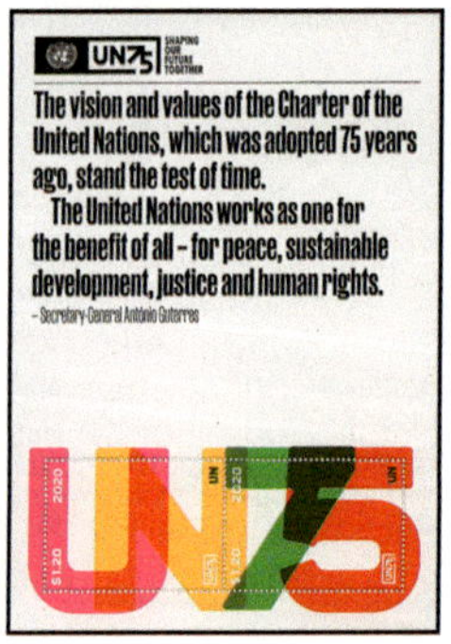

United Nations, 75th Anniv. A557

No. 1256: a, Pink "U," yellow "N." b, Green "7," red "5."

**2020, Oct. 24 Litho. *Perf. 13¼***

**1256** A557 Sheet of 2 4.80 4.80
*a.-b.* $1.20 Either single 2.40 2.40

See Offices in Geneva No. 691; Vienna No. 667.

Souvenir Sheet

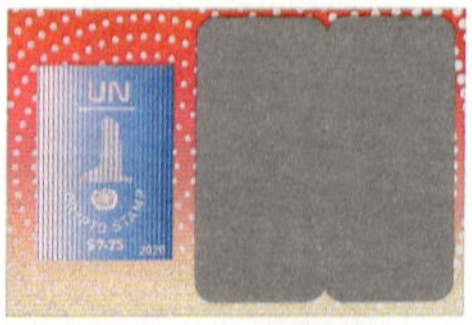
United Nations Building and Emblem A558

**Litho. With Foil Application**

**2020, Nov. 24 *Die Cut Perf. 11½***

**Self-Adhesive**

**1257** A558 $7.75 multicolored 15.50 15.50

Crypto stamp. Unused value is for sheets with unscratched panels at right. See Offices in Geneva No. 692; Vienna No. 668.

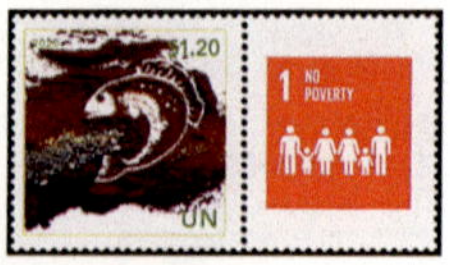

Fish A559

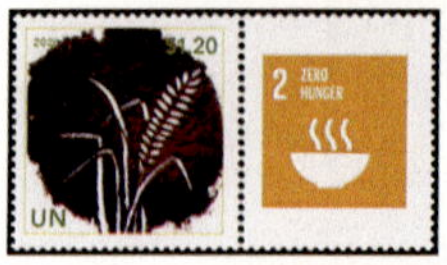

Grain Stalk A560

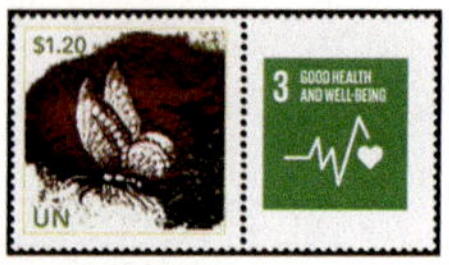

Butterfly A561

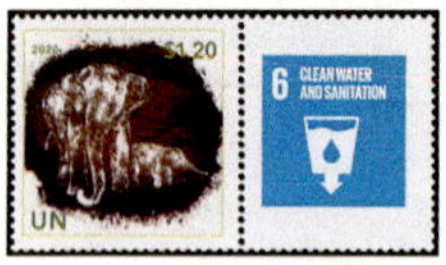

Elephants A562

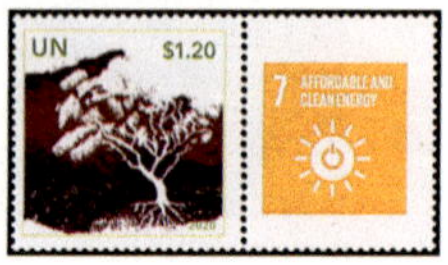

Tree A563

**2020, Dec. 5 Litho. *Perf. 14¾***

**1258** A559 $1.20 multi + label *3.00 3.00*
**1259** A560 $1.20 multi + label *3.00 3.00*
**1260** A561 $1.20 multi + label *3.00 3.00*
**1261** A562 $1.20 multi + label *3.00 3.00*
**1262** A563 $1.20 multi + label *3.00 3.00*
*a.* Vert. strip of 5, #1258-1262, + 5 labels *15.00 15.00*
Sheet of 10, 2 each #1258-1262, + 10 labels *30.00 30.00*
*Nos. 1258-1262 (5)* *15.00 15.00*

World Soil Day. The full sheet sold for $14.95. The generic labels are shown. Labels could be personalized. The personalization of labels was available only at UN Headquarters, and not through mail order.

**United Nations Emblem Type of 2016 Dated "2021" in Purple**

**2021, Jan. 22 Litho. *Perf. 14¾***

**1263** A490 $1.20 multicolored + label *3.00 3.00*
Sheet of 10 + 10 labels *30.00 —*

The full sheet sold for $14.95. The generic label has an ox on red background. The personalization of labels was available only at UN Headquarters, and not through mail order.

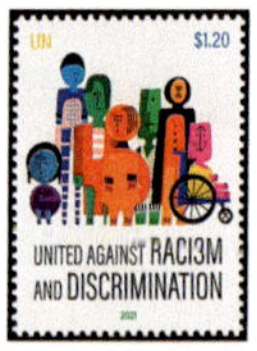

International Day for the Elimination of Racial Discrimination — A564

**2021, Mar. 19 Litho. *Perf. 13¼x13***

**1264** A564 $1.20 multicolored 2.40 2.40

See Offices in Geneva No. 693; Vienna No. 669.

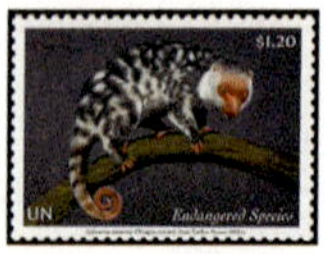

Endangered Species — A565

Designs: No. 1265, Waigeo cuscus. No. 1266, Helmeted honeyeater. No. 1267, Venus flytrap. No. 1268, American alligator.

**2021, Apr. 7 Litho. *Perf. 12¾x12½***

**1265** A565 $1.20 multicolored 2.40 2.40
**1266** A565 $1.20 multicolored 2.40 2.40
**1267** A565 $1.20 multicolored 2.40 2.40
**1268** A565 $1.20 multicolored 2.40 2.40
*a.* Block of 4, #1265-1268 9.75 9.75
*Nos. 1265-1268 (4)* 9.60 9.60

See Offices in Geneva Nos. 694-697; Vienna Nos. 670-673.

Miniature Sheet

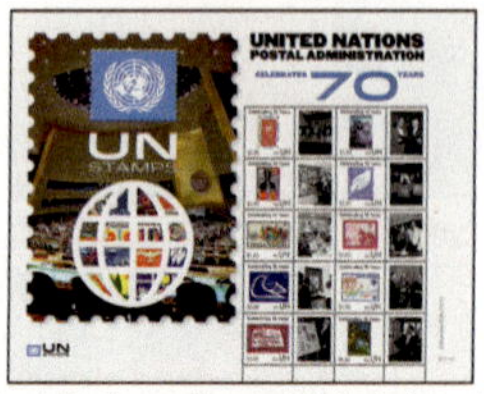

United Nations Postal Administration, 70th Anniv. — A566

No. 1269 — United Nations stamps: a, #171. b, #548. c, #873. d, #5. e, #268. f, #1. g, #249. h, #310. i, #35. j, #160.

**2021, Apr. 30 Litho. *Perf. 14¾***

**1269** A566 Sheet of 10 *30.00 30.00*
*a.-j.* $1.20 Any single + label *3.00 3.00*

The full sheet sold for $14.95. The generic labels are shown. Labels could be personalized. The personalization of labels was available only at UN Headquarters, and not through mail order.

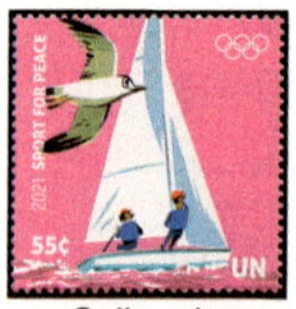

Sailors in Sailboat and Bird — A567

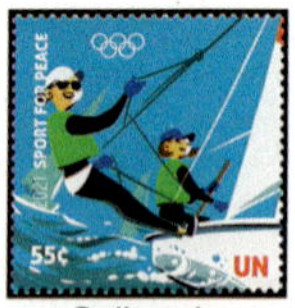

Sailors in Sailboat — A568

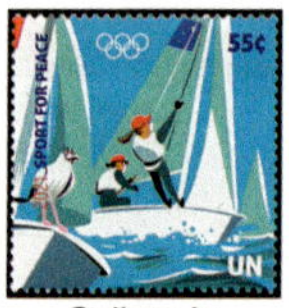

Sailors in Sailboat and Bird — A569

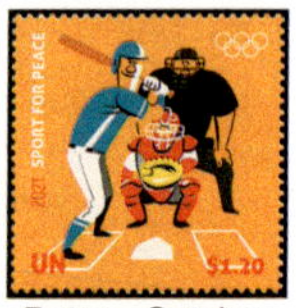

Batter, Catcher and Umpire — A570

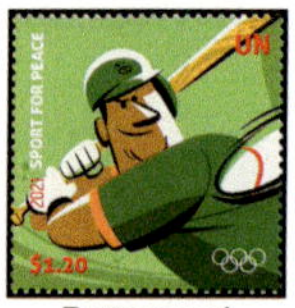

Batter and Baseball A571

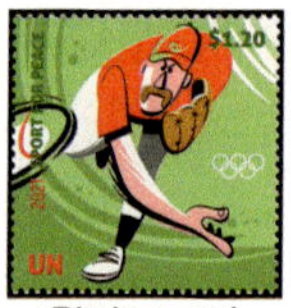
Pitcher and Baseball A572

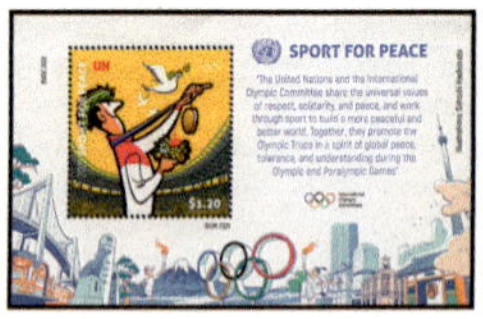

Olympic Gold Medalist and Dove A573

**2021, July 23 Litho. *Perf. 13½***

**1270** A567 55c multicolored 1.10 1.10
**1271** A568 55c multicolored 1.10 1.10
**1272** A569 55c multicolored 1.10 1.10
*a.* Horiz. strip of 3, #1270-1272 3.30 3.30
**1273** A570 $1.20 multicolored 2.40 2.40
**1274** A571 $1.20 multicolored 2.40 2.40
**1275** A572 $1.20 multicolored 2.40 2.40
*a.* Horiz. strip of 3, #1273-1275 7.20 7.20
*Nos. 1270-1275 (6)* 10.50 10.50

**Souvenir Sheet**

**1276** A573 $1.20 multicolored 2.40 2.40

Sports for Peace, 2020 Summer Olympics, Tokyo. The 2020 Summer Olympics were postponed until 2021 because of the COVID-19 pandemic. See Offices in Geneva Nos. 698-704, Vienna Nos. 674-680.

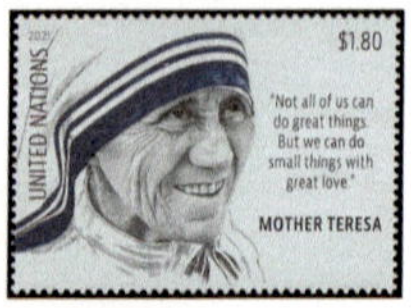

Mother Teresa (1910-97), Humanitarian A574

**2021, Aug. 12 Litho. *Perf. 14¼***

**1277** A574 $1.80 dark blue & black 3.75 3.75

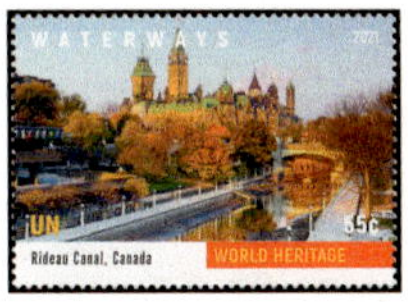


Waterway, Railway and Bridges World Heritage Sites — A575

Designs: Nos. 1278, 1280a, Rideau Canal, Canada. Nos. 1279, 1280d, Grand Canal, People's Republic of China. No. 1280b, Rhaetian Railway, Switzerland and Italy. No. 1280c, Forth Bridge, Scotland. No. 1280e, Darjeeling Himalayan Railway, India. No. 1280f, Old Bridge, Mostar, Bosnia and Herzegovina.

**2021, Aug. 25 Litho. *Perf. 14¼***

**1278** A575 55c multicolored 1.10 1.10
**1279** A575 $1.20 multicolored 2.40 2.40

### Souvenir Booklet

**1280** Booklet, #1280g-1280l 24.00
*a.-c.* A575 35c any single .75 .75
*d.-f.* A575 55c any single 1.25 1.25
*g.* Booklet pane of 4 #1280a 3.00 —
*h.* Booklet pane of 4 #1280b 3.00 —
*i.* Booklet pane of 4 #1280c 3.00 —
*j.* Booklet pane of 4 #1280d 5.00 —
*k.* Booklet pane of 4 #1280e 5.00 —
*l.* Booklet pane of 4 #1280f 5.00 —

Complete booklet sold for $12. See Offices in Geneva Nos. 705-707; Vienna Nos. 681-683.

Souvenir Sheet

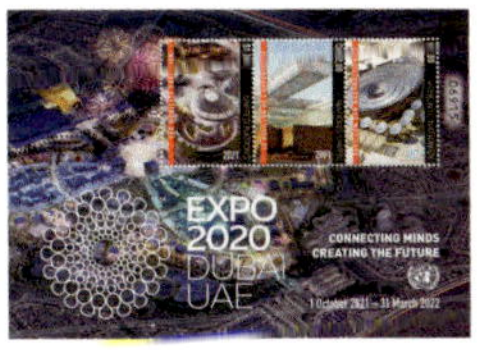


Expo 2020, Dubai A576

No. 1281: a, Mobility Pavilion. b, Opportunity Pavilion. c, Sustainability Pavilion.

**2021, Oct. 1 Litho. *Perf. 13½x13***

**1281** A576 Sheet of 3 14.50 14.50
*a.* $1.30 multi 4.75 4.75
*b.* 2fr multi 4.75 4.75
*c.* €1.80 multi 4.75 4.75

Expo 2020 was postponed until 2021 because of the COVID-19 pandemic. No. 1281 sold for $7.04.

Souvenir Sheet

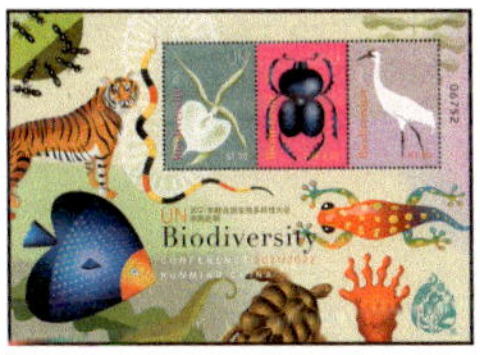


United Nations Biodiversity Conference, Kunming, People's Republic of China — A577

No. 1282: a, Flower. b, Insect. c, Bird.

**2021, Oct. 11 Litho. *Perf. 13½x13***

**1282** A577 Sheet of 3 14.50 14.50
*a.* $1.30 multi 4.75 4.75
*b.* 2fr multi 4.75 4.75
*c.* €1.80 multi 4.75 4.75

No. 1282 sold for $7.04.

Miniature Sheet

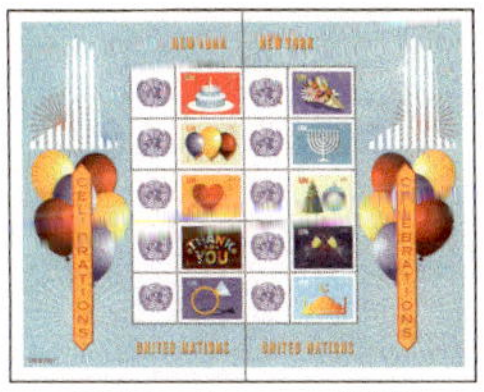

Celebrations — A578

No. 1283: a, Birthday cake. b, Flower bouquet. c, Three balloons. d, Menorah. e, Heart and arrow. f, Christmas tree and ornament. g, "Thank you." h, Champagne flutes. i, Diamond ring. j, Mosque.

**2021, Nov. 4 Litho. *Perf. 14¼***

**1283** A578 Sheet of 10 *32.50 32.50*
*a.-j.* $1.30 Any single + label *3.25 3.25*

The full sheet sold for $15.95. The generic labels are shown. Labels could be personalized. The personalization of labels was available only at UN Headquarters, and not through mail order.

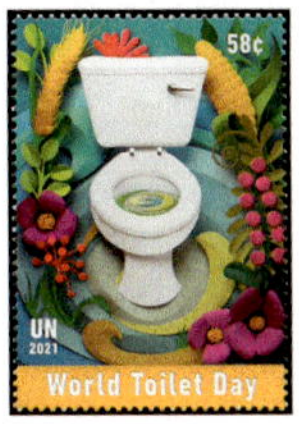


World Toilet Day — A579

**2021, Nov. 19 Litho. *Perf. 14¼***

**1284** A579 58c multicolored 1.25 1.25

Miniature Sheet

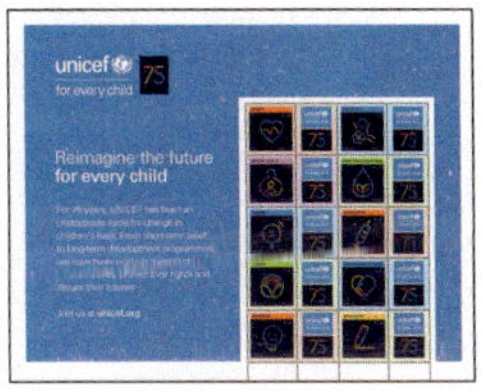


UNICEF, 75th Anniv. A580

No. 1285 — Inscription: a, Health. b, Disability. c, Mental Health. d, Water Sanitation Hygiene. e, Gender. f, Vaccination. g, Climate. h, Humanitarian Response. i, Nutrition. j, Education.

**2021, Dec. 11 Litho. *Perf. 14½***

**1285** A580 Sheet of 10 *32.50 32.50*
*a.-j.* $1.30 Any single + label *3.25 3.25*

The full sheet sold for $15.95. The generic labels are shown. Labels could be personalized. The personalization of labels was available only at UN Headquarters, and not through mail order.

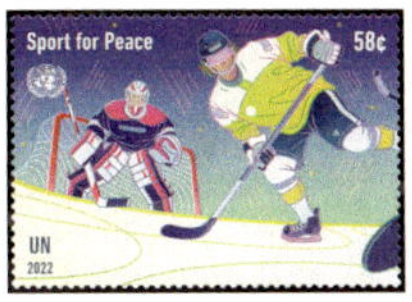


Ice Hockey Player and Goaltender A581

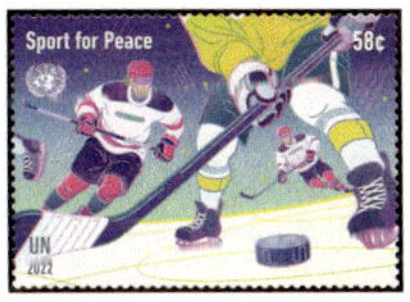


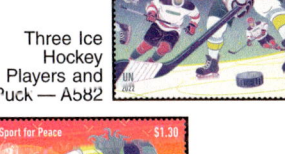

Three Ice Hockey Players and Puck — A582

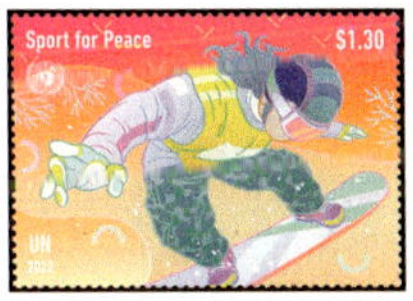


Snowboarder With Yellow Green Vest — A583

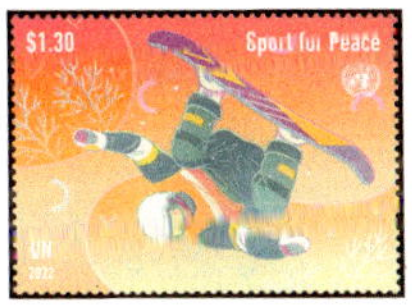


Snowboarder in Air With Orange Vest — A584

**2022, Jan. 14 Litho. *Perf. 14¼***

**1286** A581 58c multicolored 1.25 1.25
**1287** A582 58c multicolored 1.25 1.25
*a.* Horiz. pair, #1286-1287 2.50 2.50
**1288** A583 $1.30 multicolored 2.60 2.60
**1289** A584 $1.30 multicolored 2.60 2.60
*a.* Horiz. pair, #1288-1289 5.20 5.20
First day cover, #1288-1289 9.50
Inscription block of 4 10.50 —
Pane of 6 16.00 —
*Nos. 1286-1289 (4)* 7.70 7.70

Sports for Peace, 2022 Winter Olympics, Beijing. See Offices in Geneva Nos. 710-713; Vienna Nos. 687-690.

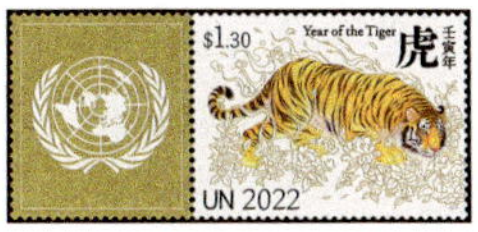


Tiger Facing Right A585

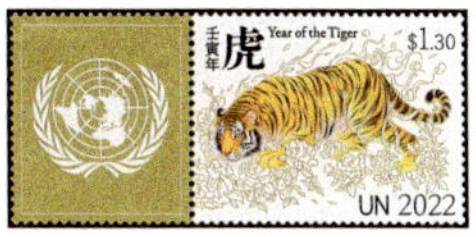


Tiger Facing Left A586

**2022, Jan. 21 Litho. *Perf. 14¼***

**1290** A585 $1.30 multi + label *3.25 3.25*
**1291** A586 $1.30 multi + label *3.25 3.25*
*a.* Horiz. pair, #1290-1291, + 2 labels *6.50 6.50*
Sheet of 10, 5 each #1290-1291, + 10 labels *32.50 32.50*

New Year 2022 (Year of the Tiger). The full sheet sold for $15.95. The generic labels are shown. Labels could be personalized. The personalization of labels was available only at UN Headquarters, and not through mail order.

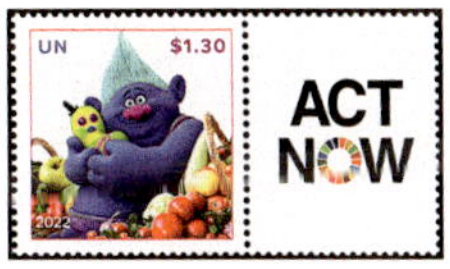


Biggie, Mr. Dinkles, Fruits and Vegetables A587

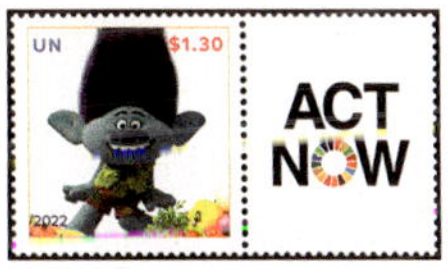


Guy Diamond, Tiny Diamond, Fruits and Vegetables A588

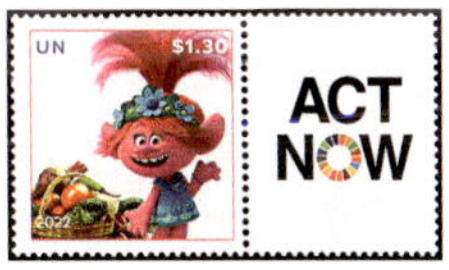


Poppy and Vegetables A589

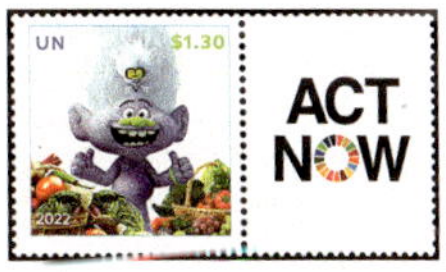


Branch, Fruits and Vegetables A590

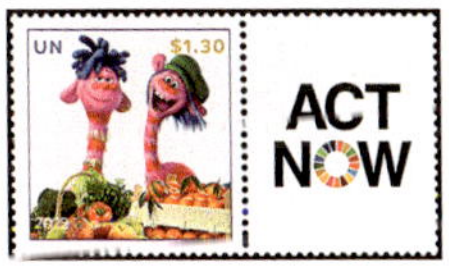


Prince Darnell, Cooper, Fruits and Vegetables A591

**2022, Feb. 22 Litho. *Perf. 14¾***

**1292** A587 $1.30 multi + label *3.25 3.25*
**1293** A588 $1.30 multi + label *3.25 3.25*
**1294** A589 $1.30 multi + label *3.25 3.25*
**1295** A590 $1.30 multi + label *3.25 3.25*
**1296** A591 $1.30 multi + label *3.25 3.25*
*a.* Vert. strip of 5, #1292-1296, + 5 labels *16.25 16.25*
Sheet of 10, 2 each #1292-1296, + 10 labels *32.50 32.50*
*Nos. 1292-1296 (5)* 16.25 16.25

Trolls Food Heroes Campaign. The full sheet sold for $15.95. The generic labels are shown. Labels could be personalized. The personalization of labels was available only at UN Headquarters, and not through mail order.

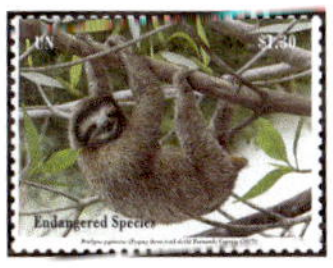


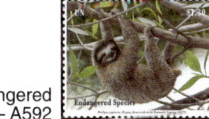

Endangered Species — A592

Designs: No. 1297, Pygmy three-toed sloth. No. 1298, Andean condor. No. 1299, Keel-billed toucan. No. 1300, Jaguar.

***Perf. 12¾x12½***

**2022, Mar. 18 Litho.**

**1297** A592 $1.30 multicolored 2.60 2.60
**1298** A592 $1.30 multicolored 2.60 2.60
**1299** A592 $1.30 multicolored 2.60 2.60
**1300** A592 $1.30 multicolored 2.60 2.60
*a.* Block of 4, #1297-1300 10.50 10.50
*Nos. 1297-1300 (4)* 10.40 10.40

See Offices in Geneva Nos. 714-717; Vienna Nos. 691-694.

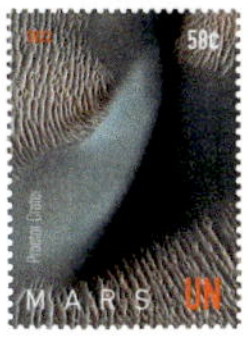


Exploration of Mars — A593

Designs: 58c, Proctor Crater. No. 1302, Mars Perseverence Rover.
No. 1303, Mars Ingenuity Helicopter.

**2022, Apr. 24 Litho. *Perf. 13¼x13***

**1301** A593 58c multicolored 1.25 1.25
**1302** A593 $1.30 multicolored 2.60 2.60

### Souvenir Sheet

***Perf. 13½***

**1303** A593 $1.30 multicolored 3.50 2.60

No. 1303 contains one 44x44mm stamp. See Offices in Geneva Nos. 718-720; Vienna Nos. 696-698.

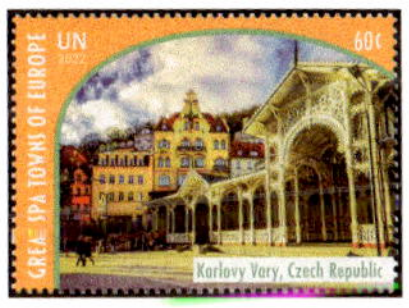


European Spa Town World Heritage Sites — A594

Designs: Nos. 1304, 1306a, Karlovy Vary, Czech Republic. Nos. 1305, 1306d, Montecatini Terme, Italy. No. 1306b, Spa, Belgium. No. 1306c, Baden-Baden, Germany. No. 1306e, Vichy, France. No. 1306f, Baden bei Wien, Austria.

**2022, Sept. 9 Litho. *Perf. 14½x14¼***

**1304** A594 60c multicolored 1.25 1.25
**1305** A594 $1.40 multicolored 3.00 3.00

### Souvenir Booklet

**1306** Booklet, #1115g-1115l 28.00
*a.-c.* A594 44c any single 1.00 1.00
*d.-f.* A594 60c any single 1.30 1.30
*g.* Booklet pane of 4 #1306a 4.00 —
*h.* Booklet pane of 4 #1306b 4.00 —
*i.* Booklet pane of 4 #1306c 4.00 —
*j.* Booklet pane of 4 #1306d 5.25 —
*k.* Booklet pane of 4 #1306e 5.25 —
*l.* Booklet pane of 4 #1306f 5.25 —

Complete booklet sold for $14. See Offices in Geneva Nos. 722-724; Vienna Nos. 700-702.

Miniature Sheet

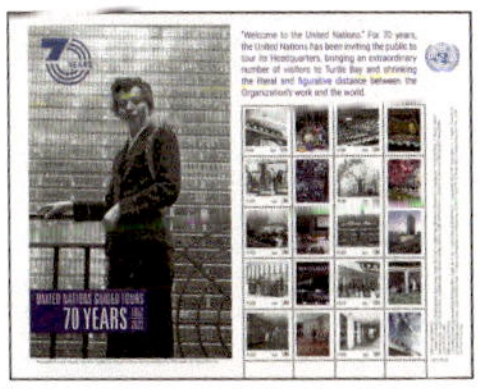


Guided Tours of United Nations Headquarters, 70th Anniv. — A595

No. 1307: a, Tourists on elevated walkway above arch. b, General Assembly chamber. c, Tourists standing in lobby. d, Tour guide touching tree branch. e, Security Council chamber. f, Tour guide standing in aisle, tourists seated in chamber. g, Children and adults at tour information counter in lobby. h, Tourists standing near circular pillars in lobby. i, Tour guide and tourists in front of mural. j, Tourists exiting doorway.

**2022, Nov. 1 Litho. *Perf. 14½***

**1307** A595 Sheet of 10 *34.00 34.00*
*a.-j.* $1.40 Any single + label *3.25 3.25*

The full sheet sold for $16.95. The generic labels are shown. Labels could be personalized. The personalization of labels was available only at UN Headquarters, and not through mail order.

# UNITED NATIONS, OFFICES IN NEW YORK

## Souvenir Sheet

Hands Reaching for Olive Branch — A596

**Litho. With Foil Application**
**2022, Nov. 18**    **Die Cut Perf. 11½**
**Self-Adhesive**
1308   A596   $4.50 multicolored   9.00   9.00

Crypto stamp. Unused value is for sheets with unscratched panels at right. See Offices in Geneva No. 725; Vienna No. 703.

Rabbit Facing Right — A597

Rabbit Facing Left — A598

**2023, Jan. 20**    **Litho.**    **Perf. 14¼**
1309   A597   $1.40 multi + label   3.50   3.50
1310   A598   $1.40 multi + label   3.50   3.50
   a. Horiz. pair, #1309-1310, + 2 labels   7.00   7.00
   Sheet of 10, 5 each #1290-1291, + 10 labels   35.00   35.00

New Year 2023 (Year of the Rabbit). The full sheet sold for $16.95. The generic labels are shown. Labels could be personalized. The personalization of labels was available only at UN Headquarters, and not through mail order.

Endangered Species — A599

Designs: No. 1311, Bighorn sheep. No. 1312, Morelet's crocodile. No. 1313, Bald eagle. No. 1314, Cape aloe.

**2023, Mar. 3**    **Litho.**    **Perf. 12¾x12½**
1311   A599   $1.45 multicolored   3.00   3.00
1312   A599   $1.45 multicolored   3.00   3.00
1313   A599   $1.45 multicolored   3.00   3.00
1314   A599   $1.45 multicolored   3.00   3.00
   a. Block of 4, #1311-1314   12.00   12.00
   Nos. 1311-1314 (4)   12.00   12.00

See Offices in Geneva Nos. 726-729; Vienna Nos. 704-707.

## Souvenir Sheet

Fifth United Nations Conference on the Least Developed Countries, Doha, Qatar — A600

No. 1315: a, "From Potential to Prosperity." b, "Du Potentiel à la Prosperite." c, "Vom Potenzial zum Wohlstand."

**2023, Mar. 5**    **Litho.**    **Perf. 13¼x14**
1315   A600   Sheet of 3   14.00   14.00
   a. $1.45 multi   4.50   4.50
   b. 2.30fr multi   4.50   4.50
   c. €1.90 multi   4.50   4.50

No. 1315 sold for $7.

United Nations Emblem, Text in English — A601

United Nations Emblem, Text in French — A602

**2023, Apr. 5**    **Litho.**    **Perf. 14¼**
1316   multi + label   6.50   6.50
   a. A601 $1.45 multicolored + label   3.25   3.25
   b. A602 1.10fr multicolored + label   3.25   3.25
   Sheet of 10, 5 each #1316a-1316b, + 10 labels   32.50   32.50

World Health Organization, 75th anniv. The full sheet sold for $16.20. The generic labels are shown. Labels could be personalized. The personalization of labels was available only at UN Headquarters, and not through mail order. Nos. 1316a-1316b also were printed in a similar sheet issued on Apr. 15 with labels and sheet margins commemorating the 60th anniversary of the United Nations Institute for Training and Research. See No. 1327.

Reclining Figure, Sculpture by Henry Moore (1898-1986) — A603

Tapestry Made by Pinton Frères of Art by Le Corbusier (1887-1965) — A604

**2023, Apr. 15**    **Litho.**    **Perf. 14½x14¼**
1317   A603   63c multicolored   1.30   1.30
1318   A604   $1.45 multicolored   3.00   3.00

World Art Day. See Offices in Geneva Nos. 730-731; Vienna Nos. 708-709.

A605

A606

A607

A608

A609

A610

A611

A612

Marine Life of Florida Reefs — A613

**2023, June 8**    **Litho.**    **Perf. 14x13¼**
1319   Sheet of 3   12.00   12.00
   a. A605 63c multicolored   1.30   1.30
   b. A606 63c multicolored   1.30   1.30
   c. A607 63c multicolored   1.30   1.30
   d. A608 63c multicolored   1.30   1.30
   e. A609 63c multicolored   1.30   1.30
   f. A610 63c multicolored   1.30   1.30
   g. A611 63c multicolored   1.30   1.30
   h. A612 63c multicolored   1.30   1.30

World Oceans Day. See Offices in Geneva No. 733; Vienna No. 710.

## Souvenir Sheet

Frankie the Dinosaur — A614

**2023, June 20**    **Litho.**    **Perf. 13¼x14**
1320   A614   $1.45 multicolored   3.00   3.00

"Don't Choose Extinction" campaign. See Offices in Geneva No. 734; Vienna No. 711.

A615

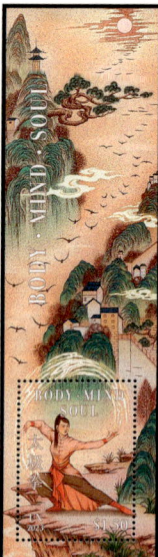

Tajiquan — A616

**2023, Aug. 10**    **Litho.**    **Perf. 14x13¼**
1321   A615   66c multicolored   1.40   1.40

## Souvenir Sheet
**Perf. 13¼x14**
1322   A616   $1.50 multicolored   3.00   3.00

UNESCO Intangible Cultural Heritage. See Offices in Geneva Nos. 735-736; Vienna Nos. 712-713.

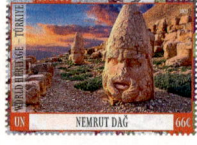

World Heritage Sites in Turkey — A617

Designs: Nos. 1323, 1325a, Nemrut Dag. Nos. 1324, 1325d, Selimiye Mosque. No. 1325b, Göreme National Park and the Rock Sites of Cappadocia. No. 1325c, Ephesus. No. 1325e, Great Mosque and Hospital of Divrigi. No. 1325f, Historic Areas of Istanbul.

**2023, Sept. 8**    **Litho.**    **Perf. 14x14¼**
1323   A617   66c multicolored   1.40   1.40
1324   A617   $1.50 multicolored   3.00   3.00

### Souvenir Booklet
1325   Booklet, #1280g-1280l   34.50
   a.-c. A617 51c any single   1.25   1.25
   d.-f. A617 66c any single   1.60   1.60
   g. Booklet pane of 4 #1325a   5.00   —
   h. Booklet pane of 4 #1325b   5.00   —
   i. Booklet pane of 4 #1325c   5.00   —
   j. Booklet pane of 4 #1325d   6.40   —
   k. Booklet pane of 4 #1325e   6.40   —
   l. Booklet pane of 4 #1325f   6.40   —

Complete booklet sold for $17.05. See Offices in Geneva Nos. 737-739; Vienna Nos. 714-716.

World Mental Health Day — A618

**2023, Oct. 10**    **Litho.**    **Perf. 13¼x14**
1326   A618   $1.50 multicolored   3.00   3.00

See Offices in Geneva No. 740; Vienna No. 717.

### United Nations Emblem Text in English Type of 2023
**2023, Nov. 30**    **Litho.**    **Perf. 14¼**
1327   Horiz. pair, #1327a, 1316b, + 2 labels   7.25   7.25
   a. A601 $1.50 multicolored + label   4.00   4.00
   Sheet of 10, 5 each #1327a, 1316b, + 10 labels   36.50   36.50

United Nations Climate Change Conference. The full sheet sold for $17.82. Labels could be personalized. The personalization of labels was available only at UN Headquarters, and not through mail order.

UNITED NATIONS, OFFICES IN NEW YORK — OFFICES IN GENEVA, SWITZERLAND

## SEMI-POSTAL STAMPS

### Souvenir Sheet

AIDS Awareness — SP1

**2002, Oct. 24    Litho.    Perf. 14½**
B1  SP1  37c + 6c multicolored  3.50  3.50
See Offices in Geneva No. B1, Vienna No. B1.

### Miniature Sheet

Campaign Against COVID-19 Pandemic — SP2

No. B2: a, Hand washing. b, Question mark in speech bubble. c, Social distancing. d, Smiling face. e, Cross in broken circle. f, Hands making heart shape.

**2020, Aug. 11    Litho.    Perf. 13¼**
B2  SP2  Sheet of 6  21.00  21.00
  a.  55c+50c multi  2.10  2.10
  b.  $1.20+50c multi  3.50  3.50
  c.  1fr+50c multi  3.50  3.50
  d.  1.50fr+50c multi  4.50  4.50
  e.  85c+50c multi  3.50  3.50
  f.  €1+50c multi  3.75  3.75

Surtax for World Health Organization COVID Solidarity Response Fund.

SP3

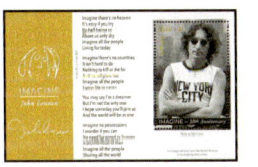

Photograph of John Lennon (1940-80), by Bob Gruen — SP4

**2021, Sept. 21    Litho.    Perf. 14¼**
B3  SP3  $1.30 multicolored  3.75  3.75

### Souvenir Sheet
### Litho. With Foil Application

B4  SP4  $2.60 multicolored  7.25  7.25
International Day of Peace. Surtax for United Nations peacekeeping efforts.

World Humanitarian Day — SP5

**2022, Aug. 19    Litho.    Perf. 13¼x13**
B5  SP5  $1.40 multicolored  4.00  4.00
Surtax for United Nations Central Emergency Response Fund. See Offices in Geneva No. B4; Vienna No. B4.

---

## AIR POST STAMPS

Plane and Gull — AP1

Swallows and UN Emblem — AP2

**1951, Dec. 14    Unwmk.    Perf. 14**
C1  AP1  6c henna brown  .25  .25
C2  AP1  10c brt blue grn  .30  .30
C3  AP2  15c deep ultra  .40  .40
  a.  15c Prussian blue  65.00
C4  AP2  25c gray black  .85  .85
Nos. C1-C4 (4)  1.80  1.80

Airplane Wing and Globe — AP3

**1957, May 27    Perf. 12½x14**
C5  AP3  4c maroon  .25  .25

### Type of 1957 and

UN Flag and Plane — AP4

**Perf. 12½x13½**
**1959, Feb. 9    Unwmk.**
C6  AP3  5c rose red  .25  .25
**Perf. 13½x14**
C7  AP4  7c ultramarine  .25  .25

Outer Space AP5

UN Emblem AP6

Bird of Laurel Leaves — AP7

**Perf. 11½**
**1963, June 17    Photo.    Unwmk.**
C8  AP5  6c blk, blue & yel grn  .25  .25
C9  AP6  8c yel, ol grn & red  .25  .25
**Perf. 12½x12**
C10  AP7  13c ultra, aquamarine, gray & carmine  .25  .25

"Flight Across Globe" AP8

Jet Plane and Envelope AP9

**Perf. 11½x12, 12x11½**
**1964, May 1    Photo.    Unwmk.**
C11  AP8  15c vio, buff, gray & pale grn  .30  .30
  a.  Gray omitted  225.00
C12  AP9  25c yel, org, gray, blue & red  .50  .50
Nos. C8-C12 (5)  1.55  1.55
See UN Offices in Geneva No. 8

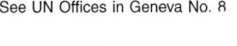

Jet Plane and UN Emblem — AP10

**1968, Apr. 18    Litho.    Perf. 13**
C13  AP10  20c multicolored  .35  .35

Wings, Envelopes and UN Emblem — AP11

**1969, Apr. 21    Litho.    Perf. 13**
C14  AP11  10c org ver, org, yel & blk  .25  .25

UN Emblem and Stylized Wing AP12

Birds in Flight AP13

Clouds — AP14

"UN" and Plane — AP15

**Litho. & Engr.**
**1972, May 1    Perf. 13x13½**
C15  AP12  9c lt blue, dk red & vio blue  .25  .25
**Photo.**
**Perf. 14x13½**
C16  AP13  11c blue & multi  .25  .25
**Perf. 13½x14**
C17  AP14  17c yel, red & org  .25  .25
**Perf. 13**
C18  AP15  21c silver & multi  .25  .25
Nos. C15-C18 (4)  1.00  1.00

Globe and Jet — AP16

Pathways Radiating from UN Emblem — AP17

Bird in Flight, UN Headquarters AP18

**Perf. 13, 12½x13 (18c)**
**1974, Sept. 16    Litho.**
C19  AP16  13c multicolored  .25  .25
C20  AP17  18c gray olive & multi  .25  .25
C21  AP18  26c blue & multi  .35  .35
Nos. C19-C21 (3)  .85  .85

Winged Airmail Letter AP19

Symbolic Globe and Plane AP20

**1977, June 27    Photo.    Perf. 14**
C22  AP19  25c greenish blue & multi  .35  .35
C23  AP20  31c magenta  .45  .45

---

## OFFICES IN GENEVA, SWITZERLAND

For use only on mail posted at the Palais des Nations (UN European Office), Geneva. Inscribed in French unless otherwise stated.

100 Centimes = 1 Franc

Catalogue values for all unused stamps in this country are for Never Hinged items.

### Types of United Nations Issues 1961-69 and

UN European Office, Geneva — G1

Designs: 5c, UN Headquarters, New York, and world map. 10c, UN flag. 20c, Three men united before globe. 50c, Opening words of UN Charter. 60c, UN emblem over globe. 70c, "un" and UN emblem. 75c, "Flight Across Globe." 80c, UN Headquarters and emblem. 90c, Abstract group of flags. 1fr, UN emblem. 2fr, Stylized globe and weather vane. 3fr, Statue by Henrik Starcke. 10fr, "Peace, Justice, Security."
The 20c, 80c and 90c are inscribed in French. The 75c and 10fr carry French inscription at top, English at bottom.

**1969-70    Photo.    Unwmk.**
**Perf. 13 (5c, 70c, 90c); 12½x12 (10c);**
1  A88  5c purple & multi  .25  .30
  a.  Green omitted
2  A52  10c salmon & multi  .25  .30
**Perf. 11½ (20c-60c, 3fr)**
3  A66  20c black & multi  .25  .30
4  G1  30c dark blue & multi  .25  .30
5  A77  50c ultra & multi  .25  .30
6  A54  60c dark brown, salmon & gold  .25  .30
7  A104  70c red, black & gold  .30  .35
**Perf. 11½x12 (75c)**
8  AP8  75c carmine rose & multi  .35  .40
**Perf 13½x14 (80c)**
9  A78  80c blue green, red & yellow  .35  .40
10  A45  90c blue & multi  .40  .45
**Litho. & Embossed**
**Perf. 14 (1fr)**
11  A79  1fr light & dark green  .40  .45
**Photo.**
**Perf. 12x11½ (2fr)**
12  A67  2fr blue & multi  .75  .85
13  A97  3fr olive & multi  1.00  1.10
**Engr.**
**Perf. 12 (10fr)**
14  A3  10fr dark blue  3.50  3.75
Nos. 1-14 (14)  8.55  9.55

## OFFICES IN GENEVA, SWITZERLAND

### Sea Bed Type of UN
**Photo. & Engr.**
1971, Jan. 25 — Perf. 13
15 A114 30c green & multi .25 .30

### Refugee Type of UN
1971, Mar. 12 — Litho. — Perf. 13x12½
16 A115 50c dp car, dp org & blk .25 .30

### World Food Program Type of UN
1971, Apr. 13 — Photo. — Perf. 14
17 A116 50c dark vio & multi .25 .30

### UPU Headquarters Type of UN
1971, May 28 — Photo. — Perf. 11½
18 A117 75c green & multi .35 .40

### Eliminate Racial Discrimination Types of UN
1971, Sept. 21 — Photo. — Perf. 13½
19 A118 30c blue & multi .25 .30
20 A119 50c yellow grn & multi .25 .30

### Picasso Type of UN
1971, Nov. 19 — Photo. — Perf. 11½
21 A122 1.10fr multicolored .75 .80

Palais des Nations, Geneva — G2

1972, Jan. 5 — Photo. — Perf. 11½
22 G2 40c ol, blue, sal & dk grn .25 .30

### Nuclear Weapons Type of UN
1972, Feb. 14 — Photo. — Perf. 13½x14
23 A124 40c yel, grn, blk, rose & gray .25 .30

### World Health Day Type of UN
**Litho. & Engr.**
1972, Apr. 7 — Perf. 13x13½
24 A125 80c black & multi .45 .50

### Human Environment Type of UN
**Lithographed & Embossed**
1972, June 5 — Perf. 12½x14
25 A126 40c ol, lemon, grn & blue .25 .30
26 A126 80c ultra, pink, grn & blue .45 .50

### Economic Commission for Europe Type of UN
1972, Sept. 11 — Litho. — Perf. 13x13½
27 A127 1.10fr red & multi 1.00 1.10

### Art at UN (Sert) Type of UN
1972, Nov. 17 — Photo. — Perf. 12x12½
28 A128 40c gold, red & brn .30 .35
29 A128 80c gold, brn & olive .60 .65

### Disarmament Decade Type of UN
1973, Mar. 9 — Litho. — Perf. 13½x13
30 A129 60c vio & multi .40 .45
31 A129 1.10fr olive & multi .85 .90

### Drug Abuse Type of UN
1973, Apr. 13 — Photo. — Perf. 13½
32 A130 60c blue & multi .45 .50

### Volunteers Type of UN
1973, May 25 — Photo. — Perf. 14
33 A131 80c gray grn & multi .35 .40

### Namibia Type of UN
1973, Oct. 1 — Photo. — Perf. 13½
34 A132 60c red & multi .35 .40

### Human Rights Type of UN
1973, Nov. 16 — Photo. — Perf. 13½
35 A133 40c ultra & multi .30 .35
36 A133 80c olive & multi .50 .55

### ILO Headquarters Type of UN
1974, Jan. 11 — Photo. — Perf. 14
37 A134 60c violet & multi .45 .50
38 A134 80c brown & multi .65 .70

### Centenary of UPU Type of UN
1974, Mar. 22 — Litho. — Perf. 12½
39 A135 30c gold & multi .25 .30
40 A135 60c gold & multi .60 .65

### Art at UN (Portinari) Type of UN
1974, May 6 — Photo. — Perf. 14
41 A136 60c dark red & multi .40 .45
42 A136 1fr green & multi .70 .75

### World Population Year Type of UN
1974, Oct. 18 — Photo. — Perf. 14
43 A140 60c brt grn & multi .50 .55
44 A140 80c brown & multi .70 .75

### Law of the Sea Type of UN
1974, Nov. 22 — Photo. — Perf. 14
45 A141 1.30fr blue & multi 1.00 1.10

### Outer Space Type of UN
1975, Mar. 14 — Litho. — Perf. 13
46 A142 60c multicolored .50 .55
47 A142 90c multicolored .75 .80

### International Women's Year Type of UN
1975, May 9 — Litho. — Perf. 15
48 A143 60c multicolored .40 .45
49 A143 90c multicolored .70 .75

### 30th Anniversary Type of UN
1975, June 26 — Litho. — Perf. 13
50 A144 60c green & multi .40 .45
51 A144 90c violet & multi .70 .75

**Souvenir Sheet**
*Imperf*
52 Sheet of 2 1.00 1.10
a. A144 60c green & multicolored .30 .35
b. A144 90c violet & multicolored .60 .65

### Namibia Type of UN
1975, Sept. 22 — Photo. — Perf. 13½
53 A145 50c multicolored .30 .35
54 A145 1.30fr multicolored .85 .90

### Peace-keeping Operations Type of UN
1975, Nov. 21 — Engr. — Perf. 12½
55 A146 60c greenish blue .35 .40
56 A146 70c bright violet .65 .65

### WFUNA Type of UN
1976, Mar. 12 — Photo. — Perf. 14
57 A152 90c multicolored .90 .95

### UNCTAD Type of UN
1976, Apr. 23 — Photo. — Perf. 11½
58 A153 1.10fr sepia & multi .90 .95

### Habitat Type of UN
1976, May 28 — Photo. — Perf. 14
59 A154 40c dull blue & multi .25 .30
60 A154 1.50fr violet & multi .75 .80

UN Emblem, Post Horn and Rainbow — G3

UN Postal Administration, 25th anniversary.

1976, Oct. 8 — Photo. — Perf. 11½
61 G3 80c tan & multi .50 .55
62 A3 1.10fr lt grn & multi 1.60 1.75

### World Food Council Type of UN
1976, Nov. 19 — Litho. — Perf. 14½
63 A156 70c multicolored .50 .55

### WIPO Type of UN
1977, Mar. 11 — Photo. — Perf. 14
64 A157 80c red & multi .60 .65

Drop of Water and Globe — G4

UN Water Conference, Mar del Plata, Argentina, Mar. 14-25.

1977, Apr. 22 — Photo. — Perf. 13½x13
65 G4 80c ultra & multi .50 .55
66 G4 1.10fr dark car & multi .80 .85

Hands Protecting UN Emblem — G5

UN Security Council.

1977, May 27 — Photo. — Perf. 11
67 G5 80c blue & multi .50 .55
68 G5 1.10fr emerald & multi .80 .85

Colors of Five Races Spun into One Firm Rope — G6

Fight against racial discrimination.

1977, Sept. 19 — Litho. — Perf. 13½x13
69 G6 40c multicolored .25 .30
70 G6 1.10fr multicolored .65 .70

Atomic Energy Turning Partly into Olive Branch — G7

Peaceful uses of atomic energy.

1977, Nov. 18 — Photo. — Perf. 14
71 G7 80c dark car & multi .55 .60
72 G7 1.10fr Prussian blue & multi .75 .80

"Tree" of Doves — G8

1978, Jan. 27 — Litho. — Perf. 14½
73 G8 35c multicolored .25 .30

Globes with Smallpox Distribution — G9

Global eradication of smallpox.

1978, Mar. 31 — Photo. — Perf. 12x11½
74 G9 80c yel & multi .60 .65
75 G9 1.10fr lt grn & multi .90 .95

### Namibia Type of UN
1978, May 5 — Photo. — Perf. 12
76 A166 80c multicolored .85 .90

Jets and Flight Patterns — G10

International Civil Aviation Organization for "Safety in the Air."

1978, June 12 — Photo. — Perf. 14
77 G10 70c multicolored .40 .45
78 G10 80c multicolored .70 .75

General Assembly, Flags and Globe — G11

1978, Sept. 15 — Photo. — Perf. 13½
79 G11 70c multicolored .45 .50
80 G11 1.10fr multicolored .85 .90

### Technical Cooperation Type of UN
1978, Nov. 17 — Photo. — Perf. 14
81 A169 80c multicolored .70 .75

Seismograph Recording Earthquake — G12

Office of the UN Disaster Relief Coordinator (UNDRO).

1979, Mar. 9 — Photo. — Perf. 14
82 G12 80c multicolored .50 .55
83 G12 1.50fr multicolored .80 .85

Children and Rainbow — G13

International Year of the Child.

1979, May 4 — Photo. — Perf. 14
84 G13 80c multicolored .35 .40
85 G13 1.10fr multicolored .65 .70

### Namibia Type of UN
1979, Oct. 5 — Litho. — Perf. 13½
86 A176 1.10fr multicolored .60 .65

International Court of Justice, Scales — G14

International Court of Justice, The Hague, Netherlands.

1979, Nov. 9 — Litho. — Perf. 13x13½
87 G14 80c multicolored .40 .45
88 G14 1.10fr multicolored .60 .65

### New Economic Order Type of UN
1980, Jan. 11 — Litho. — Perf. 15x14½
89 A179 80c multicolored .85 .90

Women's Year Emblem — G15

United Nations Decade for Women.

1980, Mar. 7 — Litho. — Perf. 14½x15
90 G15 40c multicolored .30 .35
91 G15 70c multicolored .70 .75

### Peace-keeping Operations Type of UN
1980, May 16 — Litho. — Perf. 14x13
92 A181 1.10fr blue & green .85 .90

Dove and "35" — G16

35th Anniversary of the United Nations.

1980, June 26 — Litho. — Perf. 13x13½
93 G16 40c blue grn & blk .35 .35
94 A183 70c multicolored .65 .70

**Souvenir Sheet**
*Imperf*
95 Sheet of 2 1.10 1.20
a. G16 40c blue green & black .30 .35
b. A183 70c multicolored .80 .85

### ECOSOC Type of UN and

Family Climbing Line Graph — G17

1980, Nov. 21 — Litho. — Perf. 13½x13
96 A186 40c multicolored .30 .35
97 G17 70c multicolored .60 .65

## OFFICES IN GENEVA, SWITZERLAND

### Palestinian Rights
**1981, Jan. 30**   Photo.   *Perf. 12x11½*
98   A188   80c multicolored   .55   .60

### International Year of the Disabled.
**1981, Mar. 6**   Photo.   *Perf. 14*
99   A190   40c black & blue   .25   .30
100   V4   1.50fr black & red   1.00   1.10

### Art Type of UN
**1981, Apr. 15**   Photo.   *Perf. 11½*
Granite Paper
101   A191   80c multicolored   .80   .85

### Energy Type of 1981
**1981, May 29**   Litho.   *Perf. 13*
102   A192   1.10fr multicolored   .75   .80

### Volunteers Program Type and

Volunteers Program Type and Symbols of Science, Agriculture and Industry — G18

**1981, Nov. 13**   Litho.
103   A194   40c multicolored   .45   .50
104   G18   70c multicolored   .90   .95

Fight Against Apartheid G19   Flower of Flags G20

**1982, Jan. 22**   *Perf. 11½x12*
105   G19   30c multicolored   .25   .30
106   G20   1fr multicolored   .80   .85

### Human Environment Type of UN and

Human Environment — G21

10th Anniversary of United Nations Environment Program.

**1982, Mar. 19**   Litho.   *Perf. 13½x13*
107   G21   40c multicolored   .30   .35
108   A199   1.20fr multicolored   1.10   1.40

### Outer Space Type of UN and

Satellite Applications of Space Technology — G22

Exploration and Peaceful Uses of Outer Space.

**1982, June 11**   Litho.   *Perf. 13x13½*
109   A201   80c multicolored   .60   .65
110   G22   1fr multicolored   .80   .85

### Conservation & Protection of Nature
**1982, Nov. 19**   Photo.   *Perf. 14*
111   A202   40c Bird   .45   .50
112   A202   1.50fr Reptile   1.10   1.20

### World Communications Year
**1983, Jan. 28**   Litho.   *Perf. 13*
113   A204   1.20fr multicolored   1.25   1.40

### Safety at Sea Type of UN and

Life Preserver and Radar — G23

**1983, Mar. 18**   Litho.   *Perf. 14½*
114   A205   40c multicolored   .40   .45
115   G23   80c multicolored   .80   .85

### World Food Program
**1983, Apr. 22**   Engr.   *Perf. 13½*
116   A207   1.50fr blue   1.25   1.40

### Trade Type of UN and

G24

**1983, June 6**   Litho.   *Perf. 14*
117   A208   80c multicolored   .50   .55
118   G24   1.10fr multicolored   .90   .95

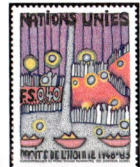

G25

35th Anniv. of the Universal Declaration of Human Rights — G26

**Photo. & Engr.**
**1983, Dec. 9**   *Perf. 13½*
119   G25   40c multicolored   .45   .50
120   G26   1.20fr multicolored   .95   1.00

### International Conference on Population Type
**1984, Feb. 3**   Litho.   *Perf. 14*
121   A212   1.20fr multicolored   .90   .95

Fishing — G27

Women Farm Workers, Africa — G28

World Food Day, Oct. 16

**1984, Mar. 15**   Litho.   *Perf. 14½*
122   G27   50c multicolored   .30   .35
123   G28   80c multicolored   .60   .65

Valletta, Malta — G29   Los Glaciares Natl. Park, Argentina — G30

World Heritage

**1984, Apr. 18**   Litho.   *Perf. 14*
124   G29   50c multicolored   .60   .65
125   G30   70c multicolored   .85   .90

G31   G32

Future for Refugees

**1984, May 29**   Photo.   *Perf. 11½*
126   G31   35c multicolored   .30   .35
127   G32   1.50fr multicolored   1.10   1.20

International Youth Year — G33

**1984, Nov. 15**   Litho.   *Perf. 13½*
128   G33   1.20fr multicolored   1.25   1.40

### ILO Type of UN and

Turin Center — G34

**1985, Feb. 1**   Engr.   *Perf. 13½*
129   A220   80c dull red   .70   .75
130   G34   1.20fr U Thant Pavilion   1.10   1.20

### UN University Type
50c, Pastoral scene, advanced communications.

**1985, Mar. 15**   Photo.   *Perf. 11½*
131   A221   50c multicolored   .60   .65
132   A221   80c like No. 131   1.00   1.10

Postman — G35   Doves — G36

**1985, May 10**   Litho.   *Perf. 14*
133   G35   20c multicolored   .25   .30
134   G36   1.20fr multicolored   1.25   1.40

### 40th Anniversary Type
*Perf. 12 x 11½*
**1985, June 26**   Photo.
135   A224   50c multicolored   .60   .65
136   A225   70c multicolored   .90   .95

**Souvenir Sheet**
*Imperf*
137   Sheet of 2   2.25   2.40
  a.   A224 50c multicolored   .85   .90
  b.   A225 70c multicolored   1.10   1.20

### UNICEF Child Survival Campaign Type
**Photo. & Engr.**
**1985, Nov. 22**   *Perf. 13½*
138   A226   50c Three girls   .40   .45
139   A226   1.20fr Infant drinking   1.10   1.20

### Africa in Crisis Type
**1986, Jan. 31**   Photo.   *Perf. 11½x12*
140   A227   1.40fr Mother, hungry children   1.25   1.40

### UN Development Program Type
Forestry.

**1986, Mar. 14**   Photo.   *Perf. 13½*
141   A228   35c Erosion control   1.60   1.75
142   A228   35c Logging   1.60   1.75
143   A228   35c Lumber transport   1.60   1.75
144   A228   35c Nursery   1.60   1.75
  a.   Block of 4, #141-144   6.50   7.50

Doves and Sun — G37

**1986, Mar. 14**   Litho.   *Perf. 15x14½*
145   G37   5c multicolored   .25   .30

### Stamp Collecting Type
Designs: 50c, UN Human Rights stamp. 80c, UN stamps.

**1986, May 22**   Engr.   *Perf. 12½*
146   A229   50c dark grn & hen brn   .60   .65
147   A229   80c dark grn & yel org   .90   .95

Flags and Globe as Dove — G38   Peace in French — G39

International Peace Year.

**Photo. & Embossed**
**1986, June 20**   *Perf. 13½*
148   G38   45c multicolored   .60   .65
149   G39   1.40fr multicolored   1.25   1.40

### WFUNA Anniversary Type
**Souvenir Sheet**
Designs: 35c, Abstract by Benigno Gomez, Honduras. 45c, Abstract by Alexander Calder (1898-1976), US. 50c, Abstract by Joan Miro (b. 1893), Spain. 70c, Sextet with Dove, by Ole Hamann, Denmark.

**1986, Nov. 14**   Litho.   *Perf. 13x13½*
150   Sheet of 4   3.75   4.00
  a.   A232 35c multicolored   .50   .55
  b.   A232 45c multicolored   .70   .75
  c.   A232 50c multicolored   .90   1.00
  d.   A232 70c multicolored   1.25   1.40

No. 150 has inscribed margin picturing UN and WFUNA emblems.

### Trygve Lie Type
**Photo. & Engr.**
**1987, Jan. 30**   *Perf. 13½*
151   A233   1.40fr multicolored   1.10   1.20

Sheaf of Colored Bands, by Georges Mathieu G40   Armillary Sphere, Palais des Nations G41

**Photo., Photo. & Engr. (#153)**
**1987, Jan. 30**   *Perf. 11½x12, 13½*
152   G40   90c multicolored   .65   .70
153   G41   1.40fr multicolored   1.25   1.40

### Shelter for the Homeless Type
Designs: 50c, Cement-making and brick-making. 90c, Interior construction and decorating.

*Perf. 13½x12½*
**1987, Mar. 13**   Litho.
154   A234   50c multicolored   .50   .55
155   A234   90c multicolored   1.00   1.10

### Fight Drug Abuse Type
Designs: 80c, Mother and child. 1.20fr, Workers in rice paddy.

**1987, June 12**   Litho.   *Perf. 14½x15*
156   A235   80c multicolored   .50   .55
157   A235   1.20fr multicolored   1.00   1.10

### UN Day Type
Designs: Multinational people in various occupations.

**1987, Oct. 23**   Litho.   *Perf. 14½x15*
158   A236   35c multicolored   .55   .60
159   A236   50c multicolored   .80   .85

### Immunize Every Child Type
Designs: 90c, Whooping cough. 1.70fr, Tuberculosis.

**1987, Nov. 20**   Litho.   *Perf. 15x14½*
160   A237   90c multicolored   1.50   1.65
161   A237   1.70fr multicolored   2.75   3.00

### IFAD Type
Designs: 35c, Flocks, dairy products. 1.40fr, Fruit.

**1988, Jan. 29**   Litho.   *Perf. 13½*
162   A238   35c multicolored   .35   .40
163   A238   1.40fr multicolored   1.40   1.50

286 OFFICES IN GENEVA, SWITZERLAND

For A Better World — G42

**1988, Jan. 29 Photo. *Perf. 14***
164 G42 50c multicolored .80 .85

### Survival of the Forests Type

Pine forest: 50c, Treetops, mountains. 1.10fr, Lake, tree trunks. Printed se-tenant in a continuous design.

**1988, Mar. 18 Litho. *Perf. 14x15***
165 A240 50c multicolored 1.25 1.40
166 A240 1.10fr multicolored 3.50 3.75
*a.* Pair, #165-166 5.50 6.00

### Intl. Volunteer Day Type

Designs: 80c, Agriculture, vert. 90c, Veterinary medicine.

***Perf. 13x14, 14x13***
**1988, May 6 Litho.**
167 A241 80c multicolored .80 .85
168 A241 90c multicolored 1.00 1.10

### Health in Sports Type

Paintings by LeRoy Neiman, American sports artist: 50c, Soccer, vert. 1.40fr, Swimming.

***Perf. 13½x13, 13x13½***
**1988, June 17 Litho.**
169 A242 50c multicolored .40 .45
170 A242 1.40fr multicolored 1.40 1.50

### Universal Declaration of Human Rights 40th Anniv. Type

**Photo. & Engr.**
**1988, Dec. 9 *Perf. 12***
171 A243 90c multicolored .70 .75

**Souvenir Sheet**
172 A243 2fr multicolored 2.75 3.00

### World Bank Type

80c, Telecommunications. 1.40fr, Industry.

**1989, Jan. 27 Litho. *Perf. 13x14***
173 A244 80c multicolored 1.00 1.10
174 A244 1.40fr multicolored 2.00 2.20

### Peace-Keeping Force Type

**1989, Mar. 17 *Perf. 14x13½***
175 A245 90c multicolored 1.25 1.40

### World Weather Watch Type

Satellite photographs: 90c, Europe under the influence of Arctic air. 1.10fr, Surface temperatures of sea, ice and land surrounding the Kattegat between Denmark and Sweden.

**1989, Apr. 21 Litho. *Perf. 13x14***
176 A247 90c multicolored 1.25 1.40
177 A247 1.10fr multicolored 2.00 2.20

G43

G44

**Photo., Photo. & Engr. (2fr)**
**1989, Aug. 23 *Perf. 14***
178 G43 50c multicolored .75 1.10
179 G44 2fr multicolored 2.50 3.75

Offices in Vienna, 10th anniv.

### Human Rights Type of 1989

Artwork: 35c, Young Mother Sewing, by Mary Cassatt. 80c, The Unknown Slave, sculpture by Albert Mangones.

**1989, Nov. 17 Litho. *Perf. 13½***
180 A250 35c multicolored .35 .40
181 A250 80c multicolored 1.00 1.10

Printed in panes of 12+12 se-tenant labels containing Articles 3 (35c) or 4 (80c) inscribed in English, French or German.
See Nos. 193-194, 209-210,34-235.

### Intl. Trade Center Type

**1990, Feb. 2 Litho. *Perf. 14½x15***
182 A251 1.50fr multicolored 2.25 2.50

G45

**1990, Feb. 2 Photo. *Perf. 14x13½***
183 G45 5fr multicolored 4.75 5.25

G46

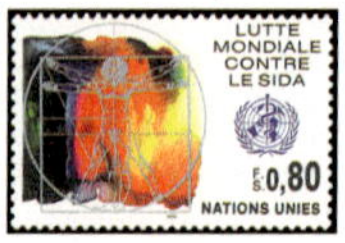


Fight AIDS Worldwide — G46a

### Fight AIDS Type

Designs: 50c, "SIDA." 80c, Proportional drawing of man like the illustration by Leonardo da Vinci.

***Perf. 13½x12½***
**1990, Mar. 16 Litho.**
184 G46 50c multicolored 1.00 1.10
185 G46a 80c multicolored 1.75 1.90

### Medicinal Plants Type

**1990, May 4 Photo. *Perf. 11½***
**Granite Paper**
186 A253 90c Plumeria rubra 1.00 1.10
187 A253 1.40fr Cinchona officinalis 2.00 2.20

### UN 45th Anniv. Type

"45," emblem and: 90c, Symbols of clean environment, transportation and industry. 1.10fr, Dove in silhouette.

**1990, June 26 Litho. *Perf. 14½x13***
188 A254 90c multicolored 1.10 1.20
189 A254 1.10fr multicolored 2.25 2.50

**Souvenir Sheet**
190 Sheet of 2, #188-189 6.00 6.50

### Crime Prevention Type

**1990, Sept. 13 Photo. *Perf. 14***
191 A255 50c Official corruption 1.25 1.40
192 A255 2fr Environmental crime 3.00 3.25

### Human Rights Type of 1989

Artwork: 35c, The Prison Courtyard by Vincent Van Gogh. 90c, Katho's Son Redeems the Evil Doer From Execution by Albrecht Durer.

**1990, Nov. 16 Litho. *Perf. 13½***
193 A250 35c multicolored .45 .50
194 A250 90c blk & brn 1.25 1.40

### Economic Commission for Europe Type

**1991, Mar. 15 Litho. *Perf. 14***
195 A256 90c Owl, gull 1.40 1.60
196 A256 90c Bittern, otter 1.40 1.60
197 A256 90c Swan, lizard 1.40 1.60
198 A256 90c Great crested grebe 1.40 1.60
*a.* Block of 4, #195-198 5.60 6.50

### Namibian Independence Type

**1991, May 10 Litho. *Perf. 14***
199 A257 70c Mountains 1.00 1.10
200 A257 90c Baobab tree 2.00 2.20

Ballots Filling Ballot Box G47

UN Emblem G48

**1991, May 10 Litho. *Perf. 15x14½***
201 G47 80c multicolored .75 .80
202 G48 1.50fr multicolored 2.00 2.20

G49

Rights of the Child — G50

**1991, June 14 Litho. *Perf. 14½***
203 G49 80c Hands holding infant 1.00 1.10
204 G50 1.10fr Children, flowers 2.00 2.20

G51

Banning of Chemical Weapons — G52

**1991, Sept. 11 Litho. *Perf. 13½***
205 G51 80c multicolored 2.00 2.20
206 G52 1.40fr multicolored 3.00 3.25

### UN Postal Administration, 40th Anniv. Type

**1991, Oct. 24 *Perf. 14x15***
207 A263 50c UN NY No. 7 .80 .85
208 A263 1.60fr UN NY No. 10 2.20 2.40

### Human Rights Type of 1989

Artwork: 50c, Early Morning in Rio...1925, by Paul Klee. 90c, Marriage of Giovanni (?) Arnolfini and Giovanna Cenami (?), by Jan Van Eyck.

**1991, Nov. 20 Litho. *Perf. 13½***
209 A250 50c multicolored .75 .80
210 A250 90c multicolored 1.25 1.40

Panes of 12+12 se-tenant labels containing Articles 15 (50c) or 16 (90c) inscribed in French, German or English.

### World Heritage Type of 1984

Designs: 50c, Sagarmatha Natl. Park, Nepal. 1.10fr, Stonehenge, United Kingdom.

**1992, Jan. 24 Litho. *Perf. 13***
**Size: 35x28mm**
211 G29 50c multicolored .80 .85
212 G29 1.10fr multicolored 1.90 2.10

G53

**1992, Jan. 24 Litho. *Perf. 15x14½***
213 G53 3fr multicolored 3.00 3.25

### Clean Oceans Type

**1992, Mar. 13 Litho. *Perf. 14***
214 A264 80c Ocean surface, diff. .90 .95
215 A264 80c Ocean bottom, diff. .90 .95
*a.* Pair, #214-215 1.80 *2.10*

### Earth Summit Type

Designs: No. 216, Rainbow. No. 217, Two clouds shaped as faces. No. 218, Two sailboats. No. 219, Woman with parasol, boat, flowers.

**1992, May 22 Photo. *Perf. 11½***
216 A265 75c multicolored 1.50 1.60
217 A265 75c multicolored 1.50 1.60
218 A265 75c multicolored 1.50 1.60
219 A265 75c multicolored 1.50 1.60
*a.* Block of 4, #216-219 6.00 6.50

### Mission to Planet Earth Type

Designs: No. 220, Space station. No. 221, Probes near Jupiter.

**1992, Sept. 4 Photo. *Rouletted 8***
**Granite Paper**
220 A266 1.10fr multicolored 2.40 2.60
221 A266 1.10fr multicolored 2.40 2.60
*a.* Pair, #220-221 5.00 5.25

### Science and Technology Type of 1992

Designs: 90c, Doctor, nurse. 1.60fr, Graduate seated before computer.

**1992, Oct. 2 Litho. *Perf. 14***
222 A267 90c multicolored 1.25 1.40
223 A267 1.60fr multicolored 3.00 3.25

### Human Rights Type of 1989

Artwork: 50c, The Oath of the Tennis Court, by Jacques Louis David. 90c, Rocking Chair I, by Henry Moore.

**1992, Nov. 20 Litho. *Perf. 13½***
224 A250 50c multicolored .75 .80
225 A250 90c multicolored 1.25 1.40

Panes of 12+12 se-tenant labels containing Articles 21 (50c) and 22 (90c) inscribed in French, German or English.

### Aging With Dignity Type

Designs: 50c, Older man coaching soccer. 1.60fr, Older man working at computer terminal.

**1993, Feb. 5 Litho. *Perf. 13***
226 A270 50c multicolored .50 .55
227 A270 1.60fr multicolored 1.50 1.65

### Endangered Species Type

Designs: No. 228, Pongidae (gorilla). No. 229, Falco peregrinus (peregrine falcon). No. 230, Trichechus inunguis (Amazonian manatee). No. 231, Panthera uncia (snow leopard).

**1993, Mar. 2 Litho. *Perf. 13x12½***
228 A271 80c multicolored 1.10 1.20
229 A271 80c multicolored 1.10 1.20
230 A271 80c multicolored 1.10 1.20
231 A271 80c multicolored 1.10 1.20
*a.* Block of 4, #228-231 4.50 4.80

### Healthy Environment Type

**1993, May 7 Litho. *Perf. 15x14½***
232 A272 60c Neighborhood .75 .80
233 A272 1fr Urban skyscrapers 1.75 1.90

### Human Rights Type of 1989

Artwork: 50c, Three Musicians, by Pablo Picasso. 90c, Voice of Space, by Rene Magritte.

**1993, June 11 Litho. *Perf. 13½***
234 A250 50c multicolored .75 .80
235 A250 90c multicolored 1.75 1.90

Printed in panes of 12 + 12 se-tenant labels containing Article 27 (50c) and 28 (90c) inscribed in French, German or English.

### Intl. Peace Day Type

Denomination at: No. 236, UL. No. 237, UR. No. 238, LL. No. 239, LR.

***Rouletted 12½***
**1993, Sept. 21 Litho. & Engr.**
236 A274 60c purple & multi 2.00 2.20
237 A274 60c purple & multi 2.00 2.20
238 A274 60c purple & multi 2.00 2.20
239 A274 60c purple & multi 2.00 2.20
*a.* Block of 4, #236-239 8.00 9.00

### Environment-Climate Type

**1993, Oct. 29 Litho. *Perf. 14½***
240 A275 1.10fr Polar bears 2.40 2.40
241 A275 1.10fr Whale sounding 2.40 2.40
242 A275 1.10fr Elephant seal 2.40 2.40
243 A275 1.10fr Penguins 2.40 2.40
*a.* Strip of 4, #240-243 9.75 10.75

### Intl. Year of the Family Type of 1993

Designs: 80c, Parents teaching child to walk. 1fr, Two women and child picking plants.

**1994, Feb. 4 Litho. *Perf. 13.1***
244 A276 80c rose vio & multi 1.00 1.10
245 A276 1fr brown & multi 1.40 1.50

### Endangered Species Type of 1993

Designs: No. 246, Mexican prairie dog. No. 247, Jabiru. No. 248, Blue whale. No. 249, Golden lion tamarin.

OFFICES IN GENEVA, SWITZERLAND 287

**1994, Mar. 18 Litho. *Perf. 12.7***

**246** A271 80c multicolored 1.10 1.20
**247** A271 80c multicolored 1.10 1.20
**248** A271 80c multicolored 1.10 1.20
**249** A271 80c multicolored 1.10 1.20
*a.* Block of 4, #246-249 4.50 5.00

### Protection for Refugees Type of 1994

Design: 1.20fr, Hand lifting figure over chasm.

**1994, Apr. 29 Litho. *Perf. 14.3x14.8***

**250** A277 1.20fr multicolored 2.25 2.40

### Intl. Decade for Natural Disaster Reduction Type of 1994

Earth seen from space, outline map of: No. 251, North America. No. 252, Eurasia. No. 253, South America. No. 254, Australia and South Pacific region.

**1994, May 27 Litho. *Perf. 13.9x14.2***

**251** A281 60c multicolored 1.75 1.90
**252** A281 60c multicolored 1.75 1.90
**253** A281 60c multicolored 1.75 1.90
**254** A281 60c multicolored 1.75 1.90
*a.* Block of 4, #251-254 7.00 7.75

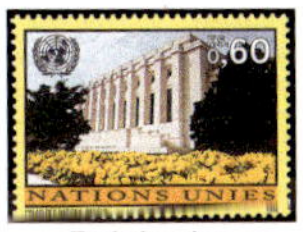

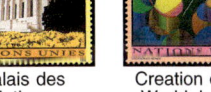

Palais des Nations, Geneva — G54

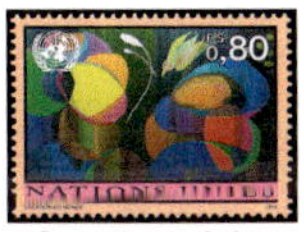

Creation of the World, by Oili Maki — G55

**1994, Sept. 1 Litho. *Perf. 14.3x14.6***

**255** G54 60c multicolored .75 .80
**256** G55 80c multicolored 1.00 1.10
**257** G54 1.80fr multi, diff. 2.25 2.50
*Nos. 255-257 (3)* 4.00 4.40

### Population and Development Type of 1994

Designs: 60c, People shopping at open-air market. 80c, People on vacation crossing bridge.

**1994, Sept. 1 Litho. *Perf. 13.2x13.6***

**258** A282 60c multicolored 1.00 1.10
**259** A282 80c multicolored 1.25 1.40

### UNCTAD Type of 1994

**1994, Oct. 28**

**260** A283 80c multi, diff. 1.10 1.20
**261** A283 1fr multi, diff. 1.50 1.65
*a.* Grayish green omitted —

### UN 50th Anniv. Type of 1995

**Litho. & Engr.**

**1995, Jan. 1 *Perf. 13.4***

**262** A284 80c multicolored 1.10 1.20

### Social Summit Type of 1995

**Photo. & Engr.**

**1995, Feb. 3 *Perf. 13.6x13.9***

**263** A285 1fr multi, diff. 1.25 1.40

### Endangered Species Type of 1993

Designs: No. 264, Crowned lemur, Lemur coronatus. No. 265, Giant Scops owl, Otus gurneyi. No. 266, Zetek's frog, Atelopus varius zeteki. No. 267, Wood bison, Bison bison athabascae.

**1995, Mar. 24 Litho. *Perf. 13x12½***

**264** A271 80c multicolored 1.10 1.20
**265** A271 80c multicolored 1.10 1.20
**266** A271 80c multicolored 1.10 1.20
**267** A271 80c multicolored 1.10 1.20
*a.* Block of 4, 264-267 4.50 5.00

### Intl. Youth Year Type of 1995

Designs: 80c, Farmer on tractor, fields at harvest time. 1fr, Couple standing by fields at night.

**1995, May 26 Litho. *Perf. 14.4x14.7***

**268** A286 80c multicolored 1.25 1.40
**269** A286 1fr multicolored 2.00 2.20

### UN, 50th Anniv. Type of 1995

Designs: 60c, Like No. 663. 1.80fr, Like No. 664.

***Perf. 13.3x13.6***

**1995, June 26 Engr.**

**270** A287 60c maroon .80 .85
**271** A287 1.80fr green 3.00 3.25

### Souvenir Sheet

**Litho. & Engr.**

***Imperf***

**272** Sheet of 2, #270-271 4.25 4.50
*a.* A287 60c maroon 1.00 1.10
*b.* A287 1.80fr green 3.25 3.40

### Conference on Women Type of 1995

Designs: 60c, Black woman, cranes flying above. 1fr, Women, dove.

**1995, Sept. 5 Photo. *Perf. 12***

**273** A288 60c multicolored 1.00 1.10

**Size: 28x50mm**

**274** A288 1fr multicolored 2.00 2.20

### UN People, 50th Anniv. Type of 1995

**1995, Oct. 24 Litho. *Perf. 14***

**275** Sheet of 12 14.00 15.00
*a.-l.* A290 30c each 1.20 1.20
**276** Souvenir booklet 15.00
*a.* A290 30c Booklet pane of 3, vert. strip of 3 from UL of sheet 3.75 3.75
*b.* A290 30c Booklet pane of 3, vert. strip of 3 from UR of sheet 3.75 3.75
*c.* A290 30c Booklet pane of 3, vert. strip of 3 from LL of sheet 3.75 3.75
*d.* A290 30c Booklet pane of 3, vert. strip of 3 from LR of sheet 3.75 3.75

### WFUNA, 50th Anniv. Type

Design: 80c, Fishing boat, fish in net.

**1996, Feb. 2 Litho. *Perf. 13x13½***

**277** A291 80c multicolored 1.25 1.40

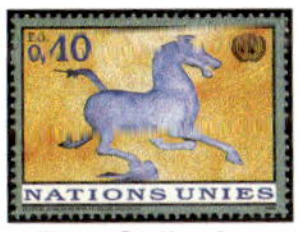

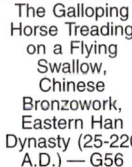

The Galloping Horse Treading on a Flying Swallow, Chinese Bronzework, Eastern Han Dynasty (25-220 A.D.) — G56

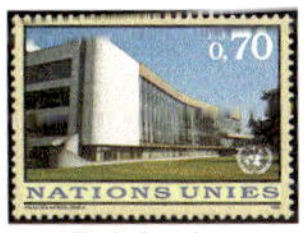

Palais des Nations, Geneva — G57

**1996, Feb. 2 Litho. *Perf. 14½x15***

**278** G56 40c multicolored .50 .55
**279** G57 70c multicolored .90 .95

### Endangered Species Type of 1993

Designs: No. 280, Paphiopedilum delenatii. No. 281, Pachypodium baronii. No. 282, Sternbergia lutea. No. 283, Darlingtonia californica.

**1996, Mar. 14 Litho. *Perf. 12½***

**280** A271 80c multicolored 1.00 1.10
**281** A271 80c multicolored 1.00 1.10
**282** A271 80c multicolored 1.00 1.10
**283** A271 80c multicolored 1.00 1.10
*a.* Block of 4, #280-283 4.00 4.50

### City Summit Type of 1996

Designs: No. 284, Asian family. No. 285, Oriental garden. No. 286, Fruit, vegetable vendor, mosque. No. 287, Boys playing ball. No. 288, Couple reading newspaper.

**1996, June 3 Litho. *Perf. 14x13½***

**284** A293 70c multicolored 1.50 1.65
**285** A293 70c multicolored 1.50 1.65
**286** A293 70c multicolored 1.50 1.65
**287** A293 70c multicolored 1.50 1.65
**288** A293 70c multicolored 1.50 1.65
*a.* Strip of 5, #284-288 7.50 8.25

### Sport and the Environment Type

Designs: 70c, Cycling, vert. 1.10fr, Sprinters.

***Perf. 14x14½, 14½x14***

**1996, July 19 Litho.**

**289** A294 70c multicolored 1.00 1.10
**290** A294 1.10fr multicolored 1.50 1.65

### Souvenir Sheet

**291** A294 Sheet of 2, #289-290 3.00 3.25

### Plea for Peace Type

Designs: 90c, Tree filled with birds, vert. 1.10fr, Bouquet of flowers in rocket tail vase, vert.

**1996, Sept. 17 Litho. *Perf. 15x14½***

**292** A295 90c multicolored 1.25 1.40
**293** A295 1.10fr multicolored 1.50 1.65

### UNICEF Type

Fairy Tales: 70c, The Sun and the Moon, South America. 1.80fr, Ananse, Africa.

**1996, Nov. 20 Litho. *Perf. 14½x15***

**294** A296 70c multicolored .80 .85
**295** A296 1.80fr multicolored 2.00 2.20

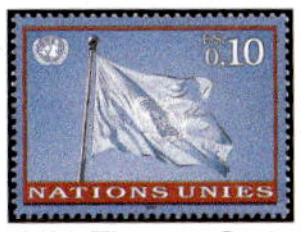

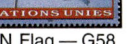

UN Flag — G58

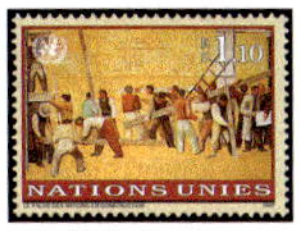

Palais des Nations Under Construction, by Massimo Campigli — G59

**1997, Feb. 12 Litho. *Perf. 14½***

**296** G58 10c multicolored .25 .30
**297** G59 1.10fr multicolored 1.25 1.40

### Endangered Species Type of 1993

Designs: No. 298, Ursus maritimus (polar bear). No. 299, Goura cristata (blue-crowned pigeon). No. 300, Amblyrhynchus cristatus (marine iguana). No. 301, Lama guanicoe (guanaco).

**1997, Mar. 13 Litho. *Perf. 12½***

**298** A271 80c multicolored .90 .95
**299** A271 80c multicolored .90 .95
**300** A271 80c multicolored .90 .95
**301** A271 80c multicolored .90 .95
*a.* Block of 4, #298-301 3.60 3.90

### Earth Summit Anniv. Type

Designs: No. 302, Person flying over mountain. No. 303, Mountain, person's face. No. 304, Person standing on mountain, sailboats. No. 305, Person, mountain, trees.

1.10fr, Combined design similar to Nos. 302-305.

**1997, May 30 Photo. *Perf. 11½***

**Granite Paper**

**302** A299 45c multicolored 1.00 1.10
**303** A299 45c multicolored 1.00 1.10
**304** A299 45c multicolored 1.00 1.10
**305** A299 45c multicolored 1.00 1.10
*a.* Block of 4, #302-305 4.00 4.50

### Souvenir Sheet

**306** A299 1.10fr multicolored 4.00 4.25

### Transportation Type of 1997

Air transportation: No. 307, Zeppelin, Fokker tri-motor. No. 308, Boeing 314 Clipper, Lockheed Constellation. No. 309, DeHavilland Comet. No. 310, Boeing 747, Illyushin jet. No. 311, Concorde.

**1997, Aug. 29 Litho. *Perf. 14x14½***

**307** A300 70c multicolored 1.00 1.10
**308** A300 70c multicolored 1.00 1.10
**309** A300 70c multicolored 1.00 1.10
**310** A300 70c multicolored 1.00 1.10
**311** A300 70c multicolored 1.00 1.10
*a.* Strip of 5, #307-311 5.00 5.50

### Philately Type

Designs: 70c, No. 146. 1.10fr, No. 147.

**1997, Oct. 14 Litho. *Perf. 13½x14***

**312** A301 70c multicolored .80 .85
**313** A301 1.10fr multicolored 1.50 1.65

### World Heritage Convention Type

Terracotta warriors of Xian: 45c, Single warrior. 70c, Massed warriors. No. 316a, like NY No. 716. No. 316b, like NY No. 717. No. 316c, like Geneva No. 314. No. 316d, like Geneva No. 315. No. 316e, like Vienna No. 230. No. 316f, like Vienna No. 231.

**1997, Nov. 19 Litho. *Perf. 13½***

**314** A302 45c multicolored 1.25 1.40
**315** A302 70c multicolored 2.25 2.50
**316** Souvenir booklet 12.00
*a.-f.* A302 10c any single .45 .50
*g.* Booklet pane of 4 #316a 2.00 2.00
*h.* Booklet pane of 4 #316b 2.00 2.00
*i.* Booklet pane of 4 #316c 2.00 2.00
*j.* Booklet pane of 4 #316d 2.00 2.00
*k.* Booklet pane of 4 #316e 2.00 2.00
*l.* Booklet pane of 4 #316f 2.00 2.00

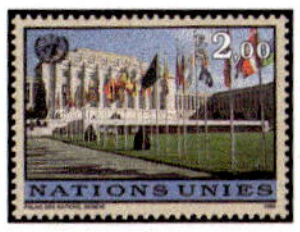

Palais des Nations, Geneva — G60

**1998, Feb. 13 Litho. *Perf. 14½x15***

**317** G60 2fr multicolored 1.50 1.65

### Endangered Species Type of 1993

Designs: No. 318, Macaca thibetana (short-tailed Tibetan macaque). No. 319, Phoenicopterus ruber (Caribbean flamingo). No. 320, Ornithoptera alexandrae (Queen Alexandra's birdwing). No. 321, Dama mesopotamica (Persian fallow deer).

**1998, Mar. 13 Litho. *Perf. 12½***

**318** A271 80c multicolored 1.00 1.10
**319** A271 80c multicolored 1.00 1.10
**320** A271 80c multicolored 1.00 1.10
**321** A271 80c multicolored 1.00 1.10
*a.* Block of 4, #318-321 4.00 4.50

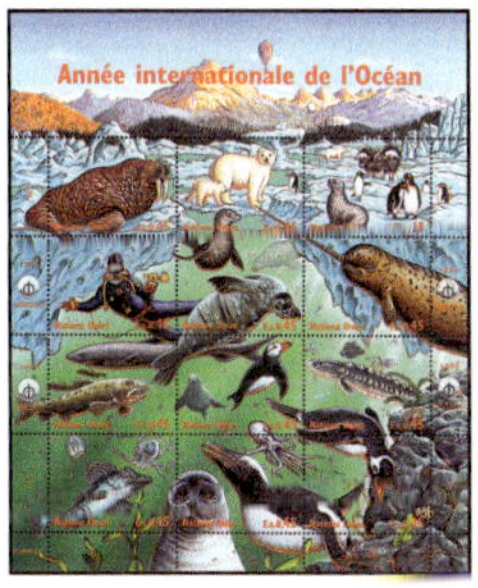

Intl. Year of the Ocean G61

**1998, May 20 Litho. *Perf. 13x13½***

**322** G61 Pane of 12 10.00 10.00
*a.-l.* 45c any single .85 .85

### Rain Forests Type

**1998, June 19 *Perf. 13x13½***

**323** A307 70c Orangutans .90 1.00

### Souvenir Sheet

**324** A307 3fr like #323 4.00 *7.50*

### Peacekeeping Type

Designs: 70c, Soldier with two children. 90c, Two soldiers, children.

**1998, Sept. 15 Photo. *Perf. 12***

**325** A308 70c multicolored .85 .90
**326** A308 90c multicolored 1.40 1.50

### Declaration of Human Rights Type of 1998

Designs: 90c, Stylized birds. 1.80fr, Stylized birds flying from hand.

**Litho. & Photo.**

**1998, Oct. 27 *Perf. 13***

**327** A309 90c multicolored .95 1.05
**328** A309 1.80fr multicolored 2.00 2.20

### Schönbrunn Palace Type

Designs: 70c, No. 331b, Great Palm House. 1.10fr, No. 331d, Blue porcelain vase, vert. No. 331a, Palace. No. 331e, The Gloriette (archway). No. 331e, Wall painting on fabric (detail), by Johann Wenzl Bergl, vert. No. 331f, Porcelain stove, vert.

**1998, Dec. 4 Litho. *Perf. 14***

**329** A310 70c multicolored .90 1.00
**330** A310 1.10fr multicolored 1.20 1.30

### Souvenir Booklet

**331** Booklet 21.50
*a.-c.* A310 10c any single .55 .55
*d.-f.* A310 30c any single 1.65 1.65
*g.* Booklet pane of 4 #331a 2.20 2.20
*h.* Booklet pane of 3 #331d 5.00 5.00
*i.* Booklet pane of 3 #331e 5.00 5.00
*k.* Booklet pane of 4 #331b 2.20 2.20
*l.* Booklet pane of 4 #331c 2.20 2.20

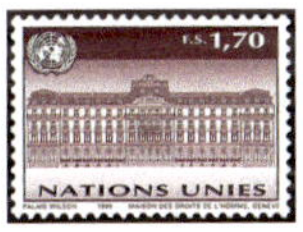

Palais Wilson, Geneva — G62

**1999, Feb. 5 Photo. *Perf. 11½***

**Granite Paper**

**332** G62 1.70fr brown red 1.75 1.90

### World Heritage, Australia Type

Designs: 90c, No. 335e, Kakadu Natl. Park. 1.10fr, No. 335c, Great Barrier Reef. No. 335a, Tasmanian Wilderness. No. 335b, Wet

tropics of Queensland. No. 335d, Uluru-Kata Tjuta Natl. Park. No. 335f, Willandra Lakes region.

**1999, Mar. 19 Litho. *Perf. 13***
**333** A313 90c multicolored 1.25 1.40
**334** A313 1.10fr multicolored 1.50 1.65

### Souvenir Booklet

**335** Booklet 16.50
*a.-c.* A313 10c any single .45 .50
*d.-f.* A313 20c any single .90 1.00
*g.* Booklet pane of 4, #335a 1.80 2.00
*h.* Booklet pane of 4, #335d 3.60 4.00
*i.* Booklet pane of 4, #335b 1.80 2.00
*j.* Booklet pane of 4, #335e 3.60 4.00
*k.* Booklet pane of 4, #335c 1.80 2.00
*l.* Booklet pane of 4, #335f 3.60 4.00

### Endangered Species Type of 1993

Designs: No. 336, Equus hemionus (Asiatic wild ass). No. 337, Anodorhynchus hyacinthinus (hyacinth macaw). No. 338, Epicrates subflavus (Jamaican boa). No. 339, Dendrolagus bennettianus (Bennetts' tree kangaroo).

**1999, Apr. 22 Litho. *Perf. 12½***
**336** A271 90c multicolored 1.00 1.10
**337** A271 90c multicolored 1.00 1.10
**338** A271 90c multicolored 1.00 1.10
**339** A271 90c multicolored 1.00 1.10
*a.* Block of 4, #336-339 4.00 4.50

### UNISPACE III Type

Designs: No. 340, Farm, satellite dish. No. 341, City, satellite in orbit. No. 342, Composite of Nos. 340-341.

**1999, July 7 Photo. *Rouletted 8***
**340** A314 45c multicolored .90 1.00
**341** A314 45c multicolored .90 1.00
*a.* Pair, #340-341 2.00 2.20

### Souvenir Sheet

***Perf. 14½***
**342** A314 2fr multicolored 4.50 5.00
*a.* Ovptd. in sheet margin 9.50 10.50

### UPU Type

Various people, early 20th century methods of mail transportation, denomination at: No. 343, UL. No. 344, UR. No. 345, LL. No. 346, LR.

**1999, Aug. 23 Photo. *Perf. 11¾***
**343** A315 70c multicolored .90 1.00
**344** A315 70c multicolored .90 1.00
**345** A315 70c multicolored .90 1.00
**346** A315 70c multicolored .90 1.00
*a.* Block of 4, #343-346 3.60 4.00

### In Memoriam Type

Designs: 1.10fr, 2fr, Armillary sphere, Palais de Nations. Size of 2fr stamp: 34x63mm.

**1999, Sept. 21 Litho. *Perf. 14½x14***
**347** A316 1.10fr multicolored 1.25 1.40

### Souvenir Sheet

***Perf. 14***
**348** A316 2fr multicolored 3.00 3.25

### Education Type

90c, Rainbow over globe. 1.80fr, Fish, tree, globe, book.

***Perf. 13½x13¾***
**1999, Nov. 18 Litho.**
**349** A317 90c multi .75 .80
**350** A317 1.80fr multi 1.75 1.90

### Intl. Year Of Thanksgiving Type

**2000, Jan 1 Litho. *Perf. 13¼x13½***
**351** A318 90c multicolored 1.00 1.10

On No. 351 portions of the design were applied by a thermographic process producing a shiny, raised effect.

### Endangered Species Type of 1993

Designs: No. 352, Hippopotamus amphibius (hippopotamus). No. 353, Coscoroba coscoroba (Coscoroba swan). No. 354, Varanus prasinus (emerald monitor). No. 355, Enhydra lutris (sea otter).

**2000, Apr. 6 Litho. *Perf. 12¾x12½***
**352** A271 90c multicolored 1.25 1.40
**353** A271 90c multicolored 1.25 1.40
**354** A271 90c multicolored 1.25 1.40
**355** A271 90c multicolored 1.25 1.40
*a.* Block of 4, #352-355 5.00 5.75

### Our World 2000 Type

Winning artwork in Millennium painting competition: 90c, The Embrace, by Rita Adaimy, Lebanon. 1.10fr, Living Single, by Richard Kimanthi, Kenya, vert.

***Perf. 13x13½, 13½x13***
**2000, May 30 Litho.**
**356** A319 90c multicolored 1.00 1.10
**357** A319 1.10fr multicolored 1.25 1.40

### 55th Anniversary Type

Designs: 90c, Trygve Lie, Harry S Truman, workers at cornerstone dedication ceremony, 1949. 1.40fr, Window cleaner on Secretariat Building, General Assembly Hall under construction, 1951.

**2000, July 7 Litho. *Perf. 13¼x13***
**358** A320 90c multicolored 1.00 1.10
**359** A320 1.40fr multicolored 1.50 1.65

### Souvenir Sheet

**360** A320 Sheet of 2, #358-359 3.50 3.75

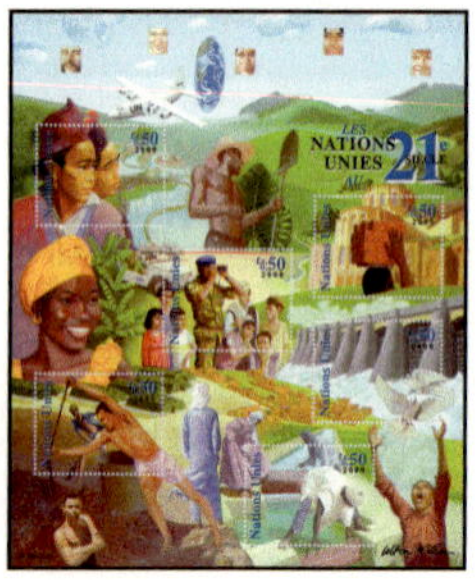

The UN in the 21st Century G63

No. 361: a, Two people, terraced rice paddy. b, Man carrying bricks on head. c, UN Peacekeeper with binoculars. d, Dam, doves. e, Men with shovels. f, People working on irrigation system.

**2000, Sept. 15 Litho. *Perf. 14***
**361** G63 Pane of 6 9.00 10.00
*a.-f.* 50c any single 1.50 1.65

### World Heritage, Spain Type

Designs: Nos. 362, 364b, Walled Town of Cuenca. Nos. 363, 364e, Toledo. No. 364a, Alhambra, Generalife and Albayzin, Granada. No. 364c, Aqueduct of Segovia. No. 364d, Amphitheater of Mérida. No. 364f, Güell Park, Barcelona.

**2000, Oct. 6 Litho. *Perf. 14¾x14½***
**362** A323 1fr multicolored 1.40 1.50
**363** A323 1.20fr multicolored 1.60 1.75

### Souvenir Booklet

**364** Booklet 11.00
*a.-c.* A323 10c any single .30 .35
*d.-f.* A323 20c any single .60 .65
*g.* Booklet pane of 4, #364a 1.20 1.40
*h.* Booklet pane of 4, #364d 2.40 2.60
*i.* Booklet pane of 4, #364b 1.20 1.40
*j.* Booklet pane of 4, #364e 2.40 2.60
*k.* Booklet pane of 4, #364c 1.20 1.40
*l.* Booklet pane of 4, #364f 2.40 2.60

### Respect for Refugees Type

Designs: 80c, 1.80fr, Refugee with cane, four other refugees.

**2000, Nov. 9 Litho. *Perf. 13¼x12¾***
**365** A324 80c multicolored 1.25 1.40

### Souvenir Sheet

**366** A324 1.80fr multicolored 2.50 2.75

### Endangered Species Type of 1993

Designs: No. 367, Felis lynx canadensis (North American lynx). No. 368, Pavo muticus (green peafowl). No. 369, Geochelone elephantopus (Galapagos giant tortoise). No. 370, Lepilemur spp. (sportive lemur).

**2001, Feb. 1 Litho. *Perf. 12¾x12½***
**367** A271 90c multicolored 1.25 1.40
**368** A271 90c multicolored 1.25 1.40
**369** A271 90c multicolored 1.25 1.40
**370** A271 90c multicolored 1.25 1.40
*a.* Block of 4, #367-370 5.00 5.75

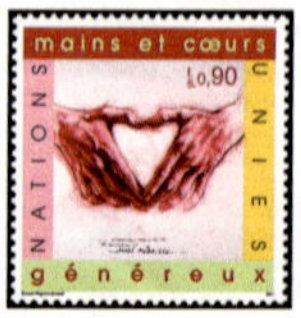


Intl. Volunteers Year — G64

Paintings by: 90c, Ernest Pignon-Ernest, France. 1.30fr, Paul Siché, France.

**2001, Mar. 29 Litho. *Perf. 13¼***
**371** G64 90c multicolored 1.10 1.20
**372** G64 1.30fr multicolored 1.60 1.75

### World Heritage, Japan Type

Designs: 1.10fr, No. 375b, Nara. 1.30fr, No. 375e, Itsukushima Shinto Shrine. No. 375a, Kyoto. No. 375c, Himeji-Jo. No. 375d, Shirakawa-Go and Gokayama. No. 375f, Nikko.

**2001, Aug. 1 Litho. *Perf. 12¾x13¼***
**373** A328 1.10fr multicolored 1.30 1.40
**374** A328 1.30fr multicolored 1.50 1.65

### Souvenir Booklet

**375** Booklet 15.00
*a.-c.* A328 10c any single .50 .55
*d.-f.* A328 30c any single .75 .80
*g.* Booklet pane of 4, #375a 2.00 2.20
*h.* Booklet pane of 4, #375d 3.00 3.20
*i.* Booklet pane of 4, #375b 2.00 2.20
*j.* Booklet pane of 4, #375e 3.00 3.20
*k.* Booklet pane of 4, #375c 2.00 2.20
*l.* Booklet pane of 4, #375f 3.00 3.20

### Dag Hammarskjöld Type

**2001, Sept. 18 Engr. *Perf. 11x11¼***
**376** A329 2fr car lake 2.50 2.75

### UN Postal Administration, 50th Anniv. Types

**2001, Oct. 18 Litho. *Perf. 13½***
**377** A330 90c Stamps, globe 1.00 1.10
**378** A330 1.30fr Stamps, horns 1.75 1.90

### Souvenir Sheet

**379** A331 Sheet of 2 12.50 13.50
*a.* 1.30fr red & light blue, 38mm diameter 5.00 5.50
*b.* 1.80fr red & light blue, 38mm diameter 7.50 8.00

### Climate Change Type

Designs: No. 380, Lizard, flowers, shoreline. No. 381, Windmills, construction workers. No. 382, Non-polluting factory. No. 383, Solar oven, city, village, picnickers.

**2001, Nov. 16 Litho. *Perf. 13¼***
**380** A332 90c multicolored 1.10 1.20
**381** A332 90c multicolored 1.10 1.20
**382** A332 90c multicolored 1.10 1.20
**383** A332 90c multicolored 1.10 1.20
*a.* Horiz. strip, #380-383 4.50 5.00

### Nobel Peace Prize Type

**2001, Dec. 10 Litho. *Perf. 13¼***
**384** A333 90c multicolored 1.10 1.20

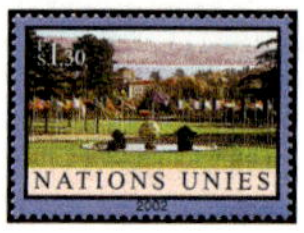


Palais des Nations — G65

**2002, Mar. 1 Litho. *Perf. 13¾***
**385** G65 1.30fr multicolored 1.40 1.50

### Endangered Species Type of 1993

Designs: No. 386, Cacajao calvus (white uakari). No. 387, Mellivora capensis (honey badger). No. 388, Otocolobus manul (manul). No. 389, Varanus exantematicus (Bosc's monitor).

**2002, Apr. 4 Litho. *Perf. 12¾x12½***
**386** A271 90c multicolored 1.50 1.65
**387** A271 90c multicolored 1.50 1.65
**388** A271 90c multicolored 1.50 1.65
**389** A271 90c multicolored 1.50 1.65
*a.* Block of 4, #386-389 6.00 6.75

### Independence of East Timor Type

Designs: 90c, Wooden statue of male figure. 1.30fr, Carved wooden container.

**2002, May 20 Litho. *Perf. 14x14½***
**390** A335 90c multicolored 1.25 1.40
**391** A335 1.30fr multicolored 1.75 1.90

### Intl. Year of Mountains Type

Designs: No. 392, Weisshorn, Switzerland. No. 393, Mt. Fuji, Japan. No. 394, Vinson Massif, Antarctica. No. 395, Mt. Kamet, India.

**2002, May 24 Litho. *Perf. 13x13¼***
**392** A336 70c multicolored 1.00 1.10
**393** A336 70c multicolored 1.00 1.10
**394** A336 1.20fr multicolored 1.75 1.90
**395** A336 1.20fr multicolored 1.75 1.90
*a.* Vert. strip or block of four, #392-395 8.50 9.50

### World Summit on Sustainable Development (Peter Max) Type

Designs: No. 396, Sun, birds, flowers, heart. No. 397, Three faceless people, diff. No. 398, Three women, diff. No. 399, Sailboat, mountain.

**2002, June 27 Litho. *Perf. 14½x14***
**396** A337 90c multicolored 1.25 1.40
**397** A337 90c multicolored 1.25 1.40
**398** A337 1.80fr multicolored 2.50 2.75
**399** A337 1.80fr multicolored 2.50 2.75
*a.* Vert. strip or block of four, #396-399 10.00 11.00

### World Heritage, Italy Type

Designs: 90c, No. 402e, Pisa. 1.30fr, No. 402b, Aeolian Islands. No. 402a, Amalfi Coast. No. 402c, Rome. No. 402d, Florence. No. 402f, Pompeii.

***Perf. 13½x13¼***
**2002, Aug. 30 Litho.**
**400** A338 90c multicolored 1.25 1.40
**401** A338 1.30fr multicolored 2.00 2.20

### Souvenir Booklet

**402** Booklet 29.00
*a.-c.* A338 10c any single .60 .80
*d.-f.* A338 20c any single 1.75 2.00
*g.* Booklet pane of 4, #402d 7.00 8.00
*h.* Booklet pane of 4, #402a 2.40 2.75
*i.* Booklet pane of 4, #402e 7.00 8.00
*j.* Booklet pane of 4, #402b 2.40 2.75
*k.* Booklet pane of 4, #402f 7.00 8.00
*l.* Booklet pane of 4, #402c 2.40 2.75

### AIDS Awareness Type

**2002, Oct. 24 Litho. *Perf. 13½***
**403** A339 1.30fr multicolored 2.00 2.20

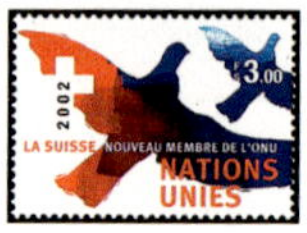


Entry of Switzerland into United Nations — G66

**2002, Oct. 24 Litho. *Perf. 14½x14¾***
**404** G66 3fr multicolored 3.50 3.75

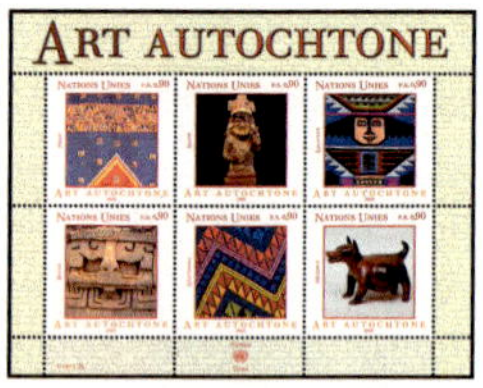


Indigenous Art — G67

No. 405: a, Detail of Inca poncho, Peru. b, Bahia culture seated figure, Brazil. c, Blanket, Ecuador. d, Mayan stone sculpture, Belize. e, Embroidered fabric, Guatemala. f, Colima terra-cotta dog sculpture, Mexico.

**2003, Jan. 31 Litho. *Perf. 14¼***
**405** G67 Pane of 6 7.50 8.50
*a.-f.* 90c Any single 1.25 1.35

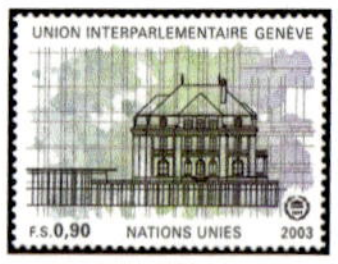


New Inter-Parliamentary Union Headquarters, Geneva — G68

**2003, Feb. 20 Litho. *Perf. 14½x14***
**406** G68 90c multicolored 1.75 1.75

### Endangered Species Type of 1993

Designs: No. 407, Branta ruficollis (red-breasted goose). No. 408, Geronticus calvus (bald ibis). No. 409, Dendrocygna bicolor (fulvous whistling duck). No. 410, Ramphastos vitellinus (channel-billed toucan).

**2003, Apr. 3 Litho. *Perf. 12¾x12½***
**407** A271 90c multicolored 1.25 1.25
**408** A271 90c multicolored 1.25 1.25
**409** A271 90c multicolored 1.25 1.25
**410** A271 90c multicolored 1.25 1.25
*a.* Block of 4, #407-410 5.00 5.00

### International Year of Freshwater Type of 2003

***Perf. 14¼x14½***
**2003, June 20 Litho.**
**411** A345 70c Waterfall 1.25 1.25
**412** A345 1.30fr People, mountain 2.25 2.25
*a.* Horiz. pair, #411-412 5.00 5.00

### Ralph Bunche Type
### Litho. With Foil Application

**2003, Aug. 7 *Perf. 13½x14***
**413** A346 1.80fr brn red & multi 2.75 2.75

OFFICES IN GENEVA, SWITZERLAND 289

### In Memoriam Type of 2003

**2003, Oct. 24 Litho. *Perf. 13¼x13***
**414** A347 85c multicolored 1.50 1.50

### World Heritage Sites, United States Type

Designs: 90c, No. 417b, Great Smoky Mountains National Park. 1.30fr, No. 417f, Yellowstone National Park. No. 417a, Yosemite National Park. No. 417c, Olympic National Park. No. 417d, Hawaii Volcanoes National Park. No. 417e, Everglades National Park.

**2003, Oct. 24 Litho. *Perf. 14½x14¼***
**415** A348 90c multicolored 1.50 1.50
**416** A348 1.30fr multicolored 2.25 2.25

### Souvenir Booklet

**417** Booklet 12.00
*a.-c.* A348 10c any single .30 .30
*d.-f.* A348 30c any single .65 .65
*g.* Booklet pane of 4 #417a 1.20 1.20
*h.* Booklet pane of 4 #417d 2.60 2.60
*i.* Booklet pane of 4 #417b 1.20 1.20
*j.* Booklet pane of 4 #417e 2.60 2.60
*k.* Booklet pane of 4 #417c 1.20 1.20
*l.* Booklet pane of 4 #417f 2.60 2.60

### Endangered Species Type of 1993

Designs: No. 418, Ursus thibetanus (Asiatic black bear). No. 419, Hippocamelus antisensis (Northern Andean deer). No. 420, Macaca silenus (Lion-tailed macaque). No. 421, Bos gaurus (Gaur).

**2004, Jan. 29 Litho. *Perf. 12¾x12½***
**418** A271 1fr multicolored 1.60 1.60
**419** A271 1fr multicolored 1.60 1.60
**420** A271 1fr multicolored 1.60 1.60
**421** A271 1fr multicolored 1.60 1.60
*a.* Block of 4, #418-421 6.50 6.50

### Indigenous Art Type of 2003

No. 422: a, Decoration for cows, Switzerland. b, Stone Age terra cotta sculpture of seated woman, Romania. c, Butter stamps, France. d, Detail of herald's tabard, United Kingdom. e, Woodcut print of medieval Cologne, Germany. f, Mesolithic era terra cotta sculpture of mother and child, Serbia and Montenegro.

**2004, Mar. 4 Litho. *Perf. 13¼***
**422** G67 Sheet of 6 7.50 7.50
*a.-f.* 1fr Any single 1.25 1.25

### Road Safety Type

Road map art with: 85c, Man on hand. 1fr, Person, seat belt, vert.

***Perf. 13x13¼, 13¼x13***
**2004, Apr. 7 Litho.**
**423** A354 85c multicolored 1.40 1.40
**424** A354 1fr multicolored 1.75 1.75

See France No. 3011.

### Japanese Peace Bell, 50th Anniv. Type

**Litho. & Engr.**
**2004, June 3 *Perf. 13¼x13***
**425** A355 1.30fr multicolored 2.00 2.00

### World Heritage Sites, Greece Type

Designs: 1fr, No. 428b, Delphi. 1.30fr, No. 428e, Pythagoreion and Heraion of Samos. No. 428a, Acropolis, Athens. No. 428c, Olympia. No. 428d, Delos. No. 428f, Mycenae and Tiryns.

**2004, Aug. 12 Litho. *Perf. 14x13¼***
**426** A356 1fr multicolored 1.50 1.50
**427** A356 1.30fr multicolored 2.00 2.00

### Souvenir Booklet

**428** Booklet 13.50
*a.-c.* A356 20c any single .30 .30
*d.-f.* A356 50c any single .80 .80
*g.* Booklet pane of 4 #428a 1.25 1.25
*h.* Booklet pane of 4 #428b 1.25 1.25
*i.* Booklet pane of 4 #428c 1.25 1.25
*j.* Booklet pane of 4 #428d 3.25 3.25
*k.* Booklet pane of 4 #428e 3.25 3.25
*l.* Booklet pane of 4 #428f 3.25 3.25

### My Dream for Peace Type

Winning designs of Lions Club International children's global peace poster contest by: 85c, Anggun Sita Rustinya, Indonesia. 1.20fr, Amanda Nunez, Belize.

**2004, Sept. 21 Litho. *Perf. 14***
**429** A357 85c multicolored 1.40 1.40
**430** A357 1.20fr multicolored 2.00 2.00

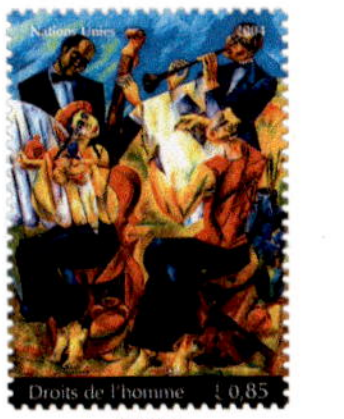

G69

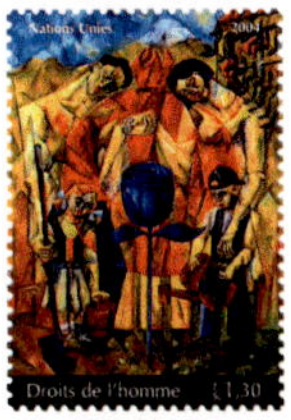

Human Rights — G70

**2004, Oct. 14 Litho. *Perf. 11¼***
**431** G69 85c multicolored 1.25 1.25
**432** G70 1.30fr multicolored 2.25 2.25

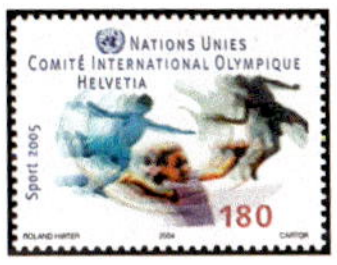

Sports — G71

**2004, Nov. 23 Litho. *Perf. 13x13½***
**433** G71 180c multicolored 3.25 3.25

See Switzerland No. 1196.

### United Nations, 60th Anniv. Type of 2005

**Litho. & Engr.**
**2005, Feb. 4 *Perf. 11x11¼***
**434** A361 1.30fr multicolored 2.50 2.50

### Souvenir Sheet

**Litho.**
***Imperf***
**435** A361 3fr multicolored 7.50 7.50

### Endangered Species Type of 1993

Designs: No. 436, Laelia milleri. No. 437, Psygmorchis pusilla. No. 438, Dendrobium cruentum. No. 439, Orchis purpurea.

**2005, Mar. 3 Litho. *Perf. 12¾x12½***
**436** A271 1fr multicolored 2.00 2.00
**437** A271 1fr multicolored 2.00 2.00
**438** A271 1fr multicolored 2.00 2.00
**439** A271 1fr multicolored 2.00 2.00
*a.* Block of 4, #436-439 8.00 8.00

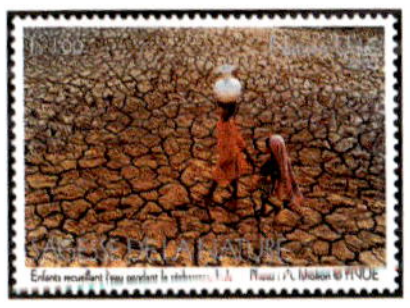

Nature's Wisdom G72

Designs: 1fr, Children collecting water, India. 80c, Ruby brittle star, Bahamas.

**2005, Apr. 21 Litho. *Perf. 13½x13¼***
**440** G72 1fr multicolored 1.75 1.75
**441** G72 1.30fr multicolored 2.00 2.00

### Intl. Year of Sport Type

**2005, June 3 Litho. *Perf. 13x13¼***
**442** A368 1fr Wheelchair racing 1.75 1.75
**443** A368 1.30fr Cycling 2.25 2.25

### World Heritage Sites, Egypt Type

Designs: Nos. 444, 446b, Philae. Nos. 445, 446c, Islamic Cairo. No. 446a, Memphis and its Necropolis. No. 446c, Abu Mena. No. 446d, Ancient Thebes. No. 446f, St. Catherine area.

**2005, Aug. 4 Litho. *Perf. 14x13¼***
**444** A369 1fr multicolored 2.00 2.00
**445** A369 1.30fr multicolored 2.50 2.50

### Souvenir Booklet

**446** Booklet, #446g-446l 16.50
*a.-c.* A369 20c any single .40 .40
*d.-f.* A369 50c any single .90 .90
*g.* Booklet pane of 4 #446a 1.60 1.60
*h.* Booklet pane of 4 #446b 1.60 1.60
*i.* Booklet pane of 4 #446c 1.60 1.60
*j.* Booklet pane of 4 #446d 3.75 3.75
*k.* Booklet pane of 4 #446e 3.75 3.75
*l.* Booklet pane of 4 #446f 3.75 3.75

### My Dream for Peace Type

Winning designs of Lions Club International children's global peace poster contest by: 1fr, Marisa Harun, Indonesia. 1.30fr, Carlos Javier Parramón Teixidó, Spain.

**2005, Sept. 21 Litho. *Perf. 14***
**447** A357 1fr multicolored 1.75 1.75
**448** A357 1.30fr multicolored 2.00 2.00

### Food for Life Type

Designs: 1fr, Rye, airplane dropping parcels, camel caravan. 1.30fr, Sorghum, people carrying grain sacks, trucks.

**2005, Oct. 20 Litho. *Perf. 13¾***
**449** A370 1fr multicolored 1.90 1.90
**450** A370 1.30fr multicolored 2.40 2.40

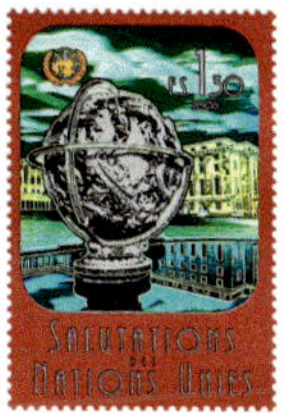

Armillary Sphere, Palais des Nations — G73

### Litho. with Hologram

**2006, Feb. 3 *Perf. 13¼x13½***
**451** G73 1.30fr multicolored 2.25 2.25

### Indigenous Art Type of 2003

No. 452 — Musical instruments: a, Bell, Benin. b, Drum, Swaziland. c, Sanza, Congo. d, Stringed instruments, Cape Verde. e, Caxixi, Ghana. f, Bells, Central Africa.

**2006, Feb. 3 Litho. *Perf. 13¼***
**452** G67 Pane of 6 12.00 12.00
*a.-f.* 1.20fr Any single 2.00 2.00

### Endangered Species Type of 1993

Designs: No. 453, Dyscophus antongilii. No. 454, Chamaeleo dilepsis. No. 455, Corallus caninus. No. 456, Phyllobates vittatus.

***Perf. 12¾x12½***
**2006, Mar. 16 Litho.**
**453** A271 1fr multicolored 1.75 1.75
**454** A271 1fr multicolored 1.75 1.75
**455** A271 1fr multicolored 1.75 1.75
**456** A271 1fr multicolored 1.75 1.75
*a.* Block of 4, #453-456 7.00 7.00

### Intl. Day of Families Type

Designs: 1fr, Family reading together. 1.30fr, Family on motorcycle.

**2006, May 27 Litho. *Perf. 14x13½***
**457** A373 1fr multicolored 1.25 1.25
**458** A373 1.30fr multicolored 1.75 1.75

### World Heritage Sites, France Type

Eiffel Tower and: Nos. 459, 461b, Provins. Nos. 460, 461e, Mont Saint-Michel. No. 461a, Banks of the Seine. No. 461c, Carcasonne. No. 461d, Roman Aqueduct. No. 446f, Chateau de Chambord.

### Litho. & Embossed with Foil Application

**2006, June 17 *Perf. 13½x13¼***
**459** A374 1fr multicolored 1.75 1.75
**460** A374 1.30fr multicolored 2.25 2.25

### Souvenir Booklet

**461** Booklet, #461g-461l 15.00
*a.-c.* A374 20c any single .35 .35
*d.-f.* A374 50c any single .85 .85
*g.* Booklet pane of 4 #461a 1.40 1.40
*h.* Booklet pane of 4 #461b 1.40 1.40
*i.* Booklet pane of 4 #461c 1.40 1.40
*j.* Booklet pane of 4 #461d 3.50 3.50
*k.* Booklet pane of 4 #461e 3.50 3.50
*l.* Booklet pane of 4 #461f 3.50 3.50

See France Nos. 3219-3220.

### My Dream for Peace Type of 2004

Winning designs of Lions Club International children's global peace poster contest by: 85c, Ariam Boaglio, Italy. 1.20fr, Sierra Spicer, US.

**2006, Sept. 21 Litho. *Perf. 13½x13***
**462** A357 85c multicolored 1.60 1.60
**463** A357 1.20fr multicolored 2.25 2.25

### Flags and Coins Type

No. 464 — Flag of: a, Uganda, 500 shilling coin. b, Luxembourg, 1 euro coin. c, Cape Verde, 20 escudo coin. d, Belgium, 1 euro coin. e, Italy, 1 euro coin. f, New Zealand, 1 dollar coin. g, Switzerland, 2 franc coin. h, Lebanon, 500 pound coin.

**2006, Oct. 5 Litho. *Perf. 13¼x13***
**464** Pane of 8 15.00 15.00
*a.-h.* A375 85c Any single 1.50 1.50

A column of rouletting in the middle of the pane separates it into two parts.

### Endangered Species Type of 1993

Designs: No. 465, Theropithecus gelada. No. 466, Cercopithecus neglectus. No. 467, Varecia variegata. No. 468, Hylobates moloch.

***Perf. 12¾x12½***
**2007, Mar. 15 Litho.**
**465** A271 1fr multicolored 1.75 1.75
**466** A271 1fr multicolored 1.75 1.75
**467** A271 1fr multicolored 1.75 1.75
**468** A271 1fr multicolored 1.75 1.75
*a.* Block of 4, #465-468 7.00 7.00

### Flags and Coins Type of 2006

No. 469 — Flag of: a, Burkina Faso, 500 franc coin. b, France, 50 cent coin. c, Moldova, 50 bani coin. d, Papua New Guinea, 1 kina coin. e, Bolivia, 1 boliviano coin. f, Myanmar, 100 kyat coin. g, Mali, 500 franc coin. h, Tunisia, 5 dinar coin.

**2007, May 3 Litho. *Perf. 13¼x13***
**469** Sheet of 8 12.50 12.50
*a.-h.* A375 85c Any single 1.50 1.50

A column of rouletting in the middle of the sheet separates it into two parts.

### Peaceful Visions Type of 2007

Designs: 1.20fr, "Harvest for All." 1.80fr, "This Dream Has Wings."

**2007, June 1 Litho. *Perf. 13x12½***
**470** A378 1.20fr multicolored 2.25 2.25
**471** A378 1.80fr multicolored 3.25 3.25

### World Heritage Sites, South America Type

Designs: Nos. 472, 474a, Tiwanaku, Bolivia. Nos. 473, 474f, Machu Picchu, Peru. No. 474b, Iguaçu National Park, Brazil. No. 474c, Galapagos Islands, Ecuador. No. 474d, Rapa Nui, Chile. No. 474e, Cueva de las Manos, Argentina.

**2007, Aug. 9 Litho. *Perf. 13¼x13***
**472** A381 1fr multicolored 1.90 1.90
**473** A381 1.80fr multicolored 3.25 3.25

### Souvenir Booklet

**474** Booklet, #474g-474l 16.00
*a.-c.* A381 20c Any single .40 .40
*d.-f.* A381 50c Any single .90 .90
*g.* Booklet pane of 4 #474a 1.60 1.60
*h.* Booklet pane of 4 #474b 1.60 1.60
*i.* Booklet pane of 4 #474c 1.60 1.60
*j.* Booklet pane of 4 #474d 3.60 3.60
*k.* Booklet pane of 4 #474e 3.60 3.60
*l.* Booklet pane of 4 #474f 3.60 3.60

### Humanitarian Mail Type

**2007, Sept. 6 Litho. *Perf. 12½x13¼***
**475** A382 1.80fr multicolored 3.00 3.00

### Space for Humanity Type

Designs: 1fr, Astronaut spacewalking. 1.80fr, International Space Station, space probe, Jupiter.
3fr, Astronauts spacewalking.

**2007, Oct. 25 Litho. *Perf. 13½x14***
**476** A383 1fr multicolored 1.90 1.90
**477** A383 1.80fr multicolored 3.25 3.25

### Souvenir Sheet

**478** A383 3fr multicolored 7.50 7.50

### Intl. Holocaust Remembrance Day Type

**2008, Jan. 27 Litho. *Perf. 13***
**479** A384 85c multicolored 3.00 3.00

### Endangered Species Type of 1993

Designs: No. 480, Odobenus rosmarus. No. 481, Platygyra daedalea. No. 482, Hippocampus bargibanti. No. 483, Delphinapterus leucas.

**2008, Mar. 6 Litho. *Perf. 12¾x12½***
**480** A271 1fr multicolored 2.00 2.00
**481** A271 1fr multicolored 2.00 2.00
**482** A271 1fr multicolored 2.00 2.00
**483** A271 1fr multicolored 2.00 2.00
*a.* Block of 4, #480-483 8.00 8.00

### Flags and Coins Type of 2006

No. 484 — Flag of: a, Madagascar, 1 ariary coin. b, Rwanda, 50 franc coin. c, Switzerland, 10 franc coin. d, Iran, 500 rial coin. e, Namibia, 5 dollar coin. f, Maldives, 1 rufiyaa coin. g, Albania, 10 lek coin. h, Turkey, 1 lira coin.

**2008, May 8 Litho. *Perf. 13¼x13***
**484** Sheet of 8 15.00 15.00
*a.-h.* A375 85c Any single 1.75 1.75

A column of rouletting in the middle of the sheet separates it into two parts.

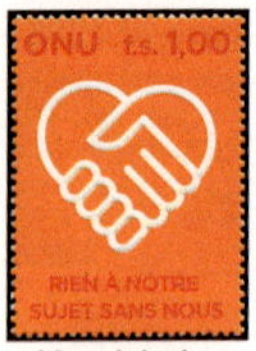

Handshake
G74

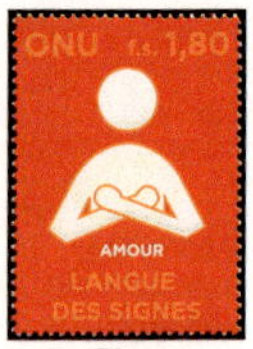

Sign Language
G75

**Litho. & Embossed**

**2008, June 6** ***Perf. 14x13¼***

**485** G74 1fr org & red 2.25 2.25
**486** G75 1.80fr red & org 4.00 4.00

Convention on the Rights of Persons with Disabilities.

### Sport for Peace Type of 2008

Designs: 1fr, 3fr, Gymnast. 1.80fr, Tennis player.

**2008, Aug. 8** **Litho.** ***Perf. 14½***

**487** A393 1fr multicolored 2.25 2.25
**488** A393 1.80fr multicolored 4.00 4.00

**Souvenir Sheet**

***Perf. 12¾x13¼***

**489** A393 3fr multicolored 9.00 9.00

2008 Summer Olympics, Beijing.

### "We Can End Poverty" Type of 2008

Winning designs in children's art contest by: 1fr, Ranajoy Banerjee, India, vert. 1.80fr, Elizabeth Elaine Chun Nig Au, Hong Kong, vert.

***Perf. 12½x12¾***

**2008, Sept. 18** **Litho.**

**490** A395 1fr multicolored 2.25 2.25
**491** A395 1.80fr multicolored 3.75 3.75

### Climate Change Types of New York and Vienna and

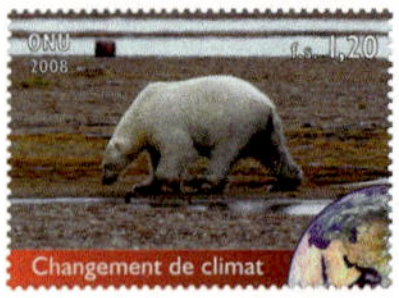

G76

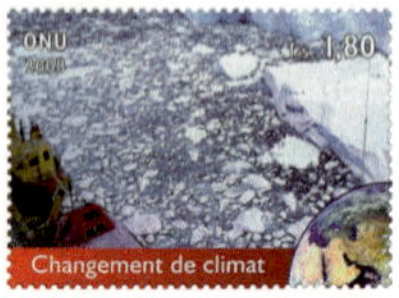

Climate Change
G77

No. 492 — Polar bear with quarter of Earth in: a, LR. b, LL. c, UR. d, UL.

No. 493 — Ship and sea ice with quarter of Earth in: a, LR. b, LL. c, UR. d, UL.

No. 494: a, Like New York #969a. b, Like New York #969b. c, Like New York #969c. d, Like New York #969d. e, Like Geneva #493a. f, Like Geneva #493b. g, Like Geneva #493c. h, Like Geneva #493d. i, Like Vienna #434a. j, Like Vienna #434b. k, Like Vienna #434c. l, Like Vienna #434d. m, Like New York #968a. n, Like New York #968b, o, Like New York #968c, p, Like New York #968d. q, Like Geneva #492a. r, Like Geneva #492b. s, Like Geneva #492c. t, Like Geneva #492d. u, Like Vienna #435a. v, Like Vienna #435b. w, Like Vienna #435c. x, Like Vienna #435d.

All stamps have red panels inscribed "Changement de climat."

**2008, Oct. 23** **Litho.** ***Perf. 13¼x13***

**492** Sheet of 4 10.50 10.50
*a.-d.* G76 1.20fr Any single 2.60 2.60
**493** Sheet of 4 15.50 15.50
*a.-d.* G77 1.80fr Any single 3.75 3.75

**Souvenir Booklet**

**494** Booklet, #494y-494ad 25.00
*a.-d.* A397 35c Any single .75 .75
*e.-h.* G77 35c Any single .75 .75
*i.-l.* V72 35c Any single .75 .75
*m.-p.* A396 50c Any single 1.00 1.00
*q.-t.* G76 50c Any single 1.00 1.00
*u.-x.* V73 50c Any single 1.00 1.00
*y.* Booklet pane of 4, #494a-494d 3.00 3.00
*z.* Booklet pane of 4, #494e-494h 3.00 3.00
*aa.* Booklet pane of 4, #494i-494l 3.00 3.00
*ab.* Booklet pane of 4, #494m-494p 4.25 4.25
*ac.* Booklet pane of 4, #494q-494t 4.25 4.25
*ad.* Booklet pane of 4, #494u-494x 4.25 4.25

### U Thant Type of 2009

**Litho. With Foil Application**

**2009, Feb. 6** ***Perf. 14x13½***

**495** A399 1.30fr red & multi 3.25 3.25

### Endangered Species Type of 1993

No. 496, Maculinea arion. No. 497, Dolomedes plantarius. No. 498, Cerambyx cerdo. No. 499, Coenagrion mercuriale.

**2009, Apr. 16** **Litho.** ***Perf. 12¾x12½***

**496** A271 1fr multicolored 1.90 1.90
**497** A271 1fr multicolored 1.90 1.90
**498** A271 1fr multicolored 1.90 1.90
**499** A271 1fr multicolored 1.90 1.90
*a.* Block of 4, #496-499 7.75 7.75
*b.* Pane of 16, imperf. 5,000.

### World Heritage Sites, Germany Type of 2009

Designs: Nos. 500, 502b, Wartburg Castle. Nos. 501, 502f, Monastic Island of Reichenau. No. 502a, Town Hall and Roland on the Marketplace, Bremen. No. 502c, Palaces and Parks of Potsdam and Berlin. No. 502d, Aachen Cathedral. No. 502e, Luther Memorials in Eisleben and Wittenberg.

**2009, May 7** **Litho.** ***Perf. 14x13½***

**500** A400 1fr multicolored 2.25 2.25
**501** A400 1.30fr multicolored 2.75 2.75

**Souvenir Booklet**

**502** Booklet, #502g-502l 18.00
*a.-c.* A400 30c any single .55 .55
*d.-f.* A400 50c any single .90 .90
*g.* Booklet pane of 4 #502a 2.25 2.25
*h.* Booklet pane of 4 #502b 2.25 2.25
*i.* Booklet pane of 4 #502c 2.25 2.25
*j.* Booklet pane of 4 #502d 3.75 3.75
*k.* Booklet pane of 4 #502e 3.75 3.75
*l.* Booklet pane of 4 #502f 3.75 3.75

### Economic and Social Council (ECOSOC) Type of 2009

Designs: 85c, Improving maternal health. 1.80fr, Access to essential medicines.

**2009, Aug. 6** ***Perf. 12¾x12½***

**503** A411 85c multicolored 2.00 2.00
**504** A411 1.80fr multicolored 4.00 4.00

### Millennium Development Goals Type of 2009

Miniature Sheet

No. 505: a, Bowl of hot food. b, Pencil. c, Female symbol. d, Teddy bear. e, Pregnant woman, heart. f, Medicine bottle. g, Stylized tree. h, Conjoined people.

**2009, Sept. 25** ***Perf. 13¼***

**505** A413 Sheet of 8 18.00 18.00
*a.-h.* 1.10fr Any single 2.25 2.25

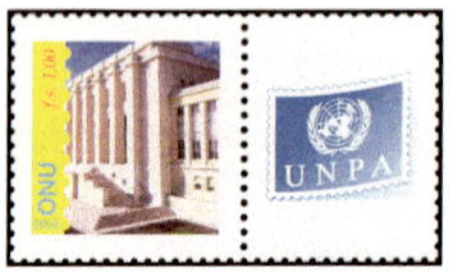

Palais des Nations
G78

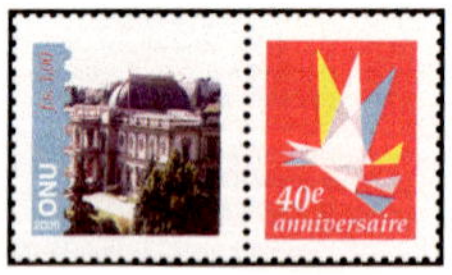

Palais des Nations
G79

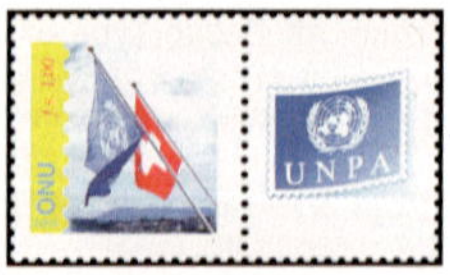

Flags of United Nations and Switzerland — G80

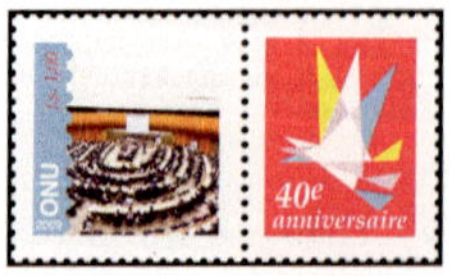

Meeting Room
G81

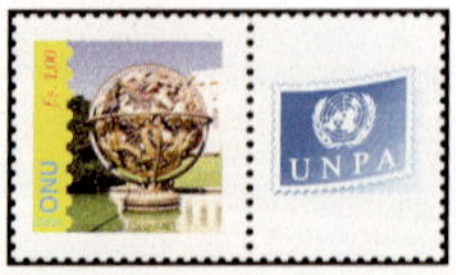

Armillary Sphere
G82

**2009, Oct. 2** ***Perf. 13¼***

**506** G78 1fr multi + label 6.00 6.00
*a.* Perf. 11¼x11 + label 5.00 5.00
**507** G79 1fr multi + label 6.00 6.00
*a.* Perf. 11¼x11 + label 5.00 5.00
**508** G80 1fr multi + label 6.00 6.00
*a.* Perf. 11¼x11 + label 5.00 5.00
**509** G81 1fr multi + label 6.00 6.00
*a.* Perf. 11¼x11 + label 5.00 5.00
**510** G82 1fr multi + label 6.00 6.00
*a.* Perf. 11¼x11 + label 5.00 5.00
*b.* Vert. strip of 5, #506-510, + 5 labels 30.00 30.00
*c.* Vert. strip of 5, #506a-510a, + 5 labels 25.00 25.00

United Nations Postal Administration in Geneva, 40th anniv. The full sheets sold for €19.90 or $14.95. Labels could not be personalized. The sheet of No. 510c has "VER. 2" in the lower right selvage.

Miniature Sheet

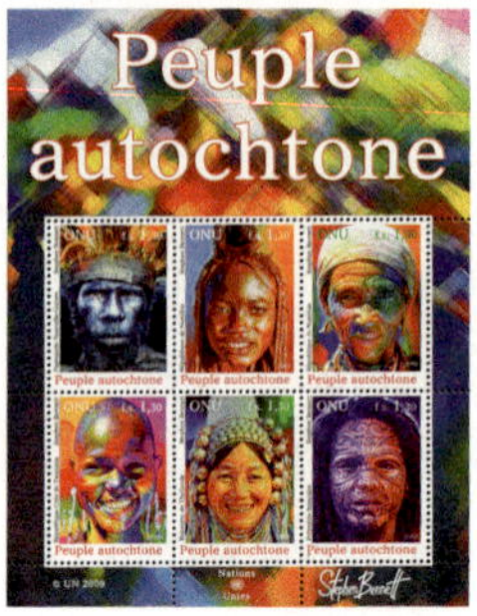

Indigenous People — G83

No. 511 — Portraits of person from: a, Papua New Guinea. b, Namibia (young woman). c, Namibia (old man). d, Tanzania. e, Thailand. f, French Polynesia.

**2009, Oct. 8** ***Perf. 12½***

**511** G83 Sheet of 6 16.00 16.00
*a.-f.* 1.30fr Any single 2.60 2.60

### Flags and Coins Type of 2006

No. 512 — Flag of: a, Equatorial Guinea, 100 franc coin. b, Laos, 20 kip coin. c, Seychelles, 5 rupee coin. d, Mauritania, 1 ougiya coin. e, Argentina, 1 peso coin. f, Morocco, 1 dirham coin. g, Sudan, 20 piaster coin. h, Brunei, 50 cent coin.

**2010, Feb. 5** **Litho.** ***Perf. 13¼x13***

**512** Sheet of 8 15.00 15.00
*a.-h.* A375 85c Any single 1.75 1.75

A column of rouletting in the middle of the sheet separates it into two parts.

### Endangered Species Type of 1993

No. 513, Fouquieria columnaris. No. 514, Aloe arborescens. No. 515, Galanthus krasnovii. No. 516, Dracaena draco.

**2010, Apr. 15** **Litho.** ***Perf. 12¾x12½***

**513** A271 1fr multicolored 2.25 2.25
**514** A271 1fr multicolored 2.25 2.25
**515** A271 1fr multicolored 2.25 2.25
**516** A271 1fr multicolored 2.25 2.25
*a.* Block of 4, #513-516 9.00 9.00

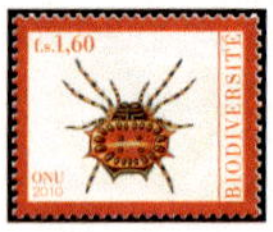

Intl. Year of Biodiversity — G84

Drawings from Art Forms from Nature, by Ernst Heinrich: 1.60fr, Arachnid. 1.90fr, Starfish.

**2010, Apr. 15** **Litho.** ***Perf. 13***

**517** G84 1.60fr multicolored 3.75 3.75
**518** G84 1.90fr multicolored 4.25 4.25

### One Planet, One Ocean Types of New York and Vienna and

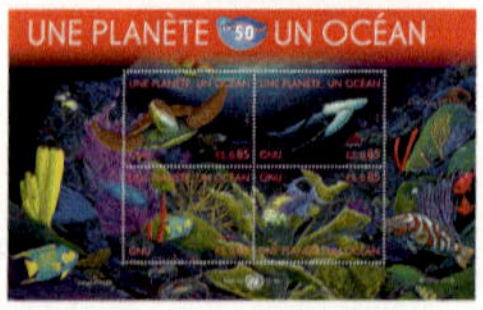

G85

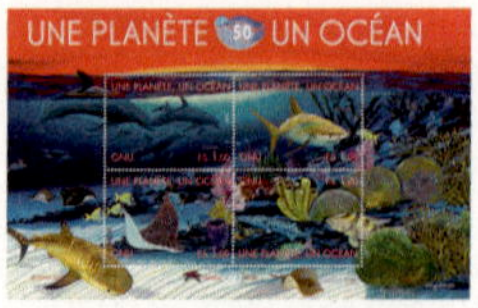

G86

No. 519: a, Turtles at left and top, fish at bottom. b, Hammerhead shark. c, Fish at left and center, corals. d, Fish at left, coral.

No. 520: a, Dolphins. b, Shark, head of fish at right, small fish in background. c, Ray and fish. d, Fish at bottom, coral and sponges.

No. 521: a, Like New York #1003a. b, Like New York #1003b, c, Like New York #1003c, d, Like New York #1003d. e, Like Vienna #471a. f, Like Vienna #471b. g, Like Vienna #471c, h, Like Vienna #471d. i, Like #519a. j, Like #519b, k, Like #519c. l, Like #519d. m, Like New York #1004a. n, Like New York #1004b. o, Like New York #1004c, p, Like New York #1004d. q, Like Vienna #472a. r, Like Vienna #472b. s, Like Vienna #472c. t, Like Vienna #472d. u, Like #520a. v, Like #520b. w, Like #520c. x, Like #520d.

**2010, May 6** **Litho.** ***Perf. 14x13¼***

**519** G85 Sheet of 4 8.00 8.00
*a.-d.* 85c Any single 2.00 2.00
**520** G86 Sheet of 4 10.00 10.00
*a.-d.* 1fr Any single 2.50 2.50

**Souvenir Booklet**

***Perf. 13¼x13***

**521** Booklet, #521y-521z, 521aa-521ad 22.00
*a.-d.* A416 30c any single .70 .70
*e.-h.* V91 30c any single .70 .70
*i.-l.* G85 30c any single .70 .70
*m.-p.* A417 50c any single 1.10 1.10
*q.-t.* V92 50c any single 1.10 1.10
*u.-x.* G86 50c any single 1.10 1.10
*y.* Booklet pane of 4 #521a-521d 2.80 2.80
*z.* Booklet pane of 4 #521e-521h 2.80 2.80
*aa.* Booklet pane of 4 #521i-521l 2.80 2.80
*ab.* Booklet pane of 4 #521m-521p 4.40 4.40
*ac.* Booklet pane of 4 #521q-521t 4.40 4.40
*ad.* Booklet pane of 4 #521u-521x 4.40 4.40

Intl. Oceanographic Commission, 50th anniv.

### United Nations, 65th Anniv. Type of 2010

**Litho. With Foil Application**

**2010, June 28** ***Perf. 13¼***

**522** A422 1.90fr red & gold 4.00 4.00
*a.* Souvenir sheet of 2 8.00 8.00

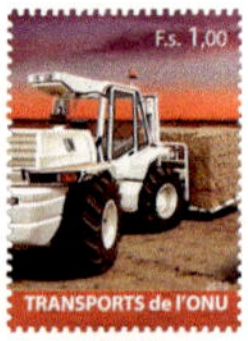

G87

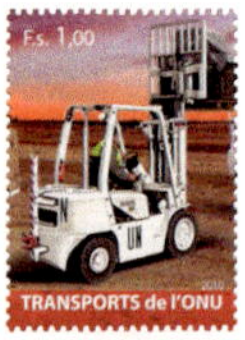

G88

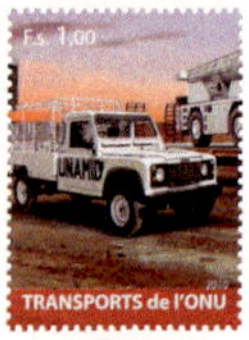

G89

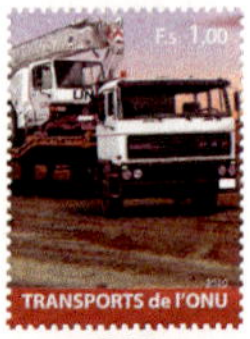

G90

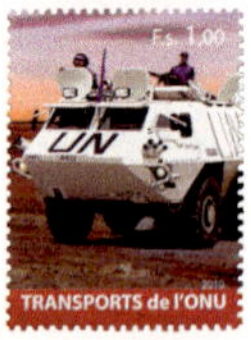

United Nations Land Transport — G91

**2010, Sept. 2** **Litho.** ***Perf. 13¼x13***

**523** G87 1fr multicolored 1.80 1.80
**524** G88 1fr multicolored 1.80 1.80
**525** G89 1fr multicolored 1.80 1.80
**526** G90 1fr multicolored 1.80 1.80
**527** G91 1fr multicolored 1.80 1.80
*a.* Horiz. strip of 5, #523-527 9.00 9.00

OFFICES IN GENEVA, SWITZERLAND 291

Miniature Sheet

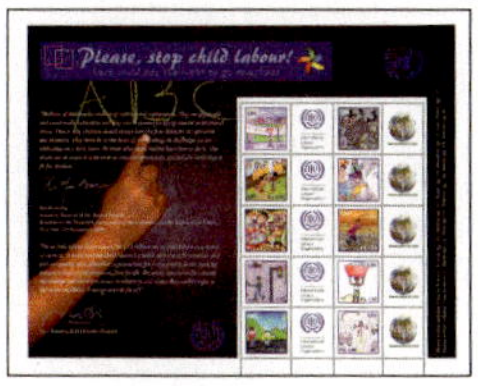


Campaign Against Child Labor — G92

No. 528: a, Child, buildings, road, burning can. b, Child with full basket on back, children playing in background. c, Child working, children on school bus. d, Child with mining helmet, three other children. e, Child near tubs, children working, child being beaten. f, Child with hoe. g, Marionette, traffic light. h, Child carrying basket on head. i, Children on rock field near hills. j, Child holding bags in road.

**2010, Sept. 2 Litho. *Perf. 14¾***

**528** G92 Sheet of 10 + 10 labels 32.50 32.50
*a.-j.* 1.90fr Any single + label 3.25 3.25

No. 528 sold for $14.95, 15fr and €11.46, each of which was far lower than the level at which 19fr, the total face value of the stamps on the sheet, was worth on the day of issue. Labels could not be personalized.

Miniature Sheet

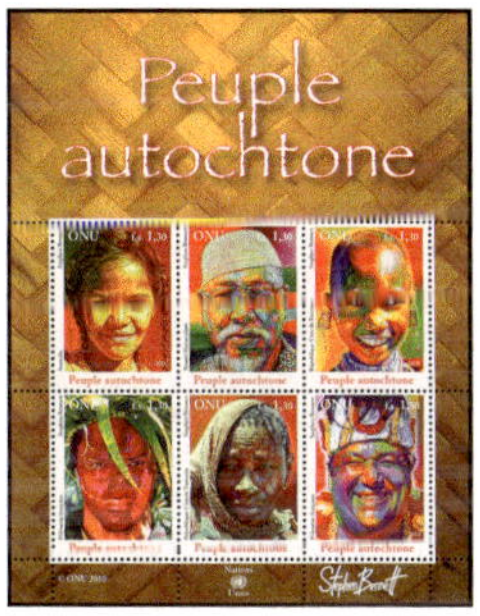


Indigenous People — G93

No. 529 — Portraits of person from: a, Australia. b, Brunei. c, Tanzania (girl with bald head). d, French Polynesia (man with headdress of leaves). e, Tanzania (man with headdress). f, French Polynesia (man with white headdress).

**2010, Oct. 21 Litho. *Perf. 13***

**529** G93 Pane of 6 14.50 14.50
*a.-f.* 1.30fr Any single 2.40 2.40

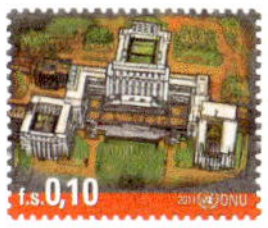

United Nations Headquarters, Geneva — G94

United Nations Headquarters, Geneva: 10c, Aerial view. 50c, Ground-level view.

**2011, Feb. 4 Litho. *Perf. 13***

**530** G94 10c multicolored .35 .35
**531** G94 50c multicolored 1.25 1.25

### Flags and Coins Type of 2006

No. 532 — Flag of: a, Mongolia, 500 tugrik coin. b, Senegal, 500 franc coin. c, Egypt, 100 piaster coin. d, Congo, 100 franc coin. e, Nicaragua, 1 Córdoba coin. f, Central African Republic, 100 franc coin. g, Algeria, 5 dinar coin. h, Ukraine, 5 hryvnia coin.

**2011, Mar. 3 Litho. *Perf. 13¼x13***

**532** Sheet of 8 15.00 15.00
*a.-h.* A375 85c Any single 1.75 1.75

A column of rouletting in the middle of the sheet separates it into two parts.

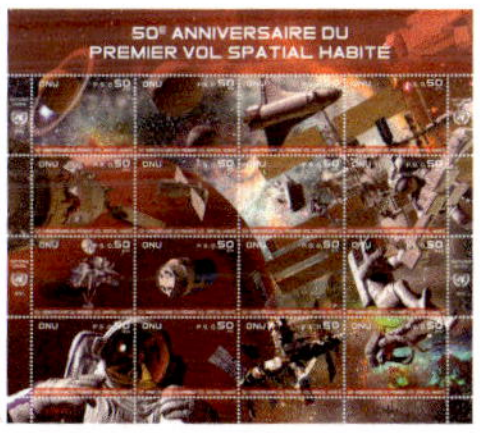


Human Space Flight, 50th Anniv. G95

No. 533: Various parts of outer space scene.

No. 534, vert.: a, International Space Station. b, International Space Station, diff.

**2011, Apr. 12 Litho. *Perf. 13x13¼***

**533** G95 Sheet of 16 18.00 18.00
*a.-p.* 50c any single 1.10 1.10

### Souvenir Sheet

**534** G95 Sheet of 2 15.00 15.00
*a.* 85c multi 6.50 6.50
*b.* 1fr multi 8.50 8.50

No. 534 contains two 40x48mm stamps that were printed as part of a larger sheet of six stamps, Vienna No. 485c, which was broken up into its component two-stamp souvenir sheets, and also sold as one unit. Value, $90, complete unit.

### UNESCO World Heritage Sites in Nordic Countries Type of 2011

Designs: 85c, Kronborg Castle, Denmark. 1fr, Suomenlinna Fortress, Finland.

**2011, May 5 Litho. *Perf. 14x13½***

**535** A433 85c multicolored 1.90 1.90
**536** A433 1fr multicolored 2.25 2.25

### AIDS Ribbon Type of 2011

**2011, June 3 Litho. *Die Cut***

**Self-Adhesive**

**537** A434 1.30fr red & orange 5.00 5.00

### ECOSOC Type of 2011

**2011, July 1 Litho. *Perf. 14¼***

**538** A435 1fr multicolored 3.00 3.00
**539** A435 1.30fr multicolored 4.00 4.00

### Endangered Species Type of 1993

Designs: No. 540, Strigops habroptilus (Kakapo). No. 541, Lophophorus impejanus (Himalayan monal). No. 542, Ciconia nigra (Black stork). No. 543, Pithecophaga jeffreyi (Philippine eagle).

**2011, Sept. 7 Litho. *Perf. 12¾x12½***

**540** A271 1fr multicolored 2.60 2.60
**541** A271 1fr multicolored 2.60 2.60
**542** A271 1fr multicolored 2.60 2.60
**543** A271 1fr multicolored 2.60 2.60
*a.* Block of 4, #540-543 10.40 10.40

### Intl. Year of Forests Type of 2011

Designs: 85c, Birds and butterflies, tree tops. 1.40fr, Fish and coral.

**Litho. With Foil Application**

**2011, Oct. 13 *Perf. 12½***

**544** 85c multicolored 2.25 2.25
**545** 1.40fr multicolored 3.75 3.75
*a.* A436 Vert. pair, #544-545 6.00 6.00

### Flags and Coins Type of 2006

No. 546 — Flag of: a, Saudi Arabia, 100 halala coin. b, Georgia, 2 lari coin. c, Democratic People's Republic of Korea, 50 won coin. d, Lesotho, 50 lisente coin. e, Serbia, 5 dinar coin. f, Djibouti, 20 franc coin. g, Belize, 1 dollar coin. h, Liechtenstein, 20 centime coin.

**2012, Feb. 3 Litho. *Perf. 13¼x13***

**546** Sheet of 8 16.50 16.50
*a.-h.* A375 85c Any single 2.00 2.00

A column of rouletting in the middle of the sheet separates it into two parts.

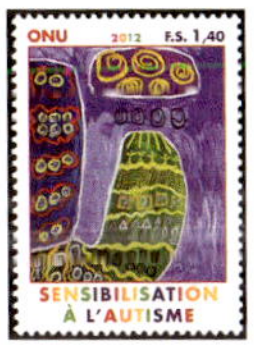


G96

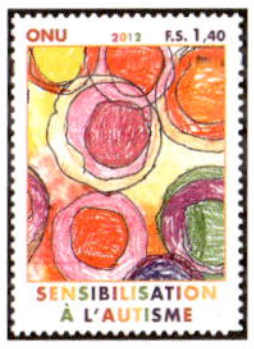


Autism Awareness — G97

Drawings by autistic people: No. 547, Victory, by J.A Tan, Canada. No. 548, Untitled drawing, by Michael Augello, U.S.

**2012, Apr. 2 Litho. *Perf. 14x13½***

**547** G96 1.40fr multicolored 3.50 3.50
**548** G97 1.40fr multicolored 3.50 3.50
*a.* Pair, #547-548 7.00 7.00

### Endangered Species Type of 1993

Designs: No. 549, Panthera tigris altaica. No. 550, Psitacella picta. No. 551, Iguana iguana. No. 552, Propithecus tattersalli.

**2012, Apr. 19 Litho. *Perf. 12¾x12½***

**549** A271 1fr multicolored 2.40 2.40
**550** A271 1fr multicolored 2.40 2.40
**551** A271 1fr multicolored 2.40 2.40
**552** A271 1fr multicolored 2.40 2.40
*a.* Block of 4, #549-552 9.75 9.75

### Rio + 20 Type of 2012

**2012, June 1 Litho. *Perf. 13x13¼***

**553** A443 1.40fr multicolored 4.00 4.00

### Sport for Peace Type of 2012

2012 Paralympics events: 1fr, Track. 1.40fr, Archery.

**Litho. With Foil Application**

**2012, Aug. 17 *Perf. 14½***

**554** A444 1fr multicolored 2.40 2.40
**555** A444 1.40fr multicolored 3.50 3.50
*a.* Souvenir sheet of 1 3.50 3.50

### UNESCO World Heritage Sites in Africa Type of 2012

Designs: 85c, Virunga National Park, Congo Democratic Republic. 1fr, Amphitheater of El Jem, Tunisia.

**2012, Sept. 5 Litho. *Perf. 13¼***

**556** A445 85c multicolored 2.00 2.00
**557** A445 1fr multicolored 2.40 2.40

Miniature Sheet

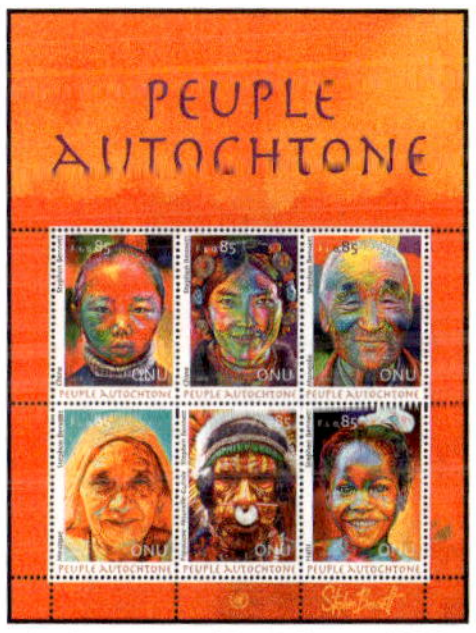


Indigenous People — G98

No. 558 — Portrait of person from: a, China. b, Tibet, China. c, Mongolia. d, Mexico. e, Papua New Guinea. f, Haiti.

**2012, Oct. 11 Litho. *Perf. 13¼x13***

**558** G98 Sheet of 6 13.50 13.50
*a.-f.* 85c Any single 2.25 2.25

### World Radio Day Type of 2013

Designs: 1.40fr, Reporter with microphone and tape recorder. 1.90fr, Engineers in studio.

**2013, Feb. 13 Litho. *Perf. 13¼x13***

**559** A448 1.40fr multicolored 3.50 3.50
**560** A448 1.90fr multicolored 4.50 4.50

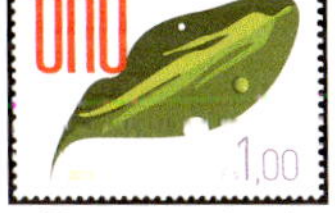


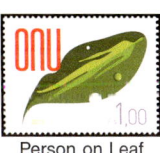

Person on Leaf G99

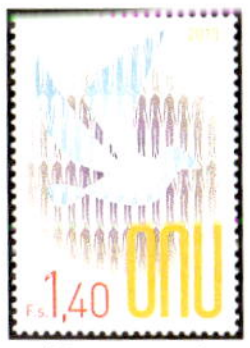


Dove and People G100

**2013, Mar. 5 Litho. *Perf. 14x13½***

**561** G99 1fr multicolored 2.40 2.40

***Perf. 13¼x14***

**562** G100 1.40fr multicolored 3.50 3.50

### World Heritage Sites, China, Type of 2013

Designs: Nos. 563, 565b, Potala Palace, Lhasa. Nos. 564, 565e, Mount Huangshan. No. 565a, Mogao Caves. No. 565c, Great Wall of China. No. 565d, Imperial Palace, Beijing. No. 565f, Mausoleum of the First Qing Emperor.

**2013, Apr. 11 Litho. *Perf. 14x13½***

**563** A452 1.40fr multicolored 3.50 3.50
**564** A452 1.90fr multicolored 4.50 4.50

### Souvenir Booklet

**565** Booklet, #565g-565l 24.00
*a.-c.* A452 30c any single .75 .75
*d.-f.* A452 50c any single 1.25 1.25
*g.* Booklet pane of 4 #565a 3.00 —
*h.* Booklet pane of 4 #565b 3.00 —
*i.* Booklet pane of 4 #565c 3.00 —
*j.* Booklet pane of 4 #565d 5.00 —
*k.* Booklet pane of 4 #565e 5.00 —
*l.* Booklet pane of 4 #565f 5.00 —

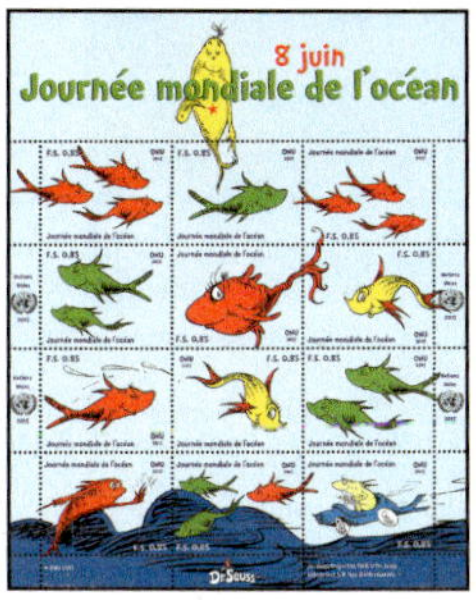


World Oceans Day G101

No. 566 — Fish from *One Fish, Two Fish, Red Fish, Blue Fish,* by Dr. Seuss: a, Three red fish facing right. b, Green fish, tail of yellow fish. c, Three red fish facing right, part of tail of red fish. d, Two entire green fish facing left, tail of bottom fish ends above "n" in "océan." e, Red fish with eye open facing left. f, Tail of red fish, yellow and red fish facing left. g, Red fish facing right, water droplets. h, Yellow and red fish facing right. i, Two green fish facing left, tail of bottom fish ends to right of "océan." j, Red fish and wave. k, Two green fish, red fish, wave. l, Yellow fish in car, wave.

**2013, May 31 Litho. *Perf. 13***

**566** G101 Sheet of 12 20.00 20.00
*a.-l.* 85c any single 1.60 1.60

### Nebulae Type of 2013

Designs: No. 567, NGC 2346. No. 568, Sh 2-106.

1fr, Messier 16.

**2013, Aug. 9 Litho. *Perf. 13¼***

**567** A454 1.40fr multicolored 3.50 3.50
**568** A454 1.40fr multicolored 3.50 3.50
*a.* Pair, #567-568 7.00 7.00

### Souvenir Sheet

**569** A454 1fr multicolored 2.40 2.40

No. 569 contains one 44x44mm stamp.

### Works of Disabled Artists Type of 2013

Designs: 1.40fr, See the Girl with the Red Dress On, by Sargy Mann, United Kingdom. 1.90fr, Performers in China Disabled People's Performing Art Troupe, People's Republic of China.

**2013, Sept. 20 Litho. *Perf. 13¼x13***

**570** A456 1.40fr multicolored 3.50 3.50
**571** A456 1.90fr multicolored 4.50 4.50

### Endangered Species Type of 1993

Designs: No. 572, Smutsia temminckii. No. 573, Perodicticus potto. No. 574, Tarsius syrichta. No. 575, Pteropus livingstonii.

**2013, Oct. 10 Litho. *Perf. 12¾x12½***

**572** A271 1.40fr multicolored 3.25 3.25
**573** A271 1.40fr multicolored 3.25 3.25
**574** A271 1.40fr multicolored 3.25 3.25
**575** A271 1.40fr multicolored 3.25 3.25
*a.* Block of 4, #572-575 13.00 13.00

### Flags and Coins Type of 2006

No. 576 — Flag of: a, Ivory Coast, 100 franc coin. b, Marshall Islands, 10 cent coin. c, Andorra, 20 cent coin. d, Guinea-Bissau, 100 franc coin. e, Kenya, 20 shilling coin. f, Antigua and Barbuda, 5 cent coin. g, Tajikistan, 50 diram coin. h, Micronesia, 5 cent coin.

**2013, Nov. 6 Litho. *Perf. 13¼x13***

**576** Sheet of 8 26.00 26.00
*a.-h.* A375 1.40fr Any single 3.25 3.25

A column of rouletting in the middle of the sheet separates it into two parts.

### International Day of Happiness Type of 2014

Designs: 1fr, A Sweet Dog's Muzzle, photograph by Jaymi Heimbuch, "Heureux." 1.40fr, Two women making heart with hands, photograph by Glow Images, Chinese characters for "Happy."

**2014, Mar. 17 Litho. *Perf. 13¼x13***

**577** A459 1fr multicolored 2.50 2.50
**578** A459 1.40fr multicolored 3.50 3.50

292 OFFICES IN GENEVA, SWITZERLAND

Miniature Sheet

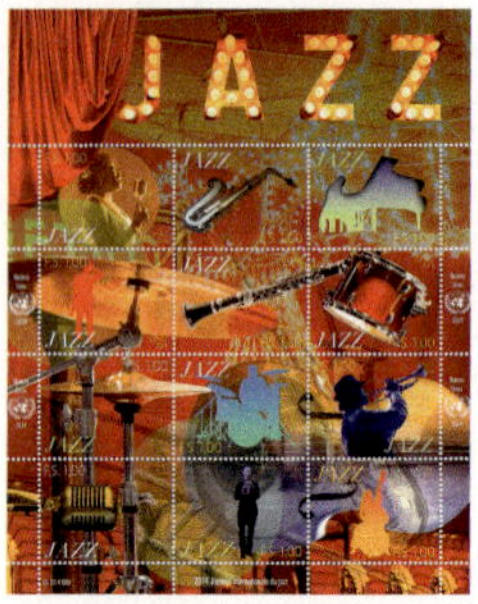


International Year of Jazz — G102

No. 579: a, Woman behind microphone. b, Saxophone. c, Silhouette of pianist at grand piano. d, Cymbal and silhouette of man holding trumpet. e, Cymbal and clarinet. f, Clarinet and drum. g, Hi-hat. h, Silhouette of drummer and drum set. i, Trumpeter with hat. j, Microphone and cymbal stands. k, Clarinetist. l, Bass player.

**2014, Apr. 30 Litho. *Perf. 13x13¼***

**579** G102 Sheet of 12 29.50 29.50
First day cover 31.00
*a.-l.* 1fr Any single 2.40 2.40

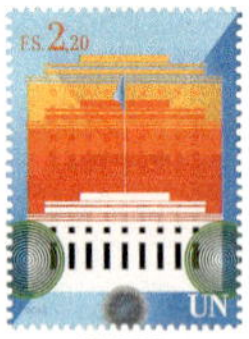


G103

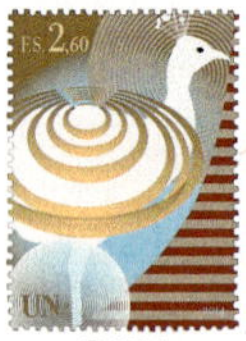


G104

**2014, June 6 Litho. *Perf. 13¼x13***

**580** G103 2.20fr multicolored 5.50 5.50
**581** G104 2.60fr multicolored 6.50 6.50

**Taj Mahal Types of 2014**

**2014, July 16 Engr. *Perf. 13¼x13***

**582** A465 1.40fr multicolored 3.50 3.50
**583** A467 1.90fr multicolored 4.75 4.75

**Souvenir Booklet**

**584** Booklet, #584g-584l 20.00
*a.* A463 30c multi .75 .75
*b.* A465 30c multi .75 .75
*c.* A466 50c multi 1.25 1.25
*d.* A464 50c multi 1.25 1.25
*e.* A467 30c multi .75 .75
*f.* A468 50c multi 1.25 1.25
*g.* Booklet pane of 4 #584a 2.50 —
*h.* Booklet pane of 4 #584b 2.50 —
*i.* Booklet pane of 4 #584c 2.50 —
*j.* Booklet pane of 4 #584d 4.00 —
*k.* Booklet pane of 4 #584e 4.00 —
*l.* Booklet pane of 4 #584f 4.00 —

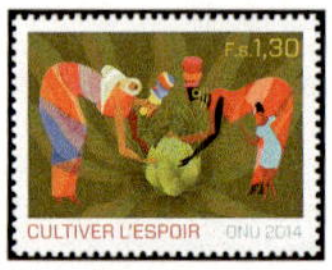


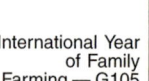

International Year of Family Farming — G105

**2014, Aug. 21 Litho. *Perf. 13x13¼***

**585** G105 1.30fr multicolored 3.25 3.25
**586** G105 1.60fr multicolored 4.00 4.00

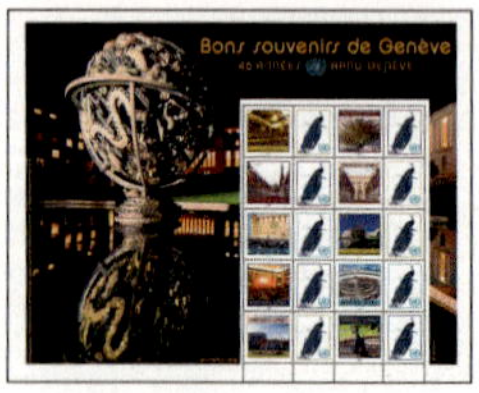


G106

No. 587: a, Room with painted ceiling. b, Peacock with spread tail. c, Rows of flags, brown panel at bottom. d, Rows of flags near Palais des Nations, tan panel at top. e, Meeting hall with United nations emblem on rear wall. f, Armillary sphere and Palais des Nations. g, Meeting hall with movie screen on rear wall. h, Circular meeting hall. i, Farm animals on grass near buildings. j, Peacock with tail down.

**2014, Sept. 12 Litho. *Perf. 14¾***

**587** G106 Sheet of 10 *35.00 35.00*
*a.-j.* 1.30fr Any single + label *3.50 3.50*

The full sheet sold for 14.95fr. The generic labels are shown. Labels could be personalized.

**Global Education First Initiative Type of 2014**

Designs: No. 588, Students in art museum. No. 589, Student in library.

**2014, Sept. 18 Litho. *Perf. 13x13¼***

**588** A470 1.90fr multicolored 4.75 4.75

**Souvenir Sheet**

***Perf. 12½***

**589** A470 1.90fr multicolored 4.75 4.75

No. 589 contains one 32x32mm stamp.

**Endangered Species Type of 2014**

Maps and: No. 590, Arapaima gigas. No. 591, Cetorhinus maximus. No. 592, Pristis pristis. No. 593, Acipenser baerii.

**2014, Oct. 23 Litho. *Perf. 12¾x12½***

**590** A471 1.40fr multicolored 3.50 3.50
**591** A471 1.40fr multicolored 3.50 3.50
**592** A471 1.40fr multicolored 3.50 3.50
**593** A471 1.40fr multicolored 3.50 3.50
*a.* Block of 4, #590-593 14.00 14.00

**Flags and Coins Type of 2006**

No. 594 — Flag of: a, Vanuatu, 10 vatu coin. b, Nauru, 1 dollar coin. c, Eritrea, 100 cent coin. d, El Salvador, 1 colon coin. e, Mozambique, 50 centavo coin. f, Burundi, 1 franc coin. g, Turkmenistan, 10 tenge coin. h, Guinea, 1 franc coin.

**2015, Feb. 6 Litho. *Perf. 13¼x13***

**594** Sheet of 8 16.50 16.50
*a.-h.* A375 90c Any single 2.00 2.00

A column of rouletting in the middle of the sheet separates it into two parts.

Miniature Sheets

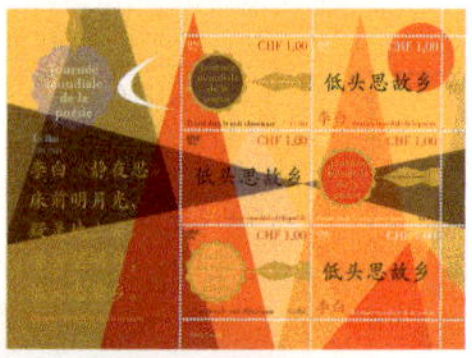

G107

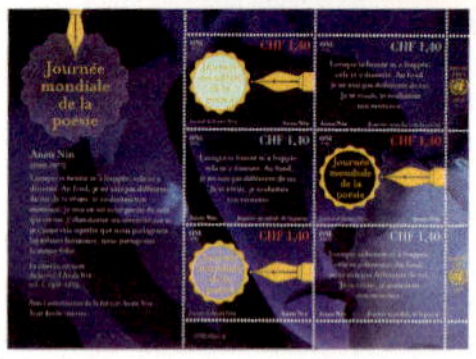


World Poetry Day G108

No. 595: a, Pen and gray circle. b, Li Bai quotation in Chinese, denomination in light blue green. c, Li Bai quotation in Chinese, denomination in red. d, Pen and red circle. e, Pen and orange circle. f, Li Bai quotation in Chinese, denomination in white.

No. 596: a, Pen and light green circle. b, Anais Nin quotation, denomination and "Journée mondiale de poésie" in light blue. c, As "b," with "Journée mondiale de poésie" in white, dark blue area below and to left of date. d, Pen and black circle. e, Pen and lilac circle. f, As "c," with dark blue area below and to right of date.

***Perf. 14½x14¼***

**2015, Mar. 20 Litho.**

**595** G107 Sheet of 6 14.00 14.00
*a.-f.* 1fr Any single 2.25 2.25
**596** G108 Sheet of 6 19.50 19.50
*a.-f.* 1.40fr Any single 3.25 3.25

**Endangered Species Type of 2015**

Designs: No. 597, Diphyllodes respublica. No. 598, Ptiloris paradiseus. No. 599, Semioptera wallacii. No. 600, Paradisaea decora.

**2015, Apr. 16 Litho. *Perf. 12½x12¾***

**597** A476 1.40fr multicolored 3.25 3.25
**598** A476 1.40fr multicolored 3.25 3.25
**599** A476 1.40fr multicolored 3.25 3.25
**600** A476 1.40fr multicolored 3.25 3.25
*a.* Block of 4, #597-600 13.00 13.00
*Nos. 597-600 (4)* 13.00 13.00

**World Heritage Sites, Southeast Asia, Type of 2015**

Designs: Nos. 601, 603b, Angkor Wat, Cambodia. Nos. 602, 603e, Cordillera, Philippines. No. 603a, Luang Prabang, Laos. No. 603c, Ayutthaya, Thailand. No. 565d, Borobudur Temple, Indonesia. No. 603f, Hué Monuments, Viet Nam.

**2015, June 5 Litho. *Perf. 14x13½***

**601** A480 1.40fr multicolored 3.25 3.25
**602** A480 1.90fr multicolored 4.50 4.50

**Souvenir Booklet**

**603** Booklet, #603g-603l 23.50
*a.-c.* A480 30c any single .70 .70
*d.-f.* A480 50c any single 1.25 1.25
*g.* Booklet pane of 4 #603a 2.80 —
*h.* Booklet pane of 4 #603b 2.80 —
*i.* Booklet pane of 4 #603c 2.80 —
*j.* Booklet pane of 4 #603d 5.00 —
*k.* Booklet pane of 4 #603e 5.00 —
*l.* Booklet pane of 4 #603f 5.00 —

**End Violence Against Children Type of 2015**

Designs: 1fr, Child marriage. 1.40fr, Child trafficking.

***Perf. 14½x14¼***

**2015, Aug. 20 Litho.**

**604** A481 1fr multicolored 2.40 2.40
**605** A481 1.40fr multicolored 3.25 3.25

Miniature Sheet

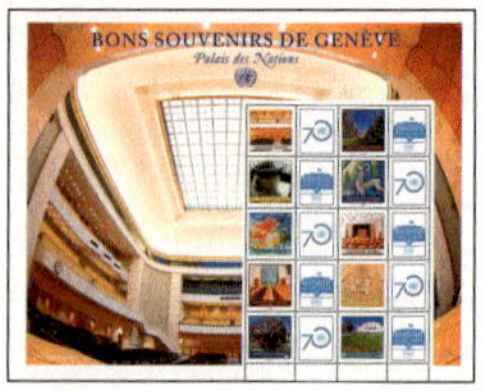


G109

No. 606: a, Balcony above auditorium seats. b, Flags. c, Spiral staircase. d, Stylized horned mammal. e, Painting of trees. f, Auditorium seats facing stage with dais. g, Side view of auditorium seats, painting on wall. h, United Nations emblem. i, Armillary Sphere. j, Palais des Nations and flowers.

**2015, Sept. 3 Litho. *Perf. 14¾***

**606** G109 Sheet of 10 + 10 labels *35.00 35.00*
*a.-j.* 1.40fr Any single + label *3.50 3.50*

The full sheet sold for $18.39 or 14.95fr. The generic labels are shown. Labels could be personalized. The personalization of labels was available only at UN Headquarters, and not through mail order.

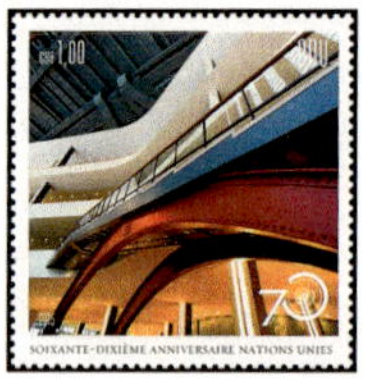


Visitors Lobby — G110

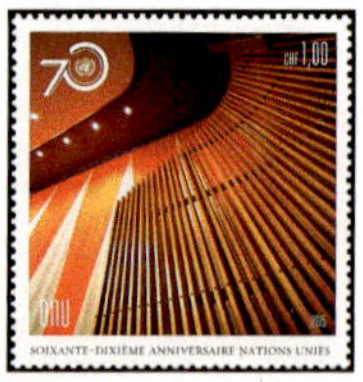


ECOSOC Chamber G111

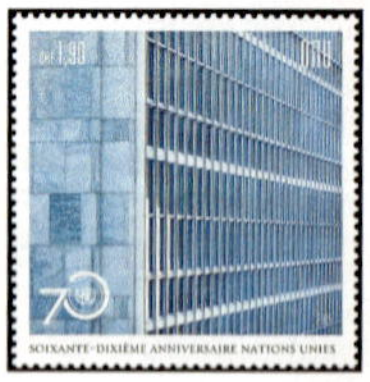


Façade of Secretariat G112

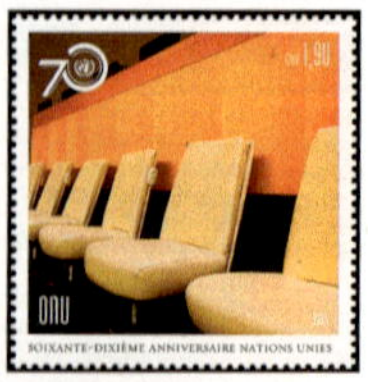


Chairs in ECOSOC Chamber G113

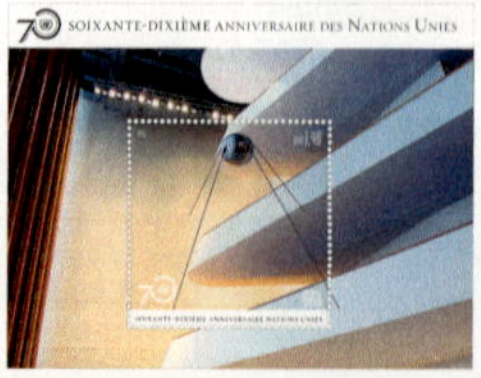


Visitors Lobby G114

Printed by Cartor Security Printing, France. Panes of 6. Designed by Rorie Katz, U.S.

**2015, Oct. 25 Litho. *Perf. 13¾***

**607** G110 1fr multicolored 2.40 2.40
**608** G111 1fr multicolored 2.40 2.40
*a.* Pair, #607-608 4.80 4.80
**609** G112 1.90fr multicolored 4.50 4.50
**610** G113 1.90fr multicolored 4.50 4.50
*a.* Pair, #609-610 9.00 9.00
*Nos. 607-610 (4)* 13.80 13.80

**Souvenir Sheet**

***Perf. 13½***

**611** G114 1.40fr multicolored 4.50 4.50

United Nations, 70th anniv.

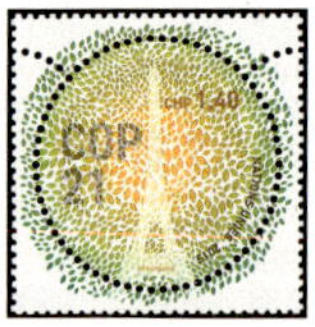


21st United Nations Climate Change Conference, Paris — G115

**2015, Nov. 24 Litho. *Perf. 13¼***

**612** G115 1.40fr multicolored 3.25 3.25

Values are for stamps with surrounding selvage.

**Free and Equal Type of 2016**

Designs: 1fr, Lesbians. 1.50fr, Gay family.

**2016, Feb. 5 Litho. *Perf. 13½x13¼***

**613** A491 1fr multicolored 2.25 2.25
**614** A491 1.50fr multicolored 3.50 3.50

**HeForShe Type of 2016**

Designs: 1fr, Man, blue background. 2fr, Woman, mauve background.

**2016, Mar. 8 Litho. *Perf. 12½x13***

**615** A492 1fr multicolored 2.25 2.25
**616** A492 2fr multicolored 4.50 4.50

Miniature Sheets

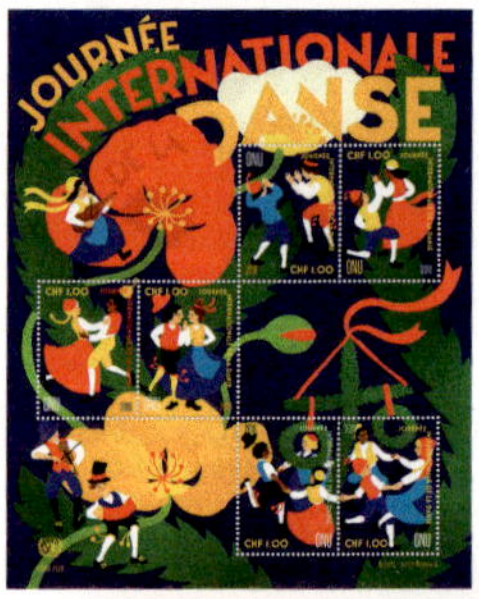


G116

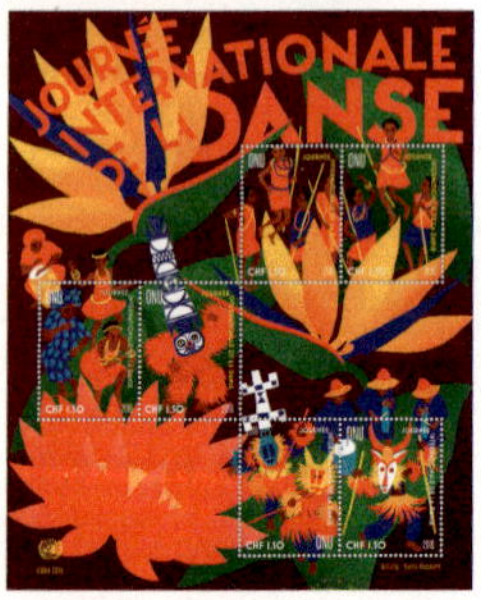


International Dance Day — G117

No. 617 — Illustration of Swedish dancers by Karin Römark: a, Two male dancers. b, Male dancer on one knee with female dancer. c, Male dancer with yellow cap and female dancer. d, Male dancer with red cap and vest with female dancer. e, Three dancers, with woman with red skirt at LR. f, Three dancers, with woman with blue skirt at LR.

No. 618 — Illustration of African dancers by Rönmark: a, Four dancers with sticks. b, Three dancers with sticks. c, Dancers without sticks. d, Dancer with blue and white mask. e, Two masked dancers with sticks. f, Masked dancer with two sticks.

**2016, Apr. 29 Litho. *Perf. 13¼x13***

**617** G116 Sheet of 6 13.50 13.50
*a.-f.* 1fr Any single 2.25 2.25
**618** G117 Sheet of 6 20.00 20.00
*a.-f.* 1.50fr Any single 3.25 3.25

OFFICES IN GENEVA, SWITZERLAND 293

### International Day of United Nations Peacekeepers Type of 2016

Designs: 1fr, Helmeted peacekeepers. 1.50fr, Peacekeeper with African women.

**Litho. With Foil Application**

**2016, May 29** *Perf. 13¼x13*

**619** A496 1fr multicolored 2.25 2.25
**620** A496 1.50fr multicolored 3.50 3.50

### Sport for Peace Type of 2016

Olympic rings and: No. 621, Rowers, denomination at UR. No. 622, Rowers, denomination at UL. No. 623, Rhythmic gymnast facing forward, eyes open. No. 624, Rhythmic gymnast facing left, eyes closed.

**2016, July 22** **Litho.** *Perf. 14¼*

**621** A498 1fr multicolored 2.25 2.25
**622** A498 1fr multicolored 2.25 2.25
*a.* Pair, #621-622 4.50 4.50
**623** A498 2fr multicolored 4.50 4.50
**624** A498 2fr multicolored 4.50 4.50
*a.* Pair, #623-624 9.00 9.00
*Nos. 621-624 (4)* 13.50 13.50

Listings for items containing stamps from New York and stamps from Geneva and/or Vienna, will be found only in the listings for New York.

### World Heritage Sites, Czech Republic Type of 2016

Designs: Nos. 625, 627b, Gardens and Castle at Kroměríz. Nos. 626, 627e, Lednice-Valtice Cultural Landscape. No. 627a, Historic Center of Prague. No. 627d, Holy Trinity Column, Olomouc. No. 627c, Historic Town Center of Kutná Hora. No. 627f, Historic Center of Cesky Krumlov.

**2016, Sept. 8** **Litho.** *Perf. 14¼*

**625** A500 1fr multicolored 2.25 2.25
**626** A500 1.50fr multicolored 3.50 3.50

**Souvenir Booklet**

**627** Booklet, #627g-627l 22.00
*a.-c.* A500 30c any single .65 .65
*d.-f.* A500 50c any single 1.10 1.10
*g.* Booklet pane of 4 #627a 2.75 —
*h.* Booklet pane of 4 #627b 2.75 —
*i.* Booklet pane of 4 #627c 2.75 —
*j.* Booklet pane of 4 #627d 4.50 —
*k.* Booklet pane of 4 #627e 4.50 —
*l.* Booklet pane of 4 #627f 4.50 —

Miniature Sheet

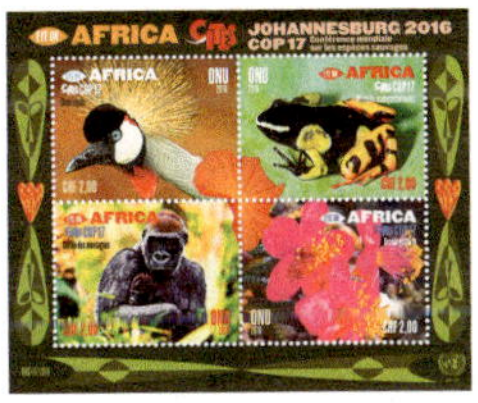

World Wildlife Conference, Johannesburg — G118

No. 628 — Part of map of Africa and: a, Grue royale (gray-crowned crane). b, Mantella madagascariensis. c, Gorille des montagnes (mountain gorilla). d, Avonia quinaria.

**2016, Sept. 24** **Litho.** *Perf. 13x13½*

**628** G118 Sheet of 4 18.00 18.00
*a.-d.* 2fr Any single 4.50 4.50

### Sustainable Development Goals Type of 2016

No. 629 — Inscription: a, 1 Pas de pauvreté. b, 2 Faim "zéro." c, 3 Bonne santé et bien-être. d, 4 Education de qualité. e, 5 Egalité entre les sexes. f, 6 Eau propre et assainissement. g, 7 Energie propre et d'un coût abordable. h, 8 Travail décent et croissance économique. i, 9 Industrie, innovation et infrastructure. j, 10 Inégalités réduites. k, 11 Villes et communautés durables. l, 12 Consommation et production responsables. m, 13 Mesures relatives à la lutte contre les changements climatiques. n, 14 Vie aquatique. o, 15 Vie terrestre. p, 16 Paix, justice et institutions efficaces. q, 17 Partneriats pour la réalisation des objectifs.

**2016, Oct. 24** **Litho.** *Perf. 13¼*

**629** Sheet of 17 + label 39.00 39.00
*a.-q.* A503 1fr Any single 2.25 2.25

Miniature Sheets

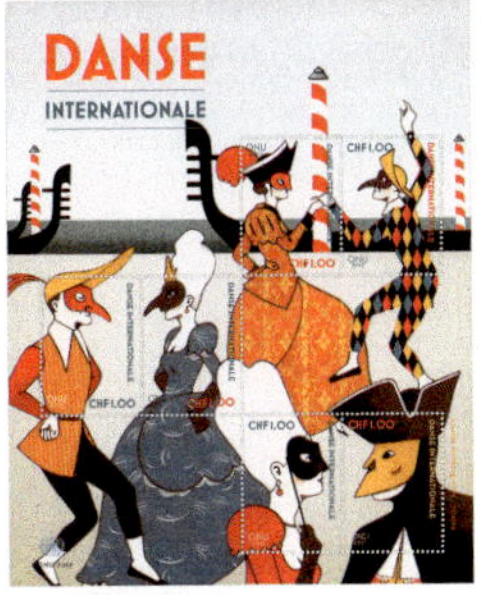

G119

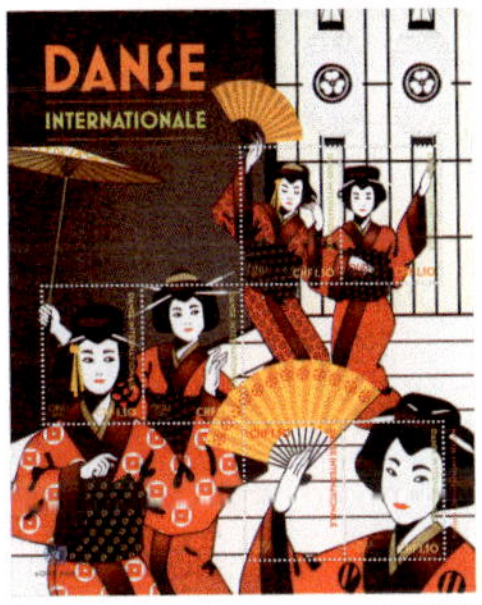

International Dance — G120

No. 630 — Illustration of Quadrille dancers by Jean François Martin: a, Female dancer wearing red mask facing right, striped pole. b, Male dancer wearing brown mask, harlequin costume, facing right. c, Masked male dancer with red mask facing right. d, Female dancer with brown mask facing left. e, Woman holding black mask facing right. f, Man wearing tan mask facing left.

No. 631 — Illustration of Japanese fan dancers by Martin: a, Dancer holding fan and other hand near her hair. b, Dancer with arm upraised at UR. c, Head of dancer, part of fan. d, Dancer holding umbrella. d, Dancer, part of fan at LR. e, Dancer's hand holding fan. f, Face of dancer, no hands visible.

**2017, Mar. 23** **Litho.** *Perf. 13¼x13*

**630** G119 Sheet of 6 13.00 13.00
*a.-f.* 1fr Any single 2.10 2.10
**631** G120 Sheet of 6 19.50 19.50
*a.-f.* 1.50fr Any single 3.25 3.25

### Endangered Species Type of 2017

Designs: No. 632, Rhampholeon spp. No. 633, Mobula spp. No. 634, Adansonia grandidieri. No. 635, Scaphiophryne marmorata.

**2017, May 11** **Litho.** *Perf. 12¾x12½*

**632** A509 1.50fr multicolored 3.25 3.25
**633** A509 1.50fr multicolored 3.25 3.25
**634** A509 1.50fr multicolored 3.25 3.25
**635** A509 1.50fr multicolored 3.25 3.25
*a.* Block of 4, #632-635 13.00 13.00
*Nos. 632-635 (4)* 13.00 13.00

### World Environment Day Type of 2017

Designs: 1fr, Snowy owl, Quebec, Canada. 2fr, Red maple and aspen trees, Canada.

**2017, June 5** **Litho.** *Perf. 13¼*

**636** A510 1fr multicolored 2.25 2.25
**637** A510 2fr multicolored 4.50 4.50

### World Heritage Sites Along the Silk Roads Type of 2017

Designs: Nos. 638, 640b, Historic Center of Bukhara, Uzbekistan. Nos. 639, 640e, Kunya Urgench, Turkmenistan. No. 640a, Longmen Grottoes, People's Republic of China. No. 640c, Tabriz Historic Bazaar Complex, Iran. No. 640d, Sulaiman-Too Sacred Mountain, Kyrgyzstan. No. 640f, Safranbolu, Turkey.

**2017, Aug. 3** **Litho.** *Perf. 14¼*

**638** A512 1fr multicolored 2.40 2.40
**639** A512 1.50fr multicolored 3.50 3.50

**Souvenir Booklet**

**640** Booklet, #640g-640l 26.50
*a.-c.* A512 30c any single .80 .80
*d.-f.* A512 50c any single 1.40 1.40
*g.* Booklet pane of 4 #640a 3.20 —
*h.* Booklet pane of 4 #640b 3.20 —
*i.* Booklet pane of 4 #640c 3.20 —
*j.* Booklet pane of 4 #640d 5.60 —
*k.* Booklet pane of 4 #640e 5.60 —
*l.* Booklet pane of 4 #640f 5.60 —

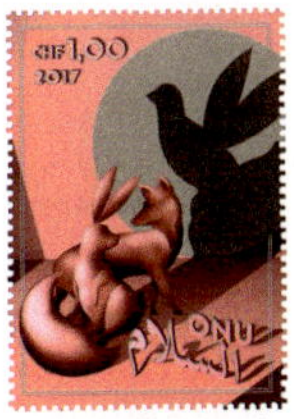

Hare, Fox and Dove — G121

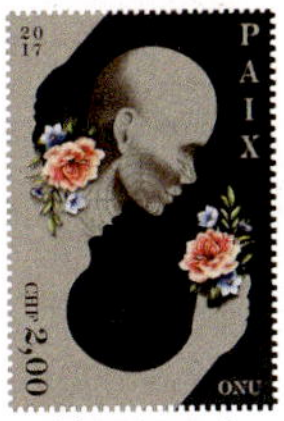

Heads and Flowers — G122

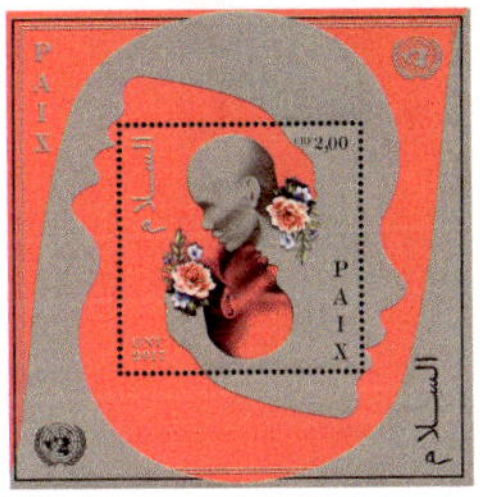

Heads and Flowers G123

Designs: 1fr, Snowy owl, Quebec, Canada. 2fr, Red maple and aspen trees, Canada.

**2017, Sept. 21** **Litho.** *Perf. 14¼x14*

**641** G121 1fr multicolored 2.40 2.40
**642** G122 2fr multicolored 4.75 4.75

**Souvenir Sheet**

*Perf. 14¼x13¾*

**643** G123 2fr multicolored 4.75 4.75

International Day of Peace.

### World Food Day Type of 2017

Designs: 1fr, Milk, yogurt and cheeses. 1.50fr, Fruits.

**2017, Oct. 16** **Litho.** *Perf. 13¼x14*

**644** A516 1fr multicolored 2.40 2.40
**645** A516 1.50fr multicolored 3.50 3.50

### Endangered Species Type of 2018

Designs: No. 646, Saiga tatarica. No. 647, Uncarina grandidieri. No. 648, Polymita picta. No. 649, Carcharhinus falciformis.

**2018, Mar. 2** **Litho.** *Perf. 12¾x12½*

**646** A519 1.50fr multicolored 3.50 3.50
**647** A519 1.50fr multicolored 3.50 3.50
**648** A519 1.50fr multicolored 3.50 3.50
**649** A519 1.50fr multicolored 3.50 3.50
*a.* Block of 4, #646-649 14.00 14.00
*Nos. 646-649 (4)* 14.00 14.00

### World Health Day Type of 2018

Designs: 1fr, Microbes and microscope. 2fr, Child, apple, pencil, triangle, numbers, glass of milk.

**2018, Apr. 6** **Litho.** *Perf. 13x13¼*

**650** A520 1fr multicolored 2.25 2.25
**651** A520 2fr multicolored 4.50 4.50

Miniature Sheet

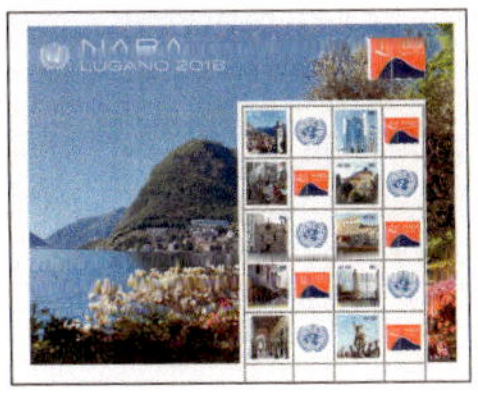

G124

No. 652: a, Cathedral of St. Lawrence belltower and buildings on hillside. b, Bank with curved glass facade. c, Table and chairs along footpath in city. d, Villa Saroli (yellow building). e, People near door of Santa Maria degli Angioli Church. f, Lugano Arts and Cultural Center (building with four large windows). g, Storefronts along hill on Via Cattedrale. h, Gates of Villa Ciani. i, Arches along Via della Posta. j, William Tell Monument.

**2018, May 17** **Litho.** *Perf. 14¾*

**652** G124 Sheet of 10 + 10 labels *35.00 35.00*
*a.-j.* 1.50fr Any single + label *3.50 3.50*

The full sheet sold for $19.06 or 16.95fr. The generic labels are shown. Labels could be personalized. The personalization of labels was available only at UN Headquarters, and not through mail order.

### UNISPACE + 50 Conferences Type of 2018

Designs: 1fr, View of Earth from space. 1.50fr, Launch of Tiangong 1.

2fr, Widefield Infrared Survey Explorer photograph of Comet 65P/Gunn.

**2018, June 20** **Litho.** *Perf. 14x14¼*

**653** A523 1fr multicolored 2.25 2.25
**654** A523 1.50fr multicolored 3.50 3.50

**Souvenir Sheet**

*Perf. 13¾*

**655** A523 2fr multicolored 4.50 4.50

No. 655 contains one 45x45mm stamp.

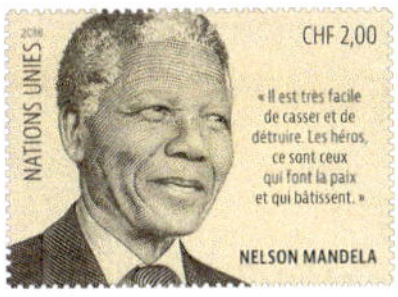

Nelson Mandela (1918-2013), President of South Africa G125

Printed by Lowe-Martin Group, Canada. Panes of 20. Designed by Martin Morck, Norway.

**2018, July 18** **Litho.** *Perf. 13¼*

**656** G125 2fr buff & black 4.50 4.50

### World Heritage Sites in the United Kingdom Type of 2016

Designs: Nos. 657, 659b, Stonehenge. Nos. 658, 659e, Edinburgh. No. 659a, Giant's Causeway. No. 659c, Conwy Castle. No. 659d, Palace of Westminster. No. 659f, Maritime Greenwich.

**2018, Aug. 15** **Litho.** *Perf. 14¼*

**657** A524 1fr multicolored 2.25 2.25
**658** A524 1.50fr multicolored 3.50 3.50

**Souvenir Booklet**

**659** Booklet, #659g-659l 23.50
*a.-c.* A524 30c any single .75 .75
*d.-f.* A524 50c any single 1.10 1.10
*g.* Booklet pane of 4 #659a 3.00 —
*h.* Booklet pane of 4 #659b 3.00 —
*i.* Booklet pane of 4 #659c 3.00 —
*j.* Booklet pane of 4 #659d 4.75 —
*k.* Booklet pane of 4 #659e 4.75 —
*l.* Booklet pane of 4 #659f 4.75 —

Miniature Sheet

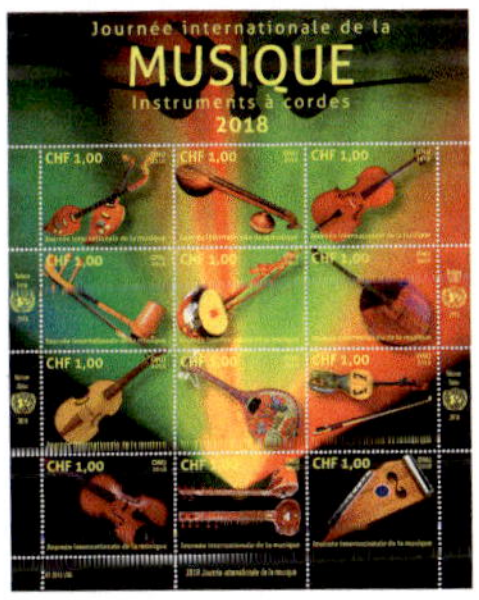

International Music Day — G126

No. 660: a, Electric guitars with carved necks. b, Veena. c, Cello. d, Erhu. e, Ektara. f, Domra. g, Viola da gamba. h, Bazouki. i, Stringed instrument with bow. j, Violin with chin rest. k, Sitars. l, Zither.

**2018, Oct. 1** **Litho.** *Perf. 14x13¼*

**660** G126 Sheet of 12 27.00 27.00
*a.-l.* 1fr Any single 2.25 2.25

Miniature Sheet

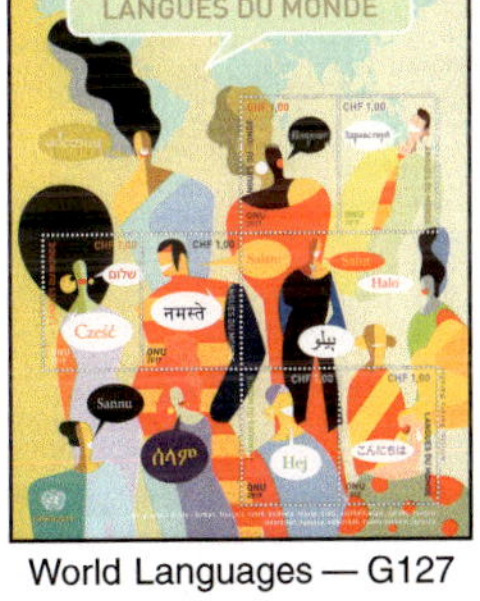

World Languages — G127

No. 661 — Word bubbles with word for "Hello" in: a, French (Bonjour). b, Russian ("Langues du Monde" in lilac). c, Hebrew and Polish (Czesc), d, Hindi ("Langues du Monde"

# OFFICES IN GENEVA, SWITZERLAND

in white). e, Danish or Swedish (Hej). f, Japanese ("Langues du Monde" in dark gray).

**2019, Feb. 21  Litho.  Perf. 13¼x13**
| 661 | G127 | Sheet of 6 | 13.50 | 13.50 |
| a.-f. | | 1fr Any single | 2.25 | 2.25 |

Gender Equality — G128

Printed by Lowe-Martin Group, Canada. Panes of 20. Designed by Chris Gash, U.S.

**2019, Mar.15  Litho.  Perf. 13¼x13**
| 662 | G128 | 1.50fr multicolored | 3.50 | 3.50 |

**Endangered Species Type of 2019**

Designs: No. 663, Hippocampus kuda. No. 664, Dugong dugon. No. 665, Stylophora pistillata. No. 666, Lamna nasus.

**2019, Apr. 26  Litho.  Perf. 12¾x12½**
| 663 | A534 | 1.50fr multicolored | 3.25 | 3.25 |
| 664 | A534 | 1.50fr multicolored | 3.25 | 3.25 |
| 665 | A534 | 1.50fr multicolored | 3.25 | 3.25 |
| 666 | A534 | 1.50fr multicolored | 3.25 | 3.25 |
| a. | | Block of 4, #663-666 | 13.50 | 13.50 |
| | | Nos. 663-666 (4) | 13.00 | 13.00 |

Souvenir Sheet

Bumblebee and Lobelia Cardinalis — G129

**Litho. With Foil Application**
**2019, May 20        Perf. 13**
| 667 | G129 | 2.60fr multicolored | 6.00 | 6.00 |

World Bee Day.

G130     G131

G132     G133

International Labor Organization, Cent. — G134

**2019, June 28  Litho.  Perf. 13½x14**
| 668 | G130 | 1fr multicolored | 2.25 | 2.25 |
| 669 | G131 | 1fr multicolored | 2.25 | 2.25 |
| 670 | G132 | 1fr multicolored | 2.25 | 2.25 |
| 671 | G133 | 1fr multicolored | 2.25 | 2.25 |
| 672 | G134 | 1fr multicolored | 2.25 | 2.25 |
| a. | | Horiz. strip of 5, #668-672 | 11.25 | 11.25 |
| | | Nos. 668-672 (5) | 11.25 | 11.25 |

**Climate Change Type of 2019**

Designs: 1fr, Fruit tree and burnt forest. 1.50fr, Field of flowers and traffic jam. 2fr, Clouds.

**2019, Sept. 23  Litho.  Perf. 14¼**
| 673 | A543 | 1fr multicolored | 2.25 | 2.25 |
| 674 | A543 | 1.50fr multicolored | 3.50 | 3.50 |

Souvenir Sheet
Perf.
| 675 | A543 | 2fr multicolored | 4.50 | 4.50 |

2019 United Nations Climate Change Conference, Madrid. No. 675 contains one 47mm diameter stamp.

Miniature Sheet

United Nations Postal Administration in Geneva, 50th Anniv. — G135

No. 676: a, Palais des Nations and Armillary Sphere, green panels. b, Palais des Nations and flags, gray panels. c, Assembly Hall, Palais des Nations, violet blue panels. d, Meeting room of Human Rights Council, light blue panels. e, Armillary Sphere in reflecting pond and Lake Geneva, violet black panels. f, Palais des Nations and flags, red panels. g, Palais des Nations and flags, orange yellow panels. h, Palais des Nations and United Nations flag, dark green panels. i, Peacock, blue green panels. j, Council Chamber, blue gray panels.

**2019, Oct. 18  Litho.  Perf. 14¾**
| 676 | G135 | Sheet of 10 + 10 labels | 38.00 | 38.00 |
| a.-j. | | 1.50fr Any single + label | 3.75 | 3.75 |

The full sheet sold for $18.80 or 16.95fr. The generic labels are shown. Labels could be personalized. The personalization of labels was available only at UN Headquarters, and not through mail order.

**World Heritage Sites in Cuba Type of 2019**

Designs: Nos. 677, 679b, Trinidad. Nos. 678, 679e, Cienfuegos. No. 679a, Morro Castle. No. 679c, Camagüey. No. 679d, Vinales Valley. No. 679f, San Pedro de la Rosa Castle.

**Litho. With Foil Application**
**2019, Oct. 24        Perf. 14¼**
| 677 | A545 | 1fr multicolored | 2.25 | 2.25 |
| 678 | A545 | 1.50fr multicolored | 3.50 | 3.50 |

**Souvenir Booklet**
| 679 | | Booklet, #679g-679l | 24.50 | |
| a.-c. | | A545 30c Any single | .75 | .75 |
| d.-f. | | A545 50c Any single | 1.25 | 1.25 |
| g. | | Booklet pane of 4 #679a | 3.00 | — |
| h. | | Booklet pane of 4 #679b | 3.00 | — |
| i. | | Booklet pane of 4 #679c | 3.00 | — |
| j. | | Booklet pane of 4 #679d | 5.00 | — |
| k. | | Booklet pane of 4 #679e | 5.00 | — |
| l. | | Booklet pane of 4 #679f | 5.00 | — |

Complete booklet sold for $12.20.

**Endangered Species Type of 2020**

Designs: No. 680, Leucogeranus leucogeranus. No. 681, Addax nasomaculatus. No. 682, Falco cherrug. No. 683, Monodon monoceros.

**Perf. 12¾x12½**
**2020, Feb. 17                Litho.**
| 680 | A546 | 1.50fr multicolored | 3.50 | 3.50 |
| 681 | A546 | 1.50fr multicolored | 3.50 | 3.50 |
| 682 | A546 | 1.50fr multicolored | 3.50 | 3.50 |
| 683 | A546 | 1.50fr multicolored | 3.50 | 3.50 |
| a. | | Block of 4, #680-683 | 14.00 | 14.00 |
| | | Nos. 680-683 (4) | 14.00 | 14.00 |

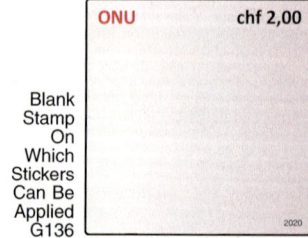

Blank Stamp On Which Stickers Can Be Applied G136

Designs: No. 1212, Hawksbill turtle. No. 1213, Queen conch. No. 1214, Mushroom coral. No. 1215, Humpback whale.

**2020, Mar. 19  Litho.  Die Cut**
**Self-Adhesive**
| 684 | G136 | 2fr multicolored with rounded corners | 4.75 | 4.75 |
| a. | | With perpendicular corners and black frame line | 4.75 | 4.75 |
| b. | | Booklet pane of 6 #1236a | 28.50 | |

No. 684 was issued as a souvenir sheet having two different sheet margins, each with different stickers. No. 684a was issued in a booklet containing six panes of one stamp, with each pane having different margins and stickers. Each booklet pane contained one sticker depicting Hello Kitty, a color wheel with Hello Kitty at the center, one of six different Sustainable Development Goal emblems, along with a variety of other stickers. The two souvenir sheets had the same sheet margin and stickers found on two of the panes of No. 684b. No. 684b was sold folded, without any means of separation between the individual panes.

Terre, Artwork by Mathilde Roussel G137

Mermaids Hate Plastic, Photograph by Benjamin Von Wong G138

**2020, Apr. 22  Litho.  Perf. 13¼**
| 685 | G137 | 1fr multicolored | 2.25 | 2.25 |
| 686 | G138 | 2fr multicolored | 4.50 | 4.50 |

Earth Day, 50th anniv. Because of the COVID-19 pandemic, Nos. 685-686 were not available for sale on day of issue stated on the first-day covers as they had not yet been printed and delivered.

Eradication of Smallpox, 40th Anniv. — G139

Printed by Cartor Security Printing, France. Panes of 20. Designed by Sergio Baradat, U.S., and World Health Organization.

**2020, May 8  Litho.  Perf. 13x13¼**
| 687 | G139 | 1.70fr multicolored | 4.00 | 4.00 |

**World Heritage Sites in Russia Type of 2020**

Designs: Nos. 688, 690b, Kazan Kremlin. Nos. 689, 690e, Saint Petersburg. No. 690a, Lake Baikal. No. 690c, Novodevichy Convent. No. 690d, Kremlin and Red Square, Moscow. No. 690f, Kizhi Pogost.

**Perf. 14½x14¼**
**2020, Sept. 11                Litho.**
| 688 | A556 | 1fr multicolored | 2.40 | 2.40 |
| 689 | A556 | 1.50fr multicolored | 3.75 | 3.75 |

**Souvenir Booklet**
| 690 | | Booklet, #690g-690l | 28.00 | |
| a.-c. | | A556 30c any single | .85 | .85 |
| d.-f. | | A556 50c any single | 1.40 | 1.40 |
| g. | | Booklet pane of 4 #690a | 3.50 | — |
| h. | | Booklet pane of 4 #690b | 3.50 | — |
| i. | | Booklet pane of 4 #690c | 3.50 | — |
| j. | | Booklet pane of 4 #690d | 5.75 | — |
| k. | | Booklet pane of 4 #690e | 5.75 | — |
| l. | | Booklet pane of 4 #690f | 5.75 | — |

Complete booklet sold for $13.21 or 11fr.

Souvenir Sheet

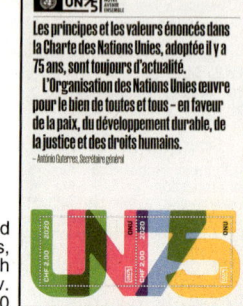

United Nations, 75th Anniv. G140

No. 691: a, Green "U," pink "N." b, Blue "7," yellow "5."

**2020, Oct. 24  Litho.  Perf. 13¼**
| 691 | G140 | Sheet of 2 | 10.00 | 10.00 |
| a.-b. | | 2fr Either single | 5.00 | 5.00 |

Souvenir Sheet

Palais des Nations and Emblem G141

**Litho. With Foil Application**
**2020, Nov. 24    Die Cut Perf. 11½**
**Self-Adhesive**
| 692 | G141 | 8fr multicolored | 19.50 | 19.50 |

Crypto stamp. Unused value is for sheets with unscratched panels at right.

International Day for the Elimination of Racial Discrimination — G142

**2021, Mar. 19  Litho.  Perf. 13¼x13**
| 693 | G142 | 2fr multicolored | 5.00 | 5.00 |

**Endangered Species Type of 2021**

Designs: No. 694, Leontopithecus chrysomelas. No. 695, Macrotis lagotis. No. 696, Lemur catta. No. 697, Caladenia huegellii.

**2021, Apr. 7  Litho.  Perf. 12¾x12½**
| 694 | A565 | 1.50fr multicolored | 3.75 | 3.75 |
| 695 | A565 | 1.50fr multicolored | 3.75 | 3.75 |
| 696 | A565 | 1.50fr multicolored | 3.75 | 3.75 |
| 697 | A565 | 1.50fr multicolored | 3.75 | 3.75 |
| a. | | Block of 4, #694-697 | 15.00 | 15.00 |
| | | Nos. 694-697 (4) | 15.00 | 15.00 |

Two Judokas — G143

Judoka in Blue Judogi — G144

Judoka in White Judogi — G145

Female Diver — G146

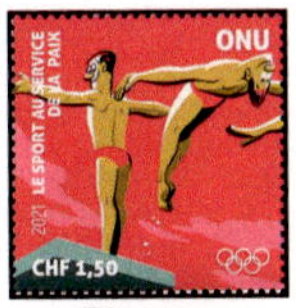

Diver on Platform G147

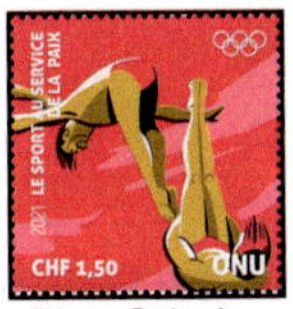

Diver Spinning G148

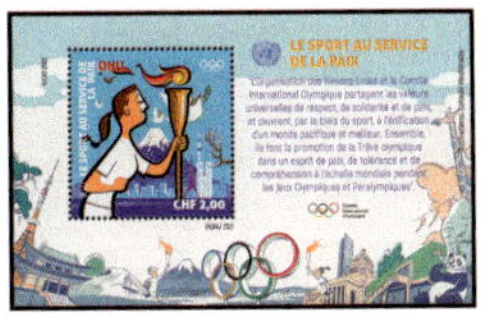

Athlete Carrying Olympic Torch G149

**2021, July 23 Litho. *Perf. 13½***

| | | | | |
|---|---|---|---|---|
| **698** | G143 | 1fr multicolored | 2.50 | 2.50 |
| **699** | G144 | 1fr multicolored | 2.50 | 2.50 |
| **700** | G145 | 1fr multicolored | 2.50 | 2.50 |
| *a.* | | Horiz. strip of 3, #698-700 | 7.50 | 7.50 |
| **701** | G146 | 1.50fr multicolored | 3.75 | 3.75 |
| **702** | G147 | 1.50fr multicolored | 3.75 | 3.75 |
| **703** | G148 | 1.50fr multicolored | 3.75 | 3.75 |
| *a.* | | Horiz. strip of 3, #701-703 | 11.25 | 11.25 |
| | | *Nos. 698-703 (6)* | 18.75 | 18.75 |

**Souvenir Sheet**

| | | | | |
|---|---|---|---|---|
| **704** | G149 | 2fr multicolored | 5.00 | 5.00 |

Sports for Peace, 2020 Summer Olympics, Tokyo. The 2020 Summer Olympics were postponed until 2021 because of the COVID-19 pandemic.

### Waterways, Railways and Bridges World Heritage Sites Type of 2020

Designs: Nos. 705, 707b, Rhaetian Railway, Switzerland and Italy. Nos. 706, 707e, Darjeeling Himalayan Railway, India. No. 707a, Rideau Canal, Canada. No. 707c, Forth Bridge, Scotland. No. 707d, Grand Canal, People's Republic of China. No. 707f, Old Bridge, Mostar, Bosnia and Herzegovina.

**2021, Aug. 25 Litho. *Perf. 14¼***

| | | | | |
|---|---|---|---|---|
| **705** | A575 | 1fr multicolored | 2.50 | 2.50 |
| **706** | A575 | 1.50fr multicolored | 3.75 | 3.75 |
| | | First day cover | | 6.00 |

**Souvenir Booklet**

| | | | |
|---|---|---|---|
| **707** | Booklet, #707g-707l | 28.00 | |
| *a.-c.* | A575 30c any single | .85 | .85 |
| *d.-f.* | A575 50c any single | 1.40 | 1.40 |
| *g.* | Booklet pane of 4 #707a | 3.50 | — |
| *h.* | Booklet pane of 4 #707b | 3.50 | — |
| *i.* | Booklet pane of 4 #707c | 3.50 | — |
| *j.* | Booklet pane of 4 #707d | 5.75 | — |
| *k.* | Booklet pane of 4 #707e | 5.75 | — |
| *l.* | Booklet pane of 4 #707f | 5.75 | — |

Complete booklet sold for $13.21 or 10.95fr.

Miniature Sheet

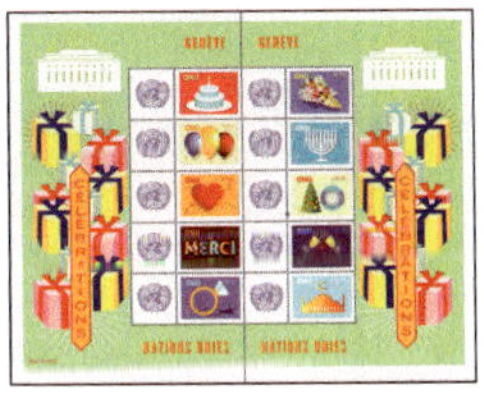

Celebrations — G150

No. 708: a, Birthday cake. b, Flower bouquet. c, Three balloons. d, Menorah. e, Heart and arrow. f, Christmas tree and ornament. g, "Merci." h, Champagne flutes. i, Diamond ring. j, Mosque.

**2021, Nov. 4 Litho. *Perf. 14¼***

| | | | | |
|---|---|---|---|---|
| **708** | G150 | Sheet of 10 + 10 labels | *41.00* | *41.00* |
| *a.-j.* | | 1.50fr Any single + label | *4.00* | *4.00* |

The full sheet sold for $20.28 or 16.95fr. The generic labels are shown. Labels could be personalized. The personalization of labels was available only at UN Headquarters, and not through mail order.

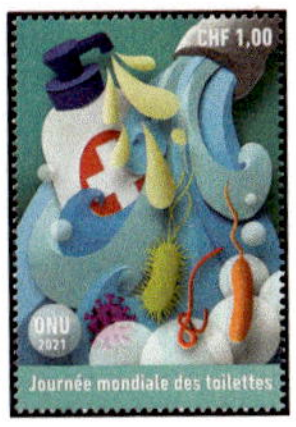

World Toilet Day — G151

**2021, Nov. 19 Litho. *Perf. 14¼***

| | | | | |
|---|---|---|---|---|
| **709** | G151 | 1fr multicolored | 2.40 | 2.40 |

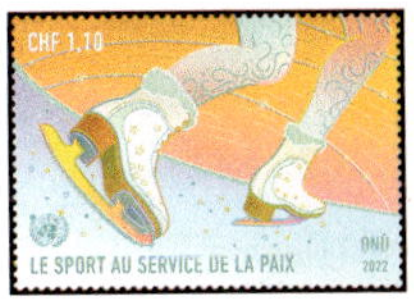

Feet of Figure Skater G152

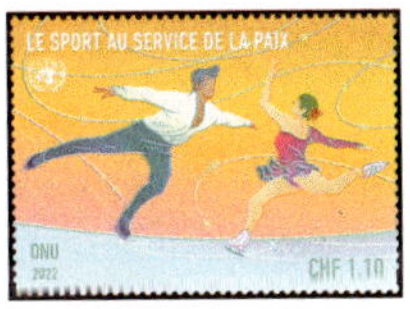

Figure Skaters G153

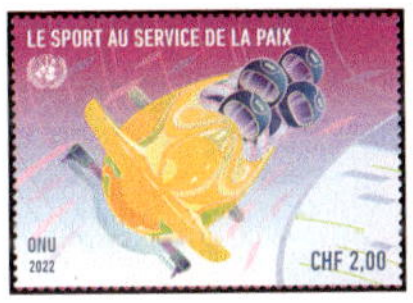

Four man Bobsled G154

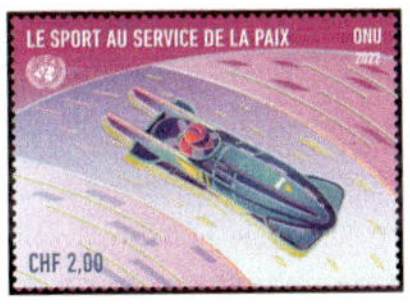

Monobob G155

**2022, Jan. 14 Litho. *Perf. 14¼***

| | | | | |
|---|---|---|---|---|
| **710** | G152 | 1.10fr multicolored | 2.25 | 2.25 |
| **711** | G153 | 1.10fr multicolored | 2.25 | 2.25 |
| *a.* | | Horiz. pair, #710-711 | 5.50 | 5.50 |
| **712** | G154 | 2fr multicolored | 5.00 | 5.00 |
| **713** | G155 | 2fr multicolored | 5.00 | 5.00 |
| *a.* | | Horiz. pair, #712-713 | 10.00 | 10.00 |
| | | *Nos. 710-713 (4)* | 14.50 | 14.50 |

Sports for Peace, 2022 Winter Olympics, Beijing.

### Endangered Species Type of 2022

Designs: No. 714, Acropora cervicornis. No. 715, Gonatodes daudini. No. 716, Mobula munkiana. No. 717, Oophaga arborea.

***Perf. 12¾x12½***

**2022, Mar. 18 Litho.**

| | | | | |
|---|---|---|---|---|
| **714** | A592 | 1.50fr multicolored | 3.75 | 0.75 |
| **715** | A592 | 1.50fr multicolored | 3.75 | 3.75 |
| **716** | A592 | 1.50fr multicolored | 3.75 | 3.75 |
| **717** | A592 | 1.50fr multicolored | 3.75 | 3.75 |
| *a.* | | Block of 4, #714-717 | 15.00 | 15.00 |
| | | *Nos. 714-717 (4)* | 15.00 | 15.00 |

### Exploration of Mars Type of 2022

Designs: 58c, Proctor Crater. No. 1302, Mars Perseverence Rover. No. 1303, Mars Ingonuity Helicopter.

**2022, Apr. 24 Litho. *Perf. 13¼x13***

| | | | | |
|---|---|---|---|---|
| **718** | A593 | 1.10fr multicolored | 2.75 | 2.75 |
| **719** | A593 | 1.50fr multicolored | 3.75 | 3.75 |

**Souvenir Sheet**

***Perf. 13½***

| | | | | |
|---|---|---|---|---|
| **720** | A593 | 2fr multicolored | 5.00 | 5.00 |

No. 720 contains one 44x44mm stamp.

Miniature Sheet

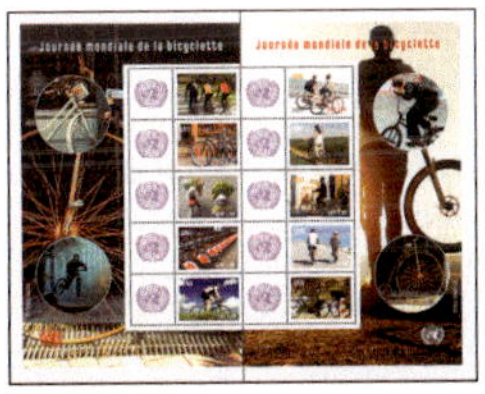

World Bicycle Day G156

No. 721: a, Three cyclists on road. b, Two cyclists near water, facing right. c, Two bicycles in front of store. d, Cyclist on dirt path. e, Two cyclists transporting flowers. f, Cyclist wearing hat, facing left. g, Row of identical bicycles. h, Backs of two cyclists near water. i, Cyclist and grass. j, Bicycles leaning on bridge railing.

**2022, June 3 Litho. *Perf. 14¼***

| | | | | |
|---|---|---|---|---|
| **721** | G156 | Sheet of 10 + 10 labels | *45.00* | *45.00* |
| *a.-j.* | | 1.50fr Any single + label | *4.50* | *4.50* |

The full sheet sold for $22.12 or €18.40. The generic labels are shown. Labels could be personalized.

### European Spa Town World Heritage Sites Type of 2022

Designs: Nos. 722, 724b, Spa, Belgium. Nos. 723, 724e, Vichy, France. No. 724a, Karlovy Vary, Czech Republic. No. 724c, Baden-Baden, Germany. No. 724d, Montecatini Terme, Italy. No. 724f, Baden bei Wien, Austria.

**2022, Sept. 9 Litho. *Perf. 14½x14¼***

| | | | | |
|---|---|---|---|---|
| **722** | A594 | 1.10fr multicolored | 2.60 | 2.60 |
| **723** | A594 | 1.50fr multicolored | 3.50 | 3.50 |

**Souvenir Booklet**

| | | | |
|---|---|---|---|
| **724** | Booklet, #690g-690l | 25.50 | |
| *a.-c.* | A594 30c any single | .80 | .80 |
| *d.-f.* | A594 50c any single | 1.30 | 1.30 |
| *g.* | Booklet pane of 4 #724a | 3.25 | — |
| *h.* | Booklet pane of 4 #724b | 3.25 | — |
| *i.* | Booklet pane of 4 #724c | 3.25 | — |
| *j.* | Booklet pane of 4 #724d | 5.25 | — |
| *k.* | Booklet pane of 4 #724e | 5.25 | — |
| *l.* | Booklet pane of 4 #724f | 5.25 | — |

Complete booklet sold for $12.63 or 10.10fr.

Souvenir Sheet

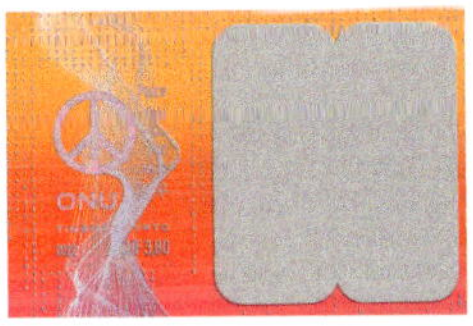

Peace Sign G157

**Litho. With Foil Application**

**2022, Nov. 18 *Die Cut Perf. 11½***

**Self-Adhesive**

| | | | | |
|---|---|---|---|---|
| **725** | G157 | 3.80fr multicolored | 8.75 | 8.75 |

Crypto stamp. Unused value is for sheets with unscratched panels at right.

### Endangered Species Type of 2023

Designs: No. 726, Equus przewalskii. No. 727, Chelonia mydas. No. 728, Gymnogyps californianus. No. 729, Dalbergia saxatilis.

**2023, Mar. 3 Litho. *Perf. 12¾x12½***

| | | | | |
|---|---|---|---|---|
| **726** | A599 | 1.80fr multicolored | 4.25 | 4.25 |
| **727** | A599 | 1.80fr multicolored | 4.25 | 4.25 |
| **728** | A599 | 1.80fr multicolored | 4.25 | 4.25 |
| **729** | A599 | 1.80fr multicolored | 4.25 | 4.25 |
| *a.* | | Block of 4, #726-729 | 17.00 | 17.00 |
| | | *Nos. 726-729 (4)* | 17.00 | 17.00 |

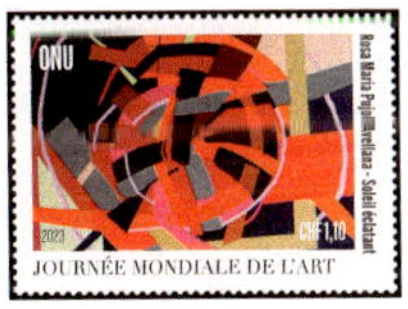

Soleil Eclatant (Bright Sun), Painting by Rosa Maria Pujol-Avellana — G158

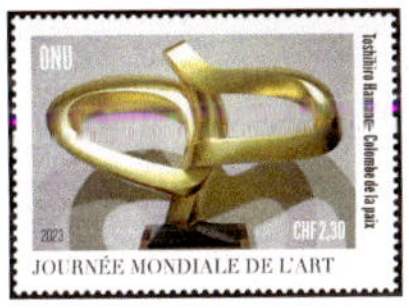

Colombe de la Paix (Dove of Peace), Sculpture by Toshihiro Hamano G159

Printed by Cartor Security Printing, France. Panes of 15. Designed by Sergio Baradat, U.S.

**2023, Apr. 15 Litho. *Perf. 14½x14¼***

| | | | | |
|---|---|---|---|---|
| **730** | G158 | 1.10fr multicolored | 2.75 | 2.75 |
| **731** | G159 | 2.30fr multicolored | 5.50 | 5.50 |

World Art Day.

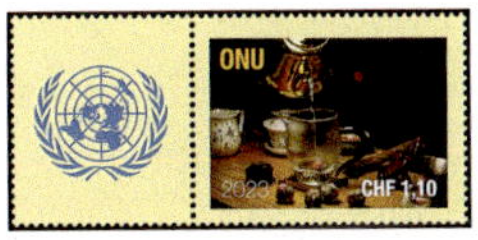

G160

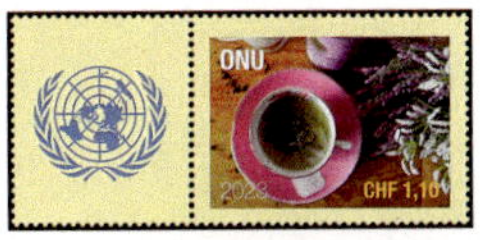

G161

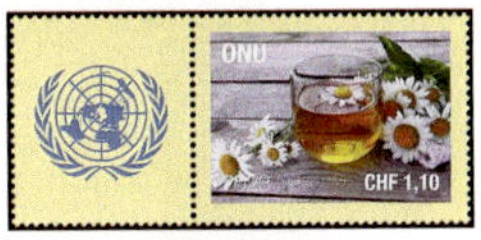

G162

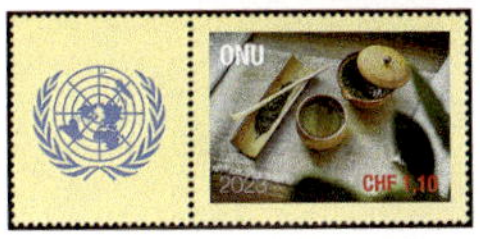

G163

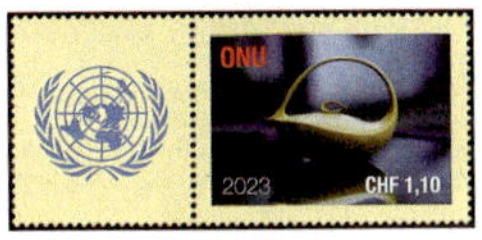

G164

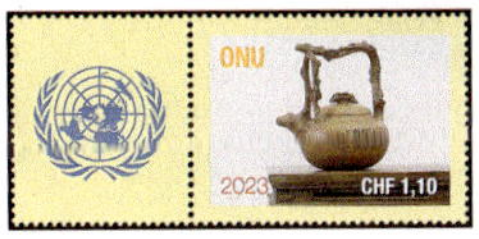

G165

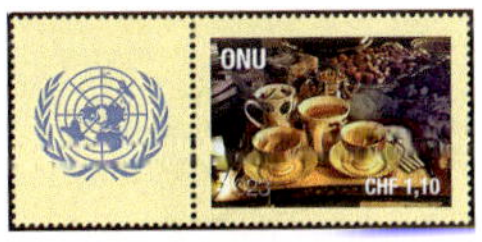

G166

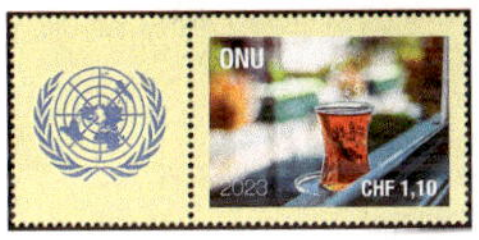

G167

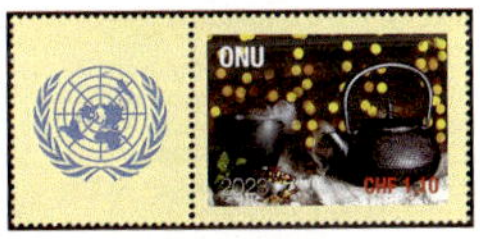

G168

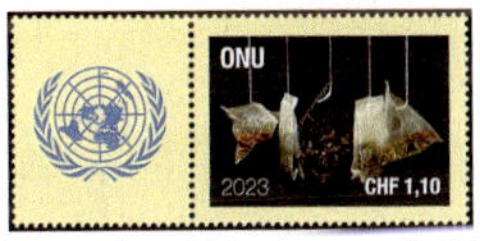

International Tea Day — G169

**2023, May 21 Litho. *Perf. 14¼***

| | | | | |
|---|---|---|---|---|
| **732** | | Sheet of 10 + 10 labels | *35.00* | *35.00* |
| *a.* | G160 | 1.10fr multicolored + label | *3.50* | *3.50* |
| *b.* | G161 | 1.10fr multicolored + label | *3.50* | *3.50* |
| *c.* | G162 | 1.10fr multicolored + label | *3.50* | *3.50* |
| *d.* | G163 | 1.10fr multicolored + label | *3.50* | *3.50* |
| *e.* | G164 | 1.10fr multicolored + label | *3.50* | *3.50* |
| *f.* | G165 | 1.10fr multicolored + label | *3.50* | *3.50* |
| *g.* | G166 | 1.10fr multicolored + label | *3.50* | *3.50* |
| *h.* | G167 | 1.10fr multicolored + label | *3.50* | *3.50* |
| *i.* | G168 | 1.10fr multicolored + label | *3.50* | *3.50* |
| *j.* | G169 | 1.10fr multicolored + label | *3.50* | *3.50* |

The full sheet sold for $16.69 or 14fr. The generic labels are shown. Labels could be personalized.

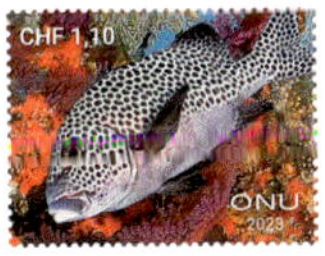

G170

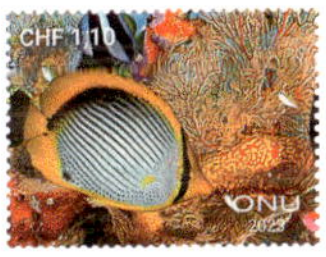

G171

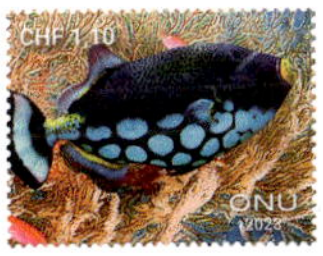

G172

# OFFICES IN GENEVA, SWITZERLAND — OFFICES IN VIENNA, AUSTRIA

 G173

 G174

 G175

 G176

 G177

Marine Life of Tubbataha Reef, Philippines — G178

**2023, June 8    Litho.    Perf. 14x13¼**
733    Sheet of 3    24.00   24.00
  a.  G170 1.10fr multicolored    2.60    2.60
  b.  G171 1.10fr multicolored    2.60    2.60
  c.  G172 1.10fr multicolored    2.60    2.60
  d.  G173 1.10fr multicolored    2.60    2.60
  e.  G174 1.10fr multicolored    2.60    2.60
  f.  G175 1.10fr multicolored    2.60    2.60
  g.  G176 1.10fr multicolored    2.60    2.60
  h.  G177 1.10fr multicolored    2.60    2.60
  i.  G178 1.10fr multicolored    2.60    2.60
World Oceans Day.

**Souvenir Sheet**

Frankie the Dinosaur — G179

**2023, June 20    Litho.    Perf. 13¼x14**
734    G179 2.30fr multicolored    5.50   5.50
"Don't Choose Extinction" campaign.

G180

Chinese Calligraphy — G181

**2023, Aug. 10    Litho.    Perf. 14x13¼**
735    G180 1.10fr multicolored    2.75   2.75

**Souvenir Sheet**
**Perf. 13¼x14**
736    G181 2.30fr multicolored    5.50   5.50
UNESCO Intangible Cultural Heritage.

**World Heritage Sites in Turkey Type of 2023**
Designs: Nos. 737, 739b, Göreme National Park and the Rock Sites of Cappadocia. Nos. 738, 739e, Great Mosque and Hospital of Divriği. No. 739a, Nemrut Dağ. No. 739c, Ephesus. No. 739d, Selimiye Mosque. No. 739f, Historic Areas of Istanbul.

**2023, Sept. 8    Litho.    Perf. 14x14¼**
737    A617 1.10fr multicolored    2.75   2.75
738    A617 1.80fr multicolored    4.50   4.50

**Souvenir Booklet**
739    Booklet, #1280g-1280l  29.50
  a.-c.  A617 35c any single    .95    .95
  d.-f.  A617 55c any single    1.50   1.50
  g.  Booklet pane of 4 #739a    3.80    —
  h.  Booklet pane of 4 #739b    3.80    —
  i.  Booklet pane of 4 #739c    3.80    —
  j.  Booklet pane of 4 #739d    6.00    —
  k.  Booklet pane of 4 #739e    6.00    —
  l.  Booklet pane of 4 #739f    6.00    —
Complete booklet sold for $14.75 or 12fr.

World Mental Health Day — G182

**2023, Oct. 10    Litho.    Perf. 13¼x14**
740    G182 1.80fr multicolored    4.50   4.50

Marie Curie (1867-1934), Physicist and Chemist — G183

**2023, Nov. 7    Litho.    Perf. 14x14¼**
741    G183 2.30fr black    5.75   5.75

## SEMI-POSTAL STAMPS

**AIDS Awareness Semi-postal Type**
**Souvenir Sheet**
**2002, Oct. 24    Litho.    Perf. 14½**
B1    GSP1 90c + 30c multicolored    4.00   4.00

GSP2

Photograph of John Lennon (1940-80), by Iain Macmillan — GSP3

**2021, Sept. 21    Litho.    Perf. 14¼**
B2    GSP2 1.50fr multicolored    5.00   5.00

**Souvenir Sheet**
**Litho. With Foil Application**
B3    GSP3 2.60fr multicolored    8.75   8.75
International Day of Peace. Surtax for United Nations peacekeeping efforts.

World Humanitarian Day — GSP4

**2022, Aug. 19    Litho.    Perf. 13¼x13**
B4    GSP4 2fr multicolored    6.00   6.00
Surtax for United Nations Central Emergency Response Fund.

## OFFICES IN VIENNA, AUSTRIA

For use only on mail posted at the Vienna International Center for the UN and the International Atomic Energy Agency.

100 Groschen = 1 Schilling
100 Cents = 1 Euro (2002)

Catalogue values for all unused stamps in this country are for Never Hinged items.

**Type of Geneva, 1978, UN Types of 1961-72 and**

Donaupark, Vienna — V1

Aerial View — V2

**1979, Aug. 24    Photo.    Perf. 11½**
**Granite Paper**
1    G8   50g multicolored    .25    .30
2    A52  1s multicolored    .25    .30
3    V1   4s multicolored    .25    .30
4    AP13 5s multicolored    .30    .35
5    V2   6s multicolored    .35    .35
6    A45  10s multicolored    .60    .70
      Nos. 1-6 (6)    2.00   2.30
No. 6 has no frame.

**New Economic Order Type of UN**
**1980, Jan. 11    Litho.    Perf. 15x14½**
7    A178 4s multicolored    .60    .70

**Dove Type of UN**
**1980, Jan. 11    Litho.    Perf. 14x13½**
8    A147 2.50s multicolored    .25    .30

Women's Year Emblem on World Map — V3

**United Nations Decade for Women**
**1980, Mar. 7    Litho.    Perf. 14½x15**
9    V3   4s light green & dark green    .40    .45
10   V3   6s bister brown    .75    .85

**Peace-keeping Operations Type of UN**
**1980, May 16    Litho.    Perf. 14x13**
11   A182 6s multicolored    .40    .45

**35th Anniversary Types of Geneva and UN**
**1980, June 26    Litho.    Perf. 13x13½**
12   G16  4s carmine rose & black    .35    .40
13   A184 6s multicolored    .60    .65

**Souvenir Sheet**
**Imperf**
14      Sheet of 2    .90   1.00
  a.   G16  4s carmine rose & black    .25    .30
  b.   A184 6s multicolored    .65    .30

**ECOSOC Types of UN and Geneva**
**1980, Nov. 21    Litho.    Perf. 13½x13**
15   A187 4s multicolored    .30    .35
16   G17  6s multicolored    .60    .30

**Palestinian Rights Type of UN**
**1981, Jan. 30    Photo.    Perf. 12x11½**
17   A188 4s multicolored    .45    .50

**Disabled Type of UN and**

Interlocking Stitches — V4

**1981, Mar. 6    Photo.    Perf. 14**
18   A189 4s multicolored    .40    .45
19   V4   6s black & orange    .60    .70

**Art Type of UN**
**1981, Apr. 15    Photo.    Perf. 11½**
**Granite Paper**
20   A191 6s multicolored    .75    .85

**Energy Type of UN**
**1981, May 29    Litho.    Perf. 13**
21   A193 7.50s multicolored    .70    .80

**Volunteers Program Types**
**1981, Nov. 13    Litho.**
22   A195 5s multicolored    .40    .45
23   G18  7s multicolored    .90   1.00

"For a Better World" — V5

**1982, Jan. 22    Perf. 11½x12**
24   V5   3s multicolored    .35    .40

**Human Environment Types of UN and Geneva**
**1982, Mar. 19    Litho.    Perf. 13½x13**
25   A200 5s multicolored    .40    .45
26   G21  7s multicolored    .80    .90

**Outer Space Type of Geneva**
**1982, June 11    Litho.    Perf. 13x13½**
27   G22  5s multicolored    .60    .70

**Conservation & Protection of Nature Type**
**1982, Nov. 16    Photo.    Perf. 14**
28   A202 5s Fish    .50    .60
29   A202 7s Animal    .70    .80

**World Communications Year Type**
**1983, Jan. 28    Litho.    Perf. 13**
30   A203 4s multicolored    .40    .45

### Safety at Sea Types of Geneva and UN

**1983, Mar. 18 Litho. *Perf. 14½***

**31** G23 4s multicolored .40 .45
**32** A206 6s multicolored .65 .75

### World Food Program Type

**1983, Apr. 22 Engr. *Perf. 13½***

**33** A207 5s green .45 .50
**34** A207 7s brown .70 .80

### UN Conference on Trade and Development Types of Geneva and UN

**1983, June 6 Litho. *Perf. 14***

**35** G24 4s multicolored .30 .35
**36** A209 8.50s multicolored .75 .85

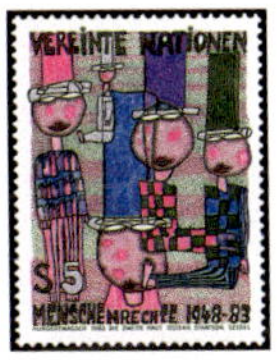

V6

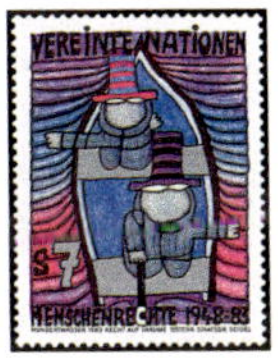

35th Anniv. of the Universal Declaration of Human Rights — V7

**Photo. & Engr.**

**1983, Dec. 9 *Perf. 13½***

**37** V6 5s multicolored .40 .45
**38** V7 7s multicolored .65 .75

### International Conference on Population Type

**1984, Feb. 3 Litho. *Perf. 14***

**39** A212 7s multicolored .65 .75

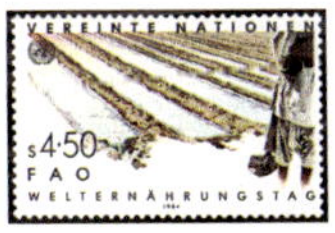

Field Irrigation — V8

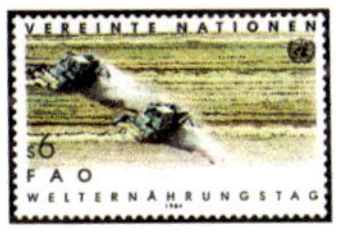

Harvesting Machine — V9

### World Food Day, Oct. 16

**1984, Mar. 15 Litho. *Perf. 14½***

**40** V8 4.50s multicolored .40 .45
**41** V9 6s multicolored .65 .75

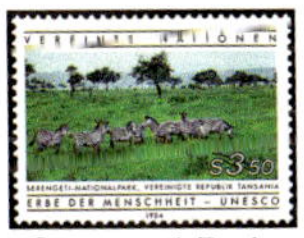

Serengeti Park, Tanzania — V10

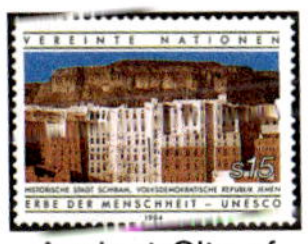

Ancient City of Shiban, People's Democratic Rep. of Yemen — V11

### World Heritage

**1984, Mar. 15 Litho. *Perf. 14***

**42** V10 3.50s multicolored .25 .30
**43** V11 15s multicolored 1.25 1.40

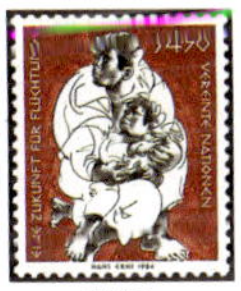

V12

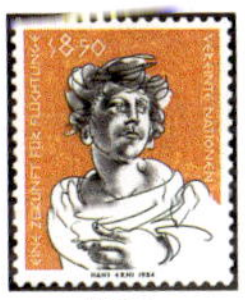

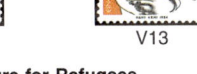

V13

### Future for Refugees

**1984, May 29 Photo. *Perf. 11½***

**44** V12 4.50s multicolored .45 .50
**45** V13 8.50s multicolored 1.25 1.40

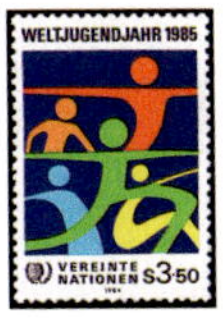

International Youth Year — V14

**1984, Nov. 15 Litho. *Perf. 13½***

**46** V14 3.50s multicolored .45 .50
**47** V14 6.50s multicolored .70 .80

### ILO Type of Geneva

**1985, Feb. 1 Engr. *Perf. 13½***

**48** G34 7.50s U Thant Pavilion .75 .85

### UN University Type

**1985, Mar. 15 Photo. *Perf. 11½***

**49** A221 8.50s Rural scene, lab researcher .75 .85

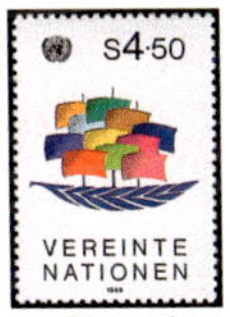

Ship of Peace V15

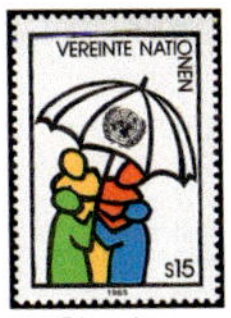

Sharing Umbrella V16

**1985, May 10 Litho. *Perf. 14***

**50** V15 4.50s multicolored .30 .35
**51** V16 15s multicolored 2.00 2.25

### 40th Anniversary Type

***Perf. 12 x 11½***

**1985, June 26 Photo.**

**52** A224 6.50s multicolored .90 1.00
**53** A225 8.50s multicolored 1.40 1.60

**Souvenir Sheet**

***Imperf***

**54** Sheet of 2 2.50 2.75
*a.* A224 6.50s multi 1.00 1.10
*b.* A225 8.50s multi 1.40 1.50

### UNICEF Child Survival Campaign Type

4s, Spoonfeeding children. 6s, Mother hugging infant.

**Photo. & Engr.**

**1985, Nov. 22 *Perf. 13½***

**55** A226 4s multicolored .75 .85
**56** A226 6s multicolored 1.40 1.60

### Africa in Crisis Type

**1986, Jan. 31 Photo. *Perf. 11½x12***

**57** A227 8s multicolored .80 .90

### UN Development Program Type

Agriculture: No. 58, Developing crop strains. No. 59, Animal husbandry. No. 60, Technical instruction. No. 61, Nutrition education.

**1986, Mar. 14 Photo. *Perf. 13½***

**58** A228 4.50s multicolored 1.40 1.60
**59** A228 4.50s multicolored 1.40 1.60
**60** A228 4.50s multicolored 1.40 1.60
**61** A228 4.50s multicolored 1.40 1.60
*a.* Block of 4, #58-61 6.25 7.00

No. 61a has a continuous design.

### Stamp Collecting Type

Designs: 3.50s, UN stamps. 6.50s, Engraver.

**1986, May 22 Engr. *Perf. 12½***

**62** A229 3.50s dk ultra & dk brown .40 .45
**63** A229 6.50s int blue & brt rose .90 1.00

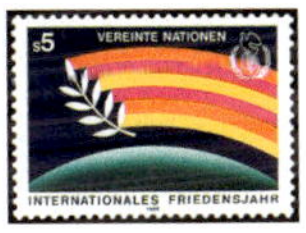

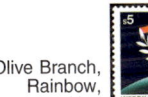

Olive Branch, Rainbow, Earth — V17

### Photogravure & Embossed

**1986, June 20 *Perf. 13½***

**64** V17 5s shown .75 .85
**65** V17 6s Doves, UN emblem 1.00 1.10

### WFUNA Anniversary Type

**Souvenir Sheet**

Designs: 4s, White stallion by Elisabeth von Janota-Bzowski, Germany. 5s, Surrealistic landscape by Ernst Fuchs, Austria. 6s, Geometric abstract by Victor Vasarely (b. 1908), France. 7s, Mythological abstract by Wolfgang Hutter (b. 1928), Austria.

**1986, Nov. 14 Litho. *Perf. 13x13½***

**66** Sheet of 4 4.00 4.25
*a.* A232 4s multicolored .75 .80
*b.* A232 5s multicolored .85 .90
*c.* A232 6s multicolored 1.00 1.10
*d.* A232 7s multicolored 1.25 1.40

No. 66 has inscribed margin picturing UN and WFUNA emblems.

### Trygve Lie Type

**Photogravure & Engraved**

**1987, Jan. 30 *Perf. 13½***

**67** A233 8s multicolored .70 .80

### Shelter for the Homeless Type

Designs: 4s, Family and homes. 9.50s, Family entering home.

***Perf. 13½x12½***

**1987, Mar. 13 Litho.**

**68** A234 4s multicolored .50 .55
**69** A234 9.50s multicolored 1.10 1.25

### Fight Drug Abuse Type

Designs: 5s, Soccer players. 8s, Family.

**1987, June 12 Litho. *Perf. 14½x15***

**70** A235 5s multicolored .40 .45
**71** A235 8s multicolored .90 1.00

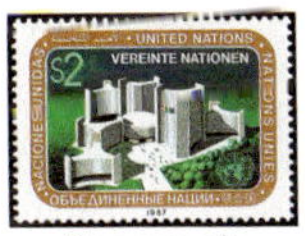

Donaupark, Vienna — V18

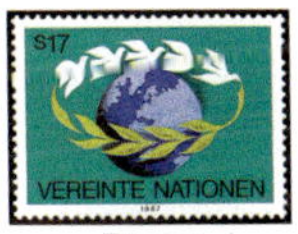

Peace Embracing the Earth — V19

**1987, June 12 Litho. *Perf. 14½x15***

**72** V18 2s multicolored .30 .35
**73** V19 17s multicolored 1.60 1.75

### UN Day Type

Designs: Multinational people in various occupations.

**1987, Oct. 23 Litho. *Perf. 14½x15***

**74** A236 5s multicolored .75 .85
**75** A236 6s multicolored .90 1.00

### Immunize Every Child Type

Designs: 4s, Poliomyelitis. 9.50s, Diphtheria.

**1987, Nov. 20 Litho. *Perf. 15x14½***

**76** A237 4s multicolored .75 .85
**77** A237 9.50s multicolored 2.00 2.25

### IFAD Type

Designs: 4s, Grains. 6s, Vegetables.

**1988, Jan. 29 Litho. *Perf. 13½***

**78** A238 4s multicolored .40 .45
**79** A238 6s multicolored .90 1.00

### Survival of the Forests Type

Deciduous forest in fall: 4s, Treetops, hills and dales. 5s, Tree trunks. Printed se-tenant in a continuous design.

**1988, Mar. 18 Litho. *Perf. 14x15***

**80** A240 4s multicolored 2.25 2.40
**81** A240 5s multicolored 3.00 3.25
*a.* Pair, #80-81 5.25 5.75

### Intl. Volunteer Day Type

Designs: 6s, Medical care, vert. 7.50s, Construction.

***Perf. 13x14, 14x13***

**1988, May 6 Litho.**

**82** A241 6s multicolored .75 .85
**83** A241 7.50s multicolored 1.00 1.10

### Health in Sports Type

Paintings by LeRoy Neiman, American Sports artist: 6s, Skiing, vert. 8s, Tennis.

***Perf. 13½x13, 13x13½***

**1988, June 17 Litho.**

**84** A242 6s multicolored .90 1.00
**85** A242 8s multicolored 1.40 1.60

### Universal Declaration of Human Rights 40th Anniv. Type

**Photo. & Engr.**

**1988, Dec. 9 *Perf. 11½***

**86** A243 5s multicolored .50 .55

**Souvenir Sheet**

**87** A243 11s multicolored 1.25 1.40

No. 87 has multicolored decorative margin inscribed with preamble to the human rights declaration in German.

### World Bank Type

**1989, Jan. 27 Litho. *Perf. 13x14***

**88** A244 5.50s Transportation 1.10 1.25
**89** A244 8s Health care, education 1.75 1.90

### Peace-Keeping Force Type

**1989, Mar. 17 *Perf. 14x13½***

**90** A245 6s multicolored .85 .95

### World Weather Watch Type

Satellite photograph and radar image: 4s, Helical cloud formation over Italy, the eastern Alps, and parts of Yugoslavia. 9.50s, Rainfall in Tokyo, Japan.

**1989, Apr. 21 Litho. *Perf. 13x14***

**91** A247 4s multicolored 1.00 1.10
**92** A247 9.50s multicolored 2.10 2.25

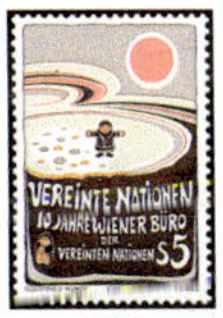

V20

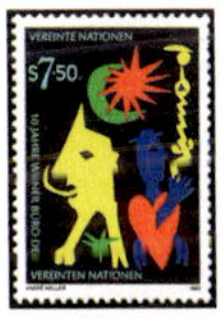

V21

**Photo. & Engr., Photo. (7.50s)**

**1989, Aug. 23 *Perf. 14***

**93** V20 5s multicolored 1.25 1.50
**94** V21 7.50s multicolored 1.25 1.50

### Human Rights Type of 1989

Paintings: 4s, The Prisoners, by Kathe Kollwitz. 6s, Justice, by Raphael.

**1989, Nov. 17 Litho. *Perf. 13½***

**95** A250 4s multicolored .50 .55
**96** A250 6s multicolored .75 .85

See Nos. 108-109, 123-124, 150-151.

### Intl. Trade Center Type

**1990, Feb. 2 Litho. *Perf. 14½x15***

**97** A251 12s multicolored 1.25 1.40

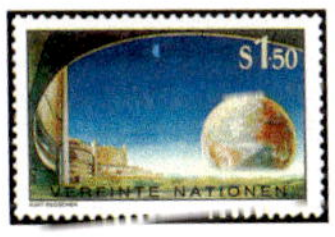

Painting by Kurt Hegschek — V22

**1990, Feb. 2 Litho *Perf. 13x13½***

**98** V22 1.50s multicolored .30 .35

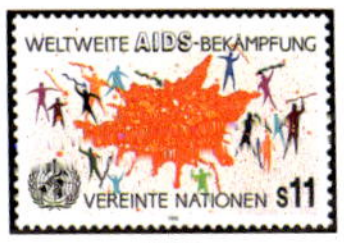

V23

Designs: 5s, "SIDA." 11s, Stylized figures, ink blot.

***Perf. 13½x12½***

**1990, Mar. 16 Litho.**

**99** V23 5s multicolored 1.00 1.10
**100** V23 11s multicolored 2.25 2.40

### Medicinal Plants Type

**1990, May 4 Photo. *Perf. 11½***

**Granite Paper**

**101** A253 4.50s Bixa orellana 1.25 1.40
**102** A253 9.50s Momordica charantia 2.50 2.75

### UN 45th Anniv. Type

Designs: 7s, 9s, "45" and emblem.

# OFFICES IN VIENNA, AUSTRIA

**1990, June 26**    Litho.    *Perf. 14½x13*
103 A254 7s multicolored    1.40 1.60
104 A254 9s multicolored, diff.    2.40 2.75

**Souvenir Sheet**
105    Sheet of 2, #103-104    5.00 5.50

**Crime Prevention Type**
**1990, Sept. 13**    Photo.    *Perf. 14*
106 A255 6s Domestic violence    1.00 1.10
107 A255 8s Crimes against cultural heritage    2.25 2.50

**Human Rights Type of 1989**
Paintings: 4.50s, Before the Judge, by Sandor Bihari. 7s, Young Man Greeted by a Woman Writing a Poem, by Suzuki Harunobu.

**1990, Nov. 16**    Litho.    *Perf. 13½*
108 A250 4.50s multicolored    .30 .35
109 A250    7s multicolored    .90 1.00

**Economic Commission for Europe Type**
**1991, Mar. 15**    Litho.    *Perf. 14*
110 A256 5s Weasel, hoopoe    1.40 1.60
111 A256 5s Warbler, swans    1.40 1.60
112 A256 5s Badgers, squirrel    1.40 1.60
113 A256 5s Fish    1.40 1.60
a.    Block of 4, #110-113    5.60 6.50

**Namibian Independence Type**
**1991, May 10**    Litho.    *Perf. 14*
114 A257    6s Mountains, clouds    1.00 1.25
115 A257 9.50s Dune, Namib Desert    2.25 2.50

V24

**1991, May 10**    Litho.    *Perf. 15x14½*
116 V24 20s multicolored    1.75 2.00

V25

Rights of the Child — V26

**1991, June 14**    Litho.    *Perf. 14½*
117 V25 7s Stick drawings    1.00 1.25
118 V26 9s Child, clock, fruit    1.50 1.75

V27

Banning of Chemical Weapons — V28

**1991, Sept. 11**    Litho.    *Perf. 13½*
119 V27 5s multicolored    .75 .90
120 V28 10s multicolored    1.75 2.00

**UN Postal Administration, 40th Anniv. Type**
**1991, Oct. 24**    Litho.    *Perf. 14x15*
121 A263 5s UN NY No. 8    .75 .90
122 A263 8s UN NY No. 5    1.50 1.75

**Human Rights Type of 1989**
Artwork: 4.50s, Pre-columbian Mexican pottery. 7s, Windows, by Robert Delaunay.

**1991, Nov. 20**    Litho.    *Perf. 13½*
123 A250 4.50s black & brown    .50 .55
124 A250 7s multicolored    .80 .90

**World Heritage Type of 1984**
Designs: 5s, Iguacu Natl. Park, Brazil. 9s, Abu Simbel, Egypt.

**1992, Jan. 24**    Litho.    *Perf. 13*
Size: 35x28mm
125 V10 5s multicolored    .75 .90
126 V10 9s multicolored    1.60 1.80

**Clean Oceans Type**
**1992, Mar. 13**    Litho.    *Perf. 14*
127 A264 7s Ocean surface, diff.    1.00 1.10
128 A264 7s Ocean bottom, diff.    1.00 1.10
a.    Pair, #127-128    2.25 2.50

**Earth Summit Type**
**1992, May 22**    Photo.    *Perf. 11½*
129 A265 5.50s Man in space    1.30 1.50
130 A265 5.50s Sun    1.30 1.50
131 A265 5.50s Man fishing    1.30 1.50
132 A265 5.50s Sailboat    1.30 1.50
a.    Block of 4, #129-132    5.50 6.00

**Mission to Planet Earth Type**
Designs: No. 133, Satellite, person's mouth. No. 134, Satellite, person's ear.

**1992, Sept. 4**    Photo.    *Rouletted 8*
Granite Paper
133 A266 10s multicolored    3.00 3.25
134 A266 10s multicolored    3.00 3.25
a.    Pair, #133-134    6.00 6.50

**Science and Technology Type of 1992**
Designs: 5.50s, Woman emerging from computer screen. 7s, Green thumb growing flowers.

**1992, Oct. 2**    Litho.    *Perf. 14*
135 A267 5.50s multicolored    .75 .85
136 A267 7s multicolored    1.40 1.60

V29

Intl. Center, Vienna — V30

**1992, Oct. 2**    Litho.    *Perf. 13x13½*
137 V29 5.50s multicolored    .90 1.00

*Perf. 13½x13*
138 V30 7s multicolored    1.25 1.40

**Human Rights Type of 1989**
Artwork: 6s, Les Constructeurs, by Fernand Leger. 10s, Sunday Afternoon on the Island of Le Grande Jatte, by Georges Seurat.

**1992, Nov. 20**    Litho.    *Perf. 13½*
139 A250 6s multicolored    .75 .85
140 A250 10s multicolored    1.25 1.40

**Aging With Dignity Type**
Designs: 5.50s, Elderly couple, family working in garden. 7s, Older woman teaching.

**1993, Feb. 5**    Litho.    *Perf. 13*
141 A270 5.50s multicolored    .75 .85
142 A270 7s multicolored    1.40 1.60

**Endangered Species Type**
Designs: No. 143, Equus grevyi (Grevy's zebra). No. 144, Spheniscus humboldti (Humboldt's penguins). No. 145, Varanus griseus (desert monitor). No. 146, Canis lupus (gray wolf).

**1993, Mar. 2**    Litho.    *Perf. 13x12½*
143 A271 7s multicolored    .90 1.00
144 A271 7s multicolored    .90 1.00
145 A271 7s multicolored    .90 1.00
146 A271 7s multicolored    .90 1.00
a.    Block of 4, #143-146    3.60 4.00

**Healthy Environment Type**
**1993, May 7**    Litho.    *Perf. 15x14½*
147 A272 6s Wave in ocean    1.25 1.40
148 A272 10s Globe    2.00 2.25

V31

**1993, May 7**    Photo.    *Perf. 11½*
Granite Paper
149 V31 13s multicolored    2.00 2.25

**Human Rights Type of 1989**
Artwork: 5s, Lower Austrian Peasants' Wedding, by Ferdinand G. Waldmüller. 6s, Outback, by Sally Morgan.

**1993, June 11**    Litho.    *Perf. 13½*
150 A250 5s multicolored    .80 .90
151 A250 6s multicolored    1.00 1.10

**Intl. Peace Day Type**
Denomination at: No. 152, UL. No. 153, UR. No. 154, LL. No. 155, LR.

*Rouletted 12½*
**1993, Sept. 21**    Litho. & Engr.
152 A274 5.50s green & multi    1.80 2.00
153 A274 5.50s green & multi    1.80 2.00
154 A274 5.50s green & multi    1.80 2.00
155 A274 5.50s green & multi    1.80 2.00
a.    Block of 4, #152-155    7.25 8.25

**Environment-Climate Type**
Designs: No. 156, Monkeys. No. 157, Bluebird, industrial pollution, volcano. No. 158, Volcano, nuclear power plant, tree stumps. No. 159, Cactus, tree stumps, owl.

**1993, Oct. 29**    Litho.    *Perf. 14½*
156 A275 7s multicolored    2.50 2.75
157 A275 7s multicolored    2.50 2.75
158 A275 7s multicolored    2.50 2.75
159 A275 7s multicolored    2.50 2.75
a.    Strip of 4, #156-159    10.00 11.00

**Intl. Year of the Family Type of 1993**
Designs: 5.50s, Adults, children holding hands. 8s, Two adults, child planting crops.

**1994, Feb. 4**    Litho.    *Perf. 13.1*
160 A276 5.50s blue green & multi    1.00 1.10
161 A276 8s red & multi    1.25 1.40

**Endangered Species Type of 1993**
Designs: No. 162, Ocelot. No. 163, White-breasted silver-eye. No. 164, Mediterranean monk seal. No. 165, Asian elephant.

**1994, Mar. 18**    Litho.    *Perf. 12.7*
162 A271 7s multicolored    1.00 1.10
163 A271 7s multicolored    1.00 1.10
164 A271 7s multicolored    1.00 1.10
165 A271 7s multicolored    1.00 1.10
a.    Block of 4, #162-165    4.00 4.40

**Protection for Refugees Type**
Design: 12s, Protective hands surround group of refugees.

**1994, Apr. 29**    Litho.    *Perf. 14.3x14.8*
166 A277 12s multicolored    1.50 1.75

V32

V33

V34

**1994, Apr. 29**    Litho.    *Perf. 12.9*
167 V32 50g multicolored    .25 .30
168 V33 4s multicolored    .40 .45
169 V34 30s multicolored    4.00 4.50
   Nos. 167-169 (3)    4.65 5.25

**Intl. Decade for Natural Disaster Reduction Type**
Earth seen from space, outline map of: No. 170, North America. No. 171, Eurasia. No. 172, South America. No. 173, Australia and South Asia.

**1994, May 27**    Litho.    *Perf. 13.9x14.2*
170 A281 6s multicolored    1.75 1.90
171 A281 6s multicolored    1.75 1.90
172 A281 6s multicolored    1.75 1.90
173 A281 6s multicolored    1.75 1.90
a.    Block of 4, #170-173    7.00 7.75

**Population and Development Type**
Designs: 5.50s, Women teaching, running machine tool, coming home to family. 7s, Family on tropical island.

**1994, Sept. 1**    Litho.    *Perf. 13.2x13.6*
174 A282 5.50s multicolored    .90 1.00
175 A282 7s multicolored    1.50 1.75

**UNCTAD Type**
**1994, Oct. 28**
176 A283 6s multi, diff.    .90 1.00
177 A283 7s multi, diff.    1.50 1.75

**UN 50th Anniv. Type**
**1995, Jan. 1**    Litho. & Engr.    *Perf. 13.4*
178 A284 7s multicolored    1.25 1.40

**Social Summit Type**
**1995, Feb. 3**    Photo. & Engr.    *Perf. 13.6x13.9*
179 A285 14s multi, diff.    2.00 2.25

**Endangered Species Type of 1993**
Designs: No. 180, Black rhinoceros, Diceros bicornis. No. 181, Golden conure, Aratinga guarouba. No. 182, Douc langur, Pygathrix nemaeus. No. 183, Arabian oryx, Oryx leucoryx.

**1995, Mar. 24**    Litho.    *Perf. 13x12½*
180 A271 7s multicolored    1.00 1.10
181 A271 7s multicolored    1.00 1.10
182 A271 7s multicolored    1.00 1.10
183 A271 7s multicolored    1.00 1.10
a.    Block of 4, 180-183    4.00 4.50

**Intl. Youth Year Type**
Designs: 6s, Village in winter. 7s, Teepees.

**1995, May 26**    Litho.    *Perf. 14.4x14.7*
184 A286 6s multicolored    .80 .90
185 A286 7s multicolored    1.00 1.10

**UN, 50th Anniv. Type**
Designs: 7s, Like No. 663. 10s, Like No. 664.

*Perf. 13.3x13.6*
**1995, June 26**    Engr.
186 A287 7s green    1.20 1.30
187 A287 10s black    1.75 1.90

**Souvenir Sheet**
Litho. & Engr.
*Imperf*
188    Sheet of 2, #186-187    2.75 3.10
a.    A287 7s green    1.10 1.25
b.    A287 10s black    1.60 1.80

**Conference on Women Type**
Designs: 5.50s, Women amid tropical plants. 6s, Woman reading, swans on lake.

**1995, Sept. 5**    Photo.    *Perf. 12*
189 A288 5.50s multicolored    .80 .90
   Size: 28x50mm
190 A288    6s multicolored    1.20 1.30

**UN People, 50th Anniv. Type**
**1995, Oct. 24**    Litho.    *Perf. 14*
191    Sheet of 12    9.00 10.00
a.-l. A290 3s any single    .75 .85
192    Souvenir booklet    9.00
a.    A290 3s Booklet pane of 3, vert. strip of 3 from UL of sheet    2.25 2.75
b.    A290 3s Booklet pane of 3, vert. strip of 3 from UR of sheet    2.25 2.75
c.    A290 3s Booklet pane of 3, vert. strip of 3 from LL of sheet    2.25 2.75
d.    A290 3s Booklet pane of 3, vert. strip of 3 from LR of sheet    2.25 2.75

**WFUNA, 50th Anniv. Type**
Design: 7s, Harlequin holding dove.

**1996, Feb. 2**    Litho.    *Perf. 13x13½*
193 A291 7s multicolored    1.00 1.10

UN Flag
V35

Abstract, by Karl Korab
V36

**1996, Feb. 2**    Litho.    *Perf. 15x14½*
194 V35 1s multicolored    .25 .30
195 V36 10s multicolored    1.60 1.75

OFFICES IN VIENNA, AUSTRIA 299

### Endangered Species Type of 1993

Designs: No. 196, Cypripedium calceolus. No. 197, Aztekium ritteri. No. 198, Euphorbia cremersii. No. 199, Dracula bella.

**1996, Mar. 14 Litho. *Perf. 12½***

**196** A271 7s multicolored .75 .85
**197** A271 7s multicolored .75 .85
**198** A271 7s multicolored .75 .85
**199** A271 7s multicolored .75 .85
*a.* Block of 4, #196-199 3.00 3.40

### City Summit Type

Designs: No. 200, Arab family selling fruits, vegetables. No. 201, Women beside stream, camels. No. 202, Woman carrying bundle on head, city skyline. No. 203, Woman threshing grain, yoke of oxen in field. No. 204, Native village, elephant.

**1996, June 3 Litho. *Perf. 14x13½***

**200** A293 6s multicolored 1.50 1.75
**201** A293 6s multicolored 1.50 1.75
**202** A293 6s multicolored 1.50 1.75
**203** A293 6s multicolored 1.50 1.75
**204** A293 6s multicolored 1.50 1.75
*a.* Strip of 5, #200-204 7.50 9.00

### Sport and the Environment Type

6s, Men's parallel bars (gymnastics), vert. 7s, Hurdles.

***Perf. 14x14½, 14½x14***

**1996, July 19 Litho.**

**205** A294 6s multicolored .80 .90
**206** A294 7s multicolored .90 1.00

**Souvenir Sheet**

**207** A294 Sheet of 2, #205-206 1.75 1.90

### Plea for Peace Type

Designs: 7s, Dove and butterflies. 10s, Stylized dove, diff.

**1996, Sept. 17 Litho. *Perf. 14½x15***

**208** A295 7s multicolored .80 .90
**209** A295 10s multicolored 1.20 1.40

### UNICEF Type

Fairy Tales: 5.50s, Hansel and Gretel, by the Brothers Grimm. 8s, How Maui Stole Fire from the Gods, South Pacific.

**1996, Nov. 20 Litho. *Perf. 14½x15***

**210** A296 5.50s multicolored .90 1.00
**211** A296 8s multicolored 1.40 1.60

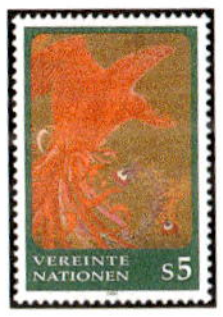
V37

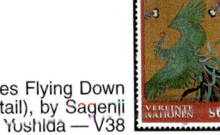

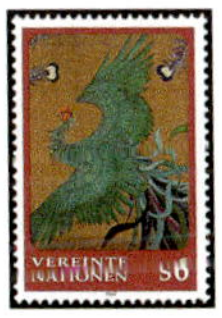
Phoenixes Flying Down (Detail), by Sagenji Yoshida — V38

**1997, Feb. 12 Litho. *Perf. 14½***

**212** V37 5s multicolored .80 .90
**213** V38 6s multicolored .90 1.00

### Endangered Species Type of 1993

Designs: No. 214, Macaca sylvanus (Barbary macaque). No. 215, Anthropoides paradisea (blue crane). No. 216, Equus przewalskii (Przewalski horse). No. 217, Myrmecophaga tridactyla (giant anteater).

**1997, Mar. 13 Litho. *Perf. 12½***

**214** A271 7s multicolored .75 .85
**215** A271 7s multicolored .75 .85
**216** A271 7s multicolored .75 .85
**217** A271 7s multicolored .75 .85
*a.* Block of 4, #214-217 3.00 3.40

### Earth Summit Anniv. Type

Designs: No. 218, Person running. No. 219, Hills, stream, trees. No. 220, Tree with orange leaves. No. 221, Tree with pink leaves.

11s, Combined design similar to Nos. 218-221.

**1997, May 30 Photo. *Perf. 11.5***

**Granite Paper**

**218** A299 3.50s multicolored 1.50 1.75
**219** A299 3.50s multicolored 1.50 1.75
**220** A299 3.50s multicolored 1.50 1.75
**221** A299 3.50s multicolored 1.50 1.75
*a.* Block of 4, #218-221 6.00 7.00

**Souvenir Sheet**

**222** A299 11s multicolored 2.40 2.60

### Transportation Type

Ground transportation: No. 223, 1829 Rocket, 1901 Darraque. No. 224, Steam engine from Vladikawska Railway, trolley. No. 225, Double-decker bus. No. 226, 1950s diesel locomotive, semi-trailer. No. 227, High-speed train, electric car.

**1997, Aug. 29 Litho. *Perf. 14x14½***

**223** A300 7s multicolored 1.25 1.40
**224** A300 7s multicolored 1.25 1.40
**225** A300 7s multicolored 1.25 1.40
**226** A300 7s multicolored 1.25 1.40
**227** A300 7s multicolored 1.25 1.40
*a.* Strip of 5, #223-227 6.25 7.00

No. 227a has continuous design.

### Philately Type

Designs: 6.50s, No. 62. 7s, No. 63.

**1997, Oct. 14 Litho. *Perf. 13½x14***

**228** A301 6.50s multicolored .80 .90
**229** A301 7s multicolored .90 1.00

### World Heritage Convention Type

Terracotta warriors of Xian: 3s, Single warrior. 6s, Massed warriors. No. 232a, like No. 716. No. 232b, like No. 717. No. 232c, like Geneva No. 314. No. 232d, like Geneva No. 315. No. 232e, like Vienna No. 230. No. 232f, like Vienna No. 231.

**1997, Nov. 19 Litho. *Perf. 13½***

**230** A302 3s multicolored 1.00 1.10
**231** A302 6s multicolored 2.00 2.25
**232** Souvenir booklet 12.00
*a.-f.* A302 1s any single .50 .55
*g.* Booklet pane of 4 #232a 2.00 2.25
*h.* Booklet pane of 4 #232b 2.00 2.25
*i.* Booklet pane of 4 #232c 2.00 2.25
*j.* Booklet pane of 4 #232d 2.00 2.25
*k.* Booklet pane of 4 #232e 2.00 2.25
*l.* Booklet pane of 4 #232f 2.00 2.25

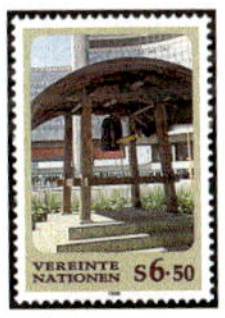
Japanese Peace Bell, Vienna V39

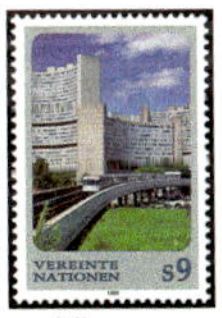
Vienna Subway, Vienna Intl. Center V40

**1998, Feb. 13 Litho. *Perf. 15x14½***

**233** V39 6.50s multicolored .80 .90
**234** V40 9s multicolored 1.00 1.10

### Endangered Species Type of 1993

Designs: No. 235, Chelonia mydas (green turtle). No. 236, Speotyto cunicularia (burrowing owl). No. 237, Trogonoptera brookiana (Rajah Brooke's birdwing). No. 238, Ailurus fulgens (lesser panda).

**1998, Mar. 13 Litho. *Perf. 12½***

**235** A271 7s multicolored .75 .85
**236** A271 7s multicolored .75 .85
**237** A271 7s multicolored .75 .85
**238** A271 7s multicolored .75 .85
*a.* Block of 4, #235-238 3.00 3.40

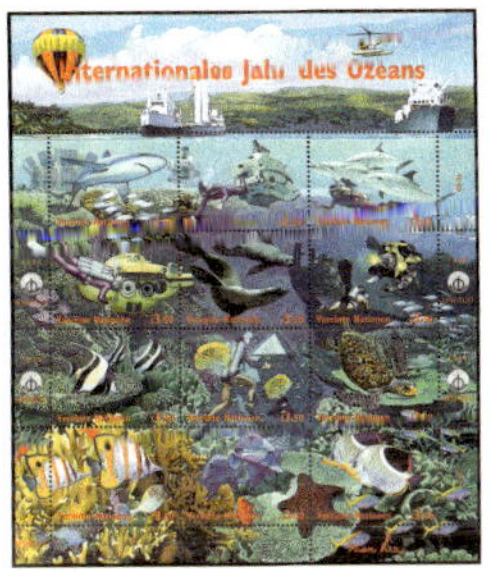

Intl. Year of the Ocean V41

**1998, May 20 Litho. *Perf. 13x13½***

**239** V41 Sheet of 12 9.00 9.00
*a.-l.* 3.50s any single .75 .75

### Rain Forests Type

**1998, June 19 *Perf. 13x13½***

**240** A307 6.50s Ocelot .90 1.00

**Souvenir Sheet**

**241** A307 22s like #240 3.00 3.25

### Peacekeeping Type of 1998

Designs: 4s, Soldier passing out relief supplies. 7.50s, UN supervised voting.

**1998, Sept. 15 Photo. *Perf. 12***

**242** A308 4s multicolored .50 .60
**243** A308 7.50s multicolored 1.00 1.10

### Declaration of Human Rights Type

Designs: 4.50s, Stylized person. 7s, Gears.

**Litho. & Photo.**

**1998, Oct. 27 *Perf. 13***

**244** A309 4.50s multicolored .80 .90
**245** A309 7s multicolored 1.25 1.40

### Schönbrunn Palace Type

Designs: 3.50s, No. 248d, Palace. 7s, No. 248c, Porcelain stove, vert. No. 248a, Blue porcelain vase, vert. No. 248b, Wall painting on fabric (detail), by Johann Wenzl Bergl, vert. No. 248e, Great Palm House (conservatory). No. 248f, The Glorlette (archway).

**1998, Dec. 4 Litho. *Perf. 14***

**246** A310 3.50s multicolored .60 .70
**247** A310 7s multicolored 1.10 1.25

**Souvenir Booklet**

**248** Booklet 20.00
*a.-c.* A310 1s any single .60 .70
*d.-f.* A310 2s any single 1.20 1.30
*g.* Booklet pane of 4 #248d 4.80 5.25
*h.* Booklet pane of 3 #248a 1.80 2.00
*i.* Booklet pane of 3 #248b 1.80 2.00
*j.* Booklet pane of 3 #248c 1.80 2.00
*k.* Booklet pane of 4 #248e 4.80 5.25
*l.* Booklet pane of 4 #248f 4.80 5.25

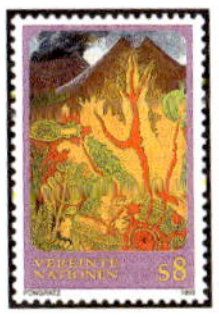
Volcanic Landscape — V42

**1999, Feb. 5 Litho. *Perf. 13x13½***

**249** V42 8s multicolored 1.25 1.40

### World Heritage, Australia Type

Designs: 4.50s, No. 252d, Uluru-Kata Tjuta Natl. Park. 6.50s, No. 252a, Tasmanian Wilderness. No. 252b, Wet tropics of Queensland. No. 252c, Great Barrier Reef. No. 252e, Kakadu Natl. Park. No. 252f, Willandra Lakes region.

**1999, Mar. 19 Litho. *Perf. 13***

**250** A313 4.50s multicolored .75 .85
**251** A313 6.50s multicolored 1.10 1.25

**Souvenir Booklet**

**252** Booklet 12.00
*a.-c.* A313 1s any single .35 .40
*d.-f.* A313 2s any single .65 .70
*g.* Booklet pane of 4, #252a 1.40 1.60
*h.* Booklet pane of 4, #252d 2.60 2.80
*i.* Booklet pane of 4, #252b 1.40 1.60
*j.* Booklet pane of 4, #252e 2.60 2.80
*k.* Booklet pane of 4, #252c 1.40 1.60
*l.* Booklet pane of 4, #252f 2.60 2.80

### Endangered Species Type of 1993

Designs: No. 253, Pongo pygmaeus (orangutan). No. 254, Pelecanus crispus (Dalmatian pelican). No. 255, Eunectes notaeus (yellow anaconda). No. 256, Caracal.

**1999, Apr. 22 Litho. *Perf. 12½***

**253** A271 7s multicolored .75 .85
**254** A271 7s multicolored .75 .85
**255** A271 7s multicolored .75 .85
**256** A271 7s multicolored .75 .85
*a.* Block of 4, #253-256 3.00 3.40

### UNISPACE III Type

Designs: No. 257, Satellite over ships. No. 258, Satellite up close. No. 259, Composite of Nos. 257-258.

**1999, July 7 Photo. *Rouletted 8***

**257** A314 3.50s multicolored .75 .85
**258** A314 3.50s multicolored .75 .85
*a.* Pair, #257-258 1.60 1.70

**Souvenir Sheet**

***Perf. 14½***

**259** A314 13s multicolored 4.50 5.00

### UPU Type

Various people, late 20th century methods of mail transportation, denomination at: No. 260, UL. No. 261, UR. No. 262, LL. No. 263, LR.

**1999, Aug. 23 Photo. *Perf. 11¾***

**260** A315 6.50s multicolored 1.00 1.10
**261** A315 6.50s multicolored 1.00 1.10
**262** A315 6.50s multicolored 1.00 1.10
**263** A315 6.50s multicolored 1.00 1.10
*a.* Block of 4, #260-263 4.00 4.50

### In Memoriam Type

Designs: 6.50s, 14s, Donaupark. Size of 14s stamp: 34x63mm.

**1999, Sept. 21 Litho. *Perf. 14½x14***

**264** A316 6.50s multicolored .90 1.00

**Souvenir Sheet**

***Perf. 14***

**265** A316 14s multicolored 3.00 3.25

### Education Type

***Perf. 13½x13¾***

**1999, Nov. 18 Litho.**

**266** A317 7s Boy, girl, book .75 .85
**267** A317 13s Group reading 1.75 1.90

### Intl. Year of Thanksgiving Type

**2000, Jan. 1 Litho. *Perf. 13¼x13½***

**268** A318 7s multicolored .80 .90

On No. 268 parts of the design were applied by a thermographic process producing a shiny, raised effect.

### Endangered Species Type of 1993

Designs: No. 269, Panthera pardus (leopard). No. 270, Platalea leucorodia (white spoonbill). No. 271, Hippocamelus bisulcus (huemal). No. 272, Orcinus orca (killer whale).

**2000, Apr. 6 Litho. *Perf. 12¾x12½***

**269** A271 7s multicolored 1.10 1.25
**270** A271 7s multicolored 1.10 1.25
**271** A271 7s multicolored 1.10 1.25
**272** A271 7s multicolored 1.10 1.25
*a.* Block of 4, #269-272 4.50 5.00

### Our World 2000 Type

Winning artwork in Millennium painting competition: 7s, Tomorrow's Dream, by Voltaire Perez, Philippines. 8s, Remembrance, by Dimitris Nalbandis, Greece, vert.

***Perf. 13x13½, 13½x13***

**2000, May 30 Litho.**

**273** A319 7s multicolored .60 .70
**274** A319 8s multicolored .75 .85

### 55th Anniversary Type

Designs: 7s, Secretariat Building, unfinished dome of General Assembly Hall, 1951. 9s, Trygve Lie and Headquarters Advisory Committee at topping-out ceremony, 1949.

**2000, July 7 Litho. *Perf. 13¼x13***

**275** A320 7s multicolored .90 1.00
**276** A320 9s multicolored 1.25 1.40

**Souvenir Sheet**

**277** A320 Sheet of 2, #275-276 2.75 3.25

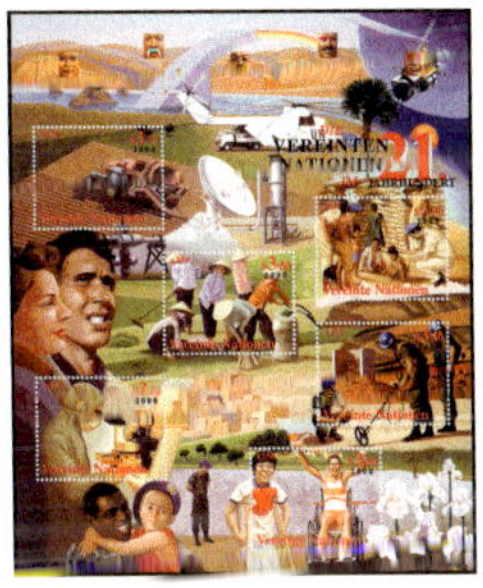
The UN in the 21st Century V43

No. 278: a, Farm machinery. b, UN Peacekeepers and children. c, Oriental farm workers. d, Peacekeepers searching for mines. e, Medical research. f, Handicapped people.

**2000, Sept. 15 Litho. *Perf. 14***

**278** V43 Sheet of 6 7.50 8.50
*a.-f.* 3.50s any single 1.25 1.40

### World Heritage, Spain Type

Designs: Nos. 279, 281c, Aqueduct of Segovia. Nos. 280, 281f, Güell Park, Barcelona. No. 281a, Alhambra, Generalife and Albayzin, Granada. No. 281b, Walled Town of Cuenca. No. 281d, Amphitheater of Mérida. No. 281e, Toledo.

**2000, Oct. 6 Litho. *Perf. 14¾x14½***

**279** A323 4.50s multicolored .80 .90
**280** A323 6.50s multicolored 1.20 1.40

### Souvenir Booklet

**281** Booklet 9.00
*a.-c.* A323 1s any single .25 .30
*d.-f.* A323 2s any single .50 .55
*g.* Booklet pane of 4, #281a 1.00 1.10
*h.* Booklet pane of 4, #281d 2.00 2.25
*i.* Booklet pane of 4, #281b 1.00 1.10
*j.* Booklet pane of 4, #281e 2.00 2.25
*k.* Booklet pane of 4, #281c 1.00 1.10
*l.* Booklet pane of 4, #281f 2.00 2.25

### Respect for Refugees Type

Designs: 7s, 25s, Refugee with hat, three other refugees.

**2000, Nov. 9 Litho. *Perf. 13¼x12¾***
**282** A324 7s multicolored 1.10 1.25

### Souvenir Sheet

**283** A324 25s multicolored 3.75 4.25

### Endangered Species Type of 1993

Designs: No. 284, Tremarctos ornatus (spectacled bear). No. 285, Anas laysanensis (Laysan duck). No. 286, Proteles cristatus (aardwolf). No. 287, Trachypithecus cristatus (silvered leaf monkey).

**2001, Feb. 1 Litho. *Perf. 12¾x12½***
**284** A271 7s multicolored 1.10 1.25
**285** A271 7s multicolored 1.10 1.25
**286** A271 7s multicolored 1.10 1.25
**287** A271 7s multicolored 1.10 1.25
*a.* Block of 4, #284-287 4.50 5.00

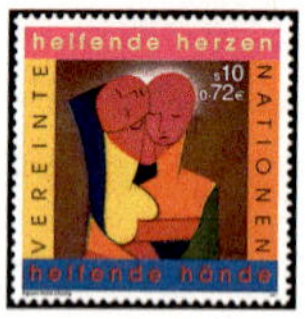

Intl. Volunteers Year — V44

Paintings by: 10s, Nguyen Thanh Chuong, Viet Nam. 12s, Ikko Tanaka, Japan.

**2001, Mar. 29 Litho. *Perf. 13¼***
**288** V44 10s multicolored 1.40 1.60
**289** V44 12s multicolored 1.75 1.90

### World Heritage, Japan Type

Designs: 7s, No. 290c, Himeji-Jo. 15s, No. 291f, Nikko. No. 292a, Kyoto. No. 292b, Nara. No. 292d, Shirakawa-Go and Gokayama. No. 292e, Itsukushima Shinto Shrine.

**2001, Aug. 1 Litho. *Perf. 12¾x13¼***
**290** A328 7s multicolored 1.00 1.10
**291** A328 15s multicolored 2.10 2.25

### Souvenir Booklet

**292** Booklet 11.50
*a.-c.* A328 1s any single .30 .35
*d.-f.* A328 2s any single .60 .70
*g.* Booklet pane of 4, #292a 1.20 1.40
*h.* Booklet pane of 4, #292d 2.40 2.75
*i.* Booklet pane of 4, #292b 1.20 1.40
*j.* Booklet pane of 4, #292e 2.40 2.75
*k.* Booklet pane of 4, #292c 1.20 1.40
*l.* Booklet pane of 4, #292f 2.40 2.75

### Dag Hammarskjöld Type

**2001, Sept. 18 Engr. *Perf. 11x11¼***
**293** A329 7s green 1.00 1.10

### UN Postal Administration, 50th Anniv. Types

**2001, Oct. 18 Litho. *Perf. 13½***
**294** A330 7s Stamps, balloons 1.00 1.10
**295** A330 8s Stamps, cake 1.10 1.25

### Souvenir Sheet

**296** A331 Sheet of 2 7.50 8.00
*a.* 7s green & light blue, 38mm diameter 2.50 2.75
*b.* 21s green & light blue, 38mm diameter 5.00 5.50

### Climate Change Type

Designs: No. 297, Solar panels, automobile at pump. No. 298, Blimp, bicyclists, horse and rider. No. 299, Balloon, sailboat, lighthouse, train. No. 300, Bird, train, traffic signs.

**2001, Nov. 16 Litho. *Perf. 13¼***
**297** A332 7s multicolored 1.00 1.10
**298** A332 7s multicolored 1.00 1.10
**299** A332 7s multicolored 1.00 1.10
**300** A332 7s multicolored 1.00 1.10
*a.* Horiz. strip, #297-300 5.00 5.50

### Nobel Peace Prize Type

**2001, Dec. 10 Litho. *Perf. 13¼***
**301** A333 7s multicolored 1.00 .55

### 100 Cents = 1 Euro (€)

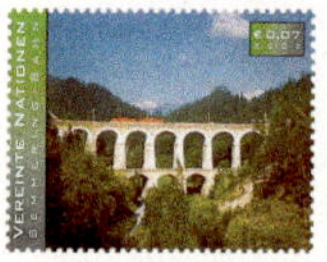
Austrian Tourist Attractions — V45

Designs: 7c, Semmering Railway. 51c, Pferdschwemme, Salzburg. 58c, Aggstein an der Donau Ruins. 73c, Hallstatt. 87c, Melk Abbey. €2.03, Kapitelschwemme, Salzburg.

**2002, Mar. 1 Litho. *Perf. 14½x14***
**302** V45 7c multicolored .25 .30
**303** V45 51c multicolored .90 1.25
**304** V45 58c multicolored 1.00 1.10
**305** V45 73c multicolored 1.25 1.40
**306** V45 87c multicolored 1.75 2.00
**307** V45 €2.03 multicolored 3.50 3.75
*Nos. 302-307 (6)* 8.65 9.80

### Endangered Species Type of 1993

Designs: No. 308, Hylobates syndactylus (siamang). No. 309, Spheniscus demersus (jackass penguin). No. 310, Prionodon linsang (banded linsang). No. 311, Bufo retiformis (Sonoran green toad).

**2002, Apr. 4 Litho. *Perf. 12¾x12½***
**308** A271 51c multicolored 1.25 1.25
**309** A271 51c multicolored 1.25 1.25
**310** A271 51c multicolored 1.25 1.25
**311** A271 51c multicolored 1.25 1.25
*a.* Block of 4, #308-311 5.00 5.00

### Independence of East Timor Type

Designs: 51c, Deer horn container with carved wooden stopper. €1.09, Carved wooden tai weaving loom.

**2002, May 20 Litho. *Perf. 14x14½***
**312** A335 51c multicolored 1.00 1.00
**313** A335 €1.09 multicolored 2.25 2.25

### Intl. Year of Mountains Type

Designs: No. 314, Mt. Cook, New Zealand. No. 315, Mt. Robson, Canada. No. 316, Mt. Rakaposhi, Pakistan. No. 317, Mt. Everest (Sagarmatha), Nepal.

**2002, May 24 Litho. *Perf. 13x13¼***
**314** A336 22c multicolored .40 .40
**315** A336 22c multicolored .40 .40
**316** A336 51c multicolored 1.00 1.00
**317** A336 51c multicolored 1.00 1.00
*a.* Vert. strip or block of four, #314-317 12.50 12.50

### World Summit on Sustainable Development (Peter Max) Type

Designs: No. 318, Rainbow. No. 319, Three women, diff. No. 320, Three faceless people. No. 321, Birds, wave.

**2002, June 27 Litho. *Perf. 14½x14***
**318** A337 51c multicolored 1.00 1.00
**319** A337 51c multicolored 1.00 1.00
**320** A337 58c multicolored 1.25 1.25
**321** A337 58c multicolored 1.25 1.25
*a.* Vert. strip or block of four, #318-321 10.00 8.50

### World Heritage, Italy Type

Designs: 51c, No. 324f, Pompeii. 58c, No. 324c, Rome. No. 324a, Amalfi Coast. No. 324b, Aeolian Islands. No. 324d, Florence. No. 324e, Pisa.

***Perf. 13½x13¼***
**2002, Aug. 30 Litho.**
**322** A338 51c multicolored 1.10 1.10
**323** A338 58c multicolored 1.25 1.25

### Souvenir Booklet

**324** Booklet 15.00
*a.-c.* A338 7c any single .40 .40
*d.-f.* A338 15c any single .85 .85
*g.* Booklet pane of 4, #324d 3.40 3.40
*h.* Booklet pane of 4, #324a 1.60 1.60
*i.* Booklet pane of 4, #324e 3.40 3.40
*j.* Booklet pane of 4, #324b 1.60 1.60
*k.* Booklet pane of 4, #324f 3.40 3.40
*l.* Booklet pane of 4, #324c 1.60 1.60

### AIDS Awareness Type

**2002, Oct. 24 Litho. *Perf. 13½***
**325** A339 €1.53 multicolored 2.50 2.75

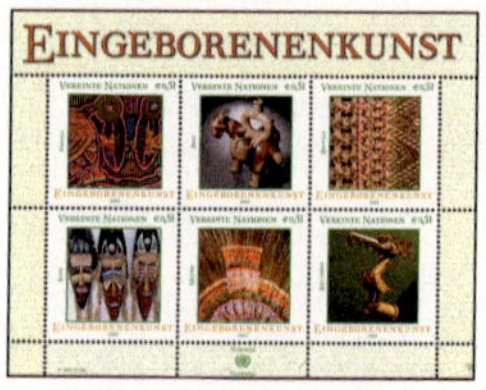

Indigenous Art — V46

No. 326: a, Mola, Panama. b, Mochican llama-shaped spouted vessel, Peru. c, Tarabuco woven cloth, Bolivia. d, Masks, Cuba. e, Aztec priest's feather headdress, Mexico. f, Bird-staffed shaped staff head, Colombia.

**2003, Jan. 31 Litho. *Perf. 14¼***
**326** V46 Sheet of 6 7.50 7.50
*a.-f.* 51c Any single 1.25 1.25

### Austrian Tourist Attractions Type of 2002

Designs: 25c, Kunsthistorisches Museum, Vienna. €1, Belvedere Palace, Vienna.

**2003, Mar. 28 Litho. *Perf. 14½x14***
**327** V45 25c multicolored .55 .55
**328** V45 €1 multicolored 2.25 2.25

### Endangered Species Type of 1993

Designs: No. 329, Anas formosa (Baikal teal). No. 330, Bostrychia hagedash (Hadada ibis). No. 331, Ramphastos toco (toco toucan). No. 332, Alopochen aegyptiacus (Egyptian goose).

**2003, Apr. 3 Litho. *Perf. 12¾x12½***
**329** A271 51c multicolored 1.25 1.25
**330** A271 51c multicolored 1.25 1.25
**331** A271 51c multicolored 1.25 1.25
**332** A271 51c multicolored 1.25 1.25
*a.* Block of 4, #329-332 5.00 5.00

### International Year of Freshwater Type of 2003

***Perf. 14¼x14½***
**2003, June 20 Litho.**
**333** A345 55c Bridge, bird 3.00 3.00
**334** A345 75c Horse, empty river 5.00 5.00
*a.* Horiz. pair, #333-334 8.00 8.00

### Austrian Tourist Attractions Type of 2002

Design: 4c, Schloss Eggenberg, Graz.

**2003, Aug. 7 Litho. *Perf. 14x13¼***
**335** V45 4c multicolored .45 .45

### Ralph Bunche Type

**Litho. With Foil Application**

**2003, Aug. 7 *Perf. 13½x14***
**336** A346 €2.10 olive green & multicolored 3.50 3.50

### In Memoriam Type of 2003

**2003, Oct. 24 Litho. *Perf. 13¼x13***
**337** A347 €2.10 multicolored 5.00 5.00

### World Heritage Sites, United States Type

Designs: 55c, No. 340c, Olympic National Park. 75c, No. 340e, Everglades National Park. No. 340a, Yosemite National Park. No. 340b, Great Smoky Mountains National Park. No. 340d, Hawaii Volcanoes National Park. No. 340f, Yellowstone National Park.

**2003, Oct. 24 Litho. *Perf. 14½x14¼***
**338** A348 55c multicolored 1.50 .75
**339** A348 75c multicolored 2.00 1.00

### Souvenir Booklet

**340** Booklet 14.50
*a.-c.* A348 15c any single .55 .55
*d.-f.* A348 20c any single .65 .65
*g.* Booklet pane of 4 #340a 2.10 2.10
*h.* Booklet pane of 4 #340d 2.60 2.60
*i.* Booklet pane of 4 #340b 2.10 2.10
*j.* Booklet pane of 4 #340e 2.60 2.60
*k.* Booklet pane of 4 #340c 2.10 2.10
*l.* Booklet pane of 4 #340f 2.60 2.60

### Austrian Tourist Attractions Type of 2002

Design: 55c, Schloss Schönbrunn, Vienna.

**2004, Jan. 29 Litho. *Perf. 13x13¼***
**341** V45 55c multicolored 1.50 1.50

### Endangered Species Type of 1993

Designs: No. 342, Melursus ursinus (Sloth bear). No. 343, Cervus eldi (Eld's deer). No. 344, Cercocebus torquatus (Cherry-crowned mangabey). No. 345, Bubalus arnee (Wild water buffalo).

**2004, Jan. 29 Litho. *Perf. 12¾x12½***
**342** A271 55c multicolored 1.50 1.50
**343** A271 55c multicolored 1.50 1.50
**344** A271 55c multicolored 1.50 1.50
**345** A271 55c multicolored 1.50 1.50
*a.* Block of 4, #342-345 6.00 6.00

### Indigenous Art Type of 2003

No. 346: a, Illuminated illustration from the Book of Kells, Ireland. b, Easter eggs, Ukraine. c, Venus of Willendorf, Paleolithic age limestone statue, Austria. d, Flatatunga panel, Iceland. e, Neolithic era idol, Hungary. f, Illuminated illustration from medical treatise, Portugal.

**2004, Mar. 4 Litho. *Perf. 13¼***
**346** V46 Sheet of 6 12.00 12.00
*a.-f.* 55c Any single 2.00 2.00

### Road Safety Type

Road map art with: 55c, Automobile, alcohol bottles. 75c, Road, clouds in traffic light colors, vert.

***Perf. 13x13¼, 13¼x13***
**2004, Apr. 7 Litho.**
**347** A354 55c multicolored 1.25 1.25
**348** A354 75c multicolored 1.75 1.75

### Japanese Peace Bell, 50th Anniv. Type

**Litho. & Engr.**

**2004, June 3 *Perf. 13¼x13***
**349** A355 €2.10 multicolored 4.50 4.50

### World Heritage Sites, Greece Type

Designs: 55c, No. 352f, Mycenae and Tiryns. 75c, No. 352e, Olympia. No. 352a, Acropolis, Athens. No. 352b, Delos. No. 352c, Delphi. No. 352d, Pythagoreion and Heraion of Samos.

**2004, Aug. 12 Litho. *Perf. 14x13¼***
**350** A356 55c multicolored 1.75 1.75
**351** A356 75c multicolored 2.25 2.25

### Souvenir Booklet

**352** Booklet 16.00
*a.-d.* A356 25c any single .60 .60
*e.-f.* A356 30c either single .70 .70
*g.* Booklet pane of 4 #352a 2.40 2.40
*h.* Booklet pane of 4 #352b 2.40 2.40
*i.* Booklet pane of 4 #352c 2.40 2.40
*j.* Booklet pane of 4 #352d 2.40 2.40
*k.* Booklet pane of 4 #352e 2.80 2.80
*l.* Booklet pane of 4 #352f 2.80 2.80

### My Dream for Peace Type

Winning designs of Lions Club International children's global peace poster contest by: 55c, Henry Ulfe Renteria, Peru. €1, Michelle Fortaliza, Philippines.

**2004, Sept. 21 Litho. *Perf. 14***
**353** A357 55c multicolored 1.40 1.40
**354** A357 €1 multicolored 2.50 2.50

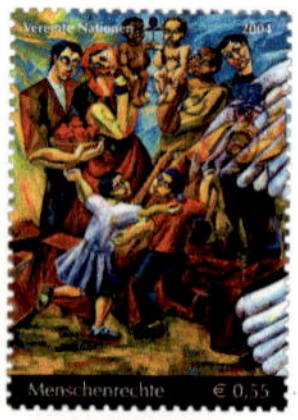

V47

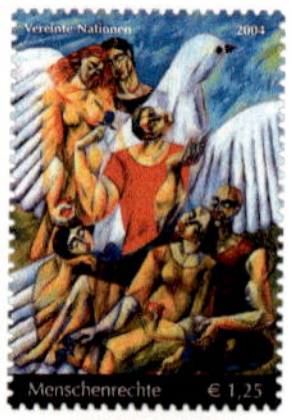

Human Rights — V48

**2004, Oct. 14 Litho. *Perf. 11¼***
**355** V47 55c multicolored 1.00 1.00
**356** V48 €1.25 multicolored 3.00 3.00

### United Nations, 60th Anniv. Type of 2005

**Litho. & Engr.**

**2005, Feb. 4 *Perf. 11x11¼***
**357** A361 55c multicolored 2.50 2.50

### Souvenir Sheet

**Litho.**

***Imperf***

**358** A361 €2.10 multicolored 6.50 6.50

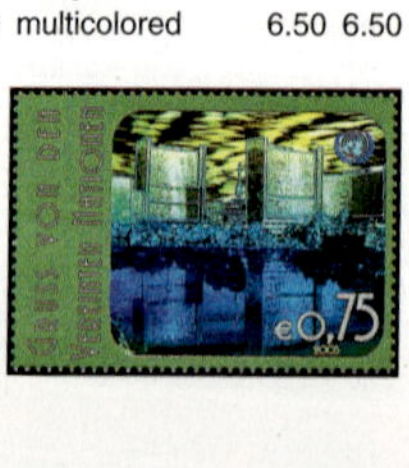
International Center, Vienna V49

### Litho. with Hologram

**2005, Feb. 4** *Perf. 13½x13¼*
**359** V49 75c multicolored 2.25 2.25

### Endangered Species Type of 1993

Designs: No. 360, Ansellia africana. No. 361, Phragmipedium kovachii. No. 362, Cymbidium ensifolium. No. 363, Renanthera imschootiana.

**2005, Mar. 3** **Litho.** *Perf. 12¾x12½*
**360** A271 55c multicolored 1.40 1.40
**361** A271 55c multicolored 1.40 1.40
**362** A271 55c multicolored 1.40 1.40
**363** A271 55c multicolored 1.40 1.40
*a.* Block of 4, #360-363 6.00 6.00

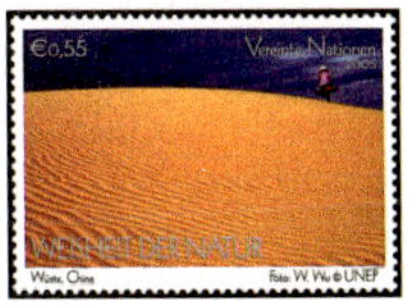

Nature's Wisdom
V50

Designs: 55c, Desert landscape, China. 80c, Cheetah family, Africa.

**2005, Apr. 21** **Litho.** *Perf. 13½x13¼*
**364** V50 55c multicolored 1.60 1.60
**365** V50 75c multicolored 2.25 2.25

### Intl. Year of Sport Type

**2005, June 3** **Litho.** *Perf. 13x13¼*
**366** A368 55c Equestrian 1.60 1.60
**367** A368 €1.10 Soccer 3.25 3.25

### World Heritage Sites, Egypt Type

Designs: Nos. 368, 370c, Abu Mena. Nos. 369, 370f, St. Catherine area. No. 370a, Memphis and its Necropolis. No. 370b, Philae. No. 370d, Ancient Thebes. No. 370e, Islamic Cairo.

**2005, Aug. 4** **Litho.** *Perf. 14x13¼*
**368** A369 55c multicolored 1.60 1.60
**369** A369 75c multicolored 2.25 2.25

### Souvenir Booklet

**370** Booklet, #370g-370l 19.50
*a.-c.* A369 25c any single .75 .75
*d.-f.* A369 30c any single .85 .85
*g.* Booklet pane of 4 #370a 3.00 3.00
*h.* Booklet pane of 4 #370b 3.00 3.00
*i.* Booklet pane of 4 #370c 3.00 3.00
*j.* Booklet pane of 4 #370d 3.50 3.50
*k.* Booklet pane of 4 #370e 3.50 3.50
*l.* Booklet pane of 4 #370f 3.50 3.50

No. 370 sold for €6.80.

### My Dream for Peace Type

Winning designs of Lions Club International children's global peace poster contest by: 55c, Lee Min Gi, Republic of Korea. €1, Natalie Chan, US.

**2004, Sept. 21** **Litho.** *Perf. 14*
**371** A357 55c multicolored 1.60 1.60
**372** A357 €1 multicolored 2.75 2.75

### Food for Life Type

Designs: 55c, Corn, people with food bowls, teacher and students. €1.25, Rice, helicopter dropping food, elephant caravan.

**2005, Oct. 20** **Litho.** *Perf. 13¾*
**373** A370 55c multicolored 1.60 1.60
**374** A370 €1.25 multicolored 3.50 3.50

### Indigenous Art Type of 2003

No. 375 — Musical instruments: a, Drum, Guinea. b, Whistle, Congo. c, Horn, Botswana. d, Drums, Burundi. e, Harp, Gabon. f, Bell, Nigeria.

**2006, Feb. 3** **Litho.** *Perf. 13¼*
**375** V46 Sheet of 6 12.00 12.00
*a.-f.* 55c Any single 2.00 2.00

### Endangered Species Type of 1993

Designs: No. 376, Dendrobates pumilio. No. 377, Furcifer lateralis. No. 378, Corallus hortulanus. No. 379, Dendrobates leucomelas.

*Perf. 12¾x12½*
**2006, Mar. 16** **Litho.**
**376** A271 55c multicolored 1.50 1.50
**377** A271 55c multicolored 1.50 1.50
**378** A271 55c multicolored 1.50 1.50
**379** A271 55c multicolored 1.50 1.50
*a.* Block of 4, #376-379 6.00 6.00

### Intl. Day of Families Type

Designs: 55c, Family at water pump. €1.25, Family preparing food.

**2006, May 27** **Litho.** *Perf. 14x13½*
**380** A373 55c multicolored 1.25 1.25
**381** A373 €1.25 multicolored 2.50 2.50

### World Heritage Sites, France Type

Eiffel Tower and: Nos. 382, 384c, Carcasonne. Nos. 383, 384f, Chateau de Chambord. No. 384a, Banks of the Seine. No. 384b, Provins. No. 384d, Roman Aqueduct. No. 384e, Mont Saint-Michel.

### Litho. & Embossed with Foil Application

**2006, June 17** *Perf. 13½x13¼*
**382** A374 55c multicolored 1.50 1.50
**383** A374 75c multicolored 2.00 2.00

### Souvenir Booklet

**384** Booklet, #384g-384l 18.00
*a.-c.* A374 25c any single .65 .65
*d.-f.* A374 30c any single .80 .80
*g.* Booklet pane of 4 #384a 2.60 2.60
*h.* Booklet pane of 4 #384b 2.60 2.60
*i.* Booklet pane of 4 #384c 2.60 2.60
*j.* Booklet pane of 4 #384d 3.25 3.25
*k.* Booklet pane of 4 #384e 3.25 3.25
*l.* Booklet pane of 4 #384f 3.25 3.25

No. 384 sold for €6.80.

### My Dream for Peace Type of 2004

Winning designs of Lions Club International children's global peace poster contest by: 55c, Klara Thein, Germany. €1, Laurensia Levina, Indonesia.

**2006, Sept. 21** **Litho.** *Perf. 13½x13*
**385** A357 55c multicolored 1.60 1.60
**386** A357 €1 multicolored 3.00 3.00

### Flags and Coins Type

No. 387 — Flag of: a, Gambia, 1 dalasi coin. b, Pakistan, 1 rupee coin. c, Afghanistan, 2 afghani coin. d, Austria, 1 euro coin. e, Germany, 50 cent coin. f, Haiti, 50 centimes coin. g, Denmark, 20 krone coin. h, Netherlands, 1 euro coin.

**2006, Oct. 5** **Litho.** *Perf. 13¼x13*
**387** Sheet of 8 14.00 14.00
*a.-h.* A375 55c Any single 1.75 1.75

A column of rouletting in the middle of the sheet separates it into two parts.

### Endangered Species Type of 1993

Designs: No. 388, Chlorocebus aethiops. No. 389, Nasalis larvatus. No. 390, Papio hamadryas. No. 391, Erythrocebus patas.

*Perf. 12¾x12½*
**2007, Mar. 15** **Litho.**
**388** A271 55c multicolored 1.60 1.60
**389** A271 55c multicolored 1.60 1.60
**390** A271 55c multicolored 1.60 1.60
**391** A271 55c multicolored 1.60 1.60
*a.* Block of 4, #388-391 6.40 6.40

### Flags and Coins Type of 2006

No. 392 — Flag of: a, Trinidad and Tobago, 50 cent coin. b, Sierra Leone, 10 cent coin. c, Hungary, 100 forint coin. d, San Marino, 2 euro coin. e, Croatia, 1 kuna coin. f, Spain, 1 euro coin. g, Kazakhstan, 100 tenge coin. h, Ireland, 5 cent coin.

**2007, May 3** **Litho.** *Perf. 13¼x13*
**392** Sheet of 8 13.00 13.00
*a.-h.* A375 55c Any single 1.60 1.60

A column of rouletting in the middle of the sheet separates it into two parts.

Five 55c stamps depicting views of the Vienna International Center and the United Nations flag were released May 3, 2007. The editors have reason to believe that these stamps were not sold at the UN Post Office in Vienna. Value, strip of 5 with labels $45, sheet of 10 $90.

### Peaceful Visions Type of 2007

Designs: 55c, "The Sowers." €1.25, "We All Thrive Under the Same Sky."

**2007, June 1** **Litho.** *Perf. 13x12½*
**398** A378 55c multicolored 1.60 1.60
**399** A378 €1.25 multicolored 3.75 3.75

### World Heritage Sites, South America Type

Designs: Nos. 400, 402e, Iguaçu National Park, Brazil. Nos. 401, 402b, Cueva de las Manos, Argentina. No. 402a, Rapa Nui, Chile. No. 402c, Machu Picchu, Peru. No. 402d, Tiwanaku, Bolivia. No. 474f, Galapagos Islands, Ecuador.

**2007, Aug. 9** **Litho.** *Perf. 13¼x13*
**400** A381 55c multicolored 2.00 2.00
**401** A381 75c multicolored 2.75 2.75

### Souvenir Booklet

**402** Booklet, #402g-402l 20.00
*a.-c.* A381 25c Any single .75 .75
*d.-f.* A381 30c Any single .90 .90
*g.* Booklet pane of 4 #402a 3.00 3.00
*h.* Booklet pane of 4 #402b 3.00 3.00
*i.* Booklet pane of 4 #402c 3.00 3.00
*j.* Booklet pane of 4 #402d 3.60 3.60
*k.* Booklet pane of 4 #402e 3.60 3.60
*l.* Booklet pane of 4 #402f 3.60 3.60

### Humanitarian Mail Type

**2007, Sept. 6** **Litho.** *Perf. 12½x13¼*
**403** A382 75c multicolored 2.25 2.25

Five 65c stamps depicting the International Space Station, astronauts and planets were released Oct. 1, 2007. The editors have reason to believe that these stamps were not sold at the UN Post Office in Vienna. Value, strip of 5 with labels $35, sheet of 10 $65.

### Space for Humanity Type

Designs: 65c, Space stations. €1.15, Space Station.
€2.10, Space probe, Jupiter.

**2007, Oct. 25** **Litho.** *Perf. 13½x14*
**409** A383 65c multicolored 2.00 2.00
**410** A383 €1.15 multicolored 3.50 3.50

### Souvenir Sheet

**411** A383 €2.10 multicolored 8.00 8.00

### Intl. Holocaust Remembrance Day Type

**2008, Jan. 27** **Litho.** *Perf. 13*
**412** A384 65c multicolored 3.00 3.00

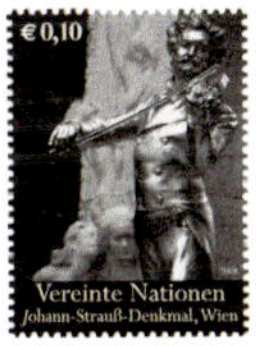

Johann Strauss Memorial, Vienna — V61

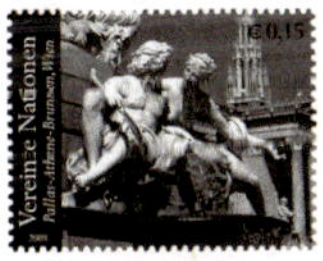

Pallas Athene Fountain, Vienna — V62

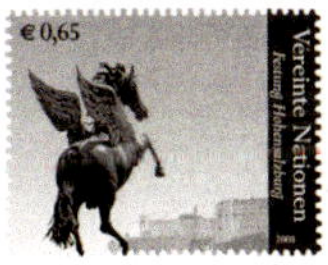

Pegasus Fountain, Salzburg — V63

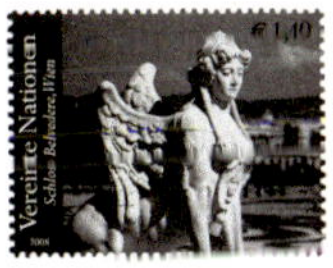

Statue, Belvedere Palace Gardens, Vienna — V64

**2008, Jan. 28** **Litho.** *Perf. 13½x14*
**413** V61 10c black .35 .35

*Perf. 14x13½*
**414** V62 15c black .50 .50
**415** V63 65c black 2.25 2.25
**416** V64 €1.40 black 4.75 4.75
*Nos. 413-416 (4)* 7.85 7.85

### Endangered Species Type of 1993

Designs: No. 4170, Mirounga angustirostris. No. 418, Millepora alcicornis. No. 419, Hippocampus histrix. No. 420, Physeter catodon.

**2008, Mar. 6** **Litho.** *Perf. 12¾x12½*
**417** A271 65c multicolored 2.50 2.50
**418** A271 65c multicolored 2.50 2.50
**419** A271 65c multicolored 2.50 2.50
**420** A271 65c multicolored 2.50 2.50
*a.* Block of 4, #417-420 10.00 10.00

### Flags and Coins Type of 2006

No. 421 — Flag of: a, Poland, 5 zloty coin. b, Latvia, 1 lat coin. c, Portugal, 1 euro coin. d, Armenia, 500 dram coin. e, Sweden, 1 krona coin. f, Cyprus, 1 euro coin. g, Slovakia, 1 koruna coin. h, Qatar, 50 dirham coin.

**2008, May 8** **Litho.** *Perf. 13¼x13*
**421** Sheet of 8 18.00 18.00
*a.-h.* A375 65c Any single 2.25 2.25

A column of rouletting in the middle of the sheet separates it into two parts.

Five 65c stamps depicting the Vienna International Center and its artwork were released May 12, 2008. The editors have reason to believe that these stamps were not sold at the UN Post Office in Vienna. Value, strip of 5 with labels $30, sheet of 10 $60.

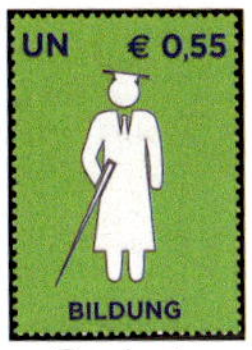


Graduate
V70

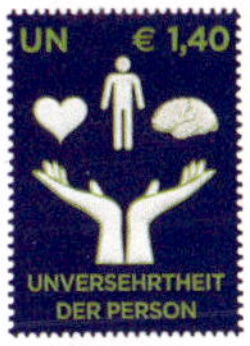


Stylized Person, Heart, Brain, Hands
V71

### Litho. & Embossed

**2008, June 6** *Perf. 14x13¼*
**427** V70 55c green & violet 2.00 2.00
**428** V71 €1.40 violet & green 5.00 5.00

Convention on the Rights of Persons with Disabilities.

### Sport for Peace Type of 2008

Designs: 65c, Man on rings. €1.30, €2.10, Swimmer.

**2008, Aug. 8** **Litho.** *Perf. 14½*
**429** A393 65c multicolored 2.25 2.25
**430** A393 €1.30 multicolored 4.50 4.50

### Souvenir Sheet

*Perf. 12¾x13¼*
**431** A393 €2.10 multicolored 9.00 9.00
*a.* Overprinted in sheet margin 10.00 10.00

2008 Summer Olympics, Beijing. No. 431a is overprinted in black "Peking 2008" and medals with UN emblem.

### "We Can End Poverty" Type of 2008

Winning designs in children's art contest: 65c, By Mariam Marukian, Armenia. 75c, By Rufaro Duri, Zimbabwe, vert.

*Perf. 12¾x12½*
**2008, Sept. 18** **Litho.**
**432** A395 65c multicolored 2.25 2.25

*Perf. 12½x12¾*
**433** A395 75c multicolored 2.60 2.60

Five €1.40 stamps depicting views of the Vienna International Center and its artwork were released Sept. 18, 2008. The editors have reason to believe that these stamps were not sold at the UN Post Office in Vienna. Value, strip of 5 with labels $40, sheet of 10 $80.

### Climate Change Types of New York and Geneva and

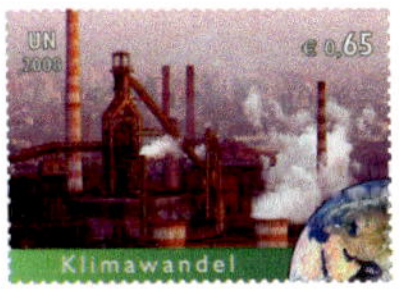


V72

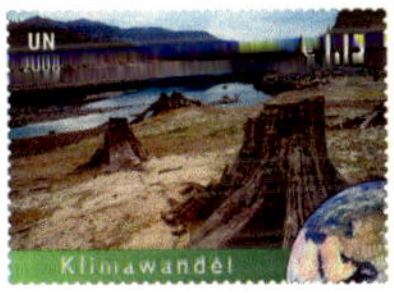


Climate Change
V73

No. 434 — Smokestacks with quarter of Earth in: a, LR. b, LL. c, UR. d, UL.

No. 435 — Cut trees with quarter of Earth in: a, LR. b, LL. c, UR. d, UL.

No. 436: a, Like New York #969a. b, Like New York #969b. c, Like New York #969c. d, Like New York #969d. e, Like Geneva #493a. f, Like Geneva #493b. g, Like Geneva #493c. h, Like Geneva #493d. i, Like Vienna #434a. j, Like Vienna #434b. k, Like Vienna #434c. l, Like Vienna #434d. m, Like New York #968a. n, Like New York #968b, o, Like New York #968c, p, Like New York #968d. q, Like Geneva #492a. r, Like Geneva #492b. s, Like Geneva #492c. t, Like Geneva #492d. u, Like Vienna #435a. v, Like Vienna #435b. w, Like Vienna #435c. x, Like Vienna #435d.

302 OFFICES IN VIENNA, AUSTRIA

All stamps have green panels inscribed "Klimawandel."

**2008, Oct. 23 Litho. *Perf. 13¼x13***

**434** Sheet of 4 9.00 9.00
*a.-d.* V72 65c Any single 2.25 2.25
**435** Sheet of 4 16.00 16.00
*a.-d.* V73 €1.15 Any single 4.00 4.00

### Souvenir Booklet

**436** Booklet, #436y-436ad 27.00
*a.-d.* A397 30c Any single 1.00 1.00
*e.-h.* G77 30c Any single 1.00 1.00
*i.-l.* V72 30c Any single 1.00 1.00
*m.-p.* A396 35c Any single 1.10 1.10
*q.-t.* G76 35c Any single 1.10 1.10
*u.-x.* V73 35c Any single 1.10 1.10
*y.* Booklet pane of 4, #436a-436d 4.25 4.25
*z.* Booklet pane of 4, #436e-436h 4.25 4.25
*aa.* Booklet pane of 4, #436i-436l 4.25 4.25
*ab.* Booklet pane of 4, #436m-436p 4.75 4.75
*ac.* Booklet pane of 4, #436q-436t 4.75 4.75
*ad.* Booklet pane of 4, #436u-436x 4.75 4.75

### U Thant Type of 2009

### Litho. With Foil Application

**2009, Feb. 6 *Perf. 14x13½***

**437** A399 €1.15 green & multi 4.50 4.50

### Endangered Species Type of 1993

Designs: No. 438, Trogonoptera brookiana. No. 439, Pandinus imperator. No. 440, Carabus intricatus. No. 441, Brachypelma smithi.

**2009, Apr. 16 Litho. *Perf. 12¾x12½***

**438** A271 65c multicolored 2.00 2.00
**439** A271 65c multicolored 2.00 2.00
**440** A271 65c multicolored 2.00 2.00
**441** A271 65c multicolored 2.00 2.00
*a.* Block of 4, #438-441 8.00 8.00

### World Heritage Sites, Germany Type of 2009

Designs: Nos. 442, 444c, Palaces and Parks of Potsdam and Berlin. Nos. 443, 444e, Luther Memorials in Eisleben and Wittenberg. No. 444a, Town Hall and Roland on the Marketplace, Bremen. No. 444b, Wartburg Castle. No. 444d, Aachen Cathedral. No. 444f, Monastic Island of Reichenau.

**2009, May 7 Litho. *Perf. 14x13½***

**442** A400 65c multicolored 1.90 1.90
**443** A400 €1.40 multicolored 4.00 4.00

### Souvenir Booklet

**444** Booklet, #444g-444l 20.00
*a.-c.* A400 30c any single .75 .75
*d.-f.* A400 35c any single .90 .90
*g.* Booklet pane of 4 #444a 3.00 3.00
*h.* Booklet pane of 4 #444b 3.00 3.00
*i.* Booklet pane of 4 #444c 3.00 3.00
*j.* Booklet pane of 4 #444d 3.60 3.60
*k.* Booklet pane of 4 #444e 3.60 3.60
*l.* Booklet pane of 4 #444f 3.60 3.60

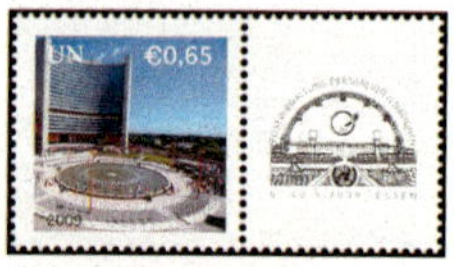

Memorial Plaza, Vienna International Center — V74

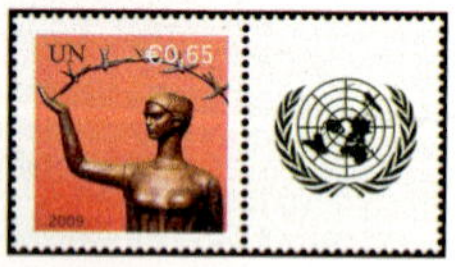

The First Swallows, Sculpture by Juozas Mikenas V75

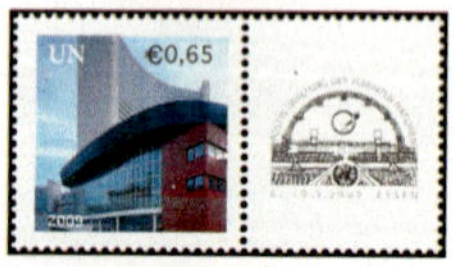

Conference Building, Vienna International Center — V76

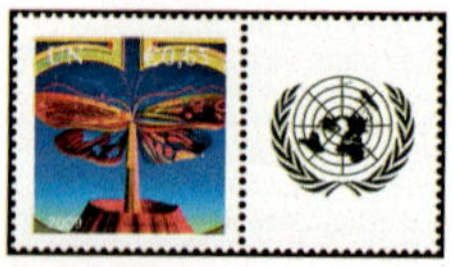

Butterfly Tree, by Rudolf Hausner V77

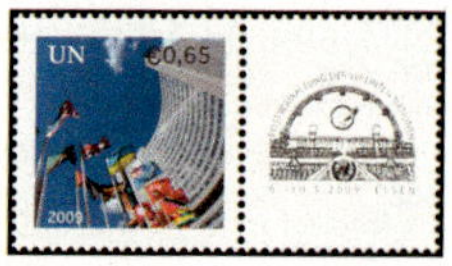

Flags in Memorial Plaza V78

**2009, May 7 *Perf. 13¼***

**445** V74 65c multi + label *5.00 5.00*
*a.* Perf. 11¼x11 *10.00 10.00*
**446** V75 65c multi + label *5.00 5.00*
*a.* Perf. 11¼x11 *10.00 10.00*
**447** V76 65c multi + label *5.00 5.00*
*a.* Perf. 11¼x11 *10.00 10.00*
**448** V77 65c multi + label *5.00 5.00*
*a.* Perf. 11¼x11 *10.00 10.00*
**449** V78 65c multi + label *5.00 5.00*
*a.* Perf. 11¼x11 *10.00 10.00*
*b.* Vert. strip of 5, #445-449, + 5 labels *25.00 25.00*
*c.* Vert. strip of 5, #445a-449a, + 5 labels *50.00 50.00*

The sheet of No. 449c has "ver. 2" in the lower right selvage.

### Economic and Social Council (ECOSOC) Type of 2009

Designs: 55c, Combat HIV/AIDS, malaria and other diseases. 65c, Reduce child mortality.

**2009, Aug. 6 Litho. *Perf. 12¾x12½***

**450** A411 55c multicolored 2.25 2.25
**451** A411 65c multicolored 3.50 3.50

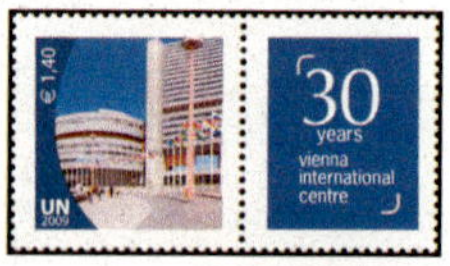


V79

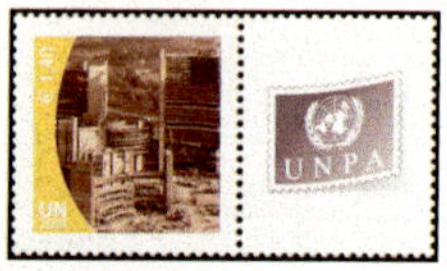

V80

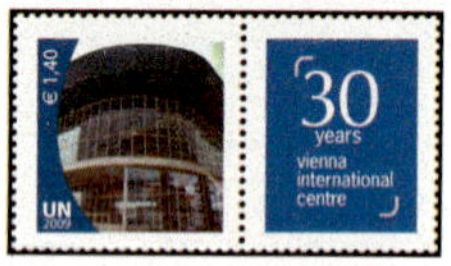


V81

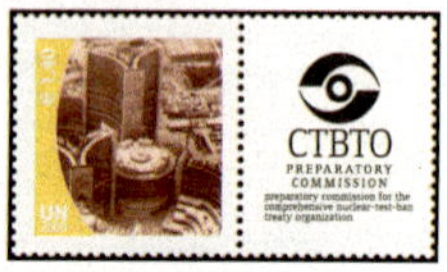


V82

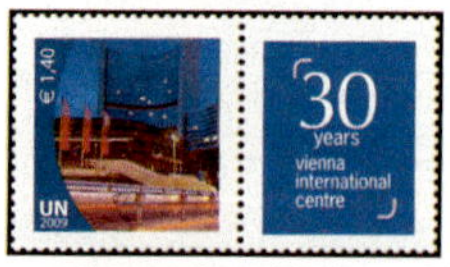


Vienna International Center, 30th Anniv. — V83

**2009, Aug. 24 *Perf. 13¼***

**452** V79 €1.40 multi + label *6.00 6.00*
*a.* Perf. 11¼x11 *20.00 20.00*
**453** V80 €1.40 multi + label *6.00 6.00*
*a.* Perf. 11¼x11 *20.00 20.00*
**454** V81 €1.40 multi + label *6.00 6.00*
*a.* Perf. 11¼x11 *20.00 20.00*
**455** V82 €1.40 multi + label *6.00 6.00*
*a.* Perf. 11¼x11 *20.00 20.00*
**456** V83 €1.40 multi + label *6.00 6.00*
*a.* Perf. 11¼x11 *20.00 20.00*
*b.* Vert. strip of 5, #452-456, + 5 labels *30.00 30.00*
*c.* Vert. strip of 5, #452a-456a, + 5 labels *100.00 100.00*

The sheet of No. 456c has "ver. 2" in the lower right selvage.

### Millennium Development Goals Type of 2009

Miniature Sheet

No. 457: a, Bowl of hot food. b, Pencil. c, Female symbol. d, Teddy bear. e, Pregnant woman, heart. f, Medicine bottle. g, Stylized tree. h, Conjoined people.

**2009, Sept. 25**

**457** A413 Sheet of 8 16.00 16.00
*a.-h.* 65c Any single 2.00 2.00

Miniature Sheet

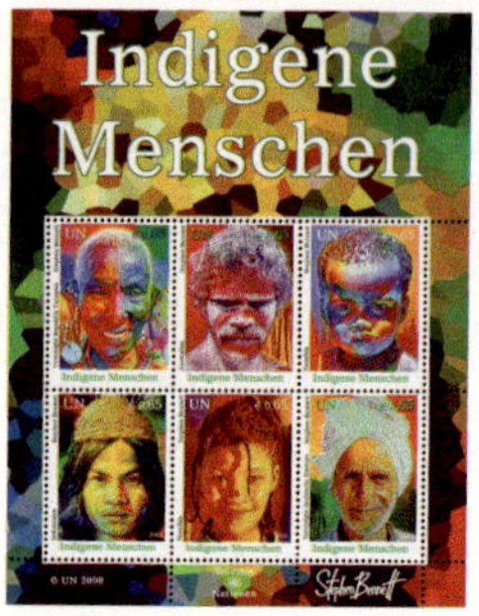


Indigenous People — V84

No. 458 — Portraits of person from: a, Tanzania. b, Australia. c, Namibia (small child). d, Indonesia. e, Namibia (young girl). f, Untied Arab Emirates.

**2009, Oct. 8 *Perf. 12½***

**458** V84 Sheet of 6 12.00 12.00
*a.-f.* 65c Any single 2.00 2.00

### Flags and Coins Type of 2006

No. 459 — Flag of: a, Romania, 1 ban coin. b, Slovenia, 5 cent coin. c, Azerbaijan, 10 giapik coin. d, Bangladesh, 5 taka coin. e, Belarus, 1 ruble coin. f, Malta, 1 euro coin. g, Swaziland, 1 lilangeni coin. h, Jordan, 10 piaster coin.

**2010, Feb. 5 Litho. *Perf. 13¼x13***

**459** Sheet of 8 16.00 16.00
*a.-h.* A375 65c Any single 2.00 2.00

A column of rouletting in the middle of the sheet separates it into two parts.

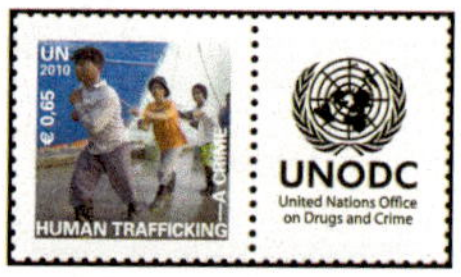


People Pulling Rope V85

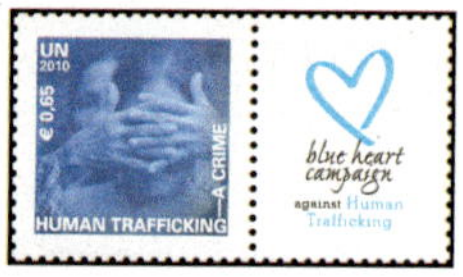


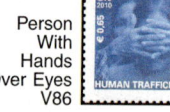

Person With Hands Over Eyes V86

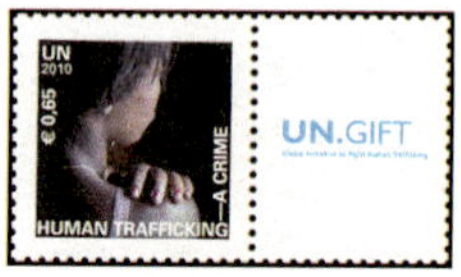


Woman Touching Her Shoulder V87

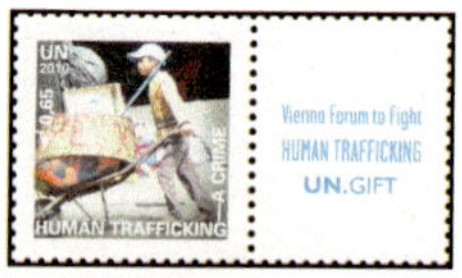


Man With Wheelbarrow — V88

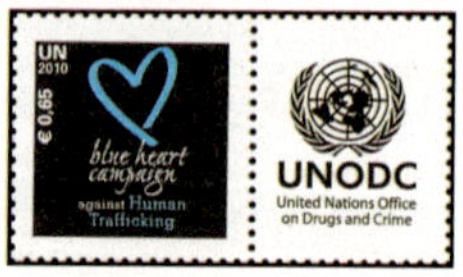


Blue Heart V89

Designed by Rorie Katz, US.

**2010, Feb. 5 Litho. *Perf. 11¼x11***

**460** V85 65c multi + label *4.50 4.50*
**461** V86 65c multi + label *4.50 4.50*
**462** V87 65c multi + label *4.50 4.50*
**463** V88 65c multi + label *4.50 4.50*
**464** V89 65c multi + label *4.50 4.50*
*a.* Vert. strip of 5, #460-464, + 5 labels *22.50 22.50*

The full sheet sold for $14.95 or €19.90. The labels could not be personalized.

### Endangered Species Type of 1993

Designs: No. 465, Mammillaria zeilmanniana. No. 466, Hoodia gordonii. No. 467, Welwitschia mirabilis. No. 468, Euphorbia milii.

**2010, Apr. 15 Litho. *Perf. 12¾x12½***

**465** A271 65c multicolored 2.25 2.25
**466** A271 65c multicolored 2.25 2.25
**467** A271 65c multicolored 2.25 2.25
**468** A271 65c multicolored 2.25 2.25
*a.* Block of 4, #465-468 9.00 9.00

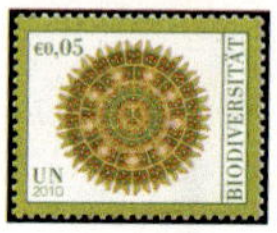


Intl. Year of Biodiversity — V90

Drawings from Art Forms from Nature, by Ernst Heinrich: 5c, Colonial algae. 20c, Boxfish.

**2010, Apr. 15 Litho. *Perf. 13***

**469** V90 5c multicolored .25 .25
**470** V90 20c multicolored .70 .70

### One Planet, One Ocean Types of New York and Geneva and

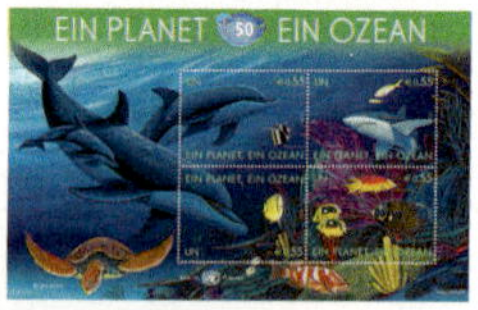


V91

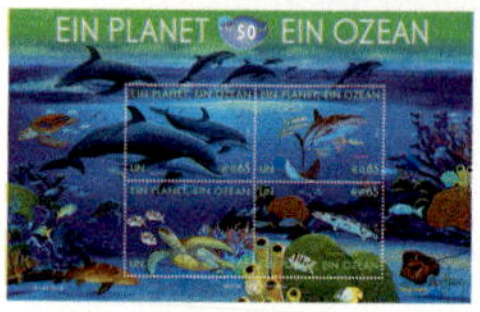


V92

No. 471: a, Dolphin at left, fish at right. b, Fish at top, shark in center. c, Dolphin at left, fish at right and bottom. d, Fish at left, top and right.

No. 472: a, Dolphins. b, Shark and fish at center, ray at bottom. c, Fish at left, turtle at bottom. d, Fish and coral.

No. 473: a, Like New York #1003a. b, Like New York #1003b, c, Like New York #1003c, d, Like New York #1003d. e, Like #471a. f, Like #471b. g, Like #471c, h, Like #471d. i, Like Geneva #519a. j, Like Geneva #519b, k, Like Geneva #519c. l, Like Geneva #519d. m, Like New York #1004a. n, Like New York #1004b. o, Like New York #1004c, p, Like New York #1004d. q, Like #472a. r, Like #472b. s, Like #472c. t, Like #472d. u, Like Geneva #520a. v, Like Geneva #520b. w, Like Geneva #520c. x, Like Geneva #520d.

**2010, May 6 Litho. *Perf. 14x13¼***

**471** V91 Sheet of 4 7.75 7.75
*a.-d.* 55c Any single 1.90 1.90
**472** V92 Sheet of 4 9.00 9.00
*a.-d.* 65c Any single 2.25 2.25

### Souvenir Booklet

***Perf. 13¼x13***

**473** Booklet, #473y-473z, 473aa-473ad 27.00
*a.-d.* A416 30c any single 1.00 1.00
*e.-h.* V91 30c any single 1.00 1.00
*i.-l.* G85 30c any single 1.00 1.00
*m.-p.* A417 35c any single 1.25 1.25
*q.-t.* V92 35c any single 1.25 1.25
*u.-x.* G86 35c any single 1.25 1.25
*y.* Booklet pane of 4 #473a-473d 4.00 4.00
*z.* Booklet pane of 4 #473e-473h 4.00 4.00
*aa.* Booklet pane of 4 #473i-473l 4.00 4.00
*ab.* Booklet pane of 4 #473m-473p 5.00 5.00
*ac.* Booklet pane of 4 #473q-473t 5.00 5.00
*ad.* Booklet pane of 4 #473u-473x 5.00 5.00

Intl. Oceanographic Commission, 50th anniv.

### United Nations, 65th Anniv. Type of 2010

### Litho. With Foil Application

**2010, June 28 *Perf. 13¼***

**474** A422 75c green & gold 3.00 3.00
*a.* Souvenir sheet of 2 6.00 6.00

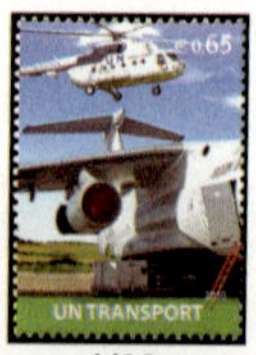


V93

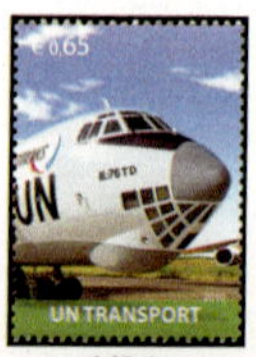


V94

OFFICES IN VIENNA, AUSTRIA 303

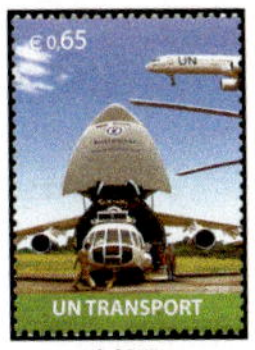


V95

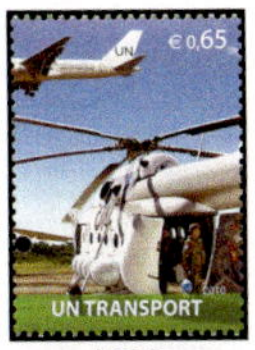


V96

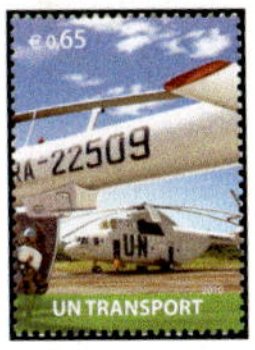


V97

**2010, Sept. 2 Litho. *Perf. 13¼x13***

| | | | | |
|---|---|---|---|---|
| 475 | V93 | 65c multicolored | 1.90 | 1.90 |
| 476 | V94 | 65c multicolored | 1.90 | 1.90 |
| 477 | V95 | 65c multicolored | 1.90 | 1.90 |
| 478 | V96 | 65c multicolored | 1.90 | 1.90 |
| 479 | V97 | 65c multicolored | 1.90 | 1.90 |
| *a.* | | Horiz. strip of 5, #475-479 | 9.50 | 9.50 |

Miniature Sheet

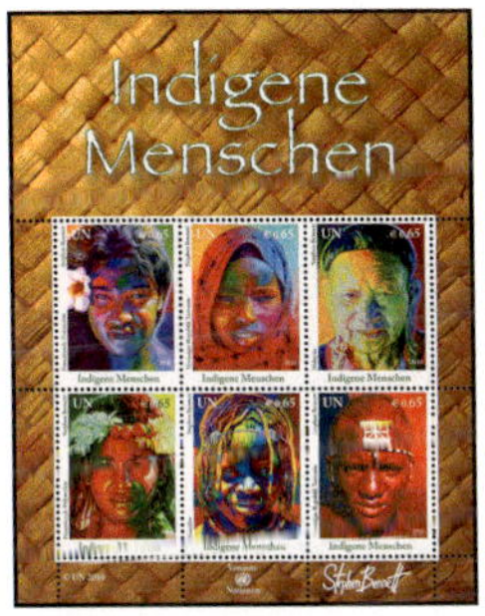


Indigenous People — V98

No. 480 — Portraits of person from: a, French Polynesia (denomination in white). b, Tanzania (child with cloth head covering). c, Malaysia. d, French Polynesia (denomination in white and green). e, Namibia. f, Tanzania (man with band around forehead).

**2010, Oct. 21 Litho. *Perf. 13***

| | | | | |
|---|---|---|---|---|
| 480 | V98 | Pane of 6 | 11.50 | 11.50 |
| *a.-f.* | | 65c Any single | 1.90 | 1.90 |

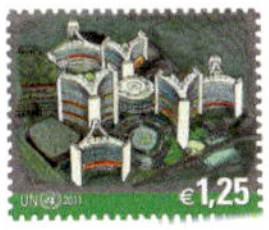

United Nations Headquarters, Vienna — V99

United Nations Headquarters, Geneva: €1.25, Aerial view. €2.85, Ground-level view.

**2011, Feb. 4 Litho. *Perf. 13***

| | | | | |
|---|---|---|---|---|
| 481 | V99 | €1.25 multicolored | 3.75 | 3.75 |
| 482 | V99 | €2.85 multicolored | 8.25 | 8.25 |

### Flags and Coins Type of 2006

No. 483 — Flag of: a, Lithuania, 2 lita coin. b, Greece, 1 euro coin. c, Kyrgyzstan, 50 tyiyn coin. d, Oman, 100 baisa coin. e, Estonia, 2 euro coin. f, Czech Republic, 5 koruna coin. g, Uzbekistan, 100 som coin. h, Monaco, 1 euro coin.

**2011, Mar. 3 Litho. *Perf. 13¼x13***

| | | | | |
|---|---|---|---|---|
| 483 | | Sheet of 8 | 15.00 | 15.00 |
| *a.-h.* | A375 | 65c Any single | 1.75 | 1.75 |

A column of rouletting in the middle of the sheet separates it into two parts.

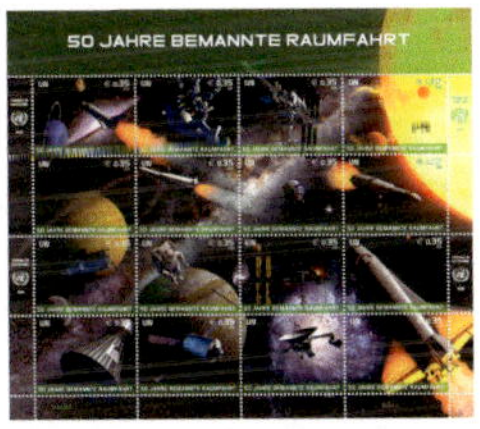


Human Space Flight, 50th Anniv. V100

No. 484: Various parts of outer space scene.

No. 485, vert.: a, Space Shuttle. b, Space Station.

**2011, Apr. 12 Litho. *Perf. 13x13¼***

| | | | | |
|---|---|---|---|---|
| 484 | V100 | Sheet of 16 | 16.50 | 16.50 |
| *a.-p.* | | 35c any single | 1.00 | 1.00 |

**Souvenir Sheet**

| | | | | |
|---|---|---|---|---|
| 485 | V100 | Sheet of 2 | 12.00 | 12.00 |
| *a.* | | 55c multi | 5.50 | 5.50 |
| *b.* | | 65c multi | 6.50 | 6.50 |
| *c.* | | Souvenir sheet of 6, New York #1025a-1025b, Geneva #534a-b, Vienna #485a-485b | 42.50 | 42.50 |

No. 485 contains two 40x48mm stamps that were printed as part of a larger sheet of six stamps, No. 485c, which was broken up into its component two-stamp souvenir sheets, and also sold as one unit. Value $90, complete unit.

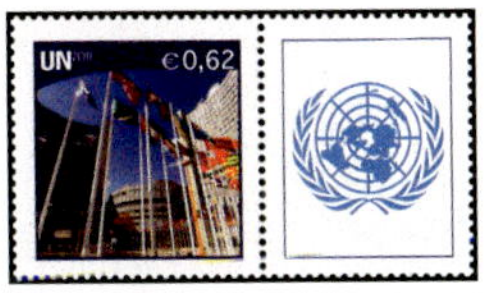

Vienna International Center and Flagpoles — V101

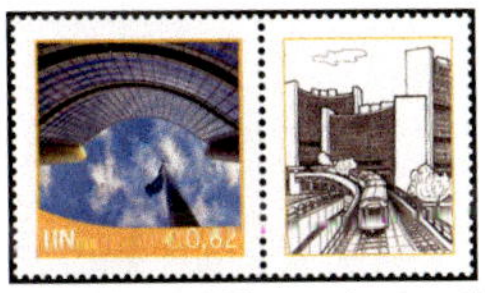

Fish-eye View of Vienna International Center and Flagpole — V102

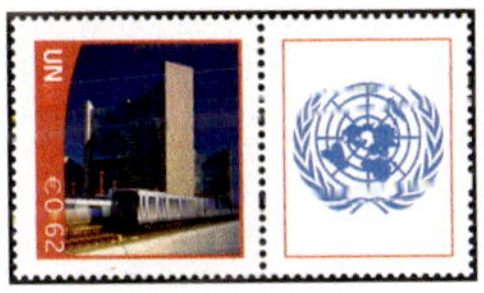

Vienna International Center and Train — V103

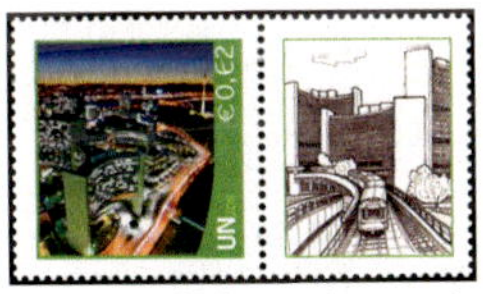

Aerial View of Vienna International Center — V104

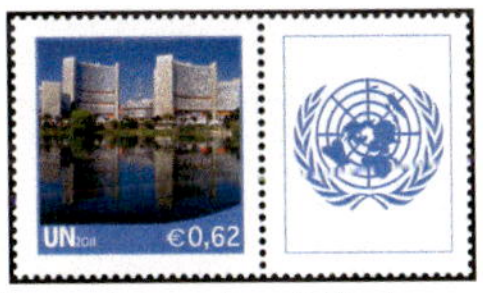

Vienna International Center and Water — V105

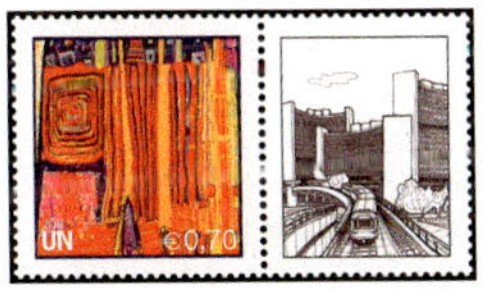

Detail From La Pioggia, Stadt Unter de Regen, by Friedensreich Hundertwasser — V106

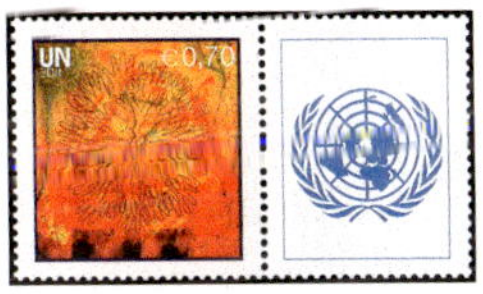

Hand In Hand, by Hans Dietrich V107

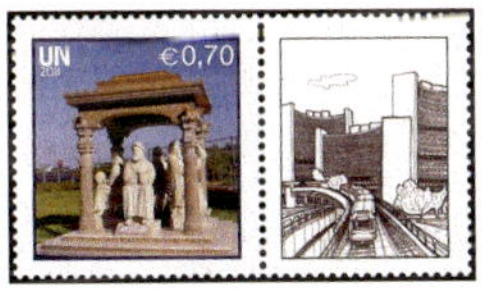

The Scholars Pavilion V108

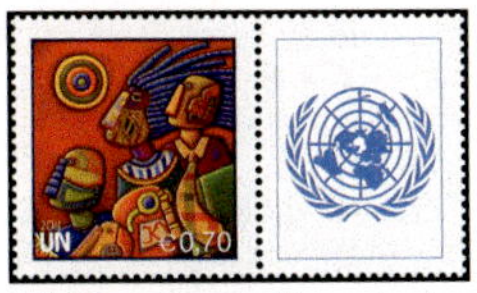

Detail From Grupo Expectante, by Alfredo Sosabravo — V109

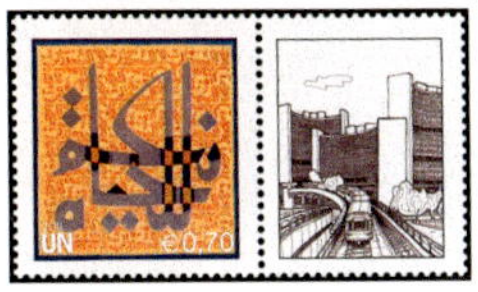

Yes to Life, No to Drugs, by Sami Burhan V110

**2011, May 1 Litho. *Perf. 14¾***

| | | | | |
|---|---|---|---|---|
| 486 | V101 | 62c multi + label | *2.50* | *2.50* |
| 487 | V102 | 62c multi + label | *2.50* | *2.50* |
| 488 | V103 | 62c multi + label | *2.50* | *2.50* |
| 489 | V104 | 62c multi + label | *2.50* | *2.50* |
| 490 | V105 | 62c multi + label | *2.50* | *2.50* |
| *a.* | | Vert. strip of 5, #486-490, + 5 labels | *15.00* | *15.00* |
| 491 | V106 | 70c multi + label | *3.00* | *3.00* |
| 492 | V107 | 70c multi + label | *3.00* | *3.00* |
| 493 | V108 | 70c multi + label | *3.00* | *3.00* |
| 494 | V109 | 70c multi + label | *3.00* | *3.00* |
| 495 | V110 | 70c multi + label | *3.00* | *3.00* |
| *a.* | | Vert. strip of 5, #491-495, + 5 labels | *17.50* | *17.50* |
| | | *Nos. 486-495 (10)* | *25.50* | *25.50* |

The full sheet of Nos. 486-490 sold for $21.45 or €12.40. The full sheet of Nos. 491-495 sold for $14.26 or €9.90. The labels could be personalized.

### UNESCO World Heritage Sites in Nordic Countries Type of 2011

Designs: 62c, Urnes Stave Church, Norway. 1fr, Struve Geodetic Arc, Norway, Finland and Sweden.

**2011, May 5 Litho. *Perf. 14x13½***

| | | | | |
|---|---|---|---|---|
| 496 | A433 | 62c multicolored | 1.90 | 1.90 |
| 497 | A433 | 70c multicolored | 2.10 | 2.10 |

### AIDS Ribbon Type of 2011

**2011, June 3 Litho. *Die Cut***

**Self-Adhesive**

| | | | | |
|---|---|---|---|---|
| 498 | A434 | 70c red & green | 2.40 | 2.40 |

### ECOSOC Type of 2011

**2011, July 1 Litho. *Perf. 14¼***

| | | | | |
|---|---|---|---|---|
| 499 | A435 | 62c multicolored | 3.00 | 3.00 |
| 500 | A435 | 70c multicolored | 4.00 | 4.00 |

### Endangered Species Type of 1993

Designs: No. 501, Cyanoramphus novaezelandiae (Red-fronted parakeet). No. 502, Haliaeetus albicilla (White-tailed eagle). No. 503, Probosciger aterrimus (Black palm cockatoo). No. 504, Caloenas nicobarica (Nicobar pigeon).

**2011, Sept. 7 Litho. *Perf. 12¾x12½***

| | | | | |
|---|---|---|---|---|
| 501 | A271 | 70c multicolored | 2.50 | 2.50 |
| 502 | A271 | 70c multicolored | 2.50 | 2.50 |
| 503 | A271 | 70c multicolored | 2.50 | 2.50 |
| 504 | A271 | 70c multicolored | 2.50 | 2.50 |
| *a.* | | Block of 4, #501-504 | 10.00 | 10.00 |

### Intl. Year of Forests Type of 2011

Designs: 62c, Tree top, crosses, circles and ovals. 70c, Stylized people and trees.

**Litho. With Foil Application**

**2011, Oct. 13 *Perf. 12½***

| | | | | |
|---|---|---|---|---|
| 505 | | 62c multicolored | 2.00 | 2.00 |
| 506 | | 70c multicolored | 2.25 | 2.25 |
| *a.* | A436 | Vert. pair, #505-506 | 4.25 | 4.25 |

### Flags and Coins Type of 2006

No. 507 — Flag of: a, Cameroun, 100 franc coin. b, Samoa, 2 tala coin. c, Surinam, 5 cent coin. d, Macedonia, 50 denar coin. e, Bulgaria, 50 stotinka coin. f, Tanzania, 100 shilling coin. g, Finland, 1 euro coin. h, Cuba, 1 peso coin.

**2012, Feb. 3 Litho. *Perf. 13¼x13***

| | | | | |
|---|---|---|---|---|
| 507 | | Sheet of 8 | 16.50 | 16.50 |
| *a.-h.* | A375 | 70c Any single | 2.00 | 2.00 |

A column of rouletting in the middle of the sheet separates it into two parts.

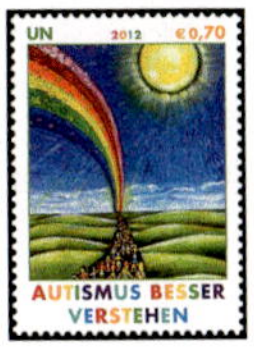


V111

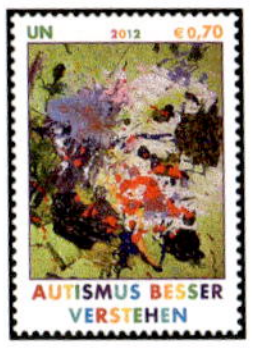


Autism Awareness — V112

Drawings by autistic people: No. 508, The Path, by Ryan Smoluk, Canada. No. 509, Untitled drawing, by Colm Isherwood, Ireland.

**2012, Apr. 2 Litho. *Perf. 14x13½***

| | | | | |
|---|---|---|---|---|
| 508 | V111 | 70c multicolored | 2.25 | 2.25 |
| 509 | V112 | 70c multicolored | 2.25 | 2.25 |
| *a.* | | Pair, #508-509 | 4.50 | 4.50 |

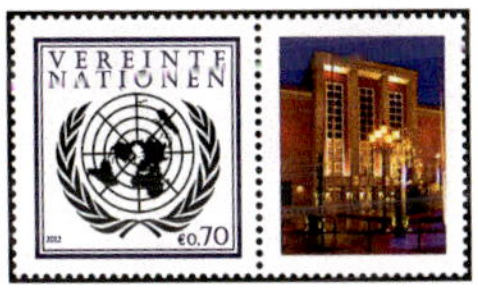


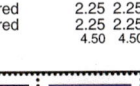

UN Emblem V113

**2012, Apr. 12 Litho. *Perf. 14½***

| | | | | |
|---|---|---|---|---|
| 510 | V113 | 70c pur, blk + label | *3.50* | *3.50* |
| | | Sheet of 10 + 10 labels | *35.00* | *35.00* |

The full sheet sold for $14.52 or €9.90. The labels could be personalized.

### Endangered Species Type of 1993

Designs: No. 511, Panthera uncia. No. 512, Polyplectron schleiermacheri. No. 513, Tyto novaehollandiae. No. 514, Ambystoma mexicanum.

**2012, Apr. 19 Litho. *Perf. 12¾x12½***

| | | | | |
|---|---|---|---|---|
| 511 | A271 | 70c multicolored | 2.25 | 2.25 |
| 512 | A271 | 70c multicolored | 2.25 | 2.25 |
| 513 | A271 | 70c multicolored | 2.25 | 2.25 |
| 514 | A271 | 70c multicolored | 2.25 | 2.25 |
| *a.* | | Block of 4, #511-514 | 9.00 | 9.00 |

### Rio + 20 Type of 2012

**2012, June 1 Litho. *Perf. 13x13¼***

| | | | | |
|---|---|---|---|---|
| 515 | A443 | 70c multicolored | 2.10 | 2.10 |

### Sport for Peace Type of 2012

**Litho. With Foil Application**

**2012, Aug. 17 *Perf. 14½***

| | | | | |
|---|---|---|---|---|
| 516 | A444 | 62c multicolored | 1.00 | 1.90 |
| 517 | A444 | 70c multicolored | 2.10 | 2.10 |
| *a.* | | Souvenir sheet of 1 | 2.10 | 2.10 |

### UNESCO World Heritage Sites in Africa Type of 2012

Designs: 62c, Kenya Lake System, Kenya. 70c, Medina of Marrakesh, Morocco.

**2012, Sept. 5 Litho. *Perf. 13¼***

| | | | | |
|---|---|---|---|---|
| 518 | A445 | 62c multicolored | 1.75 | 1.75 |
| 519 | A445 | 70c multicolored | 2.00 | 2.00 |

Miniature Sheet

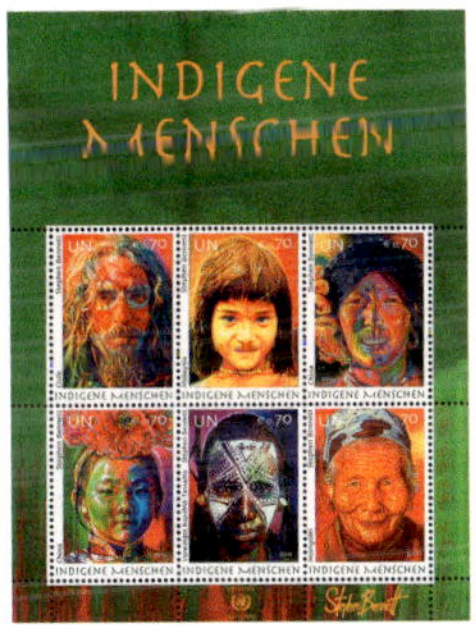


Indigenous People — V114

No. 520 — Portrait of person from: a, Chile. b, Malaysia. c, China (woman with black hair). d, China (woman with flower in hair). e, Tanzania. f, Mongolia.

**2012, Oct. 11 Litho. *Perf. 13¼x13***

| | | | | |
|---|---|---|---|---|
| 520 | V114 | Sheet of 6 | 11.50 | 11.50 |
| *a.-f.* | | 70c Any single | 1.90 | 1.90 |

304 OFFICES IN VIENNA, AUSTRIA

### World Radio Day Type of 2013

Designs: 70c, Microphone and scripts. €1.70, Boy with radio.

**2013, Feb. 13 Litho. *Perf. 13¼x13***
**521** A448 70c multicolored 2.00 2.00
**522** A448 €1.70 multicolored 5.00 5.00

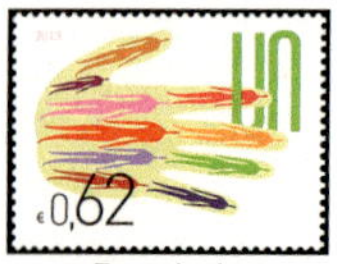
People in Handprint — V115

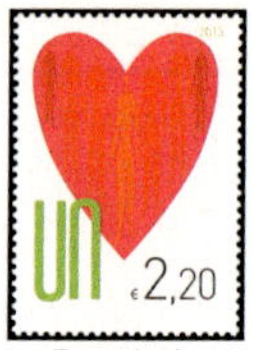
People in Heart — V116

**2013, Mar. 5 Litho. *Perf. 14x13½***
**523** V115 62c multicolored 1.90 1.90
***Perf. 13½x14***
**524** V116 €2.20 multicolored 6.50 6.50

### World Heritage Sites, China, Type of 2013

Designs: Nos. 525, 527c, Great Wall of China. Nos. 526, 527f, Mausoleum of the First Qing Emperor. No. 527a, Mogao Caves. No. 527b, Potala Palace, Lhasa. No. 527d, Imperial Palace, Beijing. No. 527e, Mount Huangshan.

**2013, Apr. 11 Litho. *Perf. 14x13½***
**525** A452 70c multicolored 2.00 2.00
**526** A452 €1.70 multicolored 5.00 5.00

**Souvenir Booklet**

**527** Booklet, #527g-527l 25.00
*a.-c.* A452 30c any single .85 .85
*d.-f.* A452 40c any single 1.10 1.10
*g.* Booklet pane of 4 #527a 3.50 —
*h.* Booklet pane of 4 #527b 3.50 —
*i.* Booklet pane of 4 #527c 3.50 —
*j.* Booklet pane of 4 #527d 4.75 —
*k.* Booklet pane of 4 #527e 4.75 —
*l.* Booklet pane of 4 #527f 4.75 —

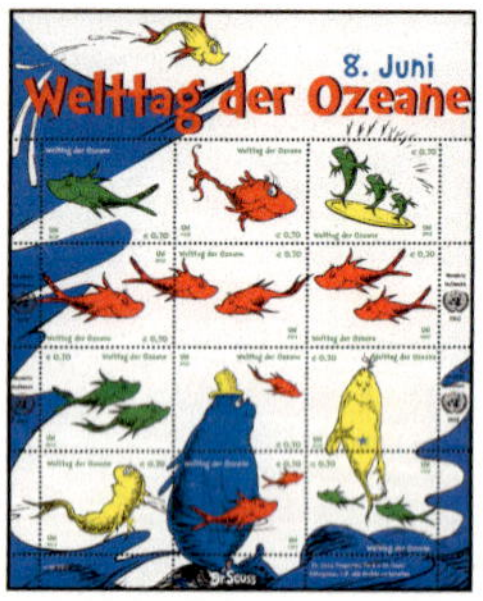

World Oceans Day V117

No. 528 — Fish from *One Fish, Two Fish, Red Fish, Blue Fish,* by Dr. Seuss: a, Green fish facing left, wave. b, Red fish facing right. c, Three green fish on plate. d, Red fish, back half of red fish, wave. e, Red fish facing left, front half of red fish facing right. f, Two red fish facing left. g, Two green fish facing right, wave. h, Red fish facing right, head of blue fish wearing hat. i, Yellow fish with green star, wave. j, Yellow fish, back of blue fish, wave. k, Two red fish, body of blue fish. l, Tail of yellow fish, two green fish facing left, wave.

**2013, May 31 Litho. *Perf. 13***
**528** V117 Sheet of 12 24.00 24.00
*a.-l.* 70c any single 2.00 2.00

### Nebulae Type of 2013

Designs: No. 567, NGC 2346. No. 568, Sh 2-106.
1fr, Messier 16.

**2013, Aug. 9 Litho. *Perf. 13¼***
**529** A454 €1.70 multicolored 5.00 5.00
**530** A454 €1.70 multicolored 5.00 5.00
*a.* Pair, #529-530 10.00 10.00

**Souvenir Sheet**

**531** A454 62c multicolored 1.90 1.90

No. 531 contains one 44x44mm stamp.

### Works of Disabled Artists Type of 2013

Designs: 70c, Electro Man, by Pete Eckert, U.S. €1.70, Dive Bomb, by Matt Sesow, U.S.

**2013, Sept. 20 Litho. *Perf. 13¼x13***
**532** A456 70c multicolored 2.00 2.00
**533** A456 €1.70 multicolored 5.00 5.00

### Endangered Species Type of 1993

Designs: No. 534, Hemigalus derbyanus. No. 535, Bubo ascalaphus. No. 536, Nycticebus coucang. No. 537, Zaglossus spp.

**2013, Oct. 10 Litho. *Perf. 12¾x12½***
**534** A271 70c multicolored 2.00 2.00
**535** A271 70c multicolored 2.00 2.00
**536** A271 70c multicolored 2.00 2.00
**537** A271 70c multicolored 2.00 2.00
*a.* Block of 4, #534-537 8.00 8.00

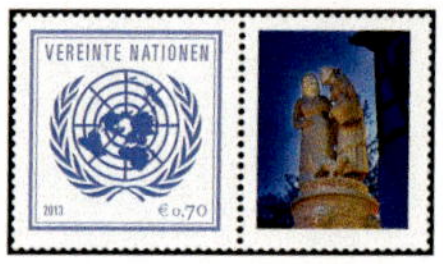

UN Emblem V118

**2013, Oct. 24 Litho. *Perf. 14½***
**538** V118 70c gray blue & blue + label *4.00 4.00*

The full sheet sold for $14.20 or €9.90. The labels could be personalized.

### Flags and Coins Type of 2006

No. 539 — Flag of: a, Malaysia, 50 sen coin. b, Nigeria, 1 naira coin. c, Zambia, 20 ngwee coin. d, Togo, 100 franc coin. e, Dominica, 5 cent coin. f, Chad, 100 franc coin. g, St. Vincent and the Grenadines, 5 cent coin. h, Syria, 25 pound coin.

**2013, Nov. 6 Litho. *Perf. 13¼x13***
**539** Sheet of 8 16.00 16.00
*a.-h.* A375 70c Any single 2.00 2.00

A column of rouletting in the middle of the sheet separates it into two parts.

### International Day of Happiness Type of 2014

Designs: 90c, Happy Asian Boy at the Park, photograph by Alan Levenson, Russian word for "Happy." €1.70, Barbary Macacque with Baby, photograph by Gerhard Schulz, Arabic word for "Happy."

**2014, Mar. 17 Litho. *Perf. 13¼x13***
**540** A459 90c multicolored 2.75 2.75
**541** A459 €1.70 multicolored 5.25 5.25

**Miniature Sheet**

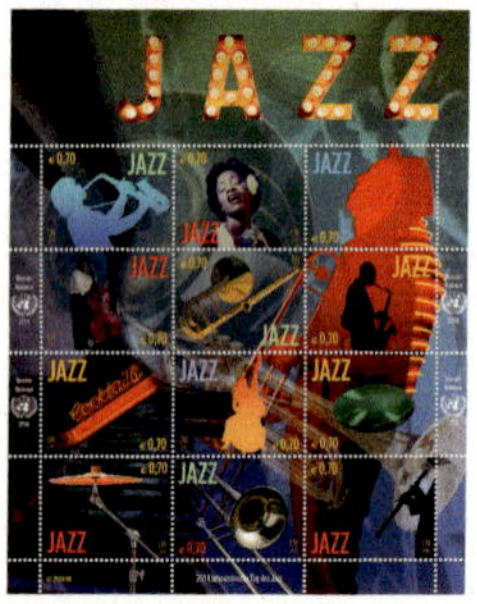

International Year of Jazz — V119

No. 542: a, Silhouette of saxophonist in blue. b, Woman singing. c, Silhouette of man in red, neon lights. d, Bass player. e, Trombone in gold. f, Silhouette of saxophonist in black, silhouette of man holding trombone. g, "Cocktails" neon sign . h, Silhouette of bass player in orange. i, Stack of record albums. j, Cymbal. k, Trombone in silver. l, Silhouette of clarinetist in black.

**2014, Apr. 30 Litho. *Perf. 13x13¼***
**542** V119 Sheet of 12 24.00 24.00
*a.-l.* 70c Any single 2.00 2.00

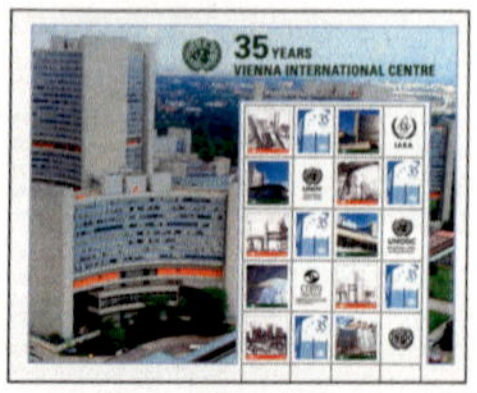
Vienna International Center, 35th Anniv. — V120

No. 543: a, Vienna International Center under construction (towers and shadows), red panel. b, Vienna International Center, street light at left, green panel. c, Vienna International Center, curved building at left, green panel. d, Vienna International Center under construction (arch in foreground, cranes at right), red panel. e, Vienna International Center under construction (cranes at left, center and right), red panel. f, Doorway to Vienna International Center, green panel. g, View of curved buildings of Vienna International Center looking up from ground, green panel. h, Vienna International Center under construction (two cranes on central tower), red panel. i, Completed Vienna International Center, red panel. j, Flags in front of Vienna International Center.

**2014, May 8 Litho. *Perf. 14¾***
**543** V120 Sheet of 10 + 10 labels *30.00 30.00*
*a.-j.* 70c Any single + label *3.00 3.00*

The full sheet sold for $14.80 or €9.90. The generic labels are shown. Labels could be personalized.

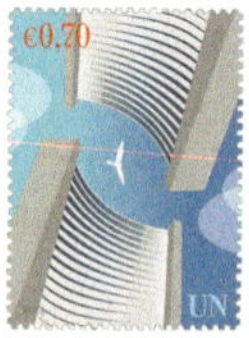
V121

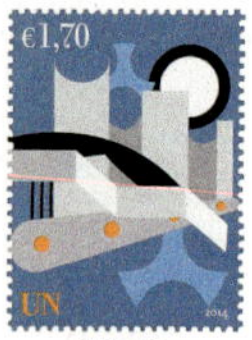
V122

Printed by Lowe-Martin Group, Canada. Panes of 20. Designed by Sergio Baradat, U.S.

**2014, June 6 Litho. *Perf. 13¼x13***
**544** V121 70c multicolored 2.10 2.10
**545** V122 €1.70 multicolored 5.25 5.25

### Taj Mahal Types of 2014

**2014, July 16 Engr. *Perf. 13¼x13***
**546** A466 90c multicolored 2.75 2.75
**547** A468 €1.70 multicolored 5.25 5.25

**Souvenir Booklet**

**548** Booklet, #548g-548l 25.00
*a.* A463 30c multi .85 .85
*b.* A465 30c multi .85 .85
*c.* A466 30c multi .85 .85
*d.* A464 40c multi 1.20 1.20
*e.* A467 40c multi 1.20 1.20
*f.* A468 40c multi 1.20 1.20
*g.* Booklet pane of 4 #548a 3.40 —
*h.* Booklet pane of 4 #548b 3.40 —
*i.* Booklet pane of 4 #548c 3.40 —
*j.* Booklet pane of 4 #548d 4.80 —
*k.* Booklet pane of 4 #548e 4.80 —
*l.* Booklet pane of 4 #548f 4.80 —

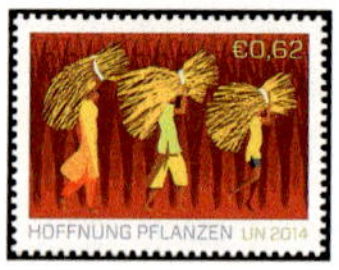

International Year of Family Farming — V123

**2014, Aug. 21 Litho. *Perf. 13x13¼***
**549** V123 62c multi 1.90 1.90
**550** V123 €1.70 multi 5.25 5.25

### Global Education First Initiative Type of 2014

Designs: €1.70, Children boarding school bus. €2, Tree growing from book held by students.

**2014, Sept. 18 Litho. *Perf. 13x13¼***
**551** A470 €1.70 multicolored 5.25 5.25

**Souvenir Sheet**
***Perf. 12½***

**552** A470 €2 multicolored 6.00 6.00

No. 552 contains one 32x32mm stamp.

### Endangered Species Type of 2014

Maps and: No. 553, Cheilinus undulatus. No. 554, Carcharodon carcharias. No. 555, Manta birostris. No. 556, Polyodon spathula.

**2014, Oct. 23 Litho. *Perf. 12¾x12½***
**553** A471 70c multicolored 2.10 2.10
**554** A471 70c multicolored 2.10 2.10
**555** A471 70c multicolored 2.10 2.10
**556** A471 70c multicolored 2.10 2.10
*a.* Block of 4, #553-556 8.50 8.50

**Miniature Sheet**

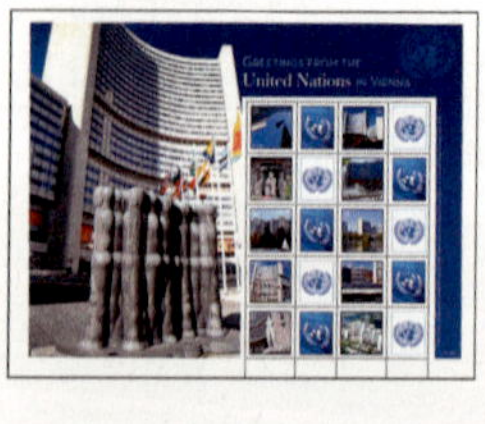
V124

No. 557: a, Flag on pole as seen from base of pole. b, Vienna International Center, structure in shadow at bottom. c, Persian Scholars Pavilion. d, Vienna International Center and fountain. e, Sailboat and Vienna International Center. f, Rowboat on water near Vienna International Center. g, Vienna International Center, flags and sculpture. h, Entrance to Vienna International Center. i, Woman Free sculpture near Vienna International Center. j, Aerial view of Vienna International Center.

**2015, Jan. 23 Litho. *Perf. 14¾***
**557** V124 Sheet of 10 *30.00 30.00*
*a.-j.* 80c Any single + label *3.00 3.00*

The full sheet sold for $15 or €10.90. The generic labels are shown. Labels could be personalized.

### Flags and Coins Type of 2006

No. 558 — Flag of: a, Tuvalu, 10 cent coin. b, Malawi, 1 kwacha coin. c, Iraq, 50 dinar coin. d, St. Thomas and Prince Islands, 250 dobra coin. e, Botswana, 10 thebe coin. f, Uruguay, 5 peso coin. g, Bosnia and Herzegovina, 20 pfennig coin. h, Somalia, 25 shilling coin.

**2015, Feb. 6 Litho. *Perf. 13¼x13***
**558** Sheet of 8 18.00 18.00
*a.-h.* A375 80c Any single 2.25 2.25

A column of rouletting in the middle of the sheet separates it into two parts.

**Miniature Sheets**

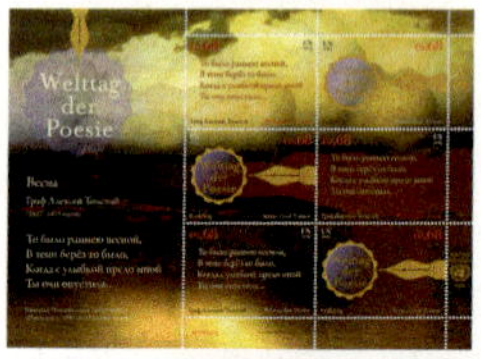
V125

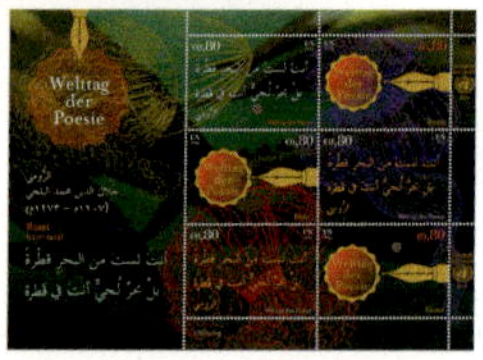
World Poetry Day V126

No. 559: a, Aleksey Tolstoy quotation in Russian in red brown, date in purple, "Welttag der Poesie" in red. b, Pen and circle, date in black, "Frühling" in purple. c, Pen and circle, date and "Frühling" in white, clouds above land in background. d, Tolstoy quotation in Russian in white, date in white, "Welttag der Poesie" in red. e, Tolstoy quotation in white, date and "Welttag der Poesie" in white. f, As "c," brown background.

No. 560: a, Rumi quotation in Arabic in light blue. b, Pen and red brown circle, denomination in red, purple jellyfish in background. c, Pen and red brown circle, denomination in white. d, Rumi quotation in orange, purple jellyfish tentacles in background. e, Rumi quotation in orange, red jellyfish tentacles in background. f, Pen and red brown circle, red denomination, red and purple jellyfish tentacles in background.

***Perf. 14½x14¼***
**2015, Mar. 20 Litho.**
**559** V125 Sheet of 6 11.50 11.50
*a.-f.* 68c Any single 1.90 1.90
**560** V126 Sheet of 6 13.50 13.50
*a.-f.* 80c Any single 2.25 2.25

### Endangered Species Type of 2015

Designs: No. 561, Pteridophora alberti. No. 562, Astrapia splendidissima. No. 563, Paradisaea apoda. No. 564, Lophorina superba.

**2015, Apr. 16 Litho. *Perf. 12½x12¾***
**561** A476 80c multicolored 2.00 2.00
**562** A476 80c multicolored 2.00 2.00
**563** A476 80c multicolored 2.00 2.00
**564** A476 80c multicolored 2.00 2.00
*a.* Block of 4, #561-564 8.00 8.00
*Nos. 561-564 (4)* 8.00 8.00

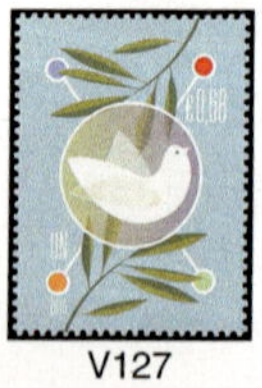
V127

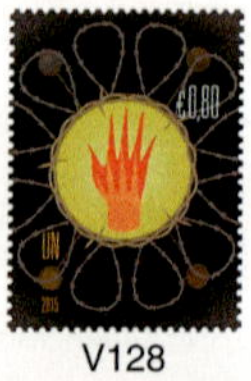
V128

# OFFICES IN VIENNA, AUSTRIA

**2015, May 7    Litho.    Perf. 13¼x13**
| 565 | V127 | 68c multicolored | 1.75 | 1.75 |
|---|---|---|---|---|
| 566 | V128 | 80c multicolored | 2.00 | 2.00 |

### World Heritage Sites, Southeast Asia Type of 2015

Designs: Nos. 567, 569c, Ayutthaya, Thailand. Nos. 568, 569f, Hué Monuments, Viet Nam. No. 569a, Luang Prabang, Laos. No. 569b, Angkor Wat, Cambodia. No. 569d, Borobudur Temple, Indonesia. No. 569e, Cordillera, Philippines.

**2015, June 5    Litho.    Perf. 14x13½**
| 567 | A480 | 80c multicolored | 2.00 | 2.00 |
|---|---|---|---|---|
| 568 | A480 | €1.70 multicolored | 4.25 | 4.25 |

### Souvenir Booklet
| 569 |  | Booklet, #569g-569l | 21.00 |  |
|---|---|---|---|---|
| a.-c. |  | A480 30c any single | .75 | .75 |
| d.-f. |  | A480 40c any single | 1.00 | 1.00 |
| g. |  | Booklet pane of 4 #569a | 3.00 | — |
| h. |  | Booklet pane of 4 #569b | 3.00 | — |
| i. |  | Booklet pane of 4 #569c | 3.00 | — |
| j. |  | Booklet pane of 4 #569d | 4.00 | — |
| k. |  | Booklet pane of 4 #569e | 4.00 | — |
| l. |  | Booklet pane of 4 #569f | 4.00 | — |

### End Violence Against Children Type of 2015

Designs: 68c, Gender-based violence. 80c, Child labor.

**Perf. 14½x14¼**
**2015, Aug. 20**        **Litho.**
| 570 | A481 | 68c multicolored | 1.75 | 1.75 |
|---|---|---|---|---|
| 571 | A481 | 80c multicolored | 2.00 | 2.00 |

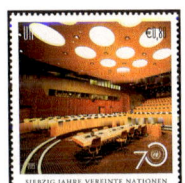

ECOSOC Chamber — V129

Trusteeship Council — V130

Visitors Lobby — V131

General Assembly Hall — V132

Trusteeship Council — V133

Printed by Cartor Security Printing, France. Panes of 6. Designed by Rorie Katz, U.S.

**2015, Oct. 25    Litho.    Perf. 13¾**
| 572 | V129 | 80c multicolored | 2.00 | 2.00 |
|---|---|---|---|---|
| 573 | V130 | 80c multicolored | 2.00 | 2.00 |
| a. |  | Pair, #572-573 | 4.00 | 4.00 |
| 574 | V131 | €1.70 multicolored | 4.25 | 4.25 |
| 575 | V132 | €1.70 multicolored | 4.25 | 4.25 |
| a. |  | Pair, #574-575 | 8.50 | 8.50 |
|  |  | Nos. 572-575 (4) | 12.50 | 12.50 |

### Souvenir Sheet
**Perf. 13½**
| 576 | V133 | €1.70 multicolored | 4.25 | 4.25 |
|---|---|---|---|---|

United Nations, 70th anniv.

### United Nations, 70th Anniv. Type of 2015

Designed by Sergio Baradat, U.S.

**2015, Nov. 5    Litho.    Perf. 14¾**
| 577 | A482 | 80c multi + label | 4.00 | 4.00 |
|---|---|---|---|---|
|  |  | Sheet of 10 + 10 labels | 40.00 | — |

The full sheet sold for $13.45 or €10.90. The sheet contains ten different generic labels. Labels could be personalized. The personalization of labels was available only at UN Headquarters, and not through mail order.

21st United Nations Climate Change Conference, Paris — V134

**2015, Nov. 24    Litho.    Perf. 13¼**
| 578 | V134 | 80c multicolored | 3.00 | 3.00 |
|---|---|---|---|---|

Values are for stamps with surrounding selvage.

### Free and Equal Type of 2016

Designs: 68c, Person coming out of closet. 80c, Gay men.

**2016, Feb. 5    Litho.    Perf. 13½x13¼**
| 579 | A491 | 68c multicolored | 1.75 | 1.75 |
|---|---|---|---|---|
| 580 | A491 | 80c multicolored | 2.00 | 2.00 |

### HeForShe Type of 2016

Designs: 1fr, Man, red background. 2fr, Woman, orange brown background.

**2016, Mar. 8    Litho.    Perf. 12½x13**
| 581 | A492 | 68c multicolored | 1.75 | 1.75 |
|---|---|---|---|---|
| 582 | A492 | 80c multicolored | 2.00 | 2.00 |

### Miniature Sheets

V135

International Dance Day — V136

No. 583 — Illustration of Spanish dancers by Allison Seiffer: a, Female dancer with fan. b, Male dancer with crossed arms. c, Red dress of dancer. d, Female dancer with male guitarist. e, Feet of dancer in ochre and green dress. f, Feet of male and female dancers, rose on floor.

No. 584 — Illustration of Middle Eastern dancers by Seiffer: a, Head of female dancer, "Welttanztag" in red, denomination in yellow. b, Head of female dancer, "Welttanztag" and denomination in red. c, Torso of dancer. d, Dancer, "Welttanztag" in black, denomination in yellow. e, Feet of dancer, "Welttanztag" in black. f, Feet of dancer and drum, "Welttanztag" in yellow.

**2016, Apr. 29    Litho.    Perf. 13¼x13**
| 583 | V135 | Sheet of 6 | 10.00 | 10.00 |
|---|---|---|---|---|
| a.-f. |  | 68c Any single | 1.60 | 1.60 |
| 584 | V136 | Sheet of 6 | 12.00 | 12.00 |
| a.-f. |  | 80c Any single | 2.00 | 2.00 |

United Nations Industrial Development Organization, 50th Anniv. — V137

**2016, May 12    Litho.    Perf. 14¾**
| 585 | V137 | 80c multi + label | 2.60 | 2.60 |
|---|---|---|---|---|
|  |  | Sheet of 10 + 10 labels | 26.50 | — |

The full sheet sold for $13.12 and €10.90. One of the ten different generic labels is shown. Labels could be personalized. The personalization of labels was available only at UN Headquarters, and not through mail order.

### International Day of United Nations Peacekeepers Type of 2016

Designs: 68c, Peacekeepers and African children. 80c, Peacekeepers in tank, Africans.

**Litho. With Foil Application**
**2016, May 29        Perf. 13¼x13**
| 586 | A496 | 68c multicolored | 1.75 | 1.75 |
|---|---|---|---|---|
| 587 | A496 | 80c multicolored | 2.00 | 2.00 |

### Sport for Peace Type of 2016

Olympic rings and: No. 588, Weight lifting, denomination at LR. No. 589, Weight lifting, denomination at LL. No. 590, Fencing, denomination at UR. No. 591, Fencing, denomination at UL.

**2016, July 22    Litho.    Perf. 14¼**
| 588 | A498 | 68c multicolored | 1.75 | 1.75 |
|---|---|---|---|---|
| 589 | A498 | 68c multicolored | 1.75 | 1.75 |
| a. |  | Pair, #588-589 | 3.50 | 3.50 |
| 590 | A498 | €1.70 multicolored | 4.25 | 4.25 |
| 591 | A498 | €1.70 multicolored | 4.25 | 4.25 |
| a. |  | Pair, #590-591 | 8.50 | 8.50 |
|  |  | Nos. 588-591 (4) | 12.00 | 12.00 |

Listings for items containing stamps from New York and stamps from Geneva and/or Vienna, will be found only in the listings for New York.

### World Heritage Sites, Czech Republic Type of 2016

Designs: Nos. 592, 594c, Historic Town Center of Kutná Hora. Nos. 593, 594f, Historic Center of Ceský Krumlov. No. 594a, Historic Center of Prague. No. 594b, Gardens and Castle at Kromeríz. No. 594d, Holy Trinity Column, Olomouc. Nos. 594e, Lednice-Valtice Cultural Landscape.

**2016, Sept. 8    Litho.    Perf. 14¼**
| 592 | A500 | 68c multicolored | 1.75 | 1.75 |
|---|---|---|---|---|
| 593 | A500 | €1.70 multicolored | 4.25 | 4.25 |

### Souvenir Booklet
| 594 |  | Booklet, #594g-594l | 20.50 |  |
|---|---|---|---|---|
| a.-c. |  | A500 30c any single | .65 | .65 |
| d.-f. |  | A500 40c any single | 1.00 | 1.00 |
| g. |  | Booklet pane of 4 #594a | 2.75 | — |
| h. |  | Booklet pane of 4 #594b | 2.75 | — |
| i. |  | Booklet pane of 4 #594c | 2.75 | — |
| j. |  | Booklet pane of 4 #594d | 4.00 | — |
| k. |  | Booklet pane of 4 #594e | 4.00 | — |
| l. |  | Booklet pane of 4 #594f | 4.00 | — |

### Comprehensive Nuclear Test-Ban Treaty Organization, 20th Anniv. — V138

**2016, Sept. 23    Litho.    Perf. 14¾**
| 595 | V138 | 80c multi + label | 4.00 | 4.00 |
|---|---|---|---|---|

The full sheet sold for $13.27 and €10.90. One of the ten different generic labels is shown. Labels could be personalized. The personalization of labels was available only at UN Headquarters, and not through mail order.

### Miniature Sheet

World Wildlife Conference, Johannesburg — V139

No. 596 — Part of map of Africa and: a, Nilkrokodil (Nile crocodile). b, Kapgeier (Cape vulture). c, Steppenschuppentier (Cape pangolin). d, Mystacidium capense.

**2016, Sept. 24    Litho.    Perf. 13x13¼**
| 596 | V139 | Sheet of 4 | 17.00 | 17.00 |
|---|---|---|---|---|
| a.-d. |  | €1.70 Any single | 4.25 | 4.25 |

### Sustainable Development Goals Type of 2016

No. 597 — Inscription: a, 1 Keine armut. b, 2 Kein hunger. c, 3 Gesundheit und wohlergehen. d, 4 Hochwertige bildung. e, 5 Geschlechter-gleichheit. f, 6 Sauberes wasser und sanitär-einrichtungen. g, 7 Bezalbare und saubere energie. h, 8 Menschenwürdige arbeit und wirtschafts-wachstum. i, 9 Industrie, innovation und infrastruktur. j, 10 Weniger ungleichheiten. k, 11 Nachhaltige städte und gemeinden. l, 12 Nachhaltige/r konsum und produktion. m, 13 Massnahmen zum klimaschutz. n, 14 Leben unter wasser. o, 15 Leben an land. p, 16 Frieden, gerechtigkeit und starke institutionen. q, 17 Partnerschaften zur erreichung der ziele.

**2016, Oct. 24    Litho.    Perf. 13¼**
| 597 |  | Sheet of 17 + label | 28.50 | 28.50 |
|---|---|---|---|---|
| a.-q. |  | A503 68c Any single | 1.60 | 1.60 |

### Miniature Sheet

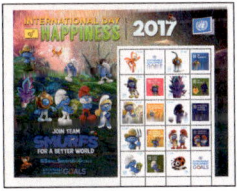

V140

No. 598: a, Insect. b, Smurf wearing diving helmet. c, Smurf holding archery bow. d, Flower with eyes. e, Smurf in park. f, Smurf with police hat, whistle and baton. g, Smurf holding pitchfork. h, Two Smurfs wearing red caps. i, Smurf holding garbage can. j, Ladybug.

**2017, Mar. 20    Litho.    Perf. 14¾**
| 598 | V140 | Sheet of 10 + 10 labels | 30.00 | 30.00 |
|---|---|---|---|---|
| a.-j. |  | 80c Any single + label | 3.00 | 3.00 |

The full sheet sold for $14.95. The generic labels are shown. Labels could be personalized.

## OFFICES IN VIENNA, AUSTRIA

### Miniature Sheets

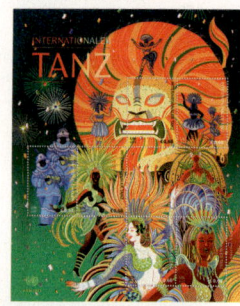

V141

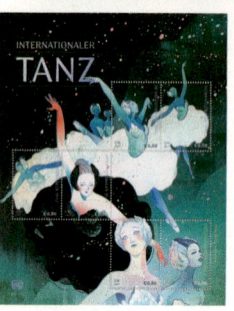

International Dance — V142

No. 599 — Illustration of Samba dancers by Victo Ngai: a, Lion's head. b, Black and tan female dancers. c, Dancers holding drums. d, Black female dancer. e, White female dancer. f, Brown female dancer.

No. 600 — Illustration of Ballet dancers by Ngai: a, Blue dancer with hand bent downward. b, Blue dancer with arm raised above head. c, Blue dancer with arms extended to side. d, Dancer with black dress. e, Head of dancer, tip of dress at bottom. f, Head of dancer facing right.

**2017, Mar. 23   Litho.   Perf. 13¼x13**
599  V141   Sheet of 6            9.75  9.75
a.-f.        68c Any single      1.60  1.60
g.           As #599, with Brasilia 2017 World Stamp Exhibition emblem overprinted in sheet margin        10.50 10.50
600          Sheet of 6          11.50 11.50
a.-f.        80c Any single      1.90  1.90

**Endangered Species Type of 2017**

Designs: No. 601, Capra caucasica. No. 602, Nautilidae spp. No. 603, Siphonochilus aethiopicus. No. 604, Lygodactylus williamsi.

**2017, May 11   Litho.   Perf. 12¾x12½**
601  A509  80c multicolored    1.90  1.90
602  A509  80c multicolored    1.90  1.90
603  A509  80c multicolored    1.90  1.90
604  A509  80c multicolored    1.90  1.90
a.    Block of 4, #601-604      7.75  7.75
      Nos. 601-604 (4)          7.60  7.60

**World Environment Day Type of 2017**

Designs: 68c, Supreme Court, Ottawa, Ontario, Canada. €1.70, Moraine Lake, Canada.

**2017, June 5   Litho.   Perf. 13¼**
605  A510  68c multicolored    1.60  1.60
606  A510  €1.70 multicolored  4.00  4.00

**World Heritage Sites Along the Silk Roads Type of 2017**

Designs: Nos. 607, 609c, Tabriz Historic Bazaar Complex, Iran. Nos. 608, 609f, Safranbolu, Turkey. No. 609a, Longmen Grottoes, People's Republic of China. No. 609b, Historic Center of Bukhara, Uzbekistan. No. 609d, Sulaiman-Too Sacred Mountain, Kyrgyzstan. No. 609e, Kunya-Urgench, Turkmenistan.

**2017, Aug. 3   Litho.   Perf. 14¼**
607  A512  80c multicolored    2.00  2.00
608  A512  €1.70 multicolored  4.25  4.25

**Souvenir Booklet**
609    Booklet, #609g-609l     23.50
a.-c.  A512 30c any single     .85   .85
d.-f.  A512 40c any single    1.10  1.10
g.     Booklet pane of 4 #609a 3.40   —
h.     Booklet pane of 4 #609b 3.40   —
i.     Booklet pane of 4 #609c 3.40   —
j.     Booklet pane of 4 #609d 4.40   —
k.     Booklet pane of 4 #609e 4.40   —
l.     Booklet pane of 4 #609f 4.40   —

### Miniature Sheet

V143

No. 610: a, Traunsee with ships and lakeshore buildings. b, Ort Castle and bridge at dusk. c, Aerial view of Cumberland Castle. d, Street in Gmunden, Austria. e, Gmunden City Hall. f, Ort Castle and bridge. g, Sailboat near Ort Castle. h, Villa Toscana. i, Aerial view of Traunsee. j, Ships on Traunsee.

**2017, Aug. 24   Litho.   Perf. 14¾**
610   V143   Sheet of 10 + 10 labels           27.50 27.50
a.-j.        68c Any single + label   2.75  2.75

United Nations Postal Administration on the Traunsee, 35th anniv. The full sheet sold for $13.64. The generic labels are shown. Labels could be personalized.

Hands and Flower V144

Handshake and Flowers V145

Handshake and Flowers — V146

Printed by Johann Enschedé and Sons, the Netherlands. Panes of 20. Designed by Stranger and Stranger, U.S.

**2017, Sept. 21   Litho.   Perf. 14x14¼**
611  V144  68c multicolored     1.75  1.75
612  V145  €1.70 multicolored   4.25  4.25

**Souvenir Sheet**
**Perf. 14¼x13¾**
613  V146  €1.70 multicolored   4.25  4.25

International Day of Peace.

**World Food Day Type of 2017**

Designs: 68c, Breads and grains. 80c, Steak, fish, chicken drumstick, shrimp, egg, beans, lemon slice.

**2017, Oct. 16   Litho.   Perf. 13¼x14**
614  A516  68c multicolored     1.75  1.75
615  A516  80c multicolored     2.00  2.00

**Endangered Species Type of 2018**

Designs: No. 616, Hoodia pilifera. No. 617, Mantella madagascariensis. No. 618, Pangshua sylhetensis. No. 619, Hippocampus zebra.

**2018, Mar. 2   Litho.   Perf. 12¾x12½**
616  A519  80c multicolored    2.00  2.00
617  A519  80c multicolored    2.00  2.00
618  A519  80c multicolored    2.00  2.00
619  A519  80c multicolored    2.00  2.00
a.    Block of 4, #616-619     8.00  8.00
      Nos. 616-619 (4)         8.00  8.00

**World Health Day Type of 2018**

Designs: 68c, Medical worker, people, globe, caduceus. €1.70, Coins entering piggy bank with white cross.

**2018, Apr. 6   Litho.   Perf. 13x13¼**
620  A520  68c multicolored    1.90  1.90
621  A520  €1.70 multicolored  4.50  4.50

United Nations Emblem V147

**2018   Litho.   Perf. 14¾**
622   V147  80c multi + label    2.75  2.75
a.    Less distinct year date and frame, lighter blue emblem   2.75  2.75

Issued: No. 622, 5/26; No. 622a, 7/30. The full sheet sold for $14.32 and €10.90. One of the ten different generic labels is shown. Labels could be personalized. The personalization of labels was available only at UN Headquarters, and not through mail order.

**UNISPACE + 50 Conferences Type of 2018**

Designs: 68c, Great Red Spot of Jupiter. 80c, Aurora Australis from International Space Station.
€1.70, View of river delta from Copernicus Sentinel satellite.

**2018, June 20   Litho.   Perf. 14x14¼**
623  A523  68c multicolored    1.90  1.90
624  A523  80c multicolored    2.25  2.25

**Souvenir Sheet**
**Perf. 13¾**
625  A523  €1.70 multicolored   4.50  4.50

No. 625 contains one 45x45mm stamp.

**World Heritage Sites In the United Kingdom Type of 2018**

Designs: Nos. 626, 628c, Conwy Castle. Nos. 627, 628f, Maritime Greenwich. No. 628a, Giant's Causeway. No. 628b, Stonehenge. No. 628d, Palace of Westminster. No. 628e, Edinburgh.

**2018, Aug. 15   Litho.   Perf. 14¼**
626  A524  90c multicolored    2.40  2.40
627  A524  €1.80 multicolored  4.75  4.75

**Souvenir Booklet**
628    Booklet, #609g-609l     25.50
a.-c.  A524 35c any single     1.00  1.00
d.-f.  A524 40c any single     1.10  1.10
g.     Booklet pane of 4 #628a 4.00   —
h.     Booklet pane of 4 #628b 4.00   —
i.     Booklet pane of 4 #628c 4.00   —
j.     Booklet pane of 4 #628d 4.50   —
k.     Booklet pane of 4 #628e 4.50   —
l.     Booklet pane of 4 #628f 4.50   —

### Miniature Sheet

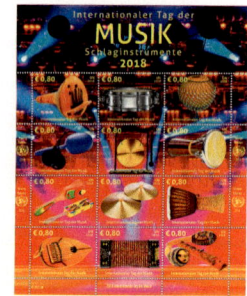

International Music Day — V148

No. 629: a, Kalimba with three holes. b, Snare drum. c, Shekere. d, Castanets. e, Gong. f, Hourglass drum. g, Castanet with handles and tambourine stick. h, Cymbals. i, Djembe drum. j, Kalimba with one hole. k, Button accordion. l, Maracas and decorated stick.

**2018, Oct. 1   Litho.   Perf. 14x13¼**
629   V148   Sheet of 12       24.50 24.50
a.-l.        80c Any single    2.00  2.00

V149

Non-Violence, Sculpture by Carl Fredrik Reuterswärd — V150

Printed by Johann Enschedé Stamps BV, the Netherlands. Panes of 20. Designed by Martin Mörck, Norway.

**2018, Oct. 2   Litho.   Perf. 14x14¼**
630  V149  90c multicolored    2.40  2.40
631  V150  €2.30 multicolored  6.00  6.00

### Miniature Sheet

World Languages — V151

No. 632 — Word bubbles with word for "Hello" in: a, Serbian or Croatian ("Sprachen der Welt" and denomination in red). b, Arabic ("Sprachen der Welt" and denomination in white). c, Korean ("Sprachen der Welt" in white, denomination in black), d, Dutch or German or Norwegian (Hallo). e, Greek and Turkish (Merhaba). f, Spanish (Hola).

**2019, Feb. 21   Litho.   Perf. 13¼x13**
632   V151   Sheet of 6         12.50 12.50
a.-f.        80c Any single     2.00  2.00

Migration — V152

Printed by Lowe-Martin Group, Canada. Panes of 20. Designed by Chris Gash, U.S.

**2019, Mar.15   Litho.   Perf. 13¼x13**
633  V152  €1.80 multicolored  4.75  4.75

**Endangered Species Type of 2019**

Designs: No. 634, Anguilla anguilla. No. 635, Dermochelys coriacea. No. 636, Acropora spp. No. 637, Huso huso.

**2019, Apr. 26   Litho.   Perf. 12¾x12½**
634  A534  90c multicolored    2.25  2.25
635  A534  90c multicolored    2.25  2.25
636  A534  90c multicolored    2.25  2.25
637  A534  90c multicolored    2.25  2.25
a.    Block of 4, #634-637     9.25  9.25
      Nos. 634-637 (4)         9.00  9.00

### Souvenir Sheet

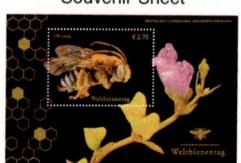

Long-horned Bee and Scutellaria Lateriflora — V153

**Litho. With Foil Application**
**2019, May 20                Perf. 13**
638  V153  €2.70 multicolored  7.00  7.00

World Bee Day.

V154        V155

OFFICES IN VIENNA, AUSTRIA 307

V156

V157

International Labor Organization, Cent. — V158

**2019, June 28 Litho.** ***Perf. 13½x14***

639 V154 80c multicolored 2.00 2.00
640 V155 80c multicolored 2.00 2.00
641 V156 80c multicolored 2.00 2.00
642 V157 80c multicolored 2.00 2.00
643 V158 80c multicolored 2.00 2.00
*a.* Horiz. strip of 5, #639-643 10.00 10.00
*Nos. 639-643 (5)* 10.00 10.00

V159

V160

V161

V162

United Nations Postal Administration in Vienna, 40th Anniv. — V163

**2019, Aug. 23 Litho.** ***Perf. 14¾***

644 V159 90c multi + label *3.00 3.00*
645 V160 90c multi + label *3.00 3.00*
646 V161 90c multi + label *3.00 3.00*
647 V162 90c multi + label *3.00 3.00*
648 V163 90c multi + label *3.00 3.00*
*a.* Vert. strip of 5, #644-648, + 5 labels *15.00 15.00*
*Nos. 644-648 (5)* *15.00 15.00*

The full sheets sold for $14.04 or €15.33. The generic labels are shown. Labels could be personalized. The personalization of labels was available only at UN Headquarters, and not through mail order.

### Climate Change Type of 2019

Designs: 80c, Canyon and mining operation. 90c, Clouds and smokestack. €1.80, Fish and corals.

**2019, Sept. 23 Litho.** ***Perf. 14¼***

649 A543 80c multicolored 2.00 2.00
650 A543 90c multicolored 2.25 2.25

**Souvenir Sheet**

***Perf.***

651 A543 €1.80 multicolored 4.50 4.50

2019 United Nations Climate Change Conference, Madrid. No. 651 contains one 47mm diameter stamp.

### World Heritage Sites in Cuba Type of 2019

Designs: Nos. 652, 654c, Camagüey. Nos. 653, 654f, San Pedro de la Rosa Castle. No. 654a, Morro Castle. No. 664b, Trinidad. No. 654d, Vinales Valley. No. 654e, Cienfuegos.

**Litho. With Foil Application**

**2019, Oct. 24** ***Perf. 14¼***

652 A545 90c multicolored 2.25 2.25
653 A545 €1.80 multicolored 4.50 4.50

**Souvenir Booklet**

654 Booklet, #1115g-1115l 25.00
*a.-c.* A545 35c Any single .95 .95
*d.-f.* A545 40c Any single 1.10 1.10
*g.* Booklet pane of 4 #654a 3.80 —
*h.* Booklet pane of 4 #654b 3.80 —
*i.* Booklet pane of 4 #654c 3.80 —
*j.* Booklet pane of 4 #654d 4.40 —
*k.* Booklet pane of 4 #654e 4.40 —
*l.* Booklet pane of 4 #654f 4.40 —

Complete booklet sold for $12.27.

### Endangered Species Type of 2020

Designs: No. 655, Panthera leo. No. 656, Pelecanus crispus. No. 657, Phocoena phocoena. No. 658, Equus africanus.

***Perf. 12¾x12½***

**2020, Feb. 17 Litho.**

655 A546 90c multicolored 2.25 2.25
656 A546 90c multicolored 2.25 2.25
657 A546 90c multicolored 2.25 2.25
658 A546 90c multicolored 2.25 2.25
*a.* Block of 4, #655-658 9.00 9.00
*Nos. 655-658 (4)* 9.00 9.00

Blank Stamp On Which Stickers Can Be Applied V164

Designs: No. 1212, Hawksbill turtle. No. 1213, Queen conch. No. 1214, Mushroom coral. No. 1215, Humpback whale.

**2020, Mar. 19 Litho.** ***Die Cut***

**Self-Adhesive**

659 V164 €1.80 multicolored with rounded corners 4.50 4.50
*a.* With perpendicular corners and black frame line 4.50 4.50
*b.* Booklet pane of 6 #1236a 27.00

No. 659 was issued as a souvenir sheet having two different sheet margins, each with different stickers. No. 659a was issued in a booklet containing six panes of one stamp, with each pane having different margins and stickers. Each booklet pane contained one sticker depicting Hello Kitty, a color wheel with Hello Kitty at the center, one of six different Sustainable Development Goal emblems, along with a variety of other stickers. The two souvenir sheets had the same sheet margin and stickers found on two of the panes of No. 659b. No. 659b was sold folded, without any means of separation between the individual panes.

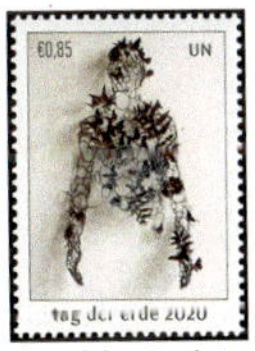

Lepidopterist, Artwork by Paul Villinski V165

Ruth, Costume by Nicole Dextras V166

**2020, Apr. 22 Litho.** ***Perf. 13¼***

660 V165 85c multicolored 2.10 2.10
661 V166 €1.35 multicolored 3.50 3.50

Earth Day, 50th anniv. Because of the COVID-19 pandemic, Nos. 660-661 were not available for sale on day of issue stated on the first-day covers as they had not yet been printed and delivered.

Florence Nightingale (1820-1910), Nurse V167

**2020, May 12 Litho.** ***Perf. 14***

662 V167 €1.35 multicolored 3.50 3.50

International Year of the Nurse and the Midwife.

### World Heritage Sites in Russia Type of 2020

Designs: Nos. 663, 665c, Novodevichy Convent. Nos. 664, 665f, Kizhi Pogost. No. 665a, Lake Baikal. No. 665b, Kazan Kremlin. No. 665d, Kremlin and Red Square, Moscow. No. 665e, Saint Petersburg.

***Perf. 14½x14¼***

**2020, Sept. 11 Litho.**

663 A556 €1 multicolored 2.60 2.60
664 A556 €1.80 multicolored 4.75 4.75

**Souvenir Booklet**

665 Booklet, #1115g-1115l 27.00
*a.-c.* A556 35c any single 1.00 1.00
*d.-f.* A556 40c any single 1.25 1.25
*g.* Booklet pane of 4 #665a 4.00 —
*h.* Booklet pane of 4 #665b 4.00 —
*i.* Booklet pane of 4 #665c 4.00 —
*j.* Booklet pane of 4 #665d 5.00 —
*k.* Booklet pane of 4 #665e 5.00 —
*l.* Booklet pane of 4 #665f 5.00 —

Complete booklet sold for $12.94 or €10.

United Nations Emblem V168

**2020, Oct. 2 Litho.** ***Perf. 14¾***

666 V168 €1 multi + label *3.25 3.25*
Sheet of 10 + 10 labels *33.50* —

The full sheet sold for $16.70 or €12.90. One of the ten different generic labels is shown. Labels could be personalized. The personalization of labels was available only at UN Headquarters, and not through mail order.

Souvenir Sheet

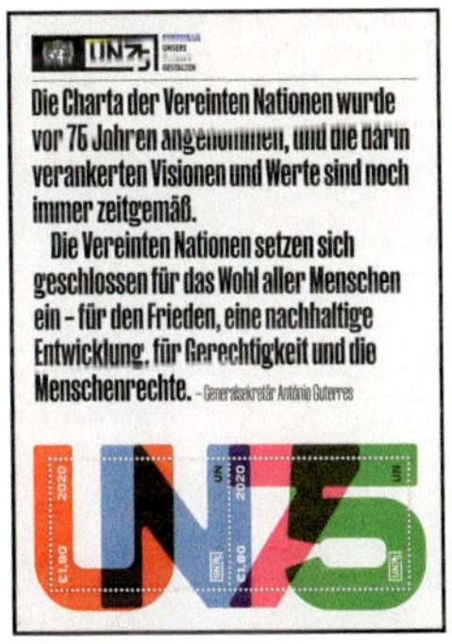

United Nations, 75th Anniv. V169

No. 667: a, Red "U," blue "N." b, Pink "7," green "5."

**2020, Oct. 24 Litho.** ***Perf. 13¼***

667 V169 Sheet of 2 9.50 9.50
*a.-b.* €1.80 Either single 4.75 4.75

Souvenir Sheet

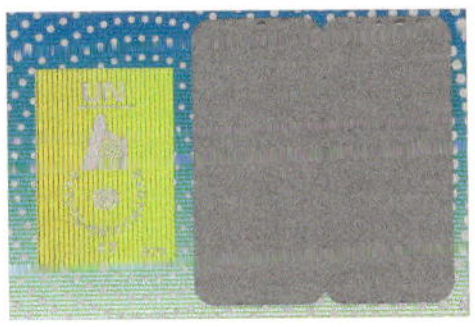
Vienna International Center and Emblem — V170

**Litho. With Foil Application**

**2020, Nov. 24** ***Die Cut Perf. 11½***

**Self-Adhesive**

668 V170 €7 multicolored 18.50 18.50

Crypto stamp. Unused value is for stamp with unscratched panels at right.

International Day for the Elimination of Racial Discrimination — V171

**2021, Mar. 19 Litho.** ***Perf. 13¼x13***

669 V171 €1.80 multicolored 5.00 5.00

### Endangered Species Type of 2021

Designs: No. 670, Neophema chrysogaster. No. 671, Babyrousa babyrussa. No. 672, Onychogalea fraenata. No. 673, Lepanthes telipogoniflora.

**2021, Apr. 7 Litho.** ***Perf. 12¾x12½***

670 A565 90c multicolored 2.50 2,50
671 A565 90c multicolored 2.50 2.50
672 A565 90c multicolored 2.50 2.50
673 A565 90c multicolored 2.50 2,50
*a.* Block of 4, #670-673 10.00 10.00
*Nos. 670-673 (4)* 10.00 5.50

Rider on Orange Horse — V172

Rider on Brown Horse — V173

Rider on White Horse — V174

Golfer Contemplating Putt — V175

Golfer and Ball on Hill — V176

Female Golfer — V177

Doves and Olympic Flame V178

**2021, July 23 Litho.** ***Perf. 13½***

674 V172 85c multicolored 2.25 2.25
675 V173 85c multicolored 2.25 2.25
676 V174 85c multicolored 2.25 2.25
*a.* Horiz. strip of 3, #674-676 6.75 6.75
677 V175 €1 multicolored 2.75 2.75
678 V176 €1 multicolored 2.75 2.75
679 V177 €1 multicolored 2.75 2.75
*a.* Horiz. strip of 3, #677-679 8.25 8.25
*Nos. 674-679 (6)* 15.00 15.00

**Souvenir Sheet**

680 V178 €1.80 multicolored 5.00 5.00

Sports for Peace, 2020 Summer Olympics, Tokyo. The 2020 Summer Olympics were postponed until 2021 because of the COVID-19 pandemic.

### Waterways, Railways and Bridges World Heritage Sites Type of 2020

Designs: Nos. 681, 683c, Forth Bridge, Scotland. Nos. 682, 683f, Old Bridge, Mostar, Bosnia and Herzegovina. No. 683a, Rideau Canal, Canada. No. 683b, Rhaetian Railway, Switzerland and Italy. No. 683d, Grand Canal, People's Republic of China. No. 683e, Darjeeling Himalayan Railway, India.

**2021, Aug. 25 Litho.** ***Perf. 14¼***

681 A575 €1 multicolored 2.75 2.75
682 A575 €1.80 multicolored 5.00 5.00

**Souvenir Booklet**

683 Booklet, #683g-683l 27.00
*a.-c.* A575 35c any single 1.00 1.00
*d.-f.* A575 40c any single 1.25 1.25
*g.* Booklet pane of 4 #683a 4.00 —
*h.* Booklet pane of 4 #683b 4.00 —
*i.* Booklet pane of 4 #683c 4.00 —
*j.* Booklet pane of 4 #683d 5.00 —
*k.* Booklet pane of 4 #683e 5.00 —
*l.* Booklet pane of 4 #683f 5.00 —

Complete booklet sold for $12.94 or €10.

Miniature Sheet

Comprehensive Nuclear Test Ban Treaty, 25th Anniv. — V179

# OFFICES IN VIENNA, AUSTRIA

No. 684: a, Hydroacoustic Station HA4, Crozet Islands, and penguins. b, Hydroacoustic Station HA3, Chile, with red sphere. c, Radionuclide Station RN68, Tristan da Cunha, in fenced enclosure. d, Radionuclide Station RN33, Germany, with green base. e, Large group of technicians at Infrasound Station IS33, Madagascar. f, Two technicians near antenna at Infrasound Station IS55, Antarctica. g, Two technicians at Auxiliary Seismic Station AS74, Oman. h, Vehicle and technician at Auxiliary Seismic Station AS69, New Zealand. i, Technician in protective clothing carrying equipment for field exercise, Kazakhstan. j, Technician for field exercise in aircraft above Jordan.

**2021, Aug. 27    Litho.    Perf. 14½**
| 684 | V179 | Sheet of 10 + 10 labels | 24.00 | 24.00 |
| a.-j. | | €1 Any single + label | 2.40 | 2.40 |

The full sheet sold for $12.00 or €12.90. The generic labels are shown. Labels could be personalized.

### Miniature Sheet

Celebrations — V180

No. 685: a, Birthday cake. b, Flower bouquet. c, Three balloons. d, Menorah. e, Heart and arrow. f, Christmas tree and ornament. g, "Danke." h, Champagne flutes. i, Diamond ring. j, Mosque.

**2021, Nov. 4    Litho.    Perf. 14¼**
| 685 | V180 | Sheet of 10 | 34.00 | 34.00 |
| a.-j. | | €1 Any single + label | 3.25 | 3.25 |

The full sheet sold for $16.93 or €12.90. The generic labels are shown. Labels could be personalized. The personalization of labels was available only at UN Headquarters, and not through mail order.

World Toilet Day — V181

**2021, Nov. 19    Litho.    Perf. 14¼**
| 686 | V181 | €1 multicolored | 2.75 | 2.75 |

Curler Delivering Stone V182

Curling Stones and Brooms V183

Skier in Air — V184

Skier On Snow V185

**2022, Jan. 14    Litho.    Perf. 14¼**
| 687 | V182 | 85c multicolored | 2.10 | 2.10 |
| 688 | V183 | 85c multicolored | 2.10 | 2.10 |
| a. | | Horiz. pair, #687-688 | 4.25 | 4.25 |
| 689 | V184 | €1.80 multicolored | 4.50 | 4.50 |
| 690 | V185 | €1.80 multicolored | 4.50 | 4.50 |
| a. | | Horiz. pair, #689-690 | 9.00 | 9.00 |
| | | Nos. 687-690 (4) | 13.20 | 13.20 |

Sports for Peace, 2022 Winter Olympics, Beijing.

### Endangered Species Type of 2022

Designs: No. 691, Dynastes satanas. No. 692, Hylocereus triangularis. No. 693, Cedrela odorata. No. 694, Acanthocereus tetragonus.

**Perf. 12¾x12½    Litho.**
**2022, Mar. 18    Litho.**
| 691 | A592 | €1 multicolored | 2.50 | 2.50 |
| 692 | A592 | €1 multicolored | 2.50 | 2.50 |
| 693 | A592 | €1 multicolored | 2.50 | 2.50 |
| 694 | A592 | €1 multicolored | 2.50 | 2.50 |
| a. | | Block of 4, #691-694 | 10.00 | 10.00 |
| | | Nos. 691-694 (4) | 10.00 | 10.00 |

Wangari Maathai (1940-2011), 2004 Nobel Peace Laureate V186

**2022, Apr. 1    Litho.    Perf. 14¼**
| 695 | V186 | 85c multicolored | 2.25 | 2.25 |

### Exploration of Mars Type of 2022

Designs: 85c, Landing area for People's Republic of China's Tianwen-1 Lander. €1, Zhurong Rover on Mars. €1.80, Zhurong Rover Landing Platform.

**2022, Apr. 24    Litho.    Perf. 13¼x13**
| 696 | A593 | 85c multicolored | 2.25 | 2.25 |
| 697 | A593 | €1 multicolored | 2.50 | 2.50 |

### Souvenir Sheet
**Perf. 13½**
| 698 | A593 | €1.80 multicolored | 4.50 | 4.50 |

No. 698 contains one 44x44mm stamp.

### Miniature Sheet

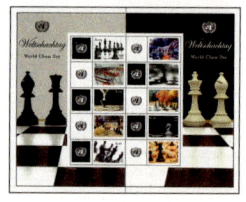

World Chess Day V187

No. 699: a, Chess board with black pieces, two pawns in forward positions. b, Player moving white king. c, Chairs and chess set on round table. d, Black pawn on chess board. e, Player toppling black king. f, Player moving black pawn. g, Table with chess boards and timers. h, Black and white knights. i, Chess board with black pieces, knight next to king. j, Chess board with black and white pieces, with toppled white king.

**2022, July 20    Litho.    Perf. 14¼**
| 699 | V187 | Sheet of 10 + 10 labels | 32.50 | 32.50 |
| a.-j. | | €1 Any single + label | 3.25 | 3.25 |

The full sheet sold for $16.10 or €12.90. The generic labels are shown. Labels could be personalized.

### European Spa Towns World Heritage Sites Type of 2022

Designs: Nos. 700, 702c, Baden-Baden, Germany. Nos. 701, 702f, Baden bei Wien, Austria. No. 702a, Karlovy Vary, Czech Republic. No. 702b, Spa, Belgium. No. 702d, Montecatini Terme, Italy. No. 702e, Vichy, France.

**2022, Sept. 9    Litho.    Perf. 14½x14¼**
| 700 | A594 | €1 multicolored | 2.40 | 2.40 |
| 701 | A594 | €1.80 multicolored | 4.25 | 4.25 |

### Souvenir Booklet
| 702 | | Booklet, #1115g-1115l | 23.50 | |
| a.-c. | | A594 35c any single | .90 | .90 |
| d.-f. | | A594 40c any single | 1.00 | 1.00 |
| g. | | Booklet pane of 4 #702a | 3.75 | — |
| h. | | Booklet pane of 4 #702b | 3.75 | — |
| i. | | Booklet pane of 4 #702c | 3.75 | — |
| j. | | Booklet pane of 4 #702d | 4.00 | — |
| k. | | Booklet pane of 4 #702e | 4.00 | — |
| l. | | Booklet pane of 4 #702f | 4.00 | — |

Complete booklet sold for $11.59 or €10.

### Souvenir Sheet

Peace Dove V188

**Litho. With Foil Application**
**2022, Nov. 18    Die Cut Perf. 11½ Self-Adhesive**
| 703 | V188 | €3.65 multicolored | 8.50 | 8.50 |

Crypto stamp. Unused value is for sheets with unscratched panels at right.

### Endangered Species Type of 2023

Designs: No. 704, Megaptera novaeangliae. No. 705, Saiga tatarica. No. 706, Lynx pardinus. No. 707, Galanthus elwesii.

**2023, Mar. 3    Litho.    Perf. 12¾x12½**
| 704 | A599 | €1.20 multicolored | 3.00 | 3.00 |
| 705 | A599 | €1.20 multicolored | 3.00 | 3.00 |
| 706 | A599 | €1.20 multicolored | 3.00 | 3.00 |
| 707 | A599 | €1.20 multicolored | 3.00 | 3.00 |
| a. | | Block of 4, #704-707 | 12.00 | 12.00 |
| | | Nos. 704-707 (4) | 12.00 | 12.00 |

Der Fall des Ikarus (The Fall of Icarus), Painting by Pablo Picasso (1881-1973) V189

Die Geister der Ahnen (The Spirits of the Ancestors), by Yves Pèdé (1959-2019) V190

**2023, Apr. 15    Litho.    Perf. 14½x14¼**
| 708 | V189 | €1 multicolored | 2.40 | 2.40 |
| 709 | V190 | €1.90 multicolored | 4.50 | 4.50 |

World Art Day.

V191

V192

V193

V194

V195

V196

V197

V198

Marine Life of Great Barrier Reef, Australia — V199

**2023, June 8    Litho.    Perf. 14x13¼**
| 710 | | Sheet of 3 | 21.50 | 21.50 |
| a. | V191 | €1 multicolored | 2.25 | 2.25 |
| b. | V192 | €1 multicolored | 2.25 | 2.25 |
| c. | V193 | €1 multicolored | 2.25 | 2.25 |
| d. | V194 | €1 multicolored | 2.25 | 2.25 |
| e. | V195 | €1 multicolored | 2.25 | 2.25 |
| f. | V196 | €1 multicolored | 2.25 | 2.25 |
| g. | V197 | €1 multicolored | 2.25 | 2.25 |
| h. | V198 | €1 multicolored | 2.25 | 2.25 |
| i. | V199 | €1 multicolored | 2.25 | 2.25 |

World Oceans Day.

### Souvenir Sheet

Frankie the Dinosaur V200

**2023, June 20    Litho.    Perf. 13¼x14**
| 711 | V200 | €1.90 multicolored | 4.50 | 4.50 |

"Don't Choose Extinction" campaign.

V201

Guqin and Its Music — V202

**2023, Aug. 10    Litho.    Perf. 14x13¼**
| 712 | V201 | €1 multicolored | 2.40 | 2.40 |
| | | First day cover | | 5.25 |

OFFICES IN VIENNA, AUSTRIA — U.N. TEMPORARY EXECUTIVE AUTHORITY, WEST NEW GUINEA

### Souvenir Sheet
Perf. 13¼x14

| 713 | V202 | €1.90 multicolored | 4.50 | 4.50 |

UNESCO Intangible Cultural Heritage.

### World Heritage Sites in Turkey Type of 2023

Designs: Nos. 714, 716c, Ephesus. Nos. 715, 716f, Historic Areas of Istanbul. No. 716a, Nemrut Dag. No. 716b, Göreme National Park and the Rock Sites of Cappadocia. No. 716d, Selimiye Mosque. No. 716e, Great Mosque and Hospital of Divrigi.

**2023, Sept. 8  Litho.  Perf. 14x14¼**

| 714 | A617 | €1.20 multicolored | 3.00 | 3.00 |
| 715 | A617 | €2.10 multicolored | 5.25 | 5.25 |

### Souvenir Booklet

| 716 | Booklet, #1280g-1280l | 32.00 | |
| a.-c. | A617 45c any single | 1.25 | 1.25 |
| d.-f. | A617 50c any single | 1.40 | 1.40 |
| g. | Booklet pane of 4 #716a | 5.00 | — |
| h. | Booklet pane of 4 #716b | 5.00 | — |
| i. | Booklet pane of 4 #716c | 5.00 | — |
| j. | Booklet pane of 4 #716d | 5.60 | — |
| k. | Booklet pane of 4 #716e | 5.60 | — |
| l. | Booklet pane of 4 #716f | 5.60 | — |

Complete booklet sold for $15.66 or €13.

World Mental Health Day — V203

**2023, Oct. 10  Litho.  Perf. 13¼x14**

| 717 | V203 | €1.20 multicolored | 3.00 | 3.00 |

---

### SEMI-POSTAL STAMPS

### AIDS Awareness Semi-postal Type
Souvenir Sheet

**2002, Oct. 24  Litho.  Perf. 14½**

| B1 | VSP1 | 51c + 25c multicolored | 3.50 | 3.50 |

VSP2

Photograph of John Lennon (1940-80), by David Nutter — VSP3

**2021, Sept. 21  Litho.  Perf. 14¼**

| B2 | VSP2 | €1 multicolored | 4.00 | 4.00 |

### Souvenir Sheet
Litho. With Foil Application

| B3 | VSP3 | €2.85 multicolored | 10.50 | 10.50 |

International Day of Peace. Surtax for United Nations peacekeeping efforts.

World Humanitarian Day — VSP4

**2022, Aug. 19  Litho.  Perf. 13¼x13**

| B4 | VSP4 | €1.80 multicolored | 5.75 | 5.75 |

Surtax for United Nations Central Emergency Response Fund.

---

## U.N. TEMPORARY EXECUTIVE AUTHORITY, WEST NEW GUINEA
### Temporary Executive Authority

LOCATION — Western half of New Guinea, southwest Pacific Ocean
GOVT. — Province of Indonesia
AREA — In 1958, the size was 151,789 sq. mi.
POP. — estimated at 730,000 in 1958
CAPITAL — Hollandia

The former Netherlands New Guinea became a territory under the administration of the United Nations Temporary Executive Authority on Oct. 1, 1962.

The territory came under Indonesian administration on May 1, 1963. For stamps issued by Indonesia see West Irian in Volume 3.

100 Cents = 1 Gulden
100 Cents = 1 Gulden

> Catalogue values for all unused stamps in this country are for Never Hinged items.

### First Printing (Hollandia)

Netherlands New Guinea Stamps of 1950-60 Overprinted

Overprint size: 17x3½mm. Top of "N" is slightly lower than the "U," and the base of the "T" is straight, or nearly so.

Photo.; Litho. (#4, 6, 8)
Perf. 12½x12, 12½x13½

**1962, Oct. 1                             Unwmk.**

| 1 | A4 | 1c vermilion & yellow | .25 | .25 |
| 2 | A1 | 2c deep orange | .25 | .25 |
| 3 | A4 | 5c chocolate & yellow | .25 | .25 |
| 4 | A5 | 7c org red, bl & brn vio | .25 | .35 |
| 5 | A4 | 10c aqua & red brown | .25 | .35 |
| 6 | A5 | 12c green, bl & brn vio | .25 | .35 |
| 7 | A4 | 15c deep yel & red brn | .45 | .45 |
| 8 | A5 | 17c brown violet & blue | .55 | .70 |
| 9 | A4 | 20c lt bl grn & red brn | .60 | .75 |
| 10 | A6 | 25c red | .40 | .55 |
| 11 | A6 | 30c deep blue | .75 | .75 |
| 12 | A6 | 40c deep orange | .75 | .75 |
| 13 | A6 | 45c dark olive | 1.00 | 1.00 |
| 14 | A6 | 55c slate blue | 25.00 | 2.25 |
| 15 | A6 | 80c dull gray violet | 5.00 | 5.00 |
| 16 | A6 | 85c dark violet brown | 2.50 | 2.50 |
| 17 | A6 | 1g plum | 8.75 | 3.00 |

Engr.

| 18 | A3 | 2g reddish brown | 11.75 | 30.00 |
| 19 | A3 | 5g green | 8.75 | 8.00 |
| | | Nos. 1-19 (19) | 67.75 | 57.50 |

Overprinted locally and sold in West New Guinea. Stamps of the second printing were used to complete sets sold to collectors.

### Second Printing (Haarlen, Netherlands)

Overprint size: 17x3½mm. Top of the "N" is slightly higher than the "U," and the base of the "T" is concave.

Photo.; Litho. (#4a, 6a, 8a)
Perf. 12½x12, 12½x13½

**1962                                   Unwmk.**

| 1a | A4 | 1c vermilion & yellow | .25 | .25 |
| 2a | A1 | 2c deep orange | .25 | .25 |
| 3a | A4 | 5c chocolate & yellow | .25 | .25 |
| 4a | A5 | 7c org red, bl & brn vio | .25 | .25 |
| 5a | A4 | 10c aqua & red brown | .25 | .25 |
| 6a | A5 | 12c green, bl & brn vio | .25 | .25 |
| 7a | A4 | 15c deep yel & red brn | .50 | .25 |
| 8a | A5 | 17c brown violet & blue | .60 | .40 |
| 9a | A4 | 20c lt blue grn & red brn | .60 | .40 |
| 10a | A6 | 25c red | .35 | .35 |
| 11a | A6 | 30c deep blue | .90 | .40 |
| 12a | A6 | 40c deep orange | .90 | .40 |
| 13a | A6 | 45c dark olive | 1.75 | .75 |
| 14a | A6 | 55c slate blue | 5.00 | 1.00 |
| 15a | A6 | 80c dull gray violet | 7.00 | 9.00 |
| 16a | A6 | 85c dark violet brown | 3.75 | 4.75 |
| 17a | A6 | 1g plum | 4.25 | 2.00 |

Engr.

| 18a | A3 | 2g reddish brown | 16.00 | 27.50 |
| 19a | A3 | 5g green | 8.00 | 6.50 |
| | | Nos. 1a-19a (19) | 51.10 | 55.20 |

---

### Third Printing
Overprint 14mm long.

Photo.; Litho. (#4b, 6b, 8b)
Perf. 12½x12

**1963, Mar.     Photo.      Unwmk.**

| 1b | A4 | 1c vermilion & yellow | 5.00 | 3.00 |
| 3b | A4 | 5c chocolate & yellow | 6.00 | 4.00 |
| 4b | A5 | 7c org red, bl & brn vio | 20.00 | 20.00 |
| 5b | A4 | 10c aqua & red brown | 6.00 | 4.00 |
| 6b | A5 | 12c green, bl & brn vio | 35.00 | 35.00 |
| 7b | A4 | 15c deep yel & red brn | 130.00 | 130.00 |
| 8b | A5 | 17c brown violet & blue | 15.00 | 12.00 |
| 9b | A4 | 20c lt blue grn & red brn | 7.50 | 5.00 |
| | | Nos. 1b-9b (8) | 224.50 | 213.00 |

The third printing was applied in West New Guinea and it is doubtful whether it was regularly issued. Used values are for canceled to order stamps.

### Fourth Printing
Overprint 19mm long.

Photogravure

**1963, Mar.   Unwmk.   Perf. 12½x12**

| 1c | A4 | 1c vermilion & yellow | 50.00 | 50.00 |
| 5c | A4 | 10c aqua & red brown | 150.00 | 150.00 |

The fourth printing was applied in West New Guinea and it is doubtful whether it was regularly issued. Used values are for canceled to order stamps.

---

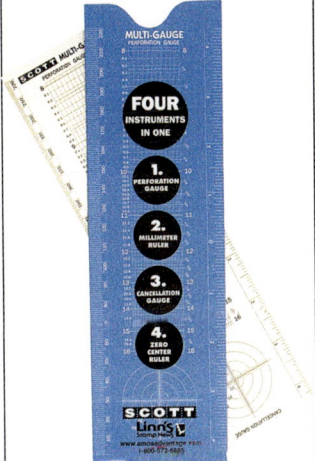

### Scott Multi-Gauge
Item No. LIN01

**$9.89** *AA* price*
$10.99 Retail

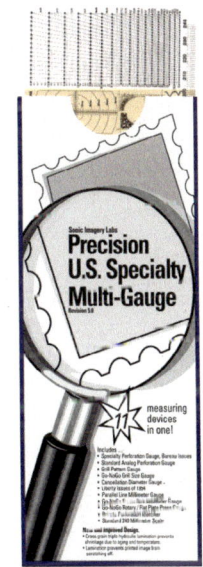

### U.S. Specialized Multi-Gauge
Item No. USSMG02

**$13.59** *AA* price*
$15.99 Retail

**AmosAdvantage.com**
**1-800-572-6885**

ORDERING INFORMATION: *AA prices apply to paid subscribers of Amos Media titles, or for orders placed online. Prices, terms and product availability subject to change.

## U.N. TRANSITIONAL AUTHORITY IN EAST TIMOR

100 cents = 1 U.S. Dollar

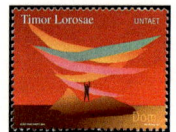

A30

**2000, Apr. 29  Litho.  Perf. 12x11¾**
| 350 | A30 | Dom. red & multi | 35.00 | 102.50 |
| 351 | A30 | Int. blue & multi | 47.50 | 112.50 |

No. 350 sold for 10c and No. 351 sold for 50c on day of issue.

---

## U.N. INTERIM ADMINISTRATION, KOSOVO

These stamps were issued by the United Nations Interim Administration Mission in Kosovo and the Post & Telecommunications of Kosovo. Service was local for the first two months, with international use to start in mid-May.

100 pfennigs = 1 mark
100 cents = €1 (2002)

Catalogue values for all unused stamps in this country are for Never Hinged items.

Peace in Kosovo — A1

Designs: 20pf, Mosaic depicting Orpheus, c. 5th-6th cent., Podujeve. 30pf, Dardinian idol, Museum of Kosovo. 50pf, Silver coin of Damastion from 4th cent. B.C. 1m, Statue of Mother Teresa, Prizren. 2m, Map of Kosovo.

**Perf. 13½x13, 13½x13¼ (30pf)**
**2000, Mar. 14  Litho.  Unwmk.**
| 1 | A1 | 20pf multicolored | .65 | .65 |
| 2 | A1 | 30pf multicolored | 1.25 | 1.25 |
| 3 | A1 | 50pf multicolored | 1.60 | 1.60 |
| 4 | A1 | 1m multicolored | 2.00 | 1.80 |
| 5 | A1 | 2m multicolored | 3.75 | 3.50 |
|   |    | Nos. 1-5 (5) | 9.25 | 8.80 |

Nos. 1-5 were demonetized July 1, 2002.

Beginning with No. 6, Kosovan stamps were not available to collectors through the United Nations Postal Administration.

Peace in Kosovo — A2

Designs: 20pf, Bird. 30pf, Street musician. 50pf, Butterfly and pear. 1m, Children and stars. 2m, Globe and handprints.

**2001, Nov. 12  Litho.  Perf. 14**
| 6 | A2 | 20pf multicolored | 1.00 | 1.00 |
| 7 | A2 | 30pf multicolored | 1.25 | 1.25 |
| 8 | A2 | 50pf multicolored | 2.00 | 2.00 |
| 9 | A2 | 1m multicolored | 4.00 | 4.00 |
| 10 | A2 | 2m multicolored | 7.50 | 7.50 |
|    |    | Nos. 6-10 (5) | 15.75 | 15.75 |

**Peace in Kosovo Type of 2001 With Denominations in Euros Only**
**2002, May 2  Litho.  Perf. 14**
| 11 | A2 | 10c Like #6 | .75 | .75 |
| 12 | A2 | 15c Like #7 | 1.00 | 1.00 |
| 13 | A2 | 26c Like #8 | 1.50 | 1.50 |
| 14 | A2 | 51c Like #9 | 4.50 | 4.50 |
| 15 | A2 | €1.02 Like #10 | 8.00 | 8.00 |
|    |    | Nos. 11-15 (5) | 15.75 | 15.75 |

Christmas — A3

Designs: 50c, Candles and garland. €1, Stylized men.

**2003, Dec. 20  Litho.  Perf. 14**
| 16 | A3 | 50c multicolored | 7.50 | 7.50 |
| 17 | A3 | €1 multicolored | 14.50 | 14.50 |

Return of Refugees A4    Five Years of Peace A5

**2004, June 29  Litho.  Perf. 13¼x13**
| 18 | A4 | €1 multicolored | 7.00 | 7.00 |
| 19 | A5 | €2 multicolored | 16.00 | 16.00 |

Musical Instruments — A6

**2004, Aug. 31  Litho.  Perf. 13¼x13**
| 20 | A6 | 20c Flute | 5.00 | 5.00 |
| 21 | A6 | 30c Ocarina | 10.00 | 10.00 |

Aprons — A7

Vests — A8

Designs: 20c, Apron from Prizren. 30c, Apron from Rugova. 50c, Three vests. €1, Two vests.

**2004, Oct. 28  Litho.  Perf. 13x13¼**
| 22 | A7 | 20c multicolored | 5.50 | 5.50 |
| 23 | A7 | 30c multicolored | 8.50 | 8.50 |
| 24 | A8 | 50c multicolored | 12.00 | 12.00 |
| 25 | A8 | €1 multicolored | 26.00 | 26.00 |
|    |    | Nos. 22-25 (4) | 52.00 | 52.00 |

Mirusha Waterfall — A9

**2004, Nov. 26  Litho.  Perf. 13x13¼**
| 26 | A9 | €2 multicolored | 7.50 | 7.50 |

House — A10

**2004, Dec. 14  Litho.  Perf. 13x13¼**
| 27 | A10 | 50c multicolored | 4.50 | 4.50 |

Flowers — A11

**2005, June 29  Litho.  Perf. 13½**
| 28 | A11 | 15c Peony | 2.25 | 2.25 |
| 29 | A11 | 20c Poppies | 3.25 | 3.25 |
| 30 | A11 | 30c Gentian | 5.00 | 5.00 |
|    |     | Nos. 28-30 (3) | 10.50 | 10.50 |

A12

Handicrafts — A13

**2005, July 20  Perf. 13¼x13**
| 31 | A12 | 20c shown | 2.50 | 2.50 |
| 32 | A12 | 30c Cradle | 3.00 | 3.00 |
| 33 | A13 | 50c shown | 3.25 | 3.25 |
| 34 | A12 | €1 Necklace | 4.25 | 4.25 |
|    |     | Nos. 31-34 (4) | 13.00 | 13.00 |

Village — A14

Town — A15

City — A16

**2005, Sept. 15  Perf. 13x13½**
| 35 | A14 | 20c multicolored | 2.00 | 2.00 |
| 36 | A15 | 50c multicolored | 3.00 | 3.00 |
| 37 | A16 | €1 multicolored | 6.00 | 6.00 |
|    |     | Nos. 35-37 (3) | 11.00 | 11.00 |

Archaeological Artifacts — A17

**2005, Nov. 2  Perf. 13½x13**
| 38 | A17 | 20c shown | 1.25 | 1.25 |
| 39 | A17 | 30c Statue | 1.75 | 1.75 |
| 40 | A17 | 50c Sculpture | 2.50 | 2.50 |
| 41 | A17 | €1 Helmet | 7.50 | 7.50 |
|    |     | Nos. 38-41 (4) | 13.00 | 13.00 |

Minerals — A18

**2005, Dec. 10  Perf. 13x13½**
| 42 | A18 | €2 multicolored | 10.00 | 10.00 |

A19

Europa — A20

**2006, July 20  Perf. 13¼x13**
| 43 | A19 | 50c multicolored | 2.25 | 2.25 |
| 44 | A20 | €1 multicolored | 4.25 | 4.25 |

Exists Imperf. Value set of two, $75.

Fauna — A21

**2006, May 23  Litho.  Perf. 13**
| 45 | A21 | 15c Wolf | 1.00 | 1.00 |
| 46 | A21 | 20c Cow | 1.25 | 1.25 |
| 47 | A21 | 30c Pigeon | 1.40 | 1.40 |
| 48 | A21 | 50c Swan | 1.60 | 1.60 |
| 49 | A21 | €1 Dog | 2.75 | 2.75 |
| a. |  | Souvenir sheet, #45-49, + label | 8.75 | 8.75 |
|    |     | Nos. 45-49 (5) | 8.00 | 8.00 |

Nos. 45-49 are inscribed CPU. Stamps with "Leoprint" imprint are from No. 63a.
No. 49a exists in two shades of green selvage.

Children — A22

Designs: 20c, Children in cradle. 30c, Children reading. 50c, Girls dancing. €1, Child in water.

**2006, June 30  Litho.  Perf. 13**
| 50 | A22 | 20c multicolored | 1.00 | 1.00 |
| 51 | A22 | 30c multicolored | 1.25 | 1.25 |
| 52 | A22 | 50c multicolored | 1.75 | 1.75 |
| 53 | A22 | €1 multicolored | 3.50 | 3.50 |
| a. |  | Souvenir sheet, #50-53 | 7.75 | 7.75 |
|    |     | Nos. 50-53 (4) | 7.50 | 7.50 |

Nos. 50-53 were printed by CPU & Moare. No. 53a was printed by two printers: 7,500 inscribed "CPU&Moare," and 5,000 inscribed "Leoprint."
Nos. 50-53 from CPO & Moare exists imperforate. Value, set, $75.
No. 53a by CPU & Moare exists imperforate. Value $75.

A23

A24

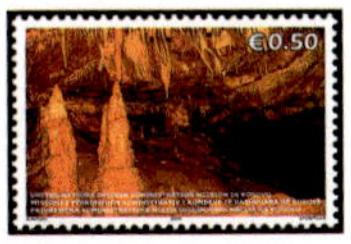

A25

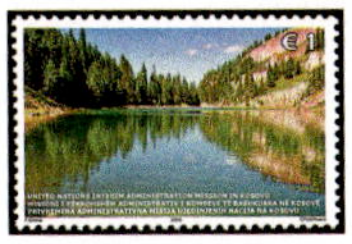

Tourist Attractions A26

**2006, Sept. 1 Litho. *Perf. 13***

| | | | | |
|---|---|---|---|---|
| 54 | A23 | 20c multicolored | 1.00 | 1.00 |
| 55 | A24 | 30c multicolored | 1.25 | 1.25 |
| 56 | A25 | 50c multicolored | 1.75 | 1.75 |
| 57 | A26 | €1 multicolored | 3.25 | 3.25 |
| *a.* | | Souvenir sheet, #54-57 | 9.50 | 9.50 |
| | | *Nos. 54-57 (4)* | 7.25 | 7.25 |

Nos. 54-57 were printed by CPU & Moare. No. 57a was printed by two printers: 7,500 inscribed "CPU&Moare," and 5,000 inscribed "Leoprint."

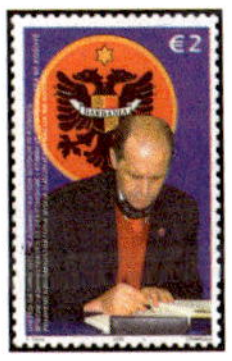

Intl. Peace Day — A27

**2006, Sept. 21 Litho. *Perf. 13***

| | | | | |
|---|---|---|---|---|
| 58 | A27 | €2 multicolored | 7.00 | 7.00 |

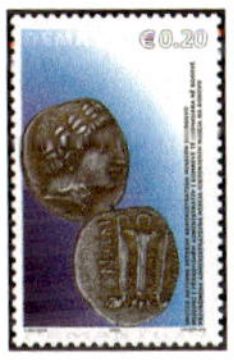

Ancient Coins — A28

Various coins.

**2006, Nov. 1 Litho. *Perf. 13***

| | | | | |
|---|---|---|---|---|
| 59 | A28 | 20c multicolored | 1.00 | 1.00 |
| 60 | A28 | 30c multicolored | 1.50 | 1.50 |
| 61 | A28 | 50c multicolored | 1.75 | 1.75 |
| 62 | A28 | €1 multicolored | 3.25 | 3.25 |
| *a.* | | Souvenir sheet, #59-62 | 9.50 | 9.50 |
| | | *Nos. 59-62 (4)* | 7.50 | 7.50 |

Nos. 59-62 are inscribed CPU. Stamps with "Leoprint" imprint are from No. 63a.

No. 62a exists imperforate. Value, $75.

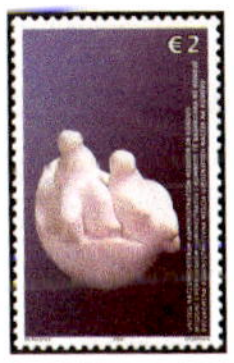

Sculpture — A29

**2006, Dec. 1 Litho. *Perf. 13***

| | | | | |
|---|---|---|---|---|
| 63 | A29 | €2 multicolored | 8.00 | 8.00 |
| *a.* | | Miniature sheet, #45-57, 59-63, + 2 labels | 80.00 | 80.00 |

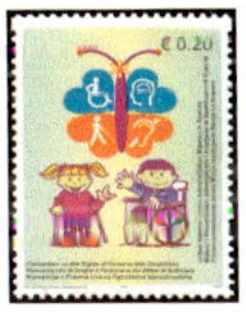

Convention on the Rights of Persons With Disabilities — A30

Emblems of handicaps and: 20c, Children and butterfly. 50c, Handicapped women. 70c, Map of Kosovo. €1, Stylized flower.

**2007, Apr. 23 Litho. *Perf. 14x14¼***

| | | | | |
|---|---|---|---|---|
| 64 | A30 | 20c multicolored | 1.25 | 1.25 |
| 65 | A30 | 50c multicolored | 2.50 | 2.50 |
| 66 | A30 | 70c multicolored | 3.00 | 3.00 |
| 67 | A30 | €1 multicolored | 3.75 | 3.75 |
| *a.* | | Souvenir sheet, #64-67 | 12.50 | 12.50 |
| | | *Nos. 64-67 (4)* | 10.50 | 10.50 |

Color shades vary widely. Printer's waste of this issue exists in the marketplace, including partial prints, missing design elements, and missing colors.

Two varieties of No. 67a, exist differing in text surrounding the stamps. It has not been established if both varieties were officially issued.

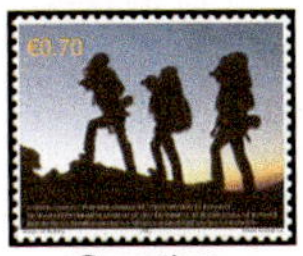

Scouting, Cent. — A31

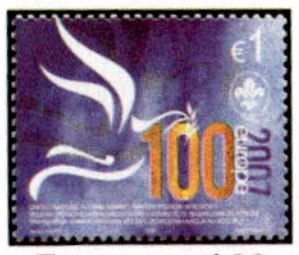

Europa — A32

**2007, May 12 Litho. *Perf. 13¼***

| | | | | |
|---|---|---|---|---|
| 68 | A31 | 70c multicolored | 4.25 | 4.25 |
| 69 | A32 | €1 multicolored | 6.25 | 6.25 |
| *a.* | | Souvenir sheet, #68-69 | 90.00 | 90.00 |

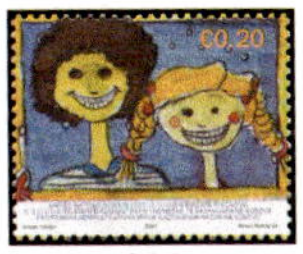

A33

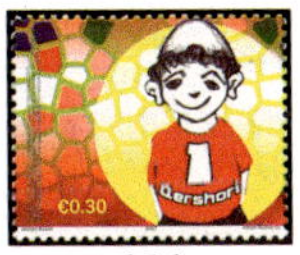

A34

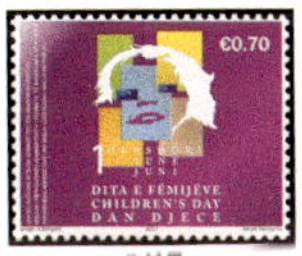

A35

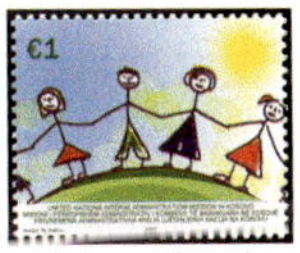

International Children's Day — A36

**2007, June 1 Litho. *Perf. 13¼***

| | | | | |
|---|---|---|---|---|
| 70 | A33 | 20c multicolored | 1.25 | 1.25 |
| 71 | A34 | 30c multicolored | 1.50 | 1.50 |
| 72 | A35 | 70c multicolored | 2.50 | 2.50 |
| 73 | A36 | €1 multicolored | 4.00 | 4.00 |
| | | *Nos. 70-73 (4)* | 9.25 | 9.25 |

Nos. 70-73 exist imperf. Value, set $45

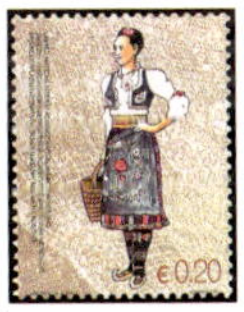

Native Costumes — A37

Designs: 20c, Serbian woman. 30c, Prizren Region woman. 50c, Sword dancer. 70c, Drenica Region woman. €1, Shepherd, Rugova.

**2007, July 6 Litho. *Perf. 13½x13¼***

| | | | | |
|---|---|---|---|---|
| 74 | A37 | 15c multicolored | 1.25 | 1.25 |
| 75 | A37 | 30c multicolored | 1.75 | 1.75 |
| 76 | A37 | 50c multicolored | 2.00 | 2.00 |
| 77 | A37 | 70c multicolored | 2.50 | 2.50 |
| 78 | A37 | €1 multicolored | 3.25 | 3.25 |
| *a.* | | Souvenir sheet, #74-78, + label | 12.50 | 12.50 |
| | | *Nos. 74-78 (5)* | 10.75 | 10.75 |

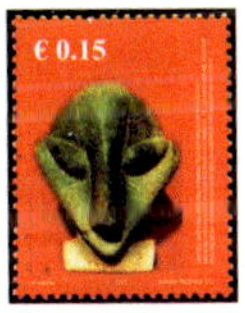

Masks — A38

Various masks.

**2007, Sept. 11 *Perf. 13½x13¼* Litho.**

| | | | | |
|---|---|---|---|---|
| 79 | A38 | 15c multicolored | .75 | .75 |
| 80 | A38 | 30c multicolored | 1.00 | 1.00 |
| 81 | A38 | 50c multicolored | 2.00 | 2.00 |
| 82 | A38 | €1 multicolored | 3.00 | 3.00 |
| | | *Nos. 79-82 (4)* | 6.75 | 6.75 |

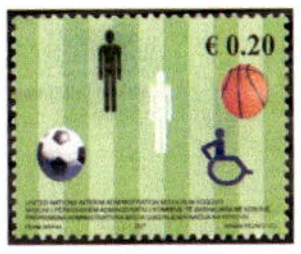

Sports — A39

Designs: 20c, Soccer ball, basketball, two people standing, person in wheelchair. 50c, Wrestlers. €1, Symbols of 24 sports.

**2007, Oct. 2 Litho. *Perf. 13¼x13½***

| | | | | |
|---|---|---|---|---|
| 83 | A39 | 20c multicolored | 1.00 | 1.00 |
| 84 | A39 | 50c multicolored | 2.25 | 2.25 |
| 85 | A39 | €1 multicolored | 4.00 | 4.00 |
| | | *Nos. 83-85 (3)* | 7.25 | 7.25 |

Nos. 83-85 exist imperf. Value, set $65.

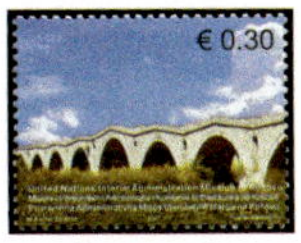

Architecture — A40

Designs: 30c, Stone bridge, Vushtrri. 50c, Hamam, Prizren. 70c, Tower. €1, Tower, diff.

**2007, Nov. 6 Litho. *Perf. 13¼***

| | | | | |
|---|---|---|---|---|
| 86 | A40 | 30c multicolored | 1.50 | 1.50 |
| 87 | A40 | 50c multicolored | 2.00 | 2.00 |
| 88 | A40 | 70c multicolored | 2.50 | 2.50 |
| 89 | A40 | €1 multicolored | 3.50 | 3.50 |
| | | *Nos. 86-89 (4)* | 9.50 | 9.50 |

Nos. 86-89 exist imperf. Value, set $85.

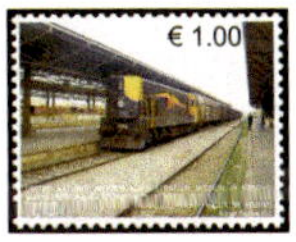

Locomotives — A41

Designs: €1, Diesel locomotive. €2, Steam locomotive

**2007, Dec. 7 Litho. *Perf. 13¼***

| | | | | |
|---|---|---|---|---|
| 90 | A41 | €1 multicolored | 4.00 | 4.00 |
| 91 | A41 | €2 multicolored | 8.00 | 8.00 |

Nos. 90-91 exist imperf. Value, set $125.

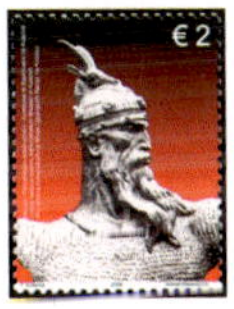

Skanderbeg (1405-68), Albanian National Hero — A42

**2008, Jan. 17 Litho. *Perf. 13¼***

| | | | | |
|---|---|---|---|---|
| 92 | A42 | €2 multicolored | 7.50 | 7.50 |

No. 92 exists imperf. Value, $35.

Kosovo declared its independence from Serbia on Feb. 17, 2008, ending the United Nations Interim Administration. Stamps issued after Feb. 17, 2008, by the Republic of Kosovo will be listed under Kosovo in the *Scott Standard Postage Stamp Catalogue.*

## ABU DHABI

ˌä-bü-ˈthä-bē

LOCATION — Arabia, on Persian Gulf
GOVT. — Sheikdom under British protection
POP. — 25,000 (estimated)
CAPITAL — Abu Dhabi

Abu Dhabi is one of six Persian Gulf sheikdoms to join the United Arab Emirates, which proclaimed its independence Dec. 2, 1971. See United Arab Emirates.

100 Naye Paise = 1 Rupee
1000 Fils = 1 Dinar (1966)

**Catalogue values for all unused stamps in this country are for Never Hinged items.**

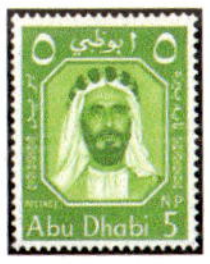

Sheik Shakbut bin Sultan — A1

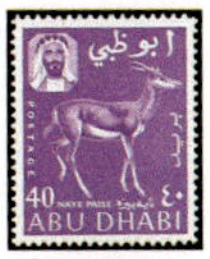

Gazelle — A1a

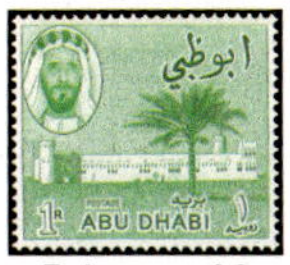

Palace — A2

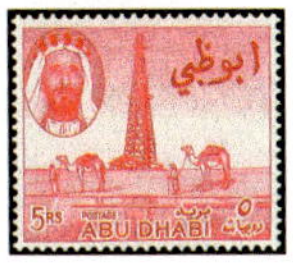

Oil Rig and Camels — A2a

***Perf. 14½***

**1964, Mar. 30 Photo. Unwmk.**

| | | | | |
|---|---|---|---|---|
| 1 | A1 | 5np brt yellow green | 4.00 | 3.75 |
| 2 | A1 | 15np brown | 3.00 | 2.00 |
| 3 | A1 | 20np brt ultra | 3.25 | 1.75 |
| *a.* | | Perf 13x13½ | 575.00 | |
| 4 | A1 | 30np red orange | 3.25 | 1.25 |
| 5 | A1a | 40np brt violet | 6.00 | 1.00 |
| 6 | A1a | 50np brown olive | 6.50 | 2.25 |
| 7 | A1a | 75np dk gray | 9.00 | 6.75 |

**Engr. *Perf. 13x13½***

| | | | | |
|---|---|---|---|---|
| 8 | A2 | 1r light green | 5.00 | 2.50 |
| 9 | A2 | 2r black | 9.00 | 6.00 |
| 10 | A2a | 5r carmine rose | 20.00 | 13.00 |
| 11 | A2a | 10r blue | 26.00 | 15.00 |
| | | *Nos. 1-11 (11)* | 95.00 | 54.25 |

For surcharges see Nos. 15-25.

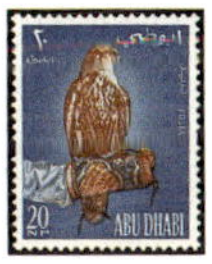

Falcon Perched on Wrist — A3

40np, Falcon facing left. 2r, Falcon facing right.

**1965, Mar. 30 Photo. *Perf. 14½***

| | | | | |
|---|---|---|---|---|
| 12 | A3 | 20np chlky blue & brn | 13.50 | 2.75 |
| 13 | A3 | 40np ultra & brown | 17.00 | 3.50 |
| 14 | A3 | 2r brt blue grn & gray brn | 29.00 | 16.00 |
| | | *Nos. 12-14 (3)* | 59.50 | 22.25 |

**Nos. 1-11 Surcharged**

a

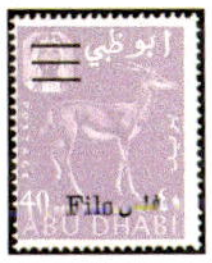

b

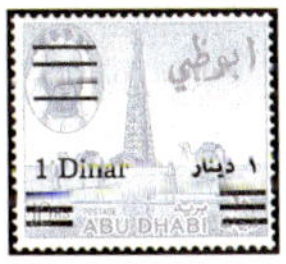

c

**1966, Oct. 1 Photo. *Perf. 14½***

| | | | | |
|---|---|---|---|---|
| 15 | A1 (a) | 5f on 5np | 10.00 | 5.00 |
| 16 | A1 (a) | 15f on 15np | 12.00 | 9.00 |
| 17 | A1 (a) | 20f on 20np, perf 13x13½ (#3a) | 14.00 | 7.00 |
| *a.* | | Perf 14½ (#3) | 275.00 | 300.00 |
| *b.* | | As "a," inverted surcharge | 700.00 | *1,000.* |
| 18 | A1 (a) | 30f on 30np | 14.00 | *16.50* |
| *a.* | | Double surcharge | 400.00 | |
| *b.* | | Arabic surcharge "20f" instead of "00f" | *11,000.* | |
| 19 | A1a (b) | 40f on 40np | 13.00 | 1.50 |
| 20 | A1a (b) | 50f on 50np | 35.00 | *32.50* |
| 21 | A1a (b) | 75f on 75np | 35.00 | *32.50* |
| *a.* | | Double surcharge | 400.00 | |

**Engr.**

***Perf. 13x13½***

| | | | | |
|---|---|---|---|---|
| 22 | A2 (c) | 100f on 1r | 17.00 | 4.00 |
| 23 | A2 (c) | 200f on 2r | 17.50 | 13.00 |
| 24 | A2a (c) | 500f on 5r | 42.50 | *47.50* |
| 25 | A2a (c) | 1d on 10r | 62.50 | *72.50* |
| | | *Nos. 15-25 (11)* | 272.50 | 241.00 |

Overprint on No. 25 has "1 Dinar" on 1 line and 3 bars through old denomination.

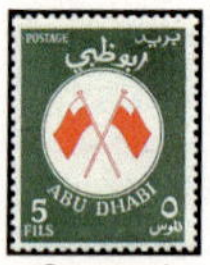

Crossed Flags of Abu Dhabi — A4

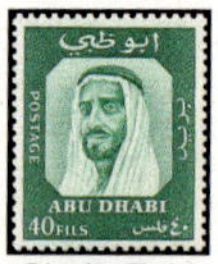

Sheik Zaid bin Sultan al Nahayan — A4a

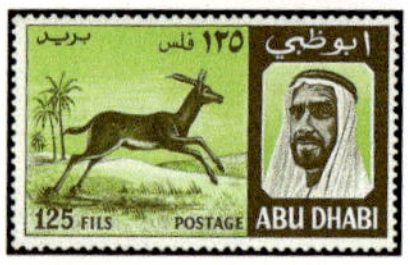

Dorcas Gazelle — A5

200f, Falcon. 500f, 1d, Palace.

**Engr.; Flags Litho.**

**1967, Apr. 1** ***Perf. 13x13½***

| | | | | |
|---|---|---|---|---|
| **26** | A4 | 5f dpl grn & red | .40 | .30 |
| **27** | A4 | 15f dk brown & red | .60 | .30 |
| **28** | A4 | 20f Prus blue & red | 1.00 | .75 |
| **29** | A4 | 35f purple & red | 1.25 | 1.00 |
| | | **Engr.** | | |
| **30** | A4a | 40f blue green | 1.50 | 1.20 |
| **31** | A4a | 50f lt brown | 1.90 | 1.50 |
| **32** | A4a | 60f blue | 2.10 | 1.60 |
| **33** | A4a | 100f car rose | 3.50 | 2.75 |
| | | **Litho.** | | |
| **34** | A5 | 125f brt yel grn & brn ol | 7.50 | 6.50 |
| **35** | A5 | 200f lt blue & lt brn | 32.00 | 27.50 |
| **36** | A5 | 500f dull org & brt redsh vio | 22.50 | 17.50 |
| **37** | A5 | 1d brt yel grn & bluish vio | 60.00 | 50.00 |
| | | *Nos. 26-37 (12)* | 134.25 | 110.90 |

For surcharge, see No. 55A.

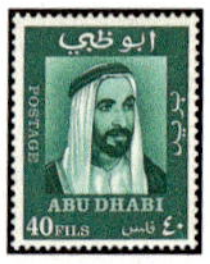

Sheik Zaid bin Sultan al Nahayan — A6

**1967, Aug. 6 Photo.** ***Perf. 14½x14***

| | | | | |
|---|---|---|---|---|
| **38** | A6 | 40f blue green | 4.50 | 2.75 |
| **39** | A6 | 50f org brown | 5.50 | 2.25 |
| **40** | A6 | 60f Prus blue | 19.00 | 4.50 |
| **41** | A6 | 100f carmine rose | 28.00 | 11.00 |
| | | *Nos. 38-41 (4)* | 57.00 | 20.50 |

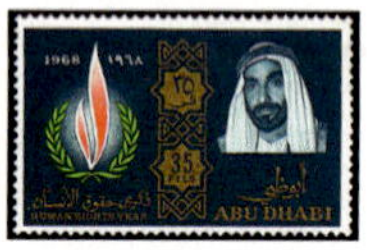

Human Rights Flame and Sheik Zaid — A6a

***Perf. 14½x14***

**1968, Apr. 1 Photo. Unwmk.**

**Emblem in Red and Green**

| | | | | |
|---|---|---|---|---|
| **42** | A6a | 35f peacock bl & gold | 2.25 | .90 |
| **43** | A6a | 60f dk blue & gold | 3.50 | 1.25 |
| **44** | A6a | 150f dk brown & gold | 9.00 | 3.00 |
| | | *Nos. 42-44 (3)* | 14.75 | 5.15 |

International Human Rights Year.

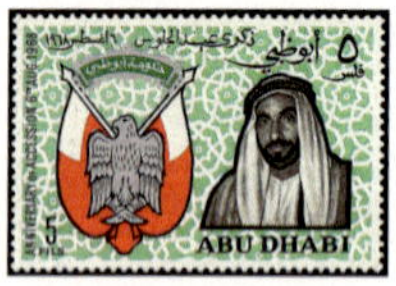

Sheik Zaid and Coat of Arms — A7

***Perf. 14x14½***

**1968, Aug. 6 Photo. Unwmk.**

| | | | | |
|---|---|---|---|---|
| **45** | A7 | 5f multicolored | 4.00 | .60 |
| **46** | A7 | 10f multicolored | 4.00 | .85 |
| **47** | A7 | 100f multicolored | 11.00 | 3.25 |
| **48** | A7 | 125f multicolored | 16.00 | 4.75 |
| | | *Nos. 45-48 (4)* | 35.00 | 9.45 |

Accession of Sheik Zaid, 2nd anniversary.

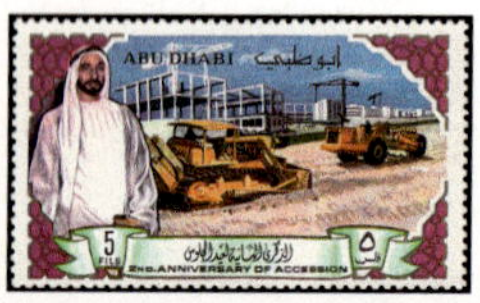

Abu Dhabi Airport A8

5f, Buildings under construction and earth-moving equipment. 35f, New bridge and falcon. Each stamp shows different portrait of Sheik Zaid.

***Perf. 12, 12½x13 (10f)***

**1969, Mar. 28 Litho.**

**Size: 5f, 35f, 59x34mm; 10f, 47x34mm**

| | | | | |
|---|---|---|---|---|
| **49** | A8 | 5f multicolored | 3.00 | .55 |
| **50** | A8 | 10f multicolored | 7.50 | 1.00 |
| **51** | A8 | 35f multicolored | 32.50 | 8.00 |
| | | *Nos. 49-51 (3)* | 43.00 | 9.55 |

Issued to publicize progress made in Abu Dhabi during preceding 2 years.

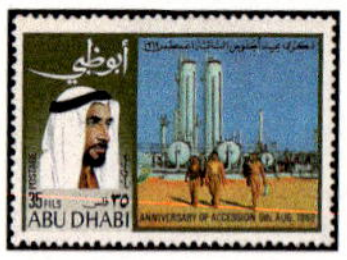

Sheik Zaid and Abu Dhabi Petroleum Co. — A9

Designs: 60f, Abu Dhabi Marine Areas drilling platform and helicopter. 125f, Zakum Field separator at night. 200f, Tank farm.

**1969, Aug. 6 Litho.** ***Perf. 14x13½***

| | | | | |
|---|---|---|---|---|
| **52** | A9 | 35f olive grn & multi | 2.00 | .85 |
| **53** | A9 | 60f yel brn & multi | 9.50 | 2.25 |
| **54** | A9 | 125f mag & multi | 11.00 | 4.00 |
| **55** | A9 | 200f org brn & multi | 15.00 | 7.00 |
| | | *Nos. 52-55 (4)* | 37.50 | 14.10 |

Accession of Sheik Zaid, 3rd anniversary.

No. 27 Surcharged "25" in Arabic

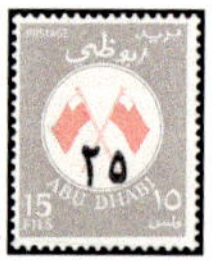

**1969, Dec. 13**

| | | | | |
|---|---|---|---|---|
| **55A** | A4 | 25f on 15f dk brn & red | *250.00* | *160.00* |

Because of local demand for 25f stamps for mailing Christmas greeting cards abroad, the Director of Posts ordered that 20,000 examples of No. 27 be surcharged "25" in Arabic for emergency use. This surcharge was applied locally, using a hand numbering machine. All stamps were sold at post office counters between Dec. 13 and Dec. 24, and the majority were used on mail during this period. Stamps remained valid and exist on covers into 1970. Double overprints exist.

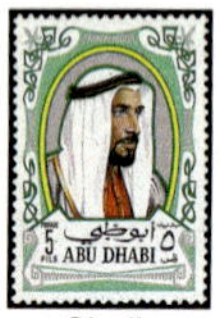

Sheik Zaid — A10

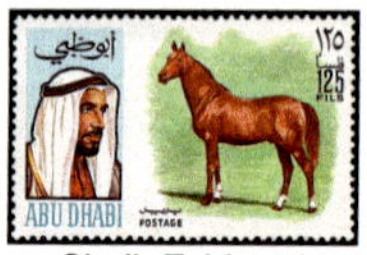

Sheik Zaid and Stallion — A11

5f, 25f, 60f, 90f, Oval frame around portrait. 150f, Gazelle and Sheik. 500f, Fort Jahili and Sheik. 1d, Grand Mosque and Sheik.

**1970-71 Litho.** ***Perf. 14***

| | | | | |
|---|---|---|---|---|
| **56** | A10 | 5f lt green & multi | 1.00 | .25 |
| **57** | A10 | 10f bister & multi | 1.25 | .25 |
| **58** | A10 | 25f lilac & multi | 2.00 | .25 |
| **59** | A10 | 35f dl blue vio & multi | 2.25 | .25 |
| **60** | A10 | 50f sepia & multi | 3.25 | .40 |
| **61** | A10 | 60f blue & multi | 3.75 | .50 |
| **62** | A10 | 70f rose red & multi | 6.00 | .65 |
| **63** | A10 | 90f magenta & multi | 8.25 | 1.00 |
| **64** | A11 | 125f multi ('71) | 12.00 | 2.00 |
| **65** | A11 | 150f multi ('71) | 15.00 | 2.50 |
| **66** | A11 | 500f multi ('71) | 85.00 | 11.00 |
| **67** | A11 | 1d multi ('71) | 85.00 | 22.50 |
| | | *Nos. 56-67 (12)* | 189.75 | 41.55 |

For surcharge see No. 80.

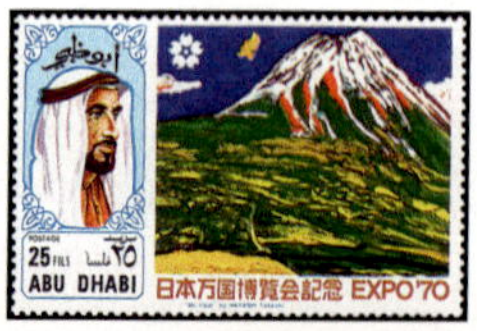

Sheik Zaid and Mt. Fuji A12

**1970, Aug. Litho.** ***Perf. 13½x13***

| | | | | |
|---|---|---|---|---|
| **68** | A12 | 25f multicolored | 4.25 | 1.25 |
| **69** | A12 | 35f multicolored | 6.00 | 2.00 |
| **70** | A12 | 60f multicolored | 11.00 | 4.00 |
| | | *Nos. 68-70 (3)* | 21.25 | 7.25 |

Issued to publicize EXPO '70 International Exhibition, Osaka, Japan, Mar. 15-Sept. 13.

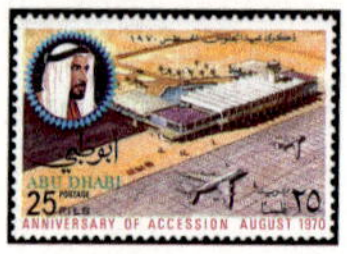

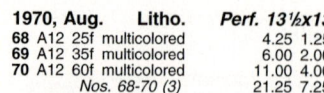

Abu Dhabi Airport — A13

Designs: 60f, Airport entrance. 150f, Aerial view of Abu Dhabi Town, vert.

***Perf. 14x13½, 13½x14***

**1970, Sept. 22 Litho.**

| | | | | |
|---|---|---|---|---|
| **71** | A13 | 25f multicolored | 4.75 | .85 |
| **72** | A13 | 60f multicolored | 9.00 | 2.00 |
| **73** | A13 | 150f multicolored | 20.00 | 5.25 |
| | | *Nos. 71-73 (3)* | 33.75 | 8.10 |

Accession of Sheik Zaid, 4th anniversary.

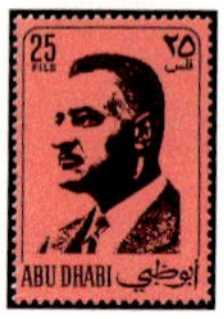

Gamal Abdel Nasser — A14

**1971, May 3 Litho.** ***Perf. 14***

| | | | | |
|---|---|---|---|---|
| **74** | A14 | 25f deep rose & blk | 6.00 | 3.50 |
| **75** | A14 | 35f rose violet & blk | 8.00 | 5.25 |

In memory of Gamal Abdel Nasser (1918-1970), President of UAR.

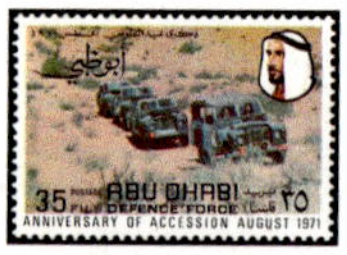

Scout Cars — A15

Designs: 60f, Patrol boat. 125f, Armored car in desert. 150f, Meteor jet fighters.

**1971, Aug. 6 Litho.** ***Perf. 13***

| | | | | |
|---|---|---|---|---|
| **76** | A15 | 35f multicolored | 6.25 | 1.50 |
| **77** | A15 | 60f multicolored | 8.50 | 2.25 |
| **78** | A15 | 125f multicolored | 18.00 | 3.75 |
| **79** | A15 | 150f multicolored | 22.50 | 7.50 |
| | | *Nos. 76-79 (4)* | 55.25 | 15.00 |

Accession of Sheik Zaid, 5th anniversary.

No. 60 Surcharged in Green

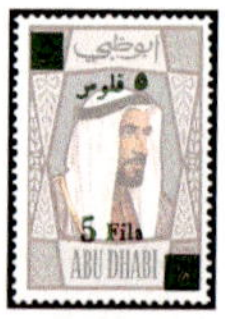

**1971, Dec. 8** ***Perf. 14***

| | | | | |
|---|---|---|---|---|
| **80** | A10 | 5f on 50f multi | *100.00* | *90.00* |

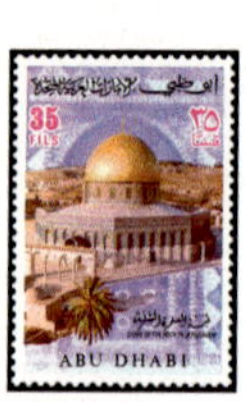

Dome of the Rock, Jerusalem — A16

Different views of Dome of the Rock.

**1972, June 3** ***Perf. 13***

| | | | | |
|---|---|---|---|---|
| **81** | A16 | 35f lt violet & multi | 30.00 | 5.75 |
| **82** | A16 | 60f lt violet & multi | 55.00 | 9.50 |
| **83** | A16 | 125f lilac & multi | 100.00 | 20.00 |
| | | *Nos. 81-83 (3)* | 185.00 | 35.25 |

Nos. 80-83 were issued after Abu Dhabi joined the United Arab Emirates Dec. 2, 1971. Stamps of UAE replaced those of Abu Dhabi. UAE Nos. 1-12 were used only in Abu Dhabi except the 10f and 25f which were issued later in Dubai and Sharjah.

# ADEN

'ā-dən

LOCATION — Southern Arabia
GOVT. — British colony and protectorate
AREA — 112,075 sq. mi.
POP. — 220,000 (est. 1964)
CAPITAL — Aden

Aden used India stamps before 1937. In January, 1963, the colony of Aden (the port) and the sheikdoms and emirates of the Western Aden Protectorate formed the Federation of South Arabia. This did not include the Eastern Aden Protectorate with Kathiri and Qu'aiti States. Stamps of Aden, except those of Kathiri and Qu'aiti States, were replaced Apr. 1, 1965, by those of the Federation of South Arabia. See South Arabia and People's Democratic Republic of Yemen, Vol. 6.

12 Pies = 1 Anna
16 Annas = 1 Rupee
100 Cents = 1 Shilling (1951)

**Catalogue values for unused stamps in this country are for Never Hinged items.**

## ISSUES UNDER BRITISH ADMINISTRATION

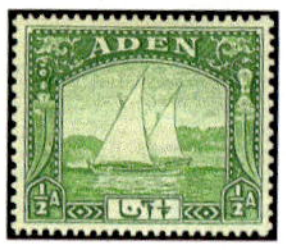

Dhow — A1

***Perf. 13x11½***

**1937, Apr. 1 Engr. Wmk. 4**

| | | | | |
|---|---|---|---|---|
| **1** | A1 | ½a lt green | 4.50 | 3.00 |
| **2** | A1 | 9p dark green | 4.25 | 3.75 |
| **3** | A1 | 1a black brown | 4.00 | 2.25 |
| **4** | A1 | 2a red | 5.00 | 3.25 |
| **5** | A1 | 2½a blue | 7.25 | 2.50 |
| **6** | A1 | 3a carmine rose | 11.00 | 8.75 |
| **7** | A1 | 3½a gray blue | 9.50 | 6.00 |
| **8** | A1 | 8a rose lilac | 27.50 | 11.50 |
| **9** | A1 | 1r brown | 62.50 | 12.50 |
| **10** | A1 | 2r orange yellow | 125.00 | 40.00 |
| **11** | A1 | 5r rose violet | 300.00 | *100.00* |
| **12** | A1 | 10r olive green | 600.00 | *400.00* |
| | | *Nos. 1-12 (12)* | 1,161. | *593.50* |
| | | Set, hinged | 775.00 | |

Common Design Types pictured following the introduction.

**Coronation Issue**

Common Design Type

**1937, May 12** ***Perf. 13½x14***

| | | | | |
|---|---|---|---|---|
| **13** | CD302 | 1a black brown | .75 | *1.25* |
| **14** | CD302 | 2½a blue | .85 | *1.40* |
| **15** | CD302 | 3½a gray blue | 1.10 | *3.00* |
| | | *Nos. 13-15 (3)* | 2.70 | *5.65* |
| | | Set, hinged | 1.75 | |

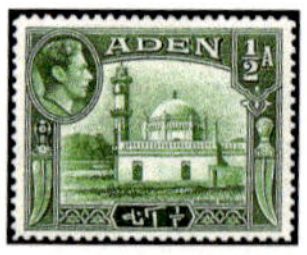

Aidrus Mosque — A2

¾a, 5r, Camel Corpsman. 1a, 2r, Aden Harbor. 1½a, 1r, Adenese dhow. 2½a, 8a, Mukalla. 3a, 14a, 10r, Capture of Aden, 1839.

**1939-48 Engr. Wmk. 4** ***Perf. 12½***

| | | | | |
|---|---|---|---|---|
| **16** | A2 | ½a green (7/42) | 1.75 | .50 |
| **17** | A2 | ¾a red brn | 2.50 | *1.10* |
| **18** | A2 | 1a brt lt blue | 1.40 | .40 |
| **19** | A2 | 1½a red | 2.50 | .60 |
| **20** | A2 | 2a dark brown | 1.60 | .25 |
| **21** | A2 | 2½a brt ultra | 1.60 | .30 |
| **22** | A2 | 3a rose car & dk brn | 1.60 | .25 |
| **23** | A2 | 8a orange | 2.00 | .40 |
| **23A** | A2 | 14a lt bl & brn blk ('45) | 3.75 | .90 |
| **24** | A2 | 1r bright green | 4.50 | 2.25 |
| **25** | A2 | 2r dp mag & bl blk ('44) | 10.00 | 3.00 |
| **26** | A2 | 5r dp ol & lake brn (1/44) | 30.00 | 20.00 |

27a A2 10r dk pur & lake brn 40.00 35.00
Nos. 16-27a (13) 103.20 64.95
Set, hinged 42.50

For shades, see the *Scott Classic Specialized Catalogue.*

**Peace Issue**
Common Design Type
***Perf. 13½x14***

**1946, Oct. 15 Engr. Wmk. 4**
28 CD303 1½a carmine .25 1.50
29 CD303 2½a deep blue .70 1.00

Return to peace at end of World War II.

**Silver Wedding Issue**
Common Design Types

**1949, Jan. 17 Photo. *Perf. 14x14½***
30 CD304 1½a scarlet .40 1.50

**Engraved; Name Typographed**
***Perf. 11½x11***
31 CD305 10r purple 40.00 55.00

25th anniv. of the marriage of King George VI and Queen Elizabeth.

**UPU Issue**
Common Design Types

Srchd. in Annas and Rupees

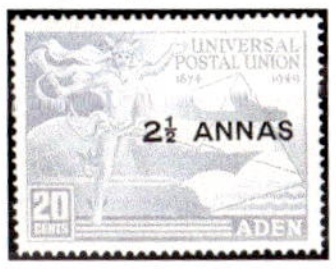


**Engr.; Name typo. on Nos. 33-34**
**1949, Oct. 10 *Perf. 13½, 11x11½***
32 CD306 2½a on 20c dp ultra .55 1.60
33 CD307 3a on 30c dp car 1.90 1.60
34 CD308 8a on 50c org 1.90 1.75
35 CD309 1r on 1sh blue 1.50 3.50
Nos. 32-35 (4) 5.85 8.45

75th anniv. of the formation of the UPU.

**Nos. 18 and 20-27 Surcharged in Black or Carmine**

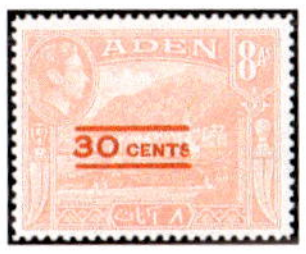


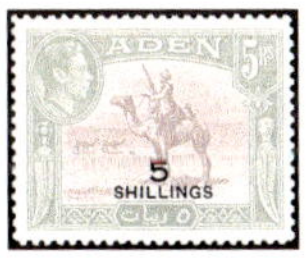


**1951, Oct. 1 Wmk. 4 *Perf. 12½***
36 A2 5c on 1a lt bl (#18a) .30 .40
37 A2 10c on 2a sepia (#20a) .25 .45
38 A2 15c on 2½a brt ultra (#21) .50 1.25
a. Double surcharge 1,600.
Hinged 1,000.
39 A2 20c on 3a rose car & dk brn (#22) .50 .50
40 A2 30c on 8a #23b (C) .85 .60
41 A2 50c on 8a #23b 1.50 .35
42 A2 70c on 14a (#23A) 2.25 1.40
43 A2 1sh on 1r #24a 3.00 .30
44 A2 2sh on 2r #25 13.00 3.50
45 A2 5sh on 5r #26 25.00 15.00
46 A2 10sh on 10r #27 35.00 15.00
Nos. 36-46 (11) 82.15 38.75
Set, hinged 42.50

Surcharge on No. 40 includes 2 bars.

**Coronation Issue**
Common Design Type

**1953, June 2 Engr. *Perf. 13½x13***
47 CD312 15c dk grn & blk 1.25 1.25

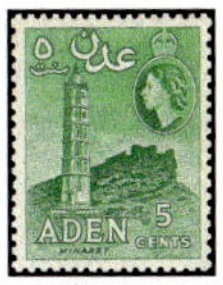
Minaret
A10

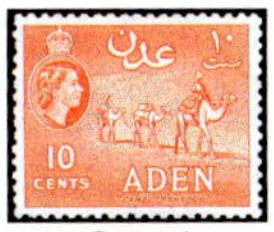
Camel Transport
A11

15c, Crater. 25c, Mosque. 35c, Dhow. 50c, Map. 70c, Salt works. 1sh, Dhow building. 1sh, 25c, Colony Badge. 2sh, Aden Protectorate levy. 5sh, Crater Pass. 10sh, Tribesman. 20sh, Aden in 1572.

***Perf. 12, 12x13½ ('56)***
**1953-59 Engr. Wmk. 4**
**Size: 29x23, 23x29mm**
48 A10 5c grn, perf 12x13½ ('56) .25 .25
a. Perf. 12 ('55) 2.25 3.00
b. 5c bluish grn, perf 12x13½ ('56) .25 1.00
49 A11 10c orange .35 .25
a. 10c vermilion ('55) 1.10 .30
50 A11 15c blue green 1.00 .55
a. 15c grayish grn ('59) 7.00 6.00
51 A11 25c carmine .75 .50
a. 25c deep rose red ('56) 5.00 1.50
52 A10 35c ultra, perf. 12 2.00 1.00
a. 35c dp bl, perf 12x13½ ('58) 5.00 5.00
b. 35c vio bl, perf 12x13½ ('59) 12.50 4.00
53 A10 50c blue, perf 12 .35 .25
a. As "b," perf 12x13½ ('56) 1.00 .25
b. 50c deep bl, perf 12 ('55) 3.00 2.00
54 A10 70c gray, perf 12 .50 .25
a. As "b," perf 12x13½ ('56) 1.75 .25
b. 70c grayish blk, perf 12 ('54) 1.40 .90
55 A11 1sh pur & sepia .50 .25
55A A11 1sh vio & blk ('56) 1.40 .25
56 A10 1sh25c blk & lt blue ('56) 11.00 .45
57 A10 2sh car rose & sep 1.25 .50
57A A10 2sh car & blk ('56) 11.50 .45
58 A10 5sh blue & sepia 2.00 1.00
58A A10 5sh dk blue & blk ('56) 12.00 1.25
59 A10 10sh olive & sepia 2.00 7.50
60 A10 10sh ol gray & blk ('54) 12.50 1.50

**Size: 36½x27mm**
***Perf. 13½x13***
61 A11 20sh rose vio & dk brn 15.00 20.00
61A A11 20sh lt vio & blk ('57) 45.00 18.00
Nos. 48-61A (18) 119.35 54.20
Set, hinged 70.00

No. 60 has heavier shading on tribesman's lower garment than No. 59.
See Nos. 66-75. For overprints see Nos. 63-64.

**Type of 1953**
Inscribed: "Royal Visit 1954"

**1954, Apr. 27 *Perf. 12***
62 A11 1sh purple & sepia .65 4.00

**Nos. 50 & 56 Overprinted in Red**

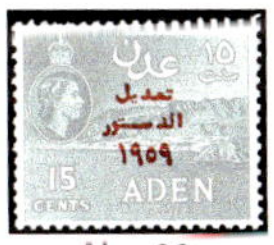
No. 63

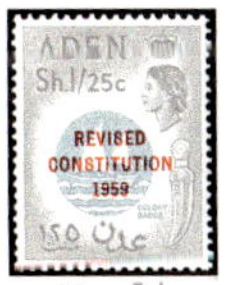

No. 64

**1959, Jan. 26 *Perf. 12, 12x13½***
63 A11 15c dark blue green .55 2.00
64 A10 1sh25c blk & light blue 1.00 1.50

Introduction of a revised constitution.

**Freedom from Hunger Issue**
Common Design Type
***Perf. 14x14½***

**1963, June 4 Photo. Wmk. 314**
65 CD314 1sh25c green 1.50 1.75

**Types of 1953-57**
***Perf. 12x13½, 12 (#67-69, 73)***

**1964-65 Engr. Wmk. 314**
66 A10 5c green ('65) 4.25 9.50
67 A11 10c orange 2.00 1.00
68 A11 15c Prus green .90 5.25
69 A11 25c carmine 3.00 .40
70 A10 35c dk blue 7.25 9.00
71 A10 50c dull blue 1.25 1.10
72 A10 70c gray 2.75 4.00
73 A11 1sh vio & black 11.00 15.00
74 A10 1sh25c blk & lt blue 16.00 2.00
75 A10 2sh car & blk ('65) 6.75 30.00
Nos. 66-75 (10) 55.15 77.25

## KATHIRI STATE OF SEIYUN

LOCATION — In Eastern Aden Protectorate
GOVT. — Sultanate
CAPITAL — Seiyun

The stamps of the Kathiri State of Seiyun were valid for use throughout Aden. Used stamps generally bear Aden GPO or Aden Camp cancels. Examples with cancels from offices in the Eastern Protectorate command a premium.

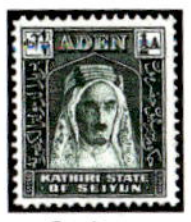
Sultan Ja'far bin Mansur al Kathiri
A1

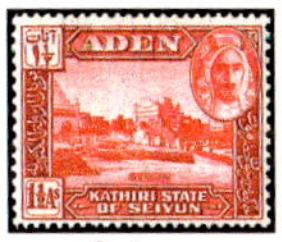
Seiyun
A2

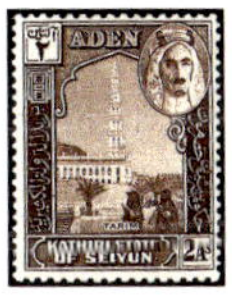
Minaret at Tarim — A3

Designs: 2½a, Mosque at Seiyun. 3a, Palace at Tarim. 8a, Mosque at Seiyun, horiz. 1r, South Gate, Tarim. 2r, Kathiri House. 5r, Mosque at Tarim.

**1942 Engr. Wmk. 4 *Perf. 13¾x14***
1 A1 ½a dark green .25 1.40
2 A1 ¾a copper brown .50 3.00
3 A1 1a deep blue .60 1.50

***Perf. 13x11½, 11½x13***
4 A2 1½a dark car rose .65 1.75
5 A3 2a sepia brown .40 1.75
6 A3 2½a deep blue 1.00 2.00
7 A2 3a dk car rose & dull brn 1.60 3.00
8 A2 8a orange red 3.00 1.25
9 A3 1r green 6.50 3.50
10 A2 2r rose vio & dk blue 13.50 18.00
11 A3 5r gray green & fawn 32.50 24.00
Nos. 1-11 (11) 60.50 61.15
Set, hinged 28.00

For surcharges see Nos. 20-27.

**Nos. 4, 6 Ovptd. in Black or Red**

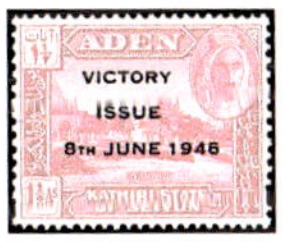

a

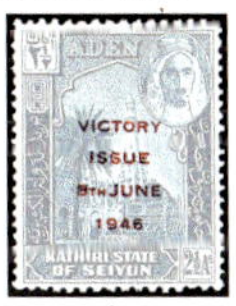

b

***Perf. 13x11½, 11½x13***
**1946, Oct. 15 Wmk. 4**
12 A2 (a) 1½a dark car rose .25 .65
13 A3 (b) 2½a deep blue (R) .25 .25
a. Inverted overprint 1,300.
Hinged 775.00
b. Double overprint 1,800.
Hinged 1,050.

Victory of the Allied Nations in WWII.
All examples of No. 13b have the 2nd overprint almost directly over the 1st.

**Silver Wedding Issue**
Common Design Types

**1949, Jan. 17 Photo. *Perf. 14x14½***
14 CD304 1½a scarlet .35 2.00

**Engraved; Name Typo.**
***Perf. 11½x11***
15 CD305 5r green 17.50 14.00

25th anniv. of the marriage of King George VI and Queen Elizabeth.

**UPU Issue**
Common Design Types

Srchd. in Annas and Rupees

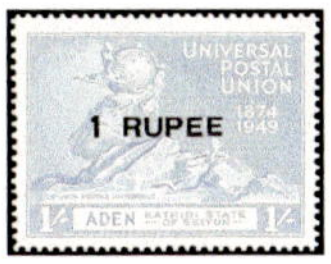


**Engr.; Name Typo. on Nos. 17-18**
**1949, Oct. 10 *Perf. 13½, 11x11½***
16 CD306 2½a on 20c dp ultra .25 4.00
17 CD307 3a on 30c dp car 1.50 4.00
18 CD308 8a on 50c orange .40 4.00
19 CD309 1r on 1sh blue .60 4.00
Nos. 16-19 (4) 2.75 16.00

75th anniv. of the formation of the UPU.

Nos. 3 and 5-11 Srchd. in Carmine or Black

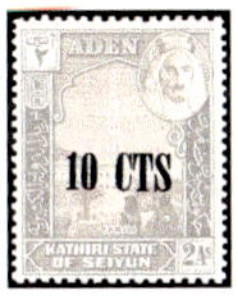


***Perf. 14, 13x11½, 11½x13***
**1951, Oct. 1 Engr. Wmk. 4**
20 A1 5c on 1a (C) .25 2.00
21 A3 10c on 2a #5a .35 1.75
22 A3 15c on 2½a .30 2.25
23 A2 20c on 3a #7 .35 2.50
24 A2 50c on 8a .80 1.60
25 A3 1sh on 1r 2.50 3.75
26 A2 2sh on 2r #10 11.50 30.00
27 A3 5sh on 5r 34.00 47.50
Nos. 20-27 (8) 50.05 91.35

**Coronation Issue**
Common Design Type

**1953, June 2 *Perf. 13½x13***
28 CD312 15c dk green & blk .75 1.50

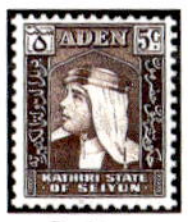
Sultan Hussein
A10

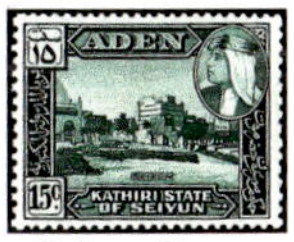
Seiyun Scene
A11

25c, Minaret at Tarim, vert. 35c, Mosque at Seiyun, vert. 50c, Palace at Tarim. 1sh, Mosque at Seiyun. 2sh, South Gate, Tarim, vert.. 5sh, Kathiri house. 10sh, Mosque entrance, Tarim, vert.

**1954, Jan. 15 Engr. *Perf. 12½***
29 A10 5c dark brown .25 .25
30 A10 10c deep blue .25 .25

***Perf. 13x11½, 11½x13***
31 A11 15c dk blue green .25 .25
32 A11 25c dk car rose .25 .25
33 A11 35c deep blue .25 .25
34 A11 50c dk car rose & dk brn .25 .25
35 A11 1sh deep orange .25 .25
36 A11 2sh gray green 4.00 2.00
37 A11 5sh vio & dk blue 9.25 8.00
38 A11 10sh vio & yel brn 10.00 8.50
Nos. 29-38 (10) 25.00 20.25

***Perf. 11½x13, 13x11½***
**1964, July 1 Wmk. 314**

Designs: 70c, Qarn Adh Dhabi. 1sh25c, Seiyun, horiz. 1sh50c, View of Gheil Omer, horiz.

39 A11 70c black 2.75 2.00
40 A11 1sh25c bright green 2.75 7.50
41 A11 1sh50c purple 2.75 8.00
Nos. 39-41 (3) 8.25 17.50

## QUAITI STATE OF SHIHR AND MUKALLA

LOCATION — In Eastern Aden Protectorate
GOVT. — Sultanate
CAPITAL — Mukalla

The stamps of the Quaiti State of Shihr and Mukalla were valid for use throughout Aden. Used stamps generally bear Aden GPO or Aden Camp cancels. Examples with cancels from offices in the Eastern Protectorate command a premium.

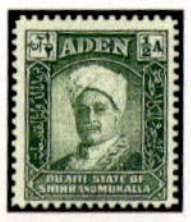

Sultan Sir Saleh bin Ghalib al Qu'aiti
A1

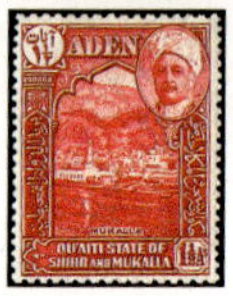

Mukalla Harbor
A2

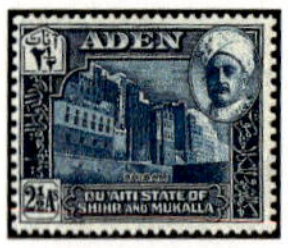

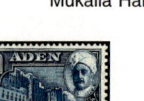

Buildings at Shibam — A3

Designs: 2a, Gateway of Shihr. 3a, Outpost of Mukalla. 8a, View of 'Einat. 1r, Governor's Castle, Du'an. 2r, Mosque in Hureidha. 5r, Meshhed.

**1942 Engr. Wmk. 4 *Perf. 13¾x14***

| | | | | |
|---|---|---|---|---|
| **1** | A1 | ½a dark green | 1.40 | .35 |
| **2** | A1 | ¾a copper brown | 2.00 | .25 |
| **3** | A1 | 1a deep blue | .80 | .80 |

***Perf. 13x11½, 11½x13***

| | | | | |
|---|---|---|---|---|
| **4** | A2 | 1½a dk car rose | 1.60 | .35 |
| **5** | A2 | 2a black brown | 1.75 | *1.25* |
| **6** | A3 | 2½a deep blue | .40 | .25 |
| **7** | A2 | 3a dk car rose & dl brn | 1.00 | .75 |
| **8** | A3 | 8a orange red | 1.10 | .35 |
| **9** | A2 | 1r green | 6.00 | 3.50 |
| *a.* | | Missing "A" in "CA" of watermark | 1,300. | *1,200.* |
| **10** | A3 | 2r rose vio & dk blue | 16.00 | 12.00 |
| **11** | A3 | 5r gray grn & fawn | 32.50 | 16.00 |
| | | *Nos. 1-11 (11)* | 64.55 | 35.85 |

For surcharges see Nos. 20-27.

### Nos. 4, 6 Ovptd. in Black or Carmine like Kathiri Nos. 12-13

**1946, Oct. 15 *Perf. 11½x13, 13x11½***

| | | | | |
|---|---|---|---|---|
| **12** | A2 (b) | 1½a dk car rose | .25 | *1.00* |
| **13** | A3 (a) | 2½a deep blue (C) | .25 | .25 |

Victory of the Allied Nations in WWII.

### Silver Wedding Issue
Common Design Types

**1949, Jan. 17 Photo. *Perf. 14x14½***

| | | | | |
|---|---|---|---|---|
| **14** | CD304 | 1½a scarlet | .55 | *2.50* |

**Engraved; Name Typo.**

***Perf. 11½x11***

| | | | | |
|---|---|---|---|---|
| **15** | CD305 | 5r green | 18.00 | 10.00 |

25th anniv. of the marriage of King George VI and Queen Elizabeth.

### UPU Issue
### Surcharged in Annas and Rupees
Common Design Types

No. 16

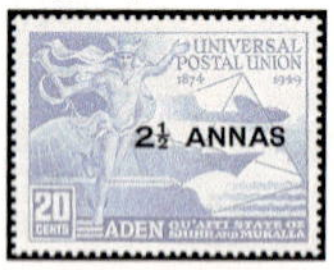


No. 17

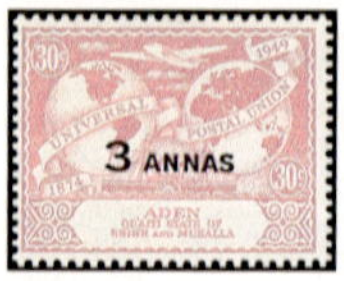


**Engr.; Name Typo. on Nos. 17 and 18**

**1949, Oct. 10 *Perf. 13½, 11x11½***

| | | | | |
|---|---|---|---|---|
| **16** | CD306 | 2½a on 20c dp ultra | .25 | *2.00* |
| **17** | CD307 | 3a on 30c dp car | 1.50 | *2.00* |
| **18** | CD308 | 8a on 50c org | .35 | *2.00* |
| **19** | CD309 | 1r on 1sh blue | .50 | *2.00* |
| *a.* | | Surcharge omitted | *4,250.* | |
| | | Hinged | *2,750.* | |
| | | *Nos. 16-19 (4)* | 2.60 | 8.00 |

### Nos. 3, 5-11 & Types Surcharged in Carmine or Black

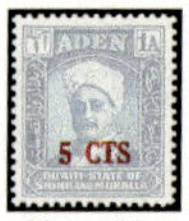


Nos. 20-21

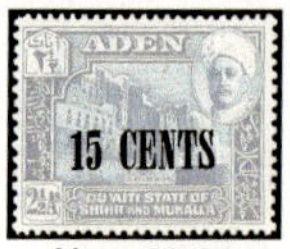


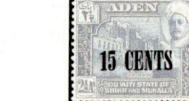

Nos. 22-24

Nos. 25-27

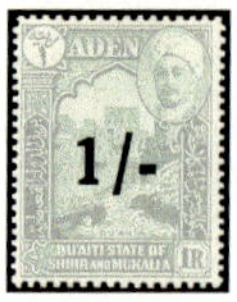


***Perf. 14, 13x11½, 11½x13***

**1951, Oct. 1 Engr. Wmk. 4**

| | | | | |
|---|---|---|---|---|
| **20** | A1 | 5c on 1a (C) | .25 | .25 |
| **21** | A2 | 10c on 2a | .25 | .25 |
| **22** | A3 | 15c on 2½a | .25 | .25 |
| **23** | A2 | 20c on 3a #7 | .30 | *.75* |
| **24** | A3 | 50c on 8a org red | .45 | *2.50* |
| **25** | A2 | 1sh on 1r | 2.00 | .55 |
| **26** | A3 | 2sh on 2r | 8.00 | *24.00* |
| **27** | A3 | 5sh on 5r | 17.00 | *34.00* |
| | | *Nos. 20-27 (8)* | 28.50 | *62.55* |

### Coronation Issue
Common Design Type

**1953, June 2 Engr. *Perf. 13½x13***

| | | | | |
|---|---|---|---|---|
| **28** | CD312 | 15c dk blue & black | 1.10 | .60 |

### Qu'aiti State in Hadhramaut

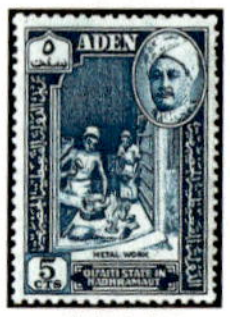

Metal Work — A10

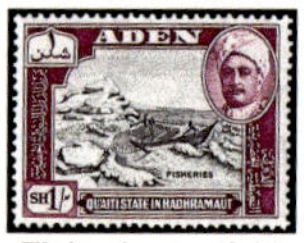

Fisheries — A11

Designs: 10c, Mat making. 15c, Weaving. 25c, Pottery. 35c, Building. 50c, Date cultivation. 90c, Agriculture. 1sh25c, 10sh, Lime burning. 2sh, Dhow building. 5sh, Agriculture.

***Perf. 11½x13, 13½x14***

**1955, Sept. 1 Engr. Wmk. 4**

| | | | | |
|---|---|---|---|---|
| **29** | A10 | 5c greenish blue | .75 | .25 |
| **30** | A10 | 10c black | 1.00 | .25 |
| **31** | A10 | 15c dk green | .75 | .25 |
| **32** | A10 | 25c carmine | .40 | .25 |
| **33** | A10 | 35c ultra | .75 | .25 |
| **34** | A10 | 50c red orange | .75 | .25 |
| **35** | A10 | 90c brown | .55 | .25 |
| **36** | A11 | 1sh purple & blk | .75 | .25 |
| **37** | A11 | 1sh25c red org & blk | .60 | .55 |
| **38** | A11 | 2sh dk blue & blk | 3.00 | .60 |
| **39** | A11 | 5sh green & blk | 4.00 | 2.25 |
| **40** | A11 | 10sh car & black | 13.50 | 7.50 |
| | | *Nos. 29-40 (12)* | 26.80 | 12.90 |

### Types of 1955 with Portrait of Sultan Awadh Bin Saleh El-Qu'aiti

Design: 70c, Agriculture. Others as before.

**1963, Oct. 20 Wmk. 314**

| | | | | |
|---|---|---|---|---|
| **41** | A10 | 5c greenish blue | .25 | *1.40* |
| **42** | A10 | 10c black | .25 | *1.15* |
| **43** | A10 | 15c dark green | .25 | *1.40* |
| **44** | A10 | 25c carmine | .25 | *.60* |
| **45** | A10 | 35c ultra | .25 | *1.50* |
| **46** | A10 | 50c red orange | .25 | *.75* |
| **47** | A10 | 70c brown | .25 | .60 |
| **48** | A11 | 1sh purple & blk | .30 | .30 |
| **49** | A11 | 1sh25c red org & blk | .50 | *5.00* |
| **50** | A11 | 2sh dk blue & blk | 2.75 | 2.25 |
| **51** | A11 | 5sh green & blk | 12.50 | *25.00* |
| **52** | A11 | 10sh car & black | 27.00 | *26.00* |
| | | *Nos. 41-52 (12)* | 44.80 | *65.95* |

## AFARS & ISSAS

French Territory of the

ä-ˌfärz and ē-ˈsäz

LOCATION — East Africa
GOVT. — French Overseas Territory
AREA — 8,880 sq. mi.
POP. — 150,000 (est. 1974)
CAPITAL — Djibouti (Jibuti)

The French overseas territory of Somali Coast was renamed the French Territory of the Afars and Issas in 1967. It became the Djibouti Republic on June 27, 1977.

100 Centimes = 1 Franc

**Catalogue values for all unused stamps in this country are for Never Hinged items.**

Imperforates

Most stamps of Afars and Issas exist imperforate in issued and trial colors, and also in small presentation sheets in issued colors.

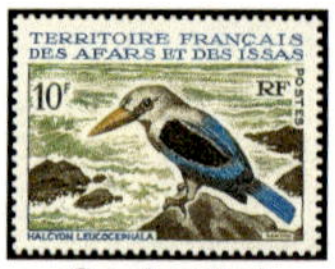

Grayheaded Kingfisher — A48

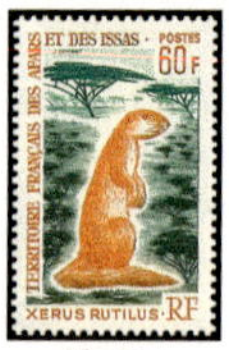

Xerus Rutilus — A48a

10fr, Halcyon leucocephala. 15fr, Haematopus ostralegus. 50fr, Tringa nebularia. 55fr, Coracias abyssinicus.

**1967 Unwmk. Engr. *Perf. 13***

| | | | | |
|---|---|---|---|---|
| **310** | A48 | 10fr multicolored | 4.00 | 3.00 |
| **311** | A48 | 15fr multicolored | 5.25 | 4.00 |
| **312** | A48 | 50fr multicolored | 12.50 | 8.00 |
| **313** | A48 | 55fr multicolored | 17.50 | 11.00 |
| **314** | A48a | 60fr multicolored | 24.00 | 17.50 |
| | | *Nos. 310-314 (5)* | 63.25 | 43.50 |
| | | *Nos. 310-314,C50 (6)* | 80.75 | 55.50 |

Issued: 10fr, 55fr, Aug. 21; 15fr, 50fr, 60fr, Sept. 25. See No. C50.

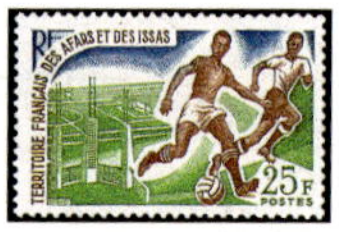

Soccer — A49

**1967, Dec. 18 Engr. *Perf. 13***

| | | | | |
|---|---|---|---|---|
| **315** | A49 | 25fr shown | 3.50 | 2.75 |
| **316** | A49 | 30fr Basketball | 4.00 | 2.75 |

Common Design Types
Pictured in section at front of book.

### WHO Anniversary Issue
Common Design Type

**1968, May 4 Engr. *Perf. 13***

| | | | | |
|---|---|---|---|---|
| **317** | CD126 | 15fr multicolored | 3.00 | 3.00 |

20th anniv. of WHO.

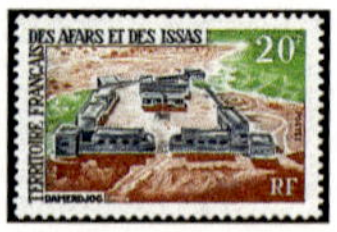

Damerdjog Fortress — A50

Administration Buildings: 25fr, Ali Adde. 30fr, Dorra. 40fr, Assamo.

**1968, May 17 Engr. *Perf. 13***

| | | | | |
|---|---|---|---|---|
| **318** | A50 | 20fr slate, brn & emer | 1.25 | 1.00 |
| **319** | A50 | 25fr brt grn, bl & brn | 1.50 | 1.25 |
| **320** | A50 | 30fr brn ol, brn org & sl | 2.00 | 1.40 |
| **321** | A50 | 40fr brn ol, sl & brt grn | 3.25 | 2.75 |
| | | *Nos. 318-321 (4)* | 8.00 | 6.40 |

### Human Rights Year Issue
Common Design Type

**1968, Aug. 10 Engr. *Perf. 13***

| | | | | |
|---|---|---|---|---|
| **322** | CD127 | 10fr purple, ver & org | 2.25 | 1.75 |
| **323** | CD127 | 70fr green, pur & org | 4.50 | 2.25 |

International Human Rights Year.

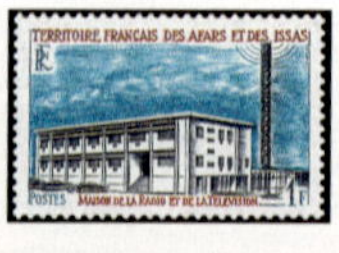

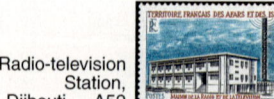

Radio-television Station, Djibouti — A52

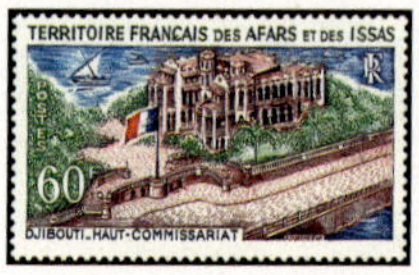

High Commission Palace, Djibouti
A53

Designs: 2fr, Justice Building. 5fr, Chamber of Deputies. 8fr, Great Mosque. 15fr, Monument of Free French Forces, vert. 40fr, Djibouti Post Office. 70fr, Residence of Gov. Léonce Lagarde at Obock. No. 332, Djibouti Harbormaster's Building. No. 333, Control tower, Djibouti Airport.

**1968-70 Engr. *Perf. 13***

| | | | | |
|---|---|---|---|---|
| **324** | A52 | 1fr multicolored | .50 | .50 |
| **325** | A52 | 2fr multicolored | .80 | .75 |
| **326** | A52 | 5fr multicolored | 1.00 | 1.00 |
| **327** | A52 | 8fr multicolored | 1.25 | 1.25 |
| **328** | A52 | 15fr multicolored | 4.50 | 3.75 |
| **329** | A52 | 40fr multicolored | 3.75 | 2.75 |
| **330** | A53 | 60fr multicolored | 3.50 | 2.40 |
| **331** | A52 | 70fr multicolored | 4.25 | 3.00 |
| **332** | A52 | 85fr multicolored | 6.25 | 3.75 |
| **333** | A52 | 85fr multicolored | 6.50 | 4.25 |
| | | *Nos. 324-333 (10)* | 32.30 | 23.40 |

Issued: No. 330, 1968; Nos. 324-328, 331-332, 1969; Nos. 329, 333, 1970.
See Nos. C54-C55.

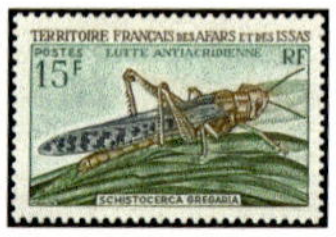

Locust — A54

Designs: 50fr, Pest control by helicopter. 55fr, Pest control by plane.

**1969, Oct. 6 Engr. *Perf. 13***

| | | | | |
|---|---|---|---|---|
| **334** | A54 | 15fr brn, grn & slate | 4.75 | 2.25 |
| **335** | A54 | 50fr dk grn, bl & ol brn | 3.00 | 2.25 |
| **336** | A54 | 55fr red brn, bl & brn | 3.50 | 2.25 |
| | | *Nos. 334-336 (3)* | 11.25 | 6.75 |

Campaign against locusts.

### ILO Issue
Common Design Type

**1969, Nov. 24 Engr. *Perf. 13***

| | | | | |
|---|---|---|---|---|
| **337** | CD131 | 30fr org, gray & lil | 2.75 | 2.00 |

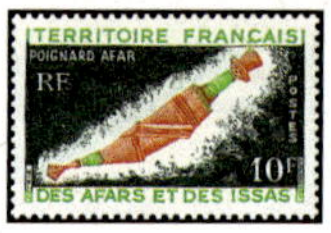

Afar Dagger in Ornamental Scabbard — A56

**1970, Apr. 3 Engr. *Perf. 13***

| | | | | |
|---|---|---|---|---|
| **338** | A56 | 10fr multicolored | 1.40 | .75 |
| **339** | A56 | 15fr multicolored | 1.75 | .75 |
| **340** | A56 | 20fr multicolored | 2.00 | 1.00 |
| **341** | A56 | 25fr multicolored | 2.25 | 1.25 |
| | | *Nos. 338-341 (4)* | 7.40 | 3.75 |

See No. 364.

### UPU Headquarters Issue
Common Design Type

**1970, May 20 Engr. *Perf. 13***

| | | | | |
|---|---|---|---|---|
| **342** | CD133 | 25fr brn, brt grn & choc | 2.50 | 1.40 |

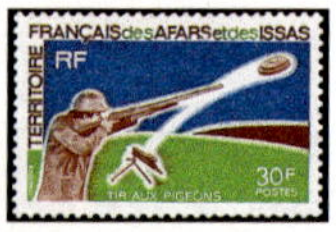

Trapshooting
A57

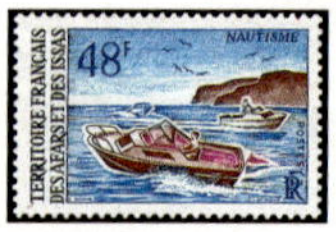

Motorboats
A58

Designs: 50fr, Steeplechase. 55fr, Sailboat, vert. 60fr, Equestrians.

**1970 Engr. *Perf. 13***

| | | | | |
|---|---|---|---|---|
| **343** | A57 | 30fr dp brn, yel grn & brt bl | 2.75 | 1.75 |
| **344** | A58 | 48fr blue & multi | 5.00 | 2.50 |
| **345** | A58 | 50fr cop red, bl & pur | 5.00 | 2.50 |
| **346** | A58 | 55fr red brn, bl & ol | 5.25 | 2.50 |
| **347** | A58 | 60fr ol, blk & red brn | 5.50 | 3.50 |
| | | *Nos. 343-347 (5)* | 23.50 | 12.75 |

Issued: 30fr, 6/5; 48fr, 10/9; 50fr, 60fr, 11/6.

# AFARS & ISSAS

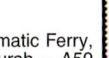
Automatic Ferry, Tadjourah — A59

**1970, Nov. 25**
348 A59 48fr blue, brn & grn   3.75   2.50

Volcanic Geode — A60

Diabase and Chrysolite — A61

10fr, Doleritic basalt. 15fr, Olivine basalt.

**1971**   **Photo.**   **Perf. 13**
349 A61 10fr black & multi   3.00   1.25
350 A61 15fr black & multi   3.50   1.75
351 A60 25fr black, crim & brn   7.00   3.25
352 A61 40fr black & multi   9.00   5.00
  Nos. 349-352 (4)   22.50   11.25

Issued: 10fr, 11/22; 15fr, 10/8; 25fr, 4/26; 40fr, 1/25.

A62

4fr, Manta birostris. 5fr, Coryphaena hippurus. 9fr, Pristis pectinatus.

**1971, July 1**   **Photo.**   **Perf. 12x12½**
353 A62 4fr mulitcolored   2.25   1.25
354 A62 5fr multicolored   2.75   1.40
355 A62 9fr multicolored   4.75   2.25
  Nos. 353-355 (3)   9.75   4.90

See No. C60.

**De Gaulle Issue**
**Common Design Type**

Designs: 60fr, Gen. Charles de Gaulle, 1940. 85fr, Pres. de Gaulle, 1970.

**1971, Nov. 9**   **Engr.**   **Perf. 13**
356 CD134 60fr ultra & blk   6.00   3.50
357 CD134 85fr dk vio bl & blk   6.50   4.00

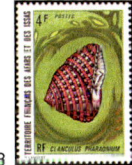
A63

Shells: 4fr, Strawberry Top. 9fr, Cypraea pantherina. 20fr, Bull-mouth helmet. 50fr, Ethiopian volute.

**1972, Mar. 8**   **Photo.**   **Perf. 12½x13**
358 A63 4fr olive & multi   1.75   1.25
359 A63 9fr dk blue & multi   2.25   1.50
360 A63 20fr dp green & multi   4.25   2.25
361 A63 50fr dp claret & multi   7.00   3.00
  Nos. 358-361 (4)   15.25   8.00

Shepherd A64

Design: 10fr, Dromedary breeding.

**1973, Apr. 11**   **Photo.**   **Perf. 13**
362 A64 9fr blue & multi   1.50   .80
363 A64 10fr blue & multi   1.75   .85

Afar Dagger — A65

**1974, Jan. 29**   **Engr.**   **Perf. 13**
364 A65 30fr slate grn & dk brn   1.50   .85

For surcharge see No. 379.

Flamingos, Lake Abbe — A66

Flamingos and different views of Lake Abbe.

**1974, Feb. 22**   **Photo.**   **Perf. 13**
370 A66 5fr multicolored   1.75   1.00
371 A66 15fr multicolored   1.50   1.25
372 A66 50fr multicolored   3.00   2.00
  Nos. 370-372 (3)   6.25   4.25

Soccer Ball — A67

**1974, May 24**   **Engr.**   **Perf. 13**
373 A67 25fr black & emerald   3.00   1.75

World Cup Soccer Championship, Munich, June 13-July 7.

Letters Around UPU Emblem — A68

**1974, Oct. 9**   **Engr.**   **Perf. 13**
374 A68 20fr multicolored   1.25   .80
375 A68 100fr multicolored   2.75   2.00

Centenary of Universal Postal Union.

Oleo Chrysophylla — A69

Designs: 15fr, Ficus species. 20fr, Solanum adoense.

**1974, Nov. 22**   **Photo.**
376 A69 10fr shown   1.75   1.00
377 A69 15fr multicolored   2.00   1.10
378 A69 20fr multicolored   3.00   1.60
  Nos. 376-378 (3)   6.75   3.60

Day Primary Forest.

No. 364 Surcharged in Red

**1975, Jan. 1**   **Engr.**   **Perf. 13**
379 A65 40fr on 30fr multi   2.00   1.25

Treasury A70

Design: 25fr, Government buildings.

**1975, Jan. 7**   **Engr.**   **Perf. 13**
380 A70 8fr blue, gray & red   .65   .50
381 A70 25fr red, blue & indigo   1.50   .45

Darioconus Textile A71

Sea Shells: No. 383, Murex palmarosa. 10fr, Conus sumatrensis. 15fr, Cypraea pulchra. No. 386, 45fr, Murex scolopax. No. 387, Cypraea exhusta. 40fr, Ranella spinosa. 55fr, Cypraea erythraensis. 60fr, Conus taeniatus.

**1975-76**   **Engr.**   **Perf. 13**
382 A71 5fr blue grn & brn   1.25   .85
383 A71 5fr blue & multi ('76)   1.25   1.00
384 A71 10fr lilac, blk & brn   2.50   .90
385 A71 15fr blue, ind & brn   3.25   1.40
386 A71 20fr purple & lt brn   5.00   3.00
387 A71 20fr brt grn & multi ('76)   2.75   1.25
388 A71 40fr green & brown   4.50   1.25
389 A71 45fr green, bl & bister   4.75   1.40
390 A71 55fr turq & multi ('76)   3.50   2.00
391 A71 60fr buff & sepia ('76)   6.50   2.75
  Nos. 382-391 (10)   35.25   15.80

Hypolimnas Misippus — A72

Butterflies: 40fr, Papilio nireus. 50fr, Acraea anemosa. 65fr, Holocerina smilax menieri. 70fr, Papilio demodocus. No. 397, Papilio dardanus. No. 398, Balachowsky gonimbrasca. 150fr, Vanessa cardui.

**1975-76**   **Photo.**   **Perf. 13**
392 A72 25fr emerald & multi   3.75   1.60
393 A72 40fr yellow & multi   4.75   2.00
394 A72 50fr ultra & multi ('76)   5.50   1.75
395 A72 65fr ol & multi ('76)   5.50   2.50
396 A72 70fr violet & multi   6.75   3.00
397 A72 100fr blue & multi   8.50   3.75
398 A72 100fr Prus bl & multi ('76)   7.00   3.50
399 A72 150fr grn & multi ('76)   8.50   3.75
  Nos. 392-399 (8)   50.25   21.85

A73

Animals: No. 400, Hyaena hyaena. No. 401, Cercopithecus aethiops. No. 402, Equus asinus somalicus. No. 403, Dorcatragus megalotis. No. 404, Ichneumia albicauda. No. 405, Hystrix galeata. No. 406, Ictonyx striatus. No. 407, Orycteropus afer.

**Perf. 13x12½, 12½x13**
**1975-76**   **Photo.**
400 A73 10fr multicolored   1.25   1.00
401 A73 15fr multicolored   1.40   1.00
402 A73 15fr multicolored   1.50   1.25
403 A73 30fr multicolored   3.00   1.50
404 A73 40fr multicolored   2.75   1.75
405 A73 60fr multicolored   4.00   2.25
406 A73 70fr multicolored   5.50   2.75
407 A73 200fr multicolored   7.50   6.50
  Nos. 400-407 (8)   27.00   17.00

Nos. 401-402, 405 are vert.
Issued: 50fr, 60fr, 70fr, 2/21; No. 401, 200fr, 10/24; 10fr, No. 402, 30fr, 2/4/76.

Birds — A74

No. 413, Vidua macroura. No. 414, Psittacula krameri. No. 415, Cinnyris venustus. No. 416, Ardea goliath. No. 417, Scopus umbretta. No. 418, Oena capensis. No. 419, Platalea alba.

**1975-76**   **Photo.**   **Perf. 12½x13**
413 A74 20fr multicolored   1.75   1.40
414 A74 25fr multicolored   2.50   .75
415 A74 50fr multicolored   3.25   1.80
416 A74 60fr multicolored   5.75   2.50
417 A74 100fr multicolored   9.25   3.00
418 A74 200fr multicolored   5.00   1.75
419 A74 300fr multicolored   12.00   4.50
  Nos. 413-419 (7)   39.50   15.70

Issued: 300fr, 6/15/76; 25fr, No. 418, 10/13/76; others 11/21 and 12/19/75.

Palms — A75

**1975, Dec. 19**   **Engr.**   **Perf. 13**
421 A75 20fr multicolored   1.10   1.00

Satellite and Alexander Graham Bell — A76

**1976, Mar. 10**   **Engr.**   **Perf. 13**
422 A70 200fr dp bl, org & sl grn   3.25   3.00

Centenary of the first telephone call by Alexander Graham Bell, Mar. 10, 1876.

Basketball — A77

**1976, July 7**   **Litho.**   **Perf. 12½**
423 A77 10fr shown   .75   .40
424 A77 15fr Bicycling   1.00   .50
425 A77 40fr Soccer   1.75   1.00
426 A77 60fr Running   2.50   1.50
  Nos. 423-426 (4)   6.00   3.40

21st Olympic Games, Montreal, Canada, July 17-Aug. 1.

Pterois Radiata A78

**1976, Aug. 10**   **Photo.**   **Perf. 13x13½**
428 A78 45fr blue & multi   3.75   1.50

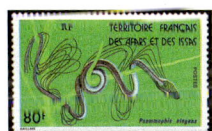
Psammophis Elegans — A79

Design: 70fr, Naja nigricollis, vert

**Perf. 13x13½, 13½x13**
**1976, Sept. 27**   **Photo.**
430 A79 70fr ocher & multi   3.50   2.25
431 A79 80fr emerald & multi   6.00   2.75

# AFARS & ISSAS

Motorcyclist — A80

**1977, Jan. 27   Litho.   Perf. 12x12½**
432  A80  200fr multicolored          6.00  3.00
Moto-Cross motorcycle race.

Conus Betulinus A81

Sea Shells: 5fr, Cyprea tigris. 70fr, Conus striatus. 85fr, Cyprea mauritiana.

**1977   Engr.   Perf. 13**
433  A81   5fr multicolored          2.50  1.00
434  A81  30fr multicolored          2.75  1.00
435  A81  70fr multicolored          7.00  2.50
436  A81  85fr multicolored          6.00  3.75
   Nos. 433-436 (4)                 18.25  8.25

Gaterin Gaterinus — A82

**1977, Apr. 15   Photo.   Perf. 13x12½**
437  A82  15fr shown                 1.50  1.00
438  A82  65fr Barracudas            3.00  1.50

---

## AIR POST STAMPS

AP16

200fr, Aquila rapax belisarius.

**1967, Aug. 21   Unwmk.**
**Engr.   Perf. 13**
C50  AP16  200fr multicolored       17.50 12.00

AP17

48fr, Parachutists. 85fr, Water skier & skin diver.

**1968   Engr.   Perf. 13**
C51  AP17  48fr multicolored         5.50  2.50
C52  AP17  85fr multicolored         7.00  4.50
Issue dates: 48fr, Jan. 5; 85fr, Mar. 15.

Aerial Map of the Territory AP18

**1968, Nov. 15   Engr.   Perf. 13**
C53  AP18  500fr bl, dk brn & ocher
                                    23.00 13.00

**Buildings Type of Regular Issue**
100fr, Cathedral. 200fr, Sayed Hassan Mosque.

**1969   Engr.   Perf. 13**
C54  A53  100fr multi, vert.         5.50  2.50
C55  A53  200fr multi, vert.         8.50  5.50
Issue dates: 100fr, Apr. 4; 200fr, May 8.

**Concorde Issue**
**Common Design Type**

**1969, Apr. 17**
C56  CD129  100fr org red & ol     26.00 16.00

Arta Ionospheric Station — AP19

**1970, May 8   Engr.   Perf. 13**
C57  AP19  70fr multicolored         4.00  3.25

Japanese Sword Guard, Fish Design — AP20

200fr, Japanese sword guard, horse design.

**Gold embossed**
**1970, Oct. 26   Perf. 12½**
C58  AP20  100fr multicolored        9.50  7.50
C59  AP20  200fr multicolored       12.50  9.00
EXPO '70 International Exposition, Osaka, Japan, Mar. 15-Sept. 13.

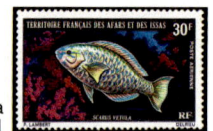

Scarus vetula AP21

**1971, July 1   Photo.   Perf. 12½**
C60  AP21  30fr black & multi        6.00  3.75

Djibouti Harbor AP22

**1972, Feb. 3**
C61  AP22  100fr blue & multi        4.50  3.00
New Djibouti harbor.

AP23

30fr, Pterocles lichtensteini. 49fr, Uppupa epops. 66fr, Capella media. 500fr, Francolinus ochropectus.

**1972   Photo.   Perf. 12½x13**
C62  AP23  30fr multi                3.75  2.75
C63  AP23  49fr multi                6.25  3.75
C64  AP23  66fr multi                8.50  5.00
C65  AP23  500fr multi              30.00 17.50
   Nos. C62-C65 (4)                 48.50 29.00
Issue dates: No. C65, Nov. 3; others Apr. 21.

AP24

Olympic Rings and: 5fr, Running. 10fr, Basketball. 55fr, Swimming, horiz. 60fr, Olympic torch and Greek frieze, horiz.

**1972, June 8   Engr.   Perf. 13**
C66  AP24   5fr multicolored          .90   .90
C67  AP24  10fr multicolored         1.00   .95
C68  AP24  55fr multicolored         2.25  1.75
C69  AP24  60fr multicolored         3.25  2.00
   Nos. C66-C69 (4)                  7.40  5.60
20th Olympic Games, Munich, 8/26-9/11.

Louis Pasteur AP25

100fr, Albert Calmette and C. Guérin.

**1972, Oct. 5   Engr.   Perf. 13**
C70  AP25  20fr multicolored         2.75  1.10
C71  AP25  100fr multicolored        5.50  4.00
Pasteur, Calmette, Guerin, chemists and bacteriologists, benefactors of mankind.

Map and Views of Territory AP26

200fr, Woman and Mosque of Djibouti, vert.

**1973, Jan. 15   Photo.   Perf. 13**
C72  AP26  30fr brown & multi        6.00  4.25
C73  AP26  200fr multicolored       11.00  8.50
Visit of Pres. Georges Pompidou of France, Jan. 15-17.

AP27

30fr, Oryx beisa. 50fr, Madoqua saltiana. 66fr, Felis caracal.

**1973, Feb. 26   Photo.   Perf. 13x12½**
C74  AP27  30fr multicolored         3.00  1.50
C75  AP27  50fr multicolored         4.25  2.75
C76  AP27  66fr multicolored         6.25  3.25
   Nos. C74-C76 (3)                 13.50  7.50
See Nos. C94-C96.

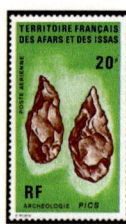

Celts — AP28

Various pre-historic flint tools. 40fr, 60fr, horiz.

**1973   Perf. 13**
C77  AP28  20fr yel grn, blk & brn   4.50  2.50
C78  AP28  40fr yellow & multi       4.75  3.00
C79  AP28  49fr lilac & multi        8.75  3.75
C80  AP28  60fr blue & multi         6.25  5.00
   Nos. C77-C80 (4)                 24.25 14.25
Issued: 20fr, 49fr, 3/16; 40fr, 60fr, 9/7.

AP29

40fr, Octopus macropus. 60fr, Halicore dugong.

**1973, Mar. 16**
C81  AP29  40fr multicolored         3.75  2.25
C82  AP29  60fr multicolored         7.50  3.75

AP30

Copernicus: 8fr, Nicolaus Copernicus, Polish astronomer. 9fr, Wilhelm C. Roentgen, physicist, X-ray discoverer. No. C85, Edward Jenner, physician, discoverer of vaccination. No. C86, Marie Curie, discoverer of radium and polonium. 49fr, Robert Koch, physician and bacteriologist. 50fr, Clement Ader (1841-1925), French aviation pioneer. 55fr, Guglielmo Marconi, Italian electrical engineer, inventor. 85fr, Moliere, French playwright. 100fr, Henri Farman (1874-1937), French aviation pioneer. 150fr, Andre-Marie Ampere (1775-1836), French physicist. 250fr, Michelangelo Buonarroti (1475-1564), Italian sculptor, painter and architect.

**1973-75   Engr.   Perf. 13**
C83  AP30    8fr multicolored        1.00  1.00
C84  AP30    9fr multicolored        2.00  1.00
C85  AP30   10fr multicolored        2.25  1.00
C86  AP30   10fr multicolored        1.50  1.00
C87  AP30   49fr multicolored        4.00  2.50
C88  AP30   50fr multicolored        3.50  2.50
C89  AP30   55fr multicolored        2.25  2.00
C90  AP30   85fr multicolored        5.75  3.00
C91  AP30  100fr multicolored        3.75  3.00
C92  AP30  150fr multicolored        6.00  3.50
C93  AP30  250fr multicolored        9.00  6.00
   Nos. C83-C93 (11)                41.00 26.25

Issued: 8fr, 85fr, 5/9/73; 9fr, No. C85, 49fr, 10/12/73; 100fr, 1/29/74; 55fr, 3/22/74; No. C86, 8/23/74; 150fr, 7/24/75; 250fr, 6/26/75; 50fr, 9/25/75.

AP31

20fr, Papio anubis. 50fr, Genetta tigrina, horiz. 66fr, Lapus habessinicus.

**Perf. 12½x13, 13x12½**
**1973, Dec. 12   Photo.**
C94  AP31  20fr multicolored         2.25  1.40
C95  AP31  50fr multicolored         3.75  2.00
C96  AP31  66fr multicolored         5.00  2.75
   Nos. C94-C96 (3)                 11.00  6.15

Spearfishing AP32

**1974, Apr. 14   Engr.   Perf. 13**
C97  AP32  200fr multicolored        8.00  7.00

No. C97 was prepared for release in Nov. 1972, for the 3rd Underwater Spearfishing Contest in the Red Sea. Dates were obliterated with a rectangle, and the stamp was not issued without this obliteration. Value without rectangle, $400.

# AFARS & ISSAS — AFGHANISTAN

Rock Carvings, Balho AP33

**1974, Apr. 26**
C98 AP33 200fr carmine & slate    9.00  7.00

Lake Assal AP34

Designs (Lake Assal): 50fr, Rock formations on shore. 85fr, Crystallized wood.

**1974, Oct. 25   Photo.   Perf. 13**
C99  AP34 49fr multicolored    2.25  1.75
C100 AP34 50fr multicolored    2.50  2.00
C101 AP34 85fr multicolored    5.00  3.75
   Nos. C99-C101 (3)           9.75  7.50

Columba Guinea — AP35

**1975, May 23   Photo.   Perf. 13**
C102 AP35 500fr multicolored  22.50 11.00

Djibouti Airport AP36

**1977, Mar. 1   Litho.   Perf. 12**
C103 AP36 500fr multicolored  12.50  9.00
Opening of new Djibouti Airport.

Thomas A. Edison and Phonograph AP37

Design: 75fr, Alexander Volta, electric train, lines and light bulb.

**1977, May 5   Engr.   Perf. 13**
C104 AP37 55fr multicolored    4.00  2.75
C105 AP37 75fr multicolored    6.25  4.75

Famous inventors: Thomas Alva Edison and Alexander Volta (1745-1827).

## POSTAGE DUE STAMPS

Nomad's Milk Jug — D3

**Perf. 14x13**
**1969, Dec. 15   Engr.   Unwmk.**
J49 D3 1fr red brn, red lil & sl   .50   .65
J50 D3 2fr red brn, emer & sl      .60   .80
J51 D3 5fr red brn, bl & slate    1.00  1.20
J52 D3 10fr red brn, brn & slate  1.75  2.00
   Nos. J49-J52 (4)               3.85  4.65

---

# AFGHANISTAN

af-'ga-nə-ˌstan

LOCATION — Central Asia, bounded by Iran, Turkmenistan, Uzbekistan, Tajikistan, Pakistan, and China
GOVT. — Republic
AREA — 251,773 sq. mi.
POP. — 38,930,000 (2020 est.)
CAPITAL — Kabul

Afghanistan changed from a constitutional monarchy to a republic in July 1973.

12 Shahi = 6 Sanar = 3 Abasi =
2 Krans = 1 Rupee Kabuli
60 Paisas = 1 Rupee (1921)
100 Pouls = 1 Rupee Afghani (1927)

**Catalogue values for unused stamps in this country are for Never Hinged items, beginning with Scott 364 in the regular postage section, Scott B1 in the semi-postal section, Scott C7 in the airpost section, Scott O8 in officials section, and Scott RA6 in the postal tax section.**

### CHARACTERS OF VALUE.

Shahi.
1871-78, A7, A8, 1876

Sanar.   Abasi.   6 Shahi.
1871-78, 1871, 1872

1 Rupee.  ½ Rupee.
1874  1876(A8)  1876 (A7)

1 Rupee.  Rupee.
1872  1874  1876 (A8)  1877-78

From 1871 to 1892 and 1898, the Moslem year date appears on the stamp. Numerals as follows:

| 1 | 2 | 3 | 4 | 5 |
| 6 | 7 | 8 | 9 | 0 |

Until 1891, cancellation consisted of cutting or tearing a piece from the stamp. Such examples should not be considered as damaged.
Values are for cut square examples of good color. Cut to shape or faded examples sell for much less, particularly Nos. 1-10.
Nos. 1-108 are on laid paper of varying thickness except where wove is noted.
Until 1907, all stamps were issued ungummed.
The tiger's head on types A1 to A11 symbolizes the name of the contemporary amir, Sher (Tiger, or Lion) Ali.

### Kingdom of Kabul

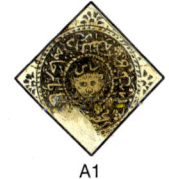
A1

Tiger's Head, Type I — A2

Tiger's Head, Type II — A2a

Both circles dotted. Thick outer circle usually measures 27.5mm-28mm in diameter. Type I: well-defined inner and outer circles with evenly spaced dots. Type II: less well-defined thin inner and outer circles, and dots are randomly spaced.

**1071   Unwmk.   Litho.   Imperf.**
**Dated "1288"**
1   A1   1sh black (30mm diameter)   1,350.  60.00
2   A2   1sh black        925.00  50.00
2A  A2a  1sh black        525.00  35.00
3   A2   1sa black        650.00  32.50
3A  A2a  1sa black        210.00  55.00
4   A2a  1ab black        150.00  60.00
   Nos. 1-4 (6)           3,810.  292.50

Nos. 1-4 are usually identified by plating. No. 1 was printed in a sheet of 15 (referred to as plate A). Nos. 2 and 3 were printing in sheets of 15 (10 of No. 2 and 5 of No. 3), referred to as plate B. Nos. 2A and 3A-4 were printed in sheets of 15 (5 of each denomination), referred to as plate C.
Similar designs without the tiger's head in the center are revenues.

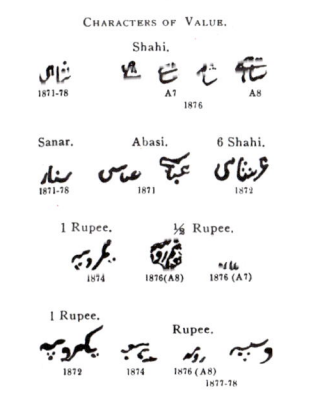
A3

Outer circle dotted; inner circle plain.
**Dated "1288"**
5   A3   1sh black        525.00  35.00
6   A3   1sa black        300.00  50.00
7   A3   1ab black        200.00  32.50
   Nos. 5-7 (3)           1,025.  117.50

Nos. 5-7 were printed in sheets of 15 (5 of each denomination), referred to as plate D.

A4

**Toned Wove Paper**
**1872   Dated "1289"**
8   A4   6sh violet       1,500.   900.
9   A4   1rup violet      1,750.  1,350.

Two varieties of each. Date varies in location. Printed in sheets of 4 (2x2) containing two of each denomination.
Most used examples are smeared with a greasy ink cancel.

A4a

**White Laid Paper**
**1873   Dated "1290"**
10   A4a  1sh black       25.00  12.00
   a. Corner ornament missing   750.00  750.00
   b. Corner ornament retouched  75.00   45.00

15 varieties. Nos. 10a, 10b are the sixth stamp on the sheet.

A5

**1873**
11   A5   1sh black       22.50  11.00

Sixty varieties of each. No. 11 in violet is believed to be a proof.

**1874   Dated "1291"**
12   A5   1ab black       90.00   55.00
13   A5   ½rup black      37.50   20.00
14   A5   1rup black      40.00   24.00
   Nos. 12-14 (3)        167.50   99.00

Five varieties of each. Nos. 12-14 were printed on the same sheet. Se-tenant varieties exist.

A6

**1875   Dated "1292"**
15   A6   1sa black       400.00  375.00
   a. Wide outer circle   1,250.  750.00
16   A6   1ab black       425.00  400.00
17   A6   1sa brown violet  75.00   30.00
   a. Wide outer circle   300.00  100.00
18   A6   1ab brown violet  80.00   60.00

Ten varieties of the sanar, five of the abasi. Nos. 15-16 and 17-18 were printed in the same sheets. Se-tenant pairs exist.

A7

**1876   Dated "1293"**
19   A7   1sh black       350.00  200.00
20   A7   1sa black       400.00  225.00
21   A7   1ab black       750.00  425.00
22   A7   ½rup black      450.00  275.00
23   A7   1rup black      875.00  275.00
24   A7   1sh violet      450.00  275.00
25   A7   1sa violet      425.00  300.00
26   A7   1ab violet      525.00  275.00
27   A7   ½rup violet     225.00   60.00
28   A7   1rup violet     225.00   75.00

12 varieties of the shahi and 3 each of the other values.

A8

**1876   Dated "1293"**
29   A8   1sh gray        16.00   10.00
29A  A8a  1sh gray        65.00   30.00
30   A8   1sa gray        20.00    8.00
31   A8   1ab gray        42.50   20.00
32   A8   ½rup gray       50.00   25.00
33   A8   1rup gray       50.00   17.50
34   A8   1sh olive blk   140.00   80.00
35   A8   1sa olive blk   190.00  100.00
36   A8   1ab olive blk   400.00  250.00
37   A8   ½rup olive blk  275.00  275.00

| | | | | | |
|---|---|---|---|---|---|
| **38** | A8 | 1rup | olive blk | 375.00 | 400.00 |
| **39** | A8 | 1sh | green | 30.00 | 8.00 |
| **40** | A8 | 1sa | green | 40.00 | 25.00 |
| **41** | A8 | 1ab | green | 85.00 | 60.00 |
| **42** | A8 | ½rup | green | 125.00 | 80.00 |
| **43** | A8 | 1rup | green | 110.00 | 125.00 |
| **44** | A8 | 1sh | ocher | 32.50 | 15.00 |
| **45** | A8 | 1sa | ocher | 40.00 | 24.00 |
| **46** | A8 | 1ab | ocher | 80.00 | 50.00 |
| **47** | A8 | ½rup | ocher | 100.00 | 65.00 |
| **48** | A8 | 1rup | ocher | 140.00 | 125.00 |
| **49** | A8 | 1sh | violet | 37.50 | 15.00 |
| **50** | A8 | 1sa | violet | 37.50 | 15.00 |
| **51** | A8 | 1ab | violet | 50.00 | 15.00 |
| **52** | A8 | ½rup | violet | 70.00 | 27.50 |
| **53** | A8 | 1rup | violet | 100.00 | 40.00 |

24 varieties of the shahi, 4 of which show denomination written:

A8a

12 varieties of the sanar, 6 of the abasi and 3 each of the ½ rupee and rupee.

A9

**1877** **Dated "1294"**

| | | | | | |
|---|---|---|---|---|---|
| **54** | A8a | 1sh | gray | 10.00 | *15.00* |
| **55** | A9 | 1sa | gray | 10.00 | 9.00 |
| **56** | A9 | 1ab | gray | 11.00 | 9.00 |
| **57** | A9 | ½rup | gray | 14.50 | *20.00* |
| **58** | A9 | 1rup | gray | 16.00 | *20.00* |
| **59** | A9 | 1sh | black | 14.50 | *20.00* |
| **60** | A9 | 1sa | black | 25.00 | *10.00* |
| **61** | A9 | 1ab | black | 42.50 | *15.00* |
| **62** | A9 | ½rup | black | 45.00 | *30.00* |
| **63** | A9 | 1rup | black | 45.00 | *30.00* |
| **64** | A9 | 1sh | green | 32.50 | 32.50 |
| **65** | A9 | 1sa | green | 15.00 | *12.00* |
| **66** | A9 | 1ab | green | 17.50 | *16.00* |
| **67** | A9 | ½rup | green | 30.00 | *30.00* |
| **68** | A9 | 1rup | green | 27.50 | *32.50* |
| **69** | A9 | 1sh | ocher | 12.50 | 5.25 |
| **70** | A9 | 1sa | ocher | 12.50 | 7.25 |
| **71** | A9 | 1ab | ocher | 32.50 | 24.50 |
| **72** | A9 | ½rup | ocher | 40.00 | 35.00 |
| **73** | A9 | 1rup | ocher | 50.00 | 35.00 |
| **74** | A9 | 1sh | violet | 15.00 | 8.00 |
| **75** | A9 | 1sa | violet | 12.50 | 5.00 |
| **76** | A9 | 1ab | violet | 19.00 | 12.00 |
| **77** | A9 | ½rup | violet | 27.50 | 30.00 |
| **78** | A9 | 1rup | violet | 27.50 | 30.00 |

25 varieties of the shahi, 8 of the sanar, 3 of the abasi and 2 each of the ½ rupee and rupee.

Some examples of Nos. 54-78 show a "94" year date. These are valued less.

Nos. 64-68 in sage green on wove paper are proofs.

A10

A11

**1878** **Dated "95"**

| | | | | | |
|---|---|---|---|---|---|
| **79** | A10 | 1sh | gray | 5.00 | 10.00 |
| **80** | A10 | 1sa | gray | 8.00 | 10.00 |
| **81** | A10 | 1ab | gray | 12.50 | 10.00 |
| **82** | A10 | ½rup | gray | 15.00 | 15.00 |
| **83** | A10 | 1rup | gray | 15.00 | 15.00 |
| **84** | A10 | 1sh | black | 10.00 | |
| **85** | A10 | 1sa | black | 10.00 | |
| **86** | A10 | 1ab | black | 37.50 | |
| **87** | A10 | ½rup | black | 35.00 | |
| **88** | A10 | 1rup | black | 35.00 | |
| **89** | A10 | 1sh | green | 32.50 | *55.00* |
| **90** | A10 | 1sa | green | 10.00 | 9.00 |
| **91** | A10 | 1ab | green | 35.00 | 30.00 |
| **92** | A10 | ½rup | green | 32.50 | 30.00 |
| **93** | A10 | 1rup | green | 60.00 | 40.00 |
| **94** | A10 | 1sh | ocher | 27.50 | 10.00 |
| **95** | A10 | 1sa | ocher | 12.00 | *15.00* |
| **96** | A10 | 1ab | ocher | 45.00 | 35.00 |
| **97** | A10 | ½rup | ocher | 65.00 | 45.00 |
| **98** | A10 | 1rup | ocher | 27.50 | *30.00* |
| **99** | A10 | 1sh | violet | 10.00 | *15.00* |
| **100** | A10 | 1sa | violet | 30.00 | 25.00 |
| **101** | A10 | 1ab | violet | 17.50 | 15.00 |
| **102** | A10 | ½rup | violet | 55.00 | 35.00 |
| **103** | A10 | 1rup | violet | 45.00 | 30.00 |
| **104** | A11 | 1sh | gray | 7.00 | 7.00 |
| **105** | A11 | 1sh | black | *100.00* | 50.00 |
| **106** | A11 | 1sh | green | 10.00 | 5.00 |
| **107** | A11 | 1sh | ocher | 10.00 | 9.00 |
| **108** | A11 | 1sh | violet | 8.00 | 8.00 |

40 varieties of the shahi, 30 of the sanar, 6 of the abasi and 2 each of the ½ rupee and 1 rupee.

The 1876, 1877 and 1878 issues were printed in separate colors for each main post office on the Peshawar-Kabul-Khulm (Tashkurghan) postal route. Some specialists consider the black printings to be proofs, trial colors or reprints from the original plates.

There are many shades of these colors.

1ab, Type I (26mm)
A12

1ab, Type II (28mm)
A13

A14

A15

Dated "1298", numerals scattered through design

**Handstamped, in watercolor**

**1881-90**

**Thin White Laid Batonne Paper**

| | | | | | |
|---|---|---|---|---|---|
| **109** | A12 | 1ab | violet | 5.00 | 3.00 |
| **109A** | A13 | 1ab | violet | 8.00 | 3.00 |
| **110** | A12 | 1ab | black brn | 8.00 | 3.00 |
| *a.* | | | Ordinary thin wove paper | — | 20.00 |
| **111** | A12 | 1ab | rose | 12.00 | 3.00 |
| *b.* | | | Se-tenant with No. 111A | 16.00 | — |
| **111A** | A13 | 1ab | rose | 9.00 | 3.00 |
| **112** | A14 | 2ab | violet | 10.00 | 3.00 |
| **113** | A14 | 2ab | black brn | 12.00 | 6.00 |
| **114** | A14 | 2ab | rose | 20.00 | 10.00 |
| **115** | A15 | 1rup | violet | 12.00 | 12.00 |
| **116** | A15 | 1rup | black brn | 14.00 | 10.00 |
| **117** | A15 | 1rup | rose | 12.50 | 7.50 |

**Thin White Wove Batonne Paper**

| | | | | | |
|---|---|---|---|---|---|
| **118** | A12 | 1ab | violet | 15.00 | 5.00 |
| **119** | A12 | 1ab | vermilion | 30.00 | 10.00 |
| **120** | A12 | 1ab | rose | 30.00 | 25.00 |
| **121** | A14 | 2ab | violet | 30.00 | 25.00 |
| **122** | A14 | 2ab | vermilion | 30.00 | 16.00 |
| **122A** | A14 | 2ab | black brn | | |
| **123** | A15 | 1rup | violet | 15.00 | 8.00 |
| **124** | A15 | 1rup | vermilion | 14.00 | 7.50 |
| **125** | A15 | 1rup | black brn | 19.00 | 8.00 |

**Thin White Laid Batonne Paper**

| | | | | | |
|---|---|---|---|---|---|
| **126** | A12 | 1ab | brown org | 20.00 | 8.00 |
| **126A** | A13 | 1ab | brn org (II) | 22.50 | 9.00 |
| **127** | A12 | 1ab | carmine lake | 20.00 | 8.00 |
| *a.* | | | Laid paper | 22.50 | 10.00 |
| **128** | A14 | 2ab | brown org | 22.50 | 8.00 |
| **129** | A14 | 2ab | carmine lake | 20.00 | 8.00 |
| **130** | A15 | 1rup | brown org | 35.00 | 15.00 |
| **131** | A15 | 1rup | car lake | 37.50 | 15.00 |

**Yellowish Laid Batonne Paper**

| | | | | | |
|---|---|---|---|---|---|
| **132** | A12 | 1ab | purple | 10.00 | 10.00 |
| **133** | A12 | 1ab | red | 12.50 | 10.00 |

**1884** **Colored Wove Paper**

| | | | | | |
|---|---|---|---|---|---|
| **133A** | A13 | 1ab | purple, *yel* (II) | 17.50 | 17.50 |
| **134** | A12 | 1ab | purple, *grn* | 20.00 | |
| **135** | A12 | 1ab | purple, *blue* | 32.50 | 21.00 |
| **136** | A12 | 1ab | red, *grn* | 37.50 | |
| **137** | A12 | 1ab | red, *yel* | 30.00 | |
| **139** | A12 | 1ab | red, *rose* | 50.00 | |
| **140** | A14 | 2ab | red, *yel* | 30.00 | |
| **142** | A14 | 2ab | red, *rose* | 30.00 | |
| **143** | A15 | 1rup | red, *yel* | 55.00 | 20.00 |
| **145** | A15 | 1rup | red, *rose* | 65.00 | 25.00 |

**Thin Colored Ribbed Paper**

| | | | | |
|---|---|---|---|---|
| **146** | A14 | 2ab | red, *yellow* | 40.00 |
| **147** | A15 | 1rup | red, *yellow* | 80.00 |
| **148** | A12 | 1ab | lake, *lilac* | 40.00 |
| **149** | A14 | 2ab | lake, *lilac* | 40.00 |
| **150** | A15 | 1rup | lake, *lilac* | 40.00 |
| **151** | A12 | 1ab | lake, *green* | 40.00 |
| **152** | A14 | 2ab | lake, *green* | 40.00 |
| **153** | A15 | 1rup | lake, *green* | 40.00 |

**1886-88** **Colored Wove Paper**

| | | | | |
|---|---|---|---|---|
| **155** | A12 | 1ab | black, *magenta* | 60.00 |
| **156** | A12 | 1ab | claret brn, *org* | 50.00 |
| **156A** | A12 | 1ab | red, *org* | 40.00 |
| **156B** | A14 | 2ab | red, *org* | 40.00 |
| **156C** | A15 | 1rup | red, *org* | 40.00 |

**Laid Batonné Paper**

| | | | | |
|---|---|---|---|---|
| **157** | A12 | 1ab | black, *lavender* | 40.00 |
| **158** | A12 | 1ab | cl brn, *grn* | 40.00 |
| **159** | A12 | 1ab | black, *pink* | 60.00 |
| **160** | A14 | 2ab | black, *pink* | 100.00 |
| **161** | A15 | 1rup | black, *pink* | 70.00 |

**Laid Paper**

| | | | | |
|---|---|---|---|---|
| **162** | A12 | 1ab | black, *pink* | 80.00 |
| **163** | A14 | 2ab | black, *pink* | 80.00 |
| **164** | A15 | 1rup | black, *pink* | 80.00 |
| **165** | A12 | 1ab | brown, *yel* | 80.00 |
| **166** | A14 | 2ab | brown, *yel* | 80.00 |
| **167** | A15 | 1rup | brown, *yel* | 80.00 |
| **168** | A12 | 1ab | blue, *grn* | 80.00 |
| **169** | A14 | 2ab | blue, *grn* | 80.00 |
| **170** | A15 | 1rup | blue, *grn* | 80.00 |

**1891** **Colored Wove Paper**

| | | | | |
|---|---|---|---|---|
| **175** | A12 | 1ab | green, *rose* | 100.00 |
| **176** | A15 | 1rup | pur, *grn batonne* | 100.00 |

Nos. 109-176 fall into three categories:

1. Those regularly issued and in normal postal use from 1881 on, handstamped on thin white laid or wove paper in strip sheets containing 12 or more impressions of the same denomination arranged in two irregular rows, with the impressions often touching or overlappng.

2. The 1884 postal issues provisionally printed on smooth or ribbed colored wove paper as needed to supplement low stocks of the normal white paper stamps.

3. The "special" printings made in a range of colors on several types of laid or wove colored papers, most of which were never used for normal printings. These were produced periodically from 1886 to 1891 to meet philatelic demands. Although nominally valid for postage, most of the special printings were exported directly to fill dealers' orders, and few were ever postally used. Many of the sheets contained all three denominations with impressions separated by ruled lines. Sometimes different colors were used, so se-tenant multiples of denomination or color exist. Many combinations of stamp and paper colors exist besides those listed.

Various shades of each color exist.

Type A12 is known dated "1297."

Counterfeits, lithographed or typographed, are plentiful.

**Kingdom of Afghanistan**

A16

A17

A18

**Dated "1309"**

**1891** **Pelure Paper** **Litho.**

| | | | | | |
|---|---|---|---|---|---|
| **177** | A16 | 1ab | slate blue | 2.00 | 2.00 |
| *a.* | | | Tete beche pair | 19.00 | |
| **178** | A17 | 2ab | slate blue | 12.00 | 12.00 |
| **179** | A18 | 1rup | slate blue | 27.50 | — |
| | | | *Nos. 177-179 (3)* | 41.50 | 14.00 |

Revenue stamps of similar design exist in various colors.

Nos. 177-179 were printed in panes on the same sheet, so se-tenant gutter pairs exist. Examples in black or red are proofs.

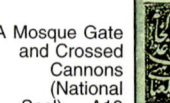

A Mosque Gate and Crossed Cannons (National Seal) — A19

**Dated "1310" in Upper Right Corner**

**1892** **Flimsy Wove Paper**

| | | | | | |
|---|---|---|---|---|---|
| **180** | A19 | 1ab | black, *green* | 3.50 | 3.00 |
| **181** | A19 | 1ab | black, *orange* | 4.50 | 4.50 |
| **182** | A19 | 1ab | black, *yellow* | 3.50 | 3.00 |
| **183** | A19 | 1ab | black, *pink* | 4.00 | 3.25 |
| **184** | A19 | 1ab | black, *lil rose* | 4.00 | 4.00 |
| **185** | A19 | 1ab | black, *blue* | 6.00 | 5.50 |
| **186** | A19 | 1ab | black, *salmon* | 4.50 | 3.75 |
| **187** | A19 | 1ab | black, *magenta* | 4.00 | 4.00 |
| **188** | A19 | 1ab | black, *violet* | 4.00 | 4.00 |
| **188A** | A19 | 1ab | black, *scarlet* | 4.00 | 3.00 |

Many shades exist.

A20

A21

**Undated**

**1894** **Flimsy Wove Paper**

| | | | | | |
|---|---|---|---|---|---|
| **189** | A20 | 2ab | black, *green* | 12.00 | 8.00 |
| **190** | A21 | 1rup | black, *green* | 14.50 | 13.00 |

24 varieties of the 2 abasi and 12 varieties of the rupee.

Nos. 189-190 and F3 were printed se-tenant in the same sheet. Pairs exist.

A21a

**Dated "1316"**

**1898** **Flimsy Wove Paper**

| | | | | | |
|---|---|---|---|---|---|
| **191** | A21a | 2ab | black, *pink* | 3.00 | |
| **192** | A21a | 2ab | black, *magenta* | 3.00 | |
| **193** | A21a | 2ab | black, *yellow* | 1.40 | |
| **193A** | A21a | 2ab | black, *salmon* | 3.50 | |
| **194** | A21a | 2ab | black, *green* | 1.75 | |
| **195** | A21a | 2ab | black, *purple* | 2.40 | |
| **195A** | A21a | 2ab | black, *blue* | 22.50 | |
| | | | *Nos. 191-195A (7)* | 37.55 | |

Nos. 191-195A were not regularly issued. Genuinely used examples are scarce. No. 195A was found in remainder stocks and probably was never released.

A22

A23

A24

**1907** **Engr.** ***Imperf.***

**Medium Wove Paper**

| | | | | | |
|---|---|---|---|---|---|
| **196** | A22 | 1ab | blue green | 50.00 | 30.00 |
| *a.* | | | 1ab emerald | — | 30.00 |
| *b.* | | | Double impression | *500.00* | |
| *c.* | | | Printed on both sides | | 450.00 |
| **197** | A22 | 1ab | brt blue | 30.00 | 25.00 |
| **198** | A23 | 2ab | deep blue | 30.00 | 25.00 |
| *a.* | | | Double impression | *550.00* | |
| **199** | A24 | 1rup | green | 100.00 | 50.00 |
| *a.* | | | 1rup blue green | 100.00 | 75.00 |

***Zigzag Roulette 10***

| | | | | | |
|---|---|---|---|---|---|
| **200** | A22 | 1ab | green | *2,750.* | 450.00 |
| *a.* | | | Double impression | | *1,500.* |
| *b.* | | | Printed on both sides | | *1,750.* |
| *c.* | | | Double impression and printed on both sides | | *2,500.* |
| *d.* | | | 1ab blue green | *2,750.* | 450.00 |
| **201** | A23 | 2ab | blue | *2,500.* | — |

**1908** ***Serrate Roulette 13***

| | | | | | |
|---|---|---|---|---|---|
| **201A** | A22 | 1ab | green | | |
| *b.* | | | 1ab emerald green | | |
| **201B** | A23 | 2ab | blue | *3,500.* | |

Nos. 201A and 201Ab are only known used on cover.

No. 201B is known only unused.

**Perf. 12 on 2, 3 or 4 Sides**

| | | | | | |
|---|---|---|---|---|---|
| **202** | A22 | 1ab | green | — | 65.00 |
| **203** | A23 | 2ab | deep blue | 35.00 | 20.00 |
| *a.* | | | Horiz. pair, imperf between | 450.00 | |
| **204** | A24 | 1rup | blue green | 125.00 | 65.00 |
| *c.* | | | Pair, imperf. between | 400.00 | |
| | | | *Nos. 202-204 (3)* | 160.00 | 150.00 |

Twelve varieties of the 1 abasi, 6 of the 2 abasi, 4 of the 1 rupee.

Nos. 196-204 were issued in small sheets containing 3 or 4 panes. Gutter pairs, normal and tete beche, exist.

Two plates were used for the 1 abasi: plate I, inner vert. lines extend into lower left panel; plate II, inner vert. lines do not extend into lower left panel.

A25

A26

A27

**1909-19 Typo. *Perf. 12***

| | | | | |
|---|---|---|---|---|
| 205 | A25 1ab ultra | | 5.00 | 2.00 |
| | a. Imperf., pair | | 48.00 | |
| 206 | A25 1ab red ('16) | | 1.60 | 1.25 |
| | a. Imperf. | | 30.00 | |
| 207 | A25 1ab rose ('18) | | 1.60 | 1.00 |
| 208 | A26 2ab green | | 2.75 | 2.25 |
| | a. Imperf., pair | | 48.00 | |
| | b. Horiz. pair, imperf. btwn. | | | |
| 208C | A26 2ab yellow ('16) | | 3.25 | 2.75 |
| 209 | A26 2ab bis ('18-'19) | | 3.25 | *3.25* |
| 210 | A27 1rup lilac brn | | 7.50 | 6.50 |
| | a. 1rup red brown | | 7.50 | 7.50 |
| 211 | A27 1rup ol bis ('16) | | 10.00 | 8.00 |
| | *Nos. 205-211 (8)* | | 34.95 | 27.00 |

A28

**1913**

| | | | |
|---|---|---|---|
| 212 | A28 2pa drab brown | 20.00 | *12.00* |
| | a. 2pa red brown | 20.00 | *12.00* |

No. 212 is inscribed "Tiket waraq dak" (Postal card stamps). It was usable only on postcards and not accepted for postage on letters.

Nos. 196-212 sometimes show letters of a papermaker's watermark, "Howard & Jones London."

Royal Star A29

**1920, Aug. 24 *Perf. 12***

**Size: 39x46mm**

| | | | |
|---|---|---|---|
| 214 | A29 10pa rose | 200.00 | 110.00 |
| 215 | A29 20pa red brown | 300.00 | 190.00 |
| 216 | A29 30pa green | 400.00 | 325.00 |
| | *Nos. 214-216 (3)* | 900.00 | 625.00 |

Independence Day. Issued to commemorate the first and second anniversaries of the signing of the armistice (Aug. 24, 1919) that ended the war of independence (Third Afghan War).

Issued in sheets of two settings: wide gutter, with 19mm between stamps, narrow gutter, with 12mm to 13mm between stamps.

No. 214 exists in two sizes: 38.5mmx46mm, position 1 in the wide gutter sheet; 38.5mmx46mm, position 2, in the wide gutter and position 1 in the narrow gutter sheet.

**1921, Mar. Size: 22½x28¼mm**

| | | | |
|---|---|---|---|
| 217 | A29 10pa rose | 2.50 | 1.25 |
| | a. Perf. 11 ('27) | 22.50 | 13.00 |
| 218 | A29 20pa red brown | 4.50 | 2.50 |
| 219 | A29 30pa yel green | 6.50 | 3.00 |
| | a. Tete beche pair | 55.00 | 32.50 |
| | b. 30pa green | 6.50 | 3.50 |
| | c. As "b," Tete beche pair | 55.00 | 32.50 |
| | *Nos. 217-219 (3)* | 13.50 | 6.75 |

3rd Independence Day.

Two types of the 10pa, three of the 20pa.

Hstmpd. in black on Nos. 217-219

**1923, Feb. 26**

| | | | |
|---|---|---|---|
| 219D | A29a 10pa rose | — | 125.00 |
| 219E | A29a 20pa red brown | — | 125.00 |
| 219F | A29a 30pa yel green | 400.00 | — |

5th Independence Day.

Two types of handstamp exist.

Forgeries exist.

See No. Q13B-Q13E.

These handstamps were used by the Kabul post office on incoming foreign mail from 1921 until Afghanistan joined the Universal Postal Union April 1, 1928. Afghan stamps were applied to foreign mail arriving in the country and were canceled with these postage-due handstamps to indicate that postage was to be collected from the addressee. The handstamps were applied primarily to Nos. 217-219, 227-235, 236, and 237-246. Values are the same as for stamps with postal cancellations. A third type of handstamp exists with no distinctive outer border.

A30

**1924, Feb. 26 *Perf. 12***

| | | | |
|---|---|---|---|
| 220 | A30 10pa chocolate | 45.00 | 30.00 |
| | a. Tete beche pair | 150.00 | 100.00 |

6th Independence Day.

Printed in sheets of four consisting of two tete beche pairs, and in sheets of two. Two types exist.

Some authorities believe that Nos. Q15-Q16 were issued as regular postage stamps.

Crest of King Amanullah — A32

**Size: 29x37mm**

**1925, Feb. 26 *Perf. 12***

| | | | |
|---|---|---|---|
| 222 | A32 10pa light brown | 75.00 | 35.00 |

7th Independence Day.

Printed in sheets of 8 (two panes of 4).

**Wove Paper**

**1926, Feb. 28 Size: 26x33mm**

| | | | |
|---|---|---|---|
| 224 | A32 10pa dark blue | 8.00 | 8.00 |
| | a. Imperf., pair | 32.50 | |
| | b. Horiz. pair, imperf. btwn. | 75.00 | |
| | c. Vert. pair, imperf. btwn. | | |
| | d. Laid paper | 40.00 | 13.00 |

7th anniv. of Independence. Printed in sheets of 4, and in sheets of 8 (two panes of 4). Tete beche gutter pairs exist.

Tughra and Crest of Amanullah — A33

**1927, Feb.**

| | | | |
|---|---|---|---|
| 225 | A33 10pa magenta | 14.00 | 12.00 |
| | a. Vertical pair, imperf. between | 75.00 | |

**Dotted Background**

| | | | |
|---|---|---|---|
| 226 | A33 10pa magenta | 20.00 | 13.00 |
| | a. Horiz. pair, imperf. between | 75.00 | |

The surface of No. 226 is covered by a net of fine dots.

8th anniv. of Independence. Printed in sheets of 8 (two panes of 4).

Tete-beche gutter pairs exist. Value, pair $85.

National Seal — A34

A35

A36

**1927, Oct. *Imperf.***

| | | | |
|---|---|---|---|
| 227 | A34 15p pink | 1.40 | 1.40 |
| 228 | A35 30p Prus green | 2.75 | 1.25 |
| 229 | A36 60p light blue | 3.75 | 3.25 |
| | *Nos. 227-229 (3)* | 7.90 | 5.90 |

**1927, Nov. *Perf. 11, 11¾***

| | | | |
|---|---|---|---|
| 230 | A34 15p pink | 1.75 | 1.40 |
| 231 | A35 30p Prus green | 3.25 | 1.40 |
| 232 | A36 60p bright blue | 3.50 | 2.00 |
| | a. Tete beche pair | 17.50 | 17.50 |
| | *Nos. 230-232 (3)* | 8.50 | 4.80 |

A37

A38

A39

A40

**1928, Feb. *Perf. 11, 11¾***

| | | | |
|---|---|---|---|
| 233 | A37 10p gray green | 1.25 | .40 |
| | a. Tete beche pair | 14.00 | 6.50 |
| | b. Vert. pair, imperf. horiz. | 11.00 | 11.00 |
| | c. Vertical pair, imperf. between | | |
| 234 | A38 25p car rose | 1.50 | .40 |
| 235 | A39 40p ultra | 2.00 | .75 |
| | a. Tete beche pair | 15.00 | *16.00* |
| 236 | A40 50p red | 2.50 | 1.00 |
| | *Nos. 233-236 (4)* | 7.25 | 2.55 |

Nos. 230-232 are usually imperforate on one or two sides. The sheets of these stamps are often imperforate at the outer margin. No. 233 was printed in sheets of nine and sheets of 20.

Tughra and Crest of Amanullah A41

**1928, Feb. 27**

| | | | |
|---|---|---|---|
| 236D | A41 15p pink | 5.00 | 5.00 |
| | a. Tete beche pair | 12.00 | 10.00 |
| | b. Horiz. pair, imperf. vert. | 22.50 | 19.00 |
| | c. As "a," imperf. vert., block of 4 | 75.00 | |

9th anniv. of Independence. This stamp is always imperforate on one or two sides.

A 15p blue of somewhat similar design was prepared for the 10th anniv., but was not issued due to Amanullah's dethronement. Value, $15.

**Types of 1927 in New Colors**

A42

**1929-30**

| | | | |
|---|---|---|---|
| 236E | A34 15p ultra | 1.75 | 1.40 |
| 236F | A42 30p dp green ('30) | 1.75 | 1.25 |
| 236G | A36 60p black ('29) | 4.00 | 2.25 |
| | *Nos. 236E-236G (3)* | 7.50 | 4.90 |

No. 236F has been redrawn. A narrow border of pearls has been added and "30," in European and Arabic numerals, inserted in the upper spandrels.

A43

**1928-30 *Perf. 11, 12***

| | | | |
|---|---|---|---|
| 237 | A43 2p dull blue | 7.75 | 4.50 |
| | a. Vertical pair, imperf. between | 20.00 | |
| 238 | A43 2p lt rose ('30) | .65 | .55 |
| 240 | A37 10p choc ('30) | 3.00 | 1.25 |
| | a. 10p brown purple ('29) | 8.50 | 8.50 |
| 242 | A38 25p Prus green ('30) | 4.00 | 1.25 |
| 244 | A30 40p rose ('29) | 3.50 | 1.25 |
| | a. Tete beche pair | 14.50 | |
| | b. Vert. pair, imperf. horiz. | 11.00 | |
| 246 | A40 50p dk blue ('29) | 5.00 | 1.50 |
| | *Nos. 237-246 (6)* | 23.90 | 10.30 |

The sheets of these stamps are often imperforate at the outer margins.

Nos. 237-238 are newspaper stamps.

This handstamp was used for 10 months by the Revolutionary Gov't in Kabul as a control mark on outgoing mail. It occasionally fell on the stamps but there is no evidence that it was officially used as an overprint. Unused examples were privately made. Forgeries exist.

Independence Monument — A46

**Laid Paper**

**Without Gum**

**Wmk. Large Seal in the Sheet**

**1931, Aug. Litho. *Perf. 12***

| | | | |
|---|---|---|---|
| 262 | A46 20p red | 2.50 | 1.25 |

13th Independence Day.

National Assembly Chamber — A47

A48

# AFGHANISTAN

National Assembly Building — A49

A50

National Assembly Chamber — A51

National Assembly Building — A52

**Wove Paper**

| 1932 | Unwmk. | Typo. | Perf. 12 |
|---|---|---|---|
| 263 | A47 | 40p olive | 1.15 .40 |
| 264 | A48 | 60p violet | 1.50 .80 |
| 265 | A49 | 80p dark red | 2.00 1.25 |
| 266 | A50 | 1af black | 16.00 7.50 |
| 267 | A51 | 2af ultra | 7.00 4.00 |
| 268 | A52 | 3af gray green | 7.50 3.50 |
|  | Nos. 263-268 (6) |  | 35.15 17.45 |

Formation of the Natl. Council. Imperforate or perforated examples on ungummed chalky paper are proofs. Covers of No. 263 imperf proofs are known used in May 1999.
See Nos. 304-305.

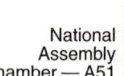

Mosque at Balkh — A53

Kabul Fortress — A54

Parliament House, Darul Funun — A55

Parliament House, Darul Funun — A56

Arch of Qalai Bist — A57

Memorial Pillar of Knowledge and Ignorance — A58

Independence Monument A59

Minaret at Herat A60

Arch of Paghman — A61

Ruins at Balkh — A62

Minarets of Herat A63

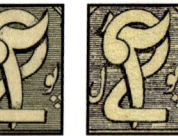

Great Buddha at Bamian A64

| 1932 |  | Typo. | Perf. 12 |
|---|---|---|---|
| 269 | A53 | 10p brown | .80 .25 |
| 270 | A54 | 15p dk brown | .60 .30 |
| 271 | A55 | 20p red | .95 .25 |
| 272 | A56 | 25p dk green | 1.35 .25 |
| 273 | A57 | 30p red | 1.35 .25 |
| 274 | A58 | 40p orange | 1.75 .50 |
| 275 | A59 | 50p blue | 2.40 1.40 |
|  | a. Tete beche pair |  | 12.00 |
| 276 | A60 | 60p blue | 2.25 .90 |
| 277 | A61 | 80p violet | 4.00 2.00 |
| 278 | A62 | 1af dark blue | 7.00 .80 |
| 279 | A63 | 2af dk red violet | 7.75 3.00 |
| 280 | A64 | 3af claret | 9.50 4.00 |
|  | Nos. 269-280 (12) |  | 39.70 13.90 |

Counterfeits of types A53-A65 exist.
See Nos. 290-295, 298-299, 302-303.

Entwined 2's — A65

Type I    Type II

Two types:
Type I — Numerals shaded. Size about 21x29mm.
Type II — Numerals unshaded. Size about 21¾x30mm.

| 1931-38 |  |  | Perf. 12, 11x12 |
|---|---|---|---|
| 281 | A65 | 2p red brn (I) | .40 .50 |
| 282 | A65 | 2p olive blk (I) ('34) | .30 .80 |
| 283 | A65 | 2p grnsh gray (I) ('34) | .40 .75 |
| 283A | A65 | 2p black (I) ('36) | .25 .75 |
| 284 | A65 | 2p salmon (II) ('38) | .50 .75 |
| 284A | A65 | 2p rose (I) ('38) | .50 .90 |
|  | b. Imperf., pair |  | 10.00 |

**Imperf**

| 285 | A65 | 2p black (II) ('37) | .75 .75 |
| 286 | A65 | 2p salmon (II) ('38) | .75 .75 |
|  | Nos. 281-286 (8) |  | 3.85 5.95 |

The newspaper rate was 2 pouls.

Independence Monument — A66

**1932, Aug.**         **Perf. 12**
287  A66  1af carmine         5.50  15.00
14th Independence Day.

A67

1929 Liberation Monument, Kabul.

**1932, Oct.**         **Typo.**
288  A67  80p red brown       2.00  7.50

Arch of Paghman A68

**1933, Aug.**
289  A68  50p light ultra     3.00  7.50
15th Independence Day.
No. 289 exists imperf. Value, $5.

**Types of 1932 and**

Royal Palace, Kabul — A69

Darrah-Shikari Pass, Hindu Kush — A70

| 1934-38 |  | Typo. | Perf. 12 |
|---|---|---|---|
| 290 | A53 | 10p deep violet | .30 .25 |
| 291 | A54 | 15p turq green | .50 .25 |
| 292 | A55 | 20p magenta | .50 .25 |
| 293 | A56 | 25p deep rose | .60 .25 |
| 294 | A57 | 30p orange | .65 .30 |
| 295 | A58 | 40p blue black | .75 .30 |
| 296 | A69 | 45p dark blue | 2.75 1.50 |
| 297 | A69 | 45p red ('38) | .50 .25 |
| 298 | A59 | 50p orange | .80 .25 |
| 299 | A60 | 60p purple | 1.00 .45 |
| 300 | A70 | 75p red | 4.00 2.00 |
| 301 | A70 | 75p dk blue ('38) | 1.00 .65 |
| 302 | A61 | 80p brown vio | 1.60 .80 |
| 303 | A62 | 1af red violet | 3.25 1.60 |
| 304 | A51 | 2af gray black | 5.25 2.40 |
| 305 | A52 | 3af ultra | 6.00 3.00 |
|  | Nos. 290-305 (16) |  | 29.45 14.50 |

Nos. 290, 292, 300, 304, 305 exist imperf.

Independence Monument — A71

**1934, Aug.**   **Litho.**   **Without Gum**
306  A71  50p pale green        3.25  2.75
   a. Tete beche pair          11.50  11.50
16th year of Independence. Each sheet of 40 (4x10) included 4 tete beche pairs as lower half of sheet was inverted.

Independence Monument — A74

**1935, Aug. 15**        **Laid Paper**
309  A74  50p dark blue         3.50  2.40
17th year of Independence.

Fireworks Display — A75

**Wove Paper**

**1936, Aug. 15**        **Perf. 12**
310  A75  50p red violet        3.25  2.50
18th year of Independence.

Independence Monument and Nadir Shah — A76

**1937**
311  A76  50p vio & bis brn     2.75  2.10
   a. Imperf., pair            9.50  9.50
19th year of Independence.

Mohammed Nadir Shah — A77

**1938**   **Without Gum**   **Perf. 11x12**
315  A77  50p brt blue & sepia  2.75  2.40
   a. Imperf. pair             24.00  19.00
20th year of Independence.

Mohammed Nadir Shah — A78

**1939**        **Perf. 11, 12x11**
317  A78  50p deep salmon       2.40  1.50
21st year of Independence.

National Arms — A79

Parliament House, Darul Funun — A80

Royal Palace, Kabul A81

Independence Monument A82

# AFGHANISTAN

Independence Monument and Nadir Shah — A83

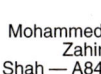

Mohammed Zahir Shah — A84

Mohammed Zahir Shah — A85

**Perf. 11, 11x12, 12x11, 12**

**1939-61**            Typo.
318   A79   2p intense blk      .30   .70
318A   A79   2p brt pink ('61)    .30   .70
      *Size: 36.5x24mm*
319   A80   10p brt purple      .30   .25
      *Size: 31.5x21mm*
320   A80   15p brt green       .35   .25
      *Size: 34x22.5mm*
321   A80   20p red lilac        .50   .25
322   A81   25p rose red       .60   .30
322A   A81   25p green ('41)    .35   .25
323   A81   30p orange         .50   .25
   a. Vert. pair, imperf between
324   A81   40p dk gray       1.00   .50
325   A82   45p brt carmine   1.00   .40
326   A82   50p dp orange     .80   .25
327   A82   60p violet         1.00   .25
328   A83   75p ultra          3.00   .80
328A   A83   75p red vio ('41)   2.25   1.60
328C   A83   75p brt red ('44)   4.00   3.00
328D   A83   75p ebnt brn ('49)   4.00   3.00
329   A83   80p chocolate     2.00   1.00
   a. 80p dull red violet (error)
330   A84   1af brt red violet    2.25   .80
330A   A84   1af brt red vio ('44)   2.25   .90
331   A85   2af copper red   3.00   .80
   2af deep rose red         4.25   1.75
332   A84   3af deep blue      5.00   2.40
     Nos. 318-332 (21)   34.75   18.65

Many shades exist in this issue.
On No. 332, the King faces slightly left.
No. 318A issued with and without gum.
See Nos. 795A-795B. For similar design see No. 907A.

Mohammed Nadir Shah — A86

**1940, Aug. 23**         *Perf. 11*
333   A86   50p gray green    2.00   1.50
     22nd year of Independence.

Independence Monument A87      Arch of Paghman A88

**1941, Aug. 23**         *Perf. 12*
334   A87   15p gray green   25.00   5.00
335   A88   50p red brown   2.50   2.10
     23rd year of Independence.

Sugar Factory, Baghlan — A89

**1942, Apr.**           *Perf. 12*
336   A89   1.25af blue (shades)   2.00   1.50
   a. 1.25af ultra          2.50   1.75

In 1949, a 1.50af brown, type A89, was sold for 3af by the Philatelic Office, Kabul. It was not valid for postage. Value $6.

Independence Monument A90     Mohammed Nadir Shah and Arch of Paghman A91

**1942, Aug. 23**         *Perf. 12*
337   A90   35p bright green   3.75   3.50
338   A91   125p chalky blue   3.00   2.00
     24th year of Independence.

Independence Monument and Nadir Shah — A92     Mohammed Nadir Shah — A93

**Perf. 11x12, 12x11**

**1943, Aug. 25**    *Typo.*    *Unwmk.*
339   A92   35p carmine   17.50   15.00
340   A93   1.25af dark blue   3.50   2.50
     25th year of Independence.

Tomb of Gohar Shad, Herat A94     Ruins of Qalai Bist A95

**1944, May 1**      *Perf. 12, 11x12*
341   A94   35p orange    1.50   .80
342   A95   70p violet     2.00   .80
   a. 70p rose lilac     2.00   .80

A96      A97

**1944, Aug.**         *Perf. 12*
343   A96   35p crimson   1.25   .65
344   A97   1.25af ultra    2.25   1.75
     26th year of Independence.

**Catalogue values for unused stamps in this section, from this point to the end of the section, are for Never Hinged items.**

A98      A99

**1945, July**
345   A98   35p deep red lilac   2.50   .80
346   A99   1.25af blue       4.00   2.00
     27th year of Independence.

Mohammed Zahir Shah A100     Independence Monument A101

Mohammed Nadir Shah — A102

**1946, July**
347   A100   15p emerald    1.25   .70
348   A101   20p dp red lilac   2.00   .85
349   A102   125p blue      3.75   2.00
     Nos. 347-349 (3)   7.00   3.55
     28th year of Independence.

Zahir Shah and Ruins of Qalai Bist — A103     A104

A105

**1947, Aug.**
350   A103   15p yellow green   .80   .55
351   A104   35p plum        1.00   .65
352   A105   125p deep blue   2.75   1.60
     Nos. 350-352 (3)   4.55   2.80
     29th year of Independence.

Begging Child — A106

A107

**1948, May**    *Unwmk.*   *Typo.*   *Perf. 12*
353   A100   35p yel green   4.75   4.00
354   A107   125p gray blue   4.75   4.00

Children's Day, May 29, 1948, and valid only on that day. Proceeds were used for Child Welfare.

A108      A109

A110

**1948, Aug.**
355   A108   15p green      .65   .30
356   A109   20p magenta    .80   .30
357   A110   125p dark blue   1.60   .80
     Nos. 355-357 (3)   3.05   1.40
     30th year of Independence.

United Nations Emblem A111

**1948, Oct. 24**
358   A111   125p dk violet blue   9.50   8.00
     UN, 3rd anniv. Valid one day only. Sheets of 9.

Maiwand Victory Column, Kandahar A112     Zahir Shah and Ruins of Qalai Bist A113

Independence Monument and Nadir Shah — A114

**1949, Aug. 24**    *Typo.*    *Perf. 12*
359   A112   25p green     1.25   .50
360   A113   35p magenta   1.50   .65
361   A114   1.25af blue     2.50   1.25
     Nos. 359-361 (3)   5.25   2.40
     31st year of Independence.

Nadir Shah — A117

**1950, Aug.**
364   A117   35p red brown   .75   .30
365   A117   125p blue      2.00   .50
     32nd year of Independence.

Medical School and Nadir Shah — A119

     *Size: 38x25mm*
**1950, Dec. 22**    *Typo.*    *Perf. 12*
367   A119   35p emerald   1.25   .65
     *Size: 46x30mm*
368   A119   1.25af deep blue   4.00   2.00
   a. 1.25af black (error)   7.00   2.00

19th anniv. of the founding of Afghanistan's Faculty of Medicine. On sale and valid for use on Dec. 22-28, 1950.
See Nos. RA9-RA10.

Minaret, Herat A120     Zahir Shah A121

# AFGHANISTAN

Mosque of Khodja Abu Parsar, Balkh — A122

A123   A124

20p, Buddha at Bamian. 40p, Ruined arch. 45p, Maiwand Victory monument. 50p, View of Kandahar. 60p, Ancient tower. 70p, Afghanistan flag. 80p, 1af, Profile of Zahir Shah in uniform.

Imprint: "Waterlow & Sons Limited, London"

**Photogravure, Engraved, Engraved and Lithographed**
*Perf. 12, 12½, 13x12½, 13½*

**1951, Mar. 21**                                 Unwmk.
369 A120  10p yellow & brn        .30    .25
370 A120  15p blue & brn          .55    .25
371 A120  20p black              8.00   7.00
372 A121  25p green               .50    .25
373 A122  30p cerise              .65    .25
374 A121  35p violet              .70    .25
375 A122  40p chestnut brn        .70    .25
376 A120  45p deep blue           .70    .25
377 A122  50p olive black        2.00    .25
378 A120  60p black              1.60    .30
379 A122  70p dk grn, blk,
              red & grn           .90    .
380 A123  75p cerise             1.25    .50
381 A123  80p carmine & blk      2.10    .90
382 A123  1af dp grn & vio       1.60    .65
383 A124  1.25af rose lil & blk  1.90   1.00
384 A124  2af ultra              2.75    .80
385 A124  3af ultra & blk        6.00   1.25
     Nos. 369-385 (17)          32.20  14.65

Nos. 372, 374 and 381 to 385 are engraved, No. 379 is engraved and lithographed.
Imperfs. exist of the photogravure stamps. See Nos. 445-451, 453, 552A-552D. For surcharges see Nos. B1-B2.

Arch of Paghman A125   Nadir Shah and Independence Monument A126

Overprint in Violet

*Perf. 13½x13, 13*
**1951, Aug. 25**                              Engr.
386 A125  35p dk green & blk     1.10    .65
387 A126  1.25af deep blue       3.00   1.40

Overprint reads "Sol 33 Istiqlal" or "33rd Year of Independence." Overprint measures about 11mm wide.
See Nos. 398-399B, 441-442.

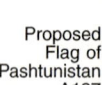
Proposed Flag of Pashtunistan A127

Design: 125p, Flag and Pashtunistan warrior.

**1951, Sept. 2**   Litho.    *Perf. 11½*
388 A127  35p dull chocolate     1.50    .75
389 A127  125p blue              3.00   1.25

Issued to publicize "Free Pashtunistan" Day. Exist Imperf.

### Imperforates

From 1951 to 1958, quantities of nearly all locally-printed stamps were left imperforate and sold by the government at double face. From 1959 until March, 1964, many of the imperforates were sold for more than face value.

Avicenna — A128

**1951, Nov. 4**   Typo.    *Perf. 11½*
390 A128  35p deep claret        7.50   1.50
391 A128  125p blue              3.00   4.00

20th anniv. of the founding of the national Graduate School of Medicine.
Exist imperf. Value $27.50.

A129

Dove and UN Symbols — A130

**1951, Oct. 24**
392 A129  35p magenta             .90    .40
393 A130  125p blue              2.25   1.75

7th anniv. of the UN. Exist imperf.

Amir Sher Ali Khan and Tiger Head Stamp — A131

Nos. 395, 397, Zahir Shah and stamp.

**1951, Dec. 23**              Litho.
394 A131  35p chocolate           .85    .40
395 A131  35p rose lilac          .85    .40
396 A131  125p ultra             1.25    .80
   a. Cliche of 35p in plate of
      125p                     110.00 200.00
397 A131  125p aqua              1.25    .80
     Nos. 394-397 (4)            4.20   2.40

76th anniv. of the UPU. Exist imperf. Values, set: unused $9; used $17.50.

### Stamps of 1951 Without Overprint
*Perf. 13½x13, 13*
**1952, Aug. 24**              Engr.
398 A125  35p dk green & blk     1.50    .55
399 A126  1.25af deep blue       3.25   1.25

For overprints see Nos. 399A-399B, 441-442.

### Same Overprinted in Violet

399A A125  35p dk grn & blk      4.00   2.25
399B A126  1.25af deep blue      4.00   2.25

Nos. 398-399B issued for 34th Independence Day.

Globe A132

*Perf. 11½*
**1952, Oct. 25**  Unwmk.    Litho.
400 A132  35p rose                .80    .65
401 A132  125p aqua              1.60   1.10

Issued to honor the United Nations. Exist Imperf. Values, set: unused $6; used $7.25.

Symbol of Medicine — A134

**1952, Nov.**               *Perf. 11½*
403 A134  35p chocolate           .70    .50
404 A134  125p violet blue       2.00   1.40

21st anniv. of the natl. Graduate School of Medicine.
No. 404 is inscribed in French with white letters on a colored background.
Exist Imperf. Values, set: unused $3.50; used $4.50.

Tribal Warrior, Natl. Flag — A135

**1952, Sept. 1**            *Perf. 11*
405 A135  35p red                 .80    .80
406 A135  125p dark blue         1.25   1.25

No. 406 is inscribed in French "Pashtunistan Day, 1952."
Exist Imperf. Values, set, unused or used, $2.75.

Flags of Afghanistan & Pashtunistan A139   Badge of Pashtunistan A140

*Perf. 10½x11, 11*
**1953, Sept. 1**             Unwmk.
411 A139  35p vermilion           .80    .80
412 A140  125p blue               .80    .80

Issued to publicize "Free Pashtunistan" Day. Exist Imperf. Values, set: unused $3.50; used, $4.

Nadir Shah and Flag Bearer — A141   A142

**1953, Aug. 24**             *Perf. 11*
413 A141  35p green               .40    .25
414 A142  125p violet             .80    .55

35th anniv. of Independence.
Exist imperf. Values, set: unused $3.50; used $4.

United Nations Emblem — A143

**1953, Oct. 24**
415 A143  35p lilac              1.00    .80
416 A143  125p violet blue       2.00   1.50

United Nations Day, 1953.
Exist imperf. Values, set, unused or used, $9.

A144   Nadir Shah — A145

**1953, Nov. 29**
417 A144  35p orange             1.50   1.50
418 A145  125p chalky blue       3.00   3.00

22nd anniv. of the founding of the Natl. Graduate School of Medicine.
Exist imperf. Values, set: unused, $9; used, $12.50.

35p. Original — Right character in second line of Persian inscription

Redrawn — Persian character

Original

Redrawn

**1953**
419 A144  35p deep orange        9.50   9.50
420 A145  125p chalky blue       9.50   9.50

Exist imperf.

Nadir Shah and Symbols of Independence A146

**1954, Aug.**   Typo.    *Perf. 11*
421 A146  35p carmine rose        .70    .40
422 A146  125p violet blue       2.00    .80

36th year of Independence.
Exist imperf. Values, set: unused $6; used, $7.

Raising Flag of Pashtunistan A147

**1954, Sept.**              *Perf. 11½*
423 A147  35p chocolate           .70    .40
424 A147  125p blue              2.00    .80

Issued to publicize "Free Pashtunistan" Day. Exist imperf. Values, set: unused $4.75; used, $6.50.

UN Flag and Map — A148

**1954, Oct. 24**            *Perf. 11*
425 A148  35p carmine rose       1.25   1.25
426 A148  125p dk violet blue    3.25   2.25

9th anniv. of the United Nations.
Exist imperf. Values, set: unused, $9; used, $10.

# AFGHANISTAN

UN Symbols — A149

Design: 125p, UN emblem & flags.

**1955, June 26   Litho.   Perf. 11**
**Size: 26½x36mm**
427  A149  35p dark green       1.10   .55
**Size: 28½x36mm**
428  A149  125p aqua            2.00  1.00

10th anniv. of the UN charter.
Exist imperf. Values, set: unused, $12; used, $12.50.

Nadir Shah (center) and Brothers — A150

1929 Civil War Scene and Zahir Shah — A151

**1955, Aug.   Unwmk.   Perf. 11**
429  A150  35p brt pink         .65    .40
430  A150  35p violet blue      .65    .40
431  A151  125p rose lilac     1.40    .90
432  A151  125p light violet   1.40    .90
Nos. 429-432 (4)                4.10   2.60

37th anniv. of Independence.
Exist imperf. Values, set: unused, $12; used, $13.50.

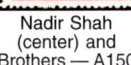

Tribal Elders' Council and Pashtun Flag — A152

**1955, Sept. 5**
433  A152  35p orange brown     .60    .25
434  A152  125p yellow green   2.00    .55

Issued for "Free Pashtunistan" Day.
Exist imperf. Values, set: unused, $7; used, $9.

UN Flag — A153

**1955, Oct. 24   Unwmk.   Perf. 11**
435  A153  35p orange brown    1.10    .60
436  A153  125p brt ultra      2.00   1.10

10th anniv. of the United Nations.
Exist imperf. Value for set: unused, $15; used, $17.50.

A154

**1956, Aug.   Litho.**
437  A154  35p lt green         .55    .30
438  A154  140p lt violet blue 2.25    .90

38th year of Independence.
Exist imperf. Value for set: unused, $3; used, $4.

Jesh'n Exhibition Hall — A155

**1956, Aug. 25**
439  A155  50p chocolate        .90    .40
440  A155  50p lt violet blue   .90    .40

International Exposition at Kabul.
Of the 50p face value, only 35p paid postage. The remaining 15p went to the Exposition.
Exist imperf. Value for set: unused, $7; used, $8.

**Nos. 398-399 Handstamped in Violet**

a  b

**1957, Aug.   Engr.   Perf. 13½x13, 13**
441  A125 (a)  35p dk green & blk   .65   .30
442  A126 (b)  1.25af deep blue    1.00   .70

Arabic overprint measures 19mm.
39th year of independence.

Pashtunistan Flag — A156

**1957, Sept. 1   Litho.   Perf. 11**
443  A156  50p pale lilac rose  1.00   .50
444  A156  155p light violet   1.50   1.00

Issued for "Free Pashtunistan" Day. French inscription on No. 444. 15p of each stamp went to the Pashtunistan Fund.
Exist imperf. Values, set: unused, $4; used, $4.50.

**Types of 1951 and**

Game of Buzkashi — A157

**Perf. 12, 12½, 12½x13, 13, 13x12, 13x12½, 13x14**
**Photo., Engr., Engr.& Litho.**
**1957, Nov. 23   Unwmk.**
Imprint: "Waterlow & Sons Limited, London"
445  A122  30p brown            .40    .25
446  A122  40p rose red         .55    .25
447  A122  50p yellow           .65    .25
448  A120  60p ultra            .80    .25
449  A123  75p brt violet      1.00    .25
450  A123  80p violet & brn    1.10    .25
451  A123  1af carmine & ultra 1.75    .25
452  A157  140p olive & dp claret 2.75  .65
453  A124  3af orange & blk    2.75    .90
Nos. 445-453 (9)               11.75   3.00

No. 452 lacks imprint.

Nadir Shah and Flag-bearer A158

**1958, Aug. 25   Perf. 13½x14**
454  A158  35p dp yellow green  .50    .25
455  A158  140p brown          1.25   1.00

40th year of Independence.

Exposition Buildings — A159

**1958, Aug. 23   Litho.   Perf. 11**
456  A159  35p brt blue green   .50    .25
457  A159  140p vermilion      1.25   1.00

International Exposition at Kabul.
Exist imperf. Value set, unused or used, $4.

Pres. Celal Bayar of Turkey — A160

**1958, Sept. 13   Unwmk.**
458  A160  50p lt blue          .30    .25
459  A160  100p brown           .65    .30

Visit of President Celal Bayar of Turkey.
Exists Imperf. Values, set: unused, $2.25; used, $3.25.

Flags of UN and Afghanistan — A161

**1958, Oct. 24   Photo.   Perf. 14x13½**
**Flags in Original Colors**
460  A161  50p dark gray        .65    .65
461  A161  100p green          1.40   1.10

United Nations Day, Oct. 24.
Exist imperf. Value set, unused or used, $4.

Atomic Energy Encircling the Hemispheres — A162

**1958, Oct. 20   Perf. 13½x14**
462  A162  50p blue             .55    .50
463  A162  100p dp red lilac    .90    .65

Issued to promote Atoms for Peace.
Exist imperf. Value set, unused or used, $3.

UNESCO Building, Paris — A163

**1958, Nov. 3**
464  A163  50p dp yellow grn    .70    .60
465  A163  100p brown olive     .70    .70

UNESCO Headquarters in Paris opening, Nov. 3.
Exist imperf. Value set, unused or used, $5.

Globe and Torch — A164

**Perf. 13½x14**
**1958, Dec. 10   Unwmk.**
466  A164  50p lilac rose       .40    .40
467  A164  100p maroon          .90   1.00

10th anniv. of the signing of the Universal Declaration of Human Rights.
Exist imperf. Value set, unused or used, $3.50.

Nadir Shah and Flags — A165

**1959, Aug.   Litho.   Perf. 11 Rough**
468  A165  35p light vermilion  .55    .50
469  A165  165p light violet   1.50    .65

41st year of Independence.
Exist imperf. Value set, unused or used, $2.50.

Uprooted Oak Emblem — A166

**1960, Apr. 7    Perf. 11**
470  A166  50p deep orange      .25    .25
471  A166  165p blue            .35    .25

World Refugee Year, 7/1/59-6/30/60.
Two imperf. souvenir sheets exist. Both contain a 50p and a 165p, type A166, with marginal inscriptions and WRY emblem in maroon. On one sheet the stamps are in the colors of Nos. 470-471 (size 108x81mm). Value $4.50. On the other, the 50p is blue and the 165p is deep orange (size 107x80mm). Value $6.
For surcharges see Nos. B35-B36.
Exist imperf. Value set, unused or used, $3.50.

Buzkashi — A167

**1960, May 4    Perf. 11, Imperf.**
472  A167  25p rose red         .55    .25
473  A167  50p bluish green    1.40    .55
a.  Cliche of 25p in plate of 50p  27.50  27.50

Exist imperf. Value set, unused or used, $2.50.
See Nos. 549-550A.

Independence Monument — A168

**1960, Aug.   Perf. 11, 12**
474  A168  50p light blue       .40    .25
475  A168  175p bright pink    1.00    .40

42nd Independence Day.
Exist imperf. Value set, unused or used, $1.75.

Globe and Flags — A169

**1960, Oct. 24   Litho.   Perf. 11, 12**
476  A169  50p rose lilac       .25    .25
477  A169  175p ultra          1.00    .65

UN Day.
Exist imperf. Value set, unused or used, $2.25.
An imperf. souvenir sheet contains one each of Nos. 476-477 with marginal inscriptions ("La Journée des Nations Unies 1960" in French and Persian) and UN emblem in light bluc. Size: 127x85½mm. Value $5.50.
This sheet was surcharged "120ps" in 1962. Value $5.50.

Teacher Pointing to Globe — A170

**1960, Oct. 23    Perf. 11**
478  A170  50p brt pink         .40    .30
479  A170  100p brt green      1.00    .50

Issued to publicize Teacher's Day.
Exist imperf. Value set, unused or used, $2.50.

Mohammed Zahir Shah — A171

# AFGHANISTAN

**1960, Oct. 15**
480 A171 50p red brown .65 .25
481 A171 150p dk car rose 1.60 .55

Honoring the King on his 46th birthday. Exist imperf. Value set, unused or used, $2.50.

Buzkashi — A172

**1960, Nov. 9**    *Perf. 11*
482 A172 175p lt red brown 2.40 .50

Exists imperf. Value, unused or used, $3. See Nos. 551-552.

No. 482 Overprinted in Bright Green

**1960, Dec. 24**
483 A172 175p red brown 2.00 2.00
   a. Souv. sheet of 1, imperf. 6.00 8.00

17th Olympic Games, Rome, 8/25-9/11. Exists imperf. Value, unused or used, $4.

Mir Wais — A173

**1961, Jan. 5**    *Unwmk.*    *Perf. 10½*
484 A173 50p brt rose lilac .65 .40
485 A173 175p ultra 1.10 .50
   a. Souv. sheet, #484-485, imperf. 3.25 3.25

Mir Wais (1665-1708), national leader. Exist imperf. Value set, unused or used, $2.25.

**No Postal Need** existed for the 1p-15p denominations issued with sets of 1961-63 (between Nos. 486 and 649, B37 and B65).
The lowest denomination actually used for non-philatelic postage in that period was 25p (except for the 2p newspaper rate for which separate stamps were provided).

Horse, Sheep and Camel — A174

Designs: No. 487, 175p, Rock partridge. 10p, 100p, Afghan hound. 15p, 150p, Grain & grasshopper, vert.

**1961, Mar. 29**    *Photo.*    *Perf. 13½x14*
486 A174 2p maroon & buff .25 .25
487 A174 2p ultra & org .25 .25
488 A174 5p brown & yel .25 .25
489 A174 10p black & salmon .25 .25
490 A174 15p blue grn & yel .25 .25
491 A174 25p black & pink .25 .25
492 A174 50p black & citron .30 .30
493 A174 100p black & pink .45 .40
494 A174 150p green & yel .65 .65
495 A174 175p ultra & pink .80 .65
   Nos. 486-495 (10) 3.70 3.50

Two souvenir sheets, perf. and imperf., contain 2 stamps, 1 each of No. 492-493. Value $3 each.

Afghan Fencing — A175

Designs: No. 497, 5p, 25p, 50p, Wrestlers. 10p, 100p, Man with Indian clubs. 15p, 150p, Afghan fencing. 175p, Children skating.

**1961, July 6**    *Perf. 13½x14*
496 A175 2p green & rose lil .25 .25
497 A175 2p brown & citron .25 .25
498 A175 5p gray & rose .25 .25
499 A175 10p blue & bister .25 .25
500 A175 15p sl bl & dl lil .25 .25
501 A175 25p black & dl bl .25 .25
502 A175 50p sl grn & bis brn .25 .25
503 A175 100p brown & bl grn .55 .55
504 A175 150p brown & org yel .90 .90
505 A175 175p black & blue .95 .95
   Nos. 496-505 (10) 4.15 4.15

Issued for Children's Day. A souvenir sheet exists, perf. and imperf., containing one each of Nos. 502-503. Values: perf $3.75; imperf $5.
For surcharges see Nos. B37-B41.

Bande Amir Lakes — A176

**1961, Aug. 7**    *Photo.*    *Perf. 13½x14*
506 A176 3af brt blue .50 .25
507 A176 10af rose claret 1.25 1.25

Nadir Shah — A177

**1961, Aug. 23**    *Perf. 14x13½*
508 A177 50p rose red & blk .55 .50
509 A177 175p brt grn & org brn .90 .70

43rd Independence Day. Exist imperf. Value set, unused or used, $2.50.
Two souvenir sheets, perf. and imperf., contain one each of Nos. 508-509. Value, each $2.50.

Girl Scout — A178

*Perf. 14x13½*
**1961, July 23**    *Unwmk.*
510 A178 50p dp car & dk gray .40 .25
511 A178 175p dp grn & rose brn 1.25 .50

Issued for Women's Day. Exist imperf. Value set, unused or used, $4.50.
Two souvenir sheets exist, perf. and imperf., containing one each of Nos. 510-511. Value $5 each.

Exhibition Hall, Kabul — A179

**1961, Aug. 23**    *Perf. 13½x14*
512 A179 50p yel brn & yel grn .25 .25
513 A179 175p blue & brn .70 .50

International Exhibition at Kabul.

Pathan with Pashtunistan Flag — A180

**1961, Aug. 31**    *Photo.*    *Perf. 14x13½*
514 A180 50p blk, lil & red .30 .25
515 A180 175p brn, grnsh bl & red .65 .55

Issued for "Free Pashtunistan Day." Exist imperf. Value set, unused or used, $1.60.
Souvenir sheets exist perf. and imperf. containing one each of Nos. 514-515. Value $2.25 each.

Assembly Building — A181

**1961, Sept. 10**    *Perf. 12*
516 A181 50p dk gray & brt grn .25 .25
517 A181 175p ultra & brn .65 .50

Anniv. of the founding of the Natl. Assembly. Exist imperf. Value set, unused or used, $1.25.
Souvenir sheets exist, perf. and imperf., containing one each of Nos. 516-517. Value $1.50 each.

Exterminating Anopheles Mosquito — A182

**1961, Oct. 5**    *Perf. 13½x14*
518 A182 50p blk & brn lil .60 .30
519 A182 175p maroon & brt grn 1.25 .90

Anti-Malaria campaign. Exist imperf. Value set, unused or used, $4. Souvenir sheets exist, perf. and imperf., containing one each of Nos. 518-519. Value $4.50 each.

Zahir Shah — A183

**1961, Oct. 15**    *Perf. 13½*
520 A183 50p rose lilac & grnish black .30 .25
521 A183 175p emerald & red brn .90 .50

Issued to honor King Mohammed Zahir Shah on his 47th birthday. See Nos. 609-612.

Pomegranates A184

Fruit: No. 523, 5p, 25p, 50p, Grapes. 10p, 150p, Apples. 15p, 175p, Pomegranates. 100p, Melons.

**1961, Oct. 16**    *Perf. 13½x14*
**Fruit in Natural Colors**
522 A184 2p black .25 .25
523 A184 2p green .25 .25
524 A184 5p lilac rose .25 .25
525 A184 10p lilac .25 .25
526 A184 15p dk blue .25 .25
527 A184 25p dull red .25 .25
528 A184 50p purple .25 .25
529 A184 100p brt blue .55 .55
530 A184 150p brown .90 .90
531 A184 175p olive gray .95 .95
   Nos. 522-531 (10) 4.15 4.15

For Afghan Red Crescent Society. Souvenir sheets exist, perf. and imperf., containing one each of Nos. 528-529. Value $2.25 each.
For surcharges see Nos. B42-B46.

UN Headquarters, NY — A185

**1961, Oct. 24**    *Perf. 13½x14*
**Vertical Borders in Emerald, Red and Black**
532 A185 1p rose lilac .25 .25
533 A185 2p slate .25 .25
534 A185 3p brown .25 .25
535 A185 4p ultra .25 .25
536 A185 50p rose red .25 .25
537 A185 75p gray .25 .25
538 A185 175p brt green .55 .55
   Nos. 532-538 (7) 2.05 2.05

16th anniv. of the UN. Nos. 536-538 exist imperf. Values, unused or used: 50p, 40c; 75p, 65c; 175p, $1.40. Souvenir sheets exist, perf. and imperf., containing one each of Nos. 536-538. Value $3 each.

Children Giving Flowers to Teacher — A186

Designs: No. 540, 5p, 25p, 50p, Tulips. 10p, 100p, Narcissus. 15p, 150p, Children giving flowers to teacher. 175p, Teacher with children in front of school.

**1961, Oct. 26**    *Photo.*    *Perf. 12*
539 A186 2p multicolored .25 .25
540 A186 2p multicolored .25 .25
541 A186 5p multicolored .25 .25
542 A186 10p multicolored .25 .25
543 A186 15p multicolored .25 .25
544 A186 25p multicolored .25 .25
545 A186 50p multicolored .25 .25
546 A186 100p multicolored .50 .50
547 A186 150p multicolored .80 .80
548 A186 175p multicolored .90 .90
   Nos. 539-548 (10) 3.95 3.95

Issued for Teacher's Day. Souvenir sheets exist, perf. and imperf., containing one each of Nos. 545-546. Value, 2 sheets, $4.50.
For surcharges see Nos. B47-B51.

### Buzkashi Types of 1960

**1961-72**    *Litho.*    *Perf. 10½, 11*
549 A167 25p violet 1.40 .25
   b. 25p brt vio, typo. ('72) .25 .25
549A A167 50p citron ('63) 2.50 .25
550 A167 50p blue 2.00 .25
550A A167 50p yel org ('69) .50 .30
551 A172 100p citron .80 .25
551A A172 150p orange ('64) .65 .30
552 A172 2af lt green 1.50 1.00
   Nos. 549-552 (7) 9.35 2.60

### Zahir Shah Types of 1951

Imprint: "Thomas De La Rue & Co. Ltd."

**1962**    *Photo., Engr., Engr. & Litho.*    *Perf. 13x12, 13*
552A A123 75p brt purple 2.75 .25
552B A123 1af car & ultra 3.50 .30
552C A124 2af blue 7.25 .80
552D A124 3af orange & blk 10.00 1.00
   Nos. 552A-552D (4) 23.50 2.35

People Raising UNESCO Symbol — A187

**1962, July 2**    *Photo.*    *Perf. 14x13½*
553 A187 2p rose lil & brn .25 .25
554 A187 2p ol bis & brn .25 .25
555 A187 5p dp org & dk grn .25 .25
556 A187 10p gray & mag .25 .25
557 A187 15p blue & brn .25 .25
558 A187 25p org yel & pur .25 .25
559 A187 50p lt grn & pur .25 .25
560 A187 75p brt cit & brn .25 .25
561 A187 100p dp org & brn .30 .30
   Nos. 553-561 (9) 2.30 2.30

15th anniv. of UNESCO. Souvenir sheets exist, perf. and imperf. One contains Nos. 558-559; the other contains Nos. 560-561. Value, $3.25 each perforated, $2.40 each imperf.
For surcharges see Nos. B52-B60.

# AFGHANISTAN

Ahmad Shah — A188

**1962, Feb. 24**    Photo.    Perf. 13½
562 A188   50p red brn & gray   .25   .25
563 A188   75p green & salmon   .30   .25
564 A188   100p claret & bister   .40   .30
    Nos. 562-564 (3)   .95   .80

Ahmad Shah (1724-73), founded the Afghan kingdom in 1747 and ruled until 1773.

Afghan Hound — A189

Designs: 5p, 75p, Afghan cock. 10p, 100p, Kondjid plant. 15p, 125p, Astrakhan skins.

**1962, Apr. 21**    Perf. 14x13½
565 A189   2p rose & brn   .25   .25
566 A189   2p lt green & brn   .25   .25
567 A189   5p dp rose & claret   .25   .25
568 A189   10p lt grn & sl grn   .25   .25
569 A189   15p blue grn & blk   .25   .25
570 A189   25p blue & brn   .25   .25
571 A189   50p gray & brn   .30   .25
572 A189   75p rose lil & lil   .50   .30
573 A189   100p gray & dl grn   .55   .40
574 A189   125p rose brn & blk   .65   .50
    Nos. 565-574 (10)   3.50   2.95

Agriculture Day.
Perf. and imperf. souvenir sheets exist. Set of 4 sheets, value $11.00.
Exist imperf. Value, set $5.50.

Athletes with Flag and Nadir Shah — A190

**1962, Aug. 23**    Perf. 12
575 A190   25p multicolored   .25   .25
576 A190   50p multicolored   .25   .25
577 A190   150p multicolored   .40   .30
    Nos. 575-577 (3)   .90   .80

44th Independence Day.

Woman in National Costume — A191

**1962, Aug. 30**    Perf. 11½x12
578 A191   25p lilac & brn   .25   .25
579 A191   50p green & brn   .25   .25
    Nos. 578-579,C15-C16 (4)   1.90   1.90

Issued for Women's Day. A souvenir sheet exists containing one each of Nos. 578-579, C15-C16. Value $4.50.

Man and Woman with Flag — A192

**1962, Aug. 31**    Photo.
580 A192   25p black, pale bl & red   .25   .25
581 A192   50p black, grn & red   .25   .25
582 A192   150p black, pink & red   .55   .40
    Nos. 580-582 (3)   1.05   .90

Issued for "Free Pashtunistan Day."

Malaria Eradication Emblem and Swamp — A193

**1962, Sept. 5**    Perf. 14x13½
583 A193   2p dk grn & ol gray   .25   .25
584 A193   2p dk green & sal   .25   .25
585 A193   5p red brn & ol   .25   .25
586 A193   10p red brn & brt grn   .25   .25
587 A193   15p red brn & gray   .25   .25
588 A193   25p brt bl & bluish grn   .25   .25
589 A193   50p brt bl & rose lil   .25   .25
590 A193   75p black & blue   .25   .25
591 A193   100p black & brt pink   .30   .25
592 A193   150p black & bis brn   .50   .40
593 A193   175p black & orange   .55   .50
    Nos. 583-593 (11)   3.35   3.15

WHO drive to eradicate malaria.
Perf. and imperf. souvenir sheets exist. Set of 4 sheets, value $14.
Exist imperf. Value, set $10.
For surcharges see Nos. B61-B71.

National Assembly Building — A194

**Perf. 10½, 11 (100p)**
**1962, Sept. 10**   Unwmk.   Litho.
594 A194   25p lt green   .25   .25
595 A194   50p blue   .45   .45
596 A194   75p rose   .60   .60
597 A194   100p violet   .75   .75
598 A194   125p ultra   1.00   1.00
    Nos. 594-598 (5)   3.05   3.05

Establishment of the National Assembly.

Horse Racing — A195

Designs: 2p, Horse racing. 3p, Wrestling. 4p, Weight lifting. 5p, Soccer.

**1962, Sept. 22**    Photo.    Perf. 12
**Black Inscriptions**
599 A195   1p lt ol & red brn   .25   .25
600 A195   2p lt grn & red brn   .25   .25
601 A195   3p yellow & dk pur   .25   .25
602 A195   4p pale bl & grn   .25   .25
603 A195   5p bluish grn & dk brn   .25   .25
    Nos. 599-603,C17-C22 (11)   4.85   4.85

4th Asian Games, Djakarta, Indonesia.
Exist imperf. Value, set of 11, unused or used, $17.50.
Two souvenir sheets exist. A perforated one contains a 125p blue, dark blue and brown stamp in horse racing design. An imperf. one contains a 2af buff, purple and black stamp in soccer design. Value, $3.50 each.

Runners — A196

1p, 2p, Diver, vert. 4p, Peaches. 5p, Iris, vert.

**Perf. 11½x12, 12x11½**
**1962, Oct. 2**   Unwmk.
604 A196   1p rose lil & brn   .25   .25
605 A196   2p blue & brn   .25   .25
606 A196   3p brt blue & lil   .25   .25
607 A196   4p ol gray & multi   .25   .25
608 A196   5p gray & multi   .25   .25
    Nos. 604-608,C23-C25 (8)   4.45   4.45

Issued for Children's Day.
Exist imperf. Value, set of 8, unused or used, $27.50.

## Zahir Shah Type of 1961, Dated "1962"

**1962, Oct. 15**    Perf. 13½
**Various Frames**
609 A183   25p lilac rose & brn   .25   .25
610 A183   50p orange brn & grn   .30   .25
611 A183   75p blue & lake   .50   .25
612 A183   100p green & red brn   .55   .25
    Nos. 609-612 (4)   1.60   1.00

Issued to honor King Mohammed Zahir Shah on his 48th birthday.

Grapes — A197

**1962, Oct. 16**    Perf. 12
613 A197   1p shown   .25   .25
614 A197   2p Grapes   .25   .25
615 A197   3p Pears   .25   .25
616 A197   4p Wistaria   .25   .25
617 A197   5p Blossoms   .25   .25
    Nos. 613-617,C26-C28 (8)   2.45   2.45

For the Afghan Red Crescent Society.
Exist imperf. Value, set of 8, unused or used, $20.

UN Headquarters, NY and Flags of UN and Afghanistan A198

**1962, Oct. 24**    Unwmk.
618 A198   1p multicolored   .25   .25
619 A198   2p multicolored   .25   .25
620 A198   3p multicolored   .25   .25
621 A198   4p multicolored   .25   .25
622 A198   5p multicolored   .25   .25
    Nos. 618-622,C29-C31 (8)   2.60   2.60

UN Day.
Exist imperf. Value, set of 8, unused or used, $9.50.
Souvenir sheets exist. One contains a single 4af ultramarine stamp, perforated; the other, a 4af ocher stamp, imperf. Value, 2 sheets, $9.25.

Boy Scout — A199

**1962, Oct. 18**    Photo.    Perf. 12
623 A199   1p yel, dk grn & sal   .25   .25
624 A199   2p yel, slate & sal   .25   .25
625 A199   3p rose, blk & sal   .25   .25
626 A199   4p multicolored   .25   .25
    Nos. 623-626,C32-C35 (8)   3.05   3.05

Issued to honor the Boy Scouts.
Exist imperf. Value, set of 8, unused or used, $27.50.

Pole Vault — A200

2p, Pole Vault. 3p, High jump. 4p, 5p, Different blossoms.

**1962, Oct. 25**   Unwmk.   Perf. 12
627 A200   1p lilac & dk grn   .25   .25
628 A200   2p yellow grn & brn   .25   .25
629 A200   3p bister & vio   .25   .25
630 A200   4p sal pink, grn & ultra   .25   .25
631 A200   5p yellow, grn & bl   .25   .25
    Nos. 627-631,C36-C37 (7)   2.75   2.75

Issued for Teacher's Day.
Exist imperf. Value, set of 7, unused or used, $12.

Rockets — A201

**1962, Nov. 29**
632 A201   50p pale lil & dk bl   .50   .50
633 A201   100p lt blue & red brn   1.25   1.25

UN World Meteorological Day.
Exist imperf. Value, set, unused or used, $25.
A souvenir sheet contains one 5af pink and green stamp. Value $6.

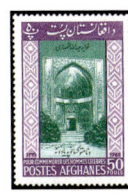
Ansari Mausoleum, Herat — A202

**Perf. 13½**
**1963, Jan. 3**   Unwmk.   Photo.
634 A202   50p purple & green   .25   .25
635 A202   75p gray & magenta   .25   .25
636 A202   100p orange brn & brn   .35   .35
    Nos. 634-636 (3)   .85   .85

Khwaja Abdullah Ansari, Sufi, religious leader and poet, on the 900th anniv. of his death.

Sheep — A203

Silkworm, Cocoons, Moth and Mulberry Branch — A204

**1963, Mar. 1**    Perf. 12
637 A203   1p grnsh blue & blk   .25   .25
638 A203   2p dl yel grn & blk   .25   .25
639 A203   3p lilac rose & blk   .25   .25
640 A204   4p gray, grn & brn   .25   .25
641 A204   5p red lil, grn & brn   .25   .25
    Nos. 637-641,C42-C44 (8)   3.10   3.10

Issued for the Day of Agriculture.
Exist imperf. Value, set of 8, unused or used, $12.

Rice — A205

Designs: 3p, Corn. 300p, Wheat emblem.

**1963, Mar. 27**   Unwmk.   Perf. 14
642 A205   2p gray, claret & grn   .25   .25
643 A205   3p ol green, yel & ocher   .25   .25
644 A205   300p dk blue & yel   .60   .60
    Nos. 642-644,C45 (4)   2.20   2.20

FAO "Freedom from Hunger" campaign.

Meteorological Measuring Instrument A206

Designs: 3p, 10p, Weather station. 4p, 5p, Rockets in space.

**1963, May 23**   Photo.   Perf. 13½x14
645 A206   1p dp magenta & brn   .25   .25
646 A206   2p brt blue & brn   .25   .25
647 A206   3p red & brown   .25   .25
648 A206   4p orange & lilac   .25   .25

326 AFGHANISTAN

**649** A206 5p green & dl vio .25 *.25*

**Imperf**

**650** A206 10p red brn & grn .45 .40
*Nos. 645-650,C46-C50 (11)* 11.15 10.50

3rd UN World Meteorological Day, Mar. 23.

Independence Monument — A207

**1963, Aug. 23 Litho. *Perf. 10½***

**651** A207 25p lt green .25 .25
**652** A207 50p orange .35 .25
**653** A207 150p rose carmine .50 .30
*Nos. 651-653 (3)* 1.10 .80

45th Independence Day.

Pathans in Forest — A208

**1963, Aug. 31 Unwmk. *Perf. 10½***

**654** A208 25p pale violet .25 .25
**655** A208 50p sky blue .25 .25
**655A** A208 150p dull red brn .60 .40
*Nos. 654-655A (3)* 1.10 .90

Issued for "Free Pashtunistan Day."

4th Asian Games, Djakarta — A208a

2p, 250p, 300p, Wrestling. 3p, 10p, Tennis. 4p, 500p, Javelin. 5p, 9af, Shot put.

**1963, Sept. 3 Litho. *Perf. 12***

**656** A208a 2p rose vio & brn .25 .25
**656A** A208a 3p olive grn & brn .25 .25
**656B** A208a 4p blue & brn .25 .25
**656C** A208a 5p yel grn & brn .25 .25
**656D** A208a 10p lt bl grn & brn .25 .25
**656E** A208a 300p yellow & vio .45 .45
**656F** A208a 500p lt yel bis & brn .85 .85
**656G** A208a 9af pale grn & vio 1.40 1.40
*Nos. 656-656G (8)* 3.95 3.95

**Souvenir Sheets**

**656H** A208a 250p lilac & vio 2.00 2.00
**656I** A208a 300p blue & blk 2.00 2.00

Nos. 656E-656F are airmail. Nos. 656-656I exist imperf. Values, unused or used: set, $12; souvenir sheets, each $11.

National Assembly Building A209

**1963, Sept. 10 *Perf. 11***

**657** A209 25p gray .25 .25
**658** A209 50p dull red .25 .25
**659** A209 75p brown .25 .25
**660** A209 100p olive .25 .25
**661** A209 125p lilac .40 .25
*Nos. 657-661 (5)* 1.40 1.25

Issued to honor the National Assembly.

Balkh Gate — A210

**1963, Oct. 8**

**662** A210 3af choc (screened margins) 1.00 .30
*a.* White margins 2.50 .55

In the original printing a halftone screen extended across the plate, covering the space between the stamps. A retouch removed the screen between the stamps (No. 662a).

Intl. Red Cross, Cent. — A210a

4p, 5p, 200p, 3af, Nurse holding patient, vert. 10p, 4af, 6af, Crown Prince Ahmed Shah.

**1963, Oct. 9 *Perf. 13½***

**662B** A210a 2p olive, blk & red .25 .25
**662C** A210a 3p blue, blk & red .25 .25
**662D** A210a 4p lt grn, blk & red .25 .25
**662E** A210a 5p lt vio, blk & red .25 .25
**662F** A210a 10p gray grn, red & blk .25 .25
**662G** A210a 100p dull bl grn, red & blk .25 .25
**662H** A210a 200p lt brn, blk & red .25 .25
**662I** A210a 4af brt bl grn, red & blk .25 .25
*m.* Souvenir sheet of 1 1.75 1.60
**662J** A210a 6af lt brn, red & blk .25 .25
*Nos. 662B-662J (9)* 2.25 2.25

**Souvenir Sheet**

**662K** A210a 3af dl blue, blk & red 1.75

Nos. 662G-662K are airmail.
Nos. 662B-662K exist imperf. Values, unused or used: set, $12; souvenir sheets, each $11.

Zahir Shah — A211

**1963, Oct. 15 *Perf. 10½***

**663** A211 25p green .25 .25
**663A** A211 50p gray .25 .25
**663B** A211 75p carmine rose .30 .25
**663C** A211 100p dull redsh brn .50 .25
*Nos. 663-663C (4)* 1.30 1.00

King Mohammed Zahir Shah, 49th birthday.

Kemal Ataturk — A212

**1963, Oct. 10 *Perf. 10½***

**664** A212 1af blue .25 .25
**665** A212 3af rose lilac .65 .50

25th anniv. of the death of Kemal Ataturk, president of Turkey.

Protection of Nubian Monuments A213

Designs: 5af, 7.50af, 10af, Ruins, vert.

***Perf. 12, Imperf. (150p, 250p, 10af)***

**1963, Nov. 16 Photo.**

**666** A213 100p lil rose & blk .25 .25
**666A** A213 150p rose lil & blk .25 *.30*
**666B** A213 200p brown & blk .40 .40
**666C** A213 250p ultra & blk .50 .50
**666D** A213 500p green & blk 1.00 1.00
**666E** A213 5af greenish blue & gray bl 1.00 1.00
**666F** A213 7.50af red brn & gray bl 1.75 1.75
**666G** A213 10af ver & gray bl 1.90 1.90
*Nos. 666-666G (8)* 7.05 7.10

Nos. 666E-666G are airmail. No. 666D exists imperf. Value, unused or used, 95¢.

Women's Day — A213a

**1964, Jan. 5 *Perf. 14x13½***

**667** A213a 2p multicolored .25 .25
**667A** A213a 3p multicolored .25 .25
**667B** A213a 4p multicolored .25 .25
**667C** A213a 5p multicolored .25 .25
**667D** A213a 10p multicolored .25 .25
*Nos. 667-667D (5)* 1.25 1.25

Exist imperf. Value set, unused or used, $2.40.

A213b

Boy and Girl Scouts — A213c

Nos. 668F-668G, 668K-668M, Girl with flag.

**1964, Jan. 5 *Perf. 13½x14, 14x13½***

**668** A213b 2p multi .25 .25
**668A** A213b 3p multi .25 .25
**668B** A213b 4p multi .25 .25
**668C** A213b 5p multi .25 .25
**668D** A213b 10p multi .25 .25
**668E** A213c 2af multi .25 .25
**668F** A213c 2af multi .25 .25
**668G** A213c 2.50af multi .25 .25
**668H** A213c 3af multi .30 .30
**668I** A213c 4af multi .40 .40
**668J** A213c 5af multi .50 .50
**668K** A213c 12af multi 1.25 1.25
*Nos. 668-668K (12)* 4.45 4.45

**Souvenir Sheets**

**668L** A213c 5af multi 1.25 1.25
**668M** A213c 6af multi 1.25 2.00
**668N** A213c 6af multi 2.50 2.50
**668O** A213c 10af multi 2.50 2.50

Nos. 668E-668O are airmail.
Nos 668-668K, 668N-668O exist imperf. Values, unused or used: set, $15; souvenir sheets, each $7.

Children — A213d

2p, Playing ball. 4p, Swinging, jumping rope, vert. 5p, Skiing, vert.

**1964, Jan. 22 *Perf. 12***

**669** A213d 2p multi .25 .25
**669A** A213d 3p like #669 .25 .25
**669B** A213d 4p multi .25 .25
**669C** A213d 5p multi .25 .25
**669D** A213d 10p like #669 .25 .25
**669E** A213d 200p like #669C .75 .75
**669F** A213d 300p like #669B 1.10 1.10
*Nos. 669-669F (7)* 3.10 3.10

Nos. 669E-669F are airmail.
Nos. 669-669F exist imperf. Value set, unused or used, $27.50.

Red Crescent Society — A213e

Designs: 100p, 200p, Pierre and Marie Curie, physicists. 2.50af, 7.50af Nurse examining child. 3.50af, 5af, Nurse and patients.

***Perf. 14, Imperf. (#670A, 670C-670D)***

**1964, Feb. 8**

**670** A213e 100p multi .50 .50
**670A** A213e 100p multi .50 .50
**670B** A213e 200p multi .80 .80
**670C** A213e 2.50af multi 1.25 1.25
**670D** A213e 3.50af multi 1.90 1.90
**670E** A213e 5af multi 2.10 2.10
**670F** A213e 7.50af multi 3.00 3.00
*Nos. 670-670F (7)* 10.05 10.05

Nos. 670A and 670E-F are airmail.

Teachers' Day — A213f

Flowers: 2p, 3p, 3af, 4af, Tulips. 4p, 5p, 3.50af, 6af, Flax. 10p, 1.50af, 2af, Iris.

***Perf. 12, Imperf. (1.50af, 2af)***

**1964, Mar. 3**

**671** A213f 2p multicolored .25 .25
**671A** A213f 3p multicolored .25 .25
**671B** A213f 4p multicolored .25 .25
**671C** A213f 5p multicolored .25 .25
**671D** A213f 10p multicolored .25 .25
**671E** A213f 1.50af multicolored 2.25 2.25
**671F** A213f 2af multicolored 3.00 3.00
**671G** A213f 3af multicolored .90 .90
**671H** A213f 3.50af multicolored 1.10 1.10
*Nos. 671-671H (9)* 8.50 8.50

**Souvenir Sheets**

**671I** A213f 4af multi 2.40 2.40
**671J** A213f 6af multi, imperf 5.00 5.00

Nos. 671E-671J are airmail. Nos. 671-671D exist imperf. Value, each 20¢.

A213g

UN Day: 5p, 10p, 2af, 3af, 4af, Doctor and nurse, vert.

**1964, Mar. 9 *Perf. 14***

**672** A213g 2p multicolored .25 .25
**672A** A213g 3p multicolored .25 .25
**672B** A213g 4p multicolored .25 .25
**672C** A213g 5p multicolored .25 .25
**672D** A213g 10p multicolored .25 .25
**672E** A213g 100p multicolored .65 .65
**672F** A213g 2af multicolored 1.20 1.20
**672G** A213g 3af multicolored 1.75 1.75
*Nos. 672-672G (8)* 4.85 4.85

**Souvenir Sheets**

**672H** A213g 4af multi, imperf. 14.50 14.50
**672I** A213g 5af multi 3.25 3.25

Nos. 672E-672G are airmail.
Nos. 672-672G exist imperf. Value set, unused or used, $20.
For surcharges see Nos. B71A-B71J.

UNICEF — A213h

Design: 5af, 7.50af, 10af, Children eating.

***Perf. 14x13½, Imperf. (150p, 250p, 10af)***

**1964, Mar. 15**

**673** A213h 100p multi .30 .30
**673A** A213h 150p multi 1.75 1.75
**673B** A213h 200p multi .65 .65
**673C** A213h 250p multi 3.00 3.00
**673D** A213h 5af multi 1.50 1.50
**673E** A213h 7.50af multi 2.40 2.40
**673F** A213h 10af multi 12.50 12.50
*Nos. 673-673F (7)* 22.10 22.10

Nos. 673D-673F are airmail.

Eradication of Malaria — A213i

# AFGHANISTAN

4p, 5p, 5af, 10af Spraying mosquitoes.

| 1964, Mar. 15 | | | Perf. 13½ | |
|---|---|---|---|---|
| 674 | A213i | 2p lt red brn & yel grn | .25 | .25 |
| 674A | A213i | 3p olive grn & buff | .25 | .25 |
| 674B | A213i | 4p dk vio & bl grn | .25 | .25 |
| 674C | A213i | 5p brn & grn | .25 | .25 |
| 674D | A213i | 2af Prus bl & ver | .65 | .30 |
| | h. | Souvenir sheet of 1 | 4.75 | 4.75 |
| 674E | A213i | 5af dk grn & lt red brn, imperf. | 5.25 | 5.25 |
| | i. | Souv. sheet of 1, imperf. | 14.50 | 14.50 |
| 674F | A213i | 10af red brn & grnsh bl | 2.75 | 1.75 |
| | | Nos. 674-674F (7) | 9.65 | 8.30 |

**Stamp Like No. 674B Surcharged in Black**

| 674G | A213i | 10p on 4p Prus bl & rose | .90 | .25 |

No. 674G not issued without surcharge.
Nos. 674D-674F are airmail.
Nos. 674-674C, 674G exist imperf. Values, each $2.75.

"Tiger's Head" of 1878 — A214

| 1964, Mar. 22 | | Photo. | Perf. 12 | |
|---|---|---|---|---|
| 675 | A214 | 1.25af gold, grn & blk | .25 | .25 |
| 676 | A214 | 5af gold, rose car & blk | .55 | .35 |

Issued to honor philately.

Unisphere and Flags — A215

| 1964, May 3 | | | Perf. 13½x14 | |
|---|---|---|---|---|
| 677 | A215 | 6af crimson, gray & grn | .25 | .25 |

New York World's Fair, 1964-65.

Hand Holding Torch — A216

| 1964, May 12 | | Photo. | Perf. 14x13½ | |
|---|---|---|---|---|
| 678 | A216 | 3.75af multicolored | .25 | .25 |

1st UN Seminar on Human Rights in Kabul, May 1964. The denomination in Persian at right erroneously reads "3.25" but the stamp was sold and used as 3.75af.

Kandahar Airport — A217

| 1964, Apr. | | Litho. | Perf. 10½, 11 | |
|---|---|---|---|---|
| 679 | A217 | 7.75af dk red brown | .65 | .40 |
| 680 | A217 | 9.25af lt blue | .90 | .80 |
| 681 | A217 | 10.50af lt green | 1.10 | .95 |
| 682 | A217 | 13.75af carmine rose | 1.40 | 1.00 |
| | | Nos. 679-682 (4) | 4.05 | 3.15 |

Inauguration of Kandahar Airport.

Snow Leopard — A218

50p, Ibex, vert. 75p, Head of argali. 5af, Yak.

| 1964, June 25 | | Photo. | Perf. 12 | |
|---|---|---|---|---|
| 683 | A218 | 25p yellow & blue | 1.75 | .25 |
| 684 | A218 | 50p dl red & grn | 2.00 | .25 |
| 685 | A218 | 75p Prus bl & lil | 2.40 | .25 |
| 686 | A218 | 5af brt grn & dk brn | 2.50 | .90 |
| | | Nos. 683-686 (4) | 8.65 | 1.65 |

View of Herat A219

Flag and Map of Afghanistan A220

Tourist publicity: 75p, Tomb of Queen Gowhar Shad, vert.

| 1964, July 12 | | Perf. 13½x14, 14x13½ | | |
|---|---|---|---|---|
| 687 | A219 | 25p sepia & bl | .25 | .25 |
| 688 | A219 | 75p dp blue & buff | .30 | .25 |
| 689 | A220 | 3af red, blk & grn | .55 | .25 |
| | | Nos. 687-689 (3) | 1.10 | .75 |

Wrestling — A221

25p, Hurdling, vert. 1af, Diving, vert. 5af, Soccer.

| 1964, July 26 | | | Perf. 12 | |
|---|---|---|---|---|
| 690 | A221 | 25p ol bis, blk & car | .25 | .25 |
| 691 | A221 | 1af bl grn, blk & car | .25 | .25 |
| 692 | A221 | 3.75af yel grn, blk & car | .40 | .25 |
| 693 | A221 | 5af brn, blk & car | .50 | .30 |
| | a. | Souv. sheet, #690-693, imperf. | 1.25 | 1.25 |
| | | Nos. 690-693 (4) | 1.40 | 1.05 |

18th Olympic Games, Tokyo, Oct. 10-25, 1964. No. 693a sold for 15af. The additional 5af went to the Afghanistan Olympic Committee.

Flag and Outline of Nadir Shah's Tomb — A222

| 1964, Aug. 24 | | | Photo. | |
|---|---|---|---|---|
| 695 | A222 | 25p multicolored | .25 | .25 |
| 696 | A222 | 75p multicolored | .30 | .25 |

Independence Day. The stamps were printed with an erroneous inscription in upper left corner: "33rd year of independence." This was locally obliterated on all stamps with a typographed gold bar. Value for set with gold bar omitted, $10.

Pashtunistan Flag — A223

| 1964, Sept. 1 | | | Unwmk. | |
|---|---|---|---|---|
| 697 | A223 | 100p gold, blk, red, bl & grn | .55 | .25 |

Issued for "Free Pashtunistan Day."

Zahir Shah — A225

| 1964, Oct. 17 | | | Perf. 14x13½ | |
|---|---|---|---|---|
| 699 | A225 | 1.25af gold & yel grn | .25 | .25 |
| 700 | A225 | 3.75af gold & rose | .40 | .40 |
| 701 | A225 | 50af gold & gray | 3.50 | 2.25 |
| | | Nos. 699-701 (3) | 4.15 | 2.90 |

King Mohammed Zahir Shah, 50th birthday.

Coat of Arms of Afghanistan and UN Emblem — A226

| 1964, Oct. 24 | | | Perf. 13½x14 | |
|---|---|---|---|---|
| 702 | A226 | 5af gold, blk & dl bl | .25 | .25 |

Issued for United Nations Day.

Emblem of Afghanistan Women's Association A227

| 1964, Nov. 9 | | Photo. | Unwmk. | |
|---|---|---|---|---|
| 703 | A227 | 25p pink, dk bl & emer | .55 | .30 |
| 704 | A227 | 75p aqua, dk bl & emer | .85 | .40 |
| 705 | A227 | 1af sil, dk bl & emer | 1.10 | .50 |
| | | Nos. 703-705 (3) | 2.50 | 1.20 |

Issued for Women's Day.

Poet Mowlana Nooruddin Abdul Rahman Jami (1414-1492) — A228

| | | Perf. 11 Rough | | Litho. |
|---|---|---|---|---|
| 1964, Nov. 23 | | | | |
| 706 | A228 | 1.50af blk, emer & yel | .95 | .95 |

No. 706 also exists clean-cut perf 10½.

Woodpecker A229

Birds: 3.75af, Black-throated jay, vert. 5af, Impeyan pheasant, vert.

| 1965, Apr. 20 | | Photo. | Perf. 13½x14, 14x13½ | Unwmk. |
|---|---|---|---|---|
| 707 | A229 | 1.25af multi | 2.25 | .40 |
| 708 | A229 | 3.75af multi | 4.00 | .85 |
| 709 | A229 | 5af multi | 5.50 | 1.75 |
| | | Nos. 707-709 (3) | 12.65 | 3.00 |

ITU Emblem, Old and New Communication Equipment — A230

| 1965, May 17 | | | Perf. 13½x14 | |
|---|---|---|---|---|
| 710 | A230 | 5af lt bl, blk & red | .50 | .35 |

Cent. of the ITU.

"Red City," Bamian — A231

Designs: 3.75af, Ruins of ancient Bamian city. 5af, Bande Amir, mountain lakes.

| 1965, May 30 | | | Perf. 13x13½ | |
|---|---|---|---|---|
| 711 | A231 | 1.25af pink & multi | .40 | .25 |
| 712 | A231 | 3.75af lt blue & multi | .65 | .25 |
| 713 | A231 | 5af yellow & multi | .95 | .25 |
| | | Nos. 711-713 (3) | 2.00 | .75 |

Issued for tourist publicity.

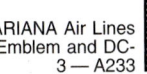

ICY Emblem — A232

| 1965, June 25 | | | Perf. 13½x13 | |
|---|---|---|---|---|
| 714 | A232 | 5af multicolored | .50 | .30 |

International Cooperation Year, 1965.

ARIANA Air Lines Emblem and DC-3 — A233

5af, Airplane at right. 10af, Airplane on top.

| 1965, July 15 | | Photo. | Perf. 13½x14 | Unwmk. |
|---|---|---|---|---|
| 715 | A233 | 1.25af brt bl, gray & blk | .30 | .25 |
| 716 | A233 | 5af red lil, blk & bl | .90 | .55 |
| 717 | A233 | 10af bis, blk, bl gray & grn | 1.50 | .55 |
| | a. | Souv. sheet, #715-717, imperf | 3.00 | 3.00 |
| | | Nos. 715-717 (3) | 2.70 | 1.05 |

10th anniv. of Afghan Air Lines, ARIANA.

Nadir Shah — A234

| 1965, Aug. 23 | | | Perf. 14x13½ | |
|---|---|---|---|---|
| 718 | A234 | 1af dl grn, blk & red brn | .40 | .25 |

For the 47th Independence Day.

Flag of Pashtunistan A235

| 1965, Aug. 31 | | Photo. | Perf. 13½x14 | Unwmk. |
|---|---|---|---|---|
| 719 | A235 | 1af multicolored | .40 | .25 |

Issued for "Free Pashtunistan Day."

Zahir Shah Signing Constitution A236

| 1965, Sept. 11 | | | Perf. 13x13½ | |
|---|---|---|---|---|
| 720 | A236 | 1.50af brt grn & blk | .40 | .25 |

Promulgation of the new Constitution.

Zahir Shah and Oak Leaves — A237

| 1965, Oct. 14 | | | Perf. 14x13½ | |
|---|---|---|---|---|
| 721 | A237 | 1.25af blk, ultra & salmon | .25 | .25 |
| 722 | A237 | 6af blu, lt bl & rose lil | .40 | .35 |

King Mohammed Zahir Shah, 51st birthday.

# AFGHANISTAN

Flags of UN and
Afghanistan
A238

**1965, Oct. 24**    **Perf. 13½x14**
723 A238 5af multicolored    .25   .25
Issued for United Nations Day.

Dappled Ground
Gecko — A239

Designs: 4af, Caucasian agamid (lizard).
8af, Horsfield's tortoise.

**Perf. 13½x14**
**1966, May 10**    **Photo.**    **Unwmk.**
724 A239 3af tan & multi    .90   .25
725 A239 4af brt grn & multi    1.10   .30
726 A239 8af violet & multi    1.75   .65
Nos. 724-726 (3)    3.75   1.20

Soccer Player and
Globe — A240

**1966, July 31**    **Litho.**    **Perf. 14x13½**
727 A240 2af rose red & blk    .60   .25
728 A240 6af violet bl & blk    1.00   .30
729 A240 12af bister brn & blk    1.60   .60
Nos. 727-729 (3)    3.20   1.15

World Cup Soccer Championship, Wembley, England, July 11-30.

Cotton Flower and
Boll — A241

5af, Silkworm. 7af, Farmer plowing with oxen.

**1966, July 31**    **Perf. 13½x14**
730 A241 1af multicolored    .85   .25
731 A241 5af multicolored    1.60   .30
732 A241 7af multicolored    2.50   .50
Nos. 730-732 (3)    4.95   1.05
Issued for the Day of Agriculture.

Independence
Monument — A242

**1966, Aug. 23**    **Photo.**    **Perf. 13½x14**
733 A242 1af multicolored    .30   .25
734 A242 3af multicolored    .85   .30
Issued to commemorate Independence Day.

Flag of
Pashtunistan
A243

**Perf. 11 Rough**
**1966, Aug. 31**    **Litho.**
735 A243 1af bright blue    .50   .25
"Free Pashtunistan Day."

Bagh-i-Bala Park
Casino — A244

Tourist publicity: 2af, Map of Afghanistan. 8af, Tomb of Abd-er-Rahman. The casino on 4af is the former summer palace of Abd-er-Rahman near Kabul.

**1966, Oct. 3**    **Photo.**    **Perf. 13½x14**
736 A244 2af red & multi    .40   .25
737 A244 4af multicolored    .80   .35
738 A244 8af multicolored    1.20   .80
  a. Souvenir sheet of 3, #736-738, imperf.    3.50   3.50
Nos. 736-738 (3)    2.40   1.40

Zahir Shah — A245

**1966, Oct. 14**    **Perf. 14x13½**
739 A245 1af dk slate grn    .25   .25
740 A245 5af red brown    .55   .30
King Mohammed Zahir Shah, 52nd birthday. See Nos. 760-761.

UNESCO
Emblem — A246

**1967, Mar. 6**    **Litho.**    **Perf. 12**
741 A246 2af multicolored    .30   .25
742 A246 6af multicolored    .40   .25
743 A246 12af multicolored    .90   .25
Nos. 741-743 (3)    1.60   .75
20th anniv. of UNESCO.

Zahir Shah and
UN Emblem — A247

**1967**    **Photo.**
744 A247 5af multicolored    .40   .25
745 A247 10af multicolored    .80   .30
UN Intl. Org. for Refugees, 20th anniv.

New Power
Station — A248

5af, Carpet, vert. 8af, Cement factory.

**1967, Jan. 7**    **Photo.**    **Perf. 13½x14**
746 A248 2af red lil & ol grn    .30   .25
747 A248 5af multicolored    .30   .25
748 A248 8af blk, dk bl & tan    .60   .30
Nos. 746-748 (3)    1.20   .80
Issued to publicize industrial development.

International Tourist
Year Emblem — A249

Designs: 6af, International Tourist Year emblem and map of Afghanistan.

**1967, May 11**    **Photo.**    **Perf. 12**
749 A249 2af yel, blk & lt bl    .40   .25
750 A249 6af bis brn, blk & lt bl    .65   .25
  a. Souv. sheet of #749-750, imperf    2.00   1.25
Intl. Tourist Year, 1967. No. 750a sold for 10af.

Power Dam,
Dorunta — A250

6af, Sirobi Dam, vert. 8af, Reservoir at Jalalabad.

**1967, July 2**    **Photo.**    **Perf. 12**
751 A250 1af dk green & lil    .40   .25
752 A250 6af red brn & grnsh bl    .80   .25
753 A250 8af plum & dk bl    1.20   .40
Nos. 751-753 (3)    2.40   .90
Progress in agriculture through electricity.

Macaque — A251

Designs: 6af, Striped hyena, horiz. 12af, Persian gazelles, horiz.

**1967, July 28**    **Photo.**    **Perf. 12**
754 A251 2af dull yel & indigo    .75   .25
755 A251 6af lt green & sepia    1.50   .30
756 A251 12af lt bl & red brn    2.25   .80
Nos. 754-756 (3)    4.50   1.35

Pashtun
Dancers — A252

**1967, Sept. 1**    **Photo.**    **Perf. 12**
757 A252 2af magenta & violet    .70   .25
Issued for "Free Pashtunistan Day."

Retreat of British at
Maiwand — A253

**1967, Aug. 24**
758 A253 1af dk brn & org ver    .40   .25
759 A253 2af dk brn & brt pink    .80   .25
Issued to commemorate Independence Day.

**King Type of 1966**
**1967, Oct. 15**    **Photo.**    **Perf. 14x13½**
760 A245 2af brown red    .25   .25
761 A245 8af dark blue    .65   .30
Issued to honor King Mohammed Zahir Shah on his 53rd birthday.

Fireworks and UN
Emblem — A254

**1967, Oct. 24**    **Litho.**    **Perf. 12**
762 A254 10af violet bl & multi    .70   .40
Issued for United Nations Day.

Greco-Roman
Wrestlers — A255

Design: 6af, Free style wrestlers.

**1967, Nov. 20**    **Photo.**
763 A255 4af ol grn & rose lil    .40   .25
764 A255 6af dp carmine & brn    .85   .25
  a. Souv. sheet of #763-764, imperf    1.75   1.75
1968 Olympic Games.

Said Jamalluddin
Afghan — A256

**1967, Nov. 27**
765 A256 1af magenta    .25   .25
766 A256 5af brown    .40   .25
Said Jamalluddin Afghan, politician (1839-97).

Bronze Vase, 11th-12th
Centuries — A257

Design: 7af, Bronze vase, Ghasnavide era, 11th-12th centuries.

**1967, Dec. 23**    **Photo.**    **Perf. 12**
767 A257 3af lt green & brn    .55   .25
768 A257 7af yel & slate grn    1.00   .25
  a. Souv. sheet, #767-768, imperf    2.75   2.75

WHO
Emblem — A258

**1968, Apr. 7**    **Photo.**    **Perf. 12**
769 A258 2af citron & brt bl    .25   .25
770 A258 7af rose & brt bl    .40   .30
20th anniv. of the WHO.

Karakul — A259

**1968, May 20**    **Photo.**    **Perf. 12**
771 A259 1af yellow & blk    .25   .25
772 A259 6af lt blue & blk    .85   .30
773 A259 12af ultra & dk brn    1.25   .50
Nos. 771-773 (3)    2.35   1.05
Issued for the Day of Agriculture.

Map of      Victory
Afghanistan     Tower,
A260         Ghazni
                A261

Design: 16af, Mausoleum, Ghazni.

**1968, June 3**    **Perf. 13½x14, 12**
774 A260 2af red, blk, lt bl & grn    .35   .25
775 A261 3af yel, dk brn & lt bl    .45   .25
776 A261 16af pink & multi    1.50   .50
Nos. 774-776 (3)    2.30   1.00
Issued for tourist publicity.

Cinereous
Vulture — A262

6af, Eagle owl. 7af, Greater flamingoes.

**1968, July 3**    **Perf. 12**
777 A262 1af sky blue & multi    1.75   .65
778 A262 6af yellow & multi    4.00   2.00
779 A262 7af multicolored    6.00   2.25
Nos. 777-779 (3)    11.75   4.90

Game of
"Pegsticking"
A263

2af, Olympic flame & rings, vert. 12af, Buzkashi.

**1968, July 20**    **Photo.**    **Perf. 12**
780 A263 2af multicolored    .35   .25
781 A263 8af orange & multi    .50   .35
782 A263 12af multicolored    1.00   .60
Nos. 780-782 (3)    1.85   1.20
19th Olympic Games, Mexico City, 10/12-27.

# AFGHANISTAN

Flower-decked Armored Car — A264

**1968, Aug. 23**
783 A264 6af multicolored .60 .25
Issued to commemorate Independence Day.

Flag of Pashtunistan A265

**1968 Aug. 31** Photo. Perf. 12
784 A265 3af multicolored .35 .25
Issued for "Free Pashtunistan Day."

Zahir Shah — A266

**1968, Oct. 14** Photo. Perf. 12
785 A266 2af ultra .25 .25
786 A266 8af brown .55 .30
King Mohammed Zahir Shah, 54th birthday.

Human Rights Flame — A267

**1968, Oct. 24**
787 A267 1af multicolored .25 .25
788 A267 2af violet, bis & blk .25 .25
789 A267 6af vio blk, bis & vio .60 .25
Nos. 787-789 (3) 1.10 .75

**Souvenir Sheet**
*Imperf*
790 A267 10af plum, bis & red org 1.75 1.75
International Human Rights Year.

Maolana Djalalodine Balkhi — A268

**1968, Nov. 26** Photo. Perf. 12
791 A268 4af dk green & mag .35 .25
Balkhi (1207-73), historian.

Kushan Mural — A269

Design: 3af, Jug shaped like female torso.

**1969, Jan. 2** Perf. 12
792 A269 1af dk grn, mar & yel .55 .25
793 A269 3af violet, gray & mar 1.20 .25
 a. Souv. sheet, #792-793, imperf 2.40 1.75
Archaeological finds at Bagram, 1st cent. B.C. to 2nd cent. A.D.

ILO Emblem — A270

**1969, Mar. 23** Photo. Perf. 12
794 A270 5af lt yel, lemon & blk .30 .25
795 A270 8af lt bl, grnsh bl & blk .55 .30
50th anniv. of the ILO.

National Arms — A270a

***Rough Perf. 11***
**1969, May (?)** Typo.
795A A270a 100p dark green .40 .25
795B A270a 150p deep brown .55 .25
Nos. 795A-795B were normally used as newspaper stamps. See Nos. 318-318A, 907A.

Badakhshan Scene — A271

Tourist Publicity: 2af, Map of Afghanistan. 7af, Three men on mules ascending the Pamir Mountains.

**1969, July 6** Photo. Perf. 13½x14
796 A271 2af ocher & multi .70 .25
797 A271 4af multicolored .90 .30
798 A271 7af multicolored 1.40 .65
 a. Souv. sheet, #796-798, imperf 3.00 2.40
Nos. 796-798 (3) 3.00 1.20
No. 798a sold for 15af.

Bust, from Hadda Treasure, 3rd-5th Centuries — A272

Designs: 5af, Vase and jug. 10af, Statue of crowned woman. 5af and 10af from Bagram treasure, 1st-2nd centuries.

**1969, Aug. 3** Photo. Perf. 14x13½
799 A272 1af olive grn & gold .40 .25
800 A272 5af purple & gold .70 .25
801 A272 10af dp blue & gold 1.10 .30
Nos. 799-801 (3) 2.20 .80

Zahir Shah and Queen Humeira — A273

**1969, Aug. 23** Perf. 12
802 A273 5af gold, dk bl & red brn .45 .25
803 A273 10af gold, dp lil & bl grn .80 .40
Issued to commemorate Independence Day

Map of Pashtunistan and Rising Sun — A274

**1969, Aug. 31** Typo. Perf. 10½
804 A274 2af lt blue & red .40 .25
Issued for "Free Pashtunistan Day."

Zahir Shah — A275

**1969, Oct. 14** Photo. Perf. 12
Portrait in Natural Colors
805 A275 2af dk brown & gold .25 .25
806 A275 6af brown & gold .55 .25
King Mohammed Zahir Shah, 55th birthday.

UN Emblem and Flag of Afghanistan A276

**1969, Oct. 24** Litho. Perf. 13½
807 A276 5af blue & multi .30 .25
Issued for United Nations Day.

ITU Emblem — A277

**1969, Nov. 12**
808 A277 6af ultra & multi .30 .25
809 A277 12af rose & multi .70 .40
Issued for World Telecommunications Day.

Crested Porcupine — A278

1af, Long-tailed porcupine. 8af, Red deer.

**1969, Dec. 7** Photo. Perf. 12
810 A278 1af yellow & multi .50 .30
811 A278 3af blue & multi 1.10 .50
812 A278 8af pink & multi 2.00 1.00
Nos. 810-812 (3) 3.60 1.80

Man's First Footprints on Moon, and Earth — A279

**1969, Dec. 28** Perf. 13½x14
813 A279 1af yel grn & multi .25 .25
814 A279 3af yellow & multi .30 .25
815 A279 6af blue & multi .45 .25
816 A279 10af rose & multi .60 .40
Nos. 813-816 (4) 1.60 1.15
Moon landing. See note after Algeria No. 427.

Anti-cancer Symbol — A280

**1970, Apr. 7** Photo. Perf. 14
817 A280 2af dk grn & rose car .25 .25
818 A280 6af dk bl & rose claret .50 .25
Issued to publicize the fight against cancer.

Mirza Abdul Quader Bedel — A281

**1970, May 6** Perf. 14x13½
819 A281 5af multicolored .40 .25
Mirza Abdul Quader Bedel (1643-1720), poet.

Education Year Emblem — A282

**1970, June 7** Photo. Perf. 12
820 A282 1af black .25 .25
821 A282 6af deep rose .30 .25
822 A282 12af green .75 .40
Nos. 820-822 (3) 1.30 .90
International Education Year 1970.

Mother and Child — A283

**1970, June 15** Perf. 13½
823 A283 6af yellow & multi .30 .25
Issued for Mother's Day.

UN Emblem, Scales of Justice, Spacecraft — A284

**1970, June 26**
824 A284 4af yel, dk bl & dp bl .25 .25
825 A284 6af pink, dk bl & brt bl .35 .25
25th anniversary of United Nations.

Mosque of the Amir of the two Swords, Kabul — A285

2af, Map of Afghanistan. 7af, Arch of Paghman.

**1970, July 6** Perf. 12
**Size: 30½x30½mm**
826 A285 2af lt bl, blk & citron .30 .25
**Size: 36x26mm**
827 A285 3af pink & multi .50 .25
828 A285 7af yellow & multi .95 .25
Nos. 826-828 (3) 1.75 .75
Issued for tourist publicity.

Zahir Shah Reviewing Troops — A286

**1970, Aug. 23** Photo. Perf. 13½
829 A286 8af multicolored .40 .25
Issued to commemorate Independence Day.

# AFGHANISTAN

Pathans — A287

**1970, Aug. 31    Typo.    Perf. 10½**
830  A287  2af ultra & red    .40  .25
Issued for "Free Pashtunistan Day."

Quail — A288

4af, Golden eagle. 6af, Ringnecked pheasant.

**1970, Sept.    Photo.    Perf. 12**
831  A288  2af multicolored    2.10  .65
832  A288  4af multicolored    4.00  .95
833  A288  6af multicolored    5.25  1.60
  Nos. 831-833 (3)    11.35  3.20

Zahir Shah — A289

**1970, Oct. 14    Photo.    Perf. 14x13½**
834  A289  3af green & vio    .25  .25
835  A289  7af dk bl & vio brn    .70  .30
King Mohammed Zahir Shah, 56th birthday.

Red Crescents — A290

**1970, Oct. 16    Typo.    Perf. 10½**
836  A290  2af black, gold & red    .30  .25
Issued for the Red Crescent Society.

UN Emblem and Charter — A291

**1970, Oct. 24    Photo.    Perf. 14**
837  A291  1af gold & multi    .25  .25
838  A291  5af gold & multi    .30  .25
United Nations Day.

Tiger Heads of 1871 — A292

**1970, Nov. 10    Perf. 12**
839  A292  1af sal, lt grnsh bl & blk    .30  .25
840  A292  4af lt ultra, yel & blk    .55  .25
841  A292  12af lilac, lt bl & blk    .95  .40
  Nos. 839-841 (3)    1.80  .90
Cent. of the 1st Afghan postage stamps. The postal service was established in 1870, but the 1st stamps were issued in May, 1871.

Globe and Waves — A293

**1971, May 17    Photo.    Perf. 13½**
842  A293  12af green, blk & bl    .70  .40
3rd World Telecommunications Day.

Callimorpha Principalis — A294

Designs: 3af, Epizygaenella species. 5af, Parnassius autocrator.

**1971, May 30    Perf. 13½x14**
843  A294  1af vermilion & multi    1.25  .55
844  A294  3af yellow & multi    2.50  1.10
845  A294  5af ultra & multi    3.50  1.75
  Nos. 843-845 (3)    7.25  3.40

"UNESCO" and Half of Ancient Kushan Statue — A295

**1971, June 26    Photo.    Perf. 13½**
846  A295  6af ocher & vio    .50  .25
847  A295  10af lt blue & mar    .80  .35
UNESCO-sponsored Intl. Kushani Seminar.

Tughra and Independence Monument A296

**1971, Aug. 23**
848  A296  7af rose red & multi    .55  .25
849  A296  9af red orange & multi    .90  .35
Independence Day.

Pashtunistan Square, Kabul — A297

**1971, Aug. 31    Typo.    Perf. 10½**
850  A297  5af deep rose lilac    .50  .25
"Free Pashtunistan Day."

Zahir Shah — A298

**1971, Oct. 14    Photo.    Perf. 12½x12**
851  A298  9af lt green & multi    .55  .30
852  A298  17af yellow & multi    1.10  .65
King Mohammed Zahir Shah, 57th birthday.

A299

Design: Map of Afghanistan, red crescent, various activities.

**1971, Oct. 16    Perf. 14x13½**
853  A299  8af lt bl, red, grn & blk    .50  .30
For Afghan Red Crescent Society.

Equality Year Emblem — A300

**1971, Oct. 24    Perf. 12**
854  A300  24af brt blue    1.50  .80
International Year Against Racial Discrimination and United Nations Day.

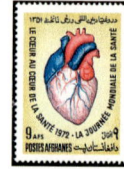
"Your Heart is your Health" — A301

**1972, Apr. 7    Photo.    Perf. 14**
855  A301  9af pale yel & multi    .90  .30
856  A301  12af gray & multi    1.75  .40
World Health Day.

Tulip — A302

Designs: 10af, Rock partridge, horiz. 12af, Lynx, horiz. 18af, Allium stipitatum (flower).

**1972, June 5    Photo.    Perf. 14**
857  A302  7af green & multi    1.25  .70
858  A302  10af blue & multi    7.50  1.60
859  A302  12af lt green & multi    2.40  1.25
860  A302  18af blue grn & multi    2.40  1.40
  Nos. 857-860 (4)    13.55  4.95

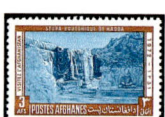
Buddhist Shrine, Hadda — A302a

Designs: 7af, Greco-Bactrian animal seal, 250 B.C. 9af, Greco-Oriental temple, Ai-Khanoum, 3rd-2nd centuries B.C.

**1972, July 16    Photo.    Perf. 12**
861  A302a  3af brown & dl bl    .65  .25
862  A302a  7af rose claret & dl grn    .95  .30
863  A302a  9af green & lilac    1.40  .40
  Nos. 861-863 (3)    3.00  .95
Tourist publicity.

King and Queen Reviewing Parade A303

**1972, Aug. 23    Photo.    Perf. 13½**
864  A303  25af gold & multi    4.50  1.25
Independence Day.
Used as a provisional in 1978 with king and queen portion removed.

Wrestling A304

10af, 19af, 21af, Wrestling, different hold.

**1972, Aug. 26**
865  A304  4af ol bis & multi    .25  .25
866  A304  8af lt blue & multi    .45  .25
867  A304  10af yel grn & multi    .60  .30
868  A304  19af multicolored    1.20  .45
869  A304  21af lilac & multi    1.25  .50
  a.  Souv. sheet, #865-869, imperf    3.25  3.25
  Nos. 865-869 (5)    3.75  1.75
20th Olympic Games, Munich, Aug. 26-Sept. 11. No. 869a sold for 60af.

Pathan and View of Tribal Territory — A305

**1972, Aug. 31    Perf. 12½x12**
870  A305  5af ultra & multi    .50  .25
Pashtunistan day.

Zahir Shah — A306

**1972, Oct. 14    Photo.    Perf. 14x13½**
871  A306  7af gold, blk & Prus bl    .65  .25
872  A306  14af gold, blk & lt brn    1.00  .40
58th birthday of King Mohammed Zahir Shah.

City Destroyed by Earthquake, Refugees A307

**1972, Oct. 16    Perf. 13½**
873  A307  7af lt bl, red & blk    .60  .25
For Afghan Red Crescent Society.

UN Emblem — A308

**1972, Oct. 24**
874  A308  12af lt ultra & blk    .60  .30
UN Economic Commission for Asia and the Far East (ECAFE), 25th anniv.

Ceramics — A309

Designs: 9af, Leather coat, vert. 12af, Metal ware, vert. 16af, Inlaid artifacts.

**1972, Dec. 10    Photo.    Perf. 12**
875  A309  7af gold & multi    .40  .25
876  A309  9af gold & multi    .65  .30
877  A309  12af gold & multi    .70  .35
878  A309  16af gold & multi    1.00  .45
  a.  Souv. sheet, #875-878, imperf    3.50  3.50
  Nos. 875-878 (4)    2.75  1.35
Handicraft industries. No. 878a sold for 45af.

WMO and National Emblems A310

**1973, Apr. 3    Photo.    Perf. 14**
879  A310  7af lt lil & dk grn    .55  .25
880  A310  14af lt bl & dp claret    1.40  .40
Cent. of intl. meteorological cooperation.

# AFGHANISTAN

Abu Rayhan al-Biruni — A311

**1973, June 16**    Photo.    Perf. 13½
881 A311 10af multicolored    .50   .40
Millennium of birth (973-1048), philosopher and mathematician.

Family — A312

**1973, June 30**    Photo.    Perf. 13½
882 A312 9af orange & red lil    .65   .25
Intl. Family Planning Fed., 21st anniv.

## Republic

Impeyan Pheasant — A313

Birds: 9af, Great crested grebe. 12af, Himalayan snow cock.

**1973, July 29**    Photo.    Perf. 12x12½
883 A313 8af yellow & multi    2.75   1.75
884 A313 9af blue & multi    3.25   2.25
885 A313 12af multicolored    4.00   3.00
Nos. 883-885 (3)    10.00   7.00

Stylized Buzkashi Horseman A314

**1973, Aug.**    Perf. 13½
886 A314 8af black    .55   .30
Tourist publicity.

Fireworks A315

**1973, Aug. 23**    Photo.    Perf. 12
887 A315 12af multicolored    .60   .30
55th Independence Day.

Lake Abassine, Pashtunistan Flag — A316

**1973, Aug. 31**    Perf. 14x13½
888 A316 9af multicolored    .55   .25
Pashtunistan Day.

Red Crescent — A317

**1973, Oct. 16**    Perf. 13½
889 A317 10af red, blk & gold    .90   .25
Red Crescent Society.

Kemal Ataturk — A318

**1973, Oct. 28**    Litho.    Perf. 10½
890 A318 1af blue    .25   .25
891 A318 7af reddish brown    1.10   .25
50th anniversary of the Turkish Republic.

Human Rights Flame, Arms of Afghanistan A319

**1973, Dec. 10**    Photo.    Perf. 12
892 A319 12af sil, blk & lt bl    .45   .35
25th anniversary of the Universal Declaration of Human Rights.

Asiatic Black Bears — A320

**1974, Mar. 26**    Litho.    Perf. 12
893 A320 5af shown    .65   .25
894 A320 7af Afghan hound    1.00   .40
895 A320 10af Persian goat    1.40   .50
896 A320 12af Leopard    1.75   .55
a. Souv. sheet, #893-896, imperf    10.00   10.00
Nos. 893-896 (4)    4.80   1.70

Worker and Farmer — A321

**1974, May 1**    Photo.    Perf. 13½x12½
897 A321 9af rose red & multi    .60   .30
International Labor Day, May 1.

Independence Monument and Arch — A322

**1974, May 27**    Photo.    Perf. 12
898 A322 4af blue & multi    .40   .25
899 A322 11af gold & multi    .55   .25
56th Independence Day.

Arms of Afghanistan and Symbol of Cooperation A323

Pres. Mohammad Daoud Khan A324

5af, Flag of Republic of Afghanistan. 15af, Soldiers, coat of arms of the Republic.

**Sizes: 4af, 15af, 36x22mm; 5af, 7af, 36x26, 26x36mm**

**1974, July 25**    Perf. 13½x12½, 14
900 A323 4af multicolored    .40   .25
901 A323 5af multicolored    .55   .25
902 A323 7af green, brn & blk    .65   .25
a. Souv. sheet, #901-902, imperf    1.75   1.75
903 A323 15af multicolored    1.25   .30
a. Souv. sheet, #900, 903, imperf    2.00   2.00
Nos. 900-903 (4)    2.85   1.05
1st anniv. of the Republic of Afghanistan.

Lesser Spotted Eagle — A325

Birds: 6af, White-fronted goose, ruddy shelduck and gray-lag goose. 11af, European coots and European crane.

**1974, Aug. 6**    Photo.    Perf. 13½x13
904 A325 1af car rose & multi    2.00   .50
905 A325 6af blue & multi    4.50   .80
906 A325 11af yellow & multi    7.00   1.40
a. Strip of 3, #904-906    14.00   14.00

Flags of Pashtunistan and Afghanistan A326

**1974, Aug. 31**    Photo.    Perf. 14
907 A326 5af multicolored    .30   .25
Pashtunistan Day.

Coat of Arms — A326a

**1974, Aug.**    Typo.    Rough Perf. 11
907A A326a 100p green    4.00   .80
See Nos. 318-318A, 795A-795B.

Coat of Arms — A327

**1974, Oct. 9**
908 A327 7af gold, grn & blk    .30   .25
Centenary of Universal Postal Union.

"un" and UN Emblem A328

**1974, Oct. 24**    Photo.    Perf. 14
909 A328 5af lt ultra & dk bl    .40   .25
United Nations Day.

Minaret of Jam — A329    Buddha, Hadda — A330

14af, Lady riding griffin, 2nd century, Bagram.

**1975, May 5**    Photo.    Perf. 13½
910 A329 7af multicolored    .40   .25
911 A330 14af multicolored    .75   .40
912 A330 15af multicolored    .95   .40
a. Souv. sheet, #910-912, imperf.    3.50   3.50
Nos. 910-912 (3)    2.10   1.05
South Asia Tourism Year 1975.

New Flag of Afghanistan A331

**1975, May 27**    Photo.    Perf. 12
913 A331 16af multicolored    .80   .25
57th Independence Day.

Celebrating Crowd — A332

**1975, July 17**    Photo.    Perf. 13¼
914 A332 9af blue & multi    .50   .25
915 A332 12af carmine & multi    .65   .30
Second anniversary of the Republic.

Women's Year Emblems — A333

**1975, Aug. 24**    Photo.    Perf. 12
916 A333 9af car, lt bl & blk    .50   .25
International Women's Year 1975.

Pashtunistan Flag, Sun Rising Over Mountains — A334

**1975, Aug. 31**    Perf. 13½
917 A334 10af multicolored    .40   .25
Pashtunistan Day.

Mohammed Akbar Khan — A335

**1976, Feb. 4**    Photo.    Perf. 14
918 A335 15af lt brown & multi    .55   .40
Mohammed Akbar Khan (1816-1846), warrior son of Amir Dost Mohammed Khan.

A336

Pres. Mohammad Daoud Khan — A337

**1974-78**    Photo.    Perf. 14
919 A336 10af multi    .65   .25
920 A336 16af multi ('78)    2.40   .90
921 A336 19af multi    .90   .50
922 A336 21af multi    1.40   .55
923 A336 22af multi ('78)    3.50   1.90
924 A336 30af multi ('78)    4.75   2.75
925 A337 50af multi ('75)    2.75   1.40
926 A337 100af multi ('75)    5.50   2.40
Nos. 919-926 (8)    21.85   10.65

# AFGHANISTAN

Arms of Republic, Independence Monument — A338

**1976, June 1**    Photo.    Perf. 14
927 A338 22af blue & multi    .70   .50
58th Independence Day.

Flag Raising — A339

**1976, July 17**    Photo.    Perf. 14
928 A339 30af multicolored    .80   .55
Republic Day.

Mountain Peaks and Flag of Pashtunistan — A340

**1976, Aug. 31**    Photo.    Perf. 14
929 A340 16af multicolored    .65   .50
Pashtunistan Day.

Coat of Arms — A340a

**1976, Sept.**    Litho.    Perf. 11 Rough
930 A340a 25p salmon    25.00   —
931 A340a 50p lt green    .55   .25
932 A340a 1af ultra    .55   .25
    Nos. 930-932 (3)    26.10   .50

Flag and Views on Open Book — A341

**1977, May 27**    Photo.    Perf. 14
937 A341 20af green & multi    .70   .60
59th Independence Day.

Pres. Daoud and National Assembly A342

President Taking Oath of Office — A343

Designs: 10af, Inaugural address. 18af, Promulgation of Constitution.

**1977, June 22**
938 A342 7af multicolored    .80   .55
939 A343 8af multicolored    .90   .70
940 A343 10af multicolored    1.10   .90
941 A342 18af multicolored    1.90   1.50
   a.   Souvenir sheet of 4    3.50   3.50
    Nos. 938-941 (4)    4.70   3.65
Election of 1st Pres. and promulgation of Constitution. No. 941a contains 4 imperf. stamps similar to Nos. 938-941.

Jamalluddin Medal — A344

**1977, July 6**    Photo.    Perf. 14
942 A344 12af blue, blk & gold    .40   .30
Sajo Jamalluddin Afghani, reformer, 80th death anniversary.

Afghanistan Flag over Crowd — A345

**1977, July 17**
943 A345 22af multicolored    .70   .55

Dancers, Fountain, Pashtunistan Flag — A346

**1977, Aug. 31**
944 A346 30af multicolored    1.10   .90
Pashtunistan Day.

Arms and Carrier Pigeon — A346a

**1977, Oct. 30**    Litho.    Perf. 11
944A A346a 1af black & blue    5.00   2.50

Members of Parliament Congratulating Pres. Daoud — A347

**1978, Feb. 5**    Litho.    Perf. 14
945 A347 20af multicolored    2.00   1.10
Election of first president, first anniversary.

Map of Afghanistan, UPU Emblem — A348

**1978, Apr. 1**    Photo.    Perf. 14
946 A348 10af green, blk & gold    .40   .25
Afghanistan's UPU membership, 50th anniv.

Wall Telephone and Satellite Station — A349

**1978, Apr. 12**
947 A349 8af multicolored    .40   .25
Afghanistan's ITU membership, 50th anniv.

## Democratic Republic

Arrows Pointing to Crescent, Cross and Lion — A350

**1978, July 6**    Litho.    Perf. 11 Rough
948 A350 3af black    1.25   .65
50th anniv. of Afghani Red Crescent Soc.

Khalq Party Emblem — A350a

**1978, Aug.**    Litho.    Perf. 11
948A A350a 1af rose red & gold    1.50   .65
948B A350a 4af rose red & gold    2.10   .90

Qalai Bist Arch — A351

Hazara Women — A351a

16af, Bamian Buddha.

**1978, Aug. 19**    Perf. 14
949 A351 16af multicolored    1.25   .50
949A A351 22af shown    1.50   .65
949B A351a 30af shown    2.10   1.10
    Nos. 949-949B (3)    4.85   2.25

Men with Pashtunistan Flag — A352

**1978, Aug. 31**    Perf. 11 Rough
950 A352 7af ultra & red    .50   .25
Pashtunistan Day.

Coat of Arms and Emblems — A353

**1978, Sept. 8**    Perf. 11
951 A353 20af rose red    .90   .40
World Literacy Day.

A354

**Perf. 11½ Rough**
**1978, Oct. 25**    Litho.
952 A354 18af light green    .95   .40
Hero of Afghanistan.

Khalq Party Flag — A355

**1978, Oct. 19**    Photo.    Perf. 11½
953 A355 8af black, red & gold    .65   .25
954 A355 9af black, red & gold    .95   .25
"The mail serving the people."

Nour Mohammad Taraki — A356

**1979, Jan. 1**    Litho.    Perf. 12
955 A356 12af multicolored    .70   .25
Nour Mohammad Taraki, founder of People's Democratic Party of Afghanistan, installation as president.

Woman Breaking Chain — A357

**1979, Mar. 8**    Litho.    Perf. 11
956 A357 14af red & ultra    1.25   .50
Women's Day. Inscribed "POSSTES."

Map of Afghanistan, Census Emblem — A358

**1979, Mar. 25**    Litho.    Perf. 12
957 A358 3af multicolored    .90   .70
First comprehensive population census.

Farmers — A359

**1979, Mar. 21**
958 A359 1af multicolored    .65   .30
Agricultural advances.

Pres. Taraki Reading First Issue of Khalq A360

**1979, Apr. 11**    Perf. 12½x12
959 A360 2af multicolored    .65   .25
Khalq, newspaper of People's Democratic Republic of Afghanistan.

Pres. Noor Mohammad Taraki — A361

Plaza with Tank Monument and Fountain A362

# AFGHANISTAN 333

House where Revolution Started — A363

Designs: 50p, Taraki, tank. 12af, House where 1st Khalq Party Congress was held.

**Perf. 12, 12½x12 (A362)**
**1979, Apr. 27**    Litho.
| | | | | |
|---|---|---|---|---|
| 959A | A363 | 50p multicolored | .65 | .25 |
| 960 | A361 | 4af multicolored | .40 | .25 |
| 961 | A362 | 5af multicolored | .55 | .25 |
| 962 | A363 | 6af multicolored | .70 | .25 |
| 963 | A363 | 12af multicolored | .80 | .25 |

Nos. 959A-963 (5)    3.10 1.25
1st anniversary of revolution.

Carpenter and Blacksmith A364

**1979, May 1**    Perf. 12
964 A364 10af multicolored    1.10 .25
Int'l Labor Day.

Children, Flag and Map of Afghanistan A366

**1979, June 1**    Litho.    Perf. 12½x12
966 A366 16af multicolored    2.00 .90
International Year of the Child.

Doves Circling Asia in Globe A366a

**1979**    Litho.    Perf. 11x10½
966A A366a 2af red & blue    1.25 .25

Armed Afghans, Kabul Memorial and Arch — A367

**1979, Aug. 19**    Litho.    Perf. 12
967 A367 30af multicolored    1.50 .90
60th independence day.

Pashtunistan Citizens, Flag — A368

**1979, Aug. 31**
968 A368 9af multicolored    .70 .25
Pashtunistan Day.

UPU Day — A369

**1979, Oct. 9**    Litho.    Perf. 12
969 A369 15af multicolored    .65 .25

Tombstone — A369a

**1979, Oct. 25**    Litho.    Perf. 12½x12
969A A369a 22af multicolored    2.40 1.25

International Women's Day — A370

**1980, Mar. 8**    Litho.    Perf. 12
970 A370 8af multicolored    1.50 .50

Farmers' Day A371

**1980, Mar. 21**    Litho.    Perf. 11½x12
971 A371 2af multicolored    2.25 .70

Non-smoker and Smoker — A372

**1980, Apr. 7**    Perf. 11½
972 A372 5af multicolored    1.75 .70
Anti-smoking campaign; World Health Day.

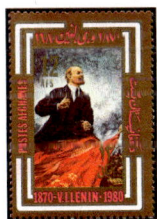

Lenin, 110th Birth Anniversary A373

**1980, Apr. 22**    Perf. 12x12½
973 A373 12af multicolored    2.50 .85

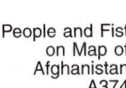

People and Fist on Map of Afghanistan A374

**1980, Apr. 27**    Litho.    Perf. 12½x12
974 A374 1af multicolored    .70 .25
Saur Revolution, 2nd anniversary.

International Workers' Solidarity Day — A375

**1980, May 1**
975 A375 9af multicolored    .50 .25

Wrestling, Moscow '80 Emblem — A376

**1980, July 19**    Perf. 12x12½, 12½x12
| | | | | |
|---|---|---|---|---|
| 976 | A376 | 3af Soccer, vert. | .60 | .25 |
| 977 | A376 | 6af shown | .70 | .25 |
| 978 | A376 | 9af Buzkashi | .80 | .25 |
| 979 | A376 | 10af Pegsticking | .95 | .25 |

Nos. 976-979 (4)    3.05 1.00
22nd Summer Olympic Games, Moscow, July 19-Aug. 3.

61st Anniversary of Independence A377

**1980, Aug. 19**    Litho.    Perf. 12½x12
980 A377 3af multicolored    .85 .25

Pashtunistan Day — A378

**1980, Aug. 30**
981 A378 25af multicolored    1.00 .45

Intl. UPU Day — A379

**1980, Oct. 9**    Litho.    Perf. 12½x12
982 A379 20af multicolored    1.00 .45

The resistance group headed by Amin Wardak released some stamps in 1980. Some of these are inscribed "WARDAK AFGHANISTAN," others "Solidarite Internationale Avec la Resistance Afghane." The status of these labels is questionable.

International Women's Day — A381

**1981, Mar. 9**    Litho.    Perf. 12½x12
984 A381 15af multicolored    1.25 .35

Farmers' Day — A382

**1981, Mar. 20**    Litho.    Perf. 12½x12
985 A382 1af multicolored    1.00 .25

Bighorn Mountain Sheep (Protected Species) — A383

**1981, Apr. 4**    Perf. 12x12½
986 A383 12af multicolored    2.40 .70

Saur Revolution, 3rd Anniversary — A384

**1981, Apr. 27**    Perf. 11
987 A384 50p brown    .70 .25

Intl. Workers' Solidarity Day — A385

**1981, May 1**    Perf. 12½x12
988 A385 10af multicolored    .95 .35

13th World Telecommunications Day — A387

**1981, May 17**    Litho.    Perf. 12½x12
990 A387 9af multicolored    .70 .25

Intl. Children's Day — A388

**1981, June 1**    Perf. 12x12½
991 A388 15af multicolored    .95 .45

People's Independence Monument 62nd Anniv. of Independence A389

**1981, Aug. 19**
992 A389 4af multicolored    1.10 .30

Pashtunistan Day — A390

**1981, Aug. 31**    Litho.    Perf. 12
992A A390 2af multicolored    .70 .25

# AFGHANISTAN

Intl. Tourism
Day — A391

**1981, Sept. 27**     **Perf. 12½x12**
993   A391   5af multicolored    .70   .25

World Food
Day — A392

**1981, Oct. 16**
995   A392   7af multicolored    .85   .25

Asia-Africa
Solidarity
Meeting
A393

**1981, Nov. 18**    **Litho.**    **Perf. 11**
996   A393   8af blue    .80   .25

Struggle Against
Apartheid — A394

**1981, Dec. 1**     **Perf. 12½x12**
997   A394   4af multicolored    1.00   .25

1300th Anniv. of
Bulgaria — A395

**1981, Dec. 9**     **Perf. 12x12½**
998   A395   20af multicolored    1.75   .50

Buzkashi Game
— A395a

**1980**    **Photo.**    **Perf. 14**
998A   A395a   50af multicolored    2.25   1.25
998B   A395a   100af multicolored    4.50   1.75

Intl. Women's
Day — A396

**1982, Mar. 8**    **Litho.**    **Perf. 12**
999   A396   6af multicolored    .60   .25

Farmers'
Day — A397

**1982, Mar. 21**
1000   A397   4af multicolored    .70   .25

Judas Trees — A398

Designs: Various local plants.

**1982, Apr. 9**    **Litho.**    **Perf. 12**
1001   A398   3af shown    .40   .25
1002   A398   4af Rose of Sharon    .70   .25
1003   A398   16af Rhubarb plant    1.60   .35
Nos. 1001-1003 (3)    2.70   .85

Saur Revolution, 4th
Anniv. — A399

**1982, Apr. 27**
1004   A399   1af multicolored    1.50   .25

George Dimitrov (1882-
1947), First Prime
Minister of
Bulgaria — A400

**1982, Apr. 30**
1005   A400   30af multicolored    2.40   .85

Intl. Workers'
Solidarity
Day — A401

**1982, May 1**
1006   A401   10af multicolored    .85   .25

Storks — A402

Nightingales — A402a

**1982, May 31**
1007   A402   6af multicolored    1.75   .50
1008   A402a   11af multicolored    2.75   .60

Hedgehogs
A403

**1982, July 6**    **Litho.**    **Perf. 12**
1009   A403   3af shown    .75   .25
1010   A403   14af Cobra    1.75   .25
See Nos. 1020-1022.

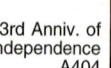

63rd Anniv. of
Independence
A404

**1982, Aug. 19**
1011   A404   20af multicolored    1.25   .50

Pashtunistan
Day — A405

**1982, Aug. 31**
1012   A405   32af multicolored    2.50   .75

World Tourism
Day — A406

**1982, Sept. 27**    **Litho.**    **Perf. 12**
1013   A406   9af multicolored    .85   .35

UPU Day — A407

**1982, Oct. 9**
1014   A407   4af multicolored    .95   .25

World Food
Day — A408

**1982, Oct. 16**
1015   A408   9af multicolored    1.50   .35

37th Anniv. of
UN — A409

**1982, Oct. 24**
1016   A409   15af multicolored    1.00   .45

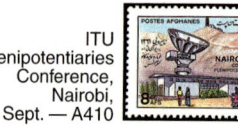

ITU
Plenipotentiaries
Conference,
Nairobi,
Sept. — A410

**1982, Oct. 26**
1017   A410   8af multicolored    .80   .25

TB Bacillus
Centenary — A411

**1982, Nov. 24**    **Litho.**    **Perf. 12**
1018   A411   7af multicolored    .50   .25

Human Rights
Declaration, 34th
Anniv. — A412

**1982, Dec. 10**
1019   A412   5af multicolored    .45   .25

**Animal Type of 1982**

**1982, Dec. 16**
1020   A403   2af Lions    .50   .25
1021   A403   7af Donkeys    1.00   .35
1022   A403   12af Marmots, vert.    2.25   .50
Nos. 1020-1022 (3)    3.75   1.10

Intl. Women's
Day — A413

**1983, Mar. 8**
1023   A413   3af multicolored    .25   .25

Mir Alicher Nawai
Research
Decade — A414

**1983, Mar. 19**
1024   A414   22af multicolored    .95   .35

Farmers'
Day — A415

**1983, Mar. 21**    **Litho.**    **Perf. 12**
1025   A415   10af multicolored    .75   .25

5th Anniv. of Saur
Revolution
A416

**1983, Apr. 27**    **Litho.**    **Perf. 12**
1026   A416   15af multicolored    .70   .35

Intl. Workers'
Solidarity
Day — A417

**1983, May 1**
1027   A417   2af multicolored    .70   .25

World
Communications
Year — A418

4af, Modes of communication. 11af, Building.

**1983, May 17**
1028   A418   4af multicolored    .45   .25
1029   A418   11af multicolored    .75   .25

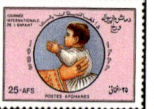

Intl. Children's
Day — A419

**1983, June 1**    **Litho.**    **Perf. 12**
1030   A419   25af multicolored    .80   .35

# AFGHANISTAN

2nd Anniv. of National Front — A420

**1983, June 15**
1031 A420 1af multicolored .35 .25

Local Butterflies A421

Various butterflies. 9af, 13af vert.

**1983, July 6**
1032 A421 9af multicolored 1.10 .80
1033 A421 13af multicolored 2.50 1.40
1034 A421 21af multicolored 3.25 1.75
 Nos. 1032-1034 (3) 6.85 3.95

Struggle Against Apartheid — A422

**1983, Aug. 1 Litho. Perf. 12**
1035 A422 10af multicolored .55 .25

64th Anniv of Independence A423

**1983, Aug. 19**
1036 A423 6af multicolored .45 .25

Parliament House — A423a

100af, Afghan Woman, Camel.

**1983, Sept. Litho. Perf. 12**
1036A A423a 50af shown 1.75 .35
1036B A423a 100af multi 4.25 .45

A424

World Tourism Day — A425

**1983, Sept. 27 Litho. Perf. 12**
1037 A424 5af shown .45 .25
1038 A425 7af shown .60 .25
1039 A424 12af Golden statues .95 .25
1040 A425 16af Stone carving 1.25 .25
 Nos. 1037-1040 (4) 3.25 1.00

World Communications Year — A426

14af, Dish antenna, dove. 15af, Building, flag.

**1983, Oct. 9 Litho. Perf. 12**
1041 A426 14af multicolored .90 .25
1042 A426 15af multicolored .90 .25

World Food Day — A427

**1983, Oct. 16 Litho. Perf. 12**
1043 A427 14af multicolored .90 .25

Sports — A428

**1983, Nov. 1 Litho. Perf. 12**
1044 A428 1af Soccer .25 .25
1045 A428 18af Boxing 1.00 .35
1046 A428 21af Wrestling 1.25 .35
 Nos. 1044-1046 (3) 2.50 .95

Pashtunistan Day — A428a

3af, Pathans Waving Flag.

**1983, Nov. Litho. Perf. 12**
1046A A428a 3af multicolored .45 .25

Handicrafts A429

2af, Jewelry. 8af, Stone ashtrays, dishes. 19af, Furniture. 30af, Leather goods.

**1983, Nov. 22**
1047 A429 2af multicolored .25 .25
1048 A429 8af multicolored .35 .25
1049 A429 19af multicolored .60 .25
1050 A429 30af multicolored 1.50 .40
 Nos. 1047-1050 (4) 2.70 1.15

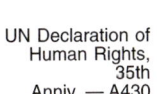

UN Declaration of Human Rights, 35th Anniv. — A430

**1983, Dec. 10 Litho. Perf. 12**
1051 A430 20af multicolored .95 .25

Kabul Polytechnical Institute, 20th Anniv. — A431

**1983, Dec. 28 Perf. 12½x12**
1052 A431 30af multicolored 1.25 .35

1984 Winter Olympics — A432

**1984, Jan. Perf. 12**
1053 A432 5af Figure skating .25 .25
1054 A432 9af Skiing .35 .25
1055 A432 11af Speed skating .50 .25
1056 A432 15af Hockey .60 .25
1057 A432 18af Biathlon .70 .25
1058 A432 20af Ski jumping .85 .25
1059 A432 22af Bobsledding 1.00 .25
 Nos. 1053-1059 (7) 4.25 1.75

Intl. Women's Day — A433

**1984, Mar. 8**
1060 A433 4af multicolored .50 .25

Farmers' Day — A434

Various agricultural scenes.

**1984, Mar. 21 Litho. Perf. 12**
1061 A434 2af multicolored .25 .25
1062 A434 4af multicolored .25 .25
1063 A434 7af multicolored .25 .25
1064 A434 9af multicolored .25 .25
1065 A434 15af multicolored .45 .25
1066 A434 18af multicolored .50 .25
1067 A434 20af multicolored .70 .25
 Nos. 1061-1067 (7) 2.65 1.75

World Aviation Day — A435

**1984, Apr. 12**
1068 A435 5af Luna 1 .35 .25
1069 A435 8af Luna 2 .45 .25
1070 A435 11af Luna 3 .55 .25
1071 A435 17af Apollo 11 .70 .25
1072 A435 22af Soyuz 6 .90 .35
1073 A435 28af Soyuz 7 .90 .35
1074 A435 34af Soyuz 6, 7, 8 1.10 .45
 Nos. 1068-1074 (7) 4.95 2.15

**Souvenir Sheet**
**Perf. 12x12½**
1075 A435 25af S. Koroliov 1.50 .90
No. 1075 contains one 30x41mm stamp.

Saur Revolution, 6th Anniv. — A436

**1984, Apr. 27 Perf. 12**
1076 A436 3af multicolored .45 .25

65th Anniv. of Independence A437

**1984, Aug. 19 Litho. Perf. 12**
1077 A437 6af multicolored .65 .25

Pashto's and Balutchi's Day — A438

3af, Symbolic sun, tribal tent.

**1984, Aug. 31**
1078 A438 3af multicolored .45 .25

Wildlife — A439

1af, Cape hunting dog, vert. 2af, Argali sheep, vert. 6af, Przewalski's horse. 8af, Wild boar, vert. 17af, Snow leopard. 19af, Tiger. 22af, Indian elephant, vert.

**Perf. 12½x12, 12x12½**
**1984, May 5 Litho.**
1079 A439 1af multicolored .25 .25
1080 A439 2af multicolored .25 .25
1081 A439 6af multicolored .60 .25
1082 A439 8af multicolored .90 .25
1083 A439 17af multicolored 1.75 .25
1084 A439 19af multicolored 3.00 .25
1085 A439 22af multicolored 3.25 .35
 Nos. 1079-1085 (7) 10.00 1.85

19th UPU Congress, Hamburg — A440

25af, German postman, 17th cent. 35af, Postrider, 16th cent. 40af, Carrier pigeon, letter.
50af, Hamburg No. 3 in black.

**1984, June 18 Perf. 12x12½**
1086 A440 25af multicolored .95 .30
1087 A440 35af multicolored 1.50 .45
1088 A440 40af multicolored 1.90 .55
 Nos. 1086-1088 (3) 4.35 1.30

**Souvenir Sheet**
1089 A440 50af multicolored 2.75 1.75
No. 1089 contains one 30x40mm stamp.

Natl. Aviation, 40th Anniv. — A441

Soviet civil aircraft.

**1984, June 29**
1090 A441 1af Antonov AN-2 .25 .25
1091 A441 4af Ilyushin IL-12 .25 .25
1092 A441 9af Tupolev TU-104 .60 .25
1093 A441 10af Ilyushin IL-18 .90 .25
1094 A441 13af Tupolev TU-134 1.10 .25
1095 A441 17af Ilyushin IL-62 1.50 .30
1096 A441 21af Ilyushin IL-28 1.75 .40
 Nos. 1090-1096 (7) 6.35 1.95

Ettore Bugatti (1881-1947), Type 43, Italy — A442

Classic automobiles and their designers: 5af, Henry Ford, 1903 Model A, US. 8af, Rene Panhard (1841-1908), 1899 Landau, France. 11af, Gottlieb Daimler (1834-1900), 1935 Daimler-Benz, Germany. 12af, Carl Benz (1844-1929), 1893 Victoris, Germany. 15af, Armand Peugeot (1849-1915), 1892 Vis-a-Vis, France. 22af, Louis Chevrolet (1879-1941), 1925 Sedan, US.

**1984, June 30**
1097 A442 2af multicolored .25 .25
1098 A442 5af multicolored .35 .25
1099 A442 8af multicolored .60 .25
1100 A442 11af multicolored .75 .25
1101 A442 12af multicolored 1.00 .25
1102 A442 15af multicolored 1.10 .25
1103 A442 22af multicolored 1.50 .25
 Nos. 1097-1103 (7) 5.55 1.85

Qalai Bist Arch — A443

World Tourism Day: 2af, Ornamental buckled harness. 5af, Victory Monument and Memorial Arch, Kabul. 9af, Standing sculpture of Afghani ruler and attendants. 15af, Buffalo riders in snow. 19af, Camel driver, tent, camel in caparison. 21af, Horsemen playing buzkashi.

**1984, Sept. 27**
1104 A443 1af multicolored .25 .25
1105 A443 2af multicolored .25 .25
1106 A443 5af multicolored .25 .25
1107 A443 9af multicolored .25 .25
1108 A443 15af multicolored .45 .25
1109 A443 19af multicolored .90 .25
1110 A443 21af multicolored 1.00 .25
 Nos. 1104-1110 (7) 3.35 1.75

# AFGHANISTAN

UN World Food Day — A444

Fruit-bearing trees.

**1984, Oct. 16**
| 1111 | A444 | 2af multicolored | .25 | .25 |
| 1112 | A444 | 4af multicolored | .25 | .25 |
| 1113 | A444 | 6af multicolored | .35 | .25 |
| 1114 | A444 | 9af multicolored | .50 | .25 |
| 1115 | A444 | 13af multicolored | .60 | .25 |
| 1116 | A444 | 15af multicolored | .75 | .25 |
| 1117 | A444 | 26af multicolored | 1.25 | .25 |
|  |  | Nos. 1111-1117 (7) | 3.95 | 1.75 |

People's Democratic Party, 20th Anniv. — A445

**1985, Jan. 1**
| 1118 | A445 | 25af multicolored | 1.25 | .45 |

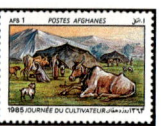

Farmer's Day — A446

1af, Oxen. 3af, Mare, foal. 7af, Brown horse. 8af, White horse, vert. 15af, Sheep, sheepskins. 16af, Shepherd, cattle, sheep. 25af, Family, camels.

**1985, Mar. 2**
| 1119 | A446 | 1af multicolored | .35 | .25 |
| 1120 | A446 | 3af multicolored | .35 | .25 |
| 1121 | A446 | 7af multicolored | .35 | .25 |
| 1122 | A446 | 8af multicolored | .60 | .25 |
| 1123 | A446 | 15af multicolored | .95 | .25 |
| 1124 | A446 | 16af multicolored | 1.10 | .35 |
| 1125 | A446 | 25af multicolored | 1.60 | .45 |
|  |  | Nos. 1119-1125 (7) | 5.30 | 2.05 |

Geologist's Day — A447

**1985, Apr. 5**
| 1126 | A447 | 4af multicolored | .35 | .25 |

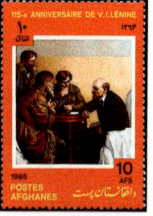

Lenin and Peasant Petitioners — A448

Lenin and: 10af, Lenin and Peasant Petitioners. 15af, Revolutionaries, 1917, Leningrad. 25af, Lenin leading Revolutionary Guards, 1917. 50af, Portrait.

**1985, Apr. 21**     *Perf. 12x12½*
| 1127 | A448 | 10af multicolored | .70 | .25 |
| 1128 | A448 | 15af multicolored | .85 | .25 |
| 1129 | A448 | 25af multicolored | 1.50 | .40 |
|  |  | Nos. 1127-1129 (3) | 3.05 | .90 |

**Souvenir Sheet**
| 1130 | A448 | 50af multicolored | 2.50 | 1.50 |

Saur Revolution, 7th Anniv. — A449

**1985, Apr. 27**
| 1131 | A449 | 21af multicolored | 1.00 | .30 |

Berlin-Treptow Soviet War Memorial, Red Army at Siege of Berlin, 1945 — A450

9af, Victorious Motherland monument, fireworks over Kremlin. 10af, Caecilienhof, site of Potsdam Treaty signing, Great Britain, USSR & US flags.

**1985, May 9**     *Perf. 12½x12*
| 1132 | A450 | 6af multicolored | .60 | .25 |
| 1133 | A450 | 9af multicolored | .85 | .25 |
| 1134 | A450 | 10af multicolored | 1.10 | .25 |
|  |  | Nos. 1132-1134 (3) | 2.55 | .75 |

End of World War II, defeat of Nazi Germany, 40th anniv.

INTELSAT, 20th Anniv. — A451

Designs: 6af, INTELSAT I satellite orbiting Earth. 9af, INTELSAT VI. 10af, Delta D rocket launch, Cape Canaveral, vert.

*Perf. 12x12½, 12½x12*     *Litho.*

**1985, Apr. 6**
| 1135 | A451 | 6af multicolored | .50 | .25 |
| 1136 | A451 | 9af multicolored | .70 | .25 |
| 1137 | A451 | 10af multicolored | .95 | .25 |
|  |  | Nos. 1135-1137 (3) | 2.15 | .75 |

12th World Youth Festival, Moscow — A452

7af, Olympic stadium, Moscow. 12af, Festival emblem. 13af, Kremlin. 18af, Folk doll, emblem.

**1985, May 5**
| 1138 | A452 | 7af multicolored | .25 | .25 |
| 1139 | A452 | 12af multicolored | .45 | .25 |
| 1140 | A452 | 13af multicolored | .55 | .35 |
| 1141 | A452 | 18af multicolored | .70 | .60 |
|  |  | Nos. 1138-1141 (4) | 1.95 | 1.45 |

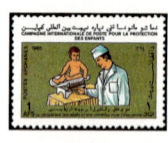

Intl. Child Survival Campaign — A453

**1985, June 1**
| 1142 | A453 | 1af Weighing child | .25 | .25 |
| 1143 | A453 | 2af Immunization | .25 | .25 |
| 1144 | A453 | 4af Breastfeeding | .35 | .25 |
| 1145 | A453 | 5af Mother, child | .40 | .25 |
|  |  | Nos. 1142-1145 (4) | 1.25 | 1.00 |

Flowers — A454

2af, Oenothera affinis. 4af, Erythrina cristagalli. 8af, Tillandsia aeranthos. 13af, Vinca major. 18af, Mirabilis jalapa. 25af, Cypella herbertii. 30af, Clytostoma callistegioides. 75af, Sesbania punicea, horiz.

**1985, July 5**
| 1146 | A454 | 2af multicolored | .25 | .25 |
| 1147 | A454 | 4af multicolored | .25 | .25 |
| 1148 | A454 | 8af multicolored | .45 | .25 |
| 1149 | A454 | 13af multicolored | .75 | .25 |
| 1150 | A454 | 18af multicolored | 1.00 | .30 |
| 1151 | A454 | 25af multicolored | 1.40 | .30 |
| 1152 | A454 | 30af multicolored | 1.75 | .30 |
|  |  | Nos. 1146-1152 (7) | 5.85 | 1.90 |

**Souvenir Sheet**
*Perf. 12½x11½*
| 1153 | A454 | 75af multicolored | 4.50 | .75 |

ARGENTINA '85.

Independence, 66th Anniv. — A455

**1985, Aug. 19**     *Perf. 12x12½*
| 1154 | A455 | 33af Mosque | 1.50 | .45 |

Pashto's and Balutchi's Day — A456

**1985, Aug. 30**
| 1155 | A456 | 25af multicolored | 1.50 | .25 |

UN Decade for Women — A457

**1985, Sept. 22**
| 1156 | A457 | 10af Emblems | 2.50 | .25 |

World Tourism Day, 10th Anniv. — A457a

1af, Guldara Stupa. 2af, Mirwais Tomb, vert. 10af, Statue of Bamyan, vert. 13af, No Gumbad Mosque, vert. 14af, Pule Kheshti Mosque. 15af, Bost Citadel. 20af, Ghazni Minaret, vert.

**1985, Sept. 27**     *Litho.*     *Perf. 12*
| 1156A | A457a | 1af multi | .25 | .25 |
| 1156B | A457a | 2af multi | .25 | .25 |
| 1156C | A457a | 10af multi | .60 | .25 |
| 1156D | A457a | 13af multi | .85 | .25 |
| 1156E | A457a | 14af multi | .95 | .25 |
| 1156F | A457a | 15af multi | 1.00 | .25 |
| 1156G | A457a | 20af multi | 1.40 | .25 |
|  |  | Nos. 1156A-1156G (7) | 5.30 | 1.75 |

Sports — A457b

*Perf. 12x12½, 12½x12*

**1985, Oct. 3**     *Litho.*
| 1156H | A457b | 1af Boxing | .25 | .25 |
| 1156I | A457b | 2af Volleyball | .25 | .25 |
| 1156J | A457b | 3af Soccer, vert. | .50 | .25 |
| 1156K | A457b | 12af Buzkashi | .75 | .25 |
| 1156L | A457b | 14af Weight lifting | .95 | .25 |
| 1156M | A457b | 18af Wrestling | 1.00 | .25 |
| 1156N | A457b | 25af Peg sticking | 1.25 | .35 |
|  |  | Nos. 1156H-1156N (7) | 4.95 | 1.85 |

World Food Day — A457c

**1985, Oct. 16**
| 1156O | A457c | 25af multicolored | .95 | .30 |

UN 40th Anniv. — A458

**1985, Oct. 24**     *Perf. 12½x12*
| 1157 | A458 | 22af multicolored | 1.10 | .30 |

A459       A459a

A459b       A459c

Birds — A459d

2af, Jay. 4af, Plover, hummingbird. 8af, Pheasant. 13af, Hoopoe. 18af, Falcon. 25af, Partridge. 30af, Pelicans, horiz. 75af, Parakeets.

**1985, Oct. 25**     *Perf. 12½x12, 12x12½*
| 1158 | A459 | 2af multicolored | .25 | .25 |
| 1159 | A459a | 4af multicolored | .85 | .45 |
| 1160 | A459b | 8af multicolored | .90 | .45 |
| 1161 | A459a | 13af multicolored | 1.40 | .75 |
| 1162 | A459 | 18af multicolored | 1.60 | .85 |
| 1163 | A459b | 25af multicolored | 2.40 | 1.25 |
| 1164 | A459c | 30af multicolored | 3.00 | 1.50 |
|  |  | Nos. 1158-1164 (7) | 10.40 | 5.50 |

**Souvenir Sheet**
*Perf. 12x12½*
| 1165 | A459d | 75af multicolored | 5.00 | .75 |

Mushrooms — A460

3af, Tricholomopsis rutilans. 4af, Boletus miniatoporus. 7af, Amanita rubescens. 11af, Boletus scaber. 12af, Coprinus atramentarius. 18af, Hypholoma. 20af, Boletus aurantiacus.

# AFGHANISTAN

**1985, June 10  Litho.  Perf. 12½x12**
| 1165A | A460 | 3af multicolored | .25 | .25 |
|---|---|---|---|---|
| 1166 | A460 | 4af multicolored | .40 | .25 |
| 1167 | A460 | 7af multicolored | .55 | .30 |
| 1168 | A460 | 11af multicolored | .80 | .50 |
| 1169 | A460 | 12af multicolored | 1.00 | .50 |
| 1170 | A460 | 18af multicolored | 1.40 | .65 |
| 1171 | A460 | 20af multicolored | 1.60 | .70 |
|  |  | Nos. 1165A-1171 (7) | 6.00 | 3.15 |

World Wildlife Fund — A461

**1985, Nov. 25**
| 1172 | A461 | 2af Leopard, cubs | .40 | .25 |
|---|---|---|---|---|
| 1173 | A461 | 9af Adult's head | 1.25 | .40 |
| 1174 | A461 | 11af Adult | 2.40 | .75 |
| 1175 | A461 | 15af Cub | 3.75 | 1.10 |
|  |  | Nos. 1172-1175 (4) | 7.80 | 2.50 |

Motorcycle, Cent. A462

Designs: Different makes and landmarks.

**1985, Dec. 16**
| 1176 | A462 | 2af multicolored | .25 | .25 |
|---|---|---|---|---|
| 1177 | A462 | 4af multicolored | .30 | .25 |
| 1178 | A462 | 8af multicolored | .50 | .25 |
| 1179 | A462 | 13af multicolored | .80 | .25 |
| 1180 | A462 | 18af multicolored | .90 | .25 |
| 1181 | A462 | 25af multicolored | 1.25 | .25 |
| 1182 | A462 | 30af multicolored | 1.25 | .25 |
|  |  | Nos. 1176-1182 (7) | 5.25 | 1.75 |

**Souvenir Sheet  Perf. 11½x12½**
| 1183 | A462 | 75af multicolored | 5.00 | .75 |

People's Democratic Party, 21st Anniv. A463

**1986, Jan. 1  Perf. 12½x12**
| 1184 | A463 | 2af multicolored | .35 | .25 |

27th Soviet Communist Party Congress A464

**1986, Mar. 31**
| 1185 | A464 | 25af Lenin | .75 | .40 |

First Man in Space, 25th Anniv. A465

Designs: 3af, Spacecraft. 7af, Soviet space achievement medal, vert. 9af, Rocket lift-off, vert. 11af, Yuri Gagarin, military decorations, vert. 13af, Gagarin, cosmonaut. 15af, Gagarin, politician. 17af, Gagarin wearing flight suit, vert.

**Perf. 12½x12, 12x12½**
**1986, Apr. 12  Litho.**
| 1186 | A465 | 3af multicolored | .25 | .25 |
|---|---|---|---|---|
| 1187 | A465 | 7af multicolored | .25 | .25 |
| 1188 | A465 | 9af multicolored | .35 | .25 |
| 1189 | A465 | 11af multicolored | .45 | .25 |
| 1190 | A465 | 13af multicolored | .50 | .25 |
| 1191 | A465 | 15af multicolored | .50 | .25 |
| 1192 | A465 | 17af multicolored | .75 | .25 |
|  |  | Nos. 1186-1192 (7) | 3.05 | 1.75 |

A465a

Loya Jirgah (Grand Assembly) of the People's Democratic Republic, 1st anniv.

**1986, Apr. 23  Litho.  Perf. 12x12½**
| 1192A | A465a | 3af multicolored | .25 | .25 |

Intl. Day of Labor Solidarity — A465b

**1986, May 1  Perf. 12½x12**
| 1192B | A465b | 5af multicolored | .35 | .25 |

Intl. Red Crescent Day — A465c

**1986, May 8  Perf. 12x12½**
| 1192C | A465c | 7af multicolored | .45 | .25 |

Intl. Children's Day — A466

1af, Mother, children, vert. 3af, Mother, child, vert. 9af, Children, map

**1986, June 1  Perf. 12**
| 1193 | A466 | 1af multicolored | .25 | .25 |
|---|---|---|---|---|
| 1194 | A466 | 3af multicolored | .25 | .25 |
| 1195 | A466 | 9af multicolored | .40 | .25 |
|  |  | Nos. 1193-1195 (3) | .90 | .75 |

World Youth Day — A466a

**1986, July 31  Perf. 12x12½**
| 1195A | A466a | 15af multicolored | .70 | .45 |

Pashtos' and Baluchis' Day — A467

**1986, Aug. 31**
| 1196 | A467 | 4af multicolored | .25 | .25 |

Intl. Peace Year — A468

**1986, Sept. 30  Photo.  Perf. 12x12½**
| 1197 | A468 | 12af black & Prus blue | .60 | .25 |

A469

1986 World Cup Soccer Championships, Mexico — A470

Various soccer plays.

**1986, Apr. 15  Litho.  Perf. 12**
| 1198 | A469 | 3af multi, vert. | .25 | .25 |
|---|---|---|---|---|
| 1199 | A469 | 4af multicolored | .35 | .25 |
| 1200 | A469 | 7af multicolored | .40 | .25 |
| 1201 | A469 | 11af multi, vert. | .70 | .25 |
| 1202 | A469 | 12af multi, vert. | .85 | .25 |
| 1203 | A469 | 18af multi, vert. | 1.25 | .25 |
| 1204 | A469 | 20af multi, vert. | 1.50 | .25 |
|  |  | Nos. 1198-1204 (7) | 5.30 | 1.75 |

**Souvenir Sheet  Perf. 12½x12**
| 1205 | A470 | 75af multicolored | 4.75 | 3.00 |

Lenin — A471

**1986, Apr. 21  Perf. 12½x12**
| 1206 | A471 | 16af multicolored | .75 | .45 |

A472

**1986, Apr. 27  Litho.  Perf. 12½x12**
| 1207 | A472 | 8af multicolored | .60 | .25 |

Saur revolution, 8th anniv.

Natl. Independence, 67th Anniv. — A473

**1986, Aug. 19  Litho.  Perf. 12½x12**
| 1208 | A473 | 10af multicolored | .50 | .25 |

Literacy Day — A474

**1986, Sept. 18  Perf. 12½x12**
| 1209 | A474 | 2af multicolored | .25 | .25 |

Dogs — A475

5af, St. Bernard. 7af, Collie. 8af, Pointer. 9af, Golden retriever. 11af, German shepherd. 15af, Bulldog. 20af, Afghan hound.

**1986, May 19  Litho.  Perf. 12x12½**
| 1210 | A475 | 5af multicolored | .25 | .25 |
|---|---|---|---|---|
| 1211 | A475 | 7af multicolored | .40 | .25 |
| 1212 | A475 | 8af multicolored | .50 | .25 |
| 1213 | A475 | 9af multicolored | .60 | .25 |
| 1214 | A475 | 11af multicolored | .70 | .25 |
| 1215 | A475 | 15af multicolored | .95 | .25 |
| 1216 | A475 | 20af multicolored | 1.25 | .30 |
|  |  | Nos. 1210-1216 (7) | 4.65 | 1.80 |

Lizards — A476

**1986, July 7  Perf. 12x12½, 12½x12**
| 1217 | A476 | 3af Cobra | .25 | .25 |
|---|---|---|---|---|
| 1218 | A476 | 4af shown | .25 | .25 |
| 1219 | A476 | 5af Praying mantis | .35 | .25 |
| 1220 | A476 | 8af Beetle | .50 | .25 |
| 1221 | A476 | 9af Tarantula | .60 | .30 |
| 1222 | A476 | 10af Python | .70 | .35 |
| 1223 | A476 | 11af Scorpions | .85 | .35 |
|  |  | Nos. 1217-1223 (7) | 3.50 | 2.00 |

Nos. 1217, 1219, 1221-1223 horiz.

STOCKHOLMIA '86 — A477

Ships.

**1986, Aug. 28  Perf. 12½x12**
| 1224 | A477 | 4af multicolored | .40 | .25 |
|---|---|---|---|---|
| 1225 | A477 | 5af multicolored | .60 | .25 |
| 1226 | A477 | 6af multicolored | .70 | .25 |
| 1227 | A477 | 7af multicolored | .85 | .25 |
| 1228 | A477 | 8af multicolored | 1.00 | .25 |
| 1229 | A477 | 9af multicolored | 1.10 | .25 |
| 1230 | A477 | 11af multicolored | 1.40 | .25 |
|  |  | Nos. 1224-1230 (7) | 6.05 | 1.75 |

**Souvenir Sheet**
| 1231 | A477 | 50af Galley | 4.25 | 2.00 |

A479

**1986, Sept. 14  Perf. 12**
| 1232 | A479 | 3af lt blue, blk & olive gray | .40 | .25 |

Reunion of Afghan tribes under the Supreme Girgah.

A480

**1986, Oct. 25  Perf. 12½x12**
| 1233 | A480 | 3af black & brt ver | .40 | .25 |

Natl. youth solidarity.

Locomotives A481

**1986, June 21  Perf. 12½x12**
| 1234 | A481 | 4af multicolored | .25 | .25 |
|---|---|---|---|---|
| 1235 | A481 | 5af multicolored | .35 | .25 |
| 1236 | A481 | 6af multicolored | .45 | .25 |
| 1237 | A481 | 7af multicolored | .50 | .25 |
| 1238 | A481 | 8af multicolored | .65 | .25 |
| 1239 | A481 | 9af multicolored | .85 | .25 |
| 1240 | A481 | 11af multicolored | 1.25 | .25 |
|  |  | Nos. 1234-1240 (7) | 4.30 | 1.75 |

# AFGHANISTAN

Fish — A482

Various fish.

**1986, May 25**

| 1241 | A482 | 5af multicolored | .25 | .25 |
|---|---|---|---|---|
| 1242 | A482 | 7af multicolored | .40 | .25 |
| 1243 | A482 | 8af multicolored | .50 | .25 |
| 1244 | A482 | 9af multicolored | .60 | .25 |
| 1245 | A482 | 11af multicolored | .85 | .25 |
| 1246 | A482 | 15af multicolored | 1.10 | .35 |
| 1247 | A482 | 20af multicolored | 1.50 | .35 |
| | | Nos. 1241-1247 (7) | 5.20 | 1.95 |

Saur Revolution, 9th Anniv. — A483

**1987, Apr. 27**     Perf. 12

| 1248 | A483 | 3af multicolored | .25 | .25 |

Natl. Reconciliation A484

**1987, May 27**     Perf. 12x12½

| 1249 | A484 | 3af multicolored | .25 | .25 |

A485      A486

UN Child Survival Campaign — A487

**1987, June 1**     Perf. 12

| 1250 | A485 | 1af multicolored | .25 | .25 |
| 1251 | A486 | 5af multicolored | .25 | .25 |
| 1252 | A487 | 9af multicolored | .35 | .25 |
| | | Nos. 1250-1252 (3) | .85 | .75 |

Conference of Clergymen and Ulema, 1st Anniv. — A488

**1987, June 30**

| 1253 | A488 | 5af multicolored | .35 | .25 |

Butterflies — A489

**1987, July 3**

| 1254 | A489 | 7af multicolored | .60 | .35 |
| 1255 | A489 | 9af multi, diff. | .75 | .35 |
| 1256 | A489 | 10af multi, diff. | 1.00 | .50 |
| 1257 | A489 | 12af multi, diff. | 1.50 | .50 |
| 1258 | A489 | 15af multi, diff. | 1.60 | .70 |
| 1259 | A489 | 22af multi, diff. | 2.25 | .95 |
| 1260 | A489 | 25af multi, diff. | 2.50 | .95 |
| | | Nos. 1254-1260 (7) | 10.20 | 4.30 |

10af, 15af and 22af horiz.

A490

**1987, Aug. 11**

| 1261 | A490 | 1af multicolored | .25 | .25 |

1st election of local representatives for State Power and Administration.

Natl. Independence, 68th Anniv. — A490a

**1987, Aug. 19**

| 1261A | A490a | 3af multicolored | .25 | .25 |

1st Artificial Satellite (Sputnik), 30th Anniv. — A491

**1987, Oct. 4**     Litho.     Perf. 12½x12

| 1262 | A491 | 10af Sputnik | .40 | .25 |
| 1263 | A491 | 15af Rocket launch | .60 | .25 |
| 1264 | A491 | 25af Soyuz | .85 | .25 |
| | | Nos. 1262-1264 (3) | 1.85 | .75 |

World Post Day — A492

**1987, Oct. 9**     Perf. 12½x12

| 1265 | A492 | 22af multicolored | 1.10 | .60 |

Intl. Communications and Transport Day — A493

**1987, Oct. 24**     Perf. 12½x12

| 1266 | A493 | 42af multicolored | 4.75 | 1.00 |

October Revolution in Russia, 70th Anniv. — A494

**1987, Nov. 7**

| 1267 | A494 | 25af Lenin | 1.25 | .70 |

Mice — A495

Various mice. Nos. 1269-1272 horiz.

**1987, Dec. 6**     Perf. 12½x12, 12x12½

| 1268 | A495 | 2af multicolored | .40 | .25 |
| 1269 | A495 | 4af multi, diff. | .50 | .25 |
| 1270 | A495 | 8af multi, diff. | .60 | .25 |
| 1271 | A495 | 16af multi, diff. | 1.00 | .25 |
| 1272 | A495 | 20af multi, diff. | 1.25 | .25 |
| | | Nos. 1268-1272 (5) | 3.75 | 1.25 |

Medicinal Plants — A496

**1987, Nov. 11**     Litho.     Perf. 12

| 1273 | A496 | 3af Castor bean | .25 | .25 |
| 1274 | A496 | 6af Licorice | .45 | .25 |
| 1275 | A496 | 9af Chamomile | .75 | .25 |
| 1276 | A496 | 14af Datura | 1.00 | .25 |
| 1277 | A496 | 18af Dandelion | 1.25 | .25 |
| | | Nos. 1273-1277 (5) | 3.70 | 1.30 |

Pashto's and Baluchis' Day — A497

**1987, Aug. 30**

| 1278 | A497 | 4af multicolored | .25 | .25 |

Dinosaurs A498

3af, Mesosaurus. 5af, Styracosaurus. 10af, Uinatherium. 15af, Protoceratops. 20af, Stegosaurus. 25af, Ceratosaurus. 30af, Dinornis maximus.

    Perf. 12½x12, 12x12½

**1988, June 6**     Litho.

| 1279 | A498 | 3af multicolored | .25 | .25 |
| 1280 | A498 | 5af multicolored | .25 | .25 |
| 1281 | A498 | 10af multicolored | .50 | .25 |
| 1282 | A498 | 15af multicolored | .75 | .25 |
| 1283 | A498 | 20af multicolored | 1.00 | .30 |
| 1284 | A498 | 25af multicolored | 1.40 | .35 |
| 1285 | A498 | 30af multicolored | 1.90 | .60 |
| | | Nos. 1279-1285 (7) | 6.05 | 2.25 |

Nos. 1280-1283 horiz.

Pashtos' and Baluchis' Day — A499

**1988, Aug. 30**     Perf. 12½x12

| 1286 | A499 | 23af multicolored | .95 | .60 |

Afghan-Soviet Joint Space Flight — A500

**1988, Aug. 30**

| 1287 | A500 | 32af multicolored | 1.25 | .50 |

Valentina Tereshkova, 1st Woman in Space, 25th Anniv. — A501

10af, Portrait, rocket, horiz. 15af, Lift-off, dove. 25af, Spacecraft, Earth, horiz.

**1988, Oct. 16**     Perf. 12x12½, 12½x12

| 1288 | A501 | 10af multicolored | .85 | .35 |
| 1289 | A501 | 15af multicolored | .85 | .30 |
| 1290 | A501 | 25af multicolored | 1.00 | .45 |
| | | Nos. 1288-1290 (3) | 2.70 | 1.10 |

Traditional Crafts — A502

    Perf. 12x12½, 12½x12

**1988, Nov. 9**     Litho.

| 1291 | A502 | 2af Pitcher, bowls | .25 | .25 |
| 1292 | A502 | 4af Vases | .25 | .25 |
| 1293 | A502 | 5af Dress | .25 | .25 |
| 1294 | A502 | 9af Mats, napkins | .35 | .25 |
| 1295 | A502 | 15af Pocketbooks | .60 | .25 |
| 1296 | A502 | 23af Jewelry | .95 | .25 |
| 1297 | A502 | 50af Furniture | 1.90 | .25 |
| | | Nos. 1291-1297 (7) | 4.55 | 1.75 |

Nos. 1291-1292, 1294-1297 horiz.

Precious and Semiprecious Gems — A503

**1988, Dec. 5**     Perf. 12½x12

| 1298 | A503 | 13af Emeralds | 1.00 | .25 |
| 1299 | A503 | 37af Lapiz lazuli | 2.25 | .60 |
| 1300 | A503 | 40af Rubies | 2.50 | .75 |
| | | Nos. 1298-1300 (3) | 5.75 | 1.60 |

1988 Winter Olympics, Calgary — A504

2af, Women's figure skating. 5af, Skiing. 9af, Bobsledding. 22af, Biathlon. 37af, Speed skating.

75af, Ice hockey.

**1988, Dec. 25**

| 1301 | A504 | 2af multicolored | .25 | .25 |
| 1301A | A504 | 5af multicolored | .25 | .25 |
| 1301B | A504 | 9af multicolored | .50 | .25 |
| 1301C | A504 | 22af multicolored | 1.00 | .35 |
| 1301D | A504 | 37af multicolored | 2.25 | .65 |

**Size: 80x60mm**

| 1302 | A504 | 75af multicolored | 4.50 | 3.50 |
| | | Nos. 1301-1302 (6) | 8.75 | 5.25 |

A510

A511

A512      A513

# AFGHANISTAN

A513a

Flowers
A514

Various flowering plants.

**Perf. 12x12½, 12½x12**

**1988, Jan. 27**      Litho.
| | | | | |
|---|---|---|---|---|
| 1303 | A510 | 3af multicolored | .25 | .25 |
| 1304 | A511 | 5af multicolored | .35 | .25 |
| 1305 | A511 | 7af multi, vert. | .50 | .25 |
| 1306 | A512 | 9af multicolored | .70 | .25 |
| 1307 | A513 | 12af multicolored | 1.25 | .35 |
| 1308 | A513a | 15af multicolored | 1.60 | .35 |
| 1309 | A514 | 24af multicolored | 2.25 | .35 |
| | Nos. 1303-1309 (7) | | 6.90 | 2.05 |

Traditional Musical Instruments
A515

String and percussion instruments.

**1988, Jan. 15**    **Litho.**    **Perf. 12**
| | | | | |
|---|---|---|---|---|
| 1310 | A515 | 1af shown | .25 | .25 |
| 1311 | A515 | 3af drums | .25 | .25 |
| 1312 | A515 | 5af multi, diff. | .30 | .25 |
| 1313 | A515 | 15af multi, diff. | .70 | .25 |
| 1314 | A515 | 18af multi, diff. | 1.00 | .30 |
| 1315 | A515 | 25af multi, diff. | 1.40 | .30 |
| 1316 | A515 | 33af multi, diff. | 1.90 | .30 |
| | Nos. 1310-1316 (7) | | 5.80 | 1.90 |

Admission of Afghanistan to the ITU and UPU, 60th Anniv. — A516

**1988, Apr. 13**    **Litho.**    **Perf. 12**
| | | | | |
|---|---|---|---|---|
| 1317 | A516 | 20af multicolored | .85 | .50 |

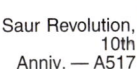

Saur Revolution, 10th Anniv. — A517

**1988, Apr. 23**
| | | | | |
|---|---|---|---|---|
| 1318 | A517 | 10af multicolored | .50 | .35 |

Fruit — A518

2af, Baskets, compote. 4af, Four baskets. 7af, Basket. 8af, Grapes, vert. 16af, Market. 22af, Market, diff. 25af, Vendor, vert.

**1988, July 18**    **Litho.**    **Perf. 12**
| | | | | |
|---|---|---|---|---|
| 1319 | A518 | 2af multicolored | .25 | .25 |
| 1320 | A518 | 4af multicolored | .35 | .25 |
| 1321 | A518 | 7af multicolored | .45 | .25 |
| 1322 | A518 | 8af multicolored | .50 | .25 |
| 1323 | A518 | 16af multicolored | .85 | .35 |
| 1324 | A518 | 22af multicolored | 1.25 | .35 |
| 1325 | A518 | 25af multicolored | 1.90 | .35 |
| | Nos. 1319-1325 (7) | | 5.55 | 2.05 |

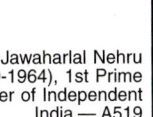

Jawaharlal Nehru (1889-1964), 1st Prime Minister of Independent India — A519

**1988, Nov. 14**
| | | | | |
|---|---|---|---|---|
| 1326 | A519 | 40af multicolored | 2.25 | .85 |

Natl. Independence, 69th Anniv. — A520

**1988, Aug. 1**
| | | | | |
|---|---|---|---|---|
| 1327 | A520 | 24af multicolored | 1.25 | .70 |

Intl. Red Cross and Red Crescent Organizations, 125th Anniv. — A521

**1988, Sept. 26**
| | | | | |
|---|---|---|---|---|
| 1328 | A521 | 10af multicolored | .85 | .50 |

Natl. Reconciliation Institute, 2nd Anniv. — A522

**1989, Jan. 4**
| | | | | |
|---|---|---|---|---|
| 1329 | A522 | 4af multicolored | .25 | .25 |

Chess — A523

Boards, early matches and hand-made chessmen.

**1989, Feb. 2**    **Litho.**    **Perf. 12x12½**
| | | | | |
|---|---|---|---|---|
| 1330 | A523 | 2af Bishop | .25 | .25 |
| 1331 | A523 | 3af Queen | .35 | .25 |
| 1332 | A523 | 4af King (bust) | .45 | .25 |
| 1333 | A523 | 7af King, diff. | .70 | .25 |
| 1334 | A523 | 16af Knight | 1.10 | .25 |
| 1335 | A523 | 24af Pawn | 1.60 | .35 |
| 1336 | A523 | 45af Bishop, diff. | 2.75 | .45 |
| | Nos. 1330-1336 (7) | | 7.20 | 2.05 |

Paintings by Picasso — A524

Designs: 4af, The Old Jew. 6af, The Two Mountebanks. 8af, Portrait of Ambrouse Vollar. 22af, Woman of Majorca. 35af, Acrobat on the Ball. 75af, Using a Horta de Ebro.

**1989, Feb. 13**    **Litho.**    **Perf. 12½x12**
| | | | | |
|---|---|---|---|---|
| 1341 | A524 | 4af multicolored | .35 | .25 |
| 1342 | A524 | 6af multicolored | .45 | .25 |
| 1343 | A524 | 8af multicolored | .55 | .25 |
| 1344 | A524 | 22af multicolored | 1.25 | .25 |
| 1345 | A524 | 35af multicolored | 2.50 | .25 |

**Size: 71x90mm**
**Imperf**
| | | | | |
|---|---|---|---|---|
| 1346 | A524 | 75af multicolored | 4.75 | 1.25 |
| | Nos. 1341-1346 (6) | | 9.85 | 2.50 |

Fauna — A525

3af, Allactaga euphratica. 4af, Equus hemionus. 14af, Felis lynx. 35af, Gypaetus barbatus. 44af, Capra falconeri. 100af, Naja oxiana.

**1989, Feb. 20**    **Litho.**    **Perf. 12½x12**
| | | | | |
|---|---|---|---|---|
| 1347 | A525 | 3af multicolored | .35 | .25 |
| 1348 | A525 | 4af multicolored | .35 | .25 |
| 1349 | A525 | 14af multicolored | 1.00 | .35 |
| 1350 | A525 | 35af multicolored | 3.75 | 1.60 |
| 1351 | A525 | 44af multicolored | 2.50 | 1.25 |

**Size: 71x91mm**
**Imperf**
| | | | | |
|---|---|---|---|---|
| 1352 | A525 | 100af multicolored | 7.75 | 3.00 |
| | Nos. 1347-1352 (6) | | 15.70 | 6.70 |

Intl. Women's Day — A526

**1989, Mar. 8**    **Perf. 12½x12**
| | | | | |
|---|---|---|---|---|
| 1353 | A526 | 8af multicolored | .45 | .25 |

Restoration and Development of San'a, Yemen — A527

**1988, Dec. 27**    **Litho.**    **Perf. 12**
| | | | | |
|---|---|---|---|---|
| 1354 | A527 | 32af multicolored | 1.60 | 1.10 |

Agriculture Day — A528

1af, Cattle. 2af, Old and new plows. 3af, Field workers.

**1989, Mar. 21**
| | | | | |
|---|---|---|---|---|
| 1355 | A528 | 1af multicolored | .25 | .25 |
| 1356 | A528 | 2af multicolored | .25 | .25 |
| 1357 | A528 | 3af multicolored | .25 | .25 |
| | Nos. 1355-1357 (3) | | .75 | .75 |

World Meteorology Day — A529

32af, Emblems. 40af, Weather station, balloon, vert.

**1989, Mar. 23**
| | | | | |
|---|---|---|---|---|
| 1358 | A529 | 27af shown | 1.25 | .25 |
| 1359 | A529 | 32af multicolored | 1.75 | .25 |
| 1360 | A529 | 40af multicolored | 2.25 | .25 |
| | Nos. 1358-1360 (3) | | 5.25 | .75 |

Saur Revolution, 11th Anniv. — A530

**1989, Apr. 27**
| | | | | |
|---|---|---|---|---|
| 1361 | A530 | 20af multicolored | 1.10 | .25 |

Classic Automobiles A531

5af, 1910 Duchs, Germany. 10af, 1911 Ford, US. 20af, 1911 Renault, France. 25af, 1911, Russo-Balte, Russia. 30af, 1926 Fiat, Italy.

**1989, Dec. 30**    **Litho.**    **Perf. 12½x12**
| | | | | |
|---|---|---|---|---|
| 1362 | A531 | 5af multi | .45 | .25 |
| 1363 | A531 | 10af multi | .75 | .25 |
| 1364 | A531 | 20af multi | 1.40 | .25 |
| 1365 | A531 | 25af multi | 1.60 | .35 |
| 1366 | A531 | 30af multi | 1.90 | .35 |
| | Nos. 1362-1366 (5) | | 6.10 | 1.45 |

Asia-Pacific Telecommunity, 10th Anniv. — A532

27af, Emblem, satellite dish.

**1989, Aug. 3**    **Perf. 12**
| | | | | |
|---|---|---|---|---|
| 1367 | A532 | 3af shown | .25 | .25 |
| 1368 | A532 | 27af multicolored | 1.10 | .25 |

Teacher's Day — A533

**1989, May 30**    **Litho.**    **Perf. 12**
| | | | | |
|---|---|---|---|---|
| 1369 | A533 | 42af multicolored | 2.25 | .35 |

French Revolution, Bicent. — A534

**1989, July**    **Litho.**    **Perf. 12**
| | | | | |
|---|---|---|---|---|
| 1370 | A534 | 25af multicolored | 1.60 | .95 |

Natl. Independence, 70th Anniv. — A535

**1989, Aug. 18**    **Litho.**    **Perf. 12**
| | | | | |
|---|---|---|---|---|
| 1371 | A535 | 25af multicolored | 1.25 | .35 |

A536

**1989, Aug. 30**
| | | | | |
|---|---|---|---|---|
| 1372 | A536 | 3af multicolored | .25 | .25 |

Pashtos' and Baluchis' Day.

Birds — A537

3af, Platalea leucorodia. 5af, Porphyrio porphyrio. 10af, Botaurus stellaris, horiz. 15af, Pelecanus onocrotalus. 20af, Netta rufina. 25af, Cygnus olor. 30af, Phalacrocorax carbo, horiz.

**1989, Dec. 5**    **Litho.**    **Perf. 12**
| | | | | |
|---|---|---|---|---|
| 1373 | A537 | 3af multicolored | .25 | .25 |
| 1374 | A537 | 5af multicolored | .50 | .25 |
| 1375 | A537 | 10af multicolored | .95 | .45 |
| 1376 | A537 | 15af multicolored | 1.25 | .55 |
| 1377 | A537 | 20af multicolored | 1.60 | .60 |
| 1378 | A537 | 25af multicolored | 2.25 | .70 |
| 1379 | A537 | 30af multicolored | 2.50 | .95 |
| | Nos. 1373-1379 (7) | | 9.30 | 3.75 |

# AFGHANISTAN

Tourism — A538

1af, Mosque. 2af, Minaret. 3af, Buzkashi, horiz. 4af, Jet over Hendo Kush, horiz.

**1989, Dec.**

| 1380 | A538 | 1af multicolored | 1.60 | 3.25 |
|---|---|---|---|---|
| 1381 | A538 | 2af multicolored | 3.25 | 6.50 |
| 1382 | A538 | 3af multicolored | 4.75 | 9.50 |
| 1383 | A538 | 4af multicolored | 6.50 | 13.00 |
|  |  | Nos. 1380-1383 (4) | 16.10 | 32.25 |

Mavlavi Allahdad Balkhi, President of Post of the Afghanistan Postal Administration, has declared that "the stamps which have been printed after year 1989 are false stamps."

The following stamps have been condemned as unauthorized by the Afghan Ministry of Communications:

**Dated 1996:** *Mushrooms*, 6 stamps + souvenir sheet. *Bears*, 5 stamps + souvenir sheet. *1998 Word Soccer Cup Championships*, 6 stamps + souvenir sheet. *Silkworms*, 6 stamps + souvenir sheet. *Domestic Cats*, 6 stamps + souvenir sheet. *Horses*, 5 stamps + souvenir sheet. *Islamic Revolution*, 6 stamps. *Independence Anniv./Honoring Prophet Mohammed*, 2 stamps.

**Dated 1997:** *Tulips*, 6 stamps + souvenir sheet. *Llamas & Camels*, 6 stamps + souvenir sheet. *Domestic Cats*, 6 stamps + souvenir sheet. *Wildflowers*, 6 stamps + souvenir sheet. *Early Sailing Ships* (triangles), 6 stamps + souvenir sheet. *1998 Word Soccer Cup Championships*, 6 stamps + souvenir sheet. *Mushrooms*, 6 stamps + souvenir sheet.

**Dated 1998:** *Mushrooms*, 6 stamps + souvenir sheet. *Butterflies*, 6 stamps + souvenir sheet. *Princess Diana*, 9 stamps in a miniature sheet. *WWF (Wild Sheep)*, strip of 4 stamps. *Wildlife*, 12 stamps. *Dogs*, 6 stamps + souvenir sheet. *Locomotives*, 6 stamps + souvenir sheet. *Prehistoric Animals*, 6 stamps + souvenir sheet. *Antique Cars*, 6 stamps + souvenir sheet. *Fish*, 6 stamps + souvenir sheet. *Birds*, 6 stamps + souvenir sheet.

**Dated 1999:** *Chess*, 6 stamps + souvenir sheet. *Mushrooms*, 6 stamps + souvenir sheet. *Locomotives*, 6 stamps + souvenir sheet. *Dogs*, 6 stamps + souvenir sheet. *Minerals*, 6 stamps + souvenir sheet. *Snails*, 6 stamps + souvenir sheet. *Vintage Race Cars*, 6 stamps + souvenir sheet. *China '99*, 12 stamps in a miniature sheet. *Cacti*, 6 stamps + souvenir sheet. *Horses*, 6 stamps + souvenir sheet. *Ferrari Automobiles*, 6 stamps + souvenir sheet. *Orchids*, 6 stamps + souvenir sheet. *Parrots*, 6 stamps + souvenir sheet. *Sailing Ships*, 6 stamps + souvenir sheet.

**Dated 2000:** *Cats*, 6 stamps + souvenir sheet. *WIPA 2000 (Birds)*, 6 stamps + souvenir sheet.

**Dated 2001:** *Mushrooms*, 6 stamps + souvenir sheet. *Locomotives*, 6 stamps + souvenir sheet.

In addition to these sets, a number of bogus illegal issues have appeared. These issues include:

*Beetles:* miniature sheet of 9 different stamps.
*Birds:* 2 miniature sheets of 9 different stamps each.
*Boats:* 3 miniature sheets of 9 different stamps each.
*Cars (Vintage):* 3 miniature sheets of 9 different stamps each.
*Cats:* 3 miniature sheets of 9 different stamps each.
*Chess:* 3 miniature sheets of 9 different stamps each.
*Dinosaurs:* 3 miniature sheets of 9 different stamps each.
*Dogs:* 3 miniature sheets of 9 different stamps each.
*Eagles & Owls:* miniature sheet of 9 different stamps.
*Eagles:* miniature sheet of 9 different stamps.
*Elvis Presley:* 3 miniature sheets of 9 different stamps each.
*Fauna of Afghanistan:* miniature sheet of 9 different stamps.
*Fish:* miniature sheet of 9 different stamps.
*Great People of the 20th Century:* miniature sheet of 9 different stamps.
*Horses:* 2 miniature sheets of 9 different stamps each.
*Korea/Japan World Soccer Cup:* 2 souvenir sheets.
*Locomotives:* 2 souvenir sheets inscribed "Trains."
*Locomotives:* miniature sheet of 9 different stamps, inscribed "English Trains."
*Marilyn Monroe:* 3 miniature sheets of 9 different stamps each.
*Marilyn Monroe:* Block of 4 different stamps.
*Mother Teresa & Pope John Paul II:* 3 miniature sheets of 6 different stamps each + 3 souvenir sheets.
*Osama Ben Laden Wanted Poster:* 1 stamp in miniature sheet of 9.
*Owls:* 3 miniature sheets of 9 different stamps each + 2 souvenir sheets.
*Paintings (Classic Posters):* miniature sheet of 9 different stamps.
*Paintings (Impressionists):* 3 miniature sheets of 6 different stamps each + 3 souvenir sheets.
*Plants:* miniature sheet of 9 different stamps + souvenir sheet depicting orchid.
*Princess Diana:* miniature sheet of 9 different stamps.
*Sports:* 4 miniature sheets of 9 different stamps each, inscribed "Formula 2000."

## Transitional Islamic State

Ahmed Shah Masood (1953?-2001), Military Leader — A539

**2002**    Litho.    Perf. 13½x13
1384   A539   14,000af multi    7.50   10.00

National Understanding A540

**2002, July 18**    Litho.    Perf. 13x13½
1385   A540   11,000af multi    6.50   6.50

Destruction of Bamyan Buddha Statue by Taliban Government — A541

**2002, July 18**    Perf. 13½x13
1386   A541   25,000af multi    7.50   10.00

On Oct. 8, 2002, a new currency was introduced. Old stamps not formerly authorized were issued and sold at face value without the zeros. The same was done with Nos. 1384-1386. Because there was no obliteration they can only be recognized with dated cancels.

Fourth Anniversary of the Islamic Revolution — A541a

**2002**    Litho.    Perf. 12¾
1386A   A541a   800af multi    .75   —

No. 1386A was originally "issued" Dec. 20, 1996 but was not authorized for postal use until 2002. It was sold and valid for 8af.

Farmers' Day — A541b

**2002**    Litho.    Perf. 12¾
1386B   A541b   1,500af multi    1.50

No. 1386B was originally "issued" Dec. 20, 1996 but was not authorized for postal use until 2002. It was sold and valid for 15af.

Mohammed's Birthday — A541c

**2002**    Litho.    Perf. 12½x12¾
1386C   A541c   1,500af multi    1.50

No. 1386C was originally "issued" Dec. 26, 1996 but was not authorized for postal use until 2002. It was sold and valid for 15af.

77th Independence Day — A541d

**2002**    Litho.    Perf. 12½x12¾
1386D   A541d   1,500af multi    .75

No. 1386D was originally "issued" Dec. 28, 1996 but was not authorized for postal use until 2002. It was sold and valid for 7af.

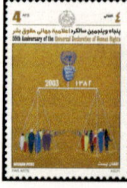

Universal Declaration of Human Rights, 55th Anniv. — A542

**2002, Dec. 10**    Litho.    Perf. 13x12¾
1387   A542   4af multi    3.50   3.50

Farmer's Day — A543

Designs: 3af, Tractor. 6af, Oxen pulling plow.

**2003, Mar. 21**    Litho.    Perf. 12¾x13
1388   A543   3af shown    5.00   —
1389   A453   6af multi    10.00   —

### Miniature Sheet

Orchids A544

No. 1390: a, 9af, Calanthe veitchii. b, 13af, Eulanthe sanderiana. c, 17af, Ordontioda vuylstekeae. d, 20af, Dendrobium infundibulum. e, 30af, Miltoniopsis roezlii. f, 40af, Cattleya labiata. g, 100af, Vanda coerulea.

**2003, Apr. 17**    Litho.    Perf. 13x12¾
1390   A544   Sheet of 7, #a-g, + 2 labels    22.50   22.50

No. 1390 exists in vertical (pictured) and horizontal formats. Value is the same.

Birthday of Mohammed A545

**2003, May 14**    Litho.    Perf. 12¾x13
1391   A545   10af multi    6.00   6.00

World Tuberculosis Day — A546

Designs: 1af, Boy and girl holding sign. 4af, Caricatures of doctors and patients, horiz. 9af, Caricatures of patients, horiz.

Perf. 13x12¾, 12¾x13
**2003, May 18**    Litho.
1392-1394   A546   Set of 3    6.00   6.00

Loya Jurga — A547

**2003, June 16**    Litho.    Perf. 12¾x13
1395   A547   20af multi    4.00   4.00

Day Against Narcotics A548

Designs: 1af, Map of Afghanistan, poppy. 2af, Poppy capsule, skulls, vert. 5af, Farmer and tractor in poppy field. 10af, Poppy capsule, skulls.

# AFGHANISTAN

**Perf. 12¾x13, 13x12¾**
**2003, June 25** Litho.
1396-1398 A548 Set of 3    3.50 3.50
**Souvenir Sheet**
1398A A548 10af multi    2.75 2.75

Dogs — A549

Designs: 10af, Rottweiler. 20af, Cocker spaniel. 30af, Doberman pinscher. 40af, Afghan hound. 50af, Giant schnauzer. 60af, Boxer.
150af, Afghan hound, diff.

**2003, July 4** Litho. Perf. 13x12¾
1399-1404 A549 Set of 6    20.00 —
**Souvenir Sheet**
1405 A549 150af multi    14.50

Lighthouses — A550

Designs: 10af, Bird Island, South Africa. 20af, Cordouan, France. 30af, Mahota Pagoda, China. 50af, Bay Canh, Viet Nam. 60af, Cap Roman Rock, South Africa. 100af, Mikomoto Shima, Japan.
150af, Bell Rock, Great Britain.

**2003, Aug. 5**
1406-1411 A550 Set of 6    22.50
**Souvenir Sheet**
1412 A550 150af multi    14.50

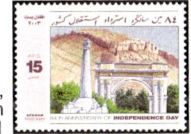

Independence, 84th Anniv. — A551

**2003, Aug. 19** Litho. Perf. 12¾x13
1413 A551 15af multi    3.50 3.50

Intl. Literacy Day — A552

**2003, Sept. 8** Litho. Perf. 12¾x13
1414 A552 2af multi    1.00 1.00

**Miniature Sheet**

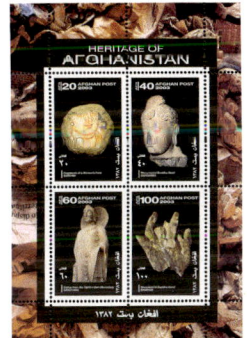

Heritage of Afghanistan — A553

No. 1415: a, 20af, Fragments of rock drawing depicting a woman, Bamiyan. b, 40af, Head of Buddha, Gandhara. c, 60af, Statue from Takht-i-Bahi Monastery, Gandhara. d, 100af, Hand of Buddha, Bamiyan.

**2003, Oct. 10** Litho. Perf. 13x12¾
1415 A553 Sheet of 4, #a-d    22.50 —

Revelation of the Koran to Mohammed A554

**2003, Nov. 23** Litho. Perf. 12¾x13
1416 A554 9af multi    6.50 6.50

A555

Afghanistan Tourism Day—A555a

Designs: 8af, 25af, Fort. 12af, Bust, jar, historical artifacts.

**2003, Dec. 10** Litho. Perf. 12¾x13
1417 A555 4af shown    .75 .75
1418 A555a 8af ol grn & multi    1.00 1.00
1418A A555 12af multi    1.25 1.25
   Nos. 1417-1418A (3)    3.00 3.00
**Souvenir Sheet**
1418B A555a 25af lil & multi    3.00 3.00

Animals A556

Designs: 6af, Leopard. 11af, Jackal. 15af, Wild goat.
40af, Leopard facing left.

**2003** Litho. Perf. 12¾
1419-1421 A556 Set of 3    5.00 5.00
**Souvenir Sheet**
1422 A556 40af multi    8.25 8.25

World Post Day — A557

**2003, Oct. 9** Litho. Perf. 12¾x13
1423 A557 8af multi    2.50 2.50

Int'l. Women's Day — A558

**2004** Litho. Perf. 12¾x13
1424 A558 6af multi    1.50 1.50

World Tuberculosis Day — A559

Designs: 1af, Woman, hands holding medicine and bloody tissue. 4af, Woman wearing mask, child. 9af, Eight men. 12af, Man, map of Afghanistan, vert. 15af, Doctor touching patient, people in white in background, vert.

**Perf. 12¾x13, 13x12¾**
**2004, Mar. 23** Litho.
1425 A559 1af multi    .35 .35
1426 A559 4af multi    .75 .75
1427 A559 9af multi    1.50 1.50
1428 A559 12af multi    2.00 2.00
1429 A559 15af multi    2.50 2.50
   Nos. 1425-1429 (5)    7.10 7.10

Pres. Hamid Karzai A560    Karzai and Map of Afghanistan A561

**2004, Oct. 7** Perf. 13x12¾
1430 A560 12af multi    3.00 3.00
1431 A561 12af multi    5.00 5.00
Oath of Pres. Karzai.

First Direct Presidential Election A562

Denominations: 15af, 25af.

**2004, Oct. 9** Litho. Perf. 12¾x13
1432-1433 A562 Set of 2    7.00 7.00
Two types of Arabic inscriptions exist on each stamp. Values the same.

Afghanistan postal officials declared a set of eight stamps depicting soccer players and a set of eight stamps depicting FIFA Presidents as "not authorized."
The editors are seeking more information about the status of a set of four Worldwide Fund for Nature stamps depicting the Himalayan musk deer.

**Souvenir Sheet**

Inauguration of Pres. Karzai — A563

**2004, Dec. 7** Litho. Perf. 13½
1434 A563 100af multi    18.00 18.00

Diplomatic Relations Between Afghanistan and People's Republic of China, 50th Anniv. A564

**2005, Jan. 20** Litho. Perf. 12
1435 A564 25af multi    3.00 3.00
**Souvenir Sheet**
**Printed On Cloth**
**Without Gum**
**Perf. 13¼x13**
1436 A564 150af multi    24.00 24.00
No. 1436 contains one 60x40mm stamp.

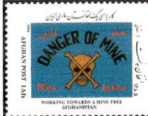

Mine Clearance Campaign A565

Designs: 1af, Mine danger warning sign. 2af, Mine clearer with dog, vert. 3af, Mine clearer with metal detector, vert.

**2006, Apr. 4** Litho. Perf. 13¼x13, 13x13¼
1437-1439 A565 Set of 3    2.00 2.00

Independence, 87th Anniv. — A566

**2006, Aug. 19** Perf. 13x13¼
1440 A566 45af multi    8.00 8.00

World Literacy Day — A567

**2006, Sept. 8**
1441 A567 12af multi    2.00 2.00

World Post Day — A568

Color of "2006": No. 1442, 15af, Light green. No. 1443, 15af, Black.

**2006, Sept. 9** Perf. 13¼x13
1442-1443 A568 Set of 2    4.50 4.50
The length of the Arabic inscription on the top of the stamp is longer on No. 1442 than on No. 1443.

World Tourism Day — A569

Designs: 15af, Lamp, pitchers, bowl, building. 30af, Pitchers, cup, mountain.

**2006, Sept. 27** Litho. Perf. 13¼x13
1444 A569 15af multi    2.50 2.50
1445 A569 30af multi    4.50 4.50

Campaign for Elimination of Violence Against Women A570

Designs: 12af, Woman behind barbed wire, chain, hands unlocking lock. 14af, Woman, roots. 19af, Eyes of woman, needle and thread closing eye hole of burqa, horiz.

**Perf. 13x13¼, 13¼x13**
**2006, Nov. 25** Litho.
1446-1448 A570 Set of 3    6.75 6.75

Mevlana Jalal ad-Din ar-Rumi (1207-73), Islamic Philosopher A571

Designs: 65af, Birthplace at Balkh. 85af, Mevlana and whirling dervishes, vert.
150af, Mevlana, whirling dervishes, birthplace at Balkh, horiz.

**Perf. 13¼x13, 13x13¼**
**2006, Nov. 26**
1449-1450 A571 Set of 2    15.00 —
**Size: 106x78mm**
**Imperf**
1451 A571 150af multi    30.00 30.00
No. 1451 contains two perforated labels lacking country name or value. See Iran No. 2911, Syria No. 1574, Turkey No. 2971.

# AFGHANISTAN

Successful Completion of Bonn Process — A572

**2007, Apr. 19**     *Perf. 13¼x13*
1452 A572 25af multi     4.00   4.00
Dated 2006.

Mevlana Jalal ad-Din ar-Rumi (1207-73), Islamic Philosopher A573

**2007, May 24**
1453 A573 40af multi     6.00   6.00

Milli Attan Dance — A574

**2007, Aug. 19**
1454 A574 38af multi     6.00   6.00

Natl. Day of Fine Arts — A575

Singers: 20af, Ustad Awal Mir. 22af, Mirmun Parwin.

**2007, Sept. 25**     *Perf. 13x13¼*
1455-1456 A575   Set of 2    7.50   7.50

Third Meeting of Economic Cooperation Organization Postal Authorities, Tehran — A576

**2007, Dec. 22**     *Perf. 13¼x13*
1457 A576 8af multi     2.00   2.00

National Unity — A577

Emperors: 25af, Ahmad Shah Baba (c. 1723-73). 30af, Mirwais Nika. 34af, Sultan Mahmood Ghaznawi (979-1030).

**2007, Dec. 22**     *Perf. 13x13¼*
1458-1460 A577   Set of 3    12.00   12.00

Red Crescent Society — A578

**2009, Jan. 21**   *Litho.*   *Perf. 13x13¼*
1461 A578 17af multi     2.40   2.40

Rudaki (c. 859-c.940), Poet — A579

**2009, Jan. 21**
1462 A579 55af multi     6.50   6.50

World Envirornmental Protection Day — A580

**2010, Jan. 1**   *Litho.*   *Perf. 13½x12¾*
1463 A580 5af multi     1.25   1.25

World Literacy Day — A581

**2011, Jan. 1**   *Litho.*   *Perf. 14*
1464 A581 22af multi     4.00   4.00

Khwaja Abdullah Ansari (1006-88), Religious Commentator — A582

**2012, Jan. 1**   *Litho.*   *Perf. 14*
1465 A582 50af multi     6.50   6.50
Dated 2009. See Iran No. 3016, Tajikistan No. 366.

Emblem and Flags of Members of South Asian Association for Regional Cooperation A583

**2012, Feb. 1**   *Litho.*   *Perf. 13½x12¾*
1466 A583 40af multi     6.50   6.50

World Peace Day — A584

**2012, Feb. 1**   *Litho.*   *Perf. 13½x12¾*
1467 A584 50af multi     6.50   6.50
Dated 2011.

---

## SEMI-POSTAL STAMPS

Catalogue values for unused stamps in this section are for Never Hinged items.

**No. 373 Surcharged in Violet**

**1952, July 12**   *Unwmk.*   *Perf. 12½*
B1 A122 40p + 30p cerise    5.25   3.00
B2 A122 125p + 30p cerise    7.75   3.50
1000th anniv. of the birth of Avicenna.

Children at Play — SP1

**1955, July 3**   *Typo.*   *Perf. 11*
B3 SP1 35p + 15p dk green    1.25   .70
B4 SP1 125p + 25p purple    2.50   1.25
The surtax was for child welfare.
Exist imperf. Values, set: unused $6.50; used $7.

Amir Sher Ali Khan, Tiger Head Stamp and Zahir Shah — SP2

**1955, July 2**     *Litho.*
B5 SP2 35p + 15p carmine    1.00   .55
B6 SP2 125p + 25p pale vio bl   1.90   1.00
85th anniv. of the Afghan post.
Exist imperf. Values, set: unused $5; used $6.

Children at Play — SP3

**1956, June 20**     *Typo.*
B7 SP3 35p + 15p brt vio bl    .90   .40
B8 SP3 140p + 15p dk org brn   2.25   .85
Issued for Children's Day. The surtax was for child welfare. No. B8 inscribed in French.
Exist imperf. Values, set: unused $8; used $8.75.

Pashtunistan Monument, Kabul — SP4

**1956, Sept. 1**     *Litho.*
B9 SP4 35p + 15p dp violet    .40   .25
B10 SP4 140p + 15p dk brown   1.10   .75
"Free Pashtunistan" Day. The surtax aided the "Free Pashtunistan" movement.
No. B9 measures 30½x19½mm; No. B10, 29x19mm. On sale and valid for use only on Sept. 1-2.
Exist imperf. Values, set: unused $6; used $7.50.

Globe and Sun — SP5

**1956, Oct. 24**     *Perf. 11*
B11 SP5 35p + 15p ultra    1.00   .90
B12 SP5 140p + 15p red brown   1.90   1.60
Afghanistan's UN admission, 10th anniv.
Exist imperf. Values, set: unused $14; used $17.50.

Children on Seesaw — SP6

**1957, June 20**     *Unwmk.*
B13 SP6 35p + 15p brt rose    .85   .55
B14 SP6 140p + 15p ultra    1.60   1.40
Children's Day. Surtax for child welfare.
Exist imperf. Values, set: unused $3.25; used $4.

UN Headquarters and Emblems — SP7

**1957, Oct. 24**     *Perf. 11 Rough*
B15 SP7 35p + 15p red brown   .60   .40
B16 SP7 140p + 15p lt ultra   1.10   1.10
United Nations Day.
Exist imperf. Values, set: unused $6; used $7.50.

Swimming Pool and Children — SP8

**1958, June 22**     *Perf. 11*
B17 SP8 35p + 15p rose    .65   .40
B18 SP8 140p + 15p dl red brn   .80   .65
Children's Day. Surtax for child welfare.
Exist imperf. Values, set: unused $5; used $6.

Pashtunistan Flag — SP9

**1958, Aug. 31**
B19 SP9 35p + 15p lt blue    .40   .25
B20 SP9 140p + 15p red brown   1.00   .65
Issued for "Free Pashtunistan Day."
Exist imperf. Values, set: unused $4; used $5.

Children Playing Tug of War — SP10

**1959, June 23**   *Litho.*   *Perf. 11*
B21 SP10 35p + 15p brown vio   .60   .35
B22 SP10 165p + 15p brt pink   1.25   .50
Children's Day. Surtax for child welfare.
Exist imperf. Value set, unused or used, $5.

Pathans in Tribal Dance — SP11

*Perf. 11 Rough*     *Unwmk.*
**1959, Sept.**
B23 SP11 35p + 15p green    .60   .35
B24 SP11 165p + 15p orange   1.25   .75
Issued for "Free Pashtunistan Day."
Exist imperf. Value set, unused or used, $2.50.

Afghan Cavalryman with UN Flag — SP12

**1959, Oct. 24**     *Perf. 11 Rough*
B25 SP12 35p + 15p orange    .35   .25
B26 SP12 165p + 15p lt bl grn   .75   .45
Issued for United Nations Day.
Exist imperf. Value set, unused or used, $2.50.

Children — SP13

# AFGHANISTAN

**1960, Oct. 23**      Litho.
| | | | |
|---|---|---|---|
| B27 | SP13 | 75p + 25p lt ultra | .90 .35 |
| B28 | SP13 | 175p + 25p lt green | 1.75 .50 |

Children's Day. Surtax for child welfare.
Exist imperf. Value set, unused or used, $2.75.

Man with Spray Gun — SP14

**1960, Sept. 6**      Perf. 11 Rough
| | | | |
|---|---|---|---|
| B29 | SP14 | 50p + 50p orange | 1.40 1.25 |
| B30 | SP14 | 175p + 50p red brown | 3.50 2.75 |

11th anniversary of the WHO malaria control program in Afghanistan.
Exist imperf. Value set, unused or used, $7.50.

SP15

**1960, Sept. 1**      Unwmk.
| | | | |
|---|---|---|---|
| B31 | SP15 | 50p + 50p rose | .60 .30 |
| B32 | SP15 | 175p + 50p dk blue | 1.40 1.10 |

Issued for "Free Pashtunistan Day."
Exist imperf. Value set, unused or used, $3.25.

Ambulance — SP16

**1960, Oct. 16**      Perf. 11
**Crescent in Red**
| | | | |
|---|---|---|---|
| B33 | SP16 | 50p + 50p violet | .65 .50 |
| B34 | SP16 | 175p + 50p blue | 1.75 1.00 |

Issued for the Red Crescent Society.
Exist imperf. Value set, unused or used, $3.25.

Nos. 470-471 Surcharged in Blue or Orange

**1960, Dec. 31**      Litho.      Perf. 11
| | | | |
|---|---|---|---|
| B35 | A166 | 50p + 25p dp org (Bl) | 1.75 1.75 |
| B36 | A166 | 165p + 25p blue (O) | 1.75 1.75 |

Exist imperf. Value set, unused or used, $11
The souvenir sheets described after No. 471 were surcharged in carmine "+25 Ps" on each stamp. Values: normal colors, unused $6, used $0.50; reversed colors, unused $7.50, used $9.50.
See general note after No. 485.

Nos. 496-500 Surcharged

**1961, July 6**    Unwmk.    Photo.    Perf. 13½x14
| | | | |
|---|---|---|---|
| B37 | A175 | 2p + 25p green & rose lil | .50 .50 |
| B38 | A175 | 2p + 25p brown & cit | .50 .50 |
| B39 | A175 | 5p + 25p gray & rose | .50 .50 |
| B40 | A175 | 10p + 25p blue & bis | .50 .50 |
| B41 | A175 | 15p + 25p sl bl & dl lil | .50 .50 |
| | | Nos. B37-B41 (5) | 2.50 2.50 |

UNICEF. The same surcharge was applied to an imperf. souvenir sheet like that noted after No. 505. Value $5.

**Nos. 522-526 Surcharged "+25PS" and Crescent in Red**

**1961, Oct. 16**      Perf. 13½x14
| | | | |
|---|---|---|---|
| B42 | A184 | 2p + 25p black | .50 .50 |
| B43 | A184 | 2p + 25p green | .50 .50 |
| B44 | A184 | 5p + 25p lilac rose | .50 .50 |
| B45 | A184 | 10p + 25p lilac | .50 .50 |
| B46 | A184 | 15p + 25p dk blue | .50 .50 |
| | | Nos. B42-B46 (5) | 2.50 2.50 |

Issued for the Red Crescent Society.

**Nos. 539-543 Surcharged in Red: "UNESCO + 25PS"**

**1962**      Perf. 12
| | | | |
|---|---|---|---|
| B47 | A186 | 2p + 25p multi | .40 .40 |
| B48 | A186 | 2p + 25p multi | .40 .40 |
| B49 | A186 | 5p + 25p multi | .40 .40 |
| B50 | A186 | 10p + 25p multi | .40 .40 |
| B51 | A186 | 15p + 25p multi | .40 .40 |
| | | Nos. B47-B51 (5) | 2.00 2.00 |

UNESCO. The same surcharge was applied to the souvenir sheets mentioned after No. 548. Value, 2 sheets, $10.

**Nos. 553-561 Surcharged: "Dag Hammarskjöld +20PS"**

**1962, Sept. 17**      Perf. 14x13½
| | | | |
|---|---|---|---|
| B52 | A187 | 2p + 20p | .25 .25 |
| B53 | A187 | 2p + 20p | .25 .25 |
| B54 | A187 | 5p + 20p | .25 .25 |
| B55 | A187 | 10p + 20p | .25 .25 |
| B56 | A187 | 15p + 20p | .25 .25 |
| B57 | A187 | 25p + 20p | .25 .25 |
| B58 | A187 | 50p + 20p | .30 .30 |
| B59 | A187 | 75p + 20p | .50 .50 |
| B60 | A187 | 100p + 20p | .80 .80 |
| | | Nos. B52-B60 (9) | 3.10 3.10 |

In memory of Dag Hammarskjold, Sec. Gen. of the UN, 1953-61. Perf. and imperf. souvenir sheets exist. Value, 2 sheets, $6.50.

**Nos. 583-593 Surcharged "+15PS"**

**1963, Mar. 15**      Perf. 14x13½
| | | | |
|---|---|---|---|
| B61 | A193 | 2p + 15p | 1.00 1.00 |
| B62 | A193 | 2p + 15p | 1.00 1.00 |
| B63 | A193 | 5p + 15p | 1.00 1.00 |
| B64 | A193 | 10p + 15p | 1.00 1.00 |
| B65 | A193 | 15p + 15p | 1.00 1.00 |
| B66 | A193 | 25p + 15p | 1.00 1.00 |
| B67 | A193 | 50p + 15p | 1.00 1.00 |
| B68 | A193 | 75p + 15p | 1.00 1.00 |
| B69 | A193 | 100p + 15p | 1.00 1.00 |
| B70 | A193 | 150p + 15p | 1.00 1.00 |
| B71 | A193 | 175p + 15p | 1.00 1.00 |
| | | Nos. B61-B71 (11) | 11.00 11.00 |

WHO drive to eradicate malaria.

**Nos. 672-672G, 672I Surcharged in Various Positions**

**1964, Mar. 9**
| | | | |
|---|---|---|---|
| B71A | A213g | 2p + 50p | .25 .25 |
| B71B | A213g | 3p + 50p | .25 .25 |
| B71C | A213g | 4p + 50p | .25 .25 |
| B71D | A213g | 5p + 50p | .25 .25 |
| B71E | A213g | 10p + 50p | .25 .25 |
| B71F | A213g | 100p + 50p | .70 .70 |
| B71G | A213g | 2af + 50p | 1.50 1.50 |
| B71H | A213g | 3af + 50p | 2.10 2.10 |
| | | Nos. B71A-B71H (8) | 5.55 5.55 |

**Souvenir Sheet**
| | | | |
|---|---|---|---|
| B71J | A213g | 5af + 50p | 4.50 4.50 |

Nos. B71E-B71G are airmail semi-postals.

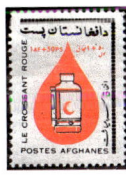

Blood Transfusion Kit — SP17

**1964, Oct. 18**      Litho.      Perf. 10½
| | | | |
|---|---|---|---|
| B72 | SP17 | 1af + 50p black & rose | .40 .30 |

Issued for the Red Crescent Society and Red Crescent Week, Oct. 18-24.

First Aid Station — SP18

**1965, Oct. 16**    Photo.    Perf. 13½x14
| | | | |
|---|---|---|---|
| B73 | SP18 | 1.50af + 50p multi | .35 .25 |

Issued for the Red Crescent Society.

Children Playing — SP19

**1966, Nov. 28**    Photo.    Perf. 13½x14
| | | | |
|---|---|---|---|
| B74 | SP19 | 1af + 1af yel grn & cl | .30 .25 |
| B75 | SP19 | 3af + 2af red & brn | .65 .50 |
| B76 | SP19 | 7af + 3af rose lil & grn | .95 .50 |
| | | Nos. B74-B76 (3) | 1.90 1.00 |

Children's Day.

Nadir Shah Presenting Society Charter — SP20

**1967, Feb. 15**    Photo.    Perf. 13x14
| | | | |
|---|---|---|---|
| B77 | SP20 | 2af + 1af red & dk grn | .35 .25 |
| B78 | SP20 | 5af + 1af lil rose & brn | .75 .35 |

Issued for the Red Crescent Society.

Vaccination — SP21

**1967, June 6**    Photo.    Perf. 12
| | | | |
|---|---|---|---|
| B79 | SP21 | 2af + 1af yellow & blk | .25 .25 |
| B80 | SP21 | 5af + 2af pink & brn | .65 .35 |

The surtax was for anti-tuberculosis work.

Red Crescent — SP22

**1967, Oct. 18**    Photo.    Perf. 12
**Crescent in Red**
| | | | |
|---|---|---|---|
| B81 | SP22 | 3af + 1af gray ol & blk | .25 .25 |
| B82 | SP22 | 5af + 1af dl bl & blk | .40 .25 |

Issued for the Red Crescent Society.

Queen Humeira — SP23

**1968, June 14**    Photo.    Perf. 12
| | | | |
|---|---|---|---|
| B83 | SP23 | 2af + 2af red brown | .35 .25 |
| B84 | SP23 | 7af + 2af dull green | .90 .60 |

Issued for Mother's Day.

Red Crescent — SP24

**1968, Oct. 16**    Photo.    Perf. 12
| | | | |
|---|---|---|---|
| B85 | SP24 | 4af + 1af yel, blk & red | .60 .25 |

Issued for the Red Crescent Society.

Red Cross, Crescent, Lion and Sun Emblems — SP25

**1969, May 5**    Litho.    Perf. 14x13½
| | | | |
|---|---|---|---|
| B86 | SP25 | 3af + 1af multicolored | .65 .35 |
| B87 | SP25 | 5af + 1af multicolored | .80 .35 |

League of Red Cross Societies, 50th anniv.

Mother and Child — SP26

**1969, June 14**    Photo.    Perf. 12
| | | | |
|---|---|---|---|
| B88 | SP26 | 1af + 1af yel org & brn | .30 .25 |
| B89 | SP26 | 4af + 1af rose lil & pur | .50 .35 |
| a. | | Souvenir sheet of 2 | 2.50 2.50 |

Mother's Day. No. B89a contains 2 imperf. stamps similar to Nos. B88-B89. Sold for 10af.

Red Crescent — SP27

**1969, Oct. 16**    Photo.    Perf. 12
| | | | |
|---|---|---|---|
| B90 | SP27 | 6af + 1af multi | .80 .30 |

Issued for the Red Crescent Society.

UN and FAO Emblems, Farmer — SP28

**1973, May 24**    Photo.    Perf. 13½
| | | | |
|---|---|---|---|
| B91 | SP28 | 14af + 7af grnsh bl & lil | 1.40 .90 |

World Food Program, 10th anniversary.

Dome of the Rock, Jerusalem — SP29

**1977, Sept. 11**    Photo.    Perf. 14
| | | | |
|---|---|---|---|
| B92 | SP29 | 12af + 3af multi | 2.10 .60 |

Surtax for Palestinian families and soldiers.

15 Cent. (lunar) of Islamic Pilgrimage (Hegira) SP30

**1981, Jan. 17**    Litho.    Perf. 12½x12
| | | | |
|---|---|---|---|
| B93 | SP30 | 13af + 2af multi | 1.75 .30 |

Red Crescent Aid Programs — SP31

**1981, May 8**      Perf. 12x12½
| | | | |
|---|---|---|---|
| B94 | SP31 | 1af + 4af multi | .65 .80 |

# AFGHANISTAN

Intl. Year of the
Disabled — SP32

**1981, Oct. 12**  **Perf. 12x12½**
B95  SP32  6af + 1af multi    .90   .50

## AIR POST STAMPS

Plane over
Kabul — AP1

*Perf. 12, 12x11, 11*

| 1939, Oct. 1 | | Typo. | Unwmk. |
|---|---|---|---|
| C1 | AP1 | 5af orange | 5.00 4.00 |
| a. | | Imperf., pair ('47) | 29.00 29.00 |
| b. | | Horiz. pair, imperf. vert. | 32.50 32.50 |
| C2 | AP1 | 10af blue | 5.00 4.00 |
| a. | | 10af lt bl | 8.00 6.00 |
| b. | | Imperf., pair ('47) | 29.00 |
| c. | | Horiz. pair, imperf. vert. | 32.50 |
| C3 | AP1 | 20af emerald | 10.00 6.00 |
| a. | | Imperf., pair ('47) | 29.00 |
| b. | | Horiz. pair, imperf. vert. | 32.50 |
| c. | | Vert. pair, imperf. horiz. | 35.00 |
| | | Nos. C1-C3 (3) | 20.00 14.00 |

These stamps come with clean-cut or rough perforations.
Exist imperf. Value, set $30.
Counterfeits exist.

> Catalogue values for unused stamps in this section, from this point to the end of the section, are for Never Hinged items.

**1948, June 14**  **Perf. 12x11½**
| C4 | AP1 | 5af emerald | 20.00 20.00 |
| C5 | AP1 | 10af red orange | 20.00 20.00 |
| C6 | AP1 | 20af blue | 20.00 20.00 |
| | | Nos. C4-C6 (3) | 60.00 60.00 |

Imperforates exist.
Forgeries exist.

Plane over Palace
Grounds,
Kabul — AP2

Imprint: "Waterlow & Sons,
Limited, London"

**1951-54**  **Engr.**  **Perf. 13½**
| C7 | AP2 | 5af henna brn | 3.00 .60 |
| C8 | AP2 | 5af dp grn ('54) | 1.60 .40 |
| C9 | AP2 | 10af gray | 6.50 1.60 |
| C10 | AP2 | 20af dark blue | 9.00 2.50 |

**1957**
| C11 | AP2 | 5af ultra | 1.75 .50 |
| C12 | AP2 | 10af dark vio | 2.50 .90 |
| | | Nos. C7-C12 (6) | 24.35 6.50 |

See No. C38.

Ariana Plane
over Hindu
Kush — AP3

*Perf. 11, Imperf.*

**1960-63**  **Litho.**  **Unwmk.**
| C13 | AP3 | 75p light vio | .55 .25 |
| C14 | AP3 | 125p blue | .75 .35 |

*Perf. 10½, 11*
| C14A | AP3 | 5af citron ('63) | 1.25 .80 |
| | | Nos. C13-C14A (3) | 2.55 1.40 |

Imperf examples of Nos. C13-C14 are valued at approx. 50 percent more than the values shown.

Girl Scout — AP4

**1962, Aug. 30**  **Photo.**  **Perf. 11½x12**
| C15 | AP4 | 100p ocher & brn | .50 .50 |
| C16 | AP4 | 175p brt yel grn & brn | .90 .90 |

Women's Day. See Nos. 578-579 and note on souvenir sheet.

### Sports Type of Regular Issue, 1962

25p, 50p, Horse racing. 75p, 100p, Wrestling. 150p, Weight lifting. 175p, Soccer.

**1962, Sept. 25**  **Unwmk.**  **Perf. 12**
### Black Inscriptions
| C17 | A195 | 25p rose & red brn | .25 .25 |
| C18 | A195 | 50p gray & red brn | .30 .30 |
| C19 | A195 | 75p pale vio & dk grn | .50 .50 |
| C20 | A195 | 100p gray ol & dk pur | .65 .65 |
| C21 | A195 | 150p rose lil & grn | .90 .90 |
| C22 | A195 | 175p sal & brn | 1.00 1.00 |
| | | Nos. C17-C22 (6) | 3.60 3.60 |

### Children's Day Type of Regular Issue

*Perf. 11½x12, 12x11½*

**1962, Oct. 14**  **Unwmk.**
| C23 | A196 | 75p Runners | .60 .60 |
| C24 | A196 | 150p Peaches | 1.10 1.10 |
| C25 | A196 | 200p Iris, vert. | 1.50 1.50 |
| | | Nos. C23-C25 (3) | 3.20 3.20 |

A souvenir sheet contains one each of Nos. C23-C25. Value $4.00.

### Red Crescent Type of Regular Issue

**1962, Oct. 16**  **Perf. 12**
### Fruit and Flowers in Natural Colors; Carmine Crescent
| C26 | A197 | 25p Grapes | .25 .25 |
| C27 | A197 | 50p Pears | .30 .30 |
| C28 | A197 | 100p Wistaria | .65 .65 |
| | | Nos. C26-C28 (3) | 1.20 1.20 |

Two souvenir sheets exist. One contains a 150p gray brown stamp in blossom design, the other a 200p gray stamp in wistaria design, imperf. Value, each $5.00.

### UN Type of Regular Issue

**1962, Oct. 24**  **Photo.**
### Flags in Original Colors, Black Inscriptions
| C29 | A198 | 75p blue | .30 .30 |
| C30 | A198 | 100p lt brn | .45 .45 |
| C31 | A198 | 125p brt grn | .60 .60 |
| | | Nos. C29-C31 (3) | 1.35 1.35 |

### Boy Scout Type of Regular Issue

**1962, Oct. 25**  **Unwmk.**  **Perf. 12**
| C32 | A199 | 25p gray, blk, dl grn & sal | .30 .30 |
| C33 | A199 | 50p grn, brn & sal | .55 .55 |
| C34 | A199 | 75p bl grn, red brn & sal | .80 .80 |
| C35 | A199 | 100p bl, slate & sal | 1.00 1.00 |
| | | Nos. C32-C35 (4) | 2.65 2.65 |

### Teacher's Day Type of Regular Issue

**1962, Oct. 25**
| C36 | A200 | 100p Pole vault | .60 .60 |
| C37 | A200 | 150p High jump | .90 .90 |

A souvenir sheet contains one 250p pink and slate green stamp in design of 150p. Values: perf $2.50; imperf $21.

### Type of 1951-54
Imprint: "Thomas De La Rue & Co. Ltd."

**1962**  **Engr.**  **Perf. 13½**
| C38 | AP2 | 5af ultra | 12.00 .90 |

### Agriculture Types of Regular Issue
**Unwmk.**

**1963, Mar. 1**  **Photo.**  **Perf. 12**
| C42 | A204 | 100p dk car, grn & brn | .35 .35 |
| C43 | A203 | 150p ocher & blk | .60 .60 |
| C44 | A204 | 200p ultra, grn & brn | .90 .90 |
| | | Nos. C42-C44 (3) | 1.85 1.85 |

Hands Holding
Wheat
Emblem — AP5

**1963, Mar. 27**  **Photo.**  **Perf. 14**
| C45 | AP5 | 500p lil, lt brn & brn | 1.10 1.10 |

FAO "Freedom from Hunger" campaign.
Two souvenir sheets exist. One contains a 1000p blue green, light brown and brown, type AP5, imperf. The other contains a 200p brown and green and 300p ultramarine, yellow and ocher in rice and corn designs, type A205. Values $5.50 and $4.

### Meteorological Day Type of Regular Issue

Designs: 100p, 500p, Meteorological measuring instrument. 200p, 400p, Weather station. 300p, Rockets in space.

**1963, May 23**  **Imperf.**
| C46 | A206 | 100p brn & bl | 3.00 3.00 |

*Perf. 13½x14*
| C47 | A206 | 200p brt grn & lil | .90 .90 |
| C48 | A206 | 300p dk bl & rose | 1.40 1.20 |
| C49 | A206 | 400p bl & dl red brn | 1.90 1.75 |
| C50 | A206 | 500p car rose & gray grn | 2.25 2.00 |
| | | Nos. C47-C50 (4) | 6.45 5.85 |

Nos. C47 and C50 printed se-tenant.
Nos. C47, C50 exist imperf. Values, unused or used: 200p, $6; 500p, $16.
Two souvenir sheets exist. One contains a 125p red and brown stamp in rocket design. The other contains a 100p blue and dull red brown in "rockets in space" design. Values $4.50 and $11.

Kabul
International
Airport — AP8

*Perf. 12x11½*

**1964, Apr.**  **Unwmk.**  **Photo.**
| C57 | AP8 | 10af red lil & grn | .75 .25 |
| C58 | AP8 | 20af dk grn & red lil | .90 .35 |
| a. | | Perf. 12 ('68) | 5.00 3.00 |
| C59 | AP8 | 50af dk bl & grnsh bl | 2.50 1.00 |
| a. | | Perf. 12 ('68) | 8.00 1.60 |
| | | Nos. C57-C59 (3) | 4.15 1.60 |

Inauguration of Kabul Airport Terminal.
Nos. C58a-C59a are 36mm wide. Nos. C58-C59 are 35½mm wide.

Zahir Shah
and Kabul
Airport
AP9

100af, Zahir Shah and Ariana Plane.

**1971**  **Photo.**  **Perf. 12½x13½**
| C60 | AP9 | 50af multi | 4.00 4.00 |
| C61 | AP9 | 100af blk, red & grn | 5.00 3.00 |

Remainders of No. C60 were used, summer in 1978, with king's portrait torn or cut off.

## REGISTRATION STAMPS

Dated "1309"
Pelure Paper

**1891**  **Unwmk.**  **Litho.**  **Imperf.**
| F1 | R1 | 1r slate blue | 2.40 |
| a. | | Tete beche pair | 13.50 |

Genuinely used examples of No. F1 are rare. Counterfeit cancellations exist.

Dated "1311"

**1893**  **Thin Wove Paper**
| F2 | R2 | 1r black, green | 2.00 |

Genuinely used examples of No. F2 are rare. Counterfeit cancellations exist.

**1894**  **Undated**
| F3 | R3 | 2ab black, green | 9.50 11.00 |

12 varieties. See note below Nos. 189-190.

**1898-1900**  **Undated**
| F4 | R4 | 2ab black, deep rose | 4.50 4.50 |
| F5 | R4 | 2ab black, lilac rose | 6.50 5.00 |
| F6 | R4 | 2ab black, magenta | 8.00 5.00 |
| F7 | R4 | 2ab black, salmon | 4.50 4.50 |
| F8 | R4 | 2ab black, orange | 4.50 4.50 |
| F9 | R4 | 2ab black, yellow | 4.50 3.50 |
| F10 | R4 | 2ab black, green | 4.50 3.50 |
| | | Nos. F4-F10 (7) | 37.00 30.50 |

Many shades of paper.
Nos. F4-F10 come in two sizes, measured between outer frame lines: 52x36mm, 1st printing; 46x33mm, 2nd printing. The outer frame line (not pictured) is 3-6mm from inner frame line.
Used on P.O. receipts.

## OFFICIAL STAMPS

Coat of
Arms — O1

**1909**  **Unwmk.**  **Typo.**  **Perf. 12**
**Wove Paper**
| O1 | O1 | red | 1.25 1.25 |
| a. | | Carmine ('19?) | 2.50 6.50 |

Later printings of No. O1 in scarlet, vermilion, claret, etc., on various types of paper, were issued until 1927.

Coat of Arms — O2

**1939-68?**  **Typo.**  **Perf. 11, 12**
| O3 | O2 | 15p emerald | 1.10 .80 |
| O4 | O2 | 30p ocher ('40) | 1.50 1.50 |
| O5 | O2 | 45p dark carmine | 1.25 1.25 |

# AFGHANISTAN

| | | | |
|---|---|---|---|
| O6 | O2 50p brt car ('68) | .70 | .70 |
| a. | 50p carmine rose ('55) | 1.25 | .70 |
| O7 | O2 1af brt red violet | 2.00 | 1.75 |
| | Nos. O3-O7 (5) | 6.55 | 6.00 |

Size of 50p, 24x31mm, others 22½x28mm.

**Catalogue values for unused stamps in this section, from this point to the end of the section, are for Never Hinged items.**

**1964-65**    Litho.    Perf. 11
| | | | |
|---|---|---|---|
| O8 | O2 50p rose | .90 | .90 |
| a. | 50p salmon ('65) | 2.00 | 2.00 |

Stamps of this type are revenues.

## PARCEL POST STAMPS

Coat of Arms — PP1

PP2

PP3

PP4

**1909**    Unwmk.    Typo.    Perf. 12
| | | | |
|---|---|---|---|
| Q1 | PP1 3sh bister | 1.25 | 2.25 |
| a. | Imperf., pair | | |
| Q2 | PP2 1kr olive gray | 3.50 | 3.50 |
| a. | Imperf., pair | | |
| Q3 | PP3 1r orange | 3.25 | 3.25 |
| Q4 | PP3 1r olive green | 24.00 | 4.50 |
| Q5 | PP4 2r red | 4.00 | 4.00 |
| | Nos. Q1-Q5 (5) | 36.00 | 17.50 |

Type I

Type II

A 1909 undenominated dull olive green Official parcel post stamp exists with two types. Type I has thinner and more rays below the crest; Type II has fewer and wider rays. Values: $450 each. A pair, imperf between, exists.

Value, $1,500. A complete sheet of two is known perforated on all sides.

**1916-18**
| | | | |
|---|---|---|---|
| Q6 | PP1 3sh green | 1.75 | 3.50 |
| Q7 | PP2 1kr pale red | 3.00 | 1.50 |
| a. | 1kr rose red ('18) | 4.00 | 4.00 |
| Q8 | PP3 1r brown org | 3.50 | 1.75 |
| a. | 1r deep brown ('18) | 12.00 | 3.00 |
| Q9 | PP4 2r blue | 6.25 | 6.50 |
| | Nos. Q6-Q9 (4) | 14.50 | 13.25 |

Nos. Q1-Q9 sometimes show letters of the papermaker's watermark "HOWARD & JONES LONDON."
Ungummed stamps are remainders. They sell for one-third the price of mint stamps.

Old Habibia College, Near Kabul — PP5

**1921**            Wove Paper
| | | | |
|---|---|---|---|
| Q10 | PP5 10pa chocolate | 5.00 | 5.75 |
| a. | Tete beche pair | 22.50 | 22.50 |
| Q11 | PP5 15pa light brn | 7.00 | 7.50 |
| a. | Tete beche pair | 27.50 | 27.50 |
| Q12 | PP5 30pa red violet | 12.50 | 7.50 |
| a. | Tete beche pair | 40.00 | 40.00 |
| b. | Laid paper | 15.00 | 15.00 |
| Q13 | PP5 1r brt blue | 14.00 | 14.00 |
| a. | Tete beche pair | 65.00 | 65.00 |
| | Nos. Q10-Q13 (4) | 38.50 | 34.75 |

Stamps of this issue are usually perforated on one or two sides only.
The laid paper of No. Q12b has a papermaker's watermark in the sheet.

**Handstamped in black on Nos. Q10-Q13**

PP5a

**1923, Feb. 26**
| | | |
|---|---|---|
| Q13B | PP5a 10pa chocolate | — — |
| Q13C | PP5a 15pa light brn | — — |
| Q13D | PP5a 30pa red violet | — — |
| Q13E | PP5a 1r brt blue | — — |

5th Independence Day.
Two types of handstamp exist.
Forgeries exist.
The existence of No. Q13E has been questioned. The editors are seeking information on this stamp.

PP6

**1924-26**            Wove Paper
| | | | |
|---|---|---|---|
| Q15 | PP6 5kr ultra ('26) | 400.00 | 400.00 |
| Q16 | PP6 5r lilac | 20.00 | 25.00 |

PP7

A 15r rose exists, but is not known to have been placed in use. Value, unused $400.

PP8

**1928-29**    Perf. 11, 11 Horizontally
| | | | |
|---|---|---|---|
| Q17 | PP7 2r yellow orange | 8.00 | 7.00 |
| Q18 | PP7 2r green ('29) | 7.50 | 7.50 |
| Q19 | PP8 3r deep green | 10.50 | 10.50 |
| Q20 | PP8 3r brown ('29) | 9.50 | 9.50 |
| | Nos. Q17-Q20 (4) | 35.50 | 35.50 |

A 3r violet imperforate stamp in design No. PP8 exists and is likely a proof. Value, $250.

## POSTAL TAX STAMPS

Aliabad Hospital near Kabul — PT1

Pierre and Marie Curie — PT2

          Perf. 12x11½, 12
**1938, Dec. 22**    Typo.    Unwmk.
| | | | |
|---|---|---|---|
| RA1 | PT1 10p peacock grn | 3.25 | 5.00 |
| RA2 | PT2 15p dull blue | 3.25 | 5.00 |

Obligatory on all mail Dec. 22-28, 1938. The money was used for the Aliabad Hospital. See note with CD80.

**Catalogue values for unused stamps in this section, from this point to the end of the section, are for Never Hinged items.**

PT3          Begging Child — PT4

**1949, May 28**    Typo.    Perf. 12
| | | | |
|---|---|---|---|
| RA3 | PT3 35p red orange | 3.25 | 2.10 |
| RA4 | PT4 125p ultra | 4.00 | 2.10 |

United Nations Children's Day, May 28.
Obligatory on all foreign mail on that date. Proceeds were used for child welfare.

Paghman Arch and UN Emblem — PT5

**1949, Oct. 24**
| | | | |
|---|---|---|---|
| RA5 | PT5 125p dk blue green | 15.00 | 9.00 |

4th anniv. of the UN. Valid one day only. Issued in sheets of 9 (3x3).

Zahir Shah and Map of Afghanistan PT6

**1950, Mar. 30**            Typo.
| | | | |
|---|---|---|---|
| RA6 | PT6 125p blue green | 4.50 | 1.50 |

Return of Zahir Shah from a trip to Europe for his health. Valid for two weeks. The tax was used for public health purposes.

Hazara Youth — PT7

**1950, May 28**    Typo.    Perf. 11½
| | | | |
|---|---|---|---|
| RA7 | PT7 125p dk blue green | 4.50 | 1.50 |

Tax for Child Welfare. Obligatory and valid only on May 28, 1950, on foreign mail.

Ruins of Qalai Bist and Globe PT8

**1950, Oct. 24**
| | | | |
|---|---|---|---|
| RA8 | PT8 1.25af ultramarine | 9.00 | 5.25 |

5th anniv. of the UN. Proceeds went to Afghanistan's UN Projects Committee.

Zahir Shah and Medical Center — PT9

**1950, Dec. 22**    Typo.    Perf. 11½
           Size: 38x25mm
| | | | |
|---|---|---|---|
| RA9 | PT9 35p carmine | 1.25 | .60 |

           Size: 46x30mm
| | | | |
|---|---|---|---|
| RA10 | PT9 1.25af black | 7.50 | 2.50 |

The tax was for the national Graduate School of Medicine.

Koochi Girl with Lamb — PT10

346 AFGHANISTAN — AGÜERA, LA — AITUTAKI

Kohistani Boy and Sheep — PT11

**1951, May 28**
| RA11 | PT10 | 35p emerald | 1.50 | .90 |
| RA12 | PT11 | 1.25af ultramarine | 1.50 | .90 |

The tax was for Child Welfare.

Distributing Gifts to Children PT12

Qandahari Boys Dancing the "Attan" PT13

**1952, May 28     Litho.**
| RA13 | PT12 | 35p chocolate | .80 | .65 |
| RA14 | PT13 | 125p violet | 1.60 | .95 |

The tax was for Child Welfare.
Exist imperf. Values, set: unused $6; used $9.50.

Soldier Receiving First Aid — PT14

**1952, Oct. 19**
| RA15 | PT14 | 10p light green | .80 | .65 |

Exist imperf. Value: unused $2.50; used $4.

Stretcher-bearers and Wounded — PT15

Soldier Assisting Wounded PT16

**1953, Oct.**
| RA16 | PT15 | 10p yel grn & org red | .80 | .80 |
| RA17 | PT16 | 10p vio brn & org red | .80 | .80 |

Exist imperf. Values, set: unused $4; used $5.

Prince Mohammed Nadir — PT17

**1953, May 28**
| RA18 | PT17 | 35p orange yellow | .50 | .25 |
| RA19 | PT17 | 125p chalky blue | .90 | .55 |

No. RA19 is inscribed in French "Children's Day." The tax was for child welfare.
Exist imperf. Values, set: unused $4; used $5.

Map and Young Musicians PT18

**1954, May 28     Unwmk.     Perf. 11**
| RA20 | PT18 | 35p purple | .65 | .40 |
| RA21 | PT18 | 125p ultra | 1.90 | 1.25 |

No. RA21 is inscribed in French. The tax was for child welfare.
Exist imperf. Values, set: unused $4.50; used $6.50.

PT19

**1954, Oct. 17     Perf. 11½**
| RA22 | PT19 | 20p blue & red | .75 | .35 |

Exists imperf. Values: unused $2; used $2.50.

Red Crescent — PT20

**1955, Oct. 18     Perf. 11**
| RA23 | PT20 | 20p dull grn & car | .70 | .35 |

Exists imperf. Values: unused $1.50; used $2.

Zahir Shah and Red Crescent — PT21

**1956, Oct. 18**
| RA24 | PT21 | 20p lt grn & rose car | .40 | .25 |

Exists imperf. Value, unused or used, $1.25.

Red Crescent Headquarters, Kabul — PT22

**1957, Oct. 17**
| RA25 | PT22 | 20p lt ultra & car | .90 | .60 |

Exists imperf. Values: unused $2; used $2.50.

Map and Crescent — PT23

**1958, Oct.     Unwmk.     Perf. 11**
| RA26 | PT23 | 25p yel grn & red | .40 | .30 |

Exists imperf. Values: unused 50¢; used 80¢.

PT24

**1959, Oct. 17     Litho.     Perf. 11**
| RA27 | PT24 | 25p lt violet & red | .40 | .25 |

The tax on Nos. RA15-RA17, RA22-RA27 was for the Red Crescent Society. Use of these stamps was required for one week.
Exists imperf. Values: unused 50¢; used 80¢.

## AGÜERA, LA
ä-gwä'rä

**LOCATION** — An administrative district in southern Rio de Oro on the northwest coast of Africa.
**GOVT.** — Spanish possession
**AREA** — Because of indefinite political boundaries, figures for area and population are not available.

100 Centimos = 1 Peseta

Type of 1920 Issue of Rio de Oro Overprinted

**1920, June     Typo.     Unwmk.     Perf. 13**
| 1 | A8 | 1c blue green | 2.75 | 3.25 |
| 2 | A8 | 2c olive brown | 2.75 | 3.25 |
| 3 | A8 | 5c deep green | 2.75 | 3.25 |
| 4 | A8 | 10c light red | 2.75 | 3.25 |
| 5 | A8 | 15c yellow | 2.75 | 3.25 |
| 6 | A8 | 20c lilac | 2.75 | 3.25 |
| 7 | A8 | 25c deep blue | 2.75 | 3.25 |
| 8 | A8 | 30c dark brown | 2.75 | 3.25 |
| 9 | A8 | 40c pink | 2.75 | 3.25 |
| 10 | A8 | 50c bright blue | 9.00 | 10.00 |
| 11 | A8 | 1p red brown | 15.00 | 20.00 |
| 12 | A8 | 4p dark violet | 42.50 | 50.00 |
| 13 | A8 | 10p orange | 90.00 | 115.00 |
| | Nos. 1-13 (13) | | 181.25 | 224.25 |
| | Set, never hinged | | 400.00 | |

Very fine examples of Nos. 1-13 will be somewhat off center. Well-centered examples are uncommon and will sell for more.

King Alfonso XIII — A2

**1922, June**
| 14 | A2 | 1c turquoise bl (I) | 1.00 | 1.50 |
| 15 | A2 | 2c dark green | 1.50 | 1.50 |
| 16 | A2 | 5c blue green | 1.50 | 1.50 |
| 17 | A2 | 10c red | 1.50 | 1.50 |
| 18 | A2 | 15c red brown | 1.50 | 1.50 |
| 19 | A2 | 20c yellow | 1.50 | 1.50 |
| 20 | A2 | 25c deep blue | 1.50 | 1.50 |
| 21 | A2 | 30c dark brown | 1.50 | 1.50 |
| 22 | A2 | 40c rose red | 1.75 | 2.00 |
| 23 | A2 | 50c red violet | 6.25 | 5.75 |
| 24 | A2 | 1p rose | 14.50 | 15.00 |
| 25 | A2 | 4p violet | 37.50 | 40.00 |
| 26 | A2 | 10p orange | 55.00 | 60.00 |
| | Nos. 14-26 (13) | | 126.50 | 134.75 |
| | Set, never hinged | | 200.00 | |

Nos. 1-26 with A.000.000 on reverse are specimens. For detailed listings, see the Scott Classic Specialized catalog.
For later issues, see Spanish Sahara.

## AITUTAKI
īt-ə-'täk-ē

**LOCATION** — One of the larger Cook Islands, in the South Pacific Ocean northeast of New Zealand
**GOVT.** — A dependency of New Zealand
**AREA** — 7 sq. mi.
**POP.** — 2,335 (1981)

The Cook Islands were attached to New Zealand in 1901. Stamps of Cook Islands were used in 1892-1903 and 1932-72.
Aitutaki acquired its own postal service in August 1972, though remaining part of Cook Islands.

12 Pence = 1 Shilling
100 Cents = 1 Dollar (1972)

**Catalogue values for unused stamps in this country are for Never Hinged items, beginning with Scott 37.**

## Watermark

Wmk. 61- Single-lined NZ and Star Close Together

**Stamps of New Zealand Surcharged in Red or Blue**

a     b

**1903     Engr.     Wmk. 61     Perf. 14**
| 1 | A18(a) | ½p green (R) | 5.00 | 7.00 |
| 2 | A35(b) | 1p rose (Bl) | 5.50 | 6.25 |

c     d

e     f

**Perf. 11**
| 3 | A22(c) | 2½p blue (R) | 20.00 | 14.00 |
| 4 | A23(d) | 3p yel brn (Bl) | 18.00 | 18.00 |
| 5 | A26(e) | 6p red (Bl) | 32.50 | 26.00 |
| 6 | A29(f) | 1sh scar (Bl) | 55.00 | 90.00 |
| a. | | 1sh orange red (Bl) | 72.50 | 110.00 |

**1911, Sept.     Typo.     Perf. 14x15**
| 7 | A41(a) | ½p yel grn (R) | 1.25 | 9.00 |

**Engr.     Perf. 14**
| 9 | A22(c) | 2½p dp blue (R) | 8.25 | 19.00 |

g     h

**1913-16     Typo.**
| 10 | A42(b) | 1p rose (Bl) | 3.25 | 14.00 |

**Engr.**
| 12 | A41(g) | 6p car rose (Bl) ('16) | 55.00 | 140.00 |
| 13 | A41(h) | 1sh ver (Bl) ('14) | 62.50 | 160.00 |

**1916-17     Perf. 14x13½, 14x14½**
| 17 | A45(g) | 6p car rose (Bl) | 2.00 | 18.00 |
| 18 | A45(h) | 1sh ver (Bl) ('17) | 15.00 | 100.00 |
| | Nos. 1-18 (13) | | 283.25 | 621.25 |

**New Zealand Stamps of 1909-19 Overprinted in Red or Dark Blue**

**1917-20     Typo.     Perf. 14x15**
| 19 | A43 | ½p yellow grn ('20) | 1.00 | 6.50 |
| 20 | A42 | 1p car (Bl) ('20) | 6.50 | 37.50 |
| 21 | A47 | 1½p gray black | 5.00 | 35.00 |
| 22 | A47 | 1½p brown org ('19) | .90 | 7.50 |
| 23 | A43 | 3p choc (Bl) ('19) | 4.00 | 22.50 |

**Perf. 14x13½, 14x14½     Engr.**
| 24 | A44 | 2½p dull blue ('18) | 1.75 | 18.00 |
| 25 | A45 | 3p vio brn (Bl) ('18) | 1.00 | 32.50 |
| 26 | A45 | 6p car rose (Bl) | 5.00 | 25.00 |
| 27 | A45 | 1sh vermilion (Bl) | 10.00 | 35.00 |
| | Nos. 19-27 (9) | | 35.15 | 219.50 |

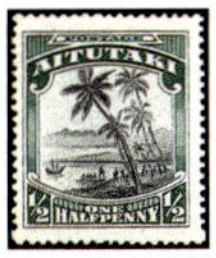

Landing of Capt. Cook A15

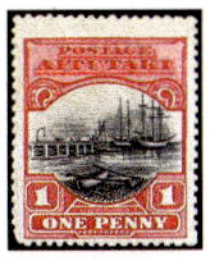

Avarua Waterfront A16

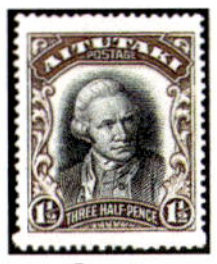

Capt. James Cook A17

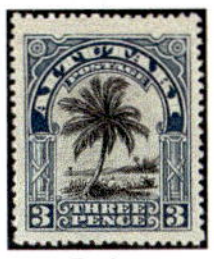

Palm A18

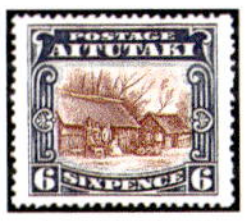

Houses at Arorangi A19

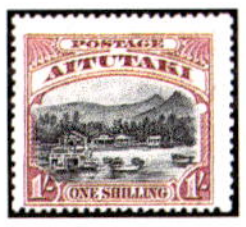

Avarua Harbor A20

**1920 Engr. Unwmk. *Perf. 14***

| | | | | |
|---|---|---|---|---|
| **28** | A15 | ½p green & black | 3.50 | *26.00* |
| **29** | A16 | 1p car & blk | 3.50 | 18.00 |
| **30** | A17 | 1½p brown & blk | 7.00 | *14.00* |
| **31** | A18 | 3p dp blue & blk | 2.75 | *16.00* |
| **32** | A19 | 6p slate & red brn | 6.25 | *16.00* |
| **33** | A20 | 1sh claret & blk | 10.00 | *16.00* |
| | | *Nos. 28-33 (6)* | 33.00 | *106.00* |

Inverted centers, double frames, etc. are from printers waste.

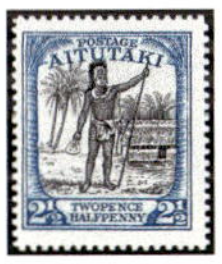

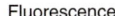

Rarotongan Chief (Te Po) — A21

**1924-27 Wmk. 61 *Perf. 14***

| | | | | |
|---|---|---|---|---|
| **34** | A15 | ½p green & blk ('27) | 3.00 | *25.00* |
| **35** | A16 | 1p carmine & blk | 7.00 | *14.00* |
| **36** | A21 | 2½p blue & blk ('27) | 10.00 | *85.00* |
| | | *Nos. 34-36 (3)* | 20.00 | *124.00* |

**Catalogue values for unused stamps in this section, from this point to the end of the section, are for Never Hinged items.**

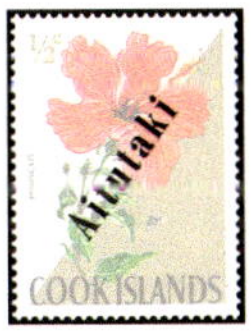

Cook Islands Nos. 199-200, 202, 205-208, 210, 212-213, 215-217 Ovptd.

**1972 Photo. Unwmk. *Perf. 14x13½***

| | | | | |
|---|---|---|---|---|
| **37** | A34 | ½c gold & multi | .40 | *.90* |
| **38** | A34 | 1c gold & multi | .85 | *1.25* |
| **39** | A34 | 2½c gold & multi | 2.50 | *7.50* |
| **40** | A34 | 4c gold & multi | .85 | *1.00* |
| **41** | A34 | 5c gold & multi | 3.00 | *8.50* |
| **42** | A34 | 10c gold & multi | 3.00 | *6.25* |
| **43** | A34 | 20c gold & multi | 3.75 | *1.10* |
| **44** | A34 | 25c gold & multi | .90 | *1.25* |
| **45** | A34 | 50c gold & multi | 2.75 | *3.25* |
| **46** | A35 | $1 gold & multi | 4.50 | *6.00* |
| **47** | A35 | $2 gold & multi | 1.00 | *1.10* |
| | | *Nos. 37-47 (11)* | 23.50 | *38.10* |

Overprint horizontal on Nos. 46-47. On $2, overprint is in capitals of different font; size: 21x3mm.

Issued: Nos. 37-46, Aug. 9; No. 47, Nov. 24.

### Same Overprint Horizontal in Silver On Cook Islands Nos. 330-332

**1972, Oct. 27 *Perf. 13½***

| | | | | |
|---|---|---|---|---|
| **48** | A53 | 1c gold & multi | .25 | .25 |
| **49** | A53 | 5c gold & multi | .25 | .25 |
| **50** | A53 | 10c gold & multi | .30 | .30 |
| | | *Nos. 48-50 (3)* | .80 | .80 |

Fluorescence

Starting in 1972, stamps carry a "fluorescent security underprinting" in a multiple pattern of New Zealand's coat of arms with "Aitutaki" above, "Cook Islands" below and two stars at each side.

### Silver Wedding Type of Cook Islands

**1972, Nov. 20 Photo. *Perf. 13½***

**Size: 29x40mm**

| | | | | |
|---|---|---|---|---|
| **51** | A54 | 5c silver & multi | 3.25 | 2.50 |

**Size: 66x40mm**

| | | | | |
|---|---|---|---|---|
| **52** | A54 | 15c silver & multi | 1.25 | 1.25 |

25th anniversary of the marriage of Queen Elizabeth II and Prince Philip. Nos. 51-52 printed in sheets of 5 stamps and one label.

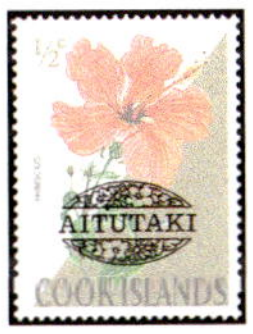

Flower Issue of Cook Islands Overprinted

**1972, Dec. 11 Photo. *Perf. 14x13½***

| | | | | |
|---|---|---|---|---|
| **53** | A34 | ½c on #199 | .25 | .25 |
| **54** | A34 | 1c on #200 | .25 | .25 |
| **55** | A34 | 2½c on #202 | .25 | .25 |
| **56** | A34 | 4c on #205 | .30 | .25 |
| **57** | A34 | 5c on #206 | .30 | .25 |
| **58** | A34 | 10c on #210 | .40 | .35 |
| **59** | A34 | 20c on #212 | 1.25 | .45 |
| **60** | A34 | 25c on #213 | .55 | *.60* |
| **61** | A34 | 50c on #215 | .85 | *.90* |
| **62** | A35 | $1 on #216 | 1.25 | *1.75* |
| | | *Nos. 53-62 (10)* | 5.65 | *5.30* |

See Nos. 73-76.

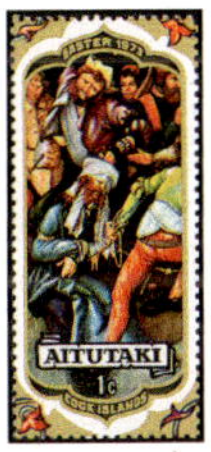

The Passion of Christ, by Mathias Grunewald — A22

Paintings: No. 63b, St. Veronica, by Rogier van der Weyden. No. 63c, Crucifixion, by Raphael. No. 63d, Resurrection, by della Francesca. No. 64a, Last Supper, by Master of Amiens. No. 64b, Condemnation of Christ, by Hans Holbein, the Elder. No. 64c, Crucifixion, by Rubens. No. 64d, Resurrection, by El Greco. No. 65a, Passion of Christ, by El Greco. No. 65b, St. Veronica, by Jakob Cornelisz. No. 65c, Crucifixion, by Rubens. No. 65d, Resurrection, by Dierik Bouts.

***Perf. 13½***

**1973, Apr. 6 Photo. Unwmk.**

| | | | | |
|---|---|---|---|---|
| **63** | | Block of 4 | 1.00 | .40 |
| *a.-d.* | | A22 1c any single | .25 | .25 |
| **64** | | Block of 4 | 1.25 | 1.00 |
| *a.-d.* | | A22 5c any single | .30 | .25 |
| **65** | | Block of 4 | 1.40 | *1.75* |
| *a.-d.* | | A22 10c any single | .35 | .25 |
| | | *Nos. 63-65 (3)* | 3.65 | 3.15 |

Easter. Printed in blocks of 4 in sheets of 40. Design descriptions in top and bottom margins.

### Coin Type of Cook Islands

Queen Elizabeth II Coins: 1c, Taro leaf. 2c, Pineapples. 5c, Hibiscus. 10c, Oranges. 20c, Fairy terns. 50c, Bonito. $1, Tangaroa, Polynesian god of creation, vert.

**1973, May 14 *Perf. 13x13½***

**Size: 37x24mm**

| | | | | |
|---|---|---|---|---|
| **66** | A55 | 1c dp car & multi | .25 | .25 |
| **67** | A55 | 2c blue & multi | .25 | .25 |
| **68** | A55 | 5c green & multi | .25 | .25 |

**Size: 46x30mm**

| | | | | |
|---|---|---|---|---|
| **69** | A55 | 10c vio blue & multi | .25 | .25 |
| **70** | A55 | 20c green & multi | .30 | .30 |
| **71** | A55 | 50c dp car & multi | .60 | .40 |

**Size: 32x54½mm**

| | | | | |
|---|---|---|---|---|
| **72** | A55 | $1 blue, blk & sil | .80 | .50 |
| | | *Nos. 66-72 (7)* | 2.70 | 2.20 |

Cook Islands coinage commemorating silver wedding anniv. of Queen Elizabeth II.

Printed in sheets of 20 stamps and label showing Westminster Abbey.

### Cook Islands Nos. 208, 210, 212 and 215 Overprinted Like Nos. 53-62 and: "TENTH ANNIVERSARY/ CESSATION/ OF/ NUCLEAR TESTING/ TREATY"

**1973, July Photo. *Perf. 14x13½***

| | | | | |
|---|---|---|---|---|
| **73** | A34 | 8c gold & multi | .25 | .25 |
| **74** | A34 | 10c gold & multi | .25 | .25 |
| **75** | A34 | 20c gold & multi | .35 | .35 |
| **76** | A34 | 50c gold & multi | .75 | .75 |
| | | *Nos. 73-76 (4)* | 1.60 | 1.60 |

Nuclear Test Ban Treaty, 10th anniv., protest against French nuclear testing on Mururoa Atoll.

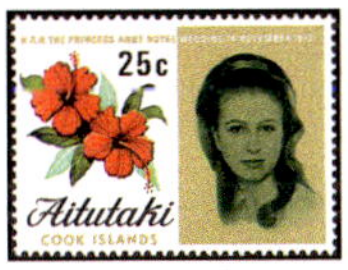

Princess Anne, Hibiscus — A23

Design: 30c, Mark Phillips and hibiscus.

**1973, Nov. 14 Photo. *Perf. 13½x14***

| | | | | |
|---|---|---|---|---|
| **77** | A23 | 25c gold & multi | .25 | .25 |
| **78** | A23 | 30c gold & multi | .30 | .30 |
| *a.* | | Souvenir sheet of 2, #77-78 | .65 | .65 |

Wedding of Princess Anne and Capt. Mark Phillips.

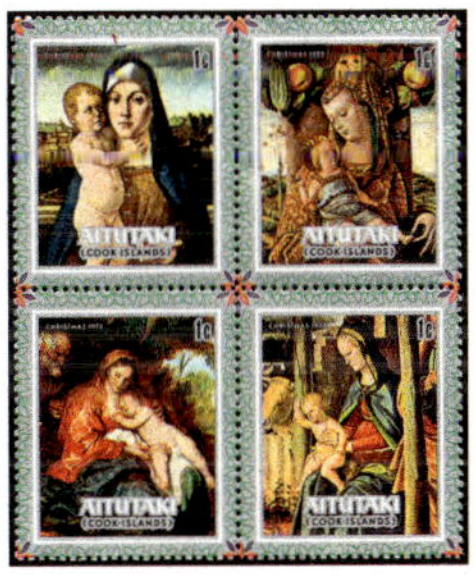

Virgin and Child, by Il Perugino A24

Paintings of the Virgin and Child by various masters — No. 79: a, Van Dyck. b, Bartolommeo Montagna. c, Carlo Crivelli. d, Il Perugino. No. 80: a, Cima da Conegliano. b, Memling. c, Veronese. d, Veronese. No. 81: a, Raphael. b, Lorenzo Lotto. c, Del Colle. d, Memling.

**1973, Dec. Photo. *Perf. 13***

| | | | | |
|---|---|---|---|---|
| **79** | A24 | 1c Block of 4, #a.-d. | .50 | .50 |
| **80** | A24 | 5c Block of 4, #a.-d. | 1.00 | 1.00 |
| **81** | A24 | 10c Block of 4, #a.-d. | 1.25 | 1.25 |
| | | *Nos. 79-81 (3)* | 2.75 | 2.75 |

Christmas. Printed in blocks of 4 in sheets of 48. Design descriptions in margins.

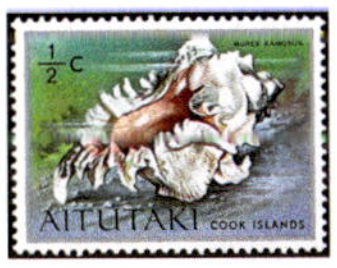

Murex Ramosus — A25

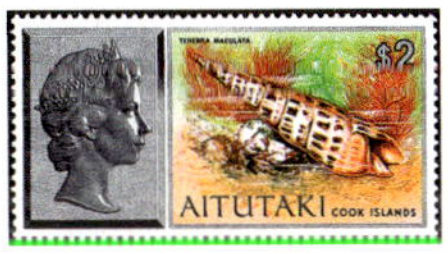

Terebra Maculata A26

Pacific Shells: 1c, Nautilus macromphalus. 2c, Harpa major. 3c, Phalium strigatum. 4c, Cypraea talpa. 5c, Mitra stictica. 8c, Charonia tritonis. 10c, Murex triremis. 20c, Oliva sericea. 25c, Tritonalia rubeta. 60c, Strombus latissimus. $1, Biplex perca. $5, Cypraea hesitata.

**1974-75 Photo. *Perf. 13***

| | | | | |
|---|---|---|---|---|
| **82** | A25 | ½c silver & multi | .95 | .95 |
| **83** | A25 | 1c silver & multi | .95 | .95 |
| **84** | A25 | 2c silver & multi | .95 | .95 |
| **85** | A25 | 3c silver & multi | .95 | .95 |
| **86** | A25 | 4c silver & multi | .95 | .95 |
| **87** | A25 | 5c silver & multi | .95 | .95 |
| **88** | A25 | 8c silver & multi | .95 | .95 |
| **89** | A25 | 10c silver & multi | .95 | .85 |
| **90** | A25 | 20c silver & multi | 1.25 | .85 |
| **91** | A25 | 25c silver & multi | 1.25 | .85 |
| **92** | A25 | 60c silver & multi | 3.75 | 1.10 |
| **93** | A25 | $1 silver & multi | 2.50 | 1.25 |

***Perf. 14***

| | | | | |
|---|---|---|---|---|
| **94** | A26 | $2 silver & multi | 6.00 | 6.00 |
| **95** | A26 | $5 silver & multi | 27.50 | 9.50 |
| | | *Nos. 82-95 (14)* | 49.85 | 27.05 |

Issued: Nos. 82-93, 1/31/74; $2, 1/20/75; $5, 2/28/75.

For overprints see Nos. O1-O16.

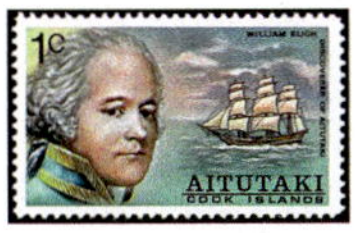

William Bligh and "Bounty" — A27

No. 96, shown. No. 97, "Bounty" at sea. No. 98, Bligh and "Bounty" off Aitutaki. No. 99, Chart of Aitutaki, 1856. No. 100, James Cook and "Resolution". No. 101, Maps of Aitutaki and Pacific Ocean.

**Size: 38x22mm**

**1974, Apr. 11 Photo. *Perf. 13***

| | | | | |
|---|---|---|---|---|
| **96** | A27 | 1c multicolored | .45 | .45 |
| **97** | A27 | 1c multicolored | .45 | .45 |
| *a.* | | Pair, #96-97 | 1.00 | 1.00 |
| **98** | A27 | 5c multicolored | 1.00 | 1.00 |
| **99** | A27 | 5c multicolored | 1.00 | 1.00 |
| *a.* | | Pair, #98-99 | 2.25 | 2.25 |
| **100** | A27 | 8c multicolored | 1.25 | 1.25 |
| **101** | A27 | 8c multicolored | 1.25 | 1.25 |
| *a.* | | Pair, #100-101 | 2.75 | 2.75 |
| | | *Nos. 96-101,C1-C6 (12)* | 10.60 | 10.10 |

Capt. William Bligh (1754-1817), European discoverer of Aitutaki, Apr. 11, 1789.

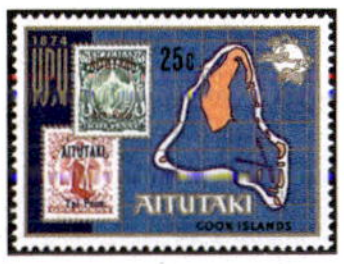

Aitutaki Nos. 1 & 2 Map and UPU Emblem — A28

Design: 50c, Aitutaki Nos. 4 and 28, map of Aitutaki and UPU emblem.

**1974, July 15 Photo. *Perf. 13½***

| | | | | |
|---|---|---|---|---|
| **102** | A28 | 25c blue & multi | .75 | .75 |
| **103** | A28 | 50c blue & multi | 1.00 | 1.00 |
| *a.* | | Souvenir sheet of 2, #102-103 | 2.00 | 2.00 |

UPU, cent. Printed in sheets of 5 plus label showing UPU emblem.

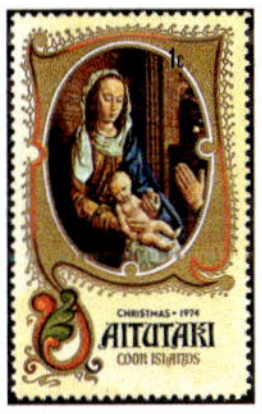

A29

Designs: Paintings of the Virgin and Child by: 1c, Van der Goes. 5c, Giovanni Bellini. 8c, Gerard David. 10c, Antonello da Messina. 25c, Joos van Cleve. 30c, Maitre de St. Catherine.

**1974, Oct. 11 Photo. *Perf. 13½***

| | | | | |
|---|---|---|---|---|
| **104** | A29 | 1c multicolored | .25 | .25 |
| **105** | A29 | 5c multicolored | .25 | .25 |
| **106** | A29 | 8c multicolored | .25 | .25 |
| **107** | A29 | 10c multicolored | .25 | .25 |
| **108** | A29 | 25c multicolored | .35 | .35 |
| **109** | A29 | 30c multicolored | .75 | .75 |
| *a.* | | Souvenir sheet of 6, #104-109 | 2.00 | 2.00 |
| | | *Nos. 104-109 (6)* | 2.10 | 2.10 |

Christmas. Nos. 104-109 printed in sheets of 15 stamps and corner label. See Nos. B1-B6.

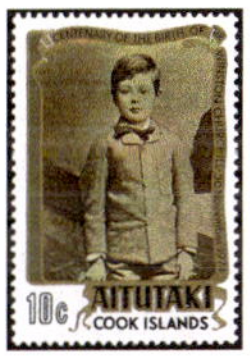

A30

Designs: Churchill portraits — 10c, Dublin, Age 5. 25c, As young man. 30c, Inspecting troops, WWII. 50c, Painting. $1, Giving V sign.

**1974, Nov. 29 Photo. *Perf. 14***

| | | | | |
|---|---|---|---|---|
| **110** | A30 | 10c multicolored | .25 | .25 |
| **111** | A30 | 25c multicolored | .25 | .25 |
| **112** | A30 | 30c multicolored | .30 | .25 |
| **113** | A30 | 50c multicolored | .50 | .50 |

**114** A30 $1 multicolored .85 .85
*a.* Souvenir sheet of 5, #110-114 + label, perf. 13½ 4.50 4.50
*Nos. 110-114 (5)* 2.15 2.10

Sir Winston Churchill (1874-1965). Nos. 110-114 printed in sheets of 5 stamps and corner label.

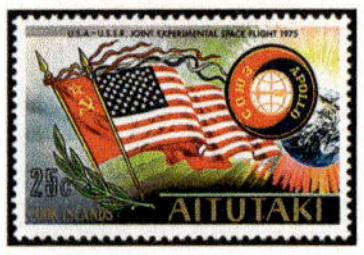

Emblem US & USSR Flags — A31

50c, Icarus and Apollo Soyuz spacecraft.

**1975, July 24 Photo.** ***Perf. 13x14½***

**115** A31 25c multicolored .30 .30
**116** A31 50c multicolored .65 .65
*a.* Souvenir sheet of 2 1.40 1.40

Apollo Soyuz space test project (Russo-American cooperation), launching July 15; link-up July 17. Nos. 115 and 116 each printed in sheets of 5 stamps and one label showing area of Apollo splash-downs. No. 116a contains one each of Nos. 115-116 with gold and black border and inscription.

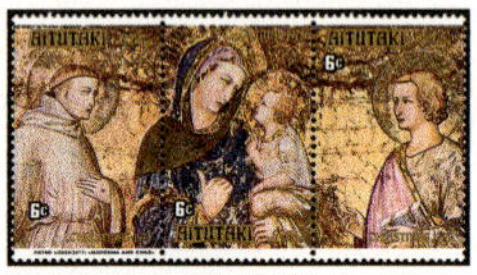

Madonna and Child, by Pietro Lorenzetti — A32

Paintings: 7c, Adoration of the Kings, by Rogier van der Weyden. 15c, Madonna and Child, by Bartolommeo Montagna. 20c, Adoration of the Shepherds.

**1975, Nov. 24 Photo.** ***Perf. 14x13½***

**117** A32 Strip of 3 .35 .35
*a.* 6c St. Francis .25 .25
*b.* 6c Madonna and Child .25 .25
*c.* 6c St. John the Evangelist .25 .25
**118** A32 Strip of 3 .40 .40
*a.* 7c One King .25 .25
*b.* 7c Madonna and Child .25 .25
*c.* 7c Two Kings .25 .25
**119** A32 Strip of 3 .75 .75
*a.* 15c St. Joseph .25 .25
*b.* 15c Madonna and Child .25 .25
*c.* 15c St. John the Baptist .25 .25
**120** A32 Strip of 3 1.10 1.10
*a.* 20c One Shepherd .25 .25
*b.* 20c Madonna and Child .25 .25
*c.* 20c Two Shepherds .25 .25
*d.* Souv. sheet of 12, #117-120, perf. 13½ 2.75 2.75
*Nos. 117-120 (4)* 2.60 2.60

Christmas. Nos. 117-120 printed in sheets of 30 (10 strips of 3).

For surcharges see Nos. B7-B10.

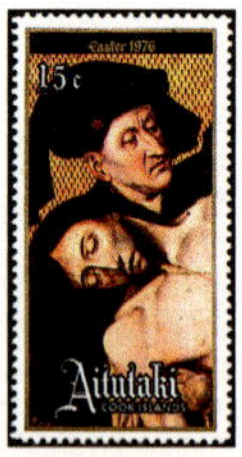

Descent from the Cross, detail — A33

Designs (Painting, Flemish School, 16th Century): 30c, Virgin Mary, disciple and body of Jesus. 35c, Mary Magdalene and disciple.

**1976, Apr. 5 Photo.** ***Perf. 13½***

**121** A33 15c gold & multi .25 .25
**122** A33 30c gold & multi .30 .30
**123** A33 35c gold & multi .45 .45
*a.* Souvenir sheet of 3 1.25 1.25
*Nos. 121-123 (3)* 1.00 1.00

Easter. No. 123a contains 3 stamps similar to Nos. 121-123, perf. 13, in continuous design without gold frames and white margins.

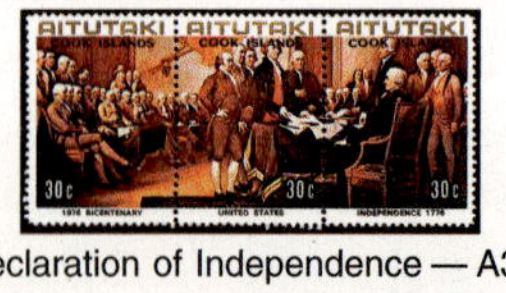

Declaration of Independence — A34

Paintings by John Trumbull: 35c, Surrender of Cornwallis at Yorktown. 50c, Washington's Farewell Address. a, "1976 BICENTENARY." b, "UNITED STATES." c, "INDEPENDENCE 1776."

**1976, June 1 Photo.** ***Perf. 13½***

**124** A34 Strip of 3 1.25 1.25
*a.-c.* 30c any single .30 .30
**125** A34 Strip of 3 1.50 1.50
*a.-c.* 35c any single .40 .40
**126** A34 Strip of 3 2.00 2.00
*a.-c.* 50c any single .55 .55
*d.* Souvenir sheet of 9 (3x3) 5.00 5.00
*Nos. 124-126 (3)* 4.75 4.75

American Bicentennial. Nos. 124-126 printed in sheets of 5 strips of 3 and 3-part corner label showing portrait of John Trumbull, commemorative inscription and portraits of Washington (30c), John Adams (35c) and Jefferson (50c). No. 126d contains 3 strips similar to Nos. 124-126.

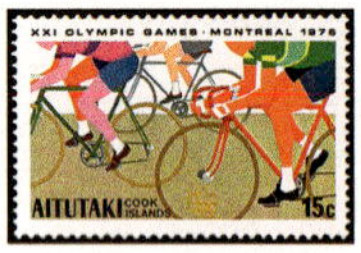

Bicycling — A35

Montreal Olympic Games Emblem and: 35c, Sailing. 60c, Field hockey. 70c, Running.

**1976, July 15 Photo.** ***Perf. 13x14***

**127** A35 15c multicolored .30 .25
**128** A35 35c multicolored .50 .45
**129** A35 60c multicolored .75 .70
**130** A35 70c multicolored 1.00 .90
*a.* Souvenir sheet of 4 3.00 3.00
*Nos. 127-130 (4)* 2.55 2.30

21st Olympic Games, Montreal, Canada, July 17-Aug. 1. Nos. 127-130 printed in sheets of 5 stamps and label showing coat of Arms and Montreal Olympic Games emblem. No. 130a contains 4 stamps similar to Nos. 127-130 with gold margin around each stamp.

**Nos. 127-130a Overprinted**

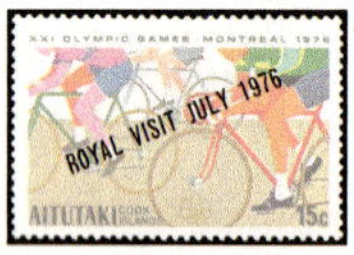


**1976, July 30**

**131** A35 15c multicolored .25 .25
**132** A35 35c multicolored .40 .40
**133** A35 60c multicolored .80 .80
**134** A35 70c multicolored .80 .80
*a.* Souvenir sheet of 4 2.50 2.50
*Nos. 131-134 (4)* 2.25 2.25

Visit of Queen Elizabeth II to Montreal and official opening of the Games. Each stamp of No. 134a has diagonal overprint. Sheet margin has additional overprint: "ROYAL VISIT OF H.M. QUEEN ELIZABETH II/OFFICIALLY OPENED 17 JULY 1976."

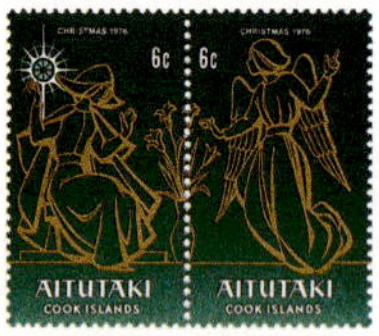

Annunciation A36

Designs: Nos. 137-138, Angel appearing to the shepherds. Nos. 139-140, Nativity. Nos. 141-142, Three Kings.

**1976, Oct. 18** ***Perf. 13½x13***

**135** 6c dk green & gold .25 .25
**136** 6c dk green & gold .25 .25
*a.* A36 Pair, #135-136 .25 .25
**137** 7c dk brown & gold .25 .25
**138** 7c dk brown & gold .25 .25
*a.* A36 Pair, #137-138 .25 .25
**139** 15c dk blue & gold .25 .25
**140** 15c dk blue & gold .25 .25
*a.* A36 Pair, #139-140 .30 .30
**141** 20c purple & gold .25 .25
**142** 20c purple & gold .25 .25
*a.* A36 Pair, #141-142 .40 .40
*b.* Souvenir sheet of 8 1.50 1.50
*Nos. 135-142 (8)* 2.00 2.00

Christmas. No. 142b contains 8 stamps similar to Nos. 135-142 with white margin around each pair of stamps.

For overprints see Nos. B11-B18.

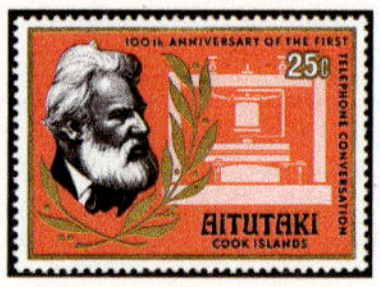

A. G. Bell and 1876 Telephone A38

Design: 70c, Satellite and radar.

**1977, Mar. 3 Photo.** ***Perf. 13½x13***

**143** A38 25c rose & multi .25 .25
**144** A38 70c violet & multi .40 .40
*a.* Souvenir sheet of 2 1.50 1.50

Centenary of first telephone call by Alexander Graham Bell, Mar. 10, 1876. No. 144a contains a 25c in colors of 70c and 70c in colors of 25c.

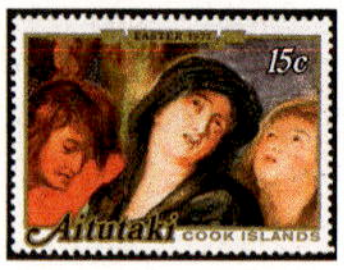

Calvary (detail), by Rubens — A39

Paintings by Rubens: 20c, Lamentation. 35c, Descent from the Cross.

**1977, Mar. 31 Photo.** ***Perf. 13½x14***

**145** A39 15c gold & multi .50 .50
**146** A39 20c gold & multi .65 .65
**147** A39 35c gold & multi .85 .85
*a.* Souv. sheet, #145-147, perf. 13 2.25 2.25
*Nos. 145-147 (3)* 2.00 2.00

Easter, and 400th birth anniv. of Peter Paul Rubens (1577-1640), Flemish painter.

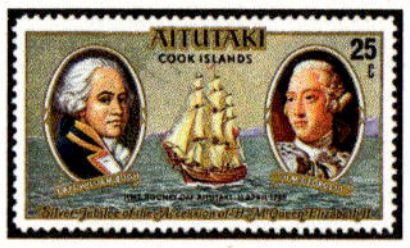

Capt. Bligh, "Bounty" and George III — A40

Designs: 35c, Rev. John Williams, George IV, First Christian Church. 50c, British flag, map of Aitutaki, Queen Victoria. $1, Elizabeth II and family on balcony after coronation.

**1977, Apr. 21** ***Perf. 13½***

**148** A40 25c gold & multi .25 .25
**149** A40 35c gold & multi .30 .30
**150** A40 50c gold & multi .50 .50
**151** A40 $1 gold & multi 1.25 1.25
*a.* Souvenir sheet of 4, #148-151 2.25 2.25
*Nos. 148-151 (4)* 2.30 2.30

Reign of Queen Elizabeth II, 25th anniv.

For overprint & surcharge see Nos. O11, O15.

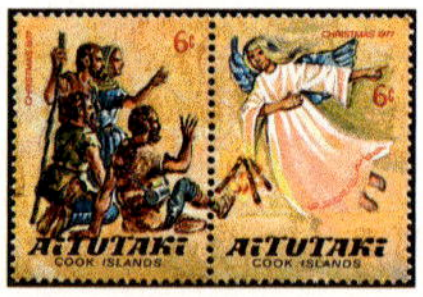

Annunciation A41

Designs: No. 154, Virgin, Child and ox. No. 155, Joseph and donkey (Nativity). No. 156, Three Kings. No. 157, Virgin and Child. No. 158, Joseph. No. 159, Virgin, Child and donkey (Flight into Egypt).

**1977, Oct. 14 Photo.** ***Perf. 13½x14***

**152** 6c multicolored .25 .25
**153** 6c multicolored .25 .25
*a.* A41 Pair, #152-153 .25 .25
**154** 7c multicolored .25 .25
**155** 7c multicolored .25 .25
*a.* A41 Pair, #154-155 .25 .25
**156** 15c multicolored .25 .25
**157** 15c multicolored .25 .25
*a.* A41 Pair, #156-157 .30 .30
**158** 20c multicolored .25 .25
**159** 20c multicolored .25 .25
*a.* A41 Pair, #158-159 .40 .40
*b.* Souvenir sheet of 8, #152-159 1.75 1.75
*Nos. 152-159 (8)* 2.00 2.00

Christmas.

For surcharges see Nos. B19-B26a.

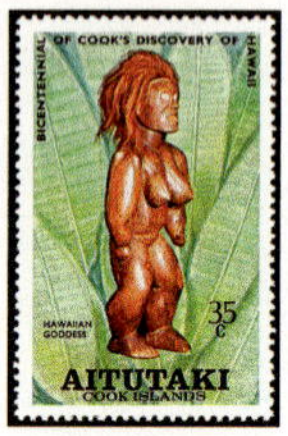

Hawaiian Wood Figurine — A43

Designs: 50c, Talbot hunting dog, figurehead of "Resolution", horiz. $1, Temple figure.

**1978, Jan. 19 Litho.** ***Perf. 13½***

**160** A43 35c multicolored .45 .45
**161** A43 50c multicolored .70 .70
**162** A43 $1 multicolored 1.00 1.00
*a.* Souvenir sheet of 3, #160-162 2.75 2.75
*Nos. 160-162 (3)* 2.15 2.15

Bicentenary of Capt. Cook's arrival in Hawaii. Nos. 160-162 issued in sheets of 6.

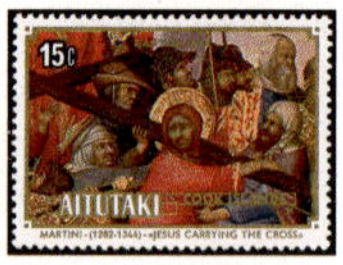

Jesus Carrying Cross, by Simone di Martini — A44

Paintings: 20c, Avignon Pietà, 15th Century. 35c, Christ at Emmaus, by Rembrandt.

**1978, Mar. 17 Photo.** ***Perf. 13½x14***

**163** A44 15c gold & multi .25 .25
**164** A44 20c gold & multi .25 .25
**165** A44 35c gold & multi .30 .30
*a.* Souvenir sheet of 3 1.00 1.00
*Nos. 163-165 (3)* .80 .80

Easter. No. 165a contains one each of Nos. 163-165, perf. 13½, and label showing Louvre, Paris. See Nos. B27-B29.

**Souvenir Sheet**

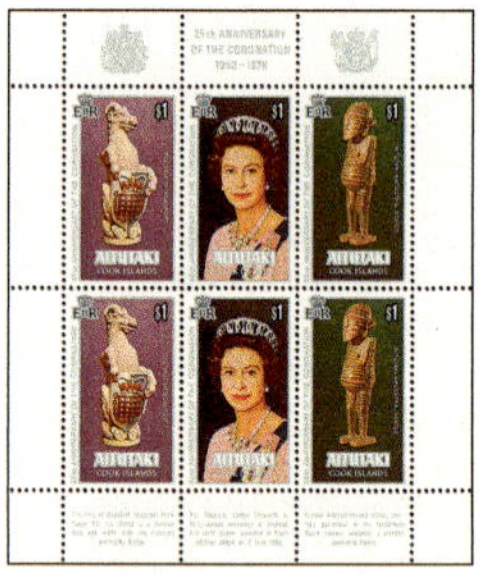

25th Anniv. of Coronation of Queen Elizabeth II. — A45

**1978, June 15 Photo.** ***Perf. 13½x13***

**166** A45 Sheet of 6 2.50 2.50
*a.* $1 Yale of Beaufort .35 .35
*b.* $1 Elizabeth II .35 .35
*c.* $1 Ancestral statue .35 .35
*d.* Souvenir sheet of 6 2.25 2.25

No. 166d contains 2 strips of Nos. 166a-166c separated by horizontal slate green gutter showing Royal family on balcony, silver marginal inscription.

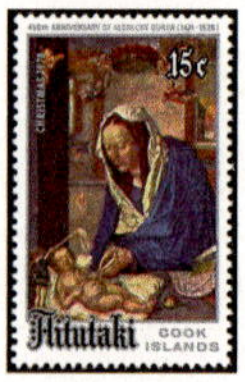

Virgin and Child, by Dürer — A46

Designs: Various paintings of the Virgin and Child by Albrecht Dürer.

**1978, Dec. 4 Photo.** ***Perf. 14½x13***

**167** A46 15c multicolored .35 .35
**168** A46 17c multicolored .40 .40
**169** A46 30c multicolored .55 .55
**170** A46 35c multicolored .65 .65
*Nos. 167-170 (4)* 1.95 1.95

Christmas; 450th death anniv. of Albrecht Dürer (1471-1528), German painter. Nos. 167-170 issued in sheets of 5 stamps and corner label. See No. B30.

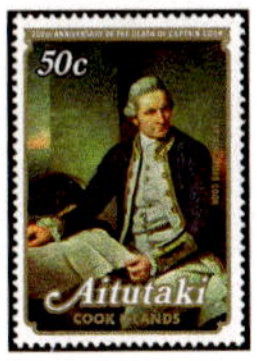

Capt. Cook, by Nathaniel Dance — A47

Design: 75c, "Resolution" and "Adventure," by William Hodges.

**1979, July 20 Photo. *Perf. 14x13½***

| | | |
|---|---|---|
| **171** A47 50c multicolored | 1.50 | 1.00 |
| **172** A47 75c multicolored | 2.00 | 1.50 |
| *a.* Souvenir sheet of 2, #171-172 | 2.75 | 2.75 |

Capt. James Cook (1728-1779), explorer, death bicentenary.

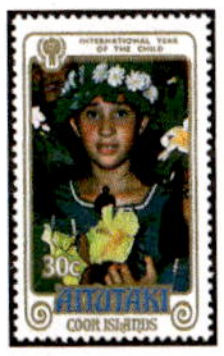

Boy Holding Hibiscus, IYC Emblem — A48

IYC Emblem and: 35c, Boy playing guitar. 65c, Boys in outrigger canoe.

**1979, Oct. 1 Photo. *Perf. 14x13½***

| | | |
|---|---|---|
| **173** A48 30c multicolored | .25 | .25 |
| **174** A48 35c multicolored | .35 | .35 |
| **175** A48 65c multicolored | .45 | .45 |
| *Nos. 173-175 (3)* | 1.05 | 1.05 |

See No. B31.

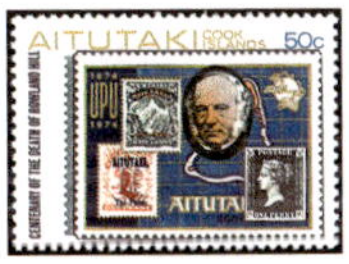

Aitutaki No. 102, Hill, Penny Black — A49

Designs: Nos. 176, 178-179, 181, paintings of letter writers, Flemish School, 17th century.

**1979, Nov. 14 Photo. *Perf. 13***

| | | |
|---|---|---|
| **176** A49 50c Gabriel Metsu | .50 | .50 |
| **177** A49 50c shown | .50 | .50 |
| **178** A49 50c Jan Vermeer | .50 | .50 |
| *a.* Strip of 3, #176-178 | 1.50 | 1.50 |
| **179** A49 65c Gerard Terborch | .60 | .60 |
| **180** A49 65c No. 103 (like No. 177) | .60 | .60 |
| **181** A49 65c Jan Vermeer | .60 | .60 |
| *a.* Strip of 3, #179-181 | 2.00 | 2.00 |
| *Nos. 176-181 (6)* | 3.30 | 3.30 |

**Souvenir Sheet**

| | | |
|---|---|---|
| **182** Sheet of 6 | 2.75 | 2.75 |
| *a.* A49 30c like No. 176 | .40 | .40 |
| *b.* A49 30c like No. 177 | .40 | .40 |
| *c.* A49 30c like No. 178 | .40 | .40 |
| *d.* A49 30c like No. 179 | .40 | .40 |
| *e.* A49 30c like No. 180 | .40 | .40 |
| *f.* A49 30c like No. 181 | .40 | .40 |

Sir Rowland Hill (1795-1879), originator of penny postage. Nos. 176-178 and 179-181 printed in sheets of 9.

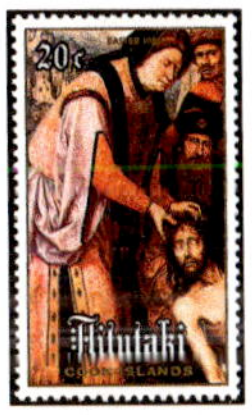

Descent from the Cross, Detail — A50

Easter: 30c, 35c, Descent from the Cross, by Quentin Metsys (details).

**1980, Apr. 3 Photo. *Perf. 13x13½***

| | | |
|---|---|---|
| **183** A50 20c multicolored | .50 | .40 |
| **184** A50 30c multicolored | .60 | .50 |
| **185** A50 35c multicolored | .70 | .60 |
| *Nos. 183-185 (3)* | 1.80 | 1.50 |

See No. B32.

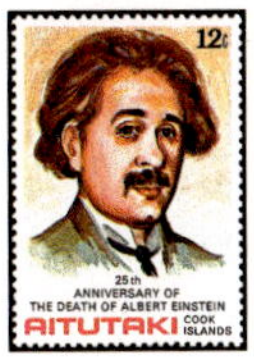

Albert Einstein — A51

No. 187, Formula, atom structure. No. 188, Portrait, diff. No. 189, Atomic blast. No. 190, Portrait, diff. No. 191, Atomic blast, trees.

**1980, July 21 Photo. *Perf. 14***

| | | |
|---|---|---|
| **186** A51 12c shown | .65 | .65 |
| **187** A51 12c multicolored | .65 | .65 |
| *a.* Pair, #186-187 | 1.50 | 1.50 |
| **188** A51 15c multicolored | .70 | .70 |
| **189** A51 15c multicolored | .70 | .70 |
| *a.* Pair, #188-189 | 1.60 | 1.60 |
| **190** A51 20c multicolored | .80 | .80 |
| **191** A51 20c multicolored | .80 | .80 |
| *a.* Pair, #190-191 | 2.00 | 2.00 |
| *b.* Souv. sheet of 6, #186-191, perf. 13 | 5.00 | 5.00 |
| *Nos. 186-191 (6)* | 4.30 | 4.30 |

Albert Einstein (1879-1955), theoretical physicist.

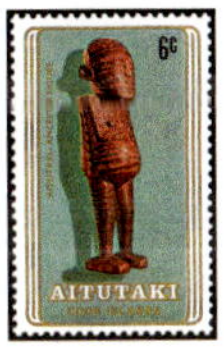

A52

No. 192, Ancestral Figure, Aitutaki. No. 193, God image staff, Rarotonga. No. 194, Trade adze, Mangaia. No. 195, Tangaroa carving, Rarotonga. No. 196, Wooden image, Aitutaki. No. 197, Hand club, Rarotonga. No. 198, Carved mace, Mangaia. No. 199, Fisherman's god, Rarotonga. No. 200, Ti'i image, Aitutaki. No. 201, Fisherman's god, diff. No. 202, Carved mace, Cook Islands. No. 203, Tangaroa, diff. No. 204, Chief's headdress, Aitutaki. No. 205, Carved mace, diff. No. 206, God image staff, diff.

**1980, Sept. 26 Photo. *Perf. 14***

| | | |
|---|---|---|
| **192** A52 6c multicolored | .25 | .25 |
| **193** A52 6c multicolored | .25 | .25 |
| **194** A52 6c multicolored | .25 | .25 |
| **195** A52 6c multicolored | .25 | .25 |
| *a.* Block of 4, #192-195 | .60 | .60 |
| **196** A52 12c multicolored | .25 | .25 |
| **197** A52 12c multicolored | .25 | .25 |
| **198** A52 12c multicolored | .25 | .25 |
| **199** A52 12c multicolored | .25 | .25 |
| *a.* Block of 4, #196-199 | .85 | .85 |
| **200** A52 15c multicolored | .25 | .25 |
| **201** A52 15c multicolored | .25 | .25 |
| **202** A52 15c multicolored | .25 | .25 |
| **203** A52 15c multicolored | .25 | .25 |
| *a.* Block of 4, #200-203 | 1.00 | 1.00 |
| **204** A52 20c multicolored | .40 | .40 |
| **205** A52 20c multicolored | .40 | .40 |
| **206** A52 20c multicolored | .40 | .40 |
| **207** A52 20c like #195 | .40 | .40 |
| *a.* Block of 4, #204-207 | 1.50 | 1.50 |
| *b.* Souvenir sheet of 16, #192-207 | 4.00 | 4.00 |

Third South Pacific Arts Festival, Port Moresby, Papua New Guinea.

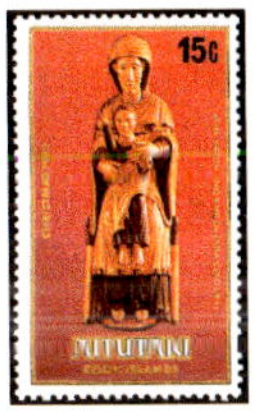

A53

Virgin and Child, Sculptures.

**1980, Nov. 21 Photo. *Perf. 13x13½***

| | | |
|---|---|---|
| **208** A53 15c 13th cent. | .25 | .25 |
| **209** A53 20c 14th cent. | .25 | .25 |
| **210** A53 25c 15th cent. | .30 | .30 |
| **211** A53 35c 15th cent., diff. | .40 | .40 |
| *Nos. 208-211 (4)* | 1.20 | 1.20 |

Christmas. See No. B33.

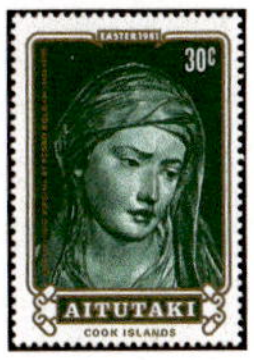

Mourning Virgin, by Pedro Roldan — A54

Easter (Roldan Sculptures): 40c, Christ. 50c, Mourning St. John.

**1981, Mar. 31 Photo. *Perf. 14***

| | | |
|---|---|---|
| **212** A54 30c green & gold | .35 | .35 |
| **213** A54 40c brt purple & gold | .40 | .40 |
| **214** A54 50c dk blue & gold | .45 | .45 |
| *Nos. 212-214 (3)* | 1.20 | 1.20 |

See No. B34.

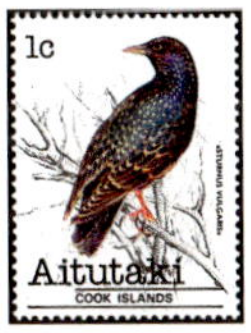

Sturnus Vulgaris — A55

No. 216, Poephila gouldiae. No. 217, Petroica multicolor. No. 218, Pachycephala pectoralis. No. 219, Falco peregrinus. No. 220, Rhipidura rufifrons. No. 221, Tyto alba. No. 222, Padda oryzivora. No. 223, Artamus leucorhynchus. No. 224, Vini peruviana. No. 225, Columba livia. No. 226, Porphyrio porphyria. No. 227, Geopelia striata. No. 228, Lonchura castaneothorax. No. 229, Acridotheres tristis. No. 230, Egretta sacra. No. 231, Diomeda melanophris. No. 232, Numenius phaeopus. No. 233, Gygis alba. No. 234, Pluvialis dominica. No. 235, Sula leucogaster. No. 236, Anas superciliosa. No. 237, Anas acuta. No. 238, Fregata minor. No. 239, Stercorarius pomarinus. No. 240, Conopoderas caffra. No. 241, Lalage maculosa. No. 242, Gallirallus philippensis. No. 243, Vini stepheni. No. 244, Diomedea epomophora. No. 245, Ptilinopus victor. No. 246, Erythrura cyaneovirens. $1, Myiagra azureocapilla. $2, Myiagra vanikorensis. $4, Amandava amandava. $5, Halcyon recurvirostris.

**1981-82 *Perf. 14x13½, 13½x14***

| | | |
|---|---|---|
| **215** A55 1c shown | .40 | .25 |
| **216** A55 1c multicolored | .40 | .25 |
| *a.* Pair, #215-216 | 1.00 | .30 |
| **217** A55 2c multicolored | .45 | .25 |
| **218** A55 2c multicolored | .45 | .25 |
| *a.* Pair, #217-218 | 1.10 | .30 |
| **219** A55 3c multicolored | .55 | .25 |
| **220** A55 3c multicolored | .55 | .25 |
| *a.* Pair, #219-220 | 1.25 | .30 |
| **221** A55 4c multicolored | .65 | .25 |
| **222** A55 4c multicolored | .65 | .25 |
| *a.* Pair, #221-222 | 1.50 | .35 |
| **223** A55 5c multicolored | .70 | .25 |
| **224** A55 5c multicolored | .70 | .25 |
| *a.* Pair, #223-224 | 1.00 | .40 |
| **225** A55 6c multicolored | .75 | .25 |
| **226** A55 6c multicolored | .75 | .25 |
| *a.* Pair, #225-226 | 1.75 | .40 |
| **227** A55 10c multicolored | .85 | .25 |
| **228** A55 10c multicolored | .85 | .25 |
| *a.* Pair, #227-228 | 2.00 | .75 |
| **229** A55 12c multicolored | .90 | .30 |
| **230** A55 12c multicolored | .90 | .30 |
| *a.* Pair, #229-230 | 2.10 | .85 |
| **231** A55 15c multicolored | 1.00 | .40 |
| **232** A55 15c multicolored | 1.00 | .40 |
| *a.* Pair, #231-232 | 2.75 | *1.25* |
| **233** A55 20c multicolored | 1.25 | .50 |
| **234** A55 20c multicolored | 1.25 | .50 |
| *a.* Pair, #233-234 | 3.25 | *1.50* |
| **235** A55 25c multicolored | 1.40 | .60 |
| **236** A55 25c multicolored | 1.40 | .60 |
| *a.* Pair, #235-236 | 3.75 | *1.60* |
| **237** A55 30c multicolored | 1.50 | .65 |
| **238** A55 30c multicolored | 1.50 | .65 |
| *a.* Pair, #237-238 | 4.00 | *2.00* |
| **239** A55 35c multicolored | 1.60 | .75 |
| **240** A55 35c multicolored | 1.60 | .75 |
| *a.* Pair, #239-240 | 4.25 | *3.00* |
| **241** A55 40c multicolored | 1.75 | .90 |
| **242** A55 40c multicolored | 1.75 | .90 |
| *a.* Pair, #241-242 | 4.50 | *3.25* |
| **243** A55 50c multicolored | 2.00 | 1.00 |
| **244** A55 50c multicolored | 2.00 | 1.00 |
| *a.* Pair, #243-244 | 5.00 | *3.50* |
| **245** A55 70c multicolored | 4.25 | 2.00 |
| **246** A55 70c multicolored | 4.25 | 2.00 |
| *e.* Pair, #245-246 | 11.00 | *7.50* |

**Size: 35x47mm**

**Photo. *Perf. 13½***

| | | |
|---|---|---|
| **246A** A55 $1 multicolored | 5.00 | 3.75 |
| **246B** A55 $2 multicolored | 5.50 | *7.50* |
| **246C** A55 $4 multicolored | 9.00 | *13.50* |
| **246D** A55 $5 multicolored | 11.00 | *17.50* |
| *Nos. 215-246D (36)* | 70.50 | 59.95 |

Issued: Nos. 215-230, 4/6; Nos. 231-238, 5/8; Nos. 239-246, 1/14/82; Nos. 246A-246B, 2/15/82.

Nos. 231-246 horiz.

For surcharges and overprint see Nos. 293-306, 452-454, O40-O41.

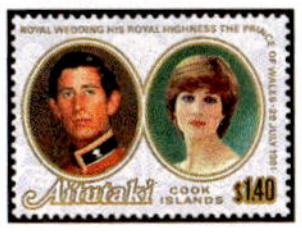

Prince Charles and Lady Diana — A56

***Perf. 13x13½, 13½x13***

**1981, June 10 Photo.**

| | | |
|---|---|---|
| **247** A56 60c Charles, vert. | .40 | .40 |
| **248** A56 80c Lady Diana, vert. | .50 | .50 |
| Complete booklet, one sheet of 4 each #247-248 | 6.00 | |
| **249** A56 $1.40 Shown | .60 | .60 |
| *Nos. 247-249 (3)* | 1.50 | 1.50 |

Royal Wedding. Issued in sheets of 4.

For overprints and surcharges see Nos. 265-267, 307, 309, 355, 405-407, B35-B37.

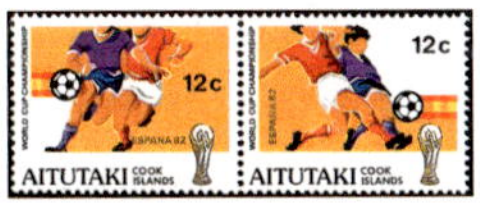

1982 World Cup Soccer A57

Designs: Various soccer players.

**1981, Nov. 30 Photo. *Perf. 14***

| | | |
|---|---|---|
| **250** A57 12c Pair, #250a-250b | 1.10 | 1.00 |
| **251** A57 15c Pair, #251a-251b | 1.25 | 1.10 |
| **252** A57 20c Pair, #252a-252b | 1.50 | 1.25 |
| **253** A57 25c Pair, #253a-253b | 1.75 | 1.40 |
| *Nos. 250-253 (4)* | 5.60 | 4.75 |

See No. B38.

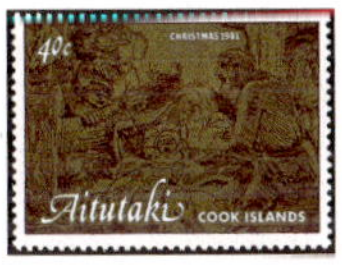

Christmas — A58

Rembrandt Etchings: 15c, Holy Family, 1632, vert. 30c, Virgin with Child, 1634, vert. 40c, Adoration of the Shepherds, 1654. 50c, Holy Family with Cat, 1644.

**1981, Dec. 10 *Perf. 14***

| | | |
|---|---|---|
| **254** A58 15c gold & dk brown | .50 | .50 |
| **255** A58 30c gold & dk brown | .65 | .60 |
| **256** A58 40c gold & dk brown | .75 | .75 |
| **257** A58 50c gold & dk brown | 1.00 | 1.00 |
| *Nos. 254-257 (4)* | 2.90 | 2.85 |

**Souvenir Sheets**

| | | |
|---|---|---|
| **258** A58 80c + 5c like #254 | .80 | .75 |
| **259** A58 80c + 5c like #255 | .80 | .75 |
| **260** A58 80c + 5c like #256 | .80 | .75 |
| **261** A58 80c + 5c like #257 | .80 | .75 |

Nos. 258-261 have multicolored margins showing entire etching. Surtax on Nos. 258-261 was for local charities.

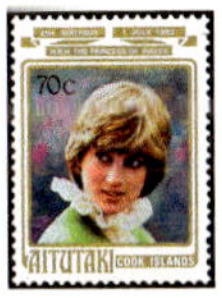

21st Birthday of Princess Diana — A59

**1982, June 24 Photo. *Perf. 14***

| | | |
|---|---|---|
| **262** A59 70c shown | 1.75 | .75 |
| **263** A59 $1 Wedding portrait | 1.75 | .90 |
| **264** A59 $2 Diana, diff. | 2.75 | 1.50 |
| *a.* Souvenir sheet of 3, #262-264 | 6.00 | 6.00 |
| *Nos. 262-264 (3)* | 6.25 | 3.15 |

See Nos. 268-270a. For surcharges see Nos. 308, 310.

**Nos. 247-249 Overprinted**

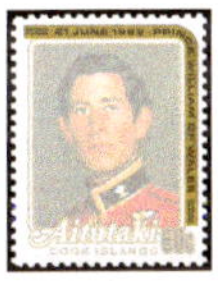

a

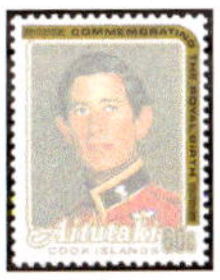

b

**1982, July 13 *Perf. 13x13½, 13½x13***

| | | |
|---|---|---|
| **265** A56 60c Pair, #a.-b. | 1.50 | 1.25 |
| **266** A56 80c Pair, #a.-b. | 2.25 | 2.00 |
| **267** A56 $1.40 Pair, #a.-b. | 3.75 | 3.25 |
| *Nos. 265-267 (3)* | 7.50 | 6.50 |

Nos. 265-267 were overprinted with alternating inscriptions within the sheet.

350 AITUTAKI

Nos. 262-264a Inscribed: "Royal Birth 21 June 1982 Prince William Of Wales"

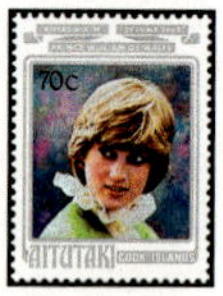


**1982, Aug. 5** **Perf. 14**

**268** A59 70c multicolored .70 .70
**269** A59 $1 multicolored 1.50 1.50
**270** A59 $2 multicolored 2.00 2.00
*a.* Souvenir sheet of 3 5.00 5.00
*Nos. 268-270 (3)* 4.20 4.20

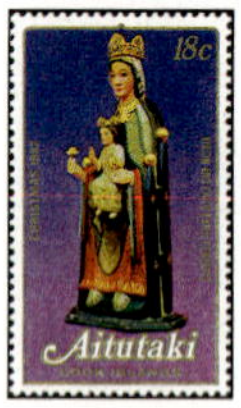


Christmas — A60

Madonna and Child Sculptures, 12th-15th Cent.

**1982, Dec. 10** **Photo.** **Perf. 13**

**271** A60 18c multicolored .65 .65
**272** A60 36c multicolored .75 .75
**273** A60 48c multicolored .90 .90
**274** A60 60c multicolored 1.25 1.25
*Nos. 271-274 (4)* 3.55 3.55

**Souvenir Sheet**

**275** Sheet of 4 4.50 4.50
*a.* A60 18c + 2c like 18c .70 .70
*b.* A60 36c + 2c like 36c .80 .80
*c.* A60 48c + 2c like 48c 1.00 1.00
*d.* A60 60c + 2c like 60c 1.25 1.25

Surtax was for children's charities.

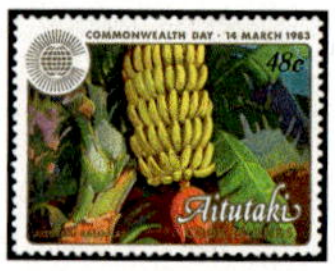


Commonwealth Day — A61

**1983, Mar. 14** **Photo.** **Perf. 13x13½**

**276** A61 48c Bananas .95 .95
**277** A61 48c Ti'i statuette .95 .95
**278** A61 48c Boys canoeing .95 .95
**279** A61 48c Capt. Bligh, Bounty .95 .95
*a.* Block of 4, #276-279 4.75 4.75

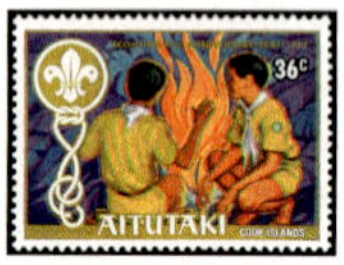


Scouting Year — A62

**1983, Apr. 18** **Photo.** **Perf. 14**

**280** A62 36c Campfire .50 .50
**281** A62 48c Salute .60 .60
**282** A62 60c Hiking .70 .70
*Nos. 280-282 (3)* 1.80 1.80

**Souvenir Sheet**

**Perf. 13½**

**283** Sheet of 3 2.50 2.50
*a.* A62 36c + 3c like #280 .60 .60
*b.* A62 48c + 3c like #281 .70 .70
*c.* A62 60c + 3c like #282 .90 .90

Surtax was for benefit of Scouting.

**Nos. 280-283 Overprinted**

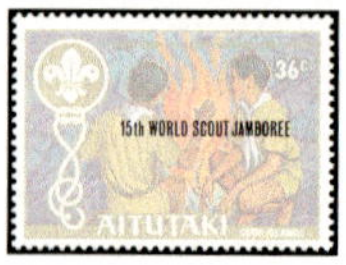


**1983, July 11** **Photo.** **Perf. 14**

**284** A62 36c multicolored .85 .85
**285** A62 48c multicolored 1.00 1.00
**286** A62 60c multicolored 1.25 1.25
*Nos. 284-286 (3)* 3.10 3.10

**Souvenir Sheet**

**287** Sheet of 3 3.00 3.00
*a.* A62 36c + 3c like #284 .65 .65
*b.* A62 48c + 3c like #285 .80 .80
*c.* A62 60c + 3c like #286 1.00 1.00

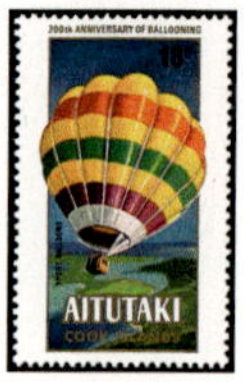


A63

Manned Flight Bicentenary: Modern sport balloons.

**1983, July 22** **Photo.** **Perf. 14x13**

**288** A63 18c multicolored .60 .60
**289** A63 36c multicolored .75 .75
**290** A63 48c multicolored 1.00 1.00
**291** A63 60c multicolored 1.25 1.25
*Nos. 288-291 (4)* 3.60 3.60

**Souvenir Sheet**

**292** A63 $2.50 multicolored 3.25 3.25

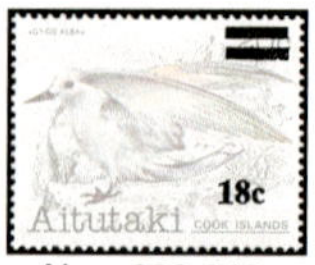


Nos. 233-246, 246D, 248-249 Surcharged in Black

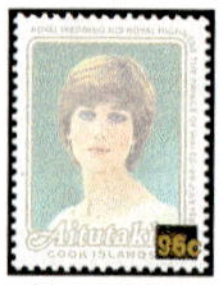


Nos. 263-264 Surcharged in Black and Gold

**1983, Sept. 22**

**293** A55 18c on 20c, #233 2.75 1.00
**294** A55 18c on 20c, #234 2.75 1.00
*a.* Pair, #293-294 6.00 2.25
**295** A55 36c on 25c, #235 3.25 1.25
**296** A55 36c on 25c, #236 3.25 1.25
*a.* Pair, #295-296 7.25 3.00
**297** A55 36c on 30c, #237 3.25 1.25
**298** A55 36c on 30c, #238 3.25 1.25
*a.* Pair, #297-298 7.25 3.00
**299** A55 36c on 35c, #239 3.50 1.40
**300** A55 36c on 35c, #240 3.50 1.40
*a.* Pair, #299-300 7.50 3.25
**301** A55 48c on 40c, #241 4.50 1.40
**302** A55 48c on 40c, #242 4.50 1.40
*a.* Pair, #301-302 10.00 3.25
**303** A55 48c on 50c, #243 4.50 1.40
**304** A55 48c on 50c, #244 4.50 1.40
*a.* Pair, #303-304 10.00 3.25
**305** A55 72c on 70c, #245 7.50 2.50
**306** A55 72c on 70c, #246 7.50 2.50
*a.* Pair, #305-306 16.50 7.50
**307** A56 96c on 80c, #248 3.00 2.25
**308** A59 96c on $1, #263 2.75 2.00
**309** A56 $1.20 on $1.40, #249 3.00 2.25
**310** A59 $1.20 on $2, #264 2.75 2.00

**Size: 35x47mm**

**311** A55 $5.60 on $5, #246D 20.00 10.00
*Nos. 293-311 (19)* 90.00 38.90

Nos. 307-308, 310-311 vert.

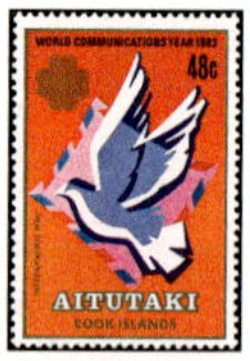


A64

60, Global coverage. 96c, Communications satellite.

**1983, Sept. 29** **Photo.** **Perf. 14**

**312** A64 48c shown .80 .55
**313** A64 60c multicolored 1.25 .70
**314** A64 96c multicolored 1.50 1.25
*a.* Souvenir sheet of 3, #312-314 3.25 3.25
*Nos. 312-314 (3)* 3.55 2.50

World Communications Year.

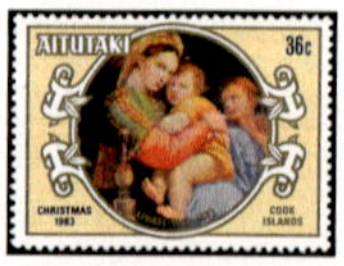


Christmas — A65

Raphael Paintings — 36c, Madonna of the Chair. 48c, Alba Madonna. 60c, Connestabile Madonna.

**1983, Nov. 21** **Photo.** **Perf. 13½x14**

**315** A65 36c multicolored .75 .40
**316** A65 48c multicolored 1.00 .80
**317** A65 60c multicolored 1.50 1.00
*Nos. 315-317 (3)* 3.25 2.20

**Souvenir Sheet**

**318** Sheet of 3 3.50 3.50
*a.* A65 36c + 3c like #315 1.00 1.00
*b.* A65 48c + 3c like #316 1.10 1.10
*c.* A65 60c + 3c like #317 1.25 1.25

**1983, Dec. 15** **Imperf.**

**Size: 46x46mm**

**319** A65 85c + 5c like #315 1.50 1.50
**320** A65 85c + 5c like #316 1.50 1.50
**321** A65 85c + 5c like #317 1.50 1.50
*Nos. 319-321 (3)* 4.50 4.50

Surtax was for children's charities.

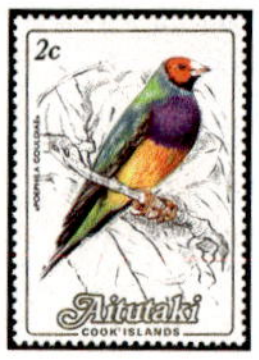


Local Birds — A66

**1984** **Photo.** **Perf. 14**

**322** A66 2c as No. 216 1.75 .90
**323** A66 3c as No. 215 1.75 .90
**324** A66 5c as No. 217 1.75 1.00
**325** A66 10c as No. 218 2.50 1.00
**326** A66 12c as No. 220 2.50 1.00
**327** A66 18c as No. 219 2.50 1.25
**328** A66 24c as No. 221 2.50 1.25
**329** A66 30c as No. 222 2.50 1.25
**330** A66 36c as No. 223 2.50 1.25
**331** A66 48c as No. 224 2.50 1.25
**332** A66 50c as No. 225 2.75 1.75
**333** A66 60c as No. 226 2.75 1.75
**334** A66 72c as No. 227 3.25 1.75
**335** A66 96c as No. 228 3.25 1.75
**336** A66 $1.20 as No. 229 3.25 2.50
**337** A66 $2.10 as No. 230 3.75 3.50
**338** A66 $3 as No. 246A 5.25 4.50
**339** A66 $4.20 as No. 246B 4.00 *5.75*
**340** A66 $5.60 as No. 246C 5.25 *7.00*
**341** A66 $9.60 as No. 246D 8.00 *10.00*
*Nos. 322-341 (20)* 64.25 51.30

For overprints and surcharges see Nos. O17-O39.

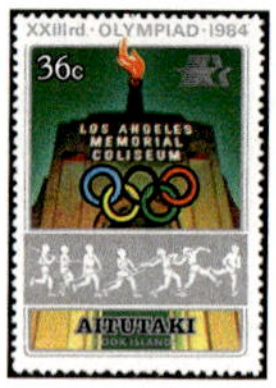


1984 Summer Olympics — A67

**1984, July 24** **Photo.** **Perf. 13x13½**

**342** A67 36c Javelin .50 .50
**343** A67 48c Shot put .60 .60
**344** A67 60c Hurdles .70 .70
**345** A67 $2 Handball 2.00 2.00
*Nos. 342-345 (4)* 3.80 3.80

**Souvenir Sheet**

**346** Sheet of 4 3.50 3.50
*a.* A67 36c + 5c like #342 .40 .40
*b.* A67 48c + 5c like #343 .55 .55
*c.* A67 60c + 5c like #344 .65 .65
*d.* A67 $2 + 5c like #345 1.50 1.50

Surtax was for benefit of local sports.

Nos. 342-345 Overprinted in Gold and Black

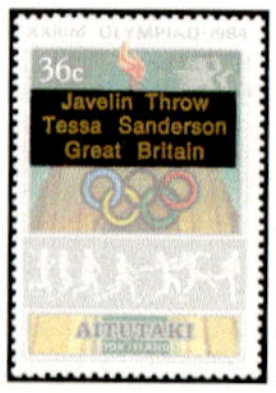


**1984, Aug. 21** **Photo.** **Perf. 13x13½**

**347** A67 36c multicolored .40 .40
**348** A67 48c multicolored .50 .50
**349** A67 60c multicolored .60 .60
**350** A67 $2 multicolored 1.75 1.75
*Nos. 347-350 (4)* 3.25 3.25

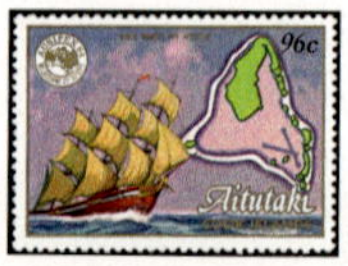


Ausipex '84 — A68

60c, William Bligh, map. 96c, Bounty, map. $1.40, Stamps, map.

**1984, Sept. 14** **Photo.** **Perf. 14**

**351** A68 60c multicolored 3.75 3.75
**352** A68 96c multicolored 3.75 3.75
**353** A68 $1.40 multicolored 3.75 3.75
*Nos. 351-353 (3)* 11.25 11.25

**Souvenir Sheet**

**354** Sheet of 3 8.00 8.00
*a.* A68 60c + 5c like #351 1.75 1.75
*b.* A68 96c + 5c like #352 2.25 2.25
*c.* A68 $1.40 + 5c like #353 3.50 3.50

For overprint see No. 399.

No. 247 Surcharged

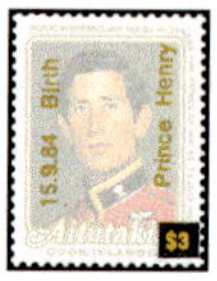


**1984, Oct. 10** **Photo.** **Perf. 13x13½**

**355** A56 $3 on 60c multi 2.75 3.00

Issued in sheets of 4.

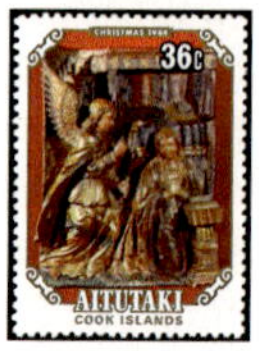


A69

**1984, Nov. 16** **Photo.** **Perf. 13**

**356** A69 36c Annunciation .45 .45
**357** A69 48c Nativity .55 .55
**358** A69 60c Epiphany .65 .65
**359** A69 96c Flight into Egypt .85 .85
*Nos. 356-359 (4)* 2.50 2.50

**Souvenir Sheets**

**Size: 45x53mm**

***Imperf***

**360** A69 90c + 7c like #356 1.10 1.10
**361** A69 90c + 7c like #357 1.10 1.10
**362** A69 90c + 7c like #358 1.10 1.10
**363** A69 90c + 7c like #359 1.10 1.10

Christmas.

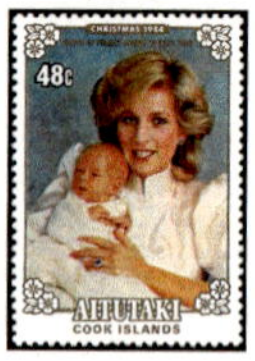


A70

**1984, Dec. 10** **Photo.** **Perf. 13½x14**

**364** A70 48c Diana, Henry 2.25 2.25
**365** A70 60c William, Henry 2.25 2.25
**366** A70 $2.10 Family 3.00 3.00
*Nos. 364-366 (3)* 7.50 7.50

**Souvenir Sheet**

**367** Sheet of 3 6.00 6.00
*a.* A70 96c + 7c like #364 2.00 2.00
*b.* A70 96c + 7c like #365 2.00 2.00
*c.* A70 96c + 7c like #366 2.00 2.00

Christmas, Birth of Prince Henry, Sept. 15.
Surtax was for benefit of local children's charities.

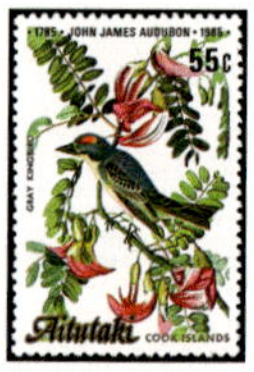


Audubon Birth Bicentenary — A71

Illustrations of bird species by John J. Audubon — 55c, Gray kingbird. 65c, Bohemian waxwing. 75c, Summer tanager. 95c, Cardinal. $1.15, White-winged crossbill.

**1985, Mar. 22** **Litho.** **Perf. 13**

**368** A71 55c multicolored 1.10 1.10
**369** A71 65c multicolored 1.25 1.25
**370** A71 75c multicolored 1.50 1.50
**371** A71 95c multicolored 1.75 1.75
**372** A71 $1.15 multicolored 2.25 2.25
*Nos. 368-372 (5)* 7.85 7.85

# AITUTAKI 351

Queen Mother, 85th Birthday — A72

Photographs: 55c, Lady Elizabeth Bowes-Lyon, age 7. 65c, Engaged to the Duke of York. 75c, Duchess of York with daughter, Elizabeth. $1.30, Holding the infant Prince Charles. $3, Portrait taken on 63rd birthday.

**1985-86**   *Perf. 13½x13*
| | | | | |
|---|---|---|---|---|
| 373 | A72 | 55c multicolored | .55 | .55 |
| 374 | A72 | 65c multicolored | .65 | .65 |
| 375 | A72 | 75c multicolored | .75 | .75 |
| 376 | A72 | $1.30 multicolored | 1.25 | 1.25 |
| a. | | Souvenir sheet of 4, #373-376 | 8.25 | 8.25 |
| | | Nos. 373-376 (4) | 3.20 | 3.20 |

**Souvenir Sheet**
| | | | | |
|---|---|---|---|---|
| 377 | A72 | $3 multicolored | 3.50 | 3.50 |

Nos. 373-376 printed in sheets of 4. Issued: No. 376a, 8/4/86; others, 6/14/85. For overprint see No. 446.

Intl. Youth Year — A73

Designs: 75c, The Calmady Children, by Thomas Lawrence (1769-1830). 90c, Madame Charpentier's Children, by Renoir (1841-1919). $1.40, Young Girls at Piano, by Renoir.

**1985, Sept. 16**   *Photo.*   *Perf. 13*
| | | | | |
|---|---|---|---|---|
| 378 | A73 | 75c multicolored | 2.50 | 2.50 |
| 379 | A73 | 90c multicolored | 2.50 | 2.50 |
| 380 | A73 | $1.40 multicolored | 3.00 | 3.00 |
| | | Nos. 378-380 (3) | 8.00 | 8.00 |

**Souvenir Sheet**
| | | | | |
|---|---|---|---|---|
| 381 | | Sheet of 3 | 6.50 | 6.50 |
| a. | A73 75c + 10c like #378 | | 1.50 | 1.50 |
| b. | A73 90c + 10c like #379 | | 1.75 | 1.75 |
| c. | A73 $1.40 + 10c like #380 | | 2.50 | 2.50 |

Surcharged for children's activities.

Adoration of the Magi, by Giotto di Bondone (1276-1337) A74

Nos. 382, 384, Giotto probe. Nos. 383, 385, Planet A probe.

**1985, Nov. 15**   *Photo.*   *Perf. 13½x13*
| | | | | |
|---|---|---|---|---|
| 382 | A74 | 95c multicolored | 1.50 | 1.50 |
| 383 | A74 | 95c multicolored | 1.50 | 1.50 |
| a. | Pair, #382-383 | | 3.50 | 3.50 |
| 384 | A74 | $1.15 multicolored | 1.50 | 1.50 |
| 385 | A74 | $1.15 multicolored | 1.50 | 1.50 |
| a. | Pair, #384-385 | | 3.50 | 3.50 |
| | | Nos. 382-385 (4) | 6.00 | 6.00 |

**Souvenir Sheet**
*Imperf*
| | | | | |
|---|---|---|---|---|
| 386 | A74 | $6.40 multicolored | 13.50 | 13.50 |

Christmas, return of Halley's Comet, 1985-86.

Halley's Comet — A75

Designs: 90c, Halley's Comet, A.D. 684, wood engraving, Nuremberg Chronicles. $1.25, Sighting of 1066, Bayeux Tapestry, detail, c. 1092, France. $1.75, The Comet Inflicting Untold Disasters, 1456, Lucerne Chronicles, by Diebolt Schilling. $4.20, Melancolia I, engraving by Durer.

**1986, Feb. 25**   *Photo.*   *Perf. 13½x13*
| | | | | |
|---|---|---|---|---|
| 387 | A75 | 90c multicolored | 1.25 | 1.25 |
| 388 | A75 | $1.25 multicolored | 1.50 | 1.50 |
| 389 | A75 | $1.75 multicolored | 2.25 | 2.25 |
| | | Nos. 387-389 (3) | 5.00 | 5.00 |

**Souvenir Sheets**
| | | | | |
|---|---|---|---|---|
| 390 | | Sheet of 3 + label | 6.50 | 6.50 |
| a. | A75 95c like #387 | | 2.00 | 2.00 |
| b. | A75 95c like #388 | | 2.00 | 2.00 |
| c. | A75 95c, like #389 | | 2.00 | 2.00 |

*Imperf*
| | | | | |
|---|---|---|---|---|
| 391 | A75 | $4.20 multicolored | 5.75 | 5.75 |

Elizabeth II, 60th Birthday — A76

**1986, Apr. 21**   *Perf. 14*
| | | | | |
|---|---|---|---|---|
| 392 | A76 | 95c Coronation portrait | 1.10 | 1.10 |

**Souvenir Sheet**
*Perf. 13½*
| | | | | |
|---|---|---|---|---|
| 393 | A76 | $4.20 Portrait, diff. | 5.25 | 5.25 |

No. 392 printed in sheets of 5 with label picturing U.K. flag and Queen's flag for New Zealand.

Statue of Liberty, Cent. — A77

**1986, June 27**   *Photo.*   *Perf. 14*
| | | | | |
|---|---|---|---|---|
| 394 | A77 | $1 Liberty head | 1.50 | 1.50 |
| 395 | A77 | $2.75 Statue | 3.00 | 3.00 |

**Souvenir Sheet**
*Perf. 13½*
| | | | | |
|---|---|---|---|---|
| 396 | | Sheet of 2 | 3.25 | 3.25 |
| a. | A77 $1.25 like $1 | | 1.50 | 1.50 |
| b. | A77 $1.25 like $2.75 | | 1.50 | 1.50 |

For surcharges see Nos B45, B49.

Wedding of Prince Andrew and Sarah Ferguson — A78

**1986, July 23**   *Perf. 14*
| | | | | |
|---|---|---|---|---|
| 397 | A78 | $2 multicolored | 2.60 | 2.60 |

**Souvenir Sheet**
*Perf. 13½*
| | | | | |
|---|---|---|---|---|
| 398 | A78 | $5 multicolored | 6.00 | 6.00 |

No. 397 printed in sheets of 5 plus label picturing Westminster Abbey. For surcharge see No. B48.

### No. 354 Overprinted

**1986, Aug. 4**   *Photo.*   *Perf. 14*
| | | | | |
|---|---|---|---|---|
| 399 | | Sheet of 3 | 13.00 | 13.00 |
| a. | A68 60c + 5c like #351 | | 3.00 | 3.00 |
| b. | A68 96c + 5c like #352 | | 3.50 | 3.50 |
| c. | A68 $1.40 + 5c like #353 | | 6.00 | 6.00 |

STAMPEX '86, Adelaide, Aug. 4-10.

Christmas — A79

Paintings by Albrecht Durer: 75c, No. 404a, St. Anne with Virgin and Child. $1.35, No. 404b, Virgin and Child. $1.95, No. 404c, Adoration of the Magi. $2.75, No. 404d, Rosary Festivity.

**1986, Nov. 21**   *Litho.*   *Perf. 13½*
| | | | | |
|---|---|---|---|---|
| 400 | A79 | 75c multicolored | 1.25 | 1.25 |
| 401 | A79 | $1.35 multicolored | 2.00 | 2.00 |
| 402 | A79 | $1.95 multicolored | 3.00 | 3.00 |
| 403 | A79 | $2.75 multicolored | 4.25 | 4.25 |
| | | Nos. 400-403 (4) | 10.50 | 10.50 |

**Souvenir Sheet**
| | | | | |
|---|---|---|---|---|
| 404 | | Sheet of 4 | 14.00 | 14.00 |
| a.-d. | A79 $1.65 any single | | 3.25 | 3.25 |

For surcharges see Nos. B39-B44, B46-B47, B50-B54.

### Nos. 247-249 Srchd. in Gold and Black

**1987, Nov. 20**   *Photo.*   *Perf. 13x12½*
| | | | | |
|---|---|---|---|---|
| 405 | A56 | $2.50 on 60c No. 247 | 2.40 | 2.40 |
| 406 | A56 | $2.50 on 80c No. 248 | 2.40 | 2.40 |
| 407 | A56 | $2.50 on $1.40 No. 249 | 2.40 | 2.40 |
| | | Nos. 405-407 (3) | 7.20 | 7.20 |

Issued in sheets of 4 with margin inscriptions overprinted with gold bar and "40th Anniversary of the Royal Wedding / 1947-1987" in black; "OVERPRINTED BY NEW ZEALAND GOVERNMENT PRINTER, / WELLINGTON, NOVEMBER 1987" at left.

A80

The Virgin with Garland, by Rubens A81

Painting details.

**1987, Dec. 10**   *Photo.*   *Perf. 13x13½*
| | | | | |
|---|---|---|---|---|
| 408 | A80 | 70c UL | 2.00 | 2.00 |
| 409 | A80 | 85c UR | 2.10 | 2.10 |
| 410 | A80 | $1.50 LL | 2.25 | 2.25 |
| 411 | A80 | $1.85 LR | 3.00 | 3.00 |
| | | Nos. 408-411 (4) | 9.35 | 9.35 |

**Souvenir Sheets**
| | | | | |
|---|---|---|---|---|
| 412 | | Sheet of 4 | 13.00 | 13.00 |
| a. | A80 95c like No. 408 | | 3.00 | 3.00 |
| b. | A80 95c like No. 409 | | 3.00 | 3.00 |
| c. | A80 95c like No. 410 | | 3.00 | 3.00 |
| d. | A80 95c like No. 411 | | 3.00 | 3.00 |

*Perf. 13*
| | | | | |
|---|---|---|---|---|
| 413 | A81 | $6 multicolored | 14.00 | 14.00 |

Christmas.

1988 Summer Olympics, Seoul A82

Flags of Korea, Aitutaki, ancient and modern events, and Seoul Games emblem or $50 silver coin issued to commemorate the participation of Aitutaki athletes in the Olympics for the 1st time: 70c, No. 418a, Obverse of silver coin, chariot race, running. 85c, Emblem, running, soccer. 95c, Emblem, boxing, handball. $1.40, No. 418b, Reverse of coin, spearmen, women's tennis.

**1988, Aug. 22**   *Photo.*   *Perf. 14½x15*
| | | | | |
|---|---|---|---|---|
| 414 | A82 | 70c multicolored | 2.00 | 2.00 |
| 415 | A82 | 85c multicolored | 2.25 | 2.25 |
| 416 | A82 | 95c multicolored | 2.50 | 2.50 |
| 417 | A82 | $1.40 multicolored | 3.00 | 3.00 |
| | | Nos. 414-417 (4) | 9.75 | 9.75 |

**Souvenir Sheet**
| | | | | |
|---|---|---|---|---|
| 418 | | Sheet of 2 | 7.50 | 7.50 |
| a.-b. | A82 $2 any single | | 3.25 | 3.25 |

### Nos. 414-417 Ovptd. with Names of 1988 Olympic Gold Medalists

a

b

c

d

**1988, Oct. 10**   *Litho.*   *Perf. 14½x15*
| | | | | |
|---|---|---|---|---|
| 419 | A82 (a) | 70c on No. 414 | 1.75 | 1.75 |
| 420 | A82 (b) | 85c on No. 415 | 1.75 | 1.75 |
| 421 | A82 (c) | 95c on No. 416 | 2.75 | 2.75 |
| 422 | A82 (d) | $1.40 on No. 417 | 2.75 | 2.75 |
| | | Nos. 419-422 (4) | 9.00 | 9.00 |

Griffith is spelled incorrectly on No. 419.

Christmas A83

Paintings by Rembrandt: 55c, Adoration of the Shepherds (detail), National Gallery, London. 70c, Holy Family, Alte Pinakothek, Munich. 85c, Presentation in the Temple, Kunsthalle, Hamburg. 95c, The Holy Family, Louvre, Paris. $1.15, Presentation in the Temple, diff., Mauritshuis, The Hague. $4.50, Adoration of the Shepherds (entire painting).

**1988, Nov. 2**   *Photo.*   *Perf. 13½*
| | | | | |
|---|---|---|---|---|
| 423 | A83 | 55c multicolored | 1.75 | 1.75 |
| 424 | A83 | 70c multicolored | 1.90 | 1.90 |
| 425 | A83 | 85c multicolored | 2.00 | 2.00 |
| 426 | A83 | 95c multicolored | 2.25 | 2.25 |
| 427 | A83 | $1.15 multicolored | 2.50 | 2.50 |
| | | Nos. 423-427 (5) | 10.40 | 10.40 |

**Souvenir Sheet**
*Perf. 14*
| | | | | |
|---|---|---|---|---|
| 428 | A83 | $4.50 multicolored | 8.00 | 8.00 |

No. 428 contains one 52x34mm stamp.

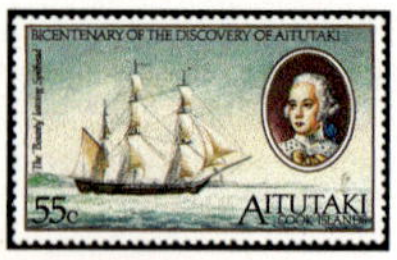


A84

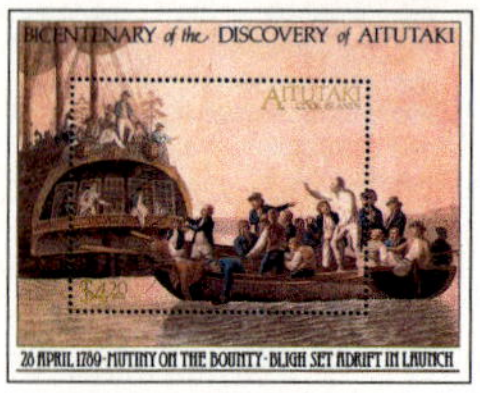


Mutiny on the *Bounty,* 200th Anniv. A85

55c, Ship, Capt. Bligh. 65c, Breadfruit. 75c, Bligh, chart. 95c, Bounty off Aitutaki. $1.65, Christian, Bligh.
$4.20, Castaways.

**1989, July 3 Photo. *Perf. 13½***

| | | | | |
|---|---|---|---|---|
| 429 | A84 | 55c multicolored | 2.00 | 2.00 |
| 430 | A84 | 65c multicolored | 2.25 | 2.25 |
| 431 | A84 | 75c multicolored | 2.50 | 2.50 |
| 432 | A84 | 95c multicolored | 2.75 | 2.75 |
| 433 | A84 | $1.65 multicolored | 3.75 | 3.75 |
| | | *Nos. 429-433 (5)* | 13.25 | 13.25 |

**Souvenir Sheet**

| | | | | |
|---|---|---|---|---|
| 434 | A85 | $4.20 multicolored | 11.00 | 11.00 |

Discovery of Aitutaki by William Bligh, bicent.

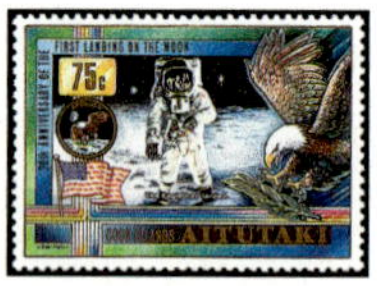


1st Moon Landing, 20th Anniv. — A86

Apollo 11 mission emblem, American flag, eagle, "The Eagle has landed" and: 75c, Astronaut standing on the lunar surface. $1.15, Conducting an experiment in front of the lunar module. $1.80, Carrying equipment. $6.40, Raising the flag.

**1989, July 28 Photo. *Perf. 13½x13***

| | | | | |
|---|---|---|---|---|
| 435 | A86 | 75c multicolored | 2.50 | 2.50 |
| 436 | A86 | $1.15 multicolored | 3.25 | 3.25 |
| 437 | A86 | $1.80 multicolored | 3.75 | 3.75 |
| | | *Nos. 435-437 (3)* | 9.50 | 9.50 |

**Souvenir Sheet**

***Perf. 13½***

| | | | | |
|---|---|---|---|---|
| 438 | A86 | $6.40 multicolored | 9.50 | 9.50 |

No. 438 contains one 42x31mm stamp.

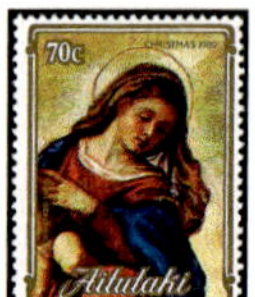


Christmas — A87

Details from *Virgin in Glory,* by Titian: 70c, Virgin. 85c, Christ child. 95c, Angel. $1.25, Cherubs. $6, Entire painting.

**1989, Nov. 20 Photo. *Perf. 13½x13***

| | | | | |
|---|---|---|---|---|
| 439 | A87 | 70c multicolored | 2.10 | 2.10 |
| 440 | A87 | 85c multicolored | 2.25 | 2.25 |
| 441 | A87 | 95c multicolored | 2.40 | 2.40 |
| 442 | A87 | $1.25 multicolored | 3.50 | 3.50 |
| | | *Nos. 439-442 (4)* | 10.25 | 10.25 |

**Souvenir Sheet**

***Perf. 13½***

| | | | | |
|---|---|---|---|---|
| 443 | A87 | $6 multicolored | 11.00 | 11.00 |

No. 443 contains one 45x60mm stamp.

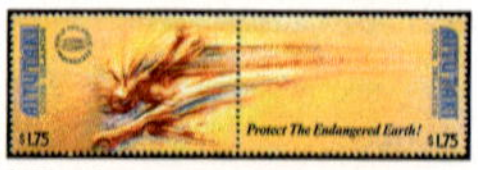


World Environmental Protection — A88

Designs: a, Human comet, World Philatelic Programs emblem. b, Comet tail and "Protect The Endangered Earth!" $3, Human comet, emblem and inscription.

**1990, Feb. 16 Photo. *Perf. 13½x13***

| | | | | |
|---|---|---|---|---|
| 444 | A88 | Pair | 5.75 | 5.75 |
| *a.-b.* | | $1.75 any single | 2.50 | 2.50 |

**Souvenir Sheet**

| | | | | |
|---|---|---|---|---|
| 445 | A88 | $3 multicolored | 7.00 | 7.00 |

**No. 376a Overprinted**

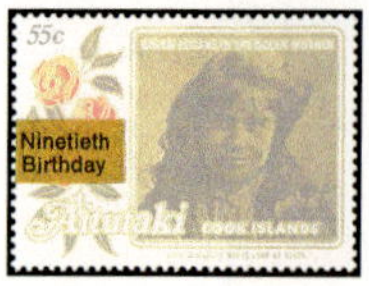


Designs: 55c, Lady Elizabeth Bowes-Lyon, 1907. 65c, Lady Elizabeth engaged to Duke of York. 75c, As Duchess of York with daughter Elizabeth. $1.30, As Queen Mother with grandson.

**1990, July 16 Litho. *Perf. 13½x13***

| | | | | |
|---|---|---|---|---|
| 446 | | Sheet of 4 | 13.00 | 13.00 |
| *a.* | | A72 55c multicolored | 2.75 | 2.75 |
| *b.* | | A72 65c multicolored | 3.00 | 3.00 |
| *c.* | | A72 75c multicolored | 3.25 | 3.25 |
| *d.* | | A72 $1.30 multicolored | 3.50 | 3.50 |

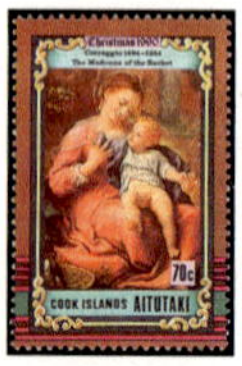


Christmas — A89

Paintings: 70c, Madonna of the Basket by Correggio. 85c, Virgin and Child by Morando. 95c, Adoration of the Child by Tiepolo. $1.75, Mystic Marriage of St. Catherine by Memling. $6, Donne Triptych by Memling.

**1990, Nov. 28 Litho. *Perf. 14***

| | | | | |
|---|---|---|---|---|
| 447 | A89 | 70c multicolored | 1.50 | 1.50 |
| 448 | A89 | 85c multicolored | 1.60 | 1.60 |
| 449 | A89 | 95c multicolored | 1.75 | 1.75 |
| 450 | A89 | $1.75 multicolored | 2.50 | 2.50 |
| | | *Nos. 447-450 (4)* | 7.35 | 7.35 |

**Souvenir Sheet**

| | | | | |
|---|---|---|---|---|
| 451 | A89 | $6 multicolored | 13.00 | 13.00 |

Nos. 246A-246B Overprinted

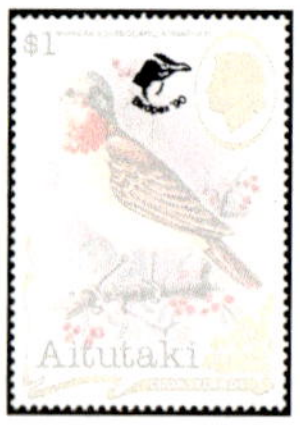


**1990, Dec. 5 Photo. *Perf. 13½***

| | | | | |
|---|---|---|---|---|
| 452 | A55 | $1 multicolored | 4.75 | 4.75 |
| 453 | A55 | $2 multicolored | 5.75 | 5.75 |

Birdpex '90, 20 Intl. Ornithological Congress, New Zealand.

No. 246D Overprinted

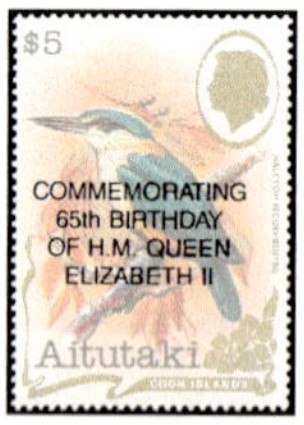


**1991, Apr. 22 Photo. *Perf. 13***

| | | | | |
|---|---|---|---|---|
| 454 | A55 | $5 multicolored | 11.00 | 11.00 |

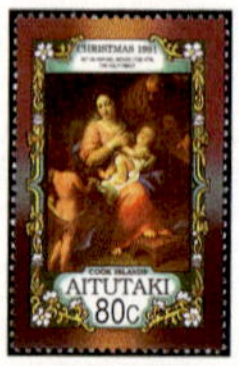


Christmas — A90

Paintings: 80c, The Holy Family, by Mengs. 90c, Virgin and Child, by Fra Filippo Lippi. $1.05, Virgin and Child, by Durer. $1.75, Adoration of the Shepherds, by De La Tour. $6, The Holy Family, by Michelangelo.

**1991, Nov. 13 Litho. *Perf. 14***

| | | | | |
|---|---|---|---|---|
| 455 | A90 | 80c multicolored | 1.75 | 1.75 |
| 456 | A90 | 90c multicolored | 1.90 | 1.90 |
| 457 | A90 | $1.05 multicolored | 2.00 | 2.00 |
| 458 | A90 | $1.75 multicolored | 2.50 | 2.50 |
| | | *Nos. 455-458 (4)* | 8.15 | 8.15 |

**Souvenir Sheet**

| | | | | |
|---|---|---|---|---|
| 459 | A90 | $6 multicolored | 13.00 | 13.00 |

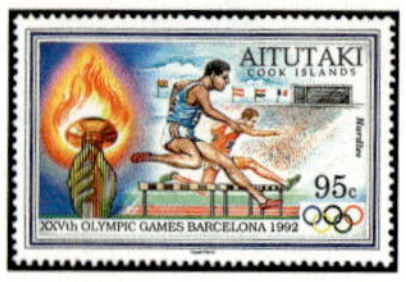


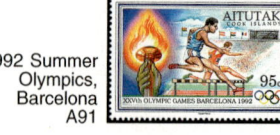

1992 Summer Olympics, Barcelona A91

**1992, July 29 Litho. *Perf. 14***

| | | | | |
|---|---|---|---|---|
| 460 | A91 | 95c Hurdles | 2.00 | 2.00 |
| 461 | A91 | $1.25 Weight lifting | 2.25 | 2.25 |
| 462 | A91 | $1.50 Judo | 2.75 | 2.75 |
| 463 | A91 | $1.95 Soccer | 3.25 | 3.25 |
| | | *Nos. 460-463 (4)* | 10.25 | 10.25 |

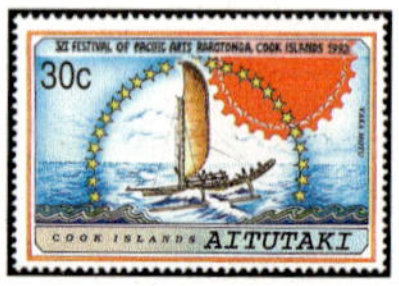


6th Festival of Pacific Arts, Rarotonga A92

Canoes: 30c, Vaka Motu. 50c, Hamatafua. 95c, Alia Kalia Ndrua. $1.75, Hokule'a Hawaiian. $1.95, Tuamotu Pahi.

**1992, Oct. 16 Litho. *Perf. 14x15***

| | | | | |
|---|---|---|---|---|
| 464 | A92 | 30c multicolored | .85 | .85 |
| 465 | A92 | 50c multicolored | 1.00 | 1.00 |
| 466 | A92 | 95c multicolored | 2.00 | 2.00 |
| 467 | A92 | $1.75 multicolored | 3.00 | 3.00 |
| 468 | A92 | $1.95 multicolored | 3.50 | 3.50 |
| | | *Nos. 464-468 (5)* | 10.35 | 10.35 |

For overprints see Nos. 524-528.

**Nos. 464-468 Overprinted**

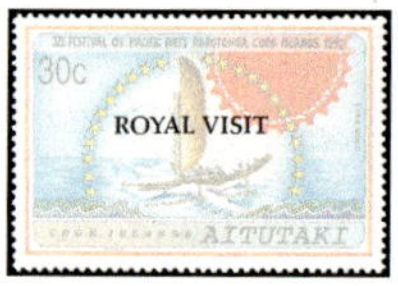


**1992, Oct. 16**

| | | | | |
|---|---|---|---|---|
| 469 | A92 | 30c on #464 | 1.00 | 1.00 |
| 470 | A92 | 50c on #465 | 1.75 | 1.75 |
| 471 | A92 | 95c on #466 | 2.75 | 2.75 |
| 472 | A92 | $1.75 on #467 | 3.75 | 3.75 |
| 473 | A92 | $1.95 on #468 | 4.50 | 4.50 |
| | | *Nos. 469-473 (5)* | 13.75 | 13.75 |

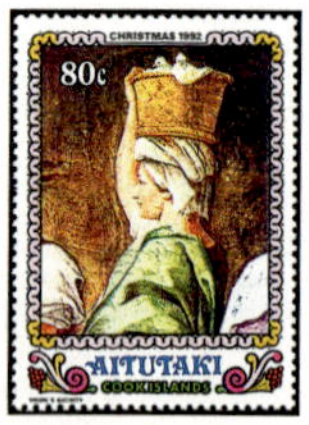


Christmas — A93

Designs: Different details from Virgin's Nativity, by Guido Reni.

**1992, Nov. 19 Litho. *Perf. 13½***

| | | | | |
|---|---|---|---|---|
| 474 | A93 | 80c multicolored | 1.90 | 1.90 |
| 475 | A93 | 90c multicolored | 2.00 | 2.00 |
| 476 | A93 | $1.05 multicolored | 2.10 | 2.10 |
| 477 | A93 | $1.75 multicolored | 2.50 | 2.50 |
| | | *Nos. 474-477 (4)* | 8.50 | 8.50 |

**Souvenir Sheet**

| | | | | |
|---|---|---|---|---|
| 478 | A93 | $6 like #476 | 8.00 | 8.00 |

No. 478 contains one 39x50mm stamp.

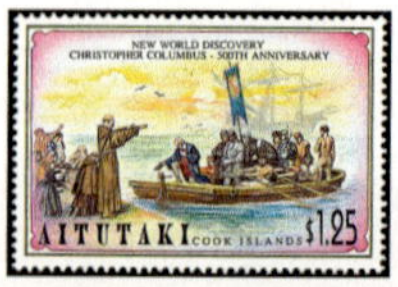


Discovery of America, 500th Anniv. — A94

Designs: $1.25, Columbus being blessed as he departs from Spain. $1.75, Map of Columbus' four voyages. $1.95, Columbus landing in New World.

**1992, Dec. 11 *Perf. 14x15***

| | | | | |
|---|---|---|---|---|
| 479 | A94 | $1.25 multicolored | 2.75 | 2.75 |
| 480 | A94 | $1.75 multicolored | 3.50 | 3.50 |
| 481 | A94 | $1.95 multicolored | 3.75 | 3.75 |
| | | *Nos. 479-481 (3)* | 10.00 | 10.00 |

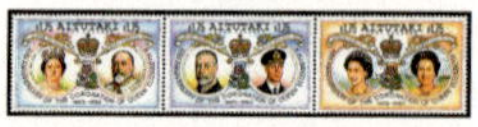

Coronation of Queen Elizabeth II, 40th Anniv. — A95

Designs: a, Victoria, Edward VII. b, George V, George VI. c, Elizabeth II.

**1993, June 4 Litho. *Perf. 14***

| | | | | |
|---|---|---|---|---|
| 482 | A97 | $1.75 Strip of 3, #a.-c. | 10.00 | 10.00 |

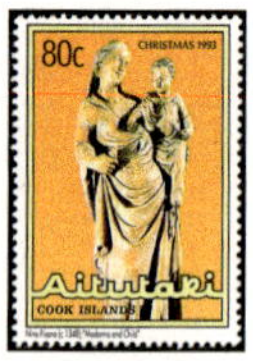


Christmas — A96

Religious sculpture: 80c, Madonna and Child, by Nino Pisano. 90c, Virgin on Rosebush, by Luca Della Robbia. $1.15, Virgin with Child and St. John, by Juan Francisco Rustici. $1.95, Virgin with Child, by Michelangelo. $3, Madonna and Child, by Jacopo Della Quercia.

**1993, Oct. 29 Litho. *Perf. 14***

| | | | | |
|---|---|---|---|---|
| 483 | A96 | 80c multicolored | 1.00 | 1.00 |
| 484 | A96 | 90c multicolored | 1.25 | 1.25 |
| 485 | A96 | $1.15 multicolored | 1.75 | 1.75 |
| 486 | A96 | $1.95 multicolored | 2.50 | 2.50 |

**Size: 32x47mm**

***Perf. 13½***

| | | | | |
|---|---|---|---|---|
| 487 | A96 | $3 multicolored | 3.50 | 3.50 |
| | | *Nos. 483-487 (5)* | 10.00 | 10.00 |

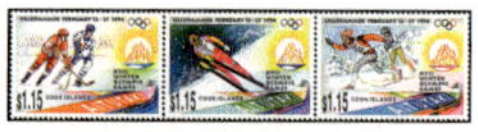

1994 Winter Olympics, Lillehammer — A97

Designs: a, Ice hockey. b, Ski jumping. c, Cross-country skiing.

**1994, Feb. 11 Litho. *Perf. 14***

| | | | | |
|---|---|---|---|---|
| 488 | A97 | $1.15 Strip of 3, #a.-c. | 12.00 | 12.00 |

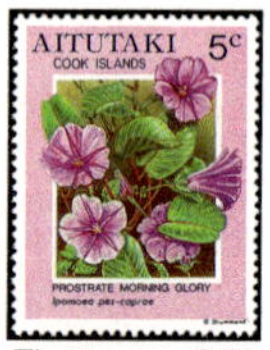


Flowers — A98

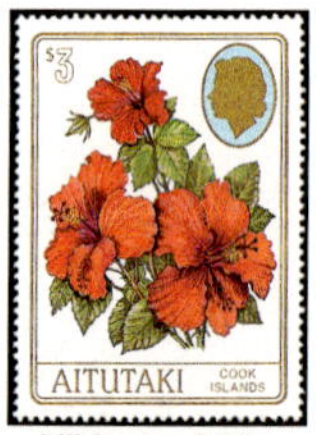


Hibiscus A98a

**1994-97 Litho. *Perf. 13½***

| | | | | |
|---|---|---|---|---|
| 489 | A98 | 5c Prostrate morning glory | .50 | .50 |
| 490 | A98 | 10c White frangipani | .60 | .60 |
| 491 | A98 | 15c Red hibiscus | .75 | .75 |
| 492 | A98 | 20c Yellow allamanda | .85 | .85 |
| 493 | A98 | 25c Royal poinciana | .85 | .85 |
| 494 | A98 | 30c White gardenia | .85 | .85 |
| 495 | A98 | 50c Pink frangipani | 1.00 | 1.00 |
| 496 | A98 | 80c Morning glory | 1.25 | 1.25 |
| 497 | A98 | 85c Yellow mallow | 1.50 | 1.50 |
| 498 | A98 | 90c Red coral tree | 1.50 | 1.50 |
| 499 | A98 | $1 Cup of gold | 1.60 | 1.60 |
| 500 | A98 | $2 Red cordia | 2.00 | 2.00 |
| 501 | A98a | $3 multicolored | 4.25 | 4.25 |
| 502 | A98a | $5 multicolored | 5.00 | 5.00 |
| 503 | A98a | $8 multicolored | 8.00 | 8.00 |
| | | *Nos. 489-503 (15)* | 30.50 | 30.50 |

Issued: 5c-90c, 2/17; $1, $2, 4/29; $3, $5, 11/18; $8, 11/21/97.

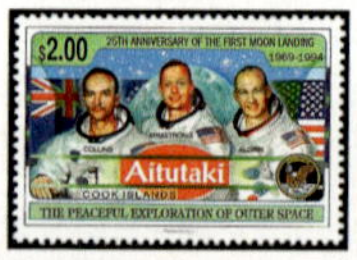


First Manned Moon Landing, 25th Anniv. — A99

# AITUTAKI

Designs: No. 506, Astronauts Collins, Armstrong, Aldrin. No. 507, Splash down in South Pacific.

**1994, July 20**   Litho.   *Perf. 14*
| | | | | |
|---|---|---|---|---|
|506|A99|$2 multicolored|6.50|6.50|
|507|A99|$2 multicolored|6.50|6.50|

Christmas — A100

Paintings: No. 508a, The Madonna of the Basket, by Corregio. b, Virgin & Child with Saints, by Hans Memling. c, The Virgin & Child with Flowers, by Dolci. d, Virgin & Child with Angels, by Bergognone.
No. 509a, The Adoration of the Kings, by Dosso. b, The Virgin & Child, by Bellini. c, The Virgin & Child, by Schiavone. d, Adoration of the Kings, by Dolci.

**1994, Nov. 30**   Litho.   *Perf. 14*
| | | | | |
|---|---|---|---|---|
|508|A100|85c Block of 4, #a-d|4.75|4.75|
|509|A100|90c Block of 4, #a-d|5.50|5.50|

End of World War II, 50th Anniv. — A101

Designs: a, Battle of Britain, 1940. b, Battle of Midway, June 1942.

**1995, Sept. 4**   Litho.   *Perf. 13½x13*
| | | | | |
|---|---|---|---|---|
|510|A101|$4 Pair, #a.-b.|20.00|20.00|

No. 510 issued in sheets of 4 stamps.

Queen Mother, 95th Birthday — A102

**1995, Sept. 14**   Litho.   *Perf. 13x13½*
| | | | | |
|---|---|---|---|---|
|511|A102|$4 multicolored|9.50|9.50|

UN, 50th Anniv. A103

**1995, Oct. 18**   Litho.   *Perf. 13½*
| | | | | |
|---|---|---|---|---|
|512|A103|$4.25 multicolored|7.50|7.50|

Year of the Sea Turtle — A104

**1995, Dec. 1**   Litho.   *Perf. 14x13½*
| | | | | |
|---|---|---|---|---|
|513|A104|95c Green|2.25|2.25|
|514|A104|$1.15 Leatherback|2.75|2.75|
|515|A104|$1.50 Olive Ridley|3.00|3.00|
|516|A104|$1.75 Loggerhead|3.25|3.25|
| |Nos. 513-516 (4)| |11.25|11.25|

Queen Elizabeth II, 70th Birthday — A105

**1996, June 24**   Litho.   *Perf. 14*
| | | | | |
|---|---|---|---|---|
|517|A105|$4.50 multicolored|8.25|8.25|

No. 517 was issued in sheets of 4.

Modern Olympic Games, Cent. — A106

Designs: No. 518, Pierre de Coubertin, Olympic torch, parading athletes, 1896. No. 519, Modern sprinters, US flag, Atlanta, 1996.

**1996, July 11**   Litho.   *Perf. 14*
| | | | | |
|---|---|---|---|---|
|518|A106|$2 multicolored|4.50|4.50|
|519|A106|$2 multicolored|4.50|4.50|
|a.| |Pair, #518-519|10.00|10.00|

Queen Elizabeth II and Prince Philip, 50th Wedding Anniv. — A107

Designs: $2.50, Queen Elizabeth II, Prince Philip, Queen Mother, and King George VI. $6, like No. 520, close-up.

**1997, Nov. 20**   Litho.   *Perf. 14*
| | | | | |
|---|---|---|---|---|
|520|A107|$2.50 multicolored|3.75|3.75|
| | |**Souvenir Sheet**| | |
|521|A107|$6 multicolored|8.00|8.00|

No. 520 was issued in sheets of 4.

Diana, Princess of Wales (1961-97) — A108

**1998, Apr. 15**   Litho.   *Perf. 14*
| | | | | |
|---|---|---|---|---|
|522|A108|$1 multicolored|1.00|1.00|
| | |**Souvenir Sheet**| | |
|523|A108|$4 like #522|5.00|5.00|

No. 522 was issued in sheets of 5 + label. No. 523 is a continuous design. For surcharge see No. B55.

**Nos. 464-468 Overprinted**

**1999, Dec. 31**   Litho.   *Perf. 14x15*
| | | | | |
|---|---|---|---|---|
|524|A92|30c on #464|.55|.55|
|525|A92|50c on #465|.70|.70|
|526|A92|95c on #466|1.00|1.00|
|527|A92|$1.75 on #467|1.50|1.50|
|528|A92|$1.95 on #468|1.75|1.75|
| |Nos. 524-528 (5)| |5.50|5.50|

Queen Mother, 100th Birthday A109

No. 529: a, Wearing crown, blue-toned photograph. b, Wearing crown, color photograph. c, Wearing hat. d, With King George VI.

**2000, Oct. 20**   Litho.   *Perf. 14*
| | | | | |
|---|---|---|---|---|
|529|A109|$3 Sheet of 4, #a-d|11.00|11.00|
| | |**Souvenir Sheet**| | |
|530|A109|$7.50 With flowers|7.00|7.00|

2000 Summer Olympics, Sydney — A110

No. 531: a, Ancient wrestling. b, Wrestling. c, Ancient boxer. d, Boxing.

**2000, Dec. 14**   Litho.   *Perf. 14*
| | | | | |
|---|---|---|---|---|
|531|A110|$2 Sheet of 4, #a-d|7.25|7.25|
| | |**Souvenir Sheet**| | |
|532|A110|$2.75 Torch relay|3.00|3.00|

Worldwide Fund for Nature (WWF) — A111

Various views of two blue lorikeets: 80c, 90c, $1.15, $1.95.

**2002, Sept. 3**   Litho.   *Perf. 14*
| | | | | |
|---|---|---|---|---|
|533-536|A111|Set of 4|5.75|5.75|

Nos. 533-536 were each issued in sheets of four with a label featuring an enlarged design of the stamp. Value, set of four sheets $24.

United We Stand — A112

**2003, Sept. 30**   Litho.   *Perf. 14*
| | | | | |
|---|---|---|---|---|
|537|A112|$1.15 multi|1.50|1.50|

Printed in sheets of 4.

Pope John Paul II (1920-2005) — A113

**2005, Nov. 11**   Litho.   *Perf. 14*
| | | | | |
|---|---|---|---|---|
|538|A113|$1.95 multi|3.75|3.75|

Printed in sheets of 5 + label.

Worldwide Fund for Nature (WWF) — A114

Blue moon butterfly: 80c, Caterpillar and chrysalis. 90c, Female. $1.15, Male. $1.95, Male, diff.

**2008, Nov. 18**   Litho.   *Perf. 13½*
| | | | | |
|---|---|---|---|---|
|539-542|A114|Set of 4|6.00|6.00|

Nos. 539-542 were each issued in sheets of four with a label featuring an enlarged design of the stamp. Value, set of four sheets $25.

Worldwide Fund for Nature (WWF) — A115

Designs: 80c, Tomato grouper. 90c, Peacock grouper. $1.10, Pair of Tomato groupers. $1.20, Head of Peacock grouper.

**2010, Dec. 9**     *Perf. 14*
| | | | | |
|---|---|---|---|---|
|543-546|A115|Set of 4|5.00|5.00|

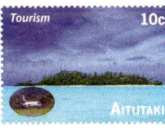

Tourism — A116

Designs: 10c, Airplane, island. 20c, Bent palm tree, sun on horizon. 30c, Beach. 40c, Ship, islands. 50c, Road in forest. 60c, Huts. 70c, People fishing. 80c, Bent palm tree. 90c, Huts. $1, Islands and beach (at left). $1.10, Fence near beach. $1.20, Sun at horizon. $1.50, Moon above island. $2, Mountain on island. $3, Building and courtyard.

**2010, Dec. 10**
| | | | | |
|---|---|---|---|---|
|547|A116|10c multi|.30|.30|
|548|A116|20c multi|.35|.35|
|549|A116|30c multi|.40|.40|
|550|A116|40c multi|.90|.90|
|551|A116|50c multi|.70|.70|
|552|A116|60c multi|.85|.85|
|553|A116|70c multi|1.00|1.00|
|554|A116|80c multi|1.10|1.10|
|555|A116|90c multi|1.15|1.15|
|556|A116|$1 multi|1.25|1.25|
|557|A116|$1.10 multi|1.40|1.40|
|558|A116|$1.20 multi|1.50|1.50|
|559|A116|$1.50 multi|1.75|1.75|
|560|A116|$2 multi|2.25|2.25|
|561|A116|$3 multi|3.75|3.75|
|a.| |Sheet of 15, #547-561|19.50|19.50|
| |Nos. 547-561 (15)| |18.65|18.65|

A117

Engagement of Prince William and Catherine Middleton — A118

## AITUTAKI

Designs: Nos. 562, 565a, 567, 50c, Middleton. Nos. 563, 565b, 568, $5, Prince playing polo.
No. 564: a, Prince in military uniform. b, Prince playing polo. c, Middleton, fence. d, Prince, man and woman in background. e, Middleton, woman in background. f, Couple, Prince at left. g, Middleton with black hat. h, Prince. i, Couple, Middleton at left. j, Hands of couple, engagement ring.
$8.10, Couple, Prince in uniform at left.

**2011, Jan. 14**   **Perf. 14**
| 562 | A117 | 50c multi | .75 | .75 |
| 563 | A117 | $5 multi | 7.00 | 7.00 |

**Miniature Sheets**
| 564 | A118 | $1 Sheet of 10, #a-j | 12.50 | 12.50 |

**Perf. 13¾x13½**
| 565 | A117 | Sheet of 2, #a-b + label | 8.00 | 8.00 |

**Souvenir Sheets**
**Perf. 14¼**
| 566 | A117 | $8.10 multi | 11.00 | 11.00 |
| 567 | A117 | $11 multi | 16.00 | 16.00 |
| 568 | A117 | $11 multi | 16.00 | 16.00 |
| | | Nos. 566-568 (3) | 43.00 | 43.00 |

No. 565 contains two 28x44mm stamps. Nos. 566-568 each contain one 38x50mm stamp.

Peonies — A119

**2011, Apr. 8**   **Litho.**   **Perf. 13¼**
| 569 | A119 | 90c multi | 1.25 | 1.25 |

**Souvenir Sheet**
**Perf. 14¾x14**
| 570 | A119 | $6.60 Peonies in vase, horiz. | 10.50 | 10.50 |

No. 569 was printed in sheets of 6. No. 570 contains one 48x42mm stamp.

**Souvenir Sheet**

Wedding of Prince William and Catherine Middleton — A120

No. 571 — Bride and groom: a, $1.10, Walking down aisle. b, $1.20, Kneeling.

**2011, July 15**   **Perf. 15x14¼**
| 571 | A120 | Sheet of 2, #a-b | 4.00 | 4.00 |

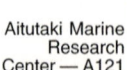 

Aitutaki Marine Research Center — A121

Designs: 10c, Suspended cages underwater. 20c, Station manager Richard Story. 80c, Tridacna maxima. 90c, Tridacna maxima. $1.10, Tridacna derasa. $1.20, Tridacna derasa, diff.
No. 578, vert.: a, $2, Researcher underwater. b, $3, Researcher lifting cage on boat.

**2011, July 25**   **Perf. 14¼x14**
| 572-577 | A121 | Set of 6 | 7.25 | 7.25 |

**Souvenir Sheet**
**Perf. 13¾**
| 578 | A121 | Sheet of 2, #a-b | 8.50 | 8.50 |

Nos. 572-577 each were printed in sheets of 4. No. 578 contains two 30x38mm stamps.

Christmas — A122

No. 579 — Items from Christmas song "The Twelve Days of Christmas": a, Nine ladies dancing. b, Ten lords a leaping. c, Eleven pipers piping. d, Twelve drummers drumming.

**2011, Dec. 24**   **Litho.**   **Perf. 13¼**
| 579 | | Horiz. strip of 4 | 8.25 | 8.25 |
| a. | | A122 90c multi | 1.50 | 1.50 |
| b. | | A122 $1 multi | 1.60 | 1.60 |
| c. | | A122 $1.20 multi | 1.90 | 1.90 |
| d. | | A122 $2 multi | 3.25 | 3.25 |
| e. | | Souvenir sheet of 4, #579a-579d | 8.25 | 8.25 |

No. 579 was printed in sheets containing three strips.

Beatification of Pope John Paul II — A123

No. 580: a, $1.10, Pope Benedict XVI. b, $5.10, Pope John Paul II.

**2012, Jan. 10**   **Perf. 13¾**
| 580 | A123 | Horiz. pair, #a-b | 10.50 | 10.50 |

No. 580 was printed in sheets containing two pairs.

Cetaceans — A124

Designs: Nos. 581, 593a, 20c, Humpback whale. Nos. 582, 593b, 30c, Humpback whale tail. Nos. 583, 593c, 50c, Humpback whale, diff. Nos. 584, 593d, 80c, Striped dolphins. Nos. 585, 593e, 90c, Striped dolphins, diff. Nos. 586, 593f, $1, Striped dolphins, diff. Nos. 587, 593g, $1.10, Striped dolphin. Nos. 588, 593h, $1.20, Striped dolphins, diff. Nos. 589, 593i, $5, Striped dolphins, diff. Nos. 590, 593j, $6, Humpback whale tail, diff. Nos. 591, 593k, $7.50, Humpback whale, diff. Nos. 592, 593l, $10, Humpback whale, diff.

**2012, June 22**   **Perf. 14**
**Stamps Without Dark Blue Frame Near Denomination**
| 581-592 | A124 | Set of 12 | 55.00 | 55.00 |

**Stamps With Dark Blue Frame All Around**
| 593 | A124 | Sheet of 12, #a-l | 55.00 | 55.00 |

Entombment of Christ, by Pietro Lorenzetti A125

The Last Supper, by Lorenzetti — A126

Madonna with St. Francis and St. John the Evangelist, by Lorenzetti — A127

Deposition of Christ from the Cross, by Lorenzetti — A128

The Flagellation of Christ, by Lorenzetti — A129

Entry of Christ Into Jerusalem, by Lorenzetti — A130

**Perf. 14¾x14¼**

**2012, Nov. 16**   **Litho.**
**Stamps With White Frames**
| 594 | | Horiz. pair | 2.80 | 2.80 |
| a. | | A125 80c multi | 1.40 | 1.40 |
| b. | | A126 80c multi | 1.40 | 1.40 |
| 595 | | Horiz. pair | 3.00 | 3.00 |
| a. | | A127 90c multi | 1.50 | 1.50 |
| b. | | A128 90c multi | 1.50 | 1.50 |
| 596 | | Horiz. pair | 10.00 | 10.00 |
| a. | | A129 $3 multi | 5.00 | 5.00 |
| b. | | A130 $3 multi | 5.00 | 5.00 |
| | | Nos. 594-596 (3) | 15.80 | 15.80 |

**Miniature Sheet**
**Stamps Without White Frame**
| 597 | | Sheet of 6 | 16.00 | 16.00 |
| a. | | A125 80c multi | 1.40 | 1.40 |
| b. | | A126 80c multi | 1.40 | 1.40 |
| c. | | A127 90c multi | 1.50 | 1.50 |
| d. | | A128 90c multi | 1.50 | 1.50 |
| e. | | A129 $3 multi | 5.00 | 5.00 |
| f. | | A130 $3 multi | 5.00 | 5.00 |

Christmas.

Personalizable Stamp — A131

A131a    A131b

**2012, Dec. 21**   **Litho.**   **Perf. 14x14¾**
| 598 | A131 | $4 multi | 6.75 | 6.75 |
| a. | | A131a 50c multi | .70 | .70 |
| b. | | A131b $1 multi | 1.40 | 1.40 |

Christmas (#598a, 598b). Issued: Nos. 598a, 598b, 12/16/19. Nos. 598a-598b have the same frame as the personalizable stamp No. 598, but have different denominations. The editors do not know if 50c and $1 stamps having these frames were made available to the public that may have different personalized images other than the images shown above placed in the vignette area. The editors also do not know if there are stamps of type A131 that are available in denominations other than 50c, $1, or $4.

**Miniature Sheet**

New Year 2013 (Year of the Snake) A132

No. 599 — Snake with background color of: a, Green. b, Yellow, c, Pink. d, Violet.

**2013, Feb. 21**   **Litho.**   **Perf. 14¾x14**
| 599 | A132 | $1.20 Sheet of 4, #a-d | 8.00 | 8.00 |

Cetaceans A133

Various boats and: Nos. 600, 612a, 10c, Humpback whale. Nos. 601, 612b, 40c, Humpback whale, diff. Nos. 602, 612c, 60c, Humpback whale, diff. Nos. 603, 612d, 70c, Striped dolphin. Nos. 604, 612e, $1.50, Striped dolphin, diff. Nos. 605, 612f, $1.80, Striped dolphin, diff. Nos. 606, 612g, $2, Striped dolphin, diff. Nos. 607, 612h, $2.25, Striped dolphin, diff. Nos. 608, 612i, $2.50, Striped dolphin, diff. Nos. 609, 612j, Humpback whale, diff. Nos. 610, 612k, $4, Humpback whale, diff. Nos. 611, 612l, $20, Humpback whale, diff.

**2013, June 5**   **Litho.**   **Perf. 14**
**Stamps With White Frames**
| 600-611 | A133 | Set of 12 | 62.50 | 62.50 |

**Miniature Sheet**
**Stamps Without White Frames**
| 612 | A133 | Sheet of 12, #a-l | 62.50 | 62.50 |

**Souvenir Sheet**

Birth of Prince George of Cambridge — A134

No. 613: a, $1.30, Duchess of Cambridge. b, $1.50, Duchess of Cambridge reviewing Scouts, Duchess and Duke of Cambridge kissing. c, $1.70, Duchess of Cambridge, diff.

**2013, Aug. 1**   **Litho.**   **Perf. 13½**
| 613 | A134 | Sheet of 3, #a-c | 7.25 | 7.25 |

**Souvenir Sheet**

China International Collection Expo — A135

No. 614: a, $1.50, Painting by Paul Gauguin. b, $1.70, Beijing Exhibition Center.

**2013, Sept. 26**   **Litho.**   **Perf. 12**
| 614 | A135 | Sheet of 2, #a-b | 5.50 | 5.50 |

Pres. John F. Kennedy (1917-63) — A136

Designs: $2.50, Kennedy and quotation. $2.90, Kennedy.

**2013, Nov. 8**   **Litho.**   **Perf. 14¼**
| 615-616 | A136 | Set of 2 | 9.00 | 9.00 |

Christmas — A137

Religious paintings by: $1, William Brassey Hole. $1.30, Bernardino Luini.
No. 619 — Religious paintings by: a, $2, Gentile da Fabriano. b, $2.40, Marten de Vos. c, $2.60, Pietro Perugino.

# AITUTAKI

355

**2013, Nov. 18     Litho.     Perf. 13¼**
617-618  A137    Set of 2                4.00   4.00
**Souvenir Sheet**
619  A137    Sheet of 3, #a-c          11.50  11.50

**Miniature Sheet**

New Year 2014 (Year of the Horse) — A138

No. 620 — Color of horse: a, $1, Purple. b, $1.30, White, horiz. c, $1.50, Dark blue. d, $1.70, Yellow, horiz.

**2014, Jan. 10     Litho.     Perf. 13¾**
620  A138    Sheet of 4, #a-d           9.00   9.00

**Miniature Sheet**

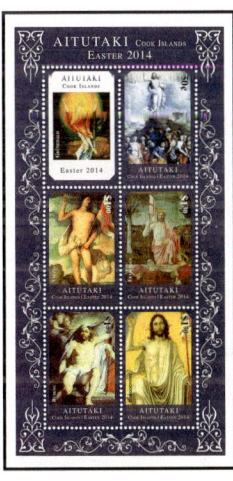

Easter — A139

No. 621 — Religious paintings by: a, 50c, Benvenuto Garofalo. b, $1, Tiziano Vecelli (Titian). c, $1.30, Piero della Francesca. d, $1.50, Peter Paul Rubens. e, $1.70, Ambrogio Dorgognone. $9.50, Painting by Paolo Veronese.

**2014, Apr. 9     Litho.     Perf. 13¼**
621  A139    Sheet of 5, #a-e, + label      10.50  10.50
**Souvenir Sheet**
622  A139    $9.50 multi               16.50  16.50

Worldwide Fund for Nature (WWF) — A140

Various depictions of spotted reef crab. $1, $1.30, $1.70, $2.10.

**2014, Nov. 28     Litho.     Perf. 14**
623-626  A140    Set of 4             9.75   9.75
626a    Souvenir sheet of 4, #623-626   9.75   9.75

Nos. 623-626 were each printed in sheets of 4.

**Souvenir Sheet**

Christmas — A141

No. 627 — Religious paintings by: a, Fra Angelico. b, Pieter Breugel, the Elder. c, Paolo Schiavo.

**Perf. 14¾x14¼**
**2014, Dec. 12     Litho.**
627  A141    $1.50 Sheet of 3, #a-c    7.00   7.00

**Souvenir Sheet**

New Year 2015 (Year of the Sheep) — A142

No. 628 — Sheep with background color of: a, $3.80, Green. b, $4.10, Orange.

**2015, Jan. 5     Litho.     Perf. 13¼**
628  A142    Sheet of 2, #a-b         11.50  11.50

**Miniature Sheet**

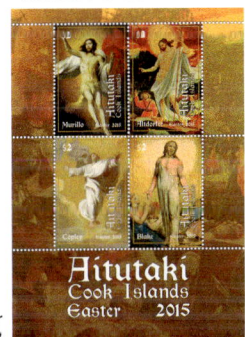

Easter — A143

No. 629 — Paintings depicting Jesus Christ by: a, Bartolomé Esteban Murillo. b, Albrecht Altdorfer. c, John Singleton Copley. d, William Blake.

**2015, Mar. 31     Litho.     Perf. 14x14¼**
629  A143    $2 Sheet of 4, #a-d       12.50  12.50

**Souvenir Sheet**

Birth of Princess Charlotte of Cambridge — A144

No. 630: a, Duchess of Cambridge holding Princess Charlotte. b, Duke of Cambridge and Prince George.

**Perf. 14¾x14¼**
**2015, June 23     Litho.**
630  A144    $4.50 Sheet of 2, #a-b    12.00  12.00

New Year 2016 (Year of the Monkey) — A145

Designs: $2.60, Monkey and red chop mark. $3, Monkey, diff.
No. 633: a, $3.80, Monkey and red chop mark. b, $4.10, Monkey, diff.

**2015, Sept. 25     Litho.     Perf. 13¼**
631-632  A145    Set of 2             7.25   7.25
**Souvenir Sheet**
633  A145    Sheet of 2, #a-b        10.50  10.50

No. 633 contains two 50x50mm diamond-shaped stamps.

**Miniature Sheet**

Queen Elizabeth II, Longest-Reigning British Monarch — A146

No. 634 — Various photographs of Queen Elizabeth II: a, $1.30. b, $1.50. c, $1.70. d, $2.

**2015, Nov. 20     Litho.     Perf. 14x14¼**
634  A146    Sheet of 4, #a-d          8.75   8.75

**Souvenir Sheet**

Christmas — A147

No. 635 — Details from *The Nativity*, by Lorenzo Monaco: a, Virgin Mary. b, Infant Jesus and farm animals. c, St. Joseph.

**2015, Dec. 9     Litho.     Perf. 13¼**
635  A147    $1 Sheet of 3, #a-c       4.00   4.00

**Souvenir Sheet**

Queen Elizabeth II, 90th Birthday — A148

No. 636 — Queen Elizabeth II: a, Without hat. b, With hat.

**2016, May 10     Litho.     Perf. 13¼**
636  A148    $3 Sheet of 2, #a-b       8.25   8.25

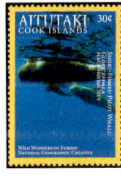

Marae Moana Marine Park — A149

Designs: 30c, Short-finned pilot whales. 50c, Whitetip reef shark. 80c, Common dolphins. $1, Emblem of Marae Moana Marine Park. $1.10, Humpback whales. $1.30, Blue shark. $1.50, Tiger shark. $1.70, Spinner dolphin. $2, Killer whale.

**2016, May 27     Litho.     Perf. 14¼x14¾**
637  A149    30c multi                 .40    .40
638  A149    50c multi                 .70    .70
639  A149    80c multi                1.10   1.10
640  A149    $1 multi                 1.40   1.40
641  A149    $1.10 multi              1.75   1.75
642  A149    $1.30 multi              1.90   1.90
643  A149    $1.50 multi              2.10   2.10
644  A149    $1.70 multi              2.40   2.40
645  A149    $2 multi                 2.75   2.75
    Nos. 637-645 (9)                 14.50  14.50

New Year 2017 (Year of the Rooster) — A150

Designs: $2.30, Rooster, green & orange tail feathers. $4.50, Rooster, green tail feathers.

**2016, Aug. 10     Litho.     Perf. 13½**
646-647  A150    Set of 2            10.00  10.00
647a    Souvenir sheet of 2, #646-647  10.00  10.00

Worldwide Fund for Nature (WWF) — A151

Chatham albatrosses: Nos. 648, 652a, $1, Two on cliff, one in flight. Nos. 649, 652b, $1.70, Adult and juvenile. Nos. 650, 652c, $2, Bird in flight. Nos. 651, 652d, $2.40, Two adults and nest.

**2016, Dec. 6     Litho.     Perf. 14¾x14¼**
**Stamps With White Frames**
648-651  A151    Set of 4            10.00  10.00
**Stamps Without White Frames**
652  A151    Block or horiz.
              strip of 4, #a-d       10.00  10.00

For surcharges, see Nos. 682-687.

A152

Christmas A153

No. 653 — Stained-glass window depicting: a, Adoration of the Shepherds. b, Holy Family.
No. 654 — Stained-glass window depicting: a, Holy Family and cows. b, Holy Family, diff.

**2016, Dec. 19     Litho.     Perf. 13¼**
653  A152    50c Horiz. pair, #a-b     1.40   1.40
654  A153    $1 Horiz. pair, #a-b      2.75   2.75

**Miniature Sheet**

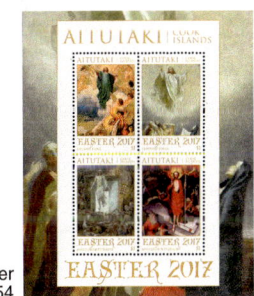

Easter A154

No. 655 — Paintings of the Resurrection of Christ by: a, Gustave Doré. b, Gebhard Fugel. c, James Jacques Tissot. d, Master of Wittingau.

**2017, Apr. 12     Litho.     Perf. 13**
655  A154    $1 Sheet of 4, #a-d       5.50   5.50

**Miniature Sheet**

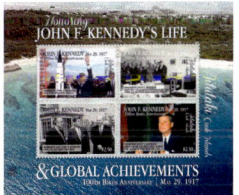

Pres. John F. Kennedy (1917-63) — A155

No. 656 — Pres. Kennedy: a, $1, With Werner von Braun. b, $1, With others watching television coverage of first U.S. manned space flight. c, $2.50, With W. Averill Harriman

# AITUTAKI

and Dean Rusk. d, $2.50, Delivering speech on Nuclear Test Ban Treaty.

**2017, July 3**    Litho.    *Perf. 13*
656   A155   Sheet of 4, #a-d    10.50   10.50

### Miniature Sheet

Reign of Queen Elizabeth II, 65th Anniv. — A156

No. 657 — Queen Elizabeth II: a, Holding handbag. b, Standing near railing. c, Holding paper. d, Wearing turquoise green hat and jacket.

**2017, July 17**    Litho.    *Perf. 13*
657   A156   $2.50 Sheet of 4, #a-d    15.00   15.00

New Year 2018 (Year of the Dog) — A157

Designs: $3, Dog. $3.80, Figurine of dog.

**2017, Nov. 1**    Litho.    *Perf. 13¼*
658-659   A157   Set of 2    9.50   9.50
659a   Souvenir sheet of 2, #658-659    9.50   9.50

Christmas — A158

No. 660, $1: a, Moon and palm trees. b, Sailboat.
No. 661, $2.40: a, Scallop shell. b, Holly and sea turtle.

**2017, Dec. 5**    Litho.    *Perf. 12½*
Horiz. pairs, #a-b
660-661   A158   Set of 2    9.75   9.75

Butterflies — A159

No. 662: a, Great eggfly butterfly. b, Blue-spotted Charaxes butterfly. c, Karner blue butterfly. d, Monarch butterfly.

**2017, Dec. 8**    Litho.    *Perf. 12½*
662   A159   $2.50 Block of 4, #a-d    14.50   14.50

### Miniature Sheet

Easter — A160

No. 663: a, $1, Tulip. b, $1, Church, chalice and bread. c, $2.40, Sun, cross and dove. d, $2.40, Easter eggs, shells and butterflies.

**2018, Mar. 19**    Litho.    *Perf. 13*
663   A160   Sheet of 4, #a-d    10.00   10.00

Birdpex Philatelic Exhibition, Mondorf-les-Bains, Luxembourg — A161

No. 664: a, $1, Hawaiian petrel. b, $4.80, Juan Fernandez petrels.

**2018, May 4**    Litho.    *Perf. 13*
664   A161   Horiz. pair, #a-b    8.25   8.25

Wedding of Prince Harry and Meghan Markle — A162

No. 665: a, Prince Charles bringing bride to groom. b, Couple kissing.
$8, Bride and groom on church steps.

**2018, Aug. 2**    Litho.    *Perf. 13*
665   A162   $4.80 Sheet of 2, #a-b    13.00   13.00

### Souvenir Sheet

666   A162   $8 multi    11.00   11.00

New Year 2019 (Year of the Pig) — A163

Pig facing: $3, Right. $3.80, Left.

**2018, Dec. 10**    Litho.    *Perf. 13¼*
667-668   A163   Set of 2    9.00   9.00

Birds of Prey — A164

Designs: Nos. 669, 681a, 20c, Bonelli's eagle. Nos. 670, 681b, 30c, Pearl kite. Nos. 671, 681c, 40c, Black-breasted buzzard kite. Nos. 672, 681d, 50c, Brahminy kite. Nos. 673, 681e, $1, Oriental honey buzzard. Nos. 674, 681f, $2, Henst's goshawk. Nos. 675, 681g, $2.40, Cuban black hawk. Nos. 676, 681h, $2.60, Double-toothed kite. Nos. 677, 681i, $4.50, Crowned eagle. Nos. 678, 681j, $5, African marsh harrier. Nos. 679, 681k, $7.50, White-bellied sea eagle. Nos. 680, 681l, $10, Pacific baza.

**2018, Dec. 27**    Litho.    *Perf. 13*
### Stamps With White Frames
669   A164   20c multi    .25   .25
670   A164   30c multi    .40   .40
671   A164   40c multi    .55   .55
672   A164   50c multi    .65   .65
673   A164   $1 multi    1.40   1.40
674   A164   $2 multi    2.75   2.75
   a.   Souvenir sheet of 6, #669-674    6.00   6.00
675   A164   $2.40 multi    3.25   3.25
676   A164   $2.60 multi    3.50   3.50
677   A164   $4.50 multi    6.00   6.00
678   A164   $5 multi    6.75   6.75
679   A164   $7.50 multi    10.00   10.00
680   A164   $10 multi    13.50   13.50
   a.   Souvenir sheet of 6, #675-680    43.00   43.00
Nos. 669-680 (12)    49.00   49.00

### Miniature Sheet
### Stamps Without White Frames
681   A164   Sheet of 12, #a-l    49.00   49.00

Stamps on Nos. 674a and 680a have white frames on one or two sides. See Nos. 690-695.

### Nos. 649-651 Surcharged

### Methods and Perfs. As Before
**2019, Aug. 5**
682   A151   50c on $1.70 #649    .65   .65
683   A151   50c on $2 #650    .65   .65
684   A151   50c on $2.40 #651    .65   .65
685   A151   $1 on $1.70 #649    1.25   1.25
686   A151   $1 on $2 #650    1.25   1.25
687   A151   $1 on $2.40 #651    1.25   1.25
Nos. 682-687 (6)    5.70   5.70

New Year 2020 (Year of the Rat) — A165

Rat facing: $3, Right. $3.80, Left.

**2019, Oct. 11**    Litho.    *Perf. 13¼*
688-689   A165   Set of 2    8.75   8.75

### Birds of Prey Type of 2018
Designs: Nos. 690, 694a, $2.50, Long-crested eagle. Nos. 691, 694b, $3, Spanish imperial eagle. Nos. 692, 694c, $4, Tawny eagle. Nos. 693, 694d, $6, Verreaux's eagle.

**2019, Nov. 15**    Litho.    *Perf. 13*
690   A164   $2.50 multi    3.25   3.25
691   A164   $3 multi    4.00   4.00
692   A164   $4 multi    5.25   5.25
693   A164   $6 multi    8.00   8.00
Nos. 690-693 (4)    20.50   20.50

### Stamps Without White Frames
### Stamp Size: 48x40mm
*Perf. 13¼x13*
694   A164   Block or vert. strip of 4, #a-d    20.50   20.50
   e.   Souvenir sheet of 4, #694a-694d    20.50   20.50

Nos. 694a-694d were printed in sheets of 8 containing two of each stamp. Stamps on No. 694e have white frames on two adjacent sides.

Owls — A166

Designs: Nos. 695, 699a, $5.50, Barred owl. Nos. 696, 699b, $6.70, Little owl. Nos. 697, 699c, $22.40, Whiskered screech owl. Nos. 698, 699d, $29.90, Verreaux's eagle owl.

**2019, Nov. 20**    Litho.    *Perf. 13*
695   A166   $5.50 multi    7.25   7.25
696   A166   $6.70 multi    8.75   8.75
697   A166   $22.40 multi    29.00   29.00
698   A166   $29.90 multi    39.00   39.00
Nos. 695-698 (4)    84.00   84.00

### Stamps Without White Frames
### Stamp Size: 48x40mm
*Perf. 13¼x13*
699   A166   Block or vert. strip of 4, #a-d    84.00   84.00
   e.   Souvenir sheet of 4, #699a-699d    84.00   84.00

Nos. 699a-699d were printed in sheets of 8 containing two of each stamp. Stamps on No. 699e have white frames on two adjacent sides.

Turtles — A167

Designs: Nos. 700, 708a, 50c, Olive ridley sea turtle in water. Nos. 701, 708b, $1, Olive ridley sea turtle exiting water. Nos. 702, 708c, $5, Olive ridley sea turtle hatchling on beach. Nos. 703, 708d, $7, Olive ridley sea turtle in water, diff. Nos. 704, 709a, $10, Loggerhead sea turtle in water. Nos. 705, 709b, $20, Loggerhead sea turtle hatchling on beach. Nos. 706, 709c, $30, Loggerhead sea turtle in water, diff. Nos. 707, 709d, $34.70, Head of Loggerhead sea turtle.

**2020, Jan. 15**    Litho.    *Perf. 13*
### Stamps With White Frames
700   A167   50c multi    .65   .65
701   A167   $1 multi    1.30   1.30
702   A167   $5 multi    6.50   6.50
703   A167   $7 multi    9.00   9.00
704   A167   $10 multi    13.00   13.00
705   A167   $20 multi    26.00   26.00
706   A167   $30 multi    39.00   39.00
707   A167   $34.70 multi    45.00   45.00
Nos. 700-707 (8)    140.45   140.45

### Stamps Without White Frames
### Stamp Size: 48x40mm
*Perf. 13¼x13*
708   A167   Block or vert. strip of 4, #a-d    17.50   17.50
   e.   Souvenir sheet of 4, #708a-708d    17.50   17.50
709   A167   Block or vert. strip of 4, #a-d    125.00   125.00
   e.   Souvenir sheet of 4, #709a-709d    125.00   125.00

Nos. 708a-708d and 709a-709d were printed in sheets of 8 containing two of each stamp. Stamps on Nos. 708e and 709e have white frames on two adjacent sides.

Birds of Paradise — A168

Designs: Nos. 710, 714a, $2.50, Greater bird-of-paradise. Nos. 711, 714b, $3, Standardwing bird-of-paradise. Nos. 712, 714c, $4, Red bird-of-paradise. Nos. 713, 714d, $6, King of Saxony bird-of-paradise.

**2020, May 8**    Litho.    *Perf. 13*
### Stamps With White Frames
710   A168   $2.50 multi    3.25   3.25
711   A168   $3 multi    3.75   3.75
712   A168   $4 multi    5.00   5.00
713   A168   $6 multi    7.50   7.50
Nos. 710-713 (4)    19.50   19.50

### Stamps Without White Frames
### Stamp Size: 48x40mm
*Perf. 13¼x13*
714   A168   Block or vert. strip of 4, #a-d    19.50   19.50
   e.   Souvenir sheet of 4, #714a-714d    19.50   19.50

Nos. 714a-714d were printed in sheets of 8 containing two of each stamp. Stamps on No. 714e have white frames on two adjacent sides.

Geese — A169

Designs: Nos. 715, 719a, $5.50, Nene geese. Nos. 716, 719b, $6.70, Red-breasted geese. Nos. 717, 719c, $22.40, Bar-headed geese. Nos. 718, 719d, $29.90, Kelp geese.

# AITUTAKI

**2020, May 20 Litho. Perf. 13**
**Stamps With White Frames**
| 715 | A169 | $5.50 multi | 7.00 | 7.00 |
| 716 | A169 | $6.70 multi | 8.50 | 8.50 |
| 717 | A169 | $22.40 multi | 28.00 | 28.00 |
| 718 | A169 | $29.90 multi | 37.50 | 37.50 |
| | | Nos. 715-718 (4) | 81.00 | 81.00 |

**Stamps Without White Frames**
**Stamp Size: 48x40mm**
**Perf. 13¼x13**
| 719 | A169 | Block or vert. strip of 4, #a-d | 81.00 | 81.00 |
| | e. | Souvenir sheet of 4, #719a-719d | 81.00 | 81.00 |

Nos. 719a-719d were printed in sheets of 8 containing two of each stamp. Stamps on No. 719e have white frames on two adjacent sides.

Butterflies
A170

Designs: Nos. 720, 728a, 50c, Great purple hairstreak butterfly. Nos. 721, 728b, $1, Red admiral butterfly. Nos. 722, 728c, $5, Holly blue butterfly. Nos. 723, 728d, $7, Cryptic wood white butterfly. Nos. 724, 729a, $10, Silver-washed fritillary butterfly. Nos. 725, 729b, $20, Painted lady butterfly. Nos. 726, 729c, $30, Checkered skipper butterfly. Nos. 727, 729d, $34.70, Large white butterfly.

**2020, June 15 Litho. Perf. 13**
**Stamps With White Frames**
| 720 | A170 | 50c multi | .65 | .65 |
| 721 | A170 | $1 multi | 1.30 | 1.30 |
| 722 | A170 | $5 multi | 6.50 | 6.50 |
| 723 | A170 | $7 multi | 9.00 | 9.00 |
| 724 | A170 | $10 multi | 13.00 | 13.00 |
| 725 | A170 | $20 multi | 26.00 | 26.00 |
| 726 | A170 | $30 multi | 39.00 | 39.00 |
| 727 | A170 | $34.70 multi | 45.00 | 45.00 |
| | | Nos. 720-727 (8) | 140.45 | 140.45 |

**Stamps Without White Frames**
**Stamp Size: 48x40mm**
**Perf. 13¼x13**
| 728 | A170 | Block or vert. strip of 4, #a-d | 17.50 | 17.50 |
| | e. | Souvenir sheet of 4, #728a-728d | 17.50 | 17.50 |
| 729 | A170 | Block or vert. strip of 4, #a-d | 125.00 | 125.00 |
| | e. | Souvenir sheet of 4, #729a-729d | 125.00 | 125.00 |

Nos. 728a-728d and 729a-729d were printed in sheets of 8 containing two of each stamp. Stamps on Nos. 728e and 729e have white frames on two adjacent sides.

**Souvenir Sheet**

New Year 2021 (Year of the Ox)
A171

**2021, Apr. 7 Litho. Perf. 13¼x13**
| 730 | A171 | $5.30 multi | 7.75 | 7.75 |

Elephants
A172

Various photographs of elephants at the Smithsonian Institution National Zoological Park Conservation Biology Institute: 50c, Two elephants. $1, One elephant. $2, Elephant spraying itself with water. $4.50, Elephant with trunk raised. $10, Elephant spraying itself with dirt.

**2021, May 5 Litho. Perf. 13**
| 731-734 | A172 | Set of 4 | 12.00 | 12.00 |

**Souvenir Sheet**
**Perf. 13¼x13**
| 735 | A172 | $10 multi | 14.50 | 14.50 |

No. 735 contains one 48x40mm stamp.

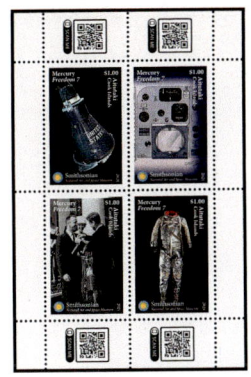
A173

A174

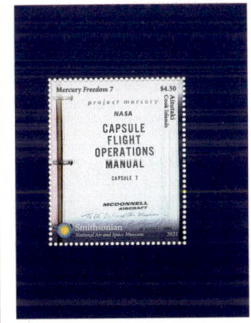

Project Mercury
A175

No. 736: a, Freedom 7 capsule. b, Drawing of instrument panel of Freedom 7. c. Pres. John F. Kennedy awarding Distinguished Service Medal to Freedom 7 astronaut Alan B. Shepard, Jr. d, Shepard's spacesuit. $2.50, Launch of Freedom 7. $4.50, Front page of Freedom 7's Capsule Flight Operations Manual.

**2021, May 5 Litho. Perf. 13**
| 736 | A173 | $1 Sheet of 4, #a-d | 6.00 | 6.00 |

**Souvenir Sheets**
**Perf. 13x13¼**
| 737 | A174 | $2.50 multi | 3.75 | 3.75 |
| 738 | A175 | $4.50 multi | 6.50 | 6.50 |

**Souvenir Sheets**

Observation Tower of Steven F. Udvar-Hazy Center of Smithsonian Institution's National Air and Space Museum — A176

Owlets From Smithsonian Institution's National Zoo Named "Increase" and "Diffusion" — A177

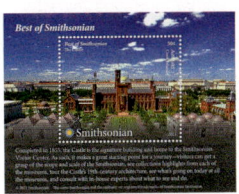

The Castle, Visitor's Center of the Smithsonian Institution — A178

Katherine Dulin Folger Rose Garden of the Smithsonian Institution — A179

Arts and Industries Building of the Smithsonian Institution — A180

Sculpture at the Smithsonian Institution's National Museum of the American Indian — A181

**2021, May 5 Litho. Perf. 13¼x13**
| 739 | A176 | 30c multi | .45 | .45 |
| 740 | A177 | 40c multi | .60 | .60 |
| 741 | A170 | 50c multi | .75 | .75 |
| 742 | A179 | 70c multi | 1.00 | 1.00 |

**Perf. 13x13¼**
| 743 | A180 | 80c multi | 1.25 | 1.25 |
| 744 | A181 | 90c multi | 1.30 | 1.30 |
| | | Nos. 739-744 (6) | 5.35 | 5.35 |

**Souvenir Sheet**

New Year 2022 (Year of the Tiger)
A182

**2022, Feb. 23 Litho. Perf. 13x13¼**
| 745 | A182 | $6.50 multi | 8.75 | 8.75 |

**Miniature Sheet**

Reign of Queen Elizabeth II, 70th Anniv.
A183

No. 746 — Queen Elizabeth II (1926-2022): a, Wearing tiara and large earrings. b, Riding in coach, waving. c, Passing by Union Jacks. d, Standing next to Archbishop of Canterbury Justin Welby. e, Seated at desk. f, Wearing tiara and strapless gown.

**2022, June 20 Litho. Perf. 13**
| 746 | A183 | $3.50 Sheet of 6, #a-f | 26.50 | 26.50 |

For overprints, see No. 750.

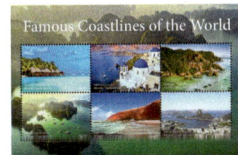

Coastlines of the World — A184

No. 747: a, Aitutaki. b, Santorini, Greece. c, La Digue, Seychelles. d, Halong Bay, Viet Nam. e, Legzira Beach, Morocco. f, Rio de Janeiro, Brazil. $9.50, Big Sur, California.

**2022, Aug. 3 Litho. Perf. 13**
| 747 | A184 | $2.50 Sheet of 6, #a-f | 18.50 | 18.50 |

**Souvenir Sheet**
**Perf. 13¼x13**
| 748 | A184 | $9.50 multi | 11.50 | 11.50 |

No. 748 contains one 48x40mm stamp.

**Souvenir Sheet**

South Island Pied Oystercatcher — A185

**2022, Aug. 18 Litho. Perf. 13¼x13**
| 749 | A185 | $9 multi | 11.00 | 11.00 |

Birdpex 9 Philatelic Exhibition, Gmunden, Austria.

**No. 746 With "IN LOVING MEMORY / 1926-2022" Overprinted on Each Stamp**

Designs as before.

**2022, Sept. 19 Litho. Perf. 13**
| 750 | A183 | $3.50 Sheet of 6, #a-f | 24.00 | 24.00 |

**Souvenir Sheet**

Giant Clam
A186

**2023, Feb. 10 Litho. Perf. 13¼x13**
| 751 | A186 | $9.50 multi | 12.00 | 12.00 |

Azure Kingfisher
A187

# AITUTAKI

Various photographs of Azure kingfisher: Nos. 752, 756a, $6.70, On branch. Nos. 753, 756b, $15, On branch, diff. Nos. 754, 756c, $20, On curved branch. Nos. 755, 756d, $25, on branch with wings spread.
No. 757, Like No. 752, vert. No. 758, Like No. 754, vert.

**2023, Aug. 16    Litho.    Perf. 13¼x13**
**Stamps With White Frames**
| 752-755 | A187 | Set of 4 | 78.50 | 78.50 |

**Stamps Without White Frames**
| 756 | A187 | Block or vert. strip of 4, #a-d | 78.50 | 78.50 |
| e. | | Souvenir sheet of 1 #756b | 17.50 | 7.50 |
| f. | | Souvenir sheet of 1 #756d | 29.50 | 29.50 |

**Souvenir Sheets**
**Perf. 13x13¼**
| 757 | A187 | $6.70 multi | 8.00 | 8.00 |
| 758 | A187 | $20 multi | 23.50 | 23.50 |

No. 756 was printed in sheets of 8 containing two of each stamp.

**Miniature Sheet**

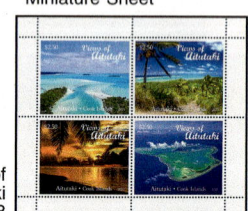
Views of Aitutaki A188

No. 759: a, Aerial view of recreational vehicle at water's edge of inlet. b, Dirt path. c, Clouds at twilight. d, Aerial view of atoll.

**2023, Sept. 27    Litho.    Perf. 13¼x13**
| 759 | A188 | $2.50 Sheet of 4, #a-d | 12.00 | 12.00 |

## SEMI-POSTAL STAMPS

### Christmas Type of 1974

Designs: 1c+1c, like No. 104. 5c+1c, like No. 105. 8c+1c, like No. 106. 10c+1c, like No. 107. 25c+1c, like No. 108. 30c+1c, like No. 109.

**1974, Dec. 2    Photo.    Perf. 13½**
| B1 | A29 | 1c + 1c multicolored | .25 | .25 |
| B2 | A29 | 5c + 1c multicolored | .25 | .25 |
| B3 | A29 | 8c + 1c multicolored | .25 | .25 |
| B4 | A29 | 10c + 1c multicolored | .25 | .25 |
| B5 | A29 | 25c + 1c multicolored | .30 | .30 |
| B6 | A29 | 30c + 1c multicolored | .30 | .30 |
| | | Nos. B1-B6 (6) | 1.60 | 1.60 |

Surtax was for child welfare.

Nos. 117-120 Surcharged in Silver

**1975, Dec. 19    Photo.    Perf. 14x13½**
| B7 | A32 | Strip of 3 | .45 | .45 |
| a.-c. | | 6c+1c any single | .25 | .25 |
| B8 | A32 | Strip of 3 | .50 | .50 |
| a.-c. | | 7c+1c any single | .25 | .25 |
| B9 | A32 | Strip of 3 | 1.00 | 1.00 |
| a.-c. | | 15c+1c any single | .30 | .30 |
| B10 | A32 | Strip of 3 | 1.50 | 1.50 |
| a.-c. | | 20c+1c any single | .45 | .45 |
| | | Nos. B7-B10 (4) | 3.45 | 3.45 |

Christmas. The surtax was for children's activities during holiday season.

Nos. 135-142a Surcharged in Silver

**1976, Nov. 19    Photo.    Perf. 13½x13**
| B11 | | 6c + 1c multicolored | .25 | .25 |
| B12 | | 6c + 1c multicolored | .25 | .25 |
| a. | | A36 Pair, #B11-B12 | .25 | .25 |
| B13 | | 7c + 1c multicolored | .25 | .25 |
| B14 | | 7c + 1c multicolored | .25 | .25 |
| a. | | A36 Pair, #B13-B14 | .25 | .25 |
| B15 | | 15c + 1c multicolored | .25 | .25 |
| B16 | | 15c + 1c multicolored | .25 | .25 |
| a. | | A36 Pair, #B15-B16 | .45 | .45 |
| B17 | | 20c + 1c multicolored | .30 | .30 |
| B18 | | 20c + 1c multicolored | .50 | .50 |
| a. | | A36 Pair, #B17-B18 | 1.00 | 1.00 |
| b. | | Souvenir sheet of 8 | 2.00 | 2.00 |

Surtax was for child welfare. Stamps of No. B18b each surcharged 2c.

Nos. 152-159a Surcharged in Black

**1977, Nov. 15    Perf. 13½x14**
| B19 | | 6c + 1c multicolored | .25 | .25 |
| B20 | | 6c + 1c multicolored | .25 | .25 |
| a. | | A41 Pair, #B19-B20 | .25 | .25 |
| B21 | | 7c + 1c multicolored | .25 | .25 |
| B22 | | 7c + 1c multicolored | .25 | .25 |
| a. | | A41 Pair, #B21-B22 | .25 | .25 |
| B23 | | 15c + 1c multicolored | .25 | .25 |
| B24 | | 15c + 1c multicolored | .25 | .25 |
| a. | | A41 Pair, #B23-B24 | .50 | .50 |
| B25 | | 20c + 1c multicolored | .30 | .30 |
| B26 | | 20c + 1c multicolored | .30 | .30 |
| a. | | A41 Pair, #B25-B26 | .65 | .65 |
| b. | | Souvenir sheet of 8 | 2.50 | 2.50 |
| | | Nos. B19-B26 (8) | 2.10 | 2.10 |

Surtax was for child welfare. Stamps of No. B26b each surcharged 2c.

### Easter Type of 1978
**Souvenir Sheets**

Paintings: No. B27, like No. 163. No. B28, like No. 164. No. B29, like No. 165.

**1978, Mar. 17    Photo.    Perf. 14**
| B27 | A44 | 50c + 5c multicolored | .55 | .55 |
| B28 | A44 | 50c + 5c multicolored | .55 | .55 |
| B29 | A44 | 50c + 5c multicolored | .55 | .55 |

Nos. B27-B29 contain one stamp 33x25mm.

### Christmas Type of 1978
**Souvenir Sheet**

**1978, Dec. 4    Photo.    Perf. 14½x13**
| B30 | | Sheet of 4 | 2.25 | 2.25 |
| a. | | A46 15c + 2c like #167 | .25 | .25 |
| b. | | A46 17c + 2c like #168 | .30 | .30 |
| c. | | A46 30c + 2c like #169 | .45 | .45 |
| d. | | A46 35c + 2c like #170 | .60 | .60 |

### Year of the Child Type
**Souvenir Sheet**

**1979, Oct. 1    Photo.    Perf. 14x13½**
| B31 | | Sheet of 3 | 1.25 | 1.25 |
| a. | | A48 30c + 3c like #173 | .30 | .30 |
| b. | | A48 35c + 3c like #174 | .35 | .35 |
| c. | | A48 65c + 3c like #175 | .45 | .45 |

### Easter Type of 1980
**Souvenir Sheet**

No. B32 shows entire painting in continuous design. Nos. B32a-B32c similar to Nos. 183-185. Size of Nos. B32a-B32c: 25x50mm.

**1980, Apr. 3    Photo.    Perf. 13x13½**
| B32 | | Sheet of 3 | 1.90 | 1.90 |
| a. | | A50 20c + 2c multicolored | .45 | .45 |
| b. | | A50 30c + 2c multicolored | .60 | .60 |
| c. | | A50 35c + 2c multicolored | .75 | .75 |

### Christmas Type of 1980
**Souvenir Sheet**

**1980, Nov. 21    Photo.    Perf. 13x13½**
| B33 | | Sheet of 4 | 1.50 | 1.50 |
| a. | | A53 15c + 2c like #208 | .25 | .25 |
| b. | | A53 20c + 2c like #209 | .30 | .30 |
| c. | | A53 25c + 2c like #210 | .35 | .35 |
| d. | | A53 35c + 2c like #211 | .45 | .45 |

### Easter Type of 1981
**Souvenir Sheet**

**1981, Mar. 31    Photo.    Perf. 13½**
| B34 | | Sheet of 3 | 1.65 | 1.65 |
| a. | | A54 30c + 2c like #212 | .35 | .35 |
| b. | | A54 40c + 2c like #213 | .50 | .50 |
| c. | | A54 50c + 2c like #214 | .65 | .65 |

Nos. 247-249 Surcharged

**1981, Nov. 23    Photo.    Perf. 13x13½**
| B35 | A56 | 60 + 5c multi | .65 | .65 |
| B36 | A56 | 80 + 5c multi | .70 | .70 |
| B37 | A56 | $1.40 + 5c multi | .90 | .90 |
| | | Nos. B35-B37 (3) | 2.25 | 2.25 |

Intl. Year of the Disabled. Surtax was for the handicapped.

### Soccer Type of 1981
**Souvenir Sheet**

a-b, 12c+2c. c-d, 15c+2c. e-f, 20c+2c. g-h, 25c+2c.

**1981, Nov. 30    Perf. 14**
| B38 | A57 | Sheet of 8, multi | 6.00 | 6.00 |

No. B38 contains stamps with 2c surtax similar to Nos. 250-253. Surtax was for local sports.

Nos. 400-404 Surcharged

**1986, Nov. 25    Litho.    Perf. 13½**
| B39 | A79 | 75c + 10c multi | 3.00 | 3.00 |
| B40 | A79 | $1.35 + 10c multi | 3.50 | 3.50 |
| B41 | A79 | $1.95 + 10c multi | 4.25 | 4.25 |
| B42 | A79 | $2.75 + 10c multi | 5.25 | 5.25 |
| | | Nos. B39-B42 (4) | 16.00 | 16.00 |

**Souvenir Sheet**
| B43 | | | 16.50 | 16.50 |
| a.-d. | | A79 $1.65 +10c on #404a-404d, each | 4.00 | 4.00 |

State visit of Pope John Paul II.
For surcharges see Nos. B51-B54.

Nos. 394-395, 397 and 400-403 Surcharged in Silver or Black

**1987, Apr. 29    Litho.    Perf. 13½, 14**
| B44 | A79 | 75c + 50c #400 | 3.50 | 2.50 |
| B45 | A77 | $1 + 50c #394 (B) | 4.25 | 3.50 |
| B46 | A79 | $1.35 + 50c #401 | 5.75 | 5.00 |
| B47 | A79 | $1.95 + 50c #402 | 6.25 | 5.00 |
| B48 | A78 | $2 + 50c #397 | 6.50 | 5.00 |
| B49 | A77 | $2.75 + 50c #395 (B) | 8.00 | 6.25 |
| B50 | A79 | $2.75 + 50c #403 | 8.50 | 7.25 |
| | | Nos. B44-B50 (7) | 42.75 | 34.50 |

Nos. B39-B42 Surcharged in Silver

**1987, Apr. 29    Litho.    Perf. 13½**
| B51 | A79 | 75c + 50c No. B39 | 4.00 | 4.00 |
| B52 | A79 | $1.35 + 50c No. B40 | 4.50 | 4.50 |
| B53 | A79 | $1.95 + 50c No. B41 | 4.75 | 4.75 |
| B54 | A79 | $2.75 + 50c No. B42 | 6.00 | 6.00 |
| | | Nos. B51-B54 (4) | 19.25 | 19.25 |

No. 523 Surcharged in Silver

**Souvenir Sheet**
**1998, Nov. 19    Litho.    Perf. 14**
| B55 | A108 | $4 + $1 multicolored | 6.25 | 6.25 |

## AIR POST STAMPS

### Capt. Bligh Type of 1974

**1974, Sept. 9    Litho.    Perf. 13**
**Size: 46x26mm**
| C1 | A27 | 10c Bligh and "Bounty" | .75 | .60 |
| C2 | A27 | 10c "Bounty" at sea | .75 | .60 |
| a. | | Pair, #C1-C2 | 1.75 | 1.75 |
| C3 | A27 | 25c Bligh and "Bounty" | .85 | .75 |
| C4 | A27 | 25c Chart, 1856 | .85 | .75 |
| a. | | Pair, #C3-C4 | 2.00 | 2.00 |
| C5 | A27 | 30c Cook and "Resolution" | 1.00 | 1.00 |
| C6 | A27 | 30c Maps | 1.00 | 1.00 |
| a. | | Pair, #C5-C6 | 2.75 | 2.75 |
| | | Nos. C1-C6 (6) | 5.20 | 4.70 |

See note after No. 101.

## OFFICIAL STAMPS

**Nos. 83-90, 92-95, 150-151 Ovptd. or Srchd. in Black, Silver or Gold**

**1978-79    Photo.    Perf. 13x13½**
| O1 | A25 | 1c multi | 1.10 | .25 |
| O2 | A25 | 2c multi | 1.75 | .25 |
| O3 | A25 | 3c multi | 1.75 | .25 |
| O4 | A25 | 4c multi (G) | 1.75 | .25 |
| O5 | A25 | 5c multi | 1.75 | .25 |
| O6 | A25 | 8c multi | 1.75 | .25 |
| O7 | A25 | 10c multi | 2.00 | .25 |
| O8 | A25 | 15c on 60c multi | 3.50 | .25 |
| O9 | A25 | 18c on 60c multi | 3.50 | .25 |
| O10 | A25 | 20c multi (G) | 3.50 | .25 |
| O11 | A40 | 50c multi | 1.50 | .70 |
| O12 | A25 | 60c multi | 12.00 | .80 |
| O13 | A25 | $1 multi | 12.00 | 1.00 |
| O14 | A26 | $2 multi | 11.00 | .80 |
| O15 | A40 | $4 on $1 multi (S) | 2.50 | .80 |
| O16 | A25 | $5 multi | 13.00 | 1.00 |
| | | Nos. O1-O16 (16) | 74.35 | 8.10 |

Overprint on 4c, 20c, $1 diagonal.
Issued: Nos. O14-O16, 2/20/79; others, 11/3/78.

**Stamps of 1983-84 Ovptd. or Surcharged in Green**

or Gold (#O29-O32)

| 1985, Aug. 9 | | | Perf. 14, 13x13½ | |
|---|---|---|---|---|
| O17 | A66 | 2c No. 322 | 2.10 | 2.10 |
| O18 | A66 | 5c No. 324 | 2.50 | 2.50 |
| O19 | A66 | 10c No. 325 | 3.00 | 3.00 |
| O20 | A66 | 12c No. 326 | 3.25 | 3.00 |
| O21 | A66 | 18c No. 327 | 4.00 | 3.50 |
| O22 | A66 | 20c on 24c No. 328 | 4.50 | 3.75 |
| O23 | A66 | 30c No. 329 | 3.50 | 2.50 |
| O24 | A66 | 40c on 36c No. 330 | 3.50 | 2.50 |
| O25 | A66 | 50c No. 332 | 3.50 | 2.50 |
| O26 | A66 | 55c on 48c No. 331 | 3.50 | 2.50 |
| O27 | A66 | 60c No. 333 | 4.00 | 2.75 |
| O28 | A66 | 65c on 72c No. 334 | 4.00 | 2.75 |
| O29 | A61 | 75c on 48c No. 276 | 2.50 | 2.10 |
| O30 | A61 | 75c on 48c No. 277 | 2.50 | 2.10 |
| O31 | A61 | 75c on 48c No. 278 | 2.50 | 2.10 |
| O32 | A61 | 75c on 48c No. 279 | 2.50 | 2.10 |
| a. | | Block of 4, Nos. O29-O32 | 11.00 | 11.00 |
| O33 | A66 | 80c on 96c No. 335 | 4.00 | 3.75 |
| | | *Nos. O17-O33 (17)* | 55.35 | 45.50 |

**Nos. 336-341 Overprinted Like Nos. O17-O21, O23, O25, O27 in Metallic Green**

| 1986, Oct. 1 | | | Perf. 14 | |
|---|---|---|---|---|
| O34 | A66 | $3 multi | 8.50 | 6.50 |
| O35 | A66 | $4.20 multi | 11.00 | 8.50 |
| O36 | A66 | $5.60 multi | 12.00 | 10.00 |
| O37 | A66 | $9.60 multi | 15.00 | 12.00 |

| 1988-91 | | | Perf. 14 | |
|---|---|---|---|---|
| O38 | A66 | $1.20 multi | 5.00 | 2.50 |
| O39 | A66 | $2.10 multi | 7.50 | 4.00 |

Nos. 246C-246D Surcharged in Metallic Blue

| | | | | |
|---|---|---|---|---|
| O40 | A55 | $14 on $4 (B) | 17.50 | 14.00 |
| O41 | A55 | $18 on $5 (B) | 22.50 | 19.00 |
| | | *Nos. O34-O41 (8)* | 99.00 | 76.50 |

Issue dates: July 2, 1991; others, June 15.

## AJMAN

äj-'man

LOCATION — Oman Peninsula, Arabia, on Persian Gulf
GOVT. — Sheikdom under British Protection
AREA — 100 sq. mi.
POP. — 4,400
CAPITAL — Ajman

Ajman is one of six Persian Gulf sheikdoms to join the United Arab Emirates, which proclaimed its independence Dec. 2, 1971. See United Arab Emirates.

100 Naye Paise = 1 Rupee

**Catalogue values for all unused stamps in this country are for Never Hinged items.**

Sheik Rashid bin Humaid al Naimi & Arab Stallion — A1

Designs: 2np, 50np, Regal angelfish. 3np, 70np, Camel. 4np, 1r, Angelfish. 5np, 1.50r, Green turtle. 10np, 2r, Jewelfish. 15np, 3r, White storks. 20np, 5r, White-eyed gulls. 30np, 10r, Lanner falcon. 40np as 1np.

**Photo. & Litho.**

| 1964 | | Unwmk. | Perf. 14 | |
|---|---|---|---|---|
| | | **Size: 35x22mm** | | |
| 1 | A1 | 1np gold & multi | .25 | .25 |
| 2 | A1 | 2np gold & multi | .25 | .25 |
| 3 | A1 | 3np gold & multi | .25 | .25 |
| 4 | A1 | 4np gold & multi | .25 | .25 |
| 5 | A1 | 5np gold & multi | .25 | .25 |
| 6 | A1 | 10np gold & multi | .25 | .25 |
| 7 | A1 | 15np gold & multi | .25 | .25 |
| 8 | A1 | 20np gold & multi | .25 | .25 |
| 9 | A1 | 30np gold & multi | .25 | .25 |
| | | **Size: 42x27mm** | | |
| 10 | A1 | 40np gold & multi | .25 | .25 |
| 11 | A1 | 50np gold & multi | .25 | .25 |
| 12 | A1 | 70np gold & multi | .25 | .25 |
| 13 | A1 | 1r gold & multi | .40 | .25 |
| 14 | A1 | 1.50r gold & multi | .80 | .35 |
| 15 | A1 | 2r gold & multi | 1.00 | .50 |
| | | **Size: 53x33½mm** | | |
| 16 | A1 | 3r gold & multi | 1.50 | 1.00 |
| 17 | A1 | 5r gold & multi | 4.00 | 2.40 |
| 18 | A1 | 10r gold & multi | 7.50 | 3.75 |
| | | *Nos. 1-18 (18)* | 18.20 | 11.25 |

Issued: Nos. 1-9, 6/20; Nos. 10-15, 9/7; Nos. 16-18, 11/4. Exist imperf. Value, set $30.

Pres. and Mrs. John F. Kennedy with Caroline — A2

Pres. Kennedy: 10np, As a boy in football uniform. 15np, Diving. 50np, As navy lieutenant, receiving Navy and Marine Corps Medal from Capt. Frederic L. Conklin. 1r, Sailing with Jacqueline Kennedy. 2r, With Eleanor Roosevelt. 5r, With Lyndon B. Johnson and Hubert H. Humphrey. 10r, Portrait.

| 1964, Dec. 15 | | Photo. | Perf. 13½x14 | |
|---|---|---|---|---|
| 19 | A2 | 10np grn & red lil | .25 | .25 |
| 20 | A2 | 15np Prus bl & vio | .25 | .25 |
| 21 | A2 | 50np org brn & dk bl | .25 | .25 |
| 22 | A2 | 1r brn & Prus grn | .50 | .30 |
| 23 | A2 | 2r red lil & dp ol | .75 | .50 |
| 24 | A2 | 3r grn & red brn | 1.50 | .75 |
| 25 | A2 | 5r vio & brn | 2.75 | 2.00 |
| 26 | A2 | 10r dk bl & red brn | 5.50 | 3.50 |
| | | *Nos. 19-26 (8)* | 11.75 | 7.80 |

John F. Kennedy (1917-63). Exist imperf. Value, set $17.50. A souvenir sheet contains one each of Nos. 23-26. Value, perf or imperf, $25.

Runners at Start — A3

10np, 1.50r, Boxing. 25np, 2r, Judo. 50np, 5r, Gymnast on vaulting horse. 1r, 3r, Sailing yacht.

| 1965, Jan. 12 | | Photo. | Perf. 13½x14 | |
|---|---|---|---|---|
| 27 | A3 | 5np red brn, brt pink & Prus grn | .25 | .25 |
| 28 | A3 | 10np dk ol grn, bl gray & red brn | .25 | .25 |
| 29 | A3 | 15np dk vio, grn & sep | .25 | .25 |
| 30 | A3 | 25np bl cal pink & blk | .25 | .25 |
| 31 | A3 | 50np mar, bl & ind | .25 | .25 |
| 32 | A3 | 1r dk grn, lil & ultra | .50 | .25 |
| 33 | A3 | 1.50r lil, grn & brn | .75 | .50 |
| 34 | A3 | 2r red org, bis & dk bl | 1.25 | .70 |
| 35 | A3 | 3r dk brn, grnsh bl & lil | 2.00 | 1.25 |
| 36 | A3 | 5r grn, yel & red brn | 3.25 | 1.75 |
| | | *Nos. 27-36 (10)* | 9.00 | 5.70 |

18th Olympic Games, Tokyo, Oct. 10-25, 1964. Exist imperf. Value, set $12. A souvenir sheet contains four stamps similar to Nos. 33-36 in changed colors. Values: perf $10; imperf $14.

Stanley Gibbons Catalogue, 1865, U.S. No. 1X2 — A4

Designs: 10np, Austria, Scarlet Mercury 1856. 15np, British Guiana 1c, 1856. 25np, Canada 12p, 1851. 50np, Hawaii 2c, 1851. 1r, Mauritius 2p, 1847. 3r, Switzerland, Geneva 10c, 1843. 5r, Tuscany 31, 1860. 5np, 15np, 50np and 3r show first edition of Stanley Gibbons Catalogue; 10np, 25np, 1r and 5r show 1965 Elizabethan Catalogue.

| 1965, May 6 | | Unwmk. | Perf. 13 | |
|---|---|---|---|---|
| 37 | A4 | 5np multi | .25 | .25 |
| 38 | A4 | 10np multi | .25 | .25 |
| 39 | A4 | 15np multi | .25 | .25 |
| 40 | A4 | 25np multi | .25 | .25 |
| 41 | A4 | 50np multi | .25 | .25 |
| 42 | A4 | 1r multi | .50 | .25 |
| 43 | A4 | 3r multi | 1.50 | .50 |
| a. | | Souv. sheet of 4, #38-39, 42-43 | 4.50 | |
| 44 | A4 | 5r multi | 3.00 | 1.10 |
| a. | | Souv. sheet of 4, #37, 40-41, 44 | 4.00 | |
| | | *Nos. 37-44 (8)* | 6.25 | 3.10 |

Gibbons Catalogue Cent. Exhib., London, Feb. 17-20. Nos. 43a and 44a for 125th anniv. of 1st postage stamp. Exist imperf. Value, set $9. Sheets exist imperf. Value for both sheets, $7.

Stamps of Ajman were replaced in 1972 by those of United Arab Emirates.

### AIR POST STAMPS

**Type of Regular Issue, 1964**

Designs: 15np, Arab stallion. 25np, Regal angelfish. 35np, Camel. 50np, Angelfish. 75np, Green turtle. 1r, Jewelfish. 2r, White storks. 3r, White-eyed gulls. 5r, Lanner falcon.

**Photo. & Litho.**

| 1965 | | Unwmk. | Perf. 14 | |
|---|---|---|---|---|
| | | **Size: 42x25½mm** | | |
| C1 | A1 | 15np silver & multi | .25 | .25 |
| C2 | A1 | 25np silver & multi | .25 | .25 |
| C3 | A1 | 35np silver & multi | .25 | .25 |
| C4 | AI | 50np silver & multi | .50 | .25 |
| C5 | A1 | 75np silver & multi | .75 | .25 |
| C6 | A1 | 1r silver & multi | 1.00 | .25 |
| | | **Size: 53x33½mm** | | |
| C7 | A1 | 2r silver & multi | 1.50 | .75 |
| C8 | A1 | 3r silver & multi | 3.00 | 1.00 |
| C9 | A1 | 5r silver & multi | 4.50 | 1.75 |
| | | *Nos. C1-C9 (9)* | 12.00 | 5.00 |

Issued: Nos. C1-C6, 11/15; Nos. C7-C9, 12/18. Exist imperf. Value, set $25.

### AIR POST OFFICIAL STAMPS

Type of Regular Issue, 1964

Designs: 75np, Jewelfish. 2r, White storks. 3r, White-eyed gulls. 5r, Lanner falcon.

**Photo. & Litho.**

| 1965, Dec. 18 | | Unwmk. | Perf. 14 | |
|---|---|---|---|---|
| | | **Size: 42x25½mm** | | |
| CO1 | A1 | 75np gold & multi | .75 | .35 |
| | | **Size: 53x33½mm** | | |
| CO2 | A1 | 2r gold & multi | 2.25 | .50 |
| CO3 | A1 | 3r gold & multi | 3.00 | 1.00 |
| CO4 | A1 | 5r gold & multi | 5.00 | 1.40 |
| | | *Nos. CO1-CO4 (4)* | 11.00 | 3.25 |

### OFFICIAL STAMPS

Type of Regular Issue, 1964

25np, Arab stallion. 40np, Regal angelfish. 50np, Camel. 75np, Angelfish. 1r, Green turtle.

**Photo. & Litho.**

| 1965, Dec. 1 | | Unwmk. | Perf. 14 | |
|---|---|---|---|---|
| | | **Size: 42x25½mm** | | |
| O1 | A1 | 25np gold & multi | .30 | .25 |
| O2 | A1 | 40np gold & multi | .40 | .25 |
| O3 | A1 | 50np gold & multi | .50 | .30 |
| O4 | A1 | 75np gold & multi | .60 | .35 |
| O5 | A1 | 1r gold & multi | .90 | .40 |
| | | *Nos. O1-O5 (5)* | 2.70 | 1.55 |

## ALAOUITES

'al-au-ˌwïtz

LOCATION — A division of Syria, in Western Asia
GOVT. — Under French Mandate
AREA — 2,500 sq. mi.
POP. — 278,000 (approx. 1930)
CAPITAL — Latakia

This territory became an independent state in 1924, although still administered under the French Mandate. In 1930, it was renamed Latakia, and Syrian stamps overprinted "Lattaquie" superseded the stamps of Alaouites. For these and subsequent issues, see Latakia and Syria.

100 Centimes = 1 Piaster

**Issued under French Mandate**

Stamps of France Surcharged

Nos. 1-6, 16-18

Nos. 7-15, 19-21

| 1925 | | Unwmk. | Perf. 14x13½ | |
|---|---|---|---|---|
| 1 | A16 | 0.10p on 2c vio brn | 4.00 | 4.00 |
| 2 | A22 | 0.25p on 5c orange | 4.00 | 4.00 |
| 3 | A20 | 0.75p on 15c gray grn | 7.25 | 7.25 |
| 4 | A22 | 1p on 20c red brn | 4.00 | 4.00 |
| 5 | A22 | 1.25p on 25c blue | 4.50 | 4.50 |
| 6 | A22 | 1.50p on 30c red | 14.50 | 14.50 |
| 7 | A22 | 2p on 35c violet | 4.75 | *4.75* |
| 8 | A18 | 2p on 40c red & pale bl | 5.50 | 5.50 |
| 9 | A18 | 2p on 45c grn & bl | 19.00 | 19.00 |
| 10 | A18 | 3p on 60c vio & ultra | 8.75 | 8.75 |
| 11 | A20 | 3p on 60c lt vio | 14.00 | 14.00 |
| b. | | Double surcharge | 165.00 | 165.00 |
| 12b | A20 | 4p on 85c vermilion | 4.00 | *4.00* |
| c. | | As "b," inverted surcharge | 60.00 | 60.00 |
| 13 | A18 | 5p on 1fr cl & ol grn | 8.50 | 8.50 |
| 14 | A18 | 10p on 2fr org & pale bl | 13.00 | 13.00 |
| 15 | A18 | 25p on 5fr bl & buff | 16.00 | 16.00 |
| | | *Nos. 1-15 (15)* | 131.75 | 131.75 |

Two types of surcharge exist on the 4p and on the 5p-25p. For detailed listings, see the *Scott Classic Specialized Catalogue of Stamps and Covers 1840-1940.*

For overprints, see Nos. C1-C4.

Same Surcharges on Pasteur Stamps of France

| | | | | |
|---|---|---|---|---|
| 16 | A23 | 0.50p on 10c green | 3.00 | 3.00 |
| 17 | A23 | 0.75p on 15c green | 3.75 | 3.75 |
| 18 | A23 | 1.50p on 30c red | 3.00 | 3.00 |
| 19 | A23 | 2p on 45c red | 3.75 | 3.75 |
| 20 | A23 | 2.50p on 50c blue | 5.25 | 5.25 |
| 21 | A23 | 4p on 75c blue | 9.00 | 9.00 |
| | | *Nos. 16-21 (6)* | 27.75 | 27.75 |

Two types of overprints exist on No. 21. For detailed listings, see *Scott Classic Specialized Catalogue of Stamps and Covers 1840-1940.*

**Inverted Surcharges**

| | | | |
|---|---|---|---|
| *1a* | A16 | 0.10p on 2c vio brn | 50.00 |
| *2a* | A22 | 0.25p on 5c orange | 50.00 |
| *3a* | A20 | 0.75p on 15c gray grn | 50.00 |
| *4a* | A22 | 1p on 20c red brn | 50.00 |
| *5a* | A22 | 1.25p on 25c blue | 50.00 |
| *6a* | A22 | 1.50p on 30c red | 60.00 |
| *7a* | A22 | 2p on 35c violet | 50.00 |
| *8a* | A18 | 2p on 40c red & pale bl | 50.00 |
| *9a* | A18 | 2p on 45c grn & bl | 60.00 |
| *10a* | A18 | 3p on 60c vio & ultra | 50.00 |
| *11a* | A20 | 3p on 60c lt vio | 60.00 |
| *12a* | A20 | 4p on 85c vermilion | 50.00 |
| *13a* | A18 | 5p on 1fr cl & ol grn | 80.00 |
| *14a* | A18 | 10p on 2fr org & pale bl | 100.00 |
| *15a* | A18 | 25p on 5fr bl & buff | 120.00 |
| *16a* | A23 | 0.50p on 10c green | 40.00 |
| *17a* | A23 | 0.75p on 15c green | 40.00 |
| *18a* | A23 | 1.50p on 30c red | 45.00 |
| *19a* | A23 | 2p on 45c red | 40.00 |
| *20a* | A23 | 2.50p on 50c blue | 40.00 |
| *21a* | A23 | 4p on 75c blue | 40.00 |

### Stamps of Syria, 1925, Overprinted in Red, Black or Blue

On A3, A5

On A4

**1925, Mar. 1** ***Perf. 12½, 13½***

| | | | |
|---|---|---|---|
| 25 | A3 0.10p dk violet (R) | 1.50 | *2.25* |
| a. | Double overprint | 42.50 | 42.50 |
| b. | Inverted overprint | 45.00 | |
| c. | Black overprint | 37.50 | 37.50 |
| e. | "ALAOUITE," instead of "ALAOUITES" | 30.00 | *30.00* |
| 26 | A4 0.25p olive black (R) | 2.25 | *3.00* |
| a. | Inverted overprint | 40.00 | |
| b. | Blue overprint | 50.00 | 50.00 |
| 27 | A4 0.50p yellow green | 1.75 | 1.75 |
| a. | Inverted overprint | 40.00 | 40.00 |
| b. | Blue overprint | 50.00 | 50.00 |
| c. | Red overprint | 50.00 | 50.00 |
| d. | "ALAOUITE," instead of "ALAOUITES" | 50.00 | 50.00 |
| e. | Double overprint | 50.00 | 50.00 |
| 28 | A4 0.75p brown orange | 4.25 | *2.25* |
| a. | Inverted overprint | 45.00 | *60.00* |
| b. | Double overprint | 47.50 | *65.00* |
| 29 | A5 1p magenta | 2.75 | 2.75 |
| a. | Inverted overprint | 40.00 | *47.50* |
| 30 | A4 1.25p deep green | 3.25 | *3.50* |
| a. | Red overprint | 50.00 | 50.00 |
| b. | Double overprint | | 75.00 |
| 31 | A4 1.50p rose red (Bl) | 2.75 | *3.00* |
| a. | Inverted overprint | 45.00 | 45.00 |
| b. | Black overprint | 40.00 | 40.00 |
| c. | As "b", inverted | 80.00 | |
| 32 | A4 2p dk brown (R) | 2.75 | *3.50* |
| a. | Blue overprint | 65.00 | 65.00 |
| b. | Inverted overprint | 40.00 | 40.00 |
| 33 | A4 2.50p pck blue (R) | 4.25 | *4.50* |
| a. | Black overprint | 65.00 | 65.00 |
| 34 | A4 3p orange brown | 2.50 | *2.75* |
| a. | Inverted overprint | 40.00 | 40.00 |
| b. | Blue overprint | 70.00 | 70.00 |
| c. | Double overprint | | 90.00 |
| 35 | A4 5p violet | 3.75 | *4.00* |
| a. | Red overprint | 70.00 | 70.00 |
| b. | Inverted overprint | 42.50 | |
| 36 | A4 10p violet brown | 5.50 | *6.00* |
| 37 | A4 25p ultra (R) | 9.00 | *10.00* |
| | *Nos. 25-37 (13)* | 46.25 | *49.25* |

For overprints see Nos. C5-C19.

### Stamps of Syria, 1925, Surcharged in Black or Red

Nos. 38-42

Nos. 43-45

**1926**

| | | | |
|---|---|---|---|
| 38 | A4 3.50p on 0.75p brn org | 2.50 | *2.75* |
| a. | Surcharged on face and back | 25.00 | 25.00 |
| 39 | A4 4p on 0.25p ol blk | 2.50 | *2.50* |
| 40 | A4 6p on 2.50p pck bl (R) | 3.00 | *3.25* |
| 41 | A4 12p on 1.25p dp grn | 3.25 | *3.50* |
| a. | Inverted surcharge | 35.00 | 35.00 |
| 42 | A4 20p on 1.25p dp grn | 5.25 | 5.25 |
| 43 | A4 4.50p on 0.75p brn org | 5.25 | 3.25 |
| a. | Inverted surcharge | 60.00 | 60.00 |
| b. | Double surcharge | 55.00 | 55.00 |
| 44 | A4 7.50p on 2.50p pck bl | 4.75 | 3.25 |
| 45 | A4 15p on 25p ultra | 8.75 | 5.50 |
| a. | Inverted surcharge | 50.00 | |
| | *Nos. 38-45 (8)* | 35.25 | *29.25* |

Two types of overprints exist on No. 39. For detailed listings, see *Scott Classic Specialized Catalogue of Stamps and Covers 1840-1940.*

For overprint, see No. C21.

### Syria No. 199 Ovptd. in Red like No. 25

**1928**

| | | | |
|---|---|---|---|
| 46 | A3 5c on 0.10p dk violet | 2.00 | 1.75 |
| a. | Double surcharge | 50.00 | |

### Syria Nos. 178 and 174 Surcharged like Nos. 43-45 in Red

| | | | |
|---|---|---|---|
| 47 | A4 2p on 1.25p dp green | 16.00 | 8.00 |
| a. | Double surcharge | 60.00 | |
| b. | Inverted surcharge | 50.00 | 50.00 |
| 48 | A4 4p on 0.25p olive black | 11.00 | 6.50 |
| a. | Double surcharge | 50.00 | 50.00 |
| b. | Inverted surcharge | 50.00 | 50.00 |

For overprint see No. C20.

| | | | |
|---|---|---|---|
| 49 | A4 4p on 0.25p olive black | 82.50 | 50.00 |
| a. | Double impression | 150.00 | |
| | *Nos. 46-49 (4)* | 111.50 | 66.25 |

## AIR POST STAMPS

Nos. 8, 10, 13 & 14 with Additional Ovpt. in Black

**1925, Jan. 1** **Unwmk.** ***Perf. 14x13½***

| | | | |
|---|---|---|---|
| C1b | A18 2p on 40c | 17.00 | 15.00 |
| C2 | A18 3p on 60c | 22.50 | *20.00* |
| a. | Inverted overprint | 125.00 | 125.00 |
| C3 | A18 5p on 1fr | 17.00 | 14.00 |
| a. | Inverted overprint | 37.50 | *37.50* |
| C4 | A18 10p on 2fr | 22.00 | 15.00 |
| a. | Inverted overprint | 35.00 | *35.00* |
| | *Nos. C1-C4 (4)* | 78.50 | *64.00* |

Two types of overprints exist on Nos. C1-C4. For detailed listings, see *Scott Classic Specialized Catalogue of Stamps and Covers 1840-1940.*

Nos. 32, 34, 35 & 36 With Additional Ovpt. in Green

**1925, Mar. 1** ***Perf. 13½***

| | | | |
|---|---|---|---|
| C5 | A4 2p dark brown | 7.50 | 6.00 |
| a. | Inverted overprint | 75.00 | 75.00 |
| b. | Red overprint | 125.00 | |
| C6 | A4 3p orange brown | 7.50 | 6.00 |
| a. | Inverted overprint | 75.00 | 75.00 |
| b. | Red overprint | 100.00 | |
| C7 | A4 5p violet | 7.50 | 6.00 |
| a. | Inverted overprint | 75.00 | 75.00 |
| b. | Red overprint | 100.00 | |
| C8 | A4 10p violet brown | 7.50 | 6.00 |
| a. | Inverted overprint | 75.00 | 75.00 |
| b. | Red overprint | 100.00 | |
| | *Nos. C5-C8 (4)* | 30.00 | 24.00 |

Nos. 32, 34, 35 & 36 With Additional Ovpt. in Red

**1926, May 1**

| | | | |
|---|---|---|---|
| C9 | A4 2p dark brown | 7.50 | 6.50 |
| a. | Red overprint double | 175.00 | 175.00 |
| b. | Black overprint double | 175.00 | 175.00 |
| c. | Black overprint inverted | 70.00 | 70.00 |
| C10 | A4 3p orange brown | 7.50 | 6.50 |
| a. | Black overprint inverted | 70.00 | 70.00 |
| C11 | A4 5p violet | 8.50 | 7.50 |
| a. | Black overprint inverted | 70.00 | 70.00 |
| C12 | A4 10p violet brown | 8.50 | 7.50 |
| a. | Black overprint inverted | 70.00 | 70.00 |
| | *Nos. C9-C12 (4)* | 32.00 | 28.00 |

No. C9 has the original overprint in black.

Double or inverted overprints, original or plane, are known on most of Nos. C9-C12. Value, each $75. Value for example with both original and plane overprint inverted, each $150.

The red plane overprint was also applied to Nos. C5-C8. These are believed to have been essays, and were not regularly issued. Value, each $100.

### Nos. 27c, 37 and Syria No. 177 With Addtl. Ovpt. of Airplane in Red or Black

**1929, June-July**

| | | | |
|---|---|---|---|
| C17 | A4 0.50p yel grn (R) | 5.00 | 5.00 |
| a. | Plane overprint double | 250.00 | |
| b. | Plane ovpt. on face and back | 60.00 | |
| c. | Pair with plane overprint Tête-bêche | 325.00 | |
| d. | Double overprint | 225.00 | 225.00 |
| e. | Overprint inverted | 125.00 | |
| f. | Plane only inverted | 250.00 | |
| C18 | A5 1p magenta (Bk) | 9.00 | 9.00 |
| a. | Red overprint | 50.00 | |
| C19 | A4 25p ultra (R) | 52.50 | 40.00 |
| a. | Plane overprint inverted | 125.00 | 125.00 |
| b. | Surcharge double | 150.00 | 150.00 |
| | *Nos. C17-C19 (3)* | 66.50 | 54.00 |

Nos. 28 and 30 exist with additional overprint of airplane in red. These stamps were never issued. Value, each $100.

Nos. 47 and 45 With Additional Ovpt. of Airplane in Red

**1929-30**

| | | | |
|---|---|---|---|
| C20 | A4 2p on 1.25p ('30) | 7.25 | 7.25 |
| a. | Surcharge inverted | 60.00 | 60.00 |
| b. | Double surcharge | 85.00 | 85.00 |
| c. | Triple surcharge | 200.00 | |
| C21 | A4 15p on 25p (Bk + R) | 57.50 | 50.00 |
| a. | Plane overprint inverted | 225.00 | 225.00 |

## POSTAGE DUE STAMPS

### Postage Due Stamps of France, 1893-1920, Surcharged Like No. 1 (Nos. J1-J2) or No. 7 (Nos. J3-J5)

**1925** **Unwmk.** ***Perf. 14x13½***

| | | | |
|---|---|---|---|
| J1 | D2 0.50p on 10c choc | 9.00 | 9.00 |
| J2 | D2 1p on 20c ol grn | 9.00 | 9.00 |
| J3 | D2 2p on 30c red | 9.50 | 9.50 |
| J4 | D2 3p on 50c vio brn | 9.50 | 9.50 |
| J5 | D2 5p on 1fr red brn, *straw* | 10.00 | 10.00 |
| | *Nos. J1-J5 (5)* | 47.00 | *47.00* |

Two types of overprints exist on No. J5. For detailed listings, see *Scott Classic Specialized Catalogue of Stamps and Covers 1840-1940.*

### 1925 Syria Postage Due Stamps Overprinted in Black, Blue or Red

**1925** ***Perf. 13½***

| | | | |
|---|---|---|---|
| J6 | D5 0.50p brown, *yel* | 5.50 | *5.50* |
| a. | Blue overprint | 45.00 | |
| b. | Red overprint | 45.00 | |
| c. | Overprint inverted | 37.50 | 37.50 |
| J7 | D6 1p vio, *rose* (Bl) | 5.00 | *5.00* |
| a. | Black overprint | 155.00 | 155.00 |
| b. | Double overprint (Bk + Bl) | 175.00 | 175.00 |
| c. | Overprint inverted | 40.00 | 40.00 |
| J8 | D5 2p blk, *blue* (R) | 6.75 | 6.75 |
| a. | Blue overprint | 45.00 | |
| J9 | D5 3p blk, *red org* (Bl) | 9.00 | 9.00 |
| a. | Overprint inverted | 35.00 | |
| J10 | D5 5p blk, *bl grn* (R) | 11.00 | 11.00 |
| a. | Overprint inverted | 30.00 | 30.00 |
| b. | Black overprint | 45.00 | |
| | *Nos. J6-J10 (5)* | 37.25 | 37.25 |

The stamps of Alaouites were superseded in 1930 by those of Latakia.

# ALBANIA

al-ˈbā-nē-ə

LOCATION — Southeastern Europe
GOVT. — Republic
AREA — 11,101 sq. mi.
POP. — 2,880,000 (2020 est.)
CAPITAL — Tirana

After the outbreak of World War I, the country fell into a state of anarchy when the Prince and all members of the International Commission left Albania. Subsequently General Ferrero in command of Italian troops declared Albania an independent country. A constitution was adopted and a republican form of government was instituted which continued until 1928 when, by constitutional amendment, Albania was declared to be a monarchy. The President of the republic, Ahmed Zogu, became king of the new state. Many unlisted varieties or surcharges and lithographed labels are said to have done postal duty in Albania and Epirus during this unsettled period.

On April 7, 1939, Italy invaded Albania. King Zog fled but did not abdicate. The King of Italy acquired the crown.

Germany occupied Albania from September, 1943, until late 1944 when it became an independent state. The People's Republic began in January, 1946.

40 Paras = 1 Piaster = 1 Grossion
100 Centimes = 1 Franc (1917)
100 Qintar = 1 Franc
100 Qintar (Qindarka) = 1 Lek (1947)

**Catalogue values for unused stamps in this country are for Never Hinged items, beginning with Scott 458 in the regular postage section, Scott B34 in the semi-postal section, and Scott C67 in the airpost section.**

### Watermarks

Wmk. 125 — Lozenges

Wmk. 220 — Double Headed Eagle

Issues of 1908 Turkey Stamps Handstamped

***Perf. 12, 13½ and Compound***

**1913, June** **Unwmk.**

| | | | |
|---|---|---|---|
| 1 | A19 2½pi violet brown | 750.00 | 900.00 |

With Additional Overprint in Carmine

| | | | |
|---|---|---|---|
| 2 | A19 10pa blue green | 675.00 | 650.00 |

Handstamped on Issue of 1909

| | | | |
|---|---|---|---|
| 4 | A21 5pa ocher | 450.00 | 450.00 |
| 5 | A21 10pa blue green | 350.00 | 225.00 |
| 6 | A21 20pa car rose | 350.00 | 250.00 |
| 7 | A21 1pi ultra | 325.00 | 250.00 |
| 8 | A21 2pi blue black | 500.00 | 450.00 |
| 10 | A21 5pi dark violet | 1,400. | 1,500. |
| 11 | A21 10pi dull red | *5,000.* | *4,750.* |

For surcharge see No. 19.

Additional values of 25pi dark green and 50pi red brown were overprinted and sold only to dealers. Values, 25pi $8,000, 50pi $16,000.

With Additional Overprint in Blue or Carmine

13A A21 10pa blue green 900.00 850.00
14 A21 20pa car rose (Bl) 800.00 850.00
15 A21 1pi brt blue (C) 1,900. 1,750.
15A A21 2pi brt blue (C) 3,750. 3,500.

**Handstamped on Newspaper Stamp of 1911**

17 A21 2pa olive green 425.00 425.00

**Handstamped on Postage Due Stamp of 1908**

18 A19 1pi black, *dp rose* 3,000. 2,500.
*a.* Inverted overprint — —

No. 18 was used for regular postage.

**No. 6 Surcharged With New Value**

19 A21 10pa on 20pa car rose 1,250. 1,250.
*a.* "11" instead of "10" — —
*b.* Inverted surchage 3,250. —
*c.* Double surcharge — —

A1

**Handstamped on White Laid Paper Without Eagle and Value Issued Without Gum**

**1913, July** ***Imperf.***
20 A1 (1pi) black 325.00 *525.00*
Cut to shape 190.00 *275.00*
*a.* Sewing machine perf. 575.00 *725.00*

**Value Typewritten in Violet Issued Without Gum**

**1913, Aug.** **With Eagle**
21 A1 10pa violet 12.00 12.00
*a.* Double impression — —
22 A1 20pa red & black 16.00 13.50
*a.* "2p para" — —
23 A1 1gr black 16.00 16.00
24 A1 2gr blue & violet 20.00 16.00
25 A1 5gr violet & blue 24.00 21.00
26 A1 10gr blue 24.00 21.00
*Nos. 21-26 (6)* 112.00 99.50

Nos. 21-26 exist with the eagle inverted or omitted and with numerous errors in the figures of value and the spelling of the word "grosh."

A2

**Handstamped on White Laid Paper Eagle and Value in Black Issued Without Gum**

**1913, Nov.** ***Perf. 11½***
27 A2 10pa green 4.00 3.25
*b.* Eagle and value in green 1,750. 1,750.
*c.* 10pa red (error) 32.50 32.50
*d.* 10pa violet (error) 32.50 32.50
29 A2 20pa red 6.00 4.75
*b.* 20pa green (error) 42.50 32.50
30 A2 30pa violet 6.00 4.75
*a.* 30pa ultramarine (error) 32.50 32.50
*b.* 30pa red (error) 32.50 32.50
31 A2 1gr ultramarine 8.00 7.25
*a.* 1gr green (error) 32.50 32.50
*b.* 1gr black (error) 32.50 32.50
*c.* 1gr violet (error) 32.50 32.50
33 A2 2gr black 12.00 8.00
*a.* 2gr violet (error) 40.00 40.00
*b.* 2gr blue (error) 40.00 40.00
*Nos. 27-33 (5)* 36.00 28.00

The stamps of this issue are known with eagle or value inverted or omitted.
1st anniv. of Albanian independence.
Counterfeits exist.

Skanderbeg (George Castriota) — A3

**1913, Dec.** **Typo.** ***Perf. 14***
35 A3 2q orange brn & buff 3.50 1.75
36 A3 5q green & blue grn 3.50 1.75
37 A3 10q rose red 3.50 1.75
38 A3 25q dark blue 3.50 1.75
39 A3 50q violet & red 8.50 3.50
40 A3 1fr deep brown 20.00 10.50
*Nos. 35-40 (6)* 42.50 *21.00*

For overprints and surcharges see Nos. 41-52, 105, J1-J9.

Nos. 35-40 Handstamped in Black or Violet

**1914, Mar. 7**
41 A3 2q orange brn & buff 50.00 *65.00*
42 A3 5q grn & bl grn (V) 50.00 *65.00*
43 A3 10q rose red 50.00 *65.00*
44 A3 25q dark blue (V) 50.00 *65.00*
45 A3 50q violet & red 50.00 *65.00*
46 A3 1fr deep brown 50.00 *65.00*
*Nos. 41-46 (6)* 300.00 390.00

Issued to celebrate the arrival of Prince Wilhelm zu Wied on Mar. 7, 1914.

**Nos. 35-40 Surcharged in Black**

a

b

**1914, Apr. 2**
47 A3 (a) 5pa on 2q 2.10 2.10
48 A3 (a) 10pa on 5q 2.10 2.10
49 A3 (a) 20pa on 10q 3.50 2.75
50 A3 (b) 1gr on 25q 3.50 3.50
51 A3 (b) 2gr on 50q 3.50 3.50
52 A3 (b) 5gr on 1fr 14.00 10.50
*Nos. 47-52 (6)* 28.70 24.45

For overprints see Nos. 105, J6-J9.

**Inverted Surcharge**

*47a* A3 (a) 5pa on 2q 24.00 24.00
*48a* A3 (a) 10pa on 5q 22.50 22.50
*49a* A3 (a) 20pa on 10q 24.00 24.00
*50a* A3 (b) 1gr on 25q 24.00 24.00
*51a* A3 (b) 2gr on 50q 28.00 28.00
*52b* A3 (b) 5gr on 1fr 90.00 90.00
*Nos. 47a-52b (6)* 212.50 212.50

**Korce (Korytsa) Issues**

A4

**1914** **Handstamped** ***Imperf.***
52A A4 10pa violet & red 200.00 200.00
*c.* 10pa black & red 325.00 325.00
53 A4 25pa violet & red 200.00 200.00
*a.* 25pa black & red 425.00 425.00

Nos. 52A-53a were handstamped directly on the cover, so the paper varies. They were also produced in sheets; these are rarely found. Nos. 52A-53a were issued by Albanian military authorities.
Counterfeits exists of Nos. 52A and 53.

A5

**1917** **Typo. & Litho.** ***Perf. 11½***
54 A5 1c dk brown & grn 17.50 12.00
55 A5 2c red & green 17.50 12.00
56 A5 3c gray grn & grn 17.50 12.00
57 A5 5c green & black 16.00 8.00
58 A5 10c rose red & black 16.00 8.00
59 A5 25c blue & black 16.00 8.00
60 A5 50c violet & black 16.00 10.00
61 A5 1fr brown & black 16.00 10.00
*Nos. 54-61 (8)* 132.50 80.00

A6

**1917-18**
62 A6 1c dk brown & grn 2.75 2.40
63 A6 2c red brown & grn 2.75 2.40
*a.* "CTM" for "CTS" 72.50 120.00
64 A6 3c black & green 2.75 2.40
*a.* "CTM" for "CTS" 80.00 135.00
65 A6 5c green & black 4.00 4.00
66 A6 10c dull red & black 4.00 4.00
67 A6 50c violet & black 7.25 6.50
68 A6 1fr red brn & black 20.00 17.50
*Nos. 62-68 (7)* 43.50 39.20

Counterfeits abound of Nos. 54-68, 80-81.

No. 65 Surcharged in Red

**1918**
80 A6 25c on 5c green & blk 275.00 *325.00*

A7

**1918**
81 A7 25c blue & black 72.50 95.00

**General Issue**

A8

A9

Handstamped in Rose or Blue XV I MCMXIX

**1919** ***Perf. 12½***
84 A8 (2)q on 2h brown 7.50 7.50
85 A8 5q on 16h green 7.50 7.50
86 A8 10q on 8h rose (Bl) 7.50 7.50
87 A8 25q on 64h blue 8.50 8.50
88 A9 25q on 64h blue *300.00 300.00*
89 A8 50q on 32h violet 7.50 7.50
90 A8 1fr on 1.28k org, *bl* 9.00 9.00
*Nos. 84-90 (7)* *347.50 347.50*

See Nos. J10-J13. Compare with types A10-A14. For overprints see Nos 91-104.

Handstamped in Rose or Blue

**1919, Jan. 16**
91 A8 (2)q on 2h brown 14.00 14.00
92 A8 5q on 16h green 10.50 10.50
93 A8 10q on 8h rose (Bl) 10.50 10.50
94 A8 25q on 64h blue 140.00 140.00
95 A9 25q on 64h blue 45.00 60.00
96 A8 50q on 32h violet 14.00 14.00
97 A8 1fr on 1.28k org, *bl* 14.00 14.00
*Nos. 91-97 (7)* 248.00 263.00

Handstamped in Violet

**1919**
98 A8 (2)q on 2h brown 17.50 17.50
99 A8 5q on 16h green 17.50 17.50
100 A8 10q on 8h rose 17.50 17.50
101 A8 25q on 64h blue 17.50 17.50
102 A9 25q on 64h blue 140.00 140.00
103 A8 50q on 32h violet 17.50 17.50
104 A8 1fr on 1.28k org, *bl* 17.50 17.50
*Nos. 98-104 (7)* 245.00 245.00

No. 50 Overprinted in Violet

**1919** ***Perf. 14***
105 A3 1gr on 25q blue 32.50 25.00

A10

A11

**1919, June 5** ***Perf. 11½, 12½***
106 A10 10q on 2h brown 7.00 7.00
107 A11 15q on 8h rose 7.00 7.00
108 A11 20q on 10h green 7.00 7.00
109 A10 25q on 64h blue 7.00 7.00
110 A11 50q on 32h violet 7.00 7.00
111 A11 1fr on 96h orange 7.00 7.00
112 A10 2fr on 1.60k vio, *buff* 25.00 21.00
*Nos. 106-112 (7)* 67.00 63.00

Nos. 106-108, 110 exist with inverted surcharge.

A12

A13

**Surcharged in Black or Violet**

**1919**
113 A12 10q on 8h car 7.00 7.00
114 A12 15q on 8h car (V) 7.00 7.00
115 A13 20q on 16h green 7.00 7.00
116 A13 25q on 32h violet 7.00 7.00
117 A13 50q on 64h blue 20.00 14.00
118 A13 1fr on 96h orange 8.50 7.00
119 A12 2fr on 1.60k vio, *buff* 14.00 10.50
*Nos. 113-119 (7)* 70.50 59.50

A14

**Overprinted in Blue or Black Without New Value**

**1920** ***Perf. 12½***
120 A14 1q gray (Bl) 100.00 95.00
121 A14 10q rose (Bk) 14.00 *32.50*
*a.* Double overprint 150.00 *150.00*
122 A14 20q brown (Bl) 45.00 40.00
123 A14 25q blue (Bk) 525.00 *600.00*
124 A14 50q brown vio (Bk) 60.00 *80.00*
*Nos. 120-124 (5)* 744.00 *847.50*

Counterfeit overprints exist of Nos. 120-128.

**Surcharged in Color Noted with New Value**

125 A14 2q on 10q rose (R) 14.00 *21.00*
126 A14 5q on 10q rose (G) 14.00 *17.50*
127 A14 25q on 10q rose (Bl) 14.00 *21.00*
128 A14 50q on 10q rose (Br) 14.00 *35.00*
*Nos. 125-128 (4)* 56.00 94.50

Stamps of type A14 (Portrait of the Prince zu Wied) were not placed in use without overprint or surcharge.

A15

**Post Horn Overprinted in Black**

**1920** ***Perf. 14x13***
129 A15 2q orange 10.50 8.50
130 A15 5q deep green 17.50 15.00
131 A15 10q red 32.50 32.50

| | | | | |
|---|---|---|---|---|
| 132 | A15 | 25q light blue | 55.00 | 30.00 |
| 133 | A15 | 50q gray green | 12.50 | 10.50 |
| 134 | A15 | 1fr claret | 12.50 | 10.50 |
| | | *Nos. 129-134 (6)* | 140.50 | 107.00 |

Type A15 was never placed in use without post horn or "Besa" overprint.

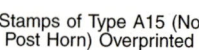

Stamps of Type A15 (No Post Horn) Overprinted

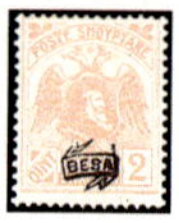

**1921**

| | | | | |
|---|---|---|---|---|
| 135 | A15 | 2q orange | 7.00 | 7.00 |
| 136 | A15 | 5q deep green | 7.00 | 7.00 |
| 137 | A15 | 10q red | 14.00 | 12.00 |
| 138 | A15 | 25q light blue | 25.00 | 21.00 |
| 139 | A15 | 50q gray green | 14.00 | 12.00 |
| 140 | A15 | 1fr claret | 14.00 | 12.00 |
| | | *Nos. 135-140 (6)* | 81.00 | 71.00 |

For surcharge & overprints see Nos. 154, 156-157.

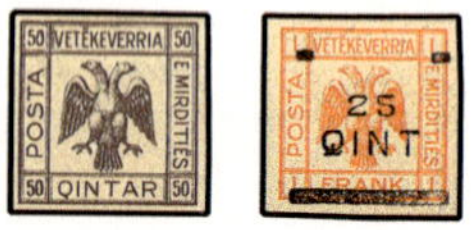

Stamps of these types, and with "TAKSE" overprint, were unauthorized and never placed in use. They are common.

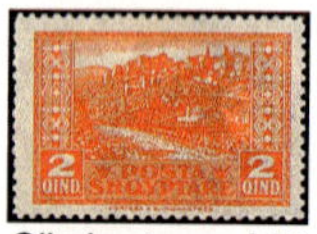

Gjirokaster — A18

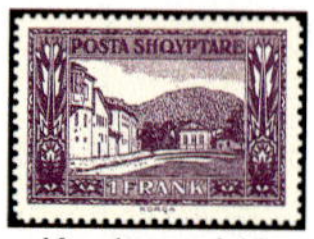

Korcha — A19

Designs: 5q, Kanina. 10q, Berati. 25q, Bridge at Vezirit. 50q, Rozafat. 2fr, Dursit.

**1923 Typo. *Perf. 12½, 11½***

| | | | | |
|---|---|---|---|---|
| 147 | A18 | 2q orange | .70 | *1.40* |
| 148 | A18 | 5q yellow green | .70 | *1.10* |
| 149 | A18 | 10q carmine | .70 | *1.10* |
| 150 | A18 | 25q dark blue | .70 | *1.10* |
| 151 | A18 | 50q dark green | .70 | *1.10* |
| 152 | A19 | 1fr dark violet | .70 | *2.75* |
| 153 | A19 | 2fr olive green | 4.25 | *8.00* |
| | | *Nos. 147-153 (7)* | 8.45 | *16.55* |

For overprints & surcharges see Nos. 158-185, B1-B8.

No. 135 Surcharged

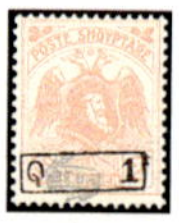

**1922 *Perf. 14x13***

| | | | | |
|---|---|---|---|---|
| 154 | A15 | 1q on 2q orange | 3.25 | *8.50* |

Stamps of Type A15 (No Post Horn) Overprinted

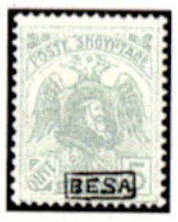

**1922**

| | | | | |
|---|---|---|---|---|
| 156 | A15 | 5q deep green | 5.00 | *8.00* |
| 157 | A15 | 10q red | 5.00 | *8.00* |

Nos. 147-151 Ovptd. in Black and Violet

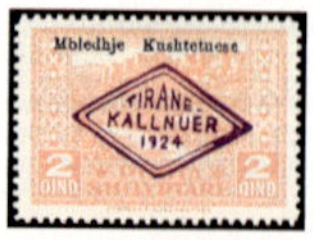


**1924, Jan. *Perf. 12½***

| | | | | |
|---|---|---|---|---|
| 158 | A18 | 2q red orange | 12.50 | *20.00* |
| 159 | A18 | 5q yellow green | 12.50 | *20.00* |
| 160 | A18 | 10q carmine | 9.00 | *14.50* |
| 161 | A18 | 25q dark blue | 9.00 | *14.50* |
| 162 | A18 | 50q dark green | 15.00 | *20.00* |
| | | *Nos. 158-162 (5)* | 58.00 | 89.00 |

The words "Mbledhje Kushtetuese" are in taller letters on the 25q than on the other values. Opening of the Constituent Assembly.

Counterfeits of Nos. 158 and 161 are plentiful.

No. 147 Surcharged

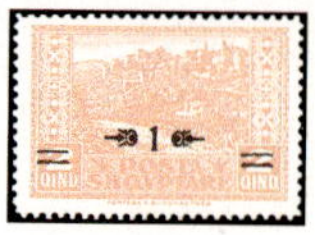

**1924**

| | | | | |
|---|---|---|---|---|
| 163 | A18 | 1q on 2q red orange | 3.00 | *8.00* |

Nos. 163, 147-152 Overprinted

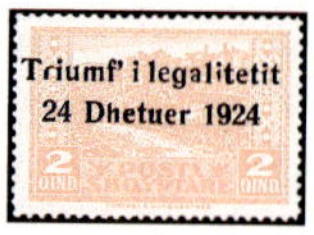


**1924**

| | | | | |
|---|---|---|---|---|
| 164 | A18 | 1q on 2q orange | 2.75 | *7.25* |
| 165 | A18 | 2q orange | 2.75 | *7.25* |
| 166 | A18 | 5q yellow green | 2.75 | *7.25* |
| 167 | A18 | 10q carmine | 2.75 | *7.25* |
| 168 | A18 | 25q dark blue | 2.75 | *7.25* |
| 169 | A18 | 50q dark green | 6.25 | *14.00* |
| 170 | A19 | 1fr dark violet | 6.25 | *17.50* |
| | | *Nos. 164-170 (7)* | 26.25 | *67.75* |

Issued to celebrate the return of the Government to the Capital after a revolution.

Nos. 163, 147-152 Overprinted

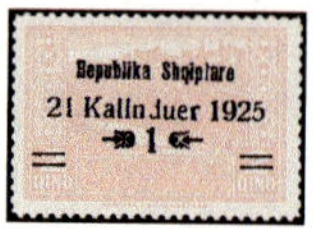


**1925**

| | | | | |
|---|---|---|---|---|
| 171 | A18 | 1q on 2q orange | 3.25 | *8.00* |
| 172 | A18 | 2q orange | 3.25 | *8.00* |
| 173 | A18 | 5q yellow green | 3.25 | *8.00* |
| 174 | A18 | 10q carmine | 3.25 | *8.00* |
| 175 | A18 | 25q dark blue | 3.25 | *8.00* |
| 176 | A18 | 50q dark green | 3.25 | *12.00* |
| 177 | A19 | 1fr dark violet | 6.25 | *16.00* |
| | | *Nos. 171-177 (7)* | 25.75 | *68.00* |

Proclamation of the Republic, Jan. 21, 1925. The date "1921" instead of "1925" occurs once in each sheet of 50.

Counterfeits exist.

Nos. 163, 147-153 Overprinted

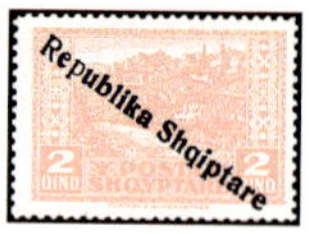


**1925**

| | | | | |
|---|---|---|---|---|
| 178 | A18 | 1q on 2q orange | 1.10 | *1.60* |
| *a.* | | Inverted overprint | 12.50 | 12.50 |
| 179 | A18 | 2q orange | 1.10 | *1.60* |
| 180 | A18 | 5q yellow green | 1.10 | *1.60* |
| *a.* | | Inverted overprint | 12.50 | 12.50 |
| 181 | A18 | 10q carmine | 1.10 | *1.60* |
| 182 | A18 | 25q dark blue | 1.10 | *1.60* |
| 183 | A18 | 50q dark green | 1.10 | *1.60* |
| 184 | A19 | 1fr dark violet | 5.00 | *4.00* |
| 185 | A19 | 2fr olive green | 7.50 | *4.00* |
| | | *Nos. 178-185 (8)* | 19.10 | 17.60 |

Counterfeits exist.

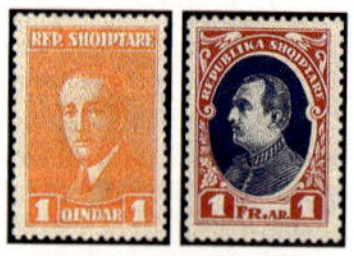

President Ahmed Zogu
A25 A26

**1925 *Perf. 13½, 13½x13***

| | | | | |
|---|---|---|---|---|
| 186 | A25 | 1q orange | .25 | .25 |
| 187 | A25 | 2q red brown | .25 | 2.00 |
| 188 | A25 | 5q green | .25 | .25 |
| 189 | A25 | 10q rose red | .25 | .25 |
| *a.* | | Perf 11½ | 20.00 | 10.00 |
| 190 | A25 | 15q gray brown | .75 | *2.00* |
| 191 | A25 | 25q dark blue | .25 | .25 |
| 192 | A25 | 50q blue green | .85 | *1.50* |
| 193 | A26 | 1fr red & ultra | 1.75 | 2.00 |
| 194 | A26 | 2fr green & orange | 1.90 | *2.00* |
| 195 | A26 | 3fr brown & violet | 4.00 | *5.00* |
| 196 | A26 | 5fr violet & black | 5.00 | 6.75 |
| | | *Nos. 186-196 (11)* | 15.50 | 22.25 |

No. 193 in ultramarine and brown, and No. 194 in green and brown were not regularly issued. Value, set $15.

For overprints & surcharges see Nos. 197-209, 238-248.

Nos. 186-196 Overprinted in Various Colors

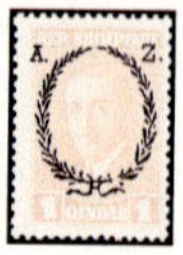


**1927**

| | | | | |
|---|---|---|---|---|
| 197 | A25 | 1q orange (V) | .60 | 1.00 |
| 198 | A25 | 2q red brn (G) | .25 | .30 |
| 199 | A25 | 5q green (R) | 1.25 | .50 |
| 200 | A25 | 10q rose red (Bl) | .25 | .30 |
| *a.* | | Perf 11½ | 25.00 | 20.00 |
| 201 | A25 | 15q gray brn (G) | 7.00 | *12.50* |
| 202 | A25 | 25q dk blue (R) | .50 | 1.00 |
| 203 | A25 | 50q blue grn (Bl) | .50 | .40 |
| 204 | A26 | 1fr red & ultra (Bk) | 1.40 | *.55* |
| 205 | A26 | 2fr green & org (Bk) | 1.50 | *.80* |
| 206 | A26 | 3fr brown & vio (Bk) | 3.50 | *1.60* |
| 207 | A26 | 5fr violet & blk (Bk) | 3.50 | *2.75* |
| | | *Nos. 197-207 (11)* | 20.25 | 21.70 |

No. 200 exists perf. 11.

For surcharges see Nos. 208-209, 238-240.

Nos. 200, 202 Surcharged in Black or Red

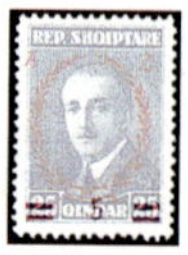

**1928**

| | | | | |
|---|---|---|---|---|
| 208 | A25 | 1q on 10q rose red | .50 | .55 |
| *a.* | | Inverted surcharge | 4.00 | 4.00 |
| 209 | A25 | 5q on 25q dk blue (R) | .50 | .55 |
| *a.* | | Inverted surcharge | 4.00 | 4.00 |

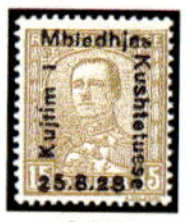


A27

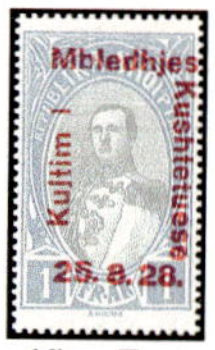


King Zog I — A28

**Black Overprint**

**1928 *Perf. 14x13½***

| | | | | |
|---|---|---|---|---|
| 210 | A27 | 1q orange brown | 5.00 | *9.50* |
| 211 | A27 | 2q slate | 5.00 | *9.50* |
| 212 | A27 | 5q blue green | 5.00 | *12.00* |
| 213 | A27 | 10q rose red | 4.00 | *12.00* |
| 214 | A27 | 15q bister | 15.00 | *47.50* |
| 215 | A27 | 25q deep blue | 6.00 | *12.00* |
| 216 | A27 | 50q lilac rose | 10.00 | *15.00* |

**Red Overprint**

***Perf. 13½x14***

| | | | | |
|---|---|---|---|---|
| 217 | A28 | 1fr blue & slate | 10.00 | 12.00 |
| | | *Nos. 210-217 (8)* | 60.00 | *129.50* |

Compare with types A29-A32.

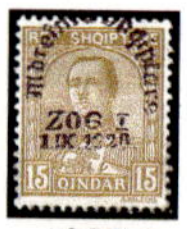

A29

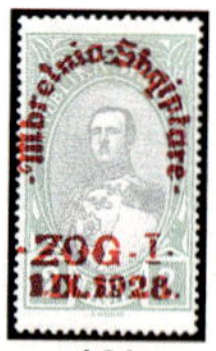


A30

**Black or Red Overprint**

**1928 *Perf. 14x13½***

| | | | | |
|---|---|---|---|---|
| 218 | A29 | 1q orange brown | 12.50 | *25.00* |
| 219 | A29 | 2q slate (R) | 12.50 | *25.00* |
| 220 | A29 | 5q blue green | 10.00 | *20.00* |
| 221 | A29 | 10q rose red | 10.00 | *16.00* |
| 222 | A29 | 15q bister | 15.00 | *27.50* |
| 223 | A29 | 25q deep blue (R) | 10.00 | *16.00* |
| 224 | A29 | 50q lilac rose | 10.00 | *16.00* |

***Perf. 13½x14***

| | | | | |
|---|---|---|---|---|
| 225 | A30 | 1fr blue & slate (R) | 12.50 | *20.00* |
| 226 | A30 | 2fr green & slate (R) | 12.50 | *20.00* |
| | | *Nos. 218-226 (9)* | 105.00 | 185.50 |

Proclamation of Ahmed Zogu as King of Albania.

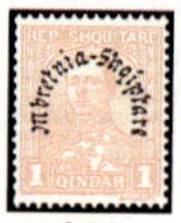

A31

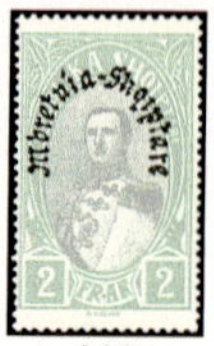


A32

**Black Overprint**

**1928 *Perf. 14x13½***

| | | | | |
|---|---|---|---|---|
| 227 | A31 | 1q orange brown | .40 | *1.25* |
| 228 | A31 | 2q slate | .40 | *1.25* |
| 229 | A31 | 5q blue green | 2.75 | *3.50* |
| 230 | A31 | 10q rose red | .40 | *1.25* |
| 231 | A31 | 15q bister | 15.00 | *24.00* |
| 232 | A31 | 25q deep blue | .40 | *1.25* |
| 233 | A31 | 50q lilac rose | .75 | *2.00* |

***Perf. 13½x14***

| | | | | |
|---|---|---|---|---|
| 234 | A32 | 1fr blue & slate | 1.50 | *2.50* |
| 235 | A32 | 2fr green & slate | 1.50 | *4.00* |
| 236 | A32 | 3fr dk red & ol bis | 7.50 | *12.00* |
| 237 | A32 | 5fr dull vio & gray | 7.50 | *16.00* |
| | | *Nos. 227-237 (11)* | 38.10 | 69.00 |

The overprint reads "Kingdom of Albania."

Nos. 203, 202, 200 Surcharged in Black

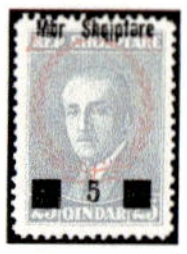

**1929 *Perf. 13½x13, 11½***

| | | | | |
|---|---|---|---|---|
| 238 | A25 | 1q on 50q blue green | .40 | *.55* |
| 239 | A25 | 5q on 25q dark blue | .40 | *.55* |
| 240 | A25 | 15q on 10q rose red | .60 | *1.00* |
| | | *Nos. 238-240 (3)* | 1.40 | 2.10 |

Nos. 186-189, 191-194 Overprinted in Black or Red

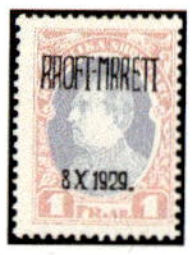


**1929 *Perf. 11½, 13½***

| | | | | |
|---|---|---|---|---|
| 241 | A25 | 1q orange | 8.00 | *20.00* |
| 242 | A25 | 2q red brown | 8.00 | *20.00* |
| 243 | A25 | 5q green | 8.00 | *20.00* |
| 244 | A25 | 10q rose red | 8.00 | *20.00* |
| 245 | A25 | 25q dark blue | 8.00 | *20.00* |
| 246 | A25 | 50q blue green (R) | 11.00 | *24.00* |
| 247 | A26 | 1fr red & ultra | 15.00 | *35.00* |
| 248 | A26 | 2fr green & orange | 15.00 | *35.00* |
| | | *Nos. 241-248 (8)* | 81.00 | 194.00 |

34th birthday of King Zog. The overprint reads "Long live the King."

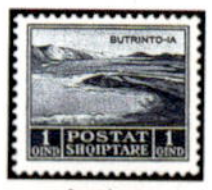

Lake Butrinto A33

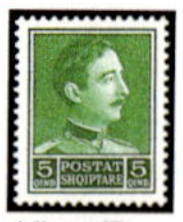

King Zog I A34

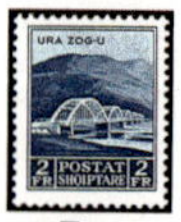

Zog Bridge A35

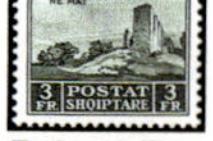

Ruin at Zog Manor A36

***Perf. 14, 14½***

**1930, Sept. 1 Photo. Wmk. 220**

| | | | | |
|---|---|---|---|---|
| 250 | A33 | 1q slate | .25 | .25 |
| 251 | A33 | 2q orange red | .25 | .25 |
| 252 | A34 | 5q yellow green | .25 | .25 |
| 253 | A34 | 10q carmine | .25 | .25 |
| 254 | A34 | 15q dark brown | .25 | .25 |
| 255 | A34 | 25q dark ultra | .25 | .25 |
| 256 | A33 | 50q slate green | .70 | .55 |
| 257 | A35 | 1fr violet | 1.10 | 1.00 |
| 258 | A35 | 2fr indigo | 1.50 | 1.10 |
| 259 | A36 | 3fr gray green | 3.50 | 2.25 |
| 260 | A36 | 5fr orange brown | 4.50 | 3.50 |
| | | *Nos. 250-260 (11)* | 12.80 | 9.90 |

2nd anniversary of accession of King Zog I.

For overprints see Nos. 261-270, 299-309, J39. For surcharges see Nos. 354-360.

Nos. 250-259 Overprinted in Black

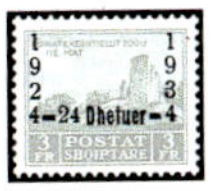

**1934, Dec. 24**

| | | | | |
|---|---|---|---|---|
| 261 | A33 | 1q slate | 7.00 | 12.00 |
| 262 | A33 | 2q orange red | 7.00 | 12.00 |
| 263 | A34 | 5q yellow green | 7.00 | 9.50 |
| 264 | A34 | 10q carmine | 9.25 | 12.00 |
| 265 | A34 | 15q dark brown | 9.25 | 12.00 |
| 266 | A34 | 25q dark ultra | 9.25 | 12.00 |
| 267 | A33 | 50q slate green | 10.00 | 16.00 |
| 268 | A35 | 1fr violet | 11.00 | 20.00 |
| 269 | A35 | 2fr indigo | 12.00 | 25.00 |
| 270 | A36 | 3fr gray green | 15.00 | 35.00 |
| | | *Nos. 261-270 (10)* | 96.75 | 165.50 |

Tenth anniversary of the Constitution.

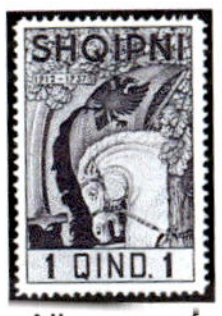


Allegory of Death of Skanderbeg A37

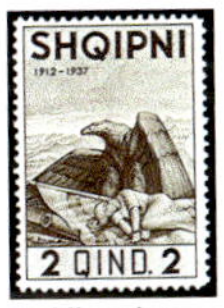


Albanian Eagle in Turkish Shackles A38

5q, 25q, 40q, 2fr, Eagle with wings spread.

**1937 Unwmk. *Perf. 14***

| | | | | |
|---|---|---|---|---|
| 271 | A37 | 1q brown violet | .25 | .25 |
| 272 | A38 | 2q brown | .50 | .35 |
| 273 | A38 | 5q lt green | .50 | .50 |
| 274 | A37 | 10q olive brown | .50 | .80 |
| 275 | A38 | 15q rose red | .80 | 1.00 |
| 276 | A38 | 25q blue | 1.50 | 2.00 |
| 277 | A37 | 50q deep green | 3.75 | 3.25 |
| 278 | A38 | 1fr violet | 9.00 | 6.00 |
| 279 | A38 | 2fr orange brown | 12.00 | 9.00 |
| | | *Nos. 271-279 (9)* | 28.80 | 23.15 |

**Souvenir Sheet**

| | | | | |
|---|---|---|---|---|
| 280 | | Sheet of 3 | 17.50 | 125.00 |
| *a.* | A37 | 20q red violet | 3.50 | 6.25 |
| *b.* | A38 | 30q olive brown | 3.50 | 6.25 |
| *c.* | A38 | 40q red | 3.50 | 6.25 |

25th anniv. of independence from Turkey, proclaimed Nov. 28, 1912.

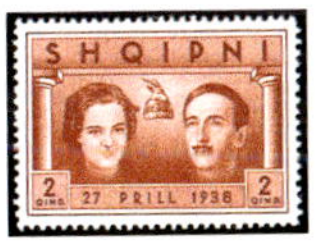


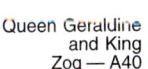

Queen Geraldine and King Zog — A40

**1938 *Perf. 14***

| | | | | |
|---|---|---|---|---|
| 281 | A40 | 1q slate violet | .30 | .40 |
| 282 | A40 | 2q red brown | .30 | .40 |
| 283 | A40 | 5q green | .30 | .40 |
| 284 | A40 | 10q olive brown | 1.10 | .80 |
| 285 | A40 | 15q rose red | 1.10 | .80 |
| 286 | A40 | 25q blue | 2.75 | 2.00 |
| 287 | A40 | 50q Prus green | 5.75 | 4.00 |
| 288 | A40 | 1fr purple | 11.50 | 8.00 |
| | | *Nos. 281-288 (8)* | 23.10 | 16.80 |

**Souvenir Sheet**

| | | | | |
|---|---|---|---|---|
| 289 | | Sheet of 4 | 32.50 | 125.00 |
| *a.* | A40 | 20q dark red violet | 7.75 | 9.75 |
| *b.* | A40 | 30q brown olive | 7.75 | 9.75 |

Wedding of King Zog and Countess Geraldine Apponyi, Apr. 27, 1938.
No. 289 contains 2 each of Nos. 289a, 289b.

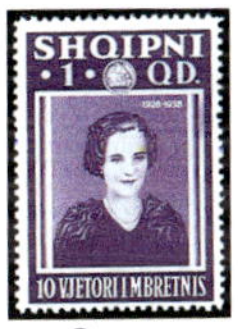


Queen Geraldine A42

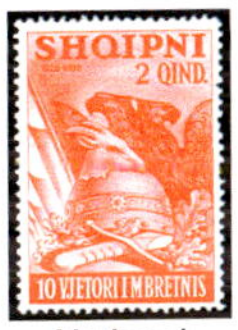


National Emblems A43

Designs: 10q, 25q, 30q, 1fr, King Zog.

**1938**

| | | | | |
|---|---|---|---|---|
| 290 | A42 | 1q dp red violet | .25 | .55 |
| 291 | A43 | 2q red orange | .25 | .55 |
| 292 | A42 | 5q deep green | .50 | .50 |
| 293 | A42 | 10q red brown | .50 | 1.00 |
| 294 | A42 | 15q deep rose | 1.00 | 1.25 |
| 295 | A42 | 25q deep blue | 1.40 | 1.40 |
| 296 | A43 | 50q gray black | 8.50 | 6.00 |
| 297 | A42 | 1fr slate green | 12.50 | 9.00 |
| | | *Nos. 290-297 (8)* | 24.90 | 20.25 |

**Souvenir Sheet**

| | | | | |
|---|---|---|---|---|
| 298 | | Sheet of 3 | 22.50 | 75.00 |
| *b.* | A43 | 20q Prussian green | 7.00 | 12.00 |
| *c.* | A42 | 30q deep violet | 7.00 | 12.00 |

10th anniv. of royal rule. They were on sale for 3 days (Aug. 30-31, Sept. 1) only, during which their use was required on all mail.
No. 298 contains Nos. 294, 298b, 298c.

## Issued under Italian Dominion

Nos. 250-260 Overprinted in Black

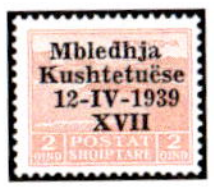


**1939 Wmk. 220 *Perf. 14***

| | | | | |
|---|---|---|---|---|
| 299 | A33 | 1q slate | 1.25 | 1.25 |
| 300 | A33 | 2q orange red | 1.25 | 1.25 |
| 301 | A34 | 5q yellow green | 1.25 | 1.25 |
| 302 | A34 | 10q carmine | 1.25 | 1.25 |
| 303 | A34 | 15q dark brown | 2.00 | 3.75 |
| 304 | A34 | 25q dark ultra | 2.00 | 3.75 |
| 305 | A33 | 50q slate green | 2.50 | 5.00 |
| 306 | A35 | 1fr violet | 2.50 | 5.00 |
| 307 | A35 | 2fr indigo | 3.25 | 9.50 |
| 308 | A36 | 3fr gray green | 7.75 | 22.50 |
| 309 | A36 | 5fr orange brown | 10.00 | 25.00 |
| | | *Nos. 299-309 (11)* | 35.00 | 79.50 |

Resolution adopted by the Natl. Assembly, Apr. 12, 1939, offering the Albanian Crown to Italy.

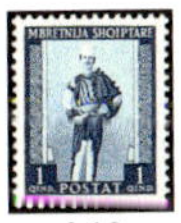

A46

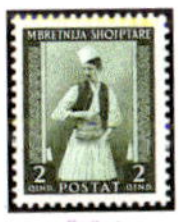

A47

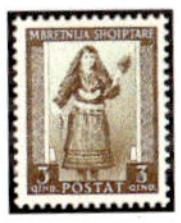

Native Costumes — A48

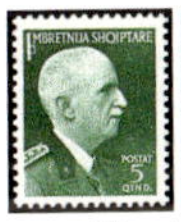

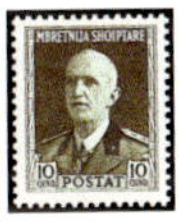

King Victor Emmanuel III A49 A50

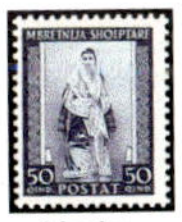

Native Costume A51

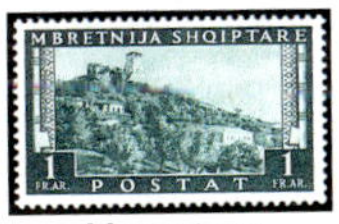


Monastery A52

Designs: 2fr, Bridge at Vezirit. 3fr, Ancient Columns. 5fr, Amphitheater.

**1939 Unwmk. Photo. *Perf. 14***

| | | | | |
|---|---|---|---|---|
| 310 | A46 | 1q blue gray | 1.25 | .50 |
| 311 | A47 | 2q olive green | 1.25 | .50 |
| 312 | A48 | 3q golden brown | 1.25 | .50 |
| 313 | A49 | 5q green | 1.25 | .25 |
| 314 | A50 | 10q brown | 1.25 | .25 |
| 315 | A50 | 15q crimson | 1.25 | .25 |
| 316 | A50 | 25q sapphire | 2.00 | .80 |
| 317 | A50 | 30q brt violet | 2.50 | 1.40 |
| 318 | A51 | 50q dull purple | 3.25 | 3.25 |
| 319 | A49 | 65q red brown | 5.00 | 11.50 |
| 320 | A52 | 1fr myrtle green | 7.50 | 9.50 |
| 321 | A52 | 2fr brown lake | 11.50 | 19.00 |
| 322 | A52 | 3fr brown black | 19.00 | 35.00 |
| 323 | A52 | 5fr gray violet | 25.00 | 50.00 |
| | | *Nos. 310-323 (14)* | 83.25 | 132.70 |

For overprints and surcharges see Nos. 331-353.

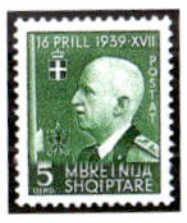

King Victor Emmanuel III — A56

**1942 Photo.**

| | | | | |
|---|---|---|---|---|
| 324 | A56 | 5q green | 1.25 | 2.00 |
| 325 | A56 | 10q brown | 1.25 | 2.00 |
| 326 | A56 | 15q rose red | 1.25 | 2.00 |
| 327 | A56 | 25q blue | 1.25 | 2.00 |
| 328 | A56 | 65q red brown | 3.50 | 4.00 |
| 329 | A56 | 1fr myrtle green | 3.50 | 4.00 |
| 330 | A56 | 2fr gray violet | 3.50 | 4.00 |
| | | *Nos. 324-330 (7)* | 15.50 | 20.00 |

Conquest of Albania by Italy, 3rd anniv.

No. 311 Surcharged in Black

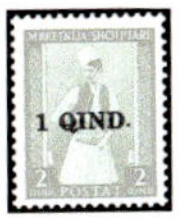


| | | | | |
|---|---|---|---|---|
| 331 | A47 | 1q on 2q olive green | 1.60 | 4.00 |

## Issued under German Administration

Stamps of 1939 Overprinted in Carmine or Brown

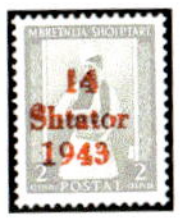


**1943**

| | | | | |
|---|---|---|---|---|
| 332 | A47 | 2q olive green | 1.00 | 4.00 |
| 333 | A48 | 3q golden brown | 1.00 | 4.00 |
| 334 | A49 | 5q green | 1.00 | 4.00 |
| 335 | A50 | 10q brown | 1.00 | 4.00 |
| 336 | A50 | 15q crimson (Br) | 1.00 | 4.00 |
| 337 | A50 | 25q sapphire | 1.00 | 4.00 |
| 338 | A50 | 30q brt violet | 1.00 | 4.00 |
| 339 | A49 | 65q red brown | 1.50 | 8.00 |
| 340 | A52 | 1fr myrtle green | 6.25 | 24.00 |
| 341 | A52 | 2fr brown lake | 7.75 | 80.00 |
| 342 | A52 | 3fr brown black | 60.00 | 200.00 |

**Surcharged with New Values**

| | | | | |
|---|---|---|---|---|
| 343 | A48 | 1q on 3q gldn brn | 1.00 | 8.00 |
| 344 | A49 | 50q on 65q red brn | 1.50 | 12.00 |
| | | *Nos. 332-344 (13)* | 85.00 | 360.00 |

Proclamation of Albanian independence.
The overprint "14 Shtator 1943" on Nos. 324 to 328 is private and fraudulent.

## Independent State

Nos. 312 to 317 and 319 to 321 Surcharged with New Value and Bars in Black or Carmine, and:

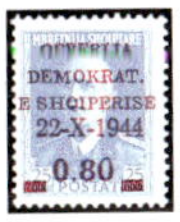


**1945**

| | | | | |
|---|---|---|---|---|
| 345 | A48 | 30q on 3q gldn brn | 3.00 | 12.00 |
| 346 | A49 | 40q on 5q green | 3.00 | 12.00 |
| 347 | A50 | 50q on 10q brown | 3.00 | 12.00 |
| 348 | A50 | 60q on 15q crimson | 3.00 | 12.00 |
| 349 | A50 | 80q on 25q saph (C) | 3.00 | 12.00 |
| 350 | A50 | 1fr on 30q brt violet | 3.00 | 12.00 |
| 351 | A49 | 2fr on 65q red brn | 3.00 | 12.00 |
| 352 | A52 | 3fr on 1fr myr green | 3.00 | 12.00 |
| 353 | A52 | 5fr on 2fr brown lake | 3.00 | 12.00 |
| | | *Nos. 345-353 (9)* | 27.00 | 108.00 |

"DEMOKRATIKE" is not abbreviated on Nos. 352 and 353.

Nos. 250, 251, 256 and 258 Surcharged in Black or Carmine, and

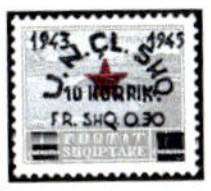

**1945 Wmk. 220**

| | | | | |
|---|---|---|---|---|
| 354 | A33 | 30q on 1q slate | 2.00 | 6.00 |
| 355 | A33 | 60q on 1q slate | 2.00 | 6.00 |
| 356 | A33 | 80q on 1q slate | 2.00 | 6.00 |
| 357 | A33 | 1fr on 1q slate | 4.00 | 12.00 |
| 358 | A33 | 2fr on 2q org red | 5.00 | 13.50 |
| 359 | A33 | 3fr on 50q sl grn | 10.00 | 25.00 |
| 360 | A35 | 5fr on 2fr indigo | 12.50 | 40.00 |
| | | *Nos. 354-360 (7)* | 37.50 | 108.50 |

Albanian Natl. Army of Liberation, 2nd anniv.
The surcharge on No. 360 is condensed to fit the size of the stamp.

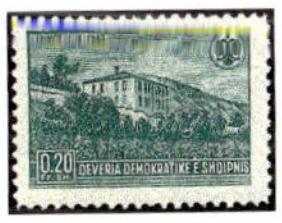

Country House, Labinot — A57

40q, 60q, Bridge at Berat. 1fr, 3fr, Permet.

***Perf. 11½***
**1945, Nov. 28 Unwmk. Typo.**

| | | | | |
|---|---|---|---|---|
| 361 | A57 | 20q bluish green | .30 | 1.20 |
| 362 | A57 | 30q deep orange | .40 | 1.75 |
| 363 | A57 | 40q brown | .40 | 1.75 |
| 364 | A57 | 60q red violet | .60 | 2.50 |
| 365 | A57 | 1fr rose red | 1.50 | 5.00 |
| 366 | A57 | 3fr dark blue | 10.00 | 21.00 |
| | | *Nos. 361-366 (6)* | 13.20 | 33.20 |

Counterfeits: lithographed; genuine: typographed.
For overprints and surcharges see Nos. 367-378, 418-423, B28-B33.

Nos. 361 to 366 Overprinted in Black

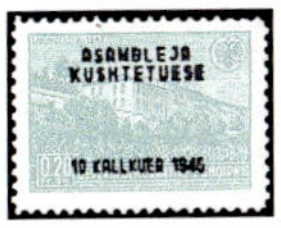

**1946**

| | | | | |
|---|---|---|---|---|
| 367 | A57 | 20q bluish green | .60 | 1.40 |
| 368 | A57 | 30q deep orange | .80 | 1.75 |
| 369 | A57 | 40q brown | 1.00 | 2.10 |
| 370 | A57 | 60q red violet | 1.60 | 3.50 |
| 371 | A57 | 1fr rose red | 6.00 | 12.50 |
| 372 | A57 | 3fr dark blue | 10.00 | 21.00 |
| | | *Nos. 367-372 (6)* | 20.00 | 42.25 |

Convocation of the Constitutional Assembly, Jan. 10, 1946.

## People's Republic

#361-366 Overprinted in Black

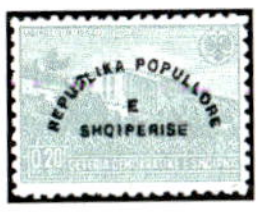

**1946 *Perf. 11***

| | | | | |
|---|---|---|---|---|
| 373 | A57 | 20q bluish green | .40 | 1.10 |
| 374 | A57 | 30q deep orange | .60 | 1.40 |
| 375 | A57 | 40q brown | 1.00 | 2.75 |
| 376 | A57 | 60q red violet | 2.00 | 5.25 |
| 377 | A57 | 1fr rose red | 6.00 | 14.00 |
| 378 | A57 | 3fr dark blue | 10.00 | 21.00 |
| | | *Nos. 373-378 (6)* | 20.00 | 45.50 |

Proclamation of the Albanian People's Republic.
Some values exist perf 11½.
For surcharges see Nos. 418-423.

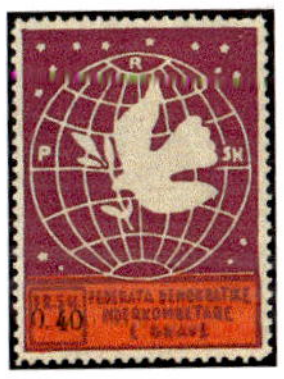

Globe, Dove and Olive Branch — A60

***Perf. 11½, Imperf.***
**1946, Mar. 8 Typo.**
**Denomination in Black**

| | | | | |
|---|---|---|---|---|
| 379 | A60 | 20q lilac & dull red | .25 | 1.25 |
| 380 | A60 | 40q dp lilac & dull red | .45 | 1.75 |
| 381 | A60 | 50q violet & dull red | .90 | 2.50 |
| 382 | A60 | 1fr lt blue & red | 1.60 | 5.00 |
| 383 | A60 | 2fr dk blue & red | 2.00 | 8.00 |
| | | *Nos. 379-383 (5)* | 5.20 | 18.50 |

International Women's Congress.
Counterfeits exist.

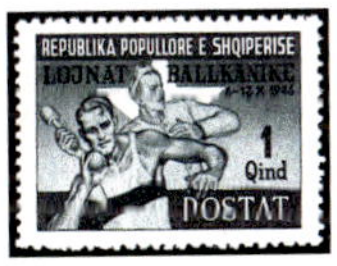


Athletes with Shot and Indian Club — A61

***Perf. 11½***
**1946, Oct. 6 Litho. Unwmk.**

| | | | | |
|---|---|---|---|---|
| 384 | A61 | 1q grnsh black | 5.00 | 8.50 |
| 385 | A61 | 2q green | 5.00 | 8.50 |
| 386 | A61 | 5q brown | 5.00 | 8.50 |
| 387 | A61 | 10q crimson | 5.00 | 8.50 |
| 388 | A61 | 20q ultra | 5.00 | 8.50 |
| 389 | A61 | 40q rose violet | 5.00 | 8.50 |
| 390 | A61 | 1fr deep orange | 12.50 | 25.00 |
| | | *Nos. 384-390 (7)* | 42.50 | 76.00 |

Balkan Games, Tirana, Oct. 6-13.

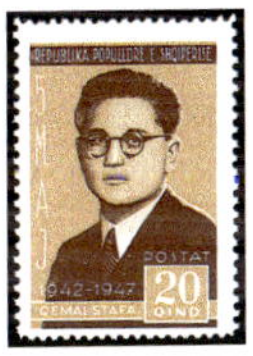

Qemal Stafa — A62

**1947, May 5 *Perf. 12½x11½***

| | | | | |
|---|---|---|---|---|
| 391 | A62 | 20q brn & yel brn | 5.00 | 11.00 |
| 392 | A62 | 28q dk blue & blue | 5.00 | 11.00 |
| 393 | A62 | 40q brn blk & gray brn | 5.00 | 11.00 |
| *a.* | | Souvenir sheet, #391-393 | 90.00 | 110.00 |
| | | *Nos. 391-393 (3)* | 15.00 | 33.00 |

5th anniv. of the death of Qemal Stafa.

Young Railway Laborers — A64

**1947, May 16** *Perf. 11½*

| | | | | | |
|---|---|---|---|---|---|
| **395** | A64 | 1q | brn blk & gray brn | 2.00 | 1.40 |
| **396** | A64 | 4q | dk green & green | 2.00 | 1.40 |
| **397** | A64 | 10q | blk brn & bis brn | 2.00 | 1.60 |
| **398** | A64 | 15q | dk red & red | 2.00 | 1.60 |
| **399** | A64 | 20q | indigo & bl gray | 4.00 | 3.00 |
| **400** | A64 | 28q | dk blue & blue | 6.00 | 2.50 |
| **401** | A64 | 40q | brn vio & rose vio | 12.50 | 14.50 |

*Perf. 13x12½*

| | | | | | |
|---|---|---|---|---|---|
| **402** | A64 | 68q | dk brn & org brn | 15.00 | *25.00* |
| | | | *Nos. 395-402 (8)* | 45.50 | 51.00 |

Issued to publicize the construction of the Durres Elbasan Railway by Albanian youths.

The 4q, 20q, 28q and 40q exist perf 13x12½.

Citizens Led by Hasim Zeneli A65

Enver Hoxha and Vasil Shanto A66

Inauguration of Vithkuq Brigade — A67

Vojo Kushi — A68

**1947, July 10** **Litho.**

| | | | | | |
|---|---|---|---|---|---|
| **403** | A65 | 16q | brn org & red brn | 4.00 | *7.00* |
| **404** | A66 | 20q | org brn & dk brn | 4.00 | *7.00* |
| **405** | A67 | 28q | blue & dk blue | 4.00 | *7.00* |
| **406** | A68 | 40q | lilac & dk brn | 4.00 | *7.00* |
| | | | *Nos. 403-406 (4)* | 16.00 | *28.00* |

4th anniv. of the formation of Albania's army, July 10, 1943.

Conference Building Ruins, Peza — A69

**1947, Sept. 16**

| | | | | | |
|---|---|---|---|---|---|
| **407** | A69 | 2 l | red violet | 2.50 | *5.25* |
| **408** | A69 | 2.50 l | deep blue | 2.50 | *5.25* |

Peza Conf., Sept. 16, 1942, 5th anniv.

Disabled Soldiers — A70

**1947, Nov. 17** *Perf. 12½x11½*

| | | | | | |
|---|---|---|---|---|---|
| **408A** | A70 | 1 l | red | 7.00 | *11.00* |

Disabled War Veterans Cong., 11/14-20/47.

A71

A73

2 l, Banquet. 2.50 l, Peasants rejoicing.

*Perf. 11½x12½, 12½x11½*

**1947, Nov. 17** **Unwmk.**

| | | | | | |
|---|---|---|---|---|---|
| **409** | A71 | 1.50 l | dull violet | 3.50 | *7.00* |
| **410** | A71 | 2 l | brown | 3.50 | *7.00* |
| **411** | A71 | 2.50 l | blue | 3.50 | *7.00* |
| **412** | A73 | 3 l | rose red | 3.50 | *7.00* |
| | | | *Nos. 409-412 (4)* | 14.00 | *28.00* |

Agrarian reform law of 11/17/46, 1st anniv.

Burning Farm Buildings — A74

Designs: 2.50 l, Trench scene. 5 l, Firing line. 8 l, Winter advance. 12 l, Infantry column.

**1947, Nov. 29** *Perf. 11½x12½*

| | | | | | |
|---|---|---|---|---|---|
| **413** | A74 | 1.50 l | red | 2.00 | *3.00* |
| **414** | A74 | 2.50 l | rose brown | 2.00 | *3.00* |
| **415** | A74 | 5 l | blue | 4.00 | *6.00* |
| **416** | A74 | 8 l | purple | 6.00 | *9.00* |
| **417** | A74 | 12 l | brown | 10.00 | *14.00* |
| | | | *Nos. 413-417 (5)* | 24.00 | *35.00* |

3rd anniv. of Albania's liberation.

**Nos. 373 to 378 Surcharged with New Value and Bars in Black**

**1948, Feb. 22** *Perf. 11*

| | | | | | |
|---|---|---|---|---|---|
| **418** | A57 | 50q | on 30q dp org | .25 | *.50* |
| **419** | A57 | 1 l | on 20q bluish grn | .40 | .85 |
| **420** | A57 | 2.50 l | on 60q red vio | 1.00 | *2.50* |
| **421** | A57 | 3 l | on 1fr rose red | 1.40 | *3.25* |
| **422** | A57 | 5 l | on 3fr dk bl | 3.00 | *5.25* |
| **423** | A57 | 12 l | on 40q brown | 8.00 | *14.00* |
| | | | *Nos. 418-423 (6)* | 14.05 | *26.35* |

The two bars consist of four type squares each set close together.

Some values exist perf 11½.

Map, Train and Construction Workers — A75

**1948, June 1** **Litho.** *Perf. 11½*

| | | | | | |
|---|---|---|---|---|---|
| **424** | A75 | 50q | dk car rose | 1.00 | 1.10 |
| **425** | A75 | 1 l | lt green & blk | 1.00 | 1.10 |
| **426** | A75 | 1.50 l | deep rose | 1.60 | 1.75 |
| **427** | A75 | 2.50 l | org brn & dk brn | 2.50 | 2.25 |
| **428** | A75 | 5 l | dull blue | 4.00 | 4.25 |
| **429** | A75 | 8 l | sal & dk brn | 7.00 | 7.00 |
| **430** | A75 | 12 l | red vio & dk vio | 12.00 | 8.50 |
| **431** | A75 | 20 l | olive gray | 16.00 | 17.50 |
| | | | *Nos. 424-431 (8)* | 45.10 | 43.45 |

Issued to publicize the construction of the Durres-Tirana Railway.

Marching Soldiers — A76

Design: 8 l, Battle scene.

**1948, July 10**

| | | | | | |
|---|---|---|---|---|---|
| **432** | A76 | 2.50 l | yellow brown | 2.00 | 3.50 |
| **433** | A76 | 5 l | dark blue | 2.75 | 5.00 |
| **434** | A76 | 8 l | violet gray | 5.25 | 7.00 |
| | | | *Nos. 432-434 (3)* | 10.00 | 15.50 |

5th anniv. of the formation of Albania's army.

Bricklayer, Flag, Globe and "Industry" — A77

**1949, May 1** **Photo.** *Perf. 12½x12*

| | | | | | |
|---|---|---|---|---|---|
| **435** | A77 | 2.50 l | olive brown | .60 | *1.75* |
| **436** | A77 | 5 l | blue | 1.20 | *1.75* |
| **437** | A77 | 8 l | violet brown | 2.25 | *4.50* |
| | | | *Nos. 435-437 (3)* | 4.05 | *8.00* |

Issued to publicize Labor Day, May 1, 1949.

Map and Soldier — A78

**1949, July 10** **Unwmk.**

| | | | | | |
|---|---|---|---|---|---|
| **438** | A78 | 2.50 l | brown | .60 | *1.75* |
| **439** | A78 | 5 l | light ultra | 1.20 | *2.75* |
| **440** | A78 | 8 l | brown orange | 2.25 | *5.25* |
| | | | *Nos. 438-440 (3)* | 4.05 | 9.75 |

6th anniv. of the formation of Albania's army.

Enver Hoxha — A79

**1949, Oct. 16** **Engr.** *Perf. 12½*

| | | | | | |
|---|---|---|---|---|---|
| **441** | A79 | 50q | purple | .25 | .25 |
| **442** | A79 | 1 l | dull green | .25 | .25 |
| **443** | A79 | 1.50 l | car lake | .25 | .25 |
| **444** | A79 | 2.50 l | brown | .35 | .25 |
| **445** | A79 | 5 l | violet blue | .80 | .70 |
| **446** | A79 | 8 l | sepia | 1.50 | 2.10 |
| **447** | A79 | 12 l | rose lilac | 4.00 | 3.50 |
| **448** | A79 | 20 l | gray blue | 4.75 | 5.25 |
| | | | *Nos. 441-448 (8)* | 12.15 | 12.55 |

Albanian Citizen and Spasski Tower, Kremlin — A80

**1949, Sept. 10** **Photo.** *Perf. 12½x12*

| | | | | | |
|---|---|---|---|---|---|
| **449** | A80 | 2.50 l | orange brown | .60 | *1.50* |
| **450** | A80 | 5 l | deep ultra | 1.50 | *3.50* |

Albanian-Soviet friendship.

Albanian Soldier and Flag — A81

Battle Scene — A82

**1949, Nov. 29** **Unwmk.** *Perf. 12*

| | | | | | |
|---|---|---|---|---|---|
| **451** | A81 | 2.50 l | brown | .40 | *1.10* |
| **452** | A82 | 3 l | dark red | .40 | *2.10* |
| **453** | A81 | 5 l | violet | 1.25 | *2.75* |
| **454** | A82 | 8 l | black | 2.50 | *5.25* |
| | | | *Nos. 451-454 (4)* | 4.55 | *11.20* |

Fifth anniversary of Albania's liberation.

Joseph V. Stalin — A83

**1949, Dec. 21**

| | | | | | |
|---|---|---|---|---|---|
| **455** | A83 | 2.50 l | dark brown | .40 | *1.40* |
| **456** | A83 | 5 l | violet blue | 1.00 | *2.50* |
| **457** | A83 | 8 l | rose brown | 2.75 | *6.00* |
| | | | *Nos. 455-457 (3)* | 4.15 | *9.90* |

70th anniv. of the birth of Joseph V. Stalin.

Canceled to Order

Beginning in 1950, Albania sold some issues in sheets canceled to order. Values in second column, when much less than unused, are for "CTO" examples. Postally used stamps are valued at slightly less than, or the same as, unused.

**Catalogue values for unused stamps in this section, from this point to the end of the section, are for Never Hinged items.**

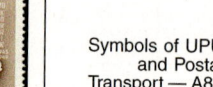

Symbols of UPU and Postal Transport — A84

**1950, July 1** **Photo.** *Perf. 12x12½*

| | | | | | |
|---|---|---|---|---|---|
| **458** | A84 | 5 l | blue | 2.00 | 1.40 |
| **459** | A84 | 8 l | rose brown | 4.00 | 1.90 |
| **460** | A84 | 12 l | sepia | 8.00 | 2.40 |
| | | | *Nos. 458-460 (3)* | 14.00 | 5.70 |

75th anniv. (in 1949) of the UPU.

Sami Frasheri — A85

Authors: 2.50 l, Andon Zako. 3 l, Naim Frasheri. 5 l, Kostandin Kristoforidhi.

**1950, Nov. 5** *Perf. 14*

| | | | | | |
|---|---|---|---|---|---|
| **461** | A85 | 2 l | dark green | 1.00 | .40 |
| **462** | A85 | 2.50 l | red brown | 1.40 | .45 |
| **463** | A85 | 3 l | brown carmine | 3.00 | .65 |
| **464** | A85 | 5 l | deep blue | 3.50 | .80 |
| | | | *Nos. 461-464 (4)* | 8.90 | 2.30 |

"Jubilee of the Writers of the Renaissance."

Arms and Albanian Flags — A86

**1951, Jan. 11** **Engr.** *Perf. 14x13½*

| | | | | | |
|---|---|---|---|---|---|
| **465** | A86 | 2.50 l | brown carmine | 1.60 | .30 |
| **466** | A86 | 5 l | deep blue | 3.25 | .65 |
| **467** | A86 | 8 l | sepia | 5.25 | 1.25 |
| | | | *Nos. 465-467 (3)* | 10.10 | 2.20 |

5th anniv. of the formation of the Albanian People's Republic.

Skanderbeg — A87

**1951, Mar. 1**

| | | | | | |
|---|---|---|---|---|---|
| **468** | A87 | 2.50 l | brown | 1.75 | .30 |
| **469** | A87 | 5 l | violet | 3.25 | .55 |
| **470** | A87 | 8 l | olive bister | 5.25 | 1.10 |
| | | | *Nos. 468-470 (3)* | 10.25 | 1.95 |

483rd anniv. of the death of George Castriota (Skanderbeg).

Enver Hoxha and Congress of Permet — A88

**1951, May 24** **Photo.** *Perf. 12*

| | | | | | |
|---|---|---|---|---|---|
| **471** | A88 | 2.50 l | dark brown | .70 | .25 |
| **472** | A88 | 3 l | rose brown | .70 | .35 |
| **473** | A88 | 5 l | violet blue | 1.75 | .55 |
| **474** | A88 | 8 l | rose lilac | 3.25 | .85 |
| | | | *Nos. 471-474 (4)* | 6.40 | 2.00 |

Congress of Permet, 7th anniversary.

Child and Globe A89

Weighing Baby A90

**1951, July 16**

| | | | | |
|---|---|---|---|---|
| **475** | A89 | 2 l green | 1.75 | .80 |
| **476** | A90 | 2.50 l brown | 2.50 | .95 |
| **477** | A90 | 3 l red | 3.25 | 1.25 |
| **478** | A89 | 5 l blue | 5.00 | 1.40 |
| | | *Nos. 475-478 (4)* | 12.50 | 4.40 |

Intl. Children's Day, June 1, 1951.

Enver Hoxha and Birthplace of Albanian Communist Party — A91

**1951, Nov. 8 Photo. *Perf. 14***

| | | | | |
|---|---|---|---|---|
| **479** | A91 | 2.50 l olive brown | .50 | .25 |
| **480** | A91 | 3 l rose brown | .50 | .40 |
| **481** | A91 | 5 l dark slate blue | 1.10 | .65 |
| **482** | A91 | 8 l black | 2.10 | .90 |
| | | *Nos. 479-482 (4)* | 4.20 | 2.20 |

Albanian Communist Party, 10th anniv.

Battle Scene — A92

Designs: 5 l, Schoolgirl, "Agriculture and Industry." 8 l, Four portraits.

**1951, Nov. 28 *Perf. 12x12½***

| | | | | |
|---|---|---|---|---|
| **483** | A92 | 2.50 l brown | .70 | .25 |
| **484** | A92 | 5 l blue | 1.40 | .50 |
| **485** | A92 | 8 l brown carmine | 3.25 | .85 |
| | | *Nos. 483-485 (3)* | 5.35 | 1.60 |

Albanian Communist Youth Org., 10th anniv.

Albanian Heroes (Haxhija, Lezha, Giylbogaj, Mazi and Deda) — A93

Designs: Nos. 486-489 each show 5 "Heroes of the People"; No. 490 shows 2 (Stafa and Shanto).

**1950, Dec. 25 Unwmk. *Perf. 14***

| | | | | |
|---|---|---|---|---|
| **486** | A93 | 2 l dark green | .75 | .25 |
| **487** | A93 | 2.50 l purple | 1.10 | .25 |
| **488** | A93 | 3 l scarlet | 2.25 | .35 |
| **489** | A93 | 5 l brt blue | 3.75 | .45 |
| **490** | A93 | 8 l olive brown | 7.50 | 1.25 |
| | | *Nos. 486-490 (5)* | 15.35 | 2.55 |

6th anniv. of Albania's liberation.

Tobacco Factory, Shkoder — A94

Composite, Lenin Hydroelectric Plant — A95

Designs: 1 l, Canal. 2.50 l, Textile factory. 3 l, "8 November" Cannery. 5 l, Motion Picture Studio, Tirana. 8 l, Stalin Textile Mill, Tirana. 20 l, Central Hydroelectric Dam.

**1953, Aug. 1 *Perf. 12x12½, 12½x12***

| | | | | |
|---|---|---|---|---|
| **491** | A94 | 50q red brown | .45 | .25 |
| **492** | A94 | 1 l dull green | .85 | .25 |
| **493** | A94 | 2.50 l brown | .85 | .25 |
| **494** | A94 | 3 l rose brown | 1.25 | .50 |
| **495** | A94 | 5 l blue | 2.10 | .75 |
| **496** | A94 | 8 l brown olive | 2.50 | 1.00 |
| **497** | A95 | 12 l deep plum | 4.25 | 1.50 |
| **498** | A94 | 20 l slate blue | 6.00 | 3.25 |
| | | *Nos. 491-498 (8)* | 18.25 | 7.75 |

Liberation Scene — A96

**1954, Nov. 29 *Perf. 12x12½***

| | | | | |
|---|---|---|---|---|
| **499** | A96 | 50q brown violet | .25 | .25 |
| **500** | A96 | 1 l olive green | .55 | .25 |
| **501** | A96 | 2.50 l yellow brown | .80 | .25 |
| **502** | A96 | 3 l carmine rose | 1.60 | .35 |
| **503** | A96 | 5 l gray blue | 2.40 | .50 |
| **504** | A96 | 8 l rose brown | 4.00 | 1.00 |
| | | *Nos. 499-504 (6)* | 9.60 | 2.60 |

10th anniversary of Albania's liberation.

School — A97

Pandeli Sotiri, Petro Nini Luarasi, Nuci Naci — A98

**1956, Feb. 23 Unwmk.**

| | | | | |
|---|---|---|---|---|
| **505** | A97 | 2 l rose violet | .40 | .25 |
| **506** | A98 | 2.50 l lt green | .55 | .35 |
| **507** | A98 | 5 l ultra | 1.40 | .60 |
| **508** | A97 | 10 l brt grnsh blue | 4.75 | 1.00 |
| | | *Nos. 505-508 (4)* | 7.10 | 2.20 |

Opening of the 1st Albanian school, 70th anniv.

Flags — A99

Designs: 5 l, Labor Party headquarters, Tirana. 8 l, Marx and Lenin.

**1957, June 1 Engr. *Perf. 11½x11***

| | | | | |
|---|---|---|---|---|
| **509** | A99 | 2.50 l brown | .35 | .25 |
| **510** | A99 | 5 l lt violet blue | 1.00 | .25 |
| **511** | A99 | 8 l rose lilac | 1.40 | 1.00 |
| | | *Nos. 509-511 (3)* | 2.75 | 1.50 |

Albania's Labor Party, 15th anniv.

Congress Emblem — A100

**1957, Oct. 4 Unwmk. *Perf. 11½***

| | | | | |
|---|---|---|---|---|
| **512** | A100 | 2.50 l gray brown | .50 | .25 |
| **513** | A100 | 3 l rose red | .50 | .25 |
| **514** | A100 | 5 l dark blue | .50 | .25 |
| **515** | A100 | 8 l green | 2.50 | .65 |
| | | *Nos. 512-515 (4)* | 4.00 | 1.40 |

4th Intl. Trade Union Cong., Leipzig, 10/4-15.

Lenin and Cruiser "Aurora" — A101

**1957, Nov. 7 Litho. *Perf. 10½***

| | | | | |
|---|---|---|---|---|
| **516** | A101 | 2.50 l violet brown | .50 | .25 |
| **517** | A101 | 5 l violet blue | 1.50 | .25 |
| **518** | A101 | 8 l gray | 1.50 | .35 |
| | | *Nos. 516-518 (3)* | 3.50 | .85 |

40th anniv. of the Russian Revolution.

Albanian Fighter Holding Flag — A102

**1957, Nov. 28 *Perf. 10½***

| | | | | |
|---|---|---|---|---|
| **519** | A102 | 1.50 l magenta | .45 | .30 |
| **520** | A102 | 2.50 l brown | .85 | .30 |
| **521** | A102 | 5 l blue | 1.25 | .90 |
| **522** | A102 | 8 l green | 3.50 | 1.25 |
| | | *Nos. 519-522 (4)* | 6.05 | 2.75 |

Proclamation of independence, 45th anniv.

Naum Veqilharxhi — A103

**1958, Feb. 1 Unwmk.**

| | | | | |
|---|---|---|---|---|
| **523** | A103 | 2.50 l dark brown | .45 | .25 |
| **524** | A103 | 5 l violet blue | .90 | .25 |
| **525** | A103 | 8 l rose lilac | 2.75 | .60 |
| | | *Nos. 523-525 (3)* | 4.10 | 1.10 |

160th anniv. of the birth of Naum Veqilharxhi, patriot and writer.

Luigj Gurakuqi (1879-1925), Writer & Politician — A104

**1958, Apr. 15 Photo. *Perf. 10½***

| | | | | |
|---|---|---|---|---|
| **526** | A104 | 1.50 l dark green | .40 | .25 |
| **527** | A104 | 2.50 l brown | .40 | .25 |
| **528** | A104 | 5 l blue | .40 | .25 |
| **529** | A104 | 8 l sepia | 3.50 | .75 |
| | | *Nos. 526-529 (4)* | 4.70 | 1.50 |

Transfer of the ashes of Luigj Gurakuqi.

Soldiers — A105

2.50 l, 11 l, Airman, sailor, soldier and tank.

**1958, July 10 Litho.**

| | | | | |
|---|---|---|---|---|
| **530** | A105 | 1.50 l blue green | .25 | .25 |
| **531** | A105 | 2.50 l dark red brown | .25 | .25 |
| **532** | A105 | 8 l rose red | .90 | .35 |
| **533** | A105 | 11 l bright blue | 2.00 | .60 |
| | | *Nos. 530-533 (4)* | 3.40 | 1.45 |

15th anniversary of Albanian army.

Cerciz Topulli and Mihal Grameno A106

Buildings and Tree A107

**1958, July 1**

| | | | | |
|---|---|---|---|---|
| **534** | A106 | 2.50 l dk olive bister | .35 | .25 |
| **535** | A107 | 3 l green | .35 | .25 |
| **536** | A106 | 5 l blue | 1.25 | .60 |
| **537** | A107 | 8 l red brown | 2.00 | .70 |
| | | *Nos. 534-537 (4)* | 3.95 | 1.00 |

50th anniversary, Battle of Mashkullore.

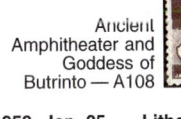

Ancient Amphitheater and Goddess of Butrinto — A108

**1959, Jan. 25 Litho. *Perf. 10½***

| | | | | |
|---|---|---|---|---|
| **538** | A108 | 2.50 l redsh brown | .45 | .25 |
| **539** | A108 | 6.50 l lt blue green | 1.40 | .30 |
| **540** | A108 | 11 l dark blue | 2.75 | .75 |
| | | *Nos. 538-540 (3)* | 4.60 | 1.30 |

Cultural Monuments Week.

Frederic Joliot-Curie and World Peace Congress Emblem — A109

**1959, July 1 Unwmk.**

| | | | | |
|---|---|---|---|---|
| **541** | A109 | 1.50 l carmine rose | 1.75 | .25 |
| **542** | A109 | 2.50 l rose violet | 3.50 | .30 |
| **543** | A109 | 11 l blue | 9.00 | 1.50 |
| | | *Nos. 541-543 (3)* | 14.25 | 2.05 |

10th anniv. of the World Peace Movement.

Basketball — A110

Sports: 2.50 l, Soccer, 5 l, Runner. 11 l, Man and woman runners with torch and flags.

**1959, Nov. 20 *Perf. 10½***

| | | | | |
|---|---|---|---|---|
| **544** | A110 | 1.50 l bright violet | .90 | .25 |
| **545** | A110 | 2.50 l emerald | .90 | .25 |
| **546** | A110 | 5 l carmine rose | 1.75 | .25 |
| **547** | A110 | 11 l ultra | 5.50 | 1.75 |
| | | *Nos. 544-547 (4)* | 9.05 | 2.50 |

1st Albanian Spartacist Games.

Fighter and Flags — A111

Designs: 2.50 l, Miner with drill standing guard. 3 l, Farm woman with sheaf of grain. 6.50 l, Man and woman in laboratory.

**1959, Nov. 29**

| | | | | |
|---|---|---|---|---|
| **548** | A111 | 1.50 l brt carmine | .90 | .25 |
| **549** | A111 | 2.50 l red brown | 1.20 | .25 |
| **550** | A111 | 3 l brt blue green | 1.75 | .30 |
| **551** | A111 | 6.50 l bright red | 3.50 | .50 |
| *a.* | | Souvenir sheet | 8.00 | 11.00 |
| | | *Nos. 548-551 (4)* | 7.35 | 1.30 |

15th anniversary of Albania's liberation.

No. 551a contains one each of Nos. 548-551, imperf. and all in bright carmine. Inscribed ribbon frame of sheet and frame lines for each stamp are blue green.

Mother and Child, UN Emblem — A112

**1959, Dec. 5 Unwmk.**

| | | | | |
|---|---|---|---|---|
| **552** | A112 | 5 l lt grnsh blue | 4.00 | 1.00 |
| *a.* | | Miniature sheet | 6.50 | 9.50 |

10th anniv. (in 1958) of the signing of the Universal Declaration of Human Rights.

No. 552a contains one imperf. stamp similar to No. 552; ornamental border.

Woman with Olive Branch — A113

**1960, Mar. 8 Litho. *Perf. 10½***

| | | | | |
|---|---|---|---|---|
| **553** | A113 | 2.50 l chocolate | .75 | .25 |
| **554** | A113 | 11 l rose carmine | 3.00 | .50 |

50th anniv. of Intl. Women's Day, Mar. 8.

Alexander Moissi — A114

**1960, Apr. 20**

| | | | | |
|---|---|---|---|---|
| **555** | A114 | 3 l deep brown | .35 | .25 |
| **556** | A114 | 11 l Prus green | 1.40 | .35 |

80th anniversary of the birth of Alexander Moissi (Moisiu) (1880-1935), German actor.

Lenin — A115

**1960, Apr. 22**

| | | | | |
|---|---|---|---|---|
| **557** | A115 | 4 l Prus blue | 1.40 | .25 |
| **558** | A115 | 11 l lake | 3.50 | .40 |

90th anniversary of birth of Lenin.

# ALBANIA

School Building — A116

**1960, May 30    Litho.    Perf. 10½**
559 A116  5 l green          1.50  .50
560 A116  6.50 l plum        1.50  .50

1st Albanian secondary school, 50th anniv.

Soldier on Guard Duty — A117

**1960, May 12    Unwmk.    Perf. 10½**
561 A117  1.50 l carmine rose   .35  .25
562 A117  11 l Prus blue       2.00  .40

15th anniversary of the Frontier Guards.

Liberation Monument, Tirana, Family and Policeman — A118

**1960, May 14**
563 A118  1.50 l green    .35  .25
564 A118  8.50 l brown   2.50  .40

15th anniversary of the People's Police.

Congress Site — A119

**1960, Mar. 25**
565 A119  2.50 l sepia    .45  .25
566 A119  7.50 l dull blue  1.10  .25

40th anniversary, Congress of Louchnia.

Pashko Vasa — A120

Designs: 1.50 l, Jani Vreto. 6.50 l, Sami Frasheri. 11 l, Page of statutes of association.

**1960, May 5**
567 A120  1 l gray olive   .35  .25
568 A120  1.50 l brown    .35  .25
569 A120  6.50 l blue    1.10  .25
570 A120  11 l rose red  3.50  .35
  Nos. 567-570 (4)      5.30 1.30

80th anniv. (in 1959) of the Association of Albanian Authors.

Albanian Fighter and Cannon — A121

**1960, Aug. 2    Litho.    Perf. 10½**
571 A121  1.50 l olive brown  .35  .25
572 A121  2.50 l maroon     .75  .35
573 A121  5 l dark blue    1.50  .45
  Nos. 571-573 (3)       2.60 1.05

Battle of Viona (against Italian troops), 40th anniv.

TU-104 Plane, Clock Tower, Tirana, and Kremlin, Moscow — A122

**1960, Aug. 18**
574 A122  1 l redsh brown   .75  .25
575 A122  7.50 l brt grnsh blue  2.50  .35
576 A122  11.50 l gray    4.50  .60
  Nos. 574-576 (3)     7.75 1.20

TU-104 flights, Moscow-Tirana, 2nd anniv.

Rising Sun and Federation Emblem — A123

**1960, Nov. 10    Unwmk.    Perf. 10½**
577 A123  1.50 l ultra    .35  .25
578 A123  8.50 l red    1.50  .35

Intl. Youth Federation, 15th anniv.

Ali Kelmendi — A124

**1960, Dec. 5    Litho.    Perf. 10½**
579 A124  1.50 l pale gray grn  .35  .25
580 A124  11 l dull rose lake  1.50  .30

Ali Kelmendi, communist leader, 60th birthday.

Flags of Russia and Albania and Clasped Hands — A125

**1961, Jan. 10    Unwmk.    Perf. 10½**
581 A125  2 l violet    .35  .25
582 A125  8 l dull red brown  1.50  .35

15th anniv. of the Albanian-Soviet Friendship Society.

Marx and Lenin — A126

**1961, Feb. 13    Litho.**
583 A126  2 l rose red    .35  .25
584 A126  8 l violet blue  1.50  .25

Fourth Communist Party Congress.

Man from Shkoder — A127

Costumes: 1.50 l, Woman from Shkoder. 6.50 l, Man from Lume. 11 l, Woman from Mirdite.

**1961, Apr. 28    Perf. 10½**
585 A127  1 l slate    .75  .30
586 A127  1.50 l dull claret  .75  .40
587 A127  6.50 l ultra   3.00  1.00
588 A127  11 l red    5.00  2.50
  Nos. 585-588 (4)    9.50  4.20

Otter — A128

Designs: 6.50 l, Badger. 11 l, Brown bear.

**1961, June 25    Unwmk.    Perf. 10½**
589 A128  2.50 l grayish blue  3.00  .35
590 A128  6.50 l blue green   6.00  1.00
591 A128  11 l dark red brown  13.50  5.00
  Nos. 589-591 (3)      22.50  6.35

Dalmatian Pelicans — A129

**1961, Sept. 30    Perf. 14**
592 A129  1.50 l shown    3.50  .50
593 A129  7.50 l Gray herons  5.00  1.50
594 A129  11 l Little egret  9.00  2.00
  Nos. 592-594 (3)    17.50  4.00

Cyclamen — A130

**1961, Oct. 27    Litho.**
595 A130  1.50 l shown    1.50  .30
596 A130  8 l Forsythia   5.00  1.50
597 A130  11 l Lily     6.50  2.00
  Nos. 595-597 (3)    13.00  3.80

Milosh G. Nikolla — A131

**1961, Oct. 30    Perf. 14**
598 A131  50q violet brown  .35  .30
599 A131  8.50 l Prus green  1.40  .80

50th anniv. of the birth of Milosh Gjergi Nikolla, poet.

Flag with Marx and Lenin — A132

**1961, Nov. 8**
600 A132  2.50 l vermilion  .65  .30
601 A132  7.50 l dull red brown  2.50  .85

20th anniv. of the founding of Albania's Communist Party.

Worker, Farm Woman and Emblem — A133

**1961, Nov. 23    Unwmk.    Perf. 14**
602 A133  2.50 l violet blue  .45  .30
603 A133  7.50 l rose claret  1.75  1.25

20th anniv. of the Albanian Workers' Party.

Yuri Gagarin and Vostok 1 — A134

**1962, Feb. 15    Unwmk.    Perf. 14**
604 A134  50q blue    .90  1.40
605 A134  4 l red lilac   3.50  3.50
606 A134  11 l dk slate grn  9.00  10.00
  Nos. 604-606 (3)    13.40  14.90

1st manned space flight, made by Yuri A. Gagarin, Soviet astronaut, Apr. 12, 1961.
Nos. 604-606 were overprinted with an overall yellow tint and with "POSTA AJRORE" (Air Mail) in maroon or black in 1962. Value: set, maroon ovpt., $90 mint, $130 used; set, black ovpt. $300 mint, $400 used.

Petro Nini Luarasi — A135

**1962, Feb. 28    Litho.**
607 A135  50q Prus blue   .40  .30
608 A135  8.50 l olive gray  3.00  1.00

50th anniv. (in 1961) of the death of Petro Nini Luarasi, Albanian patriot.

Malaria Eradication Emblem — A136

**1962, Apr. 30    Unwmk.    Perf. 14**
609 A136  1.50 l brt green   .45  .25
610 A136  2.50 l brown red   .45  .25
611 A136  10 l red lilac    .90  .60
612 A136  11 l blue      .90  .35
  Nos. 609-612 (4)    2.70  1.10

WHO drive to eradicate malaria. Souvenir sheets, perf. and imperf., contain one each of Nos. 609-612. Value $30 each. Nos. 609-612 imperf., value, set $25.

Camomile — A137

Medicinal plants.

**1962, May 10**
613 A137  50q shown    .30  .30
614 A137  8 l Linden    1.25  .60
615 A137  11.50 l Garden sage  2.00  .90
  Nos. 613-615 (3)    3.55  1.80

Value, imperf. set $30 mint, $40 used.

Woman Diver — A138

2.50 l, Pole vault. 3 l, Mt. Fuji & torch, horiz. 9 l, Woman javelin thrower. 10 l, Shot putting.

**1962, May 31    Perf. 14**
616 A138  50q brt grnsh bl & blk   .25  .25
617 A138  2.50 l gldn brn & sepia  .25  .25
618 A138  3 l blue & gray     .35  .25
619 A138  9 l rose car & dk brn  1.75  .25
620 A138  10 l olive & blk    1.75  .30
  Nos. 616-620 (5)       4.35 1.30

1964 Olympic Games, Tokyo. Value, imperf set, $50 mint, $70 used. A 15 l (like 3 l) exists in souv. sheet, perf. and imperf. Value, each $35 mint, $50 used.

Globe and Orbits A139 — Dog Laika and Sputnik 2 A140

Designs: 1.50 l, Rocket to the sun. 20 l, Lunik 3 photographing far side of the moon.

**1962, June    Unwmk.    Perf. 14**
621 A139  50q violet & org   .40  .25
622 A140  1 l blue grn & brn   .75  .30
623 A140  1.50 l yellow & ver  1.25  .40
624 A139  20 l magenta & bl  8.00  5.50
  Nos. 621-624 (4)    10.40 6.45

Russian space explorations.

Nos. 621-624 exist imperf in changed colors. Value, mint $65, used $75.

Two miniature sheets exist, containing one 14-lek picturing Sputnik 1. The perforated 14-lek is yellow and brown; the imperf. red and brown. Value, each mint $65, used $75.

Soccer Game, Map of South America — A141

2.50 l, 15 l, Soccer game and globe as ball.

**1962, July** **Litho.**

| | | | | |
|---|---|---|---|---|
| 625 | A141 | 1 l org & dk pur | .35 | .25 |
| 626 | A141 | 2.50 l emer & bluish grn | .70 | .25 |
| 627 | A141 | 6.50 l lt brn & pink | .70 | .25 |
| 628 | A141 | 15 l bluish grn & mar | 1.75 | .40 |
| | | *Nos. 625-628 (4)* | 3.50 | 1.15 |

World Soccer Championships, Chile, 5/30-6/17.

Exist imperforate in changed colors. Value, mint $40, used $75.

Two miniature sheets exist, each containing a single 20-lek in design similar to A141. The perf. sheet is brown and green; the imperf., brown and orange. Value, mint $40, used $75.

Map of Europe and Albania — A142

Designs: 1 l, 2.50 l, Map of Adriatic Sea and Albania and Roman statue.

**1962, Aug.**

| | | | | |
|---|---|---|---|---|
| 630 | A142 | 50q multicolored | .40 | *.75* |
| 631 | A142 | 1 l ultra & red | .80 | *2.00* |
| 632 | A142 | 2.50 l blue & red | 6.50 | *8.50* |
| 633 | A142 | 11 l multicolored | 9.00 | *17.50* |
| | | *Nos. 630-633 (4)* | 16.70 | *28.75* |

Tourist propaganda. Imperforates in changed colors exist. Value, mint $35, used $70.

Miniature sheets containing a 7 l and 8 l stamp, perf. and imperf., exist. Value, mint $40, used $75.

Woman of Dardhe — A143

Regional Costumes: 1 l, Man from Devoll. 2.50 l, Woman from Lunxheri. 14 l, Man from Gjirokaster.

**1962, Sept.**

| | | | | |
|---|---|---|---|---|
| 635 | A143 | 50q car, bl & pur | .35 | .25 |
| 636 | A143 | 1 l red brn & ocher | .35 | .25 |
| 637 | A143 | 2.50 l vio, yel grn & blk | 1.10 | .60 |
| 638 | A143 | 14 l red brn & pale grn | 5.25 | 1.60 |
| | | *Nos. 635-638 (4)* | 7.05 | 2.70 |

Exist imperf. Value, set, mint $40, used $60.

Chamois — A144

Animals: 1 l, Lynx, horiz. 1.50 l, Wild boar, horiz. 15 l, 20 l, Roe deer.

**1962, Oct. 24** **Unwmk.** ***Perf. 14***

| | | | | |
|---|---|---|---|---|
| 639 | A144 | 50q sl grn & dk pur | .35 | .25 |
| 640 | A144 | 1 l orange & blk | 1.40 | .25 |
| 641 | A144 | 1.50 l red brn & blk | 1.75 | .25 |
| 642 | A144 | 15 l yel ol & red brn | 15.00 | 1.00 |
| | | *Nos. 639-642 (4)* | 18.50 | 1.75 |

**Miniature Sheet**

| | | | | |
|---|---|---|---|---|
| 643 | A144 | 20 l yel ol & red brn | 135.00 | 145.00 |

Imperfs. in changed colors, value Nos. 639-642 $60, No. 643 $125.

Ismail Qemali — A145

Designs: 1 l, Albania eagle. 16 l, Eagle over fortress formed by "RPSH."

**1962, Dec. 28** **Litho.**

| | | | | |
|---|---|---|---|---|
| 644 | A145 | 1 l red & red brn | .45 | .25 |
| 645 | A145 | 3 l org brn & blk | 2.50 | .25 |
| 646 | A145 | 16 l dk car rose & blk | 4.00 | .50 |
| | | *Nos. 644-646 (3)* | 6.95 | 1.00 |

50th anniv. of independence. Imperfs. in changed colors, value, set $40 mint, $60 used.

Monument of October Revolution — A146

**1963, Jan. 5** **Unwmk.** ***Perf. 14***

| | | | | |
|---|---|---|---|---|
| 647 | A146 | 5 l shown | .85 | .25 |
| 648 | A146 | 10 l Lenin statue | 2.00 | .35 |

October Revolution (Russia, 1917), 45th anniv.

Henri Dunant, Cross, Globe and Nurse — A147

**1963, Jan 25** **Unwmk.** ***Perf. 14***

| | | | | |
|---|---|---|---|---|
| 649 | A147 | 1.50 l rose lake, red & blk | .35 | .25 |
| 650 | A147 | 2.50 l lt bl, red & blk | .70 | .25 |
| 651 | A147 | 6 l emerald, red & blk | 1.75 | .25 |
| 652 | A147 | 10 l dull yel, red & blk | 2.75 | .60 |
| | | *Nos. 649-652 (4)* | 5.55 | 1.35 |

Cent. of the Geneva Conf., which led to the establishment of the Intl. Red Cross in 1864. Imperfs. in changed colors, value, set $60.

Stalin and Battle of Stalingrad — A148

**1963, Feb. 2**

| | | | | |
|---|---|---|---|---|
| 653 | A148 | 8 l dk green & slate | 7.00 | 1.00 |

Battle of Stalingrad, 20th anniv. See No. C67.

Andrian G. Nikolayev — A149

Designs: 7.50 l, Vostoks 3 and 4 and globe, horiz. 20 l, Pavel R. Popovich. 25 l, Nikolayev, Popovich and globe with trajectories.

**1963, Feb. 28** **Litho.**

| | | | | |
|---|---|---|---|---|
| 654 | A149 | 2.50 l vio bl & sepia | .35 | .35 |
| 655 | A149 | 7.50 l lt blue & blk | 1.10 | .70 |
| 656 | A149 | 20 l violet & sepia | 2.75 | 2.25 |
| | | *Nos. 654-656 (3)* | 4.20 | 3.30 |

**Miniature Sheet**

| | | | | |
|---|---|---|---|---|
| 657 | A149 | 25 l vio bl & sepia | 35.00 | 35.00 |

1st group space flight of Vostoks 3 and 4, Aug. 11-15, 1962. Imperfs in changed colors, value: Nos. 654-656 $45 mint or used; No. 657 perf, $45 mint or used; No. 657 imperf, $50 mint or used.

"Albania" Decorating Police Officer — A150

**1963, Mar. 20** **Unwmk.** ***Perf. 14***

| | | | | |
|---|---|---|---|---|
| 658 | A150 | 2.50 l crim, mag & blk | .70 | .25 |
| 659 | A150 | 7.50 l org ver, dk red & blk | 2.50 | .25 |

20th anniversary of the security police.

Polyphylla Fullo — A151

Beetles: 1.50 l, Lucanus cervus. 8 l, Procerus gigas. 10 l, Cicindela albanica.

**1963, Mar. 20**

| | | | | |
|---|---|---|---|---|
| 660 | A151 | 50q ol grn & brn | .85 | .35 |
| 661 | A151 | 1.50 l blue & brn | 1.10 | .35 |
| 662 | A151 | 8 l dl rose & blk vio | 6.00 | 1.25 |
| 663 | A151 | 10 l brt citron & blk | 8.00 | 1.40 |
| | | *Nos. 660-663 (4)* | 16.25 | 3.35 |

1913 Stamp and Postmark — A152

10 l, Stamps of 1913, 1937 and 1962.

**1963, May 5**

| | | | | |
|---|---|---|---|---|
| 664 | A152 | 5 l yel, buff, bl & blk | 1.40 | .25 |
| 665 | A152 | 10 l car rose, grn & blk | 2.50 | .45 |

50th anniversary of Albanian stamps.

Boxer — A153

Designs: 3 l, Basketball baskets. 5 l, Volleyball. 6 l, Bicyclists. 9 l, Gymnast. 15 l, Hands holding torch, and map of Japan.

**1963, May 25** ***Perf. 13½***

| | | | | |
|---|---|---|---|---|
| 666 | A153 | 2 l yel, blk & red brn | .40 | *.70* |
| 667 | A153 | 3 l ocher, brn & bl | .50 | *1.40* |
| 668 | A153 | 5 l gray bl, red brn & brn | .85 | *1.40* |
| 669 | A153 | 6 l gray, dk gray & grn | 1.10 | *3.50* |
| 670 | A153 | 9 l rose, red brn & bl | 1.75 | *6.50* |
| | | *Nos. 666-670 (5)* | 4.60 | *13.50* |

**Miniature Sheet**

| | | | | |
|---|---|---|---|---|
| 671 | A153 | 15 l lt bl, car, blk & brn | 13.50 | 13.50 |

1964 Olympic Games in Tokyo. Value, imperfs. Nos. 666-670 $15, No. 671 $20.

Crested Grebe — A154

Birds: 3 l, Golden eagle. 6.50 l, Gray partridges. 11 l, Capercaillie.

**1963, Apr. 20** **Litho.** ***Perf. 14***

| | | | | |
|---|---|---|---|---|
| 672 | A154 | 50q multicolored | 1.10 | .25 |
| 673 | A154 | 3 l multicolored | 2.00 | .50 |
| 674 | A154 | 6.50 l multicolored | 5.25 | 1.25 |
| 675 | A154 | 11 l multicolored | 7.00 | 2.00 |
| | | *Nos. 672-675 (4)* | 15.35 | 4.00 |

Soldier and Building — A155

2.50 l, Soldier with pack, ship, plane. 5 l, Soldier in battle. 6 l, Soldier, bulldozer.

**1963, July 10** **Unwmk.** ***Perf. 12***

| | | | | |
|---|---|---|---|---|
| 676 | A155 | 1.50 l brick red, yel & blk | .45 | .25 |
| 677 | A155 | 2.50 l bl, ocher & brn | .90 | .25 |
| 678 | A155 | 5 l bluish grn, gray & blk | 1.25 | .25 |
| 679 | A155 | 6 l red brn, buff & bl | 1.75 | .25 |
| | | *Nos. 676-679 (4)* | 4.35 | 1.00 |

Albanian army, 20th anniversary.

Maj. Yuri A. Gagarin — A156

Designs: 5 l, Maj. Gherman Titov. 7 l, Maj. Andrian G. Nikolayev. 11 l, Lt. Col. Pavel R. Popovich. 14 l, Lt. Col. Valeri Bykovski. 20 l, Lt. Valentina Tereshkova.

**1963, July 30**

**Portraits in Yellow and Black**

| | | | | |
|---|---|---|---|---|
| 680 | A156 | 3 l brt purple | .70 | .25 |
| 681 | A156 | 5 l dull blue | .70 | .25 |
| 682 | A156 | 7 l gray | .95 | .25 |
| 683 | A156 | 11 l deep claret | 2.10 | .35 |
| 684 | A156 | 14 l blue green | 3.00 | .60 |
| 685 | A156 | 20 l ultra | 4.75 | 1.10 |
| | | *Nos. 680-685 (6)* | 12.20 | 2.80 |

Man's conquest of space. Value, imperf. set $40.

Volleyball — A157

**1963, Aug. 31** ***Perf. 12x12½***

| | | | | |
|---|---|---|---|---|
| 686 | A157 | 2 l shown | — | — |
| 687 | A157 | 3 l Weight lifting | — | — |
| 688 | A157 | 5 l Soccer | — | — |
| 689 | A157 | 7 l Boxing | — | — |
| 690 | A157 | 8 l Rowing | — | — |

European championships. Imperfs. in changed colors, value set $35.

Papilio Podalirius — A158

**1963, Sept. 29** **Litho.**

**Various Butterflies and Moths in Natural Colors**

| | | | | |
|---|---|---|---|---|
| 691 | A158 | 1 l red | .35 | .25 |
| 692 | A158 | 2 l blue | .70 | .25 |
| 693 | A158 | 4 l dull lilac | 1.40 | .60 |
| 694 | A158 | 5 l pale green | 1.60 | .60 |
| 695 | A158 | 8 l bister | 3.25 | 1.25 |
| 696 | A158 | 10 l light blue | 4.00 | 1.75 |
| | | *Nos. 691-696 (6)* | 11.30 | 4.70 |

Oil Refinery, Cerrik — A159

2.50 l, Food processing plant, Tirana, horiz. 30 l, Fruit canning plant. 50 l, Tannery, horiz.

**1963, Nov. 15** **Unwmk.** ***Perf. 14***

| | | | | |
|---|---|---|---|---|
| 697 | A159 | 2.50 l rose red, *pnksh* | .75 | .25 |
| 698 | A159 | 20 l slate grn, *grnsh* | 3.00 | .25 |
| 699 | A159 | 30 l dull pur, *grysh* | 7.50 | .55 |
| 700 | A159 | 50 l ocher, *yel* | 7.50 | .85 |
| | | *Nos. 697-700 (4)* | 18.75 | 1.90 |

Industrial development in Albania.

For surcharges see Nos. 841-846.

Flag and Shield — A160

**1963, Nov. 24** *Perf. 12½x12*

**701** A160 2 l grnsh bl, blk, ocher & red .45 .25
**702** A160 8 l blue, blk, ocher & red 1.75 .50

1st Congress of Army Aid Assn.

Chinese, Caucasian and Negro Men — A161

**1963, Dec. 10** *Perf. 12x11½*

**703** A161 3 l bister & blk .40 .25
**704** A161 5 l bister & ultra .75 .25
**705** A161 7 l bister & vio 1.90 .30
*Nos. 703-705 (3)* 3.05 .80

15th anniv. of the Universal Declaration of Human Rights.

Slalom Ascent — A162

Designs: 50q, Bobsled, horiz. 6.50 l, Ice hockey, horiz. 12.50 l, Women's figure skating. No. 709A, Ski jumper.

**1963, Dec. 25** *Perf. 14*

**706** A162 50q grnsh bl & blk .35 .25
**707** A162 2.50 l red, gray & blk .45 .25
**708** A162 6.50 l yel, blk & gray .90 .25
**709** A162 12.50 l red, blk & yel grn 1.75 .55
*Nos. 706-709 (4)* 3.45 1.30

**Miniature Sheet**

**709A** A162 12.50 l multi 20.00 20.00

9th Winter Olympic Games, Innsbruck, Jan. 29-Feb. 9, 1964. Imperfs. in changed colors, value Nos. 706-709 $75, No. 709A $50.

Lenin — A163

**1964, Jan. 21** *Perf. 12½x12*

**710** A163 5 l gray & bister .90 .25
**711** A163 10 l gray & ocher 2.00 .30

40th anniversary, death of Lenin.

Hurdling — A164

Designs: 3 l, Track, horiz. 6.50 l, Rifle shooting, horiz. 8 l, Basketball.

*Perf. 12½x12, 12x12½*

**1964, Jan. 30** **Litho.**

**712** A164 2.50 l pale vio & ultra .40 .25
**713** A164 3 l lt grn & red brn .75 .35
**714** A164 6.50 l blue & claret 1.10 1.00
**715** A164 8 l lt blue & ocher 2.25 1.60
*Nos. 712-715 (4)* 4.50 3.20

1st Games of the New Emerging Forces, GANEFO, Jakarta, Indonesia, Nov. 10-22, 1963.

Fish — A165

**1964, Feb. 26** **Unwmk.** *Perf. 14*

**716** A165 50q Sturgeon .40 .25
**717** A165 1 l Gilthead .75 .25
**718** A165 1.50 l Striped mullet 1.10 .25
**719** A165 2.50 l Carp 1.50 .25
**720** A165 6.50 l Mackerel 2.25 .40
**721** A165 10 l Lake Ohrid trout 3.75 .50
*Nos. 716-721 (6)* 9.75 1.90

Wild Animals A166

**1964, Mar. 28** *Perf. 12½x12*

**722** A166 1 l Red Squirrel .45 .25
**723** A166 1.50 l Beech marten .85 .25
**724** A166 2 l Red fox .85 .40
**725** A166 2.50 l Hedgehog 1.25 .40
**726** A166 3 l Hare 1.75 .60
**727** A166 5 l Jackal 1.75 .60
**728** A166 7 l Wildcat 3.50 .60
**729** A166 8 l Wolf 4.50 .95
*Nos. 722-729 (8)* 14.90 4.05

Lighting Olympic Torch — A167

5 l, Torch, globes. 7 l, 15 l, Olympic flag, Mt. Fuji. 10 l, National Stadium, Tokyo.

**1964, May 18** *Perf. 12x12½*

**730** A167 3 l lt yel grn, yel & buff .45 .70
**731** A167 5 l red & vio blue .65 1.00
**732** A167 7 l lt bl, ultra & yel .90 1.50
**733** A167 10 l orange, bl & vio 1.25 2.50
*Nos. 730-733 (4)* 3.25 5.70

**Miniature Sheet**

**734** A167 15 l lt bl, ultra & org 20.00 20.00

18th Olympic Games, Tokyo, Oct. 10-25, 1964. No. 734 contains one 49x62mm stamp. Imperfs. in changed colors, value Nos. 730-733 $17.50, No. 734 $22.50.
See No. 745.

Partisans A168

5 l, Arms of Albania. 8 l, Enver Hoxha.

*Perf. 12½x12*

**1964, May 24** **Litho.** **Unwmk.**

**735** A168 2 l orange, red & blk 1.10 .25
**736** A168 5 l multicolored 2.75 .30
**737** A168 8 l red brn, blk & red 5.50 .90
*Nos. 735-737 (3)* 9.35 1.45

20th anniv. of the Natl. Anti-Fascist Cong. of Liberation, Permet, May 24, 1944. The label attached to each stamp, without perforations between, carries a quotation from the 1944 Congress.

Albanian Flag and Revolutionists — A169

*Perf. 12½x12*

**1964, June 10** **Litho.** **Unwmk.**

**738** A169 2.50 l red & gray .40 .25
**739** A169 7.50 l lilac rose & gray 1.10 .25

Albanian revolution of 1924, 40th anniv.

Full Moon — A170

Designs: 5 l, New moon. 8 l, Half moon. 11 l, Waning moon. 15 l, Far side of moon.

**1964, June 27** *Perf. 12x12½*

**740** A170 1 l purple & yel .25 .25
**741** A170 5 l violet & yel .50 .25
**742** A170 8 l blue & yel .75 .30
**743** A170 11 l green & yel 3.00 .45
*Nos. 740-743 (4)* 4.50 1.25

**Miniature Sheet**

***Perf. 12 on 2 sides***

**744** A170 15 l ultra & yel 12.50 12.50

No. 744 contains one stamp, size: 35x36mm, perforated at top and bottom. Imperfs. in changed colors, value Nos. 740-743 $16, No. 744 $15.

**No. 733 with Added Inscription "Rimini 25-VI-64"**

**1964** *Perf. 12x12½*

**745** A167 10 l orange, bl & vio 7.00 7.00

"Toward Tokyo 1964" Phil. Exhib. at Rimini, Italy, June 25-July 6.

Wren — A171

Birds: 1 l, Penduline titmouse. 2.50 l, Green woodpecker. 3 l, Tree creeper.4 l, Nuthatch. 5 l, Great titmouse. 6 l, Goldfinch. 18 l, Oriole.

**1964, July 31** *Perf. 12x12½*

**746** A171 50q multi .45 .25
**747** A171 1 l orange & multi .90 .25
**748** A171 2.50 l multi 1.25 .40
**749** A171 3 l blue & multi 1.75 .40
**750** A171 4 l yellow & multi 2.25 .80
**751** A171 5 l blue & multi 2.75 .80
**752** A171 6 l lt vio & multi 3.00 1.25
**753** A171 18 l pink & multi 5.50 2.75
*Nos. 746-753 (8)* 17.85 6.90

Running and Gymnastics — A172

Sport: 2 l, Weight lifting, judo. 3 l, Equestrian, bicycling. 4 l, Soccer, water polo. 5 l, Wrestling, boxing. 6 l, Pentathlon, hockey. 7 l, Swimming, sailing. 8 l, Basketball, volleyball. 9 l, Rowing, canoeing. 10 l, Fencing, pistol shooting. 20 l, Three winners.

*Perf. 12x12½*

**1964, Sept. 25** **Litho.** **Unwmk.**

**754** A172 1 l lt bl, rose & emer .25 .25
**755** A172 2 l bis brn, bluish grn & vio .25 .25
**756** A172 3 l vio, red org & ol bis .25 .25
**757** A172 4 l grnsh bl, ol & ultra .45 .35
**758** A172 5 l grnsh bl, car & pale lil .45 .35
**759** A172 6 l dk bl, org & lt bl .70 .75
**760** A172 7 l dk bl, lt ol & org .70 .75
**761** A172 8 l emer, gray & yel .90 .75
**762** A172 9 l bl, yel & lil rose .90 .75
**763** A172 10 l brt grn, org brn & yel grn 1.25 1.00
*Nos. 754-763 (10)* 6.10 5.45

**Miniature Sheet**

***Perf. 12***

**764** A172 20 l violet & lemon 15.00 15.00

18th Olympic Games, Tokyo, Oct. 10-25. No. 764 contains one stamp, size: 41x68mm. Imperfs in changed colors, value: Nos. 754-763, $17.50 mint, $25 used; No. 764, $20 mint, $25 used.

Arms of People's Republic of China A173

Mao Tse-tung and Flag A174

**1964, Oct. 1** *Perf. 11½x12, 12x11½*

**765** A173 7 l black, red & yellow *10.00* *4.50*
**766** A174 8 l black, red & yellow *10.00* *6.00*

People's Republic of China, 15th anniv.

Karl Marx — A175

Designs: 5 l, St. Martin's Hall, London. 8 l, Friedrich Engels.

**1964, Nov. 5** *Perf. 12x11½*

**767** A175 2 l red, lt vio & blk .90 .45
**768** A175 5 l gray blue 2.25 1.40
**769** A175 8 l ocher, blk & red 4.00 1.75
*Nos. 767-769 (3)* 7.15 3.60

Centenary of First Socialist International.

Jeronim de Rada — A176

**1964, Nov. 15** *Perf. 12½x11½*

**770** A176 7 l slate green 1.10 .35
**771** A176 8 l dull violet 1.90 .60

Birth of Jeronim de Rada, poet, 150th anniv.

Arms of Albania A177

Factories A178

Designs: 3 l, Combine harvester. 4 l, Woman chemist. 10 l, Hands holding Communist Party book, hammer and sickle.

*Perf. 11½x12, 12x11½*

**1964, Nov. 29**

**772** A177 1 l multicolored .45 .40
**773** A178 2 l red, yel & vio bl .80 .80
**774** A178 3 l red, yel & brn 1.20 1.25
**775** A178 4 l red, yel & gray grn 1.50 1.60
**776** A177 10 l red, bl & blk 3.50 4.00
*Nos. 772-776 (5)* 7.45 8.05

20th anniversary of liberation.

Planet Mercury — A179

Planets: 2 l, Venus and rocket. 3 l, Earth, moon and rocket. 4 l, Mars and rocket. 5 l, Jupiter. 6 l, Saturn. 7 l, Uranus. 8 l, Neptune. 9 l, Pluto. 15 l, Solar system and rocket.

**1964, Dec. 15** *Perf. 12x12½*

**777** A179 1 l yellow & pur .25 .25
**778** A179 2 l multicolored .25 .25
**779** A179 3 l multicolored .40 .40
**780** A179 4 l multicolored .40 .40
**781** A179 5 l yel, dk pur & brn .80 .60
**782** A179 6 l lt grn, vio brn & yel 1.20 .60
**783** A179 7 l yellow & grn 1.40 .90

# ALBANIA 369

| 784 | A179 | 8 l yellow & vio | 1.60 | 1.00 |
| 785 | A179 | 9 l lt grn, yel & blk | 1.75 | 1.25 |
| | | Nos. 777-785 (9) | 8.05 | 5.65 |

**Miniature Sheet**
*Perf. 12 on 2 sides*

| 786 | A179 | 15 l car, bl, yel & grn | 25.00 | 35.00 |

No. 786 contains one stamp, size: 62x51mm, perforated at top and bottom. Imperfs. in changed colors. Value Nos. 777-785, $30; No. 786, $25.

European Chestnut — A180

**1965, Jan. 25** — *Perf. 11½x12*

| 787 | A180 | 1 l shown | .25 | .25 |
| 788 | A180 | 2 l Medlars | .35 | .25 |
| 789 | A180 | 3 l Persimmon | .55 | .25 |
| 790 | A180 | 4 l Pomegranate | .75 | .40 |
| 791 | A180 | 5 l Quince | 1.50 | .50 |
| 792 | A180 | 10 l Orange | 3.00 | 1.00 |
| | | Nos. 787-792 (6) | 6.40 | 2.65 |

Symbols of Industry — A181

Designs: 5 l, Books, triangle and compass. 8 l, Beach, trees and hotel.

**1965, Feb. 20**

| 793 | A181 | 2 l blk, car rose & pink | 7.50 | 7.00 |
| 794 | A181 | 5 l yel, gray & blk | 12.00 | 10.50 |
| 795 | A181 | 8 l blk, vio bl & lt bl | 15.00 | 13.00 |
| | | Nos. 793-795 (3) | 34.50 | 30.50 |

Professional trade associations, 20th anniv.

Water Buffalo — A182

Various designs: Water buffalo.

**1965, Mar.** — *Perf. 12x11½*

| 796 | A182 | 1 l lt yel grn, yel & brn blk | .75 | .35 |
| 797 | A182 | 2 l lt bl, dk gray & blk | 1.50 | .65 |
| 798 | A182 | 3 l yellow, brn & grn | 2.25 | 1.10 |
| 799 | A182 | 7 l brt grn, yel & brn blk | 5.25 | 1.50 |
| 800 | A182 | 12 l pale lil, dk brn & ind | 9.00 | 1.75 |
| | | Nos. 796-800 (5) | 18.75 | 5.35 |

Mountain View, Valbona A183

1.50 l, Seashore. 3 l, Glacier and peak. 4 l, Gorge. 5 l, Mountain peaks. 9 l, Lake and hills.

**1965, Mar.** *Litho.* — *Perf. 12*

| 801 | A183 | 1.50 l multi | 1.10 | .35 |
| 802 | A183 | 2.50 l multi | 2.75 | .70 |
| 803 | A183 | 3 l multi, vert. | 2.75 | .70 |
| 804 | A183 | 4 l multi, vert. | 3.50 | 1.25 |
| 805 | A183 | 5 l multi | 4.00 | 1.50 |
| 806 | A183 | 9 l multi | 11.00 | 3.00 |
| | | Nos. 801-806 (6) | 25.10 | 7.50 |

Frontier Guard — A184

**1965, Apr. 25** — *Unwmk.*

| 807 | A184 | 2.50 l lt blue & multi | 1.25 | .25 |
| 808 | A184 | 12.50 l lt ultra & multi | 7.25 | .90 |

20th anniversary of the Frontier Guards.

Small-bore Rifle Shooting, Prone — A185

Designs: 2 l, Rifle shooting, standing. 3 l, Target over map of Europe, showing Bucharest. 4 l, Pistol shooting. 15 l, Rifle shooting, kneeling.

**1965, May 10**

| 809 | A185 | 1 l lil, car rose, blk & brn | .35 | .25 |
| 810 | A185 | 2 l bl, blk, brn & vio bl | .35 | .25 |
| 811 | A185 | 3 l pink & car rose | .70 | .25 |
| 812 | A185 | 4 l bis, blk & vio brn | 1.40 | .25 |
| 813 | A185 | 15 l brt grn, brn & vio brn | 4.25 | .50 |
| | | Nos. 809-813 (5) | 7.05 | 1.50 |

European Shooting Championships, Bucharest.

ITU Emblem, Old and New Communications Equipment — A186

**1965, May 17** — *Perf. 12½x12*

| 814 | A186 | 2.50 l brt grn, blk & lil rose | .75 | .25 |
| 815 | A186 | 12.50 l vio, blk & brt bl | 4.25 | .30 |

Centenary of the ITU.

Col. Pavel Belyayev — A187

Designs: 2 l, Voskhod II. 6.50 l, Lt. Col. Alexei Leonov. 20 l, Leonov floating in space.

**1965, June 15** — *Perf. 12*

| 816 | A187 | 1.50 l lt blue & brn | .25 | .25 |
| 817 | A187 | 2 l dk bl, lt vio & lt ultra | .25 | .25 |
| 818 | A187 | 6.50 l lilac & brn | .30 | .25 |
| 819 | A187 | 20 l chlky bl, yel & blk | 3.00 | .40 |
| | | Nos. 816-819 (4) | 3.80 | 1.15 |

**Miniature Sheet**
*Perf. 12 on 2 sides*

| 820 | A187 | 20 l brt bl, org & blk | 11.00 | 11.00 |

Space flight of Voskhod II and 1st man walking in space, Lt. Col. Alexei Leonov. No. 820 contains one stamp, size: 51x59½mm, perforated at top and bottom. Imperf., brt grn background, value $12.

Marx and Lenin — A188

**1965, June 21** — *Perf. 12*

| 821 | A188 | 2.50 l dk brn, red & yel | .60 | .25 |
| 822 | A188 | 7.50 l sl grn, org ver & buff | 2.40 | .25 |

6th Conf. of Postal Ministers of Communist Countries, Peking, June 21-July 15.

Mother and Child — A189

2 l, Pioneers. 3 l, Boy and girl at play, horiz. 4 l, Child on beach. 15 l, Girl with book.

*Perf. 12½x12, 12x12½*

**1965, June 29** *Litho.* — *Unwmk.*

| 823 | A189 | 1 l brt bl, rose lil & blk | .25 | .25 |
| 824 | A189 | 2 l salmon, vio & blk | .25 | .25 |
| 825 | A189 | 3 l green, org & vio | .30 | .25 |
| 826 | A189 | 4 l multicolored | .70 | .25 |
| 827 | A189 | 15 l lil rose, brn & ocher | 3.25 | .50 |
| | | Nos. 823-827 (5) | 4.75 | 1.50 |

Issued for International Children's Day.

Statue of Magistrate — A190

Designs: 1 l, Amphora. 2 l, Illyrian armor. 3 l, Mosaic, horiz. 15 l, Torso, Apollo statue.

**1965, July 20** — *Perf. 12*

| 828 | A190 | 1 l lt ol, org & brn | .25 | .25 |
| 829 | A190 | 2 l gray grn, grn & brn | .25 | .25 |
| 830 | A190 | 3 l tan, brn, car & lil | .30 | .25 |
| 831 | A190 | 4 l green, bis & brn | 1.10 | .25 |
| 832 | A190 | 15 l gray & pale claret | 2.75 | .65 |
| | | Nos. 828-832 (5) | 4.65 | 1.65 |

Flowers — A191

**1965, Aug. 11** — *Perf. 12½x12*

| 833 | A191 | 1 l Fuchsia | .25 | .25 |
| 834 | A191 | 2 l Cyclamen | .50 | .25 |
| 835 | A191 | 3 l Tiger lily | .75 | .25 |
| 836 | A191 | 3.50 l Iris | 1.10 | .25 |
| 837 | A191 | 4 l Dahlia | 1.10 | .25 |
| 838 | A191 | 4.50 l Hydrangea | 1.50 | .25 |
| 839 | A191 | 5 l Rose | 1.50 | .30 |
| 840 | A191 | 7 l Tulips | 2.25 | .35 |
| | | Nos. 833-840 (8) | 8.95 | 2.15 |

**Nos. 698-700 Surcharged New Value and Two Bars**

**1965, Aug. 16** — *Perf. 14*

| 841 | A159 | 5q on 30 l | .60 | .60 |
| 842 | A159 | 15q on 30 l | .60 | .60 |
| 843 | A159 | 25q on 50 l | 1.00 | 1.00 |
| 844 | A159 | 80q on 50 l | 2.00 | 2.00 |
| 845 | A159 | 1.10 l on 20 l | 3.00 | 3.00 |
| 846 | A159 | 2 l on 20 l | 5.00 | 5.00 |
| | | Nos. 841-846 (6) | 12.20 | 12.20 |

White Stork — A192

Migratory Birds: 20q, Cuckoo. 30q, Hoopoe. 40q, European bee-eater. 50q, European nightjar. 1.50 l, Quail.

**1965, Aug. 31** — *Perf. 12*

| 847 | A192 | 10q yel, blk & gray | .35 | .35 |
| 848 | A192 | 20q brt pink, blk & dk bl | .75 | .35 |
| 849 | A192 | 30q violet, blk & bis | 1.10 | .50 |
| 850 | A192 | 40q emer, blk yel & org | 1.50 | .70 |
| 851 | A192 | 50q ultra, brn & red brn | 1.90 | .95 |
| 852 | A192 | 1.50 l bis, red brn & dp org | 5.50 | 2.75 |
| | | Nos. 847-852 (6) | 11.10 | 5.60 |

"Homecoming," by Bukurosh Sejdini — A193

**1965, Sept. 26** *Litho.* — *Perf. 12x12½*

| 853 | A193 | 25q olive black | 1.75 | .40 |
| 854 | A193 | 65q blue black | 5.25 | 1.60 |
| 855 | A193 | 1.10 l black | 7.50 | 3.25 |
| | | Nos. 853-855 (3) | 14.50 | 5.25 |

Second war veterans' meeting.

Hunting — A194

**1965, Oct. 6** *Litho.* — *Unwmk.*

| 856 | A194 | 10q Capercaillie | .35 | .25 |
| 857 | A194 | 20q Deer | .65 | .25 |
| 858 | A194 | 30q Pheasant | .75 | .25 |
| 859 | A194 | 40q Mallards | 1.25 | .25 |
| 860 | A194 | 50q Boar | 1.40 | .25 |
| 861 | A194 | 1 l Rabbit | 3.25 | .55 |
| | | Nos. 856-861 (6) | 7.65 | 1.80 |

Oleander — A195

Flowers: 20q, Forget-me-nots. 30q, Pink. 40q, White water lily. 50q, Bird's foot. 1 l, Corn poppy.

**1965, Oct. 26** — *Perf. 12½x12*

| 862 | A195 | 10q brt bl, grn & car rose | .25 | .25 |
| 863 | A195 | 20q org red, bl, brn & grn | .35 | .25 |
| 864 | A195 | 30q vio, car rose & grn | .45 | .25 |
| 865 | A195 | 40q emerald, yel & blk | .65 | .30 |
| 866 | A195 | 50q org brn, yel & grn | 1.10 | .40 |
| 867 | A195 | 1 l yel grn, blk & rose red | 2.50 | 1.60 |
| | | Nos. 862-867 (6) | 5.30 | 3.05 |

Hotel Turizmi, Fier — A196

Buildings: 10q, Hotel, Peshkopi. 15q, Sanatorium, Tirana. 25q, Rest home, Pogradec. 65q, Partisan Sports Arena, Tirana. 80q, Rest home, Mali Dajt. 1.10 l, Culture House, Tirana. 1.60 l, Hotel Adriatik, Durres. 2 l, Migjeni Theater, Shkoder. 3 l, Alexander Moissi House of Culture, Durres.

**1965, Oct. 27** — *Perf. 12x12½*

| 868 | A196 | 5q blue & blk | .25 | .25 |
| 869 | A196 | 10q ocher & blk | .25 | .25 |
| 870 | A196 | 15q dull grn & blk | .25 | .25 |
| 871 | A196 | 25q violet & blk | .25 | .25 |
| 872 | A196 | 65q lt brn & blk | .70 | .50 |
| 873 | A196 | 80q yel grn & blk | 1.40 | .50 |
| 874 | A196 | 1.10 l lilac & blk | 2.00 | .50 |
| 875 | A196 | 1.60 l lt vio bl & blk | 2.75 | 1.40 |
| 876 | A196 | 2 l dull rose & blk | 3.50 | 1.40 |
| 877 | A196 | 3 l gray & blk | 6.25 | 2.50 |
| | | Nos. 868-877 (10) | 17.60 | 7.80 |

Freighter "Teuta" — A197

Ships: 20q, Raft. 30q, Sailing ship, 19th cent. 40q, Sailing ship, 18th cent. 50q, Freighter "Vlora." 1 l, Illyric galleys.

**1965, Nov. 16**

| 878 | A197 | 10q brt grn & dk grn | .30 | .25 |
| 879 | A197 | 20q ol bis & dk grn | .30 | .25 |
| 880 | A197 | 30q lt & dp ultra | .35 | .25 |
| 881 | A197 | 40q vio & dp vio | .45 | .25 |

**882** A197 50q pink & dk red 1.25 .25
**883** A197 1 l bister & brn 3.25 .45
*Nos. 878-883 (6)* 5.90 1.70

Brown Bear — A198

Various Albanian bears. 50q, 55q, 60q, horiz.

**1965, Dec. 7** ***Perf. 11½x12***
**884** A198 10q bister & dk brn .35 .25
**885** A198 20q pale brn & dk brn .35 .25
**886** A198 30q bis, dk brn & car .70 .25
**887** A198 35q pale brn & dk brn .85 .25
**888** A198 40q bister & dk brn 1.00 .25
**889** A198 50q bister & dk brn 1.75 .25
**890** A198 55q bister & dk brn 2.25 .30
**891** A198 60q pale brn, dk brn & car 3.75 .50
*Nos. 884-891 (8)* 11.00 2.30

Basketball and Players — A199

10q, Games' emblem (map of Albania and basket). 30q, 50q, Players with ball (diff. designs). 1.40 l, Basketball medal on ribbon.

**1965, Dec. 15** **Litho.** ***Perf. 12½x12***
**892** A199 10q blue, yel & car .25 .25
**893** A199 20q rose lil, lt brn & blk .25 .25
**894** A199 30q bis, lt brn, red & blk .30 .25
**895** A199 50q lt grn, lt brn & blk 1.00 .25
**896** A199 1.40 l rose, blk, brn & yel 2.25 .50
*Nos. 892-896 (5)* 4.05 1.50

7th Balkan Basketball Championships, Tirana, Dec. 15-19.

Arms of Republic and Smokestacks — A200

Arms and: 10q, Book. 30q, Wheat. 60q, Book, hammer & sickle. 80q, Factories.

**1966, Jan. 11** **Litho.** ***Perf. 11½x12***
**Coat of Arms in Gold**
**897** A200 10q crimson & brn .25 .25
**898** A200 20q blue & vio bl .25 .25
**899** A200 30q org yel & brn .50 .25
**900** A200 60q yel grn & brt grn 1.20 .25
**901** A200 80q crimson & brn 1.40 .25
*Nos. 897-901 (5)* 3.60 1.25

Albanian People's Republic, 20th anniv.

Cow — A201

**1966, Feb. 25** ***Perf. 12½x12, 12x12½***
**902** A201 10q shown .25 .25
**903** A201 20q Pig .40 .25
**904** A201 30q Ewe & lamb .75 .30
**905** A201 35q Ram 1.20 .30
**906** A201 40q Dog 1.50 .30
**907** A201 50q Cat, vert. 1.75 .30
**908** A201 55q Horse, vert. 2.00 .40
**909** A201 60q Ass, vert. 4.00 .60
*Nos. 902-909 (8)* 11.85 2.70

Soccer Player and Map of Uruguay — A202

5q, Globe in form of soccer ball. 15q, Player, map of Italy. 20q, Goalkeeper, map of France. 25q, Player, map of Brazil. 30q, Player, map of Switzerland. 35q, Player, map of Sweden. 40q, Player, map of Chile. 50q, Player, map of Great Britain. 70q, World Championship cup & ball.

**1966, Mar. 20** **Litho.** ***Perf. 12***
**910** A202 5q gray & dp org .25 .25
**911** A202 10q lt brn, bl & vio .25 .25
**912** A202 15q cit, dk bl & brt bl .25 .25
**913** A202 20q org, vio bl & brt bl .25 .25
**914** A202 25q salmon & sepia .25 .25
**915** A202 30q lt yel grn & brn .35 .25
**916** A202 35q lt ultra & emer .50 .25
**917** A202 40q pink & brown .55 .25
**918** A202 50q pale grn, mag & rose red .75 .25
**919** A202 70q gray, brn, yel & blk 1.25 .30
*Nos. 910-919 (10)* 4.65 2.55

World Cup Soccer Championship, Wembley, England, July 11-30.

Andon Zako Cajupi — A203

**1966, Mar. 27** **Unwmk.**
**920** A203 40q bluish blk .65 .25
**921** A203 1.10 l dark green 2.00 .40

Andon Zako Cajupi, poet, birth centenary.

Painted Lady — A204

Designs: 20q, Blue dragonfly. 30q, Cloudless sulphur butterfly. 35q, 40q, Splendid dragonfly. 50q, Machaon swallow-tail. 55q, Sulphur butterfly. 60q, Whitemarbled butterfly.

**1966, Apr. 21** **Litho.** ***Perf. 11½x12***
**922** A204 10q multicolored .45 .25
**923** A204 20q yellow & multi .55 .25
**924** A204 30q yellow & multi .75 .25
**925** A204 35q sky blue & multi 1.10 .25
**926** A204 40q multicolored 1.60 .25
**927** A204 50q rose & multi 2.25 .25
**928** A204 55q multicolored 2.75 .25
**929** A204 60q multicolored 7.00 .35
*Nos. 922-929 (8)* 16.45 2.10

WHO Headquarters, Geneva, and Emblem — A205

Designs (WHO Emblem and): 35q, Ambulance and stretcher bearers, vert. 60q, Albanian mother and nurse weighing infant, vert. 80q, X-ray machine and hospital.

***Perf. 12x12½, 12½x12***
**1966, May 3** **Litho.**
**930** A205 25q lt blue & blk .40 .25
**931** A205 35q salmon & ultra .75 .25
**932** A205 60q lt grn, bl & red 1.20 .25
**933** A205 80q yel, bl, grn & lt brn 1.50 .25
*Nos. 930-933 (4)* 3.85 1.00

Inauguration of the WHO Headquarters, Geneva.

Bird's Foot Starfish — A206

Designs: 25q, Starfish. 35q, Brittle star. 45q, But-thorn starfish. 50q, Starfish. 60q, Sea cucumber. 70q, Sea urchin.

**1966, May 10** ***Perf. 12x12½***
**934** A206 15q multicolored .25 .25
**935** A206 25q multicolored .45 .30
**936** A206 35q multicolored .75 .40
**937** A206 45q multicolored 1.00 .45
**938** A206 50q multicolored 1.10 .55
**939** A206 60q multicolored 1.60 .75
**940** A206 70q multicolored 2.00 1.90
*Nos. 934-940 (7)* 7.15 4.60

Luna 10 — A207

30q, 80q, Trajectory of Luna 10, earth & moon.

**1966, June 10** ***Perf. 12x12½***
**941** A207 20q blue, yel & blk .35 .25
**942** A207 30q yel grn, blk & bl .70 .25
**943** A207 70q vio, yel & blk 1.40 .25
**944** A207 80q yel, vio, grn & blk 2.50 .50
*Nos. 941-944 (4)* 4.95 1.25

Launching of the 1st artificial moon satellite, Luna 10, Apr. 3, 1966.

Jules Rimet Cup and Soccer — A208

Designs: Various scenes of soccer play.

**1966, July 12** **Litho.** ***Perf. 12x12½***
**Black Inscriptions**
**945** A208 10q ocher & lilac .30 .25
**946** A208 20q lt blue & cit .35 .25
**947** A208 30q brick red & Prus bl .50 .25
**948** A208 35q lt ultra & rose .70 .25
**949** A208 40q yel grn & lt red brn .70 .25
**950** A208 50q lt red brn & yel grn .85 .25
**951** A208 55q rose lil & yel grn .85 .25
**952** A208 60q dp rose & ocher 1.75 .25
*Nos. 945-952 (8)* 6.00 2.00

World Cup Soccer Championship, Wembley, England, July 11-30.

Water Level Map of Albania — A209

30q, Water measure & fields. 70q, Turbine & pylon. 80q, Hydrological decade emblem.

**1966, July** ***Perf. 12½x12***
**953** A209 20q brick red, blk & org .50 .25
**954** A209 30q emer, blk & lt brn .50 .25
**955** A209 70q brt violet & blk 1.50 .25
**956** A209 80q brt bl, org, yel & blk 2.50 .45
*Nos. 953-956 (4)* 5.00 1.20

Hydrological Decade (UNESCO), 1965-74.

Greek Turtle A210

Designs: 15q, Grass snake. 25q, European pond turtle. 30q, Wall lizard. 35q, Wall gecko. 45q, Emerald lizard. 50q, Slowworm. 90q, Horned viper (or sand viper).

**1966, Aug. 10** **Litho.** ***Perf. 12½x12***
**957** A210 10q gray & multi .25 .25
**958** A210 15q yellow & multi .30 .25
**959** A210 25q ultra & multi .35 .25
**960** A210 30q multicolored .45 .25
**961** A210 35q multicolored .70 .25
**962** A210 45q multicolored .85 .25
**963** A210 50q orange & multi 1.00 .30
**964** A210 90q lilac & multi 1.75 .55
*Nos. 957-964 (8)* 5.65 2.35

Persian Cat — A211

Cats: 10q, Siamese, vert. 15q, European tabby, vert. 25q, Black kitten. 60q, 65q, 80q, Various Persians.

***Perf. 12x12½, 12½x12***
**1966, Sept. 20** **Litho.**
**965** A211 10q multicolored .35 .25
**966** A211 15q blk, sepia & car .35 .25
**967** A211 25q blk, dk & lt brn .70 .25
**968** A211 45q blk, org & yel 1.00 .25
**969** A211 60q blk, brn & yel 1.75 .30
**970** A211 65q multicolored 1.75 .40
**971** A211 80q blk, gray & yel 2.50 .50
*Nos. 965-971 (7)* 8.40 2.20

Pjeter Budi, Writer — A212

**1966, Oct. 5** ***Perf. 12x12½***
**972** A212 25q buff & slate grn .75 .25
**973** A212 1.75 l gray & dull claret 2.25 .45

UNESCO Emblem — A213

Designs (UNESCO Emblem and): 15q, Open book, rose and school. 25q, Male folk dancers. 1.55 l, Jug, column and old building.

**1966, Oct. 20** **Litho.** ***Perf. 12***
**974** A213 5q lt gray & multi .25 .25
**975** A213 15q dp blue & multi .25 .25
**976** A213 25q gray & multi .30 .25
**977** A213 1.55 l multi 2.25 .50
*Nos. 974-977 (4)* 3.05 1.25

20th anniv. of UNESCO.

A214

Designs: 15q, Hand holding book with pictures of Marx, Engels, Lenin and Stalin. 25q, Map of Albania, hammer and sickle, symbols of agriculture and industry. 65q, Symbolic grain and factories. 95q, Fists holding rifle, spade, axe, sickle and book.

**1966, Nov. 1** **Litho.** ***Perf. 11½x12***
**978** A214 15q vermilion & gold .25 .25
**979** A214 25q multicolored .25 .25
**980** A214 65q brn, brn org & gold 1.20 .25
**981** A214 95q yellow & multi 1.50 .40
*Nos. 978-981 (4)* 3.20 1.15

Albanian Communist Party, 5th Cong.

A215

Designs: 15q, Hammer and sickle, Party emblem in sunburst. 25q, Partisan and sunburst. 65q, Steel worker and blast furnace. 95q, Combine harvester, factories, and pylon.

**1966, Nov. 8**

**982** A215 15q orange & multi .40 .25
**983** A215 25q red & multi .40 .25
**984** A215 65q multicolored 1.20 .25
**985** A215 95q blue & multi 1.20 .40
*Nos. 982-985 (4)* 3.20 1.15

25th anniv. of the founding of the Albanian Workers Party.

Russian Wolfhound A216

Dogs: 15q, Sheep dog. 25q, English setter. 45q, English springer spaniel. 60q, Bulldog. 65q, Saint Bernard. 80q, Dachshund.

**1966, Oct. 30 Litho. *Perf. 12½x12***

**986** A216 10q green & multi .40 .25
**987** A216 15q multicolored .65 .25
**988** A216 25q lilac & multi .80 .25
**989** A216 45q rose & multi 1.20 .35
**990** A216 60q brown & multi 1.60 .40
**991** A216 65q ultra & multi 1.75 .45
**992** A216 80q blue grn & multi 3.25 .50
*Nos. 986-992 (7)* 9.65 2.45

Ndre Mjeda — A217

**1966 *Perf. 12½x12***

**993** A217 25q brt bl & dk brn .35 .25
**994** A217 1.75 l brt grn & dk brn 2.40 .65

Birth Centenary of the priest Ndre Mjeda.

Proclamation — A218

Designs: 10q, Banner, man and woman holding gun and axe, horiz. 1.85 l, man with axe and banner and partisan with gun.

**1966, Dec. 25 *Perf. 11½x12, 12x11½***

**995** A218 5q lt brn, red & blk .25 .25
**996** A218 10q red, blk, gray & bl .40 .25
**997** A218 1.85 l red, blk & salmon 2.40 .30
*Nos. 995-997 (3)* 3.05 .80

Albanian Communist Party, 25th anniv.

Golden Eagle — A219

Birds of Prey: 15q, European sea eagle. 25q, Griffon vulture. 40q, Common sparrowhawk. 50q, Osprey. 70q, Egyptian vulture. 90q, Kestrel.

**1966, Dec. 20 Litho. *Perf. 11½x12***

**998** A219 10q gray & multi .35 .25
**999** A219 15q multicolored .35 .25
**1000** A219 25q citron & multi .70 .25
**1001** A219 40q multicolored 1.00 .25
**1002** A219 50q multicolored 1.40 .30
**1003** A219 70q yellow & multi 2.00 .40
**1004** A219 90q multicolored 3.00 .50
*Nos. 998-1004 (7)* 8.80 2.20

Hake — A220

Fish: 15q, Red mullet. 25q, Opah. 40q, Atlantic wolf fish. 65q, Lumpfish. 80q, Swordfish. 1.15 l, Shorthorn sculpin.

**1967, Jan. 20 Photo. *Perf. 12x11½***

**Fish in Natural Colors**

**1005** A220 10q blue .35 .25
**1006** A220 15q lt yellow grn .35 .25
**1007** A220 25q Prus blue .65 .25
**1008** A220 40q emerald .65 .25
**1009** A220 65q brt blue grn 1.00 .30
**1010** A220 80q blue 1.60 .40
**1011** A220 1.15 l brt green 2.50 .65
*Nos. 1005-1011 (7)* 7.10 2.35

White Pelican — A221

Designs: Various groups of pelicans.

**1967, Feb. 22 Litho. *Perf. 12***

**1012** A221 10q pink & multi .25 .25
**1013** A221 15q pink & multi .25 .25
**1014** A221 25q pink & multi 1.00 .25
**1015** A221 50q pink & multi 2.00 .25
**1016** A221 2 l pink & multi 5.00 .75
*Nos. 1012-1016 (5)* 8.50 1.75

Camellia — A222

Flowers: 10q, Chrysanthemum. 15q, Hollyhock. 25q, Flowering Maple. 35q, Peony. 65q, Gladiolus. 80q, Freesia. 1.15 l, Carnation.

**Unwmk.**

**1967, Apr. 12 Litho. *Perf. 12***

**Flowers in Natural Colors**

**1017** A222 5q pale brown .25 .25
**1018** A222 10q lt lilac .25 .25
**1019** A222 15q gray .25 .25
**1020** A222 25q ultra .45 .25
**1021** A222 35q lt blue .70 .25
**1022** A222 65q lt blue grn 1.40 .25
**1023** A222 80q lt bluish gray 1.75 .30
**1024** A222 1.15 l dull yellow 2.10 .45
*Nos. 1017-1024 (8)* 7.15 2.25

Congress Emblem and Power Station — A223

**1967, Apr. 24 Litho. *Perf. 12***

**1025** A223 25q multi .75 .25
**1026** A223 1.75 l multi 2.25 .55

Cong. of the Union of Professional Workers, Tirana, Apr. 24.

Rose — A224

Various Roses in Natural Colors.

**1967, May 15 *Perf. 12x12½***

**1027** A224 5q blue gray .35 .25
**1028** A224 10q brt blue .35 .25
**1029** A224 15q rose violet .35 .25
**1030** A224 25q lemon .35 .25
**1031** A224 35q brt grnsh blue .70 .25
**1032** A224 65q gray 1.00 .25
**1033** A224 80q brown 1.00 .30
**1034** A224 1.65 l gray green 2.75 .50
*Nos. 1027-1034 (8)* 6.85 2.30

Seashore, Bregdet Borsh A225

Views: 15q, Buthrotum, vert. 25q, Shore, Fshati Piqeras. 45q, Shore, Bregdet. 50q, Shore, Bregdet Himare. 65q, Ship, Sarande (Santi Quaranta). 80q, Shore, Dhermi. 1 l, Sunset, Bregdet, vert.

***Perf. 12x12½, 12½x12***

**1967, June 10**

**1035** A225 15q multicolored .40 .25
**1036** A225 20q multicolored .40 .25
**1037** A225 25q multicolored .80 .35
**1038** A225 45q multicolored .80 .35
**1039** A225 50q multicolored .80 .35
**1040** A225 65q multicolored 1.50 .50
**1041** A225 80q multicolored 1.50 .70
**1042** A225 1 l multicolored 2.40 1.00
*Nos. 1035-1042 (8)* 8.60 3.75

Fawn — A226

Roe Deer: 20q, Stag, vert. 25q, Doe, vert. 30q, Young stag and doe. 35q, Doe and fawn. 40q, Young stag, vert. 65q, Stag and doe, vert. 70q, Running stag and does.

***Perf. 12½x12, 12x12½***

**1967, July 20 Litho.**

**1043** A226 15q multicolored .35 .25
**1044** A226 20q multicolored .35 .25
**1045** A226 25q multicolored .70 .25
**1046** A226 30q multicolored .70 .25
**1047** A226 35q multicolored 1.00 .25
**1048** A226 40q multicolored 1.00 .25
**1049** A226 65q multicolored 2.10 .35
**1050** A226 70q multicolored 2.75 .55
*Nos. 1043-1050 (8)* 8.95 2.40

Man and Woman from Madhe — A227

Regional Costumes: 20q, Woman from Zadrimes. 25q, Dancer and drummer, Kukesit. 45q, Woman spinner, Dardhes. 50q, Farm couple, Myseqese. 65q, Dancer with tambourine, Tirana. 80q, Man and woman, Dropullit. 1 l, Piper, Laberise.

**1967, Aug. 25 *Perf. 12***

**1051** A227 15q tan & multi .40 .25
**1052** A227 20q lt yellow grn .40 .25
**1053** A227 25q multicolored .40 .25
**1054** A227 45q sky blue & multi .80 .25
**1055** A227 50q lemon & multi .80 .30
**1056** A227 65q pink & multi .80 .40
**1057** A227 80q multicolored 1.60 .45
**1058** A227 1 l gray & multi 1.60 .60
*Nos. 1051-1058 (8)* 6.80 2.75

Fighters and Newspaper — A228

75q, Printing plant, newspapers, microphone. 2 l, People holding newspaper.

**1967, Aug. 25 *Perf. 12½x12***

**1059** A228 25q multicolored .35 .25
**1060** A228 75q pink & multi 1.00 .50
**1061** A228 2 l multicolored 2.75 1.25
*Nos. 1059-1061 (3)* 4.10 2.00

Issued for the Day of the Press.

Street Scene, by Kole Idromeno A229

Hakmarrja Battalion, by Sali Shijaku A230

Designs: 20q, David, fresco by Onufri, 16th century, vert. 45q, Woman's head, ancient mosaic, vert. 50q, Men on horseback from 16th century icon, vert. 65q, Farm Women, by Zef Shoshi. 80q, Street Scene, by Vangjush Mio. 1 l, Bride, by Kolé Idromeno, vert.

***Perf. 12, 12x12½, (A230)***

**1967, Oct. 25 Litho.**

**1062** A229 15q multicolored .45 .25
**1063** A229 20q multicolored .45 .25
**1064** A230 25q multicolored 1.00 .25
**1065** A229 45q multicolored 1.00 .25
**1066** A229 50q multicolored 1.00 .25
**1067** A230 65q multicolored 1.75 .25
**1068** A230 80q multicolored 1.75 .30
**1069** A230 1 l multicolored 4.00 .35
*Nos. 1062-1069 (8)* 11.40 2.15

Lenin at Storming of Winter Palace — A231

Designs: 15q, Lenin and Stalin, horiz. 50q, Lenin and Stalin addressing meeting. 1.10 l, Storming of the Winter Palace, horiz.

**1967, Nov. 7 *Perf. 12***

**1070** A231 15q red & multi .30 .25
**1071** A231 25q slate grn & blk .55 .25
**1072** A231 50q brn, blk & brn vio .75 .25
**1073** A231 1.10 l lilac, gray & blk 1.50 .30
*Nos. 1070-1073 (4)* 3.10 1.05

50th anniv. of the Russian October Revolution.

Rabbit — A232

Designs: Various hares and rabbits. The 15q, 25q, 35q, 40q and 1 l are horizontal.

**1967, Sept. 30**

**1074** A232 15q orange & multi .25 .25
**1075** A232 20q brt yel & multi .35 .25
**1076** A232 25q lt brn & multi .35 .25
**1077** A232 35q multicolored .75 .25
**1078** A232 40q yellow & multi .75 .25
**1079** A232 50q pink & multi 2.25 .25
**1080** A232 65q multicolored 2.25 .35
**1081** A232 1 l lilac & multi 3.00 .55
*Nos. 1074-1081 (8)* 9.95 2.40

University, Torch and Book — A233

**1967, Sept. 15 Litho. *Perf. 12***

**1082** A233 25q multi .35 .25
**1083** A233 1.75 l multi 2.25 .35

10th anniv. of the founding of the State University, Tirana.

Coat of Arms and Soldiers — A234

65q, Arms, Factory, grain, flag, gun, radio tower. 1.20 l, Arms, hand holding torch.

**1967, Sept. 16** ***Perf. 12x11½***

| | | | | |
|---|---|---|---|---|
| **1084** | A234 | 15q multi | .30 | .25 |
| **1085** | A234 | 65q multi | .75 | .25 |
| **1086** | A234 | 1.20 l multi | 1.50 | .25 |
| | | *Nos. 1084-1086 (3)* | 2.55 | .75 |

25th anniversary of the Democratic Front.

Turkey — A235

Designs: 20q, Duck. 25q, Hen. 45q, Rooster. 50q, Guinea fowl. 65q, Goose, horiz. 80q, Mallard, horiz. 1 l, Chicks, horiz.

***Perf. 12x12½, 12½x12***

**1967, Nov. 25** **Photo.**

| | | | | |
|---|---|---|---|---|
| **1087** | A235 | 15q gold & multi | .25 | .25 |
| **1088** | A235 | 20q gold & multi | .25 | .25 |
| **1089** | A235 | 25q gold & multi | .30 | .25 |
| **1090** | A235 | 45q gold & multi | 1.00 | .25 |
| **1091** | A235 | 50q gold & multi | 1.00 | .25 |
| **1092** | A235 | 65q gold & multi | 1.00 | .25 |
| **1093** | A235 | 80q gold & multi | 1.75 | .35 |
| **1094** | A235 | 1 l gold & multi | 3.25 | .45 |
| | | *Nos. 1087-1094 (8)* | 8.80 | 2.30 |

Skanderbeg A236

Designs: 10q, Arms of Skanderbeg. 25q, Helmet and sword. 30q, Kruje Castle. 35q, Petreles Castle. 65q, Berati Castle. 80q, Skanderbeg addressing national chiefs. 90q, Battle of Albulenes.

**1967, Dec. 10 Litho.** ***Perf. 12x12½***

**Medallion in Bister and Dark Brown**

| | | | | |
|---|---|---|---|---|
| **1095** | A236 | 10q gold & violet | .25 | .25 |
| **1096** | A236 | 15q gold & rose car | .25 | .25 |
| **1097** | A236 | 25q gold & vio bl | .30 | .25 |
| **1098** | A236 | 30q gold & dk blue | .40 | .25 |
| **1099** | A236 | 35q gold & maroon | .50 | .25 |
| **1100** | A236 | 65q gold & green | .80 | .25 |
| **1101** | A236 | 80q gold & gray brn | 1.60 | .30 |
| **1102** | A236 | 90q gold & ultra | 1.60 | .35 |
| | | *Nos. 1095-1102 (8)* | 5.70 | 2.15 |

500th anniv. of the death of Skanderbeg (George Castriota), national hero.

10th Winter Olympic Games, Grenoble, France, Feb. 6-18 — A237

Designs: 15q, 2 l, Winter Olympics emblem. 25q, Ice hockey. 30q, Women's figure skating. 50q, Slalom. 80q, Downhill skiing. 1 l, Ski jump.

**1967-68**

| | | | | |
|---|---|---|---|---|
| **1103** | A237 | 15q multicolored | .25 | .25 |
| **1104** | A237 | 25q multicolored | .25 | .25 |
| **1105** | A237 | 30q multicolored | .25 | .25 |
| **1106** | A237 | 50q multicolored | .30 | .25 |
| **1107** | A237 | 80q multicolored | .75 | .25 |
| **1108** | A237 | 1 l multicolored | 1.60 | .25 |
| | | *Nos. 1103-1108 (6)* | 3.40 | 1.50 |

**Miniature Sheet**

***Imperf***

| | | | | |
|---|---|---|---|---|
| **1109** | A237 | 2 l red, gray & brt bl ('68) | 6.50 | 4.50 |

Nos. 1103-1108 issued Dec. 29, 1967.

Skanderbeg Monument, Kruje — A238

Designs: 10q, Skanderbeg monument, Tirana. 15q, Skanderbeg portrait, Uffizi Galleries, Florence. 25q, engraved portrait of Gen. Tanush Topia. 35q, Portrait of Gen. Gjergj Arianti, horiz. 65q, Portrait bust of Skanderbeg by O. Paskali. 80q, Title page of "The Life of Skanderbeg." 90q, Skanderbeg battling the Turks, painting by S. Rrota, horiz.

***Perf. 12x12½, 12½x12***

**1968, Jan. 17** **Litho.**

| | | | | |
|---|---|---|---|---|
| **1110** | A238 | 10q multicolored | .35 | .25 |
| **1111** | A238 | 15q multicolored | .35 | .25 |
| **1112** | A238 | 25q blk, yel & lt bl | .75 | .25 |
| **1113** | A238 | 30q multicolored | .75 | .25 |
| **1114** | A238 | 35q lt vio, pink & blk | .75 | .25 |
| **1115** | A238 | 65q multicolored | 1.50 | .30 |
| **1116** | A238 | 80q pink, blk & yel | 2.25 | .50 |
| **1117** | A238 | 90q beige & multi | 2.25 | .65 |
| | | *Nos. 1110-1117 (8)* | 8.95 | 2.70 |

500th anniv. of the death of Skanderbeg (George Castriota), national hero.

Carnation — A239

**1968, Feb. 15** ***Perf. 12***

**Various Carnations in Natural Colors**

| | | | | |
|---|---|---|---|---|
| **1118** | A239 | 15q green | .25 | .25 |
| **1119** | A239 | 20q dk brown | .25 | .25 |
| **1120** | A239 | 25q brt blue | .25 | .25 |
| **1121** | A239 | 50q gray olice | .70 | .25 |
| **1122** | A239 | 80q bluish gray | .90 | .25 |
| **1123** | A239 | 1.10 l violet gray | 1.50 | .40 |
| | | *Nos. 1118-1123 (6)* | 3.85 | 1.65 |

"Electrification" — A240

65q, Farm tractor, horiz. 1.10 l, Cow & herd.

**1968, Mar. 5** **Litho.** ***Perf. 12***

| | | | | |
|---|---|---|---|---|
| **1124** | A240 | 25q multi | .35 | .25 |
| **1125** | A240 | 65q multi | 1.10 | .30 |
| **1126** | A240 | 1.10 l multi | 1.40 | .40 |
| | | *Nos. 1124-1126 (3)* | 2.85 | .95 |

Fifth Farm Cooperatives Congress.

Goat — A241

Various goats. 15q, 20q, 25q are vertical.

**1968, Mar. 25** ***Perf. 12x12½, 12½x12***

| | | | | |
|---|---|---|---|---|
| **1127** | A241 | 15q multi | .25 | .25 |
| **1128** | A241 | 20q multi | .25 | .25 |
| **1129** | A241 | 25q multi | .35 | .25 |
| **1130** | A241 | 30q multi | .35 | .25 |
| **1131** | A241 | 40q multi | .50 | .25 |
| **1132** | A241 | 50q multi | .50 | .25 |
| **1133** | A241 | 80q multi | 1.50 | .25 |
| **1134** | A241 | 1.40 l multi | 2.25 | .40 |
| | | *Nos. 1127-1134 (8)* | 5.95 | 2.15 |

Zef N. Jubani — A242

**1968, Mar. 30** ***Perf. 12***

| | | | | |
|---|---|---|---|---|
| **1135** | A242 | 25q yellow & choc | .35 | .25 |
| **1136** | A242 | 1.75 l lt violet & blk | 1.90 | .50 |

Sesquicentennial of the birth of Zef N. Jubani, writer and scholar.

Physician and Hospital — A243

Designs (World Health Organization Emblem and): 65q, Hospital and microscope, horiz. 1.10 l, Mother feeding child.

***Perf. 12½x12, 12x12½***

**1968, Apr. 7** **Litho.**

| | | | | |
|---|---|---|---|---|
| **1137** | A243 | 25q green & claret | .25 | .25 |
| **1138** | A243 | 65q black, yel & bl | .90 | .30 |
| **1139** | A243 | 1.10 l black & dp org | 1.10 | .40 |
| | | *Nos. 1137-1139 (3)* | 2.25 | .95 |

20th anniv. of WHO.

Scientist — A244

Women: 15q, Militia member. 60q, Farm worker. 1 l, Factory worker.

**1968, Apr. 14** ***Perf. 12***

| | | | | |
|---|---|---|---|---|
| **1140** | A244 | 15q ver & dk red | .35 | .25 |
| **1141** | A244 | 25q blue grn & grn | .35 | .25 |
| **1142** | A244 | 60q dull yel & brn | 1.10 | .25 |
| **1143** | A244 | 1 l lt vio & vio | 1.90 | .40 |
| | | *Nos. 1140-1143 (4)* | 3.70 | 1.15 |

Albanian Women's Organization, 25th anniv.

Karl Marx — A245

Designs: 25q, Marx lecturing to students. 65q, "Das Kapital," "Communist Manifesto" and marching crowd. 95q, Full-face portrait.

**1968, May 5** **Litho.** ***Perf. 12***

| | | | | |
|---|---|---|---|---|
| **1144** | A245 | 15q gray, dk bl & bis | .45 | .25 |
| **1145** | A245 | 25q brn vio, dk brn & dl yel | .60 | .25 |
| **1146** | A245 | 65q gray, blk, brn & car | 1.25 | .25 |
| **1147** | A245 | 95q gray, ocher & blk | 3.00 | .50 |
| | | *Nos. 1144-1147 (4)* | 5.30 | 1.25 |

Karl Marx, 150th birth anniversary.

Heliopsis — A246

Flowers: 20q, Red flax. 25q, Orchid. 30q, Gloxinia. 40q, Turk's-cap lily. 80q, Amaryllis. 1.40 l, Red magnolia.

**1968, May 10** ***Perf. 12x12½***

| | | | | |
|---|---|---|---|---|
| **1148** | A246 | 15q gold & multi | .25 | .25 |
| **1149** | A246 | 20q gold & multi | .25 | .25 |
| **1150** | A246 | 25q gold & multi | .30 | .25 |
| **1151** | A246 | 30q gold & multi | .35 | .25 |
| **1152** | A246 | 40q gold & multi | .35 | .25 |
| **1153** | A246 | 80q gold & multi | 1.10 | .40 |
| **1154** | A246 | 1.40 l gold & multi | 1.90 | .60 |
| | | *Nos. 1148-1154 (7)* | 4.50 | 2.25 |

Proclamation of Prizren — A247

25q, Abdyl Frasheri. 40q, House in Prizren.

**1968, June 10** **Litho.** ***Perf. 12***

| | | | | |
|---|---|---|---|---|
| **1155** | A247 | 25q emerald & blk | .40 | .25 |
| **1156** | A247 | 40q multicolored | .75 | .25 |
| **1157** | A247 | 85q yellow & multi | 1.10 | .30 |
| | | *Nos. 1155-1157 (3)* | 2.25 | .80 |

League of Prizren against the Turks, 90th anniv.

Shepherd, by A. Kushi — A248

Paintings from Tirana Art Gallery: 20q, View of Tirana, by V. Mio, horiz. 25q, Mountaineer, by G. Madhi. 40q, Refugees, by A. Buza. 80q, Guerrillas of Shahin Matrakut, by S. Xega. 1.50 l, Portrait of an Old Man, by S. Papadhimitri. 1.70 l, View of Scutari, by S. Rrota. 2.50 l, Woman in Scutari Costume, by Z. Colombi.

**1968, June 20** ***Perf. 12x12½***

| | | | | |
|---|---|---|---|---|
| **1158** | A248 | 15q gold & multi | .25 | .25 |
| **1159** | A248 | 20q gold & multi | .25 | .25 |
| **1160** | A248 | 25q gold & multi | .25 | .25 |
| **1161** | A248 | 40q gold & multi | .25 | .25 |
| **1162** | A248 | 80q gold & multi | .55 | .25 |
| **1163** | A248 | 1.50 l gold & multi | 1.40 | .30 |
| **1164** | A248 | 1.70 l gold & multi | 2.25 | .55 |
| | | *Nos. 1158-1164 (7)* | 5.20 | 2.10 |

**Miniature Sheet**

***Perf. 12½xImperf.***

| | | | | |
|---|---|---|---|---|
| **1165** | A248 | 2.50 l multi | 2.75 | 2.50 |

No. 1165 contains one stamp, size: 50x71mm.

Soldier and Guns A249

25q, Sailor, warships. 65q, Aviator, planes, vert. 95q, Militiamen, woman.

**1968, July 10** **Litho.** ***Perf. 12***

| | | | | |
|---|---|---|---|---|
| **1166** | A249 | 15q multicolored | .35 | .25 |
| **1167** | A249 | 25q multicolored | .35 | .25 |
| **1168** | A249 | 65q multicolored | 1.50 | .25 |
| **1169** | A249 | 95q multicolored | 2.25 | .25 |
| | | *Nos. 1166-1169 (4)* | 4.45 | 1.00 |

25th anniversary of the People's Army.

Squid — A250

Designs: 20q, Crayfish. 25q, Whelk. 50q, Crab. 70q, Spiny lobster. 80q, Shore crab. 90q, Norway lobster.

**1968, Aug. 20**

| | | | | |
|---|---|---|---|---|
| **1170** | A250 | 15q multicolored | .35 | .25 |
| **1171** | A250 | 20q multicolored | .35 | .25 |
| **1172** | A250 | 25q multicolored | .35 | .25 |
| **1173** | A250 | 50q multicolored | .35 | .25 |
| **1174** | A250 | 70q multicolored | .75 | .30 |
| **1175** | A250 | 80q multicolored | 1.90 | .35 |
| **1176** | A250 | 90q multicolored | 1.90 | .40 |
| | | *Nos. 1170-1176 (7)* | 5.95 | 2.05 |

Women's Relay Race A251

# ALBANIA

Sport: 20q, Running. 25q, Women's discus. 30q, Equestrian. 40q, High jump. 50q, Women's hurdling. 80q, Soccer. 1.40 l, Woman diver. 2 l, Olympic stadium.

**1968, Sept. 23**    Photo.    *Perf. 12*
| 1177 | A251 | 15q multicolored | .25 | .25 |
|---|---|---|---|---|
| 1178 | A251 | 20q multicolored | .25 | .25 |
| 1179 | A251 | 25q multicolored | .25 | .25 |
| 1180 | A251 | 30q multicolored | .25 | .25 |
| 1181 | A251 | 40q multicolored | .30 | .25 |
| 1182 | A251 | 50q multicolored | .30 | .25 |
| 1183 | A251 | 80q multicolored | .75 | .25 |
| 1184 | A251 | 1.40 l multicolored | 1.50 | .35 |
| | Nos. 1177-1184 (8) | | 3.85 | 2.10 |

### Souvenir Sheet
*Perf. 12½ Horizontally*
| 1185 | A251 | 2 l multicolored | 3.00 | 2.50 |
|---|---|---|---|---|

19th Olympic Games, Mexico City, Oct. 12-27. No. 1185 contains one rectangular stamp, size: 64x54mm. Value of imperfs., Nos. 1177-1184 $10.50, No. 1185 $7.50.

Enver Hoxha — A252

**1968, Oct. 16**    Litho.    *Perf. 12*
| 1186 | A252 | 25q blue gray | .40 | .25 |
|---|---|---|---|---|
| 1187 | A252 | 35q rose brown | .40 | .25 |
| 1188 | A252 | 80q violet | .80 | .35 |
| 1189 | A252 | 1.10 l brown | 1.20 | .50 |
| | Nos. 1186-1189 (4) | | 2.80 | 1.35 |

### Souvenir Sheet
*Imperf*
| 1190 | A252 | 1.50 l rose red, bl vio & gold | 75.00 | 75.00 |
|---|---|---|---|---|

60th birthday of Envor Hoxha, First Secretary of the Central Committee of the Communist Party of Albania.

Book and Pupils — A253

**1968, Nov. 14**    Photo.
| 1191 | A253 | 15q mar & slate grn | .40 | .25 |
|---|---|---|---|---|
| 1192 | A253 | 85q gray olive & sepia | 2.50 | .35 |

60th anniv. of the Congress of Monastir, Nov. 14-22, 1908, which adopted a unified Albanian alphabet.

Waxwing A254

Birds: 20q, Rose-colored starling. 25q, Kingfishers. 50q, Long-tailed tits. 80q, Wallcreeper. 1.10 l, Bearded tit.

**1968, Nov. 15**    Litho.
### Birds in Natural Colors
| 1193 | A254 | 15q lt blue & blk | .25 | .25 |
|---|---|---|---|---|
| 1194 | A254 | 20q bister & blk | .25 | .25 |
| 1195 | A254 | 25q pink & blk | .40 | .25 |
| 1196 | A254 | 50q lt yel grn & blk | 1.00 | .25 |
| 1197 | A254 | 80q bis brn & blk | 2.00 | .35 |
| 1198 | A254 | 1.10 l pale grn & blk | 3.00 | .55 |
| | Nos. 1193-1198 (6) | | 6.90 | 1.90 |

Mao Tse-tung A255

**1968, Dec. 26**    Litho.    *Perf. 12½x12*
| 1199 | A255 | 25q gold, red & blk | 1.00 | .40 |
|---|---|---|---|---|
| 1200 | A255 | 1.75 l gold, red & blk | 6.50 | 3.50 |

75th birthday of Mao Tse-tung.

Adem Reka and Crane — A256

Portraits: 10q, Pjeter Lleshi and power lines. 15q, Mohammed Shehu and Myrteza Kepi. 25q, Shkurte Vata and women railroad workers. 65q, Agron Elezi, frontier guard. 80q, Ismet Bruçaj and mountain road. 1.30 l, Fuat Cela, blind revolutionary.

**1969, Feb. 10**    Litho.    *Perf. 12x12½*
| 1201 | A256 | 5q multicolored | .35 | .25 |
|---|---|---|---|---|
| 1202 | A256 | 10q multicolored | .35 | .25 |
| 1203 | A256 | 15q multicolored | .70 | .25 |
| 1204 | A256 | 25q multicolored | 1.00 | .25 |
| 1205 | A256 | 65q multicolored | 1.40 | .25 |
| 1206 | A256 | 80q multicolored | 1.40 | .25 |
| 1207 | A256 | 1.30 l multicolored | 2.10 | .25 |
| | Nos. 1201-1207 (7) | | 7.30 | 1.75 |

Contemporary heroine and heroes.

Meteorological Instruments A257

Designs: 25q, Water gauge. 1.60 l, Radar, balloon and isobars.

**1969, Feb. 25**    *Perf. 12*
| 1208 | A257 | 15q multicolored | .50 | .25 |
|---|---|---|---|---|
| 1209 | A257 | 25q ultra, org & blk | .50 | .25 |
| 1210 | A257 | 1.60 l rose vio, yel & blk | 2.75 | .60 |
| | Nos. 1208-1210 (3) | | 3.75 | 1.10 |

20th anniv. of Albanian hydrometeorology.

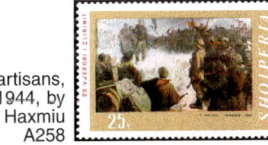

Partisans, 1944, by F. Haxmiu A258

Paintings: 5q, Student Revolutionists, by P. Mele, vert. 65q, Steel Mill, by C. Ceka. 80q, Reconstruction, by V. Kilica. 1.10 l, Harvest, by N. Jonuzi. 1.15 l, Terraced Landscape, by S. Kaceli. 2 l, Partisans' Meeting.

*Perf. 12x12½, 12½x12*
**1969, Apr. 25**    Litho.
*Size: 31½x41½mm*
| 1211 | A258 | 25q buff & multi | .25 | .25 |
|---|---|---|---|---|

*Size: 51½x30½mm*
| 1212 | A258 | 25q buff & multi | .25 | .25 |
|---|---|---|---|---|

*Size: 40½x32mm*
| 1213 | A258 | 65q buff & multi | .30 | .25 |
|---|---|---|---|---|

*Size: 51½x30½mm*
| 1214 | A258 | 80q buff & multi | .35 | .25 |
|---|---|---|---|---|
| 1215 | A258 | 1.10 l buff & multi | .75 | .25 |
| 1216 | A258 | 1.15 l buff & multi | .75 | .25 |
| | Nos. 1211-1216 (6) | | 2.65 | 1.50 |

### Miniature Sheet
*Imperf*
*Size: 111x90mm*
| 1217 | A258 | 2 l ocher & multi | 2.00 | 1.50 |
|---|---|---|---|---|

Leonardo da Vinci, Self-portrait — A259

Designs (after Leonardo da Vinci): 35q, Lilies. 40q, Design for a flying machine, horiz. 1 l, Portrait of Beatrice. No. 1222, Portrait of a Noblewoman. No. 1223, Mona Lisa.

*Perf. 12x12½, 12½x12*
**1969, May 2**    Litho.
| 1218 | A259 | 25q gold & sepia | .25 | .25 |
|---|---|---|---|---|
| 1219 | A259 | 35q gold & sepia | .35 | .25 |
| 1220 | A259 | 40q gold & sepia | .50 | .25 |
| 1221 | A259 | 1 l gold & multi | 1.40 | .25 |
| 1222 | A259 | 2 l gold & sepia | 2.75 | .55 |
| | Nos. 1218-1222 (5) | | 5.25 | 1.55 |

### Miniature Sheet
*Imperf*
| 1223 | A259 | 2 l gold & multi | 5.50 | 2.50 |
|---|---|---|---|---|

Leonardo da Vinci (1452-1519), painter, sculptor, architect and engineer.

First Congress Meeting Place — A260

Designs: 1 l, Albanian coat of arms. 2.25 l, Two partisans with guns and flag.

**1969, May 24**    *Perf. 12*
| 1224 | A260 | 25q lt grn, blk & red | .35 | .25 |
|---|---|---|---|---|
| 1225 | A260 | 2.25 l multi | 2.75 | 1.00 |

### Souvenir Sheet
| 1226 | A260 | 1 l gold, bl, blk & red | 35.00 | 35.00 |
|---|---|---|---|---|

25th anniversary of the First Anti-Fascist Congress of Permet, May 24, 1944.

Albanian Violet — A261

Designs: Violets and Pansies.

**1969, June 30**    Litho.    *Perf. 12x12½*
| 1227 | A261 | 5q gold & multi | .25 | .25 |
|---|---|---|---|---|
| 1228 | A261 | 10q gold & multi | .25 | .25 |
| 1229 | A261 | 15q gold & multi | .30 | .25 |
| 1230 | A261 | 20q gold & multi | .35 | .25 |
| 1231 | A261 | 25q gold & multi | .35 | .25 |
| 1232 | A261 | 80q gold & multi | 1.10 | .35 |
| 1233 | A261 | 1.95 l gold & multi | 1.90 | .65 |
| | Nos. 1227-1233 (7) | | 4.50 | 2.25 |

Plum, Fruit and Blossoms — A262

Designs: Blossoms and Fruits.

**1969, Aug. 10**    Litho.    *Perf. 12*
| 1234 | A262 | 10q shown | .25 | .25 |
|---|---|---|---|---|
| 1235 | A262 | 15q Lemon | .25 | .25 |
| 1236 | A262 | 25q Pomegranate | .30 | .25 |
| 1237 | A262 | 50q Cherry | .75 | .25 |
| 1238 | A262 | 80q Peach | 1.10 | .25 |
| 1239 | A262 | 1.20 l Apple | 1.90 | .40 |
| | Nos. 1234-1239 (6) | | 4.55 | 1.65 |

Basketball — A263

Designs: 10q, 80q, 2.20 l, Various views of basketball game. 25q, Hand aiming ball at basket and map of Europe, horiz.

**1969, Sept. 15**    Litho.    *Perf. 12*
| 1240 | A263 | 10q multi | .35 | .25 |
|---|---|---|---|---|
| 1241 | A263 | 15q buff & multi | .35 | .25 |
| 1242 | A263 | 25q blue & multi | .35 | .25 |
| 1243 | A263 | 80q multi | 1.00 | .25 |
| 1244 | A263 | 2.20 l multi | 2.00 | .50 |
| | Nos. 1240-1244 (5) | | 4.05 | 1.50 |

16th European Basketball Championships, Naples, Italy, Sept. 27-Oct. 5.

Runner — A264

Designs: 5q, Games' emblem. 10q, Woman gymnast. 20q, Pistol shooting. 25q, Swimmer at start. 80q, Bicyclist. 95q, Soccer.

**1969, Sept. 30**
| 1245 | A264 | 5q multicolored | .25 | .25 |
|---|---|---|---|---|
| 1246 | A264 | 10q multicolored | .25 | .25 |
| 1247 | A264 | 15q multicolored | .30 | .25 |
| 1248 | A264 | 20q multicolored | .35 | .25 |
| 1249 | A264 | 25q multicolored | .35 | .25 |
| 1250 | A264 | 80q multicolored | 1.00 | .25 |
| 1251 | A264 | 95q multicolored | 1.40 | .25 |
| | Nos. 1245-1251 (7) | | 3.90 | 1.75 |

Second National Spartakiad.

Electronic Technicians, Steel Ladle — A265

25q, Mao Tse-tung with microphones. 1.40 l, Children holding Mao's red book.

**1969, Oct. 1**    Litho.    *Perf. 12*
| 1252 | A265 | 25q multi, vert. | 2.50 | .60 |
|---|---|---|---|---|
| 1253 | A265 | 85q multi | 7.50 | 2.25 |
| 1254 | A265 | 1.40 l multi, vert. | 12.00 | 4.00 |
| | Nos. 1252-1254 (3) | | 22.00 | 6.85 |

People's Republic of China, 20th anniv.

Enver Hoxha — A266

Designs: 80q, Pages from Berat resolution. 1.45 l, Partisans with flag.

**1969, Oct. 20**    Litho.    *Perf. 12*
| 1255 | A266 | 25q multicolored | .25 | .25 |
|---|---|---|---|---|
| 1256 | A266 | 80q gray & multi | .55 | .25 |
| 1257 | A266 | 1.45 l ocher & multi | 1.60 | .45 |
| | Nos. 1255-1257 (3) | | 2.40 | .95 |

25th anniv. of the 2nd reunion of the Natl. Antifascist Liberation Council, Berat.

Soldiers A267

Designs: 30q, Oil refinery. 35q, Combine harvester. 45q, Hydroelectric station and dam. 55q, Militia woman, man and soldier. 1.10 l, Dancers and musicians.

**1969, Nov. 29**
| 1258 | A267 | 25q multi | .30 | .25 |
|---|---|---|---|---|
| 1259 | A267 | 30q multi | .35 | .25 |
| 1260 | A267 | 35q multi | .50 | .25 |
| 1261 | A267 | 45q multi | .85 | .25 |
| 1262 | A267 | 55q multi | 1.20 | .30 |
| 1263 | A267 | 1.10 l multi | 2.00 | .45 |
| | Nos. 1258-1263 (6) | | 5.20 | 1.75 |

25th anniv. of the socialist republic.

Joseph V. Stalin, (1879-1953), Russian Political Leader — A268

**1969, Dec. 21** **Litho.** ***Perf. 12***

| | | | | | |
|---|---|---|---|---|---|
| **1264** | A268 | 15q | lilac | .25 | .25 |
| **1265** | A268 | 25q | slate blue | .40 | .25 |
| **1266** | A268 | 1 l | brown | 1.40 | .25 |
| **1267** | A268 | 1.10 l | violet blue | 1.60 | .25 |
| | | | *Nos. 1264-1267 (4)* | 3.65 | 1.00 |

Head of Woman — A269

Greco-Roman Mosaics: 25q, Geometrical floor design, horiz. 80q, Bird and tree, horiz. 1.10 l, Floor with birds and grapes, horiz. 1.20 l, Fragment with corn within oval design.

**1969, Dec. 25** ***Perf. 12½x12***

| | | | | | |
|---|---|---|---|---|---|
| **1268** | A269 | 15q | gold & multi | .25 | .25 |
| **1269** | A269 | 25q | gold & multi | .25 | .25 |
| **1270** | A269 | 80q | gold & multi | .75 | .25 |
| **1271** | A269 | 1.10 l | gold & multi | 1.00 | .25 |
| **1272** | A269 | 1.20 l | gold & multi | 1.50 | .35 |
| | | | *Nos. 1268-1272 (5)* | 3.75 | 1.35 |

Cancellation of 1920 — A270

25q, Proclamation and congress site.

**1970, Jan. 21** **Litho.** ***Perf. 12***

| | | | | | |
|---|---|---|---|---|---|
| **1273** | A270 | 25q | red, gray & blk | .35 | .25 |
| **1274** | A270 | 1.25 l | dk grn, yel & blk | 2.25 | .25 |

Congress of Louchnia, 50th anniversary.

Worker, Student and Flag — A271

**1970, Feb. 11** ***Perf. 12½x12***

| | | | | | |
|---|---|---|---|---|---|
| **1275** | A271 | 25q | red & multi | .35 | .25 |
| **1276** | A271 | 1.75 l | red & multi | 2.25 | .50 |

Vocational organizations in Albania, 25th anniv.

Turk's-cap Lily — A272

Lilies: 5q, Cernum, vert. 15q, Madonna, vert. 25q, Royal, vert. 1.10 l, Tiger. 1.15 l, Albanian.

***Perf. 11½x12, 12x11½***

**1970, Mar. 10** **Litho.**

| | | | | | |
|---|---|---|---|---|---|
| **1277** | A272 | 5q | multi | .25 | .25 |
| **1278** | A272 | 15q | multi | .25 | .25 |
| **1279** | A272 | 25q | multi | .75 | .25 |
| **1280** | A272 | 80q | multi | 1.50 | .25 |
| **1281** | A272 | 1.10 l | multi | 2.25 | .25 |
| **1282** | A272 | 1.15 l | multi | 2.60 | .30 |
| | | | *Nos. 1277-1282 (6)* | 7.60 | 1.55 |

Lenin — A273

Designs (Lenin): 5q, Portrait, vert. 25q, As volunteer construction worker. 95q, Addressing crowd. 1.10 l, Saluting, vert.

**1970, Apr. 22** **Litho.** ***Perf. 12***

| | | | | | |
|---|---|---|---|---|---|
| **1283** | A273 | 5q | multi | .25 | .25 |
| **1284** | A273 | 15q | multi | .25 | .25 |
| **1285** | A273 | 25q | multi | .35 | .25 |
| **1286** | A273 | 95q | multi | .90 | .25 |
| **1287** | A273 | 1.10 l | multi | 1.60 | .25 |
| | | | *Nos. 1283-1287 (5)* | 3.35 | 1.25 |

Centenary of birth of Lenin (1870-1924).

Frontier Guard — A274

**1970, Apr. 25**

| | | | | | |
|---|---|---|---|---|---|
| **1288** | A274 | 25q | multi | .40 | .25 |
| **1289** | A274 | 1.25 l | multi | 2.00 | .50 |

25th anniversary of Frontier Guards.

Soccer Players A275

Designs: 5q, Jules Rimet Cup and globes. 10q, Aztec Stadium, Mexico City. 25q, Defending goal. 65q, 80q, No. 1296, Two soccer players in various plays. No. 1297, Mexican horseman and volcano Popocatepetl.

**1970, May 15** **Litho.** ***Perf. 12½x12***

| | | | | | |
|---|---|---|---|---|---|
| **1290** | A275 | 5q | multicolored | .25 | .25 |
| **1291** | A275 | 10q | multicolored | .25 | .25 |
| **1292** | A275 | 15q | multicolored | .25 | .25 |
| **1293** | A275 | 25q | lt green & multi | .25 | .25 |
| **1294** | A275 | 65q | pink & multi | .55 | .25 |
| **1295** | A275 | 80q | lt blue & multi | .75 | .40 |
| **1296** | A275 | 2 l | yellow & multi | 1.50 | .45 |
| | | | *Nos. 1290-1296 (7)* | 3.80 | 2.10 |

**Souvenir Sheet**

***Perf 12 x Imperf***

| | | | | | |
|---|---|---|---|---|---|
| **1297** | A275 | 2 l | multicolored | 2.75 | 2.75 |

World Soccer Championships for the Jules Rimet Cup, Mexico City, May 31-June 21, 1970. No. 1297 contains one large horizontal stamp. Nos. 1290-1297 exist imperf. Value: Nos. 1290-1296, mint or used, $12; No. 1297, mint $10, used $5.

UPU Headquarters and Monument, Bern — A276

**1970, May 30** **Litho.** ***Perf. 12½x12***

| | | | | | |
|---|---|---|---|---|---|
| **1298** | A276 | 25q | ultra, gray & blk | .25 | .25 |
| **1299** | A276 | 1.10 l | org, buff & blk | 1.00 | .25 |
| **1300** | A276 | 1.15 l | grn, gray & blk | 1.25 | .30 |
| | | | *Nos. 1298-1300 (3)* | 2.50 | .80 |

Inauguration of the new UPU Headquarters in Bern.

Bird and Grapes Mosaic — A277

Mosaics, 5th-6th centuries, excavated near Pogradec: 10q, Waterfowl and grapes. 20q, Bird and tree stump. 25q, Bird and leaves. 65q, Fish. 2.25 l, Peacock, vert.

**1970, July 10** ***Perf. 12½x12, 12x12½***

| | | | | | |
|---|---|---|---|---|---|
| **1301** | A277 | 5q | multi | .25 | .25 |
| **1302** | A277 | 10q | multi | .25 | .25 |
| **1303** | A277 | 20q | multi | .30 | .25 |
| **1304** | A277 | 25q | multi | .35 | .25 |
| **1305** | A277 | 65q | multi | .75 | .25 |
| **1306** | A277 | 2.25 l | multi | 2.60 | .35 |
| | | | *Nos. 1301-1306 (6)* | 4.50 | 1.60 |

Fruit Harvest and Dancers — A278

Designs: 25q, Contour-plowed fields and conference table. 80q, Cattle and newspapers. 1.30 l, Wheat harvest.

**1970, Aug. 28** **Litho.** ***Perf. 12x11½***

| | | | | | |
|---|---|---|---|---|---|
| **1307** | A278 | 15q | brt violet & blk | .35 | .25 |
| **1308** | A278 | 25q | dp blue & blk | .35 | .25 |
| **1309** | A278 | 80q | dp brown & blk | 1.00 | .25 |
| **1310** | A278 | 1.30 l | org brn & blk | 1.40 | .25 |
| | | | *Nos. 1307-1310 (4)* | 3.10 | 1.00 |

25th anniv. of the agrarian reform law.

Attacking Partisans — A279

Designs: 25q, Partisans with horses and flag. 1.60 l, Partisans.

**1970, Sept. 3** ***Perf. 12***

| | | | | | |
|---|---|---|---|---|---|
| **1311** | A279 | 15q | org brn & blk | .25 | .25 |
| **1312** | A279 | 25q | brn, yel & blk | .50 | .25 |
| **1313** | A279 | 1.60 l | dp grn & blk | 1.50 | .35 |
| | | | *Nos. 1311-1313 (3)* | 2.25 | .85 |

50th anniversary of liberation of Vlona.

Miners, by Nexhmedin Zajmi A280

Paintings from the National Gallery, Tirana: 5q, Bringing in the Harvest, by Isuf Sulovari, vert. 15q, The Activists, by Dhimitraq Trebicka, vert. 65q, Instruction of Partisans, by Hasan Nallbani. 95q, Architectural Planning, by Vilson Kilica. No. 1319, Woman Machinist, by Zef Shoshi, vert. No. 1320, Partisan Destroying Tank, by Sali Shijaku, vert.

***Perf. 12½x12, 12x12½***

**1970, Sept. 25** **Litho.**

| | | | | | |
|---|---|---|---|---|---|
| **1314** | A280 | 5q | multicolored | .25 | .25 |
| **1315** | A280 | 15q | multicolored | .25 | .25 |
| **1316** | A280 | 25q | multicolored | .25 | .25 |
| **1317** | A280 | 65q | multicolored | .25 | .25 |
| **1318** | A280 | 95q | multicolored | .95 | .25 |
| **1319** | A280 | 2 l | multicolored | 1.75 | .35 |
| | | | *Nos. 1314-1319 (6)* | 3.70 | 1.60 |

**Miniature Sheet**

***Imperf***

| | | | | | |
|---|---|---|---|---|---|
| **1320** | A280 | 2 l | multicolored | 2.50 | 1.50 |

Electrification Map of Albania — A281

Designs: 25q, Light bulb, hammer and sickle emblem, map of Albania and power graph. 80q, Linemen at work. 1.10 l, Use of electricity on the farm, in home and business.

**1970, Oct. 25** **Litho.** ***Perf. 12***

| | | | | | |
|---|---|---|---|---|---|
| **1321** | A281 | 15q | multi | .25 | .25 |
| **1322** | A281 | 25q | multi | .35 | .25 |
| **1323** | A281 | 80q | multi | 1.00 | .25 |
| **1324** | A281 | 1.10 l | multi | 1.20 | .25 |
| | | | *Nos. 1321-1324 (4)* | 2.80 | 1.00 |

Albanian village electrification completion.

Friedrich Engels — A282

Designs: 1.10 l, Engels as young man. 1.15 l, Engels addressing crowd.

**1970, Nov. 28** **Litho.** ***Perf. 12x12½***

| | | | | | |
|---|---|---|---|---|---|
| **1325** | A282 | 25q | bister & dk bl | .35 | .25 |
| **1326** | A282 | 1.10 l | bis & dp claret | .95 | .25 |
| **1327** | A282 | 1.15 l | bis & dk ol grn | 1.20 | .30 |
| | | | *Nos. 1325-1327 (3)* | 2.50 | .80 |

150th anniv. of the birth of Friedrich Engels (1820-95), German socialist, collaborator with Karl Marx.

Factories — A282a

Designs: 10q, Tractor factory, Tirana, horiz. 15q, Fertilizer factory, Fier, horiz. 20q, Superphosphate factory, Lac. 25q, Cement factory, Elbasan, horiz. 80q, Coking plant, Qyteti Stalin, horiz.

**1970-71** **Litho.** ***Perf. 12***

| | | | | | |
|---|---|---|---|---|---|
| **1327A** | A282a | 10q | multi | 250.00 | 160.00 |
| **1327B** | A282a | 15q | multi | 250.00 | 160.00 |
| **1327C** | A282a | 20q | multi | 250.00 | 160.00 |
| **1327D** | A282a | 25q | multi | 250.00 | 160.00 |
| **1327E** | A282a | 80q | multi | 250.00 | 160.00 |
| | | | *Nos. 1327A-1327E (5)* | 1,250. | 800.00 |

Issue dates: 15q, 12/4/70. 10q, 20q, 25q, 80q, 1/20/71.

Ludwig van Beethoven — A283

Designs: 5q, Birthplace, Bonn. 25q, 65q, 1.10 l, various portraits. 1.80 l, Scene from Fidelio, horiz.

**1970, Dec. 16** **Litho.** ***Perf. 12***

| | | | | | |
|---|---|---|---|---|---|
| **1328** | A283 | 5q | dp plum & gold | .25 | .25 |
| **1329** | A283 | 15q | brt rose lil & sil | .25 | .25 |
| **1330** | A283 | 25q | green & gold | .35 | .25 |
| **1331** | A283 | 65q | magenta & sil | .85 | .25 |
| **1332** | A283 | 1.10 l | dk blue & gold | 1.75 | .30 |
| **1333** | A283 | 1.80 l | black & sil | 2.75 | .50 |
| | | | *Nos. 1328-1333 (6)* | 6.20 | 1.80 |

Ludwig van Beethoven (1770-1827), composer.

Coat of Arms — A284

Designs: 25q, Proclamation. 80q, Enver Hoxha reading proclamation. 1.30 l, Young people and proclamation.

**1971, Jan. 11** **Litho.** ***Perf. 12***

| | | | | | |
|---|---|---|---|---|---|
| **1334** | A284 | 15q | lt bl, gold, blk & red | .25 | .25 |
| **1335** | A284 | 25q | rose lil, blk, gold & gray | .25 | .25 |
| **1336** | A284 | 80q | emerald, blk & gold | .85 | .25 |
| **1337** | A284 | 1.30 l | yel org, blk & gold | 1.20 | .30 |
| | | | *Nos. 1334-1337 (4)* | 2.55 | 1.05 |

Declaration of the Republic, 25th anniv.

# ALBANIA

"Liberty" — A285

Designs: 50q, Women's brigade. 65q, Street battle, horiz. 1.10 l, Execution, horiz.

**Perf. 12x11½, 11½x12**
| 1971, Mar. 18 | | | Litho. | |
|---|---|---|---|---|
| 1338 | A285 | 25q dk bl & bl | .35 | .25 |
| 1339 | A285 | 50q slate green | .50 | .25 |
| 1340 | A285 | 65q dk brn & chest | .75 | .25 |
| 1341 | A285 | 1.10 l purple | 1.25 | .25 |
| | | Nos. 1338-1341 (4) | 2.85 | 1.00 |

Centenary of the Paris Commune.

Black Men — A286

1.10 l, Men of 3 races. 1.15 l, Black protest.

| 1971, Mar. 21 | | | **Perf. 12x12½** | |
|---|---|---|---|---|
| 1342 | A286 | 25q blk & bis brn | .25 | .25 |
| 1343 | A286 | 1.10 l blk & rose car | .75 | .25 |
| 1344 | A286 | 1.15 l blk & ver | .90 | .25 |
| | | Nos. 1342-1344 (3) | 1.90 | .75 |

Intl. year against racial discrimination.

Tulip — A287

Designs: Various tulips.

| 1971, Mar. 25 | | | | |
|---|---|---|---|---|
| 1345 | A287 | 5q multi | .25 | .25 |
| 1346 | A287 | 10q yellow & multi | .25 | .25 |
| 1347 | A287 | 15q pink & multi | .30 | .25 |
| 1348 | A287 | 20q lt blue & multi | .35 | .25 |
| 1349 | A287 | 25q multi | .35 | .25 |
| 1350 | A287 | 80q multi | 1.00 | .25 |
| 1351 | A287 | 1 l multi | 1.75 | .25 |
| 1352 | A287 | 1.45 l citron & multi | 2.10 | .30 |
| | | Nos. 1345-1352 (8) | 6.35 | 2.05 |

Horseman, by Dürer — A288

Art Works by Dürer: 15q, Three peasants. 25q, Dancing peasant couple. 45q, The bag piper. 65q, View of Kalkreut, horiz. 2.40 l, View of Trent, horiz. 2.50 l, Self-portrait.

**Perf. 11½x12, 12x11½**
| 1971, May 15 | | | Litho. | |
|---|---|---|---|---|
| 1353 | A288 | 10q blk & pale grn | .30 | .25 |
| 1354 | A288 | 15q black & pale lil | .30 | .25 |
| 1355 | A288 | 25q blk & pale bl | .35 | .25 |
| 1356 | A288 | 45q blk & pale rose | .90 | .25 |
| 1357 | A288 | 65q black & multi | 1.75 | .25 |
| 1358 | A288 | 2.40 l black & multi | 6.60 | .70 |
| | | Nos. 1353-1358 (6) | 9.10 | 1.65 |

**Miniature Sheet**
**Imperf**
| 1359 | A288 | 2.50 l multi | 3.50 | 2.50 |

Albrecht Dürer (1471-1528), German painter and engraver.

Satellite Orbiting Globe — A289

Designs: 1.20 l, Government Building, Tirana, and Red Star emblem. 2.20 l, like 60q, 2.50 l, Flag of People's Republic of China forming trajectory around globe.

| 1971, June 10 | | | Litho. | **Perf. 12x12½** |
|---|---|---|---|---|
| 1360 | A289 | 60q purple & multi | .60 | .25 |
| 1361 | A289 | 1.20 l ver & multi | 1.40 | .30 |
| 1362 | A289 | 2.20 l green & multi | 2.50 | .50 |

**Imperf**
| 1363 | A289 | 2.50 l vio blk & multi | 5.00 | 2.75 |
| | | Nos. 1360-1363 (4) | 9.50 | 3.80 |

Space developments of People's Republic of China.

Mao Tse-tung — A290

Designs: 1.05 l, House where Communist Party was founded, horiz. 1.20 l, Peking crowd with placards, horiz.

| 1971, July 1 | | | **Perf. 12x12½, 12½x12** | |
|---|---|---|---|---|
| 1364 | A290 | 25q silver & multi | .85 | .25 |
| 1365 | A290 | 1.05 l silver & multi | 2.25 | 2.00 |
| 1366 | A290 | 1.20 l silver & multi | 3.25 | 2.25 |
| | | Nos. 1364-1366 (3) | 6.35 | 4.50 |

50th anniv. of Chinese Communist Party.

Crested Titmouse A291

| 1971, Aug. 15 | | | Litho. | **Perf. 12½x12** |
|---|---|---|---|---|
| 1367 | A291 | 5q shown | .25 | .25 |
| 1368 | A291 | 10q European serin | .30 | .25 |
| 1369 | A291 | 15q Linnet | .45 | .25 |
| 1370 | A291 | 25q Firecrest | .70 | .25 |
| 1371 | A291 | 45q Rock thrush | 1.00 | .25 |
| 1372 | A291 | 60q Blue tit | 1.75 | .50 |
| 1373 | A291 | 2.40 l Chaffinch | 6.25 | 2.75 |
| a. | | Block of 7, #1367-1373 + label | 17.50 | 15.00 |
| | | Nos. 1367-1373 (7) | 10.70 | 4.50 |

Continuous design with bird's nest label at upper left.
Nos. 1367-1372 exist in blocks of 6, with two labels. Value: unused $55; used $25.

Olympic Rings and Running A292

Designs (Olympic Rings and): 10q, Hurdles. 15q, Shooting. 25q, Gymnastics. 80q, Fencing. 1.05 l, Soccer. 2 l, Runner at finish line. 3.60 l, Diving, women's.

| 1971, Sept. 15 | | | | |
|---|---|---|---|---|
| 1374 | A292 | 5q green & multi | .25 | .25 |
| 1375 | A292 | 10q multicolored | .25 | .25 |
| 1376 | A292 | 15q blue & multi | .25 | .25 |
| 1377 | A292 | 25q violet & multi | .25 | .25 |
| 1378 | A292 | 80q lilac & multi | .75 | .25 |
| 1379 | A292 | 1.05 l multicolored | .95 | .25 |
| 1380 | A292 | 3.60 l multicolored | 3.00 | .50 |
| | | Nos. 1374-1380 (7) | 5.70 | 2.00 |

**Souvenir Sheet**
**Imperf**
| 1381 | A292 | 2 l brt blue & multi | 3.25 | 1.50 |

20th Olympic Games, Munich, Aug. 26-Sept. 10, 1972.

Workers with Flags — A293

Designs: 1.05 l, Party Headquarters, Tirana, and Red Star. 1.20 l, Rifle, star, flag and "VI."

| 1971, Nov. 1 | | | **Perf. 12** | |
|---|---|---|---|---|
| 1382 | A293 | 25q multi | .35 | .25 |
| 1383 | A293 | 1.05 l multi | 1.00 | .25 |
| 1384 | A293 | 1.20 l multi, vert. | 1.40 | .30 |
| | | Nos. 1382-1384 (3) | 2.75 | .80 |

6th Congress of Workers' Party.

Factories and Workers — A294

Designs: 80q, "XXX" and flag, vert. 1.55 l, Enver Hoxha and flags.

| 1971, Nov. 8 | | | | |
|---|---|---|---|---|
| 1385 | A294 | 15q gold, sil, lil & yel | .25 | .25 |
| 1386 | A294 | 80q gold, sil & red | .90 | .25 |
| 1387 | A294 | 1.55 l gold, sil, red & brn | 1.90 | .30 |
| | | Nos. 1385-1387 (3) | 3.05 | .80 |

30th anniversary of Workers' Party.

Construction Work, by M. Fushekati — A295

Contemporary Albanian Paintings: 5q, Young Man, by R. Kuci, vert. 25q, Partisan, by D. Jukniu, vert. 80q, Fliers, by S. Kristo. 1.20 l, Girl in Forest, by A. Sadikaj. 1.55 l, Warriors with Spears and Shields, by S. Kamberi. 2 l, Freedom Fighter, by I. Lulani.

**Perf. 12x12½, 12½x12**
| 1971, Nov. 20 | | | | |
|---|---|---|---|---|
| 1388 | A295 | 5q gold & multi | .25 | .25 |
| 1389 | A295 | 15q gold & multi | .25 | .25 |
| 1390 | A295 | 25q gold & multi | .25 | .25 |
| 1391 | A295 | 80q gold & multi | .75 | .25 |
| 1392 | A295 | 1.20 l gold & multi | .85 | .25 |
| 1393 | A295 | 1.55 l gold & multi | 1.00 | .30 |
| | | Nos. 1388-1393 (6) | 3.35 | 1.55 |

**Miniature Sheet**
**Imperf**
| 1394 | A295 | 2 l gold & multi | 2.75 | 1.75 |

Young Workers' Emblem A296

| 1971, Nov. 23 | | | **Perf. 12x12½** | |
|---|---|---|---|---|
| 1395 | A296 | 15q lt blue & multi | .25 | .25 |
| 1396 | A296 | 1.05 l grnsh gray & multi | 1.25 | .30 |

Albanian Young Workers' Union, 30th anniv.

"Halili and Hajria" Ballet A297

Scenes from "Halili and Hajria" Ballet: 10q, Brother and sister. 15q, Hajria before Sultan Suleiman. 50q, Hajria and husband. 80q, Execution of Halili. 1.40 l, Hajria killing her husband.

| 1971, Dec. 27 | | | **Perf. 12½x12** | |
|---|---|---|---|---|
| 1397 | A297 | 5q silver & multi | .25 | .25 |
| 1398 | A297 | 10q silver & multi | .25 | .25 |
| 1399 | A297 | 15q silver & multi | .25 | .25 |
| 1400 | A297 | 50q silver & multi | .60 | .25 |
| 1401 | A297 | 80q silver & multi | 1.00 | .50 |
| 1402 | A297 | 1.40 l silver & multi | 2.00 | .90 |
| | | Nos. 1397-1402 (6) | 4.35 | 2.40 |

Albanian ballet Halili and Hajria after drama by Kol Jakova.

Biathlon and Olympic Rings A298

Designs (Olympic Rings and): 10q, Sledding. 15q, Ice hockey. 20q, Bobsledding. 50q, Speed skating. 1 l, Slalom. 2 l, Ski jump. 2.50 l, Figure skating, pairs.

| 1972, Feb. 10 | | | | |
|---|---|---|---|---|
| 1403 | A298 | 5q lt olive & multi | .25 | .25 |
| 1404 | A298 | 10q lt violet & multi | .25 | .25 |
| 1405 | A298 | 15q multicolored | .25 | .25 |
| 1406 | A298 | 20q pink & multi | .25 | .25 |
| 1407 | A298 | 50q lt blue & multi | .50 | .25 |
| 1408 | A298 | 1 l ocher & multi | .80 | .25 |
| 1409 | A298 | 2 l lilac & multi | 1.75 | .40 |
| | | Nos. 1403-1409 (7) | 4.05 | 1.90 |

**Souvenir Sheet**
**Imperf**
| 1410 | A298 | 2.50 l blue & multi | 3.00 | 1.75 |

11th Winter Olympic Games, Sapporo, Japan, Feb. 3-13.

Wild Strawberries A299

Wild Fruits and Nuts: 10q, Blackberries. 15q, Hazelnuts. 20q, Walnuts. 25q, Strawberry-tree fruit. 30q, Dogwood berries. 2.40 l, Rowan berries.

| 1972, Mar. 20 | | | Litho. | **Perf. 12** |
|---|---|---|---|---|
| 1411 | A299 | 5q lt grn & multi | .25 | .25 |
| 1412 | A299 | 10q yellow & multi | .25 | .25 |
| 1413 | A299 | 15q lt vio & multi | .25 | .25 |
| 1414 | A299 | 20q pink & multi | .25 | .25 |
| 1415 | A299 | 25q multi | .25 | .25 |
| 1416 | A299 | 30q multi | .35 | .25 |
| 1417 | A299 | 2.40 l multi | 3.00 | .50 |
| | | Nos. 1411-1417 (7) | 4.60 | 2.00 |

"Your Heart is Your Health" — A300

World Health Day: 1.20 l, Cardiac patient and electrocardiogram.

| 1972, Apr. 7 | | | **Perf. 12x12½** | |
|---|---|---|---|---|
| 1418 | A300 | 1.10 l multicolored | 1.25 | .40 |
| 1419 | A300 | 1.20 l rose & multi | 1.40 | .85 |

Worker and Student — A301

7th Trade Union Cong., May 8: 2.05 l, Assembly Hall, dancers and emblem.

| 1972, Apr. 24 | | | Litho. | **Perf. 11½x12½** |
|---|---|---|---|---|
| 1420 | A301 | 25q multi | .50 | .25 |
| 1421 | A301 | 2.05 l blue & multi | 2.00 | .40 |

Qemal Stafa — A302

Designs: 15q, Memorial flame. 25q, Monument "Spirit of Defiance," vert.

**1972, May 5** ***Perf. 12½x12, 12x12½***

| | | | | | |
|---|---|---|---|---|---|
| 1422 | A302 | 15q | gray & multi | .25 | .25 |
| 1423 | A302 | 25q | sal rose, blk & gray | .30 | .25 |
| 1424 | A302 | 1.90 l | dull yel & blk | 1.75 | .35 |
| | | | *Nos. 1422-1424 (3)* | 2.30 | .85 |

30th anniversary of the murder of Qemal Stafa and of Martyrs' Day.

Camellia — A303

Designs: Various camellias.

**1972, May 10** ***Perf. 12x12½***

**Flowers in Natural Colors**

| | | | | | |
|---|---|---|---|---|---|
| 1425 | A303 | 5q | lt blue & blk | .25 | .25 |
| 1426 | A303 | 10q | citron & blk | .25 | .25 |
| 1427 | A303 | 15q | grnsh gray & blk | .25 | .25 |
| 1428 | A303 | 25q | pale sal & blk | .25 | .25 |
| 1429 | A303 | 45q | gray & blk | .45 | .25 |
| 1430 | A303 | 50q | sal pink & blk | .85 | .25 |
| 1431 | A303 | 2.50 l | bluish gray & blk | 3.25 | .90 |
| | | | *Nos. 1425-1431 (7)* | 5.55 | 2.40 |

High Jump A304

Designs (Olympic and Motion Emblems and): 10q, Running. 15q, Shot put. 20q, Bicycling. 25q, Pole vault. 50q, Hurdles, women's. 75q, Hockey. 2 l, Swimming. 2.50 l, Diving, women's.

**1972, June 30** **Litho.** ***Perf. 12½x12***

| | | | | | |
|---|---|---|---|---|---|
| 1432 | A304 | 5q | multicolored | .25 | .25 |
| 1433 | A304 | 10q | lt brn & multi | .25 | .25 |
| 1434 | A304 | 15q | lt lil & multi | .25 | .25 |
| 1435 | A304 | 20q | multicolored | .30 | .25 |
| 1436 | A304 | 25q | lt vio & multi | .30 | .25 |
| 1437 | A304 | 50q | lt grn & multi | .50 | .25 |
| 1438 | A304 | 75q | multicolored | 1.00 | .25 |
| 1439 | A304 | 2 l | multicolored | 3.00 | .35 |
| | | | *Nos. 1432-1439 (8)* | 5.85 | 2.10 |

**Miniature Sheet**

***Imperf***

| | | | | | |
|---|---|---|---|---|---|
| 1440 | A304 | 2.50 l | multi | 3.50 | 2.50 |

20th Olympic Games, Munich, Aug. 26-Sept. 11. Nos. 1432-1439 each issued in sheets of 8 stamps and one label (3x3) showing Olympic rings in gold.

Autobus — A305

25q, Electric train. 80q, Ocean liner Tirana. 1.05 l, Automobile. 1.20 l, Trailer truck.

**1972, July 25** **Litho.** ***Perf. 12***

| | | | | | |
|---|---|---|---|---|---|
| 1441 | A305 | 15q | org brn & multi | .25 | .25 |
| 1442 | A305 | 25q | gray & multi | .35 | .25 |
| 1443 | A305 | 80q | dp grn & multi | .50 | .25 |
| 1444 | A305 | 1.05 l | multi | .70 | .25 |
| 1445 | A305 | 1.20 l | multi | 1.40 | .25 |
| | | | *Nos. 1441-1445 (5)* | 3.20 | 1.25 |

Arm Wrestling — A306

Folk Games: 10q, Piggyback ball game. 15q, Women's jumping. 25q, Rope game (srum). 90q, Leapfrog. 2 l, Women throwing pitchers.

**1972, Aug. 18**

| | | | | | |
|---|---|---|---|---|---|
| 1446 | A306 | 5q | multi | .25 | .25 |
| 1447 | A306 | 10q | lt bl & multi | .25 | .25 |
| 1448 | A306 | 15q | rose & multi | .25 | .25 |
| 1449 | A306 | 25q | lt bl & multi | .25 | .25 |
| 1450 | A306 | 90q | ocher & multi | .85 | .25 |
| 1451 | A306 | 2 l | lt grn & multi | 1.60 | .30 |
| | | | *Nos. 1446-1451 (6)* | 3.45 | 1.55 |

1st National Festival of People's Games.

Mastheads A307

30th Press Day: 25q, Printing press. 1.90 l, Workers reading paper.

**1972, Aug. 25**

| | | | | | |
|---|---|---|---|---|---|
| 1452 | A307 | 15q | lt bl & blk | .25 | .25 |
| 1453 | A307 | 25q | red, grn & blk | .25 | .25 |
| 1454 | A307 | 1.90 l | lt vio & blk | 1.40 | .40 |
| | | | *Nos. 1452-1454 (3)* | 1.90 | .90 |

Map of Peza Area, Memorial Tablet — A308

25q, Guerrillas with flag. 1.90 l, Peza Conference memorial.

**1972, Sept. 16**

| | | | | | |
|---|---|---|---|---|---|
| 1455 | A308 | 15q | shown | .25 | .25 |
| 1456 | A308 | 25q | multicolored | .35 | .25 |
| 1457 | A308 | 1.90 l | multicolored | 1.90 | .40 |
| | | | *Nos. 1455-1457 (3)* | 2.50 | .90 |

30th anniversary, Conference of Peza.

Partisans, by Sotir Capo A309

Paintings: 10q, Woman, by Ismail Lulani, vert. 15q, "Communists," by Lec Shkreli, vert. 20q, View of Nendorit, 1941, by Sali Shijaku, vert. 50q, Woman with Sheaf, by Zef Shoshi, vert. 1 l, Landscape with Children, by Dhimitraq Trebicka. 2 l, Women on Bicycles, by Vilson Kilica. 2.30 l, Folk Dance, by Abdurrahim Buza.

***Perf. 12½x12, 12x12½***

**1972, Sept. 25** **Litho.**

| | | | | | |
|---|---|---|---|---|---|
| 1458 | A309 | 5q | gold & multi | .25 | .25 |
| 1459 | A309 | 10q | gold & multi | .25 | .25 |
| 1460 | A309 | 15q | gold & multi | .25 | .25 |
| 1461 | A309 | 20q | gold & multi | .25 | .25 |
| 1462 | A309 | 50q | gold & multi | .25 | .25 |
| 1463 | A309 | 1 l | gold & multi | .70 | .25 |
| 1464 | A309 | 2 l | gold & multi | 1.75 | .40 |
| | | | *Nos. 1458-1464 (7)* | 3.70 | 1.90 |

**Miniature Sheet**

***Imperf***

| | | | | | |
|---|---|---|---|---|---|
| 1465 | A309 | 2.30 l | gold & multi | 2.75 | 1.75 |

No. 1465 contains one 41x68mm stamp.

Congress Emblem — A310

Design: 2.05 l, Young worker with banner.

**1972, Oct. 23** **Litho.** ***Perf. 12***

| | | | | | |
|---|---|---|---|---|---|
| 1466 | A310 | 25q | silver, red & gold | .50 | .25 |
| 1467 | A310 | 2.05 l | silver & multi | 1.90 | .50 |

Union of Working Youth, 6th Congress.

Hammer and Sickle — A311

Design: 1.20 l, Lenin as orator.

**1972, Nov. 7** **Litho.** ***Perf. 11½x12***

| | | | | | |
|---|---|---|---|---|---|
| 1468 | A311 | 1.10 l | multi | 1.10 | .25 |
| 1469 | A311 | 1.20 l | multi | 2.25 | .30 |

Russian October Revolution, 55th anniv.

Ismail Qemali — A312

Designs: 15q, Albanian fighters, horiz. 65q, Rally, horiz. 1.25 l, Coat of arms.

***Perf. 12x11½, 11½x12***

**1972, Nov. 29**

| | | | | | |
|---|---|---|---|---|---|
| 1470 | A312 | 15q | red, brt bl & blk | .25 | .25 |
| 1471 | A312 | 25q | yel, blk & red | .25 | .25 |
| 1472 | A312 | 65q | red, sal & blk | .50 | .25 |
| 1473 | A312 | 1.25 l | dl red & blk | 1.60 | .25 |
| | | | *Nos. 1470-1473 (4)* | 2.60 | 1.00 |

60th anniv. of independence.

Cock, Mosaic — A313

Mosaics, 2nd-5th centuries, excavated near Buthrotium and Apollonia: 10q, Bird, vert. 15q, Partridges, vert. 25q, Warrior's legs. 45q, Nymph riding dolphin, vert. 50q, Fish, vert. 2.50 l, Warrior with helmet.

**1972, Dec. 10** ***Perf. 12½x12, 12x12½***

| | | | | | |
|---|---|---|---|---|---|
| 1474 | A313 | 5q | silver & multi | .25 | .25 |
| 1475 | A313 | 10q | silver & multi | .25 | .25 |
| 1476 | A313 | 15q | silver & multi | .25 | .25 |
| 1477 | A313 | 25q | silver & multi | .25 | .25 |
| 1478 | A313 | 45q | silver & multi | .40 | .25 |
| 1479 | A313 | 50q | silver & multi | .55 | .25 |
| 1480 | A313 | 2.50 l | silver & multi | 2.10 | .80 |
| | | | *Nos. 1474-1480 (7)* | 4.05 | 2.30 |

Nicolaus Copernicus — A314

Designs: 10q, 25q, 80q, 1.20 l, Various portraits of Copernicus. 1.60 l, Heliocentric solar system.

**1973, Feb. 19** **Litho.** ***Perf. 12x12½***

| | | | | | |
|---|---|---|---|---|---|
| 1481 | A314 | 5q | lil rose & multi | .25 | .25 |
| 1482 | A314 | 10q | dull ol & multi | .25 | .25 |
| 1483 | A314 | 25q | multicolored | .25 | .25 |
| 1484 | A314 | 80q | lt violet & multi | .25 | .25 |
| 1485 | A314 | 1.20 l | blue & multi | 1.40 | .30 |
| 1486 | A314 | 1.60 l | gray & multi | 2.25 | .40 |
| | | | *Nos. 1481-1486 (6)* | 4.65 | 1.70 |

500th anniversary of the birth of Nicolaus Copernicus (1473-1543), Polish astronomer.

Flowering Cactus A315

Designs: Various flowering cacti.

**1973, Mar. 25** **Litho.** ***Perf. 12***

| | | | | | |
|---|---|---|---|---|---|
| 1487 | A315 | 10q | multicolored | .30 | .25 |
| 1488 | A315 | 15q | multicolored | .30 | .25 |
| 1489 | A315 | 20q | beige & multi | .30 | .25 |
| 1490 | A315 | 25q | gray & multi | .30 | .25 |
| 1491 | A315 | 30q | beige & multi | 4.25 | 1.50 |
| 1492 | A315 | 65q | gray & multi | 1.40 | .25 |
| 1493 | A315 | 80q | multicolored | 1.40 | .25 |
| 1494 | A315 | 2 l | multicolored | 1.75 | .60 |
| *a.* | | | Block of 8, #1487-1494 | 16.00 | 8.00 |
| | | | *Nos. 1487-1494 (8)* | 10.00 | 3.60 |

A block containing Nos. 1487-1490, 1492-1494 and a label exists.

Guard and Factories A316

1.80 l, Guard and guards with prisoner.

**1973, Mar. 20** **Litho.** ***Perf. 12½x12***

| | | | | | |
|---|---|---|---|---|---|
| 1495 | A316 | 25q | ultra & blk | .35 | .25 |
| 1496 | A316 | 1.80 l | dk red & multi | 2.00 | .40 |

30th anniv. of the State Security Branch.

Common Tern — A317

Sea Birds: 15q, White-winged black terns, vert. 25q, Black-headed gull, vert. 45q, Great black-headed gull. 80q, Slender-billed gull, vert. 2.40 l, Sandwich terns.

**1973, Apr. 30** ***Perf. 12½x12, 12x12½***

| | | | | | |
|---|---|---|---|---|---|
| 1497 | A317 | 5q | gold & multi | .25 | .25 |
| 1498 | A317 | 15q | gold & multi | .25 | .25 |
| 1499 | A317 | 25q | gold & multi | .30 | .25 |
| 1500 | A317 | 45q | gold & multi | .75 | .25 |
| 1501 | A317 | 80q | gold & multi | 1.90 | .25 |
| 1502 | A317 | 2.40 l | gold & multi | 3.75 | .55 |
| | | | *Nos. 1497-1502 (6)* | 7.20 | 1.80 |

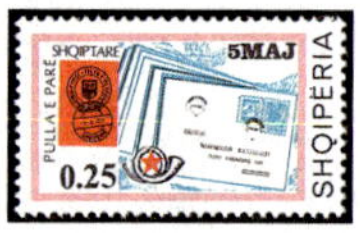


Letters, 1913 Cancellation and Post Horn — A318

Design: 1.80 l, Mailman, 1913 cancel.

**1973, May, 5** **Litho.** ***Perf. 12x11½***

| | | | | | |
|---|---|---|---|---|---|
| 1503 | A318 | 25q | red & multi | .70 | .25 |
| 1504 | A318 | 1.80 l | red & multi | 2.75 | .55 |

60th anniversary of Albanian stamps.

Farmer, Worker, Soldier — A319

Design: 25q, Woman and factory, vert.

**1973, June 4** ***Perf. 12***

| | | | | | |
|---|---|---|---|---|---|
| 1505 | A319 | 25q | carmine rose | .35 | .25 |
| 1506 | A319 | 1.80 l | yel, dp org & blk | 2.00 | .50 |

7th Congress of Albanian Women's Union.

Creation of General Staff, by G. Madhi A320

Designs: 40q, "August 1949," sculpture by Sh. Haderi, vert. 60q, "Generation after Generation," sculpture by H. Dule, vert. 80q, "Defend Revolutionary Victories," by M. Fushekati.

**1973, July 10 Litho. *Perf. 12½x12***

**1507** A320 25q gold & multi *8.00 10.00*
**1508** A320 40q gold & multi *8.00 10.00*
**1509** A320 60q gold & multi *8.00 10.00*
**1510** A320 80q gold & multi *8.00 10.00*
*Nos. 1507-1510 (4)* *32.00 40.00*

30th anniversary of the People's Army.

"Electrification," by S. Hysa — A321

Albanian Paintings: 10q, Woman Textile Worker, by N. Nallbani. 15q, Gymnasts, by M. Fushekati. 50q, Aviator, by F. Stamo. 80q, Fascist Prisoner, by A. Lakuriqi. 1.20 l, Workers with Banner, by P. Mele. 1.30 l, Farm Woman, by Zef Shoshi. 2.05 l, Battle of Tenda, by F. Haxhiu. 10q, 50q, 80q, 1.20 l, 1.30 l, vertical.

***Perf. 12½x12, 12x12½***

**1973, Aug. 10**

**1511** A321 5q gold & multi .25 .25
**1512** A321 10q gold & multi .25 .25
**1513** A321 15q gold & multi .25 .25
**1514** A321 50q gold & multi .25 .25
**1515** A321 80q gold & multi .25 .25
**1516** A321 1.20 l gold & multi 1.00 .25
**1517** A321 1.30 l gold & multi 2.00 .25
*Nos. 1511-1517 (7)* 4.25 1.75

**Souvenir Sheet**

***Imperf***

**1518** A321 2.05 l multi 2.75 1.75

Mary Magdalene, by Caravaggio — A322

Paintings by Michelangelo da Caravaggio: 10q, The Lute Player, horiz. 15q, Self-portrait. 50q, Boy Carrying Fruit and Flowers. 80q, Still Life, horiz. 1.20 l, Narcissus. 1.30 l, Boy Peeling Apple. 2.05 l, Man with Feathered Hat.

***Perf. 12x12½, 12½x12***

**1973, Sept. 28**

**1519** A322 5q gold & multi .25 .25
**1520** A322 10q gold & multi .25 .25
**1521** A322 15q gold, blk & gray .25 .25
**1522** A322 50q gold & multi .25 .25
**1523** A322 80q gold & multi .55 .25
**1524** A322 1.20 l gold & multi .70 .30
**1525** A322 1.30 l gold & multi 1.40 .30
*Nos. 1519-1525 (7)* 3.65 1.85

**Souvenir Sheet**

***Imperf***

**1526** A322 2.05 l multi 5.00 3.50

Michelangelo da Caravaggio (Merisi; 1573?-1609), Italian painter. No. 1526 contains one stamp, size: 63x73mm.

Soccer A323

Designs: 5q-1.25 l, Various soccer scenes. 2.05 l, Ball in goal and list of cities where championships were held.

**1973, Oct. 30 Litho. *Perf. 12½x12***

**1527** A323 5q multi .25 .25
**1528** A323 10q multi .25 .25
**1529** A323 15q multi .25 .25
**1530** A323 20q multi .25 .25
**1531** A323 25q multi .25 .25
**1532** A323 90q multi .40 .25
**1533** A323 1.20 l multi .80 .25
**1534** A323 1.25 l multi 1.25 .25
*Nos. 1527-1534 (8)* 3.70 2.00

**Minature Sheet**

***Imperf***

**1535** A323 2.05 l multi 3.00 2.00

World Soccer Cup, Munich 1974.

Weight Lifter — A324

Designs: Various stages of weight lifting. 1.20 l, 1.60 l, horiz.

**1973, Oct. 30 Litho. *Perf. 12***

**1536** A324 5q multi .25 .25
**1537** A324 10q multi .25 .25
**1538** A324 25q multi .25 .25
**1539** A324 90q multi .25 .25
**1540** A324 1.20 l multi .65 .25
**1541** A324 1.60 l multi 1.60 .25
*Nos. 1536-1541 (6)* 3.25 1.50

Weight Lifting Championships, Havana, Cuba.

Cement Factory, Kavaje A325

Harvester Combine A326

Skiers and Hotel — A326a

Mountain Lake — A326b

Designs: 10q, Ali Kelmendi truck factory and tank cars, horiz. 15q, Ballet. 25q, "Communication." 60q, Resort, horiz. 1 l, Mao Tse-tung textile mill. 1.20 l, Steel workers. 2.40 l, Welder and pipe. 3 l, Skanderbeg Monument, Tirana. 5 l, Roman arches, Durres.

***Perf. 12½x12, 12x12½***

**1973-74 Litho.**

**1543** A325 5q gold & multi .25 .25
**1544** A325 10q gold & multi .25 .25
**1545** A325 15q gold & multi .40 .25
**1545A** A326 20q gold & multi .25 .25
**1546** A325 25q gold & multi .25 .25
**1547** A326a 35q gold & multi .30 .25
**1548** A325 60q gold & multi .80 .25
**1549** A326b 80q gold & multi 1.40 .25
**1549A** A325 1 l gold & multi .25 .25
**1549B** A325 1.20 l gold & multi .95 .25
**1549C** A326b 2.40 l gold & multi 1.90 .35
**1550** A326b 3 l gold & multi 3.50 .35
**1551** A325 5 l gold & multi 3.50 .60
*Nos. 1543-1551 (13)* 14.00 3.80

Issue dates: Nos. 1545-1546, 1549-1550, Dec. 5, 1973; others, 1974.

Mao Tse-tung — A327

80th birthday of Mao Tse-tung: 1.20 l, Mao Tse-tung addressing crowd.

**1973, Dec. 26 *Perf. 12***

**1552** A327 85q multicolored *11.00 1.25*
**1553** A327 1.20 l multicolored *17.00 2.25*

Old Man and Dog, by Gericault — A328

Paintings by Jean Louis André Theodore Gericault: 10q, Horse's Head. 15q, Male Model. 25q, Head of Black Man. 1.20 l, Self-portrait. 2.05 l, Raft of the Medusa, horiz. 2.20 l, Battle of the Giants.

***Perf. 12x12½, 12½x12***

**1974, Jan. 18 Litho.**

**1554** A328 10q gold & multi .25 .25
**1555** A328 15q gold & multi .25 .25
**1556** A328 20q gold & multi .25 .25
**1557** A328 25q gold & blk .25 .25
**1558** A328 1.20 l gold & multi 1.40 .25
**1559** A328 2.20 l gold & multi 2.60 .40
*Nos. 1554-1559 (6)* 5.00 1.65

**Souvenir Sheet**

***Imperf***

**1560** A328 2.05 l gold & multi 3.00 1.90

No. 1560 contains one 87x78mm stamp.

Lenin, by Pandi Mele — A329

Designs: 25q, Lenin with Sailors on Cruiser Aurora, by Dhimitraq Trebicka, horiz. 1.20 l, Lenin, by Vilson Kilica.

**1974, Jan. 21 *Perf. 12½x12, 12x12½***

**1561** A329 25q gold & multi *.90 .25*
**1562** A329 60q gold & multi *2.10 .25*
**1563** A329 1.20 l gold & multi *6.00 .55*
*Nos. 1561-1563 (3)* *9.00 1.05*

50th anniv. of the death of Lenin.

Swimming Duck, Mosaic A330

Designs: Mosaics from the 5th-6th Centuries A.D., excavated near Buthrotium, Pogradec and Apollonia.

**1974, Feb. 20 Litho. *Perf. 12½x12***

**1564** A330 5q shown .25 .25
**1565** A330 10q Bird, flower .25 .25
**1566** A330 15q Vase, grapes .25 .25
**1567** A330 25q Duck .25 .25
**1568** A330 40q Donkey, bird .25 .25
**1569** A330 2.50 l Sea horse 1.25 .40
*Nos. 1564-1569 (6)* 2.50 1.65

Soccer A331

Various scenes from soccer. 2.05 l, World Soccer Cup & names of participating countries.

**1974, Apr. 25 Litho. *Perf. 12½x12***

**1570** A331 10q gold & multi .25 .25
**1571** A331 15q gold & multi .25 .25
**1572** A331 20q gold & multi .25 .25
**1573** A331 25q gold & multi .25 .25
**1574** A331 40q gold & multi .25 .25
**1575** A331 80q gold & multi .55 .25
**1576** A331 1 l gold & multi .70 .30
**1577** A331 1.20 l gold & multi 1.20 .40
*Nos. 1570-1577 (8)* 3.70 2.20

**Souvenir Sheet**

***Imperf***

**1578** A331 2.05 l gold & multi 4.00 1.75

World Cup Soccer Championship, Munich, June 13-July 7. No. 1578 contains one stamp (60x60mm) with simulated perforations. Nos. 1570-1577 exist imperf, No. 1578 with simulated perfs omitted. Values $10 and $20, respectively.

Arms of Albania, Soldier — A332

Design: 1.80 l, Soldier and front page of 1944 Congress Book.

**1974, May 24 Litho. *Perf. 12***

**1579** A332 25q multicolored .35 .25
**1580** A332 1.80 l multicolored 1.40 .30

30th anniversary of the First Anti-Fascist Liberation Congress of Permet.

Medicinal Plants — A333

10q, Bittersweet. 15q, Arbutus. 20q, Lilies of the valley. 25q, Autumn crocus. 40q, Borage, horiz. 80q, Soapwort, horiz. 2.20 l, Gentian, horiz.

**1974, May 5 *Perf. 12x12½***

**1581** A333 10q multicolored .25 .25
**1582** A333 15q multicolored .25 .25
**1583** A333 20q multicolored .25 .25
**1584** A333 25q multicolored .25 .25
**1585** A333 40q multicolored .45 .25
**1586** A333 80q multicolored .85 .25
**1587** A333 2.20 l multicolored 2.50 .45
*Nos. 1581-1587 (7)* 4.80 1.95

Revolutionaries with Albanian Flag — A334

1.80 l, Portraits of 5 revolutionaries, vert.

***Perf. 12½x12, 12x12½***

**1974, June 10**

**1588** A334 25q red, blk & lil .35 .25
**1589** A334 1.80 l yel, red & blk 1.40 .45

50th anniversary Albanian Bourgeois Democratic Revolution.

European Redwing A335

Designs: Songbirds; Nos. 1597-1600 vert.

***Perf. 12½x12, 12x12½***

**1974, July 15 Litho.**

**1594** A335 10q shown .25 .25
**1595** A335 15q European robin .25 .25
**1596** A335 20q Greenfinch .25 .25
**1597** A335 25q Bullfinch .25 .25
**1598** A335 40q Hawfinch .35 .25
**1599** A335 80q Blackcap 1.40 .25
**1600** A335 2.20 l Nightingale 2.75 .50
*Nos. 1594-1600 (7)* 5.50 2.00

# 378 ALBANIA

Globe — A336

Cent. of UPU: 1.20 l, UPU emblem. 2.05 l, Jet over globe.

**1974, Aug. 25    Litho.    Perf. 12x12½**
| 1601 | A336 | 85q grn & multi | 1.20 | .25 |
| 1602 | A336 | 1.20 l vio & ol grn | 1.75 | .25 |

**Miniature Sheet**
*Imperf*
| 1603 | A336 | 2.05 l blue & multi | 15.00 | 25.00 |

Widows, by Sali Shijaku A337

Albanian Paintings: 15q, Drillers, by Danish Jukniu, vert. 20q, Workers with Blueprints, by Clirim Ceka. 25q, Call to Action, by Spiro Kristo, vert. 40q, Winter Battle, by Sabaudin Xhaferi. 80q, Comrades, by Clirim Ceka, vert. 1 l, Aiding the Partisans, by Guri Madhi. 1.20 l, Teacher with Pupils, by Kleo Nini Brezat. 2.05 l, Comrades in Arms, by Guri Madhi.

**Perf. 12½x12, 12x12½**
**1974, Sept. 25**
| 1604 | A337 | 10q silver & multi | .25 | .25 |
| 1605 | A337 | 15q silver & multi | .25 | .25 |
| 1606 | A337 | 20q silver & multi | .25 | .25 |
| 1607 | A337 | 25q silver & multi | .25 | .25 |
| 1608 | A337 | 40q silver & multi | .30 | .25 |
| 1609 | A337 | 80q silver & multi | .70 | .25 |
| 1610 | A337 | 1 l silver & multi | 1.00 | .25 |
| 1611 | A337 | 1.20 l silver & multi | 1.40 | .25 |
| | | Nos. 1604-1611 (8) | 4.40 | 2.00 |

**Miniature Sheet**
*Imperf*
| 1612 | A337 | 2.05 l silver & multi | 2.75 | 1.75 |

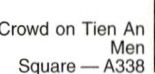

Crowd on Tien An Men Square — A338

Design: 1.20 l, Mao Tse-tung, vert.

**1974, Oct. 1    Perf. 12**
| 1613 | A338 | 85q gold & multi | 6.00 | 1.50 |
| 1614 | A338 | 1.20 l gold & multi | 9.50 | 2.50 |

25th anniversary of the proclamation of the People's Republic of China.

Women's Volleyball — A339

Spartakiad Medal and: 15q, Women hurdlers. 20q, Women gymnasts. 25q, Mass exercises in Stadium. 40q, Weight lifter. 80q, Wrestlers. 1 l, Military rifle drill. 1.20 l, Soccer.

**1974, Oct. 9    Perf. 12x12½**
| 1615 | A339 | 10q multi | .25 | .25 |
| 1616 | A339 | 15q multi | .25 | .25 |
| 1617 | A339 | 20q multi | .25 | .25 |
| 1618 | A339 | 25q gray & multi | .25 | .25 |
| 1619 | A339 | 40q multi | .25 | .25 |
| 1620 | A339 | 80q multi | .35 | .25 |
| 1621 | A339 | 1 l multi | .70 | .25 |
| 1622 | A339 | 1.20 l tan & multi | 1.00 | .25 |
| | | Nos. 1615-1622 (8) | 3.30 | 2.00 |

National Spartakiad, Oct. 9-17.

View of Berat — A340

Designs: 80q, Enver Hoxha addressing Congress, bas-relief, horiz. 1 l, Hoxha and leaders leaving Congress Hall.

**Perf. 12x12½, 12½x12**
**1974, Oct. 20    Litho.**
| 1623 | A340 | 25q rose car & blk | .35 | .25 |
| 1624 | A340 | 80q yel, brn & blk | 1.00 | .25 |
| 1625 | A340 | 1 l dp lilac & blk | 2.00 | .30 |
| | | Nos. 1623-1625 (3) | 3.35 | .80 |

30th anniversary of 2nd Congress of Berat.

Anniversary Emblem, Factory Guards A341

35q, Chemical industry. 50q, Agriculture. 80q, Arts. 1 l, Atomic diagram & computer. 1.20 l, Youth education. 2.05 l, Crowd & History Book.

**1974, Nov. 29    Litho.    Perf. 12½x12**
| 1626 | A341 | 25q green & multi | .25 | .25 |
| 1627 | A341 | 35q ultra & multi | .25 | .25 |
| 1628 | A341 | 50q brown & multi | .25 | .25 |
| 1629 | A341 | 80q multicolored | .35 | .25 |
| 1630 | A341 | 1 l violet & multi | .85 | .25 |
| 1631 | A341 | 1.20 l multicolored | 1.00 | .30 |
| | | Nos. 1626-1631 (6) | 2.95 | 1.55 |

**Miniature Sheet**
*Imperf*
| 1632 | A341 | 2.05 l gold & multi | 2.75 | 1.50 |

30th anniv. of liberation from Fascism.

Artemis, from Apolloni — A342

**1974, Dec. 25    Photo.    Perf. 12x12½**
| 1633 | A342 | 10q shown | .25 | .25 |
| 1634 | A342 | 15q Zeus statue | .25 | .25 |
| 1635 | A342 | 20q Poseidon statue | .30 | .25 |
| 1636 | A342 | 25q Illyrian helmet | .35 | .25 |
| 1637 | A342 | 40q Amphora | .70 | .25 |
| 1638 | A342 | 80q Agrippa | 1.00 | .25 |
| 1639 | A342 | 1 l Demosthenes | 1.40 | .30 |
| 1640 | A342 | 1.20 l Head of Bilia | 2.00 | .35 |
| | | Nos. 1633-1640 (8) | 6.25 | 2.15 |

**Miniature Sheet**
*Imperf*
| 1641 | A342 | 2.05 l Artemis & amphora | 3.50 | 2.10 |

Archaeological discoveries in Albania.

Workers and Factories — A343

25q, Handshake, tools and book, vert.

**1975, Feb. 11    Litho.    Perf. 12**
| 1642 | A343 | 25q brown & multi | .35 | .25 |
| 1643 | A343 | 1.80 l yellow & multi | 1.40 | .35 |

Albanian Trade Unions, 30th anniversary.

Chicory — A344

**1975, Feb. 15**
| 1644 | A344 | 5q shown | .25 | .25 |
| 1645 | A344 | 10q Houseleek | .25 | .25 |
| 1646 | A344 | 15q Columbine | .25 | .25 |
| 1647 | A344 | 20q Anemone | .25 | .25 |
| 1648 | A344 | 25q Hibiscus | .25 | .25 |
| 1649 | A344 | 30q Gentian | .35 | .25 |
| 1650 | A344 | 35q Hollyhock | .35 | .25 |
| 1651 | A344 | 2.70 l Iris | 1.10 | .45 |
| | | Nos. 1644-1651 (8) | 3.05 | 2.20 |

Protected flowers.

Jesus, from Doni Madonna — A345

Works by Michelangelo: 10q, Slave, sculpture. 15q, Head of Dawn, sculpture. 20q, Awakening Giant, sculpture. 25q, Cumaenian Sybil, Sistine Chapel. 30q, Lorenzo di Medici, sculpture. 1.20 l, David, sculpture. 2.05 l, Self-portrait. 3.90 l, Delphic Sybil, Sistine Chapel.

**1975, Mar. 20    Litho.    Perf. 12x12½**
| 1652 | A345 | 5q gold & multi | .25 | .25 |
| 1653 | A345 | 10q gold & multi | .25 | .25 |
| 1654 | A345 | 15q gold & multi | .25 | .25 |
| 1655 | A345 | 20q gold & multi | .25 | .25 |
| 1656 | A345 | 25q gold & multi | .25 | .25 |
| 1657 | A345 | 30q gold & multi | .25 | .25 |
| 1658 | A345 | 1.20 l gold & multi | .55 | .25 |
| 1659 | A345 | 3.90 l gold & multi | 1.60 | .50 |
| | | Nos. 1652-1659 (8) | 3.65 | 2.25 |

**Miniature Sheet**
*Imperf*
| 1660 | A345 | 2.05 l gold & multi | 3.50 | 2.00 |

Michelangelo Buonarroti (1475-1564), Italian sculptor, painter and architect.

Two-wheeled Cart — A346

Albanian Transportation of the Past: 5q, Horseback rider. 15q, Lake ferry. 20q, Coastal three-master. 25q, Phaeton. 3.35 l, Early automobile on bridge.

**1975, Apr. 15    Litho.    Perf. 12½x12**
| 1661 | A346 | 5q bl grn & multi | .25 | .25 |
| 1662 | A346 | 10q ol & multi | .25 | .25 |
| 1663 | A346 | 15q lil & multi | .25 | .25 |
| 1664 | A346 | 20q multi | .25 | .25 |
| 1665 | A346 | 25q multi | .25 | .25 |
| 1666 | A346 | 3.35 l ocher & multi | 1.90 | .50 |
| | | Nos. 1661-1666 (6) | 3.15 | 1.75 |

Guard at Frontier Stone — A347

Guardsman and Militia — A348

**1975, Apr. 25    Perf. 12**
| 1667 | A347 | 25q multi | .30 | .25 |
| 1668 | A348 | 1.80 l multi | 1.25 | .35 |

30th anniversary of Frontier Guards.

Posting Illegal Poster A349

Designs: 60q, Partisans in battle. 1.20 l, Partisan killing German soldier, and Albanian coat of arms.

**1975, May 9    Perf. 12½x12**
| 1669 | A349 | 25q multi | .25 | .25 |
| 1670 | A349 | 60q multi | .50 | .25 |
| 1671 | A349 | 1.20 l red & multi | 1.00 | .30 |
| | | Nos. 1669-1671 (3) | 1.75 | .80 |

30th anniversary of victory over Fascism.

European Widgeons A350

Waterfowl: 5q, Anas penelope. 10q, Netta rufina. 15q, Anser albifrons. 20q, Anas acuta. 25q, Mergus serrator. 30q, Pata somateria. 35q, Cignus cignus. 2.70 l, Spatula clypeata.

**1975, June 15    Litho.    Perf. 12**
| 1672 | A350 | 5q brt blue & multi | .25 | .25 |
| 1673 | A350 | 10q yel grn & multi | .25 | .25 |
| 1674 | A350 | 15q brt rose lil & multi | .25 | .25 |
| 1675 | A350 | 20q bl grn & multi | .25 | .25 |
| 1676 | A350 | 25q multicolored | .25 | .25 |
| 1677 | A350 | 30q multicolored | .30 | .25 |
| 1678 | A350 | 35q orange & multi | .45 | .25 |
| 1679 | A350 | 2.70 l multi | 2.75 | .90 |
| | | Nos. 1672-1679 (8) | 4.75 | 2.65 |

Shyqyri Kanapari, by Musa Qarri — A351

Albanian Paintings: 10q, Woman Saving Children in Sea, by Agim Faja. 15q, "November 28, 1912" (revolution), by Petrit Ceno, horiz. 20q, "Workers Unite," by Sali Shijaku. 25q, The Partisan Shota Galica, by Ismail Lulani. 30q, Victorious Resistance Fighters, 1943, by Nestor Jonuzi. 80q, Partisan Couple in Front of Red Flag, by Vilson Halimi. 2.05 l, Dancing Procession, by Abdurahim Buza. 2.25 l, Republic Day Celebration, by Fatmir Haxhiu, horiz.

**Perf. 12x12½, 12½x12**
**1975, July 15    Litho.**
| 1680 | A351 | 5q gold & multi | .25 | .25 |
| 1681 | A351 | 10q gold & multi | .25 | .25 |
| 1682 | A351 | 15q gold & multi | .25 | .25 |
| 1683 | A351 | 20q gold & multi | .25 | .25 |
| 1684 | A351 | 25q gold & multi | .25 | .25 |
| 1685 | A351 | 30q gold & multi | .25 | .25 |
| 1686 | A351 | 80q gold & multi | .30 | .25 |
| 1687 | A351 | 2.25 l gold & multi | 1.40 | .45 |
| | | Nos. 1680-1687 (8) | 3.20 | 2.20 |

**Miniature Sheet**
*Imperf*
| 1688 | A351 | 2.05 l gold & multi | 2.50 | 1.75 |

Nos. 1680-1687 issued in sheets of 8 stamps and gold center label showing palette and easel.

Farmer Holding Reform Law — A352

Design: 2 l, Produce and farm machinery.

**1975, Aug. 28** *Perf. 12*

| | | | | | |
|---|---|---|---|---|---|
| **1689** | A352 | 15q | multicolored | .40 | .25 |
| **1690** | A352 | 2 l | multicolored | 2.00 | .50 |

Agrarian reform, 30th anniversary.

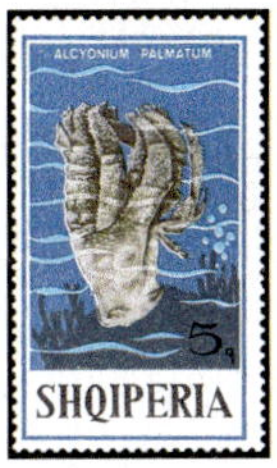

Alcyonium Palmatum — A353

Corals: 10q, Paramuricea chamaeleon. 20q, Coralium rubrum. 25q, Eunicella covalini. 3.70 l, Cladocora cespitosa.

**1975, Sept. 25** **Litho.** *Perf. 12*

| | | | | | |
|---|---|---|---|---|---|
| **1691** | A353 | 5q | blue, ol & blk | .30 | .25 |
| **1692** | A353 | 10q | blue & multi | .30 | .25 |
| **1693** | A353 | 20q | blue & multi | .30 | .25 |
| **1694** | A353 | 25q | blue & blk | .30 | .25 |
| **1695** | A353 | 3.70 l | blue & blk | 3.00 | .80 |
| | | | *Nos. 1691-1695 (5)* | 4.20 | 1.80 |

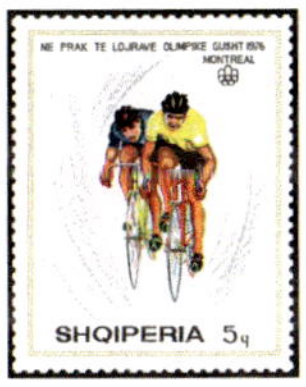

Bicycling — A354

Designs (Montreal Olympic Games Emblem and): 10q, Canoeing. 15q, Fieldball. 20q, Basketball. 25q, Water polo. 30q, Hockey. 1.20 l, Pole vault. 2.05 l, Fencing. 2.15 l, Montreal Olympic Games emblem and various sports.

**1975, Oct. 20** **Litho.** *Perf. 12½*

| | | | | | |
|---|---|---|---|---|---|
| **1696** | A354 | 5q | multi | .25 | .25 |
| **1697** | A354 | 10q | multi | .25 | .25 |
| **1698** | A354 | 15q | multi | .25 | .25 |
| **1699** | A354 | 20q | multi | .40 | .25 |
| **1700** | A354 | 25q | multi | .45 | .25 |
| **1701** | A354 | 30q | multi | .55 | .25 |
| **1702** | A354 | 1.20 l | multi | 1.50 | .30 |
| **1703** | A354 | 2.05 l | multi | 2.75 | .45 |
| | | | *Nos. 1696-1703 (8)* | 6.40 | 2.25 |

**Miniature Sheet**

***Imperf***

| | | | | | |
|---|---|---|---|---|---|
| **1704** | A354 | 2.15 l | org & multi | 4.00 | 4.00 |

21st Olympic Games, Montreal, July 18-Aug. 8, 1976. Nos. 1696-1703 exist imperf. Value $10.

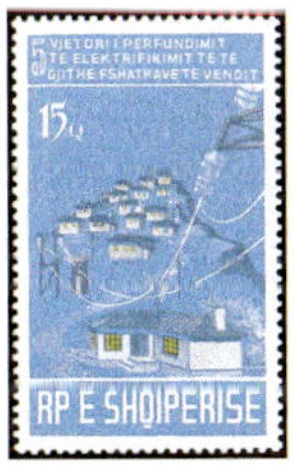

Power Lines Leading to Village — A355

Designs: 25q, Transformers and insulators. 80q, Dam and power station. 85q, Television set, power lines, grain and cogwheel.

**1975, Oct. 25** *Perf. 12x12½*

| | | | | | |
|---|---|---|---|---|---|
| **1705** | A355 | 15q | ultra & yel | .25 | .25 |
| **1706** | A355 | 25q | brt vio & pink | .25 | .25 |
| **1707** | A355 | 80q | lt grn & gray | .60 | .25 |
| **1708** | A355 | 85q | ocher & brn | 1.40 | .45 |
| | | | *Nos. 1705-1708 (4)* | 2.50 | 1.20 |

General electrification, 5th anniversary.

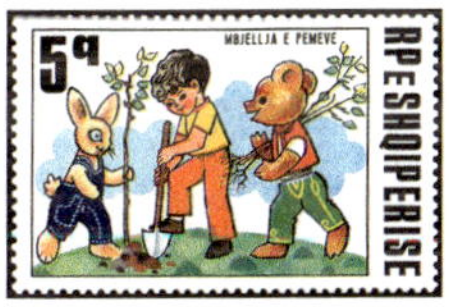

Child, Rabbit and Teddy Bear Planting Tree A356

Fairy Tales: 10q, Mother fox. 15q, Ducks in school. 20q, Little pigs building house. 25q, Animals watching television. 30q, Rabbit and bear at work. 35q, Working and playing ants. 2.70 l, Wolf in sheep's clothes.

**1975, Dec. 25** **Litho.** *Perf. 12½x12*

| | | | | | |
|---|---|---|---|---|---|
| **1709** | A356 | 5q | black & multi | .25 | .25 |
| **1710** | A356 | 10q | black & multi | .25 | .25 |
| **1711** | A356 | 15q | black & multi | .25 | .25 |
| **1712** | A356 | 20q | black & multi | .30 | .25 |
| **1713** | A356 | 25q | black & multi | .40 | .25 |
| **1714** | A356 | 30q | black & multi | .50 | .25 |
| **1715** | A356 | 35q | black & multi | .55 | .25 |
| **1716** | A356 | 2.70 l | black & multi | 3.00 | .75 |
| | | | *Nos. 1709-1716 (8)* | 5.50 | 2.50 |

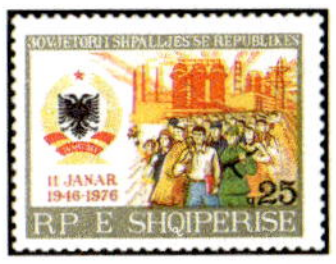

Arms, People, Factories — A357

Design: 1.90 l, Arms, government building, celebrating crowd.

**1976, Jan. 11** **Litho.** *Perf. 12*

| | | | | | |
|---|---|---|---|---|---|
| **1717** | A357 | 25q | gold & multi | .35 | .25 |
| **1718** | A357 | 1.90 l | gold & multi | 2.25 | .35 |

30th anniversary of proclamation of Albanian People's Republic.

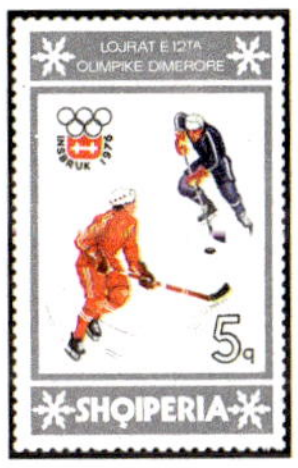

Ice Hockey, Olympic Games' Emblem — A358

Designs: 10q, Speed skating. 15q, Biathlon. 50q, Ski jump. 1.20 l, Slalom. 2.15 l, Figure skating, pairs. 2.30 l, One-man bobsled.

**1976, Feb. 4**

| | | | | | |
|---|---|---|---|---|---|
| **1719** | A358 | 5q | silver & multi | .25 | .25 |
| **1720** | A358 | 10q | silver & multi | .25 | .25 |
| **1721** | A358 | 15q | silver & multi | .25 | .25 |
| **1722** | A358 | 50q | silver & multi | .25 | .25 |
| **1723** | A358 | 1.20 l | silver & multi | .75 | .25 |
| **1724** | A358 | 2.30 l | silver & multi | 1.00 | .40 |
| | | | *Nos. 1719-1724 (6)* | 2.75 | 1.65 |

**Miniature Sheet**

***Perf. 12 on 2 sides x Imperf.***

| | | | | | |
|---|---|---|---|---|---|
| **1725** | A358 | 2.15 l | silver & multi | 2.50 | 2.00 |

12th Winter Olympic Games, Innsbruck, Austria, Feb. 4-15.

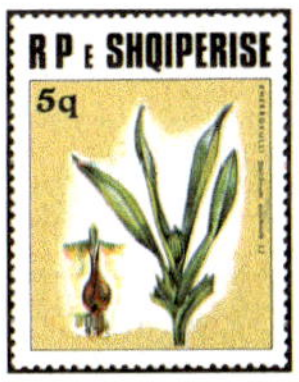

Meadow Saffron — A359

Medicinal Plants: 10q, Deadly night-shade. 15q, Yellow gentian. 20q, Horse chestnut. 70q, Shield fern. 80q, Marshmallow. 2.30 l, Thorn apple.

**1976, Apr. 10** **Litho.** *Perf. 12x12½*

| | | | | | |
|---|---|---|---|---|---|
| **1726** | A359 | 5q | black & multi | .25 | .25 |
| **1727** | A359 | 10q | black & multi | .25 | .25 |
| **1728** | A359 | 15q | black & multi | .25 | .25 |
| **1729** | A359 | 20q | black & multi | .25 | .25 |
| **1730** | A359 | 70q | black & multi | .35 | .25 |
| **1731** | A359 | 80q | black & multi | .60 | .25 |
| **1732** | A359 | 2.30 l | black & multi | 1.75 | .35 |
| | | | *Nos. 1726-1732 (7)* | 3.70 | 1.85 |

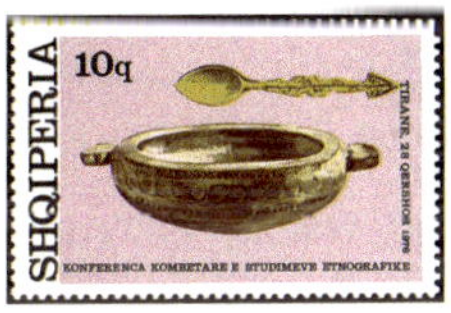

Bowl and Spoon A360

15q, Flask, vert. 20q, Carved handles, vert. 25q, Pistol and dagger. 80q, Wall hanging, vert. 1.20 l, Earrings and belt buckle. 1.40 l, Jugs, vert.

**1976** **Litho.** *Perf. 12½x12, 12x12½*

| | | | | | |
|---|---|---|---|---|---|
| **1733** | A360 | 10q | lilac & multi | .25 | .25 |
| **1734** | A360 | 15q | gray & multi | .25 | .25 |
| **1735** | A360 | 20q | multi | .25 | .25 |
| **1736** | A360 | 25q | car & multi | .25 | .25 |
| **1737** | A360 | 80q | yellow & multi | .25 | .25 |
| **1738** | A360 | 1.20 l | multi | .75 | .30 |
| **1739** | A360 | 1.40 l | tan & multi | 1.50 | .40 |
| | | | *Nos. 1733-1739 (7)* | 3.50 | 1.95 |

Natl. Ethnographic Conf., Tirana, June 28.
For surcharge see No. 1873.

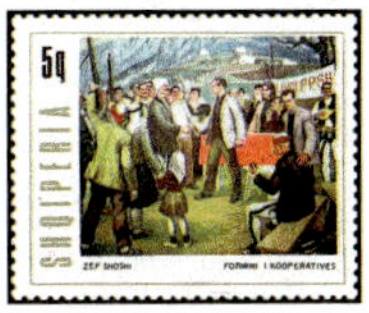

Founding of Cooperatives, by Zef Shoshi — A361

Paintings: 10q, Going to Work, by Agim Zajmi, vert. 25q, Crowd Listening to Loudspeaker, by Vilson Kilica. 40q, Woman Welder, by Sabaudin Xhaferi, vert. 50q, Factory, by Isuf Sulovari, vert. 1.20 l, 1942 Revolt, by Lec Shkreli, vert. 1.60 l, Coming Home from Work, by Agron Dine. 2.05 l, Honoring a Young Pioneer, by Andon Lakuriqi.

***Perf. 12½x12, 12x12½***

**1976, Aug. 8** **Litho.**

| | | | | | |
|---|---|---|---|---|---|
| **1740** | A361 | 5q | gold & multi | .25 | .25 |
| **1741** | A361 | 10q | gold & multi | .25 | .25 |
| **1742** | A361 | 25q | gold & multi | .25 | .25 |
| **1743** | A361 | 40q | gold & multi | .25 | .25 |
| **1744** | A361 | 50q | gold & multi | .25 | .25 |
| **1745** | A361 | 1.20 l | gold & multi | .75 | .55 |
| **1746** | A361 | 1.60 l | gold & multi | 1.00 | .85 |
| | | | *Nos. 1740-1746 (7)* | 3.00 | 2.65 |

**Miniature Sheet**

***Perf. 12 on 2 sides x Imperf.***

| | | | | | |
|---|---|---|---|---|---|
| **1747** | A361 | 2.05 l | gold & multi | 2.50 | 1.50 |

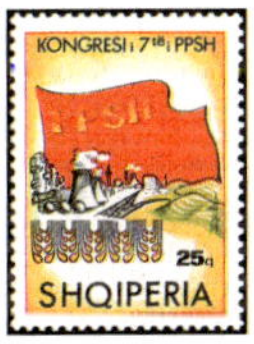

Red Flag, Agricultural Symbols — A362

Design: 1.20 l, Red flag and raised pickax.

**1976, Nov. 1**

| | | | | | |
|---|---|---|---|---|---|
| **1748** | A362 | 25q | multi | .30 | .25 |
| **1749** | A362 | 1.20 l | multi | 1.75 | .50 |

7th Workers Party Congress.

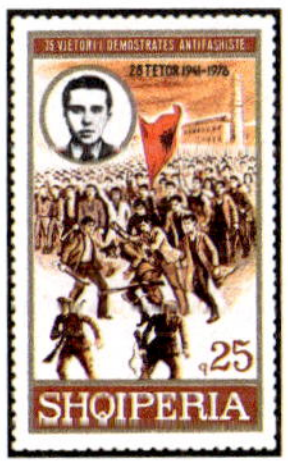

Enver Hoxha, Partisans and Albanian Flag — A363

1.90 l, Demonstrators with Albanian flag.

**1976, Oct. 28** *Perf. 12x12½*

| | | | | | |
|---|---|---|---|---|---|
| **1750** | A363 | 25q | multi | .40 | .25 |
| **1751** | A363 | 1.90 l | multi | 1.60 | .65 |

Anti-Fascist demonstrations, 35th anniv.

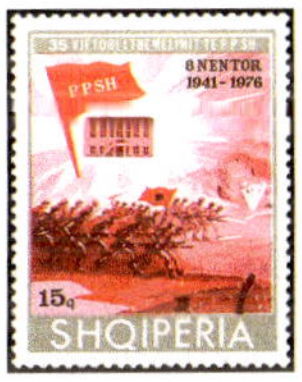

Attacking Partisans, Meeting House — A364

Designs (Red Flag and): 25q, Partisans, pickax and gun. 80q, Workers, soldiers, pickax and gun. 1.20 l, Agriculture and industry. 1.70 l, Dancers, symbols of science and art.

**1976, Nov. 8** **Litho.** *Perf. 12x12½*

| | | | | | |
|---|---|---|---|---|---|
| **1752** | A364 | 15q | gold & multi | .25 | .25 |
| **1753** | A364 | 25q | gold & multi | .25 | .25 |
| **1754** | A364 | 80q | gold & multi | .70 | .25 |
| **1755** | A364 | 1.20 l | gold & multi | 1.00 | .25 |
| **1756** | A364 | 1.70 l | gold & multi | 1.40 | .25 |
| | | | *Nos. 1752-1756 (5)* | 3.60 | 1.25 |

35th anniv. of 1st Workers Party Congress.

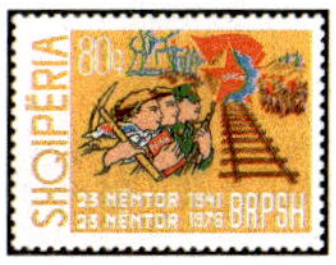

Young Workers and Track — A365

1.25 l, Young soldiers and Albanian flag.

**1976, Nov. 23** *Perf. 12*

| | | | | | |
|---|---|---|---|---|---|
| **1757** | A365 | 80q | yellow & multi | *1.25* | *.35* |
| **1758** | A365 | 1.25 l | carmine & multi | *2.25* | *.50* |

Union of Young Communists, 35th anniv.

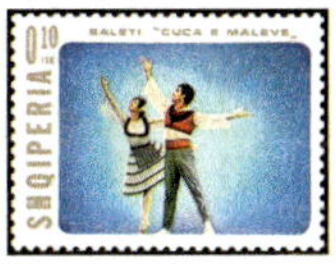

"Cuca e Maleve" Ballet — A366

Scenes from ballet "Mountain Girl."

**1976, Dec. 14** *Perf. 12*

| | | | | | |
|---|---|---|---|---|---|
| **1759** | A366 | 10q | gold & multi | .25 | *.50* |
| **1760** | A366 | 15q | gold & multi | .25 | *.50* |
| **1761** | A366 | 20q | gold & multi | .25 | *1.00* |
| **1762** | A366 | 25q | gold & multi | .30 | *2.00* |
| **1763** | A366 | 80q | gold & multi | .85 | *3.00* |
| **1764** | A366 | 1.20 l | gold & multi | 1.00 | *4.00* |
| **1765** | A366 | 1.40 l | gold & multi | 1.40 | *4.00* |
| | | | *Nos. 1759-1765 (7)* | 4.30 | *15.00* |

**Miniature Sheet**

***Perf. 12 on 2 sides x Imperf.***

| | | | | | |
|---|---|---|---|---|---|
| **1766** | A366 | 2.05 l | gold & multi | 3.25 | 2.75 |

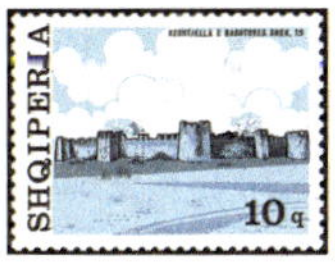

Bashtove Castle — A367

Albanian Castles: 15q, Gjirokaster. 20q, Ali Pash Tepelene. 25q, Petrele. 80q, Berat. 1.20 l, Durres. 1.40 l, Kruje.

**1976, Dec. 30** **Litho.** *Perf. 12*

| | | | | | |
|---|---|---|---|---|---|
| **1767** | A367 | 10q | black & dull bl | .25 | .25 |
| **1768** | A367 | 15q | black & grn | .25 | .25 |
| **1769** | A367 | 20q | black & gray | .25 | .25 |
| **1770** | A367 | 25q | black & brn | .25 | .25 |
| **1771** | A367 | 80q | black & rose | .80 | .35 |
| **1772** | A367 | 1.20 l | black & vio | 1.00 | .50 |
| **1773** | A367 | 1.40 l | black & brn red | 1.50 | .55 |
| | | | *Nos. 1767-1773 (7)* | 4.30 | 2.40 |

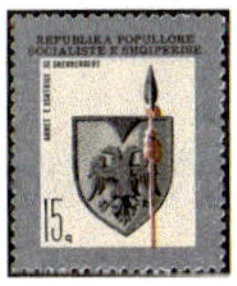

Skanderbeg's Shield and Spear — A368

Skanderbeg's Weapons: 80q, Helmet, sword and scabbard. 1 l, Halberd, quiver with arrows, crossbow and spear.

**1977, Jan. 28** **Litho.** *Perf. 12*

| | | | | | |
|---|---|---|---|---|---|
| **1774** | A368 | 15q | silver & multi | 1.25 | .40 |
| **1775** | A368 | 80q | silver & multi | 4.25 | 2.50 |
| **1776** | A368 | 1 l | silver & multi | 6.50 | 5.00 |
| | | | *Nos. 1774-1776 (3)* | 12.00 | 7.90 |

Skanderbeg (1403-1468), national hero.

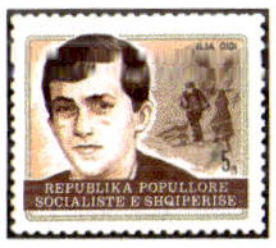

Ilia Qiqi, Messenger in Storm — A369

Modern Heroes: 10q, Ilia Dashi, sailor in battle. 25q, Fran Ndue Ivanaj, fisherman in storm. 80q, Zeliha Allmetaj, woman rescuing child. 1 l, Ylli Zaimi, rescuing goats from flood. 1.90 l, Isuf Plloci, fighting forest fire.

**1977, Feb. 28** **Litho.** *Perf. 12x12½*

| | | | | | |
|---|---|---|---|---|---|
| **1777** | A369 | 5q | brown & multi | .25 | .25 |
| **1778** | A369 | 10q | ultra & multi | .25 | .25 |
| **1779** | A369 | 25q | blue & multi | .40 | .25 |
| **1780** | A369 | 80q | ocher & multi | .90 | .35 |

| | | | | | |
|---|---|---|---|---|---|
| **1781** | A369 | 1 l | brown & multi | 1.25 | .45 |
| **1782** | A369 | 1.90 l | brown & multi | 2.60 | 1.40 |
| | | | *Nos. 1777-1782 (6)* | 5.65 | 2.95 |

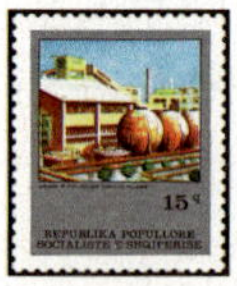

Polyvinylchloride Plant, Vlore — A370

6th Five-year plan: 25q, Naphtha fractioning plant, Ballsh. 65q, Hydroelectric station and dam, Fjerzes. 1 l, Metallurgical plant and blast furance, Elbasan.

**1977, Mar. 29 Litho. *Perf. 12½x12***

| | | | | | |
|---|---|---|---|---|---|
| **1783** | A370 | 15q | silver & multi | .35 | .25 |
| **1784** | A370 | 25q | silver & multi | .40 | .25 |
| **1785** | A370 | 65q | silver & multi | 1.10 | .35 |
| **1786** | A370 | 1 l | silver & multi | 1.60 | .65 |
| | | | *Nos. 1783-1786 (4)* | 3.45 | 1.50 |

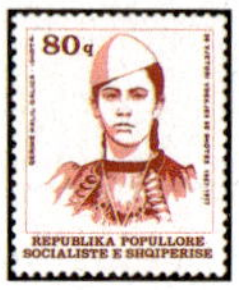

Qerime Halil Galica — A371

Design: 1.25 l, Qerime Halil Galica "Shota" and father Azem Galica.

**1977, Apr. 20 Litho. *Perf. 12***

| | | | | | |
|---|---|---|---|---|---|
| **1787** | A371 | 80q | dark red | 1.10 | .30 |
| **1788** | A371 | 1.25 l | gray blue | 1.60 | .70 |

"Shota" Galica, communist fighter.

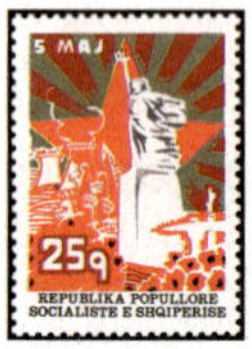

Victory Monument, Tirana — A372

Red Star and: 80q, Clenched fist, Albanian flag. 1.20 l, Bust of Qemal Stafa, poppies.

**1977, May 5 Litho. *Perf. 12***

| | | | | | |
|---|---|---|---|---|---|
| **1789** | A372 | 25q | multi | .35 | .25 |
| **1790** | A372 | 80q | multi | 1.25 | .45 |
| **1791** | A372 | 1.20 l | multi | 2.00 | .85 |
| | | | *Nos. 1789-1791 (3)* | 3.60 | 1.55 |

35th anniversary of Martyrs' Day.

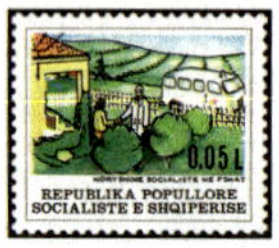

Physician Visiting Farm, Mobile Clinic — A373

10q, Cowherd, cattle ranch. 20q, Militia woman helping with harvest, rifle, combine. 80q, Modern village, highway, power lines. 2.95 l, Tractor, greenhouses.

**1977, June 18**

| | | | | | |
|---|---|---|---|---|---|
| **1792** | A373 | 5q | multi | .25 | .25 |
| **1793** | A373 | 10q | multi | .25 | .25 |
| **1794** | A373 | 20q | multi | .30 | .25 |
| **1795** | A373 | 80q | multi | 1.00 | .25 |
| **1796** | A373 | 2.95 l | multi | 3.50 | .75 |
| | | | *Nos. 1792-1796 (5)* | 5.30 | 1.75 |

"Socialist transformation of the villages."

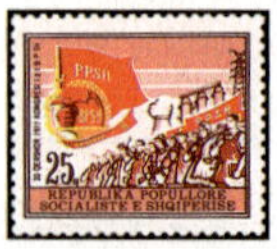

Armed Workers, Flag and Factory — A374

1.80 l, Workers with proclamation and flags.

**1977, June 20**

| | | | | | |
|---|---|---|---|---|---|
| **1797** | A374 | 25q | multi | 1.00 | .25 |
| **1798** | A374 | 1.80 l | multi | 1.50 | .80 |

9th Labor Unions Congress.

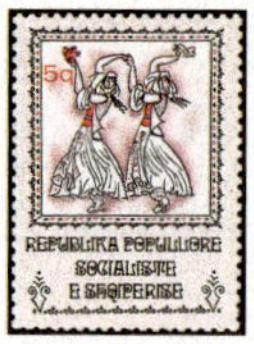

Kerchief Dance — A375

Designs: Various folk dances.

**1977, Aug. 20 Litho. *Perf. 12***

| | | | | | |
|---|---|---|---|---|---|
| **1799** | A375 | 5q | multi | .25 | .25 |
| **1800** | A375 | 10q | multi | .25 | .25 |
| **1801** | A375 | 15q | multi | .25 | .25 |
| **1802** | A375 | 25q | multi | .25 | .25 |
| **1803** | A375 | 80q | multi | .25 | .25 |
| **1804** | A375 | 1.20 l | multi | .70 | .35 |
| **1805** | A375 | 1.55 l | multi | 1.00 | .45 |
| | | | *Nos. 1799-1805 (7)* | 2.95 | 2.05 |

**Miniature Sheet**

***Perf. 12 on 2 sides x Imperf.***

| | | | | | |
|---|---|---|---|---|---|
| **1806** | A375 | 2.05 l | multi | 3.50 | 2.00 |

See Nos. 1836-1840, 1884-1888.

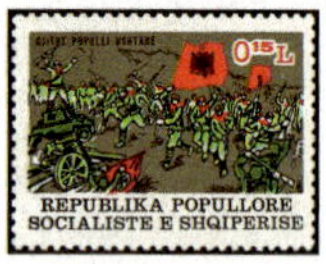

Attack — A376

Designs: 25q, Enver Hoxha addressing Army. 80q, Volunteers and riflemen. 1 l, Volunteers, hydrofoil patrolboat and MiG planes. 1.90 l, Volunteers and Albanian flag.

**1977, July 10 Litho. *Perf. 12***

| | | | | | |
|---|---|---|---|---|---|
| **1807** | A376 | 15q | gold & multi | .30 | .25 |
| **1808** | A376 | 25q | gold & multi | .30 | .25 |
| **1809** | A376 | 80q | gold & multi | .90 | .35 |
| **1810** | A376 | 1 l | gold & multi | 1.50 | .50 |
| **1811** | A376 | 1.90 l | gold & multi | 2.50 | .90 |
| | | | *Nos. 1807-1811 (5)* | 5.50 | 2.25 |

"One People-One Army."

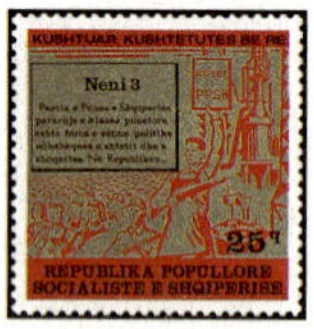

Armed Workers, Article 3 of Constitution A377

Design: 1.20 l, Symbols of farming and fertilizer industry, Article 25 of Constitution.

**1977, Oct.**

| | | | | | |
|---|---|---|---|---|---|
| **1812** | A377 | 25q | red, gold & blk | .40 | .25 |
| **1813** | A377 | 1.20 l | red, gold & blk | 1.50 | .50 |

New Constitution.

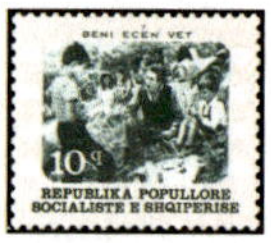

Picnic — A378

Film Frames: 15q, Telephone lineman in winter. 25q, Two men and a woman. 80q, Workers. 1.20 l, Boys playing in street. 1.60 l, Harvest.

**1977, Oct. 25 Litho. *Perf. 12½x12***

| | | | | | |
|---|---|---|---|---|---|
| **1814** | A378 | 10q | blue green | .35 | .35 |
| **1815** | A378 | 15q | multi | .35 | .35 |
| **1816** | A378 | 25q | black | .35 | .35 |
| **1817** | A378 | 80q | multi | 1.40 | 1.40 |
| **1818** | A378 | 1.20 l | deep claret | 2.00 | 2.00 |
| **1819** | A378 | 1.60 l | multi | 2.25 | 2.25 |
| | | | *Nos. 1814-1819 (6)* | 6.70 | 6.70 |

Albanian films.

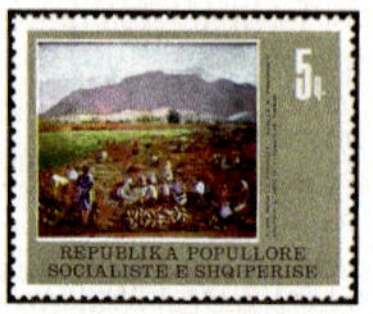

Farm Workers in Field, by V. Mio — A379

Paintings by V. Mio: 10q, Landscape in Snow. 15q, Grazing Sheep under Walnut Tree in Spring. 25q, Street in Korce. 80q, Horseback Riders on Mountain Pass. 1 l, Boats on Shore. 1.75 l, Tractors Plowing Fields. 2.05 l, Self-portrait.

**1977, Dec. 25 Litho. *Perf. 12½x12***

| | | | | | |
|---|---|---|---|---|---|
| **1820** | A379 | 5q | gold & multi | .25 | .25 |
| **1821** | A379 | 10q | gold & multi | .25 | .25 |
| **1822** | A379 | 15q | gold & multi | .25 | .25 |
| **1823** | A379 | 25q | gold & multi | .25 | .25 |
| **1824** | A379 | 80q | gold & multi | .35 | .25 |
| **1825** | A379 | 1 l | gold & multi | .60 | .25 |
| **1826** | A379 | 1.75 l | gold & multi | 1.00 | .25 |
| | | | *Nos. 1820-1826 (7)* | 2.95 | 1.75 |

**Miniature Sheet**

***Imperf.; Perf. 12 Horiz. between Vignette and Value Panel***

| | | | | | |
|---|---|---|---|---|---|
| **1827** | A379 | 2.05 l | gold & multi | 3.50 | 2.25 |

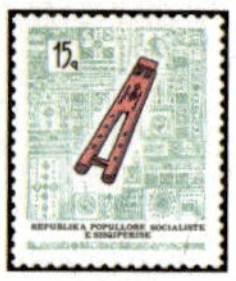

Pan Flute — A380

Folk Musical Instruments: 25q, Single-string goat's-head fiddle. 80q, Woodwind. 1.20 l, Drum. 1.70 l, Bagpipe. Background shows various woven folk patterns.

**1978, Jan. 20 *Perf. 12x12½***

| | | | | | |
|---|---|---|---|---|---|
| **1828** | A380 | 15q | multi | .40 | .25 |
| **1829** | A380 | 25q | multi | .75 | .25 |
| **1830** | A380 | 80q | multi | 2.00 | 1.00 |
| **1831** | A380 | 1.20 l | multi | 3.50 | 2.00 |
| **1832** | A380 | 1.70 l | multi | 9.00 | 3.50 |
| | | | *Nos. 1828-1832 (5)* | 15.65 | 7.00 |

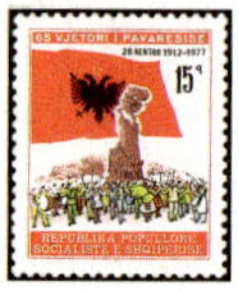

Albanian Flag, Monument and People — A381

25q, Ismail Qemali, fighters, horiz. 1.65 l, People dancing around Albanian flag, horiz.

***Perf. 12½x12, 12x12½***

**1977, Nov. 28**

| | | | | | |
|---|---|---|---|---|---|
| **1833** | A381 | 15q | multi | .25 | .25 |
| **1834** | A381 | 25q | multi | .30 | .25 |
| **1835** | A381 | 1.65 l | multi | 1.50 | 1.25 |
| | | | *Nos. 1833-1835 (3)* | 2.05 | 1.75 |

65th anniversary of independence.

**Folk Dancing Type of 1977**

Designs: Various dances.

**1978, Feb. 15 Litho. *Perf. 12***

| | | | | | |
|---|---|---|---|---|---|
| **1836** | A375 | 5q | multi | .25 | .25 |
| **1837** | A375 | 25q | multi | .25 | .25 |
| **1838** | A375 | 80q | multi | .75 | .30 |
| **1839** | A375 | 1 l | multi | .75 | .40 |
| **1840** | A375 | 2.30 l | multi | 1.75 | 1.40 |
| | | | *Nos. 1836-1840 (5)* | 3.75 | 2.60 |

Nos. 1836-1840 have white background around dancers, Nos. 1799-1805 have pinkish shadows.

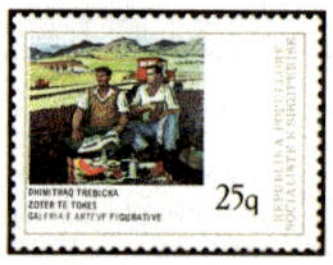

Tractor Drivers, by Dhimitraq Trebicka — A382

Working Class Paintings: 80q, Steeplejack, by Spiro Kristo. 85q, "A Point in the Discussion," by Skender Milori. 90q, Oil rig crew, by Anesti Cini, vert. 1.60 l, Metal workers, by Ramadan Karanxha. 2.20 l, Political discussion, by Sotiraq Sholla.

**1978, Mar. 25 Litho. *Perf. 12***

| | | | | | |
|---|---|---|---|---|---|
| **1841** | A382 | 25q | multi | .25 | .25 |
| **1842** | A382 | 80q | multi | .35 | .25 |
| **1843** | A382 | 85q | multi | .45 | .25 |
| **1844** | A382 | 90q | multi | .50 | .30 |
| **1845** | A382 | 1.60 l | multi | 1.40 | .90 |
| | | | *Nos. 1841-1845 (5)* | 2.95 | 1.95 |

**Miniature Sheet**

***Perf. 12 on 2 sides x Imperf.***

| | | | | | |
|---|---|---|---|---|---|
| **1846** | A382 | 2.20 l | multi | 7.00 | 2.75 |

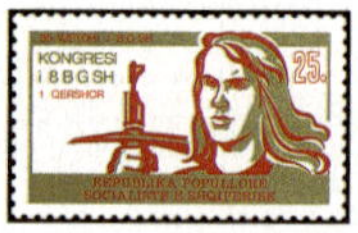

Woman with Rifle and Pickax — A383

1.95 l, Farm & Militia women, industrial plant.

**1978, June 1 Litho. *Perf. 12***

| | | | | | |
|---|---|---|---|---|---|
| **1847** | A383 | 25q | gold & red | .35 | .25 |
| **1848** | A383 | 1.95 l | gold & red | 5.25 | 1.50 |

8th Congress of Women's Union.

Children and Flowers — A384

Designs: 10q, Children with rifle, ax, book and flags. 25q, Dancing children in folk costume. 1.80 l, Children in school.

**1978, June 1 Litho.**

| | | | | | |
|---|---|---|---|---|---|
| **1849** | A384 | 5q | multi | .25 | .25 |
| **1850** | A384 | 10q | multi | .25 | .25 |
| **1851** | A384 | 25q | multi | .45 | .25 |
| **1852** | A384 | 1.80 l | multi | 3.00 | .90 |
| | | | *Nos. 1849-1852 (4)* | 3.95 | 1.65 |

International Children's Day.

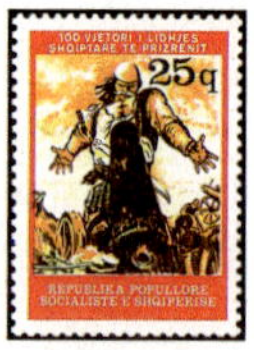

Spirit of Skanderbeg as Conqueror — A385

10q, Battle at Mostar Bridge. 80q, Marchers, Albanian flag. 1.20 l, Riflemen in winter battle. 1.65 l, Abdyl Frasheri (1839-92). 2.20 l, Rifles, scroll, pen, League building. 2.60 l, League headquarters, Prizren.

**1978, June 10 Litho. *Perf. 12***

| | | | | | |
|---|---|---|---|---|---|
| **1853** | A385 | 10q | multi | .25 | .25 |
| **1854** | A385 | 25q | multi | .25 | .30 |
| **1855** | A385 | 80q | multi | .90 | .30 |
| **1856** | A385 | 1.20 l | multi | 1.25 | .65 |
| **1857** | A385 | 1.65 l | multi | 2.00 | 1.00 |
| **1858** | A385 | 2.60 l | multi | 3.25 | 1.50 |
| | | | *Nos. 1853-1858 (6)* | 7.90 | 4.00 |

**Miniature Sheet**

***Perf. 12 on 2 sides x Imperf.***

| | | | | | |
|---|---|---|---|---|---|
| **1859** | A385 | 2.20 l | multi | 3.25 | 2.25 |

Centenary of League of Prizren.

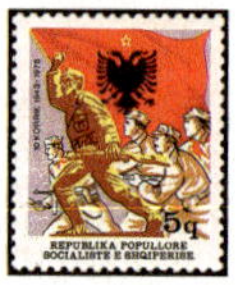

Guerrillas and Flag, 1943 — A386

Designs: 25q, Soldier, sailor, airman, militiaman, horiz. 1.90 l, Members of armed forces, civil guards, and Young Pioneers.

**1978, July 10 *Perf. 11½x12½***

| | | | | | |
|---|---|---|---|---|---|
| **1860** | A386 | 5q | multi | .35 | .25 |
| **1861** | A386 | 25q | multi | .70 | .25 |
| **1862** | A386 | 1.90 l | multi | 4.50 | 1.50 |
| | | | *Nos. 1860-1862 (3)* | 5.55 | 2.00 |

35th anniversary of People's Army.

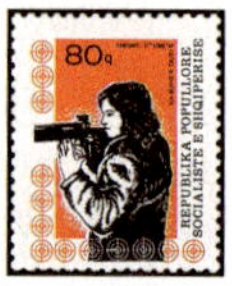

Woman with Machine Carbine — A387

25q, Man with target rifle, horiz. 95q, Man shooting with telescopic sights, horiz. 2.40 l, Woman target shooting with pistol.

***Perf. 12½x12, 12x12½***

**1978, Sept. 20 Litho.**

| | | | | | |
|---|---|---|---|---|---|
| **1863** | A387 | 25q | black & yel | .25 | .25 |
| **1864** | A387 | 80q | orange & blk | .50 | .35 |
| **1865** | A387 | 95q | red & blk | .75 | .50 |
| **1866** | A387 | 2.40 l | carmine & blk | 1.90 | 1.50 |
| | | | *Nos. 1863-1866 (4)* | 3.40 | 2.60 |

32nd National Rifle-shooting Championships, Sept. 20.

# ALBANIA

Kerchief Dance — A388

15q, Musicians. 25q, Fiddler with single-stringed instrument. 80q, Dancers, men. 1.20 l, Saber dance. 1.90 l, Singers, women.

**1978, Oct. 6    Perf. 12**
| 1867 | A388 | 10q multi | .25 | .25 |
|---|---|---|---|---|
| 1868 | A388 | 15q multi | .25 | .25 |
| 1869 | A388 | 25q multi | .25 | .25 |
| 1870 | A388 | 80q multi | .25 | .25 |
| 1871 | A388 | 1.20 l multi | .65 | .25 |
| 1872 | A388 | 1.90 l multi | 1.60 | 1.25 |
|  | Nos. 1867-1872 (6) | | 3.25 | 2.50 |

National Folklore Festival.
See Nos. 2082-2085, 2289-2290.

**No. 1736 Surcharged with New Value, 2 Bars and "RICCIONE 78"**

**1978    Litho.    Perf. 12½x12**
| 1873 | A360 | 3.30 l on 25q multi | 10.00 | 10.00 |
|---|---|---|---|---|

Riccione 78 Philatelic Exhibition.

Enver Hoxha — A389

**1978, Oct. 16    Litho.    Perf. 12x12½**
| 1874 | A389 | 80q red & multi | .40 | .35 |
|---|---|---|---|---|
| 1875 | A389 | 1.20 l red & multi | .75 | .35 |
| 1876 | A389 | 2.40 l red & multi | 1.50 | 1.00 |
|  | Nos. 1874-1876 (3) | | 2.65 | 1.70 |

**Miniature Sheet**
**Perf. 12½ on 2 sides x Imperf.**
| 1877 | A389 | 2.20 l red & multi | 3.50 | 2.00 |
|---|---|---|---|---|

70th birthday of Enver Hoxha, First Secretary of Central Committee of the Communist Party of Albania.

Woman and Wheat — A390

25q, Woman with egg crates. 80q, Shephord, choop. 2.60 l, Milkmaid, cows

**1978, Dec. 15    Perf. 12x12½**
| 1878 | A390 | 15q multicolored | .40 | .40 |
|---|---|---|---|---|
| 1879 | A390 | 25q multicolored | .55 | .40 |
| 1880 | A390 | 80q multicolored | 2.00 | 1.60 |
| 1881 | A390 | 2.60 l multicolored | 7.50 | 5.00 |
|  | Nos. 1878-1881 (4) | | 10.45 | 7.30 |

Dora d'Istria — A391

Design: 1.10 l, Full portrait of Dora d'Istria, author; birth sesquicentennial.

**1979, Jan. 22    Litho.    Perf. 12**
| 1882 | A391 | 80q lt grn & blk | 1.10 | .75 |
|---|---|---|---|---|
| 1883 | A391 | 1.90 l vio brn & blk | 1.90 | 1.50 |

**Folk Dancing Type of 1977**
Designs: Various folk dances.

**1979, Feb. 25**
| 1884 | A375 | 15q multi | .35 | .25 |
|---|---|---|---|---|
| 1885 | A375 | 25q multi | .35 | .25 |
| 1886 | A375 | 80q multi | 1.50 | .99 |
| 1887 | A375 | 1.20 l multi | 1.75 | 1.00 |
| 1888 | A375 | 1.40 l multi | 2.00 | 1.40 |
|  | Nos. 1884-1888 (5) | | 5.95 | 3.65 |

Nos. 1884-1888 have white background. Denomination in UL on No. 1885, in UR on No. 1802; LL on No.1886, UL on No. 1803.

Tower House — A392

Traditional Houses: 15q, Stone gallery house, horiz. 80q, House with wooden galleries, horiz. 1.20 l, Galleried tower house. 1.40 l, 1.90 l, Tower houses, diff.

**1979, Mar. 20**
| 1889 | A392 | 15q multi | .25 | .25 |
|---|---|---|---|---|
| 1890 | A392 | 25q multi | .25 | .25 |
| 1891 | A392 | 80q multi | .75 | .25 |
| 1892 | A392 | 1.20 l multi | 1.00 | .45 |
| 1893 | A392 | 1.40 l multi | 1.50 | .65 |
|  | Nos. 1889-1893 (5) | | 3.75 | 1.85 |

**Miniature Sheet**
**Perf. 12 on 2 sides x Imperf.**
| 1894 | A392 | 1.90 l multi | 6.00 | 3.75 |
|---|---|---|---|---|

See Nos. 2015-2018.

Soldier, Factories, Wheat — A393

1.65 l, Soldiers, workers and coat of arms.

**1979, May 14    Litho.    Perf. 12**
| 1895 | A393 | 25q multi | .75 | .35 |
|---|---|---|---|---|
| 1896 | A393 | 1.65 l multi | 3.50 | 2.00 |

Congress of Permet, 35th anniversary.

Albanian Flag — A394

**1979, June 4**
| 1897 | A394 | 25q multi | .75 | .35 |
|---|---|---|---|---|
| 1898 | A394 | 1.65 l multi | 3.50 | 2.25 |

5th Congress of Albanian Democratic Front.

Alexander Moissi, (1880-1935), Actor — A395

**1979, Apr 2**
| 1899 | A395 | 80q multi | 1.00 | .35 |
|---|---|---|---|---|
| 1900 | A395 | 1.10 l multi, diff. | 1.50 | 1.00 |

Vasil Shanto, (1913-44) — A396

Design: 25q, 90q, Qemal Stafa (1921-42).

**1979, May 5**
| 1901 | A396 | 15q multi | .25 | .25 |
|---|---|---|---|---|
| 1902 | A396 | 25q multi | .35 | .25 |
| 1903 | A396 | 60q multi | 1.20 | .60 |
| 1904 | A396 | 90q multi | 2.10 | 1.25 |
|  | Nos. 1901-1904 (4) | | 3.90 | 2.35 |

Shanto and Stafa, anti-Fascist fighters.
For similar design see A410.

Winter Campaign, by Arben Basha A397

Paintings of Military Scenes by: 25q, Ismail Lulani. 80q, Myrteza Fushekati. 1.20 l, Muhamet Deliu. 1.40 l, Jorgji Gjikopulli. 1.90 l, Fatmir Haxhiu.

**1979, July 15    Litho.    Perf. 12½x12**
| 1905 | A397 | 15q multi | .25 | .25 |
|---|---|---|---|---|
| 1906 | A397 | 25q multi | .25 | .25 |
| 1907 | A397 | 80q multi | .75 | .25 |
| 1908 | A397 | 1.20 l multi | 1.00 | .45 |
| 1909 | A397 | 1.40 l multi | 1.50 | .70 |
|  | Nos. 1905-1909 (5) | | 3.75 | 1.95 |

**Miniature Sheet**
**Perf. 12 on 2 sides x Imperf.**
| 1910 | A397 | 1.90 l multi | 3.00 | 2.00 |
|---|---|---|---|---|

Athletes Surrounding Flag — A398

**1979, Oct. 1    Litho.    Perf. 12**
| 1911 | A398 | 15q shown | .25 | .25 |
|---|---|---|---|---|
| 1912 | A398 | 25q Shooting | .25 | .25 |
| 1913 | A398 | 80q Dancing | .70 | .25 |
| 1914 | A398 | 1.20 l Soccer | .85 | .60 |
| 1915 | A398 | 1.40 l High jump | 1.20 | .85 |
|  | Nos. 1911-1915 (5) | | 3.25 | 2.20 |

Liberation Spartakiad, 35th anniversary.

Literary Society Headquarters — A399

Albanian Literary Society Centenary: 25q, Seal and charter. 80q, Founder. 1.55 l, 1879 Headquarters.
1.90 l, Founders.

**1979, Oct. 12**
| 1916 | A399 | 25q multi | .25 | .25 |
|---|---|---|---|---|
| 1917 | A399 | 80q multi | .75 | .35 |
| 1918 | A399 | 1.20 l multi | 1.00 | .60 |
| 1919 | A399 | 1.55 l multi | 1.25 | .75 |
|  | Nos. 1916-1919 (4) | | 3.25 | 1.95 |

**Miniature Sheet**
**Perf. 12½ on 2 sides x Imperf.**
| 1920 | A399 | 1.90 l multi | 2.75 | 2.00 |
|---|---|---|---|---|

Congress Statute, Coat of Arms — A400

**1979, Oct. 20    Photo.    Perf. 12x12½**
| 1921 | A400 | 25q multi | 1.00 | .75 |
|---|---|---|---|---|
| 1922 | A400 | 1.65 l multi | 4.00 | 2.50 |

2nd Congress of Berat, 35th anniversary.

Industry and Culture — A401

5q, Children Entering School, Books. 10q, Communications. 15q, Steel workers. 20q, Dancers, instruments. 25q, Newspapers, radio, television. 60q, Textile worker. 80q, Armed forces. 1.20 l, Industry. 1.60 l, Transportation. 2.40 l, Agriculture. 3 l, Medicine.

**1979    Litho.    Perf. 12½x12**
| 1923 | A401 | 5q shown | .25 | .25 |
|---|---|---|---|---|
| 1924 | A401 | 10q multi | .25 | .25 |
| 1925 | A401 | 15q multi | .25 | .25 |
| 1926 | A401 | 20q multi | .25 | .25 |
| 1927 | A401 | 25q multi | .25 | .25 |
| 1928 | A401 | 60q multi | 1.00 | .25 |
| 1929 | A401 | 80q multi | 1.40 | |
| 1930 | A401 | 1.20 l multi | 2.40 | |
| 1931 | A401 | 1.60 l multi | 3.25 | .40 |
| 1932 | A401 | 2.40 l multi | 5.00 | .45 |
| 1932A | A401 | 3 l multi | 6.75 | .60 |
|  | Nos. 1923-1932A (11) | | 21.05 | 3.45 |

Workers and Factory — A402

Worker, Red Flag and: 80q, Hand holding sickle and rifle. 1.20 l, Red star and open book. 1.55 l, Open book and cogwheel.

**1979, Nov. 29**
| 1933 | A402 | 25q multi | .25 | .25 |
|---|---|---|---|---|
| 1934 | A402 | 80q multi | .75 | .35 |
| 1935 | A402 | 1.20 l multi | .90 | .75 |
| 1936 | A402 | 1.55 l multi | 1.50 | .90 |
|  | Nos. 1933-1936 (4) | | 3.40 | 2.25 |

35th anniversary of independence.

Joseph Stalin — A403

Design: 1.10 l, Stalin on dais, horiz.

**1979, Dec. 21    Litho.    Perf. 12**
| 1937 | A403 | 80q red & dk bl | 1.10 | .75 |
|---|---|---|---|---|
| 1938 | A403 | 1.10 l red & dk bl | 1.50 | 1.50 |

Joseph Stalin (1879-1953), birth centenary.

Fireplace and Pottery, Korcar — A404

Home Furnishings: 80q, Cupboard bed, dagger, pistol, ammunition pouch, Shkodar. 1.20 l, Stool, pot, chair, Mirdit. 1.35 l, Chimney, dagger, jacket, Gjirokaster.

**1980, Feb. 27    Litho.    Perf. 12**
| 1939 | A404 | 25q multi | .25 | .25 |
|---|---|---|---|---|
| 1940 | A404 | 80q multi | .50 | .50 |
| 1941 | A404 | 1.20 l multi | 1.10 | .75 |
| 1942 | A404 | 1.35 l multi | 1.50 | 1.50 |
|  | Nos. 1939-1942 (4) | | 3.35 | 3.00 |

See Nos. 1985-1988.

Pipe, Painted Flask — A405

80q, Leather handbags. 1.20 l, Carved eagle, embroidered rug. 1.35 l, Lace.

**1980, Mar. 4**
| 1943 | A405 | 25q shown | .25 | .25 |
|---|---|---|---|---|
| 1944 | A405 | 80q multi | .50 | .50 |
| 1945 | A405 | 1.20 l multi | 1.10 | .75 |
| 1946 | A405 | 1.35 l multi | 1.50 | 1.50 |
|  | Nos. 1943-1946 (4) | | 3.35 | 3.00 |

Prof. Aleksander Xhuvanit Birth Centenary — A406

**1980, Mar. 14**
| 1947 | A406 | 80q multi | 1.40 | 1.00 |
|---|---|---|---|---|
| 1948 | A406 | 1 l multi | 1.75 | 1.75 |

Revolutionaries on Horseback A407

Insurrection at Kosove, 70th Anniversary: 1 l, Battle scene.

**1980, Apr. 4**

| | | | |
|---|---|---|---|
| 1949 | A407 80q red & black | 1.50 | 1.10 |
| 1950 | A407 1 l red & black | 2.25 | 1.90 |

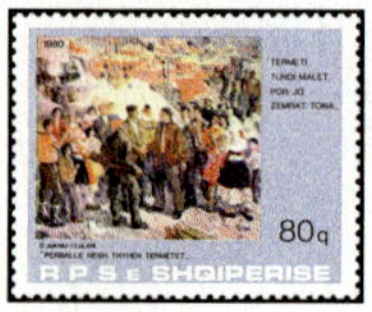

Soldiers and Workers Laboring to Aid the Stricken Populations, by D. Jukniu and I. Lulani — A408

**1980, Apr. 15 Litho. *Perf. 12½***

| | | | |
|---|---|---|---|
| 1951 | A408 80q lt blue & multi | 1.50 | 1.10 |
| 1952 | A408 1 l lt blue grn & multi | 2.25 | 1.90 |

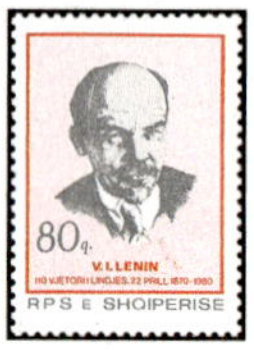

Lenin, 110th Birth Anniversary — A409

**1980, Apr. 22**

| | | | |
|---|---|---|---|
| 1953 | A409 80q multi | 1.50 | 1.10 |
| 1954 | A409 1 l multi | 2.25 | 1.90 |

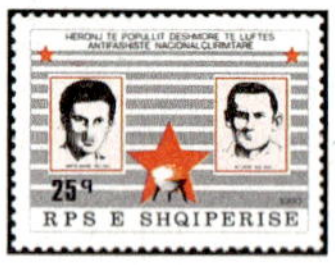

Misto Mame and Ali Demi, War Martyrs — A410

War Martyrs: 80q, Sadik Staveleci, Vojo Kusji, Hoxhi Martini. 1.20 l, Bule Naipi, Persefoni Kokedhima. 1.35 l, Ndoc Deda, Hydajet Lezha, Naim Gyylbegu, Ndoc Mazi, Ahmed Haxha.

**1980, May 5**

| | | | |
|---|---|---|---|
| 1955 | A410 25q multi | .25 | .25 |
| 1956 | A410 80q multi | .70 | .50 |
| 1957 | A410 1.20 l multi | 1.20 | .70 |
| 1958 | A410 1.35 l multi | 1.40 | 1.40 |
| | *Nos. 1955-1958 (4)* | 3.55 | 2.85 |

See Nos. 2012A-2012D, 2025-2028, 2064-2067, 2122-2125, 2171-2174, 2207-2209.

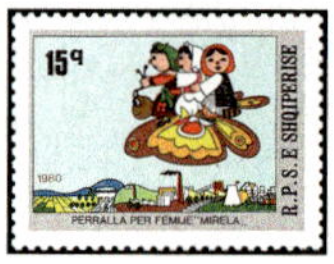

Scene from "Mirela" — A411

**1980, June 7**

| | | | |
|---|---|---|---|
| 1959 | A411 15q shown | .25 | .25 |
| 1960 | A411 25q The Scribbler | .25 | .25 |
| 1961 | A411 80q Circus Bears | .80 | .80 |
| 1962 | A411 2.40 l Waterdrops | 2.75 | 2.75 |
| | *Nos. 1959-1962 (4)* | 4.05 | 4.05 |

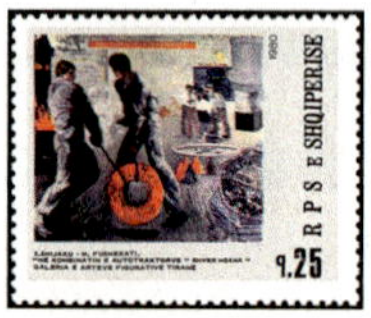

Carrying Iron Castings in the Enver Hoxha Tractor Combine, by S. Shijaku and M. Fushekati A412

Paintings (Gallery of Figurative Paintings, Tirana): 80q, The Welder, by Harilla Dhima. 1.20 l, Steel Erectors, by Petro Kokushta. 1.35 l, Pandeli Lena, 1.80 l Communists, by Vilson Kilica.

**1980, July 22**

| | | | |
|---|---|---|---|
| 1963 | A412 25q multi | .25 | .25 |
| 1964 | A412 80q multi | .70 | .70 |
| 1965 | A412 1.20 l multi | 1.20 | 1.20 |
| 1966 | A412 1.35 l multi | 1.40 | 1.40 |
| | *Nos. 1963-1966 (4)* | 3.55 | 3.55 |

***Imperf***

| | | | |
|---|---|---|---|
| 1967 | A412 1.80 l multi | 3.00 | 2.50 |

No. 1967 measures 66x82mm and has a row of perforations above and below the vignette.

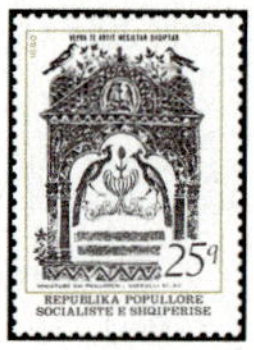

Gate, Parchment Miniature, 11th Cent. — A413

Bas reliefs of the Middle Ages: 80q, Eagle, 13th cent. 1.20 l, Heraldic lion, 14th cent. 1.35 l, Pheasant, 14th cent.

**1980, Sept. 27 Litho. *Perf. 12***

| | | | |
|---|---|---|---|
| 1968 | A413 25q gold & blk | .25 | .25 |
| 1969 | A413 80q gold & blk | .55 | .55 |
| 1970 | A413 1.20 l gold & blk | 1.20 | 1.20 |
| 1971 | A413 1.35 l gold & blk | 1.20 | 1.20 |
| | *Nos. 1968-1971 (4)* | 3.20 | 3.20 |

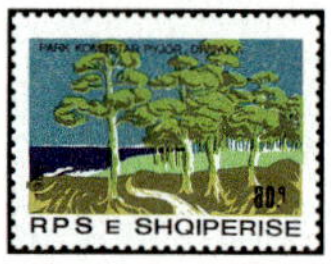

Divjaka National Park — A414

**1980, Nov. 6 Photo.**

| | | | |
|---|---|---|---|
| 1972 | A414 80q shown | .75 | .60 |
| 1973 | A414 1.20 l Lura | 1.10 | 1.10 |
| 1974 | A414 1.60 l Thethi | 1.90 | 1.60 |
| | *Nos. 1972-1974 (3)* | 3.75 | 3.30 |

**Souvenir Sheet**

***Perf. 12½ Horiz.***

| | | | |
|---|---|---|---|
| 1975 | A414 1.80 l Llogara Park | 3.50 | 3.50 |

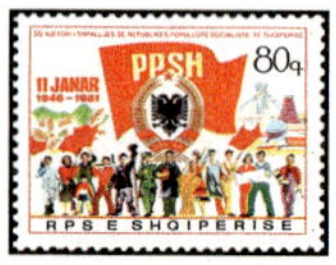

Citizens, Flag and Arms of Albania — A415

1 l, People's Party Headquarters, Tirana.

**1981, Jan. 11 Litho. *Perf. 12***

| | | | |
|---|---|---|---|
| 1976 | A415 80q multicolored | 1.00 | .70 |
| 1977 | A415 1 l multicolored | 1.40 | .70 |

35th anniversary of the Republic.

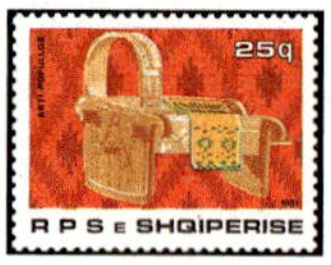

Child's Bed — A416

80q, Wooden bucket, brass bottle. 1.20 l, Shoes. 1.35 l, Jugs.

**1981, Mar. 20 Litho. *Perf. 12***

| | | | |
|---|---|---|---|
| 1978 | A416 25q multicolored | .25 | .25 |
| 1979 | A416 80q multicolored | .50 | .40 |
| 1980 | A416 1.20 l multicolored | .80 | .70 |
| 1981 | A416 1.35 l multicolored | 1.00 | .90 |
| | *Nos. 1978-1981 (4)* | 2.55 | 2.25 |

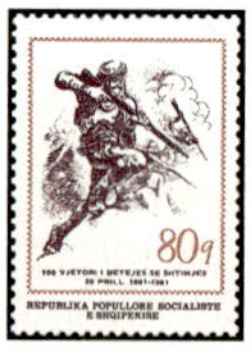

A417

80q, Soldiers. 1 l, Sword combat. 1.80 l, Soldier with pistol.

**1981, Apr. 20**

| | | | |
|---|---|---|---|
| 1982 | A417 80q multicolored | .70 | .70 |
| 1983 | A417 1 l multicolored | .85 | .70 |

**Souvenir Sheet**

***Perf. 12½ Vert.***

| | | | |
|---|---|---|---|
| 1984 | A417 1.80 l multicolored | 2.75 | 2.00 |

Battle of Shtimje centenary.

**Home Furnishings Type of 1980**

25q, House interior, Labara. 80q, Labara, diff. 1.20 l, Mat. 1.35 l, Dibres.

**1981, Feb. 25 Litho. *Perf. 12***

| | | | |
|---|---|---|---|
| 1985 | A404 25q multicolored | .25 | .25 |
| 1986 | A404 80q multicolored | .35 | .25 |
| 1987 | A404 1.20 l multicolored | .85 | .40 |
| 1988 | A404 1.35 l multicolored | 1.00 | .90 |
| | *Nos. 1985-1988 (4)* | 2.45 | 1.80 |

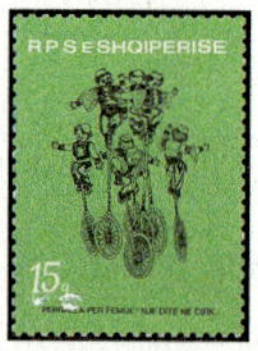

A419

Designs: Children's circus.

**1981, June *Perf. 12***

| | | | |
|---|---|---|---|
| 1989 | A419 15q multi | .25 | .25 |
| 1990 | A419 25q multi | .50 | .40 |
| 1991 | A419 80q multi | .80 | .65 |
| 1992 | A419 2.40 l multi | 1.00 | .90 |
| | *Nos. 1989-1992 (4)* | 2.55 | 2.20 |

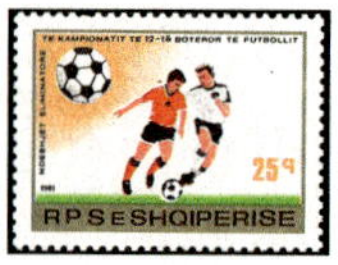

Soccer Players — A420

1982 World Cup Soccer Elimination Games: Various soccer players.

**1981, Mar. 31 Litho. *Perf. 12***

| | | | |
|---|---|---|---|
| 1993 | A420 25q multi | .70 | .35 |
| 1994 | A420 80q multi | 2.50 | 1.50 |
| 1995 | A420 1.20 l multi | 3.50 | 2.60 |
| 1996 | A420 1.35 l multi | 4.25 | 3.00 |
| | *Nos. 1993-1996 (4)* | 10.95 | 7.45 |

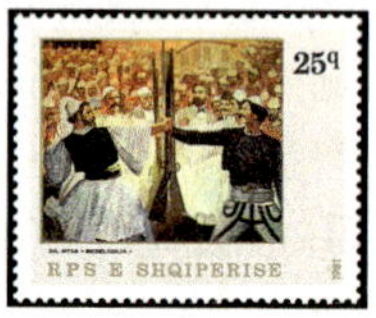

Allies, by S. Hysa — A421

Paintings: 80q, Warriors, by A. Buza. 1.20 l, Rallying to the Flag, Dec. 1911, by A. Zajmi, vert. 1.35 l, My Flag is My Heart, by L. Cefa, vert. 1.80 l, Circling the Flag in a Common Cause, by N. Vasia.

**1981, July 10 *Perf. 12½x12***

| | | | |
|---|---|---|---|
| 1997 | A421 25q multi | .25 | .25 |
| 1998 | A421 80q multi | .75 | .35 |
| 1999 | A421 1.20 l multi | .85 | .75 |
| 2000 | A421 1.35 l multi | 1.50 | .85 |
| | *Nos. 1997-2000 (4)* | 3.35 | 2.20 |

**Souvenir Sheet**

***Perf. 12½ Horiz.***

| | | | |
|---|---|---|---|
| 2001 | A421 1.80 l multi | 2.75 | 2.50 |

No. 2001 contains one 55x55mm stamp.

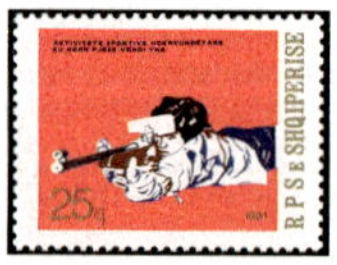

Rifleman — A422

**1981, Aug. 30 *Perf. 12***

| | | | |
|---|---|---|---|
| 2002 | A422 25q shown | .25 | .25 |
| 2003 | A422 80q Weight lifting | .50 | .35 |
| 2004 | A422 1.20 l Volleyball | .75 | .65 |
| 2005 | A422 1.35 l Soccer | 1.00 | .75 |
| | *Nos. 2002-2005 (4)* | 2.50 | 2.00 |

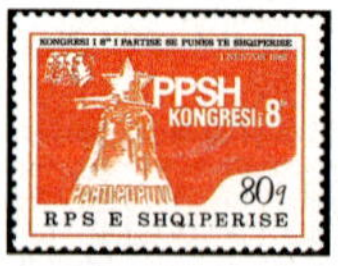

Albanian Workers' Party, 8th Congress — A423

80q, Flag, star. 1 l, Flag, hammer & sickle.

**1981, Nov. 1**

| | | | |
|---|---|---|---|
| 2006 | A423 80q multicolored | .60 | .45 |
| 2007 | A423 1 l multicolored | .85 | .75 |

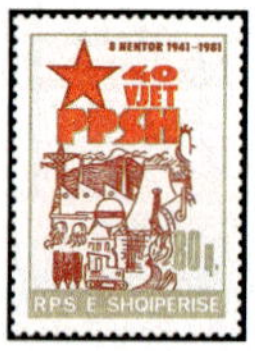

Albanian Workers' Party, 40th Anniv. — A424

80q, Symbols of industrialization. 2.80 l, Fist, emblem.
1.80 l, Enver Hoxha, Memoirs.

**1981, Nov. 8**

| | | | |
|---|---|---|---|
| 2008 | A424 80q multicolored | .35 | .35 |
| 2009 | A424 2.80 l multicolored | 1.75 | 1.40 |

**Souvenir Sheet**

***Perf. 12 Horiz.***

| | | | |
|---|---|---|---|
| 2010 | A424 1.80 l multicolored | 3.75 | 3.75 |

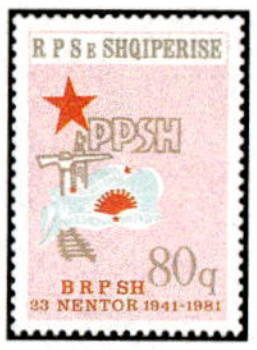

Communist Youth Org., 40th Anniv. — A425

**1981, Nov. 23**

| | | | |
|---|---|---|---|
| 2011 | A425 80q Star, ax, map | .75 | .75 |
| 2012 | A425 1 l Flags, star | 1.50 | 1.40 |

**War Martyrs Type of 1980**

25q, Perlat Rexhepi (1919-42) and Branko Kadia (1921-42). 80q, Xheladin Beqiri (1908-44) and Hajdar Dushi (1916-44). 1.20 l, Koci Bako (1905-41), Vasil Laci (1923-41) and Mujo Ulqinaku (1898-1939). 1.35 l, Mine Peza (1875-1942) and Zoja Cure (1920-44).

**1981, May 5 Litho. *Perf. 12***

| | | | |
|---|---|---|---|
| 2012A | A410 25q silver & multi | .25 | .25 |
| 2012B | A410 80q gold & multi | .65 | .35 |
| 2012C | A410 1.20 l silver & multi | .80 | .75 |
| 2012D | A410 1.35 l gold & multi | 1.40 | .85 |
| | *Nos. 2012A-2012D (4)* | 3.10 | 2.20 |

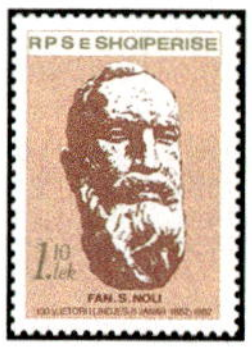

Fan S. Noli, Writer, Birth Centenary — A426

**1982, Jan. 6 Litho. *Perf. 12***

| | | | |
|---|---|---|---|
| 2013 | A426 80q lt ol grn & gold | 1.00 | .50 |
| 2014 | A426 1.10 l lt red brn & gold | 1.25 | .75 |

**Traditional Houses Type of 1979**

**1982, Feb. *Perf. 12½x12***

| | | | |
|---|---|---|---|
| 2015 | A392 25q Bulqize | .25 | .25 |
| 2016 | A392 80q Lebush | .90 | .65 |
| 2017 | A392 1.20 l Bicaj | 1.30 | .90 |
| 2018 | A392 1.55 l Klos | 1.75 | 1.10 |
| | *Nos. 2015-2018 (4)* | 4.20 | 2.90 |

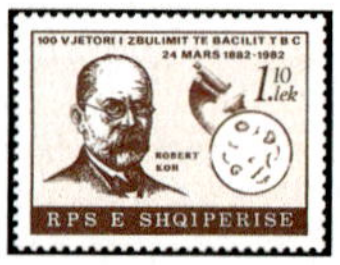

TB Bacillus Centenary A428

**1982, Mar. 24 *Perf. 12***

| | | | |
|---|---|---|---|
| 2019 | A428 80q Globe | 3.75 | 1.50 |
| 2020 | A428 1.10 l Koch | 5.25 | 2.50 |

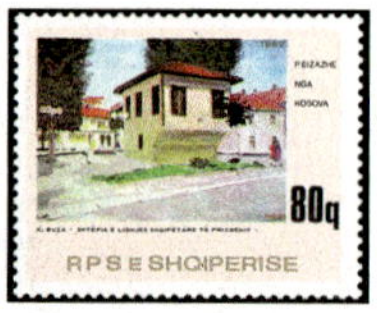

Albanian League House, Prizren, by K. Buza — A429

Kosova Landscapes: 25q, Castle at Prizrenit, by G. Madhi. 1.20 l, Mountain Gorge at Rogove, by K. Buza. 1.55 l, Street of the Hadhji at Zekes, by G. Madhi. 25q, 1.20 l, 1.55 l vert.

***Perf. 12x12½, 12½x12***

**1982, Apr. 15 Litho.**

| | | | |
|---|---|---|---|
| 2021 | A429 25q multi | .35 | .25 |
| 2022 | A429 80q multi | 1.10 | .90 |
| 2023 | A429 1.20 l multi | 1.90 | 1.10 |
| 2024 | A429 1.55 l multi | 2.75 | 1.25 |
| | *Nos. 2021-2024 (4)* | 6.10 | 3.50 |

**War Martyrs Type of 1980**

Designs: 25q, Hibe Palikuqi, Liri Gero. 80q, Mihal Duri, Kajo Karafili. 1.20 l, Fato Dudumi, Margarita Tutulani, Shejnaze Juka. 1.55 l, Memo Meto, Gjok Doci.

# ALBANIA

**1982, May**    *Perf. 12*
| | | | | |
|---|---|---|---|---|
| 2025 | A410 | 25q multi | .35 | .25 |
| 2026 | A410 | 80q multi | .85 | .60 |
| 2027 | A410 | 1.20 l multi | 1.25 | .75 |
| 2028 | A410 | 1.55 l multi | 1.75 | 1.00 |
| | Nos. 2025-2028 (4) | | 4.20 | 2.60 |

Loading Freighter — A430

Children's Paintings.

**1982, June 15**    *Perf. 12½x12*
| | | | | |
|---|---|---|---|---|
| 2029 | A430 | 15q shown | .40 | .25 |
| 2030 | A430 | 80q Forest | .85 | .45 |
| 2031 | A430 | 1.20 l City | 1.25 | .90 |
| 2032 | A430 | 1.65 l Park | 2.50 | 1.25 |
| | Nos. 2029-2032 (4) | | 5.00 | 2.85 |

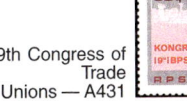

9th Congress of Trade Unions — A431

80q, Workers, factories. 1.10 l, Emblem, flag.

**1982, June 6**    *Litho.*    *Perf. 12*
| | | | | |
|---|---|---|---|---|
| 2033 | A431 | 80q multicolored | 2.00 | 1.25 |
| 2034 | A431 | 1.10 l multicolored | 2.75 | 1.50 |

Alpine Village Festival, by Danish Jukniu — A432

Industrial Development Paintings: 80q, Hydroelectric Station Builders, by Ali Miruku. 1.20 l, Steel Workers, by Clirim Ceka. 1.55 l, Oil drillers, by Pandeli Lena. 1.90 l, Trapping the Furnace, by Jorgji Gjikopulli.

**1982, July**    *Perf. 12½*
| | | | | |
|---|---|---|---|---|
| 2035 | A432 | 25q multi | .30 | .25 |
| 2036 | A432 | 80q multi | 1.00 | 1.00 |
| 2037 | A432 | 1.20 l multi | 1.50 | 1.20 |
| 2038 | A432 | 1.55 l multi | 2.25 | 1.50 |
| | Nos. 2035-2038 (4) | | 5.05 | 3.95 |

**Souvenir Sheet**
*Perf. 12 Horiz.*
| | | | | |
|---|---|---|---|---|
| 2039 | A432 | 1.90 l multi | | 3.50 2.50 |

No. 2039 contains one 54x48mm stamp.

Communist Party Newspaper "Voice of the People," 40th Anniv. — A432a

80q, Newspapers. 1.10 l, Paper, press.

**1982, Aug. 25**    *Litho.*    *Perf. 12*
| | | | | |
|---|---|---|---|---|
| 2039A | A432a | 80q multi | 75.00 | 70.00 |
| 2039B | A432a | 1.10 l multi | 75.00 | 70.00 |

40th Anniv. of Democratic Front — A433

80q, Glory to the Heroes of Peza Monument. 1.10 l, Marchers.

**1982, Sept. 16**    *Perf. 12*
| | | | | |
|---|---|---|---|---|
| 2040 | A433 | 80q multi | 6.00 | 2.50 |
| 2041 | A433 | 1.10 l multi | 8.50 | 3.50 |

8th Youth Congress — A434

**1982, Oct. 4**
| | | | | |
|---|---|---|---|---|
| 2042 | A434 | 80q multi | 2.50 | 2.00 |
| 2043 | A434 | 1.10 l multi | 4.00 | 3.00 |

Handmade Shoulder Bags — A435

25q, Rug, horiz. 1.20 l, Wooden pots, bowls, horiz. 1.55 l, Jug.

**1982, Nov.**
| | | | | |
|---|---|---|---|---|
| 2044 | A435 | 25q multi | .40 | .25 |
| 2045 | A435 | 80q multi | .90 | .50 |
| 2046 | A435 | 1.20 l multi | 1.25 | .75 |
| 2047 | A435 | 1.55 l multi | 2.00 | 1.10 |
| | Nos. 2044-2047 (4) | | 4.55 | 2.60 |

70th Anniv. of Independence — A436

20q, Ishmail Qemali. 1.20 l, Partisans. 2.40 l, Partisans, diff. 1.90 l, Independence Monument, Tirana.

**1982, Nov. 28**
| | | | | |
|---|---|---|---|---|
| 2048 | A436 | 20q multicolored | .30 | .25 |
| 2049 | A436 | 1.20 l multicolored | 1.40 | .85 |
| 2050 | A436 | 2.40 l multicolored | 7.50 | 1.50 |
| | Nos. 2048-2050 (3) | | 9.20 | 2.60 |

**Souvenir Sheet**
| | | | | |
|---|---|---|---|---|
| 2051 | A436 | 1.90 l multicolored | | 3.75 3.00 |

Dhermi Beach — A437

**1982, Dec. 20**
| | | | | |
|---|---|---|---|---|
| 2052 | A437 | 25q shown | .25 | .25 |
| 2053 | A437 | 80q Sarande | .75 | .45 |
| 2054 | A437 | 1.20 l Ksamil | 1.00 | .90 |
| 2055 | A437 | 1.55 l Lukove | 1.50 | 1.00 |
| | Nos. 2052-2055 (4) | | 3.50 | 2.60 |

Handkerchief Dancers — A438

Folkdancers — 80q, With kerchief, drum. 1.20 l, With guitar, flute, tambourine. 1.55 l, Women.

**1983, Feb. 20**    *Litho.*    *Perf. 12*
| | | | | |
|---|---|---|---|---|
| 2056 | A438 | 25q multi | .25 | .25 |
| 2057 | A438 | 80q multi | .50 | .25 |
| 2058 | A438 | 1.20 l multi | .90 | .75 |
| 2059 | A438 | 1.55 l multi | 1.20 | 1.00 |
| | Nos. 2056-2059 (4) | | 2.85 | 2.25 |

A439

**1983, Mar. 14**    *Litho.*    *Perf. 12*
| | | | | |
|---|---|---|---|---|
| 2060 | A439 | 80q multi | 1.50 | .75 |
| 2061 | A439 | 1.10 l multi | 1.90 | 1.00 |

Karl Marx (1818-83).

A440

80q, Electricity generation. 1.10 l, Gas & oil production.

**1983, Apr. 20**
| | | | | |
|---|---|---|---|---|
| 2062 | A440 | 80q multi | 1.00 | .60 |
| 2063 | A440 | 1.10 l multi | 1.25 | .90 |

Energy development.

**War Martyrs Type of 1980**

Designs: 25q, Asim Zeneli (1916-43), Nazmi Rushiti (1919-42). 80q, Shyqyri Ishmi (1922-42), Shyqyri Alimerko (1923-43), Myzafer Asqeriu (1918-42). 1.20 l, Qybra Sokoli (1924-44), Qeriba Derri (1905-44), Ylbere Bilibashi (1928-44). 1.55 l, Themo Vasi (1915-43), Abaz Shehu (1905-42).

**1983, May 5**    *Litho.*    *Perf. 12*
| | | | | |
|---|---|---|---|---|
| 2064 | A410 | 25q multi | .25 | .25 |
| 2065 | A410 | 80q multi | .75 | .30 |
| 2066 | A410 | 1.20 l multi | 1.25 | .75 |
| 2067 | A410 | 1.55 l multi | 1.90 | 1.00 |
| | Nos. 2064-2067 (4) | | 4.15 | 2.30 |

Women's Union, 9th Congress — A441

**1983, June 1**    *Litho.*    *Perf. 12x12½*
| | | | | |
|---|---|---|---|---|
| 2068 | A441 | 80q red & gold | 1.25 | .75 |
| 2069 | A441 | 1.10 l blue & gold | 1.50 | 1.00 |

Bicycling — A442

**1983, June 20**    *Perf. 12*
| | | | | |
|---|---|---|---|---|
| 2070 | A442 | 25q shown | .25 | .25 |
| 2071 | A442 | 80q Chess | .75 | .25 |
| 2072 | A442 | 1.20 l Gymnastics | 1.25 | .75 |
| 2073 | A442 | 1.55 l Wrestling | 1.50 | 1.00 |
| | Nos. 2070-2073 (4) | | 3.75 | 2.25 |

40th Anniv. of People's Army — A443

20q, Armed services. 1.20 l, Soldier, gun barrels. 2.40 l, Factory guard, crowd.

**1983, July 10**
| | | | | |
|---|---|---|---|---|
| 2074 | A443 | 20q multicolored | .25 | .25 |
| 2075 | A443 | 1.20 l multicolored | 1.25 | .75 |
| 2076 | A443 | 2.40 l multicolored | 2.25 | 1.25 |
| | Nos. 2074-2076 (3) | | 3.75 | 2.25 |

Sunny Day, by Myrteza Fushekati — A444

Paintings: 80q, Messenger of the Grasp, by Niko Progi. 1.20 l, 29 November 1944, by Harilla Dhimo. 1.55 l, Fireworks, by Pandi Mele. 1.90 l, Partisan Assault, by Sali Shijaku and M. Fushekati.

**1983, Aug. 28**    *Litho.*    *Perf. 12½x12*
| | | | | |
|---|---|---|---|---|
| 2077 | A444 | 25q multi | .25 | .25 |
| 2078 | A444 | 80q multi | .85 | .40 |
| 2079 | A444 | 1.20 l multi | 1.00 | .75 |
| 2080 | A444 | 1.55 l multi | 1.50 | .85 |
| | Nos. 2077-2080 (4) | | 3.60 | 2.25 |

**Souvenir Sheet**
*Perf. 12*
| | | | | |
|---|---|---|---|---|
| 2081 | A444 | 1.90 l multi | | 8.50 6.00 |

**Folklore Festival Type of 1978**

Gjirokaster Folklore Festival: folkdances: 25q, Sword dance. 80q, Kerchief dance. 1.20 l, Shepherd flautists. 1.55 l, Garland dance.

**1983, Oct. 6**    *Litho.*    *Perf. 12*
| | | | | |
|---|---|---|---|---|
| 2082 | A388 | 25q multicolored | .25 | .25 |
| 2083 | A388 | 80q multicolored | 1.50 | .75 |
| 2084 | A388 | 1.20 l multicolored | 1.50 | .90 |
| 2085 | A388 | 1.55 l multicolored | 3.00 | 2.00 |
| | Nos. 2082-2085 (4) | | 6.25 | 3.90 |

World Communications Year — A446

**1983, Nov. 10**
| | | | | |
|---|---|---|---|---|
| 2086 | A446 | 60q multicolored | .45 | .35 |
| 2087 | A446 | 1.20 l multicolored | 1.30 | 1.00 |

75th Birthday of Enver Hoxha — A447

**1983, Oct. 16**    *Litho.*    *Perf. 12½*
| | | | | |
|---|---|---|---|---|
| 2088 | A447 | 80q multi | .90 | .75 |
| 2089 | A447 | 1.20 l multi | 1.50 | 1.25 |
| 2090 | A447 | 1.80 l multi | 2.00 | 1.75 |
| | Nos. 2088-2090 (3) | | 4.40 | 3.75 |

**Souvenir Sheet**
*Perf. 12 Horiz.*
| | | | | |
|---|---|---|---|---|
| 2091 | A447 | 1.90 l multi | | 3.50 3.00 |

The Right to a Joint Triumph, by J. Keraj — A448

Era of Skanderbeg in Figurative Art: 80q, The Heroic Center of the Battle of Krujes, by N. Bakalli. 1.20 l, The Rights of the Enemy after our Triumph, by N. Progri. 1.55 l, The Discussion at Lezhes, by B. Ahmeti. 1.90 l, Victory over the Turks, by G. Madhi.

**1983, Dec. 10**    *Perf. 12½x12*
| | | | | |
|---|---|---|---|---|
| 2092 | A448 | 25q multi | .35 | .25 |
| 2093 | A448 | 80q multi | 1.10 | .75 |
| 2094 | A448 | 1.20 l multi | 1.50 | .90 |
| 2095 | A448 | 1.55 l multi | 2.25 | 1.10 |
| | Nos. 2092-2095 (4) | | 5.20 | 3.00 |

**Souvenir Sheet**
*Perf. 12 Horiz.*
| | | | | |
|---|---|---|---|---|
| 2096 | A448 | 1.90 l multi | | 6.00 6.00 |

Greco-Roman Ruins of Illyria — A449

80q, Amphitheater, Buthroxtum. 1.20 l, Colonnade, Apollonium. 1.80 l, Vaulted gallery, amphitheater at Epidamnus.

**1983, Dec. 28**    *Perf. 12*
| | | | | |
|---|---|---|---|---|
| 2097 | A449 | 80q multicolored | 1.50 | 1.10 |
| 2098 | A449 | 1.20 l multicolored | 2.25 | 1.50 |
| 2099 | A449 | 1.80 l multicolored | 2.25 | 1.75 |
| | Nos. 2097-2099 (3) | | 6.00 | 4.35 |

# ALBANIA

Archeological Discoveries — A450

Designs: Apollo, 3rd cent. 25q, Tombstone, Korce, 3rd cent. 80q, Apollo, diff. 1st cent. 1.10 l, Earthenware pot (child's head), Tren, 1st cent. 1.20 l, Man's head, Dyrrah, 2.20 l, Eros with Dolphin, statue Bronze Dyrrah, 3rd cent.

| 1984, Feb. 25 | | | Perf. 12x12½ | |
|---|---|---|---|---|
| 2100 | A450 | 15q multi | .25 | .25 |
| 2101 | A450 | 25q multi | .25 | .25 |
| 2102 | A450 | 80q multi | .80 | .50 |
| 2103 | A450 | 1.10 l multi | 1.20 | .75 |
| 2104 | A450 | 1.20 l multi | 1.60 | .85 |
| 2105 | A450 | 2.20 l multi | 2.50 | 1.00 |
| Nos. 2100-2105 (6) | | | 6.60 | 3.60 |

Clock Towers — A451

| 1984, Mar. 30 | | Litho. | Perf. 12 | |
|---|---|---|---|---|
| 2106 | A451 | 15q Gjirokaster | .25 | .25 |
| 2107 | A451 | 25q Kavaje | .25 | .25 |
| 2108 | A451 | 80q Elbasan | .80 | .50 |
| 2109 | A451 | 1.10 l Tirana | 1.00 | .75 |
| 2110 | A451 | 1.20 l Peqin | 1.25 | .90 |
| 2111 | A451 | 2.20 l Kruje | 2.25 | 1.50 |
| Nos. 2106-2111 (6) | | | 5.80 | 4.15 |

40th Anniv. of Liberation — A452

15q, Student & microscope. 25q, Guerrilla with flag. 80q, Children with flag. 1.10 l, Soldier. 1.20 l, Workers with flag. 2.20 l, Militia at dam.

| 1984, Apr. 20 | | Litho. | Perf. 12 | |
|---|---|---|---|---|
| 2112 | A452 | 15q multi | .25 | .25 |
| 2113 | A452 | 25q multi | .25 | .25 |
| 2114 | A452 | 80q multi | .90 | .45 |
| 2115 | A452 | 1.10 l multi | 1.20 | .75 |
| 2116 | A452 | 1.20 l multi | 1.50 | .90 |
| 2117 | A452 | 2.20 l multi | 2.25 | 1.10 |
| Nos. 2112-2117 (6) | | | 6.35 | 3.70 |

Children — A453

15q, Children reading. 25q, Young pioneers. 60q, Gardening. 2.80 l, Kite flying.

| 1984, May | | Litho. | Perf. 12 | |
|---|---|---|---|---|
| 2118 | A453 | 15q multicolored | .45 | .25 |
| 2119 | A453 | 25q multicolored | 1.00 | .25 |
| 2120 | A453 | 60q multicolored | 1.75 | .90 |
| 2121 | A453 | 2.80 l multicolored | 3.25 | 1.60 |
| Nos. 2118-2121 (4) | | | 6.45 | 3.00 |

**War Martyrs Type of 1980**

Designs: 15q, Manush Almani, Mustafa Matohiti, Kastriot Muco. 25q, Zaho Koka, Reshit Collaku, Maliq Muco. 1.20 l, Lefter Talo, Tom Kola, Fuat Babani. 2.20 l, Myslysm Shyri, Dervish Hexali, Skender Caci.

| 1984, May 5 | | Litho. | Perf. 12 | |
|---|---|---|---|---|
| 2122 | A410 | 15q multi | .45 | .25 |
| 2123 | A410 | 25q multi | .90 | .25 |
| 2124 | A410 | 1.20 l multi | 1.60 | .90 |
| 2125 | A410 | 2.20 l multi | 3.00 | 2.00 |
| Nos. 2122-2125 (4) | | | 5.95 | 3.40 |

A454

80q, Enver Hoxha. 1.10 l, Resistance fighter.

| 1984, May 24 | | Litho. | Perf. 12 | |
|---|---|---|---|---|
| 2126 | A454 | 80q multicolored | 2.25 | 1.50 |
| 2127 | A454 | 1.10 l multicolored | 2.75 | 1.75 |

40th anniv. of Permet Congress.

A455

15q, Goalkeeper. 25q, Referee. 1.20 l, Map of Europe. 2.20 l, Field diagram.

| 1984, June 12 | | Litho. | Perf. 12 | |
|---|---|---|---|---|
| 2128 | A455 | 15q multicolored | 1.00 | .25 |
| 2129 | A455 | 25q multicolored | 1.00 | .25 |
| 2130 | A455 | 1.20 l multicolored | 3.00 | .75 |
| 2131 | A455 | 2.20 l multicolored | 3.50 | 1.50 |
| Nos. 2128-2131 (4) | | | 8.50 | 2.75 |

European soccer championships.

Freedom Came, by Myrteza Fushekati A456

Paintings, Tirana Gallery of Figurative Art: 25q, Morning, by Zamir Mati, vert. 80q, My Darling, by Agim Zajmi, vert. 2.60 l, For the Partisans, by Arben Basha. 1.90 l, Eagle, by Zamir Mati, vert.

| 1984, June 12 | | | Perf. 12½ | |
|---|---|---|---|---|
| 2132 | A456 | 15q multi | .40 | .25 |
| 2133 | A456 | 25q multi | .80 | .35 |
| 2134 | A456 | 80q multi | 2.00 | 1.10 |
| 2135 | A456 | 2.60 l multi | 3.25 | 1.75 |
| Nos. 2132-2135 (4) | | | 6.45 | 3.45 |

**Souvenir Sheet**
*Perf. 12 Horiz.*

| 2136 | A456 | 1.90 l multi | 7.00 | 3.50 |
|---|---|---|---|---|

Flora — A457

15q, Moraceae L. 25q, Plantaginaceae L. 1.20 l, Hypericaceae L. 2.20 l, Leontopodium alpinum.

| 1984, Aug. 20 | | Litho. | Perf. 12 | |
|---|---|---|---|---|
| 2137 | A457 | 15q multicolored | 2.25 | .60 |
| 2138 | A457 | 25q multicolored | 3.00 | 1.10 |
| 2139 | A457 | 1.20 l multicolored | 8.25 | 3.50 |
| 2140 | A457 | 2.20 l multicolored | 17.00 | 6.50 |
| Nos. 2137-2140 (4) | | | 30.50 | 11.70 |

AUSIPEX '84, Melbourne, Sept. 21-30 — A458

*Perf. 12 Horiz.*

| 1984, Sept. 21 | | | Litho. | |
|---|---|---|---|---|
| 2141 | A458 | 1.90 l Sword dancers, emblem | 3.50 | 3.50 |

A459

Forestry, logging, UNFAO emblem — 15q, Beech trees, transport. 25q, Pine forest, logging cable. 1.20 l, Firs, sawmill. 2.20 l, Forester clearing woods.

| 1984, Sept. 25 | | | Perf. 12 | |
|---|---|---|---|---|
| 2142 | A459 | 15q multi | .80 | .45 |
| 2143 | A459 | 25q multi | 1.25 | .75 |
| 2144 | A459 | 1.20 l multi | 4.00 | 2.50 |
| 2145 | A459 | 2.20 l multi | 6.00 | 3.25 |
| Nos. 2142-2145 (4) | | | 12.05 | 6.95 |

View of Gjirokaster — A460

| 1984, Oct. 13 | | | Perf. 12½ | |
|---|---|---|---|---|
| 2146 | A460 | 1.20 l multicolored | 2.00 | 2.00 |

EURPHILA '84, Rome.

5th National Spartakiad — A461

15q, Soccer. 25q, Women's track & field. 80q, Weight lifting. 2.20 l, Pistol shooting. 1.90 l, Opening ceremony, red flags.

| 1984, Oct. 19 | | | Perf. 12 | |
|---|---|---|---|---|
| 2147 | A461 | 15q multicolored | .25 | .25 |
| 2148 | A461 | 25q multicolored | .30 | .25 |
| 2149 | A461 | 80q multicolored | .75 | .30 |
| 2150 | A461 | 2.20 l multicolored | 2.10 | 1.50 |
| Nos. 2147-2150 (4) | | | 3.40 | 2.30 |

**Souvenir Sheet**
*Perf. 12 Horiz.*

| 2151 | A461 | 1.90 l multicolored | 3.50 | 2.25 |
|---|---|---|---|---|

November 29 Revolution, 40th Anniv. — A462

80q, Industrial reconstruction. 1.10 l, Natl. flag, partisans. 1.90 l, Gen. Enver Hoxha reading 1944 declaration.

| 1984, Nov. 29 | | | Perf. 12 | |
|---|---|---|---|---|
| 2152 | A462 | 80q multicolored | 2.00 | .75 |
| 2153 | A462 | 1.10 l multicolored | 2.50 | 1.00 |

**Souvenir Sheet**
*Perf. 12 Horiz.*

| 2154 | A462 | 1.90 l multicolored | 3.50 | 3.50 |
|---|---|---|---|---|

Archaeological Discoveries from Illyria — A463

Designs: 15q, Iron Age water container. 80q, Terra-cotta woman's head, 6th-7th cent. B.C. 1.20 l, Aphrodite, bust, 3rd cent. B.C. 1.70 l, Nike, A.D. 1st-2nd cent. bronze statue.

| 1985, Feb. 25 | | | Perf. 12x12½ | |
|---|---|---|---|---|
| 2155 | A463 | 15q multi | .40 | .25 |
| 2156 | A463 | 80q multi | 1.50 | .75 |
| 2157 | A463 | 1.20 l multi | 2.00 | .90 |
| 2158 | A463 | 1.70 l multi | 3.00 | 1.50 |
| Nos. 2155-2158 (4) | | | 6.90 | 3.40 |

Hysni Kapo (1915-1980), Natl. Labor Party Leader — A464

| 1985, Mar. 4 | | | Perf. 12 | |
|---|---|---|---|---|
| 2159 | A464 | 90q red & blk | 1.40 | 1.00 |
| 2160 | A464 | 1.10 l chlky bl & blk | 1.75 | 1.50 |

OLYMPHILEX '85, Lausanne A465

25q, Women's track & field. 60q, Weight lifting. 1.20 l, Soccer. 1.50 l, Women's pistol shooting.

| 1985, Mar. 18 | | | | |
|---|---|---|---|---|
| 2161 | A465 | 25q multicolored | .25 | .25 |
| 2162 | A465 | 60q multicolored | .65 | .35 |
| 2163 | A465 | 1.20 l multicolored | 1.10 | .90 |
| 2164 | A465 | 1.50 l multicolored | 2.00 | 1.00 |
| Nos. 2161-2164 (4) | | | 4.00 | 2.50 |

Johann Sebastian Bach — A466

80q, Portrait, manuscript. 1.20 l, Eisenach, birthplace.

| 1985, Mar. 31 | | | | |
|---|---|---|---|---|
| 2165 | A466 | 80q multicolored | 16.00 | 8.00 |
| 2166 | A466 | 1.20 l multicolored | 20.00 | 10.00 |

Gen. Enver Hoxha (1908-1985) A467

| 1985, Apr. 11 | | | Perf. 12½ | |
|---|---|---|---|---|
| 2167 | A467 | 80q multicolored | 2.25 | 1.90 |

**Souvenir Sheet**
*Imperf.*

| 2168 | A467 | 1.90 l multicolored | 3.25 | 3.25 |
|---|---|---|---|---|

# ALBANIA

Natl. Frontier Guards, 40th Anniv. — A468

25q, Guardsman, family. 80q, At frontier post.

**1985, Apr. 25**    **Perf. 12**
| | | | | |
|---|---|---|---|---|
| 2169 | A468 | 25q multicolored | 1.00 | .75 |
| 2170 | A468 | 80q multicolored | 2.75 | 2.00 |

### War Martyrs Type of 1980

25q, Mitro Xhani (1916-44), Nimete Progonati (1929-44), Kozma Nushi (1909-44). 40q, Ajet Xhindoli (1922-43), Mustafa Kacaci (1903-44), Estref Caka Osaja (1919-44). 60q, Celo Sinani (1929-44), Lt. Ambro Andoni (1920-44), Meleq Gosnishti (1913-44). 1.20 l, Thodhori Mastora (1920-44), Fejzi Micoli (1919-45), Hysen Cino (1920-44).

**1985, May 5**
| | | | | |
|---|---|---|---|---|
| 2171 | A410 | 25q multi | .55 | .35 |
| 2172 | A410 | 40q multi | .85 | .70 |
| 2173 | A410 | 60q multi | 1.40 | .85 |
| 2174 | A410 | 1.20 l multi | 2.50 | 2.00 |
| | Nos. 2171-2174 (4) | | 5.30 | 3.90 |

Victory over Fascism — A469

25q, Rifle, red flag, inscribed May 9. 80q, Hand holding rifle, globe, broken swastika.

**1985, May 9**
| | | | | |
|---|---|---|---|---|
| 2175 | A469 | 25q multi | 22.50 | 35.00 |
| 2176 | A469 | 80q multi | 60.00 | 90.00 |

End of World War II, 40th anniv.

Primary School, by Thoma Malo — A470

Paintings, Tirana Gallery of Figurative Art: 80q, The Heroes, by Hysen Devolli, vert. 90q, In Our Days, by Angjelin Dodmasej, vert. 1.20 l, Going Off to Sow, by Ksenofon Dilo. 1.90 l, Foundry Workers, by Mikel Gurashi.

**1985, June 25**    **Perf. 12½**
| | | | | |
|---|---|---|---|---|
| 2177 | A470 | 25q multi | .25 | .25 |
| 2178 | A470 | 80q multi | 1.00 | .75 |
| 2179 | A470 | 90q multi | 1.25 | 1.00 |
| 2180 | A470 | 1.20 l multi | 1.60 | 1.25 |
| | Nos. 2177-2180 (4) | | 4.10 | 3.25 |

**Souvenir Sheet**
**Perf. 12 Horiz.**
| | | | | |
|---|---|---|---|---|
| 2181 | A470 | 1.90 l multi | 3.25 | 2.75 |

Basketball Championships, Spain — A471

Various plays.

**1985, July 20**    **Litho.**    **Perf. 12**
| | | | | |
|---|---|---|---|---|
| 2182 | A471 | 25q dull bl & blk | .30 | .25 |
| 2183 | A471 | 80q dull grn & blk | 1.10 | .35 |
| 2184 | A471 | 1.20 l dl vio & blk | 1.40 | .90 |
| 2185 | A471 | 1.60 l dl rose & blk | 2.25 | 1.50 |
| | Nos. 2182-2185 (4) | | 5.05 | 3.00 |

Fruits — A472

**1985, Aug. 20**
| | | | | |
|---|---|---|---|---|
| 2186 | A472 | 25q Oranges | .40 | .25 |
| 2187 | A472 | 80q Plums | 2.00 | 1.10 |
| 2188 | A472 | 1.20 l Apples | 3.25 | 1.50 |
| 2189 | A472 | 1.60 l Cherries | 4.00 | 2.25 |
| | Nos. 2186-2189 (4) | | 9.65 | 5.10 |

Architecture A473

**1985, Sept. 20**
| | | | | |
|---|---|---|---|---|
| 2190 | A473 | 25q Kruja | .40 | .40 |
| 2191 | A473 | 80q Gjirokastra | 1.90 | 1.10 |
| 2192 | A473 | 1.20 l Berati | 2.25 | 1.50 |
| 2193 | A473 | 1.60 l Shkodera | 3.00 | 1.75 |
| | Nos. 2190-2193 (4) | | 7.55 | 4.75 |

Natl. Folk Theater Festival — A474

Various scenes from folk plays.

**1985, Oct. 6**
| | | | | |
|---|---|---|---|---|
| 2194 | A474 | 25q multi | .40 | .25 |
| 2195 | A474 | 80q multi | 1.10 | .75 |
| 2196 | A474 | 1.20 l multi | 1.50 | .90 |
| 2197 | A474 | 1.60 l multi | 2.00 | 1.40 |

**Size: 56x82mm**
**Imperf**
| | | | | |
|---|---|---|---|---|
| 2198 | A474 | 1.90 l multi | 3.00 | 2.25 |
| | Nos. 2194-2198 (5) | | 8.00 | 5.55 |

Socialist People's Republic, 40th Anniv. — A475

25q, Natl. crest, vert. 80q, Proclamation, 1946.

**1986, Jan. 11**    **Litho.**    **Perf. 12½**
| | | | | |
|---|---|---|---|---|
| 2199 | A475 | 25q multicolored | 1.50 | .75 |
| 2200 | A475 | 80q multicolored | 3.00 | 1.50 |

A476

Designs: 25q, Dam, River Drin, Melgun. 80q, Bust of Enver Hoxha, dam power house.

**1986, Feb. 20**    **Perf. 12**
| | | | | |
|---|---|---|---|---|
| 2201 | A476 | 25q multi | 5.50 | 2.00 |
| 2202 | A476 | 80q multi | 12.00 | 7.00 |

Enver Hoxha hydro-electric power station, Koman.

A477

Flowers: 25q, Gymnospermium shqipetarum. 1.20 l, Leucojum valentinum.

**1986, Mar. 20**    **Litho.**    **Perf. 12**
| | | | | |
|---|---|---|---|---|
| 2203 | A477 | 25q multi | 2.00 | 1.00 |
| 2204 | A477 | 1.20 l multi | 8.00 | 4.00 |
| a. | | Pair, #2203-2204 | 12.00 | 12.00 |

Nos. 2203-2204 exist imperf. Value, pair: mint $40, used $35.

A478

Famous Men A479

Designs: 25q, Maxim Gorky, Russian author. 80q, Andre Marie Ampere, French physicist. 1.20 l, James Watt, English inventor of modern steam engine. 2.40 l, Franz Liszt, Hungarian composer.

**1986, Apr. 20**
| | | | | |
|---|---|---|---|---|
| 2205 | | Strip of 4 | 10.00 | 6.50 |
| a. | | A478 25q dull red brown | .40 | .40 |
| b. | | A478 80q dull violet | 1.60 | 1.00 |
| c. | | A478 1.20 l blue green | 3.00 | 1.60 |
| d. | | A478 2.40 l dull lilac rose | 5.75 | 3.75 |

**Size: 88x72mm**
**Imperf**
| | | | | |
|---|---|---|---|---|
| 2206 | A479 | 1.90 l multi | 5.00 | 3.00 |

No. 2206 has central area picturing Gorky, Ampere, Watt and Liszt, perf. 12½.

### War Martyrs Type of 1980

25q, Ramiz Aranitasi (1923-43), Inajete Dumi (1924-44) and Laze Nuro Ferraj (1897-1944). 80q, Dine Kalenja (1919-44), Kozma Naska (1921-44), Mot Hasa (1929-44) and Fahri Ramadani (1920-44). 1.20 l, Hiqmet Buzi (1927-44), Bairam Tusha (1922-42), Mumin Selami (1923-42) and Hajridin Bylyshi (1920-42).

**1986, May 5**    **Perf. 12**
| | | | | |
|---|---|---|---|---|
| 2207 | A410 | 25q multi | 1.25 | 1.00 |
| 2208 | A410 | 80q multi | 3.25 | 1.60 |
| 2209 | A410 | 1.20 l multi | 5.25 | 3.25 |
| | Nos. 2207-2209 (3) | | 9.75 | 5.85 |

A480

1986 World Cup Soccer Championships, Mexico — A481

25q, Globe, world cup. 1.20 l, Player, soccer ball.

**1986, May 31**    **Litho.**    **Perf. 12**
| | | | | |
|---|---|---|---|---|
| 2210 | A480 | 25q multicolored | .40 | .30 |
| 2211 | A480 | 1.20 l multicolored | 2.00 | 1.50 |

**Size: 97x64mm**
**Imperf**
| | | | | |
|---|---|---|---|---|
| 2212 | A481 | 1.90 l multicolored | 3.00 | 2.25 |
| | Nos. 2210-2212 (3) | | 5.40 | 4.05 |

No. 2212 has central label, perf. 12½.

Transportation Workers' Day, 40th Anniv. — A482

**1986, Aug. 10**    **Litho.**    **Perf. 12**
| | | | | |
|---|---|---|---|---|
| 2213 | A482 | 1.20 l multi | 11.00 | 6.50 |

Prominent Albanians A483

Designs: 30q, Naim Frasheri (1846-1900), poet. 60q, Ndre Mjeda (1866-1937), poet. 90q, Petro Nini Luarasi (1865-1911), poet, journalist. 1 l, Andon Zako Cajupi (1866-1930), poet. 1.20 l, Millosh Gjergj Nikolla Migjeni (1911-1938), novelist. 2.60 l, Urani Rumbo (1884-1936), educator.

**1986, Sept. 20**    **Litho.**    **Perf. 12**
| | | | | |
|---|---|---|---|---|
| 2214 | A483 | 30q multi | .55 | .30 |
| 2215 | A483 | 60q multi | .90 | .75 |
| 2216 | A483 | 90q multi | 1.50 | 1.00 |
| 2217 | A483 | 1 l multi | 1.90 | 1.25 |
| 2218 | A483 | 1.20 l multi | 2.25 | 1.50 |
| 2219 | A483 | 2.60 l multi | 6.00 | 2.50 |
| | Nos. 2214-2219 (6) | | 13.10 | 7.30 |

Albanian Workers' Party, 9th Congress, Tirana — A484

**1986, Nov. 3**    **Litho.**    **Perf. 12**
| | | | | |
|---|---|---|---|---|
| 2220 | A484 | 30q multi | 7.50 | 5.50 |

No. 2220 exists with country name misspelled "SHQIPERSIE." Value, mint, $150.

A485

Albanian Workers' Party, 45th Anniv.: 30q, Handstamp, signature of Hoxha. 1.20 l, Marx, Engels, Lenin and Stalin, party building.

**1986, Nov. 8**
| | | | | |
|---|---|---|---|---|
| 2221 | A485 | 30q multi | 4.00 | 1.00 |
| 2222 | A485 | 1.20 l multi | 11.00 | 3.00 |

A486

Statue of Mother Albania.

**1986, Nov. 29**    **Perf. 12x12½**
| | | | | |
|---|---|---|---|---|
| 2223 | A486 | 10q peacock blue | .25 | .25 |
| 2224 | A486 | 20q henna brn | .25 | .25 |
| 2225 | A486 | 30q vermilion | .25 | .25 |
| 2226 | A486 | 50q dk olive bis | .25 | .25 |
| 2227 | A486 | 60q lt olive grn | .35 | .25 |
| 2228 | A486 | 80q rose | .25 | .25 |
| 2229 | A486 | 90q ultra | .50 | .25 |
| 2230 | A486 | 1.20 l green | 1.00 | .50 |
| 2231 | A486 | 1.60 l red vio | 1.25 | .60 |
| 2232 | A486 | 2.20 l myrtle grn | 2.00 | 1.25 |
| 2233 | A486 | 3 l brn org | 2.50 | 1.75 |
| 2234 | A486 | 6 l yel bister | 5.00 | 3.25 |
| | Nos. 2223-2234 (12) | | 13.85 | 9.10 |

For surcharges see Nos. 2435-2439.

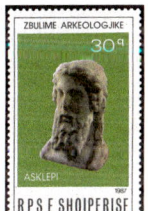

Artifacts — A487

Designs: 30q, Head of Aesoulaplus, 5th cent. B.C. Byllis, marble. 80q, Aphrodite, 3rd cent. B.C., Fier, terracotta. 1 l, Pan, 3rd-2nd cent. B.C., Byllis, bronze. 1.20 l, Jupiter, A.D. 2nd cent., Tirana, limestone.

## ALBANIA

**1987, Feb. 20**
| 2235 | A487 | 30q multi | 1.00 | .60 |
| 2236 | A487 | 80q multi | 2.00 | 1.00 |
| 2237 | A487 | 1 l multi | 3.00 | 1.40 |
| 2238 | A487 | 1.20 l multi | 4.00 | 2.50 |
| | Nos. 2235-2238 (4) | | 10.00 | 5.50 |

A488

Gun, quill pen, book of the alphabet and: 30q, Monument, vert. 80q, School, Korca. 1.20 l, Students.

**1987, Mar. 7** — Perf. 12
| 2239 | A488 | 30q multi | .40 | .25 |
| 2240 | A488 | 80q multi | 1.25 | .50 |
| 2241 | A488 | 1.20 l multi | 1.75 | 1.25 |
| | Nos. 2239-2241 (3) | | 3.40 | 2.00 |

First Albanian school, cent.

A489

Famous Men: 30q, Victor Hugo, French author. 80q, Galileo Galilei, Italian mathematician, philosopher. 90q, Charles Darwin, British biologist. 1.30 l, Miguel Cervantes, Spanish novelist.

**1987, Apr. 20**
| 2242 | A489 | 30q multi | .45 | .25 |
| 2243 | A489 | 80q multi | 1.10 | .50 |
| 2244 | A489 | 90q multi | 1.60 | 1.10 |
| 2245 | A489 | 1.30 l multi | 2.25 | 1.75 |
| | Nos. 2242-2245 (4) | | 5.40 | 3.60 |

World Food Day — A490

30q, Forsythia europaea. 90q, Moltkia doerfleri. 2.10 l, Wulfenia baldacii.

**1987, May 20**
| 2246 | A490 | 30q multicolored | .55 | .30 |
| 2247 | A490 | 90q multicolored | 1.10 | .75 |
| 2248 | A490 | 2.10 l multicolored | 2.40 | 2.10 |
| | Nos. 2246-2248 (3) | | 4.05 | 3.15 |

10th Trade Unions Cong. — A491

**1987, June 25**
| 2249 | A491 | 1.20 l multi | 4.00 | 3.00 |

Sowing, by Bujar Asllani A492

Paintings in the Eponymous Museum, Tirana: 30q, The Sustenance of Industry, by Myrteza Fushekati, vert. 80q, The Gifted Partisan, by Skender Kokobobo, vert. 1.20 l, At the Forging Block, by Clirim Ceka.

**Perf. 12x12½, 12½x12**
**1987, July 20** — Litho.
| 2250 | A492 | 30q multi | .50 | .40 |
| 2251 | A492 | 80q multi | .80 | .80 |
| 2252 | A492 | 1 l shown | 1.20 | 1.00 |
| 2253 | A492 | 1.20 l multi | 1.60 | 1.40 |
| | Nos. 2250-2253 (4) | | 4.10 | 3.60 |

A493

OLYMPHILEX '87, Rome, Aug. 29-Sept. 6 — A494

**1987, Aug. 29** — Litho. Perf. 12½
| 2254 | A493 | 30q Hammer throw | .40 | .40 |
| 2255 | A493 | 90q Running | 1.25 | .80 |
| 2256 | A493 | 1.10 l Shot put | 1.25 | 1.00 |

Size: 85x60mm
| 2257 | A494 | 1.90 l Runner, globe | 2.50 | 2.00 |
| | Nos. 2254-2257 (4) | | 5.40 | 4.20 |

Famous Men — A495

Designs: 30q, Themistokli Germenji (1871-1917), author, politician. 80q, Bajram Curri (1862-1925), founder of the Albanian League. 90q, Aleks Stavre Drenova (1872-1947), poet. 1.30 l, Gjerasim D. Qiriazi (1861-1894), teacher, journalist.

**1987, Sept. 30** — Perf. 12
| 2258 | A495 | 30q multi | .25 | .25 |
| 2259 | A495 | 80q multi | .90 | .30 |
| 2260 | A495 | 90q multi | 1.10 | .75 |
| 2261 | A495 | 1.30 l multi | 1.90 | 1.50 |
| | Nos. 2258-2261 (4) | | 4.15 | 2.80 |

Albanian Labor Party Congress, Tirana — A496

**1987, Oct. 22** — Litho. Perf. 12
| 2262 | A496 | 1.20 l multi | 5.00 | 3.50 |

Natl. Independence, 75th Anniv. — A497

**1987, Nov. 27**
| 2263 | A497 | 1.20 l State flag | 5.50 | 4.00 |

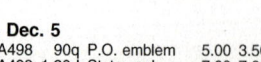
Postal Administration, 75th Anniv. — A498

**1987, Dec. 5**
| 2264 | A498 | 90q P.O. emblem | 5.00 | 3.50 |
| 2265 | A498 | 1.20 l State seal | 7.00 | 7.00 |

Art & Literature — A499

Portraits: 30q, Lord Byron (1788-1824), English Poet. 1.20 l, Eugene Delacroix (1798-1863), French painter.

**1988, Mar. 10**
| 2266 | A499 | 30q org brn & blk | 4.00 | 3.25 |
| 2267 | A499 | 1.20 l pale vio & blk | 16.00 | 12.50 |

WHO, 40th Anniv. — A500

**1988, Apr. 7**
| 2268 | A500 | 90q multi | 22.50 | 20.00 |
| 2269 | A500 | 1.20 l multi | 30.00 | 25.00 |

Flowers — A501

Designs: 30q, Sideritis raeseri. 90q, Lunaria telekiana. 2.10 l, Sanguisorba albanica.

**1988, May 20** — Booklet Stamps
| 2270 | A501 | 30q multicolored | 8.00 | 5.00 |
| 2271 | A501 | 90q multicolored | 16.00 | 11.00 |
| 2272 | A501 | 2.10 l multicolored | 24.00 | 16.00 |
| a. | Bklt. pane of 3, plus label | | 50.00 | 50.00 |
| | Nos. 2270-2272 (3) | | 48.00 | 32.00 |

10th Women's Federation Congress — A502

**1988, June 6**
| 2273 | A502 | 90q blk, red & dark org | 21.00 | 19.00 |

European Soccer Championships A503

Various athletes.
1.90 l, Goalie designs of Nos. 2274-2276.

**1988, June 10**
| 2274 | A503 | 30q multicolored | 2.00 | 2.00 |
| 2275 | A503 | 80q multicolored | 3.00 | 3.00 |
| 2276 | A503 | 1.20 l multicolored | 5.00 | 5.00 |

Size: 79x68mm
**Imperf**
| 2277 | A503 | 1.90 l multicolored | 12.00 | 12.00 |
| | Nos. 2274-2277 (4) | | 22.00 | 22.00 |

League of Prizren, 110th Anniv. — A504

**1988, June 10** — Litho. Perf. 12
| 2278 | A504 | 30q Hands | 40.00 | 40.00 |
| 2279 | A504 | 1.20 l House | 70.00 | 70.00 |

People's Army, 45th Anniv. — A505

**1988, July 10**
| 2280 | A505 | 60q shown | 40.00 | 40.00 |
| 2281 | A505 | 90q Soldier statue | 70.00 | 70.00 |

Famous Albanians — A506

Designs: 30q, Mihal Grameno (1871-1931), author. 90q, Bajo Topulli (1868-1930), freedom fighter. 1 l, Murat Toptani (1868-1917), poet. 1.20 l, Jul Variboba, poet.

**1988, Aug. 15**
| 2282 | A506 | 30q multi | 15.00 | 15.00 |
| 2283 | A506 | 90q multi | 25.00 | 25.00 |
| 2284 | A506 | 1 l multi | 30.00 | 30.00 |
| 2284A | A506 | 1.20 l multi | 40.00 | 40.00 |
| | Nos. 2282-2284A (4) | | 110.00 | 110.00 |

Migjeni (1911-1938), Poet — A507

**1988, Aug. 26** — Litho. Perf. 12
| 2285 | A507 | 90q silver & brown | 12.00 | 12.00 |

Ballads — A508

**1988, Sept. 5**
| 2286 | A508 | 30q Dede Skurra | 10.00 | 8.00 |
| 2287 | A508 | 90q Omeri Iri | 25.00 | 21.00 |
| 2288 | A508 | 1.20 l Gjergj Elez Alia | 30.00 | 25.00 |
| | Nos. 2286-2288 (3) | | 65.00 | 54.00 |

**Folklore Festival Type of 1978**
30q, Kerchief Dance. 1.20 l, Dancers with raised arm.

**1988, Oct. 6**
| 2289 | A388 | 30q multi | 30.00 | 30.00 |
| 2290 | A388 | 1.20 l multi | 110.00 | 90.00 |

Enver Hoxha Museum A510

**Perf. 12x12½, 12½x12**
**1988, Oct. 16** — Litho.
| 2291 | A510 | 90q Portrait, vert. | 4.00 | 4.00 |
| 2292 | A510 | 1.20 l shown | 6.00 | 6.00 |

Hoxha (1908-85), Communist leader.

Monastir Congress, 80th Anniv. — A511

**1988, Nov. 14** — Litho. Perf. 12
| 2293 | A511 | 60q Scroll | 22.50 | 20.00 |
| 2294 | A511 | 90q Book, building | 35.00 | 30.00 |

# ALBANIA

Locomotives, Map Showing Rail Network — A512

**1989, Feb. 28    Litho.    Perf. 12½x12**
| 2295 | A512 | 30q 1947 | .25 | .25 |
|---|---|---|---|---|
| 2296 | A512 | 90q 1949 | .75 | .35 |
| 2297 | A512 | 1.20 l 1978 | 1.00 | .60 |
| 2298 | A512 | 1.80 l 1985 | 1.60 | .75 |
| 2299 | A512 | 2.40 l 1988 | 3.75 | 1.50 |
| | | Nos. 2295-2299 (5) | 7.35 | 3.45 |

Archaeological Treasures — A513

30q, Illyrian grave. 90q, Warrior on horseback.

**1989, Mar. 10    Litho.    Perf. 12**
| 2300 | A513 | 30q blk & tan | .25 | .25 |
|---|---|---|---|---|
| 2301 | A513 | 90q blk & dl grn | .90 | .75 |
| 2302 | A513 | 2.10 l shown | 1.50 | 1.25 |
| | | Nos. 2300-2302 (3) | 2.65 | 2.25 |

Folklore — A514

**1989, Apr. 5    Litho.    Perf. 12x12½**
| 2303 | A514 | 30q multicolored | .45 | .25 |
|---|---|---|---|---|
| 2304 | A514 | 80q multi, diff. | .90 | .50 |
| 2305 | A514 | 1 l multi, diff. | .90 | .75 |
| 2306 | A514 | 1.20 l multi, diff. | 1.25 | 1.10 |
| | | Nos. 2303-2306 (4) | 3.50 | 2.60 |

Flowers — A515

Designs: 30q, Aster albanicus. 90q, Orchis x paparisti. 2.10 l, Orchis albanica.

**1989, May 10    Perf. 12**
| 2307 | A515 | 30q multicolored | .75 | .30 |
|---|---|---|---|---|
| 2308 | A515 | 90q multicolored | 3.25 | 1.10 |
| 2309 | A515 | 2.10 l multicolored | 5.25 | 1.75 |
| | | Nos. 2307-2309 (3) | 9.25 | 3.15 |

Famous People — A516

Designs: 30q, Johann Strauss the Younger (1825-1899), composer. 80q, Marie Curie (1867-1934), chemist. 1 l, Federico Garcia Lorca (1898-1936), poet. 1.20 l, Albert Einstein (1879-1955), physicist.

**1989, June 3**
| 2310 | A516 | 30q gold & blk brn | .35 | .25 |
|---|---|---|---|---|
| 2311 | A516 | 80q gold & blk brn | .75 | .45 |
| 2312 | A516 | 1 l gold & blk brn | 1.10 | .90 |
| 2313 | A516 | 1.20 l gold & blk brn | 1.50 | 1.25 |
| a. | | Block of 4, #2310-2313 | 5.50 | 4.75 |
| | | Nos. 2310-2313 (4) | 3.70 | 2.85 |

6th Congress of Albanian Democratic Front — A517

**1989, June 26**
| 2314 | A517 | 1.20 l multicolored | 7.25 | 4.00 |
|---|---|---|---|---|

French Revolution, Bicent. — A518

90q, Storming of the Bastille. 1.20 l, Statue.

**1989, July 7    Litho.    Perf. 12½**
| 2315 | A518 | 90q multicolored | .65 | .45 |
|---|---|---|---|---|
| 2316 | A518 | 1.20 l shown | 1.20 | .75 |

Illyrian Ship — A519

80q, Caravel. 90q, 3-masted schooner. 1.30 l, Modern cargo ship.

**1989, July 25    Perf. 12**
| 2317 | A519 | 30q shown | .35 | .25 |
|---|---|---|---|---|
| 2318 | A519 | 80q multicolored | .70 | .50 |
| 2319 | A519 | 90q multicolored | .70 | .70 |
| 2320 | A519 | 1.30 l multicolored | 1.00 | 1.00 |
| | | Nos. 2317-2320 (4) | 2.75 | 2.45 |

A520

Famous Men: 30q, Pjeter Bogdani (1625-1689), writer. 80q, Gavril Dara (1826-1889), poet. 90q, Thimi Mitko (1820-1890), writer. 1.30 l, Kole Idromeno (1860-1939), painter.

**1989, Aug. 30    Litho.    Perf. 12**
| 2321 | A520 | 30q multicolored | .25 | .25 |
|---|---|---|---|---|
| 2322 | A520 | 80q multicolored | .55 | .30 |
| 2323 | A520 | 90q multicolored | .95 | .60 |
| 2324 | A520 | 1.30 l multicolored | 1.60 | .75 |
| | | Nos. 2321-2324 (4) | 3.35 | 1.90 |

A521

**1989, Sept. 29**
| 2325 | A521 | 90q shown | .70 | .60 |
|---|---|---|---|---|
| 2326 | A521 | 1.20 l Workers | 1.00 | .50 |

First Communist International, 125th anniv.

Spartakiad Games — A522

**1989, Oct. 27    Perf. 12x12½**
| 2327 | A522 | 30q Gymnastics | .25 | .25 |
|---|---|---|---|---|
| 2328 | A522 | 80q Soccer | .50 | .25 |
| 2329 | A522 | 1 l Cycling | .55 | .45 |
| 2330 | A522 | 1.20 l Running | .85 | .75 |
| | | Nos. 2327-2330 (4) | 2.15 | 1.70 |

Miniature Sheet

45th Anniv. of Liberation — A523

**1989, Nov. 29    Perf. 12x12½**
| 2331 | A523 | Sheet of 4 | 4.25 | 4.25 |
|---|---|---|---|---|
| a. | | 30q Revolutionary | .50 | .25 |
| b. | | 80q "45" | 1.00 | .30 |
| c. | | 1 l Coat of arms | 1.00 | .50 |
| d. | | 1.20 l Workers | 1.00 | .85 |

Rupicapra Rupicapra — A524

**1990, Mar. 15    Perf. 12**
| 2332 | A524 | 10q Two adults | .25 | .25 |
|---|---|---|---|---|
| 2333 | A524 | 30q Adult, kid | .55 | .25 |
| 2334 | A524 | 80q Adult | 1.60 | .75 |
| 2335 | A524 | 90q Adult head | 1.60 | 1.00 |
| a. | | Block of 4, #2332-2335 | 6.00 | 6.00 |

World Wildlife Fund.

Tribal Masks — A525

**1990, Apr. 4    Perf. 12x12½**
| 2336 | A525 | 30q shown | .30 | .30 |
|---|---|---|---|---|
| 2337 | A525 | 90q multi, diff. | .65 | .40 |
| 2338 | A525 | 1.20 l multi, diff. | .90 | .55 |
| 2339 | A525 | 1.80 l multi, diff. | 1.40 | .80 |
| | | Nos. 2336-2339 (4) | 3.25 | 2.05 |

Mushrooms A526

30q, Amanita caesarea. 90q, Lepiota procera. 1.20 l, Boletus edulis. 1.80 l, Clathrus cancelatus.

**1990, Apr. 28    Litho.    Perf. 12**
| 2340 | A526 | 30q multicolored | .25 | .25 |
|---|---|---|---|---|
| 2341 | A526 | 90q multicolored | .50 | .40 |
| 2342 | A526 | 1.20 l multi | .85 | .80 |
| 2343 | A526 | 1.80 l multi | 1.20 | 1.00 |
| | | Nos. 2340-2343 (4) | 2.80 | 2.45 |

First Postage Stamp, 150th Anniv. — A527

**1990, May 6    Perf. 12**
| 2344 | A527 | 90q shown | .45 | .45 |
|---|---|---|---|---|
| 2345 | A527 | 1.20 l Post rider | .90 | .90 |
| 2346 | A527 | 1.80 l Carriage | 1.70 | 1.25 |
| a. | | Bklt. pane of 3, #2344-2346 + label | 3.50 | |
| | | Nos. 2344-2346 (3) | 3.10 | 2.60 |

World Cup Soccer, Italy — A528

**1990, June    Litho.    Perf. 12**
| 2347 | A528 | 30q multicolored | .30 | .30 |
|---|---|---|---|---|
| 2348 | A528 | 90q multi, diff. | .65 | .65 |
| 2349 | A528 | 1.20 l multi, diff. | 1.10 | .90 |

**Size: 80x63mm**
*Imperf*
| 2350 | A528 | 3.30 l multi, diff. | 3.25 | 3.25 |
|---|---|---|---|---|
| | | Nos. 2347-2350 (4) | 5.30 | 5.10 |

Vincent Van Gogh, Death Cent. — A529

Self portraits and: 30q, Details from various paintings. 90q, Woman in field. 2.10 l, Asylum. 2.40 l, Self-portrait.

**1990, July 27**
| 2351 | A529 | 30q multicolored | .40 | .40 |
|---|---|---|---|---|
| 2352 | A529 | 90q multicolored | .80 | .80 |
| 2353 | A529 | 2.10 l multicolored | 1.75 | 1.75 |

**Size: 87x73mm**
*Imperf*
| 2354 | A529 | 2.40 l multicolored | 4.00 | 4.00 |
|---|---|---|---|---|
| | | Nos. 2351-2354 (4) | 6.95 | 6.95 |

Albanian Folklore A530

Scenes from medieval folktale of "Gjergj Elez Alia": 30q, Alia lying wounded. 90q, Alia being helped onto horse. 1.20 l, Alia fighting Bajloz. 1.80 l, Alia on horseback over severed head of Bajloz.

**1990, Aug. 30    Perf. 12½x12**
| 2355 | A530 | 30q multicolored | .30 | .30 |
|---|---|---|---|---|
| 2356 | A530 | 90q multicolored | .70 | .40 |
| 2357 | A530 | 1.20 l multicolored | 1.00 | .80 |
| 2358 | A530 | 1.80 l multicolored | 1.50 | 1.00 |
| | | Nos. 2355-2358 (4) | 3.50 | 2.50 |

Founding of Berat, 2400th Anniv. — A531

Designs: 30q, Xhamia E Plumbit. 90q, Kisha E Shen Triadhes. 1.20 l, Ura E Beratit. 1.80 l, Onufri-Piktor Mesjetar. 2.40 l, Nikolla-Piktor Mesjetar.

**1990, Sept. 20    Perf. 12½**
| 2359 | | Block of 5 + 4 labels | 5.00 | 5.00 |
|---|---|---|---|---|
| a. | A531 | 30q multi | .25 | .25 |
| b. | A531 | 90q multi | .25 | .25 |
| c. | A531 | 1.20 l multi | .60 | .60 |
| d. | A531 | 1.80 l multi | 1.00 | 1.00 |
| e. | A531 | 2.40 l multi | 1.25 | 1.25 |

No. 2359 was sold in souvenir folders for 9.90 l.

Illyrian Heroes — A532

**1990, Oct. 20    Perf. 12**
| 2360 | A532 | 30q Pirroja | .25 | .25 |
|---|---|---|---|---|
| 2361 | A532 | 90q Teuta | .50 | .50 |
| 2362 | A532 | 1.20 l Bato | .75 | .75 |
| 2363 | A532 | 1.80 l Bardhyli | 1.00 | 1.00 |
| | | Nos. 2360-2363 (4) | 2.50 | 2.50 |

Intl. Literacy Year — A533

**1990, Oct. 30**
| 2364 | A533 | 90q lt bl & multi | .65 | .60 |
|---|---|---|---|---|
| 2365 | A533 | 1.20 l pink & multi | .90 | .90 |

# ALBANIA

Albanian Horseman by Eugene Delacroix — A534

Designs: 1.20 l, Albanian Woman by Camille Corot. 1.80 l, Skanderbeg by unknown artist.

| 1990, Nov. 30 | | | Perf. 12x12½ | |
|---|---|---|---|---|
| 2366 | A534 | 30q multicolored | .30 | .30 |
| 2367 | A534 | 1.20 l multicolored | .90 | .70 |
| 2368 | A534 | 1.80 l multicolored | 1.25 | 1.00 |
| | | Nos. 2366-2368 (3) | 2.45 | 2.00 |

A535

1.20 l, Boletini standing.

| 1991, Jan. 23 | | Litho. | Perf. 12x12½ | |
|---|---|---|---|---|
| 2369 | A535 | 90q shown | .60 | .50 |
| 2370 | A535 | 1.20 l multicolored | .90 | .70 |

Isa Boletini (1864-1916), freedom fighter.

A536

| 1991, Jan. 30 | | Litho. | Perf. 12 | |
|---|---|---|---|---|
| | | Background Color | | |
| 2371 | A536 | 90q pale yellow | .60 | .50 |
| 2372 | A536 | 1.20 l pale gray | .90 | .70 |

Arberi State, 800th anniv.

Pierre Auguste Renoir (1841-1919), Painter — A537

Paintings: 30q, Girl Reading, 1876, vert. 90q, The Swing, 1876, vert. 1.20 l, Boating Party, 1868-1869. 1.80 l, Flowers and grapes, 1878. 3 l, Self-portrait.

| 1991, Feb. 25 | | | Perf. 12½x12 | |
|---|---|---|---|---|
| 2373 | A537 | 30q multicolored | .50 | .25 |
| 2374 | A537 | 90q multicolored | .75 | .50 |
| 2375 | A537 | 1.20 l multicolored | 1.10 | .90 |
| 2376 | A537 | 1.80 l multicolored | 1.75 | 1.40 |

Size: 95x75mm
Imperf

| 2377 | A537 | 3 l multicolored | 4.00 | 4.00 |
|---|---|---|---|---|
| | | Nos. 2373-2377 (5) | 8.10 | 7.05 |

Flowers — A538

30q, Cistus albanicus. 90q, Trifolium pilczii. 1.80 l, Lilium albanicum.

| 1991, Mar. 30 | | | Perf. 12 | |
|---|---|---|---|---|
| 2378 | A538 | 30q multicolored | .30 | .30 |
| 2379 | A538 | 90q multicolored | .70 | .70 |
| 2380 | A538 | 1.80 l multicolored | 1.40 | 1.00 |
| | | Nos. 2378-2380 (3) | 2.40 | 2.00 |

Legend of Rozafa — A539

Various scenes from legend.

| 1991, Sept. 30 | | Litho. | Perf. 12x12½ | |
|---|---|---|---|---|
| 2381 | A539 | 30q multicolored | .30 | .30 |
| 2382 | A539 | 90q multicolored | .50 | .30 |
| 2383 | A539 | 1.20 l multicolored | 1.00 | .70 |
| 2384 | A539 | 1.80 l multicolored | 1.40 | 1.20 |
| | | Nos. 2381-2384 (4) | 3.20 | 2.50 |

For surcharges see Nos. 2586, 2604.

Wolfgang Amadeus Mozart, Death Bicent. — A540

| 1991, Oct. 5 | | Litho. | Perf. 12 | |
|---|---|---|---|---|
| 2385 | A540 | 90q Conducting | .75 | .45 |
| 2386 | A540 | 1.20 l Portrait | 1.00 | .70 |
| 2387 | A540 | 1.80 l Playing piano | 1.60 | 1.20 |

Size: 89x70mm
Imperf

| 2388 | A540 | 3 l Medal, score | 4.00 | 4.00 |
|---|---|---|---|---|
| | | Nos. 2385-2388 (4) | 7.35 | 6.35 |

Airplanes A541

Designs: 30q, Glider, Otto Lilienthal, 1896. 80q, Avion III, Clement Ader, 1897. 90q, Flyer, Wright Brothers, 1903. 1.20 l, Concorde. 1.80 l, Tupolev 114. 2.40 l, Dornier 31 E.

| 1992, Jan. 27 | | Litho. | Perf. 12½x12 | |
|---|---|---|---|---|
| 2389 | A541 | 30q multicolored | .30 | .30 |
| 2390 | A541 | 80q multicolored | .45 | .35 |
| 2391 | A541 | 90q multicolored | .65 | .55 |
| 2392 | A541 | 1.20 l multicolored | .90 | .65 |
| 2393 | A541 | 1.80 l multicolored | .90 | .65 |
| 2394 | A541 | 2.40 l multicolored | 1.40 | 1.20 |
| | | Nos. 2389-2394 (6) | 4.60 | 3.70 |

No. 2393 misidentifies a Tupolev 144.

Explorers A542

1992, Jan. 10

| 2395 | A542 | 30q Bering | .30 | .30 |
|---|---|---|---|---|
| 2396 | A542 | 90q Columbus | .70 | .30 |
| 2397 | A542 | 1.80 l Magellan | 1.50 | .90 |
| | | Nos. 2395-2397 (3) | 2.50 | 1.50 |

1992 Winter Olympics, Albertville — A543

30q, Ski jumping. 90q, Cross country skiing. 1.20 l, Pairs figure skating. 1.80 l, Luge.

| 1992, Feb. 15 | | Litho. | Perf. 12½ | |
|---|---|---|---|---|
| 2398 | A543 | 30q multicolored | .30 | .30 |
| 2399 | A543 | 90q multicolored | .60 | .45 |
| 2400 | A543 | 1.20 l multicolored | .90 | .60 |
| 2401 | A543 | 1.80 l multicolored | 1.40 | 1.00 |
| | | Nos. 2398-2401 (4) | 3.20 | 2.35 |

For surcharge see No. 2598.

Participation of Albania in Conference on Security and Cooperation in Europe, Berlin (1991) — A544

| 1992, Mar. 31 | | Litho. | Perf. 12½x12 | |
|---|---|---|---|---|
| 2402 | A544 | 90q shown | .85 | .85 |
| 2403 | A544 | 1.20 l Flags, map | 1.10 | 1.10 |
| a. | | Pair, #2402-2403 | 3.50 | 3.50 |

Dated 1991. Issued in sheets containing 2 No. 2403a, 3 each Nos. 2402-2403 + 2 labels. No. 2402 was also issued in sheets of 16.

Albanian Admission to CEPT — A545

90q, Envelopes, CEPT emblem.

| 1992, Apr. 25 | | Litho. | Perf. 12½ | |
|---|---|---|---|---|
| 2404 | A545 | 90q blk, blue & red lil | .90 | .90 |
| 2405 | A545 | 1.20 l blk, pur & red lil | 1.20 | 1.20 |
| a. | | Pair, #2404-2405 | 2.25 | 2.25 |

Issued in sheets containing 2 No. 2405a, 3 each Nos. 2404-2405 and 2 labels.

Martyrs' Day A546

90q, Freedom flame, vert. 4.10 l, Flowers.

| 1992, May 5 | | | Perf. 12x12½ | |
|---|---|---|---|---|
| 2406 | A546 | 90q multicolored | .50 | .50 |

Perf. 12½x12

| 2407 | A546 | 4.10 l multicolored | 2.50 | 2.00 |
|---|---|---|---|---|

European Soccer Championships, Sweden '92 A547

Various stylized designs of soccer plays.

| 1992, June 10 | | Litho. | Perf. 12 | |
|---|---|---|---|---|
| 2408 | A547 | 30q green & lt grn | .50 | .25 |
| 2409 | A547 | 90q blue & pink | 1.00 | .50 |
| 2410 | A547 | 10.80 l henna & tan | 6.00 | 3.75 |

Size: 90x70mm
Imperf

| 2411 | A547 | 5 l tan, lt green & pink | 4.00 | 4.00 |
|---|---|---|---|---|
| | | Nos. 2408-2411 (4) | 11.50 | 8.50 |

1992 Summer Olympics, Barcelona A548

| 1992, June 14 | | Litho. | Perf. 12 | |
|---|---|---|---|---|
| 2412 | A548 | 30q Tennis | .35 | .35 |
| 2413 | A548 | 90q Baseball | 1.00 | .55 |
| 2414 | A548 | 1.80 l Table tennis | 2.00 | 1.50 |

Size: 90x70mm
Imperf

| 2415 | A548 | 5 l Torch bearer | 4.00 | 4.00 |
|---|---|---|---|---|
| | | Nos. 2412-2415 (4) | 7.35 | 6.40 |

United Europe — A549

| 1992, July 10 | | Litho. | Perf. 12 | |
|---|---|---|---|---|
| 2416 | A549 | 1.20 l multicolored | 1.10 | .75 |

Horses — A550

30q, Native. 90q, Nonius. 1.20 l, Arabian, vert. 10.60 l, Haflinger, vert.

| 1992, Aug. 10 | | Litho. | Perf. 12 | |
|---|---|---|---|---|
| 2417 | A550 | 30q multicolored | .25 | .25 |
| 2418 | A550 | 90q multicolored | .40 | .40 |
| 2419 | A550 | 1.20 l multicolored | .55 | .55 |
| 2420 | A550 | 10.60 l multicolored | 5.25 | 4.25 |
| | | Nos. 2417-2420 (4) | 6.45 | 5.45 |

For surcharge, see No. 2781.

Discovery of America, 500th Anniv. — A551

Map of North and South America and: 60q, Columbus, sailing ships. 3.20 l, Columbus meeting natives. 5 l, Map, Columbus.

| 1992, Aug. 20 | | | | |
|---|---|---|---|---|
| 2421 | A551 | 60q blk, bl & gray | .45 | .45 |
| 2422 | A551 | 3.20 l blk, brn & gray | 3.25 | 3.25 |

Size: 90x70mm
Imperf

| 2423 | A551 | 5 l multi | 70.00 | 70.00 |
|---|---|---|---|---|

Mother Theresa, Infant — A552

| 1992, Oct. 4 | | Litho. | Perf. 12x12½ | |
|---|---|---|---|---|
| 2424 | A552 | 40q fawn | .30 | .30 |
| 2425 | A552 | 60q brown | .30 | .30 |
| 2426 | A552 | 1 l violet | .30 | .30 |
| 2427 | A552 | 1.80 l gray | .30 | .30 |
| 2428 | A552 | 2 l red | .30 | .30 |
| 2429 | A552 | 2.40 l green | .30 | .30 |
| 2430 | A552 | 3.20 l blue | .40 | .40 |
| 2431 | A552 | 5.60 l rose violet | .60 | .60 |
| 2432 | A552 | 7.20 l olive | 1.00 | 1.00 |
| 2433 | A552 | 10 l org brn | 1.25 | 1.25 |
| | | Nos. 2424-2433 (10) | 5.05 | 5.05 |

See Nos. 2472-2476.
For surcharge, see No. 2786.

A553

| 1993, Apr. 25 | | Litho. | Perf. 12 | |
|---|---|---|---|---|
| 2434 | A553 | 16 l multicolored | 2.50 | 2.50 |

Visit of Pope John Paul II.

Nos. 2223-2226, 2229 Surcharged

| 1993, May 2 | | Litho. | Perf. 12x12½ | |
|---|---|---|---|---|
| 2435 | A486 | 3 l on 10q | .25 | .25 |
| 2436 | A486 | 6.50 l on 20q | .55 | .55 |
| 2437 | A486 | 13 l on 30q | 1.60 | 1.60 |

# ALBANIA

| | | | | |
|---|---|---|---|---|
| 2438 | A486 | 20 l on 90q | 2.40 | 2.40 |
| 2439 | A486 | 30 l on 50q | 3.25 | 3.25 |
| | Nos. 2435-2439 (5) | | 8.05 | 8.05 |

Lef Nosi (1873-1945), Minister of Posts — A554

**1993, May 5** Litho. Perf. 12
2440 A554 6.50 l ol brn & bister .90 .90

First Albanian postage stamps, 80th anniv.

Europa — A555

Contemporary paintings by: 3 l, A. Zajmi, vert. 7 l, E. Hila. 20 l, B. Ahmeti-Peizazh.

**1993, May 28** Litho. Perf. 12
2441 A555 3 l multicolored .90 .90
2442 A555 7 l multicolored 3.50 3.50
Size: 116x122mm
2443 A555 20 l multicolored 6.50 6.50
Nos. 2441-2443 (0) 10.90 10.90

1993 Mediterranean Games, France — A556

3 l, Running. 16 l, Kayaking. 21 l, Cycling. 20 l, Mediterranean map.

**1993, June 20** Litho. Perf. 12
2444 A556 3 l multicolored .30 .30
2445 A556 16 l multicolored 1.75 1.75
2446 A556 21 l multicolored 2.40 2.40
Size: 111x78mm
Imperf
2447 A556 20 l multicolored 3.25 3.25
Nos. 2444-2447 (4) 7.70 7.70

For surcharge, see No. 2789.

Frang Bardhi, Author, 350th Death Anniv. — A557

**1993, Aug. 20** Litho. Perf. 12x12½
2448 A557 6.50 l shown 1.10 1.10
Size: 89x101mm
Imperf
2449 A557 20 l Writing at desk 3.50 3.50

A558

68 l, Mascot, ball, US map.

**1994, July 17** Litho. Perf. 12
2450 A558 42 l shown 1.10 1.10
2451 A558 68 l multicolored 1.60 1.60

1994 World Cup Soccer Championships, US.

A559

European Inventors, Discoveries: 50 l, Gjovalin Gjadri, engineer. 100 l, Karl von Ghega, Austrian engineer. 150 l, Sketch of road project.

**1994, Dec. 31** Litho. Perf. 14
2452 A559 50 l multicolored 1.50 1.50
2453 A559 100 l multicolored 2.25 2.25
Size: 50x70mm
Imperf
2454 A559 150 l multicolored 3.75 3.75
Nos. 2452-2454 (3) 7.50 7.50

Europa (No. 2454).

Ali Pasa of Tepelene (Lion of Janina) (1744-1822) A560

**1995, Jan. 28** Perf. 14
2455 A560 60 l shown 1.40 1.40
Size: 70x50mm
Imperf
2456 A560 100 l Tepelene Palace 2.50 2.50

Intl. Olympic Committee, Cent. — A561

**1995, Feb. 2** Imperf.
2457 A561 80 l multicolored 2.25 2.25

Karl Benz (1844-1929), Automobile Pioneer — A562

Designs: 5 l, Automobile company emblem, Benz. 10 l, Modern Mercedes Benz automobile. 60 l, First four-wheel Benz 1886 motor car. 125 l, Pre-war Mercedes touring car.

**1995, Jan. 21** Litho. Perf. 14
2458 A562 5 l multicolored .30 .30
2459 A562 10 l multicolored .30 .30
2460 A562 60 l multicolored .90 .90
2461 A562 125 l multicolored 3.00 3.00
Nos. 2458-2461 (4) 4.50 4.50

Liberation, 50th Anniv. (in 1994) — A563

**1995, Jan. 28** Litho. Perf. 14
2462 A563 50 l black, gray & red 1.25 1.25

Dated 1994.

## Miniature Sheet

Albania '93 A564

Composers: a, 3 l, Wagner. b, 6.50 l, Grieg. c, 11 l, Gounod. d, 20 l, Tchaikovsky.

**1995, Jan. 26** Perf. 12
2463 A564 Sheet of 4, #a.-d. 2.50 2.50

Voskopoja Academy, 250th Anniv. — A565

Buildings of Voskopoja.

**1995, Feb. 2**
2464 42 l multicolored .90 .90
2465 68 l multicolored 2.25 2.25
a. A565 Pair, #2464-2465 3.50 3.50

Bleta Apricula — A566

5 l, On flower. 10 l, Honeycomb, bee. 25 l, Emerging from cell of honeycomb.

**1995, Aug. 20** Litho. Perf. 12
2466 A566 5 l multicolored .30 .30
2467 A566 10 l multicolored .30 .30
2468 A566 25 l multicolored 1.25 1.25
Nos. 2466-2468 (3) 1.85 1.85

Peace & Freedom — A567

Stylized hands reaching for: 50 l, Olive branch. 100 l, Peace dove. 150 l, Stylized person.

**1995, Aug. 10** Perf. 13½x14
2469 A567 50 l multicolored 1.75 1.75
2470 A567 100 l multicolored 3.50 3.50
Size: 80x60mm
Imperf
2471 A567 150 l multicolored 5.00 5.00
Nos. 2469-2471 (3) 10.25 10.25

Europa.
For surcharges, see Nos. B39-B40.

### Mother Teresa Type of 1992

**1994-95** Litho. Perf. 12x12½
2472 A552 5 l violet .30 .30
2473 A552 18 l orange 1.10 1.10
2474 A552 20 l rose lilac .45 .45
2475 A552 25 l green 1.75 1.75
2476 A552 60 l olive 1.75 1.75
Nos. 2472-2476 (5) 5.35 5.35

Issued: 20 l, 1994; 60 l, 1995; others, 7/94.

Arctic Explorers — A568

Designs: a, Fridtjof Nansen (1861-1930), Norway. b, James Cook (1728-79), England. c, Roald Amundsen (1872-1928), Norway. d, Robert F. Scott (1872-1928), Great Britain.

**1995, Sept. 14** Litho. Perf. 13½x14
2477 A568 25 l Block of 4, #a.-d. 3.50 3.50

For surcharges, see No. 2790.

UN, 50th Anniv. — A569

100 l, Like #2478, flags streaming to right.

**1995, Sept. 14** Litho. Perf. 14x13½
2478 A569 2 l shown .25 .25
2479 A569 100 l multicolored 2.40 1.90

For surcharge, see No. 2782.

Poets — A570

**1995** Perf. 13½x14
2480 A570 25 l Paul Éluard .65 .65
2481 A570 50 l Sergei Yesenin 1.25 1.25
a. Pair, #2480-2481 2.00 2.00

Entry into Council of Europe — A571

Designs: 25 l, Doves flying from headquarters, Strasbourg. 85 l, Albanian eagle over map of Europe.

**1995** Perf. 14x13½
2482 A571 25 l multicolored .90 .90
2483 A571 85 l multicolored 3.25 3.25

For surcharge see No. 2583

Jan Kukuzeli, Composer — A572

Stylized figure: 18 l, Writing. 20 l, Holding hand to head. 100 l, Holding up scroll of paper.

**1995, Oct. 17** Perf. 13½x14
2484 A572 18 l multicolored .50 .50
2485 A572 20 l multicolored .50 .50
Size: 74x74mm
2486 A572 100 l multicolored 2.75 2.75
Nos. 2484-2486 (3) 3.75 3.75

For surcharge, see No. 2787.

# ALBANIA

World Tourism Organization, 20th Anniv. — A573

Stylized designs: 18 l, Church, saint holding scroll. 20 l, City, older buildings. 42 l, City, modern buildings.

**1995, Oct. 17**
| 2487 | A573 | 18 l multicolored | .50 | .50 |
| 2488 | A573 | 20 l multicolored | .70 | .65 |
| 2489 | A573 | 42 l multicolored | 1.50 | 1.40 |
|  | Nos. 2487-2489 (3) |  | 2.70 | 2.55 |

For surcharge, see No. 2788.

Fables of Jean de la Fontaine (1621-95) — A574

Designs: 2 l, Raptor, turtle, wolf, goose, mouse, lion, rats. 3 l, Crow, goose, dog, foxes. 25 l, Insect, doves, frogs. 60 l, Drawings of Da la Fontaine, animals, birds.

**1995, Aug. 20   Litho.   Perf. 14x13½**
| 2490 | A574 | 2 l multicolored | .25 | .25 |
| 2491 | A574 | 3 l multicolored | .25 | .25 |
| 2492 | A574 | 25 l multicolored | .50 | .50 |

**Imperf**
**Size: 73x56mm**
| 2493 | A574 | 60 l multicolored | 2.00 | 2.00 |
|  | Nos. 2490-2493 (4) |  | 3.00 | 3.00 |

For surcharges, see Nos. 2783, 2784, 2791.

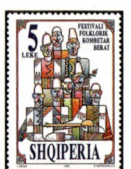

Folklore Festival, Berat — A575

Stylized designs: 5 l, Men's choir. 50 l, Costumed woman seated in chair.

**1995, Oct. 17   Litho.   Perf. 13½x14**
| 2494 | A575 | 5 l multicolored | .25 | .25 |
| 2495 | A575 | 50 l multicolored | 1.20 | 1.20 |

Motion Pictures, Cent. — A576

**1995, Nov. 17**
| 2496 | A576 | 10 l Louis Lumiere | .25 | .25 |
| 2497 | A576 | 85 l Auguste Lumiere | 1.50 | 1.50 |
| a. | Pair, #2496-2497 |  | 2.00 | 2.00 |

Elvis Presley (1935-77) — A577

**1995, Nov. 20   Litho.   Perf. 14x13½**
| 2498 | A577 | 3 l orange & multi | .30 | .30 |
| 2499 | A577 | 60 l green & multi | 1.75 | 1.75 |

For surcharge, see No. 2785.

A578

**1995, Nov. 25   Perf. 13½x14**
| 2500 | A578 | 10 l 1925 Bank notes | .30 | .30 |
| 2501 | A578 | 25 l 1995 Bank notes | .80 | .80 |

National Bank, 70th anniv.

A579

50 l, Maiden planting tree.

**1995, Nov. 27   Litho.   Perf. 13½x14**
| 2502 | A579 | 5 l shown | .25 | .25 |
| 2503 | A579 | 50 l multicolored | 1.50 | 1.50 |

Democracy, 5th anniv.

A580

Designs: 25 l, Soccer ball, British flag, map of Europe, stadium. 100 l, Soccer ball, player.

**1996, June 4   Perf. 14**
| 2504 | A580 | 25 l multicolored | .50 | .50 |
| 2505 | A580 | 100 l multicolored | 2.25 | 2.25 |

Euro '96, European Soccer Championships, Great Britain.
For surcharge, see No. 2792.

Mother Teresa — A581

150 l, Mother Teresa, diff.

**1996, May 5   Perf. 13½x14**
| 2506 | A581 | 25 l blue & multi | 1.00 | 1.00 |
| 2507 | A581 | 100 l red & multi | 2.50 | 2.50 |

**Size: 52x74mm**
**Imperf**
| 2508 | A581 | 150 l multi | 6.25 | 6.25 |
|  | Nos. 2506-2508 (3) |  | 9.75 | 9.75 |

Europa. For overprints see Nos. 2551, 2582.

GSM Cellular Telephone Transmission A582

Designs: 10 l, Satellite transmitting signals. 60 l, Uses for cellular telephone, vert.

**Perf. 13x13½, 13½x13**
**1996, Aug. 1   Litho.**
| 2509 | A582 | 10 l multicolored | .25 | .25 |
| 2510 | A582 | 60 l multicolored | 1.50 | 1.50 |

1996 Summer Olympic Games, Atlanta — A583

Stylized designs: 5 l, Runners. 25 l, Throwers. 60 l, Jumpers. 100 l, Emblem, US flag.

**1996, Aug. 3   Litho.   Perf. 13x14**
| 2511 | A583 | 5 l multicolored | .25 | .25 |
| 2512 | A583 | 25 l multicolored | .55 | .55 |
| 2513 | A583 | 60 l multicolored | 1.50 | 1.50 |

**Size: 52x37mm**
**Imperf**
| 2514 | A583 | 100 l multicolored | 2.25 | 2.25 |
|  | Nos. 2511-2514 (4) |  | 4.55 | 4.55 |

Gottfried Wilhelm Leibniz (1646-1716), Mathematician A584

85 l, René Descartes (1596-1650), mathematician.

**1996, Sept. 20   Litho.   Perf. 14**
| 2515 | A584 | 10 l multicolored | .40 | .40 |
| 2516 | A584 | 85 l multicolored | 2.00 | 2.00 |

Paintings by Francisco Goya (1746-1828) A585

Designs: 10 l, The Naked Maja. 60 l, Dona Isabel Cobos de Porcel. 100 l, Self portrait.

**1996, Sept. 25   Perf. 14x13½**
| 2517 | A585 | 10 l multicolored | .30 | .30 |
| 2518 | A585 | 60 l multicolored | 1.40 | 1.40 |

**Souvenir Sheet**
| 2519 | A585 | 100 l multicolored | 2.50 | 2.50 |

Religious Engravings — A586

Designs: a, 5 l, Book cover showing crucifixion, angels. b, 25 l, Medallion of crucifixion. c, 85 l, Book cover depicting life of Christ.

**1996, Nov. 5   Perf. 13x13½**
| 2520 | A586 | Block of 3, #a.-c. + label | 2.75 | 2.75 |

UNICEF, 50th Anniv. — A587

Children's paintings: 5 l, Fairy princess. 10 l, Doll, sun. 25 l, Sea life. 50 l, House, people.

**1996, Nov. 11   Perf. 13½**
| 2521 | A587 | 5 l multicolored | .25 | .25 |
| 2522 | A587 | 10 l multicolored | .25 | .25 |
| 2523 | A587 | 25 l multicolored | .80 | .80 |
| 2524 | A587 | 50 l multicolored | 1.20 | 1.20 |
|  | Nos. 2521-2524 (4) |  | 2.50 | 2.50 |

Gjergj Fishta (1871-1940), Writer, Priest — A588

60 l, Battle scene, portrait.

**1996, Dec. 20   Perf. 13½x14**
| 2525 | A588 | 10 l shown | .25 | .25 |
| 2526 | A588 | 60 l multicolored | 1.40 | 1.40 |

Omar Khayyam — A589

**1997, Mar. 6   Perf. 14**
| 2527 | A589 | 20 l shown | .50 | .50 |
| 2528 | A589 | 50 l Portrait, diff. | 1.10 | 1.10 |

A590

**1997, Mar. 20   Perf. 14x14½**
| 2529 | A590 | 20 l Portrait | .40 | .40 |
| 2530 | A590 | 60 l Printing press | 1.20 | 1.20 |
| a. | Pair, #2529-2530 |  | 1.75 | 1.75 |

Johannes Gutenberg (1397?-1468).

A591

The Azure Eye (Stories and Legends): 30 l, Dragon on rock looking at warrior, donkey. 100 l, Dragon drinking water from pond, warrior.

**1997, May 5   Litho.   Perf. 13x14**
| 2531 | A591 | 30 l multicolored | .70 | .70 |
| 2532 | A591 | 100 l multicolored | 2.25 | 2.25 |

Europa.

A592

**1997, Apr. 10   Perf. 14**
| 2533 | | 10 l Pelicanus crispus | .25 | .25 |
| 2534 | | 80 l Pelicans, diff. | 1.40 | 1.40 |
| a. | A592 Pair, #2533-2534 |  | 2.50 | 2.50 |

No. 2534a is a continuous design.

A593

**1997, June 25   Litho.   Perf. 14**
| 2535 | A593 | 10 l blk & dark brn | .25 | .25 |
| 2536 | A593 | 25 l blk & blue blk | .75 | .75 |

**Souvenir Sheet**
| 2537 | A593 | 80 l gray brown | 2.00 | 2.00 |

Faik Konica (1875-1942), writer and politician.
No. 2537 contains one 22x26mm stamp.

A594

1997 Mediterranean Games, Bari: 20 l, Man running. 30 l, Woman running, 3-man canoe. 100 l, Man breaking finish line, silhouettes of man and woman.

# ALBANIA

**1997, June 13**
| | | | | |
|---|---|---|---|---|
| 2538 | A594 | 20 l multicolored | .40 | .40 |
| 2539 | A594 | 30 l multicolored | .80 | .80 |

*Size: 52x74mm*
***Imperf***
| | | | | |
|---|---|---|---|---|
| 2540 | A594 | 100 l multicolored | 2.00 | 2.00 |

Skanderbeg — A595

**1997, Aug. 25**    Litho.    *Perf. 13*
| | | | | |
|---|---|---|---|---|
| 2541 | A595 | 5 l red brn & red | .25 | .25 |
| 2542 | A595 | 10 l dp ol & ol | .25 | .25 |
| 2543 | A595 | 20 l dp grn & grn | .40 | .40 |
| 2544 | A595 | 25 l dp mag & red lil | .50 | .50 |
| 2545 | A595 | 30 l dk vio & vio | .60 | .60 |
| 2546 | A595 | 50 l black | .85 | .85 |
| 2547 | A595 | 60 l brn & lt brn | 1.00 | 1.00 |
| 2548 | A595 | 80 l dk brown & brn | 1.60 | 1.60 |
| 2549 | A595 | 100 l dk red brown & red brn | 1.90 | 1.90 |
| 2550 | A595 | 110 l dark blue | 2.10 | 2.10 |
| | | Nos. 2541-2550 (10) | 9.45 | 9.45 |

**No. 2507 Ovptd. in Silver "HOMAZH / 1910-1997"**

**1997**    *Perf. 13½x14*
| | | | | |
|---|---|---|---|---|
| 2551 | A581 | 100 l red & multi | 2.50 | 2.50 |

Religious Manuscripts — A596

Albanian Codex: a, 10 l, 11th cent. b, 25 l, 6th cent. c, 60 l, 6th cent., diff.

**1997, Nov. 15**    Litho.    *Perf. 13x14*
| | | | | |
|---|---|---|---|---|
| 2552 | A596 | Block of 3, #a.-c. + label | 2.25 | 2.25 |

See No. 2575.

Post and Telecommunications Administration, 85th Anniv. — A597

**1997, Dec. 4**    *Perf. 13½*
| | | | | |
|---|---|---|---|---|
| 2553 | A597 | 10 l multi | .25 | .25 |
| 2554 | A597 | 30 l multi, diff. | .75 | .75 |

A598

**1998, Mar. 25**    Litho.    *Perf. 14*
| | | | | |
|---|---|---|---|---|
| 2555 | A598 | 30 l red brn & multi | .60 | .60 |
| 2556 | A598 | 100 l tan & multi | 1.90 | 1.90 |
| a. | | Pair, #2555-2556 | 2.50 | 2.50 |

Nikete Dardani, musician.

A599

Legends of Pogradec Ohrid Lake: a, 30 l, Old man seated at table. b, 50 l, Three Graces. c, 60 l, Two women, fountain. d, 80 l, Iceman.

**1998, Apr. 15**
| | | | | |
|---|---|---|---|---|
| 2557 | A599 | Block of 4, #a.-d. | 3.50 | 3.50 |

A600

**1998, May 5**    Litho.    *Perf. 13x14*
| | | | | |
|---|---|---|---|---|
| 2558 | A600 | 60 l shown | 1.50 | 1.50 |
| 2559 | A600 | 100 l multi, diff. | 2.25 | 2.25 |

*Size: 50x72mm*
***Imperf***
| | | | | |
|---|---|---|---|---|
| 2560 | A600 | 150 l multi, diff. | 3.50 | 3.50 |

Europa (folk festivals).

A601

Albanian League of Prizren, 120th anniv.: a, 30 l, Abdyl Frasheri. b, 50 l, Sulejman Vokshi. c, 60 l, Iljaz Pashe Dibra. d, 80 l, Ymer Prizreni.

**1998, June 10**    Litho.    *Perf. 13½x13*
| | | | | |
|---|---|---|---|---|
| 2561 | A601 | Block of 4, #a.-d. | 2.75 | 2.75 |

1998 World Cup Soccer Championships, France — A602

Stylized soccer players.

**1998, June 10**    *Perf. 13½*
| | | | | |
|---|---|---|---|---|
| 2562 | A602 | 60 l multicolored | 1.00 | 1.00 |
| 2563 | A602 | 100 l multicolored | 2.00 | 2.00 |

*Size: 50x73mm*
***Imperf***
| | | | | |
|---|---|---|---|---|
| 2564 | A602 | 120 l Mascot | 2.25 | 2.25 |

European Youth Greco-Roman Wrestling Championships, Albania — A603

**1998, July 5**    *Perf. 13½*
| | | | | |
|---|---|---|---|---|
| 2565 | A603 | 30 l shown | .50 | .50 |
| 2566 | A603 | 60 l Wrestlers, diff. | 1.00 | 1.00 |
| a. | | Pair, #2565-2566 | 1.60 | 1.60 |

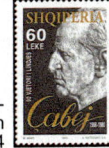

Eqerem Cabej (1908-1980), Albanian Etymologist — A604

**1998, Aug. 7**    *Perf. 14*
| | | | | |
|---|---|---|---|---|
| 2567 | A604 | 60 l yel brn & multi | .80 | .80 |
| 2568 | A604 | 80 l brn red & multi | 1.20 | 1.20 |
| a. | | Pair, #2567-2568 | 2.25 | 2.25 |

Paul Gauguin (1848-1903) — A605

Paintings (details): 60 l, The Vision after the Sermon. 80 l, Ea Haere Ia Oe. 120 l, Stylized design to resemble self-portrait.

**1998, Sept. 10**    *Perf. 13½*
| | | | | |
|---|---|---|---|---|
| 2569 | A605 | 60 l multicolored | 1.00 | 1.00 |
| 2570 | A605 | 80 l multicolored | 1.40 | 1.40 |
| a. | | Pair, #2569-2570 | 2.25 | 2.25 |

*Size: 50x73mm*
***Imperf***
| | | | | |
|---|---|---|---|---|
| 2571 | A605 | 120 l multicolored | 2.25 | 2.25 |

Epitaph of Gllavenica, 14th Cent. Depiction of Christ — A606

Designs: 30 l, Entire cloth showing artwork. 80 l, Closer view. 100 l, Upper portion of cloth, vert.

**1998, Oct. 5**    *Perf. 14½x14*
| | | | | |
|---|---|---|---|---|
| 2572 | A606 | 30 l multicolored | .50 | .50 |
| 2573 | A606 | 80 l multicolored | 1.50 | 1.50 |

**Souvenir Sheet**
*Perf. 13*
| | | | | |
|---|---|---|---|---|
| 2574 | A606 | 100 l multicolored | 1.75 | 1.75 |

No. 2574 contains one 25x29mm stamp.

**Religious Manuscripts Type of 1997**

Illustrations from Purple Codex, Gold Codex: a, 30 l, Manuscript, columns on sides, arched top. b, 50 l, Manuscript cover with embossed pictures of icons. c, 80 l, Manuscript picturing cathedral, birds.

**1998, Oct. 15**    *Perf. 13x14*
| | | | | |
|---|---|---|---|---|
| 2575 | A596 | Block of 3, #a.-c. + label | 3.00 | 3.00 |

Mikel Koliqi (1902-97), First Albanian Cardinal — A607

**1998, Nov. 28**    *Perf. 14*
| | | | | |
|---|---|---|---|---|
| 2576 | A607 | 30 l shown | .50 | .50 |
| 2577 | A607 | 100 l Portrait, facing | 1.75 | 1.75 |
| a. | | Pair, #2576-2577 | 2.50 | 2.50 |

Mother Teresa (1910-97) — A608

60 l, With child, horiz.

*Perf. 14x13½, 13½x14*
**1998, Sept. 5**    *Photo.*
| | | | | |
|---|---|---|---|---|
| 2578 | A608 | 60 l multicolored | 1.50 | 1.50 |
| 2579 | A608 | 100 l shown | 2.50 | 2.50 |

See Italy Nos. 2254-2255.

Diana, Princess of Wales (1961-97) — A609

100 l, With Mother Teresa.

**1998, Aug. 31**    Litho.    *Perf. 13½*
| | | | | |
|---|---|---|---|---|
| 2580 | A609 | 60 l shown | 2.00 | 2.00 |
| 2581 | A609 | 100 l multicolored | 3.00 | 3.00 |

**No. 2508 Overprinted in Blue**

**1998, Oct. 23**    Litho.    ***Imperf***
| | | | | |
|---|---|---|---|---|
| 2582 | A581 | 150 l multicolored | 8.00 | 8.00 |

**No. 2482 Surcharged**

**1999, Apr. 20**    Litho.    *Perf. 14x13½*
| | | | | |
|---|---|---|---|---|
| 2583 | A571 | 150 l on 25 l multi | 3.25 | 3.25 |

Famous Americans — A610

a, Washington. b, Lincoln. c, Martin Luther King, Jr.

**1999, Mar. 15**    *Perf. 14*
| | | | | |
|---|---|---|---|---|
| 2584 | A610 | 150 l Block of 3, #a.-c. + label | 9.00 | 9.00 |

Monachus Albiventer — A611

Seals: a, 110 l, One looking left, one looking right. b, 150 l, Both looking right. c, 110 l, Mirror image of No. 2585b. d, 150 l, Mirror image of No. 2585a.

**1999, Apr. 10**
| | | | | |
|---|---|---|---|---|
| 2585 | A611 | Sheet of 4, #a.-d. | 10.00 | 10.00 |

# ALBANIA

No. 2382
Surcharged

**1999, Apr. 24     Litho.     Perf. 12x12¼**
2586  A539  150 l on 90 l multi      3.25  3.25
IBRA '99, Nuremburg.

A612

**1999, Apr. 25     Litho.     Perf. 13½x13¾**
2587  A612   10 l blue & multi        .75   .75
2588  A612  100 l green & multi      4.00  4.00

**Souvenir Sheet**
**Perf. 13**
2589  A612  250 l green & multi      5.00  5.00
NATO, 50th anniv. No. 2589 contains one 30x50mm stamp.

A613

Cartoon mouse: a, 80 l, Writing. b, 110 l, Holding chin. c, 150 l, Wearing bow tie. d, 160 l, Pointing.

**1999, Apr. 30     Litho.     Perf. 13x13¾**
2590  A613   Strip of 4, #a.-d.      8.50  8.50
Animated films.

Europa — A614

**1999, May 1      Litho.     Perf. 13¾x13**
2591  A614   90 l Thethi Park        2.00  2.00
2592  A614  310 l Lura Park          4.50  4.50

**Imperf**
**Size: 80x60mm**
2592A A614  350 l Kombetare
              Park                   6.50  6.50
Nos. 2591-2592A (3)                 13.00 13.00

Illyrian Coins — A615

Designs: a, 200 l, Kings of Illyria — Monumiou c. 300-280 BC cow suckling calf, square containing double stellate pattern, and Epidamos-Dyrrachium c. 623 BC, square with double stellate. b, 20 l, Damastion c. 395-380 BC siver drachm portable ingot, Byllis c. 238-168 BC AE13 serpent entwined around cornucopia, Skodra after 168 BC, AE17 war galley, and other war galley coin. c, 10l, Epirote Republic before 238 BC silver tetraobol with jugate busts of Zeus and Dione on obverse and thunderbolt within oak wreath reverse.

310 l, Kings of Illyria — Genthos c. 197-168 BC head wearing kausia.

**1999, June 1     Litho.     Perf. 13¾x13¼**
2593  A615  Strip of 3, #a.-c.       5.00  5.00

**Souvenir Sheet**
**Perf. 13**
2594  A615  310 l multicolored       6.50  6.50

Charlie Chaplin — A616

Designs: 30 l, Holding cigarette. 50 l, Tipping hat. 250 l, Dancing.

**1999, June 20    Litho.     Perf. 14x14¼**
2595  A616   30 l multicolored        .75   .75
2596  A616   50 l multicolored       1.50  1.50
2597  A616  250 l multicolored       6.00  6.00
  a. Booklet pane, 2 each
     #2595-2597, perf. 14¼
     vert.                          70.00
     Complete booklet               70.00
Nos. 2595-2597 (3)                   8.25  8.25

In No. 2597a, the 30 l stamps are at the ends of the pane and the 250 l stamps are in the middle.

No. 2398
Surcharged

**1999, July 2     Litho.     Perf. 12½**
2598  A543  150 l on 30q multi       3.00  3.00
PhilexFrance 99.

Holocaust — A617

**1999, July 6     Litho.     Perf. 14x14¼**
2599  A617   30 l brown & multi       .60   .60
2600  A617  150 l gray & multi       3.25  3.25

First Manned Moon Landing, 30th
Anniv.
A618

No. 2601: a, 30 l, Astronaut, earth. b, 150 l, Lunar Module. c, 300 l, Astronaut, flag. 280 l, Lift-off.

**1999, July 25    Litho.     Perf. 13¼x14**
2601  A618   Strip of 3, #a.-c.     10.00 10.00

**Souvenir Sheet**
**Perf. 13**
2602  A618  280 l multicolored       6.00  6.00
No. 2602 contains one 25x29mm stamp.

UPU, 125th
Anniv.
A619

Background colors: a, 20 l, aquamarine and brown. b, 60 l, bister and dark blue.

**1999, Aug. 1     Litho.     Perf. 14x14¼**
2603  A619   Pair, #a.-b.            2.00  2.00

No. 2383
Surcharged in
Brown, Symbol in
Red and Green

**1999     Method & Perf. as Before**
2604  A539  150 l on 1.20 l multi    3.00  3.00
China 1999 World Philatelic Exhibition.

A620

Background colors: a, 10 l, Yellow. b, 20 l, Orange. c, 200 l, Green.

**1999, Sept. 2    Litho.     Perf. 14x14¼**
2605  A620  Strip of 3, #a.-c.       5.00  5.00
First Natl. Track & Field Championships, 70th anniv.

A621

30 l, Madonna and Child.

**1999, Oct. 30               Perf. 14**
2606  A621   30 l multicolored        .50   .50
2607  A621  300 l shown              6.00  6.00
  a. Souv. sheet, 2 ea #2606-
     2607                           12.00 12.00
Art by Onufri of Elbasan.

Famous Albanians — A622

Designs: a, 10 l, Bilal Golemi (1899-1955), veterinarian. b, 20 l, Azem Galica (1889-1924), freedom fighter. c, 50 l, Viktor Eftimiu (1889-1972), writer. d, 300 l, Lasgush Poradeci (1900-87), poet.

**1999, Nov. 28    Litho.     Perf. 14¼x14**
2608  A622  Block of 4, #a.-d.       8.00  8.00

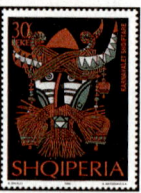
Carnival
Masks — A623

**1999, Dec. 1                Perf. 13¾**
2609  A623   30 l shown               .50   .50
2610  A623  300 l Turkey head        6.50  6.50

Millennium — A624

**2000, Mar. 27    Litho.     Perf. 13½x14**
2611  A624   40 l red & multi         .75   .75
2612  A624   90 l blue & multi       2.00  2.00

Native Costumes — A625

a, 5 l, Librazhdi. b, 10 l, Malesia e Madhe woman. c, 15 l, Malesia e Madhe man. d, 20 l, Tropoje. e, 30 l, Dumrea. f, 35 l, Tirana man. g, 40 l, Tirana woman. h, 45 l, Arbereshe. i, 50 l, Gjirokaster. j, 55 l, Lunxheri. k, 70 l, Cameria. l, 90 l, Laberia.

**2000, Mar. 28               Perf. 13x13¾**
2613  A625  Booklet pane of 12       9.00  9.00
            Booklet, #2613          12.00

Gustave Mayer (1850-1900), Student
of Albanian Culture — A626

Colors: a, 50 l, olive green. b, 130 l, carmine lake.

**2000, Mar. 30               Perf. 13½x14**
2614  A626  Pair, #a-b               3.50  3.50

Cartoon Duck — A627

Duck with: a, 250 l, Top hat. b, 10 l, Tengallon hat. c, 30 l, Cap. d, 90 l, Bow.

**2000, Apr. 6     Litho.     Perf. 13x13¾**
2615  A627  Strip of 4, #a-d         7.50  7.50

Grand Prix Race
Cars — A628

Various cars.

**2000, Apr. 10    Litho.     Perf. 14¼x14**
2616        Bklt. pane of 10 + 2 la-
            bels                    12.50 12.50
  a.-j. A628  30 l any single        1.25  1.25
            Booklet, #2616          15.00

Holy Year
2000 — A629

Designs: 15 l, Church with bell tower. 40 l, Church with conical roof. 90 l, Ruins. 250 l, Aerial view of ruins.

**2000, Apr. 22    Litho.     Perf. 13¾x14**
2617-2619 A629 Set of 3              4.00  4.00

**Souvenir Sheet**
**Perf. 13¾**
2620  A629  250 l multi              4.50  4.50
No. 2620 contains one 38x38mm stamp.

**Europa, 2000**
**Common Design Type**
**2000, May 9                Perf. 13x13¾**
2621  CD17  130 l multi              3.00  3.00

## ALBANIA

### Souvenir Sheet
**Perf. 13**
2622 CD17 300 l Detail of #2621 6.50 6.50
No. 2622 contains one 25x29mm stamp.

### Miniature Sheet

Wild Animals A630

No. 2623: a, 10 l, Canis lupus. b, 40 l, Ursus arctos. c, 90 l, Sus scrofa. d, 220 l, Vulpes vulpes.

**2000, May 17**    **Perf. 14¼x13¾**
2623 A630 Sheet of 4, #a-d 7.50 7.50

Gustav Mahler (1860-1911), Composer — A631

**2000, May 30**    **Perf. 13½x14**
2624 A631 130 l multi 2.50 2.50
WIPA 2000 Stamp Exhibition, Vienna.

European Soccer Championships A632

10 l, Goalie. 120 l, Player heading ball. 260 l, Player kicking ball.

**2000, June 1**    **Perf. 13¾x13¼**
2625-2626 A632 Set of 2 2.50 2.50

**Imperf**
**Size: 81x60mm**
2627 A632 260 l multi 5.00 5.00

Paintings by Pablo Picasso A633

Various unnamed paintings or self-portraits: 30 l, Brown panel. 40 l, Green panel. 130 l, Self portrait, with Espana 2000 philatelic exhibition emblem, vert. 250 l, Blue panel.

**2000**    **Litho.**    **Perf. 13¾**
2628-2631 A633 Set of 4 6.50 6.50

### Souvenir Sheet
**Perf. 13**
2632 A633 400 l Self-portrait 8.00 8.00
No. 2632 contains one 25x29mm stamp.
Issued: 130 l, 10/6; others 6/7.

2000 Summer Olympics, Sydney — A634

No. 2633: a, 10 l, Basketball. b, 40 l, Soccer. c, 90 l, Runner. d, 250 l, Cycling.

**2000, July 1**    **Perf. 14x14¼**
2633 A634 Block of 4, #a-d 8.00 8.00

First Zeppelin Flight, Cent. A635

No. 2634: a, 15 l, LZ-1 over Friedrichshafen. b, 30 l, Airship over Paris. c, 300 l, R34 over New York.
No. 2635, Ferdinand von Zeppelin.

**2000, July 2**    **Perf. 13¾x13**
2634 A635 Sheet of 3, #a-c 7.50 7.50

### Souvenir Sheet
**Perf. 13**
2635 A635 300 l multi 6.50 6.50
No. 2634 contains three 40x28mm stamps.

Flowers A636

No. 2636: a, 50 l, Gentiana lutea. b, 70 l, Gentiana cruciata.

**2000, Oct. 10**    **Perf. 13¼x14**
2636 A636 Pair, #a-b 2.75 2.75

Famous Albanians — A637

a, 30 l, Naim Frasheri, writer (1845-1900). b, 50 l, Bajram Curri, politician (1862-1925).

**2000, Nov. 28**    **Perf. 14¼x13¾**
2637 A637 Pair, #a-b 2.00 2.00

UN High Commissioner on Refugees, 50th Anniv. — A638

50 l, Mother & child. 90 l, Mother & child, diff.

**2000, Dec. 14**    **Perf. 13¾x14¼**
2638-2639 A638 Set of 2 3.00 3.00

Famous Albanians — A639

No. 2640: a, Ahmed Myftar Dede. b, Sali Njazi Dede.

**2001, Feb. 22**    **Litho.**    **Perf. 14¼x14**
2640 A639 90 l Horiz. pair, #a-b 4.50 4.50

Native Costumes — A640

No. 2641: a, Man from Tropoje. b, Woman from Lume. c, Woman from Mirdite. d, Man from Lume. e, Woman from Zadrime. f, Woman from Shpati. g, Man from Kruje. h, Woman from Macukulli. i, Woman from Dardhe. j, Man from Lushnje. k, Woman from Dropulli. l, Woman from Shmili.

**2001, Mar. 15**    **Perf. 13x13¾**
2641 A640 20 l Sheet of 12, #a-l 9.00 9.00
Booklet, #2641 11.00 11.00
See Nos. 2669, 2701, 2760, 2770.

Flowers A641

No. 2642: a, 10 l, Magnolia grandiflora. b, 20 l, Rosa virginiana. c, 90 l, Dianthus barbatus. d, 140 l, Syringa vulgaris.

**2001, Mar. 30**    **Perf. 14x14¼**
2642 A641 Block of 4, #a-d 5.00 5.00

Cartoon Dog A642

Denominations: a, 50 l. b, 90 l. c, 140 l, d, 20 l.

**2001, Apr. 6**    **Perf. 13x13¾**
2643 A642 Strip of 4, #a-d 5.00 5.00

Opera Composers A643

Designs: No. 2644, 90 l, Vincenzo Bellini (1801-35). No. 2645, 90 l, Giuseppe Verdi (1813-1901).
300 l, Bellini and Verdi.

**2001, Apr. 20**    **Perf. 13¾x13**
2644-2645 A643 Set of 2 3.50 3.50

### Souvenir Sheet
**Perf. 13¾**
2646 A643 300 l multi 5.00 5.00

Europa — A644

Designs: 40 l, Waterfall, cliffs. 110 l, Waterfall, boulders. 200 l, Water, shoreline. 350 l, Ripples in water, vert.

**2001, Apr. 29**    **Perf. 13¾x14**
2647-2649 A644 Set of 3 6.50 6.50

### Souvenir Sheet
**Perf. 12¾x13**
2650 A644 350 l multi 7.00 7.00
No. 2650 contains one 25x29mm stamp.

Domestic Animals A645

No. 2651: a, 10 l, Horse. b, 15 l, Donkey. c, 80 l, Cat. d, 90 l, Dog. 300 l, Cat.

**2001, May 17**    **Perf. 14¼x14**
2651 A645 Sheet of 4, #a-d 4.00 4.00

### Souvenir Sheet
**Perf. 12¾x13**
2652 A645 300 l shown 5.00 5.00
No. 2651 contains four 42x26mm stamps.

2001 Mediterranean Games, Tunis, Tunisia — A646

No. 2653: a, 10 l, Swimmer. b, 90 l, Runners. c, 140 l, Cyclists. 260 l, Discus thrower.

**2001, June 1**    **Perf. 14¼x14**
2653 A646 Vert. strip of 3, #a-c 5.00 5.00

### Souvenir Sheet
**Perf. 13x12¾**
2654 A646 260 l multi 9.00 9.00
No. 2654 contains one 29x25mm stamp.

History of Aviation A647

No. 2655: a, Clement Ader's flight of Eole, Oct. 9, 1890. b, Louis Blériot's flight of Blériot IX over English Channel, July 25, 1909. c, Charles Lindbergh's solo transatlantic flight of Spirit of St. Louis, May, 1927. d, Flight over Tirana, May 30, 1925. e, Antonov AN 10, 1956. f, First Concorde flight, Feb. 9, 1969. g, First Boeing 747 flight, Jan. 22, 1970. h, First flight of Space Shuttle Columbia, Apr. 12, 1981.

**2001, June 20**    **Perf. 13¾x13**
2655 A647 40 l Sheet of 8, #a-h 8.00 8.00

Bridges A648

No. 2656: a, 10 l, Tabakeve. b, 20 l, Kamares. c, 40 l, Golikut. d, 90 l, Mesit. 250 l, Tabakeve.

**2001, July 20**    **Perf. 13¾x13¼**
2656 A648 Sheet of 4, #a-d 3.25 3.25

# ALBANIA

**Souvenir Sheet**
*Perf. 12¾x13*
2657 A648 250 l shown  5.00 5.00
No. 2656 contains four 38x30mm stamps.

Coats of Arms — A649

Arms of: 20 l, Dimitri of Arber. 45 l, Balsha. 50 l, Muzaka. 90 l, George Castrioti (Skanderbeg).

**2001, Sept. 12**  *Perf. 12¾x13*
2658 A649 20 l multi  .50 .50
 a. Booklet pane of 4  2.00
2659 A649 45 l multi  1.00 1.00
 a. Booklet pane of 4  9.00
2660 A649 50 l multi  1.10 1.10
 a. Booklet pane of 4  4.50
2661 A649 90 l multi  2.00 2.00
 a. Booklet pane of 4  8.00
 Booklet, #2658a-2661a  24.00
 Nos. 2658-2661 (4)  4.60 4.60

See Nos. 2681-2684, 2709-2712, 2775, 2797-2800, 2801-2804.

Year of Dialogue Among Civilizations — A650

Colors of denomination: 45 l, Green. 50 l, Black. 120 l, White.

**2001, Oct. 6**  *Perf. 13½x14*
2662-2664 A650  Set of 3  5.00 5.00

Nobel Prizes, Cent. — A651

Laureates: 10 l, Doctors Without Borders, Peace, 1999. 20 l, Wilhelm C. Roentgen, Physics, 1901. 90 l, Ferid Murad, Physiology or Medicine, 1988. 200 l, Mother Teresa, Peace, 1979.

**2001, Dec. 1**  *Perf. 13¾x13¼*
2665-2668 A651  Set of 4  7.50 7.50

**Costumes Type of 2001**

No. 2669: a, Man from Gjakova. b, Woman from Prizren. c, Man from Shkoder. d, Woman from Shkoder. e, Man from Berat. f, Woman from Berat. g, Woman from Elbasan. h, Man from Elbasan. i, Woman from Vlore. j, Man from Vlore. k, Woman from Gjirokaster. l, Woman from Delvina.

**2002, Mar. 20**  Litho.  *Perf. 13x13¾*
2669 A640 30 l Sheet of 12, #a-l  8.75 8.75
 Complete booklet, #2669  9.75

Cartoon Deer A652

No. 2670: a, 50 l, Deer. b, 90 l, Deer and rabbit. c, 140 l, Deer, diff. d, 20 l, Deer and rabbit, diff.

**2002, Apr. 8**  *Perf. 13x13¾*
2670 A652 Horiz. strip of 4, #a-d  5.50 5.50

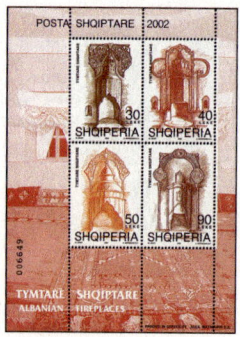

Fireplaces — A653

Fireplace color: a, 30 l, Deep brown. b, 40 l, Henna brown. 50 l, Orange brown. 90 l, Chestnut.

**2002, Apr. 15**  Litho.  *Perf. 14*
2671 A653  Sheet of 4, #a-d  4.00 4.00

Europa — A654

Designs: 40 l, High wire act. 90 l, Acrobats. 220 l, Contortionist. 350 l, Trained horse act.

**2002, May 1**  Litho.  *Perf. 13x13¾*
2672-2674 A654  Set of 3  6.50 6.50

**Souvenir Sheet**
*Perf. 13¾*
2675 A654 350 l multi  7.50 7.50
No. 2675 contains one 37x37mm stamp.

2002 World Cup Soccer Championships, Japan and Korea — A655

Emblem, soccer ball and stylized players: 20 l, 30 l, 90 l, 120 l. 360 l, Stylized player and emblem.

**2002, May 6**  Litho.  *Perf. 13¾x13¼*
2676-2679 A655  Set of 4  5.00 5.00

**Souvenir Sheet**
*Perf. 13*
2680 A655 360 l multi  7.00 7.00
No. 2680 contains one 50x29mm stamp.

**Arms Type of 2001**

**2002, May 12**  *Perf. 13*
2681 A649 20 l Gropa  .40 .40
 a. Booklet pane of 4  1.75
2682 A649 45 l Skurra  .90 .40
 a. Booklet pane of 4  4.00
2683 A649 50 l Bua  1.00 1.00
 a. Booklet pane of 4  4.50
2684 A649 90 l Topia  2.00 2.00
 a. Booklet pane of 4  9.00
 Complete booklet, #2681a-2684a  20.00
 Nos. 2681-2684 (4)  4.30 3.80

Cacti A656

No. 2685: a, Opuntia catingola. b, Neoporteria pseudoreicheana. c, Lobivia shaferi. d, Hylocereus undatus. e, Borzicactus madisoniorum.

**2002, May 17**  *Perf. 14*
2685 A656 50 l Sheet of 5, #a-e  5.00 5.00

Blood Donation — A657

Letters "A," "B," and "O" with: No. 2686, 90 l, Stylized people. No. 2687, 90 l, Wings.

**2002, June 16**  *Perf. 13¾x14¼*
2686-2687 A657  Set of 2  4.00 4.00

Sportsmen A658

No. 2688: a, Naim Kryeziu, soccer player. b, Riza Lushta, soccer player. c, Ymer Pampuri, weight lifter.
300 l, Loro Borici, soccer player, vert.

**2002, July 3**  *Perf. 14¼x14*
2688  Horiz. strip of 3  3.50 3.50
a.-c. A658 50 l Any single  1.10 1.10
**Size: 60x80mm**
**Imperf**
2689 A658 300 l multi  6.00 6.00

Intl. Federation of Stamp Dealers Associations, 50th Anniv. — A659

Designs: 50 l, Man, #2471. 100 l, Map of Albania, Europe, cube of blue spheres.

**2002, Sept. 1**  Litho.  *Perf. 13¾x13¼*
2690-2691 A659  Set of 2  3.00 3.00

Anti-Terrorism A660

Designs: 100 l, Statue of Liberty. 150 l, World Trade Center on fire.
350 l, Statue of Liberty and World Trade Center, vert.

**2002, Sept. 11**  *Perf. 13¾x13*
2692-2693 A660  Set of 2  5.00 5.00

**Souvenir Sheet**
*Perf. 13*
2694 A660 350 l multi  7.00 7.00
No. 2694 contains one 29x50mm stamp.

Mediterranean Sealife — A661

No. 2695: a, Caretta caretta. b, Delphinus delphis. c, Prionace glauca. d, Balaenoptera physalus. e, Torpedo torpedo. f, Octopus vulgaris.

*Perf. 14¼x14¾*
**2002, Sept. 12**  Litho.
2695 A661 50 l Sheet of 6, #a-f  6.00 6.00

Famous Albanians — A662

No. 2696: a, Tefta Tashko Koço (1910-47), singer. b, Naim Frasheri (1923-75), actor. c, Kristaq Antoniu (1909-79), singer. d, Panajot Kanaçi (1923-96), choreographer.

**2002, Oct. 6**  *Perf. 13¾*
2696 A662 50 l Block of 4, #a-d  4.00 4.00

Independence, 90th Anniv. — A663

Designs: 20 l, Flags of Albania and other nations. 90 l, People, Albanian flag.

**2002, Nov. 28**  Litho.  *Perf. 13½x14*
2697-2698 A663  Set of 2  2.00 2.00

Post and Telecommunications Administration, 90th Anniv. — A664

Designs: 20 l, Satellite dish. 90 l, Telegraph, air mail envelope.

**2002, Dec. 4**
2699-2700 A664  Set of 2  2.00 2.00

**Costumes Type of 2001**

No. 2701: a, Woman from Kelmendi. b, Man from Zadrime. c, Woman from Zerqani. d, Man from Peshkopi. e, Man from Malesia e Tiranes. f, Woman from Malesia e Tiranes. g, Woman from Fushe Kruje. h, Man from Shpati. i, Woman from Myzeqe. j, Woman from Labinoti. k, Man from Korce. l, Woman from Laberi.

**2003, Apr. 1**  Litho.  *Perf. 13¼*
2701 A640 30 l Sheet of 12, #a-l  8.00 8.00
 Booklet, #2701  10.00 10.00

Characterizations of Popeye — A665

No. 2702: a, 80 l, Popeye and Olive Oyl. b, 150 l, Popeye smoking pipe. c, 40 l, Popeye and Brutus. d, 50 l, Popeye walking.

**2003, Apr. 6**
2702 A665  Strip of 4, #a-d  7.00 7.00

Castles A666

No. 2703: a, 10 l, Porto Palermo. b, 20 l, Petrela. c, 50 l, Kruja. d, 120 l, Preza.

**2003, Apr. 15**  Litho.  *Perf. 13¼*
2703 A666  Sheet of 4, #a-d  6.00 6.00

Europa — A667

Poster art: 150 l, Onufri. 200 l, Various posters.
350 l, Face from Onufri poster.

**2003, Apr. 30**  *Perf. 14*
2704-2705 A667  Set of 2  6.00 6.00

**Souvenir Sheet**
2706 A667 350 l multi  8.00 8.00

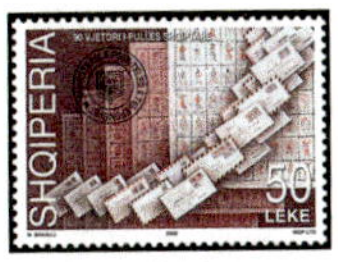


First Albanian Stamps, 90th Anniv. — A668

Designs: 50 l, Stamped envelopes, sheets of stamps. 1000 l, Seal of Post, Telegraph and Telephone Ministry.

**2003, May 12** *Perf. 13¼*
**2707-2708** A668 Set of 2 *22.50 22.50*

### Arms Type of 2001

Family arms: 10 l, Arianiti. 20 l, Jonima. 70 l, Dukagjini. 120 l, Kopili.

**2003, May 12**
**2709** A649 10 l multi .30 .30
*a.* Booklet pane of 4 1.25 —
**2710** A649 20 l multi .50 .50
*a.* Booklet pane of 4 2.25 —
**2711** A649 70 l multi 1.50 1.50
*a.* Booklet pane of 4 7.00 —
**2712** A649 120 l multi 2.50 2.50
*a.* Booklet pane of 4 11.00 —
Complete booklet, #2709a, 2710a, 27111a, 2712a 24.00
*Nos. 2709-2712 (4)* 4.80 4.80

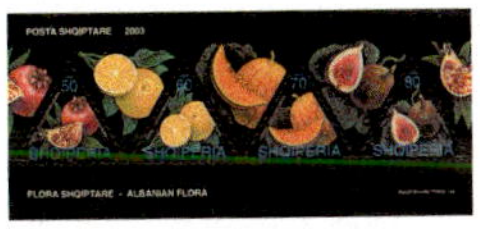

Fruit A669

No. 2713: a, 50 l, Punica gramatunil. b, 60 l, Citrus medica. c, 70 l, Cucumis melo. d, 80 l, Ficus.

***Serpentine Die Cut 6¼***
**2003, May 17** **Self-Adhesive**
**2713** A669 Sheet of 4, #a-d 5.50 5.50

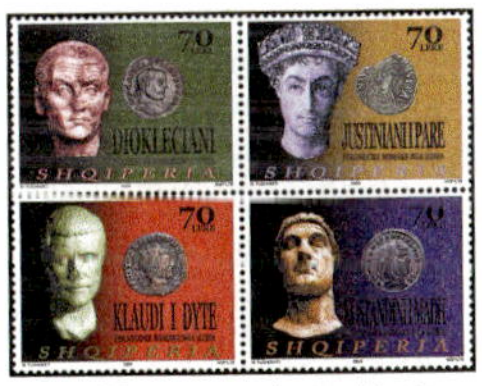


Roman Emperors from Illyria and Coins Depicting Them — A670

No. 2714: a, Diocletian (c. 245-c. 313). b, Justinian I (483-565). c, Claudius II (214-70). d, Constantine I (the Great) (d. 337).

**2003, June 20** **Litho.** *Perf. 13¼*
**2714** A670 70 l Block of 4, #a-d 6.00 6.00

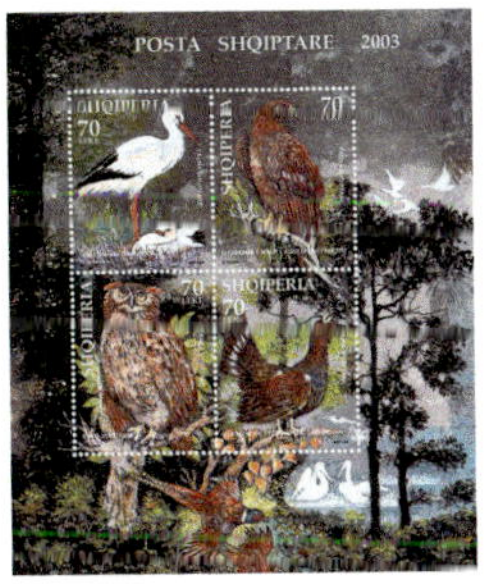


Birds A671

No. 2715: a, Ciconia ciconia. b, Aquilia chrysaetos. c, Bubo bubo. d, Tetrao urogallos.

**2003, Aug. 20** *Perf. 14¼x14¼*
**2715** A671 70 l Sheet of 4, #a-d 6.00 6.00

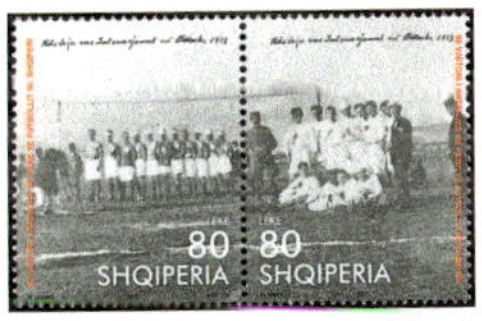


First International Soccer Match in Albania, 90th Anniv. — A672

No. 2716: a, Denomination at right. b, Denomination at left.

**2003, Sept. 2**
**2716** A672 80 l Horiz. pair, #a-b 3.50 3.50

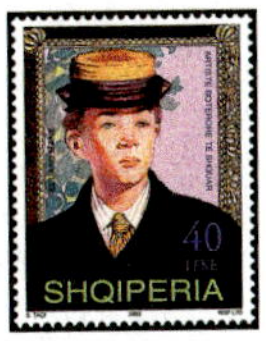


Paintings by Edouard Manet — A673

Designs: 40 l, Lunch in the Workshop (detail). 100 l, The Fifer. 250 l, Manet, horiz.

**2003, Sept. 20** *Perf. 14½x14¼*
**2717-2718** A673 Set of 2 3.00 3.00

### Souvenir Sheet
*Perf. 14¼x14½*

**2719** A673 250 l multi 4.50 4.50

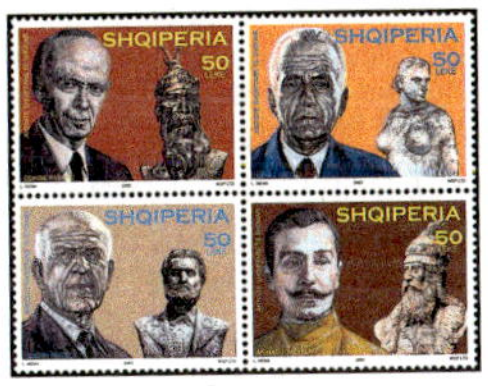


Sculptors A674

No. 2720: a, Odhise Paskali. b, Janaq Paco. c, Llazar Nikolla. d, Murat Toptani.

**2003, Oct. 6** *Perf. 13¼*
**2720** A674 50 l Block of 4, #a-d 4.00 4.00

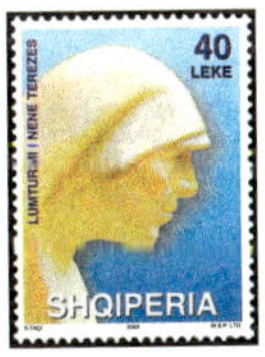


Beatification of Mother Teresa — A675

Sculptures of Mother Teresa: 40 l, Profile. 250 l, Front view. 350 l, Mother Teresa praying

**2003, Oct. 19** *Perf. 13¼*
**2721-2722** A675 Set of 2 6.00 6.00

### Souvenir Sheet
*Perf.*

**2723** A675 350 l multi 7.00 7.00

No. 2723 contains one 40mm diameter stamp.

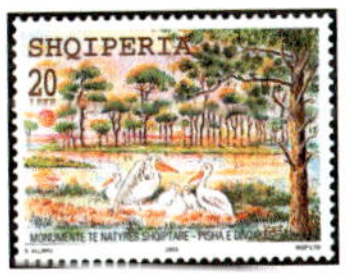


Natural Monuments A676

Designs: 20 l, Divjaka Forest Park. 30 l, Fir trees, Hotova. 200 l, Fir tree, Drenova.

**2003, Oct. 20** *Perf. 13¼*
**2724-2726** A676 Set of 3 5.00 5.00

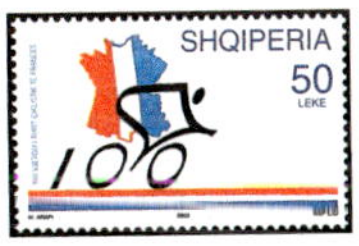


Tour de France Bicycle Race, Cent. — A677

Designs: 50 l, Cyclist, "100," map of France. 100 l, Cyclists, French flag.

**2003, Nov. 1** *Perf. 14¼x14½*
**2727-2728** A677 Set of 2 3.00 3.00

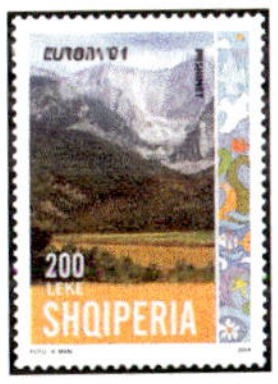


Europa — A678

Various vacation spots with country name in: No. 2729, 200 l, White. No. 2730, 200 l, Light blue.
350 l, Orange.

**2004, June 23** **Litho.** *Perf. 13½*
**2729-2730** A678 Set of 2 9.00 9.00
*a.* Booklet pane, 4 each #2729-2730, perf. 13½ on 3 sides 46.00 —
Complete booklet, #2730a 46.00

### Souvenir Sheet
*Perf. 14¼x13½*

**2731** A678 350 l multi 9.00 9.00

No. 2731 contains one 29x37mm stamp.
In No. 2730a, the two columns in the middle are tete-beche pairs of Nos. 2729-2730.

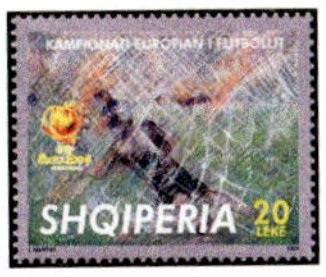


European Soccer Championships, Portugal — A679

Various players: 20 l, 40 l, 50 l, 200 l. 350 l, Player (37mm diameter stamp).

**2004, June 24** *Perf. 14*
**2732-2735** A679 Set of 4 7.00 7.00

### Souvenir Sheet
*Perf.*

**2736** A679 350 l multi 8.00 8.00

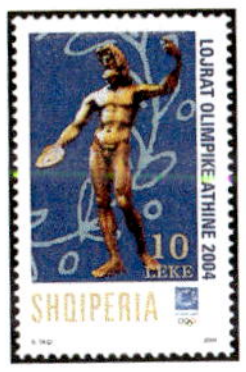


2004 Summer Olympics, Athens — A680

Designs: 10 l, Statue of discus thrower. 200 l, Bust.
350 l, Torch bearer.

**2004, Aug. 12** *Perf. 13½*
**2737-2738** A680 Set of 2 4.50 4.50

### Souvenir Sheet
*Perf. 13½x13¾*

**2739** A680 350 l multi 8.00 8.00

No. 2739 contains one 38x54mm stamp

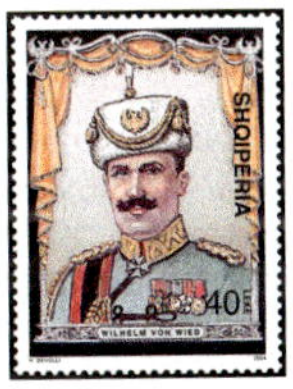


Prince Wilhelm zu Wied (1876-1945), Appointed Ruler of Albania — A681

Designs: 40 l, With hat. 150 l, Without hat.

**2004, Aug. 30** **Litho.** *Perf. 13½*
**2740-2741** A681 Set of 2 4.00 4.00

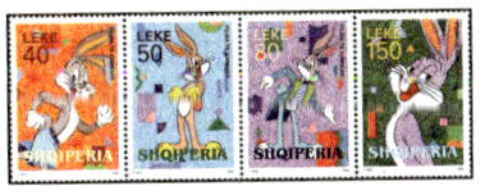

Characterizations of Bugs Bunny — A682

No. 2742 — Background color: a, 40 l, Orange. b, 50 l, Light blue. c, 80 l, Purple. d, 150 l, Green.

**2004, Sept. 15**
**2742** A682 Horiz. strip of 4, #a-d 7.00 7.00

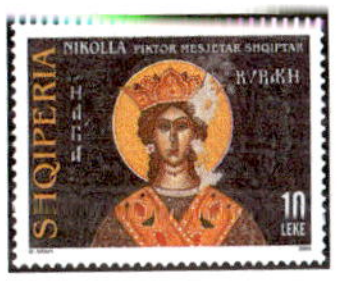


Icons Painted by Nikolla Onufri — A683

Various saints: 10 l, 20 l, 1000 l.

**2004, Oct. 3** *Perf. 14*
**2743-2745** A683 Set of 3 22.50 22.50

### Souvenir Sheet
*Perf. 13½x14¼*

**2746** A683 400 l Saint, diff. 9.00 9.00

### Souvenir Sheet

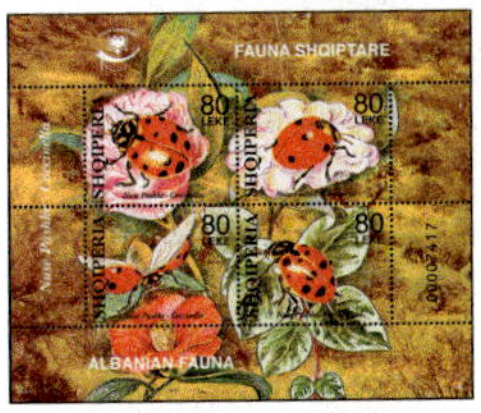


Ladybugs — A684

No. 2747: a, With 12 spots, on flower. b, With 5 spots, on flower. c, With wings extended. d, On leaves.

**2004, Oct. 10** *Perf. 14*
**2747** A684 80 l Sheet of 4, #a-d 7.00 7.00

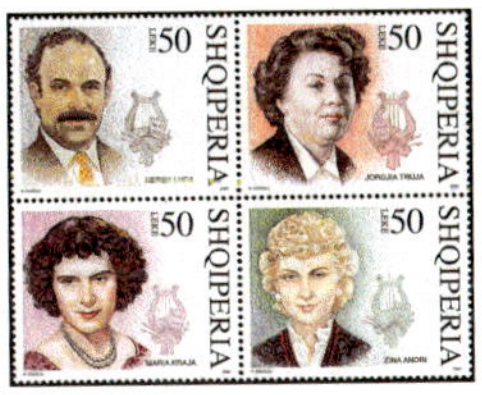


Entertainment Personalities — A685

No. 2748: a, Ndrek Luca (1924-93), actor. b, Jorgjia Truja (1909-94), singer, film director. c, Maria Kraja (1911-99), opera singer. d, Zina Andri (1924-80), actress, theater director.

**2004, Oct. 12** *Perf. 13¾x13½*
**2748** A685 50 l Block of 4, #a-d 4.50 4.50

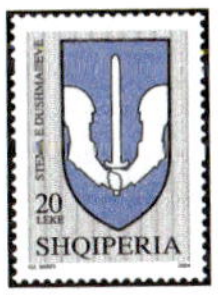


Coats of Arms — A686

Designs: 20 l, Spani. 40 l, Gjuraj. 80 l, Zahariaj. 150 l, Dushmani.

**2004, Oct. 25** *Perf. 13¾x14*
**2749** A686 20 l multi .50 .50
*a.* Booklet pane of 4 2.00 —
**2750** A686 40 l multi .80 .80
*a.* Booklet pane of 4 3.50 —
**2751** A686 80 l multi 2.00 2.00
*a.* Booklet pane of 4 8.00 —
**2752** A686 150 l multi 3.25 3.25
*a.* Booklet pane of 4 14.00 —
Complete booklet, #2749a-2752a 29.00
*Nos. 2749-2752 (4)* 6.55 6.55

### Souvenir Sheet

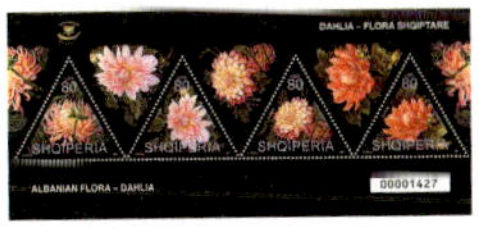

Dahlias A687

No. 2753: a, Pink flower with small petals, large bud in front. b, Bud in back. c, Small flower at right. d, Red flower with large petals, small bud in front.

**2004, Nov. 1** *Perf. 14*
**2753** A687 80 l Sheet of 4, #a-d 7.00 7.00

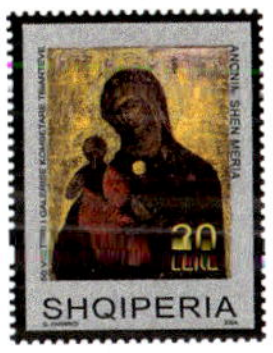


Art in National Gallery — A688

No. 2745 — Art by: a, Unknown artist (Madonna and Child). b, Mihal Anagnosti. c, Onufer Qiprioti. d, Cetiret. e, Onuferi. f, Kel Kodheli. g, Vangjush Mio. h, Abdurahim Buza. i, Mustafa Arapi. j, Guri Madhi. k, Janaq Paço. l, Zef Kolombi. m, Hasan Reçi. n, Vladimir Jani. o, Halim Beqiri. p, Edison Gjergo. q, Naxhi Bakalli. r, Agron Bregu. s, Edi Hila. t, Artur Muharremi. u, Rembrandt. v, Gazmend Leka. w, Damien Hirst. x, Edvin Rama. y, Ibrahim Kodra.

**2004, Nov. 20** *Perf. 14*
**2754** Sheet of 25 12.50 12.50
*a.-y.* A688 20 l Any single .50 .50

# 396 ALBANIA

NATO in Kosovo, 5th Anniv. — A689

NATO emblem and: 100 l, Pennants and stars. 200 l, Doves, UN flag. 350 l, Buildings, Albanian flag.

**2004, Nov. 28**    Perf. 14¼x13½
2755-2756 A689   Set of 2   7.00   7.00

**Souvenir Sheet**
2757 A689 350 l multi   8.00   8.00

Liberation From Nazi Occupation, 60th Anniv. — A690

Designs: 50 l, Two doves. 200 l, One dove.

**2004, Nov. 29**    Perf. 13¾x13½
2758-2759 A690   Set of 2   6.00   6.00

**Native Costumes Type of 2001**

No. 2760: a, Woman from Gramshi (showing back). b, Woman from Gramshi (showing front). c, Woman from Korça with blue skirt. d, Man from Kolonja. e, Woman from Korça with red dress. f, Woman from Librazhdi. g, Woman from Permeti. h, Woman from Pogradeci. i, Man from Skrapari. j, Woman from Skrapari. k, Woman from Tepelena. l, Woman from Vlora.

**2004, Dec. 4**    Perf. 13½
2760 A640 30 l Sheet of 12, #a-l   10.00   10.00
   Complete booklet, #2760   11.50

Europa Stamps, 50th Anniv. (in 2006) — A691

Vignettes similar to: 200 l, #2558. 250 l, #2471, horiz. 500 l, #2675.

**2005, Oct. 1**    Litho.   Perf. 13¾
2761-2762 A691   Set of 2   10.00   10.00

**Souvenir Sheet**
2763 A691 500 l multi   10.00   10.00
No. 2763 contains one 38x38mm stamp.

A692

Europa — A693

**2005, Oct. 5**    Perf. 14x13¾
2764 A692 200 l multi   5.00   5.00
   a. Perf. 13¼x13¾ on 2 or 3 sides   5.00   5.00
2765 A693 200 l multi   5.00   5.00
   a. Perf. 13¼x13¾ on 2 or 3 sides   5.00   5.00

**Souvenir Sheet**
*Perf. 12¾x13*
2766 A633 350 l Stuffed cabbage   9.00   9.00
   a. Booklet pane, #2766, 3 each #2764a, 2765a   40.00   —
     Complete booklet, #2766a   55.00

No. 2766 contains one 25x30mm stamp. Serial number is at top right of sheet margin on No. 2766, and on binding stub on No. 2766a. No. 2766a sold for 1650 l.

Admission to the United Nations, 50th Anniv. — A694

**2005, Oct. 19**    Perf. 12¾
2767 A694 40 l multi   .80   .80

Cartoon Characters: — A695

No. 2768 — Tom & Jerry: a, 150 l, Tom. b, 40 l, Tom & Jerry. c, 50 l, Tom & Jerry, diff. d, 80 l, Jerry.

**2005, Oct. 20**    Perf. 14
2768 A695 Horiz. strip of 4, #a-d   6.00   6.00

Paintings — A696

Various unattributed paintings: a, Mountain, town and river. b, Castle and aqueduct. c, Crowd, minaret. d, Castle on mountain, people near river.

**2005, Oct. 21**
2769 Horiz. strip of 4   20.00   20.00
   a. A696 10 l multi   .30   .30
   b. A696 20 l multi   .30   .30
   c. A696 30 l multi   .60   .60
   d. A696 1000 l multi   17.50   17.50

**Costumes Type of 2001**

No. 2770: a, Man, Tirana. b, Woman, Bende Tirana. c, Woman, Zall Dajt. d, Man, Kavaje-Durres. e, Woman, Has. f, Man, Mat. g, Woman, Liqenas. h, Woman, Klenje. i, Woman, Maleshove. j, Woman, German. k, Woman, Kruje. l, Man, Reç.

**2005, Oct. 24**    Perf. 14x13¾
2770 A640 30 l Sheet of 12, #a-l   8.00   8.00
   Complete booklet, #2770   13.00
Complete booklet sold for 460 l.

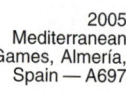

2005 Mediterranean Games, Almería, Spain — A697

**2005, Oct. 25**    Perf. 14¼x13¾
2771 Horiz. strip of 3   5.00   5.00
   a. A697 20 l Runner in blocks   .40   .40
   b. A697 60 l Gymnastics   1.00   1.00
   c. A697 120 l Relay race   2.00   2.00

**Souvenir Sheet**
*Perf. 12¾x13*
2772 A697 300 l Diver   7.50   7.50
No. 2772 contains one 50x30mm stamp.

Rotary International, Cent. — A698

Rotary International emblem and: 30 l, Map of North America. 150 l, Rays and "100 Vjet," vert.

**2005, Nov. 11**    Perf. 13¾
2773-2774 A698   Set of 2   4.00   4.00

**Arms Type of 2001**

No. 2775 — Arms of: a, Bua Despots. b, Karl Topia. c, Dukagjini II. d, Engjej.

**2005, Nov. 14**    Perf. 12¾
2775 Horiz. strip of 4   5.00   5.00
   a. A649 10 l multi   .30   .30
   b. A649 30 l multi   .50   .50
   c. A649 100 l multi   1.50   1.50
   d. A649 150 l multi   2.50   2.50
   e. Booklet pane, 4 #2775a   1.30
   f. Booklet pane, 4 #2775b   2.50   —
   g. Booklet pane, 4 #2775c   7.00   —
   h. Booklet pane, 4 #2775d   11.00   —
     Complete booklet, #2775e-2775h   25.00

**Souvenir Sheet**

Portulaca Flowers A699

No. 2776: a, Yellow flowers. b, Three white flowers. c, Red and bright yellow flowers. d, Pink flower. e, Red flower.

**2005, Nov. 17**    Perf. 14
2776 A699 70 l Sheet of 5, #a-e   10.50   10.50

Cycling in Albania, 80th Anniv. — A700

**2005, Nov. 20**    Perf. 13¼x13¾
2777 Strip of 3   6.50   6.50
   a. A700 50 l blue & multi   1.25   1.25
   b. A700 60 l red & multi   1.75   1.75
   c. A700 120 l bright red & multi   3.25   3.25

**Souvenir Sheet**

Skanderbeg (1405-68), National Hero — A701

No. 2778 — Various scenes of warriors in battle: a, 40 l (50x30mm). b, 50 l (50x30mm). c, 60 l (50x30mm). d, 70 l (50x30mm). e, 80 l (30mm diameter). f, 90 l (30mm diameter).

**2005, Nov. 28**    Perf. 13
2778 A701 Sheet of 6, #a-f   12.00   12.00

End of World War II, 60th Anniv. A702

No. 2779: a, 50 l, Doves, roses, army helmet. b, 200 l, Statues, flags, dove.

**2005, Nov. 29**    Perf. 14x13¾
2779 A702 Horiz. pair, #a-b   5.25   5.25

Marubi Family Artists — A703

No. 2780: a, Matia Kodheli-Marubi. b, Gege Marubi. c, Pjeter Marubi. d, Kel Marubi.

**2005, Dec. 4**
2780 Horiz. strip of 4   7.50   7.50
   a. A703 10 l multi   .30   .30
   b. A703 20 l multi   .50   .50
   c. A703 70 l multi   1.75   1.75
   d. A703 200 l multi   5.00   5.00

**Nos. 2417, 2433, 2446, 2477, 2478, 2484, 2487, 2490-2492, 2498 and 2504 Surcharged**

**Methods and Perfs as Before**
**2006**
2781 A550 on 30q #2417   25.00   25.00
2782 A569 on 2 l #2478   15.00   15.00
2783 A574 on 2 l #2490   15.00   15.00
2784 A574 on 3 l #2491   15.00   15.00
2785 A577 on 3 l #2498   15.00   15.00
2786 A552 on 10 l #2433   30.00   30.00
2787 A572 on 18 l #2484   20.00   20.00
2788 A573 on 18 l #2487   20.00   20.00
2789 A556 on 21 l #2446   20.00   20.00
2790 A568 on 25 l #2477 (block of 4, #a-d)   150.00   150.00
2791 A574 on 25 l #2492   30.00   30.00
2792 A580 on 25 l #2504   30.00   30.00
   Nos. 2781-2789, 2791-2792 (11)   235.00   235.00

Location of surcharge varies.

Visit of Pres. George W. Bush to Albania A704

No. 2793 — Photograph of Bush in: a, 20 l, Blue. b, 40 l, Green. c, 80 l, Full color. 200 l, Statue of Liberty, flags of US and Albania, horiz.

**2007, June 10**    Perf. 13¼x13½   Litho.
2793 A704 Horiz. strip of 3, #a-c   3.50   3.50

**Souvenir Sheet**
*Perf. 13½x13¼*
2794 A704 200 l multi   4.50   4.50

Italian Delegation of Experts in Albania, 10th Anniv. — A705

**2007, Sept. 15**    Perf. 13¼x13½   Litho.
**Granite Paper**
2795 A705 40 l multi   1.25   1.25

**Miniature Sheet**

Albanian Flag A706

No. 2796 — Various depictions of Albanian flag blowing in wind: a, 5 l. b, 10 l. c, 20 l. d, 30 l. e, 40 l. f, 50 l. g, 60 l. h, 70 l. i, 80 l. j, 100 l. k, 1000 l. l, 2000 l.

**2007, Oct. 5**    Litho.   Perf. 13¼x13
2796 A706 Sheet of 12, #a-l   90.00   90.00

**Arms Type of 2001**

Arms of: 20 l, Despot Andrea II Muzaka. 40 l, Matrenga family. 80 l, Leke Dukagjini. 150 l, Konstantin Kastrioti.

**2007, Oct. 15**    Litho.   Perf. 12¾x13¼
2797 A649 20 l multi   1.75   1.75
2798 A649 40 l multi   3.50   3.50
2799 A649 80 l multi   6.50   6.50
2800 A649 150 l multi   12.00   12.00
   a. Vert. strip of 4, #2797-2800   150.00
     Nos. 2797-2800 (4)   23.75   23.75

Nos. 2797-2800 are dated 2006.

# ALBANIA

**Arms Type of 2001**

Arms of: 10 l, Lança family. 20 l, Riki family. 60 l, Kokini family. 100 l, Zako family.

| 2007, Oct. 17 | Litho. | Perf. 12¾x13¼ | | |
|---|---|---|---|---|
| 2801 | A649 | 10 l multi | .50 | .50 |
| 2802 | A649 | 20 l multi | 1.00 | 1.00 |
| 2803 | A649 | 60 l multi | 3.00 | 3.00 |
| 2804 | A649 | 100 l multi | 5.50 | 5.50 |
| a. | Vert. strip of 4, #2801-2804 | | 150.00 | 150.00 |
| | Nos. 2801-2804 (4) | | 10.00 | 10.00 |

Europa — A707

Men and women and: No. 2805, 200 l, Flag of European Union, map of Europe. No. 2806, 200 l, Flag and map of Albania.
350 l, Men, women, flags of Albania and European Union, horiz.

| 2007, Oct. 23 | Litho. | Perf. 13x13¼ | | |
|---|---|---|---|---|
| 2805-2806 | A707 | Set of 2 | 10.00 | 10.00 |

**Souvenir Sheet**
Perf. 13¼x13

| 2807 | A707 | 350 l multi | 9.00 | 9.00 |

No. 2807 contains one 30x25mm stamp. Dated 2006.

Europa — A708

Designs: 100 l, Scouts, flags, mountain. 150 l, Scouts, flags, mountain, diff. 250 l, Knot, horiz.

| 2007, Oct. 24 | | Perf. 13¼x13 | | |
|---|---|---|---|---|
| 2808-2809 | A708 | Set of 2 | 5.00 | 5.00 |

**Souvenir Sheet**

| 2810 | A708 | 250 l multi | 5.75 | 5.75 |

Scouting, cent. No. 2810 contains one 30x25mm stamp.

Pink Panther — A709

No. 2811 — Pink Panther: a, 150 l, Wearing uniform. b, 40 l, Wearing bowtie. c, 50 l, With inspector. d, 80 l, With elbow resting on orange panel.

| 2007, Oct. 25 | | Perf. 13 | | |
|---|---|---|---|---|
| 2811 | A709 | Horiz. strip of 4, #a-d | 7.00 | 7.00 |

Children's Art — A710

No. 2812 — Art by: a, 10 l, Arkida Lema. b, 40 l, Amarilda Prifti. c, 50 l, Iliaz Kasa. d, 80 l, Klaudia Mezini, horiz.

| 2007, Oct. 29 | | Perf. 13 | | |
|---|---|---|---|---|
| 2812 | A710 | Horiz. strip of 4, #a-d | 7.00 | 7.00 |

Frescoes — A712

Designs: 70 l, sower, by David Selenices. 110 l, Floral mural, Et'hem Bey Mosque, Tirana.

| 2007, Oct. 31 | Litho. | Perf. 13 | | |
|---|---|---|---|---|
| 2814-2815 | A712 | Set of 2 | 6.00 | 6.00 |

**Miniature Sheet**

Native Costumes — A713

No. 2816: a, German woman. b, Kurbin man. c, Golloborde woman. d, Kerrabe Malesi man. e, Gur i Bardhe woman. f, Martanesh woman. g, Puke woman. h, Serice Labinot woman. i, Shen Gjergj woman. j, Tirane Qytet woman. k, Zalle Dajt man. l, Zaranike Godolesh woman.

| 2008, Nov. 1 | Litho. | Perf. 13 | | |
|---|---|---|---|---|
| 2816 | A713 | 40 l Sheet of 12, #a-l | 12.00 | 12.00 |

Dated 2006. A sheet of 20 l stamps depicting native costumes with country name at left was issued on Nov. 2 in limited quantities to those with reservations to purchase the sheet, and later was sold at an inflated price. Value, $100.

Tourism — A714

No. 2817: a, Thethi National Park (Parku Kombetar Thethit). b, Lures Lake (Liqenet e Lures). c, Kanina Castle (Kalaja e Kanines). d, Karavasta Lagoon (Laguna e Karavastase).

| 2007, Nov. 5 | | | | |
|---|---|---|---|---|
| 2817 | | Horiz. strip of 4 | 7.00 | 7.00 |
| a. | A714 40 l green & multi | | 1.00 | 1.00 |
| b. | A714 50 l red violet & multi | | 1.25 | 1.25 |
| c. | A714 60 l red & multi | | 1.50 | 1.50 |
| d. | A714 70 l blue violet & multi | | 2.25 | 2.25 |

Trees of Elbasan — A715

Designs: 70 l, Tree and pond. 90 l, Hollowed-out tree.

| 2007, Nov. 8 | | Perf. 13x13¼ | | |
|---|---|---|---|---|
| 2818-2819 | A715 | Set of 2 | 4.50 | 4.50 |

Dated 2006.

Pope Clement XI (1649-1721) — A716

No. 2820: a, 30 l, Red background. b, 120 l, Blue background.

| 2007, Nov. 9 | | Perf. 13¼x13 | | |
|---|---|---|---|---|
| 2820 | A716 | Vert. pair, #a-b | 4.50 | 4.50 |

Dated 2006.

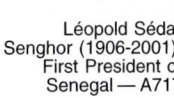 

Léopold Sédar Senghor (1906-2001), First President of Senegal — A717

Color of photograph: 40 l, Sepia. 80 l, Black.

| 2007, Nov. 10 | | | | |
|---|---|---|---|---|
| 2821-2822 | A717 | Set of 2 | 4.00 | 4.00 |

Dated 2006.

Albania as Balkan Soccer Champions, 60th Anniv. (in 2006) — A718

Background colors: 10 l, Buff and red. 80 l, Light and dark blue.

| 2007, Nov. 11 | | Perf. 13x13¼ | | |
|---|---|---|---|---|
| 2823-2824 | A718 | Set of 2 | 10.00 | 10.00 |

Dated 2006.

**Miniature Sheet**

Gjirokaster UNESCO World Heritage Site — A719

No. 2825: a, 10 l, Cannons. b, 20 l, Wall decoration. c, 30 l, Building. d, 60 l, Bridge. e, 80 l, Aerial view of town. f, 90 l, Castle atop cliff.

| 2007, Nov. 12 | | Perf. 13¼x13 | | |
|---|---|---|---|---|
| 2825 | A719 | Sheet of 6, #a-f | 9.00 | 9.00 |

Dated 2006.

Participation of Albanian Military in International Missions, 10th Anniv. (in 2006) — A720

Designs: 10 l, Soldier in gas mask. 100 l, Soldiers in raft.

| 2008, Nov. 13 | | | | |
|---|---|---|---|---|
| 2826-2827 | A720 | Set of 2 | 3.00 | 3.00 |

Dated 2006.

Mother Teresa (1910-97), 1978 Nobel Peace Laureate — A721

Background color: 60 l, Orange yellow. 130 l, Brown. 200 l, Red.

| 2007, Nov. 15 | | Perf. 13¼x13 | | |
|---|---|---|---|---|
| 2828-2829 | A721 | Set of 2 | 7.50 | 7.50 |

**Souvenir Sheet**

| 2830 | A721 | 200 l multi | — | — |

Statue of Gaia Found Near Durres — A722

No. 2831: a, 30 l, Small image of statue. b, 120 l, Large image of statue.

| 2007, Nov. 16 | Litho. | Perf. 13¼x13 | | |
|---|---|---|---|---|
| 2831 | A722 | Vert. pair, #a-b | 10.00 | 10.00 |

A 200 l souvenir sheet issued with this set was sold in limited quantities to those with reservations to purchase the sheet, and later was sold at an inflated price. Value, $250.

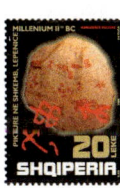

Prehistoric Cave and Rock Drawings — A723

Designs: 20 l, Rock drawings, Lepenice. 100 l, Rock drawing, Tren. 300 l, Cave drawing, Tren.

| 2007, Nov. 19 | | Perf. 13¼x13 | | |
|---|---|---|---|---|
| 2832-2833 | A723 | Set of 2 | 3.00 | 3.00 |

**Souvenir Sheet**
Perf. 13x13¼

| 2834 | A723 | 300 l multi | 6.00 | 6.00 |

Dated 2006.

Famous Men — A724

No. 2835: a, Osman Kazazi (1917-99), resistance leader. b, Pjeter Arbnori (1935-2006), politician. c, Lasgush Poradeci (1899-1987), writer. d, Cesk Zadeja (1927-97), musician.

| 2007, Nov. 22 | | Perf. 13¼x13 | | |
|---|---|---|---|---|
| 2835 | | Horiz. strip of 4 | 5.00 | 5.00 |
| a. | A724 10 l multi | | 1.25 | 1.25 |
| b. | A724 20 l multi | | 1.25 | 1.25 |
| c. | A724 60 l multi | | 1.25 | 1.25 |
| d. | A724 100 l multi | | 1.25 | 1.25 |

Famous Men — A725

No. 2836: a, Abdurrahim Buza (1905-87), painter. b, Aleks Buda (1911-93), historian. c, Thimi Mitko (1820-90), writer. d, Martin Camaj (1925-94), writer.

| 2007, Nov. 22 | | Perf. 13x13¼ | | |
|---|---|---|---|---|
| 2836 | | Horiz. strip of 4 | 5.75 | 5.75 |
| a.-d. | A725 50 l Any single | | 1.25 | 1.25 |

Dated 2006.

2006 World Cup Soccer Championships, Germany — A726

Stylized soccer players with background colors of: 30 l, Yellow. 60 l, Red. 120 l, Black. 350 l, Emblem of 2006 World Cup.

**2007, Nov. 26**

**2837-2839** A726 Set of 3 10.00 10.00

**Souvenir Sheet**

**2840** A726 350 l multi 15.00 15.00

Dated 2006.

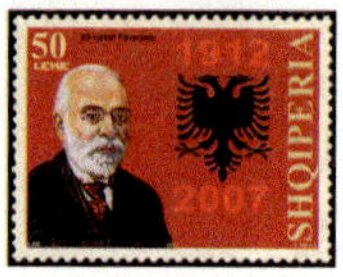

Independence, 95th Anniv. — A727

Ismail Qemali (1844-1919), first Albanian Prime Minister and: 50 l, Heraldic eagle and years. 110 l, Text.

**2007, Nov. 28** ***Perf. 13x13¼***

**2841-2842** A727 Set of 2 3.50 3.50

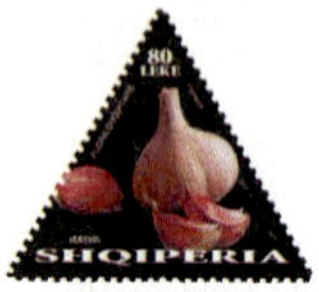

Vegetables A728

No. 2843: a, Garlic. b, Onions. c, Peppers. d, Tomatoes.

**2007, Dec. 3 Litho.** ***Perf. 12¾***

**2843** Horiz. strip of 4 + 3 labels 12.50 12.50

*a.-d.* A728 80 l Any single 3.00 3.00

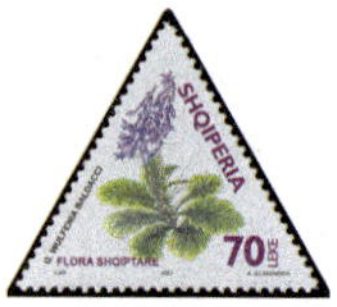

Wulfenia Baldacci — A729

**2007, Dec. 4 Litho.** ***Perf. 13***

**2844** Horiz. pair + central label 10.00 10.00

*a.* A729 70 l lilac & multi 3.75 3.75

*b.* A729 100 l buff & multi 5.25 5.25

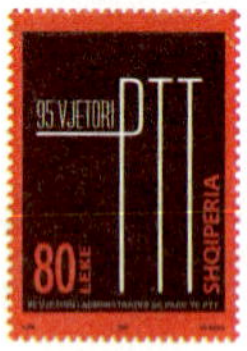

Albanian Post and Telecommunications Department, 95th Anniv. — A730

Denomination in: 80 l, Red. 90 l, Black.

**2007, Dec. 5** ***Perf. 13¼x13***

**2845-2846** A730 Set of 2 3.50 3.50

Miniature Sheet

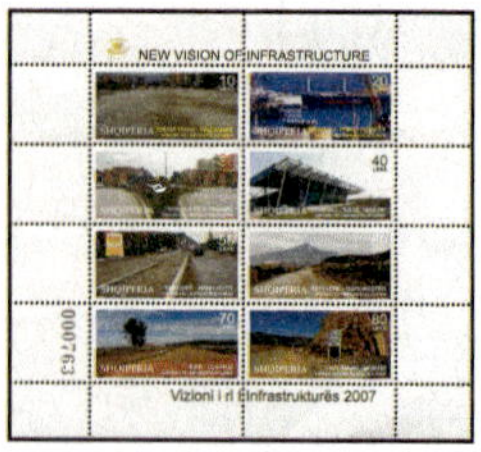

Infrastructure Development — A731

No. 2847: a, 10 l, Trans-Balkan Road. b, 20 l, Port of Durres. c, 30 l, Road, Tirana. d, 40 l, Mother Teresa Terminal. e, 50 l, Road, Shkoder. f, 60 l, Tepelene-Gjirokaster Road. g, 70 l, Fier-Lushnje Road. h, 80 l, Kalimash-Morine Road.

150 l, Mother Teresa Air Terminal, Tirana.

**2007, Dec. 7** ***Perf. 13¼x12¾***

**2847** A731 Sheet of 8, #a-h 9.50 9.50

**Souvenir Sheet**

**2848** A731 150 l multi 4.50 4.50

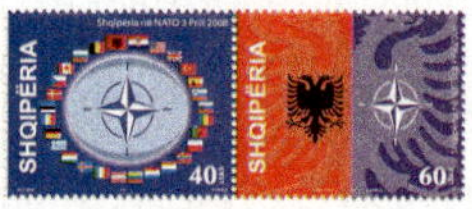

Invitation to Join NATO A732

No. 2849 — NATO emblem and: a, 40 l, Flags of member nations. b, 60 l, Heraldic eagles.

**2008, Apr. 12 Litho.** ***Perf. 13x13¼***

**2849** A732 Horiz. pair, #a-b 2.00 2.00

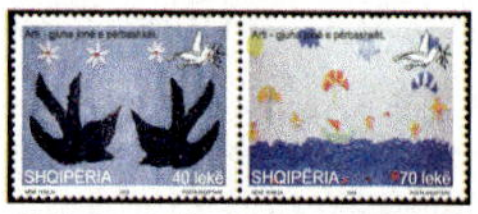

Children's Drawings — A733

No. 2850 — Dove and: a, 40 l, Black doves and flowers. b, 70 l, Boat on water.

**2008, June 1 Litho.** ***Perf. 13x13¼***

**2850** A733 Horiz. pair, #a-b 3.00 3.00

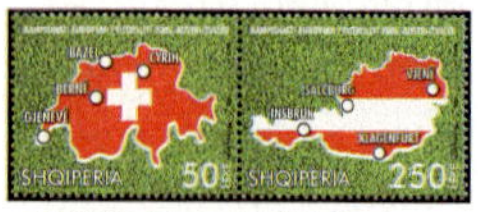

UEFA Euro 2008 Soccer Championships, Austria and Switzerland — A734

No. 2851: a, 50 l, Map of Switzerland. b, 250 l, Map of Austria

200 l, Mascots, vert.

**2008, June 16** ***Perf. 13x13¼***

**2851** A734 Horiz. pair, #a-b 8.00 8.00

**Souvenir Sheet**

***Perf. 13¼x13***

**2852** A734 200 l multi 5.00 5.00

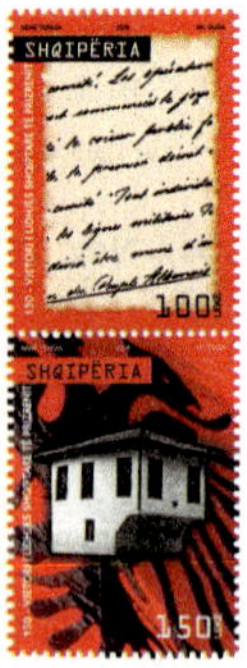

Prizren League, 130th Anniv. — A735

No. 2853: a, 100 l, Handwritten document. b, 150 l, Building, Albanian flag.

**2008, June 27** ***Perf. 13¼x13***

**Granite Paper**

**2853** A735 Vert. pair, #a-b 7.50 7.50

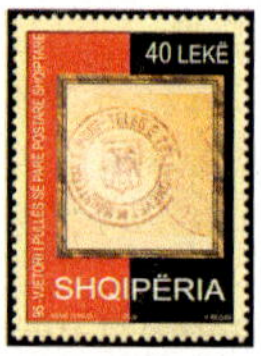

First Albanian Postage Stamps, 95th Anniv. — A736

**2008, June 30 Litho.**

**2854** A736 40 l multi 1.00 1.00

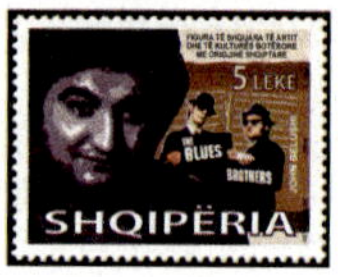

Famous People of Albanian Heritage — A737

No. 2855: a, John Belushi (1949-82), actor. b, Gjon Mili (1904-84), photographer. c, Mimar Sinan (1489-1588), architect. d, Ibrahim Kodra (1918-2006), artist.

**2008, July 9** ***Perf. 13x13¼***

**2855** Horiz. strip of 4 5.50 5.50

*a.* A737 5 l multi .30 .30

*b.* A737 10 l multi .30 .30

*c.* A737 20 l multi .30 .30

*d.* A737 200 l multi 4.00 4.00

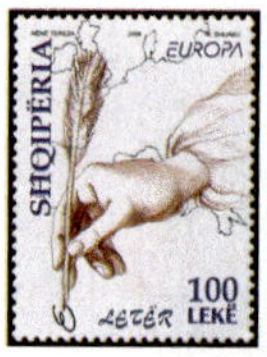

A738

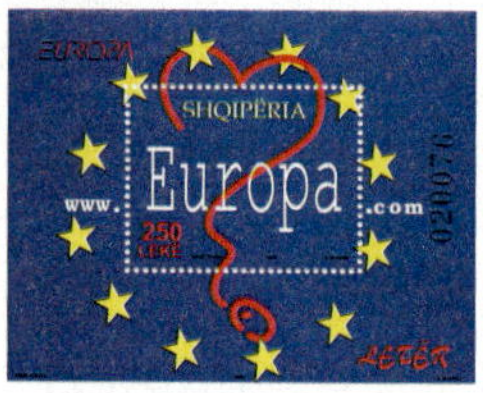

Europa A739

Hand holding quill pen and: 100 l, Map of Europe. 150 l, Map of Albania and Adriatic region.

**2008, July 15** ***Perf. 13¼x13***

**Granite Paper (#2856-2857)**

**2856-2857** A738 Set of 2 6.50 6.50

**Souvenir Sheet**

***Perf. 13x13¼***

**2858** A739 250 l multi 6.50 6.50

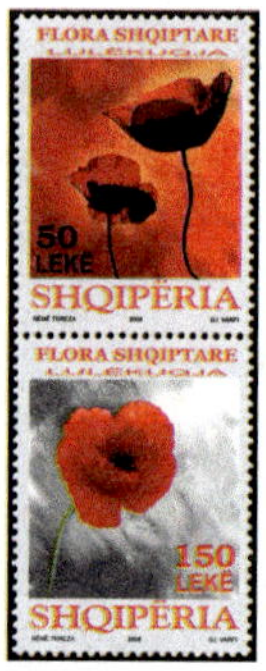

Poppies — A740

No. 2859: a, 50 l, Two poppies. b, 150 l, One poppy.

**2008, July 30** ***Perf. 13¼x13***

**Granite Paper**

**2859** A740 Vert. pair, #a-b 5.00 5.00

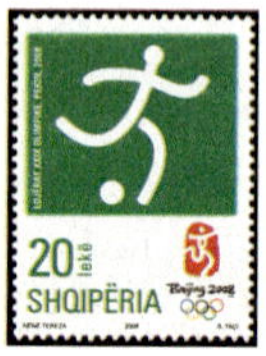

2008 Summer Olympics, Beijing — A741

No. 2860: a, Soccer. b, Water polo. c, Running. d, Cycling.

**2008, Aug. 8** ***Perf. 13x13¼***

**2860** Horiz. strip of 4 4.00 4.00

*a.* A741 20 l multi .60 .60

*b.* A741 30 l multi .80 .80

*c.* A741 40 l multi 1.00 1.00

*d.* A741 50 l multi 1.40 1.40

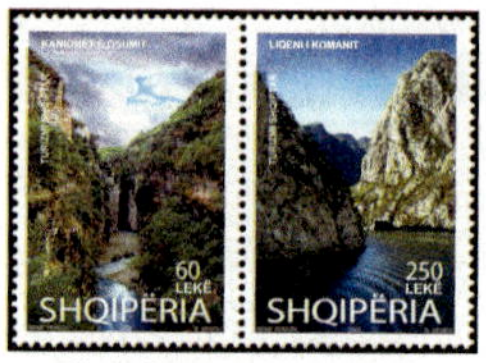

Landscapes — A742

No. 2861: a, 60 l, Osumit Canyon. b, 250 l, Komanit Lake.

**2008, Aug. 25** ***Perf. 13***

**2861** A742 Horiz. pair, #a-b 9.00 9.00

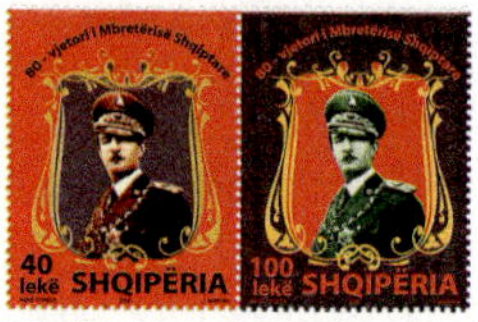

King Zog (1895-1961) — A743

No. 2862 — Denomination color: a, 40 l, Black. b, 100 l, Red.

**2008, Sept. 1** ***Perf. 13x13¼***

**2862** A743 Horiz. pair, #a-b 4.25 4.25

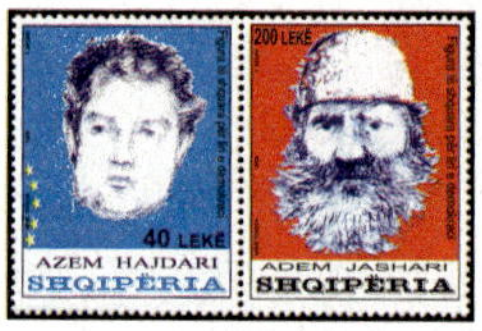

Freedom Fighters A744

No. 2863: a, 40 l, Azem Hajdari (1963-98), assassinated politician. b, 200 l, Adem Jashari (1955-98), Kosovar independence leader.

**2008, Sept. 12**

**2863** A744 Horiz. pair, #a-b 7.00 7.00

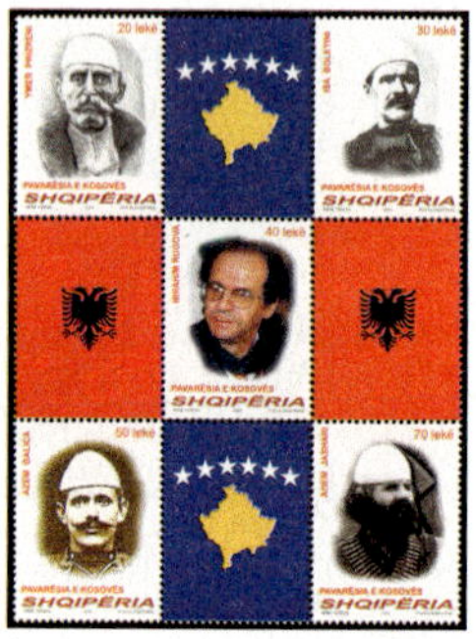

Independence of Kosovo — A745

No. 2864: a, 20 l, Ymer Prizreni (1820-87), political leader. b, 30 l, Isa Boletini (1864-1916), military leader. c, 40 l, Ibrahim Rugova (1944-2006), President of Kosovo. d, 50 l, Azem Galica (1889-1924), military leader. e, 70 l, Adem Jashari (1955-98), independence leader.

**2008, Sept. 20** ***Perf. 13¼x13***

**2864** A745 Block of 5, #a-e, + 4 labels 6.00 6.00

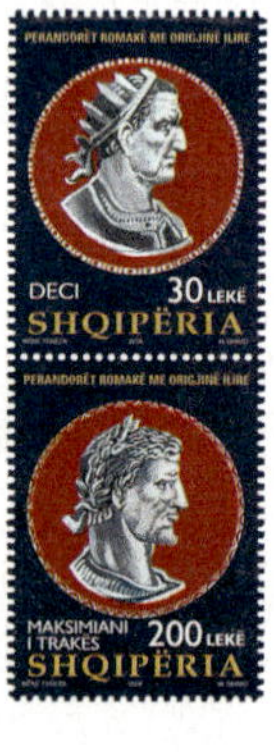

Roman Emperors of Illyrian Origin — A746

No. 2865: a, 30 l, Decius (201-51). b, 200 l, Maximinus Thrax (173-238).

**2008, Oct. 3** ***Perf. 13***

**2865** A746 Vert. pair, #a-b 6.50 6.50

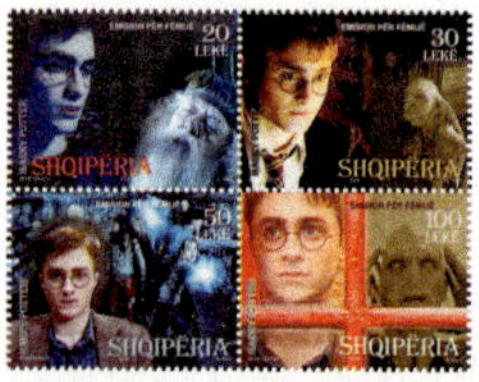

Harry Potter A747

No. 2866 — Harry Potter and: a, 20 l, Professor Dumbledore. b, 30 l, Kreacher. c, 50 l,

Hermione Granger and friends. d, 100 l, Kreacher.

**2008, Oct. 15** *Perf. 13x13¼*
**2866** A747 Block of 4, #a-d 7.50 7.50

A booklet containing a pane of Nos. 2866a-2866d sold for 550 l.

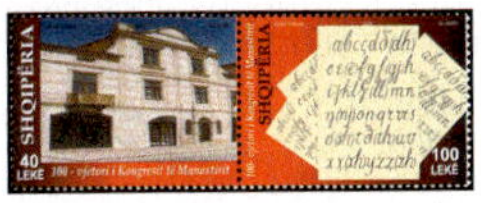

Monastir Congress, Cent. — A748

No. 2867: a, 40 l, Building. b, 100 l, Pages with handwritten Albanian alphabet.

**2008, Nov. 14** *Perf. 13*
**2867** A748 Horiz. pair, #a-b 4.50 4.50

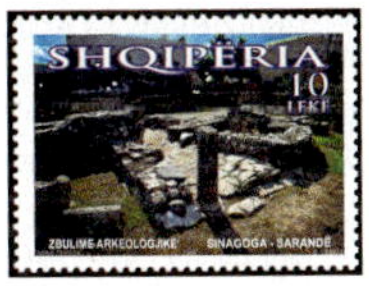

Archaeology A749

No. 2868: a, Ruins of synagogue, Sarande. b, Site at Orikumit. c, Site at Antigonese.

**2008, Dec. 5** *Perf. 13*
**2868** Horiz. strip of 3 4.50 4.50
*a.* A749 10 l multi .30 .30
*b.* A749 50 l multi 1.75 1.75
*c.* A749 80 l multi 2.25 2.25

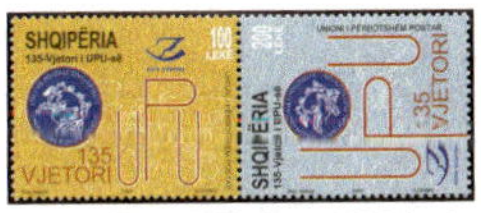

Universal Postal Union, 135th Anniv. A750

No. 2869 — Emblems of Albania Post and UPU, world map and background color of: a, 100 l, Yellow bister. b, 200 l, Light blue, vert.

***Perf. 13x13¼ (#2869a), 13¼x13 (#2869b)***

**2009, Oct. 9** **Litho.**
**2869** A750 Pair, #a-b 6.50 6.50

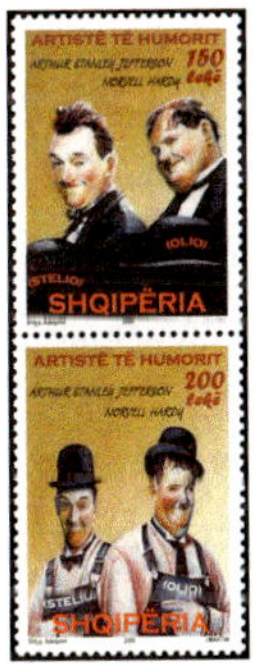

Stan Laurel (1890-1965) and Oliver Hardy (1892-1957), Comedians — A751

No. 2870 — Laurel and Hardy: a, 150 l, Holdings hats. b, 200 l, Wearing hats.
300 l, Laurel and Hardy wearing mortar-boards, horiz.

**2009, Oct. 16** **Litho.** *Perf. 13¼x13*
**2870** A751 Vert. pair, #a-b 10.00 10.00

**Souvenir Sheet**

*Perf. 13x13¼*

**2871** A751 300 l multi 8.00 8.00

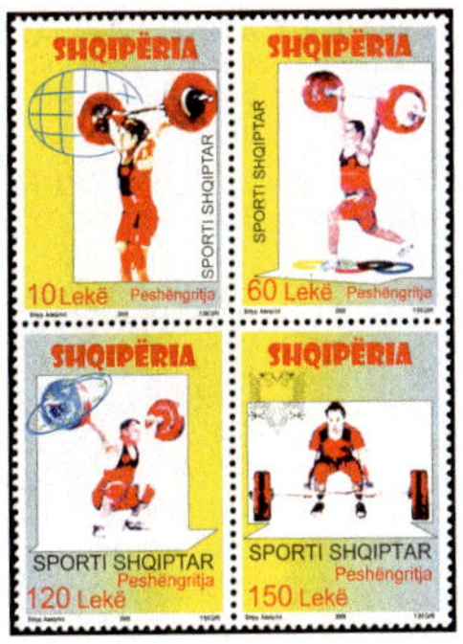

Weight Lifting A752

No. 2872 — Various weight lifters and: a, 10 l, Oval with latitudinal and longitudinal lines. b, 60 l, Olympic rings. c, 120 l, Circles and stars. d, 150 l, Double-headed eagle of Albanian arms.

**2009, Oct. 21** *Perf. 13¼x13*
**2872** A752 Block of 4, #a-d 9.00 9.00

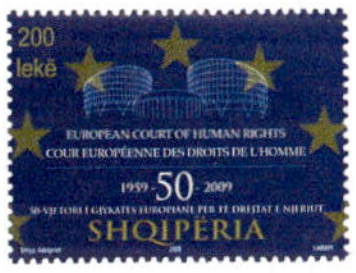

European Court of Human Rights, 50th Anniv. — A753

**2009, Oct. 30** *Perf. 13*
**2873** A753 200 l multi 5.50 5.50

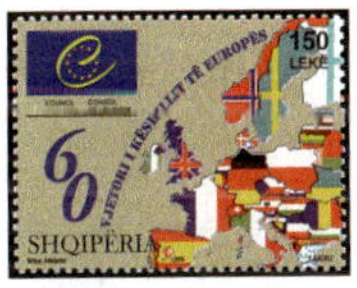

Council of Europe, 60th Anniv. — A754

**2009, Nov. 2**
**2874** A754 150 l multi 4.00 4.00

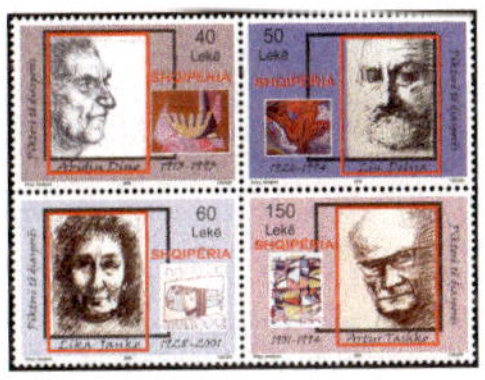
Albanian Painters A755

No. 2875: a, 40 l, Abidin Dino (1913-93). b, 50 l, Lin Delija (1926-94). c, 60 l, Lika Janko (1920-2001). d, 150 l, Artur Tashko (1901-94).

**2009, Nov. 11**
**2875** A755 Block of 4, #a-d 7.00 7.00

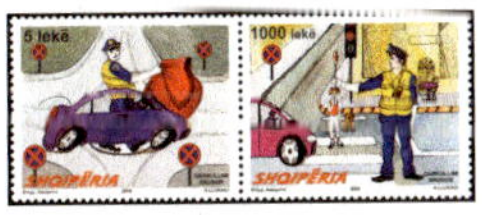
Traffic Safety A756

No. 2876 — Traffic officer: a, 5 l, Holding matador's red cape. 1000 l, Stopping traffic.

**2009, Nov. 16** *Perf. 13¼x13*
**2876** A756 Horiz. pair, #a-b *25.00 25.00*

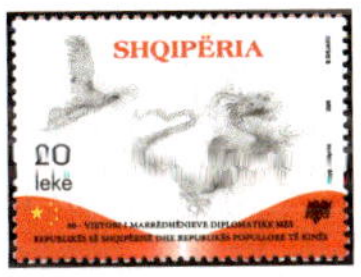

A757

**2009, Nov. 23** *Perf. 13*
**2877** A757 20 l multi .50 .50

Diplomatic relations between Albania and People's Republic of China, 60th anniv.

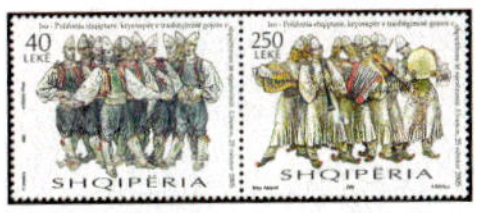

Albanian Iso-polyphonic Singers, UNESCO Intangible Cultural Heritage — A758

No. 2878: a, 40 l, Singers. b, 250 l, Musicians.

**2009, Nov. 25** *Perf. 13¼x13*
**2878** A758 Horiz. pair, #a-b 6.00 6.00

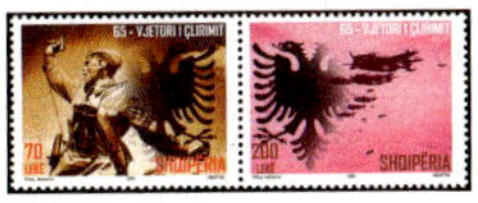

End of World War II, 65th Anniv. A759

No. 2879 — Double-headed eagle and: a, 70 l, Soldier. b, 200 l, Bombers.

**2009, Nov. 29** *Perf. 13x13¼*
**2879** A759 Horiz. pair, #a-b 6.00 6.00

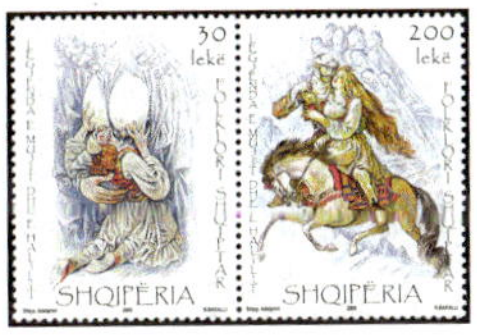

Legend of Mujit and Halitit A760

No. 2880: a, 30 l, Man being held against giant's breasts. b, 200 l, Man and woman on horse.

**2009, Dec. 5**
**2880** A760 Horiz. pair, #a-b 6.00 6.00

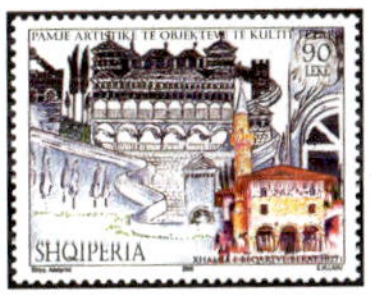

Religious Art and Buildings A761

No. 2881: a, Mosque, Berat. b, Church, Korçe. c, Church, Lezhe.

**2009, Dec. 9** *Perf. 13¼x13*
**2881** Horiz. strip of 3 7.00 7.00
*a.* A761 90 l multi 1.75 1.75
*b.* A761 100 l multi 2.00 2.00
*c.* A761 120 l multi 2.50 2.50

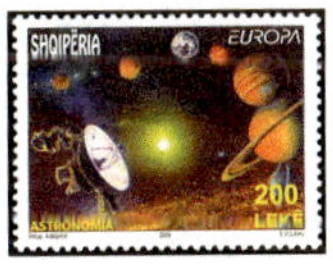

Europa — A762

Designs: 200 l, Planets, dish antenna. 250 l, Spacecraft and exploration vehicle on Mars. 350 l, Satellite above planet.

**2009, Dec. 11** *Perf. 13x13¼*
**2882** A762 200 l multi 4.00 4.00
**2883** A762 250 l multi 5.00 5.00

**Souvenir Sheet**

*Perf. 13¼x13*

**2884** A762 350 l multi 8.00 8.00
*a.* Booklet pane, #2882-2884 22.50 —
Complete booklet, #2884a 22.50

Intl. Year of Astronomy. No. 2884 contains one 30x25mm stamp.

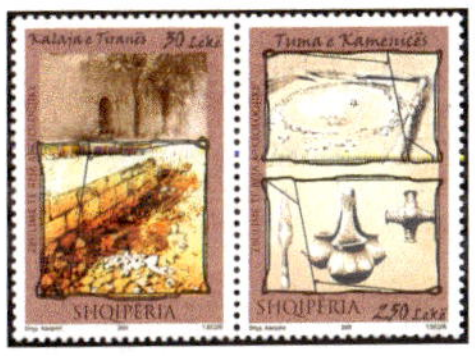

Archaeological Sites — A763

No. 2885: a, 30 l, Fort, Tirana. b, 250 l, Tomb, Kamenica.

**2009, Dec. 16** *Perf. 13*
**2885** A763 Horiz. pair, #a-b 6.00 6.00

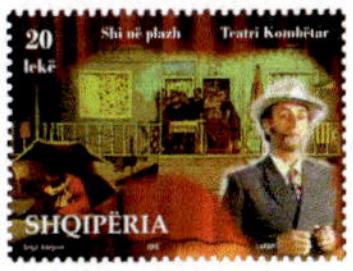

National Theater — A764

No. 2886 — Scenes from plays: a, Shi ne Plazh. b, Pallati 176. c, Apologjia e Vertete e Sokratit.

**2009, Dec. 21**
**2886** Horiz. strip of 3 7.00 7.00
*a.* A764 20 l multi .40 .40
*b.* A764 80 l multi 1.60 1.60
*c.* A764 200 l multi 4.00 4.00

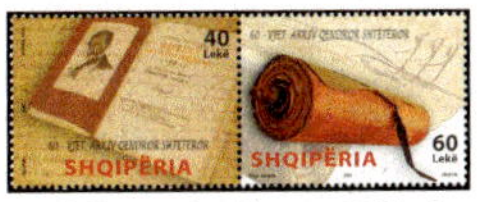

Central State Archives, 60th Anniv. A765

No. 2887: a, 40 l, Book, handwritten manuscript. b, 60 l, Scroll.

**2009, Dec. 28**
**2887** A765 Horiz. pair, #a-b 2.25 2.25

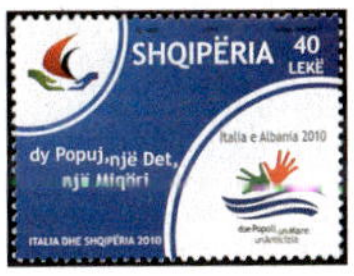

Albanian-Italian Friendship A766

**2010, Apr. 12** **Litho.** *Perf. 13*
**2888** A766 40 l multi 1.75 1.75

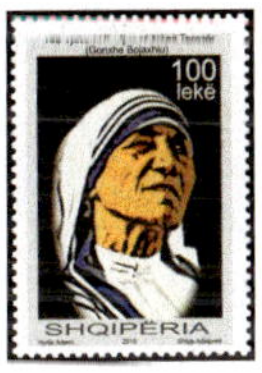

Mother Teresa (1910-97), Humanitarian — A767

**2010, Aug. 26**
**2889** A767 100 l multi 2.50 2.50

See Kosovo No. 154, Macedonia No. 529.

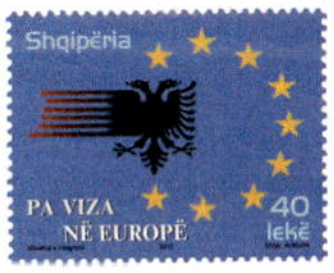

Visaless Entry Into Europe for Albanians A768

**2010, Nov. 8** *Perf. 13x13¼*
**2890** A768 40 l multi .80 .80

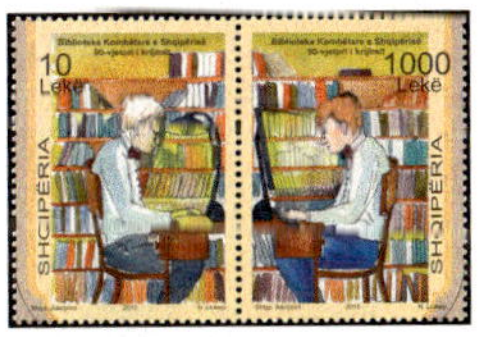

National Library, 50th Anniv. A769

No. 2891: a, 10 l, Man reading book. b, 1000 l, Man at computer.

**2011, Feb. 18**
**2891** A769 Horiz. pair, #a-b 20.00 20.00

Dated 2010.

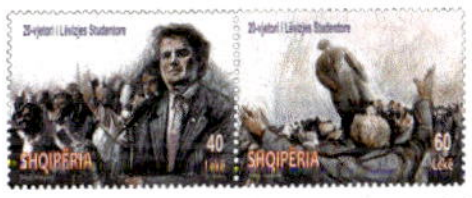

Student's Protest Movement, 20th Anniv. — A770

No. 2892: a, 40 l, Protestors, man at microphone. b, 60 l, Toppling of Enver Hoxha statue.
200 l, Students giving "V" for victory hand sign, vert.

# ALBANIA

**2011, Feb. 20** — Perf. 13
2892 A770 Horiz. pair, #a-b 2.50 2.50
**Souvenir Sheet**
2893 A770 200 l multi 4.00 4.00
Dated 2010.

Europa — A771

No. 2894 — Characters from children's stories: a, 100 l, Sun, donkey and rooster. b, 150 l, Bird and cat in balloons, girl. 250 l, Girl, stack of books, horiz.

**2011, Feb. 25** — Perf. 13¼x13
2894 A771 Vert. pair, #a-b 5.50 5.50
**Souvenir Sheet** Perf. 13x13¼
2895 A771 250 l multi 5.50 5.50
Dated 2010.

Underwater Archaeology — A772

No. 2896: a, 50 l, Close-up of underwater artifact. b, 250 l, Items on seabed.

**2011, Mar. 2** — Perf. 13¼x13
2896 A772 Horiz. pair, #a-b 6.00 6.00
Dated 2010.

2010 World Cup Soccer Championships, South Africa — A773

No. 2897 — Emblem, ball and players: a, 80 l. b, 120 l. 200 l, Two players.

**2011, Mar. 10** — Perf. 13¼x13
2897 A773 Horiz. pair, #a-b 4.00 4.00
**Souvenir Sheet**
2898 A773 200 l multi 4.00 4.00
Dated 2010.

Albanian Peacekeeping Force — A774

No. 2899: a, 50 l, Helicopter, soldiers. b, 200 l, Soldier, tank.

**2011, Mar. 21**
2899 A774 Horiz. pair, #a-b 5.25 5.25
Dated 2010.

Lushnja Congress, 90th Anniv. — A775

No. 2900: a, 70 l, Document and seal. b, 150 l, Building.

**2011, Mar. 23**
2900 A775 Horiz. pair, #a-b 4.50 4.50
Dated 2010.

National Cultural Heritage Day — A776

No. 2901: a, House, Gjirokaster. b, Apron, Dumre. c, Fortress, Tirana. d, Lute, Shkoder. 200 l, Woman, Zadrime.

**2011, Mar. 31** — Perf. 13¼x13
2901 Horiz. strip of 4 6.50 6.50
a. A776 10 l multi .25 .25
b. A776 70 l multi 1.40 1.40
c. A776 80 l multi 1.60 1.60
d. A776 120 l multi 2.50 2.50
**Souvenir Sheet**
2902 A776 200 l multi 4.25 4.25
Dated 2010.

Items Made of Silver A777

No. 2903: a, Pendant. b, Purse. c, Butterfly. d, Decorated case and cylinder with tip. 200 l, Open case and cylinder.

**2011, Apr. 6** — Perf. 13
2903 A777 Block of 4, #a-d 4.25 4.25
**Souvenir Sheet**
2904 A777 200 l multi 4.25 4.25
Dated 2010.

Durres-Kukes Road — A778

No. 2905 — Road design and: a, 40 l, Hills. b, 60 l, Construction equipment. c, 90 l, Tunnel. d, 150 l, Bridge.

**2011, Apr. 11** — Perf. 13x13¼
2905 A778 Block of 4, #a-d 7.00 7.00
Dated 2010.

**Miniature Sheet**

Historic Center of Berati UNESCO World Heritage Site — A779

No. 2906: a, 10 l, Building. b, 20 l, Buildings on hillside, street light. c, 30 l, Bridge. d, 50 l, Archway, fence on wall, buildings. e, 60 l, Buildings on hillside. 80 l, Church.

**2011, Apr. 11** — Perf. 13x13¼
2906 A779 Sheet of 6, #a-f 7.00 7.00

Europa — A780

Map of Europe with tree trunks and hills in: 200 l, Brown. 250 l, Green.

**2011, July 30** — Perf. 13¼x13
2907 A780 200 l multi 4.25 4.25
**Souvenir Sheet**
2908 A780 250 l multi 5.25 5.25
Intl. Year of Forests.

Boxing A781

No. 2909: a, 50 l, Boxers, boxer with red shirt at left. b, 100 l, Boxers, boxer with red shirt at right. 250 l, Boxer throwing punch.

**2011, Aug. 26**
2909 A781 Horiz. pair, #a-b 3.00 3.00
**Souvenir Sheet**
2910 A781 250 l multi 5.00 5.00

Multi-party Elections, 20h Anniv. — A782

**2011, Sept. 1** — Perf. 13x13¼
2911 A782 150 l multi 3.00 3.00

Ismail Kadare, Writer — A783

**2011, Sept. 12** — Perf. 13
2912 A783 40 l multi 1.00 1.00

Tourism A784

No. 2913: a, 80 l, Valbona River and mountains. b, 120 l, Rocks in Valbona River.

**2011, Sept. 27**
2913 A784 Horiz. pair, #a-b 4.00 4.00

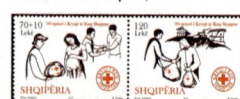

Albanian Red Cross, 90th Anniv. A785

No. 2914 — Emblem and: a, 70 l + 10 l, Aid to pregnant woman, first aid. b, 120 l, Woman receiving two bags.

**2011, Oct. 4**
2914 A785 Horiz. pair, #a-b 4.00 4.00

Carrier Pigeons A786

No. 2915 — Globe and: a, 10 l, Pigeon with mail bag. b, 1000 l, Pigeon without mail bag.

**2011, Oct. 9**
2915 A786 Horiz. pair, #a-b 22.50 22.50

Mosaics A787

No. 2916 — Mosaic from: a, 20 l, St. Michael's Basilica, Arapaj. b, 60 l, Church, Antigone. c, 120 l, Mesaplikut Basilica.

**2011, Oct. 14** — Litho.
2916 A787 Horiz. strip of 3, #a-c 4.00 4.00

Forum of States on Adriatic and Ionian Seas — A788

**2011, Nov. 18** — Perf. 13¼x13¼
2917 A788 90 l multi 1.75 1.75

Flowers A789

No. 2918: a, 30 l, Gymnospermium shqipetarum. b, 70 l, Viola kosaninii. c, 100 l, Aster albanicus subsp. paparisoi.

**2011, Dec. 5** — Perf. 13¼x13
2918 A789 Horiz. strip of 3, #a-c 4.00 4.00

Academy of Arts, 45th Anniv. — A790

**2011, Dec. 15** — Perf. 13
2919 A790 250 l multi 5.50 5.50

Nudes A791

No. 2920 — Nude: a, 10 l, Painting by Vangjush Mio. b, 90 l, Painting by Abdurrahim Buza. c, 100 l, Sculpture by Janaq Paço. 250 l, Nude sculpture by Paço, diff.

**2011, Dec. 22** — Perf. 13x13¼
2920 A791 Horiz. strip of 3, #a-c 4.00 4.00
**Souvenir Sheet**
2921 A791 250 l multi 5.50 5.50

Democracy in Albania, 20th Anniv. — A792

**2012, Mar. 22** — Perf. 13
2922 A792 100 l multi 1.90 1.90

# ALBANIA 401

Europa — A793

No. 2923 — Various tourist attractions: a, 30 l. b, 250 l.

**2012, Sept. 21**    *Perf. 13x13¼*
2923   A793   Horiz. pair, #a-b   5.25   5.25

2012 European Soccer Championships, Poland and Ukraine — A794

No. 2924 — Emblem, soccer ball, flags of European nations and large flag of: a, 100 l, Poland. b, 200 l, Ukraine.

**2012, Sept. 28**    *Perf. 13*
2924   A794   Horiz. pair, #a-b   6.00   6.00

Kin Dushi (1922-94), Writer — A795

**2012, Oct. 3**    *Perf. 13x13¼*
2925   A795   150 l multi   2.75   2.75

Albanian Membership in Universal Postal Union, 90th Anniv. — A796

**2012, Oct. 9**    *Perf. 13¼x12¾*
2926   A796   250 l multi   4.75   4.75

Revolts Against Ottoman Rule, Cent. — A797

No. 2927: a, 10 l, Rebel leader, row of rebels. b, 1000 l, Rebels.

**2012, Oct. 19**    *Perf. 13*
2927   A797   Horiz. pair, #a-b   18.50   10.50

**Souvenir Sheet**

Rock Art — A798

No. 2928 — Rock art at: a, 20 l, Rubik. b, 60 l, Boville. c, 150 l, Lepenice.

**2012, Oct. 29**    *Perf. 13¼x13*
2928   A798   Sheet of 3, #a-c   4.25   4.25

Linguists Who Have Studied Albanian Language — A799

No. 2929: a, Eric Hamp. b, Norbert Jokl (1877-1942). c, Holger Pedersen (1867-1953).

**2012, Nov. 16**    *Perf. 13*
2929   Horiz. strip of 3   3.50   3.50
   a. A799 50 l multi   .95   .95
   b. A799 60 l multi   1.10   1.10
   c. A799 70 l multi   1.40   1.40

See No. 2947.

Dancers — A800

No. 2930 — Dancers from: a, Tropoje. b, Tirana. c, Cameri. d, Lushnje.

**2012, Nov. 23**    *Perf. 13x13¼*
2930   Horiz. strip of 4   6.25   6.25
   a. A800 20 l multi   .40   .40
   b. A800 40 l multi   .75   .75
   c. A800 120 l multi   2.25   2.25
   d. A800 150 l multi   2.75   2.75

Independence, Cent. — A801

**2012, Nov. 23**    *Perf. 13¼x13*
2931   A001   40 l black & red   .75   .75

Declaration of Independence, Cent. — A802

No. 2932: a, People, Albanian flag. b, People, Albanian flag, diff. c, Flags, United Nations Headquarters. d, Flags, NATO emblem.

**2012, Nov. 28**    *Perf. 13x13¼*
2932   Horiz. strip of 4   5.50   5.50
   a. A802 50 l multi   .95   .95
   b. A802 60 l multi   1.10   1.10
   c. A802 70 l multi   1.40   1.40
   d. A802 100 l multi   1.90   1.90
   e. Booklet pane of 4, #2932a-2932d   5.50   —
   Complete booklet, #2932e   5.50

Albanian Army, Cent. — A803

No. 2933: a, 90 l, Soldiers in traditional costumes. b, 150 l, Soldiers wearing helmets.

**2012, Dec. 4**    *Litho.*
2933   A803   Horiz. pair, #a-b   4.50   4.50

Albanian Post, Telegraph and Telephone Administration, Cent. — A804

No. 2934 — Telephone, poles, wires, and: a, 80 l, Envelopes, mailbox. b, 200 l, Letter in open envelope.

**2012, Dec. 5**    *Perf. 13*
2934   A804   Horiz. pair, #a-b   5.25   5.25
   c. Booklet pane of 2, #2934a-2934b, + 2 labels   5.25
   Complete booklet, #2934c   5.25

Marine Life and Plants — A805

No. 2935: a, 10 l, Fish, sea grasses, diver. b, 250 l, Fish, sea grasses, coral.

**2012, Dec. 14**    *Perf. 13x12¾*
2935   A805   Horiz. pair, #a-b   5.00   5.00
   c. Booklet pane of 2, #2935a-2935b   5.00   —
   Complete booklet, #2935c   5.00

First Handstamped Envelope of Albania, Cent. — A806

No. 2936: a, 120 l, Front of addressed handstamped envelope. b, 150 l, Back of envelope, handstamp.

**2013, May 5**    *Perf. 13*
2936   A806   Horiz. pair, #a-b   5.25   5.25
   c. Booklet pane of 2, #2936a-2936b   5.25   —
   Complete booklet, #2936c   5.25

World Track and Field Championships, Moscow — A807

No. 2937: a, 30 l, Runner. b, 200 l, High jumper. 250 l, Pole vaulter.

**2013, Aug. 27**    *Litho.*   *Perf. 13*
2937   A807   Horiz. pair, #a-b   4.50   4.50

**Souvenir Sheet**

2938   A807   250 l multi   4.75   4.75

Vedat Kokona (1913-98), Lexicographer — A808

**2013, Aug. 30**    *Litho.*   *Perf. 13*
2939   A808   150 l multi   3.00   3.00

Europa — A809

No. 2940 — Globe, parcels, envelopes and: a, 80 l, Postal van and truck. b, 200 l, Airplane, train and ship.

**2013, Oct. 4**    *Litho.*   *Perf. 13¼x13*
2940   A809   Horiz. pair, #a-b   5.50   5.50
   c. Booklet pane of 2, #2940a-2940b   5.50   —
   Complete booklet, #2940c   5.50

Albanian Police, Cent. — A810

No. 2941 — Flag and: a, 10 l, Policewoman. b, 250 l, Policeman.

**2013, Oct. 18**    *Litho.*   *Perf. 13¼x13*
2941   A810   Horiz. pair, #a-b   5.00   5.00

Flowers — A811

No. 2942: a, Scilla albanica. b, Gymnospermium maloi. c, Tulipa albanica.

**2013, Oct. 30**    *Litho.*   *Perf. 13x13¼*
2942   Horiz. strip of 3   5.00   5.00
   a. A811 20 l multi   .40   .40
   b. A811 90 l multi   1.75   1.75
   c. A811 175 l multi   2.75   2.75

17th Mediterranean Games, Mersin, Turkey — A812

No. 2943: a, 40 l, Diving, swimming, synchronized swimming. b, 150 l, Volleyball, weight lifting, cycling. 200 l, Rowing, horiz.

**2013, Nov. 6**    *Litho.*   *Perf. 13¼x13*
2943   A812   Horiz. pair, #a-b   4.75   4.75

**Souvenir Sheet**    *Perf. 13x13¼*
2944   A812   200 l multi   4.00   4.00

International Red Cross, 150th Anniv. — A813

No. 2945 — Red cross and: a, 40 l, Aid workers helping injured man, feeding woman. b, 150 l, Worker giving bags of goods to man. 250 l, Aid workers assisting injured man.

**2013, Nov. 15**    *Litho.*   *Perf. 13*
2945   A813   Horiz. pair, #a-b   3.75   3.75

**Souvenir Sheet**

2946   A813   250 l multi   5.00   5.00

**Linguists Type of 2012**

No. 2947 — Historians: a, Milan Sufflay (1879-1931). b, Konstantin Jiracek (1854-1918). c, Ludwig von Thallóczy (1854-1916).

**2013, Nov. 25**    *Litho.*   *Perf. 13*
2947   Horiz. strip of 3   5.25   5.25
   a. A799 10 l multi   .25   .25
   b. A799 100 l multi   2.00   2.00
   c. A799 150 l multi   3.00   3.00

Recent Archaeological Finds — A814

No. 2948: a, Bronze foot, 2nd-3rd cent. b, Bronze fibula with horse design, 7th-8th cent. c, Marble statue of an aristocrat, 2nd cent. d, Relief of Heraclius and Apollo, 2nd cent.

**2013, Dec. 3**    *Litho.*   *Perf. 13*
2948   Horiz. strip of 4   6.50   6.50
   a. A814 20 l multi   .35   .35
   b. A814 90 l multi   1.75   1.75
   c. A814 100 l multi   2.00   2.00
   d. A814 120 l multi   2.40   2.40

Nikolla Naço (1843-1913), Newspaper Editor — A815

**2013, Dec. 18**    *Litho.*   *Perf. 13¼x13*
2949   A815   200 l multi   4.00   4.00

# ALBANIA

2014 World Cup Soccer Championships, Brazil — A816

No. 2950: a, Mascot. b, Mascot holding soccer ball. c, Mascot dribbling soccer ball. 140 l, Emblem, vert.

| 2014, July 9 | Litho. | Perf. 13 |
|---|---|---|
| 2950 | Horiz. strip of 3 | 3.25 3.25 |
| a. | A816 10 l multi | .25 .25 |
| b. | A816 50 l multi | 1.00 1.00 |
| c. | A816 100 l multi | 2.00 2.00 |

**Souvenir Sheet**

| 2951 | A816 140 l multi | 2.75 2.75 |

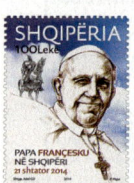

Visit to Albania of Pope Francis — A817

| 2014, Sept. 21 | Litho. | Perf. 13 |
|---|---|---|
| 2952 | A817 100 l multi | 1.90 1.90 |

Europa A818

No. 2953: a, 100 l, Gajdja (bagpipes). b, 150 l, Lodra (drum).

| 2014, Oct. 9 | Litho. | Perf. 13¼x13 |
|---|---|---|
| 2953 | A818 Horiz. pair, #a-b | 4.50 4.50 |
| c. | Souvenir sheet of 2, #2953a-2953b + central label | 4.50 4.50 |
|  | Complete booklet, #2953c | 4.50 |

Kuçi Assembly, 400th Anniv. — A819

No. 2954: a, 80 l, Participants examining document. b, 150 l, Participants. 200 l, Participants, diff.

| 2014, Oct. 14 | Litho. | Perf. 13x13¼ |
|---|---|---|
| 2954 | A819 Horiz. pair, #a-b | 4.25 4.25 |

**Souvenir Sheet**

| 2955 | A819 200 l multi | 3.75 3.75 |

Relations Between Albania and Kuwait A820

No. 2956: a, 100 l, Shiekh Sabah, emir of Kuwait. b, Handshake, flags of Albania and Kuwait.

| 2014, Nov. 11 | Litho. | Perf. 13¼x13 |
|---|---|---|
| 2956 | A820 100 l Sheet of 2, #a-b | 3.50 3.50 |

Sulejman Pashe Delvina (1884-1933), Prime Minister — A821

| 2014, Nov. 18 | Litho. | Perf. 13¼x13 |
|---|---|---|
| 2957 | A821 150 l multi | 2.75 2.75 |

Reptiles and Amphibians — A822

No. 2958: a, 80 l, Caretta caretta. b, 170 l, Hyla arborea.

| 2014, Nov. 22 | Litho. | Perf. 13 |
|---|---|---|
| 2958 | A822 Horiz. pair, #a-b | 4.50 4.50 |

**Miniature Sheet**

Coronation of Prince William of Wied, Cent. — A823

No. 2959: a, 60 l, Princess Sophie (1885-1936), wife of Prince William. b, 70 l, Crown, arms of Albania. c, 80 l, Star with eagle in circle. d, 90 l, Prince William of Wied (1876-1945).

| 2014, Nov. 26 | Litho. | Perf. 13¼x13 |
|---|---|---|
| 2959 | A823 Sheet of 4, #a-d | 5.50 5.50 |

World War II Liberation of Albania, 70th Anniv. — A824

| 2014, Nov. 29 | Litho. | Perf. 13 |
|---|---|---|
| 2960 | A824 40 l multi | .70 .70 |

Archaeological Items From Dyrrachium (Dürres) — A825

No. 2961 — Depictions of Artemis: a, 50 l, Statue, 4th cent. B.C. b, 60 l, Bust, 4th cent. B.C. c, 70 l, Marble bust, 4th cent. B.C. d, 90 l, Bronze statue, 3rd cent. B.C.

| 2014, Dec. 5 | | Perf. 13 |
|---|---|---|
| 2961 | Horiz. strip of 4 | 4.75 4.75 |
| a. | A825 50 l multi | .90 .90 |
| b. | A825 60 l multi | 1.00 1.00 |
| c. | A825 70 l multi | 1.25 1.25 |
| d. | A825 90 l multi | 1.60 1.60 |

Albanian Candidacy for European Union Membership A826

| 2014, Dec. 8 | Litho. | Perf. 13x13¼ |
|---|---|---|
| 2962 | A826 40 l multi | .70 .70 |

William Shakespeare (1564-1616), Writer — A827

| 2014, Dec. 12 | Litho. | Perf. 13 |
|---|---|---|
| 2963 | A827 150 l multi | 2.60 2.60 |

Wooden Handicrafts — A828

No. 2964: a, 40 l, Chair, Mirdite. b, 50 l, Cradle, Rreshen. c, 60 l, Shepherd's crook, Laberi. d, 70 l, Spoons, Tirana. 180 l, Ceiling decorations, Leuse.

| 2014, Dec. 19 | Litho. | Perf. 13 |
|---|---|---|
| 2964 | A828 Block of 4, #a-d | 4.00 4.00 |

**Souvenir Sheet**

| 2965 | A828 180 l multi | 3.25 3.25 |

Icons in Museums — A829

No. 2966 — Icon from: a, 10 l, Himare. b, 30 l, Dhermi. c, 40 l, Dhermi, diff. d, 70 l, Vuno. e, 90 l, Deme. f, 100 l, Vuno, diff.

| 2014, Dec. 24 | Litho. | Perf. 13¼x13 |
|---|---|---|
| 2966 | A829 Sheet of 6, #a-f | 6.00 6.00 |
| g. | Booklet pane of 6, #2966a-2966f | 6.00 |
|  | Complete booklet, #2966g | 6.00 |

No. 2966g has a decorative, curved pane margin.

Elez Isufi (1861-1924), Guerrilla Leader — A830

| 2014, Dec. 29 | Litho. | Perf. 13¼x13 |
|---|---|---|
| 2967 | A830 1000 l multi | 17.50 17.50 |

Europa — A831

| 2015, Sept. 2 | Litho. | Perf. 13¼x13 |
|---|---|---|
| 2968 | A831 130 l multi | 2.10 2.10 |

**Souvenir Sheet**

| 2969 | A831 250 l multi | 4.00 4.00 |
| a. | Booklet pane of 2, #2968-2969 | 6.25 — |
|  | Complete booklet, #2969a | 6.25 |

National Parks — A832

No. 2970: a, Shebenik-Jabllanice National Park. b, Bredhi i Hotoves National Park. c, Dajti National Park.

| 2015, Sept. 16 | Litho. | Perf. 13¼x13 |
|---|---|---|
| 2970 | Horiz. strip of 3 | 5.00 5.00 |
| a. | A832 50 l multi | .80 .80 |
| b. | A832 100 l multi | 1.60 1.60 |
| c. | A832 150 l multi | 2.50 2.50 |

Early Locomotives and Their Inventors — A833

No. 2971: a, 50 l, New Castle, Richard Trevithick (1771-1833). b, 60 l, Salamanca, Matthew Murray (1765-1826). c, 90 l, Rocket, Robert Stephenson (1803-59). d, 100 l, Locomotion, George Stephenson (1781-1848).

| | Perf. 13¼x12¾ | |
|---|---|---|
| 2015, Sept. 27 | | Litho. |
| 2971 | A833 Block of 4, #a-d | 5.00 5.00 |

Locomotives, 190th anniv.

Famous Men A834

No. 2972: a, 40 l, Dhimiter Shuteriqi (1915-2003), writer. b, 50 l, Zef Skiroi (1865-1927), poet. c, 60 l, Mahir Domi (1915-2000), linguist. d, 100 l, Gaqo Avrazi (1915-85), composer.

| 2015, Sept. 28 | Litho. | Perf. 13¼x13 |
|---|---|---|
| 2972 | A834 Block of 4, #a-d | 4.00 4.00 |

Albanian Soccer Federation, 85th Anniv. — A835

No. 2973 — Federation emblem and: a, 5 l, Soccer ball, goaltender and net. b, 10 l, Grass. c, 1000 l, Soccer ball and player making scissor kick.

| 2015, Oct. 8 | Litho. | Perf. 13¼x13 |
|---|---|---|
| 2973 | A835 Horiz. strip of 3, #a-c | 16.00 16.00 |

Famous Men — A836

No. 2974: a, Nicéphore Niépce (1765-1833), inventor of photography, b, Carl Patsch (1865-1945), historian. c, Boris Pasternak (1890-1960), 1958 Nobel laureate in Literature. d, Norman Wisdom (1915-2010), comedian and actor.

| 2015, Oct. 9 | Litho. | Perf. 13 |
|---|---|---|
| 2974 | Horiz. strip of 4 | 4.25 4.25 |
| a. | A836 10 l multi | .25 .25 |
| b. | A836 60 l multi | .95 .95 |
| c. | A836 80 l multi | 1.25 1.25 |
| d. | A836 100 l multi | 1.60 1.60 |

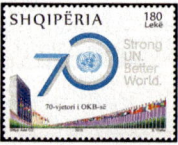

United Nations, 70th Anniv. — A837

| 2015, Oct. 24 | Litho. | Perf. 13¼x13 |
|---|---|---|
| 2975 | A837 180 l multi | 3.00 3.00 |

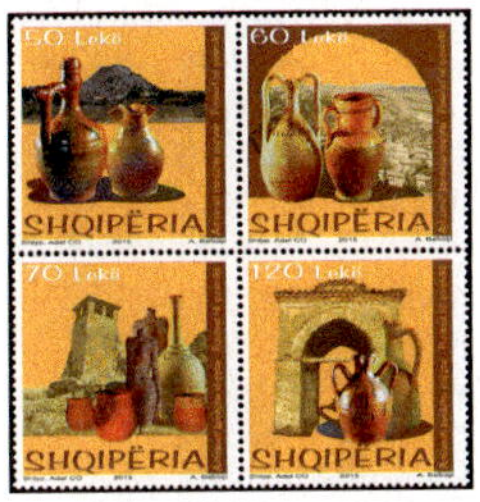

Ceramic Vessels A838

No. 2976 — Various vessels: a, 50 l. b, 60 l. c, 70 l. d, 120 l
200 l, Various ceramic vessels, diff.

**2015, Nov. 6 Litho. *Perf. 13***
**2976** A838 Block of 4, #a-d 4.75 4.75

**Souvenir Sheet**

**2977** A838 200 l multi 3.25 3.25

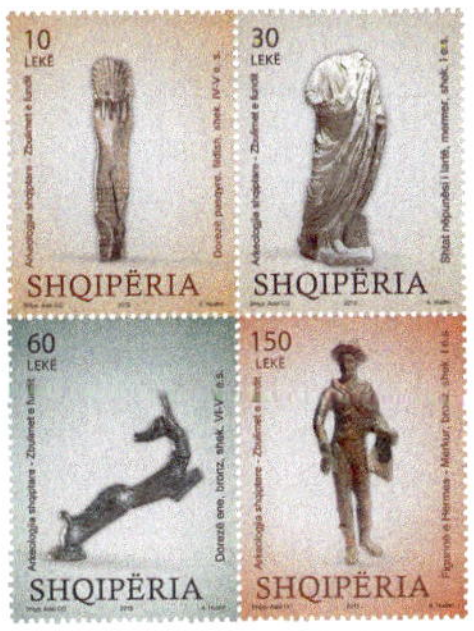

Recent Archaeological Discoveries — A839

No. 2978: a, 10 l, Ivory mirror handle, 4th-5th cent. B.C. b, 30 l, Marble statue of officer, 1st cent. B.C. c, 60 l, Bronze utensil handle, 6th-7th cent. B.C. d, 150 l, Bronze statue of Hermes, 1st cent. B.C.

**2015, Nov. 16 Litho. *Perf. 13***
**2978** A839 Block of 4, #a-d 4.00 4.00

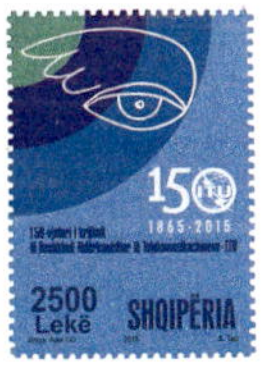

International Telecommunication Union, 150th Anniv. — A840

**2015, Dec. 5 Litho. *Perf. 13***
**2979** A840 2500 l multi 40.00 40.00

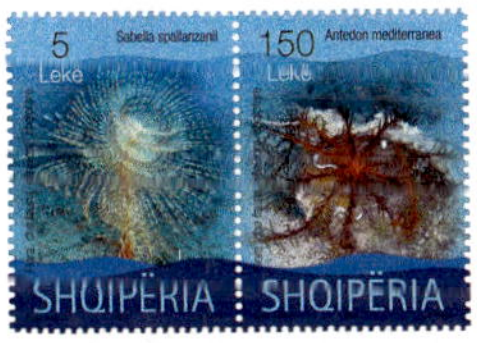

Marine Life A841

No. 2980: a, 5 l, Sabella spallanzanii. b, 150 l, Antedon mediterranea.
250 l, Cotylorhiza tuberculata.

**2015, Dec. 23 Litho. *Perf. 13¼x13***
**2980** A841 Horiz. pair, #a-b 2.50 2.50

**Souvenir Sheet**

**2981** A841 250 l multi 4.00 4.00

2016 European Soccer Championships, France — A842

No. 2982 — Emblem and player with denomination at: a, 70 l, UL. b, 100 l, UR.

**2016, June 10 Litho. *Perf. 13x13¼***
**2982** A842 Horiz. pair, #a-b 2.75 2.75

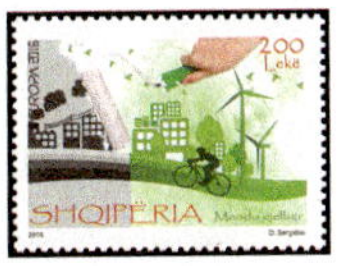

Europa — A843

**2016, July 9 Litho. *Perf. 13x13¼***
**2983** A843 200 l multi 3.25 3.25

Think Green Issue.

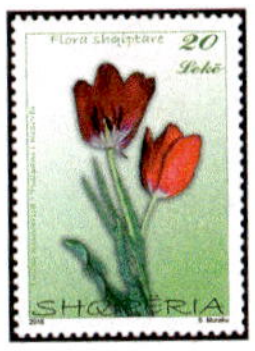

Flowers — A844

No. 2984: a, Tulipa kosovarica. b, Campanula comosiformis. c, Solenanthus albanicus.

**2016, July 27 Litho. *Perf. 13¼x13***
**2984** Horiz. strip of 3 4.00 4.00
*a.* A844 20 l multi .35 .35
*b.* A844 30 l multi .50 .50
*c.* A844 190 l multi 3.00 3.00

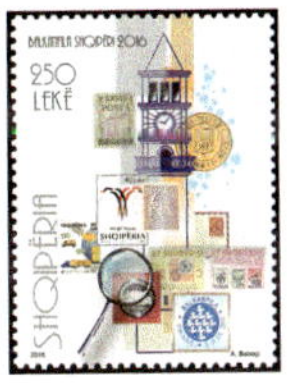

Balkanfila 2016 Intl. Stamp Exhibition, Tirana — A845

**2016, Aug. 9 Litho. *Perf. 13x13¼***
**2985** A845 250 l multi 4.25 4.25

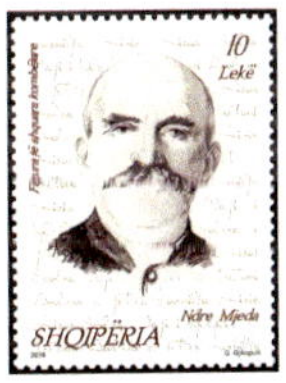

Famous Men — A846

No. 2986: a, Ndre Mjeda (1866-1937), poet. b, Kole Jakova (1916-2002), writer. c, Jusuf Vrioni (1916-2001), diplomat and translator.

**2016, Aug. 17 Litho. *Perf. 13x13¼***
**2986** Horiz. strip of 3 3.50 3.50
*a.* A846 10 l multi .25 .25
*b.* A846 50 l multi .80 .80
*c.* A846 150 l multi 2.40 2.40

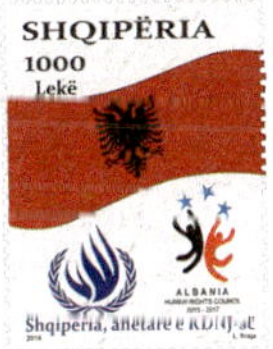

Albania, 2015-17 Member of United Nations Human Rights Council — A847

**2016, Aug. 29 Litho. *Perf. 13x13¼***
**2987** A847 1000 l multi 16.50 16.50

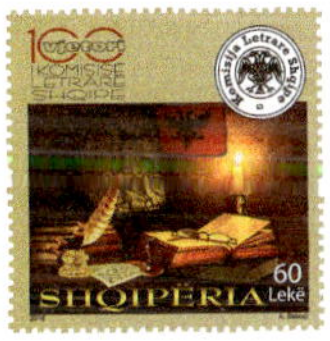

Albanian Literary Commission, Cent. — A848

**2016, Sept. 1 Litho. *Perf. 13***
**2988** A848 60 l multi 1.00 1.00

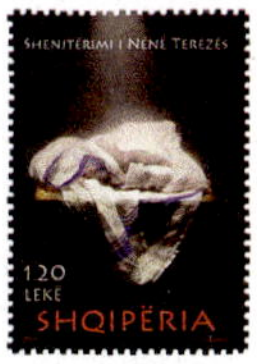

Canonization of St. Teresa of Calcutta (Mother Teresa) — A849

**2016, Sept. 4 Litho. *Perf. 13x13¼***
**2989** A849 120 l multi 2.00 2.00
*a.* Booklet pane of 1 2.00 —
Complete booklet, #2989a 2.00

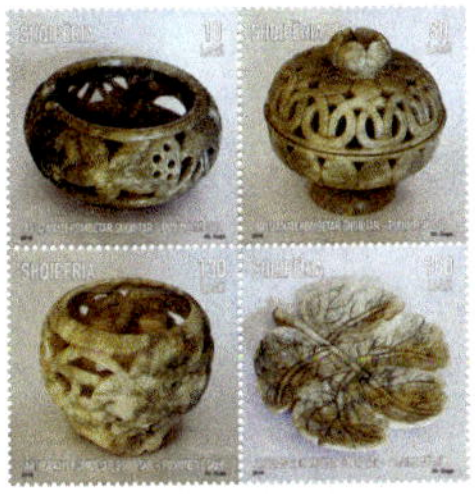

Carved Stone Containers — A850

No. 2990 — Various containers: a, 10 l. b, 80 l. c, 130 l. d, 180 l.
250 l, Bowl with lid.

**2016, Sept. 27 Litho. *Perf. 13***
**2990** A850 Block of 4, #a-d 6.50 6.50

**Souvenir Sheet**

**2991** A850 250 l multi 4.25 4.25

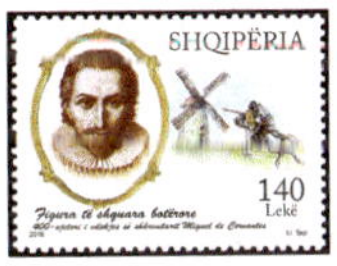

Miguel de Cervantes (1547-1616), Writer — A851

Designs: 140 l, Cervantes, Don Quixote on horse, windmill.
200 l, Don Quixoto and Sancho Panza, vert.

**2016, Oct. 9 Litho. *Perf. 13x13¼***
**2992** A851 140 l multi 2.25 2.25

**Souvenir Sheet**

**2993** A851 200 l multi 3.25 3.25

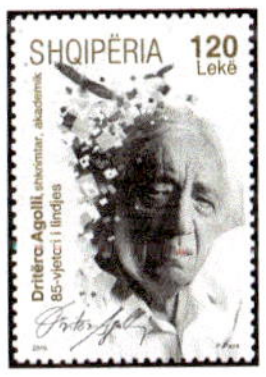

Dritero Agolli (1931-2017), Writer — A852

**2016, Oct. 13 Litho. *Perf. 13***
**2994** A852 120 l multi 2.00 2.00

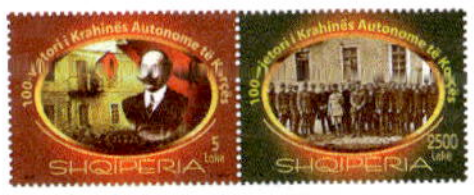

Autonomous Republic of Korçe, Cent. — A853

No. 2995: a, 5 l, Themistokli Germenji (1871-1917), prefect, flag and building. b, 2500 l, Soldiers and civilians.

**2016, Dec. 10 Litho. *Perf. 13***
**2995** A853 Horiz. pair, #a-b 39.00 39.00

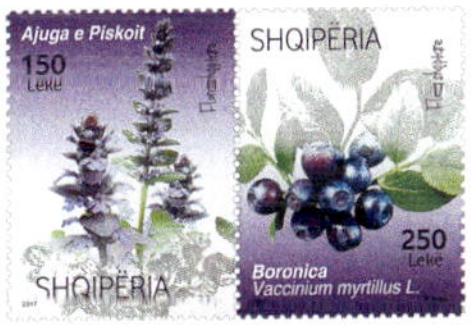

Flora A854

No. 2996: a, 150 l, Ajuga reptans. b, 250 l, Vaccinium myrtillus.

**2017, Nov. 1 Litho. *Perf. 13¼x13***
**2996** A854 Horiz. pair, #a-b 7.00 7.00

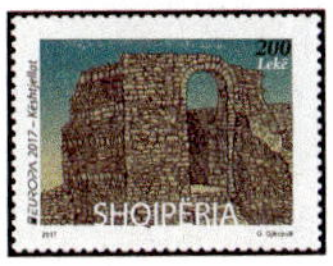

Berat Castle Ruins — A855

**2017, Nov. 18 Litho. *Perf. 13x13¼***
**2997** A855 200 l multi 3.75 3.75

**Souvenir Sheet**

**2998** A855 250 l multi 4.50 4.50

Europa.

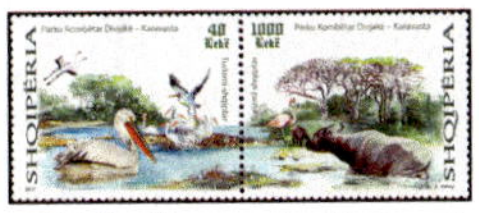

Divjake-Karavasta National Park — A856

No. 2999: a, 40 l, Various birds. b, 1000 l, Flamingo and water buffalos.

**2017, Nov. 24 Litho. *Perf. 13¼x13***
**2999** A856 Horiz. pair, #a-b 18.50 18.50

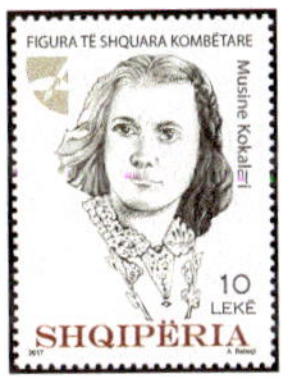

Famous Albanians — A857

No. 3000: a, Musine Kokalari (1917-83), writer. b, Zef Kolombi (1907-49), painter. c, Prenke Jakova (1917-69), composer. d, Dom Nikolle Kaçorri (1862-1917), politician.

**2017, Dec. 5 Litho. *Perf. 13x13¼***
**3000** Horiz. strip of 4 4.00 4.00
*a.* A857 10 l multi .25 .25
*b.* A857 40 l multi .75 .75
*c.* A857 70 l multi 1.25 1.25
*d.* A857 90 l multi 1.75 1.75

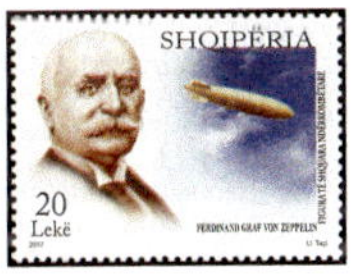

Famous Men — A858

No. 3001: a, Ferdinand von Zeppelin (1838-1917), manufacturer of Zeppelin airships. b, Edgar Degas (1834-1917), painter. c, Stefan Zweig (1881-1942), writer.

**2017, Dec. 12 Litho. *Perf. 13***
**3001** Horiz. strip of 3 4.75 4.75
*a.* A858 20 l multi .40 .40
*b.* A858 90 l multi 1.75 1.75
*c.* A858 140 l multi 2.60 2.60

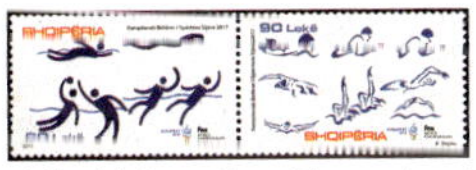

2017 World Aquatics Championships, Budapest, Hungary — A859

No. 3002: a, 60 l, Swimming, water polo, synchronized swimming. b, 90 l, Synchronized swimming and various swimming strokes.

**2017, Dec. 15 Litho. *Perf. 13¼x13***
**3002** A859 Horiz. pair, #a-b 2.75 2.75

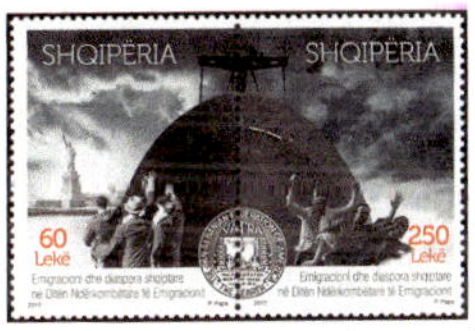

International Immigration Day — A860

No. 3003 — Emigrants, ship, emblem of Pan-Albanian Federation of America and: a, 60 l, Statue of Liberty. b, 250 l, Map of Europe.

**2017, Dec. 18 Litho. *Perf. 13x13¼***
**3003** A860 Horiz. pair, #a-b 5.75 5.75

# ALBANIA

Lynx — A861

Lynx facing: 120 l, Right. 1.90 l, Left.

| 2017, Dec. 21 | Litho. | Perf. 13x13¼ |
|---|---|---|
| 3004 A861 | 120 l multi | 2.25 2.25 |

**Souvenir Sheet**

| 3005 A861 | 190 l multi | 3.50 3.50 |

Glassware — A862

No. 3006: a, 5 l, Three bottles with caps. b, 40 l, Vase and three small glasses. c, 90 l Pitcher with lid and two bowls. d, 130 l, Two pitchers.
200 l, Five glasses and two vases.

| 2017, Dec. 23 | Litho. | Perf. 13 |
|---|---|---|
| 3006 A862 | Block of 4, #a-d | 4.75 4.75 |

**Souvenir Sheet**

| 3007 A862 | 200 l multi | 3.75 3.75 |

Albanian Art — A863

Inscriptions: 30 l, Portreti i Skenderbeut (Portrait of Skanderbeg). 40 l, Skice, studim (Study sketch), horiz. 50 l, Kaloresi (Cavalry), horiz. 80 l, Leningradi ne shi (Leningrad in the Rain), horiz. 90 l, Skice, studim (Study sketch of girl). 100 l, Ne gjume (Asleep). 180 l, Rrobaqepesja (Seamstress). 190 l, Varrimi i shokut (Burial of a Friend).

| 2017, Dec. 27 | Litho. | Perf. 13 |
|---|---|---|
| 3008-3015 A863 | Set of 8 | 14.00 14.00 |

European Day of Personal Data Protection — A864

| 2017, Dec. 28 | Litho. | Perf. 13x13¼ |
|---|---|---|
| 3016 A864 | 2500 l multi | 45.00 45.00 |

Year of Skanderbeg A865

| 2018, May 5 | Litho. | Perf. 13 |
|---|---|---|
| 3017 A865 | 250 l multi | 4.75 4.75 |

Skanderbeg (1405-68), Albanian national hero.

Europa — A866

Designs: 200 l, Gorica Bridge, Berat. 250 l, Mesi Bridge, Shkoder.

| 2018, Oct. 25 | Litho. | Perf. 13x13¼ |
|---|---|---|
| 3018 A866 | 200 l multi | 3.75 3.75 |

**Souvenir Sheet**

| 3019 A866 | 250 l multi | 4.50 4.50 |
| a. | Booklet pane of 2, #3018-3019 | 8.25 |
| | Complete booklet, #3019a | 8.25 |

**Souvenir Sheet**

Skanderbeg (1405-68), Albanian National Hero — A867

No. 3020: a, 150 l, 16th cent. engraving of Skanderbeg by Dominicus Custos. b, 250 l, Skanderbeg with sword.

| 2018, Nov. 6 | Litho. | Perf. 13x13¼ |
|---|---|---|
| 3020 A867 | Sheet of 2, #a-b | 7.50 7.50 |

Famous Men A868

No. 3021: a, 90 l, Claude Debussy (1862-1918), composer. b, 180 l, Gustav Klimt (1862-1918), painter.

| 2018, Nov. 16 | Litho. | Perf. 13 |
|---|---|---|
| 3021 A868 | Horiz. pair, #a-b | 5.00 5.00 |

Flowers A869

No. 3022: a, 40 l, Abelmoschus esculentus. b, 1000 l, Hypericum perforatum.

| 2018, Dec. 7 | Litho. | Perf. 13¼x13 |
|---|---|---|
| 3022 A869 | Horiz. pair, #a-b | 19.50 19.50 |

Fish A870

No. 3023: a, 5 l, Acipenser sturio. b, 190 l, Salmo trutta.

| 2018, Dec. 14 | Litho. | Perf. 13¼x13 |
|---|---|---|
| 3023 A870 | Horiz. pair, #a-b | 3.75 3.75 |

Historical Anniversaries A871

No. 3024: a, Publication of Dottrina Christiana, 400th anniv. b, Fourteen Points of Pres. Woodrow Wilson, cent. c, Committee for the National Defense of Kosovo, cent.

| 2018, Dec. 14 | Litho. | Perf. 13¼x13 |
|---|---|---|
| 3024 | Horiz. strip of 3 | 5.75 5.75 |
| a. | A871 50 l multi | .90 .90 |
| b. | A871 120 l multi | 2.25 2.25 |
| c. | A871 140 l multi | 2.60 2.60 |

Tourism A872

No. 3025: a, 40 l, Hills and waterfall near Permet. b, 2500 l, Katiu Bridge near Permet.

| 2018, Dec. 22 | Litho. | Perf. 13 |
|---|---|---|
| 3025 A872 | Horiz. pair, #a-b | 47.50 47.50 |

Embrodery Patterns — A873

No. 3026 — Various embroidery patterns: a, 40 l. b, 80 l. c, 90 l. d, 130 l.
200 l, Embroidery pattern, diff.

| 2018, Dec. 27 | Litho. | Perf. 13 |
|---|---|---|
| 3026 A873 | Block of 4, #a-d | 6.25 6.25 |

**Souvenir Sheet**

| 3027 A873 | 200 l multi | 3.75 3.75 |

Albanian Art — A874

Designs: 10 l, Erdhi Liria (Freedom came). 20 l, Fshatarja (Rustic scene of farmwoman drinking) (43x31mm). 30 l, Portret Punetoreje (Work portrait) (31x43mm). 40 l, Toke e Begate (Prosperous Land). 60 l, Vagonisti (Miner pushing rail car) (31x43mm). 70 l, Te Korrurat (Harvested), horiz. 90 l, Vjitja (Woman and plants) (31x43mm). 100 l, Mik-pritja (Woman holding dish) (40x40mm).

| 2018, Dec. 29 | Litho. | Perf. 13 |
|---|---|---|
| 3028-3035 A874 | Set of 8 | 7.75 7.75 |

Albanian Parliamentarism, Cent. — A875

Designs: 200 l, Republic of Albania Assembly Building.
No. 3037: a, Congress of Lushnja Building, 1920. b, National Council Building, 1920-25. c, Albanian parliamentarism centenary emblem. d, Chamber of Deputies Building, 1925-44.

| 2020, Jan. 21 | Litho. | Perf. 13¼x13 |
|---|---|---|
| 3036 A875 | 200 l multi | 3.75 3.75 |

**Miniature Sheet**

| 3037 | Sheet of 5, #3036, 3037a-3037d, + 4 labels | 6.50 6.50 |
| a. | A875 20 l multi | .35 .35 |
| b. | A875 30 l multi | .55 .55 |
| c. | A875 40 l multi | .75 .75 |
| d. | A875 60 l multi | 1.10 1.10 |

**Souvenir Sheet**

Liberation of Albania, 75th Anniv. — A876

No. 3038: a, 50 l, Mother Albania statue, Tirana. b, 250 l, Poppies.

| 2020, Feb. 10 | Litho. | Perf. 13x13¼ |
|---|---|---|
| 3038 A876 | Sheet of 2, #a-b | 5.50 5.50 |

Messenger on Via Egnatia and Ship — A877

Post Rider on Via Egnatia A878

| 2021, Feb. 22 | Litho. | Perf. 13x13¼ |
|---|---|---|
| 3039 A877 | 150 l multi | 3.00 3.00 |

**Souvenir Sheet**

| 3040 A878 | 250 l multi | 5.00 5.00 |
| a. | Booklet pane of 2, #3039-3040 | 8.00 |
| | Complete booklet, #3040a | 8.00 |

Europa. Ancient Postal Routes.

Ludwig van Beethoven (1770-1827), Composer — A879

Designs: 180 l, Face of Beethoven. 200 l, Half of Beethoven's face.

| 2021, Mar. 5 | Litho. | Perf. 13½x13 |
|---|---|---|
| 3041 A879 | 180 l multi | 3.50 3.50 |

**Souvenir Sheet**

| 3042 A879 | 200 l multi | 4.00 4.00 |

Trees and Their Blossoms — A880

No. 3043: a, 60 l, Laurus nobilis. b, 130 l, Aesculus hippocastanum.

| 2021, Mar. 15 | Litho. | Perf. 13½x13 |
|---|---|---|
| 3043 A880 | Horiz. pair, #a-b | 3.75 3.75 |

Traditional Cuisine — A881

No. 3044: a, 10 l, Lekror ne saç (vegetable pie). b, 80 l, Tave kosi (baked lamb and yogurt). c, 90 l, Tave krapi (carp casserole). d, 120 l, Fasule te kuqe (red beans).

| 2021, Mar. 30 | Litho. | Perf. 13 |
|---|---|---|
| 3044 A881 | Block of 4, #a-d | 5.75 5.75 |

Bazaars A882

No. 3045 — Craftsman and bazaar site in: a, 10 l, Korçe. b, 40 l, Kruje. c, 50 l, Shkoder. d, 200 l, Tirana.

| 2021, Apr. 11 | Litho. | Perf. 13¼x13 |
|---|---|---|
| 3045 A882 | Block of 4, #a-d | 6.00 6.00 |

# ALBANIA

Robotics
A883

No. 3046 — Craftsman and bazaar site in: a, 140 l, Robot. b, 190 l, Robotic hand.

**2021, Apr. 19    Litho.    Perf. 13x13¼**
3046  A883    Horiz. pair, #a-b    6.50 6.50

Bank Buildings
A884

No. 3047 — Various banks with background color of: a, 20 l, Lilac. b, 30 l, Yellow. c, 80 l, Green. d, 120 l, Salmon.

**2021, Apr. 28    Litho.    Perf. 13¼x13**
3047  A884    Block of 4, #a-d    5.00 5.00

Miniature Sheet

Famous Men
A885

No. 3048: a, 10 l, Vexhi Buharaja (1920-87), writer and translator. b, 20 l, Ramadan Sokoli (1920-2008), composer. c, 40 l, Kristo Frasheri (1920-2016), historian. d, 90 l, Shaban Demiraj (1920-2014), linguist. e, 100 l, Sander Prosi (1920-85), actor.

**2021, May 10    Litho.    Perf. 13**
3048  A885    Sheet of 5, #a-e, +
               4 labels            5.25 5.25

Souvenir Sheet

Tirana as Capital of Albania, Cent.
A886

**2021, May 24    Litho.    Perf. 13x13¼**
3049  A886    100 l multi    2.00 2.00

Ancient Coins
A887

No. 3050: a, 30 l, Epirus silver coin, 234-168 B.C. b, 70 l, Apollonia silver coin, 44-27 B.C. c, 90 l, Shkoder bronze coin, 168 B.C. d, 250 l, Dürres silver coin, 350-250 B.C.

**2021, June 2    Litho.    Perf. 13**
3050  A887    Block of 4, #a-d    8.75 8.75
               Dated 2020.

2020 European Soccer Championships — A888

No. 3051 — Map of Europe, 2020 European Soccer Championships emblem, soccer player and denomination: a, 20 l. b, 200 l.

**2021, June 11    Litho.    Perf. 13**
3051  A888    Horiz. pair, #a-b    4.25 4.25

The 2020 European Soccer Championships were postponed until 2021 because of the COVID-19 pandemic.

Souvenir Sheet

Ecotourism — A889

No. 3052: a, 80 l, Otok and Lake Cerknica, Slovenia. b, 100 l, Zvernec Island and Narta Lagoon, Albania.

**2021, Dec. 22    Litho.    Perf. 14¼**
3052  A889    Sheet of 2, #a-b    4.00 4.00

Joint issue between Albania and Slovenia. See Slovenia No. 1474.

Endangered Animals — A890

**2022, Mar. 30    Litho.    Perf. 13¼x13**
3053  A890    150 l multi    2.75 2.75

Souvenir Sheet
3054  A890    250 l multi    4.50 4.50
  a.   Booklet pane fo 2, #3053-3054   7.25  —
       Complete booklet, #3054a        7.25

Europa. Dated 2021.

Flora
A891

No. 3055: a, 5 l, Rosmarinus officinalis. b, 30 l, Origanum heracleoticum. c, 200 l, Lilium albanicum.

**2022, Apr. 4    Litho.    Perf. 13¼x13**
3055  A891    Horiz. strip of 3, #a-c    4.25 4.25
               Dated 2021.

Souvenir Sheets

Famous Men
A892

Designs: 10 l, Ali Pasha of Gusinje (1828-88), military commander. 20 l, Naum Naçi (1871-1927), teacher and writer. 50 l, Mustafa Krantja (1921-2002), composer and conductor. 100 l, Guri Madhi (1921-88), painter. 140 l, Andrea Mano (1919-2000), sculptor. 180 l, Pandi Raidhi (1931-99), actor.

**2022, Apr. 11    Litho.    Perf. 13¼x13**
3056-3061  A892  Set of 6    8.75 8.75
                  Dated 2021.

Egyptian Vulture
A893

No. 3062: a, 50 l, Two vultures. b, 250 l, Two vultures, diff.

**2022, Apr. 14    Litho.    Perf. 13¼x13**
3062  A893    Horiz. pair, #a-b    5.25 5.25
               Dated 2021.

Vehicles of Rally Albania
A894

No. 3063: a, 20 l, Motorcycle. b, 40 l, Truck. c, 80 l, Off-road vehicle. d, 130 l, All-terrain vehicle.

**2022, Apr. 18    Litho.    Perf. 13¼x13**
3063  A894    Block of 4, #a-d    4.75 4.75
               Dated 2021.

Souvenir Sheet

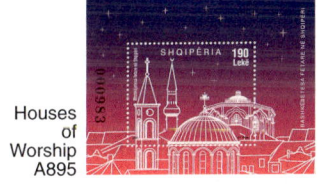

Houses of Worship
A895

**2022, Apr. 25    Litho.    Perf. 13**
3064  A895    190 l multi    3.50 3.50
               Dated 2021.

Rights of Children
A896

No. 3065: a, 40 l, Six children. b, 120 l, Five children.

**2022, Apr. 28    Litho.    Perf. 13**
3065  A896    Horiz. pair, #a-b    6.00 6.00
               Dated 2021.

Gjipe Canyon
A897

No. 3066 — Various views of canyon: a, 100 l. b, 150 l.

**2022, May 2    Litho.    Perf. 13**
3066  A897    Horiz. pair, #a-b    4.50 4.50
               Tourism. Dated 2021.

Ancient Coins
A898

No. 3067: a, 60 l, Bronze Illyrian coin, 181-168 B.C. b, 90 l, Bronze coin of Oricum, 234-168 B.C. c, 100 l, Silver stater from mint at Dyrrachium (Durres), 375-280 B.C. d, 150 l, Bronze coin of Apollonia, 168 B.C.

**2022, May 6    Litho.    Perf. 13**
3067  A898    Block of 4, #a-d    7.25 7.25
               Dated 2021.

Handmade Jewelry — A899

No. 3068 — Various pieces of jewelry with denomination of: a, 20 l. b, 60 l. c, 70 l. d, 100 l.

**2022, May 11    Litho.    Perf. 13**
3068  A899    Block of 4, #a-d    4.50 4.50
               Dated 2021.

Souvenir Sheet

Independence of Kosovo, 15th Anniv. — A900

No. 3069: a, 200 l, 15th anniversary emblem. b, 250 l, Monument.

**2023, Apr. 27    Litho.    Perf. 13x13¼**
3069  A900    Sheet of 2, #a-b    9.00 9.00

Autocephalous Orthodox Church of Albania, Cent. — A901

No. 3070 — Various unnamed clergymen with denominations of: a, 20 l. b, 30 l. c, 200 l.

**2023, Sept. 12    Litho.    Perf. 13**
3070  A901    Horiz. strip of 3, #a-c    5.00 5.00

Miniature Sheet

Motor Vehicles
A902

No. 3071: a, 10 l, 1948 Dnepr M-72 motorcycle with sidecar. b, 50 l, 1937 Fiat 1100 automobile. c, 60 l, 1954 GAZ 69 light truck. d, 70 l, 1946-56 ZIS-110 limousine. e, 80 l, MBI 1 Shekull automobile. f, 90 l, Fiat 900T police van. g, 100 l, Skoda 701 MT truck. h, 120 l, 1958-72 Skoda 706 RTO bus. i, 190 l, 1967 Jiefang CA 10 fire truck.

**2023, Oct. 5    Litho.    Perf. 13**
3071  A902    Sheet of 9, #a-i    16.00 16.00
               Dated 2022.

# ALBANIA

## Miniature Sheet

Famous Albanians Active in Italy — A903

No. 3072: a, 20 l, Jeronim de Rada (1814-1903), writer. b, 30 l, Dhimiter Kamarda (1821-82), linguist. c, 50 l, Gavril Dara the Younger (1826-85), poet. d, 60 l, Nikolle Keta (1741-1803), priest and writer. e, 90 l, Zef Skiroi (1865-1927), writer. f, 140 l, Zef Serembe (1844-1901), poet.

**2023, Oct. 13    Litho.    Perf. 13¼x13**
| 3072 | A903 | Sheet of 6, #a-f | 7.75 | 7.75 |

Dated 2022.

Underwater Archaeology — A905

No. 3074 — Various ancient pottery vessels at bottom of sea with denominations of: a, 10 l. b, 50 l. c, 90 l. d, 100 l.

**2023, Oct. 26    Litho.    Perf. 13x13¼**
| 3074 | A905 | Block of 4, #a-d | 5.00 | 5.00 |

Dated 2022.

A906

Diplomatic Relations Between Albania and the United States, Cent. (in 2022) — A907

**2023, Oct. 26    Litho.    Perf. 13¼x13**
| 3075 | A906 | 100 l multi | 2.00 | 2.00 |

**Souvenir Sheet Perf. 13x13¼**
| 3076 | A907 | 250 l multi | 5.00 | 5.00 |
| a. | | Booklet pane of 2, #3075-3076 | 8.50 | — |
| | | Complete booklet, #3076a | 8.50 | |

Dated 2022. Complete booklet sold for 420 l.

## SEMI-POSTAL STAMPS

Nos. 148-151 Surcharged in Red and Black

**1924, Nov. 1**
| B1 | A18 | 5q + 5q yel grn | 11.00 | 30.00 |
| B2 | A18 | 10q + 5q carmine | 11.00 | 30.00 |
| B3 | A18 | 25q + 5q dark blue | 11.00 | 30.00 |
| B4 | A18 | 50q + 5q dark grn | 11.00 | 30.00 |
| | | Nos. B1-B4 (4) | 44.00 | 120.00 |

Nos. B1 to B4 with Additional Surcharge in Red and Black

**1924**
| B5 | A18 | 5q + 5q + 5q yel grn | 11.00 | 26.00 |
| B6 | A18 | 10q + 5q + 5q car | 11.00 | 26.00 |
| B7 | A18 | 25q + 5q dk bl | 11.00 | 26.00 |
| B8 | A18 | 50q + 5q + 5q dk grn | 11.00 | 26.00 |
| | | Nos. B5-B8 (4) | 44.00 | 104.00 |

### Issued under Italian Dominion

Nurse and Child — SP1

**Unwmk.**
**1943, Apr. 1    Photo.    Perf. 14**
| B9 | SP1 | 5q + 5q dark grn | 1.00 | 1.50 |
| B10 | SP1 | 10q + 10q olive brn | 1.00 | 1.50 |
| B11 | SP1 | 15q + 10q rose red | 1.00 | 1.50 |
| B12 | SP1 | 25q + 15q saphire | 1.00 | 2.75 |
| B13 | SP1 | 30q + 20q violet | 1.00 | 2.75 |
| B14 | SP1 | 50q + 25q dk org | 1.00 | 2.75 |
| B15 | SP1 | 65q + 30q grnsh blk | 1.40 | 4.00 |
| B16 | SP1 | 1fr + 40q chestnut | 3.00 | 5.25 |
| | | Nos. B9-B16 (8) | 10.40 | 22.00 |

The surtax was for the control of tuberculosis.
For surcharges see Nos. B24-B27.

### Issued under German Administration

War Victims — SP2

**1944, Sept. 22**
| B17 | SP2 | 5g + 5(q) dp grn | 2.50 | 17.00 |
| B18 | SP2 | 10g + 5(q) dp brn | 2.50 | 17.00 |
| B19 | SP2 | 15g + 5(q) car lake | 2.50 | 17.00 |
| B20 | SP2 | 25g + 10(q) dp blue | 2.50 | 17.00 |
| B21 | SP2 | 1fr + 50q dk olive | 2.50 | 17.00 |
| B22 | SP2 | 2fr + 1(fr) purple | 2.50 | 17.00 |
| B23 | SP2 | 3fr + 1.50(fr) dk org | 2.50 | 17.00 |
| | | Nos. B17-B23 (7) | 17.50 | 119.00 |

Surtax for victims of World War II.

### Independent State

Nos. B9 to B12 Surcharged in Carmine

**1945, May 4    Unwmk.    Perf. 14**
| B24 | SP1 | 30q +15q on 5q+5q | 5.00 | 13.00 |
| B25 | SP1 | 50q +20q on 10q+10q | 7.50 | 13.00 |
| B26 | SP1 | 1fr +50q on 15q+10q | 12.50 | 27.50 |
| B27 | SP1 | 2fr +1fr on 25q+15q | 17.50 | 37.50 |
| | | Nos. B24-B27 (4) | 42.50 | 91.00 |

The surtax was for the Albanian Red Cross.

### People's Republic

Nos. 361 to 366 Overprinted in Red (cross) and Surcharged in Black

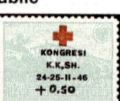

**1946, July 16    Perf. 11**
| B28 | A57 | 20q + 10q bluish grn | 11.00 | 30.00 |
| B29 | A57 | 30q + 15q dp org | 11.00 | 30.00 |
| B30 | A57 | 40q + 20q brown | 11.00 | 30.00 |
| B31 | A57 | 60q + 30q red vio | 11.00 | 30.00 |
| B32 | A57 | 1fr + 50q rose red | 11.00 | 30.00 |
| B33 | A57 | 3fr + 1.50fr dk bl | 11.00 | 30.00 |
| | | Nos. B28-B33 (6) | 66.00 | 180.00 |

To honor and benefit the Congress of the Albanian Red Cross.
Counterfeits: lithographed; genuine: typographed.

**Catalogue values for unused stamps in this section, from this point to the end of the section, are for Never Hinged items.**

SP3

**1967, Dec. 1    Litho.    Perf. 11½x12**
| B34 | SP3 | 15q + 5q blk, red & brn | .75 | .35 |
| B35 | SP3 | 25q + 5q multi | 1.50 | .80 |
| B36 | SP3 | 65q + 25q multi | 5.00 | 2.75 |
| B37 | SP3 | 80q + 40q multi | 7.00 | 4.00 |
| | | Nos. B34-B37 (4) | 14.25 | 7.90 |

6th congress of the Albanian Red Cross.

SP4

**1996, Aug. 5    Litho.    Perf. 13½x13**
| B38 | SP4 | 50 l +10 l multi | 1.60 | 1.60 |

Albanian Red Cross, 75th anniv.

Nos. 2469-2470 Surcharged

**Methods and Perfs as Before**
**2001, Mar. 12**
| B39 | A567 | 80 l +10 l on 50 l multi | 4.50 | 4.50 |
| B40 | A567 | 130 l +20 l on 100 l multi | 7.50 | 7.50 |

## AIR POST STAMPS

Airplane Crossing Mountains — AP1

**Wmk. 125**
**1925, May 30    Typo.    Perf. 14**
| C1 | AP1 | 5q green | 2.25 | 3.50 |
| C2 | AP1 | 10q rose red | 2.25 | 3.50 |
| C3 | AP1 | 25q deep blue | 2.25 | 3.50 |
| C4 | AP1 | 50q dark green | 3.50 | 6.00 |
| C5 | AP1 | 1fr dk vio & blk | 6.25 | 10.50 |
| C6 | AP1 | 2fr ol grn & vio | 10.50 | 17.50 |
| C7 | AP1 | 3fr brn org & dk grn | 12.50 | 17.50 |
| | | Nos. C1-C7 (7) | 39.50 | 62.00 |

Nos. C1-C7 exist imperf. Value $3,000.
For overprint see Nos. C8-C28.

Nos. C1-C7 Overprinted

**1927, Jan. 18**
| C8 | AP1 | 5q green | 5.25 | 10.50 |
| a. | | Dbl. overprint, one invtd. | 50.00 | |
| C9 | AP1 | 10q rose red | 5.25 | 10.50 |
| a. | | Inverted overprint | 45.00 | |
| b. | | Dbl. overprint, one invtd. | 50.00 | |
| C10 | AP1 | 25q deep blue | 4.75 | 9.50 |
| C11 | AP1 | 50q dark grn | 3.25 | 6.50 |
| a. | | Inverted overprint | 45.00 | |
| C12 | AP1 | 1fr dk vio & blk | 3.25 | 6.50 |
| a. | | Inverted overprint | 45.00 | |
| b. | | Double overprint | 45.00 | |
| C13 | AP1 | 2fr ol grn & vio | 7.50 | 10.50 |
| C14 | AP1 | 3fr brn org & dk grn | 10.50 | 15.00 |
| | | Nos. C8-C14 (7) | 39.75 | 69.00 |

Nos. C1-C7 Overprinted

**1928, Apr. 21**
| C15 | AP1 | 5q green | 5.25 | 10.50 |
| a. | | Inverted overprint | 70.00 | |
| C16 | AP1 | 10q rose red | 5.25 | 10.50 |
| C17 | AP1 | 25q deep blue | 5.25 | 10.50 |
| C18 | AP1 | 50q dark green | 10.00 | 21.00 |
| C19 | AP1 | 1fr dk vio & blk | 55.00 | 110.00 |
| C20 | AP1 | 2fr ol grn & vio | 55.00 | 110.00 |
| C21 | AP1 | 3fr brn org & dk grn | 55.00 | 110.00 |
| | | Nos. C15-C21 (7) | 190.75 | 382.50 |

First flight across the Adriatic, Valona to Brindisi, Apr. 21, 1928.
The variety "SHQYRTARE" occurs once in the sheet for each value. Value 3 times normal.

Nos. C1-C7 Overprinted in Red Brown

**1929, Dec. 1**
| C22 | AP1 | 5q green | 6.00 | 8.75 |
| C23 | AP1 | 10q rose red | 6.00 | 8.75 |
| C24 | AP1 | 25q deep blue | 6.00 | 8.75 |
| C25 | AP1 | 50q dk grn | 125.00 | 175.00 |
| C26 | AP1 | 1fr dk vio & blk | 250.00 | 200.00 |
| C27 | AP1 | 2fr ol grn | 250.00 | 375.00 |
| C28 | AP1 | 3fr brn org & dk grn | 250.00 | 375.00 |
| | | Nos. C22-C28 (7) | 893.00 | 1,151. |

Excellent counterfeits exist.

King Zog and Airplane over Tirana — AP2

AP3

**1930, Oct. 8    Photo.    Unwmk.**
| C29 | AP2 | 5q yellow green | 1.00 | 1.75 |
| C30 | AP2 | 15q rose red | 1.00 | 1.75 |
| C31 | AP2 | 20q slate blue | 1.00 | 1.75 |
| C32 | AP2 | 50q olive green | 2.00 | 2.75 |
| C33 | AP3 | 1fr dark blue | 3.00 | 5.25 |
| C34 | AP3 | 2fr olive brown | 10.00 | 17.50 |
| C35 | AP3 | 3fr purple | 22.50 | 17.50 |
| | | Nos. C29-C35 (7) | 40.50 | 48.25 |

For overprints and surcharges see Nos. C36-C45.

Nos. C29-C35 Overprinted

**1931, July 6**
| C36 | AP2 | 5q yellow grn | 5.25 | 10.50 |
| a. | | Double overprint | 140.00 | |
| C37 | AP2 | 15q rose red | 5.25 | 10.50 |
| C38 | AP2 | 20q slate blue | 5.25 | 10.50 |
| C39 | AP2 | 50q olive grn | 5.25 | 10.50 |
| C40 | AP3 | 1fr dark blue | 30.00 | 60.00 |
| C41 | AP3 | 2fr olive brn | 30.00 | 60.00 |
| C42 | AP3 | 3fr purple | 30.00 | 60.00 |
| a. | | Inverted overprint | 275.00 | |
| | | Nos. C36-C42 (7) | 111.00 | 222.00 |

1st air post flight from Tirana to Rome. Only a very small part of this issue was sold to the public. Most of the stamps were given to the Aviation Company to help provide funds for conducting the service.

### Issued under Italian Dominion

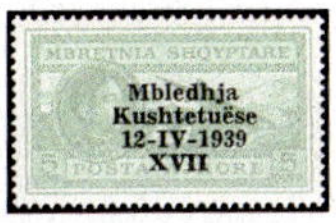


Nos. C29-C30 Overprinted in Black

**1939, Apr. 19 Unwmk. *Perf. 14***

**C43** AP2 5q yel green 3.00 *7.00*
**C44** AP2 15q rose red 3.00 *7.00*

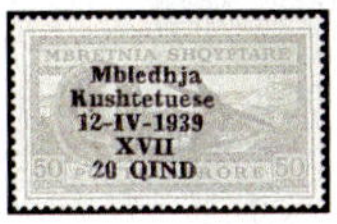


No. C32 With Additional Surcharge

**C45** AP2 20q on 50q ol grn 5.00 *11.50*
*a.* Inverted overprint
*Nos. C43-C45 (3)* 11.00 *25.50*

See note after No. 309.

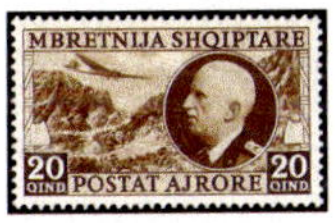


King Victor Emmanuel III and Plane over Mountains — AP4

**1939, Aug. 4 Photo.**

**C46** AP4 20q brown 35.00 15.00

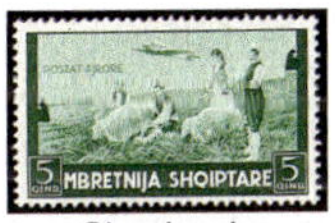


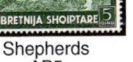

Shepherds AP5

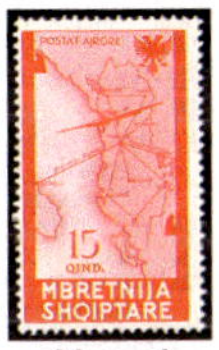


Map of Albania Showing Air Routes AP6

Designs: 20q, Victor Emmanuel III and harbor view. 50q, Woman and river valley. 1fr, Bridge at Vezirit. 2fr, Ruins. 3fr, Women waving to plane.

**1940, Mar. 20 Unwmk.**

**C47** AP5 5q green 1.25 *1.25*
**C48** AP6 15q rose red 1.25 *1.90*
**C49** AP5 20q deep blue 2.50 *3.25*
**C50** AP6 50q brown 3.25 *9.50*
**C51** AP5 1fr myrtle green 6.50 *12.50*
**C52** AP6 2fr brown black 9.50 *19.00*
**C53** AP6 3fr rose violet 16.00 *25.00*
*Nos. C47-C53 (7)* 40.25 *72.40*

### People's Republic

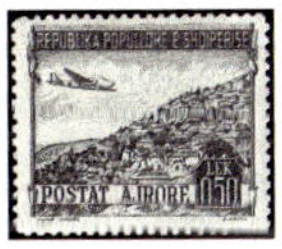


Vuno-Himare — AP12

Albanian Towns: 1 l, 10 l, Rozafat-Shkoder. 2 l, 20 l, Keshtjelle-Butrinto.

**1950, Dec. 15 Engr. *Perf. 12½x12***

**C54** AP12 50q gray black .25 *1.00*
**C55** AP12 1 l red brown 1.00 .80
**C56** AP12 2 l ultra .50 *1.60*
**C57** AP12 5 l deep green 2.00 *3.00*
**C58** AP12 10 l deep blue 4.50 *5.50*
**C59** AP12 20 l purple 10.00 11.00
*Nos. C54-C59 (6)* 18.25 *22.90*

**Nos. C50-C59 Surcharged with New Value and Bars in Red or Black**

**1952-53**

**C60** AP12 50q on 2 l (R) 90.00 *150.00*
**C61** AP12 50q on 5 l 22.50 *30.00*
**C62** AP12 2.50 l on 5 l (R) 150.00 *175.00*
**C63** AP12 2.50 l on 10 l 25.00 *45.00*
*Nos. C60-C63 (4)* 287.50 *400.00*

Issued: Nos. C60, C62, 12/26/52; Nos. C61, C63, 3/14/53.

**Catalogue values for unused stamps in this section, from this point to the end of the section, are for Never Hinged items.**

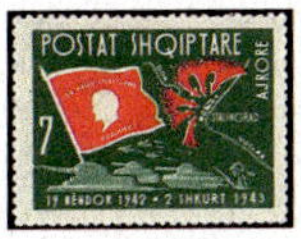


Banner with Lenin, Map of Stalingrad and Tanks — AP13

**1963, Feb. 2 Litho. *Perf. 14***

**C67** AP13 7 l grn & dp car 8.00 3.00

20th anniversary, Battle of Stalingrad.

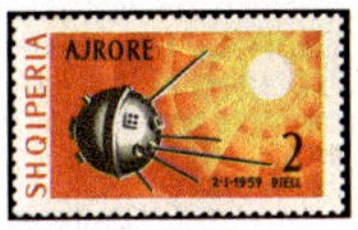


Sputnik and Sun — AP14

Designs: 3 l, Lunik 4. 5 l, Lunik 3 photographing far side of the Moon. 8 l, Venus space probe. 12 l, Mars 1.

**1963, Oct. 31 Unwmk. *Perf. 12***

**C68** AP14 2 l org, yel & blk .35 .35
**C69** AP14 3 l multi .70 .35
**C70** AP14 5 l rose lil, yel & blk 1.00 .35
**C71** AP14 8 l multi 1.75 .70
**C72** AP14 12 l blue & org 3.50 2.75
*Nos. C68-C72 (5)* 7.30 4.50

Russian interplanetary explorations.

**Nos. C68 and C71 Overprinted "Riccione 23-8-1964"**

**1964, Aug. 23**

**C73** AP14 2 l org, yel & blk 7.00 *14.00*
**C74** AP14 8 l multicolored 14.00 *21.00*

Intl. Space Exhib. in Riccione, Italy.

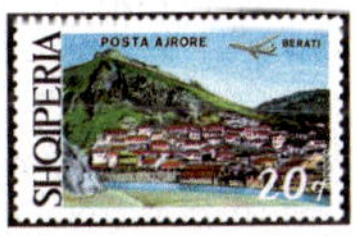


Plane over Berat — AP15

**1975, Nov. 25 Litho. *Perf. 12***

**C75** AP15 20q multi .25 .25
**C76** AP15 40q Gjirokaster .30 .25
**C77** AP15 60q Sarande .55 .30
**C78** AP15 90q Durres 1.10 .35
**C79** AP15 1.20 l Kruje 1.40 .70
**C80** AP15 2.40 l Boga 2.75 1.40
**C81** AP15 4.05 l Tirana 4.25 2.10
*Nos. C75-C81 (7)* 10.60 5.35

## SPECIAL DELIVERY STAMPS

### Issued under Italian Dominion

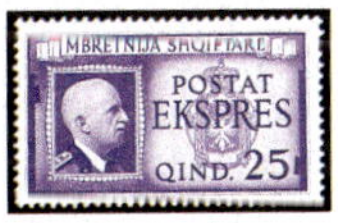


King Victor Emmanuel III — SD1

**1940 Unwmk. Photo. *Perf. 14***

**E1** SD1 25q bright violet 4.50 *7.50*
**E2** SD1 50q red orange 11.50 *18.00*

### Issued under German Administration

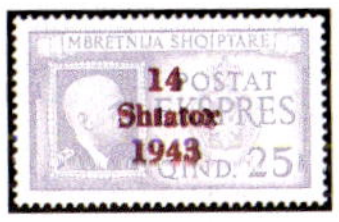


No. E1 Overprinted in Carmine

**1943**

**E3** SD1 25q bright violet 12.50 *24.00*

Proclamation of Albanian independence.

## POSTAGE DUE STAMPS

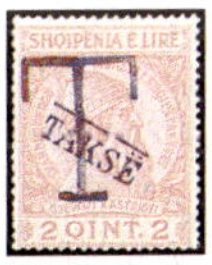


Nos. 35-39 Handstamped in Various Colors

**1914, Feb. 23 Unwmk. *Perf. 14***

**J1** A3 2q org brn & buff (Bl) 10.50 4.50
*a.* Violet ovpt. 30.00 26.00
*b.* Black ovpt. 30.00 30.00
**J2** A3 5q green (R) 10.50 4.50
*a.* Violet ovpt. 37.50 37.50
*b.* Blue ovpt. 30.00 30.00
**J3** A3 10q rose red (Bl) 15.00 4.50
*a.* Violet ovpt. 30.00 26.00
**J4** A3 25q dark blue (R) 17.50 4.50
**J5** A3 50q vio & red (Bk) 26.00 14.00
*Nos. J1-J5 (5)* 79.50 32.00

The two parts of the overprint are handstamped separately. Stamps exist with one or both handstamps inverted, double or omitted.

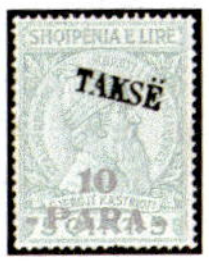


Nos. 48-51 Overprinted in Black

**1914, Apr. 16**

**J6** A3 (a) 10pa on 5q green 5.25 4.50
**J7** A3 (a) 20pa on 10q rose red 5.25 4.50
**J8** A3 (b) 1gr on 25q blue 5.25 4.50
**J9** A3 (b) 2gr on 50q vio & red 5.25 4.50
*Nos. J6-J9 (4)* 21.00 18.00

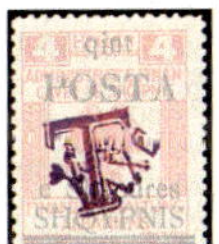


Same Design as Regular Issue of 1919, Overprinted

**1919, Feb. 10 *Perf. 11½, 12½***

**J10** A8 (4)q on 4h rose 13.00 10.50
**J11** A8 (10)q on 10k red, *grn* 13.00 10.50
**J12** A8 20q on 2k org, *gray* 13.00 10.50
**J13** A8 50q on 5k brn, *yel* 13.00 10.50
*Nos. J10-J13 (4)* 52.00 42.00

Nos. J10-J12 exist with overprint in red. Value, each $50.

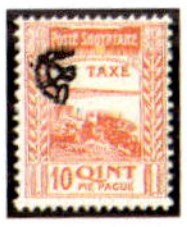


Fortress at Scutari — D3

**Post Horn Overprinted in Black**

**1920, Apr. 1 *Perf. 14x13***

**J14** D3 4q olive green .75 *4.50*
**J15** D3 10q rose red 1.50 *6.50*
**J16** D3 20q bister brn 1.50 *6.50*
**J17** D3 50q black 4.00 *17.50*
*Nos. J14-J17 (4)* 7.75 *35.00*

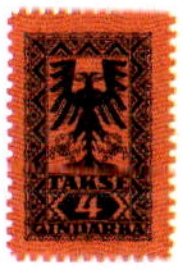


D5

**Background of Red Wavy Lines**

**1922 *Perf. 12½, 11½***

**J23** D5 4q black, *red* 1.10 *4.50*
**J24** D5 10q black, *red* 1.10 *4.50*
**J25** D5 20q black, *red* 1.10 *4.50*
**J26** D5 50q black, *red* 1.10 *4.50*
*Nos. J23-J26 (4)* 4.40 *18.00*

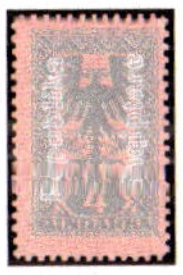

Nos. J23-J26 Overprinted in White

**1925**

**J27** D5 4q black, *red* 1.90 *4.50*
**J28** D5 10q black, *red* 1.90 *4.50*
**J29** D5 20q black, *red* 1.90 *4.50*
**J30** D5 50q black, *red* 1.90 *4.50*
*Nos. J27-J30 (4)* 7.60 *18.00*

The 10q with overprint in gold was a trial printing. It was not put in use.

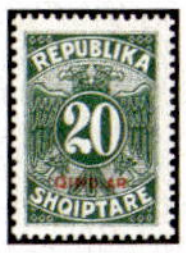


D7

**Overprinted "QIND. AR" in Red**

**1926, Dec. 24 *Perf. 13½x13***

**J31** D7 10q dark blue .75 3.50
**J32** D7 20q green .75 3.50
**J33** D7 30q red brown 1.50 *7.00*
**J34** D7 50q dark brown 2.75 *13.00*
*Nos. J31-J34 (4)* 5.75 *27.00*

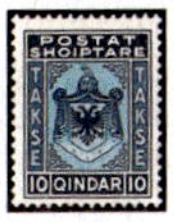


Coat of Arms — D8

**Wmk. Double Headed Eagle (220)**

**1930, Sept. 1 Photo. *Perf. 14, 14½***

**J35** D8 10q dark blue 6.75 *21.00*
**J36** D8 20q rose red 2.75 *13.00*
**J37** D8 30q violet 2.75 *13.00*
**J38** D8 50q dark green 2.75 *13.00*
*Nos. J35-J38 (4)* 15.00 *60.00*

Nos. J36-J38 exist with overprint "14 Shtator 1943" (see Nos. 332-344) which is private and fraudulent on these stamps.

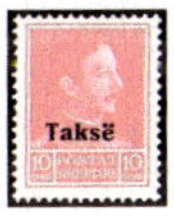


No. 253 Overprinted

**1936 *Perf. 14***

**J39** A34 10q carmine 10.00 *15.00*
*a.* Hyphens on each side of "Takse" ('39) 100.00 *200.00*

### Issued under Italian Dominion

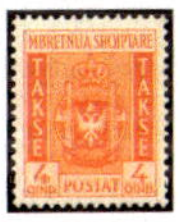


Coat of Arms — D9

**1940 Unwmk. Photo. *Perf. 14***

**J40** D9 4q red orange *20.00* *45.00*
**J41** D9 10q bright violet *20.00* *45.00*
**J42** D9 20q brown *20.00* *45.00*
**J43** D9 30q dark blue *20.00* *45.00*
**J44** D9 50q carmine rose *20.00* *45.00*
*Nos. J40-J44 (5)* *100.00* *225.00*

## CENTRAL ALBANIA

After the departure of Prince Wilhelm of Wied Oct. 2, 1914, Essad Pasha established a regime in Durres, which, with Serbian support, soon included much of central Albania. The regime issued stamps, overprinted on previously issued Albanian regular postage, postage due, and revenue stamps, and on unissued stamps commissioned in 1913 by an earlier government, which were in use during 1915/1916. Essad's Central Albania collapsed with the Austro-Hungarian invasion of the area in the spring of 1916.

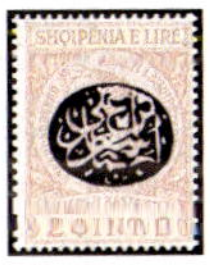


Albania Nos. 35-37, 47-52 Handstamped in Black, Blue, Red or Violet

**1915 *Perf. 14***

**1** A3 2q orange brn & buff 28.00 27.00
**2** A3 5q green & bl grn 60.00 60.00
**3** A3 10q rose red 40.00 37.50
**4** A3 25q dark blue 55.00 65.00
**5** A3 50q violet & red 55.00 65.00
**6** A3(a) 5pa on 2q org brn & buff 40.00 37.50
**7** A3(a) 10pa on 5q grn & bl grn 17.00 17.00
**8** A3(a) 20pa on 10q rose red 17.00 17.00
**9** A3(b) 1gr on 25q dk bl 17.00 17.00
**10** A3(b) 2gr on 50q vio & red 17.00 17.00

11 A3(b) 5gr on 1r dp brown 37.50 50.00
*Nos. 1-11 (11)* 383.50 410.00

**Crescent Handstamp in Black or Violet on Unissued Stamps of Albania**

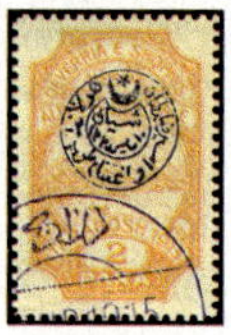

| | | | | |
|---|---|---|---|---|
| 12 | A1 | 2pa orange | 9.25 | 6.25 |
| 13 | A1 | 5pa violet | 9.25 | 8.75 |
| 14 | A1 | 10pa green | 9.25 | 9.25 |
| 15 | A1 | 20pa red | 9.25 | 6.25 |
| 16 | A1 | 40pa blue | 12.00 | 6.25 |
| 17 | A1 | 100pa pink | 28.00 | 11.50 |
| 18 | A1 | 5pi black | 80.00 | 32.00 |
| | | *Nos. 12-18 (7)* | 157.00 | 80.25 |

**Handstamp on Albania Fiscal Stamps**

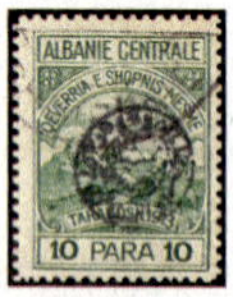

| | | | | |
|---|---|---|---|---|
| 19 | A2 | 10pa green | 11.00 | *11.50* |
| 20 | A2 | 20pa red | 11.00 | 8.75 |
| 21 | A2 | 50pa blue | 7.50 | 6.25 |
| 22 | A2 | 3pi rose | 7.50 | 6.25 |
| 23 | A2 | 6pi chocolate | 17.00 | 13.50 |
| | | *Nos. 19-23 (5)* | 54.00 | 46.25 |

**POSTAGE DUE STAMPS**
**Large "T" Handstamp on Albania Nos. 47-52**

| | | | | |
|---|---|---|---|---|
| J1 | A3 | 2q orange brn & buff | 45.00 | 42.50 |
| J2 | A3(a) | 10pa on 5q grn & bl grn | 28.00 | 27.00 |
| J3 | A3(a) | 20pa on 10q rose red | 28.00 | 27.00 |
| J4 | A3(b) | 1gr on 25q dk bl | 28.00 | 27.00 |
| J5 | A3(b) | 2gr on 50q vio & red | 28.00 | 27.00 |
| | | *Nos. J1-J5 (5)* | 157.00 | 150.50 |

## ALEXANDRETTA

ˌa-lig-ˌzan-ˈdre-tə

LOCATION — A political territory in northern Syria, bordering on Turkey
GOVT. — French mandate
AREA — 10,000 sq. mi. (approx.)
POP. — 270,000 (approx.)

Included in the Syrian territory mandated to France under the Versailles Treaty, the name was changed to Hatay in 1938. The following year France returned the territory to Turkey in exchange for certain concessions. See Hatay.

100 Centimes = 1 Piaster

**Stamps of Syria, 1930-36, Overprinted or Surcharged in Black or Red**

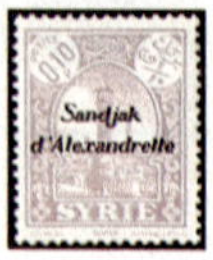
a

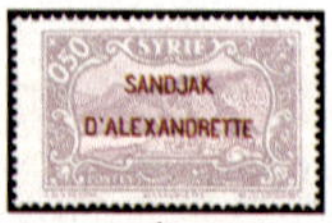
b

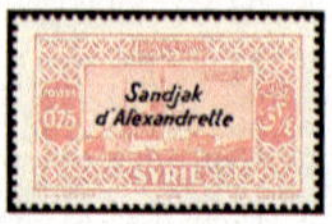
c

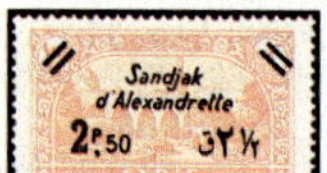
d

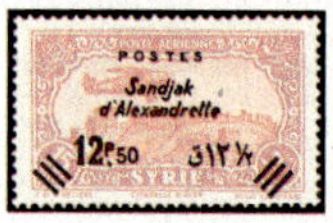
e

**1938 Unwmk. *Perf. 12x12½***

| | | | | |
|---|---|---|---|---|
| 1 | A6 (a) | 0.10p vio brn | 3.50 | 3.50 |
| 2 | A6 (a) | 0.20p brn org | 3.50 | 3.00 |

***Perf. 13½***

| | | | | |
|---|---|---|---|---|
| 3 | A9 (b) | 0.50p vio (R) | 4.50 | 3.50 |
| 4 | A10 (b) | 1p bis brn | 4.50 | 3.00 |
| 5 | A9 (b) | 2p dk vio (R) | 5.75 | 3.50 |
| 6 | A13 (b) | 3p yel grn (R) | 9.00 | 7.00 |
| 7 | A10 (b) | 4p yel org | 10.00 | 7.00 |
| 8 | A16 (b) | 6p grnsh blk (R) | 12.00 | 8.00 |
| 9 | A18 (b) | 25p vio brn | 25.00 | 25.00 |
| 10 | A15 (c) | 0.75p org red | 9.00 | 9.00 |
| 11 | A10 (d) | 2.50p on 4p yel org | 7.50 | 4.00 |
| 12 | AP2 (e) | 12.50p on 15p org red | 20.00 | 15.00 |
| | | *Nos. 1-12 (12)* | 114.25 | 91.50 |
| | | Set, never hinged | 275.00 | |

Issue dates: Nos. 1-9, Apr. 14, Nos. 10-12, Sept. 2.

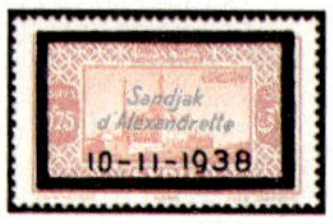
Nos. 4, 7, 10-12 Ovptd. in Black

**1938, Nov. 10**

| | | | | |
|---|---|---|---|---|
| 13 | A15 | 75c | 60.00 | 60.00 |
| *a.* | | Overprint inverted | 500.00 | |
| 14 | A10 | 1p | 37.50 | 37.50 |
| *a.* | | "Sandjah d'Alexandrette" omitted | 325.00 | |
| 15 | A10 | 2.50p on 4p | 32.50 | 32.50 |
| 16 | A10 | 4p | 37.50 | 37.50 |
| *a.* | | "Sandjah d'Alexandrette" omitted | 325.00 | |
| 17 | AP2 | 12.50p on 15p | 80.00 | 80.00 |
| *a.* | | "Sandjah d'Alexandrette" omitted | 1,500. | |
| | | *Nos. 13-17 (5)* | 247.50 | 247.50 |
| | | Set, never hinged | 500.00 | |

Death of Kemal Ataturk, pres. of Turkey.

**AIR POST STAMPS**

**Air Post Stamps of Syria, 1937, Overprinted Type "b" in Red or Black**

**1938, Apr. 14 Unwmk. *Perf. 13***

| | | | | |
|---|---|---|---|---|
| C1 | AP14 | ½p dark vio (R) | 4.50 | *5.00* |
| C2 | AP15 | 1p black (R) | 4.50 | *5.50* |
| C3 | AP14 | 2p blue grn (R) | 5.50 | *7.50* |
| C4 | AP15 | 3p deep ultra | 6.00 | *8.00* |
| C5 | AP14 | 5p rose lake | 11.00 | *18.00* |
| C6 | AP15 | 10p red brown | 11.50 | *20.00* |
| C7 | AP14 | 15p lake brown | 14.50 | *23.50* |
| C8 | AP15 | 25p dk blue (R) | 20.00 | *31.00* |
| | | *Nos. C1-C8 (8)* | 77.50 | *118.50* |
| | | Set, never hinged | 225.00 | |

**POSTAGE DUE STAMPS**

**Postage Due Stamps of Syria, 1925-31, Ovptd. Type "b" in Black or Red**

**1938, Apr. 14 Unwmk. *Perf. 13½***

| | | | | |
|---|---|---|---|---|
| J1 | D5 | 0.50p brown, *yel* | 6.50 | 5.75 |
| J2 | D6 | 1p violet, *rose* | 7.50 | 6.50 |
| J3 | D5 | 2p blk, *blue* (R) | 8.50 | 8.00 |
| J4 | D5 | 3p blk, *red org* | 10.00 | 9.00 |
| J5 | D5 | 5p blk, *bl grn* (R) | 16.00 | 14.50 |
| J6 | D7 | 8p blk, *gray bl* (R) | 22.50 | 20.00 |
| | | *Nos. J1-J6 (6)* | 71.00 | 63.75 |
| | | Set, never hinged | 225.00 | |

On No. J2, the overprint is vertical, reading up, other denominations, horizontal.
Stamps of Alexandretta were discontinued in 1938 and replaced by those of Hatay.

## ALGERIA

al-ˈjir-ē-ə

LOCATION — North Africa
GOVT. — Republic
AREA — 919,595 sq. mi.
POP. — 43,850,000 (2020 est.)
CAPITAL — Algiers

The former French colony of Algeria became an integral part of France on Sept. 1, 1958, when French stamps replaced Algerian stamps. Algeria became an independent country July 3, 1962.

100 Centimes = 1 Franc
100 Centimes = 1 Dinar (1964)

**Catalogue values for unused stamps in this country are for Never Hinged items, beginning with Scott 109 in the regular postage section, Scott B27 in the semi-postal section, Scott C1 in the air-post section, Scott CB1 in the air-post semi-postal section, Scott J25 in the postage due section, and Scott Q73 in the parcel post section.**

**Stamps of France Overprinted in Red, Blue or Black**

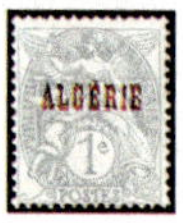
a

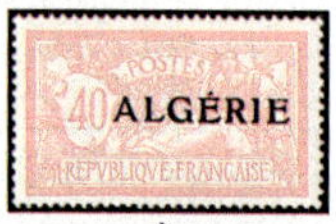
b

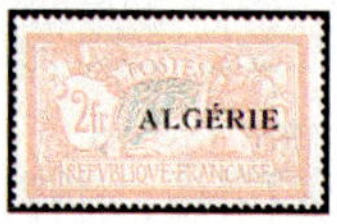
c

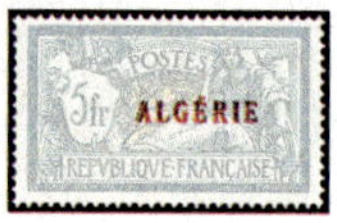
d

**1924-26 Unwmk. *Perf. 14x13½***

| | | | | |
|---|---|---|---|---|
| 1 | A16(a) | 1c dk gray (R) | .40 | .40 |
| 2 | A16(a) | 2c vio brn | .40 | .40 |
| 3 | A16(a) | 3c orange | .40 | .40 |
| 4 | A16(a) | 4c yel brn (Bl) | .40 | .40 |
| 5 | A22(a) | 5c org (Bl) | .40 | .40 |
| 6 | A16(a) | 5c grn ('25) | .80 | .80 |
| 7 | A23(a) | 10c green | .80 | .40 |
| *b.* | | Booklet pane of 10 | — | |
| | | Complete booklet, 2 #7b | 300.00 | |
| 8 | A22(a) | 10c grn ('25) | .80 | .40 |
| *a.* | | Pair, one without overprint | 1,500. | |
| 9 | A20(a) | 15c slate grn | .40 | .40 |
| 10 | A23(a) | 15c grn ('25) | 1.20 | .40 |
| 11 | A22(a) | 15c red brn (Bl) ('26) | .40 | .40 |
| 12 | A22(a) | 20c red brn (Bl) | .40 | .40 |
| *a.* | | Pair, one without overprint | 1,500. | |
| 13 | A22(a) | 25c blue (R) | .80 | .40 |
| *a.* | | Booklet pane of 10 | — | |
| | | Complete booklet, 2 #13a | 1,450. | |
| *b.* | | Pair, one without overprint | 1,750. | |
| 14 | A23(a) | 30c red (Bl) | 2.40 | .80 |
| 15 | A22(a) | 30c cerise ('25) | .80 | .80 |
| *a.* | | "ALGERIE" double | 225.00 | 150.00 |
| 16 | A22(a) | 30c lt bl (R) ('25) | .80 | .80 |
| *a.* | | Booklet pane of 10 | — | |
| | | Complete booklet, 2 #16a | 550.00 | |
| 17 | A22(a) | 35c violet | .80 | .80 |
| 18 | A18(b) | 40c red & pale bl | 1.20 | .80 |
| 19 | A22(a) | 40c ol brn (R) ('25) | 1.20 | .80 |
| 20 | A18(b) | 45c grn & bl (R) | 1.20 | .80 |
| *a.* | | Double overprint | 350.00 | |
| 21 | A23(a) | 45c red (Bl) ('25) | 1.25 | .80 |
| 22 | A23(a) | 50c blue (R) | 1.20 | .80 |
| 23 | A20(a) | 60c lt violet | 1.20 | .80 |
| *a.* | | Inverted overprint | | *2,900.* |
| 24 | A20(a) | 65c rose (Bl) | 1.20 | .80 |
| 25 | A23(a) | 75c blue (R) | 1.25 | .75 |
| *a.* | | Double overprint | 300.00 | 300.00 |
| 26 | A20(a) | 80c ver ('26) | 2.00 | 1.20 |
| 27 | A20(a) | 85c ver (Bl) | 1.20 | 1.20 |
| 28 | A18(b) | 1fr cl & ol grn | 2.00 | 1.20 |
| *a.* | | Olive green omitted | 325.00 | 325.00 |
| 29 | A22(a) | 1.05fr ver ('26) | 1.60 | 1.60 |
| 30 | A18(c) | 2fr org & pale bl | 2.40 | 1.60 |
| 31 | A18(b) | 3fr vio & bl ('26) | 5.50 | 2.40 |
| *a.* | | Blue omitted | 325.00 | |
| 32 | A18(d) | 5fr bl & buff (R) | 16.00 | 12.00 |
| | | *Nos. 1-32 (32)* | 52.80 | 36.35 |

No. 15 was issued precanceled only. Values for precanceled stamps in first column are for those which have not been through the post and have original gum. Values in second column are for postally used, gumless stamps.
For surcharges see Nos. 75, P1.

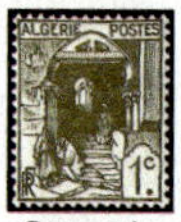
Street in Kasbah, Algiers
A1

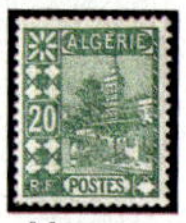
Mosque of Sidi Abd-er-Rahman
A2

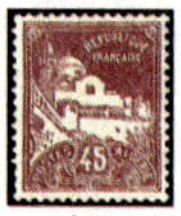
La Pêcherie Mosque
A3

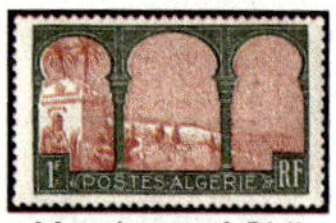
Marabout of Sidi Yacoub
A4

**1926-39 Typo. *Perf. 14x13½***

| | | | | |
|---|---|---|---|---|
| 33 | A1 | 1c olive | .25 | .25 |
| *a.* | | Imperforate | 110.00 | |
| 34 | A1 | 2c red brown | .25 | .25 |
| 35 | A1 | 3c orange | .25 | .25 |
| 36 | A1 | 5c blue green | .25 | .25 |
| 37 | A1 | 10c brt violet | .40 | .25 |
| *a.* | | Booklet pane of 10 | — | |
| | | Complete booklet, 2 #37a | 400.00 | |
| 38 | A2 | 15c orange brn | .40 | .25 |
| *a.* | | Imperforate | 110.00 | |
| *b.* | | Booklet pane of 10 | — | |
| | | Complete booklet, 2 #38b | 350.00 | |
| 39 | A2 | 20c green | .40 | .25 |
| 40 | A2 | 20c deep rose | .25 | .25 |
| *a.* | | Imperforate | 120.00 | |
| 41 | A2 | 25c blue grn | .40 | .25 |
| 42 | A2 | 25c blue ('27) | .80 | .40 |
| *a.* | | Imperforate | 120.00 | |
| 43 | A2 | 25c vio bl ('39) | .25 | .25 |
| 44 | A2 | 30c blue | .40 | .40 |
| *a.* | | Imperforate | 120.00 | |
| 45 | A2 | 30c bl grn ('27) | 1.25 | .80 |
| 46 | A2 | 35c dp violet | 1.60 | 1.20 |
| 47 | A2 | 40c olive green | .40 | .25 |
| *a.* | | Booklet pane of 10 | — | |
| | | Complete booklet, 2 #47a | 325.00 | |
| *b.* | | Imperforate | 120.00 | |
| 48 | A3 | 45c violet brn | .80 | .40 |
| 49 | A3 | 50c blue | .40 | .40 |
| *a.* | | Booklet pane of 10 | — | |
| | | Complete booklet, 2 #49a | 400.00 | |
| *b.* | | Imperforate | 125.00 | |
| *c.* | | Vert. pair, #49 and 49b | 225.00 | |
| 50 | A3 | 50c dk red ('30) | .40 | .25 |
| *a.* | | Booklet pane of 10 | — | |
| | | Complete booklet, 2 #50a | 450.00 | |
| *b.* | | Imperforate | 120.00 | |
| 51 | A3 | 60c yellow grn | .40 | .40 |
| 52 | A3 | 65c blk brn ('27) | 3.25 | 2.40 |
| 53 | A1 | 65c ultra ('38) | .40 | .40 |
| *a.* | | Booklet pane of 10 | — | |
| | | Complete booklet, 2 #53a | 160.00 | |
| 54 | A3 | 75c carmine | 1.20 | .80 |
| *a.* | | Imperforate | 125.00 | |
| *b.* | | Vert. pair, #54 and 54a | 225.00 | |
| 55 | A3 | 75c blue ('29) | 4.75 | .80 |
| 56 | A3 | 80c orange red | 1.20 | .80 |
| 57 | A3 | 90c red ('27) | 8.00 | 4.00 |
| *a.* | | Imperforate | 120.00 | |
| 58 | A4 | 1fr gray grn & red brn | 1.20 | .80 |
| *a.* | | Imperforate | 175.00 | |
| 59 | A3 | 1.05fr lt brown | 1.20 | .80 |
| 60 | A3 | 1.10fr mag ('27) | 8.00 | 4.00 |
| 61 | A4 | 1.25fr dk bl & ultra | 1.60 | 1.20 |
| 62 | A4 | 1.50fr dk bl & ultra ('27) | 5.50 | .80 |
| *a.* | | Imperforate | 400.00 | |
| 63 | A4 | 2fr prus bl & blk brn | 4.75 | 1.20 |
| *a.* | | Imperforate | 125.00 | |
| 64 | A4 | 3fr violet & org | 8.00 | 1.60 |
| 65 | A4 | 5fr red & violet | 16.00 | 4.75 |
| 66 | A4 | 10fr ol brn & rose ('27) | 80.00 | 47.50 |
| *a.* | | Imperforate | 725.00 | |
| 67 | A4 | 20fr vio & grn ('27) | 8.00 | 8.00 |
| | | *Nos. 33-67 (35)* | 162.60 | 86.85 |

A 90c red, design A1, was prepared but not issued. Values: unused $950, never hinged $1,350.
Type A4, 50c blue and rose red, inscribed "CENTENAIRE-ALGERIE" is France No. 255.
See design A24. For stamps and types surcharged see Nos. 68-74, 131, 136, 187, B1-B13, J27, P2.

Stamps of 1926 Surcharged

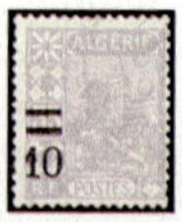

**1927**

| | | | | |
|---|---|---|---|---|
| **68** | A2 | 10c on 35c dp violet | .25 | .25 |
| **69** | A2 | 25c on 30c blue | .25 | .25 |
| **70** | A2 | 30c on 25c blue grn | .40 | .25 |
| **71** | A3 | 65c on 60c yel grn | 1.60 | 1.20 |
| **72** | A3 | 90c on 80c org red | 1.40 | .95 |
| **73** | A3 | 1.10fr on 1.05fr lt brn | 1.00 | .50 |
| **74** | A4 | 1.50fr on 1.25fr dk bl & ultra | 3.25 | 1.50 |
| | | *Nos. 68-74 (7)* | 8.15 | 4.90 |

Bars cancel the old value on Nos. 68, 69, 73, 74.

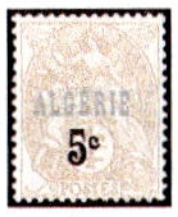

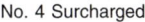

No. 4 Surcharged

**1927**

| | | | | |
|---|---|---|---|---|
| **75** | A16 | 5c on 4c yellow brown | .40 | .40 |
| *a.* | | Blue surcharge | 1,250. | *1,400.* |

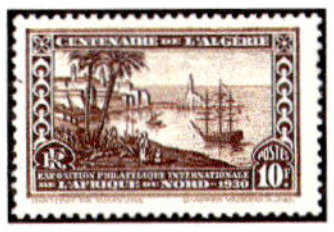

Bay of Algiers — A5

**1930, May 4** **Engr.** ***Perf. 12½***

| | | | | |
|---|---|---|---|---|
| **78** | A5 | 10fr red brown | 21.00 | 21.00 |
| *a.* | | Imperf., pair | 150.00 | |

Cent. of Algeria and for Intl. Phil. Exhib. of North Africa, May, 1930.

One example of No. 78 was sold with each 10fr admission.

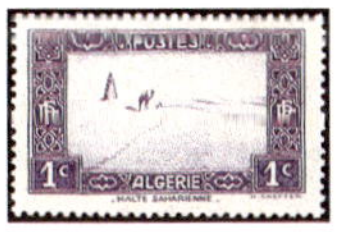

Travel across the Sahara — A6

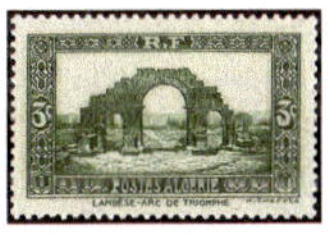

Arch of Triumph, Lambese — A7

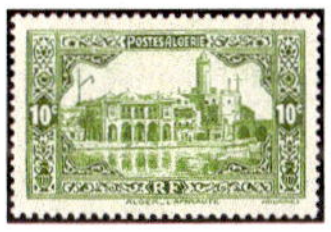

Admiralty Building, Algiers — A8

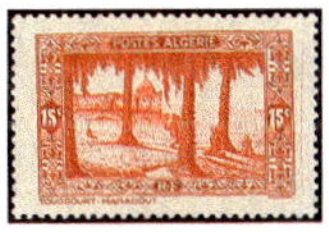

Kings' Tombs near Touggourt — A9

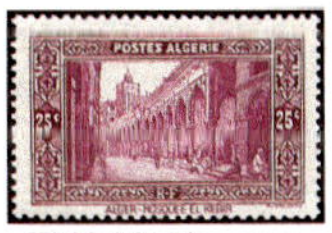

El-Kebir Mosque, Algiers A10

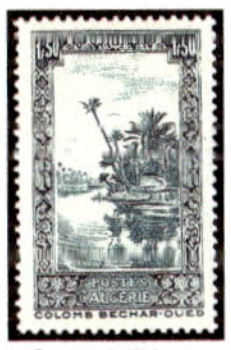

Oued River at Colomb-Bechar A11

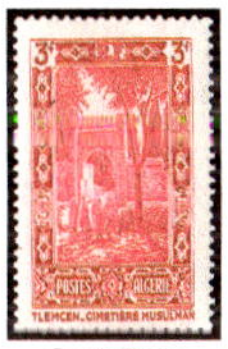

Sidi Bon Medine Cemetery at Tlemcen A13

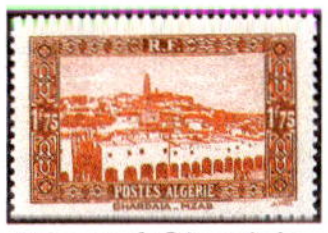

View of Ghardaia A12

**1936-41** **Engr.** ***Perf. 13***

| | | | | |
|---|---|---|---|---|
| **79** | A6 | 1c ultra | .25 | .40 |
| **80** | A11 | 2c dk violet | .25 | .40 |
| **81** | A7 | 3c dk blue grn | .25 | .40 |
| **82** | A12 | 5c red violet | .40 | .25 |
| **83** | A8 | 10c emerald | .25 | .40 |
| **84** | A9 | 15c red | .25 | .40 |
| **85** | A13 | 20c dk blue grn | .40 | .40 |
| **86** | A10 | 25c rose vio | 1.20 | .80 |
| **87** | A12 | 30c yellow grn | .80 | .40 |
| **88** | A9 | 40c brown vio | .40 | .40 |
| **89** | A13 | 45c deep ultra | 2.00 | 1.20 |
| | | On cover | | 4.50 |
| **90** | A8 | 50c red | 1.20 | .40 |
| **91** | A6 | 65c red brn | 8.00 | 4.00 |
| **92** | A6 | 65c rose car ('37) | .80 | .80 |
| **93** | A6 | 70c red brn ('39) | .40 | .40 |
| **94** | A11 | 75c slate bl | .80 | .40 |
| **95** | A7 | 90c henna brn | 2.40 | 1.60 |
| **96** | A10 | 1fr brown | .80 | .40 |
| **97** | A8 | 1.25fr lt violet | 1.20 | .80 |
| **98** | A8 | 1.25fr car rose ('39) | .80 | .40 |
| **99** | A11 | 1.50fr turq blue | 2.40 | .80 |
| **99A** | A11 | 1.50fr rose ('40) | .80 | .80 |
| **100** | A12 | 1.75fr henna brn | .40 | .40 |
| **101** | A7 | 2fr dk brown | .80 | .40 |
| **102** | A6 | 2.25fr yellow grn | 20.00 | 13.50 |
| **103** | A12 | 2.50fr dk ultra ('41) | .80 | .80 |
| **104** | A13 | 3fr magenta | 1.20 | .80 |
| **105** | A10 | 3.50fr pck blue | 6.50 | 4.00 |
| **106** | A8 | 5fr slate blue | 1.60 | .80 |
| **107** | A11 | 10fr henna brn | 1.20 | .80 |
| **108** | A9 | 20fr turq blue | 1.60 | 1.20 |
| | | *Nos. 79-108 (31)* | 60.15 | 38.95 |

See Nos. 124-125, 162.

Nos. 82 and 100 with surcharge "E. F. M. 30frs" (Emergency Field Message) were used in 1943 to pay cable tolls for US and Canadian servicemen.

For other surcharges see Nos. 122, B27.

**Catalogue values for unused stamps in this section, from this point to the end of the section, are for Never Hinged items.**

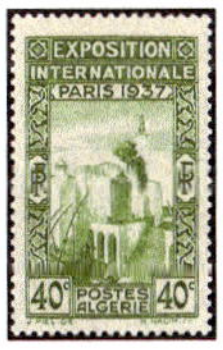

Algerian Pavilion — A14

**1937** ***Perf. 13***

| | | | | |
|---|---|---|---|---|
| **109** | A14 | 40c brt green | 2.00 | 1.20 |
| **110** | A14 | 50c rose carmine | 2.00 | .80 |
| **111** | A14 | 1.50fr blue | 2.75 | 1.20 |
| **112** | A14 | 1.75fr brown black | 2.75 | 1.60 |
| | | *Nos. 109-112 (4)* | 9.50 | 4.80 |

Paris International Exposition.

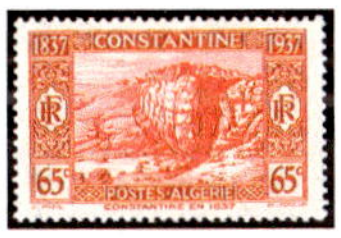

Constantine in 1837 — A15

**1937**

| | | | | |
|---|---|---|---|---|
| **113** | A15 | 65c deep rose | 1.20 | .80 |
| **114** | A15 | 1fr brown | 12.00 | 1.60 |
| **115** | A15 | 1.75fr blue green | 1.60 | .80 |
| **116** | A15 | 2.15fr red violet | 1.60 | .80 |
| | | *Nos. 113-116 (4)* | 16.40 | 4.00 |

Taking of Constantine by the French, cent.

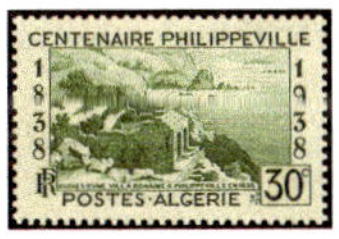

Ruins of a Roman Villa — A16

**1938**

| | | | | |
|---|---|---|---|---|
| **117** | A16 | 30c green | 2.00 | .80 |
| **118** | A16 | 65c ultra | .80 | .80 |
| **119** | A16 | 75c rose violet | 2.00 | .80 |
| **120** | A16 | 3fr carmine rose | 5.50 | 4.00 |
| **121** | A16 | 5fr yellow brown | 8.00 | 5.50 |
| | | *Nos. 117-121 (5)* | 18.30 | 11.90 |

Centenary of Philippeville.

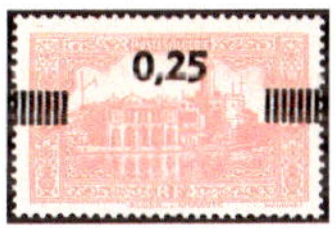

No. 90 Surcharged in Black

**1938**

| | | | | |
|---|---|---|---|---|
| **122** | A8 | 25c on 50c red | .80 | .40 |
| *a.* | | Double surcharge | 100.00 | 60.00 |
| *b.* | | Inverted surcharge | 72.50 | 47.50 |
| *c.* | | Pair, one without surcharge | 400.00 | |

**Types of 1936**
**Numerals of Value on Colorless Background**

**1939**

| | | | | |
|---|---|---|---|---|
| **124** | A7 | 90c henna brown | 1.20 | .40 |
| **125** | A10 | 2.25fr blue green | 1.20 | .80 |

For surcharge see No. B38.

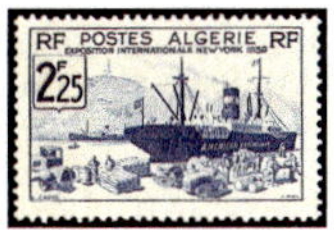

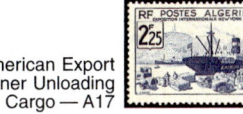

American Export Liner Unloading Cargo — A17

**1939**

| | | | | |
|---|---|---|---|---|
| **126** | A17 | 20c green | 4.00 | 1.60 |
| **127** | A17 | 40c red violet | 4.00 | 1.60 |
| **128** | A17 | 90c brown black | 2.40 | .80 |
| **129** | A17 | 1.25fr rose | 9.50 | 4.00 |
| **130** | A17 | 2.25fr ultra | 4.00 | 2.40 |
| | | *Nos. 126-130 (5)* | 23.90 | 10.40 |

New York World's Fair.

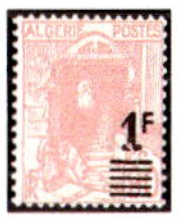

Type of 1926, Surcharged in Black

Two types of surcharge:
I — Bars 6mm
II — Bars 7mm

**1939-40** ***Perf. 14x13½***

| | | | | |
|---|---|---|---|---|
| **131** | A1 | 1fr on 90c crimson (I) | .80 | .40 |
| *a.* | | Booklet pane of 10 | — | |
| | | Complete booklet, 2 #131a | 625.00 | |
| *b.* | | Double surcharge (I) | 175.00 | |
| *c.* | | Inverted surcharge (I) | 87.50 | |
| *d.* | | Pair, one without surch. (I) | *1,800.* | |
| *e.* | | Type II ('40) | 8.00 | 1.60 |
| *f.* | | Inverted surcharge (II) | 95.00 | |
| *g.* | | Pair, one without surch. (II) | *1,800.* | |

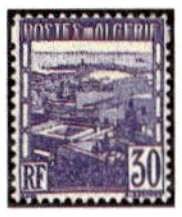

View of Algiers — A18

**1941** **Typo.**

| | | | | |
|---|---|---|---|---|
| **132** | A18 | 30c ultra | .50 | .30 |
| **133** | A18 | 70c sepia | .50 | .30 |
| **134** | A18 | 1fr carmine rose | .50 | .30 |
| | | *Nos. 132-134 (3)* | 1.50 | .90 |

See No. 163.

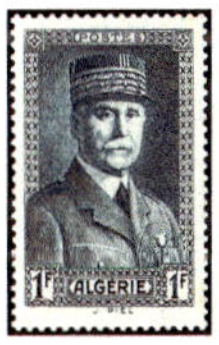

Marshal Pétain — A19

**1941** **Engr.** ***Perf. 13***

| | | | | |
|---|---|---|---|---|
| **135** | A19 | 1fr dark blue | .50 | .30 |

For stamp and type surcharged see Nos. B36-B37.

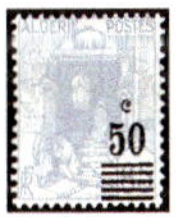

No. 53 Surcharged in Black

**1941** ***Perf. 14x13½***

| | | | | |
|---|---|---|---|---|
| **136** | A1 | 50c on 65c ultra | .70 | .25 |
| *a.* | | Booklet pane of 10 | — | |
| | | Complete booklet, 2 #136a | 120.00 | |
| *b.* | | Inverted surcharge | 95.00 | |
| *c.* | | Pair, one without surch. | 225.00 | |

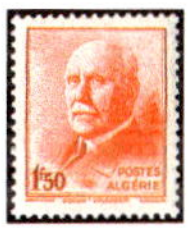

Marshal Pétain — A20

**1942** ***Perf. 14x13***

| | | | | |
|---|---|---|---|---|
| **137** | A20 | 1.50fr orange red | .30 | .25 |

Four other denominations of type A20 exist but were not placed in use. Values: 4fr, $1,300; 5fr, $1,100; 10fr, 20fr, each $600.

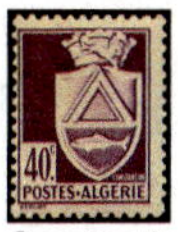

Constantine A21

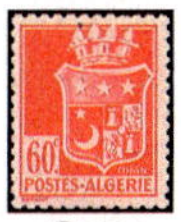

Oran A22

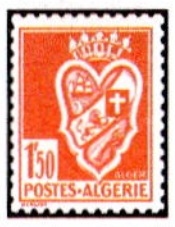

Arms of Algiers — A23

**Engraver's Name at Lower Left**

**1942-43** **Photo.** ***Perf. 12***

| | | | | |
|---|---|---|---|---|
| **138** | A21 | 40c dark vio ('43) | .70 | .40 |
| **139** | A22 | 60c rose ('43) | .55 | .25 |
| **140** | A21 | 1.20fr yel grn ('43) | .30 | .25 |
| **141** | A23 | 1.50fr car rose | .30 | .25 |
| **142** | A22 | 2fr sapphire | .80 | .25 |
| **143** | A21 | 2.40fr rose ('43) | .55 | .25 |
| **144** | A23 | 3fr sapphire | .95 | .25 |
| **145** | A21 | 4fr blue ('43) | .70 | .25 |
| **146** | A22 | 5fr yel grn ('43) | .65 | .30 |
| | | *Nos. 138-146 (9)* | 5.50 | 2.45 |

For type surcharged see No. 166.

No. 142 exists in green and violet. Value, each $60.

---

Imperforates

Nearly all of Algeria Nos. 138-285, B39-B96, C1-C12 and CB1-CB3 exist imperforate. See note after France No. 395.

---

**Without Engraver's Name**

**1942-45** **Typo.** ***Perf. 14x13½***

| | | | | |
|---|---|---|---|---|
| **147** | A23 | 10c dull brn vio ('45) | .30 | .25 |
| **148** | A22 | 30c dp bl grn ('45) | .30 | .25 |
| **149** | A21 | 40c dull brn vio ('45) | .30 | .25 |
| **150** | A22 | 60c rose ('45) | .30 | .25 |
| **151** | A21 | 70c deep bl ('45) | .30 | .25 |
| **152** | A23 | 80c dk bl grn ('43) | 1.25 | .90 |
| **153** | A21 | 1.20fr dp bl grn ('45) | .50 | .30 |
| **154** | A23 | 1.50fr brt rose ('43) | .30 | .25 |
| **155** | A22 | 2fr dp blue ('45) | .30 | .25 |
| **156** | A21 | 2.40fr rose ('45) | .80 | .65 |
| **157** | A23 | 3fr dp blue ('45) | .55 | .40 |
| **158** | A22 | 4.50fr brown vio | .30 | .25 |
| | | *Nos. 147-158 (12)* | 5.50 | 4.25 |

For surcharge see No. 190.

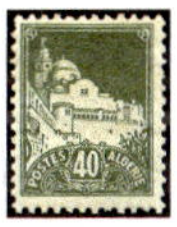

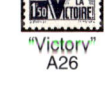

La Pêcherie Mosque — A24

**1942** **Typo.**

| | | | | |
|---|---|---|---|---|
| **159** | A24 | 50c dull red | .55 | .25 |
| *a.* | | Booklet pane of 10 | — | |
| | | Complete booklet, 2 #159a | 325.00 | |

**1942** **Photo.** ***Perf. 12***

| | | | | |
|---|---|---|---|---|
| **160** | A24 | 40c gray green | .55 | .25 |
| **161** | A24 | 50c red | .55 | .25 |

**Types of 1936-41, Without "RF"**

**1942** **Engr.** ***Perf. 13***

| | | | | |
|---|---|---|---|---|
| **162** | A11 | 1.50fr rose | .55 | .25 |

**Typo.** ***Perf. 14x13½***

| | | | | |
|---|---|---|---|---|
| **163** | A18 | 30c ultra | .55 | .25 |

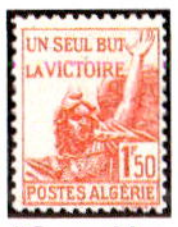

"One Aim Alone" A25

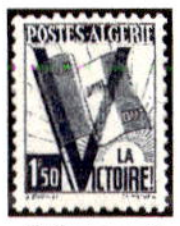

"Victory" A26

**1943** **Litho.** ***Perf. 12***

| | | | | |
|---|---|---|---|---|
| **164** | A25 | 1.50fr deep rose | .55 | .25 |
| **165** | A26 | 1.50fr dark blue | .55 | .25 |

**Type of 1942-3 Surcharged with New Value in Black**

**1943** **Photo.**

| | | | | |
|---|---|---|---|---|
| **166** | A22 | 2fr on 5fr red orange | .30 | .25 |
| *a.* | | Surcharge omitted | 325.00 | |

# ALGERIA

Summer Palace, Algiers — A27

**1944, Dec. 1**     Litho.
| 167 | A27 | 15fr slate | 2.00 | 1.75 |
| 168 | A27 | 20fr lt blue grn | 2.00 | .80 |
| 169 | A27 | 50fr dk carmine | 1.60 | .80 |
| 170 | A27 | 100fr deep blue | 4.00 | 2.50 |
| 171 | A27 | 200fr dull bis brn | 5.50 | 2.75 |
|  | | Nos. 167-171 (5) | 15.10 | 8.60 |

Marianne A28

Gallic Cock A29

**1944-45**
| 172 | A28 | 10c gray | .55 | .30 |
| 173 | A28 | 30c red violet | .30 | .25 |
| 174 | A29 | 40c rose car ('45) | .50 | .30 |
| 175 | A28 | 50c red | .50 | .30 |
| 176 | A28 | 80c emerald | .30 | .25 |
| 177 | A29 | 1fr green ('45) | .30 | .25 |
| 178 | A28 | 1.20fr rose lilac | .30 | .25 |
| 179 | A28 | 1.50fr dark blue | .30 | .25 |
| a. | | Double impression | 70.00 | |
| 180 | A28 | 2fr red | .30 | .25 |
| a. | | Double impression | 85.00 | |
| 181 | A29 | 2fr dk brown ('45) | .30 | .25 |
| 182 | A28 | 2.40fr rose red | .55 | .25 |
| 183 | A28 | 3fr purple | .55 | .40 |
| 184 | A29 | 4fr ultra ('45) | .30 | .25 |
| 185 | A28 | 4.50fr olive blk | .95 | .70 |
| 186 | A29 | 10fr grnsh blk ('45) | 1.90 | .95 |
|  | | Nos. 172-186 (15) | 7.90 | 5.20 |

No. 38 Surcharged in Black

**1944**     Perf. 14x13½
| 187 | A2 | 30c on 15c orange brn | 1.20 | .50 |
| a. | | Inverted surcharge | 70.00 | |

This stamp exists precanceled only. See note below No. 32.

No. 154 Surcharged

**1945**
| 190 | A23 | 50c on 1.50fr brt rose | .55 | .40 |
| a. | | Inverted surcharge | 72.50 | |

**Stamps of France, 1944, Overprinted Type "a" of 1924 in Black**

**1945-46**
| 191 | A99 | 80c yellow grn | .65 | .25 |
| 192 | A99 | 1fr grnsh blue | .50 | .25 |
| 193 | A99 | 1.20fr violet | .70 | .25 |
| 194 | A99 | 2fr violet brown | .90 | .25 |
| 195 | A99 | 2.40fr carmine rose | 1.20 | .40 |
| 196 | A99 | 3fr orange | 1.00 | .30 |
|  | | Nos. 191-196 (6) | 4.95 | 1.70 |

**Stamps of France, 1945-47, Overprinted in Black, Red or Carmine**

**1945-47**
| 197 | A145 | 40c lilac rose | .30 | .25 |
| 198 | A145 | 50c violet bl (R) | .30 | .25 |
| 199 | A146 | 60c brt ultra (R) | .95 | .25 |
| 200 | A146 | 1fr rose red ('47) | .50 | .25 |
| 201 | A146 | 1.50fr rose lilac ('47) | .50 | .25 |
| 202 | A147 | 2fr myr grn (R) ('46) | .30 | .25 |
| 203 | A147 | 3fr deep rose | .70 | .25 |
| 204 | A147 | 4.50fr ultra (C) ('47) | 2.00 | .25 |
| 205 | A147 | 5fr lt green ('46) | .50 | .25 |
| 206 | A147 | 10fr ultra | 1.75 | .50 |
|  | | Nos. 197-206 (10) | 7.80 | 2.75 |

France No. 383 Surcharged and Overprinted in Black

**1946**
| 207 | A99 | 2fr on 1.50fr henna brn | .50 | .25 |
| a. | | Without "2F" | 525.00 | |

**France Nos. 562 and 564 Overprinted in Carmine or Blue**

**1947**
| 208 | A153 | 10c dp ultra & blk (C) | .30 | .25 |
| 209 | A155 | 50c brown, yel & red (Bl) | .80 | .30 |

Constantine A30

Algiers A31

Arms of Oran — A32

**Perf. 14x13½**
**1947-49**     Unwmk.     Typo.
| 210 | A30 | 10c dk grn & brt red | .30 | .25 |
| 211 | A31 | 50c black & orange | .30 | .25 |
| 212 | A32 | 1fr ultra & yellow | .30 | .25 |
| 213 | A30 | 1.30fr blk & grnsh bl | 1.90 | 1.25 |
| 214 | A31 | 1.50fr pur & org yel | .50 | .25 |
| 215 | A32 | 2fr blk & brt grn | .30 | .25 |
| 216 | A30 | 2.50fr blk & brt red | 1.20 | .80 |
| 217 | A31 | 3fr vio brn & grn | .55 | .25 |
| 218 | A32 | 3.50fr lt grn & rose lil | .55 | .25 |
| 219 | A30 | 4fr dk brn & brt grn | .45 | .25 |
| 220 | A31 | 4.50fr ultra & scar | .55 | .25 |
| 221 | A31 | 5fr blk & grnsh bl | .30 | .25 |
| 222 | A32 | 6fr brown & scarlet | 1.00 | .30 |
| 223 | A32 | 8fr choc & ultra ('48) | .65 | .25 |
| 224 | A30 | 10fr car & choc ('48) | 1.00 | .40 |
| 225 | A31 | 15fr black & red ('49) | 1.10 | .25 |
|  | | Nos. 210-225 (16) | 10.95 | 5.75 |

See Nos. 274-280, 285.

Peoples of the World — A33

**1949, Oct. 24**     Engr.     Perf. 13
| 226 | A33 | 5fr green | 2.75 | 2.00 |
| 227 | A33 | 15fr scarlet | 3.50 | 2.00 |
| 228 | A33 | 25fr ultra | 6.00 | 5.25 |
|  | | Nos. 226-228 (3) | 12.25 | 9.25 |

75th anniv. of the UPU.

Grapes — A34

25fr, Dates. 40fr, Oranges and lemons.

**1950, Feb. 25**
| 229 | A34 | 20fr multicolored | 2.75 | .80 |
| 230 | A34 | 25fr multicolored | 3.25 | 1.25 |
| 231 | A34 | 40fr multicolored | 7.25 | 1.60 |
|  | | Nos. 229-231 (3) | 13.25 | 3.65 |

Apollo of Cherchell — A35

Designs: 12fr, 18fr, Isis statue, Cherchell. 15fr, 20fr, Child with eagle.

**1952**     Unwmk.     Perf. 14x13
| 240 | A35 | 10fr gray black | .65 | .25 |
| 241 | A35 | 12fr orange brn | 1.25 | .40 |
| 242 | A35 | 15fr deep blue | 1.10 | .25 |
| 243 | A35 | 18fr rose red | 1.10 | .40 |
| 244 | A35 | 20fr deep green | 1.60 | .25 |
| 245 | A35 | 30fr deep blue | 1.90 | .95 |
|  | | Nos. 240-245 (6) | 7.60 | 2.50 |

War Memorial, Algiers — A38

**1952, Apr. 11**
| 246 | A38 | 12fr dark green | 2.00 | .80 |

Issued to honor the French Africa Army.

Fossilized Nautilus A39

Phonolite Dike A40

**1952, Aug. 11**
| 247 | A39 | 15fr brt crimson | 6.50 | 2.75 |
| 248 | A40 | 30fr deep ultra | 3.50 | 1.60 |

19th Intl. Geological Cong., Algiers, 9/8-15.

French and Algerian Soldiers and Camel — A41

**1952, Nov. 30**
| 249 | A41 | 12fr chestnut brown | 2.50 | 1.75 |

50th anniv. of the establishment of the Sahara Companies.

Eugène Millon A42

François C. Maillot A43

Portrait: 50fr, Alphonse Laveran.

**Unwmk.**
**1954, Jan. 4**     Engr.     Perf. 13
| 250 | A42 | 25fr dk grn & choc | 2.00 | .80 |
| 251 | A43 | 40fr org brn & brn car | 3.00 | 1.20 |
| 252 | A42 | 50fr ultra & indigo | 3.00 | .80 |
|  | | Nos. 250-252 (3) | 8.00 | 2.80 |

Military Health Service.

Oranges — A44

**1954, May 8**
| 253 | A44 | 15fr indigo & blue | 2.00 | 1.20 |

3rd Intl. Cong. on Agronomy, Algiers, 1954.

**Type of France, 1954 Overprinted type "a" in Black**
**Unwmk.**
**1954, June 6**     Engr.     Perf. 13
| 254 | A240 | 15fr rose carmine | 2.00 | 1.20 |

Liberation of France, 10th anniversary.

Darguinah Hydroelectric Works — A45

**1954, June 19**
| 255 | A45 | 15fr lilac rose | 1.60 | 1.20 |

Opening of Darguinah hydroelectric works.

Patio of Bardo Museum — A46

**1954**     Typo.     Perf. 14x13½
| 257 | A46 | 12fr red brn & brn org | .80 | .30 |
| 258 | A46 | 15fr dk blue & blue | .70 | .25 |

See Nos. 267-271.

**Type of France, 1954, Overprinted type "a" in Carmine**
**1954**     Engr.     Perf. 13
| 260 | A247 | 12fr dark green | 2.00 | 1.00 |

150th anniv. of the 1st Legion of Honor awards at Camp de Boulogne.

St. Augustine — A47

**1954, Nov. 11**
| 261 | A47 | 15fr chocolate | 1.60 | 1.25 |

1600th anniv. of the birth of St. Augustine.

Aesculapius Statue and El Kattar Hospital, Algiers — A48

**1955, Apr. 3**     Unwmk.     Perf. 13
| 262 | A48 | 15fr red | 1.60 | .80 |

Issued to publicize the 30th French Congress of Medicine, Algiers, April 3-6, 1955.

Chenua Mountain and View of Tipasa — A49

**1955, May 31**
| 263 | A49 | 50fr brown carmine | 1.50 | .95 |

2000th anniv. of the founding of Tipasa.

**Type of France, 1955 Overprinted type "a" in Red**
**1955, June 13**
| 264 | A251 | 30fr deep ultra | 2.00 | 1.20 |

Rotary Intl., 50th anniv.

Marianne — A50

**Perf. 14x13½**
**1955, Oct. 3**     Typo.     Unwmk.
| 265 | A50 | 15fr carmine | .80 | .25 |

See No. 284.

# ALGERIA

Great Kabylia Mountains — A51

**1955, Dec. 17**  Engr.  Perf. 13
266  A51  100fr indigo & ultra  6.50  .80

**Bardo Type of 1954, "Postes" and "Algerie" in White**
Perf. 14x13½
**1955-57**  Unwmk.  Typo.
267  A46  10fr dk brn & lt brn  .80  .25
268  A46  12fr red brn & brn org ('56)  .40  .25
269  A46  18fr crimson & ver ('57)  1.00  .30
270  A46  20fr grn & yel grn ('57)  .90  .50
271  A46  25fr purple & brt purple  1.00  .25
Nos. 267-271 (5)  4.10  1.55

Marshal Franchet d'Esperey — A52

**1956, May 25**  Engr.  Perf. 13
272  A52  15fr sapphire & indigo  2.00  1.20
Birth cent. of Marshal Franchet d'Esperey.

Marshal Jacques Leclerc — A53

**1956, Nov. 29**
273  A53  15fr red brown & sepia  2.00  1.60
Death of Marshal Leclerc.
For design surcharged see No. B90.

**Type of 1947-49 and**

Arms of Bône — A54

Arms: 2fr, Tizi-Quzou. 3fr, Mostaganem. 5fr, Tlemcen. 10fr, Setif. 12fr, Orleansville.

**1956-58**  Typo.  Perf. 14x13½
274  A54  1fr green & ver  .30  .25
275  A54  2fr ver & ultra ('58)  1.00  .55
276  A54  3fr ultra & emer ('58)  1.40  .30
277  A54  5fr ultra & yellow  .80  .25
278  A31  6fr red & grn ('57)  1.40  .80
279  A54  10fr dp cl & emer ('58)  1.50  .90
280  A54  12fr ultra & red ('58)  1.75  .90
Nos. 274-280 (7)  8.15  3.95
Nos. 275 and 279 are inscribed "Republique Francaise." See No. 285.

View of Oran — A55

**1956-58**  Engr.  Perf. 13
281  A55  30fr dull purple  1.20  .40
282  A55  35fr car rose ('58)  2.40  .80

Electric Train Crossing Bridge — A56

**1957, Mar. 25**
283  A56  40fr dk blue grn & emer  2.40  .55

**Marianne Type of 1955 Inscribed "Algerie" Vertically**
Perf. 14x13½
**1957, Dec. 2**  Typo.  Unwmk.
284  A50  20fr ultra  .95  .25

**Arms Type of 1947-49 Inscribed "Republique Francaise"**
**1958, July**
285  A31  6fr red & green  37.50  28.00

## Independent State
France Nos. 939, 968, 945-946 & 1013 Ovptd. in Black or Red

No. 286

No. 288

No. 289

No. 290

**1962, July 2**
**Typographed Overprint**
286  A336  10c brt green  .80  .45
287  A349  25c lake & gray  .80  .45
288  A339  45c brt vio & ol gray  7.50  3.75
289  A330  50c ol grn & lt claret  7.50  3.75
290  A372  1fr dk bl, sl & bis  4.75  1.75
Nos. 286-290 (5)  21.35  10.15

**Handstamped Overprint**
286a  A336  10c bright green  1.00  .45
287a  A349  25c lake & gray  1.00  .45
288a  A339  45c brt vio & ol gray  30.00  22.50
289a  A339  50c sl grn & lt claret  30.00  22.50
290a  A372  1fr dk bl, sl & bis  7.00  3.00
Nos. 286a-290a (5)  69.00  48.90

Post offices were authorized to overprint their stock of these 5 French stamps. The size of the letters was specified as 3x6mm each, but various sizes were used. The post offices had permission to make their own rubber stamps. Typography, pen or pencil were also used. Many types exist. Colors of handstamped overprints include black, red, blue, violet. "EA" stands for Etat Algerien.

Mosque, Tlemcen A57

Roman Gates of Lodi, Médéa A58

5c, Kerrata Gorge. 10c, Dam at Foum el Gherza. 95c, Oil field, Hassi Messaoud.

**1962, Nov. 1**  Engr.  Perf. 13
291  A57  5c Prus grn, grn & choc  .25  .25
292  A58  10c ol blk & dk bl  .25  .25
293  A57  25c sl grn, brn & ver  .50  .25
294  A57  95c dk bl, blk & bis  2.75  .95
295  A58  1fr green & blk  2.40  1.50
Nos. 291-295 (5)  6.15  3.20

The designs of Nos. 291-295 are similar to French issues of 1959-61 with "Republique Algerienne" replacing "Republique Francaise."

Flag, Rifle, Olive Branch — A59

Design: Nos. 300-303, Broken chain, dove, and rifle added to design A59.

**1963, Jan. 6**  Litho.  Perf. 12½
**Flag in Green and Red**
296  A59  5c bister brown  .25  .25
297  A59  10c blue  .25  .25
298  A59  25c vermilion  1.75  .75
299  A59  95c violet  1.35  .75
300  A59  1fr green  1.20  .35
301  A59  2fr brown  3.00  .75
302  A59  5fr lilac  5.25  3.00
303  A59  10fr gray  20.00  14.00
Nos. 296-303 (8)  33.05  19.60
Nos. 296-299 for the successful revolution and Nos. 300-303 the return of peace.

Men of Various Races, Wheat Emblem and Globe — A60

**1963, Mar. 21**  Engr.  Perf. 13
304  A60  25c maroon, dl grn & yel  .65  .25
FAO "Freedom from Hunger" campaign.

Map of Algeria and Emblems — A61

**1963, July 5**  Unwmk.  Perf. 13
305  A61  25c bl, dk brn, grn & red  .65  .25
1st anniv. of Algeria's independence.

Physicians from 13th Century Manuscript — A62

**1963, July 29**  Engr.
306  A62  25c brn red, grn & bis  2.00  .55
2nd Congress of the Union of Arab physicians.

Orange and Blossom — A63

**1963**  Perf. 14x13
307  A63  8c gray grn & org  .25  .25
308  A63  20c slate & org red  .25  .25
309  A63  40c grnsh bl & org  .70  .30
310  A63  55c ol grn & org red  1.00  .55
Nos. 307-310 (4)  2.20  1.35
Nos. 307-310 issued precanceled only. See note below No. 32.

Scales and Scroll — A64

**1963, Oct. 13**  Unwmk.  Perf. 13
311  A64  25c blk, grn & rose red  .65  .35
Issued to honor the new constitution.

Guerrillas — A65

**1963, Nov. 1**
312  A65  25c dk brn, yel grn & car  .65  .35
9th anniversary of Algerian revolution.

Centenary Emblem — A66

**1963, Dec. 8**  Photo.  Perf. 12
313  A66  25c lt vio bl, yel & dk red  .90  .60
Centenary of International Red Cross.

UNESCO Emblem, Scales and Globe — A67

**1963, Dec. 16**  Unwmk.  Perf. 12
314  A67  25c lt blue & blk  .65  .25
15th anniv. of the Universal Declaration of Human Rights.

Workers — A68

**1964, May 1**  Engr.  Perf. 13
315  A68  50c dull red, red org & bl  1.25  .40
Issued for the Labor Festival.

Map of Africa and Flags — A69

**1964, May 25**  Unwmk.  Perf. 13
316  A69  45c blue, orange & car  1.00  .35
Africa Day on the 1st anniv. of the Addis Ababa charter on African unity.

Ramses II Battling the Hittites (from Abu Simbel) A70

Design: 30c, Two statues of Ramses II.

**1964, June 28**  Engr.  Perf. 13
317  A70  20c choc, red & vio bl  .90  .40
318  A70  30c brn, red & grnsh bl  1.05  .55
UNESCO world campaign to save historic monuments in Nubia.

A71

5c, 25c, 85c, Tractors. 10c, 30c, 65c, Men working with lathe. 12c, 15c, 45c, Electronics center & atom symbol. 20c, 50c, 95c, Draftsman & bricklayer.

**1964-65**  Typo.  Perf. 14x13½
319  A71  5c red lilac  .25  .25
320  A71  10c brown  .25  .25
321  A71  12c emerald ('65)  .45  .25
322  A71  15c dk blue ('65)  .30  .25
323  A71  20c yellow  .45  .25
324  A71  25c red  .45  .25
325  A71  30c purple ('65)  .35  .25
326  A71  45c rose car  .65  .25
327  A71  50c ultra  .65  .25
328  A71  65c orange  .70  .25
329  A71  85c green  1.40  .25
330  A71  95c car rose  1.75  .35
Nos. 319-330 (12)  7.65  3.10
For surcharges see Nos. 389, 424.

A72

**1964, Aug. 30**  Engr.  Perf. 13
331  A72  85c Communications tower  1.90  .75
Inauguration of the Hertzian cable telephone line Algiers-Annaba.

# ALGERIA

Industrial & Agricultural Symbols — A73

**1964, Sept. 26  Typo.  Perf. 13½x14**
332 A73 25c lt ultra, yel & red   .60  1.25
1st Intl. Fair at Algiers, Sept. 26-Oct. 11.

Gas Flames and Pipes — A74

**1964, Sept. 27**
333 A74 30c violet, blue & yel   .85  .50
Arzew natural gas liquification plant opening.

Planting Trees — A75

**1964, Nov. 29   Unwmk.**
334 A75 25c slate grn, yel & car   .50  .25
National reforestation campaign.

Children and UNICEF Emblem — A76

**1964, Dec. 13   Perf. 13½x14**
335 A76 15c pink, vio bl & lt grn   .50  .25
Issued for Children's Day.

Decorated Camel Saddle — A77

**1965, May 29  Typo.  Perf. 13½x14**
336 A77 20c blk, red, emer & brn   .70  .25
Handicrafts of Sahara.

ICY Emblem — A78

**1965, Aug. 29  Engr.  Perf. 13**
337 A78 30c blk, mar & bl grn   .90  .40
338 A78 60c blk, brt bl & bl grn  1.25  .50
International Cooperation Year, 1965.

ITU Emblem — A79

**1965, Sept. 19**
339 A79 60c purple, emer & buff   .90  .50
340 A79 95c dk brn, mar & buff  1.25  .55
Cent. of the ITU.

Musicians — A80

Miniatures by Mohammed Racim: 60c, Two female musicians. 5d, Algerian princess and antelope.

**1965, Dec. 27  Photo.  Perf. 11½**
341 A80 30c multicolored   1.75  .65
342 A80 60c multicolored   2.50  1.25
343 A80 5d multicolored  14.00  7.50
 Nos. 341-343 (3)  18.25  9.40

Bulls, Painted in 6000 B.C. — A81

Wall Paintings from Tassili-N-Ajjer, c. 6000 B.C.: No. 345, Shepherd, vert. 2d, Fleeing ostriches. 3d, Two girls, vert.

**1966, Jan. 29  Photo.  Perf. 11½**
344 A81 1d brn, bis & red brn   4.50  2.75
345 A81 1d gray, blk, ocher & dk brn   4.50  2.75
346 A81 2d brn, ocher & red brn  10.00  4.75
347 A81 3d buff, blk, ocher & brn red  10.00  4.75
 Nos. 344-347 (4)  29.00  15.00
See Nos. 365-368.

Pottery — A82

Handicrafts from Great Kabylia: 50c, Weaving, woman at loom, horiz. 70c, Jewelry.

**1966, Feb. 26  Engr.  Perf. 13**
348 A82 40c Prus bl, brn red & blk   .50  .35
349 A82 50c dk red, ol & ocher   .75  .40
350 A82 70c vio bl, blk & red  1.25  .55
 Nos. 348-350 (3)  2.50  1.30

Weather Balloon, Compass Rose and Anemometer A83

**1966, Mar. 23  Engr.  Unwmk.**
351 A83 1d claret, brt bl & grn  1.25  .50
World Meteorological Day.

Book, Grain, Cogwheel and UNESCO Emblem — A84

Design: 60c, Grain, cogwheel, book and UNESCO emblem.

**1966, May 2  Typo.  Perf. 13x14**
352 A84 30c yellow bis & blk   .45  .25
353 A84 60c dk red, gray & blk   .70  .40
Literacy as basis for development.

WHO Headquarters, Geneva — A85

**1966, May 30  Engr.  Perf. 13**
354 A85 30c multicolored   .45  .35
355 A85 60c multicolored   .85  .40
Inauguration of the WHO Headquarters, Geneva.

Algerian Scout Emblem A86

Arab Jamboree Emblem A87

**1966, July 23  Photo.  Perf. 12x12½**
356 A86 30c multicolored   1.25  .60
357 A87 1d multicolored   1.75  .65
No. 356 commemorates the 30th anniv. of the Algerian Mohammedan Boy Scouts. No. 357, the 7th Arab Boy Scout Jamboree, held at Good Daim, Libya, Aug. 12.

Map of Palestine and Victims — A88

**1966, Sept. 26  Typo.  Perf. 10½**
358 A88 30c red & black   .60  .25
Deir Yassin Massacre, Apr. 9, 1948.

Abd-el-Kader — A89

**1966, Nov. 2  Photo.  Perf. 11½**
359 A89 30c multicolored   .25  .25
360 A89 95c multicolored  1.05  .40
Transfer from Damascus to Algiers of the ashes of Abd-el-Kader (1807?-1883), Emir of Mascara. See Nos. 382-387.

UNESCO Emblem — A90

**1966, Nov. 19  Typo.  Perf. 10½**
361 A90 1d multicolored  1.05  .40
20th anniv. of UNESCO.

Horseman — A91

Miniatures by Mohammed Racim: 1.50d, Woman at her toilette. 2d, The pirate Barbarossa in front of the Admiralty.

**1966, Dec. 17  Photo.  Perf. 11½**
**Granite Paper**
362 A91 1d multicolored   3.25  1.50
363 A91 1.50d multicolored  5.25  1.75
364 A91 2d multicolored   6.50  3.50
 Nos. 362-364 (3)  15.00  6.75

**Wall Paintings Type of 1966**
Wall Paintings from Tassili-N-Ajjer, c. 6000 B.C.: 1d, Cow. No. 366, Antelope. No. 367, Archers. 3d, Warrior, vert.

**1967, Jan. 28  Photo.  Perf. 11½**
365 A81 1d brn, bis & dl vio   3.25  1.90
366 A81 2d brn, ocher & red   5.00  3.75
367 A81 2d brn, yel & red brn  5.00  3.75
368 A81 3d blk, gray, yel & red brn  7.00  5.25
 Nos. 365-368 (4)  20.25  14.65

Bardo Museum A92

La Kalaa Minaret A93

Design: 1.30d, Ruins at Sedrata.

**1967, Feb. 27  Photo.  Perf. 13**
369 A92 35c multicolored   .40  .25
370 A93 95c multicolored   .90  .50
371 A92 1.30d multicolored  1.50  .65
 Nos. 369-371 (3)  2.80  1.40

Moretti and International Tourist Year Emblem — A94

Design: 70c, Tuareg riding camel, Tassili, and Tourist Year Emblem, vert.

**1967, Apr. 29  Litho.  Perf. 14**
372 A94 40c multi   .70  .70
373 A94 70c multi  1.40  .60
International Tourist Year, 1967.

Spiny-tailed Agamid — A95

Designs: 20c, Ostrich, vert. 40c, Slender-horned gazelle, vert. 70c, Fennec.

**1967, June 24  Photo.  Perf. 11½**
374 A95 5c bister & blk   .70  .70
375 A95 20c ocher, blk & pink  1.40  .70
376 A95 40c ol bis, blk & red brn  2.10  1.00
377 A95 70c gray, blk & dp org  2.75  1.75
 Nos. 374-377 (4)  6.95  4.15

Dancers — A96

**Typographed and Engraved**
**1967, July 4   Perf. 10½**
378 A96 50c gray vio, yel & blk   .90  .40
National Youth Festival.

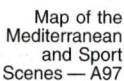

Map of the Mediterranean and Sport Scenes — A97

**1967, Sept. 2  Typo.  Perf. 10½**
379 A97 30c black, red & blue   .65  .40
Issued to publicize the 5th Mediterranean Games, Tunis, Sept. 8-17.

# ALGERIA

Skiers
A98

Olympic Emblem
and Sports
A99

**1967, Oct. 21**  Engr.  *Perf. 13*
380 A98 30c brt blue & ultra .90 .40
381 A99 95c brn org, pur & brt grn 1.65 .75
Issued to publicize the 10th Winter Olympic Games, Grenoble, Feb. 6-18, 1968.

### Abd-el-Kader Type of 1966
Lithographed, Photogravure
**1967-71**  *Perf. 13½, 11½*
382 A89 5c dull pur ('68) .25 .25
383 A89 10c green .25 .25
383A A89 10c sl grn (litho., '69) .25 .25
383B A89 25c orange ('71) .30 .25
384 A89 30c black ('68) .35 .25
385 A89 30c lt violet ('68) .45 .25
386 A89 50c rose claret .75 .25
387 A89 70c violet blue .85 .30
Nos. 382-387 (8) 3.45 2.05

No. 383, 50c and 70c, issued Nov. 13, 1967, are on granite paper, photo. The 5c, No.383A, 25c and 30c are litho., perf. 13½; others, perf. 11½.

The three 1967 stamps (No. 383, 50c, 70c) have numerals thin, narrow and close together; the Arabic inscription at lower right is 2mm high. The 5 litho. stamps are redrawn, with numerals thicker and spaced more widely; Arabic at lower right 3mm high.

Boy Scouts
Holding Jamboree
Emblem — A100

**1967, Dec. 23**  Engr.  *Perf. 13*
388 A100 1d multicolored 1.90 .70
12th Boy Scout World Jamboree, Farragut State Park, Idaho, Aug. 1-9.

### No. 324 Surcharged
**1967**  Typo.  *Perf. 14x13½*
389 A71 30c on 25c red .65 .25

Mandolin — A101

**1968, Feb. 17**  Photo.  *Perf. 12½x13*
390 A101 30c shown .55 .25
391 A101 40c Lute .75 .40
392 A101 1.30d Rebec 2.75 1.10
Nos. 390-392 (3) 4.05 1.75

Nememcha
Rug — A102

Algerian Rugs: 70c, Guergour. 95c, Djebel-Amour. 1.30d, Kalaa.

**1968, Apr. 13**  Photo.  *Perf. 11½*
393 A102 30c multi .95 .60
394 A102 70c multi 1.75 .95
395 A102 95c multi 3.00 2.00
396 A102 1.30d multi 3.50 1.50
Nos. 393-396 (4) 9.20 5.05

Human Rights
Flame — A103

**1968, May 18**  Typo.  *Perf. 10½*
397 A103 40c blue, red & yel .65 .80
International Human Rights Year, 1968.

WHO
Emblem — A104

**1968, May 18**
398 A104 70c blk, lt bl & yel .80 .40
20th anniv. of the WHO.

Welder — A105

**1968, June 15**  Engr.  *Perf. 13*
399 A105 30c gray, brn & ultra .45 .25
Algerian emigration to Europe.

Athletes, Olympic
Flame and
Rings — A106

50c, Soccer player. 1d, Mexican pyramid, emblem, Olympic flame, rings & athletes, horiz.

*Perf. 12½x13, 13x12½*
**1968, July 4**  Photo.
400 A106 30c green, red & yel .65 .50
401 A106 50c rose car & multi .95 .60
402 A106 1d dk grn, org, brn & red 1.60 .95
Nos. 400-402 (3) 3.20 2.05
19th Olympic Games, Mexico City, 10/12-27.

Scouts and
Emblem — A107

**1968, July 4**  *Perf. 13*
403 A107 30c multicolored .65 .25
8th Arab Boy Scout Jamboree, Algiers, 1968.

Barbary Sheep — A108

**1968, Oct. 19**  Photo.  *Perf. 11½*
404 A108 40c shown .90 .40
405 A108 1d Red deer 2.10 .65

Hunting Scenes,
Djemila — A109

Design: 95c, Neptune's chariot, Timgad, horiz. Both designs are from Roman mosaics.

*Perf. 12½x13, 13x12½*
**1968, Nov. 23**  Photo.
406 A109 40c gray & multi .60 .25
407 A109 95c gray & multi 1.35 .55

"Industry" — A110

Designs: No. 409, Miner with drill. 95c, "Energy" (circle and rays).

**1968, Dec. 14**  Photo.  *Perf. 11½*
408 A110 30c dp orange & sil .45 .25
409 A110 30c brown & multi .45 .25
410 A110 95c silver, red & blk 1.25 .40
Nos. 408-410 (3) 2.15 .90
Issued to publicize industrial development.

Opuntia Ficus
Indica — A111

Flowers: 40c, Carnations. 70c, Roses. 95c, Bird-of-paradise flower.

**1969, Jan.**  Photo.  *Perf. 11½*
### Flowers in Natural Colors
411 A111 25c pink & blk .65 .45
412 A111 40c yellow & blk 1.10 .60
413 A111 70c gray & blk 1.65 .75
414 A111 95c brt blue & blk 2.90 1.10
Nos. 411-414 (4) 6.30 2.90
See Nos. 496-499.

Irrigation Dam at
Djorf Torba-Oued
Guir — A112

Design: 1.50d, Truck on Highway No. 51 and camel caravan.

**1969, Feb. 22**  Photo.  *Perf. 11½*
415 A112 30c multi .55 .25
416 A112 1.50d multi 1.90 .75
Public works in the Sahara.

Mail
Coach — A113

**1969, Mar. 22**  Photo.  *Perf. 11½*
417 A113 1d multicolored 2.60 .75
Issued for Stamp Day, 1969.

Capitol,
Timgad — A114

1d, Septimius Temple, Djemila, horiz.

**1969, Apr. 5**  Photo.  *Perf. 13x12½*
418 A114 30c gray & multi .55 .25
419 A114 1d gray & multi 1.35 .50
Second Timgad Festival, Apr. 4-8.

ILO
Emblem — A115

**1969, May 24**  Photo.  *Perf. 11½*
420 A115 95c dp car, yel & blk 1.15 .45
50th anniv. of the ILO.

Arabian Saddle — A116

Algerian Handicrafts: 30c, Bookcase. 60c, Decorated copper plate.

**1969, June 28**  Photo.  *Perf. 12x12½*
### Granite Paper
421 A116 30c multicolored .45 .25
422 A116 60c multicolored .85 .35
423 A116 1d multicolored 1.50 .65
Nos. 421-423 (3) 2.80 1.25

No. 321 Surcharged

**1969**  Typo.  *Perf. 14x13½*
424 A71 20c on 12c emerald .50 .25

Pan-African Culture
Festival
Emblem — A117

**1969, July 19**  Photo.  *Perf. 12½*
425 A117 30c multicolored .60 .25
1st Pan-African Culture Festival, Algiers, 7/21-8/1.

African Development
Bank Emblem — A118

**1969, Aug. 23**  Typo.  *Perf. 10½*
426 A118 30c dull blue, yel & blk .60 .25
5th anniv. of the African Development Bank.

Astronauts and Landing
Module on
Moon — A119

*Perf. 12½x11½*
**1969, Aug. 23**  Photo.
427 A119 50c gold & multi 1.10 .50
Man's 1st landing on the moon, July 20, 1969. US astronauts Neil A. Armstrong and Col. Edwin E. Aldrin, Jr., with Lieut. Col. Michael Collins piloting Apollo 11.

Algerian
Women, by
Dinet — A120

1.50d, The Watchmen, by Etienne Dinet.

# ALGERIA

**1969, Nov. 29**   **Photo.**   **Perf. 14½**
428   A120   1d multi   2.00 .80
429   A120   1.50d multi   2.50 1.25

Mother and Child — A121

**1969, Dec. 27**   **Photo.**   **Perf. 11½**
430   A121   30c multicolored   .65 .40

Issued to promote mother and child protection.

Agricultural Growth Chart, Tractor and Dam — A122

30c, Transportation and development. 50c, Abstract symbols of industrialization.

**1970, Jan. 31**   **Photo.**   **Perf. 12½**
**Size: 37x23mm**
431   A122   25c dk brn, yel & org   .30 .25

**Litho.**   **Perf. 14**
**Size: 49x23mm**
432   A122   30c blue & multi   1.00 .25

**Photo.**   **Perf. 12½**
**Size: 37x23mm**
433   A122   50c rose lilac & blk   .60 .25
Nos. 431-433 (3)   1.90 .75

Four-Year Development Plan.

Old and New Mail Delivery — A123

**1970, Feb. 28**   **Photo.**   **Perf. 11½**
**Granite Paper**
434   A123   30c multicolored   .70 .25

Issued for Stamp Day.

Spiny Lobster — A124

Designs: 40c, Mollusks. 75c, Retepora cellulosa. 1d, Red coral.

**1970, Mar. 28**
435   A124   30c ocher & multi   .55 .25
436   A124   40c multicolored   .80 .40
437   A124   75c ultra & multi   1.35 .55
438   A124   1d lt blue & multi   2.10 .80
Nos. 435-438 (4)   4.80 2.00

Oranges, EXPO '70 Emblem — A125

Designs (EXPO '70 Emblem and): 60c, Algerian pavilion. 70c, Grapes.

**1970, Apr. 25**   **Photo.**   **Perf. 12½x12**
439   A125   30c lt blue, grn & org   .65 .30
440   A125   60c multicolored   .65 .40
441   A125   70c multicolored   1.30 .60
Nos. 439-441 (3)   2.60 1.25

EXPO '70 International Exhibition, Osaka, Japan, Mar. 15-Sept. 13, 1970.

Olives, Oil Bottle — A126

**1970, May 16**   **Photo.**   **Perf. 12½x12**
442   A126   1d yellow & multi   2.00 .80

Olive Year, 1969-1970.

Common Design Types pictured following the introduction.

**UPU Headquarters Issue**
**Common Design Type**
**1970, May 30**   **Perf. 13**
**Size: 36x26mm**
443   CD133   75c multicolored   1.10 .40

Saber — A127

Designs: 40c, Guns, 18th century, horiz. 1d, Pistol, 18th century, horiz.

**1970, June 27**   **Photo.**   **Perf. 12½**
444   A127   40c yellow & multi   1.10 .60
445   A127   75c red & multi   1.50 .80
446   A127   1d multicolored   2.10 1.10
Nos. 444-446 (3)   4.70 2.50

Map of Arab Countries and Arab League Flag — A128

**Typographed and Engraved**
**1970, July 25**   **Perf. 10½**
447   A128   30c grn, ocher & lt bl   .55 .25

25th anniversary of the Arab League.

Vladimir Lenin — A129

**1970, Aug. 29**   **Litho.**   **Perf. 11½x12**
448   A129   30c brown & buff   2.50 .40

Lenin (1870-1924), Russian communist leader.

Exhibition Hall and Algiers Fair Emblem A130

**1970, Sept. 11**   **Engr.**   **Perf. 14x13½**
449   A130   60c lt olive green   .65 .30

New Exhibition Hall for Algiers Intl. Fair.

Education Year Emblem, Blackboard, Atom Symbol — A131

Koran Page — A132

**1970, Oct. 24**   **Photo.**   **Perf. 14**
450   A131   30c pink, blk, gold & lt bl   .50 .25
451   A132   3d multicolored   4.00 1.75

Issued for International Education Year.

Great Mosque, Tlemcen — A133

Design: 40c, Ketchaoua Mosque, Algiers, vert. 1d, Mosque, Sidi-Okba, vert.

**1970-71**   **Litho.**   **Perf. 14**
456   A133   30c multicolored   .40 .25
457   A133   40c sepia & lemon ('71)   .50 .25
458   A133   1d multicolored   1.00 .40
Nos. 456-458 (3)   1.90 .90

Symbols of the Arts — A134

**1970, Dec. 26**   **Photo.**   **Perf. 13x12½**
459   A134   1d grn, lt grn & org   1.00 .50

Main Post Office, Algiers — A135

**1971, Jan. 23**   **Perf. 11½**
460   A135   30c multicolored   1.00 .40

Stamp Day, 1971.

Hurdling — A136

40c, Vaulting, vert. 75c, Basketball, vert.

**1971, Mar. 7**   **Photo.**   **Perf. 11½**
461   A136   20c lt blue & slate   .45 .25
462   A136   40c lt ol grn & slate   .55 .40
463   A136   75c salmon pink & slate   .95 .60
Nos. 461-463 (3)   1.95 1.25

Mediterranean Games, Izmir, Turkey, Oct. 1971.

Symbolic Head — A137

**1971, Mar. 27**   **Perf. 12½**
464   A137   60c car rose, blk & sil   .65 .30

Intl. year against racial discrimination.

Emblem and Technicians A138

**1971, Apr. 24**   **Photo.**   **Perf. 12½x12**
465   A138   70c cl, org & bluish blk   .75 .30

Founding of the Institute of Technology.

Woman from Aurès — A139

Regional Costumes: 70c, Man from Oran. 80c, Man from Algiers. 90c, Woman from Amour Mountains.

**1971, Oct. 16**   **Perf. 11½**
466   A139   50c gold & multi   1.10 .50
467   A139   70c gold & multi   1.40 .80
468   A139   80c gold & multi   1.75 .95
469   A139   90c gold & multi   2.10 1.00
Nos. 466-469 (4)   6.35 3.25

See Nos. 485-488, 534-537.

UNICEF Emblem, Birds and Plants — A140

**1971, Dec. 6**   **Perf. 11½**
470   A140   60c multicolored   .75 .50

25th anniv. of UNICEF.

Lion of St. Mark — A141

1.15d, Bridge of Sighs, Venice, vert.

**1972, Jan. 24**   **Litho.**   **Perf. 12**
471   A141   80c multi   1.10 .55
472   A141   1.15d multi   2.25 .95

UNESCO campaign to save Venice.

Javelin — A142

Designs: 25c, Bicycling, horiz. 60c, Wrestling. 1d, Gymnast on rings.

**1972, Mar. 25**   **Photo.**   **Perf. 11½**
473   A142   25c maroon & multi   .40 .25
474   A142   40c ocher & multi   .50 .25
475   A142   60c ultra & multi   1.10 .50
476   A142   1d rose & multi   1.50 .55
Nos. 473-476 (4)   3.50 1.55

20th Olympic Games, Munich, 8/26-9/11.

Book and Book Year Emblem — A143

**1972, Apr. 15**
477   A143   1.15d bister, brn & red   .80 .50

International Book Year 1972.

Mailmen — A144

**1972, Apr. 22**
478   A144   40c gray & multi   .70 .25

Stamp Day 1972.

# ALGERIA

Flowers — A145

**1972, May 27**
| 479 | A145 | 50c Jasmine | .65 | .40 |
|---|---|---|---|---|
| 480 | A145 | 60c Violets | .65 | .50 |
| 481 | A145 | 1.15d Tuberose | 1.75 | .65 |
| | | Nos. 479-481 (3) | 3.05 | 1.55 |

Olympic Stadium, Chéraga — A146

**1972, June 10**
| 482 | A146 | 50c gray, choc & grn | .70 | .40 |

New Day, Algerian Flag — A147

**1972, July 5**
| 483 | A147 | 1d green & multi | 1.15 | .60 |

10th anniversary of independence.

Festival Emblem — A148

**1972, July 5** Litho. Perf. 10½
| 484 | A148 | 40c grn, dk brn & org | .60 | .25 |

1st Arab Youth Festival, Algiers, July 5-11.

### Costume Type of 1971

Regional Costumes: 50c, Woman from Hoggar. 60c, Kabyle woman. 70c, Man from Mzab. 90c, Woman from Tlemcen.

**1972, Nov. 18** Photo. Perf. 11½
| 485 | A139 | 50c gold & multi | 1.40 | .65 |
| 486 | A139 | 60c gold & multi | 1.75 | .65 |
| 487 | A139 | 70c gold & multi | 1.90 | .95 |
| 488 | A139 | 90c gold & multi | 2.25 | 1.10 |
| | | Nos. 485-488 (4) | 7.30 | 3.35 |

Mailing a Letter — A149

**1973, Jan. 20** Photo. Perf. 11
| 489 | A149 | 40c orange & multi | .60 | .25 |

Stamp Day.

Ho Chi Minh, Map of Viet Nam — A150

**1973, Feb. 17** Photo. Perf. 11½
| 490 | A150 | 40c multicolored | .90 | .35 |

To honor the people of Viet Nam.

Embroidery from Annaba — A151

Designs: 60c, Tree of Life pattern from Algiers. 80c, Constantine embroidery.

**1973, Feb. 24**
| 491 | A151 | 40c gray & multi | .55 | .30 |
| 492 | A151 | 60c blue and multi | .80 | .50 |
| 493 | A151 | 80c dk red, gold & blk | 1.25 | .65 |
| | | Nos. 491-493 (3) | 2.60 | 1.45 |

Stylized Globe and Wheat — A152

**1973, Mar. 26** Photo. Perf. 11½
| 494 | A152 | 1.15d brt rose lil, org & grn | .80 | .35 |

World Food Program, 10th anniversary.

Soldier and Flag — A153

**1973, Apr. 23** Photo. Perf. 14x13½
| 495 | A153 | 40c multicolored | .60 | .25 |

Honoring the National Service.

### Flower Type of 1969

30c, Opuntia ficus indica. 40c, Roses. 1d, Carnations. 1.15d, Bird-of-paradise flower.

**1973, May 21** Photo. Perf. 11½
### Flowers in Natural Colors
| 496 | A111 | 30c pink & blk | .75 | .25 |
| 497 | A111 | 40c gray & blk | .90 | .40 |
| 498 | A111 | 1d yellow & multi | 2.00 | .65 |
| 499 | A111 | 1.15d multi | 3.25 | .95 |
| | | Nos. 496-499 (4) | 6.90 | 2.25 |

For overprints and surcharges see Nos. 518-519, 531.

OAU Emblem — A154

**1973, May 28** Photo. Perf. 12½x13
| 500 | A154 | 40c multicolored | .60 | .25 |

Org. for African Unity, 10th anniv.

Desert and Fruitful Land, Farmer and Family — A155

**1973, June 18** Perf. 11½
| 501 | A155 | 40c gold & multi | .70 | .25 |

Agricultural revolution.

Map of Africa, Scout Emblem — A156

**1973, July 16** Litho. Perf. 10½
| 502 | A156 | 80c purple | .80 | .40 |

24th Boy Scout World Conference (1st in Africa), Nairobi, Kenya, July 16-21.

Algerian PTT Emblem — A157

**1973, Aug. 6** Perf. 14
| 503 | A157 | 40c blue & orange | .60 | .25 |

Adoption of new emblem for Post, Telegraph and Telephone System.

Conference Emblem — A158

**Perf. 13½x12½**

**1973, Sept. 5** Photo.
| 504 | A158 | 40c dp rose & multi | .40 | .30 |
| 505 | A158 | 80c blue grn & multi | .75 | .40 |

4th Summit Conference of Non-aligned Nations, Algiers, Sept. 5-9.

Port of Skikda — A159

**1973, Sept. 29** Photo. Perf. 11½
| 506 | A159 | 80c ocher, blk & ultra | .70 | .40 |

New port of Skikda.

Young Workers — A160

**1973, Oct. 22** Photo. Perf. 13
| 507 | A160 | 40c multicolored | .60 | .25 |

Voluntary work service.

Arms of Algiers — A161

**1973, Dec. 22** Photo. Perf. 13
| 508 | A161 | 2d gold & multi | 2.75 | 1.40 |

Millennium of Algiers.

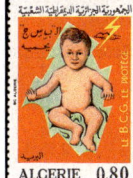

Infant — A162

**1974, Jan. 7** Litho. Perf. 10½x11
| 509 | A162 | 80c orange & multi | .70 | .50 |

Fight against tuberculosis.
No. 509 exists with 1973 year date. Value $60.

Man and Woman, Industry and Transportation — A163

**1974, Feb. 18** Photo. Perf. 11½
| 510 | A163 | 80c multicolored | .85 | .40 |

Four-year plan.

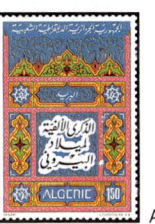

A164

**1974, Feb. 25** Photo. Perf. 11½
| 511 | A164 | 1.50d multi | 2.75 | 1.40 |

Millennium of the birth of abu-al-Rayhan al-Biruni (973-1048), philosopher and mathematician.

Map and Colors of Algeria, Tunisia, Morocco — A165

**1974, Mar. 4** Photo. Perf. 13
| 512 | A165 | 40c gold & multi | .60 | .25 |

Maghreb Committee for Coordination of Posts and Telecommunications.

Hand Holding Rifle — A166

**1974, Mar. 25** Perf. 11½
| 513 | A166 | 80c red & black | .70 | .25 |

Solidarity with the struggle of the people of South Africa.

Mother and Children — A167

**1974, Apr. 8** Perf. 13½
| 514 | A167 | 85c multicolored | .70 | .25 |

Honoring Algerian mothers.

Village — A168

# ALGERIA

Designs: 80c, Harvest. 90c, Tractor and sun. Designs after children's drawings.

**1974, June 15**    Size: 45x26mm
515 A168 70c multicolored .65 .25

Size: 48x33mm
516 A168 80c multicolored .85 .40
517 A168 90c multicolored 1.05 .60
Nos. 515-517 (3) 2.55 1.25

Nos. 498-499 Overprinted

**1974, June 22**    Photo.    Perf. 11½
518 A111 1d multi 1.65 .80
519 A111 1.15d multi 2.25 1.25
1974 Flower Show.

Stamp Vending Machine — A169

**1974, Oct. 7**    Photo.    Perf. 13
520 A169 80c multicolored .85 .25
Stamp Day 1974.

UPU Emblem and Globe — A170

**1974, Oct. 14**    Perf. 14
521 A170 80c multicolored 1.00 .40
Centenary of Universal Postal Union.

"Revolution" A171    Soldiers and Mountains A172

Raising New Flag — A173

Design: 1d, Algerian struggle for independence (people, sun and fields).

**1974, Nov. 4**    Photo.    Perf. 14
522 A171 40c multicolored .50 .25
523 A172 70c multicolored .70 .25
524 A173 95c multicolored .90 .35
525 A171 1d multicolored 1.15 .40
Nos. 522-525 (4) 3.25 1.25
20th anniv. of the start of the revolution.

"Horizon 1980" — A174

**1974, Nov. 23**    Photo.    Perf. 13
526 A174 95c ocher, dk red & blk .70 .40
10-year development plan, 1971-1980.

Ewer and Basin — A175

**1974, Dec. 21**    Perf. 11½
527 A175 50c shown .55 .30
528 A175 60c Coffee pot .75 .40
529 A175 95c Sugar bowl 1.00 .55
530 A175 1d Bath tub 1.40 .65
Nos. 527-530 (4) 3.70 1.90
17th century Algerian copperware.

No. 497 Surcharged in Black

**1975, Jan. 4**
531 A111 50c on 40c multi 2.50 .55

Mediterranean Games' Emblem — A176

**1975, Jan. 27**    Perf. 13½
532 A176 50c purple, yel & grn .45 .25
533 A176 1d orange, bl & mar .80 .35
Mediterranean Games, Algiers, 1975.

**Costume Type of 1971**

Regional Costumes: No. 534, Woman from Hoggar. No. 535, Woman from Algiers. No. 536, Woman from Oran. No. 537, Man from Tlemcen.

**1975, Feb. 22**    Photo.    Perf. 11½
534 A139 1d gold & multi 1.50 .75
535 A139 1d gold & multi 1.50 .75
536 A139 1d gold & multi 1.50 .75
537 A139 1d gold & multi 1.50 .75
Nos. 534-537 (4) 6.00 3.00

Map of Arab Countries, ALO Emblem — A177

**1975, Mar. 10**    Litho.    Perf. 10½x11
538 A177 50c red brown .60 .30
Arab Labor Organization, 10th anniversary.

Blood Transfusion — A178

**1975, Mar. 15**    Perf. 14
539 A178 50c car rose & multi .75 .40
Blood donation and transfusions.

Post Office, Al-Kantara — A179

**1975, May 10**    Photo.    Perf. 11½
Granite Paper
540 A179 50c multicolored .65 .25
Stamp Day 1975.

Policeman and Map of Algeria — A180

**1975, June 1**    Photo.    Perf. 13
541 A180 50c multicolored 1.00 .40
Natl. Security and 10th Natl. Police Day.

Ground Receiving Station — A181

Designs: 1d, Map of Algeria with locations of radar sites, transmission mast and satellite. 1.20d, Main and subsidiary stations.

**1975, June 28**    Photo.    Perf. 13
542 A181 50c blue & multi .50 .25
543 A181 1d blue & multi .85 .25
544 A181 1.20d blue & multi 1.10 .40
Nos. 542-544 (3) 2.45 .90
National satellite telecommunications network.

Revolutionary with Flag — A182

**1975, Aug. 20**    Photo.    Perf. 11½
545 A182 1d multicolored .65 .35
August 20th Revolutionary Movement (Skikda), 20th anniversary.

Swimming and Games' Emblem — A183

**Perf. 13x13½, 13½x13**
**1975, Aug. 23**    Photo.
546 A183 25c shown .25 .25
547 A183 50c Judo, map .40 .25
548 A183 70c Soccer, vert. .60 .30
549 A183 1d Running, vert. .80 .40
550 A183 1.20d Handball, vert. 1.00 .60
   a. Souv. sheet, #546-550, perf 13 6.75 6.75
Nos. 546-550 (5) 3.05 1.80
7th Mediterranean Games, Algiers, 8/23-9/46.
No. 550a sold for 4.50d. Exists imperf., same value.

Setif, Guelma, Kherrata — A184

**1975**    Litho.    Perf. 13½x14
551 A184 5c orange & blk .25 .25
552 A184 10c emerald & brn .25 .25
553 A184 25c dl blue & blk .25 .25
554 A184 30c lemon & blk .40 .25
555 A184 50c brt grn & blk .40 .25
556 A184 70c fawn & blk .45 .25
557 A184 1d vermilion & blk .75 .35
Nos. 551-557 (7) 2.75 1.85
30th anniv. of victory in World War II. Issued: 50c, 1d, Nov. 3; others, Dec. 17. For surcharge see No. 611.

Map of Maghreb and APU Emblem — A185

**1975, Nov. 20**    Photo.    Perf. 11½
558 A185 1d multicolored .70 .40
10th Cong. of Arab Postal Union, Algiers.

Mosaic, Bey Constantine's Palace — A186

Dey-Alger Palace A187

Famous buildings: 2d, Prayer niche, Medersa Sidi-Boumediene, Tlemcen.

**1975, Dec. 22**
559 A186 1d lt blue & multi 1.05 .40
560 A186 2d buff & multi 2.10 .95
561 A187 2.50d buff & blk 2.75 1.40
Nos. 559-561 (3) 5.90 2.75

Al-Azhar University — A188

**Perf. 11½x12½**
**1975, Dec. 29**    Litho.
562 A188 2d multicolored 2.10 .80
Millennium of Al-Azhar University.

Red-billed Firefinch — A189

Birds: 1.40d, Black-headed bush shrike, horiz. 2d, Blue tit. 2.50d, Blackbellied sandgrouse, horiz.

**1976, Jan. 24**    Photo.    Perf. 11½
563 A189 50c multi 1.75 .70
564 A189 1.40d multi 3.00 1.25
565 A189 2d multi 3.50 1.40
566 A189 2.50d multi 4.00 2.00
Nos. 563-566 (4) 12.25 5.35
See Nos. 595-598.

# ALGERIA

Telephones 1876 and 1976 — A190

**1976, Feb. 23   Photo.   Perf. 13½x13**
567   A190   1.40d rose, dk & lt bl   1.00   .55

Centenary of first telephone call by Alexander Graham Bell, Mar. 10, 1876.

Map of Africa with Angola and its Flag — A191

**1976, Feb. 23                Perf. 11½**
568   A191   50c brown & multi   .60   .25

Algeria's solidarity with the People's Republic of Angola.

A192

Sahraoui flag and child, map of former Spanish Sahara.

**1976, Mar. 15   Photo.   Perf. 11½**
569   A192   50c multicolored   .55   .25

Algeria's solidarity with Sahraoui Arab Democratic Republic, former Spanish Sahara.

Stamp Day — A193

**1976, Mar. 22**
570   A193   1.40d Mailman   1.25   .40

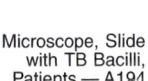

Microscope, Slide with TB Bacilli, Patients — A194

**1976, Apr. 26        Perf. 13x13½**
571   A194   50c multicolored   1.05   .30

Fight against tuberculosis.

"Setif, Guelma, Kherrata" — A195

**1976, May 24   Photo.   Perf. 13½x13**
572   A195   50c blue & yellow   .60   .25
 a.   Booklet pane of 6   8.00
 b.   Booklet pane of 10   12.00

No. 572 was issued in booklets only.

Ram's Head over Landscape — A196

**1976, June 17   Photo.   Perf. 11½**
573   A196   50c multicolored   .70   .25

Livestock breeding.

People Holding Torch, Map of Algeria — A197

**1976, June 29   Photo.   Perf. 14x13½**
574   A197   50c multicolored   .60   .25

National Charter.

Palestine Map and Flag — A198

**1976, July 12                 Perf. 11½**
**Granite Paper**
575   A198   50c multicolored   .65   .25

Solidarity with the Palestinians.

Map of Africa — A199

**1976, Oct. 3   Litho.   Perf. 10½x11**
576   A199   2d dk blue & multi   1.50   .65

2nd Pan-African Commercial Fair, Algiers.

Blind Brushmaker A200

The Blind, by Dinet — A201

**1976, Oct. 23   Photo.   Perf. 14½**
577   A200   1.20d blue & multi   .95   .50
578   A201   1.40d gold & multi   .95   .65

Rehabilitation of the blind.

"Constitution 1976" A202

**1976, Nov. 19   Photo.   Perf. 11½**
579   A202   2d multicolored   1.50   .65

New Constitution.

Soldiers Planting Seedlings — A203

**1976, Nov. 25   Litho.   Perf. 12**
580   A203   1.40d multicolored   1.50   .55

Green barrier against the Sahara.

Ornamental Border and Inscription A204

**1976, Dec. 18   Photo.   Perf. 11½**
**Granite Paper**
581   A204   2d multicolored   1.50   .65

Re-election of Pres. Houari Boumediene. See No. 627.

Map with Charge Zones and Dials — A205

**1977, Jan. 22               Perf. 13**
582   A205   40c silver & multi   .50   .25

Inauguration of automatic national and international telephone service.

People and Buildings — A206

**1977, Jan. 29   Photo.   Perf. 11½**
583   A206   60c on 50c multi   .60   .25

2nd General Population and Buildings Census. No. 583 was not issued without the typographed red brown surcharge, date, and bars.

Sahara Museum, Uargla — A207

**1977, Feb. 12   Litho.   Perf. 14**
584   A207   60c multicolored   .60   .40

El-Kantara Gorge — A208

**Perf. 12½x13½**
**1977, Feb. 19                Photo.**
585   A208   20c green & yellow   .25   .25
 a.   Bklt. pane, 3 #585, 4 #586 + label   6.00
 b.   Bklt. pane, 5 #585, 2 #587 + label   7.00
586   A208   60c brt lilac & yel   .25   .25
587   A208   1d brown & yellow   .65   .25
    Nos. 585-587 (3)   1.15   .75

National Assembly A209

**1977, Feb. 27                Perf. 11½**
588   A209   2d multicolored   1.30   .55

People and Flag A210    Soldier and Flag A211

**Perf. 13½, 11½ (3d)**
**1977, Mar. 12                Photo.**
589   A210   2d multicolored   1.30   .55
590   A211   3d multicolored   2.10   .80

Solidarity with the peoples of Zimbabwe (Rhodesia), 2d; Namibia, 3d.

Winter, Roman Mosaic — A212

The Seasons from Roman Villa, 2nd century A.D.: 1.40d, Fall. 2d, Summer. 3d, Spring.

**1977, Apr. 21   Photo.   Perf. 11½**
**Granite Paper**
591   A212   1.20d multi   1.50   .75
592   A212   1.40d multi   1.50   .75
593   A212   2d multi   2.40   1.15
594   A212   3d multi   3.25   1.50
 a.   Souv. sheet, #591-594   12.00   12.00
    Nos. 591-594 (4)   8.65   4.15

No. 594a sold for 8d and exists imperf.

**Bird Type of 1976**

Birds: 60c, Tristram's warbler. 1.40d, Moussier's redstart, horiz. 2d, Temminck's horned lark, horiz. 3d, Eurasian hoopoe.

**1977, May 21   Photo.   Perf. 11½**
595   A189   60c multi   1.30   .65
596   A189   1.40d multi   1.90   .90
597   A189   2d multi   3.00   1.30
598   A189   3d multi   4.25   1.90
    Nos. 595-598 (4)   10.45   4.75

Horseman — A213

Design: 5d, Attacking horsemen, horiz.

**1977, June 25   Photo.   Perf. 11½**
599   A213   2d multicolored   2.00   .80
600   A213   5d multicolored   5.00   2.00

# ALGERIA

Flag Colors, Games Emblem A214

Wall Painting, Games Emblem A215

**1977, Sept. 24**  Photo.  *Perf. 11½*
601  A214  60c multi  .55  .25
602  A215  1.40d multi  1.30  .60
3rd African Games, Algiers 1978.

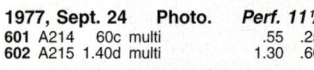

Village and Tractor — A216

**1977, Nov. 12**  *Perf. 14x13*
603  A216  1.40d multi  1.00  .40
Socialist agricultural village.

Almohades Dirham, 12th Century A217

Ancient Coins: 1.40d, Almohades coin, 12th century. 2d, Almoravides dinar, 11th century.

**1977, Dec. 17**  Photo.  *Perf. 11½*
604  A217  60c ultra, sil & blk  .55  .40
605  A217  1.40d grn, gold & brn  1.30  .60
606  A217  2d red brn, gold & brn  1.75  .90
Nos. 604-606 (3)  3.60  1.90

Flowering Trees — A218

**1978, Feb. 11**  Photo.  *Perf. 11½*
607  A218  60c Cherry  .55  .25
608  A218  1.20d Peach  1.05  .70
609  A218  1.30d Almond  1.20  .75
610  A218  1.40d Apple  1.45  .80
Nos. 607-610 (4)  4.25  2.50

No. 555 Surcharged in Black

**1978, Feb. 11**  Litho.  *Perf. 13½x14*
611  A184  60c on 50c  .80  .25

Children with Traffic Signs and Car — A219

**1978, Apr. 29**  Photo.  *Perf. 11½*
612  A219  60c multicolored  .80  .25
Road safety and protection of children.

Sports and Games Emblems — A220

Designs (Games Emblem and): 40c, Volleyball. 60c, Rowing, vert. 1.20d, Basketball. 1.30d, Hammer throwing, vert. 1.40d, Map of Africa and boxers, vert.

**1978, July 13**  Photo.  *Perf. 11½*
613  A220  40c multi  .25  .25
614  A220  60c multi  .45  .25
615  A220  1.20d multi  1.00  .40
616  A220  1.30d multi  1.00  .50
617  A220  1.40d multi  1.40  .60
Nos. 613-617 (5)  4.10  2.00
3rd African Games, Algiers, July 13-28.

TB Patient Returning to Family — A221

**1978, Oct. 5**  Photo.  *Perf. 13½x14*
618  A221  60c multicolored  .70  .25
Anti-tuberculosis campaign.

Holy Kaaba — A222

**1978, Oct. 28**  Photo.  *Perf. 11½*
619  A222  60c multicolored  .80  .25
Pilgrimage to Mecca.

National Servicemen Building Road — A223

**1978, Nov. 4**
620  A223  60c multicolored  .80  .25
African Unity Road from El Goleah to In Salah, inauguration.

Fibula — A224

Jewelry: 1.35d, Pendant. 1.40d, Ankle ring.

**1978, Dec. 21**  Photo.  *Perf. 12x11½*
621  A224  1.20d multi  1.20  .50
622  A224  1.35d multi  1.45  .60
623  A224  1.40d multi  1.75  .75
Nos. 621-623 (3)  4.40  1.85

Pres. Boumediene — A225

**1979, Jan. 7**  Photo.  *Perf. 12x11½*
624  A225  60c green, red & brown  .55  .25
Houari Boumediene, pres. of Algeria 1965-1978.

Torch and Books — A226

**1979, Jan. 27**  Photo.  *Perf. 11½*
625  A226  60c multicolored  .55  .25
Natl. Front of Liberation Party Cong.

Pres. Boumediene A227

**1979, Feb. 4**  Photo.  *Perf. 11½*
626  A227  1.40d multi  1.25  .55
40 days after death of Pres. Houari Boumediène.

### Ornamental Type of 1976

Proclamation of new President.

**1979, Feb. 10**
627  A204  2d multicolored  1.50  .40
Election of Pres. Chadli Bendjedid.

A229

**1979, Apr. 18**  Photo.  *Perf. 11½*
628  A229  60c multicolored  .50  .25
Sheik Abdul-Hamid Ben Badis (1889-1940).

A230

Designs: 1.20d, Telephone dial, map of Africa. 1.40d, Symbolic Morse key and waves.

**1979, May 19**  Photo.  *Perf. 13½x14*
629  A230  1.20d multi  .85  .30
630  A230  1.40d multi  1.05  .50
Telecom '79 Exhib., Geneva, Sept. 20-26.

Harvest, IYC Emblem — A231

1.40d, Dancers and IYC emblem, vert.

*Perf. 11½x11, 11x11½*
**1979, June 21**
631  A231  60c multi  .55  .25
632  A231  1.40d multi  1.10  .50
International Year of the Child.

Nuthatch — A232

**1979, Oct. 20**  Photo.  *Perf. 11½*
633  A232  1.40d multicolored  2.40  1.25

A233

Designs: 1.40d, Flag, soldiers and workers. 3d, Revolutionaries and emblem.

**1979, Nov. 1**  Photo.  *Perf. 12½*
634  A233  1.40d multi  1.00  .30
Size: 37x48mm
*Perf. 11½*
635  A233  3d multi  1.90  .85
November 1 revolution, 25th anniversary.

Hegira, 1500 Anniv. — A234

**1979, Dec. 2**  Photo.  *Perf. 11½*
636  A234  3d multicolored  2.00  .75

Camels, Lion, Men and Slave — A235

Dionysian Procession (Setif Mosaic): 1.35d, Elephants, tigers and women. 1.40d, Men in tiger-drawn cart. No. 639a has continuous design.

### Granite Paper

**1980, Feb. 16**  Photo.  *Perf. 11½*
637  A235  1.20d multi  1.50  .40
638  A235  1.35d multi  1.50  .55
639  A235  1.40d multi  1.75  .80
a.  Strip of 3, #637-639  5.75  5.75

Science Day — A236

**1980, Apr. 19**  Photo.  *Perf. 12*
640  A236  60c multicolored  .65  .25

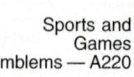 

# ALGERIA

419

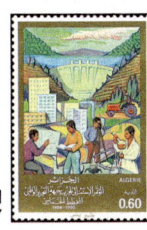

Dam and Workers — A237

**1980, June 17    Photo.    Perf. 11½**
641  A237  60c multicolored        .60  .25
Extraordinary Congress of the National Liberation Front Party.

Olympic Sports, Moscow '80 Emblem — A238

50c, Flame, rings, vert.

**1980, June 28**
642  A238  50c multicolored        .45  .25
643  A238  1.40d shown              .90  .50
22nd Summer Olympic Games, Moscow, July 19-Aug. 3.

20th Anniversary of OPEC A239

60c, Men holding OPEC emblem, vert.

**Perf. 11x10½, 10½x11**
**1980, Sept. 15                Engr.**
644  A239  60c multicolored        .60  .25
645  A239  1.40d shown             1.40  .50

Aures Valley — A240

**1980, Sept. 25  Litho.   Perf. 13½x14**
646  A240  50c shown               .45  .25
647  A240  1d El Oued Oasis        .85  .25
648  A240  1.40d Tassili Rocks    1.25  .40
649  A240  2d View of Algiers     2.10  .70
    Nos. 646-649 (4)              4.65  1.60
World Tourism Conf., Manila, Sept. 27.

Avicenna (980-1037), Philosopher and Physician — A241

**1980, Oct. 25    Photo.    Perf. 12**
650  A241  2d multicolored        2.25  .80

Ruins of El Asnam A242

**1980, Nov. 13    Photo.    Perf. 12**
651  A242  3d multicolored        2.10  .55
Earthquake relief.

Crown — A243

No. 652, Necklace, vert. No. 653, Earrings, bracelet, vert. No. 654, Crown.

**Granite Paper**
**1980, Dec. 20   Photo.    Perf. 12**
652  A243  60c multi               .60  .25
653  A243  1.40d multi            1.00  .50
654  A243  2d multi               1.50  .65
    Nos. 652-654 (3)              3.10  1.40
See Nos. 705-707.

1980-1984 Five-Year Plan — A244

**1981, Jan. 29   Litho.   Perf. 14**
655  A244  60c multicolored        .60  .25

Basket Weaving A245

**Granite Paper**
**1981, Feb. 10   Photo.   Perf. 12½**
656  A245  40c shown               .40  .25
657  A245  60c Rug weaving         .50  .25
658  A245  1d Coppersmith          .80  .25
659  A245  1.40d Jeweler          1.10  .45
    Nos. 656-659 (4)              2.80  1.20

Cedar Tree — A246

Arbor Day: 1.40d, Cypress tree, vert.

**Granite Paper**
**1981, Mar. 19   Photo.    Perf. 12**
660  A246  60c multi               .40  .25
661  A246  1.40d multi            1.10  .60

Mohamed Bachir el Ibrahimi (1869-1965) A247

Children Going to School A248

**1981, Apr. 16             Granite Paper**
662  A247  60c multicolored        .60  .25
663  A248  60c multicolored        .60  .25
Science Day.

12th International Hydatidological Congress, Algiers — A249

**1981, Apr. 23              Perf. 14x13½**
664  A249  2d multicolored        2.00  .50

13th World Telecommunications Day — A250

**1981, May 14    Photo.   Perf. 14x13½**
665  A250  1.40d multi            1.25  .25

Disabled People and Hand Offering Flower A251

1.20d, Symbolic globe, vert.

**Perf. 12½x13, 13x12½**
**1981, June 20                   Litho.**
666  A251  1.20d multicolored      .95  .25
667  A251  1.40d shown            1.10  .30
Intl. Year of the Disabled.

Papilio Machaon — A252

1.20d, Rhodocera rhamni. 1.40d, Charaxes jasius. 2d, Papilio podalirius.

**1981, Aug. 20   Photo.   Perf. 11½**
**Granite Paper**
668  A252  60c shown               .90  .35
669  A252  1.20d multicolored     1.60  .50
670  A252  1.40d multicolored     2.00  .90
671  A252  2d multicolored        2.50  .90
    Nos. 668-671 (4)              7.00  2.65

Monk Seal — A253

**1981, Sept. 17             Perf. 14x13½**
672  A253  60c shown               .90  .40
673  A253  1.40d Macaque          1.90  .80

World Food Day — A254

**1981, Oct. 16   Photo.   Perf. 14x14½**
674  A254  2d multicolored        1.25  .50

Cave Drawings of Tassili — A255

Various cave drawings. 1.60d, 2d horiz.

**1981, Nov. 21              Perf. 11½**
675  A255  60c multi               .60  .25
676  A255  1d multi               1.20  .40
677  A255  1.60d multi            1.65  .55
678  A255  2d multi               2.25  .80
    Nos. 675-678 (4)              5.70  2.00

Galley, 17-18th Cent. — A256

**1981, Dec. 17   Photo.   Perf. 11½**
679  A256  60c shown               .70  .50
680  A256  1.60d Ship, diff.      1.90  .95

1982 World Cup Soccer — A257

Designs: Various soccer players.

**Perf. 13x12½x 12½x13**
**1982, Feb. 25                   Litho.**
681  A257  80c multi, vert.        .65  .25
682  A257  2.80d multi            2.00  .80

TB Bacillus Centenary — A258

**1982, Mar. 20   Photo.   Perf. 14½x14**
683  A258  80c multi               .60  .25

Painted Stand — A259

**1982, Apr. 24   Photo.   Perf. 11½**
**Granite Paper**
684  A259  80c Mirror, vert.       .50  .25
685  A259  2d shown               1.25  .45
**Size:  48x33mm**
686  A259  2.40d Chest            1.75  .60
    Nos. 684-686 (3)              3.50  1.30

Djamaael Djadid Mosque, Algiers — A260

No. 688, Sidi Doumediene Mosque, Tlemcen. No. 689, Garden of Dey, Algiers.

**1982, May 15   Litho.   Perf. 14**
**Size:  32x22mm**
687  A260  80c brown               .50  .25
    a.  Size: 30½x21mm           3.50  .75
688  A260  2.40d purple           1.50  .50
    a.  Size: 30½x21mm           5.00  1.25
689  A260  3d olato               2.00  .80
    Nos. 687-689 (3)              4.00  1.35
See Nos. 701-704, 745-747, 774, 778-783.

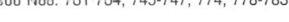

A261

Medicinal plants: No. 690, Callitris articulata. No 691, Artemisia herba-alba. No. 692, Ricinus communis. No. 693, Thymus fontanesii.

**1982, May 27   Photo.   Perf. 11½**
**Granite Paper**
690  A261  50c multi               .40  .25
691  A261  80c multi               .60  .25
692  A261  1d multi                .90  .40
693  A261  2.40d multi            1.75  .75
    Nos. 690-693 (4)              3.65  1.65

420 ALGERIA

A262

No. 694, Riflemen. No. 695, Soldiers, horiz. No. 696, Symbols, citizens, horiz. No. 697, Emblem.

**1982, July 5**     **Granite Paper**
694 A262 50c multi    .45 .25
695 A262 80c multi    .55 .25
696 A262 2d multi    1.40 .75
    Nos. 694-696 (3)    2.40 1.25
    **Souvenir Sheet**
697 A262 5d multi    5.50 5.50
Independence, 20th anniv.
No. 697 contains one 32x39mm stamp.

Soummam Congress — A263

**1982, Aug. 20**     Litho.
698 A263 80c Congress building    .60 .25

Scouting Year — A264

**1982, Oct. 21**     Photo.
    **Granite Paper**
699 A264 2.80d multi    2.00 .60

Palestinian Child — A265

**1982, Nov. 25**     Litho.    Perf. 10½
700 A265 1.60d multi    .95 .30

Chlamydotis Undulata — A266

Protected birds: No. 701, Geronticus eremita, horiz. No. 702, Chlamydotis Undulata. No. 703, Aquila rapax, horiz. No. 704, Gypaetus barbatus.

    *Perf. 15x14, 14x15*
**1982, Dec. 23**     Photo.
701 A266 50c mutli    .75 .55
702 A266 80c multi    1.15 .75
703 A266 2d multi    2.10 1.50
704 A266 2.40d multi    2.75 1.90
    Nos. 701-704 (4)    6.75 4.70

    **Jewelry Type of 1980**
**1983, Feb. 10**     Perf. 11½
    **Granite Paper**
705 A243 50c Picture frame    .35 .25
706 A243 1d Flaska    .60 .40
707 A243 2d Brooch, horiz.    1.25 .65
    Nos. 705-707 (3)    2.20 1.30

A267

80c, Abies numidica, vert. 2.80d, Acacia raddiana.

**1983, Mar. 17**     Photo.
    **Granite Paper**
708 A267 80c multicolored    .70 .25
709 A267 2.80d multicolored    2.25 .80
Intl. Arbor Day.

Various Minerals — A268

1.20d, 2.40d horiz.

    **Granite Paper**
    *Perf. 12x12½, 12½x12*
**1983, Apr. 21**     Photo.
710 A268 70c multi    1.25 .35
711 A268 80c multi    1.40 .50
712 A268 1.20d multi    1.60 .65
713 A268 2.40d multi    2.50 1.25
    Nos. 710-713 (4)    6.75 2.75

30th Anniv. of Intl. Customs Cooperation Council — A269

**1983, May 14**     Photo.    Perf. 11½
    **Granite Paper**
714 A269 80c multi    .70 .25

Emir Abdelkader Death Centenary A270

**1983, May 22**     Photo.    Perf. 12
    **Granite Paper**
715 A270 4d multi    2.40 .90

Local Mushrooms — A271

No. 716, Amanita muscaria. No. 717, Amanita phalloides. No. 718, Pleurotus eryngii. No. 719, Tefezia leonis.

**1983, July 21**     Perf. 14x15
716 A271 50c multi    1.00 .35
717 A271 80c multi    1.45 .75
718 A271 1.40d multi    3.00 1.10
719 A271 2.80d multi    4.50 2.10
    Nos. 716-719 (4)    9.95 4.30

A272

**1983, Sept. 1**     Photo.    Perf. 11½
720 A272 80c multi    .70 .25
ibn-Khaldun, historian, philosopher.

World Communications Year — A273

80c, Post Office, Algiers. 2.40d, Telephone, circuit box.

    *Perf. 11½x12½*
**1983, Sept. 22**     Litho.
721 A273 50c multicolored    .55 .25
722 A273 2.40d multicolored    1.40 .60

Goat and Tassili Mountains A274

80c, Tuaregs in native costume. 2.40d, Animals, rock painting. 2.80d, Rock formation.

**1983, Oct. 20**     Litho.    Perf. 12½x13
723 A274 50c shown    .40 .25
724 A274 80c multicolored    .50 .25
725 A274 2.40d multicolored    1.40 .55
726 A274 2.80d multicolored    1.75 .75
    Nos. 723-726 (4)    4.05 1.80

Sloughi Dog — A275

    *Perf. 14x14½, 14½x14*
**1983, Nov. 24**     Photo.
727 A275 80c shown    1.10 .35
728 A275 2.40d Sloughi, horiz.    2.75 .95

Natl. Liberation Party, 5th Congress A276

80c, Symbols of development. 5d, Emblem.

**1983, Dec. 19**     Photo.    Perf. 11½
729 A276 80c multicolored    .80 .40
    **Souvenir Sheet**
730 A276 5d multicolored    5.00 5.00
No. 730 contains one 32x38mm stamp.

    **View Type of 1982**
10c, View of Oran, 1830. 1d, Sidi Abderahman and Taalibi Mosques. 2d, Bejaia, 1830. 4d, Constantine, 1830.

**1984, Jan. 26**     Litho.    Perf. 14
    **Size: 32x22mm**
731 A260 10c multicolored    .25 .25
   a.   Size: 30½x21mm    .80 .40
732 A260 1d multicolored    .50 .25
   a.   Size: 30½x21mm    1.50 .80
733 A260 2d multicolored    1.00 .50
   a.   Size: 30½x21mm    3.00 1.50
734 A260 4d multicolored    2.50 .65
   a.   Size: 30½x21mm    6.00 1.50
    Nos. 731-734 (4)    4.25 1.65

Pottery — A278

    *Perf. 11½x12, 12x11½*
**1984, Feb. 23**     Photo.
    **Granite Paper**
735 A278 80c Jug, vert.    .50 .25
736 A278 1d Platter    .65 .40
737 A278 2d Oil lamp, vert.    1.40 .60
738 A278 2.40d Pitcher    1.75 .75
    Nos. 735-738 (4)    4.30 2.00

Fountains of Old Algiers — A279

Various fountains.

**1984, Mar. 22**     Photo.    Perf. 11½
    **Granite Paper**
739 A279 50c multi    .25 .25
740 A279 80c multi    .55 .40
741 A279 2.40d multi    1.40 .65
    Nos. 739-741 (3)    2.20 1.30

1984 Summer Olympics — A280

**1984, May 19**     Photo.    Perf. 11½
    **Granite Paper**
742 A280 1d multi    1.25 .40

Brown Stallion — A281

**1984, June 14**     Photo.    Perf. 11½
    **Granite Paper**
743 A281 80c shown    .80 .40
744 A281 2.40d White mare    2.10 .95

    **View Type of 1982**
**1984**     Litho.    Perf. 14
    **Size: 32x22mm**
745 A260 5c Mustapha Pacha    .50 .25
   a.   Size: 30½x21mm    .80 .40
746 A260 20c Bab Azzoun    .50 .25
   d.   Size: 30½x21mm    1.00 .60
746A A260 30c Algiers    .50 .25
   d.   Size: 30½x21mm    1.50 .50
746B A260 40c Kolea    .50 .25
746C A260 50c Algiers    .50 .25
   e.   Size: 30½x21mm    1.50 .50
747 A260 70c Mostaganem    .60 .25
   a.   Size: 30½x21mm    2.00 1.00
    Nos. 745-747 (6)    3.10 1.50
Issued: Nos. 745, 746, 747, 7/19; Nos. 746A-746C, 10/20.

Lute — A282

Native musical instruments.

**1984, Sept. 22**     Litho.    Perf. 15x14
748 A282 80c shown    .60 .25
749 A282 1d Drum    .90 .40
750 A282 2.40d Fiddle    1.75 .75
751 A282 2.80d Bagpipe    2.00 .95
    Nos. 748-751 (4)    5.25 2.35

30th Anniv. of Algerian Revolution A284

80c, Partisans. 5d, Algerian flags, vert.

**1984, Nov. 3**     Photo.    Perf. 11½x12
757 A284 80c multicolored    .85 .25
    **Souvenir Sheet**
758 A284 5d multicolored    5.50 5.50

M'Zab Valley — A285

80c, Map of valley. 2.40d, Town of M'Zab, vert.

**1984, Dec. 15**     Perf. 15x14, 14x15
759 A285 80c multicolored    .75 .25
760 A285 2.40d multicolored    1.75 .60

18th and 19th Century Metalware — A286

# ALGERIA

**1985, Jan. 26**   **Photo.**   *Perf. 11½*
761 A286 80c Coffee pot .60 .25
762 A286 2d Bowl, horiz. 1.25 .65
763 A286 2.40d Covered bowl 1.75 .85
    Nos. 761-763 (3) 3.60 1.75

Fish — A287

50c, Thunnus thynnus. 80c, Sparus aurata. 2.40d, Epinephelus guaza. 2.80d, Mustelus mustelus.

**1985, Feb. 23**   **Photo.**   *Perf. 15x14*
764 A287 50c multicolored .50 .25
765 A287 80c multicolored .90 .40
766 A287 2.40d multicolored 2.25 1.10
767 A287 2.80d multicolored 2.75 1.25
    Nos. 764-767 (4) 6.40 3.00

National Games — A288

**1985, Mar. 20**   *Perf. 11½x12*
**Granite Paper**
768 A288 80c Doves, emblem .80 .25

Environmental Conservation A289

**1985, Apr. 25**   *Perf. 13½*
769 A289 80c Stylized trees .70 .25
770 A289 1.40d Stylized waves 1.00 .40

**View Type of 1982 and**

The Casbah — A290

View of Constantine A290a

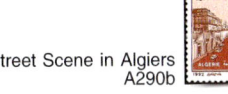
Street Scene in Algiers A290b

Designs: 2.50d, Djamaael Djadid Mosque, Algiers. 2.90d, like No. 746. 5d, like No. 746A. 1.50d, like No. 746B. 4.20d, like No. 764.

   *Perf. 13½x12½, 13 (#774, 4.20d),*
   *Perf. 13½x14 (#775)*
   *Perf. 14½x14 (2d)*
**Photo., Litho. (2d, 6,20d, 7.50d, #775)**
**1985-94**
771 A290 20c dk blue & buff .25 .25
772 A290 80c sage grn & buff .60 .25
773 A290a 1d dk olive grn .50 .25
  a. Bklt. pane of 5 + label 4.00
774 A260 1.50d dull red .55 .25
775 A290b 1.50d red brn & brn .40 .25
  a. Booklet pane of 6 2.75
776 A290b 2d dk bl & lt bl .40 .25
  a. Booklet pane of 5 + label 3.00
777 A290 2.40d chestnut & buff 1.75 .25
  a. Bklt. pane of 5 (20c, 3 80c, 2.40d) + label 5.75
778 A260 2.50d bluish green 1.00 .25
779 A260 2.90d slate 1.25 .25
780 A260 4.20d gray green 1.40 .35
781 A260 5d dp bis & blk 2.10 .40

   *Perf. 14*
782 A260 6.20d like #731 1.10 .30
783 A260 7.50d like #745 1.75 .30
    Nos. 771-783 (13) 13.05 3.60

Nos. 771-772, 777 issued only in booklet panes.
Issued: 20c, 80c, 2.40d, 6/1/85; 1d, 1/26/89; 2.50d, 2.90d, 5d, 2/23/89; No. 774, 4.20d, 3/21/91; No. 775, 5/20/92; 6.20d, 7.50d, 4/22/92; 2d, 10/21/93; No. 776a, 10/21/94.
See No. 1010.

UN, 40th Anniv. — A291

**1985, June 26**   **Photo.**   *Perf. 14*
784 A291 1d Dove, emblem, 40 .90 .25

Natl. Youth Festival — A292

**1985, July 5**   **Litho.**   *Perf. 13½*
785 A292 80c multicolored .70 .25

Intl. Youth Year — A293

80c, Silhouette, globe, emblem, vert. 1.40d, Doves, globe.

**1985, July 5**
786 A293 80c multicolored .90 .25
787 A293 1.40d multicolored .90 .40

World Map, OPEC — A294

**1985, Sept. 14**   **Photo.**   *Perf. 12½x13*
788 A294 80c multicolored .80 .25

Organization of Petroleum Exporting Countries, 25th anniv.

Family Planning — A295

**1985, Oct. 3**   **Litho.**   *Perf. 14*
789 A295 80c Mother and sons .60 .25
790 A295 1.40d Weighing infant .90 .40
791 A295 1.70d Breast-feeding 1.30 .50
    Nos. 789-791 (3) 2.80 1.15

El-Meniaa Township — A296

80c, Chetaibi Bay, horiz. 2.40d, Bou Noura Town, horiz.

**1985, Oct. 24**   **Engr.**   *Perf. 13*
792 A296 80c multicolored .50 .25
793 A296 2d shown 1.40 .40
794 A296 2.40d multicolored 1.60 .60
    Nos. 792-794 (3) 3.50 1.25

The Palm Grove, by N. Dinet — A297

**1985, Nov. 21**   **Photo.**   *Perf. 11½x12*
**Granite Paper**
795 A297 2d multicolored 1.50 .75
796 A297 3d multi, diff. 2.10 1.10

Tapestries — A298

Various designs.

**1985, Dec. 19**   **Granite Paper**
797 A298 80c multi .70 .50
798 A298 1.40d multi 1.40 .75
799 A298 2.40d multi 2.00 1.25
800 A298 2.80d multi 2.50 1.75
    Nos. 797-800 (4) 6.60 4.25

Wildcats — A299

80c, Felis margarita. 1d, Felis caracal. 2d, Felis sylvestris. 2.40d, Felis serval, vert.

**1986, Jan. 23**   *Perf. 12x11½, 11½x12*
**Granite Paper**
801 A299 80c multicolored 1.40 .60
802 A299 1d multicolored 1.75 .70
803 A299 2d multicolored 2.50 .90
804 A299 2.40d multicolored 3.50 1.60
    Nos. 801-804 (4) 9.15 3.80

UN Child Survival Campaign — A300

80c, Oral vaccine. 1.40d, Mother, child, sun. 1.70d, Three children.

**1986, Feb. 13**   **Litho.**   *Perf. 13½*
805 A300 80c multicolored .55 .25
806 A300 1.40d multicolored 1.10 .65
807 A300 1.70d multicolored 1.60 .85
    Nos. 805-807 (3) 3.25 1.75

Algerian General Worker's Union, 30th Anniv. — A301

**1986, Feb. 24**   *Perf. 12½*
**Granite Paper**
808 A301 2d multicolored 1.50 .60

National Charter — A302

**Granite Paper**
**1986, Mar. 6**   **Photo.**   *Perf. 11½*
809 A302 4d multicolored 3.00 1.25

Natl. Day of the Disabled — A303

**1986, Mar. 15**   *Perf. 12½x13*
810 A303 80c multicolored .70 .30

A304

**1986, Apr. 17**   **Litho.**   *Perf. 14x15*
811 A304 80c multicolored .75 .40
Anti-Tuberculosis campaign.

A305

2d, Soccer ball, sombrero. 2.40d, Soccer players.

**1986, Apr. 24**   *Perf. 14*
812 A305 2d multicolored 1.50 .55
813 A305 2.40d multicolored 1.75 .65
1986 World Cup Soccer Championships, Mexico.

Inner Courtyards — A306

**Granite Paper**
**1986, May 15**   **Photo.**   *Perf. 11½*
814 A306 80c multicolored .70 .30
815 A306 2.40d multi, diff. 1.90 .95
816 A306 3d multi, diff. 2.40 1.25
    Nos. 814-816 (3) 5.00 2.50

Blood Donation Campaign — A307

**1986, June 26**   **Litho.**   *Perf. 13½*
817 A307 80c multicolored 1.40 .40

Southern District Radio Communication Inauguration — A308

**1986, July**   *Perf. 13*
818 A308 60c multicolored .50 .25

# ALGERIA

422

Mosque Gateways — A309

2d, Door. 2.40d, Ornamental arch.

**Granite Paper**

**1986, Sept. 27  Photo.  Perf. 12x11½**
| 819 | A309 | 2d multicolored | 1.40 | .60 |
| 820 | A309 | 2.40d multicolored | 1.60 | .85 |

Intl. Peace Year — A310

**Perf. 13½x14½**
**1986, Oct. 16  Photo.**
| 821 | A310 | 2.40d multi | 1.60 | .60 |

Folk Dancing — A311

**1986, Nov. 22  Litho.  Perf. 14x13½**
| 822 | A311 | 80c Woman, scarf | .70 | .25 |
| 823 | A311 | 2.40d Woman, diff. | 1.75 | .70 |
| 824 | A311 | 2.80d Man, sword | 1.90 | .80 |
| | | Nos. 822-824 (3) | 4.35 | 1.75 |

Flowers — A312

80c, Narcissus tazetta. 1.40d, Iris unguicularis. 2.40d, Capparis spinosa. 2.80d, Gladiolus segetum.

**1986, Dec. 18  Photo.  Perf. 14**
| 825 | A312 | 80c multicolored | .70 | .30 |
| 826 | A312 | 1.40d multicolored | 1.25 | .60 |
| 827 | A312 | 2.40d multicolored | 1.75 | 1.00 |
| 828 | A312 | 2.80d multicolored | 2.10 | 1.25 |
| | | Nos. 825-828 (4) | 5.80 | 3.15 |

See Nos. 936-938.

Abstract Paintings by Mohammed Issia Khem — A313

2d, Man and woman, vert. 5d, Man and books.

**Perf. 11½x12, 12x11½**
**1987, Jan. 29  Litho.**
| 829 | A313 | 2d multicolored | 1.50 | .85 |
| 830 | A313 | 5d multicolored | 3.25 | 2.00 |

Jewelry from Aures — A314

**Granite Paper**

**1987, Feb. 27  Photo.  Perf. 12**
| 831 | A314 | 1d Earrings | .75 | .45 |
| 832 | A314 | 1.80d Bracelets | 1.20 | .70 |
| 833 | A314 | 2.90d Nose rings | 1.75 | 1.10 |
| 834 | A314 | 3.30d Necklace | 2.10 | 1.25 |
| | | Nos. 831-834 (4) | 5.80 | 3.50 |

Nos. 831-833 vert.

Petroglyphs, Atlas — A315

**1987, Mar. 26  Litho.  Perf. 12x11½**
**Granite Paper**
| 835 | A315 | 1d Man and woman | 1.10 | .70 |
| 836 | A315 | 2.90d Goat | 2.50 | 1.40 |
| 837 | A315 | 3.30d Horse, bull | 2.75 | 1.40 |
| | | Nos. 835-837 (3) | 6.35 | 3.50 |

Syringe as an Umbrella — A316

**Granite Paper**

**1987, Apr. 7  Perf. 11½**
| 838 | A316 | 1d multicolored | .80 | .25 |

Child Immunization Campaign, World Health Day.

Volunteers — A317

**1987, Apr. 23  Perf. 10½**
| 839 | A317 | 1d multicolored | .55 | .30 |

Third General Census — A318

**1987, May 21  Perf. 13½**
| 840 | A318 | 1d multicolored | .70 | .30 |

Algerian Postage, 25th Anniv. A319

War Orphans' Fund label (1fr + 9fr) of 1962.

**Granite Paper**

**1987, July 5  Photo.  Perf. 11½x12**
| 841 | A319 | 1.80d multicolored | 2.75 | .70 |

A320

A321

**1987, July 5**  **Granite Paper**
| 842 | A320 | 1d multicolored | .60 | .25 |

**Souvenir Sheet**
| 843 | A321 | 5d multicolored | 5.50 | 5.50 |

Natl. independence, 25th anniv.

Amateur Theater Festival, Mostaganem A322

**Granite Paper**

**1987, July 20  Perf. 12x11½**
| 844 | A322 | 1d Actors on stage | .55 | .25 |
| 845 | A322 | 1.80d Theater | .95 | .60 |
| a. | | Pair, #844-845 | 1.50 | 1.50 |

No. 845a has continuous design.

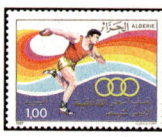

Mediterranean Games, Latakia — A323

**1987, Aug. 6  Perf. 13x12½, 12½x13**
| 846 | A323 | 1d Discus | .60 | .30 |
| 847 | A323 | 2.90d Tennis, vert. | 1.50 | .85 |
| 848 | A323 | 3.30d Team handball | 1.75 | 1.00 |
| | | Nos. 846-848 (3) | 3.85 | 2.15 |

Birds — A324

1d, Phoenicopterus ruber roseus. 1.80d, Porphyrio porphyrio. 2.50d, Elanus caeruleus. 2.90d, Milvus milvus.

**1987  Litho.  Perf. 13½**
| 849 | A324 | 1d multicolored | .85 | .50 |
| 850 | A324 | 1.80d multicolored | 1.40 | 1.00 |
| 851 | A324 | 2.50d multicolored | 2.25 | 1.25 |
| 852 | A324 | 2.90d multicolored | 2.50 | 1.50 |
| | | Nos. 849-852 (4) | 7.00 | 4.25 |

Agriculture A325

No. 853, Planting. No. 854, Reservoir. No. 855, Harvesting crop, vert. No. 856, Produce, vert.

**Perf. 10½x11, 11x10½**
**1987, Nov. 26  Litho.**
| 853 | A325 | 1d multicolored | .65 | .25 |
| 854 | A325 | 1d multicolored | .65 | .25 |
| 855 | A325 | 1d multicolored | .65 | .25 |
| 856 | A325 | 1d multicolored | .65 | .25 |
| | | Nos. 853-856 (4) | 2.60 | 1.00 |

African Telecommunications Day — A326

**1987, Dec. 7  Perf. 10½**
| 857 | A326 | 1d multicolored | .90 | .25 |

Transportation A327

**1987, Dec. 18  Litho.  Perf. 10½x11**
| 858 | A327 | 2.90d shown | 1.50 | .70 |
| 859 | A327 | 3.30d Diesel train | 3.00 | 1.50 |

Algerian Universities A328

Various campuses.

**1987, Dec. 26  Perf. 10½x11, 11x10½**
| 860 | A328 | 1d shown | .50 | .25 |
| 861 | A328 | 2.50d multi, diff. | 1.30 | .50 |
| 862 | A328 | 2.90d multi, diff. | 1.50 | .60 |
| 863 | A328 | 3.30d multi, diff., vert. | 1.75 | .70 |
| | | Nos. 860-863 (4) | 5.05 | 2.05 |

Intl. Rural Development Fund, 10th Anniv. — A329

**1988, Jan. 27  Perf. 10½x11**
| 864 | A329 | 1d multicolored | .80 | .25 |

Autonomy of State-owned Utilities — A330

**1988, Feb. 27  Litho.  Perf. 11x10½**
| 865 | A330 | 1d multicolored | .60 | .25 |

Intl. Women's Day — A331

**1988, Mar. 10  Litho.  Perf. 11x10½**
| 866 | A331 | 1d multicolored | .70 | .25 |

Arab Scouts, 75th Anniv. — A332

**1988, Apr. 7  Litho.  Perf. 10½**
| 867 | A332 | 2d multicolored | 1.20 | .50 |

1988 Summer Olympics, Seoul — A333

**1988, July 23  Litho.  Perf. 10½**
| 868 | A333 | 2.90d multicolored | 1.60 | .85 |

Hot Springs — A334

2.90d, Caverns, horiz. 3.30d, Gazebo, fountain, horiz.

**1988, July 16**
| 869 | A334 | 1d shown | .45 | .25 |
| 870 | A334 | 2.90d multicolored | 1.50 | .60 |
| 871 | A334 | 3.30d multicolored | 1.75 | .70 |
| | | Nos. 869-871 (3) | 3.70 | 1.55 |

# ALGERIA 423

**World Wildlife Fund — A335**

Barbary apes, Macaca sylvanus: 50c, Adult. 90c, Family. 1d, Close-up, vert. 1.80d, Seated on branch, vert.

**1988, Sept. 17**    Litho.    *Perf. 10½*
| | | | |
|---|---|---|---|
| 872 | A335 | 50c multicolored | 1.00 .45 |
| 873 | A335 | 90c multicolored | 1.25 .65 |
| 874 | A335 | 1d multicolored | 1.75 .90 |
| 875 | A335 | 1.80d multicolored | 3.00 1.60 |
| | | Nos. 872-875 (4) | 7.00 3.60 |

**Intl. Literacy Day — A336**

**1988, Sept. 10**    Photo.    *Perf. 10½*
876   A336   2.90d multicolored    1.50 .85

**WHO, 40th Anniv. — A337**

**1988, Oct. 15**
877   A337   2.90d multicolored    1.50 .70

**Fight Apartheid — A338**

**1988, Nov. 19**    Litho.    *Perf. 10½x11*
878   A338   2.50d multicolored    1.25 .50

**Natl. Front Congress — A339**

**1988, Nov. 29**    *Perf. 11x10½*
879   A339   1d multicolored    .60 .25

**Agriculture A340**

No. 880, Irrigation. No. 881, Orchard, fields, livestock.

**1988, Dec. 24**    *Perf. 10½*
880   A340   1d multicolored    .55 .25
881   A340   1d multicolored    .55 .25

**Natl. Goals — A342**

No. 887, Ancient fort. No. 888, Telecommunications. No. 889, Modern buildings.

**1989, Mar. 9**    Litho.    *Perf. 11½*
**Granite Paper**
886   A342   1d shown    .50 .25
887   A342   1d multicolored    .50 .25
888   A342   1d multicolored    .50 .25
889   A342   1d multicolored    .50 .25
     Nos. 886-889 (4)    2.00 1.00
Nos. 887-889 horiz.

**Airports — A343**

2.90d, Oran Es Senia, horiz. 3.30d, Tebessa, horiz.

**1989, Mar. 23**    *Perf. 10½x11, 11x10½*
890   A343   2.90d multicolored    1.20 .55
891   A343   3.30d multicolored    1.40 .70
892   A343   5d shown    2.10 1.25
     Nos. 890-892 (3)    4.70 2.50

**Development of the South — A344**

1d, Irrigation. 1.80d, Building. 2.50d, Fossil fuel extraction, vert.

**1989, Apr. 24**    Litho.    *Perf. 13½*
893   A344   1d multicolored    .50 .25
894   A344   1.80d multicolored    .70 .40
895   A344   2.50d multicolored    1.05 .55
     Nos. 893-895 (3)    2.25 1.20

**Eradicate Locusts — A345**

**1989, May 25**    *Perf. 10½*
896   A345   1d multicolored    .50 .25

**National Service — A346**

**1989, May 11**    Litho.    *Perf. 13½*
897   A346   2d multicolored    1.40 .70

**1st Moon Landing, 20th Anniv. — A347**

4d, Astronaut, lunar module, Moon's surface.

**1989, July 23**    Litho.    *Perf. 13½*
898   A347   2.90d shown    1.25 .60
899   A347   4d multi, vert.    1.60 .90

**Interparliamentary Union, Cent. — A348**

**1989, Sept. 4**    *Perf. 10½*
900   A348   2.90d gold, brt rose lil & blk    1.20 .40

**Produce — A349**

**1989, Sept. 23**    Litho.    *Perf. 11½*
**Granite Paper**
901   Strip of 3    4.00 4.00
  a. A349 2d multi, diff.    .75 .50
  b. A349 3d multi, diff.    1.20 .65
  c. A349 5d shown    1.90 1.20

**Fish — A350**

1d, Sarda sarda. 1.80d, Zeus faber. 2.90d, Pagellus bogaraveo. 3.30d, Xiphias gladius.

**1989, Oct. 27**    Litho.    *Perf. 13½*
902   A350   1d multicolored    .70 .30
903   A350   1.80d multicolored    1.25 .50
904   A350   2.90d multicolored    1.90 .70
905   A350   3.30d multicolored    2.25 .90
     Nos. 902-905 (4)    6.10 2.40

**Algerian Revolution, 35th Anniv. — A351**

**1989, Nov. 4**    Litho.    *Perf. 13½*
906   A351   1d multicolored    .50 .25

**African Development Bank, 25th Anniv. — A352**

**1989, Nov. 18**    *Perf. 10½*
907   A352   1d multicolored    .50 .25

**Mushrooms — A353**

No. 908, Boletus satanas. No. 909, Psalliota xanthoderma. No. 910, Lepiota procera. No. 911, Lactarius deliciosus.

**1989, Dec. 16**    *Perf. 13½*
908   A353   1d multi    1.00 .30
909   A353   1.80d multi    1.50 .75
910   A353   2.90d multi    2.40 1.00
911   A353   3.30d multi    3.25 1.25
     Nos. 908-911 (4)    8.15 3.30

**A354**

**1990, Jan. 18**    Litho.    *Perf. 10½*
912   A354   1d multicolored    .50 .25
Pan-African Postal Union, 10th anniv.

**Energy Conservation — A355**

**1990, Feb. 22**    Litho.    *Perf. 14*
913   A355   1d multicolored    .60 .25

**A356**

**1990, Mar. 2**    Photo.    *Perf. 11½*
914   A356   3d multicolored    1.30 .60
African Soccer Championships.

**A357**

**1990, May 17**    Litho.    *Perf. 13½*
917   A357   2.90d shown    1.10 .60
918   A357   5d Trophy    2.00 1.10
World Cup Soccer Championships, Italy.

**Rural Electrification A358**

**1990, June 21**
919   A358   2d multicolored    .90 .30

**Youth A359**    **Youth Holding Rainbow A360**

**1990, July 6**    *Perf. 13½*
920   A359   2d multicolored    .85 .30
921   A360   3d multicolored    1.25 .50

**Maghreb Arab Union — A361**

**1990**    *Perf. 14x13½*
922   A361   1d multicolored    .50 .25

**Vocations — A362**

**1990, Apr. 26**    Litho.    *Perf. 12½*
923   A362   2d Craftsmen    .75 .40
924   A362   2.90d Auto mechanics    1.00 .60
925   A362   3.30d Deep sea fishing    1.75 .75
     Nos. 923-925 (3)    3.50 1.75

# ALGERIA

Organization of Petroleum Exporting Countries (OPEC), 30th Anniv. — A363

**1990**     *Perf. 13½*
926 A363 2d multicolored    1.50 .30

Savings Promotion — A364

**1990, Oct. 31**   *Litho.*   *Perf. 14*
927 A364 1d multicolored    .50 .25

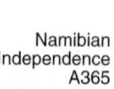

Namibian Independence A365

**1990, Nov. 8**
928 A365 3d multicolored    1.00 .30

Farm Animals — A366

**1990, Nov. 29**     *Perf. 13½*
929 A366   1d   Duck    .50 .25
930 A366   2d   Rabbit, horiz.    1.00 .40
931 A366   2.90d Turkey    1.30 .65
932 A366   3.30d Rooster, horiz.    1.60 .85
Nos. 929-932 (4)    4.40 2.15

Anti-French Riots, 30th Anniv. — A367

**1990, Dec. 11**
933 A367 1d multicolored    .65 .25

A368

**1990, Dec. 20**     *Perf. 14*
934 A368 1d multicolored    .40 .25
Fight against respiratory diseases.

Constitution, 2nd Anniv. — A369

**1991, Feb. 24**   *Litho.*   *Perf. 13½*
935 A369 1d multicolored    .55 .25

**Flower Type of 1986**
2d, Jasminum fruticans. 4d, Dianthus crinitus. 5d, Cyclamen africanum.

**1991, May 23**   *Litho.*   *Perf. 13½*
Size: 26x36mm
936 A312 2d multicolored    .80 .30
937 A312 4d multicolored    1.90 .70
938 A312 5d multicolored    2.25 1.00
Nos. 936-938 (3)    4.95 2.00

Children's Drawings — A370

**1991, June 3**   *Litho.*   *Perf. 13½*
939 A370 3d shown    1.20 .50
940 A370 4d Children playing    1.20 .50

Maghreb Arab Union Summit — A371

**1991, June 10**
941 A371 1d multicolored    .45 .25

Geneva Convention on Refugees, 40th Anniv. — A372

**1991, July 28**   *Litho.*   *Perf. 14½x13½*
942 A372 3d multicolored    1.00 .35

Postal Service — A373

4.20d, Expo emblem, vert.

**1991, Oct. 12**     *Perf. 14*
943 A373 1.50d shown    .60 .25
944 A373 4.20d multicolored    1.25 .50
Telecom '91, 6th World Forum and Exposition on Telecommunications, Geneva, Switzerland (No. 944).

Butterflies A374

2d, Zerynthia rumina. 4d, Melitaea didyma. 6d, Vanessa atalanta. 7d, Nymphalis polychloros.

**Granite Paper**
**1991, Nov. 21**   *Litho.*   *Perf. 11½*
945 A374 2d multicolored    .85 .35
946 A374 4d multicolored    1.20 .50
947 A374 6d multicolored    1.65 .75
948 A374 7d multicolored    2.00 1.10
Nos. 945-948 (4)    5.70 2.70

A375

3d, Necklace. 4d, Jewelry of Southern Tuaregs. 5d, Brooch. 7d, Rings, horiz.

**Granite Paper**
**1991, Dec. 21**     *Perf. 12*
949 A375 3d multicolored    .75 .30
950 A375 4d multicolored    .85 .45
951 A375 5d multicolored    1.00 .70
952 A375 7d multicolored    1.75 1.10
Nos. 949-952 (4)    4.35 2.55

Algerian Women — A376

**1992, Mar. 8**   *Litho.*   *Perf. 14*
953 A376 1.50d multicolored    .50 .25

Gazelles — A377

Designs: 1.50d, Gazella dorcas. 6.20d, Gazella cuvieri. 8.60d, Gazella dama.

**1992, May 13**     *Perf. 14½x13*
954 A377 1.50d multicolored    .50 .35
955 A377 6.20d multicolored    1.10 .75
956 A377 8.60d multicolored    1.75 1.10
Nos. 954-956 (3)    3.35 2.20

1992 Summer Olympics, Barcelona — A379

**1992, June 24**   *Litho.*   *Perf. 14*
958 A379 6.20d Runners    1.25 .50

Independence, 30th Anniv. — A381

**1992, July 7**   *Litho.*   *Perf. 14*
960 A381 5d multicolored    1.00 .30

Medicinal Plants — A382

No. 961, Ajuga iva. No. 962, Rhamnus alaternus. No. 963, Silybum marianum. No. 964, Lavandula stoechas.

**1992, Sept. 23**   *Litho.*   *Perf. 14*
961 A382 1.50d multi    .50 .25
962 A382 5.10d multi    1.20 .50
963 A382 6.20d multi    1.30 .60
964 A382 8.60d multi    1.60 .85
Nos. 961-964 (4)    4.60 2.20

Post Office Modernization — A383

**1992, Oct. 10**   *Litho.*   *Perf. 14*
965 A383 1.50d multicolored    .40 .25

Marine Life — A384

Designs: 1.50d, Hippocampus hippocampus. 2.70d, Caretta caretta. 6.20d, Muraena helena. 7.50d, Palinurus elephas.

**1992, Dec. 23**
966 A384 1.50d multicolored    .60 .25
967 A384 2.70d multicolored    .90 .25
968 A384 6.20d multicolored    1.90 .65
969 A384 7.50d multicolored    2.10 .85
Nos. 966-969 (4)    5.50 2.00

Pres. Mohammad Boudiaf (1919-92) — A385

**Granite Paper**
**1992, Nov. 3**   *Litho.*   *Perf. 11½*
970 A385   2d green & multi    .35 .25
971 A385 8.60d blue & multi    1.60 .85

Coins — A386

1.50d, Numidia, 2nd cent. BC. 2d, Dinar, 14th cent. 5.10d, Dinar, 11th cent. 6.20d, Abdelkader, 19th cent.

**Granite Paper**
**1992, Dec. 16**   *Litho.*   *Perf. 11½*
972 A386 1.50d multicolored    .30 .25
973 A386   2d multicolored    .40 .25
974 A386 5.10d multicolored    .90 .35
975 A386 6.20d multicolored    1.15 .50
Nos. 972-975 (4)    2.75 1.35

Door Knockers — A387

**1993, Feb. 17**   *Litho.*   *Perf. 14*
976 A387   2d Algiers    .30 .25
977 A387 5.60d Constantine    .80 .40
978 A387 8.60d Tlemcen    1.50 .65
Nos. 976-978 (3)    2.60 1.30

Flowering Trees — A388

4.50d, Neflier (medlar), horiz. 8.60d, Cognassier (quince). 11d, Abricotier (apricot).

**Granite Paper**
**1993, Mar. 17**   *Perf. 12x11½, 11½x12*
979 A388 4.50d multicolored    .85 .40
980 A388 8.60d multicolored    1.75 .75
981 A388   11d multicolored    2.25 1.00
Nos. 979-981 (3)    4.85 2.15

Natl. Coast Guard Service, 20th Anniv. — A389

**1993, Apr. 3**   *Litho.*   *Perf. 14*
982 A389 2d multicolored    1.10 .30

Traditional Grain Processing — A390

# ALGERIA

**1993, May 19**   Litho.   *Perf. 14*
| 983 | A390 | 2d Container | .45 | .25 |
| --- | --- | --- | --- | --- |
| 984 | A390 | 5.60d Millstone | .90 | .50 |
| 985 | A390 | 8.60d Press | 1.40 | .65 |
|  |  | Nos. 983-985 (3) | 2.75 | 1.40 |

Royal Mausoleums — A391

**1993, June 16**   Litho.   *Perf. 14*
| 986 | A391 | 8.60d Mauretania | 1.25 | .60 |
| --- | --- | --- | --- | --- |
| 987 | A391 | 12d El Khroub | 2.00 | .85 |

Ports — A392

**1993, Oct. 20**   Litho.   *Perf. 14x13½*
| 988 | A392 | 2d Annaba | .35 | .25 |
| --- | --- | --- | --- | --- |
| 989 | A392 | 8.60d Arzew | 1.50 | .55 |

Varanus Griseus — A393

Design: 2d, Chamaeleo vulgaris, vert.

*Perf. 13½x14, 14x13½*

**1993, Nov. 20**
| 990 | A393 | 2d multicolored | .50 | .25 |
| --- | --- | --- | --- | --- |
| 991 | A393 | 8.60d multicolored | 1.75 | .80 |

Tourism — A394

**1993, Dec. 18**   Litho.   *Perf. 14x13½*
| 992 | A394 | 2d Tipaza | .35 | .25 |
| --- | --- | --- | --- | --- |
| 993 | A394 | 8.60d Kerzaz | 1.10 | .50 |

A395

**1994, Jan. 2**   *Perf. 13½x14*
| 994 | A395 | 2d multicolored | .60 | .25 |
| --- | --- | --- | --- | --- |

SONATRACH (Natl. Society for Research, Transformation, and Commercialization of Hydrocarbons), 30th anniv.

Chahid Day — A396

**1994, Feb. 18**   Litho.   *Perf. 13½x14*
| 995 | A396 | 2d multicolored | .60 | .25 |
| --- | --- | --- | --- | --- |

1994 World Cup Soccer Championships, US — A397

**1994, Mar. 16**   *Perf. 14x13½*
| 996 | A397 | 8.60d multicolored | 2.25 | .85 |
| --- | --- | --- | --- | --- |

Orchids — A398

5.60d, Orchis simia lam. 8.60d, Ophrys lutea cavan. 11d, Ophrys apifera huds.

**1994, Apr. 20**   Litho.   *Perf. 11½*
Granite Paper
| 997 | A398 | 5.60d multicolored | 1.50 | .60 |
| --- | --- | --- | --- | --- |
| 998 | A398 | 8.60d multicolored | 1.75 | .85 |
| 999 | A398 | 11d multicolored | 2.75 | 1.25 |
|  |  | Nos. 997-999 (3) | 6.00 | 2.70 |

Ancient Petroglyphs — A399

3d, Inscriptions. 10d, Man on horse.

**1994, May 21**   Litho.   *Perf. 13x14*
| 1000 | A399 | 3d multicolored | .95 | .25 |
| --- | --- | --- | --- | --- |
| 1001 | A399 | 10d multicolored | 2.10 | .75 |

A400

**1994, June 25**
| 1002 | A400 | 12d multicolored | 1.90 | .65 |
| --- | --- | --- | --- | --- |

Intl. Olympic Committee, cent.

World Population Day — A401

**1994, July 13**
| 1003 | A401 | 3d multicolored | .50 | .25 |
| --- | --- | --- | --- | --- |

**Views of Algiers Type of 1992**

Design: 3d, like No. 775.

**1994, July 13**   Litho.   *Perf. 14*
| 1010 | A290b | 3d dk blue & lt blue | .75 | .25 |
| --- | --- | --- | --- | --- |

Jewelry from Saharan Atlas Region — A402

*Perf. 13½x14, 14x13½*   Litho.

**1994, Oct. 18**
| 1019 | A402 | 3d Fibules, vert. | .60 | .25 |
| --- | --- | --- | --- | --- |
| 1020 | A402 | 5d Belt | .90 | .30 |
| 1021 | A402 | 12d Bracelets | 2.40 | .85 |
|  |  | Nos. 1019-1021 (3) | 3.90 | 1.40 |

Algerian Revolution, 40th Anniv. — A403

**1994, Nov. 3**   Litho.   *Perf. 13½x14*
| 1022 | A403 | 3d multicolored | .40 | .25 |
| --- | --- | --- | --- | --- |

A404

**1994, Nov. 16**   Litho.   *Perf. 13½x14*
| 1023 | A404 | 3d Ladybugs | .50 | .25 |
| --- | --- | --- | --- | --- |
| 1024 | A404 | 12d Beetles | 2.00 | .75 |

Fight Against AIDS — A405

**1994, Dec. 1**   Litho.   *Perf. 14x13½*
| 1025 | A405 | 3d multicolored | 1.00 | .25 |
| --- | --- | --- | --- | --- |

Folk Dances — A406

**1994, Dec. 17**   Litho.   *Perf. 13½x14*
| 1026 | A406 | 3d Algeroise | .40 | .30 |
| --- | --- | --- | --- | --- |
| 1027 | A406 | 10d Constantinoise | 1.20 | .75 |
| 1028 | A406 | 12d Alaoui | 1.40 | .90 |
|  |  | Nos. 1026-1028 (3) | 3.00 | 1.95 |

See Nos. 1170-1172.

Minerals — A407

**1994, Sept. 21**
| 1029 | A407 | 3d Gres lite-erode | .60 | .25 |
| --- | --- | --- | --- | --- |
| 1030 | A407 | 5d Cipolin | 1.00 | .50 |
| 1031 | A407 | 10d Marne a turitella | 2.40 | .95 |
|  |  | Nos. 1029-1031 (3) | 4.00 | 1.70 |

World Tourism Organization, 20th Anniv. — A408

**1995, Jan. 28**   Litho.   *Perf. 14x13½*
| 1032 | A408 | 3d multicolored | .40 | .25 |
| --- | --- | --- | --- | --- |

Honey Bees — A409

**1995, Feb. 22**   *Perf. 13½x14, 14x13½*
| 1033 | A409 | 3d shown | .40 | .30 |
| --- | --- | --- | --- | --- |
| 1034 | A409 | 13d On flower, horiz. | 1.60 | .90 |

Flowers — A410

Granite Paper

**1995, Mar. 29**   Photo.   *Perf. 11½*
| 1035 | A410 | 3d Dahlias | .50 | .30 |
| --- | --- | --- | --- | --- |
| 1036 | A410 | 10d Zinnias | 1.50 | .80 |
| 1037 | A410 | 13d Lilacs | 1.75 | .90 |
|  |  | Nos. 1035-1037 (3) | 3.75 | 2.00 |

Decorative Stonework — A411

Various patterns.

**1995, Apr. 19**   *Perf. 14*
| 1039 | A411 | 3d brown | .60 | .30 |
| --- | --- | --- | --- | --- |
| 1040 | A411 | 4d green | .75 | .30 |
| 1041 | A411 | 5d deep claret | .90 | .30 |
|  |  | Nos. 1039-1041 (3) | 2.25 | .90 |

End of World War II, 50th Anniv. — A413

**1995, May 3**   *Perf. 14x13½*
| 1048 | A413 | 3d multicolored | .70 | .30 |
| --- | --- | --- | --- | --- |

Souvenir Sheet

VE Day, 50th Anniv. A414

**1995, May 10**   Litho.   *Perf. 13½x14*
| 1049 | A414 | 13d multicolored | 7.00 | 7.00 |
| --- | --- | --- | --- | --- |

Volleyball, Cent. — A415

**1995, June 14**
| 1050 | A415 | 3d multicolored | .65 | .30 |
| --- | --- | --- | --- | --- |

Environmental Protection — A416

3d, Air, water pollution. 13d, Air pollution.

**1995, June 5**
| 1051 | A416 | 3d multicolored | .40 | .30 |
| --- | --- | --- | --- | --- |
| 1052 | A416 | 13d multicolored | 1.60 | .85 |

General Electrification — A417

**1995, July 5**   Litho.   *Perf. 13½x14*
| 1053 | A417 | 3d multicolored | .65 | .30 |
| --- | --- | --- | --- | --- |

UN, 50th Anniv. — A418

**1995, Oct. 24**   *Perf. 14x13½*
| 1054 | A418 | 13d multicolored | 2.50 | 1.00 |
| --- | --- | --- | --- | --- |

# 426 ALGERIA

Pottery — A419

10d, Pot, Lakhdaria. 20d, Pitcher, Aokas. 21d, Jar, Larbaa Nath Iraten. 30d, Vase, Ouadhia.

**1995, Nov. 14   Litho.   Perf. 14**
| 1055 | A419 | 10d dark brown | 1.00 | .50 |
| --- | --- | --- | --- | --- |
| 1056 | A419 | 20d dull maroon | 2.10 | 1.00 |
| 1057 | A419 | 21d golden brown | 2.10 | 1.00 |
| 1058 | A419 | 30d dark rose brown | 3.25 | 1.25 |
| | | Nos. 1055-1058 (4) | 8.45 | 3.75 |

Aquatic Birds — A420

**1995, Dec. 20   Litho.   Perf. 14x13½**
| 1059 | A420 | 3d Tadorna tadorna | .70 | .25 |
| --- | --- | --- | --- | --- |
| 1060 | A420 | 5d Gallinago gallinago | 1.20 | .40 |

1996 Summer Olympics, Atlanta — A421

**1996, Jan. 24   Litho.   Perf. 14x13½**
| 1061 | A421 | 20d multicolored | 2.10 | 1.00 |
| --- | --- | --- | --- | --- |

Touareg Leather Crafts — A422

**Perf. 14x13½, 13½x14**
**1996, Feb. 14   Litho.**
| 1062 | A422 | 5d shown | 1.00 | .30 |
| --- | --- | --- | --- | --- |
| 1063 | A422 | 16d Saddle bag, vert. | 1.50 | 1.00 |

Pasteur Institute of Algeria — A423

**1996, Mar. 20   Litho.   Perf. 13½x14**
| 1064 | A423 | 5d multicolored | .75 | .25 |
| --- | --- | --- | --- | --- |

Youm El Ilm — A424

Designs: 16d, Dove, stylus, vert. 23d, Open book showing pencil, stylus, compass, satellite in earth orbit, vert.

**Perf. 14x13½, 13½x14**
**1996, Apr. 16   Litho.**
| 1065 | A424 | 5d multicolored | .55 | .30 |
| --- | --- | --- | --- | --- |
| 1066 | A424 | 16d multicolored | 1.40 | .80 |
| 1067 | A424 | 23d multicolored | 2.50 | 1.25 |
| | | Nos. 1065-1067 (3) | 4.45 | 2.35 |

Minerals — A425

Mineral, region: 10d, Iron, Djebel-Ouenza. 20d, Gold, Tirek-Amesmessa.

**1996, May 6   Litho.   Perf. 14x13½**
| 1068 | A425 | 10d multicolored | 1.15 | .55 |
| --- | --- | --- | --- | --- |
| 1069 | A425 | 20d multicolored | 2.10 | 1.00 |

Butterflies A426

Designs: 5d, Pandoriana pandora. 10d, Coenonympha pamphilus. 20d, Cynthia cardui. 23d, Melanargia galathea.

**1996, June 12   Litho.   Perf. 11½**
**Granite Paper**
| 1070 | A426 | 5d multicolored | .75 | .30 |
| --- | --- | --- | --- | --- |
| 1071 | A426 | 10d multicolored | 1.25 | .60 |
| 1072 | A426 | 20d multicolored | 2.75 | 1.00 |
| 1073 | A426 | 23d multicolored | 3.00 | 1.50 |
| | | Nos. 1070-1073 (4) | 7.75 | 3.40 |

Civil Protection — A427

5d, Giving medical aid, ambulance. 23d, Prevention of natural disasters, vert.

**Perf. 14x13½, 13½x14**
**1996, Oct. 9   Litho.**
| 1074 | A427 | 5d multicolored | .60 | .30 |
| --- | --- | --- | --- | --- |
| 1075 | A427 | 23d multicolored | 2.75 | 1.25 |

World Day Against Use of Illegal Drugs — A428

**1996, June 26   Litho.   Perf. 14x13½**
| 1076 | A428 | 5d multicolored | .70 | .30 |
| --- | --- | --- | --- | --- |

UNICEF, 50th Anniv. — A429

Stylized designs: 5d, Two children, wreath, pencils, flowers. 10d, Five children, pencil, key, flower, flag, hypodermic.

**1996, Nov. 20   Litho.   Perf. 13½x14**
| 1077 | A429 | 5d multicolored | .40 | .30 |
| --- | --- | --- | --- | --- |
| 1078 | A429 | 10d multicolored | .80 | .45 |

4th General Census — A430

**1997, Feb. 12   Litho.   Perf. 14x13½**
| 1079 | A430 | 5d multicolored | .50 | .30 |
| --- | --- | --- | --- | --- |

Protest at Ouargla, 35th Anniv. — A431

**1997, Feb. 27   Perf. 13½x14**
| 1080 | A431 | 5d multicolored | .50 | .30 |
| --- | --- | --- | --- | --- |

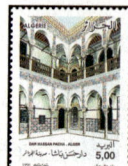
Interior Courts of Algerian Dwellings — A432

Designs: 5d, Palace of Hassan Pasha. 10d, Khedaouj El-Amia, Algiers. 20d, Palace of Light. 30d, Abdellatif Villa.

**1996, Dec. 18   Litho.   Perf. 13½x14**
| 1081 | A432 | 5d multicolored | .40 | .25 |
| --- | --- | --- | --- | --- |
| 1082 | A432 | 10d multicolored | .80 | .45 |
| 1083 | A432 | 20d multicolored | 1.75 | 1.00 |
| 1084 | A432 | 30d multicolored | 2.50 | 1.40 |
| | | Nos. 1081-1084 (4) | 5.45 | 3.10 |

Paintings by Ismail Samsom (1934-88) — A433

20d, Woman with Pigeons. 30d, Interrogation.

**1996, Dec. 25   Perf. 14**
| 1085 | A433 | 20d multicolored | 1.25 | 1.00 |
| --- | --- | --- | --- | --- |
| 1086 | A433 | 30d multicolored | 1.75 | 1.50 |

Victory Day, 35th Anniv. — A434

**1997, Mar. 19   Perf. 14x13½**
| 1087 | A434 | 5d multicolored | .50 | .25 |
| --- | --- | --- | --- | --- |

Flowers — A435

Designs: 5d, Ficaria verna. 16d, Lonicera arborea. 23d, Papaver rhoeas.

**1997, Apr. 23   Litho.   Perf. 13½x14**
| 1088 | A435 | 5d multicolored | .50 | .30 |
| --- | --- | --- | --- | --- |
| 1089 | A435 | 16d multicolored | 1.40 | .90 |
| 1090 | A435 | 23d multicolored | 2.00 | 1.50 |
| | | Nos. 1088-1090 (3) | 3.90 | 2.70 |

World Day to Stop Smoking — A436

**1997, May 31   Litho.   Perf. 13½x14**
| 1091 | A436 | 5d multicolored | .65 | .25 |
| --- | --- | --- | --- | --- |

Legislative Elections — A437

**1997, June 4**
| 1092 | A437 | 5d multicolored | .45 | .25 |
| --- | --- | --- | --- | --- |

Scorpions — A438

Designs: 5d, Buthus occitanus tunetanus. 10d, Androctonus australis hector.

**1997, June 18   Perf. 14x13½**
| 1093 | A438 | 5d multicolored | .55 | .30 |
| --- | --- | --- | --- | --- |
| 1094 | A438 | 10d multicolored | .95 | .60 |

Natl. Independence, 35th Anniv. — A439

Designs: 5d, Crowd celebrating, flags. 10d, Doves, broken chain, "35," flag.

**1997, July 5   Litho.   Perf. 14x13½**
| 1095 | A439 | 5d multicolored | .50 | .25 |
| --- | --- | --- | --- | --- |

**Souvenir Sheet**
**Perf. 14**
| 1096 | A439 | 10d multicolored | 2.75 | 2.75 |
| --- | --- | --- | --- | --- |

No. 1096 contains one 30x40mm stamp.

Wood Carvings — A440

Designs: 5d, Inscription, Nedroma Mosque. 23d, Door, Ketchaoua Mosque.

**1997, Jan. 15   Litho.   Perf. 13½x14**
| 1097 | A440 | 5d multicolored | .50 | .30 |
| --- | --- | --- | --- | --- |
| 1098 | A440 | 23d multicolored | 1.75 | 1.10 |

Moufdi Zakaria (1908-77), poet. — A441

**1997, Aug. 17   Litho.   Perf. 13½x14**
| 1099 | A441 | 5d multicolored | .50 | .25 |
| --- | --- | --- | --- | --- |

Textile Patterns — A442

**1997, Sept. 17   Litho.   Perf. 14**
| 1100 | A442 | 3d Dokkali | .40 | .30 |
| --- | --- | --- | --- | --- |
| 1101 | A442 | 5d Tellis | .50 | .30 |
| 1102 | A442 | 10d Bou-Taleb | .90 | .60 |
| 1103 | A442 | 20d Ddil | 1.75 | 1.25 |
| | | Nos. 1100-1103 (4) | 3.55 | 2.45 |

Natl. Police Force, 25th Anniv. — A443

**1997, Oct. 6   Perf. 14x13½**
| 1104 | A443 | 5d multicolored | .60 | .25 |
| --- | --- | --- | --- | --- |

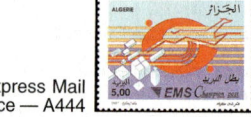
Express Mail Service — A444

**1997, Oct. 9**
| 1105 | A444 | 5d multicolored | .60 | .25 |
| --- | --- | --- | --- | --- |

# ALGERIA

Local Elections — A445

**1997, Oct. 23**    *Perf. 13½x14*
1106   A445   5d multicolored    .50   .25

Lighthouses A446

5d, Tenes. 10d, Cape Caxine, vert.

*Perf. 14x13½, 13½x14*
**1997, Nov. 5**    *Litho.*
1107   A446   5d multicolored    .65   .25
1108   A446   10d multicolored    1.50   .70

New Airpost Service, 1st Anniv. — A447

**1997, Nov. 17**    *Perf. 14x13½*
1109   A447   5d multicolored    .60   .25

Shells — A448

Designs: 5d, Chlamys varia. 10d, Bolinus brandaris. 20d, Hinia reticulata, vert.

*Perf. 14x13½, 13½x14*
**1997, Dec. 17**    *Litho.*
1110   A448   5d multicolored    .90   .25
1111   A448   10d multicolored    1.50   .60
1112   A448   20d multicolored    3.00   1.20
   Nos. 1110-1112 (3)    5.40   2.05

A449

**1997, Dec. 25**    *Perf. 13½x14*
1113   A449   5d multicolored    .60   .25

Election of the Natl. Council.

A450

Completion of Government Reforms: a, Natl. flag, people, book, ballot box. b, People, open book, torch. c, Ballot box. d, Flag, rising sun, flower. e, Ballots, building, flag.

**1997, Dec. 30**    *Litho.*    *Perf. 13½x14*
1114   A450   5d Strip of 5, #a.-e.    2.50   2.50

Bombing of Sakiet Sidi Youcef, 40th Anniv. — A451

**1998, Feb. 8**    *Litho.*    *Perf. 14x13½*
1115   A451   5d multicolored    .70   .25

National Archives — A452

**1998, Feb. 16**
1116   A452   5d multicolored    .50   .25

Intl. Women's Day — A453

**1998, Mar. 8**    *Litho.*    *Perf. 14x13½*
1117   A453   5d multicolored    .50   .25

Expo '98, Lisbon — A454

**1998, Jan. 21**    *Litho.*    *Perf. 14x13½*
1118   A454   5d shown    .50   .25
   *Size: 80x75mm*
   *Imperf*
1119   A454   24d Mosaic    3.25   3.25

1998 World Cup Soccer Championships, Paris — A455

**1998, Apr. 15**    *Litho.*    *Perf. 13½x14*
1120   A455   24d multi    2.40   1.25

Algiers Casbah — A456

Designs: 5d, Aerial view, vert. 10d, Buildings, vert. 24d, Aerial view, diff.

**1998, Apr. 22**    *Perf. 13½x14, 14x13½*
1121   A456   5d multi    .40   .25
1122   A456   10d multi    .75   .60
1123   A456   24d multi    1.75   1.25
   Nos. 1121-1123 (3)    2.90   2.10

Zaatcha Resistance A457

**1998, May 20**    *Perf. 13¼x13*
1124   A457   5d multi    .50   .25

Tourism — A458

5d, Mountains, farm, desert, vert. 10d, Youths, modes of transportation. 24d, Taghit.

*Perf. 13½x14, 14x13½*
**1998, June 4**    *Litho.*
1125   A458   5d multi    .40   .25
1126   A458   10d multi    .80   .50
1127   A458   24d multi    1.75   1.25
   Nos. 1125-1127 (3)    2.95   2.00

Arab Post Day — A459

**1998, Aug. 3**    *Litho.*    *Perf. 14x13½*
1128   A459   5d multi    .75   .25

Interpol, 75th Anniv. — A460

**1998, Sept. 7**    *Litho.*    *Perf. 14x13½*
1129   A460   5d multi    .60   .25

Creation of Provisional Government, 40th Anniv. A461

**1998, Sept. 19**    *Perf. 13¼x13*
1130   A461   5d multi    .60   .25

Natl. Diplomacy Day — A462

**1998, Oct. 8**    *Perf. 14*
1131   A462   5d multi    .50   .25

Algerian Olympic Committee, 35th Anniv. — A463

**1998, Oct. 18**    *Perf. 14x13½*
1132   A463   5d multi    .60   .25

Birds — A464

Designs: 5d, Pandion haliaetus. 10d, Larus audouinii. 24d, Phalacrocorax aristotelis, vert. 30d, Phalacrocorax carbo, vert.

*Perf. 14x13½, 13½x14*
**1998, Nov. 11**
1133   A464   5d multi    .70   .25
1134   A464   10d multi    1.40   .60
1135   A464   24d multi    2.75   1.25
1136   A464   30d multi    3.50   1.75
   Nos. 1133-1136 (4)    8.35   3.85

See Nos. 1204-1207, 1325-1326.

Universal Declaration of Human Rights, 50th Anniv. — A465

**1998, Dec. 10**    *Litho.*    *Perf. 14x13½*
1137   A465   5d Profiles, emblem    .60   .25
1138   A465   24d shown    2.25   1.00

Spinning and Weaving Tools — A466

Designs: 5d, Comb, vert. 10d, Cards. 20d, Spindle, vert. 24d, Loom, vert.

**1999, Jan. 20**    *Perf. 13½x14, 14x13½*
1139   A466   5d multi    .55   .25
1140   A466   10d multi    1.00   .50
1141   A466   20d multi    2.10   1.00
1142   A466   24d multi    2.50   1.25
   Nos. 1139-1142 (4)    6.15   3.00

Natl. Chahid Day — A467

**1999, Feb. 18**    *Perf. 13x13¼*
1143   A467   5d multi    .50   .25

Flowering Trees — A468

**1999, Mar. 17**    *Perf. 14x13½, 13½x14*
1144   A468   5d Pear    .50   .25
1145   A468   10d Plum    .90   .50
1146   A468   24d Orange, vert.    2.10   1.25
   Nos. 1144-1146 (3)    3.50   2.00

Presidential Elections — A469

**1999, Apr. 15**    *Perf. 13x13¼*
1147   A469   5d multi    .50   .25

Handicrafts A470

Designs: 5d, Tlemcen mosaic, 14th cent., vert. 10d, Mosaic, Al Qal'a of Beni Hammad, 11th cent, vert. 20d, Cradle. 24d, Table.

**1999, Apr. 18**    *Perf. 13¼x14, 14x13¼*
1148   A470   5d multi    .55   .25
1149   A470   10d multi    .90   .60
1150   A470   20d multi    1.75   1.00
1151   A470   24d multi    2.10   1.25
   Nos. 1148-1151 (4)    5.30   3.10

7th African Games, Johannesburg A471

Stylized athletes and: 5d, Map of Africa, vert. 10d, South African flag.

**1999, May 12**    *Perf. 13¼x14, 14x13¼*
1152   A471   5d multi    .45   .25
1153   A471   10d multi    .80   .50

Rocks — A472

**1999, June 6**    *Perf. 13¼x14*
1154   A472   5d Gneiss    .45   .25
1155   A472   20d Granite    1.60   1.00
1156   A472   24d Schist    2.00   1.25
   Nos. 1154-1156 (3)    4.05   2.50

# ALGERIA

A473

**1999, July 12**    **Perf. 13x13¼**
1157 A473 5d multi    .50 .25
Organization of African Unity, 35th summit.

A474

**1999, July 12**    **Perf. 13¼x14**
1158 A474 5d multi    .50 .25
Organization of African Unity Convention on Refugees.

Police Day — A475

**1999, July 22**    **Perf. 13x13¼**
1159 A475 5d multicolored    1.00 .25

Intl. Year of Culture and Peace (in 2000) — A476

**1999, Sept. 14**    **Litho.**    **Perf. 14**
1160 A476 5d multi    .50 .25

Fish — A477

Designs: 5d, Dentex dentex. 10d, Mullus surmuletus. 20d, Dentex gibbosus. 24d, Diplodus sargus.

**1999, Sept. 15**    **Perf. 14x13¼**
1161 A477 5d multi    .65 .25
1162 A477 10d multi    1.25 .50
1163 A477 20d multi    2.25 1.00
1164 A477 24d multi    3.25 1.25
   Nos. 1161-1164 (4)    7.40 3.00

Civil Peace Referendum — A478

**1999, Sept. 16**    **Perf. 13¼x14**
1165 A478 5d multi    .50 .25

UPU, 125th Anniv. — A479

**1999, Oct. 9**    **Perf. 14x13¼**
1166 A479 5d multi    .55 .25

World Post Day — A480

**1999, Oct. 9**    **Litho.**    **Perf. 14x13½**
1167 A480 5d multi    .55 .25

Intl. Rural Women's Day — A481

**1999, Oct. 14**    **Litho.**    **Perf. 14x13¼**
1168 A481 5d multi    .55 .25

Algerian Revolution, 45th Anniv. — A482

Soldiers and: a, Helicopters, burning flag. b, Burning flag.

**1999, Nov. 1**    **Perf. 13x13¼**
1169 A482 5d Pair, #a.-b.    1.25 1.25

**Folk Dances Type of 1994**
**1999, Dec. 15**    **Perf. 13¼x14**
1170 A406 5d Chaoui    .60 .25
1171 A406 10d Targuie    1.10 .50
1172 A406 24d Mzab    2.25 1.25
   Nos. 1170-1172 (3)    3.95 2.00

Millennium — A483

No. 1173: a, Doves, UN emblem. b, Sun, plant, trees. c, Umbrella over wheat and corn plants. d, Microscope and flasks. e, Crane, ship, truck. f, Train, Concorde, satellite dish, satellite, Moon. g, Windmills. h, Globe, ballot box. i, Apollo 15 astronauts on Moon. j, Film, inkwell, musical instrument and notes.
No. 1174: a, Dove with olive branch. b, Hand, flora, fauna. c, Satellites, computer, map of Africa and Europe. d, Heart, staff of Aesculapius, Red Cross, Red Crescent. e, Stylized globe and arrows. f, Animals, film, violin, painting, book. g, Flame, sun, water. h, Hand holding plant. i, symbols of democracy. j, Satellite, planets, space shuttle, astronaut.

**Sawtooth Die Cut 6¼ Vert.**
**2000, Jan. 19**    **Self-Adhesive**
**Booklet Stamps**
1173    Bklt. pane of 10 + 2 labels    10.00
   a.-j. A483 5d any single    .50 .50
1174    Bklt. pane of 10 + 2 labels    10.00
   a.-j. A483 5d any single    .50 .50

Birds — A484

Designs: No. 1175, 5d, Canary (serin cini). No. 1176, 5d, Finch (pinson), vert. 10d, Bullfinch (bouvreuil). 24d, Goldfinch (chardonneret), vert.

**Perf. 14x13¼, 13¼x14**
**2000, Jan. 19**    **Litho.**
1175-1178 A484 Set of 4    5.50 5.50

Expo 2000, Hanover — A485

**2000, Feb. 16**    **Litho.**    **Perf. 14x13¼**
1179 A485 5d multi    .60 .30

2000 Summer Olympics, Sydney — A486

**2000, Mar. 22**
1180 A486 24d multi    2.50 1.25

Telethon 2000 — A487

**2000, Apr. 8**    **Perf. 13¼x14**
1181 A487 5d multi    .75 .25

Civil Concord — A488

Designs: 5d, Dove, handshake, crowd, vert. 10d, Handshake, hands releasing dove. 20d, Handshake, doves, flowers. 24d, Doves, flowers, handshake, vert.

**Perf. 11½x11¾, 11¾x11½**
**2000, Apr. 15**
1182-1185 A488 Set of 4    6.50 3.25

National Library A489

**2000, Apr. 16**    **Perf. 13½x13**
1186 A489 5d multi    .60 .25

Blood Donation — A490

**2000, May 2**    **Perf. 13¼x14**
1187 A490 5d multi    .60 .25

Tuareg Handicrafts A491

Background colors: 5d, Rose. 10d, Buff, vert.

**2000, May 17**    **Perf. 14**
1188-1189 A491 Set of 2    1.60 .75

Famous Men — A492

No. 1190, Mohammed Dib (b. 1920), writer. No. 1191, Mustapha Kateb (1920-89), actor. No. 1192, Ali Maachi (1927-58), musician. No. 1193, Mohamed Racim (1896-1975), artist.

**2000, June 8**    **Perf. 13¼x13**
1190-1193 A492 10d Set of 4    4.25 2.00

Insects — A493

No. 1194, 5d, Hanneton. No. 1195, 5d, Anthrene. 10d, Vrillete du pain. 24d, Carabe.

**2000, Sept. 20**    **Perf. 13¼x14**
1194-1197 A493 Set of 4    5.25 2.50

Roman Cinerary Urns Found at Tipasa — A494

**2000, Oct. 18**    **Litho.**    **Perf. 14**
1198-1200 A494 Set of 3, 5d, 10d, 24d    4.25 2.25

Orchids — A495

Designs: 5d, Limodorum abortivum. 10d, Orchis papilionacea. 24d, Orchis provincialis.

**2000, Dec. 13**    **Litho.**    **Perf. 14**
1201-1203 A495 Set of 3    4.50 2.50

**Bird Type of 1998**
Designs: No. 1204, 5d, Anser anser. No. 1205, 5d, Recurvirostra avosetta, vert. 10d, Botaurus stellaris, vert. 24d, Numenius arquata.

**2001, Jan. 24**
1204-1207 A464 Set of 4    5.00 2.75

Handicrafts A496

Designs: 5d, Skampla, vert. 10d, Etagere. 24d, Mirror, vert.

**2001, Feb. 21**
1208-1210 A496 Set of 3    4.50 2.50

National Parks — A497

Designs: 5d, Belezma, vert. 10d, Gouraya. 20d, Théniet el Had. 24d, El Kala, vert.

**2001, Mar. 21**    **Perf. 13¼x14, 14x13¼**
1211-1214 A497 Set of 4    7.00 3.25

# ALGERIA

1st Intl. Colloquium on St. Augustine of Hippo A498

Designs: 5d, Statue of St. Augustine (25x37mm). 24d, Mosaic.

**Perf. 13¼x14, 13¼x13 (24d)**
**2001, Mar. 31**
1215-1216  A498  Set of 2  3.50  1.60

Silver Coins A499

Designs: 5d, 1830 Ryal boudjou. 10d, 1826 Double boudjou. 24d, 1771 Ryal drahem.

**2001, Apr. 25  Litho.  Perf. 13½x13**
1217-1219  A499  Set of 3  4.50  2.25

Natl. Scouting Day — A500

**2001, May 27  Litho.  Perf. 14**
1220  A500  5d multi  .60  .25

Palestinian Intifada — A501

**2001, June 2**
1221  A501  5d multi  .60  .25

Children's Games — A502

Designs: No. 1222, 5d, Jacks. No. 1223, 5d, Hopscotch. No. 1224, 5d, Top spinning. No. 1225, 5d, Marbles.

**2001, June 2**
1222-1225  A502  Set of 4  2.50  .90

Natl. Asthma Day — A503

**2001, June 9**
1226  A503  5d multi  .50  .25

14th Mediterranean Games, Tunis, Tunisia A504

Designs: No. 1227, 5d, Map, "50." No. 1228, 5d, Runners, emblem.

**2001, July 25  Litho.  Perf. 14**
1227-1228  A504  Set of 2  1.00  .50

15th World Festival of Youth and Students — A505

**2001, Aug. 8**
1229  A505  5d multi  .50  .25

Natl. Mujahedeen Day — A506

**2001, Aug. 20  Perf. 13¼x14**
1230  A506  5d multi  .50  .25

Intl. Teachers' Day — A507

**2001, Oct. 6  Litho.  Perf. 13¼x14**
1231  A507  5d multi  .50  .25

Year of Dialogue Among Civilizations — A508

**2001, Oct. 9**
1232  A508  5d multi  .75  .30

Natl. Emigration Day — A509

**2001, Oct. 17  Perf. 14x13¼**
1233  A509  5d multi  .50  .25

19th Cent. Revolt Leaders — A510

Designs: No. 1234, 5d, Sheik El-Mokrani, 1871-73. No. 1235, 5d, Sheik Bouamama, 1881-1908.

**2001, Nov. 1  Perf. 13¼x14**
1234-1235  A510  Set of 2  1.10  .50

Jewelry From Aurès Region — A511

Designs: No. 1236, 5d, Fibula. No. 1237, 5d, Earring. 24d, Pendant.

**2002, Jan. 23**
1236-1238  A511  Set of 3  3.00  3.00

2002 World Cup Soccer Championships, Japan and Korea — A512

Designs: 5d, Goalie, ball, net, pagoda. 24d, Oriental man, ball, vert.

**2002, Feb. 27  Perf. 14x13¼, 13¼x14**
1239-1240  A512  Set of 2  2.75  2.00

Ceasefire With French Forces, 40th Anniv. — A513

**2002, Mar. 19  Perf. 13x13½**
1241  A513  5d multi  .70  .40

Villages — A514

Designs: No. 1242, 5d, Sidi-Ouali. No. 1243, 5d, Casbah of Ighzar.

**2002, Apr. 17  Litho.  Perf. 14x13¼**
1242-1243  A514  Set of 2  1.00  .80

World Basketball Championships, Indianapolis — A515

**2002, May 15  Perf. 13¼x14**
1244  A515  5d multi  .75  .45

Children's Day — A516

Children's art: No. 1245, 5d, Shown. No. 1246, 5d, Two girls, one waving.

**2002, June 1  Perf. 14x13¼**
1245-1246  A516  Set of 2  1.00  .80

Mohamed Temmam (1915-88), Artist — A517

Designs: No. 1247, 10d, Self-portrait. No. 1248, 10d, Tailor.

**2002, June 8  Perf. 13x13¼**
1247-1248  A517  Set of 2  2.00  1.50

Independence, 40th Anniv. — A518

Designs: 5d, Emblem. 24d, People with flag.

**2002, July 5  Litho.  Perf. 14**
1249-1250  A518  Set of 2  2.50  2.00

Rocks and Minerals — A519

Designs: No. 1251, 5d, Conglomerate rock. No. 1252, 5d, Galena. No. 1253, 5d, Calcite, vert. No. 1254, 5d, Feldspar, vert.

**2002, July 24**
1251-1254  A519  Set of 4  2.00  2.00

Lighthouses A520

Designs: 5d, Cherchell. 10d, Cap de Fer. 24d, Ile de Rachgoun.

**2002, Sept. 11**
1255-1257  A520  Set of 3  3.25  3.25

Reorganization of Postal Service — A521

**2002, Oct. 9**
1258  A521  5d multi  .50  .50

Pottery — A522

Designs: No. 1259, 5d, Oil lamp. No. 1260, 5d, Jar with handles, Iraten. No. 1261, 5d, Jar, Miliana. No. 1262, 5d, Cooking pot and couscousier, Lakhdaria.

**2002, Oct. 23**
1259-1262  A522  Set of 4  2.00  2.00

Intl. Day for Tolerance — A523

**2002, Nov. 16  Litho.  Perf. 14**
1263  A523  24d multi  2.00  2.00

Shells — A524

Designs: No. 1264, 5d, Acanthocardia aculeata. No. 1265, 5d, Venus verrucosa. No. 1266, 5d, Epitonium commune. No. 1267, 5d, Xenophora crispa.

**2002, Dec. 4  Litho.  Perf. 14**
1264-1267  A524  Set of 4  2.50  2.50

Medicinal Plants — A525

Designs: 5d, Eucalyptus globulus. 10d, Malva sylvestris. 24d, Laurus nobilis.

**2002, Dec. 21**
1268-1270  A525  Set of 3  3.25  3.25

# ALGERIA

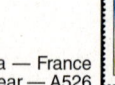

Algeria — France Year — A526

Designs: 5d, Eiffel Tower, Paris and Martyr's Monument, Algiers, vert. 24d, Flags of Algeria and France.

**2003, Feb. 19**
1271-1272  A526  Set of 2     2.50  2.50

10th Arab Games — A527

**2003, Feb. 26**
1273  A527  5d multi          .40   .40

Intl. Year of Water — A528

Designs: 5d, El Maadjen, Relizane. 10d, Well, M'zab Valley. 24d, Kesria, Timimoun.

**2003, Mar. 22**   Litho.   Perf. 14
1274-1276  A528  Set of 3    3.50  3.50

Vandal Tablets — A529

Designs: 10d, Slave sale document, 494. 24d, Tablet for calculations, 493, vert.

*Perf. 13x13¼, 13¼x13*
**2003, Apr. 23**                        Litho.
1277-1278  A529  Set of 2    3.00  3.00

Portions of the designs were applied by a thermographic process producing a shiny, raised effect.

Natl. Students Day — A530

**2003, May 19**   Litho.   Perf. 14
1279  A530  5d multi          .40   .40

Snails — A531

Designs: 5d, Rumina decollata. 24d, Heix aspersa.

**2003, May 21**   Litho.   Perf. 14
1280-1281  A531  Set of 2    2.50  2.50

African Union, 1st Anniv. — A532

**2003, July 9**             Perf. 13¼x14
1282  A532  5d multi          .50   .50

Seaweeds — A533

Designs: 5d, Ulva lactuca. 24d, Gymnogongrus crenulatus.

**2003, July 30**   Litho.   Perf. 14
1283-1284  A533  Set of 2    2.50  2.50

Roman Mosaics — A534

Designs: 5d, Farm Work. 10d, Ulysses and the Sirens. 24d, Hunting Scene.

**2003, Sept. 17**            Perf. 13½x14
1285-1287  A534  Set of 3    3.00  3.00

Algerian Olympic Committee, 40th Anniv. — A535

**2003, Oct. 18**   Litho.   Perf. 14x13½
1288  A535  5d multi          .50   .50

World Diabetes Prevention Day — A536

**2003, Nov. 14**            Perf. 13½x14
1289  A536  5d multi          .50   .50

Architectural Decorations — A537

Designs: 5d, Door, Hassan Pacha Palace, Algiers. 10d, Window, Hassan Pacha Palace. 24d, Ceiling, Djamaa Edjedid, Algiers.

**2003, Dec. 17**   Litho.   Perf. 13x13¼
1290-1292  A537  Set of 3    3.00  3.00

Algeria — People's Republic of China Diplomatic Relations, 45th Anniv. — A538

**2003, Dec. 22**            Perf. 12
1293  A538  5d multi          .50   .50

2004 Summer Olympics, Athens — A539

Olympic rings, Parthenon and: 5d, Hurdler. 10d, Torch bearer.

**2004, Feb. 29**            Perf. 13¼x14
1294-1295  A539  Set of 2   1.25  1.25

Intl. Women's Day — A540

**2004, Mar. 8**
1296  A540  5d multi          .50   .50

Arbor Day — A541

Trees: 5d, Olive. 10d, Date palm, vert.

*Perf. 14x13¼, 13¼x14*
**2004, Mar. 21**                        Litho.
1297-1298  A541  Set of 2   1.25  1.25

Numidian Kings — A542

Designs: No. 1299, 5d, Massinissa (r. 203 BC-148 BC). No. 1300, 5d, Micipsa (r. 148 BC-118 BC). No. 1301, 5d, Jugurtha (r. 118 BC-105 BC). No. 1302, 5d, Juba I (r. 63 BC-50 to 46 BC). No. 1303, 5d, Juba II (r. 29 BC- 25 BC).

**2004, Mar. 31**   Litho.   Perf. 13¼x14
1299-1303  A542  Set of 5   2.25  2.25

2004 Presidential Elections — A543

**Litho. & Embossed**
**2004, Apr. 8**             Perf. 13¼x13
1304  A543  24d multi        2.25  2.25

FIFA (Fédération Internationale de Football Association), Cent. — A544

"100" and: 5d, Goalie. 24d, Soccer balls, world map.

*Perf. 14, 14x13¼ (24d)*
**2004, May 21**                         Litho.
1305-1306  A544  Set of 2   2.50  2.50

Dromedary A545

**2004, June 9**   Litho.   Perf. 14x13¼
1307  A545  24d multi       2.25  2.25

Blood Donation Day — A546

**2004, June 14**            Perf. 14
1308  A546  5d multi          .50   .50

Professional Training — A547

**2004, June 23**
1309  A547  5d multi          .50   .50

Intl. Chess Federation (FIDE), 80th Anniv. — A548

**2004, July 21**   Litho.   Perf. 14
1310  A548  5d multi        1.20   .50

CNEP Bank, 40th Anniv. — A549

Bank emblems and: 5d, Bank notes. 24d, Algiers.

**2004, Aug. 10**   Litho.   Perf. 14
1311-1312  A549  Set of 2   2.50  2.50

Roses — A550

**2004, Oct. 20**   Litho.   Perf. 14
**Color of Rose**
1313  A550  15d yellow       1.00  1.00
1314  A550  20d yellow, diff. 2.00  2.00
1315  A550  30d red          3.00  3.00
1316  A550  50d pink         4.00  4.00
  Nos. 1313-1316 (4)        10.00 10.00

Sixth Pan-African Conference of Red Cross and Red Crescent, Algiers — A551

**2004, Sept. 8**   Litho.   Perf. 14
1317  A551  24d multi       2.25  2.25

Sahara Desert Landmarks A552

Designs: 5d, In Téhaq. 24d, Ekanassay, vert.

*Perf. 14, 14¼x14 (24d)*
**2004, Sept. 15**
1318-1319  A552  Set of 2   2.50  2.50

Revolutionary Committee of Unity and Action, 50th Anniv. A553

**2004, Nov. 1**   Litho.   Perf. 13¼x13
1320  A553  15d multi       1.75  1.75

# ALGERIA

Souvenir Sheet

Start of Algerian Revolution, 50th Anniv. — A554

**2004, Nov. 1  Litho.**
1321 A554 30d multi   2.50 2.50

Launch of ALSAT 1 Satellite, 2nd Anniv. — A555

**2004, Nov. 28  Litho.  Perf. 14x13½**
1322 A555 30d multi   2.50 2.50

Environmental Protection A556

**2004, Dec. 22**
1323 A556 15d multi   1.25 1.25

Rabah Bitat (1925-2000), Politician — A557

**2004, Dec. 29  Litho.  Perf. 14x13½**
1324 A557 15d multi   1.25 1.25

**Bird Type of 1998**

Designs: 10d, Columba palumbus. 15d, Columba livia.

**2005, Jan. 26  Litho.  Perf. 14x13¼**
1325-1326 A464  Set of 2   2.25 2.25

Flowers — A559

Designs: 15d, Echium australis. 30d, Borago officinalis.

**2005, Feb. 23  Litho.  Perf. 13½x14**
1327-1328 A559  Set of 2   3.50 3.50

Day of the Handicapped A560

**2005, Mar. 14  Perf. 14x13½**
1329 A560 15d multi   1.10 1.10

Arab League Emblem and Algerian Flag — A561

Inscription commemorating: 15d, 17th Arab Summit, Algiers. 30d, Arab League, 60th anniv., vert.

**2005, Mar. 22  Perf. 14x13½, 13½x14**
1330-1331 A561  Set of 2   3.50 3.50

National Reconciliation A562

**2005, Apr. 8  Perf. 14x13½**
1332 A562 15d multi   1.25 1.25

Madrases A563

Madras in: 10d, Algiers. 15d, Constantine. 30d, Tlemcen.

**2005, Apr. 16**
1333-1335 A563  Set of 3   4.50 4.50

Science Day.

Intl. Day of Intellectual Property — A564

**2005, Apr. 26**
1336 A564 15d multi   1.25 1.25

Intl. Day of Work Safety and Health — A565

**2005, Apr. 28  Perf. 13½x14**
1337 A565 15d multi   1.25 1.25

Massacres of May 8, 1945, 60th Anniv. — A566

**2005, May 8  Litho.  Perf. 14x13¼**
1338 A566 15d multi   1.25 1.25

15th Mediterranean Games, Almeria, Spain — A567

Games emblem and: 15d, Medal, stylized athletes. 30d, Mediterranean Sea and "2005," horiz.

**2005, May 28  Perf. 13¼x14, 14x13¼**
1339-1340 A567  Set of 2   3.50 3.50

Poets — A568

Designs: 10d, Lakhdar Ben Khlouf. 15d, Mohamed Ben M'sayeb. 20d, Si Mohand-Ou-M'hand. 30d, Aissa El-Djermouni.

**2005, June 8  Litho.  Perf. 13x13½**
1341-1344 A568  Set of 4   6.50 6.50

World Day Against Drug Abuse — A569

**2005, June 26  Perf. 14x13½**
1345 A569 15d multi   1.50 1.50

General Algerian Muslim Student's Union, 50th Anniv. — A570

**2005, July 9  Litho.  Perf. 13½x14**
1346 A570 15d multi   1.25 1.25

Leopards — A571

Leopard: 15d, Sitting. 30d, Standing.

**2005, July 21  Perf. 14x13½**
1347-1348 A571  Set of 2   3.50 3.50

World Summit on the Information Society, Tunis — A572

**2005, July 27  Perf. 13½x14**
1349 A572 15d multi   1.75 1.75

Moudjahid Day — A573

**2005, Aug. 20**
1350 A573 15d multi   1.25 1.25

Uprising at Constantine and Philippeville, 50th anniv.

Intl. Year of Sports and Physical Education — A574

**2005, Sept. 7  Litho.  Perf. 13¼x14**
1351 A574 30d multi   2.40 2.40

Forts — A575

Designs: 10d, Lighthouse Fort, Algiers. 15d, Cap Matifou Fort, Algiers. 30d, Santa Cruz Fort, Oran.

**2005, Sept. 15  Perf. 14x13¼**
1352-1354 A575  Set of 3   4.50 4.50

September 29, 2005 Referendum A576

**2005  Litho.  Perf. 14x13½**
1355 A576 15d multi   1.15 1.15

Acquisition of Control of Broadcasting, 43rd Anniv. — A577

**2005, Oct. 28**
1356 A577 30d multi   2.25 2.25

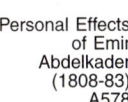 

Personal Effects of Emir Abdelkader (1808-83) A578

Designs: 15d, Saddle. 30d, Boots. 40d, Voot, vert. 50d, Signet, vert.

**2005, Nov. 1  Perf. 14x13½, 13½x14**
1357-1360 A578  Set of 4   10.50 10.50

Miguel de Cervantes (1547-1616), Writer — A579

**2005, Nov. 16  Litho.  Perf. 13½x14**
1361 A579 30d multi   2.25 2.25

Public Destruction of Mines — A580

**2005, Nov.  Litho.  Perf. 13½x14**
1362 A580 30d multi   2.25 2.25

World AIDS Day — A581

**2005, Dec. 1  Litho.  Perf. 13½x14**
1363 A581 30d multi   2.50 2.50

Numidian Kings — A582

Designs: 15d, Ptolemy of Mauretania, ruler from 23-40 A.D. 30d, Syphax, ruler from 220-203 B.C.

**2005, Dec. 14  Litho.  Perf. 13¼x14**
1364-1365 A582  Set of 2   3.25 3.25

# ALGERIA

Emblem and Headquarters of Algeria Post — A583

**2006, Jan. 14**    *Perf. 14x13¼*
1366 A583 30d multi    2.25   2.25

Birds — A584

Designs: 10d, Ciconia ciconia. 15d, Ciconia nigra. 20d, Platalea leucorodia. 30d, Grus grus.

**2006, Jan. 25**    *Perf. 13x13½*
1367-1370 A584   Set of 4   5.50   5.50

2006 Winter Olympics, Turin — A585

**2006, Feb. 1**    *Perf. 14x13¼*
1371 A585 15d multi    1.10   1.10

General Union of Algerian Workers, 50th Anniv. — A586

**2006, Feb. 24**    *Perf. 13¼x14*
1372 A586 15d multi    1.10   1.10

2006 World Cup Soccer Championships, Germany — A587

**2006, Mar. 22**
1373 A587 30d multi    2.25   2.25

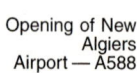
Opening of New Algiers Airport — A588

**2006, Apr. 8**    *Perf. 14x13¼*
1374 A588 30d multi    2.25   2.25

Student's Day, 50th Anniv. — A589

**2006, May 19**    *Perf. 13x13½*
1375 A589 20d multi    1.40   1.40

World Environment Day — A590

**2006, June 5**    *Perf. 14*
1376 A590 30d multi    2.25   2.25

Soummam Congress, 50th Anniv. — A591

**2006, Aug. 20**    *Perf. 13x13½*
1377 A591 20d multi    1.50   1.50

16th Arab Scholars' Games — A592

**2006, Sept. 2**    *Perf. 13¼x14*
1378 A592 30d multi    2.25   2.25

Intl. Year of Deserts and Desertifcation A593

Designs: No. 1379, 15d, Oasis. No. 1380, 15d, Oasis, sand dunes and water.

**2006, Sept. 20**   *Litho.*   *Perf. 14*
1379-1380 A593   Set of 2   2.25   2.25

World Teachers Day — A594

**2006, Oct. 5**
1381 A594 20d multi    1.40   1.40

Arbor Day — A595

Trees: 20d, Atlas pistachio. 30d, Pomagranate.

**2006, Oct. 25**
1382-1383 A595   Set of 2   3.75   3.75

Sino-African Cooperation Summit, Beijing — A596

**2006, Nov. 4**    *Perf. 12*
1384 A596 30d multi    2.25   2.25

19th Century Powder Flasks — A597

Background color: 15d, Pink. 20d, Pale green.

**2006, Nov. 22**   *Litho.*   *Perf. 13½x14*
1385-1386 A597   Set of 2   3.00   3.00

Transitory Arab Parliament, 1st Anniv. A598

**2006, Dec. 17**    *Perf. 13½x13*
1387 A598 15d multi    1.10   1.10

El Moudjahid Newspaper, 50th Anniv. — A599

**2006, Dec. 18**    *Perf. 14*
1388 A599 30d multi    2.25   2.25

Desalinization of Sea Water — A600

**2006, Dec. 20**
1389 A600 20d multi    1.50   1.50

A601

Algiers, 2007 Arab Cultural Capital A602

**2007, Jan. 12**   *Litho.*   *Perf. 13½x13*
1390 A601 15d multi    1.25   1.25
1391 A602 30d multi    2.25   2.25

Lighthouses A603

Lighthouse at: 15d, Ilot d'Arzew. 20d, Cap Sigli. 38d, Ras-atia.

**2007, Feb. 14**   *Litho.*   *Perf. 14*
1392-1394 A603   Set of 3   5.25   5.25

Employment of Women — A604

**2007, Mar. 8**   *Litho.*   *Perf. 14*
1395 A604 15d multi    1.25   1.25

Sheikh Mohamed Ameziane Belhaddad (1790-1873), Leader of 1871 Rebellion — A605

**2007, Apr. 8**    *Perf. 13x13¼*
1396 A605 15d multi    1.25   1.25

Ksars A606

Village scenes: No. 1397, 15d, Kenadsa. No. 1398, 15d, Temacine, vert.

**2007, Apr. 21**   *Perf. 13¼x13, 13x13¼*
1397-1398 A606   Set of 2   2.25   2.25

2nd Afro-Asiatic Games, Algiers — A607

**2007, May 18**   *Litho.*   *Perf. 14*
1399 A607 15d multi    1.10   1.10

9th All-African Games, Algiers — A608

**2007, May 18**
1400 A608 15d multi    1.10   1.10

Gardens A609

Designs: 15d, Landon Gardens, Biskra. 20d, Ibn Badis Gardens, Oran. 38d, Essai du Hamma Gardens, Algiers.

**2007, June 5**    *Perf. 13½x13*
1401-1403 A609   Set of 3   5.50   5.50

National Gendarmerie, 45th Anniv. — A610

Designs: 15d, Gendarmerie emblem. 38d, Gendarmerie emblem, gendarme and automobile.

**2007, June 25**   *Litho.*   *Perf. 14*
1404-1405 A610   Set of 2   4.00   4.00

Independence, 45th Anniv. — A611

Designs: 15d, People, flags and dove. 20d, Anniversary emblem, vert.

**2007, July 5**    *Perf. 13¼x13*
1406 A611 15d multi    1.25   1.25

# ALGERIA

**Imperf**
Size: 60x77mm
1407 A611 20d multi 3.00 3.00

Ceramics — A612

Designs: No. 1408, 15d, Jar with handles. No. 1409, 15d, Glazed jar without handles. 20d, Censer. 38d, Lamp, horiz.

**2007, Aug. 5** Litho. **Perf. 14**
1408-1411 A612 Set of 4 6.00 6.00

Endangered Animals A613

Designs: 15d, Striped hyena. 38d, White-tailed fox.

**2007, Sept. 12** **Perf. 13¼x13**
1412-1413 A613 Set of 2 3.25 3.25

Theaters — A614

Theater in: No. 1414, 15d, Sétif. No. 1415, 15d, Oran. 20d, Annaba, horiz. 38d, Algiers.

**Perf. 13x13¼, 13¼x13**
**2007, Oct. 24** Litho.
1414-1417 A614 Set of 4 5.75 5.75

Encyclopedia of Algerian Postage Stamps — A615

**2007, Nov. 1** **Perf. 13x13¼**
1418 A615 15d multi 1.40 1.40

Bey Ahmed de Constantine (1784-1850), Leader of 1836-48 Resistance Against French — A616

**2007, Nov. 7**
1419 A616 15d multi 1.25 1.25

National Artisan's Day — A617

**2007, Nov. 9** **Perf. 13¼x14**
1420 A617 15d multi 1.40 1.40

Tilapia — A618

**2007, Dec. 12** Litho. **Perf. 14**
1421 A618 15d multi 1.50 1.50

**Miniature Sheet**

Emir Abdelkader (1808-83) — A619

No. 1422: a, Abdelkader seated. b, Abdelkader standing. c, Abdelkader, diff.

**2007, Dec. 15**
1422 A619 Sheet of 3 5.00 5.00
a.-b. 15d Either single 1.10 1.10
c. 38d multi 2.75 2.75

Fifth General Census — A620

**2008, Jan. 16** **Perf. 14x13¼**
1423 A620 15d multi 1.25 1.25

French Air Raid on Sakiet Sidi Youssef, Tunisia, 50th Anniv. — A621

**2008, Feb. 8** Litho. **Perf. 13x13¼**
1424 A621 15d multi 1.25 1.25

**Miniature Sheet**

Fountains — A621a

**2008, Feb. 23** **Perf. 14**
1425 A621a Sheet of 4 5.50 5.50
a. 10d Ain de la Grande Rue .65 .65
b. 15d Ain Bir Djebbah 1.00 1.00
c. 20d Ain Sidi Abdellah 1.35 1.35
d. 30d Ain Dir Chebana 2.60 2.60

**Miniature Sheet**

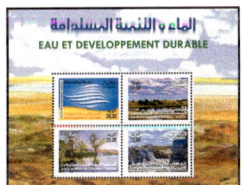

Water and Sustainable Development — A622

No. 1428: a, Issakarssen Wetlands. b, Reghaia Wetlands. c, Guerbes Wetlands. d, Emblem of Expo Zaragoza 2008.

**2008, Mar. 22** Litho. **Perf. 14**
1428 A622 Sheet of 4, #a-d 5.50 5.50
a. 10d multi .65 .65
b. 15d multi 1.00 1.00
c. 20d multi 1.35 1.35
d. 38d multi 2.60 2.60

**Souvenir Sheet**

National Liberation Front Soccer Team, 50th Anniv. — A623

**2008, Apr. 12** Litho. **Perf.**
1429 A623 38d multi 2.75 2.75

No. 1429 contains one 36mm diameter stamp.

Writers — A624

No. 1430: a, Redha Houhou (1911-56). b, Abdelhamid Benhadouga (1925-96). c, Malek Bennabi (1905-73). d, Kateb Yacine (1929-89).

**2008, Apr. 16** Litho. **Perf. 14x13½**
1430 Horiz. strip of 4 4.25 4.25
a.-d. A624 15d Any single 1.00 1.00

Children and New Technologies — A625

**2008, June 1** **Perf. 13½x14**
1431 A625 15d multi 1.05 1.05

**Souvenir Sheet**

Baya Mahieddine (1931-98), Artist — A626

No. 1432: a, 15d, Mahieddine. b, 38d, Painting by Mahieddine.

**2008, June 8** **Perf. 14**
1432 A626 Sheet of 2, #a-b 4.00 4.00

Kassamen, Algerian National Anthem, by Moufdi Zakaria — A627

**2008, July 3** **Perf. 13x13¼**
1433 A627 15d multi 1.05 1.05

Railway Stations — A628

Station in: 10d, Algiers. 15d, Constantine. 20d, Oran. 38d, Skikda.

**2008, July 9** **Perf. 14x13½**
1434-1437 A628 Set of 4 5.00 5.00

Ferhat Abbas (1899-1985), President of First Algerian Temporary Government — A629

**2008, Sept. 19** **Perf. 13x13¼**
1438 A629 15d multi 1.10 1.10

2008 Summer Olympics, Beijing — A630

Designs: No. 1439, 15d, Fencing. No. 1440, 15d, Wrestling.

**2008, July 23** Litho. **Perf. 14x13½**
1439-1440 A630 Set of 2 2.10 2.10

National Popular Army — A631

**2008, Nov. 1**
1441 A631 15d multi 1.05 1.05

12th Session of Government Postage Stamp Printers Assoc., Algiers — A632

**2008, Nov. 5** **Perf. 13x13¼**
1442 A632 15d multi 1.05 1.05

**Miniature Sheet**

Bridges in Constantine — A633

No. 1443: a, 10d, Sidi M'Cid Bridge. b, 15d, Sidi Rached Bridge. c, 20d, El Kantara Bridge. d, 38d, La Medersa Bridge.

**2008, Nov. 26** **Perf. 14**
1443 A633 Sheet of 4, #a-d 5.00 5.00

Universal Declaration of Human Rights, 60th Anniv. — A634

**2008, Dec. 10** **Perf. 14x13½**
1444 A634 15d multi 1.05 1.05

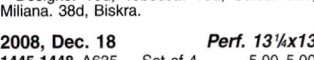

Cities — A635

Designs: 10d, Tebessa. 15d, Saida. 20d, Miliana. 38d, Biskra.

**2008, Dec. 18** **Perf. 13¼x13**
1445-1448 A635 Set of 4 5.00 5.00

Diplomatic Relations Between Algeria and People's Republic of China, 50th Anniv. — A636

**2008, Dec. 20** ***Perf. 12***
**1449** A636 15d multi 1.10 1.10

Louis Braille (1809-52), Educator of the Blind — A637

**2009, Jan. 4** ***Perf. 13½x14***
**1450** A637 15d multi 1.10 1.10

Mausoleums — A638

Mausoleum of: 15d, Sidi Abderrahmane, Algiers. 20d, Sidi Ibrahim El Atteuf, Ghardaia, horiz.

**2009, Feb. 25** ***Perf. 13½x14, 14x13½***
**1451-1452** A638 Set of 2 2.25 2.25

Natl. Day of the Handicapped — A639

Designs: 15d, Silhouettes of man with raised arm and man in wheelchair. 20d, Athlete in wheelchair, hand prints.

**2009, Mar. 14** ***Perf. 13½x14***
**1453-1454** A639 Set of 2 2.25 2.25

Protection of Polar Regions and Glaciers — A640

**2009, Mar. 28** **Litho.**
**1455** A640 38d multi 2.75 2.75

Presidential Elections — A641

**2009, Apr. 9** ***Perf. 13x13¼***
**1456** A641 15d multi 1.00 1.00

Items in National Museum — A642

Designs: 15d, Wooden sandals. 20d, Fragment of silver brooch. 30d, Vest.

**2009, Apr. 18** ***Perf. 14x13½***
**1457-1459** A642 Set of 3 4.50 4.50

University of Algiers, Cent. — A643

**2009, May 11**
**1460** A643 15d multi 1.00 1.00

Jewelry of Southern Algeria — A644

Designs: 1d, Silver fibulas. 5d, Amulet necklace. 9d, Pectoral jewelry and chain. 10d, Circular fibula.

**2009, May 13** ***Perf. 13¾***
**1461-1464** A644 Set of 4 1.75 1.75

Protection of Children From Cyberspace Dangers — A645

**2009, May 17** ***Perf. 14x13½***
**1465** A645 15d multi 1.10 1.10

16th Mediterranean Games, Pescara, Italy — A646

Designs: 15d, Sailboarding. 20d, Equestrian, horiz.

***Perf. 13½x14, 14x13½***
**2009, June 3** **Litho.**
**1466-1467** A646 Set of 2 2.40 2.40

Roman Era Archaeological Sites — A647

Designs: 15d, Madaure archaeological site. 20d, Khemissa archaeological site. 30d, Old Theater, Guelma.

**2009, June 14** ***Perf. 13½x14***
**1468-1470** A647 Set of 3 4.25 4.25

Second Panafrican Cultural Festival of Algiers A648

Designs: 15d, Shown. 20d, Map of Africa, antelope, geometric designs.

**2009, July 4** ***Perf. 13¼x13***
**1471-1472** A648 Set of 2 2.25 2.25

"The Child of Today, the Man of Tomorrow" A649

"I Love My Country" A650

**2009, June 26** ***Perf. 13½x14***
**1473** A649 15d multi 1.00 1.00
**1474** A650 20d multi 1.25 1.25

Algerian Electricity and Gas Company, 40th Anniv. — A651

**2009, July 28**
**1475** A651 15d multi 1.00 1.00

Traffic Safety — A652

**2009, Aug. 6**
**1476** A652 15d multi 1.00 1.00

Fishing Ports — A653

Designs: 15d, Bouharoun. 20d, Béni Saf. 30d, Stora.

**2009, Sept. 2** **Litho.** ***Perf. 13½x13***
**1477-1479** A653 Set of 3 4.25 4.25

Protection of the Aged — A654

**2009, Oct. 10** ***Perf. 13½x14***
**1480** A654 15d multi 1.00 1.00

National Armed Forces — A655

**2009, Nov. 1** **Litho.** ***Perf. 13x13¼***
**1481** A655 15d multi 1.00 1.00

Olive Oil Production A656

Designs: 15d, Picking olives. 20d, Pressing olives, vert.

***Perf. 13¼x13, 13x13¼***
**2009, Nov. 25**
**1482-1483** A656 Set of 2 2.40 2.40

Folktales — A657

No. 1484: a, Loundja, la Fille de l'Ogre. b, Badra. c, La Fée Colombe. d, La Rose Rouge.

**2009, Dec. 7** **Litho.** ***Perf. 13x13¼***
**1484** Block or strip of 4 4.25 4.25
***a.-d.*** A657 15d Any single .95 .95

Birds of Prey — A658

Designs: 15d, Aquila chrysaetos. 20d, Falco biarmicus, vert. 30d, Falco peregrinus, vert.

**2010, Jan. 27** ***Perf. 13¼x13, 13x13¼***
**1485-1487** A658 Set of 3 4.50 4.50

Victims of French Nuclear Testing in Algeria A659

**2010, Feb. 10** ***Perf. 13¼x13***
**1488** A659 15d multi 1.60 1.60

Forts — A660

Designs: 15d, Fort de l'Empereur, Bordj Moulay Hassan, Algiers. 20d, Gouraya Fort, Béjaia.

**2010, Feb. 15**
**1489-1490** A660 Set of 2 2.50 2.50

Expo 2010, Shanghai A661

Designs: 15d, Stylized people, flowers, buildings. 38d, Algeria Pavilion.

**2010, Mar. 24** **Litho.** ***Perf. 13¼x13***
**1491-1492** A661 Set of 2 3.75 3.75

16th Intl. Conference on Liquified Gas, Oran — A662

Conference emblem, world map and: 15d, Gas plant. 20d, Port, horiz.

**2010, Apr. 18** ***Perf. 13x13½, 13½x13***
**1493-1494** A662 Set of 2 2.50 2.50

# ALGERIA

May 8, 1945 Massacres, 65th Anniv. — A663

**2010, May 8**    Perf. 13¼
1495 A663 15d multi    1.00 1.00

2010 World Cup Soccer Championships, South Africa — A664

Designs: No. 1496, 15d, World Cup trophy, flags of participating countries. No. 1497, 15d, Player, crowd holding Algerian flags. No. 1498: a, Fox playing soccer. b, Player, soccer ball.

**2010, May 8**    Perf. 13x13¼
1496-1497 A664 Set of 2    2.00 2.00

**Souvenir Sheet**
*Imperf*
1498 A664 15d Sheet of 2, #a-b    2.00 2.00

 A665

Design: Ahellil of Gourara UNESCO World Intangible Cultural Heritage.

**2010, June 2**    Perf. 13¼x13
1499 A665 15d multi    1.15 1.15

Martyr's Sanctuary, Algiers — A666

**2010, June 20**
1500 A666 (15d) multi    1.10 1.10

African Year of Peace and Security — A667

**2010, July 19**    Perf. 13x13¼
1501 A667 15d multi    1.10 1.10

Caves A668

Designs: No. 1502, 15d, Béni Add Cave, Ain Fezza. No. 1503, 15d, Ziama Cave, Mansouriah.

**2010, July 25**    Perf. 13¼x13
1502-1503 A668 Set of 2    2.10 2.10

Organization of the Petroleum Exporting Countries, 50th Anniv. A669

Designs: 15d, Emblem. 38d, Emblem, world map, oil tanker.

**2010, Sept. 14**    Litho.    Perf. 13¼x13
1504-1505 A669 Set of 2    3.75 3.75

Mosques — A670

Designs: 15d, El Hanafi Mosque, Blida. 20d, Sidi Ali Dib Mosque, Skikda. 30d, Grand Mosque, Nedroma.

**2010, Sept. 15**    Perf. 13x13¼
1506-1508 A670 Set of 3    4.50 4.50

 Dates — A671

Date varieties: No. 1509, 15d, Degla Beida. No. 1510, 15d, Akerbuch. No. 1511, 15d, Ghars, vert. No. 1512, 15d, Deglet Nour, vert.

**2010, Oct. 6**    Perf. 13¼x13, 13x13¼
1509-1512 A671 Set of 4    4.50 4.50

Handcrafted Items — A672

Designs: 15d, Candlestick holder. 20d, Quanoun (musical instrument). 30d, Leather-covered chest with handles, horiz.

**Perf. 13¼x14, 14x13¼**
**2010, Nov. 30**    Litho.
1513-1515 A672 Set of 3    4.50 4.50

 Trees — A673

Designs: 15d, Cork oak. 20d, Carob tree. 30d, Soapberry tree. 38d, Argan tree.

**2011, Jan. 29**    Perf. 13¼x13
1516-1519 A673 Set of 4    6.25 6.25

Tlemcen, 2011 Capital of Islamic Culture — A674

Designs: 15d, Minaret of Mansoura. 20d, Door knocker, Side Boumedienne Mosque.

**2011, Feb. 15**    Litho.    Perf. 13x13¼
1520-1521 A674 Set of 2    2.10 2.10

Snakes — A675

Designs: No. 1522, 15d, Couleuvre a diademe (diadem snake). No. 1523, 15d, Vipere a cornes (Saharan horned viper).

**2011, Mar. 13**
1522-1523 A675 Set of 2    2.00 2.00

First Economic Census — A676

**2011, Apr. 12**    Perf. 13½x14
1524 A676 15d multi    .90 .90

18th Cent. Tableware From Algiers A677

Designs: 15d, Couscous dish. 30d, Butter dish.

**2011, Apr. 19**    Perf. 13¼x13
1525-1526 A677 Set of 2    2.75 2.75

Telecenters A678

**2011, May 17**    Perf. 14x13½
1527 A678 15d multi    1.10 1.10

Campaign Against Human Immunodeficiency Virus — A679

**2011, June 30**    Perf. 13½x14
1528 A679 15d multi    1.10 1.10

Benyoucef Benkhedda (1920-2003), Politician A680

**2011, Sept. 19**    Perf. 13x13¼
1529 A680 15d multi    .90 .90

A681    Comic Strips — A682

**2011, Sept. 25**    Perf. 13¼x14
1530 A681 15d multi    .90 .90
1531 A682 15d multi    .90 .90

World Post Day — A683

Main post office in: No. 1532, 15d, Constantine. No. 1533, 15d, Oran.

**2011, Oct. 9**    Perf. 14x13¼
1532-1533 A683 Set of 2    1.90 1.90

Paris Massacre of Algerian Protestors, 50th Anniv. — A684

**2011, Oct. 17**    Perf. 13x13¼
1534 A684 15d multi    .90 .90

Algerian Press Service, 50th Anniv. — A685

**2011, Oct. 25**    Perf. 14x13¼
1535 A685 15d multi    .90 .90

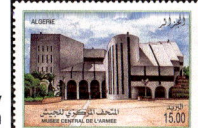

Army Museum A686

**2011, Nov. 1**    Perf. 13¼x13
1536 A686 15d multi    .90 .90

**Souvenir Sheet**

Algiers Metro A687

No. 1537: a, Train at station, people on platform. b, Train in tunnel.

**2011, Nov. 14**    Perf. 14
1537 A687 15d Sheet of 2, #a-b    2.00 2.00

Sheep A688

Sheep breeds: No. 1538, 15d, Ouled Djallal. No. 1539, 15d, El Hamra.

**2011, Nov. 16**    Perf. 13¼x13
1538-1539 A688 Set of 2    2.00 2.00

Ornamental Plants — A689

# ALGERIA

Designs: 15d, Bougainvillea. 20d, Glycine (wisteria). 30d, Mimosa, horiz. 38d, Galant de nuit (night-blooming cestrum), horiz.

**2011, Dec. 26**    Perf. 13x13¼, 13¼x13
1540-1543 A689 Set of 4    6.25 6.25

Ceasefire Between Algeria and France, 50th Anniv. — A690

**2012, Mar. 19**    Litho.    Perf. 13x13¼
1544 A690 15d multi    .90 .90

Expo 2012, Yeosu, South Korea A691

**2012, Mar. 21**    Perf. 13¼x13
1545 A691 15d multi    .90 .90

Wainscoting — A692

Designs: 15d, Door, Dar Aziza, Algiers. 20d, Ceiling, Dar Aziza. 30d, Window, Hassen Pacha Palace, Algiers.

**2012, Mar. 26**    Perf. 13x13¼
1546-1548 A692 Set of 3    3.75 3.75

Snails — A693

Designs: 15d, Theba pisana. 20d, Eobania vermiculata.

**2012, Mar. 28**
1549-1550 A693 Set of 2    2.10 2.10

Ulemas — A694

Designs: 15d, Sheikh Larbi Djedri Tebessi (1895-1957). 20d, Sheikh Embarek El-Mili (1898-1945). 30d, Sheikh Ahmed Hamani (1915-98).

**2012, Apr. 16**    Litho.    Perf. 13x13¼
1551-1553 A694 Set of 3    3.75 3.75

City Scenes — A695

Designs: 15d, Casbah of Dellys. 20d, Saracen Gate, Bejaia. 30d, Casbah of Constantine.

**2012, June 26**
1554-1556 A695 Set of 3    3.75 3.75

2012 Summer Olympics, London — A696

Designs: 15d, Judo, London Eye. 38d, Rowing, Tower Bridge, vert.

**Perf. 14x13¼, 13¼x14**
**2012, June 27**
1557-1558 A696 Set of 2    1.40 1.40

Algerian Armed Forces, 50th Anniv. — A697

Designs: No. 1559, 15d, Gendarme on motorcycle. No. 1560, 15d, Tank. No. 1561, 15d, Missiles. No. 1562, 15d, Airplane in flight. No. 1563, 15d, Member of Republican Guard on horse. No. 1564, 15d, Naval vessel.

**2012, July 5**    Perf. 14
Stamps With Year and Inscriptions At Bottom
1559-1564 A697 Set of 6    2.25 2.25
1561a    Souvenir sheet of 3, #1559-1561, with year and inscriptions at bottom of stamp removed    1.10 1.10
1564a    Souvenir sheet of 3, #1562-1564, with year and inscriptions at bottom of stamp removed    1.10 1.10

Souvenir Sheet

Algerian Independence, 50th Anniv. — A698

**2012, July 5**    Imperf.
1565 A698 15d multi    .40 .40

Wheat Varieties — A699

Designs: 15d, Bousselam. 20d, Mohamed Ben Bachir. 30d, Hedba 03.

**2012, Sept. 29**    Perf. 13x13¼
1566-1568 A699 Set of 3    1.75 1.75

Algerian Radio and Television, 50th Anniv. A700

**2012, Oct. 28**    Perf. 13¼x13
1569 A700 15d multi    .40 .40

Postage Stamps of Independent Algeria, 50th Anniv. A701

**2012, Nov. 1**
1570 A701 15d multi    .40 .40

Medicinal Plants — A702

Designs: 15d, Globularia vulgaris. 20d, Glycyrrhiza glabra. 30d, Menyanthes trifoliata.

**2012, Dec. 11**    Litho.    Perf. 13x13¼
1571-1573 A702 Set of 3    1.75 1.75

Diplomatic Relations Between Algeria and Russia, 50th Anniv. A703

**2012, Dec. 18**    Litho.    Perf. 13¼x13
1574 A703 15d multi    .40 .40

Roman Mosaics — A704

Mosaic depicting: 15d, Muse. 20d, Hunting scene.

**2012, Dec. 18**    Litho.    Perf. 13x13¼
1575-1576 A704 Set of 2    .90 .90

Yennayer Festival (Berber New Year) — A705

**2013, Jan. 12**    Litho.    Perf. 13x13¼
1577 A705 15d multi    .40 .40

Lighthouses A706

Designs: 15d, Srigina Island Lighthouse. 20d, Cap Bougaroun Lighthouse. 30d, Cap Ivi Lighthouse.

**2013, Feb. 27**    Litho.    Perf. 13¼x13
1578-1580 A706 Set of 3    3.75 3.75

Fruit and Blossoms A707

Designs: 15d, Apricots. 20d, Cherries.

**2013, Mar. 3**    Litho.    Perf. 13¼x13
1581-1582 A707 Set of 2    1.90 1.90

First Chinese Medical Team in Algeria, 50th Anniv. — A708

**2013, Apr. 16**    Litho.    Perf. 12
1583 A708 15d multi    .40 .40

**Souvenir Sheet**
1584 A708 50d multi    1.25 1.25

National Copyright Office, 40th Anniv. — A709

**2013, Apr. 26**    Litho.    Perf. 13x13¼
1585 A709 15d multi    .40 .40

National Administration School A710

**2013, Apr. 29**    Litho.    Perf. 13¼x13
1586 A710 15d multi    .40 .40

Roman Pottery — A711

Designs: No. 1587, 15d, Two-handled urn with lid, denomination at LL (shown). No. 1588, 15d, Two-handled urn without lid, denomination at LL. No. 1589, 15d, Single-handled urn without lid, denomination at LR.

**2013, May 5**    Litho.    Perf. 13x13¼
1587-1589 A711 Set of 3    1.25 1.25

Improvements in Road Safety With Global Positioning Satellite Technology — A712

**2013, May 17**    Litho.    Perf. 13x13¼
1590 A712 15d multi    .40 .40

Algerian Insurance and Re-insurance Company, 50th Anniv. — A713

**2013, June 8**    Litho.    Perf. 13x13¼
1591 A713 15d multi    .40 .40

# ALGERIA

Police Day — A714

**2013, July 22   Litho.   Perf. 13x13¼**
1592   A714   15d multi   .40   .40

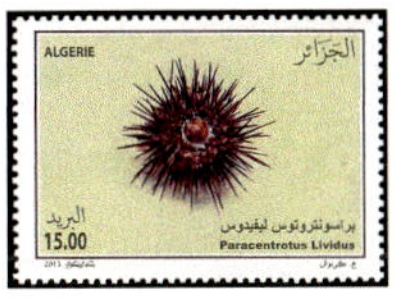

Marine Life — A715

Designs: No. 1593, 15d, Paracentrotus lividus. No. 1594, 15d, Bathynectes maravigna. No. 1595, 15d, Haliotis tuberculata.

**2013, Aug. 3   Litho.   Perf. 13¼x13**
1593-1595   A715   Set of 3   1.25   1.25

Flowers — A716

Designs: No. 1596, 15d, Carnations. No. 1597, 15d, Petunias.

**2013, Aug. 5   Litho.   Perf. 13x13¼**
1596-1597   A716   Set of 2   .75   .75

22nd African Regional Conference of Interpol, Oran — A717

**2013, Sept. 10   Litho.   Perf. 13¼x13**
1598   A717   38d multi   .95   .95

Algerian Olympic Committee, 50th Anniv. — A718

Olympic rings, "50," and: 15d, Stylized bird. 30d, Stylized bird and torch, vert.

**2013, Oct. 28   Litho.   Perf. 14**
1599-1600   A718   Set of 2   1.10   1.10

Transportation A719

Designs: 15d, Cable cars, Constantine. 20d, Tram, Oran.

**2013, Oct. 30   Litho.   Perf. 13¼x13**
1601-1602   A719   Set of 2   .90   .90

Diplomatic Relations Between Algeria and People's Republic of China, 55th Anniv. — A720

**2013, Dec. 20   Litho.   Perf. 12**
1603   A720   15d multi   .40   .40

Fish Farming — A721

Designs: 15d, Floating cages. 20d, Clenopharyngodon idella.

**2013, Dec. 24   Litho.   Perf. 14**
1604-1605   A721   Set of 2   .90   .90

Sonatrach (State-owned Oil and Gas Corporation), 50th Anniv. — A722

**2013, Dec. 31   Litho.   Perf. 13x13¼**
1606   A722   15d multi   .40   .40

**Souvenir Sheet**
1607   A722   50d multi   1.40   1.40
No. 1607 contains one 35x48mm stamp.

Flowers — A723

Designs: 15d, Ornithogalum arabicum. 20d, Bellis sylvestris. 30d, Calendula arvensis.

**2014, Jan. 29   Litho.   Perf. 14**
1608-1610   A723   Set of 3   1.75   1.75

Constitutional Council Building, Algiers, 25th Anniv. A724

**2014, Feb. 23   Litho.   Perf. 13¼x13**
1611   A724   15d multi   .40   .40

Coins — A725

Obverse and reverse of Almohad dinar from: 15d, 524-58. 20d, 580-95.

**2014, Feb. 26   Litho.   Perf. 13¼x13**
1612-1613   A725   Set of 2   .90   .90

Supreme Court, 50th Anniv. — A726

**2014, Mar. 2   Litho.   Perf. 14**
1614   A726   15d multi   .40   .40

National Day of Handicapped Persons — A727

**2014, Mar. 14   Litho.   Perf. 13x13¼**
1615   A727   15d multi   .40   .40

Intl. Day of Anti Personnel Mine Victims — A728

**2014, Apr. 4   Litho.   Perf. 13x13¼**
1616   A728   15d multi   .40   .40

2014 Presidential Election A729

**2014, Apr. 16   Litho.   Perf. 13¼x13**
1617   A729   15d multi   .40   .40

19th Century Kitchen Tools — A730

Designs: 15d, Coffee mill, Algiers. 20d, Tuareg sugar hammer, horiz. 30d, Tuareg sugar shears, horiz.

**Perf. 13x13¼, 13¼x13**
**2014, Apr. 28   Litho.**
1618-1620   A730   Set of 3   1.75   1.75

Amazigh High Commission, 19th Anniv. — A731

**2014, May 27   Litho.   Perf. 13¼x14**
1621   A731   15d multi   .40   .40

17th Ministerial Conference of the Non-Aligned Movement, Algiers — A732

Designs: No. 1622, 15d, Stylized dove with olive branch, globe with Algeria highlighted. No. 1623, 15d, Conference emblem.

**2014, May 28   Litho.   Perf. 13x13¼**
1622-1623   A732   Set of 2   .75   .75
1623a   Souvenir sheet of 2, #1622-1623   .75   .75

2014 World Cup Soccer Championships, Brazil — A733

Algerian soccer player dribbling ball with country name in: 15d, White. 38d, Green.

**2014, June 26   Litho.   Perf. 13x13¼**
1624-1625   A733   Set of 2   1.40   1.40

Olympic Complex, Oran — A734

**2014, July 5   Litho.   Perf. 13¼x13**
1626   A734   15d multi   .40   .40

Traditional Women's Veils — A735

Designs: 15d, Haik. 30d, M'laya.

**2014, Aug. 27   Litho.   Perf. 13x13¼**
1627-1628   A735   Set of 2   1.10   1.10

Prehistoric Art — A736

Designs: 15d, Painting on rock of horse-drawn chariot. 20d, Head of ram. 30d, Baetulus, vert.

**2014, Sept. 1   Litho.   Perf. 14**
1629-1631   A736   Set of 3   1.60   1.60

**Souvenir Sheet**

Rugs A737

No. 1632: a, Rug from Serbia ("Radomir Bojanic" inscribed at LR). b, Rug from Algeria (Arabic script at LR).

**2014, Oct. 7   Litho.   Perf. 13¼x14**
1632   A737   15d Sheet of 2, #a-b   .75   .75
See Serbia No. 647.

World Post Day — A738

**2014, Oct. 9   Litho.   Perf. 13¼x14**
1633   A738   15d multi   .35   .35

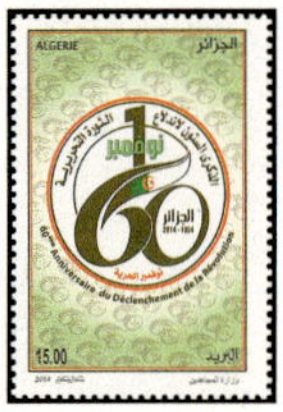

Algerian War of Independence, 60th Anniv. — A739

**2014, Nov. 1 Litho.** ***Perf. 13x13¼***
**1634** A739 15d multi .35 .35

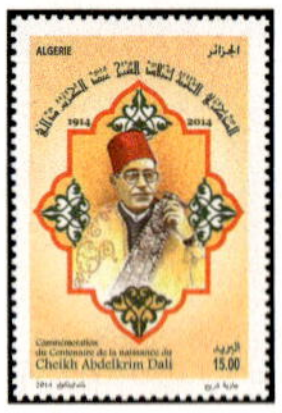

Sheikh Abdelkrim Dali (1914-78), Musician — A740

**2014, Nov. 16 Litho.** ***Perf. 13x13¼***
**1635** A740 15d multi .35 .35

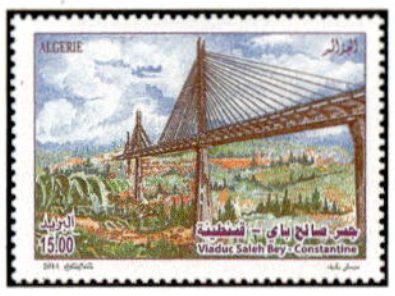

Bridges A741

Designs: No. 1636, 15d, Saleh Bey Viaduct, Constantine. No. 1637, 15d, Highway bridge and Algerian flag, vert.

***Perf. 13¼x13, 13x13¼***
**2014, Nov. 19 Litho.**
**1636-1637** A741 Set of 2 .70 .70

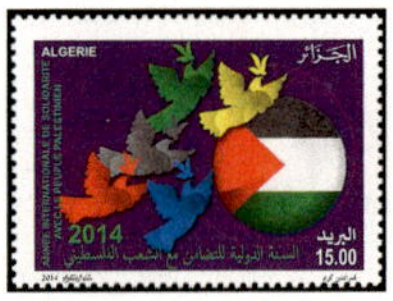

Intl. Year of Solidarity With the Palestinian People A742

**2014, Dec. 13 Litho.** ***Perf. 13¼x13***
**1638** A742 15d multi .35 .35

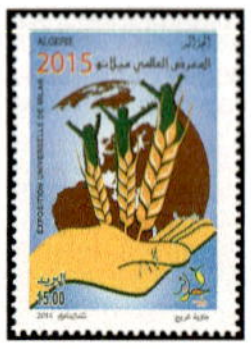

Expo 2015, Milan — A743

Designs: 15d, Globe, hand holding wheat stalks, silhouettes of people. 38d, Stylized fish and fruit, horiz.

**2014, Dec. 22 Litho.** ***Perf. 14***
**1639-1640** A743 Set of 2 1.25 1.25

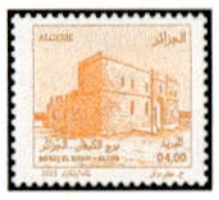

Bordj el Kifan, Algiers — A744

**2015 Litho.** ***Perf. 14x13¾***
**1641** A744 4d pale orange .25 .25
**1642** A744 10d lt blue .25 .25
**1643** A744 25d green .55 .55

Issued: 4d, 10d, 8/5; 25d, 1/4.

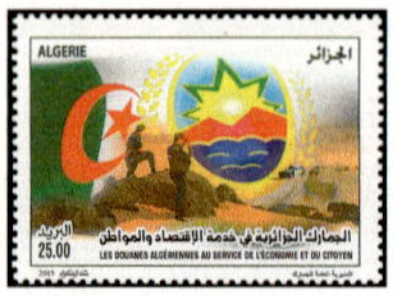

Algerian Customs A745

**2015, Jan. 26 Litho.** ***Perf. 13¼x13***
**1644** A745 25d multi .55 .55

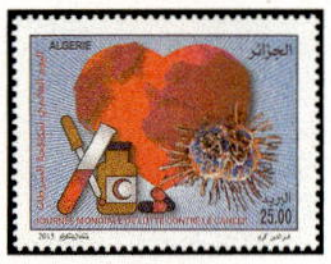

Intl. Day of the Fight Against Cancer — A746

**2015, Feb. 4 Litho.** ***Perf. 14***
**1645** A746 25d multi .55 .55

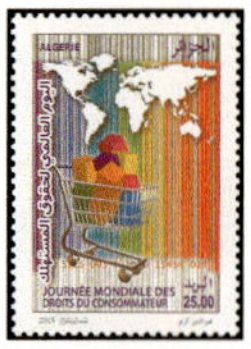

World Consumer Rights Day — A747

World map, bar code and: 25d, Shopping cart. 30d, Umbrella.

**2015, Mar. 15 Litho.** ***Perf. 13½x14***
**1646-1647** A747 Set of 2 1.25 1.25

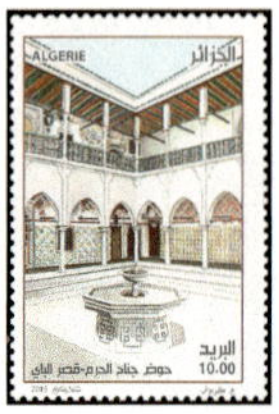

A748

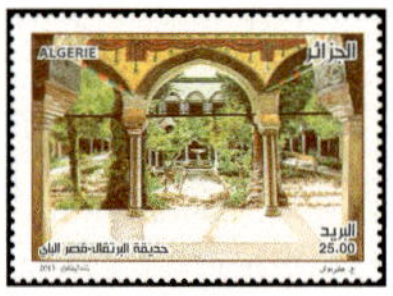

A749

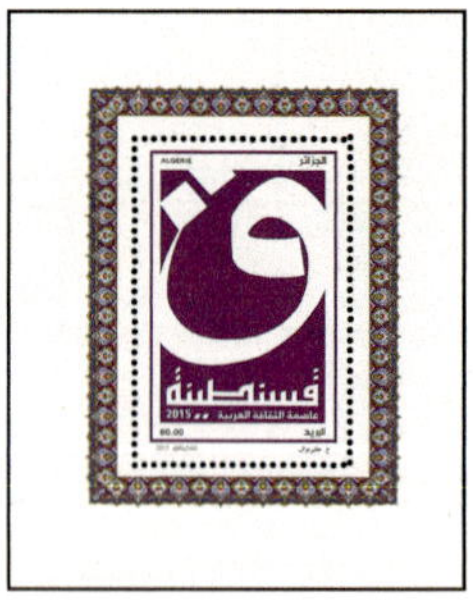

Constantine, 2015 Capital of Arab Culture — A750

***Perf. 13x13¼, 13¼x13***
**2015, Apr. 16 Litho.**
**1648** A748 10d multi .25 .25
**1649** A749 25d multi .55 .55

**Souvenir Sheet**

**1650** A750 60d purple & blk 1.25 1.25

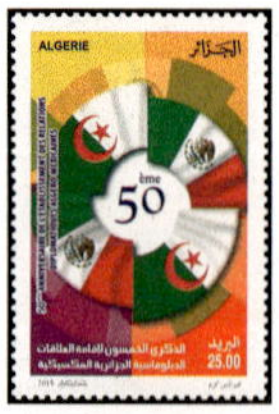

Diplomatic Relations Between Algeria and Mexico, 50th Anniv. — A751

**2015, Apr. 23 Litho.** ***Perf. 13x13¼***
**1651** A751 25d multi .55 .55

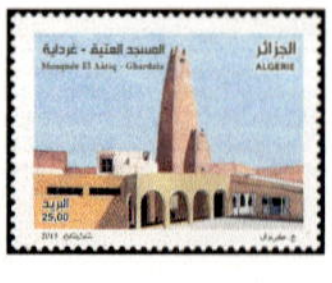

Mosques — A752

El Aatiq Mosque in: No. 1652, 25d, Ghardaia. No. 1653, 25d, Metlili, vert.

***Perf. 14x13½, 13½x14***
**2015, May 28 Litho.**
**1652-1653** A752 Set of 2 1.00 1.00

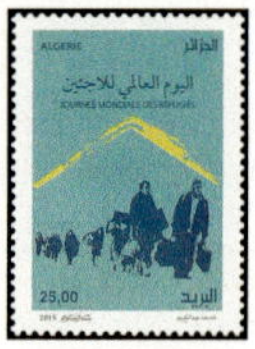

World Refugee Day — A753

**2015, June 20 Litho.** ***Perf. 13½x14***
**1654** A753 25d multi .50 .50

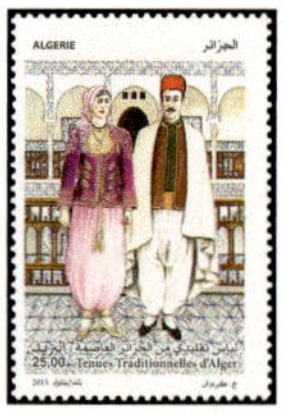

Traditional Costumes — A754

Man and woman from: 25d, Algiers. 30d, Kabylie.

**2015, July 15 Litho.** ***Perf. 13x13¼***
**1655-1656** A754 Set of 2 1.10 1.10

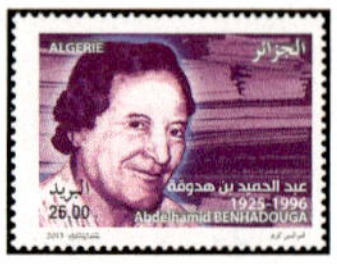

Famous Men — A755

Designs: No. 1657, 25d, Abdelhamid Benhadouga (1925-96), writer. No. 1658, 25d, M'hamed Issiakhem (1928-85), painter. No. 1659, 25d, Ismail Samsom (1934-88), painter, vert. No. 1660, 25d, Mouloud Feraoun (1913-62), writer, vert.

***Perf. 14x13½, 13½x14***
**2015, Sept. 21 Litho.**
**1657-1660** A755 Set of 4 1.90 1.90

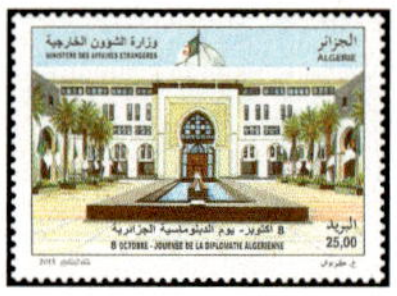

Day of Algerian Diplomacy A756

**2015, Oct. 8 Litho.** ***Perf. 13¼x13***
**1661** A756 25d multi .50 .50

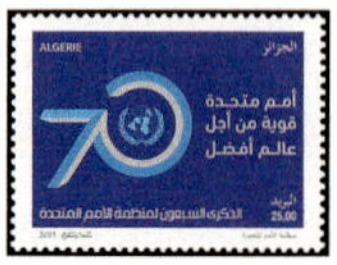

United Nations, 70th Anniv. — A757

**2015, Oct. 24 Litho.** ***Perf. 14x13½***
**1662** A757 25d multi .50 .50

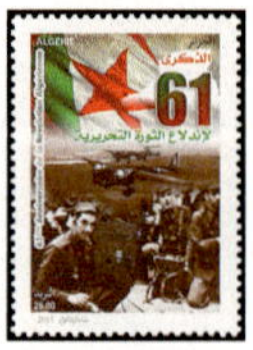

Algerian Revolution, 61st Anniv. — A758

**2015, Nov. 1 Litho.** ***Perf. 13½x14***
**1663** A758 25d multi .50 .50

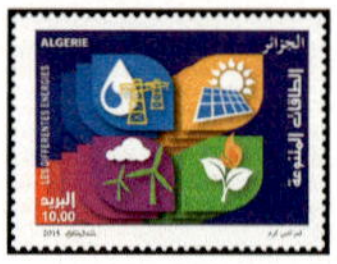

A759

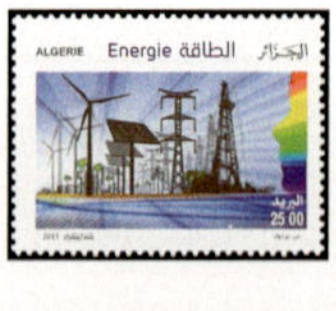

Energy — A760

**2015, Nov. 11 Litho.** ***Perf. 14x13½***
**1664** A759 10d multi .25 .25
**1665** A760 25d multi .50 .50

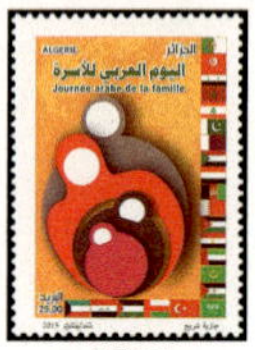

A761

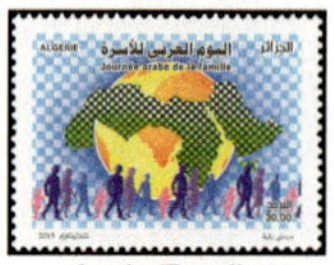

Arab Family Day — A762

**2015, Dec. 7 Litho.** ***Perf. 13½x14***
**1666** A761 25d multi .50 .50

***Perf. 14x13½***

**1667** A762 30d multi .60 .60

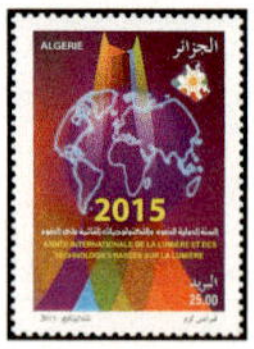

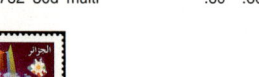

International Year of Light — A763

**2015, Dec. 20 Litho.** ***Perf. 13½x14***
**1668** A763 25d multi .50 .50

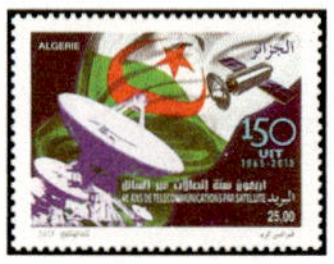

International Telecommunication Union, 150th Anniv. — A764

**2015, Dec. 22 Litho.** ***Perf. 14x13½***
**1669** A764 25d multi .50 .50

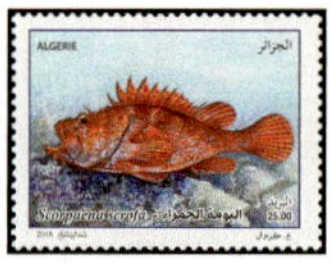

Fish — A765

Designs: 25d, Scorpaena scrofa. 50d, Mugil cephalus.

**2016, Jan. 20 Litho.** ***Perf. 14x13½***
**1670-1671** A765 Set of 2 1.40 1.40

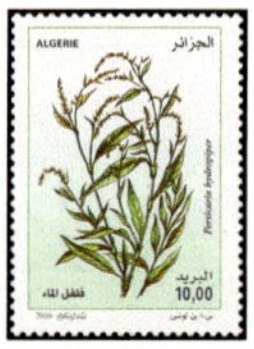

Medicinal Plants — A766

Designs: 10d, Persicaria hydropiper. 25d, Eupatorium cannabinum.

**2016, Feb. 10 Litho.** ***Perf. 13½x14***
**1672-1673** A766 Set of 2 .65 .65

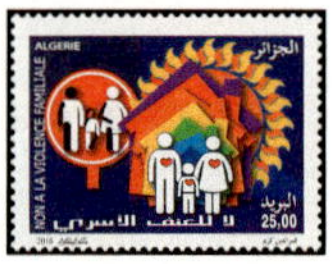

Campaign Against Domestic Violence — A767

**2016, Feb. 24 Litho.** ***Perf. 14x13½***
**1674** A767 25d multi .45 .45

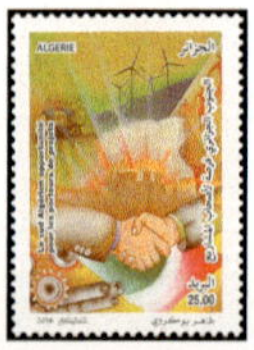

Southern Algeria Development — A768

**2016, Mar. 16 Litho.** ***Perf. 13½x14***
**1675** A768 25d multi .50 .50

# ALGERIA 439

Beni Haroun Dam — A769

**2016, Mar. 22  Litho.  Perf. 13¼x13**
1676  A769  25d multi  .50  .50

World Autism Day — A770

Children's art: 25d, City. 50d, Flowers.

**2016, Apr. 2  Litho.  Perf. 13¼x13**
1677-1678  A770  Set of 2  1.40  1.40

Museums A771

Designs: No. 1679, 25d, Ahmed Zabana National Public Museum, Oran. No. 1680, 25d, Cirta National Public Museum, Constantine. No. 1681, 25d, Nasreddine Dinet National Public Museum, Boussaada.

**2016, Apr. 18  Litho.  Perf. 13¼x13**
1679-1681  A771  Set of 3  1.40  1.40

Gun — A772

Gorgon's Mask — A773

**2016, May 18  Litho.  Perf. 13¼x13**
1682  A772  25d multi  .45  .45
**Perf. 13x13¼**
1683  A773  50d multi  .90  .90

2016 Summer Olympics, Rio de Janeiro — A774

Statue of Christ the Redeemer, Rio de Janeiro, and: 10d, Weight lifting. 25d, Boxing. 50d, Statue of Christ the Redeemer, soccer.

**2016, June 1  Litho.  Perf. 13x13¼**
1684-1685  A774  Set of 2  .65  .65
**Souvenir Sheet**
1686  A774  50d multi  .90  .90

Harbors — A775

Harbor of: 10d, El Djamila. 25d, Sidi Fredj. 50d, Tigzirt.

**2016, June 22  Litho.  Perf. 14x13½**
1687-1689  A775  Set of 3  1.60  1.60

Dances — A776

Designs: 10d, Baba Merzoug-Karkabo. 25d, El Baroude. 50d, El Hadra.

**2016, July 20  Litho.  Perf. 14x13½**
1690-1692  A776  Set of 3  1.60  1.60

Cities — A777

Designs: No. 1693, 25d, Mostaganem. No. 1694, 25d, Djelfa.

**2016, Aug. 3  Litho.  Perf. 13¼x13**
1693-1694  A777  Set of 2  .95  .95

Soummam Conference, 60th Anniv. — A778

**2016, Aug. 20  Litho.  Perf. 13x13¼**
1695  A778  25d multi  .45  .45

Architecture A779

Designs: 25d, Faculty of Medicine Building, Laghouat. 50d, Faculty of Law Building, Algiers.

**2016, Sept. 7  Litho.  Perf. 13¼x13**
1696-1697  A779  Set of 2  1.40  1.40

Emblem of Professional Education and Job Training — A780

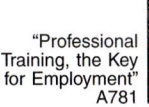
"Professional Training, the Key for Employment" A781

**2016, Oct. 5  Litho.  Perf. 14**
1698  A780  10d multi  .25  .25
1699  A781  25d multi  .45  .45

Institute of Diplomacy and International Relations — A782

**2016, Oct. 24  Litho.  Perf. 14x13½**
1700  A782  25d multi  .45  .45

Mohammed Aissa Messaoudi (1931-94), Journalist — A783

**2016, Oct. 28  Litho.  Perf. 13x13¼**
1701  A783  25d multi  .45  .45

"Taxation To Build the Algeria of Tomorrow" A784

Land Registry A785

**2016, Nov. 9  Litho.  Perf. 13½x14**
1702  A784  10d multi  .25  .25
**Perf. 14x13½**
1703  A785  25d multi  .45  .45

Atlas Lion — A786

**2016, Dec. 14  Litho.  Perf. 13¼x13**
1704  A786  50d multi  .90  .90

Modernization of Justice System A787

**2017, Jan. 15  Litho.  Perf. 13¼x13**
1705  A787  25d multi  .45  .45

Spas — A788

Designs: 5d, Hammam Essalihine. 20d, Hammam Bouhadjar. 25d, Hammam Zelfana.

**2017, Jan. 29  Litho.  Perf. 14x13¼**
1706-1708  A788  Set of 3  .95  .95

Berber as an Official Language in Algeria, 1st Anniv. — A789

**2017, Feb. 7  Litho.  Perf. 13x13¼**
1709  A789  25d multi  .45  .45

Campaign Against Food Wastage A790

Prevention of Food Poisoning A791

**2017, Mar. 15  Litho.  Perf. 14x13¼**
1710  A790  25d multi  .45  .45
**Perf. 13¼x14**
1711  A791  25d multi  .45  .45

International Trisomy 21 (Down Syndrome) Day — A792

**2017, Mar. 21  Litho.  Perf. 13¼x13**
1712  A792  25d multi  .45  .45

**Souvenir Sheet**

Tinhinan Jewelry A793

No. 1713: a, 10d, Necklace. b, 20d, Gold bracelets. c, 20d, Gold pendant.

**2017, Apr. 18  Litho.  Perf. 14**
1713  A793  Sheet of 3, #a-c  .95  .95

Second Session of the Specialized Technical Committee on Social Development, Labor and Employment of the African Union — A794

**2017, Apr. 26  Litho.  Perf. 13¼x14**
1714  A794  25d multi  .45  .45

Theaters — A795

Theater in: No. 1715, 25d, Sidi Bel Abbes. No. 1716, 25d, Tizi Ouzou. No. 1717, 25d, Bejaia.

**2017, May 18  Litho.  Perf. 13¼x14**
1715-1717  A795  Set of 3  .95  .95

Warda Al-Jazairia (1939-2012), Singer — A796

Fadila Dziria (1917-70), Singer — A797

**2017, June 8  Litho.  Perf. 13x13¼**
1718  A796  50d multi  .95  .95
1719  A797  50d multi  .95  .95

**Miniature Sheet**

Waterfalls — A798

No. 1720: a, Oued El Bared Waterfall, Setif. b, Tifrit Waterfall, Saida. c, Sidi Ouadah Waterfall, Tiaret. d, Lakhdaria Waterfall, Bouira.

**2017, June 24 Litho. *Perf. 14x13¼***
**1720** A798 25d Sheet of 4, #a-d 1.90 1.90

Miniature Sheet

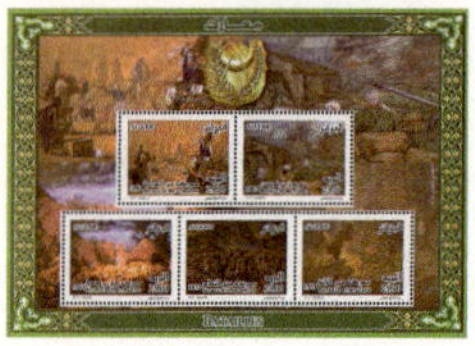

Battles A799

No. 1721: a, Battle of Bir El Gharama, 1881. b, Battle of Bir Teskift, 1957. c, Battle of Djbel Bouk'hil, 1961. d, Battle of Kheng Ennetah, 1832. e, Battle of Ain Zana, 1959.

**2017, July 5 Litho. *Perf. 14x13¼***
**1721** A799 25d Sheet of 5, #a-e 2.40 2.40

Souvenir Sheet

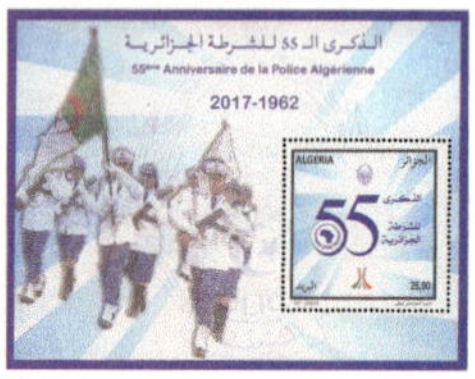

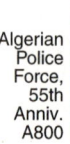

Algerian Police Force, 55th Anniv. A800

**2017, July 23 Litho. *Perf. 14***
**1722** A800 25d multi .50 .50

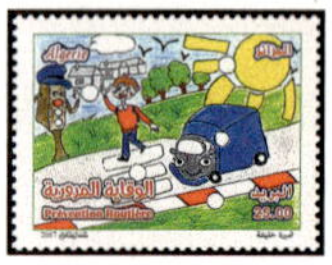

Road Safety — A801

**2017, Aug. 6 Litho. *Perf. 14x13¼***
**1723** A801 25d multi .45 .45

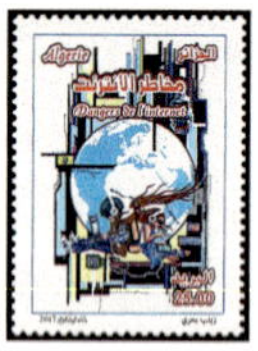

Dangers of the Internet — A802

**2017, Aug. 6 Litho. *Perf. 13¼x14***
**1724** A802 25d multi .45 .45

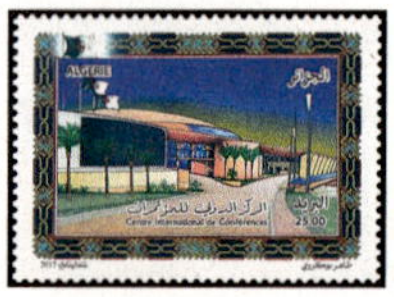

Algiers Architecture A803

Designs: No. 1725, 25d, International Conference Center. No. 1726, 25d, Opera House.

**2017, Sept. 10 Litho. *Perf. 13¼x13***
**1725-1726** A803 Set of 2 .90 .90

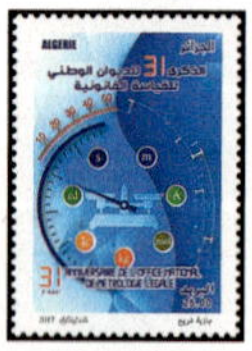

National Office of Weights and Measures, 31st Anniv. — A804

**2017, Sept. 29 Litho. *Perf. 13¼x14***
**1727** A804 25d multi .45 .45

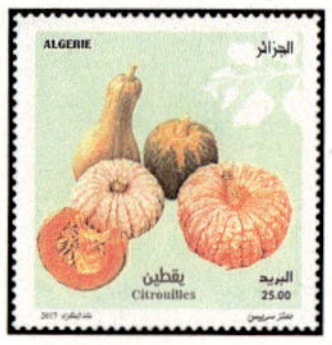

Fruits and Vegetables A805

Designs: No. 1728, 25d, Citrouilles (squashes). No. 1729, 25d, Aubergines (eggplants). No. 1730, 25d, Clementines. No. 1731, 25d, Pêches (peaches).

**2017, Oct. 16 Litho. *Perf. 14***
**1728-1731** A805 Set of 4 1.75 1.75

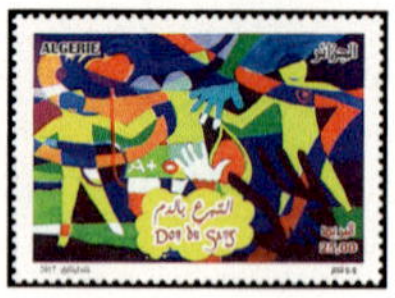

Blood Donation A806

**2017, Oct. 25 Litho. *Perf. 13¼x13***
**1732** A806 25d multi .45 .45

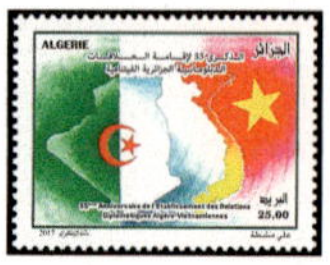

Diplomatic Relations Between Algeria and Viet Nam, 55th Anniv. — A807

**2017, Oct. 28 Litho. *Perf. 14x13¼***
**1733** A807 25d multi .45 .45

Souvenir Sheet

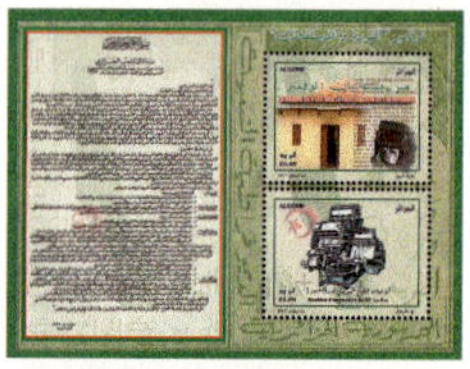

National Liberation Front Proclamation of November 1, 1954 — A808

No. 1734: a, House from which proclamation was made, and printing press. b, Printing press.

**2017, Nov. 1 Litho. *Perf. 14x13¼***
**1734** A808 25d Sheet of 2, #a-b .90 .90

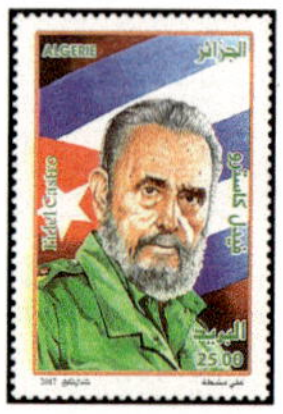

Fidel Castro (1926-2016), President of Cuba — A809

**2017, Nov. 26 Litho. *Perf. 13x13¼***
**1735** A809 25d multi .45 .45

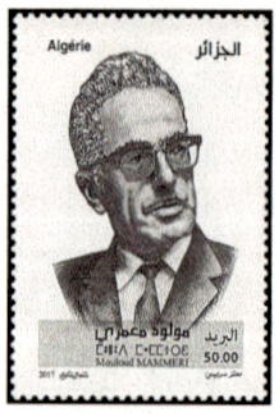

Mouloud Mammeri (1917-89), Writer — A810

**Litho. & Engr.**
**2017, Dec. 28 *Perf. 13x13¼***
**1736** A810 50d black .90 .90

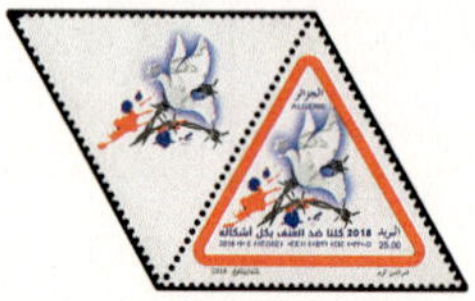

Campaign Against Violence — A811

**2018, Jan. 2 Litho. *Perf. 14¼***
**1737** A811 25d multi + label .45 .45

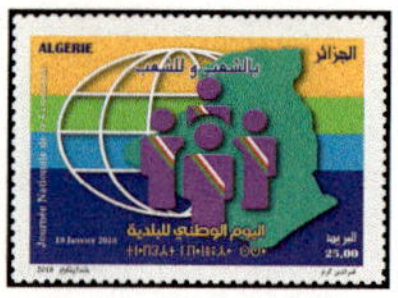

National Day of Municipalities A812

**2018, Jan. 18 Litho. *Perf. 13¼x13***
**1738** A812 25d multi .45 .45

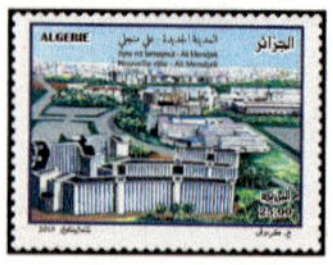

New Cities — A813

Designs: No. 1739, 25d, Ali Mendjeli. No. 1740, 25d, Sidi Abdellah.

**2018, Jan. 28 Litho. *Perf. 14x13¼***
**1739-1740** A813 Set of 2 .90 .90

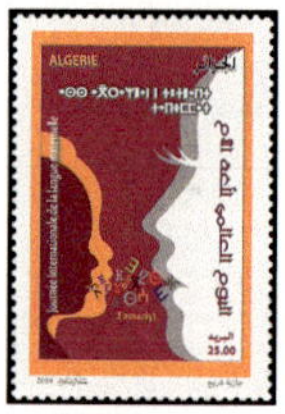

International Mother Language Day — A814

**2018, Feb. 21 Litho. *Perf. 13x13¼***
**1741** A814 25d multi .45 .45

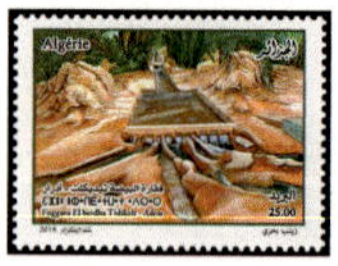

International Decade of Water for Sustainable Development A815

Foggaras (water systems) in Adrar Province: No. 1742, 25d, Foggara El Beidha, Tidikelt Region. No. 1743, 25d, Foggara El Kbira, Gourara Region. No. 1744, 25d, Foggara Armoul, Touât Region.

**2018, Mar. 22 Litho. *Perf. 14x13¼***
**1742-1744** A815 Set of 3 1.40 1.40

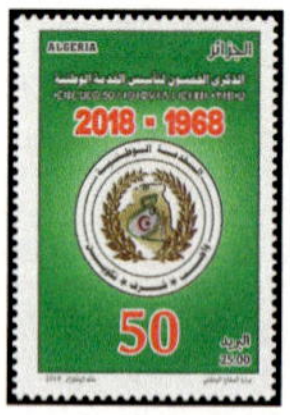

National Service, 50th Anniv. — A816

**2018, Apr. 8 Litho. *Perf. 13x13¼***
**1745** A816 25d multi .45 .45

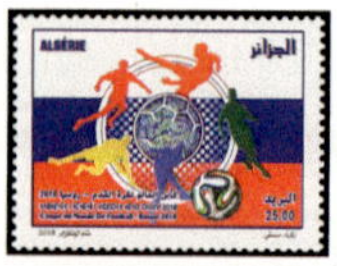

2018 World Cup Soccer Championships, Russia — A817

**2018, Apr. 21 Litho. *Perf. 14x13¼***
**1746** A817 25d multi .45 .45

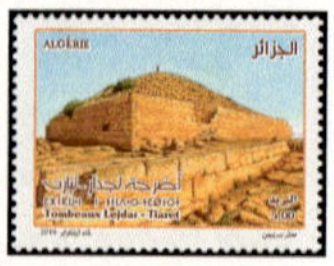

Historical Sites — A818

Designs: 5d, Jedar near Tiaret. 10d, Ruins of Tiddis, vert. 20d, Cedias Mausoleum, Khenchela, vert. 25d, El Mokrani Castle, Bordj Bou Arreridj.

***Perf. 14x13¼, 13¼x14***
**2018, May 12 Litho.**
**1747-1750** A818 Set of 4 1.10 1.10

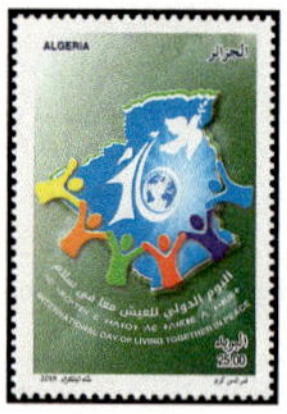

International Day of Living Together in Peace — A819

**2018, May 16 Litho. *Perf. 13x13¼***
**1751** A819 25d multi .45 .45

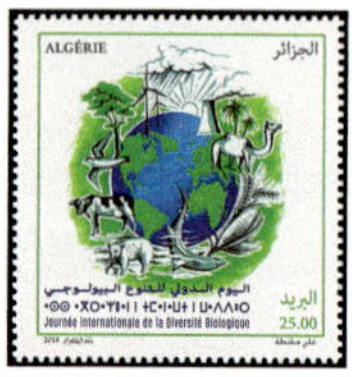

International Day of Biological Diversity — A820

**2018, May 22 Litho. *Perf. 14***
**1752** A820 25d multi .45 .45

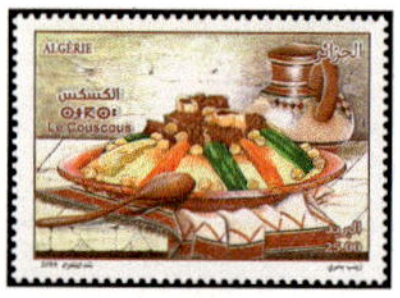

Couscous A821

**2018, June 12 Litho. *Perf. 13¼x13***
**1753** A821 25d multi .45 .45

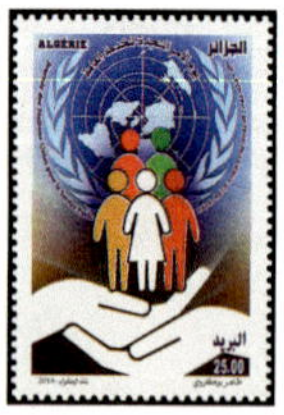

United Nations Day for Public Service — A822

**2018, June 23 Litho. *Perf. 13x13¼***
**1754** A822 25d multi .45 .45

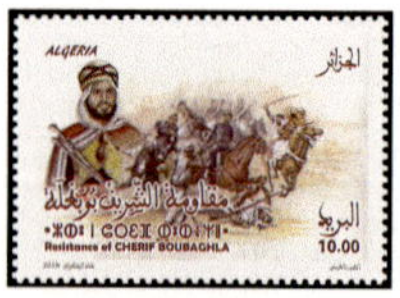

Freedom Fighters A823

Designs: 10d, Cherif Boubaghla (?-1854). 20d, Sheikh Amoud (1859-1929), vert. 25d, Bennacer Ben Chohra (1804-84), vert.

***Perf. 13¼x13, 13x13¼***
**2018, July 5 Litho.**
**1755-1757** A823 Set of 3 .95 .95

# ALGERIA

Blaoui el Houari (1926-2017), Singer — A824

**2018, July 19**    Litho.    Perf. 13x13¼
1758   A824   50d multi      .85   .85

### Souvenir Sheet

Nelson Mandela (1918-2013), President of South Africa — A825

**2018, July 18**    Litho.    Perf. 13¼
1759   A825   100d multi      1.75   1.75

A826

Third African Youth Games, Algeria — A827

**2018, July 19**    Litho.    Perf. 13¼x14
1760   A826   25d multi      .45   .45
1761   A827   25d multi      .45   .45

Zaouia (Islamic School) A828

Dome of Zaouia, Map of Algeria, Muslim Man and Calligrapher A829

**2018, Sept. 1**    Litho.    Perf. 14
1762   A828   25d multi      —   —
                        Perf. 13¼
1763   A829   25d multi      —   —

Sbiba Festival A830

No. 1764: a, Four Tuareg dancers. b, Tuareg dancers and festival attendees.

**2018, Sept. 27**    Litho.    Perf. 14x13½
1764   A830   25d Horiz. pair, #a-b      —   —

Honeycomb, Bees and Eucalyptus Blossoms A831

Honeycomb, Bees and Jujube Blossoms A832

**2018, Oct. 16**    Litho.    Perf. 14¼
1765   A831   25d multi      —   —
1766   A832   25d multi      —   —

National Press Day — A833

**2018, Oct. 22**    Litho.    Perf. 13x13½
1767   A833   25d multi      —   —

Green City — A834

**2018, Oct. 25**    Litho.    Perf. 13x13½
1768   A834   25d multi      —   —

Mostefa Ben Boulaid (1917-56), Revolution Leader A835

Mourad Didouche (1927-55), Revolution Leader A836

Larbi Ben M'hidi (1923-57), Revolution Leader A837

Colonel Amirouchené Ait Hamouda (1926-59), Revolution Leader A838

Colonel Youcef Zighoud (1921-56), Revolution Leader — A839

**2018, Nov. 1**    Litho.    Perf. 13½x14
1769   A835   25d multi      —   —
1770   A836   25d multi      —   —
1771   A837   25d multi      —   —
1772   A838   25d multi      —   —
1773   A839   25d multi      —   —

Martyrs of the Algerian Revolution.

### Souvenir Sheet

Proclamation Declaring the Formation of the State of Palestine, 30th Anniv. — A840

**2018, Nov. 15**    Litho.    Perf. 13½x13
1774   A840   70d multi      —   —

Women's Entrepreneurship Day — A841

**2018, Nov. 21**    Litho.    Perf. 14x13¼
1775   A841   25d multi      .45   .45

Launch of Alcomsat-1, 1st Anniv. — A842

**2018, Dec. 11**    Litho.    Perf. 13½x14
1776   A842   25d multi      —   —

World Arabic Language Day — A843

**2018, Dec. 18**    Litho.    Perf. 13x13½
1777   A843   50d multi      —   —

Diplomatic Relations Between Algeria and People's Republic of China, 60th Anniv. A844

**2018, Dec. 20**    Litho.    Perf. 13½x13
1778   A844   25d multi      —   —

Pres. Houari Boumédiène (1932-78) — A845

**2018, Dec. 27**    Litho.    Perf. 13x13½
1779   A845   50d multi      —   —

International Year of the Periodic Table of Elements A846

**2019, Jan. 2**    Litho.    Perf. 13¼x13
1780   A846   25d multi      .45   .45

Women in Health Services in the Algerian Revolution — A847

No. 1781: a, Female health care worker treating standing soldier in forest. b, Male and female health care workers treating soldiers sitting against rock face.

**2019, Feb. 18**    Litho.    Perf. 14x13½
1781   A847   25d Horiz. pair, #a-b      —   —

Mar. 8, 1974, Crash of Airplane Carrying Algerian Journalists in Hanoi, Viet Nam — A848

**2019, Mar. 8**    Litho.    Perf. 13½x13
1782   A848   25d multi      —   —

International Labor Organization, Cent. — A849

**2019, Mar. 9**    Litho.    Perf. 13½x13
1783   A849   25d multi      —   —

Emiliano Zapata (1879-1919), Leader of Mexican Revolution A850

**2019, Apr. 10**    Litho.    Perf. 13½x13
1784   A850   25d multi      —   —

### Souvenir Sheet

Science Day A851

**2019, Apr. 16**    Litho.    Imperf.
1785   A851   50d multi

# ALGERIA

### Souvenir Sheet

Protected Species — A852

No. 1786: a, Oryx dammah. b, Cobra from North Africa.

**2019, May 11    Litho.    Perf. 14x13½**
1786  A852  25d  Sheet of 2, #a-b  — —

2019 Africa Cup of Nations Soccer Tournament, Egypt — A853

**2019, May 15    Litho.    Perf.**
1787  A853  25d  multi  — —

Traditional Costumes — A854

Designs: No. 1788, 25d, Woman wearing Tlemcenian scarf. No. 1789, 25d, Man wearing burnous of Southern Algeria. No. 1790, 25d, Woman wearing Kabyle dress. No. 1791, 25d, Man wearing clothing of Aurès.

**2019, July 8    Litho.    Perf. 13x13½**
1788-1791  A854  Set of 4  — —

National Society for Electricity and Gas (Sonelgaz), 50th Anniv. — A855

**2019, July 28    Litho.    Perf. 13x13½**
1792  A855  25d  multi  — —

Ahmed Zabana (1926-56), Revolution Leader A856

Ali Ammar (1930-57), Revolution Leader A857

Malika Gaid (1933-58), Revolutionary Hero and Nurse A858

Hassiba Ben Bouali (1938-57), Revolutionary Hero A859

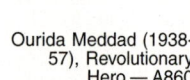

Ourida Meddad (1938-57), Revolutionary Hero — A860

**2019, Oct. 3    Litho.    Perf. 13½x14**
1793     Vert. strip of 5  — —
   a.  A856  25d  multi  — —
   b.  A857  25d  multi  — —
   c.  A858  25d  multi  — —
   d.  A859  25d  multi  — —
   e.  A860  25d  multi  — —

Martyrs of the Algerian Revolution.

Mohamed Seddik Ben Yahia (1932-82), Politician — A861

**2019, Oct. 8    Litho.    Perf. 13x13½**
1794  A861  50d  multi  — —

Dome of the Rock, Jerusalem, Doves and Palestinian Authority Flag — A862

**2019, Oct. 9    Litho.    Perf. 13½x13**
1795  A862  100d  multi  — —

Jerusalem, capital of the Palestinian Authority.

World Organ Donation and Transplantation Day — A863

**2019, Oct. 20    Litho.    Perf. 14x13½**
1796  A863  25d  multi  — —

24th Algiers International Book Fair — A864

**2019, Nov. 2    Litho.    Perf. 13x13½**
1797  A864  25d  multi  — —

### Souvenir Sheet

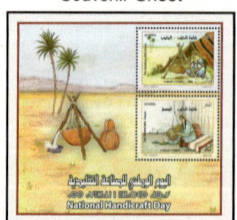

National Handicrafts Day — A865

No. 1798: a, Southern milk churn. b, Central milk churn.

**2019, Nov. 11    Litho.    Perf. 14x13½**
1798  A865  50d  Sheet of 2, #a-b  — —

Algerian Sign Language Dictionary — A866

**2019, Dec. 5    Litho.    Perf. 13x13½**
1799  A866  25d  multi  — —

Stone Engravings, Sfissifa Station A867

Ain El Haneche Archaeological Site — A868

Abou Al Mouhajir Dinar Mosque, Mila — A869

**2020, Jan. 25    Litho.    Perf. 13½x13**
1800  A867  25d  multi  — —
1801  A868  25d  multi  — —
1802  A869  25d  multi  — —

Archaeological sites and treasures.

Myotis Nattereri — A870

Hirundo Rustica — A871

Bubo Ascalaphus — A872

**2020, Feb. 22    Litho.    Perf. 13¼**
1803  A870  20d  multi  — —
1804  A871  25d  multi  — —
    **Perf. 13¼x14**
1805  A872  30d  multi  — —

Repatriation From France of Skulls of 24 Zaatcha Resistance Fighters A873

**2020, Aug. 20    Litho.    Perf. 13¼x13**
1806  A873  25d  multi  — —

Campaign Against COVID-19 Pandemic — A874

No. 1807 — COVID-19 viruses and: a, Stylized people on globe. b, Ways to prevent spread of virus, protective mask over house with stylized people.

**2021, Feb. 27    Litho.    Perf. 14x13¼**
1807  A874  25d  Horiz. pair, #a-b  — —

Promotion of Consumption of Algerian Goods — A875

**2021, Mar. 15    Litho.    Perf. 13¼x14**
1808  A875  25d  multi  — —

Campaign Against Forest Fires — A876

**2021, Mar. 21    Litho.    Perf. 14¼**
1809  A876  50d  multi  — —

People Playing Khargba A877

People Playing Sig — A878

**2021, Apr. 18    Litho.    Perf. 13¼x13**
1810  A877  25d  multi  — —
    **Perf. 14**
1811  A878  50d  multi  — —

Fruits — A879

Designs: 25d, Blackberries. 50d, Strawberry.

**2021, May 16    Litho.    Perf. 14**
1812-1813  A879  Set of 2  — —

Algerian Cuisine A880

Designs: 25d, Rechta (noodles). 50d, Harira (soup).

**2021, May 18    Litho.    Perf. 13¼x13**
1814-1815  A880  Set of 2  — —

Recycling Economy — A881

**2021, June 6    Litho.    Perf. 13¼x14**
1816  A881  25d  multi  — —

# ALGERIA

People Celebrating Independence Day — A882

**2021, July 5**  Litho.  Perf. 13¼x13
1817  A882  25d  multi

Chamassa (Brooch) — A883

Skhab (Necklace of Scented Beads) — A884

**2021, July 14**  Litho.  Perf. 14
1818  A883  50d  multi
1819  A884  50d  multi

2020 Summer Olympics, Tokyo — A885

Designs: 25d, Kayaker and Mount Fuji. 50d, Karatekas and torii.

**2021, July 15**  Litho.  Perf. 14
1820-1821  A885  Set of 2

The 2020 Summer Olympics were postponed until 2021 because of the COVID-19 pandemic.

Tambourine A886

Goblet Drum — A887

**2021, Oct. 1**  Litho.  Perf. 14
1822  A886  25d  multi
Perf. 14x13½
1823  A887  50d  multi

World Teacher's Day — A888

**2021, Oct. 5**  Litho.  Perf. 13½x13
1824  A888  50d  multi

Djamaa El Djazair Mosque, Muhammadia A889

**2021, Oct. 19**  Litho.  Perf. 13½x13
1825  A889  50d  multi

Medjerda River — A890

**2021, Oct. 24**  Litho.  Perf. 13½x13
1826  A890  50d  multi

Joint issue between Algeria and Tunisia. See Tunisia No. 1769.

Group of 22, House of Lyes Deriche and Algerian Flags A891

**2021, Nov. 1**  Litho.  Imperf.
1827  A891  100d  multi

Start of Algerian War of Independence and Declaration of November 1, 1954, 67th anniv.

Saddlemaking — A892

No. 1828: a, Decorated saddle. b, Saddle and saddlemaking tools.

**2021, Nov. 9**  Litho.  Perf. 14x13½
1828  A892  25d  Horiz. pair, #a-b

2021 Africa Cup of Nations Soccer Tournament, Cameroun — A893

**2022, Jan. 9**  Litho.  Perf. 13x13½
1829  A893  25d  multi

The 2021 Africa Cup of Nations Soccer Tournament was postponed until 2022 because of the COVID-19 pandemic.

Mohamed Balouizdad (1924-52), President of Special Organization — A894

**2022, Feb. 15**  Litho.  Perf. 13x13½
1830  A894  25d  multi

Special Organization, 75th anniv.

Cohesion Between the Algerian People and Their Army — A895

**2022, Feb. 23**  Litho.  Perf. 13½x13
1831  A895  25d  multi

Algerian Pavilion at EXPO 2020, Dubai — A896

Designs: 25d, Pavilion entrance. 50d, Entire pavilion.

**2022, Mar. 1**  Litho.  Perf. 13¼x14
1832  A896  25d  multi  .35  .35
Size: 58x58mm
Imperf
1833  A896  50d  multi  .70  .70

EXPO 2020 was postponed until 2021 because of the COVID-19 pandemic.

National Remembrance Day — A897

**2022, May 8**  Litho.  Perf. 13¼x13
1834  A897  25d  multi

Great Mosque of Oran — A898

**2022, May 17**  Litho.  Perf. 13½x13
1835  A898  25d  multi  .35  .35

Traditional Costumes from Oran — A899    Gallal — A900

**2022, May 18**  Litho.  Perf. 13¼x14
1836  A899  25d  multi
Perf. 14x13¼
1837  A900  25d  multi

Athmane Bali (1953-2005), Singer A901

Mohamed Tahar el Fergani (1928-2016), Singer — A902

**2022, June 11**  Litho.  Perf. 13½x13
1838  A901  25d  multi
Perf. 13x13½
1839  A902  25d  multi

A903

2022 Mediterranean Games, Oran — A904

Designs: No. 1840, 25d, Volleyball. No. 1841, 25d, Table tennis. No. 1842, 25d, High jump. No. 1843, 25d, Fencing. 100d, Oran, flag of Algeria, emblem of 2022 Mediterranean Games.

**2022, June 25**  Litho.  Perf. 14
1840-1843  A903  Set of 4  1.40  1.40
Imperf
1844  A904  100d  multi  1.40  1.40

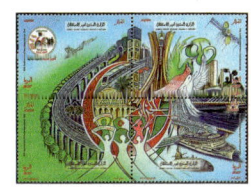

Independence, 60th Anniv. — A905

No. 1845: a, 60th anniversary emblem, military aircraft, highway, train. b, Martyr's Memorial, Algiers, buildings, doves, satellite. c, Highway, people with banners and Algerian flag. d, Highway, bridges, ship, submarine.

**2022, July 7**  Litho.  Perf. 13½x13
1845  A905  25d  Block of 4, #a-d

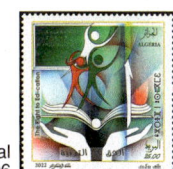

Educational Rights — A906

**2022, July 17**  Litho.  Perf. 14
1846  A906  25d  multi  .35  .35

Arab League Summit, Algiers — A907

**2022, Aug. 22**  Litho.  Perf.
1847  A907  25d  multi  .35  .35

Man Weaving Fishing Net — A908    Woman Shaping Pottery — A909

**2022, Sept. 4 Litho. *Perf. 14***
**1848** A908 25d multi .35 .35

***Perf. 13x13½***
**1849** A909 25d multi .35 .35

Sheikh Sidi Mohamed Belkebir (1911-2000), Religious Scholar A910

**2022, Sept. 18 Litho. *Perf. 13½x13***
**1850** A910 25d multi .35 .35

National Imam Day.

Sixth Population and Housing Census — A911

**2022, Sept. 25 Litho. *Perf. 13¼x14***
**1851** A911 25d multi — —

Sea Mammals — A912

Designs: No. 1852, 25d, Stenella coeruleoalba. No. 1853, 25d, Delphinus delphis.

**2022, Oct. 1 Litho. *Perf. 14x13¼***
**1852-1853** A912 Set of 2 — —

World Post Day — A913

**2022, Oct. 9 Litho. *Perf. 13x13¼***
**1854** A913 25d multi .35 .35

Olive Varieties A914

No. 1855: a, Sigoise. b, Chemlal.

**2022, Oct. 18 Litho. *Perf. 13½x13***
**1855** A914 25d Vert. pair, #a-b — —

Diplomatic Relations Between Algeria and Cuba, 60th Anniv. — A915

**2022, Oct. 17 Litho. *Perf. 13¼x13***
**1857** A915 25d multi .35 .35

Algerian Soccer Federation, 60th Anniv. — A916

**2022, Oct. 21 Litho. *Perf. 13x13¼***
**1858** A916 25d multi .35 .35

Islamic Banking — A917

**2022, Nov. 2 Litho. *Perf. 13x13½***
**1859** A917 25d multi .35 .35

Choukri Mesli (1931-2017), Postage Stamp Designer A918

Ali Mechta (1953-2021), Postage Stamp Designer A919

Kamar Eddine Krim (1952-2020), Postage Stamp Designer A920

Ali Ali-Khodja (1923-2010), Postage Stamp Designer A921

**2022, Nov. 3 Litho. *Perf. 13¼x14***
**1860** A918 25d multi .35 .35
**1861** A919 25d multi .35 .35
**1862** A920 25d multi .35 .35
**1863** A921 25d multi .35 .35
*Nos. 1860-1863 (4)* 1.40 1.40

Achievements of Handicapped Athletes — A922

**2022, Dec. 5 Litho. *Perf. 13x13½***
**1864** A922 25d multi — —

National Innovation Day — A923

**2022, Dec. 7 Litho. *Perf. 14***
**1865** A923 25d multi .40 .40

Bank of Algeria, 60th Anniv. A924

**2022, Dec. 15 Litho. *Perf. 13¼x13***
**1866** A924 25d multi .40 .40

2022 Africa Cup of Nations Soccer Championships, Algeria — A925

**2023, Jan. 17 Litho. *Perf. 13x13¼***
**1867** A925 50d multi .75 .75

The 2022 Africa Cup of Nations Soccer Championships were postponed to 2023 because of the COVID-19 pandemic.

Preparation of First Program Budget — A926

**2023, Jan. 30 Litho. *Perf.***
**1868** A926 25d multi — —

17th Session of the Parliamentary Union of the Organization of Islamic Cooperation A927

**2023, Jan. 31 Litho. *Perf. 13½x13***
**1869** A927 25d multi — —

Tribute to Martyrs of the Algerian Revolution A928

**2023, Feb. 18 Litho. *Perf. 14***
**1870** A928 50d multi .75 .75

Preventive Health Care Week — A929

**2023, Mar. 7 Litho. *Perf. 13x13¼***
**1871** A929 25d multi .40 .40

International Day of Women Judges — A930

**2023, Mar. 12 Litho. *Imperf.***
**1872** A930 100d multi 1.50 1.50

Public Accessibilty for the Handicapped A931

**2023, Mar. 14 Litho. *Perf. 13¼x13***
**1873** A931 25d multi .40 .40

Brass Items — A932

Designs: No. 1874, 25d, Mahbes (bucket). No. 1875, 25d, Mehres (mortar and pestle).

**2023, Apr. 18 Litho. *Perf. 13¼x14***
**1874-1875** A932 multi .75 .75

Honey Cones A933

Makrout With Almonds A934

**2023, Apr. 24 Litho. *Perf. 13¼x13***
**1876** A933 50d multi .75 .75
**1877** A934 50d multi .75 .75

Partition of Palestine, 75th Anniv. A935

**2023, May 24 Litho. *Perf. 13¼x13***
**1878** A935 68d multi 1.00 1.00

## SEMI-POSTAL STAMPS

Regular Issue of 1926 Surcharged in Black or Red

**1927 Unwmk. *Perf. 14x13½***

| | | | | | |
|---|---|---|---|---|---|
| **B1** | A1 | 5c | +5c bl grn | 1.75 | 1.75 |
| **B2** | A1 | 10c | +10c lilac | 1.75 | 1.75 |
| **B3** | A2 | 15c | +15c org brn | 1.75 | 1.75 |
| **B4** | A2 | 20c | +20c car rose | 1.75 | 1.75 |
| **B5** | A2 | 25c | +25c bl grn | 1.75 | 1.75 |
| **B6** | A2 | 30c | +30c lt bl | 1.75 | 1.75 |

# ALGERIA

| | | | |
|---|---|---|---|
| B7 | A2 35c +35c dp vio | 1.75 | 1.75 |
| B8 | A2 40c +40c ol grn | 1.75 | 1.75 |
| B9 | A3 50c +50c dp bl (R) | 1.75 | 1.75 |
| a. | Double surcharge | 425.00 | 425.00 |
| B10 | A3 80c +80c red org | 1.75 | 1.75 |
| B11 | A4 1fr +1fr gray grn & red brn | 1.75 | 1.75 |
| B12 | A4 2fr +2fr Prus bl & blk brn | 35.00 | 35.00 |
| B13 | A4 5fr +5fr red & vio | 45.00 | 45.00 |
| | Nos. B1-B13 (13) | 99.25 | 99.25 |

The surtax was for the benefit of wounded soldiers. Government officials speculated in this issue.

Railroad Terminal, Oran — SP1

Ruins at Djemila — SP2

Mosque of Sidi Abd-er-Rahman — SP3

Designs: 10c+10c, Rummel Gorge, Constantine. 15c+15c, Admiralty Buildings, Algiers. 25c+25c, View of Algiers. 30c+30c, Trajan's Arch, Timgad. 40c+40c, Temple of the North, Djemila. 75c+75c Mansourah Minaret, Tlemcen. 1f+1f, View of Ghardaia. 1.50f+1.50f, View of Tolga. 2f+2f, Tuareg warriors. 3f+3f, Kasbah, Algiers.

| 1930 | | Engr. | | Perf. 12½ |
|---|---|---|---|---|
| B14 | SP1 | 5c +5c orange | 12.00 | 12.00 |
| B15 | SP1 | 10c +10c ol grn | 12.00 | 12.00 |
| B16 | SP1 | 15c +15c dk brn | 12.00 | 12.00 |
| B17 | SP1 | 25c +25c black | 12.00 | 12.00 |
| B18 | SP1 | 30c +30c dk red | 12.00 | 12.00 |
| B19 | SP1 | 40c +40c ap grn | 12.00 | 12.00 |
| B20 | SP2 | 50c +50c ultra | 10.00 | 10.00 |
| B21 | SP2 | 75c +75c red pur | 10.00 | 10.00 |
| B22 | SP2 | 1fr +1fr org red | 10.00 | 10.00 |
| B23 | SP2 | 1.50fr +1.50fr deep ultra | 10.00 | 10.00 |
| B24 | SP2 | 2fr +2fr dk car | 10.00 | 10.00 |
| B25 | SP2 | 3fr +3fr dk car | 10.00 | 10.00 |
| B26 | SP3 | 5fr +5fr grn & car | 25.00 | 25.00 |
| a. | | Center inverted | 750.00 | |
| | Nos. B14-B26 (13) | 157.00 | 157.00 |

Centenary of the French occupation of Algeria. The surtax on the stamps was given to the funds for the celebration.

Nos. B14-B26 exist imperf. Value, set in pairs, $800.

**Catalogue values for unused stamps in this section, from this point to the end of the section, are for Never Hinged items.**

No. 102 Surcharged in Red

| 1938 | | | Perf. 13 |
|---|---|---|---|
| B27 | A6 65c +35c on 2.25fr yel grn | 1.60 | 1.20 |
| a. | Inverted surcharge | 350.00 | |
| b. | Pair, one without surcharge | 1,875. | |

20th anniversary of Armistice.
No. 79 with surcharge is considered an essay. Values: unused $260, never hinged $350.

René Caillié, Charles Lavigerie and Henri Duveyrier — SP14

| 1939 | | | Engr. | |
|---|---|---|---|---|
| B28 | SP14 | 30c +20c dk bl grn | 2.40 | 2.40 |
| B29 | SP14 | 90c +60c car rose | 2.40 | 2.40 |

| B30 | SP14 2.25fr +75c ultra | 20.00 | 16.00 |
| B31 | SP14 5fr +5fr brn blk | 40.00 | 32.50 |
| | Nos. B28-B31 (4) | 64.80 | 53.30 |

Pioneers of the Sahara.

French and Algerian Soldiers — SP15

| 1940 | | Photo. | | Perf. 12 |
|---|---|---|---|---|
| B32 | SP15 1fr +1fr bl & car | 1.60 | 1.20 |
| a. | Double surcharge | 260.00 | |
| B33 | SP15 1fr +2fr brn rose & blk | 1.60 | 1.20 |
| B34 | SP15 1fr +4fr dp grn & red | 2.40 | 2.00 |
| B35 | SP15 1fr +9fr brn & car | 4.00 | 2.75 |
| | Nos. B32-B35 (4) | 9.60 | 7.15 |

The surtax was used to assist the families of mobilized men.
Nos. B32-B35 exist without surcharge. Value set, $325.

Type of Regular Issue, 1941 Surcharged in Carmine

| 1941 | | Engr. | | Perf. 13 |
|---|---|---|---|---|
| B36 | A19 1fr +4fr black | .70 | .30 |

No. 135 Surcharged in Carmine

| B37 | A19 1fr +4fr dark blue | .70 | .30 |

The surtax was for National Relief.

No. 124 Surcharged in Black

| 1942 | | | | |
| B38 | A7 90c +60c henna brn | .60 | .25 |
| a. | Double surcharge | 175.00 | |

The surtax was used for National Relief. The stamp could also be used as 1.50 francs for postage.

Mother and Child — SP16

| 1943, Dec. 1 | | Litho. | | Perf. 12 |
|---|---|---|---|---|
| B39 | SP16 50c +4.50fr brt pink | 1.00 | 1.30 |
| B40 | SP16 1.50fr +8.50fr lt grn | 1.00 | 1.30 |
| B41 | SP16 3fr +12fr dp bl | 1.00 | 1.30 |
| B42 | SP16 5fr +15fr vio brn | 1.00 | 1.40 |
| | Nos. B39-B42 (4) | 4.00 | 5.30 |

The surtax was for the benefit of soldiers and prisoners of war.

Planes over Fields — SP17

| 1945, July 2 | | Engr. | | Perf. 13 | | Unwmk. |
|---|---|---|---|---|
| B43 | SP17 1.50fr +3.50fr lt ultra, red org & blk | 1.15 | .85 |

The surtax was for the benefit of Algerian airmen and their families.

**France No. B192 Overprinted Type "a" of 1924 in Black**

| 1945 | | | |
|---|---|---|---|
| B44 | SP146 4fr +6fr dk vio brn | 1.15 | .85 |

The surtax was for war victims of the P.T.T.

**Overprinted in Blue on Type of France, 1945**

| 1945, Oct. 15 | | | |
|---|---|---|---|
| B45 | SP150 2fr +3fr dk brn | 1.15 | .85 |

For Stamp Day.

**Overprinted in Blue on Type of France, 1946**

| 1946, June 29 | | | |
|---|---|---|---|
| B46 | SP160 3fr +2fr red | 1.70 | 1.25 |

For Stamp Day.

Children Playing by Stream — SP18

Girl — SP19

Athlete — SP20

Repatriated Prisoner and Bay of Algiers — SP21

| 1946, Oct. 2 | | Engr. | | Perf. 13 |
|---|---|---|---|---|
| B47 | SP18 3fr +17fr dark grn | 2.75 | 2.25 |
| B48 | SP19 4fr +21fr red | 2.75 | 2.25 |
| B49 | SP20 8fr +27fr rose lilac | 7.25 | 6.25 |
| B50 | SP21 10fr +35fr dark blue | 3.25 | 2.50 |
| | Nos. B47-B50 (4) | 16.00 | 13.25 |

**Type of France, 1947, Overprinted type "a" of 1924 in Carmine**

| 1947, Mar. 15 | | | |
|---|---|---|---|
| B51 | SP172 4.50fr +5.50fr dp ultra | 1.75 | 1.25 |

For Stamp Day.

**Same on Type of France, 1947, Surcharged Like No. B36 in Carmine**

| 1947, Nov. 13 | | | |
|---|---|---|---|
| B52 | A173 5fr +10fr dk Prus grn | 1.60 | 1.25 |

Type of France, 1948, Overprinted in Dark Green — f

| 1948, Mar. 6 | | | |
|---|---|---|---|
| B53 | SP176 6fr +4fr dk grn | 1.75 | 1.25 |

For Stamp Day.

**Type of France, 1948, Overprinted in Blue**

| 1948, May | | | |
|---|---|---|---|
| B54 | A176 6fr +4fr red | 1.70 | 1.25 |

Aircraft Carrier Arromanches — SP23

**Unwmk.**

| 1949, Jan. 15 | | Engr. | | Perf. 13 |
|---|---|---|---|---|
| B55 | SP22 10fr +15fr dp blue | 10.00 | 8.00 |
| B56 | SP23 18fr +22fr red | 10.00 | 8.00 |

The surtax was for naval charities.

Type of France, 1949, Overprinted in Blue — g

| 1949, Mar. 26 | | | |
|---|---|---|---|
| B57 | SP180 15fr +5fr lilac rose | 3.25 | 2.25 |

For Stamp Day, Mar. 26-27.

**Type of France, 1950, Overprinted type "f" in Green**

| 1950, Mar. 11 | | | |
|---|---|---|---|
| B58 | SP183 12fr +3fr blk brn | 3.25 | 2.75 |

For Stamp Day, Mar. 11-12.

Foreign Legionary — SP24

| 1950, Apr. 30 | | | |
|---|---|---|---|
| B59 | SP24 15fr +5fr dk grn | 3.00 | 2.40 |

Charles de Foucauld and Gen. J. F. H. Laperrine — SP25

| 1950, Aug. 21 | | Unwmk. | | Perf. 13 |
|---|---|---|---|---|
| B60 | SP25 25fr +5fr brn ol & brn blk | 8.00 | 6.25 |

50th anniversary of the presence of the French in the Sahara.

Emir Abd-el-Kader and Marshal T. R. Bugeaud — SP26

| 1950, Aug. 21 | | | |
|---|---|---|---|
| B61 | SP26 40fr +10fr org brn & blk brn | 8.00 | 6.25 |

Unveiling of a monument to Emir Abd-el-Kader at Cacheron.

Col. Colonna d'Ornano and Fine Arts Museum, Algiers — SP27

| 1951, Jan. 11 | | | |
|---|---|---|---|
| B62 | SP27 15fr +5fr blk brn, vio brn & red brn | 1.40 | 1.25 |

Death of Col. Colonna d'Ornano, 10th anniv.

**Type of France, 1951, Overprinted type "a" of 1924 in Black**

| 1951, Mar. 10 | | | |
|---|---|---|---|
| B63 | SP186 12fr +3fr brown | 2.75 | 2.50 |

For Stamp Day.

# ALGERIA

### Type of France, 1952, Overprinted type "g" in Dark Blue
**1952, Mar. 8**    Unwmk.    *Perf. 13*
B64 SP190 12fr +3fr dk bl    2.75   2.50
For Stamp Day.

French Military Medal — SP28

**Unwmk.**
**1952, July 5**    Engr.    *Perf. 13*
B65 SP28 15fr +5fr grn, yel & brn   3.50   2.75
Centenary of the creation of the French Military Medal.

### Type of France 1952, Surcharged type "g" and Surtax in Black
**1952, Sept. 15**
B66 A222 30fr +5fr dp ultra    4.00   3.25
10th anniv. of the defense of Bir-Hakeim.

View of El Oued — SP29

Design: 12fr+3fr, View of Bou-Noura.
**1952, Nov. 15**    Engr.
B67 SP29 8fr +2fr ultra & red   3.25   3.00
B68 SP29 12fr +3fr red    6.50   4.75
The surtax was for the Red Cross.

### Type of France, 1953, Overprinted type "a" of 1924 in Black
**1953, Mar. 14**    Engr.
B69 SP193 12fr +3fr purple   2.50   2.40
For Stamp Day. Surtax for Red Cross.

Victory of Cythera — SP30

**Unwmk.**
**1953, Dec. 18**    Engr.    *Perf. 13*
B70 SP30 15fr +5fr blk brn & brn   1.60   1.25
The surtax was for army welfare work.

### Type of France, 1954, Overprinted type "a" of 1924 in Black
**1954, Mar. 20**    Unwmk.    *Perf. 13*
B71 SP196 12fr +3fr scarlet   2.25   2.00
For Stamp Day.

Soldiers and Flags — SP31

**1954, Mar. 27**
B72 SP31 15fr +5fr dk brn   2.00   1.25
The surtax was for old soldiers.

Foreign Legionary — SP32

**1954, Apr. 30**
B73 SP32 15fr +5fr dk grn   3.00   2.50
The surtax was for the welfare fund of the Foreign Legion.

Nurses and Verdun Hospital, Algiers — SP33

15fr+5fr, J. H. Dunant & ruins at Djemila.
**1954, Oct. 30**
B74 SP33 12fr +3fr indigo & red   6.50   5.50
B75 SP33 15fr +5fr pur & red   7.50   6.25
The surtax was for the Red Cross.

 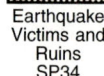

Earthquake Victims and Ruins SP34    First Aid SP35

Design: Nos. B80-B81, Removing wounded.
**1954, Dec. 5**
B76 SP34 12fr +4fr dk vio brn   3.50   2.75
B77 SP34 15fr +5fr dp bl   3.50   2.75
B78 SP35 18fr +6fr lil rose   4.50   3.50
B79 SP35 20fr +7fr violet   4.50   3.50
B80 SP35 25fr +8fr rose brn   4.50   3.50
B81 SP35 30fr +10fr brt bl grn   4.50   3.50
Nos. B76-B81 (6)   25.00   19.50
The surtax was for victims of the Orleansville earthquake disaster of September 1954.

### Type of France, 1955, Overprinted type "a" of 1924 in Black
**1955, Mar. 19**
B82 SP199 12fr +3fr dp ultra   2.75   2.25
For Stamp Day, Mar. 19-20.

Women and Children — SP36

**1955, Nov. 5**
B83 SP36 15fr +5fr blue & indigo   1.40   1.25
The tax was for war victims.

Cancer Victim — SP37

**1956, Mar. 3**    Unwmk.    *Perf. 13*
B84 SP37 15fr +5fr dk brn   2.00   1.60
The surtax was for the Algerian Cancer Society. The male figure in the design is Rodin's "Age of Bronze."

### Type of France, 1956, Overprinted type "a" of 1924 in Black
**1956, Mar.**
B85 SP202 12fr +3fr red   2.50   2.00
For Stamp Day, Mar. 17-18.

Foreign Legion Rest Home — SP38

**1956, Apr. 29**
B86 SP38 15fr +5fr dk bl grn   2.50   2.00
Honoring the French Foreign Legion.

### Type of France, 1957, Overprinted type "f" in Black
**1957, Mar. 16**    Engr.    *Perf. 13*
B87 SP204 12fr +3fr dull purple   2.00   1.60
For Stamp Day and to honor the Maritime Postal Service.

Fennec — SP39

Design: 15fr+5fr, Stork flying over roofs.
**1957, Apr. 6**
B88 SP39 12fr +3fr red brn & red   9.00   7.25
B89 SP39 15fr +5fr sepia & red   9.00   7.25
The surtax was for the Red Cross.

Regular Issue of 1956 Srchd. in Dark Blue

**1957, June 18**
B90 A53 15fr +5fr scar & rose red   2.50   1.60
17th anniv. of General de Gaulle's appeal for a Free France.

The Giaour, by Delacroix SP40    On the Banks of the Oued, by Fromentin SP41

Design: 35fr+10fr, Dancer, by Chasseriau.
**Unwmk.**
**1957, Nov. 30**    Engr.    *Perf. 13*
B91 SP40 15fr +5fr dk car   8.00   7.00
B92 SP41 20fr +5fr grn   8.00   7.00
B93 SP40 35fr +10fr dk bl   9.00   7.25
Nos. B91-B93 (3)   25.00   21.25
Surtax for army welfare organizations.

### Type of France Overprinted type "f" in Blue
**1958, Mar. 15**    Unwmk.    *Perf. 13*
B94 SP206 15fr +5fr org brn   2.00   1.60
For Stamp Day.

Bird-of-Paradise Flower — SP42

**1958, June 14**    Engr.    *Perf. 13*
B95 SP42 20fr +5fr grn, org & vio   5.50   4.00
The surtax was for Child Welfare.

Arms & Marshal's Baton — SP43

**1958, July 20**
B96 SP43 20fr +5fr ultra, car & grn   2.50   2.00
Marshal de Lattre Foundation.

### Independent State

Clasped Hands, Wheat, Olive Branch — SP44

**1963, May 27**    Unwmk.    *Perf. 13*
B97 SP44 50c +20c sl grn, brt grn & car   1.10   .65
Surtax for the Natl. Solidarity Fund.

Burning Books — SP45

**1965, June 7**    Engr.    *Perf. 13*
B98 SP45 20c +5c ol grn, red & blk   .50   .40
Burning of the Library of Algiers, 6/7/62.

Soldiers and Woman Comforting Wounded Soldier — SP46

**1966, Aug. 20**    Photo.    *Perf. 11½*
B99 SP46 30c +10c multi   1.25   .70
B100 SP46 95c +10c multi   1.75   1.25
Day of the Moudjahid (Moslem volunteers).

Red Crescent, Boy and Girl — SP47

**1967, May 27**    Litho.    *Perf. 14*
B101 SP47 30c +10c brt grn, brn & car   .85   .50
Algerian Red Crescent Society.

SP48    Flood Victims — SP48a

**1969, Nov. 15**    Typo.    *Perf. 10½*
B102 SP48 30c +10c multi   .70   .50
**Litho.**
B103 SP48a 95c +25c multi   1.60   .95

Red Crescent Flag — SP49

# ALGERIA

**1971, May 17    Engr.    Perf. 10½**
B104 SP49 30c +10c slate grn & car    .70 .40
Algerian Red Crescent Society.

Intl. Children's Day — SP50

**1989, June 1    Litho.    Perf. 10½x11**
B105 SP50 1d +30c multi    .70 .55
Surtax for child welfare.

Solidarity with Palestinians — SP51

**1990, Dec. 9    Litho.    Perf. 10½x11**
B106 SP51 1d +30c multi    .70 .45

Natl. Solidarity with Education — SP52

**1995, Sept. 20    Litho.    Perf. 13x14**
B107 SP52 3d +50c multi    .60 .30

Red Crescent Society — SP53

**1998, May 2    Litho.    Perf. 13x13¼**
B108 SP53 5d +1d multi    .50 .30

World Children's Day — SP54

No. B110, Flower, child, adult, vert.

**1998, June 1    Perf. 14x13½, 13½x14**
B109 SP54 5d +1d shown    .50 .25
B110 SP54 5d +1d multi    .50 .25

Flood Victim Relief — SP55

**2001, Dec. 24    Litho.    Perf. 13¼x14**
B111 SP55 5d +5d multi    1.00 .75

Earthquake Relief — SP56

**2003, Dec. 3    Litho.    Perf. 13¼x14**
B112 SP56 5d +5d multi    .90 .90

TeleFood — SP57

Children's drawings with: No. B113, 5d+1d, Blue frame. No. B114, 5d+1d, Pink frame.

**Perf. 14, 14x13½ (#B114)**
**2004, Oct. 16    Litho.**
B113-B114 SP57 Set of 2    1.00 1.00

## AIR POST STAMPS

Catalogue values for unused stamps in this section are for Never Hinged items.

Plane over Algiers Harbor — AP1

Two types of 20fr:
Type I — Monogram "F" without serifs. "POSTE" indented 3mm.
Type II — Monogram "F" with serifs. "POSTE" indented 4½mm.

**Unwmk.**
**1946, June 20    Engr.    Perf. 13**
C1 AP1 5fr red    .30 .25
C2 AP1 10fr deep blue    .30 .25
C3 AP1 15fr deep green    1.20 .40
C4 AP1 20fr brown (II)    1.10 .25
C4A AP1 20fr brown (I)    225.00 140.00
C5 AP1 25fr violet    1.40 .25
C6 AP1 40fr gray black    1.60 .65
  Nos. C1-C4,C5-C6 (6)    5.90 2.05
For surcharges see Nos. C7, CB1-CB2.

No. C1 Surcharged in Black

**1947, Jan. 18**
C7 AP1 (4.50fr) on 5fr red    .35 .25
  a. Inverted surcharge    800.00 600.00
  b. Double surcharge    1,000. 700.00
  c. Pair, one without surcharge    1,200.

Storks over Mosque AP2

Plane over Village AP3

**1949-53**
C8 AP2 50fr green    4.50 .90
C9 AP3 100fr brown    3.50 .65
C10 AP2 200fr bright red    10.50 5.25
C11 AP3 500fr ultra ('53)    32.50 20.00
  Nos. C8-C11 (4)    51.00 26.80

Beni Bahdel Dam — AP4

**1957, July 1    Unwmk.    Perf. 13**
C12 AP4 200fr dark red    9.50 2.00

### Independent State

Caravelle over Ghardaia AP5

Designs: 2d, Caravelle over El Oued. 5d, Caravelle over Tipasa.

**1967-68    Engr.    Perf. 13**
C13 AP5 1d lil, org brn & emer    1.40 .60
C14 AP5 2d brt bl, org brn & emer    3.25 1.40
C15 AP5 5d brt bl, grn & org brn ('68)    8.50 3.25
  Nos. C13-C15 (3)    13.15 5.25

Plane over Casbah, Algiers — AP6

Designs: 3d, Plane over Oran. 4d, Plane over Rhumel Gorge.

**1971-72    Photo.    Perf. 12½**
C16 AP6 2d grysh blk & multi    2.50 1.00
C17 AP6 3d violet & blk    3.75 1.60
C18 AP6 4d blk & multi    4.25 2.00
  Nos. C16-C18 (3)    10.50 4.60
Issued: 2d, 6/12/71; 3d, 4d, 2/28/72.

Storks and Plane — AP7

**1979, Mar. 24    Photo.    Perf. 11½**
C19 AP7 10d multi    6.50 2.50

Plane Approaching Coastal City — AP8

**1991, Apr. 26    Litho.    Perf. 13½**
C20 AP8 10d shown    3.00 1.50
C21 AP8 20d Plane over city    6.00 3.00

Plane Over Djidjelli Corniche — AP9

**1993, Sept. 25    Engr.    Perf. 13½x14**
C22 AP9 50d blue, grn & brn    6.75 3.25

## AIR POST SEMI-POSTAL STAMPS

Catalogue values for unused stamps in this section are for Never Hinged items.

No. C2 Surcharged in Carmine

**1947, June 18    Perf. 13**
CB1 AP1 10fr +10fr deep blue    2.50 1.75
7th anniv. of Gen. Charles de Gaulle's speech in London, June 18, 1940.

No. C1 Surcharged in Blue

**1948, June 18**
CB2 AP1 5fr +10fr red    2.50 1.75
8th anniv. of Gen. Charles de Gaulle's speech in London, June 18, 1940.

Monument, Clock Tower and Plane — SPAP1

**1949, Nov. 10    Engr.    Unwmk.**
CB3 SPAP1 15fr +20fr dk brn    7.00 5.25
25th anniv. of Algeria's 1st postage stamps.

## POSTAGE DUE STAMPS

D1

**Perf. 14x13½**
**1926-27    Typo.    Unwmk.**
J1 D1 5c light blue    .40 .30
J2 D1 10c dk brn    .40 .30
J3 D1 20c olive grn    .80 .30
J4 D1 25c car rose    .80 .65
J5 D1 30c rose red    1.20 .50
J6 D1 45c blue grn    1.60 .65
J7 D1 50c brn vio    .80 .25
J8 D1 60c green ('27)    3.25 .90
J9 D1 1fr red brn, straw    .40 .30
J10 D1 2fr lil rose ('27)    .80 .30
J11 D1 3fr deep blue ('27)    .80 .30
  Nos. J1-J11 (11)    11.25 4.75
See Nos. J25-J26, J28-J32. For surcharges, see Nos. J18-J20.

D2

**1926-27**
J12 D2 1c olive grn    .40 .40
J13 D2 10c violet    1.60 .80
J14 D2 30c bister    1.60 .80
J15 D2 60c dull red    1.20 .80
J16 D2 1fr brt vio ('27)    20.00 4.00
J17 D2 2fr lt bl ('27)    16.00 1.60
  Nos. J12-J17 (6)    40.80 8.40
See note below France No. J51.
For surcharges, see Nos. J21-J24.

Stamps of 1926 Surcharged

**1927**
J18 D1 60c on 20c olive grn    2.00 .80
J19 D1 2fr on 45c blue grn    2.75 1.60
J20 D1 3fr on 25c car rose    1.60 .80
  Nos. J18-J20 (3)    6.35 3.20

# ALGERIA

## Recouvrement Stamps of 1926 Surcharged

### 1927-32

| | | | | |
|---|---|---|---|---|
| J21 | D2 | 10c on 30c bis ('32) | 5.50 | 4.00 |
| J22 | D2 | 1fr on 1c olive grn | 4.00 | 1.60 |
| J23 | D2 | 1fr on 60c dl red ('32) | 24.00 | .80 |
| J24 | D2 | 2fr on 10c violet | 16.00 | 12.00 |
| | | Nos. J21-J24 (4) | 49.50 | 18.40 |

*Catalogue values for unused stamps in this section, from this point to the end of the section, are for Never Hinged items.*

### Type of 1926, Without "R F"

**1942**    Typo.    Perf. 14x13½

| J25 | D1 | 30c dark red | 1.25 | 1.25 |
|---|---|---|---|---|
| J26 | D1 | 2fr magenta | 1.75 | 2.75 |

### Type of 1926 Surcharged in Red

**1944**    Perf. 14x13½

| J27 | A2 | 50c on 20c yel grn | 1.00 | .70 |
|---|---|---|---|---|
| a. | | Inverted surcharge | 27.50 | |
| b. | | Double surcharge | 70.00 | |

No. J27 was issued precanceled only. See note after No. 32.

### Type of 1926

**1944**    Litho.    Perf. 12

| J28 | D1 | 1.50fr brt rose lilac | 1.00 | .50 |
|---|---|---|---|---|
| J29 | D1 | 2fr greenish blue | 1.25 | .90 |
| J30 | D1 | 5fr rose carmine | 1.25 | 1.10 |
| | | Nos. J28-J30 (3) | 3.50 | 2.50 |

### Type of 1926

**1947**    Typo.    Perf. 14x13½

| J32 | D1 | 5fr green | 2.50 | 1.25 |
|---|---|---|---|---|

### France Nos. J80-J81 Overprinted in Carmine or Black

### 1947

| J33 | D5 | 10c sepia (C) | .50 | .25 |
|---|---|---|---|---|
| J34 | D5 | 30c bright red violet | .65 | .25 |

D3

**Perf. 14x13**

**1947-55**    Unwmk.    Engr.

| J35 | D3 | 20c red | .70 | .35 |
|---|---|---|---|---|
| J36 | D3 | 60c ultra | 1.00 | .45 |
| J37 | D3 | 1fr dk org brn | .50 | .35 |
| J38 | D3 | 1.50fr dull green | 1.50 | 1.10 |
| J39 | D3 | 2fr red | .70 | .35 |
| J40 | D3 | 3fr violet | .75 | .45 |
| J41 | D3 | 5fr ultra ('49) | 1.10 | .35 |
| J42 | D3 | 6fr black | .85 | .45 |
| J43 | D3 | 10fr lil rose | 1.40 | .45 |
| J44 | D3 | 15fr ol grn ('55) | 1.40 | 1.25 |
| J45 | D3 | 20fr brt grn | 1.10 | .85 |
| J46 | D3 | 30fr red org ('55) | 2.50 | 1.50 |
| J47 | D3 | 50fr indigo ('51) | 4.75 | 2.75 |
| J48 | D3 | 100fr brt bl ('53) | 17.50 | 8.50 |
| | | Nos. J35-J48 (14) | 35.75 | 19.15 |

### Independent State

### France Nos. J93-J97 Overprinted in Black

**Perf. 14x13½**

**1962, July 2**    Typo.    Unwmk.

**Handstamped Overprint**

| J49 | D6 | 5c bright pink | 7.00 | 7.00 |
|---|---|---|---|---|
| J50 | D6 | 10c red orange | 7.00 | 7.00 |
| J51 | D6 | 20c olive bister | 7.00 | 7.00 |
| J52 | D6 | 50c dark green | 10.00 | 10.00 |
| J53 | D6 | 1fr deep green | 14.00 | 14.00 |
| | | Nos. J49-J53 (5) | 45.00 | 45.00 |

### Typographed Overprint

| J49a | D6 | 5c bright pink | 23.00 | 17.00 |
|---|---|---|---|---|
| J50a | D6 | 10c red orange | 23.00 | 17.00 |
| J51a | D6 | 20c olive bister | 23.00 | 17.00 |
| J52a | D6 | 50c dark green | 50.00 | 35.00 |
| J53a | D6 | 1fr deep green | 70.00 | 55.00 |
| | | Nos. J49a-J53a (5) | 189.00 | 141.00 |

See note after No. 290.

Scales — D4

**1963, June 25**    Perf. 14x13½

| J54 | D4 | 5c car rose & blk | .25 | .25 |
|---|---|---|---|---|
| J55 | D4 | 10c olive & car | .25 | .25 |
| J56 | D4 | 20c ultra & blk | .55 | .30 |
| J57 | D4 | 50c bister brn & grn | 1.25 | .80 |
| J58 | D4 | 1fr lilac & org | 2.25 | 2.00 |
| | | Nos. J54-J58 (5) | 4.55 | 3.60 |

### No. J58 Surcharged with New Value & 3 Bars

**1968, Mar. 28**    Typo.    Perf. 14x13½

| J59 | D4 | 60c on 1fr lilac & org | 1.25 | 1.00 |
|---|---|---|---|---|

Grain — D5

**1972-93**    Litho.    Perf. 13½x14

| J60 | D5 | 10c bister | .25 | .25 |
|---|---|---|---|---|
| J61 | D5 | 20c deep brown | .25 | .25 |
| J62 | D5 | 40c orange | .25 | .25 |
| J63 | D5 | 50c dk vio blue | .30 | .25 |
| J64 | D5 | 80c dk olive gray | .75 | .30 |
| J65 | D5 | 1d green | .90 | .55 |
| a. | | yel green, perf. 14¼x14 | .25 | .25 |
| J66 | D5 | 2d blue | 1.75 | 1.00 |
| a. | | Prus bl, perf. 14¼x14 | .25 | .25 |
| J67 | D5 | 3d violet | .50 | .25 |
| J68 | D5 | 4d lilac rose | .65 | .35 |
| | | Nos. J60-J68 (9) | 5.60 | 3.45 |

Issued: 3d, 4d, 1/21/93; others, 10/21/72. Nos. J65a is inscribed "B ALGERIE" at bottom right. No. J66a is inscribed "B ALGERIE" or "BC ALGERIE."

Main Post Office, Algiers — D6

**2006, Mar. 28**    Litho.    Perf. 13¾x14

| J69 | D6 | 5d green | .90 | .90 |
|---|---|---|---|---|
| J70 | D6 | 10d blue | 1.60 | 1.60 |

## NEWSPAPER STAMPS

### Nos. 1 and 33 Surcharged in Red

**1924-26**    Unwmk.    Perf. 14x13½

| P1 | A16 | ½c on 1c dk gray | .40 | .40 |
|---|---|---|---|---|
| a. | | Triple surcharge | 300.00 | |
| P2 | A1 | ½c on 1c olive ('26) | .40 | .40 |

## PARCEL POST STAMPS

Inscribed "I APPORT A LA GARE" — PP1

**1899**    Typo.    Perf. 11½x11

| Q1 | PP1 | 25c blue, bl | 28.00 | 22.50 |
|---|---|---|---|---|
| | | Never hinged | 67.50 | |

Inscribed "II VALEUR DECLAREE" — PP2

**1899**    Typo.    Perf. 11½x11

| Q2 | PP2 | 10c black, yelsh | 125.00 | 75.00 |
|---|---|---|---|---|
| | | Never hinged | 275.00 | |

Inscribed "III LIVRAISON PAR EXPRESS" — PP3

**1899**    Typo.    Perf. 11½x11

| Q3 | PP3 | 25c lilac | 16.00 | 10.00 |
|---|---|---|---|---|
| | | Never hinged | 35.00 | |
| | | Nos. Q1-Q3 (3) | 169.00 | 107.50 |

Nos. Q1-Q3 were reprinted with minor design and color variations in 1912, 1916 (just the 10c), 1918-20 (25c blue and 10c black), and 1921-23.

### Types of 1899 Overprinted in Blue or Black

**1924**

| Q4 | PP1 | 25c blue, bl (Blk) | 3.75 | 3.75 |
|---|---|---|---|---|
| Q5 | PP2 | 15c black (Bl) | 2.75 | 2.75 |
| Q6 | PP3 | 60c brown (Blk) | 3.75 | 3.75 |
| | | Nos. Q4-Q6 (3) | 10.25 | 10.25 |

Nos. Q4, Q5 and Q6 were not issued without overprint. Nos. Q4 and Q5 were reprinted with minor design and color variations in 1926.

### Type of 1899

**1924**

| Q7 | PP1 | 60c blue | 350.00 | |
|---|---|---|---|---|
| | | Never hinged | 550.00 | |
| a. | | Tete beche pair | 3,000. | |

### Overprinted "CONTROLE REPARTITEUR" in Blue or Black

PP4

**1924-27**

| Q8 | PP4 | 5c green (Blk) | 1.80 | 1.80 |
|---|---|---|---|---|
| Q9 | PP4 | 15c yellow (Bl) | 1.80 | 1.80 |
| Q10 | PP4 | 35c vermilion (Blk) | 1.80 | 1.80 |
| Q11 | PP4 | 60c violet (Bl) | 2.25 | 1.80 |
| Q12 | PP4 | 1fr black (Bl) | 2.25 | 1.80 |
| | | Nos. Q8-Q12 (5) | 9.90 | 9.00 |

Nos. Q8-Q12 were not issued without overprint. "Majoration" indicates an increase in the postal rate.

### No. Q6 Surcharged in Black

No. Q13

No. Q14

No. Q13 — Two wide-spaced bars over value, in black.
No. Q14 — Two narrow-spaced bars over value, in black.

**1927**

| Q13 | PP3 | 65c on 60c brown | 20.00 | 20.00 |
|---|---|---|---|---|
| Q14 | PP3 | 65c on 60c brown | 7.00 | 7.00 |

### New Designs With "CONTROLE REPARTITEUR" Overprint in Blue or Black

PP5

### No. Q15 Surcharged in Black

PP6     PP7

### No. Q22 Surcharged in Black

**1927**

| Q15 | PP5 | 50c black (Bl) | 5.00 | 5.00 |
|---|---|---|---|---|
| Q16 | PP5 | 1.50fr on 50c black | 5.00 | 5.00 |
| Q17 | PP5 | 2fr on 50c black | 5.00 | 5.00 |
| Q18 | PP5 | 2.50fr on 50c black | 5.00 | 5.00 |
| Q19 | PP6 | 95c green (Blk) | 7.00 | 6.00 |
| Q20 | PP6 | 1.40fr green (Blk) | 7.00 | 6.00 |
| Q21 | PP6 | 1.55fr green (Blk) | 7.00 | 6.00 |
| Q22 | PP7 | 50c rose (Blk) | 8.00 | 8.00 |
| Q23 | PP7 | 1.50fr on 50c rose (Blk) | 5.00 | 5.00 |
| Q24 | PP7 | 2fr on 50c rose (Blk) | 8.00 | 8.00 |
| Q25 | PP7 | 2.50fr on 50c rose (Blk) | 8.00 | 8.00 |
| | | Nos. Q15-Q25 (11) | 70.00 | 62.50 |

Nos. Q15-Q25 were not issued without overprint.

# ALGERIA

Nos. Q19-Q21 Surcharged in Black

**1929, Jan.**
| | | | | |
|---|---|---|---|---|
| Q26 | PP6 | 1fr on 95c grn (Blk) | 4.50 | 3.50 |
| Q27 | PP6 | 1.50fr on 1.40fr grn (Blk) | 4.50 | 3.50 |
| Q28 | PP6 | 1.65fr on 1.55fr grn (Blk) | 4.50 | 4.50 |
| | | Nos. Q26-Q28 (3) | 13.50 | 11.50 |

**1929, July**
| | | | | |
|---|---|---|---|---|
| Q29 | PP6 | 1.05fr on 95c grn (Blk) | 6.00 | 6.00 |
| Q30 | PP6 | 1.60fr on 1.40fr grn (Blk) | 6.00 | 6.00 |
| Q31 | PP6 | 1.75fr on 1.55fr grn (Blk) | 6.00 | 6.00 |
| | | Nos. Q29-Q31 (3) | 18.00 | 18.00 |

**1930**

Three types of the 1.15fr surcharge and two types of the 1.85fr surcharge exist.
1.15fr SURCHARGE:
Type I — slanted serif on "1" of "15".
Type II — straight serif on "1" of "15".
Type III — heavily curved serif on "5" of "15".
1.85fr SURCHARGE:
Type I — narrow curved top on "5" of "85".
Type II — heavily curved top on "5" of "85".

| | | | | |
|---|---|---|---|---|
| Q32 | PP6 | 1.15fr on 95c grn (Blk) (I) | 3.50 | 3.50 |
| a. | | Type II | 13.00 | 13.00 |
| b. | | Type III | 45.00 | 45.00 |
| Q33 | PP6 | 1.70fr on 1.40fr grn (Blk) | 6.00 | 6.00 |
| Q34 | PP6 | 1.85fr on 1.55fr grn (Blk) (I) | 4.50 | 4.50 |
| b. | | Type III | 45.00 | 45.00 |
| | | Nos. Q32-Q34 (3) | 14.00 | 14.00 |

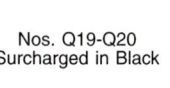

Nos. Q19-Q20 Surcharged in Black

Two types of the 2fr surcharge exist.
Type I — narrow "2".
Type II — thick "2".
Three types of the 2.25fr surcharge exist.
Type I — narrow "2.25".
Type II — raised "25".
Type III — thick "2.25".

**1932**
| | | | | |
|---|---|---|---|---|
| Q35 | PP6 | 1.50fr on 95c grn (Blk) | 35.00 | 35.00 |
| Q36 | PP6 | 2fr on 1.40fr grn (Blk) (I) | 32.50 | 32.50 |
| a. | | Type II | 72.50 | 72.50 |
| Q37 | PP6 | 2.25fr on 1.55fr grn (Blk) | 35.00 | 35.00 |
| a. | | Type II | 72.50 | 72.50 |
| b. | | Type III | 82.50 | 82.50 |
| | | Nos. Q35-Q37 (3) | 102.50 | 102.50 |

 PP8

**1935**
| | | | | |
|---|---|---|---|---|
| Q38 | PP8 | 2c blue | 22.50 | 22.50 |
| Q39 | PP8 | 3.50fr blue | 22.50 | 22.50 |

Nos. Q38-Q39 were not issued without overprint.

**No. Q15 Surcharged**

**1937**
| | | | | |
|---|---|---|---|---|
| Q40 | PP5 | 60c on 50c black | 14.00 | 14.00 |
| Q41 | PP5 | 1.80fr on 50c black | 20.00 | 20.00 |
| Q42 | PP5 | 2.40fr on 50c black | 20.00 | 20.00 |
| Q43 | PP5 | 3fr on 50c black | 20.00 | 20.00 |
| | | Nos. Q40-Q43 (4) | 74.00 | 74.00 |

**Type of 1927 Overprinted "CONTROLE REPARTITEUR" in Black**
| | | | | |
|---|---|---|---|---|
| Q44 | PP6 | 1.50fr green | 35.00 | 35.00 |
| Q45 | PP6 | 2fr green | 35.00 | 35.00 |
| Q46 | PP6 | 2.25fr green | 35.00 | 35.00 |
| | | Nos. Q44-Q46 (3) | 105.00 | 105.00 |

Nos. Q44-Q46 were not issued without overprint.

**Nos. Q38-Q39 Surcharged**
| | | | | |
|---|---|---|---|---|
| Q47 | PP8 | 2.25fr on 2fr blue | 14.50 | 14.50 |
| a. | | 2.25fr on 3.50fr blue (error) | 1,450. | 1,200. |
| Q48 | PP8 | 4.25fr on 3.50fr blue | 14.50 | 14.50 |
| a. | | 4.25fr on 2fr blue (error) | 1,450. | 1,200. |

**Stamps Inscribed "VALEUR DECLAREE" Overprinted "CONTROLE REPARTITEUR" in Blue**

 PP9

**1938**
| | | | | |
|---|---|---|---|---|
| Q49 | PP9 | 60c black | 25.00 | 25.00 |
| Q50 | PP9 | 1.80fr black | 25.00 | 25.00 |
| Q51 | PP9 | 2.40fr black | 25.00 | 25.00 |
| Q52 | PP9 | 3fr black | 25.00 | 25.00 |
| | | Nos. Q49-Q52 (4) | 100.00 | 100.00 |

Nos. Q49-Q52 were not issued without overprint.

Nos. Q44-Q46 Surcharged in Black and Overprinted "CONTROLE REPARTITEUR" in Blue or Black

**1938**
| | | | | |
|---|---|---|---|---|
| Q53 | PP6 | 2fr on 1.50fr grn | 10.00 | 10.00 |
| Q54 | PP6 | 2.50fr on 2fr grn | 9.00 | 9.00 |
| Q55 | PP6 | 3fr on 2.25fr grn | 9.00 | 9.00 |
| | | Nos. Q53-Q55 (3) | 28.00 | 28.00 |

**Overprinted "CONTROLE REPARTITEUR" in Blue**

**1938**
| | | | | |
|---|---|---|---|---|
| Q56 | PP8 | 2.25fr dk blue | 26.00 | 26.00 |
| Q57 | PP8 | 4.25fr dk blue | 26.00 | 26.00 |

Nos. Q56-Q57 were not issued without overprint.

**Type of 1938 Overprinted "CONTROLE" in Violet**

**1939**
| | | | | |
|---|---|---|---|---|
| Q58 | PP9 | 60c black | 18.00 | 18.00 |
| Q59 | PP9 | 1.80fr black | 26.00 | 26.00 |
| Q60 | PP9 | 2.40fr black | 26.00 | 26.00 |
| Q61 | PP9 | 3fr black | 26.00 | 26.00 |
| | | Nos. Q58-Q61 (4) | 96.00 | 96.00 |

Nos. Q58-Q61 were not issued without overprint.

**Type of 1938 Surcharged in Black and Overprinted "CONTROLE" in Violet**

**1939**
| | | | | |
|---|---|---|---|---|
| Q62 | PP6 | 2fr on 1.50fr grn | 22.50 | 22.50 |
| Q63 | PP6 | 2.50fr on 2fr grn | 22.50 | 22.50 |
| Q64 | PP6 | 3fr on 2.25fr grn | 22.50 | 22.50 |
| | | Nos. Q62-Q64 (3) | 67.50 | 67.50 |

Nos. Q62-Q64 were not issued without overprint.

**Overprinted "CONTROLE" in Violet**

Inscribed "C.F.A. COLIS POSTAL REMBOURSEMENT DOMICILE" — PP10

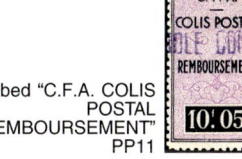

Inscribed "C.F.A. COLIS POSTAL REMBOURSEMENT" PP11

**1939**
| | | | | |
|---|---|---|---|---|
| Q65 | PP10 | 2fr yel & org | 18.00 | 18.00 |
| Q66 | PP11 | 3.80fr vio & blk | 18.00 | 18.00 |
| Q67 | PP11 | 5.05fr vio & blk | 18.00 | 18.00 |
| Q68 | PP11 | 7.55fr vio & blk | 18.00 | 18.00 |
| Q69 | PP11 | 10.05fr vio & blk | 18.00 | 18.00 |
| Q70 | PP11 | 15.05fr vio & blk | 18.00 | 18.00 |
| | | Nos. Q65-Q70 (6) | 108.00 | 108.00 |

Nos. Q65-Q70 were not issued without overprint.

**Type of 1935 Overprinted "CONTROLE" in Violet**

**1939**
| | | | | |
|---|---|---|---|---|
| Q71 | PP8 | 2.25fr dk blue | 26.00 | 26.00 |
| Q72 | PP8 | 4.25fr dk blue | 26.00 | 26.00 |
| | | Nos. Q65-Q70 (6) | 108.00 | 108.00 |

Nos. Q71-Q72 were not issued without overprint.

**Catalogue values for unused stamps in this section, from this point to the end of the section, are for Never Hinged items.**

No. Q58 Surcharged in Black or Red

**1941**
| | | | | |
|---|---|---|---|---|
| Q73 | PP9 | 1.80fr on 60c blk (Blk) | 10.00 | 5.00 |
| a. | | Tete beche pair | 140.00 | |
| Q74 | PP9 | 1.80fr on 60c blk (R) | 10.00 | 5.00 |

**No. Q45-Q46 Surcharged in Violet**

**1941**
| | | | | |
|---|---|---|---|---|
| Q75 | PP6 | 2.20fr on 2fr grn | 35.00 | 20.00 |
| Q76 | PP6 | 2.80fr on 2fr grn | 28.00 | 17.50 |
| a. | | Imperf. | 100.00 | |
| Q77 | PP6 | 3.30fr on 2fr grn | — | 325.00 |
| Q78 | PP6 | 2.20fr on 2.25fr grn | 210.00 | 130.00 |
| Q79 | PP6 | 2.80fr on 2.25fr grn | 425.00 | 280.00 |
| a. | | Imperf. | 500.00 | |
| Q80 | PP6 | 3.30fr on 2.25fr grn | 42.50 | 25.00 |
| a. | | Imperf. | 105.00 | |
| | | Nos. Q75-Q80 (6) | 740.50 | 797.50 |

Nos. Q65-Q70 Surcharged in Black or Red

**1941**
| | | | | |
|---|---|---|---|---|
| Q81 | PP10 | 2.20fr on 2fr yel & org | 11.00 | 6.00 |
| Q82 | PP11 | 4.15fr on 3.80fr vio & blk (Blk) | 7.00 | 3.50 |
| Q83 | PP11 | 4.15fr on 3.80fr vio & blk (R) | 10.00 | 6.00 |
| Q84 | PP11 | 5.55fr on 5.05fr vio & blk | 21.00 | 14.00 |
| Q85 | PP11 | 8.25fr on 7.55fr vio & blk | 22.00 | 14.00 |
| Q86 | PP11 | 11.05fr on 10.05fr vio & blk | 70.00 | 42.50 |
| Q87 | PP11 | 16.55fr on 15.05fr vio & blk | 70.00 | 42.50 |
| | | Nos. Q81-Q87 (7) | 211.00 | 128.50 |

Nos. Q71, Q72 Surcharged in Black

**1941**
| | | | | |
|---|---|---|---|---|
| Q88 | PP8 | 2.40fr on 2.25fr dk bl | 15.00 | 10.00 |
| Q89 | PP8 | 7.20fr on 4.25fr dk bl | 15.00 | 10.00 |

Nos. Q88 and Q89 were intended for use on bulky packages.

Nos. Q90-Q102, Q105-Q111, Q112-Q116, Q118-Q133, Q137-Q144 were not issued without the control overprint, although examples exist without the overprint. These examples are considered remainders or missing-overprint varieties.

**Overprinted "Controle des Recettes" in Violet**

Philippeville Railway Station — PP12

**1941-42**
| | | | | |
|---|---|---|---|---|
| Q90 | PP12 | 60c black | 10.00 | 7.00 |
| a. | | Imperf. | 32.50 | |
| Q91 | PP12 | 1.80fr black | 5.00 | 3.00 |
| a. | | Imperf. | 32.50 | |
| Q92 | PP12 | 2.40fr black | 22.00 | 15.00 |
| a. | | Imperf. | 60.00 | |
| Q93 | PP12 | 3fr black | 17.50 | 10.00 |
| a. | | Imperf. | 42.50 | |
| | | Nos. Q90-Q93 (4) | 54.50 | 35.00 |

**Overprinted "Controle des Recettes" in Violet**

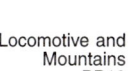

Locomotive and Mountains PP13

**1941-42**
| | | | | |
|---|---|---|---|---|
| Q94 | PP13 | 2.20fr yel grn | 15.00 | 10.00 |
| a. | | Imperf. | 42.50 | |
| Q95 | PP13 | 2.80fr yel grn | 7.00 | 4.00 |
| Q96 | PP13 | 3.30fr yel grn | 7.00 | 4.00 |
| a. | | Double impression | 75.00 | |
| | | Nos. Q94-Q96 (3) | 29.00 | 18.00 |

Nos. Q94-Q96 were intended for use on parcels delivered by autorail.

**Overprinted "Controle des Recettes" in Violet**

Viaduct over Chiffa Gorge — PP14

Locomotive and passenger cars crossing M'raier Oasis — PP15

**1941-42**
| | | | | |
|---|---|---|---|---|
| Q97 | PP14 | 2.20fr orange | 25.00 | 17.50 |
| a. | | Imperf. | 75.00 | |
| b. | | Double impression | 75.00 | |
| Q98 | PP15 | 4.15fr lilac | 9.00 | 6.00 |
| a. | | Double impression | 75.00 | |
| Q99 | PP15 | 5.55fr lilac | 7.00 | 4.00 |
| a. | | Imperf. | 37.50 | |
| Q100 | PP15 | 8.25fr lilac | 14.00 | 10.00 |
| a. | | Imperf. | 42.50 | |
| Q101 | PP15 | 11.05fr lilac | 22.00 | 14.00 |
| a. | | Double impression | 42.50 | |
| Q102 | PP15 | 16.55fr lilac | 7.00 | 5.00 |
| a. | | Imperf. | 37.50 | |
| b. | | Double impression | 65.00 | |
| c. | | 16.55fr black (error) | 950.00 | |
| | | Nos. Q97-Q102 (6) | 84.00 | 56.50 |

No. Q102c is an error of color; 100 examples were printed.

450 ALGERIA

### Type of 1935 Overprinted "Controle des Recettes" in Black

**1941-42**

**Q103** PP8 2.40fr dk bl 5.00 3.00
*a.* Imperf. 32.50
**Q104** PP8 7.20fr dk bl 5.00 3.00
*a.* Imperf. 32.50

Nos. Q103-Q104 were intended for bulky packages.

### No. Q90, Q92, Q93 With Manuscript Surcharge in Red

**1943**

**Q105** PP12 90c on 60c blk 90.00 55.00
**Q106** PP12 2.70fr on 2.40fr blk 90.00 55.00
**Q107** PP12 6.30fr on 2.40fr blk 90.00 55.00
**Q108** PP12 9.90fr on 2.40fr blk 90.00 55.00
**Q109** PP12 13.50fr on 3fr blk 90.00 55.00
**Q110** PP12 17.10fr on 3fr blk 105.00 55.00
**Q111** PP12 20.70fr on 3fr blk 105.00 55.00
*a.* Imperf. 950.00
*Nos. Q105-Q111 (7)* 660.00 385.00

Two horizontal bars in red obliterate original denominations.

### Q97-Q101 Surcharged With Manuscript Numerals in Red

**1943**

**Q112** PP14 2.70fr on 2.20fr yel brn 90.00 55.00
**Q113** PP13 5.80fr on 4.15fr lil 105.00 55.00
**Q114** PP13 8fr on 5.55fr lil 105.00 55.00
**Q115** PP13 10.30fr on 8.25fr lil 105.00 55.00
**Q116** PP13 12.50fr on11.05fr lil 105.00 55.00
*Nos. Q112-Q116 (5)* 510.00 275.00

Two horizontal bars in red obliterate original denominations.

### Type of 1924 Overprinted "Controle Des Recettes" in Black

**1943**

**Q117** PP4 45c lilac 15.00 10.00
*a.* Imperf. 45.00

"Majoration" indicates an increase in the postal rate.

### Type of 1941-42 Overprinted "Controle des Recettes" in Violet

**1943**

**Q118** PP12 90c orange 4.00 2.50
*a.* Imperf. 18.00
**Q119** PP12 1.80fr orange 4.00 2.50
*a.* Imperf. 18.00
**Q120** PP12 2.70fr orange 4.00 2.50
*a.* Imperf. 18.00
**Q121** PP12 6.30fr orange 4.00 2.50
*a.* Imperf. 18.00
**Q122** PP12 9.90fr orange 4.00 2.50
*a.* Imperf. 18.00
**Q123** PP12 13.50fr orange 4.00 2.50
*a.* Imperf. 18.00
**Q124** PP12 17.10fr orange 4.00 2.50
*a.* Imperf. 18.00
**Q125** PP12 20.70fr orange 4.00 3.00
*a.* Imperf. 18.00
*Nos. Q118-Q125 (8)* 32.00 20.50

### Types of 1941-42 Overprinted "Controle des Recettes" in Violet

**1943**

**Q126** PP13 2.70fr green 15.00 10.00
*a.* Imperf. 28.00
**Q127** PP13 3.90fr green 11.00 7.00
*a.* Imperf. 30.00
**Q128** PP13 4.20fr green 15.00 10.00
*a.* Imperf. 30.00
**Q129** PP15 5.80fr lilac 15.00 10.00
*a.* Imperf. 30.00
**Q130** PP15 8fr lilac 15.00 10.00
*a.* Imperf. 30.00
**Q131** PP15 10.30fr lilac 15.00 10.00
*a.* Imperf. 30.00
**Q132** PP15 12.50fr lilac 15.00 10.00
*a.* Imperf. 30.00
**Q133** PP15 17.40fr lilac 15.00 10.00
*a.* Imperf. 30.00
*Nos. Q126-Q133 (8)* 116.00 77.00

Nos. Q126-Q128 were for delivery by autorail. Nos. Q129-Q133 were for delivery by Michelin train.

### Type of 1935 Overprinted "Controle des Recettes" in Violet

**1943**

**Q134** PP8 6.50fr dk bl 15.00 10.00
*a.* Imperf. 30.00
**Q135** PP8 9.70fr dk bl 15.00 10.00
*a.* Imperf. 30.00
**Q136** PP8 12.20fr dk bl 18.00 14.00
*a.* Imperf. 30.00
*Nos. Q134-Q136 (3)* 48.00 34.00

Nos. Q134-Q136 were intended for use on bulky parcels.

### Nos. Q126-Q133 Surcharged in Black

**1944**

**Q137** PP13 3.20fr on 2.70fr grn 11.00 7.00
*a.* Imperf. 30.00
**Q138** PP13 4.60fr on 3.90fr grn 21.00 15.00
**Q139** PP13 4.90fr on 4.20fr grn 15.00 10.00
**Q140** PP15 6.20fr on 5.80fr lil 25.00 15.00
**Q141** PP15 8.40fr on 8fr lil 25.00 15.00
*a.* Surcharge inverted 60.00
*b.* Dbl. surch., one invtd. 70.00
**Q142** PP15 10.70fr on 10.30fr lil 25.00 15.00
**Q143** PP15 12.90fr on 12.50fr lil 15.00 10.00
**Q144** PP15 18.60fr on 17.40fr lil 4.00 2.50
*Nos. Q137-Q144 (8)* 141.00 89.50

Four vertical bars obliterate the original denominations of Nos. Q137-Q144.

Nos. Q137-Q139 were for delivery by autorail. Nos. Q140-Q144 were for delivery by Michelin train.

### Nos. Q134-Q136 Surcharged in Black

**1944**

**Q145** PP8 7.60fr on 6.50fr dk bl 15.00 10.00
*a.* Imperf. 30.00
**Q146** PP8 11.30fr on 9.70fr dk bl 11.00 7.00
*a.* Imperf. 30.00
**Q147** PP8 14.20fr on 12.20fr dk bl 11.00 7.00
*a.* Imperf. 30.00
*Nos. Q145-Q147 (3)* 37.00 24.00

Nos. Q145-Q147 were intended for use on bulky parcels. Four vertical bars obliterate the original denominations.

### Nos. Q126-Q133 Surcharged in Black

No. Q148

No. Q151

**1945**

**Q148** PP13 4.10fr on 2.70fr grn 3.00 2.00
**Q149** PP13 5.20fr on 3.90fr grn 3.00 2.00
**Q150** PP13 6.20fr on 4.20fr grn 3.00 2.00
*a.* Imperf. 18.00
**Q151** PP14 7.40fr on 5.80fr lil 3.00 2.00
*a.* Imperf. 22.00
**Q152** PP14 9.60fr on 8fr lil 3.00 2.00
*a.* Imperf. 22.00
**Q153** PP14 11.90fr on 10.30fr lil 3.00 2.00
*a.* Imperf. 22.00
*b.* Dbl.surch., one invtd. 75.00
**Q154** PP14 14.10fr on 12.50fr lil 3.00 2.00
*a.* Imperf. 22.00
*Nos. Q148-Q154 (7)* 21.00 14.00

Four vertical bars obliterate the orginal denominations of Nos. Q148-Q154.

Nos. Q148-Q150 were for delivery by autorail. Nos. Q151-Q154 were for delivery by Michelin train.

### Nos. Q134-Q136 Surcharged in Black

No. Q155

**1944**

**Q155** PP8 8.80fr on 6.50fr dk bl 3.00 2.00
*a.* Imperf. 22.00
**Q156** PP8 13.40fr on 9.70fr dk bl 3.00 2.00
*a.* Imperf. 22.00
**Q157** PP8 18fr on 12.20fr dk bl 3.00 2.00
*a.* Imperf. 22.00
*Nos. Q155-Q157 (3)* 9.00 6.00

Nos. Q155-Q157 were for use on bulky packages. Four vertical bars obliterate the original denominations.

### Type of 1941-42 Overprinted "Controle des Recettes" in Violet

No. Q158

No. Q160

**1945-46**

**Q158** PP13 5.20fr green 3.00 2.00
*a.* Imperf. 18.00
**Q159** PP13 9fr green 3.00 2.00
*a.* Imperf. 18.00
**Q160** PP15 7.30fr lilac 3.00 2.00
*a.* Imperf. 18.00
**Q161** PP15 9.50fr lilac 3.00 2.00
*a.* Imperf. 18.00
**Q162** PP15 11.80fr lilac 3.00 2.00
*a.* Imperf. 18.00
**Q163** PP15 11.80fr lilac 3.00 2.00
*a.* Imperf. 18.00
**Q164** PP15 18.60fr lilac 3.50 2.00
*a.* Imperf. 18.00
**Q165** PP15 25fr lilac 3.50 2.00
*a.* Imperf. 18.00
*Nos. Q160-Q165 (6)* 19.00 12.00

Nos. Q158-Q159 were for delivery by autorail. Nos. Q160-Q165 were for delivery by Michelin train.

### Overprinted "Controle des Recettes" in Violet

Bon Train Station PP16

**1945-46**

**Q166** PP16 12.40fr pale bl, rough impression 3.50 2.00
*a.* Imperf. 18.00
**Q167** PP16 12.40fr pale bl, fine impression 18.00 12.00
*a.* Imperf. 32.00
**Q168** PP16 18.80fr pale bl, rough impression 4.00 3.00
*a.* Imperf. 18.00
**Q169** PP16 18.80fr pale bl, fine impression 15.00 10.00
*a.* Imperf. 32.00
**Q170** PP16 25.20fr pale bl, rough impression 4.00 3.00
*a.* Imperf. 18.00
**Q171** PP16 25.20fr bl, fine impression 17.00 10.00
*a.* Imperf. 32.00
*Nos. Q166-Q171 (6)* 61.50 40.00

Nos. Q166-Q171 were intended for use on bulky parcels.

### Nos. Q158, Q164, Q166-Q171 Surcharged in Black

No. Q178

**1946**

**Q172** PP13 7fr on 5.20fr grn 3.00 2.00
*a.* Imperf. 18.00
**Q173** PP15 18.50fr on 18.60fr lil 3.00 2.00
*a.* Imperf. 18.00
*b.* Double surcharge 60.00
*c.* Doule surch., one invtd. 70.00
**Q174** PP15 20fr on 18.60fr lil 210.00
**Q175** PP16 15fr on 12.40fr pale bl 3.00 2.00
*a.* Imperf. 18.00
**Q176** PP16 15fr on 12.40fr bl 16.00 10.00
*a.* Imperf. 32.00
**Q177** PP16 20fr on 18.80fr pale bl 3.00 2.00
*a.* Imperf. 18.00
**Q178** PP16 20fr on 18.80fr bl 16.00 10.00
*a.* Imperf. 32.00
**Q179** PP16 30fr on 25.20fr pale bl 3.00 2.00
*a.* Imperf. 18.00
**Q180** PP16 30fr on 25.20fr bl 16.00 10.00
*a.* Imperf. 32.00
*Nos. Q172-Q180 (9)* 273.00 40.00

Four vertical bars obliterate the original denominations of Nos. Q172-Q180.

No. Q172 was for delivery by autorail. Nos. Q173-Q174 were for delivery by Michelin train. Nos. Q175-Q180 were intended for use on bulky packages.

### Nos. Q158, Q164, Q166-Q171 Surcharged in Black

No. Q181

No. Q183

No. Q189

**1947**

**Q181** PP13 8fr on 7fr on 5.20fr grn 3.00 2.00
*a.* Imperf. 25.00
**Q182** PP13 10fr on 9fr grn 3.00 2.00
*a.* Imperf. 25.00
**Q183** PP15 8.30fr on 7.30fr lil 3.00 2.00
*a.* Imperf. 25.00
**Q184** PP15 10.50fr on 9.50fr lil 4.00 2.00
*a.* Imperf. 25.00
**Q185** PP15 12.80fr on 11.80fr lil 3.00 2.00
*a.* Imperf. 25.00
**Q186** PP15 15fr on 14fr lil 4.00 2.00
*a.* Imperf. 25.00
**Q187** PP15 19.50fr on 18.50fr on 18.60fr lil 3.00 2.00
*a.* Imperf. 25.00
**Q188** PP15 26fr on 25fr lil 4.00 2.00
*a.* Imperf. 25.00
**Q189** PP16 17fr on 15fr on 12.40fr pale bl 3.00 2.00
*a.* Imperf. 25.00
**Q190** PP16 17fr on 15fr on 12.40fr bl 16.00 11.00
*a.* Imperf. 39.00
**Q191** PP16 23fr on 20fr on 18.80fr pale bl 3.00 2.00
**Q192** PP16 23fr on 20fr on 18.80fr bl 16.00 11.00
**Q193** PP16 35fr on 30fr on 25.20fr pale bl 3.00 2.00
**Q194** PP16 35fr on 30fr on 25.20fr bl 16.00 11.00
*Nos. Q181-Q194 (14)* 84.00 55.00

Four vertical bars obliterate the original denominations of Nos. Q181-Q194.

Nos. Q181-Q182 were for delivery by autorail. Nos. Q183-Q188 were for delivery by Michelin train. Nos. Q189-Q194 were intended for use on bulky packages.

**Nos. Q158, Q164, Q166-Q171 Surcharged in Black**

No. Q195 
CHEMINS DE FER ALGERIENS
10F
COLIS POSTAL

No. Q197 
CHEMINS DE FER ALGERIENS
10F3

No. Q203 
CHEMINS DE FER ALGERIENS
22F

**1947**

| | | | | |
|---|---|---|---|---|
| **Q195** | PP13 | 10fr on 7fr on 5.20fr grn | 3.00 | 2.00 |
| *a.* | | Imperf. | 25.00 | |
| **Q196** | PP13 | 13fr on 9fr grn | 3.00 | 2.00 |
| *a.* | | Imperf. | 25.00 | |
| **Q197** | PP15 | 10.30fr on 7.30fr lil | 3.00 | 2.00 |
| *a.* | | Imperf. | 32.50 | |
| **Q198** | PP15 | 12.50fr on 9.50fr lil | 3.00 | 2.00 |
| *a.* | | Imperf. | 32.50 | |
| **Q199** | PP15 | 14.80fr on 11.80fr lil | 3.00 | 2.00 |
| **Q200** | PP15 | 17fr on 14fr lil | 3.00 | 2.00 |
| *a.* | | Double surcharge | 42.00 | |
| **Q201** | PP15 | 21.50fr on 18.50fr on 18.60fr lil | 3.00 | 2.00 |
| *a.* | | Inverted surcharge | 60.00 | |
| **Q202** | PP15 | 28fr on 25fr lil | 4.00 | 2.00 |
| **Q203** | PP16 | 22fr on 15fr on 12.40fr pale bl | 3.00 | 2.00 |
| **Q204** | PP16 | 22fr on 15fr on 12.40fr bl | 16.00 | 11.00 |
| **Q205** | PP16 | 30fr on 20fr on 18.80fr pale bl | 3.00 | 2.00 |
| **Q206** | PP16 | 30fr on 20fr on 18.80fr bl | 16.00 | 11.00 |
| **Q207** | PP16 | 46fr on 30fr on 25.20fr pale bl | 3.00 | 2.00 |
| *a.* | | Double surcharge | 32.50 | |
| **Q208** | PP16 | 46fr on 30fr on 25.20fr bl | 16.00 | 11.00 |
| | | *Nos. Q195-Q208 (14)* | 82.00 | 55.00 |

Four vertical bars obliterate the original denominations of Nos. Q181-Q194.

Nos. Q195-Q196 were for delivery by autorail. Nos. Q197-Q202 were for delivery by Michelin train. Nos. Q203-Q208 were intended for use on bulky packages.

**Nos. Q158, Q164, Q166-Q171 Surcharged in Black**

 No. Q209
CHEMINS DE FER ALGERIENS
1F

No. Q218 
CHEMINS DE FER ALGERIENS
13F

 No. Q223
CHEMINS DE FER ALGERIENS
14F
COLIS POSTAL

**1948-49**

| | | | | |
|---|---|---|---|---|
| **Q209** | PP12 | 1fr on 90c yel | 3.00 | 2.00 |
| *a.* | | Imperf. | 14.00 | |
| **Q210** | PP12 | 1fr on 13.50fr org | 4.00 | 2.00 |
| *a.* | | Imperf. | 14.00 | |
| **Q211** | PP12 | 2fr on 1.80fr org | 3.00 | 2.00 |
| **Q212** | PP12 | 3fr on 2.70fr org | 3.00 | 2.00 |
| **Q213** | PP12 | 7fr on 6.30fr org | 3.00 | 2.00 |
| **Q214** | PP12 | 11fr on 9.90fr org | 3.00 | 2.00 |
| **Q215** | PP12 | 15fr on 13.50fr org | 3.00 | 2.00 |
| *a.* | | Imperf. | 14.00 | |
| *b.* | | Inverted surcharge | 27.50 | |
| **Q216** | PP12 | 19fr on 17.10fr org | 3.00 | 2.00 |
| *a.* | | Imperf. | 14.00 | |
| **Q217** | PP12 | 23fr on 20.70fr org | 3.00 | 2.00 |
| *a.* | | Imperf. | 14.00 | |
| *b.* | | Double surcharge | 39.00 | |
| *c.* | | Double surch., one inverted | 30.00 | |
| **Q218** | PP15 | 13fr on 10.30fr on 7.30fr lil | 3.00 | 2.00 |
| **Q219** | PP15 | 15fr on 12.50fr on 9.50fr lil | 3.00 | 2.00 |
| **Q220** | PP15 | 19fr on 14.80fr on 11.80fr lil | 3.00 | 2.00 |
| *a.* | | Imperf. | 15.00 | |
| **Q221** | PP15 | 24fr on 14fr lil | 3.00 | 2.00 |
| *a.* | | Imperf. | 15.00 | |
| **Q222** | PP15 | 30fr on 28fr on 25fr lil | 3.00 | 2.00 |
| *a.* | | Imperf. | 15.00 | |
| **Q223** | PP13 | 14fr on 4.10fr on 2.70fr grn | 3.00 | 2.00 |
| *a.* | | Imperf. | 25.00 | |
| *b.* | | Double surcharge | 42.00 | |
| **Q224** | PP13 | 17fr on 10fr on 9fr grn | 3.00 | 2.00 |
| *a.* | | Imperf. | 25.00 | |
| **Q225** | PP13 | 19fr on 9fr grn | 3.00 | 2.00 |
| *a.* | | Imperf. | 25.00 | |
| | | *Nos. Q209-Q225 (17)* | 52.00 | 34.00 |

Four vertical bars obliterate the original denominations of Nos. Q209-Q225.

Nos. Q218-Q222 were for delivery by Michelin train. Nos. Q223-Q225 were for delivery by autorail.

## ALLENSTEIN

ˈa-lən-ˌshtīn

LOCATION — In East Prussia
AREA — 4,457 sq. mi.
POP. — 540,000 (estimated 1920)
CAPITAL — Allenstein

Allenstein, a district of East Prussia, held a plebiscite in 1920 under the Versailles Treaty, voting to join Germany rather than Poland. Later that year, Allenstein became part of the German Republic.

100 Pfennig = 1 Mark

Stamps of Germany, 1906-20, Overprinted 
PLÉBISCITE
OLSZTYN
ALLENSTEIN

***Perf. 14, 14½, 14x14½, 14½x14***

**1920** **Wmk. 125**

| | | | | |
|---|---|---|---|---|
| **1** | A16 | 5pf green | .45 | *1.20* |
| **2** | A16 | 10pf carmine | .45 | *1.20* |
| **3** | A22 | 15pf dk vio | .45 | *1.20* |
| **4** | A22 | 15pf vio brn | 5.50 | *12.00* |
| **5** | A16 | 20pf bl vio | .45 | *1.75* |
| **6** | A16 | 30pf org & blk, *buff* | .45 | *1.75* |
| **7** | A16 | 40pf lake & blk | .45 | *1.20* |
| **8** | A16 | 50pf pur & blk, *buff* | .45 | *1.20* |
| **9** | A16 | 75pf grn & blk | .45 | *1.20* |
| **10** | A17 | 1m car rose | 1.60 | *5.00* |
| *a.* | | Double overprint | *250.00* | *1,000.* |
| **11** | A17 | 1.25m green | 1.60 | 5.25 |
| *a.* | | Double overprint | — | — |
| **12** | A17 | 1.50m yel brn | 1.00 | *4.00* |
| **13** | A21 | 2.50m lilac rose | 2.50 | *10.50* |
| **14** | A19 | 3m blk vio | 2.50 | *5.25* |
| *a.* | | Double overprint | 300.00 | *1,050.* |
| | | Never hinged | 575.00 | |
| *b.* | | Inverted overprint | — | — |
| | | *Nos. 1-14 (14)* | 18.30 | *52.70* |
| | | Set, never hinged | 52.00 | |

Overprinted 
TRAITÉ
DE
VERSAILLES
DEUTSCHES REICH

| | | | | |
|---|---|---|---|---|
| **15** | A16 | 5pf green | .40 | *1.00* |
| **16** | A16 | 10pf carmine | .40 | *1.00* |
| **17** | A22 | 15pf dark vio | .40 | *1.00* |
| **18** | A22 | 15pf vio brn | 20.00 | *40.00* |
| **19** | A16 | 20pf blue vio | .65 | *1.50* |
| **20** | A16 | 30pf org & blk, *buff* | .40 | *1.00* |
| **21** | A16 | 40pf lake & blk | .40 | *1.00* |
| **22** | A16 | 50pf pur & blk, *buff* | .40 | *1.00* |
| **23** | A16 | 75pf grn & blk | .65 | *1.50* |
| **24** | A17 | 1m car rose | 1.60 | 3.00 |
| *a.* | | Inverted overprint | 600.00 | *800.00* |
| | | Never hinged | 800.00 | |
| **25** | A17 | 1.25m green | 1.60 | *3.00* |
| **26** | A17 | 1.50m yel brn | 1.25 | *3.00* |
| **27** | A21 | 2.50m lilac rose | 2.75 | *7.50* |
| **28** | A19 | 3m blk vio | 1.75 | 3.00 |
| *a.* | | Inverted overprint | 400.00 | *975.00* |
| | | Never hinged | 725.00 | |
| *b.* | | Double overprint | 200.00 | *600.00* |
| | | Never hinged | 600.00 | |
| | | *Nos. 15-28 (14)* | 32.65 | *68.50* |
| | | Set, never hinged | 80.00 | |

The 40pf carmine rose (Germany No. 124) exists with this oval overprint, but it is doubtful whether it was regularly issued. Value $110 hinged, $210 never hinged.

## ANDORRA, SPANISH ADMINISTRATION

an-ˈdor-ə

LOCATION — On the southern slope of the Pyrenees Mountains between France and Spain.
GOVT. — Co-principality
AREA — 179 sq. mi.
POP. — 77,000 (2020 est.)
CAPITAL — Andorra la Vella

Andorra was subject to the joint control of France and the Spanish Bishop of Urgel and paid annual tribute to both. In 1993, Andorra became a constitutional coprincipality, governed by its own parliament.

100 Centimos = 1 Peseta
100 Centimes = 1 Franc
100 Cents = 1 Euro (2002)

**Catalogue values for unused stamps in the Spanish Administration for this country are for Never Hinged items, beginning with Scott 50 in the regular postage section and Scott C2 in the airpost section; for the French Administration of this country, Never Hinged items begin at Scott 78 for regular postage, Scott B1 for the semi-postal section, Scott C1 for the airpost section, and Scott J21 for the postage due section.**

A majority of the Spanish Andorra stamps issued to about 1950 are poorly centered. The fine examples that are valued will be somewhat off center. Very poorly centered examples (perfs cutting design) sell for less. Well centered very fine stamps are scarce and sell for approximately twice the values shown (Nos. 1-24, F1-F3), or 50% more (Nos. 25-49, E4-E5).

Stamps of Spain, 1922-26, Overprinted in Red or Black 
CORREOS
ANDORRA

***Perf. 13½x12½, 12½x11½, 14***

**1928** **Unwmk.**

| | | | | |
|---|---|---|---|---|
| **1** | A49 | 2c olive green | .55 | .55 |

**Control Numbers on Back**

| | | | | |
|---|---|---|---|---|
| **2** | A49 | 5c car rose (Bk) | .80 | .80 |
| **3** | A49 | 10c green | .80 | .80 |
| **4** | A49 | 15c slate blue | 3.25 | 3.25 |
| **5** | A49 | 20c reddish vio | 3.25 | 3.50 |
| **6** | A49 | 25c rose red (Bk) | 3.25 | 3.50 |
| *b.* | | Inverted ovpt., perf 14 | 130.00 | — |
| **7** | A49 | 30c black brown | 18.00 | 16.50 |
| *b.* | | Inverted ovpt., perf 12½x11½ | 130.00 | 50.00 |
| **8** | A49 | 40c deep blue | 18.00 | 11.00 |
| **9** | A49 | 50c orange (Bk) | 18.00 | 14.50 |
| *c.* | | Inverted ovpt., perf 14 | 130.00 | — |
| **10** | A49a | 1p blue blk | 23.00 | *23.50* |
| **11** | A49a | 4p lake (Bk) | 150.00 | *175.00* |
| **12** | A49a | 10p brown (Bk) | 275.00 | 275.00 |
| *a.* | | Double overprint | *700.00* | |
| | | *Nos. 1-12 (12)* | 513.90 | 527.90 |
| | | Set, never hinged | 1,200. | |

Counterfeit overprints exist.

Nos. 1-12 perf 14 are worth much more. See the *Scott Classic Specialized Catalogue.*

ANDORRA
CORREOS
2
CENTIMOS

La Vall
A1

ANDORRA
5 CENTIMOS

St. Juan de Caselles
A2

ANDORRA
10

St. Julia de Loria
A3

ANDORRA
15

St. Coloma
A4

ANDORRA
1 PESETA

General Council — A5

**1929, Nov. 25** **Engr.** ***Perf. 14***

| | | | | |
|---|---|---|---|---|
| **13** | A1 | 2c olive green | 1.10 | .60 |

**Control Numbers on Back**

| | | | | |
|---|---|---|---|---|
| **14** | A2 | 5c carmine lake | 3.50 | 1.25 |
| **15** | A3 | 10c yellow green | 3.50 | *4.50* |
| **16** | A4 | 15c slate green | 3.50 | *4.50* |
| **17** | A3 | 20c violet | 3.50 | *4.50* |
| **18** | A4 | 25c carmine rose | 7.75 | 6.25 |
| **19** | A1 | 30c olive brown | 115.00 | *175.00* |
| **20** | A2 | 40c dark blue | 4.50 | 3.00 |
| **21** | A3 | 50c deep orange | 5.50 | 4.50 |
| **22** | A5 | 1p slate | 12.50 | 14.50 |
| **23** | A5 | 4p deep rose | 90.00 | *110.00* |
| **24** | A5 | 10p bister brown | 100.00 | *140.00* |
| | | *Nos. 13-24 (12)* | 350.35 | *468.60* |
| | | Set, never hinged | 800.00 | |

Nos. 13-24 exist imperforate with control numbers on the back. Value, $2,200 unused; $3,150 never hinged.

**1931-38** ***Perf. 11½***

| | | | | |
|---|---|---|---|---|
| *13a* | A1 | 2c | 6.25 | .80 |

**Control Numbers on Back**

| | | | | |
|---|---|---|---|---|
| *14a* | A2 | 5c | 10.00 | 2.25 |
| *15a* | A3 | 10c | 10.00 | 2.00 |
| *16a* | A4 | 15c | 30.00 | 25.00 |
| *17a* | A3 | 20c | 10.00 | 6.00 |
| *18a* | A4 | 25c | 10.00 | 6.00 |
| *19a* | A1 | 30c ('33) | 175.00 | 65.00 |
| *20a* | A2 | 40c ('35) | 17.00 | 13.00 |
| *22a* | A5 | 1p ('38) | 40.00 | 25.00 |
| | | *Nos. 13a-22a (9)* | 308.25 | 145.05 |
| | | Set, never hinged | 500.00 | |

**Without Control Numbers**

**1936-43** ***Perf. 11½x11***

| | | | | |
|---|---|---|---|---|
| **25** | A1 | 2c red brown ('37) | 2.00 | 1.60 |
| **26** | A2 | 5c dark brown | 2.00 | 1.60 |
| **27** | A3 | 10c blue green | 13.00 | 3.25 |
| *a.* | | 10c yellow green | 150.00 | 80.00 |
| | | Never hinged | 200.00 | |
| **28** | A4 | 15c blue green ('37) | 7.50 | 3.50 |
| *a.* | | 15c yellow green | 8.00 | 5.75 |
| **29** | A3 | 20c violet | 7.00 | 3.50 |
| **30** | A4 | 25c deep rose ('37) | 3.25 | *3.25* |
| **31** | A1 | 30c carmine | 5.50 | 3.25 |
| **31A** | A2 | 40c dark blue | *750.00* | — |
| | | Never hinged | 1,250. | |
| **32** | A1 | 45c rose red ('37) | 2.00 | 1.60 |
| **33** | A3 | 50c deep orange | 10.00 | 5.75 |
| **34** | A1 | 60c deep blue ('37) | 7.00 | 3.50 |
| **34A** | A5 | 1p slate | *1,000.* | — |
| | | Never hinged | 2,000. | |
| **35** | A5 | 4p deep rose ('43) | 40.00 | *47.50* |
| **36** | A5 | 10p bister brn ('43) | 52.50 | *57.50* |
| | | *Nos. 25-31,32-34,35-36 (12)* | 151.75 | 135.80 |
| | | Set, never hinged | 925.00 | |

Exist imperforate. Value hinged, $275.

Beware of counterfeits of Nos. 31A and 34A. Purchase of stamps with certificates is strongly advised.

ANDORRA
2
CTS CORREOS

Edelweiss
A6

ANDORRA
20
CTS CORREOS

Provost
A7

# ANDORRA, SPANISH ADMINISTRATION

Coat of Arms
A8

Plaza of Ordino
A9

Chapel of Meritxell
A10

Map
A11

**1948-53   Unwmk.   Photo.   Perf. 12½**
| 37 | A6 | 2c brn olive ('51) | .35 | .35 |
| 38 | A6 | 5c orange ('53) | .35 | .35 |
| 39 | A6 | 10c blue ('53) | .35 | .35 |

**Engr.   Perf. 9½x10**
| 40 | A7 | 20c brown vio | 4.25 | 2.75 |
| 41 | A7 | 25c org, perf. 12½ ('53) | 3.00 | 2.10 |
| 42 | A8 | 30c dk slate grn | 4.25 | 3.25 |
| 43 | A9 | 50c deep green | 5.00 | 4.75 |
| 44 | A10 | 75c dark blue | 6.50 | 4.75 |
| 45 | A9 | 90c dp car rose | 3.50 | 3.50 |
| 46 | A10 | 1p brt orange ver | 5.00 | 4.25 |
| 47 | A8 | 1.35p dk blue vio | 3.50 | 3.50 |

**Perf. 10**
| 48 | A11 | 4p ultra ('53) | 4.75 | 8.50 |
| 49 | A11 | 10p dk vio brn ('51) | 11.00 | 11.00 |
| | | Nos. 37-49 (13) | 51.80 | 49.40 |
| | | Set, never hinged | 120.00 | |

*Catalogue values for unused stamps in this section, from this point to the end of the section, are for Never Hinged items.*

Bridge of St. Anthony
A12

Madonna of Meritxell, 8th Century
A13

Designs: 70c, Aynos pasture. 1p, View of Canillo. 2p, St. Coloma. 2.50p, Arms of Andorra. 3p, Old Andorra, horiz. 5p, View of Ordino, horiz.

**1963-64   Unwmk.   Engr.   Perf. 13**
| 50 | A12 | 25c dk gray & sepia | .30 | .25 |
| 51 | A12 | 70c dk sl grn & brn blk | .40 | .35 |
| 52 | A12 | 1p slate & dull pur | .85 | .45 |
| 53 | A12 | 2p violet & dull pur | .85 | .50 |
| 54 | A12 | 2.50p rose claret | .85 | .70 |
| 55 | A12 | 3p blk & grnsh gray | 1.60 | .80 |
| 56 | A12 | 5p dk brn & choc | 2.50 | 1.25 |
| 57 | A13 | 6p sepia & car | 3.50 | 2.75 |
| | | Nos. 50-57 (8) | 10.85 | 7.05 |

Issued: 25c-2p, 7/20/63; 2.50p-6p, 2/29/64.

Narcissus — A14

**1966, June 10   Engr.   Perf. 13**
| 58 | A14 | 50c shown | .85 | .50 |
| 59 | A14 | 1p Pinks | .85 | .50 |
| 60 | A14 | 5p Jonquils | 2.50 | 1.50 |
| 61 | A14 | 10p Hellebore | 1.75 | 1.00 |
| | | Nos. 58-61 (4) | 5.95 | 3.50 |

Common Design Types pictured following the introduction.

**Europa Issue 1972**
Common Design Type
**1972, May 2   Photo.   Perf. 13**
Size: 25½x38mm
| 62 | CD15 | 8p multicolored | 60.00 | 60.00 |

Encamp Valley — A15

Tourist publicity: 1.50p, Massana (village). 2p, Skiing on De La Casa Pass. 5p, Pessons Lake, horiz.

**1972, July 4   Photo.   Perf. 13**
| 63 | A15 | 1p multicolored | .50 | .40 |
| 64 | A15 | 1.50p multicolored | .75 | .40 |
| 65 | A15 | 2p multicolored | 2.25 | 1.00 |
| 66 | A15 | 5p multicolored | 3.00 | 1.10 |
| | | Nos. 63-66 (4) | 6.50 | 2.90 |

Butterfly Stroke — A16

Design: 2p, Volleyball, vert.

**1972, Oct.   Photo.   Perf. 13**
| 67 | A16 | 2p lt blue & multi | .35 | .35 |
| 68 | A16 | 5p multicolored | .55 | .55 |

20th Olympic Games, Munich, 8/26-9/11.

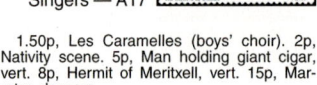
St. Anthony Singers — A17

1.50p, Les Caramelles (boys' choir). 2p, Nativity scene. 5p, Man holding giant cigar, vert. 8p, Hermit of Meritxell, vert. 15p, Marratxa dancers.

**1972, Dec. 5   Photo.   Perf. 13**
| 69 | A17 | 1p multicolored | .35 | .25 |
| 70 | A17 | 1.50p multicolored | .35 | .25 |
| 71 | A17 | 2p multicolored | .45 | .35 |
| 72 | A17 | 5p multicolored | .60 | .45 |
| 73 | A17 | 8p multicolored | .90 | .50 |
| 74 | A17 | 15p multicolored | 1.75 | 1.10 |
| | | Nos. 69-74 (6) | 4.40 | 2.90 |

Andorran customs. No. 71 is for Christmas.

**Europa Issue 1973**
Common Design Type and

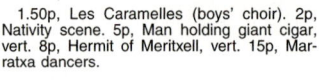
Symbol of Unity — A18

**1973, Apr. 30   Photo.   Perf. 13**
| 75 | A18 | 2p ultra, red & blk | .40 | .25 |

Size: 37x25mm
| 76 | CD16 | 8p tan, red & blk | 1.25 | .85 |

Nativity — A19

Christmas: 5p, Adoration of the Kings. Designs are from altar panels of Meritxell Parish Church.

**1973, Dec. 14   Photo.   Perf. 13**
| 77 | A19 | 2p multicolored | .40 | .30 |
| 78 | A19 | 5p multicolored | 1.25 | 1.00 |

Virgin of Ordino — A20

Europa: 8p, Les Banyes Cross.

**1974, Apr. 29   Photo.   Perf. 13**
| 79 | A20 | 2p multicolored | .90 | .70 |
| 80 | A20 | 8p slate & brt blue | 2.75 | 1.75 |

Cupboard
A21

Crowns of Virgin and Child of Roser
A22

**1974, July 30   Photo.   Perf. 13**
| 81 | A21 | 10p multicolored | 2.00 | 1.60 |
| 82 | A22 | 25p dark red & multi | 3.75 | 3.25 |

UPU Monument, Bern — A23

**1974, Oct. 9   Photo.   Perf. 13**
| 83 | A23 | 15p multicolored | 1.75 | 1.75 |

Centenary of Universal Postal Union.

Nativity — A24

Christmas: 5p, Adoration of the Kings.

**1974, Dec. 4   Photo.   Perf. 13**
| 84 | A24 | 2p multicolored | .80 | .70 |
| 85 | A24 | 5p multicolored | 1.90 | 1.60 |

Mail Delivery, Andorra, 19th Century — A25

**1975, Apr. 4   Photo.   Perf. 13**
| 86 | A25 | 3p multicolored | .45 | .45 |

Espana 75 Intl. Philatelic Exhibition, Madrid, 4/4-13.

12th Century Painting, Ordino Church — A26

Design: 12p, Christ in Glory, 12th century Romanesque painting, Ordino church.

**1975, Apr. 28   Photo.   Perf. 13**
| 87 | A26 | 3p multicolored | 1.25 | .70 |
| 88 | A26 | 12p multicolored | 2.25 | 1.40 |

Urgel Cathedral and Document — A27

**1975, Oct. 4   Photo.   Perf. 13**
| 89 | A27 | 7p multicolored | 1.75 | 1.25 |

Millennium of consecration of Urgel Cathedral, and Literary Festival 1975.

Nativity, Ordino — A28

Christmas: 7p, Adoration of the Kings, Ordino.

**1975, Dec. 3   Photo.   Perf. 13**
| 90 | A28 | 3p multicolored | .40 | .40 |
| 91 | A28 | 7p multicolored | .85 | .85 |

Caldron and CEPT Emblem — A29

Europa: 12p, Chest and CEPT emblem.

**1976, May 3   Photo.   Perf. 13**
| 92 | A29 | 3p bister & multi | .40 | .25 |
| 93 | A29 | 12p yel & multi, horiz. | 1.00 | .50 |

Slalom and Montreal Olympic Emblem — A30

Design: 15p, One-man canoe and Montreal Olympic emblem, horiz.

**1976, July 9   Photo.   Perf. 13**
| 94 | A30 | 7p multicolored | .45 | .25 |
| 95 | A30 | 15p multicolored | .90 | .40 |

21st Olympic Games, Montreal, Canada, July 17-Aug. 1.

Nativity — A31

Christmas: 25p, Adoration of the Kings. Wall paintings in La Massana Church.

**1976, Dec. 7   Photo.   Perf. 13**
| 96 | A31 | 3p multicolored | .50 | .25 |
| 97 | A31 | 25p multicolored | 1.00 | .35 |

View of Ansalonge
A32

Europa: 12p, Xuclar, valley, mountains.

**1977, May 2   Litho.   Perf. 13**
| 98 | A32 | 3p multicolored | .35 | .25 |
| 99 | A32 | 12p multicolored | .90 | .40 |

# ANDORRA, SPANISH ADMINISTRATION

Cross of Terme — A33

Christmas: 12p, Church of St. Miguel d'Engolasters.

**1977, Dec. 2    Photo.    Perf. 13x12½**
100  A33  5p multicolored          .45   .35
101  A33  12p multicolored        1.10   .65

### Souvenir Sheet

A34

Designs: 5p, Map of Post Offices. 10p, Mail delivery. 20p, Post Office, 1928. 25p, Andorran coat of arms.

**1978, Mar. 31    Photo.    Perf. 13x13½**
102  A34  Sheet of 4              1.60  1.60
  a.  5p multicolored              .35   .35
  b.  10p multicolored             .35   .35
  c.  20p multicolored             .35   .35
  d.  25p multicolored             .35   .35

Spanish postal service in Andorra, 50th anniv.

La Vall — A35

Europa: 12p, St. Juan de Caselles.

**1978, May 2    Perf. 13**
103  A35  5p multicolored          .40   .25
104  A35  12p multicolored         .90   .40

Crown, Bishop's Mitre and Staff — A36

**1978, Sept. 24    Photo.    Perf. 13**
105  A36  5p brown, car & yel      .85   .40

700th anniversary of the signing of treaty establishing Co-Principality of Andorra.

Holy Family — A37

Christmas: 25p, Adoration of the Kings. Both designs after frescoes in the Church of St. Mary d'Encamp.

**1978, Dec. 5    Photo.    Perf. 13**
106  A37  5p multicolored          .25   .25
107  A37  25p multicolored         .65   .35

Young Woman — A38

Designs: 5p, Young man. 12p, Bridegroom and bride riding mule.

**1979, Feb. 14    Photo.    Perf. 13**
108  A38  3p multicolored          .25   .25
109  A38  5p multicolored          .25   .25
110  A38  12p multicolored         .40   .30
     Nos. 108-110 (3)              .90   .80

Old Mail Truck — A39

Europa: 12p, Stampless covers of 1846 & 1854.

**1979, Apr. 30    Engr.    Perf. 13**
111  A39  5p yel grn & dk blue     .40   .25
112  A39  12p dk red & violet      .85   .40

Children Holding Hands — A40

**1979, Oct. 18    Photo.    Perf. 13**
113  A40  19p multicolored         .90   .35

International Year of the Child.

St. Coloma's Church — A41

Christmas: 25p, Agnus Dei roundel, St. Coloma's Church.

**1979, Nov. 28    Photo.    Perf. 13½**
114  A41  8p multicolored          .25   .25
115  A41  25p multicolored         .70   .40

Bishop Pere d'Arg — A42

Bishops of Urgel: 5p, Josep Caixal. 13p, Joan Benlloch.

**1979, Dec. 27    Engr.**
116  A42  1p dk blue & brown       .30   .25
117  A42  5p rose lake & purple    .30   .25
118  A42  13p brown & dk green     .30   .30
     Nos. 116-118 (3)              .90   .80
     See Nos. 132-133, 159, 175, C4.

Antoni Fiter, Magistrate — A43

Europa: 19p, Francesc Cairat, magistrate.

**1980, Apr. 28    Photo.    Perf. 13x13½**
119  A43  8p bister, blk & brn     .35   .25
120  A43  19p lt green & blk       .85   .40

Boxing, Moscow '80 Emblem — A44

**1980, July 23    Photo.    Perf. 13½x12½**
121  A44  5p Downhill skiing       .25   .25
122  A44  8p shown                 .25   .25
123  A44  50p Target shooting      .80   .40
     Nos. 121-123 (3)             1.30   .90

12th Winter Olympic Games, Lake Placid, NY, Feb. 12-24 (5p); 22nd Summer Olympic Games, Moscow, July 19-Aug. 3.

Nativity — A45

**1980, Dec. 12    Litho.    Perf. 13**
124  A45  10p Nativity, vert.      .25   .25
125  A45  22p shown                .65   .30

Christmas 1980.

Children Dancing at Santa Anna Feast — A46

Europa: 30p, Going to church on Aplec de la Verge de Canolich Day.

**1981, May 7    Photo.    Perf. 13**
126  A46  12p multicolored         .40   .25
127  A46  30p multicolored         .85   .40

50th Anniv. of Police Force — A47

**1981, July 2    Photo.    Perf. 13½x13**
128  A47  30p multicolored         .85   .35

Intl. Year of the Disabled — A48

**1981, Oct. 8    Photo.    Perf. 13½**
129  A48  50p multicolored        1.25   .40

Christmas 1981 — A49

Designs: Encamp Church retable.

**1981, Dec. 3    Photo.    Perf. 13½**
130  A49  12p Nativity             .40   .25
131  A49  30p Adoration            .80   .45

### Bishops of Urgel Type of 1979

**1981, Dec. 12    Engr.    Perf. 13½**
132  A42  7p Salvador Casanas      .30   .25
133  A42  20p Josep de Boltas      .55   .25

Natl. Arms — A51

**1982, Feb. 17    Photo.    Perf. 13x13½**
134  A51  1p bright pink           .25   .25
135  A51  3p bister brown          .25   .25
136  A51  7p red orange            .25   .25
137  A51  12p lake                 .25   .25
138  A51  15p ultra                .30   .25
139  A51  20p blue green           .40   .40
140  A51  30p crimson rose         .80   .40

**Perf. 13½x12½**
**1982, Sept. 30    Engr.    Size: 25½x30½mm**
141  A51  50p dark green          1.00   .40
142  A51  100p dark blue          1.75   .80
     Nos. 134-142 (9)             5.25  3.25

For type A51 without "PTA" see Nos. 192-198.

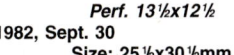

Europa 1982 — A52

14p, New Reforms, 1866, vert. 33p, Reform of Institutions, 1981.

**1982, May 12    Photo.    Perf. 13**
143  A52  14p multicolored         .35   .25
144  A52  33p multicolored        1.00   .40

1982 World Cup — A53

Designs: Various soccer players.

**1982, June 13    Photo.    Perf. 13x13½**
145  A53  14p multicolored        1.05  1.05
146  A53  33p multicolored        1.90  1.90
  a.  Pair, #145-146 + label      3.25  3.25

A54

Anniversaries: 9p, Permanent Spanish and French delegations, cent. 14p, 50th anniv. of Andorran stamps, horiz. 23p, St. Francis of Assisi (1182-1226). 33p, Anyos Pro-Vicarial District membership centenary (Relacio sobre la Vall de Andorra titlepage).

**1982, Sept. 7    Engr.    Perf. 13**
147  A54  9p dk blue & brown       .30   .25
148  A54  14p black & green        .80   .40
149  A54  23p dk blue & brown      .60   .25
150  A54  33p black & olive grn    .60   .40
     Nos. 147-150 (4)             2.30  1.30

A55    A55a

Christmas: 14p, Madonna and Child, Andorra la Vieille Church, vert. 33p, El Tio de Nadal (children in traditional costumes striking hollow tree).

**Perf. 13x13½, 13½x13**
**1982, Dec. 9    Photo.**
151  A55  14p multicolored         .40   .25
152  A55a 33p multicolored         .85   .40

Europa 1983 — A56

16, La Cortinada Church, architect, 12th cent. 38p, Water mill, 16th cent.

**1983, June 7    Photo.    Perf. 13**
153  A56  16p multicolored         .40   .25
154  A56  38p multicolored         .85   .40

# ANDORRA, SPANISH ADMINISTRATION

Local Mushrooms — A57

16p, Lactarius sanguifluus.

**1983, July 20　Photo.　Perf. 13x12½**
155　A57　16p multicolored　　.80　.60
　　See Nos. 165, 169, 172.

Universal Suffrage, 50th Anniv. — A58

**Photogravure and Engraved**
**1983, Sept. 6　　　　Perf. 13**
156　A58　10p multicolored　　.40　.25

Visit of Monsignor Jacinto Verdaguer Bishop and Co-Prince — A59

**1983, Sept. 6**
157　A59　50p multicolored　　1.00　.55

Christmas 1983 — A60

Saint Cerni de Nagol, Romanesque fresco, Church of San Cerni de Nagol.

**1983, Nov. 24　Photo.　Perf. 13½**
158　A60　16p multicolored　　.45　.25

**Bishops of Urgel Type of 1979**

26p, Joan J. Laguarda Fenollera.

**1983, Dec. 7　Engr.　Perf. 13**
159　A42　26p multicolored　　.80　.40

1984 Winter Olympics — A62

**1984, Feb. 17　Litho.　Perf. 13½x14**
160　A62　16p Ski jumping　　.80　.25

ESPAÑA '84 — A63

**1984, Apr. 27　Photo.　Perf. 13**
161　A63　26p Emblems　　.80　.40

Europa (1959-84) — A64

**1984, May 5　　　　Engr.**
162　A64　16p brown　　.60　.25
163　A64　38p blue　　　.90　.40

1984 Summer Olympics — A65

**1984, Aug. 9　Litho.　Perf. 13½x14**
164　A65　40p Running　　1.25　.60

**Mushroom Type of 1983**

11p, Morchella esculenta.

**1984, Sept. 27　Photo.　Perf. 13x12½**
165　A57　11p multicolored　　7.25　2.00

Christmas 1984 — A66

**1984, Dec. 6　Photo.　Perf. 13½**
166　A66　17p Nativity carving　　.50　.25

Europa 1985 — A67

18p, Mossen Enric Arfany, composer, natl. hymn score. 45p, Musician Playing Viol, Romanesque fresco detail, La Cortinada Church, vert.

**1985, May 3　Engr.　Perf. 13½**
167　A67　18p dk vio, grn & chocolate　　.45　.25
168　A67　45p green & chocolate　　1.40　.40

**Mushroom Type of 1983**
**Perf. 13½x12½**
**1985, Sept. 19　　　　Photo.**
169　A57　30p Gyromitra esculenta　1.10　.40

Pal Village — A68

**1985, Nov. 7　Engr.　Perf. 13½**
170　A68　17p brt ultra & dk blue　　.50　.25

Christmas 1985 — A69

Fresco: Angels Playing Trumpet and Psaltery, St. Bartholomew Chapel.

**1985, Dec. 11　Photo.　Perf. 13½x13**
171　A69　17p multicolored　　.50　.25

**Mushroom Type of 1983**
**Perf. 13½x12½**
**1986, Apr. 10　　　　Photo.**
172　A57　30p Marasmius oreades　.90　.40

Europa 1986 — A70

**1986, May 5　Engr.　Perf. 13**
173　A70　17p Water　　.40　.30
174　A70　45p Soil and air　　1.60　.60

**Bishops of Urgel Type of 1979**
**1986, Sept. 11　Engr.　Perf. 13½**
175　A42　35p Justi Guitart　　.80　.40

Christmas — A72

Santa Roma de Les Bons Church bell.

**1986, Dec. 11　Litho.　Perf. 14**
176　A72　19p multicolored　　.50　.25

A73

Contemporary Natl. Coat of Arms.

**1987, Mar. 27　Photo.　Perf. 14**
177　A73　48p multicolored　　.90　.40

Visit of the co-princes: the Bishop of Urgel and president of France, September 26, 1986.

Europa 1987 — A74

Modern architecture: 19p, Meritxell Sanctuary interior. 48p, Sanctuary exterior, vert.

**1987, May 15　Engr.　Perf. 14x13½**
178　A74　19p dark blue & brown　.40　.40
179　A74　48p dark blue & brown　1.60　.60

**Souvenir Sheet**

1992 Summer Olympics, Barcelona — A75

20p, House of the Valleys. 50p, Bell tower, Chapel of the Archangel Michael, and torchbearer.

**1987, July 20　Photo.　Perf. 14**
180　A75　Sheet of 2　　4.00　4.00
　a.　20p multicolored　1.20　1.20
　b.　50p multicolored　2.25　2.25

Local Mushrooms — A76

**1987, Sept. 11　　Perf. 13½x12½**
181　A76　100p Boletus edulis　2.25　1.25

Christmas — A77

Design: Detail from a Catalan manuscript, De Nativitat, by R. Llull.

**1987, Nov. 18　Litho.　Perf. 14**
182　A77　20p multicolored　　.50　.25

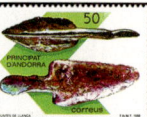

Lance and Arrowhead (Bronze Age) — A78

**1988, Mar. 25　Photo.　Perf. 14**
183　A78　50p multicolored　　.90　.40

Europa 1988 — A79

Transport and communications: 20p, Les Bons, a medieval road. 45p, Trader and pack mules, early 20th cent.

**1988, May 5　Engr.　Perf. 14x13½**
184　A79　20p dark bl & dark red　.45　.25
185　A79　45p dark bl & dark red　1.50　.40

Pyrenean Mastiff — A80

**1988, July 26　Litho.　Perf. 14x13½**
186　A80　20p multicolored　　1.50　.60

Bishop of Urgel and Seigneur of Caboet Confirming Co-Principality, 700th Anniv. — A81

**1988, Oct. 24　Litho.　Perf. 14x13½**
187　A81　20p gold, blk & int blue　.60　.30

Christmas 1988 — A82

**1988, Nov. 30　Litho.　Perf. 14x13½**
188　A82　20p multicolored　　.50　.25

**Arms Type of 1982 Without "PTA"**
**1988, Dec. 2　Photo.　Perf. 13½x13½**
192　A51　20p brt blue green　　.50　.25
　　**Size: 25x30½mm**
　　**Perf. 13½x12½**
　　**Engr.**
194　A51　50p grnsh black　　1.00　.40
196　A51　100p dark blue　　2.25　.80
198　A51　500p dark brown　　8.25　3.00
　　Nos. 192-198 (4)　12.00　4.45

Europa 1989 — A83

**Perf. 14x13½, 13½x14**
**1989, May 8　　Litho. & Engr.**
200　A83　20p Leapfrog, vert.　.55　.40
201　A83　45p Tug of war　　1.50　.80

Santa Roma Church, Les Bons — A84

**Litho. & Engr.**
**1989, June 20　　Perf. 13½x14**
202　A84　50p blk, dp bl & grn bl　1.25　.40

## ANDORRA, SPANISH ADMINISTRATION

Anniv. Emblem — A85

**1989, Oct. 26  Litho.  Perf. 14x13½**
203  A85  20p multicolored   .80   .40

Intl. Red Cross and Red Crescent societies, 125th annivs.; Year for the Protection of Human Life.

Christmas — A86

The Immaculate Conception.

**1989, Dec. 1**
204  A86  20p multicolored   .50   .25

Europa 1990 — A87

Post offices.

**Perf. 13½x14, 14x13½**
**1990, May 17     Photo.**
205  A87  20p shown         .55   .25
206  A87  50p Post office, vert.  1.40  .40

Gomphidius Rutilus — A88

**1990, June 21   Litho.   Perf. 13x13½**
207  A88  45p multicolored  1.50   .60

Plandolit House — A89

**Litho. & Engr.**
**1990, Oct. 17     Perf. 13x12½**
208  A89  20p brown & org yel   .50   .25

Christmas — A90

**1990, Nov. 26    Litho.    Perf. 14x13½**
209  A90  25p lake, brn & bister   .60   .30

4th Games of the Small European States — A91

**1991, Apr. 29    Photo.    Perf. 13½x14**
210  A91  25p Discus           .60   .30
211  A91  45p High jump, runner  1.00  .40

Europa — A92

**Perf. 14x13½, 13½x14**
**1991, May 10    Litho.**
212  A92  25p Olympus-1 satellite   .70   .40
213  A92  55p Olympus-1, horiz.   2.50   .80

Macrolepiota Procera — A93

**1991, Sept. 20   Litho.   Perf. 13x12½**
214  A93  45p multicolored   1.40   .40

Christmas — A94

**1991, Nov. 29    Photo.    Perf. 14x13½**
215  A94  25p multicolored   1.00   .40

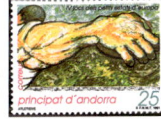

Woman Carrying Water Pails — A95

**1992, Feb. 14    Photo.    Perf. 13½x14**
216  A95  25p multicolored    .80   .40

European Discovery of America, 500th Anniv. — A96

**Perf. 14x13½, 13½x14**
**1992, May 8       Photo.**
217  A96  27p Santa Maria, vert.   .65   .40
218  A96  45p King Ferdinand  2.25   .40

Europa.

1992 Summer Olympics, Barcelona — A97

**1992, July 22    Photo.    Perf. 13½x14**
219  A97  27p Kayak            .00   .40

Nativity Scene, by Fra Angelico — A98

**1992, Nov. 18    Photo.    Perf. 14**
220  A98  27p multicolored    .80   .40

Natl. Automobile Museum — A99

**Litho. & Engr.**
**1992, Sept. 10            Perf. 13½x14**
221  A99  27p 1894 Benz       1.00   .40

Cantharellus Cibarius — A100

**1993, Mar. 25    Photo.    Perf. 13½x14**
222  A100  28p multicolored   1.00   .40

Contemporary Paintings — A101

Europa: 28p, Upstream, by John Alan Morrison. 45p, Rhythm, by Angel Calvente, vert.

**Perf. 13½x14, 14x13½**
**1993, May 20    Litho.**
223  A101  28p multicolored    .75   .40
224  A101  45p multicolored   1.50   .80

Art and Literature Society, 25th Anniv. — A102

**1993, Sept. 23   Litho.   Perf. 14**
225  A102  28p multicolored    .80   .40

Christmas — A103

**Litho. & Engr.**
**1993, Nov. 25            Perf. 14x13½**
226  A103  28p multicolored    .80   .40

Souvenir Sheet

Constitution, 1st Anniv. — A104

**1994, Mar. 14    Photo.    Perf. 14**
227  A104  29p multicolored   1.00   .75

Sir Alexander Fleming (1881-1955), Co-discoverer of Penicillin — A105

**1994, May 6     Photo.    Perf. 13½x14**
228  A105  29p Portrait         .60   .40
229  A105  55p AIDS virus      1.50   .80

Europa.

Hygrophorus Gliocyclus A106

**1994, Sept. 27    Photo.    Perf. 14**
230  A106  29p multicolored   1.00   .50

Christmas — A107

**1994, Nov. 29    Photo.    Perf. 14x13½**
231  A107  29p multicolored   1.00   .50

Nature Conservation in Europe — A108

**1995, Mar. 23    Photo.    Perf. 14**
232  A108  30p Farm in valley   .70   .45
233  A108  60p Stone fence, valley  1.35  .75

Europa — A109

**1995, May 8     Photo.    Perf. 14**
234  A109  60p multicolored   1.60   .80

Christmas — A110

**1995, Nov. 8    Photo.    Perf. 14**
235  A110  30p Flight to Egypt  1.00   .40

Entrance Into Council of Europe — A111

**1995, Nov. 10**
236  A111  30p multicolored   1.10   .40

Mushrooms A112

30p, Ramaria aurea. 60p, Tuber melanosporum.

**1996, Apr. 30    Photo.    Perf. 14**
237  A112  30p multicolored    .90   .35
238  A112  60p multicolored   1.60   .80

Isabelle Sandy (1884-1975), Writer — A113

**1996, May 7**
239  A113  60p brown & violet  1.75   .80

Europa.

Intl. Museum Day — A114

Design: Antique coal-heated iron.

**1996, Sept. 12    Photo.    Perf. 14**
240  A114  60p multicolored   1.10   .55

455

# 456 ANDORRA, SPANISH ADMINISTRATION

 Christmas A115

The Annunciation, by Andrew Martin, 1753, St. Eulalia d'Encamp Church.

**1996, Nov. 26**   **Photo.**   **Perf. 14**
241   A115   30p multicolored   .90   .40

 Museums of Andorra — A116

Early bicycles designed by: 32p, Karl Drais, 1818. 65p, Pierre Michaux, 1861.

**1997, Apr. 28**   **Photo.**   **Perf. 14**
242   A116   32p multicolored   .70   .35
243   A116   65p multicolored   1.40   .70

See Nos. 248-249.

 A117

Europa (Stories and Legends): Hikers watching family of bears crossing over river on fallen tree.

**1997, May 6**   **Photo.**   **Perf. 14**
244   A117   65p multicolored   1.75   .80

 UNESCO — A118

**1997, Sept. 30**   **Photo.**   **Perf. 14**
245   A118   32p multicolored   .80   .35

 Christmas — A119

**1997, Nov. 25**   **Photo.**   **Perf. 14**
246   A119   32p multicolored   .75   .35

 1998 Winter Olympic Games, Nagano — A120

**1998, Feb. 23**   **Photo.**   **Perf. 14**
247   A120   35p Slalom skier   .80   .35

**Museums of Andorra Type of 1997**

Early bicycles: 35p, Kangaroo, 1878. 70p, Hirondelle, 1889.

**1998, Apr. 24**   **Photo.**   **Perf. 13½x14**
248   A116   35p multicolored   .60   .35
249   A116   70p multicolored   1.25   .70

 Harlequins, Canillas Carnival — A121

**1998, May 22**   **Photo.**   **Perf. 14**
250   A121   70p multicolored   1.50   .70

Europa.

 Manual Digest, 250th Anniv. — A122

**1998, Sept. 30**   **Photo.**   **Perf. 14**
251   A122   35p multicolored   .70   .40

Inauguration of the Postal Museum of Andorra — A123

**1998, Nov. 19**   **Photo.**   **Perf. 14**
252   A123   70p multicolored   1.25   .75

Christmas A124

**1998, Nov. 26**
253   A124   35p multicolored   .80   .40

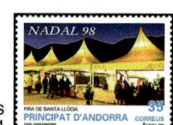 Museums of Andorra — A125

Early bicycles designed by: 35p, Salvo, 1878, vert. 70p, Rudge, 1883.

**1999, Jan. 29**   **Photo.**   **Perf. 14**
254   A125   35p multicolored   .70   .40
255   A125   70p multicolored   1.10   .75

Council of Europe, 50th Anniv. — A126

**1999, Apr. 29**   **Photo.**   **Perf. 14**
256   A126   35p multicolored   .80   .40

 Incles Valley — A127

**1999, May 6**
257   A127   70p multicolored   1.60   .80

Europa.

 Transporting Mail on Horseback A128

**1999, Feb. 18**   **Photo.**   **Perf. 14**
258   A128   35p black & sepia   1.00   .50

 Restoration of Casa Rull, Sispony, La Massana — A129

**1999, Sept. 22**   **Photo.**   **Perf. 13½x14**
259   A129   35p multicolored   .90   .45

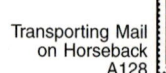 Christmas — A130

**1999, Nov. 10**   **Engr.**   **Perf. 14x13½**
260   A130   35p orange brn & brn   .90   .45

 St. Coloma's Church — A131

**1999, Nov. 12**   **Photo.**
261   A131   35p multicolored   .80   .40

European heritage.

**Europa, 2000**
**Common Design Type**

**2000, May 11**   **Photo.**   **Perf. 13¾**
262   CD17   70p multicolored   1.75   .80

 Angonella Lakes — A132

**2000, June 29**   **Photo.**   **Perf. 13¾x14**
263   A132   35p multicolored   .90   .45

 Casa Lacruz — A133

**2000, July 20**   **Photo.**   **Perf. 13¾x14**
264   A133   35p multicolored   .90   .45

 China, Areny-Plandolit Museum — A134

**2000, July 27**   **Perf. 14x13¾**
265   A134   70p multicolored   1.50   .75

 2000 Summer Olympics, Sydney — A135

**2000, Sept. 29**   **Photo.**   **Perf. 14x13½**
266   A135   70p multicolored   1.50   .75

 European Convention on Human Rights, 50th Anniv. — A136

**2000, Nov. 3**     **Perf. 13½x14**
267   A136   70p multicolored   1.60   .75

 Natl. Archives, 25th Anniv. — A137

**2000, Nov. 14**     **Perf. 14x13½**
268   A137   35p multicolored   .80   .40

 Christmas — A138

**2000, Nov. 22**
269   A138   35p multicolored   1.00   .40

 Rec de Solà — A139

**2001, Mar. 30**   **Photo.**   **Perf. 14x13¾**
270   A139   40p multicolored   .80   .60

 Europa — A140

**2001, May 16**     **Perf. 13¾x14**
271   A140   75p multicolored   1.50   .85

 Casa Palau, Sant Julià de Lòria — A141

**2001, June 20**   **Photo.**   **Perf. 14x13¾**
272   A141   75p multi   1.25   .75

 Chapel of the Virgin of Meritxell, 25th Anniv. of Rebuilding — A142

**2001, Sept. 7**   **Photo.**   **Perf. 14x13¾**
273   A142   40p multi   .90   .60

 Natl. Auditorium, 10th Anniv. — A143

**2001, Sept. 20**     **Perf. 13¾x14**
274   A143   75p multi   1.50   1.00

# ANDORRA, SPANISH ADMINISTRATION

Christmas — A144

**2001, Nov. 20 Photo. Perf. 13¾x14**
275 A144 40p multi    1.00 .55

**100 Cents = 1 Euro (€)**

Coat of Arms — A145

**2002, Jan. 2 Photo. Perf. 12¾x13¼**
276 A145 25c brown orange    .85 .60
277 A145 50c claret    1.40 1.10

Birds — A146

Designs: 25c, Prunella collaris. 50c, Montifringilla nivalis.

**2002, Mar. 27 Perf. 13¾x14**
278-279 A146 Set of 2    2.50 2.00

Intl. Year of Mountains — A147

**2002, Apr. 5**
280 A147 50c multi    1.75 1.10

Europa — A148

**2002, May 9**
281 A148 50c multi    14.00 3.50

Architectural Heritage — A149

Designs: €1.80, Casa Fusilé, Escaldes-Engordany. €2.10, Farga Rossell Centre, La Massana.

**2002, June 14 Photo. Perf. 14x13¾**
282-283 A149 Set of 2    11.00 9.00

Historic Automobiles — A150

Designs: 25c, Pinette. 50c, Rolls-Royce, horiz.

**2002, Oct. 8 Perf. 14x13¾, 13¾x14**
284-285 A150 Set of 2    2.25 2.00

Christmas — A151

**2002, Nov. 26 Perf. 13¾x14**
286 A151 25c multi    .90 .70

Artistic Heritage A152

Various religious murals from Santa Coloma Church: a, 25c. b, 75c. c, 50c.

**2002, Nov. 28 Perf. 14x13¾**
287 A152 Horiz. strip of 3, #a-c    4.25 3.50

Sassanat Bridge — A153

**Perf. 13½x13¾**
**2003, Feb. 27 Photo.**
288 A153 26c multi    1.40 .60

Constitution, 10th Anniv. — A154

**2003, Mar. 14 Photo. Perf. 13¾x14**
289 A154 76c multi    2.50 1.75

Europa — A155

**2003, Apr. 24**
290 A155 76c multi    2.25 1.10

Oenanthe Oenanthe — A156

**2003, June 11 Photo. Perf. 14x13¾**
291 A156 26c multi    1.25 .90

Admission to United Nations, 10th Anniv. — A157

**2003, July 28 Photo. Perf. 13¾x14**
292 A157 76c multi    2.50 1.75

Automobiles A158

Designs: 51c, 1908 Carter, vert. 76c, 1928 Peugeot.

**2003, Oct. 15 Perf. 14x13¾, 13¾x14**
293-294 A158 Set of 2    7.00 7.00

Christmas A159

**2003, Nov. 20 Perf. 13¾x14**
295 A159 26c multi    .90 .60

Coat of Arms — A160

**2004, Jan. 2 Perf. 12¾x13¼**
296 A160 27c bright blue    .70 .60
297 A160 52c olive green    1.40 1.25
298 A160 77c red orange    2.00 1.75
   Nos. 296-298 (3)    4.10 3.60
See Nos. 308-310, 319-320, 327-328.

Art by Joaquim Mir — A161

Designs: 27c, Fira del Bestiar. 52c, L'Escorxador, vert.

**2004 Perf. 13¾x14, 14x13¾**
299-300 A161 Set of 2    2.25 1.75
Issued: 27c, 2/20; 52c, 3/18.

Europa — A162

**2004, Apr. 29 Photo. Perf. 14x13¾**
301 A162 77c black    2.00 1.60

Fringilla Coelebs — A163

**2004, June 15 Photo. Perf. 13¾x14**
302 A163 27c multi    1.00 .60

Automobiles A164

Designs: €1.90, 1939 Simca 508-C. €2.19, 1955 Messerschmitt KR-1.

**2004, Oct. 15 Photo. Perf. 13¾x14**
303-304 A164 Set of 2    11.00 9.50

Postal Code — A165

**2004, Oct. 25 Perf. 14x13¾**
305 A165 52c multi    1.00 1.05

Admission to Council of Europe, 10th Anniv. — A166

**2004, Nov. 10 Perf. 13¾x14**
306 A166 52c multi    1.50 1.25

Christmas A167

**2004, Nov. 22**
307 A167 27c multi    1.00 .75

**Arms Type of 2004**

**2005, Jan. 28 Litho. Perf. 12¾x13¼**
308 A160 28c blue    .70 .65
309 A160 53c yel green    1.35 1.25
310 A160 78c brt pink    2.00 1.75
   Nos. 308-310 (3)    4.05 3.65

Selection of Madriu-Peralita-Claror Valley as UNESCO World Heritage Site — A168

**2005, Mar. 7 Photo. Perf. 14x13¾**
311 A168 28c multi    .90 .90

Endless, Sculpture by Mark Brusse — A169

**2005, Mar. 14 Perf. 13¾x14**
312 A169 53c multi    1.50 1.10

Europa — A170

**2005, Apr. 15 Photo. Perf. 13¾x14**
313 A170 78c multi    2.50 1.60

9th Games of Small European States — A171

**2005, May 20 Photo. Perf. 14x13¾**
314 A171 €1.95 multi    5.50 4.25

Caritas Andorra, 25th Anniv. — A172

**2005, June 15**
315 A172 28c multi    .70 .70

Cinclus Cinclus — A173

**2005, July 11 Photo. Perf. 13¾x14**
316 A173 €2.21 multi    6.25 6.25

Christmas A174

**2005, Nov. 2 Photo. Perf. 13¾x14**
317 A174 28c blk & org    1.00 .65

# ANDORRA, SPANISH ADMINISTRATION

2006 Winter Olympics, Turin — A175

**2006, Feb. 6**
318  A175  29c multi  1.00  .70

**Arms Type of 2004**
**2006, Mar. 1  Litho.  Perf. 12¾x13¼**
319  A160  29c yel brown  .75  .65
320  A160  57c blue  1.50  1.25

Earth, Fire, Water and Wind, Sculpture by Satoru Sato — A176

**2006, Apr. 10  Photo.  Perf. 14x13¾**
321  A176  78c multi  2.50  1.75

Europa — A177

**2006, May 16  Perf. 13¾x14**
322  A177  57c multi  1.75  1.75

Perdix Perdix — A178

**2006, June 6**
323  A178  €2.39 multi  6.75  6.75

Fulbright Scholarships A179

**2006, Aug. 8  Photo.  Perf. 13¾x14**
324  A179  57c multi  1.75  1.45

UNESCO, 60th Anniv., Andorran National UNESCO Committee, 10th Anniv. — A180

**2006, Oct. 2  Perf. 14x13¾**
325  A180  €2.33 multi  6.50  6.50

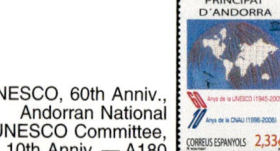
Christmas A181

**2006, Nov. 2  Photo.  Perf. 13¾x14**
326  A181  29c multi  1.00  .80

**Arms Type of 2004**
**2007, Jan. 19  Litho.  Perf. 12¾x13¼**
327  A160  30c red  .75  .75
328  A160  58c gray  1.50  1.50

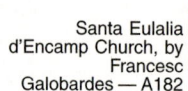
Santa Eulalia d'Encamp Church, by Francesc Galobardes — A182

**2007, Feb. 12  Photo.  Perf. 14x13¾**
329  A182  30c multi  .80  .80

Europa — A183

**2007, Apr. 23  Photo.  Perf. 14x13¾**
330  A183  58c multi  1.60  1.60
Scouting, cent.

Jordino Family, Sculptures by Rachid Khimoune — A184

**2007, May 21**
331  A184  €2.43 multi  6.75  6.75

Tetrao Urogallus A185

**2007, July 4  Photo.  Perf. 13¾x14**
332  A185  €2.49 multi  7.00  7.00

Casa de la Vall, by Francesc Galobardes A186

**2007, Sept. 10**
333  A186  78c multi  2.25  2.25

Andorran Red Cross, 25th Anniv. — A187

**2007, Oct. 15  Photo.  Perf. 13¾x14**
334  A187  30c black & red  .90  .90

Christmas A188

**2007, Nov. 2**
335  A188  30c multi  .90  .90

Gypaetus Barbatus — A189

**2008, Jan. 24  Photo.  Perf. 13¾**
336  A189  31c multi  .90  .90

Carro Votiu, Sculpture by Jordi Casamajor — A190

**2008, Jan. 24  Perf. 12¾x13**
337  A190  60c multi  1.60  1.60

Constitution, 15th Anniv. — A191

**2008, Mar. 12  Photo.  Perf. 14x13¾**
338  A191  31c multi  .90  .90

Europa — A192

**2008, Apr. 23**
339  A192  60c black & deep blue  1.90  1.90

Andorran Science Society, 25th Anniv. — A193

**2008, May 14**
340  A193  78c blue & black  2.25  2.25

*Souvenir Sheet*

Expo Zaragoza 2008 A194

**2008, June 13  Photo.  Perf. 13¾**
341  A194  €2.60 multi  7.50  7.50

2008 Summer Olympics, Beijing — A195

**2008, July 8  Litho.  Perf. 14x13¾**
342  A195  60c multi  1.90  1.90

Vall del Comapedrosa — A196

**2008, Sept. 15**
343  A196  €2.44 multi  6.25  6.25

Sispony, by Carme Massana A197

**2008, Oct. 13  Photo.  Perf. 12¾**
344  A197  31c multi  .90  .90

La Missa del Gallo, by Sergi Mas — A198

**2008, Nov. 11**
345  A198  31c multi  .90  .90
Christmas.

Narcissus — A199

**Die Cut Perf. 13**
**2009, Jan. 17  Litho.**
**Self-Adhesive**
346  A199  32c multi  .85  .85

Andorran School, 25th Anniv. — A200

**2009, Feb. 9  Perf. 14x13¾**
347  A200  62c multi  1.60  1.60

Mercè Rodoreda (1908-83), Writer — A201

**2009, Mar. 6**
348  A201  78c black  2.00  2.00

Council of Europe, 60th Anniv. — A202

**2009, Apr. 6  Litho.  Perf. 14x13¾**
349  A202  32c multi  1.00  1.00

Europa — A203

**2009, Apr. 23**
350  A203  62c multi  1.75  1.75
Intl. Year of Astronomy.

# ANDORRA, SPANISH ADMINISTRATION

**Souvenir Sheet**

Madrid Bridge — A204

**2009, May 18**    Photo.
351   A204   €2.70 multi    6.50   6.50

Eurasian Sparrowhawk — A205

**2009, Sept. 10**   Photo.   Perf. 14x13¾
352   A205   €2.47 multi    6.75   6.75

Paintings — A206

Designs: 62c, El Tarter, by Francesc Galobardes. 78c, Contrallum a Canillo, by Carme Massana.

**2009, Oct. 8**   Photo.   Perf. 13¾x14
353-354   A206   Set of 2    4.00   4.00

Christmas A207

**2009, Nov. 2**    Litho.
355   A207   32c multi    .95   .95

Pyrenees Iris — A208

    *Die Cut Perf. 13*
**2010, Jan. 12**    Litho.
    Self-Adhesive
356   A208   34c multi    .90   .90

Jacint Verdaguer (1845-1902), Poet — A209

    *Litho. & Engr.*
**2010, Feb. 8**   Perf. 14x13¾
357   A209   64c black & red    1.75   1.75

Paris Bridge, Andorra la Vella — A210

**2010, Mar. 5**    Litho.
358   A210   €2.75 multi    7.00   7.00

Europa — A211

**2010, May 6**   Photo.   Perf. 13¼x13¾
359   A211   64c multi    1.75   1.75

Bonfire — A212

**2010, June 1**   Perf. 13¾x13¼
360   A212   64c multi    1.60   1.60

2010 World Cup Soccer Championships, South Africa — A213

**2010, June 1**
361   A213   78c multi    1.90   1.90

Recycling A214

    Perf. 13¾x13¼
**2010, Sept. 6**    Photo.
362   A214   €2.49 multi    7.00   7.00

Churches — A215

Nos. 363: a, Sant Joan de Caselles Church, b, Sant Romà de Les Bons Church, horiz.

    Perf. 13¼x13, 13x13¼
**2010, Oct. 6**    Engr.
363   A215   78c Sheet of 2, #a-b    4.50   4.50
See Andorra, French Administration No. 679.

Christmas A216

**2010, Nov. 2**   Photo.   Perf. 13¾x13¼
364   A216   34c multi    .95   .95

Escaldes-Engordany Parish, 2011 Capital of Catalan Culture — A217

    *Die Cut Perf. 13*
**2011, Jan. 12**    Litho.
    Self-Adhesive
365   A217   35c multi    .95   .95

Miquel Marti i Pol (1929-2003), Writer — A218

**2011, Feb. 7**   Perf. 14x13¾
366   A218   65c black & gray    1.75   1.75

Europa — A219

**2011, Apr. 4**
367   A219   65c multi    1.75   1.75
Intl. Year of Forests.

Casa Farràs — A220

**2011, May 3**   Perf. 13¾x14
368   A220   80c multi    2.40   2.40

Painted Keystone, Sant Esteve Church — A221

**2011, June 1**
369   A221   €2.55 multi    7.00   7.00

Venice Biennale — A222

Artwork by: 80c, Helena Guàrdia. €2.55, Francisco Sánchez.

**2011, July 1**
370-371   A222   Set of 2    0.26   9.25

Equality of the Sexes — A223

**2011, Sept. 8**   Perf. 14x13¾
372   A223   80c multi    2.25   2.25

America Issue, Mailbox — A224

**2011, Oct. 11**   Perf. 13¾x14
373   A224   80c multi    2.25   2.25

Christmas A225

**2011, Nov. 3**
374   A225   35c multi    1.10   1.10
   a.   Tete-beche pair    2.50   2.50

Rossell Forge Interpretive Center, La Massana, 10th Anniv. — A226

**2012, Jan. 9**   Litho.   *Die Cut Perf. 13*
    Self-Adhesive
375   A226   36c multi    1.10   1.10

Agustí Bartra (1908-82), Poet — A227

**2012, Feb. 27**   Perf. 14x13¾
376   A227   51c black    1.40   1.40

Europa — A228

**2012, Apr. 4**   Perf. 13¾x14
377   A228   70c multi    1.90   1.90

CIAM Building, Escaldes-Engordany — A229

**2012, May 3**
378   A229   85c multi    2.25   2.25

Wood Carving, Sant Marti de la Cortinada Church, Ordino — A230

**2012, June 1**   Perf. 14x13¾
379   A230   85c multi    2.25   2.25

A231      Art — A232

**2012, July 2**   Perf. 13¾x14
380   A231   €2.90 multi    7.50   7.50
    Perf. 14x13¾
381   A232   €2.90 multi    7.50   7.50

Civic Values — A233

**2012, Sept. 10**   Perf. 14x13¾
382   A233   85c multi    2.25   2.25

# ANDORRA, SPANISH ADMINISTRATION

America Issue, Cosmological Legend — A234

**2012, Oct. 11**
383   A234   85c multi   1.75   1.75

Christmas — A235

**2012, Nov. 5**
384   A235   36c multi   .95   .95

Salvador Espriu (1913-85), Poet — A236

**2013, Jan. 10    Die Cut Perf. 13**
**Self-Adhesive**
385   A236   37c multi   1.00   1.00

A237

**2013, Feb. 21    Perf. 13¾x14**
386   A237   75c multi   2.00   2.00
Road between Andorra and La Seu d'Urgell, Spain, cent.

Areny-Plandolit Museum, Ordino — A238

**2013, Mar. 4    Perf. 14x13¾**
387   A238   52c multi   1.40   1.40

**Souvenir Sheet**

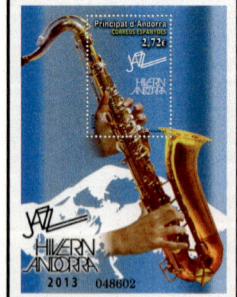

Winter Jazz Festival A239

**2013, Apr. 1    Perf. 13¼x13¾**
388   A239   €2.72 multi   7.00   7.00

Europa — A240

**2013, Apr. 23    Perf. 13¾x13¼**
389   A240   75c multi   2.00   2.00

Women in Portuguese Costumes A241

**2013, May 6    Perf. 13½x13¼**
390   A241   90c multi   2.40   2.40

Casa dels Russos — A242

**2013, June 3**
391   A242   75c multi   2.00   2.00

**Souvenir Sheet**

School Correspondence — A243

**Perf. 13¼x13¾**
**2013, Sept. 16    Litho.**
392   A243   €2.72 multi   7.50   7.50

Diversity and Anti-Discrimination — A244

**2013, Oct. 3    Litho.    Perf. 13¾x13¼**
393   A244   90c multi   2.50   2.50

A245

Christmas — A246

**2013, Nov. 4    Litho.    Perf. 13¼x13¾**
394   A245   37c multi   1.00   1.00
395   A246   75c multi   2.00   2.00

14th Intl. Winter Road Conference, Andorra — A247

**2014, Jan. 13    Litho.    Perf. 13¼x13¾**
396   A247   38c multi   1.10   1.10

Coat of Arms — A248

**2014, Feb. 3    Litho.    Perf. 13¼x13¾**
397         Vert. strip of 5   4.50   4.50
  a. A248   1c gray          .25    .25
  b. A248   2c brown         .25    .25
  c. A248   5c blue          .25    .25
  d. A248   50c dull green   1.40   1.40
  e. A248   €1 red           2.75   2.75

Sculpture by Samantha Bosque — A249

**2014, Mar. 3    Litho.    Perf. 13¼x13¾**
398   A249   54c multi   1.50   1.50

Closure of Radio Andorra, 30th Anniv. — A250

**2014, Apr. 7    Litho.    Perf. 13¾x13¼**
399   A250   92c multi   2.60   2.60

Accordion — A251

**2014, Apr. 23    Litho.    Perf. 13¼x13¾**
400   A251   76c multi   2.10   2.10
Europa.

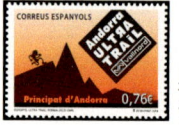

Andorra Ultra Trail, Vallnord — A252

**2014, June 9    Litho.    Perf. 13¾x13¼**
401   A252   76c red & black   2.10   2.10

Filipinos in Andorra — A253

**2014, July 7    Litho.    Perf. 13¾x13¼**
402   A253   92c multi   2.50   2.50

Intl. Year of Family Farming — A254

**Perf. 13¾x13¼**
**2014, Sept. 15    Litho.**
403   A254   76c multi   2.00   2.00

**Souvenir Sheet**

Mural in Sant Martí de la Cortinada Church — A255

**2014, Oct. 6    Litho.    Perf. 13¼x13¾**
404   A255   €2.72 multi   6.75   6.75

Christmas A256

**2014, Nov. 5    Litho.    Perf. 13¾x13¼**
405   A256   38c multi   .95   .95

Casa Felipó — A257

**Perf. 13¼x13¾**
**2014, Nov. 10    Litho.**
406   A257   €2.72 multi   6.75   6.75

Virgin of Meritxell — A258

**2015, Jan. 13    Litho.    Perf. 14x13¾**
407   A258   A multi   .95   .95
No. 407 sold for 42c on day of issue.

Chamois — A259

**2015, Feb. 9    Litho.    Perf. 13¾x14**
408   A259   €1 multi   2.25   2.25

Higher Education in Andorra, 25th Anniv. — A260

**2015, Mar. 2    Litho.    Perf. 13¾x13¼**
409   A260   55c multi   1.25   1.25

Europa — A261

**2015, Apr. 23    Litho.    Perf. 13¾x13¼**
410   A261   90c multi   2.10   2.10

Between, Sculpture by Agustí Roqué — A262

**2015, May 1    Litho.    Perf. 13¾x13¼**
411   A262   €2.84 multi   6.50   6.50
Venice Biennale.

2015 World Motorcycling Trial Grand Prix, Andorra — A263

**Perf. 13¾x13¼**
**2015, June 10    Litho.**
412   A263   €1 multi   2.25   2.25

# ANDORRA, SPANISH ADMINISTRATION

English Community in Andorra — A264

**2015, July 8   Litho.   Perf. 13¼x13¾**
413  A264  90c multi           2.00  2.00

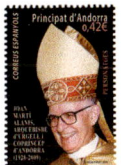
Joan Martí Alanis (1929-2009), Bishop of Urgel and Co-Prince — A265

**2015, Sept. 8   Litho.   Perf. 13¼x13¾**
414  A265  42c multi            .95   .95

Age of Majority at 18, 30th Anniv. — A266

**2015, Sept. 8   Litho.   Perf. 13¾**
415  A266  €1 multi            2.25  2.25

### Souvenir Sheet

Hotel Rosaleda, Encamp — A267

**2015, Oct. 15   Litho.   Perf. 13¼x13¾**
416  A267  €2.84 multi         6.25  6.25

Christmas A268

**2015, Nov. 2   Litho.   Perf. 13¾x13¼**
417  A268  42c multi            .95   .95

Dolors Parella i Fivaller (d. 1855), Murdered Baroness — A269

**2015, Nov. 4   Litho.   Perf. 13¼x13¾**
418  A269  90c multi           1.90  1.90

Coat of Arms — A270

**2016, Jan. 13   Litho.   Perf. 14x13½**
419  A270  A magenta & black  1.00  1.00
No. 419 sold for 45c on day of issue. See No. 431.

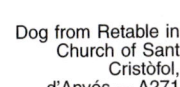 
Dog from Retable in Church of Sant Cristòfol, d'Anyós — A271

**2016, Feb. 9   Litho.   Perf. 14x13½**
420  A271  €1.30 multi         3.00  3.00

Interpretive Center for Romanesque Art, Pal, 10th Anniv. — A272

**2016, Mar. 2   Litho.   Perf. 13¼x13¾**
421  A272  57c multi           1.25  1.25
No. 421 has two die cut openings in the interior of the arches.

Europa — A273

**2016, Apr. 22   Litho.   Perf. 13¾x13¼**
422  A273  €1.15 multi         2.75  2.75
Think Green Issue.

Anima Compartida, by Joan Xandri — A274

**2016, May 11   Litho.   Perf. 13¾x13¼**
423  A274  €2.95 multi         6.75  6.75
2015 Venice Biennale.

Andorra la Vella, 2016 Ibero-American Capital of Culture — A275

**Perf. 13¾x13¼**
**2016, June 10           Litho.**
424  A275  €1.30 multi         3.00  3.00

French Community in Andorra — A276

**2016, July 8   Litho.   Perf. 13¼x13¾**
425  A276  €1.15 multi         2.60  2.60

Tree of Science — A277

**2016, Sept. 8   Litho.   Perf. 13¾x13¼**
426  A277  45c blk & brn       1.00  1.00
Ramón Llull (c. 1232-c. 1315), philosopher.

Reforms of 1866, 150th Anniv. — A278

**2016, Sept. 8   Litho.   Perf. 13¼x13¾**
427  A278  €1.30 multi         3.00  3.00

### Souvenir Sheet

Vilanova Clinic A279

**2016, Oct. 14   Litho.   Perf. 13¼x13¾**
428  A279  €2.95 multi         6.50  6.50

Christmas — A280

**2016, Nov. 4   Litho.   Perf. 13¼x13¾**
429  A280  45c Pastorets       .95   .95

Montserrat Palau Martí (1916-2004), Ethnologist A281

**2016, Nov. 8   Litho.   Perf. 13¾x13¼**
430  A281  €1.15 multi         2.50  2.50

**Coat of Arms Type of 2016**
**2017, Jan. 13   Litho.   Perf. 14x13½**
431  A270  A blue & black     1.10  1.10
No. 431 sold for 50c on day of issue.

Argentine Community in Andorra — A282

**Perf. 13¼x13¾**
**2017, Feb. 24           Litho.**
432  A282  €1.25 multi         2.75  2.75

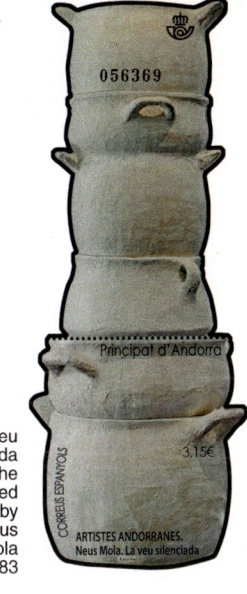
La Veu Silenciada (The Silenced Voice), by Neus Mola A283

**Perf. 13¼ Horiz. at Top**
**2017, Mar. 9           Litho.**
433  A283  €3.15 multi + label  6.75  6.75
No. 433 was sold folded.

Castell de les Bons — A284

**2017, Apr. 21   Litho.   Perf. 13¼x13¾**
434  A284  €1.25 multi         2.75  2.75
Europa.

Pere Canturri (1935-2015), Historian and Governmental Minister — A285

**2017, Apr. 28   Litho.   Perf. 13¼x13¾**
435  A285  60c multi           1.40  1.40

### Souvenir Sheet

Sculptures — A286

No. 436: a, Lost Origin, by Zoe. b, Omphalos, by Jordi Casamajor.

**2017, May 11   Litho.   Perf. 13¼x13¾**
436  A286  Sheet of 2          2.50  2.50
  a.  50c multi               1.10  1.10
  b.  60c multi               1.40  1.40

Birch Tree and Leaf — A287

**2017, June 5   Litho.   Perf. 13¾x13¼**
437  A287  €1.35 multi         3.25  3.25

# ANDORRA, SPANISH ADMINISTRATION

Estany d'Encamp
A288

**2017, July 8**   Litho.   *Perf. 13¾x13¼*
438   A288   €1.25 multi     3.00   3.00

Julià Reig i Ribó (1911-96), Politician — A289

**2017, Sept. 8**   Litho.   *Perf. 13¾x13¼*
439   A289   €1.35 multi     3.25   3.25

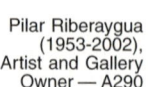 

Pilar Riberaygua (1953-2002), Artist and Gallery Owner — A290

      *Perf. 13¾x13¼*
**2017, Sept. 22**       Litho.
440   A290   €1.25 multi     3.00   3.00

### Souvenir Sheet

Arajol Chalet A291

**2017, Oct. 14**   Litho.   *Perf. 13¼x13¾*
441   A291   €3.15 multi     7.50   7.50

Bulls, Sant Miquel del Prats Altarpiece Detail — A292

**2017, Nov. 3**   Litho.   *Perf. 13¾x13¼*
442   A292   €1.35 multi     3.25   3.25

Christmas — A293

**Die Cut Perf. 13**
**2017, Nov. 8**    On Wood Veneer Self-Adhesive   Litho.
443   A293   50c multi     1.25   1.25

Coat of Arms — A294

**2018, Jan. 2**   Litho.   *Perf. 14x13¾*
444   A294   A multi     1.40   1.40
No. 444 sold for 55c on day of issue.

Dante Alighieri (c. 1265-1321), Writer — A295

**2018, Feb. 24**   Litho.   *Perf. 13¾*
445   A295   €1.35 multi     3.25   3.25
Italian Community in Andorra.

### Souvenir Sheet

Andorran Constitution, 25th Anniv. — A296

**2018, Mar. 14**   Litho.   *Perf. 13x13½*
446   A296   €3.30 multi     8.25   8.25

Escaldes-Engordany Parish, 40th Anniv. — A297

**2018, Apr. 6**   Litho.   *Perf. 13x13½*
447   A297   55c multi     1.40   1.40

Engordany Bridge — A298

**2018, Apr. 23**   Litho.   *Perf. 14¼x14*
448   A298   €1.35 multi     3.25   3.25
Europa. Stone grit is affixed to portions of the design.

Roser Jordana Mallol (1942-2014), Promoter of Andorran Tourism — A299

**2018, May 16**   Litho.   *Perf. 13½x13*
449   A299   €1.35 multi     3.25   3.25

Walnuts and Leaf of Walnut Tree — A300

**2018, May 25**   Litho.   *Perf. 13½x13*
450   A300   €1.45 multi     3.50   3.50

Bilateral Relationships Between Andorra and Spain, 25th Anniv. — A301

**2018, June 5**   Litho.   *Perf. 13½x13*
451   A301   €1.35 multi     3.25   3.25

Summer Solstice Festival, UNESCO Intangible Cultural Heritage — A302

**2018, June 22**   Litho.   *Perf. 13½x13*
452   A302   €1.45 multi     3.50   3.50

European Year of Cultural Heritage — A303

**2018, July 5**   Litho.   *Perf. 13¼x13¾*
453   A303   €1.45 multi     3.50   3.50

Privada Tutelar Foundation, 10th Anniv. — A304

**2018, Aug. 9**   Litho.   *Perf. 13¼x13¾*
454   A304   65c multi     1.50   1.50

View of Escaldes From Els Vilars — A305

**2018, Sept. 17**   Litho.   *Perf. 13½x13*
455   A305   €1.45 multi     3.50   3.50

Cultural Guide Courses, 25th Anniv. — A306

**2018, Oct. 10**   Litho.   *Perf. 13¾x13¼*
456   A306   €1.45 multi     3.50   3.50

### Souvenir Sheet

Christmas Diorama (unfolded) — A307

**2018, Nov. 8**   Litho.   *Perf. 13¾*
457   A307   €3.30 multi     7.50   7.50
No. 457 was sold with a fold in the sheet margin so the stamp would appear through the holes in the illustration printed on the back of the sheet margin.

Flag of Andorra — A308

**2019, Jan. 4**   Litho.   *Perf. 13½x13*
458   A308   A multi     1.40   1.40
No. 458 sold for 60c on day of issue. Compare with No. 472.

Tradition of Burning of Christmas Trees — A309

**2019, Jan. 24**   Litho.   *Perf. 13½x13*
459   A309   €1.40 multi     3.25   3.25

General Council of the Valleys, 600th Anniv. — A310

**2019, Feb. 11**   Litho.   *Perf. 13½x13*
460   A310   €3.50 multi     8.00   8.00

A311

Design: Maria Lluisa de Riba (1908-93), last heir of Rossell family, and Rossell house, Ordino.

**2019, Mar. 8**   Litho.   *Perf. 13½x13*
461   A311   €1.50 multi     3.50   3.50

European Robin A312

**2019, Apr. 26**   Litho.   *Perf. 13¼x13½*
462   A312   €1.40 multi     3.25   3.25
Europa.

### Souvenir Sheet

Andorran Foods A313

No. 463: a, Chickory. b, Escudella.

**2019, May 11**   Litho.   *Perf. 13x13¾*
463   A313   Sheet of 2     6.75   6.75
   a.   €1.40 multi     3.25   3.25
   b.   €1.50 multi     3.50   3.50

### Souvenir Sheet

Hydroelectric Power in Andorra, 90th Anniv. — A314

**Litho. With Lenticular Lens Affixed**
**2019, May 31**   *Perf. 14½x14¾*
464   A314   €4 multi     9.00   9.00

Holly Leaves and Berries — A315

**Litho. With Foil Application**
**2019, July 8**   *Perf. 13¾x13¼*
465   A315   70c multi     1.60   1.60

La Purito Cycling Tour, 5th Anniv. — A316

**2019, Aug. 4**   Litho.   *Perf. 13¾x13¼*
466   A316   70c multi     1.60   1.60

# ANDORRA, SPANISH ADMINISTRATION

Goddess of Oxygen, by Philippe Shangti — A317

2019, Sept. 8 Litho. Perf. 13x13½
467 A317 €1.50 multi 3.25 3.25
Venice Art Biennale.

Molleres de Meritxell, by Francesc Galobardes A318

2019, Sept. 22 Litho. Perf. 13½x13
468 A318 €1.40 multi 3.25 3.25

The Firebird — A319

2019, Oct. 14 Litho. Perf. 13x13½
469 A319 70c multi 1.60 1.60
Russian community in Andorra.

Admission of Andorra to Council of Europe, 25th Anniv. — A320

2019, Nov. 8 Litho. Perf. 13
470 A320 €1.40 multi + label 3.25 3.25
See Andorra (French Administration) No. 815.

Christmas — A321

2019, Nov. 8 Engr. Perf. 13x13½
471 A321 60c black 1.40 1.40

Flag of Andorra — A322

2020, Jan. 3 Litho. Perf. 13½x13
472 A322 A multi 1.50 1.50
No. 472 sold for 65c on day of issue. Compare with No. 458.

27th Ibero-American Summit of Heads of State and Government, Andorra — A323

Perf. 13¼x13½
2020, Feb. 11 Litho.
473 A323 75c multi 1.75 1.75

Carolina Plandolit i Pelati (?-1902), Wife of Guillem d'Areny i Plandolit, First Syndic of the General Council — A324

2020, Mar. 6 Litho. Perf. 13x13½
474 A324 €1.55 multi 3.50 3.50

Wolf and Protective Collar for Sheepdogs — A325

2020, Mar. 19 Litho. Perf. 13x13½
475 A325 €1.45 multi 3.25 3.25

Cal Pal Manor House, La Cortinada — A326

2020, May 14 Litho. Perf. 13¾x13¼
476 A326 75c multi 1.75 1.75

Postal Carriers and Map of Andorra-La Seu d'Urgell, Spain Postal Route — A327

2020, May 14 Litho. Perf. 13¼x13¾
477 A327 €1.45 multi 3.25 3.25
Europa.

Souvenir Sheet

Andorran Woman Suffrage Decree, 50th Anniv. A328

2020, May 29 Litho. Perf. 13¼
478 A328 €3.80 multi 8.50 8.50

Beyondwalls, Painting on Land by Saype — A329

Perf. 13¾x13¼
2020, June 30 Litho.
479 A329 €1.45 multi 3.25 3.25
2019 L'Andart Biennale.

Linden Leaf and Blossom — A330

2020, July 8 Litho. Perf. 13½x13¼
480 A330 €1.45 multi 3.50 3.50

Collada dels Meners A331

2020, Aug. 4 Litho. Perf. 13x13½
481 A331 €1.40 multi 3.50 3.50

Diplomatic Relations Between Andorra and Liechtenstein, 25th Anniv. — A332

2020, Sept. 8 Litho. Perf. 13¾x13¼
482 A332 €1.55 multi 3.75 3.75

Pep Aguareles (1965-2019), Photographer A333

2020, Oct. 9 Litho. Perf. 13¾x13¼
483 A333 €1.45 multi 3.50 3.50

Souvenir Sheet

Chinese Community in Andorra — A334

2020, Oct. 21 Litho. Perf. 13¼
484 A334 €3.80 multi 9.00 9.00

Casa de la Vall A335

Litho. & Engr.
2020, Nov. 5 Perf. 13x12½
485 A335 €2.40 multi + 2 flanking labels 5.75 5.75
Candidacy of Casa de la Vall, Castell de Foix and Cathedral of the See of Urgell (shown on flanking labels) for UNESCO World Heritage Site status. See French Andorra No. 828.

Canopy of the Chapel of St. Bartholomew A336

2020, Nov. 5 Litho. Perf. 13½
486 A336 65c multi 1.60 1.60
Christmas.

Flag of Andorra — A337

2021, Jan. 18 Litho. Perf. 13¾x13¼
487 A337 A multi 1.75 1.75
No. 487 sold for 70c on day of issue.

Souvenir Sheet

Tribute to Workers During the COVID-19 Pandemic — A338

2021, Jan. 19 Litho. Perf. 13½x13¼
488 A338 €4.15 multi 10.00 10.00

Harlequins of Canillo — A339

Perf. 13½x13¼
2021, Feb. 12 Litho.
489 A339 €1.50 multi 3.75 3.75

Marcella Pelegrí, Primary School Teacher — A340

2021, Mar. 8 Litho. Perf. 13½x13¼
490 A340 €1.60 multi 3.75 3.75

Antoni Morell (1941-2020), Writer — A341

2021, Apr. 23 Litho. Perf. 13½x13¼
491 A341 70c multi 1.75 1.75

Bearded Vulture A342

2021, Apr. 30 Litho. Perf. 13¼x13½
492 A342 €1.50 multi 3.75 3.75
Europa.

Borda de l'Any de la Part Winery A343

2021, May 3 Litho. Perf. 13¼x13½
493 A343 €2.50 multi 6.00 6.00

Hiker — A344

2021, June 2 Litho. Perf. 13¾x13¼
494 A344 80c multi 1.90 1.90

Elder Blossoms A345

2021, July 8 Litho. Perf. 13¾x13¼
495 A345 €1.50 multi 3.75 3.75

# ANDORRA, SPANISH ADMINISTRATION

Publication of Travel Guide *Les Valls d'Andorra*, by Bonaventura Riberaygua Argelich, 75th Anniv. — A346

2021, Aug. 4   Litho.   Perf. 13x13¼
496  A346  €1.60 multi        3.75  3.75

Coronation of Our Lady of Meritxell, Cent. — A347

2021, Sept. 7   Litho.   Perf. 13¼x13¾
497  A347  €2 multi           4.75  4.75

Souvenir Sheet

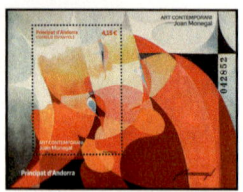

Painting by Joan Monegal (1933-81) — A348

2021, Oct. 9   Litho.   Perf. 13¾x13¼
498  A348  €4.15 multi        9.75  9.75

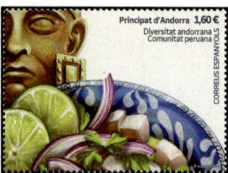

Peruvian Community in Andorra — A349

2021, Oct. 21   Litho.   Perf. 13¼x13¾
499  A349  €1.60 multi        3.75  3.75

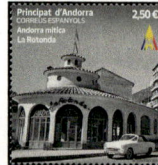

Rotonda Restaurant, c. 1960 — A350

2021, Nov. 5   Litho.   Perf. 13¼x13½
500  A350  €2.50 multi        5.75  5.75

St. Sylvester's Day Race, Sant Julia de Loria — A351

2021, Nov. 5   Litho.   Perf. 13x13¼
501  A351  70c multi          1.60  1.60

Christmas.

Flag of Andorra — A352

Litho. With Foil Application
2022, Jan. 3          Perf. 13½x13
502  A352  A sil & multi      1.75  1.75

No. 502 sold for 75c on day of issue.

Dance of the Bear — A353

2022, Feb. 11   Litho.   Perf. 13x13½
503  A353  €1.65 multi        3.75  3.75

Europa Cup 2022-23 Season Skiing Finals, Soldeu — A354

2022, Mar. 14   Litho.   Perf. 13½x13
504  A354  €1.75 multi        4.00  4.00

Eurasian Eagle-Owl — A355

2022, Mar. 25   Litho.   Perf. 13½x13
505  A355  €4.60 multi       10.50 10.50

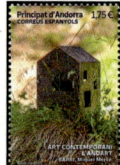

Barri, Art Installation by Miquel Mercè — A356

2022, Apr. 22   Litho.   Perf. 13x13½
506  A356  €1.75 multi        4.00  4.00

Andorra L'Andart International Biennial.

Legend of Meritxell — A357

2022, May 19   Litho.   Perf. 13¾x13¼
507  A357  €1.65 multi        3.50  3.50

Europa.

Estany de les Salamandres — A358

2022, June 2   Litho.   Perf. 13¾x13¼
508  A358  €1.75 multi        3.75  3.75

Hazelnut Tree — A359

2022, July 8   Litho.   Perf. 13¾x13¼
509  A359  €1.65 multi        3.50  3.50

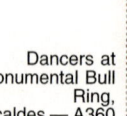

Dancers at Monumental Bull Ring, Escaldes — A360

2022, July 22   Litho.   Perf. 13½
510  A360  €1.75 multi        3.75  3.75

Souvenir Sheet

Flags of Andorra and Spain A361

2022, Sept. 7   Litho.   Perf. 13¾x13¼
511  A361  €4.60 multi        9.00  9.00

Visit of King Felipe VI of Spain to Andorra.

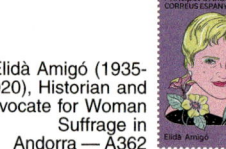

Elidà Amigó (1935-2020), Historian and Advocate for Woman Suffrage in Andorra — A362

Perf. 13¼x13¾
2022, Sept. 23        Litho.
512  A362  €1 multi           2.00  2.00

Independence of India, 75th Anniv. — A363

2022, Oct. 3   Litho.   Perf. 13¼x13¾
513  A363  €2.25 multi        4.50  4.50

Oscar Ribas (1936-2020), Prime Minister — A364

2022, Oct. 26   Litho.   Perf. 13¼x13¾
514  A364  €1.95 multi        4.00  4.00

Nov. 7, 1982 Valira River Flood, 40th Anniv. — A365

2022, Nov. 4   Litho.   Perf. 13¼x13¾
515  A365  €1.75 multi        3.75  3.75

Christmas — A366

2022, Nov. 7   Litho.   Perf. 13¼x13¾
516  A366  75c multi          1.60  1.60

Flag and Coat of Arms of Andorra — A367

Litho. With Foil Application
2023, Jan. 16         Perf. 13¼x13¾
517  A367  A sil & multi      1.75  1.75

No. 517 sold for 78c on day of issue.

Andorra Rugby Team, 60th. Anniv. — A368

Perf. 13¾x13¼
2023, Feb. 17         Litho.
518  A368  €1.65 multi        3.75  3.75

Souvenir Sheet

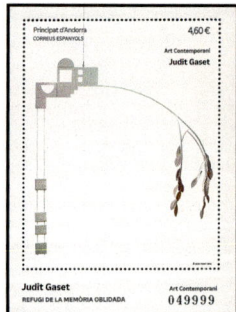

"Refuge of the Forgotten Memory," Art by Judit Gaset — A369

2023, Mar. 24   Litho.   Perf. 13½x13
519  A369  €4.60 multi       10.00 10.00

Quima Calvó, Suffragette and Chef — A370

2023, Apr. 14   Litho.   Perf. 13x13¾
520  A370  €1.75 multi        4.00  4.00

Black Redstart — A371

2023, Apr. 21   Litho.   Perf. 13½x13¼
521  A371  €1.75 multi        4.00  4.00

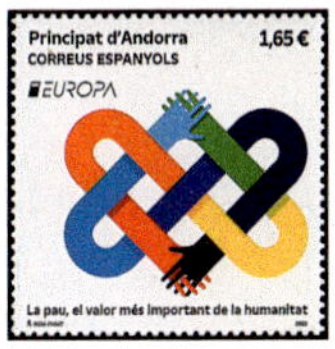


Europa — A372

**2023, May. 9 Litho. *Perf. 13¼***

522 A372 €1.65 multi 3.75 3.75

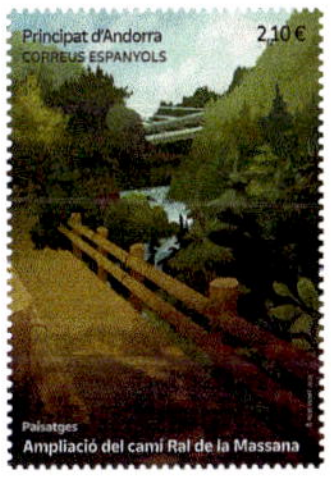


Ral de la Massana Road — A373

***Perf. 13¾x13¼***

**2023, June 12 Litho.**

523 A373 €2.10 multi 4.75 4.75

## AIR POST STAMPS

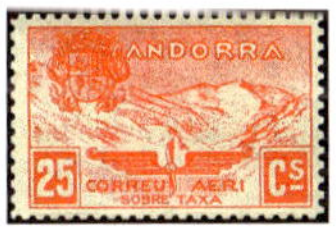


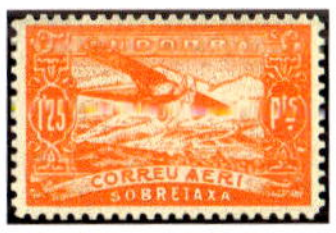


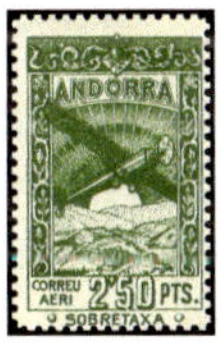


A set of 12 stamps, inscribed "CORREU AER / SOBRETAXA" was authorized in 1932 for a proposed private air service between Andorra and Barcelona. These stamps were prepared but not issued. Value, set unused $32, never hinged. $42.50. The stamps were also overprinted "FRANQUICIA DEL CONSELL" for official use. Value, set $140.

**Catalogue values for unused stamps in this section are for Never Hinged items.**

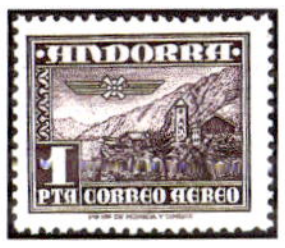


AP1

**Unwmk.**

**1951, June 27 Engr. *Perf. 11***

C1 AP1 1p dark violet brown 25.00 4.25

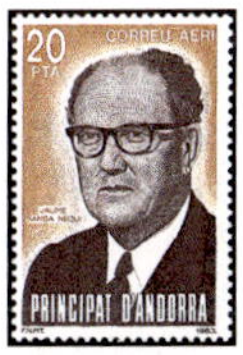


AP2

**Litho. & Engr.**

**1983, Oct. 20 *Perf. 13***

C2 AP2 20p brown & bis brn .40 .25

Jaime Sansa Nequi, Episcopal Church official.

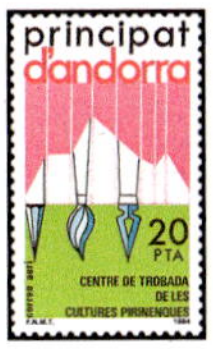


AP3

**1984, Oct. 25 Photo. *Perf. 13***

C3 AP3 20p multicolored .40 .25

Pyrenees Art Center.

**Bishops of Urgel Type of 1979**

**1985, June 13 Engr. *Perf. 13½***

C4 A42 20p Ramon Iglesias .40 .25

## SPECIAL DELIVERY STAMPS

**Special Delivery Stamp of Spain, 1905 Overprinted**

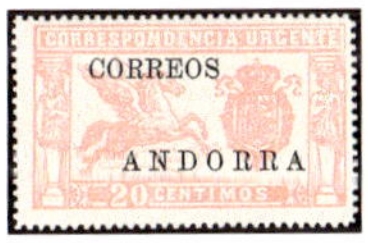


**1928 Unwmk. *Perf. 14***

**Without Control Number on Back**

E1 SD1 20c red 80.00 95.00
Never hinged 150.00

**With Control Number on Back**

E2 SD1 20c pale red 55.00 55.00
Never hinged 95.00

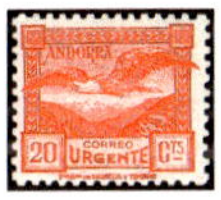


Eagle over Mountain Pass — SD2

**1929 *Perf. 14***

**With Control Number on Back**

E3 SD2 20c scarlet 25.00 20.00
Never hinged 35.00

Perf 11½ examples are numbered A000.000 and are specimens. Value, $400.

No. E3 exists imperforate with control numbers on the back. Value, $110 unused, $155 never hinged.

**1937 *Perf. 11½x11***

**Without Control Number on Back**

E4 SD2 20c red 7.75 9.50
Never hinged 8.75

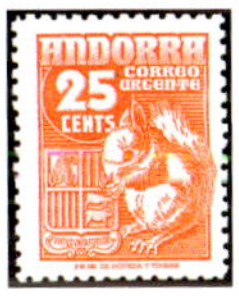


Arms and Squirrel — SD3

**1949 Unwmk. Engr. *Perf. 10x9½***

E5 SD3 25c red 5.75 4.50
Never hinged 8.25

# ANDORRA, FRENCH ADMINISTRATION

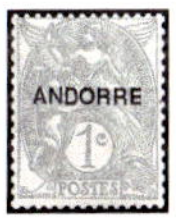


Stamps and Types of France, 1900-1929, Overprinted

***Perf. 14x13½***

**1931, June 16 Unwmk.**

| | | | | |
|---|---|---|---|---|
| 1 | A16 | 1c gray | 1.00 | *1.00* |
| *a.* | | Double overprint | 1,800. | 2,500. |
| *b.* | | Double overprint | 1,800. | |
| 2 | A16 | 2c red brown | 1.40 | *1.40* |
| 3 | A16 | 3c orange | 1.40 | *1.40* |
| 4 | A16 | 5c green | 2.10 | *2.40* |
| 5 | A16 | 10c lilac | 3.50 | *3.75* |
| 6 | A22 | 15c red brown | 5.50 | 5.50 |
| 7 | A22 | 20c red violet | 7.75 | *8.25* |
| 8 | A22 | 25c yellow brn | 9.50 | *10.00* |
| 9 | A22 | 30c green | 9.00 | *9.50* |
| 10 | A22 | 40c ultra | 10.00 | *12.00* |
| 11 | A20 | 45c lt violet | 40.00 | *40.00* |
| 12 | A20 | 50c vermilion | 45.00 | *45.00* |
| *a.* | | Pair, one without overprint | 475.00 | |
| 13 | A20 | 65c gray green | 20.00 | 20.00 |
| 14 | A20 | 75c rose lilac | 14.00 | 14.00 |
| 15 | A22 | 90c red | 26.00 | *30.00* |
| 16 | A20 | 1fr dull blue | 30.00 | *34.00* |
| 17 | A22 | 1.50fr light blue | 40.00 | *42.50* |

Overprinted

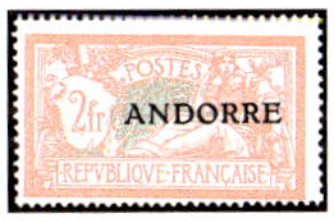


| | | | | |
|---|---|---|---|---|
| 18 | A18 | 2fr org & pale bl | 24.00 | *30.00* |
| 19 | A18 | 3fr brt vio & rose | 100.00 | *120.00* |
| 20 | A18 | 5fr dk bl & buff | 130.00 | *135.00* |
| 21 | A18 | 10fr grn & red | 275.00 | *275.00* |
| 22 | A18 | 20fr mag & grn | 375.00 | *450.00* |
| | | *Nos. 1-22 (22)* | 1,170. | *1,291.* |

See No. P1 for ½c on 1c gray.

Nos. 9, 15 and 17 were not issued in France without overprint.

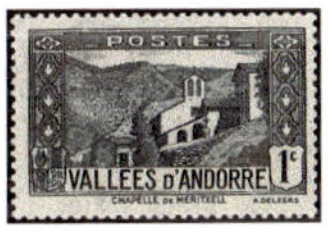


Chapel of Meritxell — A50

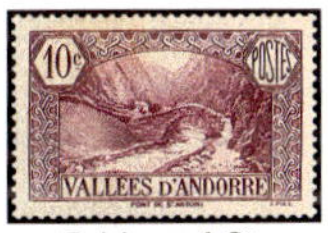


Bridge of St. Anthony A51

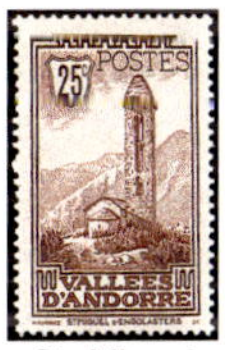


St. Miguel d'Engolasters A52

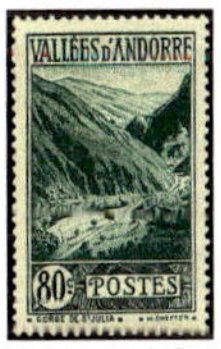


Gorge of St. Julia — A53

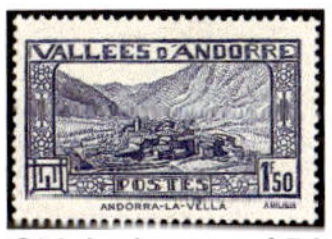


Old Andorra — A54

**1932-43 Engr. *Perf. 13***

| | | | | |
|---|---|---|---|---|
| 23 | A50 | 1c gray blk | .55 | *.55* |
| 24 | A50 | 2c violet | .95 | .80 |
| 25 | A50 | 3c brown | .80 | *.65* |
| 26 | A50 | 5c blue green | .95 | *.90* |
| 27 | A51 | 10c dull lilac | 1.30 | 1.30 |
| 28 | A50 | 15c deep red | 1.90 | 1.75 |
| 29 | A51 | 20c lt rose | 12.00 | 9.75 |
| 30 | A52 | 25c brown | 5.75 | 5.25 |
| 31 | A51 | 25c brn car ('37) | 11.00 | *14.00* |
| 32 | A51 | 30c emerald | 4.25 | 3.75 |
| 33 | A51 | 40c ultra | 12.00 | 0.75 |
| 34 | A51 | 40c brn blk ('39) | 1.45 | 1.40 |
| 35 | A51 | 45c lt red | 12.00 | 9.75 |
| 36 | A51 | 45c bl grn ('39) | 6.75 | 5.50 |
| 37 | A52 | 50c lilac rose | 13.50 | 13.00 |
| 38 | A51 | 50c lt vio ('39) | 6.50 | 5.75 |
| 38A | A51 | 50c grn ('40) | 2.00 | 1.00 |
| 39 | A51 | 55c lt vio ('38) | 23.00 | 16.50 |
| 40 | A51 | 60c yel brn ('38) | 1.50 | 1.25 |
| 41 | A52 | 65c yel grn | 55.00 | 55.00 |
| 42 | A51 | 65c blue ('38) | 17.00 | 13.50 |
| 43 | A51 | 70c red ('39) | 2.75 | 2.10 |
| 44 | A52 | 75c violet | 11.50 | 7.75 |
| 45 | A51 | 75c ultra ('39) | 5.00 | *4.75* |
| 46 | A51 | 80c green ('38) | 29.00 | 21.00 |
| 46A | A53 | 80c bl grn ('40) | .50 | .60 |
| 47 | A53 | 90c deep rose | 6.25 | 5.25 |
| 48 | A53 | 90c dk grn ('39) | 4.25 | 4.25 |
| 49 | A53 | 1fr blue grn | 20.00 | 13.50 |
| 50 | A53 | 1fr scarlet ('38) | 31.00 | 22.00 |
| 51 | A53 | 1fr dp ultra ('39) | .50 | .50 |
| 51A | A53 | 1.20fr brt vio ('42) | .50 | .50 |
| 52 | A50 | 1.25fr rose car ('33) | 55.00 | 42.50 |
| 52A | A50 | 1.25fr rose ('38) | 6.00 | 3.50 |
| 52B | A53 | 1.30fr sepia ('40) | .50 | .50 |
| 53 | A54 | 1.50fr ultra | 25.00 | 16.00 |
| 53A | A53 | 1.50fr crim ('40) | .50 | .50 |
| 54 | A53 | 1.75fr violet ('33) | 105.00 | *120.00* |
| 55 | A53 | 1.75fr dk bl ('38) | 50.00 | 47.50 |
| 56 | A53 | 2fr red violet | 11.50 | 9.50 |
| 56A | A50 | 2fr rose red ('40) | 1.60 | 1.60 |
| 56B | A50 | 2fr dk bl grn ('42) | .50 | .50 |
| 57 | A50 | 2.15fr dk vio ('38) | 60.00 | 55.00 |
| 58 | A50 | 2.25fr ultra ('39) | 9.00 | 8.00 |
| 58A | A50 | 2.40fr red ('42) | .65 | .50 |
| 59 | A50 | 2.50fr gray blk ('39) | 9.75 | 7.75 |
| 59A | A50 | 2.50fr dp ultra ('40) | 2.40 | 2.10 |
| 60 | A53 | 3fr orange brn | 14.00 | 9.00 |
| 60A | A50 | 3fr red brn ('40) | .50 | .50 |
| 60B | A50 | 4fr sl bl ('42) | .50 | .50 |
| 60C | A50 | 4.50fr dp vio ('42) | 1.75 | 1.60 |
| 61 | A54 | 5fr brown | .95 | .70 |
| 62 | A54 | 10fr violet | .95 | .70 |
| 62B | A54 | 15fr dp ultra ('42) | 1.20 | 1.00 |
| 63 | A54 | 20fr rose lake | 1.25 | .85 |
| 63A | A51 | 50fr turq bl ('43) | 1.75 | 1.50 |
| | | *Nos. 23-63A (56)* | 661.65 | 586.00 |

A 20c ultra exists but was not issued. Value: unused, $20,000; never hinged $30,000.

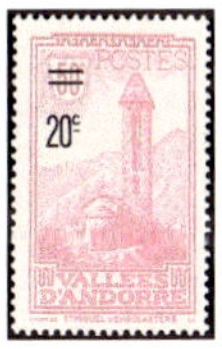


No. 37 Surcharged in Black

**1935, Sept. 18**

| | | | | |
|---|---|---|---|---|
| 64 | A52 | 20c on 50c lil rose | 18.50 | 17.00 |
| *a.* | | Double surcharge | *6,500.* | |

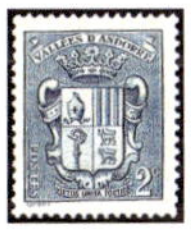


Coat of Arms — A55

**1936-42 *Perf. 14x13***

| | | | | |
|---|---|---|---|---|
| 65 | A55 | 1c black ('37) | .25 | .25 |
| 66 | A55 | 2c blue | .25 | *.25* |
| 67 | A55 | 3c brown | .25 | *.25* |
| 68 | A55 | 5c rose lilac | .25 | *.25* |
| 69 | A55 | 10c ultra ('37) | .25 | *.25* |
| 70 | A55 | 15c red violet | 2.75 | 2.25 |
| 71 | A55 | 20c emerald ('37) | .25 | *.25* |
| 72 | A55 | 30c cop red ('38) | .60 | *.70* |
| 72A | A55 | 30c blk brn ('42) | .25 | .40 |
| 73 | A55 | 35c Prus grn ('38) | 70.00 | 70.00 |
| 74 | A55 | 40c cop red ('42) | .60 | .60 |
| 75 | A55 | 50c Prus grn ('42) | .60 | .60 |
| 76 | A55 | 60c turq bl ('42) | .60 | .60 |
| 77 | A55 | 70c vio ('42) | .60 | .60 |
| | | *Nos. 65-77 (14)* | 77.50 | 77.25 |
| | | Set, never hinged | 135.00 | |

**Catalogue values for unused stamps in this section, from this point to the end of the section, are for Never Hinged items.**

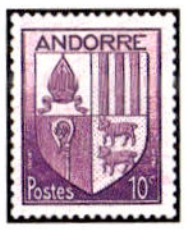


Coat of Arms — A56

**1944**

| | | | | |
|---|---|---|---|---|
| 78 | A56 | 10c violet | .30 | .30 |
| 79 | A56 | 30c deep magenta | .30 | .30 |
| 80 | A56 | 40c dull blue | .30 | .30 |
| 81 | A56 | 50c orange red | .30 | .30 |
| 82 | A56 | 60c black | .30 | .30 |
| 83 | A56 | 70c brt red violet | .30 | .30 |
| 84 | A56 | 80c blue green | .30 | .30 |
| | | *Nos. 78-84 (7)* | 2.10 | 2.10 |

See No. 114.

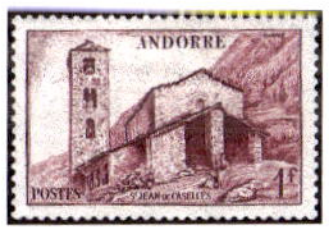


St. Jean de Caselles — A57

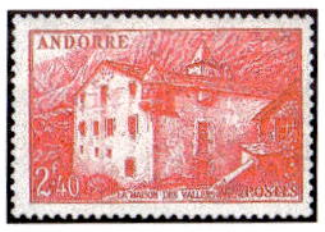


La Maison des Vallees — A58

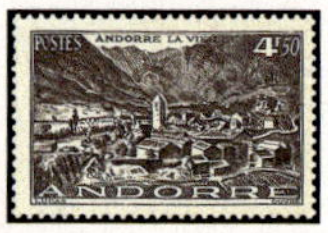
Old Andorra — A59

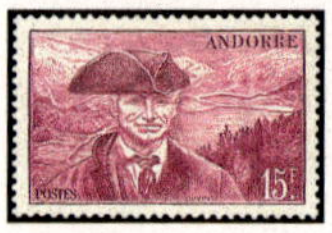
Provost — A60

**1944-47** *Perf. 13*

| | | | | | |
|---|---|---|---|---|---|
| 85 | A57 | 1fr | brown violet | .25 | .25 |
| 86 | A57 | 1.20fr | blue | .25 | .25 |
| 87 | A57 | 1.50fr | red | .25 | .25 |
| 88 | A57 | 2fr | dk blue grn | .25 | .25 |
| 89 | A58 | 2.40fr | rose red | .25 | .25 |
| 90 | A58 | 2.50fr | rose red ('46) | 7.25 | .80 |
| 91 | A58 | 3fr | sepia | .25 | .25 |
| 92 | A58 | 4fr | ultra | .40 | .25 |
| 93 | A59 | 4.50fr | brown blk | .40 | .25 |
| 94 | A58 | 4.50fr | dk bl grn ('47) | 9.50 | 5.50 |
| 95 | A59 | 5fr | ultra | .35 | .25 |
| 96 | A59 | 5fr | Prus grn ('46) | 1.40 | .50 |
| 97 | A59 | 6fr | rose car ('45) | .35 | .25 |
| 98 | A59 | 10fr | Prus green | .35 | .25 |
| 99 | A59 | 10fr | ultra ('46) | 2.40 | .40 |
| 100 | A60 | 15fr | rose lilac | .95 | .40 |
| 101 | A60 | 20fr | deep blue | .95 | .40 |
| 102 | A60 | 25fr | lt rose red ('46) | 5.50 | 1.90 |
| 103 | A60 | 40fr | dk green ('46) | 5.50 | 2.00 |
| 104 | A60 | 50fr | sepia | 1.75 | 1.40 |
| | | | *Nos. 85-104 (20)* | 38.55 | 16.05 |

**1948-49**

| | | | | | |
|---|---|---|---|---|---|
| 105 | A58 | 4fr | lt blue grn | 1.60 | .80 |
| 106 | A59 | 6fr | violet brn | .80 | .40 |
| 107 | A59 | 8fr | indigo | 1.25 | 1.20 |
| 108 | A59 | 12fr | bright red | 1.25 | 1.20 |
| 109 | A59 | 12fr | blue grn ('49) | 1.50 | .75 |
| 110 | A59 | 15fr | crimson ('49) | 1.00 | .55 |
| 111 | A60 | 18fr | deep blue | 5.00 | 2.40 |
| 112 | A60 | 20fr | dark violet | 3.50 | 2.00 |
| 113 | A60 | 25fr | ultra ('49) | 2.50 | 1.20 |
| | | | *Nos. 105-113 (9)* | 18.40 | 10.50 |

**1949-51** *Perf. 14x13, 13*

| | | | | | |
|---|---|---|---|---|---|
| 114 | A56 | 1fr | deep blue | .95 | .65 |
| 115 | A57 | 3fr | red ('51) | 7.25 | 4.75 |
| 116 | A57 | 4fr | sepia | 2.50 | 2.25 |
| 117 | A58 | 5fr | emerald | 3.75 | 2.75 |
| 118 | A58 | 5fr | purple ('51) | 13.50 | 4.75 |
| 119 | A58 | 6fr | blue grn ('51) | 7.25 | 3.25 |
| 120 | A58 | 8fr | brown | .95 | .75 |
| 121 | A59 | 15fr | blk brn ('51) | 16.00 | 3.00 |
| 122 | A59 | 18fr | rose red ('51) | 30.00 | 15.00 |
| 123 | A60 | 30fr | ultra ('51) | 40.00 | 22.50 |
| | | | *Nos. 114-123 (10)* | 122.15 | 59.65 |

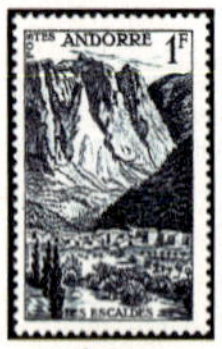
Les Escaldres Spa — A61

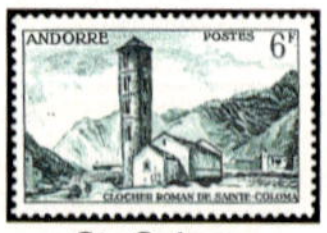
St. Coloma Belfry — A62

Designs: 15fr-25fr, Gothic cross. 30fr-75fr, Village of Les Bons.

**1955-58 Unwmk. Engr.** *Perf. 13*

| | | | | | |
|---|---|---|---|---|---|
| 124 | A61 | 1fr | dk gray bl | .25 | .25 |
| 125 | A61 | 2fr | dp green | .35 | .25 |
| 126 | A61 | 3fr | red | .35 | .25 |
| 127 | A61 | 5fr | chocolate | .35 | .25 |
| 128 | A62 | 6fr | dk bl grn | .80 | .80 |
| 129 | A62 | 8fr | rose brown | .80 | .80 |
| 130 | A62 | 10fr | brt violet | 1.25 | .80 |
| 131 | A62 | 12fr | indigo | 1.60 | .80 |
| 132 | A61 | 15fr | red | 1.60 | .85 |
| 133 | A61 | 18fr | blue grn | 2.00 | .85 |
| 134 | A61 | 20fr | dp purple | 3.50 | 2.00 |
| 135 | A61 | 25fr | sepia | 3.50 | 2.00 |
| 136 | A62 | 30fr | deep blue | 40.00 | 19.50 |
| 137 | A62 | 35fr | Prus bl ('57) | 12.00 | 7.25 |
| 138 | A62 | 40fr | dk green | 47.50 | 28.00 |
| 139 | A62 | 50fr | cerise | 4.50 | 3.25 |
| 140 | A62 | 65fr | purple ('58) | 12.00 | 6.50 |
| 141 | A62 | 70fr | chestnut ('57) | 7.25 | 6.50 |
| 142 | A62 | 75fr | violet blue | 65.00 | 45.00 |
| | | | *Nos. 124-142 (19)* | 204.60 | 125.90 |

Issued: 35fr, 70fr, 8/19; 65fr, 2/10; others, 2/15.

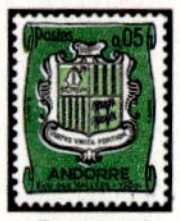
Coat of Arms A63

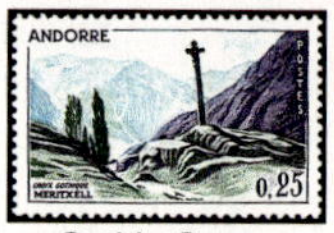
Gothic Cross, Meritxell A64

65c, 85c, 1fr, Engolasters Lake.

**1961, June 19 Typo.** *Perf. 14x13*

| | | | | | |
|---|---|---|---|---|---|
| 143 | A63 | 5c | brt green & blk | .25 | .25 |
| 144 | A63 | 10c | red, pink & blk | .25 | .25 |
| 145 | A63 | 15c | blue & black | .25 | .25 |
| 146 | A63 | 20c | yellow & brown | .40 | .30 |

**Engr.** *Perf. 13*

| | | | | | |
|---|---|---|---|---|---|
| 147 | A64 | 25c | violet, bl & grn | .60 | .30 |
| 148 | A64 | 30c | mar, ol grn & brn | .70 | .50 |
| 149 | A64 | 45c | indigo, bl & grn | 17.50 | 16.00 |
| 150 | A64 | 50c | pur, lt brn & ol grn | 1.50 | 1.25 |
| 151 | A64 | 65c | bl, ol & brn | 22.00 | 18.50 |
| 152 | A64 | 85c | rose lil, vio bl & brn | 22.00 | 18.50 |
| 153 | A64 | 1fr | grnsh bl, ind & brn | 1.50 | 1.25 |
| | | | *Nos. 143-153 (11)* | 66.95 | 57.35 |

See Nos. 161-166A.

Imperforates

Most stamps of Andorra, French Administration, from 1961 onward exist imperforate in issued and trial colors, and also in small presentation sheets in issued colors.

Common Design Types pictured following the introduction.

### Telstar Issue

Common Design Type

**1962, Sept. 29** **Engr.**

154 CD111 50c ultra & purple 2.00 1.60

1st television connection of the US and Europe through the Telstar satellite, 7/11-12.

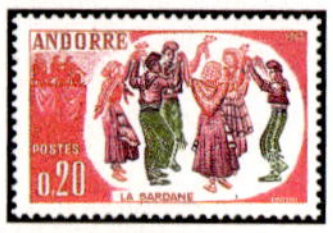
"La Sardane" — A66

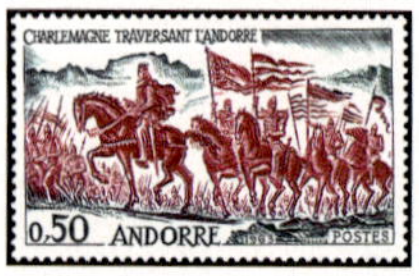
Charlemagne Crossing Andorra — A67

1fr, Louis le Debonnaire giving founding charter.

**1963, June 22 Unwmk.** *Perf. 13*

| | | | | | |
|---|---|---|---|---|---|
| 155 | A66 | 20c | lil rose, cl & ol grn | 5.00 | 5.00 |
| 156 | A67 | 50c | sl grn & dk car rose | 8.50 | 8.50 |
| 157 | A67 | 1fr | red brn, ultra & dk grn | 14.00 | 14.00 |
| | | | *Nos. 155-157 (3)* | 27.50 | 27.50 |

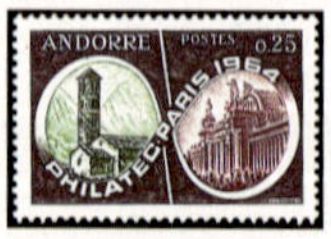
Old Andorra Church and Champs-Elysées Palace — A68

**1964, Jan. 20** **Engr.**

158 A68 25c vio brn, grn & blk 2.00 1.60

"PHILATEC," Intl. Philatelic and Postal Techniques Exhib., Paris, June 5-21, 1964.

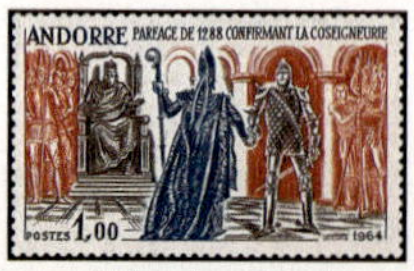
Bishop of Urgel and Seigneur of Caboet Confirming Co-Principality, 1288 — A69

Design: 60c, Napoleon re-establishing Co-principality, 1806.

**1964, Apr. 25 Engr.** *Perf. 13*

| | | | | | |
|---|---|---|---|---|---|
| 159 | A69 | 60c | dk brn, red brn & sl grn | 22.50 | 22.50 |
| 160 | A69 | 1fr | brt bl, org brn & blk | 22.50 | 22.50 |

### Arms Type of 1961

**1964, May 16 Typo.** *Perf. 14x13*

| | | | | | |
|---|---|---|---|---|---|
| 161 | A63 | 1c | dk blue & gray | .25 | .25 |
| 162 | A63 | 2c | black & orange | .25 | .25 |
| 163 | A63 | 12c | purple, emer & yel | .90 | .90 |
| 164 | A63 | 18c | black, lil & pink | 1.00 | 1.00 |
| | | | *Nos. 161-164 (4)* | 2.40 | 2.40 |

### Scenic Type of 1961

Designs: 40c, 45c, Gothic Cross, Meritxell. 60c, 90c, Pond of Engolasters.

**1965-71 Engr.** *Perf. 13*

| | | | | | |
|---|---|---|---|---|---|
| 165 | A64 | 40c | dk brn, org brn & sl grn | 1.00 | .80 |
| 165A | A64 | 45c | vio bl, ol bis & slate | 1.10 | .80 |
| 166 | A64 | 60c | org brn & dk brn | 1.60 | 1.25 |
| 166A | A64 | 90c | ultra, bl grn & bister | 2.00 | 1.00 |
| | | | *Nos. 165-166A (4)* | 5.70 | 3.85 |

Issued: 40c, 60c, Apr. 24, 1965. 45c, June 13, 1970. 90c, Aug. 28, 1971.

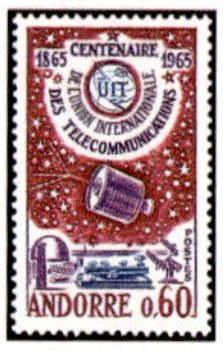
Syncom Satellite over Pleumeur-Bodou Station — A70

**1965, May 17** **Unwmk.**

167 A70 60c dp car, lil & bl 6.50 4.75

Cent. of the ITU.

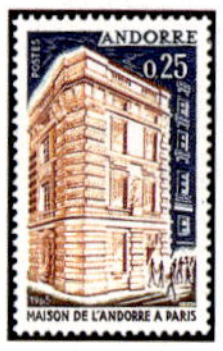
Andorra House, Paris — A71

**1965, June 5**

168 A71 25c dk bl, org brn & ol gray 1.25 .80

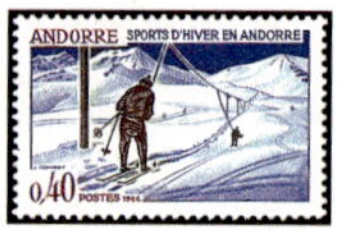
Ski Lift — A72

Design: 25c, Chair lift, vert.

**1966, Apr. 2 Engr.** *Perf. 13*

| | | | | | |
|---|---|---|---|---|---|
| 169 | A72 | 25c | brt bl, grn & dk brn | 1.60 | 1.25 |
| 170 | A72 | 40c | mag, brt ultra & sep | 2.40 | 1.60 |

Winter sports in Andorra.

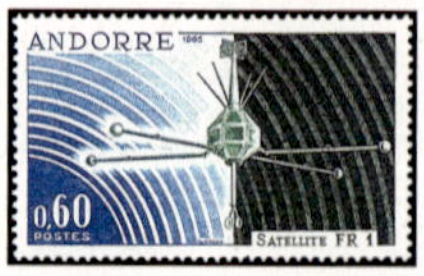
FR-1 Satellite A73

**1966, May 7** *Perf. 13*

171 A73 60c brt bl, grn & dk grn 2.10 1.60

Issued to commemorate the launching of the scientific satellite FR-1, Dec. 6, 1965.

### Europa Issue, 1966

Common Design Type

**1966, Sept. 24 Engr.** *Perf. 13*

**Size: 21½x35½mm**

172 CD9 60c brown *3.00 3.00*

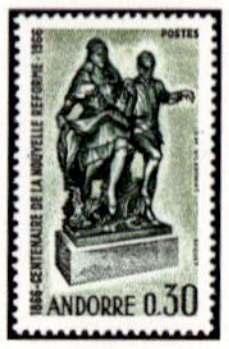
Folk Dancers, Sculpture by Josep Viladomat — A74

**1967, Apr. 29 Engr.** *Perf. 13*

173 A74 30c ol grn, dp grn & slate 1.25 .80

Cent. (in 1966) of the New Reform, which reaffirmed and strengthened political freedom in Andorra.

### Europa Issue, 1967

Common Design Type

**1967, Apr. 29**

**Size: 22x36mm**

| | | | | | |
|---|---|---|---|---|---|
| 174 | CD10 | 30c | bluish blk & lt bl | *4.25* | *1.75* |
| 175 | CD10 | 60c | dk red & brt pink | *6.50* | *4.50* |

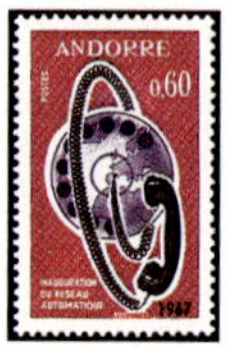
Telephone Encircling the Globe — A75

**1967, Apr. 29**

176 A75 60c dk car, vio & blk 2.00 1.25

Automatic telephone service.

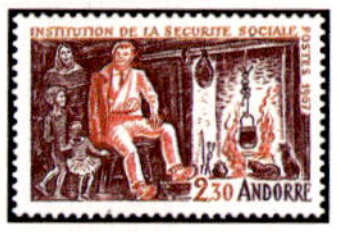
Injured Father at Home — A76

**1967, Sept. 23 Engr.** *Perf. 13*

177 A76 2.30fr ocher, dk red brn & brn red 9.75 7.50

Introduction of Social Security System.

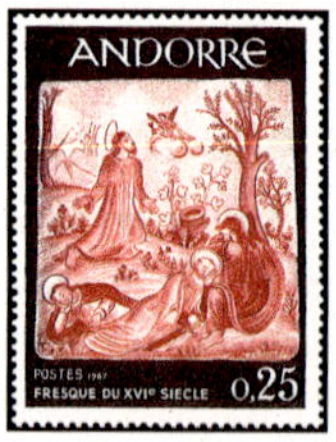
Jesus in Garden of Gethsemane A77

Designs (from 16th century frescoes in La Maison des Vallees): 30c, The Kiss of Judas. 60c, The Descent from the Cross (Pieta).

**1967, Sept. 23**

| | | | | | |
|---|---|---|---|---|---|
| 178 | A77 | 25c | black & red brn | .80 | .80 |
| 179 | A77 | 30c | purple & red lilac | .80 | .80 |
| 180 | A77 | 60c | indigo & Prus blue | 1.60 | 1.25 |
| | | | *Nos. 178-180 (3)* | 3.20 | 2.85 |

See Nos. 185-187.

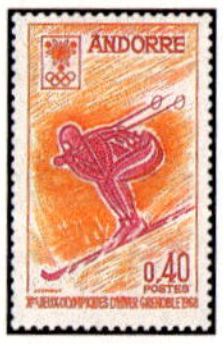
Downhill Skier — A78

**1968, Jan. 27 Engr.** *Perf. 13*

181 A78 40c org, ver & red lil 1.60 1.25

10th Winter Olympic Games, Grenoble, France, Feb. 6-18.

### Europa Issue, 1968

Common Design Type

**1968, Apr. 27 Engr.** *Perf. 13*

**Size: 36x22mm**

| | | | | | |
|---|---|---|---|---|---|
| 182 | CD11 | 30c | gray & brt bl | *6.50* | *3.00* |
| 183 | CD11 | 60c | brown & lilac | *10.00* | *7.00* |

# ANDORRA, FRENCH ADMINISTRATION

High Jump — A79

**1968, Oct. 12**    Engr.    Perf. 13
184 A79 40c brt blue & brn    1.50   1.25

19th Olympic Games, Mexico City, Oct. 12-27.

### Fresco Type of 1967

Designs (from 16th century frescoes in La Maison des Vallees): 25c, The Scourging of Christ. 30c, Christ Carrying the Cross. 60c, The Crucifixion. (All horiz.)

**1968, Oct. 12**
185 A77 25c dk grn & gray grn    .85   .80
186 A77 30c dk brown & lilac    .85   .80
187 A77 60c dk car & vio brn    1.75   1.25
     Nos. 185-187 (3)    3.45   2.85

### Europa Issue, 1969
### Common Design Type

**1969, Apr. 26**    Engr.    Perf. 13
188 CD12 40c rose car, gray & dl bl    7.50   3.50
189 CD12 70c indigo, dl red & ol    11.00   8.50

10th anniv. of the Conf. of European Postal and Telecommunications Administrations.

Kayak on Isere River — A80

**1969, Aug. 2**    Engr.    Perf. 13
190 A80 70c dk sl grn, ultra & ind    2.50   2.75

Intl. Canoe & Kayak Championships, Bourg-Saint-Maurice, Savoy, July 31-Aug. 6.

Drops of Water & Diamond — A80a

**1969, Sept. 27**    Engr.    Perf. 13
191 A80a 70c blk, dp ultra & grnsh bl    3.25   4.00

European Water Charter.

St. John, the Woman and the Dragon — A81

The Revelation (From the Altar of St. John, Caselles): 40c, St. John Hearing Voice from Heaven on Patmos. 70c, St. John and the Seven Candlesticks.

**1969, Oct. 18**
192 A81 30c brn, dp pur & brn red    .75   .75
193 A81 40c gray, dk brn & brn ol    1.10   1.10
194 A81 70c dk red, maroon & brt rose lilac    1.40   1.40
     Nos. 192-194 (3)    3.25   3.25

See Nos. 199-201, 207-209, 214-216.

Field Ball — A82

**1970, Feb. 21**    Engr.    Perf. 13
195 A82 80c multi    2.00   2.00

Issued to publicize the 7th International Field Ball Games, France, Feb. 26-Mar. 8.

### Europa Issue, 1970
### Common Design Type

**1970, May 2**    Engr.    Perf. 13
     Size: 36x22mm
196 CD13 40c orange    6.00   2.50
197 CD13 80c violet blue    14.00   6.00

Shot Put — A83

**1970, Sept. 11**    Engr.    Perf. 13
198 A83 80c bl & dk brn    2.00   2.00

1st European Junior Athletic Championships, Colombes, France, Sept. 11-13.

### Altar Type of 1969

The Revelation (from the Altar of St. John, Caselles): 30c, St. John recording angel's message. 40c, Angel erecting column symbolizing faithful in heaven. 80c, St. John's trial in kettle of boiling oil.

**1970, Oct. 24**
199 A81 30c dp car, dk brn & brt pur    .90   .90
200 A81 40c violet & slate grn    1.10   1.10
201 A81 80c ol, dk bl & car rose    1.90   1.90
     Nos. 199-201 (3)    3.90   3.90

Ice Skating — A84

**1971, Feb. 20**    Engr.    Perf. 13
202 A84 80c dk red, red lil & pur    2.00   2.00

World Figure Skating Championships, Lyons, France, Feb. 23-28.

Capercaillie — A85

Nature protection: No. 204, Brown bear.

**1971, Apr. 24**    Photo.    Perf. 13
203 A85 80c multicolored    3.25   3.25
     Engr.
204 A85 80c blue, grn & brn    2.40   2.40

### Europa Issue, 1971
### Common Design Type

**1971, May 8**    Engr.    Perf. 13
     Size: 35½x22mm
205 CD14 50c rose red    8.00   2.25
206 CD14 50c lt blue green    12.00   5.50

### Altar Type of 1969

The Revelation (from the Altar of St. John, Caselles): 30c, St. John preaching, Rev. 1:3. 50c, "The Sign of the Beast . . ." Rev. 16:1-2. 90c, The Woman, Rev. 17:1.

**1971, Sept. 18**
207 A81 30c dl grn, ol & brt grn    1.25   1.00
208 A81 50c rose car, org & ol brn    1.60   1.25
209 A81 90c blk, dp pur & bl    2.40   2.00
     Nos. 207-209 (3)    5.25   4.25

### Europa Issue 1972
### Common Design Type

**1972, Apr. 29**    Photo.    Perf. 13
     Size: 21½x37mm
210 CD15 50c brt mag & multi    7.50   2.50
211 CD15 90c multicolored    13.50   4.50

Golden Eagle — A86

**1972, May 27**    Engr.
212 A86 60c dk grn, olive & plum    5.00   3.25

Nature protection.

Shooting — A87

**1972, July 8**
213 A87 1fr dk purple    3.75   2.00

20th Olympic Games, Munich, 8/26-9/11.

### Altar Type of 1969

The Revelation (from the Altar of St. John, Caselles): 30c, St. John, bishop and servant. 50c, Resurrection of Lazarus. 90c, Angel with lance and nails.

**1972, Sept. 16**    Engr.    Perf. 13
214 A81 30c dk ol, gray & red lil    1.25   .85
215 A81 50c vio blue & slate    1.50   1.25
216 A81 90c dk Prus bl & sl grn    2.40   2.40
     Nos. 214-216 (3)    5.15   4.50

De Gaulle as Coprince of Andorra — A88

90c, De Gaulle in front of Maison des Vallées.

**1972, Oct. 23**    Engr.    Perf. 13
217 A88 50c violet blue    2.00   2.00
218 A88 90c dk carmine    3.00   3.00
   a. Pair, #217-218 + label    6.00   6.00

Visit of Charles de Gaulle to Andorra, 5th anniv.

See Nos. 399-400.

### Europa Issue 1973
### Common Design Type

**1973, Apr. 28**    Photo.    Perf. 13
     Size: 36x22mm
219 CD16 50c violet & multi    9.00   3.00
220 CD16 90c dk red & multi    11.00   8.00

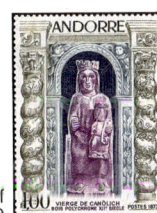
Virgin of Canolich — A89

**1973, June 16**    Engr.    Perf. 13
221 A89 1fr ol, Prus bl & vio    2.25   1.60

Lily — A90

45c, Iris. 50c, Columbine. 65c, Tobacco. No. 226, Pinks. No. 227, Narcissuses.

**1973-74**    Photo.    Perf. 13
222 A90 30c car rose & multi    .80   .80
223 A90 45c yel grn & multi    .40   .40
224 A90 50c buff & multi    1.75   1.75
225 A90 65c gray & multi    .40   .40
226 A90 70c ultra & multi    1.50   1.50
227 A90 90c grnsh bl & multi    1.25   1.25
     Nos. 222-227 (6)    6.10   6.10

Issued: 30c, 50c, No. 226, 7/7/73. 45c, 65c, No. 227, 4/6/74.
See Nos. 238-240.

Blue Titmouse — A91

Nature protection: 60c, Citril finch and mistletoe. 80c, Eurasian bullfinch. 1fr, Lesser spotted woodpecker.

**1973-74**    Photo.    Perf. 13
228 A91 60c buff & multi    4.00   1.75
229 A91 80c gray & multi    4.00   2.25
230 A91 90c gray & multi    2.75   1.25
231 A91 1fr yel grn & multi    2.75   1.60
     Nos. 228-231 (4)    13.50   6.85

Issued: 90c, 1fr, 10/27/73. 60c, 80c, 9/21/74.

### Europa Issue

Virgin of Pal — A92

90c, Virgin of Santa Coloma. Statues are polychrome 12th cent. carvings by rural artists.

**1974, Apr. 27**    Engr.    Perf. 13
232 A92 50c multicolored    9.00   3.00
233 A92 90c multicolored    12.50   7.00

Arms of Andorra and Cahors Bridge — A93

**1974, Aug. 24**    Engr.    Perf. 13
234 A93 1fr blue, vio & org    1.00   .80

First anniv. of meeting of the co-princes of Andorra: Pres. Georges Pompidou of France and Msgr. Juan Marti Alanis, Bishop of Urgel.

Mail Box, Chutes and Globe — A94

**1974, Oct. 5**    Engr.    Perf. 13
235 A94 1.20fr multi    1.25   1.25

Centenary of Universal Postal Union.

Coronation of St. Marti, 16th Century — A95

Europa: 80c, Crucifixion, 16th cent., vert.

# ANDORRA, FRENCH ADMINISTRATION

**Perf. 11½x13, 13x11½**
**1975, Apr. 26**     Photo.
236 A95   80c gold & multi    4.50   3.00
237 A95   1.20fr gold & multi   6.50   4.00

### Flower Type of 1973
Designs: 60c, Gentian. 80c, Anemone. 1.20fr, Autumn crocus.

**1975, May 10**    Photo.    Perf. 13
238 A90   60c olive & multi    .50   .40
239 A90   80c brt rose & multi   1.25   .80
240 A90   1.20fr green & multi   1.25   .80
Nos. 238-240 (3)    3.00   2.00

Abstract Design — A96

**1975, June 7**    Engr.    Perf. 13
241 A96   2fr bl, magenta & emer   1.75   1.50
ARPHILA 75 International Philatelic Exhibition, Paris, June 6-16.

A97

**1975, Aug. 23**    Engr.    Perf. 13
242 A97   80c violet bl & blk   1.00   1.00
Georges Pompidou (1911-74), pres. of France and co-prince of Andorra (1969-74).

A98

**1975, Nov. 8**    Engr.    Perf. 13
243 A98   1.20fr Costume, IWY Emblem   1.25   1.00
International Women's Year.

Skier and Snowflake — A99

**1976, Jan. 31**    Engr.    Perf. 13
244 A99   1.20fr multicolored   1.50   1.10
12th Winter Olympic Games, Innsbruck, Austria, Feb. 4-15.

Telephone and Satellite — A100

**1976, Mar. 20**    Engr.    Perf. 13
245 A100   1fr multicolored   1.00   1.00
Centenary of first telephone call by Alexander Graham Bell, Mar. 10, 1976.

Catalan Forge — A101

Europa: 1.20fr, Woolen worker.

**1976, May 8**       Perf. 13
246 A101   80c multi   3.25   1.00
247 A101   1.20fr multi   4.75   1.75

Thomas Jefferson — A102

**1976, July 3**    Engr.    Perf. 13
248 A102   1.20fr multi   1.25   1.00
American Bicentennial.

Trapshooting — A103

**1976, July 17**    Engr.    Perf. 13
249 A103   2fr multi   1.75   1.40
21st Olympic Games, Montreal, Canada, July 17-Aug. 1.

Meritxell Sanctuary and Old Chapel A104

**1976, Sept. 4**    Engr.    Perf. 13
250 A104   1fr multi   1.00   1.00
Dedication of rebuilt Meritxell Church, Sept. 8, 1976.

Apollo — A105

Design: 1.40fr, Morio butterfly.

**1976, Oct. 16**    Photo.    Perf. 13
251 A105   80c black & multi   1.90   1.25
252 A105   1.40fr salmon & multi   3.25   2.00
Nature protection.

Ermine — A106

**1977, Apr. 2**    Photo.    Perf. 13
253 A106   1fr vio bl, gray & blk   1.60   1.25
Nature protection.

St. Jean de Caselles — A107

Europa: 1.40fr, Sant Vicens Castle.

**1977, Apr. 30**    Engr.    Perf. 13
254 A107   1fr multi   3.00   1.25
255 A107   1.40fr multi   4.75   2.00

Manual Digest, 1748, Arms of Andorra — A108

**1977, June 11**    Engr.    Perf. 13
256 A108   80c grn, bl & brn   .90   .90
Establishment of Institute of Andorran Studies.

St. Romanus of Caesarea — A109

**1977, July 23**    Engr.    Perf. 12½x13
257 A109   2fr multi   1.75   1.50
Design from altarpiece in Church of St. Roma de les Bons.

General Council Chamber A110

Guillem d'Arény Plandolit A111

**1977, Sept. 24**    Engr.    Perf. 13
258 A110   1.10fr multi   1.40   1.00
259 A111   2fr car & dk brn   1.40   1.00
Andorran heritage. Guillem d'Arény Plandolit started Andorran reform movement in 1866.

Squirrel — A112

**1978, Mar. 18**    Engr.    Perf. 13
260 A112   1fr multi   .90   .75

Flag and Valira River Bridge — A113

**1978, Apr. 8**
261 A113   80c multi   .65   .65
Signing of the treaty establishing the Co-Principality of Andorra, 700th anniv.

Pal Church — A114

Europa: 1.40fr, Charlemagne's Castle, Charlemagne on horseback, vert.

**1978, Apr. 29**    Engr.    Perf. 13
262 A114   1fr multi   3.00   1.50
263 A114   1.40fr multi   5.50   2.75

Virgin of Sispony — A115

**1978, May 20**    Engr.    Perf. 12x13
264 A115   2fr multi   1.50   1.25

Visura Tribunal — A116

**1978, June 24**    Engr.    Perf. 13
265 A116   1.20fr multi   1.00   .50

Preamble of 1278 Treaty A117

**1978, Sept. 2**    Engr.    Perf. 13x12½
266 A117   1.70fr multi   1.00   .75
700th anniversary of the signing of treaty establishing Co-Principality of Andorra.

Pyrenean Chamois — A118

**1979, Mar. 26**    Engr.    Perf. 13
267 A118   1fr multi   .65   .65

White Partridges — A119

**1979, Apr. 7**    Photo.    Perf. 13
268 A119   1.20fr multi   1.50   .75
Nature protection. See Nos. 288-289.

French Mailman, 1900 — A120

Europa: 1.70fr, 1st French p.o. in Andorra.

**1979, Apr. 28**    Engr.    Perf. 13
269 A120   1.20fr multi   2.00   .75
270 A120   1.70fr multi   4.00   1.25

Falcon, Pre-Roman Painting — A121

**1979, June 2**    Engr.    Perf. 12½x13
271 A121   2fr multi   1.10   .90

# ANDORRA, FRENCH ADMINISTRATION

Child with Lambs, Church, IYC Emblem. — A122

**1979, July 7**    Photo.    Perf. 13
272 A122 1.70fr multi    1.20   .85

International Year of the Child.

Trobada Monument — A123

**1979, Sept. 29**    Engr.    Perf. 13
273 A123 2fr multi    1.25 1.00

Co-Principality of Andorra, 700th anniv

Judo Hold — A124

**1979, Nov. 24**    Engr.    Perf. 13
274 A124 1.30fr multi    .90   .75

World Judo Championships, Paris, Dec. 1979

Farm House, Cortinada — A125

**1980, Jan. 26**    Engr.    Perf. 13
275 A125 1.10fr multi    .75   .60

Cross-Country Skiing — A126

**1980, Feb. 9**
276 A126 1.80fr ultra & lil rose   1.50 1.10

13th Winter Olympic Games, Lake Placid, NY, Feb. 12-24.

A128

**1980, Aug. 30**    Engr.    Perf. 13
278 A128 1.20fr multi    .75   .75

World Bicycling championships.

A129

Europa: 1.30fr, Charlemagne (742-814). 1.80fr, Napoleon I (1769-1821).

**1980, Apr. 26**    Engr.    Perf. 13
279 A129 1.30fr multi    1.75   .60
280 A129 1.80fr gray grn & brn   2.00 1.00

Pyrenees Lily — A130

1.10fr, Dog-toothed violet.

**1980**    Photo.
281 A130 1.10fr multicolored    .75   .55
282 A130 1.30fr shown    .75   .65

Nature protection. Issue dates: 1.10fr, June 21; 1.30fr, May 17.

De La Vall House, 400th Anniversary of Restoration A131

**1980, Sept. 6**    Engr.
283 A131 1.40fr multi    .75   .65

Angel, Church of St. Cerni de Nagol, Pre-Romanesque Fresco — A132

**1980, Oct. 25**    Perf. 13x12½
284 A132 2fr multi    1.25 1.25

Bordes de Mereig Mountain Village — A133

**1981, Mar. 21**    Engr.    Perf. 13
285 A133 1.40fr bl gray & dk brn   .80   .80

**Europa Issue**

Ball de l'Ossa, Winter Game — A134

2fr, El Contrapas dance

**1981, May 16**    Engr.
286 A134 1.40fr shown    1.50   .50
287 A134 2fr multicolored    1.75 1.00

**Bird Type of 1979**

1.20fr, Phylloscopus bonelli. 1.40fr, Tichodroma muraria.

**1981, June 20**    Photo.
288 A119 1.20fr multicolored    .65   .65
289 A119 1.40fr multicolored    1.00   .65

World Fencing Championship, Clermont-Ferrand, July 2-13 — A135

**1981, July 4**    Engr.
290 A135 2fr bl & blk    .90   .80

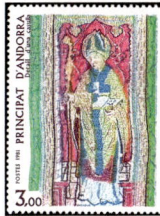

St. Martin, 12th Cent. Tapestry — A136

**1981, Sept. 5**    Engr.    Perf. 12x13
291 A136 3fr multi    1.25 1.00

Intl. Drinking Water Decade — A137

**1981, Oct. 17**    Perf. 13
292 A137 1.60fr multi    .75   .50

Intl. Year of the Disabled — A138

**1981, Nov. 7**
293 A138 2.30fr multi    1.00   .65

Europa 1982 — A139

1.60fr, Creation of Andorran govt., 1982. 2.30fr, Land Council, 1419.

**1982, May 8**    Engr.    Perf. 13
294 A139 1.60fr multi    1.50   .70
295 A139 2.30fr multi    2.00   .70

1982 World Cup A140

Various soccer players

**1982, June 12**    Engr.    Perf. 13
296   1.60fr red & dk brn    .80   .65
297   2.60fr red & dk brn    1.10   .95
  a. A140 Pair, #296-297 + label   2.25 2.25

Souvenir Sheet

No. 52 A141

**1982, Aug. 21**    Engr.
298 A141 5fr blk & rose car    2.40 2.40

1st Andorran Stamp Exhib., 8/21-9/19.

Horse, Roman Wall Painting A142

**1982, Sept. 4**    Photo.    Perf. 13x12½
299 A142 3fr multi    1.25 1.00

Wild Cat — A143

**1982, Oct. 9**    Engr.    Perf. 13
300 A143 1.80fr shown    1.10   .85
301 A143 2.60fr Pine trees    .90   .75

TB Bacillus Centenary — A144

**1982, Nov. 13**
302 A144 2.10fr Koch, lungs    .85   .65

St. Thomas Aquinas (1225-74) — A145

**1982, Dec. 4**
303 A145 2fr multi    .85   .65

Manned Flight Bicentenary A146

**1983, Feb. 26**    Engr.
304 A146 2fr multi    .90   .75

Nature Protection — A147

**1983, Apr. 16**    Engr.    Perf. 13
305 A147 1fr Birch trees    .40   .30
306 A147 1.50fr Trout    .75   .55

See Nos. 325-326.

Catalane Gold Works — A148

**1983, May 7**    Engr.    Perf. 13
307 A148 1.80fr Exterior    1.00   .50
308 A148 2.60fr Interior    1.60   .80

Europa.

30th Anniv. of Customs Cooperation Council — A149

3fr, Letter of King Louis XIII.

**1983, May 14**
309 A149 3fr multicolored    1.25 1.00

First Arms of Valleys of Andorra — A150

**1983, Sept. 3**    Engr.    Perf. 13
310 A150   5c olive grn & red    .25   .25
311 A150 10c grn & olive grn    .25   .25
312 A150 20c brt pur & red    .25   .25

## ANDORRA, FRENCH ADMINISTRATION

| | | | | |
|---|---|---|---|---|
| 313 | A150 | 30c brn vio & red | .35 | .35 |
| 314 | A150 | 40c dk bl & vio | .35 | .35 |
| 315 | A150 | 50c gray & red | .25 | .25 |
| 316 | A150 | 1fr deep magenta | .25 | .25 |
| 317 | A150 | 2fr org red & red brn | .90 | .40 |
| 318 | A150 | 5fr dk brn & red | 1.25 | .80 |
| | | Nos. 310-318 (9) | 4.10 | 3.15 |

See Nos. 329-335, 380-385, 464-465.

Painting, Cortinada Church — A151

**1983, Sept. 24**    Perf. 12x13
319 A151 4fr multi    1.75 1.00

Plandolit House — A152

**1983, Oct. 15**    Photo.    Perf. 13
320 A152 1.60fr dp ultra & brn    .75 .55

1984 Winter Olympics — A153

**1984, Feb. 18**    Engr.
321 A153 2.80fr multicolored    1.25 .90

Pyrenees Region Work Community (Labor Org.) — A154

**1984, Apr. 28**    Engr.    Perf. 13
322 A154 3fr brt blue & sepia    1.20 .90

Europa (1959-84) — A155

**1984, May 5**    Engr.
323 A155 2fr brt grn    1.60 .80
324 A155 2.80fr rose car    2.75 1.40

**Nature Protection Type of 1983**

**1984, July 7**    Engr.    Perf. 13
325 A147 1.70fr Chestnut tree    .80 .40
326 A147 2.10fr Walnut tree    1.20 .65

Pyrenees Art Center — A155a

**1984, Sept. 7**    Engr.
327 A155a 3fr multi    1.40 1.00

Romanesque Fresco, Church of St. Cerni de Nagol — A156

**1984, Nov. 17**    Perf. 12x13
328 A156 5fr multi    2.25 1.90

**First Arms Type of 1983**

**1984-87**    Engr.    Perf. 13
329 A150 1.90fr emerald    3.25 .80
330 A150 2.20fr red orange    1.25 .40
   a. Bklt. pane, 2 #329, 6 #330    15.00
331 A150 3fr bl grn & red brn    1.50 1.00
332 A150 4fr brt org & brn    3.50 1.25
333 A150 10fr brn org & blk    3.50 1.60
334 A150 15fr grn & dk grn    5.00 2.40
335 A150 20fr brt bl & red brn    7.00 2.75
   Nos. 329-335 (7)    25.00 10.20

Nos. 329-330 issued in booklets only.
Issued: 3fr, 20fr, 12/1/84; 10fr, 2/9/85; 4fr, 15fr, 4/19/86; 1.90fr, 2.20fr, 3/28/87.

Saint Julia Valley — A157

**1985, Apr. 13**    Engr.
336 A157 2fr multi    1.00 .60

Europa 1985 — A158

2.10fr, Le Val D'Andorre. 3fr, Instruments.

**1985, May 4**    Engr.
337 A158 2.10fr multicolored    1.75 .75
338 A158 3fr multicolored    4.00 1.25

Intl. Youth Year — A159

**1985, June 8**    Engr.
339 A159 3fr multicolored    1.25 .90

Wildlife Conservation A160

1.80fr, Anas platyrhynchos. 2.20fr, Carduelis carduelis.

**1985, Aug. 3**    Photo.
340 A160 1.80fr multicolored    1.00 .65
341 A160 2.20fr multicolored    1.40 .85

Two Saints, Medieval Fresco in St. Cerni de Nagol Church — A161

**1985, Sept. 14**    Engr.    Perf. 12½x13
342 A161 5fr multicolored    2.00 1.75

Postal Museum Inauguration — A162

**1986, Mar. 22**    Engr.    Perf. 13
343 A162 2.20fr like No. 269    1.00 .65

Europa 1986 — A163

**1986, May 3**    Engr.    Perf. 13
344 A163 2.20fr Ansalonga    2.50 .90
345 A163 3.20fr Isard    5.00 1.60

1986 World Cup Soccer Championships, Mexico — A164

**1986, June 14**
346 A164 3fr multi    1.50 1.00

Angonella Lake — A165

**1986, June 28**
347 A165 2.20fr multi    1.00 .70

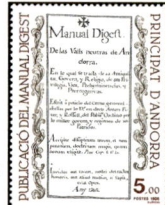

Manual Digest Frontispiece, 1748 — A166

**1986, Sept. 6**    Engr.
348 A166 5fr chnt brn, gray ol & blk    2.25 1.40

Intl. Peace Year — A167

**1986, Sept. 27**
349 A167 1.90fr bl gray & grnsh bl    1.00 .65

St. Vincenc d'Enclar — A168

**1986, Oct. 18**    Engr.    Perf. 13½x13
350 A168 1.90fr multicolored    .95 .65

Contemporary Natl. Coat of Arms — A169

**1987, Mar. 27**    Litho.    Perf. 12½x13
351 A169 2.20fr multi    1.60 1.60
Visit of the French co-prince.

Europa 1987 — A170

2.20fr, Meritxell Sanctuary. 3.40fr, Pleta D'Ordino.

**1987, May 2**    Engr.    Perf. 13
352 A170 2.20fr multicolored    2.00 .80
353 A170 3.40fr multicolored    4.50 2.00

Ransol Village — A171

**1987, June 13**    Photo.
354 A171 1.90fr multicolored    1.25 1.00

Nature — A172

1.90fr, Cavall rogenc. 2.20fr, Graellsia isabellae.

**1987, July 4**
355 A172 1.90fr multicolored    1.25 .80
356 A172 2.20fr multicolored    1.60 1.25

Aryalsu, Romanesque Painting, La Cortinada Church — A173

**Litho. & Engr.**
**1987, Sept. 5**    Perf. 12½x13
357 A173 5fr multi    2.50 1.60

Hiker Looking at Map — A174

**1987, Sept. 19**    Engr.    Perf. 13
358 A174 2fr olive, grn & dark brn vio    1.00 .60

Medieval Iron Key, La Cortinada — A175

**1987, Oct. 17**    Litho.
359 A175 3fr multi    1.25 1.00

Andorran Coat of Arms — A176

**Booklet Stamp**
**1988, Feb. 6**    Engr.    Perf. 13
360 A176 2.20fr red    1.00 .50
   a. Bklt. pane of 5    5.00
   Complete bklt., 2 #360a    10.00
See Nos. 386-388.

Shoemaker's Last from Roc de l'Oral — A177

**1988, Feb. 13**    Photo.
361 A177 3fr multi    1.50 1.10

# ANDORRA, FRENCH ADMINISTRATION

Rugby — A178

**1988, Mar. 19    Engr.    Perf. 13½x13**
362  A178  2.20fr blk, org, turq grn    1.20   .95

Europa 1988 — A179

Transport and communication: 2.20fr, Broadcast tower. 3.60fr, Computer graphics.

**1988, Apr. 30    Engr.    Perf. 13**
363  A179  2.20fr multicolored    1.75   .90
364  A179  3.60fr multicolored    3.75  1.10

Hot Springs, Escaldes — A180

**1988, May 14    Engr.**
365  A180  2.20fr Prus blue, org brn & emer    1.25   .80

Tor D'Ansalonga Farmhouse, Ansalonga Pass — A181

**1988, June 11    Engr.**
366  A181  2fr multi    1.10   .65

Sheepdog — A182

**1988, July 2    Photo.**
367  A182     2fr shown    1.50   .60
368  A182  2.20fr Hare    1.50   .60

Roman Fresco, 8th Cent., St. Steven's Church, Andorre-La-Vieille — A183

**1988, Sept. 3    Engr.    Perf. 13x12½**
369  A183  5fr multicolored    2.25  1.50

French Revolution, Bicent. — A184

**1989, Jan. 1    Litho.    Perf. 13**
370  A184  2.20fr red & vio bl    1.00  1.00

Poble de Pal Village — A185

**1989, Mar. 4    Engr.    Perf. 13**
371  A185  2.20fr indigo & lilac    1.00   .65

Europa 1989 — A186

Children's games: 2.20fr, Human tower. 3.60fr, The handkerchief.

**1989, Apr. 29    Engr.    Perf. 13**
372  A186  2.20fr multi    2.00   .80
373  A186  3.60fr multi    2.50  1.75

Red Cross — A187

**1989, May 6**
374  A187  3.60fr multi    1.75  1.25

Visigothic — Merovingian Age Cincture from a Column, St. Vicenc D'Anclar — A188

**1989, June 3    Photo.**
375  A188  3fr multi    1.40  1.10

Wildlife — A189

**1989, Sept. 16    Engr.    Perf. 13**
376  A189  2.20fr Wild boar    1.25   .90
377  A189  3.60fr Newt    2.00  1.25

Scene of Salome from the Retable of St. Michael of Mosquera, Encamp — A190

**1989, Oct. 14    Perf. 13x13½**
378  A190  5fr multi    2.50  1.25

La Margineda Bridge — A191

**1990, Feb. 26    Engr.    Perf. 13**
379  A191  2.30fr multi    1.25   .60
Tourism.

**Arms Types of 1983 and 1988**

**1990-93    Engr.    Perf. 13**
380  A150  2.10fr green    1.00   .40
381  A150  2.20fr green    1.25   .40
382  A150  2.30fr vermilion    1.00   .40
383  A150  2.40fr green    1.40   .40
384  A150  2.50fr vermilion    1.25   .40
385  A150  2.80fr vermilion    1.60   .40
      Nos. 380-385 (6)    7.50  2.80

**Booklet Stamps**
**Perf. 13**
386  A176  2.30fr red    1.00   .40
   a.   Booklet pane of 5    5.00
387  A176  2.50fr vermilion    1.25   .40
   a.   Booklet pane of 5    6.25

388  A176  2.80fr red    1.25   .40
   c.   Booklet pane of 5    6.25
        Nos. 386-388 (3)    3.50  1.20
Issued: 2.20fr, #384, 10/26/91; #387, 10/21/91; 2.40fr, 2.80fr, 8/9/93; 2.10fr, 2.30fr, 1990.

Llorts Mines — A193

**1990, Apr. 21    Engr.    Perf. 12½x13**
390  A193  3.20fr multicolored    1.75  1.00

Europa — A194

Designs: 2.30fr, Early post office. 3.20fr, Modern post office.

**1990, May 5    Perf. 13**
391  A194  2.30fr blk & scar    2.00   .75
392  A194  3.20fr scar & vio    3.00  1.50

Otter — A195

**1990, May 25    Perf. 12x13**
393  A195  2.30fr Roses, vert.    1.10   .55
394  A195  3.20fr shown    1.75  1.00

Censer of St. Roma of Les Bons — A196

**1990, June 25    Perf. 12½x13**
395  A196  3fr multicolored    1.25   .65

Tobacco Drying Sheds, Les Bons — A197

**1990, Sept. 15    Engr.    Perf. 12½x13**
396  A197  2.30fr multi    1.00   .65

St. Coloma (Detail) — A198

**1990, Oct. 8    Perf. 12½x13**
397  A198  5fr multi    2.50  1.50

Coin from Church of St. Eulalia d'Encamp — A199

**1990, Oct. 27    Litho.    Perf. 13**
398  A199  3.20fr multi    1.40   .75

**De Gaulle Type of 1972 Dated 1990**
**1990, Oct. 23    Engr.    Perf. 13**
399  A88  2.30fr vio bl    1.00   .65
400  A88  3.20fr dk car    1.25  1.10
   a.   Pair, #399-400 + label    2.50  2.50
Birth centenary of De Gaulle.

4th Games of the Small European States — A200

**1991, Apr. 8    Photo.    Perf. 13**
401  A200  2.50fr multicolored    1.00   .60

Chapel of St. Roma Dels Vilars — A201

**1991, Mar. 9    Engr.    Perf. 13**
402  A201  2.50fr multicolored    1.10   .65

Europa — A202

2.50fr, TV satellite. 3.50fr, Telescope, horiz.

**1991, Apr. 27    Perf. 13x12½, 12½x13**
403  A202  2.50fr multicolored    2.75  1.75
404  A202  3.50fr multicolored    4.50  2.25

Bottles from Tombs of St. Vincenc d'Enclar — A203

**1991, May 11    Photo.    Perf. 13**
405  A203  3.20fr multicolored    1.50  1.00

Farm Animals — A204

**1991, June 22    Engr.    Perf. 13**
406  A204  2.50fr Sheep    1.25   .80
407  A204  3.50fr Cow    2.00  1.25

Petanque World Championships A205

**1991, Sept. 14    Engr.    Perf. 13**
408  A205  2.50fr multicolored    1.25   .95

Wolfgang Amadeus Mozart, Death Bicent. — A206

**1991, Oct. 5**
409  A206  3.40fr multicolored    1.75  1.10

Virgin and Child of St. Julia and St. Germa — A207

**1991, Nov. 16    Engr.    Perf. 12½x13**
410  A207  5fr multicolored    2.00  1.00

# ANDORRA, FRENCH ADMINISTRATION

1992 Winter Olympics, Albertville — A208

**1992, Feb. 10**    Litho.    *Perf. 13*
411 A208 2.50fr Slalom skiing    1.25   1.00
412 A208 3.40fr Figure skating    1.25   1.00
   a.   Pair, #411-412 + label    2.75   2.75

Church of St. Andrew of Arinsal — A209

**1992, Mar. 21**    Engr.    *Perf. 12x13*
413 A209 2.50fr black & tan    .75   .50

Discovery of America, 500th Anniv. — A210

2.50fr, Columbus' fleet. 3.40fr, Landing in New World.

**1992, Apr. 25**    *Perf. 13*
414 A210 2.50fr multicolored    2.50   1.00
415 A210 3.40fr multicolored    5.00   2.00
Europa.

1992 Summer Olympics, Barcelona — A211

**1992, June 8**    Litho.    *Perf. 13*
416 A211 2.50fr Kayaking    1.25   1.00
417 A211 3.40fr Shooting    1.25   1.00
   a.   Pair, #416-417 + label    2.75   2.75

European Globeflower — A212

Design: 3.40fr, Vulture, horiz.

**1992, July 6**
418 A212 2.50fr multicolored    1.25   .65
419 A212 3.40fr multicolored    1.75   1.00

Martyrdom of St. Eulalia — A213

**1992, Sept. 14**    Photo.    *Perf. 13*
420 A213 4fr multicolored    1.50   .95

Sculpture by Mauro Staccioli — A214

**1992, Oct. 5**    Engr.    *Perf. 12½x13*
421 A214 5fr multicolored    2.00   1.00
Ordino Arcalis '91.

Tempest in a Tea Cup, by Dennis Oppenheim — A215

**1992, Nov. 14**    Engr.    *Perf. 13x12½*
422 A215 5fr multicolored    2.00   1.00

Skiing in Andorra — A216

Ski resorts: No. 423: a, 2.50fr, Soldeu El Tarter. b, 3.40fr, Arinsal.
No. 424: a, 2.50fr, Pas de la Casa-Grau Roig. b, 2.50fr, Ordino Arcalis. c, 3.40fr, Pal.

**1993, Mar. 13**    Litho.    *Perf. 13*
423 A216 Pair, #a.-b. + label    2.60   2.60
424 A216 Strip of 3, #a.-c.    3.75   3.75

Sculptures A217

Europa: 2.50fr, "Estructures Autogeneradores," by Jorge du Bon, vert. 3.40fr, Sculpture, "Fisicromia per Andorra," by Carlos Cruz-Diez.

**1993, May 15**    Engr.    *Perf. 12½x13*
425 A217 2.50fr multicolored    1.60   1.25
   Litho.    *Perf. 14x13½*
426 A217 3.40fr multicolored    2.00   1.50

Butterflies — A218

2.50fr, Polymmatus icarus. 4.20fr, Nymphalidae.

**1993, June 28**    Litho.    *Perf. 13*
427 A218 2.50fr multicolored    1.20   .65
428 A218 4.20fr multicolored    1.90   1.40

Tour de France Bicycle Race — A219

**1993, July 20**    Litho.    *Perf. 13*
429 A219 2.50fr multicolored    1.25   .65

Andorra School, 10th Anniv. — A220

**1993, Sept. 20**    Litho.    *Perf. 13*
430 A220 2.80fr multicolored    1.25   1.00

Un Lloc Paga, by Michael Warren — A221

**1993, Oct. 18**    Engr.    *Perf. 12½x13*
431 A221 5fr blue & black    2.00   1.50

Sculpture, by Erik Dietman — A222

**1993, Nov. 8**    Engr.    *Perf. 12½x13*
432 A222 5fr multicolored    2.00   1.50

1994 Winter Olympics, Lillehammer A223

**1994, Feb. 21**    Litho.    *Perf. 13*
433 A223 3.70fr multicolored    2.25   1.50

1st Anniversary of the Constitution — A224

Designs: 2.80fr, Monument, by Emili Armengol. 3.70fr, Stone tablet with inscription.

**1994, Mar. 15**    Litho.    *Perf. 13*
434 A224 2.80fr multicolored    1.25   1.00
435 A224 3.70fr multicolored    1.25   1.00
   a.   Pair, #434-435 + label    2.75   2.75

European Discoveries A225

Europa: 2.80fr, Discovery of AIDS virus. 3.70fr, Radio diffusion.

**1994, May 7**    Litho.    *Perf. 13*
436 A225 2.80fr multicolored    1.75   .90
437 A225 3.70fr multicolored    2.75   1.25

1994 World Cup Soccer Championships, US — A226

**1994, June 20**
438 A226 3.70fr multicolored    2.00   1.25

Tourist Sports — A227

Designs: No. 439, Mountain climbing. No. 440, Fishing. No. 441, Horseback riding. No. 442, Mountain biking.

**1994, July 11**
439 A227 2.80fr multicolored    1.20   1.00
440 A227 2.80fr multicolored    1.20   1.00
   a.   Pair, #439-440 + label    2.50   2.50
441 A227 2.80fr multicolored    1.20   1.00
442 A227 2.80fr multicolored    1.20   1.00
   a.   Pair, #441-442 + label    2.50   2.50
   Nos. 439-442 (4)    4.80   4.00

Butterflies — A228

2.80fr, Iphiclides podalirus. 4.40fr, Aglais urticae.

**1994, Sept. 5**    Litho.    *Perf. 13*
443 A228 2.80fr multicolored    1.60   .65
444 A228 4.40fr multicolored    2.25   .95

A229

**1994, Oct. 22**    Litho.    *Perf. 13*
445 A229 2.80fr multicolored    1.10   .65
Meeting of the Co-Princes, 1st anniv.

A230

**1995, Feb. 27**    Litho.    *Perf. 13*
446 A230 2.80fr multicolored    1.50   .50
European Nature Conservation Year

1995 World Cup Rugby Championships A231

**1995, Apr. 24**    Litho.    *Perf. 13*
447 A231 2.80fr multicolored    1.50   .75

Peace & Freedom — A232

Europa: 2.80fr, Dove with olive branch. 3.70fr, Flock of doves.

**1995, Apr. 29**
448 A232 2.80fr multicolored    1.90   .75
449 A232 3.70fr multicolored    3.00   1.00

Caritas in Andorra, 15th Anniv. — A233

**1995, May 15**    Litho.    *Perf. 13*
450 A233 2.80fr multicolored    1.40   .65

Caldea Health Spa — A234

**1995, June 26**    Litho.    *Perf. 13*
451 A234 2.80fr multicolored    1.20   .65

# ANDORRA, FRENCH ADMINISTRATION

Ordino Natl. Auditorium A235

**1995, July 10**    Litho. & Engr.
452 A235 3.70fr black & buff    1.50 1.00

Virgin of Meritxell A236

**1995, Sept. 11**    Litho.    Perf. 14
453 A236 4.40fr multicolored    1.75 .95

Protection of Nature — A237

Butterflies: 2.80fr, Papallona llimonera, vert. 3.70fr, Papallona melanargia galathea.

**1995, Sept. 25**    Perf. 13
454 A237 2.80fr multicolored    1.50 1.00
455 A237 3.70fr multicolored    1.75 1.25

UN, 50th Anniv. — A238

2.80fr, Flag, emblem. 3.70fr, Emblem, "50," flag.

**1995, Oct. 21**    Litho.    Perf. 13
456 A238 2.80fr multicolored    1.25 1.00
457 A238 3.70fr multicolored    1.25 1.00
   a. Pair, #456-457 + label    2.75 2.75

Andorra's Entrance into Council of Europe — A239

**1995, Nov. 4**
458 A239 2.80fr multicolored    1.40 .65

World Skiing Championships, Ordino Arcalis — A240

**1996, Jan. 29**    Litho.    Perf. 13
459 A240 2.80fr multicolored    1.10 .65

Basketball in Andorra — A241

**1996, Jan. 29**    Litho.    Perf. 13
460 A241 3.70fr multicolored    1.50 .95

Our Lady of Meritxell Special School, 25th Anniv. — A242

**1996, Feb. 17**    Litho.    Perf. 13
461 A242 2.80fr multicolored    1.10 .65

Songbirds — A243

3fr, Pit riog. 3.80fr, Mallarenga carbonera.

**1996, Mar. 25**
462 A243 3fr multicolored    1.25 .65
463 A243 3.80fr multicolored    1.75 1.40

**First Arms Type of 1983**
**1996, Apr. 17**    Engr.    Perf. 13
464 A150 2.70fr green    .95 .65
465 A150 3fr red    1.20 .35

Cross of St. James d'Engordany — A244

**1996, Apr. 20**    Litho.
466 A244 3fr multicolored    1.25 .65

Censer of St. Eulalia d'Encamp A245

**1996, Apr. 20**
467 A245 3.80fr multicolored    1.50 1.20

Europa — A246

3fr, Ermessenda de Castellbo.

**1996, May 6**
468 A246 3fr multicolored    1.90 1.00

Chess — A247

**1996, June 8**    Litho.    Perf. 13
469 A247 4.50fr multicolored    1.90 1.00

1996 Summer Olympic Games, Atlanta — A248

**1996, June 29**    Litho.    Perf. 13
470 A248 3fr multicolored    1.50 .70

Arms of the Community of Canillo — A249

**Serpentine Die Cut 7 Vert.**
**1996, June 10**    Litho.
**Self-Adhesive**
471 A249 (3fr) multicolored    1.20 .45
   a. Booklet of 10    12.00

Natl. Children's Choir, 5th Anniv. — A250

**1996, Sept. 14**    Perf. 13
472 A250 3fr multicolored    1.20 .60

Livestock Fair — A251

**1996, Oct. 26**    Engr.    Perf. 12x13
473 A251 3fr multicolored    1.20 .60

Churches — A252

Designs: No. 474, St. Romá de Les Bons. No. 475, St. Coloma.

**1996, Nov. 16**    Litho.    Perf. 13
474 A252 6.70fr multicolored    2.75 1.40
475 A252 6.70fr multicolored    2.75 1.40

A253

**1997, Jan. 7**    Litho.    Perf. 13
476 A253 3fr multicolored    1.20 .60

Pres. Francois Mitterrand (1916-96).

A254

**Sawtooth Die Cut 7 Vert. x Straight Die Cut**
**1997, Feb. 24**    Litho.
**Self-Adhesive**
477 A254 (3fr) Arms of Encamp    1.50 .45
   a. Booklet pane of 10    15.00

By its nature, No. 477a is a complete booklet. The peelable paper backing serves as a booklet cover.

A255

**1997, Mar. 22**    Perf. 13
478 A255 3fr Volleyball    1.25 .60

"The White Lady" — A256

**1997, June 10**    Litho.    Perf. 13
479 A256 3fr multicolored    1.75 .90

Europa (Stories and Legends).

Oreneta Cuablanca A257

**1997, May 31**    Litho.    Perf. 13
480 A257 3.80fr multicolored    2.40 1.25

Paintings of Mills — A258

**1997, Sept. 15**    Litho.    Perf. 13
481 A258 3fr Cal Pal, vert.    1.25 .60
482 A258 4.50fr Mas d'en Sole    2.00 1.00

Religious Artifacts — A259

Designs: 3fr, Monstrance of St. Iscle and St. Victoria. 15.50fr, Altar piece of St. Pierre d'Alxirivall.

**1997, Oct. 27**
483 A259 3fr multicolored    1.40 .60
484 A259 15.50fr multicolored    5.50 2.75
   a. Pair, #483-484 + label    7.50 7.50

Legends — A260

Designs: No. 485, Legend of Meritxell. No. 486, The cross of seven arms. 3.80fr, The fountain of Esmelicat.

**1997, Nov. 22**    Litho.    Perf. 13
485 A260 3fr multicolored    1.40 .60
486 A260 3fr multicolored    1.40 .60
487 A260 3.80fr multicolored    2.00 1.00
   a. Strip of 3, #485-487    5.00 5.00

Chapel of St. Miguel d'Engolasters — A261

**1997, Nov. 28**    Litho.    Perf. 13
488 A261 3fr multicolored    1.20 .60

Monaco Intl. Philatelic Exhibition.

Happy Anniversary — A262

**1998, Jan. 3**    Litho.    Perf. 13
489 A262 3fr Juggling candles    1.20 .60

# ANDORRA, FRENCH ADMINISTRATION

1998 Winter Olympic Games, Nagano — A263

**1998, Feb. 14**
490  A263  4.40fr multicolored        2.00  1.00

Arms of Ordino — A264

*Serpentine Die Cut Vert.*
**1998, Mar. 7   Self-Adhesive   Litho.**
**Booklet Stamp**
491  A264 (3fr) multicolored         1.25   .30
  a. Booklet pane of 10             12.50
    Complete booklet, #491a         12.50
See Nos. 504, 518, 531.

Mesa de Vila Church A265

**1998, Mar. 28**                  *Perf. 13*
492  A265  4.50fr multicolored        2.25  2.00

Rotary Club of Andorra, 20th Anniv. — A265a

**1998, Apr. 11**
493  A265a 3fr multicolored           1.20   .60

Finch — A266

**1998**          *Litho.*           *Perf. 13*
494  A266  3.80fr multicolored        2.00  1.00

1998 World Cup Soccer Championships, France — A267

**1998, June 6**   *Litho.*         *Perf. 13*
495  A267  3fr multicolored           1.60  1.25
For overprint see No. 499.

Music Festival — A268

**1998, June 20**  *Litho.*         *Perf. 13*
496  A268  3fr multicolored           1.50   .90
Europa.

Expo '98, Lisbon — A269

**1998, July 6**
497  A269  5fr multicolored           2.25  1.40

Chalice, House of the Valleys — A270

**1998, Sept. 19   Litho.**        *Perf. 13*
498  A270  4.50fr multicolored        2.25  1.00

No. 495 Overprinted

**1998, Nov. 16**
499  A267  3fr multicolored           2.75  1.50

Early Maps of Andorra — A271

**1998, Nov. 16**
500  A271    3fr 1717, vert.          2.00  1.25
501  A271   15.50fr 1777              8.00  3.50

Inauguration of the Postal Museum — A272

**1998, Nov. 19   Litho.**         *Perf. 13*
502  A272  3fr multicolored           1.20   .60

Manual Digest, 250th Anniv. — A273

**1998, Dec. 7**
503  A273  3.80fr multicolored        1.50  1.00

**Arms Type of 1998**
**Self-Adhesive**
*Serpentine Die Cut Vert.*
**1999, Jan. 18         Booklet Stamp**
504  A264 (3fr) La Massana           1.25   .55
  a. Booklet pane of 10             12.50
No. 504a is a complete booklet.

Recycling — A274

**1999, Mar. 13    Litho.**        *Perf. 13*
505  A274  5fr multicolored           2.25  1.40

Sorteny Valley A275

**1999, Apr. 10**
506  A275  3fr multicolored           2.00  1.25
Europa.

Council of Europe, 50th Anniv. — A276

**1999, May 5      Litho.**        *Perf. 13*
507  A276  3.80fr multicolored        1.60  1.00

First Stage Coach — A277

**1999, May 15**
508  A277  2.70fr multi               1.60  1.25

1999 European National Soccer Championships A278

**1999, June 10    Photo.**        *Perf. 13*
509  A278  4.50fr multicolored        2.25  1.50

PhilexFrance 99 — A279

**1999, July 2     Litho.**       *Perf. 13x13¼*
510  A279  3fr multicolored           1.20   .60

Historic View of Pal — A280

*Perf. 13x13¼, 13¼x13*
**1999, July 10               Litho.**
511  A280  3fr shown                  1.20   .60
512  A280  3fr Different view, vert.  1.40   .60

International Federation of Photographic Art, 50th Anniv. — A281

**1999, July 24    Litho.**        *Perf. 13*
513  A281  4.40fr multicolored        2.25  1.00

Casa Rull, Sispony — A282

**1999, Sept. 6    Litho.**       *Perf. 13x13¼*
514  A282  15.50fr multicolored       6.00  3.50

Chest With Six Locks A283

**1999, Oct. 9     Litho.**       *Perf. 13x13¼*
515  A283  6.70fr multicolored        2.75  1.50

Christmas A284

**1999, Nov. 27    Litho.**        *Perf. 13*
516  A284  3fr multicolored           1.20   .60

Year 2000 — A285

**2000, Jan. 5     Litho.**       *Perf. 13x13¼*
517  A285  3fr multicolored           1.20   .60

**Arms Type of 1998**
**Self-Adhesive**
*Serpentine Die Cut 6½ Vert.*
**2000, Feb. 26         Booklet Stamp**
518  A264 (3fr) Andorra-la-Vielle    1.25   .40
  a. Booklet pane of 10             12.50
No. 518a is a complete booklet.

Snowboarding — A286

**2000, Mar. 17    Litho.**        *Perf. 13*
519  A286  4.50fr multi               2.00  1.00

Montserrat Caballé Chant Competition A287

**2000, Apr. 3**                   *Perf. 13x13¼*
520  A287  3.80fr multi               2.00  1.00

Campanula Cochleariifolia — A288

**2000, Apr. 17    Litho.**        *Perf. 13*
521  A288  2.70fr multi               1.20   .60

**Europa, 2000**
**Common Design Type**
**2000, May 9**                   *Perf. 13½x13*
522  CD17  3fr multi                  2.00  1.00

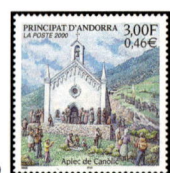

Festivals — A289

No. 523: a, Canòlic. b, Meritxell.

**2000, May 27     Litho.**        *Perf. 13*
523   Pair + central label            3.00  3.00
  a.-b. A289 3fr Any single           1.25  1.00

Pardal Comú — A290

**2000, July 7     Litho.**        *Perf. 13*
524  A290  4.40fr multi               2.00  1.00

# ANDORRA, FRENCH ADMINISTRATION

475

A291

**2000, Sept. 11**    Litho.    Perf. 13
525 A291 5fr multi    2.00   1.00
2000 Summer Olympics, Sydney.

World Tourism Day — A292

**2000, Sept. 28**
526 A292 3fr multi    1.20   .60

Expo 2000, Hanover — A293

**2000, Oct. 6**    Litho.    Perf. 13
527 A293 3fr multi    1.20   .60

"Europe, A Common Heritage" — A294

**2000, Nov. 4**    Litho.    Perf. 13½x13
528 A294 3.80fr multi    1.60   1.00

Prehistoric Pottery of Prats A295

**2000, Dec. 16**    Perf. 13x13¼
529 A295 6.70fr multi    3.00   1.50

National Archives, 25th Anniv. — A296

**2000, Dec. 22**    Perf. 13
530 A296 15.50fr multi    7.50   4.50

**Arms Type of 1998**
*Serpentine Die Cut 6½ Vert.*
**2001, Feb. 19**    Litho.
**Booklet Stamp**
**Self-Adhesive**
531 A264 (3fr) Sant Julià de Lòria    1.25   .40
   a. Booklet, 10 #531    12.50

Canillo Aliga Mountain Station — A297

**2001, Feb. 10**    Litho.    Perf. 13
532 A297 4.50fr multi    2.00   1.00

Casa Cristo Museum — A298

**2001, Feb. 17**    Perf. 13¼x13
533 A298 6.70fr multi    2.75   1.50

Andorran Heritage A299

No. 534: a, Legend of Engolasters Lake. b, Foundation of Andorra.

**2001, Mar. 23**    Perf. 13
534 A299 3fr Pair, #a-b, with central label    3.00   3.00

Intl. Book Day — A300

**2001, Apr. 23**    Litho.    Perf. 13
535 A300 3.80fr multi    1.75   1.00

Europa — A301

**2001, Apr. 28**
536 A301 3fr multi    2.00   1.00

A302

3fr, Raspberries, vert.

**2001, May 12**
537 A302    3fr multicolored    1.20   .60
538 A302    4.40fr shown    2.00   1.00

European Language Year — A303

**2001, June 16**    Litho.    Perf. 13
539 A303 3.80fr multi    1.75   1.00

Escaldes-Engordany Jazz Festival — A304

**2001, July 7**
540 A304 3fr multi    1.00   .70

General Council's Kitchen — A305

**2001, Aug. 10**
541 A305 5fr multi    2.50   1.50

A306

**2001, Sept. 7**    Litho.    Perf. 13
542 A306 3fr multi    1.50   .80
Chapel of the Virgin of Meritxell, 25th anniv. of rebuilding

Hotel Pla — A307

**2001, Oct. 12**
543 A307 15.50fr multi    6.50   3.00

Cross of Terme — A308

**2001, Nov. 17**    Litho.    Perf. 13½x13
544 A308 2.70fr multi    1.25   .75

**100 Cents = 1 Euro (€)**

National Arms — A309

Legends
A310    A311

Designs: 10c, Legend of Meritxell. 20c, Fountain of Esmelicat. 50c, The Cross with Seven Arms. €1, The Founding of Andorra. €2, Legend of Engolasters Lake. €5, The White Lady.

Perf. 13¼ (A309), 13¼x13
**2002, Jan. 2**    Photo. (A309), Litho.
545 A309    1c yel & multi    .25   .25
546 A309    2c tan & multi    .25   .25
547 A309    5c bl & multi    .25   .25
548 A310    10c multi    .25   .25
549 A310    20c multi    .50   .40
550 A309    (46c) red & multi    1.00   .40
551 A310    50c multi    2.25   .80
552 A311    €1 multi    2.50   1.00
553 A311    €2 multi    4.50   1.50
554 A311    €5 multi    12.00   5.00
Nos. 545-554 (10)    23.75   10.10

See Nos. 577, 618, 635, 661-666, 680. Compare type A309 with type A597.

Traffic Safety Education in Schools — A312

**2002, Jan. 25**    Litho.    Perf. 13½x13
555 A312 69c multi    2.25   1.00

2002 Winter Olympics, Salt Lake City — A313

**2002, Feb. 2**    Litho.    Perf. 13
556 A313 58c multi    1.50   .75

Hotel Rosaleda — A314

**2002, Mar. 16**    Litho.    Perf. 13
557 A314 46c multi    2.25   1.00

World Day for Water — A315

**2002, Mar. 22**    Litho.    Perf. 13
558 A315 67c multi    1.60   1.00

Europa — A316

**2002, May 10**    Litho.    Perf. 13
559 A316 46c multi    2.00   .40

Bilberries — A317

**2002, July 6**    Litho.    Perf. 13
560 A317 46c multi    1.60   .80

Seated Nude, Sculpture by Josep Viladomat — A318

**2002, Aug. 24**    Litho.    Perf. 13¼x13
561 A318 €2.36 multi    6.50   3.25

Envalira Tunnel — A319

**2002, Sept. 2**    Perf. 13
562 A319 46c multi    1.75   .80

# ANDORRA, FRENCH ADMINISTRATION

Piper of Ordino — A320

**2002, Sept. 27**
563 A320 41c multi     1.75   .80
   See No. 578.

Detail of Santa Coloma Wall Painting — A321

**2002, Nov. 16**   Litho.   *Perf. 13*
564 A321 €1.02 multi     3.00   1.75

Comú d'Escaldes — Engordany Coat of Arms — A322

*Serpentine Die Cut 6¾ Vert.*
**2003, Jan. 20**   Photo.
**Booklet Stamp**
**Self-Adhesive**
565 A322 (46c) multi     1.40   .50
 a.   Booklet pane of 10     14.00

Legend of the Margineda Pine — A323

**2003, Feb. 10**   Litho.   *Perf. 13*
566 A323 69c multi     2.00   1.00
   See No. 579.

Constitution, 10th Anniv. — A324

**2003, Mar. 14**   Litho.   *Perf. 13x13½*
567 A324 €2.36 multi     6.50   3.50

Buildings, Les Bons — A325

**2003, Mar. 31**    *Perf. 13*
568 A325 67c multi     2.25   1.25

Hotel Mirador — A326

**2003, Apr. 12**   Litho.   *Perf. 13*
569 A326 €1.02 multi     3.00   2.00

Europa — A327

**2003, May 17**
570 A327 46c multi     1.75   .80

Falles de San Joan — A328

**2003, June 23**   Litho.   *Perf. 13*
571 A328 50c multi     1.60   .80

A329

**2003, July 5**
572 A329 50c multi     1.75   .80
   Tour de France bicycle race, cent.

A330

**2003, Aug. 8**
573 A330 90c multi     2.50   1.50
   World Track and Field Championships, Paris.

Sparassis Crispa — A331

Currants — A332

**2003, Sept. 15**   Litho.   *Perf. 13*
574 A331 45c multi     1.50   1.00
575 A332 75c multi     2.25   1.00

Telephones in Andorra, Cent. — A333

**2003, Oct. 30**   Litho.   *Perf. 13*
576 A333 50c multi     1.75   .65

**Types of 2002-03 Inscribed "Postes"**
**2003, Nov. 29**   Photo.   *Perf. 13x13¼*
577 A309 (45c) green & multi   1.30   .80
   Litho.
   *Perf. 13*
578 A320   75c multi     3.25   2.00
579 A323   90c multi     3.25   2.25
   Nos. 577-579 (3)     7.80   5.05

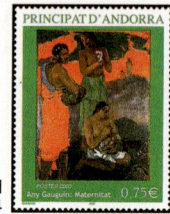

Maternity, by Paul Gauguin — A334

**2003, Nov. 29**   Litho.   *Perf. 13¼x13*
580 A334 75c multi     3.00   1.75

St. Anthony's Auction — A335

**2004, Jan. 17**   Litho.   *Perf. 13*
581 A335 50c multi     1.25   .60

Children of the World — A336

**2004, Mar. 20**   Litho.   *Perf. 13*
582 A336 50c multi     1.25   .60

Hotel Valira — A337

**2004, Apr. 17**   Litho.   *Perf. 13*
583 A337 €1.11 multi     3.00   2.50

Europa — A338

**2004, May 7**   Litho.   *Perf. 13*
584 A338 50c multi     1.40   .60

A339

**2004, May 15**
585 A339 45c multi     1.25   .65
   Legend of the Castle of St. Vincent.

A340

**2004, June 26**
586 A340 75c multi     1.75   .90
   Madriu-Peralita-Claror Valley, UNESCO World Heritage Site candidate.

Poblet de Fontenada — A341

**2004, July 3**
587 A341 50c multi     1.40   .60

2004 Summer Olympics, Athens — A342

**2004, Aug. 7**   Litho.   *Perf. 13*
588 A342 90c multi     2.50   1.75

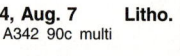

Margineda Bridge — A343

No. 589: a, €1, Black and white sketch. b, €2, Full color painting.

**2004, Oct. 2**
589 A343   Horiz. pair, #a-b, + central label     8.00   8.00

Postal Code — A344

**2004, Oct. 23**    *Perf. 13¼x13*
590 A344 50c multi     1.40   .60

Admission to Council of Europe, 10th Anniv. — A345

**2004, Nov. 6**
591 A345 €2.50 multi     6.50   4.00

Christmas — A346

**2004, Dec. 4**    *Perf. 13*
592 A346 50c multi     1.40   .60

The Magi — A347

**2005, Jan. 5**
593 A347 50c multi     1.50   .65

Selection of Madriu-Peralita-Claror Valley as UNESCO World Heritage Site — A348

**2005, Jan. 22**
594 A348 50c multi     1.40   .60

# ANDORRA, FRENCH ADMINISTRATION

Legend of Rat Pass — A349

**2005, Feb. 12**
595  A349  48c multi                      1.50   .65

Aegolius Funereus — A350

**2005, Apr. 6**   Litho.   Perf. 13
596  A350  90c multi                      2.50  2.25

Europa — A351

**2005, May 7**   Litho.   Perf. 13x13¼
597  A351  55c multi                      1.60  1.40

**Souvenir Sheet**

9th Games of Small European States — A352

No. 598: a, 53c, Shooting. b, 55c, Track and field. c, 82c, Swimming. d, €1, Basketball.

**2005, May 28**   Perf. 13¼x13
598  A352  Sheet of 4, #a-d   0.00  8.00

Bordes d'Ensegur — A353

**2005, June 11**   Litho.   Perf. 13
599  A353  €2.50 multi                    6.50  5.00

Police Motorcycle — A354

**2005, July 2**
600  A354  53c multi                      1.50  1.20

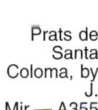

Prats de Santa Coloma, by J. Mir — A355

**2005, Aug. 10**   Perf. 13x13¼
601  A355  82c multi                      2.25  1.75

Calones Hostel — A356

**2005, Sept. 10**   Litho.   Perf. 13
602  A356  €1.98 multi                    6.00  4.50

Josep Alsina Photography Business — A357

**2005, Oct. 8**   Litho.   Perf. 13¼x13
603  A357  53c multi                      1.40  .65

Rotary International, Cent. — A358

**2005, Nov. 5**   Perf. 13
604  A358  55c multi                      1.40  .65

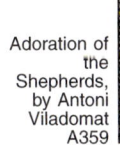

Adoration of the Shepherds, by Antoni Viladomat — A359

**2005, Dec. 7**   Litho.   Perf. 13
605  A359  €1.22 multi                    3.50  3.00

Animals — A360

Designs: No. 606, 53c, Ursus arctos. No. 607, 53c, Rupicapra pyrenaica, vert.

**2006, Jan. 16**
606-607  A360  Set of 2                   3.00  2.50
See Nos. 619-620, 633-634, 648-649, 670-671.

2006 Winter Olympics, Turin — A361

No. 608: a, 55c, Alpine skiing. b, 75c, Cross-country skiing.

**2006, Feb. 4**
608  A361  Horiz. pair, #a-b, + central label   3.50  3.50

Tobacco Museum — A362

**2006, Mar. 4**   Litho.   Perf. 13
609  A362  82c multi                      2.00  1.50

Decree of Napoleon I, Bicent. — A363

**2006, Mar. 27**
610  A363  53c multi                      1.40  .65

Legend of the Bear Cave — A364

**2006, Apr. 10**   Litho.   Perf. 13
611  A364  48c multi                      2.00  1.00

Europa — A365

**2006, May 9**   Litho.   Perf. 13x13¼
612  A365  53c multi                      1.40  .65

Sorteny Valley Nature Park — A366

**2006, June 10**   Perf. 13
613  A366  55c multi                      1.40  .65

Pablo Casals (1876-1973), Cellist — A367

**2006, July 31**   Litho.   Perf. 13
614  A367  90c multi                      2.25  2.10

Ford Model T — A368

**2006, Sept. 2**   Litho.   Perf. 13
615  A368  85c multi                      2.25  2.10

Montserrat Procession, by Josp Borrell — A369

**2006, Nov. 4**   Litho.   Perf. 13¼x13
616  A369  €1.30 multi                    3.25  3.00

Retable, St. Martin's Church, Cortinada — A370

**2006, Dec. 2**   Perf. 13
617  A370  54c multi                      1.40  .65

**Arms Type of 2002 Inscribed "Postes"**

**2007, Jan. 13**   Perf. 13x13¼
618  A309  60c multi                      1.50  .75

**Animals Type of 2006**

Designs: 54c, Marmota marmota, vert. 60c, Sciurus vulgaris.

**2007, Jan. 20**   Perf. 13
619-620  A360  Set of 2                   3.00  2.50

Legend of the Wolf's Testament — A371

**2007, Feb. 24**
621  A371  49c multi                      1.40  .65

Predelle, Prats — A372

**2007, Mar. 17**   Litho.   Perf. 13¼x13
622  A372  €1.30 multi                    3.50  3.25

Compare with types A383, A396, A414 and A420.

National Arms — A373

**Serpentine Die Cut 11**
**2007, Apr. 2**   Litho.
**Booklet Stamp**
**Self-Adhesive**
623  A373  (54c) multi                    1.60  1.60
  a.   Booklet pane of 10               16.00
  b.   Booklet pane of 12               21.00

Issued: No. 623b, 3/1/16. Stamps in No. 623b sold for 80c on day of issue.

Rose — A374

**2007, Apr. 23**   Photo.   Perf. 13¼
624  A374  86c multi                      2.25  2.00

Values are for stamps with surrounding selvage.

Europa — A375

**2007, May 5**   Litho.   Perf. 13¼x13
625  A375  54c multi                      1.75  1.60

Scouting, cent.

Joining of Meritxell and Sabart — A376

# 478  ANDORRA, FRENCH ADMINISTRATION

No. 626: a, Madonna and Child. b, Priest.

**2007, June 2**  Litho.  *Perf. 13*
626  A376  54c Horiz. pair, #a-b, + central label   3.00  3.00

Engine — A377

**2007, July 10**
627  A377  60c multi   1.50  1.25

2007 Rugby World Cup, France — A378

**2007, Sept. 1**  Litho.  *Perf. 13¼*
628  A378  85c multi   2.00  1.50

Values are for stamps with surrounding selvage.

Comapedrosa Valley — A379

**2007, Oct. 6**  Litho.  *Perf. 13¼x13*
629  A379  €3.04 multi   7.50  6.50

Prehistoric People — A380

Prehistoric people at: 60c, Marigneda Grotto. 85c, Cedre.

**2007, Nov. 10**
630-631  A380  Set of 2   4.00  3.50

Retable, St. Martin's Church, Cortinada A381

**2007, Dec. 3**  Litho.  *Perf. 13*
632  A381  54c multi   1.40  .65

**Animals Type of 2006**
Designs: 54c, Vulpes vulpes. 60c, Sus scrofa, vert.

**2008, Jan. 28**
633-634  A360  Set of 2   3.50  3.00

**Arms Type of 2002 Inscribed "Postes"**

**2008, Mar. 1**  Photo.  *Perf. 13x13¼*
635  A309  65c blue & multi   1.50  1.00

Legend of the Treasure of the Fountain of Manegó — A382

**2008, Mar. 8**  Litho.  *Perf. 13*
636  A382  50c multi   1.25  .75

Predelle, Prats — A383

**2008, Apr. 12**  *Perf. 13¼x13*
637  A383  €1.33 multi   3.50  3.50

Compare with Types A372, A396, A414 and A420.

Cartercar Automobile A384

**2008, May 3**  Litho.  *Perf. 13*
638  A384  65c multi   1.75  1.50

Europa — A385

**2008, May 17**
639  A385  55c multi   1.50  .75

**Miniature Sheet**

2008 Summer Olympics, Beijing — A386

No. 640: a, Kayaking. b, Running. c, Swimming. d, Judo.

**2008, June 16**  Litho.  *Perf. 13x13½*
640  A386  55c Sheet of 4, #a-d   6.00  6.00
Olympex 2008 Philatelic Exhibition, Beijing (#640d).

Narcissus Poeticus — A387

**2008, June 18**  *Perf. 13¼x13*
641  A387  55c multi   1.50  .75

No. 641 is impregnated with a narcissus scent.

Vall d'Incles — A388

**2008, July 5**  *Perf. 13*
642  A388  €2.80 multi   7.50  7.50

Universal Male Suffrage, 75th Anniv. — A389

**2008, Aug. 30**  Litho.  *Perf. 13*
643  A389  55c multi   1.40  .75

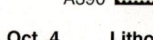
Sustainable Development A390

**2008, Oct. 4**  Litho.  *Perf. 13*
644  A390  88c multi   2.00  1.25

Roc d'Enclar — A391

**2008, Nov. 8**  *Perf. 13¼*
645  A391  85c multi   2.00  1.25

Retable of St. Mark and St. Mary — A392

**2008, Dec. 13**  *Perf. 13*
646  A392  55c multi   1.40  .75

Louis Braille (1809-52), Educator of the Blind — A393

**2009, Jan. 24**  Engr.
647  A393  88c multi   2.00  1.25

**Animals Type of 2006**
Designs: 55c, Equus mulus, vert. 65c, Bos taurus.

**2009, Feb. 14**  Litho.  *Perf. 13*
648-649  A360  Set of 2   2.75  2.00

Legend of the Devils of Aixirvall — A394

**2009, Mar. 7**
650  A394  51c multi   1.40  .75

**Souvenir Sheet**

Protection of Polar Regions and Glaciers — A395

No. 651: a, 56c, Emperor penguins. b, 85c, Boat off shore in polar regions, vert.

*Perf. 13x13¼, 13¼x13 (85c)*
**2009, Mar. 27**  Litho. & Engr.
651  A395  Sheet of 2, #a-b, + label   3.50  3.50

Predelle, Prats — A396

**2009, Apr. 18**  Litho.  *Perf. 13¼x13*
652  A396  €1.35 multi   3.50  3.50

Compare with types A372, A383, A414 and A420.

Europa — A397

**2009, May 2**  *Perf. 13*
653  A397  56c multi   1.40  .75

Intl. Year of Astronomy.

Early Renault Automobile A398

**2009, May 16**
654  A398  70c multi   1.75  1.00

St. Joan de Caselles, by Maurice Utrillo A399

**2009, May 23**  *Perf. 13x13¼*
655  A399  90c multi   2.25  1.50

Cercle des Pessons — A400

**2009, June 13**  Litho.  *Perf. 13*
656  A400  €2.80 multi   7.50  6.00

Tour de France Bicycle Race — A401

**2009, July 11**
657  A401  56c multi   1.40  .75

Arts and Letters Circle, 40th Anniv. — A402

**2009, Oct. 3**  Litho.  *Perf. 13*
658  A402  51c multi   1.40  .75

# ANDORRA, FRENCH ADMINISTRATION

Romanesque Art — A403

**2009, Nov. 7**     *Perf. 13¼x13*
659 A403 85c multi    2.00 1.50

Epiphany — A404

**2009, Dec. 12**     *Perf. 13*
660 A404 56c multi    1.40 .75

**Arms Type of 2002 Inscribed "POSTES"**

**2010, Jan. 4**   Photo.   *Perf. 13x13¼*
661 A309 1c yel & multi   .25 .25
662 A309 5c lt bl & multi   .25 .25
663 A309 10c org & multi   .25 .25
664 A309 20c lilac & multi   .45 .45
665 A309 60c ol grn & multi   1.25 1.25
666 A309 (70c) dk bl & multi   1.60 1.60
Nos. 661-666 (6)   4.05 4.05
Compare Nos. 661 and 664 to Nos. 869-870.

2010 Winter Olympics, Vancouver A405

**2010, Jan. 23**   Photo.   *Perf. 13x13¼*
667 A405 85c multi    2.00 1.50

Casamanya Peak — A406

**2010, Feb. 15**   Litho.   *Perf. 13*
668 A406 €2.80 multi    6.50 5.00

Rights of the Child Convention, 20th Anniv. — A407

**2010, Mar. 2**     Photo.
669 A407 56c multi    1.40 .75

**Animals Type of 2006**
Designs: 56c, Gyps fulvus, vert. 90c, Ovis aries.

**2010, Mar. 8**   Litho.   *Perf. 13*
670-671 A360   Set of 2    3.00 2.25

Andorran Embassy, Brussels A408

**2010, Apr. 12**   Engr.   *Perf. 13*
672 A408 70c multi + label    1.75 1.75

Legend of Charlemagne's Chair — A409

**2010, Apr. 26**   Litho.   *Perf. 13*
673 A409 51c multi    1.25 .65

Europa — A410

**Litho. & Embossed with Foil Application**
**2010, May 10**     *Perf. 13¼*
674 A410 56c multi    1.40 1.00

Radio Andorra Building — A411

**2010, May 25**   Litho.   *Perf. 13*
675 A411 56c multi    1.40 1.00

1985 Ferrari 328 GTS — A412

**2010, June 21**   Litho.   *Perf. 13*
676 A412 70c multi    1.75 1.75

Still Life, by Carme Massana — A413

**2010, July 12**     *Perf. 13¼x13*
677 A413 95c multi    2.50 2.50

Predelle, Prats — A414

**2010, Sept. 6**   Litho.   *Perf. 13¼x13*
678 A414 €1.40 multi    3.75 3.75
Compare with types A372, A383, A396 and A420.

**Souvenir Sheet**

Churches — A415

No. 679: a, Sant Joan de Caselles Church. b, Sant Romà de Les Bons Church, horiz.

*Perf. 13¼x13, 13x13¼*
**2010, Oct. 4**     Engr.
679 A415 58c Sheet of 2, #a-b    3.25 3.25
See Andorra, Spanish Administration No. 363.

**Arms Type of 2002 Inscribed "POSTES"**
**2010, Oct. 18**   Photo.   *Perf. 13x13¼*
680 A309 (58c) red & multi    1.75 1.75

Feudal Andorra — A416

681 A416 87c multi    2.40 2.40

Christmas — A417

**2010, Nov. 29**     *Perf. 13*
682 A417 58c multi    1.60 1.60

Legend of St. Joan de Caselles — A418

**2011, Feb. 12**   Litho.   *Perf. 13*
683 A418 €2.80 multi    8.00 8.00

Francophonia A419

**2011, Mar. 19**     *Perf. 13x13¼*
684 A419 87c multi    2.50 2.50

Predelle, Prats — A420

**2011, Apr. 9**     *Perf. 13¼x13*
685 A420 €1.40 multi    4.00 4.00
Compare with types A372, A383, A386 and A414.

Europa — A421

**Silk-Screened on Wood Veneer**
**2011, May 7**   Serpentine Die Cut 11 **Self-Adhesive**
686 A421 58c black & white    1.75 1.75
Intl. Year of Forests.

Councilor, by Francesc Borràs (1891-1968) A422

**2011, May 21**   Litho.   *Perf. 13*
687 A422 95c multi    2.75 2.75

Placeta de Sant Esteve A423

**2011, June 4**     Engr.
688 A423 58c multi    1.75 1.75

Soriano-Pedroso Automobile A424

**2011, June 18**     Litho.
689 A424 75c multi    2.10 2.10

Rugby — A425

**2011, July 9**   Photo.   *Perf. 13*
690 A425 89c multi    2.40 2.40
Values are for stamps with surrounding selvage.

**Souvenir Sheet**

Dance of the Seven Parishes, Plaza Benlloch A426

**2011, July 16**   Litho. & Engr.
691 A426 €1.45 multi    4.25 4.25

Flora — A427

Designs: 60c, Rhododendron ferrugineum. €1, Rosa sempervirens, horiz.

**2011, Sept. 4**   Litho.   *Perf. 13*
692-693 A427   Set of 2    4.50 4.50
See Nos. 706-707, 720-721, 751, 782.

Council of the Land — A428

**2011, Sept. 24**     *Perf. 13x13¼*
694 A428 89c multi    2.50 2.50

# ANDORRA, FRENCH ADMINISTRATION

Leaf and Coat of Arms — A429

**2011, Oct. 1**   Photo.   Perf. 13x13¼
695   A429   (57c) multi   1.60   1.60

Angel From Santa Eulalia d'Encamp Retable — A430

**2011, Nov. 26**   Litho.   Perf. 13
696   A430   60c multi   1.60   1.60

Legend of the Shop of the Sorceresses — A431

**2012, Jan. 14**
697   A431   €2.78 multi   7.50   7.50

Women's World Cup Alpine Skiing Races, Soldeu — A432

**2012, Feb. 11**   Perf. 13x13¼
698   A432   89c multi   2.40   2.40

Massana Valley, by Joaquim Mir (1873-1940) A433

**2012, Mar. 3**
699   A433   €1 multi   2.60   2.60

Souvenir Sheet

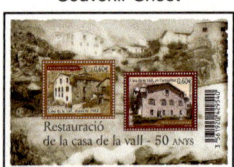

Restoration of Casa de la Vall, 50th Anniv. — A434

No. 700 — Casa de la Vall in: a, 1962. b, 2012.

**2012, Mar. 10**   Litho. & Engr.
700   A434   60c Sheet of 2, #a-b   3.25   3.25

Bugatti 37 Race Car — A435

**2012, Apr. 14**   Litho.   Perf. 13
701   A435   77c multi   2.10   2.10

Souvenir Sheet

Europa A436

**2012, May 5**   Litho.   Perf. 13¼x13
702   A436   77c multi   2.00   2.00

Noi. 702 has die cut opening in center of stamp.

Placeta de la Consòrcia, Andorra la Vella — A437

**2012, June 8**   Engr.   Perf. 13x12¾
703   A437   60c multi   1.50   1.50

Judo — A438

**2012, July 6**   Litho.   Perf. 13
704   A438   77c multi   1.90   1.90

Souvenir Sheet

Marratxa Dance — A439

**2012, July 20**   Litho. & Engr.   Perf. 13x13¼
705   A439   €1.45 multi   3.75   3.75

**Flora Type of 2011**

Designs: 60c, Sempervivum montanum. €1, Eryngium bourgatii.

**2012, Sept. 14**   Litho.   Perf. 13
706-707   A427   Set of 2   4.25   4.25

Woman Suffrage, 42nd Anniv. — A440

**2012, Oct. 5**   Perf. 13¼x13
708   A440   89c multi   2.25   2.25

Andorran Presidency of the Council of Europe — A441

**2012, Oct. 26**
709   A441   €1 multi   2.60   2.60

King Henri IV of France (1553-1610), Co-Prince of Andorra — A442

**2012, Nov. 8**   Engr.   Perf. 13x13¼
710   A442   60c multi   1.60   1.60
  a.   Sheet of 10, 5 each #710, France #4297   16.00   16.00
See France No. 4297.

Angel From Roser d'Ordino Retable — A443

**2012, Nov. 23**   Litho.   Perf. 13
711   A443   57c multi   1.50   1.50

Legend of Moixella — A444

**2013, Jan. 12**
712   A444   €2.78 multi   7.50   7.50

Souvenir Sheet

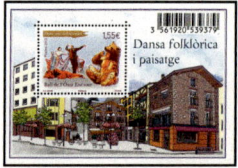

Bear Ball, Encamp A445

**2013, Feb. 23**   Perf. 13x13¼
713   A445   €1.55 multi   4.00   4.00

Constitution, 20th Anniv. — A446

**2013, Mar. 16**   Litho.   Perf. 13
714   A446   63c multi   1.60   1.60

Cord 810 Phaeton — A447

**2013, Apr. 13**
715   A447   95c multi   2.50   2.50

Plaça Rebés, Andorra la Vella A448

**2013, May 11**   Engr.   Perf. 12¾
716   A448   63c multi   1.75   1.75

Europa — A449

**2013, May 18**   Litho.   Perf. 13¼
717   A449   80c multi   2.25   2.25

Retable, Church of Sant Miquel, Prats — A450

**2013, July 6**   Litho.   Perf. 13¼x13
718   A450   €1.05 multi   2.75   2.75

Andorran School, 30th Anniv. — A451

**2013, July 27**   Litho.   Perf. 13
719   A451   63c multi   1.75   1.75

**Flora Type of 2011**

Designs: 58c, Papaver rhoeas. €1.05, Paeonia mascula, horiz.

**2013, Sept. 7**   Litho.   Perf. 13
720-721   A427   Set of 2   4.50   4.50

First French School in Canillo, Cent. — A452

**2013, Oct. 2**   Litho.   Perf. 13¼
722   A452   63c multi   1.75   1.75

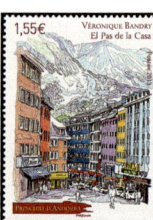

Andorran Presidency of the Working Community of the Pyrenees A453

**2013, Oct. 5**   Litho.   Perf. 13¼
723   A453   95c multi   2.60   2.60

El Pas de la Casa, Painting by Véronique Bandry — A454

**2013, Oct. 26**   Litho.   Perf. 13¼x13
724   A454   €1.55 multi   4.25   4.25

Angel, Saint Joan de Sispony Church — A455

**2013, Nov. 12**   Litho.   Perf. 13
725   A455   58c multi   1.60   1.60
Christmas.

# ANDORRA, FRENCH ADMINISTRATION

Legend of the Canòlich Sanctuary — A456

**2014, Jan. 11**  Litho.  *Perf. 13*
726  A456  €3.50 multi           9.50  9.50

Schools in Partnership With UNESCO — A457

**2014, Feb. 15**  Litho.  *Perf. 13¼*
727  A457  66c multi           1.90  1.90

1917 Hispano Guadalajara Automobile A458

**2014, Mar. 29**  Litho.  *Perf. 13*
728  A458  98c multi           2.75  2.75

Cyanistes Caeruleus A459

**2014, May 3**  Engr.  *Perf. 13¼*
729  A459  66c multi           1.90  1.90

Bagpipes — A460

**2014, May 24**  Litho.  *Perf. 13¼*
730  A460  83c multi           2.25  2.25
Europa.

Madriu-Perafita-Claror Valley — A461

**2014, June 16**  Litho.  *Perf. 13*
731  A461  98c multi           2.75  2.75

Buildings in Engordany — A462

**2014, June 16**  Engr.  *Perf. 13x12¾*
732  A462  66c multi           1.90  1.90

Fixats en la Contemporaneitat, by Javier Balmaseda — A463

**2014, July 11**  Litho.  *Perf. 13x13¼*
733  A463  €1.65 multi           4.50  4.50

Souvenir Sheet

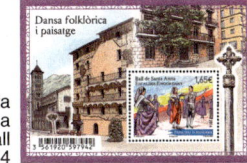
Santa Anna Ball A464

**Litho. & Engr.**
**2014, July 25**  *Perf. 13x13¼*
734  A464  €1.65 multi           4.50  4.50

Electricity Museum, Encamp — A465

**2014, July 25**  Litho.  *Perf. 13x13¼*
735  A465  €1.10 multi           3.00  3.00

Pitavola Butterfly — A466

**2014, Sept. 6**  Litho.  *Perf. 13*
736  A466  83c multi           2.10  2.10

Detail From Sant Miquel de Prats Retable — A467

**2014, Sept. 27**  Litho.  *Perf. 13¼x13*
737  A467  €1.10 multi           2.75  2.75

Skis and Ski Poles — A468

**2014, Oct. 18**  Litho.  *Perf. 13¼*
738  A468  83c multi           2.10  2.10

Esteve Albert (1914-95), Writer — A469

**2014, Nov. 9**  Engr.  *Perf. 13¼*
739  A469  66c ochre & blk           1.75  1.75

Christmas A470

**2014, Nov. 29**  Litho.  *Perf. 13*
740  A470  66c multi           1.75  1.75

Instinct of Conservation, by Javier Balmaseda — A471

**2015, Jan. 3**  Litho.  *Perf. 13x13¼*
741  A471  €1.90 multi           4.50  4.50

Legend of the First Snow — A472

**2015, Feb. 7**  Litho.  *Perf. 13*
742  A472  €3.67 multi           8.25  8.25

Citroen DS 21 — A473

**2015, Mar. 20**  Litho.  *Perf. 13*
743  A473  €1.20 multi           2.75  2.75

Departure of French Gendarmes Led by Col. René Baulard, 75th Anniv. — A474

**2015, Apr. 11**  Litho.  *Perf. 13*
744  A474  76c multi           1.75  1.75

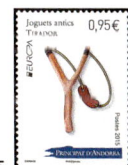
Europa — A475

**2015, May 9**  Litho.  *Perf. 13¼*
745  A475  95c multi           2.10  2.10

Trobada Monument — A476

**2015, June 13**  Engr.  *Perf. 13¼*
746  A476  €1.25 multi           2.75  2.75

Comapedrosa, Highest Peak in Andorra — A477

**2015, June 20**  Litho.  *Perf. 13¼*
747  A477  76c multi           1.75  1.75

Inside, by Agustí Roqué A478

**2015, July 4**  Litho.  *Perf. 13x13¼*
748  A478  €3.05 multi           6.75  6.75
Venice Biennale.

Souvenir Sheet

Contrapas Dance — A479

**Litho. & Engr.**
**2015, July 18**  *Perf. 13x13¼*
749  A479  €1.90 multi           4.25  4.25

UCI Mountain Bike and Trials World Championships, Vallnord — A480

**2015, Aug. 29**  Litho.  *Perf. 13¼x13*
750  A480  €1.20 multi           2.75  2.75

**Flora Type of 2011 and**

Parnassius Apollo — A481

Design. 76c, Thymus vulgaris, vert.

**2015, Oct. 2**  Engr.  *Perf. 13*
751  A427  76c multi           1.60  1.60
752  A481  95c multi           2.25  2.25

Ramon d'Areny-Plandolit, Philatelist, and Maximum Cardo — A482

**2015, Nov. 7**  Engr.  *Perf. 13x12½*
753  A482  €1.25 multi           2.75  2.75

Live Nativity Scene, Engordany A483

**2015, Nov. 27**  Litho.  *Perf. 13*
754  A483  76c multi           1.60  1.60
Christmas.

# 482 ANDORRA, FRENCH ADMINISTRATION

2014 Andorran Coinage A484

No. 755: a, 1-cent, 2-cent, 5-cent and 2-euro coins. b, 10-cent, 20-cent, 50-cent and 1-euro coins.

**2016, Jan. 8** Litho. Perf. 13
755 A484 80c Horiz. pair, #a-b 3.50 3.50

Women's Alpine Skiing World Cup Race at Soldeu-El Tarter — A485

**2016, Feb. 27** Litho. Perf. 13¼
756 A485 €1.25 multi 2.75 2.75

Donzella Cremada Rock Carving — A486

**2016, Mar. 19** Litho. Perf. 13
757 A486 €3.77 multi 8.75 8.75

Reforms of 1866, 150th Anniv. — A487

**2016, Apr. 23** Litho. Perf. 13¼
758 A487 €1 multi 2.40 2.40

The Republic, Statue by Josep Viladomat (1899-1989) and Escaldes-Engordany Art Center — A488

**2016, Apr. 6** Engr. Perf. 13¼
759 A488 80c multi 1.90 1.90

Europa — A489

**2016, May 8** Litho. Perf. 13¼
760 A489 €1 multi 2.25 2.25
Think Green Issue.

Dancing Giants of Andorra Festival — A490

**2016, June 10** Litho. Perf. 13¼
761 A490 80c multi 1.90 1.90

Souvenir Sheet

Sardana Dance A491

**Litho. & Engr.**
**2016, July 15** Perf. 13x13¼
762 A491 €1.60 multi 3.75 3.75

Intimitat Compartida, by Joan Xandri A492

**2016, July 29** Litho. Perf. 13x13¼
763 A492 €3.20 multi 7.25 7.25
2015 Venice Biennale.

Clipol Bus — A493

**2016, Sept. 2** Litho. Perf. 13
764 A493 €1.25 multi 2.75 2.75

Isabelle Sandy (1884-1975), Writer — A494

**2016, Oct. 7** Engr. Perf. 13¼
765 A494 €1.60 multi 3.50 3.50

Lavender A495 / Catalan Sheepdog A496

**Litho. & Engr.**
**2016, Nov. 5** Perf. 13
766 A495 80c multi 1.75 1.75
767 A496 €1 multi 2.25 2.25

Angels Painted by Antoni Viladomat i Manalt (1678-1755) A497

**2016, Nov. 25** Litho. Perf. 13
768 A497 80c multi 1.75 1.75

Legend of the Cave of Arans — A498

**2017, Jan. 13** Litho. Perf. 13
769 A498 €3.95 multi 8.50 8.50

Opening of Carmen Thyssen Museum, Escaldes-Engordany — A499

**2017, Feb. 3** Litho. Perf. 13¼x13
770 A499 €1.30 multi 2.75 2.75

Philandorre Philatelic Association, 40th Anniv. — A500

**2017, Mar. 9** Engr. Perf. 13
771 A500 85c multi + label 1.90 1.90

Comic Festival, La Massana — A501

**2017, Apr. 7** Litho. Perf. 13¼
772 A501 €1.70 multi 3.75 3.75

Sant Vinçenç d'Enclar Castle — A502

**2017, May 6** Litho. Perf. 13¼
773 A502 €1.10 multi 2.50 2.50
Europa.

Castellars Making Human Tower — A503

**2017, May 26** Litho. Perf. 13¼
774 A503 85c multi 1.90 1.90

Maria Assumpta D'Areny Plandolit (1860-92), Daughter of Andorran Reformer Guillem d'Areny Plandolit — A504

**2017, June 21** Engr. Perf. 13¼
775 A504 €1.10 multi 2.50 2.50

Souvenir Sheet

Stick Dancing — A505

**Litho. & Engr.**
**2017, July 8** Perf. 13x13¼
776 A505 €1.70 multi 4.00 4.00

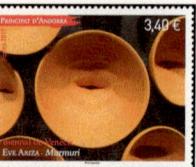

Murmuri, by Eve Ariza A506

**2017, July 22** Litho. Perf. 13
777 A506 €3.40 multi 8.00 8.00
2017 Venice Art Biennale.

Roc del Quer, Canillo A507

**2017, Sept. 2** Photo. Perf. 13x12¾
778 A507 €1.30 multi 3.00 3.00

A508

Design: Photograph of 1967 visit of French President Charles de Gaulle to Andorra, by Fèlix Peig Ballart (1917-2007).

**2017, Sept. 15** Litho. Perf. 13¼
779 A508 85c multi 2.00 2.00

Pere Canturri (1935-2015), Historian and Governmental Minister — A509

**2017, Oct. 7** Litho. Perf. 13¼
780 A509 €1.10 multi 2.60 2.60

Peugeot 172 M — A510

**2017, Nov. 10** Litho. Perf. 13
781 A510 85c multi 2.10 2.10

**Flora Type of 2011 and**

Salamandra Salamandra A511

Design: 85c, Cerastium pyrenaicum, horiz.

**2017, Nov. 13** Engr. Perf. 13
782 A427 85c multi 2.10 2.10
783 A511 €1.10 multi 2.60 2.60

Christmas A512

**2017, Nov. 24** Litho. Perf. 13
784 A512 85c multi 2.10 2.10

# ANDORRA, FRENCH ADMINISTRATION

Legend of the Snow Maiden — A513

**2018, Jan. 12**   Litho.   Perf. 13
785   A513   €4.05 multi    10.00   10.00

Tenth Conference on Snow and Mountain Tourism, Escaldes-Engordany — A514

**2018, Feb. 2**   Litho.   Perf. 13¼
786   A514   €1.30 multi    3.25   3.25

Andorran Constitution, 25th Anniv. — A515

**2018, Mar. 9**   Engr.   Perf. 13¼
787   A515   95c multi    2.40   2.40

Casa de la Vall, by Joan Miró (1893-1983) A516

**2018, Apr. 6**   Litho.   Perf. 13x13¼
788   A516   €1.20 multi    3.00   3.00

Caramelles (Singers) — A517

**2018, Apr. 20**   Litho.   Perf. 13¼
789   A517   95c multi    2.25   2.25

Tosca Bridge — A518

**2018, May 4**   Engr.   Perf. 13¼
790   A518   €1.20 multi    3.00   3.00
Europa.

### Souvenir Sheet

Summer Solstice Festival, UNESCO Intangible Cultural Heritage — A519

**2018, June 8**   Litho.   Perf. 13x13¼
791   A519   €1.90 multi    4.50   4.50

Escaldes-Engordany Parish, 40th Anniv. — A520

**2018, June 14**   Litho.   Perf. 13¼
792   A520   80c multi    1.90   1.90

Pompeu Fabra (1868-1948), Linguist — A521

**2018, July 20**   Engr.   Perf. 13
793   A521   €1.30 multi    3.00   3.00

Church of Santa Coloma and Icon — A522

**2018, Aug. 10**   Engr.   Perf. 13
794   A522   €1.20 multi    2.75   2.75
European Year of Cultural Heritage.

Sweet Candies Caramels, Sculpture by Laurence Jenkell A523

**2018, Sept. 14**   Litho.   Perf. 13x13¼
795   A523   €1.20 multi    2.75   2.75

Otter — A524

**2018, Sept. 28**   Litho.   Perf. 13
796   A524   95c multi    2.25   2.25

Lídia Armengol i Vila (1948-91), Politician — A525

**2018, Oct. 5**   Engr.   Perf. 13¼
797   A525   €1.20 choc & org red   2.75   2.75

Citroen CX — A526

**2018, Nov. 9**   Litho.   Perf. 13
798   A526   €1.90 multi    4.50   4.50

Detail From Retable of Santa Creu de Canillo Church — A527

**2018, Nov. 17**   Litho.   Perf. 13
799   A527   95c multi    2.25   2.25

Andorra Coat of Arms — A528

**2019, Jan. 2**   Photo.   Perf. 13x13¼
800   A528   (€1.30) multi    3.00   3.00

Legend of the White Horse of Solana — A529

**2019, Jan. 4**   Litho.   Perf. 13
801   A529   €4.18 multi    9.75   9.75

Escudelle of St. Anthony Festival, 50th Anniv. — A530

**2019, Jan. 17**   Litho.   Perf. 13x13¼
802   A530   88c multi    2.10   2.10

General Council of Andorra, 600th Anniv. — A531

**2019, Feb. 11**   Litho.   Perf. 13x13¼
803   A531   €1.05 multi    2.40   2.40

2019 Finals of World Alpine Skiing Championships, Soldeu — A532

**2019, Mar. 9**   Litho.   Perf. 13¼
804   A532   €1.30 multi    3.00   3.00

Estanyó del Querol Lake A533

**2019, Apr. 13**   Litho.   Perf. 13
805   A533   €1.05 multi    2.40   2.40

Lagopus Muta — A534

**2019, May 10**   Engr.   Perf. 13x13¼
806   A534   €1.30 multi    3.00   3.00
Europa.

Andorra Hydroelectric Forces (Electric Company), 90th Anniv. — A535

**2019, May 31**   Litho.   Perf. 13x13¼
807   A535   €1.05 multi    2.40   2.40

Andorra, by Eduard Arranz Bravo — A536

**2019, July 5**   Litho.   Perf. 13¼x13
808   A536   €1.05 black & red    2.40   2.40

Julia Bonet Fité (1922-2011), Businesswoman, and Her Perfume Shop — A537

**2019, July 19**   Engr.   Perf. 13x13¼
809   A537   €1.30 multi    3.00   3.00

Artifacts From La Margineda Archaeological Site — A538

**2019, Aug. 9**   Engr.   Perf. 13x13¼
810   A538   €2.10 multi    4.75   4.75

Renault 4CV — A539

**2019, Sept. 6**   Litho.   Perf. 13¼
811   A539   €1.05 multi    2.40   2.40

Argynnis Pandora — A540

Ursus Arctos — A541

**2019, Oct. 4**   Litho.   Perf. 13
812   A540   €1.05 multi    2.40   2.40
   Engr.
813   A541   €1.30 dark brown    3.00   3.00

# ANDORRA, FRENCH ADMINISTRATION

Detail From Retable of Santa Creu de Canillo Church — A542

**2019, Nov. 2    Litho.    Perf. 13**
814  A542  €1.05 multi                2.40  2.40

Admission of Andorra to Council of Europe, 25th Anniv. — A543

**2019, Nov. 8    Litho.    Perf. 13**
815  A543  €1.30 multi + label        3.00  3.00

See Andorra (Spanish Administration) No. 470.

Envalira Pass — A544

**2020, Jan. 4    Litho.    Perf. 13**
816  A544  €4.30 multi                9.50  9.50

Victoria Zorzano (1908-98), Radio Announcer — A545

**2020, Feb. 8    Engr.    Perf. 13¼**
817  A545  €1.40 multi                3.25  3.25

International Francophone Organization, 50th Anniv. — A546

**2020, Mar. 20    Litho.    Perf. 13¼x13**
818  A546  €1.16 multi                2.50  2.50

Hiking Boots — A547

**2020, Apr. 4    Litho.    Perf. 13¼x13**
819  A547  €1.16 multi                2.60  2.60

Andorra GR7 long-distance hiking trail.

Map of 19th Century Andorra la Vella-L'Ospitalet, France Postal Route — A548

**2020, May 11    Litho.    Perf. 13x13¼**
820  A548  €1.40 multi                3.25  3.25

Europa.

Espai Columba Museum, 1st Anniv. — A549

**2020, June 12    Litho.    Perf. 13x13¼**
821  A549  €1.16 multi                2.60  2.60

Oncorhynchus Mykiss — A550

**2020, June 19    Litho.    Perf. 13**
822  A550  €1.16 multi                2.60  2.60

L'Orri del Cubil Archaeological Site — A551

**2020, July 3    Engr.    Perf. 13**
823  A551  €2.32 multi                5.50  5.50

Esbalçat Pond A552

**2020, Aug. 21    Litho.    Perf. 13**
824  A552  €1.16 multi                2.75  2.75

Comte de Foix Secondary School, 40th Anniv. — A553

**2020, Sept. 11    Engr.    Perf. 13¼**
825  A553  €1.96 black & red          4.50  4.50

Jacques Chirac (1932-2019), President of France and Co-Prince of Andorra — A554

**2020, Sept. 26    Litho.    Perf. 13¼**
826  A554  €1.16 multi                2.75  2.75

Abies Alba — A555

**2020, Oct. 2    Litho.    Perf. 13**
827  A555  €1.40 multi                3.25  3.25

Casa de la Vall A556

**2020, Nov. 5    Engr.    Perf. 13¼**
828  A556  €2.32 multi + 2 flanking labels    5.75  5.75

Candidacy of Casa de la Vall, Castell de Foix and Cathedral of the See of Urgell (shown on flanking labels) for UNESCO World Heritage Site status. See Spanish Andorra No. 485.

Hartung Sparta Nature, Automobile Manufactured in Andorra — A557

**2020, Nov. 6    Litho.    Perf. 13¼**
829  A557  €1.40 multi                3.50  3.50

Tradition of Eating Grapes As Bells Ring in New Year's Day — A558

**2020, Nov. 6    Litho.    Perf. 13¼x13**
830  A558  €1.16 multi                2.75  2.75

Col de Beixalis — A559

**2021, Jan. 2    Litho.    Perf. 13**
831  A559  €4.40 multi               11.00 11.00

Tribute to Workers During the COVID-19 Pandemic — A560

**2021, Feb. 27    Litho.    Perf. 13¼**
832  A560  €1.28 multi                3.25  3.25

Opening of Prisunic Shopping Center — A561

**2021, Mar. 19    Litho.    Perf. 13¼**
833  A561  €1.28 multi                3.00  3.00

Bailen Guai Motorbike — A562

**2021, Apr. 23    Engr.    Perf. 13¼x13**
834  A562  €1.50 multi                3.75  3.75

Galemys Pyrenaicus — A563

**2021, May 14    Litho.    Perf. 13¼**
835  A563  €1.50 multi                3.75  3.75

Europa.

Pilar Maestre and Huguet Mir (1880-1957), Primary School Teachers — A564

**2021, June 4    Litho.    Perf. 13¼**
836  A564  €1.28 multi                3.00  3.00

Napoleon Bonaparte (1769-1821), Emperor of France — A565

**2021, June 17    Engr.    Perf. 13**
837  A565  €2.56 gold & blk           6.00  6.00

Stages 15 and 16 of the 2021 Tour de France in Andorra — A566

**Digital Printing**

**2021, July 13        Perf. 13¼**
838  A566  €1.50 multi                3.75  3.75

Cabana Sorda Lake A567

**2021, July 23    Litho.    Perf. 13**
839  A567  €1.28 multi                3.00  3.00

Oil Lamp From Church of Santa Eulalia d'Encamp A568

**2021, Aug. 6    Engr.    Perf. 13¼x13**
840  A568  €2.56 multi                6.00  6.00

Adoption of "El Gran Carlemany" as National Anthem, Cent. — A569

**2021, Sept. 6    Litho.    Perf. 13x13¼**
841  A569  €1.28 multi                3.00  3.00

Manuel Mas (1946-2001), Foreign Minister — A570

**2021, Sept. 24    Litho.    Perf. 13¼x13**
842  A570  €1.50 multi                3.50  3.50

# ANDORRA, FRENCH ADMINISTRATION

The Time Game, Sculpture by Judit Gaste Flinch — A571

**2021, Oct. 15**    Litho.    *Perf. 13*
843   A571   €2.56 multi      6.00   6.00

Alnus Glutinosa — A572

**2021, Nov. 5**    Engr.    *Perf. 13*
844   A572   €1.50 multi      3.50   3.50

Angel in St. Bartomeu Chapel, Sant Julià de Lòria — A573

**Digital Printing**    *Perf. 13*
**2021, Nov. 5**
845   A573   €1.28 multi      3.00   3.00

Plc de Carroi — A574

**2022, Jan. 3**    Litho.    *Perf. 13*
846   A574   €4.55 multi      10.50   10.50

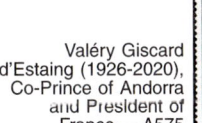

Valéry Giscard d'Estaing (1926-2020), Co-Prince of Andorra and President of France — A575

**2022, Feb. 2**    Litho.    *Perf. 13¼*
847   A575   €1.43 multi      3.25   3.25

Rosa Ferrer (1960-2018), Minister of Health, Welfare and Employment — A576

**2022, Mar. 8**    Litho.    *Perf. 13¼*
848   A576   €2.32 multi      5.25   5.25

Catalan Studies Program at Charles University, Prague, 30th Anniv. — A577

**2022, Apr. 8**    Litho.    *Perf. 13¼*
849   A577   €1.65 multi      3.50   3.50

Legends of Charlemagne (747-814) — A578

**2022, May 13**    Litho.    *Perf. 13¼*
850   A578   €1.65 multi      3.50   3.50

Europa.

Brown Cow — A579

**2022, May 27**    Litho.    *Perf. 13¼*
851   A579   €1.16 multi      2.50   2.50

Volkswagen 1303S — A580

**2022, June 23**    Engr.    *Perf. 13¼*
852   A580   €1.65 multi      3.50   3.50

Estany de l'Isla A581

**2022, July 9**    Litho.    *Perf. 13*
853   A581   €1.65 multi      3.50   3.50

Luna Park — A582

**2022, July 22**    Litho.    *Perf. 13¼*
854   A582   €1.43 multi      3.00   3.00

Execution of Joana Call for Witchcraft, 550th Anniv. — A583

**2022, Aug. 5**    Engr.    *Perf. 13*
855   A583   €2.32 multi      4.75   4.75

Destruction of Our Lady of Meritxell Icon in Meritxell Sanctuary Fire, 50th Anniv. — A584

**2022, Sept. 9**    Litho.    *Perf. 13¼*
856   A584   €1.43 multi      3.00   3.00

Trollius Europaeus A585

**2022, Sept. 30**    Litho.    *Perf. 13*
857   A585   €2.32 multi      4.50   4.50

El Voluntariat, Sculpture by Nerea Aixàs — A586

**2022, Oct. 21**    Litho.    *Perf. 13*
858   A586   €2.86 multi      5.75   5.75

Louis Pasteur (1822-95), Microbiologist — A587

**2022, Nov. 3**    Engr.    *Perf. 13¼*
859   A587   €1.65 black      3.50   3.50

Angel From Canopy in Chapel of St. Bartholomew, Sant Julià de Lòria — A588

**2022, Nov. 3**    Litho.    *Perf. 13*
860   A588   €1.43 multi      3.00   3.00

Col de Cabús — A589

**2023, Jan. 2**    Litho.    *Perf. 13¼*
861   A589   €4.83 multi      10.50   10.50

N.S.U Kettenkrad Half-Track Motorcycle — A590

**2023, Feb. 3**    Litho.    *Perf. 13¼*
862   A590   €1.16 multi      2.50   2.50

National Coat of Arms — A591

**2023, Mar. 6**    Litho.    *Perf. 13¼x13*
863   A591   50c multi      1.10   1.10

Finals of 2022-23 Alpine Skiing World Cup, Soldeu — A592

**2023, Mar. 10**    Litho.    *Perf. 13¼*
864   A592   €1.80 multi      4.00   4.00

Refuge Envalira Ski Chalet — A593

**2023, Mar. 23**    Engr.    *Perf. 13¼*
865   A593   €2.32 multi      5.00   5.00

Caterina Guerrero (1939-2020), Poet — A594

**2023, Apr. 14**    Litho.    *Perf. 13¼*
866   A594   €1.16 multi      2.60   2.60

Europa — A595

**2023, May 9**    Litho.    *Perf. 13¼*
867   A595   €1.80 multi      4.00   4.00

Moreno Pond A596

**2023, June 9**    Litho.    *Perf. 13*
868   A596   €1.80 multi      4.00   4.00

National Arms — A597

**2023, June 16**    Litho.    *Perf. 13¼x13*
869   A597   1c yel & multi      .30   .30
870   A597   20c lilac & multi      .45   .45

Compare type A597 with type A309.

Perseid Meteor Shower (Tears of St. Lawrence) A598

**2023, July 7**    Litho.    *Perf. 13¼*
871   A598   €1.16 multi      2.60   2.60

Andorran Anniversaries Pertaining to the United Nations — A599

No. 872 — Hands and text commemorating: a, 30th anniv. of Andorra in the United Nations (country name at LR). b, 30th anniv. of Andorra in UNESCO (country name at UL).

## ANDORRA, FRENCH ADMINISTRATION — ANGOLA

**2023, July 28**   Litho.   *Perf. 13*
872 A599 €1.80 Horiz. pair, #a-b   8.00 8.00

Book Restoration Fund of Casa d'Areny and Casa Rossell — A600

**2023, Aug. 11**   Litho.   *Perf. 13¼*
873 A600 €2.32 multi   5.00 5.00

Rugby, 200th Anniv. — A601

**2023, Sept. 15**   Litho.   *Perf. 13¼*
874 A601 €1.80 multi   4.00 4.00

Fragaria Vesca — A602

**2023, Sept. 22**   Engr.   *Perf. 13*
875 A602 €2.32 multi   5.00 5.00

Andorra Bicycle Museum, Andorra la Vella, 1st Anniv. — A603

**2023, Oct. 5**   Litho.   *Perf. 13¼*
876 A603 €1.16 multi   2.50 2.50

### SEMI-POSTAL STAMP

Catalogue values for unused stamps in this section are for Never Hinged items.

Virgin of St. Coloma — SP1

**Unwmk.**
**1964, July 25**   Engr.   *Perf. 13*
B1 SP1 25c + 10c multi   24.00 24.00
The surtax was for the Red Cross.

### AIR POST STAMPS

Catalogue values for unused stamps in this section are for Never Hinged items.

Chamois — AP1

**Unwmk.**
**1950, Feb. 20**   Engr.   *Perf. 13*
C1 AP1 100fr indigo   87.50 60.00

East Branch of Valira River — AP2

**1955-57**
C2 AP2 100fr dark green   16.00 10.50
C3 AP2 200fr cerise   32.50 16.00
C4 AP2 500fr dp bl ('57)   120.00 65.00
Nos. C2-C4 (3)   168.50 91.50
No. C3 in dark green was not regularly issued. Value, $3,500.

D'Inclès Valley — AP3

**1961-64**   Unwmk.   *Perf. 13*
C5 AP3 2fr red, ol gray & cl   1.25 1.25
C6 AP3 3fr bl, mar & slate grn   1.60 1.60
C7 AP3 5fr rose lil & red org   3.25 2.40
C8 AP3 10fr bl grn & slate grn   4.75 4.50
Nos. C5-C8 (4)   10.85 9.75
Issued: 10fr, 4/25/64; others, 6/19/61.

### POSTAGE DUE STAMPS

Postage Due Stamps of France, 1893-1931, Overprinted

### On Stamps of 1893-1926
**1931-33**   Unwmk.   *Perf. 14x13½*
J1 D2 5c blue   2.40 2.40
J2 D2 10c brown   2.40 2.40
J3 D2 30c rose red   1.60 1.60
J4 D2 50c violet brn   2.40 2.40
J5 D2 60c green   34.00 34.00
J6 D2 1fr red brn, *straw*   2.40 2.40
J7 D2 2fr brt violet   16.00 16.00
J8 D2 3fr magenta   3.25 3.25
Nos. J1-J8 (8)   64.45 64.45

### On Stamps of 1927-31
J9 D4 1c olive grn   3.25 3.25
J10 D4 10c rose   5.50 6.50
J11 D4 60c red   27.50 26.50
J12 D4 1fr Prus grn ('32)   110.00 120.00
J13 D4 1.20fr on 2fr bl   80.00 80.00
J14 D4 2fr ol brn ('33)   200.00 225.00
J15 D4 5fr on 1fr vio   120.00 120.00
Nos. J9-J15 (7)   546.25 581.25

 D5    D6

**1935-41**   Typo.
J16 D5 1c gray green   3.25 3.25
J17 D6 5c light blue ('37)   6.75 6.75
J18 D6 10c brown ('41)   4.00 5.50
J19 D6 2fr violet ('41)   11.00 8.75
J20 D6 5fr red orange ('41)   19.00 11.00
Nos. J16-J20 (5)   44.00 35.25

Catalogue values for unused stamps in this section, from this point to the end of the section, are for Never Hinged items.

Wheat Sheaves — D7

**1943-46**   *Perf. 14x13½*
J21 D7 10c sepia   .80 .70
J22 D7 30c brt red vio   .90 .70
J23 D7 50c blue grn   1.25 1.10
J24 D7 1fr brt ultra   1.10 .90
J25 D7 1.50fr rose red   6.75 5.50
J26 D7 2fr turq blue   1.75 1.60
J27 D7 3fr brown org   2.00 1.90
J28 D7 4fr dp vio ('45)   6.25 5.50
J29 D7 5fr brt pink   4.25 3.75
J30 D7 10fr red org ('45)   6.50 5.50
J31 D7 20fr olive brn ('46)   7.75 6.50
Nos. J21-J31 (11)   39.30 33.65

Inscribed: "Timbre Taxe"

**1946-53**
J32 D7 10c sepia ('46)   1.60 1.60
J33 D7 1fr ultra   .80 .80
J34 D7 2fr turq blue   1.25 1.25
J35 D7 3fr orange brn   2.75 2.75
J36 D7 4fr violet   3.50 3.50
J37 D7 5fr brt pink   2.75 2.75
J38 D7 10fr red orange   4.75 4.75
J39 D7 20fr olive brn   8.00 8.00
J40 D7 50fr dk green ('50)   47.50 47.50
J41 D7 100fr dp green ('53)   120.00 120.00
Nos. J32-J41 (10)   192.90 192.90

Inscribed: "Timbre Taxe"

**1961, June 19**   *Perf. 14x13½*
J42 D7 5c rose pink   4.00 4.00
J43 D7 10c red orange   8.00 8.00
J44 D7 20c olive   12.00 12.00
J45 D7 50c dark slate green   24.00 24.00
Nos. J42-J45 (4)   48.00 48.00

D8

**1964-71**   Typo.   *Perf. 14x13½*
J46 D8 5c Centaury ('65)   .25 .25
J47 D8 10c Gentian ('65)   .25 .25
J48 D8 15c Corn poppy   .25 .25
J49 D8 20c Violets ('71)   .30 .25
J50 D8 30c Forget-me-not   .40 .30
J51 D8 40c Columbine ('71)   .55 .40
J52 D8 50c Clover ('65)   .65 .55
Nos. J46-J52 (7)   2.65 2.25

D9

**1985, Oct. 21**   Engr.   *Perf. 13*
J53 D9 10c Holly   .25 .25
J54 D9 20c Blueberries   .25 .25
J55 D9 30c Raspberries   .25 .25
J56 D9 40c Bilberries   .25 .25
J57 D9 50c Blackberries   .25 .25
J58 D9 1fr Broom   .40 .40
J59 D9 2fr Rosehips   .95 .65
J60 D9 3fr Nightshade   1.25 .95
J61 D9 4fr Nabiu   1.50 1.25
J62 D9 5fr Strawberries   1.90 1.50
Nos. J53-J62 (10)   7.25 6.00

### NEWSPAPER STAMP

France No. P7 Overprinted

**1931**   Unwmk.   *Perf. 14x13½*
P1 A16 ½c on 1c gray   1.25 1.25
  a. Double overprint   2,750.
    Never Hinged   3,600.

## ANGOLA
aŋ-ˈgō-lə

LOCATION — S.W. Africa between Zaire and Namibia.
GOVT. — Republic.
AREA — 481,351 sq. mi.
POP. — 33,870,000 (2020 est.)

CAPITAL — Luanda

Angola was a Portuguese overseas territory until it became independent November 11, 1975, as the People's Republic of Angola.

1000 Reis = 1 Milreis
100 Centavos = 1 Escudo (1913, 1954)
100 Centavos = 1 Angolar (1932)
10 Lweys = 1 Kwanza (1977)

Catalogue values for unused stamps in this country are for Never Hinged items, beginning with Scott 328 in the regular postage section, Scott C26 in the airpost section, Scott J31 in the postage due section, and Scott RA7 in the postal tax section.

**Watermark**

Wmk. 232 — Maltese Cross

Portuguese Crown — A1

*Perf. 12½, 13½*
**1870-77**   Typo.   Unwmk.
**Thin to Medium Paper**
1 A1 5r gray black   4.00 2.00
2 A1 10r yellow   27.00 20.00
3 A1 20r bister   3.50 2.25
4 A1 25r red   16.00 10.00
5 A1 40r blue ('77)   225.00 160.00
6 A1 50r green   70.00 17.00
7 A1 100r lilac   13.50 5.50
8 A1 200r orange ('77)   8.00 4.50
9 A1 300r choc ('77)   23.50 14.50

**1881-85**   *Perf. 12½, 13½*
10 A1 10r green ('83)   10.00 5.25
11 A1 20r carmine rose ('85)   21.00 14.00
12 A1 25r violet ('85)   15.00 5.50
13 A1 40r buff ('82)   14.50 6.50
14 A1 50r blue   50.00 10.00
Nos. 10-15 (5)   110.50 41.25

Two types of numerals are found on #2, 11, 13, 15.

The cliche of 40r in plate of 20r error, was discovered before the stamps were issued. All examples were defaced by a blue pencil mark. Values, $2,100 unused; in pair with 20r, $2,400.

In perf. 12½, Nos. 1-4, 4a and 6, as well as 7a, were printed in 1870 on thicker paper and 1875 on normal paper. Stamps of the earlier printing sell for 2 to 5 times more than those of the 1875 printing.

Some reprints of the 1870-85 issues are on a smooth white chalky paper, ungummed and perf. 13½. Value, each $17.50.

Other reprints of these issues are on thin ivory paper with shiny white gum and clear-cut perf. 13½. Value, each $24.

King Luiz — A2

**1886**   Embossed   *Perf. 12½*
16 A2 5r black   19.00 7.50
17 A2 10r green   16.50 7.00
18 A2 20r rose   28.00 15.50
19 A2 25r red violet   20.00 5.00
20 A2 40r chocolate   22.50 8.50
21 A2 50r blue   29.00 5.00
22 A2 100r yellow brn   40.00 11.50

ANGOLA 487

| | | | | |
|---|---|---|---|---|
| **23** | A2 | 200r gray violet | 55.00 | 16.00 |
| **24** | A2 | 300r orange | 55.00 | 20.00 |
| | | *Nos. 16-24 (9)* | 285.00 | 96.00 |

For surcharges see Nos. 61-69, 172-174, 208-210.

*Reprints of 5r, 20r & 100r have cleancut perf. 13½.*

King Carlos — A3

**1893-94 Typo.** ***Perf. 11½, 12½, 13½***

| | | | | |
|---|---|---|---|---|
| **25** | A3 | 5r yellow | 2.90 | 1.50 |
| **26** | A3 | 10r redsh violet | 3.25 | 2.50 |
| **27a** | A3 | 15r chocolate | 6.75 | 3.00 |
| **28** | A3 | 20r lavender | 8.00 | 3.00 |
| **29c** | A3 | 25r green | 4.50 | 2.25 |
| **30b** | A3 | 50r light blue | 6.75 | 2.90 |
| **31** | A3 | 75r carmine | 12.50 | 9.00 |
| **32** | A3 | 80r lt green | 20.00 | 10.00 |
| **33** | A3 | 100r brown, *buff* | 20.00 | 10.00 |
| **34** | A3 | 150r car, *rose* | 25.00 | 17.00 |
| **35** | A3 | 200r dk blue, *lt bl* | 25.00 | 15.50 |
| **36** | A3 | 300r dk blue, *sal* | 25.00 | 15.50 |

For surcharges see Nos. 70-81, 175-179, 213-216, 234.

No. P1 Surcharged in Blue

**1894, Aug.** ***Perf. 13½***

| | | | | |
|---|---|---|---|---|
| **37** | N1 | 25r on 2½r brown | 85.00 | 72.50 |
| *a.* | | Double surcharge, one inverted | 175.00 | |
| *b.* | | Perf. 11½ | 110.00 | 85.00 |
| *c.* | | Perf. 12½ | 100.00 | 77.50 |
| *d.* | | As 'c,' double surcharge, one inverted | 140.00 | 125.00 |

King Carlos — A5

**1898-1903** ***Perf. 11½***

**Name and Value in Black except 500r**

| | | | | |
|---|---|---|---|---|
| **38** | A5 | 2½r gray | .65 | .50 |
| **39** | A5 | 5r orange | .65 | .50 |
| **40** | A5 | 10r yellow grn | .65 | .50 |
| **41** | A5 | 15r violet brn | 3.25 | 1.60 |
| **42** | A5 | 15r gray green ('03) | 1.60 | 1.40 |
| **43** | A5 | 20r gray violet | .70 | .50 |
| **44** | A5 | 25r sea green | 1.60 | .75 |
| **45** | A5 | 25r car ('03) | .85 | .45 |
| **46** | A5 | 50r blue | 2.75 | 1.00 |
| **47** | A5 | 50r brown ('03) | 8.00 | 3.75 |
| **48** | A5 | 65r dull blue ('03) | 8.50 | 5.75 |
| **49** | A5 | 75r rose | 11.00 | 6.00 |
| **50** | A5 | 75r red violet ('03) | 3.00 | 2.00 |
| **51** | A5 | 80r violet | 10.00 | 3.00 |
| **52** | A5 | 100r dk blue, *blue* | 2.00 | 1.40 |
| **53** | A5 | 115r org brn, *pink* ('03) | 11.00 | 7.50 |
| **54** | A5 | 130r brn, *straw* ('03) | 11.00 | 7.50 |
| **55** | A5 | 150r brn, *straw* | 11.00 | 6.00 |
| **56** | A5 | 200r red vio, *pink* | 7.50 | 1.75 |
| **57** | A5 | 300r dk blue, *rose* | 6.50 | 5.00 |
| **58** | A5 | 400r dull bl, *straw* ('03) | 12.50 | 3.50 |
| **59** | A5 | 500r blk & red, *bl* ('01) | 16.00 | 5.00 |
| **60** | A5 | 700r vio, *yelsh* ('01) | 35.00 | 17.00 |
| | | *Nos. 38-60 (23)* | 165.70 | 82.35 |

For surcharges and overprints see Nos. 83-102, 110-117, 159-171, 181-183, 217-218, 221-225.

Stamps of 1886-94 Surcharged in Black or Red

Two types of surcharge:
I — 3mm between numeral and REIS.
II — 4½mm spacing.

**1902** ***Perf. 12½***

| | | | | |
|---|---|---|---|---|
| **61** | A2 | 65r on 40r choc | 13.50 | 8.00 |
| **62** | A2 | 65r on 300r org, I | 13.50 | 8.00 |
| *a.* | | Type II | 13.50 | 8.00 |
| **63** | A2 | 115r on 10r green | 11.25 | 7.75 |
| *a.* | | Inverted surcharge | 90.00 | 50.00 |
| *b.* | | Perf. 13½ | 75.00 | 45.00 |
| **64** | A2 | 115r on 200r gray vio | 11.25 | 7.75 |
| **65** | A2 | 130r on 50r blue | 15.25 | 5.75 |
| **66** | A2 | 130r on 100r brown | 10.00 | 5.75 |
| **67** | A2 | 400r on 20r rose | 115.00 | 67.50 |
| *a.* | | Perf. 13½ | 200.00 | 125.00 |
| **68** | A2 | 400r on 25r violet | 26.00 | 13.00 |
| **69** | A2 | 400r on 5r black (R) | 22.50 | 16.00 |
| *a.* | | Double surcharge | 75.00 | 50.00 |
| | | *Nos. 61-69 (9)* | 238.25 | 139.50 |

For surcharges see Nos. 172-174, 208-210.

***Perf. 11½, 12½, 13½***

| | | | | |
|---|---|---|---|---|
| **70** | A3 | 65r on 5r yel, I, perf. 11½ | 11.00 | 7.75 |
| *a.* | | Type II | 11.00 | 7.75 |
| **71** | A3 | 65r on 10r red vio, I, perf. 12½ | 8.50 | 6.50 |
| *a.* | | Type II | 7.25 | 5.50 |
| *b.* | | Perf. 11½, I | 13.50 | 7.75 |
| *c.* | | Perf. 11½, I | 12.00 | 7.00 |
| **72** | A3 | 65r on 20r lav, perf. 11½ | 13.00 | 8.00 |
| **73** | A3 | 65r on 25r green, perf. 12½ | 14.50 | 10.00 |
| *b.* | | Perf. 13½ | 7.50 | 5.50 |
| **74** | A3 | 115r on 80r lt grn, perf. 12½ | 17.00 | 10.75 |
| **75** | A3 | 115r on 100r brn, *buff*, perf. 12½ | 17.00 | 10.00 |
| *b.* | | Perf. 13½ | 80.00 | 45.00 |
| **76** | A3 | 115r on 150r car, *rose*, perf. 11½ | 20.00 | 12.50 |
| *a.* | | Perf. 13½ | 27.00 | 15.75 |
| *b.* | | Perf. 12½ | 24.00 | 15.00 |
| **77** | A3 | 130r on 15r choc, perf. 12½ | 8.00 | 5.50 |
| *b.* | | Type II | 8.00 | 4.50 |
| **78** | A3 | 130r on 75r carmine, perf. 11½ | 67.50 | 55.00 |
| *a.* | | Perf. 13½ | 72.50 | 57.50 |
| *b.* | | Perf. 12½ | 12.50 | 10.25 |
| **79** | A3 | 130r on 300r dk bl, *sal*, perf. 12½ | 22.50 | 18.00 |
| *a.* | | Perf. 13½ | 30.00 | 16.25 |
| **80** | A3 | 400r on 50r lt bl, I, perf. 12½ | 11.50 | 6.50 |
| *a.* | | Perf. 11½ | 32.50 | 15.00 |
| *c.* | | Type II | 10.50 | 6.50 |
| **81** | A3 | 400r on 200r bl, *bl*, perf. 12½ | 11.50 | 9.00 |
| *a.* | | Perf. 13½ | 375.00 | 225.00 |
| **82** | N1 | 400r on 2½r brn, I, perf. 12½ | 2.25 | 1.75 |
| *a.* | | Type II | 1.75 | 1.60 |
| | | *Nos. 70-82 (13)* | 224.25 | 161.25 |

For surcharges see Nos. 175-180, 211-216, 234-235.

*Reprints of Nos. 65, 67, 68 and 69 have clean-cut perforation 13½.*

For detailed listings of perforation and paper varieties, see *Scott Classic Specialized Catalogue of Stamps and Covers 1840-1940.*

Stamps of 1898 Overprinted — a

**1902** ***Perf. 11½***

| | | | | |
|---|---|---|---|---|
| **83** | A5 | 15r brown | 2.50 | 1.75 |
| **84** | A5 | 25r sea green | 2.00 | 1.00 |
| **85** | A5 | 50r blue | 4.50 | 2.00 |
| **86** | A5 | 75r rose | 7.00 | 5.25 |
| | | *Nos. 83-86 (4)* | 16.00 | 10.00 |

For surcharge see No. 116.

No. 48 Surcharged in Black

**1905**

| | | | | |
|---|---|---|---|---|
| **87** | A5 | 50r on 65r dull blue | 6.75 | 3.50 |

For surcharge see No. 183.

Stamps of 1898-1903 Overprinted in Carmine or Green — b

**1911**

| | | | | |
|---|---|---|---|---|
| **88** | A5 | 2½r gray | .60 | .50 |
| **89** | A5 | 5r orange yel | .60 | .50 |
| **90** | A5 | 10r light green | .60 | .50 |
| **91** | A5 | 15r gray green | .85 | .70 |
| **92** | A5 | 20r gray violet | .90 | .75 |
| **93** | A5 | 25r car (G) | .90 | .75 |
| **94** | A5 | 50r brown | 3.25 | 1.75 |
| **95** | A5 | 75r lilac | 6.75 | 3.25 |
| **96** | A5 | 100r dk blue, *bl* | 6.75 | 3.50 |
| **97** | A5 | 115r org brn, *pink* | 3.75 | 1.75 |
| **98** | A5 | 130r brn, *straw* | 3.75 | 1.75 |
| **99** | A5 | 200r red lil, *pnksh* | 4.50 | 2.40 |
| **100** | A5 | 400r dull bl, *straw* | 4.50 | 1.75 |
| **101** | A5 | 500r blk & red, *bl* | 4.50 | 2.25 |
| **102** | A5 | 700r violet, *yelsh* | 4.50 | 2.50 |
| | | *Nos. 88-102 (15)* | 46.70 | 24.60 |

Inverted and double overprints of Nos. 88-102 were made intentionally.

For surcharges see Nos. 217-218, 221-222, 224.

King Manuel II — A6

**Overprinted in Carmine or Green**

**1912** ***Perf. 11½x12***

| | | | | |
|---|---|---|---|---|
| **103** | A6 | 2½r violet | .75 | .50 |
| **104** | A6 | 5r black | .75 | .50 |
| **105** | A6 | 10r gray green | .75 | .50 |
| **106** | A6 | 20r carmine (G) | .75 | .50 |
| **107** | A6 | 25r violet brown | .75 | .50 |
| **108** | A6 | 50r dk blue | 1.75 | 1.40 |
| **109** | A6 | 75r bister brown | 2.00 | 1.75 |
| **110** | A6 | 100r brown, *lt green* | 3.75 | 2.25 |
| **111** | A6 | 200r dk green, *salmon* | 3.75 | 2.40 |
| **112** | A6 | 300r black, *azure* | 3.75 | 2.40 |
| | | *Nos. 103-112 (10)* | 18.75 | 12.70 |

For surcharges see Nos. 219-220, 226-227.

No. 91 Surcharged in Black

**1912, June** ***Perf. 11½***

| | | | | |
|---|---|---|---|---|
| **113** | A5 | 2½r on 15r gray green | 5.00 | 2.85 |
| **114** | A5 | 5r on 15r gray green | 5.50 | 2.85 |
| **115** | A5 | 10r on 15r gray green | 4.25 | 2.85 |
| | | *Nos. 113-115 (3)* | 14.75 | 8.55 |

Inverted and double surcharges of Nos. 113-115 were made intentionally.

Nos. 86 and 50 Surcharged in Black and Overprinted in Violet — c

**1912**

| | | | | |
|---|---|---|---|---|
| **116** | A5 | 25r on 75r rose | 90.00 | 62.50 |
| **117** | A5 | 25r on 75r red violet | 6.25 | 5.50 |
| *a.* | | "REUPBLICA" | 110.00 | 77.50 |
| *b.* | | "25" omitted | 135.00 | 70.00 |
| *c.* | | "REPUBLICA" omitted | 110.00 | 77.50 |

Ceres — A7

**With Imprint**

**1914 Chalky Paper** ***Perf. 15x14***

**Name and Value in Black**

| | | | | |
|---|---|---|---|---|
| **118** | A7 | ¼c olive brown | 1.75 | .80 |
| **119** | A7 | ½c black | 1.75 | .80 |
| **120** | A7 | 1c blue green | 1.75 | .80 |
| **121** | A7 | 1½c lilac brown | 3.50 | 2.00 |
| **122** | A7 | 2c carmine | 6.25 | 2.90 |
| **123** | A7 | 2½c violet | 1.25 | .55 |
| **124** | A7 | 5c blue | 2.65 | 1.40 |
| **125** | A7 | 7½c yellow brn | 3.50 | 2.15 |
| **126** | A7 | 8c slate | 3.50 | 2.15 |
| **127** | A7 | 10c orange brn | 3.50 | 2.15 |
| **128** | A7 | 15c brown rose | 5.25 | 2.20 |
| **129** | A7 | 20c yel green | 2.65 | 1.40 |
| **130** | A7 | 30c brown, *green* | 2.65 | 2.15 |
| **131** | A7 | 40c brown, *pink* | 2.65 | 2.15 |
| **132** | A7 | 50c orange, *sal* | 9.75 | 7.35 |
| **133** | A7 | 1e green, *blue* | 7.00 | 4.25 |
| | | *Nos. 118-133 (16)* | 59.35 | 35.20 |

**1915-22 Ordinary Paper**

| | | | | |
|---|---|---|---|---|
| **134** | A7 | ¼c olive brown | .40 | .40 |
| **135** | A7 | ½c black | .40 | .40 |
| **136** | A7 | 1c blue green | .40 | .40 |
| **137** | A7 | 1c yellow green ('18) | .40 | .40 |
| **138** | A7 | 1½c lilac brown | .40 | .40 |
| **139** | A7 | 2c carmine | .50 | .40 |
| **140** | A7 | 2½c dark violet | .50 | .40 |
| **141** | A7 | 3c orange | 24.00 | 21.50 |
| **142** | A7 | 4c dull rose ('21) | .40 | .40 |
| **143** | A7 | 5c blue | 1.55 | 1.25 |
| **144** | A7 | 6c lilac ('21) | .40 | .40 |
| **145** | A7 | 7c ultra ('21) | .40 | .40 |
| **146** | A7 | 7½c yellow brn ('20) | .50 | .40 |
| **147** | A7 | 8c slate | .55 | .50 |
| **148** | A7 | 10c orange brn ('18) | .50 | .40 |
| **149** | A7 | 12c olive brown ('21) | 1.30 | .90 |
| **150** | A7 | 15c plum ('20) | .50 | .40 |
| **151** | A7 | 15c brown rose ('21) | .50 | .40 |
| **152** | A7 | 20c yel green ('18) | 5.95 | 4.50 |
| **153** | A7 | 30c gray green ('21) | .90 | .60 |
| **154** | A7 | 80c pink ('21) | 1.55 | .90 |
| **155** | A7 | 2e dark violet ('22) | 3.10 | 2.70 |
| | | *Nos. 134-155 (22)* | 45.10 | 38.45 |

**1921-26** ***Perf. 12x11½***

| | | | | |
|---|---|---|---|---|
| **156** | A7 | ¼c olive brown ('24) | .45 | .45 |
| **157** | A7 | ½c black | .45 | .45 |
| **158** | A7 | 1c blue green ('24) | .45 | .45 |
| **158C** | A7 | 1½c lilac brown ('24) | .45 | .45 |
| **158D** | A7 | 2c carmine ('24) | .45 | .45 |
| **158E** | A7 | 2c gray ('25) | .75 | .55 |
| **158F** | A7 | 2½c lt violet ('24) | .45 | .45 |
| **158G** | A7 | 3c orange | .45 | .45 |
| **158H** | A7 | 4c dull rose | .45 | .45 |
| **158I** | A7 | 4½c gray | .45 | .45 |
| **158J** | A7 | 5c blue ('24) | .45 | .45 |
| **158K** | A7 | 6c lilac | .45 | .45 |
| **158L** | A7 | 7c ultra | .45 | .45 |
| **158M** | A7 | 7½c yellow brown ('24) | .55 | .45 |
| **158N** | A7 | 8c slate ('24) | .55 | .45 |
| **158O** | A7 | 10c orange brn ('24) | .45 | .40 |
| **158P** | A7 | 12c olive brn | .75 | .60 |
| **158Q** | A7 | 12c dp green ('25) | .75 | .50 |
| **158R** | A7 | 15c plum ('24) | .45 | .35 |
| **158S** | A7 | 20c yel green | 1.75 | 1.60 |
| **158T** | A7 | 24c ultra ('25) | 1.60 | 1.20 |
| **158U** | A7 | 25c choc ('25) | 1.60 | 1.20 |
| **158V** | A7 | 30c gray grn | .75 | .60 |
| **158W** | A7 | 40c turq blue | 1.20 | .70 |
| **158X** | A7 | 50c lt violet ('25) | 1.40 | .70 |
| **158Y** | A7 | 60c dk blue ('22) | 1.50 | 1.00 |
| **158Z** | A7 | 60c dp rose ('26) | 75.00 | 47.50 |
| **159A** | A7 | 80c pink ('22) | 1.75 | 1.00 |
| **159B** | A7 | 1e rose ('22) | 1.75 | 1.00 |
| | | *Nos. 156-159B (29)* | 97.95 | 65.20 |

**Glazed Paper**

**1921-25** ***Perf. 12x11½***

| | | | | |
|---|---|---|---|---|
| **159C** | A7 | 1e rose | 1.75 | 1.75 |
| **159D** | A7 | 1e deep blue ('25) | 3.25 | 1.60 |
| **159E** | A7 | 2e dark violet ('22) | 2.25 | 1.25 |
| **159F** | A7 | 5e buff ('25) | 14.00 | 11.50 |
| **159G** | A7 | 10c pink ('25) | 30.00 | 25.00 |
| **159H** | A7 | 20e pale turq ('25) | 100.00 | 70.00 |
| | | *Nos. 159C-159H (6)* | 151.25 | 111.10 |

For surcharges see Nos. 228-229, 236-239.

**Stamps of 1898-1903 Overprinted type "c" in Red or Green**

**1914** ***Perf. 11½, 12***

| | | | | |
|---|---|---|---|---|
| **159** | A5 | 10r yel green (R) | 7.50 | 5.50 |
| **160** | A5 | 15r gray green (R) | 6.75 | 5.50 |
| **161** | A5 | 20r gray violet (G) | 2.75 | 2.00 |
| **163** | A5 | 75r red violet (G) | 2.75 | 1.40 |
| **164** | A5 | 100r blue, *blue* (R) | 4.00 | 3.75 |
| **165** | A5 | 115r org brn, *pink* (R) | 150.00 | |
| **167** | A5 | 200r red vio, *pnksh* (G) | 2.75 | 1.75 |
| **169** | A5 | 400r dl bl, *straw* (R) | 50.00 | 45.00 |
| **170** | A5 | 500r blk & red, *bl* (R) | 6.75 | 5.50 |
| **171** | A5 | 700r vio, *yelsh* (G) | 35.00 | 23.50 |

Inverted and double overprints were made intentionally. No. 165 was not regularly issued. Red overprints on the 20r, 75r, 200r were not regularly issued. The 130r was not regularly issued without surcharge (No. 225). Value, $125 mint.

**On Nos. 63-65, 74-76, 78-79, 82**

***Perf. 11½, 12½, 13½***

| | | | | |
|---|---|---|---|---|
| **172** | A2 | 115r on 10r (R) | 19.00 | 18.00 |
| *a.* | | Perf. 13½ | 19.00 | 18.00 |
| **173** | A2 | 115r on 200r (R) | 25.00 | 24.25 |
| **174** | A2 | 130r on 50r (R) | 31.50 | 30.50 |
| **175** | A3 | 115r on 80r (R) | 225.00 | 225.00 |
| **176** | A3 | 115r on 100r (R) | 290.00 | 225.00 |
| *a.* | | Perf. 11½ | [illegible] | [illegible] |
| *b.* | | Perf. 13½ | 900.00 | 850.00 |
| **177** | A3 | 115r on 150r (G) | 250.00 | 200.00 |
| *a.* | | Perf. 12½ | 270.00 | 225.00 |
| *b.* | | Perf. 13½ | 800.00 | 775.00 |
| **178** | A3 | 130r on 75r (G) | 4.50 | 3.75 |
| *a.* | | Perf. 12½ | 9.50 | 7.85 |
| **179** | A3 | 130r on 300r (R) | 10.50 | 8.25 |
| *a.* | | Perf. 12½ | 17.50 | 16.00 |
| **180** | N1 | 400r on 2½r (R) | 1.10 | .80 |
| *a.* | | Perf. 11½ | 5.50 | .80 |
| *b.* | | Perf. 13½ | 1.10 | .80 |
| | | *Nos. 172-180 (9)* | 856.60 | 735.55 |

Nos. 85-87 Overprinted in Red or Green

**On Stamps of 1902**

***Perf. 11½, 12***

| | | | | |
|---|---|---|---|---|
| **181** | A5 | 50r blue (R) | 2.50 | 2.00 |

**182** A5 75r rose (G) 5.65 4.00

### On No. 87

**183** A5 50r on 65r dull blue (R) 5.65 2.05
*Nos. 181-183 (3)* 13.80 8.05

Inverted and double surcharges of Nos. 181-183 were made intentionally.

Common Design Types pictured following the introduction.

## Vasco da Gama Issue of Various Portuguese Colonies

Common Design Types CD20-CD27 Srchd.

### On Stamps of Macao

**1913** *Perf. 12½ to 16*

**184** ¼c on ½a blue grn 2.50 2.05
**185** ½c on la red 2.50 2.05
**186** 1c on 2a red violet 2.70 2.05
**187** 2½c on 4a yel green 1.95 1.45
**188** 5c on 8a dk blue 1.95 1.45
**189** 7½c on 12a vio brn 9.00 6.40
**190** 10c on 16a bister brn 3.10 2.30
**191** 15c on 24a bister 4.20 2.30
*Nos. 184-191 (8)* 27.90 20.05

### On Stamps of Portuguese Africa

*Perf. 14 to 15*

**192** ¼c on 2½r blue grn 1.10 .70
**193** ½c on 5r red 1.10 .70
**194** 1c on 10r red violet 1.10 .70
**195** 2½c on 25r yel grn 1.10 .70
**196** 5c on 50r dk blue 1.10 .70
**197** 7½c on 75r vio brn 6.75 5.50
**198** 10c on 100r bister brn 2.65 1.65
**199** 15c on 150r bister 3.10 1.85
*Nos. 192-199 (8)* 18.00 12.50

### On Stamps of Timor

**200** ¼c on ½a blue grn 2.50 1.75
**201** ½c on 1a red 2.50 1.75
**202** 1c on 2a red vio 2.70 1.75
**203** 2½c on 4a yel grn 1.95 1.25
**204** 5c on 8a dk blue 1.95 1.25
**205** 7½c on 12a vio brn 8.95 5.50
**206** 10c on 16a bis brn 3.10 2.00
**207** 15c on 24a bister 4.20 2.00
*Nos. 200-207 (8)* 27.85 17.25
*Nos. 184-207 (24)* 73.75 49.80

Provisional Issue of 1902 Overprinted in Carmine

**1915** *Perf. 11½, 12½, 13½*

**208** A2 115r on 10r green 2.25 2.15
*a.* Perf. 12½ 2.95 2.50
**209** A2 115r on 200r gray vio 2.50 2.25
**210** A2 130r on 100r brown 2.15 2.00
**211** A3 115r on 80r lt green 1.90 1.55
**212** A3 115r on 100r brn, *buff* 2.50 2.15
*a.* Perf. 11½ 117.50 100.00
*b.* Perf. 13½ 18.00 14.50
**213** A3 115r on 150r car, *rose* 1.90 1.80
*a.* Perf. 12½ 4.25 3.60
*b.* Perf. 13½ 2.95 2.50
**214** A3 130r on 15r choc 1.90 1.70
*a.* Perf. 12½ 8.75 7.25
**215** A3 130r on 75r carmine 3.40 2.50
*a.* Perf. 13½ 5.65 4.50
*b.* Perf. 12½ 3.60 2.25
**216** A3 130r on 300r dk bl, *sal* 2.25 2.15
*a.* Perf. 13½ 4.25 2.70
*Nos. 208-216 (9)* 20.75 18.25

## Stamps of 1911-14 Surcharged in Black

d

e

### On Stamps of 1911

**1919** *Perf. 11½*

**217** A5 (d) ½c on 75r red lilac 3.40 2.50
**218** A5 (d) 2½c on 100r blue, *grysh* 3.40 2.50

### On Stamps of 1912

*Perf. 11½x12*

**219** A6 (e) ½c on 75r bis brn 1.70 1.15
**220** A6 (e) 2½c on 100r brn, *lt grn* 3.40 2.50

### On Stamps of 1914

**221** A5 (d) ½c on 75r red lil 1.80 1.55
**222** A5 (d) 2½c on 100r bl, *grysh* 2.25 1.60
*Nos. 217-222 (6)* 15.95 11.80

Inverted and double surcharges were made for sale to collectors.

Nos. 163, 98 and Type of 1914 Surcharged in Black

**1921**

**223** A5 (c) 00.5c on 75r *400.00 350.00*
**224** A5 (b) 4c on 130r (#98) 2.50 1.70
**225** A5 (c) 4c on 130r brn, *straw* 7.50 5.75
*a.* Without surcharge *240.00*

## Nos. 109 and 108 Surcharged with New Values and Bars in Black

**226** A6 00.5c on 75r 1.80 1.55
**227** A6 1c on 50r 1.90 1.70

## Nos. 146 and 150 Surcharged with New Values and Bars in Black

**228** A7 00.5c on 7½c 2.50 2.00
**229** A7 04c on 15c 2.50 1.70
*Nos. 224-229 (6)* 18.70 14.40
*Nos. 223-229 (7)* *418.70 364.40*

The 04c surcharge exists on the 15c brown rose, perf 12x11½, No. 158R.

Some authorities question the status of No. 223.

Nos. 81-82 Surcharged

**1925** *Perf. 12½*

**234** A3 40c on 400r on 200r bl, *bl* 1.15 1.00
*a.* Perf. 13½ 1.15 1.00
**235** N1 40c on 400r on 2½r brn 1.25 1.10
*a.* Perf. 13½ 6.00 4.75

Nos. 158Y, 159A, 159D-159E Surcharged

**1931** *Perf. 12x 11½*

**236** A7 50c on 60c deep rose 2.25 1.80
**237** A7 70c on 80c pink 4.50 2.70
**238** A7 70c on 1e deep blue 4.00 2.70
**239** A7 1.40e on 2e dark violet 2.50 1.80
*Nos. 236-239 (4)* 13.25 9.00

Ceres — A14

*Perf. 12x11½*

**1932-46** Typo. Wmk. 232

**243** A14 1c bister brn .30 .25
**244** A14 5c dk brown .35 .30
**245** A14 10c dp violet .35 .30
**246** A14 15c black .35 .30
**247** A14 20c gray .40 .30
**248** A14 30c myrtle grn .40 .30
**249** A14 35c yel grn ('46) 7.50 4.50
**250** A14 40c dp orange .40 .30
**251** A14 45c lt blue 1.75 1.25
**252** A14 50c lt brown .30 .25
**253** A14 60c olive grn 1.00 .30
**254** A14 70c orange brn 1.10 .30
**255** A14 80c emerald .75 .25
**256** A14 85c rose 5.50 2.00
**257** A14 1a claret 1.10 .30
**258** A14 1.40a dk blue 11.50 1.75
**258A** A14 1.75a dk blue ('46) 16.00 5.25
**259** A14 2a dull vio 5.25 .55
**260** A14 5a pale yel grn 10.50 1.75
**261** A14 10a olive bis 20.00 5.25
**262** A14 20a orange 52.50 5.25
*Nos. 243-262 (21)* 137.30 31.00
Set, never hinged 175.00

For surcharges see Nos. 263-267, 271-273, 294A-300, J31-J36.

Surcharged in Black

5½mm between bars and new value.

**1934**

**263** A14 10c on 45c lt bl 3.50 2.50
**264** A14 20c on 85c rose 3.50 2.50
**265** A14 30c on 1.40a dk bl 3.50 2.50
**266** A14 70c on 2a dl vio 5.50 2.75
**267** A14 80c on 5a pale yel grn 8.75 2.75
*Nos. 263-267 (5)* 24.75 13.00
Set, never hinged 42.50

See Nos. 294A-300.

Nos. J26, J30 Surcharged in Black

**1935** Unwmk. *Perf. 11½*

**268** D2 5c on 6c lt brown 1.80 1.60
**269** D2 30c on 50c gray 1.80 1.60
**270** D2 40c on 50c gray 1.80 1.60
*Nos. 268-270 (3)* 5.40 4.80
Set, never hinged 10.00

Inverted and double surcharges were made for sale to collectors.

No. 255 Surcharged in Black

**1938** Wmk. 232 *Perf. 12x11½*

**271** A14 5c on 80c emerald 1.10 .55
**272** A14 10c on 80c emerald 1.60 .75
**273** A14 15c on 80c emerald 2.25 .75
*Nos. 271-273 (3)* 4.95 2.05
Set, never hinged 8.25

## Vasco da Gama Issue

Common Design Types

**Engr.; Name & Value Typo. in Black**

*Perf. 13½x13*

**1938, July 26** Unwmk.

**274** CD34 1c gray green .30 .25
**275** CD34 5c orange brn .30 .25
**276** CD34 10c dk carmine .40 .25
**277** CD34 15c dk violet brn .40 .25
**278** CD34 20c slate .40 .25
**279** CD35 30c rose violet .55 .35
**280** CD35 35c brt green 1.00 .65
**281** CD35 40c brown .40 .25
**282** CD35 50c brt red vio .55 .25
**283** CD36 60c gray black 1.10 .25
**284** CD36 70c brown vio 1.10 .25
**285** CD36 80c orange 1.10 .25
**286** CD36 1a red 1.10 .25
**287** CD37 1.75a blue 2.10 .85
**288** CD37 2a brown car 3.25 1.30
**289** CD37 5a olive grn 13.50 1.30
**290** CD38 10a blue vio 28.00 1.65
**291** CD38 20a red brown 40.00 3.70
*Nos. 274-291 (18)* 95.55 12.55
Set, never hinged 150.00

For surcharges see Nos. 301-304.

Marble Column and Portuguese Arms with Cross — A20

**1938, July 29** *Perf. 12½*

**292** A20 80c blue green 3.50 2.25
**293** A20 1.75a deep blue 22.50 6.00
**294** A20 20a dk red brown 67.50 37.50
*Nos. 292-294 (3)* 93.50 45.75
Set, never hinged 155.00

Visit of the President of Portugal to this colony in 1938.

## Stamps of 1932 Surcharged with New Value and Bars

8mm between bars and new value.

**1941-45** Wmk. 232 *Perf. 12x11½*

**294A** A14 5c on 80c emer ('45) 1.00 .60
**295** A14 10c on 45c lt blue 2.00 1.25
**296** A14 15c on 45c lt blue 2.00 1.25
**297** A14 20c on 85c rose 2.00 1.25
**298** A14 35c on 85c rose 2.00 1.25
**299** A14 50c on 1.40a dk blue 2.00 1.25
**300** A14 60c on 1a claret 10.25 8.00
*Nos. 294A-300 (7)* 21.25 14.85
Set, never hinged 37.00

Nos. 285 to 287 Surcharged in Black or Red

**1945** Unwmk. *Perf. 13½x13*

**301** CD36 5c on 80c org 1.00 .60
**302** CD36 50c on 1a red 1.00 .60
**303** CD37 50c on 1.75a bl (R) 1.00 .60
**304** CD37 50c on 1.75a bl 1.00 .60
*Nos. 301-304 (4)* 4.00 2.40
Set, never hinged 5.75

Sao Miguel Fort, Luanda — A21

John IV — A22

Designs: 10c, Our Lady of Nazareth Church, Luanda. 50c, Salvador Correia de Sa e Bene vides. 1a, Surrender of Luanda. 1.75a, Diogo Cao. 2a, Manuel Cerveira Pereira. 5a, Stone Cliffs, Yelala. 10a, Paulo Dias de Novais. 20a, Massangano Fort.

*Perf. 14½*

**1948, May** Unwmk. Litho.

**305** A21 5c dk violet .30 .30
**306** A21 10c dk brown .75 .30
**307** A22 30c blue grn .30 .30
**308** A22 50c vio brown .30 .30
**309** A21 1a carmine .70 .30
**310** A22 1.75a slate blue 1.00 .45
**311** A22 2a green 1.00 .45
**312** A21 5a gray black 2.50 .90
**313** A22 10a rose lilac 8.25 1.25
**314** A21 20a gray blue 17.50 5.50
*a.* Sheet of 10, #305-314 100.00 100.00
Never hinged 145.00
*Nos. 305-314 (10)* 32.60 10.05
Set, never hinged 50.00

300th anniv. of the restoration of Angola to Portugal. No. 314a sold for 42.50a.

## Lady of Fatima Issue

Common Design Type

**1948, Dec.**

**315** CD40 50c carmine 1.50 .90
**316** CD40 3a ultra 6.00 2.70
**317** CD40 6a red orange 18.00 6.25
**318** CD40 9a dp claret 42.50 10.75
*Nos. 315-318 (4)* 68.00 20.60
Set, never hinged 125.00

Our Lady of the Rosary at Fatima, Portugal.

Chiumbe River A24

Black Rocks A25

Designs: 50c, View of Luanda. 2.50a, Sa da Bandeira. 3.50a, Mocamedes. 15a, Cubal River. 50a, Duke of Bragança Falls.

**1949** Unwmk. *Perf. 13½*

**319** A24 20c dk slate blue .45 .30
**320** A25 40c black brown .45 .30
**321** A24 50c rose brown .45 .30
**322** A24 2.50a blue violet 2.50 .70
**323** A24 3.50a slate gray 2.50 .85
**323A** A24 15a dk green 14.50 2.50
**324** A24 50a dp green 90.00 6.90
*Nos. 319-324 (7)* 110.85 11.85
Set, never hinged 180.00

# ANGOLA

Sailing Vessel — A26

**1949, Aug.** Perf. 14
325 A26 1a chocolate 6.75 .75
326 A26 4a dk Prus green 17.50 2.75
Set, never hinged 37.50

Centenary of founding of Mocamedes.

UPU Symbols — A27

**1949, Oct.**
327 A27 4a dk grn & lt grn 9.00 3.00
Never hinged 13.50

75th anniv. of the UPU.

> Catalogue values for unused stamps in this section, from this point to the end of the section, are for Never Hinged items.

Stamp of 1870 — A28

**1950, Apr. 2** Perf. 11½x12
328 A28 50c yellow green 1.75 .85
329 A28 1a red 1.75 .85
330 A28 4a black 6.25 1.26
a. Sheet of 3, #328-330 40.00 32.50
Nos. 328-330 (3) 9.75 2.65

Angola's first philatelic exhibition, marking the 80th anniversary of Angola's first stamps. No. 330a contains Nos. 328, 329 (inverted), 330, perf. 11½ and sold for 6.50a. All examples carry an oval exhibition cancellation in the margin but the stamps were valid for postage.

### Holy Year Issue
### Common Design Types

**1950, May** Perf. 13x13½
331 CD41 1a dull rose vio 1.60 .35
332 CD42 4a black 6.00 1.00

Melierax
Mechowi
A31

Merops Apiaster
A32

Designs: 10c, Coracias spatulatus. 15c, Ierathopius ecaudatus. 50c, Ceryle maxima. 1a, Buccanodon anchietae. 2a, Bucorvus cafer. 2.50a, Rhynchops flavirostris. 3a, Astur polyzonoides. 3.50a, Otis caffra. 4a, Oriolus notatus. 4.50a, Urolestes melanoleucus. 5a, Lamprocolius phoenicopterus. 6a, Heteropsar acuticaudus. 7a, Urobrachya bocadei. 10a, Alcedo semitorquata. 12.50a, Eurocephalus anguitimens. 15a, Neocichla gutturalis. 20a, Lophoceros elegans. 25a, Cinnyricinclus verreauxi. 30a, Chloropphoneus sulfureopectus modestus. 40a, Serpentarius serpentarius. 50a, Agapornis roseicollis.

### Photogravure and Lithographed
**1951** Unwmk. Perf. 11½
**Background Color**
333 A31 5c lt blue .55 .25
334 A32 10c aqua .55 .25
335 A32 15c salmon pink .75 .25
336 A32 20c pale yellow .75 .40
337 A31 50c gray blue .75 .25
338 A31 1a lilac .75 .25
339 A31 1.50a gray buff .75 .25
340 A31 2a cream 4.00 .25
341 A32 2.50a gray 1.50 .25
342 A32 3a lemon yel 1.10 .25
343 A31 3.50a lt gray 1.50 .25
344 A31 4a rose buff 1.75 .25
345 A32 4.50a rose lilac 1.75 .25
346 A31 5a green 7.50 .55
347 A31 6a blue 10.50 1.50
348 A31 7a orange 11.50 2.00
349 A31 10a lilac rose 45.00 2.75
350 A32 12.50a slate gray 13.00 3.75
351 A31 15a pale olive 11.50 3.75
352 A31 20a pale bis brn 110.00 9.00
353 A31 25a lilac rose 40.00 6.75
354 A32 30a pale salmon 40.00 9.00
355 A31 40a yellow 57.50 11.50
356 A31 50a turquoise 140.00 22.50
Nos. 333-356 (24) 502.95 76.45
Set, hinged 225.00

### Holy Year Extension Issue
### Common Design Type
**1951, Oct.** Litho. Perf. 14
357 CD43 4a orange + label 4.50 1.60

Sheets contain alternate vertical rows of stamps and labels bearing quotations from Pope Pius XII or the Patriarch Cardinal of Lisbon. Stamp without label attached sells for less.

### Medical Congress Issue
### Common Design Type
Design: Medical examination.
**1952, June** Perf. 13½
358 CD44 1a vio blue & brn blk 1.35 .45

Head of Christ — A35

**1952, Oct.** Unwmk. Perf. 13
359 A35 10c dk blue & buff .30 .25
360 A35 50c dk ol grn & ol gray 1.10 .30
361 A35 2a rose vio & cream 3.50 .75
Nos. 359-361 (3) 4.90 1.30

Exhibition of Sacred Missionary Art, Lisbon, 1951.

Leopard
A36

Sable
Antelope
A37

Animals: 20c, Elephant. 30c, Eland. 40c, African crocodile. 50c, Impala. 1a, Mountain zebra. 1.50a, Sitatunga. 2a, Black rhinoceros. 2.30a, Gomobok. 2.50a, Lion. 3a, Buffalo. 3.50a, Springbok. 4a, Brindled gnu. 5a, Hartebeest. 7a, Wart hog. 10a, Defassa waterbuck. 12.50a, Hippopotamus. 15a, Greater kudu. 20a, Giraffe.

**1953, Aug. 15** Perf. 12½
362 A36 5c multicolored .30 .25
363 A37 10c multicolored .30 .25
364 A37 20c multicolored .30 .25
365 A37 30c multicolored .30 .25
366 A36 40c multicolored .30 .25
367 A37 50c multicolored .30 .25
368 A37 1a multicolored .30 .25
369 A37 1.50a multicolored .35 .25
370 A36 2a multicolored .35 .25
371 A37 2.30a multicolored .40 .25
372 A37 2.50a multicolored .45 .25
373 A36 3a multicolored .50 .25
374 A37 3.50a multicolored .50 .25
375 A37 4a multicolored 18.00 .40
376 A37 5a multicolored .90 .25
377 A37 7a multicolored 1.35 .35
378 A37 10a multicolored 2.75 .35
379 A37 12.50a multicolored 6.75 3.00
380 A37 15a multicolored 9.00 3.00
381 A37 20a multicolored 11.75 1.90
Nos. 362-381 (20) 55.15 12.60
Set, hinged 18.00

Stamp of Portugal and Arms of Colonies — A38

**1953, Nov.** Photo. Perf. 13
**Stamp and Arms Multicolored**
382 A38 50c gray & dark gray 1.35 .55

Cent. of Portugal's 1st postage stamps.

Map and Plane — A39

### Typographed and Lithographed
**1954, May 27** Perf. 13½
383 A39 35c multicolored .30 .25
384 A39 4.50e multicolored 1.70 .75

Visit of Pres. Francisco H C. Lopes.

### Sao Paulo Issue
### Common Design Type
**1954** Litho.
385 CD46 1e bister & gray .80 .30

Map of Angola — A41

**1955, Aug.** Unwmk. Perf. 13½
386 A41 5c multicolored .30 .25
387 A41 20c multicolored .30 .25
388 A41 50c multicolored .30 .25
389 A41 1e multicolored .30 .25
390 A41 2.30e multicolored .50 .35
391 A41 4e multicolored 2.50 .25
392 A41 10e multicolored 2.50 .25
393 A41 20e multicolored 4.25 .45
Nos. 386-393 (8) 10.95 2.30

For overprints see Nos. 593, 598, 604.

Artur de Paiva — A42

**1956, Oct. 9** Perf. 13½x12½
394 A42 1e blk, dk bl & ocher .45 .30

Cent. of the birth of Col. Artur de Paiva.

Man of Malange — A43

### Various Costumes in Multicolor; Inscriptions in Black Brown
**1957, Jan. 1** Photo. Perf. 11½
**Granite Paper**
395 A43 5c gray .30 .25
396 A43 10c orange yel .30 .25
397 A43 15c lt blue grn .30 .25
398 A43 20c pale rose vio .30 .25
399 A43 30c brt rose .30 .25
400 A43 40c blue gray .30 .25
401 A43 50c pale olive .30 .25
402 A43 80c lt violet .40 .35
403 A43 1.50e buff 2.25 .35
404 A43 2.50e lt yel grn 2.95 .25
405 A43 4e salmon 1.80 .25
406 A43 10e salmon pink 2.70 .45
Nos. 395-406 (12) 12.20 3.40

Jose M. Antunes — A44

**1957, Apr.** Perf. 13½
407 A44 1e aqua & brown .90 .45

Birth cent. of Father Jose Maria Antunes.

Fair Emblem, Globe and Arms — A45

**1958, July** Litho. Perf. 12x11½
408 A45 1.50e multicolored .75 .65

World's Fair, Brussels, Apr. 17-Oct. 19.

### Tropical Medicine Congress Issue
### Common Design Type
Design: Securidaca longipedunculata.
**1958, Dec. 15** Perf. 13½
409 CD47 2.50e multicolored 3.50 1.00

Medicine Man — A47

Designs: 1.50e, Early government doctor. 2.50e, Modern medical team.

**1958, Dec. 18** Perf. 11½x12
410 A47 1e blue blk & brown .45 .25
411 A47 1.50e gray, blk & brown 1.40 .50
412 A47 2.50e multicolored 2.25 1.10
Nos. 410-412 (3) 4.10 1.85

75th anniversary of the Maria Pia Hospital, Luanda.

Welwitschia Mirabilis — A48

**1959, Oct. 1** Litho. Perf. 14½
**Various Views of Plant and Various Frames**
413 A48 1.50e lt brn, grn & blk 1.10 .65
414 A48 2.50e multicolored 1.75 .85
415 A48 5e multicolored 3.00 1.00
416 A48 10e multicolored 4.50 2.10
Nos. 413-416 (4) 10.35 4.60

Centenary of discovery of Welwitschia mirabilis, desert plant.

Map of West Africa, c. 1540, by Jorge Reinel — A49

**1960, June 25** Perf. 13½
417 A49 2.50e multicolored .55 .25

500th anniv. of the death of Prince Henry the Navigator.

Distributing Medicines — A50

**1960, Oct.** Litho. Perf. 14½
418 A50 2.50e multicolored .65 .25

10th anniv. of the Commission for Technical Co-operation in Africa South of the Sahara (C.C.T.A.).

Girl of Angola — A51

Various portraits.

**1961, Nov. 30** Unwmk. Perf. 13
419 A51 10c multicolored .30 .25
420 A51 15c multicolored .30 .25
421 A51 30c multicolored .30 .25
422 A51 50c multicolored .30 .25
423 A51 60c multicolored .30 .25
424 A51 1.50e multicolored .30 .25
425 A51 2e multicolored 1.00 .25
426 A51 2.50e multicolored 1.00 .25

| | | | | |
|---|---|---|---|---|
| **427** | A51 | 3e multicolored | 3.50 | .30 |
| **428** | A51 | 4e multicolored | 1.50 | .25 |
| **429** | A51 | 5e multicolored | 1.10 | .30 |
| **430** | A51 | 7.50e multicolored | 1.50 | .90 |
| **431** | A51 | 10e multicolored | 1.20 | .70 |
| **432** | A51 | 15e multicolored | 2.00 | .90 |
| **432A** | A51 | 25e multicolored | 2.40 | 1.25 |
| **432B** | A51 | 50e multicolored | 3.75 | 2.75 |
| | | *Nos. 419-432B (16)* | 20.75 | 9.35 |

**Sports Issue**

Common Design Type

Sports: 50c, Flying. 1e, Rowing. 1.50e, Water polo. 2.50e, Hammer throwing. 4.50e, High jump. 15e, Weight lifting.

**1962, Jan. 18** ***Perf. 13½***

**Multicolored Design**

| | | | | |
|---|---|---|---|---|
| **433** | CD48 | 50c lt blue | .30 | .25 |
| **434** | CD48 | 1e olive bister | 1.10 | .25 |
| **435** | CD48 | 1.50e salmon | .75 | .30 |
| **436** | CD48 | 2.50e lt green | .90 | .30 |
| **437** | CD48 | 4.50e pale blue | .75 | .60 |
| **438** | CD48 | 15e yellow | 1.75 | 1.50 |
| | | *Nos. 433-438 (6)* | 5.55 | 3.20 |

For overprint see No. 608.

**Anti-Malaria Issue**

Common Design Type

Design: Anopheles funestus.

**1962, April** **Litho.** ***Perf. 13½***

| | | | | |
|---|---|---|---|---|
| **439** | CD49 | 2.50e multicolored | 2.25 | .90 |

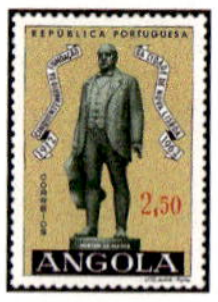

Gen. Norton de Matos — A54

**1962, Aug. 8** **Unwmk.** ***Perf. 14½***

| | | | | |
|---|---|---|---|---|
| **440** | A54 | 2.50e multicolored | .65 | .40 |

50th anniv. of the founding of Nova Lisboa.

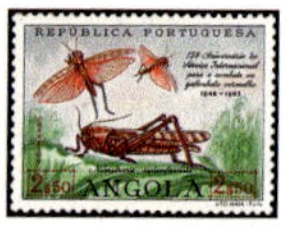

Locusts — A56

**1963, June 2** **Litho.** ***Perf. 14***

| | | | | |
|---|---|---|---|---|
| **447** | A56 | 2.50e multicolored | 1.60 | .95 |

15th anniv. of the Intl. Anti-Locust Organ.

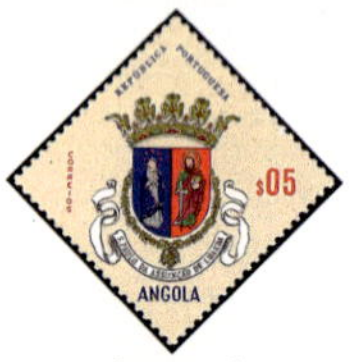

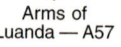

Arms of Luanda — A57

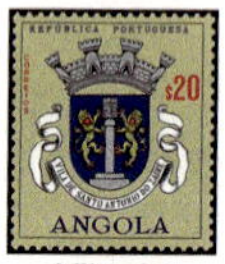

Vila de Santo Antonio do Zaire — A58

Coats of Arms (Provinces and Cities): 10c, Massangano. 15c, Sanza-Pombo. 25c, Ambriz. 30c, Muxima. 40c, Ambrizete. 50c, Carmona. 60c, Catete. 70c, Quibaxe. No. 458, Salazar. No. 459, Maquela do Zombo. 1.20e, Bembe. No. 461, Malanje. No. 462, Caxito. 1.80e, Dondo. 2e, Henrique de Carvalho. No. 465, Moçamedes. No. 466, Damba. 3e, Novo Redondo. 3.50e, S. Salvador do Congo. 4e, Cuimba. 5e, Luso. 6.50e, Negage. 7e, Quitexe. 7.50e, S. Filipe de Benguela. 8e, Mucaba. 9e, 31 de Janeiro. 10e, Lobito. 11e, Nova Caipemba. 12.50e, Gabela. 14e, Songo. 15e Sá da Bandeira. 17e, Quimbele. 17.50e, Silva Porto. 20e, Nova Lisboa. 22.50e, Cabinda. 25e, Noqui. 30e, Serpa Pinto. 35e, Santa Cruz. 50e, General Freire.

**1963** ***Perf. 13½***

**Arms in Original Colors; Red and Violet Blue Inscriptions**

| | | | | |
|---|---|---|---|---|
| **448** | A57 | 5c tan | .30 | .25 |
| **449** | A57 | 10c lt blue | .30 | .25 |
| **450** | A58 | 15c salmon | .30 | .25 |
| **451** | A58 | 20c olive | .30 | .25 |
| **452** | A58 | 25c lt blue | .30 | .25 |
| **453** | A57 | 30c buff | .30 | .25 |
| **454** | A58 | 40c gray | .30 | .25 |
| **455** | A57 | 50c lt green | .30 | .25 |
| **456** | A58 | 60c brt yellow | .30 | .25 |
| **457** | A58 | 70c dull rose | .30 | .25 |
| **458** | A57 | 1e pale lilac | .65 | .25 |
| **459** | A58 | 1e dull yellow | .30 | .25 |
| **460** | A58 | 1.20e rose | .30 | .25 |
| **461** | A57 | 1.50e pale salmon | .90 | .25 |
| **462** | A58 | 1.50e lt green | .75 | .25 |
| **463** | A58 | 1.80e yel olive | .75 | .55 |
| **464** | A57 | 2e lt yel green | .65 | .25 |
| **465** | A57 | 2.50e lt gray | 2.50 | .30 |
| **466** | A58 | 2.50e dull blue | 2.25 | .25 |
| **467** | A57 | 3e yel olive | .75 | .25 |
| **468** | A57 | 3.50e gray | .90 | .25 |
| **469** | A58 | 4e citron | .60 | .30 |
| **470** | A57 | 5e citron | .75 | .30 |
| **471** | A58 | 6.50e tan | .65 | .40 |
| **472** | A58 | 7e rose lilac | .90 | .75 |
| **473** | A57 | 7.50e pale lilac | 1.00 | .75 |
| **474** | A58 | 8e lt aqua | .90 | .75 |
| **475** | A58 | 9e yellow | 1.10 | 1.00 |
| **476** | A57 | 10e dp salmon | 1.20 | .80 |
| **477** | A58 | 11e dull yel grn | 1.25 | 1.25 |
| **478** | A57 | 12.50e pale blue | 1.50 | 1.25 |
| **479** | A58 | 14e lt gray | 1.50 | 1.25 |
| **480** | A57 | 15e lt blue | 1.50 | 1.25 |
| **481** | A58 | 17e pale blue | 1.60 | 1.50 |
| **482** | A57 | 17.50e dull yellow | 2.40 | 2.25 |
| **483** | A57 | 20e lt aqua | 2.40 | 1.75 |
| **484** | A57 | 22.50e gray | 2.50 | 2.40 |
| **485** | A58 | 25e citron | 2.10 | 1.50 |
| **486** | A57 | 30e yellow | 3.00 | 2.50 |
| **487** | A58 | 35e grysh blue | 3.25 | 3.00 |
| **488** | A58 | 50e dp yellow | 4.50 | 2.25 |
| | | *Nos. 448-488 (41)* | 48.30 | 32.80 |

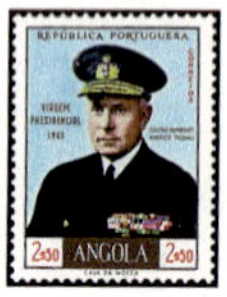

Pres. Américo Rodrigues Thomaz — A59

**1963, Sept. 16** **Litho.**

| | | | | |
|---|---|---|---|---|
| **489** | A59 | 2.50e multicolored | .65 | .30 |

Visit of the President of Portugal.

**Airline Anniversary Issue**

Common Design Type

**1963, Oct. 5** **Unwmk.** ***Perf. 14½***

| | | | | |
|---|---|---|---|---|
| **490** | CD50 | 1e lt blue & multi | 1.35 | .35 |

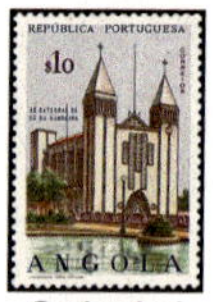

Cathedral of Sá da Bandeira A61

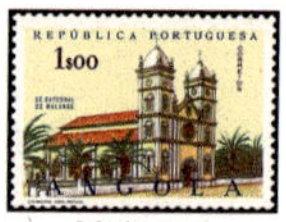

Malange Cathedral A62

Churches: 20c, Landana. 30c, Luanda Cathedral. 40c, Gabela. 50c, St. Martin's Chapel, Baia dos Tigres. 1.50e, St. Peter, Chibia. 2e, Church of Our Lady, Benguela. 2.50e, Church of Jesus, Luanda. 3e, Camabatela. 3.50e, Mission, Cabinda. 4e, Vila Folgares. 4.50e, Church of Our Lady, Lobito. 5e, Church of Cabinda. 7.50e, Cacuso Church, Malange. 10e, Lubango Mission. 12.50e, Huila Mission. 15e, Church of Our Lady, Luanda Island.

**1963, Nov. 1** **Litho.**

**Multicolored Design and Inscription**

| | | | | |
|---|---|---|---|---|
| **491** | A61 | 10c gray blue | .30 | .25 |
| **492** | A61 | 20c pink | .30 | .25 |
| **493** | A61 | 30c lt blue | .30 | .25 |
| **494** | A61 | 40c tan | .30 | .25 |
| **495** | A61 | 50c lt green | .30 | .25 |
| **496** | A62 | 1e buff | .30 | .25 |
| **497** | A61 | 1.50e lt vio blue | .30 | .25 |
| **498** | A62 | 2e pale rose | .35 | .25 |
| **499** | A61 | 2.50e gray | .35 | .25 |
| **500** | A62 | 3e buff | .35 | .25 |
| **501** | A61 | 3.50e olive | .55 | .25 |
| **502** | A62 | 4e buff | .55 | .25 |
| **503** | A62 | 4.50e pale blue | .75 | .30 |
| **504** | A61 | 5e tan | .75 | .30 |
| **505** | A62 | 7.50e gray | 1.00 | .55 |
| **506** | A61 | 10e dull yellow | 1.40 | .75 |
| **507** | A62 | 12.50e bister | 1.60 | 1.25 |
| **508** | A62 | 15e pale gray vio | 2.40 | 1.40 |
| | | *Nos. 491-508 (18)* | 12.15 | 7.55 |

**National Overseas Bank Issue**

Common Design Type

Design: Antonio Teixeira de Sousa.

**1964, May 16** ***Perf. 13½***

| | | | | |
|---|---|---|---|---|
| **509** | CD51 | 2.50e multicolored | .90 | .45 |

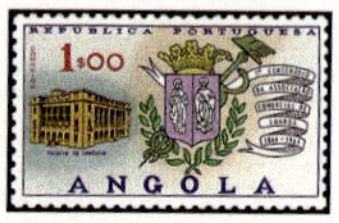

Commerce Building and Arms of Chamber of Commerce — A64

**1964, Nov.** **Litho.** ***Perf. 12***

| | | | | |
|---|---|---|---|---|
| **510** | A64 | 1e multicolored | .45 | .25 |

Luanda Chamber of Commerce centenary.

**ITU Issue**

Common Design Type

**1965, May 17** **Unwmk.** ***Perf. 14½***

| | | | | |
|---|---|---|---|---|
| **511** | CD52 | 2.50e gray & multi | 1.25 | .65 |

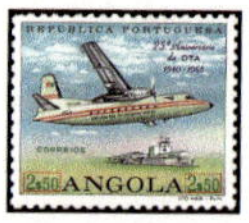

Plane over Luanda Airport — A65

**1965, Dec. 3** **Litho.** ***Perf. 13***

| | | | | |
|---|---|---|---|---|
| **512** | A65 | 2.50e multicolored | 1.25 | .60 |

25th anniv. of DTA, Direccao dos Transportes Aereos.

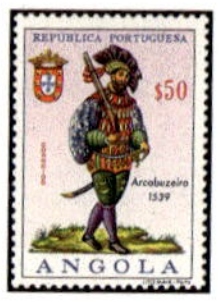

Harquebusier, 1539 — A66

50c, Harquebusier, 1539. 1e, Harquebusier, 1640. 1.50e, Infantry officer, 1777. 2e, Standard bearer, infantry, 1777. 2.50e, Infantry soldier, 1777. 3e, Cavalry officer, 1783. 4e, Cavalry soldier, 1783. 4.50e, Infantry officer, 1807. 5e, Infantry soldier, 1807. 6e, Cavalry officer, 1807. 8e, Cavalry soldier, 1807. 9e, Infantry soldier, 1873.

**1966, Feb. 25** **Litho.** ***Perf. 14½***

| | | | | |
|---|---|---|---|---|
| **513** | A66 | 50c multicolored | .30 | .25 |
| **514** | A66 | 1e multicolored | .30 | .25 |
| **515** | A66 | 1.50e multicolored | .30 | .25 |
| **516** | A66 | 2e multicolored | .30 | .25 |
| **517** | A66 | 2.50e multicolored | .40 | .25 |
| **518** | A66 | 3e multicolored | .40 | .25 |
| **519** | A66 | 4e multicolored | .60 | .25 |
| **520** | A66 | 4.50e multicolored | .65 | .25 |
| **521** | A66 | 5e multicolored | .65 | .30 |
| **522** | A66 | 6e multicolored | 1.10 | .65 |
| **523** | A66 | 8e multicolored | 1.50 | 1.10 |
| **524** | A66 | 9e multicolored | 1.60 | 1.25 |
| | | *Nos. 513-524 (12)* | 8.10 | 5.30 |

**National Revolution Issue**

Common Design Type

Design: St. Paul's Hospital and Commercial and Industrial School.

**1966, May 28** **Litho.** ***Perf. 12***

| | | | | |
|---|---|---|---|---|
| **525** | CD53 | 1e multicolored | .50 | .25 |

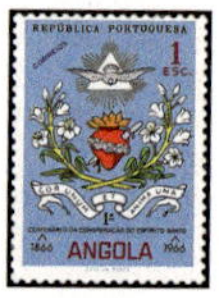

Emblem of Holy Ghost Society — A68

**1966** **Litho.** ***Perf. 13***

| | | | | |
|---|---|---|---|---|
| **526** | A68 | 1e blue & multi | .50 | .25 |

Centenary of the Holy Ghost Society.

**Navy Club Issue**

Common Design Type

Designs: 1e, Mendes Barata and cruiser Dom Carlos I. 2.50e, Capt. Augusto de Castilho and corvette Mindelo.

**1967, Jan. 31** **Litho.** ***Perf. 13***

| | | | | |
|---|---|---|---|---|
| **527** | CD54 | 1e multicolored | 1.00 | .45 |
| **528** | CD54 | 2.50e multicolored | 1.35 | .75 |

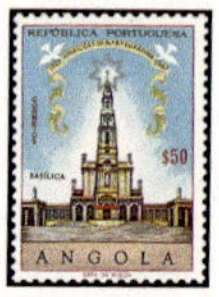

Fatima Basilica — A70

**1967, May 13** **Litho.** ***Perf. 12½x13***

| | | | | |
|---|---|---|---|---|
| **529** | A70 | 50c multicolored | .45 | .25 |

50th anniv. of the apparition of the Virgin Mary to 3 shepherd children at Fatima.

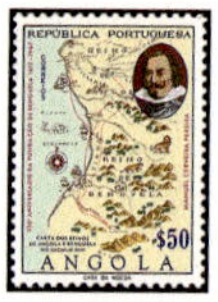

Angola Map, Manuel Cerveira Pereira — A71

**1967, Aug. 15** **Litho.** ***Perf. 12½x13***

| | | | | |
|---|---|---|---|---|
| **530** | A71 | 50c multicolored | .45 | .25 |

350th anniv. of the founding of Benguela.

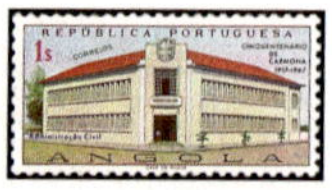

Administration Building, Carmona — A72

**1967** **Litho.** ***Perf. 12***

| | | | | |
|---|---|---|---|---|
| **531** | A72 | 1e multicolored | .30 | .25 |

50th anniv. of the founding of Carmona.

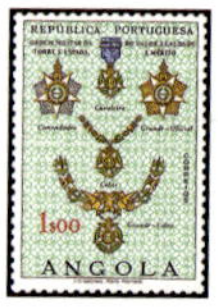

Military Order of Valor — A73

50c, Ribbon of the Three Orders. 1.50e, Military Order of Avis. 2e, Military Order of Christ. 2.50e, Military Order of St. John of Espada. 3e, Order of the Empire. 4e, Order of Prince Henry. 5e, Order of Benemerencia. 10e, Order of Public Instruction. 20e, Order for Industrial & Agricultural Merit.

**1967, Oct. 31** ***Perf. 14***

| | | | | |
|---|---|---|---|---|
| **532** | A73 | 50c lt gray & multi | .30 | .25 |
| **533** | A73 | 1e lt green & multi | .30 | .25 |
| **534** | A73 | 1.50e yellow & multi | .30 | .25 |
| **535** | A73 | 2e multicolored | .30 | .25 |
| **536** | A73 | 2.50e multicolored | .30 | .25 |
| **537** | A73 | 3e lt olive & multi | .35 | .25 |
| **538** | A73 | 4e gray & multi | .50 | .25 |
| **539** | A73 | 5e multicolored | .60 | .25 |
| **540** | A73 | 10e lilac & multi | 1.00 | .50 |
| **541** | A73 | 20e lt blue & multi | 2.25 | 1.20 |
| | | *Nos. 532-541 (10)* | 6.20 | 3.70 |

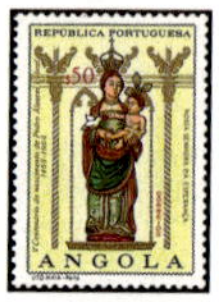

Our Lady of Hope — A74

1e, Belmonte Castle, horiz. 1.50e, St. Jerome's Convent. 2.50e, Cabral's Armada.

**1968, Apr. 22** **Litho.** ***Perf. 14***

| | | | | |
|---|---|---|---|---|
| **542** | A74 | 50c yellow & multi | .30 | .25 |
| **543** | A74 | 1e gray & multi | .50 | .25 |
| **544** | A74 | 1.50e lt blue & multi | .60 | .25 |
| **545** | A74 | 2.50e buff & multi | 1.00 | .35 |
| | | *Nos. 542-545 (4)* | 2.40 | 1.10 |

500th anniv. of the birth of Pedro Alvares Cabral, navigator who took possession of Brazil for Portugal.

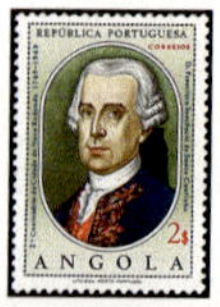

Francisco Inocencio de Souza Coutinho — A75

**1969, Jan. 7** **Litho.** ***Perf. 14***

| | | | | |
|---|---|---|---|---|
| **546** | A75 | 2e multicolored | .45 | .25 |

Founding of Novo Redondo, 200th anniv.

# ANGOLA

## Admiral Coutinho Issue
### Common Design Type
Design: Adm. Gago Coutinho and his first ship.

**1969, Feb. 17**    Litho.    *Perf. 14*
547 CD55 2.50e multicolored    .85   .35

Compass Rose — A77

**1969, Aug. 29**    Litho.    *Perf. 14*
548 A77 1e multicolored    .45   .25

500th anniv. of the birth of Vasco da Gama (1469-1524), navigator.

## Administration Reform Issue
### Common Design Type

**1969, Sept. 25**    Litho.    *Perf. 14*
549 CD56 1.50e multicolored    .30   .25

Portal of St. Jeronimo's Monastery — A79

**1969, Dec. 1**    Litho.    *Perf. 14*
550 A79 3e multicolored    .45   .25

500th anniv. of the birth of King Manuel I.

Angolasaurus Bocagei — A80

Fossils and Minerals: 1e, Ferrometeorite. 1.50e, Dioptase crystals. 2e, Gondwanidium. 2.50e, Diamonds. 3e, Estromatolite. 3.50e, Procarcharodon megalodon. 4e, Microceratodus angolensis. 4.50e, Moscovite. 5e, Barite. 6e, Nostoceras. 10e, Rotula orbiculus angolensis.

**1970, Oct. 31**    Litho.    *Perf. 13*
551 A80 50c tan & multi    .45   .40
552 A80 1e multicolored    .45   .40
553 A80 1.50e multicolored    .55   .40
554 A80 2e multicolored    .55   .40
555 A80 2.50e lt gray & multi    .55   .40
556 A80 3e multicolored    .60   .40
557 A80 3.50e blue & multi    .90   .50
558 A80 4e lt gray & multi    .90   .50
559 A80 4.50e gray & multi    1.00   .50
560 A80 5e gray & multi    1.35   .50
561 A80 6e pink & multi    2.65   1.45
562 A80 10e lt blue & multi    3.75   1.90
Nos. 551-562 (12)    13.60   7.75

## Marshal Carmona Issue
### Common Design Type

**1970, Nov. 15**    *Perf. 14*
563 CD57 2.50e multicolored    .45   .25

Arms of Malanje, Cotton Boll and Field — A82

**1970, Nov. 20**    *Perf. 13*
564 A82 2.50e multicolored    .55   .35

Centenary of the municipality of Malanje.

Mail Ships and Angola No. 1 — A83

4.50e, Steam locomotive and Angola No. 4.

**1970, Dec. 1**    *Perf. 13½*
565 A83 1.50e multicolored    .60   .30
566 A83 4.50e multicolored    2.95   2.70

Cent. of stamps of Angola. See No. C36. For overprint see No. 616B.

Map of Africa, Diagram of Seismic Tests — A84

**1971, Aug. 22**    Litho.    *Perf. 13*
567 A84 2.50e multicolored    .45   .25

5th Regional Conference of Soil and Foundation Engineers, Luanda, Aug. 22-Sept. 5.

Galleon on Congo River — A85

**1972, May 25**    Litho.    *Perf. 13*
568 A85 1e brt grn & multi    .65   .25

4th centenary of the publication of The Lusiads by Luiz Camoens.

### Olympic Games Issue
### Common Design Type

**1972, June 20**    *Perf. 14x13½*
569 CD59 50c multicolored    .65   .25

### Lisbon-Rio de Janeiro Flight Issue
### Common Design Type

**1972, Sept. 20**    Litho.    *Perf. 13½*
570 CD60 1e multicolored    .35   .25

### WMO Centenary Issue
### Common Design Type

**1973, Dec. 15**    Litho.    *Perf. 13*
571 CD61 1e dk gray & multi    .45   .25

Radar Station — A89

**1974, June 25**    Litho.    *Perf. 13*
572 A89 2e multicolored    .45   .25

Establishment of satellite communications network via Intelsat among Portugal, Angola and Mozambique.

For overprint see No. 616A

Harpa Doris — A90

Designs: Sea shells: 30c, Murex melanamathos. 50c, Venus foliacea lamellosa. 70c, Lathyrus filosus. 1e, Cymbium ciolum. 1.50e, Cassis tesselata. 2e, Cypraea stercoraria. 2.50e, Conus prometheus. 3e, Strombus latus. 3.50e, Tympanotonus fuscatus. 4e, Cardium costatum. 5e, Natica fulminea. 6e, Lyropecten nodosus. 7e, Tonna galea. 10e, Donax rugosus. 25e, Cymatium trigonum. 30e, Olivancilaria acuminata. 35e, Semifusus morio. 40e, Clavatula lineata. 50e, Solarium granulatum.

**1974, Oct. 25**    Litho.    *Perf. 12x12½*
573 A90 25c shown    .30   .25
574 A90 30c multicolored    .30   .25
575 A90 50c multicolored    .30   .25
576 A90 70c multicolored    .35   .25
577 A90 1e multicolored    .35   .25
578 A90 1.50e multicolored    .40   .25
579 A90 2e multicolored    .40   .25
580 A90 2.50e multicolored    .45   .25
581 A90 3e multicolored    .65   .45
582 A90 3.50e multicolored    .65   .45
583 A90 4e multicolored    .65   .45
584 A90 5e multicolored    .75   .45
585 A90 6e multicolored    1.25   .45
586 A90 7e multicolored    1.25   .45
587 A90 10e multicolored    1.00   .45
588 A90 25e multicolored    2.25   .90
589 A90 30e multicolored    2.50   .90
590 A90 35e multicolored    3.00   .90
591 A90 40e multicolored    3.50   1.10
592 A90 50e multicolored    5.00   1.75
Nos. 573-592 (20)    25.30   10.50

For overprints see Nos. 605-607, 617-630.

No. 386 Overprinted in Blue

**1974, Dec. 21**    Litho.    *Perf. 13½*
593 A41 5c multicolored    .35   .75

Youth philately.

## Republic

Star and Hand Holding Rifle — A91

**1975, Nov. 11**    Litho.    *Perf. 13x13½*
594 A91 1.50e red & multi    .50   .25

Independence in 1975.

Diquiche Mask — A92

Design: 3e, Bui ou Congolo mask.

**1976, Feb. 6**    *Perf. 13½*
595 A92 50c lt blue & multi    .30   .25
596 A92 3e multicolored    .55   .25

Workers — A93

**1976, May 1**    Litho.    *Perf. 12*
597 A93 1e red & multi    .75   .25

International Workers' Day.

No. 392 Overprinted

**1976, June 15**    Litho.    *Perf. 13½*
598 A41 10e multicolored    1.10   .75

Stamp Day.

President Agostinho Neto — A94

**1976, Nov. 11**    Litho.    *Perf. 13*
599 A94 50c yel & dk brown    .30   .25
600 A94 2e lt gray & plum    .30   .25
601 A94 3e gray & indigo    .40   .25
602 A94 5e buff & brown    .40   .25
603 A94 10e tan & sepia    .55   .25
  a. Souv. sheet of 1, imperf.    4.00   4.00
Nos. 599-603 (5)    1.95   1.25

First anniversary of independence.

Nos. 393, 588-589, 592 Overprinted

**1977, Feb. 9**    *Perf. 13½, 12x12½*
604 A41 20e multicolored    1.75   .50
605 A90 25e multicolored    2.25   .60
606 A90 30e multicolored    2.60   .75
607 A90 50e multicolored    4.25   1.25
Nos. 604-607 (4)    10.85   3.10

Overprint in 3 lines on No. 604, in 2 lines on others.

### No. 438 Overprinted

**1976, Dec. 31**    *Perf. 13½*
608 CD48 15e multicolored    2.00   .65

Child and WHO Emblem — A95

**1977**    Litho.    *Perf. 10½*
609 A95 2.50k blk & lt blue    .65   .25

Campaign for vaccination against poliomyelitis.

Map of Africa, Flag of Angola — A96

**1977**    Photo.
610 A96 6k blk, red & blue    .60   .35

First Congress of Popular Movement for the Liberation of Angola.

Anti-Apartheid Emblem — A97

**1979, June 20**    Litho.    *Perf. 13½*
611 A97 1k multicolored    .30   .25

Anti-Apartheid Year.

Human Rights Emblem — A98

**1979, June 15**    Litho.    *Perf. 13½*
612 A98 2.50k multicolored    .75   .25

Declaration of Human Rights, 30th anniv. (in 1975).

# ANGOLA

Child Flowers, Globe, IYC Emblem — A99

**1980, May 1    Litho.    Perf. 14x14½**
613  A99  3.50k multicolored     .75  .25
International Year of the Child (1979).

Running, Moscow '80 Emblem — A100

**1980, Dec. 15    Litho.    Perf. 13½**
614  A100  9k shown              .70  .25
615  A100  12k Swimming, horiz.  .80  .35
22nd Summer Olympic Games, Moscow, July 19-Aug. 3.

5th Anniv. of Independence A101

**1980, Nov. 11**
616  A101  5.50k multicolored    .75  .25

Nos. 572, 566 Overprinted

**1980-81    Litho.    Perf. 13½x13**
616A  A89  2e multi (bar only)   1.25  .25
616B  A83  4.50e multicolored    2.75  1.50
Issued: 2e, 5/17/81; 4.50e, 6/15/80.
See No. C37.

Nos. 577-580, 582-591 Overprinted

**1981, June 15    Litho.    Perf. 12x12½**
617  A90  1e multicolored      .30  .25
618  A90  1.50e multicolored   .30  .25
619  A90  2e multicolored      .30  .25
620  A90  2.50e multicolored   .30  .25
621  A90  3.50e multicolored   .30  .25
622  A90  4e multicolored      .30  .25
623  A90  5e multicolored      .35  .25
624  A90  6e multicolored      .40  .25
625  A90  7e multicolored      .55  .25
626  A90  10e multicolored     .65  .30
627  A90  25e multicolored    1.40  .50
628  A90  30e multicolored    1.75  .75
629  A90  35e multicolored    2.00  .90
630  A90  40e multicolored    2.50  1.25
Nos. 617-630 (14)             11.40  5.95

Man Walking with Canes, Tchibinda Ilunga Statue — A102

**1981, Sept. 5    Litho.    Perf. 13½**
631  A102  9k multicolored     .50  .30
Turipex '81 tourism exhibition.

M.P.L.A. Workers' Party Congress — A103

**1980, Dec. 23    Litho.    Perf. 14**
632  A103  50 l Millet         .30  .25
633  A103  5k Coffee           .35  .25
634  A103  7.50k Sunflowers    .40  .25
635  A103  13.50k Cotton       .65  .30
636  A103  14k Oil             .80  .35
637  A103  16k Diamonds        .95  .45
Nos. 632-637 (6)               3.45  1.85

People's Power — A104

**1980, Nov. 11**
638  A104  40k lt blue & blk   1.75  .65

Natl. Heroes' Day — A105

4.50k, Former Pres. Neto. 50k, Neto, diff.

**1980, Sept. 17    Perf. 14x13½**
639  A105  4.50k multicolored  .30  .25
640  A105  50k multicolored    2.75  .75

Soweto Uprising, 5th Anniv. — A106

**1981**
641  A106  4.50k multicolored  .35  .25

2nd Central African Games A107

50 l, Bicycling, tennis. 5k, Judo, boxing. 6k, Basketball, volleyball. 10k, Handball, soccer.

**1981, Sept. 3    Litho.    Perf. 13½**
642  A107  50 l multicolored   .30  .25
643  A107  5k multicolored     .65  .25
644  A107  6k multicolored     .85  .25
645  A107  10k multicolored   1.40  .35
Nos. 642-645 (4)               3.20  1.10

**Souvenir Sheet**
*Imperf*
646  A107  15k multicolored   3.00  3.00

Charaxes Kahldeni — A108

1k, Abantis zambesiaca. 5k, Catacroptera cloanthe. 9k, Myrina ficedula, vert. 10k, Colotis danae. 15k, Acraea acrita. 100k, Precis hierta.

**1982, Feb. 26    Litho.    Perf. 13½**
647  A108  50 l shown          .30  .25
648  A108  1k multicolored     .30  .25
649  A108  5k multicolored     .40  .25
650  A108  9k multicolored    1.00  .25
651  A108  10k multicolored   1.00  .25
652  A108  15k multicolored   1.25  .40
653  A108  100k multicolored  8.00  3.00
  a.  Souvenir sheet         12.00  12.00
Nos. 647-653 (7)              12.25  4.65
No. 653a contains Nos. 647-653, imperf., and sold for 30k (stamps probably not valid individually).

5th Anniv. of UN Membership A109

5.50k, The Silence of the Night, by Musseque Catambor. 7.50k, Cotton picking, Catete.

**1982, Sept. 22    Litho.**
654  A109  5.50k multicolored  .40  .25
655  A109  7.50k multicolored  .55  .25

20th Anniv. of Engineering Laboratory A110

**1982, Dec. 21    Litho.    Perf. 14**
656  A110  9k Lab              .65  .30
657  A110  13k Worker, vert.   .65  .40
658  A110  100k Equipment, vert.  6.75  3.50
Nos. 656-658 (3)               8.05  4.20

Local Flowers A111

5k, Dichrostachys glomerata. 12k, Amblygonocarpus obtusangulus. 50k, Albizzia versicolor.

**1983, Feb. 18    Perf. 13½**
659  A111  5k multicolored     .40  .25
660  A111  12k multicolored    .75  .30
661  A111  50k multicolored   3.50  1.40
Nos. 659-661 (3)               4.65  1.95

Women's Org., First Congress — A112

**1983    Litho.    Perf. 13½**
662  A112  20k multicolored   1.25  .50

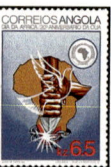

Africa Day — A113

**1983, June 30    Perf. 13**
663  A113  6.5k multicolored   .65  .35

World Communications Year — A114

**1983, June 30    Litho.    Perf. 13½**
664  A114  6.5k M'pungi        .75  .35
665  A114  12k Mondu          1.25  .55

BRASILIANA '83 Stamp Exhibition, Rio de Janeiro, July 29-Aug. 7 — A115

Crop-eating insects: 4.50k, Antestiopsis lineaticollis. 6.5k, Stephanoderes hampei ferr. 10k, Zonocerus variegatus.

**1983, July 29    Litho.    Perf. 13**
666  A115  4.5k multicolored   .50  .25
667  A115  6.5k multicolored   .55  .35
668  A115  10k multicolored   1.00  .60
Nos. 666-668 (3)               2.05  1.20

25th Anniv. of Economic Commission for Africa — A116

**1983, Aug. 2**
669  A116  10k Map, emblem    .70  .50

185th Anniv. of Post Office — A117

50 l, Mail collection, vert. 3.5k, Unloading mail plane. 5k, Sorting mail. 15k, Mailing letter, vert. 30k, Post office box delivery.

**1983, Dec. 7    Litho.    Perf. 13½**
670  A117  50 l multicolored   .30  .25
671  A117  3.5k multicolored   .35  .25
672  A117  5k multicolored     .55  .40
673  A117  15k multicolored   1.50  .90
674  A117  30k multicolored   2.90  1.60
  a.  Min. sheet of 3, #671-672, 674   8.00  8.00
Nos. 670-674 (5)               5.60  3.40
No. 674a sold for 100k.

Local Butterflies A118

50 l, Parasa karschi. 1k, Diaphone angolensis. 3.5k, Choeropasis jucunda. 6.5k, Hespagarista rendalli. 15k, Euchromia guineensis. 17.5k, Mazuca roseistriga. 20k, Utetheisa callima.

**1984, Jan. 20    Litho.    Perf. 13½**
675  A118  50 l multicolored   .30  .25
676  A118  1k multicolored     .30  .25
677  A118  3.5k multicolored   .55  .25
678  A118  6.5k multicolored   .95  .35
679  A118  15k multicolored   1.60  .90
680  A118  17.5k multicolored 1.90  1.00
681  A118  20k multicolored   2.75  1.25
Nos. 675-681 (7)               8.35  4.25

A119

**1984, Apr. 11    Litho.    Perf. 13½**
682  A119  30k multicolored   2.50  1.75
First Natl. Worker's Union Congress, Apr. 11-16.

Local Birds — A120

10.50k, Bucorvus leadbeateri. 14k, Gypohierax angolensis. 16k, Ardea goliath. 19.50k, Pelecanus onocrotalus. 22k, Platalea alba. 26k, Balearica pavonnia.

**1984, Oct. 24    Litho.    Perf. 13½**
683  A120  10.50k multicolored  .80  .40
684  A120  14k multicolored   1.00  .50
685  A120  16k multicolored   1.20  .65
686  A120  19.50k multicolored 1.60  .65
687  A120  22k multicolored   1.75  .75
688  A120  26k multicolored   2.50  1.00
Nos. 683-688 (6)               8.85  3.95

Local Animals — A121

# ANGOLA

1k, Tragelaphus strepsiceros. 4k, Antidorcas marsupialis angolensis. 5k, Pan troglodytes. 10k, Syncerus caffer. 15k, Hippotragus niger variani. 20k, Orycteropus afer. 25k, Crocuta crocuta.

**1984, Nov. 12**
| 689 | A121 | 1k multicolored | .35 | .25 |
|---|---|---|---|---|
| 690 | A121 | 4k multicolored | .45 | .25 |
| 691 | A121 | 5k multicolored | .60 | .25 |
| 692 | A121 | 10k multicolored | 1.75 | .30 |
| 693 | A121 | 15k multicolored | 2.10 | .45 |
| 694 | A121 | 20k multicolored | 2.50 | .60 |
| 695 | A121 | 25k multicolored | 3.00 | .65 |
| | | Nos. 689-695 (7) | 10.75 | 2.75 |

Angolese Monuments A122

5k, San Pedro da Barra. 12.5k, Nova Oeiras. 18k, M'Banza Kongo. 26k, Massangano. 39k, Escravatura Museum.

**1985, Feb. 21**    Litho.    Perf. 13½
| 696 | A122 | 5k multicolored | .35 | .25 |
|---|---|---|---|---|
| 697 | A122 | 12.5k multicolored | .90 | .50 |
| 698 | A122 | 18k multicolored | 1.20 | .75 |
| 699 | A122 | 26k multicolored | 1.90 | .90 |
| 700 | A122 | 39k multicolored | 2.60 | 1.50 |
| | | Nos. 696-700 (5) | 6.95 | 3.90 |

United Workers' Party, 25th Anniv. — A123

**1985, May**    Litho.    Perf. 12
| 701 | A123 | 77k XXV, red flags | 7.00 | 4.00 |
|---|---|---|---|---|

Printed in sheets of 5.

A124

1k, Flags. 11k, Oil drilling platform, Cabinda. 57k, Conference.

**1985, May**
| 702 | A124 | 1k multicolored | .30 | .25 |
|---|---|---|---|---|
| 703 | A124 | 11k multicolored | 1.00 | .80 |
| 704 | A124 | 57k multicolored | 2.60 | 1.25 |
| a. | | Strip of 3, #702-704 | 4.50 | 4.50 |

Southern African Development Council, 5th anniv.

Medicinal plants — A125

No. 705, Lonchocarpus sericeus. No. 706, Gossypium. No. 707, Cassia occidentalis. No. 708, Gloriosa superba. No. 709, Cochlospermum angolensis.

**Lithographed and Typographed**
**1985, July 5**    Perf. 11
| 705 | A125 | 1k multi | .30 | .25 |
|---|---|---|---|---|
| 706 | A125 | 4k multi | .40 | .30 |
| 707 | A125 | 11k multi | 1.00 | .70 |
| 708 | A125 | 25.50k multi | 2.00 | 1.00 |
| 709 | A125 | 55k multi | 3.50 | 2.50 |
| | | Nos. 705-709 (5) | 7.20 | 4.75 |

ARGENTINA '85 exhibition.

5th Natl. Heroes Day — A126

Natl. flag and: 10.50k, Portrait of Agostinho Neto, party leader. 36.50k, Neto working.

**1985**    Litho.    Perf. 13½
| 710 | A126 | 10.50k multicolored | 12.00 | 7.50 |
|---|---|---|---|---|
| 711 | A126 | 36.50k multicolored | 16.00 | 10.00 |

Ministerial Conference of Non-Aligned Countries, Luanda — A127

**1985, Sept. 4**    Photo.    Perf. 11
| 712 | A127 | 35k multicolored | 2.50 | 1.75 |
|---|---|---|---|---|

UN, 40th Anniv. — A128

**1985, Oct. 29**    Litho.    Perf. 11
| 713 | A128 | 12.50k multicolored | 1.25 | .75 |
|---|---|---|---|---|

Industry and Natural Resources A129

**1985, Nov. 11**
| 714 | A129 | 50 l Cement Factory | .30 | .25 |
|---|---|---|---|---|
| 715 | A129 | 5k Logging | .35 | .25 |
| 716 | A129 | 7k Quartz | .50 | .40 |
| 717 | A129 | 10k Iron mine | .85 | .50 |
| a. | | Souvenir sheet of 4, #714-717, imperf. | 3.50 | 3.50 |
| | | Nos. 714-717 (4) | 2.00 | 1.40 |

Natl. independence, 10th anniv.

2nd Natl. Workers' Party Congress (MPLA) — A130

**1985, Nov. 28**    Perf. 13½
| 718 | A130 | 20k multicolored | 1.50 | 1.00 |
|---|---|---|---|---|

Demostenes de Almelda Clington Races, 30th Anniv. — A131

Various runners.

**1985, Dec. 13**
| 719 | A131 | 50 l multicolored | .30 | .25 |
|---|---|---|---|---|
| 720 | A131 | 5k multicolored | .40 | .25 |
| 721 | A131 | 6.50k multicolored | .60 | .25 |
| 722 | A131 | 10k multicolored | .80 | .30 |
| | | Nos. 719-722 (4) | 2.10 | 1.05 |

1986 World Cup Soccer Championships, Mexico — A132

Map, soccer field and various plays.

**1986, May 6**    Litho.    Perf. 11½x11
| 723 | A132 | 50 l multi | .30 | .25 |
|---|---|---|---|---|
| 724 | A132 | 3.50k multi | .40 | .25 |
| 725 | A102 | 5k multi | .65 | .25 |
| 726 | A132 | 7k multi | .80 | .25 |
| 727 | A132 | 10k multi | 1.25 | .40 |
| 728 | A132 | 18k multi | 2.10 | .60 |
| | | Nos. 723-728 (6) | 5.50 | 2.00 |

Struggle Against Portugal, 25th Anniv. — A133

**1986, May 6**    Perf. 11x11½
| 729 | A133 | 15k multicolored | 1.40 | .50 |
|---|---|---|---|---|

First Man in Space, 25th Anniv. — A134

50 l, Skylab, US. 1k, Spacecraft. 5k, A. Leonov space-walking. 10k, Lunokhod on Moon. 13k, Apollo-Soyuz link-up.

**1986, Aug. 21**    Litho.    Perf. 11x11½
| 730 | A134 | 50 l multicolored | .30 | .25 |
|---|---|---|---|---|
| 731 | A134 | 1k multicolored | .30 | .25 |
| 732 | A134 | 5k multicolored | .40 | .25 |
| 733 | A134 | 10k multicolored | .90 | .35 |
| 734 | A134 | 13k multicolored | .95 | .40 |
| | | Nos. 730-734 (5) | 2.85 | 1.50 |

Admission of Angola to UN, 10th Anniv. — A135

**1986, Dec. 1**    Litho.    Perf. 11x11½
| 735 | A135 | 22k multi | 1.60 | 1.10 |
|---|---|---|---|---|

Liberation Movement, 30th Anniv. — A136

Angolese at work, fighting and: No. 736a, "1956." No. 736b, Congress emblem, "1980." No. 736c, Labor Party emblem, "1985."

**1986, Dec. 3**    Perf. 11½x11
| 736 | A136 | Strip of 3 | 1.50 | 1.50 |
|---|---|---|---|---|
| a.-c. | | 5k any single | .45 | .25 |

Agostinho Neto University, 10th Anniv. — A137

**1986, Dec. 30**    Litho.    Perf. 11x11½
| 737 | A137 | 50 l Mathematics | .30 | .25 |
|---|---|---|---|---|
| 738 | A137 | 1k Law | .50 | .25 |
| 739 | A137 | 10k Medicine | .85 | .60 |
| | | Nos. 737-739 (3) | 1.65 | 1.20 |

Tribal Hairstyles — A138

**1987, Apr. 15**    Litho.    Perf. 11½x11
| 740 | A138 | 1k Quioca | .30 | .25 |
|---|---|---|---|---|
| 741 | A138 | 1.50k Luanda | .35 | .25 |
| 742 | A138 | 5k Humbe | .65 | .25 |
| 743 | A138 | 7k Muila | .80 | .25 |
| 744 | A138 | 20k Muila, diff. | 2.00 | .45 |
| 745 | A138 | 30k Dilolo | 3.75 | .80 |
| | | Nos. 740-745 (6) | 7.85 | 2.25 |

Landscapes — A139

**1987, July 7**    Perf. 11½x12, 12x11½    Litho.
| 746 | A139 | 50 l Pambala Shore | .30 | .25 |
|---|---|---|---|---|
| 747 | A139 | 1.50k Dala Waterfalls | .30 | .25 |
| 748 | A139 | 3.50k Black Stones | .30 | .25 |
| 749 | A139 | 5k Cuango River | .45 | .25 |
| 750 | A139 | 10k Luanda coast | .95 | .35 |
| 751 | A139 | 20k Hills of Leba | 1.90 | .45 |
| | | Nos. 746-751 (6) | 4.20 | 1.80 |

Nos. 746-747, 749 and 751 horiz.

Lenin — A140

**1987, Nov. 25**    Perf. 12x12½
| 752 | A140 | 15k multi | 1.25 | .45 |
|---|---|---|---|---|

October Revolution, Russia, 70th anniv.

2nd Congress of the Organization of Angolan Women (OMA) — A141

10k, Soldier, nurse, technician, student

**1988, May 30**    Litho.    Perf. 13x13½
| 753 | A141 | 2k shown | .35 | .25 |
|---|---|---|---|---|
| 754 | A141 | 10k multicolored | .85 | .25 |

Victory Carnival, 10th Anniv. — A142

Various carnival scenes.

**1988, June 15**    Litho.    Perf. 13½x13
| 755 | A142 | 5k shown | .40 | .25 |
|---|---|---|---|---|
| 756 | A142 | 10k multi, diff. | .70 | .30 |

Augusto N'Gangula (1956-1968), Youth Pioneer Killed by Portuguese Colonial Army — A143

Agostinho Neto Pioneers' Organization (OPA), 25th Anniv. — A144

**1989, Oct. 2**    Litho.    Perf. 12x11½
| 757 | A143 | 12k multicolored | 1.10 | .65 |
|---|---|---|---|---|
| 758 | A144 | 15k multicolored | 1.40 | .80 |

Pioneer Day.

10th Natl. Soccer Championships, Benguela, May 1 — A145

**1989, Oct. 16**
| 759 | A145 | 5k shown | .50 | .40 |
|---|---|---|---|---|
| 760 | A145 | 5k Luanda, 3 years | .50 | .40 |
| 761 | A145 | 5k Luanda, 5 years | .50 | .40 |
| a. | | Strip of 3, #759-761 | 1.60 | 1.60 |
| | | Nos. 759-761 (3) | 1.50 | 1.20 |

# ANGOLA

Intl. Fund for Agricultural Development, 10th Anniv. — A146

**1990, Feb. 15**    Litho.    *Perf. 11½x12*
762   A146   10k multicolored    1.10   .45

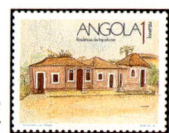

Ingombotas' Houses — A147

Architecture: 2k, Alta Train Station. 5k, National Museum of Anthropology. 15k, Ana Joaquina Palace. 23k, Iron Palace. 36k, Meteorological observatory, vert. 50k, People's Palace.

**1990, Feb. 20**    *Perf. 12x11½, 11½x12*
763   A147   1k shown    .30   .25
764   A147   2k multicolored    .30   .25
765   A147   5k multicolored    .40   .25
766   A147   15k multicolored    1.10   .60
767   A147   23k multicolored    1.90   .90
768   A147   36k multicolored    3.00   1.25
769   A147   50k multicolored    4.00   1.75
    Nos. 763-769 (7)    11.00   5.25

Luanda and Benguela Railways — A148

Various maps and locomotives.

**1990, Mar. 1**    *Perf. 12x11½*
770   A148   5k shown    .40   .25
771   A148   12k Garrat T (left)    1.25   .45
772   A148   12k Garrat T (right)    1.25   .45
    a.   Pair, #771-772    2.75   2.75
773   A148   14k Mikado    1.25   .75
    Nos. 770-773 (4)    4.15   1.90

**Souvenir Sheet**
774   A148   25k Diesel electric    3.00   3.00

No. 772a has a continuous design.

Southern Africa Development Coordinating Conf. (SADCC), 10th Anniv. — A149

**1990, Apr. 1**    Litho.    *Perf. 14*
775   A149   5k shown    .40   .25
776   A149   9k Floating oil rig    1.00   .45

Pan-African Postal Union (PAPU), 10th Anniv. — A150

10k, Simulated stamp, map.

**1990, Apr. 6**
777   A150   4k shown    .45   .25
778   A150   10k multicolored    1.00   .65

Paintings by Raul Indipwo — A151

6k, Tres Gracas. 9k, Muxima, vert.

**1990, Apr. 24**
779   A151   6k multicolored    .45   .25
780   A151   9k multicolored    1.00   .35

Stamp World London 90.

Hippotragus Niger Variani, Adult Male and Female — A152

**1990, May 9**    *Perf. 14x13½*
781   A152   5k Adult male    1.50   1.50
782   A152   5k shown    1.50   1.50
783   A152   5k Adult female    1.50   1.50
784   A152   5k Female, calf    1.50   1.50
    Nos. 781-784 (4)    6.00   6.00

World Wildlife Fund. Various combinations available in blocks or strips of four.

Rosa de Porcelana — A153

**1990, June 2**    Litho.    *Perf. 14*
785   A153   5k shown    .40   .25
786   A153   8k Cravo burro    .80   .35
787   A153   10k Alamandra    .95   .45
    Nos. 785-787 (3)    2.15   1.05

**Souvenir Sheet**
788   A153   40k Hibiscus    5.00   5.00

Belgica '90.

**Miniature Sheet**

Intl. Literacy Year A154

Various animals and forest scenes.

**1990, July 26**    Litho.    *Perf. 14*
789   A154   Sheet of 30    10.00   10.00
    a.-ad.   1k any single    .30   .30
790   A154   5k Zebra    1.00   1.00
791   A154   5k Butterfly    1.00   1.00
792   A154   5k Horse    1.00   1.00
    a.   Block of 3, #790-792 + label    4.00   4.00

People's Assembly, 10th Anniv. — A155

**1990, Nov. 11**    *Perf. 14*
793   A155   10k multicolored    .90   .90

3rd Natl. Labor Congress — A156

**1990**    Litho.    *Perf. 13½*
794   A156   14k multicolored    1.00   .50

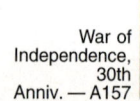 

War of Independence, 30th Anniv. — A157

Uniforms: No. 795, Machete, 1961. No. 796, Rifle, 1962-63. No. 797, Rifle, 1968. No. 798, Automatic rifle, 1972.

**1991, Feb. 28**    Litho.    *Perf. 14*
795   A157   6k multicolored    .65   .25
    a.   Perf. 13½ vert.    1.20   .75
796   A157   6k multicolored    .65   .25
    a.   Perf. 13½ vert.    1.20   .75
797   A157   6k multicolored    .65   .25
    a.   Perf. 13½ vert.    1.20   .75
798   A157   6k multicolored    .65   .25
    a.   Perf. 13½ vert.    1.20   .75
    b.   Bklt. pane of 4, #795a-798a
    Nos. 795-798 (4)    2.60   1.00

Musical Instruments — A158

Designs: a, Marimba. b, Mucupela. c, Ngoma la Txina. d, Kissange.

**1991, Apr. 5**    Litho.    *Perf. 14*
799   A158   6k Block or strip of 4, #799a-799d    2.50   2.50

Tourism — A159

Designs: 3k, Iona National Park. 7k, Kalandula Waterfalls. 35k, Lobito Bay. 60k, Weltwitschia Mirabilis plant.

**1991, June 25**    Litho.    *Perf. 14*
800   A159   3k multi    .30   .25
801   A159   7k multi    .30   .40
802   A159   35k multi    .95   .80
803   A159   60k multi    1.60   1.50
    Nos. 800-803 (4)    3.15   2.95

**Souvenir Sheet**

Design: 30k, Map details.

**1991, June 25**    *Perf. 13¼*
803A   A159   30k multi    4.00   4.00

Dogs — A160

**1991, July 5**    Litho.    *Perf. 14*
804   A160   5k Kabir of dembos    .50   .50
805   A160   7k Ombua    .55   .55
806   A160   11k Kabir massongo    .90   .40
807   A160   12k Kawa tchowe    .90   .50
    Nos. 804-807 (4)    2.85   1.95

1992 Summer Olympics, Barcelona — A161

**1991, July 26**    *Perf. 13*
808   A161   4k Judo    .30   .25
809   A161   6k Sailing    .30   .25
810   A161   10k Running    .45   .25
811   A161   100k Swimming    3.50   2.25
    Nos. 808-811 (4)    4.55   3.00

Navigation Aids — A162

**1991, Nov. 8**    Litho.    *Perf. 12*
812   A162   5k Quadrant    .30   .25
813   A162   15k Astrolabe    .55   .55
814   A162   20k Cross-staff    .75   .40
815   A162   50k Portolano    1.75   1.00
    Nos. 812-815 (4)    3.35   2.20

Iberex '91.

Rays — A163

**1992, Mar. 30**    Litho.    *Perf. 14*
816   A163   40k Myliobatis aquila    .90   .30
817   A163   50k Aetobatus narinari    .90   .40
818   A163   66k Manta birostris    1.10   .50
819   A163   80k Raja miraletus    1.50   .65
    Nos. 816-819 (4)    4.40   1.85

**Souvenir Sheet**
    *Perf. 13½*
820   A163   25k Manta birostris, diff.    5.00   5.00

Quioca Masks — A164

**1992, Apr. 30**    Litho.    *Perf. 13½*
821   A164   60k Kalelwa    .30   .25
822   A164   100k Mukixe Wa Kino    .45   .35
823   A164   150k Cikunza    .75   .55
824   A164   250k Mukixi Wa Mbwesu    1.20   .70
    Nos. 821-824 (4)    2.70   1.85

See Nos. 854-857, 868-871, 883-886, 895-898.

Lubrapex '92 — A165

Medicinal Plants: 200k, Ptaeroxylon obliquum. 300k, Spondias mombin. 500k, Parinari curatellifolia. 600k, Cochlospermum angolense.

**1992, May 8**    *Perf. 14*
825   A165   200k brown & pale yel    .75   .55
826   A165   300k brown & pale yel    1.10   .90
827   A165   500k brown & pale yel    2.00   1.60
828   A165   600k brown & pale yel    2.10   1.75
    a.   Block or strip of 4, #825-828    6.00   6.00

Evangelization of Angola, 500th Anniv. — A166

150k, King, missionaries. 420k, Ruins of M'banza Congo. 470k, Maxima Church. 500k, Faces of people.

**1992, May 10**    *Perf. 13½*
829   A166   150k multicolored    .55   .45
830   A166   420k multicolored    1.60   1.25
831   A166   470k multicolored    1.75   1.40
832   A166   500k multicolored    2.00   1.60
    Nos. 829-832 (4)    5.90   4.70

Traditional Houses — A167

150k, Dimbas. 330k, Cokwe. 360k, Mbali. 420k, Ambwelas. 500k, Upper Zambezi.

# ANGOLA

## Perf. 14, 13½ Vert. (#832A)
**1992, May 22**
| | | | | |
|---|---|---|---|---|
| 832A | A167 | 150k multi | 1.25 | 1.00 |
| b. | | Bklt. pane of 4, #832A, 833a-835a | 7.50 | |
| 833 | A167 | 330k multi | 1.40 | 1.10 |
| a. | | Perf. 13½ vert. | 1.60 | 1.60 |
| 834 | A167 | 360k multi | 1.60 | 1.25 |
| a. | | Perf. 13½ vert. | 1.60 | 1.60 |
| 835 | A167 | 420k multi | 2.00 | 1.60 |
| a. | | Perf. 13½ vert. | 2.00 | 2.00 |
| 836 | A167 | 500k multi | 2.00 | 1.60 |
| | | Nos. 832A-836 (5) | 8.25 | 6.55 |

Expo '92, Seville.

Agapornis Roseicollis A168

150k, Two birds on branch. 200k, Birds feeding. 250k, Hand holding bird. 300k, Bird on perch.

**1992, June 2** — Perf. 12x11½
| 837 | A168 | 150k multicolored | 1.00 | .50 |
|---|---|---|---|---|
| 838 | A168 | 200k multicolored | 1.40 | .65 |
| 839 | A168 | 250k multicolored | 1.75 | .80 |
| 840 | A168 | 300k multicolored | 2.10 | 1.00 |
| a. | | Strip of 4, #837-840 | 6.50 | 6.50 |

Expo '92, Seville.

### Souvenir Sheet

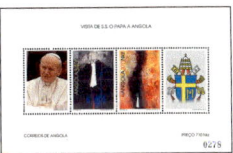

Visit of Pope John Paul II to Angola — A169

Abstract paintings: a, 340k, The Crucifixion. b, 370k, The Resurrection.

**1992, June 4** — Litho. — Perf. 13½
| 841 | A169 | Sheet of 2, #a.-b. + 2 labels | 4.00 | 4.00 |

1992 Summer Olympics, Barcelona A170

**1992, July 30** — Perf. 14
| 842 | A170 | 120k Hurdles | .55 | .40 |
|---|---|---|---|---|
| 843 | A170 | 180k Cycling | .80 | .55 |
| 844 | A170 | 240k Roller hockey | .95 | .75 |
| 845 | A170 | 360k Basketball | 1.50 | 1.10 |
| | | Nos. 842-845 (4) | 3.80 | 2.80 |

Native Fishing — A171

**1992, Aug. 5** — Perf. 11½x12
| 846 | A171 | 65k Building traps | .50 | .25 |
|---|---|---|---|---|
| 847 | A171 | 90k Using nets | .65 | .35 |
| 848 | A171 | 100k Laying traps | .80 | .40 |
| 849 | A171 | 120k Fisherman in boats | .95 | .50 |
| | | Nos. 846-849 (4) | 2.90 | 1.50 |

### Souvenir Sheet

Discovery of America, 500th Anniv. — A172

**1992, Sept. 18** — Litho. — Perf. 12
| 850 | A172 | 500k multicolored | 4.00 | 4.00 |

Genoa '92.

First Free Elections in Angola — A173

Designs: 120k, People voting. 150k, Map, ballot box, peace doves. 200k, People, dove, hand dropping ballot into ballot box.

**1992, Oct. 27** — Litho. — Perf. 11½x12
| 851 | A173 | 120k multicolored | .35 | .25 |
|---|---|---|---|---|
| 852 | A173 | 150k multicolored | .40 | .30 |
| 853 | A173 | 200k multicolored | .55 | .40 |
| | | Nos. 851-853 (3) | 1.30 | .95 |

### Quioca Mask Type of 1992

**1992, Nov. 6** — Perf. 13½
| 854 | A164 | 72k Cihongo | .30 | .25 |
|---|---|---|---|---|
| 855 | A164 | 80k Mbwasu | .35 | .25 |
| 856 | A164 | 120k Cinhanga | .40 | .35 |
| 857 | A164 | 210k Kalewa | .75 | .65 |
| | | Nos. 854-857 (4) | 1.80 | 1.50 |

Inauguration of Express Mail Service — A174

**1992, Dec. 14** — Litho. — Perf. 12x11½
| 858 | A174 | 450k Truck | 1.40 | 1.20 |
|---|---|---|---|---|
| 859 | A174 | 550k Airplane | 1.75 | 1.40 |

Meteorological Instruments — A175

**1993, Mar. 23** — Litho. — Perf. 11½x12
| 860 | A175 | 250k Weather balloon | .95 | .80 |
|---|---|---|---|---|
| 861 | A175 | 470k Actinometer | 1.90 | 1.40 |
| 862 | A175 | 500k Rain gauge | 1.90 | 1.60 |
| | | Nos. 860-862 (3) | 4.75 | 3.80 |

Seashells — A176

210k, Trochita trochiformis. 330k, Strombus latus. 400k, Aporrhais pesgallinae. 500k, Fusos aff. albinus. 1000k, Pusionella nifat.

**1993, Apr. 6** — Perf. 12x11½
| 863 | A176 | 210k multicolored | .75 | .75 |
|---|---|---|---|---|
| 864 | A176 | 330k multicolored | 1.10 | 1.10 |
| 865 | A176 | 400k multicolored | 1.50 | 1.50 |
| 866 | A176 | 500k multicolored | 1.75 | 1.75 |
| | | Nos. 863-866 (4) | 5.10 | 5.10 |

### Souvenir Sheet

| 867 | A176 | 1000k multicolored | 4.00 | 4.00 |

### Quioca Art Type of 1992

**1993, June 7** — Litho. — Perf. 12
| 868 | A164 | 72k Men with vehicles | .30 | .25 |
|---|---|---|---|---|
| 869 | A164 | 210k Cavalier | 1.10 | .50 |
| 870 | A164 | 420k Airplane | 2.25 | .90 |
| 871 | A164 | 600k Men carrying stretcher | 3.00 | 1.25 |
| | | Nos. 868-871 (4) | 6.65 | 2.90 |

Flowering Plants — A177

360k, Sansevieria cylindrica. 400k, Euphorbia tirucalli. 500k, Opuntia ficus-indica. 600k, Dracaena aubryana.

**1993, June 28** — Perf. 11½x12
| 872 | A177 | 360k multicolored | 1.20 | .90 |
|---|---|---|---|---|
| 873 | A177 | 400k multicolored | 1.40 | 1.00 |
| 874 | A177 | 500k multicolored | 1.50 | 1.00 |
| 875 | A177 | 600k multicolored | 2.00 | 1.40 |
| | | Nos. 872-875 (4) | 6.10 | 4.30 |

### Souvenir Sheet

Africa Day A178

**1993, May 31** — Perf. 12
| 876 | A178 | 1500k Leopard | 6.00 | 6.00 |

Tribal Pipes — A179

**1993, Aug. 16** — Litho. — Perf. 11½x12
| 877 | A179 | 72k Vimbundi | .30 | .25 |
|---|---|---|---|---|
| 878 | A179 | 200k Vimbundi, diff. | .75 | .40 |
| 879 | A179 | 420k Mutopa | 1.40 | .90 |
| 880 | A179 | 600k Pexi | 2.00 | 1.25 |
| | | Nos. 877-880 (4) | 4.45 | 2.80 |

### Souvenir Sheet

Union of Portuguese Speaking Capitals — A180

**1993, July 30** — Perf. 12x11½
| 881 | A180 | 1500k multicolored | 5.50 | 5.50 |

Turtles — A181

Designs: a, 180k, Chelonia mydas. b, 450k, Eretmochelys imbricata. c, 550k, Dermochelys coriacea. d, 630k, Caretta caretta.

**1993, July 9** — Litho. — Perf. 12½x12
| 882 | A181 | Block of 4, #a.-d. | 7.00 | 7.00 |

### Quioca Art Type of 1992

**1993, Sept. 1** — Litho. — Perf. 12
| 883 | A164 | 300k Leopard | .95 | .65 |
|---|---|---|---|---|
| 884 | A164 | 600k Malhado | 1.90 | 1.25 |
| 885 | A164 | 800k Birds | 2.50 | 1.75 |
| 886 | A164 | 1000k Chickens | 3.25 | 2.10 |
| | | Nos. 883-886 (4) | 8.60 | 5.75 |

Mushrooms — A182

300k, Tricholoma georgii. 500k, Amanita phalloides. 600k, Amanita vaginata. 1000k, Macrolepiota procera.

**1993, Dec. 5** — Litho. — Perf. 12
| 887 | A182 | 300k multicolored | .95 | .55 |
|---|---|---|---|---|
| a. | | Perf. 11½ vert. | 1.60 | 1.60 |
| 888 | A182 | 500k multicolored | 1.60 | .95 |
| a. | | Perf. 11½ vert. | 2.40 | 1.60 |
| 889 | A182 | 600k multicolored | 1.90 | 1.20 |
| a. | | Perf. 11½ vert. | 3.25 | 3.25 |
| 890 | A182 | 1000k multicolored | 3.25 | 2.00 |
| a. | | Perf. 11½ vert. | 4.75 | 4.75 |
| b. | | Booklet pane of 4, #887a-890a | 12.00 | |
| | | Nos. 887-890 (4) | 7.70 | 4.70 |

A183

Natl. Culture Day: 500k, Cinganji, wood carving of dancer. 1000k, Ohunya yo soma, staff with woman's face. 1200k, Ongende, sculpture of man on donkey. 2200k, Upi, corn pestle.

**1994, Jan. 10** — Litho. — Perf. 12
| 891 | A183 | 500k multicolored | .80 | .50 |
|---|---|---|---|---|
| 892 | A183 | 1000k multicolored | 1.50 | .95 |
| 893 | A183 | 1200k multicolored | 2.00 | 1.25 |
| 894 | A183 | 2200k multicolored | 3.50 | 2.25 |
| | | Nos. 891-894 (4) | 7.80 | 4.95 |

Hong Kong '94.

### Quioca Art Type of 1992

**1994, Feb. 21** — Litho. — Perf. 12
| 895 | A164 | 500k Bird on flower | .50 | .40 |
|---|---|---|---|---|
| 896 | A164 | 2000k Plant with roots | 2.25 | 1.60 |
| 897 | A164 | 2500k Feto | 2.75 | 2.00 |
| 898 | A164 | 3000k Plant | 3.50 | 2.40 |
| | | Nos. 895-898 (4) | 9.00 | 6.40 |

Social Responsibilities of AIDS — A184

500k, Mass of people. 1000k, Witchdoctor receiving AIDS through needle, people being educated. 3000k, Stylized man, woman.

**1994, May 5** — Litho. — Perf. 12
| 899 | A184 | 500k multicolored | .55 | .40 |
|---|---|---|---|---|
| 900 | A184 | 1000k multicolored | 1.10 | .55 |
| 901 | A184 | 3000k multicolored | 3.50 | 2.40 |
| | | Nos. 899-901 (3) | 5.15 | 3.35 |

1994 World Cup Soccer Championships, US — A185

500k, Large arrows, small ball. 700k, Small arrows, large ball. 2200k, Ball in goal. 2500k, Ball, foot.

**1994, June 17** — Perf. 14
| 902 | A185 | 500k multicolored | .55 | .40 |
|---|---|---|---|---|
| 903 | A185 | 700k multicolored | .80 | .55 |
| 904 | A185 | 2200k multicolored | 2.50 | 1.75 |
| 905 | A185 | 2500k multicolored | 3.00 | 2.00 |
| | | Nos. 902-905 (4) | 6.85 | 4.70 |

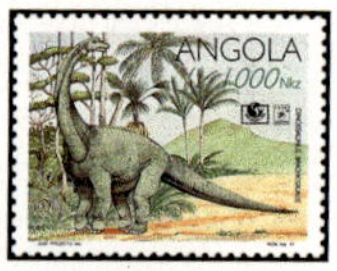


Dinosaurs A186

1000k, Brachiosaurus. 3000k, Spinosaurus. 5000k, Ouranosaurus. 10,000k, Lesothosaurus.
19,000k, Lesothosaurus, map of Africa.

**1994, Aug. 16 Litho. *Perf. 12***

| | | | | |
|---|---|---|---|---|
| **906** | A186 | 1000k multi | .30 | .25 |
| **907** | A186 | 3000k multi | .75 | .55 |
| **908** | A186 | 5000k multi | 1.25 | .95 |
| **909** | A186 | 10,000k multi | 2.50 | 2.00 |
| | | *Nos. 906-909 (4)* | 4.80 | 3.75 |

**Souvenir Sheet**

| | | | | |
|---|---|---|---|---|
| **910** | A186 | 19,000k multi | 7.50 | 7.50 |

PHILAKOREA '94, SINGPEX '94. No. 910 contains one 44x34mm stamp.

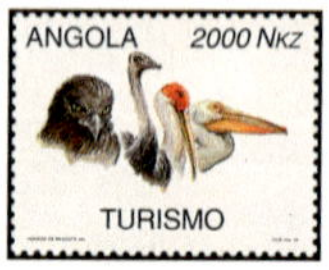


Tourism — A187

2000k, Birds. 4000k, Wild animals. 8000k, Native women. 10,000k, Native men.

**1994, Sept. 27 Litho. *Perf. 12x11½***

| | | | | |
|---|---|---|---|---|
| **911** | A187 | 2000k multi | .50 | .40 |
| **912** | A187 | 4000k multi | .95 | .80 |
| **913** | A187 | 8000k multi | 2.00 | 1.60 |
| **914** | A187 | 10,000k multi | 2.50 | 2.00 |
| | | *Nos. 911-914 (4)* | 5.95 | 4.80 |

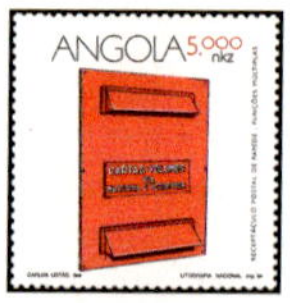


Post Boxes — A188

Designs: 5000k, Letters, bundled mail wall box. 7500k, Wall box for letters. 10,000k, Pillar box. 21,000k, Multi-function units.

**1994, Oct. 7 *Perf. 14½***

| | | | | |
|---|---|---|---|---|
| **915** | A188 | 5000k multicolored | .75 | .40 |
| **916** | A188 | 7500k multicolored | 1.00 | .55 |
| **917** | A188 | 10,000k multicolored | 1.40 | .90 |
| **918** | A188 | 21,000k multicolored | 3.00 | 1.75 |
| | | *Nos. 915-918 (4)* | 6.15 | 3.50 |

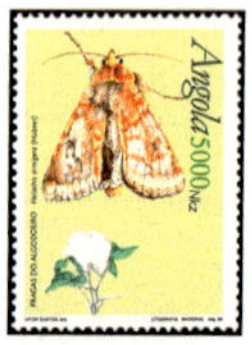


Cotton Pests — A189

Insects: 5000k, Heliothis armigera. 6000k, Bemisia tabasi. 10,000k, Dysdercus. 27,000k, Spodoptera exigua.

**1994, Nov. 11 Litho. *Perf. 14***

| | | | | |
|---|---|---|---|---|
| **919** | A189 | 5000k multicolored | 1.10 | .40 |
| **920** | A189 | 6000k multicolored | 1.35 | .50 |
| **921** | A189 | 10,000k multicolored | 2.15 | .90 |
| **922** | A189 | 27,000k multicolored | 5.40 | 2.10 |
| | | *Nos. 919-922 (4)* | 10.00 | 3.90 |

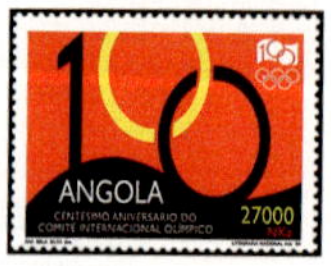


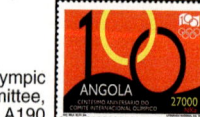

Intl. Olympic Committee, Cent. — A190

**1994, Dec. 15**

| | | | | |
|---|---|---|---|---|
| **923** | A190 | 27,000k multicolored | 4.50 | 4.50 |

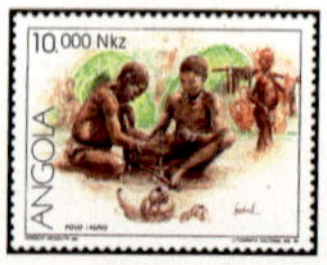


Tribal Culture — A191

Designs: 10,000k, Rubbing sticks to start fire. 15,000k, Extracting sap from tree. 20,000k, Smoking tribal pipe. 25,000k, Shooting bow & arrow. 28,000k, Mothers, children. 30,000k, Cave art.

**1995, Jan. 6 Litho. *Perf. 14***

| | | | | |
|---|---|---|---|---|
| **924** | A191 | 10,000k multicolored | .50 | .35 |
| **925** | A191 | 15,000k multicolored | .75 | .50 |
| **926** | A191 | 20,000k multicolored | 1.00 | .65 |
| **927** | A191 | 25,000k multicolored | 1.25 | .80 |
| **928** | A191 | 28,000k multicolored | 1.25 | .90 |
| **929** | A191 | 30,000k multicolored | 1.50 | 1.20 |
| | | *Nos. 924-929 (6)* | 6.25 | 4.40 |

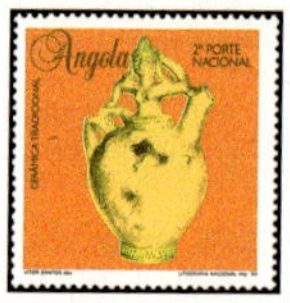


Traditional Ceramics — A192

Designs: No. 930, Pitcher with bust of a woman as stopper. No. 931, Cone-shaped vase. No. 932, Bird-shaped vase. No. 933, Pitcher with bust of a man as stopper.

**1995, Jan. 2 Litho. *Perf. 14½***

| | | | | |
|---|---|---|---|---|
| **930** | A192 | (2) 2nd class natl. | .55 | .25 |
| **931** | A192 | (1) 1st class natl. | .80 | .35 |
| **932** | A192 | (2) 2nd class intl. | 1.10 | .55 |
| **933** | A192 | (1) 1st class intl. | 1.50 | 1.25 |
| | | *Nos. 930-933 (4)* | 3.95 | 2.40 |

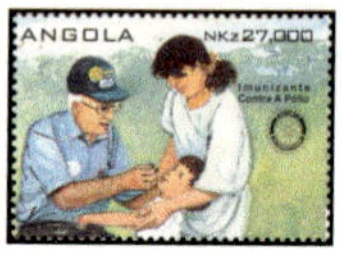


Rotary Intl., 90th Anniv. — A193

a, Immunizing boy against polio. b, Medical examination. c, Immunizing girl against polio.
No. 936, Dove over map.

**1995, Feb. 23 Litho. *Perf. 14***

| | | | | |
|---|---|---|---|---|
| **934** | | Strip of 3 | 6.00 | 6.00 |
| *a.-c.* | | A193 27,000k any single | 2.00 | 1.25 |
| **935** | | Strip of 3 | 6.00 | 6.00 |
| *a.-c.* | | A193 27,000k any single | 2.00 | 1.25 |

**Souvenir Sheet**

| | | | | |
|---|---|---|---|---|
| **936** | A193 | 81,000k multicolored | 7.50 | 7.50 |
| *a.* | | English inscription | 7.50 | 7.50 |

No. 934 has Portuguese inscriptions. No. 935 has English inscriptions. Both were issued in sheets of 9 stamps.
No. 936 contains Portuguese inscription in sheet margin.

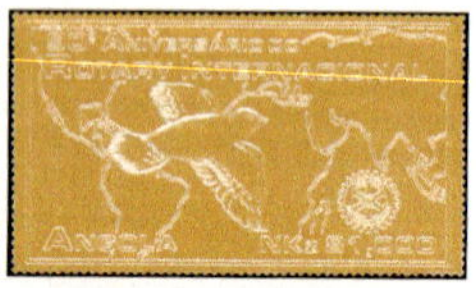

Rotary Intl., 90th Anniv. A194

**Litho. & Embossed**

**1995, Feb. 23 *Perf. 11½x12***

| | | | | |
|---|---|---|---|---|
| **937** | A194 | 81,000k gold | 60.00 | |

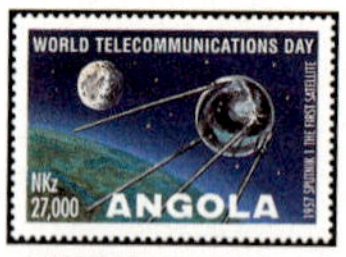


World Telecommunications Day — A195

Designs: No. 938, 1957 Sputnik 1. No. 939, Shuttle, Intelsat satellite.

**1995 Litho. *Perf. 14***

| | | | | |
|---|---|---|---|---|
| **938** | A195 | 27,000k multicolored | 2.00 | 2.00 |
| **939** | A195 | 27,000k multicolored | 2.00 | 2.00 |
| *a.* | | Souvenir sheet, #938-939 | 4.50 | 4.50 |

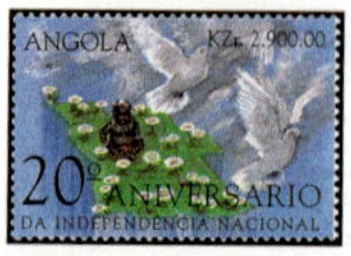


Independence, 20th Anniv. — A196

**1995, Nov. 11 Litho. *Perf. 14***

| | | | | |
|---|---|---|---|---|
| **940** | A196 | 2900k multicolored | 1.60 | 1.60 |

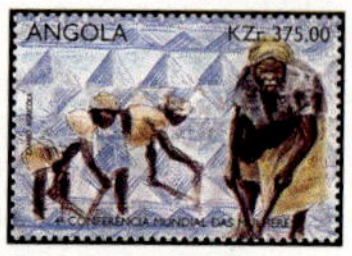


4th World Conference on Women, Beijing — A197

Designs: 375k, Women working in fields. 1106k, Woman teaching, girls with book. 1265k, Woman in industry, career woman. 2900k, Woman in native headdress, vert.
1500k, Native mother, children, vert.

**1996, Jan. 29 Litho. *Perf. 14***

| | | | | |
|---|---|---|---|---|
| **941** | A197 | 375k multicolored | .30 | .25 |
| **942** | A197 | 1106k multicolored | .80 | .80 |
| **943** | A197 | 1265k multicolored | 1.50 | 1.50 |
| **944** | A197 | 2900k multicolored | 3.00 | 3.00 |
| | | *Nos. 941-944 (4)* | 5.60 | 5.55 |

**Souvenir Sheet**

| | | | | |
|---|---|---|---|---|
| **945** | A197 | 1500k multicolored | 12.50 | 12.50 |

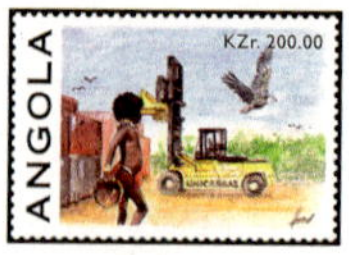


UN Assistance Programs A198

Designs: 200k, Boy, highlift moving supplies. 1265k, Supply ship arriving. No. 948, Two high lifts. No. 949, Tractor-trailer traveling past vultures, native girl.
No. 950, Man, ship.

**1996 Litho. *Perf. 14***

| | | | | |
|---|---|---|---|---|
| **946** | A198 | 200k multicolored | .30 | .25 |
| **947** | A198 | 1265k multicolored | 1.00 | 1.00 |
| **948** | A198 | 2583k multicolored | 2.25 | 2.25 |
| **949** | A198 | 2583k multicolored | 2.50 | 2.50 |
| | | *Nos. 946-949 (4)* | 6.05 | 6.00 |

**Souvenir Sheet**

| | | | | |
|---|---|---|---|---|
| **950** | A198 | 1265k multicolored | *6.50* | *6.50* |

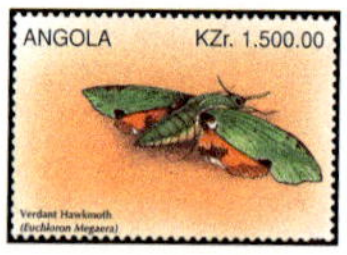


Flora and Fauna — A199

1500k, Verdant hawkmoth. 4400k, Water lily. 5100k, Panther toad. 6000k, African wild dog.
1500k: a, Western honey buzzard. b, Bateleuer. c, Common kestrel.
4400k; d, Red-crested turaco. e, Giraffe. f, Elephant.
5100k: g, Hippopotamus. h, Cattle egret. i, Lion.
6000k: j, Helmeted turtle. k, African pygmy goose. l, Egyptian plover.
12,000k, Spotted hyena.

**1996, Apr. 20 Litho. *Perf. 14***

| | | | | |
|---|---|---|---|---|
| **951-954** | A199 | Set of 4 | 5.00 | 5.00 |
| **955** | A199 | Sheet of 12, #a.-l. | 7.50 | 7.50 |

**Souvenir Sheet**

| | | | | |
|---|---|---|---|---|
| **956** | A199 | 12,000k multicolored | 3.00 | 3.00 |

Sheets of 12, #a-i.

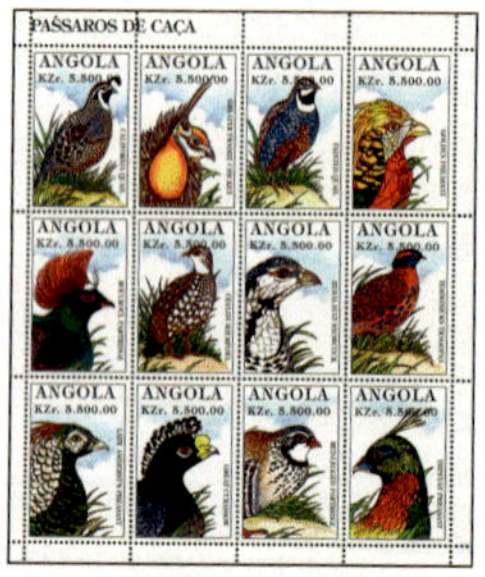


Birds — A200

Fowl, each 5500k: No. 957a, California quail. b, Greater prairie chicken. c, Painted quail. d, Golden pheasant. e, Roulroul partridge. f, Ceylon sourfowl. g, Himalayan snowcock. h, Temminicks tragopan. i, Lady Amherst's pheasant. j, Great curassow. k, Red-legged partridge. l, Impeyan pheasant.
Hummingbirds, each 5500k: No. 958a, Anna's. b, Blue-throated. c, Broad-tailed. d, Costa's. e, White-eared. f, Calliope. g, Violet-crowned. h, Rufous. i, Crimson topaz. j, Broad-billed. k, Frilled coquette. l, Ruby-throated.
No. 959, 12,000k, Ring-necked pheasant. No. 960, 12,000k, Racquet-tail hummingbird.

**1996, Apr. 20**

| | | | | |
|---|---|---|---|---|
| **957-958** | A200 | Set of 2 | 20.00 | 20.00 |

**Souvenir Sheets**

| | | | | |
|---|---|---|---|---|
| **959-960** | A200 | Set of 2 | 5.50 | 5.50 |

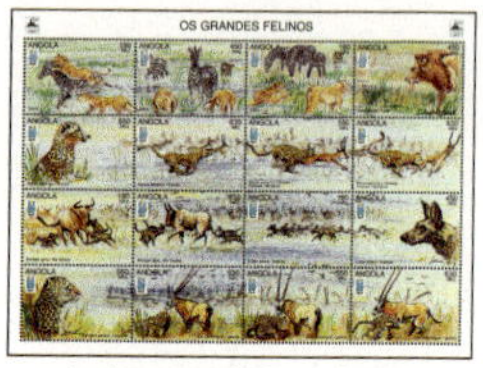


Lubrapex '96 — A201

Wild animals: a, 180k, Lions attacking zebra. b, 450k, Zebras, lions, diff. c, 180k, Zebras grazing, lions stalking. d, 450k, Panthera leo. e, 550k, Cheetah. f, 630k, Cheetah running. g, 550k, Cheetah chasing antilope. h, 630k, Cheetah attacking antelope. i, 180k, Antilope (gnu) being attacked by wild dogs. j, 450k, Antelope, wild dogs. k, 180k, Pack of wild dogs. l, 450k, Licaon pictus. m, 550k, Panthera pardus. n, 630k, Oryx. o, 550k, Oryx, diff. p, 630k, Leopard attacking oryx.

**1996, Apr. 27**

| | | | | |
|---|---|---|---|---|
| **961** | A201 | Sheet of 16, #a.-p. | 9.00 | 9.00 |

Sheets of 6, #a.-f.

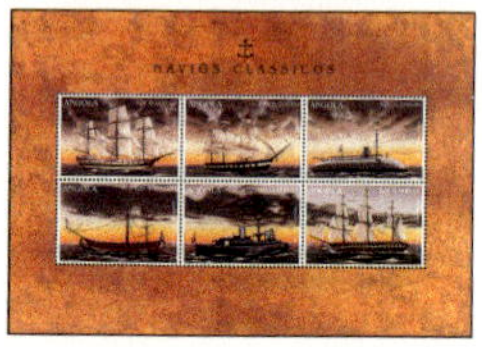


Ships — A202

Designs, each 6000k: No. 962a, Styrbjorn, Sweden, 1789. b, Constellation, US, 1797. c, Taureau, France, 1865. d, Bomb Ketch, France, 1682. e, Sardegna, Italy, 1881. f, HMS Glasgow, England, 1867.
No. 963a, Essex, US, 1812. b, HMS Inflexible, England, 1881. c, HMS Minotaur, England, 1863. d, Napoleon, France, 1854. e, Sophia Amalia, Denmark, 1650. f, Massena, France, 1887.
No. 964, 12,000k, HMS Tremendous, England, 1806, vert. No. 965, 12,000k, Royal Prince, England, 1666.

**1996, May 4**

| | | | | |
|---|---|---|---|---|
| **962-963** | A202 | Set of 2 | 10.00 | 10.00 |

**Souvenir Sheets**

| | | | | |
|---|---|---|---|---|
| **964-965** | A202 | Set of 2 | 6.00 | 6.00 |

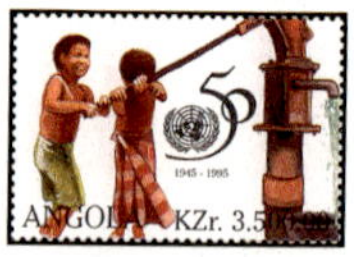


UN, 50th Anniv. (in 1995) — A203

Designs: No. 966, Boys pumping water. No. 967, Man, woman with girl.
8000k, Unloading supplies from ship.

**1996, Apr. 27 Litho. *Perf. 14***

| | | | | |
|---|---|---|---|---|
| **966** | A203 | 3500k multicolored | 1.25 | 1.25 |
| **967** | A203 | 3500k multicolored | 1.25 | 1.25 |

**Souvenir Sheet**

| | | | | |
|---|---|---|---|---|
| **968** | A203 | 8000k multicolored | 2.75 | 2.75 |

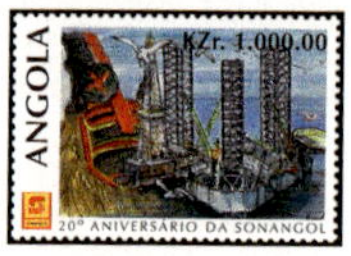


Sonangol, 20th Anniv. — A204

Face in traditional mask, costume, native birds, and: No. 969, Oil derricks. No. 970, Oil storage tanks, ship. 2500k, Refinery equipment. 5000k, Cargo shipment, jet.

**1996, May 12**

| | | | | |
|---|---|---|---|---|
| **969** | A204 | 1000k multicolored | .30 | .25 |
| **970** | A204 | 1000k multicolored | .30 | .25 |
| **971** | A204 | 2500k multicolored | 1.60 | 1.60 |
| **972** | A204 | 5000k multicolored | 2.75 | 2.75 |
| | | *Nos. 969-972 (4)* | 4.95 | 4.85 |

# ANGOLA

Brapex '96 — A205

Designs: No. 973, Slaves in hold. No. 974, Slaves fleeing ship as it's overturned. No. 975, Slave boats approaching ship. No. 976, Slaves talking with captain.
50,000k, like No. 975.

**1996, Oct. 19**    Litho.    Perf. 14

| 973 | A205 | 20,000k multicolored | 1.60 | 2.25 |
|---|---|---|---|---|
| 974 | A205 | 20,000k multicolored | 1.60 | 2.25 |
| 975 | A205 | 30,000k multicolored | 2.15 | 3.00 |
| 976 | A205 | 30,000k multicolored | 2.15 | 3.00 |
|  | Nos. 973-976 (4) |  | 7.50 | 10.50 |

**Souvenir Sheet**

| 977 | A205 | 50,000k multicolored | 4.50 | 4.50 |
|---|---|---|---|---|

Churches — A206

Designs: 5,000k, Mission, Huila. No. 979, Church of the Nazarene. No. 980, Church of Our Lady of Pó Pulo. 25,000k, St. Adriáo Church.

**1996, Dec. 6**    Litho.    Perf. 14

| 978 | A206 | 5,000k multicolored | .40 | .40 |
|---|---|---|---|---|
| 979 | A206 | 10,000k multicolored | .90 | .90 |
| 980 | A206 | 10,000k multicolored | .90 | .90 |
| 981 | A206 | 25,000k multicolored | 2.10 | 2.10 |
|  | Nos. 978-981 (4) |  | 4.30 | 4.30 |

1996 Summer Olympic Games, Atlanta — A207

5,000k, Handball, vert. 10,000k, Swimming. 25,000k, Track & field, vert. 35,000k, Shooting. 65,000k, Basketball.

**1996, Dec. 9**

| 982 | A207 | 5,000k multi | .60 | .60 |
|---|---|---|---|---|
| 983 | A207 | 10,000k multi | 1.25 | 1.25 |
| 984 | A207 | 25,000k multi | 3.25 | 3.25 |
| 985 | A207 | 35,000k multi | 4.50 | 4.50 |
|  | Nos. 982-985 (4) |  | 9.60 | 9.60 |

**Souvenir Sheet**

| 986 | A207 | 65,000k multi | 6.00 | 6.00 |
|---|---|---|---|---|

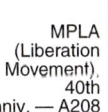 

MPLA (Liberation Movement), 40th Anniv. — A208

**1996, Dec. 10**    Litho.    Perf. 14

| 987 | A208 | 30,000k Dolphins, map | 3.50 | 3.50 |
|---|---|---|---|---|

Trains — A209

Trains — A209a

No. 988: a, AVE, Spain. b, Bullet Train, Japan. c, GM F7 Warbonnet, US. d, Deltic, Great Britain. e, Eurostar, France/Great Britain. f, ETR 450, Italy.
No. 989: a, Class E1300, Morocco. b, ICE, Germany. c, X2000, Sweden. d, TGV Duplex, France.
No. 989E, each 250,000k: f, Steam engine. g, Garrat. h, General Electric.
No. 990, 110,000k, Canadian Pacific 4-4-0, Canada. No. 991, 110,000k, Via Rail Canadian, Canada.

**1997, May 29**    Litho.    Perf. 14
**Sheets of 6, 4 or 3**

| 988 | A209 | 100,000k #a.-f. | 8.00 | 8.00 |
|---|---|---|---|---|
| 989 | A209 | 140,000k #a.-d | 8.00 | 8.00 |
| 989E | A209a | Sheet of 3, #f.-h. | 14.00 | 14.00 |

**Souvenir Sheets**
**Perf. 13½**

| 990-991 | A209 | Set of 2 | 8.00 | 8.00 |
|---|---|---|---|---|

Nos. 990-991 contain one 38x50 or 50x38mm stamp, respectively.
PACIFIC 97.

Horses A210

No. 992: a, Thoroughbred. b, Palomino, appaloosa. c, Arabians. d, Arabian colt. e, Thoroughbred colt. f, Mustang. g, Mustang, diff. h, Furioso.
No. 993: a, Thoroughbred. b, Arabian, palomino. c, Arabian, chincoteague. d, Pintoo. e, Przewalski's horse. f, Thoroughbred colt. g, Arabians. h, New forest pony.
No. 994: a, Selle Francais. b, Fjord. c, Percheron. d, Italian heavy draft. e, Shagya Arab. f, Avelignese. g, Czechoslovakian warmblood. h, New forest pony.
215,000k, Thoroughbreds. 220,000k, Thoroughbreds, diff.

**1997, July 5**    Litho.    Perf. 14
**Sheets of 8**

| 992 | A210 | 100,000k #a.-h. | 8.50 | 8.50 |
|---|---|---|---|---|
| 993 | A210 | 120,000k #a.-h. | 10.00 | 10.00 |
| 994 | A210 | 140,000k #a.-h. | 12.50 | 12.50 |

**Souvenir Sheets**

| 995 | A210 | 215,000k multi | 6.00 | 6.00 |
|---|---|---|---|---|
| 996 | A210 | 220,000k multi | 6.00 | 6.00 |

PACIFIC 97.

1998 World Cup Soccer Championships, France — A211

Winners holding World Cup trophy: No. 997: a, Uruguay, 1930. b, Germany, 1954. c, Brazil, 1970. d, Argentina, 1986. e, Brazil, 1994.

Winning team pictures: No. 998a, Germany, 1954. b, Uruguay, 1958. c, Italy, 1938. d, Brazil, 1962. e, Brazil, 1970. f, Uruguay, 1930. 220,000k, Angolan team members standing. 250,000k, 1997 Angolan team picture.

**1997, July 5**    Litho.    Perf. 14
**Sheets of 5 or 6**

| 997 | A211 | 100,000k #a.-e. + label | 9.00 | 9.00 |
|---|---|---|---|---|
| 998 | A211 | 100,000k #a.-f. | 10.00 | 10.00 |

**Souvenir Sheets**

| 999 | A211 | 220,000k multi | 5.50 | 5.50 |
|---|---|---|---|---|
| 1000 | A211 | 250,000k multi | 5.50 | 5.50 |

ENSA (Security System), 20th Anniv. — A212

"Star" emblem, and stylized protection of "egg," each 240,000k: No. 1001, Industry. No. 1002, Recreation. No. 1003, Homes, shelters. No. 1004, Accident prevention.
350,000k, Emblem.

**1998**    Litho.    Perf. 13½

| 1001-1004 | A212 | Set of 4 | 8.00 | 8.00 |
|---|---|---|---|---|

**Souvenir Sheet**
**Perf. 13½x13**

| 1005 | A212 | 350,000k multi | 4.00 | 4.00 |
|---|---|---|---|---|

No. 1005 contains one 60x40mm stamp.

GURN (Natl. Unity & Reconciliation Government), 1st Anniv. — A213

Emblem, portion of country map and: 100,000k, Sea, swordfish, ships, oil derrick. b, Sea, ships, swordfish. c, Sea, swordfish, ships, mining car on railroad track. d, Sea, power lines.
200,000k: e, Train on track, antelope. f, Mining cars on track, tractor pulling cart. g, Railroad track across rivers, tractor plowing. h, Power lines. i, UR corner of map, crystals. j, Train on track. k, Elephant, tree. l, Trunk of tree, bottom edge of map.

**1998**

| 1006 | A213 | Sheet of 12, #a.-l. | 18.00 | 18.00 |
|---|---|---|---|---|

**Souvenir Sheet**

Education in Angola — A214

**1998**

| 1007 | A214 | 400,000k multi | 8.00 | 8.00 |
|---|---|---|---|---|

Diana, Princess of Wales (1961-97) — A215

Various portraits, each 100,000k, color of sheet margin: No. 1008, pale green. No. 1009, pale yellow.
400,000k, Wearing protective clothing.

**1998, May 21**    Litho.    Perf. 14
**Sheets of 6, #a.-f.**

| 1008-1009 | A215 | Set of 2 | 12.00 | 12.00 |
|---|---|---|---|---|

**Souvenir Sheet**

| 1010 | A215 | 400,000k multi | 5.00 | 5.00 |
|---|---|---|---|---|

See No. 1028.

Expo '98, Lisbon — A216

Marine life: No. 1011, 100,000k, Anemones. No. 1012, 100,000k, Sea urchin. No. 1013, 100,000k, Sea horses. No. 1014, 100,000k, Coral (Caravela). No. 1015, 240,000k, Sea slug. No. 1016, 240,000k, Worms (Tunicados).

**1998, May 21**    Perf. 13½

| 1011-1016 | A216 | Set of 6 | 10.00 | 10.00 |
|---|---|---|---|---|

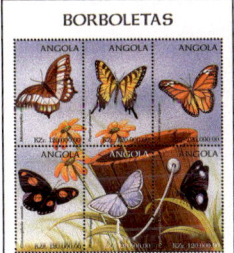

Butterflies — A217

No. 1017, each 120,000k: a, Metamorpha stelene. b, Papilio glaucus. c, Danaus plexippus. d, Catonephele numilli. e, Plebejus argus. f, Hypolimnas bolina.
No. 1018, each 120,000k: a, Terinos terpander. b, Rematistes aganice. c, Hebomoia glaucippe. d, Colias eurytheme. e, Pereute leucodrosime. f, Lycaena dispar.
No. 1019, each 120,000k, horiz.: a, Dynastor napolean. b, Zeuxidia amethystus. c, Battus philenor. d, Phoebis philea. e, Danaus chrysippus. f, Glaucopsyche alexis.
Each 250,000k: No. 1020, Euphaedra neophron. No. 1021, Thecla betulae, horiz. No. 1022, Uraneis ucubis, armiliaria staminea.

**1998, May 21**    Perf. 14
**Sheets of 6, #a.-f.**

| 1017-1019 | A217 | Set of 3 | 20.00 | 20.00 |
|---|---|---|---|---|

**Souvenir Sheets**

| 1020-1022 | A217 | Set of 3 | 16.00 | 16.00 |
|---|---|---|---|---|

Cats and Dogs — A218

Cats, each 140,000k: No. 1023a, British tortoiseshell. b, Chinchilla. c, Russian blue. d, Black Persian (longhair). e, British red tabby. f, Birman.
Dogs, each 140,000k: No. 1024a, West Highland terrier. b, Irish setter. c, Dachshund. d, St. John water dog. e, Shetland sheep dog. f, Dalmatian.
Each 500,000k: No. 1025, Turkish van (swimming cat). No. 1026, Labrador retriever.

**1998, May 21**    Litho.    Perf. 14x13½
**Sheets of 6, #a.-f.**

| 1023-1024 | A218 | Set of 2 | 15.00 | 15.00 |
|---|---|---|---|---|

**Souvenir Sheets**

| 1025-1026 | A218 | Set of 2 | 12.00 | 12.00 |
|---|---|---|---|---|

498 ANGOLA

Wild Animals — A219

100,000k: a, Panthera leo. b, Hippopotamus amphibius. c, Loxodonta africana. d, Giraffa camelopardalis.
220,000k: e, Syncerus caffer-caffer. f, Gorilla gorilla. g, Ceratotherim simum. h, Oryx gazella.

| 1998, July 24 | Litho. | | Perf. 14 | |
|---|---|---|---|---|
| 1027 | A219 | Sheet of 8, #a.-h. | 12.00 | 12.00 |

**Diana, Princes of Wales Type of 1998**

Pictures showing Diana's campaign to ban land mines, each 150,000k: a, With girl. b, With two boys. c, Wearing protective clothing.

| 1998, Aug. 31 | Litho. | | Perf. 14 | |
|---|---|---|---|---|
| 1028 | A215 | Strip of 3, #a.-c. | 7.00 | 7.00 |

No. 1028 was issued in sheets of 6 stamps.

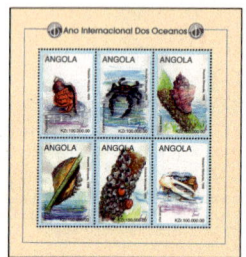

Intl. Year of the Ocean — A220

Marine life: No. 1029a, Pagurites. b, Callinectes marginatus. c, Thais forbesi. d, Ostrea tulipa. e, Balanus amohitrite. f, Uca tangeri.
No. 1030: a, Littorina angulifera. b, Semifusus morio. c, Thais coronata. d, Cerithium atratum (red branch). e, Ostrea tulipa. f, Cerithium atratum (green branch).
Each 300,000k: No. 1031, Goniopsis, horiz. No. 1032, Unidentified shell.

| 1998, Sept. 4 | | Sheets of 6 | |
|---|---|---|---|
| 1029 | A220 | 100,000k #a.-f. | 5.00 5.00 |
| 1030 | A220 | 170,000k #a.-f. | 7.00 7.00 |
| **Souvenir Sheets** | | | |
| 1031-1032 | A220 | Set of 2 | 11.00 11.00 |

Battle Against Polio in Angola A221

| 1998, Aug. 28 | Litho. | Perf. 13½ |
|---|---|---|
| 1033 | A221 | 500,000k multicolored | 3.75 3.75 |

Traditional Boats — A222

Designs: No. 1034, 250,000k, Boat, Bimba. No. 1035, 250,000k, Canoe with sail, Ndongo. 500,000k, Constructing boat, Ndongo.

| 1998, Sept. 4 | | Perf. 14 |
|---|---|---|
| 1034-1036 | A222 | Set of 3 | 7.50 7.50 |

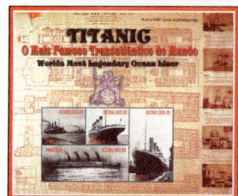

Titanic — A223

Views of Titanic, each 350,000k: a, Under tow. b, Stern. c, Starboard side at night. d, At dock.

| 1998, Sept. 4 | | | |
|---|---|---|---|
| 1037 | A223 | Sheet of 4, #a.-d. | 9.00 9.00 |

No. 1037c is 76x30mm, No. 1037d is 38x61mm.

Angolan Food — A224

Various vegetables, fruits: No. 1038, 100,000k, 4 fruits. No. 1039, 100,000k, Squash sliced in half. No. 1040, 120,000k, Ears of corn. No. 1041, 120,000k, Green beans. No. 1042, 140,000k, Fruit with red seeds sliced in half. No. 1043, 140,000k, Sliced bananas.

| 1998 | | | |
|---|---|---|---|
| 1038-1043 | A224 | Set of 6 | 7.00 7.00 |

Portugal '98.

Airplanes A225

No. 1044, IL-62 M. No. 1045, B737 100.
No. 1046: a, Ultralight. b, Gyroplane. c, Business jet. d, onvertible plane (e). e, Chuterplane (a, b, d). f, Twin rotors (e). g, Skycrane. h, Aerospatiale Concorde (i). i, Flying boat.
No. 1047: a, Pedal power (b). b, Sail plane (a, e). c, Aerobatic (f). d, Hang gliding (g). e, Balloon (h). f, Glidercraft (e, i). g, Model airplane. h, Air racing (i). i, Solar cells.
No. 1048, 1,000,000k, Boeing 777. No. 1049, 1,000,000k, Columbia Space Shuttle, vert. No. 1049A, 1,000,000k, Boeing 737-200. No. 1049B, 1,000,000k, Boeing 747-300.

| 1998-99 | Litho. | | Perf. 14 | |
|---|---|---|---|---|
| 1044 | A225 | 200,000k multi | 1.75 | 1.75 |
| 1045 | A225 | 200,000k multi | 1.75 | 1.75 |
| **Sheets of 9** | | | | |
| 1046 | A225 | 150,000k #a.-i. | 5.00 | 5.00 |
| 1047 | A225 | 250,000k #a.-i. | 8.00 | 8.00 |
| **Souvenir Sheets** | | | | |
| 1048-1049B | A225 | Set of 4 | 26.00 | 26.00 |

Nos. 1048-1049B each contain one 85x28mm stamp.
Issued: Nos. 1049A-1049B, 3/25/99; others 12/24/98.

Dinosaurs — A226

Designs, vert., each 120,000k: No. 1050, Parasaurolophus. No. 1051, Maiasaura. No. 1052, Iguanodon. No. 1053, Elaphosaurus.
No. 1054, vert, 120,000k: a, Brontosaurus. b, Plateosaurus. c, Brachiosaurus. d, Anatosaurus. e, Tyrannosaurus. f, Carnotaurus. g, Corythosaurus. h, Stegosaurus. i, Iguanodon, diff.
No. 1055, 120,000k: a, Hadrosaurus. b, Ouranosaurus. c, Hypsilophodon. d, Brachiosaurus. e, Shunosaurus. f, Amargasaurus. g, Tuojiangosaurus. h, Monoclonius. i, Struthiosaurus.
Each 550,000k: No. 1056, Triceratops, vert. No. 1057, Tyrannosaurus, vert.

| 1998, Dec. 28 | | | |
|---|---|---|---|
| 1050-1053 | A226 | Set of 4 | 7.00 6.00 |
| **Sheets of 9, #a.-i.** | | | |
| 1054-1055 | A226 | Set of 2 | 9.50 9.50 |
| **Souvenir Sheets** | | | |
| 1056-1057 | A226 | Set of 2 | 5.00 5.00 |

World Wildlife Fund — A227

Lesser flamingo: a, Facing left. b, Body facing forward. c, Head and neck. d, With wings spread.

| | | **Strip of 4** | | |
|---|---|---|---|---|
| 1999 | Litho. | | Perf. 14 | |
| 1058 | A227 | 300,000k #a.-d. | 5.00 | 5.00 |

No. 1058 was issued in sheets of 16 stamps.

Fauna — A228

Designs, each 300,000k: No. 1059, Equis caballus przewalski. No. 1060, Spheniscciformes, vert. No. 1061, Haliaeetus leucocephalus, vert. No. 1062, Anodorhynchus hyacinthinus.
No. 1063, 300,000k: a, Vulpes velox hebes. b, Odocoileus. c, Pongo pygmaeus. d, Leontopitecus rosalia. e, Panthera tigris. f, Tragelaphus eurycerus.
No. 1064, 300,000k: a, Tremarctos ornatus. b, Aphelocoma. c, Otus insularis. d, Balaeniceps rex. e, Lepidochelys kempii. f, Lutra canadensis.
Each 1,000,000k: No. 1065, Ailuropoda melanoleuca, vert. No. 1066, Ursus arctos horribilis.

| 1999 | | | |
|---|---|---|---|
| 1059-1062 | A228 | Set of 4 | 5.00 5.00 |
| **Sheets of 6, #a.-f.** | | | |
| 1063-1064 | A228 | Set of 2 | 15.00 15.00 |
| **Souvenir Sheets** | | | |
| 1065-1066 | A228 | Set of 2 | 12.00 12.00 |

These Flora and Fauna stamps, formerly Nos. 1067-1078, were not authorized by Angola postal authorities.
Other items inscribed "Angola" that were not authorized but which have appeared on the market include sheets with the themes of Disney and History of Animation, Millennium, Animals, Trains, Flora, Muhammad Ali & Lennox Lewis, Bruce Lee, Albert Einstein / Moon Landing, Elvis Presley and other entertainers, Great Personalities, John Kennedy and Marilyn Monroe, Martin Luther King, Jr., Payne Stewart, Colin Montgomerie, Babe Ruth, Cardinal John O'Connor, Pope John Paul II / Mother Teresa and Queen Elizabeth II / Winston Churchill.

World Telecommunications Day — A230

| 1999, May 17 | Litho. | Perf. 14 |
|---|---|---|
| 1079 | A230 | 500,000k multi | .75 .75 |

Waterfalls — A231

a, Andulo. b, Chiumbo. c, Ruacaná. d, Coemba.

| 1999, June 5 | | Sheet of 4 |
|---|---|---|
| 1080 | A231 | 500,000k #a.-d. | 3.00 3.00 |

A232

African Men's Basketball Championships — No. 1081: a, Poster. b, Basketball, hoop, tan background. c, Basketball, hoop, green background. d, Welwitschia plant holding basketball.
2,500,000k, Similar to No. 1081c.

| 1999, July 29 | Sheet of 4 | Perf. 13½ |
|---|---|---|
| 1081 | A232 | 1,500,000k #a.-d. | 4.00 4.00 |
| **Souvenir Sheet** | | |
| **Perf. 13x13½** | | |
| 1082 | A232 | 2,500,000k multi | 2.50 2.50 |

No. 1082 contains one 40x30mm stamp. Stamps have one "0" too many in the denominations. Correct denominations would be 1.500.000.00

A233

| 1999, Aug. 17 | | Perf. 14 |
|---|---|---|
| 1083 | A233 | 1,000,000k multi | 1.25 1.25 |

Southern African Development Community. Issued in sheets of 4. Value $5.

Tribal Kings — A234

No. 782: a, Ekuikui II. b, Mvemba Nzinga. c, Mwata Yamvu Naweji II. d, Njinga Mbande. 1,000,000k, Mandume Ndemufayo.

| 1999, Sept. 17 | | Sheet of 4 |
|---|---|---|
| 1084 | A234 | 500,000k #a.-d. | 7.50 7.50 |
| **Souvenir Sheet** | | |
| 1085 | A234 | 1,000,000k multi | 4.00 4.00 |

A235

Queen Mother (b. 1900) — No. 1086: a, With King George VI. b, Wearing brooch. c, Wearing tiara. d, Wearing hat.
500,000k, Wearing academic gown.

ANGOLA 499

**Sheet of 4**
**1999, Sept. 17**    Litho.    *Perf. 14*
1086   A235   200,000k   #a.-d.    8.00   8.00
**Souvenir Sheet**
*Perf. 13¾*
1087   A235   500,000k multi    5.50   5.50
No. 1087 contains one 38x51mm stamp.

Ships — A236

No. 1088, each 950,000k: a, Egyptian bark, 1300 B.C. b, Flemish carrack, 1480. c, Beagle, 1830. d, North Star, 1852. e, Fram, 1892. f, Unyon Maru, 1909. g, Juan Sebastian de Elcano, 1927. h, Tovarishch, 1933.
No. 1089, each 950,000k: a, Bucentauro, 1728. b, Clermont, 1807. c, Savannah, 1819. d, Dromedary, 1844. e, Iberia, 1881. f, S.S. Gluckauf, 1886. g, City of Paris, 1888. h, Mauretania, 1906.
No. 1090, each 950,000k: a, Gloire, 1859. b, L'Ocean, 1868. c, Dandalo, 1870, stern of HMS Dreadnought, 1906. d, Bow of Dreadnought. e, Bismarck, 1939, stern of USS Cleveland, 1946. f, Bow of Cleveland. g, USS Boston, 1942, stern of USS Long Beach, 1959. h, Bow of Long Beach.
Each 5,000,000k: No. 1091, Chinese junk. No. 1092, Madre de Deus, 1609. No. 1093, Catamaran, 1861. No. 1094, Natchez, 1870.

**1999, Sept. 23**    Litho.    *Perf. 14*
**Sheets of 8**
1088-1090   A236   Set of 3    27.00   27.00
**Souvenir Sheets**
1091-1094   A236   Set of 4    22.00   22.00

Mushrooms — A237

No. 1095, Amanita caesarea. No. 1096, Psalliota xanthoderma. No. 1097, Hygrocybe conica. No. 1098, Boletus chrysenteron. No. 1099, Coprinus comatus. No. 1100, Boletus luteus.
No. 1101. a, Morchella crassipes. b, Boletus rufescens. c, Amanita phalloides. d, Collybia iocephala. e, Tricholoma aurantium. f, Cortinarius violaceus. g, Mycena polygramma. h, Psalliota augusta.
No. 1102: a, Amanita muscaria. b, Boletus aereus. c, Coprinus comatus. d, Amanita rubescens. e, Cortinarius collinitus. f, Boletus satanas. g, Lepiota procera. h, Clitocybe geotropa.
No. 1103: a, Russula nigricans. b, Boletus granulatus. c, Mycena strobilinoides. d, Amanita caesarea. e, Amanita muscaria. f, Boletus, crocipodius. g, Russula virescens. h, Lactarius deliciosus.
No. 1104, Psalliota haemorrhoidaria.
No. 1105, Mycena lilacifolia.

**1999, Sept. 23**    Litho.    *Perf. 14*
1095   A237   1,250,000k multi    1.25   1.00
1096   A237   1,250,000k multi    1.25   1.00
1097   A237   1,250,000k multi    1.25   1.00
1098   A237   1,250,000k multi    1.25   1.00
1099   A237   1,250,000k multi    1.25   1.00
1100   A237   1,250,000k multi    1.25   1.00
Nos. 1095-1100 (6)    7.50   6.00
**Sheets of 8**
1101   A237   1,000,000k #a-h    8.00   8.00
1102   A237   1,000,000k #a-h    8.00   8.00
1103   A237   1,000,000k #a-h    8.00   8.00
**Souvenir Sheets**
1104   A237   5,000,000k multi    5.50   5.50
1105   A237   5,000,000k multi    5.50   5.50

A238

First Manned Moon Landing, 30th Anniv. — A239

No. 1107: a, Astronaut spacewalking. b, Mariner 8. c, Viking 10. d, GINGA satellite. e, Soyuz 19. f, Voyager.
No. 1108, vert.: a, Space telescope. b, Space shuttle Atlantis. c, Uhuru satellite. d, Mir space station. e, Gemini 7. f, Venera 7.
No. 1109: a, Mercury, Venus. b, Jupiter. c, Neptune, Pluto. d, Earth, Mars. e, Saturn. f, Uranus.
No. 1110: a, Explorer 17. b, Intelsat 4A. c, GOES-D Satellite. d, Intelsat 2. e, Navstar. f, S.M.S.
No. 1111, 6,000,000k, Lunar rover, vert. No. 1112, 6,000,000k, Apollo 17 astronaut on moon, vert. No. 1113, 12,000,000k, Neil Armstrong, vert. No. 1114, 12,000,000k, Space shuttle Columbia. No. 1115, 12,000,000k, SBS-4, vert.

*Perf. 13¾ (A238), 14 (A239)*
**1999, Nov. 15**    Litho.
**Sheets of 6, #a.-f.**
1107-1108   A238   3,500,000k    10.00   10.00
1109-1110   A239   3,500,000k    10.00   10.00
**Souvenir Sheets**
1111-1112   A238   Set of 2    8.00   8.00
1113-1115   A239   Set of 3    16.00   16.00

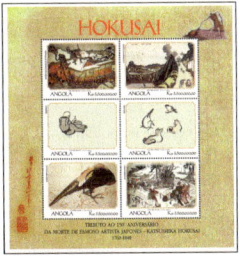

Hokusai Paintings — A240

No. 1116, each 3,500,000k: a, Night attack. b, Usigafuchi No Kudan. c, Drawing of man and bowl. d, Wildlife. e, Pheasant. f, People on bridge.
No. 1117, each 3,500,000k: a, Tree and shoreline. b, Kabuki theater. c, Hen. d, Cooper. e, Trip to Enoshima. f, Sumida River landscape.
Each 12,000,000k: No. 1118, Yama-uba and Kintori, vert. No. 1119, Woman, vert.

**1999, Dec. 13**    Litho.    *Perf. 13¾*
**Sheets of 6, #a.-f.**
1116-1117   A240   Set of 2    18.00   18.00
**Souvenir Sheets**
1118-1119   A240   Set of 2    12.00   12.00

On Dec. 13, the date of issue of these stamps, Angola devalued its currency, with approximately 1,000,000k being the equivalent of 1k after the devaluation.

**Souvenir Sheets**

PhilexFrance 99 — A241

No. 1120, 4-8-4 Linder Compound express. No. 1121, Hovertrain prototype.

**2000, Mar. 13**    Litho.    *Perf. 13¾*
1120-1121   A241   12k Set of 2    11.00   11.00

A242

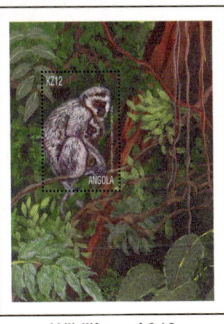

Wildlife — A243

1.50k, Zebra. 2k, Fruit bat. 3k, California condor. 5.50k, Lion.
No. 1126, horiz.: a, Equus zebra. b, Ploceus xanthops. c, Lycaon protus. d, Acinonyx jubatus. e, Oryx gazella. f, Nursing Otocyon megalotis. g, Giraffa camelopardalio. h, Ovis adustus. i, Perodicticus potto. j, Panthera leo. k, Coracius caudata. l, Pair of Otocyon megalotis.
No. 1127, horiz.: a, Struthio camelus. b, Felis lybica. c, Aepyceros melampus. d, Cercopithecus aethiops. e, Diceros bicornis. f, Papio sp. g, Felis caracal. h, Sagittarius serpentarius. i, Phacochoerus aethiopicus. j, Arctocephalus pusillus. k, Alcedo cristata. l, Hippopotamus amphibius.
No. 1128, 3.50k: a, Deer. b, Turkey. c, Beaver. d, Frog. e, Manatee. f, Trout.
No. 1129, 3.50k: a, Macaque. b, Toucan. c, Bothriopsis bilineata. d, Hyla leucopyliata. e, Tamarin. f, Eagle.
No. 1130, 3.50k, vert.: a, Mountain gorilla. b, Rhinoceros. c, Water buffalo. d, Chameleon. e, Cobra. f, Meerkats.
No. 1131, 3.50k, vert.: a, Kangaroo. b, Koala. c, Kingfishers. d, Frog on tree root. e, Three fish. f, Turtle.
No. 1132, 12k, Sloth. No. 1133, 12k, Lemur, vert. No. 1134, 12k, Cheetah, vert. No. 1135, 12k, Orangutan, vert. No. 1136, 12k, Cercopithecus aethiops, diff. No. 1137, 12k, Loxodonta africana.

**2000, Apr. 7**    *Perf. 14*
1122-1125   A242   Set of 4    6.00   6.00
1126   A243   1.50k Sheet of 12, #a-l    9.00   9.00
1127   A243   2k Sheet of 12, #a-l    13.00   13.00
**Sheets of 6, #a-f**
1128-1131   A242   Set of 4    40.00   40.00
**Souvenir Sheets**
1132-1135   A242   Set of 4    24.00   24.00
1136-1137   A243   Set of 2    12.00   12.00

Birds of Prey — A244

1.50k, Harpy eagle. 2k, Unidentified bird. 3k, Vulture, vert. 5.50k, King vulture, vert.
No. 1142, 3.50k: a, Accipiter gentilis. b, Surnia ulula. c, Falco peregrinus. d, Otus asio. e, Haliaeetus vocifer. f, Herpetotheres cachinnans.
No. 1143, 3.50k: a, Falco sparverius. b, Pulsetrix perspicillata. c, Elomus leucurus. d, Ninox novaeseelandiae. e, Polemaetus bellicosus. f, Polyborus plancus.
No. 1144, 6.50k: a, Verreaux's eagle. b, Aguia gigante. c, Aguia peixe.
No. 1145, 6.50k, vert.: a, Aguia despeida. b, Aguia dourada. c, Aguia devoradora de macacos.
No. 1146, 12k, King vulture, diff. No. 1147, 12k, Falcon, vert. No. 1148, 15k, Sagittarius serpentarius. No. 1149, 15k, Aquila chrysaetos.

**2000, Apr. 10**
1138-1141   A244   Set of 4    5.50   5.50
**Sheets of 6, #a-f**
1142-1143   A244   Set of 2    19.00   19.00
**Sheets of 3, #a-c**
1144-1145   A244   Set of 2    18.00   18.00
**Souvenir Sheets**
1146-1147   A244   Set of 2    12.00   12.00
1148-1149   A244   Set of 2    13.00   13.00

Millennium — A245

Highlights of the 16th Century: a, Paintings by Lai-Ji. b, The Last Judgment, by Luca Signorelli. c, Garden of Earthly Delights by Hieronymus Bosch. d, The Prince, written by Niccolò Machiavelli. e, Utopia, written by Sir Thomas More. f, Nursing Otocyon megalotis. g, Charles I of Spain becomes Holy Roman Emperor Charles V. h, The School of Athens, by Raphael. i, Juan Sebastián de Elcano circumnavigates globe. j, Henry VIII of England. k, Spanish conquest of Aztecs and Incas. l, Placentia Cathedral. m, Potatoes introduced to Europe. n, Heliocentric theory of Copernicus. o, Portuguese reach Japan. p, Death of Albrecht Dürer (60x40mm). q, Bartolomé de Las Casas promotes rights for Indians.

**2000, Oct. 2**    Litho.    *Perf. 12¾x12½*
1150   A245   2.50k Sheet of 17, #a-q, + label    24.00   24.00

War Damage in Angola — A246

Designs: No. 1151, 3k, B.N.A. Building, Kuito. No. 1152, 3k, Kunje St., Kuito. No. 1153, 4k, Post office. No. 1154, 4k, Police headquarters. No. 1155, 5k, Apartment house. No. 1156, 5k, Independence Square. No. 1157, 6k, Child waving from upper floor of apartment house. No. 1158, 6k, Building, man carrying pack.

**2000, Sept. 29**    Litho.    *Perf. 14*
1151-1158   A246   Set of 8    18.00   18.00

The Popes of the Millennium — A247

No. 1159, 3k: a, Nicholas II, 1059-61. b, Paschal II, 1099-1118. c, Sergius IV, 1009-1012. d, Victor II, 1055-57. e, Victor III, 1086-87. f, Urban III, 1185-87.
No. 1160, 3k: a, Innocent II, 1130-43. b, John XIII, 965-72. c, Agapetus II, 946-55. d, John XV, 985-96. e, John XVIII, 1003-09. f, Lucius II, 1144-45.
No. 1161, 3k: a, Celestine II, 1143-44. b, Clement II, 1046-47. c, Clement III, 1187-91. d, Gelasius II, 1118-19. e, Benedict VII, 974-83. f, Gregory V, 996-99.
No. 1162, 12k, Leo IX, 1049-54. No. 1163, 12k, Gregory VII, 1073-85. No. 1164, 12k, Leo XIII, 1878-1903.

**2000, Oct. 2**    *Perf. 12x12¼*
**Sheets of 6, #a-f**
1159-1161   A247   Set of 3    27.00   27.00
**Souvenir Sheets**
1162-1164   A247   Set of 3    18.00   18.00

# ANGOLA

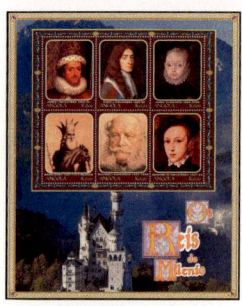

Monarchs — A248

No. 1165, 3k: a, Henry II, King of Germany and Holy Roman Emperor, 1002-24. b, Marina Mniszek, wife of false Russian czar Dmitri, 1605-06. c, Ivan IV of Russia, 1533-84. d, Ivan III of Russia, 1462-1505.

No. 1166, 3k: a, Charles II of Great Britain, 1660-85. b, Lady Jane Grey of England, 1533. c, Leopold III of Belgium, 1934-51. d, Louis XV of France, 1715-74.

No. 1167, 3k: a, James I of Great Britain, 1603-25. b, James II of Great Britain, 1685-88. c, James IV of Scotland, 1567-1625. d, Brian Boru of Ireland, 1002-14. e, Wilhelm I, King of Prussia and German Emperor, 1861-88. f, Edward VI of England, 1547-53.

No. 1168, 12k, Feodor I of Russia, 1584-98. No. 1169, 12k, False Russian czar Dmitri, 1605-06. No. 1170, 12k, William IV of Great Britain, 1830-37.

| 2000, Oct. 2 | | Sheets of 4, #a-d | |
|---|---|---|---|
| 1165-1166 | A248 | Set of 2 | 12.50 12.50 |
| 1167 | A248 | Sheet of 6, #a-f | 9.50 9.50 |

**Souvenir Sheets**

| 1168-1170 | A248 | Set of 3 | 18.00 18.00 |

Children's Drawings A249

Various designs. Denominations: 3k, 4k, 5k.

| 2000, Nov. 7 | | | Perf. 14 |
|---|---|---|---|
| 1171-1173 | A249 | Set of 3 | 4.75 4.75 |

Post Office Buildings A250

Designs: No. 1174, 5k, Former Secretary of Communications Building, Luanda. No. 1175, 5k, Mbanza Congo Post Office. No. 1176, 5k, Namibe Post Office. No. 1177, 8k, Facade of Luanda Post Office. No. 1178, 8k, Luanda Post Office, diff. No. 1179, 8k, Lobito Post Office.

| 2000, Sept. 29 | | Litho. | Perf. 14 |
|---|---|---|---|
| 1174-1179 | A250 | Set of 6 | 8.50 8.50 |

National Radio and Television, 25th Anniv. — A251

No. 1180, 9.50k: a, Woman at computer in newsroom. b, Reporter with tape recorder reporting on tank battle. c, Rescuing victims from airplane crash.

No. 1181, 9.50k: a, People and equipment in newsroom. b, Cameraman filming tank battle. c, Refugees.

No. 1182, 20k, Reporter with tape recorder. No. 1183, 20k, Cameraman, vert.

**Perf. 13¼x13½, 13½x13¼**

| 2000, Dec. 7 | | Sheets of 3, #a-c | |
|---|---|---|---|
| 1180-1181 | A251 | Set of 2 | 12.00 12.00 |

**Souvenir Sheets**

| 1182-1183 | A251 | Set of 2 | 8.00 8.00 |

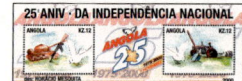

Independence, 25th Anniv. — A252

No. 1184: a, Tank, rifle, dove. b, Dove, hoe, tractor.

| 2001, Feb. 13 | | Litho. | Perf. 14¼x14 |
|---|---|---|---|
| 1184 | A252 | 12k Sheet of 2, #a-b | 5.00 5.00 |

Africa Day — A253

Designs: No. 1185, 10k, Shown. No. 1186, 10k, Xylophone.

30k, Map, musical instruments, native with mask, elephant, satellite dishes and computer.

| 2001, May 25 | | | Perf. 13x13¼ |
|---|---|---|---|
| 1185-1186 | A253 | Set of 2 | 4.00 4.00 |

**Souvenir Sheet**

| 1187 | A253 | 30k multi | 6.00 6.00 |

Flowers — A254

Butterfly and: 8k, Nicolaia speciosa. 9k, Allamanda cathartica. 10k, Welwitschia mirabilis. No. 1191, 10k, Tagetes patula. 30k, Welwitschia mirabilis.

| 2001, June 9 | | | |
|---|---|---|---|
| 1188-1191 | A254 | Set of 4 | 7.75 7.75 |

**Souvenir Sheet**

| 1192 | A254 | 30k multi | 6.50 6.50 |

Belgica 2001 Intl. Stamp Exhibition, Brussels (No. 1192).

Total Solar Eclipse, June 21 A255

| 2001, June 21 | | | |
|---|---|---|---|
| 1193 | A255 | 30k multi | 6.50 6.50 |

Fish — A256

Designs: 11k, Protopterus annectens. 17k, Protopterus amphibius. 18k, Tilapia ruweti. 36k, Tilapia rendalli.

**Perf. 13½x13¼**

| 2001, Sept. 28 | | Litho. | |
|---|---|---|---|
| 1194-1196 | A256 | Set of 3 | 7.75 7.75 |

**Souvenir Sheet**
**Perf. 13x13¼**

| 1197 | A256 | 36k multi | 6.00 6.00 |

Traditional Dances and Costumes A257

Designs: No. 1198, 11k, Massemba. No. 1199, 11k, Ovambo Efundula. 17k, Macolo Batuque. No. 1201, 18k, Humbi Puberty. No. 1202, 18k, Mukixi. 36k, Carneval.

| 2001, Nov. 12 | | | Perf. 13x13¼ |
|---|---|---|---|
| 1198-1202 | A257 | Set of 5 | 11.00 11.00 |

**Souvenir Sheet**

| 1203 | A257 | 36k multi | 5.50 5.50 |

**Souvenir Sheet**

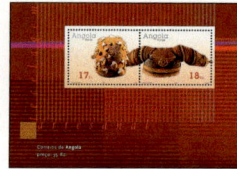

Handmade Weaving — A258

No. 1204: a, 17k, Banda. b, 18k, Kijinga.

| 2001, Dec. 7 | | | |
|---|---|---|---|
| 1204 | A258 | Sheet of 2, #a-b | 5.25 5.25 |

Minerals — A259

Designs: No. 1205, 11k, Hematite. No. 1206, 11k, Malachite. No. 1207, 18k, Psilomelane. No. 1208, 18k, Diamond.

| 2001, Dec. 14 | | | Perf. 13½x13¼ |
|---|---|---|---|
| 1205-1208 | A259 | Set of 4 | 8.50 8.50 |

Masks — A260

Designs: 10k, Mwana Mpwevo. No. 1210, 11k, Mukixi. No. 1211, 11k, Mbunda. 17k, Mwana Pwo. 18k, Likisi-Cinganji. 36k, Ndemba, horiz.

| 2002, Jan. 8 | | | Perf. 13¼x13½ |
|---|---|---|---|
| 1209-1213 | A260 | Set of 5 | 10.00 10.00 |

**Souvenir Sheet**
**Perf. 13x13¼**

| 1214 | A260 | 36k multi | 5.50 5.50 |

2002 World Cup Soccer Championships, Japan and Korea — A261

Two players and: 35k, Ball in air. 37k, Ball on ground.

| 2002, June 28 | | | Perf. 13x13¼ |
|---|---|---|---|
| 1215-1216 | A261 | Set of 2 | 6.50 6.50 |
| 1216a | | Souvenir sheet, #1215-1216 | 10.00 10.00 |

Meeting of African Committee of International Socialists — A262

Designs: No. 1217, 10k, Fight against poverty (red and orange map of Africa). No. 1218, 10k, Abolition of the death penalty (man with target on chest). No. 1219, 10k, End to violence against women (stylized woman). No. 1220, 10k, Fight against poverty (masks). No. 1221, 10k, Annulment of foreign debt (map of Africa with dollar sign).

| 2002, July 12 | | | |
|---|---|---|---|
| 1217-1221 | A262 | Set of 5 | 5.50 5.50 |
| 1221a | | Souvenir sheet, #1218-1221 | 6.00 6.00 |

National Peace and Reconciliation A263

| 2002, Oct. 9 | | | |
|---|---|---|---|
| 1222 | A263 | 35k multi | 2.75 2.75 |

Reptiles — A264

Designs: 21k, Pithon anchietae. 35k, Lacerta sp. 37k, Naja nigricollis. 40k, Crocodylus niloticus.

| 2002, Oct. 15 | | | Perf. 13x13¼ |
|---|---|---|---|
| 1223-1226 | A264 | Set of 4 | 10.00 10.00 |

Lighthouses and Buoys — A265

Designs: No. 1227, 45k, Tafe. No. 1228, 45k, Red buoy, Luanda Bay. No. 1229, 45k, Green buoy, Luanda Bay. No. 1230, 45k, Cabeça da Cobra. No. 1231, 45k, Barra do Dande. No. 1232, 45k, Moita Seca.

| 2002, Nov. 22 | | Set of 6 | 20.00 20.00 |
|---|---|---|---|
| 1227-1232 | A265 | | |

**Souvenir Sheet**

Dec. 4, 2002 Total Solar Eclipse A266

No. 1233: a, 21k, Sun partially eclipsed. b, 35k, Sun mostly eclipsed. c, 37k, Sun totally eclipsed.

| 2002, Dec. 4 | | | |
|---|---|---|---|
| 1233 | A266 | Sheet of 3, #a-c | 7.00 7.00 |

Angola - Italy Friendship — A267

António Manuel, Prince of N'Funta and Ambassador of Congo to Rome (d. 1608), and: 35k, Lion. 45k, Plaque with Italian inscription.

| 2002, Dec. 6 | | | |
|---|---|---|---|
| 1234-1235 | A267 | Set of 2 | 6.00 6.00 |
| 1235a | | Souvenir sheet, #1234-1235 | 6.00 6.00 |

Pottery — A268

Designs: 27k, Omolingui. 45k, Mulondo. 47k, Ombya yo Tuma. 51k, Sanga.

| 2002, Dec. 7 | | Litho. | |
|---|---|---|---|
| 1236-1238 | A268 | Set of 3 | 8.50 8.50 |

**Souvenir Sheet**

| 1239 | A268 | 51k multi | 4.00 4.00 |

United Nations 3rd Meeting on Science, Technology and Development A269

| 2003, May 30 | | | Perf. 13x13¼ |
|---|---|---|---|
| 1240 | A269 | 50k multi | 3.75 3.75 |

ANGOLA 501

Powered Flight, Cent. — A270

**2003, Aug. 21 Litho. Perf. 13x13½**
1241 A270 25k multi 1.90 1.90
Printed in sheets of 3 stamps + label.

Poets — A271

Designs: No. 1242, 27k, António Jacinto (1924-91) and poem. No. 1243, 45k, Agostinho Neto (1922-79) and poem.
No. 1244: a, 27k, Jacinto. b, 45k, Neto.

**2003, Sept. 18 Litho. Perf. 13x13¼**
1242-1243 A271 Set of 2 5.00 5.00
**Souvenir Sheet**
1244 A271 Sheet of 2, #a-b 4.25 4.25

Hippotragus Niger — A272

Designs: 27k, Pair with curved horns. 45k, Pair with straight horns. 47k, With herd in background.

**2003, Oct. 9**
1245-1247 A272 Set of 3 8.50 8.50

Women's Hairstyles — A273

No. 1248: a, Mbunda. b, Soyo. c, Huila. d, Humbi. e, Cabinda. f, Quipungu.

**2003, Nov. 10 Perf. 13¼x13**
1248 A273 25k Sheet of 6, #a-f 10.00 10.00

Whales — A274

Designs: 27k, Balaenoptera edeni. 45k, Cephalorhynchus heavisidii.
No. 1251: a, 47k, Giobiocephaia melaena.

**2003, Dec. 5 Perf. 14¾x14¼**
1249-1250 A274 Set of 2 5.00 5.00
**Souvenir Sheet**
1251 A274 Sheet, #1249, 1251a 5.50 5.50

Christmas — A275

No. 1252, 27k: a, The Ascension, attributed to Jorge Afonso. b, Adoration of the Shepherds, by André Reinoso.
No. 1253, 45k: a, Adoration of the Shepherds, detail showing Holy Family, by Josefa de Obidos. b, Adoration of the Shepherds, detail showing angels, by de Obidos.

**2003, Dec. 5 Perf. 13¼x13¾**
**Horiz. Pairs, #a-b**
1252-1253 A275 Set of 2 10.00 10.00
1253c Souvenir sheet, #1252a-1252b, 1253a-1253b 10.00 10.00

Chess A276

No. 1254: a, Chess pieces. b, Chess pieces and board.

**2003, Dec. 10**
1254 A276 45k Horiz. pair, #a-b 6.50 6.50

Eagles — A277

Designs: No. 1255, 20k, Aquila rapax. No. 1256, 20k, Polemaetus bellicosus. No. 1257, 25k, Haliaeetus vocifer. No. 1258, 25k, Terathopius ecaudatus. 45k, Aquila verreauxi.

**2003, Dec. 10 Perf. 14¾x14¼**
1255-1258 A277 Set of 4 6.50 6.50
**Souvenir Sheet**
1259 A277 45k multi 3.25 3.25

Election of Pope John Paul II, 25th Anniv. A278

No. 1260: a, Portrait. b, Pope waving.

**2003, Dec. 15 Perf. 13¼x13¾**
1260 A278 27k Horiz. pair, #a-b, + central label 4.00 4.00

Flora — A279

Designs: No. 1261, 27k, Psidium guayava. No. 1262, 27k, Adansonia digitata. No. 1263, 45k, Cymbopogon citratus. No. 1264, 45k, Carica papaya.

**2004, Aug. 17 Litho. Perf. 14x13½**
1261-1264 A279 Set of 4 6.00 6.00
1264a Souvenir sheet, #1261-1264 6.00 6.00

2004 Summer Olympics, Athens — A280

Designs: No. 1265, 27k, Handball. No. 1266, 27k, Basketball. No. 1267, 45k, Track. No. 1268, 45k, Volleyball.

**2004, Sept. 30 Perf. 13¾**
1265-1268 A280 Set of 4 6.00 6.00

Marine Mammals A281

No. 1269: a, Megaptera novaeangliae. b, Cephalorhynchus heavisidii. c, Tursiops truncatus. 99k, Megaptera novaeangliae, diff.

**2004, Oct. 9 Perf. 14x13½**
1269 Horiz. strip of 3 4.00 4.00
a.-b. A281 27k Either single 1.10 1.10
c. A281 45k multi 1.75 1.75
**Souvenir Sheet**
1270 A281 99k multi 4.00 4.00

A sheetlet of eight hexagonal 15k depicting the national birds of South African Postal Operators Association (SAPOA) countries was produced in extremely limited quantities. Sheetlet inscribed Angola, value $450.

Trains — A282

Designs: No. 1271, 27k, shown. No. 1272, 27k, Benguela Locomotive 225. No. 1273, 27k, Moçamedes locomotive.

**2004, Nov. 30 Perf. 13¾**
1271-1273 A282 Set of 3 3.25 3.25

Fire Fighting — A283

Telephone, emergency number and: No. 1274, 27k, Fire fighter with hose. No. 1275, 27k, Fire truck. 45k, Fire truck, diff.

**2004, Nov. 30**
1274-1276 A283 Set of 3 4.00 4.00
1276a Souvenir sheet, #1274-1276 4.00 4.00

FIFA (Fédération Internationale de Football Association), Cent. — A284

**2004, Dec. 7**
1277 A284 45k multi 1.90 1.90

Christmas — A285

No. 1278: a, 27k, Magi. b, 45k, Holy Family.

**2004, Dec. 14 Litho. Perf. 13¾**
1278 A285 Horiz. pair, #a-b 3.00 3.00

Worldwide Fund for Nature (WWF) — A286

No. 1279 — Colobus angolensis: a, Pair of adults. b, Adult and juvenile. c, Close-up of adult's face. d, Adult on rock.

**2004, Dec. 29 Litho. Perf. 13¾**
1279 A286 27k Block of 4, #a-d 4.00 4.00

Rotary International, Cent. — A287

Woman and: 45k, City. 51k, Ostriches.

**2005, Feb. 23 Litho. Perf. 13x13¼**
1280-1281 A287 Set of 2 4.00 4.00
1281a Souvenir sheet, #1280-1281 4.00 4.00

Basketry — A288

Designs: No. 1282, 27k, Kinda Kya Kuzambuila. No. 1283, 27k, Ngyendu. No. 1284, 45k, Ngombo Ya Cisuka. No. 1285, 45k, Silo. 90k, Kinda Kya Kuzambuila, diff.

**2005, Sept. 6 Litho. Perf. 12x12½**
1282-1285 A288 Set of 4 12.00 12.00
**Souvenir Sheet**
1286 A288 90k multi 20.00 20.00
Expo 2005, Aichi, Japan.

Independence, 30th Anniv. — A289

Designs: 27k, Capanda Hydroelectric Dam. 45k, Presidents Agostinho Neto and José Eduardo dos Santos, Angolan flag and dove.

**2005, Nov. 8 Litho. Perf. 12x12½**
1287-1288 A289 Set of 2 5.50 5.50

**Souvenir Sheet**

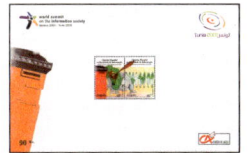

World Summit on the Information Society, Tunis — A290

No. 1289: a, Mail box, map of Africa, dish antenna, Angolan. b, Computer, world map, dish antenna.

**2005, Nov. 14 Litho. Perf. 12**
1289 A290 45k Sheet of 2, #a-b 20.00 20.00

**Souvenir Sheet**

23rd Ministerial Conference of the African Oil Producing Countries — A291

Design: 51p, Off-shore oil rig.

**2006, Apr. 24 Litho. Perf. 12x12½**
1294 A291 51k multi — —

Four additional stamps were issued in this set. The editors would like to examine any examples.

A292

2006 World Cup Soccer Championships, Germany — A293

# ANGOLA

**2006, Aug. 30**    *Perf. 12x11¾*
1295 A292 45k shown    3.00 3.00
1296 A293 45k shown    3.00 3.00
**Souvenir Sheet**
1297 A293 90k Player dribbling    4.50 4.50
Nos. 1295-1297 lack country name.

Community of Portuguese Language Nations, 10th Anniv. — A294

Anniversary emblem, emblem of 2006 Lubrapex Intl. Stamp Exhibition and: 27k, Dogs. No. 1299, 45k, Vultures. No. 1300, 45k, Parrots.

**2006, Oct. 30**    *Litho.*    *Perf. 12x11¾*
1298-1300 A294 Set of 3    6.00 6.00
Nos. 1298-1300 lack country name.

National Bank of Angola, 30th Anniv. — A295

Designs: No. 1301, 27k, Bird in flight, people in boat, ship, Katanga cross currency. No. 1302, 27k, Men, cowrie shells. No. 1303, 45k, Early automobile, coins. No. 1304, 45k, Building, banknotes.
90k, Dome, luggage

**2006, Nov. 7**
1301-1304 A295 Set of 4    7.50 7.50
**Souvenir Sheet**
1305 A295 90k multi    7.00 7.00

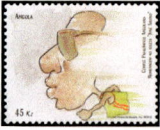

José Sayovo, First Angolan Paralympian Gold Medalist — A296

**2006, Dec. 29**    *Litho.*    *Perf. 12x11¾*
1306 A296 45k multi    1.10 1.10

Peace, 5th Anniv. — A297

**2007, Apr. 20**    *Litho.*    *Perf. 13x13½*
1307 A297 51k multi    1.75 1.75

52nd Venice Art Biennale — A298

Designs: 65k, Entire painting. 155k, Painting detail.

**2007, Apr. 20**    *Perf. 13x13½*
1308 A298 65k multi    1.90 1.90
**Souvenir Sheet**    *Perf. 13½x13*
1309 A298 155k multi    4.50 4.50
No. 1309 contains one 60x40mm stamp.

**Souvenir Sheet**

Africa Day A299

**2007, Apr. 20**    *Perf. 13½x13*
1310 A299 130k multi    9.00 9.00

Scouting, Cent. A300

No. 1311: a, 30k, Scouts sitting in fleur-de-lis pattern. b, 30k, Scouts sitting at desks. c, 55k, Scouts sitting on ground. d, 65k, Scouts saluting.
130k, Group of scouts standing on steps.

**2007, June 1**    *Perf. 13x13½*
1311 A300 Sheet of 4, #a-d    5.50 5.50
**Souvenir Sheet**    *Perf. 13½x13*
1312 A300 130k multi    4.00 4.00
No. 1312 contains one 60x40mm stamp.

**Souvenir Sheet**

Southern African Development Community, 27th Anniv. — A301

**2007, Aug. 17**    *Perf. 12½x13*
1313 A301 150k multi    8.00 8.00

**Souvenir Sheet**

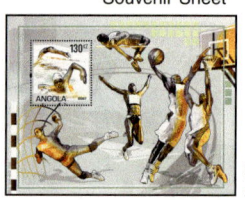

Sports A302

*Perf. 13¼ Syncopated*
**2007, Sept. 20**
1314 A302 130k multi    4.00 4.00

**Souvenir Sheet**

World Post Day A303

No. 1315 — Post office at: a, Malange. b, Huamba.

**2007, Oct. 9**    *Perf. 12¾x13½*
1315 A303 45k Sheet of 2, #a-b    4.50 4.50

Sea Turtles A304

No. 1316: a, 27k, Caretta caretta. b, 27k, Chelonia mydas. c, 45k, Eretmochelys imbricata. d, 45k, Lepidochelys olivacea.
130k, Dermochelys coriacea, vert.

**2007, Nov. 11**    *Perf. 13x13¼*
1316 A304 Sheet of 4, #a-d    4.50 4.50
**Souvenir Sheet**    *Perf. 13¼ Syncopated*
1317 A304 130k multi    6.00 6.00
No. 1317 contains one 38x39mm stamp.

Angolan Cuisine — A305

Various unnamed Angolan dishes: 37k, 40k, 59k, 153k.

**2008, May 30**    *Perf. 13x13½*
1318-1320 A305 Set of 3    7.00 7.00
**Souvenir Sheet**
1321 A305 153k multi    13.00 13.00

Water Resources A306

Designs: No. 1322, 37k, Kuebe River. No. 1323, 37k, Kuanza Rapids. No. 1324, 40k, Kuanza River. No. 1325, 40k, Mouth of Mbridge River.
153k, Kalandula Waterfalls.

**2008, June 30**    *Perf. 13x13½*
1322-1325 A306 Set of 4    8.00 8.00
**Souvenir Sheet**
1326 A306 153k multi    8.00 8.00

**Miniature Sheet**

Lwini Fund, 10th Anniv. A307

No. 1327: a, 37k, Land mine removal, vert. b, 40k, Wooden box and books. c, 40k, Princess Diana and Angolan woman. d, 59k, Children in wheelchairs. e, 59k, Men making baskets.

*Perf. 13½x13, 13x13½ (37k)*
**2008, June 30**
1327 A307 Sheet of 5, #a-e, + label    10.00 10.00

Water Jugs — A308

Designs: No. 1328, 37k, Jug with head on top. No. 1329, 37k, Two-handled jug. No. 1330, 40k, Jug with handle and spout. No. 1331, 40k, Jug with woman on top.

**2008, July 30**    *Perf. 13½x13*
1328-1331 A308 Set of 4    8.50 8.50

Mangroves on Chiloango River — A309

Designs: No. 1332, 37k, Roots. No. 1333, 37k, Trees along river. 59k, Roots, diff.

**2008, Aug. 30**    *Perf. 13x13½*
1332-1334 A309 Set of 3    7.00 7.00

**Miniature Sheet**

2008 Summer Olympics, Beijing — A310

No. 1335: a, Basketball. b, Handball. c, Running. d, Canoeing.

**2008, Sept. 20**    *Perf. 12¾x13½*
1335 A310 30k Sheet of 4, #a-d    3.75 3.75

Coffee — A311

Designs: 37k, Coffee berries. No. 1337, 45k, Woman picking berries, horiz. No. 1338, 45k, Tree with berries.

*Perf. 13¼x13, 13x13¼*
**2009, Dec. 7**    *Litho.*
**Granite Paper**
1336-1338 A311 Set of 3    4.00 4.00

Pres. Antonio Agostinho Neto (1922-79) — A312

Pres. Neto: 40k, Behind lectern. 50k, In army uniform.
150k, Pres. Neto with school children, horiz.

**2009, Dec. 7**    *Granite Paper*
1339-1340 A312 Set of 2    2.75 2.75
**Souvenir Sheet**
1341 A312 150k multi    10.00 10.00

**Souvenir Sheet**

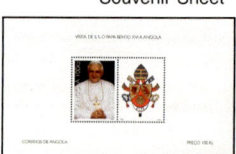

Pope Benedict XVI A313

**2009, Dec. 7**    *Perf. 13¼x13*
**Granite Paper**
1342 A313 100k multi + label    4.00 4.00

2010 Africa Cup of Nations Soccer Tournament, Angola — A314

Stadiums in: No. 1343, 40k, Benguela. No. 1344, 40k, Cabinda. No. 1345, 50k, Luanda. No. 1346, 50k, Huíla.

**2010, Jan. 8**    *Perf. 13x13¼*
**Granite Paper**
1343-1346 A314 Set of 4    5.00 5.00

Africa Day — A315

Designs: 40k, People from Uige and Zaire Provinces. 60k, People from Lunda and Moxico Provinces.
120k, People from Luanda Province.

**2010** ***Perf. 13x13¼***
**1348-1349** A315 Set of 2 2.75 2.75

**Souvenir Sheet**

***Perf. 13¼ Syncopated***

**1350** A315 120k multi 3.75 3.75

Expo 2010, Shanghai. No. 1350 contains one 50x39mm stamp.

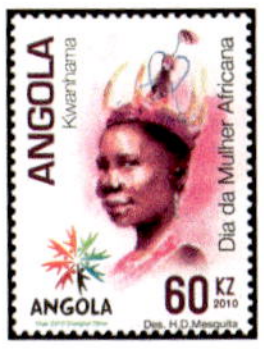


African Women's Day — A316

Designs: No. 1351, 60k, Kwanhama woman. No. 1352, 60k, Quipungo woman.
150k, Mucubal woman.

**2010** ***Perf. 13¼x13***
**1351-1352** A316 Set of 2 3.25 3.25

**Souvenir Sheet**

***Perf. 13¼ Syncopated***

**1353** A316 150k multi 4.00 4.00

Expo 2010, Shanghai. No. 1353 contains one 39x50mm stamp.

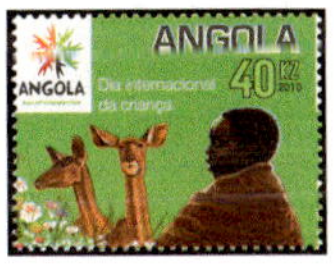


Intl. Children's Day — A317

Children, flowers and wildlife with background color of: No. 1354, 40k, Green. No. 1355, 40k, Orange. No. 1356, 60k, Blue. No. 1357, 60k, Green.
150k, Orange.

**2010** ***Perf. 13x13¼***
**1354-1357** A317 Set of 4 5.00 5.00

**Souvenir Sheet**

***Perf. 13¼ Syncopated***

**1358** A317 150k multi 4.25 4.25

Expo 2010, Shanghai. No. 1358 contains one 50x39mm stamp.

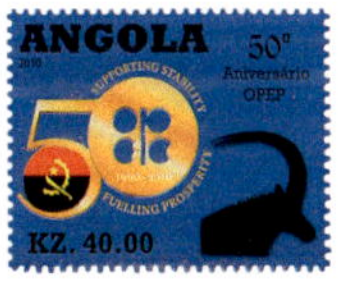


Organization of Petroleum Exporting Countries, 50th Anniv. — A318

50th anniversary emblem with Angolan flag and: 40k, Antelope. 50k, Statue. 60k, Off-shore oil drilling platform.
150k, Off-shore oil drilling platform and other equipment.

**2010, Oct.** ***Perf. 13x13¼***
**1359-1361** A318 Set of 3 3.25 3.25

**Souvenir Sheet**

***Perf. 13½ Syncopated***

**1362** A318 150k multi 3.25 3.25

No. 1362 contains one 50x39mm stamp.

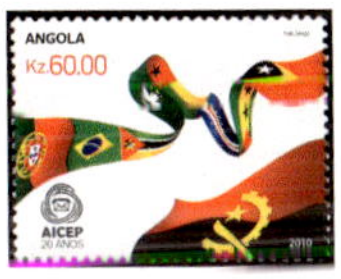


Portuguese Agency for External Investment and Commerce, 20th Anniv. — A319

**2010, Nov.** ***Perf. 13x13¼***
**1363** A319 60k multi 1.40 1.40

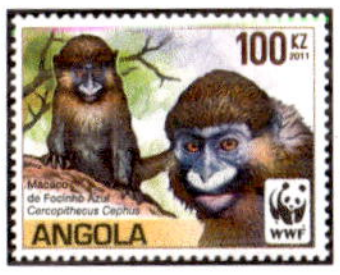


Worldwide Fund for Nature (WWF) — A320

No. 1364: a, Two Cercopithecus cephus, one on rock at left. b, Three Cercopithecus ascanius. c, Two Cercopithecus ascanius. d, Two Cercopithecus cephus, one on branch at right.
350k, Cercopithecus cephus and Cercopithecus ascanius, vert.

**2011, Aug. 31** ***Perf. 13x13¼***
**1364** Strip of 4, #a-d 9.00 9.00
*a.-d.* A320 100k Any single 2.25 2.25
*e.* Souvenir sheet of 8, 2 each #1364a-1364d 18.00 18.00

**Souvenir Sheet**

***Perf. 13¼***

**1365** A320 350k multi 7.50 7.50

No. 1365 contains one 39x45mm stamp.

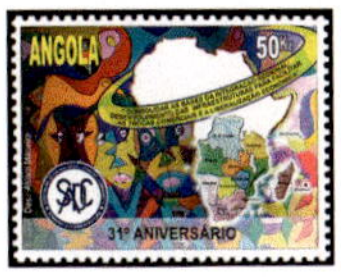


A321

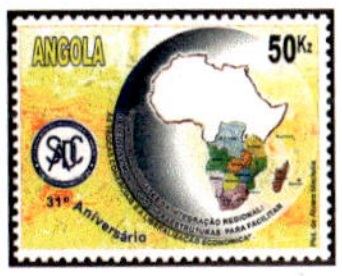


A322

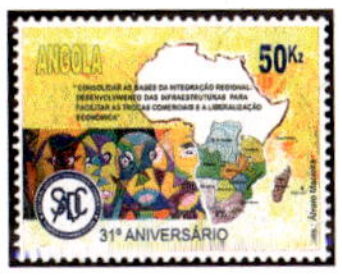


A323

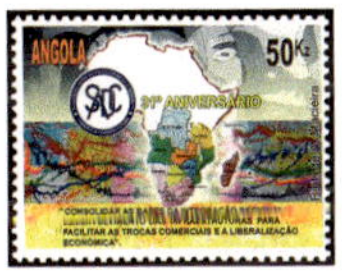


Southern African Development Community, 31st Anniv. — A324

Design: 150k, Emblem and map of Africa, diff.

**2011, Aug. 12** ***Perf. 13x13¼***
**1366** A321 50k multi 1.10 1.10
**1367** A322 50k multi 1.10 1.10
**1368** A323 50k multi 1.10 1.10
**1369** A324 50k multi 1.10 1.10
*Nos. 1366-1369 (4)* 4.40 4.40

**Souvenir Sheet**

***Perf. 13½***

**1370** A324 150k multi 3.25 3.25

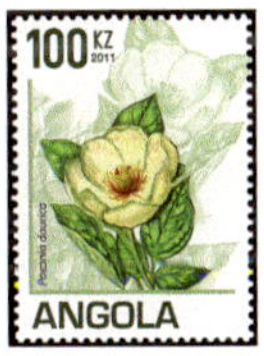


Peonies — A325

No. 1371: a, Paeonia daurica. b, Paeonia mlokosewitschii. c, Paeonia veitchii. d, Paeonia broteri.
350k, Paeonia officinalis salmonea.

**2011, Apr. 31** ***Perf. 13¼x13***
**1371** Horiz. strip of 4 9.00 9.00
*a.-d.* A325 100k Any single 2.25 2.25
*e.* Souvenir sheet of 4, #1371a-1371d 9.00 9.00

**Souvenir Sheet**

***Perf. 13½***

**1372** A325 350k multi 7.50 7.50

China 2011 International Stamp Exhibition, Wuxi. No. 1372 contains one 39x45mm stamp.

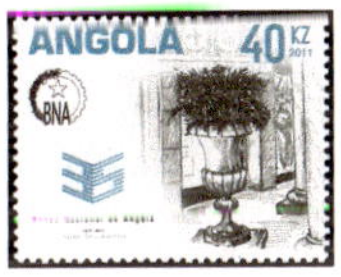


National Bank of Angola, 35th Anniv. — A326

Emblem and: 40k, Ornamental planter. 50k, Crest on exterior wall. No. 1375, 60k, Roof ornament. No. 1376, 60k, Windows near corner of building.
150k, Aerial view of building.

**2011, Nov. 4** ***Perf. 13x13¼***
**1373-1376** A326 Set of 4 4.50 4.50

**Souvenir Sheet**

***Perf. 13x13¼ Syncopated***

**1377** A326 150k multi 3.25 3.25

No. 1377 contains one 50x39mm stamp.

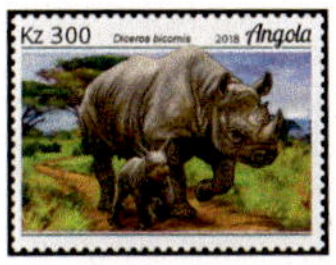


Fauna, Flora and Mushrooms A344

Designs: No. 1420, 300k, Adult and juvenile Diceros bicornis. No. 1421, 300k, Adult Diceros bicornis facing right. No. 1422, 300k, One Ceratotherium simum. No. 1423, 300k, Two Ceratotherium simum. No. 1424, 300k, Head of Giraffa camelopardalis angolensis. No. 1425, 300k, Front view of Giraffa camelopardalis angolensis drinking water. No. 1426, 300k, Side view of Giraffa camelopardalis angolensis with head lowered. No. 1427, 300k, Six adult and juvenile Giraffa camelopardalis angolensis. No. 1428, 300k, Galagoides demidoff. No. 1429, 300k, Allenopithecus nigroviridis. No. 1430, 300k, Lophocebus aterrimus. No. 1431, 300k, Colobus angolensis. No. 1432, 300k, Hypsignathus monstrosus. No. 1433, 300k, Mops condylurus. No. 1434, 300k, Epomops franqueti. No. 1435, 300k, Epomophorus crypturus. No. 1436, 300k, Acinonyx jubatus. No. 1437, 300k, Panthera pardus pardus. No. 1438, 300k, Caracal caracal. No. 1439, 300k, Panthera leo bleyenberghi. No. 1440, 300k, Loxodonta africana walking left. No. 1441, 300k, Loxodonta africana facing right. No. 1442, 300k, Two Loxodonta africana with hindquarters touching. No. 1443, 300k, Two Loxodonta africana facing right. No. 1444, 300k, Stenella attenuata. No. 1445, 300k, Stenella longirostris. No. 1446, 300k, Stenella frontalis. No. 1447, 300k, Lagenodelphis hosei. No. 1448, 300k, Globicephala macrorhynchus. No. 1449, 300k, Megaptera novaeangliae. No. 1450, 300k, Eubalaena australis. No. 1451, 300k, Kogia breviceps. No. 1452, 300k, Treron calvus. No. 1453, 300k, Oena capensis. No. 1454, 300k, Columba guinea. No. 1455, 300k, Streptopelia capicola. No. 1456, 300k, Bubo africanus. No. 1457, 300k, Bubo leucostictus. No. 1458, 300k, Otus senegalensis. No. 1459, 300k, Scotopelia peli. No. 1460, 300k, Agapornis pullarius. No. 1461, 300k, Poicephalus meyeri reichenowi. No. 1462, 300k, Poicephalus robustus. No. 1463, 300k, Poicephalus ruepellii. No. 1464, 300k, Halcyon senegalensis. No. 1465, 300k, Corythornis cristatus. No. 1466, 300k, Ispidina picta. No. 1467, 300k, Ceryle rudis. No. 1468, 300k, Merops variegatus. No. 1469, 300k, Merops albicollis. No. 1470, 300k, Merops bullockoides. No. 1471, 300k, Merops nubicoides. No. 1472, 300k, Dendropicos fuscescens. No. 1473, 300k, Campethera abingoni. No. 1474, 300k, Dendropicos elliotii. No. 1475, 300k, Chloropicus xantholophus. No. 1476, 300k, Tockus leucomelas. No. 1477, 300k, Bycanistes fistulator. No. 1478, 300k, Lophoceros alboterminatus. No. 1479, 300k, Bucorvus leadbeateri. No. 1480, 300k, Sylvietta ruficapilla. No. 1481, 300k, Acrocephalus gracilirostris. No. 1482, 300k, Sylvietta rufescens. No. 1483, 300k, Hylia prasina. No. 1484, 300k, Trichlolaema leucomelas and Pogoniulus subsulphureus. No. 1485, 300k, Pogoniulus chrysoconus. No. 1486, 300k, Trachyphonus vaillantii. No. 1487, 300k, Lybius minor. No. 1488, 300k, Centropus monachus. No. 1489, 300k, Chrysococcyx klaas. No. 1490, 300k, Chrysococcyx caprius. No. 1491, 300k, Clamator glandarius. No. 1492, 300k, Ardea purpurea. No. 1493, 300k, Pelecanus onocrotalus. No. 1494, 300k, Hydroprogne caspia. No. 1495, 300k, Sarkidiornis melanotos. No. 1496, 300k, Haliaeetus vocifer. No. 1497, 300k, Aquila nipalensis. No. 1498, 300k, Aquila rapax. No. 1499, 300k, Gypohierax angolensis. No. 1500, 300k, Papilio phorcas congoanus. No. 1501, 300k, Hypolycaena antifaunus. No. 1502, 300k, Charaxes numenes. No. 1503, 300k, Charaxes eupale. No. 1504, 300k, Barbus fasciolatus. No. 1505, 300k, Schilbe mystus. No. 1506, 300k, Trachinus araneus. No. 1507, 300k, Synodontis woosnami and Chelonia mydas. No. 1508, 300k, Euspira grossularia. No. 1509, 300k, Tonna galea. No. 1510, 300k, Cardium costatum. No. 1511, 300k, Marginella glabella. No. 1512, 300k, Osteolaemus tetraspis, head at LL. No. 1513, 300k, Osteolaemus tetraspis, head at LR. No. 1514, 300k, Crocodylus niloticus, head at right. No. 1515, 300, Crocodylus niloticus, head at left. No. 1516, 300k, Dendroaspis jamesoni. No. 1517, 300k, Bitis caudalis. No. 1518, 300k, Bitis arietans. No. 1519, 300k, Naja anchietae. No. 1520, 300k, Caretta caretta. No.1521, 3 00k, Dermochelys coriacea. No. 1522, 300k, Lepidochelys olivacea. No. 1523, 300k, Eretmochelys imbricata. No. 1524, 300k, Diplodocus longus and amethyst. No. 1525, 300k, Rhamphorhynchus longicaudus and pyroxenite. No. 1526, 300k, Hatzegopteryx thambema and quartz. No. 1527, 300k, Yangchuanosaurus shangyouensis, atacamite and libethenite. No. 1528, 300k, Adult Diceros bicornis facing left. No. 1529, 300k, Hippotragus niger variani. No. 1530, 300k, Lycaon pictus. No. 1531, 300k, Gyps africanus. No. 1532, 300k, Laelia purpurata "Miss Scarlet." No. 1533, 300k, Cymbidium "Sandy Tiger." No. 1534, 300k, Laeliocattleya "Trick or Treat Sweety." No. 1535, 300k, Brassolaeliocattleya Momilani Rainbow "The Gypsy." No. 1536, 300k, Amanita muscaria. No. 1537, 300k, Coprinellus micaceus. No. 1538, 300k, Amanita rubescens. No. 1539, 300k, Agaricus xanthodermus.

No. 1540, 1200k, Adult and juvenile Ceratotherium simum. No. 1541, 1200k, Giraffa camelopardalis angolensis, diff. No. 1542, 1200k, Ceratopithecus ascanius. No. 1543, 1200k, Cistugo seabrae. No. 1544, 1200k, Leptailurus serval. No. 1545, 1200k, Loxodonta africana facing left. No. 1546, 1200k, Steno bredanensis. No. 1547, 1200k, Balaenoptera musculus. No. 1548, 1200k, Spilopelia senegalensis. No. 1549, 1200k, Bubo lacteus. No. 1550, 1200k, Psittacus erithacus. No. 1551, 1200k, Halcyon leucocephala. No. 1552, 1200k, Merops malimbicus. No. 1553, 1200k, Campethera bennettii. No. 1554, 1200k, Bycanistes bucinator. No. 1555, 1200k, Hyliota flavigaster. No. 1556, 1200k, Trachyphonus purpuratus. No. 1557, 1200k, Chrysococcyx cupreus. No. 1558, 1200k, Netta rufina. No. 1559, 1200k, Terathopius ecaudatus. No. 1560, 1200k, Junonia sophia. No. 1561, 1200k, Synodontis nigromaculatus. No. 1562, 1200k, Architectonica perspectiva. No. 1563, 1200k, Crocodylus niloticus, diff. No. 1564, 1200k, Bitis caudalis, diff. No. 1565, 1200k, Chelonia mydas. No. 1566, 1200k, Austroraptor cabazai and rhodochrosite. No. 1567, 1200k, Mecistops cataphractus. No. 1568, 1200k, Laelia anceps "SanBar Bounty." No. 1569, 1200k, Gliophorus psittacinus

**2018, Dec. 10** **Litho.** ***Perf. 13x13¼***
**1420-1539** A344 Set of 120 235.00 235.00

**Souvenir Sheets**

**1540-1569** A344 Set of 30 235.00 235.00

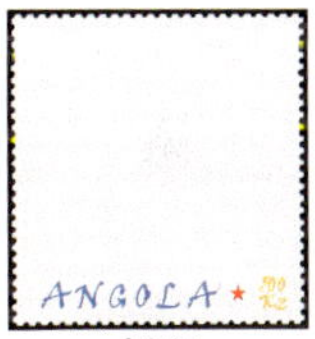


A345

A346

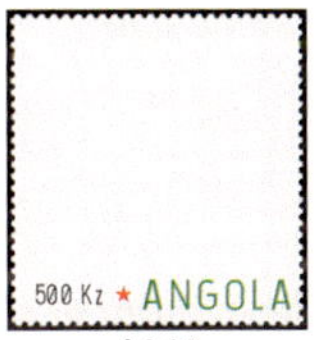


A347

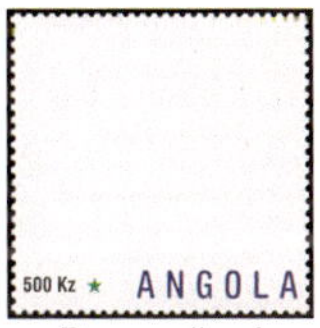


Personalized Stamps — A348

**2019, May 15** **Litho.** ***Perf. 12¾x13¼***
**1570** A345 500k multi 3.00 3.00
**1571** A346 500k multi 3.00 3.00
**1572** A347 500k multi 3.00 3.00

***Perf. 13¼x12¾***

**1573** A348 500k multi 3.00 3.00
*Nos. 1570-1573 (4)* 12.00 12.00

The vignette portions of Nos. 1570-1570 could be personalized.

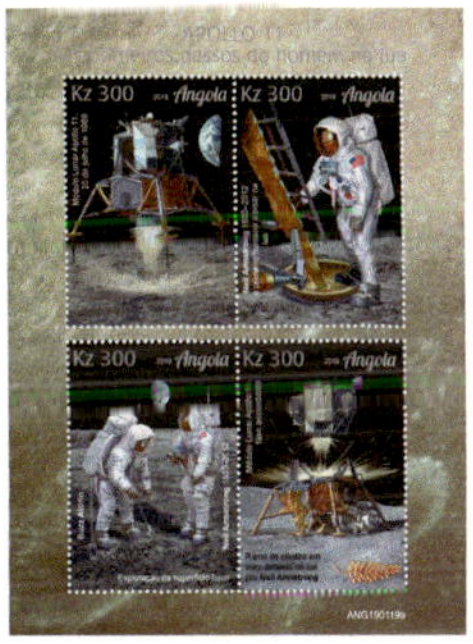


First Man on the Moon, 50th Anniv. A349

No. 1574: a, Apollo 11 Lunar Module approaching Moon's surface. b, Neil Armstrong's first step on the Moon. c, Armstrong and Buzz Aldrin on Moon. d, Lunar Module leaving Moon.
1200k, Armstrong and U.S. flag on Moon.

**Litho. With Foil Application**

**2019, May 15** ***Perf. 13¼***

**1574** A349 300k Sheet of 4, #a-d 7.25 7.25

**Souvenir Sheet**

**1575** A349 1200k multi 7.25 7.25

No. 1575 contains one 45x51mm stamp.

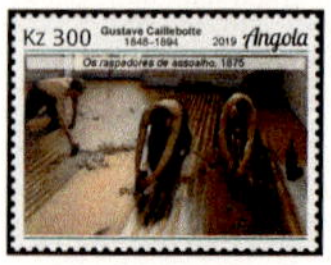


A350

No. 1576, 300k, The Floor Scrapers, by Gustave Caillebotte (1848-94). No. 1577, 300k, The Luncheon on the Grass, by Edouard Manet (1832-83). No. 1578, 300k, Pont Boieldieu in Rouen, Rainy Weather, by Camille Pissarro (1830-1903). No. 1579, 300k, Dance at Le Moulin de la Galette, by Pierre-Auguste Renoir (1841-1919).

No. 1580, 300k, Oshkosh Striker 8x8 fire truck. No. 1581, 300k, 1980 Seagrave fire truck. No. 1582, 300k, Spartan KME fire truck. No. 1583, 300k, American LaFrance Pioneer fire truck.

No. 1584, 300k, U-127 class 4-6-0 locomotive. No. 1585, 300k, London North Eastern Railway class A4 2509 Silver Link. No. 1586, 300k, London North Eastern Railway class A3 4472 Flying Scotsman. No. 1587, 300k, South African class 25NC 4-8-4 locomotive.

No. 1588, 300k, South African class 33-400 locomotive. No. 1589, 300k, South African class GMA 4-8-2+2-8-4 locomotive. No. 1590, 300k, South African class 43-000 locomotive. No. 1591, 300k, South African class 26 4-8-4 locomotive.

No. 1592, 300k, Prototype Russian rescue vehicle, vert. No. 1593, 300k, 1991 Land Rover Defender ambulance, vert. No. 1594, 300k, RMMV Survivor R, vert. No. 1595, 300k, Scania P 93ML fire truck, vert.

No. 1596, 300k, BMW R1200GS motorcycle, vert. No. 1597, 300k, KTM 950 Adventure motorcycle, vert. No. 1598, 300k, Suzuki TL1000R motocycle, vert. No. 1599, 300k, 2009 Yamaha R1 motorcycle, vert.

No. 1600, 300k, Fairchild Republic A-10 Thunderbolt II, vert. No. 1601, 300k, McDonnell Douglas F/A-18 Hornet, vert. No. 1602, 300k, Alenia Aermacchi M-346 Master, vert. No. 1603, 300k, Lockheed F-117 Nighthawk, vert.

No. 1604, 300k, Pres. John F. Kennedy (1917-63) and Apollo mission emblem, vert. No. 1605, 300k, Apollo 11 Command and Service Modules, Apollo 11 emblems and "50," vert. No. 1606, 300k, Saturn V SA-506 rocket, vert. No. 1607, Neil Armstrong (1930-2012), first man on Moon, vert.

No. 1608, 300k, Thalassa and flag of Netherlands, vert. No. 1609, 300k, Juan Sebastián de Elcano and flag of Spain, vert. No. 1610, 300k, Christian Radich and flag of Norway, vert. No. 1611, 300k, Gorch Fock and flag of Germany, vert.

No. 1612, 300k, Portland Head Lighthouse, Maine, and flag of United States, vert. No. 1613, 300k, Portland Bill Lighthouse, and flag of Great Britain, vert. No. 1614, 300k, Slettnes Lighthouse, and flag of Norway, vert. No. 1615, 300k, Rubjerg Knude Lighthouse, and flag of Denmark, vert.

No. 1616, 300k, Equus quagga and flag of Botswana, vert. No. 1617, 300k, Loxodonta africana and flag of Central African Republic, vert. No. 1618, 300k, Aquila chrysaetos and flag of Egypt, vert. No. 1619, 300k, Panthera leo and flag of Kenya, vert.

No. 1620, 300k, World map, child and parched land, vert. No. 1621, 300k, Sea level measurement posts, vert. No. 1622, 300k, Corals in acidified ocean, vert. No. 1623, 300k, Polar bears on ice, vert.

No. 1624, 300k, Egyptian Mau cat, vert. No. 1625, 300k, Siamese cat, vert. No. 1626, 300k, Russian Blue cat and flag of Russia, vert. No. 1627, 300k, Japanese bobtail cats, vert.

No. 1628, 300k, Cyclostoma purum, vert. No. 1629, 300k, Tegula gallina, vert. No. 1630, 300k, Calyptraea spirata and Labyrinthus plicatus, vert. No. 1631, 300k, Hindsia nivea and Micrarionta kelletti, vert.

No. 1632, 300k, Ichthyosaurus communis, vert. No. 1633, 300k, Liopleurodon ferox, vert. No. 1634, 300k, Eromangasaurus australis, vert. No. 1635, 300k, Dinichthys terrelli, vert.

No. 1636, 300k, Parasaurolophus walkeri, vert. No. 1637, 300k, Ceratops horridus, vert. No. 1638, 300k, Tyrannosaurus rex and Charles Darwin (1809-82), naturalist, vert. No. 1639, 300k, Darwin, map and dinosaur skeleton, vert.

No. 1640, 300k, Two Girl Scouts and tent, vert. No. 1641, 300k, Boy and Girl Scout at campfire, vert. No. 1642, 300k, Boy and Girl Scout with map and flag, vert. No. 1643, 300k, Three Scouts and campfire, vert.

No. 1644, 300k, Pope John Paul II (1920-2005) with arms raised, vert. No. 1645, 300k, Pope John Paul II holding cross, vert. No. 1646, 300k, Pope John Paul II and bishop, vert. No. 1647, 300k, Pope John Paul II standing in automobile, vert.

No. 1648, 300k, Princess Diana (1961-97) in wedding dress, vert. No. 1649, 300k, Princess Diana with Indian children, vert. No. 1650, 300k, Princess Diana riding horse, vert. No. 1651, 300k, Princess Diana holding roses, coat of arms, vert.

No. 1652, 300k, Nelson Mandela (1918-2013), President of South Africa, prison and his prisoner number, vert. No. 1653, 300k, Nobel medal, Mandela wearing tribal costume, vert. No. 1654, 300k, Mandela and election campaign crowd, vert. No. 1655, 300k, Mandela casting ballot, flag and coat of arms of South Africa, vert.

No. 1656, 300k, Mohandas K. Gandhi (1869-1948), Indian nationalist leader, his signature and Taj Mahal, vert. No. 1657, 300k, Taj Mahal, Gandhi holding walking stick, vert. No. 1658, 300k, Gandhi, flag and emblem of India, vert. No. 1659, 300k, Gandhi and crowd, vert.

No. 1660, 300k, Henri Dunant (1828-1910), founder of International Red Cross, and Red Cross volunteers and flag, vert. No. 1661, 300k, Dodge WC54 ambulance and Red Cross tent, vert. No. 1662, 300k, Barkas V 901/2 ambulance and AW139 helicopter, vert. No. 1663, 300k, World War I Red Cross nurses, vert.

No. 1664, 300k, Sick child and mosquito, vert. No. 1665, 300k, Child, hand with hypodermic needle and mosquito, vert. No. 1666, 300k, Children under mosquito netting, vert. No. 1667, 300k, Man spraying insecticide, mosquito, vert.

No. 1668, 300k, Rotary International emblem and Rotary founder Paul P. Harris (1868-1947), seated, vert. No. 1669, 300k, Rotary International emblem and Harris, standing, vert. No. 1670, 300k, Rotary International emblem, Harris and his wife, Jean (1881-1963), vert. No. 1671, 300k, Rotary International emblem, Harris and Luther Burbank (1849-1926), botanist.

No. 1672, 300k, 2018 Nobel laureates in Physiology or Medicine, Tasuku Honjo and James P. Allison, vert. No. 1673, 300k, 2018 Nobel laureates in Chemistry, George P. Smith, Frances H. Arnold, and Sir Gregory P. Winter, vert. No. 1674, 300k, 2018 Nobel laureates in Physics, Arthur Ashkin, Gérard A. Mourou, and Donna T. Strickland, vert. No. 1675, 300k, 2018 Nobel laureates in Economics, William D. Nordhaus and Paul M. Romer, vert.

No. 1676, 300k, Magnus Carlsen, World chess champion, flag and reversed map of Norway, vert. No. 1677, 300k, Fabiano Caruana, second-ranked chess player in world, flag and map of United States, vert. No. 1678, 300k, Ding Liren, fourth-ranked chess player in world, flag and map of People's Republic of China, vert. No. 1679, 300k, Sergey Karjakin, youngest chess player to achieve Grand Master status, flag and map of Russia, vert.

No. 1680, 300k, Omakola, vert. No. 1681, 300k, Tambor falante, vert. No. 1682, 300k, Lamelofone, vert. No. 1683, 300k, Mucupela, vert.

No. 1684, 300k, Pig with tulip, vert. No. 1685, 300k, Pig with pear, vert. No. 1686, 300k, Pig balancing on ball, vert. No. 1687, 300k, Pig jumping rope, vert.

No. 1688, 1200k, Water Lilies, by Claude Monet (1840-1926). No. 1689, 1200k, Mount Arlington, New Jersey 1939 Model VC fire truck. No. 1690, 1200k, Great Western Railway class 7800 locomotive. No. 1691, 1200k, South African class 19D 4-8-2 locomotive. No. 1692, 1200k, Canadair CL-415 firefighting airplane, vert. No. 1693, 1200k, Gilera CX motorcycle, vert. No. 1694, 1200k, Dornier Alpha Jet and Lockheed Martin F-35 Lightning II, vert. No. 1695, 1200k, Apollo 11 Command, Service and Lunar Modules and medal, vert. No. 1696, 1200k, Dar Mlodziedzy and flag of Poland, vert. No. 1697, 1200k, Split Rock Lighthouse, Minnesota, and flag of United States, vert. No. 1698, 1200k, Hippotragus niger and flag of Angola, vert. No. 1699, 1200k, Thermometer and changing landscape, vert. No. 1700, 1200k, Peterbald cat, vert. No. 1701, 1200k, Succinea putris, Fusus kelletii, and Labyrinthus leucodon, vert. No. 1702, 1200k, Helicoprion beswsonowi, vert. No. 1703, 1200k, Darwin and Stegosaurus stenops, vert. No. 1704, 1200k, Two Scouts, tent and lantern, vert. No. 1705, 1200k, Pope John Paul II holding cross, diff., vert. No. 1706, 1200k, Princess Diana and Queen Elizabeth II, vert. No. 1707, 1200k, Mandela standing in automobile, vert. No. 1708, 1200k, Gandhi holding microphone, vert. No. 1709, 1200k, Dunant and horse-drawn ambulance, vert. No. 1710, 1200k, Plasmodium malariae and medical worker, vert. No. 1711, 1200k, Rotary International emblem and bust of Harris, vert. No. 1712, 1200k, Dove and 2018 Nobel Peace laureates, Denis Mukwege and Nadia Murad, vert. No. 1713, 1200k, Shakhriyar Mamedyarov, third-ranked chess player in world, flag and map of Azerbaijan, vert. No. 1714, 1200k, Balafon and marimba, vert. No. 1715, 1200k, Pig blowing bubbles, vert.

***Perf. 13x13¼, 13¼x13***

**2019, May 15** **Litho.**

**1576-1687** A350 Set of 112 200.00 200.00

**Souvenir Sheets**

**1688-1715** A350 Set of 28 200.00 200.00

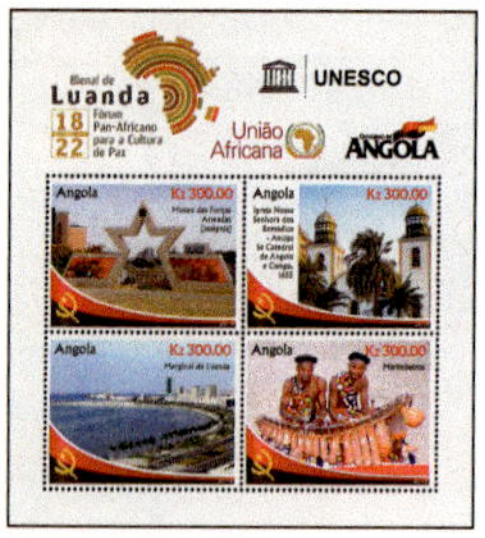


A351

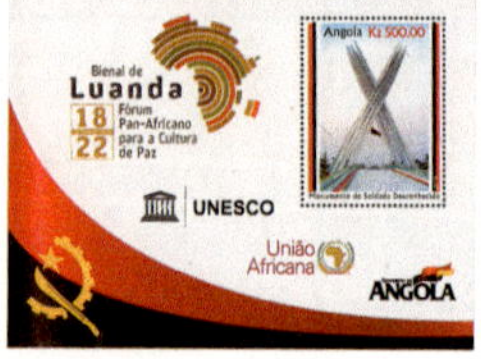


Luanda Biennale
A352

No. 1716: a, Star gateway at Armed Forces Museum, Luanda. b, Cathedral of the Holy Savior, Luanda. c, Luanda Waterfront. d, Marimba players.

500k, Monument to the Unknown Soldier, Luanda.

***Perf. 12¾x13¼***

**2019, Sept. 18** **Litho.**

**1716** A351 300k Sheet of 4, #a-d 6.50

**Souvenir Sheet**

***Perf. 13¼x12¾***

**1717** A352 500k multi 2.75 2.75

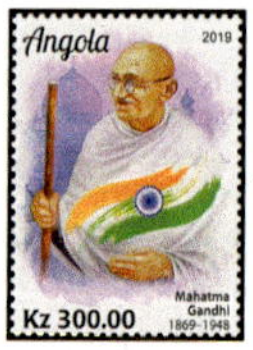


Flag of India and Mohandas K. Gandhi (1869-1948), Indian Nationalist Leader — A353

**2019, Dec. 20** **Litho.** ***Perf. 13¼x13***

**1718** A353 300k multi 1.25 1.25

No. 1718 was printed in sheets of 10 + 2 central labels.

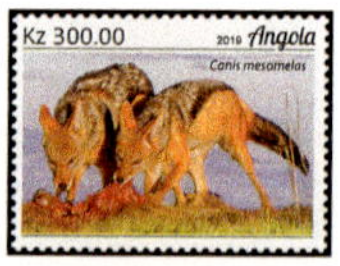


A354

Designs: No. 1719, 300k, Two Canis mesomelas eating. No. 1720, 300k, Two Canis mesomelas on grass. No. 1721, 300k, One Canis mesomelas on rock. No. 1722, 300k, Canis adustas.

No. 1723, 300k, Atelerix frontalis on ground facing right, Latin name at UR in white. No. 1724, 300k, Atelerix frontalis on ground facing right, Latin name at UR in black. No. 1725, 300k, Atelerix frontalis on log facing right, Latin name in UR in black. No. 1726, 300k, Atelerix frontalis facing left.

No. 1727, 300k, Smutsia temminckii facing left. No. 1728, 300k, Smutsia temminckii facing right. No. 1729, 300k, Phataginus tricuspis facing left. No. 1730, 300k, Phataginus tricuspis facing right.

No. 1731, 300k, Two Aonyx capensis. No. 1732, 300k, One Aonyx capensis facing left. No. 1733, 300k, Head of Aonyx capensis. No. 1734, 300k, Three Hydrictis maculicollis.

No. 1735, 300k, One seated Vulpes chama. No. 1736, 300k, One standing Vulpes chama. No. 1737, 300k, Two Vulpes chama. No. 1738, 300k, Three Vulpes chama.

No. 1739, 300k, Oreotragus oreotragus. No. 1740, 300k, Kobus ellipsiprymnus. No. 1741, 300k, Damaliscus lunatus. No. 1742, 300k, Hippotragus equinus.

No. 1743, 300k, Head of Hippopotamus amphibius in water, hippopotami in background. No. 1744, 300k, Three Hippopotamus amphibius walking through shallow water. No. 1745, 300k, One Hippopotamus amphibius on land. No. 1746, Two Hippopotamus amphibius standing in water.

No. 1747, 300k, Male Panthera leo facing left. No. 1748, 300k, Male Panthera leo carrying food in mouth. No. 1749, 300k, Female Panthera leo. No. 1750, 300k, Three Panthera leo cubs.

No. 1751, 300k, One Panthera pardus resting on rock. No. 1752, 300k, Adult and juvenile Panthera pardus on tree limb. No. 1753, 300k, One Panthera pardus resting on tree limb. No. 1754, 300k, One Panthera pardus standing.

No. 1755, 300k, Caracal aurata standing at left, head at right. No. 1756, 300k, Head of Caracal aurata at left, standing at right. No. 1757, 300k, Caracal aurata facing right. No. 1758, 300k, Caracal aurata facing left.

No. 1759, 300k, One Trichechus senegalensis, Latin name at UL in one line. No. 1760, 300k, Two Trichechus senegalensis, Latin name at LL. No. 1761, 300k, Two Trichechus senegalensis, Latin name at LR. No. 1762, 300k, One Trichechus senegalensis, Latin name in UL in two lines.

No. 1763, 300k, Two Orcinus orca. No. 1764, 300k, One Orcinus orca facing right with open mouth. No. 1765, 300k, One Orcinus orca facing left with open mouth. No. 1766, 300k, Three Orcinus orca.

No. 1767, 300k, Caprimulgus natalensis. No. 1768, 300k, Caprimulgus pectoralis. No. 1769, 300k, Caprimulgus europaeus. No. 1770, 300k, Caprimulgus rufigena.

No. 1771, 300k, Actophilornis africanus in water, facing left, Latin name at top center. No. 1772, 300k, Actophilornis africanus in water facing left, Latin name at UR in two lines. No. 1773, 300k, Actophilornis africanus near water, facing left, Latin name at UL. No. 1774, 300k, Actophilornis africanus in flight.

No. 1775, 300k, Terathopius ecaudatus. No. 1776, 300k, Stephanoaetus coronatus. No. 1777, 300k, Aquilla verreauxii. No. 1778, 300k, Haliaeetus vocifer.

No. 1779, 300k, Junonia sophia. No. 1780, 300k, Graphium angolanus. No. 1781, 300k, Papilio zalmoxis. No. 1782, 300k, Papilio antimachus.

No. 1783, 300k, Connochaetes taurinus, Cameia National Park. No. 1784, 300k, Diceros bicornis, Iona National Park. No. 1785, 300k, Panthera leo, Bicuar National Park. No. 1786, 300k, Lycaon pictus, Quissama National Park.

No. 1787, 300k, Giraffa giraffa angolensis and Rio Cuanza. No. 1788, 300k, Smutsia temminckii and Quissama National Park. No. 1789, 300k, Antidorcas marsupialis angolensis and Iona National Park. No. 1790, 300k, Epomophorus angolensis and Tundavala Gap.

No. 1791, 300k, SDD6A locomotive. No. 1792, 300k, GE C30ACi locomotive. No. 1793, 300k, GE U20C locomotive. No. 1794, 300k, CKD8F locomotive.

No. 1795, 300k, Pan troglodytes, vert. No. 1796, 300k, Cercopithecus ascanius, vert. No. 1797, 300k, Cercopithecus neglectus, vert. No. 1798, 300k, Papio ursinus, vert.

No. 1799, 300k, One Orycteropus afer facing forward, vert. No. 1800, 300k, One Orycteropus afer facing right, vert. No. 1801, 300k, One Orycteropus afer behind rock, facing right, vert. No. 1802, 300k, Two Orycteropus afer, vert.

No. 1803, 300k, Crocuta crocuta facing left, vert. No. 1804, 300k, Crocuta crocuta facing right, vert. No. 1805, 300k, Crocuta crocuta in water, vert. No. 1806, 300k, Four Crocuta crocuta, vert.

No. 1807, 300k, Equus quagga chapmani on its back, vert. No. 1808, 300k, Three Equus quagga chapmani, vert. No. 1809, 300k, Adult nursing juvenile Equus quagga chapmani, vert. No. 1810, 300k, Two adult Equus quagga chapmani, vert.

No. 1811, 300k, Lycaon pictus pictus facing right, vert. No. 1812, 300k, Lycaon pictus pictus running in shallow water, vert. No. 1813, 300k, Two Lycaon pictus pictus at play, vert. No. 1814, 300k, Two Lycaon pictus pictus eating dead animal, vert.

No. 1815, 300k, Lepus capensis on hind legs, facing left, vert. No. 1816, 300k, Lepus capensis facing right, with front legs bent, vert. No. 1817, 300k, Lepus capensis facing right, with front legs straight, vert. No. 1818, 300k, Lepus capensis drinking water, vert.

No. 1819, 300k, Pterocles bicinctus facing right, vert. No. 1820, 300k, Pterocles bicinctus facing left, vert. No. 1821, 300k, Pterocles burchelli facing right, vert. No. 1822, 300k, Pterocles burchelli facing left, vert.

No. 1823, 300k, Gold (ouro), vert. No. 1824, 300k, Bayldonite, vert. No. 1825, 300k, Quartz, vert. No. 1826, 300k, Kaolinite (caulinta), vert.

No. 1827, 300k, Back of Chokwe chair (encosto da cadeira Chokwe), vert. No. 1828, 300k, Chokwe mask (máscara Chokwe), vert. No. 1829, 300k, Ceramic vessel (vaso de cerâmica), vert. No. 1830, 300k, Top of scepter (topo de ceptro), vert.

No. 1831, 300k, Rat with tuba, vert. No. 1832, 300k, Rat carrying barrel, vert. No. 1833, 300k, Rat playing with top, vert. No. 1834, 300k, Rat delivering mail to mailbox, vert.

No. 1835, 1200k, Canis mesomelas, vert. No. 1836, 1200k, Atelerix frontalis, vert. No. 1837, 1200k, Smutsia temminckii, vert. No. 1838, 1200k, Aonyx capensis, vert. No. 1839, 1200k, Vulpes chama, vert. No. 1840, 1200k, Hippotragus niger variani, vert. No. 1841, 1200k, Hippopotamus amphibius, vert. No. 1842, 1200k, Panthera leo, vert. No. 1843, 1200k, Panthera pardus, vert. No. 1844, 1200k, Caracal aurata, vert. No. 1845, 1200k, Trichechus senegalensis, vert. No. 1846, 1200k, Orcinus orca, vert. No. 1847, 1200k, Caprimulgus rufigena, vert. No. 1848, 1200k, Actophilornis africanus, vert. No. 1849, 1200k, Polemaetus bellicosus, vert. No. 1850, 1200k, Eurema hecabe, vert. No. 1851, 1200k, Hippotragus niger, Cangandala National Park, vert. No. 1852, 1200k, Aviceda cuculoides and Calandula Falls, vert. No. 1853, 1200k, SDD6 Diesel locomotive. No. 1854, 1200k, Cercopithecus mitis, vert. No. 1855, 1200k, Orycteropus afer, diff., vert. No. 1856, 1200k, Two Crocuta crocuta, vert. No. 1857, 1200k, Equus quagga chapmani standing, vert. No. 1858, 1200k, Lycaon pictus pictus, diff., vert. No. 1859, 1200k, Lepus capensis, diff., vert. No. 1860, 1200k, Pterocles namaqua, vert. No. 1861, 1200k, Opal, vert. No. 1862, 1200k, Chikwe statue, vert. No. 1863, 1200k, Rat holding gift, vert.

***Perf. 13x13¼, 13¼x13***

**2019, Dec. 20** **Litho.**

**1719-1834** A354 Set of 116 145.00 145.00

**Souvenir Sheets**

**1835-1863** A354 Set of 29 145.00 145.00

## SEMI-POSTAL STAMPS

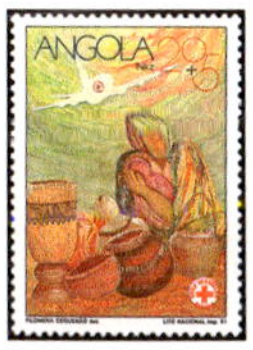


Angolan Red Cross — SP1

No. B1, Mother and child. No. B2, Zebra and foal.

**1991, Sept. 19** **Litho.** ***Perf. 14***

**B1** SP1 20k +5k multi 1.25 1.25
**B2** SP1 40k +5k multi 2.25 2.25

## AIR POST STAMPS

**Plane Over Globe**
Common Design Type

***Perf. 13½x13***

**1938, July 26** **Engr.** **Unwmk.**

**Name and Value in Black**

| | | | | |
|---|---|---|---|---|
| **C1** | CD39 | 10c red orange | .45 | .40 |
| **C2** | CD39 | 20c purple | .45 | .40 |
| **C3** | CD39 | 50c orange | .45 | .40 |
| **C4** | CD39 | 1a ultra | .45 | .40 |
| **C5** | CD39 | 2a lilac brn | .95 | .40 |
| **C6** | CD39 | 3a dk green | 1.90 | .60 |
| **C7** | CD39 | 5a red brown | 4.50 | .90 |
| **C8** | CD39 | 9a rose carmine | 7.00 | 1.90 |
| **C9** | CD39 | 10a magenta | 9.75 | 3.00 |
| | | *Nos. C1-C9 (9)* | 25.90 | 8.40 |
| | | Set, Never Hinged | 36.00 | |

No. C7 exists with overprint "Exposicao Internacional de Nova York, 1939-1940" and Trylon and Perisphere. Value; unused and used $110, never hinged, $160.

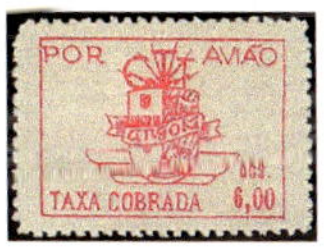


AP2

**Issued Without Gum**

***Rough Perf. 10½***

**1947, Aug. 6** **Litho.**

| | | | | |
|---|---|---|---|---|
| **C10** | AP2 | 1a red brown | 15.25 | 4.75 |
| **C11** | AP2 | 2a yellow grn | 17.25 | 6.00 |
| **C12** | AP2 | 3a orange | 17.25 | 6.00 |
| **C13** | AP2 | 3.50a orange | 31.00 | 6.00 |
| **C14** | AP2 | 5a olive grn | 105.00 | 27.00 |
| **C15** | AP2 | 6a rose | 105.00 | 26.00 |
| **C16** | AP2 | 9a red | 360.00 | 270.00 |
| **C17** | AP2 | 10a green | 237.50 | 102.50 |
| **C18** | AP2 | 20a blue | 335.00 | 112.50 |
| **C19** | AP2 | 50a black | 425.00 | 270.00 |
| **C20** | AP2 | 100a yellow | 600.00 | 525.00 |
| | | *Nos. C10-C20 (11)* | 2,248. | 1,356. |

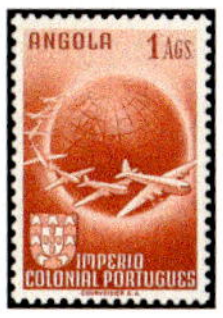


Planes Circling Globe — AP3

**1949, May 1** **Photo.** ***Perf. 11½***

| | | | | |
|---|---|---|---|---|
| **C21** | AP3 | 1a henna brown | .40 | .25 |
| **C22** | AP3 | 2a red brown | .85 | .25 |
| **C23** | AP3 | 3a plum | 1.15 | .25 |
| **C24** | AP3 | 6a dull green | 2.25 | .85 |
| **C25** | AP3 | 9a violet brown | 3.10 | 2.25 |
| | | *Nos. C21-C25 (5)* | 7.75 | 3.85 |
| | | Set, Never Hinged | 15.50 | |

**Catalogue values for unused stamps in this section, from this point to the end of the section, are for Never Hinged items.**

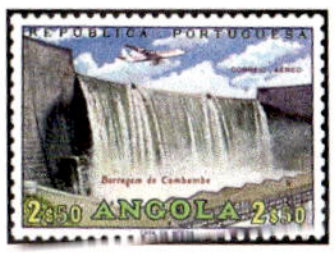


Cambambe Dam — AP4

Designs: 1.50e, Oil refinery, vert. 3e, Salazar Dam. 4e, Capt. Teófilo Duarte Dam. 4.50e, Craveiro Lopes Dam. 5e, Cuango Dam. 6e, Quanza River Bridge. 7e, Capt. Teófilo Duarte Bridge. 8.50e, Oliveira Salazar Bridge. 12.50e, Capt. Silva Carvalho Bridge.

***Perf. 11½x12, 12x11½***

**1965, July 12** **Litho.** **Unwmk.**

| | | | | |
|---|---|---|---|---|
| **C26** | AP4 | 1.50e multicolored | 2.50 | .25 |
| **C27** | AP4 | 2.50e multicolored | 1.50 | .25 |
| **C28** | AP4 | 3e multicolored | 2.50 | .25 |
| **C29** | AP4 | 4e multicolored | 1.00 | .25 |
| **C30** | AP4 | 4.50e multicolored | 1.00 | .25 |
| **C31** | AP4 | 5e multicolored | 1.60 | .25 |
| **C32** | AP4 | 6e multicolored | 1.60 | .25 |
| **C33** | AP4 | 7e multicolored | 2.50 | .25 |
| **C34** | AP4 | 8.50e multicolored | 3.25 | 1.40 |
| **C35** | AP4 | 12.50e multicolored | 3.75 | 1.60 |
| | | *Nos. C26-C35 (10)* | 21.20 | 5.00 |

**Stamp Centenary Type**

Design: 2.50e, Boeing 707 jet & Angola #2.

**1970, Dec. 1** **Litho.** ***Perf. 13½***

**C36** A83 2.50e multicolored 2.00 .85
*a.* Souv. sheet of 3, #565-566, C36 13.50 13.00

No. C36a sold for 15e.

No. C36 Ovptd.

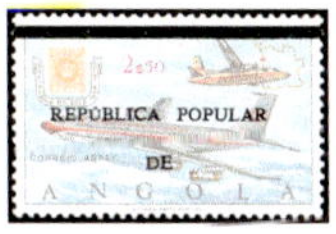


**1980, June 15** **Litho.** ***Perf. 13½***

**C37** A83 2.50e multicolored 1.40 .45

## POSTAGE DUE STAMPS

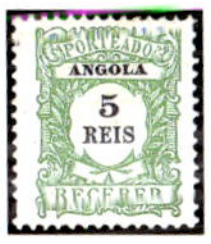


D1

**1904** **Unwmk.** **Typo.** ***Perf. 11½x12***

| | | | | |
|---|---|---|---|---|
| **J1** | D1 | 5r yellow grn | .50 | .45 |
| **J2** | D1 | 10r slate | .50 | .45 |
| **J3** | D1 | 20r yellow brn | .95 | .50 |
| **J4** | D1 | 30r orange | .95 | .50 |
| **J5** | D1 | 50r gray brown | 1.15 | .85 |
| **J6** | D1 | 60r red brown | 11.50 | 5.50 |
| **J7** | D1 | 100r lilac | 2.25 | 2.75 |
| **J8** | D1 | 130r dull blue | 2.25 | 2.75 |
| **J9** | D1 | 200r carmine | 13.50 | 7.50 |
| **J10** | D1 | 500r gray violet | 12.00 | 6.00 |
| | | *Nos. J1-J10 (10)* | 45.55 | 27.25 |
| | | Set, never hinged | 100.00 | |

Postage Due Stamps of 1904 Overprinted in Carmine or Green

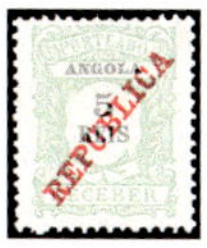


**1911**

| | | | | |
|---|---|---|---|---|
| **J11** | D1 | 5r yellow grn | .35 | .30 |
| **J12** | D1 | 10r slate | .35 | .30 |
| **J13** | D1 | 20r yellow brn | .35 | .30 |
| **J14** | D1 | 30r orange | .50 | .30 |
| **J15** | D1 | 50r gray brown | .50 | .30 |
| **J16** | D1 | 60r red brown | 1.55 | 1.00 |
| **J17** | D1 | 100r lilac | 1.60 | 1.00 |
| **J18** | D1 | 130r dull blue | 1.75 | 1.40 |
| **J19** | D1 | 200r carmine (G) | 2.25 | 1.40 |
| **J20** | D1 | 500r gray violet | 2.60 | 2.60 |
| | | *Nos. J11-J20 (10)* | 11.80 | 8.90 |
| | | Set, never hinged | 70.00 | |

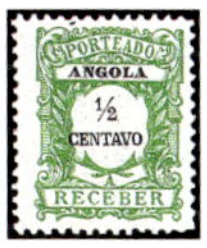


D2

**1921** ***Perf. 11½***

| | | | | |
|---|---|---|---|---|
| **J21** | D2 | ½c yellow green | .35 | .30 |
| **J22** | D2 | 1c slate | .35 | .30 |
| **J23** | D2 | 2c orange brown | .35 | .30 |
| **J24** | D2 | 3c orange | .35 | .30 |
| **J25** | D2 | 5c gray brown | .35 | .30 |
| **J26** | D2 | 6c lt brown | .45 | .30 |
| **J27** | D2 | 10c red violet | .60 | .45 |
| **J28** | D2 | 13c dull blue | 1.00 | .85 |
| **J29** | D2 | 20c carmine | 1.00 | .85 |
| **J30** | D2 | 50c gray | 1.00 | .85 |
| | | *Nos. J21-J30 (10)* | 5.80 | 4.80 |
| | | Set, never hinged | 7.50 | |

For surcharges see Nos. 268-270.

**Catalogue values for unused stamps in this section, from this point to the end of the section, are for Never Hinged items.**

Stamps of 1932 Surcharged in Black

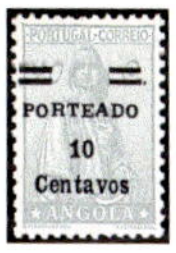


**1949, Feb.** **Wmk. 232** ***Perf. 12x11½***

| | | | | |
|---|---|---|---|---|
| **J31** | A14 | 10c on 20c gray | .40 | .30 |
| **J32** | A14 | 20c on 30c myrtle grn | .80 | .50 |
| **J33** | A14 | 30c on 50c lt brown | 1.10 | .80 |
| **J34** | A14 | 40c on 1a claret | 1.60 | 1.20 |
| **J35** | A14 | 50c on 2a dull vio | 2.70 | 2.10 |
| **J36** | A14 | 1a on 5a pale yel grn | 2.90 | 2.50 |
| | | *Nos. J31-J36 (6)* | 9.50 | 7.40 |

Common Design Type

**Photogravure and Typographed**

**1952** **Unwmk.** ***Perf. 14***

**Numeral in Red, Frame Multicolored**

| | | | | |
|---|---|---|---|---|
| **J37** | CD45 | 10c red brown | .30 | .30 |
| **J38** | CD45 | 30c olive green | .30 | .30 |
| **J39** | CD45 | 50c chocolate | .30 | .30 |
| **J40** | CD45 | 1a dk vio blue | .65 | .55 |
| **J41** | CD45 | 2a red brown | .80 | .75 |
| **J42** | CD45 | 5a black brown | .80 | .75 |
| | | *Nos. J37-J42 (6)* | 3.15 | 2.95 |

## NEWSPAPER STAMP

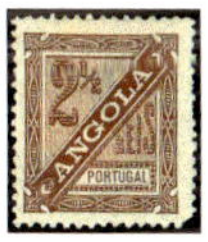


N1

**1893** **Typo.** **Unwmk.** ***Perf. 11½***

**P1** N1 2½r brown 3.50 1.75
*a.* Perf. 12½ 3.50 1.75
*b.* Perf. 13½ 3.15 1.75

No. P1 was also used for ordinary postage.
For surcharges see Nos. 37, 82, 180, 235.

## POSTAL TAX STAMPS

**Pombal Issue**
Common Design Types

**1925, May 8** **Unwmk.** ***Perf. 12½***

| | | | | |
|---|---|---|---|---|
| **RA1** | CD28 | 15c lilac & black | 1.10 | .90 |
| **RA2** | CD29 | 15c lilac & black | 1.10 | .90 |
| **RA3** | CD30 | 15c lilac & black | 1.10 | .90 |
| | | *Nos. RA1-RA3 (3)* | 3.30 | 2.70 |

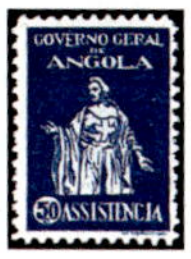


"Charity" — PT1

**1929** **Litho.** ***Perf. 11***

**Without Gum**

**RA4** PT1 50c dark blue 6.75 2.25

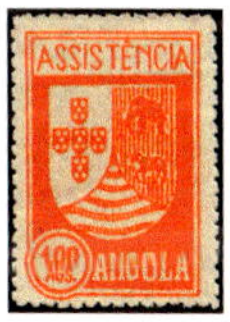


Coat of Arms — PT2

**1939** **Without Gum** ***Perf. 10½***

**RA5** PT2 50c turq green 3.75 .35
**RA6** PT2 1a red 8.00 2.50

A 1.50a, type PT2, was issued for fiscal use. Value, $7.50.

**Catalogue values for unused stamps in this section, from this point to the end of the section, are for Never Hinged items.**

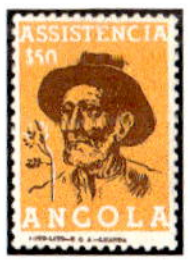


Old Man — PT3

Designs: 1e, Boy. 1.50e, Girl.

**Imprint: "Foto-Lito-E.G.A.-Luanda"**

**Heads in dark brown**

**1955** **Unwmk.** ***Perf. 13***

| | | | | |
|---|---|---|---|---|
| **RA7** | PT3 | 50c dk ocher | .45 | .30 |
| **RA8** | PT3 | 1e orange ver | 1.00 | .45 |
| **RA9** | PT3 | 1.50e brt yel grn | .90 | .45 |
| | | *Nos. RA7-RA9 (3)* | 2.35 | 1.20 |

A 2.50e, type PT3 showing an old woman, was issued for revenue use. Value $1.45.

No. RA7 Surcharged in Red or Black

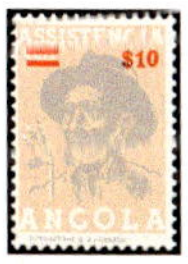


**1957-58** **Head in dark brown**

| | | | | |
|---|---|---|---|---|
| **RA11** | PT3 | 10c on 50c dk ocher (R) | .35 | .30 |
| **RA12** | PT3 | 10c on 50c dk ocher ('58) | .35 | .30 |
| **RA13** | PT3 | 30c on 50c dk ocher | .35 | .30 |
| | | *Nos. RA11-RA13 (3)* | 1.05 | .90 |

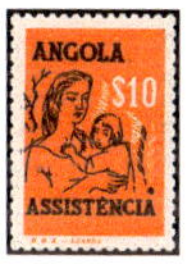


Mother and Child — PT4

Design: 30c, Boy and girl.

**1959** **Litho.** ***Perf. 13***

**RA14** PT1 10c orange & blk .30 .25
**RA15** PT4 30c slate & blk .30 .25

**Type of 1955 Redrawn**

Design: 1e, Boy.

**1961, Nov.** ***Perf. 13***

**RA16** PT3 1e salmon pink & dk brn .30 .30

Denomination in italics.

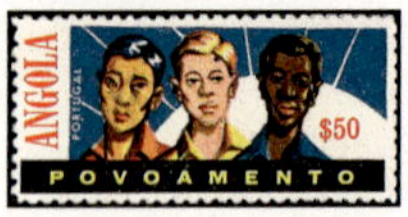


Yellow, White and Black Men — PT5

**1962, July 1 Typo. *Perf. 10½***

**Without Gum**

| | | | | |
|---|---|---|---|---|
| RA17 | PT5 | 50c multicolored | .70 | .60 |
| *a.* | | Perf. 11½ | 1.00 | .85 |
| RA18 | PT5 | 1e multicolored | .60 | .35 |

Issued for the Provincial Settlement Committee (Junta Provincial do Povoamento). The tax was used to promote Portuguese settlement in Angola, and to raise educational and living standards of recent immigrants.

Denominations higher than 1e were used for revenue purposes.

### Head Type of 1955

Designs: 50c, Old man. 1e, Boy. 1.50e, Girl.

**Without Imprint**
**Heads in dark brown**

**1964-65 Litho. *Perf. 11½***

| | | | | |
|---|---|---|---|---|
| RA19 | PT3 | 50c orange | .35 | .25 |
| RA20 | PT3 | 1e dull red org ('65) | .35 | .25 |
| RA21 | PT3 | 1.50e yel grn ('65) | .35 | .35 |
| | | *Nos. RA19-RA21 (3)* | 1.05 | .85 |

No. RA20 is the second redrawing of 1e, with bolder lettering. Space between "Assistencia" and denomination on RA20-RA21 is ½mm; on the 1955 issue space is 2¼mm and 1¾mm, respectively.

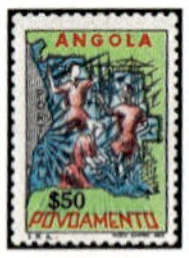


Map of Angola, Industrial and Farm Workers — PT6

**1965, Sept. 1 Litho. *Perf. 13***

| | | | | |
|---|---|---|---|---|
| RA22 | PT6 | 50c multicolored | .50 | .25 |
| RA23 | PT6 | 1e multicolored | .50 | .25 |

The 2e was used for revenue purposes. Value 50c.

### Head Type of 1955

Designs: 50c, Old man. 1e, Boy. 1.50e, Girl.

**Imprint: "I.N.A." or "INA" (1e)**

**1966 Heads in dark brown**

| | | | | |
|---|---|---|---|---|
| RA25 | PT3 | 50c dull orange | .30 | .25 |
| RA26 | PT3 | 1e dull brick red | .30 | .25 |
| RA27 | PT3 | 1.50e lt yel grn | .60 | .35 |
| | | *Nos. RA25-RA27 (3)* | 1.20 | .85 |

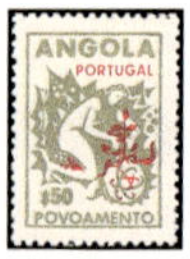


Woman Planting Tree — PT7

**1972 Litho. *Perf. 13***

| | | | | |
|---|---|---|---|---|
| RA28 | PT7 | 50c shown | .35 | .25 |
| RA29 | PT7 | 1e Workers | .35 | .25 |
| RA30 | PT7 | 2e Produce | .35 | .25 |
| | | *Nos. RA28-RA30 (3)* | 1.05 | .75 |

### POSTAL TAX DUE STAMPS

**Pombal Issue**

Common Design Types

**1925, May 8 Unwmk. *Perf. 12½***

| | | | | |
|---|---|---|---|---|
| RAJ1 | CD28 | 30c lilac & black | 1.10 | .90 |
| RAJ2 | CD29 | 30c lilac & black | 1.10 | .90 |
| RAJ3 | CD30 | 30c lilac & black | 1.10 | .90 |
| | | *Nos. RAJ1-RAJ3 (3)* | 3.30 | 2.70 |

See note after Portugal No. RAJ4.

## ANGRA

'aŋ-grə

LOCATION — An administrative district of the Azores, consisting of the islands of Terceira, Sao Jorge and Graciosa.
GOVT. — A district of Portugal
AREA — 275 sq. mi.
POP. — 70,000 (approx.)
CAPITAL — Angra do Heroismo

1000 Reis = 1 Milreis

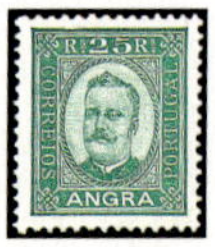


King Carlos — A1

**1892-93 Typo. Unwmk. *Perf. 12½***

| | | | | |
|---|---|---|---|---|
| 1 | A1 | 5r yellow | 5.75 | 3.25 |
| *a.* | | Perf 11½ | 17.00 | 9.00 |
| *b.* | | Perf 13½ | 5.00 | 3.25 |
| 2 | A1 | 10r redsh violet | 5.75 | 3.00 |
| *a.* | | Perf 13½ | 6.25 | 4.25 |
| 3 | A1 | 15r chocolate | 6.25 | 4.50 |
| *a.* | | Perf 13½ | 6.25 | 4.75 |
| 4 | A1 | 20r lavender | 6.25 | 4.50 |
| *a.* | | Perf 13½ | 6.00 | 4.75 |
| 5 | A1 | 25r green | 8.75 | 2.25 |
| *a.* | | Perf 13½ | 13.75 | 8.50 |
| *b.* | | Perf 11½ | 8.25 | 2.00 |
| 7 | A1 | 50r blue | 12.75 | 6.50 |
| *a.* | | Perf 13½ | 17.50 | 10.00 |
| 8 | A1 | 75r carmine | 14.75 | 8.50 |
| 9 | A1 | 80r yellow green | 17.50 | 16.50 |
| 10 | A1 | 100r brown, *yel*, perf 13½ ('93) | 62.50 | 24.00 |
| *a.* | | Perf 12½ | 260.00 | 210.00 |
| 11 | A1 | 150r car, *rose* ('93) | 87.50 | 67.50 |
| *a.* | | Perf 13½ | 100.00 | 85.00 |
| 12 | A1 | 200r dk blue, *bl* ('93) | 87.50 | 67.50 |
| | | Never hinged | 140.00 | |
| *a.* | | Perf 13½ | 100.00 | 85.00 |
| 13 | A1 | 300r dk blue, *sal* ('93) | 87.50 | 67.50 |
| | | Never hinged | 120.00 | |
| *a.* | | Perf 13½ | 97.50 | 85.00 |
| | | *Nos. 1-13 (12)* | 402.75 | 275.50 |

*Reprints of 50r, 150r, 200r and 300r, made in 1900, are perf. 11½ and ungummed. Value, each $75. Reprints of all values, made in 1905, have shiny white gum and clean-cut perf. Value, each $30.*

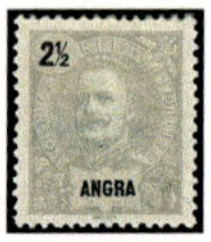


King Carlos — A2

**Name and Value in Black except Nos. 26 and 35**

**1897-1905 *Perf. 11½***

| | | | | |
|---|---|---|---|---|
| 14 | A2 | 2½r gray | 1.25 | .80 |
| 15 | A2 | 5r orange | 1.25 | .80 |
| *a.* | | Diagonal half used as 2½r on newspaper or circular | | *50.00* |
| 16 | A2 | 10r yellow grn | 1.25 | .80 |
| 17 | A2 | 15r brown | 15.00 | 10.00 |
| 18 | A2 | 15r gray grn ('99) | 1.40 | 1.00 |
| 19 | A2 | 20r gray violet | 3.00 | 2.20 |
| 20 | A2 | 25r sea green | 5.00 | 2.00 |
| 21 | A2 | 25r car rose ('99) | 1.10 | 1.00 |
| 22 | A2 | 50r dark blue | 9.00 | 3.00 |
| 23 | A2 | 50r ultra ('05) | 22.00 | 18.00 |
| 24 | A2 | 65r slate bl ('98) | 2.10 | 1.00 |
| 25 | A2 | 75r rose | 5.75 | 2.75 |
| 26 | A2 | 75r gray brn & car, *straw* ('05) | 22.00 | 18.00 |
| 27 | A2 | 80r violet | 2.50 | 2.20 |
| 28 | A2 | 100r dk blue, *bl* | 4.50 | 3.00 |
| 29 | A2 | 115r org brn, *pink* ('98) | 4.50 | 3.50 |
| 30 | A2 | 130r gray brn, *straw* ('98) | 4.50 | 3.50 |
| 31 | A2 | 150r lt brn, *straw* | 4.50 | 3.00 |
| 32 | A2 | 180r sl, *pnksh* ('98) | 5.50 | 5.00 |
| 33 | A2 | 200r red vio, *pnksh* | 9.00 | 8.00 |
| 34 | A2 | 300r blue, *rose* | 13.50 | 10.00 |
| 35 | A2 | 500r blk & red, *bl* | 27.50 | 22.00 |
| *a.* | | Perf. 12½ | 37.50 | 29.00 |
| | | *Nos. 14-35 (22)* | 166.10 | 121.55 |

Azores stamps were used in Angra from 1906 to 1931, when they were superseded by those of Portugal.

## ANGUILLA

aŋ-ˌgwi-lə

LOCATION — In the West Indies southeast of Puerto Rico
GOVT. — British territory
AREA — 60 sq. mi.
POP. — 13,572 (2011)
CAPITAL — The Valley

Anguilla separated unilaterally from the Associated State of St. Kitts-Nevis-Anguilla in 1967, formalized in 1980 following direct United Kingdom intervention some years before. A British Commissioner exercises executive authority.

100 Cents = 1 Eastern Caribbean Dollar

**Catalogue values for all unused stamps in this country are for Never Hinged items.**

**St. Kitts-Nevis Nos. 145-160 Overprinted**

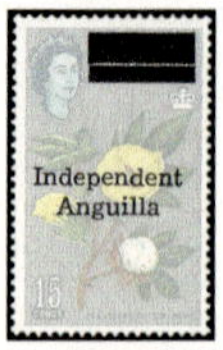


On Type A14

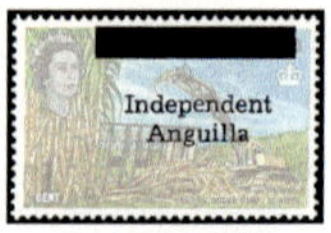


On Type A15

**Wmk. 314**

**1967, Sept. 4 Photo. *Perf. 14***

| | | | | |
|---|---|---|---|---|
| 1 | A14 | ½c blue & dk brn | 75.00 | 21.00 |
| 2 | A15 | 1c multicolored | 85.00 | 9.00 |
| 3 | A14 | 2c multicolored | 75.00 | 2.90 |
| 4 | A14 | 3c multicolored | 75.00 | 7.00 |
| 5 | A15 | 4c multicolored | 90.00 | 5.25 |
| 6 | A15 | 5c multicolored | 375.00 | 40.00 |
| 7 | A15 | 6c multicolored | 160.00 | 16.00 |
| 8 | A15 | 10c multicolored | 90.00 | 9.00 |
| 9 | A14 | 15c multicolored | 180.00 | 14.00 |
| 10 | A15 | 20c multicolored | 375.00 | 21.00 |
| 11 | A14 | 25c multicolored | 300.00 | 40.00 |
| 12 | A15 | 50c multicolored | *5,500.* | *725.00* |
| 13 | A14 | 60c multicolored | *6,500.* | *1,850.* |
| 14 | A14 | $1 multicolored | *4,500.* | *625.00* |
| 15 | A15 | $2.50 multicolored | *3,500.* | *375.00* |
| 16 | A14 | $5 multicolored | *4,000.* | *400.00* |
| | | *Nos. 1-16 (16)* | 25,880. | 4,160. |

Counterfeit overprints exist.

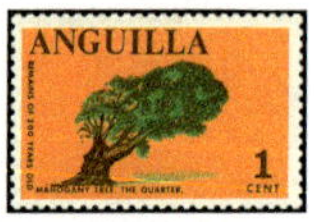


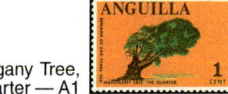

Mahogany Tree, The Quarter — A1

Designs: 2c, Sombrero Lighthouse. 3c, St. Mary's Church. 4c, Valley Police Station. 5c, Old Plantation House, Mt. Fortune. 6c, Valley Post Office. 10c, Methodist Church, West End. 15c, Wall-Blake Airport. 20c, Plane over Sandy Ground. 25c, Island Harbor. 40c, Map of Anguilla. 60c, Hermit crab and starfish. $1, Hibiscus. $2.50, Coconut harvest. $5, Spiny lobster.

***Perf. 12½x13***

**1967-68 Litho. Unwmk.**

| | | | | |
|---|---|---|---|---|
| 17 | A1 | 1c orange & multi | .25 | .80 |
| 18 | A1 | 2c gray green & blk | .25 | 1.00 |
| 19 | A1 | 3c emerald & blk | .25 | .25 |
| 20 | A1 | 4c brt blue & blk | .25 | .25 |
| 21 | A1 | 5c lt blue & multi | .25 | .25 |
| 22 | A1 | 6c ver & black | .25 | .25 |
| 23 | A1 | 10c multicolored | .25 | .25 |
| 24 | A1 | 15c multicolored | 2.10 | .25 |
| 25 | A1 | 20c multicolored | 1.25 | 1.75 |
| 26 | A1 | 25c multicolored | .60 | .25 |
| 27 | A1 | 40c blue & multi | 1.00 | .50 |
| 28 | A1 | 60c yellow & multi | 4.50 | 4.00 |
| 29 | A1 | $1 lt green & multi | 1.75 | 2.75 |
| 30 | A1 | $2.50 multicolored | 2.00 | 5.50 |
| 31 | A1 | $5 multicolored | 2.75 | 3.50 |
| | | *Nos. 17-31 (15)* | 17.70 | 21.55 |

Issued: 1c, 5c, 10c, 20c, 25c, 40c, 11/27/67; 3c, 4c, 15c, 60c, $1, $5, 2/10/68; 2c, 6c, $2.50, 3/21/68.

For overprints see Nos. 53-67, 78-82.

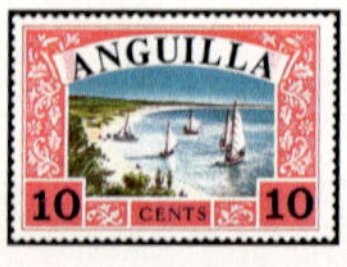


Sailboats — A2

Designs: 15c, Boat building. 25c, Schooner Warspite. 40c, Yacht Atlantic Star.

**1968, May 11 *Perf. 14***

| | | | | |
|---|---|---|---|---|
| 32 | A2 | 10c rose & multi | .35 | .25 |
| 33 | A2 | 15c olive & multi | .40 | .25 |
| 34 | A2 | 25c lilac rose & multi | .60 | .25 |
| 35 | A2 | 40c dull blue & multi | .65 | .35 |
| | | *Nos. 32-35 (4)* | 2.00 | 1.10 |

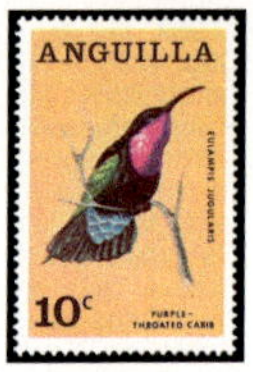


Purple-throated Carib — A3

Anguillan Birds: 15c, Bananaquit. 25c, Black-necked stilt, horiz. 40c, Royal tern, horiz.

**1968, July 8**

| | | | | |
|---|---|---|---|---|
| 36 | A3 | 10c dull yel & multi | .75 | .25 |
| 37 | A3 | 15c yel green & multi | 1.00 | .25 |
| 38 | A3 | 25c multicolored | 1.40 | .25 |
| 39 | A3 | 40c multicolored | 1.75 | .35 |
| | | *Nos. 36-39 (4)* | 4.90 | 1.10 |

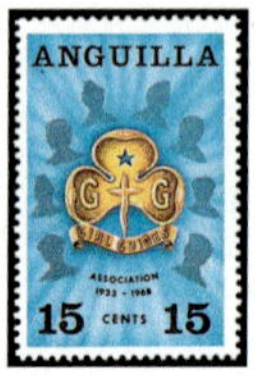


Girl Guide Badge — A4

10c, Girl Guide badge, horiz. 25c, Badge and Headquarters, horiz. 40c, Merit Badges.

**1968, Oct. 14 *Perf. 13x13½, 13½x13***

| | | | | |
|---|---|---|---|---|
| 40 | A4 | 10c lt green & multi | .25 | .25 |
| 41 | A4 | 15c lt blue & multi | .25 | .25 |
| 42 | A4 | 25c multicolored | .25 | .25 |
| 43 | A4 | 40c multicolored | .30 | .25 |
| | | *Nos. 40-43 (4)* | 1.05 | 1.00 |

Anguillan Girl Guides, 35th anniversary.

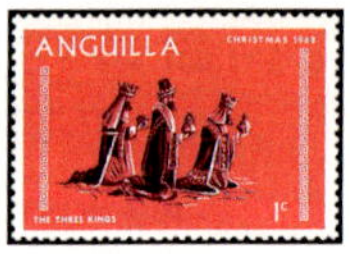


Three Kings — A5

Christmas: 10c, Three Kings seeing Star, vert. 15c, Holy Family, vert. 40c, Shepherds seeing Star. 50c, Holy Family and donkey.

**1968, Nov. 18**

| | | | | |
|---|---|---|---|---|
| 44 | A5 | 1c lilac rose & black | .25 | .25 |
| 45 | A5 | 10c blue & black | .25 | .25 |
| 46 | A5 | 15c brown & black | .25 | .25 |
| 47 | A5 | 40c brt ultra & black | .25 | .25 |
| 48 | A5 | 50c green & black | .30 | .25 |
| | | *Nos. 44-48 (5)* | 1.30 | 1.25 |

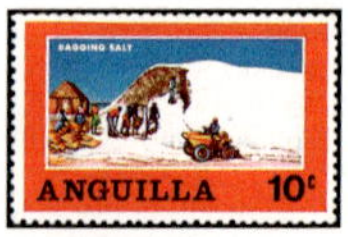


Bagging Salt — A6

Salt Industry: 15c, Packing salt. 40c, Salt pond. 50c, Loading salt.

**1969, Jan. 4 *Perf. 13***

| | | | | |
|---|---|---|---|---|
| 49 | A6 | 10c red & multi | .25 | .25 |
| 50 | A6 | 15c lt blue & multi | .30 | .25 |
| 51 | A6 | 40c emerald & multi | .30 | .25 |
| 52 | A6 | 50c purple & multi | .35 | .25 |
| | | *Nos. 49-52 (4)* | 1.20 | 1.00 |

Nos. 17-31 Overprinted

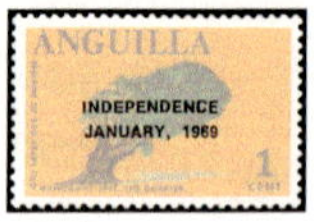


**1969, Jan. 9 *Perf. 12½x13***

| | | | | |
|---|---|---|---|---|
| 53 | A1 | 1c orange & multi | .25 | .25 |
| 54 | A1 | 2c gray green & blk | .25 | .25 |
| 55 | A1 | 3c emerald & blk | .25 | .25 |
| 56 | A1 | 4c brt blue & blk | .25 | .25 |
| 57 | A1 | 5c lt blue & multi | .25 | .25 |
| 58 | A1 | 6c vermilion & blk | .25 | .25 |
| 59 | A1 | 10c multicolored | .25 | .25 |
| 60 | A1 | 15c multicolored | .25 | .30 |

| | | | | |
|---|---|---|---|---|
| 61 | A1 | 20c multicolored | .30 | .35 |
| 62 | A1 | 25c multicolored | .40 | .50 |
| 63 | A1 | 40c blue & multi | .70 | *.70* |
| 64 | A1 | 60c yellow & multi | .80 | *.80* |
| 65 | A1 | $1 lt green & multi | 1.25 | *1.50* |
| 66 | A1 | $2.50 multicolored | 3.75 | *4.50* |
| 67 | A1 | $5 multicolored | 8.25 | *9.50* |
| | | *Nos. 53-67 (15)* | 17.45 | 19.90 |

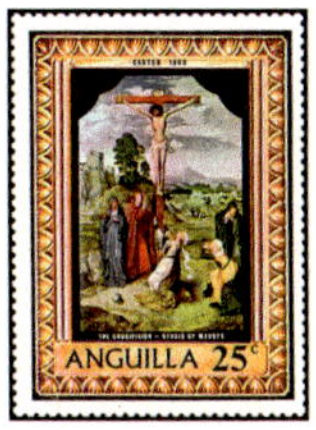

Crucifixion, School of Quentin Massys — A7

Easter: 40c, The Last Supper, ascribed to Roberti.

**1969, Mar. 31 Litho. *Perf. 13½***

| | | | | |
|---|---|---|---|---|
| 68 | A7 | 25c multicolored | .25 | .25 |
| 69 | A7 | 40c multicolored | .35 | .25 |

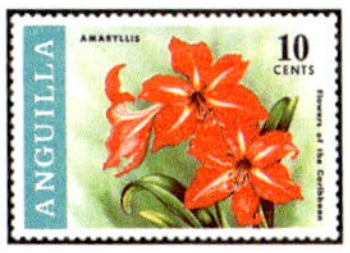

Amaryllis — A8

**1969, June 10 *Perf. 14***

| | | | | |
|---|---|---|---|---|
| 70 | A8 | 10c shown | .25 | .25 |
| 71 | A8 | 15c Bougainvillea | .35 | .35 |
| 72 | A8 | 40c Hibiscus | .55 | .55 |
| 73 | A8 | 50c Cattleya orchid | 1.75 | 1.25 |
| | | *Nos. 70-73 (4)* | 2.90 | 2.40 |

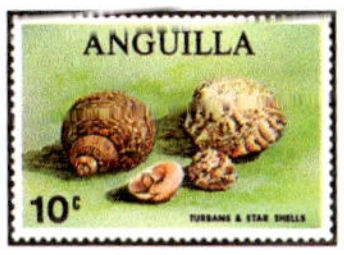

Turban and Star Shells — A9

Sea Shells: 15c, Spiny oysters. 40c, Scotch, royal and smooth bonnets. 50c, Triton trumpet.

**1969, Sept. 22**

| | | | | |
|---|---|---|---|---|
| 74 | A9 | 10c multicolored | .25 | .25 |
| 75 | A9 | 15c multicolored | .35 | .30 |
| 76 | A9 | 40c multicolored | .70 | .35 |
| 77 | A9 | 50c multicolored | .80 | .40 |
| | | *Nos. 74-77 (4)* | 2.10 | 1.30 |

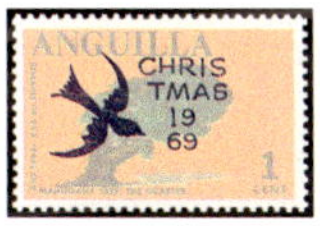

No. 17 Ovptd.

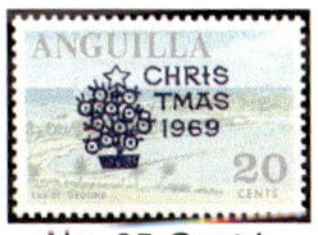

No. 25 Ovptd.

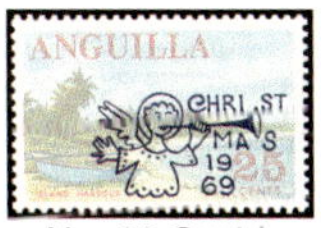

No. 26 Ovptd.

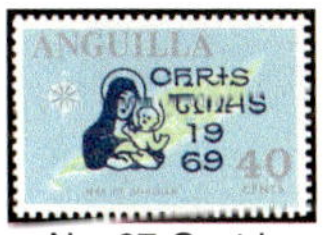

No. 27 Ovptd.

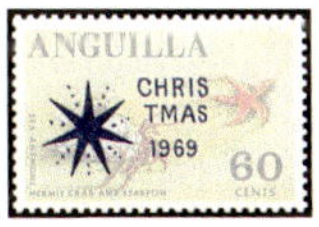

No. 28 Ovptd.

**1969, Oct. 27 *Perf. 12½x13***

| | | | | |
|---|---|---|---|---|
| 78 | A1 | 1c orange & multi | .25 | .25 |
| 79 | A1 | 20c multicolored | .25 | .25 |
| 80 | A1 | 25c multicolored | .25 | .25 |
| 81 | A1 | 40c blue & multi | .50 | .25 |
| 82 | A1 | 60c yellow & multi | .75 | .30 |
| | | *Nos. 78-82 (5)* | 2.00 | 1.30 |

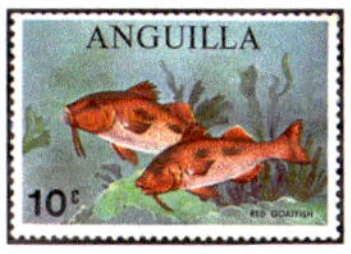

Red Goatfish — A10

Designs: 15c, Blue-striped grunts. 40c, Mutton grouper. 50c, Banded butterfly-fish.

**1969, Dec. 1 *Perf. 14***

| | | | | |
|---|---|---|---|---|
| 83 | A10 | 10c multicolored | .40 | .25 |
| 84 | A10 | 15c multicolored | .50 | .25 |
| 85 | A10 | 40c multicolored | .95 | .45 |
| 86 | A10 | 50c multicolored | 1.25 | .60 |
| | | *Nos. 83-86 (4)* | 3.10 | 1.55 |

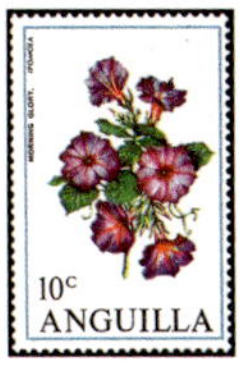

Morning Glory — A11

**1970, Feb. 23**

| | | | | |
|---|---|---|---|---|
| 87 | A11 | 10c shown | .40 | .25 |
| 88 | A11 | 15c Blue petrea | .55 | .25 |
| 89 | A11 | 40c Hibiscus | .75 | .30 |
| 90 | A11 | 50c Flamboyant | .95 | .35 |
| | | *Nos. 87-90 (4)* | 2.65 | 1.15 |

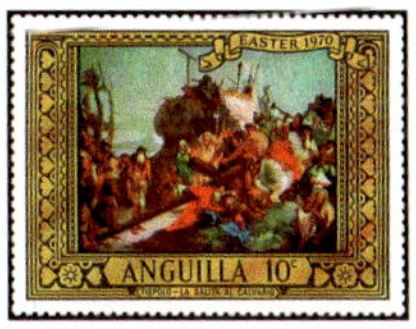

The Way to Calvary, by Tiepolo A12

Easter: 20c, Crucifixion, by Masaccio, vert. 40c, Descent from the Cross, by Rosso Fiorentino, vert. 60c, Jesus Carrying the Cross, by Murillo.

**1970, Mar. 26 *Perf. 13½***

| | | | | |
|---|---|---|---|---|
| 91 | A12 | 10c multicolored | .25 | .25 |
| 92 | A12 | 20c multicolored | .25 | .25 |
| 93 | A12 | 40c multicolored | .30 | .25 |
| 94 | A12 | 60c multicolored | .40 | .30 |
| | | *Nos. 91-94 (4)* | 1.20 | 1.05 |

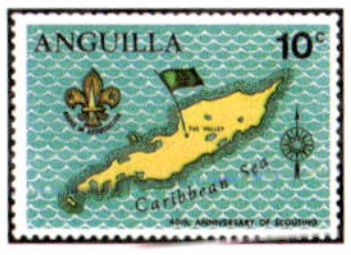

Anguilla Map, Scout Badge — A13

Designs: 15c, Cub Scouts practicing first aid. 40c, Monkey bridge. 50c, Scout Headquarters, The Valley, and Lord Baden-Powell.

**1970, Aug. 10 *Perf. 13***

| | | | | |
|---|---|---|---|---|
| 95 | A13 | 10c multicolored | .25 | .25 |
| 96 | A13 | 15c multicolored | .25 | .25 |
| 97 | A13 | 40c multicolored | .30 | .25 |
| 98 | A13 | 50c multicolored | .40 | .30 |
| | | *Nos. 95-98 (4)* | 1.20 | 1.05 |

Anguilla Boy Scouts, 40th anniversary.

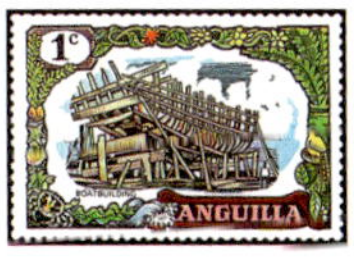

Boat Building — A14

Designs: 2c, Road construction. 3c, Blowing Point dock, 4c, Radio announcer. 5c, Cottage Hospital extension. 6c, Valley secondary school. 10c, Hotel extension. 15c, Sandy Ground. 20c, Supermarket and movie house. 25c, Bananas and mangoes. 40c, Wall-Blake airport. 60c, Sandy Ground jetty. $1, Administration building. $2.50, Cow and calf. $5, Sandy Hill Bay.

**1970, Nov. 23 Litho. *Perf. 14***

| | | | | |
|---|---|---|---|---|
| 99 | A14 | 1c multicolored | .30 | *.40* |
| 100 | A14 | 2c multicolored | .30 | *.40* |
| 101 | A14 | 3c multicolored | .30 | .25 |
| 102 | A14 | 4c multicolored | .30 | *.50* |
| 103 | A14 | 5c multicolored | .50 | .50 |
| 104 | A14 | 6c multicolored | .40 | *.50* |
| 105 | A14 | 10c multicolored | .40 | .30 |
| 106 | A14 | 15c multicolored | .40 | .30 |
| 107 | A14 | 20c multicolored | .75 | .30 |
| 108 | A14 | 25c multicolored | .40 | *1.00* |
| 109 | A14 | 40c multicolored | 4.00 | 3.00 |
| 110 | A14 | 60c multicolored | .70 | *3.00* |
| 111 | A14 | $1 multicolored | 1.25 | 1.25 |
| 112 | A14 | $2.50 multicolored | 1.75 | *4.00* |
| 113 | A14 | $5 multicolored | 3.75 | 4.00 |
| | | *Nos. 99-113 (15)* | 15.50 | 19.70 |

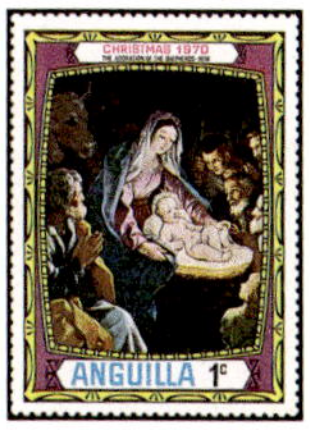

Adoration of the Shepherds, by Guido Reni — A15

Christmas: 20c, Virgin and Child, by Benozzo Gozzoli. 25c, Nativity, by Botticelli. 40c, Santa Margherita Madonna, by Mazzola. 50c, Adoration of the Kings, by Tiepolo.

**1970, Dec. 11 *Perf. 13½***

| | | | | |
|---|---|---|---|---|
| 114 | A15 | 1c multicolored | .25 | .25 |
| 115 | A15 | 20c multicolored | .25 | .25 |
| 116 | A15 | 25c multicolored | .30 | .25 |
| 117 | A15 | 40c multicolored | .45 | .35 |
| 118 | A15 | 50c multicolored | .50 | .40 |
| | | *Nos. 114-118 (5)* | 1.75 | 1.50 |

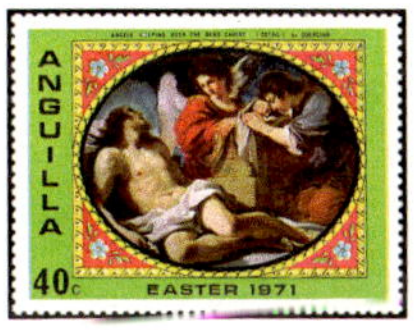

Angels Weeping over the Dead Christ, by Guercino A16

Easter: 10c, Ecce Homo, by Correggio, vert. 15c, Christ Appearing to St. Peter, by Carracci, vert. 50c, The Supper at Emmaus, by Caravaggio.

**1971, Mar. 29**

| | | | | |
|---|---|---|---|---|
| 119 | A16 | 10c pink & multi | .25 | .25 |
| 120 | A16 | 15c lt blue & multi | .25 | .25 |
| 121 | A16 | 40c yel green & multi | .40 | .25 |
| 122 | A16 | 50c violet & multi | .50 | .25 |
| | | *Nos. 119-122 (4)* | 1.40 | 1.00 |

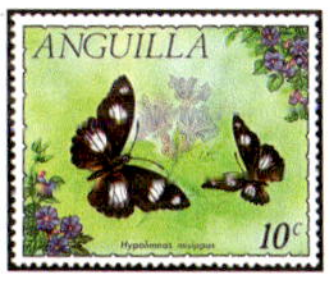

Hypolimnas Misippus — A17

Butterflies: 15c, Junonia lavinia. 40c, Agraulis vanillae. 50c, Danaus plexippus.

**1971, June 21 *Perf. 14x14½***

| | | | | |
|---|---|---|---|---|
| 123 | A17 | 10c multicolored | 2.00 | 1.00 |
| 124 | A17 | 15c multicolored | 2.00 | 1.25 |
| 125 | A17 | 40c multicolored | 2.50 | 1.50 |
| 126 | A17 | 50c multicolored | 2.50 | 2.00 |
| | | *Nos. 123-126 (4)* | 9.00 | 5.75 |

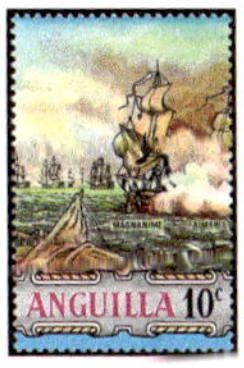

Magnanime and Aimable in Battle — A18

Ships: 15c, HMS Duke and Agamemnon against Glorieux. 25c, HMS Formidable and Namur against Ville de Paris. 40c, HMS Canada. 50c, HMS St. Albans and wreck of Hector.

**1971, Aug. 30 Litho. *Perf. 14***

| | | | | |
|---|---|---|---|---|
| 127 | A18 | 10c multicolored | 1.10 | 1.10 |
| 128 | A18 | 15c multicolored | 1.40 | 1.40 |
| 129 | A18 | 25c multicolored | 1.50 | 1.50 |
| 130 | A18 | 40c multicolored | 1.60 | 1.60 |
| 131 | A18 | 50c multicolored | 1.75 | 1.75 |
| *a.* | | Strip of 5, #127-131 | 8.25 | 8.25 |
| | | *Nos. 127-131 (5)* | 7.35 | 7.35 |

West Indies sea battles.

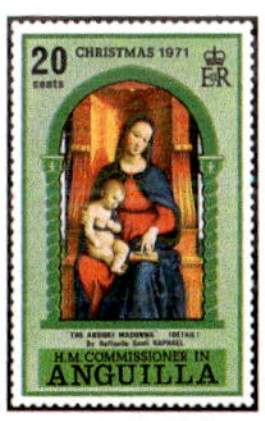

Ansidei Madonna, by Raphael — A19

Christmas: 25c, Mystic Nativity, by Botticelli. 40c, Virgin and Child, School of Seville, inscribed Murillo. 50c, Madonna of the Iris, ascribed to Dürer.

**1971, Nov. 29 *Perf. 14x13½***

| | | | | |
|---|---|---|---|---|
| 132 | A19 | 20c green & multi | .30 | .30 |
| 133 | A19 | 25c blue & multi | .30 | .30 |
| 134 | A19 | 40c lilac rose & multi | .35 | *.40* |
| 135 | A19 | 50c violet & multi | .40 | *.60* |
| | | *Nos. 132-135 (4)* | 1.35 | *1.60* |

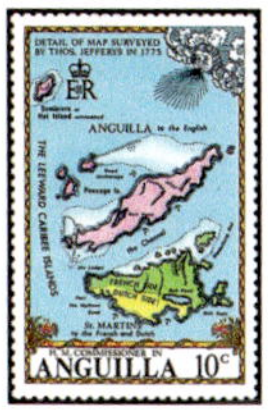

Map of Anguilla and St. Maarten, by Jefferys, 1775 — A20

Maps of Anguilla by: 15c, Samuel Fahlberg, 1814. 40c, Thomas Jefferys, 1775, horiz. 50c, Capt. E. Barnett, 1847, horiz.

**1972, Jan. 24 *Perf. 14x13½, 13½x14***

| | | | | |
|---|---|---|---|---|
| 136 | A20 | 10c lt blue & multi | .25 | .25 |
| 137 | A20 | 15c lt green & multi | .35 | .30 |
| 138 | A20 | 40c lt green & multi | .55 | .40 |
| 139 | A20 | 50c lt ultra & multi | .80 | .40 |
| | | *Nos. 136-139 (4)* | 1.95 | 1.35 |

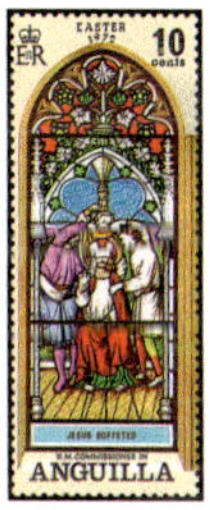

Jesus Buffeted, Stained-glass Window — A21

Easter (19th cent. Stained-glass Windows, Bray Church): 15c, Jesus Carrying the Cross. 25c, Crucifixion. 40c, Descent from the Cross. 50c, Burial.

**1972, Mar. 14 *Perf. 14x13½***

| | | | | |
|---|---|---|---|---|
| 140 | A21 | 10c multicolored | .30 | .30 |
| 141 | A21 | 15c multicolored | .35 | .35 |
| 142 | A21 | 25c multicolored | .35 | .35 |
| 143 | A21 | 40c multicolored | .40 | .40 |
| 144 | A21 | 50c multicolored | .50 | .50 |
| *a.* | | Strip of 5, #140-144 | 2.50 | 2.50 |
| | | *Nos. 140-144 (5)* | 1.90 | 1.90 |

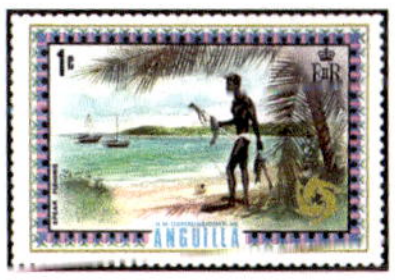

Spear Fishing — A22

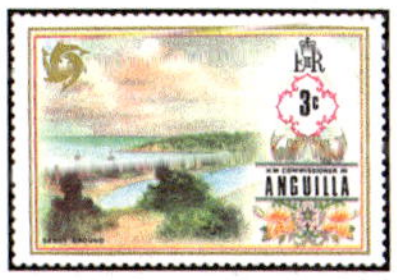

Sandy Ground A23

2c, Loblolly tree, vert. 4c, Ferry, Blowing Point, vert. 5c, Agriculture. 6c, St. Mary's Church, vert. 10c, St. Gerard's Church. 15c, Cottage Hospital. 20c, Public Library. 25c, Sunset, Blowing Point. 40c, Boat building. 60c, Hibiscus. $1, Man-o-war bird. $2.50, Frangipani. $5, Brown pelican. $10, Green-back turtle.

**1972-75 *Perf. 13½***

| | | | | |
|---|---|---|---|---|
| 145 | A22 | 1c shown | .25 | .50 |
| 146 | A23 | 2c multicolored | .25 | .50 |
| 147 | A23 | 3c shown | .25 | .50 |
| 148 | A23 | 4c multicolored | 1.75 | .25 |
| 149 | A23 | 5c multicolored | .25 | *1.25* |
| 150 | A23 | 6c multicolored | .35 | .25 |
| 151 | A23 | 10c multicolored | .35 | .50 |
| 152 | A22 | 15c multicolored | .35 | .40 |
| 153 | A23 | 20c multicolored | .35 | .45 |
| 154 | A23 | 25c multicolored | .50 | *2.00* |
| 155 | A22 | 40c multicolored | 5.00 | 1.25 |
| 156 | A22 | 60c multicolored | 4.25 | 4.25 |
| 157 | A23 | $1 multicolored | 10.00 | 8.50 |
| 158 | A23 | $2.50 multicolored | 6.00 | *11.00* |
| 159 | A23 | $5 multicolored | 18.00 | *19.00* |
| 160 | A22 | $10 multicolored | 17.00 | 20.00 |
| | | *Nos. 145-160 (16)* | 64.90 | 70.60 |

Issued: $10, 5/20/75; others 10/30/72.
For overprints see Nos. 229-246.

Common Design Types pictured following the introduction.

### Silver Wedding Issue, 1972
Common Design Type

Design: Queen Elizabeth II, Prince Philip, schooner and dolphin.

***Perf. 14x14½***

| **1972, Nov. 20** | **Photo.** | **Wmk. 314** | | |
|---|---|---|---|---|
| **161** | CD324 | 25c olive & multi | .55 | *.75* |
| **162** | CD324 | 40c maroon & multi | .55 | *.75* |

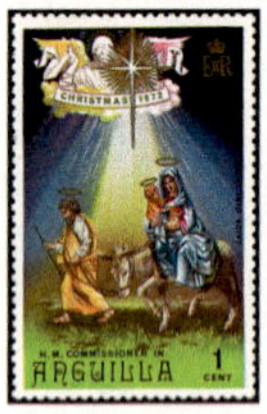


Flight into Egypt — A24

20c, Star of Bethlehem. 25c, Nativity. 40c, Three Kings. 50c, Adoration of the Kings.

***Perf. 13½***

| **1972, Dec. 4** | **Litho.** | **Unwmk.** | | |
|---|---|---|---|---|
| **163** | A24 | 1c shown | .25 | .25 |
| **164** | A24 | 20c multicolored | .25 | .25 |
| **165** | A24 | 25c multicolored | .25 | .25 |
| **166** | A24 | 40c multicolored | .25 | .25 |
| **167** | A24 | 50c multicolored | .25 | .25 |
| *a.* | | Vert. strip of 4, #164-167 | 1.40 | 1.40 |
| | | *Nos. 163-167 (5)* | 1.25 | 1.25 |

Christmas.

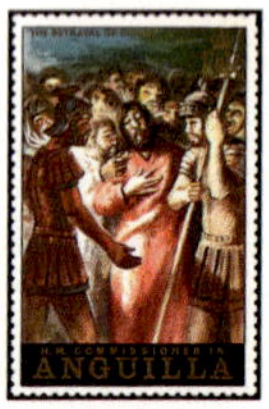


Betrayal of Jesus — A25

10c, Man of Sorrow. 20c, Jesus Carrying Cross. 25c, Crucifixion. 40c, Descent from Cross. 50c, Resurrection.

| **1973, Mar. 26** | | | | |
|---|---|---|---|---|
| **168** | A25 | 1c shown | .25 | .25 |
| **169** | A25 | 10c multicolored | .25 | .25 |
| **170** | A25 | 20c multicolored | .25 | .25 |
| **171** | A25 | 25c multicolored | .25 | .25 |
| **172** | A25 | 40c multicolored | .25 | .25 |
| **173** | A25 | 50c multicolored | .25 | .35 |
| *a.* | | Souvenir sheet of 6 | 1.10 | *1.50* |
| *b.* | | Vert. strip of 5, #169-173 | 1.00 | 1.00 |
| | | *Nos. 168-173 (6)* | 1.50 | 1.60 |

Easter. No. 173a contains 6 stamps similar to Nos. 168-173 with bottom panel in lilac rose.

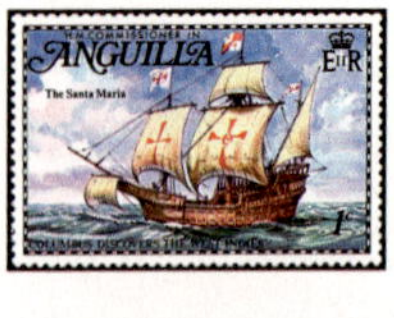


Santa Maria — A26

20c, Old West Indies map. 40c, Map of voyages. 70c, Sighting land. $1.20, Columbus landing.

| **1973, Sept. 10** | | | | |
|---|---|---|---|---|
| **174** | A26 | 1c multicolored | .25 | .25 |
| **175** | A26 | 20c multicolored | 1.60 | 1.60 |
| **176** | A26 | 40c multicolored | 1.90 | 1.90 |
| **177** | A26 | 70c multicolored | 2.00 | 2.00 |
| **178** | A26 | $1.20 multicolored | 2.75 | 2.75 |
| *a.* | | Souvenir sheet of 5, #174-178 | 8.00 | 8.00 |
| *b.* | | Horiz. strip of 4, #175-178 | 8.00 | 8.00 |
| | | *Nos. 174-178 (5)* | 8.50 | 8.50 |

Discovery of West Indies by Columbus.

### Princess Anne's Wedding Issue
Common Design Type

| **1973, Nov. 14** | **Wmk. 314** | ***Perf. 13½*** | | |
|---|---|---|---|---|
| **179** | CD325 | 60c blue grn & multi | .25 | .25 |
| **180** | CD325 | $1.20 lilac & multi | .30 | .30 |

Wedding of Princess Anne and Capt. Mark Phillips, Nov. 14, 1973.

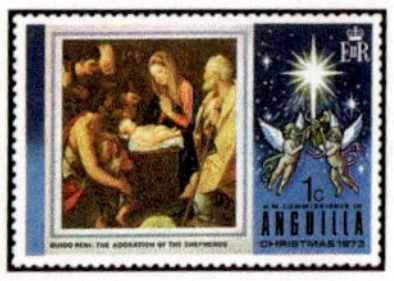


Adoration of the Shepherds, by Guido Reni — A27

Paintings: 10c, Virgin and Child, by Filippino Lippi. 20c, Nativity, by Meester Van de Brunswijkse Diptiek. 25c, Madonna of the Meadow, by Bellini. 40c, Virgin and Child, by Cima. 50c, Adoration of the Kings, by Geertgen Tot Sint Jans.

| **1973, Dec. 2** | | **Unwmk.** | | |
|---|---|---|---|---|
| **181** | A27 | 1c multicolored | .25 | .25 |
| **182** | A27 | 10c multicolored | .25 | .25 |
| **183** | A27 | 20c multicolored | .25 | .25 |
| **184** | A27 | 25c multicolored | .25 | .25 |
| **185** | A27 | 40c multicolored | .25 | .25 |
| **186** | A27 | 50c multicolored | .25 | .25 |
| *a.* | | Souvenir sheet of 6, #181-186 | 1.50 | 1.50 |
| *b.* | | Horiz. strip of 5, #182-186 | 1.00 | 1.00 |
| | | *Nos. 181-186 (6)* | 1.50 | 1.50 |

Christmas.

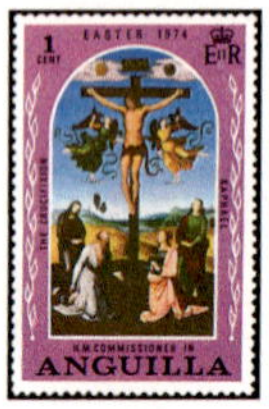


Crucifixion, by Raphael — A28

Easter (Details from Crucifixion by Raphael): 15c, Virgin Mary and St. John. 20c, The Two Marys. 25c, Left Angel. 40c, Right Angel. $1, Christ on the Cross.

| **1974, Mar. 30** | | | | |
|---|---|---|---|---|
| **187** | A28 | 1c lilac & multi | .25 | .25 |
| **188** | A28 | 15c gray & multi | .25 | .25 |
| **189** | A28 | 20c salmon & multi | .25 | .25 |
| **190** | A28 | 25c yel green & multi | .25 | .25 |
| **191** | A28 | 40c orange & multi | .25 | .25 |
| **192** | A28 | $1 lt blue & multi | .25 | .25 |
| *a.* | | Souvenir sheet of 6, #187-192 | 1.50 | *1.75* |
| *b.* | | Vert. strip of 5, #188-192 | 1.00 | 1.00 |
| | | *Nos. 187-192 (6)* | 1.50 | 1.50 |

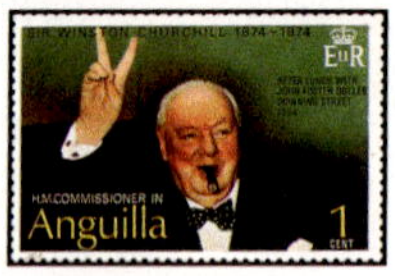


Churchill Making Victory Sign — A29

20c, Roosevelt, Churchill, US, British flags. 25c, Churchill broadcasting during the war. 40c, Blenheim Palace. 60c, Churchill Statue & Parliament. $1.20, Chartwell.

| **1974, June 24** | | | | |
|---|---|---|---|---|
| **193** | A29 | 1c multicolored | .25 | .25 |
| **194** | A29 | 20c multicolored | .25 | .25 |
| **195** | A29 | 25c multicolored | .25 | .25 |
| **196** | A29 | 40c multicolored | .30 | .30 |
| **197** | A29 | 60c multicolored | .35 | .35 |
| **198** | A29 | $1.20 multicolored | .50 | .50 |
| *a.* | | Souvenir sheet of 6, #193-198 | 1.75 | 1.75 |
| *b.* | | Horiz. strip of 5, #194-198 | 2.00 | 2.00 |
| | | *Nos. 193-198 (6)* | 1.90 | 1.90 |

Sir Winston Spencer Churchill (1874-1965).

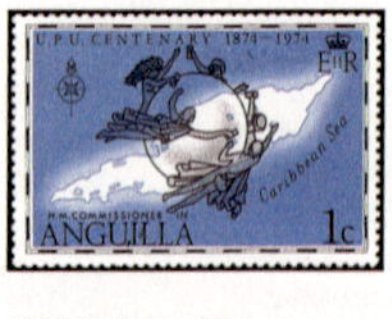


UPU Emblem, Map of Anguilla A30

| **1974, Aug. 27** | | | | |
|---|---|---|---|---|
| **199** | A30 | 1c black & ultra | .25 | .25 |
| **200** | A30 | 20c black & orange | .25 | .25 |
| **201** | A30 | 25c black & yellow | .25 | .25 |
| **202** | A30 | 40c black & brt lilac | .25 | .25 |
| **203** | A30 | 60c black & lt green | .30 | .30 |
| **204** | A30 | $1.20 black & blue | .45 | .45 |
| *a.* | | Souvenir sheet of 6 | 1.60 | *2.00* |
| *b.* | | Horiz. strip of 5, #200-204 | 1.50 | 1.50 |
| | | *Nos. 199-204 (6)* | 1.75 | 1.75 |

UPU, centenary. No. 204a contains one each of Nos. 199-204 with second row (40c, 60c, $1.20) perf. 15 at bottom.

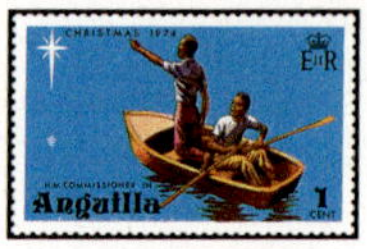


Fishermen Seeing Star — A31

Christmas: 20c, Nativity. 25c, King offering gift. 40c, Star over map of Anguilla. 60c, Family looking at star. $1.20, Two angels with star and "Peace."

| **1974, Dec. 16** | **Litho.** | ***Perf. 14½*** | | |
|---|---|---|---|---|
| **205** | A31 | 1c brt blue & multi | .25 | .25 |
| **206** | A31 | 20c dull grn & multi | .25 | .25 |
| **207** | A31 | 25c gray & multi | .25 | .25 |
| **208** | A31 | 40c car & multi | .25 | .25 |
| **209** | A31 | 60c dp blue & multi | .25 | .25 |
| **210** | A31 | $1.20 ultra & multi | .25 | .25 |
| *a.* | | Souvenir sheet of 6, #205-210 | 1.60 | *2.25* |
| *b.* | | Horiz. strip of 5, #206-210 | 1.25 | 1.25 |
| | | *Nos. 205-210 (6)* | 1.50 | 1.50 |

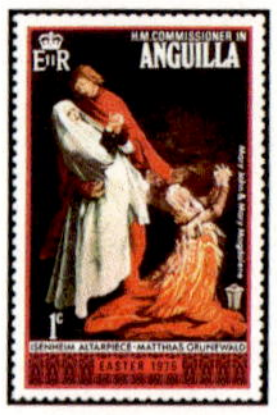


Virgin Mary, St. John, Mary Magdalene — A32

Paintings from Isenheim Altar, by Matthias Grunewald: 10c, Crucifixion. 15c, John the Baptist. 20c, St. Sebastian and Angels. $1, Burial of Christ, horiz. $1.50, St. Anthony, the Hermit.

| **1975, Mar. 25** | | ***Perf. 13½*** | | |
|---|---|---|---|---|
| **211** | A32 | 1c multicolored | .25 | .25 |
| **212** | A32 | 10c multicolored | .25 | .25 |
| **213** | A32 | 15c multicolored | .25 | .25 |
| **214** | A32 | 20c multicolored | .25 | .25 |
| **215** | A32 | $1 multicolored | .25 | *.35* |
| **216** | A32 | $1.50 multicolored | .30 | *.45* |
| *a.* | | Souvenir sheet of 6 | 1.60 | *2.00* |
| *b.* | | Horiz. strip of 5, #212-216 | 1.25 | 1.25 |
| | | *Nos. 211-216 (6)* | 1.55 | 1.80 |

Easter. No. 216a contains 6 stamps similar to Nos. 211-216 with simulated perforations.

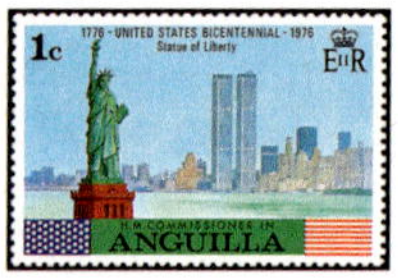


Statue of Liberty, N.Y. Skyline — A33

10c, Capitol, Washington, DC. 15c, Congress voting independence. 20c, Washington, map & his battles. $1, Boston Tea Party. $1.50, Bicentennial emblem, historic US flags.

| **1975, Nov. 10** | | | | |
|---|---|---|---|---|
| **217** | A33 | 1c multicolored | .25 | .25 |
| **218** | A33 | 10c multicolored | .25 | .25 |
| **219** | A33 | 15c multicolored | .25 | .25 |
| **220** | A33 | 20c multicolored | .25 | .25 |
| **221** | A33 | $1 multicolored | .50 | .40 |
| **222** | A33 | $1.50 multicolored | .60 | *.60* |
| *a.* | | Souvenir sheet of 6 | 1.75 | *2.50* |
| *b.* | | Horiz. strip of 5, #218-222 | 2.00 | *2.00* |
| | | *Nos. 217-222 (6)* | 2.10 | 2.00 |

American Bicentennial. No. 222a contains one each of Nos. 217-222 with second row (20c, $1, $1.50) perf. 15 at bottom.

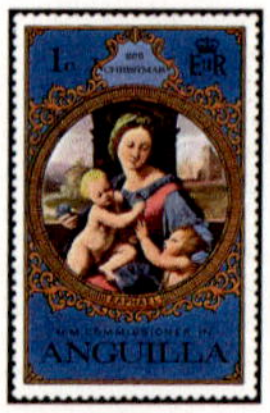


Virgin and Child with St. John, by Raphael — A34

Paintings, Virgin and Child by: 10c, Cima. 15c, Dolci. 20c, Durer. $1, Bellini. $1.50, Botticelli.

| **1975, Dec. 8** | | ***Perf. 14x13½*** | | |
|---|---|---|---|---|
| **223** | A34 | 1c ultra & multi | .25 | .25 |
| **224** | A34 | 10c Prus blue & multi | .25 | .25 |
| **225** | A34 | 15c plum & multi | .25 | .25 |
| **226** | A34 | 20c car rose & multi | .25 | .25 |
| **227** | A34 | $1 brt grn & multi | .30 | .25 |
| **228** | A34 | $1.50 blue grn & multi | .45 | .40 |
| *a.* | | Souvenir sheet of 6, #223-228 | 2.25 | *2.75* |
| *b.* | | Horiz. strip of 5, #224-228 | 1.75 | 1.50 |
| | | *Nos. 223-228 (6)* | 1.75 | 1.65 |

Christmas.

### Nos. 145-146, 148, 150-160 Surcharged and/or Overprinted

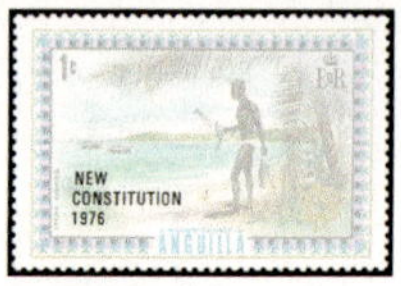


(a)

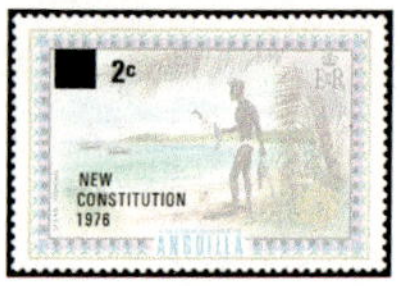


(b)

| **1976** | | **Litho.** | ***Perf. 13½*** | |
|---|---|---|---|---|
| **229** | A22 (a) | 1c #145 | .35 | *.50* |
| **230** | A22 (b) | 2c on 1c #145 | .35 | *.50* |
| **231** | A23 (a) | 2c #146 | 7.75 | 1.75 |
| **232** | A22 (b) | 3c on 40c #155 | .90 | .75 |
| **233** | A23 (a) | 4c #148 | 1.10 | *1.25* |
| **234** | A22 (b) | 5c on 40c #155 | .35 | *.65* |
| **235** | A23 (a) | 6c #150 | .35 | *.65* |
| **236** | A23 (b) | 10c on 20c #153 | .35 | *.65* |
| **237** | A23 (a) | 10c #151 | 8.25 | 5.50 |
| **238** | A22 (a) | 15c #152 | .35 | *1.25* |
| **239** | A23 (a) | 20c #153 | .35 | *.60* |
| **240** | A23 (a) | 25c #154 | .35 | *.60* |
| **241** | A22 (a) | 40c #155 | 1.10 | .80 |
| **242** | A22 (a) | 60c #156 | .75 | .80 |
| **243** | A23 (a) | $1 #157 | 6.75 | 2.50 |
| **244** | A23 (a) | $2.50 #158 | 2.25 | 2.50 |
| **245** | A23 (a) | $5 #159 | 8.50 | *10.00* |
| **246** | A22 (a) | $10 #160 | 3.25 | *7.00* |
| | | *Nos. 229-246 (18)* | 43.40 | 38.25 |

Nos. 229-246 exist with second "o" of "Constitution" in italic type. Value, set *$175.*

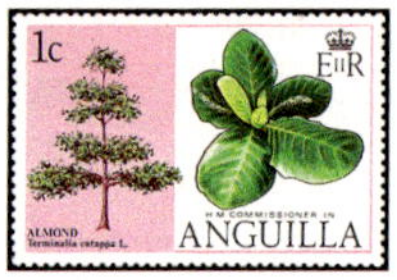


Flowering Trees — A35

| **1976, Feb. 16** | | ***Perf. 13½x14*** | | |
|---|---|---|---|---|
| **247** | A35 | 1c Almond | .25 | .25 |
| **248** | A35 | 10c Clusia rosea | .25 | .25 |
| **249** | A35 | 15c Calabash | .25 | .25 |
| **250** | A35 | 20c Cordia | .25 | .25 |
| **251** | A35 | $1 Papaya | .50 | .40 |
| **252** | A35 | $1.50 Flamboyant | .70 | .55 |
| *a.* | | Souvenir sheet of 6, #247-252 | 2.50 | 2.50 |
| *b.* | | Horiz. strip of 5, #248-252 | 2.50 | 2.50 |
| | | *Nos. 247-252 (6)* | 2.20 | 1.95 |

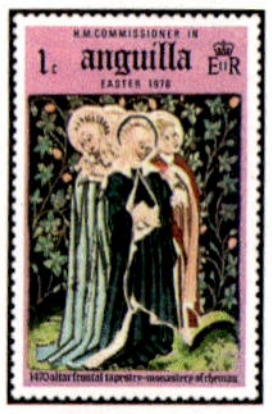


The Three Marys — A36

Designs: 10c, Crucifixion. 15c, Two soldiers. 20c, Annunciation. $1, Altar tapestry, 1470, Monastery of Rheinau, Switzerland, horiz. $1.50, "Noli me Tangere" (Jesus and Mary Magdalene). Designs of vertical stamps show details from tapestry shown on $1 stamp.

| **1976, Apr. 5** | | ***Perf. 14x13½, 13½x14*** | | |
|---|---|---|---|---|
| **253** | A36 | 1c multicolored | .25 | .25 |
| **254** | A36 | 10c multicolored | .25 | .25 |
| **255** | A36 | 15c multicolored | .25 | .25 |
| **256** | A36 | 20c multicolored | .25 | .25 |
| **257** | A36 | $1 multicolored | .45 | .45 |
| **258** | A36 | $1.50 multicolored | .55 | .55 |
| *a.* | | Souvenir sheet of 6 | 2.25 | *2.75* |
| *b.* | | Horiz. strip of 5, #254-258 | 2.25 | 2.25 |
| | | *Nos. 253-258 (6)* | 2.00 | 2.00 |

Easter. No. 258a contains 6 stamps similar to Nos. 253-258 with simulated perforations.

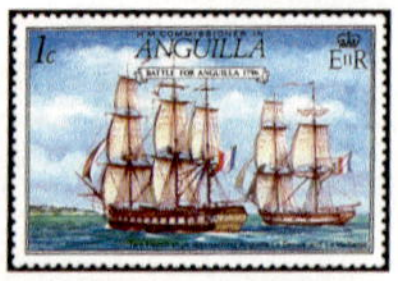


Le Desius and La Vaillante Approaching Anguilla A37

Sailing Ships: 3c, Sailboat leaving Anguilla for Antigua to get help. 15c, HMS Lapwing in battle with frigate Le Desius and brig La Vaillante. 25c, La Vaillante aground off St. Maarten. $1, Lapwing. $1.50, Le Desius burning.

**1976, Nov. 8 Litho. *Perf. 13½x14***

| | | | | |
|---|---|---|---|---|
| **259** | A37 | 1c multicolored | .25 | .25 |
| **260** | A37 | 3c multicolored | 1.40 | .50 |
| **261** | A37 | 15c multicolored | 1.50 | .70 |
| **262** | A37 | 25c multicolored | 1.50 | .95 |
| **263** | A37 | $1 multicolored | 2.00 | 1.40 |
| **264** | A37 | $1.50 multicolored | 2.25 | 1.90 |
| *a.* | | Souvenir sheet of 6, #259-264 | 7.75 | 7.75 |
| *b.* | | Strip of 5, #260-264 | 9.50 | 9.50 |
| | | *Nos. 259-264 (6)* | 8.90 | 5.70 |

Bicentenary of Battle of Anguilla between French and British ships.

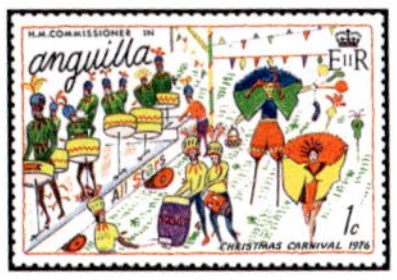

Christmas Carnival A38

Children's Paintings: 3c, 3 children dreaming of Christmas gifts. 15c, Caroling. 25c, Candlelight procession. $1, Going to Church on Christmas Eve. $1.50, Airport, coming home for Christmas.

**1976, Nov. 22**

| | | | | |
|---|---|---|---|---|
| **265** | A38 | 1c multicolored | .25 | .25 |
| **266** | A38 | 3c multicolored | .25 | .25 |
| **267** | A38 | 15c multicolored | .25 | .25 |
| **268** | A38 | 25c multicolored | .25 | .25 |
| **269** | A38 | $1 multicolored | .30 | .30 |
| **270** | A38 | $1.50 multicolored | .40 | .40 |
| *a.* | | Souvenir sheet of 6, #265-270 | 2.25 | 2.25 |
| *b.* | | Strip of 5, #266-270 | 1.75 | 1.75 |
| | | *Nos. 265-270 (6)* | 1.70 | 1.70 |

Christmas. For overprints and surcharges see Nos. 305-310a.

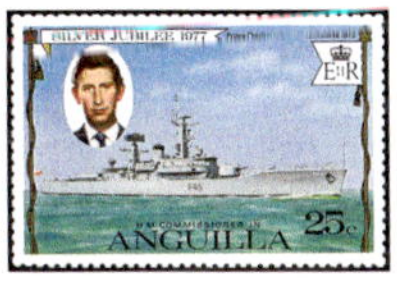

Prince Charles and HMS Minerva, 1973 — A39

Designs: 40c, Prince Philip landing at Road Bay, 1964. $1.20, Homage to Queen at Coronation. $2.50, Coronation regalia and map of Anguilla.

**1977, Feb. 9**

| | | | | |
|---|---|---|---|---|
| **271** | A39 | 25c multicolored | .25 | .25 |
| **272** | A39 | 40c multicolored | .25 | .25 |
| **273** | A39 | $1.20 multicolored | .25 | .25 |
| **274** | A39 | $2.50 multicolored | .35 | .30 |
| *a.* | | Souvenir sheet of 4, #271-274 | 1.00 | *1.50* |
| | | Complete booklet, 2 each #271-274 | 3.00 | |
| | | Complete booklet, 2 each #271-274 with vert. selvage at right | 5.00 | |
| | | *Nos. 271-274 (4)* | 1.10 | 1.05 |

25th anniv. of reign of Queen Elizabeth II.

The booklets with thin vert. selvage at right were from a separate printing.

For overprints see Nos. 297-300.

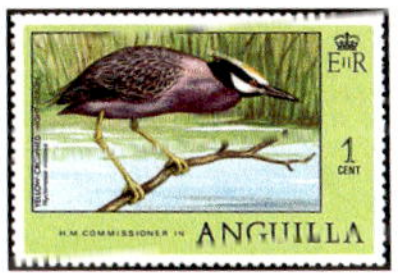

Yellow-crowned Night Heron — A40

Designs: 2c, Great barracuda. 3c, Queen conch. 4c, Spanish bayonet (Yucca). 5c, Trunkfish. 6c, Cable and telegraph building. 10c, American sparrow hawk. 15c, Ground orchids. 20c, Parlorfish. 22c, Lobster fishing boat. 35c, Boat race. 50c Sea bean (flowers). $1, Sandy Island with palms. $2.50, Manchineel (fruit). $5, Ground lizard. $10, Red-billed tropic bird.

**1977-78 Litho. *Perf. 13½x14***

| | | | | |
|---|---|---|---|---|
| **275** | A40 | 1c multicolored | .35 | *1.00* |
| **276** | A40 | 2c multicolored | .35 | *2.50* |
| **277** | A40 | 3c multicolored | 2.00 | *3.50* |
| **278** | A40 | 4c multicolored | .40 | *.70* |
| **279** | A40 | 5c multicolored | 1.75 | *.45* |
| **280** | A40 | 6c multicolored | .35 | *.45* |
| **281** | A40 | 10c multicolored | 5.50 | 4.50 |
| **282** | A40 | 15c multicolored | 3.75 | 2.00 |
| **283** | A40 | 20c multicolored | 3.75 | 1.00 |
| **284** | A40 | 22c multicolored | .60 | *1.00* |
| **285** | A40 | 35c multicolored | 1.50 | 1.00 |
| **286** | A40 | 50c multicolored | 1.00 | .90 |
| **287** | A40 | $1 multicolored | .70 | .90 |
| **288** | A40 | $2.50 multicolored | 1.10 | 1.00 |
| **289** | A40 | $5 multicolored | 2.25 | 2.25 |
| **290** | A40 | $10 multicolored | 9.00 | 6.50 |
| | | *Nos. 275-290 (16)* | 34.35 | 29.65 |

Issued: Nos. 275-280, 290, 4/18/77; others 2/20/78.

For overprints and surcharges see Nos. 319-324, 337-342, 387-390, 402-404, 407-415, 417-423.

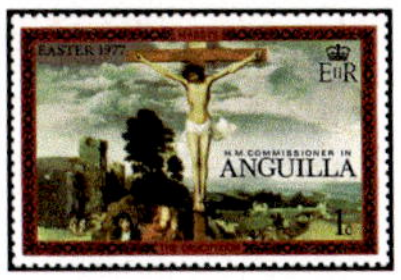

Crucifixion, by Quentin Massys A41

Easter (Paintings): 3c, Betrayal of Christ, by Ugolino. 22c, Way to Calvary, by Ugolino. 30c, The Deposition, by Ugolino. $1, Resurrection, by Ugolino. $1.50, Crucifixion, by Andrea del Castagno.

**1977, Apr. 25**

| | | | | |
|---|---|---|---|---|
| **291** | A41 | 1c multicolored | .25 | .25 |
| **292** | A41 | 3c multicolored | .25 | .25 |
| **293** | A41 | 22c multicolored | .25 | .25 |
| **294** | A41 | 30c multicolored | .35 | .30 |
| **295** | A41 | $1 multicolored | .60 | .55 |
| **296** | A41 | $1.50 multicolored | .90 | .80 |
| *a.* | | Souvenir sheet of 6, #291-296 | 2.50 | 2.50 |
| *b.* | | Strip of 5, #292-296 | 2.50 | 2.50 |
| | | *Nos. 291-296 (6)* | 2.60 | 2.40 |

**Nos. 271-274, 274a Overprinted**

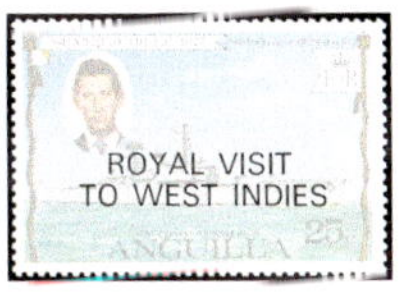


**1977, Oct. 26 Litho. *Perf. 13½x14***

| | | | | |
|---|---|---|---|---|
| **297** | A39 | 25c multicolored | .25 | .25 |
| **298** | A39 | 40c multicolored | .25 | .25 |
| **299** | A39 | $1.20 multicolored | .40 | *.50* |
| **300** | A39 | $2.50 multicolored | .75 | *1.00* |
| *a.* | | Souvenir sheet of 4 | 1.40 | *2.00* |
| | | *Nos. 297-300 (4)* | 1.65 | 2.00 |

Visit of Queen Elizabeth II to West Indies.

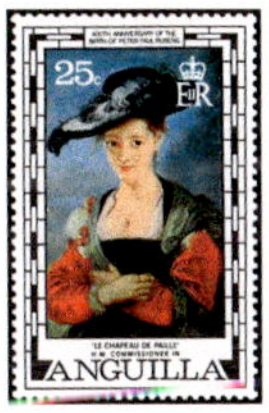

Suzanne Fourment in Velvet Hat, by Rubens — A42

Rubens Paintings: 40c, Helena Fourment with her Children. $1.20, Rubens with his wife. $2.50, Marchesa Brigida Spinola-Doria.

**1977, Nov. 1 *Perf. 14x13½***

| | | | | |
|---|---|---|---|---|
| **301** | A42 | 25c black & multi | .25 | .25 |
| **302** | A42 | 40c black & multi | .30 | .30 |
| **303** | A42 | $1.20 multicolored | .80 | .80 |
| **304** | A42 | $2.50 black & multi | 1.10 | *1.35* |
| *a.* | | Souvenir sheet of 4, #301-304 | 2.50 | *2.75* |
| | | *Nos. 301-304 (4)* | 2.45 | 2.70 |

Peter Paul Rubens, 400th birth anniv. Nos. 301-304 printed in sheets of 5 stamps and blue label with Rubens' portrait.

For overprint, see Nos. 311-314.

**Nos. 265-270b Ovptd. & Srchd.**

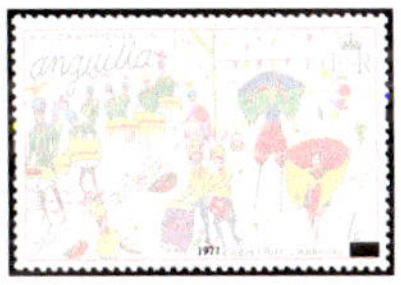

**1977, Nov. 7 *Perf. 13½x14***

| | | | | |
|---|---|---|---|---|
| **305** | A38 | 1c multicolored | .25 | .25 |
| **306** | A38 | 5c on 3c multi | .25 | .25 |
| **307** | A38 | 12c on 15c multi | .25 | .25 |
| **308** | A38 | 18c on 25c multi | .30 | .30 |
| **309** | A38 | $1 multicolored | .60 | .60 |
| **310** | A38 | $2.50 on $1.50 multi | 1.25 | 1.25 |
| *a.* | | Souvenir sheet of 6, #305-310 | 3.50 | 3.50 |
| *b.* | | Strip of 5, #306-310 | 3.00 | 3.00 |
| | | *Nos. 305-310 (6)* | 2.90 | 2.90 |

Christmas. Stamps and souvenir sheets have "1976" and old denomination obliterated with variously shaped rectangles.

Nos. 301-304a Ovptd. in Gold

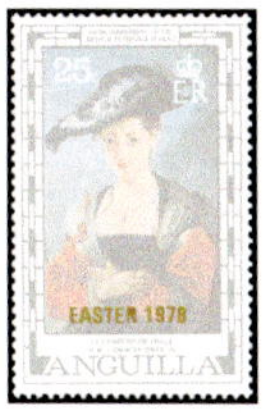


**1978, Mar. 6 *Perf. 14x13½***

| | | | | |
|---|---|---|---|---|
| **311** | A42 | 25c black & multi | .25 | .25 |
| **312** | A42 | 40c black & multi | .25 | .25 |
| **313** | A42 | $1.20 black & multi | .60 | .60 |
| **314** | A42 | $2.50 black & multi | .70 | .70 |
| *a.* | | Souvenir sheet of 4, #311-314 | 2.25 | *2.50* |
| | | *Nos. 311-314 (4)* | 1.80 | 1.80 |

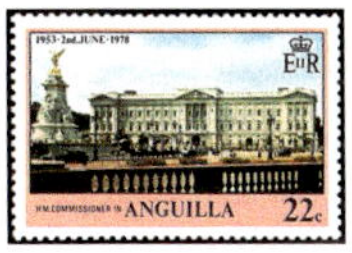

Buckingham Palace — A43

Designs: 50c, Coronation procession. $1.50, Royal family on balcony. $2.50, Royal coat of arms.

**1978, Apr. 6 *Perf. 14***

| | | | | |
|---|---|---|---|---|
| **315** | A43 | 22c multicolored | .25 | .25 |
| **316** | A43 | 50c multicolored | .25 | .25 |
| **317** | A43 | $1.50 multicolored | .40 | .40 |
| **318** | A43 | $2.50 multicolored | .60 | .60 |
| *a.* | | Souvenir sheet of 4, #315-318 | 1.60 | 1.60 |
| | | Complete booklet, 2 each #315-318 | 3.25 | |
| | | Complete booklet, 2 each #315-318 with thin vert. selvage at right | 4.00 | |
| | | *Nos. 315-318 (4)* | 1.50 | 1.50 |

25th anniv. of coronation of Queen Elizabeth II.

The booklets with thin vert. selvage at right were from a separate printing.

**Nos. 284-285 and 288 Ovptd. and Surcharged**

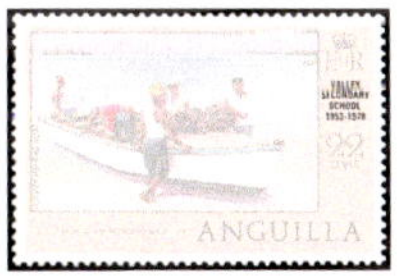

**1978, Aug. 14 Litho. *Perf. 13½x14***

| | | | | |
|---|---|---|---|---|
| **319** | A40 | 22c multicolored | .50 | .50 |
| **320** | A40 | 35c multicolored | .70 | .70 |
| **321** | A40 | $1.50 on $2.50 multi | 1.30 | 1.30 |
| | | *Nos. 319-321 (3)* | 2.50 | 2.50 |

Valley Secondary School, 25th anniv. Surcharge on No. 321 includes heavy bar over old denomination.

**Nos. 286-287, 289 Ovptd. and Surcharged**

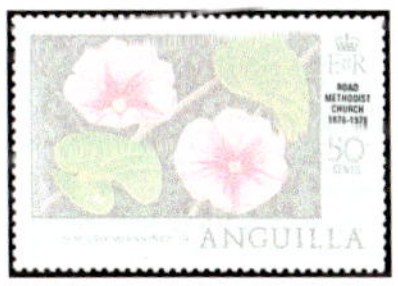

**1978, Aug. 14**

| | | | | |
|---|---|---|---|---|
| **322** | A40 | 50c multicolored | 1.00 | 1.00 |
| **323** | A40 | $1 multicolored | 1.25 | 1.25 |
| **324** | A40 | $1.20 on $5 multi | 2.00 | 2.00 |
| | | *Nos. 322-324 (3)* | 4.25 | 4.25 |

Road Methodist Church, centenary. Surcharge on No. 324 includes heavy bar over old denomination.

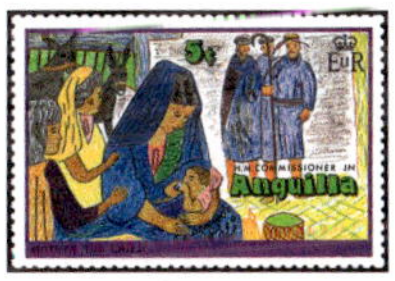

Mother and Child — A44

Christmas: 12c, Christmas masquerade. 18c, Christmas dinner. 22c, Serenade. $1, Star over manger. $2.50, Family going to church.

**1978, Dec. 11 Litho. *Perf. 13½***

| | | | | |
|---|---|---|---|---|
| **325** | A44 | 5c multicolored | .25 | .25 |
| **326** | A44 | 12c multicolored | .25 | .25 |
| **327** | A44 | 18c multicolored | .25 | .25 |
| **328** | A44 | 22c multicolored | .25 | .25 |
| **329** | A44 | $1 multicolored | .30 | .30 |
| **330** | A44 | $2.50 multicolored | .60 | .60 |
| *a.* | | Souvenir sheet of 6, #325-330 | 2.00 | *2.25* |
| | | *Nos. 325-330 (6)* | 1.90 | 1.90 |

**Type A44 in Changed Colors with IYC Emblem and Inscription**

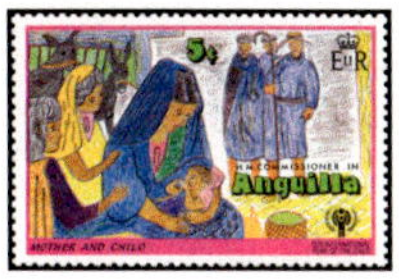

**1979, Jan. 15 Litho. *Perf. 13½***

| | | | | |
|---|---|---|---|---|
| **331** | A44 | 5c multicolored | .25 | .25 |
| **332** | A44 | 12c multicolored | .25 | .25 |
| **333** | A44 | 18c multicolored | .25 | .25 |
| **334** | A44 | 22c multicolored | .25 | .25 |
| **335** | A44 | $1 multicolored | .30 | .30 |
| **336** | A44 | $2.50 multicolored | .50 | .50 |
| *a.* | | Souvenir sheet of 6, #331-336 | 2.75 | *3.25* |
| | | *Nos. 331-336 (6)* | 1.80 | 1.80 |

Intl. Year of the Child. For overprint see No. 416

**Nos. 275-278, 280-281 Surcharged**

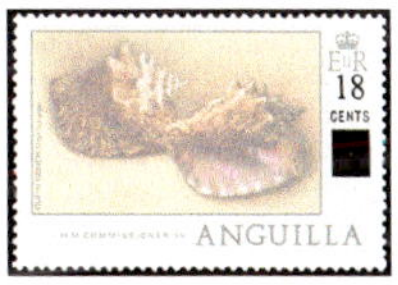

**1979, Feb. 8 Litho. *Perf. 13½x14***

| | | | | |
|---|---|---|---|---|
| **337** | A40 | 12c on 2c multi | *.60* | *.50* |
| **338** | A40 | 14c on 4c multi | *.50* | *.60* |
| **339** | A40 | 18c on 3c multi | *1.10* | *.90* |
| **340** | A40 | 25c on 6c multi | *.70* | *.55* |
| **341** | A40 | 38c on 10c multi | *2.75* | *1.10* |
| **342** | A40 | 40c on 1c multi | *3.00* | *1.10* |
| | | *Nos. 337-342 (6)* | 8.65 | 4.75 |

No. 338 exists with surcharge inverted. Value, *$30*.

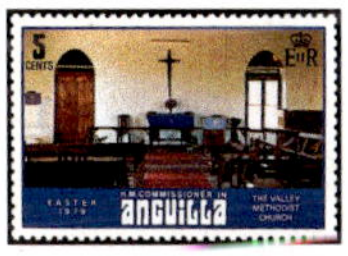

Valley Methodist Church — A45

Church Interiors: 12c, St. Mary's Anglican Church, The Valley. 18c, St. Gerard's Roman Catholic Church, The Valley. 22c, Road Methodist Church. $1.50, St. Augustine's Anglican Church, East End. $2.50, West End Methodist Church.

**1979, Mar. 30 Litho. *Perf. 14***

| | | | | |
|---|---|---|---|---|
| **343** | A45 | 5c multicolored | .25 | .25 |
| **344** | A45 | 12c multicolored | .25 | .25 |
| **345** | A45 | 18c multicolored | .25 | .25 |
| **346** | A45 | 22c multicolored | .25 | .25 |
| **347** | A45 | $1.50 multicolored | .40 | .40 |
| **348** | A45 | $2.50 multicolored | .60 | .60 |
| *a.* | | Souvenir sheet of 6 | 2.25 | 2.25 |
| *b.* | | Strip of 6, #343-348 | 2.00 | 2.00 |
| | | *Nos. 343-348 (6)* | 2.00 | 2.00 |

Easter. No. 348a contains Nos. 343-348 in 2 horizontal rows of 3.

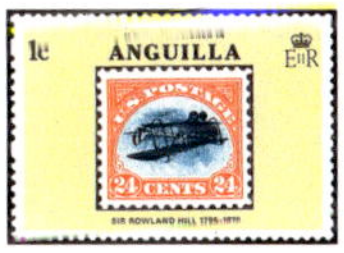

US No. C3a — A46

No. 350, Cape of Good Hope #1. No. 351, Penny Black. No. 352, Germany #C36. No. 353, US #245. No. 354, Great Britain #93.

**1979, Apr. 23 Litho. *Perf. 14***

| | | | | |
|---|---|---|---|---|
| **349** | A46 | 1c multicolored | .25 | .25 |
| **350** | A46 | 1c multicolored | .25 | .25 |
| **351** | A46 | 22c multicolored | .25 | .25 |
| **352** | A46 | 35c multicolored | .25 | .25 |
| **353** | A46 | $1.50 multicolored | .50 | .50 |

| | | | | |
|---|---|---|---|---|
| **354** | A46 | $2.50 multicolored | .75 | .75 |
| *a.* | | Souvenir sheet of 6, #349-353 | 2.00 | *2.75* |
| | | Complete booklet, 2 each #349-354 | 4.50 | |
| | | *Nos. 349-354 (6)* | 2.25 | 2.25 |

Sir Rowland Hill (1795-1879), originator of penny postage.

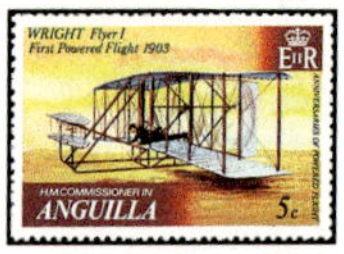

Wright's Flyer A — A47

History of Aviation: 12c, Louis Bleriot landing at Dover, 1909. 18c, Vickers Vimy, 1919. 22c, Spirit of St. Louis, 1927. $1.50, LZ127 Graf Zeppelin, 1928. $2.50, Concorde, 1979.

**1979, May 21 Litho. *Perf. 14***

| | | | | |
|---|---|---|---|---|
| **355** | A47 | 5c multicolored | .25 | .25 |
| **356** | A47 | 12c multicolored | .30 | .25 |
| **357** | A47 | 18c multicolored | .35 | .25 |
| **358** | A47 | 22c multicolored | .40 | .30 |
| **359** | A47 | $1.50 multicolored | .95 | .95 |
| **360** | A47 | $2.50 multicolored | 3.50 | 1.50 |
| *a.* | | Souvenir sheet of 6, #355-360 | 6.50 | 6.50 |
| | | *Nos. 355-360 (6)* | 5.75 | 3.50 |

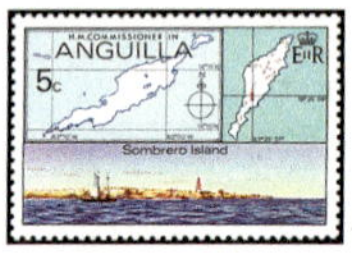

Map of Anguilla, Map and View of Sombrero Island — A48

Map of Anguilla, Map and View of: 12c, Anguillita Island. 18c, Sandy Island. 25c, Prickly Pear Cays. $1, Dog Island. $2.50, Scrub Island.

**1979 Litho. *Perf. 14***

| | | | | |
|---|---|---|---|---|
| **361** | A48 | 5c multicolored | .25 | .25 |
| **362** | A48 | 12c multicolored | .25 | .25 |
| **363** | A48 | 18c multicolored | .25 | .25 |
| **364** | A48 | 25c multicolored | .25 | .25 |
| **365** | A48 | $1 multicolored | .45 | *.55* |
| **366** | A48 | $2.50 multicolored | .70 | *.95* |
| *a.* | | Souvenir sheet of 6, #361-366 | 3.00 | 3.00 |
| | | *Nos. 361-366 (6)* | 2.15 | 2.50 |

Anguilla's Outer Islands.

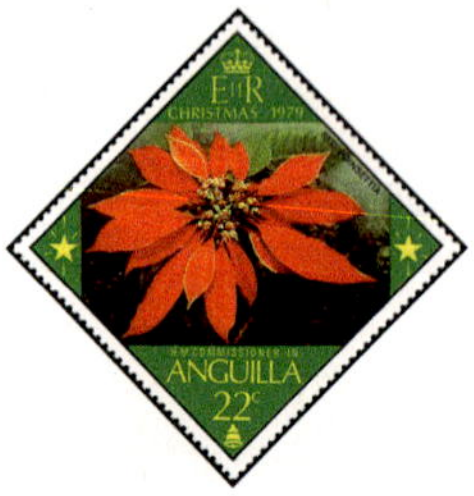

Red Poinsettia — A49

35c, Kalanchoe. $1.50, Cream poinsettia. $2.50, White poinsettia.

**1979, Oct. 22 Litho. *Perf. 14½***

| | | | | |
|---|---|---|---|---|
| **367** | A49 | 22c shown | .25 | .25 |
| **368** | A49 | 35c multicolored | .25 | .25 |
| **369** | A49 | $1.50 multicolored | .40 | .40 |
| **370** | A49 | $2.50 multicolored | .65 | .65 |
| *a.* | | Souvenir sheet of 4, #367-370 | 2.50 | 2.50 |
| | | *Nos. 367-370 (4)* | 1.55 | 1.55 |

Christmas.

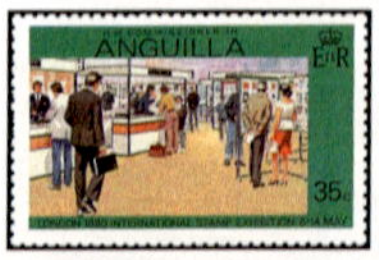

Booths and Frames — A50

Designs: 50c, Earls Court Exhibition Hall. $1.50, Penny Black, Great Britain #2. $2.50, Exhibition emblem.

**1979, Dec. 10 Litho. *Perf. 13***

| | | | | |
|---|---|---|---|---|
| **371** | A50 | 35c multicolored | .25 | .25 |
| **372** | A50 | 50c multicolored | .25 | .25 |
| **373** | A50 | $1.50 multicolored | .40 | .40 |
| **374** | A50 | $2.50 multicolored | .70 | .70 |
| *b.* | | Souvenir sheet of 4, #371-374 | 1.75 | 1.75 |
| | | Complete booklet, 2 each #371-374 | 4.00 | |
| | | *Nos. 371-374 (4)* | 1.60 | 1.60 |

***Perf. 14½***

| | | | | |
|---|---|---|---|---|
| *371a* | A50 | 35c | .25 | .25 |
| *372a* | A50 | 50c | .25 | .25 |
| *373a* | A50 | $1.50 | .45 | .45 |
| *374a* | A50 | $2.50 | .80 | .80 |
| *c.* | | Souvenir sheet of 4, #371-374 | 2.00 | 2.00 |
| | | *Nos. 371a-374a (4)* | 1.75 | 1.75 |

London 1980 Intl. Stamp Exhibition, May 6-14, 1980.

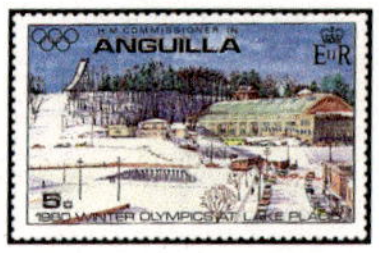

Lake Placid and Olympic Rings — A51

Olympic Rings and: 18c, Ice Hockey. 35c, Figure skating. 50c, Bobsledding. $1, Downhill skiing. $2.50, Luge.

**1980, Jan. Litho. *Perf. 13½, 14½***

| | | | | |
|---|---|---|---|---|
| **375** | A51 | 5c multicolored | .25 | .25 |
| **376** | A51 | 18c multicolored | .25 | .25 |
| **377** | A51 | 35c multicolored | .25 | .25 |
| **378** | A51 | 50c multicolored | .30 | .25 |
| **379** | A51 | $1 multicolored | .45 | *.65* |
| **380** | A51 | $2.50 multicolored | .80 | *1.10* |
| *a.* | | Souvenir sheet of 6, #375-380 | 2.25 | *3.00* |
| | | *Nos. 375-380 (6)* | 2.30 | 2.75 |

13th Winter Olympic Games, Lake Placid, NY, Feb. 12-24.

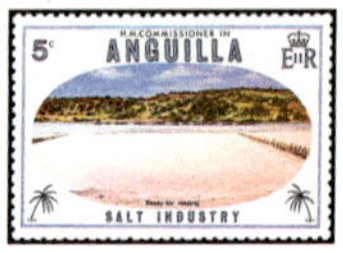

Salt Field — A52

12c, Tallying salt. 18c, Unloading salt flats. 22c, Storage pile. $1, Bagging and grinding. $2.50, Loading onto boats.

**1980, Apr. 14 Litho. *Perf. 14***

| | | | | |
|---|---|---|---|---|
| **381** | A52 | 5c multicolored | .25 | .25 |
| **382** | A52 | 12c multicolored | .25 | .25 |
| **383** | A52 | 18c multicolored | .25 | .25 |
| **384** | A52 | 22c multicolored | .25 | .25 |
| **385** | A52 | $1 multicolored | .40 | .40 |
| **386** | A52 | $2.50 multicolored | .85 | .85 |
| *a.* | | Souvenir sheet of 6, #381-386 | 2.25 | 2.25 |
| | | *Nos. 381-386 (6)* | 2.25 | 2.25 |

Salt industry.

**Nos. 281, 288 Overprinted**

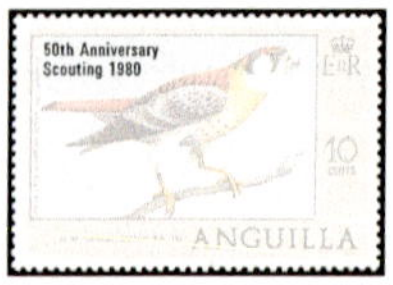

**1980, Apr. 16 *Perf. 13½x14***

| | | | | |
|---|---|---|---|---|
| **387** | A40 | 10c multicolored | 3.25 | .30 |
| **388** | A40 | $2.50 multicolored | 3.25 | 2.00 |

**Nos. 283, 289 Overprinted**

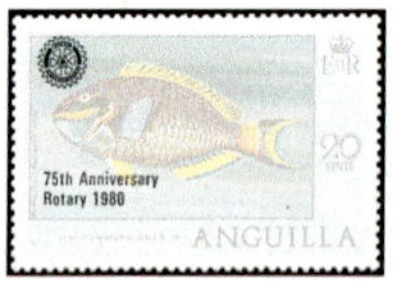

**1980, Apr. 16 *Perf. 13½x14***

| | | | | |
|---|---|---|---|---|
| **389** | A40 | 20c multicolored | 2.50 | .30 |
| **390** | A40 | $5 multicolored | 5.00 | 3.00 |

Rotary International, 75th anniversary.

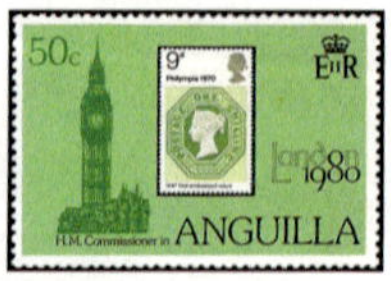

Big Ben, Great Britain No. 643, London 1980 Emblem A53

Designs: $1.50, Canada No. 756. $2.50, Statue of Liberty, US No. 1632.

**1980, May**

| | | | | |
|---|---|---|---|---|
| **391** | A53 | 50c multicolored | .45 | .45 |
| **392** | A53 | $1.50 multicolored | .65 | .65 |
| **393** | A53 | $2.50 multicolored | 1.15 | 1.15 |
| *a.* | | Souvenir sheet of 3, #391-393 | 2.25 | 2.25 |
| | | *Nos. 391-393 (3)* | 2.25 | 2.25 |

London 1980 International Stamp Exhibition, May 6-14.

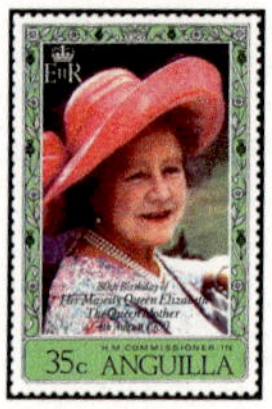

Queen Mother Elizabeth, 80th Birthday — A54

**1980, Aug. 4 Litho. *Perf. 14***

| | | | | |
|---|---|---|---|---|
| **394** | A54 | 35c multicolored | .55 | .35 |
| **395** | A54 | 50c multicolored | .70 | .40 |
| **396** | A54 | $1.50 multicolored | 1.25 | 1.00 |
| **397** | A54 | $3 multicolored | 1.50 | 1.50 |
| *a.* | | Souvenir sheet of 4, #394-397 | 5.00 | 4.25 |
| | | *Nos. 394-397 (4)* | 4.00 | 3.25 |

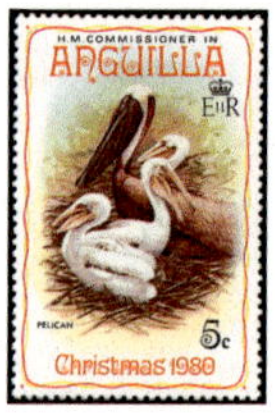

Pelicans — A55

22c, Great gray herons. $1.50, Swallows. $3, Hummingbirds.

**1980, Nov. 10 Litho. *Perf. 14***

| | | | | |
|---|---|---|---|---|
| **398** | A55 | 5c multicolored | .40 | .25 |
| **399** | A55 | 22c multicolored | 1.10 | .30 |
| **400** | A55 | $1.50 multicolored | 2.40 | .95 |
| **401** | A55 | $3 multicolored | 3.00 | 2.10 |
| *a.* | | Souvenir sheet of 4, #398-401 | 12.00 | 12.00 |
| | | *Nos. 398-401 (4)* | 6.90 | 3.60 |

Christmas. For overprints see Nos. 405-406.

**Nos. 275, 278, 280-290, 334, 400-401 Overprinted**

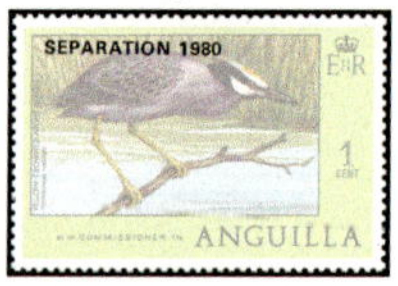

***Perf. 13½x14, 14 (A55)***

**1980, Dec. 18 Litho.**

| | | | | |
|---|---|---|---|---|
| **402** | A40 | 1c #275 | .25 | .80 |
| **403** | A40 | 2c on 4c #278 | .25 | .80 |
| **404** | A40 | 5c on 15c #282 | 1.25 | .80 |
| **405** | A55 | 5c on $1.50 #400 | 1.25 | .80 |
| **406** | A55 | 5c on $3 #401 | 1.25 | .80 |
| **407** | A40 | 10c #281 | 1.90 | .80 |
| **408** | A40 | 12c on $1 #287 | .30 | .80 |
| **409** | A40 | 14c on $2.50 #288 | .30 | .80 |
| **410** | A40 | 15c #282 | 1.50 | .80 |
| **411** | A40 | 18c on $5 #289 | .35 | .80 |
| **412** | A40 | 20c #283 | .35 | .80 |
| **413** | A40 | 22c #284 | .35 | .80 |
| **414** | A40 | 25c on 15c #282 | 1.50 | .95 |
| **415** | A40 | 35c #285 | .40 | *.95* |
| **416** | A44 | 38c on 22c #334 | .40 | *.95* |
| **417** | A40 | 40c on 1c #275 | .40 | *.95* |
| **418** | A40 | 50c #286 | .45 | *1.10* |
| **419** | A40 | $1 #287 | .60 | *1.40* |
| **420** | A40 | $2.50 #288 | 1.50 | *3.50* |
| **421** | A40 | $5 #289 | 2.75 | *4.50* |
| **422** | A40 | $10 #290 | 5.50 | *6.50* |
| **423** | A40 | $10 on 6c #280 | 5.50 | *6.50* |
| | | *Nos. 402-423 (22)* | 28.30 | 36.90 |

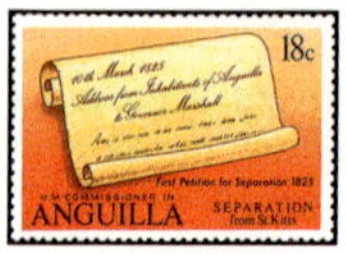

Petition for Separation, 1825 — A56

22c, Referendum ballot, 1967. 35c, Airport blockade, 1967. 50c, Anguilla flag. $1, Separation celebration, 1980.

**1980, Dec. 18 *Perf. 14***

| | | | | |
|---|---|---|---|---|
| **424** | A56 | 18c multicolored | .25 | .25 |
| **425** | A56 | 22c multicolored | .25 | .25 |
| **426** | A56 | 35c multicolored | .30 | .30 |
| **427** | A56 | 50c multicolored | .35 | .35 |
| **428** | A56 | $1 multicolored | .60 | *.80* |
| *a.* | | Souvenir sheet of 5, #424-428 | 1.75 | *2.00* |
| | | *Nos. 424-428 (5)* | 1.75 | 1.95 |

Separation from St. Kitts-Nevis.

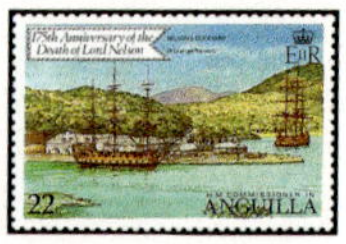

Nelson's Dockyard, by R. Granger Barrett — A57

Ship Paintings: 35c, Agamemnon, Vanguard, Elephant, Captain and Victory, by Nicholas Pocock. 50c, Victory, by Monamy Swaine. $3, Battle of Trafalgar, by Clarkson Stanfield. $5, Lord Nelson, by L.F. Abbott and Nelson's arms.

**1981, Mar. 2 Litho. *Perf. 14***

| | | | | |
|---|---|---|---|---|
| **429** | A57 | 22c multicolored | 2.10 | .90 |
| **430** | A57 | 35c multicolored | 2.40 | 1.25 |
| **431** | A57 | 50c multicolored | 2.75 | 1.50 |
| **432** | A57 | $3 multicolored | 3.75 | *5.50* |
| | | *Nos. 429-432 (4)* | 11.00 | 9.15 |

**Souvenir Sheet**

| | | | | |
|---|---|---|---|---|
| **433** | A57 | $5 multicolored | 4.75 | 4.75 |

Lord Horatio Nelson (1758-1805), 175th death anniversary (1980).

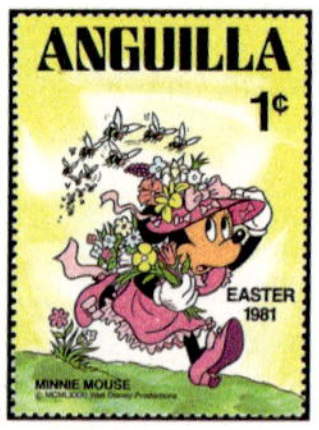

Minnie Mouse — A58

Easter: Various Disney characters in Easter outfits.

**1981, Mar. 30 Litho. *Perf. 13½***

| | | | | |
|---|---|---|---|---|
| **434** | A58 | 1c multicolored | .25 | .25 |
| **435** | A58 | 2c multicolored | .25 | .25 |
| **436** | A58 | 3c multicolored | .25 | .25 |
| **437** | A58 | 5c multicolored | .25 | .25 |
| **438** | A58 | 7c multicolored | .25 | .25 |
| **439** | A58 | 9c multicolored | .25 | .25 |
| **440** | A58 | 10c multicolored | .25 | .25 |
| **441** | A58 | $2 multicolored | 1.50 | 1.50 |
| **442** | A58 | $3 multicolored | 2.00 | 2.00 |
| | | *Nos. 434-442 (9)* | 5.25 | 5.25 |

**Souvenir Sheet**

| | | | | |
|---|---|---|---|---|
| **443** | A58 | $5 multicolored | 5.50 | 5.50 |

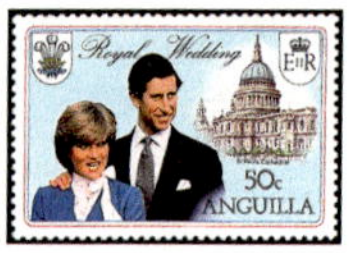

Prince Charles, Lady Diana, St. Paul's Cathedral — A59

$2.50, Althorp. $3, Windsor Castle. $5, Buckingham Palace.

**1981, June 15 Litho. *Perf. 14***

| | | | | |
|---|---|---|---|---|
| **444** | A59 | 50c shown | .25 | .25 |
| *a.* | | Souvenir sheet of 2 | .30 | .30 |
| *b.* | | Wmk. 380 | .25 | .25 |
| *c.* | | Booklet pane of 4 #444b | 1.00 | 1.00 |
| **445** | A59 | $2.50 multicolored | .45 | .60 |
| *a.* | | Souvenir sheet of 2 | 1.60 | 1.60 |
| **446** | A59 | $3 multicolored | .55 | .75 |
| *a.* | | Souvenir sheet of 2 | 2.00 | 2.00 |
| *b.* | | Wmk. 380 | 1.25 | 1.25 |
| *c.* | | Booklet pane of 4 #446b | 5.00 | 5.00 |
| | | Complete booklet, #444c, 446c | 6.00 | |
| | | *Nos. 444-446 (3)* | 1.25 | 1.60 |

**Souvenir Sheet**

| | | | | |
|---|---|---|---|---|
| **447** | A59 | $5 multicolored | 1.50 | 1.50 |

Royal Wedding. Nos. 444a-446a contain stamps in different colors.

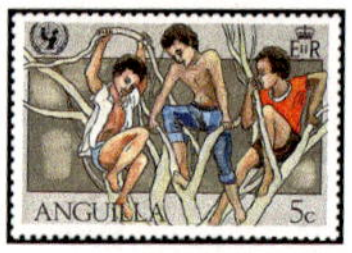

Boys Climbing Tree — A60

10c, Boys sailing boats. 15c, Children playing instruments. $3, Children with animals. $4, Boys playing soccer, vert.

**1981 Litho. *Perf. 14***

| | | | | |
|---|---|---|---|---|
| **448** | A60 | 5c multicolored | .25 | .25 |
| **449** | A60 | 10c multicolored | .30 | .30 |
| **450** | A60 | 15c multicolored | .40 | *.45* |
| **451** | A60 | $3 multicolored | 2.75 | *3.50* |
| | | *Nos. 448-451 (4)* | 3.70 | 4.50 |

**Souvenir Sheet**

| | | | | |
|---|---|---|---|---|
| **452** | A60 | $4 multicolored | 4.25 | 4.25 |

UNICEF, 35th anniv.
Issued: 5c-15c, July 31; $3-$4, Sept. 30.

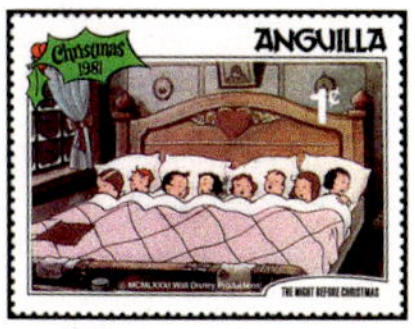


"The Children were Nestled all Snug in their Beds" — A61

Christmas: Scenes from Walt Disney's The Night Before Christmas.

**1981, Nov. 2 Litho. *Perf. 13½***

| | | | | |
|---|---|---|---|---|
| **453** A61 | 1c multicolored | .25 | .25 |
| **454** A61 | 2c multicolored | .25 | .25 |
| **455** A61 | 3c multicolored | .25 | .25 |
| **456** A61 | 5c multicolored | .30 | .25 |
| **457** A61 | 7c multicolored | .30 | .25 |
| **458** A61 | 10c multicolored | .30 | .25 |
| **459** A61 | 12c multicolored | .30 | .25 |
| **460** A61 | $2 multicolored | 3.25 | 2.10 |
| **461** A61 | $3 multicolored | 3.25 | 2.50 |
| | *Nos. 453-461 (9)* | 8.45 | 6.35 |

**Souvenir Sheet**

| | | | |
|---|---|---|---|
| **462** A61 | $5 multicolored | 7.00 | 7.00 |

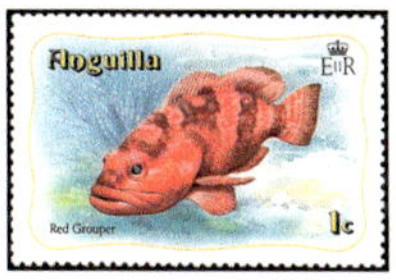


Red Grouper A62

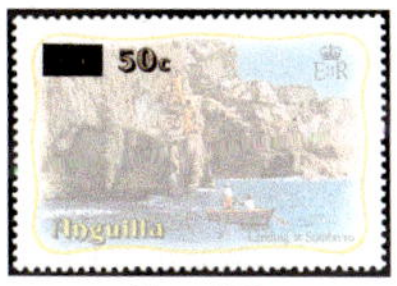

No. 473

5c, Ferries, Blowing Point. 10c, Racing boats. 15c, Majorettes. 20c, Launching boat, Sandy Hill. 25c, Coral. 30c, Little Bay cliffs. 35c, Fountain Cave. 40c, Sandy Isld. 45c, Landing, Sombrero. 60c, Seine fishing. 75c, Boat race, Sandy Ground. $1, Bagging lobster, Island Harbor. $5, Pelicans. $7.50, Hibiscus. $10, Queen triggerfish.

**1982, Jan. 1 Litho. *Perf. 14***

| | | | |
|---|---|---|---|
| **463** A62 | 1c multi | .25 | *.90* |
| **464** A62 | 5c multi | .35 | *.90* |
| **465** A62 | 10c multi | .25 | *.00* |
| **466** A62 | 15c multi | .25 | *.90* |
| **467** A62 | 20c multi | .45 | *.90* |
| **468** A62 | 25c multi | 1.75 | .90 |
| **469** A62 | 30c multi | .35 | *1.10* |
| **470** A62 | 35c multi | 1.75 | 1.25 |
| **471** A62 | 40c multi | .35 | *1.10* |
| **472** A62 | 45c multi | .55 | *1.25* |
| **473** A62 | 50c on 45c, #472 | .60 | .55 |
| **474** A62 | 60c multi | 3.50 | 3.50 |
| **475** A62 | 75c multi | 1.10 | *2.50* |
| **476** A62 | $1 multi | 2.50 | 2.50 |
| **477** A62 | $5 multi | 18.00 | 18.00 |
| **478** A62 | $7.50 multi | 14.00 | *20.00* |
| **479** A62 | $10 multi | 18.00 | *20.00* |
| | *Nos. 463-479 (17)* | 64.00 | *77.15* |

For overprints & surcharges see Nos. 507-510, 546A-546D, 578-582, 606-608, 640-647.

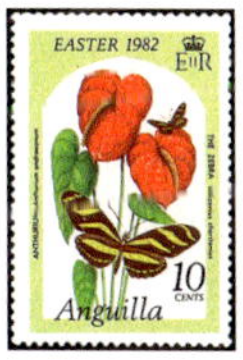


Easter — A63

Butterflies on flowers: 10c, Zebra, anthurium. 35c, Caribbean buckeye. 75c, Monarch, allamanda. $3, Red rim, orchid. $5, Flambeau, amaryllis.

**1982, Apr. 5**

| | | | |
|---|---|---|---|
| **480** A63 | 10c multicolored | 1.00 | .25 |
| **481** A63 | 35c multicolored | 1.75 | .55 |
| **482** A63 | 75c multicolored | 2.00 | .80 |
| **483** A63 | $3 multicolored | 3.50 | 2.40 |
| | *Nos. 480-483 (4)* | 8.25 | 4.00 |

**Souvenir Sheet**

| | | | |
|---|---|---|---|
| **484** A63 | $5 multicolored | 5.75 | 5.75 |

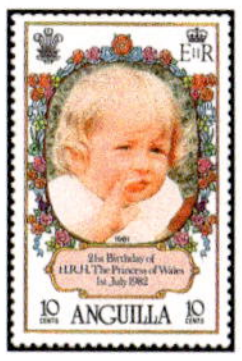


Princess Diana, 21st Birthday — A64

Designs: Portraits, 1961-1981.

**1982, May 17**

| | | | |
|---|---|---|---|
| **485** A64 | 10c 1961 | .60 | .25 |
| **486** A64 | 30c 1968 | 1.35 | .25 |
| **487** A64 | 40c 1970 | .70 | .30 |
| **488** A64 | 60c 1974 | .70 | .40 |
| **489** A64 | $2 1981 | 1.10 | 1.50 |
| **490** A64 | $3 1981 | 5.00 | 2.10 |
| *a.* | Souvenir sheet of 6, #485-490 | 9.75 | 9.75 |
| | Complete booklet, 4 each #485, 487-489 | 10.00 | |
| | *Nos. 485-490 (6)* | 9.45 | 4.80 |

**Souvenir Sheet**

| | | | |
|---|---|---|---|
| **491** A64 | $5 1981 | 9.75 | 9.75 |

For overprints see Nos. 639A-639G.

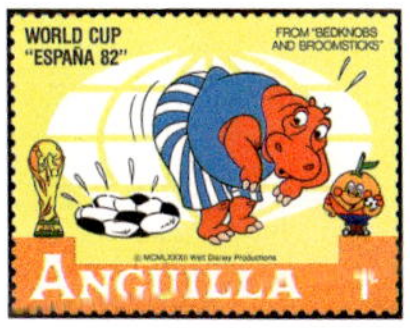


1982 World Cup — A65

Various Disney characters playing soccer.

**1982, Aug. 3 Litho. *Perf. 11***

| | | | |
|---|---|---|---|
| **492** A65 | 1c multicolored | .25 | .25 |
| **493** A65 | 3c multicolored | .25 | .25 |
| **494** A65 | 4c multicolored | .25 | .25 |
| **495** A65 | 5c multicolored | .25 | .25 |
| **496** A65 | 7c multicolored | .25 | .25 |
| **497** A65 | 9c multicolored | .25 | .25 |
| **498** A65 | 10c multicolored | .25 | .25 |
| **499** A65 | $2.50 multicolored | 2.50 | 2.25 |
| **500** A65 | $3 multicolored | 2.50 | 2.25 |
| | *Nos. 492-500 (9)* | 6.75 | 6.25 |

**Souvenir Sheet**

***Perf. 14***

| | | | |
|---|---|---|---|
| **501** A65 | $5 multicolored | 8.00 | 8.00 |

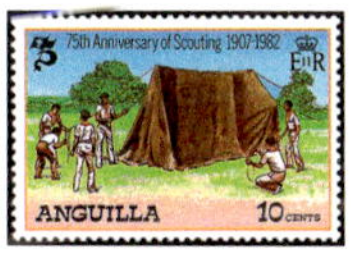


Scouting Year — A66

**1982, July 5**

| | | | |
|---|---|---|---|
| **502** A66 | 10c Pitching tent | .60 | .50 |
| **503** A66 | 35c Marching band | 1.00 | .70 |
| **504** A66 | 75c Sailing | 1.40 | 1.25 |
| **505** A66 | $3 Flag bearers | 3.75 | 2.75 |
| | *Nos. 502-505 (4)* | 6.75 | 5.20 |

**Souvenir Sheet**

| | | | |
|---|---|---|---|
| **506** A66 | $5 Camping | 6.25 | 6.25 |

**Nos. 465, 474-475, 477 Overprinted**

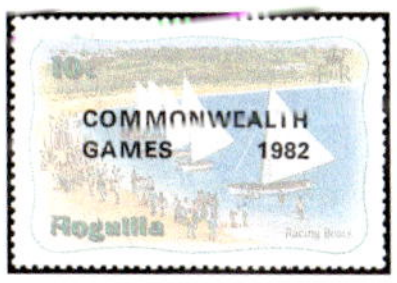


**1982, Oct. 18 Litho. *Perf. 14***

| | | | |
|---|---|---|---|
| **507** A62 | 10c multicolored | .30 | .30 |
| **508** A62 | 60c multicolored | .70 | .70 |
| **509** A62 | 75c multicolored | .90 | .90 |
| **510** A62 | $5 multicolored | 5.00 | 5.00 |
| | *Nos. 507-510 (4)* | 6.90 | 6.90 |

12th Commonwealth Games, Brisbane, Australia, Sept. 30-Oct. 9.

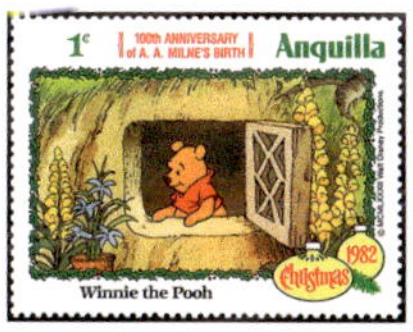


Christmas A67

Scenes from Walt Disney's Winnie the Pooh.

**1982, Nov. 29**

| | | | |
|---|---|---|---|
| **511** A67 | 1c multicolored | .25 | .25 |
| **512** A67 | 2c multicolored | .25 | .25 |
| **513** A67 | 3c multicolored | .25 | .25 |
| **514** A67 | 5c multicolored | .40 | .25 |
| **515** A67 | 7c multicolored | .40 | .25 |
| **516** A67 | 10c multicolored | .50 | .25 |
| **517** A67 | 12c multicolored | .60 | .30 |
| **518** A67 | 20c multicolored | 1.35 | .35 |
| **519** A67 | $5 multicolored | 8.50 | 8.50 |
| | *Nos. 511-519 (9)* | 12.50 | 10.65 |

**Souvenir Sheet**

| | | | |
|---|---|---|---|
| **520** A67 | $5 multicolored | 11.50 | 11.50 |

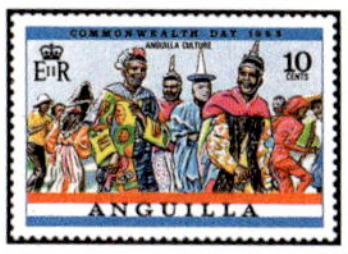


Commonwealth Day (Mar. 14) — A68

10c, Carnival procession. 35c, Flags. 75c, Economic cooperation. $2.50, Salt pond. $5, Map showing Commonwealth.

**1983, Feb. 28 Litho. *Perf. 14***

| | | | |
|---|---|---|---|
| **521** A68 | 10c multicolored | .25 | .25 |
| **522** A68 | 35c multicolored | .45 | .50 |
| **523** A68 | 75c multicolored | .85 | 1.00 |
| **524** A68 | $2.50 multicolored | 5.25 | 5.25 |
| | *Nos. 521-524 (4)* | 6.80 | 7.00 |

**Souvenir Sheet**

| | | | |
|---|---|---|---|
| **525** A68 | $5 multicolored | 7.00 | 7.00 |

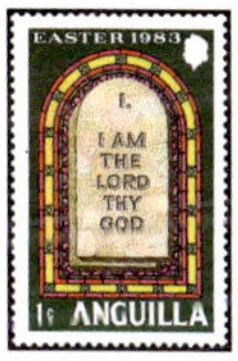


Easter A69

Ten Commandments.

**1983, Mar. 31 Litho. *Perf. 14***

| | | | |
|---|---|---|---|
| **526** A69 | 1c multicolored | .25 | .25 |
| **527** A69 | 2c multicolored | .25 | .25 |
| **528** A69 | 3c multicolored | .25 | .25 |
| **529** A69 | 10c multicolored | .25 | .25 |
| **530** A69 | 35c multicolored | .55 | .30 |
| **531** A69 | 60c multicolored | 1.00 | .50 |
| **532** A69 | 75c multicolored | 1.10 | .55 |
| **533** A69 | $2 multicolored | 2.75 | 2.10 |
| **534** A69 | $2.50 multicolored | 3.00 | 2.10 |
| **535** A69 | $5 multicolored | 4.25 | 3.25 |
| | *Nos. 526-535 (10)* | 13.65 | 9.80 |

**Souvenir Sheet**

| | | | |
|---|---|---|---|
| **536** A69 | $5 Moses Taking Tablets | 4.50 | 4.50 |

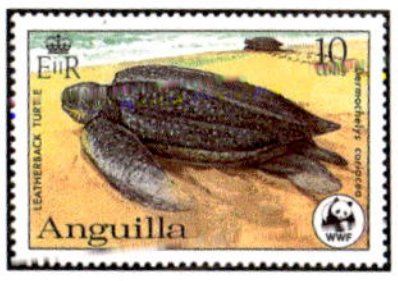


Local Turtles and World Wildlife Fund Emblem A70

**1983, Aug. 10 Litho. *Perf. 13½***

| | | | |
|---|---|---|---|
| **537** A70 | 10c Leatherback | *5.00* | *2.10* |
| **538** A70 | 35c Hawksbill | *8.25* | 3.25 |
| **539** A70 | 75c Green | *12.00* | *4.75* |
| **540** A70 | $1 Loggerhead | *13.50* | *6.50* |
| | *Nos. 537-540 (4)* | 38.75 | 16.60 |

**Souvenir Sheet**

| | | | |
|---|---|---|---|
| **541** A70 | $5 Leatherback, diff. | *30.00* | *8.25* |

**1983, Aug. 10 Litho. *Perf. 12***

| | | | |
|---|---|---|---|
| *537a* A70 | 10c Leatherback | *3.50* | *2.40* |
| *538a* A70 | 35c Hawksbill | *11.00* | *4.75* |
| *539a* A70 | 75c Green | *14.50* | *10.50* |
| *540a* A70 | $1 Loggerhead | *22.00* | *13.00* |
| | *Nos. 537a-540a (4)* | 51.00 | 30.65 |

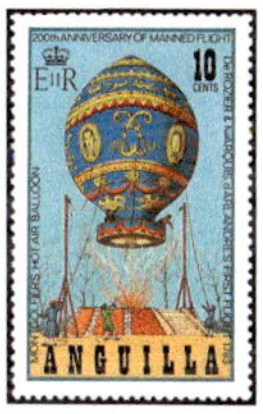


Manned Flight Bicentenary — A71

10c, Montgolfiere, 1783. 60c, Blanchard & Jeffries, 1785. $1, Giffard's airship, 1852. $2.50, Lilienthal's glider, 1890. $5, Wright Brothers' plane, 1909.

**1983, Aug. 22 *Perf. 14***

| | | | |
|---|---|---|---|
| **542** A71 | 10c multicolored | .60 | .40 |
| **543** A71 | 60c multicolored | 1.90 | .90 |
| **544** A71 | $1 multicolored | 2.00 | 1.10 |
| **545** A71 | $2.50 multicolored | 3.00 | 3.00 |
| | *Nos. 542-545 (4)* | 7.50 | 5.40 |

**Souvenir Sheet**

| | | | |
|---|---|---|---|
| **546** A71 | $5 multicolored | 6.50 | *6.50* |

**Nos. 465, 471, 476-477 Overprinted**

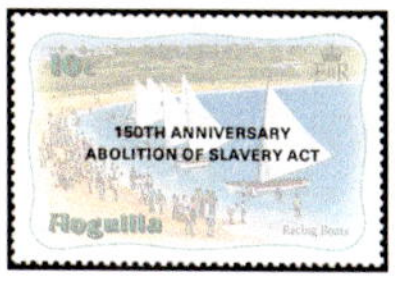


10c, Racing boats. 40c, Sandy Isld. $1, Bagging lobster, Island Harbor. $5, Pelicans.

**1983, Oct. 24 Litho. *Perf. 14***

| | | | |
|---|---|---|---|
| **546A** A62 | 10c multicolored | .30 | .25 |
| **546B** A62 | 40c multicolored | .45 | .35 |
| **546C** A62 | $1 multicolored | 1.00 | .65 |
| **546D** A62 | $5 multicolored | 7.75 | 3.75 |
| | *Nos. 546A-546D (4)* | 9.50 | 5.00 |

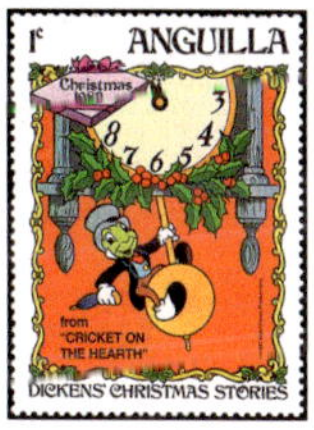


Jiminy Cricket — A72

Various Disney productions: 2c, Jiminy Cricket, kettle. 3c, Jiminy Cricket, toys. 4c, Mickey and Morty. 5c, Scrooge McDuck. 6c, Minnie and Goofy. 10c, Goofy and Elf. $2, Scrooge McDuck, diff. $3, Disney characters. $5, Scrooge McDuck.

**1983, Nov. 14 *Perf. 13½***

| | | | |
|---|---|---|---|
| **547** A72 | 1c shown | .25 | .25 |
| **548** A72 | 2c multicolored | .25 | .25 |
| **549** A72 | 3c multicolored | .25 | .25 |
| **550** A72 | 4c multicolored | .25 | .25 |
| **551** A72 | 5c multicolored | .25 | .25 |
| **552** A72 | 6c multicolored | .25 | .25 |
| **553** A72 | 10c multicolored | .25 | .25 |
| **554** A72 | $2 multicolored | 4.50 | 3.25 |
| **555** A72 | $3 multicolored | 5.00 | 3.00 |
| | *Nos. 547-555 (9)* | 11.25 | 8.00 |

**Souvenir Sheet**

| | | | |
|---|---|---|---|
| **556** A72 | $5 multicolored | 8.00 | 8.00 |

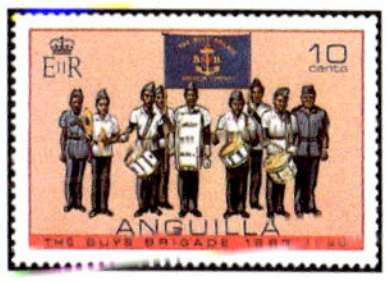


Boys' Brigade Centenary A73

10c, Anguilla company, banner. $5, Marching with drummer.

**1983, Sept. 12 Litho. *Perf. 14***

| | | | |
|---|---|---|---|
| **557** A73 | 10c multicolored | .50 | .35 |
| **558** A73 | $5 multicolored | 3.75 | 3.25 |
| *a.* | Souvenir sheet of 2, #557-558 | 4.75 | 4.75 |

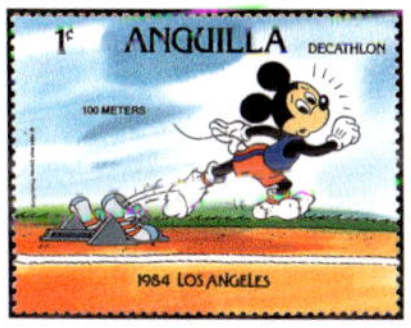


1984 Olympics, Los Angeles A74

Mickey Mouse Competing in Decathlon.

**1984, Feb. 20 Litho. *Perf. 14***

| | | | |
|---|---|---|---|
| **559** A74 | 1c 100-meter run | .25 | .25 |
| **560** A74 | 2c Long jump | .25 | .25 |
| **561** A74 | 3c Shot put | .25 | .25 |
| **562** A74 | 4c High jump | .25 | .25 |
| **563** A74 | 5c 400-meter run | .25 | .25 |
| **564** A74 | 6c Hurdles | .25 | .25 |
| **565** A74 | 10c Discus | .25 | .25 |
| **566** A74 | $1 Pole vault | 3.25 | 3.00 |
| **567** A74 | $4 Javelin | 6.75 | 4.75 |
| | *Nos. 559-567 (9)* | 11.75 | 9.50 |

**Souvenir Sheet**

| | | | |
|---|---|---|---|
| **568** A74 | $5 1500-meter run | 12.50 | 12.50 |

512 ANGUILLA

**1984, Apr. 24** ***Perf. 12½x12***

| | | | | |
|---|---|---|---|---|
| *559a* | A74 | 1c | .25 | .25 |
| *560a* | A74 | 2c | .25 | .25 |
| *561a* | A74 | 3c | .25 | .25 |
| *562a* | A74 | 4c | .25 | .25 |
| *563a* | A74 | 5c | .25 | .25 |
| *564a* | A74 | 6c | .25 | .25 |
| *565a* | A74 | 10c | .25 | .25 |
| *566a* | A74 | $1 | 4.75 | 3.75 |
| *567a* | A74 | $4 | 6.25 | *9.50* |
| | | *Nos. 559a-567a (9)* | 12.75 | 15.00 |

**Souvenir Sheet**

| | | | | |
|---|---|---|---|---|
| *568a* | A74 | $5 With Olympic rings emblem | 11.00 | 11.00 |

Nos. 559a-567a inscribed with Olympic rings emblem. Printed in sheets of 5 plus label.

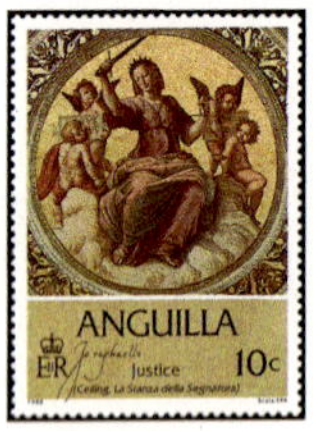


Easter — A75

Ceiling and Wall Frescoes, La Stanze della Segnatura, by Raphael (details).

**1984, Apr. 19** **Litho.** ***Perf. 13½x14***

| | | | | |
|---|---|---|---|---|
| **569** | A75 | 10c Justice | .25 | .25 |
| **570** | A75 | 25c Poetry | .30 | .30 |
| **571** | A75 | 35c Philosophy | .40 | .40 |
| **572** | A75 | 40c Theology | .40 | .40 |
| **573** | A75 | $1 Abraham & Paul | .90 | .90 |
| **574** | A75 | $2 Moses & Matthew | 1.75 | 1.75 |
| **575** | A75 | $3 John & David | 2.50 | 2.50 |
| **576** | A75 | $4 Peter & Adam | 3.00 | 3.00 |
| | | *Nos. 569-576 (8)* | 9.50 | 9.50 |

**Souvenir Sheet**

| | | | | |
|---|---|---|---|---|
| **577** | A75 | $5 Astronomy | 5.25 | 5.25 |

**Nos. 463, 469, 477-479 Surcharged**

**1984** **Litho.** ***Perf. 14***

| | | | | |
|---|---|---|---|---|
| **578** | A62 | 25c on $7.50 #478 | .85 | .45 |
| **579** | A62 | 35c on 30c #469 | .70 | .55 |
| **580** | A62 | 60c on 1c #463 | .75 | .60 |
| **581** | A62 | $2.50 on $5 #477 | 3.75 | 1.90 |
| **582** | A62 | $2.50 on $10 #479 | 2.75 | 1.90 |
| | | *Nos. 578-582 (5)* | 8.80 | 5.40 |

Issue dates: 25c, May 17, others, Apr. 24.

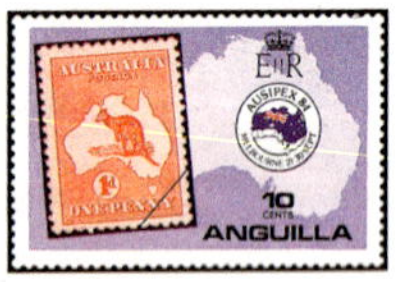


Ausipex '84 — A76

Australian stamps.

**1984, July 16** **Litho.** ***Perf. 13½***

| | | | | |
|---|---|---|---|---|
| **583** | A76 | 10c No. 2 | .60 | .45 |
| **584** | A76 | 75c No. 18 | 1.75 | 1.40 |
| **585** | A76 | $1 No. 130 | 2.25 | 1.90 |
| **586** | A76 | $2.50 No. 178 | 3.50 | 3.50 |
| | | *Nos. 583-586 (4)* | 8.10 | 7.25 |

**Souvenir Sheet**

| | | | | |
|---|---|---|---|---|
| **587** | A76 | $5 Nos. 378, 379 | 6.75 | 6.75 |

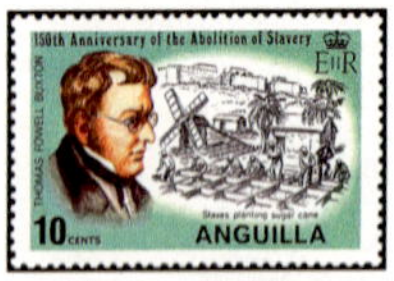


Slavery Abolition Sesquicentennial — A77

Abolitionists and Vignettes: 10c, Thomas Fowell Buxton, planting sugar cane. 25c, Abraham Lincoln, cotton field. 35c, Henri Christophe, armed slave revolt. 60c, Thomas Clarkson, addressing Anti-Slavery Society. 75c, William Wilberforce, Slave auction. $1, Olaudah Equiano, slave raid on Benin coast. $2.50, General Gordon, slave convoy in Sudan. $5, Granville Sharp, restraining ship captain from boarding slave.

**1984, Aug. 1** ***Perf. 12***

| | | | | |
|---|---|---|---|---|
| **588** | A77 | 10c multicolored | .25 | .25 |
| **589** | A77 | 25c multicolored | .45 | .45 |
| **590** | A77 | 35c multicolored | .55 | .55 |
| **591** | A77 | 60c multicolored | .70 | .70 |
| **592** | A77 | 75c multicolored | .90 | .90 |
| **593** | A77 | $1 multicolored | 1.00 | 1.00 |
| **594** | A77 | $2.50 multicolored | 1.90 | 1.90 |
| **595** | A77 | $5 multicolored | 3.75 | 3.75 |
| *a.* | | Miniature sheet of 8, #588-595 | 9.50 | *11.00* |
| | | *Nos. 588-595 (8)* | 9.50 | 9.50 |

For overprints see Nos. 688-695a.

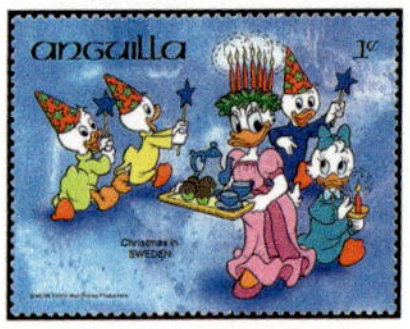


Christmas A78

Various Disney characters and celebrations.

***Perf. 14, 12½x12 ($2)***

**1984, Nov. 12** **Litho.**

| | | | | |
|---|---|---|---|---|
| **596** | A78 | 1c multicolored | .25 | .25 |
| **597** | A78 | 2c multicolored | .25 | .25 |
| **598** | A78 | 3c multicolored | .25 | .25 |
| **599** | A78 | 4c multicolored | .25 | .25 |
| **600** | A78 | 5c multicolored | .25 | .25 |
| **601** | A78 | 10c multicolored | .25 | .25 |
| **602** | A78 | $1 multicolored | 3.75 | 3.00 |
| **603** | A78 | $2 multicolored | 4.75 | *5.00* |
| **604** | A78 | $4 multicolored | 6.00 | *9.50* |
| | | *Nos. 596-604 (9)* | 16.00 | 19.00 |

**Souvenir Sheet**

| | | | | |
|---|---|---|---|---|
| **605** | A78 | $5 multicolored | 8.50 | 8.50 |

**Nos. 464-465, 477 Ovptd. or Srchd.**

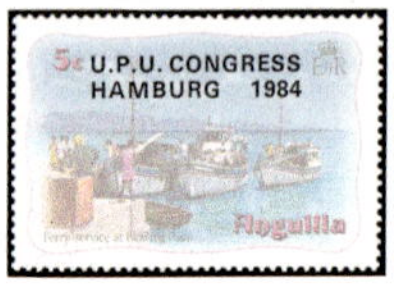


**1984, Aug. 13**

| | | | | |
|---|---|---|---|---|
| **606** | A62 | 5c #464 | .35 | .25 |
| **607** | A62 | 20c on 10c #465 | .50 | .30 |
| **608** | A62 | $5 #477 | 7.00 | 4.25 |
| | | *Nos. 606-608 (3)* | 7.85 | 4.80 |

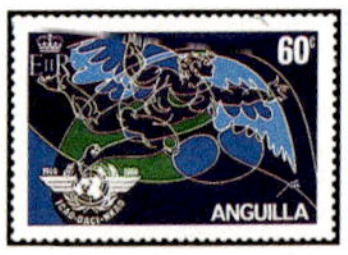


Intl. Civil Aviation Org., 40th Anniv. — A79

60c, Icarus, by Hans Erni. 75c, Sun Princess, by Sadiou Diouf. $2.50, Anniv. emblem, vert.

$5, Map of the Caribbean.

**1984, Dec. 3** **Litho.** ***Perf. 14***

| | | | | |
|---|---|---|---|---|
| **609** | A79 | 60c multicolored | .90 | *1.00* |
| **610** | A79 | 75c multicolored | 1.40 | *1.60* |
| **611** | A79 | $2.50 multicolored | 4.00 | *4.25* |
| | | *Nos. 609-611 (3)* | 6.30 | *6.85* |

**Souvenir Sheet**

| | | | | |
|---|---|---|---|---|
| **612** | A79 | $5 multicolored | 6.00 | *7.00* |

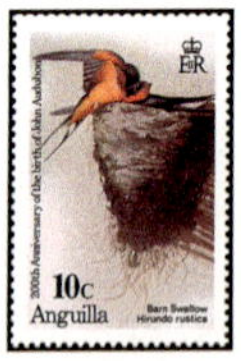


Audubon Birth Bicent. — A80

Illustrations by artist and naturalist J. J. Audubon (1785-1851) — 10c, Hirundo rustica. 60c, Mycteria americana. 75c, Sterna dougallii. $5, Pandion haliaetus.

No. 617, Vireo solitarus, horiz. No. 618, Piranga ludoviciana, horiz.

**1985, Apr. 30** **Litho.** ***Perf. 14***

| | | | | |
|---|---|---|---|---|
| **613** | A80 | 10c multicolored | 1.25 | 1.00 |
| **614** | A80 | 60c multicolored | 2.10 | 2.10 |
| **615** | A80 | 75c multicolored | 2.10 | 2.10 |
| **616** | A80 | $5 multicolored | 7.75 | 7.75 |
| | | *Nos. 613-616 (4)* | 13.20 | 12.95 |

**Souvenir Sheets**

| | | | | |
|---|---|---|---|---|
| **617** | A80 | $4 multicolored | 7.00 | 7.00 |
| **618** | A80 | $4 multicolored | 7.00 | 7.00 |

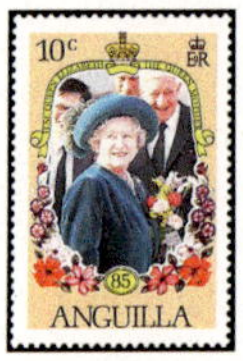


Queen Mother 85th Birthday — A81

Photographs: 10c, Visiting the children's ward at King's College Hospital. $2, Inspecting Royal Marine Volunteer Cadets at Deal. $3, Outside Clarence House in London. $5, In an open carriage at Ascot.

**1985, July 2**

| | | | | |
|---|---|---|---|---|
| **619** | A81 | 10c multicolored | .25 | .25 |
| **620** | A81 | $2 multicolored | 1.00 | 1.00 |
| **621** | A81 | $3 multicolored | 1.75 | 1.75 |
| | | *Nos. 619-621 (3)* | 3.00 | 3.00 |

**Souvenir Sheet**

| | | | | |
|---|---|---|---|---|
| **622** | A81 | $5 multicolored | 2.75 | 2.75 |

Nos. 619-621 printed in sheetlets of 5.

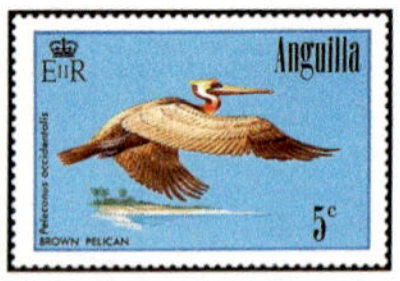


Birds — A82

5c, Brown pelican. 10c, Turtle dove. 15c, Man-o-war. 20c, Antillean crested hummingbird. 25c, White-tailed tropicbird. 30c, Caribbean elaenia. No. 629, 35c, Black-whiskered vireo. No. 629A, 35c, Lesser Antillean bullfinch ('86). 40c, Yellow-crowned night heron. 45c, Pearly-eyed thrasher. 50c, Laughing bird. 65c, Brown booby. 80c, Gray kingbird. $1, Audubon's shearwater. $1.35, Roseate tern. $2.50, Bananaquit. $5, Belted kingfisher. $10, Green heron.

**1985-86** **Litho.** ***Perf. 13½x14***

| | | | | |
|---|---|---|---|---|
| **623** | A82 | 5c multi | 3.00 | 2.00 |
| **624** | A82 | 10c multi | 3.00 | 2.00 |
| **625** | A82 | 15c multi | 3.00 | 2.00 |
| **626** | A82 | 20c multi | 3.00 | 2.00 |
| **627** | A82 | 25c multi | 3.00 | 2.50 |
| **628** | A82 | 30c multi | 3.00 | 2.50 |
| **629** | A82 | 35c multi | 13.00 | 10.00 |
| **629A** | A82 | 35c multi | 3.00 | 2.50 |
| **630** | A82 | 40c multi | 3.00 | 2.50 |
| **631** | A82 | 45c multi | 3.00 | 2.50 |
| **632** | A82 | 50c multi | 3.00 | 2.50 |
| **633** | A82 | 65c multi | 3.00 | 2.50 |
| **634** | A82 | 80c multi | 4.00 | *5.00* |
| **635** | A82 | $1 multi | 4.00 | *5.00* |
| **636** | A82 | $1.35 multi | 3.00 | *5.00* |
| **637** | A82 | $2.50 multi | 10.00 | *11.00* |
| **638** | A82 | $5 multi | 7.75 | *13.50* |
| **639** | A82 | $10 multi | 13.00 | *17.50* |
| | | *Nos. 623-639 (18)* | 87.75 | 92.50 |

Issued: 25c, 65c, $1.35, $5, 7/22; 45c, 50c, 80c, $1, $10, 9/30; 5c-20c, 30c, No. 629, 40c, $2.50, 11/11; No. 629A, 3/10.

For overprints & surcharges see Nos. 678-682, 713-716, 723-739, 750-753, 764-767, 783-786.

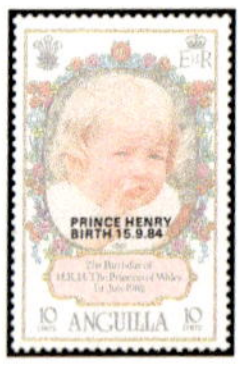


Nos. 485-491 Overprinted

**1985, Oct. 31** **Litho.** ***Perf. 14***

| | | | | |
|---|---|---|---|---|
| **639A** | A64 | 10c multicolored | .25 | .25 |
| **639B** | A64 | 30c multicolored | .25 | .25 |
| **639C** | A64 | 40c multicolored | .30 | .30 |
| **639D** | A64 | 60c multicolored | .45 | .45 |
| **639E** | A64 | $2 multicolored | 1.50 | 1.50 |
| **639F** | A64 | $3 multicolored | 3.50 | 3.50 |
| *h.* | | Souv. sheet of 6, #639A-639F | 4.25 | 4.25 |
| | | Complete booklet, 4 each #639A, 639C-639E | 11.00 | |
| | | *Nos. 639A-639F (6)* | 6.25 | 6.25 |

**Souvenir Sheet**

| | | | | |
|---|---|---|---|---|
| **639G** | A64 | $5 multicolored | 4.50 | 4.50 |

**Nos. 464, 469, 475 and 477 Ovptd.**

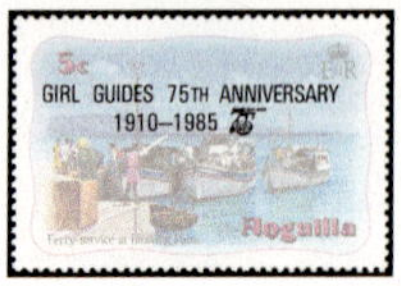


**1985, Oct. 14** **Litho.** ***Perf. 14***

| | | | | |
|---|---|---|---|---|
| **640** | A62 | 5c multicolored | .45 | .25 |
| **641** | A62 | 30c multicolored | .75 | .55 |
| **642** | A62 | 75c multicolored | 1.10 | .90 |
| **643** | A62 | $5 multicolored | 10.50 | 10.50 |
| | | *Nos. 640-643 (4)* | 12.80 | 12.20 |

**Nos. 465 and 469 Ovptd. or Srchd.**

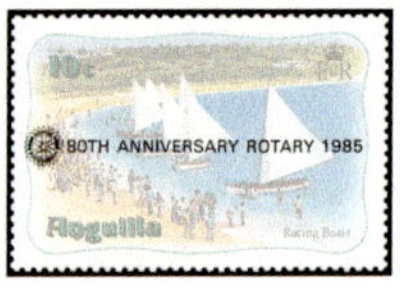


**1985, Nov. 18**

| | | | | |
|---|---|---|---|---|
| **644** | A62 | 10c multicolored | .65 | .25 |
| **645** | A62 | 35c on 30c multi | 1.40 | .50 |

**Nos. 476, 469 Srchd. or Ovptd.**

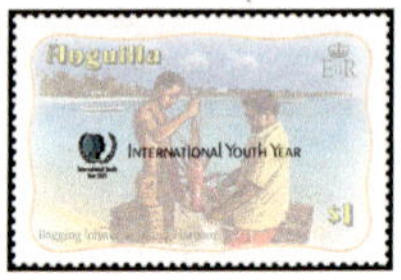


**1985, Nov. 18**

| | | | | |
|---|---|---|---|---|
| **646** | A62 | $1 multicolored | 2.25 | 1.25 |
| **647** | A62 | $5 on 30c multi | 6.75 | 6.75 |

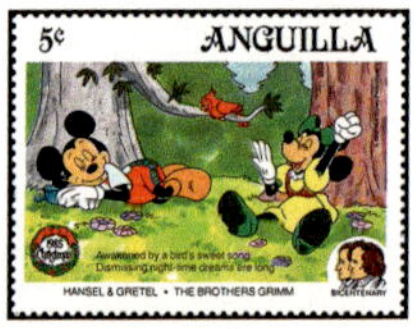


Brothers Grimm A83

Christmas: Disney characters in Hansel and Gretel.

**1985, Nov. 11** **Litho.** ***Perf. 14***

| | | | | |
|---|---|---|---|---|
| **648** | A83 | 5c multicolored | .55 | .55 |
| **649** | A83 | 50c multicolored | 1.75 | .80 |
| **650** | A83 | 90c multicolored | 2.25 | 1.25 |
| **651** | A83 | $4 multicolored | 4.00 | 4.00 |
| | | *Nos. 648-651 (4)* | 8.55 | 6.60 |

**Souvenir Sheet**

| | | | | |
|---|---|---|---|---|
| **652** | A83 | $5 multicolored | 8.00 | 8.00 |

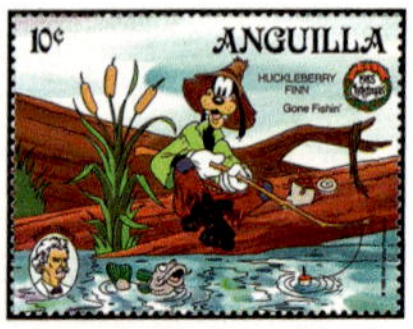


Mark Twain (1835-1910), Author A84

Disney characters in Huckleberry Finn.

**1985, Nov. 11**

| | | | | |
|---|---|---|---|---|
| **653** | A84 | 10c multicolored | .70 | .35 |
| **654** | A84 | 60c multicolored | 2.25 | 1.10 |
| **654A** | A84 | $1 multicolored | 3.00 | 1.60 |
| **655** | A84 | $4 multicolored | 4.00 | 4.00 |
| | | *Nos. 653-655 (4)* | 9.95 | 7.05 |

**Souvenir Sheet**

| | | | | |
|---|---|---|---|---|
| **656** | A84 | $5 multicolored | 9.00 | 9.00 |

Christmas. No. 654A printed in sheets of 8.

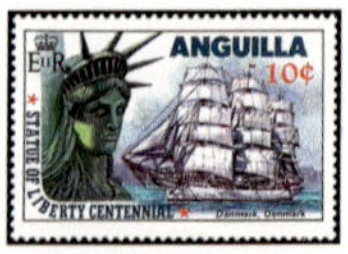


Statue of Liberty Centennial A85

10c, Danmark, Denmark. 20c, Eagle, USA. 60c, Amerigo Vespucci, Italy. 75c, Sir Winston Churchill, G.B. $2, Nippon Maru, Japan. $2.50, Gorch, Germany.

$5, Statue of Liberty, vert.

**1985, Nov. 25**

| | | | | |
|---|---|---|---|---|
| **657** | A85 | 10c multicolored | .85 | .70 |
| **658** | A85 | 20c multicolored | 1.25 | .95 |
| **659** | A85 | 60c multicolored | 1.60 | 1.60 |
| **660** | A85 | 75c multicolored | 1.60 | 1.50 |
| **661** | A85 | $2 multicolored | 1.60 | *3.00* |
| **662** | A85 | $2.50 multicolored | 2.10 | *3.00* |
| | | *Nos. 657-662 (6)* | 9.00 | 10.75 |

**Souvenir Sheet**

| | | | | |
|---|---|---|---|---|
| **663** | A85 | $5 multicolored | 9.00 | 9.00 |

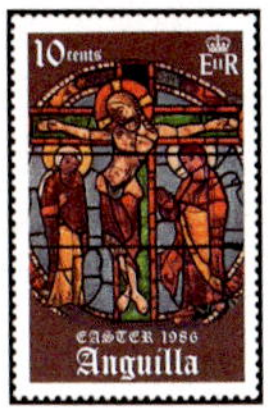


Easter — A86

Stained glass windows.

**1986, Mar. 27 Litho. *Perf. 14***

| | | | | |
|---|---|---|---|---|
| **664** | A86 | 10c multicolored | .25 | .25 |
| **665** | A86 | 25c multicolored | .50 | .50 |
| **666** | A86 | 45c multicolored | .90 | .90 |
| **667** | A86 | $4 multicolored | 4.25 | *5.25* |
| | | *Nos. 664-667 (4)* | 5.90 | 6.90 |

**Souvenir Sheet**

| | | | | |
|---|---|---|---|---|
| **668** | A86 | $5 multi, horiz. | 7.00 | 7.00 |

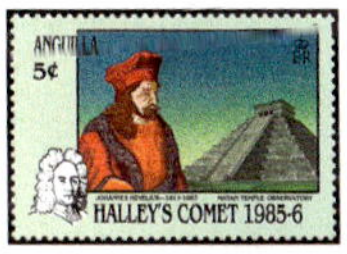


Halley's Comet — A87

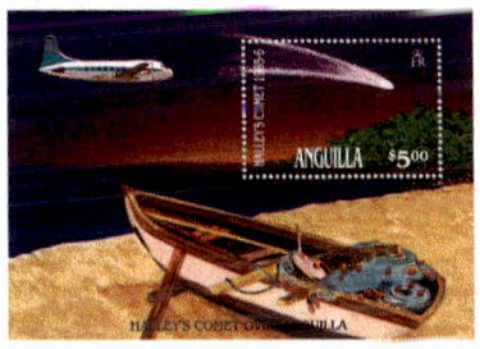


A88

Designs: 5c, Johannes Hevolius (1611-1687), Mayan temple observatory. 10c, US Viking probe landing on Mars, 1976. 60c, Theatri Cosmicum (detail), 1668. $4, Sighting, 1835. $5, Comet over Anguilla.

**1986, Mar. 24**

| | | | | |
|---|---|---|---|---|
| **669** | A87 | 5c multicolored | .45 | .45 |
| **670** | A87 | 10c multicolored | .50 | .50 |
| **671** | A87 | 60c multicolored | 1.50 | 1.10 |
| **672** | A87 | $4 multicolored | 6.25 | 6.25 |
| | | *Nos. 669-672 (4)* | 8.70 | 8.30 |

**Souvenir Sheet**

| | | | | |
|---|---|---|---|---|
| **673** | A88 | $5 multicolored | 5.50 | *6.25* |

**Queen Elizabeth II, 60th Birthday**

Common Design Type

20c, Inspecting guards, 1946. $2, Garter Ceremony, 1985. $3, Trooping the color. $5, Christening, 1926.

**1986, Apr. 21**

| | | | | |
|---|---|---|---|---|
| **674** | CD339 | 20c multicolored | .25 | .25 |
| **675** | CD339 | $2 multicolored | 1.50 | 1.50 |
| **676** | CD339 | $3 multicolored | 2.25 | 2.25 |
| | | *Nos. 674-676 (3)* | 4.00 | 4.00 |

**Souvenir Sheet**

| | | | | |
|---|---|---|---|---|
| **677** | CD339 | $5 multicolored | 4.00 | 4.00 |

**Nos. 623, 631, 635, 637 and 639 Ovptd.**

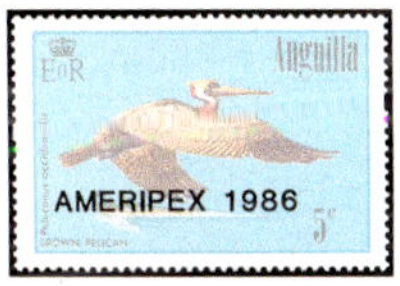


**1986, May 22 *Perf. 13½x14***

| | | | | |
|---|---|---|---|---|
| **678** | A82 | 5c multicolored | .90 | *1.10* |
| **679** | A82 | 45c multicolored | 2.00 | .75 |
| **680** | A82 | $1 multicolored | 3.50 | 1.60 |
| **681** | A82 | $2.50 multicolored | 3.50 | *4.25* |
| **682** | A82 | $10 multicolored | 10.00 | *11.00* |
| | | *Nos. 678-682 (5)* | 19.90 | 18.70 |

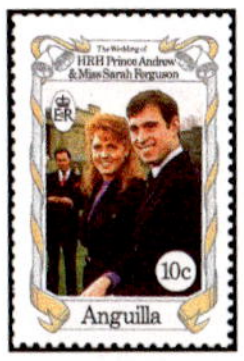


Wedding of Prince Andrew and Sarah Ferguson — A89

**1986, July 23 Litho. *Perf. 14***

| | | | | |
|---|---|---|---|---|
| **683** | A89 | 10c Couple | .25 | .25 |
| **684** | A89 | 35c Andrew | .30 | .30 |
| **685** | A89 | $2 Sarah | 1.10 | *1.60* |
| **686** | A89 | $3 Couple, diff. | 1.75 | *2.75* |
| | | *Nos. 683-686 (4)* | 3.40 | *4.90* |

**Souvenir Sheet**

| | | | | |
|---|---|---|---|---|
| **687** | A89 | $6 Westminster Abbey | 5.25 | *6.00* |

***Perf. 12***

| | | | | |
|---|---|---|---|---|
| *683a* | A89 | 10c Couple | .40 | .25 |
| *684a* | A89 | 35c Andrew | .65 | .30 |
| *685a* | A89 | $2 Sarah | 1.60 | 1.25 |
| *686a* | A89 | $3 Couple, diff. | 2.00 | 1.90 |
| | | *Nos. 683a-686a (4)* | 4.65 | 3.70 |

**Souvenir Sheet**

| | | | | |
|---|---|---|---|---|
| *687a* | A89 | $6 Westminster Abbey | 5.25 | *6.00* |

**Nos. 588-595 Overprinted**

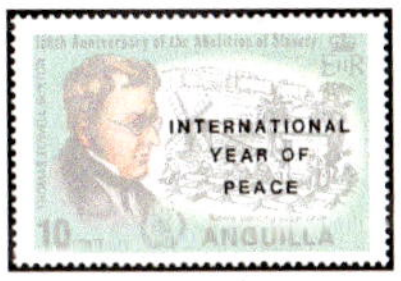


**1986, Sept. 29 Litho. *Perf. 12***

| | | | | |
|---|---|---|---|---|
| **688** | A77 | 10c multicolored | .65 | .35 |
| **689** | A77 | 25c multicolored | 1.00 | .55 |
| **690** | A77 | 35c multicolored | 1.25 | .65 |
| **691** | A77 | 60c multicolored | 2.00 | .95 |
| **692** | A77 | 75c multicolored | 2.00 | 1.25 |
| **693** | A77 | $1 multicolored | 2.00 | 1.40 |
| **694** | A77 | $2.50 multicolored | 3.50 | *5.00* |
| **695** | A77 | $5 multicolored | 4.75 | *6.50* |
| *a.* | | Miniature sheet, #688-695 | 19.00 | *20.00* |
| | | *Nos. 688-695 (8)* | 17.15 | 16.65 |

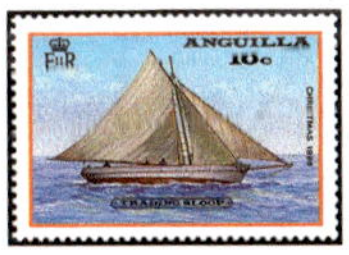


Ships — A90

**1986, Nov. 29 Litho. *Perf. 14***

| | | | | |
|---|---|---|---|---|
| **696** | A90 | 10c Trading Sloop | 1.75 | .45 |
| **697** | A90 | 45c Lady Rodney | 3.25 | .60 |
| **698** | A90 | 80c West Derby | 4.50 | 3.00 |
| **699** | A90 | $3 Warspite | 7.75 | 6.00 |
| | | *Nos. 696-699 (4)* | 17.25 | 10.05 |

**Souvenir Sheet**

| | | | | |
|---|---|---|---|---|
| **700** | A90 | $6 Boat Race Day, vert. | 20.00 | 20.00 |

Christmas.

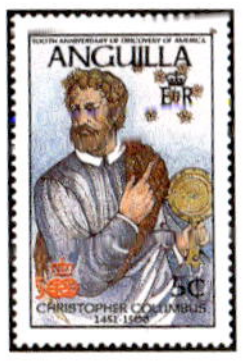


Discovery of America, 500th Anniv. (in 1992) — A91

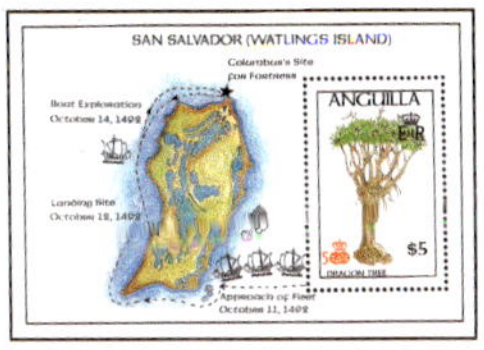


Dragon Tree A92

5c, Christopher Columbus, astrolabe. 10c, Aboard ship. 35c, Santa Maria. 80c, Ferdinand, Isabella. $4, Indians. No. 707, Caribbean manatee.

**1986, Dec. 22**

| | | | | |
|---|---|---|---|---|
| **701** | A91 | 5c multi | .85 | .85 |
| **702** | A91 | 10c multi | 1.40 | .90 |
| **703** | A91 | 35c multi | 2.75 | 1.60 |
| **704** | A91 | 80c multi, horiz. | 2.00 | *2.25* |
| **705** | A91 | $4 multi | 4.50 | *5.00* |
| | | *Nos. 701-705 (5)* | 11.50 | 10.60 |

**Souvenir Sheets**

| | | | | |
|---|---|---|---|---|
| **706** | A92 | $5 shown | 9.00 | 9.00 |
| **707** | A92 | $5 multi, horiz. | 9.00 | 9.00 |

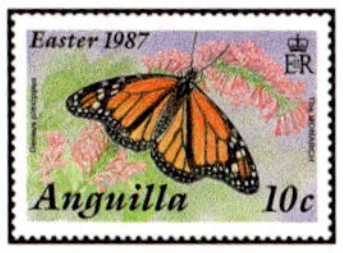


Butterflies — A93

10c, Monarch. 80c, White peacock. $1, Zebra. $2, Caribbean buckeye. $6, Flambeau.

**1987, Apr. 14 Litho. *Perf. 14***

| | | | | |
|---|---|---|---|---|
| **708** | A93 | 10c multicolored | 2.00 | .90 |
| **709** | A93 | 80c multicolored | 5.50 | 2.75 |
| **710** | A93 | $1 multicolored | 6.50 | 3.25 |
| **711** | A93 | $2 multicolored | 10.00 | *11.00* |
| | | *Nos. 708-711 (4)* | 24.00 | 17.90 |

**Souvenir Sheet**

| | | | | |
|---|---|---|---|---|
| **712** | A93 | $6 multicolored | 20.00 | 20.00 |

Easter.

**Nos. 629A, 631, 634 and 639 Ovptd in Red**

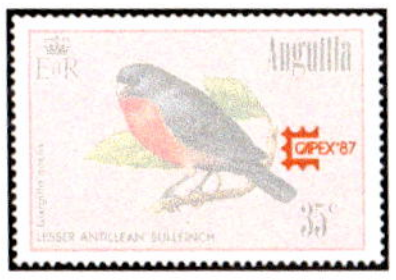


**1987, May 25 Litho. *Perf. 13½x14***

| | | | | |
|---|---|---|---|---|
| **713** | A82 | 35c on No. 629A | 2.25 | 1.00 |
| **714** | A82 | 45c on No. 631 | 2.25 | 1.10 |
| **715** | A82 | 80c on No. 634 | 3.25 | 1.60 |
| **716** | A82 | $10 on No. 639 | 12.00 | *16.00* |
| | | *Nos. 713-716 (4)* | 19.75 | *19.70* |

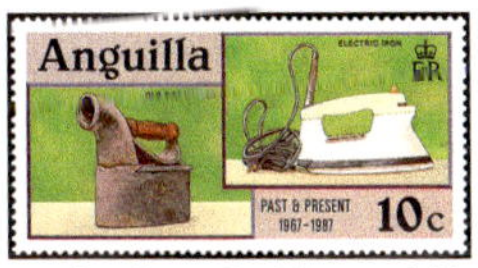


Separation from St. Kitts and Nevis, 20th Anniv. — A94

10c, Old goose iron, electric iron. 35c, Old East End School, Albena Lake-Hodge Comprehensive College. 45c, Old market place, People's Market. 80c, Old ferries & modern ferry at Blowing Point. $1, Old & new cable & wireless offices. $2, Public meeting at Burrowes Park, House of Assembly.

**1987, May 25 *Perf. 14***

| | | | | |
|---|---|---|---|---|
| **717** | A94 | 10c multicolored | .75 | .50 |
| **718** | A94 | 35c multicolored | .85 | .65 |
| **719** | A94 | 45c multicolored | 1.00 | .80 |
| **720** | A94 | 80c multicolored | 2.25 | 1.00 |
| **721** | A94 | $1 multicolored | 1.75 | 1.25 |
| **722** | A94 | $2 multicolored | 2.50 | *2.75* |
| *a.* | | Souvenir sheet of 6, #717-722 | 12.50 | 12.50 |
| | | *Nos. 717-722 (6)* | 9.10 | 6.95 |

**Nos. 623, 625-628, 629A-639 Ovptd. In Red or Srchd. in Red & Black**

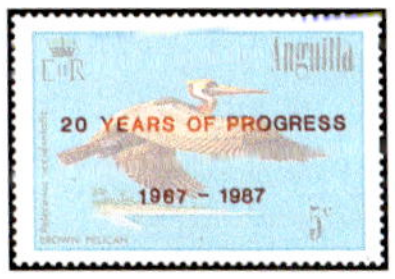


**1987, Sept. 4 Litho. *Perf. 13½x14***

| | | | | |
|---|---|---|---|---|
| **723** | A82 | 5c No. 623 | 3.50 | 3.00 |
| **724** | A82 | 10c on 15c No. 625 | 3.50 | 3.00 |
| **725** | A82 | 15c No. 625 | 3.50 | 3.00 |
| **726** | A82 | 20c No. 626 | 3.50 | 3.00 |
| **727** | A82 | 25c No. 627 | 3.50 | 3.00 |
| **728** | A82 | 30c No. 628 | 3.50 | 3.00 |
| **729** | A82 | 35c No. 629A | 3.50 | 3.00 |
| **730** | A82 | 40c No. 630 | 3.50 | 3.00 |
| **731** | A82 | 45c No. 631 | 3.50 | 3.00 |
| **732** | A82 | 50c No. 632 | 3.50 | 3.00 |
| **733** | A82 | 65c No. 633 | 3.75 | 3.25 |
| **734** | A82 | 80c No. 634 | 3.50 | 3.00 |
| **735** | A82 | $1 No. 635 | 4.00 | *4.00* |
| **736** | A82 | $1.35 No. 636 | 4.75 | 4.75 |
| **737** | A82 | $2.50 No. 637 | 5.50 | *6.50* |
| **738** | A82 | $5 No. 638 | 7.50 | *9.00* |
| **739** | A82 | $10 No. 639 | 11.00 | *13.50* |
| | | *Nos. 723-739 (17)* | 75.00 | 74.00 |

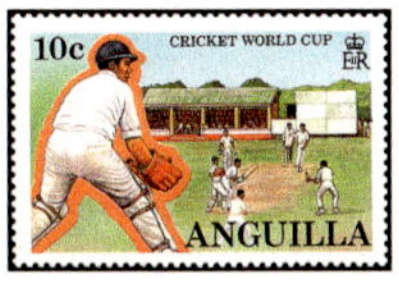


Cricket World Cup — A95

Various action scenes.

**1987, Oct. 5 *Perf. 14***

| | | | | |
|---|---|---|---|---|
| **740** | A95 | 10c multicolored | 1.75 | .90 |
| **741** | A95 | 35c multicolored | 2.50 | .90 |
| **742** | A95 | 45c multicolored | 2.50 | .95 |
| **743** | A95 | $2.50 multicolored | 5.00 | *7.50* |
| | | *Nos. 740-743 (4)* | 11.75 | 10.25 |

**Souvenir Sheet**

| | | | | |
|---|---|---|---|---|
| **744** | A95 | $6 multicolored | 15.00 | 15.00 |

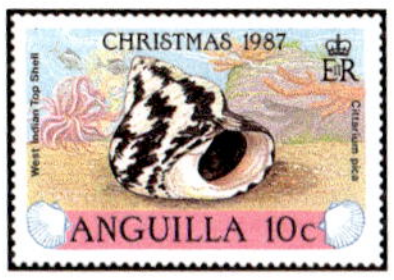


Sea Shells, Crabs — A96

10c, West Indian top shell. 35c, Ghost crab. 50c, Spiny Caribbean vase. $2, Great land crab. $6, Queen conch.

**1987, Nov. 2**

| | | | | |
|---|---|---|---|---|
| **745** | A96 | 10c multicolored | 1.75 | .70 |
| **746** | A96 | 35c multicolored | 2.25 | 1.10 |
| **747** | A96 | 50c multicolored | 4.00 | 2.10 |
| **748** | A96 | $2 multicolored | 6.00 | *10.50* |
| | | *Nos. 745-748 (4)* | 14.00 | 14.40 |

**Souvenir Sheet**

| | | | | |
|---|---|---|---|---|
| **749** | A96 | $6 multicolored | 14.00 | 14.00 |

Christmas.

**Nos. 629A, 635-636 and 639 Ovptd. in Scarlet**

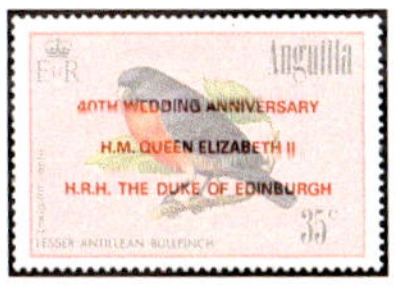


**1987, Dec. 14 Litho. *Perf. 13½x14***

| | | | | |
|---|---|---|---|---|
| **750** | A82 | 35c multicolored | .30 | .30 |
| **751** | A82 | $1 multicolored | .70 | .75 |
| **752** | A82 | $1.35 multicolored | 1.00 | 1.00 |
| **753** | A82 | $10 multicolored | 7.00 | *8.50* |
| | | *Nos. 750-753 (4)* | 9.00 | 10.55 |

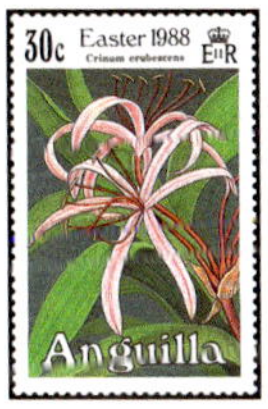


Easter (Lilies) — A97

30c, Crinum erubescens. 45c, Hymenocallis caribaea. $1, Crinum macowanii. $2.50, Hemerocallis fulva. $6, Lilium longiflorum.

**1988, Mar. 28 Litho. *Perf. 14***

| | | | | |
|---|---|---|---|---|
| **754** | A97 | 30c multicolored | .65 | .35 |
| **755** | A97 | 45c multicolored | .85 | .35 |
| **756** | A97 | $1 multicolored | 2.25 | 1.00 |
| **757** | A97 | $2.50 multicolored | 2.50 | *4.00* |
| | | *Nos. 754-757 (4)* | 6.25 | 5.70 |

**Souvenir Sheet**

| | | | | |
|---|---|---|---|---|
| **758** | A97 | $6 multicolored | 5.75 | *7.25* |

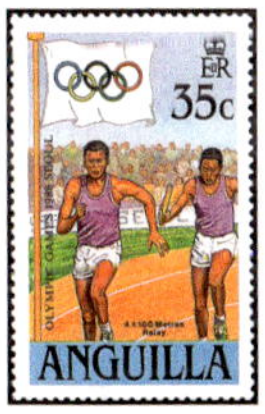


1988 Summer Olympics, Seoul — A98

# ANGUILLA

**1988, July 25**    **Litho.**    *Perf. 14*
| | | | | |
|---|---|---|---|---|
| 759 | A98 | 35c 4x100-Meter relay | .70 | .35 |
| 760 | A98 | 45c Windsurfing | .80 | .50 |
| 761 | A98 | 50c Tennis | 2.25 | 1.60 |
| 762 | A98 | 80c Basketball | 5.00 | 4.25 |
| | | Nos. 759-762 (4) | 8.75 | 6.70 |

**Souvenir Sheet**
| 763 | A98 | $6 Women's 200 meters | 5.75 | 5.75 |

**Nos. 629A, 634-635 and 637 Ovptd.**

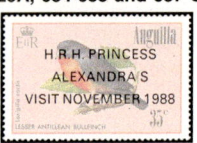

**1988, Dec. 14**    **Litho.**    *Perf. 13½x14*
| 764 | A82 | 35c multicolored | 1.90 | .85 |
| 765 | A82 | 80c multicolored | 2.75 | 1.75 |
| 766 | A82 | $1 multicolored | 2.75 | 2.10 |
| 767 | A82 | $2.50 multicolored | 4.75 | 5.75 |
| | | Nos. 764-767 (4) | 12.15 | 10.45 |

Marine Life — A99

35c, Common sea fan. 80c, Coral crab. $1, Grooved brain coral. $1.60, Old wife. $6, West Indies spiny lobster.

**1988, Nov. 28**    **Litho.**    *Perf. 14*
| 768 | A99 | 35c multicolored | 1.50 | .45 |
| 769 | A99 | 80c multicolored | 2.25 | .95 |
| 770 | A99 | $1 multicolored | 3.25 | 1.60 |
| 771 | A99 | $1.60 multicolored | 3.50 | 4.50 |
| | | Nos. 768-771 (4) | 10.50 | 7.50 |

**Souvenir Sheet**
| 772 | A99 | $6 multicolored | 6.75 | 6.75 |

Christmas.

Lizards A100

**1989, Feb. 20**    **Litho.**    *Perf. 13½x14*
| 773 | A100 | 45c Wood slave | 1.50 | .70 |
| 774 | A100 | 80c Slippery back | 2.40 | 1.25 |
| 775 | A100 | $2.50 Iguana | 5.50 | 6.50 |
| | | Nos. 773-775 (3) | 9.40 | 8.45 |

**Souvenir Sheet**
| 776 | A100 | $6 Tree lizard | 16.00 | 16.00 |

Easter — A101

Paintings: 35c, Christ Crowned with Thorns, by Hieronymous Bosch (c. 1450-1516. 80c, Christ Bearing the Cross, by David. $1, The Deposition, by David. $1.60, Pieta, by Rogier van der Weyden (1400-1464). $6, Crucified Christ with the Virgin Mary and Saints, by Raphael.

**1989, Mar. 23**    **Litho.**    *Perf. 14x13½*
| 777 | A101 | 35c multicolored | .50 | .35 |
| 778 | A101 | 80c multicolored | .90 | .75 |
| 779 | A101 | $1 multicolored | 1.00 | .80 |
| 780 | A101 | $1.60 multicolored | 1.60 | 2.25 |
| | | Nos. 777-780 (4) | 4.00 | 4.15 |

**Souvenir Sheet**
| 781 | A101 | $6 multicolored | 4.50 | 5.00 |

University of the West Indies, 40th Anniv. — A102

**1989, Apr. 24**    **Litho.**    *Perf. 14x13½*
| 782 | A102 | $5 Coat of arms | 3.50 | 4.50 |

**Nos. 634-636 and 638 Ovptd.**

**1989, July 3**    **Litho.**    *Perf. 13½X14*
| 783 | A82 | 80c multicolored | 2.75 | 1.25 |
| 784 | A82 | $1 multicolored | 2.75 | 1.60 |
| 785 | A82 | $1.35 multicolored | 3.25 | 2.50 |
| 786 | A82 | $5 multicolored | 9.25 | 12.00 |
| | | Nos. 783-786 (4) | 18.00 | 17.35 |

Christmas A103

Well-known and historic houses: 5c, Lone Star, 1930. 35c, Whitehouse, 1906. 45c, Hodges House. 80c, Warden's Place. $6, Wallblake House, 1787.

**1989, Dec. 4**    **Litho.**    *Perf. 13½x14*
| 787 | A103 | 5c multicolored | .45 | 1.10 |
| 788 | A103 | 35c multicolored | .75 | .55 |
| 789 | A103 | 45c multicolored | .90 | .65 |
| 790 | A103 | 80c multicolored | 1.60 | 2.10 |
| | | Nos. 787-790 (4) | 3.70 | 4.40 |

**Souvenir Sheet**
| 791 | A103 | $6 multicolored | 5.00 | 5.00 |

Fish — A104

5c, Blear eye. 10c, Redman. 15c, Speckletail. 25c, Grunt. 30c, Amber jack. 35c, Red hind. 40c, Goatfish. 45c, Old wife. 50c, Butter fish. 65c, Shell fish. 80c, Yellowtail snapper. $1, Katy. $1.35, Mutton grouper. $2.50, Doctor fish. $5, Angelfish. $10, Barracuda.

**1990, Apr. 2**    **Litho.**    *Perf. 13½x14*
| 792 | A104 | 5c multicolored | 1.10 | 1.50 |
| 793 | A104 | 10c multicolored | 1.10 | 1.50 |
| 794 | A104 | 15c multicolored | 1.10 | .90 |
| 795 | A104 | 25c multicolored | 1.25 | 1.10 |
| 796 | A104 | 30c multicolored | 1.25 | 1.10 |
| 797 | A104 | 35c multicolored | 1.25 | 1.10 |
| 798 | A104 | 40c multicolored | 1.50 | 1.10 |
| 799 | A104 | 45c multicolored | 1.50 | .80 |
| 800 | A104 | 50c multicolored | 1.75 | 1.25 |
| 801 | A104 | 65c multicolored | 2.25 | 1.25 |
| 802 | A104 | 80c multicolored | 2.10 | 1.50 |
| 803 | A104 | $1 multicolored | 2.25 | 1.50 |
| 804 | A104 | $1.35 multicolored | 2.50 | 2.25 |
| 805 | A104 | $2.50 multicolored | 4.00 | 4.75 |
| 806 | A104 | $5 multicolored | 5.75 | 7.75 |
| 807 | A104 | $10 multicolored | 9.25 | 11.50 |
| | | Nos. 792-807 (16) | 39.90 | 40.85 |

**Inscribed "1992"**
| 792a | A104 | 5c Blear eye | .90 | 1.25 |
| 793a | A104 | 10c Redman | .90 | 1.25 |
| 797a | A104 | 35c Red hind | 1.00 | 1.00 |
| | | Nos. 792a-797a (3) | 2.80 | 3.50 |

For overprints and surcharge see Nos. 821-824, 849. For booklet see No. 890.

Easter — A105

35c, Last Supper. 45c, Trial. $1.35, Calvary. $2.50, Empty tomb. $6, The Resurrection.

**1990, Apr. 2**       *Perf. 14x13½*
| 811 | A105 | 35c multicolored | 1.25 | .25 |
| 812 | A105 | 45c multicolored | 1.25 | .35 |
| 813 | A105 | $1.35 multicolored | 3.00 | 3.00 |
| 814 | A105 | $2.50 multicolored | 3.75 | 3.75 |
| | | Nos. 811-814 (4) | 9.25 | 7.35 |

**Souvenir Sheet**
| 815 | A105 | $6 multicolored | 11.50 | 11.50 |

See Nos. 834-838.

Cape of Good Hope No. 7 — A106

Stamps of Great Britain and exhibition emblem: 25c, No. 1, vert. 50c, No. 2, vert. $2.50, No. 93. $6, Nos. 1-2.

**1990, Apr. 30**       *Perf. 14*
| 816 | A106 | 25c multicolored | 1.00 | .40 |
| 817 | A106 | 50c multicolored | 1.75 | .70 |
| 818 | A106 | $1.50 shown | 3.00 | 3.00 |
| 819 | A106 | $2.50 multicolored | 4.00 | 4.75 |
| | | Nos. 816-819 (4) | 9.75 | 8.85 |

**Souvenir Sheet**
| 820 | A106 | $6 multicolored | 13.00 | 15.00 |

Stamp World London '90, Penny Black 150th anniv.

**Nos. 803-806 Overprinted**

a

b

c

d

$1, Katy. $1.35, Mutton grouper. $2.50, Doctor fish. $5, Angelfish.

**1990, Sept. 24**    **Litho.**    *Perf. 13½x14*
| 821 | A104(a) | $1 multi | 2.25 | 1.40 |
| 822 | A104(b) | $1.35 multi | 2.50 | 1.60 |
| 823 | A104(c) | $2.50 multi | 6.00 | 6.00 |
| 824 | A104(d) | $5 multi | 11.50 | 11.50 |
| | | Nos. 821-824 (4) | 22.25 | 20.50 |

Birds — A107

10c, Laughing gull. 35c, Brown booby. $1.50, Bridled tern. $3.50, Brown pelican. $6, Least tern.

**1990, Dec. 3**       *Perf. 14*
| 825 | A107 | 10c multicolored | .95 | .55 |
| 826 | A107 | 35c multicolored | 1.60 | .55 |
| 827 | A107 | $1.50 multicolored | 2.25 | 2.75 |
| 828 | A107 | $3.50 multicolored | 5.00 | 5.00 |
| | | Nos. 825-828 (4) | 9.80 | 8.85 |

**Souvenir Sheet**
| 829 | A107 | $6 multicolored | 10.00 | 11.50 |

Christmas.

Flags — A108

50c, Mermaid. 80c, New Anguilla official. $1, Three dolphins. $5, Governor's official.

**1990, Nov. 5**    **Litho.**    *Perf. 13½x14*
| 830 | A108 | 50c multicolored | 1.75 | .65 |
| 831 | A108 | 80c multicolored | 2.75 | 1.25 |
| 832 | A108 | $1 multicolored | 2.90 | 1.50 |
| 833 | A108 | $5 multicolored | 8.25 | 9.50 |
| | | Nos. 830-833 (4) | 15.65 | 12.90 |

Nos. 811-815 Inscribed or Overprinted

**1991, Apr. 30**    **Litho.**    *Perf. 14x13½*
| 834 | A105 | 35c like #811 | 1.25 | .75 |
| 835 | A105 | 45c like #812 | 1.50 | .75 |
| 836 | A105 | $1.35 like #813 | 3.00 | 3.00 |
| 837 | A105 | $2.50 like #814 | 4.75 | 5.25 |
| | | Nos. 834-837 (4) | 10.50 | 9.75 |

**Souvenir Sheet**
| 838 | A105 | $6 like #815 | 13.50 | 13.50 |

Easter. "1990" obliterated by black bar in souvenir sheet margin.

Christmas A109

5c, Angel, vert. 35c, Santa, vert. $1, Palm trees, poinsettias. $5, Homes, holly.

*Perf. 14x13½, 13½x14*

**1991, Dec.**       **Litho.**
| 839 | A109 | 5c multicolored | .75 | .90 |
| 840 | A109 | 35c multicolored | 2.00 | .75 |
| 841 | A109 | 80c shown | 3.00 | 2.75 |
| 842 | A109 | $1 multicolored | 3.00 | 2.75 |
| | | Nos. 839-842 (4) | 8.75 | 7.15 |

**Souvenir Sheet**
| 843 | A109 | $5 multicolored | 10.00 | 10.00 |

Easter A110

Designs: 35c, Church, angels holding palms, vert. 45c Church, angels singing, vert. 80c, Village. $1, People going to church, vert. $5, People at beach, sailboats.

**1992**    **Litho.**    *Perf. 14*
| 844 | A110 | 35c multicolored | 1.00 | .65 |
| 845 | A110 | 45c multicolored | 1.25 | .65 |
| 846 | A110 | 80c multicolored | 2.25 | 1.10 |

**847** A110 $1 multicolored 2.25 1.60
**848** A110 $5 multicolored 6.25 *12.00*
*Nos. 844-848 (5)* 13.00 16.00

### No. 796 Surcharged

**1992, June 10 Litho. *Perf. 13½x14***
**849** A104 $1.60 on 30c #796 4.00 2.75

No. 849 inscribed "1992."

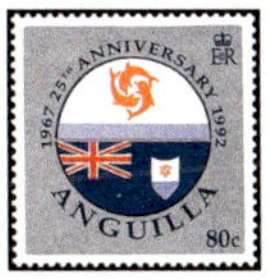


Independence, 25th Anniv. — A111

80c, Official seal, flag. $1, Official seal. $1.60, Flags, airport. $2, First seal. $10, Nos. 1, 8-11, 15-16.

**1992, Aug. 10 Litho. *Perf. 14***
**850** A111 80c multicolored 2.50 1.50
**851** A111 $1 multicolored 2.50 1.50
**852** A111 $1.60 multicolored 4.75 4.75
**853** A111 $2 multicolored 4.75 4.75
*Nos. 850-853 (4)* 14.50 12.50

### Souvenir Sheet

**854** A111 $10 multicolored 15.00 15.00

No. 854 contains one 85x85mm stamp. For booklet see No. 970.

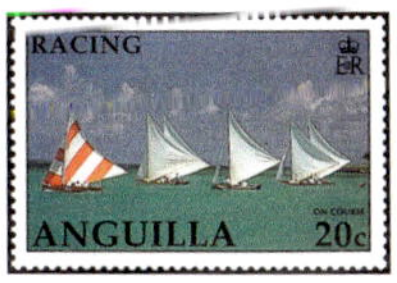


Sailboat Racing A112

Designs: 20c, On course. 35c, Stylized boat poster. 45c, Start of race. No. 858, Blue Bird, 1971, vert. No. 859, Construction plans for Blue Bird, vert. $1, Stylized boat poster, diff. $6, Like Nos. 855 & 857.

***Perf. 13½x14, 14x13½***
**1992, Oct. 12 Litho.**
**855** A112 20c multicolored 1.90 .60
**856** A112 35c multicolored 2.40 .50
**857** A112 45c multicolored 2.75 .50
**858** A112 80c multicolored 3.75 *4.25*
**859** A112 80c multicolored 3.75 *4.25*
***a.*** Pair, #858-859 8.00 *10.00*
**860** A112 $1 multicolored 3.75 2.50
*Nos. 855-860 (6)* 18.30 12.60

### Souvenir Sheet

**861** A112 $6 multicolored 10.00 *12.50*

No. 861 contains one 96x31mm stamp.

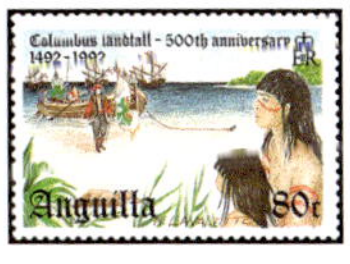


Discovery of America, 500th Anniv. — A113

80c, Landfall. $1, Columbus, vert. $2, Fleet. $3, Pinta. $6, Map of voyage, vert.

**1992, Dec. 15 Litho. *Perf. 14***
**862** A113 80c multicolored 3.00 1.75
**863** A113 $1 multicolored 3.00 1.75
**864** A113 $2 multicolored 4.75 5.50
**865** A113 $3 multicolored 5.50 *7.00*
*Nos. 862-865 (4)* 16.25 16.00

### Souvenir Sheet

**866** A113 $6 multicolored 15.00 15.00

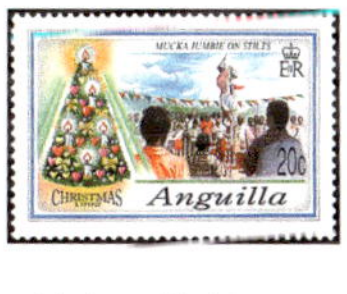


Christmas A114

Various Christmas trees and: 20c, Mucka Jumbie on stilts. 70c, Masquerading house to house. $1.05, Christmas baking, old oven style. $2.40, $5, Collecting presents.

**1992, Dec. 7**
**867** A114 20c multicolored .90 .65
**868** A114 70c multicolored 2.00 .95
**869** A114 $1.05 multicolored 2.25 1.75
**870** A114 $2.40 multicolored 4.25 *6.00*
*Nos. 867-870 (4)* 9.40 9.35

### Souvenir Sheet

**871** A114 $5 Sheet of 1 + 3 labels 7.00 7.00

Labels on No. 871 are similar to Nos. 867-869, but without denomination.

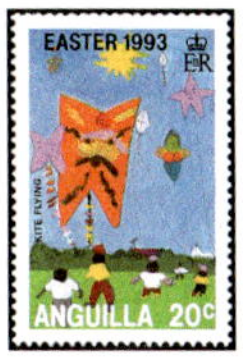


Easter — A115

Children's drawings: 20c, Kite flying. 45c, Cliff top village service. 80c, Morning devotion on Sombrero. $1.50, Hilltop church service. $5, Good Friday kites.

**1993, Mar. 29 Litho. *Perf. 14***
**872** A115 20c multicolored 1.75 .90
**873** A115 45c multicolored 2.75 .90
**874** A115 80c multicolored 4.00 2.10
**875** A115 $1.50 multicolored 4.50 *7.00*
*Nos. 872-875 (4)* 13.00 10.90

### Souvenir Sheet

**876** A115 $5 multicolored 9.00 9.00

No. 876 contains one 42x56mm stamp.

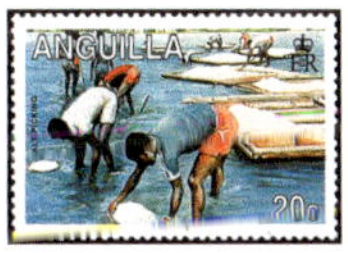


Native Industries A116

20c, Salt. 80c, Tobacco, $1, Cotton. $2, Sugar cane.

**1993, June 23 Litho. *Perf. 14***
**877** A116 20c multicolored 3.25 1.10
**878** A116 80c multicolored 3.00 1.75
**879** A116 $1 multicolored 3.00 1.75
**880** A116 $2 multicolored 4.25 *6.50*
*Nos. 877-880 (4)* 13.50 11.10

### Souvenir Sheet

**881** A116 $6 Fishing 14.00 14.00

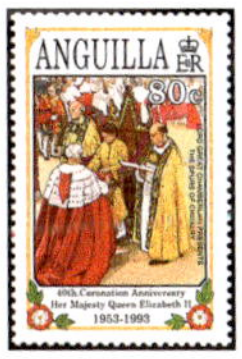


Coronation of Queen Elizabeth II, 40th Anniv. — A117

Designs: 80c, Lord Great Chamberlain presents the spurs of chivalry. $1, The benediction. $2, Queen Elizabeth II, coronation photograph. $3, St. Edward's Crown. $6, Queen, Prince Philip in Gold State Coach.

**1993, Aug. 16 Litho. *Perf. 14***
**882** A117 80c multicolored 2.25 1.00
**883** A117 $1 multicolored 2.50 1.10
**884** A117 $2 multicolored 3.25 3.25
**885** A117 $3 multicolored 3.75 *4.75*
*Nos. 882-885 (4)* 11.75 10.10

### Souvenir Sheet

**886** A117 $6 multicolored 14.00 *16.00*

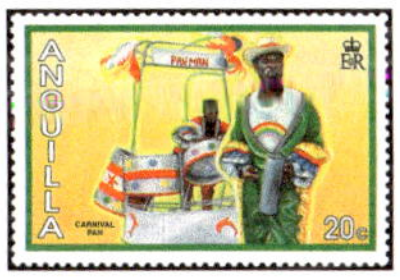


Anguilla Carnival A118

20c, Pan musician. 45c, Pirates. 80c, Stars. $1, Playing mas. $2, Masqueraders. $3, Commandos. $5, Carnival fantasy.

**1993, Aug. 23 Litho. *Perf. 14***
**887** A118 20c multicolored .70 .50
**888** A118 45c multicolored 1.25 .50
**889** A118 80c multicolored 2.40 1.10
**890** A118 $1 multicolored 2.40 1.25
Booklet, 5 ea #796, 890 14.00
**891** A118 $2 multicolored 3.75 *5.50*
**892** A118 $3 multicolored 4.00 *6.25*
*Nos. 887-892 (6)* 14.50 15.10

### Souvenir Sheet

**893** A118 $5 multicolored 14.00 14.00

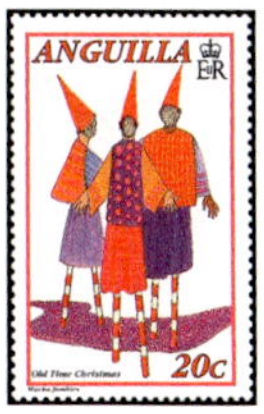


Christmas — A119

Traditional Christmas customs: 20c, Mucka Jumbies. 35c, Serenaders. 45c, Baking. $3, Five-fingers Christmas tree. $4, Mucka Jumbies and serenaders.

**1993, Dec. 7 Litho. *Perf. 14x13½***
**894** A119 20c multicolored 1.10 .90
**895** A119 35c multicolored 1.50 .90
**896** A119 45c multicolored 1.75 .90
**897** A119 $3 multicolored 5.75 *8.00*
*Nos. 894-897 (4)* 10.10 10.70

### Souvenir Sheet
### *Perf. 14*

**898** A119 $4 multicolored 5.75 5.75

No. 898 contains one 51x42mm stamp.

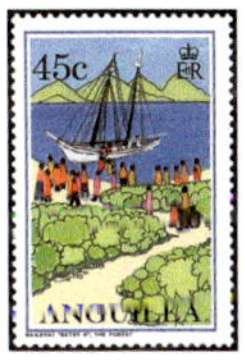


Mail Delivery — A120

Designs: 20c, Traveling Branch mail van, Sandy Ground, horiz. 45c, Mail boat, Betsy R, The Forest. 80c, Old post office, horiz. $1, Mail by jeep, Island Harbor. $4, New post office, 1993, horiz.

**1994, Feb. 11 Litho. *Perf. 14***
**899** A120 20c multicolored 2.00 .95
**900** A120 45c multicolored 2.75 .95
**901** A120 80c multicolored 3.50 1.90
**902** A120 $1 multicolored 3.50 1.90
**903** A120 $4 multicolored 5.50 *8.75*
*Nos. 899-903 (5)* 17.25 14.45

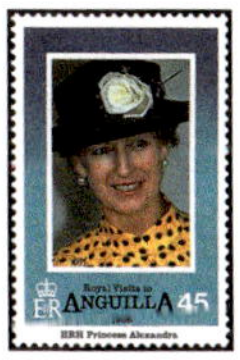


Royal Visits — A121

45c, Princess Alexandra. 50c, Princess Alice. 80c, Prince Philip. $1, Prince Charles. $2, Queen Elizabeth II.

**1994, Feb. 18**
**904** A121 45c multicolored 2.00 .80
**905** A121 50c multicolored 2.25 .80
**906** A121 80c multicolored 3.00 1.75
**907** A121 $1 multicolored 3.50 1.75
**908** A121 $2 multicolored 4.75 *5.50*
***a.*** Souvenir sheet of 4, #904-908 15.00 15.00
*Nos. 904-908 (5)* 15.50 10.60

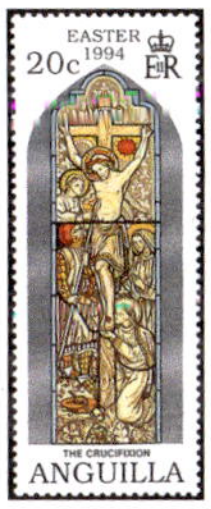


Easter — A122

Stained glass windows: 20c, Crucifixion. 45c, Empty tomb. 80c, Resurrection. $3, Risen Christ with disciples.

**1994, Apr. 6 Litho. *Perf. 14x15***
**909** A122 20c multicolored .90 .65
**910** A122 45c multicolored 1.10 .80
**911** A122 80c multicolored 2.10 1.10
**912** A122 $3 multicolored 5.50 *6.25*
*Nos. 909-912 (4)* 9.60 8.80

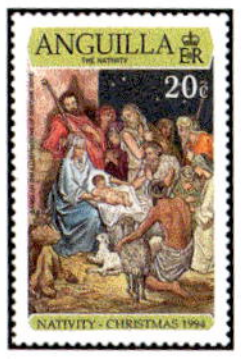


Christmas — A123

Designs: 20c, Adoration of the shepherds. 30c, Magi, shepherds. 35c, The Annunciation. 45c, Nativity Scene. $2.40, Flight into Egypt.

**1994, Nov. 22 Litho. *Perf. 14***
**913** A123 20c multicolored 1.00 .80
**914** A123 30c multicolored 1.25 .80
**915** A123 35c multicolored 1.25 .80
**916** A123 45c multicolored 1.50 .80
**917** A123 $2.40 multicolored 5.00 *6.00*
*Nos. 913-917 (5)* 10.00 9.20

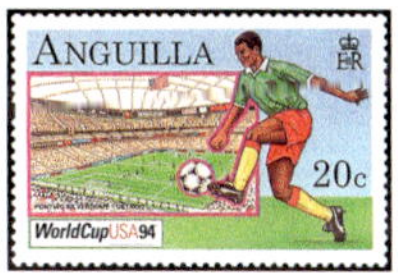


1994 World Cup Soccer Championships, US — A124

Soccer player and: 20c, Pontiac Silverdome, Detroit. 70c, Foxboro Stadium, Boston. $1.80, RFK Memorial Stadium, Washington. $2.40, Soldier Field, Chicago. $6, Two players.

**1994, Oct. 3 Litho. *Perf. 13½x14***
**918** A124 20c multicolored 1.00 .50
**919** A124 70c multicolored 1.50 1.10
**920** A124 $1.80 multicolored 3.00 *3.25*
**921** A124 $2.40 multicolored 3.50 *4.00*
*Nos. 918-921 (4)* 9.00 8.85

### Souvenir Sheet

**922** A124 $6 multicolored 13.00 13.00

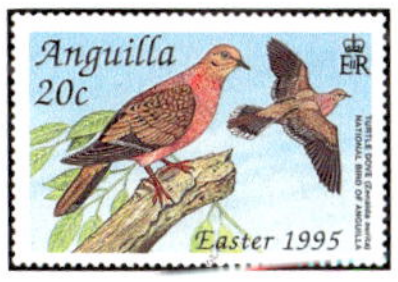


Easter A125

Turtle dove: 45c, One on tree branch. 50c, One on nest, one on branch. $5, Mother with young.

**1995, Apr. 10 Litho. *Perf. 14***
**923** A125 20c multicolored .70 .60
**924** A125 45c multicolored 1.10 .90
**925** A125 50c multicolored 1.25 1.10
**926** A125 $5 multicolored 7.00 *10.00*
*Nos. 923-926 (4)* 10.05 12.60

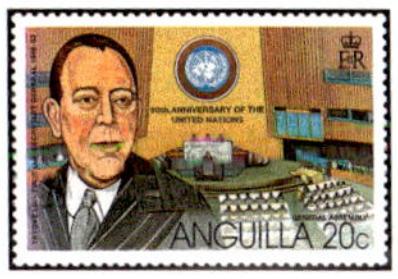


UN, 50th Anniv. A126

Secretaries general and: 20c, Trygve Lie (1946-53), general assembly. 80c, UN flag, UN headquarters with "50" (no portrait). $1, Dag Hammarskjold (1953-61), charter, U Thant (1961-71). $5, UN complex, New York, vert. (no portrait).

***Perf. 13½x14, 14x13½***
**1995, June 26 Litho.**
**927** A126 20c multicolored .40 .40
**928** A126 80c multicolored .80 .80
**929** A126 $1 multicolored 1.00 1.00
**930** A126 $5 multicolored 5.00 5.00
*Nos. 927-930 (4)* 7.20 7.20

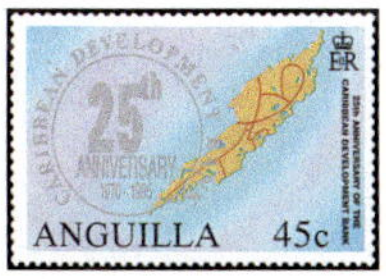


Caribbean Development Bank, 25th Anniv. — A127

Designs: 45c, Emblem, map of Anguilla. $5, Local headquarters along waterfront.

**1995, Aug. 15 Litho. *Perf. 13½x14***

**931** A127 45c multicolored 2.50 2.50
**932** A127 $5 multicolored 4.75 4.75
*a.* Pair, #931-932 7.50 7.50

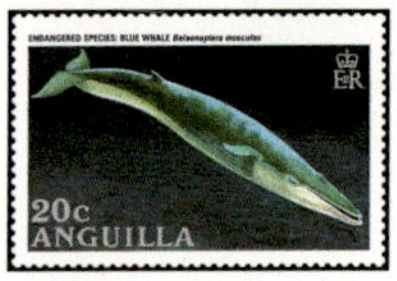


Whales A128

20c, Blue whale. 45c, Right whale, vert. $1, Sperm whale. $5, Humpback whale.

***Perf. 13½x14, 14x13½***

**1995, Nov. 24 Litho.**

**933** A128 20c multicolored 2.75 .95
**934** A128 45c multicolored 3.00 .80
**935** A128 $1 multicolored 3.75 2.10
**936** A128 $5 multicolored 8.50 10.50
*Nos. 933-936 (4)* 18.00 14.35

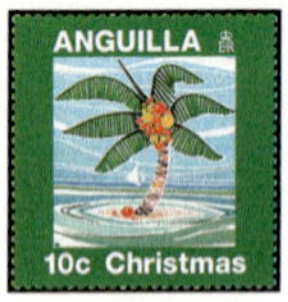


Christmas — A129

10c, Palm tree. 25c, Fish net floats. 45c, Sea shells. $5, Fish.

**1995, Dec. 12 *Perf. 14½***

**937** A129 10c multicolored .80 .80
**938** A129 25c multicolored 1.10 .65
**939** A129 45c multicolored 1.25 .65
**940** A129 $5 multicolored 9.50 12.00
*Nos. 937-940 (4)* 12.65 14.10

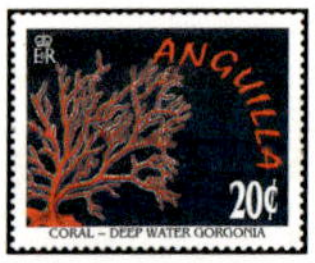


Corals — A130

20c, Deep water gorgonia. 80c, Common sea fan. $5, Venus sea fern.

**1996, June 21 Litho. *Perf. 14x14½***

**941** A130 20c multicolored 2.00 .95
**942** A130 80c multicolored 3.25 1.40
**943** A130 $5 multicolored 9.00 11.00
*Nos. 941-943 (3)* 14.25 13.35

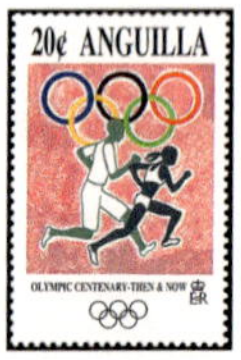


A131

1996 Summer Olympic Games, Atlanta: 20c, Running. 80c, Javelin, wheelchair basketball. $1, High jump. $3.50, Olympic torch, Greek, US flags.

**1996, Dec. 12 Litho. *Perf. 14***

**944** A131 20c multicolored .95 .75
**945** A131 80c multicolored 3.25 1.50
**946** A131 $1 multicolored 2.25 1.50
**947** A131 $3.50 multicolored 6.00 6.00
*Nos. 944-947 (4)* 12.45 9.75

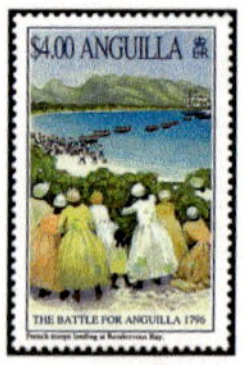


A132

Battle for Anguilla, bicent.: 60c, Sandy Hill Fort, HMS Lapwing. 75c, French troops destroy church, horiz. $1.50, HMS Lapwing defeats Valiant, Decius, horiz. $4, French troops land, Rendezvous Bay.

**1996, Dec. 12**

**948** A132 60c multicolored 1.25 1.25
**949** A132 75c multicolored 1.25 1.25
**950** A132 $1.50 multicolored 2.50 2.50
**951** A132 $4 multicolored 4.00 5.00
*Nos. 948-951 (4)* 9.00 10.00

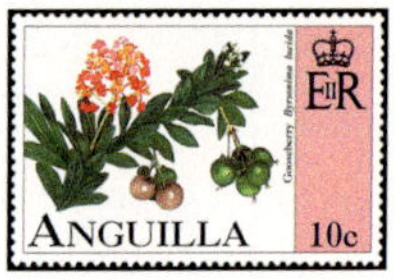


Fruits and Nuts — A133

10c, Gooseberry. 20c, West Indian cherry. 40c, Tamarind. 50c, Pomme-surette. 60c, Sea almond. 75c, Sea grape. 80c, Banana. $1, Genip. $1.10, Coco plum. $1.25, Pope. $1.50, Papaya. $2, Sugar apple. $3, Soursop. $4, Pomegranate. $5, Cashew. $10, Mango.

**1997, Apr. 30 Litho. *Perf. 14***

**952** A133 10c multicolored .50 .75
**953** A133 20c multicolored .60 .40
**954** A133 40c multicolored .75 .40
**955** A133 50c multicolored 1.00 .50
**956** A133 60c multicolored 1.00 .60
**957** A133 75c multicolored 1.25 .80
**958** A133 80c multicolored 1.25 .90
**959** A133 $1 multicolored 1.50 1.25
**960** A133 $1.10 multicolored 1.50 1.75
**961** A133 $1.25 multicolored 1.75 1.90
**962** A133 $1.50 multicolored 2.00 2.25
**963** A133 $2 multicolored 2.50 3.00
**964** A133 $3 multicolored 4.00 4.00
**965** A133 $4 multicolored 5.25 5.50
**966** A133 $5 multicolored 6.25 6.50
**967** A133 $10 multicolored 10.00 10.50
*Nos. 952-967 (16)* 41.10 41.00

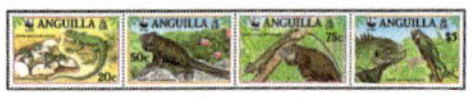

Iguanas — A134

World Wildlife Fund: a, 20c, Baby iguanas emerging from eggs, juvenile iguana. b, 50c, Adult on rock. c, 75c, Two iguanas on tree limbs. d, $3, Adult up close, adult on tree branch.

**1997, Oct. 13 Litho. *Perf. 13½x14***

**968** A134 Strip of 4, #a.-d. 10.00 10.00

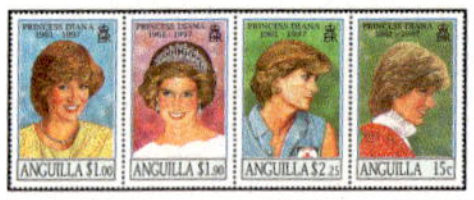

Diana, Princess of Wales (1961-97) — A135

Designs: a, 15c, In red & white. b, $1, In yellow. c, $1.90, Wearing tiara. d, $2.25, Wearing blouse with Red Cross emblem.

**1998, Apr. 14 Litho. *Perf. 14***

**969** A135 Strip of 4, #a.-d. 9.50 9.50

No. 969 was issued in sheets of 16 stamps.

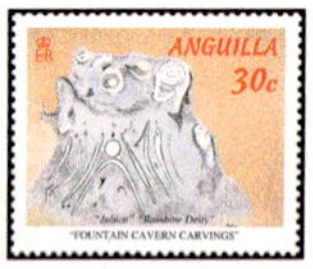


Fountain Cavern Carvings — A136

30c, Rainbow Deity (Juluca). $1.25, Lizard. $2.25, Solar Chieftan. $2.75, Creator.

**1997, Nov. 17 Litho. *Perf. 14x14½***

**970** A136 30c multicolored .55 .55
Booklet, 5 ea #851, 970 12.00
**971** A136 $1.25 multicolored 1.25 1.25
**972** A136 $2.25 multicolored 2.10 2.10
**973** A136 $2.75 multicolored 2.75 2.75
*Nos. 970-973 (4)* 6.65 6.65

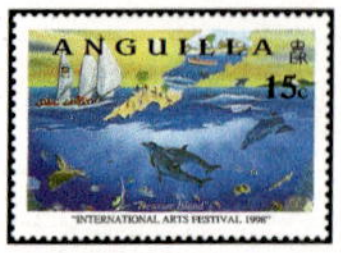


1998 Intl. Arts Festival — A137

Paintings: 15c, "Treasure Island." 30c, "Posing in the Light." $1, "Pescadores de Anguilla." $1.50, "Fresh Catch." $1.90, "The Bell Tower of St. Mary's."

**1998, Aug. 24 Litho. *Perf. 14***

**974** A137 15c multi .65 .65
**975** A137 30c multi, vert. .80 .80
**976** A137 $1 multi, vert. 1.40 1.40
Booklet, 5 ea #975-976 10.00
**977** A137 $1.50 multi 1.40 1.60
**978** A137 $1.90 multi, vert. 1.75 2.00
*Nos. 974-978 (5)* 6.00 6.45

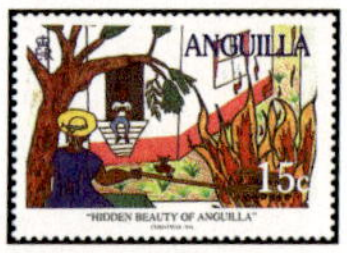


Christmas A138

Paintings of "Hidden beauty of Anguilla": 15c, Woman cooking over open fire, girl seated on steps. $1, Person looking over fruits and vegetables. $1.50, Underwater scene. $3, Cacti growing along shore.

**1998, Nov. 18**

**979** A138 15c multicolored .50 .50
**980** A138 $1 multicolored 1.00 1.00
**981** A138 $1.50 multicolored 1.40 1.40
**982** A138 $3 multicolored 2.10 2.10
*Nos. 979-982 (4)* 5.00 5.00

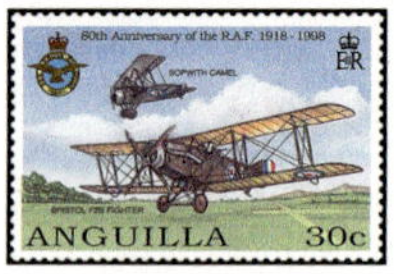


Royal Air Force, 80th Anniv. — A139

Designs: 30c, Sopwith Camel, Bristol F2B. $1, Supermarine Spitfire II, Hawker Hurricane Mk1. $1.50, Avro Lancaster. $1.90, Harrier GR7, Panavia Tornado F3.

**1998, Dec. 31 Litho. *Perf. 13½***
**Granite Paper (No. 983)**

**983** A139 30c multicolored 1.25 .60
**984** A139 $1 multicolored 2.00 1.00
**985** A139 $1.50 multicolored 2.50 2.25
**986** A139 $1.90 multicolored 4.00 3.25
Booklet, 5 ea #983-984 16.50
*Nos. 983-986 (4)* 9.75 7.10

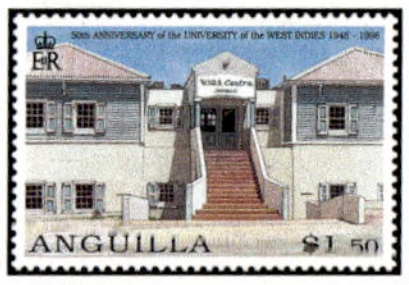


University of the West Indies, 50th Anniv. A140

Designs: $1.50, Anguilla campus. $1.90, Anguilla campus, torchbearer, University arms.

**1998, Dec. 31 Litho. *Perf. 13¼***
**Granite Paper (#988)**

**987-988** A140 Set of 2 3.00 3.50

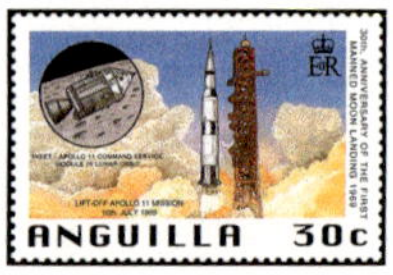


First Manned Moon Landing, 30th Anniv. — A141

Designs: 30c, Lift-off of Apollo 11, Command and Service Modules in lunar orbit. $1, Buzz Aldrin on Moon, footprint. $1.50, Lunar Module leaving Moon. $1.90, Splashdown.

**1999, May 6 Litho. *Perf. 13¾***

**989** A141 30c multi .80 .50
**990** A141 $1 multi 1.40 .90
**991** A141 $1.50 multi 1.50 1.75
**992** A141 $1.90 multi 2.50 3.25
*Nos. 989-992 (4)* 6.20 6.40

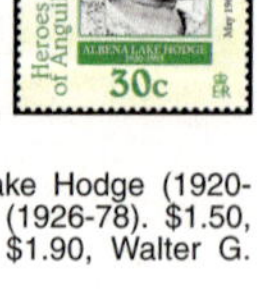


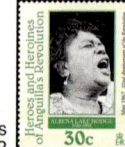

Heroes of Anguilla's Revolution — A142

Designs: 30c, Albena Lake Hodge (1920-85). $1, Collins O. Hodge (1926-78). $1.50, Edwin W. Rey (1906-80). $1.90, Walter G. Hodge (1920-89).

**1999, July 5 *Perf. 14½x14¼***

**993** A142 30c multi .50 .30
**994** A142 $1 multi .90 .60
**995** A142 $1.50 multi 1.25 1.25
**996** A142 $1.90 multi 1.90 2.00
*Nos. 993-996 (4)* 4.55 4.15

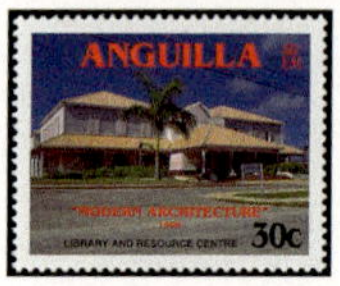


Modern Architecture A143

Designs: No. 997, 30c, Library and resource center. No. 998, 65c, Parliamentary building and court house. No. 999, $1, Caribbean Commercial Bank. No. 999A, $1.50, Police headquarters. No. 1000, $1.90, Post office.

**1999 Litho. *Perf. 14x14½***

**997-1000** A143 Set of 5 7.50 7.50

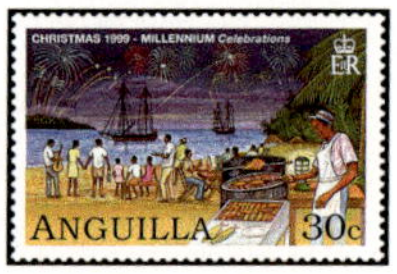


Christmas and Millennium Celebrations A144

Designs: 30c, Fireworks display and barbecue. $1, Globe, musicians. $1.50, Family dinner. $1.90, Decorated tree.

**1999 Litho. *Perf. 13¼***

**1001** A144 30c multi .55 .50
**1002** A144 $1 multi 1.40 .90
**1003** A144 $1.50 multi 2.10 2.10
**1004** A144 $1.90 multi 2.25 3.75
*Nos. 1001-1004 (4)* 6.30 7.25

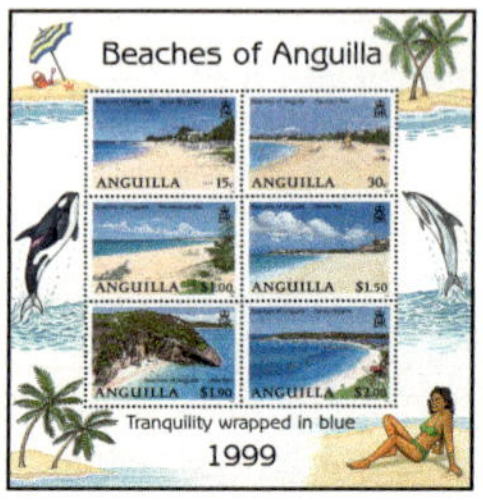


Beaches A145

1005, 15c, Shoal Bay. 1006, 30c, Maundys Bay. 1007, $1, Rendezvous Bay. 1008, $1.50, Meads Bay. 1009, $1.90, Little Bay. 1010, $2, Sandy Ground.

**1999 *Perf. 12***

**1005-1010** A145 Set of 6 8.25 8.25
*1010a* Sheet of 6, #1005-1010 8.25 8.25
*1010b* As "a," with show emblem in margin 8.25 8.00

The Stamp Show 2000, London (No. 1010b). Issued: No. 1010b, 5/22/00.

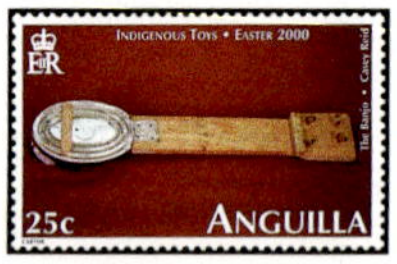


Easter A146

Toys: 25c, Banjo. 30c, Top. $1.50, Slingshot. $1.90, Roller. $2.50, Killy ban.

No. 1016: a, 75c, Rag doll. b, $1, Kite. c, $1.25, Cricket ball. d, $4, Pond boat.

**2000 *Perf. 13¼***

**1011** A146 25c multi .25 .25
**1012** A146 30c multi .35 .35
**1013** A146 $1.50 multi 1.25 1.25
**1014** A146 $1.90 multi 1.60 2.25
**1015** A146 $2.50 multi 2.60 3.00
*Nos. 1011-1015 (5)* 6.05 7.10

**Souvenir Sheet**

**1016** A146 Sheet of 4, #a-d 6.25 6.25

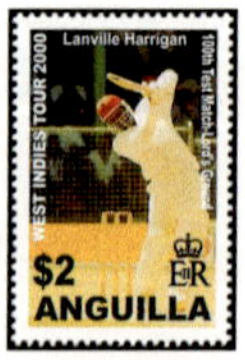


100th Test Match at Lord's Ground — A147

$2, Lanville Harrigan. $4, Cardigan Connor. $6, Lord's Ground, horiz.

**2000, May 5 Litho. *Perf. 13¾x13¼***

**1017-1018** A147 Set of 2 7.75 7.75

**Souvenir Sheet**

**1018A** A147 $6 multi 12.00 12.00

# ANGUILLA

Prince William, 18th Birthday — A148

Prince William and: 30c, Queen Elizabeth II, Princes Philip and Charles. $1, Princess Diana, Princes Harry and Charles. $1.90, Princes Harry and Charles. $2.25, Princes Charles and Harry, in winter wear. $8, Prince William, vert.

| 2000, July 20 | | | Perf. 13¼ | |
|---|---|---|---|---|
| 1019-1022 | A148 | Set of 4 | 9.25 | 9.25 |

**Souvenir Sheet**

| 1023 | A148 | $8 multicolored | 9.50 | 9.50 |
|---|---|---|---|---|

Queen Mother, 100th Birthday A149

Queen Mother and. 30c, Prince William. $1.50, Anguilla shoreline. $1.90, Clarence House. $5, Castle of Mey.

| 2000, Aug. 4 | | | | |
|---|---|---|---|---|
| 1024-1027 | A149 | Set of 4 | 8.75 | 8.75 |

Intl. Arts Festival — A150

Artwork: 15c, Anguilla Montage, by Weme Caster. 30c, Serenity, by Damien Carty. 65c, Inter-island Cargo, by Paula Walden. $1.50, Rainbow City Where Spirits Find Form, by Fiona Percy. $1.90, Sailing Silver Seas, by Valerie Carpenter. $7, Historic Anguilla, by Melsadis Fleming.

| 2000, Sept. 21 | | | Perf. 14¼x14½ | |
|---|---|---|---|---|
| 1028-1032 | A150 | Set of 5 | 5.75 | 5.75 |

**Souvenir Sheet** Perf. 14¼

| 1033 | A150 | $7 multi | 7.25 | 7.25 |
|---|---|---|---|---|

No. 1033 contains one 43x28mm stamp.

Christmas — A151

Flower and Garden Show flower arrangements by: 15c, Rowena Carty. 25c, Yvonda Hodge. 30c, Carty, diff. $1, Simon Rogers. $1.50, Lady Josephine Gumbs $1.90, Carty, diff.

| 2000, Nov. 22 | | | Perf. 13¼ | |
|---|---|---|---|---|
| 1034-1039 | A151 | Set of 6 | 6.75 | 6.75 |

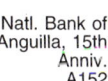

Natl. Bank of Anguilla, 15th Anniv. A152

Designs: 30c, Soccer team in annual primary school tournament. $1, Sponsored sailboat, De Chan, vert. $1.50, Bank's crest, vert. $1.90, New bank building.

| 2000, Nov. 27 | | | | |
|---|---|---|---|---|
| 1040-1043 | A152 | Set of 4 | 5.25 | 5.25 |

Ebenezer Methodist Church, 170th Anniv. A153

Church in: 30c, Sepia tones. $1.90, Full color.

| 2000, Dec. 4 | | | | |
|---|---|---|---|---|
| 1044-1045 | A153 | Set of 2 | 2.75 | 2.75 |

UN Women's Human Rights Campaign A154

Designs: 25c, Soroptimist Day Care Center. 30c, Britannia Idalia Gumbs, vert. $2.25, Woman, vert.

| 2001 | | Litho. | Perf. 13¼ | |
|---|---|---|---|---|
| 1046-1048 | A154 | Set of 3 | 4.00 | 4.00 |

American Revolution, 225th Anniv. — A155

Designs: 30c, John Paul Jones, USS Ranger. $1, George Washington, Battle of Yorktown. $1.50, Thomas Jefferson, Submission of Declaration of Independence. $1.90, John Adams, Adams and Benjamin Franklin signing peace treaty.

| 2001, July 4 | | Litho. | Perf. 13¼ | |
|---|---|---|---|---|
| 1049-1052 | A155 | Set of 4 | 8.75 | 8.75 |

Birds — A156

Designs: 30c, White-cheeked pintail. $1, Black-faced grassquits, vert. $1.50, Brown noddy. $2, Black-necked stilts, vert. $3, Snowy plovers.
No. 1058: a, 25c, Snowy egret. b, 65c, Red-billed tropicbird. $1.35, Greater yellowlegs. $2.25, Sooty tern.

| 2001, Aug. 7 | | | | |
|---|---|---|---|---|
| 1053-1057 | A156 | Set of 5 | 14.00 | 14.00 |

**Souvenir Sheet**

| 1058 | A156 | Sheet of 4, #a-d | 11.00 | 11.00 |
|---|---|---|---|---|

Year of Dialogue Among Civilizations — A157

| 2001, Oct. 9 | | | Perf. 13¼x13 | |
|---|---|---|---|---|
| 1059 | A157 | $1.90 multi | 3.00 | 3.00 |

Christmas A158

Musical instruments: 15c, Triangle. 25c, Maracas. 30c, Guiro, vert. $1.50, Marimba. $1.90, Tambu, vert. $2.50, Bath pan, vert.
No. 1066, vert.: a, 75c, Banjo. b, $1, Quatro. c, $1.25, Ukulele. d, $3, Cello.

| 2001, Nov. 5 | | Litho. | Perf. 13¼ | |
|---|---|---|---|---|
| 1060-1065 | A158 | Set of 6 | 10.00 | 10.00 |

**Souvenir Sheet**

| 1066 | A158 | Sheet of 4, #a-d | 9.00 | 9.00 |
|---|---|---|---|---|

Sombrero Lighthouse A159

Designs: 30c, Lighhouse in 1960s, vert. $1.50, Comparison of old and new lighthouses. $1.90, New lighthouse, 2001, vert.

| 2002, Apr. 2 | | Litho. | Perf. 13¼ | |
|---|---|---|---|---|
| 1067-1069 | A159 | Set of 3 | 7.00 | 7.00 |

Social Security Board, 20th Anniv. — A160

Social Security: 30c, Community service, vert. 75c, Benefits all ages, vert. $2.50, Benefits employees.

| 2002, May 28 | | Litho. | Perf. 13¼ | |
|---|---|---|---|---|
| 1070-1072 | A160 | Set of 3 | 5.00 | 5.00 |

Royal Navy Ships — A161

Designs: 30c, HMS Antrim, 1967. 50c, HMS Formidable, 1939. $1.50, HMS Dreadnought, 1906. $2, HMS Warrior, 1860.
$7, HMS Ark Royal, 1981, vert.

| 2002, June 24 | | Litho. | Perf. 13¼ | |
|---|---|---|---|---|
| 1073-1076 | A161 | Set of 4 | 6.25 | 6.25 |

**Souvenir Sheet**

| 1077 | A161 | $7 multi | 10.00 | 10.00 |
|---|---|---|---|---|

Reign of Queen Elizabeth II, 50th Anniv. — A162

Designs: 30c, Holding baby. $1.50, Wearing white dress. $1.90, Wearing tiara. $5, Wearing yellow hat.
$8, At desk.

| 2002, Oct. 14 | | Litho. | Perf. 13¼ | |
|---|---|---|---|---|
| 1078-1081 | A162 | Set of 4 | 8.50 | 8.50 |

**Souvenir Sheet**

| 1082 | A162 | $8 multi | 10.00 | 10.00 |
|---|---|---|---|---|

Pan-American Health Organization, Cent — A163

Designs: 30c, The Valley Health Center. $1.50, Emblem, "100".

| 2002, Nov. 11 | | | | |
|---|---|---|---|---|
| 1083-1084 | A163 | Set of 2 | 2.75 | 2.75 |

Ships — A164

15c, Finance. 30c, Tiny Gull. 65c, Lady Laurel. 75c, Spitfire. $1, Liberator $1.35, Excelsior. $1.50, Rose Millicent. $1.90, Betsy R. $2, Ounream R. $2.25, New London. $3, Ismay. $10, Warspite.

| 2003, June 10 | | Litho. | Perf. 14 | |
|---|---|---|---|---|
| 1085 | A164 | 15c multi | .50 | .50 |
| 1086 | A164 | 30c multi | .60 | .30 |
| 1087 | A164 | 65c multi | 1.00 | .65 |
| 1088 | A164 | 75c multi | 1.00 | .75 |
| 1089 | A164 | $1 multi | 1.25 | 1.00 |
| 1090 | A164 | $1.35 multi | 1.50 | 1.50 |
| 1091 | A164 | $1.50 multi | 1.75 | 1.60 |
| 1092 | A164 | $1.90 multi | 2.00 | 1.90 |
| 1093 | A164 | $2 multi | 2.25 | 2.00 |
| 1094 | A164 | $2.25 multi | 3.00 | 2.50 |
| 1095 | A164 | $3 multi | 3.25 | 3.25 |
| 1096 | A164 | $10 multi | 10.00 | 11.00 |
| Nos. 1085-1096 (12) | | | 28.10 | 26.95 |

Artifacts — A165

Designs: 30c, Stone pestle. $1, Frog-shaped shell ornament. $1.50, Pottery. $1.90, Mask.

| 2003, Aug. 18 | | Litho. | Perf. 13¼ | |
|---|---|---|---|---|
| 1097-1100 | A165 | Set of 4 | 5.75 | 5.75 |

Hotels — A166

Designs: 75c, Frangipani Beach Club. $1, Pimms, Cap Juluca. $1.35, Cocoloba Beach Resort. $1.50, Malliouhana Hotel. $1.90, Carimar Beach Club. $3, Covecastles.

| 2003 | | Litho. | Perf. 13¼ | |
|---|---|---|---|---|
| 1101-1106 | A166 | Set of 6 | 9.50 | 9.50 |

2002 International Arts Festival A167

Paintings: 15c, Eudice's Garden, by Eunice Summer. 30c, Hammocks, by Lisa Davenport. $1, Conched Out, by Richard Shaffett. $1.50, Island Rhythms, by Carol Gavin. $1.90, Party at the Beach, by Jean-Pierre Ballagny. $3, Shoal Bay Before Luis, by Jacqueline Mariethoz, vert.

**Perf. 13½x13¼, 13¼x13½**

| 2004, Aug. 23 | | | Litho. | |
|---|---|---|---|---|
| 1107-1112 | A167 | Set of 6 | 12.50 | 12.50 |

2004 Summer Olympics, Athens — A168

2004 Athens Olympics emblem and: 30c, Runners. $1, Yachting. $1.50, Gymnastics. $1.90, Acropolis, Pierre de Coubertin, Dimitrios Vikelas, horiz.

**Perf. 13½x13¼, 13¼x13½**

| 2004, Sept. 20 | | | Litho. | |
|---|---|---|---|---|
| 1113-1116 | A168 | Set of 4 | 7.00 | 7.00 |

Goats A169

Various goats: 30c, 50c, $1, $1.50, $1.90, $2.25. $1, $1.90 are vert.

**Perf. 13¼x13½, 13½x13¼**

| 2004, Oct. 4 | | | | |
|---|---|---|---|---|
| 1117-1122 | A169 | Set of 6 | 10.50 | 10.50 |

Development of the Telephone — A170

Types of telephones: 30c, Cordless. $1, Touch-tone. $1.50, Cellular. $1.90, Rotary dial, horiz. $3.80, Magneto.

# ANGUILLA

**Perf. 13¼x13, 13x13¼**
2004, Nov. 8    Litho.
1123-1127  A170  Set of 5    8.75  8.75

Christmas — A171

Santa Claus: 30c, Baking with rock oven. $1.50, Climbing coconut tree. $1.90, With string band. $3.80, Delivering gifts by donkey. $8, Delivering gifts by boat.

2004, Nov. 15    **Perf. 13x13¼**
1128-1131  A171  Set of 4    7.25  7.25
**Souvenir Sheet**
1132  A171  $8 multi    7.50  7.50

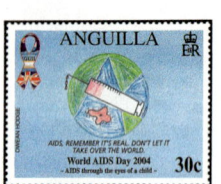
World AIDS Day — A172

Children's drawings by: 30c, Owean Hodge. $1.50, Lydia Fleming. $1.90, Nina Rodriguez. No. 1136: a, 15c, Kenswick Richardson. b, 75c, Toniquewah Ruan. c, $1, Elizabeth Anne Orchard. d, $2, Tricia Watty-Beard.

2005, Jan. 18    **Perf. 13**
1133-1135  A172  Set of 3    5.00  5.00
**Souvenir Sheet**
1136  A172  Sheet of 4, #a-d    5.00  5.00

Rotary International, Cent. — A173

Designs: 30c, Emblem of Anguilla Rotary Club. $1, Pelican and palm tree. $1.50, Rotary International founder Paul Harris. $1.90, Children at playground.

**Perf. 14¾x14¼**
2005, Mar. 23    Litho.
1137-1140  A173  Set of 4    4.75  4.75

Dogs — A174

Designs: 30c, Dog in field. $1.50, Two dogs sitting, vert. $1.90, Dog sitting, vert. $2.25, Dog.

**Perf. 14¼x14¾, 14¾x14¼**
2005, June 1
1141-1144  A174  Set of 4    5.50  5.50

Commercial Airplanes — A175

Designs: 30c, Air Anguilla Cessna 402. 40c, LIAT DHC Dash 8. 60c, Winair Foxtrot-DHC Twin Otter. $1, Anguilla Airways Piper Aztec. $1.50, St. Thomas Air Transport Piper Aztec. $1.90, Carib Air Service Piper Aztec.

2006, Mar. 13    Litho.    **Perf. 13¼**
1145-1150  A175  Set of 6    7.00  7.00

Butterflies — A176

Designs: 30c, Appias drusillia. $1.50, Danaus plexippus megalippe. $1.90, Phoebis sennae. $2.75, Papilio demoleus. No. 1155: a, 40c, Aphrissa statira. b, 60c, Eurema elathea. c, $1, Danaus plexippus megalippe, diff. d, $3, Agraulis vanillae.

2006, Oct. 9    Litho.    **Perf. 13¼**
1151-1154  A176  Set of 4    7.25  7.25
**Miniature Sheet**
1155  A176  Sheet of 4, #a-d    5.75  5.75

Anguilla Soroptomist Club, 25th Anniv. — A177

Designs: $1.90, Soroptomist International emblem. $2.75, Alecia Ballin.

2007, Jan. 29
1156-1157  A177  Set of 2    5.25  5.25

Bronze Devotional Medallions From El Buen Consuelo Shipwreck — A178

Medallions depicting: 30c, St. Bruno. $1.50, Our Lady of Sorrows. $1.90, Five Wounds of Jesus. $2.75, Virgin and Child.

2007, Mar. 19    Litho.    **Perf. 13¼**
1158-1161  A178  Set of 4    6.25  6.25

Anguilla Revolution, 40th Anniv. — A179

Participants: 30c, Hyacinth Carty. $1, Edward Duncan. $1.50, Connell Harrigan. $1.90, Rev. Leonard Carty. $2.25, Jeremiah Gumbs. $3.75, Atlin Harrigan.

2007, July 18    Litho.    **Perf. 13¼**
1162-1167  A179  Set of 6    10.00  10.00

Historical Architecture — A180

Designs: 30c, Building with lean-to and gabled roof, by Melsadis Fleming. $1, Building with lean-to and gabled roof, by Daryl Thompson. $1.25, Building with double-hipped roof, by Fleming. $1.50, Building with hipped roof, by Susan Croft. $1.90, Building with double-gabled roof, by Fleming. $2.40, Building with double-hipped roof, by Fleming, diff. $2.75, Building with hipped roof, by Fleming. $3.75, Building with gabled roof, by Fleming.

2008, Oct. 6    **Perf. 14x14¾**
1168-1175  A180  Set of 8    10.00  10.00

Traditional Household Items — A181

Designs: 30c, Three-legged pot. $1, Mortar and pestle. $1.50, Gas and coal irons. $1.90, Oil and gas lamps. $2, Coal pots. $2.25, Enamel and aluminum utensils.

2009, June 18    **Perf. 13¼**
1176-1181  A181  Set of 6    6.75  6.75

Wild Flowers — A182

Designs: 30c, Tabebulia heterophylla. $1, Argemone mexicana. $1.50, Catharanthus roseus. $1.90, Datura stramonium. $2, Centrosena virginiatum. $2.25, Tetramicra canaliculata.

2009, Sept. 12
1182-1187  A182  Set of 6    6.75  6.75

Endemic Flora and Fauna — A183

Designs: $1.50, Sombrero Island ground lizard. $2, Little Scrub Island ground lizard. $2.25, Anguilla bush.

2010, Aug. 10    **Perf. 13¼**
1188-1190  A183  Set of 3    4.50  4.50

Wedding of Prince William and Catherine Middleton — A184

Designs: $4, Couple. $5, Couple, horiz. $6, Couple, diff. $10, Couple and royal arms, horiz.

2011, June 20    Litho.    **Perf. 13¼**
1191-1194  A184  Set of 4    18.50  18.50

Anguilla Revolutionary Coins — A185

Designs: 15c, 1967 Liberty dollar counterstruck on Panamanian balboa. 40c, 1967 Liberty dollar counterstruck on Mexican peso. $2.50, Obverse and reverse of 1968 silver $25 coin commemorating first year of Independence. $5, Ship, reverse of 1969 $4 coin.

2012, Feb. 28    **Perf. 13½x13¼**
1195-1198  A185  Set of 4    6.00  6.00

Royal Anguilla Police Force, 40th Anniv. — A186

Designs: 30c, Old Valley Police Station. $1, Police on parade. $1.50, Police headquarters. $1.90, Past and present police crests. $5, Lt. Col. Claudius M. Roberts, first Chief of Police, vert.

2012, Nov. 26    **Perf. 13¼**
1199-1203  A186  Set of 5    7.25  7.25

Methodism on Anguilla, 200th Anniv. — A187

Designs: 40c, Old Methodist Manse, Sandy Ground. 65c, Map of Anguilla, 200th anniversary emblem. $10, Montage of Ebenezer and Bethel Churches, by Aileen Lamond-Smith.

2013, Nov. 11    Litho.    **Perf. 13¼**
1204-1206  A187  Set of 3    8.25  8.25

Ship Captains — A188

Captains: 15c, George Richardson (1919-2003). 50c, James Woods (1908-98). 75c, Fritz Ericson Hughes (1891-1970). $1.35, Christopher John Connor (1925-94). $2, Herchel Gumbs (1884-1965). $2.25, Zilphus Fleming (1915-92). $2.50, Walter Hodge (1920-89). $5, John Franklin (1912-98).

2013, Nov. 25    Litho.    **Perf. 13¼**
1207-1214  A188  Set of 8    11.00  11.00
1214a    Sheet of 8, #1207-1214    11.00  11.00
See Nos. 1219-1226.

Secondary Education, 60th Anniv. — A189

Designs: 15c, Boy's shirt and tie, 1950s. $1.35, Girl's uniform, 1950s. $2, James T. Thorn, first principal of Valley Secondary School. $2.50, Valley Secondary School crest.

2013, Dec. 31    Litho.    **Perf. 13¼**
1215-1218  A189  Set of 4    4.50  4.50

**Ship Captains Type of 2013**

Designs: 50c, Harry S. Franklin (1926-2006). 65c, John A. Edwards (1910-75). 75c, Amos Richardson (1924-2004). 80c, George Joshua Gumbs (1926-2012). $2, Ivan Richardson (1917-67). $2.50, Edward Camile Connor (1910-2000). $3, Henry E. Richardson (1890-1990). $6, Malcolm C. Wathey (1905-84).

2014, July 7    Litho.    **Perf. 13¼**
1219-1226  A188  Set of 8    12.00  12.00
1226a    Souvenir sheet of 8, #1219-1226    12.00  12.00

Day Around the Island Boat Race Winning Sailboats — A190

Designs: 50c, Real Deal, champion in 2011, 2012. 60c, Superstar, champion in 2004, 2007, 2009, horiz. 80c, Nathalie, champion in 1993, 1994, 1995. $1.35, UFO, champion in 1997, 1998, 2003, 2005, horiz. $3, De Tree, champion in 2001, 2006, 2008, 2010, 2013, horiz. $10, De Chan, champion in 1982-84, 1986, 1991-92, 1996, 2002. No. 1233: a, 15c, Sonic, champion in 2014. b, 40c, Satellite, champion in 2000. c, 65c, Viagra, champion in 1999. d, 75c, Saga Boy, champion in 1990. e, $4, Wasp, champion in 1987.

2015, May 29    Litho.    **Perf. 13¼**
1227-1232  A190  Set of 6    12.00  12.00
**Souvenir Sheet**
1233  A190  Sheet of 5, #a-e    4.50  4.50

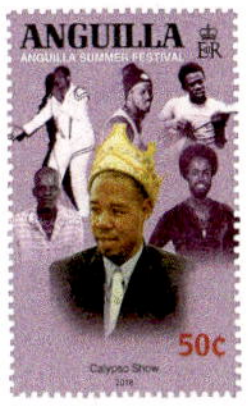

Summer Festival — A191

Designs: 50c, Calypso Show. $1, August Monday Beach Party, horiz. $1.40, Jouvert, horiz. $1.80, Woman in butterfly costume, horiz. $2.10, Parade, horiz. $3, Queen Show.

**2016, Aug. 2 Litho. *Perf. 13¼***
**1234-1239** A191 Set of 6 7.25 7.25

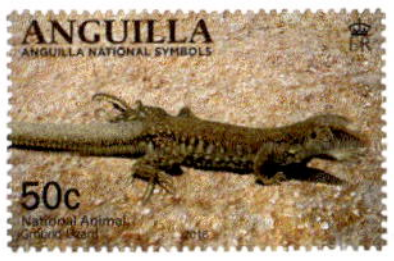

National Symbols A192

Designs: 50c, Ground lizard (national animal). 75c, White cedar flowers (national flower). $1.40, Peas and rice (national dish). $1.80, Turtle doves (national bird). $2.10, Boat racing (national sport). $3, Turquoise, white and orange (national colors). $5, White cedar tree (national tree), vert. $10, National flag.

**2016, Oct. 10 Litho. *Perf. 13¼***
**1240-1247** A192 Set of 8 18.50 18.50

## ANJOUAN

'an-jü-wän

LOCATION — One of the Comoro Islands in the Mozambique Channel between Madagascar and Mozambique.
GOVT. — French colony.
AREA — 89 sq. mi.
POP. — 20,000 (approx. 1912)
CAPITAL — Mossamondu

See Comoro Islands.

100 Centimes = 1 Franc

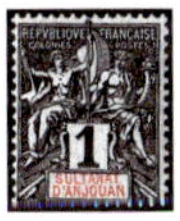

Navigation and Commerce — A1

***Perf. 14x13½***

**1892-1907 Typo. Unwmk.**

**Name of Colony in Blue or Carmine**

| | | | | | |
|---|---|---|---|---|---|
| **1** | A1 | 1c | black, *blue* | 1.75 | 1.75 |
| **2** | A1 | 2c | brown, *buff* | 2.75 | 1.75 |
| **3** | A1 | 4c | claret, *lav* | 5.50 | 4.00 |
| **4** | A1 | 5c | green, *grnsh* | 9.50 | 6.25 |
| **5** | A1 | 10c | blk, *lavender* | 11.50 | 6.75 |
| **6** | A1 | 10c | red ('00) | 67.50 | 30.00 |
| **7** | A1 | 15c | blue, quadrille paper | 17.00 | 11.50 |
| **8** | A1 | 15c | gray, *lt gray* ('00) | 32.50 | 22.50 |
| **9** | A1 | 20c | red, *green* | 17.50 | 11.00 |
| **10** | A1 | 25c | black, *rose* | 17.50 | 14.00 |
| **11** | A1 | 25c | blue ('00) | 32.50 | 22.50 |
| **12** | A1 | 30c | brn, *bister* | 35.00 | 22.50 |
| **13** | A1 | 35c | blk, *yel* ('06) | 18.00 | 10.00 |
| **14** | A1 | 40c | red, *straw* | 37.50 | 32.50 |
| **15** | A1 | 45c | blk, *gray grn* ('07) | 150.00 | 115.00 |
| **16** | A1 | 50c | car, *rose* | 45.00 | 32.50 |
| **17** | A1 | 50c | brn, *az* ('00) | 32.50 | 32.50 |
| **18** | A1 | 75c | vio, *orange* | 37.50 | 27.50 |
| **19** | A1 | 1fr | brnz grn, *straw* | 90.00 | 77.50 |
| | | | *Nos. 1-19 (19)* | 631.00 | 482.00 |

Perf 13½x14 stamps are counterfeits.

**Issues of 1892-1907 Surcharged in Black or Carmine**

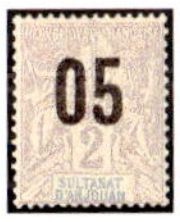

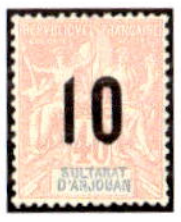

**1912**

| | | | | | |
|---|---|---|---|---|---|
| **20** | A1 | 5c on 2c brn, *buff* | | 1.25 | 1.25 |
| **21** | A1 | 5c on 4c cl, *lav* (C) | | 1.40 | *1.50* |
| | *a.* | Pair, one without surcharge | | *1,000.* | *1,100.* |
| **22** | A1 | 5c on 15c blue (C) | | 1.40 | 1.40 |
| | *a.* | Pair, one without surcharge | | *1,100.* | *1,000.* |
| **23** | A1 | 5c on 20c red, *green* | | 1.40 | 1.40 |
| | *a.* | Pair, one without surcharge | | *1,100.* | *1,100.* |
| **24** | A1 | 5c on 25c blk, *rose* (C) | | 1.50 | *1.75* |
| **25** | A1 | 5c on 30c brn, *bis* (C) | | 2.00 | *2.10* |
| **26** | A1 | 10c on 40c red, *straw* | | 2.00 | *2.25* |
| **27** | A1 | 10c on 45c black, *gray green* (C) | | 2.40 | 2.40 |
| **28** | A1 | 10c on 50c car, *rose* | | 6.00 | *6.50* |
| **29** | A1 | 10c on 75c vio, *org* | | 4.00 | *4.50* |
| **30** | A1 | 10c on 1fr brnz grn, *straw* | | 5.50 | *5.75* |
| | *a.* | Pair, one without surcharge | | *1,250.* | *1,200.* |
| | | *Nos. 20-30 (11)* | | 28.85 | 30.80 |

Two spacings between the surcharged numerals are found on Nos. 20-30. See the *Scott Classic Specialized Catalogue of Stamps and Covers* for detailed listings.

Nos. 20-30 were available for use in Madagascar and the Comoro archipelago.

The stamps of Anjouan were superseded by those of Madagascar, and in 1950 by those of Comoro Islands.

## ANNAM & TONKIN

a-'nam and 'tan-'kin

LOCATION — In French Indo-China bordering on the China Sea on the east and Siam on the west.
GOVT. — French Protectorate
AREA — 97,503 sq. mi.
POP. — 14,124,000 (approx. 1890)
CAPITAL — Annam: Hue; Tonkin: Hanoi

For administrative purposes, the Protectorates of Annam, Tonkin, Cambodia, Laos and the Colony of Cochin-China were grouped together and were known as French Indo-China.

100 Centimes = 1 Franc

Catalogue values for unused stamps are for examples without gum as most stamps were issued in that condition.

**Stamps of French Colonies, 1881-86 Handstamped Surcharged in Black**

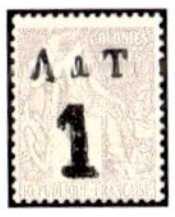

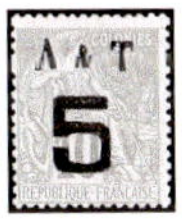

***Perf. 14x13½***

**1888, Jan. 21 Unwmk.**

| | | | | |
|---|---|---|---|---|
| **1** | A9 | 1c on 2c brn, *buff* | 47.50 | *50.00* |
| | *a.* | Inverted surcharge | 200.00 | *200.00* |
| | *b.* | Sideways surcharge | 200.00 | *210.00* |
| **2** | A9 | 1c on 4c claret, *lav* | 37.50 | 45.00 |
| | *a.* | Inverted surcharge | 200.00 | *210.00* |
| | *b.* | Double surcharge | 275.00 | 225.00 |
| | *c.* | Sideways surcharge | 200.00 | *210.00* |
| **3** | A9 | 5c on 10c blk, *lav* | 47.50 | 37.50 |
| | *a.* | Inverted surcharge | 200.00 | 200.00 |
| | *b.* | Double surcharge | 225.00 | 225.00 |
| **4** | A9 | 5c on 2c brn, *buff* | *8,500.* | |

**Hyphen between "A" and "T"**

| | | | | |
|---|---|---|---|---|
| **7** | A9 | 1c on 2c brn, *buff* | 325.00 | *425.00* |
| | *a.* | Inverted surcharge | 750.00 | *775.00* |
| | *b.* | Sideways surcharge | 750.00 | *775.00* |
| | *c.* | Pair, Nos. 1, 7 | 9,000. | |
| **8** | A9 | 1c on 4c claret, *lav* | 525.00 | *625.00* |
| **9** | A9 | 5c on 10c blk, *lav* | 220.00 | *240.00* |

A 5c on 2c with surcharge in blue was prepared but not issued.

In these surcharges there are different types of numerals and letters.

There are numerous other errors in the placing of the surcharges, including double one inverted, double both inverted, double one sideways, and pair one without surcharge.

Such varieties command substantial premiums.

These stamps were superseded in 1892 by those of Indo-China.

## ANTIGUA

an-'tēg-ˌwə

LOCATION — In the West Indies, southeast of Puerto Rico
GOVT. — Independent state
AREA — 171 sq. mi.
POP. — 98,000 (2020 est.)
CAPITAL — St. John's

Antigua was one of the presidencies of the former Leeward Islands colony until becoming a Crown Colony in 1956. It became an Associated State of the United Kingdom in 1967 and an independent nation on November 1, 1981, taking the name of Antigua and Barbuda.

Antigua stamps were discontinued in 1890 and resumed in 1903. In the interim, stamps of Leeward Islands were used. Between 1903-1956, stamps of Antigua and Leeward Islands were used concurrently.

12 Pence = 1 Shilling
20 Shillings = 1 Pound
100 Cents = 1 Dollar (1951)

**Catalogue values for unused stamps in this country are for Never Hinged items, beginning with Scott 96.**

**Watermark**

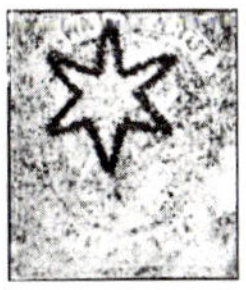

Wmk. 5 — Star

Values for unused stamps are for examples with original gum as defined in the catalogue introduction. Any exceptions will be noted. Very fine examples of Nos. 1-8, 11, 18-20 will have perforations touching the design on at least one frameline due to the narrow spacing of the stamps on the plates. Stamps with perfs clear of the framelines on all four sides are extremely scarce and will command higher prices.

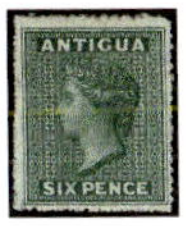

Queen Victoria — A1

***Rough Perf. 14-16***

**1862 Engr. Unwmk.**

| | | | | |
|---|---|---|---|---|
| **1** | A1 | 6p blue green | 950.00 | 600.00 |
| | *a.* | Perf. 11-13 | *8,500.* | |
| | *b.* | Perf. 11-13x14-16 | *3,750.* | |
| | *c.* | Perf. 11-13 compound with 14-16 | *3,750.* | |

There is a question whether Nos. 1a-1c ever did postal duty.

Values for No. 1 are for stamps with perfs. cutting into the design. Values for No. 1b are for examples without gum.

**1863-67 Wmk. 5**

| | | | | |
|---|---|---|---|---|
| **2** | A1 | 1p dull rose | 135.00 | 60.00 |
| | *a.* | Vert. pair, imperf. btwn. | *37,500.* | |
| | *b.* | Imperf., pair | | 2,750. |
| | *c.* | 1p lilac rose | 150.00 | 82.50 |
| **3** | A1 | 1p vermilion ('67) | 275.00 | 32.50 |
| | *a.* | Horiz. pair, imperf. btwn. | *37,500.* | |
| **4** | A1 | 6p green | 775.00 | 30.00 |
| | *a.* | 6p yellow green | *4,750.* | 120.00 |
| | *b.* | Pair, imperf. btwn. | | — |

**1872 Wmk. 1 *Perf. 12½***

| | | | | |
|---|---|---|---|---|
| **5** | A1 | 1p lake | 220.00 | 22.50 |
| **6** | A1 | 1p vermilion | 225.00 | 26.50 |
| **7** | A1 | 6p blue green | 600.00 | 12.50 |

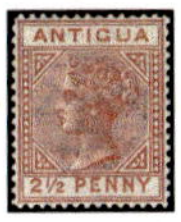

Queen Victoria — A2

**1873-79 *Perf. 14***

| | | | | |
|---|---|---|---|---|
| **8** | A1 | 1p lake | 250.00 | 12.50 |
| | *a.* | Half used as ½p on cover | | *9,500.* |

**Typo.**

| | | | | |
|---|---|---|---|---|
| **9** | A2 | 2½p red brown ('79) | 700.00 | 210.00 |
| **10** | A2 | 4p blue ('79) | 290.00 | 18.00 |

**Engr.**

| | | | | |
|---|---|---|---|---|
| **11** | A1 | 6p blue green ('76) | 450.00 | 22.50 |

**1882-87 Typo. Wmk. 2**

| | | | | |
|---|---|---|---|---|
| **12** | A2 | ½p green | 5.00 | *20.00* |
| **13** | A2 | 2½p red brown | 225.00 | 67.50 |
| **14** | A2 | 2½p ultra ('87) | 8.50 | *17.00* |
| **15** | A2 | 4p blue | 350.00 | 19.00 |
| **16** | A2 | 4p brown org ('87) | 2.50 | *3.75* |
| **17** | A2 | 1sh violet ('86) | 190.00 | 175.00 |

**Engr.**

| | | | | |
|---|---|---|---|---|
| **18** | A1 | 1p carmine ('84) | 2.60 | *4.50* |
| **19** | A1 | 6p deep green | 77.50 | *150.00* |

No. 18 was used for a time in St. Christopher and is identified by the "A12" cancellation.

**1884 *Perf. 12***

| | | | | |
|---|---|---|---|---|
| **20** | A1 | 1p rose red | 65.00 | 20.00 |

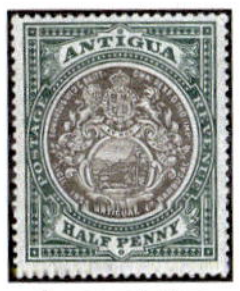

Seal of the Colony — A3

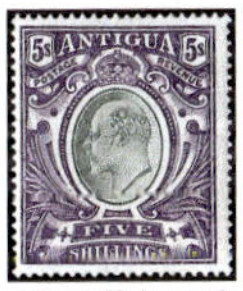

King Edward VII — A4

**1903 Typo. Wmk. 1 *Perf. 14***

| | | | | |
|---|---|---|---|---|
| **21** | A3 | ½p blue grn & blk | 4.00 | *7.50* |
| | *a.* | Bluish paper ('09) | 100.00 | 100.00 |
| **22** | A3 | 1p car & black | 14.00 | 1.50 |
| | *a.* | Bluish paper ('09) | 92.50 | 92.50 |
| **23** | A3 | 2p org brn & vio | 8.25 | *27.50* |
| **24** | A3 | 2½p ultra & black | 18.00 | *25.00* |
| **25** | A3 | 3p ocher & gray green | 12.00 | *24.00* |
| **26** | A3 | 6p black & red vio | 35.00 | *60.00* |
| **27** | A3 | 1sh violet & ultra | 57.50 | *70.00* |
| **28** | A3 | 2sh pur & gray green | 95.00 | *125.00* |
| **29** | A3 | 2sh6p red vio & blk | 30.00 | *75.00* |
| **30** | A4 | 5sh pur & gray green | 115.00 | *165.00* |
| | | *Nos. 21-30 (10)* | 388.75 | *580.50* |

The 2½p, 1sh and 5sh exist on both ordinary and chalky paper.

**1908-20 Wmk. 3**

| | | | | |
|---|---|---|---|---|
| **31** | A3 | ½p green | 5.25 | *5.25* |
| **32** | A3 | 1p scarlet ('15) | 8.00 | 3.75 |
| **33** | A3 | 2p org brn & dull vio ('12) | 5.25 | *35.00* |
| **34** | A3 | 2½p ultra | 21.00 | *19.00* |
| **35** | A3 | 3p ocher & grn ('12) | 7.00 | *21.00* |
| **36** | A3 | 6p blk & red vio ('11) | 8.25 | *47.50* |
| **37** | A3 | 1sh vio & ultra | 27.50 | *80.00* |
| **38** | A3 | 2sh vio & green ('12) | 110.00 | *130.00* |
| | | *Nos. 31-38 (8)* | 195.25 | *341.50* |

Nos. 33, 35 to 38 are on chalky paper.
For overprints see Nos. MR1-MR3.

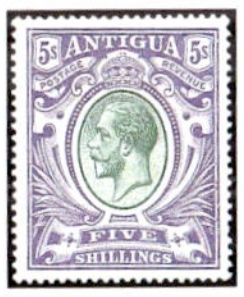

George V — A6

**1913**

| | | | | |
|---|---|---|---|---|
| **41** | A6 | 5sh violet & green | 100.00 | *160.00* |

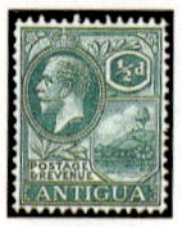

St. John's Harbor — A7

**1921-29** **Wmk. 4**

| | | | | |
|---|---|---|---|---|
| 42 | A7 | ½p green | 3.25 | .60 |
| 43 | A7 | 1p rose red | 4.50 | .60 |
| 44 | A7 | 1p dp violet ('23) | 8.75 | 1.75 |
| 45 | A7 | 1½p orange ('22) | 6.50 | 6.00 |
| 46 | A7 | 1½p rose red ('26) | 10.00 | 2.00 |
| 47 | A7 | 1½p fawn ('29) | 3.25 | .75 |
| 48 | A7 | 2p gray | 4.50 | .90 |
| 49 | A7 | 2½p ultra ('27) | 17.00 | 5.00 |
| 50 | A7 | 2½p orange ('23) | 2.75 | 20.00 |

**Chalky Paper**

| | | | | |
|---|---|---|---|---|
| 51 | A7 | 3p violet, *yel* ('25) | 16.00 | 8.00 |
| 52 | A7 | 6p vio & red vio | 8.50 | 6.00 |
| 53 | A7 | 1sh black, *emer* ('29) | 6.50 | 5.00 |
| 54 | A7 | 2sh vio & ultra, *blue* ('27) | 12.00 | 65.00 |
| 55 | A7 | 2sh6p blk & red, *blue* ('27) | 52.50 | 47.50 |
| 56 | A7 | 3sh grn & vio ('22) | 52.50 | 105.00 |
| 57 | A7 | 4sh blk & red ('22) | 52.50 | 77.50 |
| | | *Nos. 42-57 (16)* | 261.00 | 351.60 |

**Wmk. 3**

**Chalky Paper**

| | | | | |
|---|---|---|---|---|
| 58 | A7 | 3p violet, *yel* | 5.00 | 15.00 |
| 59 | A7 | 4p black & red, *yel* ('22) | 2.50 | 6.50 |
| 60 | A7 | 1sh black, *emerald* | 4.75 | 10.50 |
| 61 | A7 | 2sh vio & ultra, *bl* | 14.50 | 37.50 |
| 62 | A7 | 2sh6p blk & red, *bl* | 19.00 | 70.00 |
| 63 | A7 | 5sh grn & red, *yel* ('22) | 9.25 | 60.00 |
| 64 | A7 | £1 vio & black, *red* ('22) | 300.00 | 425.00 |
| | | *Nos. 58-64 (7)* | 355.00 | 624.50 |

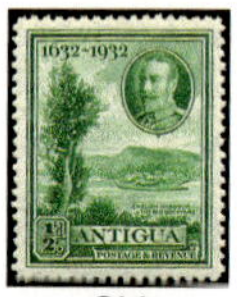

Old Dockyard, English Harbour A8

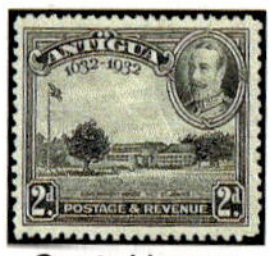

Govt. House, St. John's A9

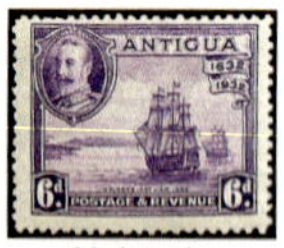

Nelson's "Victory," 1805 — A10

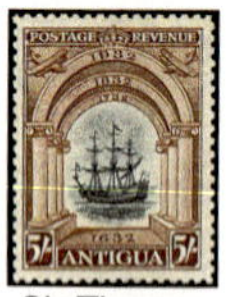

Sir Thomas Warner's Ship, 1632 — A11

***Perf. 12½***

**1932, Jan. 27** **Engr.** **Wmk. 4**

| | | | | |
|---|---|---|---|---|
| 67 | A8 | ½p green | 4.75 | 8.75 |
| 68 | A8 | 1p scarlet | 6.50 | 9.00 |
| 69 | A8 | 1½p lt brown | 4.75 | 5.50 |
| 70 | A9 | 2p gray | 9.00 | 27.50 |
| 71 | A9 | 2½p ultra | 8.75 | 9.75 |
| 72 | A9 | 3p orange | 8.75 | 14.00 |
| 73 | A10 | 6p violet | 16.00 | 14.00 |
| 74 | A10 | 1sh olive green | 21.00 | 32.50 |
| 75 | A10 | 2sh6p claret | 57.50 | 82.50 |
| 76 | A11 | 5sh red brown & black | 125.00 | 160.00 |
| | | *Nos. 67-76 (10)* | 262.00 | 363.50 |
| | | Set, never hinged | 650.00 | |

Tercentenary of the colony.

Forged cancellations abound, especially dated "MY 18 1932."

Common Design Types pictured following the introduction.

**Silver Jubilee Issue**

Common Design Type

**1935, May 6** ***Perf. 13½x14***

| | | | | |
|---|---|---|---|---|
| 77 | CD301 | 1p car & blue | 2.25 | 4.00 |
| 78 | CD301 | 1½p gray blk & ultra | 2.50 | 1.50 |
| 79 | CD301 | 2½p blue & brn | 6.50 | 1.75 |
| 80 | CD301 | 1sh brt vio & ind | 9.00 | 16.00 |
| | | *Nos. 77-80 (4)* | 20.25 | 23.25 |
| | | Set, never hinged | 32.50 | |

**Coronation Issue**

Common Design Type

**1937, May 12** ***Perf. 11x11½***

| | | | | |
|---|---|---|---|---|
| 81 | CD302 | 1p carmine | .50 | 2.75 |
| 82 | CD302 | 1½p brown | .35 | 2.50 |
| 83 | CD302 | 2½p deep ultra | 1.00 | 2.75 |
| | | *Nos. 81-83 (3)* | 1.85 | 8.00 |
| | | Set, never hinged | 2.75 | |

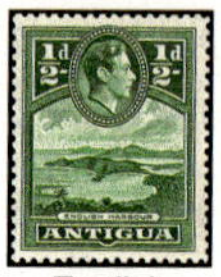

English Harbour A14

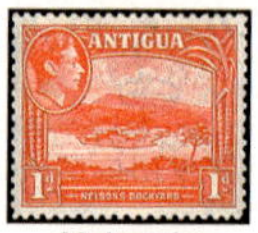

Nelson's Dockyard A15

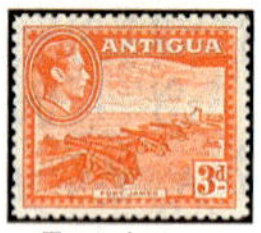

Fort James A16

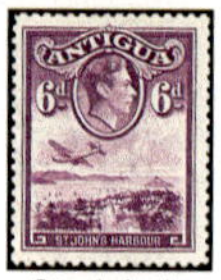

St. John's Harbor A17

**1938-51** **Engr.** ***Perf. 12½***

| | | | | |
|---|---|---|---|---|
| 84 | A14 | ½p yel green | .30 | 1.50 |
| 85 | A15 | 1p scarlet | 2.25 | 2.50 |
| 86 | A15 | 1½p red brown ('43) | 1.80 | 2.75 |
| 87 | A14 | 2p gray | .70 | 1.00 |
| 88 | A15 | 2½p ultra ('43) | .75 | .90 |
| 89 | A16 | 3p pale orange ('44) | .75 | 1.10 |
| 90 | A17 | 6p purple | 2.75 | 1.25 |
| 91 | A17 | 1sh brown & blk | 3.50 | 2.00 |
| 92 | A16 | 2sh6p dp claret ('42) | 16.00 | 20.00 |
| 93 | A17 | 5sh grayish olive green ('44) | 9.00 | 11.00 |
| 94 | A15 | 10sh red vio ('48) | 11.00 | 35.00 |
| 95 | A16 | £1 Prussian blue ('48) | 22.50 | 60.00 |
| | | *Nos. 84-95 (12)* | 71.30 | 139.00 |
| | | Set, never hinged | 105.00 | |

See Nos. 107-113, 115-116, 118-121, 136-142, 144-145.

For overprint see Nos. 125-126.

**Catalogue values for unused stamps in this section, from this point to the end of the section, are for Never Hinged items.**

**Peace Issue**

Common Design Type

**1946, Nov. 1** **Wmk. 4** ***Perf. 13½x14***

| | | | | |
|---|---|---|---|---|
| 96 | CD303 | 1½p brown | .25 | .25 |
| 97 | CD303 | 3p dp orange | .25 | .55 |

**Silver Wedding Issue**

Common Design Types

**1949, Jan. 3** **Photo.** ***Perf. 14x14½***

| | | | | |
|---|---|---|---|---|
| 98 | CD304 | 2½p bright ultra | .55 | 2.75 |

**Engraved; Name Typographed**

***Perf. 11½x11***

| | | | | |
|---|---|---|---|---|
| 99 | CD305 | 5sh dk brown olive | 13.00 | 13.00 |

**UPU Issue**

Common Design Types

***Perf. 13½, 11x11½***

**1949, Oct. 10** **Wmk. 4**

**Engr.; Name Typo. on 3p and 6p**

| | | | | |
|---|---|---|---|---|
| 100 | CD306 | 2½p deep ultra | .40 | .70 |
| 101 | CD307 | 3p orange | 1.60 | 3.25 |
| 102 | CD308 | 6p purple | .80 | 2.25 |
| 103 | CD309 | 1sh red brown | .80 | 1.50 |
| | | *Nos. 100-103 (4)* | 3.60 | 7.70 |

**University Issue**

Common Design Types

***Perf. 14x14½***

**1951, Feb. 16** **Engr.** **Wmk. 4**

| | | | | |
|---|---|---|---|---|
| 104 | CD310 | 3c chocolate & blk | .45 | 1.75 |
| 105 | CD311 | 12c purple & blk | .90 | 2.00 |

**Coronation Issue**

Common Design Type

**1953, June 2** ***Perf. 13½x13***

| | | | | |
|---|---|---|---|---|
| 106 | CD312 | 2c dk green & blk | .40 | .75 |

**Types of 1938 with Portrait of Queen Elizabeth II**

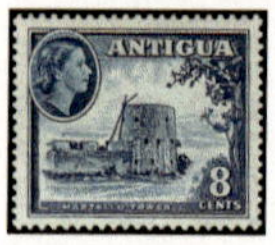

Martello Tower — A24

***Perf. 13x13½, 13½x13***

**1953-56** **Wmk. 4**

| | | | | |
|---|---|---|---|---|
| 107 | A16 | ½c dk red brn ('56) | .35 | .35 |
| 108 | A14 | 1c gray | .30 | 1.75 |
| 109 | A15 | 2c deep green | .30 | .25 |
| 110 | A15 | 3c yellow & blk | .50 | .25 |
| 111 | A14 | 4c rose red (shades) | 1.25 | .25 |
| 112 | A15 | 5c dull vio & blk | 2.40 | .45 |
| 113 | A16 | 6c orange | 2.40 | .25 |
| 114 | A24 | 8c deep blue | 2.60 | .25 |
| 115 | A17 | 12c violet | 2.60 | .25 |
| 116 | A17 | 24c chocolate & blk | 4.50 | .25 |
| 117 | A24 | 48c dp bl & rose lil | 9.50 | 3.25 |
| 118 | A16 | 60c claret | 8.50 | .75 |
| 119 | A17 | $1.20 olive green | 3.75 | .90 |
| 120 | A15 | $2.40 magenta | 17.00 | 11.50 |
| 121 | A16 | $4.80 greenish blue | 22.00 | 27.50 |
| | | *Nos. 107-121 (15)* | 77.95 | 48.20 |

See No. 143. For overprint see No. 125-126.

**West Indies Federation**

Common Design Type

***Perf. 11½x11***

**1958, Apr. 22** **Engr.** **Wmk. 314**

| | | | | |
|---|---|---|---|---|
| 122 | CD313 | 3c green | 1.50 | .30 |
| 123 | CD313 | 6c blue | 1.90 | 2.75 |
| 124 | CD313 | 12c carmine rose | 2.40 | .75 |
| | | *Nos. 122-124 (3)* | 5.80 | 3.80 |

**Nos. 110 and 115 Overprinted in Red or Black: "Commemoration Antigua Constitution 1960"**

***Perf. 13x13½, 13½x13***

**1960, Jan. 1** **Wmk. 4**

| | | | | |
|---|---|---|---|---|
| 125 | A15 | 3c yellow & black | .25 | .25 |
| 126 | A17 | 12c violet (Blk) | .25 | .25 |

Constitutional reforms effective Jan. 1, 1960.

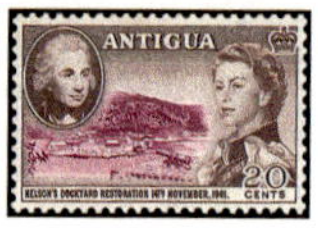

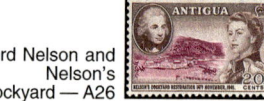

Lord Nelson and Nelson's Dockyard — A26

***Perf. 11½x11***

**1961, Nov. 14** **Wmk. 314**

| | | | | |
|---|---|---|---|---|
| 127 | A26 | 20c brown & lilac | 1.60 | 1.60 |
| 128 | A26 | 30c dk blue & green | 1.75 | 2.75 |

Completion of the restoration of Lord Nelson's headquarters, English Harbour.

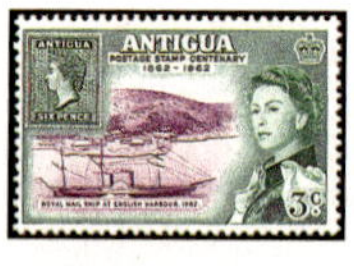

Stamp of 1862 and Royal Mail Steam Packet in English Harbour — A27

**1962, Aug. 1** **Engr.** ***Perf. 13***

| | | | | |
|---|---|---|---|---|
| 129 | A27 | 3c dull green & pur | .70 | .25 |
| 130 | A27 | 10c dull green & ultra | .80 | .25 |
| 131 | A27 | 12c dull green & blk | .90 | .25 |
| 132 | A27 | 50c dull grn & brn org | 1.50 | 2.25 |
| | | *Nos. 129-132 (4)* | 3.90 | 3.00 |

Centenary of first Antigua postage stamp.

**Freedom from Hunger Issue**

Common Design Type

***Perf. 14x14½***

**1963, June 4** **Photo.** **Wmk. 314**

| | | | | |
|---|---|---|---|---|
| 133 | CD314 | 12c green | .35 | .35 |

**Red Cross Centenary Issue**

Common Design Type

**1963, Sept. 2** **Litho.** ***Perf. 13***

| | | | | |
|---|---|---|---|---|
| 134 | CD315 | 3c black & red | .25 | .75 |
| 135 | CD315 | 12c ultra & red | .75 | 1.25 |

**Types of 1938-53 with Portrait of Queen Elizabeth II**

***Perf. 13x13½, 13½x13***

**1963-65** **Engr.** **Wmk. 314**

| | | | | |
|---|---|---|---|---|
| 136 | A16 | ½c brown ('65) | 2.50 | .85 |
| 137 | A14 | 1c gray ('65) | 1.25 | 1.00 |
| 138 | A15 | 2c deep green | .70 | .30 |
| 139 | A15 | 3c orange yel & blk | .40 | .30 |
| 140 | A14 | 4c brown red | .35 | 3.00 |
| 141 | A15 | 5c dull vio & black | .30 | .25 |
| 142 | A16 | 6c orange | .60 | .35 |
| 143 | A24 | 8c deep blue | .35 | .25 |
| 144 | A17 | 12c violet | 1.00 | .25 |
| 145 | A17 | 24c choc & black | 5.00 | .80 |
| | | *Nos. 136-145 (10)* | 12.45 | 7.35 |

For surcharge see No. 152.

**Shakespeare Issue**

Common Design Type

***Perf. 14x14½***

**1964, Apr. 23** **Photo.** **Wmk. 314**

| | | | | |
|---|---|---|---|---|
| 151 | CD316 | 12c red brown | .35 | .25 |

**No. 144 Surcharged with New Value and Bars**

***Perf. 13½x13***

**1965, Apr. 1** **Engr.** **Wmk. 314**

| | | | | |
|---|---|---|---|---|
| 152 | A17 | 15c on 12c violet | .30 | .30 |

**ITU Issue**

Common Design Type

***Perf. 11x11½***

**1965, May 17** **Litho.** **Wmk. 314**

| | | | | |
|---|---|---|---|---|
| 153 | CD317 | 2c blue & ver | .25 | .25 |
| 154 | CD317 | 50c orange & vio bl | 1.20 | 1.10 |

**Intl. Cooperation Year Issue**

Common Design Type

**1965, Oct. 25** ***Perf. 14½***

| | | | | |
|---|---|---|---|---|
| 155 | CD318 | 4c blue grn & claret | .25 | .25 |
| 156 | CD318 | 15c lt vio & green | .30 | .25 |

**Churchill Memorial Issue**

Common Design Type

**1966, Jan. 24** **Photo.** ***Perf. 14***

**Design in Black, Gold and Carmine Rose**

| | | | | |
|---|---|---|---|---|
| 157 | CD319 | ½c bright blue | .25 | 2.00 |
| 158 | CD319 | 4c green | .30 | .25 |
| 159 | CD319 | 25c brown | 1.25 | .30 |
| 160 | CD319 | 35c violet | 1.25 | .50 |
| | | *Nos. 157-160 (4)* | 3.05 | 3.05 |

**Royal Visit Issue**

Common Design Type

**1966, Feb. 4** **Litho.** ***Perf. 11x12***

**Portraits in Black**

| | | | | |
|---|---|---|---|---|
| 161 | CD320 | 6c violet blue | 1.75 | 1.10 |
| 162 | CD320 | 15c dark car rose | 1.75 | 1.50 |

**World Cup Soccer Issue**

Common Design Type

**1966, July 1** **Wmk. 314** ***Perf. 14***

| | | | | |
|---|---|---|---|---|
| 163 | CD321 | 6c multicolored | .25 | .60 |
| 164 | CD321 | 35c multicolored | .55 | .25 |

**WHO Headquarters Issue**

Common Design Type

**1966, Sept. 20** ***Perf. 14***

| | | | | |
|---|---|---|---|---|
| 165 | CD322 | 2c multicolored | .25 | .25 |
| 166 | CD322 | 15c multicolored | .90 | .30 |

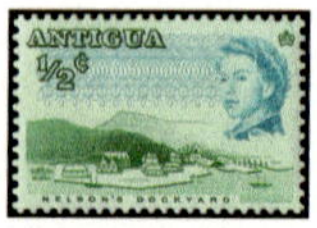

Nelson's Dockyard — A35

Designs: 1c, Old post office, St. John's. 2c, Health Center. 3c, Teachers' Training College. 4c, Martello Tower, Barbuda. 5c, Ruins of officers quarters, Shirley Heights. 6c, Government House, Barbuda. 10c, Princess Margaret School. 15c, Air terminal. 25c, General post office. 35c, Clarence House. 50c, Government House. 75c, Administration building. $1, Court House, St. John's. $2.50, Magistrates' Court. $5, St. John's Cathedral.

***Perf. 11½x11***

**1966, Nov. 1** **Engr.** **Wmk. 314**

| | | | | |
|---|---|---|---|---|
| 167 | A35 | ½c green & blue | .25 | 1.10 |
| 168 | A35 | 1c purple & rose | .25 | .30 |
| 169 | A35 | 2c slate & org | .25 | .25 |
| 170 | A35 | 3c rose red & blk | .30 | .30 |
| 171 | A35 | 4c dull vio & brn | 1.00 | .25 |
| 172 | A35 | 5c vio bl & olive | .25 | .25 |
| 173 | A35 | 6c dp org & pur | 1.00 | .30 |
| 174 | A35 | 10c brt grn & rose red | .25 | .25 |
| 175 | A35 | 15c brn & blue | 1.50 | .25 |
| | | Complete booklet, 4 ea. #172, 174, 175 | 11.00 | |
| 176 | A35 | 25c slate & brn | .55 | .25 |
| 177 | A35 | 35c dp rose & sep | 1.50 | .55 |
| 178 | A35 | 50c green & black | 2.00 | 2.25 |
| 179 | A35 | 75c Prus bl & vio blue | 3.50 | 2.25 |
| 180 | A35 | $1 dp rose & olive | 8.00 | 2.50 |

**181** A35 $2.50 black & rose 6.50 *8.00*
**182** A35 $5 ol grn & dl vio 9.00 6.50
*Nos. 167-182 (16)* 36.10 25.55

For surcharge see No. 231.

**1969** ***Perf. 13½***

*167a* A35 ½c .25 *2.25*
*168a* A35 1c .25 *1.25*
*169a* A35 2c .25 *.65*
*170a* A35 3c .25 *.25*
*171a* A35 4c .25 *.25*
*172b* A35 5c .25 .25
*173a* A35 6c .25 *.90*
*174b* A35 10c .25 .25
*175b* A35 15c .55 .25
*176a* A35 25c .45 .25
*177a* A35 35c .60 *1.00*
*178a* A35 50c .75 *2.25*
*180a* A35 $1 1.25 *5.00*
*181a* A35 $2.50 1.50 *8.00*
*182a* A35 $5 11.50 *24.00*
*Nos. 167a-182a (15)* 18.60 *46.80*

The ½c, 3c, 6c are on ordinary paper. The 15c through $5 on glazed paper. The others exist on both papers.

### UNESCO Anniversary Issue

Common Design Type

**1966, Dec. 1 Litho.** ***Perf. 14***

**183** CD323 4c "Education" .25 .25
**184** CD323 25c "Science" .40 .25
**185** CD323 $1 "Culture" 1.25 *2.00*
*Nos. 183-185 (3)* 1.90 *2.50*

### Independent State

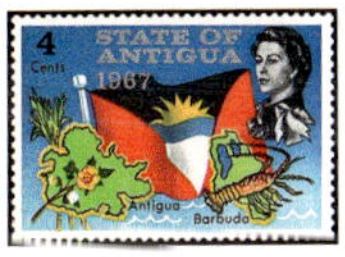

Flag of Antigua, Spiny Lobster, Maps of Antigua and Barbuda — A37

Designs: 15c, 35c, Flag of Antigua. 25c, Flag and Premier's Office Building.

**1967, Feb. 27 Photo.** ***Perf. 14***

**186** A37 4c multicolored .25 .25
**187** A37 15c multicolored .25 .25
**188** A37 25c multicolored .25 .25
**189** A37 35c multicolored .25 .25
*Nos. 186-189 (4)* 1.00 1.00

Antigua's independence, Feb. 27, 1967.

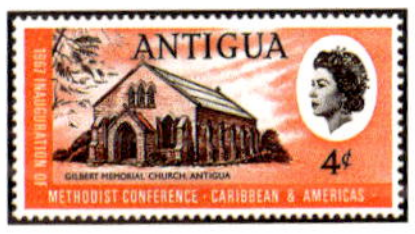

Gilbert Memorial Church, Antigua A38

25c, Nathaniel Gilbert's House. 35c, Map of the Caribbean and Central America.

***Perf. 14x13½***

**1967, May 18 Photo. Wmk. 314**

**190** A38 4c brt red & black .25 .25
**191** A38 25c emerald & black .25 .25
**192** A38 35c ultra & black .25 .25
*Nos. 190-192 (3)* .75 .75

Attainment of autonomy by the Methodist Church in the Caribbean and the Americas, and the opening of headquarters near St. John's, Antigua, May 1967.

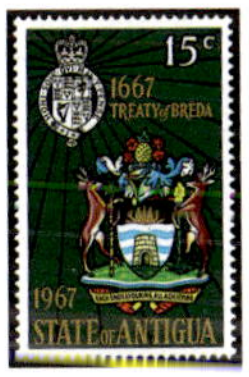

Antiguan and British Royal Arms — A39

**1967, July 21** ***Perf. 14½x14***

**193** A39 15c dark green & multi .25 .25
**194** A39 35c deep blue & multi .25 .25

Granting of a new coat of arms to the State of Antigua; 300th anniv. of the Treaty of Breda.

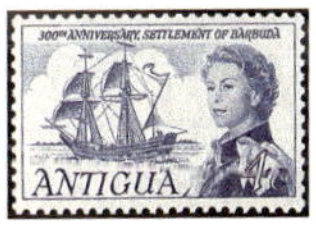

Sailing Ship, 17th Century — A40

Design: 6c, 35c, Map of Barbuda from Jan Blaeu's Atlas, 1665.

***Perf. 11½x11***

**1967, Dec. 14 Engr. Wmk. 314**

**195** A40 4c dark blue .35 .25
**196** A40 6c deep plum .35 *1.25*
**197** A40 25c green .50 .25
**198** A40 35c black .50 .30
*Nos. 195-198 (4)* 1.70 *2.05*

Resettlement of Barbuda, 300th anniv.

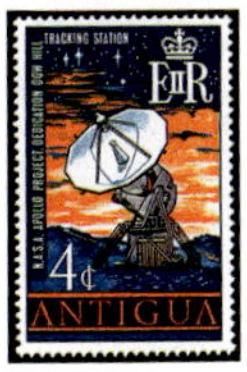

Dow Hill Antenna — A41

Designs: 15c, Antenna and rocket blasting off. 25c, Nose cone orbiting moon. 50c, Re-entry of space capsule.

***Perf. 14½x14***

**1968, Mar. 29 Photo. Wmk. 314**

**199** A41 4c dk blue, org & black .25 .25
**200** A41 15c dk blue, org & black .25 .25
**201** A41 25c dk blue, org & black .25 .25
**202** A41 50c dk blue, org & black .25 *.35*
*Nos. 199-202 (4)* 1.00 *1.10*

Dedication of the Dow Hill tracking station in Antigua for the NASA Apollo project.

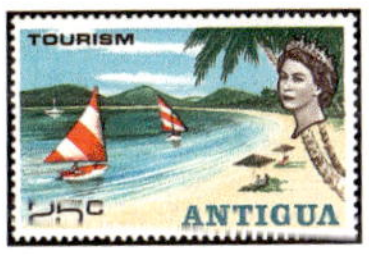

Beach and Sailfish — A42

Designs: ½c, 50c, Limbo dancer, flames and dancing girls. 15c, Three girls on a beach and water skier. 35c, Woman scuba diver, corals and fish.

**1968, July 1 Photo.** ***Perf. 14***

**203** A42 ½c red & multi .25 .25
**204** A42 15c sky blue & multi .25 .25
**205** A42 25c blue & multi .30 .25
**206** A42 35c brt blue & multi .30 .25
**207** A42 50c multicolored .50 *1.10*
*Nos. 203-207 (5)* 1.60 *2.10*

Issued for tourist publicity.

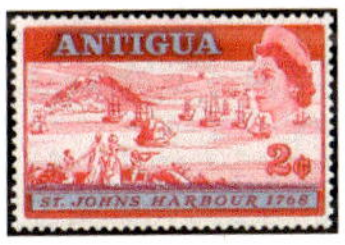

St. John's Harbor, 1768 — A43

St. John's Harbor: 15c, 1829. 25c, Map of deep-sea harbor, 1968. 35c, Dock, 1968. 2c, Like $1.

**Engr. & Litho.; Engr. ($1)**

**1968, Oct. 31 Wmk. 314** ***Perf. 13***

**208** A43 2c dp car & lt blue .25 *.30*
**209** A43 15c sepia & yel grn .35 .25
**210** A43 25c dk blue & yel .45 .25
**211** A43 35c dp green & sal .50 .25
**212** A43 $1 black .85 *1.75*
*Nos. 208-212 (5)* 2.40 *2.80*

Opening of St. John's deep-sea harbor.

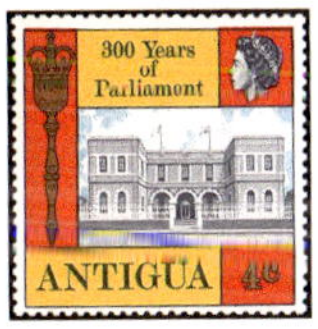

Mace and Parliament — A44

Mace and: 15c, Mace bearer. 25c, House of Representatives, interior. 50c, Antigua coat of arms and great seal.

**1969, Feb. 3 Photo.** ***Perf. 12½***

**213** A44 4c crimson & multi .25 .25
**214** A44 15c crimson & multi .25 .25
**215** A44 25c crimson & multi .25 .25
**216** A44 50c crimson & multi .30 *1.40*
*Nos. 213-216 (4)* 1.05 *2.15*

300th anniversary of Antigua Parliament.

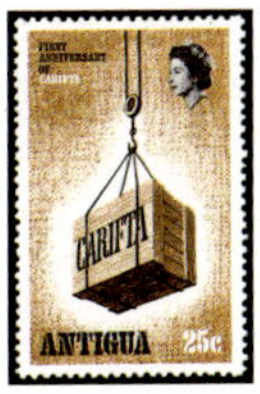

CARIFTA Cargo — A45

4c, 15c, Ship, plane and trucks, horiz.

***Perf. 13½x13, 13x13½***

**1969, Apr. 14 Litho. Wmk. 314**

**217** A45 4c blk & brt lilac rose .25 .25
**218** A45 15c blk & brt grnsh blue .25 .25
**219** A45 25c bister & black .25 .25
**220** A45 35c tan & black .25 .25
*Nos. 217-220 (4)* 1.00 1.00

1st anniv. of CARIFTA (Caribbean Free Trade Area).

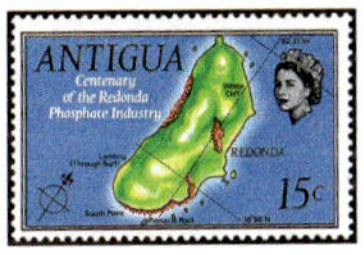

Map of Redonda Island — A46

25c, View of Redonda from the sea & seagulls.

**1969, Aug. 1 Photo.** ***Perf. 13x13½***

**221** A46 15c ultra & multi .25 .25
**222** A46 25c multicolored .25 .25
**223** A46 50c salmon & multi .40 *.60*
*Nos. 221-223 (3)* .90 *1.10*

Centenary of Redonda phosphate industry.

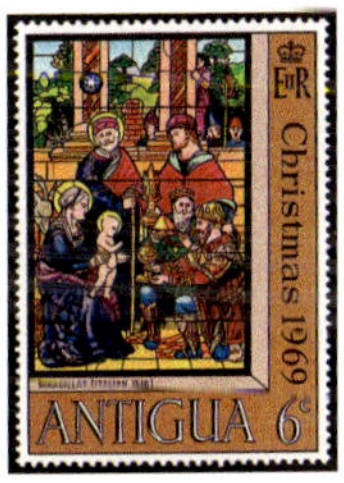

Adoration of the Kings, by Gugliemo Marcillat — A47

Christmas: 10c, 50c, Holy Family, by anonymous German artist, 15th century.

**1969, Oct. 15 Litho.** ***Perf. 13x14***

**224** A47 6c bister brn & multi .25 .25
**225** A47 10c fawn & multi .25 .25
**226** A47 35c gray olive & multi .25 .25
**227** A47 50c gray blue & multi .30 .25
*Nos. 224-227 (4)* 1.05 1.00

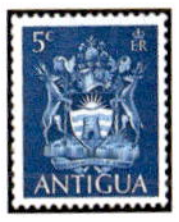

Arms of Antigua — A48

### Coil Stamps

**Wmk. 314 upright**

**1970, Jan. 30 Photo.** ***Perf. 14½x14***

**228** A48 5c bright blue .25 .25
*a.* Wmk. 373 ('77) *7.00*
**229** A48 10c bright green .25 .25
*a.* Wmk. 373, invtd. ('77) — *2.00*
**230** A48 25c deep magenta .25 .25
*a.* Wmk. 373 ('77) *12.50*
*Nos. 228-230 (3)* .75 .75

### Glazed Paper

**1973, Mar. 5 Wmk. 314 sideways**

*228b* A48 5c bright blue 1.00 *2.00*
*229b* A48 10c bright green 1.00 *2.00*
*230b* A48 25c deep magenta 1.25 *1.75*
*Nos. 228b-230b (3)* 3.25 *5.75*

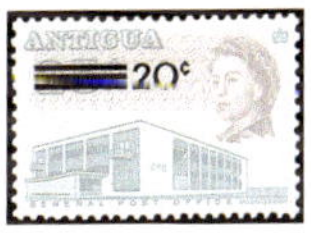

No. 176 Surcharged

**1970, Jan. 2 Engr.** ***Perf. 11½x11***

**231** A35 20c on 25c slate & brn .35 .25

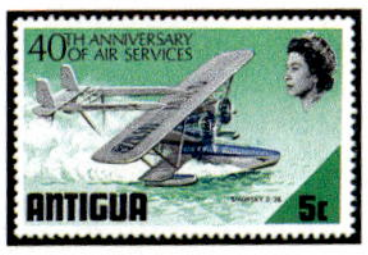

Sikorsky S-38 — A49

Aircraft: 20c, Dornier DO-X. 35c, Hawker Siddeley 748. 50c, Douglas C-124C Globemaster II. 75c, Vickers VC 10.

**1970, Feb. 16 Litho.** ***Perf. 14½***

**232** A49 5c brt green & multi .60 .25
**233** A49 20c ultra & multi 1.00 .25
**234** A49 35c blue grn & multi 1.25 .25
**235** A49 50c blue & multi 1.25 *1.50*
**236** A49 75c vio blue & multi 1.60 *2.25*
*Nos. 232-236 (5)* 5.70 *4.50*

40th anniversary of air service.

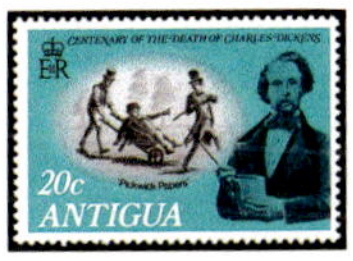

Dickens and Scene from "Pickwick Papers" — A50

Charles Dickens (1812-1870), English novelist and Scene from: 5c, "Nicholas Nickleby." 35c, "Oliver Twist." $1, "David Copperfield."

**Wmk. 314**

**1970, May 19 Litho.** ***Perf. 14***

**237** A50 5c olive & sepia .25 .25
**238** A50 20c aqua & sepia .25 .25
**239** A50 35c violet & sepia .25 .25
**240** A50 $1 scarlet & sepia .60 *.75*
*Nos. 237-240 (4)* 1.35 *1.50*

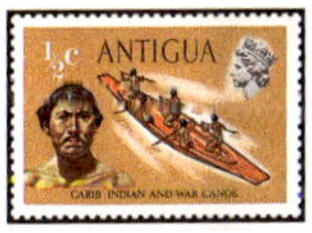

Carib Indian and War Canoe — A51

Ships: 1c, Columbus and "Nina." 2c, Sir Thomas Warner's arms and sailing ship. 3c, Viscount Hood and "Barfleur." 4c, Sir George Rodney and "Formidable." 5c, Capt. Horatio Nelson and "Boreas." 6c, King William IV and "Pegasus." 10c, Blackbeard (Edward Teach) and pirate ketch. 15c, Capt. Cuthbert Collingwood and "Pelican." 20c, Admiral Nelson and "Victoria." 25c, Paddle steamer "Solent" and Steam Packet Company emblem. 35c, King George V and corvette "Canada." 50c, Cruiser "Renown" and royal badge. 75c, S.S. "Federal Maple" and maple leaf. $1, Racing yacht "Sol-Quest" and Gallant 53 class emblem. $2.50, Missile destroyer "London" and her emblem. $5, Tug "Pathfinder" and arms of Antigua.

**Wmk. 314 Sideways**

**1970, Aug. 19 Litho.** ***Perf. 14***

**241** A51 ½c ocher & multi .25 *1.25*
**242** A51 1c Prus bl & multi .30 *1.25*
**243** A51 2c yel grn & multi .35 *3.00*
**244** A51 3c ol bis & multi .35 *3.00*
**245** A51 4c bl gray & multi .40 *2.75*
**246** A51 5c fawn & multi .50 .40
**247** A51 6c rose lil & multi 1.40 *4.25*
**248** A51 10c brn org & multi .80 .25
**249** A51 15c ultra & multi 7.00 1.00
**250** A51 20c ol grn & multi 1.15 .40
**251** A51 25c olive & multi 1.25 .40
**252** A51 35c dull red brn & multi 1.60 .80
**253** A51 50c lt brn & multi 3.50 *5.75*
**254** A51 75c beige & multi 4.50 *5.75*
**255** A51 $1 Prus green & multi 4.50 1.75
**256** A51 $2.50 gray & multi 6.25 *7.25*
**257** A51 $5 yel & multi 2.75 *6.00*
*Nos. 241-257 (17)* 36.85 *45.25*

**1972-74 Wmk. 314 Upright**

*241a* A51 ½c .30 *.45*
*242a* A51 1c .40 *1.25*
*244a* A51 3c .80 *1.75*
*245a* A51 4c .55 *2.00*
*246a* A51 5c .60 .40
*247a* A51 6c .90 *2.75*
*248a* A51 10c .60 *.60*
*249a* A51 15c 6.25 .90
*254a* A51 75c 6.25 3.00
*255a* A51 $1 2.75 1.75
*256a* A51 $2.50 2.50 *6.50*
*257a* A51 $5 3.50 *10.00*
*Nos. 241a-257a (12)* 25.40 *31.35*

For surcharge see No. 368.

**1975, Jan. 21 Wmk. 373**

*257b* A51 $5 yellow & multi 4.00 *12.00*

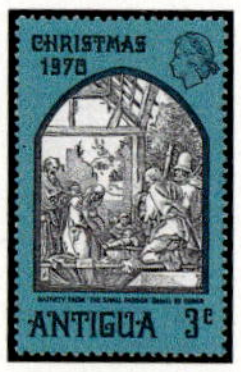


Nativity, by Albrecht Dürer — A52

Christmas: 10c, 50c, Adoration of the Magi, by Albrecht Dürer.

**Engr. & Litho.**

**1970, Oct. 28** ***Perf. 13½x14***

| | | | | |
|---|---|---|---|---|
| **258** | A52 | 3c brt grnsh blue & blk | .25 | .25 |
| **259** | A52 | 10c pink & plum | .25 | .25 |
| **260** | A52 | 35c brick red & black | .25 | .25 |
| **261** | A52 | 50c lilac & violet | .30 | .25 |
| | | *Nos. 258-261 (4)* | 1.05 | 1.00 |

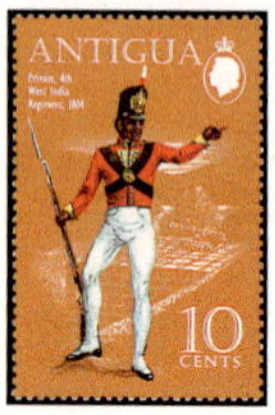


Private, 4th West India Regiment, 1804 — A53

Military Uniforms: ½c, Drummer Boy, 4th King's Own Regiment, 1759. 20c, Grenadier Company Officer, 60th Regiment, The Royal American, 1809. 35c, Light Company Officer, 93rd Regiment, The Sutherland Highlanders, 1826-1834. 75c, Private, 3rd West India Regiment, 1851.

***Perf. 14x13½***

**1970, Dec. 1 Litho. Wmk. 314**

| | | | | |
|---|---|---|---|---|
| **262** | A53 | ½c lake & multi | .25 | .25 |
| **263** | A53 | 10c brn org & multi | .45 | .25 |
| **264** | A53 | 20c Prus grn & multi | .90 | .25 |
| **265** | A53 | 35c dl pur & multi | 1.10 | .25 |
| **266** | A53 | 75c dk ol grn & multi | 2.25 | *2.75* |
| *a.* | | Souv. sheet, #262-266 + label | 6.50 | *7.00* |
| | | *Nos. 262-266 (5)* | 4.95 | *3.75* |

See Nos. 274-278, 283-287, 307-311, 329-333.

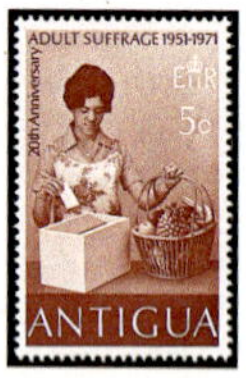


Market Woman Voting — A54

Voting by: 20c, Businessman. 35c, Mother (and child). 50c, Workman.

***Perf. 14½x14***

**1971, Feb. 1 Photo. Wmk. 314**

| | | | | |
|---|---|---|---|---|
| **267** | A54 | 5c brown | .25 | .25 |
| **268** | A54 | 20c olive black | .25 | .25 |
| **269** | A54 | 35c rose magenta | .25 | .25 |
| **270** | A54 | 50c violet blue | .25 | .25 |
| | | *Nos. 267-270 (4)* | 1.00 | 1.00 |

Adult suffrage, 20th anniversary.

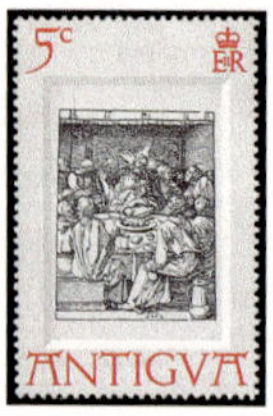


Last Supper, from The Small Passion, by Dürer — A55

Woodcuts by Albrecht Dürer: 35c, Crucifixion from Eichstatt Missal. 75c, Resurrection from The Great Passion.

***Perf. 14x13½***

**1971, Apr. 7 Litho. Wmk. 314**

| | | | | |
|---|---|---|---|---|
| **271** | A55 | 5c gray, red & black | .25 | .25 |
| **272** | A55 | 35c gray, violet & black | .25 | .25 |
| **273** | A55 | 75c gray, gold & black | .25 | .25 |
| | | *Nos. 271-273 (3)* | .75 | .75 |

Easter.

### Uniform Type of 1970

Military Uniforms: ½c, Private, Suffolk Regiment, 1704. 10c, Grenadier, South Staffordshire, 1751. 20c, Fusilier, Royal Northumberland, 1778. 35c, Private, Northamptonshire. 1793, 75c, Private, East Yorkshire, 1805.

**1971, July 12 Litho. Wmk. 314**

| | | | | |
|---|---|---|---|---|
| **274** | A53 | ½c gray grn & multi | .25 | .25 |
| **275** | A53 | 10c bluish blk & multi | .45 | .25 |
| **276** | A53 | 20c dk pur & multi | 1.15 | .25 |
| **277** | A53 | 35c dk ol & multi | 1.40 | .25 |
| **278** | A53 | 75c brown & multi | 1.75 | *2.75* |
| *a.* | | Souv. sheet, #274-278 + label | 7.00 | *8.00* |
| | | *Nos. 274-278 (5)* | 5.00 | *3.75* |

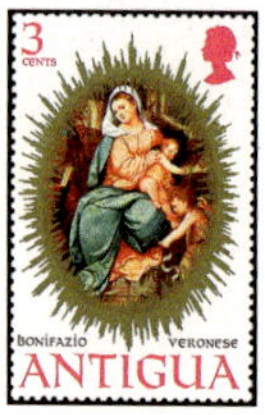


Virgin and Child, by Veronese — A56

Christmas: 5c, 50c, Adoration of the Shepherds, by Bonifazio Veronese.

**1971, Oct. 4** ***Perf. 14x13½***

| | | | | |
|---|---|---|---|---|
| **279** | A56 | 3c multicolored | .25 | .25 |
| **280** | A56 | 5c multicolored | .25 | .25 |
| **281** | A56 | 35c multicolored | .25 | .25 |
| **282** | A56 | 50c multicolored | .40 | .30 |
| | | *Nos. 279-282 (4)* | 1.15 | 1.05 |

### Uniform Type of 1970

Military Uniforms: ½c, Officer, King's Own Borderers Regiment, 1815. 10c, Sergeant, Buckinghamshire Regiment, 1837. 20c, Private, South Hampshire Regiment, 1853. 35c, Officer, Royal Artillery, 1854. 75c, Private, Worcestershire Regiment, 1870.

**1972, July 1**

| | | | | |
|---|---|---|---|---|
| **283** | A53 | ½c ol brn & multi | .25 | .25 |
| **284** | A53 | 10c dp grn & multi | .60 | .25 |
| **285** | A53 | 20c brt vio & multi | 1.10 | .25 |
| **286** | A53 | 35c mar & multi | 1.35 | .30 |
| **287** | A53 | 75c dk vio bl & multi | 1.75 | *3.00* |
| *a.* | | Souvenir sheet of 5, #283-287 + label | 7.50 | *8.50* |
| | | *Nos. 283-287 (5)* | 5.05 | *4.05* |

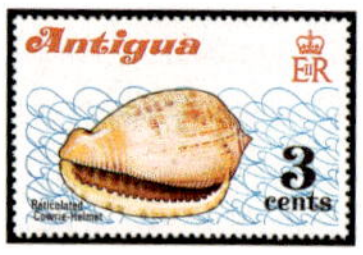


Reticulated Helmet Cowrie — A57

Sea Shells: 5c, Measled cowrie. 35c, West Indian fighting conch. 50c, Hawkwing conch.

**1972, Aug. 1** ***Perf. 14½x14***

| | | | | |
|---|---|---|---|---|
| **288** | A57 | 3c multicolored | .55 | .25 |
| **289** | A57 | 5c ver & multi | .55 | .25 |
| **290** | A57 | 35c lt vio & multi | 1.60 | .25 |
| **291** | A57 | 50c rose red & multi | 1.75 | *2.75* |
| | | *Nos. 288-291 (4)* | 4.45 | *3.50* |

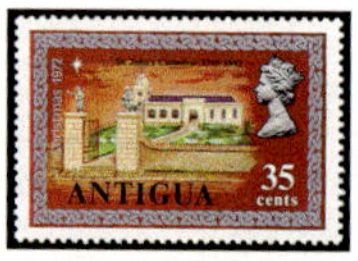


St. John's Cathedral, 1745-1843 A58

Christmas: 50c, Interior of St. John's. 75c, St. John's rebuilt.

**1972, Nov. 6 Litho.** ***Perf. 14***

| | | | | |
|---|---|---|---|---|
| **292** | A58 | 35c org brn & multi | .25 | .25 |
| **293** | A58 | 50c vio & multi | .30 | .30 |
| **294** | A58 | 75c multicolored | .50 | *.55* |
| *a.* | | Souv. sheet, #292-294, perf 15 | 1.00 | *1.25* |
| | | *Nos. 292-294 (3)* | 1.05 | *1.10* |

### Silver Wedding Issue, 1972

Common Design Type

**1972, Nov. 20 Photo.** ***Perf. 14x14½***

| | | | | |
|---|---|---|---|---|
| **295** | CD324 | 20c ultra & multi | .25 | .25 |
| **296** | CD324 | 35c steel blue & multi | .25 | .25 |

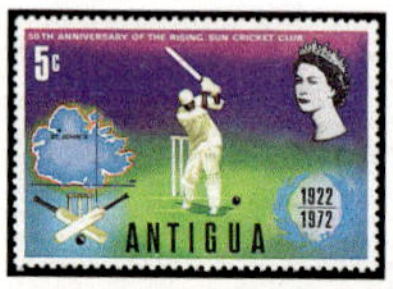


Map of Antigua, Batsman Driving Ball — A60

Designs: 35c, Batsman and wicketkeeper. $1, Emblem of Rising Sun Cricket Club.

**1972, Dec. 15** ***Perf. 13½x14***

| | | | | |
|---|---|---|---|---|
| **297** | A60 | 5c multicolored | .25 | .25 |
| **298** | A60 | 35c multicolored | .75 | .30 |
| **299** | A60 | $1 multicolored | 2.25 | *2.50* |
| *a.* | | Souvenir sheet of 3, #297-299 | 5.25 | *6.25* |
| | | *Nos. 297-299 (3)* | 3.25 | *3.05* |

Rising Sun Cricket Club, St. John's, 50th anniv.

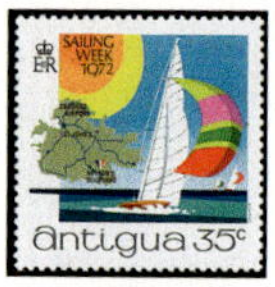


Map of Antigua and Yacht — A61

**1972, Dec. 29** ***Perf. 14½***

| | | | | |
|---|---|---|---|---|
| **300** | A61 | 35c shown | .25 | .25 |
| **301** | A61 | 50c Racing yachts | .25 | .25 |
| **302** | A61 | 75c St. John's G.P.O. | .35 | .25 |
| **303** | A61 | $1 Statue of Liberty | .40 | .25 |
| *a.* | | Souvenir sheet of 2, #301, 303 | 1.10 | *1.25* |
| | | *Nos. 300-303 (4)* | 1.25 | *1.00* |

Opening of Antigua and Barbuda Information Office in New York City.

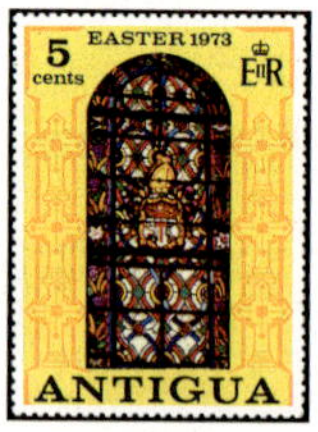


Window with Episcopal Coat of Arms — A62

Stained glass windows from Cathedral of St. John: 35c, Crucifixion. 75c, Arm of Rt. Rev. D.G. Davis, 1st bishop of Antigua.

**1973, Apr. 16 Litho.** ***Perf. 13½***

| | | | | |
|---|---|---|---|---|
| **304** | A62 | 5c yellow & multi | .25 | .25 |
| **305** | A62 | 35c brt lilac & multi | .25 | .25 |
| **306** | A62 | 75c blue & multi | .30 | .25 |
| | | *Nos. 304-306 (3)* | .80 | .75 |

Easter.

### Uniform Type of 1970

Military Uniforms: ½c, Private, Col. Zacharia Tiffin's Regiment, 1701. 10c, Private, 63rd Regiment, 1759. 20c, Officer, 35th Sussex Regiment, 1828. 35c, Private, 2nd West India Regiment, 1853. 75c, Sergeant, Princess of Wales Regiment, Hertfordshire, 1858.

***Perf. 14x13½***

**1973, July 1 Wmk. 314**

| | | | | |
|---|---|---|---|---|
| **307** | A53 | ½c dp ultra & multi | .25 | .25 |
| **308** | A53 | 10c rose lilac & multi | .35 | .25 |
| **309** | A53 | 20c gray & multi | .50 | .25 |
| **310** | A53 | 35c multicolored | .70 | .25 |
| **311** | A53 | 75c multicolored | 1.50 | 1.25 |
| *a.* | | Souv. sheet, #307-311 + label | 4.00 | 3.75 |
| | | *Nos. 307-311 (5)* | 3.30 | 2.25 |

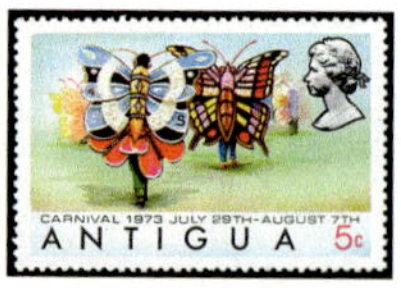


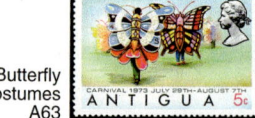

Butterfly Costumes A63

Designs: 20c, Carnival revelers. 35c, Costumed group. 75c, Carnival Queen.

***Perf. 13½x14***

**1973, July 30 Unwmk.**

| | | | | |
|---|---|---|---|---|
| **312** | A63 | 5c multicolored | .25 | .25 |
| **313** | A63 | 20c multicolored | .25 | .25 |
| **314** | A63 | 35c multicolored | .25 | .25 |
| **315** | A63 | 75c multicolored | .30 | .25 |
| *a.* | | Souvenir sheet of 4, #312-315 | 1.10 | *1.25* |
| | | *Nos. 312-315 (4)* | 1.05 | 1.00 |

Carnival, July 29-Aug. 7.

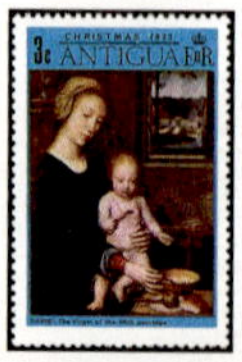


Virgin of the Porridge, by David — A64

Christmas: 5c, Adoration of the Kings, by Stomer. 20c, Virgin of the Grand Duke, by Raphael. 35c, Nativity with God the Father and Holy Ghost, by Tiepolo. $1, Madonna and Child, by Murillo.

***Perf. 14½***

**1973, Oct. 15 Photo. Unwmk.**

| | | | | |
|---|---|---|---|---|
| **316** | A64 | 3c brt blue & multi | .25 | .25 |
| **317** | A64 | 5c emerald & multi | .25 | .25 |
| **318** | A64 | 20c gold & multi | .25 | .25 |
| **319** | A64 | 35c violet & multi | .25 | .25 |
| **320** | A64 | $1 red & multi | .35 | *.55* |
| *a.* | | Souvenir sheet of 5, #316-320 | 1.40 | *1.60* |
| | | *Nos. 316-320 (5)* | 1.35 | *1.55* |

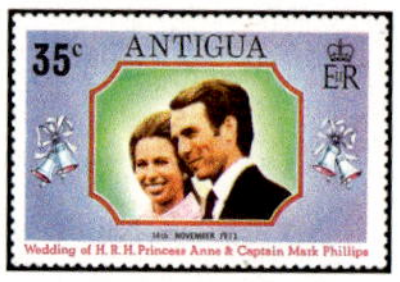


Princess Anne and Mark Phillips — A65

Design: $2, different border.

**1973, Nov. 14 Litho.** ***Perf. 13½***

| | | | | |
|---|---|---|---|---|
| **321** | A65 | 35c dull ultra & multi | .25 | .25 |
| **322** | A65 | $2 yel grn & multi | .25 | .25 |
| *a.* | | Souvenir sheet of 2, #321-322 | .65 | .65 |

Wedding of Princess Anne and Capt. Mark Phillips.

Nos. 321-322 were issued in sheets of 5 plus label.

### Nos. 321-322 and 322a Ovptd.

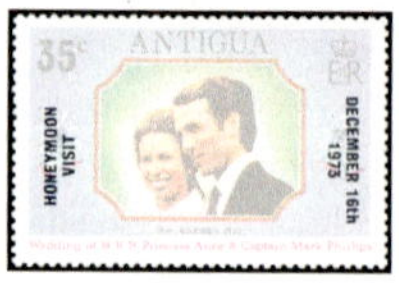


**1973, Dec. 15 Litho.** ***Perf. 13½***

| | | | | |
|---|---|---|---|---|
| **323** | A65 | 35c multicolored | .25 | .25 |
| **324** | A65 | $2 multicolored | .40 | .40 |
| *a.* | | Souvenir sheet of 2, #323-324 | .65 | .65 |

Visit of Princess Anne and Mark Phillips to Antigua, Dec. 16. Same overprint in sheet margins of Nos. 323-324 and 324a.

Overprint lithographed. Also exists typographed.

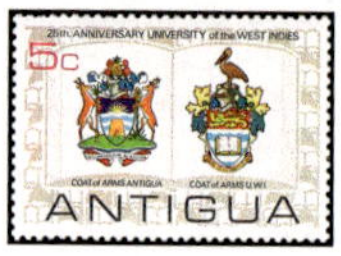


Arms of Antigua and U.W.I. — A66

Designs: 20c, Dancers. 35c, Antigua campus. 75c, Chancellor Sir Hugh Wooding.

**1974, Feb. 18 Wmk. 314**

| | | | | |
|---|---|---|---|---|
| **325** | A66 | 5c multicolored | .25 | .25 |
| **326** | A66 | 20c multicolored | .25 | .25 |
| **327** | A66 | 35c multicolored | .25 | .25 |
| **328** | A66 | 75c multicolored | .25 | .25 |
| | | *Nos. 325-328 (4)* | 1.00 | 1.00 |

University of the West Indies, 24th anniv.

### Uniform Type of 1970

Military Uniforms: ½c, Officer, 59th Foot, 1797. 10c, Gunner, Royal Artillery, 1800. 20c, Private, 1st West India Regiment, 1830. 35c, Officer, Gordon Highlanders, 1843. 75c, Private, Royal Welsh Fusiliers, 1846.

**1974, May 1** ***Perf. 14x13½***

| | | | | |
|---|---|---|---|---|
| **329** | A53 | ½c dull grn & multi | .25 | .25 |
| **330** | A53 | 10c ocher & multi | .40 | .25 |
| **331** | A53 | 20c multicolored | .75 | .25 |
| **332** | A53 | 35c gray bl & multi | .90 | .25 |
| **333** | A53 | 75c dk gray & multi | 1.25 | *1.75* |
| *a.* | | Souvenir sheet of 5, #329-333 | 3.25 | 2.50 |
| | | *Nos. 329-333 (5)* | 3.55 | 2.75 |

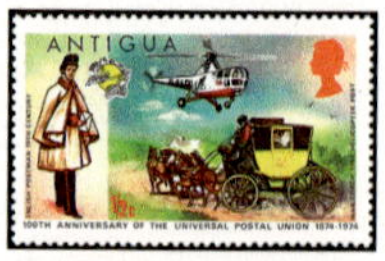


English Mailman and Coach, Helicopter A67

UPU, Cent.: 1c, English bellman, 1846; Orinoco mailboat, 1851; telecommunications satellite. 2c, English mailtrain guard, 1852; Swiss post passenger bus, 1906; Italian hydrofoil. 5c, Swiss messenger, 16th century; Wells Fargo coach, 1800; Concorde. 20c, German postilion, 1820; Japanese mailmen, 19th century; carrier pigeon. 35c, Contemporary Antiguan mailman; radar station; aquaplane. $1, Medieval French courier; American train, 1884; British Airways jet.

**1974, July 15 Litho. *Perf. 14½***

334 A67 ½c multicolored .25 .25
335 A67 1c multicolored .25 .25
336 A67 2c multicolored .25 .25
337 A67 5c multicolored .55 .40
338 A67 20c multicolored .30 .25
339 A67 35c multicolored .40 .25
340 A67 $1 multicolored 1.50 *2.00*
*a.* Souvenir sheet of 7, #334-340 + label, perf. 13 4.00 3.00
*Nos. 334-340 (7)* 3.50 3.65

For surcharges see Nos. 365-367.

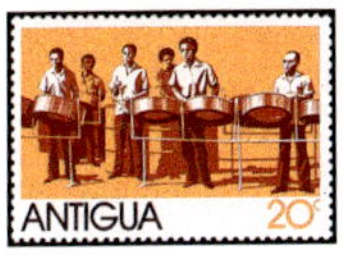


Traditional Steel Band — A68

Carnival 1974 (Steel Bands): 5c, Traditional players, vert. 35c, Modern steel band. 75c, Modern players, vert.

**1974, Aug. 1, Wmk. 314 *Perf. 14***

341 A68 5c rose red, dk red & blk .25 .25
342 A68 20c ocher, brn & blk .25 .25
343 A68 35c yel grn, grn & blk .25 .25
344 A68 75c dl bl, dk bl & blk .25 *1.00*
*a.* Souvenir sheet of 4, #341-344 .75 *1.25*
*Nos. 341-344 (4)* 1.00 *1.75*

For surcharge see No. 364.

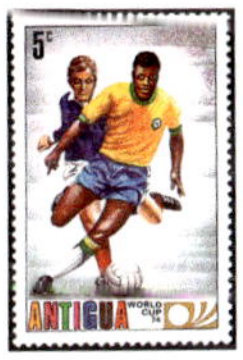


Soccer — A69

Designs: Games' emblem and soccer.

**1974, Sept. 23 Unwmk. *Perf. 14½***

345 A69 5c multicolored .25 .25
346 A69 35c multicolored .25 .25
347 A69 75c multicolored .25 .25
348 A69 $1 multicolored .30 .30
*a.* Souvenir sheet of 4 1.10 1.10
*Nos. 345-348 (4)* 1.05 1.05

World Cup Soccer Championship, Munich, June 13-July 7. Nos. 345-348 issued in sheets of 5 plus label showing Soccer Cup. No. 348a contains one each of Nos. 345-348, perf. 13½, and 2 labels.

For overprints and surcharges see Nos. 361-363.

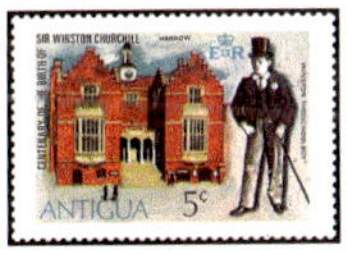


Winston Churchill (1874-1965) at Harrow — A70

Designs: 35c, St. Paul's during bombing and Churchill portrait. 75c, Churchill's coat of arms and catafalque. $1, Churchill during Boer war, warrant for arrest and map of his escape route.

**1974, Oct. 20 Unwmk. *Perf. 14½***

349 A70 5c multicolored .25 .25
350 A70 35c multicolored .25 .25
351 A70 75c multicolored .25 *.60*
352 A70 $1 multicolored .30 *1.00*
*a.* Souvenir sheet of 4, #349-352 1.10 *1.60*
*Nos. 349-352 (4)* 1.05 *2.10*

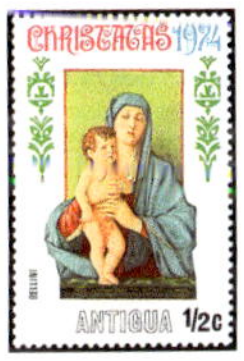


Virgin and Child, by Giovanni Bellini — A71

Christmas — Paintings of the Virgin and Child: 1c, Raphael. 2c, Van der Weyden. 3c, Giorgione. 5c, Andrea Montagna. 20c, Alvise Vivarini. 35c, Bartolommeo Montagna. 75c, Lorenzo Costa.

**1974, Nov. 18 Litho. *Perf. 14½***

353 A71 ½c shown .25 .25
354 A71 1c multicolored .25 .25
355 A71 2c multicolored .25 .25
356 A71 3c multicolored .25 .25
357 A71 5c multicolored .25 .25
358 A71 20c multicolored .25 .25
359 A71 35c multicolored .25 .25
360 A71 75c multicolored .35 *1.00*
*a.* Souv. sheet, #357-360, perf 13½ 1.00 *1.50*
*Nos. 353-360 (8)* 2.10 2.75

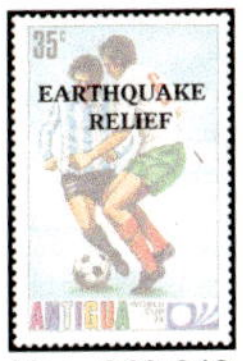


Nos. 346-348 Overprinted

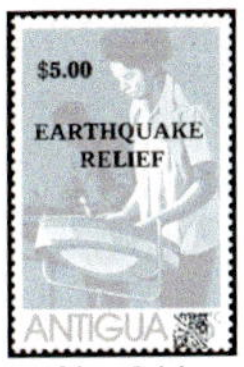


No. 344 Surcharged and Overprinted

**1974, Oct. 16 Litho. *Perf. 14½, 14***

361 A69 35c multicolored .30 .30
362 A69 75c multicolored .45 .35
363 A69 $1 multicolored .55 .45
364 A68 $5 on 75c multi 1.75 *2.50*
*Nos. 361-364 (4)* 3.05 *3.60*

Earthquake of Oct. 8, 1974.

**Nos. 338-340 and 254a Surcharged**

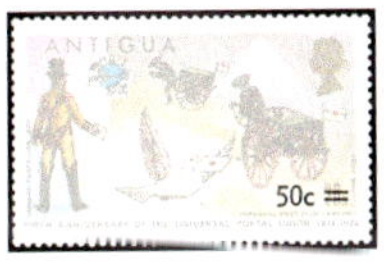


**1974-75 Wmk. 314 *Perf. 14½***

365 A67 50c on 20c 1.25 *2.00*
366 A67 $2.50 on 35c 2.75 *6.00*
367 A67 $5 on $1 6.00 *7.50*

***Perf. 14***

368 A51 $10 on 75c 2.75 *8.00*
*Nos. 365-368 (4)* 12.75 *23.50*

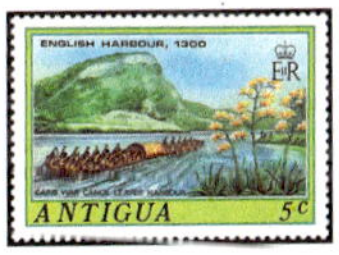


Carib War Canoe, English Harbour — A72

Designs (Nelson's Dockyard): 15c, Raising ship, 1770. 35c, Lord Nelson and "Boreas." 50c, Yachts arriving for Sailing Week, 1974. $1, "Anchorage" in Old Dockyard, 1970.

**1975, Mar. 17 Unwmk. *Perf. 14½***

369 A72 5c multicolored .30 .25
370 A72 15c multicolored .90 .25
371 A72 35c multicolored 1.25 .25
372 A72 50c multicolored 1.50 *1.75*
373 A72 $1 multicolored 1.75 *2.10*
*Nos. 369-373 (5)* 5.70 *4.60*

**Souvenir Sheet**

***Perf. 13½***

373A A72 Sheet of 5, #369-373 6.00 6.00

Stamps in No. 373A are 43x28mm.

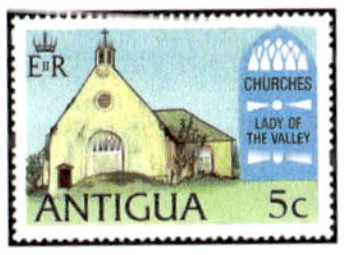


Lady of the Valley Church — A73

Churches of Antigua: 20c, Gilbert Memorial. 35c, Grace Hill Moravian. 50c, St. Phillip's. $1, Ebenezer Methodist.

**1975, May 19 Litho. *Perf. 14½***

374 A73 5c multicolored .25 .25
375 A73 20c multicolored .25 .25
376 A73 35c multicolored .25 .25
377 A73 50c multicolored .25 .25
378 A73 $1 multicolored .25 .45
*a.* Souvenir sheet of 3, #376-378, perf. 13½ 1.00 *1.40*
*Nos. 374-378 (5)* 1.25 1.45

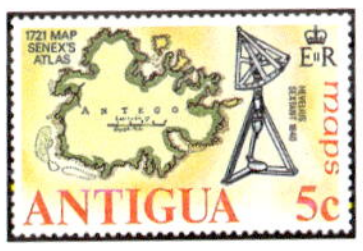


Antigua, Senex's Atlas, 1721, and Hevelius Sextant, 1640 — A74

Maps of Antigua: 20c, Jeffery's Atlas, 1775, and 18th century engraving of ship. 35c, Barbuda and Antigua, 1775 and 1975. $1, St. John's and English Harbour, 1973.

**1975, July 21 Wmk. 314**

379 A74 5c multicolored .35 .25
380 A74 20c multicolored .65 .25
381 A74 35c multicolored .85 .25
382 A74 $1 multicolored 1.75 *2.10*
*a.* Souvenir sheet of 4, #379-382 4.50 3.50
*Nos. 379-382 (4)* 3.60 2.85

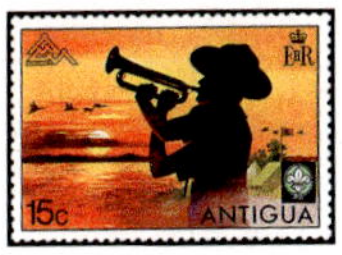


Bugler and Sunset — A75

Nordjamb 75 Emblem and: 20c, Black and white Scouts, tents and flags. 35c, Lord Baden-Powell and tents. $2, Dahomey dancers.

**Unwmk.**

**1975, Aug. 26 Litho. *Perf. 14***

383 A75 15c multicolored .30 .25
384 A75 20c multicolored .35 .25
385 A75 35c multicolored .50 .30
386 A75 $2 multicolored 2.00 2.25
*a.* Souvenir sheet of 4, #383-386 4.00 4.00
*Nos. 383-386 (4)* 3.15 3.05

Nordjamb 75, 14th Boy Scout Jamboree, Lillehammer, Norway, July 29-Aug. 7.

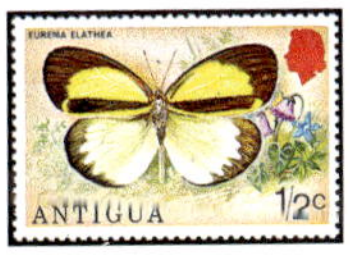


Eurema Elathea — A76

Butterflies: 1c, Danaus plexippus. 2c, Phoebis philea. 5c, Marpesia petreus thetys. 20c, Eurema proterpia. 35c, Papilio polydamas. $2, Vanessa cardui.

**1975, Oct. 30 Litho. *Perf. 14***

387 A76 ½c multicolored .25 .25
388 A76 1c multicolored .25 .25
389 A76 2c multicolored .25 .25
390 A76 5c multicolored .30 .25
391 A76 20c multicolored 1.25 .50
392 A76 35c multicolored 1.75 .75
393 A76 $2 multicolored 5.00 *8.00*
*a.* Miniature sheet of 4, #390-393 9.50 *10.00*
*Nos. 387-393 (7)* 9.05 *10.25*

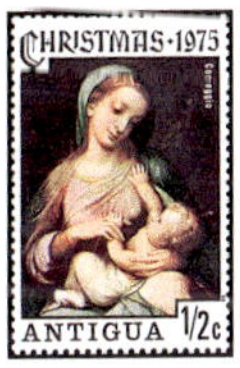


Virgin and Child, by Correggio — A77

Christmas: Virgin and Child paintings.

**1975, Nov. 17 Unwmk.**

394 A77 ½c shown .25 .25
395 A77 1c El Greco .25 .25
396 A77 2c Durer .25 .25
397 A77 3c Antonello .25 .25
398 A77 5c Bellini .25 .25
399 A77 10c Durer .25 .25
400 A77 35c Bellini .40 .25
401 A77 $2 Durer .75 .90
*a.* Souvenir sheet of 4, #398-401 2.00 2.00
*Nos. 394-401 (8)* 2.65 2.65

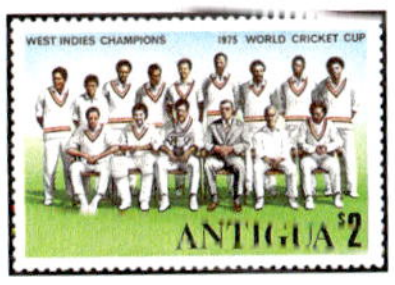


West Indies Team — A78

Designs: 5c, Batsman I.V.A. Richards and cup, vert. 35c, Bowler A.M.E. Roberts and cup, vert.

**1975, Dec. 15 Litho. *Perf. 14***

402 A78 5c multicolored 1.10 .25
403 A78 35c multicolored 2.00 .25
404 A78 $2 multicolored 4.25 *7.75*
*Nos. 402-404 (3)* 7.35 *8.55*

World Cricket Cup, victory of West Indies team.

A number of unissued items, imperfs., part perfs., missing color varieties, etc., were made available when the Format International inventory was liquidated. Imperfs of some or all of the Antigua stamps in the following sets are included: #405-422, 503-507, 515-517, 703-707, 745-749, 755-759, 808-816, 819-826, 905-909, 934-937.

See footnote after #962.

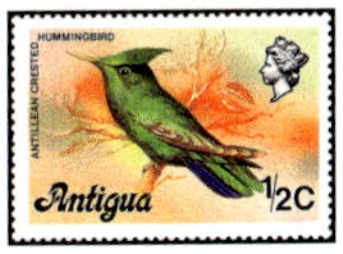


Antillean Crested Hummingbird A79

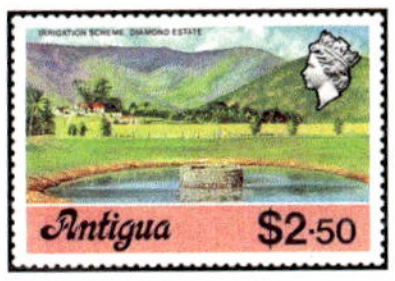


Irrigation System, Diamond Estate — A80

Designs: 1c, Imperial parrot. 2c, Zenaida dove. 3c, Loggerhead kingbird. 4c, Red-necked pigeon. 5c, Rufous-throated solitaire. 6c, Orchid tree. 10c, Bougainvillea. 15c, Geiger tree. 20c, Flamboyant. 25c, Hibiscus. 35c, Flame of the Woods. 50c, Cannon at Fort James. 75c, Premier's Office. $1, Potworks Dam. $5, Government House. $10, Coolidge International Airport.

**1976, Jan. 19 Litho. *Perf. 15***

405 A79 ½c multicolored .35 .60
406 A79 1c multicolored 1.25 .50
407 A79 2c multicolored 1.25 .50
408 A79 3c multicolored 1.25 .55
409 A79 4c multicolored 1.25 *2.00*
410 A79 5c multicolored 1.75 .25
411 A79 6c multicolored .30 *2.00*
412 A79 10c multicolored .30 .25
413 A79 15c multicolored .35 .25
414 A79 20c multicolored .35 .35
415 A79 25c multicolored .35 .25
416 A79 35c multicolored .35 .35
417 A79 50c multicolored .50 .50
418 A79 75c multicolored .60 *1.75*
419 A79 $1 multicolored .75 .95

***Perf. 13½x14***

420 A80 $2.50 rose & multi 1.50 *4.50*
421 A80 $5 lilac & multi 2.50 *5.50*
422 A80 $10 multicolored 4.25 *7.50*
*Nos. 405-422 (18)* 19.20 *28.55*

**Inscribed "1978"**

**1978**

405a A79 ½c multicolored .90 *1.10*
406a A79 1c multicolored 1.50 1.10
407a A79 2c multicolored 1.50 1.10
408a A79 3c multicolored 1.50 1.10
409a A79 4c multicolored 1.75 1.10
410a A79 5c multicolored 2.00 .90
411a A79 6c multicolored .35 *1.25*
412a A79 10c multicolored .35 .35
413a A79 15c multicolored .30 .35
414a A79 20c multicolored .30 *1.00*
415a A79 25c multicolored .35 *.65*
416a A79 35c multicolored .35 .55
417a A79 50c multicolored .55 *1.00*
418a A79 75c multicolored .55 *1.10*
419a A79 $1 multicolored .75 *1.25*

***Perf. 13½x14***

420a A80 $2.50 rose & multi 1.75 *5.50*
421a A80 $5 lilac & multi 1.90 *6.50*
422a A80 $10 multicolored 6.50 *8.50*
*Nos. 405a-422a (18)* 23.15 *34.30*

For overprints see Nos. 607-617.

Some Antigua issues from the 1970s were overprinted "Redonda." Other stamps inscribed "Redonda," but lacking any mention of Antigua, were also created in the 1970s and 1980s. These stamps are not listed because Redonda is uninhabited and has no need for stamps of its own.

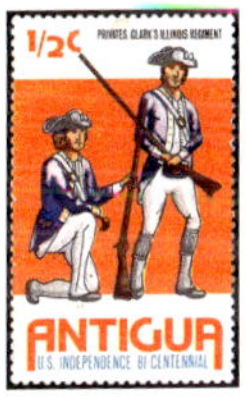


Privates, Clark's Illinois Regiment — A81

1c, Riflemen, Pennsylvania Militia. 2c, Decorated American powder horn. 5c, Water bottle of Maryland troops. 35c, "Liberty Tree" and

"Rattlesnake" flags. $1, American privateer Montgomery. $2.50, Congress Flag. $5, Continental Navy sloop Ranger.

**1976, Mar. 17 Litho. *Perf. 14½***

| | | | | |
|---|---|---|---|---|
| 423 | A81 | ½c multicolored | .25 | .25 |
| 424 | A81 | 1c multicolored | .25 | .25 |
| 425 | A81 | 2c multicolored | .25 | .25 |
| 426 | A81 | 5c multicolored | .25 | .25 |
| 427 | A81 | 35c multicolored | .45 | .25 |
| 428 | A81 | $1 multicolored | 1.25 | .30 |
| 429 | A81 | $5 multicolored | 2.25 | 2.75 |
| | | *Nos. 423-429 (7)* | 4.95 | 4.30 |

**Souvenir Sheet**

***Perf. 13***

| | | | | |
|---|---|---|---|---|
| 430 | A81 | $2.50 multicolored | 1.90 | 1.90 |

American Bicentennial.

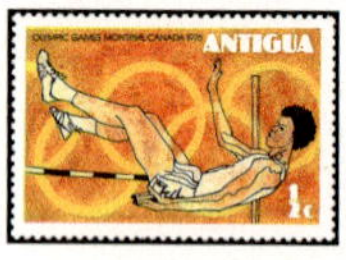


High Jump, Olympic Rings — A82

Olympic Rings and: 1c, Boxing. 2c, Pole vault. 15c, Swimming. 30c, Running. $1, Bicycling. $2, Shot put.

**1976, July 12 Litho. *Perf. 14½***

| | | | | |
|---|---|---|---|---|
| 431 | A82 | ½c yellow & multi | .25 | .25 |
| 432 | A82 | 1c purple & multi | .25 | .25 |
| 433 | A82 | 2c emerald & multi | .25 | .25 |
| 434 | A82 | 15c brt blue & multi | .25 | .25 |
| 435 | A82 | 30c olive & multi | .30 | .25 |
| 436 | A82 | $1 orange & multi | .40 | .25 |
| 437 | A82 | $2 red & multi | 1.10 | 1.10 |
| a. | | Souvenir sheet of 4 | 2.25 | 2.25 |
| | | *Nos. 431-437 (7)* | 2.80 | 2.60 |

21st Olympic Games, Montreal, Canada, July 17-Aug. 1. No. 437a contains one each of Nos. 434-437, perf. 13½.

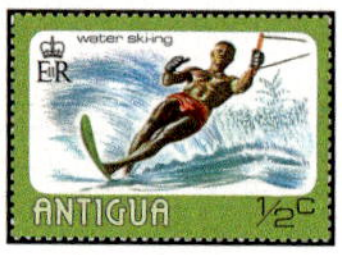


Water Skiing — A83

Water Sports: 1c, Sailfish sailing. 2c, Snorkeling. 20c, Deep-sea fishing. 50c, Scuba diving. $2, Swimming.

**1976, Aug. 26 *Perf. 14***

| | | | | |
|---|---|---|---|---|
| 438 | A83 | ½c yel grn & multi | .25 | .25 |
| 439 | A83 | 1c sepia & multi | .25 | .25 |
| 440 | A83 | 2c gray & multi | .25 | .25 |
| 441 | A83 | 20c multicolored | .25 | .25 |
| 442 | A83 | 50c brt vio & multi | .40 | .40 |
| 443 | A83 | $2 lt gray & multi | 1.10 | 1.10 |
| a. | | Souvenir sheet of 3, #441-443 | 2.00 | 2.00 |
| | | *Nos. 438-443 (6)* | 2.50 | 2.50 |

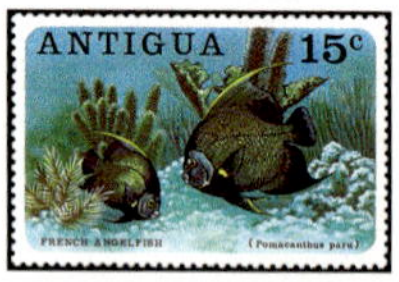


French Angelfish A84

**1976, Oct. 4 Litho. *Perf. 13½x14***

| | | | | |
|---|---|---|---|---|
| 444 | A84 | 15c shown | .45 | .25 |
| 445 | A84 | 30c Yellowfish grouper | .70 | .25 |
| 446 | A84 | 50c Yellowtail snappers | .85 | .45 |
| 447 | A84 | 90c Shy hamlet | 1.30 | .75 |
| | | *Nos. 444-447 (4)* | 3.30 | 1.70 |

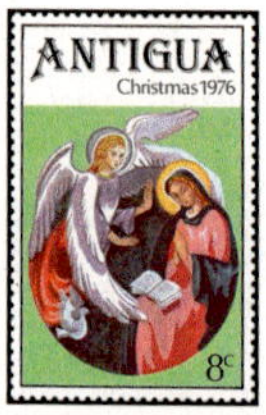


The Annunciation — A85

Christmas: 10c, Flight into Egypt. 15c, Three Kings. 50c, Shepherds and star. $1, Kings presenting gifts to Christ Child.

**1976, Nov. 15 Litho. *Perf. 14***

| | | | | |
|---|---|---|---|---|
| 448 | A85 | 8c multicolored | .25 | .25 |
| 449 | A85 | 10c multicolored | .25 | .25 |
| 450 | A85 | 15c multicolored | .25 | .25 |
| 451 | A85 | 50c multicolored | .25 | .25 |
| 452 | A85 | $1 multi | .25 | .25 |
| | | *Nos. 448-452 (5)* | 1.25 | 1.25 |

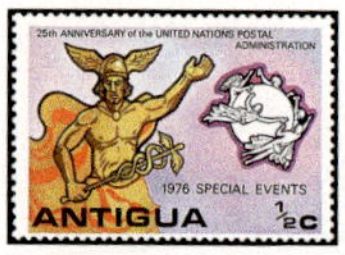


Mercury and UPU Emblem — A86

Designs: 1c, Alfred Nobel, symbols of prize categories. 10c, Viking spacecraft. 50c, Vivi Richards (batsman) and Andy Roberts (bowler). $1, Alexander G. Bell, telephones, 1876 and 1976. $2, Schooner Freelance.

**1976, Dec. 28 Litho. *Perf. 14***

| | | | | |
|---|---|---|---|---|
| 453 | A86 | ½c multicolored | .25 | .25 |
| 454 | A86 | 1c multicolored | .25 | .25 |
| 455 | A86 | 10c multicolored | .35 | .25 |
| 456 | A86 | 50c multicolored | 3.50 | 1.75 |
| 457 | A86 | $1 multicolored | .90 | *1.75* |
| 458 | A86 | $2 multicolored | 2.10 | *4.00* |
| a. | | Souvenir sheet of 4, #455-458 | 8.25 | 8.25 |
| | | *Nos. 453-458 (6)* | 7.35 | 8.25 |

Special 1976 Events: UN Postal Admin., 25th anniv. (½c); Nobel Prize, 75th anniv. (1c); Viking Space Mission to Mars (10c); World Cricket Cup victory (50c); Telephone cent. ($1); Operation Sail, American Bicent. ($2).

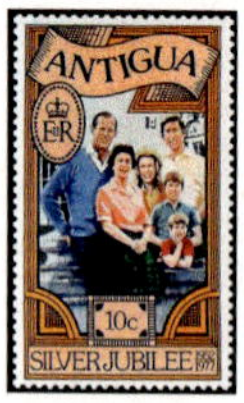


Royal Family — A87

Designs: 10c, Queen Elizabeth, Prince Philip and their children. 30c, Elizabeth II and Prince Philip touring Antigua. 50c, Queen enthroned. 90c, Queen wearing crown. $2.50, Queen and Prince Charles. $5, Queen and Prince Philip.

**1977, Feb. 7 *Perf. 13½x14***

| | | | | |
|---|---|---|---|---|
| 459 | A87 | 10c multicolored | .25 | .25 |
| 460 | A87 | 30c multicolored | .25 | .25 |
| 461 | A87 | 50c multicolored | .25 | .25 |
| 462 | A87 | 90c multicolored | .25 | .25 |
| 463 | A87 | $2.50 multicolored | .25 | *.50* |
| | | *Nos. 459-463 (5)* | 1.25 | 1.50 |

**Souvenir Sheet**

| | | | | |
|---|---|---|---|---|
| 464 | A87 | $5 multicolored | .70 | *.85* |
| | | Complete booklet, 6 #461 var., 1 #464 var., self-adhesive and in changed colors | 3.75 | |

Reign of Queen Elizabeth II, 25th anniv.

Nos. 459-463 were printed in sheets of 40. Sheets of 5 plus label, perf. 12, probably were not sold by the Antigua Post Office.

For overprints see Nos. 477-482.

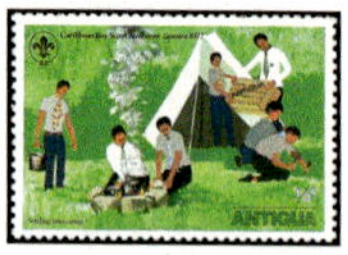

Scouts Camping — A88

Boy Scout Emblem and: 1c, Scouts on hike. 2c, Rock climbing. 10c, Cutting logs. 30c, Map and compass reading. 50c, First aid. $2, Scouts on raft.

**1977, May 23 Litho. *Perf. 14***

| | | | | |
|---|---|---|---|---|
| 465 | A88 | ½c multicolored | .25 | .25 |
| 466 | A88 | 1c multicolored | .25 | .25 |
| 467 | A88 | 2c multicolored | .25 | .25 |
| 468 | A88 | 10c multicolored | .25 | .25 |
| 469 | A88 | 30c multicolored | .30 | .25 |
| 470 | A88 | 50c multicolored | .50 | .35 |
| 471 | A88 | $2 multicolored | 1.00 | *2.00* |
| a. | | Souvenir sheet of 3, #469-471 | 3.25 | *3.75* |
| | | *Nos. 465-471 (7)* | 2.80 | 3.60 |

Caribbean Boy Scout Jamboree, Jamaica.

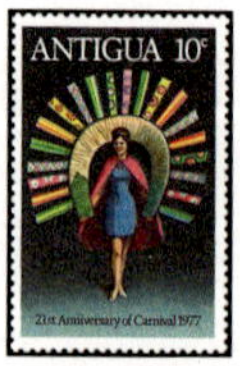


Carnival Queen Holding Horseshoe — A89

30c, Carnival Queen in feather costume. 50c, Butterfly costume. 90c, Carnival Queen with ornaments. $1, Carnival King, Queen.

**1977, July 18 Litho. *Perf. 14***

| | | | | |
|---|---|---|---|---|
| 472 | A89 | 10c multicolored | .25 | .25 |
| 473 | A89 | 30c multicolored | .25 | .25 |
| 474 | A89 | 50c multicolored | .25 | .25 |
| 475 | A89 | 90c multicolored | .35 | .30 |
| 476 | A89 | $1 multicolored | .40 | .40 |
| a. | | Souvenir sheet of 4, #473-476 | 1.50 | *1.75* |
| | | *Nos. 472-476 (5)* | 1.50 | 1.45 |

21st Summer Carnival.

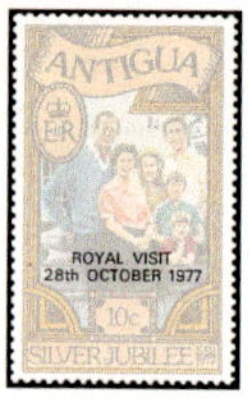


Nos. 459-464 Overprinted

***Perf. 13½x14, 12***

**1977, Oct. 17 Litho.**

| | | | | |
|---|---|---|---|---|
| 477 | A87 | 10c multicolored | .25 | .25 |
| 478 | A87 | 30c multicolored | .25 | .25 |
| 479 | A87 | 50c multicolored | .25 | .25 |
| 480 | A87 | 90c multicolored | .30 | .30 |
| 481 | A87 | $2.50 multicolored | .45 | .40 |
| | | *Nos. 477-481 (5)* | 1.50 | 1.45 |

**Souvenir Sheet**

| | | | | |
|---|---|---|---|---|
| 482 | A87 | $5 multicolored | 1.75 | 1.75 |

Visit of Queen Elizabeth II, Oct. 28.

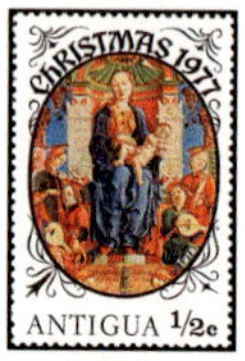


Virgin and Child, by Cosimo Tura — A90

Virgin and Child by: 1c, $2, Carlo Crivelli (different). 2c, 25c, Lorenzo Lotto (different). 8c, Jacopo da Pontormo. 10c, Tura.

**1977, Nov. 15 Litho. *Perf. 14***

| | | | | |
|---|---|---|---|---|
| 483 | A90 | ½c multicolored | .25 | .25 |
| 484 | A90 | 1c multicolored | .25 | .25 |
| 485 | A90 | 2c multicolored | .25 | .25 |
| 486 | A90 | 8c multicolored | .25 | .25 |
| 487 | A90 | 10c multicolored | .25 | .25 |
| 488 | A90 | 25c multicolored | .25 | .25 |
| 489 | A90 | $2 multicolored | .50 | *1.00* |
| a. | | Souvenir sheet of 4, #486-489 | 1.40 | *2.50* |
| | | *Nos. 483-489 (7)* | 2.00 | *2.50* |

Christmas.

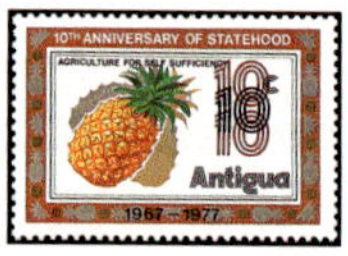


Pineapple — A91

10th anniv. of Statehood: 15c, Flag of Antigua. 50c, Police band. 90c, Prime Minister V. C. Bird. $2, Coat of Arms.

**1977, Dec. 28 Litho. *Perf. 13x13½***

| | | | | |
|---|---|---|---|---|
| 490 | A91 | 10c multicolored | .25 | .25 |
| 491 | A91 | 15c multicolored | .50 | .25 |
| 492 | A91 | 50c multicolored | 2.00 | .75 |
| 493 | A91 | 90c multicolored | .50 | .75 |
| 494 | A91 | $2 multicolored | .90 | *1.50* |
| a. | | Souv. sheet, #491-494, perf 14 | 3.50 | 3.50 |
| | | *Nos. 490-494 (5)* | 4.15 | 3.50 |

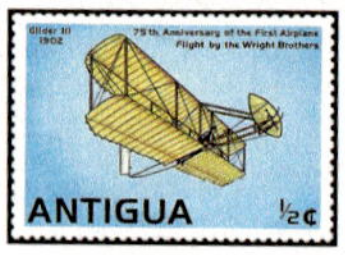


Wright Glider III, 1902 — A92

1c, Flyer I in air, 1903. 2c, Weight and derrick launch system and Wright engine, 1903. 10c, Orville Wright, vert. 50c, Flyer III, 1905. 90c, Wilbur Wright, vert. $2, Wright Model B, 1910. $2.50, Flyer I, 1903, on ground.

**1978, Mar. 28 *Perf. 14***

| | | | | |
|---|---|---|---|---|
| 495 | A92 | ½c multicolored | .25 | .25 |
| 496 | A92 | 1c multicolored | .25 | .25 |
| 497 | A92 | 2c multicolored | .25 | .25 |
| 498 | A92 | 10c multicolored | .35 | .25 |
| 499 | A92 | 50c multicolored | .55 | .25 |
| 500 | A92 | 90c multicolored | .80 | .30 |
| 501 | A92 | $2 multicolored | .80 | .80 |
| | | *Nos. 495-501 (7)* | 3.25 | 2.35 |

**Souvenir Sheet**

| | | | | |
|---|---|---|---|---|
| 502 | A92 | $2.50 multicolored | 2.10 | *2.75* |

1st powered flight by Wright brothers, 75th anniv.

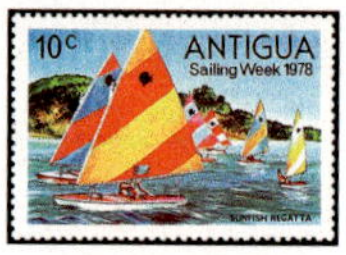


Sunfish Regatta — A93

Sailing Week 1978: 50c, Fishing and work boat race. 90c, Curtain Bluff race. $2, Powerboat rally. $2.50, Guadeloupe-Antigua race.

**1978, Apr. 29 Litho. *Perf. 14½***

| | | | | |
|---|---|---|---|---|
| 503 | A93 | 10c multicolored | .30 | .25 |
| 504 | A93 | 50c multicolored | .40 | .25 |
| 505 | A93 | 90c multicolored | .70 | .40 |
| 506 | A93 | $2 multicolored | 1.25 | .75 |
| | | *Nos. 503-506 (4)* | 2.65 | 1.65 |

**Souvenir Sheet**

| | | | | |
|---|---|---|---|---|
| 507 | A93 | $2.50 multicolored | 2.25 | 2.25 |

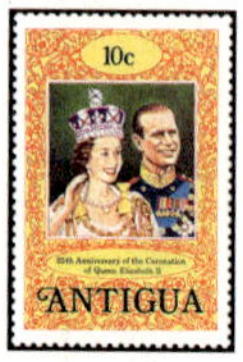


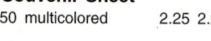

25th Anniv. of the Coronation of Queen Elizabeth II — A94

Designs: 10c, Elizabeth II and Prince Philip. 30c, Coronation. 50c, State coach. 90c, Elizabeth II and Archbishop. $2.50, Elizabeth II. $5, Elizabeth II, Prince Philip, Prince Charles and Princess Anne as children.

**1978, June 2 Litho. *Perf. 14, 12***

| | | | | |
|---|---|---|---|---|
| 508 | A94 | 10c multicolored | .25 | .25 |
| 509 | A94 | 30c multicolored | .25 | .25 |
| 510 | A94 | 50c multicolored | .25 | .25 |
| 511 | A94 | 90c multicolored | .25 | .25 |
| 512 | A94 | $2.50 multicolored | .30 | .30 |
| | | *Nos. 508-512 (5)* | 1.30 | 1.30 |

**Souvenir Sheet**

| | | | | |
|---|---|---|---|---|
| 513 | A94 | $5 multicolored | 1.25 | 1.25 |

25th anniv. of coronation of Queen Elizabeth II.

Nos. 508-512 were printed in sheets of 50 (2 panes of 25), perf. 14, and in sheets of 3 plus label, perf. 12, with frames in changed colors.

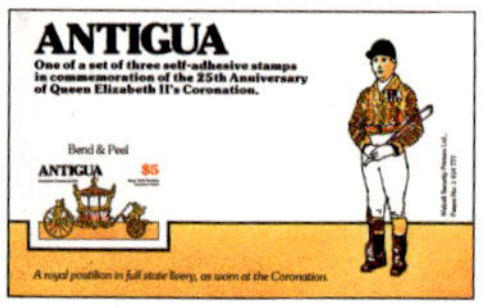


Glass Coach A95

Royal Coaches: 50c, Irish state coach. $5, Coronation coach.

**1978, June 2 Litho. *Imperf.***

**Self-adhesive**

| | | | |
|---|---|---|---|
| 514 | | Souvenir booklet | 2.50 |
| a. | A95 | Bklt. pane, 3 each 25c, 50c | 1.00 |
| b. | A95 | Bklt. pane, 1 $5 | 1.40 |

25th anniversary of coronation of Queen Elizabeth II. No. 514 contains 2 booklet panes printed on peelable paper backing showing royal processions.

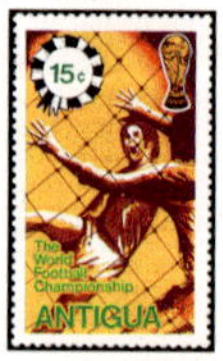


Soccer — A96

Designs: Various soccer scenes. Stamps in souvenir sheet horizontal.

**1978, Aug. 18 Litho. *Perf. 15***

| | | | | |
|---|---|---|---|---|
| 515 | A96 | 10c multicolored | .25 | .25 |
| 516 | A96 | 15c multicolored | .25 | .25 |
| 517 | A96 | $3 multicolored | 1.60 | *1.75* |
| | | *Nos. 515-517 (3)* | 2.10 | 2.25 |

**Souvenir Sheet**

**518** Sheet of 4 3.75 3.75
*a.* A96 25c multicolored .25 .25
*b.* A96 30c multicolored .40 .40
*c.* A96 50c multicolored .70 .70
*d.* A96 $2 multicolored 2.00 2.00

11th World Cup Soccer Championship, Argentina, June 1-25.

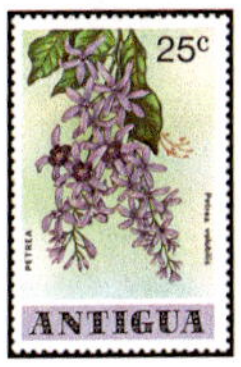


Purple Wreath — A97

**1978, Oct. Litho. *Perf. 14***
**519** A97 25c shown .25 .25
**520** A97 50c Sunflowers .40 .25
**521** A97 90c Frangipani .70 .30
**522** A97 $2 Passionflower 1.50 *1.75*
*Nos. 519-522 (4)* 2.85 2.55

**Souvenir Sheet**

**523** A97 $2.50 Red hibiscus 2.00 *2.50*

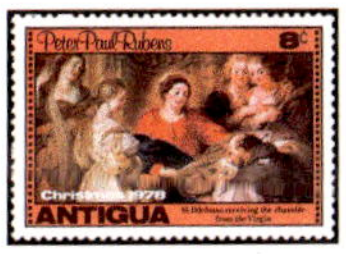


St. Ildefonso Receiving Chasuble, by Rubens — A98

Christmas: 25c, Flight of St. Barbara, by Rubens. $2, Madonna and Child with Ss. Joseph and John and a Dono, by Sebastiano del Piombo. $4, Annunciation, by Rubens.

**1978, Oct. 30 Litho. *Perf. 14***
**524** A98 8c multicolored .25 .25
**525** A98 25c multicolored .25 .25
**526** A98 $2 multicolored .65 .55
*Nos. 524-526 (3)* 1.15 1.05

**Souvenir Sheet**

**527** A98 $4 multicolored 1.90 1.90

No. 526 is incorrectly attributed to Rubens.

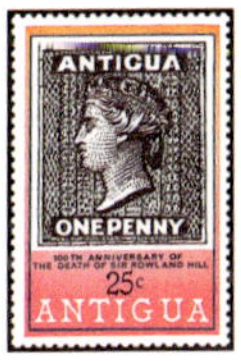


Antigua #2 — A99

Designs: 50c, Great Britain Penny Black, 1840. $1, Woman posting letter in pillar box, and coach. $2, Mail train, ship, plane and Concorde. $2.50, Rowland Hill.

**1979, Aug. 27 Litho. *Perf. 14***
**528** A99 25c multicolored .25 .25
**529** A99 50c multicolored .25 .25
**530** A99 $1 multicolored .35 .25
**531** A99 $2 multicolored .85 .50
*Nos. 528-531 (4)* 1.70 1.25

**Souvenir Sheet**

**532** A99 $2.50 multicolored 1.15 1.15

Sir Rowland Hill (1795-1879), originator of penny postage.

Nos. 528-531 were printed in sheets of 50 (2 panes of 25), perf. 14, and in sheets of 5 plus label, perf. 12, with frames in changed colors.

For overprints, see Nos. 571A-571D.

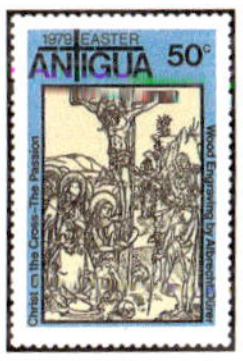


Crucifixion, by Durer — A100

Designs (after Dürer): 10c, Deposition. $2.50, Crucifixion. $4, Man of Sorrows.

**1979, Mar. 15**
**533** A100 10c multicolored .25 .25
**534** A100 50c multicolored .50 .25
**535** A100 $4 multicolored 1.10 1.10
*Nos. 533-535 (3)* 1.85 1.60

**Souvenir Sheet**

**536** A100 $2.50 multicolored 1.25 1.25

Easter.

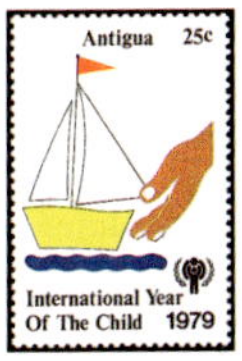


Child Playing with Sailboat — A101

IYC emblem, child's hand holding toy: 50c, Rocket. 90c, Automobile. $2, Train. $5, Plane.

**1979, Apr. 9 Litho. *Perf. 14***
**537** A101 25c multicolored .25 .25
**538** A101 50c multicolored .25 .25
**539** A101 90c multicolored .40 .30
**540** A101 $2 multicolored 1.00 1.00
*Nos. 537-540 (4)* 1.90 1.80

**Souvenir Sheet**

**541** A101 $5 multicolored 1.90 1.90

International Year of the Child.

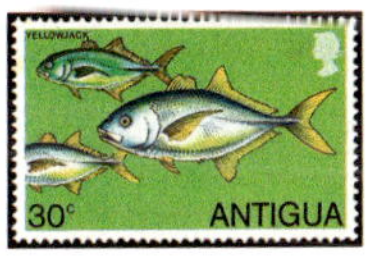


Yellowjacks A102

Sport Fish: 50c, Bluefin tunas. 90c, Sailfish. $2.50, Barracuda. $3, Wahoos.

**1979, May Litho. *Perf. 14½***
**542** A102 30c multicolored .30 .25
**543** A102 50c multicolored .40 .30
**544** A102 90c multicolored .85 .40
**545** A102 $3 multicolored 2.50 2.00
*Nos. 542-545 (4)* 4.05 2.95

**Souvenir Sheet**

**546** A102 $2.50 multicolored 2.25 2.25

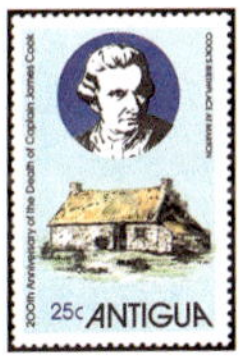


Capt. Cook and his Birthplace at Marton — A103

Capt. James Cook (1728-1779) and: 50c, HMS Endeavour. 90c, Marine timekeeper. $2.50, HMS Resolution. $3, Landing at Botany Bay.

**1979, July 2 Litho. *Perf. 14***
**547** A103 25c multicolored .55 .30
**548** A103 50c multicolored .85 .40
**549** A103 90c multicolored .00 *.75*
**550** A103 $3 multicolored 1.45 *2.75*
*Nos. 547-550 (4)* 3.45 *4.20*

**Souvenir Sheet**

**551** A103 $2.50 multicolored 2.75 2.75

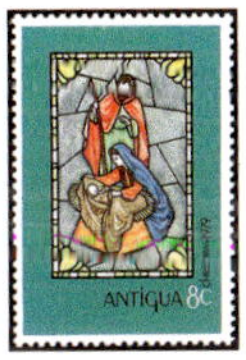

Holy Family — A104

Stained-glass Windows: 25c, Flight into Egypt. 50c, Shepherd and star. $3, Angel with trumpet. $4, Three Kings offering gifts.

**1979, Oct. 1 Litho. *Perf. 14***
**552** A104 8c multicolored .25 .25
**553** A104 25c multicolored .25 .25
**554** A104 50c multicolored .30 .25
**555** A104 $4 multicolored .80 *2.25*
*Nos. 552-555 (4)* 1.60 *3.05*

**Souvenir Sheet**

***Perf. 12x12½***

**556** A104 $3 multicolored 1.25 *1.75*

Christmas.

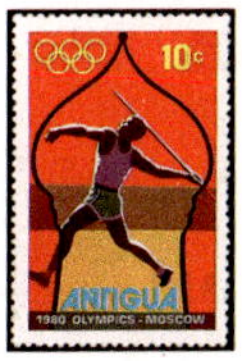


Javelin, Olympic Rings — A105

**1980, Feb. 7 Litho. *Perf. 14***
**557** A105 10c shown .25 .25
**558** A105 25c Running .30 .30
**559** A105 $1 Pole vault .50 .50
**560** A105 $2 Hurdles .60 *1.50*
*Nos. 557-560 (4)* 1.65 2.55

**Souvenir Sheet**

**561** A105 $3 Boxing, horiz. 1.25 1.25

22nd Summer Olympic Games, Moscow, July 19-Aug. 3.

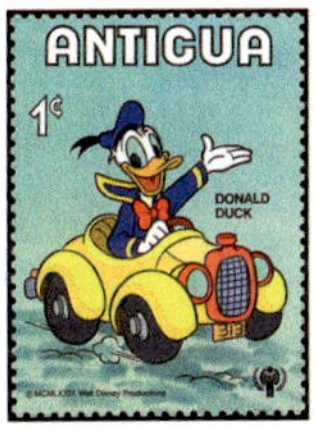


Disney Characters and IYC Emblem — A106

Transportation scenes: ½c, Mickey, plane. 1c, Donald, car. 2c, Goofy driving taxi. 3c, Mickey, Minnie in sidecar. 4c, Huey, Dewey and Louie. 5c, Grandma Duck. 10c, Mickey in jeep. $1, Chip and Dale sailing. $4, Donald on train.

$2.50, Goofy in glider.

½c, 2c, 3c, 4c, 5c, $1, $2.50, horiz.

**1980, Mar. 24 Litho. *Perf. 11***
**562** A106 ½c multicolored .25 .25
**563** A106 1c multicolored .25 .25
**564** A106 2c multicolored .25 .25
**565** A106 3c multicolored .25 .25
**566** A106 4c multicolored .25 .25
**567** A106 5c multicolored .25 .25
**568** A106 10c multicolored .25 .25
**569** A106 $1 multicolored 1.25 1.50
**570** A106 $4 multicolored 3.00 *6.00*
*Nos. 562-570 (9)* 6.00 *9.25*

**Souvenir Sheet**

**571** A106 $2.50 multicolored 7.50 7.50

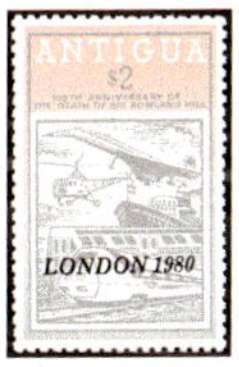


Nos. 528-531 in Changed Colors & Overprinted

**1980, May 6 Litho. *Perf. 12***
**571A** A99 25c multicolored .35 .35
**571B** A99 50c multicolored .45 .45
**571C** A99 $1 multicolored .75 .75
**571D** A99 $2 multicolored 3.00 3.00
*Nos. 571A-571D (4)* 4.55 4.55

London '80 Intl. Stamp Exhib., May 6-14.
For overprints see Barbuda Nos. 423-426.

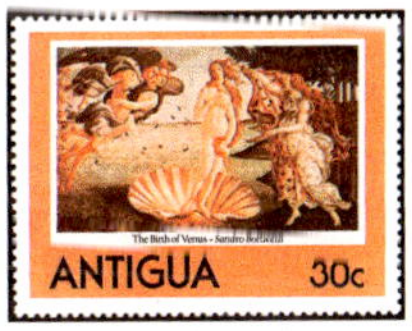


Birth of Venus, by Botticelli — A106a

10c, David, by Donatello. 50c, Reclining Couple, sarcophagus, Cerveteri. 90c, The Garden of Earthly Delights, by Hieronymus Bosch. $1, Portinari Altarpiece, by Hugo van der Goes. $4, Eleanora of Toledo and her Son Giovanni de Medici, by Bronzino. $5, The Holy Family, by Rembrandt.

***Perf. 13½x14, 14x13½***

**1980, June 23 Litho.**
**572** A106a 10c multi, vert. .25 .25
**573** A106a 30c multi .40 .25
**574** A106a 50c multi .55 .40
**575** A106a 90c multi .70 .70
**576** A106a $1 multi .80 .80
**577** A106a $4 multi, vert. 2.00 *3.00*
*Nos. 572-577 (6)* 4.70 5.40

**Souvenir Sheet**

***Perf. 14***

**578** A106a $5 multicolored 3.00 3.00

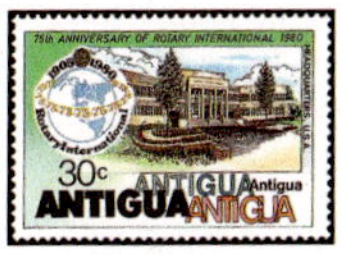


Anniversary Emblem, Intl. Headquarters, Evanston, IL — A107

50c, Antigua club banner. 90c, Map of Antigua. $3, Paul. P. Harris, emblem.
$5, Emblems, Antigua flags.

**1980, July 21 Litho. *Perf. 14***
**579** A107 30c shown .35 .25
**580** A107 50c multicolored .40 .40
**581** A107 90c multicolored .60 .60
**582** A107 $3 multicolored 1.90 *2.75*
*Nos. 579-582 (4)* 3.25 *4.00*

**Souvenir Sheet**

**583** A107 $5 multicolored 2.00 2.00

Rotary International, 75th anniv.

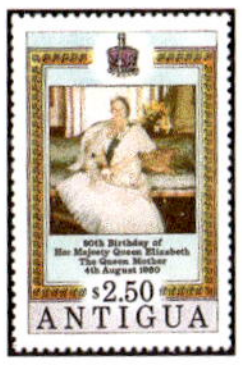


A108

**1980, Sept. 15**
**584** A108 10c multicolored .25 .25
**585** A108 $2.50 multicolored 1.25 *1.50*

**Souvenir Sheet**

***Perf. 12***

**586** A108 $3 multicolored 1.25 *2.00*

Queen Mother Elizabeth, 80th birthday.

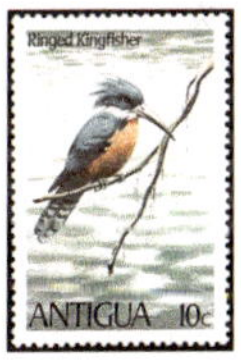


A109

No. 587, Ringed Kingfisher. No. 588, Plain pigeon. No. 889, Green-throated carib. No. 890, Black-necked stilt.
No. 591, Roseate tern.

**1980, Nov. 3 Litho. *Perf. 14***
**587** A109 10c multicolored .90 .30
**588** A109 30c multicolored 1.25 .50
**589** A109 $1 multicolored 1.75 1.75
**590** A109 $2 multicolored 2.50 *3.75*
*Nos. 587-590 (4)* 6.40 *6.30*

**Souvenir Sheet**

**591** A109 $2.50 multicolored 6.75 6.75

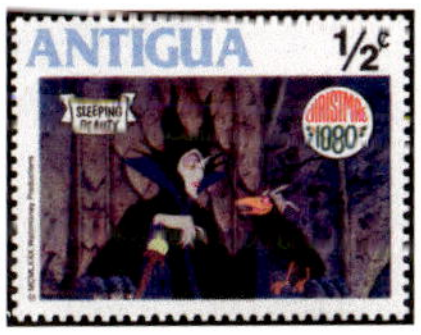


Maleficent and Diablo A110

Christmas: Various scenes from Walt Disney's Sleeping Beauty. $4 vert.

**1980, Dec. 23 *Perf. 11, 13½x14 ($4)***
**592** A110 ½c multicolored .25 .25
**593** A110 1c multicolored .25 .25
**594** A110 2c multicolored .25 .25
**595** A110 4c multicolored .25 .25
**596** A110 8c multicolored .25 .25
**597** A110 10c multicolored .25 .25
**598** A110 25c multicolored .30 .30
**599** A110 $2 multicolored 2.25 2.25
**600** A110 $2.50 multicolored 2.50 2.50
*Nos. 592-600 (9)* 6.55 6.55

**Souvenir Sheet**

**601** A110 $4 multicolored 6.50 6.50

526 ANTIGUA

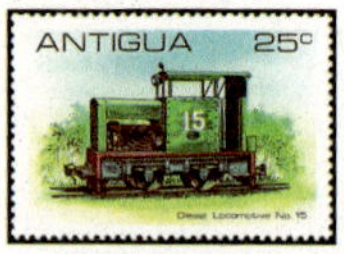


Sugar-cane Railway Diesel Locomotive No. 15 — A111

50c, Narrow-gauge steam locomotive. 90c, Diesels #1, #10. $3, Hauling sugar-cane. $2.50, Sugar factory, train yard.

**1981, Jan. 12** *Perf. 14*

**602** A111 25c shown .25 .25
**603** A111 50c multicolored .40 .40
**604** A111 90c multicolored .75 .75
**605** A111 $3 multicolored 2.10 2.10
*Nos. 602-605 (4)* 3.50 3.50

**Souvenir Sheet**

**606** A111 $2.50 multicolored 2.60 2.60

**Nos. 411-412, 414-422 Overprinted**

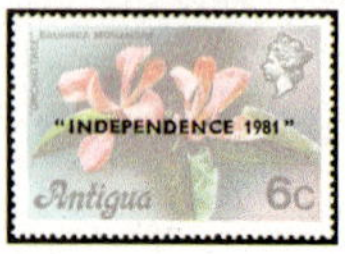


**1981, Mar. 31** **Litho.**

**607** A79 6c multicolored .25 .25
**608** A79 10c multicolored .25 .25
**609** A79 20c multicolored .25 .25
**610** A79 25c multicolored .25 .25
**611** A79 35c multicolored .30 .30
**612** A79 50c multicolored .50 .50
**613** A79 75c multicolored .60 .60
**614** A79 $1 multicolored .85 *1.25*
**615** A80 $2.50 multicolored 1.50 *2.25*
**616** A80 $5 multicolored 2.60 *3.75*
**617** A80 $10 multicolored 5.25 *7.00*
*Nos. 607-617 (11)* 12.60 *16.65*

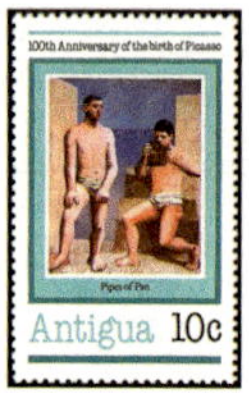


Pipes of Pan, by Picasso — A112

Paintings by Pablo Picasso (1881-1973): 50c, Seated Harlequin. 90c, Paulo as Harlequin. $4, Mother and Child. $5, Three Musicians.

**1981, May 5** **Litho.** *Perf. 14*

**618** A112 10c multicolored .25 .25
**619** A112 50c multicolored .40 .40
**620** A112 90c multicolored .75 .75
**621** A112 $4 multicolored 2.10 2.10
*Nos. 618-621 (4)* 3.50 3.50

**Souvenir Sheet**

*Perf. 14x14½*

**622** A112 $5 multicolored 2.25 *2.75*

**Royal Wedding Issue**

Common Design Type

**1981, June 16** **Litho.** *Perf. 14*

**623** CD331a 25c Couple .25 .25
**624** CD331a 50c Glamis Castle .25 .25
**625** CD331a $4 Charles .80 .80
*Nos. 623-625 (3)* 1.30 1.30

**Souvenir Sheet**

**626** CD331 $5 Glass coach 1.25 1.25
**627** CD331 Booklet 4.00
*a.* Pane of 6 (2x25c, 2x$1, 2x$2), Charles 2.50
*b.* Pane of 1, $5, Couple 1.50

No. 627 contains imperf., self-adhesive stamps.

Nos. 623-625 also printed in sheets of 5 plus label, perf. 12 in changed colors.

For surcharges see Nos. 792, 795, 802, 805.

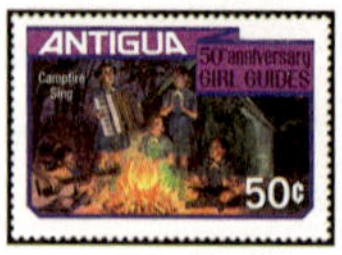


Campfire Sing — A113

**1981, Oct. 28** **Litho.** *Perf. 15*

**628** A113 10c Irene Joshua .25 .25
**629** A113 50c shown .40 .25
**630** A113 90c Sailing .65 .55
**631** A113 $2.50 Milking cow 1.60 *2.00*
*Nos. 628-631 (4)* 2.90 3.05

**Souvenir Sheet**

**632** A113 $5 Flag raising 5.25 5.25

Girl Guides, 50th anniv.

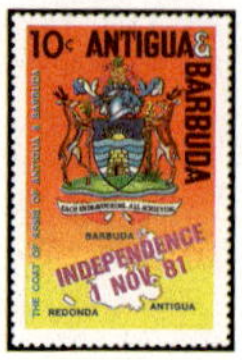


A114

10c, Arms. 50c, Flag. 90c, Prime Minister Bird. $2.50, St. John's Cathedral, horiz. $5, Map.

**1981, Nov. 1** **Litho.** *Perf. 15*

**633** A114 10c multicolored .30 .25
**634** A114 50c multicolored .85 .50
**635** A114 90c multicolored .55 .55
**636** A114 $2.50 multicolored 1.40 *2.25*
*Nos. 633-636 (4)* 3.10 *3.55*

**Souvenir Sheet**

**637** A114 $5 multicolored 4.25 3.25

Independence.
No. 637 contains one 41x41mm stamp.

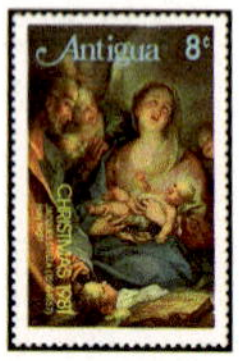


A115

Christmas (Virgin and Child Paintings by): 8c, Holy Night, by Jacques Stella (1596-1657). 30c Julius Schnorr von Carolsfeld (1794-1872). $1, Alonso Cano (1601-1667). $3, Lorenzo de Credi (1459-1537). $5, Holy Family, by Pieter von Avont (1600-1652).

**1981, Nov. 16**

**638** A115 8c multicolored .30 .25
**639** A115 30c multicolored .50 .25
**640** A115 $1 multicolored 1.20 1.20
**641** A115 $3 multicolored 1.75 *3.25*
*Nos. 638-641 (4)* 3.75 *4.95*

**Souvenir Sheet**

**642** A115 $5 multicolored 3.75 *4.50*

On No. 639, the artist's name is misspelled as "Carolfeld."

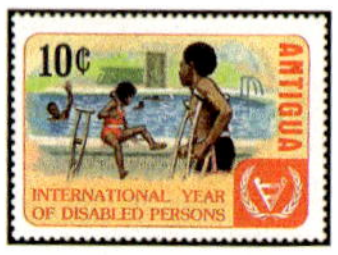


Intl. Year of the Disabled — A116

**1981, Dec. 1** **Litho.** *Perf. 15*

**643** A116 10c Swimming .25 .25
**644** A116 50c Discus .30 *.30*
**645** A116 90c Archery .45 *.55*
**646** A116 $2 Baseball 1.00 *1.40*
*Nos. 643-646 (4)* 2.00 *2.50*

**Souvenir Sheet**

**647** A116 $4 Basketball 4.50 3.25

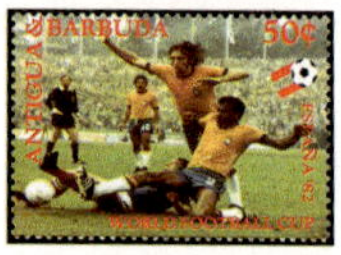


1982 World Cup Soccer — A117

Designs: Various soccer players.

**1982, Apr. 15** **Litho.** *Perf. 14*

**648** A117 10c multicolored .30 .25
**649** A117 50c multicolored .45 .30
**650** A117 90c multicolored .90 .65
**651** A117 $4 multicolored 3.00 *3.50*
*Nos. 648-651 (4)* 4.65 4.70

**Souvenir Sheet**

**652** A117 $5 multicolored 6.75 *7.50*

Also issued in sheetlets of 5 + label in changed colors, perf. 12.

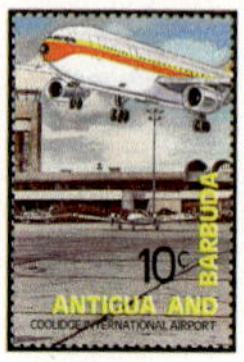


A118

No. 653, A-300 Airbus. No. 654, Hawker-Siddeley 748. No. 655, De Havilland Twin Otter DCH6. No. 656, Britten-Norman Islander.
No. 657, Jet, horiz.

**1982, June 17** **Litho.** *Perf. 14½*

**653** A118 10c multicolored .25 .25
**654** A118 50c multicolored .35 .35
**655** A118 90c multicolored .65 .65
**656** A118 $2.50 multicolored 1.75 1.75
*Nos. 653-656 (4)* 3.00 3.00

**Souvenir Sheet**

**657** A118 $5 multicolored 4.00 4.00

Coolidge Intl. Airport opening.

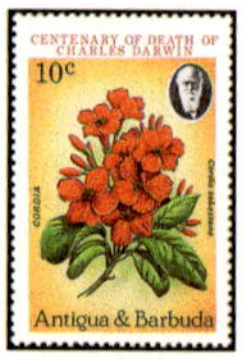


A119

No. 658, Cordia, vert. No. 659, Golden spotted mongoose. No. 660, Corallita, vert. No. 661, Bulldog bats.
No. 662, Caribbean monk seals.

**1982, June 28** **Litho.** *Perf. 14½*

**658** A119 10c multicolored .35 .25
**659** A119 50c multicolored .70 .40
**660** A119 90c multicolored 1.10 .75
**661** A119 $3 multicolored 2.50 *3.25*
*Nos. 658-661 (4)* 4.65 *4.65*

**Souvenir Sheet**

**662** A119 $5 multicolored 7.75 7.75

Charles Darwin's death centenary.

**Princess Diana Issue**

Common Design Type

90c, Greenwich Palace. $1, Wedding. $4, Diana.
$5, Diana, diff.

**1982, July 1** **Litho.** *Perf. 14½x14*

**663** CD332 90c multicolored .70 .50
**664** CD332 $1 multicolored .80 .60
**665** CD332 $4 multicolored 3.00 2.50
*Nos. 663-665 (3)* 4.50 3.60

**Souvenir Sheet**

**666** CD332 $5 multicolored 3.75 3.75

For overprints and surcharges see Nos. 672-675, 797, 799, 803, 806.

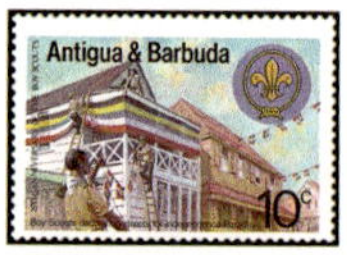


Scouting Year — A120

Independence Day celebration: 10c, Decorating buildings. 50c, Helping woman. 90c, Princess Margaret. $2.20, Cub Scout giving directions.
$5, Baden-Powell.

**1982, July 15** *Perf. 14*

**667** A120 10c multicolored .30 .25
**668** A120 50c multicolored .60 .45
**669** A120 90c multicolored .85 .65
**670** A120 $2.20 multicolored 1.50 *2.50*
*Nos. 667-670 (4)* 3.25 *3.85*

**Souvenir Sheet**

**671** A120 $5 multicolored 5.75 5.75

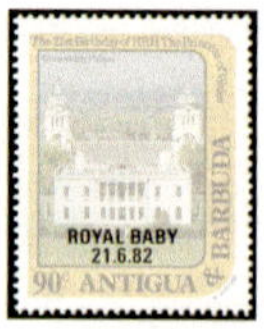


Nos. 663-666 Overprinted

**1982, Aug. 30** **Litho.** *Perf. 14½x14*

**672** CD332 90c multicolored .45 .45
**673** CD332 $1 multicolored .55 .55
**674** CD332 $4 multicolored 1.90 1.90
*Nos. 672-674 (3)* 2.90 2.90

**Souvenir Sheet**

**675** CD332 $5 multicolored 2.60 2.60

For surcharges see Nos. 798, 800, 804, 807.

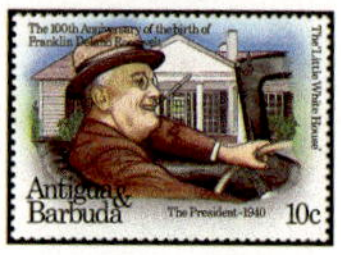


Roosevelt Driving by "The Little White House" — A121

25c, Washington as blacksmith. 45c, Churchill, Roosevelt, Stalin. 60c, Washington crossing Delaware, vert. $1, Roosevelt on train, vert. $3, Roosevelt, vert.
No. 682, Washington, vert. No. 683, Eleanor and Franklin.

**1982, Sept. 20** *Perf. 15*

**676** A121 10c shown .25 .25
**677** A121 25c multicolored .40 .25
**678** A121 45c multicolored 1.40 .35
**679** A121 60c multicolored .95 .35
**680** A121 $1 multicolored 1.35 .90
**681** A121 $3 multicolored 1.30 *2.50*
*Nos. 676-681 (6)* 5.65 *4.60*

**Souvenir Sheets**

**682** A121 $4 multicolored 3.50 3.50
**683** A121 $4 multicolored 3.50 3.50

George Washington's 250th birth anniv. and Franklin D. Roosevelt's birth centenary.

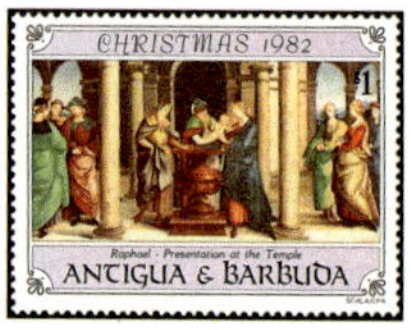


Christmas A122

Raphael Paintings: 10c, Annunciation. 30c, Adoration of the Magi. $1, Presentation at the Temple. $4, Coronation of the Virgin.
$5, Marriage of the Virgin.

**1982, Nov.** **Litho.** *Perf. 14*

**684** A122 10c multicolored .25 .25
**685** A122 30c multicolored .25 .25
**686** A122 $1 multicolored .50 .50
**687** A122 $4 multicolored 2.25 2.25
*Nos. 684-687 (4)* 3.25 *3.25*

**Souvenir Sheet**

**688** A122 $5 multicolored 3.25 3.25

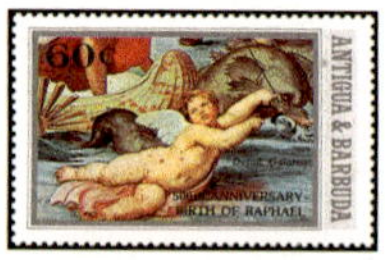


500th Birth Anniv. of Raphael A123

45c, Galatea taking Reins of Dolphins, vert. 50c, Sea Nymphs carried by Tritons, vert. 60c, Winged Angel Steering Dolphins. $4, Cupids Shooting Arrows.
$5, Galatea.

**1983, Jan. 28.** **Litho.** *Perf. 14½*

**689** A123 45c multicolored .30 .30
**690** A123 50c multicolored .40 .40
**691** A123 60c multicolored .45 .45
**692** A123 $4 multicolored 2.00 2.00
*Nos. 689-692 (4)* 3.15 3.15

**Souvenir Sheet**

**693** A123 $5 multicolored 3.00 3.00

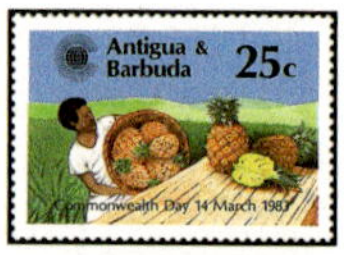


A124

**1983, Mar. 14** *Perf. 14*

**694** A124 25c Pineapple crop .25 .25
**695** A124 45c Carnival .25 .25
**696** A124 60c Tourists, sailboat .35 .35
**697** A124 $3 Control Tower 1.00 *1.50*
*Nos. 694-697 (4)* 1.85 2.35

Commonwealth Day.

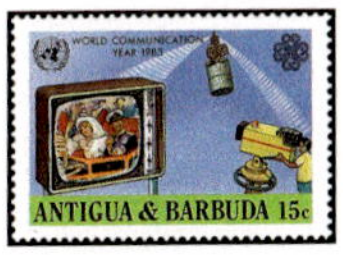

World Communications Year — A125

15c, TV screen, camera. 50c, Police radio, car. 60c, Long distance phone call. $3, Dish antenna, planets.
$5, Comsat satellite.

**1983, Apr. 5 Litho. *Perf. 14***

**698** A125 15c multicolored .50 .25
**699** A125 50c multicolored 2.10 1.25
**700** A125 60c multicolored 2.10 1.40
**701** A125 $3 multicolored 4.00 *5.00*
*Nos. 698-701 (4)* 8.70 7.90

### Souvenir Sheet

**702** A125 $5 multicolored 2.75 *3.25*

Imperforates
See note following No. 404.

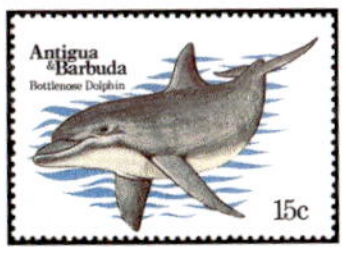

Bottlenose Dolphin — A126

50c, Finback whale. 60c, Bowhead whale. $3, Spectacled porpoise.
$5, Unicorn whale.

**1983, May 9 Litho. *Perf. 15***

**703** A126 15c shown .75 .25
**704** A126 50c multicolored 1.60 1.25
**705** A126 60c multicolored 1.75 1.25
**706** A126 $3 multicolored 3.25 *4.25*
*Nos. 703-706 (4)* 7.35 7.00

### Souvenir Sheet

**707** A126 $5 multicolored 8.50 8.50

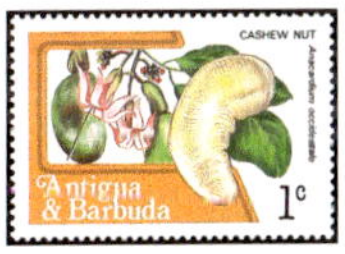

Cashew Nut — A127

**1983, July 11 *Perf. 14***

**708** A127 1c shown .25 *1.10*
**709** A127 2c Passion fruit .25 *1.10*
**710** A127 3c Mango .25 *1.10*
**711** A127 5c Grapefruit .25 *1.10*
**712** A127 10c Pawpaw .40 .25
**713** A127 15c Breadfruit .75 .25
**714** A127 20c Coconut .45 .25
**715** A127 25c Oleander .75 .35
**716** A127 30c Banana .55 .40
**717** A127 40c Pineapple .75 .40
**718** A127 45c Cordia .85 .55
**719** A127 50c Cassia .90 .60
**720** A127 60c Poui 1.75 1.00
**721** A127 $1 Frangipani 2.25 1.50
**722** A127 $2 Flamboyant 3.50 *3.75*
**723** A127 $2.50 Lemon 3.75 *6.00*
**724** A127 $5 Lignum vitae 5.00 *12.00*
**725** A127 $10 Arms 8.00 *17.00*
*Nos. 708-725 (18)* 30.65 *48.70*

**1986 *Perf. 12½x12***

*708a* A127 1c .25 *1.10*
*709a* A127 2c .25 *1.10*
*710a* A127 3c .25 *1.10*
*711a* A127 5c .30 *1.10*
*712a* A127 10c .35 .25
*713a* A127 15c .50 .25
*714a* A127 20c .60 .25
*715a* A127 25c .60 .25
*716a* A127 30c .70 .30
*717a* A127 40c .75 .30
*718a* A127 45c .80 .45
*719a* A127 50c 1.20 .45
*720a* A127 60c 1.75 1.10
*721a* A127 $1 2.00 1.25
*722a* A127 $2 3.75 *4.25*
*723a* A127 $2.50 4.25 *6.00*
*724a* A127 $5 6.75 *12.00*
*725a* A127 $10 11.00 *17.00*
*Nos. 708a-725a (18)* 36.05 *48.50*

Issue dates: $2-$5, Dec; others Mar.

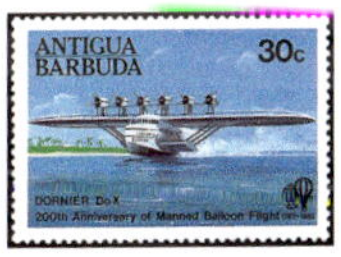

Manned Flight Bicentenary A128

30c, Dornier DoX. 50c, Supermarine S-6B. 60c, Curtiss F9C, USS Akron. $4, Pro Juventute balloon.
$5, Graf Zeppelin.

**1983, Aug. 15 *Perf. 15***

**726** A128 30c multicolored 1.00 .30
**727** A128 50c multicolored 1.25 .60
**728** A128 60c multicolored 1.40 .75
**729** A128 $4 multicolored 3.25 *5.75*
*Nos. 726-729 (4)* 6.90 *7.40*

### Souvenir Sheet

**730** A128 $5 multicolored 3.50 3.50

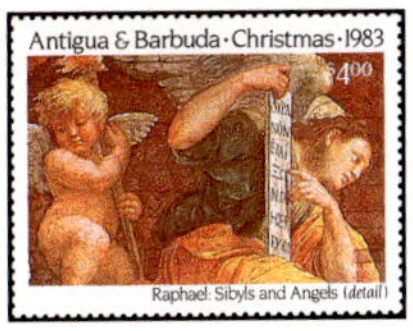

Christmas A129

Raphael Paintings: 10c, Angel flying with scroll. 30c, Angel, diff. $1, Inscribing tablet. $4, Angel showing tablet.
$5, Vision of Ezekiel.
10c, 30c, $1, $4, Sybils and Angels details.

**1983, Oct. 4 Litho. *Perf. 14***

**731** A129 10c multicolored .35 .25
**732** A129 30c multicolored .65 .40
**733** A129 $1 multicolored 1.50 1.25
**734** A129 $4 multicolored 2.75 *4.75*
*Nos. 731-734 (4)* 5.25 *6.65*

### Souvenir Sheet

**735** A129 $5 multicolored 1.60 *2.10*

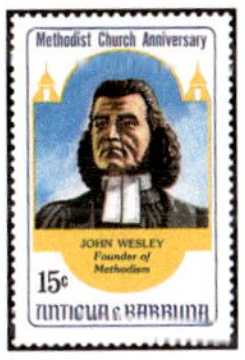

Methodist Church, Anniv. — A130

Designs: 15c, John Wesley founder of Methodism. 50c, Nathaniel Gilbert, Antiguan founder. 60c, St. John's Methodist Church Steeple. $3, Ebenezer Methodist Church.

**1983, Nov. Litho. *Perf. 14***

**736** A130 15c multicolored .25 .25
**737** A130 50c multicolored .75 .45
**738** A130 60c multicolored .80 .60
**739** A130 $3 multicolored 2.25 *3.75*
*Nos. 736-739 (4)* 4.05 *5.05*

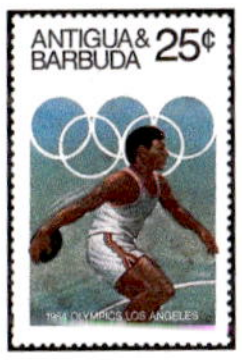

1984 Olympics, Los Angeles — A131

**1984, Jan. Litho. *Perf. 15***

**740** A131 25c Discus .25 .25
**741** A131 50c Gymnastics .30 .25
**742** A131 90c Hurdling .60 .60
**743** A131 $3 Bicycling 4.00 *3.00*
*Nos. 740-743 (4)* 5.15 *4.10*

### Souvenir Sheet

**744** A131 $5 Volleyball, horiz. 3.50 *4.00*

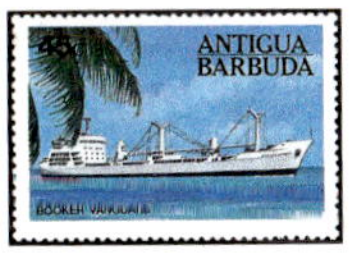

Booker Vanguard A132

**1984, June 4 Litho. *Perf. 15***

**745** A132 45c shown 1.00 .45
**746** A132 50c Canberra 1.20 .70
**747** A132 60c Yachts 1.40 .90
**748** A132 $4 Fairwind 3.00 *6.75*
*Nos. 745-748 (4)* 6.60 *8.80*

### Souvenir Sheet

**749** A132 $5 Man-of-war, vert. 2.75 *3.50*

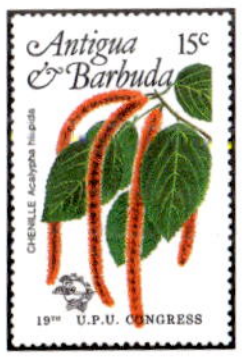

Local Flowers — A133

**1984, June 25 Litho. *Perf. 15***

**755** A133 15c multicolored .50 .25
**756** A133 50c multicolored 1.00 .75
**757** A133 60c multicolored 1.00 1.00
**758** A133 $3 multicolored 3.50 *5.50*
*Nos. 755-758 (4)* 6.00 *7.50*

### Souvenir Sheet

**759** A133 $5 multicolored 3.50 3.50

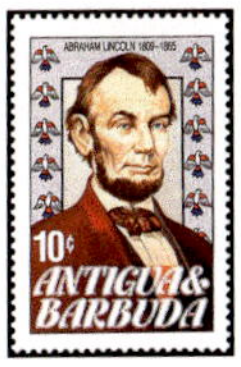

US Presidents — A134

**1984, July 18 Litho. *Perf. 14***

**760** A134 10c Lincoln .25 .25
**761** A134 20c Truman .25 .25
**762** A134 30c Eisenhower .30 .25
**763** A134 40c Reagan .50 .45
**764** A134 90c Lincoln, diff. .90 .80
**765** A134 $1.10 Truman, diff. 1.25 1.10
**766** A134 $1.50 Eisenhower, diff. 1.60 *1.75*
**767** A134 $2 Reagan, diff. 1.75 *2.00*
*Nos. 760-767 (8)* 6.80 6.85

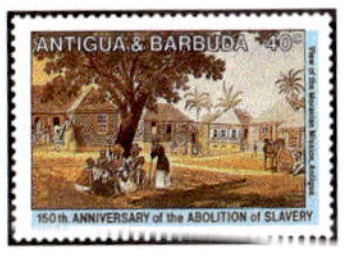

Slavery Abolition Sesquicentennial A135

40c, Moravian Mission. 50c, Antigua Courthouse, 1823. 60c, Sugar cane planting. $3, Boiling House, Delaps' Estate.
$5, Willoughby Bay.

**1984, Aug. 1**

**768** A135 40c multicolored .85 .45
**769** A135 50c multicolored .90 .60
**770** A135 60c multicolored 1.00 .70
**771** A135 $3 multicolored 3.75 *4.75*
*Nos. 768-771 (4)* 6.50 6.50

### Souvenir Sheet

**772** A135 $5 multicolored 6.25 6.25

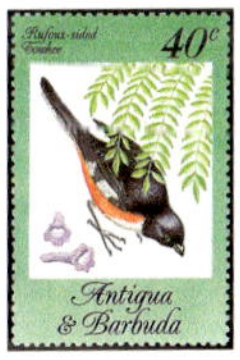

Song Birds — A136

40c, Rufous-sided towhee. 50c, Parula warbler. 60c, House wren. $2, Ruby-crowned kinglet. $3, Yellow-shafted flicker.
$5, Yellow-breasted chat.

**1984, Aug. 15 *Perf. 15***

**773** A136 40c multicolored 1.65 .70
**774** A136 50c multicolored 1.50 .90
**775** A136 60c multicolored 1.75 1.75
**776** A136 $2 multicolored 2.00 *3.50*
**777** A136 $3 multicolored 2.25 *4.75*
*Nos. 773-777 (5)* 9.15 *11.60*

### Souvenir Sheet

**778** A136 $5 multicolored 4.75 *5.75*

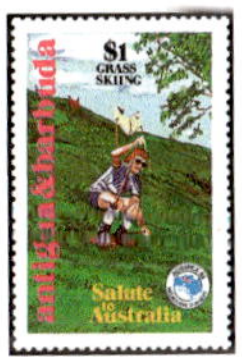

AUSIPEX '84 — A137

$1, Grass skiing. No. 780, $5, Australian rules football. No. 781, $5, Boomerang.

**1984, Sept. 21 *Perf. 15***

**779** A137 $1 multicolored 1.25 1.50
**780** A137 $5 multicolored 4.00 4.75

### Souvenir Sheet

**781** A137 $5 multicolored 3.25 3.25

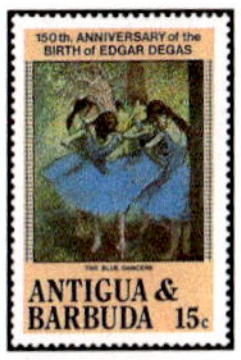

The Blue Dancers, by Degas — A137a

Paintings by Correggio: 25c, Virgin and Infant with Angels and Cherubs. 60c, The Four Saints. 90c, Saint Catherine. $3, The Campori Madonna. No. 790, St. John the Baptist.
Paintings by Degas: 50c, The Pink Dancers. 70c, Two Dancers. $4, Dancers at the Bar. No. 791, Folk Dancers.

**1984, Oct. Litho. *Perf. 15***

**782** A137a 15c multicolored .35 .25
**783** A137a 25c multicolored .40 .25
**784** A137a 50c multicolored .85 .50
**785** A137a 60c multicolored .85 .40
**786** A137a 70c multicolored 1.05 .70
**787** A137a 90c multicolored 1.05 .75
**788** A137a $3 multicolored 2.40 *4.00*
**789** A137a $4 multicolored 2.60 *4.50*
*Nos. 782-789 (8)* 9.55 *11.35*

### Souvenir Sheets

**790** A137a $5 multicolored 3.00 3.00
**791** A137a $5 multi, horiz. 3.00 3.00

### Nos. 623-626, 663-666, 672-675, 694-697 Surcharged in Black or Gold

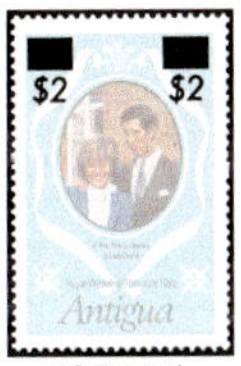

(CD331)

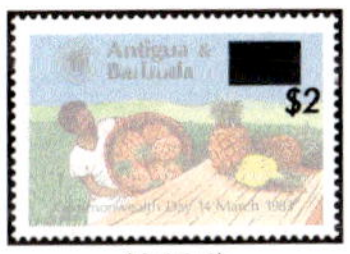

(A124)

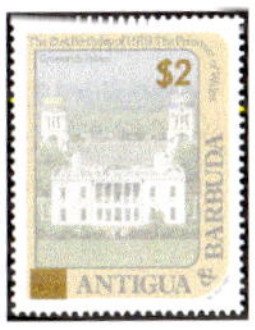

(CD332)

**1984, June *Perf. 14, 14½x14***

**792** CD331 $2 on 25c #623 3.00 *3.50*
**793** A124 $2 on 25c #694 2.25 *1.50*
**794** A124 $2 on 45c #695 2.25 *1.50*
**795** CD331 $2 on 50c #624 3.00 *3.50*
**796** A124 $2 on 60c #696 2.25 *2.75*
**797** CD332 $2 on 90c #663 (G) 2.50 *2.75*
**798** CD332 $2 on 90c #672 (G) 2.50 *2.75*
**799** CD332 $2 on $1 #664 (G) 2.50 *2.75*
**800** CD332 $2 on $1 #673 (G) 2.50 *2.75*
**801** A124 $2 on $3 #697 2.25 *1.50*
**802** CD331 $2 on $4 #625 3.00 *3.50*
**803** CD332 $2 on $4 #665 (G) 2.50 *2.75*
**804** CD332 $2 on $4 #674 (G) 2.50 *2.75*
*Nos. 792-804 (13)* 33.00 *34.25*

### Souvenir Sheets

**805** CD331 $2 on $5 #626 8.00 8.00
**806** CD332 $2 on $5 #666 6.75 6.75
**807** CD332 $2 on $5 #675 6.75 6.75

Nos. 797-800, 803-804 exist with silver surcharge.

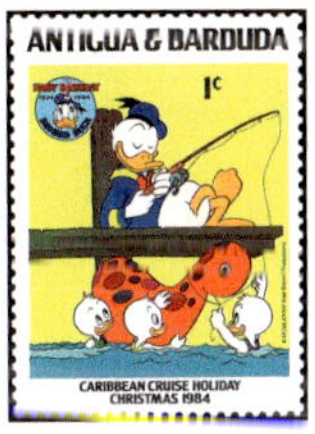

Christmas 1984 and 50th Anniv. of Donald Duck — A138

Scenes from various Donald Duck comics.

**1984, Nov. Litho. *Perf. 11***

**808** A138 1c multicolored .25 .25
**809** A138 2c multicolored .25 .25
**810** A138 3c multicolored .25 .25
**811** A138 4c multicolored .25 .25
**812** A138 5c multicolored .25 .25
**813** A138 10c multicolored .25 .25
**814** A138 $1 multicolored 1.75 1.10
**815** A138 $2 multicolored 2.00 *2.75*
**816** A138 $5 multicolored 3.75 *5.50*
*Nos. 808-816 (9)* 9.00 10.85

### Souvenir Sheets

*Perf. 14*

**817** A138 $5 multi, horiz. 6.75 6.75
**818** A138 $5 Donald on beach 6.75 6.75

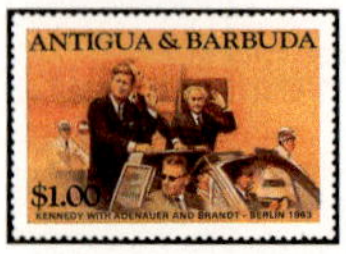


20th Century Leaders — A139

No. 819, John F. Kennedy (1917-1963), vert. No. 820, Winston Churchill (1874-1965), vert. No. 821, Mahatma Gandhi (1869-1948), vert. No. 822, Mao Tse-Tung (1883-1976), vert. No. 823, Kennedy in Berlin. No. 824, Churchill in Paris. No. 825, Gandhi in Great Britain. No. 826, Mao in Peking.

No. 827, Flags of Great Britain, India, China, USA.

**1984, Nov. 19 Litho. *Perf. 15***

**819** A139 60c multicolored 1.15 *1.40*
**820** A139 60c multicolored 1.15 *1.40*
**821** A139 60c multicolored 1.15 *1.40*
**822** A139 60c multicolored 1.15 *1.40*
**823** A139 $1 multicolored 1.25 *1.60*
**824** A139 $1 multicolored 1.25 *1.60*
**825** A139 $1 multicolored 1.25 *1.60*
**826** A139 $1 multicolored 1.25 *1.60*
*Nos. 819-826 (8)* 9.60 *12.00*

### Souvenir Sheet

**827** A139 $5 multicolored 9.25 9.25

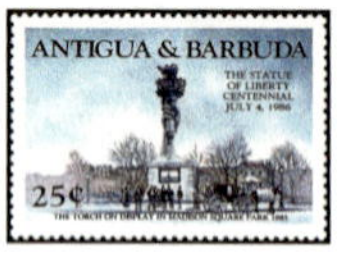


Statue of Liberty Centennial A140

25c, Torch on display, 1885. 30c, Restoration, 1984-1986, vert. 50c, Bartholdi supervising construction, 1876. 90c, Statue on Liberty Island. $1, Dedication Ceremony, 1886, vert. $3, Operation Sail, 1976, vert.

$5, Port of New York.

**1985, Jan. 7**

**828** A140 25c multicolored .25 .25
**829** A140 30c multicolored .25 .25
**830** A140 50c multicolored .40 .30
**831** A140 90c multicolored .70 .50
**832** A140 $1 multicolored 1.50 1.10
**833** A140 $3 multicolored 2.00 *2.75*
*Nos. 828-833 (6)* 5.10 5.15

### Souvenir Sheet

**834** A140 $5 multicolored 4.50 4.50

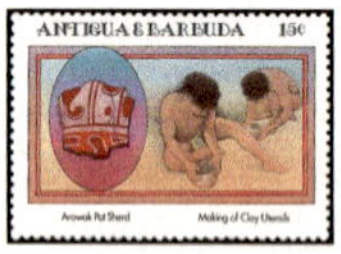


Traditional Scenes — A141

15c, Ceramics, Arawak pot shard. 50c, Tatooing, body design. 60c, Harvesting Manioc, god Yocahu. $3, Caribs in battle, war club.

$5, Tainos worshiping.

**1985, Jan. 21**

**835** A141 15c multicolored .30 .25
**836** A141 50c multicolored .40 .40
**837** A141 60c multicolored .55 .50
**838** A141 $3 multicolored 1.75 *2.50*
*Nos. 835-838 (4)* 3.00 *3.65*

### Souvenir Sheet

**839** A141 $5 multicolored 2.75 2.75

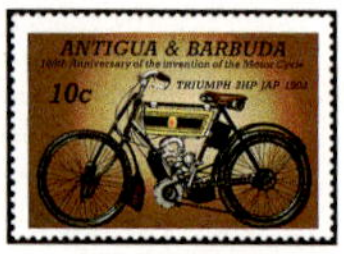


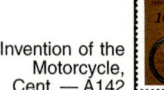

Invention of the Motorcycle, Cent. — A142

10c, Triumph 2HP Jap, 1903. 30c, Indian Arrow, 1949. 60c, BMW R100RS, 1976. $4, Harley Davidson Model II, 1916.

$5, Laverda Jota, 1975.

**1985, Mar. 7 *Perf. 14***

**840** A142 10c multicolored .60 .40
**841** A142 30c multicolored 1.10 .50
**842** A142 60c multicolored 1.40 1.25
**843** A142 $4 multicolored 5.50 *7.25*
*Nos. 840-843 (4)* 8.60 9.40

### Souvenir Sheet

**844** A142 $5 multicolored 6.00 *7.00*

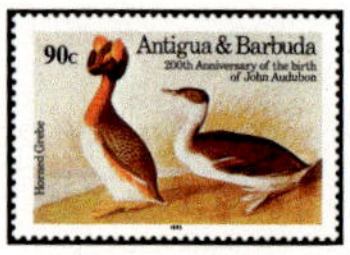


John J. Audubon, 200th Birth Anniv. — A143

90c, Horned grebe. $1, Least petrel. $1.50, Great blue heron. $3, Double-crested cormorant.

$5, White-tailed tropic bird, vert.

**1985, Mar. 25 *Perf. 14***

**845** A143 90c multicolored 1.75 1.10
**846** A143 $1 multicolored 2.00 1.10
**847** A143 $1.50 multicolored 2.75 *3.00*
**848** A143 $3 multicolored 4.50 *5.75*
*Nos. 845-848 (4)* 11.00 *10.95*

### Souvenir Sheet

**849** A143 $5 multicolored 10.00 10.00

See Nos.910-914.

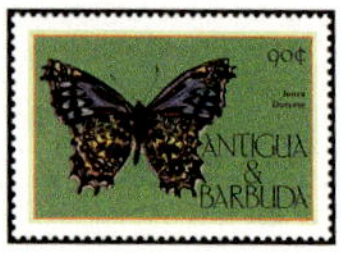


Butterflies A144

25c, Polygrapha cyanea. 60c, Leodonta dysoni. 90c, Junea doraete. $4, Prepona xenagoras.

$5, Caerois gerdrudtus.

**1985, Apr. 16 *Perf. 14***

**850** A144 25c multicolored 1.25 .25
**851** A144 60c multicolored 2.25 1.10
**852** A144 90c multicolored 3.00 1.25
**853** A144 $4 multicolored 7.50 *10.00*
*Nos. 850-853 (4)* 14.00 12.60

### Souvenir Sheet

**854** A144 $5 multicolored 6.50 6.50

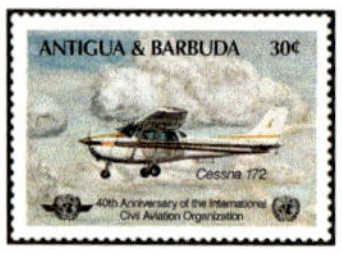


Cessna 172 — A145

90c, Fokker DVII. $1.50, Spad VII. $3, Boeing 747.

$5, Twin Otter, Coolidge Intl. Airport.

**1985, Apr. 30**

**855** A145 30c shown 1.25 .25
**856** A145 90c multicolored 2.50 1.25
**857** A145 $1.50 multicolored 3.50 3.25
**858** A145 $3 multicolored 5.25 *7.00*
*Nos. 855-858 (4)* 12.50 *11.75*

### Souvenir Sheet

**859** A145 $5 multicolored 5.25 5.25

40th anniv. of the ICAO. Nos. 855, 858-859 show the ICAO and UN emblems.

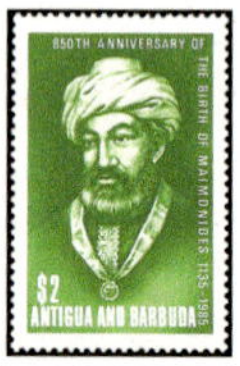


Maimonides (1135-1204), Judaic Philosopher and Physician — A146

**1985, June 17 Litho. *Perf. 14***

**860** A146 $2 yellow green 3.75 3.25

### Souvenir Sheet

**861** A146 $5 deep brown 6.75 5.00

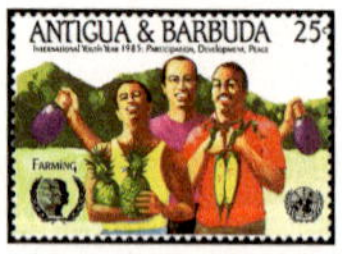


Intl. Youth Year — A147

25c, Agriculture. 50c, Hotel management. 60c, Environmental studies. $3, Windsurfing.

$5, Youths, national flag.

**1985, July 1**

**862** A147 25c multicolored .25 .25
**863** A147 50c multicolored .35 .30
**864** A147 60c multicolored 1.00 .75
**865** A147 $3 multicolored 2.10 *5.00*
*Nos. 862-865 (4)* 3.70 *6.30*

### Souvenir Sheet

**866** A147 $5 multicolored 3.25 3.25

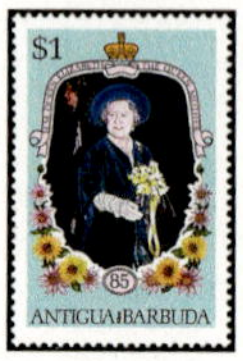


Queen Mother, 85th Birthday — A148

Designs: 90c, $1, Attending a church service. No. 867A, $1.50, Touring the London Gardens, children in a sandpit. $2.50, $3, Photograph (1979). $5, With Prince Edward at the wedding of Prince Charles and Lady Diana Spencer.

***Perf. 14, 12x12½ (90c, $1, $3)***

**1985, July 15**

**866A** A148 90c multi ('86) .55 .55
**867** A148 $1 multi .60 .60
**867A** A148 $1 multi ('86) .60 .60
**868** A148 $1.50 multi .90 .90
**869** A148 $2.50 multi 1.40 1.40
**869A** A148 $3 multi ('86) 1.60 1.60
*Nos. 866A-869A (6)* 5.65 5.65

### Souvenir Sheet

**870** A148 $5 multicolored 4.00 4.00

Nos. 866A, 867A, 869A issued in sheets of 5 plus label on Jan. 13, 1986.

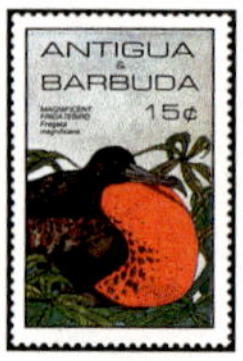


Marine Life — A149

15c, Fregata magnificens. 45c, Diploria labyrinthi-formis. 60c, Oreaster reticulatus. $3, Gymnothorax moringa.

$5, Acropora palmata.

**1985, Aug. 1 *Perf. 14***

**871** A149 15c multicolored 1.00 .25
**872** A149 45c multicolored 2.00 .85
**873** A149 60c multicolored 2.25 1.60
**874** A149 $3 multicolored 7.00 *8.50*
*Nos. 871-874 (4)* 12.25 *11.20*

### Souvenir Sheet

**875** A149 $5 multicolored 8.75 8.75

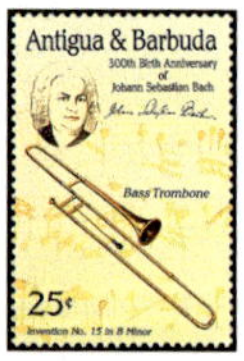


Johann Sebastian Bach — A150

**1985, Aug. 26 Litho. *Perf. 14***

**876** A150 25c Bass trombone 1.10 .40
**877** A150 50c English horn 1.40 .90
**878** A150 $1 Violino piccolo 2.75 1.50
**879** A150 $3 Bass rackett 6.00 *6.75*
*Nos. 876-879 (4)* 11.25 9.55

### Souvenir Sheet

**880** A150 $5 Portrait 5.75 5.75

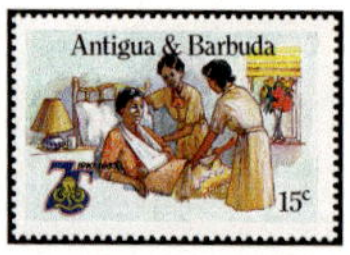


Girl Guides, 75th Anniv. — A151

Public service and growth-oriented activities: 15c, Public service. 45c, Guides meeting. 60c, Lord and Lady Baden-Powell. $3, Nature study.

$5, Barn swallow.

**1985, Sept. 10**

**881** A151 15c multicolored .75 .25
**882** A151 45c multicolored 1.25 .40
**883** A151 60c multicolored 1.60 .60
**884** A151 $3 multicolored 4.25 4.25
*Nos. 881-884 (4)* 7.85 5.50

### Souvenir Sheet

**885** A151 $5 multicolored 5.50 *8.00*

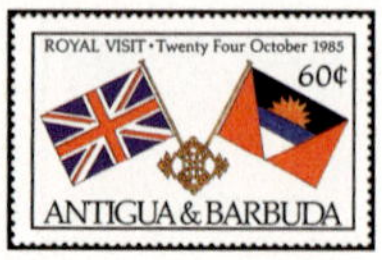


State Visit of Elizabeth II, Oct. 24 — A152

**1985, Oct. 24 Litho. *Perf. 14½***

**886** A152 60c National flags .90 .45
**887** A152 $1 Elizabeth II, vert. 1.35 .90
**888** A152 $4 HMY Britannia 3.25 *6.50*
*Nos. 886-888 (3)* 5.50 *7.85*

### Souvenir Sheet

**889** A152 $5 Map of Antigua 3.50 3.50

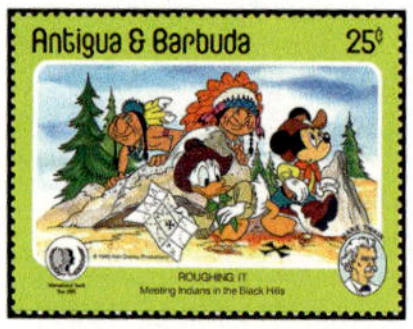


Mark Twain A153

Disney characters in Roughing It: 25c, Cowboys and Indians. 50c, Canoeing. $1.10, Pony Express. $1.50, Buffalo hunt in Missouri. $2, Nevada silver mine.

$5, Stagecoach on Kansas plains.

**1985, Nov. 4 *Perf. 14***

**890** A153 25c multicolored 1.00 .25
**891** A153 50c multicolored 1.25 .40
**892** A153 $1.10 multicolored 2.00 1.25
**893** A153 $1.50 multicolored 2.50 *3.50*
**894** A153 $2 multicolored 3.25 *4.25*
*Nos. 890-894 (5)* 10.00 9.65

### Souvenir Sheet

**895** A153 $5 multicolored 8.75 8.75

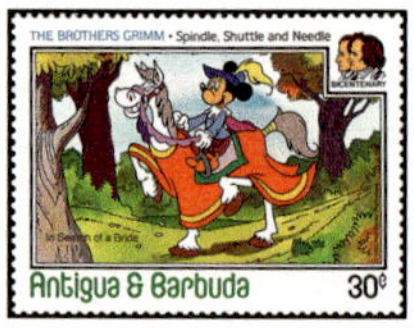


Jacob and Wilhelm Grimm, Fabulists and Philologists A154

Disney characters in Spindle, Shuttle and Needle.

**1985, Nov. 11**

**896** A154 30c multicolored 1.00 .35
**897** A154 60c multicolored 1.50 .70
**898** A154 70c multicolored 1.75 1.25
**899** A154 $1 multicolored 2.00 1.60
**900** A154 $3 multicolored 4.50 *7.00*
*Nos. 896-900 (5)* 10.75 *10.90*

### Souvenir Sheet

**900A** A154 $5 multicolored 8.75 8.75

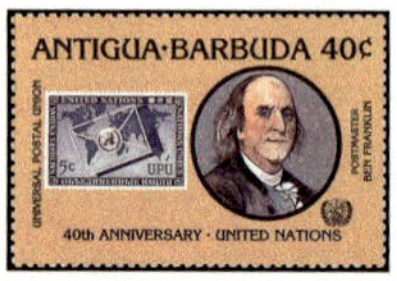


UN 40th Anniv. A155

Stamps of UN and portraits: 40c, No. 18 and Benjamin Franklin. $1, No. 391 and George Washington Carver, agricultural chemist. $3, No. 299 and Charles Lindbergh. $5, Marc Chagall, artist, vert.

**1985, Nov. 18 *Perf. 13½x14***

**901** A155 40c multicolored .90 .50
**902** A155 $1 multicolored 1.75 1.25
**903** A155 $3 multicolored 4.25 *7.00*
*Nos. 901-903 (3)* 6.90 *8.75*

### Souvenir Sheet

***Perf. 14x13½***

**904** A155 $5 multicolored 6.75 6.75

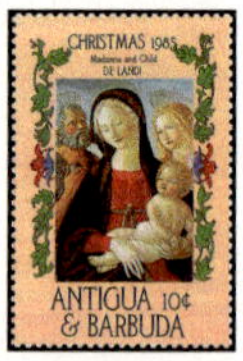


Christmas — A156

Religious paintings: 10c, Madonna and Child, by De Landi. 25c, Madonna and Child, by Bonaventura Berlingheiri (d. 1244). 60c, The Nativity, by Fra Angelico (1400-1455). $4, Presentation in the Temple, by Giovanni di

Paolo Grazia (c.1403-1482). $5, The Nativity, by Antoniazzo Romano.

**1985, Dec. 30** ***Perf. 15***

| | | | | | |
|---|---|---|---|---|---|
| **905** | A156 | 10c | multicolored | .30 | .25 |
| **906** | A156 | 25c | multicolored | .60 | .25 |
| **907** | A156 | 60c | multicolored | .85 | .45 |
| **908** | A156 | $4 | multicolored | 1.90 | *4.00* |
| | | | *Nos. 905-908 (4)* | 3.65 | *4.95* |

**Souvenir Sheet**

| | | | | | |
|---|---|---|---|---|---|
| **909** | A156 | $5 | multicolored | 3.50 | *3.75* |

**Audubon Type of 1985**

Illustrations of North American ducks: 60c, Mallard. 90c, Dusky duck. $1.50, Common pintail. $3, Widgeon.
$5, Common eider.

**1986, Jan. 6** ***Perf. 12½x12***

| | | | | | |
|---|---|---|---|---|---|
| **910** | A143 | 60c | multicolored | 1.90 | 1.00 |
| **911** | A143 | 90c | multicolored | 2.40 | 1.50 |
| **912** | A143 | $1.50 | multicolored | 3.00 | 3.50 |
| **913** | A143 | $3 | multicolored | 4.00 | *5.75* |
| | | | *Nos. 910-913 (4)* | 11.30 | 11.75 |

**Souvenir Sheet**
***Perf. 14***

| | | | | | |
|---|---|---|---|---|---|
| **914** | A143 | $5 | multicolored | 7.25 | 7.25 |

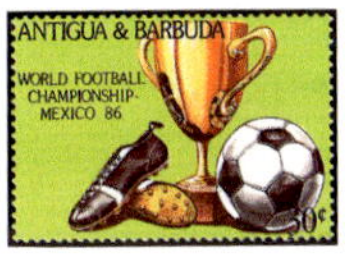

1986 World Cup Soccer Championships, Mexico — A157

**1986, Mar. 17** **Litho.** ***Perf. 14***

| | | | | | |
|---|---|---|---|---|---|
| **915** | A157 | 30c | shown | 1.30 | .25 |
| **916** | A157 | 60c | Heading the ball | 1.50 | .60 |
| **917** | A157 | $1 | Referee | 1.90 | 1.40 |
| **918** | A157 | $4 | Goal | 5.25 | *7.50* |
| | | | *Nos. 915-918 (4)* | 9.95 | 9.75 |

**Souvenir Sheet**

| | | | | | |
|---|---|---|---|---|---|
| **919** | A157 | $5 | Action | 7.50 | 7.50 |

Nos. 916-917 vert.
For overprints see Nos. 963-967.

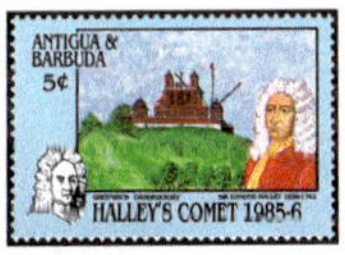

A158

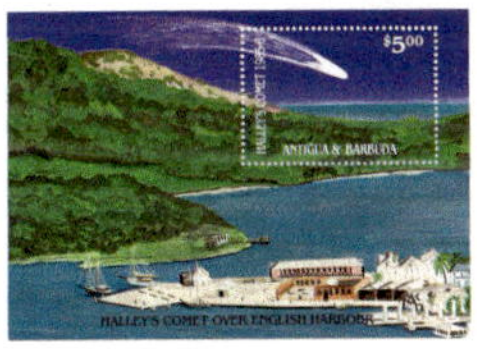

Halley's Comet A159

Designs: 5c, Edmond Halley, Greenwich Observatory. 10c, Me 163B Komet. German WWII fighter plane. 60c, Montezuma sighting comet, 1517. $4, Pocahontas saving Capt. John Smith's life, 1607 sighting as sign for Powhatan Indians to raid Jamestown. $5, Comet over Antigua.

**1986, Mar. 24**

| | | | | | |
|---|---|---|---|---|---|
| **920** | A158 | 5c | multicolored | .30 | .25 |
| **921** | A158 | 10c | multicolored | .35 | .25 |
| **922** | A158 | 60c | multicolored | 1.40 | .60 |
| **923** | A158 | $4 | multicolored | 4.25 | *5.75* |
| | | | *Nos. 920-923 (4)* | 6.30 | 6.75 |

**Souvenir Sheet**

| | | | | | |
|---|---|---|---|---|---|
| **924** | A159 | $5 | multicolored | 4.50 | 4.50 |

For overprints see Nos. 973-977.

**Queen Elizabeth II, 60th Birthday**
Common Design Type

60c, Wedding, 1947. $1, Trooping the color. $4, Visiting Scotland.
$5, Held by Queen Mary, 1927.

**1986, Apr. 21**

| | | | | | |
|---|---|---|---|---|---|
| **925** | CD339 | 60c | multicolored | .40 | .45 |
| **926** | CD339 | $1 | multicolored | .60 | .60 |
| **927** | CD339 | $4 | multicolored | 1.75 | *1.90* |
| | | | *Nos. 925-927 (3)* | 2.75 | 2.95 |

**Souvenir Sheet**

| | | | | | |
|---|---|---|---|---|---|
| **928** | CD339 | $5 | multicolored | 2.75 | *3.25* |

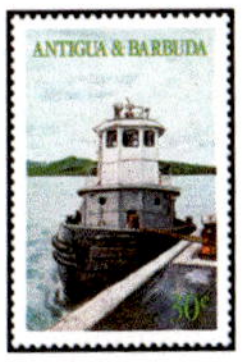

Boats — A160

30c, Tugboat. 60c, Fishing boat. $1, Sailboat 2056. $4, Lateen-rigged sailboat.
$5, Boatbuilding.

**1986, May 15**

| | | | | | |
|---|---|---|---|---|---|
| **929** | A160 | 30c | multicolored | .25 | .25 |
| **930** | A160 | 60c | multicolored | .45 | .30 |
| **931** | A160 | $1 | multicolored | .80 | .50 |
| **932** | A160 | $4 | multicolored | 3.00 | 3.00 |
| | | | *Nos. 929-932 (4)* | 4.50 | 4.05 |

**Souvenir Sheet**

| | | | | | |
|---|---|---|---|---|---|
| **933** | A160 | $5 | multicolored | 3.25 | *4.00* |

A number of unissued items, imperfs., part perfs., missing color varieties, etc., were made available when the Format International inventory was liquidated. Imperfs of some or all of the Antigua stamps in the following sets are included: Nos. 405-422, 503-507, 515-517, 703-707, 745-749, 755-759, 808-816, 819-826, 905-909, 934-937.
See footnote after No. 962.

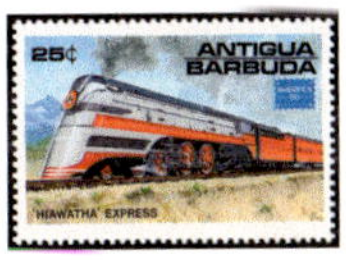

AMERIPEX '86 — A161

American trains.

**1986, May 22** ***Perf. 15***

| | | | | | |
|---|---|---|---|---|---|
| **934** | A161 | 25c | Hiawatha | 1.10 | .30 |
| **935** | A161 | 50c | Grand Canyon | 1.35 | .60 |
| **936** | A161 | $1 | Powhattan Arrow | 1.75 | 1.75 |
| **937** | A161 | $3 | Empire State | 3.00 | *5.50* |
| | | | *Nos. 934-937 (4)* | 7.20 | *8.15* |

**Souvenir Sheet**

| | | | | | |
|---|---|---|---|---|---|
| **938** | A161 | $5 | Daylight | 8.00 | *10.00* |

**Wedding of Prince Andrew and Sarah Ferguson**
Common Design Type

**1986, July 23** ***Perf. 14***

| | | | | | |
|---|---|---|---|---|---|
| **939** | CD340 | 45c | Couple | .30 | .30 |
| **940** | CD340 | 60c | Prince Andrew | .45 | .45 |
| **941** | CD340 | $4 | Princes Andrew, Philip | 2.75 | *3.75* |
| | | | *Nos. 939-941 (3)* | 3.50 | *4.50* |

**Souvenir Sheet**

| | | | | | |
|---|---|---|---|---|---|
| **942** | CD340 | $5 | Couple, diff. | 3.50 | *4.25* |

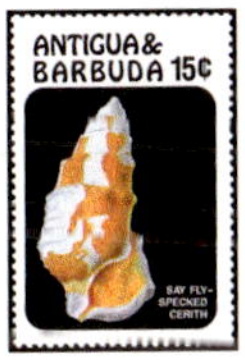

Conch Shells — A162

15c, Say fly-specked cerith. 45c, Gmelin smooth scotch bonnet. 60c, Linne West Indian crown conch. $3, Murex ciboney.
$5, Atlantic natica.

**1986, Aug. 6** **Litho.** ***Perf. 15***

| | | | | | |
|---|---|---|---|---|---|
| **943** | A162 | 15c | multicolored | .75 | .35 |
| **944** | A162 | 45c | multicolored | 1.75 | 1.25 |
| **945** | A162 | 60c | multicolored | 1.90 | 1.90 |
| **946** | A162 | $3 | multicolored | 5.75 | *9.50* |
| | | | *Nos. 943-946 (4)* | 10.15 | *13.00* |

**Souvenir Sheet**

| | | | | | |
|---|---|---|---|---|---|
| **947** | A162 | $5 | multicolored | 7.25 | *8.00* |

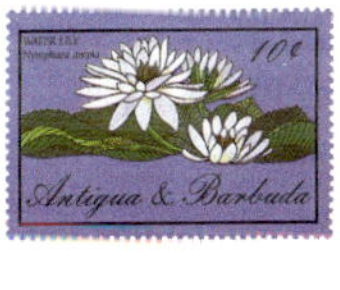

Flowers — A163

10c, Water lily. 15c, Queen of the night. 50c, Cup of gold. 60c, Beach morning glory. 70c, Golden trumpet. $1, Air plant. $3, Purple wreath. $4, Zephyr lily.
No. 956, Dozakie. No. 957, Four o'clock.

**1986, Aug. 25** **Litho.** ***Perf. 15***

| | | | | | |
|---|---|---|---|---|---|
| **948** | A163 | 10c | multicolored | .30 | .25 |
| **949** | A163 | 15c | multicolored | .30 | .25 |
| **950** | A163 | 50c | multicolored | .50 | .45 |
| **951** | A163 | 60c | multicolored | .65 | .55 |
| **952** | A163 | 70c | multicolored | .75 | .65 |
| **953** | A163 | $1 | multicolored | .85 | 1.10 |
| **954** | A163 | $3 | multicolored | 1.90 | *2.75* |
| **955** | A163 | $4 | multicolored | 2.40 | *3.50* |
| | | | *Nos. 948-955 (8)* | 7.65 | *9.50* |

**Souvenir Sheets**

| | | | | | |
|---|---|---|---|---|---|
| **956** | A163 | $4 | multicolored | 2.75 | *3.25* |
| **957** | A163 | $5 | multicolored | 3.50 | *4.00* |

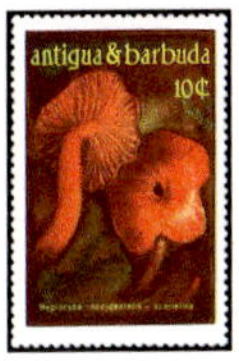

Fungi — A164

10c, Hygrocybe occidentalis scarletina. 50c, Trogia buccinalis. $1, Collybia subpruinosa. $4, Leucocoprinus brebissonii.
$5, Pyrrhoglossum pyrrhum.

**1986, Sept. 15**

| | | | | | |
|---|---|---|---|---|---|
| **958** | A164 | 10c | multicolored | .30 | .25 |
| **959** | A164 | 50c | multicolored | .65 | .55 |
| **960** | A164 | $1 | multicolored | 1.35 | 1.25 |
| **961** | A164 | $4 | multicolored | 3.25 | *4.50* |
| | | | *Nos. 958-961 (4)* | 5.55 | 6.55 |

**Souvenir Sheet**

| | | | | | |
|---|---|---|---|---|---|
| **962** | A164 | $5 | multicolored | 11.00 | 11.00 |

An unissued $3 stamp and No. 961 inscribed "4$" were made available when the Format International inventory was liquidated.

**Nos. 915-919 Ovptd. in Gold in 2 or 3 lines**

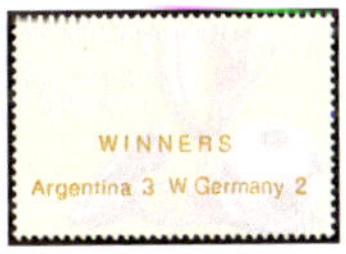


**1986, Sept. 15** ***Perf. 14***

| | | | | | |
|---|---|---|---|---|---|
| **963** | A157 | 30c | multicolored | 1.10 | .35 |
| **964** | A157 | 60c | multicolored | 1.00 | .70 |
| **965** | A157 | $1 | multicolored | 2.00 | 1.10 |
| **966** | A157 | $4 | multicolored | 3.50 | *4.50* |
| | | | *Nos. 963-966 (4)* | 8.20 | 6.65 |

**Souvenir Sheet**

| | | | | | |
|---|---|---|---|---|---|
| **967** | A157 | $5 | multicolored | 5.00 | 5.00 |

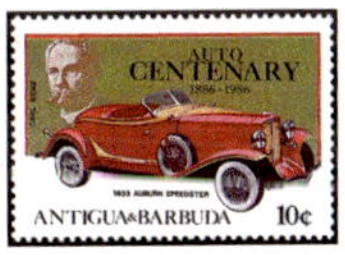

Automobile, Cent. — A165

Carl Benz and classic automobiles: 10c, 1933 Auburn Speedster. 15c, 1986 Mercury Sable. 50c, 1959 Cadillac. 60c, 1950 Studebaker. 70c, 1939 Lagonda V-12. $1, 1930 Adler Standard. $3, 1956 DKW. $4, 1936 Mercedes 500K.
No. 972, 1921 Mercedes Knight. No. 972A, 1896 Daimler.

**1986, Oct. 20**

| | | | | | |
|---|---|---|---|---|---|
| **968** | A165 | 10c | multicolored | .25 | .25 |
| **968A** | A165 | 15c | multicolored | .30 | .25 |
| **969** | A165 | 50c | multicolored | .55 | .25 |
| **970** | A165 | 60c | multicolored | .70 | .30 |
| **970A** | A165 | 70c | multicolored | .80 | .40 |
| **970B** | A165 | $1 | multicolored | 1.10 | .55 |
| **970C** | A165 | $3 | multicolored | 2.75 | 2.75 |
| **971** | A165 | $4 | multicolored | 3.25 | 3.25 |
| | | | *Nos. 968-971 (8)* | 9.70 | 8.00 |

**Souvenir Sheets**

| | | | | | |
|---|---|---|---|---|---|
| **972** | A165 | $5 | multicolored | 4.25 | 4.25 |
| **972A** | A165 | $5 | multicolored | 4.25 | 4.25 |

**Nos. 920-924 Ovptd. in Black or Silver**

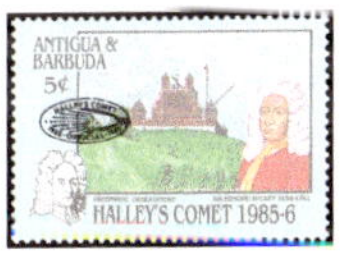


**1986, Oct. 22** **Litho.** ***Perf. 14***

| | | | | | |
|---|---|---|---|---|---|
| **973** | A158 | 5c | multicolored | 4.75 | .25 |
| **974** | A158 | 10c | multicolored | .25 | .25 |
| **975** | A158 | 60c | multicolored | 1.25 | .60 |
| **976** | A158 | $4 | multicolored | 5.50 | 4.00 |
| | | | *Nos. 973-976 (4)* | 11.75 | 5.10 |

**Souvenir Sheet**

| | | | | | |
|---|---|---|---|---|---|
| **977** | A159 | $5 | multicolored (S) | 6.00 | *6.50* |

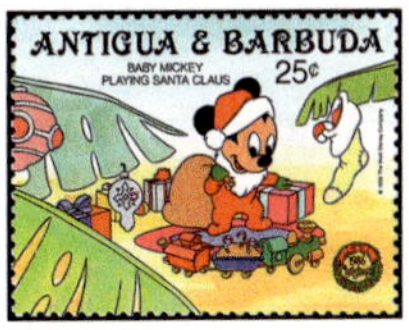

Christmas A166

Disney characters as children: 25c, Mickey. 30c, Mickey, Minnie. 40c, Aunt Matilda, Goofy. 60c, Goofy, Pluto. 70c, Pluto, Donald, Daisy. $1.50, Stringing popcorn. $3, Grandma Duck, Minnie. $4, Donald, Pete. No. 986, Playing with presents. No. 987, Reindeer.

**1986, Nov. 4** ***Perf. 11***

| | | | | | |
|---|---|---|---|---|---|
| **978** | A166 | 25c | multicolored | .55 | .25 |
| **979** | A166 | 30c | multicolored | .70 | .30 |
| **980** | A166 | 40c | multicolored | .75 | .35 |
| **981** | A166 | 60c | multicolored | .90 | .65 |
| **982** | A166 | 70c | multicolored | 1.10 | 1.00 |
| **983** | A166 | $1.50 | multicolored | 1.75 | *2.25* |
| **984** | A166 | $3 | multicolored | 2.75 | *4.25* |
| **985** | A166 | $4 | multicolored | 3.25 | *4.25* |
| | | | *Nos. 978-985 (8)* | 11.75 | *13.30* |

**Souvenir Sheets**
***Perf. 14***

| | | | | | |
|---|---|---|---|---|---|
| **986** | A166 | $5 | multicolored | 6.50 | *7.00* |
| **987** | A166 | $5 | multicolored | 6.50 | *7.00* |

Nos. 985 printed in sheets of 8.

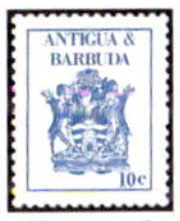

Coat of Arms A167

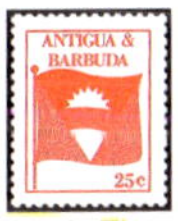

Natl. Flag A168

**1986, Nov. 25** **Litho.** ***Perf. 14x14½***

| | | | | | |
|---|---|---|---|---|---|
| **988** | A167 | 10c | bright blue | 1.00 | .90 |
| **989** | A168 | 25c | orange | 1.75 | 1.25 |

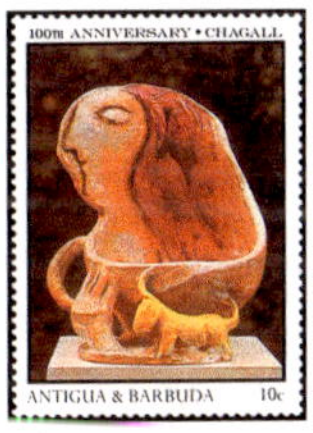

Marc Chagall (1887-1985), Artist — A169

Designs: No. 990, The Profile, 1957. No. 991, Portrait of the Artist's Sister, 1910. No. 992, Bride with Fan, 1911. No. 993, David in Profile, 1914. No. 994, Fiancee with Bouquet, 1977. No. 995, Self-portrait with Brushes, 1909. No. 996, The Walk, 1973. No. 997, Candles, 1938. No. 998, Fall of Icarus, 1975. No. 999, Myth of Orpheus, 1977.

**1987, Mar. 30** **Litho.** ***Perf. 13½x14***

| | | | | | |
|---|---|---|---|---|---|
| **990** | A169 | 10c | multicolored | .45 | .25 |
| **991** | A169 | 30c | multicolored | .60 | .30 |
| **992** | A169 | 40c | multicolored | .80 | .35 |
| **993** | A169 | 60c | multicolored | .90 | .40 |
| **994** | A169 | 90c | multicolored | 1.00 | .55 |
| **995** | A169 | $1 | multicolored | 1.00 | .60 |
| **996** | A169 | $3 | multicolored | 2.50 | 2.50 |
| **997** | A169 | $4 | multicolored | 2.75 | 2.75 |

**Size: 110x95mm**
***Imperf***

| | | | | | |
|---|---|---|---|---|---|
| **998** | A169 | $5 | multicolored | 5.75 | 5.75 |
| **999** | A169 | $5 | multicolored | 5.75 | 5.75 |
| | | | *Nos. 990-999 (10)* | 21.50 | 19.20 |

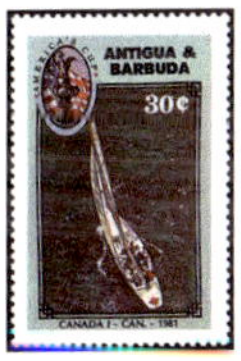

A170

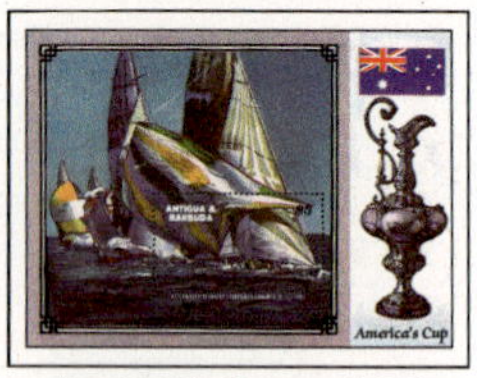


America's Cup — A171

30c, Canada I, 1981. 60c, Gretel II, 1970. $1, Sceptre, 1958. $3, Vigilant, 1893.
$5, Australia II, Liberty, 1983.

**1987, Feb. 5** ***Perf. 15***

| | | | | | |
|---|---|---|---|---|---|
| **1000** | A170 | 30c multicolored | | .55 | .25 |
| **1001** | A170 | 60c multicolored | | .70 | .35 |
| **1002** | A170 | $1 multicolored | | 1.00 | 1.00 |
| **1003** | A170 | $3 multicolored | | 2.50 | *3.00* |
| | | *Nos. 1000-1003 (4)* | | 4.75 | *4.60* |

**Souvenir Sheet**

| | | | | |
|---|---|---|---|---|
| **1004** | A171 | $5 multicolored | 5.00 | 5.00 |

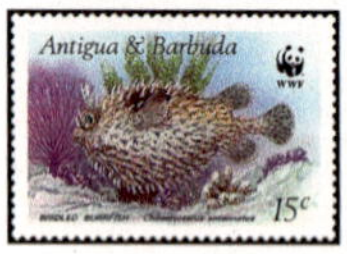


Fish, World Wildlife Fund — A172

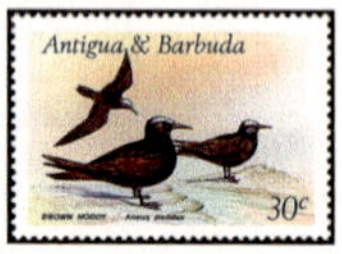


Marine Birds — A173

15c, Bridled burrfish. 30c, Brown noddy. 40c, Nassau grouper. 50c, Laughing gull. 60c, French angelfish. $1, Porkfish. $2, Royal tern. $3, Sooty tern.
No. 1013, Banded butterfly fish. No. 1014, Brown booby.

**1987, Feb. 23** **Litho.** ***Perf. 14***

| | | | | |
|---|---|---|---|---|
| **1005** | A172 | 15c multicolored | 3.00 | .45 |
| **1006** | A173 | 30c multicolored | 6.00 | .50 |
| **1007** | A172 | 40c multicolored | 3.75 | .60 |
| **1008** | A173 | 50c multicolored | 6.75 | 1.40 |
| **1009** | A172 | 60c multicolored | 4.00 | 1.40 |
| **1010** | A172 | $1 multicolored | 4.00 | 1.60 |
| **1011** | A173 | $2 multicolored | 9.00 | 5.50 |
| **1012** | A173 | $3 multicolored | 9.00 | 7.50 |
| | | *Nos. 1005-1012 (8)* | 45.50 | 18.95 |

**Souvenir Sheets**

| | | | | |
|---|---|---|---|---|
| **1013** | A172 | $5 multicolored | 10.00 | 10.00 |
| **1014** | A173 | $5 multicolored | 10.00 | 10.00 |

The 30c, 50c, $2, $3 and Nos. 1013-1014 do not picture the WWF emblem.
For overprints see Nos. 1137-1139A.

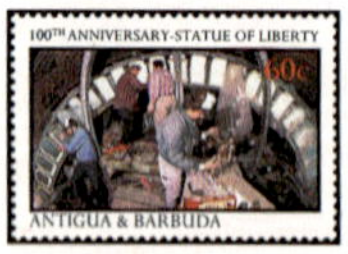


Statue of Liberty, Cent. — A174

Photographs by Peter B. Kaplan: 15c, Lee Iacocca. 30c, Statue at dusk. 45c, Crown, head. 50c, Iacocca, torch. 60c, Crown observatory. 90c, Interior restoration. $1, Head. $2, Statue at sunset. $3, Men on scaffold, flag. $5, Statue at night.

**1987, Apr. 20** ***Perf. 14***

| | | | | |
|---|---|---|---|---|
| **1015** | A174 | 15c multicolored | .25 | .25 |
| **1016** | A174 | 30c multicolored | .25 | .25 |
| **1017** | A174 | 45c multicolored | .35 | .35 |
| **1018** | A174 | 50c multicolored | .40 | .40 |
| **1019** | A174 | 60c multicolored | .40 | .40 |
| **1020** | A174 | 90c multicolored | .55 | .55 |
| **1021** | A174 | $1 multicolored | .65 | .65 |
| **1022** | A174 | $2 multicolored | 1.25 | *1.50* |
| **1023** | A174 | $3 multicolored | 1.40 | *2.00* |
| **1024** | A174 | $5 multicolored | 2.40 | *3.50* |
| | | *Nos. 1015-1024 (10)* | 7.90 | *9.85* |

Nos. 1015-1018, 1021-1022, 1024 vert.

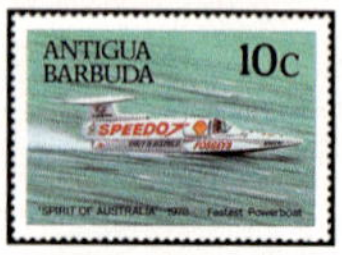


A175

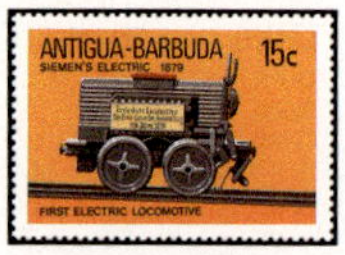


Transportation Innovations — A175a

10c, Spirit of Australia, 1978. 15c, Siemens' Electric locomotive, 1879. 30c, USS Triton, 1960. 50c, Trevithick, 1801. 60c, USS New Jersey, 1942. 70c, Draisine bicycle, 1818. 90c, SS United States, 1952. $1.50, Cierva C-4, 1923. $2, Curtiss NC-4, 1919. $3, Queen Elizabeth II, 1969.

**1987, Apr. 19** ***Perf. 15***

| | | | | |
|---|---|---|---|---|
| **1025** | A175 | 10c multi | .85 | .25 |
| **1026** | A175a | 15c multi | 1.10 | .30 |
| **1027** | A175 | 30c multi | 1.10 | .35 |
| **1028** | A175a | 50c multi | 1.25 | .45 |
| **1029** | A175 | 60c multi | 1.25 | .50 |
| **1030** | A175a | 70c multi | 1.25 | .65 |
| **1031** | A175 | 90c multi | 1.25 | .75 |
| **1032** | A175a | $1.50 multi | 1.90 | *2.50* |
| **1033** | A175a | $2 multi | 2.10 | *2.75* |
| **1034** | A175 | $3 multi | 3.25 | *4.25* |
| | | *Nos. 1025-1034 (10)* | 15.30 | *12.75* |

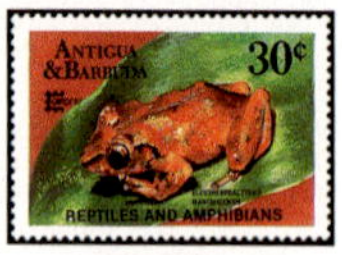


Reptiles and Amphibians A176

30c, Eleutherodactylus martinicensis. 60c, Thecadactylus rapicauda. $1, Anolis bimaculatus leachi. $3, Geochelone carbonaria.
$5, Ameiva griswoldi.

**1987, June 15** ***Perf. 14***

| | | | | |
|---|---|---|---|---|
| **1035** | A176 | 30c multicolored | .50 | .25 |
| **1036** | A176 | 60c multicolored | .75 | .35 |
| **1037** | A176 | $1 multicolored | 1.00 | .65 |
| **1038** | A176 | $3 multicolored | 2.00 | *2.75* |
| | | *Nos. 1035-1038 (4)* | 4.25 | *4.00* |

**Souvenir Sheet**

| | | | | |
|---|---|---|---|---|
| **1039** | A176 | $5 multicolored | 5.00 | 5.00 |

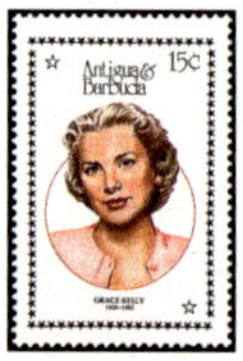


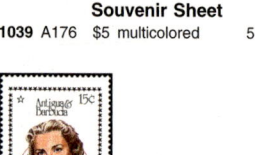

Entertainers — A177

**1987, May 11**

| | | | | |
|---|---|---|---|---|
| **1040** | A177 | 15c Grace Kelly | .90 | .30 |
| **1041** | A177 | 30c Marilyn Monroe | 2.75 | .60 |
| **1042** | A177 | 45c Orson Welles | .90 | .40 |
| **1043** | A177 | 50c Judy Garland | .90 | .45 |
| **1044** | A177 | 60c John Lennon | 4.00 | 1.00 |
| **1045** | A177 | $1 Rock Hudson | 1.50 | .90 |
| **1046** | A177 | $2 John Wayne | 2.50 | 1.75 |
| **1047** | A177 | $3 Elvis Presley | 9.00 | 4.25 |
| | | *Nos. 1040-1047 (8)* | 22.45 | 9.65 |

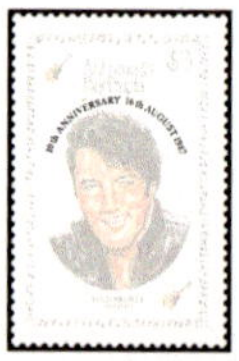

No. 1047 Overprinted

**1987, Sept. 9** **Litho.** ***Perf. 14***

| | | | | |
|---|---|---|---|---|
| **1047A** | A177 | $3 multicolored | 7.50 | 5.50 |

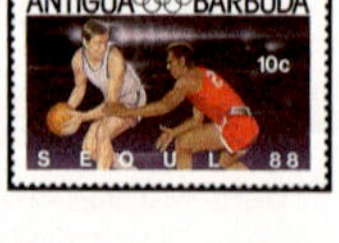


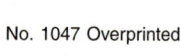

1988 Summer Olympics, Seoul — A178

10c, Basketball. 60c, Fencing. $1, Women's gymnastics. $3, Soccer.
$5, Boxing glove.

**1987, Mar. 23**

| | | | | |
|---|---|---|---|---|
| **1048** | A178 | 10c multicolored | .50 | .30 |
| **1049** | A178 | 60c multicolored | .75 | .40 |
| **1050** | A178 | $1 multicolored | 1.05 | 1.00 |
| **1051** | A178 | $3 multicolored | 2.50 | *4.00* |
| | | *Nos. 1048-1051 (4)* | 4.80 | *5.70* |

**Souvenir Sheet**

| | | | | |
|---|---|---|---|---|
| **1052** | A178 | $5 multicolored | 4.25 | *4.75* |

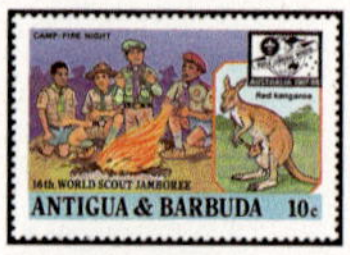


16th World Scout Jamboree, Australia, 1987-88 — A179

10c, Campfire, red kangaroo. 60c, Kayaking, blue-winged kookaburra. $1, Obstacle course, ring-tailed rock wallaby. $3, Field kitchen, koalas.
$5, Flags.

**1987, Nov. 2** **Litho.** ***Perf. 15***

| | | | | |
|---|---|---|---|---|
| **1053** | A179 | 10c multicolored | .70 | .25 |
| **1054** | A179 | 60c multicolored | 1.40 | .65 |
| **1055** | A179 | $1 multicolored | 1.15 | .75 |
| **1056** | A179 | $3 multicolored | 1.75 | *3.50* |
| | | *Nos. 1053-1056 (4)* | 5.00 | *5.15* |

**Souvenir Sheet**

| | | | | |
|---|---|---|---|---|
| **1057** | A179 | $5 multicolored | 3.50 | 3.50 |

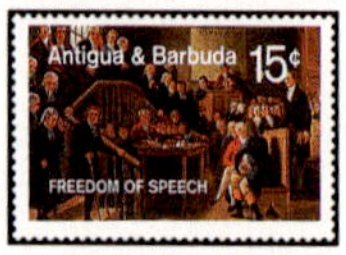


US Constitution Bicent. — A180

Designs: 15c, Virginia House of Burgesses exercising right of freedom of speech. 45c, Connecticut state seal. 60c, Delaware state seal. $4, Gouverneur Morris (1752-1816), principal writer of the Constitution, vert. $5, Roger Sherman (1721-1793), jurist and statesman, vert.

**1987, Nov. 16** **Litho.** ***Perf. 14***

| | | | | |
|---|---|---|---|---|
| **1058** | A180 | 15c multicolored | .25 | .25 |
| **1059** | A180 | 45c multicolored | .25 | .25 |
| **1060** | A180 | 60c multicolored | .30 | .30 |
| **1061** | A180 | $4 multicolored | 2.25 | 2.25 |
| | | *Nos. 1058-1061 (4)* | 3.05 | 3.05 |

**Souvenir Sheet**

| | | | | |
|---|---|---|---|---|
| **1062** | A180 | $5 multicolored | 3.25 | 3.25 |

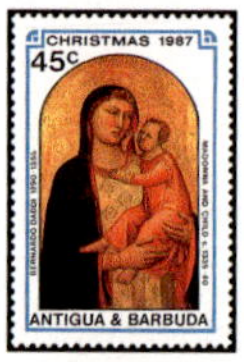


A181

Christmas (Paintings): 45c, Madonna and Child, by Bernardo Daddi (1290-1355). 60c, Joseph, detail from The Nativity, by Sano Di Pietro (1406-1481). $1, Mary, detail from Di Pietro's The Nativity. $4, Music-making Angel, by Melozzo Da Forli (1438-1494). $5, The Flight into Egypt, by Di Pietro.

**1987, Dec. 1**

| | | | | |
|---|---|---|---|---|
| **1063** | A181 | 45c multicolored | .35 | .25 |
| **1064** | A181 | 60c multicolored | .45 | .35 |
| **1065** | A181 | $1 multicolored | .75 | .55 |
| **1066** | A181 | $4 multicolored | 2.00 | *3.25* |
| | | *Nos. 1063-1066 (4)* | 3.55 | *4.40* |

**Souvenir Sheet**

| | | | | |
|---|---|---|---|---|
| **1067** | A181 | $5 multicolored | 3.00 | 3.00 |

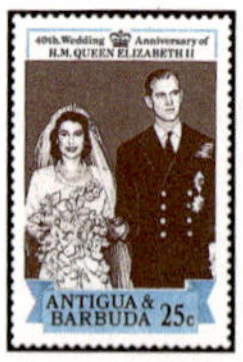


A182

No. 1068, Wedding portrait. No. 1069, Elizabeth II, c. 1970. No. 1070, Christening of Charles, 1948. No. 1071, Elizabeth II, c. 1980.
No. 1072, Royal family, c. 1951.

**1988, Feb. 8** **Litho.** ***Perf. 14***

| | | | | |
|---|---|---|---|---|
| **1068** | A182 | 25c multi | .25 | .25 |
| **1069** | A182 | 60c multi | .50 | .40 |
| **1070** | A182 | $2 multi | 1.10 | 1.10 |
| **1071** | A182 | $3 multi | 1.60 | 1.60 |
| | | *Nos. 1068-1071 (4)* | 3.45 | 3.35 |

**Souvenir Sheet**

| | | | | |
|---|---|---|---|---|
| **1072** | A182 | $5 multi | 2.75 | 2.75 |

40th wedding anniv. of Queen Elizabeth II and Prince Philip.

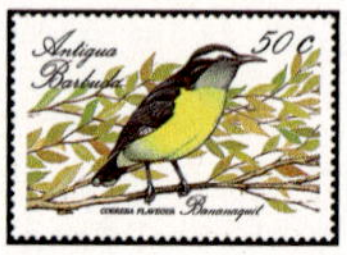


Tropical Birds — A183

10c, Great blue heron, vert. 15c, Ringed kingfisher. 50c, Bananaquit. 60c, Purple gallinule. 70c, Blue-hooded euphonia. $1, Caribbean parakeet, vert. $3, Troupial. $4, Hummingbird. No. 1081, Roseate flamingo, vert. No. 1082, Brown pelicans, vert.

**1988, Mar. 1**

| | | | | |
|---|---|---|---|---|
| **1073** | A183 | 10c multicolored | .55 | .40 |
| **1074** | A183 | 15c multicolored | .60 | .40 |
| **1075** | A183 | 50c multicolored | 1.10 | .50 |
| **1076** | A183 | 60c multicolored | 1.10 | .50 |
| **1077** | A183 | 70c multicolored | 1.25 | .55 |
| **1078** | A183 | $1 multicolored | 1.50 | .70 |
| **1079** | A183 | $3 multicolored | 3.00 | *3.50* |
| **1080** | A183 | $4 multicolored | 3.00 | *3.50* |
| | | *Nos. 1073-1080 (8)* | 12.10 | 10.05 |

**Souvenir Sheets**

| | | | | |
|---|---|---|---|---|
| **1081** | A183 | $5 multicolored | 4.50 | 4.50 |
| **1082** | A183 | $5 multicolored | 4.50 | 4.50 |

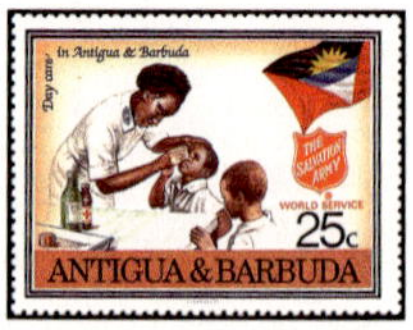


Salvation Army A184

25c, Day-care, Antigua. 30c, Penicillin inoculation, Indonesia. 40c, Day-care Center, Bolivia. 45c, Rehabilitation, India. 50c, Training the blind, Kenya. 60c, Infant care, Ghana. $1, Job training, Zambia. $2, Food distribution, Sri Lanka.
$5, General Eva Burrows.

**1988, Mar. 7**

| | | | | |
|---|---|---|---|---|
| **1083** | A184 | 25c multicolored | .80 | .45 |
| **1084** | A184 | 30c multicolored | .80 | .45 |
| **1085** | A184 | 40c multicolored | .90 | .55 |
| **1086** | A184 | 45c multicolored | .90 | .55 |
| **1087** | A184 | 50c multicolored | 1.10 | 1.10 |
| **1088** | A184 | 60c multicolored | 1.25 | 1.25 |
| **1089** | A184 | $1 multicolored | 1.50 | 1.75 |
| **1090** | A184 | $2 multicolored | 2.25 | *3.25* |
| | | *Nos. 1083-1090 (8)* | 9.50 | *9.35* |

**Souvenir Sheet**

| | | | | |
|---|---|---|---|---|
| **1091** | A184 | $5 multicolored | 5.00 | 5.00 |

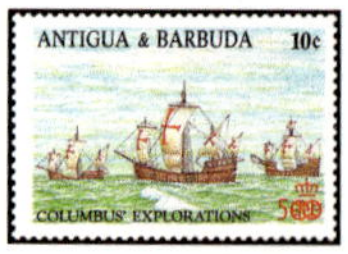


A185

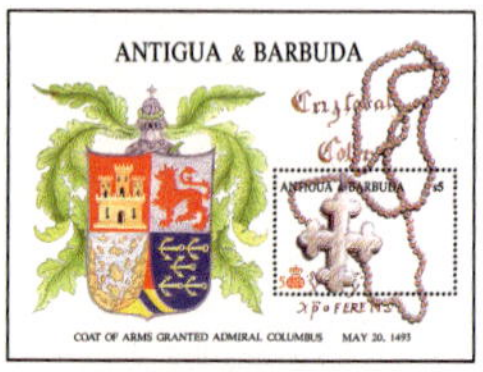


Discovery of America, 500th Anniv. (in 1992) — A186

Anniv. emblem and: 10c, Fleet. 30c, View of fleet in harbor from Paino Indian village. 45c, Caravel anchored in harbor, Paino village. 60c, Columbus, 3 Indians in canoe. 90c, Indian, parrot, Columbus. $1, Columbus in longboat. $3, Spanish guard, fleet in harbor. $4, Ships under full sail. No. 1100, Stone cross given to Columbus by Queen Isabella. No. 1101, Gold excelente.

**1988, Mar. 14** **Litho.** ***Perf. 14***

| | | | | |
|---|---|---|---|---|
| **1092** | A185 | 10c multicolored | .75 | .35 |
| **1093** | A185 | 30c multicolored | .75 | .40 |
| **1094** | A185 | 45c multicolored | .85 | .40 |
| **1095** | A185 | 60c multicolored | .85 | .40 |
| **1096** | A185 | 90c multicolored | 1.50 | .90 |
| **1097** | A185 | $1 multicolored | 1.50 | .90 |
| **1098** | A185 | $3 multicolored | 2.50 | *3.25* |
| **1099** | A185 | $4 multicolored | 2.75 | *3.25* |
| | | *Nos. 1092-1099 (8)* | 11.45 | 9.85 |

**Souvenir Sheets**

| | | | | |
|---|---|---|---|---|
| **1100** | A186 | $5 multicolored | 4.50 | 4.50 |
| **1101** | A186 | $5 multicolored | 4.50 | 4.50 |

ANTIGUA 531

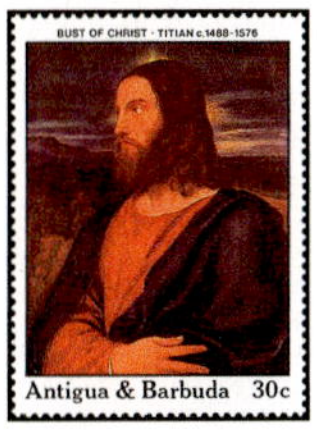

Paintings by Titian — A187

Details: 30c, Bust of Christ. 40c, Scourging of Christ. 45c, Madonna in Glory with Saints. 50c, The Averoldi Polyptych. $1, Christ Crowned with Thorns. $2, Christ Mocked. $3, Christ and Simon of Cyrene. $4, Crucifixion with Virgin and Saints. No. 1110, Ecce Homo. No. 1111, Noli Me Tangere.

**1988, Apr. 11 Litho. *Perf. 13½x14***

| | | | | | |
|---|---|---|---|---|---|
| **1102** | A187 | 30c | shown | .45 | .25 |
| **1103** | A187 | 40c | multicolored | .55 | .30 |
| **1104** | A187 | 45c | multicolored | .55 | .30 |
| **1105** | A187 | 50c | multicolored | .55 | .45 |
| **1106** | A187 | $1 | multicolored | .85 | .65 |
| **1107** | A187 | $2 | multicolored | 1.05 | *1.25* |
| **1108** | A187 | $3 | multicolored | 1.75 | *2.00* |
| **1109** | A187 | $4 | multicolored | 2.10 | *2.75* |
| | | | *Nos. 1102-1109 (8)* | 7.85 | *7.95* |

**Souvenir Sheets**

| | | | | | |
|---|---|---|---|---|---|
| **1110** | A187 | $5 | multicolored | 3.75 | 3.75 |
| **1111** | A187 | $5 | multicolored | 3.75 | 3.75 |

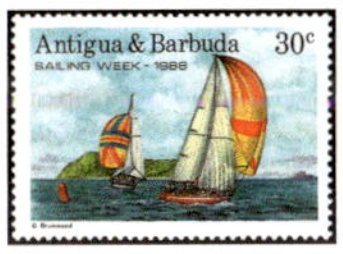

Sailing Week — A188

30c, Canada I, 1980. 60c, Gretel II, Australia, 1970. $1, Sceptre, GB, 1958. $3, Vigilant, US, 1893.
$5, Australia II, 1983.

**1988, Apr. 18 *Perf. 15***

| | | | | | |
|---|---|---|---|---|---|
| **1112** | A188 | 30c | multicolored | .25 | .25 |
| **1113** | A188 | 60c | multicolored | .45 | .45 |
| **1114** | A188 | $1 | multicolored | .60 | .60 |
| **1115** | A188 | $3 | multicolored | 1.25 | *2.25* |
| | | | *Nos. 1112-1115 (4)* | 2.55 | *3.55* |

**Souvenir Sheet**

| | | | | | |
|---|---|---|---|---|---|
| **1116** | A188 | $5 | multicolored | 2.75 | *3.25* |

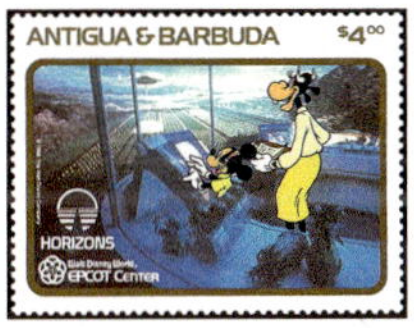

Walt Disney Animated Characters and Epcot Center, Walt Disney World A189

25c, The Living Seas. 30c, World of Motion. 40c, Spaceship Earth. 60c, Universe of Energy. 70c, Journey to Imagination. $1.50, The Land. $3, Communicore. $4, Horizons.
No. 1125, Epcot Center. No. 1126, The Contemporary Resort Hotel.

**1988, May 3 *Perf. 14x13½, 13½x14***

| | | | | | |
|---|---|---|---|---|---|
| **1116A** | A189 | 1c | like 25c | .25 | .25 |
| **1116B** | A189 | 2c | like 30c | .25 | .25 |
| **1116C** | A189 | 3c | like 40c | .25 | .25 |
| **1116D** | A189 | 4c | like 60c | .25 | .25 |
| **1116E** | A189 | 5c | like 70c | .25 | .25 |
| **1116F** | A189 | 10c | like $1.50 | .25 | .25 |
| **1117** | A189 | 25c | multi | .45 | .25 |
| **1118** | A189 | 30c | multi | .45 | .25 |
| **1119** | A189 | 40c | multi | .55 | .25 |
| **1120** | A189 | 60c | multi | .75 | .35 |
| **1121** | A189 | 70c | multi | .85 | .40 |
| **1122** | A189 | $1.50 | multi | 1.60 | 1.60 |
| **1123** | A189 | $3 | multi | 2.25 | *2.75* |
| **1124** | A189 | $4 | multi | 2.25 | *2.75* |
| | | | *Nos. 1116A-1124 (14)* | 10.65 | 10.10 |

**Souvenir Sheets**

| | | | | | |
|---|---|---|---|---|---|
| **1125** | A189 | $5 | multi | 4.00 | 4.00 |
| **1126** | A189 | $5 | multi | 4.00 | 4.00 |

30c, 40c, $1.50, $3 and No. 1126 are vert.

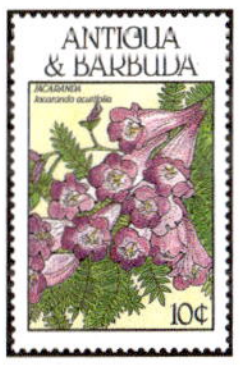

Flowering Trees — A190

**1988, May 16 *Perf. 14***

| | | | | | |
|---|---|---|---|---|---|
| **1127** | A190 | 10c | Jacaranda | .30 | .25 |
| **1128** | A190 | 30c | Cordia | .30 | .25 |
| **1129** | A190 | 50c | Orchid tree | .45 | .40 |
| **1130** | A190 | 90c | Flamboyant | .55 | .50 |
| **1131** | A190 | $1 | African tulip tree | .65 | .60 |
| **1132** | A190 | $2 | Potato tree | 1.25 | *1.60* |
| **1133** | A190 | $3 | Crepe myrtle | 1.50 | *2.00* |
| **1134** | A190 | $4 | Pitch apple | 1.75 | *2.75* |
| | | | *Nos. 1127-1134 (8)* | 6.75 | *8.35* |

**Souvenir Sheets**

| | | | | | |
|---|---|---|---|---|---|
| **1135** | A190 | $5 | Cassia | 3.25 | *3.75* |
| **1136** | A190 | $5 | Chinaberry | 3.25 | *3.75* |

Nos. 1135-1136 are continuous designs.

**Nos. 1011-1012, 1014 and 1013 Ovptd. in Black for Philatelic Exhibitions**

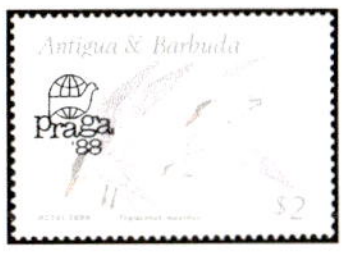

a

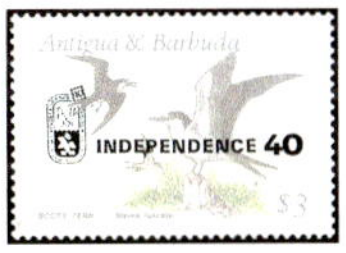

b

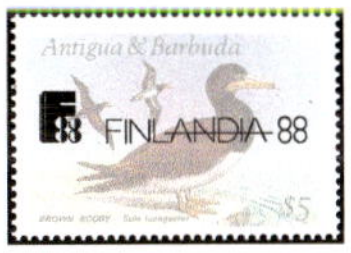

c

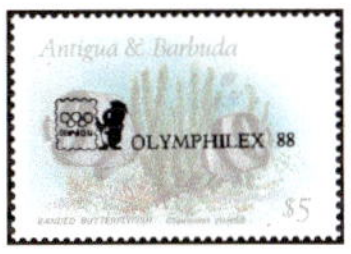

d

**1988, May 9 Litho. *Perf. 14***

| | | | | | |
|---|---|---|---|---|---|
| **1137** | A173 (a) | $2 | multi | 8.00 | 8.00 |
| **1138** | A173 (b) | $3 | multi | 8.50 | 8.50 |

**Souvenir Sheets**

| | | | | | |
|---|---|---|---|---|---|
| **1139** | A173 (c) | $5 | multi | 14.00 | 14.00 |
| **1139A** | A172 (d) | $5 | multi | 14.00 | 14.00 |

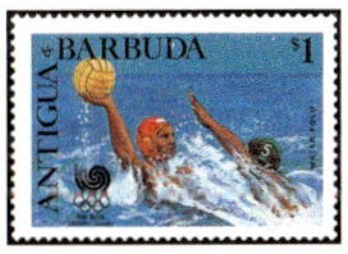

1988 Summer Olympics, Seoul — A192

40c, Gymnastic rings, vert. 60c, Weight lifting, vert. $1, Water polo. $3, Boxing.
$5, Torch-bearer, vert.

**1988, June 10**

| | | | | | |
|---|---|---|---|---|---|
| **1140** | A192 | 40c | multicolored | .35 | .30 |
| **1141** | A192 | 60c | multicolored | .40 | .30 |
| **1142** | A192 | $1 | multicolored | .80 | .45 |
| **1143** | A192 | $3 | multicolored | 1.60 | *2.25* |
| | | | *Nos. 1140-1143 (4)* | 3.15 | *3.30* |

**Souvenir Sheet**

| | | | | | |
|---|---|---|---|---|---|
| **1144** | A192 | $5 | multicolored | 3.50 | 3.50 |

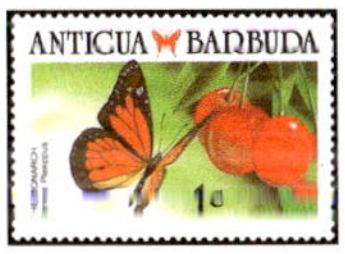

Butterflies A193

1c, Monarch. 2c, Jamaican clearwing. 3c, Yellow-barred ringlet. 5c, Cracker. 10c, Jamaican mestra. 15c, Mimic. 20c, Silver spot. 25c, Zebra. 30c, Fiery sulphur. 40c, Androgeus swallowtail. 45c, Giant brimstone. 50c, Orbed sulphur. 60c, Blue-backed skipper. $1, Common white skipper. $2, Baracoa skipper. $2.50, Mangrove skipper. $5, Silver king. $10, Pygmy skipper. $20, Parides lycimenes.

**1988-90 Litho. *Perf. 14***

| | | | | | |
|---|---|---|---|---|---|
| **1145** | A193 | 1c | multi | .50 | *1.10* |
| **1146** | A193 | 2c | multi | .65 | *1.10* |
| **1147** | A193 | 3c | multi | .65 | *1.10* |
| **1148** | A193 | 5c | multi | .80 | *1.10* |
| **1149** | A193 | 10c | multi | .95 | .35 |
| **1150** | A193 | 15c | multi | 1.25 | .35 |
| **1151** | A193 | 20c | multi | 1.40 | .35 |
| **1152** | A193 | 25c | multi | 1.40 | .35 |
| **1153** | A193 | 30c | multi | 1.40 | .35 |
| **1154** | A193 | 40c | multi | 1.40 | .35 |
| **1155** | A193 | 45c | multi | 1.40 | .35 |
| **1156** | A193 | 50c | multi | 1.50 | .45 |
| **1157** | A193 | 60c | multi | 1.60 | .60 |
| **1158** | A193 | $1 | multi | 2.00 | 1.00 |
| **1159** | A193 | $2 | multi | 3.00 | 3.50 |
| **1160** | A193 | $2.50 | multi | 4.00 | 4.75 |
| **1161** | A193 | $5 | multi | 5.00 | 7.00 |
| **1161A** | A193 | $10 | multi | 7.00 | *12.00* |
| **1162** | A193 | $20 | multi | 18.00 | *21.00* |
| | | | *Nos. 1145-1162 (19)* | 53.90 | *57.15* |

Issued: $20, Feb. 19, 1990; others, Aug. 29.

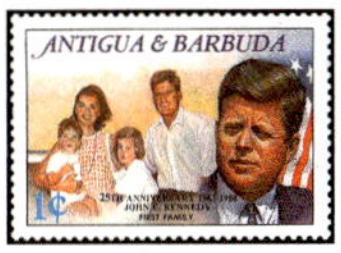

John F. Kennedy — A194

30c, First family. 60c, Motorcade, Mexico. $1, Funeral procession. $4, Aboard PT109.
$5, Taking Oath of Office.

**1988, Nov. 22 Litho. *Perf. 14***

| | | | | | |
|---|---|---|---|---|---|
| **1162A** | A194 | 1c | like 30c | .25 | .25 |
| **1162B** | A194 | 2c | like $4 | .25 | .25 |
| **1162C** | A194 | 3c | like $1 | .25 | .25 |
| **1162D** | A194 | 4c | like 60c | .25 | .25 |
| **1163** | A194 | 30c | multi | .35 | .25 |
| **1164** | A194 | 60c | multi | .70 | .40 |
| **1165** | A194 | $1 | multi | .75 | .75 |
| **1166** | A194 | $4 | multi | 2.25 | *3.25* |
| | | | *Nos. 1162A-1166 (8)* | 5.05 | *5.65* |

**Souvenir Sheet**

| | | | | | |
|---|---|---|---|---|---|
| **1167** | A194 | $5 | multi | 3.75 | 3.75 |

Miniature Sheet

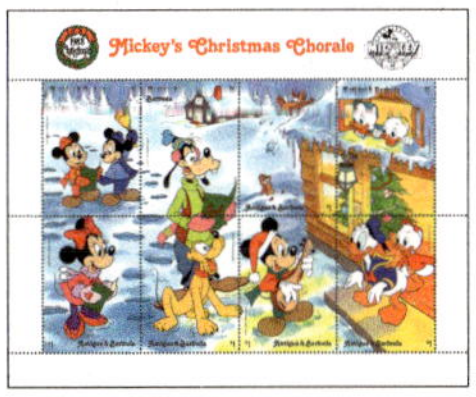

Christmas, Mickey Mouse 60th Anniv. — A195

Walt Disney characters: No. 1168: a, Morty and Ferdie. b, Goofy. c, Chip-n-Dale. d, Huey and Dewey. e, Minnie Mouse. f, Pluto. g, Mickey Mouse. h, Donald Duck and Louie.
No. 1169, Goofy driving Mickey and Minnie in a horse-drawn carriage. No. 1170, Characters on roller skates, caroling.

**1988, Dec. 1 *Perf. 13½x14, 14x13½***

| | | | | | |
|---|---|---|---|---|---|
| **1168** | A195 | | Sheet of 8 | 9.00 | 9.00 |
| *a.-h.* | | $1 | any single | .95 | .95 |

**Souvenir Sheets**

| | | | | | |
|---|---|---|---|---|---|
| **1169** | A195 | $7 | multicolored | 5.25 | 5.25 |
| **1170** | A195 | $7 | multi, horiz. | 5.25 | 5.25 |

**1988, Dec. 1 Litho. *Perf. 14***

| | | | | | |
|---|---|---|---|---|---|
| **1171** | A195 | 10c | like No. 1168e | .25 | .25 |
| **1172** | A195 | 25c | like No. 1168f | .25 | .25 |
| **1173** | A195 | 30c | like No. 1168g | .30 | .30 |
| **1174** | A195 | 70c | like No. 1168h | .60 | .60 |
| | | | *Nos. 1171-1174 (4)* | 1.40 | 1.40 |

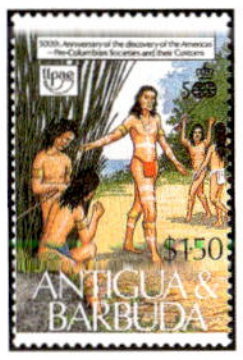

Arawak Indian Whip Dance — A196

UPAE and discovery of America emblems and: a, Five adults. b, Eight adults. c, Seven adults. d, Three adults, three children.

**1989, May 16 Litho. *Perf. 14***

| | | | | | |
|---|---|---|---|---|---|
| **1175** | | | Strip of 4 | 5.00 | 5.00 |
| *a.-d.* | A196 | $1.50 | any single | .90 | .90 |

**Souvenir Sheet**

| | | | | | |
|---|---|---|---|---|---|
| **1176** | A196 | $6 | Arawak chief | 4.00 | 4.00 |

Discovery of America 500th anniv. (in 1992), pre-Columbian societies and customs.

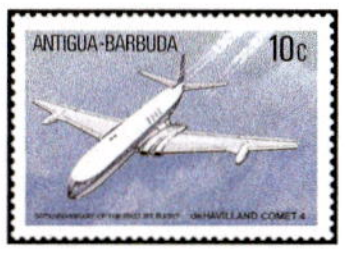

Jet Flight, 50th Anniv. — A197

Various jet aircraft: 10c, DeHavilland Comet 4. 30c, Messerschmitt Me262. 40c, Boeing 707. 60c, Canadair F-86 Sabre. $1, Lockheed F-104 Starfighter. $2, McDonnell Douglas DC-10. $3, Boeing 747. $4, McDonnell F-4 Phantom.
No. 1185, Grumman F-14 Tomcat. No. 1186, Concorde.

**1989, May 29 Litho. *Perf. 14x13½***

| | | | | | |
|---|---|---|---|---|---|
| **1177** | A197 | 10c | multicolored | 1.10 | .35 |
| **1178** | A197 | 30c | multicolored | 1.60 | .35 |
| **1179** | A197 | 40c | multicolored | 1.60 | .35 |
| **1180** | A197 | 60c | multicolored | 1.90 | .50 |
| **1181** | A197 | $1 | multicolored | 2.10 | .75 |
| **1182** | A197 | $2 | multicolored | 3.00 | 2.75 |
| **1183** | A197 | $3 | multicolored | 3.25 | *4.25* |
| **1184** | A197 | $4 | multicolored | 3.25 | *4.25* |
| | | | *Nos. 1177-1184 (8)* | 17.80 | *13.55* |

**Souvenir Sheets**

| | | | | | |
|---|---|---|---|---|---|
| **1185** | A197 | $7 | multicolored | 6.00 | *7.00* |
| **1186** | A197 | $7 | multicolored | 6.00 | *7.00* |

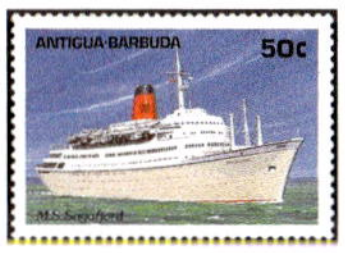

Caribbean Cruise Ships — A198

25c, TSS Festivale. 45c, M.S. Southward. 50c, M.S. Sagafjord. 60c, MTS Daphne. 75c, M.V. Cunard Countess. 90c, M.S. Song of America. $3, M.S. Island Princess. $4, S.S. Galileo.
No. 1195, S.S. Norway. No. 1196, S.S. Oceanic.

**1989, June 20 Litho. *Perf. 14***

| | | | | | |
|---|---|---|---|---|---|
| **1187** | A198 | 25c | multi | 1.30 | .35 |
| **1188** | A198 | 45c | multi | 1.50 | .35 |
| **1189** | A198 | 50c | multi | 1.50 | .35 |
| **1190** | A198 | 60c | multi | 1.50 | .40 |
| **1191** | A198 | 75c | multi | 1.75 | 1.00 |
| **1192** | A198 | 90c | multi | 2.00 | 1.10 |
| **1193** | A198 | $3 | multi | 4.00 | *5.50* |
| **1194** | A198 | $4 | multi | 4.00 | *6.00* |
| | | | *Nos. 1187-1194 (8)* | 17.55 | 15.05 |

**Souvenir Sheets**

| | | | | | |
|---|---|---|---|---|---|
| **1195** | A198 | $6 | multi | 4.50 | *5.50* |
| **1196** | A198 | $6 | multi | 4.50 | *5.50* |

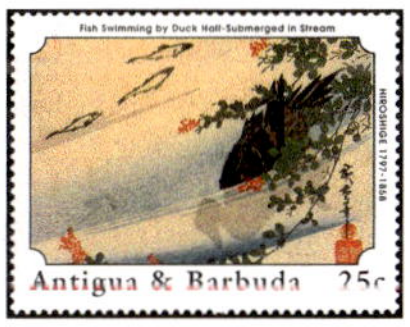

Paintings by Hiroshige A199

Designs: 25c, *Fish Swimming by Duck Half-submerged in Stream.* 45c, *Crane and Wave.* 50c, *Sparrows and Morning Glories.* 60c, *Crested Blackbird and Flowering Cherry.* $1, *Great Knot Sitting among Water Grass.* $2, *Goose on a Bank of Water.* $3, *Black Paradise Flycatcher and Blossoms.* $4, *Sleepy Owl Perched on a Pine Branch.* No. 1205, *Bullfinch Flying Near a Clematis Branch.* No. 1206, *Titmouse on a Cherry Branch.*

**1989, July 3 *Perf. 14x13½***

| | | | | | |
|---|---|---|---|---|---|
| **1197** | A199 | 25c | multicolored | .90 | .30 |
| **1198** | A199 | 45c | multicolored | 1.10 | .40 |
| **1199** | A199 | 50c | multicolored | 1.25 | .40 |
| **1200** | A199 | 60c | multicolored | 1.25 | .50 |
| **1201** | A199 | $1 | multicolored | 1.60 | .65 |
| **1202** | A199 | $2 | multicolored | 2.50 | 2.50 |
| **1203** | A199 | $3 | multicolored | 3.00 | 3.00 |
| **1204** | A199 | $4 | multicolored | 3.00 | 3.00 |
| | | | *Nos. 1197-1204 (8)* | 14.60 | 10.75 |

**Souvenir Sheets**

| | | | | | |
|---|---|---|---|---|---|
| **1205** | A199 | $5 | multicolored | 6.00 | 6.00 |
| **1206** | A199 | $5 | multicolored | 6.00 | 6.00 |

Hirohito (1901-1989) and enthronement of Akihito as emperor of Japan.

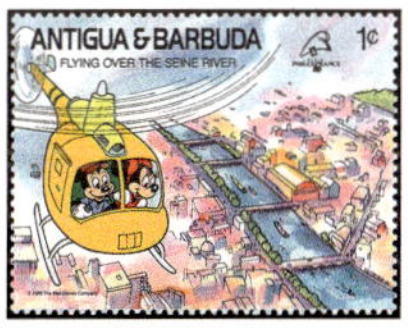

PHILEXFRANCE '89 — A200

532 ANTIGUA

Walt Disney characters, French landmarks: 1c, Helicopter over the Seine. 2c, Arc de Triomphe. 3c, Painting Notre Dame Cathedral. 4c, Entrance to the Metro. 5c, Fashion show. 10c, Follies. No. 1213, Shopping stalls on the Seine. $6, Sidewalk cafe, Left Bank. No. 1215, Hot air balloon *Ear Force One*. No. 1216, Dining.

**1989, July 7** ***Perf. 14x13½***

| | | | | |
|---|---|---|---|---|
| **1207** | A200 | 1c multicolored | .25 | .25 |
| **1208** | A200 | 2c multicolored | .25 | .25 |
| **1209** | A200 | 3c multicolored | .25 | .25 |
| **1210** | A200 | 4c multicolored | .25 | .25 |
| **1211** | A200 | 5c multicolored | .25 | .25 |
| **1212** | A200 | 10c multicolored | .25 | .25 |
| **1213** | A200 | $5 multicolored | 7.50 | 7.50 |
| **1214** | A200 | $6 multicolored | 7.50 | 7.50 |
| | | *Nos. 1207-1214 (8)* | 16.50 | 16.50 |

**Souvenir Sheets**

| | | | | |
|---|---|---|---|---|
| **1215** | A200 | $5 multicolored | 6.25 | 6.25 |
| **1216** | A200 | $5 multicolored | 6.25 | 6.25 |

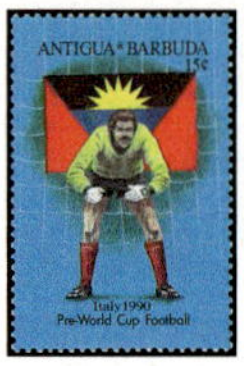

1990 World Cup Soccer Championships, Italy — A201

Natl. flag, various actions of a defending goalie.

**1989, Aug. 21** ***Perf. 14***

| | | | | |
|---|---|---|---|---|
| **1217** | A201 | 15c multicolored | .75 | .25 |
| **1218** | A201 | 25c multicolored | .80 | .25 |
| **1219** | A201 | $1 multicolored | 1.25 | 1.00 |
| **1220** | A201 | $4 multicolored | 2.50 | *4.75* |
| | | *Nos. 1217-1220 (4)* | 5.30 | *6.25* |

**Souvenir Sheets**

| | | | | |
|---|---|---|---|---|
| **1221** | A201 | $5 2 players, horiz. | 3.75 | *4.25* |
| **1222** | A201 | $5 3 players, horiz. | 3.75 | *4.25* |

For overprints see Nos. 1344-1349.

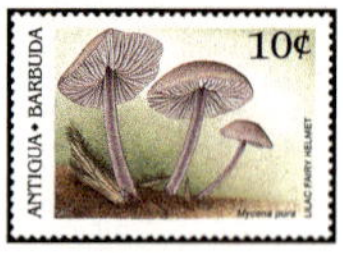

Mushrooms A202

10c, Lilac fairy helmet. 25c, Rough psathyrella, vert. 50c, Golden tops. 60c, Blue cap, vert. 75c, Brown cap, vert. $1, Green gill, vert. $3, Red pinwheel. $4, Red chanterelle.

No. 1231, Slender stalk. No. 1232, Paddy straw mushroom.

**1989, Oct. 12** **Litho.** ***Perf. 14***

| | | | | |
|---|---|---|---|---|
| **1223** | A202 | 10c multi | .75 | .35 |
| **1224** | A202 | 25c multi | 1.05 | .30 |
| **1225** | A202 | 50c multi | 1.50 | .50 |
| **1226** | A202 | 60c multi | 1.50 | .60 |
| **1227** | A202 | 75c multi | 1.75 | 1.10 |
| **1228** | A202 | $1 multi | 1.75 | 1.25 |
| **1229** | A202 | $3 multi | 2.75 | *3.75* |
| **1230** | A202 | $4 multi | 2.75 | *3.75* |
| | | *Nos. 1223-1230 (8)* | 13.80 | 11.60 |

**Souvenir Sheets**

| | | | | |
|---|---|---|---|---|
| **1231** | A202 | $6 multi | 8.50 | 8.50 |
| **1232** | A202 | $6 multi | 8.50 | 8.50 |

Nos. 1224, 1226-1228, 1231 vert.

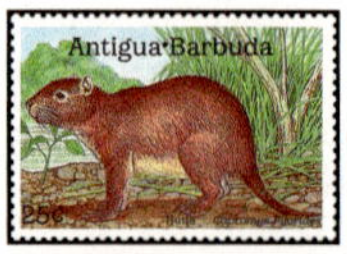

Wildlife — A203

25c, Hutia. 45c, Caribbean monk seal. 60c, Mustache bat, vert. $4, Manatee, vert.

$5, West Indies giant rice rat.

**1989, Oct. 19** **Litho.** ***Perf. 14***

| | | | | |
|---|---|---|---|---|
| **1233** | A203 | 25c multi | .80 | .35 |
| **1234** | A203 | 45c multi | 2.25 | .75 |
| **1235** | A203 | 60c multi | 1.50 | .75 |
| **1236** | A203 | $4 multi | 3.25 | *5.25* |
| | | *Nos. 1233-1236 (4)* | 7.80 | *7.10* |

**Souvenir Sheet**

| | | | | |
|---|---|---|---|---|
| **1237** | A203 | $5 multi | 8.50 | *9.00* |

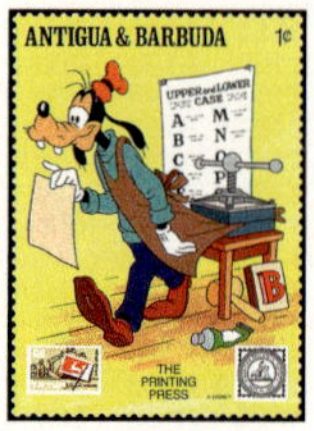

American Philatelic Soc. Emblem, Stamps on Stamps and Walt Disney Characters Promoting Philately — A204

Designs: 1c, Israel #150, printing press. 2c, Italy #1238, first day cancel. 3c, US #143L4, Pony Express recruits. 4c, Denmark #566, early radio broadcast. 5c, German Democratic Republic #702, television. 10c, Great Britain #1, stamp collector. $4, Japan #1414, integrated circuits. $6, Germany #B667, boom box. No. 1246, US #1355, C3a, and Jenny biplane over Disneyland, horiz. No. 1247, US #940, 1421 and stamps for the wounded.

**1989, Nov. 2** ***Perf. 13½x14, 14x13½***

| | | | | |
|---|---|---|---|---|
| **1238** | A204 | 1c multicolored | .25 | .25 |
| **1239** | A204 | 2c multicolored | .25 | .25 |
| **1240** | A204 | 3c multicolored | .25 | .25 |
| **1241** | A204 | 4c multicolored | .25 | .25 |
| **1242** | A204 | 5c multicolored | .25 | .25 |
| **1243** | A204 | 10c multicolored | .25 | .25 |
| **1244** | A204 | $4 multicolored | 4.00 | *5.50* |
| **1245** | A204 | $6 multicolored | 5.00 | *6.50* |
| | | *Nos. 1238-1245 (8)* | 10.50 | *13.50* |

**Souvenir Sheets**

| | | | | |
|---|---|---|---|---|
| **1246** | A204 | $5 multicolored | 5.50 | *6.50* |
| **1247** | A204 | $5 multicolored | 5.50 | *6.50* |

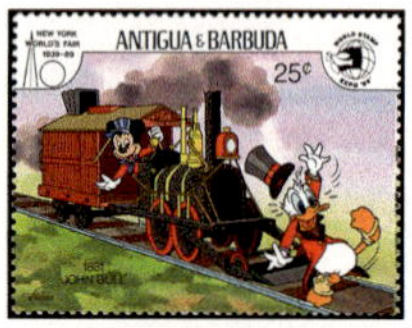

Locomotives and Walt Disney Characters A205

25c, John Bull, 1831. 45c, Atlantic, 1832. 50c, William Crook's, 1861. 60c, Minnetonka, 1869. $1, Thatcher Perkins, 1863. $2, Pioneer, 1848. $3, Peppersass, 1869. $4, Gimbels Flyer.

No. 1256, #6100 Class S-1 & 1835 Thomas Jefferson. No. 1257, Jupiter & #119.

***Perf. 14x13½, 13½x14***

**1989, Nov. 17**

| | | | | |
|---|---|---|---|---|
| **1248** | A205 | 25c multi | .85 | .40 |
| **1249** | A205 | 45c multi | .95 | .40 |
| **1250** | A205 | 50c multi | .95 | .40 |
| **1251** | A205 | 60c multi | .95 | .60 |
| **1252** | A205 | $1 multi | 1.20 | .75 |
| **1253** | A205 | $2 multi | 1.75 | 2.25 |
| **1254** | A205 | $3 multi | 2.25 | *3.75* |
| **1255** | A205 | $4 multicolored | 2.40 | *3.75* |
| | | *Nos. 1248-1255 (8)* | 11.30 | 12.30 |

**Souvenir Sheets**

| | | | | |
|---|---|---|---|---|
| **1256** | A205 | $6 multi | 12.00 | 12.00 |
| **1257** | A205 | $6 multi | 12.00 | 12.00 |

New York World's Fair, 50th anniv., and World Stamp Expo '89, Washington, DC.

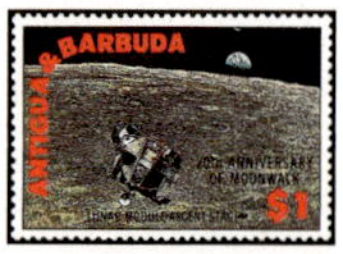

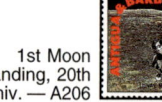

1st Moon Landing, 20th Anniv. — A206

10c, Apollo 11 liftoff. 45c, Aldrin walking on Moon. $1, Eagle ascending from Moon. $4, Recovery after splashdown.

$5, Armstrong.

**1989, Nov. 24** **Litho.** ***Perf. 14***

| | | | | |
|---|---|---|---|---|
| **1258** | A206 | 10c multicolored | .55 | .25 |
| **1259** | A206 | 45c multicolored | 1.40 | .25 |
| **1260** | A206 | $1 multicolored | 1.60 | .85 |
| **1261** | A206 | $4 multicolored | 2.50 | *4.50* |
| | | *Nos. 1258-1261 (4)* | 6.05 | *5.85* |

**Souvenir Sheet**

| | | | | |
|---|---|---|---|---|
| **1262** | A206 | $5 multicolored | 5.50 | 5.50 |

Nos. 1258-1259 and 1262, vert.

Souvenir Sheet

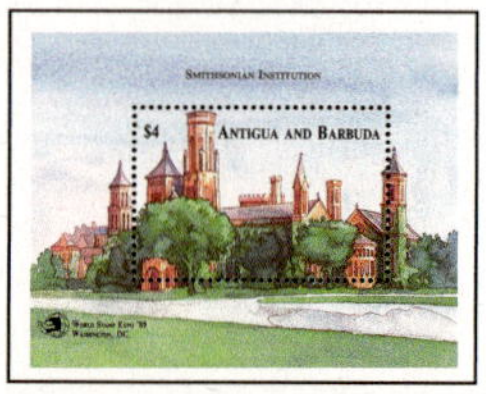

Smithsonian Institution, Washington, DC — A207

**1989, Nov. 17** **Litho.** ***Perf. 14***

| | | | | |
|---|---|---|---|---|
| **1263** | A207 | $4 multicolored | 3.00 | 3.00 |

World Stamp Expo '89.

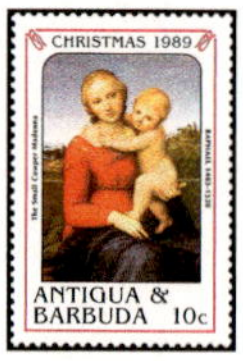

Christmas — A208

Religious paintings: 10c, *The Small Cowper Madonna*. 25c, *Madonna of the Goldfinch*. 30c, *The Alba Madonna*. 50c, *Bologna Altarpiece* (attendant). 60c, *Bologna Altarpiece* (heralding angel). 70c, *Bologna Altarpiece* (archangel). $4, *Bologna Altarpiece* (saint holding ledger). No. 1271, *Madonna of Foligno*. No. 1272, *The Marriage of the Virgin*. No. 1273, *Bologna Altarpiece* (Madonna and Child).

*Bologna Altarpiece* by Giotto. Other paintings by Raphael.

**1989, Dec. 11** **Litho.** ***Perf. 14***

| | | | | |
|---|---|---|---|---|
| **1264** | A208 | 10c multicolored | .35 | .25 |
| **1265** | A208 | 25c multicolored | .45 | .25 |
| **1266** | A208 | 30c multicolored | .45 | .25 |
| **1267** | A208 | 50c multicolored | .70 | .40 |
| **1268** | A208 | 60c multicolored | .75 | .45 |
| **1269** | A208 | 70c multicolored | .85 | .50 |
| **1270** | A208 | $4 multicolored | 2.75 | *4.25* |
| **1271** | A208 | $5 multicolored | 2.75 | *4.25* |
| | | *Nos. 1264-1271 (8)* | 9.05 | *10.60* |

**Souvenir Sheets**

| | | | | |
|---|---|---|---|---|
| **1272** | A208 | $5 multicolored | 5.00 | *6.00* |
| **1273** | A208 | $5 multicolored | 5.00 | *6.00* |

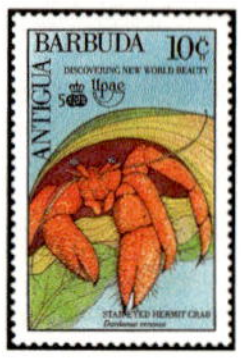

America Issue — A210

UPAE, discovery of America 500th anniv. emblems and marine life: 10c, Star-eyed hermit crab. 20c, Spiny lobster. 25c, Magnificent banded fanworm. 45c, Cannonball jellyfish. 60c, Red-spiny sea star. $2, Peppermint shrimp. $3, Coral crab. $4, Branching fire coral. No. 1283, Common sea fan. No. 1284, Portuguese man-of-war.

**1990, Mar. 26** **Litho.** ***Perf. 14***

| | | | | |
|---|---|---|---|---|
| **1275** | A210 | 10c multicolored | .50 | .25 |
| **1276** | A210 | 20c multicolored | .75 | .25 |
| **1277** | A210 | 25c multicolored | .80 | .25 |
| **1278** | A210 | 45c multicolored | .95 | .30 |
| **1279** | A210 | 60c multicolored | 1.10 | .50 |
| **1280** | A210 | $2 multicolored | 1.90 | 2.25 |
| **1281** | A210 | $3 multicolored | 2.10 | *3.50* |
| **1282** | A210 | $4 multicolored | 2.10 | *3.50* |
| | | *Nos. 1275-1282 (8)* | 10.20 | *10.80* |

**Souvenir Sheets**

| | | | | |
|---|---|---|---|---|
| **1283** | A210 | $5 multicolored | 4.25 | 4.25 |
| **1284** | A210 | $5 multicolored | 4.25 | 4.25 |

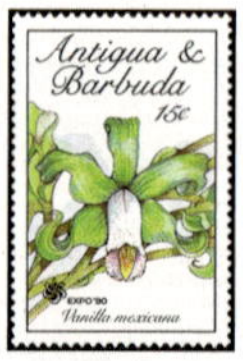

Orchids — A211

No. 1285, Vanilla mexicana. No. 1286, Epidendrum ibaguense. No. 1287, Epidendrum secundum. No. 1288, Maxillaria conferta. No. 1289, Oncidium altissimum. No. 1290, Spiranthes lanceolata. No. 1291, Tonopsis utricularioides. No. 1292, Epidendrum nocturnum.

No. 1293, Octomeria graminifolia. No. 1294, Rodriguezia lanceolata.

**1990, Apr. 17** ***Perf. 14***

| | | | | |
|---|---|---|---|---|
| **1285** | A211 | 15c multicolored | .80 | .35 |
| **1286** | A211 | 45c multicolored | 1.10 | .35 |
| **1287** | A211 | 50c multicolored | 1.25 | .40 |
| **1288** | A211 | 60c multicolored | 1.40 | .40 |
| **1289** | A211 | $1 multicolored | 1.50 | .85 |
| **1290** | A211 | $2 multicolored | 2.00 | 2.25 |
| **1291** | A211 | $3 multicolored | 2.25 | 3.25 |
| **1292** | A211 | $5 multicolored | 3.25 | *4.25* |
| | | *Nos. 1285-1292 (8)* | 13.55 | 12.10 |

**Souvenir Sheets**

| | | | | |
|---|---|---|---|---|
| **1293** | A211 | $6 multicolored | 4.00 | 4.00 |
| **1294** | A211 | $6 multicolored | 4.00 | 4.00 |

EXPO '90, Osaka.

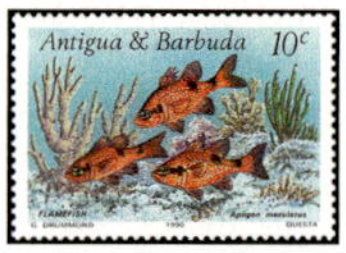

Fish — A212

10c, Flamefish. 15c, Coney. 50c, Squirrelfish. 60c, Sergeant major. $1, Yellowtail snapper. $2, Rock beauty. $3, Spanish hogfish. $4, Striped parrotfish.

No. 1303, Blackbar soldierfish. No. 1304, Foureye butterflyfish.

**1990, May 21** ***Perf. 14***

| | | | | |
|---|---|---|---|---|
| **1295** | A212 | 10c multicolored | .80 | .45 |
| **1296** | A212 | 15c multicolored | 1.10 | .45 |
| **1297** | A212 | 50c multicolored | 1.50 | .55 |
| **1298** | A212 | 60c multicolored | 1.60 | .55 |
| **1299** | A212 | $1 multicolored | 1.75 | .75 |
| **1300** | A212 | $2 multicolored | 2.50 | *2.75* |
| **1301** | A212 | $3 multicolored | 3.00 | *3.50* |
| **1302** | A212 | $4 multicolored | 3.25 | *3.50* |
| | | *Nos. 1295-1302 (8)* | 15.50 | *12.50* |

**Souvenir sheets**

| | | | | |
|---|---|---|---|---|
| **1303** | A212 | $5 multicolored | 5.50 | 5.50 |
| **1304** | A212 | $5 multicolored | 5.50 | 5.50 |

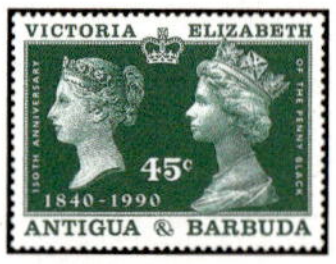

Victoria and Elizabeth II — A213

**1990, May 3** **Litho.** ***Perf. 15x14***

| | | | | |
|---|---|---|---|---|
| **1305** | A213 | 45c green | 1.00 | .30 |
| **1306** | A213 | 60c bright rose | 1.40 | .50 |
| **1307** | A213 | $5 bright ultra | 4.00 | *5.25* |
| | | *Nos. 1305-1307 (3)* | 6.40 | *6.05* |

**Souvenir Sheet**

| | | | | |
|---|---|---|---|---|
| **1308** | A213 | $6 black | 5.00 | *6.00* |

Penny Black, 150th anniv.

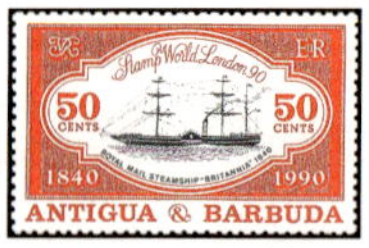

Royal Mail Transport A214

Designs: 50c, Steam packet *Britannia*, 1840. 75c, Railway mail car, 1892. $4, *Centaurus* seaplane, 1938. $6, Subway, 1927.

**1990, May 3** ***Perf. 13½***

| | | | | |
|---|---|---|---|---|
| **1309** | A214 | 50c red & deep green | 1.25 | .30 |
| **1310** | A214 | 75c red & vio brn | 1.50 | 1.00 |
| **1311** | A214 | $4 red & brt ultra | 4.00 | *5.25* |
| | | *Nos. 1309-1311 (3)* | 6.75 | 6.55 |

**Souvenir Sheet**

| | | | | |
|---|---|---|---|---|
| **1312** | A214 | $6 red & black | 5.50 | *6.25* |

Stamp World London '90.

Miniature Sheet

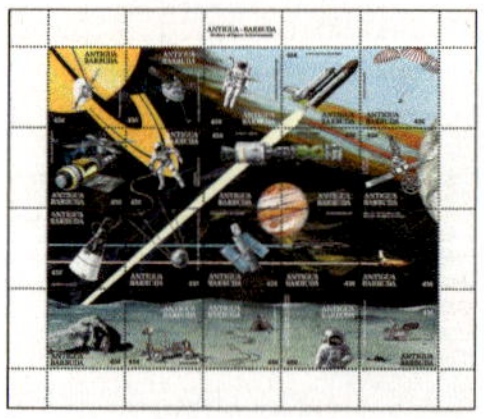

Space Achievements — A215

Designs: a, *Voyager 2* passing Saturn. b, *Pioneer 11* photographing Saturn. c, Manned maneuvering unit. d, *Columbia* space shuttle.

ANTIGUA 533

e, Splashdown of Apollo 10 command module. f, *Skylab*. g, Ed White space walking, Gemini 4 mission. h, Apollo module, Apollo-Soyuz mission. i, Soyuz module, Apollo-Soyuz mission. j, *Mariner 1* passing Venus. k, Gemini 4 module. l, *Sputnik*. m, Hubble Space Telescope. n, X-15 rocket plane. o, Bell X-1 breaking sound barrier. p, Astronaut, Apollo 17 mission. r, American lunar rover. r, Lunar module, Apollo 14 mission. s, First men on the Moon, Apollo 11 mission. t, Lunokhod, Soviet lunar rover.

**1990, June 11 Litho. *Perf. 14***

| | | | | |
|---|---|---|---|---|
| **1313** | A215 | Sheet of 20 | 16.00 | 16.00 |
| *a.-t.* | | 45c any single | .75 | .75 |

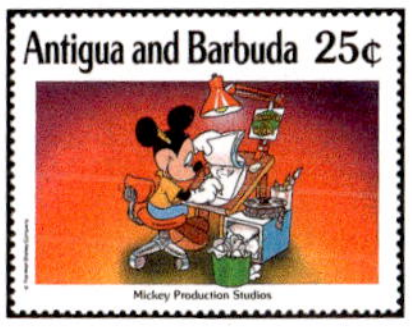


Mickey Production Studios
A216

Walt Disney characters in Hollywood: 45c, Minnie Mouse reading script. 50c, Director Mickey Mouse, take 1 of Minnie. 60c, Make-up artist Daisy Duck. $1, Clarabelle as Cleopatra. $2, Mickey, Goofy, Donald Duck. $3, Goofy destroying set. $4, Mickey, Donald editing film. No. 1322, Mickey directs surfing film. No. 1323, Minnie, Daisy, Clarabelle in musical.

**1990, Sept. 3 Litho. *Perf. 14x13½***

| | | | | | |
|---|---|---|---|---|---|
| **1314** | A216 | 25c | shown | .70 | .25 |
| **1315** | A216 | 45c | multicolored | .80 | .25 |
| **1316** | A216 | 50c | multicolored | .90 | .25 |
| **1317** | A216 | 60c | multicolored | 1.10 | .30 |
| **1318** | A216 | $1 | multicolored | 1.25 | .60 |
| **1319** | A216 | $2 | multicolored | 1.75 | 2.10 |
| **1320** | A216 | $3 | multicolored | 2.25 | 3.25 |
| **1321** | A216 | $4 | multicolored | 2.25 | 3.25 |
| | | *Nos. 1314-1321 (8)* | | 11.00 | 10.25 |

**Souvenir Sheets**

| | | | | | |
|---|---|---|---|---|---|
| **1322** | A216 | $5 | multicolored | 4.50 | 4.50 |
| **1323** | A216 | $5 | multicolored | 4.50 | 4.50 |

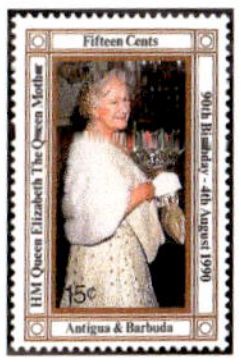


A217

**1990, Aug. 27 Litho. *Perf. 14***

| | | | | | |
|---|---|---|---|---|---|
| **1324** | A217 | 15c | multicolored | .40 | .25 |
| **1325** | A217 | 35c | multi, diff. | .65 | .25 |
| **1326** | A217 | 75c | multi, diff. | 1.10 | .65 |
| **1327** | A217 | $3 | multi, diff. | 2.00 | *3.00* |
| | | *Nos. 1324-1327 (4)* | | 4.15 | *4.15* |

**Souvenir Sheet**

| | | | | | |
|---|---|---|---|---|---|
| **1328** | A217 | $6 | multi, diff. | 5.00 | 5.00 |

Queen Mother, 90th birthday

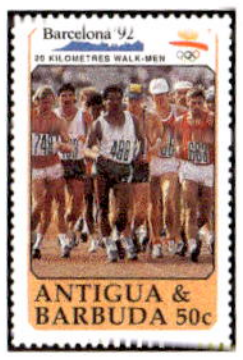


A218

No. 1329, 20-Kilometer Walk. No. 1330, Triple jump. No. 1331, 10,000 meter run. No. 1332, Javelin.
No. 1333, Opening ceremony, Los Angeles, 1984.

**1990, Oct. 1 Litho. *Perf. 14***

| | | | | | |
|---|---|---|---|---|---|
| **1329** | A218 | 50c | multicolored | .90 | .30 |
| **1330** | A218 | 75c | multicolored | 1.10 | .60 |
| **1331** | A218 | $1 | multicolored | 1.35 | .70 |
| **1332** | A218 | $5 | multicolored | 3.50 | *5.50* |
| | | *Nos. 1329-1332 (4)* | | 6.85 | *7.10* |

**Souvenir Sheet**

| | | | | | |
|---|---|---|---|---|---|
| **1333** | A218 | $6 | multicolored | 5.75 | *7.25* |

1992 Summer Olympics, Barcelona.

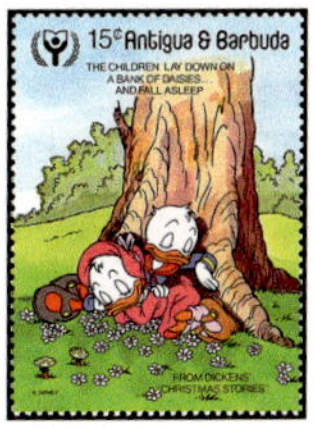


Intl. Literacy Year — A219

Walt Disney characters in scenes from books by Charles Dickens: 15c, Huey and Dewey, Christmas Stories. 45c, Donald Duck, Bleak House. 50c, Dewey, Bad Pete, Oliver Twist. 60c, Daisy Duck, Old Curiosity Shop. $1, Little Nell. $2, Scrooge McDuck, Pickwick Papers. $3, Mickey and Minnie Mouse, Dombey and Son. $5, Minnie, Our Mutual Friend. No. 1342, Mickey and friends, David Copperfield. No. 1343, Pinocchio, Oliver Twist.

**1990, Oct. 15 Litho. *Perf. 14***

| | | | | | |
|---|---|---|---|---|---|
| **1334** | A219 | 15c | multicolored | .75 | .25 |
| **1335** | A219 | 45c | multicolored | 1.00 | .35 |
| **1336** | A219 | 50c | multicolored | 1.10 | .40 |
| **1337** | A219 | 60c | multicolored | 1.25 | .45 |
| **1338** | A219 | $1 | multicolored | 1.40 | .70 |
| **1339** | A219 | $2 | multicolored | 2.00 | 2.25 |
| **1340** | A219 | $3 | multicolored | 2.25 | 3.25 |
| **1341** | A219 | $5 | multicolored | 2.75 | *4.25* |
| | | *Nos. 1334-1341 (8)* | | 12.50 | 11.90 |

**Souvenir Sheets**

| | | | | | |
|---|---|---|---|---|---|
| **1342** | A219 | $6 | multicolored | 6.00 | 6.00 |
| **1343** | A219 | $6 | multicolored | 6.00 | 6.00 |

Nos. 1217-1222 Overprinted

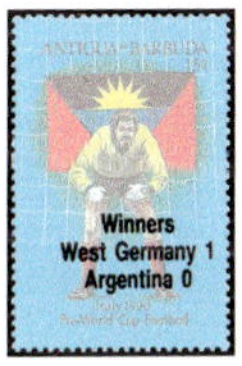


**1990, Nov. 11**

| | | | | | |
|---|---|---|---|---|---|
| **1344** | A201 | 15c | multicolored | .85 | .30 |
| **1345** | A201 | 25c | multicolored | .85 | .30 |
| **1346** | A201 | $1 | multicolored | 1.75 | 1.50 |
| **1347** | A201 | $4 | multicolored | 3.50 | *5.00* |
| | | *Nos. 1344-1347 (4)* | | 6.95 | *7.10* |

**Souvenir Sheets**

| | | | | |
|---|---|---|---|---|
| **1348** | A201 | $5 on #1221 | 5.50 | 5.50 |
| **1349** | A201 | $5 on #1222 | 5.50 | 5.50 |

Overprint on Nos. 1348-1349 is 32x13mm.

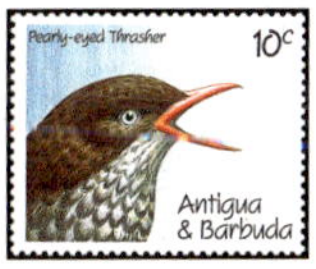


Birds — A220

10c, Pearly-eyed thrasher. 25c, Purple-throated carib. 50c, Common yellowthroat. 60c, American kestrel. $1, Yellow-bellied sapsucker. $2, Purple gallinule. $3, Yellow-crowned night heron. $4, Blue-hooded euphonia.

No. 1358, Brown pelican. No. 1359, Frigate bird.

**1990, Nov. 19 Litho. *Perf. 14***

| | | | | | |
|---|---|---|---|---|---|
| **1350** | A220 | 10c | multicolored | .50 | .35 |
| **1351** | A220 | 25c | multicolored | .60 | .40 |
| **1352** | A220 | 50c | multicolored | .70 | .45 |
| **1353** | A220 | 60c | multicolored | 1.10 | .75 |
| **1354** | A220 | $1 | multicolored | 1.25 | .80 |
| **1355** | A220 | $2 | multicolored | 2.25 | *2.50* |
| **1356** | A220 | $3 | multicolored | 2.50 | *3.00* |
| **1357** | A220 | $4 | multicolored | 2.75 | *3.25* |
| | | *Nos. 1350-1357 (8)* | | 11.65 | *11.50* |

**Souvenir Sheets**

| | | | | | |
|---|---|---|---|---|---|
| **1358** | A220 | $6 | multicolored | 7.00 | *8.75* |
| **1359** | A220 | $6 | multicolored | 7.00 | *8.75* |

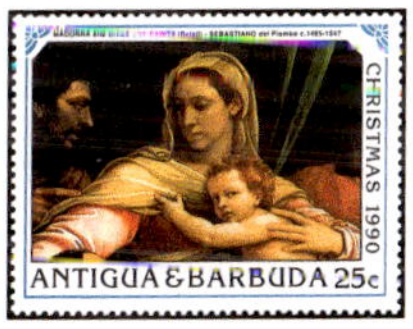


Christmas A221

Paintings: 25c, Madonna and Child with Saints by del Piombo. 30c, Virgin and Child with Angels by Grunewald, vert. 40c, Holy Family and a Shepherd by Titian. 60c, Virgin and Child by Fra Filippo Lippi, vert. $1, Jesus, St. John and Two Angels by Rubens. $2, Adoration of the Shepherds by Catena. $4, Adoration of the Magi by Giorgione. $5, Virgin and Child Adored by a Warrior by Catena. No. 1368, Allegory of the Blessings of Jacob by Rubens, vert. No. 1369, Adoration of the Magi by Fra Angelico, vert.

***Perf. 14x13½, 13½x14***

**1990, Dec. 10 Litho.**

| | | | | | |
|---|---|---|---|---|---|
| **1360** | A221 | 25c | multicolored | .85 | .40 |
| **1361** | A221 | 30c | multicolored | .85 | .40 |
| **1362** | A221 | 40c | multicolored | 1.00 | .45 |
| **1363** | A221 | 60c | multicolored | 1.25 | .50 |
| **1364** | A221 | $1 | multicolored | 1.50 | 1.00 |
| **1365** | A221 | $2 | multicolored | 2.25 | *2.50* |
| **1366** | A221 | $4 | multicolored | 3.50 | *5.00* |
| **1367** | A221 | $5 | multicolored | 3.50 | *5.00* |
| | | *Nos. 1360-1367 (8)* | | 14.70 | *15.25* |

**Souvenir Sheets**

| | | | | | |
|---|---|---|---|---|---|
| **1368** | A221 | $6 | multicolored | 4.25 | 4.25 |
| **1369** | A221 | $6 | multicolored | 4.25 | 4.25 |

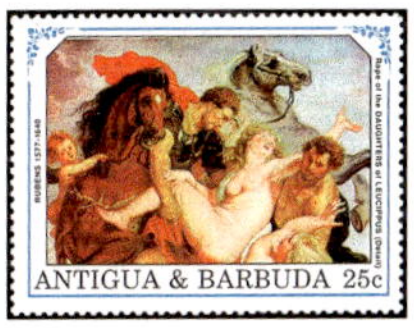


Peter Paul Rubens (1577-1640), Painter A222

Entire paintings or different details from: 25c, Rape of the Daughters of Leucippus. 45c, $2, $4, Bacchanal. 50c, $1, $3, Rape of the Sabine Women. 60c, Battle of the Amazons. No. 1378, Rape of Hippodameia. No. 1379, Battle of the Amazons.

**1991, Jan. 21 Litho. *Perf. 14***

| | | | | | |
|---|---|---|---|---|---|
| **1370** | A222 | 25c | multicolored | 1.00 | .30 |
| **1371** | A222 | 45c | multicolored | 1.25 | .45 |
| **1372** | A222 | 50c | multicolored | 1.25 | .50 |
| **1373** | A222 | 60c | multicolored | 1.50 | .65 |
| **1374** | A222 | $1 | multicolored | 1.75 | 1.00 |
| **1375** | A222 | $2 | multicolored | 2.00 | *2.50* |
| **1376** | A222 | $3 | multicolored | 2.50 | *3.75* |
| **1377** | A222 | $4 | multicolored | 2.75 | *4.75* |
| | | *Nos. 1370-1377 (8)* | | 14.00 | *13.90* |

**Souvenir Sheets**

| | | | | | |
|---|---|---|---|---|---|
| **1378** | A222 | $6 | multicolored | 4.50 | *5.25* |
| **1379** | A222 | $6 | multicolored | 4.50 | *5.25* |

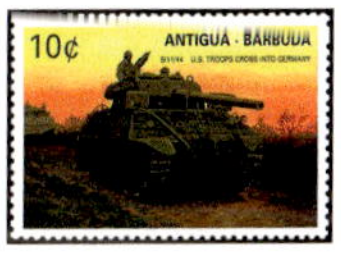


World War II Milestones A223

Designs: 10c, US troops enter Germany, Sept. 11, 1944. 15c, All axis forces surrender in North Africa, May 12, 1943. 25c, US troops invade Kwajalein, Jan. 31, 1944. 45c, Roosevelt and Churchill meet in Casablanca, Jan. 14, 1943. 50c, Marshal Badoglio signs agreement with allies, Sept. 1, 1943. $1, Mountbatten appointed Supreme Allied Commander, Southeast Asia Command, Aug. 25, 1943. $2, Major Greek tactical victory, Koritza, Nov. 22, 1940. $4, Britain and USSR sign mutual assistance pact, July 12, 1941. $5, Operation Torch, Nov. 8, 1942. No. 1389, Japanese attack on Pearl Harbor, Dec. 7, 1941. No. 1390, American bombing attack on Schweinfurt, Oct. 14, 1943.

**1991, Mar. 11 Litho. *Perf. 14***

| | | | | | |
|---|---|---|---|---|---|
| **1380** | A223 | 10c | multicolored | 1.10 | .60 |
| **1381** | A223 | 15c | multicolored | 1.25 | .50 |
| **1382** | A223 | 25c | multicolored | 1.25 | .50 |
| **1383** | A223 | 45c | multicolored | 2.50 | .65 |
| **1384** | A223 | 50c | multicolored | 1.50 | .65 |
| **1385** | A223 | $1 | multicolored | 2.75 | 1.50 |
| **1386** | A223 | $2 | multicolored | 3.00 | 2.75 |
| **1387** | A223 | $4 | multicolored | 3.00 | *4.00* |
| **1388** | A223 | $5 | multicolored | 3.25 | *4.00* |
| | | *Nos. 1380-1388 (9)* | | 19.60 | *15.15* |

**Souvenir Sheets**

| | | | | | |
|---|---|---|---|---|---|
| **1389** | A223 | $6 | multicolored | 6.75 | *7.25* |
| **1390** | A223 | $6 | multicolored | 6.75 | *7.25* |

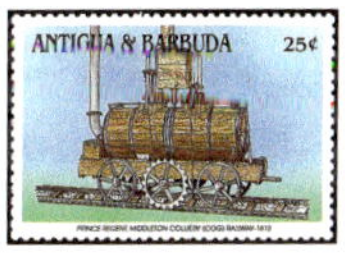


Cog Railways of the World — A224

Designs: 25c, Prince Regent, Middleton Colliery, 1812. 30c, Snowdon Mountain Railway, Wales. 40c, 1st Railcar at Hell Gate, Manitou and Pike's Peak Railway. 60c, PNKA Rack Railway, Amberawa, Java. $1, Green Mountain Railway, Mt. Desert Island, Maine, 1883. $2, Cog locomotive, Pike's Peak, 1891. $4, Vitznau-Rigi Cog Railway, Lake Lucerne. $5, Leopoldina Railway, Brazil. No. 1399, Electric Cog Donkey Engines, Panama Canal. No. 1400, Gornergratbahn, 1st electric cog railway in Switzerland, vert.

**1991, Mar. 18 Litho. *Perf. 14***

| | | | | | |
|---|---|---|---|---|---|
| **1391** | A224 | 25c | multicolored | 1.10 | .35 |
| **1392** | A224 | 30c | multicolored | 1.25 | .35 |
| **1393** | A224 | 40c | multicolored | 1.25 | .45 |
| **1394** | A224 | 60c | multicolored | 1.50 | .50 |
| **1395** | A224 | $1 | multicolored | 2.00 | .75 |
| **1396** | A224 | $2 | multicolored | 2.75 | 2.75 |
| **1397** | A224 | $4 | multicolored | 3.25 | *4.25* |
| **1398** | A224 | $5 | multicolored | 3.25 | *4.25* |
| | | *Nos. 1391-1398 (8)* | | 16.35 | *13.65* |

**Souvenir Sheets**

| | | | | | |
|---|---|---|---|---|---|
| **1399** | A224 | $6 | multicolored | 7.00 | 7.00 |
| **1400** | A224 | $6 | multicolored | 7.00 | 7.00 |

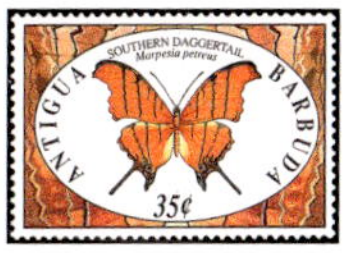


Butterflies A225

10c, Zebra. 35c, Southern daggertail. 50c, Red anartia. 75c, Malachite. $1, Polydamas swallowtail. $2, Orion. $4, Mimic. $5, Cracker.
Caterpillars: No. 1409, Monarch, vert. No. 1410, Painted lady, vert.

**1991, Apr. 15 Litho. *Perf. 14***

| | | | | | |
|---|---|---|---|---|---|
| **1401** | A225 | 10c | multicolored | .70 | .35 |
| **1402** | A225 | 35c | multicolored | 1.10 | .35 |
| **1403** | A225 | 50c | multicolored | 1.25 | .45 |
| **1404** | A225 | 75c | multicolored | 1.50 | .85 |
| **1405** | A225 | $1 | multicolored | 1.75 | 1.00 |
| **1406** | A225 | $2 | multicolored | 2.25 | *2.50* |
| **1407** | A225 | $4 | multicolored | 3.00 | *4.00* |
| **1408** | A225 | $5 | multicolored | 3.00 | *4.00* |
| | | *Nos. 1401-1408 (8)* | | 14.55 | 13.50 |

**Souvenir Sheets**

| | | | | | |
|---|---|---|---|---|---|
| **1409** | A225 | $6 | multicolored | 7.25 | *8.50* |
| **1410** | A225 | $6 | multicolored | 7.25 | *8.50* |

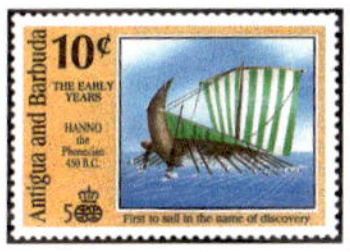


Voyages of Discovery A226

Designs: 10c, Hanno, Phoenicia, c. 450 B.C. 15c, Pytheas, Greece, 325 B.C. 45c, Eric the Red, Viking, A.D. 985. 60c, Leif Erikson, Viking, A.D. 1000. $1, Scylax, Greece, A.D. 518. $2, Marco Polo, A.D. 1259. $4, Queen Hatsheput, Egypt, 1493 B.C. $5, St. Brendan, Ireland, 500 A.D. No. 1419, Columbus, bareheaded. No. 1420, Columbus, wearing hat.

**1991, Apr. 22**

| | | | | | |
|---|---|---|---|---|---|
| **1411** | A226 | 10c | multicolored | .80 | .35 |
| **1412** | A226 | 15c | multicolored | .90 | .35 |
| **1413** | A226 | 45c | multicolored | 1.25 | .40 |
| **1414** | A226 | 60c | multicolored | 1.40 | .55 |
| **1415** | A226 | $1 | multicolored | 1.75 | .90 |
| **1416** | A226 | $2 | multicolored | 2.25 | *2.75* |
| **1417** | A226 | $4 | multicolored | 3.00 | *4.00* |
| **1418** | A226 | $5 | multicolored | 3.00 | *4.00* |
| | | *Nos. 1411-1418 (8)* | | 14.35 | *13.30* |

**Souvenir Sheets**

| | | | | | |
|---|---|---|---|---|---|
| **1419** | A226 | $6 | multicolored | 4.25 | *4.75* |
| **1420** | A226 | $6 | multicolored | 4.25 | *4.75* |

Discovery of America, 500th anniv. (in 1992).

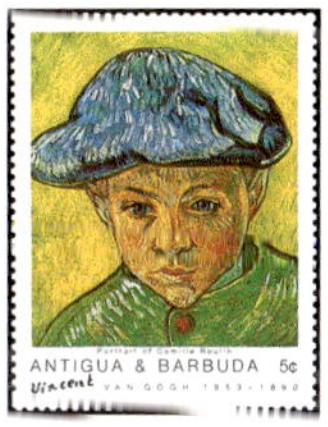


Paintings by Vincent Van Gogh — A227

Designs: 5c, Portrait of Camille Roulin. 10c, Portrait of Armand Roulin. 15c, Young Peasant Woman with Straw Hat Sitting in the Wheat. 25c, Portrait of Adeline Ravoux. 30c, The Schoolboy (Camille Roulin). 40c, Portrait of Doctor Gachet. 50c, Portrait of a Man. 75c, Two Children. $2, Portrait of Postman Joseph Roulin. $3, The Seated Zouave. $4, L'arlesienne: Madame Ginoux with Books. No. 1432, Self Portrait, November/December 1888. No. 1433, Flowering Garden. No. 1434, Farmhouse In Provence. $6, The Bridge at Trinquetaille.

**1991, May 13 *Perf. 13½***

| | | | | | |
|---|---|---|---|---|---|
| **1421** | A227 | 5c | multicolored | .60 | .75 |
| **1422** | A227 | 10c | multicolored | .60 | .55 |
| **1423** | A227 | 15c | multicolored | .70 | .45 |
| **1424** | A227 | 25c | multicolored | .80 | .45 |

**1425** A227 30c multicolored .80 .45
**1426** A227 40c multicolored .90 .45
**1427** A227 50c multicolored 1.00 .45
**1428** A227 75c multicolored 1.60 .75
**1429** A227 $2 multicolored 2.50 2.50
**1430** A227 $3 multicolored 3.00 2.75
**1431** A227 $4 multicolored 3.50 *4.25*
**1432** A227 $5 multicolored 3.50 *4.25*
*Nos. 1421-1432 (12)* 19.50 *18.05*

**Size: 102x76mm**

***Imperf***

**1433** A227 $5 multicolored 5.00 *6.00*
**1434** A227 $5 multicolored 5.00 *6.00*
**1435** A227 $6 multicolored 6.00 *7.00*

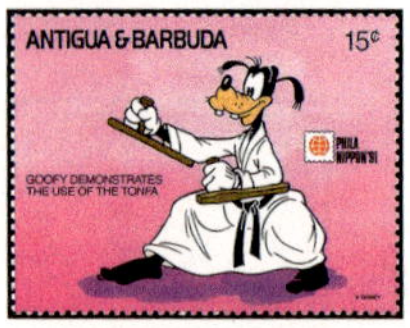


Phila Nippon '91 — A228

Walt Disney characters demonstrating Japanese martial arts: 10c, Mickey as champion sumo wrestler, vert. 15c, Goofy using tonfa. 45c, Ninja Donald in full field dress. 60c, Mickey using weapon in kung fu, vert. $1, Goofy tries kendo, vert. $2, Mickey, Donald demonstrating special technique of aikido. $4, Mickey flips Donald with judo throw. $5, Mickey demonstrates yabusame (target shooting from running horse), vert. No. 1444, Mickey using karate. No. 1445, Mickey demonstrating tamashiwara (powerbreaking), vert.

***Perf. 13½x14, 14x13½***

**1991, June 29** **Litho.**

**1436** A228 10c multicolored .70 .25
**1437** A228 15c multicolored .80 .25
**1438** A228 45c multicolored 1.35 .45
**1439** A228 60c multicolored 1.75 .60
**1440** A228 $1 multicolored 2.25 1.25
**1441** A228 $2 multicolored 2.75 3.00
**1442** A228 $4 multicolored 3.50 *4.75*
**1443** A228 $5 multicolored 3.50 *4.75*
*Nos. 1436-1443 (8)* 16.60 *15.30*

**Souvenir Sheets**

**1444** A228 $6 multicolored 5.50 *6.50*
**1445** A228 $6 multicolored 5.50 *6.50*

**Royal Family Birthday, Anniversary**
Common Design Type

**1991, July 8** **Litho.** ***Perf. 14***

**1446** CD347 10c multicolored .50 .25
**1447** CD347 15c multicolored .35 .25
**1448** CD347 20c multicolored .35 .25
**1449** CD347 40c multicolored 1.00 .30
**1450** CD347 $1 multicolored 1.25 .75
**1451** CD347 $2 multicolored 1.75 1.75
**1452** CD347 $4 multicolored 2.75 2.75
**1453** CD347 $5 multicolored 4.50 4.50
*Nos. 1446-1453 (8)* 12.45 10.80

**Souvenir Sheets**

**1454** CD347 $4 Elizabeth, Philip 3.75 3.75
**1455** CD347 $4 Charles, Diana, sons 5.50 5.50

10c, 40c, $1, $5, No. 1455, Charles and Diana, 10th wedding anniversary. Others, Queen Elizabeth II, 65th birthday.

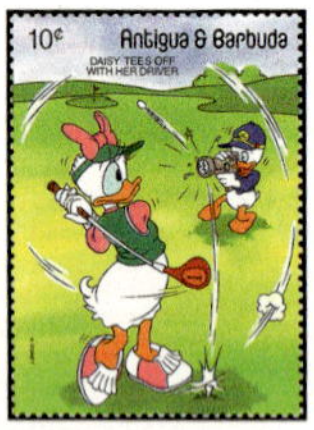


Walt Disney Characters Playing Golf — A229

Designs: 10c, Daisy Duck teeing off. 15c, Goofy using 3-Wood. 45c, Mickey using 3-Iron. 60c, Mickey missing ball using 6-Iron. $1, Donald trying 8-Iron to get out of pond. $2, Minnie using 9-Iron. $4, Donald digging hole with sand wedge. $5, Goofy trying new approach with putter. No. 1464, Grandma Duck using pitching wedge. No. 1465, Mickey cheering Minnie as she uses her 5-Wood, horiz.

***Perf. 13½x14, 14x13½***

**1991, Aug. 7** **Litho.**

**1456** A229 10c multicolored .75 .40
**1457** A229 15c multicolored .85 .40
**1458** A229 45c multicolored 1.25 .40
**1459** A229 60c multicolored 1.75 .50
**1460** A229 $1 multicolored 2.00 1.10
**1461** A229 $2 multicolored 2.50 *2.75*
**1462** A229 $4 multicolored 3.25 *4.00*
**1463** A229 $5 multicolored 3.50 *4.00*
*Nos. 1456-1463 (8)* 15.85 *13.55*

**Souvenir Sheets**

**1464** A229 $6 multicolored 6.25 *6.50*
**1465** A229 $6 multicolored 6.25 *6.50*

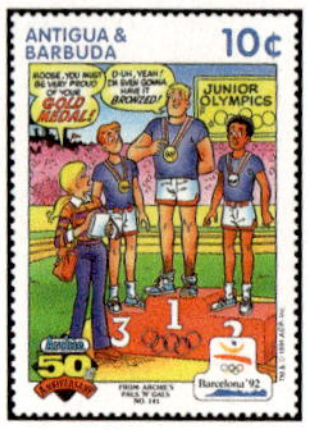


1992 Summer Olympics, Barcelona — A230

Archie Comics, 50th anniv.: 10c, Moose receiving gold medal. 25c, Archie, Veronica, Mr. Lodge, polo match, horiz. 40c, Archie & Betty, fencing. 60c, Archie, women's volleyball. $1, Archie, tennis. $2, Archie, marathon race. $4, Archie, judging women's gymnastics, horiz. $5, Archie, Betty, Veronica, basketball. No. 1474, Archie, soccer. No. 1475, Archie, Betty, baseball, horiz.

***Perf. 13½x14, 14x13½***

**1991, Aug. 19**

**1466** A230 10c multicolored .65 .30
**1467** A230 25c multicolored 1.00 .30
**1468** A230 40c multicolored 1.25 .35
**1469** A230 60c multicolored 1.50 .45
**1470** A230 $1 multicolored 1.75 1.00
**1471** A230 $2 multicolored 2.50 2.50
**1472** A230 $4 multicolored 3.75 3.75
**1473** A230 $5 multicolored 3.75 *5.00*
*Nos. 1466-1473 (8)* 16.15 *13.65*

**Souvenir Sheets**

**1474** A230 $6 multicolored 6.00 *6.75*
**1475** A230 $6 multicolored 6.00 *6.75*

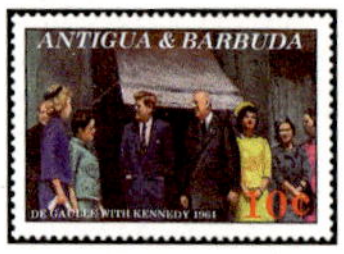


Charles de Gaulle, Birth Cent. — A231

Charles de Gaulle: 10c, and Pres. Kennedy, families, 1961. 15c, and Pres. Roosevelt, 1945, vert. 45c, and Chancellor Adenauer, 1962, vert. 60c, Liberation of Paris, 1944, vert. $1, Crossing the Rhine, 1945. $2, In Algiers, 1944. $4, and Pres. Eisenhower, 1960. $5, Returning from Germany, 1968, vert. No. 1484, and Churchill at Casablanca, 1943. No. 1485, and Citizens.

**1991, Sept. 11** **Litho.** ***Perf. 14***

**1476** A231 10c multicolored .80 .35
**1477** A231 15c multicolored .90 .35
**1478** A231 45c multicolored 1.25 .40
**1479** A231 60c multicolored 1.50 .50
**1480** A231 $1 multicolored 1.75 .90
**1481** A231 $2 multicolored 2.50 *3.00*
**1482** A231 $4 multicolored 3.25 *4.25*
**1483** A231 $5 multicolored 3.25 *4.25*
*Nos. 1476-1483 (8)* 15.20 *14.00*

**Souvenir Sheets**

**1484** A231 $6 multicolored 6.75 6.75
**1485** A231 $6 multicolored 6.75 6.75

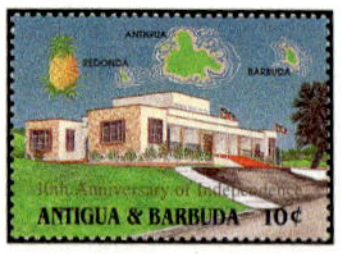


Independence, 10th Anniv. — A232

Designs: 10c, Island maps, government building. $6, Old P. O., St. Johns, #1 & #635.

**1991, Oct. 28**

**1486** A232 10c multicolored .85 .50

**Souvenir Sheet**

**1487** A232 $6 multicolored 6.75 *8.00*

No. 1487 contains one 50x38mm stamp.

Miniature Sheet

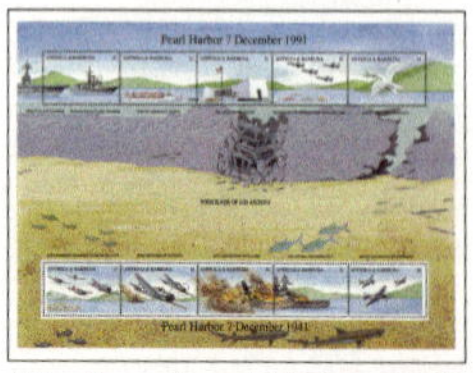

Attack on Pearl Harbor, 50th Anniv. — A233

Designs: No. 1488a, Bow of Nimitz class carrier, Ticonderoga class cruiser. b, Tourist boat to Arizona Memorial. c, USS Arizona Memorial. d, Aircraft salute to missing men. e, White tern. f, Japanese Kate torpedo bombers. g, Japanese Zero fighters. h, Battleship row in flames. i, USS Nevada breaking out. j, Zeros returning to carriers.

**1991, Dec. 9** ***Perf. 14½x15***

**1488** A233 $1 Sheet of 10, #a.-j. 22.50 22.50

Inscription for No. 1488f incorrectly describes torpedo bombers as Zekes.

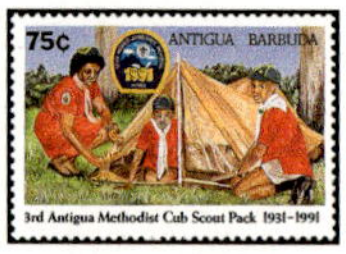


3rd Antigua Methodist Cub Scout Pack, 60th Anniv. — A234

Designs: $2, Lord Robert Baden-Powell, scouts, vert. $3.50, Scouts around campfire. $5, Antigua & Barbuda flag, Jamboree emblem, vert.

**1991, Dec. 9** ***Perf. 14***

**1489** A234 75c multicolored 1.50 .90
**1490** A234 $2 multicolored 6.00 5.00
**1491** A234 $3.50 multicolored 5.00 5.00
*Nos. 1489-1491 (3)* 12.50 10.90

**Souvenir Sheet**

**1492** A234 $5 multicolored 5.00 5.00

17th World Scout Jamboree, Korea.

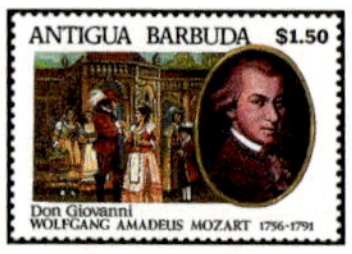


Wolfgang Amadeus Mozart, Death Bicent. — A235

Portrait of Mozart and: $1.50, Scene from opera, Don Giovanni. $4, St. Peter's Cathedral, Salzburg.

**1991, Dec. 9**

**1493** A235 $1.50 multicolored 3.50 3.50
**1494** A235 $4 multicolored 6.75 6.75

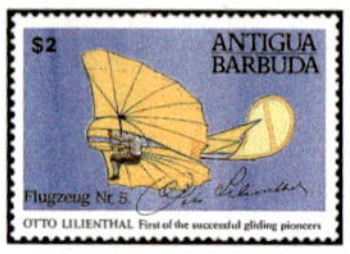


Anniversaries and Events — A236

Designs: $2, Otto Lilienthal's glider No. 5. $2.50, Locomotive cab, vert.

**1991, Dec. 9** **Litho.** ***Perf. 14***

**1495** A236 $2 multicolored 3.50 2.75
**1496** A236 $2.50 multicolored 6.50 4.00

First glider flight, cent. (No. 1495). Trans-Siberian Railway, cent. (No. 1496).

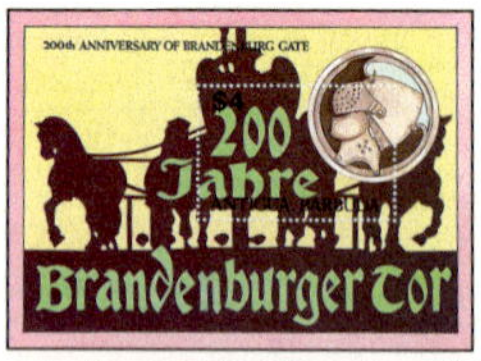


Brandenburg Gate, Bicent. — A237

25c, Demonstrators in autos, German flag. $2, Statue. $3, Portions of decorative frieze.

**1991, Dec. 9** **Litho.** ***Perf. 14***

**1499** A237 25c multicolored .25 .25
**1500** A237 $2 multicolored 1.10 *1.75*
**1501** A237 $3 multicolored 2.00 *3.00*
*Nos. 1499-1501 (3)* 3.35 *5.00*

**Souvenir Sheet**

**1502** A237 $4 multicolored 4.75 4.75

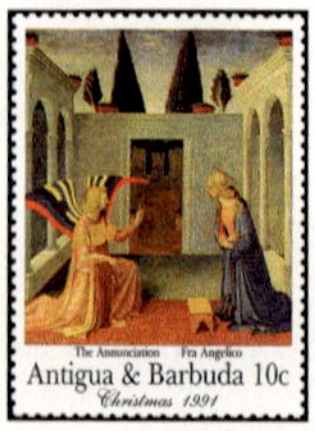


Christmas — A238

Paintings by Fra Angelico: 10c, The Annunciation. 30c, Nativity. 40c, Adoration of the Magi. 60c, Presentation in the Temple. $1, Circumcision. $3, Flight into Egypt. $4, Massacre of the Innocents. $5, Christ Teaching in the Temple. No. 1511, Adoration of the Magi, diff. No. 1512, Adoration of the Magi (Cook Tondo).

**1991, Dec. 12** ***Perf. 12***

**1503** A238 10c multicolored .40 .25
**1504** A238 30c multicolored .65 .25
**1505** A238 40c multicolored .80 .30
**1506** A238 60c multicolored 1.00 .45
**1507** A238 $1 multicolored 1.25 .75
**1508** A238 $3 multicolored 2.50 *3.00*
**1509** A238 $4 multicolored 2.75 *3.50*
**1510** A238 $5 multicolored 3.00 *3.75*
*Nos. 1503-1510 (8)* 12.35 *12.25*

**Souvenir Sheets**

**1511** A238 $6 multicolored 7.00 *8.00*
**1512** A238 $6 multicolored 7.00 *8.00*

**Queen Elizabeth II's Accession to the Throne, 40th Anniv.**
Common Design Type

Queen Elizabeth II and various island scenes.

**1992, Feb. 6** **Litho.** ***Perf. 14***

**1513** CD348 10c multicolored .90 .30
**1514** CD348 30c multicolored 1.10 .30
**1515** CD348 $1 multicolored 1.25 .75
**1516** CD348 $5 multicolored 2.75 *3.75*
*Nos. 1513-1516 (4)* 6.00 *5.10*

**Souvenir Sheets**

**1517** CD348 $6 Beach 4.50 *5.00*
**1518** CD348 $6 Flora 4.50 *5.00*

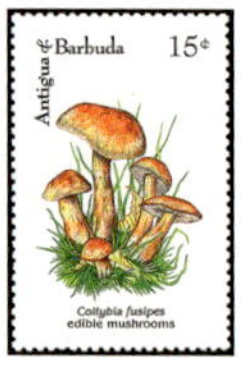


Mushrooms — A239

10c, Amanita caesarea. 15c, Collybia fusipes. 30c, Boletus aereus. 40c, Laccaria amethystina. $1, Russula virescens. $2, Tricholoma auratum. $4, Calocybe gambosa. $5, Panus tigrinus.

No. 1527, Auricularia auricula. No. 1528, Clavariadelphus truncatus.

**1992** **Litho.** ***Perf. 14***

**1519** A239 10c multicolored .75 .35
**1520** A239 15c multicolored .90 .35
**1521** A239 30c multicolored 1.25 .35
**1522** A239 40c multicolored 1.25 .45
**1523** A239 $1 multicolored 2.00 1.00
**1524** A239 $2 multicolored 2.75 2.75
**1525** A239 $4 multicolored 3.50 *4.00*
**1526** A239 $5 multicolored 3.50 *4.00*
*Nos. 1519-1526 (8)* 15.90 *13.25*

**Souvenir Sheet**

**1527** A239 $6 multicolored 6.50 *7.00*
**1528** A239 $6 multicolored 6.50 *7.00*

Issued: 10c, 30c, $1, $5, No. 1528, May 18; others, Mar.

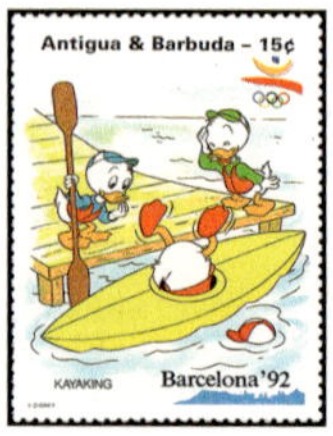


Disney Characters at Summer Olympics, Barcelona — A240

Designs: 10c, Mickey presenting gold medal to mermaid for swimming. 15c, Dewey and Huey watching Louie in kayak. 30c, Uncle McScrooge, Donald yachting. 50c, Donald, horse trying water polo. $1, Big Pete weight lifting. $2, Donald, Goofy fencing. $4, Mickey, Donald playing volleyball. $5, Goofy vaulting over horse.

No. 1537, $6, Mickey playing basketball, horiz. No. 1538, $6, Minnie Mouse on uneven parallel bars, horiz. No. 1539, $6, Mickey, Goofy, and Donald judging Minnie's floor exercise, horiz. No. 1540, $6, Mickey running after soccer ball.

**1992, Mar. 16** ***Perf. 13***

**1529** A240 10c multicolored .65 .25
**1530** A240 15c multicolored .75 .25
**1531** A240 30c multicolored .95 .30
**1532** A240 50c multicolored 1.50 .50
**1533** A240 $1 multicolored 1.75 .85
**1534** A240 $2 multicolored 2.75 2.75

ANTIGUA 535

| | | | | |
|---|---|---|---|---|
| **1535** A240 | $4 multicolored | 3.50 | *4.25* |
| **1536** A240 | $5 multicolored | 3.50 | *4.25* |
| | *Nos. 1529-1536 (8)* | 15.35 | *13.40* |

### Souvenir Sheets

| | | | |
|---|---|---|---|
| **1537-1540** A240 | Set of 4 | 16.50 | 16.50 |

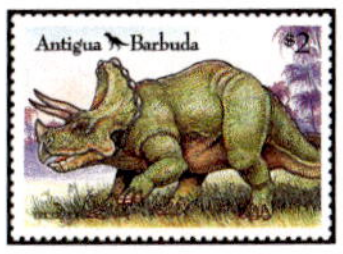
Dinosaurs A241

10c, Pteranodon. 15c, Brachiosaurus. 30c, Tyrannosaurus rex. 50c, Parasaurolophus. $1, Deinonychus. $2, Triceratops. $4, Protoceratops. $5, Stegosaurus.
No. 1549, Apatosaurus. No. 1550, Allosaurus.

**1992, Apr. 6** ***Perf. 14***

| | | | |
|---|---|---|---|
| **1541** A241 | 10c multicolored | .70 | .35 |
| **1542** A241 | 15c multicolored | .75 | .35 |
| **1543** A241 | 30c multicolored | .95 | .35 |
| **1544** A241 | 50c multicolored | 1.10 | .45 |
| **1545** A241 | $1 multicolored | 1.50 | .80 |
| **1546** A241 | $2 multicolored | 2.25 | 2.25 |
| **1547** A241 | $4 multicolored | 2.50 | *3.25* |
| **1548** A241 | $5 multicolored | 2.50 | *3.25* |
| | *Nos. 1541-1548 (8)* | 12.25 | *11.05* |

### Souvenir Sheets

| | | | |
|---|---|---|---|
| **1549** A241 | $6 multicolored | 5.50 | 5.50 |
| **1550** A241 | $6 multicolored | 5.50 | *6.50* |

Nos. 1541-1544 are vert.

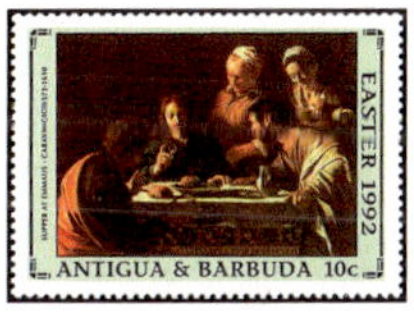
Easter A242

Paintings: 10c, Supper at Emmaus, by Caravaggio. 15c, The Vision of St. Peter, by Francisco de Zurbaran. 30c, $1, Christ Driving the Money Changers from the Templo, by Tiepolo (detail on $1). 40c, Martyrdom of St. Bartholomew (detail), by Jusepe de Ribera. $2, Crucifixion (detail), by Albrecht Altdorfer. $4, $5, The Deposition ( diff. detail), by Fra Angelico. No. 1559, Crucifixion, by Albrecht Altdorfer, vert. No. 1560, The Last Supper, by Vicente Juan Masip.

**1992, Apr. 15** ***Perf. 14x13½***

| | | | |
|---|---|---|---|
| **1551** A242 | 10c multicolored | .55 | .25 |
| **1552** A242 | 15c multicolored | .75 | .25 |
| **1553** A242 | 30c multicolored | 1.00 | .35 |
| **1554** A242 | 40c multicolored | 1.25 | .50 |
| **1555** A242 | $1 multicolored | 2.25 | 1.00 |
| **1556** A242 | $2 multicolored | 3.25 | 3.25 |
| **1557** A242 | $4 multicolored | 4.25 | *4.75* |
| **1558** A242 | $5 multicolored | 4.25 | *4.75* |
| | *Nos. 1551-1558 (8)* | 17.55 | *15.10* |

### Souvenir Sheet

***Perf. 13½x14***

| | | | |
|---|---|---|---|
| **1559** A242 | $6 multicolored | 5.50 | *6.50* |
| **1560** A242 | $6 multicolored | 5.50 | *6.50* |

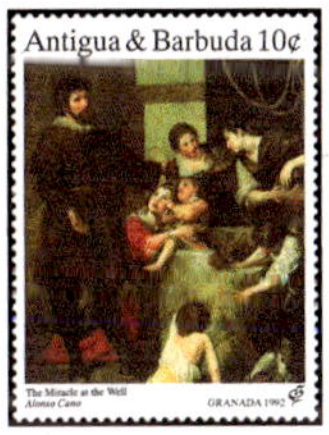
Spanish Art — A243

Designs: 10c, The Miracle at the Well, by Alonso Cano. 15c, The Poet Luis de Gongora y Argote, by Velazquez. 30c, The Painter Francisco Goya, by Vincente Lopez Portana. 40c, Maria de Las Nieves Michaela Fourdiniere, by Luis Paret y Alcazar. $1, Charles III Eating before His Court, by Paret y Alcazar, horiz. $2, A Rain Shower in Granada, by Antonio Munoz Degrain, horiz. $4, Sarah Bernhardt, by Santiago Rusinol y Prats. $5, The Hermitage Garden, by Joaquin Mir Trinxet. No. 1569, Olympus: Battle with the Giants, by Francisco Bayeu y Subias. No. 1570, The Ascent of Monsieur Boucle's Montgolfier Balloon in the Gardens of Aranjuez, by Antonio Cárnicero.

**1992, May 11**

| | | | |
|---|---|---|---|
| **1561** A243 | 10c multicolored | .45 | .25 |
| **1562** A243 | 15c multicolored | .65 | .30 |
| **1563** A243 | 30c multicolored | .90 | .35 |
| **1564** A243 | 40c multicolored | .90 | .50 |
| **1565** A243 | $1 multicolored | 1.50 | 1.25 |
| **1566** A243 | $2 multicolored | 2.25 | *4.00* |
| **1567** A243 | $4 multicolored | 3.50 | *4.00* |
| **1568** A243 | $5 multicolored | 4.25 | *4.50* |

### Size: 120x95mm

***Imperf***

| | | | |
|---|---|---|---|
| **1569** A243 | $6 multicolored | 7.50 | *8.50* |
| **1570** A243 | $6 multicolored | 7.50 | *8.50* |
| | *Nos. 1561-1570 (10)* | 29.40 | *32.15* |

Granada '92.

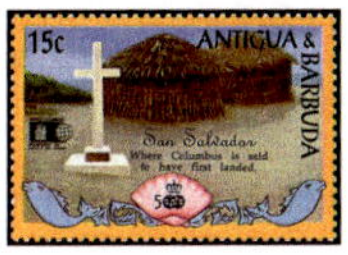
Discovery of America, 500th Anniv. — A244

Designs: 15c, San Salvador Island. 30c, Martin Alonzo Pinzon, captain of Pinta. 40c, Columbus, signature, coat of arms. $1, Pinta. $2, Nina. $4, Santa Maria. No. 1577, Sea monster. No. 1578, Map, sailing ship.

**1992, May 25** **Litho.** ***Perf. 14***

| | | | |
|---|---|---|---|
| **1571** A244 | 15c multicolored | .35 | .25 |
| **1572** A244 | 30c multicolored | .45 | .25 |
| **1573** A244 | 40c multicolored | .60 | .35 |
| **1574** A244 | $1 multicolored | 2.25 | 1.75 |
| **1575** A244 | $2 multicolored | 2.50 | *3.00* |
| **1576** A244 | $4 multicolored | 3.00 | *5.75* |
| | *Nos. 1571-1576 (6)* | 9.15 | *11.35* |

### Souvenir Sheets

| | | | |
|---|---|---|---|
| **1577** A244 | $6 multicolored | 6.00 | *6.75* |
| **1578** A244 | $6 multicolored | 6.00 | *6.75* |

World Columbian Stamp Expo '92, Chicago.

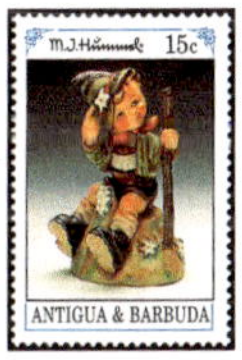
Hummel Figurines — A245

Designs 15c, No. 1587a, $1.50, Boy sitting on rock pointing to flower in cap. 30c, No. 1587b, $1.50, Girl sitting on fence. 40c, No. 1587c, $1.50, Boy holding binoculars. 50c, No. 1587d, $1.50, Boy carrying umbrella. $1, No. 1588a, $1.50, Two boys looking up at direction marker. $2, No. 1588b, $1.50, Boy carrying basket on back, walking with stick. $4, No. 1588c, $1.50, Two girls, goat. $5, No. 1588d, $1.50, Boy carrying walking stick.

**1993, Jan. 6** **Litho.** ***Perf. 14***

| | | | |
|---|---|---|---|
| **1579** A245 | 15c multicolored | .40 | .25 |
| **1580** A245 | 30c multicolored | .65 | .25 |
| **1581** A245 | 40c multicolored | .80 | .30 |
| **1582** A245 | 50c multicolored | .90 | .40 |
| **1583** A245 | $1 multicolored | 1.50 | .75 |
| **1584** A245 | $2 multicolored | 1.75 | *2.25* |
| **1585** A245 | $4 multicolored | 2.75 | *3.50* |
| **1586** A245 | $5 multicolored | 2.75 | *3.50* |
| | *Nos. 1579-1586 (8)* | 11.50 | *11.20* |

### Souvenir Sheets

| | | | |
|---|---|---|---|
| **1587** A245 | $1.50 Sheet of 4, #a.-d. | 7.00 | 7.00 |
| **1588** A245 | $1.50 Sheet of 4, #a.-d. | 7.00 | 7.00 |

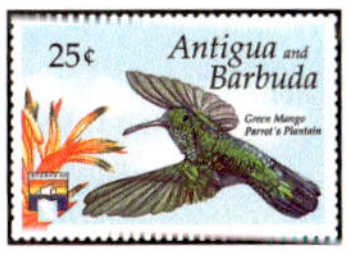
Hummingbirds and Flowers — A246

Designs: 10c, Antillean crested, wild plantain. 25c, Green mango, parrot's plantain. 45c, Purple-throated carib, lobster claws. 60c, Antillean mango, coral plant. $1, Vervain, cardinal's guard. $2, Rufous breasted hermit, heliconia. $4, Blue-headed, red ginger. $5, Green-throated carib, ornamental banana. No. 1597, Bee, jungle flame. No. 1598, Western streamertails, bignonia.

**1992, Aug. 10** **Litho.** ***Perf. 14***

| | | | |
|---|---|---|---|
| **1589** A246 | 10c multicolored | .45 | .45 |
| **1590** A246 | 25c multicolored | .60 | .30 |
| **1591** A246 | 45c multicolored | .80 | .35 |
| **1592** A246 | 60c multicolored | .90 | .45 |
| **1593** A246 | $1 multicolored | 1.25 | .75 |
| **1594** A246 | $2 multicolored | 2.00 | 2.00 |
| **1595** A246 | $4 multicolored | 3.25 | *5.75* |
| **1596** A246 | $5 multicolored | 3.50 | *5.75* |
| | *Nos. 1589-1596 (8)* | 12.75 | *15.80* |

### Souvenir Sheets

| | | | |
|---|---|---|---|
| **1597** A246 | $6 multicolored | 6.00 | *6.50* |
| **1598** A246 | $6 multicolored | 6.00 | *6.50* |

Genoa '92.

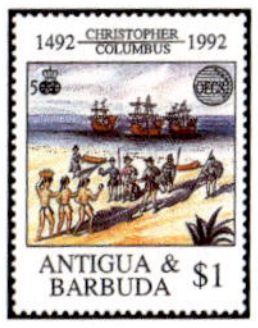
Discovery of America, 500th Anniv. — A247

**1992, Aug. 24** **Litho.** ***Perf. 14½***

| | | | |
|---|---|---|---|
| **1599** A247 | $1 Coming ashore | 1.00 | .75 |
| **1600** A247 | $2 Natives, ships | 1.75 | *2.10* |

Organization of East Caribbean States.

### Souvenir Sheet

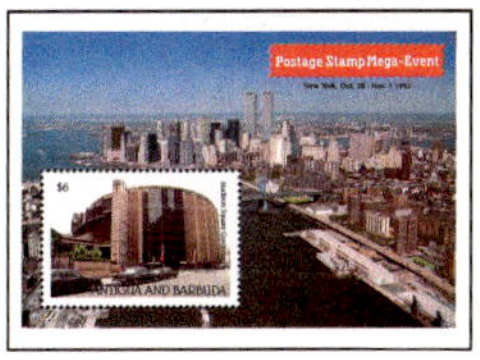
Madison Square Garden, NYC A248

**1992, Oct. 28** **Litho.** ***Perf. 14***

| | | | |
|---|---|---|---|
| **1601** A248 | $6 multicolored | 5.00 | *6.75* |

Postage Stamp Mega-Event, Jacob Javits Center, New York City.

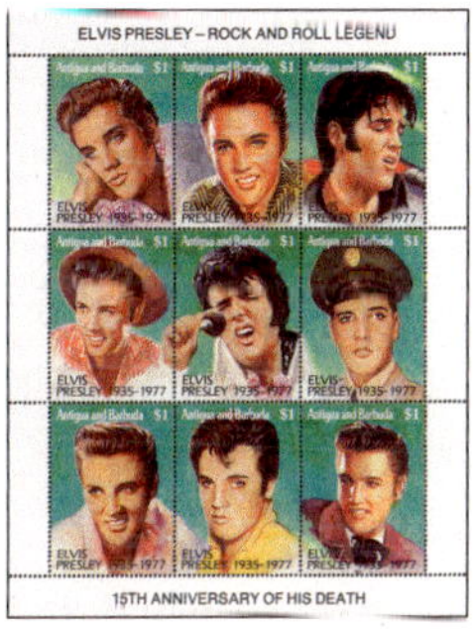
Elvis Presley (1935-1977) — A249

Various pictures of Elvis Presley.

**1992, Oct. 26** ***Perf. 13½x14***

| | | | |
|---|---|---|---|
| **1602** A249 | $1 Sheet of 9, #a.-i. | 15.00 | 13.00 |

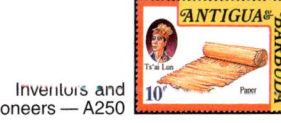

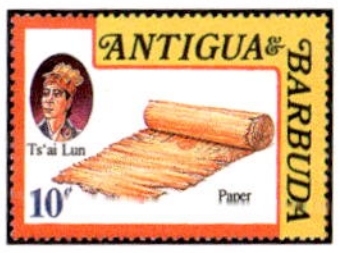
Inventors and Pioneers — A250

Designs: 10c, Ts'ai Lun, paper. 25c, Igor I. Sikorsky, 4 engine airplane. 30c, Alexander Graham Bell, telephone. 40c, Johannes Gutenberg, printing press. 60c, James Watt, steam engine. $1, Anton van Leeuwenhoek, microscope. $4, Louis Braille, Braille printing. $5, Galileo, telescope. No. 1607, Phonograph. No. 1608, Steamboat.

**1992, Oct. 19** **Litho.** ***Perf. 14***

| | | | | |
|---|---|---|---|---|
| **1603** | A250 | 10c multicolored | .25 | .25 |
| **1604** | A250 | 25c multicolored | 1.50 | .35 |
| **1605** | A250 | 30c multicolored | .60 | .40 |
| **1605A** | A250 | 40c multicolored | .60 | .40 |
| **1605B** | A250 | 60c multicolored | 3.75 | 1.00 |
| **1605C** | A250 | $1 multicolored | 2.00 | 1.50 |
| **1605D** | A250 | $4 multicolored | 4.50 | *5.75* |
| **1606** | A250 | $5 multicolored | 4.75 | *5.75* |
| | | *Nos. 1603-1606 (8)* | 17.95 | *15.40* |

### Souvenir Sheet

| | | | | |
|---|---|---|---|---|
| **1607** | A250 | $6 multicolored | 5.75 | *6.50* |
| **1608** | A250 | $6 multicolored | 5.75 | *6.50* |

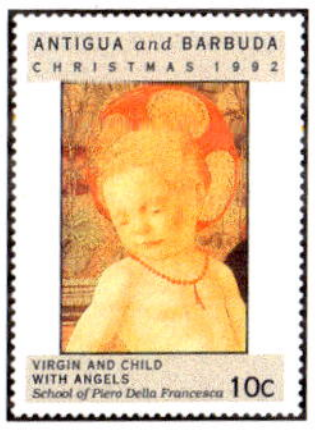
Christmas — A251

Details from Paintings: 10c, Virgin and Child with Angels, by School of Piero Della Francesca. 25c, Madonna Degli Alberelli, by Giovanni Bellini. 30c, Madonna and Child with St. Anthony Abbot and St. Sigismund, by Neroccio di Landi. 40c, Madonna and the Grand Duke, by Raphael. 60c, The Nativity, by George de la Tour. $1, Holy Family, by Jacob Jordaens. $4, Madonna and Child Enthroned, by Margaritone. $5, Madonna and Child on a Curved Throne, by Byzantine artist. No. 1617, Madonna and Child, by Domenico Ghirlandaio (both names misspelled). No. 1618, The Holy Family, by Pontormo.

**1992, Nov. 16** ***Perf. 13½x14***

| | | | |
|---|---|---|---|
| **1609** A251 | 10c multicolored | .65 | .25 |
| **1610** A251 | 25c multicolored | 1.00 | .25 |
| **1611** A251 | 30c multicolored | 1.10 | .25 |
| **1612** A251 | 40c multicolored | 1.25 | .30 |
| **1613** A251 | 60c multicolored | 1.50 | .60 |
| **1614** A251 | $1 multicolored | 1.75 | 1.00 |
| **1615** A251 | $4 multicolored | 3.75 | *4.50* |
| **1616** A251 | $5 multicolored | 3.75 | *4.50* |
| | *Nos. 1609-1616 (8)* | 14.75 | *11.65* |

### Souvenir Sheet

| | | | |
|---|---|---|---|
| **1617** A251 | $6 multicolored | 5.75 | *6.50* |
| **1618** A251 | $6 multicolored | 5.75 | *6.50* |

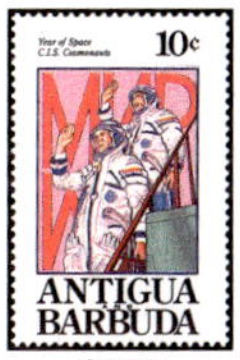
A252

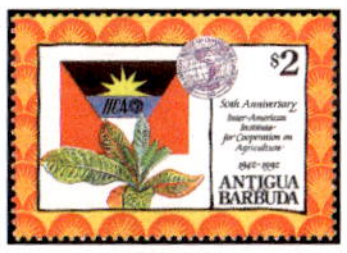
A253

Anniversaries and Events: 10c, Cosmonauts. 40c, Graf Zeppelin, Goodyear blimp. 45c, Right Rev. Daniel C. Davis, St. John's Cathedral. 75c, Konrad Adenauer. $1, Bus Mosbacher, Weatherly. $1.50, Rain forest. No. 1625, Felis tigris. No. 1626, Flag, emblems, plant. No. 1627, Women acting on stage. $2.25, Women carrying baskets of food on their heads. $3, Lions Club emblem, club member. No. 1630, West German, NATO flags. No. 1631, China's Long March Booster Rocket. No. 1632, Dr. Hugo Eckener.
No. 1633, $6, The Hindenburg. No. 1634, $6, Brandenburg Gate, German flag. No. 1635, $6, Monarch butterfly. No. 1636, $6, Hermes Shuttle, Columbus Space Station.

**1992, Dec. 14** **Litho.** ***Perf. 14***

| | | | |
|---|---|---|---|
| **1619** A252 | 10c multicolored | .80 | .50 |
| **1620** A252 | 40c multicolored | 1.75 | .55 |
| **1621** A253 | 45c multicolored | .75 | .35 |
| **1622** A252 | 75c multicolored | .90 | .60 |
| **1623** A252 | $1 multicolored | 1.25 | .75 |
| **1624** A252 | $1.50 multicolored | 1.75 | 1.10 |
| **1625** A252 | $2 multicolored | 4.25 | 2.00 |
| **1626** A253 | $2 multicolored | 2.75 | 1.50 |
| **1627** A253 | $2 multicolored | 2.50 | 1.75 |
| **1628** A252 | $2.25 multicolored | 2.50 | 2.50 |
| **1629** A252 | $3 multicolored | 3.75 | 3.75 |
| **1630** A252 | $4 multicolored | 5.00 | 5.00 |
| **1631** A252 | $4 multicolored | 5.50 | 5.50 |
| **1632** A252 | $6 multicolored | 5.00 | 5.00 |
| | *Nos. 1619-1632 (14)* | 38.45 | 30.85 |

### Souvenir Sheets

| | | | |
|---|---|---|---|
| **1633-1636** A252 | Set of 4 | 22.00 | *27.50* |

Intl. Space Year (Nos. 1619, 1631, 1636). Count Zeppelin, 75th anniv. of death (Nos. 1620, 1632-1633). Diocese of Northeast Caribbean and Aruba District, 150th anniv. (No. 1621). Konrad Adenauer, 25th anniv. of death (Nos. 1622, 1630, 1634). 1962 winner of America's Cup (No. 1623). Earth Summit, Rio (Nos. 1624-1625, 1635). Inter-American Institute for Cooperation on Agriculture, 50th anniv. (No. 1626). Cultural Development, 40th anniv. (No. 1627). WHO Intl. Conf. on Nutrition, Rome (No. 1628). Lions Club, 75th anniv. (No. 1629).
Issued: Nos. 1619, 1621-1623, 1626-1631, 1634, 1636, Nov.; Nos. 1624-1625, 1635, Dec. 14.

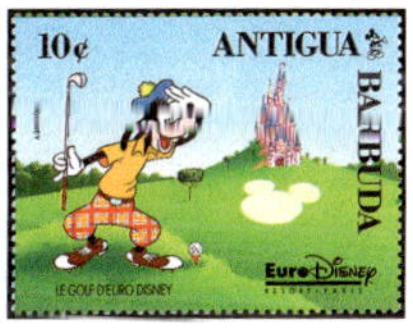
Euro Disney, Paris A254

Disney characters: 10c, Golf course. 25c, Davy Crockett Campground. 30c, Cheyenne Hotel. 40c, Santa Fe Hotel. $1, New York Hotel. $2, In car, map showing location. $4, Pirates of the Caribbean. $5, Adventureland.
No. 1645, $6, Mickey Mouse on map with star, vert. No. 1646, $6, Roof turret at entrance, Mickey Mouse in uniform. No. 1646A, $6, Mickey Mouse, colored spots on poster, vert. No. 1646B, $6, Mickey on poster, vert., diff.

**1992-93 Litho. *Perf. 14x13½***

**1637** A254 10c multicolored .70 .25
**1638** A254 25c multicolored .90 .25
**1639** A254 30c multicolored .90 .25
**1640** A254 40c multicolored 1.00 .30
**1641** A254 $1 multicolored 2.00 .75
**1642** A254 $2 multicolored 2.75 2.75
**1643** A254 $4 multicolored 3.75 *5.00*
**1644** A254 $5 multicolored 3.75 *5.00*
*Nos. 1637-1644 (8)* 15.75 *14.55*

**Souvenir Sheets**

***Perf. 13½x14***

**1645-1646B** A254 Set of 4 17.00 *20.00*

Issued: Nos. 1638-1639, 1642-1643, 1646-1646B, 2/22/93; others, 12/1992.

Miniature Sheets

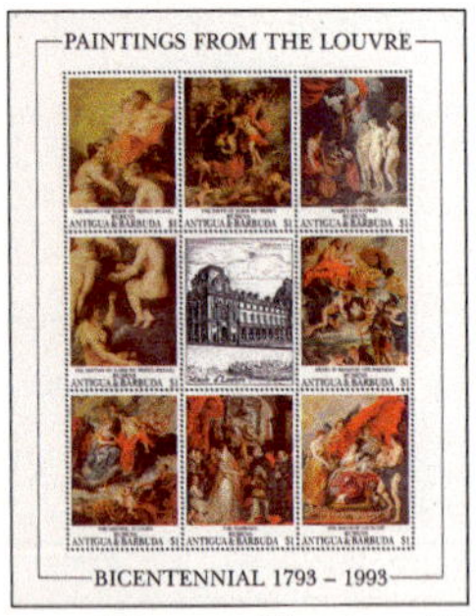

Louvre Museum, Bicent. — A255

Details or entire paintings, by Peter Paul Rubens: No. 1647a, Destiny of Marie de' Medici. b, Birth of Marie de'Medici. c, Marie's Education. d, Destiny of Marie de'Medici, diff. e, Henry IV Receives the Portrait. f, The Meeting at Lyons. g, The Marriage. h, The Birth of Louis XIII.

No. 1648a, The Capture of Juliers. b, The Exchange of Princesses. c, The Happiness of the Regency. d, The Majority of Louis XIII. e, The Flight from Blois. f, The Treaty of Angouleme. g, The Peace of Angers. h, The Queen's Reconciliation with Her Son.

$6, Helene Fourment Au Carosse.

**1993, Mar. 22 Litho. *Perf. 12***

**1647** A255 $1 Sheet of 8, #a.-h., + label 7.25 7.25
**1648** A255 $1 Sheet of 8, #a.-h., + label 7.25 7.25

**Souvenir Sheet**

***Perf. 14½***

**1649** A255 $6 multicolored 7.75 7.75

No. 1649 contains one 55x88mm stamp.

Nos. 1647-1649 exist imperf. Values about double those of normal sheets.

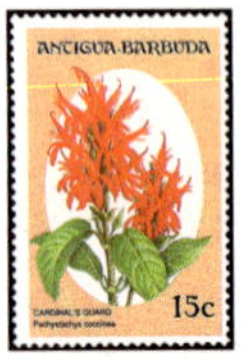

Flowers — A256

15c, Cardinal's guard. 25c, Giant granadilla. 30c, Spider flower. 40c, Gold vine. $1, Frangipani. $2, Bougainvillea. $4, Yellow oleander. $5, Spicy jatropha.

No. 1658, Bird lime tree. No. 1659, Fairy lily.

**1993, Mar. 15 Litho. *Perf. 14***

**1650** A256 15c multicolored .95 .30
**1651** A256 25c multicolored 1.10 .30
**1652** A256 30c multicolored 1.10 .35
**1653** A256 40c multicolored 1.10 .35
**1654** A256 $1 multicolored 2.10 .90
**1655** A256 $2 multicolored 2.75 2.75
**1656** A256 $4 multicolored 3.75 *4.50*
**1657** A256 $5 multicolored 3.75 *4.50*
*Nos. 1650-1657 (8)* 16.60 *13.95*

**Souvenir Sheets**

**1658** A256 $6 multicolored 5.25 *6.50*
**1659** A256 $6 multicolored 5.25 *6.50*

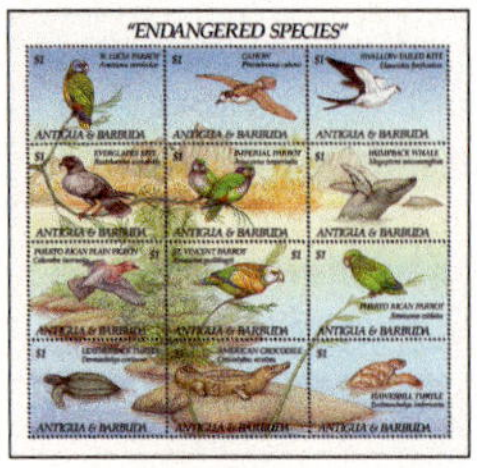

Endangered Species — A257

Designs: No. 1660a, St. Lucia parrot. b, Cahow. c, Swallow-tailed kite. d, Everglades kite. e, Imperial parrot. f, Humpback whale. g, Puerto Rican plain pigeon. h, St. Vincent parrot. i, Puerto Rican parrot. j, Leatherback turtle. k, American crocodile. l, Hawksbill turtle.

No. 1662, West Indian manatee.

**1993, Apr. 5**

**1660** A257 $1 Sheet of 12, #a.-l. 15.00 15.00

**Souvenir Sheets**

**1661** A257 $6 like #1660f 4.75 *5.50*
**1662** A257 $6 multicolored 4.75 *5.50*

Philatelic Publishing Personalities A258

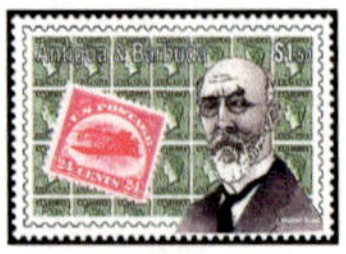

Portrait, stamp: No. 1663, J. Walter Scott (1842-1919), US "#C3a," Antigua #1. No. 1664, Theodore Champion, France #8, Antigua #1. No. 1665, E. Stanley Gibbons (1856-1913), cover of his first price list and catalogue, Antigua #1. No. 1666, Hugo Michel (1866-1944), Bavaria #1, Antigua #1. No. 1667, Alberto (1877-1944) and Giulio (1902-1987) Bolaffi, Sardinia #1, Great Britain #3. No. 1668, Richard Borek (1874-1947), Brunswick #24, Bavaria #1.

Front pages, Mekeel's Weekly Stamp News: No. 1669a, Jan. 7, 1890. b, Feb. 12, 1993.

**1993, June 14**

**1663** A258 $1.50 multicolored 1.90 1.60
**1664** A258 $1.50 multicolored 1.90 1.60
**1665** A258 $1.50 multicolored 1.90 1.60
**1666** A258 $1.50 multicolored 1.90 1.60
**1667** A258 $1.50 multicolored 1.90 1.60
**1668** A258 $1.50 multicolored 1.90 1.60
*Nos. 1663-1668 (6)* 11.40 9.60

**Souvenir Sheet**

**1669** A258 $3 Sheet of 2, #a.-b. 6.25 *7.00*

Mekeel's Weekly Stamp News, cent. (in 1891; No. 1669).

Miniature Sheets

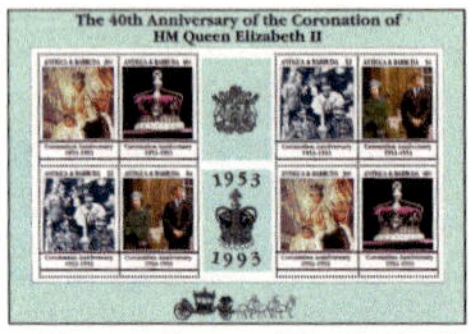

Coronation of Queen Elizabeth II, 40th Anniv. — A259

No. 1670 — Coronation: a, 30c, Official photograph. b, 40c, Crown of Queen Elizabeth, the Queen Mother. c, $2, Dignataries attending ceremony. d, $4, Queen, Prince Edward.

No. 1671, $1 — First decade, 1953-1963: a, Wedding photograph of Princess Margaret and Antony Armstrong-Jones. b, Queen opening Parliament, Prince Philip. c, Queen holding infant. d, Royal family. e, Queen Elizabeth II, formal portrait. f, Queen, Charles de Gaulle. g, Queen, Pope John XXIII. h, Queen inspecting troops.

No. 1672, $1 — Second decade, 1963-1973: a, Investiture of Charles as Prince of Wales. b, Queen opening Parliament, Prince Philip, diff. c, Queen holding infant, diff. d, Queen, Prince Philip, children. e, Wearing blue robe, diadem. f, Prince Philip, Queen seated. g, Prince Charles, Queen at microphone. h, Queen conversing, model airplane.

No. 1673, $1 — Third decade, 1973-1983: a, Wedding photograph of Prince Charles and Princess Diana. b, Queen opening Parliament, Prince Philip, diff. c, Princess Diana with infant. d, Princess Anne with infant. e, Portrait of Queen. f, Queen waving, Prince Philip. g, Queen, Pope John Paul II. h, Wedding portrait of Mark Phillips and Princess Anne.

No. 1674, $1 — Fourth decade, 1983-1993: a, Wedding photograph of Sarah Ferguson and Prince Andrew. b, Queen opening Parliament, Prince Philip, diff. c, Princess Diana holding infant, diff. d, Sarah Ferguson, infant. e, Queen wearing blue dress. f, Queen waving from carriage, Prince Philip. g, Queen wearing military uniform. h, Queen Mother.

$6, Portrait, by Denis Fildes.

**1993, June 2 Litho. *Perf. 13½x14***

**1670** A259 Sheet, 2 each #a.-d. 8.50 8.50

**Sheets of 8, #a-h**

**1671-1674** A259 Set of 4 34.00 34.00

**Souvenir Sheet**

***Perf. 14***

**1675** A259 $6 multicolored 5.00 5.00

No. 1675 contains one 28x42mm stamp.

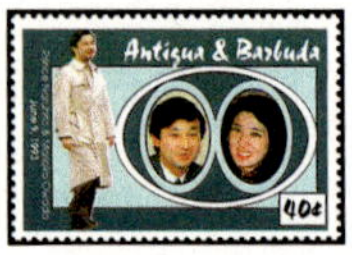

A260

Wedding of Japan's Crown Prince Naruhito and Masako Owada: Cameo photos of couple and: 40c, Crown Prince. $3, Princess.

$6, Princess wearing white coat, vert.

**1993, Aug. 16 Litho. *Perf. 14***

**1676** A260 40c multicolored .65 .40
**1677** A260 $3 multicolored 2.25 *3.25*

**Souvenir Sheet**

**1678** A260 $6 multicolored 6.00 6.00

Picasso (1881-1973) A261

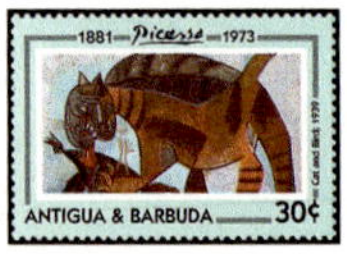

Paintings: 30c, Cat and Bird, 1939. 40c, Fish on a Newspaper, 1957. $5, Dying Bull, 1934.

$6, Woman with a Dog, 1953.

**1993, Aug. 16 Litho. *Perf. 14***

**1679** A261 30c multicolored .90 .40
**1680** A261 40c multicolored .90 .40
**1681** A261 $5 multicolored 3.75 3.75
*Nos. 1679-1681 (3)* 5.55 4.55

**Souvenir Sheet**

**1682** A261 $6 multicolored 5.75 5.75

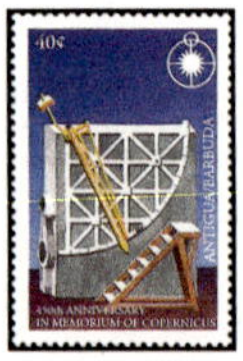

Copernicus (1473-1543) — A262

Designs: 40c, Astronomical devices. $4, Photograph of supernova.

$5, Copernicus.

**1993, Aug. 16**

**1683** A262 40c multicolored .65 .50
**1684** A262 $4 multicolored 3.25 3.25

**Souvenir Sheet**

**1685** A262 $5 multicolored 5.25 5.25

Willy Brandt (1913-1992), German Chancellor A263

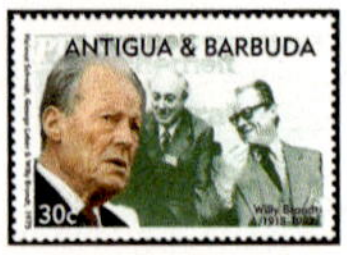

Designs: 30c, Helmut Schmidt, George Leber, Brandt. $4, Brandt, newspaper headlines.

$6, Brandt at Warsaw Ghetto Memorial, 1970.

**1993, Aug. 16**

**1686** A263 30c multicolored .75 .35
**1687** A263 $4 multicolored 3.75 3.75

**Souvenir Sheet**

**1688** A263 $6 multicolored 5.50 5.50

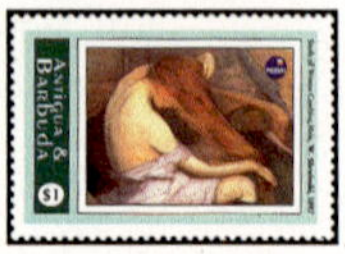

Polska '93 — A264

Paintings: $1, Study of a Woman Combing Her Hair, by Wladyslaw Slewinski, 1897. $3, Artist's Wife with Cat, by Konrad Krzyzanowski, 1912.

$6, General Confusion, by S. I. Witkiewicz, 1930, vert.

**1993, Aug. 16**

**1689** A264 $1 multicolored .90 .90
**1690** A264 $3 multicolored 2.25 2.25

**Souvenir Sheet**

**1691** A264 $6 multicolored 5.50 5.50

Inauguration of Pres. William J. Clinton — A265

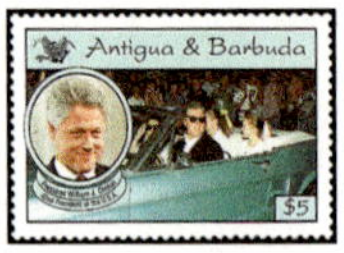

Designs: $5, Pres. Clinton driving car. $6, Pres. Clinton, inauguration ceremony, vert.

**1993, Aug. 16**

**1692** A265 $5 multicolored 3.25 3.25

**Souvenir Sheet**

**1693** A265 $6 multicolored 5.00 5.00

No. 1693 contains one 43x57mm stamp.

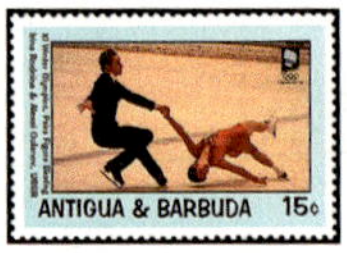

1994 Winter Olympics, Lillehammer, Norway — A266

15c, Irina Rodnina, Alexei Ulanov, gold medalists, pairs figure skating, 1972. $5, Alberto Tomba, gold medal, giant slalom, 1988, 1992.

$6, Yvonne van Gennip, Andrea Ehrig, gold, bronze medalists, speedskating, 1988.

**1993, Aug. 16**

**1694** A266 15c multicolored 1.00 .30
**1695** A266 $5 multicolored 3.25 3.25

**Souvenir Sheet**

**1696** A266 $6 multicolored 5.50 5.50

1994 World Cup Soccer Championships, US — A267

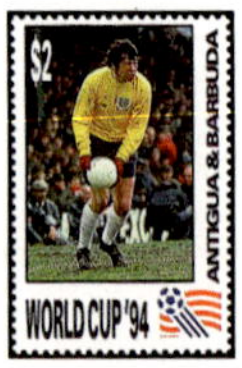

English soccer players: No. 1697, $2, Gordon Banks. Nos. 1698, $2, Bobby Moore. No. 1699, $2, Peter Shilton. No. 1700, $2, Nobby Stiles. No. 1701, $2, Bryan Robson. No. 1702, $2, Geoff Hurst. No. 1703, $2, Gary Lineker. No. 1704, $2, Bobby Charlton. No. 1705, $2, Martin Peters. No. 1706, $2, John Barnes. No. 1707, $2, David Platt. No. 1708, $2, Paul Gascoigne.

No. 1709, $6, Bobby Moore. No. 1710, $6, Player holding 1990 Fair Play Winners Trophy.

**1993, July 30 Litho. *Perf. 14***

**1697-1708** A267 Set of 12 18.00 18.00

**Souvenir Sheets**

**1709-1710** A267 Set of 2 10.00 10.00

Nos. 1697-1708 issued in sheets of five plus label identifying player.

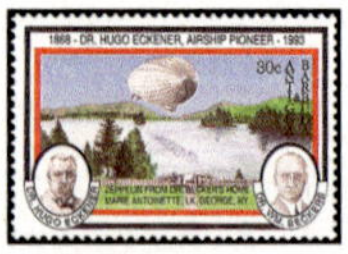

Aviation Anniversaries A268

Designs: 30c, Dr. Hugo Eckener, Dr. Wm. Beckers, zeppelin over Lake George, NY. No. 1712, Chicago Century of Progress Exhibition seen from zeppelin. No. 1713, George Washington, Blanchard's balloon, vert. No. 1714, Gloster E.28/39, first British jet plane. $4, Pres. Wilson watching take-off of first scheduled air mail plane. No. 1716, Hindenburg over

# ANTIGUA

Ebbets Field, Brooklyn, NY, 1937. No. 1717, Gloster Meteor in combat.
No. 1718, Eckener, vert. No. 1719, Alexander Hamilton, Pres. Washington, John Jay, gondola of Blanchard's balloon. No. 1720, PBY-5.

### 1993, Oct. 11
| | | | | |
|---|---|---|---|---|
| 1711 | A268 | 30c multicolored | 1.00 | .60 |
| 1712 | A268 | 40c multicolored | 1.00 | 1.00 |
| 1713 | A268 | 40c multicolored | 1.00 | 1.00 |
| 1714 | A268 | 40c multicolored | 1.00 | 1.00 |
| 1715 | A268 | $4 multicolored | 4.00 | 4.00 |
| 1716 | A268 | $5 multicolored | 4.00 | 4.00 |
| 1717 | A268 | $5 multicolored | 4.00 | 4.00 |
| | Nos. 1711-1717 (7) | | 16.00 | 15.60 |

#### Souvenir Sheets
| | | | | |
|---|---|---|---|---|
| 1718 | A268 | $6 multicolored | 5.25 | 5.25 |
| 1719 | A268 | $6 multicolored | 6.00 | 6.00 |
| 1720 | A268 | $6 multicolored | 6.00 | 6.00 |

Dr. Hugo Eckener, 125th anniv. of birth (Nos. 1711-1712, 1716, 1718). First US balloon flight, bicent. (Nos. 1713, 1715, 1719). Royal Air Force, 75th anniv. (Nos. 1714, 1717, 1720).
No. 1720 contains one 57x43mm stamp.

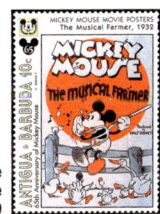

Mickey Mouse Movie Posters — A269

Nos. 1721-1729: 10c, The Musical Farmer, 1932. 15c, Little Whirlwind, 1941. 30c, Pluto's Dream House, 1940. 40c, Gulliver Mickey, 1934. 50c, Alpine Climbers, 1936. $1, Mr. Mouse Takes a Trip, 1940. $2, The Nifty Nineties, 1941. $4, Mickey Down Under, 1948. $5, The Pointer, 1939.
No. 1730, $6, The Simple Things, 1953. No. 1731, $6, The Prince and the Pauper, 1990.

### 1993, Oct. 25  Litho.  Perf. 13½x14
| | | | | |
|---|---|---|---|---|
| 1721-1729 | A269 | Set of 9 | 15.00 | 15.00 |

#### Souvenir Sheets
| | | | | |
|---|---|---|---|---|
| 1730-1731 | A269 | Set of 2 | 13.00 | 13.00 |

St. John's Lodge #492, 150th Anniv. — A270

Designs: 10c, W.K. Heath, Grand Inspector 1961-82. 15c, Present Masonic Hall. 40c, 1st Masonic Hall. 60c, J.L.E. Jeffery, Grand Inspector 1953-61, vert.

### 1993, Aug. 16  Litho.  Perf. 14
| | | | | |
|---|---|---|---|---|
| 1732-1735 | A270 | Set of 4 | 10.00 | 10.00 |

First Ford Engine and Benz's First 4-Wheel Car, Cent. — A271

30c, Lincoln Continental. 40c, 1914 Mercedes racing car. $4, 1966 Ford GT40. $5, 1954 Mercedes Benz gull wing coupe, street version.
No. 1740, $6, Mustang emblem. No. 1741, $6, US #1286A, Germany #471.

### 1993, Oct. 11  Litho.  Perf. 14
| | | | | |
|---|---|---|---|---|
| 1736-1739 | A271 | Set of 4 | 9.00 | 9.00 |

#### Souvenir Sheets
| | | | | |
|---|---|---|---|---|
| 1740-1741 | A271 | Set of 2 | 11.00 | 11.00 |

Christmas A272

Nos. 1742-1750, Disney characters in The Nutcracker: 10c, 15c, 20c, 30c, 40c, 50c, 60c, $3, $6.
No. 1751, $6, Minnie and Mickey. No. 1752, $6, Mickey, vert.

### 1993, Nov. 8  Perf. 14x13½, 13½x14
| | | | | |
|---|---|---|---|---|
| 1742-1750 | A272 | Set of 9 | 13.00 | 13.00 |

#### Souvenir Sheets
| | | | | |
|---|---|---|---|---|
| 1751-1752 | A272 | Set of 2 | 11.50 | 11.50 |

Fine Art — A273

Paintings by Rembrandt: No. 1753, 15c, Hannah and Samuel. No. 1755, 30c, Isaac & Rebecca (The Jewish Bride). No. 1756, 40c, Jacob Wrestling with the Angel. No. 1760, $5, Moses with the Tablets of the Law.
Paintings by Matisse: No. 1754, 15c, Guitarist. No. 1757, 60c, Interior with a Goldfish Bowl. No. 1758, $1, Portrait of Mlle. Yvonne Landsberg. No. 1759, $4, The Toboggan, Plate XX from Jazz.
No. 1761, $6, The Blinding of Samson by the Philistines, by Rembrandt. No. 1762, $6, The Three Sisters, by Matisse.

### 1993, Nov. 22  Perf. 13½x14
| | | | | |
|---|---|---|---|---|
| 1753-1760 | A273 | Set of 8 | 10.50 | 10.50 |

#### Souvenir Sheets
| | | | | |
|---|---|---|---|---|
| 1761-1762 | A273 | Set of 2 | 11.50 | 11.50 |

A274

Hong Kong '94 — A275

Stamps, fishing boats at Shau Kei Wan: No. 1763, Hong Kong #370, bow of boat. No. 1764, Stern of boat, #1300.
Museum of Qin figures, Shaanxi Province, Tomb of Qin First Emperor: No. 1765a, Inside museum. b, Cavalryman, horse. c, Warriors in battle formation. d, Painted bronze horses, chariot. e, Pekingese dog (not antiquity). f, Chin warrior figures, horses.

### 1994, Feb. 18  Litho.  Perf. 14
| | | | | |
|---|---|---|---|---|
| 1763 | A274 | 10c multicolored | .70 | .70 |
| 1764 | A274 | 40c multicolored | .70 | .70 |
| a. | | Pair, #1763-1764 | 1.60 | 1.60 |

#### Miniature Sheet
| | | | | |
|---|---|---|---|---|
| 1765 | A275 | 40c Sheet of 6, #a.-f. | 5.75 | 5.75 |

Nos. 1763-1764 issued in sheets of 5 pairs. No. 1764a is a continuous design.
New Year 1994 (Year of the Dog) (No. 1765e).

Hong Kong '94 — A276

Disney characters: 10c, Mickey's "Pleasure Junk." 15c, Mandarin Minnie. 30c, Donald, Daisy journey by house boat. 50c, Mickey, Birdman of Mongkok. $1, Pluto encounters a good-luck dog. $2, Minnie, Daisy celebrate Bun Festival. $4, Goofy, the noodle maker. $5, Goofy pulls Mickey in a rickshaw.
No. 1774, $5, Mickey celebrating New Year with Dragon Dance, horiz. No. 1775, $5, View of Hong Kong Harbor, horiz.

### 1994, Feb. 18  Litho.  Perf. 13½x14
| | | | | |
|---|---|---|---|---|
| 1766-1773 | A276 | Set of 8 | 14.00 | 14.00 |

#### Souvenir Sheets  Perf. 14x13½
| | | | | |
|---|---|---|---|---|
| 1774-1775 | A276 | $5 Set of 2 | 11.00 | 11.00 |

Sierra Club, Cent. — A277

No. 1776: a, Bactrian camel, emblem UR. b, Bactrian camel, emblem UL. c, African elephant, emblem UL. d, African elephant, emblem UR. e, Leopard, blue background. f, Leopard, emblem UR. g, Leopard, emblem UL. h, Club emblem.
No. 1777: a, Sumatran rhinoceros, lying on ground. b, Sumatran rhinoceros, looking straight ahead. c, Ring-tailed lemur standing. d, Ring-tailed lemur sitting on branch. e, Red-fronted brown lemur on branch. f, Red-fronted brown lemur. g, Red-fronted brown lemur, diff.
No. 1778, $1.50, Sumatran rhinoceros, horiz. No. 1779, $1.50, Ring-tailed lemur, horiz. No. 1780, $1.50, Bactrian camel, horiz. No. 1781, $1.50, African elephant, horiz.

### 1994, Mar. 1  Litho.  Perf. 14
| | | | | |
|---|---|---|---|---|
| 1776 | A277 | $1.50 Sheet of 8, #a.-h. | 12.00 | 12.00 |
| 1777 | A277 | $1.50 Sheet of 8, #a.-g, #1776i | 12.00 | 12.00 |

#### Souvenir Sheets
| | | | | |
|---|---|---|---|---|
| 1778-1781 | A277 | Set of 4 | 6.50 | 6.50 |

New Year 1994 (Year of the Dog) — A278

Small breeds of dogs: No. 1782a, West highland white terrier. b, Beagle. c, Scottish terrier. d, Pekingese. e, Dachshund. f, Yorkshire terrier. g, Pomeranian. h, Poodle. i, Shetland sheepdog. j, Pug. k, Shih tzu. l, Chihuahua.
Large breeds of dogs: No. 1783a, Mastiff. b, Border collie. c, Samoyed. d, Airedale terrier. e, English setter. f, Rough collie. g, Newfoundland. h, Weimaraner. i, English springer spaniel. j, Dalmatian. k, Boxer. l, Old English sheepdog.
No. 1784, $6, Welsh corgi. No. 1785, $6, Labrador retriever.

### 1994, Apr. 5  Perf. 14
| | | | | |
|---|---|---|---|---|
| 1782 | A278 | 50c Sheet of 12, #a.-l. | 7.75 | 7.75 |
| 1783 | A278 | 75c Sheet of 12, #a.-l. | 11.50 | 11.50 |

#### Souvenir Sheets
| | | | | |
|---|---|---|---|---|
| 1784-1785 | A278 | Set of 2 | 11.50 | 11.50 |

Orchids — A279

Designs: 10c, Spiranthes lanceolata. 20c, Ionopsis utriculariodes. 30c, Tetramicra canaliculata. 50c, Oncidium picturatum. $1, Epidendrum difforme. $2, Epidendrum ciliare. $4, Epidendrum ibaguense. $5, Epidendrum nocturnum.
No. 1794, $6, Encyclia cochleata. No. 1795, $6, Rodriguezia lanceolata.

### 1994, Apr. 11  Perf. 14
| | | | | |
|---|---|---|---|---|
| 1786-1793 | A279 | Set of 8 | 17.50 | 17.50 |

#### Souvenir Sheets
| | | | | |
|---|---|---|---|---|
| 1794-1795 | A279 | Set of 2 | 11.00 | 13.00 |

Butterflies — A280

Designs: 10c, Monarch. 15c, Florida white. 30c, Little sulphur. 40c, Troglodyte. $1, Common long-tail skipper. $2, Caribbean buckeye. $4, Polydamas swallowtail. $5, Zebra.
No. 1804, $6, Cloudless sulphur. No. 1805, $6, Hanno blue.

### 1994, June 27  Perf. 14
| | | | | |
|---|---|---|---|---|
| 1796-1803 | A280 | Set of 8 | 18.50 | 18.50 |

#### Souvenir Sheets
| | | | | |
|---|---|---|---|---|
| 1804-1805 | A280 | Set of 2 | 11.00 | 13.00 |

Marine Life — A281

No. 1806: a, Bottlenose dolphin. b, Killer whale (a). c, Spinner dolphin (b). d, Ocean sunfish (a). e, Caribbean reef shark, short fin pilot whale (d, f). f, Butterfly fish. g, Moray eel. h, Trigger fish. i, Red lobster (h).
No. 1807, $6, Blue marlin, horiz. No. 1808, $6, Sea horse.

### 1994, July 21  Litho.  Perf. 14
| | | | | |
|---|---|---|---|---|
| 1806 | A281 | 50c Sheet of 9, #a.-i. | 7.75 | 7.75 |

#### Souvenir Sheets
| | | | | |
|---|---|---|---|---|
| 1807-1808 | A281 | Set of 2 | 13.00 | 13.00 |

Intl. Year of the Family — A282

### 1994, Aug. 4
| | | | | |
|---|---|---|---|---|
| 1809 | A282 | 90c multicolored | 1.10 | 1.10 |

D-Day, 50th Anniv. — A283

Designs: 40c, Short Sunderland attacks U-boat. $2, Lockheed P-38 Lightning attacks train. $3, B-26 Marauders of 9th Air Force. $6, Hawker Typhoon Fighter Bombers.

### 1994, Aug. 4
| | | | | |
|---|---|---|---|---|
| 1810-1812 | A283 | Set of 3 | 7.00 | 7.00 |

#### Souvenir Sheet
| | | | | |
|---|---|---|---|---|
| 1813 | A283 | $6 multicolored | 7.50 | 7.50 |

A284

# ANTIGUA

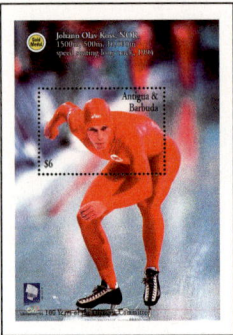

Intl. Olympic Committee, Cent. — A285

Designs: 50c, Edwin Moses, US, hurdles, 1984. $1.50, Steffi Graf, Germany, tennis, 1988. $6, Johann Olav Koss, Norway, speed skating, 1994.

**1994, Aug. 4**
| 1814 | A284 | 50c multicolored | .40 | .30 |
| 1815 | A284 | $1.50 multicolored | 2.00 | 2.00 |

**Souvenir Sheet**
| 1816 | A285 | $6 multicolored | 6.00 | 6.00 |

English Touring Cricket, Cent. — A286

35c, M.A. Atherton, England, Wisden Trophy. 75c, I.V.A. Richards, Leeward Islands, vert. $1.20, R.B. Richardson, Leeward Islands, Wisden Trophy.
$3, First English team, 1895.

**1994, Aug. 4**
| 1817-1819 | A286 | Set of 3 | 6.00 | 6.00 |

**Souvenir Sheet**
| 1820 | A286 | $3 multicolored | 3.00 | 3.00 |

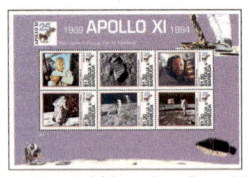

First Manned Moon Landing, 25th Anniv. — A287

No. 1821, $1.50: a, Edwin E. Aldrin, Jr. b, First footprint on Moon. c, Neil A. Armstrong. d, Aldrin descending to lunar surface. e, Aldrin deploys ALSEP (spelled ALSET in error on stamp). f, Aldrin, US flag, Tranquility Base.
No. 1822, $1.50: a, Scientific research, Tranquility Base. b, Plaque on Moon. c, Eagle ascending to docking. d, Command module in lunar orbit. e, US No. C76 made from die carried to Moon. f, Pres. Nixon, Apollo 11 crew.
$6, Armstrong, Aldrin, Postmaster General Blount.

**1994, Aug. 4** Sheets of 6, #a-f
| 1821-1822 | A287 | Set of 2 | 22.50 | 22.50 |

**Souvenir Sheet**
| 1823 | A287 | $6 multicolored | 5.25 | 5.25 |

A288

PHILAKOREA '94 — A289

40c, Entrance bridge, Songgwangsa Temple. 90c, Song-op Folk Village, Cheju. $3, Panoramic view, Port Sogwip'o.
Ceramics, Koryo & Choson Dynasties: No. 1827a, Long-necked bottle. b, Jar. c, Jar, diff. d, Ewer in form of bamboo shoot. e, Jar, diff. f, Pear-shaped bottle. g, Porcelain jar with dragon design. h, Porcelain jar with bonsai design.
$4, Ox, ox herder, vert.

**1994, Aug. 4** Perf. 14, 13½ (#1827)
| 1824-1826 | A288 | Set of 3 | 3.00 | 3.00 |
| 1827 | A289 | 75c Sheet of 8, #a-h. | 6.25 | 6.25 |

**Souvenir Sheet**
| 1828 | A288 | $4 multicolored | 4.50 | 4.50 |

Stars of Country & Western Music — A290

No. 1829, 75c: a, Patsy Cline. b, Tanya Tucker. c, Dolly Parton. d, Anne Murray. e, Tammy Wynette. f, Loretta Lynn. g, Reba McEntire. h, Skeeter Davis.
No. 1830, 75c: a, Travis Tritt. b, Dwight Yoakam. c, Billy Ray Cyrus. d, Alan Jackson. e, Garth Brooks. f, Vince Gill. g, Clint Black. h, Eddie Rabbit.
No. 1831, 75c: a, Hank Snow. b, Gene Autry. c, Jimmie Rogers. d, Ernest Tubb. e, Eddy Arnold. f, Willie Nelson. g, Johnny Cash. h, George Jones.
No. 1832, $6, Kitty Wells, horiz. No. 1833, $6, Hank Williams, Sr. No. 1834, $6, Hank Williams, Jr.

**1994, Aug. 18** Litho. Perf. 14
Sheets of 8, #a-h
| 1829-1831 | A290 | Set of 3 | 15.50 | 15.50 |

**Souvenir Sheets**
| 1832-1834 | A290 | Set of 3 | 15.50 | 15.50 |

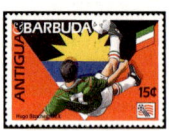

1994 World Cup Soccer Championships, US — A291

Designs: 15c, Hugo Sanchez, Mexico. 35c, Juergen Klinsmann, Germany. 65c, Antigua player. $1.20, Cobi Jones, US. $4, Roberto Baggio, Italy. $5, Bwalya Kalusha, Zambia.
No. 1841, $6, FIFA World Cup Trophy, vert. No. 1842, $6, Maldive Islands player, vert.

**1994, Sept. 19**
| 1835-1840 | A291 | Set of 6 | 13.50 | 13.50 |

**Souvenir Sheets**
| 1841-1842 | A291 | Set of 2 | 8.75 | 8.75 |

Order of the Caribbean Community A292

First award recipients: 65c, Sir Shridath Ramphal, statesman, Guyana. 90c, William Demas, economist, Trinidad & Tobago. $1.20, Derek Walcott, writer, St. Lucia.

**1994, Sept. 26**
| 1843-1845 | A292 | Set of 3 | 3.50 | 3.50 |

Herman E. Sieger (1902-54) A293

Germany No. C35, Graf Zeppelin, Sieger.

**1994, June 6** Litho. Perf. 14
| 1846 | A293 | $1.50 multicolored | 4.00 | 4.00 |

Birds — A294

Designs: 10c, Magnificent frigate birds. 15c, Bridled quail dove. 30c, Magnificent frigate bird hatchling. 40c, Purple-throated carib, vert. No. 1851, $1, Antigua broad-wing hawk, vert. No. 1852, $1, Magnificent frigate bird, vert. $3, Magnificent frigate bird, white head. $4, Yellow warbler.
No. 1855, $6, West Indian Whistling duck. No. 1856, $6, Magnificent frigate bird, diff., vert.

**1994, Dec. 12** Litho. Perf. 14
| 1847-1854 | A294 | Set of 8 | 11.00 | 11.00 |

**Souvenir Sheets**
| 1855-1856 | A294 | Set of 2 | 9.25 | 9.25 |

World Wildlife Fund (Nos. 1847, 1849, 1852-1853).

Christmas — A295

Paintings of Madonnas: 15c, The Virgin and Child by the Fireside, by Robert Campin. 35c, The Reading Madonna, by Giorgione. 40c, Madonna and Child, by Giovanni Bellini. 45c, The Litta Madonna, by da Vinci. 65c, The Virgin and Child Under the Apple Tree, by Lucas Cranach the Elder. 75c, Madonna and Child, by Master of the Female Half-Lengths. $1.20, An Allegory of the Church, by Alessandro Allori. $5, Madonna and Child Wreathed with Flowers, by Jacob Jordaens.
No. 1865, $6, The Virgin Enthroned with Child, by Bohemian Master. No. 1866, $6, Madonna and Child with (painting's) Commissioners, by Palma Vecchio.

**1994, Dec. 12** Perf. 13½x14
| 1857-1864 | A295 | Set of 8 | 14.00 | 14.00 |

**Souvenir Sheets**
| 1865-1866 | A295 | Set of 2 | 9.50 | 9.50 |

Birds — A296

Designs: 15c, Magnificent frigate bird. 25c, Blue-hooded euphonia. 35c, Meadowlark. 40c, Red-billed tropic bird. 45c, Greater flamingo. 60c, Yellow-faced grassquit. 65c, Yellow-billed cuckoo. 70c, Purple-throated carib. 75c, Bananaquit. 90c, Painted bunting. $1.20, Red-legged honeycreeper. $2, Jacana. $5, Greater antillean bullfinch. $10, Caribbean elaenia. $20, Trembler.

**1995, Feb. 6** Perf. 14½x14
| 1867 | A296 | 15c multicolored | .25 | .25 |
| 1868 | A296 | 25c multicolored | .25 | .25 |
| 1869 | A296 | 35c multicolored | .25 | .25 |
| 1870 | A296 | 40c multicolored | .30 | .30 |
| 1871 | A296 | 45c multicolored | .40 | .40 |
| 1872 | A296 | 60c multicolored | .45 | .45 |
| 1873 | A296 | 65c multicolored | .60 | .60 |
| 1874 | A296 | 70c multicolored | .60 | .60 |
| 1875 | A296 | 75c multicolored | .65 | .65 |
| 1876 | A296 | 90c multicolored | .80 | .80 |
| 1877 | A296 | $1.20 multicolored | 1.00 | 1.00 |
| 1878 | A296 | $2 multicolored | 1.75 | 1.75 |
| 1879 | A296 | $5 multicolored | 4.75 | 4.75 |
| 1880 | A296 | $10 multicolored | 9.50 | 9.50 |
| 1881 | A296 | $20 multicolored | 19.00 | 19.00 |
| Nos. 1867-1881 (15) | | | 40.55 | 40.55 |

See Nos. 2693-2694.

Prehistoric Animals — A297

Designs, vert.: 15c, Pachycephalosaurus. 20c, Afrovenator. 65c, Centrosaurus. 90c, Pentaceratops. $1.20, Tarbosaurus. $5, Styracosaurus.

No. 1888: a, Kronosaur. b, Ichthyosaur. c, Plesiosaur. d, Archelon. e, Two tyrannosaurs. f, One tyrannosaur. g, One parasaurolophus. h, Two parasaurolophuses. i, Oviraptor. j, Protoceratops with eggs. k, Pteranodon, protoceratops. l, Protoceratops.
No. 1889, $6, Carnotaurus. No. 1890, $6, Corythosaurus.

**1995, May 15** Litho. Perf. 14
| 1882-1887 | A297 | Set of 6 | 7.50 | 7.50 |
| 1888 | A297 | 75c Sheet of 12, #a-l. | 8.50 | 8.50 |

**Souvenir Sheets**
| 1889-1890 | A297 | Set of 2 | 14.50 | 14.50 |

1996 Summer Olympics, Atlanta — A298

Gold medalists: 15c, Al Oerter, US, discus. 20c, Greg Louganis, US, diving. 65c, Naim Suleymanoglu, Turkey, weight lifting. 90c, Louise Ritter, US, high jump. $1.20, Nadia Comaneci, Romania, gymnastics. $5, Olga Bondarenko, USSR, 10,000-meter run.
No. 1897, $6, Lutz Hessilch, Germany, 1000-meter sprint cycling, vert. No. 1898, $6, US team, eight-oared shell, 800-, 1500-meters.

**1995, June 6** Litho. Perf. 14
| 1891-1896 | A298 | Set of 6 | 7.25 | 7.25 |

**Souvenir Sheets**
| 1897-1898 | A298 | Set of 2 | 13.00 | 13.00 |

End of World War II, 50th Anniv. — A299

No. 1899: a, Chiang Kai-Shek. b, Gen. MacArthur. c, Gen. Chennault. d, Brigadier Orde C. Wingate. e, Gen. Stilwell. f, Field Marshall William Slim.
No. 1900: a, Map of Germany showing battle plan. b, Tanks, infantry advance. c, Red Army at gates of Berlin. d, German defenses smashed. e, Airstrikes on Berlin. f, German soldiers give up. g, Berlin falls to Russians. h, Germany surrenders.
$3, Plane, ship, Adm. Chester Nimitz. $6, Gen. Konev at command post outside Berlin, vert.

**1995, July 20**
| 1899 | A299 | $1.20 Sheet of 6, #a.-f. + label | 7.00 | 7.00 |
| 1900 | A299 | $1.20 Sheet of 8, #a.-h. + label | 10.50 | 10.50 |

**Souvenir Sheets**
| 1901 | A299 | $3 multicolored | 4.00 | 4.00 |
| 1902 | A299 | $6 multicolored | 6.00 | 6.00 |

UN, 50th Anniv. — A300

No. 1903: a, 75c, Earl of Halifax, signatures. b, 90c, Virginia Gildersleeve. c, $1.20, Harold Stassen.
$6, Franklin D. Roosevelt.

**1995, July 20** Litho. Perf. 14
| 1903 | A300 | Strip of 3, #a.-c. | 2.25 | 3.00 |

**Souvenir Sheet**
| 1904 | A300 | $6 multicolored | 4.25 | 4.25 |

No. 1903 is a continuous design.

FAO, 50th Anniv. — A301

No. 1905 — Street market scene: a, 75c, Two women, bananas. b, 90c, Women, crates, produce. c, $1.20, Women talking, one with box of food on head.
$6, Tractor.

**1995, July 20**
1905  A301  Strip of 3, #a.-c.   2.25  3.00
**Souvenir Sheet**
1906  A301  $6 multicolored   4.25  4.25
No. 1905 is a continuous design.

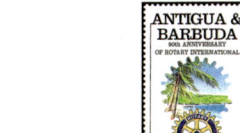
Rotary Intl., 90th Anniv. — A302

**1995, July 20**
1907  A302  $5 shown   4.50  4.50
**Souvenir Sheet**
1908  A302  $6 Natl. flag, Rotary emblem   4.50  4.50

Queen Mother, 95th Birthday — A303

No. 1909: a, Drawing. b, White & dark pink hat. c, Formal portrait. d, Blue green hat, dress.
$6, Light blue dress, pearls.

**1995, July 20**   Perf. 13½x14
1909  A303  $1.50 Strip or block of 4, #a.-d.   5.75  5.75
**Souvenir Sheet**
1910  A303  $6 multicolored   5.75  5.75
No. 1909 was issued in sheets of 2 each. Sheets of 1909-1910 exist with black frame overprinted in margin, with text "In Memoriam/1900-2002."

Ducks — A304

No. 1911: a, Ring-necked duck. b, Ruddy duck. c, Green-winged teal (I). d, Wood duck. e, Hooded merganser (I). f, Lesser scaup (g). g, West Indian tree duck (h, k, l). h, Fulvous whistling duck (I). i, Bahama pintail. j, Shoveler (i). k, Masked duck (I). l, American widgeon.
$6, Blue-winged teal.

**1995, Aug. 31**   Litho.   Perf. 14
1911  A304  75c Sheet of 12, #a.-l.   12.00  12.00
**Souvenir Sheet**
1912  A304  $6 multicolored   7.50  7.50

Bees — A305

Designs: 90c, Mining bee. $1.20, Solitary bee. $1.65, Leaf-cutter. $1.75, Honey bee.
$6, Solitary mining bee.

**1995, Sept. 7**
1913-1916  A305  Set of 4   7.50  7.50
**Souvenir Sheet**
1917  A305  $6 multicolored   6.50  6.50

Domestic Cats — A306

Designs: a, Somali. b, Persian. c, Devon rex. d, Turkish angora. e, Himalayan. f, Maine coon. g, Nonpedigree. h, American wirehair. i, British shorthair. j, American curl. k, Black nonpedigree. l, Birman.
$6, Siberian, vert.

**1995, Sept. 7**
1918  A306  45c Sheet of 12, #a.-l.   9.00  9.00
**Souvenir Sheet**
1919  A306  $6 multicolored   7.00  7.00

Tourism — A307

Stylized paintings depicting: a, Caring. b, Marketing. c, Working. d, Enjoying life.

**1995, July 31**   Litho.   Perf. 14
1920  A307  $2 Sheet of 4, #a.-d.   6.75  6.75

Greenbay Moravian Church, 150th Anniv. — A308

Designs: 20c, 1st structure, wood & stone. 60c, 1st stone, concrete building, 3/67. 75c, $2, Present structure. 90c, John A. Buckley, 1st minister of African descent. $1.20, John Ephraim Knight, longest serving minister. $6, Front of present structure.

**1995, Sept. 4**
1921-1926  A308  Set of 6   9.00  9.00
**Souvenir Sheet**
1927  A308  $6 multicolored   5.50  5.50

Flowers — A309

No. 1928: a, Narcissus. b, Camellia. c, Iris. d, Tulip. e, Poppy. f, Peony. g, Magnolia. h, Oriental lily. i, Rose. j, Pansy. k, Hydrangea. l, Azaleas.
$6, Bird of paradise, calla lily.

**1995, Sept. 7**
1928  A309  75c Sheet of 12, #a.-l.   9.25  9.25
**Souvenir Sheet**
1929  A309  $6 multicolored   5.50  5.50

1995 Boy Scout Jamboree, Netherlands A310

No. 1930, $1.20: a, Explorer tent. b, Camper tent. c, Wall tent.
No. 1931, $1.20: a, Trail tarp. b, Miner's. c, Voyager.
No. 1932, $6, Scout with camping equipment, vert. No. 1933, $6, Scout making camp fire.

**1995, Oct. 5**   Strips of 3, #a-c
1930-1931  A310  Set of 2   9.00  9.00
**Souvenir Sheets**
1932-1933  A310  Set of 2   10.00  10.00
For overprints see Nos. 1963-1966.

Trains — A311

Designs: 35c, Gabon. 65c, Canadian. 75c, US. 90c, British high-speed. No. 1938, $1.20, French high-speed. No. 1939, $6, American high-speed (Amtrak).
No. 1940: a, Australian diesel. b, Italian high-speed. c, Thai diesel. d, US steam. e, South African steam. f, Natal steam. g, US war train. h, British steam. i, British steam, diff.
No. 1941, $6, Australian diesel, vert. No. 1942, $6, Asian steam, vert.

**1995, Oct. 23**   Litho.   Perf. 14
1934-1939  A311  Set of 6   10.50  10.50
1940  A311  $1.20 Sheet of 9, #a.-i.   12.50  12.50
**Souvenir Sheets**
1941-1942  A311  Set of 2   14.00  14.00

Birds — A312

No. 1943: a, Purple-throated carib. b, Antillean crested hummingbird. c, Bananaquit (d). d, Mangrove cuckoo. e, Troupial. f, Green-throated carib (e, g). g, Yellow warbler (h). h, Blue-hooded Euphonia. i, Scally-breasted thrasher. j, Burrowing owl (i). k, Caribbean crackle (k). l, Adelaide's warbler.
$6, Purple gallinule.

**1995, Aug. 31**
1943  A312  75c Sheet of 12, #a.-l.   11.50  11.50
**Souvenir Sheet**
1944  A312  $6 multicolored   7.50  7.50

**Miniature Sheets of 9**

Establishment of Nobel Prize Fund, Cent. — A313

No. 1945, $1: a, S.Y. Agnon, literature, 1966. b, Kipling, literature, 1907. c, Aleksandr Solzhenitsyn, literature, 1970. d, Jack Steinberger, physics, 1988. e, Andrei Sakharov, peace, 1975. f, Otto Stern, physics, 1943. g, Steinbeck, literature, 1962. h, Nadine Gordimer, literature, 1991. i, Faulkner, literature, 1949.
No. 1946, $1: a, Hammarskjold, peace, 1961. b, Georg Wittig, chemistry, 1979. c, Wilhelm Ostwald, chemistry, 1909. d, Koch, physiology or medicine, 1945. e, Karl Ziegler, chemistry, 1963. f, Fleming, physiology or medicine, 1945. g, Hermann Staudinger, chemistry, 1953. h, Manfred Eigen, chemistry, 1967. i, Arno Penzias, physics, 1978.
No. 1947, $6, Elie Wiesel, peace, 1986, vert. No. 1948, $6, Dalai Lama, peace, 1989, vert.

**Sheets of 9, #a-i, + label**

**1995, Nov. 8**
1945-1946  A313  Set of 2   20.00  20.00
**Souvenir Sheets**
1947-1948  A313  Set of 2   10.00  10.00

Christmas — A314

Details or entire paintings: 15c, Rest on the Flight into Egypt, by Veronese. 35c, Madonna with The Child, by Van Dyck. 65c, Sacred Conversation Piece, by Veronese. 75c, Vision of Saint Anthony, by Van Dyck. 90c, The Virgin and the Infant, by Van Eyck. No. 1954, The Immaculate Conception, by Tiepolo.
$5, Christ Appearing to His Mother, by Van Der Weyden. $6, Infant Jesus and the Young St. John, by Murillo.

**1995, Dec. 18**   Litho.   Perf. 13½x14
1949-1954  A314  Set of 6   7.00  7.00
**Souvenir Sheets**
1955  A314  $5 multicolored   4.00  4.00
1956  A314  $6 multicolored   5.50  5.50

Elvis Presley (1935-77) — A315

Nos. 1957-1958, Various portraits depicting Presley's life.

**1995, Dec. 8**   Perf. 14
1957  A315  $1 Sheet of 9, #a.-i.   11.00  11.00
**Souvenir Sheet**
1958  A315  $6 multicolored   7.25  7.25

John Lennon (1940-80), Entertainer — A316

45c, 50c, 65c, 75c, Various portraits of Lennon.

**1995, Dec. 8**
1959-1962  A316  Set of 4   3.00  3.00
**Souvenir Sheet**
1962A  A316  $6 like 75c   6.75  6.75
Nos. 1959-1962 were each issued in miniature sheets of 16.
No. 1962A has a continuous design.

**Nos. 1930-1933 Ovptd.**

**1995, Dec. 14**
1963  A310  $1.20 Strip of 3, #a-c (#1930)   3.50  3.50
1964  A310  $1.20 Strip of 3, #a-c (#1931)   3.50  3.50
**Souvenir Sheets**
1965  A310  $6 multi (#1932)   6.50  6.50
1966  A310  $6 multi (#1933)   6.50  6.50
Size and location of overprint varies.

Mushrooms — A317

No. 1967, 75c: a, Hygrophoropsis aurantiaca. b, Hygrophorus bakerensis. c,

# ANTIGUA

Hygrophorus conicus. d, Hygrophorus miniatus.
No. 1968, 75c: a, Suillus brevipes. b, Suillus luteus. c, Suillus granulatus. d, Suillus caerulescens.
No. 1969, $6, Conocybe filaris. No. 1970, $6, Hygrocybe flavescens.

**1996, Apr. 22 — Litho. — Perf. 14**
**Strips of 4, #a-d**
1967-1968  A317  Set of 2   6.25  6.25
**Souvenir Sheets**
1969-1970  A317  Set of 2   9.00  9.00

Nos. 1967-1968 were each issued in sheets of 12 stamps.

Sailing Ships — A318

Designs: 15c, Resolution. 25c, Mayflower. 45c, Santa Maria. No. 1970D, 75c, Aemilia, Holland, 1630. No. 1970E, 75c, Sovereign of the Seas, England, 1637. 90c, HMS Victory, England, 1765.
No. 1971 — Battleships: a, Aemila, Holland, 1630. b, Sovereign of the Seas, England, 1637. c, Royal Louis, France, 1692. d, HMS Royal George, England, 1715. e, Le Protecteur, France, 1761. f, HMS Victory, England, 1765.
No. 1972 — Ships of exploration: a, Santa Maria. b, Victoria. c, Golden Hinde. d, Mayflower. e, Griffin. f, Resolution.
No. 1973, $6, Grande Hermine. No. 1974, $6 USS Constitution, 1797.

**1996, Apr. 25**
1970A-1970F  A318  Set of 6   3.50  3.50
1971  A318  $1.20 Sheet of 6, #a.-f.   8.50  8.50
1972  A318  $1.50 Sheet of 6, #a.-f.   10.00  10.00
**Souvenir Sheets**
1973-1974  A318  Set of 2   11.50  11.50

1996 Summer Olympics, Atlanta — A319

Designs: 65c, Florence Griffith Joyner, women's track, vert. 75c, Olympic Stadium, Seoul, 1988. 90c, Allison Jolly, yachting. $1.20, 2000m Tandem cycling.
No. 1979, 90c — Medalists: a, Wolfgang Nordwig, pole vault. b, Shirley Strong, women's 100m hurdles. c, Sergei Bubka, pole vault. d, Filbert Bayi, 3000m steeplechase. e, Victor Saneyev, triple jump. f, Silke Renk, women's javelin. g, Daley Thompson, decathlon. h, Bob Richards, pole vault. i, Parry O'Brien, shot put.
No. 1980, 90c — Diving medalists: a, Ingrid Kramer, women's platform. b, Kelly McCormick, women's springboard. c, Gary Tobian, men's springboard. d, Greg Louganis, men's diving. e, Michelle Mitchell, women's platform. f, Zhou Jihong, women's platform. g, Wendy Wyland, women's platform. h, Xu Yanmei, women's platform. i, Fu Mingxia, women's platform.
$5, Bill Toomey, decathlon. $6, Mark Lenzi, men's springboard.

**1996, May 6**
1975-1978  A319  Set of 4   2.50  2.50
**Sheets of 9, #a-i**
1979-1980  A319  90c Set of 2   12.50  12.50
**Souvenir Sheets**
1981  A319  $5 multicolored   4.50  4.50
1982  A319  $6 multicolored   5.50  5.50

Sea Birds — A320

No. 1983, 75c: a, Black skimmer. b, Black-capped petrel. c, Sooty tern. d, Royal tern.
No. 1984, 75c: a, Pomarina jaegger. b, White-tailed tropicbird. c, Northern gannet. d, Laughing gull.
$5, Great frigatebird. $6, Brown pelican.

**1996, May 13**
**Vertical Strips of 4, #a-d**
1983-1984  A320  Set of 2   5.50  5.50
**Souvenir Sheets**
1985  A320  $5 multicolored   4.50  4.50
1986  A320  $6 multicolored   5.50  5.50

Nos. 1983-1984 were each issued in sheets of 12 stamps with each strip in sheet having a different order.

Disney Characters In Scenes from Jules Verne's Science Fiction Novels A321

Designs: 1c, Around the World in Eighty Days. 2c, Journey to the Center of the Earth. 5c, Michel Strogoff. 10c, From the Earth to the Moon. 15c, Five Weeks in a Balloon. 20c, Around the World in Eighty Days, diff. $1, The Mysterious Island. $2, From the Earth to the Moon, diff. $3, Captain Grant's Children. $5, Twenty Thousand Leagues Under the Sea.
No. 1997, $6, Twenty Thousand Leagues Under the Sea, diff. No. 1998, $6, Journey to the Center of the Earth, diff.

**1996, June 6 — Litho. — Perf. 14x13½**
1987-1996  A321  Set of 10   12.50  12.50
**Souvenir Sheets**
1997-1998  A321  Set of 2   12.50  12.50

Bruce Lee (1940-73), Martial Arts Expert — A322

Various portraits.

**1996, June 13 — Perf. 14**
1999  A322  75c Sheet of 9, #a.-i.   6.50  6.50
**Souvenir Sheet**
2000  A322  $5 multicolored   5.75  5.75
China '96 (No. 1999).

Queen Elizabeth II, 70th Birthday A323

Designs: a, In blue dress, pearls. b, Carrying bouquet of flowers. c, In uniform.
$6, Painting as younger woman.

**1996, July 17 — Perf. 13½x14**
2001  A323  $2 Strip of 3, #a.-c.   4.00  4.00
**Souvenir Sheet**
2002  A323  $6 multicolored   4.75  4.75

No. 2001 was issued in sheets of 9 stamps.

Traditional Cavalry — A324

No. 2003: a, Ancient Egyptian. b, 13th cent. English. c, 16th cent. Spanish. d, 18th cent. Chinese.
$6, 19th cent. French.

**1996, July 24 — Litho. — Perf. 14**
2003  A324  60c Block of 4, #a.-d.   2.50  2.50
**Souvenir Sheet**
2004  A324  $6 multicolored   4.75  4.75

No. 2003 was issued in sheets of 16 stamps.

UNICEF, 50th Anniv. — A325

Designs: 75c, Girl. 90c, Children. $1.20, Woman holding baby. $6, Girl, diff.

**1996, July 30**
2005-2007  A325  Set of 3   3.00  3.00
**Souvenir Sheet**
2008  A325  $6 multicolored   4.50  4.50

Jerusalem, 3000th Anniv. — A326

Site, flower: 75c, Tomb of Zachariah, verbascum sinuatum. 90c, Pool of Siloam, hyacinthus orientalis. $1.20, Hurva Synagogue, ranunculus asiaticus.
$6, Model of Herod's Temple.

**1996, July 30**
2009-2011  A326  Set of 3   2.25  2.25
**Souvenir Sheet**
2012  A326  $6 multicolored   6.50  6.50

Radio, Cent. — A327

Entertainers: 65c, Kate Smith. 75c, Dinah Shore. 90c, Rudy Vallee. $1.20, Bing Crosby. $6, Jo Stafford.

**1996, July 30**
2013-2016  A327  Set of 4   3.50  3.50
**Souvenir Sheet**
2017  A327  $6 multicolored   4.50  4.50

Christmas — A328

Details or entire paintings, by Filippo Lippi: 60c, Madonna Enthroned. 90c, Adoration of the Child and Saints. $1, Annunciation. $1.20, Birth of the Virgin. $1.60, Adoration of the Child. $1.75, Madonna and Child.
No. 2024, $6, Madonna and Child, diff. No. 2025, $6, Circumcision.

**1996, Nov. 25 — Perf. 13½x14**
2018-2023  A328  Set of 6   7.50  7.50
**Souvenir Sheets**
2024-2025  A328  Set of 2   10.50  10.50

Disney Pals — A329

Designs: 1c, Goofy, Wilbur. 2c, Donald, Goofy. 5c, Donald, Panchito, Jose Carioca. 10c, Mickey, Goofy. 15c, Dale, Chip. 20c, Pluto, Mickey. $1, Daisy, Minnie at ice cream shop. $2, Daisy, Minnie. $3, Gus Goose, Donald.
No. 2035, $6, Donald, vert. No. 2036, $6, Goofy.

**1997, Feb. 17 — Litho. — Perf. 14x13½**
2026-2034  A329  Set of 9   5.50  5.50
**Souvenir Sheets**
**Perf. 13½x14, 14x13½**
2035-2036  A329  Set of 2   9.50  9.50

Salute to Broadway — A330

No. 2037 — Stars, show: a, Robert Preston, The Music Man. b, Michael Crawford, Phantom of the Opera. c, Zero Mostel, Fiddler on the Roof. d, Patti Lupone, Evita. e, Raul Julia, Threepenny Opera. f, Mary Martin, South Pacific. g, Carol Channing, Hello Dolly. h, Yul Brynner, The King and I. i, Julie Andrews, My Fair Lady.
$6, Mickey Rooney, Sugar Babies.

**1997 — Perf. 14**
2037  A330  $1 Sheet of 9, #a.-i.   8.00  8.00
**Souvenir Sheet**
2038  A330  $6 multicolored   5.50  5.50

Butterflies — A331

Designs: 90c, Charaxes porthos. $1.20, Aethiopana honorius. $1.60, Charaxes hadrianus. $1.75, Precis westermanni.
No. 2043, $1.10: a, Charaxes protoclea. b, Byblia ilithyia. c, Black-headed tchagra (bird). d, Charaxes nobilis. e, Pseudacraea boisduvali. f, Charaxes smaragdalis. g, Charaxes lasti. h, Pseudacraea poggei. i, Graphium colonna.
No. 2044, $1.10: a, Carmine bee-eater (bird). b, Pseudacraea eurytus. c, Hypolimnas monteironis. d, Charaxes anticlea. e, Graphium leonidas. f, Graphium illyris. g, Nepheronia argia. h, Graphium policenes. i, Papilio dardanus.
No. 2045, $6, Euxanthe tiberius, horiz. No. 2046, $6, Charaxes lactitinctus, horiz. No. 2047, $6, Euphaedra neophron.

**1997, Mar. 10**
2039-2042  A331  Set of 4   5.50  5.50
**Sheets of 9, #a-i**
2043-2044  A331  Set of 2   18.50  18.50
**Souvenir Sheets**
2045-2047  A331  Set of 3   14.50  14.50

# ANTIGUA 541

UNESCO, 50th Anniv. A332

World Heritage Sites: 60c, Convent of the Companions of Jesus, Morelia, Mexico. 90c, Fortress, San Lorenzo, Panama, vert. $1, Canaima Natl. Park, Venezuela, vert. $1.20, Huascarán Natl. Park, Peru, vert. $1.60, Church of San Francisco, Guatemala, vert. $1.75, Santo Domingo, Dominican Republic, vert.

No. 2054, vert, each $1.10: a-c, Guanajuato, Mexico. d, Jesuit missions of the Chiquitos, Bolivia. e, Huascarán Natl. Park, Peru. f, Jesuit missions, La Santisima, Paraguay. g, Cartagena, Colombia. h, Old Havana fortification, Cuba.

No. 2055, each $1.65: a, Tikal Natl. Park, Guatemala. b, Rio Platano Reserve, Honduras. c, Ruins of Copán, Honduras. d, Church of El Carmen, Antigua, Guatemala. e, Teotihuacán, Mexico.

No. 2056, $6, Teotihuacán, Mexico, diff. No. 2057, $6, Tikal Natl. Park, Guatemala, diff.

**1997, Apr. 10**   **Litho.**   **Perf. 14**
2048-2053 A332 Set of 6   4.75   4.75
2054 A332 Sheet of 8, #a.-h. + label   8.00   8.00
2055 A332 Sheet of 5, #a.-e. + label   7.50   7.50
**Souvenir Sheets**
2056-2057 A332 Set of 2   9.75   9.75

Endangered Species — A333

No. 2058, each $1.20: a, Red bishop. b, Yellow baboon. c, Superb starling. d, Ratel. e, Hunting dog. f, Serval.

No. 2059, each $1.65: a, Okapi. b, Giant forest squirrel. c, Masked weaver. d, Common genet. e, Yellow-billed stork. f, Red-headed agama.

No. 2060, $6, Malachite kingfisher. No. 2061, $6, Gray crowned crane. No. 2062, $6, Bat-eared fox.

**1997, Apr. 24**
2058 A333 Sheet of 6, #a.-f.   7.50   7.50
2059 A333 Sheet of 6, #a.-f.   9.00   9.00
**Souvenir Sheets**
2060-2062 A333 Set of 3   17.00   17.00

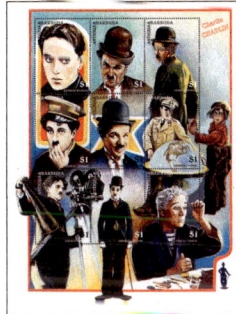

Charlie Chaplin (1889-1977), Comedian, Actor — A334

Various portraits.

**1997, Feb. 24**   **Litho.**   **Perf. 14**
2063 A334 $1 Sheet of 9, #a.-i.   6.75   6.75
**Souvenir Sheet**
2064 A334 $6 multicolored   5.25   5.25

Paul P. Harris (1868-1947), Founder of Rotary, Intl. — A335

Designs: $1.75, Service above self, James Grant, Ivory Coast, 1994, portrait of Harris. $6, Group study exchange, New Zealand.

**1997, June 12**   **Litho.**   **Perf. 14**
2065 A335 $1.75 multicolored   1.60   1.60
**Souvenir Sheet**
2066 A335 $6 multicolored   4.50   4.50

Heinrich von Stephan (1831-97) A336

No. 2067, each $1.75, Portrait of Von Stephan and: a, Kaiser Wilhelm I. b, UPU emblem. c, Pigeon Post.
$6, Von Stephan, Basel messenger, 1400's.

**1997, June 12**
2067 A336 Sheet of 3, #a.-c.   3.50   3.50
**Souvenir Sheet**
2068 A336 $6 multicolored   5.00   5.00

PACIFIC 97.

Queen Elizabeth II, Prince Philip, 50th Wedding Anniv. — A337

No. 2069: a, Queen. b, Royal arms. c, Queen, Prince in royal attire. d, Queen, King riding in open carriage. e, Balmoral Castle. f, Prince Philip.
$6, Early portrait of Queen, King in royal attire.

**1997, June 12**
2069 A337 $1 Sheet of 6, #a.-f.   6.25   6.25
**Souvenir Sheet**
2070 A337 $6 multicolored   5.25   5.25

Grimm's Fairy Tales — A338

Scenes from "Cinderella", each $1.75: No. 2071: a, Mother, stepsisters. b, Cinderella, fairy godmother. c, Cinderella, Prince Charming.
$6, Prince trying shoe on Cinderella.

**1997, June 13**   **Perf. 13½x14**
2071 A338 Sheet of 3, #a.-c.   4.75   4.75
**Souvenir Sheet**
2072 A338 $6 multicolored   5.25   5.25

Chernobyl Disaster, 10th Anniv. — A339

Designs: $1.65, UNESCO. $2, Chabad's Children of Chernobyl.

**1997, June 12**
2073 A339 $1.65 multicolored   1.50   1.50
2074 A339 $2 multicolored   1.75   1.75

Mushrooms A340

Designs: 45c, Marasmius rotula. 65c, Cantharellus cibarius. 70c, Lepiota cristata. 90c, Auricularia mesenterica. $1, Pholiota alnicola. $1.65, Leccinum aurantiacum.

No. 2081, each $1.75: a, Entoloma serrulatum. b, Panaeolus sphinctrinus. c, Volvariella bombycina. d, Conocybe percincta. e, Pluteus cervinus. f, Russula foetens.
No. 2082, $6, Panellus serotinus. No. 2083, $6, Amanita cothurnata.

**1997, Aug. 12**   **Litho.**   **Perf. 14**
2075-2080 A340 Set of 6   4.00   4.00
2081 A340 Sheet of 6, #a.-f.   8.00   8.00
**Souvenir Sheets**
2082-2083 A340 Set of 2   10.00   10.00

Orchids — A341

Designs: 45c, Odontoglossum cervantesii. 65c, Medford star. 75c, Motes resplendent. 90c, Debutante. $1, Apple blossom. $2, Dendrobium.

No. 2090, $1.65: a, Angel lace. b, Precious stones. c, Orange theope butterfly. d, Promenaea xanthina. e, Lycaste macrobulbon. f, Amesiella philippinensis. g, Machu Picchu. h, Zuma urchin.
No. 2091, $1.65: a, Sophia Martin. b, Dogface butterfly. c, Mini purple. d, Showgirl. e, Mem. Dorothy Bertsch. f, Black II. g, Leeanum. h, Paphiopedilum macranthum.
No. 2092, $6, Seine. No. 2093, $6, Paphiopedilum gratrixianum.

**1997, Aug. 19**   **Litho.**   **Perf. 14**
2084-2089 A341 Set of 6   5.75   5.75
**Sheets of 8, #a-h**
2090-2091 A341 Set of 2   17.00   17.00
**Souvenir Sheets**
2092-2093 A341 Set of 2   10.00   10.00

1998 World Cup Soccer Championships, France — A342

Designs: 60c, Maradona, Argentina, 1986. 75c, Fritz Walter, W. Germany, 1954. 90c, Zoff, Italy, 1982. $1.20, Moore, England, 1966. $1.65, Alberto, Brazil, 1970. $1.75, Matthäus, W. Germany.

No. 2100, vert: a, Ademir, Brazil, 1950. b, Eusebio, Portugal, 1966. c, Fontaine, France, 1958. d, Schillaci, Italy, 1990. e, Leonidas, Brazil, 1938. f, Stabile, Argentina, 1930. g, Nejedly, Czechoslovakia, 1934. h, Muller, W. Germany, 1970.
No. 2101, $6, Players, W. Germany, 1990. No. 2102, $6, Bebeto, Brazil, vert.

**1997, Oct. 6**   **Litho.**   **Perf. 14**
2094-2099 A342 Set of 6   5.25   5.25
2100 A342 $1 Sheet of 8, #a.-h., + label   5.25   5.25
**Souvenir Sheets**
2101-2102 A342 Set of 2   8.50   8.50

Domestic Animals — A343

No. 2103, $1.65 — Dogs: a, Dachshund. b, Staffordshire terrier. c, Sharpei. d, Beagle. e, Norfolk terrier. f, Golden retriever.
No. 2104, $1.65 — Cats: a, Scottish fold. b, Japanese bobtail. c, Tabby manx. d, Bicolor American shorthair. e, Sorrel abyssinian. f, Himalayan blue point.
No. 2105, $6, Siberian husky, vert. No. 2106, $6, Red tabby American shorthair kitten, vert.

**1997, Oct. 27**   **Litho.**   **Perf. 14**
**Sheets of 6, #a-f**
2103-2104 A343 Set of 2   18.00   18.00
**Souvenir Sheets**
2105-2106 A343 Set of 2   10.00   10.00

Early Trains — A344

No. 2107, $1.65: a, Original Trevithick drawing, 1804. b, "Puffing Billy," William Hedley, 1860. c, Crampton locomotive, Northern Railway, France, 1858. d, Twenty-five ton locomotive, Lawrence Machine Shop, 1860's. e, First locomotive, "Mississippi," built in England. f, "Coppernob," locomotive by Edward Bury, Furness Railway.
No. 2108, $1.65: a, "Jenny Lind," by David Joy for E.B. Wilson. b, "Atlantic" type locomotive, by Schenectady Locomotive Works, 1899. c, British built tank engine, Japan, by Kisons of Leeds, 1881. d, Express freight locomotive, 4-8-2 type, Pennsylvania Railroad. e, Four-cylinder locomotive, by Karl Golsdorf, Austria. f, "E" series 0-10-0 locomotive, produced by Lugansk Works, Russia, 1930.
No. 2109, $6, "Patente" George Stephenson, 1843. No. 2110, $6, Brunel's Trestle, Lynher River.

**1997, Nov. 10**   **Sheets of 6, #a-f**
2107-2108 A344 Set of 2   19.00   19.00
**Souvenir Sheets**
2109-2110 A344 Set of 2   10.00   10.00

Christmas — A345

Entire paintings or details: 15c, The Angel Leaving Tobias and His Family, by Rembrandt. 25c, The Resurrection, by Martin Knoller. 60c, Astronomy, by Raphael. 75c, Music-making Angel, by Melozzo da Forli. 90c, Amor, by Parmigianino. $1.20, Madonna and Child with Saints John the Baptist, Anthony, Stephen and Jerome, by Rosso Fiorentino.
No. 2117, $6, The Portinari Altarpiece, by Hugo Van Der Goes. No. 2118, $6, The Wedding of Tobiolo, by Gianantonio and Francesco Guardi.

**1997, Dec. 2**   **Litho.**   **Perf. 14**
2111-2116 A345 $6 Set of 6   3.75   3.75
**Souvenir Sheets**
2117-2118 A345 $6 Set of 2   9.00   9.00

Diana, Princess of Wales (1961-97) — A346

Various portraits, color of sheet margin: No. 2119, $1.65, Pale green. No. 2120, $1.65, Pale pink.
No. 2121, $6, With her sons (in margin). No. 2122, $6, With Pope John Paul II (in margin).

**1998, Jan. 19**   **Litho.**   **Perf. 14**
**Sheets of 6, #a-f**
2119-2120 A346 Set of 2   12.50   12.50
**Souvenir Sheets**
2121-2122 A346 Set of 2   9.00   9.00

Fish — A347

Designs: 75c, Yellow damselfish. 90c, Barred hamlet. $1, Jewolfish. $1.20, Bluehead wrasse. $1.50, Queen angelfish. $1.75, Queen triggerfish.
No. 2129, $1.65: a, Jack-knife fish. b, Cuban hogfish. c, Sergeant major. d, Neon goby. e, Jawfish. f, Flamefish.
No. 2130, $1.65: a, Rock beauty. b, Yellowtail snapper. c, Creole wrasse. d, Slender filefish. e, Squirrel fish. f, Fairy basslet.
No. 2131, $6, Black-capped gramma. No. 2132, $6, Porkfish.

**1998, Feb. 19**
2123-2128 A347 Set of 6   4.25   4.25

## 542 ANTIGUA

**Sheets of 6, #a-f**
2129-2130  A347  Set of 2     13.00 13.00
**Souvenir Sheets**
2131-2132  A347  Set of 2     10.00 10.00

Cedar Hall Moravian Church, 175th Anniv. — A348

Designs: 20c, First church, manse, 1822-40. 45c, Cedar Hall School, 1840. 75c, Hugh A. King, former minister. 90c, Present structure. $1.20, Water tank, 1822. $2, Former manse demolished, 1978.
$6, Present structure, diff.

**1998, Mar. 16    Litho.    Perf. 14**
2133-2138  A348  Set of 6     4.00 4.00
**Souvenir Sheet**
2139  A348  $6 multicolored   4.75 4.75
 No. 2139 contains one 50x37mm stamp.

Lighthouses A349

Lighthouse, location: 45c, Trinity, Europa Point, Gibraltar, vert. 65c, Tierra Del Fuego, Argentina. 75c, Point Loma, California, US. 90c, Groenpoint, South Africa, vert. $1, Youghal, County Cork, Ireland, vert. $1.20, Launceston, Tasmania, Australia, vert. $1.65, Point Abino, Ontario, Canada. $1.75, Great Inagua, Bahamas.
$6, Capa Hatteras, North Carolina, US.

**1998, Apr. 20**
2140-2147  A349  Set of 8     8.00 8.00
**Souvenir Sheet**
2148  A349  $6 multi, vert.  7.75 7.75

Winnie the Pooh — A350

No. 2149, $1: a, Pooh, Tigger in January. b, Pooh, Piglet in February. c, Piglet in March. d, Tigger, Pooh, Piglet in April. e, Kanga, Roo in May. f, Pooh, Owl in June.
 No. 2150, $1,: a, Pooh, Eeyore, Tigger, Piglet in July. b, Pooh, Piglet in August. c, Christopher Robin in September. d, Eeyore in October. e, Pooh, Rabbit in November. f, Pooh, Piglet in December.
 No. 2151, $6, Pooh, Rabbit holding blanket, Spring. No. 2152, $6, Pooh holding hand to mouth, Summer. No. 2153, $6, Pooh holding rake, Fall. No. 2154, $6, Eeyore, Pooh, Winter.

**1998, May 11    Litho.    Perf. 13½x14**
**Sheets of 6, #a-f**
2149-2150  A350  Set of 2    13.50 13.50
**Souvenir Sheet**
2151-2154  A350  Set of 4    19.00 19.00

Thomas Oliver Robinson Memorial High School, Cent. — A351

Designs: 20c, $6, Nellie Robinson (1880-1972), founder, vert. 45c, School picture, 1985. 65c, Former building, 1930-49. 75c, Students with present headmistress, Natalie Hurst. 90c, Ina Loving (1908-96), educator, vert. $1.20, Present building, 1950.

**1998, July 23    Litho.    Perf. 14**
2155-2160  A351  Set of 6     4.00 4.00
**Souvenir Sheet**
2161  A351  $6 multicolored   4.00 4.00
 No. 2161 is a continuous design.

Intl. Year of the Ocean — A352

No. 2162 — Marine life, "20,000 Leagues Under the Sea": a, Spotted eagle ray. b, Manta ray. c, Hawksbill turtle. d, Jellyfish. e, Queen angelfish. f, Octopus. g, Emperor angelfish. h, Regal angelfish. i, Porkfish. j, Raccoon butterfly fish. k, Atlantic barracuda. l, Sea horse. m, Nautilus. n, Trumpet fish. o, White tip shark. p, Spanish galleon. q, Black tip shark. r, Long-nosed butterfly fish. s, Green moray eel. t, Captain Nemo. u, Treasure chest. v, Hammerhead shark. w, Divers. x, Lion fish. y, Clown fish.
 No. 2163 — Wildlife and birds: a, Maroon tailed conure. b, Cocoi heron. c, Common tern. d, Rainbow lorikeet. e, Saddleback butterfly fish. f, Goatfish, cat shark. g, Blue shark, stingray. h, Majestic snapper. i, Nassau grouper. j, Black-cap gramma, blue tang. k, Stingrays. l, Stingrays, giant starfish.
 No. 2164, $6, Fiddler ray. No. 2165, $6, Humpback whale.

**1998, Aug. 17**
2162  A352  40c Sheet of 25, #a.-y.          8.25 8.25
2163  A352  75c Sheet of 12, #a.-l.  7.75 7.75
**Souvenir Sheets**
2164-2165  A352  Set of 2   9.75 9.75

Ships — A353

No. 2166, each $1.75: a, Savannah. b, Viking ship. c, Greek warship.
 No. 2167, each $1.75: a, Clipper. b, Dhow. c, Fishing cat.
 No. 2168, $6, Dory, vert. No. 2169, $6, Baltimore clipper. No. 2170, $6, English warship, 13th cent.

**1998, Aug. 18    Perf. 14x14½**
**Sheets of 3, #a-c**
2166-2167  A353  Set of 2    7.25 7.25
**Souvenir Sheets**
**Perf. 14**
2168-2170  A353  $6 Set of 3  15.00 15.00

CARICOM, 25th Anniv. — A354

**1998, Aug. 20    Litho.    Perf. 13½**
2171  A354  $1 multicolored  1.40 1.40

Antique Automobiles A355

No. 2172 $1.65: a, 1911 Torpedo. b, 1913 Mercedes 22. c, 1920 Rover. d, 1956 Mercedes Benz. e, 1934 Packard V12. f, 1924 Opel.
 No. 2173, $1.65 — Fords: a, 1896. b, 1903 Model A. c, 1928 Model T. d, 1922 Model T. e, 1929 Blackhawk. f, 1934 Sedan.
 No. 2174, $6, 1908 Ford. No. 2175, $6, 1929 Ford.

**1998, Sept. 1    Perf. 14**
**Sheets of 6, #a-f**
2172-2173  A355  Set of 2    15.00 15.00
**Souvenir Sheets**
2174-2175  A355  Set of 2     9.00 9.00
 Nos. 2174-2175 each contain one 60x40mm stamp.

Aircraft — A356

No. 2176, $1.65: a, NASA Space Shuttle. b, Saab Grippen. c, Eurofighter EF2000. d, Sukhoi SU 27. e, Northrop B-2. f, Lockheed F-117 Nighthawk.
 No. 2177, $1.65: a, Lockheed-Boeing General Dynamics Yf-22. b, Dassault-Breguet Rafale BO 1. c, MiG 29. d, Dassault-Breguet Mirage 2000D. e, Rockwell B-1B Lancer. f, McDonnell-Douglas C-17A.
 No. 2178, $6, Sukhoi SU 35. No. 2179, $6, F-18 Hornet.

**1998, Sept. 21    Sheets of 6, #a-f**
2176-2177  A356  Set of 2    14.50 14.50
**Souvenir Sheets**
2178-2179  A356  Set of 2    10.50 10.50

Inventors and Inventions — A357

No. 2180 $1: a, Rudolf Diesel (1858-1913). b, Internal combustion, diesel engines. c, Zeppelin war balloon, Intrepid. d, Ferdinand von Zeppelin (1838-1917). e, Wilhelm Conrad Röntgen (1845-1923). f, X-ray machine. g, Saturn rocket. h, Wernher von Braun (1912-77).
 No. 2181, $1: a, Carl Benz (1844-1929). b, Internal combustion engine, automobile. c, Atomic bomb. d, Albert Einstein. e, Leopold Godowsky, Jr. (1901-83) and Leopold Damrosch Mannes (1899-1964). f, Kodachrome film. g, First turbo jet airplane. h, Hans Pabst von Ohain (1911-98).
 No. 2182, $6, Hans Geiger (1882-1945), inventor of the Geiger counter. No. 2183, $6, William Shockley (1910-89), developer of transistors.

**1998, Nov. 10    Litho.    Perf. 14**
**Sheets of 8, #a-h**
2180-2181  A357  Set of 2    16.50 16.50
**Souvenir Sheets**
2182-2183  A357  Set of 2    10.50 10.50
 Nos. 2180b-2180c, 2180f-2180g, 2181b-2181c, 2181f-2181g are 53x38mm.

Diana, Princess of Wales (1961-97) — A358

Designs: a, Peach bar with country name on left side. b, Peach bar with country name on right side.

**1998, Nov. 18**
2184  A358  $1.20 Pair, #a.-b.  1.10 1.10
 No. 2184 was printed in sheets containing 3 pairs.

Gandhi — A359

Portraits: 90c, Up close, later years. $1, Seated with hands clasped. $1.20, Up close, early years. $1.65, Primary school, Rajkot, age 7. $6, With stick, walking with boy (in margin).

**1998, Nov. 18**
2185-2188  A359  Set of 4    6.00 6.00
**Souvenir Sheet**
2189  A359  $6 multicolored   5.00 5.00

Picasso — A360

Paintings: $1.20, Figures on the Seashore, 1931, horiz. $1.65, Three Figures Under a Tree, 1907. $1.75, Two Women Running on the Beach, 1922, horiz.
$6, Bullfight, 1900, horiz.

**1998, Nov. 18**
2190-2192  A360  Set of 3     3.00 3.00
**Souvenir Sheet**
2193  A360  $6 multicolored   5.00 5.00

1998 World Scouting Jamboree, Chile — A361

90c, Handshake. $1, Scouts hiking. $1.20, Sign.
$6, Lord Baden-Powell.

**1998, Oct. 8    Litho.    Perf. 14**
2194-2196  A361  Set of 3     2.25 2.25
**Souvenir Sheet**
2197  A361  $6 multicolored   4.50 4.50

Organization of American States, 50th Anniv. — A362

**1998, Nov. 18    Perf. 13½**
2198  A362  $1 multicolored   .80 .80

Enzo Ferrari (1898-1988), Automobile Manufacturer A363

No. 2199, each $1.75: a, Top view of Dino 246 GT-GTS. b, Front view of Dino 246 GT-GTS. c, 1977 365 GT4 BB.
$6, Dino 246 GT-GTS.

**1998, Nov. 18    Perf. 14**
2199  A363  Sheet of 3, #a.-c.  8.00 8.00
**Souvenir Sheet**
2200  A363  $6 multicolored   8.00 8.00
 No. 2200 contains one 92x35mm stamp.

Royal Air Force, 80th Anniv. — A364

No. 2201, each $1.75: a, McDonnell Douglas Phantom FGR1. b, Sepecat Jaguar GR1A. c, Panavia Tornado F3. d, McDonnell Douglas Phantom FGR2.
 No. 2202, $6, Eurofighter 2000, Hurricane. No. 2203, $6, Hawk, biplane.

**1998, Nov. 18**
2201  A364  Sheet of 4, #a.-d.  6.25 6.25
**Souvenir Sheets**
2202-2203  A364  Set of 2   11.00 11.00

Sea Birds — A365

Designs: 15c, Brown pelican. 25c, Dunlin. 45c, Atlantic puffin. 90c, Pied cormorant.
 No. 2208: a, King eider. b, Inca tern. c, Dovekie. d, Ross's bull. e, Brown noddy. f, Marbled murrelet. g, Northern gannet. h, Razorbill. i, Long-tailed jaeger. j, Black guillemot. k, Whimbrel. l, Oystercatcher.
 No. 2209, $6, Rhynchops niger. No. 2210, $6, Diomedea exulans.

**1998, Nov. 24**
2204-2207  A365  Set of 4    2.00 2.00

# ANTIGUA

2208 A365 75c Sheet of 12, #a.-l. 8.50 8.50
**Souvenir Sheets**
2209-2210 A365 Set of 2 11.00 11.00

Christmas — A366

Dogs with Christmas decorations: 15c, Border collie. 25c, Dalmatian. 65c, Weimaraner. 75c, Scottish terrier. 90c, Long-haired dachshund. $1.20, Golden retriever. $2, Pekingese. No. 2218, $6, Dalmatian, diff. No. 2219, $6, Jack Russell terrier.

**1998, Dec. 10**
2211-2217 A366 Set of 7 7.00 7.00
**Souvenir Sheet**
2218-2219 A366 Set of 2 9.25 9.25

Disney Characters in Water Sports — A367

No. 2220, $1 — Water skiing: a, Goofy, maroon skis. b, Mickey. c, Goofy, Mickey. d, Donald. e, Goofy, blue skis. f, Minnie.
No. 2221, $1 — Surfing: a, Goofy running with board. b, Mickey. c, Donald holding board. d, Donald, riding board. e, Minnie. f, Goofy in water.
No. 2221G, Sailing & sailboarding: h, Mickey wearing cap. i, Mickey, Goofy, counterbalancing boat. j, Goofy sailboarding. k, Mickey, seagull overhead. l, Goofy puffing at sail. m, Mickey sailboarding.
No. 2222, Mickey. No. 2223, Minnie. No. 2224, Goofy. No. 2225, Donald.

**1999, Jan. 11    Litho.    Perf. 13½x14**
**Sheets of 6, #a-f**
2220-2221 A367 Set of 2 11.00 11.00
2221G A367 $1 Sheet of 6, #h.-m. 5.50 5.50
**Souvenir Sheets**
2222-2225 A367 Set of 4 18.50 18.50
Mickey Mouse, 70th anniv.

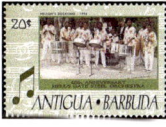
Hell's Gate Steel Orchestra, 50th Anniv. — A368

Designs: 20c, Nelson's Dockyard, 1996. 60c, Holiday Inn, Rochester, New York, 1992. 75c, Early years, 1950. 90c, World's Fair, 1964, Eustace Henry (AKA Manning). $1.20, Alston Henry playing double tenor.
No. 2231, $4, Like #2229, vert. No. 2232, $4, The early years, vert.

**1999, Feb. 1    Litho.    Perf. 14**
2226-2230 A368 Set of 5 3.25 3.25
**Souvenir Sheets**
2231-2232 A368 Set of 2 6.75 6.75

Flowers — A369

Designs, vert: 60c, Tulip. 75c, Fuschia. $1.20, Calla lily. $1.65, Sweet pea.
No. 2237: a, Morning glory. b, Geranium. c, Blue hibiscus. d, Marigolds. e, Sunflower. f, Impatiens. g, Petunia. h, Pansy. i, Saucer magnolia.
No. 2238: a, Primrose. b, Bleeding heart. c, Pink dogwood. d, Peony. e, Rose. f, Hellebores. g, Lily. h, Violet. i, Cherry blossoms.
No. 2239, $6, Lily, vert. No. 2240, $6, Zinnias, vert.

**1999, Apr. 19    Litho.    Perf. 14**
2233-2236 A369 Set of 4 3.00 3.00
2237 A369 90c Sheet of 9, #a.-i. 6.25 6.25
2238 A369 $1 Sheet of 9, #a.-i. 7.25 7.25
**Souvenir Sheets**
2239-2240 A369 Set of 2 9.25 9.25

Elle Macpherson, Model — A370

Various portraits, each $1.20.

**1999, Apr. 26    Perf. 13½**
2241 A370 Sheet of 8, #a.-h. 8.50 8.50
Australia '99 World Stamp Expo.

John Glenn's Space Flight — A371

Space Exploration — A372

No. 2242 — John Glenn, 1962, each $1.75: a, Climbing into Mercury Capsule. b, Formal portrait. c, Having helmet adjusted. d, Entering pressure chamber.
No. 2243, $1.65: a, Luna 2. b, Mariner 2. c, Giotto space probe. d, Rosat. e, Intl. Ultraviolet Explorer. f, Ulysses Space Probe.
No. 2244, $1.65: a, Mariner 10. b, Luna 9. c, Advanced X-ray Astrophysics Facility. d, Magellan Spacecraft. e, Pioneer-Venus 2. f, Infra-red Astronomy Satellite.
No. 2245, $6, Salyut 1, horiz. No. 2246, $6, MIR, horiz.

**1999, May 6    Litho.    Perf. 14**
2242 A371 Sheet of 4, #a.-d. 6.50 6.50
**Sheets of 6, #a-f**
2243-2244 A372 Set of 2 15.00 15.00
**Souvenir Sheets**
2245-2246 A372 Set of 2 9.00 9.00
Nos. 2245-2246 are incorrectly inscribed.

Prehistoric Animals — A373

Designs: 65c, Brachiosaurus. 75c, Oviraptor, vert. $1, Homotherium. $1.20, Macrauchenia, vert.
No. 2251, each $1.65: a, Leptictidium. b, Ictitherium. c, Plesictis. d, Hemicyon. e, Diacodexio. f, Stylinodon. g, Kanuites. h, Chriacus. i, Argyrolagus.
No. 2252, each $1.65: a, Struthiomimus. b, Corythosaurus. c, Dsungaripterus. d, Compognathus. e, Prosaurolophus. f, Montanoceratops. g, Stegosaurus. h, Deinonychus. i, Ouranosaurus.
No. 2253, each $6, Pteranodon. No. 2254, $6, Eurhinodelphus.

**1999, May 26**
2247-2250 A373 Set of 4 3.50 3.50
**Sheets of 9, #a-i**
2251-2252 A373 Set of 2 22.00 22.00
**Souvenir Sheets**
2253-2254 A373 Set of 2 9.00 9.00
Illustrations on Nos. 2247-2248 are switched.

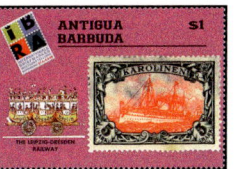
IBRA'99, World Stamp Exhibition, Nuremberg — A374

Exhibition emblem, Leipzig-Dresden Railway and: No. 2255, $1, Caroline Islands #19. No. 2257, $1.65, Caroline Islands #4.
Emblem, Gölsdorf 4-4-0 and: No. 2256, $1.20, Caroline Islands #16. No. 2258, $1.90, Caroline Islands #8, #10.
$6, Registered label on cover.

**1999, June 24    Litho.    Perf. 14**
2255-2258 A374 Set of 4 5.00 5.00
**Souvenir Sheet**
2259 A374 $6 multicolored 4.75 4.75

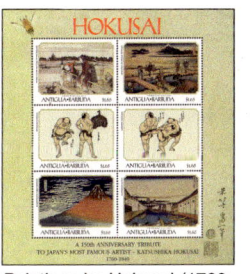
Paintings by Hokusai (1760-1849) — A375

No. 2260, $1.65 — Details or entire paintings: a, Asakusa Honganji. b, Dawn at Isawa in Kai Province. c, Samurai with Bow and Arrow (bows level). d, Samurai with Bow and Arrow (bows at different angles). e, Kajikazawa in Kai Province. f, A Great Wave.
No. 2261, $1.65: a, People on the Balcony of the Sazaido. b, Nakahara in Sagami Province. c, Defensive Positions (2 men). d, Defensive Positions (3 men). e, Mount Fuji in Clear Weather. f, Nihonbashi in Edo.
No. 2262, $6, Gotenyama At Shinagawa on Tokaido Highway, vert. No. 2263, $6, A Netsuke Workshop, vert.

**1999, June 24    Sheets of 6, #a-f**
2260-2261 A375 Set of 2 15.00 15.00
**Souvenir Sheets**
2262-2263 A375 Set of 2 9.25 9.25

Johann Wolfgang von Goethe (1749-1832), Poet — A376

No. 2264, each $1.75: a, Three archangels in "Faust." b, Portraits of Goethe and Friedrich von Schiller (1759-1805). c, Faust reclining in landscape with spirits.
$6, Profile portrait of Goethe.

**1999, June 24    Litho.    Perf. 14**
2264 A376 Sheet of 3, #a.-c. 4.50 4.50
**Souvenir Sheet**
2265 A376 $6 multicolored 4.50 4.50

**Souvenir Sheets**

Philexfrance '99, World Philatelic Exhibition — A377

Locomotives: No. 2266, Crampton 1855-69. No. 2267, 232-U1 4-Cylinder Compound 4-6-4, 1949.

**1999, June 24    Perf. 13¾**
2266 A377 $6 multicolored 5.00 5.00
2267 A377 $6 multicolored 5.00 5.00

Wedding of Prince Edward and Sophie Rhys-Jones — A378

No. 2268: a, Sophie. b, Sophie, Edward. c, Edward.
$6, Horse and carriage, couple.

**1999, June 24    Perf. 13½**
2268 A378 $3 Sheet of 3, #a.-c. 6.75 6.75
**Souvenir Sheet**
2269 A378 $6 multicolored 5.00 5.00

A379

Various white kittens: 35c, 45c, 60c, 75c, 90c, $1.
No. 2276, $1.65: a, One holding paw on another. b, Black & white. c, White kitten, black kitten. d, One with yarn. e, Two in basket. f, One looking up.
No. 2277, $1.65: a, One playing with red yarn. b, Two long-haired. c, Yellow tabby. d, One with mouse. e, Yellow tabby on pillow. f, Black & gray tabby.
No. 2278, $6, Tabby cat carrying kitten. No. 2279, $6, Yellow kitten in tree.

**1999, May 25    Litho.    Perf. 14½x14**
2270-2275 A379 Set of 6 3.00 3.00
**Sheets of 6**
2276-2277 A379 Set of 2 15.00 15.00
**Souvenir Sheets**
2278-2279 A379 Set of 2 9.25 9.25
Australia '99, World Stamp Expo (Nos. 2276-2279).

A380

UN Rights of the Child Convention, 10th Anniv. — No. 2280: a, Three children. b, Adult hand taking child's hand, silhouette of mother holding infant. c, UN Building, member flags, dove.
$6, Dove.

**1999, June 22    Perf. 14**
2280 A380 $3 Sheet of 3, #a.-c. 6.75 6.75
**Souvenir Sheet**
2281 A380 $6 multicolored 5.00 5.00

# ANTIGUA

Boats — A381

Designs: 25c, Missa Ferdie. 45c, Sailboats. 60c, Jolly Roger Pirate Ship. 90c, $4, Freewinds. $1.20, Monarch of the Seas.

**1999, June 24**    Litho.    Perf. 13x11
2282-2286   A381   Set of 5   3.25   3.25
2286a   Souvenir sheet, #2282-2286   3.75   3.75

**Souvenir Sheet**
**Perf. 13¾**
2287   A381   $4 multicolored   3.75   3.75

No. 2287 contains one 51x38mm stamp.

A382

Butterflies: 65c, Fiery jewel. 75c, Hewitson's blue hairstreak. $1.20, Scarce bamboo page, horiz. $1.65, Paris peacock, horiz.
No. 2292, horiz.: a, California dog face. b, Small copper. c, Zebra swallowtail. d, White M hairstreak. e, Old world swallowtail. f, Buckeye. g, Apollo. h, Sonoran blue. i, Purple emperor.
No. 2293, $6, Monarch. No. 2294, $6, Cairns birdwing, horiz.

**1999, Aug. 16**    Perf. 14
2288-2291   A382   Set of 4   3.75   3.75
2292   A382   $1 Sheet of 9, #a.-i.   8.50   8.50

**Souvenir Sheets**
2293-2294   A382   Set of 2   11.00   11.00

Christmas — A383

15c, Madonna and child in a Wreath of Flowers by Peter Paul Rubens. 25c, Shroud of Christ Held by Two Angels, by Albrecht Dürer. 45c, Madonna and Child Enthroned Between Two Saints, by Raphael. 60c, Holy Family with the Lamb, by Raphael. $2, The Transfiguration, by Raphael. $4, Three Putti Holding a Coat of Arms, by Dürer.
$6, The Coronation of the Holy St. Catherine, by Rubens.

**1999, Nov. 22**    Litho.    Perf. 13¾
2295-2300   A383   Set of 6   6.50   6.50

**Souvenir Sheet**
2301   A383   $6 multicolored   5.50   5.50

Famous Elderly People — A384

Designs: a, Katharine Hepburn. b, Martha Graham. c, Eubie Blake. d, Agatha Christie. e, Eudora Welty. f, Helen Hayes. g, Vladimir Horowitz. h, Katharine Graham. i, Pablo Casals. j, Pete Seeger. k, Andres Segovia. l, Frank Lloyd Wright.

**2000, Jan. 18**    Litho.    Perf. 14
2302   A384   90c Sheet of 12, #a-l   8.00   8.00

Charlie Chaplin — A385

Designs: a, "Modern Times," street scene. b, "The Gold Rush," with other actor. c, Unidentified film. d, "Modern Times," on gears. e, "The Gold Rush," arms akimbo. f, "The Gold Rush," with cane.

**2000, Jan. 18**    Perf. 13¾
2303   A385   $1.65 Sheet of 6, #a-f   7.25   7.25

Sir Cliff Richard, Rock Musician — A386

**2000, Jan. 18**    Perf. 13¼
2304   A386   $1.65 multi   1.25   1.25

Issued in sheets of 6.

Birds — A387

Designs: 75c, Streamertail. 90c, Yellow-bellied sapsucker. $1.20, Rufous-tailed jacamar. $2, Spectacled owl.
No. 2309, $1.20: a, Ground dove. b, Wood stork. c, Saffron finch. d, Green-backed heron. e, Lovely cotinga. f, St. Vincent parrot. g, Cuban grassquit. h, Red-winged blackbird.
No. 2310, $1.20: a, Scarlet macaw. b, Yellow-fronted amazon. c, Queen-of-Bavaria. d, Nanday conure. e, Jamaican tody. f, Smooth-billed ani. g, Puerto Rican woodpecker. h, Ruby-throated hummingbird.
No. 2311, $6, Vermilion flycatcher. No. 2312, $6, Red-capped manakin, vert.

**2000, Apr. 17**    Litho.    Perf. 14
2305-2308   A387   Set of 4   4.00   4.00

**Sheets of 8, #a-h**
**Perf. 13¾x14**
2309-2310   A387   Set of 2   15.00   15.00

**Souvenir Sheets**
**Perf. 13¾**
2311-2312   A387   Set of 2   9.25   9.25

The Stamp Show 2000, London (Nos. 2309-2312). Size of stamps: Nos. 2309-2310, 48x31mm; No. 2311, 50x38mm; No. 2312, 38x50mm.

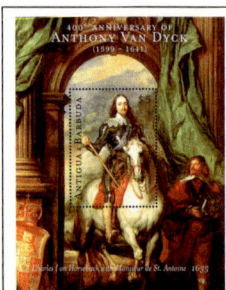

Paintings of Anthony Van Dyck A388

No. 2313, $1.20: a, Arthur Goodwin. b, Sir Thomas Wharton. c, Mary Villers (as Venus), Daughter of the Duke of Buckingham. d, Christina Bruce, Countess of Devonshire. e, James Hamilton, 3rd Marquis and 1st Duke of Hamilton. f, Henry Danvers, Earl of Danby.
No. 2314, $1.20: a, Charles I in Robes of State. b, Henrietta Maria. c, Queen Henrietta Maria with Her Dwarf Sir Jeffrey Hudson. d, Charles I in Armor. e, Henrietta Maria in Profile, facing right. f, Queen Henrietta Maria.
No. 2315, $1.20: a, Marie de Raet, Wife of Philippe le Roy. b, Jacomo de Cachiopin. c, Princess Henrietta of Lorraine Attended by a Page. d, Portrait of a Man. e, Portrait of a Woman. f, Philippe le Roy, Seigneur de Ravels.
No. 2316, $5, Charles I on Horseback with Monsieur de St. Antoine. No. 2317, $5, Le Roi a La Chasse (Charles I hunting). No. 2318, $5, Charles I in Three Positions. No. 2319, $5, Charles I and Queen Henrietta.
No. 2320, $6, Portrait of Two Young English Gentlemen, Sons of the Duke of Lenox. No. 2321, $6, George, Lord Digby, and William, Lord Russell.
Illustration reduced.

**2000, May 15**    Perf. 13¾
**Sheets of 6, #a-f**
2313-2315   A388   Set of 3   15.00   15.00

**Souvenir Sheets**
2316-2319   A388   Set of 4   15.50   15.50
2320-2321   A388   Set of 2   9.25   9.25

Butterflies — A389

No. 2322, $1.65: a, Orange theope. b, Sloane's urania. c, Gold-drop helicopis. d, Papilio velovis. e, Graphium androcles. f, Cramer's mesene.
No. 2323, $1.65, horiz.: a, Euploea miniszeki. b, Doris. c, Evenus coronata. d, Anchisiades swallowtail. e, White-spotted tadpole. f, Morpho patroclus.
No. 2324, $1.65, horiz.: a, Mesosemia loruhama. b, Bia actorion. c, Ghost brimstone. d, Blue tharops. e, Catasticta manco. f, White-tailed page.
No. 2325, $6, Reakirt's blue. No. 2326, $6, Graphium encelades, horiz. No. 2327, $6, Graphium milon, horiz.
Illustration reduced.

**2000, May 29**    Perf. 14
**Sheets of 6, #a-f**
2322-2324   A389   Set of 3   22.50   22.50

**Souvenir Sheets**
2325-2327   A389   Set of 3   14.00   14.00

Prince William, 18th Birthday A390

Prince William — No. 2328: a, With checked shirt, waving. b, In jacket and white shirt. c, With arms clasped. d, In striped shirt, waving. $6, With Prince Harry, Princess Diana and unidentified man.

**2000, June 21**    Perf. 14
2328   A390   $1.65 Sheet of 4, #a-d   4.75   4.75

**Souvenir Sheet**
**Perf. 13¾**
2329   A390   $6 multi   4.25   4.25

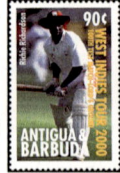

100th Test Cricket Match at Lord's Ground — A391

90c, Richie Richardson. $5, Viv Richard. $6, Lord's Ground, horiz.

**2000, June 26**    Perf. 14
2330-2331   A391   Set of 2   4.50   4.50

**Souvenir Sheet**
2332   A391   $6 multi   4.50   4.50

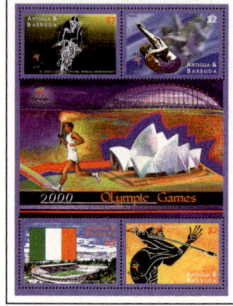

**Souvenir Sheet**

2000 Summer Olympics, Sydney — A392

Designs: a, Cyclist. b, Diver. c, Italian flag, Flaminio Stadium, Rome. d, Ancient Greek javelin thrower.

**2000, June 26**
2333   A392   $2 Sheet of 4, #a-d   6.00   6.00

First Zeppelin Flight, Cent. A393

No. 2334: a, LZ-1. b, LZ-2. c, LZ-3. $6, LZ-7.

**2000, June 26**    Perf. 13½
2334   A393   $3 Sheet of 3, #a-c   6.75   6.75

**Souvenir Sheet**
**Perf. 14¼**
2335   A393   $6 multi   4.25   4.25

No. 2334 contains three 45x27mm stamps.

Cats A394

No. 2336: a, Long-haired blue & white. b, Snow shoe. c, Persian. d, Chocolate lynx point. e, Brown & white sphynx. f, White tortoiseshell.
$6, Lavender tortie.

**2000, May 29**    Litho.    Perf. 14
2336   A394   $1.65 Sheet of 6, #a-f   7.50   7.50

**Souvenir Sheet**
2337   A394   $6 multi   4.50   4.50

**Souvenir Sheet**

Public Railways, 175th Anniv. — A395

No. 2338: a, Locomotion No. 1, George Stephenson. b, John Bull.

**2000, June 26**
2338   A395   $3 Sheet of 2, #a-b   4.50   4.50

The Stamp Show 2000, London.

ANTIGUA 545

**Souvenir Sheet**

Johann Sebastian Bach (1685-1750) — A396

**2000, June 26**
2339  A396  $6 multi   4.25  4.25

Berlin Film Festival, 50th Anniv. A397

No. 2340: a, Une Femme Est Une Femme. b, Carmen Jones. c, Die Ratten. d, Die Vier im Jeep. e, Lilies of the Field. f, Invitation to the Dance.
$6, Sense and Sensibility.

**2000, June 26**
2340  A397  $1.65 Sheet of 6, #a-f  7.25 7.25
**Souvenir Sheet**
2341  A397  $6 multi   4.50 4.50

Flowers — A398

Designs: 45c, Epidendrum pseudepidendrum. 65c, Odontoglossum cervantesii. 75c, Cattleya dowiana. 90c, Beloperone guttata. $1, Colliandra haematocephala. $1.20, Brassavola nodosa.
No. 2348, $1.65: a, Masdevallia coccinea. b, Paphinia cristata. c, Vanilla planifolia. d, Cattleya forbesii. e, Lycaste skinneri. f, Cattleya percivaliana.
No. 2349, $1.65: a, Anthurium andreanum. b, Doxantha unguiscati. c, Hibiscus rosa-sinensis. d, Canna indica. e, Heliconius umilis. f, Strelitzia reginae.
No. 2350, $1.65: a, Pseudocalymma alliaceum. b, Datura candida. c, Ipomoea tuberosa. d, Allamanda cathartica. e, Aspasia epidendroides. f, Maxillaria cucullata.
No. 2351, $6, Strelitzia reginae. No. 2352, $6, Cattleya leopoldii. No. 2353, $6, Rossioglossum grande.

**2000, May 29**    Litho.    Perf. 14
2342-2347  A398  Set of 6   3.50 3.50
**Sheets of 6, #a-f**
2348-2350  A398  Set of 3  22.50 22.50
**Souvenir Sheets**
2351-2353  A398  Set of 3  13.00 13.00

Dogs — A399

Designs: 90c, Boxer. $1, Wire-haired pointer (inscribed Alaskan malamute). $2, Alaskan malamute (inscribed Wire-haired pointer). $4, Saluki.

No. 2358: a, Bearded collie. b, Cardigan Welsh corgi. c, Saluki. d, Basset hound. e, Standard poodle. f, Boston terrier.
$6, Cavalier King Charles Spaniel.

**2000, May 29**
2354-2357  A399  Set of 4   5.50 5.50
2358  A399  $1.65 Sheet of 6, #a-f  7.00 7.00
**Souvenir Sheet**
2359  A399  $6 multi   4.50 4.50

Space Achievements — A400

No. 2360, $1.65: a, Sputnik 1. b, Explorer 1. c, Mars Express. d, Luna 1. e, Ranger 7. f, Mariner 4.
No. 2361, $1.65: a, Mariner 10. b, Soho. c, Mariner 2. d, Giotto. e, Exosat. f, Pioneer.
No. 2362, $6, Hubble Space Telescope. No. 2363, $6, Vostok 1.

**2000, June 26**  Sheets of 6, #a-f
2360-2361  A400  Set of 2  14.00 14.00
**Souvenir Sheets**
2362-2363  A400  Set of 2   9.00 9.00
World Stamp Expo 2000, Anaheim.

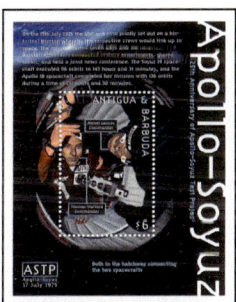

Apollo-Soyuz Mission, 25th Anniv. — A401

No. 2364: a, Alexei Leonov. b, Soyuz 19. c, Valeri Kubasov.
$6, Leonov and Thomas Stafford.

**2000, June 26**
2364  A401  $3 Sheet of 3, #a-c  6.50 6.50
**Souvenir Sheet**
2365  A401  $6 multi   4.25 4.25

Albert Einstein (1879-1955) — A402

**2000, June 26**    Perf. 14¼
2366  A402  $6 multi   4.25 4.25

Girls' Brigade — A403

Designs: 20c, Outreach program to Sunshine Home for Girls. 60c, Ullida Rawlins Gill, Intl. vice-president, vert. 75c, Officers and girls. 90c, Raising the flag, vert. $1.20, Members with 8th Antigua Company flag.
$5, Emblem, vert.

**2000, July 13**    Perf. 14
2367-2371  A403  Set of 5   2.75 2.75
**Souvenir Sheet**
2372  A403  $5 multi   3.75 3.75

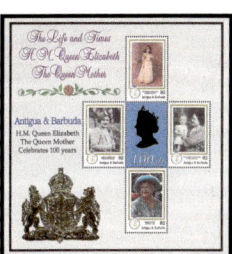

A404

Queen Mother, 100th Birthday A405

No. 2373: a, As child. b, In 1940. c, With Princess Anne, 1951. d, In Canada, 1989.
$6, Inspecting the troops. $20, In gardens.

**Litho., Margin Embossed**
**2000, Aug. 4**    Perf. 14
2373  A404  $2 Sheet of 4, #a-d, + label   6.00 6.00
**Souvenir Sheet**
**Perf. 13¾**
2374  A404  $6 multi   4.50 4.50
**Without Gum**
**Litho. & Embossed**
**Die Cut 8¾x9**
2375  A405  $20 gold & multi
No. 2374 contains one 38x51mm stamp.
See Nos. 2536-2537.

Popes A406

No. 2376, $1.65: a, Alexander VI, 1492-1503, hands clasped. b, Benedict XIII, 1724-30. c, Boniface IX, 1389-1404. d, Alexander VI, no hands. e, Clement VIII, 1592-1605. f, Clement VI, 1342-52.
No. 2377, $1.65: a, John Paul II, 1978-present. b, Benedict XV, 1914-22. c, John XXIII, 1958-63. d, Pius XI, 1922-39. e, Pius XII, 1939-58. f, Paul VI, 1963-78.
No. 2378, $6, Pius II, 1458-1464. No. 2379, $6, Pius VII, 1800-23.

**2000, Aug. 21**   Litho.   Perf. 13¾
**Sheets of 6, #a-f**
2376-2377  A406  Set of 2  15.00 15.00
**Souvenir Sheets**
2378-2379  A406  Set of 2   9.25 9.25

Monarchs — A407

No. 2380, $1.65: a, Donaldbane of Scotland, 1093-97. b, Duncan I of Scotland, 1034-40. c, Duncan II of Scotland, 1094. d, Macbeth of Scotland, 1040-57. e, Malcolm III of Scotland, 1057-93. f, Edgar of Scotland, 1097-1107.
No. 2381, $1.65: a, Charles I of Great Britain, 1625-49. b, Charles II of Great Britain, 1660-85. c, Charles Edward Stuart, the "Young Pretender," 1720-1788. d, James II of Great Britain, 1685-89. e, James II of Scotland, 1437-60. f, James III of Scotland, 1460-88.
No. 2382, $6, Robert I of Scotland, 1306-29. No. 2383, $6, Anne of Great Britain, 1702-14.
Illustration reduced.

**2000, Aug. 21**
**Sheets of 6, #a-f**
2380-2381  A407  Set of 2  15.00 15.00
**Souvenir Sheets**
2382-2383  A407  Set of 2   9.25 9.25

Millennium (#2385) — A408

No. 2384 — Chinese paintings: a, Admonitions of the Instructress to the Court Ladies, attributed to Ku K'ai-chih. b, Ink drawing on silk, 3rd cent. B.C. c, Ink and color drawing on silk, 2nd cent. B.C. d, Scholars of the Northern Qi Collating Texts (detail), attributed to Yang Zihua. e, Spring Outing (detail), attributed to Zhan Ziqian. f, Portrait of the Emperors (detail), attributed to Yen Liben. g, Sailing Boats and a Riverside Mansion, attributed to Li Sixun. h, Two Horses and a Groom (detail), by Han Kan. i, King's Portrait (detail), attributed to Wu Daozi. j, Court Ladies Wearing Flowered Headdresses (detail), attributed to Zhou Fang. k, Wintry Groves and Layered Banks, by Dong Yuan. l, Mount Kuanglu, by Jing Hao. m, Pheasant and Small Birds by a Jujube Shrub, by Huang Jucai. n, Deer Among Red Maples, by anonymous painter. o, Wintry Groves and Layered Banks, diff., by Dong Yuan. p, Literary Gathering, by Han Huang (60x40mm). q, Sketches of Birds and Insects (detail), by Huang Quan.

**Perf. 12¾x12½**
**2000, Aug. 21**    Litho.
2384  A408  25c Sheet of 17, #a-q, + label   5.00 5.00

Highlights of 1250-1300: a, Expansion of the Inquisition. b, Chartres Cathedral. c, Sculptures in Naumburg Cathedral. d, 1st English Parliament. e, The Madonna in Majesty (Maestà), by Cimabue. f, Marco Polo. g Divine wind. h, Death of St. Thomas Aquinas. i, Arezzo Cathedral. j, Margaret, Queen of Scotland. k, Jewish exodus from England. l, Fall of Acre to Muslims. m, Moses de León writes much of The Zohar. n, German Civil War. o, Death of Kublai Khan. p, Dante writes La Vita Nuova (60x40mm). q, Chao Meng-fu paints Autumn Colors on the Quiao and Hua Mountains.

**2000, Aug. 21**
2385  A408  60c Sheet of 17, #a-q, + label   9.00 9.00

# 546 ANTIGUA

Battle of Britain, 60th Anniv. A409

No. 2386, $1.20: a, Bristol Blenheim. b, Winston Churchill. c, Bristol Blenheim and barrage balloon. d, Heinkel. e, Spitfire. f, German rescue vessel. g, Messerschmitt 109. h, RAF air and sea rescue launch.
No. 2387, $1.20: a, German lookout. b, Children being evacuated. c, Youngsters evacuated from hospitals. d, Hurricane. e, Rescue workers. f, British political cartoon. g, King George VI and Queen Elizabeth inspect wreckage. h, Barrage balloon over Tower Bridge.
No. 2388, $6, Spitfires. No. 2389, $6, Junkers 87B.

| 2000, Oct. 16 | Litho. | | Perf. 14 |
|---|---|---|---|
| Sheets of 8, #a-h | | | |
| 2386-2387 | A409 Set of 2 | 14.50 | 14.50 |
| Souvenir Sheets | | | |
| 2388-2389 | A409 Set of 2 | 9.25 | 9.25 |

Rainforest Fauna — A410

Designs: 75c, Agouti. 90c, Capybara. $1.20, Basilisk lizard. $2, Heliconid butterfly.
No. 2394, $1.65: a, Green violet-ear hummingbird. b, Harpy eagle. c, Three-toed sloth. d, White uakari monkey. e, Anteater. f, Coati.
No. 2395, $1.75: a, Red-eyed tree frog. b, Black spider monkey. c, Emerald toucanet. d, Kinkajou. e, Spectacled bear. f, Tapir.
No. 2396, $6, Keel-billed toucan, horiz. No. 2397, $6, Scarlet macaw, horiz.

| 2000, Sept. 25 | Litho. | | Perf. 14 |
|---|---|---|---|
| 2390-2393 | A410 Set of 4 | 3.75 | 3.75 |
| Sheets of 6, #a-f | | | |
| 2394-2395 | A410 Set of 2 | 15.00 | 15.00 |
| Souvenir Sheets | | | |
| 2396-2397 | A410 Set of 2 | 9.25 | 9.25 |

Submarines A411

Designs: 65c, Sea Cliff. 75c, Beaver Mark IV. 90c, Reef Ranger. $1, Cubmarine. $1.20, Alvin. $3, Argus.
No. 2404, $2: a, Revenge. b, Walrus. c, Los Angeles. d, Daphne. e, USS Ohio. f, USS Skipjack.
No. 2405, $6, Trieste. No. 2406, $6, German Type 209.

| 2000, Oct. 2 | | | |
|---|---|---|---|
| 2398-2403 | A411 Set of 6 | 5.50 | 5.50 |
| 2404 | A411 $2 Sheet of 6, #a-f | 8.75 | 8.75 |
| Souvenir Sheets | | | |
| 2405-2406 | A411 Set of 2 | 9.00 | 9.00 |

Paintings from the Prado A412

No. 2407, $1.65: a, Three men. b, Man's head. c, Three women. d, Man on white horse. e, Man on brown horse. f, Man leading horse. a-c from Family Portrait, by Adriaen Thomasz Key. d-f from The Devotion of Rudolf I, by Peter Paul Rubens and Jan Wildens.
No. 2408, $1.65: a, Seated man. b, Man with sash. c, Group of men. d, Laureated figure. e, Men working at anvil. f, Two workers. a-c from The Defense of Cadiz Against the English by Francisco de Zurbaran. d-f from Vulcan's Forge, by Diego Velázquez

No. 2409, $1.65: a, Mandolin player. b, Woman with fan. c, Two men. d, Bald man. e, Two Magi. f, Jesus, Mary and Joseph. a-c from The Concert, by Vicente Palmaroli y Gonzalez. d-f from The Adoration of the Magi, by Juan Bautista Maino
No. 2410, $6, The Seller of Fans, by José del Castillo. No. 2411, $6, Portrait of a Family in a Garden, by Jan van Kessel, the Younger. No. 2412, $6, The Deliverance of St. Peter, by José de Ribera, horiz.
Illustration reduced.

| 2000, Oct. 6 | Perf. 12x12¼, 12¼x12 |
|---|---|
| Sheets of 6, #a-f | |
| 2407-2409 A412 Set of 3 | 20.00 20.00 |
| Souvenir Sheets | |
| 2410-2412 A412 Set of 3 | 13.00 13.00 |

España 2000 Intl. Philatelic Exhibition.

Christmas — A413

Designs (background): 25c, No. 2417a, Angels, full body (blue). 45c, No. 2417b, Angel's heads (orange). 90c, No. 2417c, Angel's heads (blue). $5, No. 2417d, Angels, full body (yellow).

| 2000, Dec. 4 | | | Perf. 14 |
|---|---|---|---|
| 2413-2416 | A413 Set of 4 | 4.50 | 4.50 |
| 2417 | A413 $1.75 Sheet of 4, #a-d | 5.25 | 5.25 |
| Souvenir Sheet | | | |
| 2418 | A413 $6 Jesus | 4.50 | 4.50 |

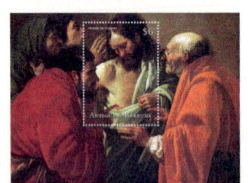

Rijksmuseum, Amsterdam, Bicent. (in 2000) — A414

No. 2419, $1: a, Dr. Ephraim Bueno, by Rembrandt. b, Woman Writing a Letter, by Frans van Mieris, the Elder. c, Mary Magdalene, by Jan van Scorel. d, Portrait of a Woman (inscribed Anna Coddle), by Maarten van Heemskerck. e, Cleopatra's Banquet, by Gerard Lairesse. f, Titus van Rijn in Friar's Habit, by Rembrandt.
No. 2420, $1.20: a, Saskia van Uylenburgh, by Rembrandt. b, In the Month of July, by Paul Joseph Constantin Gabriel. c, Maria Trip, by Rembrandt. d, Still Life with Flowers, by Jan van Huysum. e, Hesje van Cleyburgh, by Rembrandt. f, Girl in a White Kimono, by George Hendrik Breitner.
No. 2421, $1.65: a, Man and woman at spinning wheel, by Pieter Pietersz. b, Self-portrait, by Rembrandt. c, Jeremiah Lamenting the Destruction of Jerusalem, by Rembrandt. d, The Jewish Bride, by Rembrandt. e, Tobit and Anna with a Kid, by Rembrandt. f, The Prophetess Anna, by Rembrandt.
No. 2422, $6, Doubting Thomas, by Hendrick ter Brugghen. No. 2423, $6, Still Life with Cheeses, by Floris van Dijck. No. 2424, $6, Isaac Blessing Jacob, by Govert Flinck.

| 2001, Jan. 15 | Litho. | | Perf. 13¾ |
|---|---|---|---|
| Sheets of 6, #a-f | | | |
| 2419-2421 | A414 Set of 3 | 17.00 | 17.00 |
| Souvenir Sheets | | | |
| 2422-2424 | A414 Set of 3 | 13.50 | 13.50 |

Pokémon A415

No. 2425: a, Starmie. b, Misty. c, Brock. d, Geodude. e, Krabby. f, Ash.

| 2001, Feb. 13 | | | |
|---|---|---|---|
| 2425 | A415 $1.75 Sheet of 6, #a-f | 7.25 | 7.25 |
| Souvenir Sheet | | | |
| 2426 | A415 $6 Charizard | 4.25 | 4.25 |

Mushrooms — A416

Designs: 25c, Blue-toothed entoloma. 90c, Common morel. $1, Red cage fungus. $1.75, Fawn shield-cap.
No. 2431, $1.65: a, Lilac bonnet. b, Silky volvar. c, Poplar field cap. d, St. George's mushroom. e, Red-stemmed tough shank. f, Fly agaric.
No. 2432, $1.65: a, Copper trumpet. b, Meadow mushroom. c, Green-gilled parasol. d, Panther. e, Death cap. f, King bolete.
No. 2433, $6, Yellow parasol. No. 2434, Mutagen milk cap.

| 2001, Mar. 26 | | | Perf. 13¾x13¼ |
|---|---|---|---|
| 2427-2430 | A416 Set of 4 | 3.00 | 3.00 |
| Sheets of 6, #a-f | | | |
| 2431-2432 | A416 Set of 2 | 15.00 | 15.00 |
| Souvenir Sheets | | | |
| 2433-2434 | A416 Set of 2 | 9.25 | 9.25 |

Hong Kong 2001 Stamp Exhibition (2431-2434).

Population and Housing Census — A417

Map of Antigua with various graphs. Denominations: 15c, 25c, 65c, 90c.

| 2001, Apr. 2 | | | Perf. 13¾ |
|---|---|---|---|
| 2435-2438 | A417 Set of 4 | 1.50 | 1.50 |
| Souvenir Sheet | | | |
| 2439 | A417 $6 Map, emblem | 4.50 | 4.50 |

Phila Nippon '01, Japan — A418

Designs: 45c Two women facing right, from Yuna (Bath-house Women). 60c, Woman facing left, from Yuna. 65c, Two women, from

Yuna. 75c, Man with stringed instrument at top, from Hikone Screen. $1, Woman with stringed instrument at bottom, from Hikone Screen. $1.20, Two people, from Hikone Screen.
No. 2446 — Namban Screen, by Naizen Kano, each $1.65: a, Ship's stern. b, Ship's bow. c, Man with closed umbrella. d, Man with open umbrella.
No. 2447 — Merry Making Under the Cherry Blossoms, by Naganobu Kano, each $1.65: a, Steps. b, Tree. c, Four people near building. d, Four people, mountains. e, Three people. f, One person.
No. 2448, $6, Visiting a Shrine on a Rainy Night, by Harunobu Suzuki. No. 2449, $6, Courtesan on a Veranda Upstairs, by Kokan Shiba. No. 2450, $6, Daruma, by Tsujo Kano.

| 2001, May 28 | Litho. | | Perf. 14¼x14 |
|---|---|---|---|
| 2440-2445 | A418 Set of 6 | 3.50 | 3.50 |
| 2446 | A418 Sheet of 4, #a-d | 5.00 | 5.00 |
| 2447 | A418 Sheet of 6, #a-f | 7.50 | 7.50 |
| Souvenir Sheets | | | |
| Perf. 13¾ | | | |
| 2448-2450 | A418 Set of 3 | 12.50 | 12.50 |

Nos. 2448-2450 each contain one 38x51mm stamp.
No. 2449 is incorrectly inscribed. It actually depicts "Courtesan on a Veranda Upstairs," by Kokan.

Orchids — A419

Designs: 45c, Hintleya burtii. 75c, Neomoovea irrovata. 90c, Comparettia speciosa. $1, Cypripedium crapeanum.
No. 2455, $1.20, vert.: a, Trichoceuos muralis. b, Dracula rampira. c, Psychopsis papilio. d, Lycaste clenningiana. e, Telipogon nevuosus. f, Masclecallia ayahbacana.
No. 2456, $1.65, vert.: a, Rhyncholaelia glanca. b, Oncidium barbatum. c, Phaius tankervillege. d, Ghies brechtiana. e, Angraecum leonis. f, Cychnoches loddigesti.
No. 2457, $1.65, vert.: a, Cattleya dowiana. b, Dendrobium cruentum. c, Bulbophyllum lobbi. d, Chysis laevis. e, Ancistrochilus rothschildicanus. f, Angraecum sororium.
No. 2458, $6, Trichopilia fragrans, vert. No. 2459, $6, Symphalossum sanguinem, vert.

| 2001, June 11 | | | Perf. 14 |
|---|---|---|---|
| 2451-2454 | A419 Set of 4 | 2.40 | 2.40 |
| Sheets of 6, #a-f | | | |
| 2455-2457 | A419 Set of 3 | 19.00 | 19.00 |
| Souvenir Sheets | | | |
| 2458-2459 | A419 Set of 2 | 9.00 | 9.00 |

Souvenir Sheets

I Love Lucy A420

Designs: No. 2460, $6, Fred and Ricky. No. 2461, $6, Lucy and Ethel. No. 2462, $6, Lucy and fireplace. No. 2463, $6, Lucy and open door.

| 2001, Mar. 5 | Litho. | | Perf. 13¾ |
|---|---|---|---|
| 2460-2463 | A420 Set of 4 | 18.00 | 18.00 |

See Nos. 2522-2525.

Marine Life and Birds — A421

Designs: 25c, Yellowtail damselfish. 45c, Indigo hamlet. 65c, Great white shark. No. 2467, 90c, Bottlenose dolphin. No. 2468, 90c, Palette surgeonfish. $1, Octopus.
No. 2470, $1.20: a, Common dolphin. b, Franklin's gull. c, Rock beauty. d, Bicolor

# ANTIGUA

angelfish. e, Beaugregory. f, Banded butterflyfish.
No. 2471, $1.20: a, Common tern. b, Flying fish. c, Queen angelfish. d, Blue-striped grunt. e, Porkfish. f, Blue tang.
No. 2472, $1.65: a, Dugong. b, White-tailed tropicbird. c, Bull shark and Spanish grunt. d, Manta ray. e, Green turtle. f, Spanish grunt.
No. 2473, $1.65: a, Red-footed booby. b, Bottlenose dolphin. c, Hawksbill turtle. d, Monk seal. e, Bull shark and coral. f, Lemon shark.
No. 2474, $5, Sailfish. No. 2475, $5, Beaugregory and brown pelican, vert. No. 2476, $6, Hawksbill turtle. No. 2477, $6, Queen triggerfish.

**2001, June 11**     *Perf. 14*
2464-2469   A421   Set of 6   3.25   3.25
**Sheets of 6, #a-f**
2470-2473   A421   Set of 4   24.00   24.00
**Souvenir Sheets**
2474-2477   A421   Set of 4   16.00   16.00

Ship Freewinds — A422

Designs: 30c, Maiden voyage anniversary in Antigua. 45c, In St. Barthelemy. 75c, In Caribbean at sunset. 90c, In Bonaire. $1.50, In Bequia.
No. 2483, $4, With lights on during eclipse. No. 2484, $4, In Curacao.

**2001, June 15**
2478-2482   A422   Set of 5   3.00   3.00
**Souvenir Sheets**
2483-2484   A422   Set of 2   6.00   6.00

Toulouse-Lautrec Paintings — A423

No. 2485: a, Monsieur Georges-Henri Manuel Standing. b, Monsieur Louis Pascal. c, Roman Coolus. d, Monsieur Fourcade. $5, Dancing at the Moulin de la Galette.

**2001, July 3**     *Perf. 13¾*
2485   A423   $2 Sheet of 4, #a-d   6.00   6.00
**Souvenir Sheet**
2486   A423   $5 multi   3.75   3.75

Giuseppe Verdi (1813-1901), Opera Composer — A424

No. 2487: a, Verdi in hat. b, Character and score from Don Carlos. c, Conductor and score for Aida. d, Musicians and score for Rigoletto.

**2001, July 3**     *Perf. 14*
2487   A424   $2 Sheet of 4, #a-d   6.00   6.00
**Souvenir Sheet**
2488   A424   $5 Verdi, score   3.75   3.75

Marlene Dietrich — A425

No. 2489: a, With cigarette. b, On sofa. c, Color photograph. d, With piano.

**2001, July 3**     *Perf. 13¾*
2489   A425   $2 Sheet of 4, #a-d   6.00   6.00

Queen Victoria (1819-1901) — A426

No. 2490: a, Blue dress. b, Red hat. c, Crown. d, Crown and blue sash.

**2001, July 3**     *Perf. 14*
2490   A426   $2 Sheet of 4, #a-d   6.00   6.00
**Souvenir Sheet**
2491   A426   $5 As old woman   3.75   3.75

Queen Elizabeth II, 75th Birthday — A427

No. 2492: a, At birth, 1926. b, In 1938. c, In 1939. d, At coronation, 1953. e, In 1956. f, In 1985.

**2001, July 3**
2492   A427   $1 Sheet of 6, #a-f   3.75   3.75
**Souvenir Sheet**
2493   A427   $6 In 1940   4.50   4.50

Photomosaic of Queen Elizabeth II — A428

**2001, July 3**     *Litho.*     *Perf. 14*
2494   A428   $1 multi   .75   .75

Queen Elizabeth II, 75th birthday. Issued in sheets of 8.

Monet Paintings — A429

No. 2495, horiz.: a, Water Lilies. b, Rose Portals, Giverny. c, The Water Lily Pond, Harmony in Green. d, The Artist's Garden, Irises. $5, Jerusalem Artichokes.

**2001, July 3**     *Perf. 13¾*
2495   A429   $2 Sheet of 4, #a-d   6.00   6.00
**Souvenir Sheet**
2496   A429   $5 multi   3.75   3.75

Endangered Animals — A430

Designs: 25c, Collared peccary. 30c, Baird's tapir. 45c, Agouti. 75c, Bananaquit. 90c, Six-banded armadillo. $1, Roseate spoonbill.
No. 2503, each $1.80: a, Mouse opossum. b, Magnificent black frigatebird. c, Northern jacana. d, Painted bunting. e, Haitian solenodon. f, St. Lucia iguana.
No. 2504, each $2.50: a, West Indian iguana. b, Scarlet macaw. c, Cotton-topped tamarin. d, Kinkajou.
No. 2505, $6, Ocelot, vert. No. 2506, $6, King vulture, vert.

**2001, Sept. 10**     *Perf. 14*
2497-2502   A430   Set of 6   2.50   2.50
2503   A430   Sheet of 6, #a-f   8.00   8.00
2504   A430   Sheet of 4, #a-d   7.00   7.00
**Souvenir Sheets**
2505-2506   A430   Set of 2   9.00   9.00

Rudolph Valentino (1895-1926), Actor — A431

No. 2507, $1: a, Blood and Sand. b, Eyes of Youth. c, All Night. d, Last known photo of Valentino. e, Camille. f, Cobra.
No. 2508, $1: a, The Son of the Sheik. b, The Young Rajah. c, The Eagle. d, The Sheik. e, A Sainted Devil. f, Monsieur Beaucaire.
No. 2509, $6, The Four Horsemen of the Apocalypse. No. 2510, $6, Valentino with Natasha Rambova.

**2001, Oct. 2**     *Perf. 13¾*
**Sheets of 6, #a-f**
2507-2508   A431   Set of 2   9.00   9.00
**Souvenir Sheets**
2509-2510   A431   Set of 2   9.00   9.00

Scenes From Shirley Temple Movies — A432

No. 2511, $1.65 — Scenes from Baby, Take a Bow, with Temple: a, In polka dot dress. b, With man on steps. c, With man holding gun. d, With woman.
No. 2512, $1.80, horiz. — Scenes from The Little Princess, with Temple: a, With man. b, Washing floor. c, With woman and child. d, With old woman.
No. 2513, $1.50 — Scenes from The Little Princess, with Temple: a, With woman. b, In pink dress. c, Holding doll. d, On throne. e, With man. f, With birthday cake.
No. 2514, $1.65, horiz. — Scenes from Baby, Take a Bow, with Temple: a, With woman and five children. b, With arms around man. c, Being tucked in bed. d, With man. e, Standing with man and woman. f, Looking in cradle.
No. 2515, $6, In polka-dot dress, from Baby, Take a Bow. No. 2516, $6, With soldiers, from The Little Princess.

**2001, Oct. 2**     **Sheets of 4, #a-d**
2511-2512   A432   Set of 2   10.50   10.50
**Sheets of 6, #a-f**
2513-2514   A432   Set of 2   14.00   14.00
**Souvenir Sheets**
2515-2516   A432   Set of 2   8.00   8.00

Nobel Prizes, Cent. — A433

No. 2517, $1.50 — Chemistry laureates: a, Melvin Calvin, 1961. b, Linus C. Pauling, 1954. c, Vincent du Vigneaud, 1955. d, Richard Synge, 1952. e, Archer Martin, 1952. f, Alfred Werner, 1913.
No. 2518, $1.50 — Chemistry laureates: a, Robert F. Curl, Jr., 1996. b, Alan J. Heeger, 2000. c, Michael Smith, 1993. d, Sidney Altman, 1989. e, Elias James Corey, 1990. f, William Francis Giauque, 1949.
No. 2519, $6, Ernest Rutherford, Chemistry, 1908. No. 2520, $6, International Red Cross, Peace, 1944. No. 2521, $6, Ernst Otto Fischer, Chemistry, 1973.

**2001, Nov. 29**     *Perf. 14*
**Sheets of 6, #a-f**
2517-2518   A433   Set of 2   13.50   13.50
**Souvenir Sheets**
2519-2521   A433   Set of 3   13.50   13.50

**I Love Lucy Type of 2001**

Designs: No. 2522, $6, Fred at desk. No. 2523, $6, Lucy and Fred. No. 2524, $6, Lucy, closed door. No. 2525, $6, Fred and Ricky at desk, horiz.

**2001**     *Perf. 13¾*
2522-2525   A420   Set of 4   18.00   18.00

Christmas — A434

Paintings: 25c, Madonna and Child with Angels, by Filippo Lippi. 45c, Madonna of Corneto Tarquinia, by Lippi. 50c, Madonna and Child, by Domenico Ghirlandaio. 75c, Madonna and Child, by Lippi. $4, Madonna del Ceppo, by Lippi.
$6, Madonna Enthroned with Angels and Saints, by Lippi.

**2001, Dec. 4**     *Litho.*     *Perf. 14*
2526-2530   A434   Set of 5   4.50   4.50
**Souvenir Sheet**
2531   A434   $6 multi   4.50   4.50

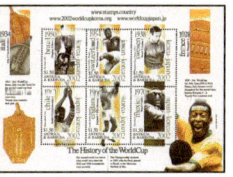

2002 World Cup Soccer Championships, Japan and Korea — A435

No. 2532, $1.50: a, Scene from final game, 1950. b, Ferenc Puskas, 1954. c, Raymond Kopa, 1958. d, Mauro, 1962. e, Gordon Banks, 1966. f, Pelé, 1970.
No. 2533, $1.50: a, Daniel Passarella, 1978. b, Karl-Heinz Rummenigge, 1982. c, World Cup trophy, 1986. d, Diego Maradona, 1990. e, Roger Milla, 1994. f, Zinedine Zidane, 1998.
No. 2534, $6, Head from Jules Rimet Cup, 1930. No. 2535, $6, Head and globe from World Cup trophy, 2002.

**2001, Dec. 17**     *Perf. 13¾x14¼*
**Sheets of 6, #a-f**
2532-2533   A435   Set of 2   12.00   12.00
**Souvenir Sheets**
*Perf. 14¼*
2534-2535   A435   Set of 2   8.00   8.00

## ANTIGUA

### Queen Mother Type of 2000 Redrawn

No. 2536, each $2: a, As child. b, In 1940. c, With Princess Anne, 1951. d, In Canada, 1989.
$6, Inspecting the troops.

**2001, Dec.**   *Perf. 14*
**Yellow Orange Frames**
2536 A404 Sheet of 4, #a-d, + label   6.00 6.00

**Souvenir Sheet**
*Perf. 13¾*
2537 A404 $6 multi   4.50 4.50

Queen Mother's 101st birthday. No. 2537 contains one 38x51mm stamp with a darker appearance than that found on No. 2374. Sheet margins of Nos. 2536-2537 lack embossing and gold arms found on Nos. 2373-2374.

US Civil War A436

No. 2538: a, Battle of Nashville. b, Battle of Atlanta. c, Battle of Spotsylvania. d, Battle of the Wilderness. e, Battle of Chickamauga Creek. f, Battle of Gettysburg. g, Battle of Chancellorsville. h, Battle of Fredericksburg. i, Battle of Antietam. j, Second Battle of Bull Run. k, Battle of Five Forks. l, Seven Days' Battle. m, Battle of Bull Run. n, Battle of Shiloh. o, Battle of Seven Pines. p, Battle of Fort Sumter. q, Battle of Chattanooga. r, Surrender at Appomattox.

No. 2539, vert.: a, Gen. Ulysses S. Grant. b, Pres. Abraham Lincoln. c, Confederate Pres. Jefferson Davis. d, Gen. Robert E. Lee. e, Gen. George A. Custer. f, Adm. Andrew Hull Foote. g, General Thomas "Stonewall" Jackson. h, Gen. J.E.B. Stuart. i, Gen. George G. Meade. j, Gen. Philip H. Sheridan. k, Gen. James Longstreet. l, Gen. John S. Mosby.

No. 2540, $6, Monitor. No. 2541, $6, Merrimack.

**2002, Jan. 28**   *Perf. 14¾*
2538 A436 45c Sheet of 18, #a-r   10.00 10.00
2539 A436 50c Sheet of 12, #a-l   8.00 8.00

**Souvenir Sheets**
*Perf. 14½x14¾ (#2540), 13¾*
2540-2541 A436 Set of 2   11.00 11.00

No. 2541 contains one 50x38mm stamp.

Reign of Queen Elizabeth II, 50th Anniv. A437

No. 2542: a, Striped dress. b, Green patterned dress. c, Orange patterned dress. d, White jacket.
$6, Queen with Princess Margaret.

**2002, Feb. 6**   *Perf. 14¼*
2542 A437 $2 Sheet of 4, #a-d   7.00 7.00

**Souvenir Sheet**
2543 A437 $6 multi   4.50 4.50

United We Stand — A438

**2002, Feb. 11**   *Perf. 13½x13¼*
2544 A438 $2 multi   1.50 1.50
Printed in sheets of 4.

Cricket Player Sir Vivian Richards, 50th Birthday — A439

Designs: 25c, Raising bat. 30c, Receiving gift. 50c, With arms raised. 75c, At bat. $1.50, Wearing sash, with woman. $1.80, Standing next to photograph of himself.
No. 2551, $6, Holding sword. No. 2552, $6, With Antigua color guard.

**2002, Mar. 7**   *Perf. 13½x13¼*
2545-2550 A439 Set of 6   4.00 4.00

**Souvenir Sheets**
2551-2552 A439 Set of 2   9.00 9.00

Flora and Fauna — A440

Designs: 50c, Thick-billed parrot. 75c, Lesser long-nosed bat. $1.50, Montserrat oriole. $1.80, Miss Perkin's blue butterfly.
No. 2557, 90c: a, Quetzals. b, Two-toed sloth. c, Lovely cotinga. d, Giant hairstrak butterfly. e, Magenta-throated woodstar. f, Bull's-eye silk moth. g, Golden toads. h, Collared peccaries. i, Tamandua anteater.
No. 2558, $1: a, St. Lucia parrot. b, Cuban kite. c, West Indian whistling duck. d, Poey's sulphur butterfly. e, Scarlet ibis. f, Blackcapped petrel. g, St. Lucia whiptail. h, Cuban Solenodon. i, False androgeus swallowtail butterfly.
No. 2559, $6, Margay. No. 2560, $6, Olive Ridley turtle.

**2002, Apr. 8**   *Perf. 14*
2553-2556 A440 Set of 4   3.50 3.50

**Sheets of 9, #a-i**
2557-2558 A440 Set of 2   14.00 14.00

**Souvenir Sheets**
2559-2560 A440 Set of 2   9.00 9.00

Antigua Community Players, 50th Anniv. — A441

Various photos: 20c, 25c, 30c, 75c, 90c, $1.50, $1.80.
No. 2568, $4, Former Pres. Edie Hill-Thibou, vert. No. 2569, $4, Acting Pres. and Music Director Yvonne Maginley, vert.

**2002, June 11**   *Perf. 13½x13¾*   *Litho.*
2561-2567 A441 Set of 7   4.25 4.25

**Souvenir Sheets**
*Perf. 14*
2568-2569 A441 Set of 2   6.00 6.00

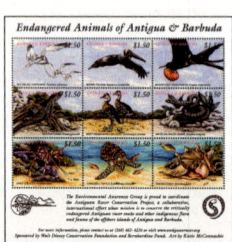
Endangered Animals — A442

No. 2570, each $1.50: a, Red-billed tropicbird. b, Brown pelican. c, Magnificent frigatebird. d, Ground lizard. e, West Indian whistling duck. f, Antiguan racer snake. g, Spiny lobster. h, Hawksbill turtle. i, Queen conch.

**2002, July 12**   *Perf. 14*
2570 A442 Sheet of 9, #a-i   12.00 12.00

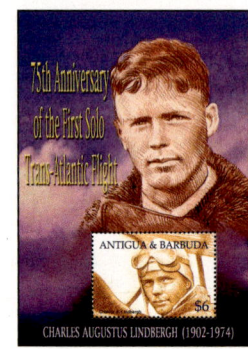
2002 Winter Olympics, Salt Lake City — A443

Designs: No. 2571, $2, Cross-country skiing. No. 2572, $2, Pairs figure skating.

**2002, July 15**   *Perf. 13½x13¼*
2571-2572 A443 Set of 2   3.50 3.50
2572a   Souvenir sheet, #2571-2572   3.50 3.50

First Solo Transatlantic Flight, 75th Anniv. — A444

No. 2573, each $2.50: a, Charles Lindbergh and The Spirit of St. Louis. b, Arrival at Le Bourget Airport, Paris. c, Lindbergh receiving hero's welcome, New York.
$6, Lindbergh in airplane.

**2002, July 15**   *Perf. 13¼x13½*
2573 A444 Sheet of 3, #a-c   5.75 5.75

**Souvenir Sheet**
2574 A444 $6 multi   4.50 4.50

Intl. Year of Mountains — A445

No. 2575: a, Mt. Fuji. b, Machu Picchu. c, Matterhorn.

**2002, July 15**   *Perf. 13½x13¼*
2575 A445 $2 Sheet of 3, #a-c   4.50 4.50

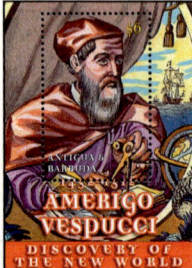
Amerigo Vespucci (1454-1512), Explorer A446

No. 2576, horiz., each $2.50: a, Vespucci with gray head covering. b, Vespucci with red head covering. c, Hands and map.
$6, Vespucci and compass.

*Perf. 13¼x13½, 13½x13¼*
**2002, July 15**
2576 A446 Sheet of 3, #a-c   6.00 6.00

**Souvenir Sheet**
2577 A446 $6 multi   4.50 4.50

Princess Diana (1961-97) — A447

No. 2578: a, Wearing seven-strand pearl necklace. b, Wearing tiara and white dress. c, Wearing hat. d, Wearing earrings and black dress. e, Wearing tiara, no dress seen. f, Wearing earrings, no dress seen.
$6, Wearing white dress.

**2002, July 29**   *Perf. 14*
2578 A447 $1.80 Sheet of 6, #a-f   7.50 7.50

**Souvenir Sheet**
2579 A447 $6 multi   4.50 4.50

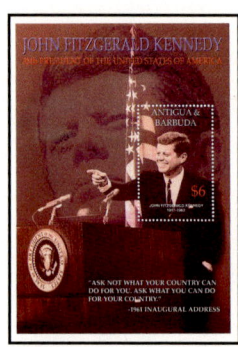
Presidents John F. Kennedy and Ronald Reagan — A448

No. 2580, $1.50, horiz.: a, John, Robert and Edward Kennedy. b, Kennedy with Danny Kaye. c, Kennedy addressing nation. d, With wife, Jacqueline. e, Shaking hands with young Bill Clinton. f, Family members at funeral.
No. 2581, $1.50, horiz.: a, Reagan with wife, Nancy, and Pope John Paul II. b, As George Gipp in movie *Knute Rockne, All American*. c, With Gen. Matthew Ridgeway at Bitburg Cemetery. d, With Vice-president George H. W. Bush and Mikhail Gorbachev. e, With Presidents Ford, Carter, and Nixon. f, On horseback, with Queen Elizabeth II.
No. 2582, $6, Kennedy and flag. No. 2583, $6, Reagan.

**2002, July 29**   *Litho.*
**Sheets of 6, #a-f**
2580-2581 A448 Set of 2   13.50 13.50

**Souvenir Sheets**
2582-2583 A448 Set of 2   9.00 9.00

Elvis Presley (1935-77) — A449

**2002, Aug. 20**   *Perf. 13¾*
2584 A449 $1 multi   1.25 1.25
Printed in sheets of 9.

# ANTIGUA 549

Teddy Bears, Cent. A450

No. 2585: a, Cheerleader bear. b, Figure skater bear. c, Ballet dancer bear. d, Aerobics instructor bear.

**2002, Aug. 26**
2585 A450 $2 Sheet of 4, #a-d    7.00 7.00

Pokémon A451

No. 2586: a, Croconau. b, Mantine. c, Feraligatr. d, Quilfish. e, Romoraid. f, Quagsire. $6, Chinchou.

**2002, Aug. 26**
2586 A451 $1.50 Sheet of 6, #a-f    6.75 6.75
           Souvenir Sheet
2587 A451    $6 multi          4.50 4.50

Lee Strasberg (1901-82), Movie Actor and Director — A452

**2002, Sept. 16**        Perf. 14
2588 A452 $1 multi          .75 .75
Printed in sheets of 9.

Charlie Chaplin (1889-1977), Actor — A453

No. 2589: a, Wearing bowler hat, facing forward. b, Wearing suit and vest. c, Wearing top hat. d, Wearing bowler hat, profile. e, Wearing bow tie and suit. f, With hand at chin. $6, Wearing bowler hat, diff.

**2002, Sept. 16**
2589 A453 $1.80 Sheet of 6, #a-f    8.25 8.25
           Souvenir Sheet
2590 A453    $6 multi          4.50 4.50

Marlene Dietrich (1901-92), Actress — A454

No. 2591: a, With hands at side of face. b, Wearing top hat. c, Facing forward. d, With hand on chin. e, Wearing black hat. f, Wearing gloves. $6, Facing forward, diff.

**2002, Sept. 16**
2591 A454 $1.50 Sheet of 6, #a-f    6.75 6.75
           Souvenir Sheet
2592 A454    $6 multi          4.50 4.50

Bob Hope A455

No. 2593: a, Wearing red cap. b, Wearing hat with strap. c, Wearing top hat. d, Wearing black cap. e, Wearing camouflage. f, Wearing white cap.

**2002, Sept. 16**
2593 A455 $1.50 Sheet of 6, #a-f    7.50 7.50

Ferrari Race Cars — A456

Designs: 20c, 1957 801. 25c, 1959 256 F1. 30c, 1960 246P F1. 90c, 1966 246 F1. $1, 1971 312 B2. $1.50, 1969 312 F1. $2, 1997 F310B. $4, 2002 F2002.

**2002, Oct. 14**        Litho.
2594-2601 A456 Set of 8      7.75 7.75

Independence, 21st Anniv. — A457

Designs: 25c, Flag. 30c, Arms, vert. $1.50, Mt. St. John's Hospital nearing completion. $1.80, Parliament Building.
No. 2606, $6, Prime Minister Lester B. Bird, vert. No. 2607, $6, Sir Vere C. Bird, vert.

**2002, Oct. 31**        Perf. 14
2602-2605 A457 Set of 4     3.50 3.50
           Souvenir Sheets
2606-2607 A457 Set of 2     9.00 9.00
Nos. 2606-2607 each contain one 38x50mm stamp.

Second Round of World Cup Soccer Championships — A458

No. 2608, $1.65: a, Pyo Lee. b, Ji Sung Park. c, Jung Hwan Ahn. d, Filippo Inzaghi. e, Paolo Maldini. f, Damiano Tommasi.
No. 2609, $1.65: a, Juan Valeron. b, Iker Casillas. c, Fernando Hierro. d, Gary Kelly. e, Damien Duff. f, Matt Holland.
No. 2610, $3: a, South Korean coach Guus Hiddink. b, Chul Sang Yoo.
No. 2611, $3: a, Francesco Totti. b, Italy coach Giovanni Trapattoni.
No. 2612, $3: a, Spain coach Jose Antonio Camacho. b, Carlos Gamarra.
No. 2613, $3: a, Robbie Keane. b, Ireland coach Mick McCarthy.

**2002, Nov. 4**        Perf. 13½x13¼
           Sheets of 6, #a-f
2608-2609 A458 Set of 2    15.00 15.00
           Souvenir Sheets, #a-b
2610-2613 A458 Set of 4    18.00 18.00

Christmas A459

Designs: 25c, Coronation of the Virgin, by Domenico Ghirlandaio. 45c, Adoration of the Magi (detail), by Ghirlandaio. 75c, Annunciation (detail), by Simone Martini, vert. 90c, Adoration of the Magi (detail, diff.) by Ghirlandaio. $5, Madonna and Child, by Giovanni Bellini. $6, Madonna and Child, by Martini.

**2002, Nov. 18**        Perf. 14
2614-2618 A459 Set of 5     5.50 5.50
           Souvenir Sheet
2619 A459    $6 multi          4.50 4.50

Worldwide Fund for Nature (WWF) — A460

Antiguan racer snake: a, Head. b, Snake with head near tail. c, Snake and dried leaves. d, Snake on rocks.

**2002, Nov. 25**
2620    Strip of 4       3.75 3.75
a.-d. A460 $1 Any single     .90 .90
Printed in sheets of 4 strips.

Flora & Fauna A461

No. 2621, $1.50: a, Magnificent frigatebird. b, Sooty tern. c, Bananaquit. d, Yellow-crowned night heron. e, Greater flamingo. f, Belted kingfisher.
No. 2622, $1.50: a, Killer whale. b, Sperm whale. c, Minke whale. d, Blainville's beaked whale. e, Blue whale. f, Cuvier's beaked whale.
No. 2623, $1.80: a, Hieroglyphic moth. b, Hypocrita dejanira. c, Snowy eupseudosoma moth. d, Composia credula. e, Giant silkworm moth. f, Diva moth.
No. 2624, $1.80: a, Epidendrum fragrans. b, Dombeya. c, Yellow poui. d, Milky wave plant. e, Cinderella plant. f, Coral orchid.
No. 2625, $5, Snowy egret. No. 2626, $5, Rothschildia orizabae. No. 2627, $6, Humpback whale. No. 2628, $6, Ionopsis utricularoides.

**2002, Nov. 25**        Litho.
           Sheets of 6, #a-f
2621-2624 A461 Set of 4    32.50 32.50
           Souvenir Sheets
2625-2628 A461 Set of 4    19.00 19.00

Pan-American Health Organization, Cent. — A462

No. 2629: a, Dr. Margaret O'Garro. b, Nurse Ineta Wallace. c, Public Health Worker Vincent Edwards.

**2002, Dec. 2**
2629 A462 $1.50 Sheet of 3, #a-c    3.50 3.50

Souvenir Sheets

Science Fiction A463

No. 2630, $6, Writings of Nostradamus. No. 2631, $6, 2001: A Space Odyssey, by Arthur C. Clarke. No. 2632, $6, Are We Alone?

**2002, Dec. 12**        Perf. 13¾
2630-2632 A463 Set of 3    13.50 13.50

A464

20th World Scout Jamboree, Thailand — A465

No. 2633, horiz.: a, Lord Robert Baden-Powell. b, Ernest Thompson Seton, first Chief Scout. c, First black troop.
No. 2634: a, Brownie with broad neckerchief "X." b, Brownie with narrow neckerchief "X." c, Brownie with incomplete neckerchief "X."
No. 2635, Seton. No. 2636, Scout salute.

**2002, Dec. 12**        Litho.    Perf. 14
2633 A464 $3 Sheet of 3, #a-c    7.00 7.00
2634 A465 $3 Sheet of 3, #a-c    7.00 7.00
           Souvenir Sheet
2635 A464    $6 multi          4.50 4.50
2636 A465    $6 multi          4.50 4.50

# ANTIGUA

Ram, by Liu Jiyou — A466

**2003, Feb. 10**     **Perf. 13¾**
2637 A466 $1.80 multi    1.40 1.40

New Year 2003 (Year of the Ram). Issued in sheets of 4.

A467

Coronation of Queen Elizabeth II, 50th Anniv. — A468

No. 2638, each $3: a, In uniform. b, With tan jacket. c, With white dress and hat.
$6, With white dress.

**2003**    **Litho.**    **Perf. 14**
2638 A467 Sheet of 3, #a-c    6.75 6.75
**Souvenir Sheet**
2639 A467 $6 multi    4.50 4.50
**Miniature Sheet**
**Litho. & Embossed**
**Perf. 13¼x13**
2640 A468 $20 gold & multi    17.50 17.50

Issued: Nos. 2638-2639, 5/14; No. 2640, 2/10.

Paintings of Lucas Cranach the Elder (1472-1553) A469

Designs: 75c, Lucretia. 90c, Venus and Cupid. $1, Judith with the Head of Holofernes, c. 1530. $1.50, Portrait of a Young Lady.
No. 2645: a, Portrait of the Wife of a Jurist. b, Portrait of a Jurist. c, Johannes Cuspinian. d, Portrait of Anna Cuspinian.
$6, Judith with the Head of Holofernes, c. 1532.

**2003, Apr. 30**    **Litho.**    **Perf. 14¼**
2641-2644 A469 Set of 4    3.25 3.25
2645 A469 $2 Sheet of 4, #a-d    6.00 6.00
**Souvenir Sheet**
2646 A469 $6 multi    4.50 4.50

Paintings of Yoshitoshi Taiso (1839-92) — A470

Designs: 25c, A High Class Maid Training in a Samurai Household. 50c, A Castle-Toppler Known as "Keisei": A Beautiful Woman Able to Seduce a Ruler So That He Forgets the Affairs of the State. $1, Stylish Young Geisha Battling a Snowstorm on Her Way to Work. $5, A Lady in Distress Being Treated With Moxa.
No. 2651: a, A Lady of the Imperial Court Wearing Four Layers of Robes. b, Young Mother Adoring Her Infant Son. c, Lady-in-waiting Looking Amused Over a Veranda in the Household of a Great Lord. d, A High-ranking Courtesan Known as "Oiran" Waiting For a Private Assignation.
$6, A Girl Teasing Her Cat.

**2003, Apr. 30**
2647-2650 A470 Set of 4    5.00 5.00
2651 A470 $2 Sheet of 4, #a-d    6.00 6.00
**Souvenir Sheet**
2652 A470 $6 multi    4.50 4.50

Paintings of Raoul Dufy (1877-1953) A471

Designs: 90c, Boats at Martigues. $1, Harvesting. $1.80, Sailboats in the Port of Le Havre. $5, The Big Bather, vert.
No. 2657: a, The Beach and the Pier at Trouville. b, Port With Sailing Ships. c, Black Cargo. d, Nice, the Bay of Anges.
No. 2658, $6, The Interior With an Open Window. No. 2659, $6, Vence.

**2003, Apr. 30**
2653-2656 A471 Set of 4    6.50 6.50
2657 A471 $2 Sheet of 4, #a-d    6.00 6.00
**Size: 96x76mm**
**Imperf**
2658-2659 A471 Set of 2    9.00 9.00

Prince William, 21st Birthday A472

No. 2660: a, With yellow and black shirt. b, With polo helmet. c, With blue shirt.
$6, In suit.

**2003, May 14**    **Perf. 14**
2660 A472 $3 Sheet of 3, #a-c    7.00 7.00
**Souvenir Sheet**
2661 A472 $6 multi    4.50 4.50

Salvation Army in Antigua, Cent. — A473

Designs: 30c, Emblem, Tamarind tree, Parham, vert. 90c, Salvation Army Pre-school, vert. $1, Meals on Wheels. $1.50, St. John's Citadel Band. $1.80, Salvation Army Citadel.
$6, Tamarind tree, Parham, vert.

**2003, May 19**    **Perf. 14¼**
2662-2666 A473 Set of 5    4.25 4.25
**Souvenir Sheet**
2667 A473 $6 multi    4.50 4.50

Antigua & Barbuda Scouts Association, 90th Anniv. — A474

Designs: 30c, First Anglican Scout troop, 1931. $1, National Scout Camp, 2002. $1.50, Woodbadge Training Course, 2000, horiz. $1.80, Men visiting National Scout Camp, 1986, horiz.
No. 2672: a, Edris George. b, Theodore George. c, Edris James.
$6, Scout with semaphore flags.

**2003, June 9**    **Perf. 14**
2668-2671 A474 Set of 4    3.75 3.75
2672 A474 90c Sheet of 3, #a-c    2.25 2.25
**Souvenir Sheet**
2673 A474 $6 multi    4.75 4.75

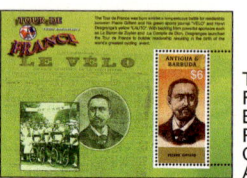

Tour de France Bicycle Race, Cent. A475

No. 2674, $2: a, Cesar Garin, 1903. b, Henri Cornet, 1904. c, Louis Trousselier, 1905. d, René Pottier, 1906.
No. 2675, $2: a, Lucien Petit-Breton, 1907. b, Petit-Breton, 1908. c, François Faber, 1909. d, Octave Lapize, 1910.
No. 2676, $2: a, Gustave Garrigou, 1911. b, Odile Defraye, 1912. c, Philippe Thys, 1913. d, Thys, 1914.
No. 2677, $6, Pierre Giffard. No. 2678, $6, Henri Desgrange. No. 2679, $6, Comte de Dion.

**2003, June 9**    **Perf. 13¼**
**Sheets of 4, #a-d**
2674-2676 A475 Set of 3    18.00 18.00
**Souvenir Sheets**
2677-2679 A475 Set of 3    13.50 13.50

Caribbean Community, 30th Anniv. — A476

**2003, July 4**    **Perf. 14**
2680 A476 $1 multi    .80 .80

Intl. Year of Fresh Water A477

No. 2681, horiz.: a, Chutes de Carbet and rocks. b, Chutes de Carbet and foliage at left and right. c, Rocks at base of Chutes de Carbet.
$6, Ocho Rios Waterfall.

**2003, July 14**    **Perf. 13¼**
2681 A477 $2 Sheet of 3, #a-c    5.25 5.25
**Souvenir Sheet**
2682 A477 $6 multi    5.00 5.00

General Motors Automobiles — A478

No. 2683, $2 — Cadillacs: a, 1955 Eldorado convertible. b, 1937 Series 60. c, 1959 Eldorado. d, 2002 Eldorado.
No. 2684, $2 — Chevrolet Corvettes: a, 1954 convertible. b, 1964 Sting Ray. c, 1964 Sting Ray convertible. d, 1998 convertible.
No. 2685, $6, 1953 Cadillac Eldorado. No. 2686, $6, 1956 Corvette convertible.

**2003, July 14**    **Perf. 13¼x13½**
**Sheets of 4, #a-d**
2683-2684 A478 Set of 2    12.00 12.00
**Souvenir Sheets**
2685-2686 A478 Set of 2    9.00 9.00

Cadillac, cent.; Corvette, 50th anniv.

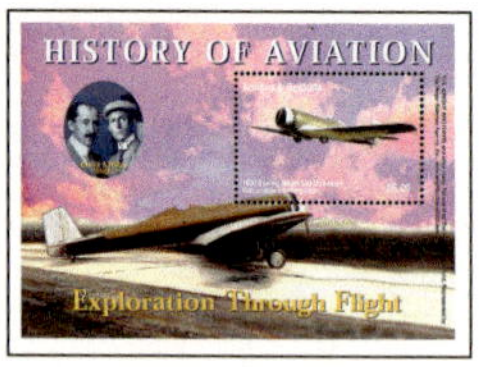

History of Aviation A479

No. 2687, $2: a, First Wright Brothers flight, 1903. b, First free flight in helicopter by Paul Cornu, 1907. c, First landing on ship, by E. B. Ely. d, Curtiss A-1, first hydroplane, 1911.
No. 2688, $2: a, Bell X-5, 1951. b, Convair XFY-1, 1954. c, North American X-15, 1959. d, Alexei Leonov, first man to walk in space, 1965.
No. 2689, $2: a, Concorde, 1969. b, Martin X-24, 1969. c, Apollo-Soyuz space mission, 1975. d, Mars probe Viking, 1976.
No. 2690, $6, Boeing Model 200 Monomail, 1930. No. 2691, $6, Breaking of sound barrier by Bell X-1, 1947. No. 2692, $6, Grumman X-29, 1984.

**2003, July 28**    **Perf. 14**
**Sheets of 4, #a-d**
2687-2689 A479 Set of 3    20.00 20.00
**Souvenir Sheets**
2690-2692 A479 Set of 3    13.50 13.50

**Bird Type of 1995**

Designs: $5, Montezuma oropendola. $10, Green jay.

**2003, Aug. 11**    **Litho.**    **Perf. 15x14**
2693 A296 $5 multi    3.75 3.75
2694 A296 $10 multi    7.50 7.50

Circus Performers — A480

No. 2695, $1.80 — Clowns: a, Apes. b, Mo Lite. c, Gigi. d, "Buttons" McBride.
No. 2696, $1.80 — Performers: a, Chun Group. b, Casselly Sisters. c, Oliver Groszer. d, Keith Nelson.

**2003, Sept. 1**    **Perf. 14**
**Sheets of 4, #a-d**
2695-2696 A480 Set of 2    11.00 11.00

Christmas — A481

Designs: 25c, Madonna and Child, by Bartolomeo Vivarini. 30c, Holy Family, by Pompeo Girolamo Batoni. 45c, Madonna and Child, by Benozzo Gozzoli. 50c, Madonna and Child (Calci Parish Church), by Gozzoli. 75c, Madonna and Child Giving Blessings, by Gozzoli. 90c, Madonna and Child, by Master of the Female Half-figures. $2.50, Benois Madonna, by Leonardo da Vinci.

$6, The Virgin and Child with Angels, by Rosso Fiorentino.

**2003, Nov. 10 Litho. *Perf. 14¼***

**2697-2703** A481 Set of 7 4.25 4.25

**Souvenir Sheet**

**2704** A481 $6 multi 4.50 4.50

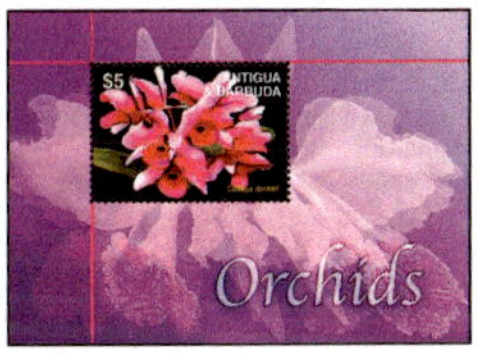
Orchids

Orchids A482

No. 2705, $2.50, vert.: a, Psychopsis papilio. b, Amesiella philippinensis. c, Maclellanara Pagan Dove Song. d, Phalaenopsis Little Hal.

No. 2706, $2.50: a, Daeliocattleya Amber Glow. b, Hygrochilus parishii. c, Dendrobium crystallinum. d, Disa hybrid.

$5, Cattleya deckeri.

**2003, Dec. 8 *Perf. 13½***

**Sheets of 4, #a-d**

**2705-2706** A482 Set of 2 17.50 17.50

**Souvenir Sheet**

**2707** A482 $5 multi 5.00 5.00

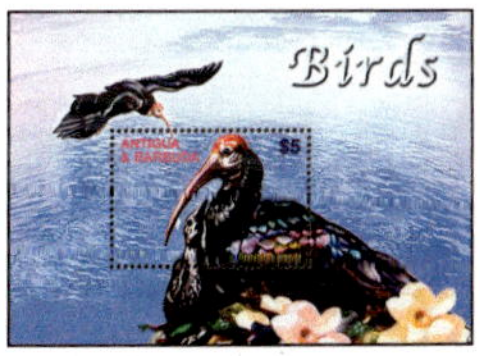
Birds

Birds A483

No. 2708, $2.50, vert.: a, Blue and gold macaw. b, Green-winged macaw. c, Green-naped lorikeet. d, Lesser sulfur-crested cockatoo.

No. 2709, $2.50: a, Severe macaw. b, Blue-headed parrot. c, Budgerigar. d, Sun conure.

$5, Bald ibis.

**2003, Dec. 8 Sheets of 4, #a-d**

**2708-2709** A483 Set of 2 19.50 19.50

**Souvenir Sheet**

**2710** A483 $5 multi 5.00 5.00

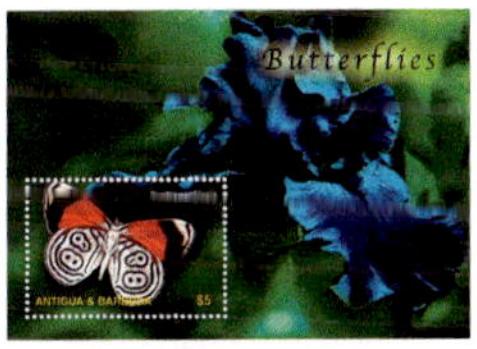
Butterflies

Butterflies — A484

No. 2711, $2: a, Esmerelda. b, Tiger pierid. c, Blue night. d, Charaxes nobilis.

No. 2712, $2.50: a, Orange-barred sulphur. b, Scarce bamboo page. c, Charaxes latona. d, Hewitson's blue hairstreak.

$5, Diaethia meridionalis.

**2003, Dec. 8 Sheets of 4, #a-d**

**2711-2712** A484 Set of 2 17.50 17.50

**Souvenir Sheet**

**2713** A484 $5 multi 5.00 5.00

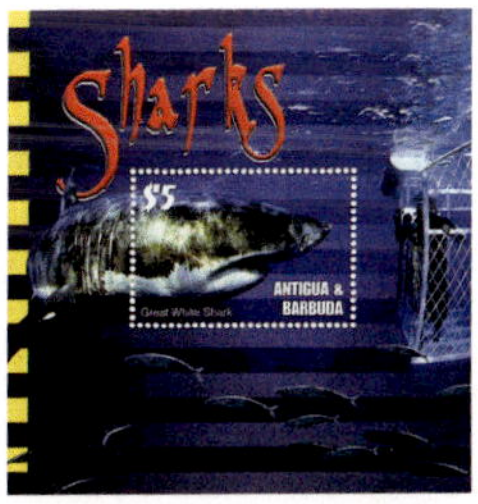
Sharks

Sharks A485

No. 2714: a, Bull. b, Gray reef. c, Black tip. d, Leopard.

$5, Great white.

**2003, Dec. 8**

**2714** A485 $2 Sheet of 4, #a-d 7.50 7.50

**Souvenir Sheet**

**2715** A485 $5 multi 4.50 4.50

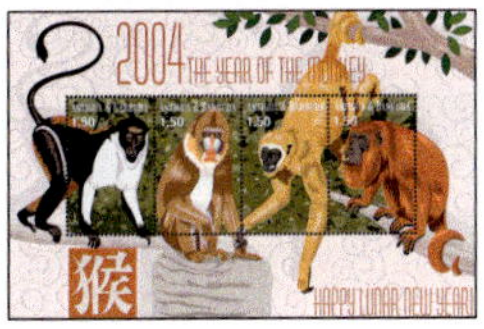

New Year 2004 (Year of the Monkey) A486

No. 2716, each $1.50: a, Monkey with black face and white chest. b, Monkey with brown face and white chest. c, Monkey with black, gray and yellow face. d, Red brown monkey on branch.

**2004, Jan. 19 *Perf. 14***

**2716** A486 Sheet of 4, #a-d 5.00 5.00

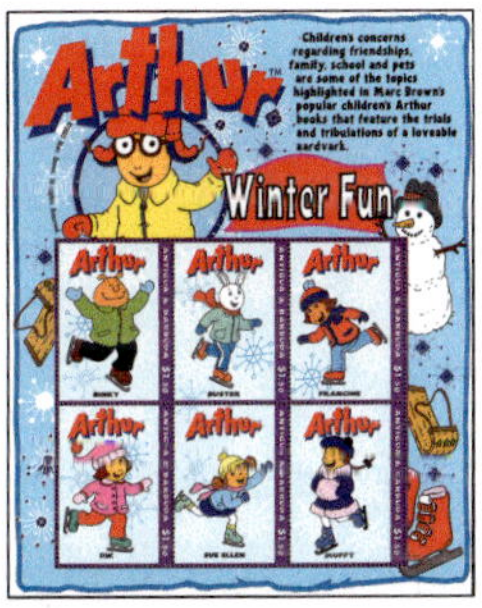
Arthur
Winter Fun

Arthur and Friends A487

No. 2717, each $1.50: a, Binky. b, Buster. c, Francine. d, D.W. e, Sue Ellen. f, Muffy.

No. 2718, each $1.80: a, Binky. b, Muffy. c, Francine. d, Buster.

No. 2719, each $2.50: a, Arthur hitting baseball. b, Sue Ellen. c, Binky. d, Arthur with foot on home plate.

**2004, Feb. 16 *Perf. 13¼***

**2717** A487 Sheet of 6, #a-f 6.75 6.75

**Sheets of 4, #a-d**

**2718-2719** A487 Set of 2 13.00 13.00

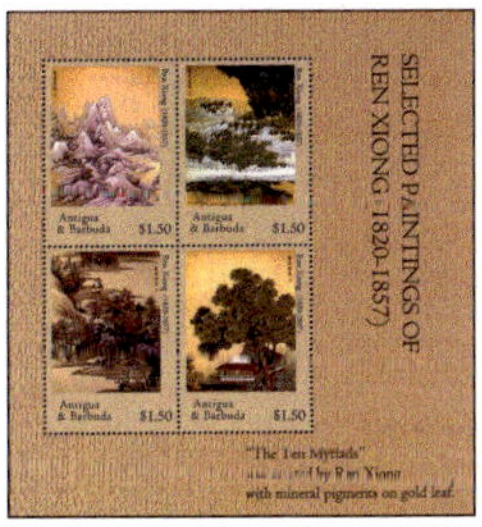
SELECTED PAINTINGS OF REN XIONG (1820-1857)

Paintings by Ren Xiong (1820-57) — A488

No. 2720, each $1.50: a, Purple hills. b, Cliffside waves. c, Hills at left, trees, Chinese text at right. d, House and tree.

No. 2721, each $1.50: a, Rocky pinnacles. b, Rocks at left and right. c, Hills, trees and bridge, Chinese text at top right. d, Waterfall at right, Chinese text at top left. e, Waterfalls, Chinese text at left. f, Rocks and flowers, Chinese text at top left.

No. 2722, each $1.50: a, Bird on flowering tree. b, Bird in tree.

**2004, Feb. 16**

**2720** A488 Sheet of 4, #a-d 4.50 4.50
**2721** A488 Sheet of 6, #a-f 6.75 6.75
**2722** A488 Sheet of 2, #a-b 4.00 4.00

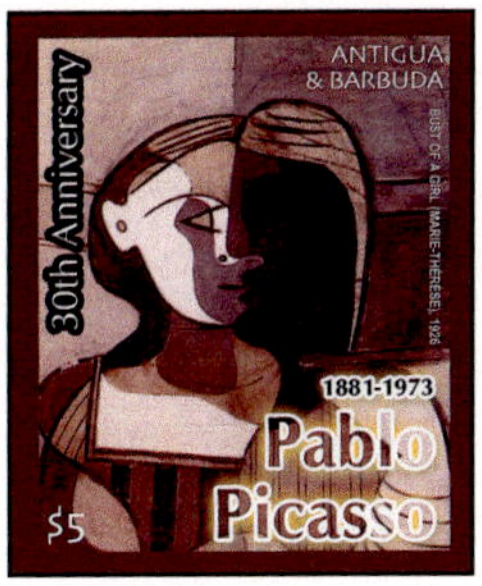
30th Anniversary
ANTIGUA & BARBUDA
1881-1973
Pablo Picasso
$5

Paintings by Pablo Picasso A489

No. 2723: a, Woman with a Flower. b, Marie-Thérèse Seated. c, The Red Armchair (Marie-Thérèse) Seated. d, The Dream (Marie-Thérèse) Seated.

$5, Bust of a Girl (Marie-Thérèse).

**2004, Mar. 8 *Perf. 14¼***

**2723** A489 $2 Sheet of 4, #a-d 6.50 6.50

***Imperf***

**2724** A489 $5 shown 4.00 4.00

No. 2723 contains four 38x50mm stamps.

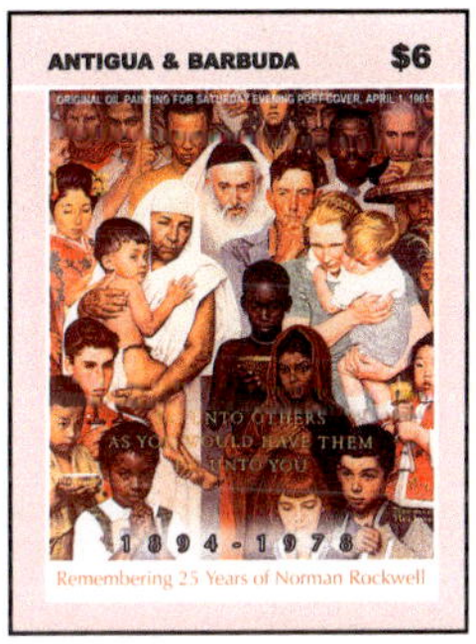
ANTIGUA & BARBUDA $6
1894-1978
Remembering 25 Years of Norman Rockwell

Paintings by Norman Rockwell A490

No. 2725: a, Freedom of Speech. b, Freedom to Worship. c, Freedom from Want. d, Freedom from Fear.

$5, Painting for cover of Apr. 1, 1961 Saturday Evening Post.

**2004, Mar. 8**

**2725** A490 $2 Sheet of 4, #a-d 6.00 6.00

***Imperf***

**2726** A490 $6 shown 4.50 4.50

No. 2725 contains four 38x50mm stamps.

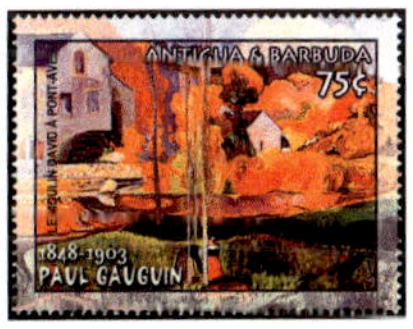
ANTIGUA & BARBUDA
75¢
1848-1903
PAUL GAUGUIN

Paintings by Paul Gauguin (1848-1903) A491

Designs: 25c, Vaite Goupil, vert. 30c, Autoportrait près de Golgotha, vert. 75c, Le Moulin David à Pont-Aver. $2.50, Moisson en Bretagne, vert.

$4, Cavaliers sur la Plage.

**2004, Mar. 8 Litho. *Perf. 14¼***

**2727-2730** A491 Set of 4 3.00 3.00

***Imperf***

**Size: 77x63mm**

**2731** A491 $4 multi 4.75 4.75

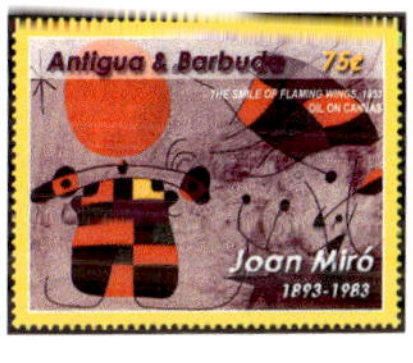
Antigua & Barbuda 75¢
Joan Miró
1893-1983

Paintings by Joan Miró (1893-1983) A492

Designs: 75c, The Smile of Flaming Wings. 90c, The Bird's Song in the Dew of the Moon. $1, Dancer II, vert. $4, Painting, 1954, vert.

No. 2736, $2 — Painting Based on a Collage, description in: a, LL. b, LR. c, UL. d, UR.

$5, Bather. $6, Flame in Space and Nude Woman, vert.

**2004, Mar. 8 Litho. *Perf. 14¼***

**2732-2735** A492 Set of 4 5.50 5.50
**2736** A492 $2 Sheet of 4, #a-d 6.50 6.50

***Imperf***

**Size: 102x83mm**

**2737** A492 $5 multi 4.00 4.00

**Size: 83x102mm**

**2738** A492 $6 multi 5.00 5.00

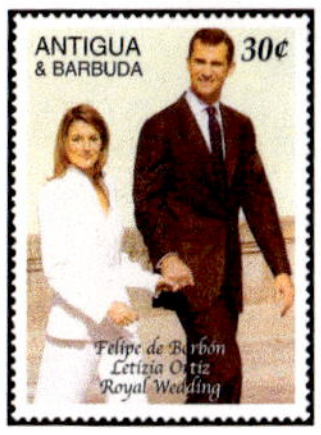
ANTIGUA & BARBUDA
30¢

Wedding of Prince Felipe de Borbón of Spain and Letizia Ortiz — A493

Designs: 30c, Couple. 50c, Couple, diff. 75c, Letizia. 90c, Prince Felipe. $1, Couple, diff. No. 2744, $5, Couple, diff.

No. 2745: a, Spanish royal family. b, Flags and Prince Felipe in uniform. c, Prince Felipe, his grandfather, Juan de Borbón y Battenberg, and his father, King Juan Carlos. d, Letizia, Prince Felipe, King Juan Carlos and Queen Sophia, horiz. e, Similar to 75c. f, Similar to 90c.

No. 2746, $5, Couple, diff. No. 2747, $5, Similar to #2745a. No. 2748, $5, Similar to #2745c. No. 2749, $6, Letizia, map of Europe. No. 2750, $6, Similar to #2745b. No. 2751, $6, Similar to #2745d, horiz.

**2004, May 21 *Perf. 13¼***

**2739-2744** A493 Set of 6 6.50 6.50
**2745** A493 $1.80 Sheet of 6, #a-f 8.50 8.50

**Souvenir Sheets**

**2746-2751** A493 Set of 6 25.00 25.00

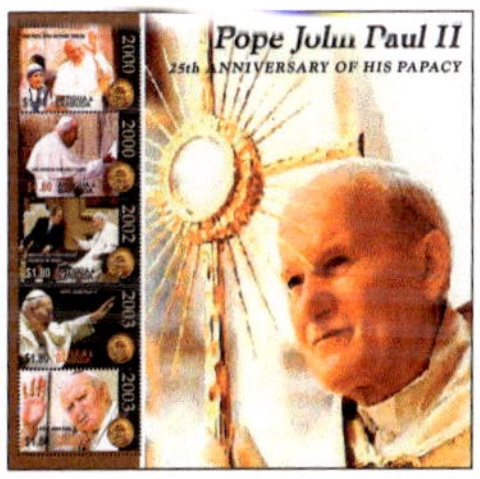
Pope John Paul II
25th ANNIVERSARY OF HIS PAPACY

Election of Pope John Paul II, 25th Anniv. (in 2003) A494

No. 2752: a, Pope with Mother Teresa. b, Pope in the Holy Land. c, Pope meeting with Pres. George W. Bush. d, Pope waving, dark background. e, Pope waving, light background.

**2004, June 17 *Perf. 14***

**2752** A494 $1.80 Sheet of 5, #a-e 7.25 7.25

Inscription of "2000" on No. 2752a is incorrect.

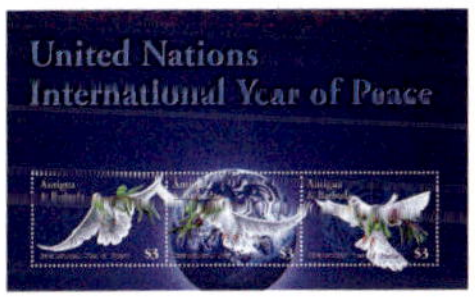
United Nations
International Year of Peace

Intl. Year of Peace A495

No. 2753 Dove and: a, Intl. Year of Peace emblem. b, Earth. c, UN emblem.

**2004, June 17**

**2753** A495 $3 Sheet of 3, #a-c 6.75 6.75

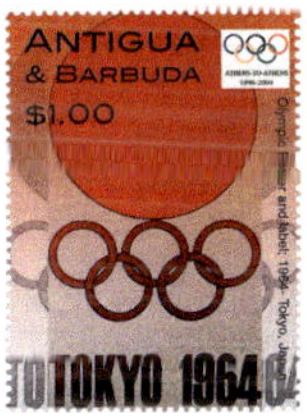
ANTIGUA & BARBUDA
$1.00
TOKYO 1964

2004 Summer Olympics, Athens — A496

Designs: $1, Poster for 1964 Tokyo Olympics. $1.65, Commemorative medal for 1964 Tokyo Olympics. $1.80, Fencing, horiz. $2, Wrestlers, horiz.

**2004, June 17 *Perf. 14¼***

**2754-2757** A496 Set of 4 5.00 5.00

# ANTIGUA

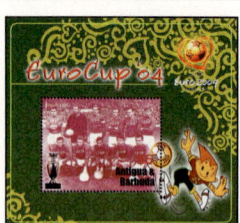

European Soccer Championships, Portugal — A497

No. 2758: a, Milan Galic. b, Slava Metreveli. c, Igor Netto. d, Parc des Princes. $6, 1960 USSR team.

| 2004, June 17 | | Perf. 14 |
|---|---|---|
| 2758 A497 $2 Sheet of 4, #a-d | | 7.50 7.50 |
| **Souvenir Sheet** | | |
| **Perf. 14¼** | | |
| 2759 A497 $6 multi | | 5.00 5.00 |

No. 2758 contains four 28x42mm stamps.

Locomotives, Signals and Stations — A498

No. 2760, $1: a, Evening Star. b, Indian Railways XC Pacific. c, German Kreigslokomotive. d, Bulleid Light Pacific. e, G. W. R. copper cap chimney. f, Tallylyn Railway. g, Preservation volunteers. h, N. E. R. Y7 0-4-0T. h, Breda 0-4-0 WT, locomotive shed, Asmara, Eritrea.
No. 2761, $1, vert.: a, King Class 4-6-0. b, Argentinian 11B Class 2-8-0. c, Baldwin Mikado. d, Round trackside signal with red horizontal band. e, Wooden box with button signal. f, Signal house, signals with red and yellow arms. g, Signal house, signal with two red arms. h, Window of signal house. i, Signal lights.
No. 2762, $1, vert.: a, 2-4-0T on Douglas to Port Erin line, Isle of Man. b, South African Railways 4-8-2S. c, China Railways SY Class 2-8-2. d, St. Pancras Station. e, Ulverston Station, f, Bolton Station. g, Liverpool St. Station. h, Cannon St. Station. i, Malvern Station.
No. 2763, $5, Settle-Carlisle line. No. 2764, $6, Douro Valley Railway. No. 2765, $6, Train over Lake Egridir, Turkey.

| 2004, June 17 | | Perf. 14 |
|---|---|---|
| | **Sheets of 9, #a-i** | |
| 2760-2762 A498 Set of 3 | | 21.00 21.00 |
| | **Souvenir Sheets** | |
| 2763-2765 A498 Set of 3 | | 14.00 14.00 |

D-Day, 60th Anniv. — A499

Designs: 30c, Derrick Tysoe. 45c, Lt. Gen. Walter Bedell Smith. $1.50, Les Perry. $3, Maj. Gen. Percy Hobart.
No. 2770, $2: a, Tiger II tank. b, Standartenfuhrer Kurt Meyer. c, Canadian infantry. d, British infantry.
No. 2771, $2: a, Hamilcar disgorges Tetrarch tank. b, Horsa glider unloads cargo. c, Beachheads established. d, Liberation begins.
No. 2772, $6, Sherman tank. No. 2773, $6, Mulberry Harbor.

| 2004, July 26 | | Perf. 14¼ |
|---|---|---|
| | **Stamp + Label (#2766-2769)** | |
| 2766-2769 A499 Set of 4 | | 4.00 4.00 |
| | **Sheets of 4, #a-d** | |
| 2770-2771 A499 Set of 2 | | 12.00 12.00 |
| | **Souvenir Sheets** | |
| 2772-2773 A499 Set of 2 | | 9.00 9.00 |

**Miniature Sheet**

Queen Juliana of the Netherlands (1909-2004) — A500

No. 2774 — Netherlands flag and: a, Juliana. b, Juliana and Prince Bernhard. c, Juliana and Princess Beatrix. d, Juliana and Princess Irene. e, Juliana and Princess Margriet. f, Juliana and Princess Christina.

| 2004, June 17 | Litho. | Perf. 13¼ |
|---|---|---|
| 2774 A500 $2 Sheet of 6, #a-f | | 9.00 9.00 |

**Miniature Sheet**

National Basketball Association Players — A501

No. 2775: a, Mike Bibby, Sacramento Kings. b, Jim Jackson, Houston Rockets. c, Tracy McGrady, Houston Rockets. d, Chris Webber, Sacramento Kings. e, Peja Stojakovic, Sacramento Kings. f, Yao Ming, Houston Rockets.

| 2004, Nov. 8 | | Perf. 12 |
|---|---|---|
| 2775 A501 $1.50 Sheet of 6, #a-f | | 6.75 6.75 |

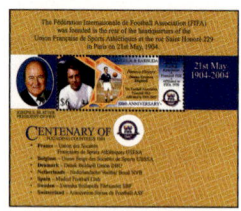

FIFA (Fédération Internationale de Football Association), Cent. — A502

No. 2776: a, Zinedine Zidane. b, Roberto Baggio. c, Franz Beckenbauer. d, Ossie Ardiles.
$6, Jimmy Greaves.

| 2004, Nov. 8 | | Perf. 12¾x12½ |
|---|---|---|
| 2776 A502 $2 Sheet of 4, #a-d | | 6.00 6.00 |
| | **Souvenir Sheet** | |
| 2777 A502 $6 multi | | 4.50 4.50 |

**Miniature Sheet**

John Denver (1943-97), Singer — A503

No. 2778, each $1.50: a, At microphone. b, Tuning guitar. c, With arm extended. d, Facing left, playing guitar.

| 2004, Nov. 22 | | Perf. 14 |
|---|---|---|
| 2778 A503 Sheet of 4, #a-d | | 4.50 4.50 |

**Miniature Sheet**

George Herman "Babe" Ruth (1895-1948), Baseball Player — A504

No. 2779, each $1.80: a, Wearing blue cap. b, Wearing crown. c, Wearing pinstriped cap. d, Holding bat.

| 2004, Nov. 22 | | |
|---|---|---|
| 2779 A504 Sheet of 4, #a-d | | 5.50 5.50 |

No. 2780, $2: a, "Billy attackled me too hard," purple panel. b, "His ears came from where his eyes are." c, "Tennessee!" d, "One candy or one bowl?"
No. 2781, $2: a, "If you had wider shoulders, Daddy, you could be a two-seater." b, "Billy attackled me too hard," red panel. c, "Who teepeed the mummies?" d, "Looking out there makes me realize it's indeed the little things that count."
No. 2782, $2: a, "Someday I might travel to another planet, but I'm not sure why." b, "Adam and Eve were lucky. They didn't have any history to learn." c, "My backpack is too full. Will somebody help me stand up?" d, "I tripped because one foot tried to hug the other foot."
No. 2783, $2: a, "If you don't put enough stamps on it the mailman will only take it part way." b, "Gee, Grandma, you have a lot of thoughts on your wall." c, "Shall I play for you pa-rum-pa-pum-pummm. . .?" d, "You have to do that when you're married."
No. 2784, $2: a, Billy. b, Jeffy. c, PJ. d, Dolly.

| | Perf. 13¼, 14¼(#2784) | |
|---|---|---|
| 2004, Nov. 22 | **Sheets of 4, #a-d** | |
| 2780-2784 A505 Set of 5 | | 30.00 30.00 |

World AIDS Day — A506

| 2004, Dec. 1 | | Perf. 14 |
|---|---|---|
| 2785 A506 $2 multi | | 1.75 1.75 |

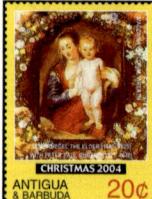

Christmas — A507

Designs: 20c, Madonna in Floral Wreath, by Jan Breughel the Elder and Peter Paul Rubens. 25c, Madonna and Child, by Jan Gossaert. 30c, Santa Claus on skis. 45c, Santa Claus with raised arms. 50c, Santa Claus, reindeer on roof. $1, Floral Wreath with Virgin and Child, by Daniel Seghers. $1.80, Madonna and Child, by Andrea Mantegna.

$6, Madonna in a Floral Wreath, by Seghers.

| 2004, Dec. 13 | | Perf. 12¼x12 |
|---|---|---|
| 2786-2792 A507 Set of 7 | | 3.50 3.50 |
| | **Souvenir Sheet** | |
| 2793 A507 $6 multi | | 5.00 5.00 |

Dogs — A508

Designs: 30c, American pit bull terrier. 90c, Maltese. $1.50, Rottweiler. $3, Australian terrier.
$6, German shepherd, horiz.

| 2005, May 23 | Litho. | Perf. 12¾ |
|---|---|---|
| 2794-2797 A508 Set of 4 | | 8.00 8.00 |
| | **Souvenir Sheet** | |
| 2798 A508 $6 multi | | 6.25 6.25 |

Cats — A509

Designs: 75c, Golden Persian. $1, Calico shorthair. $1.50, Siamese. $3, Tabby Persian. $5, Turkish.

| 2005, May 23 | | |
|---|---|---|
| 2799-2802 A509 Set of 4 | | 6.00 6.00 |
| | **Souvenir Sheet** | |
| 2803 A509 $5 multi | | 5.00 5.00 |

Insects A510

No. 2804, horiz.: a, Figure-of-eight butterfly. b, Honeybee. c, Migratory grasshopper. d, Hercules beetle.
$5, Cramer's Mesene butterfly.

| 2005, May 23 | | |
|---|---|---|
| 2804 A510 $2 Sheet of 4, #a-d | | 7.75 7.75 |
| | **Souvenir Sheet** | |
| 2805 A510 $5 multi | | 4.50 4.50 |

Marine Life A511

No. 2806: a, Yellowtail damselfish. b, French angelfish. c, Horseshoe crab. d, Emerald mithrax crab.
$6, Spanish hogfish.

| 2005, May 23 | | |
|---|---|---|
| 2806 A511 $2 Sheet of 4, #a-d | | 7.25 7.25 |
| | **Souvenir Sheet** | |
| 2807 A511 $6 multi | | 5.75 5.75 |

Prehistoric Animals — A512

No. 2808, $2: a, Mammuthus imperator. b, Brontops. c, Hyracotherium. d, Propaleotherium.
No. 2809, $2.50: a, Ceratosaur. b, Coelurosaurs. c, Ornitholestes. d, Baryonyx.
No. 2810, $3: a, Plateosaurus. b, Yangchuanosaurus. c, Ceolophysis. d, Lystrosaurus.
No. 2811, $4, Triceratops. No. 2812, $5, Stegoasurus, vert. No. 2813, $6, Coelodonta.

**2005, May 23**

**Sheets of 4, #a-d**

**2808-2810** A512 Set of 3 28.00 28.00

**Souvenir Sheets**

**2811-2813** A512 Set of 3 13.00 13.00

Miniature Sheet

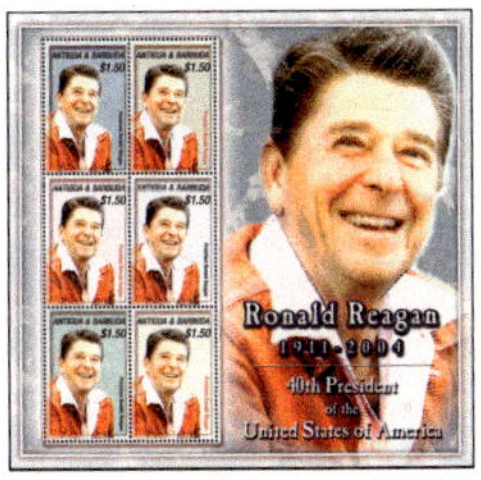
Ronald Reagan
1911-2004
40th President of the United States of America

Pres. Ronald Reagan (1911-2004) — A513

No. 2814 — Background colors: a, Gray blue. b, Gray brown. c, Pink. d, White. e, Gray green. f, Buff.

**2005, June 15** ***Perf. 14***

**2814** A513 $1.50 Sheet of 6, #a-f 7.50 7.50

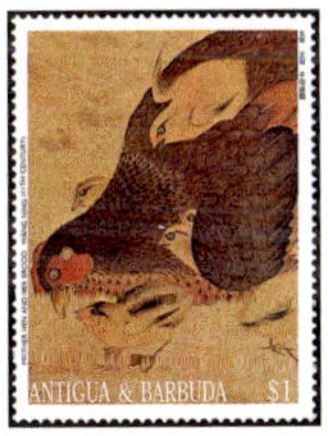
ANTIGUA & BARBUDA $1

New Year 2005 (Year of the Rooster) — A514

Mother Hen and Her Brood, by Wang Ning: $1, Detail. $4, Entire painting.

**2005, June 15** ***Perf. 14¼***

**2815** A514 $1 multi .75 .75

**Souvenir Sheet**

**2816** A514 $4 multi 4.00 4.00

No. 2815 printed in sheets of 4.

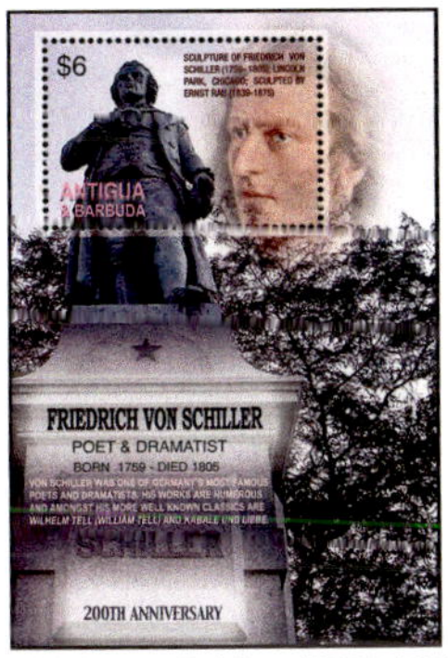
$6
ANTIGUA & BARBUDA
FRIEDRICH VON SCHILLER
POET & DRAMATIST
200TH ANNIVERSARY

Friedrich von Schiller (1759-1805), Writer — A515

No. 2817: a, Bust of Schiller, by C. L. Richter, Central Park, New York. b, Actors in "Kabale und Liebe." c, Schiller's birthplace, Marbach, Germany.
$6, Sculpture of Schiller, by Ernst Rau, Lincoln Park, Chicago.

**2005, June 15** ***Perf. 14***

**2817** A515 $3 Sheet of 3, #a-c 6.75 6.75

**Souvenir Sheet**

**2818** A515 $6 multi 5.25 5.25

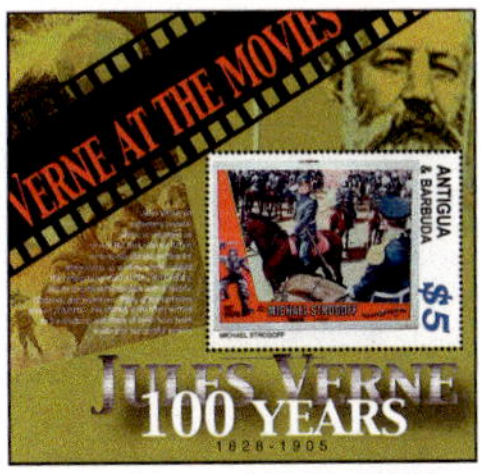
VERNE AT THE MOVIES
ANTIGUA & BARBUDA
$5
JULES VERNE
100 YEARS
1828-1905

Jules Verne (1828-1905), Writer — A516

No. 2819, vert. — Movie posters for Verne works: a, Monster Island, 1961. b, Journey to the Center of the Earth, 1961. c, From the Earth to the Moon, 1956. d, Sea Devils, 1961.
$5, Michael Strogoff, 1956.

**2005, June 15**

**2819** A516 $2 Sheet of 4, #a-d 6.00 6.00

**Souvenir Sheet**

**2820** A516 $5 multi 3.75 3.75

No. 2819 contains four 28x42mm stamps.

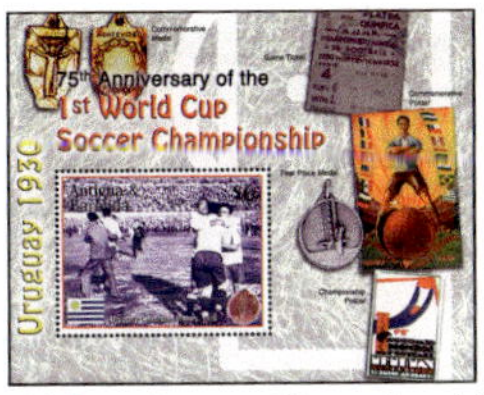
75th Anniversary of the 1st World Cup Soccer Championship
Uruguay 1930

World Cup Soccer Championships, 75th Anniv. — A517

No. 2821, each $1.50 — Uruguayan flag, first place medal and: a, 1930 Uruguay team. b, Hector Castro scoring goal against Argentina. c, Crowd in Estadio Centenario. d, Hector Castro.
$6, Uruguay team celebrating 1930 victory.

**2005, June 15** ***Perf. 14¼***

**2821** A517 Sheet of 4, #a-d 8.00 8.00

**Souvenir Sheet**

**2822** A517 $6 multi 4.50 4.50

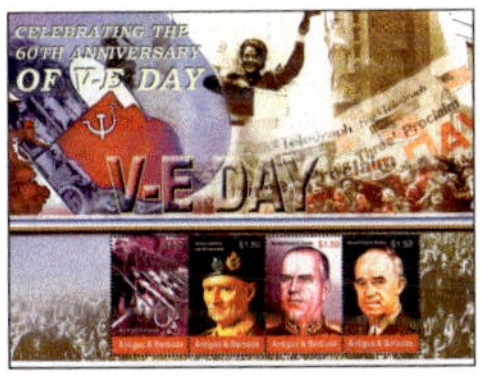
CELEBRATING THE 60TH ANNIVERSARY OF V-E DAY
V-E DAY

End of World War II, 60th Anniv. A518

No. 2823, $1.50: a, Soldiers in Red Square, Moscow, May 9, 1945. b, Gen. Bernard Law Montgomery. c, Marshal Georgi K. Zhukov. d, Gen. Omar N. Bradley.
No. 2824, $2, horiz.: a, Winston Churchill, Franklin D. Roosevelt and Joseph Stalin at Yalta Summit. b, Raising of US flag on Mount Suribachi. c, Gen. Douglas MacArthur signing Japanese surrender documents. d, Japanese officials at surrender ceremony.

**2005, June 15** ***Perf. 14***

**Sheets of 4, #a-d**

**2823-2824** A518 Set of 2 10.50 10.50

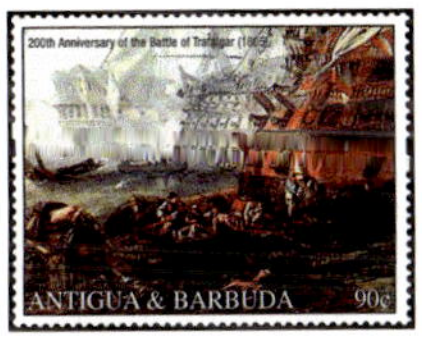
ANTIGUA & BARBUDA 90c

Battle of Trafalgar, Bicent. A519

Various ships in battle: 90c, $1, $1.50, $1.80.
$6, The Victory firing during the Battle of Trafalgar.

**2005, June 15** ***Perf. 14¼***

**2825-2828** A519 Set of 4 6.75 6.75

**Souvenir Sheet**

**2829** A519 $6 multi 7.75 7.75

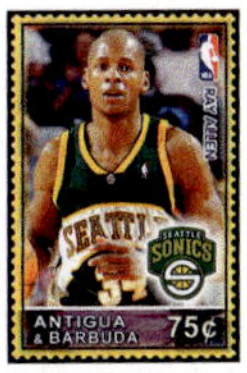
ANTIGUA & BARBUDA 75¢

National Basketball Association Players — A520

Designs: No. 2830, 75c, Ray Allen, Seattle Supersonics. No. 2831, 75c, Lucious Harris, Cleveland Cavaliers. No. 2832, 75c, Dwight Howard, Orlando Magic. No. 2833, 75c, Antonio McDyess, Detroit Pistons. No. 2834, 75c, Emeka Okafor, Charlotte Bobcats.

**2005** ***Perf. 14***

**2830-2834** A520 Set of 5 3.00 3.00

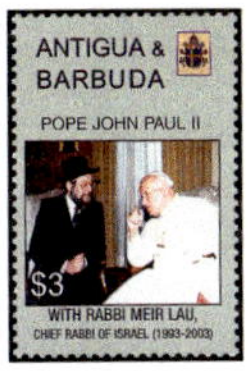
ANTIGUA & BARBUDA
POPE JOHN PAUL II
$3
WITH RABBI MEIR LAU, CHIEF RABBI OF ISRAEL (1993-2003)

Pope John Paul II (1920-2005) and Meir Lau, Chief Rabbi of Israel — A521

**2005, Oct. 10** ***Perf. 13½x13¼***

**2835** A521 $3 multi 4.25 4.25

Printed in sheets of 6.

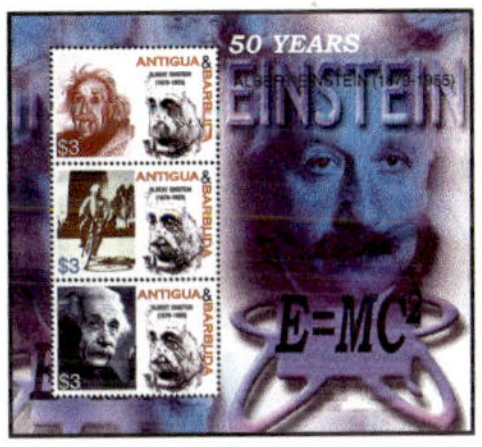
50 YEARS
EINSTEIN
E=MC²

Albert Einstein (1879-1955), Physicist — A522

No. 2836 — Photograph of Einstein in: a, Brown. b, Olive green. c, Black.

**2005, Oct. 10 Litho.** ***Perf. 13¼x13½***

**2836** A522 $3 Sheet of 3, #a-c 6.75 6.75

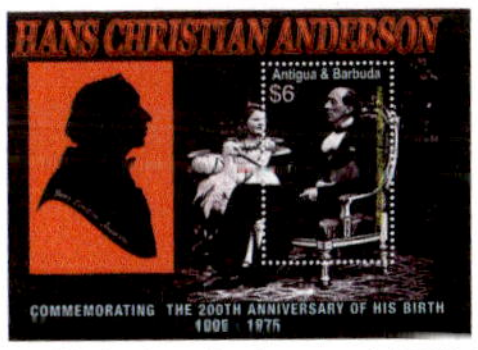
HANS CHRISTIAN ANDERSON
$6
COMMEMORATING THE 200TH ANNIVERSARY OF HIS BIRTH 1805 - 1875

Hans Christian Andersen (1805-75), Author — A523

No. 2837: a, Portrait of Andersen. b, Statue of Andersen, Central Park, New York City. c, Andersen's gravesite.
$6, Andersen seated.

**2005, Oct. 10** ***Perf. 13½x13¼***

**2837** A523 $3 Sheet of 3, #a-c 6.75 6.75

**Souvenir Sheet**

**2838** A523 $6 multi 5.25 5.25

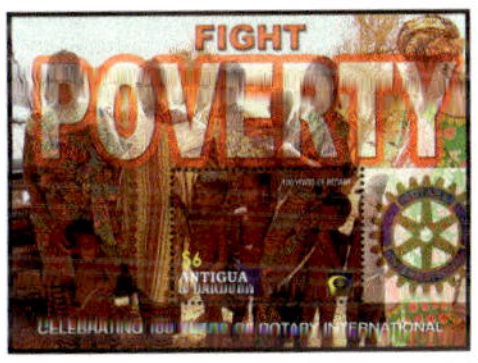
FIGHT
POVERTY

Rotary International, Cent. — A524

No. 2839, vert.: a, Italy #1372. b, Paul Harris Medallion. c, Paul P. Harris, first Rotary President.
$6, Children.

**2005, Oct. 10** ***Perf. 13½x13¼***

**2839** A524 $3 Sheet of 3, #a-c 7.25 7.25

**Souvenir Sheet**

***Perf. 13¼x13½***

**2840** A524 $6 multi 6.00 6.00

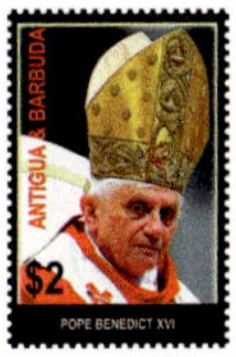
ANTIGUA & BARBUDA
$2
POPE BENEDICT XVI

Pope Benedict XVI — A525

**2005, Nov. 21** ***Perf. 13½x13¼***

**2841** A525 $2 multi 1.75 1.75

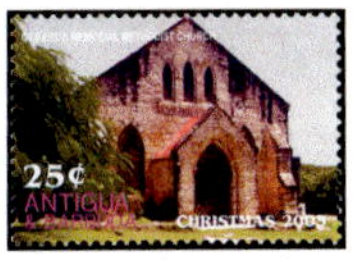
25¢
ANTIGUA
CHRISTMAS 2005

Christmas A526

Churches: 25c, Gilbert's Memorial Methodist Church. No. 2843, 30c, People's Church, Barbuda. No. 2844, 30c, Tyrell's Roman Catholic Church. 45c, St. Barnabas Anglican Church. 50c, St. Peter's Anglican Church. No. 2847, 75c, Spring Gardens Moravian Church. No. 2848, 75c, St. Steven's Anglican Church. No. 2849, 90c, Holy Family Catholic Cathedral. No. 2850, 90c, Pilgrim Holiness Church, vert. $1, Ebenezer Methodist Church.
No. 2852, $5, St. John's Cathedral. No. 2853, $5, Worship service, Spring Gardens Moravian Church, vert.

**2005, Dec. 19** ***Perf. 12¾***

**2842-2851** A526 Set of 10 6.75 6.75

**Souvenir Sheets**

**2852-2853** A526 Set of 2 8.00 8.00

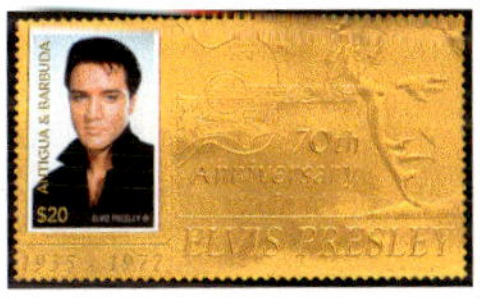
ANTIGUA & BARBUDA
$20
ELVIS PRESLEY

Elvis Presley (1935-77) — A527

***Serpentine Die Cut 8¾x9***

**2005 Litho. & Embossed**

**2854** A527 $20 gold & multi 16.00 16.00

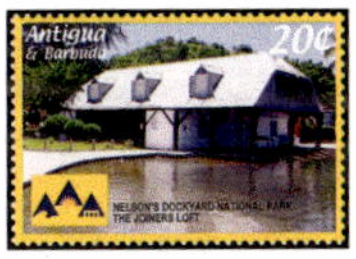
Antigua & Barbuda
20c

National Parks — A528

Designs: No. 2855, 20c, Joiner's Loft, Nelson's Dockyard Natl. Park. No. 2856, 20c, Pay Office, Nelson's Dockyard Natl. Park, vert. No. 2857, 30c, Admiral's House Museum, Nelson's Dockyard Natl. Park. No. 2858, 30c, Bakery, Nelson's Dockyard Natl. Park. No. 2859, 75c, Devil's Bridge Natl. Park. No. 2860, 75c, View from Shirley Heights Lookout, Nelson's Dockyard Natl. Park. No. 2861, 90c, Green Castle Hill Natl. Park. No. 2862, 90c, Fort Berkeley, Nelson's Dockyard Natl. Park. No. 2863, $1.50, Pigeon Point Beach, Nelson's Dockyard Natl. Park. No. 2864, $1.50, Half Moon Bay Natl. Park. $1.80, Cannon at Ft. Berkeley.
No. 2866, $5, Codrington Lagoon Natl. Park. No. 2867, $5, Museum, Nelson's Dockyard Natl. Park, vert.

**2006, Jan. 9** ***Perf. 14***

**2855-2865** A528 Set of 11 7.00 7.00

**Souvenir Sheets**

**2866-2867** A528 Set of 2 9.50 9.50

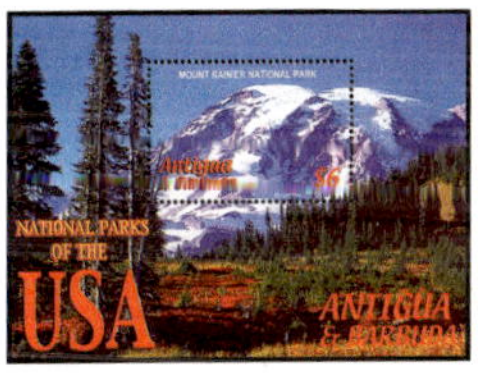
NATIONAL PARKS OF THE USA
ANTIGUA & BARBUDA

National Parks of the United States A529

No. 2868: a, Yellowstone. b, Olympic. c, Glacier. d, Grand Canyon. e, Yosemite. f, Great Smoky Mountains.
$6, Mount Rainier.

**2006, Jan. 6** ***Perf. 14¼***

**2868** A529 $1.50 Sheet of 6, #a-f 7.50 7.50

## 554 ANTIGUA

### Souvenir Sheet
### Perf. 14
| 2869 | A529 | $6 multi | | 4.75 | 4.75 |

No. 2868 contains six 50x38mm stamps.

Moravian Church Antigua Conference, 250th Anniv. — A530

Designs: 30c, Bishop John Ephraim Knight. $1, John Andrew Buckley. $1.50, Old Spring Gardens Moravian Church, horiz. No. 2873, $5, Sandbox tree. No. 2874, $5, Westerby Memorial. No. 2875, $5, Spring Gardens Teachers College, horiz.

**2006, Apr. 3**     **Perf. 12¾**
| 2870-2872 | A530 | Set of 3 | 2.25 | 2.25 |

### Souvenir Sheets
| 2873-2875 | A530 | Set of 3 | 13.00 | 13.00 |

Marilyn Monroe (1926-62), Actress — A531

**2006, Apr. 10**     **Perf. 13¼**
| 2876 | A531 | $3 multi | | 2.25 | 2.25 |

Printed in sheets of 4.

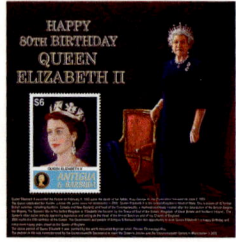

Queen Elizabeth II, 80th Birthday — A532

No. 2877: a, As young woman (black and white photo). b, Wearing pearl necklace. c, Wearing white blouse. d, Wearing crown.
$6, Wearing crown, diff.

**2006, Apr. 10**
| 2877 | A532 | $2 Sheet of 4, #a-d | 6.50 | 6.50 |

### Souvenir Sheet
| 2878 | A532 | $6 multi | | 4.75 | 4.75 |

2006 Winter Olympics, Turin — A533

Designs: No. 2879, 75c, Austria #715. No. 2880, 75c, Poster for 1972 Sapporo Winter Olympics, vert. No. 2881, 90c, Austria #714. No. 2882, 90c, Japan #1103, vert. $2, Austria #717. $3, Poster for 1964 Innsbruck Winter Olympics, vert.

**2006, May 11**    **Litho.**    **Perf. 14¼**
| 2879-2884 | A533 | Set of 6 | 7.00 | 7.00 |

### Miniature Sheets

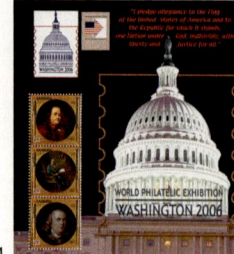

A534

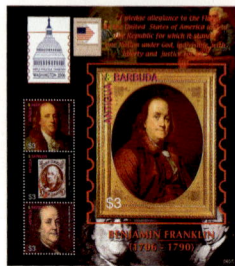

Washington 2006 World Philatelic Exhibition — A535

No. 2885: a, Framed circular portrait of Benjamin Franklin wearing red jacket with fur collar. b, Framed circular portrait of Franklin seated. c, Framed circular portrait of Franklin wearing gray jacket.
No. 2886: a, Unframed portrait of Franklin wearing jacket with fur collar. b, US #1. c, Unframed portrait of Franklin wearing black coat. d, Framed oval portrait like #2885a (73x87mm).

**2006, May 29**    **Perf. 11½**
| 2885 | A534 | $3 Sheet of 3, #a-c | 7.50 | 7.50 |

**Perf. 11½, Imperf. (#2886d)**
| 2886 | A535 | $3 Sheet of 4, #a-d | 9.50 | 9.50 |

### Miniature Sheet

Wolfgang Amadeus Mozart (1756-91), Composer — A536

No. 2887: a, Mozart's viola. b, Mozart at age 11. c, Young Mozart. d, Mozart in Verona, 1770.

**2006, July 3**    **Perf. 12¾**
| 2887 | A536 | $3 Sheet of 4, #a-d | 11.00 | 11.00 |

### Miniature Sheet

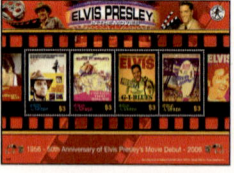

Posters of Elvis Presley Movies — A537

No. 2888: a, Charro! b, Follow That Dream. c, G.I. Blues. d, Blue Hawaii.

**2006, July 12**    **Perf. 13¼**
| 2888 | A537 | $3 Sheet of 4, #a-d | 10.00 | 10.00 |

Antigua and Barbuda Girl Guides, 75th Anniv. — A538

Designs: 25c, Leaders after garbage collection race, 2002. 30c, Girl Guides color party, horiz. 45c, Uniformed and non-uniformed members. 50c, Girl Guides marching band, horiz. $1, Leeward Islands leaders training camp, 1946.
No. 2894, $5, Assistant Commissioner Lisa Simon. No. 2895, $5, Girl Guides gathering at Fort James, 1935, horiz. No. 2896, $5, Enrollment ceremony, 2006, horiz.

**2006, July 17**    **Perf. 12¾**
| 2889-2893 | A538 | Set of 5 | 2.75 | 2.75 |

### Souvenir Sheets
| 2894-2896 | A538 | Set of 3 | 12.50 | 12.50 |

Leeward Islands Air Transport, 50th Anniv. — A539

Designs: 30c, HS-748 Hawker Siddely Avro. No. 2898, 50c, BN2 Islanders. No. 2899, 50c, BN2 Norman Islander. No. 2900, 50c, Beechcraft Twin Bonanza, vert. $1.50, BAC 111, HS-748. $2.50, DH8-300 de Havilland.
$5, Sir Frank Delisle, LIAT founder, and Beechcraft Twin Bonanza, vert.

**2006, Oct. 2**    **Litho.**    **Perf. 14¼**
| 2897-2902 | A539 | Set of 6 | 6.25 | 6.25 |

### Souvenir Sheet
| 2903 | A539 | $5 multi | | 5.25 | 5.25 |

Independence, 25th Anniv. — A540

Designs: 30c, Pineapple. $1, Flag. $1.50, Coat of arms.
No. 2907: a, One magnificent frigatebird. b, Two fallow deer. c, One fallow deer. d, Two magnificent frigatebirds.
$5, New Parliament Building, vert.

**2006, Oct. 30**    **Perf. 12¾**
| 2904-2906 | A540 | Set of 3 | 2.50 | 2.50 |
| 2907 | A540 | 25c Sheet of 4, #a-d | 1.50 | 1.50 |

### Souvenir Sheet
| 2908 | A540 | $5 multi | | 5.50 | 5.50 |

No. 2908 contains one 38x50mm stamp.

Civil Rights Leaders — A541

No. 2909, $2: a, Dalai Lama. b, Pres. Abraham Lincoln. c, Susan B. Anthony. d, Harriet Tubman.
No. 2910, $2: a, Mahatma Gandhi. b, Nelson Mandela. c, Rosa Parks.
$5, Dr. Martin Luther King, Jr.

**2006, Nov. 20**    **Perf. 12, 12½ (#2910)**
| 2909 | | Horiz. strip of 4 | 8.00 | 8.00 |
| a.-d. | A541 | $2 Any single | 1.75 | 1.75 |
| 2910 | A541 | $2 Sheet of 3, #a-c | 5.00 | 5.00 |

### Souvenir Sheet
| 2911 | A541 | $5 multi | | 5.50 | 5.50 |

Rembrandt (1606-69), Painter — A542

Designs: 50c, Landscape with the Baptism of the Eunuch. 75c, Landscape with a Coach. $1, River Landscape with Ruins. $2, Landscape with a Castle.
No. 2916, $2: a, The Holy Family (Joseph at table). b, The Good Samaritan Arriving at the Inn. c, Rebecca Taking Leave of Her Family. d, The Holy Family (Madonna and Child).
No. 2917, $2 — Samson Posting the Riddle to the Wedding Guests: a, Woman with beads in hair. b, Three men. c, Two men. d, Woman holding glass.
No. 2918, $5, Self-portrait. No. 2919, $5, Rembrandt's Mother.

**2006, Dec. 20**    **Perf. 12¼x12**
| 2912-2915 | A542 | Set of 4 | 5.00 | 5.00 |

**Sheets of 4, #a-d**
| 2916-2917 | A542 | Set of 2 | 13.50 | 13.50 |

**Imperf**
**Size: 70x100mm**
| 2918-2919 | A542 | Set of 2 | 9.00 | 9.00 |

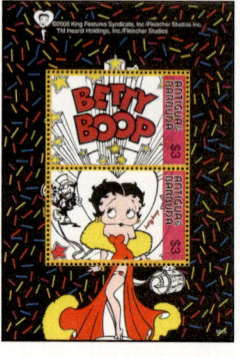

Betty Boop — A543

No. 2920, vert. — Background color: a, Yellow. b, Green. c, Red violet. d, Orange. e, Blue green. f, Purple.
No. 2921: a, Text, "Betty Boop" and stars. b, Betty Boop and cat.

**2006, Dec. 20**    **Perf. 14¼**
| 2920 | A543 | $1.50 Sheet of 6, #a-f | 7.50 | 7.50 |

### Souvenir Sheet
| 2921 | A543 | $3 Sheet of 2 | 5.00 | 5.00 |

Space Achievements — A544

No. 2922: a, JSC Shuttle mission simulator. b, STS-1 prime crew in classroom. c, STS-1 Columbia on launch pad. d, Launch of Columbia. e, Columbia landing at Edwards Air Force Base. f, Columbia on runway.
No. 2923, $3: a, Molniya 8K78M launch vehicle. b, Luna 9 flight apparatus. c, Moon images transmitted by Luna 9. d, Luna 9 capsule.
No. 2924, $3: a, Apollo crew boards transfer van. b, Handshake after Apollo-Soyuz linkup. c, Display of Apollo-Soyuz plaque. d, Recovery of Apollo command module.
No. 2925, $6, Artist's conception of NASA spaceship to orbit Moon. No. 2926, $6, Calipso Satellite. No. 2927, $6, Space Station Mir.

**2006**    **Perf. 12¾**
| 2922 | A544 | $2 Sheet of 6, #a-f | 10.00 | 10.00 |

**Sheets of 4, #a-d**
| 2923-2924 | A544 | Set of 2 | 21.00 | 21.00 |

### Souvenir Sheets
| 2925-2927 | A544 | Set of 3 | 16.00 | 16.00 |

Christmas — A545

Ornaments: 30c, Ball. 90c, Star. $1, Bell. $1.50, Christmas tree.
No. 2932: a, Ball. b, Star. c, Bell. d, Christmas tree.
$6, Santa Claus at beach.

**2006**    **Perf. 13½**
| 2928-2931 | A545 | Set of 4 | 3.00 | 3.00 |
| 2932 | A545 | $2 Sheet of 4, #a-d | 6.75 | 6.75 |

### Souvenir Sheet
| 2933 | A545 | $6 multi | | 6.00 | 6.00 |

# ANTIGUA

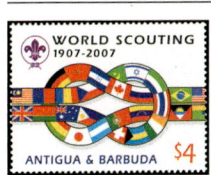

Scouting, Cent. A546

Scout emblem at: $4, UL. $6, LR.

| 2007, Jan. 18 | | | Perf. 13½ |
|---|---|---|---|
| 2934 | A546 | $4 multi | 4.00 4.00 |

**Souvenir Sheet**

| 2935 | A546 | $6 multi | 6.00 6.00 |

No. 2934 was printed in sheets of 3.

Christopher Columbus (1451-1506), Explorer — A547

Designs: 75c, Map of North and South America, Columbus on bended knee. 90c, Portrait of Columbus. $2, Portrait, diff. $3, Portrait, diff.
$6, Columbus and ships.

| 2007, Jan. 18 | | | Perf. 13¼ |
|---|---|---|---|
| 2936-2939 | A547 | Set of 4 | 7.00 7.00 |

**Souvenir Sheet**

| 2940 | A547 | $6 multi | 6.00 6.00 |

**Miniature Sheets**

Pres. John F. Kennedy (1917-63) — A548

No. 2941, $3: a, Wearing naval ensign dress uniform. b, With crew. c, On PT-109. d, Wearing light jacket in South Pacific.
No. 2942, $3: a, Campaigning on crutches. b, Wearing t-shirt. c, With John F. Fitzgerald and Joseph P. Kennedy. d, Celebrating victory with sister.

**Sheets of 4, #a-d**

| 2007, Jan. 18 | | | Litho. |
|---|---|---|---|
| 2941-2942 | A548 | Set of 2 | 22.00 22.00 |

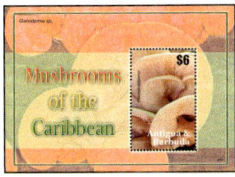

Mushrooms — A549

No. 2943: a, Cantharellus cibarius. b, Auricularia auricula-judae. c, Mycena acicula. d, Peziza vesiculosa.
$6, Pleurotus djamor.

| 2007, Apr. 2 | | Litho. | Perf. 14¼ |
|---|---|---|---|
| 2943 | A549 | $2 Sheet of 4, #a-d | 9.00 9.00 |

**Souvenir Sheet**

| 2944 | A549 | $6 multi | 6.50 6.50 |

Butterflies — A550

Designs: 75c, Figure-of-eight. 90c, Tiger pierid. $1, Purple mort bleu. $4, Mosaic.
No. 2949: a, Small lacewing. b, Clorinde. c, Common morpho. d, White peacock.

$5, Grecian shoemaker.

| 2007, Apr. 2 | | | |
|---|---|---|---|
| 2945-2948 | A550 | Set of 4 | 8.00 8.00 |
| 2949 | A550 | $2 Sheet of 4, #a-d | 7.00 7.00 |

**Souvenir Sheet**

| 2950 | A550 | $5 multi | 6.50 6.50 |

Flowers — A551

Designs: 75c, Allamanda. 90c, Bidens sulphurea. $1, Alstromeria caryophyflacea. $4, Bougainvillea.
No. 2955, $2, horiz.: a, Canna limbata. b, Gazania rigens. c, Glorlosa rothschildiana. d, Hibiscus sinensis.
No. 2956, $3, horiz.: a, Oncidium flexuosum. b, Paphiopedilum pinocchio. c, Cattleyopsis lindenii. d, Cattleyopsis cubensis.
No. 2957, $6, Caesalpinia pulcherrima. No. 2958, $6, Osmoglossum pulchellum.

| 2007, Apr. 2 | | | |
|---|---|---|---|
| 2951-2954 | A551 | Set of 4 | 8.00 8.00 |

**Sheets of 4, #a-d**

| 2955-2956 | A551 | Set of 2 | 20.00 20.00 |

**Souvenir Sheets**

| 2957-2958 | A551 | Set of 2 | 12.00 12.00 |

Cricket Players — A552

Designs: 25c, Kenneth Benjamin. 30c, Anderson Roberts. 90c, Ridley Jacobs. $1, Curtly Ambrose. $1.50, Richard Richardson. $5, Sir Vivian Richards.

| 2007, Apr. 5 | | | Perf. 12¾ |
|---|---|---|---|
| 2959-2963 | A552 | Set of 5 | 3.75 3.75 |

**Souvenir Sheet**

| 2964 | A552 | $5 multi | 6.00 6.00 |

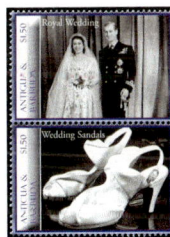

Wedding of Queen Elizabeth II and Prince Philip, 60th Anniv. — A553

No. 2965: a, Couple. b, Wedding sandals. $6, Couple, vert.

| 2007, May 1 | | | Perf. 14 |
|---|---|---|---|
| 2965 | A553 | $1.50 Pair, #a-b | 3.00 3.00 |

**Souvenir Sheet**

| 2966 | A553 | $6 multi | 6.00 6.00 |

No. 2965 was printed in sheets containing three of each stamp.

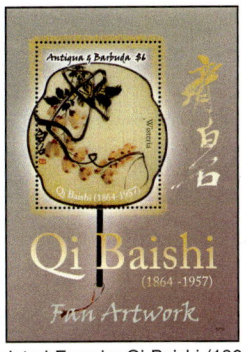

Painted Fans by Qi Baishi (1864-1957) — A554

No. 2967, horiz.: a, Camellias and butterfly. b, Two Shrimp and Arrowhead Leaves. c, Gourd and Ladybug. d, Bird. e, Landscape. f, Five Shrimp.
No. 2968: a, Chrysanthemums. b, Maple Leaves.
$6, Wisteria.

| 2007, May 1 | | | Perf. 14¼ |
|---|---|---|---|
| 2967 | A554 | $1.50 Sheet of 6, #a-f | 7.50 7.50 |
| 2968 | A554 | $3 Sheet of 2, #a-b | 6.00 6.00 |

**Souvenir Sheet**

| 2969 | A554 | $6 multi | 6.00 6.00 |

**Miniature Sheet**

Ferrari Automobiles — A555

No. 2970: a, 1969 365 GTS4. b, 2005 Superamerica. c, 1990 F1 90. d, 1976 400 Automatic. e, 1954 250 GT Coupe. f, 1960 156 F2. g, 1972 312 P. h, 1956 D 50.

| 2007, June 4 | | | Perf. 13¼ |
|---|---|---|---|
| 2970 | A555 | $1.40 Sheet of 8, #a-h | 10.00 10.00 |

Concorde — A556

No. 2971, $1.50 — Concorde O1: a, On ground, red frame. b, In air, green frame. c, On ground, blue violet frame. d, In air, red frame. e, On ground, green frame. f, In air, blue violet frame.
No. 2972, $1.50 — Concorde in flight and: a, Millennium Wheel, green denomination. b, Sydney Opera House, black denomination. c, Millennium Wheel, red violet denomination. d, Sydney Opera House, red orange denomination. e, Millennium Wheel, black denomination. f, Sydney Opera House, blue denomination.

| 2007, June 20 | | | Perf. 12¾ |
|---|---|---|---|

**Sheets of 6, #a-f**

| 2971-2972 | A556 | Set of 2 | 17.50 17.50 |

First Helicopter Flight, Cent. — A557

No. 2973, horiz.: a, NH 90. b, BO 105, black denomination at LR. c, NH 90. d, AS-61 over water. e, BO 105, black denomination at LL. f, AS-61 from below.
$6, UH-1 Iroquois.

| 2007, June 20 | | | Perf. 12¾ |
|---|---|---|---|
| 2973 | A557 | $1.50 Sheet of 6, #a-f | 9.25 9.25 |

**Souvenir Sheet**

| 2974 | A557 | $6 multi | 6.75 6.75 |

Pope Benedict XVI — A558

| 2007, July 30 | | | Perf. 13¾ |
|---|---|---|---|
| 2975 | A558 | $1.40 multi | 1.50 1.50 |

Printed in sheets of 8.

**Miniature Sheet**

Elvis Presley (1935-77) — A559

No. 2967 — Presley: a, Wearing black jacket. b, Facing left, wearing striped shirt, brown background. c, Wearing jacket and holding guitar. d, Facing forward, wearing striped shirt, brown background. e, Wearing red shirt. f, Holding guitar, purple background.

| 2007, July 30 | | | Perf. 13¼ |
|---|---|---|---|
| 2976 | A559 | $1.50 Sheet of 6, #a-f | 11.00 11.00 |

Princess Diana (1961-97) — A560

No. 2977 — Princess Diana wearing: a, Beige suit. b, Lilac dress. c, Purple jacket with black-edged collar. d, Hat.
$6, White robe.

| 2007, July 30 | | | |
|---|---|---|---|
| 2977 | A560 | $2 Sheet of 4, #a-d | 7.50 7.50 |

**Souvenir Sheet**

| 2978 | A560 | $6 multi | 5.75 5.75 |

Flora — A561

Designs: 15c, Bird of paradise. 20c, Seaside mahoe. 30c, Hibiscus. 50c, Agave. 70c, Barringtonia tree. 75c, Coconut tree. 90c, Mesquite tree, horiz. $1, Tamarind tree. $1.50,

Black willow flowers, horiz. $1.80, Baobab tree, horiz. $2, Petrea volubilis. $2.50, Opuntia cochenillifera, horiz. $5, Locust fruit, horiz. $10, Barbuda black warri. $20, Castor oil plant.

**Perf. 12½x13¼, 13¼x12½**

| 2007, Oct. 1 | | | | Litho. | |
|---|---|---|---|---|---|
| 2979 | A561 | 15c multi | | .25 | .25 |
| 2980 | A561 | 20c multi | | .25 | .25 |
| 2981 | A561 | 30c multi | | .30 | .25 |
| 2982 | A561 | 50c multi | | .45 | .40 |
| 2983 | A561 | 70c multi | | .70 | .55 |
| 2984 | A561 | 75c multi | | .75 | .60 |
| 2985 | A561 | 90c multi | | .90 | .70 |
| 2986 | A561 | $1 multi | | 1.00 | .75 |
| 2987 | A561 | $1.50 multi | | 1.40 | 1.10 |
| 2988 | A561 | $1.80 multi | | 1.75 | 1.40 |
| 2989 | A561 | $2 multi | | 2.25 | 1.50 |
| 2990 | A561 | $2.50 multi | | 2.75 | 1.90 |
| 2991 | A561 | $5 multi | | 5.00 | 3.75 |
| 2992 | A561 | $10 multi | | 8.00 | 7.50 |
| 2993 | A561 | $20 multi | | 19.00 | 15.00 |
| Nos. 2979-2993 (15) | | | | 44.75 | 35.90 |

**Miniature Sheet**

Intl. Holocaust Remembrance Day — A562

No. 2994 — United Nations delegates, each $1.40: a, John W. Ashe, Antigua & Barbuda. b, Alfred Capelle, Marshall Islands. c, Masao Nakayama, Micronesia. d, Gilles Noghes, Monaco. e, Baatar Choisuren, Mongolia. f, Filipe Chidumo, Mozambique. g, Marlene Moses, Nauru. h, Franciscus Majoor, Netherlands.

**2007, Oct. 25**  **Perf. 13¼**
2994  A562  Sheet of 8, #a-h   10.00  10.00

Christmas A563

Designs: 30c, Stylized map of Antigua & Barbuda, sailboat, candy canes. 90c, Dancers, sailboat, decorated palm tree. $1, Decorated cake. $1.50, Woman in costume.

**2007, Nov. 5**  **Perf. 14¾x14**
2995-2998  A563  Set of 4   2.75  2.75

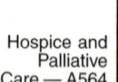

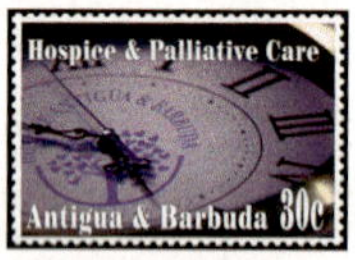

Hospice and Palliative Care — A564

Emblem of Hospice Antigua & Barbuda and: No. 2999, 30c, Clock. No. 3000, 30c, Hands.

**2007, Dec. 27**  **Perf. 13¼**
2999-3000  A564  Set of 2   .85  .85

National Heroes — A565

Designs: No. 3001, 90c, King Court (1691-1736), slave rebellion leader. No. 3002, 90c, Dame Georgianna E. (Nellie) Robinson (1880-1972), educator. $1, Sir Vivian Richards, cricket player. $1.50, Sir Vere Cornwall Bird, Sr. (1909-99), first Prime Minister.

**2008, Mar. 7**  **Litho.**  **Perf. 12¾**
3001-3004  A565  Set of 4   4.00  4.00

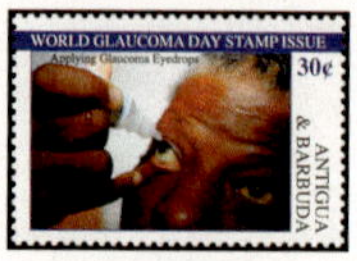

World Glaucoma Day — A566

Designs: 30c, Person applying glaucoma eyedrops. 50c, Normal and glaucomatous optic nerves. $1, Braille writing.

**2008, Mar. 7**  **Perf. 13¼**
3005-3007  A566  Set of 3   2.25  2.25

32nd America's Cup Yacht Races, Off Valencia, Spain — A567

No. 3008 — Various yachts with text "32nd America's Cup" in: a, $1.20, Yellow. b, $1.80, White. c, $3, Blue. d, $5, Orange.

**2008, Mar. 25**  **Perf. 12½**
3008  A567  Block of 4, #a-d   8.25  8.25

**Miniature Sheet**

2008 Summer Olympics, Beijing — A568

No. 3009, each $1.40: a, Pierre de Coubertin. b, Poster for 1896 Athens Olympic Games. c, Spiridon Louis, 1896 marathon gold medalist. d, Paul Masson, 1896 cycling gold medalist.

**2008, Mar. 25**  **Perf. 12¾**
3009  A568  Sheet of 4, #a-d   4.25  4.25

2008 World Stamp Championship, Israel — A569

**2008, May 14**  **Imperf.**
3010  A569  $6 multi   4.75  4.75

Visit of Pope Benedict XVI to United States — A570

**2008, June 18**  **Perf. 13¼**
3011  A570  $2 multi   1.75  1.75
Printed in sheets of 4.

**Miniature Sheet**

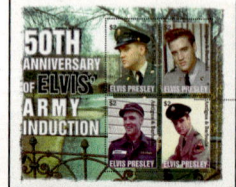

Army Induction of Elvis Presley, 50th Anniv. — A571

No. 3012 — Presley wearing: a, Dress uniform and cap. b, Dress uniform, no cap. c, Army fatigues and cap. d, Dress uniform with shoulder insignia and cap.

**2008, June 18**
3012  A571  $2 Sheet of 4, #a-d   6.50  6.50

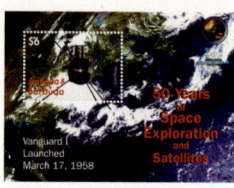

Space Achievements — A572

No. 3013, $1.50, vert. — Vanguard I: a, Against black background, with five rods showing. b, Against white and green background. c, Against black background, with six rods showing.
No. 3014, $1.50: a, Explorer III and equipment, vert. b, Explorer III and Earth, vert. c, Diagram of Van Allen radiation belts.
No. 3015, $2, vert. — Vanguard I and: a, Black background. b, Multicolored background.
No. 3016, $2, vert. — Explorer III and: a, Red and green background. b, Black background.
No. 3017, $6, Vanguard I. No. 3018, $6, Explorer III.

**2008, July 29**  **Perf. 13¼**
**Horiz. Strips of 3, #a-c**
3013-3014  A572  Set of 2   9.00  9.00
**Pairs, #a-b**
3015-3016  A572  Set of 2   8.00  8.00
**Souvenir Sheets**
3017-3018  A572  Set of 2   12.00  12.00

Nos. 3013-3014 were each printed in sheets containing two strips. Nos. 3015-3016 were each printed in sheets containing two pairs.

**Miniature Sheets**

Muhammad Ali, Boxer — A573

No. 3019 — Ali with words or letters in background: a, "ws" at UR. b, "learned" above denomination. c, "is so ugly" at UR. d, "should donate" at UR. e, "greates" at UR. f, "hat" at UR.
No. 3020 — Ali, each $2: a, Hitting punching bag. b, Wearing robe. c, With bare shoulders. d, Wearing protective headgear.

**2008, Sept. 29**  **Perf. 11½**
3019  A573  $1.50 Sheet of 6, #a-f  7.50  7.50
**Perf. 13¼**
3020  A573  Sheet of 4, #a-d   6.50  6.50
No. 3020 contains four 37x50mm stamps.

Star Trek A574

No. 3021: a, Capt. James Kirk and Mr. Spock. b, Chief Engineer Scott, Dr. Leonard McCoy, Kirk and Spock. c, Lt. Uhura, Spock. d, Actors on planetary city set. e, Uhura. f, Scott.
No. 3022: a, McCoy. b, Spock. c, Kirk. d, Hikaru Sulu.

**2008, Sept. 29**  **Perf. 11½**
3021  A574  $1.50 Sheet of 6, #a-f  8.00  8.00
**Perf. 13¼**
3022  A574  $2 Sheet of 4, #a-d   7.50  7.50
No. 3022 contains four 50x37mm stamps.

**Miniature Sheet**

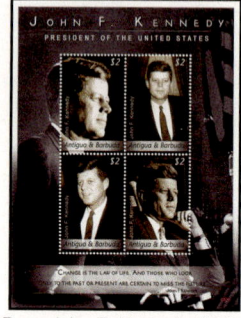

Pres. John F. Kennedy (1917-63) — A575

No. 3023 — Kennedy: a, Looking right. b, Looking forward, curtains in background. c, Looking forward, smiling with teeth showing. d, Looking right with hand at chin.

**2008, Dec. 18**  **Perf. 13¼**
3023  A575  $2 Sheet of 4, #a-d   6.75  6.75

**Miniature Sheet**

Marilyn Monroe (1926-62), Actress — A576

No. 3024 — Monroe wearing: a, Orange sweater, with arm raised. b, Orange sweater, arms at side. c, Pink sweater. d, Purple sweater.

**2008, Dec. 18**
3024  A576  $2 Sheet of 4, #a-d   8.50  8.50

Christmas A577

Stained-glass windows: 30c, Holy Family. 90c, Infant Jesus in manger. $1, Madonna and Child, vert. $1.50, Sts. Elizabeth and John the Baptist, vert.

**2009, Jan. 2**  **Perf. 14¾x14, 14x14¾**
3025-3028  A577  Set of 4   3.00  3.00

**Miniature Sheet**

China 2009 World Stamp Exhibition — A578

No. 3029: a, Baseball. b, Beach volleyball. c, Artistic gymnastics. d, Judo.

**2009, Jan. 5**  **Perf. 11¼x11½**
3029  A578  $1.40 Sheet of 4, #a-d   4.50  4.50

# ANTIGUA

## Miniature Sheet

Pres. Abraham Lincoln (1809-65) — A579

No. 3030: a, Lincoln's first inaugural address, 1861. b, Lincoln, flag. c, Lincoln's second inaugural address, 1865. d, Lincoln at right, crowd at second inaugural.

| 2009, Jan. 5 | | Perf. 11½x11¼ | | |
|---|---|---|---|---|
| 3030 | A579 | $2 Sheet of 4, #a-d | 7.25 | 7.25 |

Inauguration of US Pres. Barack Obama — A580

Pres. Obama facing: $2.75, Right. $10, Left.

| 2009, Jan. 20 | | Perf. 12¼x11¾ | | |
|---|---|---|---|---|
| 3031 | A580 | $2.75 multi | 2.75 | .275 |

**Souvenir Sheet**
**Perf. 13¼x13½**

| 3032 | A580 | $10 multi | 7.75 | 7.75 |

No. 3031 was printed in sheets of 4. No. 3032 contains one 37x51mm stamp.

New Year 2009 (Year of the Ox) — A581

| 2009, Jan. 26 | | Perf. 11½x12 | | |
|---|---|---|---|---|
| 3033 | A581 | $1 multi | 1.25 | 1.25 |

Printed in sheets of 4.

A582

A583

| 2009, Apr. 10 | | Perf. 13½x13¼ | | |
|---|---|---|---|---|
| 3034 | A582 | $1 multi | 1.10 | 1.10 |

**Souvenir Sheet**
**Perf. 13**

| 3035 | A583 | $5 multi | 4.75 | 4.75 |

No. 0031 was printed in sheets of 8.

## Miniature Sheet

Elvis Presley (1935-77) — A584

No. 3036 — Presley wearing: a, Hat. b, Suit with handkerchief in pocket. c, Black shirt and pants. d, Pink, white and black windbreaker. e, Blue shirt and lei. f, Suit without handkerchief.

| 2009, Apr. 14 | | Perf. 14x14¼ | | |
|---|---|---|---|---|
| 3036 | A584 | $1.50 Sheet of 6, #a-f | 7.75 | 7.75 |

## Miniature Sheets

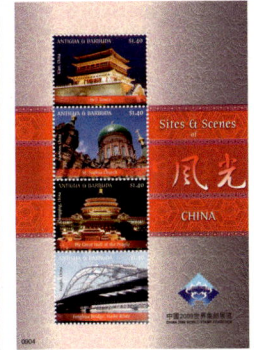

A585

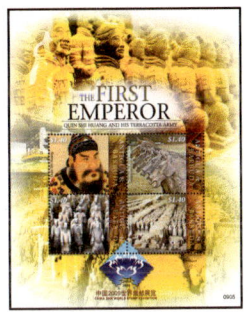

China 2009 World Stamp Exhibition — A586

No. 3037 — Landmarks in China: a, Bell Tower, Xian. b, St. Sophia Church, Harbin. c, Great Hall of the People, Chongqing. d, Fenghua Bridge, Tianjin.
No. 3038 — First emperor of China: a, Qin Shi Huang (259-210 B.C.). b, Horses of Terracotta Army. c, Soldiers of Terracotta Army. d, Excavated Terracotta Army.

| 2009, June 29 | | Litho. | Perf. 12 | |
|---|---|---|---|---|
| 3037 | A585 | $1.40 Sheet of 4, #a-d | 5.50 | 5.50 |

**Perf. 12½x12¾**

| 3038 | A586 | $1.40 Sheet of 4, #a-d | 5.50 | 5.50 |

A587

| 2009, July 9 | | Perf. 14x15 | | |
|---|---|---|---|---|
| 3039 | A587 | $4 multi | 3.50 | 3.50 |

## Miniature Sheets

Dogs A588

No. 3040, $2.50 — Labrador retrievers: a, Puppy in canoe. b, Two puppies at window. c, Two puppies with stick. d, Puppy in bucket.
No. 3041, $2.50 — Dachshunds: a, Dog and carrying case. b, Dog and flowers. c, Two dogs in flower box. d, Dog near flower pot.

| 2009, Aug. 13 | | Perf. 12 | | |
|---|---|---|---|---|
| | | Sheets of 4, #a-d | | |
| 3040-3041 | A588 | Set of 2 | 21.00 | 21.00 |

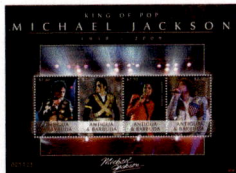

A589

Michael Jackson (1958-2009), Singer — A590

No. 3042 — Jackson: a, Holding microphone, wearing black coat with gold trim. b, Wearing black coat with gold trim, not holding microphone. c, Wearing red and black shirt. d, Wearing jacket with eagle and shield.
No. 3043 — Jackson: a, Wearing black pants, white above red orange frame at top of stamp. b, Wearing pants with buckles along leg, white above red orange frame at top of stamp. c, As "b," with black above red orange frame. d, As "a," with black above red orange frame.
$6, Jackson singing.

| 2009 | | Litho. | Perf. 11¼x11½ | |
|---|---|---|---|---|
| 3042 | A589 | $2.50 Sheet of 4, #a-d | 9.50 | 9.50 |

**Perf. 12x11½**

| 3043 | A590 | $2.50 Sheet of 4, #a-d | 9.50 | 9.50 |

**Souvenir Sheet**
**Perf. 13¼**

| 3044 | A590 | $6 multi | 4.75 | 4.75 |

Issued: Nos. 3042-3043, 9/30; No. 3044, 12/3. No. 3044 contains one 37x50mm stamp.

Meeting of US Pres. Barack Obama and Pope Benedict XVI A591

No. 3045, vert.: a, Pres. Obama. b, Pope Benedict XVI. c, Michelle Obama.
$6, Pope Benedict XVI and Pres. Obama.

| 2009, Nov. 4 | | Perf. 11¼x11½ | | |
|---|---|---|---|---|
| 3045 | A591 | $2.75 Sheet of 3, #a-c | 7.50 | 7.50 |

**Souvenir Sheet**
**Perf. 11½x12**

| 3046 | A591 | $6 multi | 5.75 | 5.75 |

Chinese Aviation, Cent. A592

No. 3047 — Aerobatic team: a, Six airplanes with blue, white and red contrails. b, Six airplanes flying right in double triangle formation. c, Six airplanes flying left in diagonal line formation. d, Five airplanes.
$6, J-7GB.

| 2009, Nov. 12 | | Perf. 14 | | |
|---|---|---|---|---|
| 3047 | A592 | $2 Sheet of 4, #a-d | 6.75 | 6.75 |

**Souvenir Sheet**
**Perf. 14¼**

| 3048 | A592 | $6 multi | 5.00 | 5.00 |

Aeropex 2009 Intl. Philatelic Exhibition, Beijing. No. 3048 contains one 50x37mm stamp.

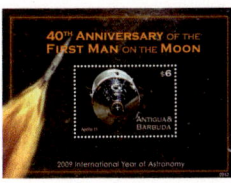

First Man on the Moon, 40th Anniv. A593

No. 3049: a, Apollo 11 patch, US flag on Moon. b, Lunar Module on Moon. c, Passive seismic experiment package. d, Apollo 11 on launch pad.
$6, Apollo 11 Command and Service Modules.

| 2009, Nov. 13 | | Perf. 12¾x12½ | | |
|---|---|---|---|---|
| 3049 | A593 | $2.50 Sheet of 4, #a-d | 9.50 | 9.50 |

**Souvenir Sheet**
**Perf. 12¾x13**

| 3050 | A593 | $6 multi | 5.50 | 5.50 |

Intl. Year of Astronomy

## Souvenir Sheets

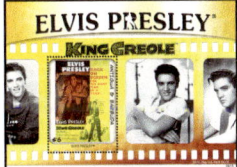

A594

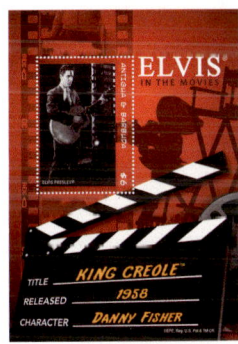

A595

A596

Elvis Presley (1935-77) — A597

| 2009, Nov. 26 | | | Perf. 13¼ | |
|---|---|---|---|---|
| 3051 | A594 | $6 multi | 5.50 | 5.50 |
| 3052 | A595 | $6 multi | 5.50 | 5.50 |
| 3053 | A596 | $6 multi | 5.50 | 5.50 |
| 3054 | A597 | $6 multi | 5.50 | 5.50 |
| | Nos. 3051-3054 (4) | | 22.00 | 22.00 |

Worldwide Fund for Nature (WWF) — A598

## ANTIGUA

No. 3055 — Caribbean coots: a, Pair in water. b, Pair taking off. c, Pair and chick. d, Adult and chick.

| | 2009, Dec. 3 | | Perf. 13¼ | |
|---|---|---|---|---|
| 3055 | | Strip of 4 | 7.50 | 7.50 |
| a.-d. | A598 | $2.65 Any single | 1.75 | 1.75 |
| e. | | Miniature sheet, 2 each #3055a-3055d | 20.00 | 20.00 |

Christmas — A599

Christmas light displays: 90c, Candles. $1, Palm tree and reindeer. $1.80, Bells. $3, Nativity scene, horiz.

| | 2009, Dec. 3 | | Perf. 14x14¾, 14¾x14 | |
|---|---|---|---|---|
| 3056-3059 | A599 | Set of 4 | 5.00 | 5.00 |

Sir Vere Cornwall Bird, Sr. (1909-99), First Chief Minister, Premier and Prime Minister — A600

Bird: 30c, In chair. 75c, With blue, white and red stripes in background. 90c, Wearing red hat. $1.50, With building in background.
No. 3064: a, Like 75c. b, Like 30c. c, Like 90c. d, Like $1.50.
$6, Bird, map of Antigua with flag.

| | 2009, Dec. 8 | | Perf. 11¼x11½ | |
|---|---|---|---|---|
| 3060-3063 | A600 | Set of 4 | 3.00 | 3.00 |
| 3064 | A600 | $2.50 Sheet of 4, #a-d | 8.00 | 8.00 |

**Souvenir Sheet**
**Perf. 12x11½**

| 3065 | A600 | $6 multi | 5.00 | 5.00 |
|---|---|---|---|---|

Birds — A601

Designs: $1.20, Glossy ibis. $1.80, Green-winged teal. No. 3068, $3, California clapper rail. $5, Cattle egret, vert.
No. 3070: a, Green heron. b, Common ground dove. c, White-tailed hawk. d, Black-faced grassquit.
No. 3071, $3: a, Bananaquit. b, Osprey.

**Perf. 11½x11¼, 11¼x11½**
**2009, Dec. 8**

| 3066-3069 | A601 | Set of 4 | 7.75 | 7.75 |
|---|---|---|---|---|

**Perf. 11½x12**

| 3070 | A601 | $2.50 Sheet of 4, #a-d | 9.00 | 9.00 |
|---|---|---|---|---|

**Souvenir Sheet**

| 3071 | A601 | $3 Sheet of 2, #a-b | 5.50 | 5.50 |
|---|---|---|---|---|

**Souvenir Sheet**

New Year 2010 (Year of the Tiger) A602

No. 3072 — Chinese bronze tigers of: a, Western Han Dynasty. b, Shang Dynasty.

| | 2010, Jan. 4 | | Perf. 11½x12 | |
|---|---|---|---|---|
| 3072 | A602 | $5 Sheet of 2, #a-b | 7.75 | 7.75 |

Ferrari Automobiles and Their Parts — A603

No. 3073, $1.25: a, Engine of 1960 246 P F1. b, 1960 246 P F1.
No. 3074, $1.25: a, Engine of 1964 158 F1. b, 1964 158 F1.
No. 3075, $1.25: a, Interior of 1966 365P Speciale. b, 1966 365P Speciale.
No. 3076, $1.25: a, Air foil and rear wheel of 1968 312 F1-68. b, 1968 312 F1-68.

| | 2010, Feb. 22 | | Perf. 12 | |
|---|---|---|---|---|
| | | **Vert. Pairs, #a-b** | | |
| 3073-3076 | A603 | Set of 4 | 8.25 | 8.25 |

Nos. 3073-3076 exist imperf. Value, set of pairs $25.

Whales and Dolphins — A604

Designs: $1.20, Risso's dolphin. $1.80, Common dolphin. $3, Humpback whale. $5, Sperm whale.
No. 3081: a, Shortsnout dolphin. b, Spotted dolphin. c, Cuvier's beaked whale. d, Shortfin pilot whale. e, Gulf Stream beaked whale. f, Rough-toothed dolphin.

| | 2010, Feb. 23 | | Litho. | |
|---|---|---|---|---|
| 3077-3080 | A604 | Set of 4 | 10.00 | 10.00 |
| 3081 | A604 | $2 Sheet of 6, #a-f | 11.00 | 11.00 |

**Miniature Sheets**

A605

A606

Princess Diana (1961-97) — A607

No. 3082 — Diana wearing: a, White dress. b, Pink dress. c, Lilac suit. d, White dress, holding flowers.
No. 3083 — Diana wearing tiara and: a, White dress, two earrings visible. b, Red dress, earring with black stone. c, Red dress, pearl earring. d, White dress with high collar.
No. 3084 — Diana wearing: a, Lei. b, Lilac dress. c, Blue and white dress and hat. d, Red orange hat and dress.

| 2010 | | Litho. | Perf. 12x11½ | |
|---|---|---|---|---|
| 3082 | A605 | $2 Sheet of 4, #a-d | 6.50 | 6.50 |
| 3083 | A606 | $2.75 Sheet of 4, #a-d | 8.25 | 8.25 |
| 3084 | A607 | $2.75 Sheet of 4, #a-d | 8.25 | 8.25 |
| | | Nos. 3082-3084 (3) | 23.00 | 23.00 |

Issued: No. 3082, 2/23; Nos. 3083-3084, 5/10.

Butterflies A608

Designs: $1.20, Common buckeye. $1.80, Red postman. $3, Red admiral. $5, Zebra longwing.
No. 3089: a, Orange sulfur. b, Blue morpho. c, Queen butterfly. d, Zebra swallowtail. e, Malachite. f, Gatekeeper butterfly.

| | 2010, Apr. 14 | | Perf. 14 | |
|---|---|---|---|---|
| 3085-3088 | A608 | Set of 4 | 10.00 | 10.00 |

**Perf. 14¾x14**

| 3089 | A608 | $2 Sheet of 6, #a-f | 10.50 | 10.50 |
|---|---|---|---|---|

No. 3089 contains six 40x30mm stamps.

Sharks — A609

Designs: $1.20, Nurse shark. $1.80, Caribbean reef shark. $3, Tiger shark. $5, Whale shark.
No. 3094: a, Caribbean sharpnose shark. b, Blacktip shark. c, Oceanic whitetip shark. d, Bull shark.

| | 2010, Apr. 14 | | Perf. 14 | |
|---|---|---|---|---|
| 3090-3093 | A609 | Set of 4 | 10.50 | 10.50 |

**Perf. 14¾x14**

| 3094 | A609 | $2.75 Sheet of 4, #a-d | 10.00 | 10.00 |
|---|---|---|---|---|

No. 3094 contains four 40x30mm stamps.

Pope John Paul II (1920-2005) — A610

| | 2010, May 10 | | Perf. 11¼x11½ | |
|---|---|---|---|---|
| 3095 | A610 | $2.75 multi | 2.10 | 2.10 |

Printed in sheets of 4, with each stamp having slight differences in background.

Boy Scouts of America, Cent. A611

No. 3096, $2.50: a, Scout at lectern. b, Scouts canoeing.
No. 3097, $2.50: a, Statue of Liberty giving Scout salute. b, Scouts using map and compass.

| | 2010, May 10 | | Perf. 13¼ | |
|---|---|---|---|---|
| | | **Pairs, #a-b** | | |
| 3096-3097 | A611 | Set of 2 | 7.50 | 7.50 |

Nos. 3096 and 3097 each were printed in sheets containing two pairs.

Girl Guides, Cent. A612

No. 3098: a, Rainbows. b, Brownies. c, Guides. d, Senior Section.
$6, Girl Guides, diff.

| | 2010, May 10 | | Perf. 11½x12 | |
|---|---|---|---|---|
| 3098 | A612 | $2.75 Sheet of 4, #a-d | 8.50 | 8.50 |

**Souvenir Sheet**
**Perf. 11½**

| 3099 | A612 | $6 multi | 4.75 | 4.75 |
|---|---|---|---|---|

**Miniature Sheet**

Expo 2010, Shanghai — A613

No. 3100: a, Dancers, Shanghai Intl. Culture and Art Festival. b, China National Grand Theater, Beijing. c, Rice terraces, Guangxi Province, China. d, Dance performance, Beijing.

| | 2010, May 10 | | Perf. 11½ | |
|---|---|---|---|---|
| 3100 | A613 | $1.50 Sheet of 4, #a-d | 4.50 | 4.50 |

**Miniature Sheet**

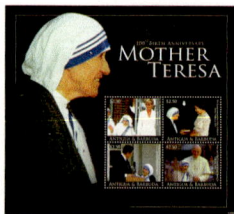

Mother Teresa (1910-97), Humanitarian — A614

No. 3101 — Mother Teresa and: a, Princess Diana. b, Queen Elizabeth II. c, Pres. Ronald Reagan. d, Pope John Paul II.

| | 2010, May 10 | | Perf. 11½x12 | |
|---|---|---|---|---|
| 3101 | A614 | $2.50 Sheet of 4, #a-d | 7.50 | 7.50 |

**Miniature Sheet**

Pres. John F. Kennedy (1917-63) — A615

No. 3102: a, Sitting in limousine. b, Standing. c, Sitting in rocking chair. d, Behind microphones.

| | 2010, May 10 | | Perf. 11¼x11½ | |
|---|---|---|---|---|
| 3102 | A615 | $2.75 Sheet of 4, #a-d | 8.25 | 8.25 |

# ANTIGUA

### Miniature Sheet

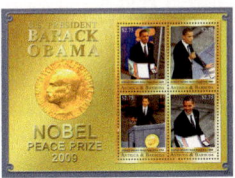

Awarding of Nobel Peace Prize to Pres. Barack Obama A616

No. 3103 — Pres. Obama: a, Holding diploma and medal, blue curtain in background. b, At lectern, with hand closed. c, At lectern, with hand open. d, Holding diploma and medal.

**2010, May 10**    *Perf. 12x11½*
3103 A616 $2.75 Sheet of 4, #a-d    8.25 8.25

### Miniature Sheets

A617

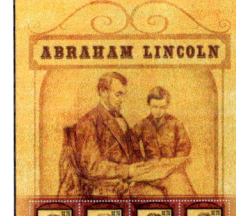

Pres. Abraham Lincoln (1809-65) — A618

Various photographs of Lincoln.

**2010, May 10**    *Perf. 11¼x11½*
3104 A617 $2.75 Sheet of 4, #a-d    8.25 8.25
3105 A618 $2.75 Sheet of 4, #a-d    8.25 8.25

### Miniature Sheets

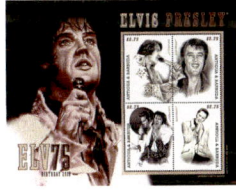

A619

Elvis Presley (1935-77) — A620

No. 3106: a, Wearing rhinestone-studded jacket, microphone in front of mouth. b, Wearing black open-neck shirt. c, Two portraits. d, Wearing white jacket with lapels and pockets with dark trim.
No. 3107: a, Presley holding guitar, parts of "E" and "L" in background. b, Presley holding guitar, parts of "L" and "V" in background. c, Presley holding guitar, parts of "V" and "7" in background. d, Three portraits.

**2010, May 10**    *Perf. 13¼*
3106 A619 $2.75 Sheet of 4, #a-d    8.25 8.25
3107 A620 $2.75 Sheet of 4, #a-d    8.25 8.25

### Miniature Sheet

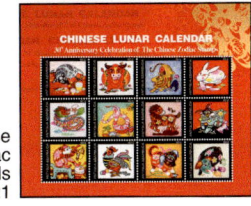

Chinese Zodiac Animals A621

No. 3108: a, Rat. b, Ox. c, Tiger. d, Rabbit. e, Dragon. f, Snake. g, Horse. h, Goat. i, Monkey. j, Cock. k, Dog. l, Pig.

**2010, Jan. 4**    *Litho.*    *Perf. 12¼*
3108 A621 60c Sheet of 12, #a-l    5.50 5.50

### Miniature Sheet

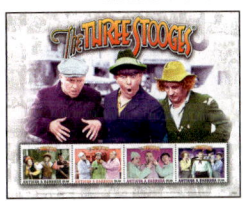

The Three Stooges A622

No. 3109: a, Moe and Larry with cowboy hats, Curly with pick. b, Moe, Larry and Curly in painter's coveralls. c, Moe and Larry in surgical garb examining Curly. d, Moe and Larry squeezing Curly's neck in giant nutcracker.

**2010, Sept. 27**    *Litho.*    *Perf. 11½x12*
3109 A622 $2.50 Sheet of 4, #a-d    7.50 7.50

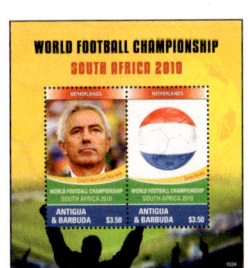

2010 World Cup Soccer Championships, South Africa — A623

No. 3110: a, Maximiliano Pereira. b, John Heitinga. c, Edinson Cavani. d, Mark Van Bommel. e, Martin Caceres. f, Giovanni van Bronckhorst.
No. 3111, $3.50: a, Netherlands Coach Bert van Marwijk. b, Netherlands flag on soccer ball.
No. 3112, $3.50: a, Uruguay Coach Oscar Tabarez. b, Uruguay flag on soccer ball.

**2010, Oct. 18**    *Perf. 12*
3110 A623 $1.50 Sheet of 6, #a-f    7.75 7.75
Souvenir Sheets of 2, #a-b
3111-3112 A623 Set of 2    11.00 11.00

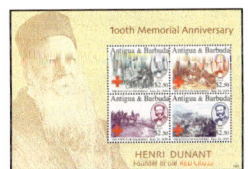

Henri Dunant (1828-1910), Founder of Red Cross — A624

No. 3113 — Red Cross, scenes from Battle of Solferino and portrait of Dunant in: a, Blue green. b, Brown. c, Lilac. d, Blue gray.
$6, Red Cross, Battle of Solferino, Dunant in lilac.

**2010, Dec. 20**
3113 A624 $2.50 Sheet of 4, #a-d    8.00 8.00
Souvenir Sheet
3114 A624 $6 multi    4.75 4.75

Cats A625

No. 3115: a, California spangled cat. b, Siamese cat. c, British shorthair cat. d, Norwegian forest cat. e, Egyptian Mau cat. f, American curl longhair cat.
$6, Manx cat.

**2010, Dec. 20**
3115 A625 $2.50 Sheet of 6, #a-f    13.00 13.00
Souvenir Sheet
3116 A625 $6 multi    5.00 5.00
No. 3115 contains six 30x40mm stamps.

A626

Pope Benedict XVI A627

No. 3118 — Pope Benedict XVI and: a, Buff area below "G" in "Antigua," brown area below "U" in "Antigua." b, Red brown area below "IG" of "Antigua," buff area below first "A" in "Antigua." c, Dark brown areas below "ANTIG" of "Antigua." d, Buff areas below first and second "A" of "Antigua."

**2010, Dec. 20**    *Litho.*    *Perf. 12*
3117 A626 $2.75 multi    2.10 2.10
3118 A627 $2.75 Sheet of 4, #a-d    8.50 8.50
No. 3117 issued in sheets of 4.

### Souvenir Sheet

New Year 2011 (Year of the Rabbit) A628

No. 3119: a, Rabbit. b, Chinese character for "rabbit."

**2011, Jan. 3**
3119 A628 $4 Sheet of 2, #a-b    6.00 6.00

Pandas A629

No. 3120: a, Panda with mouth open. b, Head of panda. c, Panda eating, large leaf partially covering head. d, Panda eating, diff.
$5, Panda, diff.

**2011, Jan. 3**
3120 A629 $2 Sheet of 4, #a-d    7.00 7.00
Souvenir Sheet
3121 A629 $5 multi    4.25 4.25
Beijing 2010 Intl. Philatelic Exhibition.

Christmas 2010 — A630

Designs: 30c, Casini Madonna, by Tommaso Masaccio. 75c, Madonna of the Stars, by Tintoretto. 90c, Wall mosaic, Basilica of Sant'Apollinaire Nuovo, Ravenna, Italy. $1.50, The Annunciation, by Fra Angelico.

**2011, Jan. 17**    *Perf. 12¾x12½*
3122-3125 A630 Set of 4    2.60 2.60

Engagement of Prince William and Catherine Middleton A631

Design: No. 3126, Couple.
No. 3127: a, Prince William. b, Middleton.
No. 3128, $6, Prince William wearing striped shirt and necktie, vert. No. 3129, $6, Prince William wearing white shirt and bow tie, vert.

**2011, Feb. 14**    *Perf. 13 Syncopated*
3126 A631 $2.50 multi    1.90 1.90
3127 A631 $2.50 Horiz. pair, #a-b    3.75 3.75
Souvenir Sheets
3128-3129 A631 Set of 2    9.00 9.00
No. 3126 printed in sheets of 4. No. 3127 printed in sheets of 2 pairs.

### Miniature Sheets

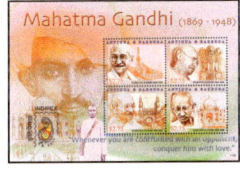

A632

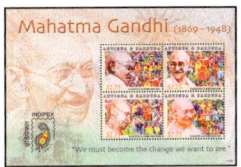

Mohandas K. Gandhi (1869-1948), Indian Nationalist — A633

No. 3130 — Gandhi and: a, Qutub Minar Tower, Delhi. b, Asoka pillar. c, Hyderabad Mosque. d, Taj Mahal.
No. 3131 — Crowd and: a, Profile of Gandhi, robe visible. b, Gandhi looking forward. c, Profile of Gandhi, robe not visible. d, Gandhi looking right.

**2011, Mar. 1**    *Perf. 12*
3130 A632 $2.75 Sheet of 4, #a-d    8.25 8.25
3131 A633 $2.75 Sheet of 4, #a-d    8.25 8.25
2011 Indipex Intl. Philatelic Exhibition, New Delhi

Beatification of Pope John Paul II — A634

No. 3132 — Pope John Paul II: a, Holding crucifix. b, Wearing red stole.
$6, Head of Pope John Paul II.

**2011, Apr. 4**    *Perf. 13 Syncopated*
3132 A634 $2 Pair, #a-b    3.00 3.00
Souvenir Sheet
*Perf. 12*
3133 A634 $6 multi    4.50 4.50

## ANTIGUA

### Miniature Sheets

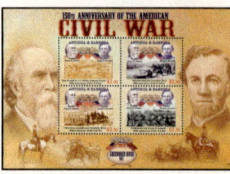

United States Civil War, 150th Anniv. A635

No. 3134, $2.50 — Eagle, shield, flags, Generals Henry R. Jackson and Joseph J. Reynolds of Battle of Greenbrier River, Oct. 3, 1861, and: a, Battle map by A. T. McRae, Quitman Guards. b, Skirmish along the Greenbrier river. c, Union forces assembling near Greenbrier River. d, Battle scene.
No. 3135, $2.50 — Eagle, shield, flags, Confederate Secretary of the navy Stephen Mallory, Union Lt. Commander Alexander Murray of Battle of Cockle Creek, Oct. 5, 1861, and: a, Warships of the Atlantic Blockading Squadron. b, Flotilla of Union warships. c, Confederate privateers near Delaware Bay. d, USS Minnesota.
No. 3136, $2.50 — Eagle, shield, flags, Confederate Brigadier General Richard H. Anderson, Union Colonel Harvey Brown of Battle of Santa Rosa Island, Oct. 9, 1861, and: a, Fort Pickens. b, Drawing of Fight at Santa Rosa Island, by John Volck. c, Boats cutting off confederate dispatch galley. d, Col. Brown commanding 3rd U.S. Infantry.

**Sheets of 4, #a-d**

| 2011, Apr. 4 | | | **Perf. 12** |
|---|---|---|---|
| 3134-3136 | A635 | Set of 3 | 22.50 22.50 |

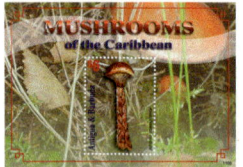

Mushrooms — A636

No. 3137: a, Tylopilus potamogeton. b, Amanita campinaranae. c, Cantharellus altratus. d, Tylopilus orsonianus. e, Boletellus ananas. f, Amanita craseoderma.
No. 3138: a, Amanita cyanopus. b, Phyllobolites miniatus. c, Chroogomphus jamaicensis. d, Coltricia cf. montagnei.
No. 3139, $6, Austroboletus rostrupii. No. 3140, $6, Austroboletus festivus.

| 2011, May 9 | | | **Litho.** |
|---|---|---|---|
| 3137 | A636 | $2 Sheet of 6, #a-f | 10.00 10.00 |
| 3138 | A636 | $2.50 Sheet of 4, #a-d | 7.50 7.50 |

**Souvenir Sheets**

| 3139-3140 | A636 | Set of 2 | 9.00 9.00 |

1997 Visit of Princess Diana To Barbuda — A637

Designs: No. 3141, $10, Princess Diana, her sons, family friend and airplane. No. 3142, $10, Princess Diana.
$50, Princess Diana, horiz.

| 2011, July 12 | | | **Perf. 12** |
|---|---|---|---|
| 3141-3142 | A637 | Set of 2 | 17.00 17.00 |

**Souvenir Sheet**

| 3143 | A637 | $50 multi | 37.50 37.50 |

Nos. 3141-3142 each were issued in sheets of 5.

Wedding of Prince William and Catherine Middleton — A638

No. 3144, $2.50 — a, Prince William wearing cap. b, Middleton, name at left in one line. c, Couple.
No. 3145, $2.50 — a, Prince William waving. b, Middleton, name at top in two lines. c, Couple kissing.
$6, Couple, diff.

| 2011, Aug. 15 | | **Perf. 13x13¼** |
|---|---|---|
| 3144 | A638 | Sheet of 4, #3144a-3144b, 2 #3144c 7.50 7.50 |
| 3145 | A638 | Sheet of 4, #3145a-3145b, 2 #3145c 7.50 7.50 |

**Souvenir Sheet**
**Perf. 12**

| 3146 | A638 | $6 multi | 4.50 4.50 |

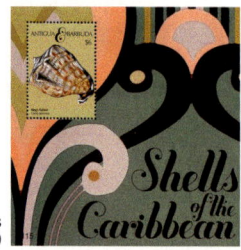

Shells A639

No. 3147: a, Bleeding tooth nerite. b, Pen shell. c, Banded tulip shell. d, Chank shell. e, Flame helmet. f, Atlantic partridge tun.
No. 3148: a, Pink conch. b, Sunrise tellin. c, Flamingo tongue. d, Queen's helmet.
No. 3149, $6, King's helmet. No. 3150, $6, Triton's trumpet, horiz.

**Perf. 13¼x13, 13x13¼**

| 2011, Aug. 15 | | | |
|---|---|---|---|
| 3147 | A639 | $2 Sheet of 6, #a-f | 9.00 9.00 |
| 3148 | A639 | $2.75 Sheet of 4, #a-d | 8.25 8.25 |

**Souvenir Sheets**

| 3149-3150 | A639 | Set of 2 | 9.00 9.00 |

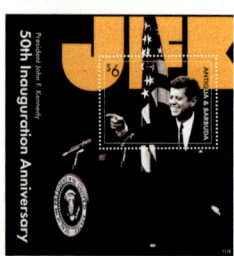

Pres. John F. Kennedy (1917-63) — A640

No. 3151, vert. — Pres. Kennedy: a, Inspecting Mercury capsule, Feb. 22, 1962. b, On Cape Canaveral tour, Nov. 16, 1963. c, At Saturn rocket briefing, Nov. 16, 1963. d, At Cape Canaveral, pointing, Nov. 16, 1963.
$6, Kennedy and flag.

| 2011, Sept. 9 | | | **Perf. 12** |
|---|---|---|---|
| 3151 | A640 | $2.75 Sheet of 4, #a-d | 8.25 8.25 |

**Souvenir Sheet**
**Perf. 12¾**

| 3152 | A640 | $6 multi | 4.50 4.50 |

No. 3151 contains four 30x40mm stamps.

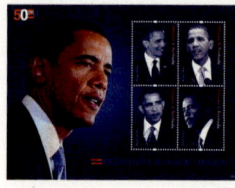

Pres. Barack Obama, 50th Birthday A641

No. 3153 — Pres. Obama: a, Looking right, wearing dark tie and flag lapel pin. b, Wearing light patterned tie, standing in front of microphone. c, Wearing dark patterned tie, standing in front of microphones. d, Looking left.
$6, Pres. Obama, diff.

| 2011, Sept. 9 | | **Perf. 13 Syncopated** |
|---|---|---|
| 3153 | A641 | $2.75 Sheet of 4, #a-d 8.25 8.25 |

**Souvenir Sheet**

| 3154 | A641 | $6 multi | 5.00 5.00 |

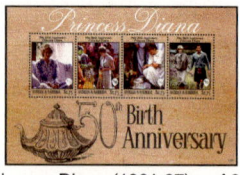

Princess Diana (1961-97) — A642

No. 3155 — Princess Diana: a, Seated on sofa. b, Wearing beige and white dress. c, Wearing white dress. d, With Prince Charles.
$6, Princess Diana, horiz.

| 2011, Sept. 9 | | | **Perf. 12** |
|---|---|---|---|
| 3155 | A642 | $2.75 Sheet of 4, #a-d | 8.25 8.25 |

**Souvenir Sheet**
**Perf. 12¾**

| 3156 | A642 | $6 multi | 4.50 4.50 |

No. 3156 contains one 51x38mm stamp.

First Man in Space, 50th Anniv. A643

No. 3157, $2.75: a, Liftoff of Vostok 1. b, Russian tracking ship named after Yuri Gagarin. c, Vostok 1 mission emblem. d, Alan Shepard, first American astronaut.
No. 3158, $2.75: a, Map of Gagarin's flightpath. b, Vostok 8K72K rocket. c, Gagarin, first cosmonaut. d, Virgil "Gus" Grissom, American astronaut, and rocket.
No. 3159, $6, Gagarin, diff. No. 3160, $6, Vostok spacecraft and Earth.

**Sheets of 4, #a-d**

| 2011, Sept. 9 | | | **Perf. 12** |
|---|---|---|---|
| 3157-3158 | A643 | Set of 2 | 16.50 16.50 |

**Souvenir Sheets**

| 3159-3160 | A643 | Set of 2 | 9.00 9.00 |

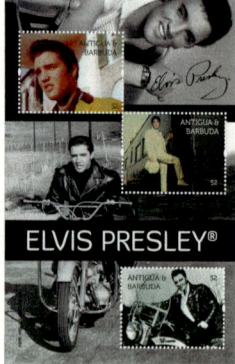

A644

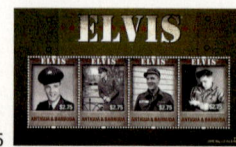

A645

A646

Elvis Presley (1935-77) — A647

No. 3161 — Presley: a, With building in background. b, On train steps. c, On motorcycle.
No. 3162 — Presley wearing: a, Army dress uniform. b, Dress uniform, standing next to railing. c, Battle fatigues. d, Battle fatigues, reading letter.
No. 3163 — Presley wearing: a, Glasses and red shirt. b, Suit, facing right. c, Sequined suit, facing forward. d, Suit, facing left.
No. 3164 — Presley: a, On stage. b, Wearing sweater.

| 2011, Sept. 9 | | **Perf. 13 Syncopated** |
|---|---|---|
| 3161 | A644 | $2 Sheet of 3, #a-c 4.50 4.50 |
| 3162 | A645 | $2.75 Sheet of 4, #a-d 8.25 8.25 |
| 3163 | A646 | $2.75 Sheet of 4, #a-d 8.25 8.25 |
| | Nos. 3161-3163 (3) | 21.00 21.00 |

**Souvenir Sheet**

| 3164 | A647 | $3 Sheet of 2, #a-b | 4.50 4.50 |

### Miniature Sheets

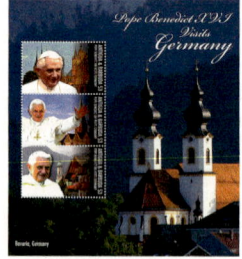

A648

Visit of Pope Benedict XVI to Germany A649

No. 3165 — Pope Benedict XVI: a, With church spires behind head. b, With arm extended, crucifix visible, hand in front of church steeple. c, With mountain behind head, chuch steeple and building with flowers at right.
No. 3166 — Pope Benedict XVI: a, Facing right, church with red roof at right. b, With arm extended, no crucifix visible, chuch at right. c, With Brandenburg Gate at left.

| 2011, Aug. 3 | | **Litho.** | **Perf. 12** |
|---|---|---|---|
| 3165 | A648 | $3 Sheet of 3, #a-c | 6.75 6.75 |
| 3166 | A649 | $3 Sheet of 3, #a-c | 6.75 6.75 |

# ANTIGUA 561

Fish
A650

No. 3167, $3.50: a, Queen angelfish. b, Ocean surgeonfish. c, Rock beauty. d, Gray angelfish.
No. 3168, $3.50: a, Foureye butterflyfish. b, French grunt. c, French angelfish. d, Spotfin butterflyfish.
No. 3169, $9, Great barracuda (80x30mm).
No. 3170, $9, Banded butterflyfish (40x40mm).

**Sheets of 4, #a-d**

**2011, Sept. 30**    *Perf. 12*
3167-3168   A650   Set of 2   21.00   21.00

**Souvenir Sheets**
3169-3170   A650   Set of 2   13.50   13.50

Hu Jintao, President of People's Republic of China — A651

Pres. Hu and flag of People's Republic of China: $3, At lower left. $6, In background.

**2011, Oct. 24**
3171   A651   $3 multi   2.25   2.25

**Souvenir Sheet**
3172   A651   $6 multi   4.50   4.50

China 2011 Intl. Philatelic Exhibition, Wuxi (No. 3172).

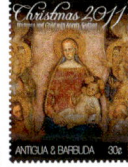

Christmas — A652

Paintings: 30c, Madonna and Child with Angels, by Giottino. 75c, The Annunciation and Two Saints, by Simone Martini. $1.50, Paradise, by Giusto de' Menabuoi. $3, Madonna, by Vitale da Bologna.

**2011, Nov. 15**    *Perf. 14*
3173-3176   A652   Set of 4   4.25   4.25

**Miniature Sheet**

Chinese Zodiac Animals
A653

No. 3177: a, Rat. b, Ox. c, Tiger. d, Rabbit. e, Dragon. f, Snake. g, Horse. h, Sheep. i, Monkey. j, Rooster. k, Dog. l, Boar.

**Litho. With Foil Application**
**2011, Nov. 15**    *Perf. 13 Syncopated*
3177   A653   65c Sheet of 12, #a-l   5.75   5.75

Pres. Abraham Lincoln (1809-65) — A654

No. 3178: a, Lincoln without beard. b, Campaign poster for Lincoln and Hannibal Hamlin. c, Eyes and nose of Lincoln. d, Linoln with beard.
$6, Lincoln, vert.

**2011, Dec. 19**    *Litho.*    *Perf. 12*
3178   A654   $2.75 Sheet of 4, #a-d   8.25   8.25

**Souvenir Sheet**
3179   A654   $6 multi   4.50   4.50

No. 3179 contains one 30x50mm stamp.

Sinking of the Titanic, Cent.
A655

No. 3180 — Titanic passengers: a, Joseph Bruce Ismay (1862-1937), chairman of White Star Line. b, William Stead (1849-1912), journalist. c, Benjamin Guggenheim (1865-1912), businessman. d, Thomas Andrews (1873-1912), naval architect of Titanic.
$9, Titanic, horiz.

**2012, Jan. 25**
3180   A655   $3.50 Sheet of 4, #a-d   10.50   10.50

**Souvenir Sheet**
3181   A655   $9 multi   6.75   6.75

No. 3181 contains one 50x30mm stamp.

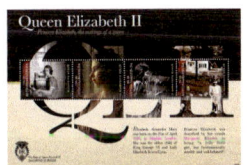

Reign of Queen Elizabeth II, 60th Anniv.
A656

No. 3182 — Queen Elizabeth II as young girl: a, At piano. b, Color photograph, looking left. c, In meadow, looking right. d, Near house and flowers.
$9, Queen Elizabeth II and flowers, vert.

**2012, Mar. 26**
3182   A656   $3.50 Sheet of 4, #a-d   10.50   10.50

**Souvenir Sheet**
3183   A656   $9 multi   6.75   6.75

First Wedding Anniversary of the Duke and Duchess of Cambridge — A657

No. 3184 — Duke and Duchess, rose and background color of: a, Dark red violet. b, Red. c, Rose. d, Pink.
No. 3185: a, Rose and Duke of Cambridge. b, Rose and Duchess of Cambridge.

**2012, May 3**    *Perf. 13 Syncopated*
3184   A657   $3.50 Sheet of 4, #a-d   10.50   10.50

**Souvenir Sheet**
3185   A657   $4.50 Sheet of 2, #a-b   6.75   6.75

**Miniature Sheet**

2012 Summer Olympics, London — A658

No. 3186: a, Rhythmic gymnastics. b, Hurdles. c, Judo. d, Three runners.

**2012, June 18**    *Perf. 12*
3186   A658   $2.20 Sheet of 4, #a-d   6.50   6.50

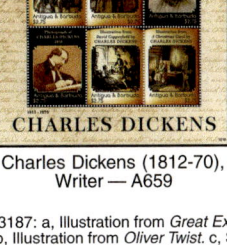

Charles Dickens (1812-70), Writer — A659

No. 3187: a, Illustration from *Great Expectations*. b, Illustration from *Oliver Twist*. c, Sketch of Dickens. d, Photograph of Dickens. e, Illustration from *David Copperfield*. f, Illustration from *A Christmas Carol*.
$9, Illustration from *A Tale of Two Cities*, horiz.

**2012, July 30**    *Perf. 14*
3187   A659   $2.75 Sheet of 6, #a-f   12.50   12.50

**Souvenir Sheet**
**Perf. 12**
3188   A659   $9 multi   6.75   6.75

Princess Diana (1961-97) — A660

No. 3189 — Princess Diana wearing: a, White gown, denomination at UL. b, White jacket, denomination at UL. c, Red dress. d, White dress and necklace, denomination at UR.
$9, Princess Diana and school children.

**2012, July 30**    *Perf. 14*
3189   A660   $3.50 Sheet of 4, #a-d   10.50   10.50

**Souvenir Sheet**
3190   A660   $9 multi   6.75   6.75

**Miniature Sheet**

Seahorses — A661

Various seahorses.

**2012, Sept. 24**    *Perf. 14*
3191   A661   $3 Sheet of 5, #a-e   11.50   11.50

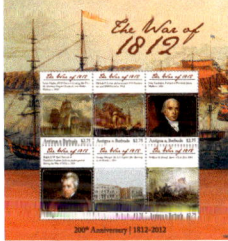

War of 1812
A662

No. 3192: a, HMS Shannon Leading Her Prize The American Frigate Chesapeake into Halifax Harbor, by Louis Haghe. b, Action Between USS Constitution and HMS Guerriere, by Michele F. Corne. c, Portrait of Pres. James Madison, by John Vanderlyn. d, Portrait of Pres. Andrew Jackson, by George E. W. Earl. e, The U.S. Capitol After Burning by the British, by George Munger. f, Battle of Lake Erie, by William H. Powerll.
$9, A View of the Bombardment of Fort McHenry, Near Baltimore, by John Bower.

**2012, Nov. 12**    *Perf. 12*
3192   A662   $2.75 Sheet of 6, #a-f   12.50   12.50

**Souvenir Sheet**
3193   A662   $9 multi   6.75   6.75

Christmas — A663

Paintings: 30c, Adoration of the Child, by Antonio da Correggio. 75c, Madonna and Child with Two Angels, by Fra Filippo Lippi. $1.50, Virgin and Child, by Peter Paul Rubens. $2, Madonna and Child, by Parmigianino. $3, The Grand Duke's Madonna, by Raphael. $3.25, Adoration of the Magi, by Sandro Botticelli.

**2012, Nov. 19**    *Perf. 12¾*
3194-3199   A663   Set of 6   8.00   8.00

**Miniature Sheet**

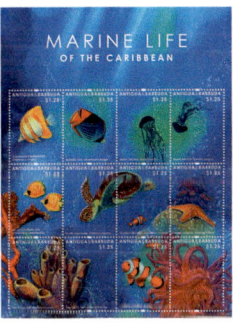

Marine life
A664

No. 3200: a, Copperband butterflyfish. b, Butterfly fish. c, Moon jellyfish, tentacles at bottom. d, Moon jellyfish, tentacles at top. e, Masked butterflyfish. f, Head of Green sea turtle. g, Rear of Green sea turtle, Ocellaris clownfish. h, Forbes sea star. i, Fan coral, red coral at left. j, Fan coral at left. k, Ocellaris clownfish and sea anemone. l, Sea anemone.

**2012, Dec. 3**    *Perf. 13 Syncopated*
3200   A664   $1.25 Sheet of 12, #a-l   11.50   11.50

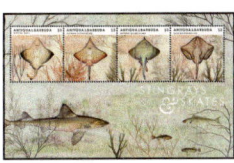

Stingrays and Skates
A665

No. 3201: a, Dipturus batis. b, Dipturus oxyrhynchus without long appendages near tail. c, Dipturus oxyrhynchus with long appendages near tail. d, Raja microocellata.
$9, Leucoraja naevus, vert.

**2012, Dec. 3**    *Perf. 13¾*
3201   A665   $3 Sheet of 4, #a-d   9.00   9.00

**Souvenir Sheet**
**Perf. 12¾**
3202   A665   $9 multi   6.75   6.75

No. 3202 contains one 38x51mm stamp.

Turtles
A666

No. 3203: a, Chelonia mydas. b, Trachemys decorata. c, Dermochelys coriacea. d, Chelonoidis carbonaria.
$9, Chelus fimbriatus.

**2012, Dec. 3**    *Perf. 14*
3203   A666   $3.50 Sheet of 4, #a-d   10.50   10.50

**Souvenir Sheet**
**Perf. 12**
3204   A666   $9 multi   6.75   6.75

# ANTIGUA

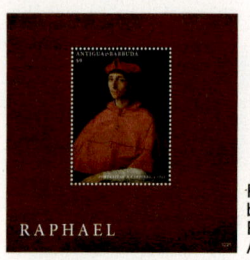

Paintings by Raphael A667

No. 3205: a, Andrea Navagero. b, La Muta. c, Self-portrait. d, La Fornarina. $9, Portrait of a Cardinal.

**2013, Feb. 20**    *Perf. 12½*
3205 A667 $3.25 Sheet of 4, #a-d    9.75 9.75

**Souvenir Sheet**
3206 A667 $9 multi    6.75 6.75

### Souvenir Sheets

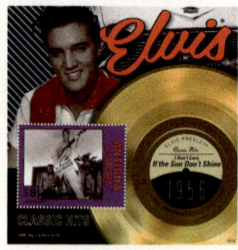

Elvis Presley (1935-77) — A668

Presley: No. 3207, $9, Standing in front of sign depicting him playing guitar, purple frame. No. 3208, $9, Wearing suit and tie, black frame. No. 3209, $9, Holding microphone, red frame. No. 3210, $9, With guitar on back, looking at music stand, red frame. No. 3211, $9, With Pres. Richard M. Nixon, gray frame.

**2013, Feb. 20**
3207-3211 A668 Set of 5    34.00 34.00

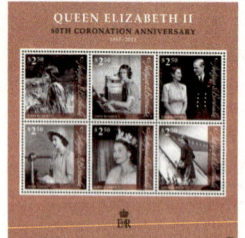

Coronation of Queen Elizabeth II, 60th Anniv. — A669

No. 3212 — Queen Elizabeth II: a, As young woman in field. b, As young woman at piano. c, With Prince Philip. d, Behind microphone. e, Wearing tiara. f, Boarding airplane. $9, Queen Eliazbeth II wearing hat, vert.

**2013, May 13**    *Litho.*    *Perf. 13¾*
3212 A669 $2.50 Sheet of 6, #a-f    11.50 11.50

**Souvenir Sheet**
*Perf. 12½*
3213 A669 $9 multi    6.75 6.75
No. 3213 contains one 38x51mm stamp.

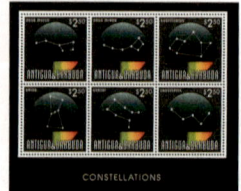

Constellations — A670

No. 3214: a, Ursa Major. b, Ursa Minor. c, Sagittarius. d, Orion. e, Gemini. f, Cassiopeia. $9, Canis Major, vert.

**2013, May 13**    *Litho.*    *Perf. 13¾*
3214 A670 $2.50 Sheet of 6, #a-f    11.50 11.50

**Souvenir Sheet**
*Perf. 12½*
3215 A670 $9 multi    6.75 6.75
No. 3215 contains one 38x51mm stamp.

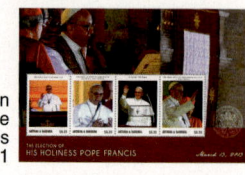

Election of Pope Francis A671

No. 3216 — Pope Francis: a, Waving, orange background. b, Behind microphone, cardinal in background. c, Waving, behind lectern and microphone. d, Facing right, waving, cardinals in background. $9, Pope Francis waving, diff.

*Perf. 13¼x12½*
**2013, June 19**    *Litho.*
3216 A671 $3.25 Sheet of 4, #a-d    9.75 9.75

**Souvenir Sheet**
*Perf. 13½*
3217 A671 $9 multi    6.75 6.75
No. 3217 contains one 38x51mm stamp.

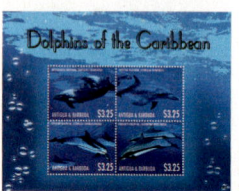

Dolphins A672

No. 3218: a, Bottlenose dolphins. b, Spotted dolphins. c, Striped dolphins. d, Fraser's dolphins. $9, Pygmy killer whale.

*Perf. 12½x13¼*
**2013, June 19**    *Litho.*
3218 A672 $3.25 Sheet of 4, #a-d    9.75 9.75

**Souvenir Sheet**
*Perf. 12½x12*
3219 A672 $9 multi    6.75 6.75

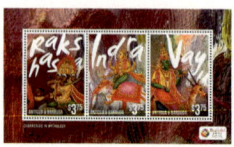

Mythological Beings of Asia — A673

No. 3220: a, Rakshasa. b, Indra. c, Vayu. $9, Garuda.

**2013, Oct. 28**    *Litho.*    *Perf. 12½*
3220 A673 $3.75 Sheet of 3, #a-c    8.50 8.50

**Souvenir Sheet**
3221 A673 $9 multi    6.75 6.75
Thailand 2013 World Stamp Exhibition, Bangkok.

Tourist Attractions in China — A674

No. 3222: a, Dazu Rock Carvings. b, Terracotta warriors. c, Seventeen-arch bridge at Summer Palace. d, Temple of Heaven. No. 3223: a, Forbidden City. b, Potala Palace.

**2013, Oct. 28**    *Litho.*    *Perf. 14*
3222 A674 $3.25 Sheet of 4, #a-d    9.75 9.75

**Souvenir Sheet**
3223 A674 $4.75 Sheet of 2, #a-b    7.00 7.00
2013 China International Collection Expo, Beijing.

Dogs A675

No. 3224: a, Chow chow. b, Japanese chin. c, Poodle. d, French bulldog. $9, Toy spaniel.

**2013, Oct. 28**    *Litho.*    *Perf. 14*
3224 A675 $3.25 Sheet of 4, #a-d    9.75 9.75

**Souvenir Sheet**
*Perf. 12*
3225 A675 $9 multi    6.75 6.75

Birth of Prince George of Cambridge — A676

No. 3226 — Duke and Duchess of Cambridge with Prince George: a, Duke holding Prince. b, Duchess holding Prince, Duke waving. c, Duke holding Prince, head of prince visible. d, Duchess holding Prince, shoulder of Duke visible. $9, Duke and Duchess of Cambridge with Prince George, diff.

**2013, Oct. 28**    *Litho.*    *Perf. 13¾*
3226 A676 $3.25 Sheet of 4, #a-d    9.75 9.75

**Souvenir Sheet**
3227 A676 $9 multi    6.75 6.75

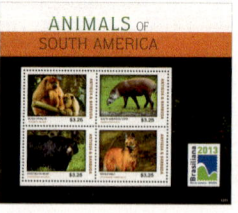

Animals of South America A677

No. 3228: a, Black howler. b, South American tapir. c, Spectacled bear. d, Maned wolf. $9, Toco toucan.

**2013, Nov. 18**    *Litho.*    *Perf. 12½x12*
3228 A677 $3.25 Sheet of 4, #a-d    9.75 9.75

**Souvenir Sheet**
3229 A677 $9 multi    6.75 6.75
2013 Brasiliana World Stamp Exhibition, Rio de Janeiro.

Christmas — A678

Paintings: 30c, Holy Family, by Alessandro Buonvicino. 75c, Christ Blessing, by Girolamo Romani (Il Romanino). 90c, Madonna, by Correggio. $1.50, The Adoration of the Shepherds, by Girolamo Savoldo. $3, Madonna and Child, by Giovanni da Pordenone.

**2013, Dec. 2**    *Litho.*    *Perf. 12½*
3230-3234 A678 Set of 5    4.75 4.75

New Year 2014 (Year of the Horse) A679

No. 3235 — Various paintings of horses, by Liu Jiyu (1918-83), with: a, Artist's name at UL, "Year of the Horse" in red at LL. b, Artist's name at LL, "Year of the Horse" in red at UR. c, Artist's name at LL, no "Year of the Horse" inscription. d, Artist's name at UL, "Year of the Horse" in tan at LL.
No. 3236, horiz. — Various paintings of horses, by Liu Jiyu, with "Year of the Horse" at: a, LR. b, LL.

**2013, Dec. 2**    *Litho.*    *Perf. 14*
3235 A679 $3.25 Sheet of 4, #a-d    9.75 9.75

**Souvenir Sheet**
*Perf. 12*
3236 A679 $3.50 Sheet of 2, #a-b    5.25 5.25

A680

A681

Nelson Mandela (1918-2013), President of South Africa — A682

No. 3237 — Mandela: a, Behind microphone. b, Wearing blue shirt with circular designs. c, Sitting in chair. d, With cap lifted. e, Wearing black shirt. f, Wearing sunglasses.
No. 3238 — Mandela: a, Wearing black-and-white patterned shirt, with red ribbon near collar. b, Wearing black-and-white patterned shirt, no red ribbon. c, Wearing white shirt and jacket with leopard-skin pattern. d, Waving. e, Wearing black, white and red patterned shirt, with red ribbon near collar. f, Wearing tasseled cap.
$9, Mandela with people in background. $13.50, Mandela, diff.

**2013, Dec. 15**    *Litho.*    *Perf. 13¾*
3237 A680 $2.50 Sheet of 6, #a-f    11.00 11.00
3238 A681 $2.50 Sheet of 6, #a-f    11.00 11.00

**Souvenir Sheets**
3239 A681 $9 multi    6.75 6.75

**Litho.; Margin Embossed With Foil Application**
*Imperf*
3240 A682 $13.50 multi    10.00 10.00

# ANTIGUA

**Characters From** *Downton Abbey* **Television Series — A683**

No. 3241: a, Mrs. Hughes. b, Miss O'Brein. c, Thomas Barrow. d, William Mason. $9, Mrs. Patmore and Daisy, horiz.

| 2014, Mar. 24 | | Litho. | | Perf. 14 |
|---|---|---|---|---|
| 3241 | A683 | $3.25 Sheet of 4, #a-d | 9.75 | 9.75 |

**Souvenir Sheet**

| 3242 | A683 | $9 multi | 6.75 | 6.75 |

**Parrots A684**

No. 3243, $4.75: a, Eclectus parrot. b, Blue-and-yellow macaw. c, Black-capped lory. d, Sun parakeet.
No. 3244, $4.75: a, Blue-and-yellow macaw, leg near beak. b, Lilac-crowned Amazon. c, Saint Vincent Amazon. d, Indian ring-necked parakeet.
No. 3245, $9.50: a, Scarlet macaw. b, Yellow-headed Amazon.
No. 3246, $9.50: a, Rainbow lorikeet. b, Hyacinth macaw.

| 2014, June 23 | | Litho. | | Perf. 14 |
|---|---|---|---|---|

**Sheets of 4, #a-d**

| 3243-3244 | A684 | Set of 2 | 28.00 | 28.00 |

**Souvenir Sheets of 2, #a-b**

| 3245-3246 | A684 | Set of 2 | 28.00 | 28.00 |

A685

A686

A687

**Aloe Vera A688**

No. 3247: a, Plant in pot. b, Plant (no pot and plus signs). c, Close-up of plant.
No. 3248: a, Plant and roots. b, Plant diagonally. c, Close-up of plant, diff.
No. 3249: a, Plant (no plus signs). b, Plant and plus signs.
No. 3250: a, Plant (no plus signs), diff. b, Plant cut into pieces and plus signs.

| 2014, June 23 | | Litho. | | Perf. 13¾ |
|---|---|---|---|---|
| 3247 | A685 | $4.75 Sheet of 4, #3247a-3247b, 2 #3247c | 14.00 | 14.00 |
| 3248 | A686 | $4.75 Sheet of 4, #3248a-3248b, 2 #3248c | 14.00 | 14.00 |

**Souvenir Sheets**

| 3249 | A687 | $9.50 Sheet of 2, #a-b | 14.00 | 14.00 |
| 3250 | A688 | $9.50 Sheet of 2, #a-b | 14.00 | 14.00 |

Christmas — A689

Paintings by Raphael: $2.25, Holy Family Below the Oak. $3.50, Madonna with the Blue Diadem. No. 3253, $5, Incoronazione della Vergine, detta Pala Oddi. No. 3254, $5, Aldobrandini Madonna.

| 2014, Dec. 29 | | Litho. | | Perf. 14¼ |
|---|---|---|---|---|
| 3251-3254 | A689 | Set of 4 | 12.00 | 12.00 |

**New Year 2015 (Year of the Ram) A690**

No. 3255 — Ram with: a, Orange horns (at right). b, Red horns (at left). c, Green horns (at left). d, Olive horns at right.
$10, Ram with red horns at right.

| 2015, Jan. 2 | | Litho. | | Perf. 14 |
|---|---|---|---|---|
| 3255 | A690 | $3.25 Sheet of 4, #a-d | 9.75 | 9.75 |

**Souvenir Sheet**

**Perf.**

| 3256 | A690 | $10 multi | 7.50 | 7.50 |

No. 3256 contains one 38mm diameter stamp.

**Rare Stamps A691**

No. 3257: a, Canada #3. b, Livingston, Alabama #51X1. c, Belgium #123B. $10, Canada #387a, horiz.

| 2015, Jan. 2 | | Litho. | Perf. 13¼x12½ |
|---|---|---|---|
| 3257 | A691 | $3.50 Sheet of 3, #a-c | 7.75 7.75 |

**Souvenir Sheet Perf. 12½x13¼**

| 3258 | A691 | $10 multi | 7.50 | 7.50 |

Hummingbirds — A692

No. 3259, $3.25: a, Broad-tailed hummingbird, flower at LL. b, Broad-billed hummingbird, beak at right. c, Rufous-tailed hummingbird. d, Allen's hummingbird in flight.
No. 3260, $3.25: a, Allen's hummingbird on perch. b, Broad-tailed hummingbird, flower at UR. c, Broad-billed hummingbird, beak and flower at left. d, Ruby-throated hummingbird.
No. 3261, $5: a, Ruby-throated hummingbird on branch. b, Buff-bellied hummingbird.
No. 3262, $5: a, Anna's hummingbird. b, Calliope hummingbird.

**Perf. 14, 12 (#3262)**

| 2015, Jan. 2 | | Litho. |
|---|---|---|

**Sheets of 4, #a-d**

| 3259-3260 | A692 | Set of 2 | 19.50 | 19.50 |

**Souvenir Sheets of 2, #a-b**

| 3261-3262 | A692 | Set of 2 | 15.00 | 15.00 |

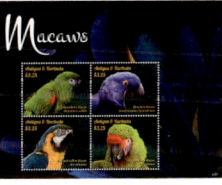

**Macaws A693**

No. 3263, $3.25: a, Red-shouldered macaw. b, Hyacinth macaw. c, Blue-and-yellow macaw. d, Military macaw.
No. 3264, $3.25, vert.: a, Blue-headed macaw. b, Blue-throated macaw. c, Catalina macaw. d, Miligold macaw.
No. 3265, $5, vert.: a, Harlequin macaw. b, Scarlet macaw.
No. 3266, $5, vert.: a, Hahn's green macaw. b, Green-winged macaw.

**Perf. 14, 12 (#3264)**

| 2015, Jan. 2 | | Litho. |
|---|---|---|

**Sheets of 4, #a-d**

| 3263-3264 | A693 | Set of 2 | 19.50 | 19.50 |

**Souvenir Sheets of 2, #a-b**

| 3265-3266 | A693 | Set of 2 | 15.00 | 15.00 |

**Ducks and Geese A694**

No. 3267, $3.25: a, Hartlaub's ducks. b, Wood ducks. c, Common shelducks. d, Mallards.
No. 3268, $3.25: a, Ruddy shelducks. b, White-backed duck and eggs in nest. c, Knob-billed ducks. d, Fulvous whistling ducks.
No. 3269, $5: a, Egyptian geese. b, Chiloé wigeons.
No. 3270, $5: a, White-face whistling ducks. b, Red-billed teals.

| 2015, Jan. 2 | | Litho. | | Perf. 14 |
|---|---|---|---|---|

**Sheets of 4, #a-d**

| 3267-3268 | A694 | Set of 2 | 19.50 | 19.50 |

**Souvenir Sheets of 2, #a-b**

| 3269-3270 | A694 | Set of 2 | 15.00 | 15.00 |

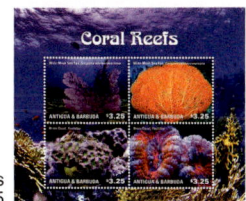

**Corals A695**

No. 3271, $3.25: a, Purple wide-mesh sea fans. b, Orange wide-mesh sea fan. c, Brain coral with green spots. d, Brain coral with red spots.
No. 3272, $3.25: a, Solitary disk coral. b, Antler coral. c, Common mushroom coral. d, Common lettuce coral.
No. 3273: a, Elkhorn coral. b, Orage cup coral.
$10, Great star coral, vert.

| 2015, Jan. 2 | | Litho. | | Perf. 14 |
|---|---|---|---|---|

**Sheets of 4, #a-d**

| 3271-3272 | A695 | Set of 2 | 10.50 | 19.50 |
| 3273 | A695 | $5 Sheet of 2, #a-b | 7.50 | 7.50 |

**Souvenir Sheet Perf. 12½**

| 3274 | A695 | $10 multi | 7.50 | 7.50 |

No. 3274 contains one 38x51mm stamp.

Prince George of Cambridge — A696

No. 3275 — Prince George in hands of: a, Duchess of Cambridge. b, Duke of Cambridge.
No. 3276, $9.50, Prince George, black panel at bottom. No. 3277, $9.50, Prince George, Duchess of Cambridge, red panel at bottom.

**Perf. 13 Syncopated**

| 2015, Jan. 2 | | Litho. |
|---|---|---|
| 3275 | A696 | $3.25 Pair, #a-b | 5.00 | 5.00 |

**Souvenir Sheets**

| 3276-3277 | A696 | Set of 2 | 14.00 | 14.00 |

No. 3275 was printed in sheets containing three pairs.

Julie Mango Tree — A697

| 2015, Jan. 16 | | Litho. | | Perf. 13¾ |
|---|---|---|---|---|
| 3278 | A697 | 25c multi | .25 | .25 |

Pink Desert Roses — A698

| 2015, Feb. 24 | | Litho. | | Perf. 14 |
|---|---|---|---|---|
| 3279 | A698 | $2.20 multi | 1.75 | 1.75 |

## ANTIGUA

### Souvenir Sheet
### Perf. 12

| 3280 | A698 | $10 Pink desert roses, diff. | 7.50 | 7.50 |

No. 3279 was printed in sheets of 8 + central label.

**Valentina Tereshkova, First Woman in Space — A699**

No. 3281: a, Space capsule and Earth, conical section of capsule at left. b, Space capsule and Earth, conical section of capsule at bottom. c, Tereshkova. d, Rocket lift-off. $10, Capsule, diff.

**2015, Mar. 24 — Litho. — Perf. 14**

| 3281 | A699 | $3.25 Sheet of 4, #a-d | 9.75 | 9.75 |

### Souvenir Sheet
### Perf. 12¾

| 3282 | A699 | $10 multi | 7.50 | 7.50 |

No. 3282 contains one 51x38mm stamp.

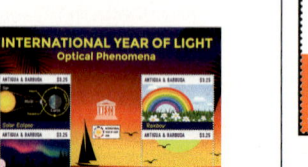

**International Year of Light — A700**

No. 3283: a, Solar eclipse. b, Rainbow. c, Aurora Borealis. d, Sunset. $10, Sunlight.

**2015, Mar. 24 — Litho. — Perf. 12¾**

| 3283 | A700 | $3.25 Sheet of 4, #a-d | 9.75 | 9.75 |

### Souvenir Sheet
### Perf.

| 3284 | A700 | $10 multi | 7.50 | 7.50 |

No. 3284 contains one 38mm diameter stamp.

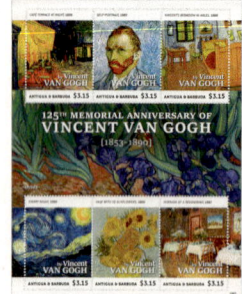

**Paintings by Vincent van Gogh (1853-90) — A701**

No. 3285: a, Cafén Terrace at Night, 1888. b, Self-portrait, 1889. c, Vincent's Bedroom in Arles, 1888. d, Starry Night, 1889. e, Vase with 12 Sunflowers, 1888. f, Interior of a Restaurant, 1887. $10, Postman Joseph Roulin, 1888.

**2015, Mar. 24 — Litho. — Perf. 12¾**

| 3285 | A701 | $3.15 Sheet of 6, #a-f | 14.00 | 14.00 |

### Souvenir Sheet

| 3286 | A701 | $10 multi | 7.50 | 7.50 |

A702

**Horses in Art A703**

No. 3287 — Various unattributed paintings depicting: a, Roundup of wild horses. b, Rider on horse, woman tending to two horses. c, Brown horse facing left. d, White horse and attendant facing left. e, Horse and colt. f, White horse facing right.
No. 3288 — Various unattributed paintings depicting: a, Horses and jockeys at race track. b, Horses and riders at seashore. c, Horse and jockey with race track grandstand in background. d, Horse and fence.
No. 3289, $10, Black horse with clipped tail facing left. No. 3290, $10, Rider on galloping horse beside running dogs.

**2015, Mar. 24 — Litho. — Perf. 12¾**

| 3287 | A702 | $3.15 Sheet of 6, #a-f | 14.00 | 14.00 |
| 3288 | A703 | $3.25 Sheet of 4, #a-d | 9.75 | 9.75 |

### Souvenir Sheets

| 3289-3290 | A703 | Set of 2 | 15.00 | 15.00 |

**Landscapes — A704**

Designs: 30c, White sand beach, Barbuda. 75c, Aerial view of St. John's, Antigua. 90c, English Harbor, Antigua. $1, Pink sand beach, Barbuda. $1.50, Green Island.

**2015, Apr. 20 — Litho. — Perf. 13¼x12½**

| 3291-3295 | A704 | Set of 5 | 3.50 | 3.50 |

**Flag of Antigua and Barbuda A705**

**Coat of Arms of Antigua and Barbuda A706**

**2015, Apr. 20 — Litho. — Perf. 13¼x12½**

| 3296 | A705 | $50 multi | 37.50 | 37.50 |
| 3297 | A706 | $100 multi | 75.00 | 75.00 |

**Queen Elizabeth II, Longest-Reigning British Monarch — A707**

No. 3298 — Queen Elizabeth II: a, As young woman. b, Wearing tiara. c, Wearing hat. d, Wearing blue dress. e, Wearing green dress. f, Wearing pink jacket.
No. 3299 — Queen Elizabeth II: a, As child. b, As older woman wearing white hat.

**2015, July 8 — Litho. — Perf. 14**

| 3298 | A707 | $3.15 Sheet of 6, #a-f | 14.00 | 14.00 |

### Souvenir Sheet
### Perf. 12

| 3299 | A707 | $5 Sheet of 2, #a-b | 7.50 | 7.50 |

### Souvenir Sheets

**Elvis Presley (1935-77) — A708**

Various photographs of Presley with panel at bottom of stamp in: No. 3300, $10, Dull green. No. 3301, $10, Purple. No. 3302, $10, Orange. No. 3303, $10, Salmon.

**2015, Aug. 31 — Litho. — Perf. 14**

| 3300-3303 | A708 | Set of 4 | 30.00 | 30.00 |

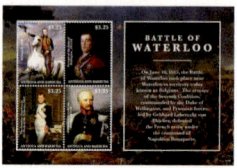

**Battle of Waterloo, 200th Anniv. — A709**

No. 3304: a, King William II of the Netherlands. b, Portrait of the Duke of Wellington. c, Emperor Napoleon in His Study at the Tuileries. d, Gebhard Lebrecht von Blücher. $10, The Battle of Waterloo, horiz.

**2015, Dec. 1 — Litho. — Perf. 12x12½**

| 3304 | A709 | $3.25 Sheet of 4, #a-d | 9.75 | 9.75 |

### Souvenir Sheet
### Perf. 13½

| 3305 | A709 | $10 multi | 7.50 | 7.50 |

No. 3305 contains one 51x38mm stamp.

**Christmas — A710**

Paintings by Sandro Botticelli: 90c, The Virgin Adoring the Sleeping Christ Child. $2.25, Madonna and Child with St. John the Baptist. $3.50, Madonna and Child. $5, Madonna and Child with an Angel.

**2015, Nov. 3 — Litho. — Perf. 12½**

| 3306-3309 | A710 | Set of 4 | 8.75 | 8.75 |

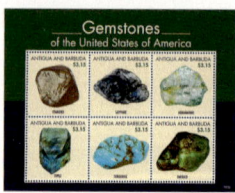

**Gemstones — A711**

No. 3310: a, Diamond. b, Sapphire. c, Aquamarine. d, Topaz. e, Turquoise. f, Emerald. $10, Opal.

**2015, Dec. 28 — Litho. — Perf. 13¾**

| 3310 | A711 | $3.15 Sheet of 6, #a-f | 14.00 | 14.00 |

### Souvenir Sheet

| 3311 | A711 | $10 multi | 7.50 | 7.50 |

**World War I Events of 1915 A712**

No. 3312: a, Zeppelins. b, Sinking of British steamer Andex. c, Diagrams of torpedoed RMS Lusitania. d, Fokker airplane. e, Serbian refugees. f, Evacuation of Gallipoli. $10, Soldier wearing gas mask.

**2015, Dec. 28 — Litho. — Perf. 12**

| 3312 | A712 | $3.15 Sheet of 6, #a-f | 14.00 | 14.00 |

### Souvenir Sheet

| 3313 | A712 | $10 multi | 7.50 | 7.50 |

**New Horizons Space Probe A713**

No. 3314: a, New Horizons above Earth, Jan. 19, 2006. b, New Horizons near Asteroid 2002 JF 56, June 12, 2006. c, Voyager 2 flying by Neptune, Summer, 1989. d, New Horizons crossing Neptune orbit, Aug. 25, 2014. $10, Rocket launch.

**2015, Dec. 28 — Litho. — Perf. 14**

| 3314 | A713 | $3.25 Sheet of 4, #a-d | 9.75 | 9.75 |

### Souvenir Sheet

| 3315 | A713 | $10 multi | 7.50 | 7.50 |

### Miniature Sheet

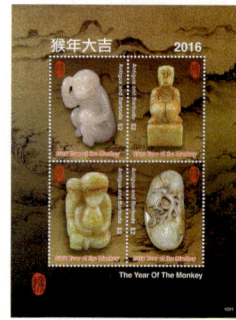

**New Year 2016 (Year of the Monkey) A714**

No. 3316 — Stone figurines: a, Monkey holding ball. b, Monkey on pedestal. c, Two monkeys. d, Monkey in tree.

**2016, Jan. 28 — Litho. — Perf. 14**

| 3316 | A714 | $2 Sheet of 4, #a-d | 6.00 | 6.00 |

**Visit of Pope Francis to New York City A715**

No. 3317 — Pope Francis in front of: a, Flags, teeth visible. b, United Nations Building and flags, waving. c, As "a," waving hand. d, As "b," no hands visible. e, As "a," teeth not visible. f, As "b", waving with hand raised above head. $10, Pope Francis waving, flags.

**2016, Jan. 28 — Litho. — Perf. 14**

| 3317 | A715 | $3.15 Sheet of 6, #a-f | 14.00 | 14.00 |

### Souvenir Sheet
### Perf. 12

| 3318 | A715 | $10 multi | 7.50 | 7.50 |

# ANTIGUA

Paintings
A716

No. 3319, $3.50 — Details of *Consequences of War*, by Peter Paul Rubens: a, Left portion. b, Center portion. c, Right portion.
No. 3320, $3.50: a, *The Death of General Wolfe*, by Benjamin West. b, *Lady with an Ermine*, by Leonardo da Vinci. c, *An Old Man and His Grandson*, by Domenico Ghirlandaio.
No. 3321, $10, The Tempest, by Giorgione.
No. 3322, $10, The Virgin and Child with St. Anne, by Leonardo.

| 2016, Feb. 2 | Litho. | Perf. 12½ |
|---|---|---|
| Sheets of 3, #a-c | | |
| 3319-3320 A716 Set of 2 | | 15.50 15.50 |
| Size: 100x100mm | | |
| Imperf | | |
| 3321-3322 A716 Set of 2 | | 15.00 15.00 |

Klingons From *Star Trek* A717

No. 3323: a, Klingon holding tangled Christmas lights. b, Three Klingons caroling. c, Klingon snowman. d, Klingon as Santa Claus. e, Klingon family and Christmas stocking. f, Two Klingon holding mugs.
$10, Klingon as Santa Claus, vert.

| 2016, Feb. 15 | Litho. | Perf. 12½ |
|---|---|---|
| 3323 A717 $3.15 Sheet of 6, #a-f | | 14.00 14.00 |
| Souvenir Sheet Perf. 11¼x11½ | | |
| 3324 A717 $10 multi | | 7.50 7.50 |

No. 3324 contains one 30x50mm stamp.

Mushrooms — A718

No. 3325: a, Weeping bolete. b, Saffron milk cap. c, Black trumpet. d, Parasol mushroom. e, Green-cracking russula. f, Common puffball.
No. 3326, vert.: a, Red-capped scaber stalk. b, Porcino. c, Fly agaric. d, Psilocybe cubensis.
$10, Chanterelle, vert.

| 2016, May 11 | Litho. | Perf. 14 |
|---|---|---|
| 3325 A718 $3.15 Sheet of 6, #a-f | | 14.00 14.00 |
| 3326 A718 $3.25 Sheet of 4, #a-d | | 9.75 9.75 |
| Souvenir Sheet Perf. 12 | | |
| 3327 A718 $10 multi | | 7.50 7.50 |

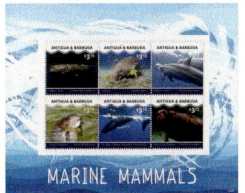

Marine Mammals — A719

No. 3328: a, Sperm whale. b, Dugong. c, Spinner dolphins. d, Harbor porpoise. e, Humpback whale. f, West Indian manatee.
No. 3329: a, California sea lion. b, Polar bear. c, Northern fur seal. d, Harp seal.
$10, Walruses, horiz.

| 2016, May 25 | Litho. | Perf. 13¾ |
|---|---|---|
| 3328 A719 $3.15 Sheet of 6, #a-f | | 14.00 14.00 |
| 3329 A719 $3.25 Sheet of 4, #a-d | | 9.75 9.75 |
| Souvenir Sheet Perf. 14 | | |
| 3330 A719 $10 multi | | 7.50 7.50 |

No. 3330 contains one 40x30mm stamp.

Reptiles A720

No. 3331: a, Ball python. b, White-lipped pit viper. c, Leatherback sea turtle. d, Green sea turtle. e, Spectacled caiman. f, American crocodile.
No. 3332: a, Carolina anole. b, Dwarf yellow-headed gecko. c, Little striped whiptail. d, Giant girdled lizard.
$10, Panther chameleon.

| 2016, May 25 | Litho. | Perf. 14 |
|---|---|---|
| 3331 A720 $3.15 Sheet of 6, #a-f | | 14.00 14.00 |
| Perf. 12 | | |
| 3332 A720 $3.25 Sheet of 4, #a-d | | 9.75 9.75 |
| Souvenir Sheet | | |
| 3333 A720 $10 multi | | 7.50 7.50 |

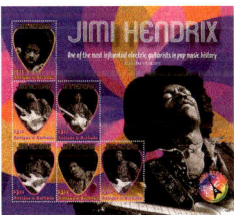

Jimi Hendrix (1942-70), Rock Musician — A721

No. 3334 — Various photographs of Hendrix, as shown.
$10, Hendrix, diff.

| 2016, May 25 | Litho. | Perf. 14 |
|---|---|---|
| 3334 A721 $3.15 Sheet of 6, #a-f | | 14.00 14.00 |
| Souvenir Sheet Perf. 12 | | |
| 3335 A721 $10 multi | | 7.50 7.50 |

No. 3335 contains one 30x50mm stamp.

A722

A723

A724

Atlantic Goliath Grouper A725

| 2016, June 8 | Litho. | Perf. 12 |
|---|---|---|
| 3336 | Strip of 4 | 9.75 9.75 |
| a. A722 $3.25 multi | | 2.40 2.40 |
| b. A723 $3.25 multi | | 2.40 2.40 |
| c. A724 $3.25 multi | | 2.40 2.40 |
| d. A725 $3.25 multi | | 2.40 2.40 |
| e. Miniature sheet of 8, 2 each #3336a-3336d | | 19.50 19.50 |

Worldwide Fund for Nature (WWF).

William Shakespeare (1564-1616), Writer — A726

No. 3337 — Various scenes from *Hamlet*: a, Hamlet and Claudius. b, Hamlet holding sword. c, Hamlet and Ophelia. d, Hamlet holding skull.
$10, Shakespeare.

| 2016, July 22 | Litho. | Perf. 14 |
|---|---|---|
| 3337 A726 $3.25 Sheet of 4, #a-d | | 9.75 9.75 |
| Souvenir Sheet Perf. 13¾ | | |
| 3338 A726 $10 multi | | 7.50 7.50 |

No. 3338 contains one 35x35mm stamp.

Sergei Korolev (1907-66), Rocket Engineer — A727

No. 3339: a, Statue depicting Korolev, Moscow. b, Luna 3 and Moon. c, Sputnik 1. d, Vostok 1.
$14, Soyuz TMA-ISS rocket launch.

| 2016, July 29 | Litho. | Perf. 14 |
|---|---|---|
| 3339 A727 $4 Sheet of 4, #a-d | | 12.00 12.00 |
| Souvenir Sheet Perf. 12 | | |
| 3340 A727 $14 multi | | 10.50 10.50 |

Queen Elizabeth II, 90th Birthday A728

No. 3341: a, Queen Elizabeth II wearing pink jacket and hat. b, Royal coat of arms. c, Queen Elizabeth II wearing blue jacket and hat. d, Queen's royal cypher.
No. 3342, vert.: a, Queen's flag. b, Queen Elizabeth II wearing white and apple green hat.

| 2016, July 29 | Litho. | Perf. 13¾ |
|---|---|---|
| 3341 A728 $4 Sheet of 4, #a-d | | 12.00 12.00 |
| Souvenir Sheet Perf. 12½ | | |
| 3342 A728 $7 Sheet of 2, #a-b | | 10.50 10.50 |

No. 3342 contains two 38x51mm stamps.

## Souvenir Sheets

Elvis Presley (1935-77) — A729

Inscriptions: No. 3343, $14, First top-billed film. No. 3344, $14, Last Ed Sullivan appearance. No. 3345, $14, Graceland welcomes Scatter. No. 3346, $14, Performs at Messick High School, horiz.

| Perf. 13¼x13, 13x13¼ | | |
|---|---|---|
| 2016, Aug. 16 | Litho. | |
| 3343-3346 A729 Set of 4 | | 42.00 42.00 |

Statue of Liberty, 130th Anniv. A730

No. 3347 — Various depictions of the Statue of Liberty, as shown.
$14, Statue of Liberty, diff.

| 2016, Aug. 29 | Litho. | Perf. 14 |
|---|---|---|
| 3347 A730 $3.15 Sheet of 6, #a-f | | 14.00 14.00 |
| Souvenir Sheet Perf. | | |
| 3348 A730 $14 multi | | 10.50 10.50 |

No. 3348 contains one 33x44mm oval stamp.

Characters From *Star Trek* Television Series — A731

No. 3349: a, Captain Kirk. b, Spock. c, Uhura. d, Chekov. e, McCoy. f, Scotty.
No. 3350, $7, horiz.: a, Captain Kirk, diff. b, Mirror Captain Kirk.
No. 3351, $7, horiz.: a, Spock, diff. b, Mirror Spock.

# ANTIGUA

**2017, Jan. 9**   Litho.   **Perf. 14**
3349 A731 $3 Sheet of 6, #a-f   13.50   13.50
**Souvenir Sheets of 2, #a-b**
  **Perf. 12½**
3350-3351 A731 Set of 2   21.00   21.00
Nos. 3350-3351 each contain two 51x38mm stamps.

Christmas
A732

Designs: No. 3352, $5.50, Christmas tree. No. 3353, $5.50, Snowflake. No. 3354, $10, Reindeer. No. 3355, $10, Angel.

**2017, Jan. 23**   Litho.   **Perf. 12½**
3352-3355 A732 Set of 4   23.00   23.00

A733

A734

New Year 2017 (Year of the Rooster)
A735

No. 3357: a, Two roosters, pale mauve background. b, One rooster, brown background. c, One rooster, head pointing left, white background. d, One rooster, head pointing right, white background with flowers.
No. 3358 — Rooster facing: a, Right. b, Left. c, Right, streak of color at LL. b, Left, streak of color at LR.

**2017, Jan. 23**   Litho.   **Perf. 12**
3356 A733 $5.50 multi   4.25   4.25
**Miniature Sheets**
  **Perf. 12½**
3357 A734 $5.50 Sheet of 4, #a-d   16.50   16.50
3358 A735 $5.50 Sheet of 4, #a-d   16.50   16.50
No. 3356 comes in sheets of 4.

A736

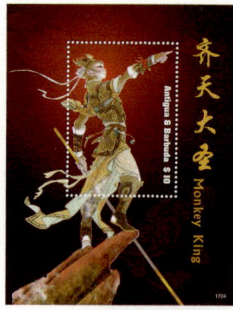

A737

Monkey King
A738

No. 3359 — Various scenes from *The Monkey King*, as shown.

**2017, Mar. 15**   Litho.   **Perf. 12½**
3359 A736 $5.50 Sheet of 4, #a-d   16.50   16.50
**Souvenir Sheets**
3360 A737 $10 multi   7.50   7.50
  **Perf. 14**
3361 A738 $10 multi   7.50   7.50

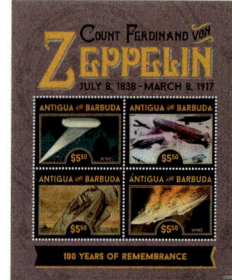

Zeppelins — A739

No. 3362: a, Spotlight on Zeppelin. b, Zeppelins and airplanes. c, Zeppelin crash in ocean, ship in background. d, Zeppelin on fire.
No. 3363: a, Z2. b, LZ 127.

**2017, Apr. 5**   Litho.   **Perf. 14**
3362 A739 $5.50 Sheet of 4, #a-d   16.50   16.50
**Souvenir Sheet**
  **Perf. 12**
3363 A739 $7.50 Sheet of 2, #a-b   11.00   11.00
Count Ferdinand von Zeppelin (1838-1917). No. 3363 contains two 50x30mm stamps.

**Miniature Sheet**

Acheivements of Pres. John F. Kennedy (1917-63) — A740

No. 3364: a, Kennedy signing copy of *Why England Slept*, 1940 (35x70mm). b, Kennedy at his inauguration, 1961 (70x35mm). c, Kennedy wearing naval uniform (35x70mm). d, Kennedy as child wearing police uniform (35x35mm). e, Kennedy graduating from Harvard, 1940 (35x35mm).

**2017, June 3**   Litho.   **Perf. 13¾**
3364 A740 $3.50 Sheet of 5, #a-e   13.00   13.00

First Man in Space, 55th Anniv. (in 2016)
A741

No. 3365: a, Vostok mission patch. b, Yuri Gagarin in military uniform. c, Gagarin in space suit. d, Vostok 1 capsule. e, Vostok mission patch with "CCCP." f, Coin depicting Gagarin.
No. 3366: a, Nose of Vostok 1 at lift-off. b, Vostok 1 engines and exhaust at lift-off.

**2017, June 3**   Litho.   **Perf. 14**
3365 A741 $3 Sheet of 6, #a-f   13.50   13.50
**Souvenir Sheet**
  **Perf. 13¼**
3366 A741 $8 Sheet of 2, #a-b   12.00   12.00
No. 3366 contains two 35x35mm stamps.

**Miniature Sheets**

Elvis Presley (1935-77) — A743

No. 3367 — Presley wearing: a, Suit and tie. b, Shirt and tie. c, Black and blue shirt d, Jacket and striped shirt.
No. 3368 — Presley: a, Wearing striped jacket. b, Holding guitar. c, Wearing striped shirt, color photograph. d, Wearing sweater. e, Wearing shirt and tie. f, Wearing ribbed shirt, black-and-white photograph.

**2017, July 25**   Litho.   **Perf. 14**
3367 A742 $3.50 Sheet of 4, #a-d   10.50   10.50
3368 A743 $3.50 Sheet of 6, #a-f   15.50   15.50

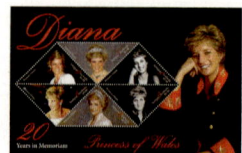

Princess Diana (1961-97) — A744

No. 3369 — Princess Diana wearing: a, White dress covering shoulders. b, Tiara and necklace. c, Black dress, hand touching face.

d, White dress not covering shoulders. e, Tiara and gown. f, Collared jacket.
No. 3370 — Princess Diana wearing: a, Black and white hat. b, Pink hat.

**2017, July 25**   Litho.   **Perf. 12**
3369 A744 $3.50 Sheet of 6, #a-f   15.50   15.50
**Souvenir Sheet**
3370 A744 $3.50 Sheet of 2, #a-b   5.25   5.25

Paintings by Edgar Degas (1834-1917) — A745

No. 3371: a, At the Cafe des Ambassadeurs. b, Young Woman with Ibis. c, The Orchestra at the Opera. d, Visit to a Museum.
No. 3372: a, The Green Dancer. b, Ballet Dancers on the Stage. c, Ballet Class.

**2017, July 25**   Litho.   **Perf. 14**
3371 A745 $5.50 Sheet of 4, #a-d   16.50   16.50
**Souvenir Sheet**
3372 A745 $5 Sheet of 3, #a-c   11.00   11.00

Piping Plovers
A746

No. 3373 — Plover: a, Facing left, beak open. b, In flight. c, Walking left, beak closed. $10, Head of plover, vert.

**2017, July 25**   Litho.   **Perf. 14**
3373 A746 $5 Sheet of 3, #a-c   11.00   11.00
**Souvenir Sheet**
3374 A746 $10 multi   7.50   7.50

Horses
A747

No. 3375: a, Two Icelandic horses running left. b, New Forest pony. c, Camargue horse. d, Hutsul horse. e, Two Icelandic horses standing. f, Orlov trotter.
No. 3376: a, Morgan horse. b, Arabian horse. c, Lippizan horse.

**2017, July 28**   Litho.   **Perf. 12½x13¼**
3375 A747 $4 Sheet of 6, #a-f   18.00   18.00
**Souvenir Sheet**
3376 A747 $7.50 Sheet of 3, #a-c   17.00   17.00

A748

Fallow Deer
A749

# ANTIGUA

No. 3377: a, Buck looking over shoulder. b, Profile of Buck. c, Doe in green foilage. d, Doe in field.
No. 3378: a, Fawn. b, Doe in grass by tree. c, Buck profile in tall grass.

**2017, Aug. 1** Litho. *Perf. 14*
3377 A748 $7.50 Sheet of 4, #a-d 22.50 22.50

**Souvenir Sheet**
3378 A749 $7 Sheet of 3, #a-c 15.50 15.50

Macaws — A750

No. 3379: a, Blue-and-yellow macaw facing right. b, Scarlet macaw facing right, on branch. c, Blue-and-yellow macaw facing left. d, Scarlet macaw facing left on branch. e, Head of Blue-and-yellow macaw. f, Scarlet macaw facing right, diff.
No. 3380: a, Military macaw. b, Scarlet macaw in flight. c, Blue-and-yellow macaw in flight.

**2017, Aug. 1** Litho. *Perf. 14*
3379 A750 $4 Sheet of 6, #a-f 18.00 18.00

**Souvenir Sheet**
3380 A750 $7 Sheet of 3, #a-c 15.50 15.50

## Miniature Sheets

A751

Hawksbill Turtles — A752

Various photographs of Hawksbill turtles, as shown.

**2017, Aug. 1** Litho. *Perf. 14*
3381 A751 $7 Sheet of 4, #a-d 21.00 21.00
3382 A752 $7 Sheet of 4, #a-d 21.00 21.00

## Miniature Sheets

Fruits and Vegetables — A753

No. 3383: a, Apple bananas. b, Malay apples. c, Sapodillas. d, Eggplants.
No. 3384: a, Papayas. b, Cacao pods. c, Spanish limes. d, Avocados.

**2017, Aug. 1** Litho. *Perf. 14*
3383 A753 $7 Sheet of 4, #a-d 21.00 21.00
*Perf. 13¾*
3384 A753 $7 Sheet of 4, #a-d 21.00 21.00
No. 3384 contains four 35x35mm stamps.

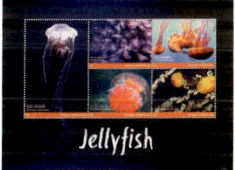

Jellyfish — A754

No. 3385: a, Pacific sea nettle (40x60mm). b, Moon jellyfish (40x30mm). c, Black sea nettle, blue background (40x30mm). d, Sea nettle jellyfish (40x30mm). e, Black sea nettle, black lilac background (40x30mm).
No. 3386, vert.: a, Blue bubbler (30x40mm). b, Brown jellyfish (30x40mm). c, Lion's mane jellyfish (30x40mm).
No. 3387, vert.: a, Barrel jellyfish (30x40mm). b, Spotted jellyfish (30x40mm).

**2017, Aug. 1** Litho. *Perf. 14*
3385 A754 $5 Sheet of 5, #a-e 18.50 18.50
3386 A754 $7 Sheet of 3, #a-c 15.50 15.50

**Souvenir Sheet**
3387 A754 $7.50 Sheet of 2, #a-b 11.00 11.00

Animals — A755

No. 3388: a, Prehensile-tailed porcupine. b, San Clemente Island fox. c, Jaguarundi. d, Grevy's zebra.
$15, Snowy owl.

**2017, Aug. 14** Litho. *Perf. 12½*
3388 A755 $6 Sheet of 4, #a-d 18.00 18.00

**Souvenir Sheet**
3389 A755 $15 multi 11.00 11.00

## Miniature Sheets

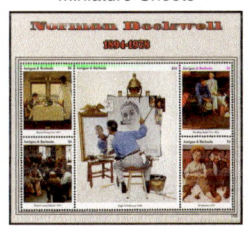

Paintings by Norman Rockwell (1894-1978) — A756

No. 3390: a, $4, Boy in Dining Car (30x40mm). b, $4, Breaking Home Ties (30x40mm). c, $4, Homecoming Marine (30x40mm). d, $4, Retribution (30x40mm). e, $10, Triple Self-portrait (60x80mm).
No. 3391: a, $4, Russian Schoolroom (30x40mm). b, $4, Southern Justice (Murder in Mississippi) (30x40mm). c, $4, The Circus Barker (30x40mm). d, $4, The Love Song (30x40mm). e, $10, Little Boy Writing a Letter (60x80mm).
No. 3392: a, $4, The Problem We All Live With (30x40mm). b, $4, The Scoutmaster (30x40mm). c, $4, They Remembered Me (30x40mm). d, $4, We, Too, Have a Job to Do (30x40mm). e, $10, The Runaway (60x80mm).

**2017, Aug. 22** Litho. *Perf. 14*
Sheets of 5, #a-e
3390-3392 A756 Set of 3 57.50 57.50

## Miniature Sheet

Seadragons — A757

No. 3393: a, Weedy seadragon facing left. b, Weedy seadragon facing right. c, Weedy seadragon facing right, diff. d, Leafy seadragon.

**2017, Aug. 22** Litho. *Perf. 14*
3393 A757 $7 Sheet of 4, #a-d 21.00 21.00

Seahorses — A758

No. 3394: a, Thorny seahorse. b, Thorny seahorse and coral. c, Yellow seahorse.

**2017, Aug. 22** Litho. *Perf. 12*
3394 A758 $7 Sheet of 3, #a-c 15.50 15.50

Horses — A759

No. 3395: a, Icelandic horses walking to left. b, New Forest pony. c, Camargue horse. d, Hutsul horse. e, Icelandic horses standing. f, Orlov trotter.
No. 3396: a, Morgan horse. b, Arabian horse. c, Lipizzan horse.

*Perf. 12½x13¼*
**2017, Sept. 26** Litho.
3395 A759 $4 Sheet of 6, #a-f 18.00 18.00

**Souvenir Sheet**
3396 A759 $7.50 Sheet of 3, #a-c 17.00 17.00

## Miniature Sheet

New Year 2018 (Year of the Dog) — A760

No. 3397: a, Rottweiler at left. b, English bulldog at right. c, English bulldog at left. d, Rottweiler at right.

**2017, Nov. 7** Litho. *Perf. 14*
3397 A760 $7 Sheet of 4, #a-d 21.00 21.00

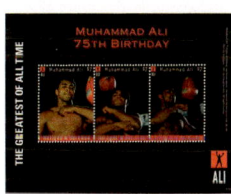

Muhammad Ali (1942-2016), Boxer — A761

No. 3398 — Ali with: a, One hand visible, punching bag at right. b, Both hands visible, punching bag at left. c, Both hands visible, punching bag at right.
$12, Ali, fist by chin.

**2018, Jan. 23** Litho. *Perf. 13¼x12½*
3398 A761 $7 Sheet of 3, #a-c 15.50 15.50

**Souvenir Sheet**
*Perf. 10¼*
3399 A761 $12 multi 9.00 9.00
No. 3399 contains one 38x51mm stamp.

## Miniature Sheet

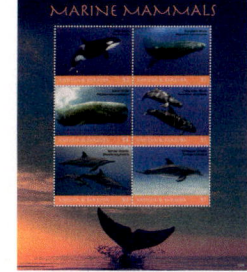

Marine Mammals — A762

No. 3400: a, $2, Killer whale. b, $3, Humpback whale. c, $4, Sperm whale. d, $5, False killer whales. e, $6, Spinner dolphins. f, $7, Bottlenose dolphin.

**2018, May 8** Litho. *Perf. 14*
3400 A762 Sheet of 6, #a-f 20.00 20.00

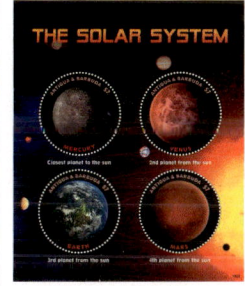

Solar System — A763

No. 3401, $7: a, Mercury. b, Venus. c, Earth. d, Mars.
No. 3402: a, $6, Jupiter. b, $6, Neptune. c, $8, Saturn. d, $8, Uranus.
$12, Sun.

**2018, May 9** Litho. *Perf.*
Sheets of 4, #a-d
3401-3402 A763 Set of 2 42.00 42.00

**Souvenir Sheet**
3403 A763 $12 multi 9.00 9.00

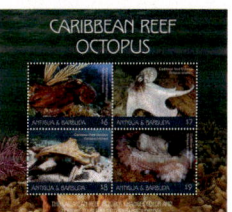

Caribbean Reef Octopus — A764

No. 3404 — Various photographs of octopus: a, $6. b, $7. c, $8. d, $9.
$10, Octopus, diff.

**2018, May 20** Litho. *Perf. 14*
3404 A764 Sheet of 4, #a-d 22.50 22.50

**Souvenir Sheet**
*Perf. 12½*
3405 A764 $10 multi 7.50 7.50
No. 3405 contains one 51x38mm stamp.

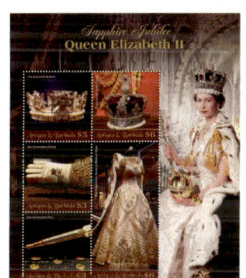

Coronation of Queen Elizabeth II, 65th Anniv. — A765

No. 3406: a, $3, Coronation pen (35x35mm). b, $3, Coronation glove (35x35mm). c, $5, Diamond diadem

(35x35mm). d, $6, Imperial State Crown (35x35mm). e, $6, Coronation gown and Robe of State (35x70mm).
No. 3407: a, Gold State Coach (40x30mm). b, Queen Elizabeth II and Prince Philip (40x30mm).

| 2018, May 29 | Litho. | | Perf. 13¾ | |
|---|---|---|---|---|
| 3406 | A765 | Sheet of 5, #a-e | 17.00 | 17.00 |

**Souvenir Sheet**
**Perf. 14**

| 3407 | A765 | $6.50 Sheet of 2, #a-b | 9.75 | 9.75 |
|---|---|---|---|---|

**Miniature Sheet**

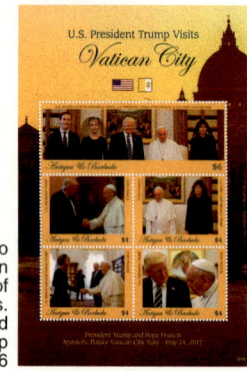

Visit to Vatican City of Pres. Donald Trump — A766

No. 3408 — Pope Francis and: a, $4, Pres. Trump, shaking hands (40x30mm). b, $4, Melania Trump (40x30mm). c, $4, Ivanka Trump (40x30mm). d, $4, Pres Trump, standing (40x30mm). e, $6, Trump family and Jared Kushner (80x30mm).
$10, Trump family and Kushner.

| 2018, July 25 | Litho. | | Perf. 14 | |
|---|---|---|---|---|
| 3408 | A766 | Sheet of 5, #a-e | 16.50 | 16.50 |

**Souvenir Sheet**
**Perf. 14**

| 3409 | A766 | $10 multi | 7.50 | 7.50 |
|---|---|---|---|---|

No. 3409 contains one 40x30mm stamp.

**Miniature Sheet**

Scalloped Hammerhead Sharks — A767

No. 3410 — Various photographs of sharks: a, $4. b, $5. c, $6. d, $7.

| 2018, July 25 | Litho. | | Perf. 12 | |
|---|---|---|---|---|
| 3410 | A767 | Sheet of 4, #a-d | 16.50 | 16.50 |

Corals and Sponges A768

No. 3411: a, $1, Elkhorn coral. b, $2, Azure vase sponge. c, $3, Giant barrel sponge. d, $4, Branching fire coral. e, $5, Staghorn coral. f, $6, Branching vase sponge.
$10, Pillar coral, vert.

| 2018, July 25 | Litho. | | Perf. 14 | |
|---|---|---|---|---|
| 3411 | A768 | Sheet of 6, #a-f | 15.50 | 15.50 |

**Souvenir Sheet**
**Perf. 12½**

| 3412 | A768 | $10 multi | 7.50 | 7.50 |
|---|---|---|---|---|

No. 3412 contains one 38x51mm stamp.

Flowers A769

No. 3413: a, $2, Desert rose. b, $3, White frangipani. c, $4, Heliconia. d, $5, Red hibiscus. e, $6, Bougainvillea. f, $7, White oleander.
$12, Dagger log, vert.

| 2018, July 25 | Litho. | | Perf. 14 | |
|---|---|---|---|---|
| 3413 | A769 | Sheet of 6, #a-f | 20.00 | 20.00 |

**Souvenir Sheet**
**Perf. 12**

| 3414 | A769 | $12 multi | 9.00 | 9.00 |
|---|---|---|---|---|

No. 3414 contains one 30x50mm stamp.

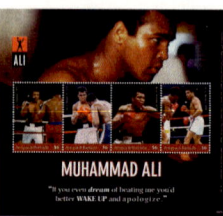

Engagement of Prince Harry and Meghan Markle — A770

No. 3415: a, Couple, Prince Harry waving. b, Hands of couple. c, Couple, Prince Harry touching suit button.
$10, Couple, horiz.

| 2018, Aug. 22 | Litho. | | Perf. 14 | |
|---|---|---|---|---|
| 3415 | A770 | $5.50 Sheet of 3, #a-c | 12.50 | 12.50 |

**Souvenir Sheet**
**Perf. 12½**

| 3416 | A770 | $10 multi | 7.50 | 7.50 |
|---|---|---|---|---|

No. 3416 contains one 51x38mm stamp.

Muhammad Ali (1942-2016), Boxer — A771

No. 3417 — Ali boxing against: a, George Foreman, 1974. b, Joe Frazier, 1975. c, Earnie Shavers, 1977. d, Leon Spinks, 1978.
$10, Ali with arms raised, horiz.

| 2018, Aug. 22 | Litho. | | Perf. 14 | |
|---|---|---|---|---|
| 3417 | A771 | $6 Sheet of 4, #a-d | 18.00 | 18.00 |

**Souvenir Sheet**

| 3418 | A771 | $10 multi | 7.50 | 7.50 |
|---|---|---|---|---|

Air Mail Centenary — A772

No. 3419: a, Charles Lindbergh in plane cockpit. b, 1929 Antigua air mail postmark. c, Antigua stamps on air mail cover. d, Lindbergh and the Spirit of St. Louis.
$10, Sikorsky S-38A.

| 2018, Aug. 22 | Litho. | | Perf. 14 | |
|---|---|---|---|---|
| 3419 | A772 | $5.50 Sheet of 4, #a-d | 16.50 | 16.50 |

**Souvenir Sheet**
**Perf. 12½**

| 3420 | A772 | $10 multi | 7.50 | 7.50 |
|---|---|---|---|---|

No. 3420 contains one 51x38mm stamp.

**Miniature Sheet**

Birth of Prince Louis of Cambridge — A773

No. 3421: a, Duke and Duchess of Cambridge with Prince Louis. b, Princess Charlotte of Cambridge. c, Prince George of Cambridge. d, Prince Louis of Cambridge in arms of his mother.

| 2018, Aug. 28 | Litho. | | Perf. 13¾ | |
|---|---|---|---|---|
| 3421 | A773 | $5.50 Sheet of 4, #a-d | 16.50 | 16.50 |

Wedding of Prince Harry and Meghan Markle A774

No. 3422: a, Groom, lamp in background. b, Bride, lamp in background. c, Groom, tile floor in background. d, Bride, tile floor in background.
$10, Bride and groom on steps, horiz.

| 2018, Aug. 28 | Litho. | | Perf. 12 | |
|---|---|---|---|---|
| 3422 | A774 | $5 Sheet of 4, #a-d | 15.00 | 15.00 |

**Souvenir Sheet**
**Perf. 12½**

| 3423 | A774 | $10 multi | 7.50 | 7.50 |
|---|---|---|---|---|

No. 3423 contains one 102x38mm stamp.

Magnificent Frigatebirds — A775

No. 3424 — Frigatebird: a, $5, On perch. b, $5, In flight. c, $6, Facing left. b, $6, Facing right.
$10, Two birds.

| 2018, Oct. 1 | Litho. | | Perf. 14 | |
|---|---|---|---|---|
| 3424 | A775 | Sheet of 4, #a-d | 16.50 | 16.50 |

**Souvenir Sheet**

| 3425 | A775 | $10 multi | 7.50 | 7.50 |
|---|---|---|---|---|

No. 3425 contains one 80x30mm stamp.

Bees A776

No. 3426: a, $2, Metallic green bee (40x30mm). b, $3, Buff-tailed bumblebee (40x30mm). c, $4, Leafcutter bee (40x30mm).

d, $5, Eastern carpenter bee (40x30mm). e, $6, Buff-tailed bumblebee, diff. (40x60mm).
$10, Honeybee, vert.

| 2018, Oct. 1 | Litho. | | Perf. 14 | |
|---|---|---|---|---|
| 3426 | A776 | Sheet of 5, #a-e | 15.00 | 15.00 |

**Souvenir Sheet**
**Perf. 12½**

| 3427 | A776 | $10 multi | 7.50 | 7.50 |
|---|---|---|---|---|

No. 3427 contains one 38x51mm stamp.

**Miniature Sheets**

United States Presidents — A777

No. 3428: a, 1c, George Washington. b, 2c, John Adams. c, 3c, Thomas Jefferson. d, 4c, James Madison. e, 5c, James Monroe. f, 6c, John Quincy Adams. g, 7c, Andrew Jackson. h, 8c, Martin Van Buren. i, 9c, William Henry Harrison. j, 10c, John Tyler. k, 11c, James Knox Polk. l, $5, Seal of the President of the United States.
No. 3429: a, 12c, Zachary Taylor. b, 13c, Millard Fillmore. c, 14c, Fanklin Pierce. d, 15c, James Buchanan. e, 16c, Abraham Lincoln. f, 17c, Andrew Johnson. g, 18c, Ulysses S. Grant. h, 19c, Rutherford B. Hayes. i, 20c, James Garfield. j, 21c, Chester A. Arthur. k, 22c, Grover Cleveland. l, $4, White House.
No. 3430: a, 23c, Benjamin Harrison. b, 24c, Grover Cleveland. c, 25c, William McKinley. d, 26c, Theodore Roosevelt. e, 27c, William Howard Taft. f, 28c, Woodrow Wilson. g, 29c, Warren G. Harding. h, 30c, Calvin Coolidge. i, 31c, Herbert Hoover. j, 32c, Franklin D. Roosevelt. k, 33c, Harry S. Truman. l, $3, U.S. Capitol.
No. 3431: a, 34c, Dwight D. Eisenhower. b, 35c, John F. Kennedy. c, 36c, Lyndon B. Johnson. d, 37c, Richard M. Nixon. e, 38c, Gerald R. Ford. f, 39c, Jimmy Carter. g, 40c, Ronald Reagan. h, 41c, George H. W. Bush. i, 42c, Bill Clinton. j, 43c, George W. Bush. k, 44c, Barack Obama. l, 45c, Donald Trump.

| 2018, Nov. 1 | Litho. | | Perf. 13¾ | |
|---|---|---|---|---|
| 3428 | A777 | Sheet of 12, #a-l | 4.25 | 4.25 |
| 3429 | A777 | Sheet of 12, #a-l | 4.50 | 4.50 |
| 3430 | A777 | Sheet of 12, #a-l | 4.50 | 4.50 |
| 3431 | A777 | Sheet of 12, #a-l | 3.50 | 3.50 |
| | | Nos. 3428-3431 (4) | 16.75 | 16.75 |

New Year 2019 (Year of the Pig) A779

No. 3432: a, Red pig. b, Black pig.

| 2018, Nov. 1 | Litho. | | Perf. 14 | |
|---|---|---|---|---|
| 3432 | A778 | $3 Pair, #a-b | 4.50 | 4.50 |

**Souvenir Sheet**
**Perf. 13¾**

| 3433 | A779 | $6 multi | 4.50 | 4.50 |
|---|---|---|---|---|

No. 3432 was printed in sheets containing two pairs.

# ANTIGUA

### Miniature Sheet

Flowers
A780

No. 3434: a, $2, Lobster claw plant. b, $3, Easter lily. c, $4, Flamingo flower. d, $5, Red frangipani. e, $6, False bird of paradise. f, $7, Flaming torch.

| 2018, Nov. 1 | Litho. | Perf. 14 |
|---|---|---|
| 3434 A780 | Sheet of 6, #a-f | 20.00 20.00 |

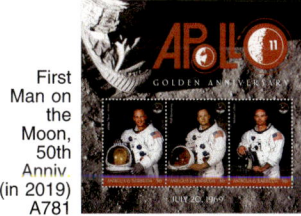

First Man on the Moon, 50th Anniv. (in 2019) A781

No. 3435 — Apollo 11 astronauts: a, Edwin "Buzz" Aldrin, Jr. b, Neil Armstrong. c, Michael Collins.
$10, Footprint on Moon.

| 2018, Nov. 1 | Litho. | Perf. 12 |
|---|---|---|
| 3435 A781 | $6 Sheet of 3, #a-c | 13.50 13.50 |

**Souvenir Sheet**
**Perf. 12½**

| 3436 A781 | $10 multi | 7.50 7.50 |
|---|---|---|

No. 3436 contains one 38x51mm stamp.

Classic Stamps
A782

Most expensive variety of the illustrated stamp: No. 3437, $6, United States #7X1. No. 3438, $6, United States #11X6. No. 3439, $6, United States #1. No. 3440, $6, United States #2. No. 3441, $6, United States #5. No. 3442, $6, United States #85E. No. 3443, $6, United States #85F. No. 3444, $6, United States #120b. No. 3445, $6, United States #121b. No. 3446, $6, United States #181. No. 3447, $6, United States #292. No. 3448, $6, United States #294a. No. 3449, $6, United States #295a. No. 3450, $6, United States #C3a. No. 3451, $6, United States #C15. No. 3452, $6, Confederate States #36X1. No. 3453, $6, Confederate States #51X1. No. 3454, $6, Confederate States #62X6. No. 3455, $6, Confederate States #66X5. No. 3456, $6, Canal Zone #157a. No. 3457, $6, Hawaii #3. No. 3458, $6, Argentina #10. No. 3459, $6, Australian States - New South Wales #2s. No. 3460, $6, Australian States - Queensland #3. No. 3461, $6, Australian States - Tasmania #8. No. 3462, $6, Australian States - Western Australia #3a. No. 3463, $6, Austria #226a. No. 3464, $6, Barbados #21c. No. 3465, $6, Belgium #1. No. 3466, $6, Belgium #123B. No. 3467, $6, Bermuda #X1. No. 3468, $6, Bermuda #1b. No. 3469, $6, Brazil #1c. No. 3470, $6, British Central Africa #A1. No. 3471, $6, British Central Africa #71. No. 3472, $6, British Central Africa #72. No. 3473, $6, British Guiana #1. No. 3474, $6, British Guiana #7. No. 3475, $6, British Guiana #13. No. 3476, $6, Canadian Provinces - New Brunswick #5. No. 3477, $6, Canadian Provinces - Newfoundland #9. No. 3478, $6, Canadian Provinces - Newfoundland #C1. No. 3479, $6, Canadian Provinces - Nova Scotia #6b. No. 3480, $6, Canada #1. No. 3481, $6, Canada #2. No. 3482, $6, Canada #3. No. 3483, $6, Canada #387a. No. 3484, $6, Cape of Good Hope #7b. No. 3485, $6, Ceylon #5. No. 3486, $6, Ceylon #7a. No. 3487, $6, Ceylon #218. No. 3488, $6, China #83. No. 3489, $6, Denmark #1. No. 3490, $6, Dominica #14. No. 3491, $6, Falkland Islands #151a. No. 3492, $6, Finland #2a. No. 3493, $6, France #9a. No. 3494, $6, France #19a. No. 3495, $6, German States - Bavaria #1b. No. 3496, $6, German States - Brunswick #9f. No. 3497, $6, German States - Lubeck #1. No. 3498, $6, German States - Saxony #1a. No. 3499, $6, Gibraltar #30a. No. 3500, $6, Gold Coast #24. No. 3501, $6, Great Britain #1c. No. 3502, $6, Great Britain #2c. No. 3503, $6, Great Britain #92. No. 3504, $6, Honduras #178. No. 3505, $6, Hong Kong #1a. No. 3506, $6, India #A3. No. 3507, $6, India #6c. No. 3508, $6, Italian States - Tuscany #23. No. 3509, $6, Italian States - Two Sicilies #8. No. 3510, $6, Jamaica #83a. No. 3511, $6, Kenya, Uganda and Tanzania #41D. No. 3512, $6, Malta #65. No. 3513, $6, Mauritius #2. No. 3514, $6, Mauritius #15. No. 3515, $6, Mexico #C74. No. 3516, $6, Nevis #13. No. 3517, $6, New Zealand #123a. No. 3518, $6, Niger Coast Protectorate #34. No. 3519, $6, Northern Nigeria #18A. No. 3520, $6, Norway #1. No. 3521, $6, Peru #1. No. 3522, $6, Reunion #1. No. 3523, $6, Romania #4. No. 3524, $6, Rhodesia #118c. No. 3525, $6, St. Helena #1. No. 3526, $6, Sierra Leone #63A. No. 3527, $6, Spain #8a. No. 3528, $6, Sweden #2. No. 3529, $6, Switzerland #1L1. No. 3530, $6, Switzerland #2L1. No. 3531, $6, Switzerland #3L1a. No. 3532, $6, Switzerland #4. No. 3533, $6, Switzerland #5. No. 3534, $6, Transvaal #3a. No. 3535, $6, Trinidad "Lady McLeod" stamp. No. 3536, $6, Uruguay #5d.

**Die Cut Perf. 9x9½, 10¾ (#3449, 3482, 3512, 3515)**

**2018, Nov. 1 — Embossed On Gold-Faced Paper**

| 3437-3536 A782 | Set of 100 | 450.00 450.00 |
|---|---|---|

Christmas 2018 — A783

Designs: 90c, Ornaments on Christmas tree. $2.25, Decorated Christmas tree. $3.50, Candles. $5, Christmas stocking and gifts near fireplace.

| 2019, Jan. 8 | Litho. | Perf. 12¾ |
|---|---|---|
| 3537-3540 A783 | Set of 4 | 8.75 8.75 |

A784

Designs: 10c, Team running. 30c, Team holding banner. 90c, Team on boat. $1.50, Team holding oars. $100, Team holding flares. $10, Team holding flares, diff.

| 2019, Mar. 20 | Litho. | Perf. 14 |
|---|---|---|
| 3541-3545 A784 | Set of 5 | 76.00 76.00 |
| 3543a | Souvenir sheet of 6, 2 each #3541-3540 | 8.00 8.00 |

**Souvenir Sheet**
**Perf. 12**

| 3546 A784 | $10 multi | 7.50 7.50 |
|---|---|---|

Team Antigua Island Girls, 13th place finishers in Talisker Whisky Atlantic Challenge.
Team Antigua Island Girls rowed from the Canary Islands to Antigua in 47 days, 8 hours and 25 minutes. No. 3546 contains one 50x30mm stamp.

### Miniature Sheet

Mohandas K. Gandhi (1869-1948), Indian Nationalist Leader — A785

No. 3547 — Various photographs of Gandhi on 1930 Salt March with "Mahatma Gandhi": a, $4, At UL, in black, reading up (40x30mm). b, $4, At UL, in white, reading horizontally (40x30mm). c, $4, At UR, in black, reading down (Gandhi holding walking stick, 40x30mm). d, $4, At UR, in black, reading down (Gandhi's walking stick not visible, 40x30mm). e, $5, Gandhi bending down to touch salt (40x60mm).

| 2019, June 11 | Litho. | Perf. 14 |
|---|---|---|
| 3547 A785 | Sheet of 5, #a-e | 15.50 15.50 |

**Souvenir Sheet**

Elvis Presley (1935-77) — A786

Inscriptions: $11, "I can sing this song all day." $12, "Started a revolution, ended up a king," horiz. $13, "It Happened at the World's Fair." $14, Elvis's iconic sunglasses.

| 2019, June 11 | Litho. | Perf. 14 |
|---|---|---|
| 3548-3551 A786 | Set of 4 | 37.00 37.00 |

### Miniature Sheet

Roses
A787

No. 3552: a, $3, Pink roses and butterfly. b, $3, White roses and pink buds. c, $4, Yellow roses. d, $4, Pale yellow roses. e, $5, White roses and butterflies. f, $5, Pink roses.

| 2019, June 1 | Litho. | Perf. 14 |
|---|---|---|
| 3552 A787 | Sheet of 6, #a-f | 18.00 18.00 |

2019 China World Stamp Exhibition, Wuhan — A788

No. 3553 — Sights in Cherry Blossom Park, Wuhan: a, $4, Cherry blossoms, pagoda. b, $5, Lanterns and cherry blossoms. c, $6, Cherry blossoms. d, $7, Pagoda, cherry trees, lake.
$14, Pagoda, cherry trees, vert.

| 2019, June 1 | Litho. | Perf. 14 |
|---|---|---|
| 3553 A788 | Sheet of 4, #a-d | 16.50 16.50 |

**Souvenir Sheet**

| 3554 A788 | $14 multi | 10.50 10.50 |
|---|---|---|

Pres. Franklin D. Roosevelt (1882-1945) — A789

No. 3555 — Roosevelt: a, At 1933 Presidential inauguration. b, Working on stamp collection, 1936. c, With wife, Eleanor, 1939. d, Making radio address, 1939. e, Signing declaration of war, 1941. f, With Winston Churchill, 1941.
$14, Official Presidential portrait, by Frank O. Salisbury, vert.

| 2019, June 1 | Litho. | Perf. 14 |
|---|---|---|
| 3555 A789 | $4 Sheet of 6, #a-f | 18.00 18.00 |

**Souvenir Sheet**
**Perf. 12½**

| 3556 A789 | $14 multi | 10.50 10.50 |
|---|---|---|

No. 3556 contains one 38x51mm stamp.

### Miniature Sheet

Beans
A790

No. 3557: a, $3, Vanilla bean and orchid. b, $3, Bowl of vanilla ice cream. c, $4, Cocoa bean. d, $4, Chocolate bar. e, $5, Coffee beans. f, $5, Cup of coffee.

| 2019, June 11 | Litho. | Perf. 14 |
|---|---|---|
| 3557 A790 | Sheet of 6, #a-f | 18.00 18.00 |

Sea Birds A791

No. 3558: a, $1, Brown pelican. b, $2, White-tailed tropicbird. c, $3, Cory's shearwater. d, $4, Brown boobies. e, $5, Red-footed booby. f, $6, Masked boobies.
No. 3559: a, $7.50, Magnificent frigatebird chick. b, $8.50, Male Magnificent frigatebird.

| 2019, June 11 | Litho. | Perf. 14 |
|---|---|---|
| 3558 A791 | Sheet of 6, #a-f | 15.50 15.50 |

**Souvenir Sheet**
**Perf. 12½**

| 3559 A791 | Sheet of 2, #a-b | 12.00 12.00 |
|---|---|---|

No. 3559 contains two 51x38mm stamps.

Beaches
A792

No. 3560: a, $2, Darkwood Beach, Antigua. b, $3, Ffryes Beach, Antigua. c, $4, Galley Bay Beach, Antigua. d, $5, Pink Sand Beach, Barbuda. e, $6, Turners Beach, Antigua. f, $7, Valley Church Beach, Antigua.
No. 3561: a, $8, Galleon Beach, Antigua. b, $9, Princess Diana Beach, Barbuda.

| 2019, June 11 | Litho. | Perf. 14 |
|---|---|---|
| 3560 A792 | Sheet of 6, #a-f | 20.00 20.00 |

**Souvenir Sheet**

| 3561 A792 | Sheet of 2, #a-b | 12.50 12.50 |
|---|---|---|

### Miniature Sheet

Leonard Bernstein (1918-90), Conductor — A793

# ANTIGUA

No. 3562 — Bernstein: a, Wearing jacket and bow tie. b, Standing near microphone stand. c, Wearing white shirt, conducting. d, Wearing black shirt, conducting.

**2019, June 17**    Litho.    **Perf. 14**
3562 A793   $5.50 Sheet of 4, #a-d    16.50   16.50

### Miniature Sheet

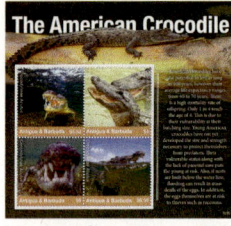

American Crocodiles — A794

No. 3563 — Various photographs of crocodiles with denominations of: a, $4. b, $5.50. c, $6. d, $6.50.

**2020, Jan. 15**    Litho.    **Perf. 13¾**
3563 A794   Sheet of 4, #a-d    16.50   16.50

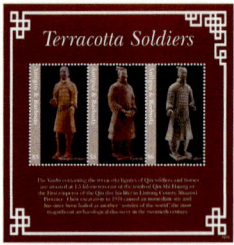

Terracotta Soldiers, People's Republic of China — A795

No. 3564: a, $3, Armored figure. b, $5, General. c, $6, Officer. $10, Head of statue.

**2020, Jan. 15**    Litho.    **Perf. 12**
3564 A795   Sheet of 3, #a-c    10.50   10.50
**Souvenir Sheet**
3565 A795   $10 multi    7.50   7.50

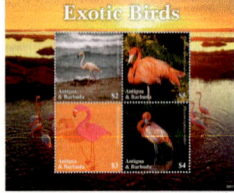

Flamingos — A796

No. 3566 — Various photographs of Phoenicopterus ruber with denominations of: a, $2. b, $3. c, $4. d, $5.
$14, Phoenicopterus ruber feeding chick, vert.

**2020, May 20**    Litho.    **Perf. 13¾**
3566 A796   Sheet of 4, #a-d    10.50   10.50
**Souvenir Sheet**    **Perf. 12**
3567 A796   $14 multi    10.50   10.50
No. 3567 contains one 30x50mm stamp.

Turkey Vultures A797

No. 3568 — Cathartes aura: a, $1, In flight. b, $1, Landing. c, $1.50, Standing in tall grass. d, $2, Head.
$14, Cathartes aura on roof, vert.

**2020, May 20**    Litho.    **Perf. 12**
3568 A797   Sheet of 4, #a-d    4.25   4.25
**Souvenir Sheet**
3569 A797   $14 multi    10.50   10.50

Sheep A798

No. 3570 — Various photographs of heads of Merino sheep with denominations of: a, $3. b, $4. c, $5.
$14, Blackface sheep.

**2020, May 20**    Litho.    **Perf. 13¾**
3570 A798   Sheet of 3, #a-c    9.00   9.00
**Souvenir Sheet**
3571 A798   $14 multi    10.50   10.50

Mallard Ducks A799

No. 3572 — Mallard duck: a, $4, Facing right. b, $5, Facing right, diff. c, $6, In flight. d, $7, Facing left.
$14, Mallard duck in flight, diff.

**2020, May 20**    Litho.    **Perf. 14**
3572 A799   Sheet of 4, #a-d    16.50   16.50
**Souvenir Sheet**    **Perf. 12½**
3573 A799   $14 multi    10.50   10.50
No. 3573 contains one 51x38mm stamp.

Spotted Cleaner Shrimp A800

No. 3574 — Various depictions of spotted cleaner shrimp: a, $4. b, $5. c, $6. d, $7.
$14, Spotted cleaner shrimp, vert.

**2020, May 20**    Litho.    **Perf. 14**
3574 A800   Sheet of 4, #a-d    16.50   16.50
**Souvenir Sheet**    **Perf. 12½**
3575 A800   $14 multi    10.50   10.50
No. 3575 contains one 38x51mm stamp.

Seashells — A801

No. 3576 — Various unnamed seashells with frame color of: a, $3, Light blue. b, $3, Brown rose. c, $4, Lilac. d, $4, Yellow brown. e, $5, Salmon. f, $5, Blue green.
$14, Conch shell, black frame.

**2020, May 20**    Litho.    **Perf. 13¾**
3576 A801   Sheet of 6, #a-f    18.00   18.00
**Souvenir Sheet**
3577 A801   $14 multi    10.50   10.50

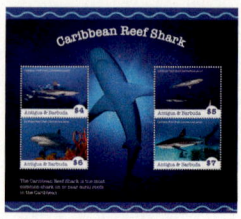

Caribbean Reef Sharks — A805

No. 3584 — Various depictions of Caribbean reef sharks: a, $4. b, $5. c, $6. d, $7.
$14, Caribbean reef shark, diff.

**2020, June 3**    Litho.    **Perf. 14**
3584 A805   Sheet of 4, #a-d    16.50   16.50
**Souvenir Sheet**
3585 A805   $14 multi    10.50   10.50
No. 3585 contains one 80x30mm stamp.

Dorje Chang Buddha III, Religious Leader — A806

**2020, Dec. 21**    Litho.    **Perf. 13¼**
3586 A806   $5 multi    3.75   3.75

### Miniature Sheet

Tribute to Workers During the COVID-19 Pandemic — A807

No. 3587: a, Health care worker with syringe and bottle. b, Gloved hand holding Earth. c, Person holding "Thank You" sign. d, Earth, gloved hand, hypodermic needle, vaccine vial.

**2020, Dec. 21**    Litho.    **Perf. 14**
3587 A807   $5 Sheet of 4, #a-d    15.00   15.00

### Miniature Sheet

Victory in Europe (V-E Day), 75th Anniv. A808

No. 3588: a, General Dwight D. Eisenhower (1890-1969). b, Neville Chamberlain (1869-1940), British Prime Minister. c, V-E Day celebrations in France. d, Franklin D. Roosevelt (1882-1945), U.S. President. e, Winston Churchill (1874-1965), British Prime Minister.

**2020, Dec. 21**    Litho.    **Perf. 12**
3588 A808   $4.50 Sheet of 5, #a-e    17.00   17.00

Paintings by Raphael (1483-1520) — A809

No. 3589 — Paintings in the Room of the Segnatura, Apostolic Palace, Vatican City: a, Cardinal and Theological Virtues, 1511. b, The Parnassua, 1509-11. c, Disputation of the Holy Sacrament, 1509. d, Ceiling of the Selling Room, 1508.
$25, The School of Athens, 1511.

**2020, Dec. 21**    Litho.    **Perf. 14**
3589 A809   $5 Sheet of 4, #a-d    15.00   15.00
**Souvenir Sheet**    **Perf. 12**
3590 A809   $25 multi    18.50   18.50
No. 3590 contains one 50x30mm stamp.

Ludwig van Beethoven (1770-1827), Composer — A810

No. 3591 — Portrait of Beethoven by: a, Carl Traugott Riedel. b, Christian Horneman. c, Joseph Williborord Mähler. d, Ferdinand Schimon.
$25, Portrait of Beethoven by Joseph Karl Stieler.

**2020, Dec. 21**    Litho.    **Perf. 14**
3591 A810   $5 Sheet of 4, #a-d    15.00   15.00
**Souvenir Sheet**    **Perf. 12½**
3592 A810   $25 multi    18.50   18.50
No. 35920 contains one 38x51mm stamp.

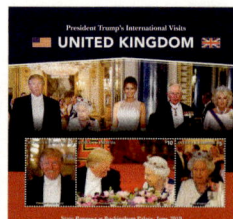

Visit to the United Kingdom of Pres. Donald Trump A811

No. 3593: a, $5, Pres. Trump (30x40mm). b, $5, Queen Elizabeth II (30x40mm). c, $10, Pres. Trump and Queen Elizabeth II (60x40mm).
$25, Pres. Trump and wife, Melania, Queen Elizabeth II, Prince Charles and his wife, the Duchess of Cornwall, horiz.

**2020, Dec. 21**    Litho.    **Perf. 14**
3593 A811   Sheet of 3, #a-c    15.00   15.00
**Souvenir Sheet**    **Perf. 12**
3594 A811   $25 multi    18.50   18.50
No. 3594 contains one 80x30mm stamp.

Sea Otters A812

No. 3595 — Various photograhphs of sea otters, as shown.
$14, Sea otter, vert.

**2020, Dec. 21**    Litho.    **Perf. 13¾**
3595 A812   $5.50 Sheet of 4, #a-d    16.50   16.50
**Souvenir Sheet**    **Perf. 12½**
3596 A812   $14 multi    10.50   10.50
No. 3596 contains one 38x51mm stamp.

# ANTIGUA

A813

Working Dogs A814

No. 3597: a, Police dog. b, Sled dogs. c, Herd dog. d, Guide dog.
$14, Military dog, vert.

**2020, Dec. 21**   Litho.   **Perf. 13¾**
3597 A813 $5.50 Sheet of 4,
#a-d   16.50 16.50
**Souvenir Sheet**
**Perf. 12**
3598 A814 $14 multi   10.50 10.50

Manatees — A815

No. 3599 — Manatee with denomination in: a, $5, Black (40x30mm). b, $5, White (40x30mm). c, $6, Black (80x30mm).
$12, Manatee, vert.

**2020, Dec. 21**   Litho.   **Perf. 14**
3599 A815   Sheet of 3, #a-c   12.00 12.00
**Souvenir Sheet**
**Perf. 12**
3600 A815 $12 multi   9.00 9.00

No. 3600 contains one 30x50mm stamp.

**Miniature Sheet**

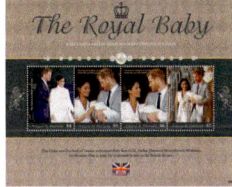

Birth of Archie Mountbatten-Windsor — A816

No. 3601: a, $4, Duke and Duchess of Sussex. b, $5, Duke and Duchess of Sussex, holding son, Archie. c, $6, Duke and Duchess of Sussex holding son, Archie, diff. d, $7, Duke and Duchess of Sussex holding son, Archie, diff.

**2021, Apr. 28**   Litho.   **Perf. 14**
3601 A816   Sheet of 4, #a-d   16.50 16.50

**Miniature Sheet**

New Year 2021 (Year of the Ox) A817

No. 3602 — Color of ox: a, Red. b, Violet. c, Pale yellow. d, Orange.

**2021, Apr. 11**   Litho.   **Perf. 13¾**
3602 A817 $5.50 Sheet of 4,
#a-d   16.50 16.50

**Miniature Sheet**

Arrival in Massachusetts of the Pilgrims, 400th Anniv. (in 2020) — A818

No. 3603: a, The Mayflower at sea. b, The First Thanksgiving at Plymouth, painting by Jennie A. Brownscombe (reversed image). c, Mayflower Compact. d, Embarkation of the Pilgrims, painting by Robert Walter Weir.

**2021, Apr. 28**   Litho.   **Perf. 14**
3603 A818 $5 Sheet of 4, #a-d   15.00 15.00

**Miniature Sheet**

United Nations, 75th Anniv. (in 2020) A819

No. 3604: a, United Nations Headquarters, Chrysler Building, and other New York City buildings. b, United Nations General Assembly Hall. c, United Nations Security Council Hall. d, United Nations Headquarters.

**2021, Apr. 28**   Litho.   **Perf. 14**
3604 A819 $5.50 Sheet of 4,
#a-d   16.50 16.50

**Miniature Sheet**

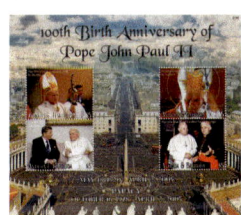

St. John Paul II (1920-2005) — A820

No. 3605: a, St. John Paul II holding papal ferula in Munich, 1980. b, Painting depicting Pope John Paul II. c, Pope John Paul II and Pres. Ronald Reagan. d, Pope John Paul II and Cardinal Joseph Ratzinger (later Pope Benedict XVI).

**2021, Apr. 28**   Litho.   **Perf. 14**
3605 A820 $5 Sheet of 4, #a-d   15.00 15.00

**Miniature Sheet**

Metropolitan Museum of Art, 150th Anniv. (in 2020) — A821

No. 3606: a, Hippopotamus sculpture (Museum's mascot). b, Opening reception. c, Ticket counter. d, European Sculpture Court.

**2021, Apr. 28**   Litho.   **Perf. 14**
3606 A821 $5.50 Sheet of 4,
#a-d   16.50 16.50

A822

Morgan Plus 4 Automobiles, 70th Anniv. (in 2020) — A823

No. 3607: a, Black 2010 Morgan Plus 4. b, White 1952 Morgan Plus 4. c, Green 1956 Morgan Plus 4. d, Black 1956 Morgan Plus 4 (reversed image).
$14, White 1957 Morgan Plus 4.

**2021, Apr. 28**   Litho.   **Perf. 14**
3607 A822 $5.50 Sheet of 4,
#a-d   16.50 16.50
**Souvenir Sheet**
**Perf. 12½**
3608 A823 $14 multi   10.50 10.50

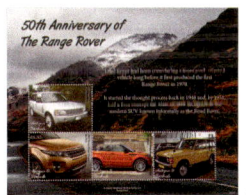

Range Rover, 50th Anniv. (in 2020) A825

No. 3609: a, White 2007 Land Range Rover. b, 2014 Range Rover Evoque. c, 2016 Land Range Rover. d, Yellow 2007 Land Range Rover.
$14, 2013 Land Range Rover.

**2021, Apr. 28**   Litho.   **Perf. 14**
3609 A824 $5.50 Sheet of 4,
#a-d   16.50 16.50
**Souvenir Sheet**
**Perf. 12½**
3610 A825 $14 multi   10.50 10.50

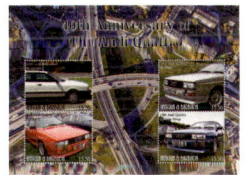

A826

Audi Quattro Automobiles, 40th Anniv. (in 2020) — A827

No. 3611: a, 1988 Audi 80 Quattro. b, 1991 Audi Quattro. c, 1985 Audi Quattro. d, 1986 Audi Quattro.
$14, 1987 Audi Quattro.

**2021, Apr. 28**   Litho.   **Perf. 14**
3611 A826 $5.50 Sheet of 4,
#a-d   16.50 16.50
**Souvenir Sheet**
**Perf. 12½**
3612 A827 $14 multi   10.50 10.50

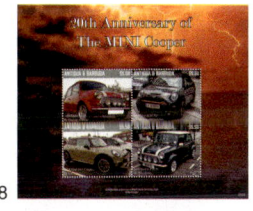

A828

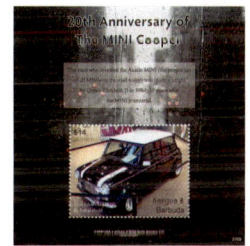

Mini Cooper Automobiles, 20th Anniv. (in 2020) — A829

No. 3613: a, 1993 Mini Cooper. b, 2019 Mini JCW F57. c, 2019 Mini John Cooper. d, 2008 Mini JCP W50.
$14, 1990 Mini Cooper.

**2021, Apr. 28**   Litho.   **Perf. 14**
3613 A828 $5.50 Sheet of 4,
#a-d   16.50 16.50
**Souvenir Sheet**
**Perf. 12½**
3614 A829 $14 multi   10.50 10.50

Rabbits A830

No. 3615: a, Netherland Dwarf rabbit. b, Omilteme Cottontail rabbit. c, Desert Cottontail rabbit. d, Satin rabbit.
$14, Fee de Marbourg rabbit, vert.

**2021, Apr. 28**   Litho.   **Perf. 14**
3615 A830 $5.50 Sheet of 4,
#a-d   16.50 16.50
**Souvenir Sheet**
3616 A830 $14 multi   10.50 10.50

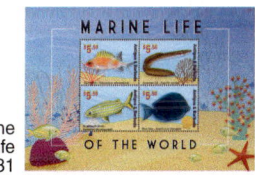

Marine Life A831

No. 3617: a, Squirrelfish. b, American eel. c, Smallmouth grunt. d, Blue tang.
$14, Southern stingray.

# ANTIGUA

**2021, Apr. 28**    Litho.    Perf. 14
3617 A831 $5.50 Sheet of 4, #a-d    16.50 16.50
**Souvenir Sheet**
3618 A831 $14 multi    10.50 10.50

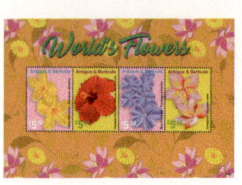

Flowers A832

No. 3619: a, Yellow allamanda. b, Hawaiian hibiscus. c, Blue plumbago. d, Frangipani.
$14, Oleander.

**2021, Apr. 28**    Litho.    Perf. 14
3619 A832 $5.50 Sheet of 4, #a-d    16.50 16.50
**Souvenir Sheet**
3620 A832 $14 multi    10.50 10.50

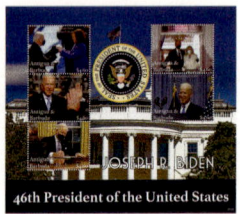

Joseph R. Biden, Jr., 46th President of the United States — A833

No. 3621 — Pres. Biden: a, And Vice-President Kamala Harris. b, And wife, Jill. c, Taking oath of office. d, And microphones. e, Sitting at desk.
$14.60, Pres. Biden wearing protective face mask, vert.

**2021, Aug. 9**    Litho.    Perf. 14
3621 A833 $4.60 Sheet of 5, #a-e    17.00 17.00
**Souvenir Sheet**
**Perf. 12½**
3622 A833 $14.60 multi    11.00 11.00
No. 3622 contains one 38x51mm stamp.

Queen Elizabeth II, 95th Birthday A834

No. 3623 — Queen Elizabeth II: a, Wearing uniform and hat. b, Wearing tiara. c, Wearing scarf. d, Without head covering.
$14, Queen Elizabeth II in 1952, horiz.

**2021, Aug. 9**    Litho.    Perf. 12½
3623 A834 $4.95 Sheet of 4, #a-d    15.00 15.00
**Souvenir Sheet**
**Perf. 14**
3624 A834 $14 multi    10.50 10.50
No. 3624 contains one 40x30mm stamp.

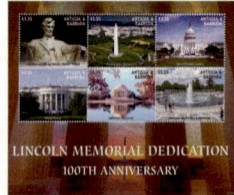

Dedication of the Lincoln Memorial, Cent. (in 2022) — A835

No. 3625 — Washington, D. C. attractions: a, Statue of Abraham Lincoln, by Daniel Chester French. b, Washington Monument. c, Untied States Capitol. d, White House. e, Jefferson Memorial. f, National World War II Memorial.
$14, Lincoln Memorial.

**2021**    Litho.    Perf. 14
3625 A835 $3.35 Sheet of 6, #a-f    15.00 15.00
**Souvenir Sheet**
**Perf. 12**
3626 A835 $15 multi    11.00 11.00
Issued: No. 3625, 10/8; No. 3626, 9/30. No. 3626 contains one 50x30mm stamp.

**Miniature Sheet**

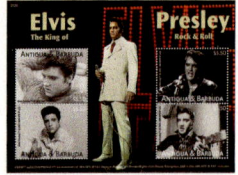

Elvis Presley (1935-77) — A836

No. 3627 — Presley: a, Wearing sweater. b, With microphone at mouth level. c, Holding guitar. d, With microphone above head.

**2021, Oct. 8**    Litho.    Perf. 14
3627 A836 $5.50 Sheet of 4, #a-d    16.50 16.50

Hummingbirds — A837

No. 3628 — Photographs of various hummingbirds with denomination of: a, $3.50. b, $4. c, $4.50. d, $5. 3, $5.50.
$14, Hummingbird, horiz.

**2021, Oct. 8**    Litho.    Perf. 14
3628 A837 Sheet of 5, #a-e    17.00 17.00
**Souvenir Sheet**
3629 A837 $14 multi    10.50 10.50

Tropical Fruits A838

No. 3630: a, Starfruits. b, Coconut. c, Passionfruits. d, Papayas. e, Dragonfruits. f, Pineapples.
No. 3631, vert.: a, Lychees. b, Mangos.

**2021, Oct. 8**    Litho.    Perf. 14
3630 A838 $4 Sheet of 6, #a-f    18.00 18.00
**Souvenir Sheet**
3631 A838 $8 Sheet of 2, #a-b    12.00 12.00

Mushrooms — A839

No. 3632: a, $2.50, Saffron milk cap. b, $3.50, Chanterelle. c, $4.50, Penny bun. d, $4.50, Fly agaric. e, $5.50, Honey fungus.
$14.50, Yellow morel, vert.

**2021, Oct. 8**    Litho.    Perf. 14
3632 A839 Sheet of 5, #a-e    15.50 15.50
**Souvenir Sheet**
**Perf. 12½**
3633 A839 $14.50 multi    11.00 11.00
No. 3633 contains one 38x51mm stamp.

Duke and Duchess of Cambridge, 10th Anniv. of Wedding — A840

No. 3634 — Various photographs of Duke and Duchess of Cambridge, with Duke at: a, Right, wearing white shirt. b, Left, wearing suit and red tie. c, Right, seated in red chair. d, Left, wearing blue shirt. e, Right, kissing Duchess at wedding. f, Right, wearing suit and red tie.
$14, Duke and Duchess of Cambridge in carriage on wedding day.

**2021, Oct. 8**    Litho.    Perf. 14
3634 A840 $4 Sheet of 6, #a-f    18.00 18.00
**Souvenir Sheet**
**Perf. 12½**
3635 A840 $14 multi    10.50 10.50
No. 3635 contains one 51x38mm stamp.

Duke and Duchess of Sussex, First Anniv. of Wedding A841

No. 3636 — Various photographs of Duke and Duchess of Sussex, with Duke at: a, Left, in coach, wearing uniform with cap on wedding day. b, Right, wearing suit and blue sweater. c, Left, wearing suit and tie. d, Left, wearing uniform without cap, on wedding day.
$14, Duke and Duchess of Sussex holding hands.

**2021, Oct. 8**    Litho.    Perf. 14
3636 A841 $5.50 Sheet of 4, #a-d    16.50 16.50
**Souvenir Sheet**
**Perf. 12½**
3637 A841 $14 multi    10.50 10.50
No. 3637 contains one 51x38mm stamp.

Prince Philip (1921-2021) — A842

No. 3638 — Prince Philip: a, At ceremony with Queen Elizabeth II, in uniform. b, Wearing bow tie and medal. c, With Princess Elizabeth on wedding day. d, Wearing striped shirt and tie, facing left. e, Wearing striped shirt and tie, facing right.
$14, Coffin of Prince Philip being brought into St. George's Chapel.

**2021, Oct. 8**    Litho.    Perf. 14
3638 A842 $4.50 Sheet of 5, #a-e    17.00 17.00
**Souvenir Sheet**
3639 A842 $14 multi    10.50 10.50

2020 Summer Olympics, Tokyo — A843

No. 3640: a, Rhythmic gymnastics and "2." b, Field hockey and "0." c, Equestrian and "2." d, Diving and "0."

**2021, Dec. 1**    Litho.    Perf. 14
3640 A843 $5.50 Sheet of 4, #a-d    16.50 16.50
The 2020 Summer Olympics were postponed until 2021 because of the COVID-19 pandemic.

A844

A845

A846

Space Exploration — A847

No. 3641: a, Apollo Command Module and Moon. b, Apollo Lunar Module. c, Rocket launch. d, Splashdown.
No. 3642: a, Apollo rocket stage with open hatches. b, Astronaut in capsule's hatchway. c, Footprint on surface of Moon. d, Astronaut saluting United States flag on Moon. e, Lunar Rover on Moon. f, View of Moon.

# ANTIGUA

No. 3643, Rocket launch under cloudy skies. No. 3644, Vehicles near rocket on launch pad.

| 2022, Feb. 9 | Litho. | Perf. 13x12¾ |
|---|---|---|
| 3641 | A844 | $4.15 Sheet of 4, #a-d | 12.50 12.50 |

**Perf. 12¾x13**

| 3642 | A845 | $4.15 Sheet of 6, #a-f | 18.50 18.50 |

**Souvenir Sheets**
**Perf. 13x13¼**

| 3643 | A846 | $14.50 multi | 11.00 11.00 |
| 3644 | A847 | $14.50 multi | 11.00 11.00 |

Reign of Queen Elizabeth (1926-2022), 70th Anniv. — A848

No. 3645 — Queen Elizabeth II: a, Wearing red hat and jacket. b, Exiting carriage at House of Parliament. c, Wearing yellow jacket at Epsom Racecourse. d, Wearing crown at coronation.
$13.70, Wearing purple hat and jacket, horiz.

| 2022, Mar. 29 | Litho. | Perf. 14 |
|---|---|---|
| 3645 | A848 | $4.70 Sheet of 4, #a-d | 14.00 14.00 |

**Souvenir Sheet**
**Perf. 12½**

| 3646 | A848 | $13.70 multi | 10.50 10.50 |

No. 3646 contains one 51x38mm stamp.

**Miniature Sheet**

New Year 2022 (Year of the Tiger) A849

No. 3647 — Tiger at: a, Left, facing forward. b, Right, facing left. c, Left, facing right. d, Right, hind leg at top. e, Left, crouching in grass. f, Right, sitting with front leg lifted.

| 2022, May 30 | Litho. | Perf. 14 |
|---|---|---|
| 3647 | A849 | $3 Sheet of 6, #a-f | 13.50 13.50 |

**Miniature Sheet**

Birds A850

No. 3648: a, Brown noddy. b, Barbuda warbler. c, Purple-throated carib. d, Magnificent frigatebirds.

| 2022, May 30 | Litho. | Perf. 14 |
|---|---|---|
| 3648 | A850 | $5 Sheet of 4, #a-d | 15.00 15.00 |

**Miniature Sheet**

Insects A851

No. 3649: a, Rutela laeta. b, European honey bee. c, Leaf cricket. d, Gopher beetle.

| 2022, May 30 | Litho. | Perf. 14 |
|---|---|---|
| 3649 | A851 | $5 Sheet of 4, #a-d | 15.00 15.00 |

**Miniature Sheet**

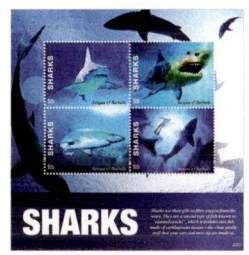

Sharks A852

No. 3650: a, Shark with mouth slightly open, country name in black. b, Shark with mouth open wide, country name in black. c, Shark facing right, country name in white. d, Sharks and diver, country name in white.

| 2022, May 30 | Litho. | Perf. 14 |
|---|---|---|
| 3650 | A852 | $5 Sheet of 4, #a-d | 15.00 15.00 |

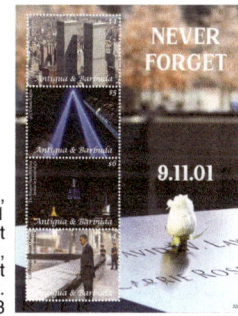

Sept. 11, 2001 Terrorist Attacks, 21st Anniv. A853

No. 3651: a, $4, World Trade Center twin towers. b, $4, Pres. Barack Obama at Sept. 11 Memorial. c, $5, Tribute in Light. d, $6, Empire State Building with blue lights.
$14, People touching Sept. 11 Memorial.

| 2022, May 30 | Litho. | Perf. 14 |
|---|---|---|
| 3651 | A853 | Sheet of 4, #a-d | 14.00 14.00 |

**Souvenir Sheet**
**Perf. 12½**

| 3652 | A853 | $14 multi | 10.50 10.50 |

No. 3652 contains one 51x38mm stamp.

**Souvenir Sheet**

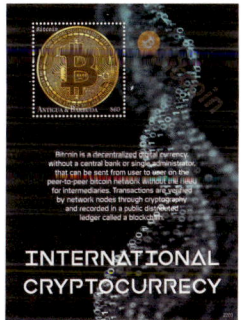

Bitcoin A854

| 2022, May 30 | Litho. | Perf. 13¾ |
|---|---|---|
| 3653 | A854 | $60 multi | 45.00 45.00 |

**Miniature Sheet**

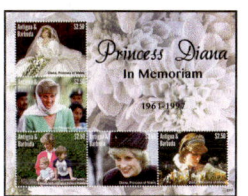

World War II Aircraft A855

No. 3654: a, Boeing B-17 Flying Fortress. b, Ilyushin Il-2 Shturmovik. c, Yakovlev Yak-3. d, Supermarine Spitfire.
$14, Douglas SBD Dauntless.

| 2022, Oct. 10 | Litho. | Perf. 14 |
|---|---|---|
| 3654 | A855 | $5.50 Sheet of 4, #a-d | 16.50 16.50 |

**Souvenir Sheet**
**Perf. 12**

| 3655 | A855 | $14 multi | 10.50 10.50 |

No. 3655 contains one 80x30mm stamp.

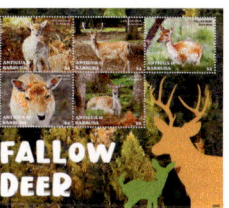

Princess Diana (1961-97) — A856

No. 3656 — Princess Diana: a, Wearing wedding gown. b, Wearing scarf on head. c, With Princes William and Harry. d, Wearing black hat. e, Wearing tiara.
$12.50, Princess Diana wearing plaid jacket.

| 2022, Oct. 10 | Litho. | Perf. 14 |
|---|---|---|
| 3656 | A856 | $2.50 Sheet of 5, #a-e | 9.25 9.25 |

**Souvenir Sheet**
**Perf. 13¾**

| 3657 | A856 | $12.50 multi | 9.25 9.25 |

No. 3657 contains one 35x35mm stamp.

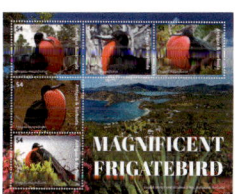

Fallow Deer A857

No. 3658: a, Fawn facing forward. b, Buck. c, Deer facing left, tree branch at left. d, Deer facing forward, legs not visible. e, Deer resting on ground.
$14, Head of deer, vert.

| 2022, Nov. 11 | Litho. | Perf. 14 |
|---|---|---|
| 3658 | A857 | $4 Sheet of 5, #a-e | 15.00 15.00 |

**Souvenir Sheet**

| 3659 | A857 | $14 multi | 10.50 10.50 |

Fregata Magnificens — A858

No. 3660 — Magnificent frigatebird: a, Facing right, denomination in black. b, Facing left, denomination in white. c, Facing left, denomination in black. d, Facing right, denomination in white. e, Facing right, with foliage partially covering bird, denomination in black.
$14, Frigatebird, diff.

| 2022, Nov. 11 | Litho. | Perf. 14 |
|---|---|---|
| 3660 | A858 | $4 Sheet of 5, #a-e | 15.00 15.00 |

**Souvenir Sheet**
**Perf. 12½**

| 3661 | A858 | $14 multi | 10.50 10.50 |

No. 3661 contains one 51x38mm stamp.

**Miniature Sheet**

Queen Elizabeth II (1926-2022) — A859

No. 3662 — Queen Elizabeth II: a, As child. b, As young woman. c, Wearing crown. d, Wearing blue dress. e, Wearing pink coat and hat.

| 2022 | Litho. | Perf. 14 |
|---|---|---|
| 3662 | A859 | $4.96 Sheet of 5, #a-e | 18.50 18.50 |

No. 3662 was alleged to have been issued on Sept. 8, 2022, which was the day Queen Elizabeth II died.

Horses A860

No. 3663: a, Haflinger horse. b, Friesian stallion. c, Arabian horse. d, Shire horse. e, American mustang. f, Appaloosa horse.
$14, American quarterhorse, vert.

| 2023, Mar. 28 | Litho. | Perf. 14 |
|---|---|---|
| 3663 | A860 | $3.50 Sheet of 6, #a-f | 15.50 15.50 |

**Souvenir Sheet**

| 3664 | A860 | $14 multi | 10.50 10.50 |

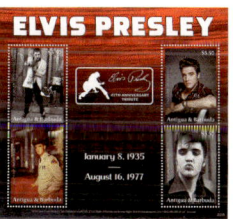

Turtles A861

No. 3665: a, Common mud turtle. b, Western pond turtle. c, Escambia map turtle. d, Smooth softshell turtle. e, Florida soft shell turtle. f, Blanding's turtle.
$14, Spiny softshell turtle.

| 2023, Mar. 28 | Litho. | Perf. 14 |
|---|---|---|
| 3665 | A861 | $3.50 Sheet of 6, #a-f | 15.50 15.50 |

**Souvenir Sheet**

| 3666 | A861 | $14 multi | 10.50 10.50 |

Elvis Presley (1935-77) — A862

No. 3667 — Presley: a, Performing. b, Wearing striped shirt. c, In army uniform. d, With puckered lips.
$14, Presley and rear-view mirror of motorcycle, horiz.

| 2023, Mar. 28 | Litho. | Perf. 14 |
|---|---|---|
| 3667 | A862 | $5.50 Sheet of 4, #a-d | 16.50 16.50 |

**Souvenir Sheet**

| 3668 | A862 | $14 multi | 10.50 10.50 |

## WAR TAX STAMPS

No. 31 and Type A3 Overprinted in Black or Red

| | 1916-18 | Wmk. 3 | | Perf. 14 |
|---|---|---|---|---|
| MR1 | A3 | ½p green | 4.75 | 3.75 |
| MR2 | A3 | ½p green (R) ('17) | 1.60 | 3.50 |
| MR3 | A3 | 1½p orange ('18) | 1.75 | 1.75 |
| | Nos. MR1-MR3 (3) | | 8.10 | 9.00 |

## ARGENTINA

ˌär-jən-ˈtē-nə

LOCATION — In South America
GOVT. — Republic
AREA — 1,084,120 sq. mi.
POP. — 45,200,000 (2020 est.)
CAPITAL — Buenos Aires

100 Centavos = 1 Peso (1858, 1992)
100 Centavos = 1 Austral (1985)

Catalogue values for unused stamps in this country are for Never Hinged items, beginning with Scott 587 in the regular postage section, Scott B12 in the semi-postal section, Scott C59 in the airpost section, Scott CB1 in the airpost semi-postal section and Scott O79 in the officials section.

### Watermarks

Wmk. 84 — Italic RA

Wmk. 85 — Small Sun, 4 ½mm

Wmk. 86 — Large Sun, 6mm

Wmk. 87 — Honeycomb

Wmk. 88 — Multiple Suns

Wmk. 89 — Large Sun

In this watermark the face of the sun is 7mm in diameter, the rays are heavier than in the large sun watermark of 1896-1911 and the watermarks are placed close together, so that parts of several frequently appear on one stamp. This paper was intended to be used for fiscal stamps and is usually referred to as "fiscal sun paper."

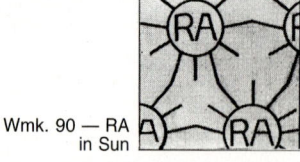
Wmk. 90 — RA in Sun

In 1928 watermark 90 was slightly modified, making the diameter of the Sun 9mm instead of 10mm. Several types of this watermark exist.

Wmk. 205 — AP in Oval

The letters "AP" are the initials of "AHORRO POSTAL." This paper was formerly used exclusively for Postal Savings stamps.

Wmk. 287 — Double Circle and Letters in Sheet

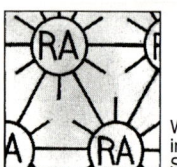
Wmk. 288 — RA in Sun with Straight Rays

Wmk. 365 — Argentine Arms, "Casa de Moneda de la Nacion" & "RA" Multiple

**Values for Unused**
Unused values for Nos. 5-17 are for examples without gum. Examples with original gum command higher prices. Unused values of Nos. 1-4B and stamps after No. 17 are for examples with original gum as defined in the catalogue introduction.

### Argentine Confederation

Symbolical of the Argentine Confederation — A1

| | | Unwmk. | | |
|---|---|---|---|---|
| **1858, May 1** | | **Litho.** | | **Imperf.** |
| 1 | A1 | 5c red | 1.75 | 40.00 |
| a. | | Colon after "5" | 2.50 | 32.50 |
| b. | | Colon after "V" | 2.50 | 32.50 |
| 2 | A1 | 10c green | 5.00 | 90.00 |
| f. | | Diagonal half used as 5c on cover | | 1,000. |
| 3 | A1 | 15c blue | 18.00 | 250.00 |
| c. | | Horiz. third used as 5c on cover | | 10,000. |
| | | Nos. 1-3 (3) | 24.75 | 380.00 |

There are nine varieties of Nos. 1, 2 and 3. Counterfeits and forged cancellations of Nos. 1-3 are plentiful.

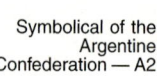 
Symbolical of the Argentine Confederation — A2

| **1860, Jan.** | | | | |
|---|---|---|---|---|
| 4 | A2 | 5c red | 6.00 | 100.00 |
| 4A | A2 | 10c green | 8.50 | — |
| 4B | A2 | 15c blue | 40.00 | — |
| | | Nos. 4-4B (3) | 54.50 | |

Nos. 4A and 4B were never placed in use. Some compositions of Nos. 4-4B contain 8 different types across the sheet. Other settings exist with minor variations. Counterfeits and forged cancellations of Nos. 4-4B are plentiful.

### Argentine Republic

Seal of the Republic — A3

**Broad "C" in "CENTAVOS," Accent on "U" of "REPUBLICA"**

| **1862, Jan. 11** | | | | |
|---|---|---|---|---|
| 5 | A3 | 5c rose | 49.00 | 37.50 |
| 6 | A3 | 10c green | 175.00 | 80.00 |
| 7 | A3 | 15c blue | 350.00 | 225.00 |
| a. | | Without accent on "U" | 8,000. | 5,000. |
| b. | | Tete beche pair | 150,000. | 120,000. |
| d. | | 15c ultramarine | 500.00 | 350.00 |
| e. | | Diagonal third used as 5c on cover | | 12,000. |

No. 6g is printed on white wove paper.
Only one used example of No. 7b is known. It has faults. Two unused examples of No. 7d are known. One is sound with origional gum, the other is in a block, without gum, and has tiny faults.
No. 7u is known only used in Mendoza.

**Broad "C" in "CENTAVOS," No Accent on "U"**

| **1863** | | | | |
|---|---|---|---|---|
| 7C | A3 | 5c rose | 20.00 | 24.00 |
| i. | | 5c rose lilac | 200.00 | 250.00 |
| 7F | A3 | 10c yellow green | 1,000. | 250.00 |

**Narrow "C" in "CENTAVOS," No Accent on "U"**

| **1864** | | | | |
|---|---|---|---|---|
| 7H | A3 | 5c rose red | 225.00 | 32.50 |

The so-called reprints of 10c and 15c are counterfeits. They have narrow "C" and straight lines in shield. Nos. 7C and 7H have been extensively counterfeited.

### Rivadavia Issue

Bernardino Rivadavia
A4    A5

Rivadavia — A6

| **1864-67** | **Engr.** | **Wmk. 84** | | **Imperf.** |
|---|---|---|---|---|
| **Clear Impressions** | | | | |
| 8 | A4 | 5c brown rose | 2,500. | 250. |
| a. | | 5c brick red ('67) | 2,500. | 250. |
| 9 | A5 | 10c green | 3,000. | 1,750. |
| 10 | A6 | 15c blue | 13,500. | 6,500. |
| **Perf. 11½** | | | | |
| **Dull to Worn Impressions** | | | | |
| 11 | A4 | 5c brown rose ('65) | 40.00 | 15.00 |
| 11B | A4 | 5c lake | 100.00 | 22.50 |
| 12 | A5 | 10c green | 150.00 | 70.00 |
| a. | | Diagonal half used as 5c on cover | | 2,000. |
| b. | | Vert. half used as 5c on cover | | 3,000. |
| c. | | Horiz. pair, imperf vert. | | 5,000. |
| 13 | A6 | 15c blue | 450.00 | 150.00 |

| **1867-72** | | **Unwmk.** | | **Imperf.** |
|---|---|---|---|---|
| 14 | A4 | 5c carmine ('72) | 350. | 100. |
| 15 | A4 | 5c rose, thin white paper | 350. | 100. |
| 15A | A5 | 10c green, medium white paper | 3,000. | 3,200. |
| 16 | A6 | 15c blue, medium white paper | 3,000. | 2,700. |

Nos. 15A-16 issued without gum.

| **1867** | | | | **Perf. 11½** |
|---|---|---|---|---|
| 17 | A4 | 5c carmine | 1,000. | 200.00 |

Rivadavia
A7

Manuel Belgrano
A8

Jose de San Martin — A9

**Groundwork of Horizontal Lines**

| **1867-68** | | | | **Perf. 12** |
|---|---|---|---|---|
| 18 | A7 | 5c vermilion | 225.00 | 17.50 |
| 18A | A8 | 10c green | 50.00 | 7.50 |
| b. | | Diag. half used as 5c on cover | | 2,500. |
| 19 | A9 | 15c blue | 100.00 | 22.50 |

**Groundwork of Crossed Lines**

| 20 | A7 | 5c vermilion | 15.00 | 1.25 |
|---|---|---|---|---|
| 21 | A9 | 15c blue | 120.00 | 15.00 |

See Nos. 27, 33-34, 39 and types A19, A33, A34, A37. For surcharges and overprints see Nos. 30-32, 41-42, 47-51, O6-O7, O26.

Gen. Antonio G. Balcarce
A10

Mariano Moreno
A11

Carlos Maria de Alvear
A12

Gervasio Antonio Posadas
A13

Cornelio Saavedra — A14

| **1873** | | | | |
|---|---|---|---|---|
| 22 | A10 | 1c purple | 6.00 | 2.25 |
| a. | | 1c gray violet | 10.00 | 2.25 |
| 23 | A11 | 4c brown | 6.00 | .75 |
| a. | | 4c red brown | 15.00 | 3.00 |
| 24 | A12 | 30c orange | 140.00 | 25.00 |
| a. | | Vert. pair, imperf horiz. | 4,000. | |
| 25 | A13 | 60c black | 160.00 | 5.00 |
| 26 | A14 | 90c blue | 60.00 | 3.00 |
| | | Nos. 22-26 (5) | 372.00 | 36.00 |

For overprints see Nos. O5, O12-O14, O19-O21, O25, O29.
Four examples of No. 24a are known. Three examples of No. 26 are known on cover.

| **1873** | | | | **Laid Paper** |
|---|---|---|---|---|
| 27 | A8 | 10c green | 325.00 | 32.50 |

**Nos.18, 18A Surcharged in Black**

Nos. 30-31    No. 32

ARGENTINA 575

**1877, Feb.** **Wove Paper**

| | | | | |
|---|---|---|---|---|
| 30 | A7 | 1c on 5c vermilion | 75.00 | 25.00 |
| *a.* | | Inverted surcharge | 1,000. | 300.00 |
| 31 | A7 | 2c on 5c vermilion | 125.00 | 75.00 |
| *a.* | | Inverted surcharge | 1,200. | 750.00 |
| 32 | A8 | 8c on 10c green | 160.00 | 40.00 |
| *b.* | | Inverted surcharge | 2,500. | 1,000. |
| | | *Nos. 30-32 (3)* | 360.00 | 140.00 |

Varieties also exist with double and triple surcharges, surcharge on reverse, 8c on No. 27, all made clandestinely from the original cliches of the surcharges.

Forgeries of these surcharges include the inverted and double varieties.

**1876-77** ***Rouletted***

| | | | | |
|---|---|---|---|---|
| 33 | A7 | 5c vermilion | 200.00 | 85.00 |
| 34 | A7 | 8c lake ('77) | 35.00 | .65 |

Belgrano A17

Dalmacio Vélez Sarsfield A18

San Martín — A19

**1878** ***Rouletted***

| | | | | |
|---|---|---|---|---|
| 35 | A17 | 16c green | 12.00 | 1.10 |
| 36 | A18 | 20c blue | 20.00 | 2.25 |
| 37 | A19 | 24c blue | 30.00 | 3.50 |
| | | *Nos. 35-37 (3)* | 62.00 | 6.85 |

See No. 56. For overprints see Nos. O9-O10, O15-O17, O22, O28.

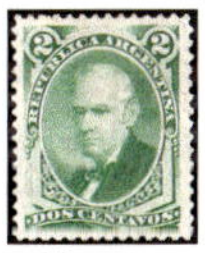
Vicente Lopez A20

Alvear A21

**1877-80** ***Perf. 12***

| | | | | |
|---|---|---|---|---|
| 38 | A20 | 2c yellow green | 5.00 | .75 |
| 39 | A7 | 8c lake ('80) | 4.50 | .75 |
| *a.* | | 8c brown lake | *52.50* | .75 |
| 40 | A21 | 25c lake ('78) | 30.00 | 6.00 |
| | | *Nos. 38-40 (3)* | 39.50 | 7.50 |

No. 38 measures 19.9 mm x 25.3 mm. No. 38a measures 19.8 mm x 25.3 mm.

For overprints see Nos. O4, O11, O18, O24.

### No. 18 Surcharged in Black

Large "P"

Small "P"

**1882**

| | | | | |
|---|---|---|---|---|
| 41 | A7 | ½c on 5c ver | 2.75 | 2.75 |
| *a.* | | Double surcharge | 100.00 | 100.00 |
| *b.* | | Inverted surcharge | 50.00 | 50.00 |
| *c.* | | "PROVISORIO" omitted | 110.00 | 110.00 |
| *d.* | | Fraction omitted | 100.00 | |
| *e.* | | "PROVISOBIO" | 50.00 | 50.00 |
| *f.* | | Pair, one without surcharge | 250.00 | |
| *g.* | | Small "P" in "PROVISORIO" | 2.75 | 2.75 |
| *h.* | | As "a," small "P" in "PROVISORIO" | 50.00 | 50.00 |
| *i.* | | As "b," small "P" in "PROVISORIO" | 75.00 | 75.00 |
| *j.* | | As "d," small "P" in "PROVISORIO" | 30.00 | 30.00 |

### Perforated across Middle of Stamp

| | | | | |
|---|---|---|---|---|
| 42 | A7 | ½c on 5c ver | 6.00 | 6.00 |
| *a.* | | "PROVISORIQ" | 50.00 | 50.00 |
| *b.* | | Large "P" in "PROVISORIO" | 10.00 | 30.00 |

A23

**1882** **Typo.** ***Perf. 12½***

| | | | | |
|---|---|---|---|---|
| 43 | A23 | ½c brown | 2.25 | 1.50 |
| *a.* | | Imperf., pair | 100.00 | 80.00 |
| 44 | A23 | 1c red | 15.00 | 6.00 |
| 45 | A23 | 12c ultra | 90.00 | 14.00 |

***Perf. 14¼***

| | | | | |
|---|---|---|---|---|
| 44A | A23 | 1c red | 3.50 | 1.50 |
| 45A | A23 | 12c ultra | 65.00 | 12.00 |

**Engr.**

| | | | | |
|---|---|---|---|---|
| 46 | A23 | 12c grnsh blue | 225.00 | 16.00 |
| | | *Nos. 43-46 (6)* | 400.75 | 51.00 |

See type A29. For overprints see Nos. O2, O8, O23, O27.

### No. 21 Surcharged in Red

a

b

c

**1884** **Engr.** ***Perf. 12***

| | | | | |
|---|---|---|---|---|
| 47 | A9 (a) | ½c on 15c blue | 3.00 | 2.00 |
| *a.* | | Groundwork of horiz. lines | 150.00 | 90.00 |
| *b.* | | Inverted surcharge | 35.00 | 25.00 |
| 48 | A9 (b) | 1c on 15c blue | 22.50 | 16.50 |
| *a.* | | Groundwork of horiz. lines | 13.00 | 11.50 |
| *b.* | | Inverted surcharge | 100.00 | 62.50 |
| *c.* | | Double surcharge | 50.00 | 40.00 |
| *d.* | | Triple surcharge | 400.00 | |

### Nos. 20-21 Surcharged in Black

| | | | | |
|---|---|---|---|---|
| 49 | A7 (a) | ½c on 5c ver | 5.00 | 4.50 |
| *a.* | | Inverted surcharge | 200.00 | 150.00 |
| *b.* | | Date omitted | 200.00 | — |
| *c.* | | Pair, one without surcharge | 500.00 | |
| *d.* | | Double surcharge | 550.00 | |
| 50 | A9 (a) | ½c on 15c blue | 15.00 | 12.00 |
| *a.* | | Groundwork of horiz. lines | 50.00 | 35.00 |
| *b.* | | Inverted surcharge | 90.00 | 70.00 |
| *c.* | | Pair, one without surcharge | 400.00 | |
| 51 | A7 (c) | 4c on 5c ver | 12.00 | 9.00 |
| *a.* | | Inverted surcharge | 35.00 | 28.00 |
| *b.* | | Double surcharge | 700.00 | 350.00 |
| *c.* | | Pair, one without surcharge but with "4" in manuscript | 750.00 | 650.00 |
| *d.* | | Pair, one without surcharge | 400.00 | |
| | | *Nos. 47-51 (5)* | 57.50 | 44.00 |

A29

**1884-85** **Engr.** ***Perf. 12***

| | | | | |
|---|---|---|---|---|
| 52 | A29 | ½c red brown | 1.50 | .65 |
| *a.* | | Horiz. pair, imperf vert. | | *1,200.* |
| 53 | A29 | 1c rose red | 7.00 | .65 |
| *a.* | | Horiz. pair, imperf vert. | *300.00* | *250.00* |
| 54 | A29 | 12c deep blue | 35.00 | 1.50 |
| *a.* | | 12c grnsh blue ('85) | 50.00 | 1.50 |
| *b.* | | Horiz. pair, imperf vert. | *300.00* | *250.00* |
| | | *Nos. 52-54 (3)* | 43.50 | 2.80 |

For overprints see Nos. O1, O3, O9.

### San Martin Type of 1878

**1887** **Engr.**

| | | | | |
|---|---|---|---|---|
| 56 | A19 | 24c blue | 20.00 | 1.40 |

Justo Jose de Urquiza A30

Lopez A31

Miguel Juarez Celman A32

Rivadavia (Large head) A33

Rivadavia (Small head) A34

Domingo F. Sarmiento A35

Nicolas Avellaneda — A36

San Martin — A37

Julio A. Roca — A37a

Belgrano — A37b

Manuel Dorrego A38

Moreno A39

Bartolome Mitre — A40

CINCO CENTAVOS.
A33 — Shows collar on left side only.
A34 — Shows collar on both sides. Lozenges in background larger and clearer than in A33.

**1888-90** **Litho.** ***Perf. 11½***

| | | | | |
|---|---|---|---|---|
| 57 | A30 | ½c blue | 1.75 | .75 |
| *b.* | | Vert. pair, imperf. horiz. | 200.00 | 200.00 |
| *c.* | | Horiz. pair, imperf. vert. | 200.00 | 200.00 |
| 58 | A31 | 2c yel grn | 20.00 | 10.00 |
| *b.* | | Vert. pair, imperf. horiz. | 130.00 | |
| *c.* | | Horiz. pair, imperf. vert. | 250.00 | |
| 59 | A32 | 3c blue green | 3.50 | 1.50 |
| *b.* | | Horiz. pair, imperf. vert. | 60.00 | |
| *c.* | | Horiz. pair, imperf. btwn. | 130.00 | |
| *d.* | | Vert. pair, imperf. btwn. | 25.00 | 25.00 |
| 60 | A33 | 5c carmine | 18.00 | .75 |
| *b.* | | Vert. pair, imperf. horiz. | 175.00 | |
| 61 | A34 | 5c carmine | 26.00 | 2.25 |
| *b.* | | Vert. pair, imperf. btwn. | *200.00* | |
| *c.* | | Vert. pair, imperf. horiz. | | 400.00 |
| 62 | A35 | 6c red | 50.00 | 20.00 |
| *b.* | | Vert. pair, imperf. btwn. | *150.00* | |
| *c.* | | Perf. 12 | 100.00 | 50.00 |
| 63 | A36 | 10c brown | 26.00 | 1.50 |
| 64 | A37 | 15c orange | 27.50 | 2.25 |
| *d.* | | Vert. pair, imperf. btwn. | | 600.00 |
| 64A | A37a | 20c green | 25.00 | 1.50 |
| 64B | A37b | 25c purple | 45.00 | 4.00 |
| 65 | A38 | 30c brown | 40.00 | 4.00 |
| *b.* | | 30c reddish chocolate brown | 400.00 | 80.00 |
| *c.* | | Horiz. pair, imperf. btwn. | 700.00 | 500.00 |
| 66 | A39 | 40c slate, perf. 12 | 150.00 | 3.00 |
| *a.* | | Perf. 11½ | 300.00 | 4.00 |
| *b.* | | Horiz. pair, imperf. btwn. (#66) | | 800.00 |
| 67 | A40 | 50c blue | 350.00 | 20.00 |
| | | *Nos. 57-67 (13)* | 782.75 | 71.50 |

In this issue there are several varieties of each value, the difference between them being in the relative position of the head to the frame.

### Imperf., Pairs

| | | | | |
|---|---|---|---|---|
| *57a* | A30 | ½c | 85.00 | 67.50 |
| *58a* | A31 | 2c | 100.00 | |
| *59a* | A32 | 3c | 45.00 | 27.50 |
| *61a* | A34 | 5c | | *100.00* |
| *62a* | A35 | 6c | *150.00* | 150.00 |
| *63a* | A36 | 10c | *55.00* | |
| *64c* | A37 | 15c | | *200.00* |
| *65a* | A38 | 30c | *325.00* | *225.00* |

Urquiza A41

Velez Sarsfield A42

Miguel Juarez Celman A43

Rivadavia (Large head) A44

Sarmiento A45

Juan Bautista Alberdi A46

**1888-89** **Engr.** ***Perf. 11½, 11½x12***

| | | | | |
|---|---|---|---|---|
| 68 | A41 | ½c ultra | .75 | .45 |
| *a.* | | Vert. pair, imperf. horiz. | — | |
| *b.* | | Imperf., pair | 30.00 | — |
| 69 | A42 | 1c brown | 1.50 | .75 |
| *a.* | | Vert. pair, imperf. horiz. | 65.00 | |
| *b.* | | Vert. pair, imperf. btwn. | — | |
| *c.* | | Imperf., pair | 30.00 | |
| *d.* | | Horiz. pair, imperf. btwn. | 100.00 | |
| 70 | A43 | 3c blue green | 6.00 | 1.75 |
| 71 | A44 | 5c rose | 4.50 | .75 |
| *a.* | | Imperf., pair | 50.00 | — |
| 72 | A45 | 6c blue black | 3.00 | .90 |
| *b.* | | Perf. 11½x12 | 15.00 | 4.50 |

Search
PHILASEARCH
www.Philasearch.com

| | | | | |
|---|---|---|---|---|
| **73** | A46 | 12c blue | 8.75 | 3.75 |
| *a.* | | Imperf., pair | 45.00 | |
| *b.* | | bluish paper | 9.50 | 3.75 |
| *c.* | | Perf. 11½ | 14.00 | 3.00 |
| | | *Nos. 68-73 (6)* | 24.50 | 8.35 |

Nos. 69-70 exist with papermakers' watermarks.

See No. 77, types A50, A61. For surcharges see Nos. 83-84.

Jose Maria Paz
A48

Santiago Derqui
A49

Rivadavia (Small head)
A50

Avellaneda
A51

Moreno
A53

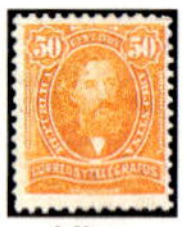

Mitre
A54

Gervasio Antonio de Posadas — A55

**1890 Engr. *Perf. 11½***

| | | | | |
|---|---|---|---|---|
| **75** | A48 | ¼c green | .65 | .45 |
| **76** | A49 | 2c violet | 1.50 | .75 |
| *a.* | | 2c purple | 2.00 | .75 |
| *b.* | | 2c slate | 2.00 | .75 |
| *c.* | | Horiz. pair, imperf. btwn. | 30.00 | 25.00 |
| *d.* | | Imperf., pair | 37.50 | |
| *e.* | | Perf. 11½x12 | 9.00 | .75 |
| **77** | A50 | 5c carmine | 3.50 | .45 |
| *a.* | | Imperf., pair | 70.00 | 32.50 |
| *b.* | | Perf. 11½x12 | 10.00 | 1.25 |
| *c.* | | Vert. pair, imperf. btwn. | 75.00 | 60.00 |
| *d.* | | Horiz. pair, imperf. btwn. | 75.00 | 60.00 |
| **78** | A51 | 10c brown | 4.50 | .75 |
| *b.* | | Imperf., pair | 150.00 | |
| *c.* | | Vert. pair, imperf. btwn. | 225.00 | |
| **80** | A53 | 40c olive green | 8.00 | 1.50 |
| *a.* | | Imperf., pair | 55.00 | |
| *b.* | | Horiz. pair, imperf. btwn. | | *250.00* |
| **81** | A54 | 50c orange | 9.00 | 1.50 |
| *a.* | | Imperf., pair | 80.00 | |
| *b.* | | Perf. 11½x12 | 40.00 | 3.00 |
| **82** | A55 | 60c black | 20.00 | 4.50 |
| *a.* | | Imperf., pair | — | |
| *b.* | | Vert. pair, imperf. btwn. | 125.00 | 100.00 |
| | | *Nos. 75-82 (7)* | 47.15 | 9.90 |

Type A50 differs from type A44 in having the head smaller, the letters of "Cinco Centavos" not as tall, and the curved ornaments at sides close to the first and last letters of "Republica Argentina."

Lithographed Surcharge on No. 73 in Black or Red

**1890 *Perf. 11½x12***

| | | | | |
|---|---|---|---|---|
| **83** | A46 | ¼c on 12c blue | .75 | .75 |
| *a.* | | Perf. 11½ | 50.00 | 40.00 |
| *b.* | | Double surcharge | 75.00 | 47.50 |
| *c.* | | Inverted surcharge | 100.00 | |
| **84** | A46 | ¼c on 12c blue (R) | .75 | .75 |
| *a.* | | Double surcharge | 55.00 | 50.00 |
| *b.* | | Perf. 11½ | 8.00 | 6.00 |

Surcharge is different on Nos. 83 and 84.

Nos. 83-84 exist as pairs, one without surcharge. These were privately produced.

Rivadavia
A57

Jose de San Martin
A58

Gregorio Araoz de Lamadrid
A59

Admiral Guillermo Brown
A60

**1891 Engr. *Perf. 11½***

| | | | | |
|---|---|---|---|---|
| **85** | A57 | 8c carmine rose | 1.50 | .65 |
| *a.* | | Imperf., pair | 130.00 | |
| **86** | A58 | 1p deep blue | 50.00 | 12.00 |
| **87** | A59 | 5p ultra | 325.00 | 45.00 |
| **88** | A60 | 20p green | 500.00 | 100.00 |
| | | *Nos. 85-88 (4)* | 876.50 | 157.65 |

A 10p brown and a 50p red were prepared but not issued. Values: 10p $1,500 for fine, 50p $1,200 with rough or somewhat damaged perfs.

Velez Sarsfield — A61

**1890 *Perf. 11½***

| | | | | |
|---|---|---|---|---|
| **89** | A61 | 1c brown | 1.25 | .65 |
| *b.* | | Horiz. pair, imperf. btwn. | | *550.00* |

Type A61 is a re-engraving of A42. The figure "1" in each upper corner has a short horizontal serif instead of a long one pointing downward. In type A61 the first and last letters of "Correos y Telegrafos" are closer to the curved ornaments below than in type A42. Background is of horizontal lines (cross-hatching on No. 69).

"Santa Maria," "Nina" and "Pinta" — A62

**1892, Oct. 12 Wmk. 85 *Perf. 11½***

| | | | | |
|---|---|---|---|---|
| **90** | A62 | 2c light blue | 8.50 | 3.00 |
| *a.* | | Double impression | 225.00 | |
| **91** | A62 | 5c dark blue | 9.50 | 4.00 |

Discovery of America, 400th anniv. Counterfeits of Nos. 90-91 are litho.

Rivadavia
A63

Belgrano
A64

San Martin — A65

**1892-95 Wmk. 85 *Perf. 11½***

| | | | | |
|---|---|---|---|---|
| **92** | A63 | ½c dull blue | 1.00 | .35 |
| *a.* | | ½c bright ultra | 80.00 | 40.00 |
| **93** | A63 | 1c brown | .65 | .50 |
| **94** | A63 | 2c green | 1.00 | .35 |
| **95** | A63 | 3c org ('95) | 1.75 | .35 |
| **96** | A63 | 5c carmine | 1.75 | .35 |
| *b.* | | 5c green (error) | 700.00 | 700.00 |
| **98** | A64 | 10c car rose | 13.50 | .60 |
| **99** | A64 | 12c dp bl ('93) | 10.00 | .60 |
| **100** | A64 | 16c gray | 16.50 | .65 |
| **101** | A64 | 24c gray brown | 16.50 | .65 |
| **102** | A64 | 50c blue green | 27.50 | .75 |
| **103** | A65 | 1p lake ('93) | 12.00 | 1.00 |
| *a.* | | 1p red brown | 20.00 | 5.00 |
| **104** | A65 | 2p dark green | 27.50 | 3.50 |
| **105** | A65 | 5p dark blue | 37.50 | 3.50 |
| | | *Nos. 92-105 (13)* | 167.15 | 13.15 |

***Perf. 12***

| | | | | |
|---|---|---|---|---|
| **92E** | A63 | ½c dull blue | 6.00 | 1.00 |
| **93E** | A63 | 1c brown | 10.00 | 2.00 |
| **94E** | A63 | 2c green | 10.00 | 3.00 |
| **95E** | A63 | 3c org ('95) | 30.00 | 5.00 |
| **96E** | A63 | 5c carmine | 35.00 | 1.00 |
| **98E** | A64 | 10c car rose | 21.00 | 3.50 |
| **99E** | A64 | 12c dp bl ('93) | 40.00 | 4.00 |
| **100E** | A64 | 16c gray | 40.00 | 4.00 |
| **101E** | A64 | 24c gray brown | 30.00 | 17.00 |
| **102E** | A64 | 50c blue green | 30.00 | 6.00 |
| **104E** | A65 | 2p dark green | 125.00 | 40.00 |
| | | *Nos. 92E-104E (11)* | 377.00 | 86.50 |

***Perf. 11½x12***

| | | | | |
|---|---|---|---|---|
| **92F** | A63 | ½c dull blue | 18.00 | 10.00 |
| **93F** | A63 | 1c brown | 15.00 | 8.00 |
| **94F** | A63 | 2c green | 40.00 | 15.00 |
| **95F** | A63 | 3c org ('95) | 55.00 | 22.50 |
| **96F** | A63 | 5c carmine | 20.00 | 4.00 |
| **98F** | A64 | 10c car rose | 30.00 | 7.50 |
| **99F** | A64 | 12c dp bl ('93) | 60.00 | 27.50 |
| **100F** | A64 | 16c gray | 60.00 | 27.50 |
| **102F** | A64 | 50c blue green | 60.00 | 10.00 |
| **103F** | A64 | 1p red brown | 60.00 | 10.00 |
| **104F** | A65 | 2p dark green | 175.00 | 75.00 |
| | | *Nos. 92F-104F (11)* | 593.00 | 217.00 |

The high values of this and succeeding issues are frequently punched with the word "INUTILIZADO," parts of the letters showing on each stamp. These punched stamps sell for only a small fraction of the catalogue values.

Examples of No. 95 in yellow shades are changelings.

*Reprints of No. 96b have white gum. The original stamp has yellowish gum. Value $125.*

**Imperf., Pairs**

| | | | |
|---|---|---|---|
| *92b* | A63 | ½c | 60.00 |
| *93a* | A63 | 1c | 60.00 |
| *94a* | A63 | 2c | 30.00 |
| *96a* | A63 | 5c | 30.00 |
| *98a* | A64 | 10c | 60.00 |
| *99a* | A64 | 12c | 60.00 |
| *100a* | A64 | 16c | 60.00 |
| *101a* | A64 | 24c | 60.00 |
| *102a* | A64 | 50c | 60.00 |
| *103b* | A65 | 1p | 60.00 |
| *105a* | A65 | 5p | 150.00 |

Nos. 102a, 103b and 105a exist only without gum; the other imperfs are found with or without gum, and values are the same for either condition.

**Vertical Pairs, Imperf. Between**

| | | | | |
|---|---|---|---|---|
| *92c* | A63 | ½c | 125.00 | |
| *93b* | A63 | 1c | 100.00 | |
| *94b* | A63 | 2c | 50.00 | |
| *95a* | A63 | 3c | 250.00 | |
| *96c* | A63 | 5c | 45.00 | — |
| *98b* | A64 | 10c | 100.00 | |
| *99b* | A64 | 12c | 100.00 | |

**Horizontal Pairs, Imperf. Between**

| | | | | |
|---|---|---|---|---|
| *93c* | A63 | 1c | 110.00 | |
| *94c* | A63 | 2c | 55.00 | |
| *96d* | A63 | 5c | 55.00 | 45.00 |
| *98c* | A64 | 10c | 110.00 | |

**1896-97 Wmk. 86 *Perf. 11½***

| | | | | |
|---|---|---|---|---|
| **106** | A63 | ½c slate | .65 | .30 |
| *a.* | | ½c gray blue | 2.00 | .35 |
| *b.* | | ½c indigo | .65 | .30 |
| **107** | A63 | 1c brown | .65 | .30 |
| **108** | A63 | 2c yellow green | .65 | .30 |
| **109** | A63 | 3c orange | .65 | .30 |
| **110** | A63 | 5c carmine | .65 | .30 |
| *a.* | | Imperf., pair | 100.00 | |
| **111** | A64 | 10c carmine rose | 10.00 | .30 |
| **112** | A64 | 12c deep blue | 5.00 | .30 |
| *a.* | | Imperf., pair | — | |
| **113** | A64 | 16c gray | 13.50 | .90 |
| **114** | A64 | 24c gray brown | 13.50 | 1.25 |
| *a.* | | Imperf., pair | 100.00 | — |
| **115** | A64 | 30c orange ('97) | 13.50 | .70 |
| **116** | A64 | 50c blue green | 13.50 | .70 |
| **117** | A64 | 80c dull violet | 20.00 | .90 |
| **118** | A65 | 1p lake | 30.00 | 1.60 |
| **119** | A65 | 1p20c black ('97) | 13.50 | 3.50 |
| **120** | A65 | 2p dark green | 20.00 | 10.00 |
| **121** | A65 | 5p dark blue | 135.00 | 13.50 |
| | | *Nos. 106-121 (16)* | 290.75 | 35.15 |

***Perf. 12***

| | | | | |
|---|---|---|---|---|
| **106E** | A63 | ½c slate | 2.00 | 1.00 |
| *a.* | | ½c gray blue | 10.00 | 4.00 |
| *b.* | | ½c indigo | 10.00 | 4.00 |
| **107E** | A63 | 1c brown | 1.75 | 1.00 |
| **108E** | A63 | 2c yellow green | 2.50 | 1.00 |
| **109E** | A63 | 3c orange | 45.00 | 2.00 |
| **110E** | A63 | 5c carmine | 3.50 | 1.00 |
| **111E** | A64 | 10c car rose | 15.00 | 1.00 |
| **112E** | A64 | 12c deep blue | 11.00 | 2.00 |
| **113E** | A64 | 16c gray | 35.00 | 5.50 |
| **114E** | A64 | 24c gray brown | 52.50 | 11.00 |
| **115E** | A64 | 30c orange ('97) | 52.50 | 2.00 |
| **116E** | A64 | 50c blue green | 65.00 | .80 |
| **117E** | A64 | 80c dull violet | 65.00 | 22.50 |
| **118E** | A65 | 1p lake | 65.00 | 3.50 |
| **119E** | A65 | 1p20c black ('97) | 65.00 | 22.50 |
| **121E** | A65 | 5p dark blue | 800.00 | 20.00 |
| | | *Nos. 106E-121E (15)* | 1,281. | 96.80 |

***Perf. 11½x12***

| | | | | |
|---|---|---|---|---|
| **106F** | A63 | ½c slate | 20.00 | 11.00 |
| **107F** | A63 | 1c brown | 30.00 | 25.00 |
| **108F** | A63 | 2c yellow green | 20.00 | 11.00 |
| **109F** | A63 | 3c orange | 13.00 | 8.00 |
| **110F** | A63 | 5c carmine | 26.00 | 4.50 |
| **111F** | A64 | 10c car rose | 45.00 | 18.00 |
| **112F** | A64 | 12c deep blue | 47.50 | 15.00 |
| **113F** | A64 | 16c gray | 60.00 | 20.00 |
| **115F** | A64 | 30c org ('97) | — | 75.00 |
| **116F** | A64 | 50c blue green | — | 75.00 |
| **117F** | A64 | 80c dull violet | — | 75.00 |
| **119F** | A65 | 1p20c black ('97) | 100.00 | 60.00 |
| | | *Nos. 106F-119F (12)* | 361.50 | 397.50 |

**Vertical Pairs, Imperf. Between**

| | | | | |
|---|---|---|---|---|
| *106c* | A63 | ½c | 200.00 | |
| *107a* | A63 | 1c | 125.00 | |
| *108a* | A63 | 2c | 125.00 | |
| *109a* | A63 | 3c | 200.00 | |
| *110b* | A63 | 5c | 125.00 | 125.00 |
| *112b* | A64 | 12c | 125.00 | 100.00 |

**Horizontal Pairs, Imperf. Between**

| | | | | |
|---|---|---|---|---|
| *107b* | A63 | 1c | 125.00 | |
| *108b* | A63 | 2c | 125.00 | |
| *110c* | A63 | 5c | 125.00 | 80.00 |
| *111a* | A64 | 10c | 125.00 | |
| *112c* | A64 | 12c | 125.00 | |

Allegory, Liberty Seated
A66 A67

**1899-1903 *Perf. 11½***

| | | | | |
|---|---|---|---|---|
| **122** | A66 | ½c yel brn | .40 | .30 |
| **123** | A66 | 1c green | .60 | .30 |
| **124** | A66 | 2c slate | .60 | .30 |
| **125** | A66 | 3c org ('01) | .80 | .50 |
| **126** | A66 | 4c yel ('03) | 1.40 | .60 |
| **127** | A66 | 5c car rose | .60 | .30 |
| **128** | A66 | 6c blk ('03) | .90 | .60 |
| **129** | A66 | 10c dk grn | 1.40 | .40 |
| **130** | A66 | 12c dull blue | .95 | .60 |
| **131** | A66 | 12c ol grn ('01) | .95 | .60 |
| **132** | A66 | 15c sea grn ('01) | 2.50 | .60 |
| **132B** | A66 | 15c dl blue ('01) | 2.50 | .60 |
| **133** | A66 | 16c orange | 8.00 | 8.00 |
| **134** | A66 | 20c claret | 1.90 | .30 |
| **135** | A66 | 24c violet | 4.00 | 1.00 |
| **136** | A66 | 30c rose | 7.25 | .60 |
| **137** | A66 | 30c ver ('01) | 4.00 | .50 |
| *a.* | | 30c scarlet | 47.50 | 3.00 |
| **138** | A66 | 50c brt blue | 4.50 | .50 |
| **139** | A67 | 1p bl & blk | 15.00 | 1.25 |
| *a.* | | Center inverted | *2,000.* | *1,000.* |
| **140** | A67 | 5p org & blk | 57.50 | 11.00 |
| | | Punch cancellation | | 3.00 |
| *a.* | | Center inverted | *2,750.* | 2,500. |
| **141** | A67 | 10p grn & blk | 70.00 | 18.00 |
| | | Punch cancellation | | 3.00 |
| *a.* | | Center inverted | *5,000.* | |
| | | Punch cancellation | | 675.00 |
| **142** | A67 | 20p red & blk | 200.00 | 35.00 |
| | | Punch cancellation | | 3.00 |
| *a.* | | Center invtd. (punch cancel) | | *4,000.* |
| | | *Nos. 122-142 (22)* | 385.75 | 81.85 |

Nos. 139-142 used are valued with violet oval or black boxed parcel cancels. Examples with letter cancels are worth ⅓rd more.

***Perf. 12***

| | | | | |
|---|---|---|---|---|
| **122E** | A66 | ½c yellow brown | 1.50 | 1.20 |
| **123E** | A66 | 1c green | 2.00 | .60 |
| **124E** | A66 | 2c slate | 1.50 | .60 |
| **125E** | A66 | 3c orange ('01) | 3.50 | 1.75 |
| **126E** | A66 | 4c yellow ('03) | 10.00 | 3.50 |
| **127E** | A66 | 5c carmine rose | 5.25 | .60 |
| **128E** | A66 | 6c black ('03) | 8.50 | 2.00 |
| **129E** | A66 | 10c dark green | 8.50 | 1.75 |
| **130E** | A66 | 12c dull blue | 8.00 | 2.00 |
| **131E** | A66 | 12c ol grn ('01) | 8.50 | 2.00 |
| **132E** | A66 | 15c sea grn ('01) | 17.00 | 1.75 |
| **133E** | A66 | 16c orange | 10.00 | 9.50 |
| **134E** | A66 | 20c claret | 12.00 | 9.50 |
| **135E** | A66 | 24c violet | 11.00 | 8.50 |
| **136E** | A66 | 30c rose | 28.00 | 3.50 |
| **137E** | A66 | 30c ver ('01) | 60.00 | 4.00 |
| *a.* | | 30c scarlet | 47.50 | 3.00 |
| **138E** | A66 | 50c brt blue | 27.50 | 3.50 |
| **139E** | A67 | 1p bl & blk | 500.00 | 160.00 |
| | | *Nos. 122E-139E (18)* | 722.75 | 216.25 |

***Perf. 11½x12***

| | | | | |
|---|---|---|---|---|
| **122F** | A66 | ½c yellow brown | 25.00 | 15.00 |
| | | Never hinged | 37.50 | |
| | | On cover, single franking | | 20.00 |
| **123F** | A66 | 1c green | 25.00 | 15.00 |
| | | Never hinged | 37.50 | |
| | | On cover | | 1.00 |
| **124F** | A66 | 2c slate | 12.00 | 3.00 |
| | | Never hinged | 18.00 | |
| | | On cover | | 1.00 |
| **125F** | A66 | 3c orange ('01) | 47.50 | 18.00 |
| | | Never hinged | 72.50 | |
| | | On cover | | 1.50 |
| **127F** | A66 | 5c carmine rose | 12.00 | 6.00 |
| | | Never hinged | 18.00 | |
| | | On cover | | 1.00 |
| **128F** | A66 | 6c black ('03) | 32.50 | 20.00 |
| | | Never hinged | 47.50 | |
| | | On cover | | 2.00 |
| **129F** | A66 | 10c dark green | 30.00 | 6.50 |
| | | Never hinged | 45.00 | |
| | | On cover | | 1.50 |
| **130F** | A66 | 12c dull blue | 50.00 | 15.00 |
| | | Never hinged | 75.00 | |
| | | On cover | | 2.00 |
| **131F** | A66 | 12c ol grn ('01) | 50.00 | 10.00 |
| | | Never hinged | 75.00 | |
| | | On cover | | 2.00 |
| **132F** | A66 | 15c sea grn ('01) | 50.00 | 8.00 |
| | | Never hinged | 75.00 | |
| | | On cover | | 2.50 |
| **134F** | A66 | 20c claret | 60.00 | 12.00 |
| | | Never hinged | 90.00 | |
| | | On cover | | 1.00 |
| **135F** | A66 | 24c violet | 50.00 | 10.00 |
| | | Never hinged | 75.00 | |
| | | On cover | | 5.00 |

| | | | | | |
|---|---|---|---|---|---|
| **136F** | A66 | 30c | rose | 120.00 | 20.00 |
| | | | Never hinged | 175.00 | |
| | | | On cover | | 5.00 |
| **137F** | A66 | 30c | ver ('01) | 140.00 | 25.00 |
| | | | Never hinged | 210.00 | |
| | | | On cover | | 5.00 |
| **138F** | A66 | 50c | brt blue | 120.00 | 20.00 |
| | | | Never hinged | 175.00 | |
| | | | On cover | | 10.00 |
| | *Nos. 122F-138F (15)* | | | 824.00 | 203.50 |

### Imperf., Pairs

| | | | |
|---|---|---|---|
| *122a* | A66 | ½c | 35.00 |
| *123a* | A66 | 1c | 50.00 |
| *124a* | A66 | 2c | 17.50 |
| *125a* | A66 | 3c | 325.00 |
| *127a* | A66 | 5c | 17.50 |
| *128a* | A66 | 6c | 60.00 |
| *129a* | A66 | 10c | 50.00 |
| *132a* | A66 | 15c | 50.00 |

### Vertical Pairs, Imperf. Between

| | | | | |
|---|---|---|---|---|
| *122b* | A66 | ½c | 10.00 | 9.50 |
| *123b* | A66 | 1c | 10.00 | 9.50 |
| *124b* | A66 | 2c | 5.00 | 4.50 |
| *125b* | A66 | 3c | 325.00 | 200.00 |
| *126a* | A66 | 4c | 400.00 | 275.00 |
| *127b* | A66 | 5c | 4.50 | 2.50 |
| *128b* | A66 | 6c | 13.50 | 10.00 |
| *129b* | A66 | 10c | 85.00 | |
| *132c* | A66 | 15c | 15.00 | 10.00 |

### Horizontal Pairs, Imperf. Between

| | | | | |
|---|---|---|---|---|
| *122c* | A66 | ½c | 30.00 | 19.00 |
| *123c* | A66 | 1c | 47.50 | 27.50 |
| *124c* | A66 | 2c | 10.00 | 5.00 |
| *125c* | A66 | 3c | 325.00 | 200.00 |
| *126b* | A66 | 4c | 400.00 | |
| *127c* | A66 | 5c | 10.00 | 5.00 |
| *128c* | A66 | 6c | 17.00 | 10.00 |
| *129c* | A66 | 10c | 17.00 | 10.00 |
| *132d* | A66 | 15c | 40.00 | 23.00 |
| *138a* | A66 | 50c | 165.00 | |

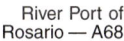

River Port of Rosario — A68

**1902, Oct. 26** *Perf. 11½, 11½x12*

| | | | | | |
|---|---|---|---|---|---|
| **143** | A68 | 5c | deep blue | 4.75 | 2.00 |
| *a.* | | | Imperf., pair | 95.00 | |
| *b.* | | | Vert. pair, imperf. btwn. | 60.00 | |
| *c.* | | | Horiz. pair, imperf. btwn. | 90.00 | |

Completion of port facilities at Rosario.

San Martin
A69 A70

**1908-09** **Typo.** *Perf. 13½x12½*

| | | | | | |
|---|---|---|---|---|---|
| **144** | A69 | ½c | violet | .50 | .30 |
| **145** | A69 | 1c | brnsh buff | .50 | .30 |
| **146** | A69 | 2c | chocolate | .60 | .30 |
| **147** | A69 | 3c | green | .65 | .40 |
| **148** | A69 | 4c | redsh violet | 1.25 | .40 |
| **149** | A69 | 5c | carmine | .60 | .30 |
| **150** | A69 | 6c | olive bister | .75 | .40 |
| **151** | A69 | 10c | gray green | 1.75 | .30 |
| **152** | A69 | 12c | yellow buff | 1.00 | .60 |
| **153** | A69 | 12c | dk blue ('09) | 1.75 | .30 |
| **155** | A69 | 20c | ultra | 1.25 | .30 |
| **156** | A69 | 24c | red brown | 3.50 | .60 |
| **157** | A69 | 30c | dull rose | 6.00 | .60 |
| **158** | A69 | 50c | black | 6.00 | .50 |
| **159** | A70 | 1p | sl bl & pink | 18.00 | 2.50 |
| | *Nos. 144-159 (15)* | | | 44.10 | 8.10 |

The 1c blue was not issued. Value $500.

Wmk. 86 appears on ½, 1, 6, 20, 24 and 50c. Other values have similar wmk. with wavy rays.

Stamps lacking wmk. are from outer rows printed on sheet margin.

*Perf. 13½*

| | | | | | |
|---|---|---|---|---|---|
| **146A** | A69 | 2c | chocolate | 1.20 | .25 |
| **147A** | A69 | 3c | green | 2.00 | 1.00 |
| **148A** | A69 | 4c | redsh violet | 1.30 | .50 |
| **149A** | A69 | 5c | carmine | 1.00 | .30 |
| **151A** | A69 | 10c | gray green | 6.25 | 2.25 |
| **152A** | A69 | 12c | yellow buff | 1.20 | .70 |
| **153A** | A69 | 12c | dk blue ('09) | 4.25 | 1.00 |
| **154A** | A69 | 15c | apple green | .60 | .50 |
| **156A** | A69 | 24c | red brown | 4.75 | 1.30 |
| **157A** | A69 | 30c | dull rose | 9.50 | 1.30 |
| **159A** | A70 | 1p | sl bl & pink | 20.00 | 3.00 |

Pyramid of May — A71

Nicolas Rodriguez Pena and Hipolito Vieytes — A72

Meeting at Pena's Home — A73

Designs: 3c, Miguel de Azcuenaga (1754-1833) and Father Manuel M. Alberti (1763-1811). 4c, Viceroy's house and Fort Buenos Aires. 5c, Cornelio Saavedra (1759-1829). 10c, Antonio Luis Beruti (1772-1842) and French distributing badges. 12c, Congress building. 20c, Juan Jose Castelli (1764-1812) and Domingo Matheu (1765-1831). 24c, First council. 30c, Manuel Belgrano (1770-1820) and Juan Larrea (1782-1847). 50c, First meeting of republican government, May 25, 1810. 1p, Mariano Moreno (1778-1811) and Juan Jose Paso (1758-1833). 5p, Oath of the Junta. 10p, Centenary Monument. 20p, Jose Francisco de San Martin (1778-1850).

### Inscribed "1810 1910"
Various Frames

**1910, May 1** **Engr.** *Perf. 11½*

| | | | | | |
|---|---|---|---|---|---|
| **160** | A71 | ½c | bl & gray bl | .30 | .25 |
| **161** | A72 | 1c | bl grn & blk | .30 | .30 |
| *b.* | | | Horiz. pair, imperf. btwn. | 65.00 | |
| **162** | A73 | 2c | olive & gray | .25 | .30 |
| **163** | A72 | 3c | green | .70 | .40 |
| **164** | A73 | 4c | dk blue & grn | .70 | .40 |
| **165** | A71 | 5c | carmine | .40 | .25 |
| **166** | A73 | 10c | yel brn & blk | 1.10 | .50 |
| **167** | A73 | 12c | brt blue | 1.10 | .50 |
| **168** | A72 | 20c | gray brn & blk | 3.25 | .60 |
| **169** | A73 | 24c | org brn & bl | 1.75 | 1.25 |
| **170** | A72 | 30c | lilac & blk | 1.75 | 1.00 |
| **171** | A71 | 50c | car & blk | 4.50 | 1.25 |
| **172** | A72 | 1p | brt blue | 9.50 | 3.25 |
| **173** | A73 | 5p | orange & vio | 72.50 | 35.00 |
| | | | Punch cancel | | 5.00 |
| **174** | A71 | 10p | orange & blk | 90.00 | 62.50 |
| | | | Punch cancel | | 10.00 |
| **175** | A71 | 20p | dp blue & ind | 160.00 | 100.00 |
| | | | Punch cancel | | 15.00 |
| | *Nos. 160-175 (16)* | | | 338.10 | 207.75 |

Centenary of the republic.

### Center Inverted

| | | | |
|---|---|---|---|
| *160a* | A71 | ½c | *1,000.* |
| *161a* | A72 | 1c | *1,000.* |
| *162a* | A73 | 2c | *800.00* |
| *164a* | A73 | 4c | *650.00* |
| *167a* | A73 | 12c | *1,000.* |
| *171a* | A71 | 50c | *1,000.* |
| *173a* | A73 | 5p | *750.00* |

Domingo F. Sarmiento — A87

**1911, May 15** **Typo.** *Perf. 13½*

| | | | | | |
|---|---|---|---|---|---|
| **176** | A87 | 5c | gray brn & blk | .80 | .40 |

Domingo Faustino Sarmiento (1811-88), pres. of Argentina, 1868-74.

Agriculture — A88

### Size: 19x25mm

### Wmk. 86, without Face

**1911** **Engr.** *Perf. 12*

| | | | | | |
|---|---|---|---|---|---|
| **177** | A88 | 5c | vermilion | .40 | .25 |
| **178** | A88 | 12c | deep blue | 5.00 | .50 |

### Size: 18x23mm

### Wmk. 86, with Face

**1911** **Typo.** *Perf. 13½x12½*

| | | | | | |
|---|---|---|---|---|---|
| **179** | A88 | ½c | violet | .50 | .30 |
| **180** | A88 | 1c | brown ocher | .30 | .30 |
| **181** | A88 | 2c | chocolate | .30 | .25 |
| *a.* | | | Perf. 13½ | 15.00 | 4.00 |
| *b.* | | | Imperf., pair | *40.00* | |
| **182** | A88 | 3c | green | .50 | .50 |
| **183** | A88 | 4c | brown violet | .50 | .30 |
| **184** | A88 | 10c | gray green | .50 | .30 |
| **185** | A88 | 20c | ultra | 1.50 | .65 |
| **186** | A88 | 24c | red brown | 6.50 | 3.75 |
| **187** | A88 | 30c | claret | 3.50 | .50 |
| **188** | A88 | 50c | black | 8.00 | .80 |
| | *Nos. 179-188 (10)* | | | 25.10 | 7.95 |

The 5c dull red is a proof. In this issue Wmk. 86 comes: straight rays (4c, 20c, 24c) and wavy rays (2c). All other values exist with both forms.

**Wmk. 87 (Horiz. or Vert.)**

**1912-14** *Perf. 13½x12½*

| | | | | | |
|---|---|---|---|---|---|
| **189** | A88 | ½c | violet | .30 | .30 |
| **190** | A88 | 1c | ocher | .30 | .30 |
| **191** | A88 | 2c | chocolate | .50 | .30 |
| **192** | A88 | 3c | green | .50 | .50 |
| **193** | A88 | 4c | brown violet | .50 | .60 |
| **194** | A88 | 5c | red | .40 | .30 |
| **195** | A88 | 10c | deep green | 1.75 | .30 |
| **196** | A88 | 12c | deep blue | .60 | .30 |
| **197** | A88 | 20c | ultra | 3.25 | .50 |
| **198** | A88 | 24c | red brown | 6.50 | 2.00 |
| **199** | A88 | 30c | claret | 5.50 | 7.00 |
| **200** | A88 | 50c | black | 10.00 | .90 |
| | *Nos. 189-200 (12)* | | | 30.10 | 13.30 |

See Nos. 208-212. For overprints see Nos. OD1-OD8, OD47-OD54, OD102-OD108, OD146-OD152, OD183-OD190, OD235-OD241, OD281-OD284, OD318-OD323.

*Perf. 13½*

| | | | | |
|---|---|---|---|---|
| *189a* | A88 | ½c | 1.00 | .50 |
| *190a* | A88 | 1c | 1.00 | .50 |
| *191a* | A88 | 2c | 1.00 | .50 |
| *192a* | A88 | 3c | 150.00 | 30.00 |
| *193a* | A88 | 4c | 2.50 | 1.25 |
| *194a* | A88 | 5c | .90 | .50 |
| *196a* | A88 | 12c | 3.50 | 1.50 |
| *197a* | A88 | 20c | 9.00 | .90 |
| | *Nos. 189a-197a (8)* | | 168.90 | 35.65 |

A89

**1912-13** *Perf. 13½*

| | | | | | |
|---|---|---|---|---|---|
| **201** | A89 | 1p | dull bl & rose | 10.00 | 1.10 |
| | | | Punch cancel | | .35 |
| **202** | A89 | 5p | slate & ol grn | 19.00 | 7.00 |
| | | | Punch cancel | | 1.00 |
| **203** | A89 | 10p | violet & blue | 75.00 | 17.50 |
| | | | Punch cancel | | 1.40 |
| **204** | A89 | 20p | blue & claret | 210.00 | 80.00 |
| | | | Punch cancel | | 2.00 |
| | *Nos. 201-204 (4)* | | | 314.00 | 105.60 |

**1915** **Unwmk.** *Perf. 13½x12½*

| | | | | | |
|---|---|---|---|---|---|
| **208** | A88 | 1c | ocher | 1.50 | .30 |
| **209** | A88 | 2c | chocolate | 1.50 | .30 |
| **212** | A88 | 5c | red | 1.50 | .30 |
| | *Nos. 208-212 (3)* | | | 4.50 | .90 |

Only these denominations were printed on paper without watermark.

Other stamps of the series are known unwatermarked but they are from the outer rows of sheets the other parts of which are watermarked.

Francisco Narciso de Laprida
A90

Declaration of Independence
A91

A92 A92a
Jose de San Martin

*Perf. 13½, 13½x12½*

**1916, July 9** **Litho.** **Wmk. 87**

| | | | | | |
|---|---|---|---|---|---|
| **215** | A90 | ½c | violet | .60 | .30 |
| **216** | A90 | 1c | buff | .50 | .30 |

*Perf. 13½x12½*

| | | | | | |
|---|---|---|---|---|---|
| **217** | A90 | 2c | chocolate | .60 | .30 |
| **218** | A90 | 3c | green | .60 | .60 |
| **219** | A90 | 4c | red violet | .60 | .60 |

*Perf. 13½*

| | | | | | |
|---|---|---|---|---|---|
| **220** | A91 | 5c | red | .50 | .30 |
| *a.* | | | Imperf., pair | *40.00* | |
| **221** | A91 | 10c | gray green | 1.60 | .30 |
| **222** | A92 | 12c | blue | .90 | .35 |
| **223** | A92 | 20c | ultra | .70 | .70 |
| **224** | A92 | 24c | red brown | 2.75 | 1.40 |
| **225** | A92 | 30c | claret | 2.75 | 1.60 |
| **226** | A92 | 50c | gray black | 6.75 | 1.60 |
| **227** | A92a | 1p | slate bl & red | 10.00 | 10.00 |
| | | | Punch cancel | | .50 |
| *a.* | | | Imperf., pair | *325.00* | |
| **228** | A92a | 5p | black & gray grn | 100.00 | 80.00 |
| | | | Punch cancel | | 15.00 |
| **229** | A92a | 10p | violet & blue | 150.00 | 135.00 |
| | | | Punch cancel | | 9.00 |
| **230** | A92a | 20p | dull blue & cl | 150.00 | 100.00 |
| | | | Punch cancel | | 7.00 |
| *a.* | | | Imperf., pair | 650.00 | |
| | *Nos. 215-230 (16)* | | | 428.75 | 333.35 |

Cent. of Argentina's declaration of independence of Spain, July 9, 1816.

The watermark is either vert. or horiz. on Nos. 215-220, 222; only vert. on No. 221, and only horiz. on Nos. 223-230.

For overprints see Nos. OD9, OD55-OD56, OD109, OD153, OD191-OD192, OD285, OD324.

A93

A94

A94a

**1917** *Perf. 13½*

| | | | | | |
|---|---|---|---|---|---|
| **231** | A93 | ½c | violet | .60 | .60 |
| *a.* | | | Imperf. pair | 70.00 | |
| **232** | A93 | 1c | buff | .60 | .30 |
| *a.* | | | Imperf. pair | 70.00 | |
| **233** | A93 | 2c | brown | .60 | .30 |
| *a.* | | | Imperf. pair | 70.00 | |
| **234** | A93 | 3c | lt green | 1.00 | .30 |
| *a.* | | | Imperf. pair | 70.00 | |
| **235** | A93 | 4c | red violet | 1.50 | .60 |
| *a.* | | | Imperf. pair | 70.00 | |
| **236** | A93 | 5c | red | 1.25 | .50 |
| | | | Never hinged | 1.90 | |
| *a.* | | | Imperf. pair | *15.00* | |
| **237** | A93 | 10c | gray green | 4.00 | .50 |
| *a.* | | | Imperf. pair | *70.00* | |
| | *Nos. 231-237 (7)* | | | 9.55 | 3.10 |

*Perf. 13½x12½*

| | | | | | |
|---|---|---|---|---|---|
| **231B** | A93 | ½c | violet | .30 | .30 |
| **232B** | A93 | 1c | buff | .40 | .40 |
| **233B** | A93 | 2c | brown | .40 | .40 |
| **234B** | A93 | 3c | lt green | 1.00 | .30 |
| **235B** | A93 | 4c | red violet | 2.00 | .50 |
| **236B** | A93 | 5c | red | .30 | .30 |
| **237B** | A93 | 10c | gray green | 3.00 | .25 |
| | *Nos. 231B-237B (7)* | | | 7.40 | 2.45 |

*Perf. 13½*

| | | | | | |
|---|---|---|---|---|---|
| **238** | A94 | 12c | blue | 1.00 | .25 |
| **239** | A94 | 20c | ultra | 2.50 | .30 |
| **240** | A94 | 24c | red brown | 6.00 | 3.00 |
| **241** | A94 | 30c | claret | 6.00 | 1.50 |
| **242** | A94 | 50c | gray black | 6.00 | .60 |
| **243** | A94a | 1p | slate bl & red | 6.00 | .60 |
| **244** | A94a | 5p | blk & gray grn | 19.00 | 3.00 |
| | | | Punch cancel | | 1.50 |
| **245** | A94a | 10p | violet & blue | 47.50 | 12.00 |
| | | | Punch cancel | | 1.50 |
| **246** | A94a | 20p | dull blue & cl | 90.00 | 50.00 |
| | | | Punch cancel | | 1.00 |
| *a.* | | | Center inverted | 1,500. | 1,500. |
| | *Nos. 231-246 (16)* | | | 193.55 | 74.35 |

The watermark is either vert. or horiz. on Nos. 231-236, 238 and 231B-236B, 238B; only vert. on No. 237 and 237B, and only horiz. on Nos. 239-246.

All known examples of No. 246a are off-center to the right.

See Nos. 292-300, 304-307A, 310-314, 318, 322.

For overprints see Nos. OD10-OD20, OD57-OD71, OD74, OD110-OD121, OD154-OD159, OD161-OD162, OD193-OD207, OD209-OD211, OD242-OD252, OD254-OD255, OD286-OD290, OD325-OD328, OD330.

Juan Gregorio Pujol — A95

**1918, June 15** **Litho.** *Perf. 13½*

| | | | | | |
|---|---|---|---|---|---|
| **247** | A95 | 5c | bister & gray | .60 | .35 |

Cent. of the birth of Juan G. Pujol (1817-61), lawyer and legislator.

**1918-19** **Unwmk.** *Perf. 13½*

| | | | | | |
|---|---|---|---|---|---|
| **248** | A93 | ½c | violet | .30 | .25 |
| **249** | A93 | 1c | buff | .30 | .25 |
| *a.* | | | Imperf., pair | 35.00 | |
| **250** | A93 | 2c | brown | .30 | .25 |
| **251** | A93 | 3c | lt green | .50 | .25 |
| **252** | A93 | 4c | red violet | .50 | .25 |
| **253** | A93 | 5c | red | .80 | .25 |
| **254** | A93 | 10c | gray green | .80 | .25 |
| **255** | A94 | 12c | blue | 1.25 | .25 |
| **256** | A94 | 20c | ultra | 2.00 | .25 |
| **257** | A94 | 24c | red brown | 2.40 | .25 |

258 A94 30c claret 3.00 .35
259 A94 50c gray black 8.00 1.25
*Nos. 248-259 (12)* 20.15 4.10

***Perf. 13½x12½***

248B A93 ½c violet .70 .50
249B A93 1c buff .70 .50
250B A93 2c brown .70 .50
251B A93 3c lt green .90 .50
252B A93 4c red violet .90 .50
253B A93 5c red .60 .50
254B A93 10c gray green 2.00 .50
*Nos. 248B-254B (7)* 6.50 3.50

The stamps of this issue sometimes show letters of papermakers' watermarks.

There were two printings, in 1918 and 1923, using different ink and paper.

**1920** **Wmk. 88**

264 A93 ½c violet .50 .25
265 A93 1c buff .50 .25
266 A93 2c brown .50 .25
267 A93 3c green 2.00 1.00
268 A93 4c red violet 2.50 1.50
269 A93 5c red .50 .25
270 A93 10c gray green 6.00 .30

***Perf. 13½***

264A A93 ½c violet .80 .30
265A A93 1c buff .80 .30
266A A93 2c brown 1.00 .30
267A A93 3c green 2.00 1.00
269A A93 5c red 4.00 .30
270A A93 10c gray green 55.00 15.00
271 A94 12c blue 3.00 .30
272 A94 20c ultra 4.25 .40
274 A94 30c claret 15.00 3.00
275 A94 50c gray black 10.00 3.00
*Nos. 264-275 (17)* 108.35 27.70

Belgrano's Mausoleum A96

Creation of Argentine Flag A97

Gen. Manuel Belgrano — A98

**1920, June 18**

280 A96 2c red 1.00 .30
*a.* Perf. 13½x12½ 3.00 1.00
281 A97 5c rose & blue 1.00 .30
282 A98 12c green & blue 2.00 1.00
*Nos. 280-282 (3)* 4.00 1.60

Belgrano (1770-1820), Argentine general, patriot and diplomat.

Gen. Justo Jose de Urquiza — A99

**1920, Nov. 11**

283 A99 5c gray blue .60 .35

Gen. Justo Jose de Urquiza (1801-70), pres. of Argentina, 1854-60. See No. 303.

Bartolome Mitre — A100

**1921, June 26** **Unwmk.**

284 A100 2c violet brown .50 .35
285 A100 5c light blue .50 .35

Bartolome Mitre (1821-1906), pres. of Argentina, 1862-65.

Allegory, Pan-America — A101

**1921, Aug. 25** ***Perf. 13½***

286 A101 3c violet 1.50 .35
287 A101 5c blue 2.00 .35
288 A101 10c vio brown 3.00 .50
289 A101 12c rose 3.50 1.00
*Nos. 286-289 (4)* 10.00 2.20

Inscribed "Buenos Aires-Agosto de 1921" A102

Inscribed "Republica Argentina" A103

**1921, Oct.** ***Perf. 13½x12½***

290 A102 5c rose 1.25 .35
291 A103 5c rose 7.00 10.50

***Perf. 13½***

290A A102 5c rose 6.00 .50
291A A103 5c rose 7.00 .60

1st Pan-American Postal Cong., Buenos Aires, Aug., 1921.

See Nos. 308-309, 319. For overprints see Nos. OD72, OD160, OD208, OD253, OD329.

**1920** **Wmk. 89** ***Perf. 13½x12½***

292 A93 ½c violet 1.60 .80
293 A93 1c buff 4.50 1.50
294 A93 2c brown 4.00 .50
297 A93 5c red 5.00 .35
298 A93 10c gray green 5.00 .35

***Perf. 13½***

294A A93 2c brown 7.00 1.50
297A A93 5c red 52.50 9.00
298A A93 10c gray green 40.00 2.00
299 A94 12c blue *6,000.* 200.00
300 A94 20c ultra 12.00 1.50

**1920** **Wmk. 89**

303 A99 5c gray blue 500.00 400.00

**1922-23** **Wmk. 90** ***Perf. 13½***

304 A93 ½c violet .60 .25
305 A93 1c buff 1.00 .30
306 A93 2c brown 1.00 .30
307 A93 3c green .60 .40
307A A93 4c red violet 1.50 1.00
308 A102 5c rose 10.00 3.00
309 A103 5c red 5.00 .80
310 A93 10c gray green 9.00 1.00
311 A94 12c blue 1.00 .40
312 A94 20c ultra 2.00 .50
313 A94 24c red brown 20.00 10.00
314 A94 30c claret 10.00 1.00

***Perf. 13½x12½***

304B A93 ½c violet .50 .30
305B A93 1c buff .50 .30
306B A93 2c brown .50 .30
307B A93 3c green 1.00 .80
307C A93 4c red violet 22.50 10.00
308B A102 5c rose 6.00 1.00
309B A103 5c red .60 .30
310B A93 10c gray green 2.25 .25
*Nos. 304-310B (20)* 95.55 32.20

**Paper with Gray Overprint RA in Sun**

**1922-23** **Unwmk.** ***Perf. 13½***

318 A93 2c brown 10.00 2.50
319 A103 5c red 15.00 2.50
322 A94 20c ultra 50.00 5.00

***Perf. 13½x12½***

318A A93 2c brown 10.00 2.50
319A A103 5c red 8.50 2.50

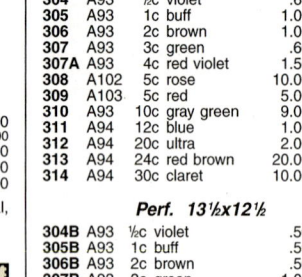

A104

San Martín — A105

**With Period after Value**

***Perf. 13½x12½***

**1923, May** **Litho.** **Wmk. 90**

323 A104 ½c red violet .50 .30
324 A104 1c buff .80 .30
325 A104 2c dark brown .60 .30
326 A104 3c lt green .80 .40
327 A104 4c red brown .80 .40
328 A104 5c red .80 .30
329 A104 10c dull green 7.00 .30
330 A104 12c deep blue .70 .30
331 A104 20c ultra 2.00 .30
332 A104 24c lt brown 5.00 3.00
333 A104 30c claret 16.00 .80
334 A104 50c black 62.00 7.00

***Perf. 13½***

323A A104 ½c red violet .80 .30
324A A104 1c buff 1.50 .30
325A A104 2c dark brown 41.00 .30
326A A104 3c lt green 3.00 1.00
327A A104 4c red brown 3.00 1.00
328A A104 5c red 3.00 .30
329A A104 10c dull green 10.00 1.00
330A A104 12c deep blue 12.50 3.00
331A A104 20c ultra 11.00 .70
332A A104 24c lt brown 20.00 5.00
333A A104 30c claret 20.00 3.00
334A A104 50c black 8.00 1.00

**Without Period after Value**

***Perf. 13½***

**Wmk. 87**

335 A105 1p blue & red 10.00 .80
336 A105 5p gray lil & grn 30.00 6.00
Punch cancel 1.00
337 A105 10p clar & blue 90.00 15.00
Punch cancel 2.00
338 A105 20p sl & brn lake 120.00 45.00
Punch cancel 1.25
*Nos. 323-338 (28)* 480.80 97.40

Nos. 335-338 and 353-356 canceled with round or oval killers in purple (revenue cancellations) sell for one-fifth to one-half as much as postally used copies.

For overprints see Nos. 399-404.

**Design of 1923**
**Without Period after Value**

***Perf. 13½x12½***

**1923-24** **Litho.** **Wmk. 90**

340 A104 ½c red violet .50 .30
341 A104 1c buff .50 .30
342 A104 2c dk brown .50 .30
343 A104 3c green .60 .30
*a.* Imperf., pair 60.00
344 A104 4c red brown .80 .30
345 A104 5c red .50 .30
346 A104 10c dull green .50 .30
347 A104 12c deep blue .80 .30
348 A104 20c ultra 1.00 .30
349 A104 24c lt brown 4.00 1.25
350 A104 25c purple 2.00 .40
351 A104 30c claret 4.00 .40
352 A104 50c black 6.00 .40

***Perf. 13½***

340B A104 ½c red violet 180.00 60.00
345B A104 5c red 75.00 30.00
346B A104 10c dull green 75.00 30.00
349B A104 24c lt brown 150.00 50.00
353 A105 1p blue & red 6.00 .70
354 A105 5p dk vio & grn 35.00 2.00
355 A105 10p claret & blue 75.00 8.00
356 A105 20p slate & lake 120.00 15.00
*Nos. 340-356 (21)* 737.70 200.85

**1931-33** **Typo.**

*343b* A104 3c 3.00 .50
*345a* A104 5c 4.50 .50
*346a* A104 10c 7.50 .50
*347a* A104 12c 15.00 3.50
*348a* A104 20c 55.00 3.50
*350a* A104 25c 40.00 2.00
*351a* A104 30c 25.00 1.50
*Nos. 343b-351a (7)* 150.00 12.00

The typographed stamps were issued only in coils and have a rough impression with heavy shading about the eyes and nose. Nos. 343 and 346 are known without watermark.

Nos. 341-345, 347-349, 351a may be found in pairs, one with period.

See note after No. 338. See Nos. 362-368. For overprints see Nos. OD21-OD33, OD75-OD87, OD122-OD133, OD163-OD175, OD212-OD226, OD256-OD268, OD291-OD304, OD331-OD345.

Rivadavia — A106

**1926, Feb. 8** ***Perf. 13½***

357 A106 5c rose .60 .35

Presidency of Bernardino Rivadavia, cent.

Rivadavia A108

San Martin A109

General Post Office, 1926 A110

General Post Office, 1826 A111

**1926, July 1** ***Perf. 13½x12½***

358 A108 3c gray green .50 .30
359 A109 5c red .50 .30

***Perf. 13½***

360 A110 12c deep blue 1.25 .40
361 A111 25c chocolate 3.25 .80
*a.* "1326" for "1826" 15.00 10.00
*Nos. 358-361 (4)* 5.50 1.80

Centenary of the Post Office.

For overprints see Nos. OD34, OD88, OD134, OD227-OD228, OD269, OD305, OD346.

**Type of 1923-31 Issue**
**Without Period after Value**

**1927** **Wmk. 205** ***Perf. 13½x12½***

362 A104 ½c red violet .70 .60
*a.* Pelure paper 2.75 2.50
363 A104 1c buff .70 .60
364 A104 2c dark brown .70 .35
*a.* Pelure paper 1.00 .70
365 A104 5c red 1.00 .35
*a.* Period after value 15.00 9.00
*b.* Pelure paper 1.00 .70
366 A104 10c dull green 6.00 3.50
367 A104 20c ultra 60.00 6.00

***Perf. 13½***

368 A105 1p blue & red 45.00 8.50
*Nos. 362-368 (7)* 114.10 19.90

Arms of Argentina and Brazil — A112

**Wmk. RA in Sun (90)**

**1928, Aug. 27** ***Perf. 12½x13***

369 A112 5c rose red 1.50 .40
370 A112 12c deep blue 2.50 .70

Cent. of peace between the Empire of Brazil and the United Provinces of the Rio de la Plata.

Allegory, Discovery of the New World A113

"Spain" and "Argentina" A114

"America" Offering Laurels to Columbus — A115

**1929, Oct. 12** **Litho.** ***Perf. 13½***

371 A113 2c lilac brown 2.00 .40
372 A114 5c light red 2.00 .40
373 A115 12c dull blue 6.00 1.00
*Nos. 371-373 (3)* 10.00 1.80

Discovery of America by Columbus, 437th anniv.

Spirit of Victory Attending Insurgents A116

March of the Victorious Insurgents A117

***Perf. 13½x12½ (A116), 12½x13 (A117)***

**1930**

| | | | | | |
|---|---|---|---|---|---|
| **374** | A116 | ½c | violet gray | 1.00 | .50 |
| **375** | A116 | 1c | myrtle green | 1.00 | .50 |
| **376** | A117 | 2c | dull violet | 1.00 | .50 |
| **377** | A116 | 3c | green | 1.00 | .50 |
| **378** | A116 | 4c | violet | 1.00 | .70 |
| **379** | A116 | 5c | rose red | 1.00 | .30 |
| **380** | A116 | 10c | gray black | 1.00 | .70 |
| **381** | A117 | 12c | dull blue | 1.75 | .80 |
| **382** | A117 | 20c | ocher | 2.00 | 1.00 |
| **383** | A117 | 24c | red brown | 6.50 | 2.50 |
| **384** | A117 | 25c | green | 7.50 | 2.50 |
| **385** | A117 | 30c | deep violet | 9.50 | 3.50 |
| **386** | A117 | 50c | black | 13.00 | 6.25 |
| **387** | A117 | 1p | sl bl & red | 25.00 | 10.00 |
| **388** | A117 | 2p | black & org | 37.50 | 14.00 |
| **389** | A117 | 5p | dull grn & blk | 100.00 | 35.00 |
| **390** | A117 | 10p | dp red brn & dull blue | 140.00 | 47.50 |
| **391** | A117 | 20p | yel grn & dl bl | 260.00 | 125.00 |
| **392** | A117 | 50p | dk grn & vio | 900.00 | 800.00 |
| | | | *Nos. 374-390 (17)* | 349.75 | 126.75 |

Revolution of 1930.

Nos. 387-392 with oval (parcel post) cancellation sell for less.

For overprint see No. 405.

**1931** ***Perf. 12½x13***

| | | | | | |
|---|---|---|---|---|---|
| **393** | A117 | ½c | red violet | 1.00 | .60 |
| **394** | A117 | 1c | gray black | 1.50 | 1.00 |
| **395** | A117 | 3c | green | 1.50 | .70 |
| **396** | A117 | 4c | red brown | 1.00 | .50 |
| **397** | A117 | 5c | red | .80 | .50 |
| *a.* | | | Plane omitted, top left corner | 10.00 | 8.00 |
| **398** | A117 | 10c | dull green | 1.90 | .80 |
| | | | *Nos. 393-398 (6)* | 7.70 | 4.00 |

Revolution of 1930.

Stamps of 1924-25 Overprinted in Red or Green

**1931, Sept. 6** ***Perf. 13½, 13½x12½***

| | | | | | |
|---|---|---|---|---|---|
| **399** | A104 | 3c | green | .50 | .50 |
| **400** | A104 | 10c | dull green | .70 | .70 |
| **401** | A104 | 30c | claret (G) | 5.00 | 3.25 |
| **402** | A104 | 50c | black | 5.00 | 3.25 |

Overprinted in Blue

| | | | | | |
|---|---|---|---|---|---|
| **403** | A105 | 1p | blue & red | 6.00 | 3.25 |
| **404** | A105 | 5p | dk violet & grn | 60.00 | 22.50 |

No. 388 Overprinted in Blue

***Perf. 12½x13***

| | | | | | |
|---|---|---|---|---|---|
| **405** | A117 | 2p | black & orange | 12.00 | 8.00 |
| | | | *Nos. 399-405 (7)* | 89.20 | 41.45 |

1st anniv. of the Revolution of 1930. See Nos. C30-C34.

Refrigeration Compressor — A118

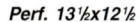

***Perf. 13½x12½***

**1932, Aug. 29** **Litho.**

| | | | | | |
|---|---|---|---|---|---|
| **406** | A118 | 3c | green | 1.25 | .50 |
| **407** | A118 | 10c | scarlet | 2.25 | .40 |
| **408** | A118 | 12c | gray blue | 7.50 | 1.10 |
| | | | *Nos. 406-408 (3)* | 11.00 | 2.00 |

6th Intl. Refrigeration Congress.

Port of La Plata A119

Pres. Julio A. Roca A120

Municipal Palace — A121

Cathedral of La Plata — A122

Dardo Rocha — A123

***Perf. 13½x13, 13x13½ (10c)***

**1933, Jan.**

| | | | | | |
|---|---|---|---|---|---|
| **409** | A119 | 3c | green & dk brn | .50 | .30 |
| **410** | A120 | 10c | orange & dk vio | .70 | .30 |
| **411** | A121 | 15c | dk bl & dp bl | 2.50 | 1.50 |
| **412** | A122 | 20c | violet & yel brn | 2.25 | 1.00 |
| **413** | A123 | 30c | dk grn & vio brn | 14.00 | 7.00 |
| | | | *Nos. 409-413 (5)* | 19.95 | 10.10 |

50th anniv. of the founding of the city of La Plata, Nov. 19th, 1882.

Christ of the Andes A124

Buenos Aires Cathedral A125

**1934, Oct. 1** ***Perf. 13x13½, 13½x13***

| | | | | | |
|---|---|---|---|---|---|
| **414** | A124 | 10c | rose & brown | 1.00 | .30 |
| **415** | A125 | 15c | dark blue | 3.00 | .60 |

32nd Intl. Eucharistic Cong., Oct. 10-14.

"Liberty" with Arms of Brazil and Argentina A126

Symbolical of "Peace" and "Friendship" A127

**1935, May 15** ***Perf. 13x13½***

| | | | | | |
|---|---|---|---|---|---|
| **416** | A126 | 10c | red | 1.00 | .30 |
| **417** | A127 | 15c | blue | 2.00 | .60 |

Visit of Pres. Getulio Vargas of Brazil.

Belgrano A128

Sarmiento A129

Urquiza A130

Louis Braille A131

San Martin A132

Brown A133

Moreno A134

Alberdi A135

Nicolas Avellaneda A136

Rivadavia A137

Mitre A138

Bull (Cattle Breeding) A139

Martin Güemes A140

Agriculture A141

Merino Sheep (Wool) — A142

Sugar Cane — A143

Oil Well (Petroleum) — A144

Map of South America A145 A146

Fruit A147

Iguacu Falls (Scenic Wonders) A148

Grapes (Vineyards) A149

Cotton A150

Two types of A140:
Type I — Inscribed Juan Martin Guemes.
Type II — Inscribed Martin Güemes.

***Perf. 13, 13½x13, 13x13½***

**1935-51** **Litho.** **Wmk. 90**

| | | | | | |
|---|---|---|---|---|---|
| **418** | A128 | ½c | red violet | .30 | .25 |
| **419** | A129 | 1c | buff | .30 | .25 |
| *a.* | | | Typo. | 3.00 | .25 |
| **420** | A130 | 2c | dark brown | .50 | .25 |
| **421** | A131 | 2½c | black ('39) | .40 | .25 |
| **422** | A132 | 3c | green | .60 | .25 |
| **423** | A132 | 3c | lt gray ('39) | .60 | .25 |
| **424** | A134 | 3c | lt gray ('46) | .50 | .25 |
| **425** | A133 | 4c | lt gray | .60 | .25 |
| **426** | A133 | 4c | sage grn ('39) | .50 | .25 |
| **427** | A134 | 5c | yel brn, typo. | .80 | .25 |
| *a.* | | | Tete beche pair, typo. | 20.00 | 10.00 |
| *b.* | | | Booklet pane of 8, typo. | | |
| *c.* | | | Booklet pane of 4, typo. | | |
| *d.* | | | Litho. | 5.00 | .50 |
| **428** | A135 | 6c | olive green | .50 | .25 |
| **429** | A136 | 8c | orange ('39) | .50 | .25 |
| **430** | A137 | 10c | car, perf. 13½ (typo.) | 4.00 | .25 |
| *a.* | | | Perf. 13½x13 | 3.00 | .35 |
| **431** | A137 | 10c | brown ('42) | .40 | .25 |
| **432** | A138 | 12c | brown | 1.00 | .25 |
| **433** | A138 | 12c | red ('39) | .40 | .25 |
| **434** | A139 | 15c | slate bl ('36) | 1.50 | .25 |
| **435** | A139 | 15c | pale ultra ('39) | 3.00 | .25 |
| **436** | A140 | 15c | lt gray bl (II) ('42) | 50.00 | 3.00 |
| **437** | A140 | 20c | lt ultra (I) | 1.00 | .25 |
| **438** | A140 | 20c | lt ultra (II) ('36) | 1.00 | .25 |
| **439** | A140 | 20c | bl gray (II) ('39) | 3.00 | .25 |
| **439A** | A139 | 20c | dk bl & pale bl, ('42) 22x33mm | 1.00 | .25 |
| **440** | A139 | 20c | blue ('51) | 1.00 | .25 |
| *a.* | | | Typo. | .35 | .35 |
| **441** | A141 | 25c | car & pink ('36) | 1.25 | .25 |
| **442** | A142 | 30c | org brn & yel brown ('36) | 1.00 | .25 |
| **443** | A143 | 40c | dk vio ('36) | 1.00 | .25 |
| **444** | A144 | 50c | red & org ('36) | 1.00 | .25 |
| **445** | A145 | 1p | brn blk & lt bl ('36) | 25.00 | 1.00 |
| **446** | A146 | 1p | brn blk & lt bl ('37) | 16.00 | .30 |
| *a.* | | | Chalky paper | 100.00 | 2.00 |
| **447** | A147 | 2p | brn lake & dk ultra ('36) | 2.50 | .25 |
| **448** | A148 | 5p | ind & ol grn ('36) | 4.00 | .25 |
| **449** | A149 | 10p | brn lake & blk | 15.00 | 1.25 |
| **450** | A150 | 20p | bl grn & brn ('36) | 25.00 | 3.00 |
| | | | *Nos. 418-450 (34)* | 165.15 | 15.80 |

See Nos. 485-500, 523-540, 659, 668. For overprints see Nos. O07-O41, O43-O51, O53-O56, O58-O78, O108, O112, OD35-OD46, OD89-OD101, OD135-OD145, OD176-OD182C, OD229-OD234F, OD270-OD280, OD306-OD317, OD347-OD357.

No. 439A exists with attached label showing medallion. Value $42.50 unused, $22.50 used.

# ARGENTINA

### Souvenir Sheet

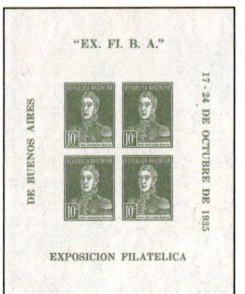
Plaque — A151

**Without Period after Value**

**1935, Oct. 17    Litho.    Imperf.**
452 A151   Sheet of 4   75.00   35.00
    a.   10c dull green   16.50   7.50

Phil. Exhib. at Buenos Aires, Oct. 17-24, 1935. The stamps were on sale during the 8 days of the exhibition only. Sheets measure 83x101mm.

Plaque — A152

**1936, Dec. 1    Perf. 13x13½**
453 A152 10c red   .80   .40

Inter-American Conference for Peace.

Domingo Faustino Sarmiento — A153

**1938, Sept. 5**
454 A153   3c sage green   .50   .50
455 A153   5c red   .50   .50
456 A153 15c deep blue   2.25   .70
457 A153 50c orange   4.25   1.00
    Nos. 454-457 (4)   7.50   2.70

50th anniv. of the death of Domingo Faustino Sarmiento, pres., educator and author.

"Presidente Sarmiento" — A154

**1939, Mar. 16**
458 A154 5c greenish blue   .80   .35

Final voyage of the training ship "Presidente Sarmiento."

Allegory of the UPU A155

Coat of Arms A157

Bonete Hill, Nahuel Huapi Park A159

Allegory of Modern Communications A160

Argentina, Land of Promise A161     Lake Frias, Nahuel Huapi Park A162

**Perf. 13x13½, 13½x13**

**1939, Apr. 1    Photo.**
459 A155   5c rose carmine   1.00   .25
460 A156 15c grnsh black   1.00   .40
461 A157 20c brt blue   1.00   .25
462 A158 25c dp blue grn   2.00   .40
463 A159 50c brown   3.00   1.00
464 A160   1p brown violet   6.50   2.75
465 A161   2p magenta   27.50   17.50
466 A162   5p purple   62.50   52.50
    Nos. 459-466 (8)   104.50   75.05

Universal Postal Union, 11th Congress.

### Souvenir Sheets

A163

A164

**1939, May 12    Wmk. 90    Imperf.**
467 A163   Sheet of 4   15.00   7.50
    a.   5c rose carmine (A155)   2.00   1.50
    b.   20c bright blue (A157)   2.00   1.50
    c.   25c deep blue green (A158)   2.00   1.50
    d.   50c brown (A159)   2.00   1.50
468 A164   Sheet of 4   15.00   7.50

**Issued in four forms:**
    a.   Unsevered horizontal pair of sheets, type A163 at left, A164 at right   30.00   16.00
    b.   Unsevered vertical pair of sheets, type A163 at top, A164 at bottom   30.00   15.00
    c.   Unsevered block of 4 sheets, type A163 at left, A164 at right   65.00   65.00
    d.   Unsevered block of 4 sheets, type A163 at top, A164 at bottom   65.00   65.00

11th Cong. of the UPU and the Argentina Intl. Phil. Exposition (C.Y.T.R.A.). No. 468 contains Nos. 467a-467d.

Family and New House — A165

**Perf. 13½x13**

**1939, Oct. 2    Litho.    Wmk. 90**
469 A165 5c bluish green   .50   .35

1st Pan-American Housing Congress.

Bird Carrying Record A166

Head of Liberty and Arms of Argentina A167

Record and Winged Letter — A168

**Perf. 13x13½, 13½x13 (#472)**

**1939, Dec. 11    Photo.**
470 A166 1.18p indigo   14.00   10.00
471 A167 1.32p bright blue   14.00   10.00
472 A168 1.50p dark brown   52.50   35.00
    Nos. 470-472 (3)   80.50   55.00

These stamps were issued for the recording and mailing of flexible phonograph records.

Map of the Americas — A169

**1940, Apr. 14    Perf. 13x13½**
473 A169 15c ultramarine   1.00   .35

50th anniv. of the Pan American Union.

### Souvenir Sheet

Reproductions of Early Argentine Stamps — A170

**Wmk. RA in Sun (90)**

**1940, May 25    Litho.    Imperf.**
474 A170   Sheet of 5   25.00   10.00
    a.   5c dark blue (Corrientes A2)   2.50   1.75
    b.   5c red (Argentina A1)   2.50   1.75
    c.   5c dark blue (Cordoba #1)   2.50   1.75
    d.   5c red (Argentina A3)   2.50   1.75
    e.   10c dark blue (Buenos Aires A1)   2.50   1.75

100th anniv. of the first postage stamp.

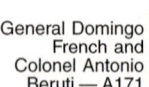

General Domingo French and Colonel Antonio Beruti — A171

**1941, Feb. 20    Perf. 13½x13**
475 A171 5c dk gray blue & lt blue   .60   .35

Issued in honor of General French and Colonel Beruti, patriots.

Marco M. de Avellaneda — A172

**1941, Oct. 3    Perf. 13x13½**
476 A172 5c dull slate blue   .60   .35

Avellaneda, (1814-41), army leader and martyr.

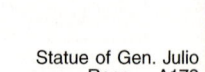
Statue of Gen. Julio Roca — A173

**1941, Oct. 19    Photo.    Wmk. 90**
477 A173 5c dark olive green   .50   .35

Dedication of a monument to Lt. Gen. Julio Argentino Roca (1843-1914).

Carlos Pellegrini and Bank of the Nation — A174

**1941, Oct. 26    Perf. 13½x13**
478 A174 5c brown carmine   .60   .35

Founding of the Bank of the Nation, 50th anniv.

Gen. Juan Lavalle — A175

**1941, Dec. 5    Perf. 13x13½**
479 A175 5c bright blue   .60   .35

Gen. Juan Galo de Lavalle (1797-1841).

National Postal Savings Bank — A176

**1942, Apr. 5    Litho.    Perf. 13½x13**
480 A176 1c pale olive   .60   .35

Jose Manuel Estrada — A177

**1942, July 13    Perf. 13x13½**
481 A177 5c brown violet   .60   .35

Jose Estrada (1842-1894), writer and diplomat.
    Exists imperf. Value, pair $45.
    No. 481 exists with label, showing medallion, attached. Value, pair $11.

### Types of 1935-51

**Perf. 13, 13x13½, 13½x13**

**1942-50    Litho.    Wmk. 288**
485 A128   ½c brown violet   10.00   2.00
486 A129   1c buff ('50)   .40   .30
487 A130   2c dk brown ('50)   .40   .25
488 A132   3c lt gray   16.00   1.25
489 A134   3c lt gray ('49)   .30   .25
490 A137 10c red brn ('49)   2.50   .25
491 A138 12c red   .50   .25
492 A140 15c lt gray blue (II)   1.00   .25
493 A139 20c dk sl bl & pale bl   4.50   .30
494 A141 25c dull rose ('49)   1.00   .25
495 A142 30c org brn ('49)   1.50   .25
496 A143 40c violet ('49)   10.00   1.00
497 A144 50c red & org ('49)   10.00   .50
498 A146   1p brn blk & lt bl   10.00   .40
499 A147   2p brn lake & bl ('49)   22.50   3.00
500 A148   5p ind & ol grn ('49)   65.00   4.00
    Nos. 485-500 (16)   155.60   14.50

No. 493 measures 22x33mm.

Post Office, Buenos Aires — A178

# ARGENTINA 581

Inscribed: "Correos y Telegrafos."

| 1942, Oct. 5 | | Litho. | Perf. 13 |
|---|---|---|---|
| 503 | A178 | 35c lt ultra | 10.00 .35 |

See Nos. 541-543.

Proposed Columbus Lighthouse — A179

| 1942, Oct. 12 | | | Wmk. 288 |
|---|---|---|---|
| 504 | A179 | 15c dull blue | 10.00 .50 |
| | | Wmk. 90 | |
| 505 | A179 | 15c dull blue | 70.00 8.00 |

450th anniv. of the discovery of America by Columbus.

Jose C. Paz — A180

| 1942, Dec. 15 | | | Wmk. 288 |
|---|---|---|---|
| 506 | A180 | 5c dark gray | .50 .35 |

Cent. of the birth of Jose C. Paz, stateman and founder of the newspaper La Prensa.

Books and Argentine Flag — A181

| 1943, Apr. 1 | | Litho. | Perf. 13 |
|---|---|---|---|
| 507 | A181 | 5c dull blue | .50 .35 |

1st Book Fair of Argentina.

Arms of Argentina Inscribed "Honesty, Justice, Duty" — A182

| 1943-50 | | Wmk. 288 | Perf. 13 |
|---|---|---|---|
| | | Size: 20x26mm | |
| 508 | A182 | 5c red ('50) | 6.00 .35 |
| | | Wmk. 90 | |
| 509 | A182 | 5c red | .60 .35 |
| a. | | 5c dull red, unsurfaced paper | 8.00 .35 |
| 510 | A182 | 15c green | .90 .35 |
| | | Perf. 13x13½ | |
| | | Size: 22x33mm | |
| 511 | A182 | 20c dark blue | .95 .35 |
| | Nos. 508-511 (4) | | 8.15 1.40 |

Change of political organization, 6/4/43.

Independence House, Tucuman — A183

| 1943-51 | | Wmk. 90 | Perf. 13 |
|---|---|---|---|
| 512 | A183 | 5c blue green | 1.00 .35 |
| | | Wmk. 288 | |
| 513 | A183 | 5c blue green ('51) | .30 .35 |

Restoration of Independence House.

Liberty Head and Savings Bank — A184

| 1943, Oct. 25 | | | Wmk. 90 |
|---|---|---|---|
| 514 | A184 | 5c violet brown | .50 .35 |
| | | Wmk. 288 | |
| 515 | A184 | 5c violet brown | 60.00 8.00 |

1st conference of National Postal Savings.

Port of Buenos Aires in 1800 — A185

| 1943, Dec. 11 | | | Wmk. 90 |
|---|---|---|---|
| 516 | A185 | 5c gray black | .50 .35 |

Day of Exports.

Warship, Merchant Ship and Sailboat — A186

| 1944, Jan. 31 | | | Perf. 13 |
|---|---|---|---|
| 517 | A186 | 5c blue | .60 .35 |

Issued to commemorate Sea Week.

Arms of Argentine Republic — A187

| 1944, June 4 | | | |
|---|---|---|---|
| 518 | A187 | 5c dull blue | .60 .35 |

1st anniv. of the change of political organization in Argentina.

St. Gabriel A188  Cross at Palermo A189

| 1944, Oct. 11 | | | |
|---|---|---|---|
| 519 | A188 | 3c yellow green | .70 .35 |
| 520 | A189 | 5c deep rose | .80 .35 |

Fourth national Eucharistic Congress.

Allegory of Savings — A190

| 1944, Oct. 24 | | | |
|---|---|---|---|
| 521 | A190 | 5c gray | .50 .35 |

20th anniv. of the National Savings Bank.

Reservists — A191

| 1944, Dec. 1 | | | |
|---|---|---|---|
| 522 | A191 | 5c blue | .50 .35 |

Day of the Reservists.

**Types of 1935-51**
Perf. 13x13½, 13½x13

| 1945-47 | | Litho. | Unwmk. |
|---|---|---|---|
| 523 | A128 | ½c brown vio ('46) | .25 .25 |
| 524 | A129 | 1c yellow brown | .25 .25 |
| 525 | A130 | 2c sepia | .25 .25 |
| 526 | A132 | 3c lt gray (San Martin) | 2.50 .25 |
| 527 | A134 | 3c lt gray (Moreno) ('46) | .25 .25 |
| 528 | A135 | 6c olive grn ('47) | .50 .35 |
| 529 | A137 | 10c brown ('46) | 2.00 .30 |
| 530 | A140 | 15c lt gray bl (II) | 1.25 .25 |
| 531 | A139 | 20c dk sl bl & pale bl | 3.00 .25 |
| 532 | A141 | 25c dull rose | 2.50 .25 |
| 533 | A142 | 30c orange brown | 1.00 .25 |
| 534 | A143 | 40c violet | 2.00 .35 |
| 535 | A144 | 50c red & orange | 3.00 .25 |
| 536 | A146 | 1p brn blk & lt bl | 4.50 .25 |
| 537 | A147 | 2p brown lake & bl | 35.00 1.00 |
| 538 | A148 | 5p ind & ol grn ('46) | 60.00 4.00 |
| 539 | A149 | 10p dp cl & int blk | 17.50 2.50 |
| 540 | A150 | 20p bl grn & brn ('46) | 15.00 2.50 |
| | Nos. 523-540 (18) | | 150.75 13.75 |

No. 531 measures 22x33mm.

**Post Office Type Inscribed**

| 1945 | | Unwmk. | Perf. 13x13½ |
|---|---|---|---|
| 541 | A178 | 35c lt ultra | 2.50 .35 |
| | | Wmk. 90 | |
| 542 | A178 | 35c lt ultra | 1.60 .35 |
| | | Wmk. 288 | |
| 543 | A178 | 35c lt ultra | .50 .35 |
| | Nos. 541-543 (3) | | 4.60 1.05 |

Nos. 541 and 543 exist imperf. Value, each, pair $10.

Bernardino Rivadavia
A192  A193

Mausoleum of Rivadavia — A194

Perf. 13½x13

| 1945, Sept. 1 | | Litho. | Unwmk. |
|---|---|---|---|
| 544 | A192 | 3c blue green | .40 .35 |
| 545 | A193 | 5c rose | .40 .35 |
| 546 | A194 | 20c blue | .50 .35 |
| | Nos. 544-546 (3) | | 1.30 1.05 |

Cent. of the death of Bernardino Rivadavia, Argentina's first president.
No. 546 exists imperf. Value, pair $20.
No. 546 exists with mute label attached Value, pair, $4.50.

San Martin — A195

| 1945-46 | | Wmk. 90 | Typo. or Litho. |
|---|---|---|---|
| 547 | A195 | 5c carmine | .35 .35 |
| a. | | Litho. ('46) | .35 .35 |
| | | Wmk. 288 | |
| 548 | A195 | 5c carmine, litho. | 125.00 30.00 |
| | | Unwmk. | |
| 549 | A195 | 5c carmine ('46) | 1.50 .35 |
| a. | | Litho. ('46) | .35 .35 |

Nos. 547 and 547a exist imperf. Values, pairs: No. 547, $17.50; No. 547a, $10.
For overprints see Nos. O42, O57.

Monument to Army of the Andes, Mendoza — A196

| 1946, Jan. 14 | | Litho. | Perf. 13½x13 |
|---|---|---|---|
| 550 | A196 | 5c violet brown | .40 .35 |

Issued to honor the Unknown Soldier of the War for Independence.

Franklin D. Roosevelt — A197

| 1946, Apr. 12 | | | |
|---|---|---|---|
| 551 | A197 | 5c dark blue | .35 .35 |

A198

Liberty Administering Presidential Oath.

| 1946, June 4 | | | Perf. 13x13½ |
|---|---|---|---|
| 552 | A198 | 5c blue | .35 .35 |

Inauguration of Pres. Juan D. Perón, 6/4/46.

Argentina Receiving Popular Acclaim — A199

| 1946, Oct. 17 | | | Perf. 13½x13 |
|---|---|---|---|
| 553 | A199 | 5c rose violet | .80 .30 |
| 554 | A199 | 10c blue green | 1.25 .40 |
| 555 | A199 | 15c dark blue | 1.75 .60 |
| 556 | A199 | 50c red brown | 2.25 .50 |
| 557 | A199 | 1p carmine rose | 3.00 1.20 |
| | Nos. 553-557 (5) | | 9.05 3.00 |

First anniversary of the political organization change of Oct. 17, 1945.

Coin Bank and World Map — A200

| 1946, Oct. 31 | | | Unwmk. |
|---|---|---|---|
| 558 | A200 | 30c dk rose car & pink | .60 .35 |

Universal Day of Savings, October 31, 1946.

Argentine Industry — A201

| 1946, Dec. 6 | | | Perf. 13x13½ |
|---|---|---|---|
| 559 | A201 | 5c violet brown | .50 .35 |

Day of Argentine Industry, Dec. 6.

International Bridge Connecting Argentina and Brazil — A202

| 1947, May 21 | | Litho. | Perf. 13½x13 |
|---|---|---|---|
| 560 | A202 | 5c green | .40 .35 |

Opening of the Argentina-Brazil International Bridge, May 21, 1947.

Map of Argentine Antarctic Claims — A203

| 1947-49 | | Unwmk. | Perf. 13x13½ |
|---|---|---|---|
| 561 | A203 | 5c violet & lilac | 1.00 .35 |
| 562 | A203 | 20c dk car rose & rose | 2.00 .35 |
| | | Wmk. 90 | |
| 563 | A203 | 20c dk car rose & rose | 4.00 .35 |
| | | Wmk. 288 | |
| 564 | A203 | 20c dk car rose & rose ('49) | 7.00 .50 |
| | Nos. 561-564 (4) | | 14.00 1.55 |

1st Argentine Antarctic mail, 43rd anniv.
Nos. 561 and 563 exist imperf. Values, pairs: No. 561, $13.50; No. 563, $27.50.

# ARGENTINA

Justice — A204

**1947, June 4**    **Unwmk.**
565 A204 5c brn vio & pale yel    .35   .35
1st anniversary of the Peron government.

Icarus Falling — A205

**1947, Sept. 25**    **Perf. 13½x13**
566 A205 15c red violet    .40   .35
Aviation Week.

Training Ship Presidente Sarmiento — A206

**1947, Oct. 5**    **Perf. 13x13½**
567 A206 5c blue    .50   .35
50th anniv. of the launching of the Argentine training frigate "Presidente Sarmiento."

Cervantes and Characters from Don Quixote — A207

**Perf. 13½x13**
**1947, Oct. 12**   **Photo.**   **Wmk. 90**
568 A207 5c olive green    .40   .35
400th anniv. of the birth of Miguel de Cervantes Saavedra, playwright and poet. Exists imperf. Value, pair $10.

Gen. Jose de San Martin — A208

**Perf. 13½x13**
**1947-49**   **Unwmk.**   **Litho.**
569 A208 5c dull green    .40   .35
        **Wmk. 288**
570 A208 5c dull green ('49)    .40   .35
Transfer of the remains of Gen. Jose de San Martin's parents.
Nos. 569 and 570 exist imperf. Value for pair, each $10.

School Children — A209

**1947-49**   **Unwmk.**   **Perf. 13x13½**
571 A209 5c green    .30   .35
        **Wmk. 90**
574 A209 20c green    .50   .35
        **Wmk. 288**
575 A209 5c green ('49)    .50   .35
  Nos. 571-575 (3)    1.30   1.05
Argentine School Crusade for World Peace. Nos. 571 and 574 exist imperf. Value for pair, each $10.

Statue of Araucanian Indian — A210

**1948, May 21**    **Wmk. 90**
576 A210 25c yellow brown    .35   .35
American Indian Day, Apr. 19. No. 576 exists imperf. Value, pair $10.

Cap of Liberty — A211

**1948, July 16**
577 A211 5c ultra    .35   .35
Revolution of June 4, 1943, 5th anniv.

Manual Stop Signal — A212

**1948, July 22**
578 A212 5c chocolate & yellow    .35   .35
Traffic Safety Day, June 10. No. 578 exists imperf. Value, pair $10.

Post Horn and Oak Leaves — A213

**1948, July 22**    **Unwmk.**
579 A213 5c lilac rose    .45   .35
200th anniversary of the establishment of regular postal service on the Plata River. No. 579 exists imperf. Value, pair $10.

Argentine Farmers — A214

**Perf. 13x13½**
**1948, Sept. 20**    **Wmk. 288**
580 A214 10c red brown    .35   .35
Agriculture Day, Sept. 8, 1948.

Liberty and Symbols of Progress — A215

**Perf. 13x13½**
**1948, Nov. 23**   **Photo.**   **Wmk. 287**
581 A215 25c red brown    .50   .35
3rd anniversary of President Juan D. Peron's return to power, October 17, 1945. No. 581 exists imperf. Value, pair $10.

## Souvenir Sheets

A216

15c, Mail coach. 45c, Buenos Aires in 18th cent. 55c, 1st train, 1857. 85c, Sailing ship, 1767.

**1948, Dec. 21**   **Unwmk.**   **Imperf.**
582 A216   Sheet of 4    12.00   5.00
  a.   15c dark green    1.00   .75
  b.   45c orange brown    1.00   .75
  c.   55c lilac brown    1.00   .75
  d.   85c ultramarine    1.00   .75

A217

Designs: 85c, Domingo de Basavilibaso (1709-75). 1.05p, Postrider. 1.20p, Sailing ship, 1798. 1.90p, Courier in the Andes, 1772.
583 A217   Sheet of 4    32.50   20.00
  a.   85c brown    4.75   3.25
  b.   1.05p dark green    4.75   3.25
  c.   1.20p dark blue    4.75   3.25
  d.   1.90p red brown    4.75   3.25
200th anniversary of the establishment of regular postal service on the Plata River.

Winged Wheel — A218

**Perf. 13½x13**
**1949, Mar. 1**    **Wmk. 288**
584 A218 10c blue    .50   .35
Railroad nationalization, 1st anniv.

Liberty — A219

**1949, June 20**   **Engr.**   **Wmk. 90**
585 A219 1p red & red violet    1.25   .35
Ratification of the Constitution of 1949.

Allegory of the UPU — A220

**1949, Nov. 19**
586 A220 25c dk grn & yel grn    .40   .35
75th anniv. of the UPU.

**Catalogue values for unused stamps in this section, from this point to the end of the section, are for Never Hinged items.**

Gen. Jose de San Martin — A221

San Martin at Boulogne sur Mer — A222

Mausoleum of San Martin — A223

20c, 50c, 75c, Different portraits of San Martin. 1p, House where San Martin died.

**Engr., Photo. (25c, 1p, 2p)**
**1950, Aug. 17**   **Wmk. 90**   **Perf. 13½**
587 A221 10c indigo & dk pur    .50   .35
588 A221 20c red brn & dk brn    .50   .35
589 A222 25c brown    .50   .35
590 A221 50c dk green & ind    .80   .35
591 A221 75c choc & dk grn    1.20   .35
  a.   Souv. sheet of 4, #587, 588, 590, 591, imperf.    6.00   3.00
592 A222 1p dark green    2.75   .40
593 A223 2p dp red lilac    3.25   .35
  Nos. 587-593 (7)    9.50   2.65
Death cent. of General Jose de San Martin.

Map Showing Antarctic Claims — A224

**1951, May 21**   **Litho.**   **Perf. 13x13½**
594 A224 1p choc & lt blue    1.40   .35
For overprint see No. O52. No. 594 exists imperf. Value, pair $25.

Pegasus and Train A225

Communications Symbols A226

Design: 25c, Ship and dolphin.
**1951, Oct. 17**   **Photo.**   **Perf. 13½**
595 A225 5c dark brown    1.60   .35
596 A225 25c Prus green    3.25   .35
597 A226 40c rose brown    3.75   .35
  Nos. 595-597 (3)    8.60   1.05
Close of Argentine Five Year Plan.

Woman Voter and "Argentina" — A227

**1951, Dec. 14**    **Perf. 13½x13**
598 A227 10c brown violet    .85   .35
Granting of women's suffrage.

# ARGENTINA

Eva Peron
A228    A229

**Litho. or Engraved (#605)**
**1952, Aug. 26    Wmk. 90    Perf. 13**
| 599 | A228 | 1c orange brown | .40 | .25 |
| 600 | A228 | 5c gray | .40 | .25 |
| 601 | A228 | 10c rose lilac | .40 | .25 |
| 602 | A228 | 20c rose pink | .40 | .25 |
| 603 | A228 | 25c dull green | .45 | .25 |
| 604 | A228 | 40c dull violet | .55 | .25 |
| 605 | A228 | 45c deep blue | .55 | .25 |
| 606 | A228 | 50c dull brown | .80 | .25 |

**Photo.**
| 607 | A229 | 1p dark brown | 1.20 | .30 |
| 608 | A229 | 1.50p deep green | 4.50 | .30 |
| 609 | A229 | 2p brt carmine | 1.20 | .30 |
| 610 | A229 | 3p indigo | 1.90 | .30 |
| | | Nos. 599-610 (12) | 12.75 | 3.20 |

For overprints see Nos. O79-O85.
Nos. 599, 601-604 and 606 exist imperf. Value for set of 6 pairs, $235.

**Inscribed: "Eva Peron"**
**1952-53    Perf. 13x13½**
| 611 | A229 | 1p dark brown | 1.20 | .35 |
| 612 | A229 | 1.50p deep green | 2.40 | .35 |
| 613 | A229 | 2p brt car ('53) | 2.40 | .40 |
| 614 | A229 | 3p indigo | 1.60 | .90 |

**Engr.**
**Perf. 13½x13**
**Size: 30x40mm**
| 615 | A229 | 5p red brown | 6.00 | 2.00 |
| 616 | A228 | 10p red | 9.50 | 4.00 |
| 617 | A228 | 20p green | 21.00 | 8.50 |
| 618 | A228 | 50p ultra | 47.50 | 20.00 |
| | | Nos. 611-618 (8) | 94.50 | 36.50 |

For overprints see Nos. O86-O93.

Indian Funeral Urn — A230

**1953, Aug. 28    Photo.    Perf. 13x13½**
| 619 | A230 | 50c blue green | .85 | .35 |

Founding of Santiago del Estero, 400th anniv.

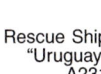

Rescue Ship "Uruguay" A231

**1953, Oct. 8    Perf. 13½**
| 620 | A231 | 50c ultra | 1.50 | .50 |

50th anniv. of the rescue of the Antarctic expedition of Otto C. Nordenskjold.

Planting Argentine Flag in the Antarctic — A232

**1954, Jan. 20    Engr.    Perf. 13½x13**
| 621 | A232 | 1.45p blue | 1.60 | .50 |

50th anniv. of Argentina's 1st antarctic p.o. and the establishing of the La Luy radio p.o. in the South Orkneys.

Wired Communications A233    Television A234

**Perf. 13x13½, 13½x13**
**1954, Apr.    Photo.    Wmk. 90**
| 622 | A233 | 1.50p shown | .55 | .35 |
| 623 | A233 | 3p Radio | 2.25 | .35 |
| 624 | A234 | 5p shown | 3.25 | .40 |
| | | Nos. 622-624 (3) | 6.05 | 1.10 |

Intl. Plenipotentiary Conf. of Telecommunications, Buenos Aires, 1952.

Pediment, Buenos Aires Stock Exchange — A235

**1954, July 13    Perf. 13½x13**
| 625 | A235 | 1p dark green | 1.00 | .35 |

Cent. of the establishment of the Buenos Aires Stock Exchange.

Eva Peron — A236

**1954    Wmk. 90**
| 626 | A236 | 3p dp car rose | 3.50 | .50 |

**Wmk. 288**
| 627 | A236 | 3p dp car rose | 250.00 | 50.00 |

2nd anniv. of the death of Eva Peron.

Jose de San Martin A237    Wheat A238

Industry — A238a    Eva Peron Foundation Building — A239

Cliffs of Humahuaca A240

Gen. Jose de San Martin — A241

Designs: 50c, Buenos Aires harbor. 1p, Cattle ranch (Ganaderia). 3p, Nihuil Dam. 5p, Iguacu Falls, vert. 20p, Mt. Fitz Roy, vert.

**Engraved (#632, 638-642),**
**Photogravure (#634-637)**
**Perf. 13½, 13x13½ (80c), 13½x13**
**(#639, 641-642)**
**1954-59    Wmk. 90**
| 628 | A237 | 20c brt red, typo. | .35 | .25 |
| 629 | A237 | 20c red, litho. ('55) | 1.10 | .25 |
| 630 | A237 | 40c red, litho. ('56) | .45 | .25 |
| 631 | A237 | 40c brt red, typo. ('55) | .45 | .25 |
| 632 | A239 | 50c blue ('56) | .45 | .25 |
| 633 | A239 | 50c bl, litho. ('59) | .35 | .25 |
| 634 | A238 | 80c brown | .45 | .25 |
| 635 | A239 | 1p brown ('58) | .45 | .25 |
| 636 | A238a | 1.50p ultra ('58) | .45 | .25 |
| 637 | A239 | 2p dk rose lake | .55 | .25 |
| 638 | A239 | 3p violet brn ('56) | .55 | .25 |
| 639 | A240 | 5p gray grn ('55) | 9.00 | .25 |
| a. | | Perf. 13½ | 10.00 | |
| 640 | A240 | 10p yel grn ('55) | 9.00 | .25 |
| 641 | A240 | 20p dull vio ('55) | 12.00 | .50 |
| a. | | Perf. 13½ | 16.00 | |
| 642 | A241 | 50p ultra & ind ('55) | 14.00 | 1.50 |
| a. | | Perf. 13½ | 15.00 | 1.00 |
| | | Nos. 628-642 (15) | 49.60 | 5.25 |

See Nos. 699-700. For similar designs inscribed "Republica Argentina" see Nos. 823-827, 890, 935, 937, 940, 990, 995, 1039, 1044, 1048.
For overprints see Nos. O94-O106, O142, O153-O157.

Allegory — A242

**1954, Aug. 26    Typo.    Perf. 13½**
| 643 | A242 | 1.50p slate black | 1.00 | .35 |

Cent. of the establishment of the Buenos Aires Grain Exchange.

Clasped Hands and Congress Medal — A243

**1955, Mar. 21    Photo.    Perf. 13½x13**
| 644 | A243 | 3p red brown | 1.75 | .35 |

Issued to publicize the National Productivity and Social Welfare Congress.

Allegory of Aviation — A244

**1955, June 18    Wmk. 90    Perf. 13½**
| 645 | A244 | 1.50p olive gray | 1.25 | .35 |

Commercial aviation in Argentina, 25th anniv.

Argentina Breaking Chains — A245

**1955, Oct. 16    Litho.**
| 647 | A245 | 1.50p olive green | .95 | .35 |

Liberation Revolution of Sept. 16, 1955.

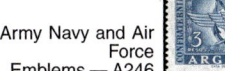

Army Navy and Air Force Emblems — A246

**Perf. 13½x13**
**1955, Dec. 31    Photo.    Wmk. 90**
| 648 | A246 | 3p blue | 1.00 | .35 |

"Brotherhood of the Armed Forces."

Justo Jose de Urquiza — A247

**1956, Feb. 3    Perf. 13½**
| 649 | A247 | 1.50p dk grn, lt grn | .95 | .35 |

Battle of Caseros, 104th anniversary.
No. 649 exists imperf. Value, pair $30.

Coin and Die — A248

**1956, July 28    Engr.    Perf. 13½x13**
| 650 | A248 | 2p multicolored | .65 | .35 |

75th anniversary of the Argentine Mint.

1856 Stamp of Corrientes A249    Juan G. Pujol A250

Design: 2.40p, Stamp of 1860-78.

**1956, Aug. 21**
| 651 | A249 | 40c dk grn & blue | .35 | .35 |
| 652 | A249 | 2.40p brn & lil rose | .60 | .35 |

**Photo.**
| 653 | A250 | 4.40p brt blue | 1.40 | .35 |
| a. | | Souv. sheet, #651-653, imperf. | 9.75 | 6.00 |
| | | Nos. 651-653 (3) | 2.35 | 1.05 |

Centenary of Argentine postage stamps.
No. 653a for the Argentine stamp cent. and Philatelic Exhib. for the Cent. of Corrientes Stamps, Oct. 12-21. The 4.40p is photo., the other two stamps and border litho. Colors of 40c and 2.40p differ slightly from engraved stamps.

Felling Trees, La Pampa A251    Mate Herb and Gourd, Misiones A252

1p, Cotton plant and harvest, Chaco.

**1956, Sept. 1    Perf. 13½**
| 654 | A251 | 50c ultra | 1.00 | .35 |
| 655 | A251 | 1p magenta | 1.00 | .35 |
| 656 | A252 | 1.50p green | 1.00 | .35 |
| | | Nos. 654-656 (3) | 3.00 | 1.05 |

Elevation of the territories of La Pampa, Chaco and Misiones to provinces.

"Liberty" — A253

# ARGENTINA

**Perf. 13½**

**1956, Sept. 15  Wmk. 90  Photo.**
657 A253 2.40p lilac rose    1.00 .35
1st anniv. of the Revolution of Liberation.

Florentino Ameghino — A254

**1956, Nov. 30**
658 A254 2.40p brown    .85 .35
Issued to honor Florentino Ameghino (1854-1911), anthropologist.
For overprint see No. O110.

**Adm. Brown Type of 1935-51**

Two types:
I. Background lines touch the left cheek, bust and lower frame in direct contact.
II. Background lines don't touch the left cheek, white line separates bust from frame line.

**Size: 19½-20½x26-27mm**

| 1956 | Litho. | | Perf. 13 |
|---|---|---|---|
| 659 | A133 20c dull purple (I) | .60 | .35 |
| a. | Type II | .60 | .35 |
| b. | Size 19½x25¼mm (I) | .75 | .35 |

For overprint see No. O108.

Benjamin Franklin — A255

**1956, Dec. 22  Photo.  Perf. 13½**
660 A255 40c intense blue    .90 .35
250th anniv. of the birth of Benjamin Franklin.

Frigate "Hercules" A256

Guillermo Brown A257

**1957, Mar. 2**
661 A256 40c brt blue    .50 .35
662 A257 2.40p gray black    .80 .35
 Nos. 661-662, C63-C65 (5)    3.00 1.75
Admiral Guillermo (William) Brown (1777-1857), founder of the Argentine navy.

Roque Saenz Pena (1851-1914) — A258

**1957, Apr. 1**
663 A258 4.40p grnsh gray    .90 .35
Roque Saenz Pena, pres. 1910-14.
For overprint see No. O111.

Church of Santo Domingo, 1807 — A259

**1957, July 6  Wmk. 90**
664 A259 40c brt blue green    .60 .35
150th anniv. of the defense of Buenos Aires.

"La Portena" — A260

**1957, Aug. 31  Wmk. 90  Perf. 13½**
665 A260 40c pale brown    1.00 .35
Centenary of Argentine railroads.

Esteban Echeverria — A261

**1957, Sept. 2   Perf. 13x13½**
666 A261 2p claret    .60 .35
Esteban Echeverria (1805-1851), poet.
For overprint see No. O109.

"Liberty" — A262

**1957, Sept. 28   Perf. 13½**
667 A262 40c carmine rose    .65 .35
Constitutional reform convention.

**Portrait Type of 1935-51**

**1957, Oct. 28  Litho.  Perf. 13½**
**Size: 16½x22mm**
668 A128 5c Jose Hernandez    .60 .35
For overprint see No. O112.

Oil Derrick and Hands Holding Oil — A263

**Perf. 13½**
**1957, Dec. 21  Wmk. 90  Photo.**
669 A263 40c bright blue    .90 .35
50th anniv. of the national oil industry.
No. 669 exists imperf. Value, pair $30.

Museum, La Plata — A264

**1958, Jan. 11**
670 A264 40c dark gray    .60 .35
City of La Plata, 75th anniversary.

A265      A266

40c, Locomotive & arms of Argentina & Bolivia. 1p, Map of Argentine-Bolivian boundary & plane.

**1958, Apr. 19  Wmk. 90  Perf. 13½**
671 A265 40c slate & dp car    .80 .35
672 A266 1p dark brown    .80 .35
Argentine-Bolivian friendship. No. 671 for the opening of the Jacuiba-Santa Cruz railroad; No. 672, the exchange of presidential visits.

Symbols of the Republic — A267

**1958, Apr. 30   Photo. & Engr.**
673 A267 40c multicolored    .55 .50
674 A267 1p multicolored    .70 .50
675 A267 2p multicolored    1.25 .50
 Nos. 673-675 (3)    2.50 1.50
Transmission of Presidential power.

Flag Monument — A268

**1958, June 21  Litho.  Wmk. 90**
676 A268 40c blue & violet bl    .60 .35
1st anniv. of the Flag Monument of Rosario.
Exists imperf. Value, pair $40.

Map of Antarctica — A269

**1958, July 12    Perf. 13½**
677 A269 40c car rose & blk    .95 .35
International Geophysical Year, 1957-58.
Exists imperf. Value, pair $80.

Stamp of Cordoba and Mail Coach — A270

**1958, Oct. 18**
678 A270 40c pale blue & slate    .65 .35
 Nos. 678, C72-C73 (3)    1.75 1.05
Centenary of Cordoba postage stamps.

"Slave" by Michelangelo and UN Emblem A271

**Engraved and Lithographed**
**1959, Mar. 14  Wmk. 90  Perf. 13½**
679 A271 40c violet brn & gray    .60 .35
10th anniv. (in 1958) of the signing of the Universal Declaration of Human Rights. No UN Emblem (error) Value, $200.
Exists imperf. Value, pair $50.

Orchids and Globe — A272

**1959, May 23  Photo.  Perf. 13½**
680 A272 1p dull claret    .75 .35
1st International Horticulture Exposition.
Exists imperf. Value, pair $50.

Pope Pius XII — A273

**1959, June 20  Engr.  Perf. 13½**
681 A273 1p yellow & black    .65 .35
Pope Pius XII, 1876-1958.
Exists imperf. Value, pair $50.

William Harvey — A274

1p, Claude Bernard. 1.50p, Ivan P. Pavlov.

**1959, Aug. 8  Litho.  Wmk. 90**
682 A274 50c green    .35 .35
683 A274 1p dark red    .35 .35
684 A274 1.50p brown    .45 .35
 Nos. 682-684 (3)    1.15 1.05
21st Intl. Cong. of Physiological Sciences, Buenos Aires.

**Type of 1958 and**

Domestic Horse A275

Jose de San Martin A276

Tierra del Fuego A277

Inca Bridge, Mendoza A278

Ski Jumper — A279

Mar del Plata — A280

Designs: 10c, Cayman. 20c, Llama. 50c, Puma. No. 690, Sunflower. 3p, Zapata Slope, Catamarca. 12p, 23p, 25p, Red Quebracho tree. 20p, Nahuel Huapi Lake. 22p, "Industry" (cogwheel and factory).

Two overall paper sizes for 1p, 5p:
I — 27x37½mm or 37½x27mm.
II — 27x39mm or 39x27mm.

**Perf. 13x13½**
**1959-70  Litho.  Wmk. 90**
685 A275 10c slate green    .40 .35
686 A275 20c dl red brn ('61)    .40 .35
687 A275 50c bister ('60)    .40 .35
688 A275 50c bis, typo. ('60)    .40 .35
689 A275 1p rose red    .40 .35

**Perf. 13½**
690 A278 1p brn, photo., I ('61)    .35 .35
a. Paper II ('69)    1.10 .35
690B A278 1p brown, I    1.10 .70
691 A276 2p rose red ('61)    .45 .35

# ARGENTINA

| | | | | |
|---|---|---|---|---|
| 692 | A276 | 2p red, typo. (19½ x 26mm) ('61) | .55 | .35 |
| a. | | Redrawn (19½ x 25mm) | 4.50 | .35 |
| 693 | A277 | 3p dk bl, photo. ('60) | .35 | .35 |
| 694 | A276 | 4p red, typo ('62) | 1.10 | .35 |
| 694A | A276 | 4p red ('62) | .65 | .35 |
| 695 | A277 | 5p gray brn, photo., I | .35 | .35 |
| e. | | 5p dark brown, paper II ('70) | 10.00 | 5.50 |
| 695A | A276 | 8p ver ('65) | 2.25 | .35 |
| 695B | A276 | 8p red, typo. ('65) | .35 | .35 |
| 695C | A276 | 10p ver ('65) | .65 | .35 |
| 695D | A276 | 10p red, typo. ('66) | .65 | .35 |

**Photo.**

| | | | | |
|---|---|---|---|---|
| 696 | A278 | 10p lt red brn ('60) | .55 | .35 |
| 697 | A278 | 12p dk brn vio ('62) | 1.10 | .35 |
| 697A | A278 | 12p dk brn, litho. ('64) | 13.00 | .40 |
| 698 | A278 | 20p Prus grn ('60) | 3.25 | .35 |
| 698A | A276 | 20p red, typo. ('67) | .35 | .35 |
| 699 | A238a | 22p ultra ('62) | 2.25 | .35 |
| 700 | A238a | 22p ultra, litho. ('62) | 27.50 | .35 |
| 701 | A278 | 23p green ('65) | 5.50 | .35 |
| 702 | A278 | 25p dp vio ('66) | 2.25 | .35 |
| 703 | A278 | 25p pur, litho. ('66) | 6.50 | .35 |
| 704 | A279 | 100p blue ('61) | 9.00 | .35 |
| 705 | A280 | 300p dp vio ('62) | 5.50 | .35 |
| | | Nos. 685-705 (29) | 87.55 | 10.55 |

Imperf and imperf between examples of some numbers exist.
See Nos. 882-887, 889, 892, 923-925, 928-930, 938, 987-989, 991.
For overprints and surcharges see Nos. 1076, C82-C83, O113-O118, O122-O124, O126-O141, O143-O145, O183.
The 300p remained on sale as a 3p stamp after the 1970 currency exchange.

Symbolic Sailboat — A281

**1959, Oct. 3   Litho.   Perf. 13½**
706  A281  1p blk, red & bl   .60   .35
Red Cross sanitary education campaign.

Child Playing with Doll — A282

**1959, Oct. 17**
707  A282  1p red & blk   .60   .35
Issued for Mother's Day, 1959.

Buenos Aires 1p Stamp of 1859 — A283

**1959, Nov. 21   Wmk. 90   Perf. 13½**
708  A283  1p gray & dk bl   .60   .35
Issued for the Day of Philately.

Bartolomé Mitre and Justo José de Urquiza — A284

**1959, Dec. 12   Photo.   Perf. 13½**
709  A284  1p purple   .60   .35
Treaty of San Jose de Flores, centenary.
Exists imperf. Value, pair $40.

WRY Emblem — A285

**1960, Apr. 7   Litho.   Wmk. 90**
710  A285  1p bister & car   .60   .35
711  A285  4.20p apple grn & dp claret   .60   .35
World Refugee Year, July 1, 1959-June 30, 1960. See No. B25.

Abraham Lincoln — A286

**1960, Apr. 14   Photo.   Perf. 13½**
712  A286  5p ultra   .70   .35
Sesquicentennial (in 1959) of the birth of Abraham Lincoln.
Exists imperf. Value, pair $70.

Cornelio Saavedra and Cabildo, Buenos Aires — A287

"Cabildo" and: 2p, Juan José Paso. 4.20p, Manuel Alberti and Miguel Azcuénaga. 10.70p, Juan Larrea and Domingo Matheu.

**1960, May 28   Wmk. 90   Photo.   Perf. 13½**
713  A287  1p rose lilac   .50   .35
714  A287  2p bluish grn   .50   .35
715  A287  4.20p gray & grn   .60   .05
716  A287  10.70p gray & ultra   .90   .35
Nos. 713-716,C75-C76 (6)   3.70   2.10
150th anniversary of the May Revolution.
Souvenir sheets are Nos. C75a and C76a.

Luis Maria Drago — A288

**1960, July 8**
717  A288  4.20p brown   .60   .35
Centenary of the birth of Dr. Luis Maria Drago, statesman and jurist.
Exists imperf. Value, pair $40.

Juan Bautista Alberdi — A289

**1960, Sept. 10   Wmk. 90   Perf. 13½**
718  A289  1p green   .60   .35
150th anniversary of the birth of Juan Bautista Alberdi, statesman and philosopher.
Exists imperf. Value, pair $40.

Map of Argentina and Antarctic Sector — A290

**1960, Sept. 24   Litho.   Perf. 13½**
719  A290  5p violet   1.00   .35
National census of 1960.
Exists imperf. Value, pair $70.

Caravel and Emblem — A291

**1960, Oct. 1   Photo.**
720  A291  1p dk olive grn   .60   .35
721  A291  5p brown   .95   .35
Nos. 720-721,C78-C79 (4)   3.30   1.40
8th Congress of the Postal Union of the Americas and Spain.

Virgin of Luján, Patroness of Argentina — A292

**1960, Nov. 12   Wmk. 90   Perf. 13½**
722  A292  1p dark blue   .85   .35
First Inter-American Marian Congress.
Exists imperf. Value, pair $30.

Argentine Boy Scout Emblem — A293

**1961, Jan. 17   Litho.**
723  A293  1p car rose & blk   .60   .35
International Patrol Encampment of the Boy Scouts, Buenos Aires.
Exists imperf. Value, pair $70.

"Shipment of Cereals," by Quinquela Martin — A294

**1961, Feb. 11   Photo.   Perf. 13½**
724  A294  1p red brown   .60   .35
Export drive: "To export is to advance."
Exists imperf. Value, pair $40.

Naval Battle of San Nicolás — A295

**1961, Mar. 2   Perf. 13½**
725  A295  2p gray   .60   .35
Naval battle of San Nicolas, 150th anniv.
Exists imperf. Value, pair $67.50.

Mariano Moreno by Juan de Dios Rivera — A296

**1961, Mar. 25   Perf. 13½**
726  A296  2p blue   .60   .35
Mariano Moreno (1778-1811), writer, politician, member of the 1810 Junta.
Exists imperf. Value, pair $40.

Emperor Trajan Statue — A297

**1961, Apr. 11**
727  A297  2p slate green   .60   .35
Visit of Pres. Giovanni Gronchi of Italy to Argentina, April 1961.
Exists imperf. Value, pair $40.

Rabindranath Tagore — A298

**1961, May 13   Photo.   Perf. 13½**
728  A298  2p purple, grysh   1.20   .35
Centenary of the birth of Rabindranath Tagore, Indian poet.

San Martin Statue, Madrid — A299

**1961, May 24   Wmk. 90**
729  A299  1p olive gray   .60   .35
Unveiling of a statue of General José de San Martin in Madrid.
Exists imperf. Value, pair $40.

Manuel Belgrano — A300

**1961, June 17   Perf. 13½**
730  A300  2p violet blue   .85   .35
Erection of a monument by Hector Rocha, to General Manuel Belgrano in Buenos Aires.
Exists imperf. Value, pair $40.

Explorers, Sledge and Dog Team — A301

**1961, Aug. 19   Photo.   Wmk. 90**
731  A301  2p black   1.10   .35
10th anniversary of the General San Martin Base, Argentine Antarctic.
Exists imperf. Value, pair $75.

Spanish Conquistador and Sword — A302

**1961, Aug. 19   Litho.**
732  A302  2p red & blk   1.00   .35
First city of Jujuy, 400th anniversary.
Exists imperf. Value, pair $40.

Sarmiento Statue by Rodin, Buenos Aires — A303

**1961, Sept. 9   Photo.**
733  A303  2p violet   .60   .35
Domingo Faustino Sarmiento (1811-88), political leader and writer.

586 ARGENTINA

Exists imperf. Value, pair $40.

Symbol of World Town Planning — A304

**1961, Nov. 25   Litho.   Perf. 13½**
734  A304  2p ultra & yel   .60   .35
World Town Planning Day, Nov. 8.

Manuel Belgrano Statue, Buenos Aires — A305

**1962, Feb. 24   Photo.**
735  A305  2p Prus blue   .60   .35
150th anniversary of the Argentine flag.
Exists imperf. Value, pair $40.

Grenadier, Flag and Regimental Emblem — A306

**1962, Mar. 31   Wmk. 90   Perf. 13½**
736  A306  2p carmine rose   .85   .35
150th anniversary of the San Martin Grenadier Guards regiment.
Exists imperf. Value, pair $40.

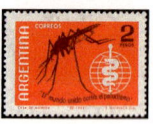

Mosquito and Malaria Eradication Emblem — A307

**1962, Apr. 7   Litho.**
737  A307  2p vermilion & blk   .60   .35
WHO drive to eradicate malaria.

Church of the Virgin of Luján — A308

**1962, May 12   Perf. 13½**
738  A308  2p org brn & blk   .60   .35
75th anniversary of the pontifical coronation of the Virgin of Lujan.

Bust of Juan Jufrè — A309

**1962, June 23   Photo.**
739  A309  2p Prus blue   .60   .35
Founding of San Juan, 4th cent.
Exists imperf. Value, pair $40.

"Soaring into Space" — A310

**1962, Aug. 18   Litho.   Perf. 13½**
740  A310  2p maroon, blk & bl   .60   .35
Argentine Air Force, 50th anniversary.

Exists imperf. Value, pair $40.

Juan Vucetich — A311

**1962, Oct. 6   Photo.   Wmk. 90**
741  A311  2p green   .60   .35
Juan Vucetich (1864-1925), inventor of the Argentine system of fingerprinting.
Exists imperf. Value, pair $40.

Domingo F. Sarmiento — A312

Design: 4p, Jose Hernandez.

**1962-66   Photo.   Perf. 13½**
742  A312  2p deep green   .75   .35
    **Litho.**
742A A312  2p lt green ('64)   .75   .35
    **Photo.**
742B A312  4p dull red ('65)   .75   .35
    **Litho.**
742C A312  4p rose red ('66)   1.75   .35
    Nos. 742-742C (4)   4.00  1.40
No. 742A exists imperf. Value, pair $40.
See No. 817-819. For overprints see Nos. O119-O121, O125, O149.

February 20th Monument, Salta — A313

**1963, Feb. 23   Photo.   Wmk. 90**
743  A313  2p dark green   .90   .35
150th anniversary of the Battle of Salta, War of Independence.
Exists imperf. Value, pair $40.

Gear Wheels — A314

**1963, Mar. 16   Litho.   Perf. 13½**
744  A314  4p gray, blk & brt rose   .85   .35
Argentine Industrial Union, 75th anniv.
Exists imperf. Value, pair $40.

National College, Buenos Aires — A315

**1963, Mar. 16   Wmk. 90**
745  A315  4p dull org & blk   .90   .35
National College of Buenos Aires, cent.
Exists imperf. Value, pair $40.

Child Draining Cup — A316

**1963, Apr. 6**
746  A316  4p multicolored   .60   .35
FAO "Freedom from Hunger" campaign.

Exists imperf. Value, pair $40.

Frigate "La Argentina," 1817, by Emilio Biggeri — A317

**1963, May 18   Photo.**
747  A317  4p bluish green   1.10   .35
Issued for Navy Day, May 17.
Exists imperf. Value, pair $40.

Seat of 1813 Assembly and Official Seal — A318

**1963, July 13   Litho.   Perf. 13½**
748  A318  4p lt blue & blk   .85   .35
150th anniversary of the 1813 Assembly.
Exists imperf. Value, pair $40.

Battle of San Lorenzo, 1813 — A319

**1963, Aug. 24**
749  A319  4p grn & blk, *grnsh*   .85   .35
Sesquicentennial of the Battle of San Lorenzo.

Queen Nefertari Offering Papyrus Flowers, Abu Simbel — A320

**1963, Sept. 14   Perf. 13½**
750  A320  4p ocher, blk & bl grn   .85   .35
Campaign to save the historic monuments in Nubia.
Exists imperf. Value, pair $40.

Government House, Buenos Aires — A321

**1963, Oct. 12   Wmk. 90   Perf. 13½**
751  A321  5p rose & brown   .85   .35
Inauguration of President Arturo Illia.
Exists imperf. Value, pair $40.

"Science" — A322

**1963, Oct. 16   Litho.**
752  A322  4p org brn, bl & blk   .90   .35
10th Latin-American Neurosurgery Congress.
Exists imperf. Value, pair $40.

Francisco de las Carreras, Supreme Court Justice — A323

**1963, Nov. 23   Photo.   Perf. 13½**
753  A323  5p bluish green   .60   .35
Centenary of judicial power.
Exists imperf. Value, pair $40.

Blackboards A324

**1963, Nov. 23   Litho.**
754  A324  5p red, blk & bl   .60   .35
Issued to publicize "Teachers for America" through the Alliance for Progress program.
Exists imperf. Value, pair $40.

Kemal Atatürk — A325

**1963, Dec. 28   Photo.   Perf. 13½**
755  A325  12p dark gray   .85   .35
25th anniversary of the death of Kemal Atatürk, president of Turkey.
Exists imperf. Value, pair $40.

"Payador" by Juan Carlos Castagnino — A326

**1964, Jan. 25   Litho.**
756  A326  4p ultra, blk & lt bl   .85   .35
Fourth National Folklore Festival.
Exists imperf. Value, pair $40.

Maps of South Georgia, South Orkney and South Sandwich Islands — A327

4p, Map of Argentina & Antarctic claims, vert.

**1964, Feb. 22   Wmk. 90   Perf. 13½**
    **Size: 33x22mm**
757  A327  2p lt & dk bl & bister   1.60   .30
    **Size: 30x40mm**
758  A327  4p lt & dk bl & ol grn   2.25   .30
    Nos. 757-758,C92 (3)   6.85  1.35
Argentina's claim to Antarctic territories, 60th anniv.
Exist imperf. Value, set of 3 pairs, $150.

Jorge Newbery in Cockpit — A328

**1964, Feb. 23   Photo.**
759  A328  4p deep green   .90   .35
Newbery, aviator, 50th death anniv.
Exists imperf. Value, pair $40.

John F. Kennedy — A329

**1964, Apr. 14   Engr.   Wmk. 90**
760  A329  4p claret & dk bl   .85   .35
President John F. Kennedy (1917-63).
Exists imperf. Value, pair $100.

# ARGENTINA

José Brochero by José Cuello — A330

**1964, May 9**    **Photo.**    **Perf. 13½**
761 A330 4p light sepia    .85   .35

50th anniversary of the death of Father Jose Gabriel Brochero.
Exists imperf. Value, pair $50.

Soldier of Patricios Regiment — A331

**1964, May 29**    **Litho.**    **Wmk. 90**
762 A331 4p blk, ultra & red    1.00   .35

Issued for Army Day. Later Army Day stamps, inscribed "Republica Argentina," are of type A340a.
Exists imperf. Value, pair $40.

Pope John XXIII — A332

**1964, June 27**    **Engr.**
763 A332 4p orange & blk    .60   .35

Issued in memory of Pope John XXIII.
Exists imperf. Value, pair $50.

University of Cordoba Arms — A333

**1964, Aug. 22**    **Litho.**    **Wmk. 90**
764 A333 4p blk, ultra & yel    .60   .35

350th anniv. of the University of Cordoba.

Pigeons and UN Building, NYC — A334

**1964, Oct. 24**    **Perf. 13½**
765 A334 4p dk blue & lt blue    .60   .35

Issued for United Nations Day.
Exists imperf. Value, pair $40.

Joaquin V. Gonzalez — A335

**1964, Nov. 14**    **Photo.**
766 A335 4p dk rose carmine    .85   .35

Centenary (in 1963) of the birth of Joaquin V. Gonzalez, writer.
Exists imperf. Value, pair $40.

Julio Argentino Roca — A336

**1964, Dec. 12**    **Perf. 13½**
767 A336 4p violet blue    .60   .35

General Julio A. Roca, (1843-1914), president of Argentina, (1880-86, 1898-1904).
Exists imperf. Value, pair $40.

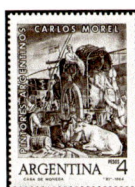

Market at Montserrat Square, by Carlos Morel — A337

**1964, Dec. 19**    **Photo.**
768 A337 4p sepia    .60   .35

19th century Argentine painter Carlos Morel.
Exists imperf. Value, pair $40.

General Belgrano Base, Antarctica — A338

4p, Icebreaker General San Martin.

**1965**    **Perf. 13½**
769 A338 2p dull purple    .75   .35
770 A338 4p ultra    1.50   .35

Issued to publicize the natl. territory of Tierra del Fuego, Antarctic and South Atlantic Isles.
Issue dates: 4p, Feb. 27; 2p, June 5.
No. 769 exists imperf. Value, pair $50.

Girl with Piggy Bank — A339

**1965, Apr. 3**    **Litho.**
771 A339 4p red org & blk    .60   .35

National Postal Savings Bank, 50th anniv.
Exists imperf. Value, pair $40.

Sun and Globe — A340

**1965, May 29**
772 A340 4p blk, org & dl bl    .75   .30
   Nos. 772, C98-C99 (3)    3.25   1.15

International Quiet Sun Year, 1964-65.
Exists imperf. Value, pair $40.

Hussar of Pueyrredon Regiment — A340a

**1965, June 5**    **Wmk. 90**    **Perf. 13½**
773 A340a 8p dp ultra, blk & red    1.00   .50

Issued for Army Day. See Nos. 796, 838, 857, 893, 944, 958, 974, 1145.
Exists imperf. Value, pair $50.

Ricardo Rojas (1882-1957) — A341

Portraits: No. 775, Ricardo Guiraldes (1886-1927). No. 776, Enrique Larreta (1873-1961). No. 777, Leopoldo Lugones (1874-1938). No. 778, Roberto J. Payro (1867-1928).

**1965, June 26**    **Photo.**
774 A341 8p brown    .60   .35
775 A341 8p brown    .60   .35
776 A341 8p brown    .60   .35
777 A341 8p brown    .60   .35
778 A341 8p brown    .60   .35
   Nos. 774-778 (5)    3.00   1.75

Issued to honor Argentine writers. Printed se-tenant in sheets of 100 (10x10); 2 horizontal rows of each design with Guiraldes in top rows and Rojas in bottom rows.
Nos. imperf. Value, strip of 5, $250.

Hipolito Yrigoyen — A342

**1965, July 3**    **Litho.**
779 A342 8p pink & black    .60   .35

Hipolito Yrigoyen (1852-1933), president of Argentina 1916-22, 1928-30.

Children Looking Through Window — A343

**1965, July 24**    **Photo.**
780 A343 8p salmon & blk    .85   .35

International Seminar on Mental Health.
Exists imperf. Value, pair $40.

Child's Funerary Urn and 16th Century Map — A344

**1965, Aug. 7**    **Litho.**
781 A344 8p lt grn, dk red, brn & ocher    .60   .35

City of San Miguel de Tucuman, 400th anniv.
Exists imperf. Value, pair $40.

Cardinal Cagliero — A345

**1965, Aug. 21**    **Photo.**
782 A345 8p violet    .55   .35

Juan Cardinal Cagliero (1839-1926), missionary to Argentina and Bishop of Magida.
Exists imperf. Value, pair $40.

Dante Alighieri — A346

**1965, Sept. 16**    **Wmk. 90**    **Perf. 13½**
783 A346 8p light ultra    .85   .35

Dante Alighieri (1265-1321), Italian poet.
Exists imperf. Value, pair $40.

Clipper "Mimosa" and Map of Patagonia — A347

**1965, Sept. 25**    **Litho.**
784 A347 8p red & black    .60   .35

Centenary of Welsh colonization of Chubut, and the founding of the city of Rawson. Exists imperf. Value, pair $40.

A348

Design: Map of Buenos Aires, cock and compass Emblem of federal police.

**1965, Oct. 30**    **Photo.**    **Perf. 13½**
785 A348 8p carmine rose    .60   .35

Issued for Federal Police Day. Exists imperf. Value, pair $40.

Child's Drawing of Children — A349

**1965, Nov. 6**    **Litho.**    **Wmk. 90**
786 A349 8p lt yel grn & blk    .60   .35

Public education law, 81st anniversary. Exists imperf. Value, pair $40.

Church of St. Francis, Catamarca — A350

**1965, Dec. 8**
787 A350 8p org yel & red brn    .60   .35

Brother Mamerto de la Asuncion Esquiu, preacher, teacher and official of 1885 Provincial Constitutional Convention.

Ruben Dario — A351

**Litho. and Photo.**
**1965, Dec. 22**    **Perf. 13½**
788 A351 15p bl vio, gray    .60   .35

Ruben Dario (pen name of Felix Ruben Garcia Sarmiento, 1867-1916), Nicaraguan poet, newspaper correspondent and diplomat. Exists imperf. Value, pair $40.

"The Orange Seller" — A352

Pueyrredon Paintings: No. 790, "Stop at the Grocery Store." No. 791, "Landscape at San Fernando" (sailboats). No. 792, "Bathing Horses at River Plata."

**1966, Jan. 29**    **Photo.**    **Perf. 13½**
789 A352 8p bluish green    .80   .50
790 A352 8p bluish green    .80   .50
791 A352 8p bluish green    .80   .50
792 A352 8p bluish green    .80   .50
   a. Block of 4, #789-792 + 2 labels    4.00   4.00

Prilidiano Pueyrredon (1823-1870), painter.

# ARGENTINA

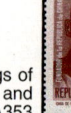

Sun Yat-sen, Flags of Argentina and China — A353

**1966, Mar. 12      Wmk. 90      Perf. 13½**
793  A353  8p dk red brown      .95  .35

Dr. Sun Yat-sen (1866-1925), founder of the Republic of China. Exists imperf. Value, pair $100.

**Souvenir Sheet**

Rivadavia Issue of 1864 — A354

**Wmk. 90**
**1966, Apr. 20      Litho.      Imperf.**
794  A354  Sheet of 3      1.90  1.10
  a.  4p gray & red brown      .35  .35
  b.  5p gray & green      .35  .35
  c.  8p gray & dark blue      .35  .35

2nd Rio de la Plata Stamp Show, Buenos Aires, Mar. 16-24. Exists with flags omitted (error). Value, $150.

People of Various Races and WHO Emblem A355

**1966, Apr. 23      Perf. 13½**
795  A355  8p brown & black      .60  .35

Opening of the WHO Headquarters, Geneva. Exists imperf. Value, pair $40.

**Soldier Type of 1965**

Army Day: 8p, Cavalryman, Guemes Infernal Regiment.

**1966, May 28      Litho.**
796  A340a  8p multicolored      1.00  .35

Exists imperf. Value, pair $40.

Coat of Arms — A356

Arms: a, National. b, Buenos Aires. c, La Rioja. d, Catamarca. e, Cordoba. f, Corrientes. g, Chaco. h, Chubut. i, Entre Rios. j, Formosa. k, Jujuy. l, La Pampa. m, Federal Capital. n, Mendoza. o, Misiones. p, Neuquen. q, Salta. r, San Juan. s, San Luis. t, Santa Cruz. u, Santa Fe. v, Santiago del Estero. w, Tucuman. x, map of Rio Negro. y, Map of Tierra del Fuego, Antarctica, South Atlantic Islands.

**1966, July 30      Wmk. 90      Perf. 13½**
797    Sheet of 25      35.00
  a.-y.  A356 10p black & multi      1.00  1.00

150th anniv. of Argentina's Declaration of Independence. Exists imperf. Value, sheet $2,000.

Three Crosses, Caritas Emblem — A357

**1966, Sept. 10      Litho.      Perf. 13½**
798  A357  10p ol grn, blk & lt bl      .60  .35

Caritas, charity organization.

Hilario Ascasubi (1807-75) — A358

Portraits: No. 800, Estanislao del Campo (1834-80). No. 801, Miguel Cane (1851-1905). No. 802, Lucio V. Lopez (1848-94). No. 803, Rafael Obligado (1851-1920). No. 804, Luis Agote (1868-1954), M.D. No. 805, Juan B. Ambrosetti (1865-1917), naturalist and archaeologist. No. 806, Miguel Lillo (1862-1931), botanist and chemist. No. 807, Francisco P. Moreno (1852-1919), naturalist and paleontologist. No. 808, Francisco J. Muñiz (1795-1871), physician.

**1966      Photo.      Wmk. 90**
799  A358  10p dk blue green      .65  .40
800  A358  10p dk blue green      .65  .40
801  A358  10p dk blue green      .65  .40
802  A358  10p dk blue green      .65  .40
803  A358  10p dk blue green      .65  .40
804  A358  10p deep violet      .65  .40
805  A358  10p deep violet      .65  .40
806  A358  10p deep violet      .65  .40
807  A358  10p deep violet      .65  .40
808  A358  10p deep violet      .65  .40
  Nos. 799-808 (10)      6.50  4.00

Nos. 799-803 issued Sept. 17 to honor Argentine writers. Printed se-tenant in sheets of 100 (10x10); 2 horizontal rows of each portrait. Nos. 804-808 issued Oct. 22 to honor Argentine scientists; 2 horizontal rows of each portrait. Scientists set has value at upper left, frame line with rounded corners.

Anchor — A359

**1966, Oct. 8      Litho.**
809  A359  4p multicolored      .60  .35

Argentine merchant marine. Exists imperf. Value, pair $40.

Flags and Map of the Americas — A360

**1966, Oct. 29      Perf. 13½**
810  A360  10p gray & multi      .60  .35

7th Conference of American Armies.

Argentine National Bank — A361

**1966, Nov. 5      Photo.**
811  A361  10p brt blue green      .60  .35

75th anniv. of the Argentine National Bank. Exists imperf. Value, pair $40.

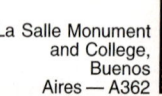

La Salle Monument and College, Buenos Aires — A362

**1966, Nov. 26      Litho.      Perf. 13½**
812  A362  10p brown org & blk      .60  .35

75th anniv. of the Colegio de la Salle, Buenos Aires, and to honor Saint Jean Baptiste de la Salle (1651-1719), educator. Exists imperf. Value, pair $125.

Map of Argentine Antarctica and Expedition Route — A363

**1966, Dec. 10      Wmk. 90**
813  A363  10p multicolored      1.00  .35

1965 Argentine Antarctic expedition, which planted the Argentine flag on the South Pole. Exists imperf. Value, pair $70.
See No. 851.

Juan Martin de Pueyrredon — A364

**1966, Dec. 17      Photo.      Perf. 13½**
814  A364  10p dull red brn      .60  .35

Issued to honor Juan Martin de Pueyrredon (1777-1850), Governor of Cordoba and of the United Provinces of the River Plata.

Gen. Juan de Las Heras — A365

**1966, Dec. 17      Engr.**
815  A365  10p black      .60  .35

Issued to honor Gen. Juan Gregorio de Las Heras (1780-1866), Peruvian field marshal and aide-de-camp to San Martin.

**Inscribed "Republica Argentina" Types of 1955-61 and**

Jose Hernandez — A366

Trout Leaping in National Park — A366a

Designs: 50p, Gen. Jose de San Martin. 90p, Guillermo Brown. 500p, Red deer in forest.

Two overall paper sizes for 6p, 50p (No. 827) and 90p:
  I — 27x37½mm
  II — 27x39mm

**Perf. 13½**
**1965-68      Wmk. 90      Photo.**
817  A366  6p rose red, litho, I ('67)      1.75  .30
818  A366  6p rose red ('67), II      6.50  .35
819  A366  6p brn, 15x22mm ('68)      .35  .30
823  A238a  43p dk car rose      8.50  .35
824  A238a  45p brn ('66)      4.25  .30
825  A238a  45p brn, litho ('67)      9.50  .35
826  A241  50p dk bl, 29x40mm      10.00  .45
827  A241  50p dk bl, 22x31½mm, I ('67)      5.25  .35
  a.  Paper II      2.25  .30

828  A366  90p ol bis, I ('67)      3.50  .35
  a.  Paper II      14.00  .35
**Engr.**
829  A495  500p yellow grn ('66)      3.00  .30
829A  A366a  1,000p vio bl ('68)      9.50  .35
  Nos. 817-829A (11)      62.10  3.75

The 500p and 1,000p remained on sale as 5p and 10p stamps after the 1970 currency exchange.
See Nos. 888, 891, 939, 992, 1031, 1045-1047. For surcharge and overprints see Nos. 1077, O153-O158, O162.

Pre-Columbian Pottery — A367

**1967, Feb. 18      Litho.      Perf. 13½**
830  A367  10p multicolored      .60  .35

20th anniv. of UNESCO. Exists imperf. Value, pair $40.

"The Meal" by Fernando Fader — A368

**1967, Feb. 25      Photo.      Wmk. 90**
831  A368  10p red brown      .60  .35

Issued in memory of the Argentine painter Fernando Fader (1882-1935). Exists imperf. Value, pair $40.

Col. Juana Azurduy de Padilla (1781-1862), Soldier — A369

Famous Argentine Women: No. 833, Juana Manuela Gorriti, writer. No. 834, Cecilia Grierson (1858-1934), physician. No. 835, Juana Paula Manso (1819-75), writer and educator. No. 836, Alfonsina Storni (1892-1938), writer and educator.

**1967, May 13      Photo.      Perf. 13½**
832  A369  6p dark brown      .65  .25
833  A369  6p dark brown      .65  .25
834  A369  6p dark brown      .65  .25
835  A369  6p dark brown      .65  .25
836  A369  6p dark brown      .65  .25
  Nos. 832-836 (5)      3.25  1.25

Printed se-tenant in sheets of 100 (10x10); 2 horizontal rows of each portrait.

Schooner "Invencible," 1811 — A370

**1967, May 20      Litho.**
837  A370  20p multicolored      1.25  .35

Issued for Navy Day. Exists imperf. Value, pair $50.

**Soldier Type of 1965**

Army Day: 20p, Highlander (Arribeños Corps).

**1967, May 27**
838  A340a  20p multicolored      .90  .35

Exists imperf. Value, pair $50.

# ARGENTINA

### Souvenir Sheet

Manuel Belgrano and José Artigas — A371

**1967, June 22**    *Imperf.*
839 A371   Sheet of 2    1.10   .65
    a.   6p gray & brown    .35   .25
    b.   22p brown & gray    .35   .25
Third Rio de la Plata Stamp Show, Montevideo, Uruguay, June 18-25.

Peace Dove and Valise — A372

**1967, Aug. 5**   *Litho.*   *Perf. 13½*
840 A372   20p multicolored    .60   .35
Issued for International Tourist Year 1967.

PADELAI Emblem — A373

**1967, Aug. 12**    *Litho.*
841 A373   20p multicolored    .55   .35
75th anniv. of the Children's Welfare Association (Patronato de la Infancia-PADELAI).

Stagecoach and Modern City — A374

**1967, Sept. 23**   *Wmk. 90*   *Perf. 13½*
842 A374   20p rose, yel & blk    .60   .35
Centenary of Villa Maria, Cordoba.

San Martin by Ibarra — A375

"Battle of Chacabuco" by P. Subercaseaux — A376

**1967, Sept. 30**    *Litho.*
843 A375   20p blk brn & pale yel    .70   .35
    *Engr.*
844 A376   40p blue black    1.10   .35
Battle of Chacabuco, 150th anniversary.

Exhibition Rooms — A377

**1967, Oct. 11**    *Photo.*
845 A377   20p blue gray    .60   .35
Government House Museum, 10th anniv.

Pedro L. Zanni, Fokker and 1924 Flight Route — A378

**1967, Oct. 21**   *Litho.*   *Perf. 13½*
846 A378   20p multicolored    .60   .35
Issued for Aviation Week and to commemorate the 1924 flight of the Fokker seaplane "Province of Buenos Aires" from Amsterdam, Netherlands, to Osaka, Japan.

Training Ship General Brown, by Emilio Biggeri — A379

**1967, Oct. 28**    *Wmk. 90*
847 A379   20p multicolored    1.25   .35
Issued to honor the Military Naval School.

Ovidio Lagos and Front Page — A380

**1967, Nov. 11**    *Photo.*
848 A380   20p sepia    .50   .35
Centenary of La Capital, Rosario newspaper. Imperf pair $40.

St. Barbara — A381

**1967, Dec. 2**    *Perf. 13½*
849 A381   20p rose red    .60   .35
St. Barbara, patron saint of artillerymen.

Portrait of his Wife, by Eduardo Sivori — A382

**1968, Jan. 27**   *Photo.*   *Perf. 13½*
850 A382   20p blue green    .60   .30
Eduardo Sivori (1847-1918), painter.

### Antarctic Type of 1966 and

Admiral Brown Scientific Station — A383

Planes over Map of Antarctica — A384

6p, Map showing radio-postal stations 1966-67.

**1968, Feb. 17**   *Litho.*   *Wmk. 90*
851 A363   6p multicolored    .65   .30
852 A383   20p multicolored    .90   .30
853 A384   40p multicolored    1.50   .50
    Nos. 851-853 (3)    3.05   1.10
Issued to publicize Argentine research projects in Argentine Antarctica.

The Annunciation, by Leonardo da Vinci — A385

**1968, Mar. 23**   *Photo.*   *Perf. 13½*
854 A385   20p lilac rose    .60   .35
Issued for the Day of the Army Communications System and its patron saint, Gabriel. Exists imperf. Value, pair $40.

Man in Wheelchair and Factory — A386

**1968, Mar. 23**    *Litho.*
855 A386   20p green & black    .60   .35
Day of Rehabilitation of the Handicapped.

Children and WHO Emblem — A387

**1968, May 11**   *Wmk. 90*   *Perf. 13½*
856 A387   20p dk vio bl & ver    .60   .35
20th anniv. of WHO.

### Soldier Type of 1965

Army Day: 20p, Uniform of First Artillery Regiment "General Iriarte."

**1968, June 8**    *Litho.*
857 A340a   20p multicolored    1.00   .35

Frigate "Libertad," Painting by Emilio Biggeri — A388

**1968, June 15**    *Wmk. 90*
858 A388   20p multicolored    1.40   .35
Issued for Navy Day. Exists imperf. Value, pair $40.

Guillermo Rawson and Old Hospital — A389

**1968, July 20**   *Photo.*   *Perf. 13½*
859 A389   6p olive bister    .60   .35
Cent. of Rawson Hospital, Buenos Aires.

Student Directing Traffic for Schoolmates A390

**1968, Aug. 10**   *Litho.*   *Perf. 13½*
860 A390   20p lt bl, blk, buff & car    .80   .35
Traffic safety and education.

O'Higgins Joining San Martin at Battle of Maipu, by P. Subercaseaux — A391

**1968, Aug. 15**    *Engr.*
861 A391   40p bluish black    .90   .35
Sesquicentennial of the Battle of Maipu.

Osvaldo Magnasco (1864-1920), Lawyer, Professor of Law and Minister of Justice — A392

**1968, Sept. 7**   *Photo.*   *Perf. 13½*
862 A392   20p brown    .65   .35

Grandmother's Birthday, by Patricia Lynch — A393

The Sea, by Edgardo Gomez — A394

**1968, Sept. 21**    *Litho.*
863 A393   20p multicolored    .60   .35
864 A394   20p multicolored    .60   .35
The designs were chosen in a competition among kindergarten and elementary school children.

Mar del Plata at Night — A395

**1968, Oct. 19**   *Litho.*   *Perf. 13½*
865 A395   20p black, ocher & bl    1.40   .25
    Nos. 865, C113-C114 (3)    4.00   1.10
4th Plenary Assembly of the Intl. Telegraph and Telephone Consultative Committee, Mar del Plata, Sept. 23-Oct. 25.

Frontier Gendarme A396

Patrol Boat A397

**1968, Oct. 26**
866 A396   20p multicolored    .60   .35
867 A397   20p blue, vio bl & blk    .60   .35
No. 866 honors the Gendarmery; No. 867 the Coast Guard.

# ARGENTINA

Aaron de Anchorena and Pampero Balloon — A398

**1968, Nov. 2**    Photo.
868 A398 20p blue & multi   .60   .35
22nd Aeronautics and Space Week.

St. Martin of Tours, by Alfredo Guido — A399

**1968, Nov. 9**    Litho.
869 A399 20p lilac & dk brn   .60   .35
St. Martin of Tours, patron saint of Buenos Aires.

Municipal Bank Emblem — A400

**1968, Nov. 16**
870 A400 20p multicolored   .60   .35
Buenos Aires Municipal Bank, 90th anniv.

Anniversary Emblem — A401

**1968, Dec. 14**   Wmk. 90   Perf. 13½
871 A401 20p car rose & dk grn   .60   .35
ALPI (Fight Against Polio Assoc.), 25th anniv.

Shovel and State Coal Fields Emblem A402

Pouring Ladle and Army Manufacturing Emblem A403

**1968, Dec. 21**    Litho.
872 A402 20p orange, bl & blk   .60   .35
873 A403 20p dl vio, dl yel & blk   .60   .35
Issued to publicize the National Coal and Steel industry at the Rio Turbio coal fields and the Zapla blast furnaces.

Woman Potter, by Ramon Gomez Cornet — A404

**1968, Dec. 21**   Photo.   Perf. 13½
874 A404 20p carmine rose   .75   .40
Centenary of the Witcomb Gallery.

View of Buenos Aires and Rio de la Plata by Ulrico Schmidl A405

**1969, Feb. 8**   Litho.   Wmk. 90
875 A405 20p yellow, blk & ver   .75   .35
Ulrico Schmidl (c. 1462-1554) who wrote "Journey to the Rio de la Plata and Paraguay."

### Types of 1955-67

Designs: 50c, Puma. 1p, Sunflower. 3p, Zapata Slope, Catamarca. 5p, Tierra del Fuego. 6p, José Hernandez. 10p, Inca Bridge, Mendoza. 50p, José de San Martin. 90p, Guillermo Brown. 100p, Ski jumper.

**Photo.; Litho. (50c, 3p, 10p)**
**1969-70**   Wmk. 365   Perf. 13½
882 A275   50c bister ('70)   1.00   .60
883 A277   5p brown   1.40   .90
884 A279 100p blue   26.00   8.00

**Unwmk.**
885 A278   1p brown ('70)   .40   .25
886 A277   3p dk blue ('70)   .65   .25
  a.   Wmk. 90   10.00   3.00
887 A277   5p brown ('70)   .75   .25
888 A366   6p red brn, 15x22mm ('70)   .90   .25
889 A278   10p dull red ('70)   .50   .25
  a.   Wmk. 90   475.00   60.00
890 A241   50p dk bl, 22x31½mm ('70)   1.50   .25
891 A366   90p ol brn, 22x32mm ('70)   4.00   .50
892 A279 100p blue ('70)   12.50   1.00
Nos. 882-892 (11)   49.60   12.50

For surcharges see Nos. 1076-1077.

### Soldier Type of 1965

Army Day: 20p, Sapper (gastador) of Buenos Aires Province, 1856.

**Wmk. 365**
**1969, May 31**   Litho.   Perf. 13½
893 A340a 20p multicolored   1.10   .35

Frigate Hercules, by Emilio Biggeri — A406

**1969, May 31**
894 A406 20p multicolored   1.75   .35
Issued for Navy Day.

"All Men are Equal" — A407

**1969, June 28**    Wmk. 90
895 A407 20p black & ocher   .60   .35
International Human Rights Year.

ILO Emblem — A408

**1969, June 28**   Litho.   Wmk. 365
896 A408 20p lt green & multi   .60   .35
50th anniv. of the ILO. Exists imperf. Value, pair $100.

Pedro N. Arata (1849-1922), Chemist — A409

Portraits: No. 898, Miguel Fernandez (1883-1950), zoologist. No. 899, Angel P. Gallardo (1867-1934), biologist. No. 900, Cristobal M. Hicken (1875-1933), botanist. No. 901, Eduardo Ladislao Holmberg, M.D. (1852-1937), natural scientist.

**1969, Aug. 9**   Wmk. 365   Perf. 13½
897 A409 6p Arata   .70   .45
898 A409 6p Fernandez   .70   .45
899 A409 6p Gallardo   .70   .45
900 A409 6p Hicken   .70   .45
901 A409 6p Holmberg   .70   .45
Nos. 897-901 (5)   3.50   2.25
Argentine scientists. See No. 778 note.

Radar Antenna, Balcarce Station and Satellite — A410

**1969, Aug. 23**    Wmk. 99
902 A410 20p yellow & blk   .60   .35
Communications by satellite through Intl. Telecommunications Satellite Consortium (INTELSAT). Exists imperf. Value, pair $40. See No. C115.

Nieuport 28, Flight Route and Map of Buenos Aires Province — A411

**1969, Sept. 13**   Litho.   Wmk. 90
903 A411 20p multicolored   .60   .35
50th anniv. of the first Argentine airmail service from El Palomar to Mar del Plata, flown Feb. 23-24, 1919, by Capt. Pedro L. Zanni.

Military College Gate and Emblem A412

**1969, Oct. 4**   Wmk. 365   Perf. 13½
904 A412 20p multicolored   .60   .35
Cent. of the National Military College, El Palomar (Greater Buenos Aires).

Gen. Angel Pacheco — A413

**1969, Nov. 8**   Photo.   Wmk. 365
905 A413 20p deep green   .60   .35
Gen. Angel Pacheco (1795-1869).

La Farola, Logotype of La Prensa — A414

Design: No. 907, Bartolomé Mitre & La Nacion logotype.

**1969, Nov. 8**   Litho.   Perf. 13½
906 A414 20p orange, yel & blk   .95   .35
907 A414 20p brt green & blk   .95   .35
Cent. of newspapers La Prensa and La Nacion.

Julian Aguirre — A415

Musicians: No. 909, Felipe Boero. No. 910, Constantino Gaito. No. 911, Carlos Lopez Buchardo. No. 912, Alberto Williams.

**Wmk. 365**
**1969, Dec. 6**   Photo.   Perf. 13½
908 A415 6p Aguirre   .85   .35
909 A415 6p Boero   .85   .35
910 A415 6p Gaito   .85   .35
911 A415 6p Buchardo   .85   .35
912 A415 6p Williams   .85   .35
Nos. 908-912 (5)   4.25   1.75
Argentine musicians. See No. 778 note.

Lt. Benjamin Matienzo and Nieuport Plane — A416

**1969, Dec. 13**    Litho.
913 A416 20p multicolored   .75   .35
23rd Aeronautics and Space Week.

High Power Lines and Map — A417

Design: 20p, Map of Santa Fe Province and schematic view of tunnel.

**1969, Dec. 13**
914 A417   6p multicolored   .60   .35
915 A417 20p multicolored   1.40   .35
Completion of development projects: 6p for the hydroelectric dams on the Limay and Neuquen Rivers, the 20p the tunnel under Rio Grande from Sante Fe to Parana. Set exists imperf.©

Lions Emblem A418

**1969, Dec. 20**   Wmk. 365   Perf. 13½
916 A418 20p black, emer & org   .95   .35
Argentine Lions Intl. Club, 50th anniv.

Madonna and Child, by Raul Soldi — A419

**1969, Dec. 27**    Litho.
917 A419 20p multicolored   .90   .35
Christmas 1969.

# ARGENTINA

Manuel Belgrano, by Jean Gericault — A420

The Creation of the Flag, Bas-relief by Jose Fioravanti — A421

**1970, July 4**    **Unwmk.**    **Photo.**    **Perf. 13½**
918 A420 20c deep brown .55 .35

    **Litho.**    **Perf. 12½**
919 A421 50c bister, blk & bl .85 .55

Gen. Manuel Belgrano (1770-1820), Argentine patriot.

San Jose Palace — A422

**1970, Aug. 9**    **Litho.**    **Perf. 13½**
920 A422 20c yellow grn & multi .60 .35

Gen. Justo Jose de Urquiza (1801-70), pres. of Argentina, 1854-60.

Schooner "Juliet" — A423

**1970, Aug. 8**    **Unwmk.**
921 A423 20c multicolored 1.25 .40

Issued for Navy Day.

Receiver of 1920 and Waves — A424

**1970, Aug. 29**
922 A424 20c lt blue & multi .70 .35

50th anniv. of Argentine broadcasting.

### Types of 1955-67 Inscribed "Republica Argentina" and

Belgrano A425      Lujan Basilica A426

Designs: 1c, Sunflower. 3c, Zapata Slope, Catamarca. 5c, Tierra del Fuego. 8c, No. 931, Belgrano. 10c, Inca Bridge, Mendoza. 25c, 50c, 70c, Jose de San Martin. 65c, 90c, 1.20p, San Martin. 1p, Ski jumper. 1.15p, 1.80p, Adm. Brown.

**1970-73**    **Photo.**    **Unwmk.**    **Perf. 13½**
923 A270 1c dk green ('71) .35 .35
924 A277 3c car rose ('71) .35 .35
925 A277 5c Prus blue ('71) .35 .35
926 A425 6c deep blue .35 .35
927 A425 8c green ('72) .35 .35
928 A278 10c dull red ('71) .45 .35
929 A278 10c brn, litho. ('71) .90 .35
930 A278 10c org brn ('72) .35 .35
931 A425 10c brown ('73) .35 .35
932 A426 18c yel & dk brn, litho ('73) .35 .35
933 A425 25c brown ('71) .50 .35
934 A425 50c scarlet ('72) 1.40 .35
935 A241 65c brn, 22x31½mm, paper II ('71) 1.25 .35
936 A425 70c dk blue ('73) .35 .35
937 A241 90c emer, 22x31½mm ('72) 3.25 .35
938 A279 1p brn, 22½x29½mm ('71) 6.00 .35
939 A366 1.15p dk bl, 22½x32mm ('71) 1.25 .35
940 A241 1.20p org, 22x31½mm ('73) 1.40 .35
941 A366 1.80p brown ('73) .45 .35
Nos. 923-941 (19) 20.00 6.65

The imprint "Casa de Moneda de la Nacion" (in capitals) appears on 3c, 5c, Nos. 928-929; 65c, 90c, 1p, 1.20p.
On type A425 only the 6c is inscribed "Ley 18.188" below denomination.
Fluorescent paper was used in printing the 25c, 50c, and 70c. The 3c, 5c, 8c, No. 931 and 65c were issued on both ordinary and fluorescent paper.
See Nos. 987-996, 1032-1038, 1042-1043, 1089-1107. For overprint and surcharge see Nos. 1010, 1078.

### Soldier Type of 1965

Galloping messenger of Field Army, 1879.

**1970, Oct. 17**    **Litho.**    **Perf. 13½**
944 A340a 20c multicolored 1.10 .35

Dome of Cathedral of Cordoba — A430

**1970, Nov. 7**    **Unwmk.**
945 A430 50c gray & blk 1.00 .35

Bishopric of Tucuman, 400th anniv. See No. C131.

People Around UN Emblem — A431

**1970, Nov. 7**
946 A431 20c tan & multi .60 .35

25th anniversary of the United Nations

State Mint and Medal — A432

**1970, Nov. 28**    **Unwmk.**    **Perf. 13½**
947 A432 20c gold, grn & blk .60 .35

Inauguration of the State Mint Building, 25th anniversary.

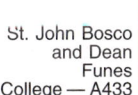

St. John Bosco and Dean Funes College — A433

**1970, Dec. 19**
948 A433 20c olive & blk .60 .35

Honoring the work of the Salesian Order in Patagonia.

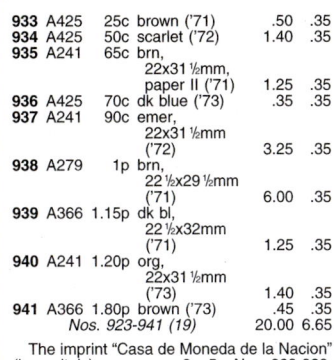

Nativity, by Horacio Gramajo Gutierrez A434

**1970, Dec. 19**
949 A434 20c multicolored .80 .35

Christmas 1970.

Argentine Flag, Map of Argentine Antarctica — A435

**1971, Feb. 20**    **Litho.**    **Perf. 13½**
950 A435 20c multicolored 1.50 .50

Argentine South Pole Expedition, 5th anniv.

Phosphorescent Sorting Code and Albert Einstein A436

**1971, Apr. 30**    **Unwmk.**    **Perf. 13½**
951 A436 25c multicolored .70 .35

Electronics in postal development.

Symbolic Road Crossing A437

**1971, May 29**    **Litho.**
952 A437 25c blue & blk .60 .35

Inter-American Regional Meeting of the Intl. Federation of Roads, Buenos Aires, 3/28-31.

Elias Alippi — A438

Actors: No. 954, Juan Aurelio Casacuberta. No. 955, Angelina Pagano. No. 956, Roberto Casaux. No. 957, Florencio Parravicini. See No. 778 note.

**1971, May 29**    **Litho.**
953 A438 15c Alippi .60 .35
954 A438 15c Casacuberta .60 .35
955 A438 15c Pagano .60 .35
956 A438 15c Casaux .60 .35
957 A438 15c Parravicini .60 .35
Nos. 953-957 (5) 3.00 1.75

### Soldier Type of 1965

Army Day, May 29; Artilleryman, 1900.

**1971, July 3**    **Unwmk.**    **Perf. 13½**
958 A340a 25c multicolored 1.50 .35

Bilander "Carmen," by Emilio Biggeri — A439

**1971, July 3**
959 A439 25c multicolored 1.50 .35

Navy Day

Peruvian Order of the Sun — A440

**1971, Aug. 28**
960 A440 31c multicolored .90 .35

Sesquicentennial of Peru's independence.

Güemes in Battle, by Lorenzo Gigli — A441

Design: No. 962, Death of Güemes, by Antonio Alice.

**1971, Aug. 28**    **Size: 39x29mm**
961 A441 25c multicolored .75 .35
     **Size: 84x29mm**
962 A441 25c multicolored .75 .35

Sesquicentennial of the death of Martin Miguel de Güemes, leader in Gaucho War, Governor and Captain General of Salta Province.

Stylized Tulip — A442

**1971, Sept. 18**
963 A442 25c tan & multi .60 .35

3rd Intl. and 8th Natl. Horticultural Exhib.

Father Antonio Saenz, by Juan Gut — A443

**1971, Sept. 18**
964 A443 25c gray & multi .60 .35

Sesquicentennial of University of Buenos Aires, and to honor Father Antonio Saenz, first Chancellor and Rector.

Fabricaciones Militares Emblem A444

**1971, Oct. 16**    **Unwmk.**    **Perf. 13½**
965 A444 25c brn, gold, bl & blk .60 .35

30th anniv. of military armament works.

Cars and Trucks — A445

Design: 65c, Tree converted into paper.

**1971, Oct. 16**
966 A445 25c dull bl & multi .65 .35
967 A445 65c green & multi 1.60 .35
Nos. 966-967,C134 (3) 3.25 1.05

Nationalized industries.

# ARGENTINA

Luis C. Candelaria and his Plane, 1918 — A446

**1971, Nov. 27**
968  A446  25c multicolored  .60  .35
25th Aeronautics and Space Week.

Observatory and Nebula of Magellan A447

**1971, Nov. 27**
969  A447  25c multicolored  .90  .35
Cordoba Astronomical Observatory, cent.

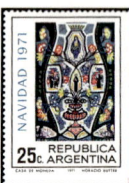

Christ in Majesty — A448

**1971, Dec. 18**  **Litho.**
970  A448  25c blk & multi  .55  .35
Christmas 1971. Design is from a tapestry by Horacio Butler in Basilica of St. Francis, Buenos Aires.

Mother and Child, by J. C. Castagnino — A449

**1972, May 6**  **Unwmk.**  **Perf. 13½**
971  A449  25c fawn & black  .65  .35
25th anniv. (in 1971) of UNICEF.

Mailman's Bag — A450

**1972, Sept. 2**  **Litho.**  **Perf. 13½**
972  A450  25c lemon & multi  .60  .35
Bicentenary of appointment of first Argentine mailman.

Adm. Brown Station, Map of Antarctica A451

**1972, Sept. 2**
973  A451  25c blue & multi  .90  .35
10th anniv. (in 1971) of Antarctic Treaty.

**Soldier Type of 1965**
Army Day:  25c, Sergeant, Negro and Mulatto Corps, 1806-1807.

**1972, Sept. 23**
974  A340a  25c multicolored  .90  .35

Brigantine "Santisima Trinidad" A452

**1972, Sept. 23**
975  A452  25c multicolored  1.10  .35
Navy Day. See No. 1006.

Oil Pump — A453

**1972, Sept. 30**  **Litho.**  **Perf. 13½**
976  A453  45c multicolored  1.00  .35
50th anniv. of the organ. of the state oil fields (Yacimientos Petroliferos Fiscales).

Sounding Balloon — A454

**1972, Sept. 30**
977  A454  25c multicolored  .60  .35
Cent. of Natl. Meteorological Service.

Trees and Globe A455

**1972, Oct. 14**  **Perf. 13x13½**
978  A455  25c bl, blk & lt bl  .85  .35
7th World Forestry Congress, Buenos Aires, Oct. 4-18.

Arms of Naval School, Frigate "Presidente Sarmiento" — A456

**1972, Oct. 14**
979  A456  25c gold & multi  .95  .35
Centenary of Military Naval School.

Early Balloon and Plane, Antonio de Marchi — A457

**1972, Nov. 4**  **Perf. 13½**
980  A457  25c multicolored  .70  .35
Aeronautics and Space Week, and in honor of Baron Antonio de Marchi (1875-1934), aviation pioneer.

Bartolomé Mitre — A458

**1972, Nov. 4**  **Engr.**
981  A458  25c dark blue  .75  .35
Pres. Bartolome Mitre (1821-1906), writer, historian, soldier.

Flower and Heart — A459

**1972, Dec. 2**  **Litho.**  **Perf. 13½**
982  A459  90c lt bl, ultra & blk  .75  .35
"Your heart is your health," World Health Day.

"Martin Fierro," by Juan C. Castagnino A460

"Spirit of the Gaucho," by Vicente Forte A461

**1972, Dec. 2**  **Litho.**  **Perf. 13½**
983  A460  50c multicolored  .50  .35
984  A461  90c multicolored  .75  .40
Intl. Book Year 1972, and cent. of publication of the poem, Martin Fierro, by Jose Hernandez (1834-86).

Iguacu Falls and Tourist Year Emblem A462

**1972, Dec. 16**  **Perf. 13x13½**
985  A462  45c multicolored  .60  .35
Tourism Year of the Americas.

King, Wood Carving, 18th Century — A463

**1972, Dec. 16**  **Perf. 13½**
986  A463  50c multicolored  .70  .35
Christmas 1972.

**Types of 1955-73 Inscribed "Republica Argentina" and**

Moon Valley, San Juan Province — A463a

Designs: 1c, Sunflower. 5c, Tierra del Fuego. 10c, Inca Bridge, Mendoza. 50c, Lujan Basilica. 65c, 22.50p, San Martin. 1p, Ski jumper. 1.15p, 4.50p, Guillermo Brown. 1.80p, Manuel Belgrano.

**Litho.; Photo. (1c, 65c, 1p)**
**Perf. 13½, 12½ (1.80p)**

**1972-75**  **Wmk. 365**
987  A278  1c dk green  .30  .30
988  A277  5c dark blue  .30  .30
989  A278  10c bister brn  .35  .30
989A A426  50c dull pur ('75)  .30  .30
990  A241  65c gray brown  4.25  .35
991  A279  1p brown  4.75  .30
992  A366  1.15p dk gray bl  1.75  .60
993  A425  1.80p blue ('75)  .35  .30
994  A366  4.50p green ('75)  .55  .30
995  A241  22.50p vio bl ('75)  1.75  .40
996  A463a  50p multi ('75)  1.60  .30
  Nos. 987-996 (11)  16.25  3.75

Paper size of 1c is 27½x39mm; others of 1972, 37x27, 27x37mm.
Size of 22.50p, 50p: 26½x38½mm.
See Nos. 1050, 1108.

Cock (Symbolic of Police) — A464

**1973, Feb. 3**  **Litho.**  **Unwmk.**
997  A464  50c lt green & multi  .60  .35
Sesqui. of Federal Police of Argentina.

First Coin of Bank of Buenos Aires — A465

**1973, Feb. 3**  **Perf. 13½**
998  A465  50c purple, yel & brn  .60  .35
Sesquicentennial of the Bank of Buenos Aires Province.

DC-3 Planes Over Antarctica A466

**1973, Apr. 28**  **Litho.**  **Perf. 13½**
999  A466  50c lt blue & multi  1.60  .50
10th anniversary of Argentina's first flight to the South Pole.

Rivadavia's Chair, Argentine Arms and Colors — A467

**1973, May 19**  **Litho.**  **Perf. 13½**
1000  A467  50c multicolored  .60  .35
Inauguration of Pres. Hector J. Campora, May 25, 1973.

San Martin, by Gil de Castro — A468

# ARGENTINA

San Martin and Bolivar — A469

**1973, July 7  Litho.  Perf. 13½**
1001  A468  50c lt green & multi   .60  .35
1002  A469  50c yellow & multi   .60  .35

Gen. San Martin's farewell to the people of Peru and his meeting with Simon Bolivar at Guayaquil July 26-27, 1822.

Eva Peron — A470

**1973, July 26  Litho.  Perf. 13½**
1003  A470  70c black, org & bl   .60  .35

Maria Eva Duarte de Peron (1919-1952), political leader.

House of Viceroy Sobremonte, by Hortensia de Virgillon — A471

**1973, July 20  Perf. 13x13½**
1004  A471  50c blue & multi   .60  .35

400th anniversary of the city of Cordoba.

Woman, by Lino Spilimbergo — A472

**1973, Aug. 28  Litho.  Perf. 13½**
1005  A472  70c multicolored   1.20  .35

Philatelists' Day. See Nos. B60-B61.

**Ship Type of 1972**

Navy Day: 70c, Frigate "La Argentina."

**1973, Oct. 27  Litho.  Perf. 13½**
1006  A452  70c multicolored   .80  .35

New and Old Telephones — A473

**1973, Oct. 27**
1007  A473  70c brt blue & multi   .60  .35

Natl. telecommunications system, 25th anniv.

Plume Made of Flags of Participants — A474

**1973, Nov. 3  Perf. 13½**
1008  A474  70c yellow bis & multi   .60  .35

12th Cong. of Latin Notaries, Buenos Aires.

No. 940 Overprinted

**1973, Nov. 30  Photo.**
1010  A241  1.20p orange   1.10  .35

Assumption of presidency by Juan Peron, Oct. 12.

Virgin and Child, Window, La Plata Cathedral — A476

Christmas: 1.20p, Nativity, by Bruno Venier, b. 1914.

**1973, Dec. 15  Litho.  Perf. 13½**
1011  A476  70c gray & multi   .50  .35
1012  A476  1.20p black & multi   1.00  .35

The Lama, by Juan Battle Planas — A477

Paintings: 50c, Houses in Boca District, by Eugenio Daneri, horiz. 90c, The Blue Grotto, by Emilio Pettoruti, horiz.

**1974, Feb. 9  Litho.  Perf. 13½**
1013  A477  50c multicolored   .75  .35
1014  A477  70c multicolored   .75  .35
1015  A477  90c multicolored   .75  .35
  Nos. 1013-1015, B64 (4)   2.70  1.40

Argentine painters.

Mar del Plata — A478

**1974, Feb. 9**
1016  A478  70c multicolored   .60  .35

Centenary of Mar del Plata.

Weather Symbols — A479

**1974, Mar. 23  Litho.  Perf. 13½**
1017  A479  1.20p multicolored   .60  .35

Cent. of intl. meteorological cooperation.

Justo Santa Maria de Oro — A480

**1974, Mar. 23**
1018  A480  70c multicolored   .60  .35

Bicentenary of the birth of Brother Justo Santa Maria de Oro (1772-1836), theologian, patriot, first Argentine bishop.

Belisario Roldan (1873-1922), Writer — A481

**1974, June 29  Photo.  Unwmk.**
1019  A481  70c bl & brn   .60  .35

Poster with Names of OAS Members A482

**1974, June 29  Litho.**
1020  A482  1.38p multicolored   .60  .35

Organization of American States, 25th anniv.

ENCOTEL Emblem — A483

**1974, Aug. 10  Litho.  Perf. 13**
1021  A483  1.20p blue, gold & blk   70  .35

ENCOTEL, Natl. Post and Telegraph Press.

Flags of Argentina, Bolivia, Brazil, Paraguay, Uruguay — A484

**1974, Aug. 16  Perf. 13½**
1022  A484  1.38p multicolored   .60  .35

6th Meeting of Foreign Ministers of Rio de la Plata Basin Countries.

El Chocon Hydroelectric Complex, Limay River — A485

Somisa Steel Mill, San Nicolas — A486

Gen. Belgrano Bridge, Chaco-Corrientes — A487

**Perf. 13½, 13x13½ (4.50p)**
**1974, Sept. 14**
1023  A485  70c multicolored   .45  .30
1024  A486  1.20p multicolored   .75  .30
1025  A487  4.50p multicolored   2.25  .45
  Nos. 1023-1025 (3)   3.45  1.05

Development projects.

Brigantine Belgrano, by Emilio Biggeri — A488

**1974, Oct. 26  Litho.  Perf. 13½**
1026  A488  1.20p multicolored   1.25  .35

Departure into exile in Chile of General San Martin, Sept. 22, 1822.

Alberto R. Mascias and Bleriot Plane — A489

**1974, Oct. 26  Unwmk.**
1027  A489  1.20p multicolored   .80  .35
  a.  Wmk 365   —  —

Air Force Day, Aug. 10, and to honor Alberto Roque Garcias (1878-1951), aviation pioneer.

Hussar, 1812, by Eleodoro Marenco — A490

**1974, Oct. 26**
1028  A490  1.20p multicolored   .80  .35

Army Day.

Post Horn and Flags — A491

**1974, Nov. 23  Unwmk.  Perf. 13½**
1029  A491  2.65p multicolored   1.00  .35
  a.  Wmk 365   45.00  22.50

Centenary of Universal Postal Union.

Franciscan Monastery A492

**1974, Nov. 23  Litho.**
1030  A492  1.20p multicolored   .60  .35

400th anniversary, city of Santa Fe.

**Trout Type of 1968**
**1974  Engr.  Unwmk.**
1031  A366a  1000p vio bl   .30  .35

Due to a shortage of 10p stamps a quantity of this 1,000p was released for use as 10p.

**Types of 1954-73 Inscribed "Republica Argentina" and**

Red Deer in Forest — A495

# ARGENTINA

Congress Building — A497

Designs: 30c, 60c, 1.80p, Manuel Belgrano. 50c, Lujan Basilica. 1.20p, 2p, 6p, San Martin (16x22 ½mm). 2.70p, 7.50p, 22.50p, San Martin (22x31 ½mm). 4.50p, 13.50p, Guillermo Brown. 10p, Leaping trout.

**1974-76  Unwmk.  Photo.  Perf. 13½**

| | | | | |
|---|---|---|---|---|
| 1032 | A425 | 30c brown vio | .40 | .35 |
| 1033 | A426 | 50c blk & brn red | .40 | .35 |
| 1034 | A426 | 50c bister & bl | .35 | .35 |
| 1035 | A425 | 60c ocher | .40 | .35 |
| 1036 | A425 | 1.20p red | .40 | .35 |
| 1037 | A425 | 1.80p deep blue | .40 | .35 |
| 1038 | A425 | 2p dark purple | .50 | .40 |
| 1039 | A241 | 2.70p dk bl, 22x31 ½mm | .40 | .35 |
| 1040 | A366 | 4.50p green | 2.00 | .35 |
| 1041 | A495 | 5p yel green | .50 | .35 |
| 1042 | A425 | 6p red orange | .40 | .35 |
| 1043 | A425 | 6p emerald | .40 | .35 |
| 1044 | A425 | 7.50p grn, 22x31 ½mm | 1.20 | .35 |
| 1045 | A366a | 10p violet blue | 2.50 | .35 |
| 1046 | A366 | 13.50p scar, 16x22 ½mm | .60 | .35 |
| 1047 | A366 | 13.50p scar, 22x31 ½mm | 1.20 | .35 |
| 1048 | A241 | 22.50p dp bl, 22x31 ½mm | 1.20 | .60 |
| 1049 | A497 | 30p yel & dk red brn | 4.50 | .35 |
| 1050 | A463a | 50p multicolored | 1.75 | .35 |
| | | Nos. 1032-1050 (19) | 19.50 | 6.95 |

Issued: 10p, 5/74; 30c, 1.20p, 2.70p, 5/15/74; 5p, 11/20/74; 30p, 12/10/74; 2p, 3/1/75; 60c, 7.50p, 4/30/75; 4.50p, 7/21/75; 1.80p, Nos. 1042, 1047, 22.50p, 8/14/75; No. 1046, 10/10/75; No. 1034, 10/30/75; No. 1043, 11/6/75; 50p, 2/76.

Fluorescent paper was used in printing No. 1036, 2p, Nos. 1044 and 1047. The 30p was issued on both ordinary and fluorescent paper.
See No. 829. For type of A495 overprinted see No. 1144.

### Miniature Sheet

A498

**1974, Dec. 7  Litho.  Perf. 13½**

| 1052 | A498 | Sheet of 6 | 4.50 | 3.00 |
|---|---|---|---|---|
| a. | | 1p Mariano Necochea | .50 | .25 |
| b. | | 1.20p Jose de San Martin | .50 | .25 |
| c. | | 1.70p Manuel Isidoro Suarez | .50 | .25 |
| d. | | 1.90p Juan Pascual Pringles | .50 | .25 |
| e. | | 2.70p Latin American flags | .50 | .25 |
| f. | | 4.50p Jose Felix Bogado | .50 | .25 |

Sesqui. of Battles of Junin and Ayacucho.

Dove, by Vito Campanella — A499

St. Anne, by Raul Soldi — A500

**1974, Dec. 21  Litho.  Perf. 13½**

| 1053 | A499 | 1.20p multicolored | .90 | .35 |
|---|---|---|---|---|
| 1054 | A500 | 2.65p multicolored | .90 | .35 |

Christmas 1974.

Boy Looking at Stamp — A501

**1974, Dec. 21**

| 1055 | A501 | 1.70p black & yel | .60 | .35 |
|---|---|---|---|---|

World Youth Philately Year.

Space Monsters, by Raquel Forner — A502

Argentine modern art: 4.50p, Dream, by Emilio Centurion.

**1975, Feb. 22  Litho.  Perf. 13½**

| 1056 | A502 | 2.70p multi | 1.00 | .30 |
|---|---|---|---|---|
| 1057 | A502 | 4.50p multi | 1.95 | .40 |

Indian Woman and Cathedral, Catamarca — A503

Tourist Publicity: No. 1059, Carved chancel and street scene. No. 1060, Logging operations and monastery yard. No. 1061, Painted pottery and power station. No. 1062, Farm cart and colonial mansion. No. 1063, Perito Moreno glacier and spinning mill. No. 1064, Lake Lapataia and scientific surveyor. No. 1065, Los Alerces National Park and oil derrick.

**1975  Litho.  Perf. 13½**
**Unwmk., Wmk 365 (6p)**

| 1058 | A503 | 1.20p shown | .50 | .35 |
|---|---|---|---|---|
| 1059 | A503 | 1.20p Jujuy | .50 | .35 |
| 1060 | A503 | 1.20p Salta | .50 | .35 |
| 1061 | A503 | 1.20p Santiago del Estero | .50 | .35 |
| 1062 | A503 | 1.20p Tucuman | .50 | .35 |
| 1063 | A503 | 6p Santa Cruz | .90 | .35 |
| 1064 | A503 | 6p Tierra del Fuego | .90 | .35 |
| 1065 | A503 | 6p Chubut | .90 | .35 |
| | | Nos. 1058-1065 (8) | 5.20 | 2.80 |

Issue dates: 1.20p, Mar. 8; 6p, Dec. 20.

"We Have Been Inoculated" — A504

**1975, Apr. 26  Unwmk.  Perf. 13½**

| 1066 | A504 | 2p multi | .70 | .35 |
|---|---|---|---|---|

Children's inoculation campaign (child's painting).

Hugo A. Acuña and South Orkney Station — A505

Designs: No. 1068, Francisco P. Moreno and Lake Nahuel Huapi. No. 1069, Lt. Col. Luis Piedra Buena and cutter, Luisito. No. 1070, Ensign José M. Sobral and Snow Hill House. No. 1071, Capt. Carlos M. Moyano and Cerro del Toro (mountain).

**1975, June 28  Litho.  Perf. 13**

| 1067 | A505 | 2p grnsh bl & multi | .60 | .35 |
|---|---|---|---|---|
| 1068 | A505 | 2p yel grn & multi | .60 | .35 |
| 1069 | A505 | 2p lt vio & multi | .60 | .35 |
| 1070 | A505 | 2p gray bl & multi | .60 | .35 |
| 1071 | A505 | 2p pale grn & multi | .60 | .35 |
| | | Nos. 1067-1071 (5) | 3.00 | 1.75 |

Pioneers of Antarctica.

Frigate "25 de Mayo" — A506

**1975, Sept. 27  Unwmk.  Perf. 13½**

| 1072 | A506 | 6p multi | 1.10 | .35 |
|---|---|---|---|---|

Navy Day 1975.

Eduardo Bradley and Balloon — A507

**1975, Sept. 27  Wmk. 365**

| 1073 | A507 | 6p multi | .70 | .35 |
|---|---|---|---|---|

Air Force Day.

Declaration of Independence, by Juan M. Blanes — A508

**1975, Oct. 25**

| 1074 | A508 | 6p multi | .95 | .35 |
|---|---|---|---|---|

Sesquicentennial of Uruguay's declaration of independence.

Flame — A509

**1975, Oct. 17  Unwmk.**

| 1075 | A509 | 6p gray & multi | .60 | .35 |
|---|---|---|---|---|

Loyalty Day, 30th anniversary of Pres. Peron's accession to power.

No. 886 Surcharged

No. 891 Surcharged

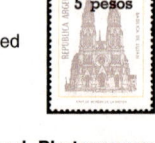

No. 932 Surcharged

**1975  Lithographed, Photogravure**

| 1076 | A277 | 6c on 3p | .50 | .35 |
|---|---|---|---|---|
| a. | | On #886a | 50.00 | |
| 1077 | A366 | 30c on 90p | .60 | .35 |
| 1078 | A426 | 5p on 18c | .70 | .35 |
| | | Nos. 1076-1078 (3) | 1.80 | 1.05 |

Issued: 6c, 10/30; 30c, 11/20; 5p, 10/24.

A510

Design: International Bridge, flags of Argentina & Uruguay.

**1975, Oct. 25  Litho.  Wmk. 365**

| 1081 | A510 | 6p multi | .60 | .35 |
|---|---|---|---|---|

Post Horn, Surcharged — A511

**1975, Nov. 8**

| 1082 | A511 | 10p on 20c multi | .75 | .35 |
|---|---|---|---|---|

Introduction of postal code. Not issued without surcharge.

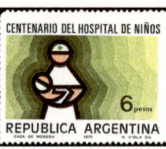

Nurse Holding Infant — A512

**1975, Dec. 13  Litho.  Perf. 13½**

| 1083 | A512 | 6p multi | .95 | .35 |
|---|---|---|---|---|

Children's Hospital, centenary.

Nativity, Nueva Pompeya Church — A513

**1975, Dec. 13  Litho.  Unwmk.**

| 1084 | A513 | 6p multicolored | .70 | .35 |
|---|---|---|---|---|

Christmas 1975.

### Types of 1970-75 and

Church of St. Francis, Salta — A515

Designs: 3p, No. 1099, 60p, 90p, Manuel Belgrano. 12p, 15p, 20p, 30p, No. 1100, 100p, 110p, 120p, 130p, San Martin. 15p, 70p, Guillermo Brown. 300p, Moon Valley (lower inscriptions italic). 500p, Adm. Brown Station, Antarctica.

**1976-78  Photo.  Unwmk.  Perf. 13½**

| 1089 | A425 | 3p slate | .50 | .30 |
|---|---|---|---|---|
| 1090 | A425 | 12p rose red | .45 | .30 |

**Perf. 12½x13  Litho.  Wmk. 365**

| 1091 | A425 | 12p rose red | .60 | .30 |
|---|---|---|---|---|
| 1092 | A425 | 12p emerald | .60 | .30 |

**Perf. 13½  Photo.  Unwmk.**

| 1093 | A425 | 12p emer ('77) | .60 | .30 |
|---|---|---|---|---|
| 1094 | A425 | 15p rose red | .50 | .30 |
| 1095 | A425 | 15p vio bl ('77) | .60 | .30 |
| 1097 | A425 | 20p rose red ('77) | .60 | .30 |
| 1098 | A425 | 30p rose red ('77) | .60 | .30 |
| 1099 | A425 | 40p dp grn | 1.75 | .30 |
| 1100 | A425 | 40p rose red ('77) | .60 | .30 |
| 1101 | A425 | 60p dk bl ('77) | 2.50 | .30 |
| 1102 | A425 | 70p dk bl ('77) | 2.50 | .35 |
| 1103 | A425 | 90p emer ('77) | 1.25 | .30 |
| 1104 | A425 | 100p red | 1.75 | .30 |
| 1105 | A425 | 110p rose red ('78) | .60 | .30 |
| 1106 | A425 | 120p rose red ('78) | .60 | .30 |
| 1107 | A425 | 130p rose red ('78) | .85 | .30 |

**Litho.**

| 1108 | A463a | 300p multi | 5.00 | .35 |
|---|---|---|---|---|
| a. | | Wmk 365 | 17.50 | 5.00 |

## ARGENTINA

| | | | | |
|---|---|---|---|---|
| 1109 | A515 | 500p multi ('77) | 8.50 | .35 |
| a. | | Wmk 365 | 120.00 | 14.00 |
| 1110 | A515 | 1000p multi ('77) | 6.75 | 8.00 |
| | | Nos. 1089-1110 (21) | 37.70 | 14.15 |

Fluorescent paper was used in printing both 12p rose red, 15p rose red, 20p, 30p, 40p rose red, 100p, 110p, 120p, 130p.

No. 1099 and the 300p were issued on both ordinary and fluorescent paper.

Nos. 1108 and 1109 exist imperf. Values, pairs: No. 1108 $250; No. 1109 $120.

See Nos. B73-B74.

A516

| 1976 | Photo. | Unwmk. | | |
|---|---|---|---|---|
| 1112 | A516 | 12c gray & blk | .35 | .30 |
| 1113 | A516 | 50c gray & grn | .35 | .30 |
| 1114 | A516 | 1p red & blk | .35 | .30 |
| 1115 | A516 | 4p bl & blk | .35 | .30 |
| 1116 | A516 | 5p org & blk | .40 | .30 |
| 1117 | A516 | 6p dp brn & blk | .40 | .30 |
| 1118 | A516 | 10p gray & vio bl | .70 | .30 |
| 1119 | A516 | 27p lt grn & blk | .50 | .30 |
| 1120 | A516 | 30p lt bl & blk | 2.50 | .30 |
| 1121 | A516 | 45p yel & blk | 1.40 | .30 |
| 1122 | A516 | 50p dl grn & blk | 1.40 | .30 |
| 1123 | A516 | 100p brt grn & red | 1.40 | .30 |

| | Perf. 13x12½ | | | |
|---|---|---|---|---|
| 1976 | Litho. | | Wmk. 365 | |
| 1124 | A516 | 5p org & blk | .45 | .30 |
| 1125 | A516 | 27p lt grn & blk | 1.00 | .30 |
| 1126 | A516 | 45p yel & blk | 1.40 | .30 |
| | | Nos. 1112-1126 (15) | 12.95 | 4.50 |

The 1p, 6p, 10p, 50p and No. 1116 were issued on both ordinary and fluorescent paper.

Jet and Airlines Emblem A517

| | Perf. 13x13½ | | | |
|---|---|---|---|---|
| 1976, Apr. 24 | Litho. | | Unwmk. | |
| 1130 | A517 | 30p bl, lt bl & dk bl | 1.35 | .35 |

Argentine Airlines, 25th anniversary.

Frigate Heroina & Map of Falkland Islands A518

**1976, Apr. 26**
| 1131 | A518 | 6p multi | 3.25 | .40 |

Argentina's claim to Falkland Islands.

Louis Braille — A519

| | Wmk. 365 | | | |
|---|---|---|---|---|
| 1976, May 22 | Engr. | | Perf. 13½ | |
| 1132 | A519 | 10.70 deep blue | .60 | .30 |

Sesquicentennial of the invention of the Braille system of writing for the blind by Louis Braille (1809-1852).

Private, 7th Infantry Regiment — A520

**1976, May 29  Litho.  Unwmk.**
| 1133 | A520 | 12p multi | .70 | .35 |

Army Day.

Schooner Rio de la Plata, by Emilio Biggeri — A521

**1976, June 19**
| 1134 | A521 | 12p multi | .95 | .35 |

Navy Day.

Dr. Bernardo Houssay A522

Argentine Nobel Prize Winners: 10p, Bernardo Houssay, medicine and physiology, 1947. 15p, Luis F. Leloir, chemistry, 1970. 20p, Carlos Saavedra Lamas, peace, 1936.

**1976, Aug. 14  Litho.  Perf. 13½**
| 1135 | A522 | 10p org & blk | .60 | .35 |
| 1136 | A522 | 15p yel & blk | .60 | .35 |
| 1137 | A522 | 20p ochre & blk | .60 | .35 |
| | | Nos. 1135-1137 (3) | 1.80 | 1.05 |

Rio de la Plata International Bridge — A523

**1976, Sept. 18  Litho.  Perf. 13½**
| 1138 | A523 | 12p multi | .95 | .35 |

Inauguration of International Bridge connecting Puerto Unzue, Argentina, and Fray Bentos, Uruguay.

Pipelines & Cooling Tower, Gen. Mosconi Plant — A524

**1976, Nov. 20  Litho.  Perf. 13½**
| 1139 | A524 | 28p multi | .70 | .35 |

Pablo Teodoro Fels & Bleriot Monoplane, 1910 — A525

**1976, Nov. 20**
| 1140 | A525 | 15p multi | .75 | .35 |

Air Force Day.

Nativity — A526

**1976, Dec. 18  Litho.  Perf. 13½**
| 1141 | A526 | 20p multi | .90 | .35 |

Christmas. Painting by Edith Chiapotto.

Water Conference Emblem — A527

**1977, Mar. 19  Litho.  Perf. 13½**
| 1142 | A527 | 70p multi | .90 | .35 |

UN Water Conf., Mar del Plata, Mar. 14-25.

Dalmacio Velez Sarsfield A528

**1977, Mar. 19  Engr.**
| 1143 | A528 | 50p blk & red brn | .95 | .35 |

Dalmacio Velez Sarsfield (1800-1875), author of Argentine civil code.

Red Deer Type of 1974 Surcharged

**1977, July 30  Photo.  Perf. 13½**
| 1144 | A495 | 100p on 5p brn | 1.60 | .35 |

Sesquicentennial of Uruguayan postal service. Not issued without surcharge.

Soldier, 16th Lancers — A529

**1977, July 30**
| 1145 | A529 | 30p multi | 1.10 | .35 |

Army Day.

Schooner Sarandi, by Emilio Biggeri — A530

**1977, July 30**
| 1146 | A530 | 30p multi | 1.10 | .50 |

Navy Day.

Soccer Games' Emblem — A531

70p, Argentina '78 emblem, flags & soccer field.

**1977, May 14**
| 1147 | A531 | 30p multi | .70 | .35 |
| 1148 | A531 | 70p multi | 1.00 | .35 |

11th World Cup Soccer Championship, Argentina, June 1-25, 1978.

The Visit, by Horacio Butler — A532

Consecration, by Miguel P. Caride — A533

**1977, Mar. 26  Litho.**
| 1149 | A532 | 50p multi | .75 | .35 |
| 1150 | A533 | 70p multi | 1.00 | .35 |

Argentine artists.

Sierra de la Ventana A534

Views: No. 1152, Civic Center, Santa Rosa. No. 1153, Skiers, San Martin de los Andes. No. 1154, Boat on Lake Fonck, Rio Negro.

**1977, Oct. 8  Litho.  Perf. 13x13½**
| 1151 | A534 | 30p multi | .60 | .35 |
| 1152 | A534 | 30p multi | .60 | .35 |
| 1153 | A534 | 30p multi | .60 | .35 |
| 1154 | A534 | 30p multi | .60 | .35 |
| | | Nos. 1151-1154 (4) | 2.40 | 1.40 |

Guillermo Brown, by R. del Villar — A535

**1977, Oct. 8  Perf. 13½**
| 1155 | A535 | 30p multi | .60 | .35 |

Adm. Guillermo Brown (1777-1857), leader in fight for independence, bicentenary of birth.

Jet — A536

Double-decker, 1926 — A537

**1977  Litho.  Perf. 13½**
| 1156 | A536 | 30p multi | .55 | .35 |
| 1157 | A537 | 40p multi | .65 | .35 |

50th anniversary of military plane production (30p); Air Force Day (40p).
Issue dates: 30p, Dec. 3; 40p, Nov. 26.

Adoration of the Kings — A538

**1977, Dec. 17**
| 1158 | A538 | 100p multi | 1.25 | .35 |

Christmas 1977.

Historic City Hall, Buenos Aires A539

Chapel of Rio Grande Museum, Tierra del Fuego A540

5p, 20p, La Plata Museum. 10p, Independence Hall, Tucuman. 40p, City Hall, Salta. No. 1165, City Hall, Buenos Aires. 100p, Columbus Theater, Buenos Aires. 200p, flag Monument, Rosario. 280p, 300p, Chapel of Rio Grande Museum, Tierra del Fuego. 480p, 520p, 800, Ruins of Jesuit Mission Church of San Ignacio, Misiones. 500p, Candonga

# ARGENTINA

Chapel, Cordoba. 1000p, G.P.O., Buenos Aires. 2000p, Civic Center, Bariloche, Rio Negro.

Three types of 10p: I. Nine vertical window bars; small imprint "E. MILIAVACA Dib." II. Nine bars; large imprint "E. MILIAVACA DIB." III. Redrawn; 5 bars; large imprint.

**1977-81   Photo.   Unwmk.   Perf. 13½**
**Size: 32x21mm, 21x32mm**

| 1159 | A540 | 5p gray & blk | .40 | .30 |
|---|---|---|---|---|
| 1160 | A540 | 10p lt ultra & blk, I | .40 | .30 |
| a. | Type II | | .60 | .35 |
| 1161 | A540 | 10p lt bl & blk, III | .40 | .30 |
| 1162 | A540 | 20p citron & blk, litho. | .40 | .30 |
| 1163 | A539 | 40p gray bl & blk | .50 | .30 |
| 1164 | A539 | 50p yel & blk | .60 | .30 |
| 1165 | A540 | 50p citron & blk | .85 | .30 |
| 1166 | A540 | 100p org & blk, litho. | .50 | .35 |
| a. | Wmk. 365 | | 100.00 | 18.00 |
| 1167 | A540 | 100p red org & blk | .50 | .30 |
| 1168 | A540 | 100p turq & blk | .40 | .30 |
| 1169 | A539 | 200p lt bl & blk | .85 | .30 |
| 1170 | A540 | 280p rose & blk | 11.00 | 1.00 |
| 1171 | A540 | 300p lemon & blk | 1.40 | .30 |
| 1172 | A540 | 480p org & blk | 1.75 | .30 |
| 1173 | A540 | 500p yel grn & blk | .60 | .30 |
| 1174 | A540 | 520p org & blk | 1.20 | .35 |
| 1175 | A540 | 800p rose lil & blk | 2.10 | .30 |
| 1176 | A540 | 1000p lem bis & blk | 1.75 | .50 |
| 1177 | A540 | 1000p gold & blk, 40x29mm | 3.00 | .30 |
| 1178 | A540 | 2000p multi | 1.40 | .50 |
| | Nos. 1159-1178 (20) | | 30.00 | 7.25 |

Nos. 1161, 1163, 1165, 1167, 1169, 1171, 1173, 1176, 1177 were issued on both ordinary and fluorescent paper. No. 1174 was issued only on fluorescent paper. All others were issued only on ordinary paper.

Issued: No. 1164, 5/30/77; 280p, 12/15/77; No. 1160, 3/14/78; 480p, 5/22/78; 5p, 7/25/78; 20p, 500p, 9/8/78; No. 1166, 9/20/78; No. 1177, 9/28/78; 520p, 9/30/78; 300p, 10/5/78; 40p, 12/1/78; No. 1161, 1979; No. 1165, 1/8/79; 800p, 3/20/79; No. 1167, 4/25/79; 200p, 6/23/79; No. 1176, 12/15/79; 2000p, 6/25/80; No. 1168, 5/26/81.

For overprints see Nos. 1253, 1315.

Soccer Games' Emblem — A544

**1978, Feb. 10   Photo.   Perf. 13½**
| 1179 | A544 | 200p yel grn & bl | 1.10 | .35 |
|---|---|---|---|---|
| a. | Wmk 365 | | 100.00 | 75.00 |

11th World Cup Soccer Championship, Argentina, June 1-25.

View of El Rio, Rosario — A545

Designs (Argentina '78 Emblem and): 100p, Rio Tercero Dam, Cordoba. 150p, Cordillera Mountains, Mendoza. 200p, City Center, Mar del Plata. 300p, View of Buenos Aires.

**1978, May 6   Litho.   Perf. 13**
| 1180 | A545 | 50p multi | .45 | .45 |
|---|---|---|---|---|
| 1181 | A545 | 100p multi | .45 | .45 |
| 1182 | A545 | 150p multi | .75 | .50 |
| 1183 | A545 | 200p multi | .75 | .50 |
| 1184 | A545 | 300p multi | 1.40 | .60 |
| | Nos. 1180-1184 (5) | | 3.80 | 2.50 |

Sites of 11th World Cup Soccer Championship, June 1-25.

Children A546

**1978, May 20**
| 1185 | A546 | 100p multi | .60 | .35 |

50th anniversary of Children's Institute.

Labor Day, by B. Quinquela Martin — A547

Design: No. 1187, Woman's torso, sculpture by Orlando Pierri.

**1978, May 20   Perf. 13½**
| 1186 | A547 | 100p multi | .75 | .35 |
|---|---|---|---|---|
| 1187 | A547 | 100p multi | .75 | .35 |

Argentina, Hungary, France, Italy and Emblem — A548

Stadium A549

Teams and Argentina '78 Emblem: 200p, Poland, Fed. Rep. of Germany, Tunisia, Mexico. 300p, Austria, Spain, Sweden, Brazil. 400p, Netherlands, Iran, Peru, Scotland.

**1978   Litho.   Perf. 13**
| 1188 | A548 | 100p multi | .45 | .45 |
|---|---|---|---|---|
| 1189 | A548 | 200p multi | 1.00 | .45 |
| 1190 | A548 | 300p multi | 1.40 | .55 |
| 1191 | A548 | 400p multi | 1.75 | .55 |
| | Nos. 1188-1191 (4) | | 4.60 | 2.00 |

**Souvenir Sheet**
**Lithographed and Engraved**
**Perf. 13½**
| 1192 | A549 | 700p buff & blk | 3.00 | 3.00 |

11th World Cup Soccer Championship, Argentina, June 1-25. Issued: Nos. 1188-1191, 6/6; No. 1192, 6/3.

Stadium Type of 1978 Inscribed in Red

**Lithographed and Engraved**
**1978, Sept. 2   Perf. 13½**
| 1193 | A549 | 1000p buff, blk & red | 4.50 | 4.50 |

Argentina's victory in 1978 Soccer Championship. No. 1193 has margin similar to No. 1192 with Rimet Cup emblem and text added in red.

Young Tree Nourished by Old Trunk, UN Emblem A550

**1978 Sept. 2   Litho.**
| 1194 | A550 | 100p multi | .60 | .35 |

Technical Cooperation among Developing Countries Conf., Buenos Aires, Sept. 1978.

Emblems of Buenos Aires & Bank — A551

**1978, Sept. 16**
| 1195 | A551 | 100p multi | .60 | .35 |

Bank of City of Buenos Aires, centenary.

General Savio & Steel Production A552

**1978, Sept. 16**
| 1196 | A552 | 100p multi | .60 | .35 |

Gen. Manuel N. Savio (1892-1948), general manager of military heavy industry.

San Martin — A553

**1978, Oct.   Engr.**
| 1197 | A553 | 2000p grnsh blk | 4.25 | .50 |

**1979   Wmk. 365**
| 1198 | A553 | 2000p grnsh blk | 5.75 | 1.00 |

Gen Jose de San Martin (1778-1850), soldier and statesman. See No. 1292.

Globe & Argentine Flag — A554

**1978, Oct. 7   Litho.   Perf. 13½**
| 1199 | A554 | 200p multi | 1.00 | .35 |

12th Intl. Cancer Cong., Buenos Aires, Oct. 5-11.

Chessboard, Queen & Pawn — A555

**1978, Oct. 7**
| 1200 | A555 | 200p multi | 4.50 | .65 |

23rd National Chess Olympics, Buenos Aires, Oct. 25-Nov. 12.

Correct Positioning of Stamps — A557

50p, Use correct postal code number.

**1978   Photo.   Perf. 13½**
| 1201 | A557 | 20p ultra | .60 | .35 |
|---|---|---|---|---|
| 1203 | A557 | 50p carmine | .60 | .35 |

No. 1201 issued on both ordinary and fluorescent paper.

A558     A559

**1978-82   Photo.   Perf. 13½**
| 1204 | A558 | 150p bl & ultra | .65 | .35 |
|---|---|---|---|---|
| 1205 | A558 | 180p bl & ultra | .65 | .35 |
| 1206 | A558 | 200p bl & ultra | .90 | .35 |
| 1207 | A559 | 240p ol bis & bl ('79) | .65 | .35 |
| 1208 | A559 | 260p blk & lt bl ('79) | .65 | .35 |
| 1209 | A559 | 290p brn & lt bl ('79) | .80 | .35 |
| 1210 | A559 | 310p mag & bl ('79) | .80 | .35 |
| 1211 | A559 | 350p ver & bl ('79) | 1.00 | .35 |
| 1212 | A559 | 450p ultra & bl | .90 | .35 |
| 1213 | A559 | 600p grn & bl ('80) | 2.00 | .35 |
| 1214 | A559 | 700p blk & bl ('80) | 1.20 | .35 |
| 1215 | A559 | 800p red & bl ('81) | .80 | .35 |
| 1216 | A559 | 1100p gray & bl ('81) | 1.60 | .35 |
| 1217 | A559 | 1500p blk & bl ('81) | .90 | .35 |
| 1218 | A559 | 1700p grn & bl ('82) | .90 | .35 |
| | Nos. 1204-1218 (15) | | 14.40 | 5.25 |

No. 1204 issued on fluorescent and ordinary paper. No. 1206 issued only on fluorescent paper.

For overprint see No. 1338.

Balsa "24" — A561

Ships: 200p, Tug Legador. 300p, River Parana tug No. 34. 400p, Passenger ship Ciudad de Parana.

**1978, Nov. 4   Litho.   Perf. 13½**
| 1220 | A561 | 100p multi | .45 | .30 |
|---|---|---|---|---|
| 1221 | A561 | 200p multi | .70 | .30 |
| 1222 | A561 | 300p multi | 1.00 | .30 |
| a. | Pair, #1221-1222 | | 2.00 | |
| 1223 | A561 | 400p multi | 1.30 | .60 |
| a. | Pair, #1220, 1223 | | 2.00 | |
| | Nos. 1220-1223 (4) | | 3.45 | 1.50 |

20th anniversary of national river fleet. Issued on fluorescent paper.

View and Arms of Bahia Blanca — A562

**1978, Nov. 25   Litho.   Perf. 13½**
| 1224 | A562 | 20p multi | .75 | .35 |

Sesquicentennial of Bahia Blanca.

"Spain," (Queen Isabella and Columbus) by Arturo Dresco — A563

**1978, Nov. 25**
| 1225 | A563 | 300p multi | 3.00 | .60 |

Visit of King Juan Carlos and Queen Sofia of Spain to Argentina, Nov. 26.

Virgin and Child, San Isidro Cathedral — A564

**1978, Dec. 16**
| 1226 | A564 | 200p gold & multi | 1.00 | .35 |

Christmas 1978.

Slope at Chacabuco, by Pedro Subercaseaux A565

Painting: 1000p, The Embrace of Maipu (San Martin and O'Higgins), by Pedro Subercaseaux, vert.

# ARGENTINA

**1978, Dec. 16**    Litho.    Perf. 13½
1227 A565 500p multi    2.25   .35
1228 A565 1000p multi    3.75   .35
José de San Martin, 200th birth anniversary.

Adolfo Alsina — A566

Design: No. 1230, Mariano Moreno.

**1979, Jan. 20**
1229 A566 200p lt bl & blk    .75   .35
1230 A566 200p yel red & blk    .75   .35
Adolfo Alsina (1828-1877), political leader, vice-president; Mariano Moreno (1778-1811), lawyer, educator, political leader.

Argentina No. 37 and UPU Emblem A567

**1979, Jan. 20**
1231 A567 200p multi    .75   .35
Centenary of Argentina's UPU membership.

Still-life, by Carcova A568

Painting: 300p, The Laundresses, by Faustino Brughetti.

**1979, Mar. 3**
1232 A568 200p multi    .90   .30
1233 A568 300p multi    .90   .35
Ernesto de la Carcova (1866-1927) and Faustino Brughetti (1877-1956), Argentine painters.

Balcarce Earth Station — A569

**1979, Mar. 3**
1234 A569 200p multicolored    .90   .35
Third Inter-American Telecommunications Conference, Buenos Aires, March 5-9.

Stamp Collecting — A570

**1979**
1235 A570 30p multicolored    .60   .35
Printed on ordinary and fluorescent paper.

European Olive — A571

**1979, June 2**    Litho.    Perf. 13½
1236 A571 100p shown    .85   .35
1237 A571 200p Tea    .85   .35
1238 A571 300p Sorghum    1.60   .45
1239 A571 400p Common flax    1.60   .55
    Nos. 1236-1239 (4)    4.90   1.70

Laurel and Regimental Emblem — A572

**1979, June 9**
1240 A572 200p gold & multi    .70   .35
Founding of Subteniente Berdina Village in memory of Sub-lieutenant Rodolfo Hernan Berdina, killed by terrorists in 1975.

"75" and Automobile Club Emblem A573

**1979, June 9**
1241 A573 200p gold & multi    .60   .35
Argentine Automobile Club, 75th anniv.

Exchange Building and Emblem A574

**1979, June 9**
1242 A574 200p bl, blk & gold    .60   .35
Grain Exchange, 125th anniversary.

Cavalry Officer, 1817 — A575

**1979, July 7**    Litho.    Perf. 13½
1243 A575 200p multi    1.25   .35
Army Day.

Corvette Uruguay and Navy Emblem A576

Design: No. 1245, Hydrographic service ship & emblem.

**1979**    Perf. 13
1244 A576 250p multi    1.65   .35
1245 A576 250p multi    1.65   .35
Navy Day; Cent. of Naval Hydrographic Service. Issued: No. 1244, July 28; No. 1245, July 7.

Tree and Man — A577

**1979, July 28**    Perf. 13½
1246 A577 250p multi    .85   .35
Protection of the Environment Day, June 5.

"Spad" Flying over Andes, and Vicente Almandos Almonacid A578

**1979, Aug. 4**
1247 A578 250p multi    1.00   .35
Air Force Day.

Gen. Julio A. Roca Occupying Rio Negro, by Juan M. Blanes — A579

**1979, Aug. 4**
1248 A579 250p multi    1.00   .35
Conquest of Rio Negro Desert, centenary.

Rowland Hill — A580

**1979, Sept. 29**    Litho.    Perf. 13½
1249 A580 300p gray red & blk    .90   .35
Sir Rowland Hill (1795-1879), originator of penny postage.

Viedma Navarez Monument — A581

**1979, Sept. 29**
1250 A581 300p multi    1.10   .35
Viedma and Carmen de Patagones towns, bicentenary.

Pope Paul VI — A582

Design: No. 1252, Pope John Paul I.

**1979, Oct. 27**    Engr.    Perf. 13½
1251 A582 500p black    1.25   .65
1252 A582 500p sepia    1.25   .35

No. 1169 Overprinted in Red

**1979, Nov. 10**    Photo.    Perf. 13½
1253 A539 200p lt blue & blk    .90   .35
Rosario Philatelic Society, 75th anniversary.

A583

**1979, Nov. 10**    Litho.
1254 A583 300p multi    1.00   .35
Frontier resettlement.

A584

**1979, Dec. 1**    Litho.    Perf. 13½
1255 A584 300p multi    1.00   .35
Military Geographic Institute centenary.

Christmas 1979 — A585

**1979, Dec. 1**
1256 A585 300p multi    .90   .40

General Mosconi Birth Centenary A586

**1979, Dec. 15**    Engr.    Perf. 13½
1257 A586 1000p blk & bl    1.75   .50

Rotary Emblem and Globe — A587

**1979, Dec. 20**    Litho.
1258 A587 300p multi    2.00   .35
Rotary International, 75th anniversary.

Child and IYC Emblem — A588

Family, by Pablo Menicucci A589

**1979, Dec. 29**
1259 A588 500p lt bl & sepia    1.00   .35
1260 A589 1000p multi    1.75   .35
International Year of the Child.

# ARGENTINA

Microphone, Waves, ITU Emblem — A590

**1980, Mar. 22   Litho.   Perf. 13x13½**
1261  A590  500p multi        1.65  .35
Regional Administrative Conference on Broadcasting by Hectometric Waves for Area 2, Buenos Aires, Mar. 10-29.

Guillermo Brown — A591

**1980           Engr.           Perf. 13½**
1262  A591  5000p black        5.25  .35
See No. 1372.

Argentine Red Cross Centenary A592

**1980, Apr. 19   Litho.   Perf. 13½**
1263  A592  500p multi          .80  .35

OAS Emblem — A593

**1980, Apr. 19**
1264  A593  500p multi          .80  .35
Day of the Americas, Apr. 14.

Dish Antennae, Balcarce A594

No. 1266, Hydroelectric Station, Salto Grande. No. 1267, Bridge, Zarate-Brazo Largo.

**1980, Apr. 26       Litho. & Engr.**
1265  A594  300p shown         .75  .35
1266  A594  300p multicolored  .75  .35
1267  A594  300p multicolored  .75  .35
   Nos. 1265-1267 (3)         2.25 1.05

Capt. Hipolito Bouchard, Frigate "Argentina" — A595

**1980, May 31   Litho.   Perf. 13x13½**
1268  A595  500p multicolored  1.40  .35
Navy Day.

"Villarino," San Martin, by Theodore Gericault — A596

**1980, May 31**
1269  A596  500p multicolored  1.40  .35
Return of the remains of Gen. Jose de San Martin to Argentina, centenary.

Buenos Aires Gazette, 1810, Signature A597

**1980, June 7       Perf. 13½**
1270  A597  500p multicolored  .80  .35
Journalism Day.

### Miniature Sheet

Coaches in Victoria Square — A598

**1980 June 14**
1271  A598  Sheet of 14       21.00 17.50
  a.-n. 500p any single        .90   .50
Buenos Aires, 400th anniv. No. 1271 shows ceramic mural of Victoria Square by Rodolfo Franco in continuous design. See No. 1285.

Gen. Pedro Aramburu — A599

**1980, July 12   Litho.   Perf. 13½**
1272  A599  500p yel & blk     .90  .35
Gen. Pedro Eugenio Aramburu (1903-1970), provisional president, 1955.

Army Day — A600

**1980, July 12**
1273  A600  500p multicolored 1.10  .35

Gen. Juan Gregorio de Las Heras (1780-1866), Hero of 1817 War of Independence A601

Grandees of Argentina Bicentenary: No. 1275, Rivadavia. No. 1276, Brig. Gen Jose Matias Zapiola (1780-1874), naval commander and statesman.

**1980, Aug. 2   Litho.   Perf. 13½**
1274  A601  500p tan & blk     .80  .35
1275  A601  500p multicolored  .80  .35
1276  A601  500p lt lilac & blk .80 .35
   Nos. 1274-1276 (3)         2.40 1.05

Avro "Gosport" Biplane, Maj. Francisco de Artega — A602

**1980, Aug. 16         Perf. 13**
1277  A602  500p multicolored  .85  .40
Air Force Day. Artega (1882-1930) was first director of Military Aircraft Factory where Avro "Gosport" was built (1927).

University of La Plata, 75th Anniversary A603

**1980, Aug. 16         Perf. 13½**
1278  A603  500p multi         .80  .35

### Souvenir Sheets

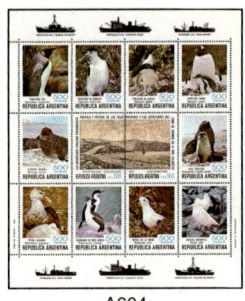

A604

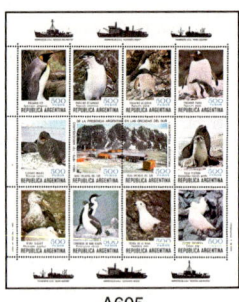

A605

**1980, Sept. 27   Litho.   Perf. 13½**
1279  A604  Sheet of 12       23.00 20.00
  a.-l. 500p, any single       .75   .60
1280  A605  Sheet of 12       23.00 20.00
  f.-g. 500p, any single       .75   .60
75th anniv. of Argentina's presence in the South Orkneys and 150th anniv. of political and military command in the Falkland Islands. Nos. 1279-1280 each contain 12 stamps (4x3) with landscape designs in center of sheets. Silhouettes of Argentine exploration ships in margins. No. 1280 contains Nos. 1279a-1279e, 1279h-1279m, 1280a-1280b.

No. 1279: a, King penguin. b, Bearded penguin. c, Adelie penguins. d, Papua penguins. e, Sea elephants. f, Puerto Soledad, 1829. g, Puerto Soledad harbor, 1829. h, Fur seals. i, Giant petrels. j, Blue-eyed cororants. k, Stormy petrels. l, Antarctic doves.
No. 1280: Letters a-e and h-l are the same as No. 1279. f, South Orkneys Argentine Base, towers and buildings. g, South Orkneys Argentine Base, buildings and mountains.

Anti-smoking Campaign — A608

**1980, Oct. 11**
1282  A608  700p multi         1.10  .40

National Census — A609

**1980, Sept.**
1283  A609  500p blk & bl      1.40  .35

Madonna and Child (Congress Emblem) A610

**1980, Oct. 1           Litho.**
1284  A610  700p multi         1.10  .35
National Marian Cong., Mendoza, Oct. 8-12.

### Mural Type of 1980
#### Miniature Sheet

**1980, Oct. 25**
1285      Sheet of 14         21.00 17.50
  a.-n. A598 500p, any single  .65   .50
Buenos Aires, 400th anniv./Buenos Aires '80 Stamp Exhib., Oct. 24-Nov. 2. No. 1285 shows ceramic mural Arte bajo la Ciudad by Alfredo Guido in continuous design.

Technical Military Academy, 50th Anniversary — A611

**1980, Nov. 1**
1286  A611  700p multi         1.00  .35

Amateur Radio Operation — A612

**1980, Nov. 1**
1287  A612  700p multi         1.00  .35

Medal — A613        Lujan Cathedral Floor Plan — A614

**1980, Nov. 29   Litho.   Perf. 13½**
1288  A613  700p multi         1.00  .35
1289  A614  700p olive & brn   1.00  .35
Christmas 1980. 150th anniv. of apparition of Holy Virgin to St. Catherine Laboure, Paris (No. 1288), 350th anniv. of apparition at Lujan.

150th Death Anniversary of Simon Bolivar — A615

**1980, Dec. 13**
1290  A615  700p multi         1.00  .40

# ARGENTINA

Soccer Gold Cup Championship, Montevideo, 1980 — A616

**1981, Jan. 3**    *Litho.*
1291 A616 1000p multi    1.35   .40

**San Martin Type of 1978**
**1981, Jan. 20**    *Engr.*    *Perf. 13½*
1292 A553 10,000p dark blue    7.75   .35

Landscape in Lujan, by Marcos Tiglio — A617

Paintings: No. 1304, Expansion of Light along a Straight Line, by Miguel Angel Vidal, vert.

**1981, Apr. 11**    *Litho.*
1303 A617 1000p multi    1.10   .45
1304 A617 1000p multi    1.10   .45

Intl. Sports Medicine Congress, June 7-12 — A618

**1981, June 6**    *Litho.*    *Perf. 13½*
1305 A618 1000p bl & dk brn    1.00   .35

Esperanza Base, Antarctica A619

Cargo Plane, Map of Vice-Commodore Marambio Island — A620

*Perf. 13½, 13x13½ (No. 1308)*
**1981, June 13**
1306 A619 1000p shown    1.60   .75
1307 A619 2000p Almirante Irizar    3.00   .85
1308 A620 2000p shown    2.90   1.35
Nos. 1306-1308 (3)    7.50   2.95

Antarctic Treaty 20th anniv.

Antique Pistols (Military Club Centenary) A621

**1981, June 27**    *Perf. 13½*
1309 A621 1000p Club building    1.10   .35
1310 A621 2000p shown    1.10   .35

Gen. Juan A. Alvarez de Arenales (1770-1831) — A622

Famous Men: No. 1312, Felix G. Frias (1816-1881), writer. No. 1313, Jose E. Uriburu (1831-1914), statesman.

**1981, Aug. 8**    *Litho.*    *Perf. 13½*
1311 A622 1000p multi    .90   .35
1312 A622 1000p multi    .90   .35
1313 A622 1000p multi    .90   .35
Nos. 1311-1313 (3)    2.70   1.05

Naval Observatory Centenary — A623

**1981, Aug. 15**    *Litho.*    *Perf. 13x13½*
1314 A623 1000p multi    1.25   .35

No. 1176 Overprinted in Red

**1981, Aug. 15**    *Photo.*    *Perf. 13½*
1315 A540 1000p lem & blk    2.00   .35

50th anniv. of Bahia Blanca Philatelic and Numismatic Society.

St. Cayetano, Stained-glass Window, Buenos Aires — A624

**1981, Sept. 5**    *Litho.*    *Perf. 13½*
1316 A624 1000p multi    .95   .35

St. Cayetano, founder of Teatino Order, 500th birth anniv.

Pablo Castaibert (1883-1909) and his Monoplane (Air Force Day) — A625

**1981, Sept. 5**    *Perf. 13x13½*
1317 A625 1000p multi    1.35   .40

Intl. Year of the Disabled A626

**1981, Sept. 10**    *Perf. 13½*
1318 A626 1000p multi    1.00   .35

22nd Latin-American Steelmakers' Congress, Buenos Aires, Sept. 21-26 — A627

**1981, Sept. 19**
1319 A627 1000p multi    .85   .35

Army Regiment No. 1 (Patricios), 175th Anniv. — A628

**1981, Oct. 10**    *Litho.*    *Perf. 13½*
1320 1500p Natl. arms    .75   .35
1321 1500p shown    .75   .35
   a. A628 Pair, #1320-1321    2.00   2.00

A629

San Martin as artillery Captain in Battle of Bailen, 1808.

**1981, Oct. 5**
1322    Sheet of 8 + 4 labels    6.75   6.75
   a. A629 1000p multi    .50   .35
   b. A629 1500p multi    .65   .55

Espamer '81 Intl. Stamp Exhib. (Americas, Spain, Portugal), Buenos Aires, Nov. 13-22. No. 1322 contains 2 each se-tenant pairs with label between.

A630

**1981, Oct. 5**
1323 A630 1000p multi    7.00   .40

Anti-indiscriminate whaling.

Espamer '81 Emblem and Ship — A631

**1981**
1324 A631 1300p multi    1.25   .40

No. 1324 Overprinted in Blue

**1981, Nov. 7**    *Photo.*    *Perf. 13½*
1325 A631 1300p multi    1.75   .40

Postal Administration philatelic training course.

Soccer Players A632

Designs: Soccer players.

**1981, Nov. 13**    *Litho.*
1326 A632    Sheet of 4 + 2 labels    9.00   9.00
   a. 2000p multi    1.50   1.25
   b. 3000p multi    1.75   1.50
   c. 5000p multi    2.00   1.75
   d. 15,000p multi    2.25   2.00

Espamer '81.

"Peso" Coin Centenary A633

2000p, Patacon, 1881. 3000p, Argentine Oro, 1881.

**1981, Nov. 21**
1327 A633 2000p multicolored    .80   .35
1328 A633 3000p multicolored    .80   .35

Christmas 1981 — A634

**1981, Dec. 12**
1329 A634 1500p multi    2.60   .50

Traffic Safety — A635

1000p, Observe traffic lights, vert. 2000p, Drive carefully, vert. 3000p, Cross at white lines. 4000p, Don't shine headlights.

**1981, Dec. 19**    *Litho.*
1330 A635 1000p multicolored    1.90   .40
1331 A635 2000p multicolored    1.00   .50
1332 A635 3000p multicolored    1.50   .45
1333 A635 4000p multicolored    1.50   .65
Nos. 1330-1333 (4)    5.90   2.00

Francisco Luis Bernardez, Ciuda Laura — A636

Writers and title pages from their works: 2000p, Lucio V. Mansilla, Excursion a los indios ranqueles. 3000p, Conrado Nale Roxlo, El Grillo. 4000p, Victoria Ocampo, Sur.

**1982, Mar. 20**    *Litho.*
1334 A636 1000p shown    2.00   .40
1335 A636 2000p multi    1.00   .40
1336 A636 3000p multi    1.00   .50
1337 A636 4000p multi    2.00   .30
Nos. 1334-1337 (4)    6.00   1.60

No. 1218 Overprinted

**1982, Apr. 17**    *Photo.*    *Perf. 13½*
1338 A559 1700p green & blue    .95   .35

Argentina's claim on Falkland Islands.

Robert Koch — A637

**1982, Apr. 17**    *Litho.*    *Wmk. 365*
1339 A637 2000p multi    1.40   .35

TB bacillus centenary and 25th Intl. Tuberculosis Conference.

American Airforces Commanders' 22nd Conf. — A638

**1982, Apr. 17**
1340 A638 2000p multi    1.50   .35

# ARGENTINA

Stone Carving, City Founder's Signature (Don Hernando de Lerma) — A639

**1982, Apr. 17**
1341 A639 2000p multi    1.75 .40
**Souvenir Sheet**
1342 A639 5000p multi    3.25 3.25
City of Salta, 400th anniv. No. 1342 contains one 43x30mm stamp.

Naval Center Centenary — A640

**1982, Apr. 24**    **Perf. 13x13½**
1343 A640 2000p multi    1.00 .35

Chorisia Speciosa — A641

200p, Zinnia peruviana. 300p, Ipomoea purpurea. 400p, Tillandsia aeranthos. 800p, Oncidium bifolium. 1000p, Erythrina cristagalli. 2000p, Jacaranda mimosi-folia. 3000p, Bauhinia candicans. 5000p, Tecoma stans. 10,000p, Tabebuia ipe. 20,000p, Passiflora coerulea. 30,000p, Aristolochia littoralis. 50,000p, Oxalis enneaphylla.

| 1982 | Unwmk. | Photo. | Perf. 13½ |
|---|---|---|---|
| 1344 | A641 | 200p multi | .40 .30 |
| 1345 | A641 | 300p multi | .40 .30 |
| 1346 | A641 | 400p multi | .40 .30 |
| 1347 | A641 | 500p shown | .35 .30 |
| 1348 | A641 | 800p multi | .35 .30 |
| 1349 | A641 | 1000p multi | .40 .30 |
| 1350 | A641 | 2000p multi | .40 .30 |
| 1351 | A641 | 3000p multi | .90 .30 |
| 1352 | A641 | 5000p multi | .85 .30 |
| 1353 | A641 | 10,000p multi | 1.40 .30 |
| 1354 | A641 | 20,000p multi | 1.75 .40 |
| 1355 | A641 | 30,000p multi | 2.50 .45 |
| 1356 | A641 | 50,000p multi | 5.00 .75 |
| | | Nos. 1344-1356 (13) | 15.10 4.60 |

Nos. 1344-1346, 1348-1350 issued on fluorescent paper. Nos. 1353-1356 issued on ordinary paper. Others issued on both fluorescent and ordinary paper.
Issued: 500p, 2000p, 5000p, 10,000p, 5/22; 200p, 300p, 1000p, 20,000p, 9/25; 400p, 800p, 30,000p, 50,000p, 12/4; 3000p, 12/18.
See Nos. 1429-1443A, 1515-1527, 1683-1691. For overprint see No. 1382.

10th Death Anniv. of Gen. Juan C. Sanchez — A641a

**1982, May 29**    **Litho.**    **Wmk. 365**
1364 A641a 5000p grn & blk    1.10 .40

Luis Vernet, First Commander — A641b

**1982, June 12**
1365 A641b 5000p org & blk    2.00 1.10
**Size: 83x28mm**
1366 A641b 5000p Map    1.25 .90
   a. Pair, Nos. 1365-1366    3.25 2.75
153rd Anniv. of Malvinas Political and Military Command District. Compare with No. 1411.

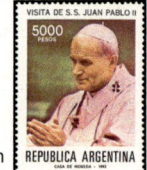

Visit of Pope John Paul II — A641c

**1982, June 12**
1367 A641c 5000p multi    2.25 .55

Organ Grinder, by Aldo Severi (b. 1928) — A641d

3000p, Still Life, by Santiago Cogorno (b. 1915).

**1982, July 3**    **Wmk. 365**
1368 A641d 2000p shown    1.00 .40
1369 A641d 3000p multi    1.00 .40

**Guillermo Brown Type of 1980 and**

Jose de San Martin — A641e

**Litho. and Engr.**
**1982**    **Unwmk.**    **Perf. 13½**
1372 A591 30,000p blk & bl    4.00 .70
1376 A641e 50,000p sepia & car    7.75 1.00
Issue dates: 30,000p, June; 50,000p, July.

Scouting Year — A641f

**Wmk. 365**
**1982, Aug. 7**    **Litho.**    **Perf. 13½**
1380 A641f 5000p multi    2.60 .50

Alconafta Fuel Campaign — A641g

**1982, Aug. 7**    **Wmk. 365**
1381 A641g 2000p multi    1.10 .40

No. 1352 Overprinted

**1982, Aug. 7**    **Photo.**    **Unwmk.**
1382 A641 5000p multi    2.60 1.00

Rio III Central Nuclear Power Plant, Cordoba A642

**Wmk. 365**
**1982, Sept. 4**    **Litho.**    **Perf. 13½**
1383 A642 2000p shown    .70 .40
1384 A642 2000p Control room    .70 .40

Namibia Day — A643

**1982, Sept. 4**
1385 A643 5000p Map    1.20 .35

Formosa Cathedral A644

Churches and Cathedrals of the Northeast: 2000p, Our Lady of Itati, Corrientes, vert. 3000p, Resistencia Cathedral, Chaco, vert. 10,000p, St. Ignatius Church ruins, Misiones.

**1982, Sept. 18**    **Litho. & Engr.**
1386 A644 2000p dk grn & blk    .70 .65
1387 A644 3000p dk brn & brn    .70 .65
1388 A644 5000p dk bl & brn    1.25 .65
1389 A644 10,000p dp org & blk    1.25 .65
   Nos. 1386-1389 (4)    3.90 2.60

Tension Sideral, by Mario Alberto Agatiello — A645

Sculpture (Espamer '81 and Juvenex '82 Exhibitions): 3000p, Sugerencia II, by Eduardo Mac Entyre. 5000p, Storm, by Carlos Silva.

**1982, Oct. 2**    **Litho.**    **Perf. 13½**
1390 A645 2000p multi    2.25 .40
1391 A645 3000p multi    2.25 .40
1392 A645 5000p multi    2.25 .45
   Nos. 1390-1392 (3)    6.75 1.25

Santa Fe Bridge — A646

**1982, Oct. 16**    **Litho. & Engr.**
1393 A646 2000p bl & blk    1.25 .40
2nd Southern Cross Games, Santa Fe and Rosario, Nov. 26-Dec. 5.

10th World Men's Volleyball Championship A647

**1982, Oct. 16**    **Litho.**    **Wmk. 365**
1394 A647 2000p multi    .75 .35
1395 A647 5000p multi    1.00 .35

Los Andes Newspaper Centenary A648

Design: Army of the Andes Monument, Hill of Glory, Mendoza.

**1982, Oct. 30**
1396 A648 5000p multi    .85 .40

A649

**1982, Oct. 30**    **Wmk. 365**
1397 A649 5000p Signs    .90 .40
50th Anniv. of Natl. Roads, Administration.

A650

A650a

La Plata City Cent., each 2500p: No. 1400: a, Cathedral, diff. b, Head, top. c, Observatory. d, City Hall, diff. e, Head, bottom. f, University.

**1982, Nov. 20**    **Litho.**
1398 A650 5000p Cathedral    1.10 .50
1399 A650 5000p City Hall    1.10 .50
1400 A650a Sheet of 6    4.00 4.00
   a.-f. 2500p Any single    .35 .25

Well, Natl. Hydrocarbon Congress Emblem A651

**1982, Nov. 20**
1401 A651 5000p multi    1.40 .40
Oil Discovery, Comodoro Rivadavia, 75th anniv.

Jockey Club of Buenos Aires Centenary A652

Design: No. 1403, Carlos Pellegrini, first president.

**1982, Dec. 4**    **Litho.**
1402 A652 5000p Emblem    1.25 .40
1403 A652 5000p multi    1.25 .40

Christmas — A653

3000p, St. Vincent de Paul. 5000p, St. Francis of Assisi.

# ARGENTINA

601

| 1982, Dec. 18 | | Perf. 13½ |
|---|---|---|
| 1404 A653 3000p multi | | 2.25 1.00 |
| **Size: 29x38mm** | | |
| 1405 A653 5000p multi | | 1.60 .50 |

Pedro B. Palacios (1854-1917), Writer — A654

Writers: 2000p, Leopoldo Marechal (1900-1970). 3000p, Delfina Bunge de Galvez (1881-1952). 4000p, Manuel Galvez (1882-1962). 5000p, Evaristo Carriego (1883-1912).

| 1983, Mar. 26 | Litho. | Perf. 13½ |
|---|---|---|
| 1406 A654 1000p multi | | .75 .40 |
| 1407 A654 2000p multi | | .75 .40 |
| 1408 A654 3000p multi | | .75 .40 |
| 1409 A654 4000p multi | | .75 .40 |
| 1410 A654 5000p multi | | .75 .40 |
| a. Strip of 5, #1406-1410 | | 4.00 4.00 |

Recovery of the Malvinas (Falkland Islands) A655

20,000p, Map, flag.

| 1983, Apr. 9 | Litho. | Perf. 13½ |
|---|---|---|
| 1411 A655 20,000p multi | | 2.00 .60 |

Compare No. 1411 with No. 1366.

Telecommunications Systems — A656

No. 1412, SITRAM, No. 1413, ARPAC network.

| 1983, Apr. 16 | | Wmk. 365 |
|---|---|---|
| 1412 A656 5000p multi | | 1.50 .65 |
| 1413 A656 5000p multi | | 1.50 .65 |

Naval League Emblem — A657

| 1983, May 14 | Litho. | Perf. 13½ |
|---|---|---|
| 1414 A657 5000p multi | | .90 .40 |

Navy Day and 50th anniv. of Naval League.

Allegory, by Victor Rebuffo — A658

| 1983, May 14 | | |
|---|---|---|
| 1415 A658 5000p multi | | .90 .40 |

Natl. Arts Fund, 25th Anniv.

75th Anniv. of Colon Opera House, Buenos Aires — A659

| 1983, May 28 | | Wmk. 365 |
|---|---|---|
| 1416 A659 5000p Main hall | | 1.00 .40 |
| 1417 A659 10000p Stage | | 1.25 .40 |

Protected Species A660

1p, Chrysocyon brachyurus. 1.50p, Ozotocerus bezoarticus. 2p, Myrmecophaga tridactyla. 2.50p, Leo onca.

| 1983, July 2 | Litho. | Perf. 13½ |
|---|---|---|
| 1418 A660 1p multicolored | | 1.20 .40 |
| 1419 A660 1.50p multicolored | | 1.75 .40 |
| 1420 A660 2p multicolored | | 1.90 .40 |
| 1421 A660 2.50p multicolored | | 2.00 .40 |
| Nos. 1418-1421 (4) | | 6.85 1.60 |

City of Catamarca, 300th Anniv. — A661

Foundation of the City of Catamarca, by Luis Varela Lezana (1900-1982).

| 1983, July 16 | Litho. | Perf. 13½ |
|---|---|---|
| 1422 A661 1p multi | | .75 .40 |

Mamerto Esquiu (1826-1883) — A662

| 1983, July 16 | | |
|---|---|---|
| 1423 A662 1p multi | | .75 .40 |

Bolivar, by Herrera Toro — A663

Bolivar, Engraving by Kepper — A664

**Perf. 13 (A663), 13½ (A664)**

| 1983 | | Unwmk. |
|---|---|---|
| 1424 A663 1p multi | | .55 .50 |
| 1425 A664 2p blk & maroon | | .75 .65 |
| 1426 A664 10p San Martin | | 4.00 .75 |
| Nos. 1424-1426 (3) | | 5.30 1.90 |

Issue dates: 1p, 2p, July 23. 10p, Aug. 20. See Nos. 1457-1462B.

Gen. Toribio de Luzuriaga (1782-1842) — A665

| 1983, Aug. 20 | Litho. | Perf. 13½ |
|---|---|---|
| 1427 A665 1p multi | | .85 .40 |

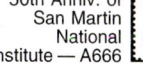

50th Anniv. of San Martin National Institute — A666

| 1983, Aug. 20 | Engr. | Unwmk. |
|---|---|---|
| 1428 A666 2p sepia | | .85 .40 |

**Flower Type of 1982 in New Currency**

| 1983-85 | | Photo. | Perf. 13½ |
|---|---|---|---|
| 1429 | A641 | 5c like #1347 | .70 .30 |
| 1430 | A641 | 10c like #1349 | .35 .30 |
| 1431 | A641 | 20c like #1350 | .35 .30 |
| 1432 | A641 | 30c like #1351 | .55 .30 |
| 1433 | A641 | 40c Eichhornia crassipes | .35 .30 |
| 1434 | A641 | 50c like #1352 | .35 .30 |
| 1435 | A641 | 1p like #1353 | .40 .30 |
| 1435A | A641 | 1.80p Mutisia retusa | .40 .30 |
| 1436 | A641 | 2p like #1354 | .50 .30 |
| 1437 | A641 | 3p like #1355 | .55 .30 |
| 1438 | A641 | 5p like #1356 | .55 .30 |
| 1439 | A641 | 10p Alstroemeria aurantiaca | 1.50 .80 |
| 1440 | A641 | 20p like #1345 | .55 .30 |
| 1441 | A641 | 30p Embothrium coccineum | 2.75 .30 |
| 1442 | A641 | 50p like #1346 | .85 .40 |
| 1443 | A641 | 100p like #1348 | 2.40 .30 |
| 1443A | A641 | 300p Cassia carnaval | 2.75 .50 |
| Nos. 1429-1443A (17) | | | 15.85 5.90 |

Issued: 20p, 8/27/84; 50p, 10/19/84; 100p, 12/84; 300p, 6/15/85.
Nos. 1429, 1433, 1435A issued on fluorescent paper. Nos. 1443, 1443A issued on ordinary paper. Others issued on both ordinary and fluorescent paper.
No. 1440 has denomination at UL.
For overprint and surcharge see Nos. 1489, 1530.

Intl. Rotary South American Regional Conference, Buenos Aires, Sept. 25-28 — A667

| 1983, Sept. 24 | | Litho. |
|---|---|---|
| 1444 A667 1p multi | | 1.25 .40 |

9th Pan American Games, Caracas, Aug. 10-28 — A668

| 1983, Sept. 24 | | |
|---|---|---|
| 1445 A668 1p Track | | .65 .40 |
| 1446 A668 2p Emblem | | .90 .40 |

World Communications Year — A669

| 1983, Oct. 8 | | Perf. 13½ |
|---|---|---|
| 1447 A669 2p multi | | .85 .40 |

Squash Peddler by Antonio Berni (1905-1981) — A670

2p, Figure in Yellow by Luis Seoane (1910-79).

| 1983, Oct. 15 | | Perf. 13½ |
|---|---|---|
| 1448 A670 1p multi | | .80 .40 |
| 1449 A670 2p multi | | .80 .40 |

World Communications Year — A671

Designs: 1p, Wagon, 18th cent. 2p, Post chaise, 19th cent. 4p, Steam locomotive, 1857. 5p, Tramway, 1910.

| 1983, Nov. 19 | Litho. | Perf. 13½ |
|---|---|---|
| 1450 A671 1p multi | | .90 .40 |
| 1451 A671 2p multi | | .90 .40 |
| 1452 A671 4p multi | | 1.25 .40 |
| 1453 A671 5p multi | | 1.25 .40 |
| Nos. 1450-1453 (4) | | 4.30 1.60 |

World Communications Year — A672

2p, General Post Office.

| 1983, Nov. 26 | Litho. | Perf. 12½x12 |
|---|---|---|
| 1454 A672 2p multicolored | | .65 .40 |

Return to Elected Government — A673

| 1983, Dec. 10 | Photo. | Perf. 13½ |
|---|---|---|
| 1455 A673 2p Coin, 1813 | | .90 .40 |

Eudyptes Crestatus — A674

Designs: b, Diomedea exulans. c, Diomedea melanophris. d, Eudyptes chrysolophus. e, Luis Piedra Buena. f, Carlos Maria Moyano. g, Luis Py. h, Augusto Lasserre. i, Phoebetria palpebrata. j, Hydrurga leptonyx k, Lobodon carcinophagus. l, Leptonychotes weddelli.

| 1983, Dec. 10 | | Litho. |
|---|---|---|
| 1456 A674 Sheet of 12 | | 12.50 12.50 |
| a.-l. 2p any single | | .40 .25 |

Southern pioneers and fauna. Margin depicts various airplanes and emblems.

**Bolivar Type of 1983**

Famous men: 10p, Angel J. Carranza (1834-99), historian. No. 1458, 500p, Guillermo Brown. No. 1459, Estanislao del Campo

# ARGENTINA

(1834-80), poet. 30p, Jose Hernandez (1834-86), author. 40p, Vicente Lopez y Planes (1784-1856), poet and patriot. 50p, San Martin. 200p, Belgrano.

**1983-85**    **Litho. & Engr.**    *Perf. 13½*

| 1457 | A664 | 10p pale bl & dk bl | .65 | .40 |
|---|---|---|---|---|
| 1458 | A664 | 20p dk bl & blk | .65 | .40 |
| 1459 | A664 | 20p dl brn ol & ol blk | .65 | .40 |
| 1460 | A664 | 30p pale bl & bluish blk | .75 | .40 |
| 1461 | A664 | 40p lt bl grn & blk | 1.25 | .40 |
| 1462 | A664 | 50p Prus grn & choc | 3.00 | 1.50 |
| 1462A | A664 | 200p int bl & blk | 2.60 | 1.00 |
| 1462B | A664 | 500p brn & int bl | 2.50 | .70 |
| | | Nos. 1457-1462B (8) | 12.05 | 5.00 |

Issued: No. 1458, 10/6; 10p, No. 1459, 30p, 40p, 3/23/85; 50p, 4/23/85; 200p, 11/2/85; 500p, 5/2/85.

Christmas 1983 — A675

Nativity Scenes: 2p, Tapestry, by Silke. 3p, Stained-glass window, San Carlos de Bariloche's Wayn Church, vert.

**1983, Dec. 17**    **Litho.**    *Perf. 13½*

| 1463 | A675 | 2p multi | .65 | .35 |
|---|---|---|---|---|
| 1464 | A675 | 3p multi | 1.25 | .45 |

Centenary of El Dia Newspaper — A676

4p, Masthead, printing roll.

**1984, Mar. 24**    **Litho.**

| 1465 | A676 | 4p multicolored | .70 | .40 |
|---|---|---|---|---|

Alejandro Carbo Teachers' College Centenary A677

**1984, June 2**    **Litho.**    *Perf. 13½*

| 1466 | A677 | 10p Building | .70 | .40 |
|---|---|---|---|---|

1984 Olympics A678

Designs: No. 1468, Weightlifting, discus, shot put. No. 1469, Javelin, fencing. No. 1470, Bicycling, swimming.

**1984, July 28**    **Litho.**    *Perf. 13½*

| 1467 | A678 | 5p shown | .65 | .45 |
|---|---|---|---|---|
| 1468 | A678 | 5p multicolored | .65 | .45 |
| 1469 | A678 | 10p multicolored | 1.10 | .55 |
| 1470 | A678 | 10p multicolored | 1.10 | .55 |
| | | Nos. 1467-1470 (4) | 3.50 | 2.00 |

Rosario Stock Exchange Centenary — A679

**1984, Aug. 11**

| 1471 | A679 | 10p multicolored | .75 | .40 |
|---|---|---|---|---|

Wheat — A680

**1984, Aug. 11**

| 1472 | A680 | 10p shown | .85 | .40 |
|---|---|---|---|---|
| 1473 | A680 | 10p Corn | .85 | .40 |
| 1474 | A680 | 10p Sunflower | .85 | .40 |
| | | Nos. 1472-1474 (3) | 2.55 | 1.20 |

18th FAO Regional Conference for Latin America and Caribbean (No. 1472); 3rd Natl. Corn Congress (No. 1473); World Food Day (No. 1474).

Wildlife Protection A681

No. 1475, Hippocamelus bisulcus. No. 1476, Vicugna vicugna. No. 1477, Aburria jacutinga. No. 1478, Mergus octosetaceus. No. 1479, Podiceps gallardoi.

**1984, Sept. 22**    **Litho.**    *Perf. 13½*

| 1475 | A681 | 20p multicolored | 1.25 | .80 |
|---|---|---|---|---|
| 1476 | A681 | 20p multicolored | 1.25 | .80 |
| 1477 | A681 | 20p multicolored | 1.25 | .80 |
| 1478 | A681 | 20p multicolored | 1.25 | .80 |
| 1479 | A681 | 20p multicolored | 1.25 | .80 |
| | | Nos. 1475-1479 (5) | 6.25 | 4.00 |

First Latin American Theater Festival, Cordoba, Oct. — A682

**1984, Oct. 13**    **Litho.**    *Perf. 13½*

| 1480 | A682 | 20p Mask | .65 | .40 |
|---|---|---|---|---|

Intl. Eucharistic Congress, 50th Anniv. — A683

Apostles' Communion, by Fra Angelico.

**1984, Oct. 13**

| 1481 | A683 | 20p multicolored | .70 | .40 |
|---|---|---|---|---|

Glaciares Natl. Park (UNESCO World Heritage List) — A684

**1984, Nov. 17**    **Litho.**

| 1482 | A684 | 20p Sea | .90 | .50 |
|---|---|---|---|---|
| 1483 | A684 | 30p Glacier | 1.40 | .50 |

City of Puerto Deseado Centenary A685

No. 1485, Ushuaia centenary.

**1984, Nov. 17**    *Perf. 13½*

| 1484 | A685 | 20p shown | .95 | .50 |
|---|---|---|---|---|
| 1485 | A685 | 20p multicolored | .95 | .50 |

Childrens' Paintings, Christmas 1984 — A686

**1984, Dec. 1**    **Litho.**    *Perf. 13½*

| 1486 | A686 | 20p Diego Aguero | .80 | .40 |
|---|---|---|---|---|
| 1487 | A686 | 30p Leandro Ruiz | 1.00 | .40 |
| 1488 | A686 | 50p Maria Castillo, vert. | 1.10 | .40 |
| | | Nos. 1486-1488 (3) | 2.90 | 1.20 |

No. 1439 Overprinted

**1984, Dec. 1**    **Photo.**    *Perf. 13½*

| 1489 | A641 | 10p multicolored | .70 | .45 |
|---|---|---|---|---|

Buenos Aires Philatelic Center, 50th anniv.

Vista Del Jardin Zoologico, by Fermin Eguia — A687

Paintings: No. 1491, El Congreso Iluminado, by Francisco Travieso. No. 1492, Galpones (La Boca), by Marcos Borio.

**1984, Dec. 15**    *Perf. 13½*

| 1490 | A687 | 20p multi | .75 | .50 |
|---|---|---|---|---|
| 1491 | A687 | 20p multi, vert. | .75 | .50 |
| 1492 | A687 | 20p multi, vert. | .75 | .50 |
| | | Nos. 1490-1492 (3) | 2.25 | 1.50 |

Gen. Martin Miguel de Guemes (1785-1821) A688

**1985, Mar. 23**    **Litho.**    *Perf. 13½*

| 1493 | A688 | 30p multicolored | .75 | .50 |
|---|---|---|---|---|

ARGENTINA '85 Exhibition A689

First airmail service from: 20p, Buenos Aires to Montevideo, 1917. 40p, Cordoba to Villa Dolores, 1925. 60p, Bahia Blanca to Comodoro Rivadavia, 1929. 80p, Argentina to Germany, 1934. 100p, naval service to the Antarctic, 1952.

**1985, Apr. 27**

| 1494 | A689 | 20p Bleriot Gnome | .40 | .40 |
|---|---|---|---|---|
| 1495 | A689 | 40p Junker F-13L | .65 | .40 |
| 1496 | A689 | 60p Latte 25 | .95 | .40 |
| 1497 | A689 | 80p L.Z. 127 Graf Zeppelin | 1.20 | .60 |
| 1498 | A689 | 100p Consolidated PBY Catalina | 1.60 | .60 |
| | | Nos. 1494-1498 (5) | 4.80 | 2.40 |

Central Bank, 50th Anniv. — A690

80p, Bank Building, Buenos Aires.

**1985, June 1**

| 1499 | A690 | 80p multicolored | .95 | .50 |
|---|---|---|---|---|

Jose A. Ferreyra (1889-1943), Director of Munequitas Portenas A691

Famous directors and their films: No. 1501, Leopoldo Torre Nilsson (1924-1978), scene from Martin Fierro.

**1985, June 1**

| 1500 | A691 | 100p shown | 1.00 | .50 |
|---|---|---|---|---|
| 1501 | A691 | 100p multi | 1.00 | .50 |

Carlos Gardel (1890-1935), Entertainer — A692

Paintings: No. 1502, Gardel playing the guitar on stage, by Carlos Alonso (b. 1929). No. 1503, Gardel in a wide-brimmed hat, by Hermenegildo Sabat (b. 1933). No. 1504, Portrait of Gardel in an ornamental frame, by Aldo Severi (b. 1928) and Martiniano Arce (b. 1939).

**1985, June 15**

| 1502 | A692 | 200p multi | 1.75 | .75 |
|---|---|---|---|---|
| 1503 | A692 | 200p multi | 1.75 | .75 |
| 1504 | A692 | 200p multi | 1.75 | .75 |
| | | Nos. 1502-1504 (3) | 5.25 | 2.25 |

The Arrival, by Pedro Figari — A693

A Halt on the Plains, by Prilidiano Pueyrredon — A693a

Oil paintings (details): 30c, The Wagon Square, by C. B. de Quiros.

**1985, July 6**    **Litho.**    *Perf. 13½*

| 1505 | A693 | 20c multi | 1.20 | .50 |
|---|---|---|---|---|
| 1506 | A693 | 30c multi | 1.60 | .50 |

**Souvenir Sheet**
*Perf. 12*

| 1507 | A693a | Sheet of 2 | 4.00 | 4.00 |
|---|---|---|---|---|
| | a. | 20c Pilgrims, vert. | .40 | .40 |
| | b. | 30c Wagon | .45 | .45 |

ARGENTINA '85. No. 1507 contains one 30x40mm and one 40x30mm stamp. See No. 1542.

Buenos Aires to Montevideo, 1917 Teodoro Fels Flight — A694

Historic flight covers: No. 1509, Villa Dolores to Cordoba, 1925. No. 1510, Buenos Aires to France, 1929 St. Exupery flight. No. 1511, Buenos Aires to Bremerhaven, 1934 Graf Zeppelin flight. No. 1512, 1st Antarctic flight, 1952.

**1985, July 13**    *Perf. 12x12½*

| 1508 | A694 | 10c emer & multi | .75 | .40 |
|---|---|---|---|---|
| 1509 | A694 | 10c ultra & multi | .75 | .40 |
| 1510 | A694 | 10c lt choc & multi | .75 | .40 |
| 1511 | A694 | 10c chnt & multi | .75 | .40 |
| 1512 | A694 | 10c ap grn & multi | .75 | .40 |
| | | Nos. 1508-1512 (5) | 3.75 | 2.00 |

ARGENTINA '85.

# ARGENTINA 603

Illuminated Fruit, by Fortunato Lacamera (1887-1951) A695

Paintings: 20c, Woman with Bird, by Juan del Prete, vert.

**1985, Sept. 7**      **Perf. 13½**
| 1513 | A695 | 20c multi | 1.10 | .60 |
| 1514 | A695 | 30c multi | 1.25 | .60 |

### Flower Types of 1982-85
Designs: 1a, Begonia micranthera var. hieronymi. 5a, Gymnocalycium bruchii.

**1985-88**      **Photo.**      **Perf. 13½**
| 1515 | A641 | ½c like #1356 | .95 | .25 |
| 1516 | A641 | 1c like #1439 | .55 | .25 |
| 1517 | A641 | 2c like #1345 | .55 | .25 |
| 1518 | A641 | 3c like #1441 | .55 | .25 |
| 1519 | A641 | 5c like #1346 | .55 | .25 |
| 1520 | A641 | 10c like #1348 | .95 | .25 |
| 1521 | A641 | 20c like #1347 | .75 | .25 |
| 1522 | A641 | 30c like #1443A | 1.50 | .30 |
| 1523 | A641 | 50c like #1344 | 2.00 | .30 |
| 1524 | A641 | 1a multi | 1.50 | .35 |
| 1525 | A641 | 2a like #1351 | 1.10 | .25 |
| 1526 | A641 | 5a multi | 6.50 | 2.50 |

**Size: 15x23mm**
| 1527 | A641 | 8½c like #1349 | .55 | .25 |
| Nos. 1515-1527 (13) | | | 18.00 | 5.70 |

Issued: ½c, 1c, 12/16; 2c, 8½c, 30c, 9/18; 3c, 5c, 10c, 50c, 1a, 9/7; 20c, 10/17; 5a, 3/21/87; 2a, 12/5/88.

### No. 1435 Surcharged
**1986, Nov. 4**      **Photo.**      **Perf. 13½**
| 1530 | A641 | 10c on 1p No. 1435 | 1.25 | .50 |

Folk Musical Instruments — A699

**1985, Sept. 14**      **Litho.**      **Perf. 13½**
| 1531 | A699 | 20c Frame drum | .85 | .60 |
| 1532 | A699 | 20c Long flute | .85 | .60 |
| 1533 | A699 | 20c Jew's harp | .85 | .60 |
| 1534 | A699 | 20c Pan flutes | .85 | .60 |
| 1535 | A699 | 20c Musical bow | .85 | .60 |
| Nos. 1531-1535 (5) | | | 4.25 | 3.00 |

Juan Bautista Alberdi (1810-1884), Historian, Politician — A700

Famous men: 20c, Nicolas Avellaneda (1836-1885), President in 1874. 30c, Fr. Luis Beltran (1784-1827), military and naval engineer. 40c, Ricardo Levene (1885-1959), historian, author.

**1985, Oct. 5**
| 1536 | A700 | 10c multi | .35 | .35 |
| 1537 | A700 | 20c multi | .60 | .35 |
| 1538 | A700 | 30c multi | .85 | .50 |
| 1539 | A700 | 40c multi | 1.60 | .60 |
| Nos. 1536-1539 (4) | | | 3.40 | 1.80 |

### Type of 1985 and

Skaters — A701

Deception, by J. H. Rivoira — A702

**1985, Oct. 19**      **Litho.**      **Perf. 13½**
| 1540 | A701 | 20c multi | 1.00 | .40 |
| 1541 | A702 | 30c multi | 1.10 | .40 |

**Size: 147x75mm Imperf**
| 1542 | A693a | 1a multi | 3.50 | 3.50 |

IYY. No. 1542 is inscribed in silver with the UN 40th anniversary and IYY emblems.

Provincial Views — A703

Designs: No. 1543, Rock Window, Buenos Aires. No. 1544, Forclaz Windmill, Entre Rios. No. 1545, Lake Potrero de los Funes, San Luis. No. 1546, Mission church, north-east province. No. 1547, Penguin colony, Punta Tombo, Chubut. No. 1548, Water Mirrors, Cordoba.

**1985, Nov. 23**      **Perf. 13½**
| 1543 | A703 | 10c multi | .95 | .40 |
| 1544 | A703 | 10c multi | .95 | .40 |
| 1545 | A703 | 10c multi | .95 | .40 |
| 1546 | A703 | 10c multi | .95 | .40 |
| 1547 | A703 | 10c multi | .95 | .40 |
| 1548 | A703 | 10c multi | .95 | .40 |
| Nos. 1543-1548 (6) | | | 5.70 | 2.40 |

Christmas 1985 — A704

Designs: 10c, Birth of Our Lord, by Carlos Cortes. 20c, Christmas, by Hector Viola.

**1985, Dec. 7**
| 1549 | A704 | 10c multi | .65 | .40 |
| 1550 | A704 | 20c multi | 1.40 | .75 |

Natl. Campaign for the Prevention of Blindness A705

**1985, Dec. 7**
| 1551 | A705 | 10c multi | .75 | .40 |

Rio Gallegos City, Cent. — A716

**1985, Dec. 21**      **Litho.**      **Perf. 13½**
| 1552 | A716 | 10c Church | 1.75 | .50 |

Natl. Grape Harvest Festival, 50th Anniv. — A717

**1986, Mar. 15**
| 1553 | A717 | 10c multi | .75 | .40 |

Exists with Wmk. 365, Value $20.

Historical Architecture in Buenos Aires — A718

Designs: No. 1554, Valentin Alsina House, Italian Period, 1860-70. No. 1555, House on Cerrito Street, French influence, 1880-1900. No. 1556, House on the Avenida de Mayo y Santiago del Estero, Art Nouveau, 1900-10. No. 1557, Customs Building, academic architecture, 1900-15. No. 1558, Isaac Fernandez Blanco Museum, house of architect Martin Noel, natl. restoration, 1910-30. Nos. 1554-1556 vert.

**1986, Apr. 19**
| 1554 | A718 | 20c multi | .85 | .50 |
| 1555 | A718 | 20c multi | .85 | .50 |
| 1556 | A718 | 20c multi | .85 | .50 |
| 1557 | A718 | 20c multi | .85 | .50 |
| 1558 | A718 | 20c multi | .85 | .50 |
| Nos. 1554-1558 (5) | | | 4.25 | 2.50 |

Antarctic Bases, Pioneers and Fauna A719

Designs: a, Base, Jubany. b, Arctocephalus gazella. c, Otaria byronia. d, Gen. Belgrano Base. e, Daption capensis. f, Diomedia melanophris. g, Apterodytes patagonica. h, Macronectes giganteus. i, Hugo Alberto Acuna (1885-1953). j, Spheniscus magellanicus. k, Gallinago gallinae. l, Capt. Agustin del Castillo (1855-89).

**1986, May 31**
| 1559 | A719 | Sheet of 12 | 20.00 | 20.00 |
| a.-l. | | 10c any single | .90 | .85 |

Famous People — A720

Designs: No. 1560, Dr. Alicia Moreau de Justo, human rights activist. No. 1561, Dr. Emilio Ravignani (1886-1954), historian. No. 1562, India Gandhi.

**1986, July 5**      **Litho.**      **Perf. 13½**
| 1560 | A720 | 10c multi | .65 | .50 |
| 1561 | A720 | 20c multi | .65 | .50 |
| 1562 | A720 | 30c multi | 1.75 | 1.00 |
| Nos. 1560-1562 (3) | | | 3.05 | 2.00 |

Statuary, Buenos Aires — A721

20c, Fountain of the Nereids, by Dolores Lola Mora (1866-1936). 30c, Lamenting at Work, by Rogelio Yrurtia (1879-1950), horiz.

**1986, July 5**
| 1563 | A721 | 20c multi | 1.25 | .45 |
| 1564 | A721 | 30c multi | 1.25 | .45 |

Famous Men — A722

Designs: No. 1565, Francisco N. Laprida (1786-1829), politician. No. 1566, Estanislao Lopez (1786-1838), brigadier general. No. 1567, Francisco Ramirez (1786-1821), general.

**1986, Aug. 9**      **Litho.**      **Perf. 13**
| 1565 | A722 | 20c dl yel, brn & blk | .75 | .50 |
| 1566 | A722 | 20c dl yel, brn & blk | .75 | .50 |
| 1567 | A722 | 20c dl yel, brn & blk | .75 | .50 |
| Nos. 1565-1567 (3) | | | 2.25 | 1.50 |

Fr. Ceferino Namuncura (1886-1905) — A723

**1986, Aug. 30**      **Perf. 13½**
| 1568 | A723 | 20c multi | .85 | .40 |

### Miniature Sheets

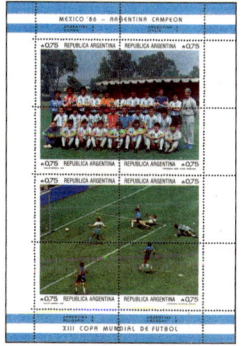

Natl. Team Victory, 1986 World Cup Soccer Championships, Mexico — A724

Designs: No. 1569a-1569d, Team. Nos. 1569e-1569h, Shot on goal. Nos. 1570a-1570d, Action close-up. Nos. 1570e-1570h, Diego Maradona holding soccer cup.

**1986, Nov. 8**      **Litho.**      **Perf. 13½**
| 1569 | A724 | Sheet of 8 | 14.50 | 14.50 |
| a.-h. | | 75c any single | 1.45 | 1.45 |
| 1570 | A724 | Sheet of 8 | 14.50 | 14.50 |
| a.-h. | | 75c any single | 1.45 | 1.45 |

San Francisco (Cordoba), Cent. — A725

20c, Municipal Building.

**1986, Nov. 8**
| 1571 | A725 | 20c multicolored | .75 | .45 |

Trelew City (Chubut), Cent. — A726

20c, Old railroad station, 1865.

**1986, Nov. 22**      **Litho.**      **Perf. 13½**
| 1572 | A726 | 20c multicolored | .75 | .45 |

Mutualism Day — A727

**1986, Nov. 22**
| 1573 | A727 | 20c multicolored | 1.00 | .50 |

Christmas A728

# ARGENTINA

Designs: 20c, Naif retable, by Aniko Szabo (b. 1945). 30c, Everyone's Tree, by Franca Delacqua (b. 1947).

**1986, Dec. 13**    Litho.    Perf. 13½
| 1574 | A728 | 20c multicolored | 1.20 | .60 |
| 1575 | A728 | 30c multicolored | 1.40 | .60 |

Santa Rosa de Lima, 400th Birth Anniv. — A729

**1986, Dec. 13**
| 1576 | A729 | 50c multicolored | 2.10 | .85 |

Rio Cuarto Municipal Building — A730

No. 1578, Court Building, Cordoba.

**1986, Dec. 20**
| 1577 | A730 | 20c shown | 1.15 | .45 |
| 1578 | A730 | 20c multicolored | 1.15 | .45 |

Rio Cuarto City, bicent. Court Building, Cordoba, 50th anniv.

Antarctic Treaty, 25th Anniv. — A731

**1987, Mar. 7**    Litho.    Perf. 13½
| 1579 | A731 | 20c Marine biologist | 1.25 | .50 |
| 1580 | A731 | 30c Ornithologist | 1.75 | .50 |

**Souvenir Sheet**
*Perf. 12*
| 1581 | | Sheet of 2 | 5.75 | 5.75 |
| a. | A731 | 20c like No. 1579 | 2.00 | 1.50 |
| b. | A731 | 30c like No. 1580 | 3.00 | 2.00 |

No. 1581 contains 2 stamps, size: 40x50mm. Exist imperf. Value $500.

Natl. Mortgage Bank, Cent. — A732

**1987, Mar. 21**    Perf. 13½
| 1582 | A732 | 20c multicolored | 1.05 | .50 |

Natl. Cooperative Associations Movement A733

**1987, Mar. 21**
| 1583 | A733 | 20c multicolored | 1.05 | .50 |

Second State Visit of Pope John Paul II — A734

**Engr., Litho. (No. 1585)**
**1987, Apr. 4**    Perf. 13½
| 1584 | A734 | 20c shown | .50 | .35 |

| 1585 | A734 | 80c Papal blessing | 1.90 | .90 |

**Souvenir Sheet**
*Perf. 12*
| 1586 | A734 | 1a like 20c | 3.75 | 3.00 |

No. 1586 contains one 40x50mm stamp.

Intl. Peace Year — A735

30c, Pigeon, abstract sculpture by Victor Kaniuka.

**1987, Apr. 11**    Litho.
| 1587 | A735 | 20c multicolored | .95 | .40 |
| 1588 | A735 | 30c multicolored | .95 | .40 |

Low Handicap World Polo Championships A736

Polo Players, painting by Alejandro Moy.

**1987, Apr. 11**
| 1589 | A736 | 20c multicolored | 1.10 | .40 |

**Miniature Sheet**

ICOM '86 — A737

Designs: a, Emblem. b, Family crest, National History Museum, Buenos Aires. c, St. Bartholomew, Enrique Larreta Museum of Spanish Art, Buenos Aires. d, Zoomorphic club, Patagonian Museum, San Carlos de Bariloche. e, Supplication, anthropomorphic sculpture, Natural Sciences Museum, La Plata. f, Wrought iron lattice from the house of J. Urquiza, president of the Confederation of Argentina, Entre Rios History Museum, Parana. g, St. Joseph, 18th cent. wood figurine, Northern History Museum, Salta. h, Funerary urn, Provincial Archaeological Museum, Santiago del Estero.

**1987, May 30**
| 1590 | A737 | Sheet of 8 | 6.00 | 6.00 |
| a.-h. | | 25c any single | .60 | .60 |

Intl. Council of Museums, 14th general conf.

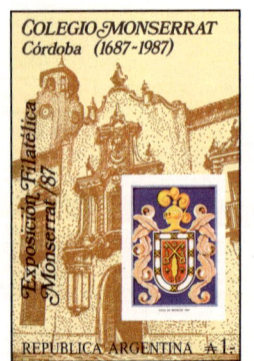

Natl. College of Monserrat, Cordoba, 300th Anniv. — A738

**1987, July 4**    Imperf.
| 1591 | A738 | 1a multicolored | 2.25 | 2.25 |

Monserrat '87 Philatelic Exposition.

Fight Drug Abuse — A739

The Proportions of Man, by da Vinci.

**1987, Aug. 15**    Perf. 13½
| 1592 | A739 | 30c multicolored | 1.40 | .50 |

Famous Men — A740

Portraits and quotations: 20c, Jorge Luis Borges (1899-1986), writer. 30c, Armando Discepolo (1887-1971), playwright. 50c, Carlos A. Pueyrredon (1887-1962), professor, Legion of Honor laureate.

**1987, Aug. 15**
| 1593 | A740 | 20c multicolored | .75 | .60 |
| 1594 | A740 | 30c multicolored | .75 | .60 |
| 1595 | A740 | 50c multicolored | .75 | .60 |
| | | Nos. 1593-1595 (3) | 2.25 | 1.80 |

Pillar Boxes
A741    A742

**1987**    Photo.    Perf. 13½
| 1596 | A741 | (30c) yel, blk & dark red | 1.15 | .40 |
| | | Booklet with 10 stamps | 11.50 | |
| 1597 | A742 | (33c) lt blue grn, blk & yel | 1.15 | .40 |
| | | Complete booklet, 10 #1597 | 11.50 | |

Issue dates: (30c), June 8; (33c), July 13.

The Sower, by Julio Vanzo — A743

**1987, Sept. 12**
| 1598 | A743 | 30c multicolored | 1.00 | .50 |

Argentine Agrarian Federation, 75th anniv.

10th Pan American Games, Indianapolis, Aug. 7-25 — A744

**1987, Sept. 26**
| 1599 | A744 | 20c Basketball | 1.10 | .50 |
| 1600 | A744 | 30c Rowing | 1.25 | .50 |
| 1601 | A744 | 50c Yachting | 1.40 | .50 |
| | | Nos. 1599-1601 (3) | 3.75 | 1.50 |

Children Playing Doctor, WHO Emblem A745

**1987, Oct. 7**
| 1602 | A745 | 30c multi | .75 | .50 |

Vaccinate every child campaign.

Heroes of the Revolution — A746

Signing of the San Nicolas Accord, 1852, by Rafael del Villar — A747

Independence anniversaries and historic events: No. 1603, Maj.-Col. Ignacio Alvarez Thomas (1787-1857). No. 1604, Col. Manuel Crispulo Bernabe Dorrego (1787-1829). No. 1606, 18th cent. Spanish map of the Falkland Isls., administered by Jacinto de Altolaguirre.

**1987, Oct. 17**
| 1603 | A746 | 25c shown | .65 | .40 |
| 1604 | A746 | 25c multi | .65 | .40 |
| 1605 | A747 | 50c shown | 1.25 | .50 |
| 1606 | A747 | 50c multi | 1.25 | .50 |
| | | Nos. 1603-1606 (4) | 3.80 | 1.80 |

Museum established in the House of the San Nicholas Accord, 50th anniv. (No. 1605); Jacinto de Altolaguirre (1754-1787), governor the Malvinas Isls. for the King of Spain (No. 1606).

Celedonio Galvan Moreno, 1st Director A748

**1987, Nov. 21**
| 1607 | A748 | 50c multicolored | 1.05 | .50 |

*Postas Argentinas* magazine, 50th anniv.

LRA National Radio, Buenos Aires, 50th Anniv. — A749

**1987, Nov. 21**
| 1608 | A749 | 50c multicolored | 1.05 | .50 |

Natl. Philatelic Society, Cent. — A750

**1987, Nov. 21**
| 1609 | A750 | 1a Jose Marco del Pont | 1.90 | .75 |

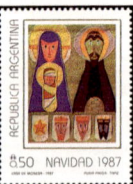

Christmas — A751

Tapestries: 50c, *Navidad*, by Alisia Frega. 1a, *Vitral*, by Silvina Trigos.

**1987, Dec. 5**
| 1610 | A751 | 50c multicolored | 1.00 | .50 |
| 1611 | A751 | 1a multicolored | 1.40 | .75 |

Natl. Parks A752

# ARGENTINA

**1987, Dec. 19**    **Perf. 13x13½**
| 1612 | A752 | 50c Baritu | 1.75 | .50 |
| 1613 | A752 | 50c Nahuel Huapi | 1.75 | .50 |
| 1614 | A752 | 50c Rio Pilcomayo | 1.75 | .50 |
| 1615 | A752 | 50c Tierra del Fuego | 1.75 | .50 |
| 1616 | A752 | 50c Iguacu | 1.75 | .50 |
| | | Nos. 1612-1616 (5) | 8.75 | 2.50 |

See Nos. 1647-1651, 1715-1719, 1742-1746.

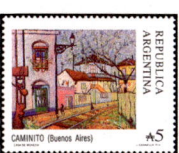

Landscapes in Buenos Aires Painted by Jose Cannella — A753

No. 1617, Caminito. No. 1618, Viejo Almacen.

**1988-89**    **Litho.**    **Perf. 13½**
| 1617 | A753 | 5a multi | 3.25 | 1.25 |
| 1618 | A753 | 10a multi | 6.50 | 2.50 |
| 1618A | A753 | 10a like No. 1618 | 1.60 | .60 |
| 1618B | A753 | 50a like No. 1617 | 1.60 | .60 |
| c. | | Wmk 365 | 150.00 | 20.00 |
| | | Nos. 1617-1618B (4) | 12.95 | 4.95 |

No. 1618 inscribed "Viejo Almacen"; No. 1618A inscribed "El Viejo Almacen."

Issue dates: 5a, No. 1618, 3/15; No. 1618A, 10/20; 50a, 5/30/89.

For overprint see No. 1635.

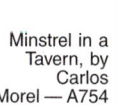

Minstrel in a Tavern, by Carlos Morel — A754

Paintings: No. 1620, Interior of Curuzu, by Candido Lopez.

**1988, Mar. 19**    **Litho.**    **Perf. 13½**
| 1619 | A754 | 1a shown | 1.25 | .50 |
| 1620 | A754 | 1a multicolored | 1.25 | .50 |

See Nos. 1640-1641.

Argentine-Brazilian Economic Cooperation and Integration Program for Mutual Growth — A755

**1988, Mar. 10**
| 1621 | A755 | 1a multicolored | .90 | .50 |

Cities of Alta Gracia and Corrientes, 400th Anniv. — A756

No. 1022, Alta Gracia Church. No. 1623, Chapel of St. Anne, Corrientes.

**1988, Apr. 9**    **Litho.**    **Perf. 13½**
| 1622 | A756 | 1a multicolored | 1.25 | .50 |
| 1623 | A756 | 1a multicolored | 1.25 | .50 |

Labor Day — A757

Grain Carriers, a tile mosaic by Alfredo Guido, Line D of Nueve de Julio station, Buenos Aires subway: a, (UL). b, (UR). c, (LL). d, (LR).

**1988, May 21**
| 1624 | A757 | Block of 4 | 5.00 | 5.00 |
| a.-d. | | 50c any single | .75 | .75 |

1988 Summer Olympics, Seoul — A758

**1988, July 16**    **Litho.**    **Perf. 13½**
| 1625 | A758 | 1a Running | .60 | .50 |
| 1626 | A758 | 2a Soccer | 1.40 | .75 |
| 1627 | A758 | 3a Field hockey | 2.00 | 1.50 |
| 1628 | A758 | 4a Tennis | 2.25 | 1.25 |
| | | Nos. 1625-1628 (4) | 6.25 | 4.00 |

Mendoza Bank, Cent. — A759

Natl. Gendarmerie, Cent. — A760

**1988, Aug. 13**
| 1629 | A759 | 2a multicolored | 1.50 | .60 |
| 1630 | A760 | 2a multicolored | 1.50 | .60 |

Sarmiento and Cathedral School to the North, Buenos Aires — A761

**1988, Sept. 10**    **Litho.**    **Perf. 13½**
| 1631 | A761 | 3a multicolored | 1.50 | .50 |

Domingo Faustino Sarmiento (1811-1888), educator, politician.

St. Cayetano, Patron of Workers — A762

El Amor, by Antonio Berni, Pacific Gallery, Buenos Aires — A763

3a, Our Lady of Carmen, Cuyo.

**1988, Sept. 10**    **Litho.**
| 1632 | A762 | 2a multicolored | .90 | .75 |
| 1633 | A762 | 3a multicolored | 1.60 | 1.25 |

**Souvenir Sheet**
**Perf. 12**
| 1634 | A763 | 5a multicolored | 3.00 | 3.00 |

Liniers Philatelic Circle and the Argentine Western Philatelic Institution (IFADO), 50th anniv.
No. 1634 contains one 40x30mm stamp.

No. 1617 Ovptd.

**1988, Oct. 29**    **Litho.**    **Perf. 13½**
| 1635 | A753 | 5a multicolored | 7.00 | 2.00 |

21st Congress of the Intl. Urology Soc.

Tourism — A763a

3a, Purmamarca, Jujuy. 20a, Ushuaia.

**1988, Nov. 1**    **Litho.**    **Perf. 13½**
| 1635A | A763a | 3a multi | .80 | .40 |

**Size: 28½x38mm**
| 1635B | A763a | 20a multi | 4.90 | 2.10 |

Buenos Aires Subway, 75th Anniv. — A764

5a, Train, c. 1913.

**1988, Dec. 17**    **Litho.**    **Perf. 13½**
| 1636 | A764 | 5a multicolored | 1.60 | .65 |

Christmas — A765

Frescoes in Ucrania Cathedral, Buenos Aires: No. 1637, Virgin Patron. No. 1638, Virgin of Tenderness.

**1988, Dec. 17**
| 1637 | A765 | 5a multicolored | 2.50 | .65 |
| 1638 | A765 | 5a multicolored | 2.50 | .65 |

St. John Bosco (1815-1888), Educator, and Church in Ushuaia — A766

**1989, Apr. 8**    **Litho.**    **Perf. 13½**
| 1639 | A766 | 5a multicolored | 1.15 | .50 |

Dated 1988.

**Art Type of 1988**

Paintings: No. 1640, Blancos, by Fernando Fader (1882-1935). No. 1641, Rincon de los Areneros, by Justo Lynch (1870-1953).

**1989, Apr. 8**
| 1640 | A754 | 5a multicolored | 2.00 | .40 |
| 1641 | A754 | 5a multicolored | 2.00 | .40 |

Holy Week — A767

Sculpture and churches: No. 1642, The Crown of Thorns, Calvary of Tandil, and Church of Our Lady Carmelite, Tandil. No. 1643, Jesus the Nazarene and Metropolitan Cathedral, Buenos Aires. No. 1644, Jesus Encounters His Mother (scene of the crucifixion), La Quebrada Village, San Luis. No. 1645, Our Lady of Sorrow and Church of Humahuaca, Jujuy.

**1989, Apr. 22**    **Litho.**    **Perf. 13½**
| 1642 | A767 | 2a multicolored | .60 | .50 |
| 1643 | A767 | 2a multicolored | .60 | .50 |
| 1644 | A767 | 3a multicolored | .80 | .50 |
| 1645 | A767 | 3a multicolored | .80 | .50 |
| a. | | Block of 4 + 2 labels | 3.50 | 3.00 |
| | | Nos. 1642-1645 (4) | 2.80 | 2.00 |

Printed in sheets of 16+4 labels containing blocks of 4 of each design. Labels picture Jesus's arrival in Jerusalem (Palm Sunday).

Prevent Alcoholism — A768

**1989, Apr. 22**
| 1646 | A768 | 5a multicolored | 1.00 | .40 |

**Natl. Park Type of 1987**

**1989, May 6**    **Perf. 13x13½**
| 1647 | A752 | 5a Lihue Calel | 1.50 | .40 |
| 1648 | A752 | 5a El Palmar | 1.50 | .40 |
| 1649 | A752 | 5a Calilegua | 1.50 | .40 |
| 1650 | A752 | 5a Chaco | 1.50 | .40 |
| 1651 | A752 | 5a Los Glaciares | 1.50 | .40 |
| | | Nos. 1647-1651 (5) | 7.50 | 2.00 |

Admission of Argentina to the ITU, Cent. — A769

**1989, May 6**    **Perf. 13½**
| 1652 | A769 | 10a multicolored | 2.00 | .40 |

World Model Aircraft Championships — A770

No. 1653, F1A glider. No. 1654, F1B rubber band motor. No. 1655, F1C gas motor.

**1989, May 27**    **Litho.**    **Perf. 13½**
| 1653 | A770 | 5a multi | .80 | .35 |
| 1654 | A770 | 5a multi | .80 | .35 |
| 1655 | A770 | 10a multi | 1.40 | .40 |
| | | Nos. 1653-1655 (3) | 3.00 | 1.10 |

French Revolution, Bicent. — A771

Designs: 10a, "All men are born free and equal." 15a, French flag and La Marianne, by Gandon. 25a, Liberty Guiding the People, by Delacroix.

**1989, July 1**    **Litho.**    **Perf. 13½**
| 1656 | A771 | 10a shown | .85 | .50 |
| 1657 | A771 | 15a multicolored | .85 | .50 |

**Souvenir Sheet**
**Perf. 12**
| 1658 | A771 | 25a multicolored | 2.40 | 2.40 |

No. 1658 contains one 40x30mm stamp.

The Republic, a Bronze Bust in the Congreso de la Nacion, Buenos Aires — A772

**1989, Aug. 12**    **Litho.**    **Perf. 13½**
| 1659 | A772 | 300a on 50a multi | 2.00 | .50 |

Peaceful transition of power (presidential office). Not issued without surcharge.

# ARGENTINA

Immigration to Argentina A773

150a, S.S. Weser, 1889. 200a, Immigrant hotel, 1889.

**1989, Aug. 19**      *Perf. 13½*
| | | | | |
|---|---|---|---|---|
| 1660 | A773 | 150a multi | 2.00 | .55 |
| 1661 | A773 | 200a multi | 2.00 | .55 |

**Souvenir Sheet**
*Perf. 12*
| | | | |
|---|---|---|---|
| 1662 | | Sheet of 2 | 3.50 3.50 |
| a. | | A773 150a like No. 1660 | 1.50 1.50 |
| b. | | A773 200a like No. 1661 | 1.50 1.50 |

No. 1662 contains 40x30mm stamps.

Famous Men — A774

Designs: No. 1663, Fr. Guillermo Furlong (1889-1974), historian, and title page of *The Jesuits*. No. 1664, Dr. Gregorio Alvarez (1889-1986), physician, and title page of *Canto a Chos Malal*. 200a, Brig.-Gen. Enrique Martinez (1789-1870) and lithograph of *La Batalla de Maipu*, by Teodoro Gericault.

**1989, Oct. 7**    *Litho.*    *Perf. 13½*
| | | | | |
|---|---|---|---|---|
| 1663 | A774 | 150a multicolored | 1.10 | .55 |
| 1664 | A774 | 150a multicolored | 1.10 | .55 |
| 1665 | A774 | 200a multicolored | 1.10 | .55 |
| | | Nos. 1663-1665 (3) | 3.30 | 1.65 |

America Issue — A775

Emblem of the Postal Union of the Americas and Spain (PUAS) and pre-Columbian art from Catamarca Province: 200a, Wooden mask from Atajo, Loma Morada. 300a, Urn of the Santa Maria Culture (Phase 3) from Punta de Balastro, Santa Maria Department.

**1989, Oct. 14**
| | | | | |
|---|---|---|---|---|
| 1666 | A775 | 200a multicolored | 1.40 | 1.20 |
| 1667 | A775 | 300a multicolored | 2.25 | 1.30 |

Federal Police Week — A776

Children's drawings: No. 1668, Diego Molinari, age 13. No. 1669, Carlos Alberto Sarago, age 8. No. 1670, Roxana Andrea Osuna, age 7. No. 1671, Pablo Javier Quaglia, age 9.

**1989, Oct. 28**    *Litho.*    *Perf. 13½*
| | | | | |
|---|---|---|---|---|
| 1668 | A776 | 100a multi | .85 | .35 |
| 1669 | A776 | 100a multi | .85 | .35 |
| 1670 | A776 | 150a multi | 1.40 | .50 |
| 1671 | A776 | 150a multi | 1.40 | .50 |
| | | Nos. 1668-1671 (4) | 4.50 | 1.70 |

Battle of Vuelta de Obligado, 1845 — A777

**1989, Dec. 2**    *Litho.*    *Perf. 13x13½*
| | | | | |
|---|---|---|---|---|
| 1672 | A777 | 300a multicolored | 1.75 | .60 |

Paintings A778

*Cristo de los Cerros*, Sculpture by Chipo Cespedes — A779

No. 1673, Gato Frias. No. 1674, Maria Carballido.

**1989, Dec. 2**     *Perf. 13½*
| | | | | |
|---|---|---|---|---|
| 1673 | A778 | 200a multi | 1.35 | .50 |
| 1674 | A778 | 200a multi | 1.35 | .50 |
| 1675 | A779 | 300a shown | 1.35 | .50 |
| | | Nos. 1673-1675 (3) | 4.05 | 1.50 |

Christmas.

Buenos Aires Port, Cent. A780

**1990, Mar. 3**    *Litho.*    *Perf. 13½*
| | | | | |
|---|---|---|---|---|
| 1676 | A780 | Strip of 4 | 16.00 | 15.00 |
| a.-d. | | 200a any single | 1.50 | .75 |

Aconcagua Intl. Fair, Mendoza — A781

Design: Aconcagua mountain, Los Horcones Lagoon and fair emblem.

**1990, Mar. 3**
| | | | | |
|---|---|---|---|---|
| 1677 | A781 | Pair, #a.-b. | 2.50 | 1.50 |

Natl. Savings and Insurance Fund, 75th Anniv. — A782

**1990, May 5**    *Litho.*    *Perf. 13½*
| | | | | |
|---|---|---|---|---|
| 1678 | A782 | 1000a multicolored | 1.05 | .50 |

**Miniature Sheet**

1990 World Cup Soccer Championships, Italy — A783

Designs: a, Athlete's torso (striped jersey). b, Athlete's torso (solid jersey). c, Players' feet, soccer ball. d, Player (knee to waist).

**1990, May 5**
| | | | | |
|---|---|---|---|---|
| 1679 | A783 | Sheet of 4 | 9.00 | 8.00 |
| a.-d. | | 2500a multicolored | 2.00 | 1.50 |

Carlos Pellegrini, Commercial High School Founder, Cent. — A784

**1990, June 2**    *Litho.*    *Perf. 13½*
| | | | | |
|---|---|---|---|---|
| 1680 | A784 | 2000a multicolored | 1.75 | .60 |

Youth Against Drugs — A785

**1990, June 2**
| | | | | |
|---|---|---|---|---|
| 1681 | A785 | 2000a multicolored | 1.75 | .60 |

Intl. Literacy Year — A786

**1990, July 14**    *Litho.*    *Perf. 13½*
| | | | | |
|---|---|---|---|---|
| 1682 | A786 | 2000a multicolored | 1.75 | .60 |

**Flower Type of 1982 in New Currency**

**1989-90**    *Photo.*    *Perf. 13½*
| | | | | |
|---|---|---|---|---|
| 1683 | A641 | 10a like #1433 | .40 | .25 |
| 1684 | A641 | 20a like #1440 | .35 | .25 |
| 1685 | A641 | 50a like #1354 | .40 | .25 |
| 1686 | A641 | 100a like #1439 | .50 | .25 |
| 1687 | A641 | 300a like #1345 | 1.75 | .50 |
| 1688 | A641 | 500a like #1441 | 2.75 | .75 |
| 1689 | A641 | 1000a like #1355 | .85 | .35 |
| 1690 | A641 | 5000a like #1349 | 4.25 | .35 |
| 1691 | A641 | 10,000a like #1350 | 7.00 | 3.25 |
| | | Nos. 1683-1691 (9) | 18.25 | 6.20 |

Issued: 20a, 100a, 300a, 500a, 8/1/89; 10a, 8/24/89; 50a, 8/30/89; 1000, 3/8/90; 5000a, 4/6/90; 10,000a, 7/2/90.

World Basketball Championships A787

**1990, Aug. 11**    *Litho.*    *Perf. 13½*
| | | | | |
|---|---|---|---|---|
| 1703 | A787 | 2000a multicolored | 2.25 | 1.50 |

**Souvenir Sheet**
*Perf. 12*
| | | | | |
|---|---|---|---|---|
| 1704 | A787 | 5000a Jump ball | 6.75 | 6.00 |

Postal Union of the Americas and Spain, 14th Congress A788

No. 1705, Arms, seal. No. 1706, Sailing ships. No. 1707, Modern freighter. No. 1708, Van, cargo plane.

**1990, Sept. 15**    *Litho.*    *Perf. 13½*
| | | | | |
|---|---|---|---|---|
| 1705 | A788 | 3000a multi | 2.00 | .75 |
| 1706 | A788 | 3000a multi | 2.00 | .75 |
| 1707 | A788 | 3000a multi | 2.00 | .75 |
| 1708 | A788 | 3000a multi | 2.00 | .75 |
| | | Nos. 1705-1708 (4) | 8.00 | 3.00 |

America Issue — A789

No. 1709, Iguacu Falls, hamelia erecta. No. 1710, Puerto Deseado, elephant seal.

**1990, Oct. 13**
| | | | | |
|---|---|---|---|---|
| 1709 | A789 | 3000a multicolored | 2.75 | 1.25 |
| 1710 | A789 | 3000a multicolored | 2.75 | 1.25 |

**Natl. Park Type of 1987**

**1990, Oct. 27**     *Perf. 13x13½*
| | | | | |
|---|---|---|---|---|
| 1715 | A752 | 3000a Lanin | 2.25 | .90 |
| 1716 | A752 | 3000a Laguna Blanca | 2.25 | .90 |
| 1717 | A752 | 3000a Perito Moreno | 2.25 | .90 |
| 1718 | A752 | 3000a Puelo | 2.25 | .90 |
| 1719 | A752 | 3000a El Rey | 2.25 | .90 |
| | | Nos. 1715-1719 (5) | 11.25 | 4.50 |

Stamp Day — A790

**1990, Oct. 27**     *Perf. 13½*
| | | | | |
|---|---|---|---|---|
| 1720 | A790 | 3000a multicolored | 1.90 | .75 |

Salvation Army, Cent. — A793

Designs: No. 1722, Natl. University of the Littoral, Santa Fe, cent.

**1990, Dec. 1**    *Litho.*    *Perf. 13½*
| | | | | |
|---|---|---|---|---|
| 1721 | A793 | 3000a multicolored | 2.25 | .90 |
| 1722 | A793 | 3000a multicolored | 2.25 | .90 |
| a. | | Pair, #1721-1722 + label | 8.00 | 7.00 |

**Miniature Sheets**

Christmas — A794

Stained glass windows: No. 1723, The Immaculate Conception. No. 1724, The Nativity. No. 1725, Presentation of Jesus at the Temple.

**1990, Dec. 1**     *Perf. 13½x13*
**Sheets of 4**
| | | | | |
|---|---|---|---|---|
| 1723 | A794 | 3000a #a.-d. | 8.50 | 7.50 |
| 1724 | A794 | 3000a #a.-d. | 8.50 | 7.50 |
| 1725 | A794 | 3000a #a.-d. | 8.50 | 7.50 |

Landscapes A795

Paintings: No. 1726, Los Sauces, by Atilio Malinverno. No. 1727, Paisaje, by Pio Collivadino, vert.

**1991, May 4**    *Litho.*    *Perf. 13½*
| | | | | |
|---|---|---|---|---|
| 1726 | A795 | 4000a multicolored | 1.75 | .90 |
| 1727 | A795 | 4000a multicolored | 1.75 | .90 |

# ARGENTINA

Return of Remains of Juan Manuel de Rosas (1793-1877) — A796

**1991, June 1**   Litho.   Perf. 13½
1728  A796  4000a multicolored   1.50  .75

Swiss Confederation, 700th Anniv. — A797

**1991, Aug. 3**   Litho.   Perf. 13½
1729  A797  4000a multicolored   1.50  .75

### Miniature Sheet

Cartoons — A798

Designs: a, Hernan, the Corsair by Jose Luis Salinas. b, Don Fulgencio by Lino Palacio. c, Medical Rules of Salerno by Oscar Esteban Conti. d, Buenos Aires Undershirt by Alejandro del Prado. e, Girls! by Jose A.G. Divito. f, Langostino by Eduardo Carlos Ferro. g, Mafalda by Joaquin Salvador Lavoro. h, Mort Cinder by Alberto Breccia.

**1991, Aug. 3**
1730  A798  4000a Sheet of 8,
              #a.-h.   21.00  19.00

City of La Rioja, 400th Anniv. — A799

**1991, Sept. 14**   Litho.   Perf. 13½
1731  A799  4000a multicolored   1.50  .75

First Balloon Flight over the Andes, 75th Anniv. A800

**1991, Sept. 14**
1732  A800  4000a multicolored   1.50  .75

America Issue — A801

Designs: No. 1733, Magellan's caravel, Our Lady of Victory. No. 1734, Ships of Juan Diaz de Solis.

**1991, Nov. 9**   Litho.   Perf. 13½
1733  A801  4000a multicolored   2.00  1.75
1734  A801  4000a multicolored   2.00  1.75

Anniversaries — A802

Designs: a, Johann Heinrich Pestalozzi, Swiss pedagogue and educational reformer, whose Argentine school, the Colegio Pestalozzi, was associated with the anti-fascist newspaper Argentinisches Tageblatt. b, Leandro N. Alem, founder of Radical People's Party. c, Man with rifle, emblem of Argentine Federal Shooting Club. d, Dr. Nicasio Etcheparebarda, emblem of College of Odontology. e, Dalmiro Huergo, emblem of Graduate School of Economics.

**1991, Nov. 30**
1735  A802  4000a Strip of 5,
              #a.-e.   9.25  8.00

Christmas — A803

Stained glass windows from Our Lady of Lourdes Basilica, Buenos Aires: Nos. 1736a-1736b, Top and bottom portions of Virgin of the Valley, Catamarca. Nos. 1736c-1736d, Top and bottom portions of Virgin of the Rosary of the Miracle, Cordoba.

**1991, Nov. 30**
1736  A803  4000a Block of 4,
              #a.-d.   7.00  6.00
       e.   Sheet of 16, 4 ea #a-d, + 4
              labels   30.00  26.00

The four labels of No. 1736a form a nativity scene across the middle of the sheet.

Famous Men — A804

Designs: a, Gen. Juan de Lavalle (1797-1841), Peruvian medal of honor. b, Brig. Gen. Jose Maria del Rosario Ciriaco Paz (1791-1854), medal. c, Marco Manuel de Avellaneda (1813-1841), lawyer. d, Guillermo Enrique Hudson (1841-1922), author.

**1991, Dec. 14**   Litho.   Perf. 13½
1737  A804  4000a Block of 4, #a.-
              d.   6.75  5.75

Birds — A805

No. 1738, Pterocnemia pennata. No. 1739, Morphnus guianensis. No. 1740, Ara chloroptera.

**1991, Dec. 28**
1738  A805  4000a multicolored   1.90  1.00
1739  A805  4000a multicolored   1.90  1.00
1740  A805  4000a multicolored   1.90  1.00
       Nos. 1738-1740 (3)        5.70  3.00

### Miniature Sheet

Arbrafex '92, Argentina-Brazil Philatelic Exhibition — A806

Traditional costumes: a, Gaucho, woman. b, Gaucho, horse. c, Gaucho in store. d, Gaucho holding lariat.

**1992, Mar. 14**   Litho.   Perf. 13½
1741  A806  38c Sheet of 4, #a.-d.   8.00  7.00

### Natl. Park Type of 1987

No. 1742, Alerces. No. 1743, Formosa Nature Reserve. No. 1744, Petrified Forest. No. 1745, Arrayanes. No. 1746, Laguna de los Pozuelos.

**1992, Apr. 4**   Litho.   Perf. 13x13½
1742  A752  38c multicolored   1.75  .50
1743  A752  38c multicolored   1.75  .50
1744  A752  38c multicolored   1.75  .70
1745  A752  38c multicolored   1.75  .50
1746  A752  38c multicolored   1.75  .50
       Nos. 1742-1746 (5)      8.75  2.70

Mushrooms — A807

10c, Psilocybe cubensis. 25c, Coprinus atramentarius. 50c, Suillus granulatus. 51c, Morchella esculenta. 61c, Amanita muscaria. 68c, Coprinus comatus. 1.77p, Stropharia aeruginosa.

**1992-94**   Photo.   Perf. 13½
1748  A807  10c multi   1.10  .30
1749  A807  25c multi   1.20  .30
       a.   Wmk. 365    30.00  4.00
1750  A807  38c like #1748   1.20  .30
1751  A807  48c like #1749   1.50  .60
1752  A807  50c multi   2.40  .30
1753  A807  51c multi   1.50  .60
1754  A807  61c multi   1.90  .75
1755  A807  68c multi   3.00  .50
1756  A807  1p like #1754   5.00  .80
1757  A807  1.25p like #1752  5.00  .50
1758  A807  1.77p multi   7.50  2.75
1759  A807  2p like #1753   10.00  2.25
       Nos. 1748-1759 (12)   41.30  9.95

No. 1758 not issued without overprint "Contro Filatelico de Neuquen y Rio Negro 50th Aniversario."
Issued: 38c, 4/4/92; 48c, 51c, 61c, 8/1/92; 1.77p, 11/7/92; 25c, 50c, 8/17/93; 1p, 2p, 8/26/93; 10c, 1/11/94; 68c, 1.25p, 10/10/92; No. 1749a, 1997.
See design A838.

Falkland Islands War, 10th Anniv. — A808

No. 1767, Pucara IA 50. No. 1768, Cruiser Gen. Belgrano. No. 1769, Soldier and truck.

**1992, May 2**   Litho.   Perf. 13½
1767  A808  38c multicolored   1.85  .80
1768  A808  38c multicolored   1.85  .80
1769  A808  38c multicolored   1.85  .80
       Nos. 1767-1769 (3)      5.55  2.40

### Miniature Sheet

Preserve the Environment — A809

a, Deer. b, Geese. c, Butterflies. d, Whale.

**1992, June 6**   Litho.   Perf. 12
1770  A809  38c Sheet of 4, #a.-d.  9.00  8.00

Paintings by Florencio Molina Campos A810

No. 1771, A La Sombra. No. 1772, Tileforo Areco, vert.

**1992, June 6**   Perf. 13½
1771  A810  38c multicolored   1.75  .90
1772  A810  38c multicolored   1.75  .90

Famous Men — A811

Designs: No. 1770, Gen. Lucio N. Mansilla (1792-1871). No. 1774, Jose Manuel Estrada (1842-1894), writer. No. 1775, Brig. Gen. Jose I. Garmendia (1842-1915).

**1992, July 4**   Litho.   Perf. 13½
1773  A811  38c multicolored   1.25  .70
1774  A811  38c multicolored   1.25  .70
1775  A811  38c multicolored   1.25  .70
       Nos. 1773-1775 (3)      3.75  2.10

Fight Against Drugs — A812

**1992, Aug. 1**   Perf. 13½x13
1776  A812  38c multicolored   1.60  .70

Col. Jose M. Calaza, 140th Birth Anniv. — A813

**1992, Sept. 5**   Litho.   Perf. 13½
1777  A813  38c multicolored   1.50  1.25

Discovery of America, 500th Anniv. — A814

Designs: a, Columbus, castle, ship. b, Native drawings, Columbus.

**1992, Oct. 10**   Litho.   Perf. 13½
1778  A814  38c Pair, #a.-b.   4.50  4.00

# ARGENTINA

Argentine Film Posters — A815

No. 1779, Dios Se Lo Pague, 1948. No. 1780, Las Aguas Bajan Turbias, 1952. No. 1781, Un Guapo Del 900, 1960. No. 1782, La Tregua, 1974. No. 1783, La Historia Oficial, 1984.

| 1992, Nov. 7 | Litho. | Perf. 13½ |
|---|---|---|
| 1779 A815 38c multicolored | 1.75 | .50 |
| 1780 A815 38c multicolored | 1.75 | .50 |
| 1781 A815 38c multicolored | 1.75 | .50 |
| 1782 A815 38c multicolored | 1.75 | .50 |
| 1783 A815 38c multicolored | 1.75 | .50 |
| Nos. 1779-1783 (5) | 8.75 | 2.50 |

Christmas — A816

**1992, Nov. 28**
1784 A816 38c multicolored  1.50  .60

### Miniature Sheet

Iberoprenfil '92 — A817

Lighthouses: a, Punta Mogotes. b, Rio Negro. c, San Antonio. d, Cabo Blanco.

**1992, Dec. 5**
1785 A817 38c Sheet of 4, #a.-d.  12.00  12.00

A818

Fight Against AIDS — A819

| 1992, Dec. 12 | Litho. | Perf. 13½ |
|---|---|---|
| 1786 A818 10c multicolored | 2.75 | 1.00 |
| 1787 A819 26c multicolored | 5.25 | 1.00 |

Intl. Space Year — A820

**1992, Dec. 19**
1788 A820 38c multicolored  1.50  .75

---

### Souvenir Sheet

Miraculous Lord Crucifix, 400th Anniv. of Arrival in America — A821

**1992, Dec. 26**  Perf. 12
1789 A821 76c multicolored  4.75  4.50

Jujuy City, 400th Anniv. — A822

| 1993, Apr. 24 | Litho. | Perf. 13½ |
|---|---|---|
| 1790 A822 38c multicolored | 1.50 | 1.25 |

Argentina Soccer Assoc., Cent. — A823

**1993, Mar. 27**
1791 A823 38c multicolored  1.50  .60

### Souvenir Sheet

Intl. Philatelic Exhibitions — A824

Designs: a, 38c, City Hall, Poznan, Poland. b, 48c, Statue of Christ the Redeemer, Rio de Janeiro, Brazil. c, 76c, Royal Palace, Bangkok, Thailand.

**1993, May 8**  Litho.  Perf. 12
1792 A824 Sheet of 3, #a.-c.  5.75  5.00
Polska '93 (No. 1792a), Brasiliana '93 (No. 1792b), Bangkok '92 (No. 1792c).

Luis C. Candelaria's Flight Over Andes Mountains, 75th Anniv. — A825

**1993, June 26**  Litho.  Perf. 13x13½
1793 A825 38c multicolored  1.75  1.50

---

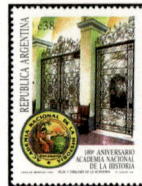 

Order of San Martin, 50th Anniv. — A826    National History Academy, Cent. — A827

| 1993, May 29 | | Perf. 13½ |
|---|---|---|
| 1794 A826 38c multicolored | 1.75 | .60 |
| 1795 A827 38c multicolored | 1.75 | .60 |

Armed Forces Memorial Day — A828

No. 1796, Natl. Gendarmerie. No. 1797, Coast Guard.

**1993, June 12**
| 1796 A828 38c multicolored | 1.75 | .60 |
| 1797 A828 38c multicolored | 1.75 | .60 |

Paintings A829

Designs: No. 1798, Old House, by Norberto Russo. No. 1799, Pa'las Casas, by Adriana Zaefferer.

| 1993, Aug. 14 | Litho. | Perf. 13½ |
|---|---|---|
| 1798 A829 38c multicolored | 1.75 | .60 |
| 1799 A829 38c multicolored | 1.75 | .60 |

Pato A830

**1993, Aug. 28**  Litho.  Perf. 12
1800 A830 1p multicolored  3.50  1.25

Nut-Bearing Trees — A831

Designs: No. 1801, Enterolobium contortisiliquum. No. 1802, Prosopis alba. No. 1803, Magnolia grandiflora. No. 1804, Erythrina falcata.

| 1993, Sept. 25 | Litho. | Perf. 13x13½ |
|---|---|---|
| 1801 A831 75c multicolored | 2.75 | 1.00 |
| 1802 A831 75c multicolored | 2.75 | 1.00 |
| 1803 A831 1.50p multicolored | 5.25 | 2.00 |
| 1804 A831 1.50p multicolored | 5.25 | 2.00 |
| Nos. 1801-1804 (4) | 16.00 | 6.00 |

America Issue — A832

Whales: 50c, Eubalaena australis. 75c, Cephalorhynchus commersonii.

---

| 1993, Oct. 9 | | Perf. 13½ |
|---|---|---|
| 1805 A832 50c multicolored | 2.00 | .80 |
| 1806 A832 75c multicolored | 3.00 | 1.25 |

### Miniature Sheet

Christmas, New Year — A833

Denomination at: a, UL. b, UR. c, LL. d, LR.

**1993, Dec. 4**  Litho.  Perf. 13½
1807 A833 75c Sheet of 4, #a.-d.  10.00  8.00

Cave of the Hands, Santa Cruz — A834

**1993, Dec. 18**
1808 A834 1p multicolored  3.25  3.00

New Emblem, Argentine Postal Service — A835

**1994, Jan. 8**  Perf. 11½
1809 A835 75c multicolored  4.75  4.50
See Nos. 1883A-1884.

A836

Players from: 25c, Germany, 1990. 50c, Brazil, 1970. 75c, 1.50p, Argentina, 1986. 1p, Italy, 1982.

| 1994, June 11 | Litho. | Perf. 13½ |
|---|---|---|
| 1810 A836 25c multicolored | .85 | .45 |
| 1811 A836 50c multicolored | 1.60 | .90 |
| 1812 A836 75c multicolored | 2.50 | 1.40 |
| 1813 A836 1p multicolored | 3.75 | 2.00 |
| Nos. 1810-1813 (4) | 8.70 | 4.75 |

### Souvenir Sheet
Perf. 12
1814 A836 1.50p multicolored  5.25  5.00

No. 1814 contains one 40x50mm stamp with continuous design.

1994 World Cup Soccer Championships, US — A837

Drawings of championships by: No. 1815, Julian Lisenberg. No. 1816, Matias Taylor, vert. No. 1817, Torcuato S. Gonzalez Agote, vert. No. 1818, Maria Paula Palma.

# ARGENTINA

**1994, July 23** — *Perf. 13½*
| 1815 | A837 | 75c multicolored | 3.25 | 1.00 |
| 1816 | A837 | 75c multicolored | 3.25 | 1.00 |
| 1817 | A837 | 75c multicolored | 3.25 | 1.00 |
| 1818 | A837 | 75c multicolored | 3.25 | 1.00 |
| | | Nos. 1815-1818 (4) | 13.00 | 4.00 |

Issued in sheet containing a block of 4 of each stamp + 4 labels.

A838

Molothrus Badius — A838a

**1994-95** — *Litho.* — *Perf. 13½*
| 1819 | A838 | 10c like #1748 | .35 | .25 |
| 1820 | A838 | 25c like #1749 | .60 | .35 |
| 1823 | A838 | 50c like #1752 | 1.25 | .60 |
| 1828 | A838 | 1p like #1754 | 2.60 | 1.25 |
| 1832 | A838 | 2p like #1753 | 5.50 | 2.50 |
| 1835 | A838a | 9.40p multicolored | 26.00 | 25.00 |
| | | Nos. 1819-1835 (6) | 36.30 | 29.95 |

See designs A807, A849.
Issued: 10c, 25c, 50c, 1p, 2p, 6/14/94; 9.40p, 4/12/95.

Wildlife of Falkland Islands — A839

Designs: 25c, Melanodera melanodera. 50c, Pygoscelis papua. 75c, Tachyeres brachypterus. 1p, Mirounga leonina.

**1994, Aug 6**
| 1839 | A839 | 25c multicolored | 1.00 | .55 |
| 1840 | A839 | 50c multicolored | 1.50 | .75 |
| 1841 | A839 | 75c multicolored | 3.00 | 1.50 |
| 1842 | A839 | 1p multicolored | 4.50 | 2.00 |
| | | Nos. 1839-1842 (4) | 10.00 | 4.80 |

City of San Luis, 400th Anniv. — A840

**1994, Aug. 20**
| 1843 | A840 | 75c multicolored | 4.00 | 1.50 |

Province of Tierra del Fuego, Antarctica and South Atlantic Islands — A841

**1994, Aug. 20**
| 1844 | A841 | 75c multicolored | 3.25 | 1.50 |

Argentine Inventors A842

Designs: No. 1845, Ladislao Jose Biro (1899-1985), ball point pen. No. 1846, Raul Pateras de Pescara (1890-1966), helicopter. No. 1847, Quirino Cristiani (1896-1984), animated drawings. No. 1848, Enrique Finochietto (1881-1948), surgical instruments.

**1994, Oct. 1**
| 1845 | A842 | 75c multicolored | 2.10 | 2.10 |
| 1846 | A842 | 75c multicolored | 2.10 | 2.10 |
| 1847 | A842 | 75c multicolored | 2.10 | 2.10 |
| 1848 | A842 | 75c multicolored | 2.10 | 2.10 |
| a. | | Block of 4, #1845-1848 | 9.50 | 9.50 |

Issued in sheets containing 4 No. 1848a + 4 labels.

UNICEF Christmas A843

75c, Bell, red ornament, star.

**1994, Nov. 26** — *Litho.* — *Perf. 11½*
| 1849 | A843 | 50c shown | 2.00 | 1.25 |
| 1850 | A843 | 75c multicolored | 2.75 | 2.50 |

Take Care of Our Planet — A844

Children's paintings: No. 1851, Boy, girl holding earth, vert. No. 1852, Children outdoors, vert. No. 1853, World as house. No. 1854, People around "world" table.

**1994, Dec. 3** — *Perf. 13½*
| 1851 | A844 | 25c multicolored | .95 | .50 |
| 1852 | A844 | 25c multicolored | .95 | .50 |
| 1853 | A844 | 50c multicolored | 1.50 | .80 |
| 1854 | A844 | 50c multicolored | 1.50 | .80 |
| | | Nos. 1851-1854 (4) | 4.90 | 2.60 |

Christmas A845

**1994, Dec. 10**
| 1855 | A845 | 50c Annunciation | 1.75 | 1.00 |
| 1856 | A845 | 75c Madonna & Child | 2.50 | 1.00 |

Nos. 1855-1856 each issued in sheets of 20 + 5 labels.

12th Pan American Games, Mar del Plata — A846

**1995** — *Litho.* — *Perf. 13½*
| 1857 | A846 | 75c Running | 2.50 | .65 |
| 1858 | A846 | 75c Cycling | 2.50 | .65 |
| 1859 | A846 | 75c Diving | 2.50 | .65 |
| 1860 | A846 | 1.25p Gymnastics, vert. | 3.75 | .75 |
| 1861 | A846 | 1.25p Soccer, vert. | 3.75 | .75 |
| | | Nos. 1857-1861 (5) | 15.00 | 3.45 |

Issued: No. 1857, 2/18; others, 3/11.

Natl. Constitution A847

Design: 75c, Natl. Congress Dome, woman from statue The Republic Triumphant.

**1995, Apr. 8**
| 1862 | A847 | 75c multicolored | 2.50 | 2.25 |

21st Intl. Book Fair A848

**1995, Apr. 8**
| 1863 | A848 | 75c multicolored | 2.50 | 2.25 |

Birds — A849

5p, Carduelis magellanica. 10p, Zonotrichia capensis.

**1995** — *Litho.* — *Perf. 13½*
| 1876 | A849 | 5p multicolored | 15.00 | 15.00 |
| 1880 | A849 | 10p multicolored | 30.00 | 30.00 |

Issued: 5p, 10p, 5/23/95.

A850

**1995, Mar. 25** — *Litho.* — *Die Cut*
**Self-Adhesive**
| 1883A | A850 | 25c multicolored | 11.00 | 1.00 |
| 1884 | A850 | 75c multicolored | 3.00 | 1.00 |
| a. | | Booklet pane, 2 #1883A, 6 #1884 | 42.00 | |
| | | Complete booklet, #1884a | 62.00 | |
| b. | | Booklet pane, 4 #1883A, 12 #1884 | 82.50 | |
| | | Complete booklet, #1884b | 106.00 | |

See Nos. 1921A-1921B.

Argentine Engineers' Center, Cent. — A851

**1995, June 3** — *Perf. 13½*
| 1885 | A851 | 75c multicolored | 2.50 | .60 |

Jose Marti (1853-95) A852

No. 1887, Antonio Jose de Sucre (1795-1830).

**1995, Aug. 12** — *Litho.* — *Perf. 13½*
| 1886 | A852 | 1p multicolored | 3.25 | 3.00 |
| 1887 | A852 | 1p multicolored | 3.25 | 3.00 |

Fauna — A853

Type I

Type II

25c Penguin:
Type I — Penguin 16mm tall, with top of penguin's head barely above blue background circle and eyes below the outer limit of the circle.
Type II — Penguin 17mm tall, with top of penguin's head well above blue background circle and eyes even with the outer limit of the circle.
50c Toucan:
Type I — Wing at left touches edge of circle and large part of beak is outside of circle.
Type II — Wing at left does not touch edge of circle and small part of beak is outside of circle.
75c Condor:
Type I — Slanted lines in "75" and the "c" in the denomination are thick.
Type II — Slanted lines in "75" and the "c" in the denomination are thin.
1p Owl:
Type I — Pupil of eye at left is on arc of the edge of the blue circle.
Type II — Pupil of eye at left is below the arc of the edge of the blue circle.
2p Bigua:
Type I — Tip of beak touches the bottom of the horizontal line in the right angle at upper left.
Type II — Tip of beak is to the right of and lower than the bottom of the horizontal line in the right angle at upper left.

**1995, Sept. 1** — *Litho.* — *Perf. 13½*
| 1888 | A853 | 5c Ostrich | .30 | .25 |
| 1889 | A853 | 25c Penguin, type I | .80 | .35 |
| 1889A | A853 | 25c Penguin, type II | — | — |
| 1890 | A853 | 50c Toucan, type I | 1.50 | .35 |
| 1890A | A853 | 50c Toucan, type II | — | — |
| 1891 | A853 | 75c Condor, type I | 2.10 | .35 |
| 1891A | A853 | 75c Condor, type II | — | — |
| 1892 | A853 | 1p Owl, type I | 4.25 | .35 |
| 1892A | A853 | 1p Owl, type II | — | — |
| 1893 | A853 | 2p Bigua, type I | 6.25 | .35 |
| 1893A | A853 | 2p Bigua, type II | — | — |
| 1894 | A853 | 2.75p Tero | 10.50 | .35 |
| | | Nos. 1888-1894 (10) | 25.70 | 2.35 |

**Booklet Stamps**
*Perf. 13½ on 2 or 3 Sides*
| 1895 | A853 | 25c Alligator | .80 | .40 |
| 1896 | A853 | 50c Fox | 1.50 | .70 |
| 1897 | A853 | 75c Anteater | 2.25 | 1.00 |
| 1898 | A853 | 75c Deer | 2.25 | 1.00 |
| 1899 | A853 | 75c Whale | 2.25 | 1.00 |
| a. | | Booklet pane, 1 each Nos. 1889, 1890, 1891, 1895-1899 | 13.50 | 13.50 |
| | | Complete booklet, #1899a | 14.50 | |
| | | Nos. 1895-1899 (5) | 9.05 | 4.10 |

See Nos. 1958, 2004-2004A.

Native Heritage A854

a, Cave drawings, shifting sands. b, Stone mask. c, Anthropomorphic vessel. d, Woven textile.

**1995, Sept. 9**
| 1900 | A854 | 75c Block of 4, #a.-d. | 10.00 | 9.00 |

Sunflower, Postal Service Emblem A855

**1995, Oct. 7**
| 1901 | A855 | 75c multicolored | 8.25 | 8.00 |

Juan D. Peron (1895-1974) A856

**1995, Oct. 7**
| 1902 | A856 | 75c lt ol bis & dk bl | 2.25 | .60 |

## ARGENTINA

### Miniature Sheet

Anniversaries — A857

Annivs: a, UN, 50th. b, ICAO, 50th (in 1994). c, FAO, 50th. d, ILO, 75th (in 1994).

| 1995, Oct. 14 | | Perf. 12 | |
|---|---|---|---|
| 1903 | A857 75c Sheet of 4, #a.-d. | 10.00 | 9.00 |

Christmas and New Year — A858

Designs: Nos. 1904, 1908, Christmas tree, presents. No. 1905, "1996." No. 1906, Champagne glasses. No. 1907, Present.

| 1995, Nov. 25 | Litho. | Perf. 13½ | |
|---|---|---|---|
| 1904 | A858 75c multicolored | 2.25 | .45 |

**Booklet Stamps**
**Perf. 13½ on 1 or 2 Sides**

| 1905 | A858 75c multicolored | 2.50 | .75 |
|---|---|---|---|
| 1906 | A858 75c multicolored | 2.50 | .75 |
| 1907 | A858 75c multicolored | 2.50 | .75 |
| 1908 | A858 75c multicolored | 2.50 | .75 |
| a. | Booklet pane, #1905-1908 + label | 10.00 | |
| | Complete booklet, #1908a | 22.00 | |
| | Nos. 1904-1908 (5) | 12.25 | 3.45 |

No. 1908a is a continuous design. Ribbon extends from edge to edge on No. 1908 and stops at edge of package on No. 1905.

### Miniature Sheet

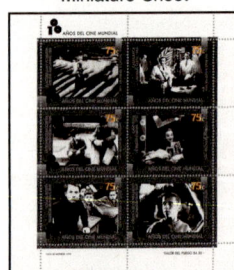

Motion Pictures, Cent. — A859

Black and white film clips, director: a, The Battleship Potemkin, Sergei Eisenstein (Soviet Union). b, Casablanca, Michael Curtiz (US). c, Bicycle Thief, Vittorio De Sica (Italy). d, Limelights, Charles Chaplin (England). e, The 400 Blows, Francois Truffaut (France). f, Chronicle of the Lonely Child, Leonardo Favio (Argentina).

| 1995, Dec. 2 | | Perf. 13½ | |
|---|---|---|---|
| 1909 | A859 75c Sheet of 6, #a.-f. | 26.00 | 25.00 |

The Sky — A860

| 1995, Dec. 16 | Perf. 13½ on 3 Sides | | |
|---|---|---|---|
| **Booklet Stamps** | | | |
| 1910 | A860 25c Dirigible | .70 | .35 |
| 1911 | A860 25c Kite | .70 | .35 |
| 1912 | A860 25c Hot air balloon | .70 | .35 |
| 1913 | A860 50c Balloons | 1.50 | .35 |
| 1914 | A860 50c Paper airplane | 1.50 | .35 |
| 1915 | A860 75c Airplane | 2.25 | .35 |
| 1916 | A860 75c Helicopter | 2.25 | .35 |
| 1917 | A860 75c Parachute | 2.25 | .35 |
| a. | Booklet pane, #1910-1917 + label | 13.00 | |
| | Complete booklet, No. 1917a | 27.00 | |

Nos. 1910-1917 do not appear in Scott number order in No. 1917a, which has a continuous design.

America Issue — A861

Postal vehicles from Postal & Telegraph Museum: No. 1918, Horse & carriage. No. 1919, Truck.

| 1995, Dec. 16 | | Perf. 13½ | |
|---|---|---|---|
| 1918 | A861 75c multicolored | 2.75 | .75 |
| 1919 | A861 75c multicolored | 2.75 | .75 |

Olympic Games, Cent. — A862

| 1996, Mar. 30 | Litho. | Perf. 13½ | |
|---|---|---|---|
| 1920 | A862 75c Running | 2.50 | .75 |
| 1921 | A862 1p Discus | 3.50 | .90 |

**Type of 1995**
**Self-Adhesive**
**Coil Stamps**
**Country Name and Denomination in Blue**

| 1996 | Litho. | Die Cut | |
|---|---|---|---|
| 1921A | A850 25c multi | 7.00 | 2.00 |
| 1921B | A850 75c multi | 14.00 | 3.00 |

Physicians A863

Designs: a, Francisco J. Muniz (1795-1871). b, Ricardo Gutierrez (1838-96). c, Ignacio Pirovano (1844-95). d, Esteban L. Maradona (1895-1995).

| 1996, Apr. 20 | Litho. | Perf. 12 | |
|---|---|---|---|
| 1922 | A863 50c Sheet of 4 | 7.00 | 6.00 |
| a.-d. | Any single | 1.00 | 1.00 |

Jerusalem, 3000th Anniv. — A864

7th cent. mosaic maps of city, denomination at: No. 1923, LL. No. 1924, LR.

| 1996, May 18 | Litho. | Perf. 13½ | |
|---|---|---|---|
| 1923 | A864 75c multicolored | 1.50 | .75 |
| 1924 | A864 75c multicolored | 1.50 | .75 |
| a. | Pair, #1923-1924 | 6.50 | 6.00 |

No. 1924a is a continuous design and was issued in sheets of 8 + 4 labels.

Endangered Fauna — A865

| 1996, June 15 | Litho. | Perf. 13½ | |
|---|---|---|---|
| 1925 | A865 75c Capybara | 2.00 | .75 |
| 1926 | A865 75c Guanaco | 2.00 | .75 |
| a. | Pair, #1925-1926 | 5.50 | 5.00 |

America Issue.

Summer Olympic Games — A866

Designs: 75c, Torch bearer, Buenos Aires, candidate for 2004 Games. 1p, Men's eight with coxswain, Atlanta, 1996.

| 1996, July 6 | | | |
|---|---|---|---|
| 1927 | A866 75c multicolored | 2.25 | .70 |
| 1928 | A866 1p multicolored | 2.75 | .90 |

National Parks — A867

Wildlife, national park: No. 1929, Mountain turkey, Diamante. No. 1930, Parrot, San Antonio Nature Reserve. No. 1931, Deer, Otamendi Natl. Reserve. No. 1932, Rabbit, El Leoncito Nature Reserve.

| 1996, Aug. 24 | Litho. | Perf. 13x13½ | |
|---|---|---|---|
| 1929 | A867 75c multicolored | 2.50 | .70 |
| 1930 | A867 75c multicolored | 2.50 | .70 |
| 1931 | A867 75c multicolored | 2.50 | .70 |
| 1932 | A867 75c multicolored | 2.50 | .70 |
| | Nos. 1929-1932 (4) | 10.00 | 2.80 |

Central Post Office, Buenos Aires — A868

| 1996, Oct. 5 | Litho. | Die Cut | |
|---|---|---|---|
| **Self-Adhesive** | | | |
| **Size: 25x35mm** | | | |
| 1933 | A868 75c multicolored | 20.00 | 8.00 |

Vignette of No. 1933 is broken by circular and rectangular die cut areas to guard against reuse.
See Nos. 1983-1984.

Carousel Figures A869

Designs: No. 1934, Hand-carved decorative ornaments. No. 1935, Child on carousel horse. No. 1936, Carousel. No. 1937, Heads of horses. No. 1938, Child in airplane. No. 1939, Carousel pig. No. 1940, Boy in car.

| 1996, Oct. 5 | | Perf. 13½ Horiz. | |
|---|---|---|---|
| **Booklet Stamps** | | | |
| 1934 | A869 25c multicolored | .50 | .30 |
| 1935 | A869 25c multicolored | .50 | .30 |
| 1936 | A869 25c multicolored | .50 | .30 |
| 1937 | A869 50c multicolored | 1.00 | .60 |
| 1938 | A869 50c multicolored | 1.00 | .60 |
| 1939 | A869 50c multicolored | 1.00 | .60 |
| 1940 | A869 75c multicolored | 1.50 | .75 |
| a. | Booklet pane, #1934-1940 | 7.00 | |
| | Complete booklet, #1940a | 9.00 | |

Sequence of stamps in No. 1940a: No. 1940, 1934, 1937, 1935, 1938, 1936, 1939.

Port Belgrano Naval Base, Cent. — A870

Designs: 25c, LST "San Antonio." 50c, Corvette Rosales. 75c, Destroyer Hercules. 1p, Aircraft carrier, "25th of May."

| 1996-97 | Litho. | Perf. 13½ | |
|---|---|---|---|
| 1941 | A870 25c multicolored | 1.50 | .50 |
| 1942 | A870 50c multicolored | 1.50 | .50 |
| 1943 | A870 75c multicolored | 3.00 | .75 |
| 1944 | A870 1p multicolored | 3.50 | 1.00 |
| | Nos. 1941-1944 (4) | 9.50 | 2.75 |

Issued: 25c, 1p, 10/5/96; 50c, 75c, 2/1/97.

Christmas A871

Tapestries: 75c, Nativity, by Gladys Angelica Rinaldi, vert. 1p, Candles, by Norma Bonet de Maekawa.

| 1996, Nov. 30 | Litho. | Perf. 13½ | |
|---|---|---|---|
| 1945 | A871 75c multicolored | 2.00 | .75 |
| 1946 | A871 1p multicolored | 2.75 | 1.00 |

Exploration of Antarctica A872

Designs: 75c, Melchior Base. 1.25p, Icebreaker ARA Alte. Irizar.

| 1996, Nov. 30 | | | |
|---|---|---|---|
| 1947 | A872 75c multicolored | 2.25 | .75 |
| 1948 | A872 1.25p multicolored | 3.25 | 1.25 |

National Gallery, Cent. — A873

Paintings of women by: 75c, Paul Gauguin, vert. No. 1950, Edouard Manet, vert. No. 1951, Amedeo Modigliani, vert. 1.25p, Pablo Picasso.

| 1996, Dec. 14 | | | |
|---|---|---|---|
| 1949 | A873 75c multicolored | 2.25 | .70 |
| 1950 | A873 1p multicolored | 3.00 | 1.00 |
| 1951 | A873 1p multicolored | 3.00 | 1.00 |
| 1952 | A873 1.25p multicolored | 4.75 | 1.25 |
| | Nos. 1949-1952 (4) | 13.00 | 3.95 |

Mining Industry A874

| 1997, Feb. 1 | Litho. | Perf. 13½ | |
|---|---|---|---|
| 1953 | A874 75c Granite | 2.00 | 1.50 |
| 1954 | A874 1.25p Borax | 3.50 | 3.50 |

Traditional Costumes A875

| 1997, Feb. 22 | Litho. | Perf. 13½ | |
|---|---|---|---|
| 1955 | A875 75c multicolored | 2.75 | 2.50 |

America issue.

Repatriation of the Curved Sword of Gen. San Martin, Cent. — A876

| 1997, Mar. 15 | Litho. | Perf. 13½ | |
|---|---|---|---|
| 1956 | A876 75c multicolored | 2.50 | 2.25 |

29th Youth Rugby World Championships A877

| 1997, Mar. 22 | Litho. | Perf. 13½ | |
|---|---|---|---|
| 1957 | A877 75c multicolored | 2.50 | 2.25 |

**Fauna Type of 1995**

| 1997, Feb. 22 | Litho. | Perf. 13½ | |
|---|---|---|---|
| 1958 | A853 10c Reddish sandpiper | 1.60 | .35 |

# ARGENTINA

Buenos Aires-Rio de Janeiro Regatta, 50th Anniv. — A879

**1997, Apr. 5**  Litho.  *Perf. 13½*
1960  A879  75c Fortuna II  2.50  2.25

Natl. History Museum, Cent. — A880

**1997, May 17**
1961  A880  75c multicolored  2.50  2.25

La Plata Natl. University, Cent. — A881

**1997, May 17**
1962  A881  75c multicolored  2.50  2.25

Lighthouses — A882

a, Cabo Vírgenes. b, Isla Pingüino. c, San Juan de Salvamento. d, Punta Delgada.

**1997, May 31**
1963  A882  75c Sheet of 4, #a.-d.  11.00  8.00

Ramón J. Cárcano (1860-1946), Developer of Postal and Telegraph System — A883

**1997, May 31**
1964  A883  75c multicolored  2.50  2.25

Buenos Aires, Candidate for 2004 Summer Olympics A884

**1997, June 21**
1965  A884  75c multicolored  2.50  2.25

First Electric Tram in Buenos Aires, Cent. A885

Designs: a, Lacroze Suburban Service Tram Co, 1912. b, Lacroze Urban Service Tram Co., 1907. c, Anglo Argentina Tram Co., 1930. d, Buenos Aires City Transportation Corp., 1942. e, Military Manufacture Tram, 1956. f, South Electric Tram, 1908.

**1997, July 12**  Sheet of 6
1966  A885  75c #a.-f. + 2 labels  14.00  12.50

Monument to Joaquín V. González (1863-1923), La Rioja — A886

**1997, Aug. 9**
1967  A886  75c multicolored  2.50  2.25

Musicians and Composers — A887

Paintings: No. 1968, Alberto Ginastera (1916-83), by Carlos Nine. No. 1969, Astor Piazzolla (1921-92), by Carlos Alonso. No. 1970, Aníbal Troilo (1914-75), by Hermenegildo Sabat. No. 1971, Atahualpa Yupanqui (b. 1908), by Luis Scafati.

**1997, Aug. 9**
1968  A887  75c multicolored  2.50  2.00
1969  A887  75c multicolored  2.50  2.00
1970  A887  75c multicolored  2.50  2.00
1971  A887  75c multicolored  2.50  2.00
  Nos. 1968-1971 (4)  10.00  8.00

Argentine Authors A888

Designs: No. 1972, Jorge Luis Borges (1899-1986), maze. No. 1973, Julio Cortázar (1914-84), hop scotch game.

**1997, Aug. 30**  Litho.  *Perf. 13*
1972  A888  1p multicolored  2.75  1.00
1973  A888  1p multicolored  2.75  1.00

Women's Political Rights Law, 50th Anniv. — A889

**1997, Sept. 6**  Litho.  *Perf. 13½*
1974  A889  75c Eva Perón  0.25  2.00

Mercosur (Common Market of Latin America) — A890

**1997, Sept. 27**  Litho.  *Perf. 13½*
1975  A890  75c multicolored  2.50  2.25

See Bolivia No. 1019, Brazil No. 2646, Paraguay No. 2564, Uruguay No. 1681.

Launching of Frigate President Sarmiento, Cent. — A891

Designs: No. 1976, Painting of ship by Hugo Leban.
No. 1977: a, Ship. b, Ship's figurehead, vert.

**1997, Oct. 4**
1976  A891  75c multicolored  2.75  2.50

**Souvenir Sheet**
*Perf. 12*
1977  A891  75c Sheet of 2, #a.-b.  5.25  4.00

No. 1977 contains one 40x30mm stamp and one 30x40mm stamp.

Ernesto "Che" Guevara (1928-67) — A892

**1997, Oct. 18**
1978  A892  75c multicolored  5.25  5.00

Ecology on Stamps A893

Children's drawings: No. 1979, Animal, by J. Chiapparo, vert. No. 1980, Vicuna, by L.L. Portal, vert. No. 1981, Seal, by A. Lloren. No. 1982, Bird in flight, by J. Saccone.

**1997, Nov. 8**  Litho.  *Perf. 13½*
1979  A893  50c multicolored  1.60  .50
1980  A893  50c multicolored  1.60  .50
1981  A893  75c multicolored  2.25  .75
1982  A893  75c multicolored  2.25  .75
  Nos. 1979-1982 (4)  7.70  2.50

**Central Post Office, Buenos Aires, Type of 1996**

**1997, July 24**  Litho.  *Die Cut*
**Self-Adhesive**
**Size: 23x35mm**
1983  A868  25c multicolored  12.00  .75
1984  A868  75c multicolored  5.00  .75
  a.  Bklt. pane, 2 #1983, 6 #1984  55.00
    Completo booklet, #1984a  62.00

Nos. 1983-1984 are broken at both the top and bottom of each stamp by three lines of wavy die cutting.

Christmas — A893a

Nativity scene tapestries by: Nos. 1984B, 1984G, Mary José. No. 1984C, Elena Aguilar. No. 1984D, Silvia Pettachi. No. 1984E, Ana Escobar. No. 1984F, Alejandra Martinez. No. 1984H, Nidia Martinez.

**1997, Nov. 22**  Litho.  *Perf. 13½*
1984B  A893a  75c multicolored  2.50  2.25

**Booklet Stamps**
**Self-Adhesive**
**Size: 44x27mm**
*Die Cut*
1984C  A893a  25c multicolored  .75  .50
1984D  A893a  25c multicolored  1.00  .50
1984E  A893a  50c multicolored  1.50  .75
1984F  A893a  50c multicolored  1.50  .75
1984G  A893a  75c multicolored  2.00  .75
1984H  A893a  75c multicolored  2.00  .75
  i.  Booklet pane, #1984C-1984H  12.00

Nos. 1984C-1984H are broken at upper right by three die cut chevrons. By its nature, No. 1984Hi is a complete booklet.

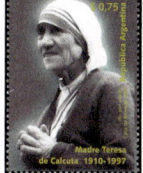

Mother Teresa (1910-97) — A893b

**1997, Dec. 27**
1984J  A893b  75c multicolored  2.50  2.25

Dr. Bernardo A. Houssay (1887-1971), 1947 Nobel Prize Winner in Medicine A894

**1998, Jan. 31**  Litho.  *Perf. 13½*
1985  A894  75c multicolored  2.50  2.25

First Ascension of Mount Aconcagua, Cent. — A895

**1998, Feb. 14**  *Perf. 12*
1986  A895  1.25p multicolored  3.75  3.50

Founding of San Martín de los Andes, Cent. — A896

**1998, Mar. 14**  Litho.  *Perf. 13½*
1987  A896  75c multicolored  2.50  2.25

Regimental Quarters of Gen. San Martín's Mounted Grenadiers — A897

Designs: a, Statue. b, Large jar with painting of San Martín. c, Regimental seal. d, Regimental quarters.

**1998, Mar. 21**  Litho.  *Perf. 13½*
1988  A897  75c Block of 4, #a.-d.  9.00  6.00

Protection of the Ozone — A898

**1998, Mar. 28**  Litho.  *Perf. 13½*
1989  A898  75c multicolored  2.50  2.25

America Issue — A899

Letter carriers: No. 1990, Wearing white uniform. No. 1991, Carrying letter bag with shoulder strap.

# ARGENTINA

**1998, Apr. 4**
1990 A899 75c multicolored 2.75 .75
1991 A899 75c multicolored 2.75 .75

Characters from Stories by Maria Elena Walsh — A900

Designs: No. 1992, El Reino Del Reves. No. 1993, Zoo Loco. No. 1994, Dailan Kifki. No. 1995, Manuelita.

**1998, Apr. 17  Litho.  Die Cut**
**Booklet Stamps**
**Self-Adhesive**
1992 A900 75c multicolored 3.75 3.00
1993 A900 75c multicolored 3.75 3.00
1994 A900 75c multicolored 3.75 3.00
1995 A900 75c multicolored 3.75 3.00
  a. Complete booklet, #1992-1995  22.00

Historic Chapels A901

Designs: No. 1996, San Pedro de Fiambalá, Catamarca. No. 1997, Huacalera, Jujuy. No. 1998, Santo Domingo, La Rioja. No. 1999, Tumbaya, Jujuy.

**1998, Apr. 25  Litho.  Perf. 13x13½**
1996 A901 75c multicolored 2.25 2.00
1997 A901 75c multicolored 2.25 2.00
1998 A901 75c multicolored 2.25 2.00
1999 A901 75c multicolored 2.25 2.00
  Nos. 1996-1999 (4)  9.00 8.00

White Helmets, A Commitment to Humanity A902

**1998, May 23  Litho.  Perf. 13½**
2000 A902 1p multicolored 3.00 2.75

Beginning with No. 2001, many Argentine stamps are inscribed "Correo Oficial," but these are not Official stamps (i.e., for government use only). The addition of "Correo Oficial" distinguishes these stamps, which are products of the Argentine Postal Service, from other stamps from a private post, OCA, which are also inscribed "Republica Argentina."

1998 World Cup Soccer Championships, France — A903

Stylized players representing: a, Argentina. b, Croatia. c, Jamaica. d, Japan.

**1998, May 30**
2001 A903 75c Block of 4, #a.-d.  8.75 7.75

Journalist's Day — A904

**1998, June 20**
2002 A904 75c multicolored 2.50 2.25

Creation of Argentine Postal System, 250th Anniv. — A905

  a, Corrientes design A2, peso coin. b, Building, post box.

**1998, June 27**
2003 A905 75c Pair, #a.-b.  5.00 4.50

**Fauna Type of 1995**
**1998  Litho.  Die Cut**
**Self-Adhesive (#2004)**
2004 A853 60c Picaflor  2.25 2.00
**Perf. 13½**
2004A A853 3.25p Tero  10.00 5.00

No. 2004 is broken at bottom right by 3 or 5 lines of wavy die cutting.
Issued: 60c, 12/12; 3.25p, 7/22.

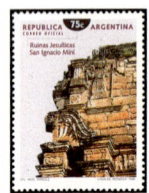

Ruins, Mission St. Ignacio — A906

**1998, July 25  Litho.  Perf. 13½**
2005 A906 75c multicolored  2.50 2.25
Mercosur.

Cattle — A907

**1998, Aug. 1**
2006 A907 25c Brahman  .80 .70
2007 A907 25c Aberdeen-Angus  .80 .70
2008 A907 50c Hereford  1.50 .90
2009 A907 50c Criolla  1.50 .90
2010 A907 75c Holland-Argentina  2.10 1.75
2011 A907 75c Shorthorn  2.10 1.75
  Nos. 2006-2011 (6)  8.80 6.70

Deception Island Base, Antarctica, 50th Anniv. — A908

**1998, Aug. 15  Litho.  Perf. 14½**
2012 A908 75c multicolored  2.60 2.40

State of Israel, 50th Anniv. — A909

**1998, Sept. 5  Litho.  Perf. 13½**
2013 A909 75c multicolored  2.50 2.25

Argentina-Japan Friendship Treaty, Cent. — A910

**1998, Oct. 3**
2014 A910 75c multicolored  2.50 2.25

Post Office Building, Buenos Aires, 70th Anniv. — A911

Designs: No. 2015, Building, clock, tile. No. 2016, Column ornamentation, tile, bench.

**1998, Oct. 3**
2015 A911 75c multicolored  2.25 2.00
2016 A911 75c multicolored  2.25 2.00
  a. Pair, #2015-2016  5.00 4.50

Cartoons — A912

Designs: a, Patoruzu, by Quinterno. b, Matias, by Sendra. c, Clemente, by Caloi. d, El Eternauta, by Oesterheld and López. e, Loco Chavez, by Trillo and Altuna. f, Inodoro Pereyra, by Fontanarrosa. g, Tia Vicenta, by Landrú. h, Gaturro, by Nik.

**1998, Oct. 17  Litho.  Perf. 13¾x13¼**
2017 A912 75c Sheet of 8, #a.-h.  24.00 22.00

Dr. Pedro de Elizalde's Children's Hospital, 220th Anniv. — A913

**1998, Oct. 24  Litho.  Perf. 13½**
2025 A913 75c multicolored  2.60 2.40

Raoul Wallenberg (1912-47), Humanitarian A914

**1998, Nov. 21**
2026 A914 75c multicolored  3.00 2.75

Espamer '98 — A915

25c, Spanish flags, arms. 75c, 18th cent. schooner. 75c+75c, Brigantine, gray sails. 1.25p+1.25p, Brigantine, white sails.

**1998, Nov. 21  Die Cut**
**Booklet Stamps**
**Self-Adhesive**
2027 A915 25c multicolored  1.10 .75
2028 A915 75c multicolored  3.50 2.00
2029 A915 75c +75c multi  6.75 4.00
2030 A915 1.25p +1.25p multi  11.00 3.25
  a. Booklet pane, #2027-2030  23.00

Nos. 2027-2030 are broken at top right of each stamp by four lines of wavy die cutting. No. 2030a is a complete booklet.

Organization of American States, 50th Anniv. — A916

**1998, Nov. 28  Perf. 13½**
2031 A916 75c multicolored  2.50 2.25

Dinosaurs of Argentina A917

Designs: a, Eoraptor. b, Gasparinisaura. c, Giganotosaurus. d, Patagosaurus.

**1998, Nov. 28**
2032 A917 75c Sheet of 4, #a.-d.  11.00 10.00

Christmas — A918

**1998, Dec. 5**
2033 A918 75c multicolored  2.50 2.25

Newspaper El Liberal, Cent. — A919

**1998, Dec. 5**
2034 A919 75c Juan A. Figueroa  2.50 2.25

La Nueva Provincia, Daily Newspaper, Cent. — A920

**1998, Dec. 12**
2035 A920 75c Enrique Julio  2.50 2.25

Universal Declaration of Human Rights, 50th Anniv. — A921

**1998, Dec. 12**
2036 A921 75c multicolored  2.50 2.25

Holocaust Memorial, Cathedral of Buenos Aires — A922

**1998, Dec. 12**
2037 A922 75c multicolored  2.50 2.25

Southern Cross — A923

Inscriptions: 8.75p, Sur postal express. 17.50p, Sur postal 24.

**1999-2000  Litho.  Die Cut**
**Self-Adhesive**
2038 A923 8.75p bl & silver  27.00 18.00
2039 A923 17.50p bl & gold  56.00 37.50

Issued: 8.75p, 7/1/99; 17.50p, 3/2/00. Nos. 2038-2039 are broken at right by five wavy lines of die cutting.

# ARGENTINA

National Fund for the Arts, 40th Anniv. — A925

**1999, Mar. 6**    **Litho.**    **Perf. 13½**
2042   A925   75c multicolored    2.25   2.00

Intl. Year of the Ocean (in 1998) — A926

**1999, Mar. 6**
2043   A926   50c Penguin, vert.    1.90   1.60
2044   A926   75c Dolphins    1.90   1.60

Postmen — A927

Designs: 25c, Early postman, city scene. 50c, Early postman, people on bicycles, factory. 75c, Modern postman, city buildings.

**1998-2001**    **Litho.**    **Die Cut**
**Self-Adhesive**
2045   A927   25c multicolored    60.00   .75
2046   A927   75c multicolored    30.00   .50
   a.   Strip of 4, 1 #2045, 3 #2046    150.00

**Booklet Stamps**
**Serpentine Die Cut 6**
2047   A927   25c multicolored    40.00   1.00
2048   A927   75c multicolored    15.00   1.00
   a.   Bklt. pane, 2 #2047, 6 #2048    175.00
   Complete booklet, #2048a    180.00

**Serpentine Die Cut 11**
2048B   A927   25c multi    2.00   .25
2048C   A927   75c multi    6.00   .50
   d.   Booklet pane, 2 #2048B, 6 #2048C    45.00
   Complete booklet, 2 #2048Cd    90.00
   Complete booklet, 4 #2048Cd    180.00

**Size: 21x27mm**
**Die Cut**
2049   A927   25c multicolored    3.50   .50
2050   A927   50c multicolored    3.50   1.00
2051   A927   75c multicolored    3.50   1.75
   a.   Bklt. pane, 2 ea #2049-2051    21.00
   Complete booklet, #2051a    32.00

Nos. 2045-2048C are broken at lower right by five lines of wavy die cutting. Nos. 2049-2051 are broken in center by five wavy lines of die cutting. Nos. 2045-2046 have darker vignettes than Nos. 2047-2048.
Issued: Nos. 2045-2048, 12/9/98. Nos. 2049-2051, 2/2/99. Nos. 2048B-2048C, Feb. 2001.

25th Book Fair — A928

Designs: a, Book. b, Obelisk, readers.

**1999, Apr. 17**    **Litho.**    **Perf. 13¾x13½**
2052   A928   75c Pair, a.-b.    4.25   3.50

Argentine Rugby Union, Cent. — A929

75c, Player, balls. 1.50p, Old, modern players.

**1999, Apr. 24**    **Litho.**    **Perf. 13¾x13½**
2054   A929   75c multicolored    2.25   1.90
**Souvenir Sheet**
2055   A929   1.50p multi + 3 labels    6.75   6.50

Cafes of Buenos Aires — A930

Designs: a, Mug, Giralda Dairy. b, Two glasses, Homero Manzi Cafe. c, Hat hanging on rack, Ideal Sweet Shop. d, Cup and saucer, Tortoni Cafe.

**Serpentine Die Cut**
**1999, Apr. 30**    **Litho.**
**Self-Adhesive**
2056    Booklet pane of 4    14.00   12.00
   a.   A930 25c multicolored    .60   .50
   b.-c.   A930 75c multi, each    1.75   1.00
   d.   A930 1.25p multicolored    3.00   1.25
   Complete booklet, #2056    15.00

Argentine Olympic Committee, 75th Anniv. — A931

**1999, May 15**    **Perf. 14x13¼**
2057   A931   75c Pierre de Coubertin    2.25   1.75

Enrico Caruso (1873-1921), Opera Singer — A932

Designs: a, Portrait of Caruso. b, Singer, various musical instruments. c, Outside of Colon Theatre, Buenos Aires. d, Scene from opera, "El Matrero."

**1999, May 15**    **Perf. 13½**
2058   A932   75c Sheet of 4, #a.-d.    10.00   9.00

Famous Women — A933

Designs: a, Rosario Vera Peñaloza (1873-1950), educator. b, Julieta Lanteri (1862-1932), physician.

**1999, June 5**    **Perf. 14x13¼**
2059   A933   75c Pair, #a.-b.    4.60   3.90

**Souvenir Sheets**

Paintings from Natl. Museum of Art, Buenos Aires — A934

No. 2060: a, Anarchy of Year 20, by Luis Felipe Noé. b, Retrato de L.E.S., by Carlos Alonso.
No. 2061: a, Typical Orchestra, by Antonio Berni. b, Untitled, (Woman seated), by Aída Carballo.

**1999, June 5**    **Perf. 14**
**Sheets of 2**
2060   A934   75c #a.-b.    5.50   5.00
2061   A934   75c #a.-b.    5.50   5.00
No. 2060b is 40x40mm, No. 2061a, 70x50mm, No. 2061b, 40x50mm.

Carrier Pigeon — A935

**1999, June 12**    **Perf. 13¾x13½**
2062   A935   75c multicolored    2.50   2.25

Maps — A936

**1999, June 12**    **Die Cut**
**Self-Adhesive**
2063   A936   35c Local highway    1.25   1.20
2064   A936   40c City street    1.35   1.20
2065   A936   50c Regional highway    1.75   1.20
   Nos. 2063-2065 (3)    4.35   3.60
Nos. 2063-2065 are broken at lower left by five wavy lines of die cutting.

Dogs — A937

Designs: a, 25c, Boxer. b, 25c, English sheepdog. c, 50c, Collie. d, 50c, St. Bernard. e, 75c, German shepherd. f, 75c, Siberian husky.

**1999, July 24**    **Litho.**    **Perf. 13½**
2066   A937   Sheet of 6, #a.-f.    12.00   10.50

Natl. Telecommunications Day — A938

**1999, July 24**    **Perf. 13½x13¾**
2067   A938   75c multicolored    2.25   1.75

Justo José de Urquiza School, Concepción del Uruguay, 150th Anniv. — A939

**1999, Aug. 7**    **Perf. 13¾x13½**
2068   A939   75c multicolored    2.25   1.75

Otto Krause Technical School, Buenos Aires, Cent. — A940

**1999, Aug. 7**    **Perf. 13½x13¾**
2069   A940   75c multicolored    2.25   1.75

Bethlehem 2000 Project — A941

**1999, Aug. 21**    **Perf. 13½**
2070   A941   75c multicolored    2.25   1.75

America Issue, A New Millennium Without Arms — A942

No. 2072, Tree of hands, vert.

**Perf. 13½x13¾, 13¾x13½**
**1999, Aug. 21**
2071   A942   75c shown    2.25   2.00
2072   A942   75c multicolored    2.25   2.00

National Parks A943

Parks and animals: No. 2073, Mburucuyá, coypu. No. 2074, Quebrada de Los Condoritos, condor. No. 2075, San Guillermo, vicuna. No. 2076, Sierra de las Quijadas, puma. No. 2077, Talampaya, gray fox.

**1999, Sept. 25**    **Litho.**    **Perf. 14x13½**
2073   A943   50c multicolored    1.60   1.40
2074   A943   50c multicolored    1.60   1.40
2075   A943   50c multicolored    1.60   1.40
2076   A943   75c multicolored    3.50   1.00
2077   A943   75c multicolored    3.50   1.90
   Nos. 2073-2077 (5)    11.80   8.00
For surcharge, see Nos. 2853A-2854.

Inter-American Development Bank, 40th Anniv. — A944

**1999, Oct. 9**    **Litho.**    **Perf. 13½x13¾**
2078   A944   75c multi    2.25   1.75

UPU, 125th Anniv. — A945

**1999, Oct. 9**    **Perf. 13¾x13½**
2079   A945   1.50p multi    4.00   3.75

Trees — A946

a, Nothofagus pumilio. b, Prosopis caldenia. c, Schinopsis balansae. d, Cordia trichotoma.

**1999, Oct. 16**    **Perf. 13½x13¾**
2080   A946   75c Strip of 4, #a-d    8.75   7.75

# ARGENTINA

Sinking of A.R.A. Fournier, 50th Anniv. — A947

**1999, Oct. 16**     Perf. 13¾x13½
2081 A947 75c multi     2.25 1.75

Aviation Anniversaries A948

Designs: No. 2082, Late 25 airplane. No. 2083, Parachutists.

**1999, Oct. 30**     Perf. 13¾x13½
2082 A948 75c multi     2.10 1.90
2083 A948 75c multi     2.10 1.90

First Argentine airmail flight, 70th anniv. (No. 2082), Hundred consecutive jumps by Argentine Parachute Club, 50th anniv.

### Souvenir Sheets

Millennium — A949

No. 2084: a, 75c, Head of soccer player. b, 50c, Machine as soccer player.
No. 2085: a, 50c, Cane, vert. b, 75c, Head of Jorge Luis Borges (1899-1986), writer.
No. 2086: a, 50c, Accordion player on bed, vert. b, 75c, Stylized tango dancers.

**1999, Oct. 30**     Perf. 14
2084 A949 Sheet of 2, #a.-b.     4.50 4.00
2085 A949 Sheet of 2, #a.-b.     4.50 4.00
2086 A949 Sheet of 2, #a.-b.     4.50 4.00

Size of 75c stamps: 40x40mm.

Argentine Soccer Teams — A950

Designs: No. 2087, Banner and flags of River Plate team. No. 2088, Banner of Boca Juniors team, balloons.

River Plate team (red and white team colors) — No. 2089: a, Stadium, emblem, soccer balls. b, Team on field. c, Fans. d, Emblem. e, Trophy. f, Banner in stadium. g, Player, ball.

Boca Juniors team (blue and yellow team colors) — No. 2090: a, Two players, ball. b, Emblem. c, Four players celebrating. d, Fans, balloons. e, Banner in stadium. f, Blurred shot of players in action. g, Blurred shot of players, diff.

**1999**     Perf. 13½x13¼
2087 A950 75c multi     2.25 2.00
2088 A950 75c multi     2.25 2.00

**Self-Adhesive**
**Die Cut**

2089 Pane of 7     39.00 37.50
   a. A950 25c multi     2.50 2.00
   b.-c. A950 50c any single     2.50 2.00
   d.-f. A950 75c any single     5.50 5.50
   g. A950 1.50p multi     11.00 10.00
2090 Pane of 7     39.00 37.50
   a. A950 25c multi     2.50 2.00
   b.-c. A950 50c any single     3.50 2.00
   d.-f. A950 75c any single     5.50 5.00
   g. A950 1.50p multi     11.00 10.00

Issued: Nos. 2087-2088, 11/13; Nos. 2089-2090, 11/15.

Sizes: Nos. 2089a-2089f, 2090a-2090f, 37x27mm; No. 2089g, 2090g, 37x37mm.

Canonization of Brother Héctor Valdivielso Sáez — A951

**1999, Nov. 20**     Perf. 13¾x13½
2091 A951 75c multi     2.25 1.90

Manuel Belgrano National Naval School, Bicent. — A952

**1999, Nov. 27**
2092 A952 75c multi     2.25 1.90

### Souvenir Sheet

Launch of Corvette Uruguay, 125th Anniv. A953

**1999, Nov. 27**     Litho.     Perf. 14
2093 A953 1.50p multi     7.00 6.75

A954

Christmas — A955

No. 2094, Figurines of Holy Family.
No. 2095: a, Magus. b, Bell. c, Two Magi, camels. d, Leaf. e, Angel with star. f, Nativity scene. g, Star. h, Ornaments.

**1999, Dec. 4**     Perf. 13¾x13½
2094 A954 75c multi     2.25 1.90

**Perf. 14**
2095 A955 Sheet of 8     13.50 11.50
   a.-b. 25c any single     1.00 .80
   c.-d. 50c any single     1.60 1.25
   e.-h. 75c any single     2.00 1.75

Sizes: Nos. 2095a, 2095b, 2095g, 2095h, 30x30mm.

Viticulture — A956

Designs: a, 25c, Grape on vine. b, 50c, Bottoms of wine bottles. c, 50c, Cork and corkscrew. d, 25c, Glass of wine, wine bottle.

**2000, Feb. 26**     Litho.     Perf. 13¼
2096 A956 Block of 4, #a-d     9.50 8.50

World Mathematics Year — A957

**2000, Mar. 18**     Perf. 13¾x13½
2097 A957 75c multi     2.25 1.90

Birds — A958

a, Leptotila verrauxi. b, Columba picazuro. c, Columbina picni. d, Zenaida auriculata.

**2000, Mar. 18**     Die Cut
**Self-Adhesive**
2098 Booklet of 4     11.00 10.00
   a.-d. A958 75c any single     2.50 1.50

### Souvenir Sheet

Bangkok 2000 Stamp Exhibition — A959

Designs: a, 25c, Vanda coerulea. b, 75c, Erythrina crista-galli.

**2000, Mar. 25**     Perf. 14
2099 A959 Sheet of 2, #a-b     4.00 3.50

### Miniature Sheet

Libraries A960

Designs: a, 25c, National Public Library Protection Commission. b, 50c, Jujuy Public Library. c, 75c, Argentine Library for the Blind. d, 1p, Argentine National Library.

**Litho., Litho. & Embossed (#2100c)**
**2000, Apr. 15**     Perf. 13½
2100 A960 Sheet of 4, #a-d     7.75 6.75

Gen. Luis Maria Campos Military School, Cent. — A961

**2000, Apr. 29**     Perf. 13¾x13½
2101 A961 75c multi     2.25 1.90

Discovery of Brazil, 500th Anniv. — A962

a, 75c, Pedro Cabral, 1558 map of Brazil coastline. b, 25c, Compass rose and ship.

**2000, Apr. 29**
2102 A962 Pair, #a-b     4.25 3.75

### Souvenir Sheet

The Stamp Show 2000, London A963

Designs: a, 25c, Great Britain #1 and design A1, La Porteña, 1st locomotive in Argentina. b, 75c, Argentina No. 7, mail box.

**2000, May 20**     Perf. 14
2103 A963 Sheet of 2, #a-b     4.00 3.50

91st Intl. Convention of Rotary International, Buenos Aires — A964

**2000, June 3**     Litho.     Perf. 13½x13¾
2104 A964 75c multi     2.25 1.90

Stampin' the Future A965

Children's Stamp Design Contest Winners: 25c, Rocío Casado. 50c, Carolina Cáceres, vert. 75c, Valeria A. Pizarro. 1p, Cristina Ayala Castro, vert.

**Perf. 13½x13¼, 13¼x13½**
**2000, June 24**
2105-2108 A965 Set of 4     7.50 6.50

America Issue — A966

AIDS Prevention: No. 2109, Handshake. No. 2110, Heart and hands.

**2000, July 8**     Perf. 13¾x13½
2109-2110 A966 75c Set of 2     4.25 3.75

Antoine de Saint-Exupéry (1900-44), Pilot, Writer — A967

Designs: Nos. 2111, 2115, Potez 25. Nos. 2112, 2116, Late 28. No. 2113, Saint-Exupéry. No. 2114, Henri Guillaumet, Vicente A. Almonacid and Jean Mermoz. No. 2117, Map of southern Argentina, tail of Late 25 plane. 1p, Nose of Late 25 plane, cover from 1st airmail flight to Trelew.

**2000, July 29**     Perf. 13½
2111 A967 25c multi     1.40 1.25
2112 A967 50c multi     3.00 2.60

**Booklet Stamps**
**Perf. 14**
**Size: 30x30mm**
2113 A967 25c multi     2.25 .50
2114 A967 50c multi     3.25 1.10
**Size: 60x20mm**
2115 A967 25c multi     2.25 .50
2116 A967 50c multi     3.25 1.10
   a. Booklet pane, #2113-2116     13.00
**Size: 40x30mm**
2117 A967 50c multi     3.25 1.10
2118 A967 1p multi     4.75 1.75
   a. Booklet pane, #2117-2118     8.75
   Booklet, #2116a, 2118a     24.00
   Nos. 2111-2118 (8)     23.40 9.90

Argentine airmail service, 73rd anniv., Aerofila 2000 Philatelic Exhibition, Buenos Aires (No. 2118a).

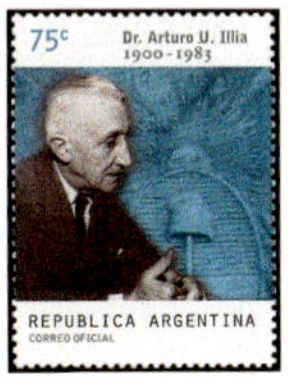

President Arturo U. Illia (1900-82) — A968

**2000, Aug. 5** *Perf. 13½x13¼*
**2119** A968 75c multi 2.25 1.75

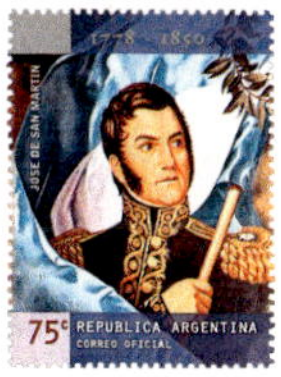

José de San Martín (1778-1850) — A969

**2000, Aug. 26** *Perf. 13½*
**2120** A969 75c multi 2.25 1.75

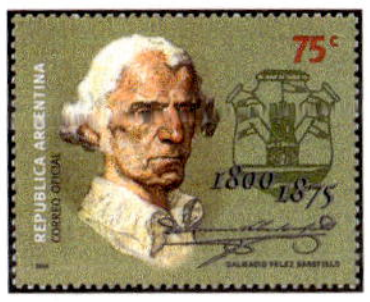

Dalmacio Vélez Sarsfield (1800-75), Writer of Civil Code — A970

*Perf. 13½x13¼*
**2000, Sept. 23** **Litho.**
**2121** A970 75c multi 2.25 1.75

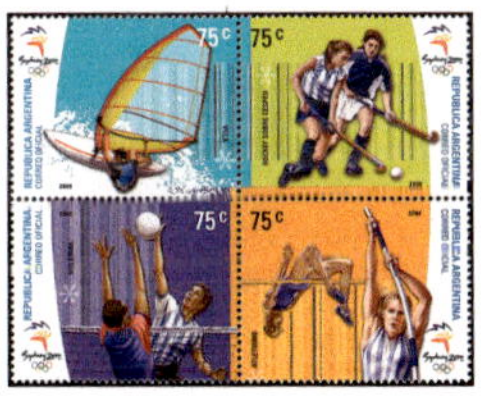

2000 Summer Olympic, Sydney A971

No. 2122: a, Windsurfing. b, Field hockey. c, Volleyball. d, Pole vault.

**2000, Sept. 23** *Perf. 13½*
**2122** A971 75c Block of 4, #a-d 8.75 7.50

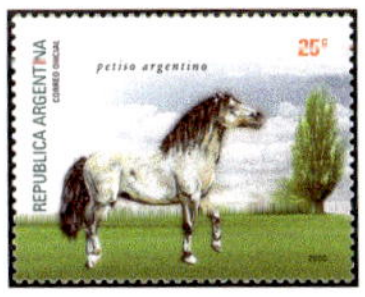

Horses — A972

No. 2123: a, Argentine Petiso. b, Argentine Carriage Horse. c, Peruvian. d, Criolla. e, Argentine Saddle Horse. f, Argentine Polo.

No. 2124: a, Horse-drawn mail coach. b, Horse's head.

**2000, Oct. 7** *Perf. 13¾x13½*
**2123** Sheet of 6 + 2 labels 9.50 8.00
*a.-b.* A972 25c Any single 1.10 1.10
*c.-d.* A972 50c Any single 1.40 1.10
*e.-f.* A972 75c Any single 2.10 2.10

**Souvenir Sheet**

*Perf. 14*

**2124** Sheet of 2 4.00 3.50
*a.* A972 25c multi 1.25 1.25
*b.* A972 75c multi 1.75 1.75

España 2000 Intl. Philatelic Exhibition.

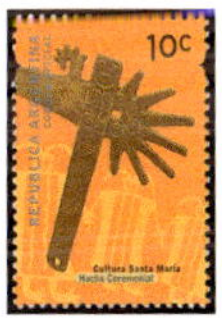

Archaeological Artifacts — A973

Designs: 10c, Ceremonial hatchet, Santa Maria culture. 25c, Musical pipes. 50c, Loom, Mapuche culture. 60c, Poncho. 75c, Funerary mask, Tafi culture. 1p, Basket, Mbayá Indians. 2p, Drum, Mapuche culture. 3.25p, Ceremonial mask, Chané culture. 5p, Funerary urn, Belén culture. 9.40p, Rhea-feather costume.

*Perf. 13½x13¾ Syncopated*

**2000** **Litho.**

| | | | | |
|---|---|---|---|---|
| **2125** | A973 | 10c multi | .25 | .25 |
| **2126** | A973 | 25c multi | .65 | .50 |
| **2127** | A973 | 50c multi | 1.00 | .80 |
| **2128** | A973 | 60c multi | 1.30 | 1.00 |
| **2129** | A973 | 75c multi | 1.60 | 1.25 |
| **2130** | A973 | 1p multi | 2.25 | 1.75 |
| **2131** | A973 | 2p multi | 4.50 | 3.00 |
| *a.* | | Inscribed "República Argentina" (with accent) | — | — |
| **2132** | A973 | 3.25p multi | 8.50 | 5.50 |
| **2133** | A973 | 5p multi | 11.00 | 7.00 |
| *a.* | | Inscribed "República Argentina" (with accent) | — | — |
| **2134** | A973 | 9.40p multi | 21.00 | 9.50 |
| | | *Nos. 2125-2134 (10)* | 52.05 | 30.55 |

Issued: 10c, 60c, 11/16; 25c, 50c, 75c, 9.40p, 10/26; 1p, 2p, 9/13; 3.25p, 5p, 8/30.

See Nos. 2495, 2670-2672. For surcharges, see Nos. 2841, 2849.

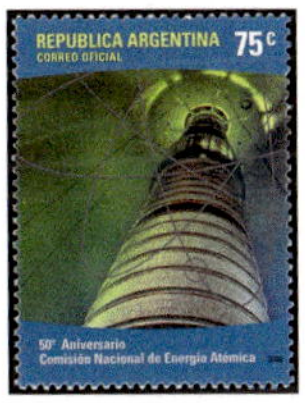

Natl. Atomic Energy Commission, 50th Anniv. — A974

**2000, Nov. 11** **Litho.** *Perf. 13½*
**2135** A974 75c multi 2.25 1.75

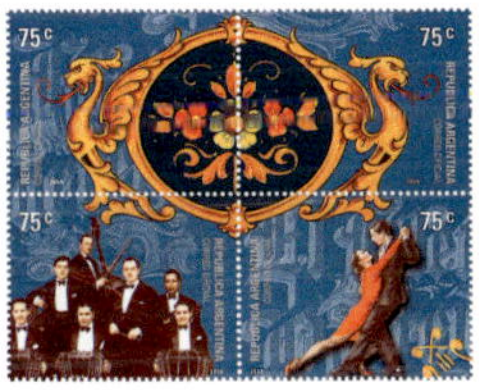

Fileteado Art Style and the Tango A975

No. 2136: a, Left side of Fileteado design. b, Right side of Fileteado design. c, Musicians. d, Tango dancers.

**2000, Nov. 11** *Perf. 13¾x13½*
**2136** A975 75c Block of 4, #a-d 11.00 10.00

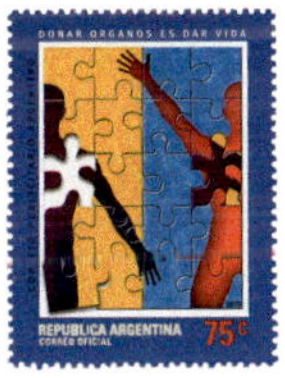

Organ Donation Campaign — A976

**2000, Nov. 25** *Perf. 13½*
**2137** A976 75c multi 2.25 1.75

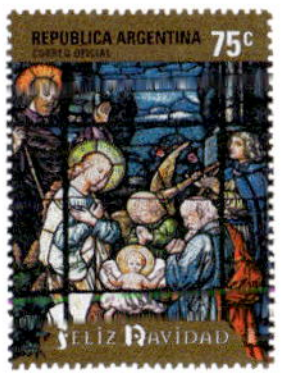

Christmas — A977

**2000, Nov. 25**
**2138** A977 75c multi 2.25 1.75

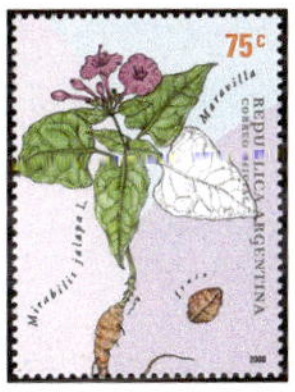

Medicinal Plants — A978

Designs: No. 2139, 75c, Mirabilis jalapa. No. 2140, 75c, Senna corymbosa. No. 2141, 75c, Eugenia uniflora. No. 2142, 75c, Commelina erecta.

**2000, Nov. 25**
**2139-2142** A978 Set of 4 8.50 7.00

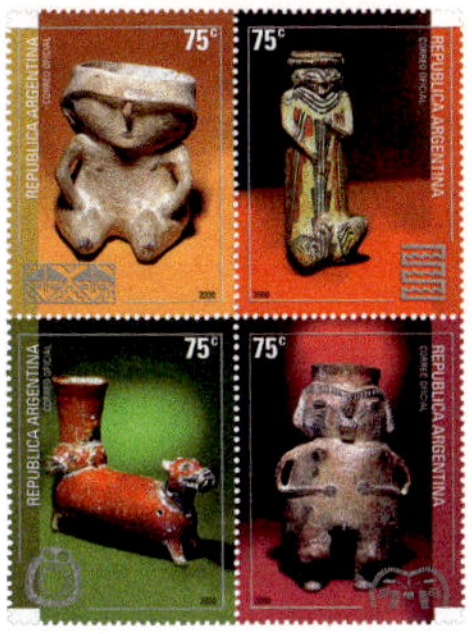

Pre-Columbian Art — A979

Various artifacts. Background colors: a, Bright orange. b, Red orange. c, Green. d, Red violet.

**2000, Dec. 9**
**2143** A979 75c Block of 4, #a-d 12.00 11.00

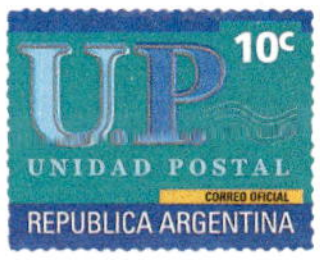

A979a

*Serpentine Die Cut 11¼x11*

**2001, Feb. 6** **Litho.** **Self-Adhesive**

**Background Color**

| | | | | |
|---|---|---|---|---|
| **2143E** | A979a | 10c blue grn | *.85* | *.30* |
| **2143F** | A979a | 25c brt green | *2.25* | *.75* |
| **2143G** | A979a | 60c orange | *4.50* | *1.90* |
| **2143H** | A979a | 75c red | *7.00* | *2.00* |
| **2143I** | A979a | 1p blue | *9.00* | *2.75* |
| **2143J** | A979a | 3p red brn | *35.00* | *8.50* |
| **2143K** | A979a | 3.25p yel green | *30.00* | *9.00* |
| **2143L** | A979a | 5.50p rose | *52.50* | *16.00* |
| | | *Nos. 2143E-2143L (8)* | *141.10* | *41.20* |

Nos. 2143E-2143L are broken at right by five die cut wavy lines. Sold at Unidad Postal outlets. See Nos. 2217-2224A.

**Miniature Sheet**

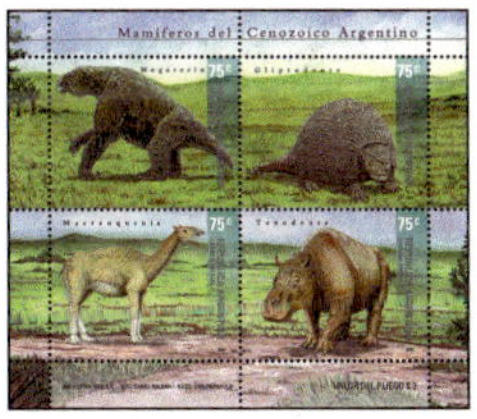

Cenozoic Mammals — A980

No. 2144: a, Megaterio (Megatherium americanum). b, Gliptodonte (Doedicurus clavicaudatus). c, Macrauquenia (Macrauchenia patachonica). d, Toxodonte (Toxodon platensis).

**2001, Mar. 10** *Perf. 13¾x13½*
**2144** A980 75c Sheet of 4, #a-d 11.00 10.00

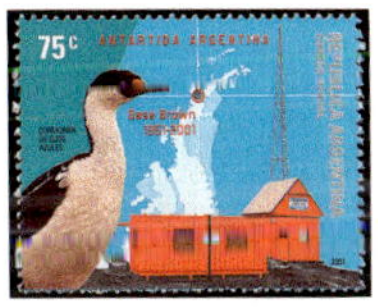

Antarctic Bases, 50th Anniv. — A981

Map and: No. 2145, 75c, Cormorant, Base Brown. No. 2146, 75c, Skua, Base San Martín.

*Perf. 13¾x13½*

**2001, Mar. 24** **Litho.**
**2145-2146** A981 Set of 2 5.00 4.00

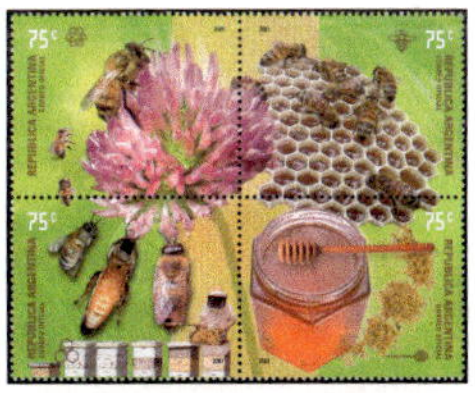

Apiculture — A982

No. 2147: a, Bee on flower. b, Bees on honeycomb. c, Bees, apiarist, and hives. d, Honey, pollen.

**2001, Apr. 7** *Perf. 13½x13¼*
**2147** A982 Block of 4 18.00 15.00
*a.-d.* 75c Any single 3.00 3.00

**Souvenir Sheet**

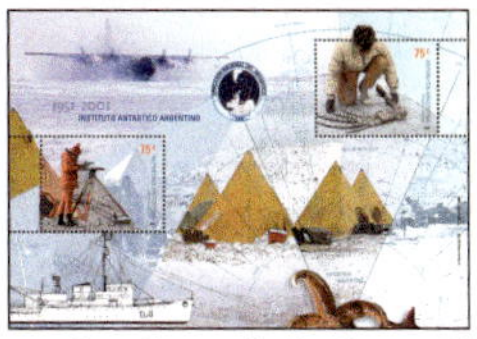

Argentine Antarctic Institute, 50th Anniv. — A983

No. 2148: a, Scientist with fossils. b, Scientist with mapping equipment.

**2001, Apr. 21** *Perf. 14*
**2148** A983 75c Sheet of 2, #a-b 8.50 8.00

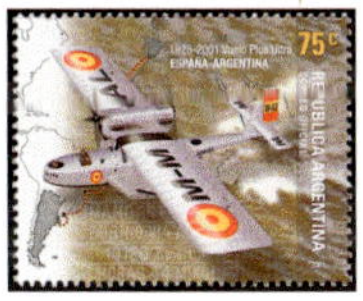

Spain to Argentina Flight of Plus Ultra Seaplane, 75th Anniv. — A984

**2001, Apr. 28** *Perf. 13¾x13¼*
**2149** A984 75c multi 2.25 1.75

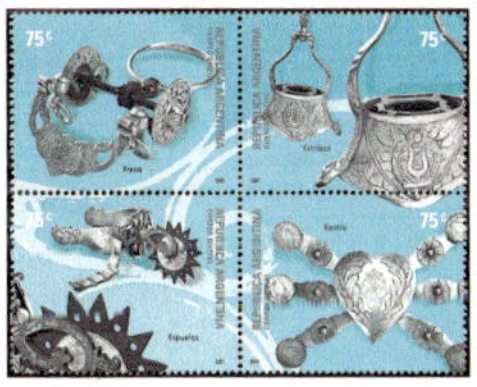

Art in Silver A985

No. 2150: a, Bridle (Freno). b, Stirrups (Estribos). c, Spurs (Espuelas). d, Gaucho's ornament (Rastra).

**2001, May 19** **Litho.** *Perf. 13¾x13½*
**2150** A985 75c Block of 4, #a-d 11.00 10.00

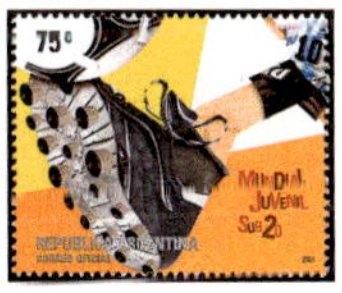

World Youth Soccer Championships A986

Designs: No. 2151, 75c, Player kicking ball. No. 2152, 75c, Goalie catching ball.

**2001, June 16**
**2151-2152** A986 Set of 2 4.50 3.25

**Souvenir Sheet**

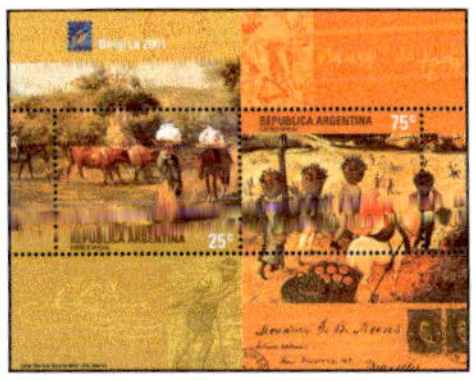

Belgica 2001 Intl. Stamp Exhibition, Brussels — A987

No. 2153: a, 25c, Washerwoman by the Banks of the Belgrano, by Prilidiano Pueyrredón. b, 75c, The Hay Harvest, by Pieter Breughel, the Elder.

**2001, June 16** *Perf. 14*
**2153** A987 Sheet of 2, #a-b 4.00 3.50

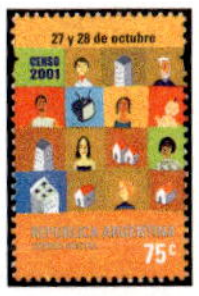

2001 Census — A988

# ARGENTINA

**Perf. 13½x13¾ Syncopated**
**2001, July 14**
2154 A988 75c multi     2.00 1.75

SAC-C Satellite, Birds and Flowers — A989

**2001, July 14**    **Perf. 13¾x13½**
2155 A989 75c multi     2.00 1.75
Environmental protection.

Bandoneón Recital — 1990, by Aldo Severi — A990

**2001, July 28**    **Perf. 13½x13¾**
2156 A990 75c multi     2.25 1.75
The tango in art.

Souvenir Sheet

Phila Nippon '01, Japan A991

No. 2157: a, Tango dancers, musical score. b, Kabuki dancer.

**2001, July 28**    **Perf. 14**
2157 A991 75c Sheet of 2, #a-b   5.50 5.00
Exists imperf. Value, pair $200.

Miniature Sheet

Wild Cats A992

No. 2158: a, 25c, Puma. b, 25c, Jaguar. c, 50c, Jaguarundi and young. d, 50c, Ocelot. e, 75c, Mountain cat. f, 75c, Huiña.

**2001, July 28**    **Perf. 13¾x13½**
2158 A992 Sheet of 6, #a-f, +2 labels    11.50 10.00

Enrique Santos Discépolo (1901-51), Tango Lyricist — A993

**2001, Aug. 4**    **Perf. 13½x13¾**
2159 A993 75c multi     2.50 2.25

America Issue — UNESCO World Heritage — A994

No. 2160 — Buildings and artifacts from Jesuit Block and Estancias of Cordoba: a, Denomination at UL. b, Denomination at UR.

**2001, Aug. 11**    **Perf. 13¾x13½**
2160 A994 75c Horiz. pair, #a-b   9.00 7.50

Prevention of Breast Cancer — A995

**2001, Sept. 1**    **Perf. 13½x13¾**
2161 A995 75c multi     2.25 1.75

World Championship Race Cars of Juan Manuel Fangio — A996

No. 2162 — Cars and track layouts: a, Alfa Romeo 159 Alfetta, Barceloná, 1951. b, Mercedes-Benz W196, Reims, France, 1954. c, Lancia-Ferrari D50, Monte Carlo, Monaco, 1956. d, Maserati 250F, Nürburgring, Germany, 1957.

**2001, Oct. 6**    **Perf. 13¾x13½**
2162 A996 75c Block of 4, #a-d   11.00 9.00

Politicians A997

Designs: No. 2163, 75c, Roque Sáenz Peña (1851-1914). No. 2164, 75c, Justo José de Urquiza (1801-70).

**2001, Oct. 20**
2163-2164 A997   Set of 2    4.50 3.50

Bulnesia Sarmientoi — A998

**2001, Oct. 20**   **Litho.**   **Perf. 13½x13¾**
2165 A998 75c multi     2.25 1.75

Souvenir Sheet

Hafnia 01 Philatelic Exhibition, Copenhagen — A999

No. 2166: a, 25c, Argentine post rider, 18th cent. b, 75c, European post rider, 17th cent.

**2001, Oct. 27**   **Litho.**   **Perf. 14**
2166 A999 Sheet of 2, #a-b   4.00 3.50

Items in Argentine Museums A1000

Designs: No. 2167, 75c, Ammonite, skeleton of Carnotaurus sastrei, from Argentine Naural Science Museum. No. 2168, 75c, Letter from Buenos Aires, stagecoach "La Pobladora," from Enrique Udaondo Graphic Museum Complex. No. 2169, 75c, Icons from Averias culture, funerary urn from Las Mercedes culture, from Emilio and Duncan Wagner Museum of Anthropological and Natural Sciences, vert. No. 2170, 75c, Crucifix of Juan Martin de Pueyrredon, and detail, from Pueyrredon Museum, vert.

**Perf. 13¾x13½, 13½x13¾**
**2001, Nov. 10**    **Litho.**
2167-2170 A1000   Set of 4   8.50 7.50

Aviators and Their Airplanes A1001

Designs: No. 2171, 75c, Carola Lorenzini (1899-1941) and Focke Wulf 44-J. No. 2172, 75c, Jean Mermoz (1901-36) and "Arc-en-Ciel."

**2001, Nov. 24**    **Perf. 13¾x13½**
2171-2172 A1001   Set of 2   4.50 3.50
No. 2171 exists imperf. Value, pair $150.

Christmas — A1002

**2001, Nov. 24**    **Perf. 13½x13¾**
2173 A1002 75c multi     2.25 1.75

Dances A1003

No. 2174: a, Flamenco. b, Waltz. c, Zamba. d, Tango.

**Perf. 13¾x13½**
**2001, Nov. 29**    **Litho.**
2174   Booklet pane of 4   11.00 —
a.-d.   A1003 75c Any single   2.00 2.00
     Booklet, #2174   11.00

Dancers' Day — A1004

**2001, Dec. 1**   **Litho.**   **Perf. 13¾x13½**
2175 A1004 75c multi     2.50 2.00

Argentine Television, 50th Anniv. — A1005

No. 2176: a, Television, camera, microphone, test pattern. b, Televisions and videotape reels. c, Television, astronaut and satellite dish. d, Televisions, cables and VCR remote control.

**2001, Dec. 1**    **Perf. 13¾x13½**
2176 A1005 75c Block of 4, #a-d   8.75 7.00

Argentina in the Antarctic A1006

Designs: No. 2177, 75c, Esperanza Base, 50th anniv. No. 2178, 75c, First air and sea courier service, 50th anniv.

**2002, Mar. 9**
2177-2178 A1006   Set of 2   4.50 3.25

America Issue — Education A1007

No. 2179: a, School and Argentine flag. b, Children playing hop scotch.

**2002, Mar. 23**
2179 A1007 75c Vert. pair, #a-b   4.50 3.50

Falkland Islands Birds — A1008

Designs: No. 2180, 50c, Charadrius falklandicus. No. 2181, 50c, Larus scoresbii. No. 2182, 75c, Chloephaga rubidiceps, vert. No. 2183, 75c, Aptenodytes patagonicus, vert.

**Perf. 13¾x13½, 13½x13¾**
**2002, Apr. 13**    **Litho.**
2180-2183 A1008   Set of 4   7.00 6.00

2002 World Cup Soccer Championships, Japan and Korea — A1009

No. 2184: a, Flags, soccer ball and field (38mm diameter). b, Soccer players, years of Argentinian championships.

**2002, Apr. 27**   **Litho.**   **Perf. 12¾**
2184 A1009 75c Horiz. pair, #a-b   4.00 3.25
See Brazil No. 2840, France No. 2891, Germany No. 2163, Italy No. 2526, Uruguay No. 1946.

Anniversaries — A1010

No. 2185, 25c: a, Rosario riverfront, Ship on Paraná River, arms. b, Rosario riverfront, National Flag Monument.
No. 2186, 50c: a, Mt. Fitzroy, Nahuel Huapi Natl. Park. b, Dr. Francisco P. Moreno.
No. 2187, 75c: a, Flower, aerial view of San Carlos de Bariloche. b, Church and town map.

**2002, May 11**   **Litho.**   **Perf. 13½x13¾**
     **Horiz. Pairs, #a-b**
2185-2187 A1010   Set of 3   7.50 6.00

# ARGENTINA

Pan-American Health Organization, Cent. — A1011

**2002, June 1**
2188  A1011  75c multi  2.25  1.75

Doctors A1012

No. 2189: a, Cosme Mariano Argerich (1758-1820), founder of Military Health Service. b, José María Ramos Mejía (1849-1914), psychiatric educator. c, Salvador Mazza (1886-1946), Chagas' disease specialist. d, Carlos Arturo Gianantonio (1926-95), pediatrician.

*Perf. 13¾x13½*
**2002, June 15**    Litho.
2189  A1012  50c Block of 4, #a-d  5.00  4.00

Landscapes — A1013

No. 2190: a, Seven-colored Mountain, Jujuy Province. b, Iguaçu Falls, Misiones Province. c, Talampaya Natl. Park, La Rioja Province. d, Mt. Aconcagua, Mendoza Province. e, Rose Garden, Buenos Aires. f, San Jorge Lighthouse, Chubut. g, Perito Moreno Glacier, Santa Cruz Province. h, Lapataia Bay, Tierra del Fuego Province.

**2002, July 29**   *Perf. 14x13½*
2190  A1013  Block of 8  14.00  12.00
a.-h.  75c Any single  1.50  1.50

For surcharge, see No. 2847.

Eva Perón (1919-52) — A1014

No. 2191: a, Official portrait. b, Embossed profile. c, At microphone. d, Painting by Nicolas Garcia Uriburu.

**Litho., Litho & Embossed (#2191b)**
**2002, July 27**   *Perf. 13½x13¾*
2191  Horiz. strip of 4  7.00  6.00
a.-d.  A1014 75c Any single  1.00  1.25

Worldwide Fund for Nature (WWF) — A1015

No. 2192: a, Ozotoceros bezoarticus. b, Vicugna vicugna. c, Pudu puda. d, Catagonus wagneri.

**2002, July 27  Litho.  *Perf. 13¾x13½***
2192  A1015  $1 Block of 4, #a-d  8.50  7.00

## Souvenir Sheet

Philakorea 2002 World Stamp Exhibition, Seoul — A1016

No. 2193: a, Argentine soccer player (blue and white shirt). b, Korean soccer player (red shirt).

**2002, Aug. 10**   *Perf. 14*
2193  A1016  1.50p Sheet of 2, #a-b  6.50  6.00

Sports — A1016a

10c, Cycling. 25c, Tennis. 50c, Auto racing. 75c, Parachuting. 1p, Horse racing. 2p, Golf. 5p, Sailing.

*Perf. 13½x13¾ Syncopated*
**2002, Sept. 6**    Litho.
2193C  A1016a  10c multi  2.40  .35
2193D  A1016a  25c multi  2.40  .35
2193E  A1016a  50c multi  2.40  .40
2193F  A1016a  75c multi  4.25  .75
2193G  A1016a  1p multi  4.25  1.05
2193H  A1016a  2p multi  7.00  2.10
2193I  A1016a  5p multi  10.25  5.25
Nos. 2193C-2193I (7)  32.95  10.25

Nos. 2193C-2193I were sold only to customers who met certain mailing requirements but could be used on mail by anyone without restrictions.

Valdés Peninsula Tourism — A1017

Whale breaching: a, Head. b, Tail.

**2002, Sept. 14**   *Perf. 13½x13¾*
2194  A1017  75c Horiz. pair, #a-b  4.00  3.50

Insects A1018

Designs: 25c, Edessa meditabunda. 50c, Elaechlora viridis. 75c, Chrysodina aurata. 1p, Steirastoma breve.

**2002, Sept. 21**   *Perf. 13¾x13½*
2195-2198  A1018  Set of 4  6.25  5.25

Men's Volleyball World Championships A1019

Various players with background colors of: No. 2199, 75c, Blue green (shown). No. 2200, 75c, Light blue. No. 2201, 75c, Bright yellow green. No. 2202, 75c, Pale orange.

*Perf. 13½x13¾*
**2002, Sept. 28**    Litho.
2199-2202  A1019  Set of 4  7.25  6.25

On Nos. 2199-2202 portions of the design were applied by a thermographic process producing a shiny, raised effect.

Argentine Highway Association, 50th Anniv. — A1020

**2002, Oct. 5**   *Perf. 13¾x13½*
2203  A1020  75c multi  1.90  1.60

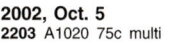

Argentine Personalities A1021

Designs: No. 2204, 75c, Roberto Arlt (1900-42), novelist. No. 2205, 75c, Beatriz Guido (1924-88), writer. No. 2206, 75c, Niní Marshall (1903-96), actress. No. 2207, 75c, Luis Sandrini (1905-80), actor.

**2002, Oct. 19**
2204-2207  A1021  Set of 4  7.00  6.00

Immigrant Agricultural Colonies — A1022

Flags of France, Switzerland, Spain and Italy and: a, Hotel for immigrants, mother and son, stamped passport. b, Two immigrants and ship. c, Two immigrants, Provisory Hotel for immigrants, French immigrant instruction book. d, Farmer plowing field, family of immigrants.

**2002, Oct. 19  Litho.  *Perf. 13½x13¾***
2200  Horiz. strip of 4  7.00  6.00
a.-d.  A1022 75c Any single  1.50  1.50

Argentine Federation of Philatelic Entities, 50th Anniv. — A1023

Designs: No. 2209, 75c, Stamped cover, stagecoach, EXFICEC '56 exhibition cancel, Head of Ceres from Corrientes issue. No. 2210, 75c, ESPAMER '98 Cancel, postman, ship and map, coat of arms.

**2002, Nov. 2**   *Perf. 13¾x13½*
2209-2210  A1023  Set of 2  3.50  2.75

Christmas A1024

**2002, Nov. 16**
2211  A1024  75c multi  1.75  .50

Folk Musicians — A1025

Designs: No. 2212, 75c, Gustavo "Cuchi" Leguizamón (1917-2000). No. 2213, 75c, Armando Tejada Gómez (1929-92). No. 2214, 75c, Carlos Vega (1898-1966). No. 2215, 75c, Andrés Chazarreta (1876-1960).

**2002, Dec. 7**   *Perf. 13½x13¾*
2212-2215  A1025  Set of 4  7.00  6.00

Puppets A1026

No. 2216: a, Marionette of woman. b, King and fish hand puppets. c, Rod puppet of man. d, Shadow theater.

**2002, Dec. 7**   *Perf. 13¾x13½*
2216  Booklet pane of 4  10.00  8.00
a.-d.  A1026 75c Any single  2.25  2.00
Booklet, #2216  10.00

## Unidad Postal Type of 2001
*Perf. 13¾x13½ Syncopated*
**2002**    Litho.
**Size: 35x24mm (10p, 35x25mm)**
**Background Color**

2217  A979a  10c blue green  .30  .25
2218  A979a  25c brt green  .65  .40
2219  A979a  50c tan  1.20  .55
2220  A979a  75c red  1.75  .85
2221  A979a  1p blue  2.75  1.20
2222  A979a  2p gray  5.50  1.75
2223  A979a  3p brown  6.50  2.00
2224  A979a  5p olive bister  10.50  2.60
2224A  A979a  10p yellow  21.00  3.50
Nos. 2217-2224A (9)  50.15  13.10

Issue dates: Nos. 2217-2224, 6/02; 10p, 8/16/02.

Nos. 2217-2224A were sold only at Unidad Postal outlets.

For surcharge, see No. 2843.

Communal Vegetable Gardens A1027

Designs: No. 2225, 75c, Cabbage. No. 2226, 75c, Corn, vert.

*Perf. 13¾x13½, 13½x13¾*
**2003, Mar. 8**
2225-2226  A1027  Set of 2  3.50  2.50

Native Handicrafts A1028

Designs: No. 2227, 75c, Sieve, by Mbyá people, fork and spoon by Wichi people. No. 2228, 75c, Woven waistband of Pilagá'ck people, Bag by Nam Qom people.

**2003, Mar. 8**   *Perf. 13¾x13½*
2227-2228  A1028  Set of 2  3.50  2.75

National Parks A1029

Animals and parks: No. 2229, 50c, Lama guanicoe, Los Cardones National Park. No. 2230, 50c, Playa Cayana, Colonia Benítez Natural Reserve. No. 2231, 50c, Mazama gouazoupira, Copo National Park. No. 2232, 75c, Tinamotis pentlandii, Campo de los Alisos National Park. No. 2233, 75c, Spheniscus magellanicus, Monte León, planned National Park

**2003, Mar. 22**   *Perf. 14x13½*
2229-2233  A1029  Set of 5  7.25  5.50

Paintings A1030

Designs: No. 2234, 25c, Composición con Trapo Rejilla, by Kenneth Kemble. No. 2235, 25c, Pintura, by Roberto Aizenberg, vert. 50c, Pantalla, by Rómulo Macció, vert. No. 2237, 75c, La Giaconda, by Guillermo Roux. No.

2238, 75c, Hacerse Humo, by Antonio Seguí.
1p, San P., by Xul Solar (with attached label).

**Perf. 13¾x13½, 13½x13¾**
**2003, Apr. 12**
2234-2239  A1030  Set of 6   9.50  8.00

Nos. 2234-2238 were each printed in sheets of 4; No. 2239 was printed in sheets of 2 + 2 labels.

Argentina, Champions of 2002 Intl. Sporting Events — A1031

Designs: No. 2240, 75c, Women's field hockey. No. 2241, 75c, Soccer for blind players.

**Litho., Litho. & Embossed (#2241)**
**2003, May 3**       **Perf. 13¾x13½**
2240-2241  A1031  Set of 2   3.50  3.00

Comic Strips A1032

No. 2242: a, 25c, Mago Fafa, by Alberto Bróccoli. b, 25c, Astronaut, by Crist (Cristóbal Reinoso). c, 50c, Hijitus, by Manuel García Ferré. d, 50c, Savarese, by Domingo Mandrafina and Robin Wood. e, 75c, Sónoman, by Oswal (Oswaldo Walter Viola). f, 75c, El Tipito, by Daniel Paz and Rudy (Marcelo E. Rudaeff). g, 75c, La Vaca Aurora, by Domingo Mirco Repetto. h, 75c, Diógenes y el Linyera, by Tabaré (Gómez Laborde), Jorge Guinzberg and Carlos Abrevaya.

**2003, May 17  Litho.   Perf. 13½x13¾**
2242  A1032  Sheet of 8, #a-h   11.50  9.50

Silver Tableware — A1033

No. 2243: a, Soup bowl with lid (sopera). b, Kettle and burner, maté kettle and drinking tube. c, Chocolate pot and jar with handle. d, Sugar bowl (azucarera).

**2003, May 24        Perf. 13¾x13½**
2243  A1033  75c  Block of 4, #a-d   7.00  5.75

Food A1034

Designs: Nos. 2244a, 2245a, Empanadas (red denomination). Nos. 2244b, 2245b, Locro (orange denomination) Nos. 2244c, 2246a, Parrillada (green denomination) Nos. 2244d, 2246b, Pastelitos (blue denomination).

**2003, June 7        Perf. 13¾x13½**
2244  A1034  75c  Vert strip of 4, #a-d, + 4 labels   9.50  8.00

**Booklet Panes**
**Perf. 14**
2245  A1034  75c  Pane of 2, #a-b, + 2 labels   16.00  15.00
2246  A1034  75c  Pane of 2, #a-b, + 2 labels   16.00  15.00
 Complete booklet, #2245-2246   32.00

Size of stamps in booklet panes: 40x30mm.

**Miniature Sheet**

Children's Games — A1035

No. 2247: a, El Elástico. b, La escondida (hide and seek). c, La mancha (tag). d, Martín Pescador.

**2003, July 12       Perf. 13¾x13½**
2247  A1035  50c  Sheet of 4, #a-d   7.50  6.50

Landscapes — A1036

No. 2248: a, Mbiguá Marsh, Formosa Province. b, Dead Man's Salt Flats, Catamarca Province. c, Quilmes Ruins, Tucumán Province. d, Iberá Marshes, Corrientes Province. e, Ischigualasto Provincial Park, San Juan Province. f, Mar del Plata, Buenos Aires Province. g, Caleu Caleu Department, La Pampa Province. h, Lanín National Park, Nequén Province.

**2003, July 19       Perf. 14x13¾**
2248  A1036  75c  Block of 8, #a-h   14.00  12.00

For surcharge, see No. 2845.

Opening of Nuestra Señora del Rosario Bridge and Roadway, Rosario-Victoria — A1037

No. 2249: a, 25c, Bridge, map of roadway. b, 75c, Bridge and cross-section.

**Perf. 13½x13¾**
**2003, Aug. 23         Litho.**
2249  A1037  Horiz. pair, #a-b   6.00  5.00

Argentine History — A1038

Designs: No. 2250, 75c, Dr. Vicente Fidel López (1815-1903), Education minister, headquarters of Province of Buenos Aires Bank. No. 2251, 75c, First page of constitution, medal and signature of Juan Bautista Alberdi. No. 2252, 75c, Emblem and squadron of General San Martín Mounted Grenadiers Regiment. No. 2253, 75c, Presidential sash and staff, Casa Rosada. No. 2254, 75c, Arms of Río Negro Province, vert.

**Perf. 13¾x13½, 13½x13¾**
**2003, Sept. 6**
2250-2254  A1038  Set of 5   8.75  7.00
Constitution, 150th anniv. (No. 2251), Revival of General San Martín Mounted Grenadiers Regiment, cent. (No. 2252), Presidential inauguration (No. 2253).

**Souvenir Sheet**

Bangkok 2003 World Philatelic Exhibition — A1039

No. 2255: a, Quebrada de Humahuacha black demon mask, Argentine flag. b, Phi Ta Khon Festival mask, Thailand flag.

**Litho. with Foil Application**
**2003, Oct. 4          Perf. 14**
2255  A1039  75c  Sheet of 2, #a-b   4.25  3.50

America Issue — Flora and Fauna — A1040

Designs: No. 2256, 75c, Nothofagus pumilio. No. 2257, 75c, Vultur gryphus.

**2003, Oct. 11  Litho.  Perf. 13¾x13½**
2256-2257  A1040  Set of 2   3.75  3.25

Jubany Base, Antarctica, 50th Anniv. — A1041

**2003, Oct. 18**
2258  A1041  75c  multi   1.90  1.60

Rescue of Swedish Scientific Expedition by A. R. A. Uruguay, Cent. — A1042

Designs: No. 2259, Welcome, (ship and penguins) by Eduardo De Martino.
No. 2260: a, A. R. A. Uruguay. b, A. R. A. Uruguay and Lt. Julián Irízar.

**2003, Oct. 18         Perf. 13¾x13½**
2259  A1042  75c  multi   1.90  1.60

**Souvenir Sheet**
**Perf. 14**
2260  A1042  75c  Sheet of 2, #a-b   4.50  4.00

No. 2260 contains two 40x30mm stamps.

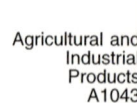 

Agricultural and Industrial Products A1043

Designs: No. 2261, 75c, Cattle. No. 2262, 75c, Soybeans. No. 2263, 75c, Aluminum. No. 2264, 75c, Teradi 800 cobalt therapy machine.

**2003, Oct. 18         Perf. 13¾x13½**
2261-2264  A1043  Set of 4   7.00  6.00

Christmas — A1044

Designs: No. 2265, 75c, Purmamarca clay creche figures. No. 2266, 75c, Gaucho Birth, carved wood creche figures by Eloy López.

**2003, Nov. 8        Perf. 13½x13¾**
2265-2266  A1044  Set of 2   3.50  1.50

20th Century Architecture A1045

Designs: No. 2267, 75c, Barolo Palace, Buenos Aires, by Mario Palanti, 1923. No. 2268, 75c, Tucumán Province Bank Building, San Miguel de Tucumán, by Alejandro Virasoro, 1928. No. 2269, 75c, Córdoba Province Savings Bank Building, Córdoba, by Jaime Roca, 1929. No. 2270, 75c, Minetti Palace, Rosario, by Juan B. Durand, Leopoldo Schwarz and José Gerbino, 1930.

**2003, Nov. 8**
2267-2270  A1045  Set of 4   7.00  5.50

Orcadas Base, Antarctica, Cent. — A1046

Designs: No. 2271, Helicopter, Orcadas Base.
No. 2272: a, #127 with 1904 South Orcadas cancel, vert. b, Meteorological observatory and weather vane.

**2004, Feb. 21       Perf. 13¾x13½**
2271  A1046  75c  multi   2.25  2.00

**Souvenir Sheet**
**Perf. 14**
2272  A1046  75c  Sheet of 2, #a-b   5.50  5.00

No. 2272 contains one 30x40mm and one 40x30mm stamp.

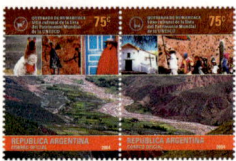

Quebrada de Humahuaca UNESCO World Heritage Site — A1047

No. 2273 — View of Rio Grande Valley and: a, Decorated llama, rock painting, person in front of door. b, Santa Rosa de Lima Church, costumed carnival participants.

**2004, Mar. 27       Perf. 13½x13¾**
2273  A1047  75c  Horiz. pair, #a-b   4.00  3.50

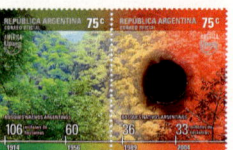

America Issue — Forest Conservation — A1048

No. 2274 — Forest and timeline charting hectares of forest with years: a, 1914, 1956. b, 1989, 2004.

**2004, Mar. 27**
2274  A1048  75c  Horiz. pair, #a-b   4.50  4.00

No. 2274b has large hole in center of stamp.

# ARGENTINA

La Voz del
Interior
Newspaper,
Cent. — A1049

| 2004, Apr. 17 | | Perf. 13¾x13½ |
|---|---|---|
| 2275 | A1049 75c multi | 2.00  1.75 |

For surcharge, see No. 2846.

Landscapes — A1050

No. 2276: a, Molinos, Salta Province. b, Pampa del Indio Provincial Park, Chaco Province. c, Rio Hondo Dam, Santiago del Estero Province. d, Bridge, Santa Fe de la Vera Cruz, Santa Fe Province. e, San Roque Lake, Córdoba Province. f, El Palmar National Park, Entre Rios Province. g, Potrero de los Funes, San Luis Province. h, Mt. Tronador, Río Negro Province.

| 2004, Apr. 17 | | Perf. 14x13½ |
|---|---|---|
| 2276 | A1050 75c Block of 8, #a-h | 17.00  15.00 |

FIFA (Fédération
Internationale de
Football
Association),
Cent. — A1051

Paintings of soccer players by Rubén Ramonda: No. 2277, 75c, The Tunnel (blue background). No. 2278, 75c, El Picado (orange background).

| 2004, May 22 | Litho. | Perf. 13¾x13½ |
|---|---|---|
| 2277-2278 | A1051  Set of 2 | 4.00  3.50 |

España 2004 World Philatelic
Exhibition — A1052

No. 2279: a, Return of the Fishing Fleet, by Joaquín Sorolla y Bastida. b, A Stop in the Pampas, by Angel Della Valle, vert.

| 2004, May 22 | | Perf. 14 |
|---|---|---|
| 2279 | A1052 75c Sheet of 2, #a-b | 5.50  5.00 |

Naval Hydrographic Service, 125th
Anniv — A1053

No. 2280 — Nautical chart and: a, Binnacle. b, Sextant. c, Cabo Vírgenes Lighthouse. d, Oceanographic ship Puerto Deseado.

| 2004, June 5 | | Perf. 13¾x13½ |
|---|---|---|
| 2280 | A1053 75c Block of 4, #a-d | 8.00  7.00 |

Printed in sheets of four blocks separated by a central column of labels.

## Souvenir Sheet

Circus
A1054

No. 2281: a, Trained dogs. b, Clown on stilts, trapeze artist. c, Clown juggling on unicycle. d, Bareback rider.

| 2004, June 12 | | |
|---|---|---|
| 2281 | A1054 50c Sheet of 4, #a-d | 8.00  7.00 |

Characters From Comic Strip
"Patoruzito," by Dante
Quinterno — A1055

No. 2282: a, 25c, Isidorito. b, 25c, Upita. c, 50c, Patoruzito. d, 50c, Malén. e, 75c, Pamperito. f, 75c, Chacha.
No. 2283: a, Patoruzito (20x60mm). b, Pamperito (20x60mm). c, Isidorito (30x30mm).
No. 2284: a, Malén (30x40mm). b, Upita (30x40mm). c, Chacha (30x40mm).

| 2004, July 10 | Litho. | Perf. 13½x13¾ |
|---|---|---|
| 2282 | A1055 Sheet of 6 + 2 labels | 9.00  7.50 |

### Booklet Panes
### Perf. 14

| 2283 | Booklet pane of 3 + label | 15.00  15.00 |
|---|---|---|
| a.-c. | A1055 75c Any single | 4.00  4.00 |
| 2284 | Booklet pane of 3 + label | 15.00  15.00 |
| a.-c. | A1055 75c Any single | 4.00  4.00 |
| | Complete booklet, #2283-2284 | 34.00 |

Fish of the
Falkland Islands
Area — A1056

Designs: No. 2285, 75c, Salilota australis. No. 2286, 75c, Patagonototheri ramsayi. No. 2287, 75c, Dissostichus eleginoides. No. 2288, 75c, Bathyraja griseocauda.

| 2004, July 17 | Litho. | Perf. 13¾x13½ |
|---|---|---|
| 2285-2288 | A1056  Set of 4 | 8.00  7.00 |

Assistance
Dogs — A1057

Designs: No. 2289, 75c, Rescue dog. No. 2290, 75c, Seeing-eye dog, vert.

### Perf. 13¾x13½, 13½x13¼
| 2004, July 17 | | |
|---|---|---|
| 2289-2290 | A1057  Set of 2 | 4.25  3.75 |

2004 Summer Olympics,
Athens — A1058

No. 2291: a, Cycling. b, Judo. c, Swimming. d, Tennis.

| 2004, Aug. 7 | | Perf. 13¾x13½ |
|---|---|---|
| 2291 | A1058 75c Block of 4, #a-d | 8.00  7.00 |

Legends
A1059

Designs: No. 2292, 75c, El Pehuén. No. 2293, 75c, La Yacumama. No. 2294, 75c, La Pachamama. No. 2295, 75c, La Difunta Correa.

| 2004, Aug. 21 | | |
|---|---|---|
| 2292-2295 | A1059  Set of 4 | 8.00  7.00 |

### Souvenir Sheet

World Stamp Championship 2004,
Singapore — A1060

No. 2296: a, Mangifera indica. b, Syagrus romanzoffiana.

| 2004, Aug. 21 | | Perf. 14 |
|---|---|---|
| 2296 | A1060 75c Sheet of 2, #a-b | 4.00  3.50 |

Centenaries
A1061

Designs: No. 2297, 75c, Agronomy and Veterinary Science Institute for Higher Learning, Buenos Aires. No. 2298, 75c, City of Neuquén. No. 2299, 75c, Philatelic Association of Rosario.

| 2004, Sept. 11 | | Perf. 13¾x13½ |
|---|---|---|
| 2297-2299 | A1061  Set of 3 | 5.75  5.00 |

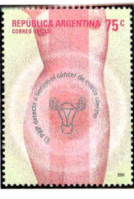

Prevention of Uterine
Cancer — A1062

| 2004, Sept. 18 | | Perf. 13½x13¾ |
|---|---|---|
| 2300 | A1062 75c multi | 2.00  1.75 |

Preservation of
Water
Resources
A1063

No. 2301: a, Hourglass with clean water. b, Hourglass with polluted water.

| 2004, Sept. 18 | | Perf. 13¾x13½ |
|---|---|---|
| 2301 | A1063 75c Vert. tete beche pair, #a-b | 3.75  3.25 |

Landmarks in
Argentina —
A1063a

Designs: 25c, Ruins of San Ignacio Miní, Misiones Province. 50c, Iruya. 1p, Buenos Aires. 2p, Aconcagua Provincial Park. 3p, Valdes Peninsula. 5p, Mina Clavero. 10p, Ushuaia.

### Perf. 13¾x13½ Syncopated
| 2004, Sept. 24 | | Litho. | |
|---|---|---|---|
| 2301C | A1063a 25c multi | .35 | .35 |
| 2301D | A1063a 50c multi | .50 | .50 |
| 2301E | A1063a 1p multi | 1.00 | 1.00 |
| 2301F | A1063a 2p multi | 2.10 | 2.00 |
| 2301G | A1063a 3p multi | 3.00 | 3.00 |
| 2301H | A1063a 5p multi | 5.25 | 5.00 |
| j. | With label | 3.50 | 3.50 |
| 2301I | A1063a 10p multi | 10.00 | 9.50 |
| | Nos. 2301D-2301I (6) | 21.85 | 21.00 |

Issued: No. 2301Hj, 5/11/10.
See Nos. 2357, 2586-2587, 2678-2679.

The Nativity   Virgin Mary
A1064         A1065

| 2004, Oct. 16 | Litho. | Perf. 13½x13¾ |
|---|---|---|
| 2302 | A1064 75c multi | 1.60  .65 |
| 2303 | A1065 75c multi | 1.60  .65 |

Christmas, Stained glass windows, St Felicitas Church, Buenos Aires.

Numismatics — A1066

No. 2304 — Halves of 1813 silver 1 real coin and 1813 gold 8 escudos coin: a, Obverse (sun). b, Reverse (coat of arms).

| 2004, Oct. 23 | | |
|---|---|---|
| 2304 | A1066 75c Horiz. pair, #a-b | 3.25  2.75 |

Andrés Bello
and Front Page
of Spanish
Grammar for
Americans
A1067

| 2004, Nov. 6 | | Perf. 13¾x13½ |
|---|---|---|
| 2305 | A1067 75c multi | 1.75  1.50 |

Third Intl. Spanish Language Congress, Rosario.

Buenos Aires
Commodities
Exchange,
150th
Anniv. — A1068

| 2004, Nov. 6 | | |
|---|---|---|
| 2306 | A1068 75c multi | 1.75  1.50 |

Medicinal
Plants — A1069

Designs: No. 2307, 75c, Aloysia citriodora. No. 2308, 75c, Minthostachys mollis. No. 2309, 75c, Lippia turbinata. No. 2310, 75c, Tagetes minuta.

| 2004, Nov. 20 | | Perf. 13½x13¾ |
|---|---|---|
| 2307-2310 | A1069  Set of 4 | 8.00  7.00 |

# ARGENTINA

**12th Pan-American Scout Jamboree** — A1070

**2005, Jan. 15**    Perf. 13¾x13½
2311   A1070   75c multi     1.50   1.10

**Argentina — Thailand Diplomatic Relations, 50th Anniv.** — A1071

Designs: No. 2312, 75c, Tango dancers, Argentina. No. 2313, 75c, Tom-tom dancers, Thailand.

**2005, Feb. 5**    Perf. 13½x13¾
2312-2313   A1071   Set of 2    3.50   3.00

**Paintings by Antonio Berni (1905-81)** — A1072

Designs: No. 2314, Woman with a Red Sweater. No. 2315 — Details from Manifestation: a, 75c, Bearded man, man looking up (40x50mm). b, 75c, Child, two men with hats in foreground, horiz. (50x40mm).

**2005, Mar. 12**    Perf. 13½x13¾
2314   A1072   75c shown    1.50   1.10
**Souvenir Sheet**
**Perf. 14**
2315   A1072   Sheet of 2, #a-b   3.50   2.75

**Rotary International, Cent.** — A1073

**2005, Mar. 19**    Perf. 13¾x13½
2316   A1073   75c multi     1.50   1.00

**Writers** — A1074

Designs: No. 2317, 75c, Silvina Ocampo (1903-93). No. 2318, 75c, Ezequiel Martínez Estrada (1895-1964).

**2005, Mar. 19**    Perf. 13½x13¾
2317-2318   A1074   Set of 2    4.25   3.75

**Argentine Motor Vehicles** — A1075

Designs: No. 2319, 75c, Graciela sedan. No. 2320, 75c, Justicialista Sport. No. 2321, 75c, Rastrojero Diesel truck. No. 2322, 75c, Siam Di Tella 1500. No. 2323, 75c, Torino 380 W.

**2005, Apr. 9**   Litho.   Perf. 13¾x13½
2319-2323   A1075   Set of 5    8.25   7.00
A portion of the design of each stamp is coated with a glossy varnish.

**Intl. Year of Physics** — A1076

Designs: No. 2324, 75c, José Antonio Balseiro, founder of Balseiro Institute, nuclear reactor. No. 2325, 75c, Albert Einstein, front page of Einstein's theory of relativity.

**2005, Apr. 23**   Litho.   Perf. 13¾x13½
2324-2325   A1076   Set of 2    3.50   3.00
Balseiro Institute, 50th anniv.

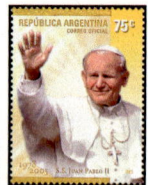

**Pope John Paul II (1920-2005)** — A1077

Designs: No. 2326, Pope waving. No. 2327: a, Pope with crucifix, Papal arms. b, Pope and crowd.

**2005, Apr. 23**    Perf. 13½x13¾
2326   A1077   75c shown    2.75   2.50
**Souvenir Sheet**
**Perf. 14**
2327   A1077   75c Sheet of 2, #a-b   5.50   4.75
No. 2327 contains two 40x50mm stamps.

**General Workers Confederation, 75th Anniv.** — A1078

**La Capital Newspaper, Mar del Plata, Cent.** — A1079

**Sunday Blue Law No. 4661, Cent.** — A1080

**2005, May 21**   Litho.   Perf. 13½x13¾
2328   A1078   75c multi     1.50   1.25
2329   A1079   75c multi     1.50   1.25
2330   A1080   75c multi     1.50   1.25
    Nos. 2328-2330 (3)    4.50   3.75

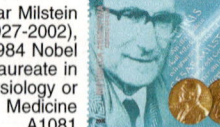

**César Milstein (1927-2002), 1984 Nobel Laureate in Physiology or Medicine** — A1081

**2005, June 4**    Perf. 13¾x13½
2331   A1081   75c multi     1.60   1.40

**Volunteer Firefighters** — A1082

Designs: No. 2332, 75c, Orestes Liberti (1860-1936), first commander of volunteer firefighter brigade, horse-drawn fire engine. No. 2333, 75c, Fire fighters in action, fire truck.

**2005, June 4**    Perf. 13½x13¾
2332-2333   A1082   Set of 2    3.00   2.50

**Argentine Red Cross, 125th Anniv.** — A1083

**2005, June 11**    Perf. 13¾x13½
2334   A1083   75c multi     1.50   1.10

**Juan Filloy (1894-2000), Writer** — A1084

**2005, July 16**
2335   A1084   75c multi     1.50   1.00

**Miniature Sheet**

**Cats** A1085

No. 2336: a, 25c, Birman. b, 25c, Siamese. c, 50c, Oriental. d, 50c, Persian. e, 75c, Abyssinian. f, 75c, European.

**2005, July 16**
2336   A1085   Sheet of 6, #a-f, + 2 labels    7.50   6.00

**Wine Regions** A1086

Glass of wine, map, vineyard in: No. 2337, 75c, Salta Province, Torrontés grapes. No. 2338, 75c, Mendoza Province, Malbec grapes. No. 2339, 75c, San Juan Province, Syrah grapes. No. 2340, 75c, Río Negro Province, Merlot grapes.

**2005, July 16**    Perf. 14x13½
2337-2340   A1086   Set of 4    6.25   5.25
Compare Nos. 2337-2340 with Nos. 2370b-2373b. For surcharges, see Nos. 2855-2857.

**Historic Houses of Worship** A1087

Designs: No. 2341, 75c, Our Lady of the Rosary of Candonga Chapel, Sierra Chicas. No. 2342, 75c, Al Ahmad Mosque, Buenos Aires. No. 2343, 75c, Temple of the Israelite Congregation, Buenos Aires. No. 2344, 75c, Vision of the Middle Buddhist Temple, Buenos Aires.

**2005, Aug. 6**    Perf. 13¾x13½
2341-2344   A1087   Set of 4    6.00   4.75

**Local Grocery Stores** — A1088

Designs: No. 2345, 75c, Pulpería de Cacho di Catarina, Mercedes. No. 2346, 75c, Pulpería El Torito, Baradero. No. 2347, 75c, Pulpería Perucho, General Lavalle. No. 2348, 75c, Pulpería Impini, Larroque.

**2005, Sept. 10**
2345-2348   A1088   Set of 4    6.00   4.75

**Antarctic Science** A1089

Designs: No. 2349, Iceberg, Antarctic Treaty emblem
No. 2350: a, Major General Hernán Pujato and members of First Argentine Polar Expedition air crew. b, Divers, raft, iceberg.

**2005, Sept. 24**    Perf. 13¾x13½
2349   A1089   75c multi     1.90   1.60
**Souvenir Sheet**
**Perf. 14**
2350   A1089   75c Sheet of 2, #a-b   4.50   4.00
No. 2350 contains two 40x30mm stamps.

**Colón Theater Companies, 80th Anniv.** — A1090

No. 2351: a, Dancer Julio Bocca, ballet dancers, Colón Theater building. b, Orchestra, choir, opera singers.

**2005, Sept. 24**    Perf. 13½x13¾
2351   A1090   75c Horiz. pair, #a-b   3.00   2.00

**Alternative Energy Sources** — A1091

Designs: 75c, Solar power. 4p, Wind power.

**2005, Oct. 15**
2352-2353   A1091   Set of 2    8.25   5.50

**Christmas** — A1092

Details from altarpiece by Elena Storni: No. 2354, Madonna and Child.
No. 2355: a, The Annunciation, Mary and Elizabeth. b, Nativity. c, Magi. d, Presentation of Jesus in the Temple.

**2005, Oct. 15**    Perf. 13½x13¾
2354   A1092   75c shown    1.50   .50
**Souvenir Sheet**
**Litho. with Foil Application**
**Perf. 14**
2355   A1092   75c Sheet of 4, #a-d   6.00   4.00
No. 2355 contains four 40x40mm stamps.

# ARGENTINA

Fourth Summit of the Americas, Mar del Plata — A1093

**2005, Oct. 29**   **Litho.**   **Perf. 13¾x13½**
2356  A1093  75c multi   1.50  1.25

### Landmarks Type of 2004

Design: Perito Moreno Glacier

**Perf. 13¾x13½ Syncopated**
**2005, Nov. 18**
2357  A1063a  4p multi   4.25  3.75

Immigrants to Argentina A1095

Designs: No. 2358, 75c, German immigrants in Cañada de Gómez, bandoneon. No. 2359, 75c, Slovakian immigrants in Buenos Aires, weather indicator. No. 2360, 75c, Welsh immigrants, Chubut Central Railway train, railway lantern. No. 2361, 75c, Jewish settlers, Moisés Ville, wheat.

**2005, Nov. 19**   **Perf. 13¾x13½**
2358-2361  A1095  Set of 4   6.00  3.75

Boxers — A1096

Designs: No. 2362, 75c, Lius Angel Firpo (1894-1960). No. 2363, 75c, Nicolino Locche (1939-2005).

**2005, Dec. 17**   **Perf. 13½x13¾**
2362-2363  A1096  Set of 2   3.00  2.00

Argentine Design A1097

Designs: No. 2364, 75c, Image and sound design. No. 2365, 75c, Clothes and textile design, vert. No. 2366, 75c, Industrial design, vert. No. 2367, 75c, Graphic design.

**Perf. 13¾x13½, 13½x13¾**
**2005, Dec. 17**
2364-2367  A1097  Set of 4   6.00  4.00

Pres. Bartolomé Mitre (1821-1906) A1098

**2006, Jan. 21**   **Perf. 13¾x13½**
2368  A1098  75c multi   1.50  1.00

Esquel, Cent. — A1099

**2006, Feb. 18**
2369  A1099  75c multi   1.50  1.00

Wine Producing Regions — A1100

No. 2370: a, Merlot grapes and wine, Alto Valle, Río Negro (70x30mm). b, Wine flowing from vat (50x30mm).
No. 2371: a, Wine barrels (50x30mm). b, Torrontés grapes and wine, Cafayate, Salta (70x30mm).
No. 2372: a, Grape harvesters (50x30mm). b, Syrah grapes and wine, Valle del Zonda, San Juan (70x30mm).
No. 2373: a, Malbec grapes and wine, Valle del Tupungato, Mendoza (70x30mm). b, Wine in glass and bottle (50x30mm).

**2006, Mar. 3**   **Litho.**   **Perf. 14**
2370  A1100  Booklet pane of 2   5.25  5.00
  a.  50c multi   .50  .45
  b.  3.50p multi   4.00  3.50
      Complete booklet, #2370   6.00
2371  A1100  Booklet pane of 2   5.25  5.00
  a.  75c multi   .85  .75
  b.  3.25p multi   3.50  3.00
      Complete booklet, #2371   6.00
2372  A1100  Booklet pane of 2   5.25  5.00
  a.  1p multi   1.10  1.00
  b.  3p multi   3.50  3.00
      Complete booklet, #2372   6.00
2373  A1100  Booklet pane of 2   6.50  6.00
  a.  1.25p multi   2.00  1.75
  b.  2.75p multi   4.00  3.50
      Complete booklet, #2373   6.50
      Nos. 2370-2373 (4)   22.25

Compare Nos. 2370b-2373b with Nos. 2337-2340.

Dr. Ramón Carrillo (1906-56), Neurologist A1101

**Perf. 13¾x13½**
**2006, Mar. 11**   **Litho.**
2374  A1101  75c multi   1.50  1.00

Musical Instruments — A1102

Designs: 75c, Charango. 3.50p, Drum.

**2006, Mar. 11**   **Perf. 13½x13¾**
2375-2376  A1102  Set of 2   6.50  5.00

### Miniature Sheet

Lighthouses — A1103

No. 2377: a, Primero de Mayo. b, Año Nuevo. c, El Rincón. d, Recalada a Bahía Blanca.

**2006, Mar. 18**
2377  A1103  Sheet of 4, #a-d   5.50  4.25

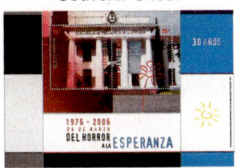

Souvenir Sheet

Start of Military Dictatorship, 30th Anniv. — A1104

No. 2378: a, Man, left side of Navy Mechanics School. b, Flower, right side of Navy Mechanics School.

**2006, Mar. 25**   **Perf. 14**
2378  A1104  75c Sheet of 2, #a-b   3.25  2.75

Silver Religious Objects A1105

No. 2379: a, Crown. b, Candelabra. c, Chalice. d, Viaticum.

**2006, Apr. 8**   **Perf. 13¾x13½**
2379  A1105  75c Block of 4, #a-d   6.00  5.00

Auto Racing — A1106

Races and winning automobiles: No. 2380, 75c, Rally Nacional A8, Toyota Corolla WRC. No. 2381, 75c, Turismo Carretera, Ford Falcon. No. 2382, 75c, Turismo Competición 2000, Ford Focus. No. 2383, 75c, Class 3 Turismo Nacional, Ford Escort.

**2006, May 6**
2380-2383  A1106  Set of 4   6.00  5.00

### Miniature Sheet

Dogs A1107

No. 2384: a, 25c, Springer spaniel. b, 25c, Yorkshire terrier. c, 50c, Argentino dog. d, 50c, Miniature schnauzer. e, 75c, Poodle. f. 75c, Chow chow.

**2006, May 20**
2384  A1107  Sheet of 6 #a-f, + 2 labels   7.75  6.00

A1108

2006 World Cup Soccer Championships — A1109

No. 2386: a, Serbia & Montenegro player. b, Argentina player, blue and white background.
No. 2387: a, Ivory Coast player. b, Netherlands player.

**2006, May 20**   **Litho.**   **Perf. 13¾x13½**
2385  A1108  4p shown   6.75  6.00

**Booklet Panes**
**Perf. 14¼**
2386       Pane of 2   3.50  3.50
  a.-b.  A1109 1p Either single   1.50  1.50
2387       Pane of 2   3.50  3.50
  a.-b.  A1109 1p Either single   1.50  1.50
      Complete booklet, #2386-2387   8.25

**Souvenir Sheet**
2388  A1109  1.50p shown   4.00  3.50

World No Tobacco Day A1110

**2006, May 27**   **Litho.**   **Perf. 14x13½**
2389  A1110  75c multi   1.50  1.25

Intl. Year of Deserts and Desertification A1111

Designs: No. 2390, 75c, Lizard and plant. No. 2391, 75c, Impression of lizard in sand, dead plant.

**Perf. 13¾x13½**
**2006, June 10**   Set of 2   **Litho.**
2390-2391  A1111   3.00  2.50

Famous Men — A1112

Designs: No. 2392, 75c, Tato Bores (1927-96), television actor. No. 2393, 75c, Rodolfo Walsh (1927-77), kidnapped journalist.

**2006, June 10**   **Perf. 13½x13¾**
2392-2393  A1112  Set of 2   3.00  2.50

Winter Sports A1113

No. 2394: a, Alpine skiing. b, Snowboarding. c, Cross-country skiing. d, Biathlon.

**2006, June 17**   **Perf. 13¾x13½**
2394  A1113  75c Block of 4, #a-d   6.00  5.00

Tango Dancing A1114

# ARGENTINA

Designs: 75c, Musician. 4p, Dancers.

**2006, June 24**
2395-2396  A1114  Set of 2  7.00  6.50
See France Nos. 3224-3225.

Patoruzito Riding Pamperito — A1115

**2006, July 8**
2397  A1115  75c multi  1.50  1.25

Endangered Animals — A1116

Designs: No. 2398, 75c, Eubalaena australis. No. 2399, 75c, Hippocamelus bisulcus. No. 2400, 75c, Hippocamelus antisensis. No. 2401, 75c, Panthera onca.

**2006, July 8**  Perf. 14x13¾
2398-2401  A1116  Set of 4  6.50  6.00
For surcharges, see Nos. 2850-2853.

30th Mercosur Common Market Council and Summit of Presidents, Córdoba — A1117

**2006, July 22**  Perf. 13¾x13½
2402  A1117  3.50p multi  5.75  5.00

**Souvenir Sheet**

First British Invasion of Buenos Aires and Reconquest, Bicent. — A1118

**2006, July 22**  Perf. 14
2403  A1118  1.50p multi  2.75  2.25

Energy Conservation A1119

Winning designs in children's art contest: No. 2404, 75c, Light bulb, house and electrical cord, by Florencia Tovi. No. 2405, 75c, Plant in sunlight, unplugged lamp, by Camila Suárez.

**2006, July 22**  Perf. 13¾x13½
2404-2405  A1119  Set of 2  3.00  2.00

First Postage Stamps of Corrientes, 150th Anniv. — A1120

Designs: 75c, August 21, 1856 Corrientes cancel. 1.50p, Corrientes #1.

**Litho. & Embossed**
**2006, Aug. 19**  Perf. 13¾x13½
2406  A1120  75c multi  1.50  1.10

**Souvenir Sheet**
**Litho. Perf. 14**
2407  A1120  1.50p multi  2.75  2.25
No. 2407 contains one 40x40mm stamp.

Interjurisdictional Committee on the Colorado River, 50th Anniv. — A1121

**Perf. 13½x13¾**
**2006, Aug. 26**  Litho.
2408  A1121  75c multi  1.50  1.25

Patricios Infantry Corps, Bicent. — A1122

**2006, Sept. 9**
2409  A1122  75c multi  1.50  1.10

Grapes, Wines and Vineyards — A1123

Designs: No. 2410, 75c, Syrah grapes and wine, Catamarca vineyards. No. 2411, 75c, Torrontés Riojano grapes and wine, La Rioja vineyards. No. 2412, 75c, Pinot Noir grapes and wine, Neuquén vineyards.

**2006, Sept. 16**  Perf. 14x13½
2410-2412  A1123  Set of 3  4.50  3.25
Compare Nos. 2410-2412 with Nos. 2426b-2428b. For surcharges, see Nos. 2840, 2842, 2844.

Col. Ramón L. Falcón Federal Police Cadet School, Cent. — A1124

**2006, Oct. 14  Litho.  Perf. 13¾x13½**
2413  A1124  75c multi  1.50  1.00

Border Bridges A1125

Designs: No. 2414, 75c, Pres. Tancredo Neves Intl. Bridge. No. 2415, 75c, San Roque González de Santa Cruz Intl. Bridge.

**2006, Oct. 14**  Perf. 14x13¾
2414-2415  A1125  Set of 2  3.00  2.00
For surcharges, see Nos. 2858-2859.

Christmas — A1126

Paintings by Alfredo Guttero: No. 2416, 75c, Madonna and Dove. No. 2417, 75c, The Annunciation, horiz.

**Perf. 13½x13¾, 13¾x13½**
**2006, Oct. 21**
2416-2417  A1126  Set of 2  3.00  2.00

Natl. Institute of Agricultural and Cattle Ranching Technology, 50th Anniv. — A1127

**Perf. 13¾x13½**
**2006, Nov. 11**  Litho.
2418  A1127  75c multi  1.50  1.25

Rock Musicians — A1128

Designs: No. 2419, 75c, Tanguito (1945-72). No. 2420, 75c, Luca Prodan (1953-87). No. 2421, 75c, Miguel Abuelo (1946-88). No. 2422, 75c, Pappo (1950-2005).

**2006, Nov. 18**  Perf. 13½x13¾
2419-2422  A1128  Set of 4  6.00  4.50

Caciques — A1129

Designs: No. 2423, 75c, Valentín Sayhueque (1823-1903), Huilliche cacique. No. 2424, 75c, Casimiro Biguá, Tehuelche cacique.

**2006, Dec. 2**
2423-2424  A1129  Set of 2  3.00  2.25

Frigate Hercules, Detail From *Battle of Martín García Island*, by Emilio Biggeri A1130

**2007, Mar. 10**  Perf. 13¾x13½
2425  A1130  75c multi  1.50  1.25
Adm. Guillermo Brown (1777-1857).

Wine-Growing Regions — A1131

No. 2426: a, Hand picking bunch of grapes. b, Vineyard, grapes, bottle of Pinot Noir, Neuquén Region (60x30mm).
No. 2427: a, Harvester cutting grapes from vine. b, Vineyard, grapes, bottle of Torrontés Riojano, La Rioja Region (60x30mm).
No. 2428: a, Harvester inspecting grapes on vine. b, Vineyard, grapes, bottle of Syrah, Catamarca Region (60x30mm).

**2007, Mar. 10**  Litho.  Perf. 14
2426  Booklet pane of 2  7.00  7.00
 a. A1131 75c multi  1.25  1.25
 b. A1131 3.25p multi  5.25  5.25
  Complete booklet, #2426  7.00
2427  Booklet pane of 2  7.00  7.00
 a. A1131 75c multi  1.25  1.25
 b. A1131 3.25p multi  5.25  5.25
  Complete booklet, #2427  7.00
2428  Booklet pane of 2  7.00  7.00
 a. A1131 75c multi  1.25  1.25
 b. A1131 3.25p multi  5.25  5.25
  Complete booklet, #2428  7.00
Complete booklets include a plastic wine bottle spout. Compare Nos. 2426b-2428b with Nos. 2410-2412.

Falkland Islands War, 25th Anniv. — A1132

Map of the Falkland Islands and: No. 2429, 75c, Argentina No. C90 in changed colors with Islas Malvinas cancel. No. 2430, 75c, IAI Dagger fighters. No. 2431, 75c, Battle cruiser ARA General Belgrano. No. 2432, 75c, Decorated war veteran. No. 2433, 75c, War decoration, vert.

**Perf. 13¾x13½, 13½x13¾**
**2007, Mar. 31**  Litho.
2429-2433  A1132  Set of 5  6.25  5.00

Postal and Telecommunications Workers Federation, 50th Anniv. — A1133

**2007, Apr. 14**  Perf. 13¾x13½
2434  A1133  75c multi  1.50  1.25

Map of Antarctica, Icebreaker Almirante Irízar — A1134

No. 2436 — Antarctic fauna: a, Phalacrocorax atriceps. b, Leptonychotes weddellii. c, Sterna vittata, denomination at UR. d, Sterna vittata, denomination at UL. e, Pygoscelis adeliae. f, Chionis alba. g, Pygoscelis papua, denomination at UR. h, Pygoscelis papua, denomination at UL.

**2007, Apr. 21**
2435  A1134 4p shown  12.00  10.00
2436  Sheet of 8  6.00  5.00
 a.-h. A1134 75c Any single  .50  .50

**Miniature Sheet**

Toys A1135

No. 2437: a, Rocking horse. b, Tea set. c, Toy train and stations. d, Toy soldiers.

**2007, May 5  Litho.  Perf. 13¾x13½**
2437  A1135  Sheet of 4  6.00  5.00
 a.-d. 75c Any single  .65  .65

Museums A1136

Designs: 75c, Latin American Art Museum, Buenos Aires. 3.25p, High Mountain Archaeological Museum, Salta.

**2007, May 5**
2438-2439  A1136  Set of 2  6.50  6.00

# ARGENTINA

Road Safety Year — A1137

**2007, May 19 Litho. Perf. 13½x13¾**
2440 A1137 75c red & silver 1.50 1.25

### Souvenir Sheet

Intl. Polar Year A1138

**2007, June 2 Perf. 14**
2441 A1138 4p multi + label 6.25 6.00

Defense of Buenos Aires From British Attack, Bicent. A1139

**2007, June 23 Perf. 13¾x13½ Litho.**
2442 A1139 75c multi 1.50 1.25

Pierre Auger Observatory A1140

**2007, July 14 Litho. Perf. 13½x13¾**
2443 A1140 75c multi 1.50 1.25

St. Joseph Calasanctius (1557-1648) A1141

**2007, July 14**
2444 A1141 1p multi 1.75 1.50

### Souvenir Sheet

Campo del Cielo Meteorite A1142

**2007, July 28 Perf. 14**
2445 A1142 6p multi 10.50 10.00

No. 2445 was sold with, but unattached to, a booklet cover, and 3-D glasses.

Homero Manzi (1907-51), Political Leader, Tango Lyricist — A1143

**Perf. 13½x13¾**
**2007, Aug. 11 Litho.**
2446 A1143 1p multi 1.50 1.25

Tourism Along Route 40 — A1144

No. 2447: a, Road to San Carlos de Bariloche (30x30mm). b, El Acay Pass (40x30mm). c, Road to Perito Moreno (70x30mm). d, La Trochita locomotive (40x30mm). e, Lanin Volcano (40x30mm). f, Rio Grande (50x30mm). g, Animals on road, San José Jachal (40x30mm). h, Cuesta de Miranda (50x30mm) i, Nuestra Senora del Tránsito Chapel (30x30mm). j, Quilmes Ruins (30x30mm). k, Road to Oratorio (40x30mm).

**2007, Aug. 25 Litho. Perf. 14**
2447 Sheet of 11 14.50 14.00
a.-b. A1144 50c Either single .65 .65
c.-k. A1144 1p Any single 1.25 1.25

### Souvenir Sheet

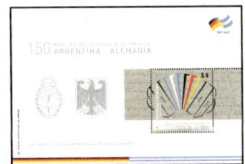
Diplomatic Relations Between Argentina and Germany, 150th Anniv. — A1145

**2007, Sept. 8**
2448 A1145 4p multi 5.25 5.00

Prevention of Carbon Monoxide Accidents A1146

Children's art by: No. 2449, 1p, Julieta Saavedra Barragán. No. 2450, 1p, Leandro Ventancour. No. 2451, 1p, Efraín Osvaldo Rost, vert. No. 2452, 1p, Camila M. Alvarez Petrone, vert.

**Perf. 13¾x13½, 13½x13¾**
**2007, Sept. 8**
2449-2452 A1146 Set of 4 6.00 5.00

San Lorenzo de Almagro Athletic Club, Cent. — A1147

**2007, Sept. 22 Perf. 13½x13¾**
2453 A1147 1p multi 1.50 1.25

Beatification of Ceferino Namuncurá (1886-1905) A1148

**2007, Oct. 13 Litho. Perf. 13¾x13½**
2454 A1148 1p multi 1.50 1.25

Contemporary Art — A1149

Designs: No. 2455, 1p, Corrientes Esquina Uruguay, photograph by Horacio Coppola. No. 2456, 1p, 0611, painting by Pablo Siquier. No. 2457, 1p, Diálogo, digital photograph by Liliana Porter, vert. No. 2458, 1p, Imaginando el Estupor, mosaic by Marta Minujin, vert.

**Perf. 13¾x13½, 13½x13¾**
**2007, Oct. 27**
2455-2458 A1149 Set of 4 6.00 5.00

Nos. 2455-2458 each were printed in sheets of 4.

Christmas — A1150

Designs: 25c, Adoration of the Magi. 1p, Holy Family.

**2007, Nov. 10 Perf. 13½x14**
2459-2460 A1150 Set of 2 3.00 2.50

First Balloon Crossing of Río de la Plata, Cent. — A1151

**Perf. 13¾x13½**
**2007, Nov. 24 Litho.**
2461 A1151 1p multi 1.50 1.25

Discovery of Oil and Gas in Argentina, Cent. — A1152

**2007, Nov. 24**
2462 A1152 1p multi 1.50 1.25

2007 Presidential Inauguration A1153

**2007, Dec. 15 Perf. 13½x13¾**
2463 A1153 1p multi 1.50 1.25

Festivals — A1154

Designs: No. 2464, 1p, National Chamamé Festival, Corrientes Province. No. 2465, 1p, National Poncho Festival, Catamarca Province. No. 2466, 1p, National Festival of Dressage and Folklore, Jesús María, Cordoba Province. No. 2467, 1p, National Snow Festival, San Carlos de Bariloche, Río Negro Province.

**2007, Dec. 15**
2464-2467 A1154 Set of 4 6.00 5.00

2008 Summer Olympics, Beijing — A1155

Designs: No. 2468, 50c, Mountain biking. No. 2469, 50c, Taekwondo. 1p, Basketball. 4p, Pole vault.

**Perf. 13½x13¾**
**2008, Mar. 29 Litho.**
2468-2471 A1155 Set of 4 6.00 5.00

Natl. Scientific and Technical Research Council, 50th Anniv. — A1156

Designs: No. 2472, 1p, Bone tissue bridges with 45S5 bioactive glass particles. No. 2473, 1p, Pollen grain of Polygonum sp. No. 2474, 1p, Remnants of Supernova W44. No. 2475, 1p, Cave paintings, Epuyén River Valley. No. 2476, 1p, Fluidodinamica (fluid dynamics).

**2008, Apr. 12 Perf. 13¾x13½**
2472-2476 A1156 Set of 5 5.75 4.50

Association of Argentine Private Radio Stations, 50th Anniv. — A1157

**2008, Apr. 26**
2477 A1157 1p multi 1.15 .90

Pres. Arturo Frondizi (1908-95), Oil Pumps A1158

**2008, Apr. 26**
2478 A1158 1p multi 1.25 1.00

Birds — A1159

Male and female: 1p, Sturnella loyca. 4p, Xanthopsar flavus.

**2008, Apr. 26 Perf. 13½x13¾**
2479-2480 A1159 Set of 2 5.50 5.00

Argentine Aero Club, Cent. — A1160

**2008, May 10 Perf. 14x13½**
2481 A1160 1p multi 1.15 .90

Colón Theater, Buenos Aires, Cent. A1161

**2008, May 24**
2482 A1161 1p multi 1.15 .90

# ARGENTINA

Aimé Bonpland (1773-1858), Founder of Corrientes Natural Sciences Museum
A1162

**2008, May 24**     **Perf. 13¾x13½**
2483   A1162   1p multi     1.15   .90

Dr. Marcos Sastre (1808-87), Textbook Writer, and Text from Reading Book, Anagnosia
A1163

**Perf. 13¾x13½**
**2008, June 21**     **Litho.**
2484   A1163   1p multi     1.15   .90

Luciano-Honorato Valette (1880-1957), Antarctic Naturalist — A1164

Disappearance of Rescue Ship ARA Guaraní, 50th Anniv. — A1165

**2008, June 28**
2485   A1164   1p multi     1.15   .90
2486   A1165   1p multi     1.15   .90

Characters From "The Mail Song," by Maria Elena Walsh
A1166

Character From "Big Brother," by Silvia Schujer
A1167

Characters From "Letters to Santa Claus," by Luis María Pescetti
A1168

Character From "Mammarachos por Carta," by Ricardo Mariño
A1169

**Perf. 13½x13¾, 13¾x13½**
**2008, July 26**
2487   A1166   1p multi     1.15   .90
2488   A1167   1p multi     1.15   .90
2489   A1168   1p multi     1.15   .90
2490   A1169   1p multi     1.15   .90
    Nos. 2487-2490 (4)    4.60 3.60
Children's songs and literature.

Scenes From "The Mail Song," by María Elena Walsh
A1170

Scenes From "Mamarrachos por Carta," by Ricardo Mariño — A1171

Characters From "Letters to Santa Claus," by Luis María Pescetti — A1172

Characters From "Big Brother," by Silvia Schujer — A1173

**2008, July 26   Litho.   Perf. 13½x13¾**
**Booklet Stamps**
2491   A1170   Block of 6    7.50   7.50
  a.-f.    1p Any single    1.20   1.20
  g.    Booklet pane, 2 #2491   15.00   15.00
2492   A1171   Block of 6    7.50   7.50
  a.-f.    1p Any single    1.20   1.20
  g.    Booklet pane, 2 #2492   15.00   15.00
**Perf. 14¼**
2493   A1172   Booklet pane of 2   10.00   10.00
  a.-b.    4p Either single    5.00   5.00
**Perf. 14**
2494   A1173   Booklet pane of 2   10.00   10.00
  a.-b.    4p Either single    5.00   5.00
    Complete booklet, #2491g, 2492g, 2493, 2494   50.00

Complete booklet is a spiral-bound book containing the four booklet panes, postal cards, text pages and pieces for a children's card game.

**Archaeological Artifacts Type of 2000**
Design: Jar, Yocavil culture.

**Perf. 13½x13¾ Syncopated**
**2008, Aug. 2**
2495   A973   10p multi     7.25   6.75

**Souvenir Sheet**

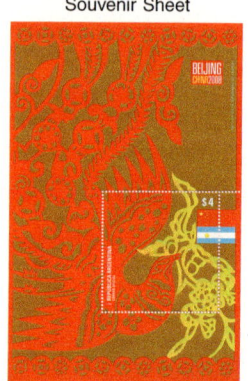

Olympex 2008 World Stamp Exhibition, Beijing — A1174

**Litho. With Foil Application**
**2008, Aug. 2**     **Perf. 14**
2496   A1174   4p multi     3.50   3.00

Immigrants to Argentina
A1175

Designs: No. 2497, 1p, Cherry blossoms, koi, immigrants from Japan. No. 2498, 1p, Metal decorative plates and immigrants from Lebanon. No. 2499, 1p, Tiles, guitar and immigrants from Portugal. No. 2500, 1p, Wooden decorative box, embroidered silk, Ugaritic alphabet and immigrants from Syria.

**Perf. 13¾x13½**
**2008, Sept. 20**     **Litho.**
2497-2500   A1175   Set of 4   4.25   3.00

**Souvenir Sheets**

National Flower Festival
A1176

Designs: No. 2501, 5p, Gerbera daisy, gardenia and rose (shown). No. 2502, 5p, Carnation, gold-banded lily and delphinium.

**2008, Sept. 27**     **Perf. 14**
2501-2502   A1176   Set of 2   8.50   8.50
Nos. 2501-2502 are impregnated with a floral scent.

**Souvenir Sheets**

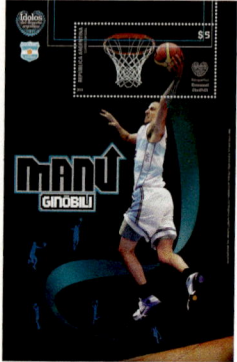

Sports Personalities — A1177

Designs: No. 2503, 5p, Hand of Manu Ginobili, basketball and hoop. No. 2504, 5p, Rugby football kicked by Hugo Porta, goal posts, silhouettes of rugby player kicking ball. No. 2505, 5p, Silhouette of golfer putting, foot of Roberto De Vicenzo, vert. No. 2506, 5p, Juan Manuel Fangio in race car, vert.

**2008, Oct. 11**     **Perf. 14**
2503-2506   A1177   Set of 4   27.50   27.50
See Nos. 2541-2544, 2632-2635.

Science Teaching Year — A1178

**2008, Oct. 25**     **Perf. 13¾x13½**
2507   A1178   1p multi     1.25   1.00

Flowers
A1179

Designs: No. 2508, 1p, Ceiba chodatii. No. 2509, 1p, Nelumbo nucifera.

**2008, Oct. 25**
2508-2509   A1179   Set of 2   3.00   2.50
See Viet Nam Nos. 3343-3344.

**Souvenir Sheet**

First Stamps of Argentina, Buenos Aires and Cordoba, 150th Anniv. — A1180

No. 2510: a, Cordoba No. 2 (30x30mm). b, Buenos Aires No. 4 (40x30mm). c, Argentina No. 3 (30x40mm).

**2008, Nov. 1**     **Perf. 14**
2510   A1180   1p Sheet of 3, #a-c   4.75   4.00

Christmas — A1181

**2008, Nov. 15**     **Perf. 13½x13¾**
2511   A1181   1p multi     1.00   .80

No. 2491: a, Bird holding Argentina #2216b in beak. b, Mailbox. c, Paper airplane, letters. d, Post office, letters. e, Smokestacks behind open envelope with letter. f, Philatelic office, Argentina #2236, #2239 and its adjacent label.
No. 2492: a, Postman holding letter. b, Postman and woman reading letter. c, Bird reading letter. d, Man with pipe. e, Birds on mail box. f, Monkey with banana.
No. 2493: a, Child writing letter to Santa Claus. b, Santa Claus reading letter from child.
No. 2494: a, Girl at table playing card game (40x50mm). b, Boy and mother, horiz. (70x40mm).

# ARGENTINA

Dances — A1182

Designs: No. 2512, 1p, Malambo sureño dancer, Argentina. No. 2513, 1p, Hoy-nazan dancers, Armenia.

**2008, Nov. 22**    Litho.
2512-2513   A1182   Set of 2    2.25   1.75
See Armenia Nos. 790-791.

El Cronista Comercial Newspaper, Cent. — A1183

**2008, Dec. 13**    Perf. 13¾x13½
2514   A1183   1p multi    1.00   .80

School of Forestry, 50th Anniv. — A1184

**2008, Dec. 13**    Perf. 13½x3¾
2515   A1184   1p multi    1.00   .80

Festivals — A1185

Designs: No. 2516, 1p, Chaya Festival, La Rioja Province. No. 2517, 1p, Natl. Grape Harvest Festival, Mendoza Province. No. 2518, 1p, Natl. Cherry Festival, Los Antiguos, Santa Cruz Province. No. 2519, 1p, Natl. Sea Festival, Mar del Plata, Buenos Aires Province.

**2009, Feb. 14**    Perf. 13½x13¾
2516-2519   A1185   Set of 4    4.25   3.25

### Souvenir Sheet

Preservation of Polar Regions and Glaciers — A1186

No. 2520: a, Retreat of Piedras Blancas Glacier. b, Retreat of Argentine Antarctic Tuntuy ice.

**2009, Mar. 7**    Perf. 14
2520   A1186   5p Sheet of 2, #a-b    7.50   7.00

Bishop Colombres Memorial Experimental Agribusiness, Cent. — A1187

**2009, Mar. 21**    Perf. 13¾x13½
2521   A1187   1p multi    1.00   .80

### Souvenir Sheet

New Year 2009 (Year of the Ox) A1188

**Litho. & Embossed, Margin With Foil Application**

**2009, Apr. 4**    Perf. 14
2522   A1188   5p multi    4.50   4.25
China 2009 World Stamp Exhibition, Luoyang.

Holy Cross Exaltation Parish, Puerto Santa Cruz, Cent. — A1189

**2009, Apr. 18**    Litho.   Perf. 13½x13¾
2523   A1189   1p multi    1.00   .80

Argentine Exports A1190

Designs: 1p, Wine. 5p, Agricultural machines.

**2009, Apr. 18**    Perf. 13¾x13½
2524-2525   A1190   Set of 2    4.50   4.00

Endangered Species — A1191

Designs: No. 2526, 1p, Harpyhaliaetus coronatus. No. 2527, 1p, Chelonoidis chilensis, horiz.

**Perf. 13½x13¾, 13¾x13½**
**2009, Apr. 18**
2526-2527   A1191   Set of 2    2.50   2.00

Pres. Raúl Ricardo Alfonsín (1927-2009) A1192

**2009, May 9**    Perf. 13½x13¾
2528   A1192   1p multi    1.00   .80

Children of the Holy Virgin of the Garden Congregation in Argentina, 150th Anniv. — A1193

**2009, May 23**
2529   A1193   1p multi    1.00   .80

Raúl Scalabrini Ortiz (1898-1959), Writer — A1194

**2009, May 23**
2530   A1194   1p multi    1.00   .80

Political and Military Command of the Malvinas (Falkland Islands), 180th Anniv. — A1195

Paintings: 1p, Luis Vernet, governor of the Malvinas, by Luisa Vernet Lavalle Lloveras. 5p, Ship and houses near cliff, by Vernet, map of Malvinas.

**2009, June 13**    Perf. 13½x13¾
2531   A1195   1p multi    1.00   .85

### Souvenir Sheet
**Perf. 14**
2532   A1195   5p multi    4.00   3.75
No. 2532 contains one 70x30mm stamp.

Water A1196

No. 2533: a, Droplets. b, Drops, clouds and hand, vert.

**2009, June 27**    Perf. 14
2533    Sheet of 2, unscratched   7.50   7.00
   a.   A1196 5p multi    3.50   2.60
   b.   A1196 5p multi, unscratched    3.50   3.50
   c.   As "b," scratched    3.50
No. 2533b and sheet margin have scratch off panels.

Flora and Fauna — A1197

Designs: No. 2534, 1p, Polybetes pythagoricus. No. 2535, 1p, Passiflora caerulea.

**2009, July 25**    Perf. 13¾x13½
2534-2535   A1197   Set of 2    2.10   1.60

Amusement Park Rides — A1198

No. 2536: a, Bumper cars. b, Roller coaster. c, Ferris wheel. d, Ghost train.

**2009, Aug. 1**
2536    Horiz. strip of 4 + flanking label    3.75   2.75
   a.-d.   A1198 1p Any single    .85   .65

### Miniature Sheet

Sheep A1199

No. 2537: a, Merino ram. b, Romney Marsh yearling. c, Corriedale ewe and lamb. d, Hampshire Down ewe and lamb. e, Lincoln ewe. f, Frisian ewe.

**2009, Aug. 22**
2537   A1199   1p Sheet of 6, #a-f, + 2 labels    6.00   4.50

Soil Erosion A1200

No. 2538 — Erosion by: a, Water. b, Wind.

**2009, Sept. 12**    Perf. 14x13½
2538    Horiz. pair    1.90   1.60
   a.-b.   A1200 1p Either single    .95   .80

A1201

America Issue, Education For All — A1202

**Perf. 13¾x13½**
**2009, Sept. 12**    Litho.
2539   A1201   1p multi    1.00   .76
2540   A1202   1p multi    1.00   .75

### Sports Personalities Type of 2008

Designs: No. 2541, 5p, Delfo Cabrera running in 1948 Summer Olympics, vert. No. 2542, 5p, Tennis ball and shorts of Guillermo Vilas (38mm diameter). No. 2543, 10p, Field hockey players, stick of Luciana Aymar, vert. No. 2544, 10p, Cyclists chasing Juan Curuchet, vert.

**Perf. 14, Perf. (No. 2542)**
**2009, Sept. 26**    Litho.
2541-2544   A1177   Set of 4    22.00   20.00
The tennis ball on No 2542 is covered with flocking.

National Technological University, 50th Anniv. — A1203

**2009, Oct. 17**    Perf. 13½x13¾
2545   A1203   1p multi    1.00   .80

# ARGENTINA

### Souvenir Sheets

A1204

Italia 2009 Intl. Philatelic Exhibition, Rome — A1205

No. 2546: a, La Scala Theater, Milan. b, Colon Theater, Buenos Aires.
No. 2547: a, Froilán González racing in Ferrari 375 (85x30mm rhomboid) b, Ferrari F60 race car (60x20mm).

**2009, Oct. 24    Litho.    Perf. 14**
2546  A1204  6p Sheet of 2, #a-b    7.50  7.00
2547  A1205  6p Sheet of 2, #a-b    7.50  7.00

Intl. Year of Astronomy A1206

Designs: 1p, Telescope, National University of Córdoba Astronomical Observatory. 10p, Galileo Galilei (1564-1642), diagram of solar system orbits.

**2009, Oct. 24    Litho.    Perf. 13¾x13½**
2548  A1206  1p multi    1.00  .80

**Souvenir Sheet**
**Perf. 14**
2549  A1206  10p multi    7.50  7.25

No. 2549 contains one 80x20mm stamp.

Children's Art — A1207

Winning art in "I Can Slow TB Down" children's stamp design contest: No. 2550, 1p, Boxing gloves hitting "TB," by Alberto Penayo Pardo. No. 2551, 1p, Lungs with bandage, by Candela Alemany Fiandrino. No. 2552, 1p, Boy coughing, doctor holding sign, by Rocío Cabrera, vert. No. 2553, 1p, Hands holding lungs, by Juliana Benzo, vert.

**Perf. 13¾x13½, 13½x13¾**
**2009, Nov. 14    Litho.**
2550-2553  A1207  Set of 4    7.00  3.25

Christmas — A1208

**2009, Nov. 21    Perf. 13½x14**
2554  A1208  1p multi    1.00  .45

Historic Buildings A1209

No. 2555, 1p — San Martín Mansion, 1910: a, Exterior. b, Interior.

No. 2556, 1p — Ortiz Basualdo Mansion, 1918: a, Exterior. b, Interior.
No. 2557, 1p — Fernandez-Anchorena Mansion, 1909: a, Exterior. b, Interior.
No. 2558, 1p — Duhau Mansion, 1934: a, Exterior. b, Interior.

**Perf. 13¾x13½**
**2009, Dec. 12    Litho.**
**Horiz. Pairs, #a-b**
2555-2558  A1209  Set of 4    7.00  6.00

Nos. 2555-2558 each were printed in sheets containing 8 pairs and 4 labels.

Festivals — A1210

Designs: No. 2559, 1.50p, National Apple Festival, General Roca, Río Negro Province. No. 2560, 1.50p, National Sun Festival, San Juan, San Juan Province. No. 2561, 1.50p, National Students Festival, San Salvador de Jujuy, Jujuy Province. No. 2562, 1.50p, National Tradition Festival, San Antonio de Areco, Buenos Aires Province.

**2010, Feb. 20    Perf. 13½x13¾**
2559-2562  A1210  Set of 4    5.25  4.25

South American Sails 2010 Regatta — A1211

Designs: 1.50p, Argentine Navy frigate Libertad.
No. 2564: a, Chilean Navy schooner Esmerelda. b, Libertad, diff.

**Perf. 13¾x13½ Syncopated**
**2010, Feb. 20**
2563  A1211  1.50p multi    1.25  1.00

**Souvenir Sheet**
**Perf. 14**
2564  A1211  6p Sheet of 2,
              #a-b, + 12 labels    7.75  7.75

No. 2564 contains two 40x50mm stamps.

May Revolution, Bicent. — A1212

**Perf. 13½x13¾ Syncopated**
**2010, Mar. 6**
2565  A1212  1.50p multi    1.25  .90

National Symbols — A1213

Designs: No. 2566, 1.50p, Coat of arms. No. 2567, 1.50p, Flag, horiz.

**Perf. 13½x13¾, 13¾x13½**
**2010, Mar. 27**
2566-2567  A1213  Set of 2    2.50  1.75

A Culture of Peace A1214

No. 2568: a, Dove. b, Map of South America.

**2010, Apr. 24    Litho.    Perf. 13½x13¾**
2568  A1214  1.50p Horiz. pair,
              #a-b    2.25  1.75

Buenos Aires City Symphony, Cent. — A1215

**2010, Apr. 24    Perf. 14x13½**
2569  A1215  1.50p multi    1.25  1.00

Argentine Army, Bicent. — A1216

**2010, May 8    Perf. 13½x13¾**
2570  A1216  1.50p multi    1.25  1.00

Argentine Naval Command, Bicent. A1217

**2010, May 29    Perf. 13¾x13½**
2571  A1217  1.50p multi    1.25  1.00

Bicentenary Mural — A1218

No. 2572: a, Cabildo, Buenos Aires (30x50mm). b, General Manuel Belgrano, flag of Argentina on pole, Casa de Tucumán, San Miguel de Tucumán (30x50mm). c, Gen. José de San Martín on horseback, raising sword (40x80mm). d, National Constitution (30x50mm). e, Ships unloading immigrants (30x50mm). f, Sword battle, people voting, "1910," horiz. (70x30mm). g, National Congress, Blind Justice (30x50mm). h, Trolley, film set, bridge, horiz. (40x30mm). i, Palm tree, crowd, banners, men with feet in fountain, baby with umbilical cord (30x60mm). j, Military with guns, cardinal, man smoking cigar, eyes, "the disappeared" in pit (30x40mm). k, Mothers of the Plaza de Mayo holding pictures of the disappeared, May Pyramid statue (40x60mm). l, Motorcyclist, men with briefcases holding cellular phones, man on computer, airplanes (40x60mm).

**2010, May 29    Litho.    Perf. 14**
2572         Sheet of 12    16.00  13.00
a.-l.  A1218  1.50p Any single    1.25  1.00

Gazeta de Buenos-Ayres, Bicent. — A1219

**2010, June 5  Litho.  Perf. 13½x13¾**
2573  A1219  1.50p multi    1.25  1.00

A1220

2010 World Cup Soccer Championships, South Africa — A1221

2010 World Cup emblem and stylized player from: No. 2574, 1.50p, Nigeria. No. 2575, 1.50p, Greece, vert. 5p, South Korea. 7p, Argentina, vert.
No. 2578, 5p, Argentina player sliding to kick ball. No. 2579, 5p, Argentina player heading ball into net. No. 2580, 5p, Argentina player making scissor kick. No. 2581, 5p, Goalie making save, vert.

**Perf. 13¾x13½, 13½x13¾**
**2010, June 5**
2574-2577  A1220  Set of 4    10.50  9.00

**Souvenir Sheets**
**Perf. 14**
2578-2581  A1221  Set of 4    14.00  12.50

Nos. 2578-2579 each contain one 70x40mm stamp, No. 2580 contains one 60x40mm stamp, and No. 2581 contains one 40x60mm stamp.

World Junior Rugby Championships, Argentina A1222

**2010, June 19    Perf. 13¾x13½**
2582  A1222  1.50p multi    1.25  1.00

**Souvenir Sheet**

First Government Junta, Bicent. — A1223

**2010, July 24    Perf. 14**
2583  A1223  5p multi    3.50  3.00

**Miniature Sheet**

Toys and Games A1224

No. 2584: a, Sulky-cycle (sulky-ciclo). b, Cup and ball (balero). c, Top (trompo). d, Hoop (aro). e, Doll (muñeca).

**Perf. 13½x13¾ Syncopated**
**2010, July 24    Litho.**
2584  A1224  2p Sheet of 5, #a-e,
              + 15 labels    7.75  6.50

The stamps and labels of No. 2584 are puzzle pieces that when separated and rearranged form a picture.

# ARGENTINA

Jorge Luis Borges (1899-1986), Writer — A1225

**Perf. 13¾x13½ Syncopated**
**2010, Aug. 14** Litho.
2585 A1225 7p multi 4.75 4.50
2010 Frankfurt Book Fair. See Germany No. 2585.

**Landmarks Type of 2004**
Designs: 1.50p, Parana River, Corrientes. 6p, Les Eclaireurs Lighthouse, Tierra del Fuego.

**Perf. 13¾x13½ Syncopated**
**2010** Litho.
2586 A1063a 1.50p multi + label 2.00 1.50
2587 A1063a 6p multi 7.00 6.50
Issued: 1.50p, 5/11; 6p, 2/12.

Mountain Lakes — A1226

Flags of Romania and Argentina and: 1.50p, Lake Ballea, Romania. 7p, Lake Nahuel Huapi, Argentina.

**2010, Aug. 14** **Perf. 13¾x13½**
2588-2589 A1226 Set of 2 6.00 5.00
See Romania Nos. 5201-5202.

Women's Field Hockey World Cup Championships, Rosario A1227

**2010, Aug. 28**
2590 A1227 1.50p multi 1.25 1.00

Games — A1228

Designs: No. 2591, 1.50p, Truco (card game). No. 2592, 1.50p, Bocce.

**2010, Aug. 28** **Perf. 13½x13¾**
2591-2592 A1228 Set of 2 2.50 1.90

2010 Census — A1229

**Perf. 13¾x13½ Syncopated**
**2010, Sept. 18**
2593 A1229 1.50p multi 1.25 1.00

Juan Bautista Alberdi (1810-84), Lawyer and Diplomat — A1230

**2010, Sept. 18** **Perf. 13½x13¾**
2594 A1230 1.50p multi 1.25 1.00

National Library, Bicent. A1231

**Perf. 13¾x13½**
**2010, Sept. 18** Litho.
2595 A1231 1.50p multi 1.25 1.00

**Souvenir Sheet**

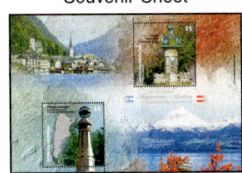

Weather Stations in Austria and Argentina — A1232

No. 2596 — Weather station in: a, Stadtpark, Vienna. b, Buenos Aires Botanical Garden.

**2010, Oct. 16** **Perf. 14**
2596 A1232 5p Sheet of 2, #a-b 7.00 6.25
See Austria No. 2283.

The Child of Bethlehem, by Aldo Severi — A1233

**2010, Nov. 13** **Perf. 13¾x13½**
2597 A1233 1.50p multi 1.25 1.00
Christmas.

Federal Electric Power Council, 50th Anniv. — A1234

**2010, Nov. 27** **Perf. 13½x13¾**
2598 A1234 1.50p multi 1.25 1.00

**Souvenir Sheets**

Lighthouses — A1235

Portuguese Ceramic Tile — A1236

No. 2599: a, Querandí Lighthouse, Argentina. b, Santa Marta Lighthouse, Portugal.

**2010, Sept. 25** **Perf. 14**
2599 A1235 5p Sheet of 2, #a-b 6.75 6.00
2600 A1236 10p multi 6.75 6.00
Portugal 2010 Intl. Philatelic Exhibition, Lisbon. Portions of the designs of Nos. 2599a-2599b were applied by a thermographic process producing a shiny, raised effect.

World Post Day — A1237

**2010, Oct. 9** Litho. **Perf. 13½x13¾**
2601 A1237 1.50p multi 1.25 1.00

A Song to Work, Sculpture by Rogelio Yrurtia — A1238

**2010, Oct. 16** **Perf. 14x13½**
2602 A1238 1.50p multi 1.25 1.00

Dakar Rally in Argentina — A1239

No. 2603 — Photographs of 2009 and 2010 Rallies: a, Starting line of Rally, Buenos Aires (60x40mm). b, Motorcycle No. 107 (50x50mm). c, Car No. 300 on dirt road (60x40mm). d, Truck No. 502 on dirt road, (50x50mm). e, Vehicles on dirt road (50x50mm). f, Quad No. 251 (40x80mm). g, Quad No. 277 (40x80mm).
No. 2604: a, Car No. 375 on dirt road (60x50mm). b, Two quad riders in sand near hill (60x40mm). c, Car No. 377 in air (60x40mm). d, Motorcycle No. 1 (40x50mm). e, Tree near Laguna del Pescado (40x50mm). f, White clouds over mountain near Tucumán (40x50mm). g, Road and bridge near Jujuy (40x50mm). h, Truck No. 500 in water (70x50mm).

**2010, Dec. 11** **Perf. 14**
2603 Booklet pane of 7 14.00 14.00
 a.-e. A1239 1.50p Any single 1.00 1.00
 f. A1239 5p multi 3.25 3.25
 g. A1239 7p multi 4.50 4.50
2604 Booklet pane of 8 14.00 14.00
 a.-g. A1239 1.50p Any single 1.00 1.00
 h. A1239 10p multi 6.50 6.50
Complete booklet, #2603-2604 + post card 28.00

Intl. Year of Forests — A1240

**2011, Mar. 19** **Perf. 13½x13¾**
2605 A1240 2p multi 1.50 1.20

Postal Union of the Americas, Spain and Portugal (UPAEP), Cent. — A1241

**2011, Mar. 19** **Perf. 13¾x13½**
2606 A1241 8p multi 5.00 4.50

Buenos Aires, 2010 World Book Capital A1242

No. 2607 — Stylized buildings spelling: a, "Buenos Aires Capital." b, "Mundial del Libro 2011."

**2011, Apr. 16** **Perf. 14x13½**
2607 Horiz. pair 2.90 2.25
 a.-b. A1242 2p Either single 1.40 1.10

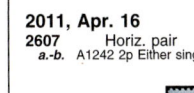

A1243

Antarctic Treaty, 50th Anniv. A1244

Designs: 2p, Iceberg and Antarctic Treaty emblem.
No. 2609: a, Pygoscelis papua. b, Scientist and equipment.

**2011, Apr. 16** **Perf. 13¾x13½**
2608 A1243 2p multi 1.40 1.00

**Souvenir Sheet**
**Perf. 14**
2609 A1244 8p Sheet of 2, #a-b 8.50 8.00
34th Antarctic Treaty Consultative Meeting, Buenos Aires.

Mariano Moreno (1778-1811), Politician A1245

**2011, May 21** **Perf. 13¾x13½**
2610 A1245 2p multi 1.40 1.00

World Blood Donor Day — A1246

**Perf. 13¾x13½ Syncopated**
**2011, May 21**
2611 A1246 5p multi 3.25 2.50

Year of Decent Labor, Health and Safety for Workers A1247

**2011, June 4** **Perf. 13¾x13½**
2612 A1247 2p multi 1.40 1.00

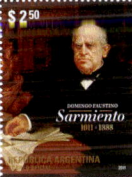

Pres. Domingo Faustino Sarmiento (1811-88) — A1248

**2011, June 25** **Perf. 13½x13¾**
2613 A1248 2.50p multi 1.75 1.50

# ARGENTINA

May Pyramid, Buenos
Aires, Bicent. — A1249

| 2011, June 25 | | Perf. 13½x14 |
|---|---|---|
| 2614 | A1249 2.50p multi | 1.75 1.50 |

America Cup Soccer
Tournament — A1250

No. 2615 — Players from Group A teams: a, Argentina and Bolivia. b, Colombia and Costa Rica.
No. 2616 — Players from Group B teams: a, Venezuela and Brazil. b, Paraguay and Ecuador.
No. 2617 — Players from Group C teams: a, Peru and Uruguay. b, Mexico and Chile.

| 2011, June 25 | | Perf. 14 |
|---|---|---|
| 2615 | Wheel with 2 sheets | 9.00 9.00 |
| a.-b. | A1250 5p Either sheet | 4.50 4.50 |
| 2616 | Wheel with 2 sheets | 9.00 9.00 |
| a.-b. | A1250 5p Either sheet | 4.50 4.50 |
| 2617 | Wheel with 2 sheets | 9.00 9.00 |
| a.-b. | A1250 5p Either sheet | 4.50 4.50 |
| | Nos. 2615-2617 (3) | 27.00 27.00 |

Nos. 2615a-2615b, 2616a-2616b and 2617a-2617b are attached to wheels with a metal grommet at the center of the wheels.

Launch of SAC-D/Aquarius
Satellite — A1251

| 2011, July 23 | Litho. | Perf. 13¾x13½ |
|---|---|---|
| 2618 | A1251 2.50p multi | 1.75 1.50 |

Mailboxes
A1252

Designs: No. 2619, 2.50p, Corneta type mailbox, cancel. No. 2620, 2.50p, Pillar box, handwritten letter, vert.

| Perf. 13¾x13½, 13½x13¾ | | |
|---|---|---|
| 2011, Aug. 20 | | |
| 2619-2620 A1252 | Set of 2 | 3.50 3.00 |

Festivals — A1253

Designs: No. 2621, 2.50p, National Beer Festival, Villa General Belgrano. No. 2622, 2.50p, National Horse Festival, San Cristóbal. No. 2623, 2.50p, Foreign Communities Fair,

Comodoro Rivadavia. No. 2624, 2.50p, National Tea Festival, Campo Viera.

| 2011, Sept. 10 | | Perf. 13½x13¾ |
|---|---|---|
| 2621-2624 A1253 | Set of 4 | 7.00 6.00 |

Orchids
A1254

Designs: No. 2625, 2.50p, Zygopetalum maxillare. No. 2626, 2.50p, Sacoila lanceolata, vert.

| Perf. 13¾x13½, 13½x13¾ | | |
|---|---|---|
| 2011, Sept. 24 | | |
| 2625-2626 A1254 | Set of 2 | 5.50 5.00 |

Train on
the
Clouds
A1255

No. 2627: a, Train cars, bridge (yellow orange panel). b, Locomotive, bridge (blue panel). c, Train on curved bridge (orange panel). d, Train on curved bridge, diff. (red panel).

| 2011, Sept. 24 | | Perf. 14 |
|---|---|---|
| 2627 | Sheet of 4 | 16.00 15.00 |
| a.-d. | A1255 5p Any single | 4.00 3.75 |

Argentine
Pediatric
Society,
Cent. — A1256

| 2011, Oct. 22 | | Perf. 13¾x13½ |
|---|---|---|
| 2628 | A1256 2.50p multi | 1.75 1.50 |

Miniature Sheet

Pig
Breeds
A1257

No. 2629: a, Landrace. b, Hampshire. c, Pietrain. d, Duroc Jersey. e, Spotted Poland. f, Yorkshire.

| 2011, Oct. 29 | | Litho. |
|---|---|---|
| 2629 A1257 2.50p Sheet of 6, #a-f, + 2 labels | | 10.00 9.00 |

Christmas — A1258

Litho. With Glitter Affixed
| 2011, Oct. 29 | Perf. 13¾ Syncopated |
|---|---|
| 2630 A1258 2.50p multi | 1.75 .75 |

Souvenir Sheet

Pres. Néstor Carlos Kirchner (1950-2010), and Casa Rosada — A1259

| 2011, Nov. 26 | Litho. | Perf. 14 |
|---|---|---|
| 2631 | A1259 5p multi | 3.25 3.00 |

**Sports Personalities Type of 2008**
Souvenir Sheets

Designs: No. 2632, 10p, Horse and mallet of Adolfo Cambiaso, polo player, vert. No. 2633, 10p, Chessboard and Miguel Najdorf (1910-97), chess player, vert. (50x60mm). No. 2634, 10p, Sailboard of Carlos Espinola, sailboarder, vert. (50x60mm). No. 2635, 10p, Roller skates of Nora Vega, roller skater (60x40mm).

| 2011, Nov. 12 | | |
|---|---|---|
| 2632-2635 A1177 | Set of 4 | 25.00 24.00 |

Rights of the
Child — A1260

Winning art in children's stamp design contest by: No. 2636, 2.50p, Nicolás Agustín Bernachea (blue panels). No. 2637, 2.50p, Sofía Panagópulo (pink panels). No. 2638, 2.50p, Ezequiel Catalano Segesso (yellow green panels). No. 2639, 2.50p, Laura Florencia Martinessi (orange panels).

| 2011, Nov. 26 | | Perf. 13½x13¾ |
|---|---|---|
| 2636-2639 A1260 | Set of 4 | 7.00 6.00 |

Souvenir Sheet

Creation of Argentine Flag and Pledge
of Allegiance, Bicent. — A1261

| 2012, Mar. 3 | Litho. | Perf. 14 |
|---|---|---|
| 2640 | A1261 5p multi | 3.00 2.75 |

First Argentine
Flight Landing
at South Pole,
50th
Anniv. — A1262

| 2012, Mar. 3 | Litho. | Perf. 13¾x13½ |
|---|---|---|
| 2641 | A1262 2.50p multi | 1.60 1.40 |

Monument to Gen. Manuel Belgrano,
Buenos Aires, and Argentine
Flag — A1263

| 2012, Mar. 31 | | Perf. 14x13¾ |
|---|---|---|
| 2642 | A1263 2.50p multi | 1.60 1.40 |

Argentine
Claims of
Sovereignty
Over British
South Atlantic
Islands
A1264

Argentine flag and map of: No. 2643, 2.50p, Falkland Islands (Isla Gran Malvina and Isla Soledad). No. 2644, 2.50p, South Georgia (Isla San Pedro). No. 2645, 2.50p, South Sandwich Islands (Islas Traverse, Islas Candelaria, Isla Saunders, Isla Jorge, Isla Blanca and Grupo Tule del Sur), vert. (28x67mm).

| Perf. 13¾x13½, 13¾x14 (#2645) | | |
|---|---|---|
| 2012, Mar. 31 | | |
| 2643-2645 A1264 | Set of 3 | 5.00 4.00 |

Presidential Staff
and Argentine
Flag — A1265

| 2012, Apr. 14 | | Perf. 13½x13¾ |
|---|---|---|
| 2646 | A1265 2.50p multi | 1.60 1.40 |

Presidential mandate of Cristina Fernández Kirchner for 2011-15.

Monument to Gen. José de San
Martín, First Deed of Río Gallegos
Town Council — A1266

| 2012, Apr. 14 | | Perf. 14x13¾ |
|---|---|---|
| 2647 | A1266 2.50p multi | 1.60 1.40 |

Río Gallegos Town Council, cent.

Alernative Energies — A1267

Designs: 2.50p, Biogas, biomass and biocombustibles. 9.50p, Solar, wind and hydroelectric energy.

| 2012, Apr. 28 | Litho. | Perf. 14x13½ |
|---|---|---|
| 2648-2649 A1267 | Set of 2 | 7.00 6.50 |

Argentine Natural
History Museum,
Bicent. — A1268

Museum emblem and: No. 2650, 2.50p, Skeleton of Dahlia the Elephant. No. 2651, 2.50p, Skull of Bonatitan reigi (dinosaur). No. 2652, 2.50p, Agrias narcissus butterflies, horiz. No. 2653, 2.50p, Display in Hall of Birds, horiz.

| Perf. 13½x13¾, 13¾x13½ | | |
|---|---|---|
| 2012, Apr. 28 | | |
| 2650-2653 A1268 | Set of 4 | 6.50 5.50 |

# ARGENTINA

Intl. Year of Cooperatives A1269

**2012, June 16**    Perf. 13¾x13½
2654 A1269 2.50p multi    1.60 1.40

Passage of Sáenz Peña Universal Male Suffrage Law, Cent. — A1270

**2012, June 16**    Perf. 13½x13¾
2655 A1270 2.50p multi    1.60 1.40

Paintings of Historical Events of 1812 — A1271

Painting of: No. 2656, 2.50p, Jujuy Exodus, by unknown artist. No. 2657, 2.50p, Battle of Tucuman, by Tomas del Villar.

**2012, June 16**    Perf. 13¾x13½
2656-2657 A1271 Set of 2    4.00 3.50

Argentine School of Military Aviation, Cent. — A1272

**2012, July 21**    Perf. 14x13½
2658 A1272 2.75p multi    1.75 1.50

Operation Southern Cross for Naval Assistance in Antarctica A1273

**2012, July 21**    Perf. 13¾x13½
2659 A1273 5p multi    3.00 2.75

### Souvenir Sheet

Eva Perón (1919-52)    A1274

**2012, Sept. 1**    Perf. 14
2660 A1274 10p multi    5.75 5.50

Alzheimer's Disease Awareness — A1275

**2012, Sept. 15**    Perf. 13½x13¾
2661 A1275 3p multi    1.90 1.75

Festivals — A1276

Designs: No. 2662, 3p, National Artisans Festival, Colón. No. 2663, 3p, Maní National Festival, Hernando. No. 2664, 3p, National Orange Festival, Bella Vista. No. 2665, 3p, National Calf Festival and Branding Day, Ayacucho.

**2012, Sept. 25**
2662-2665 A1276 Set of 4    7.50 6.50

General San Martín Mounted Grenadiers Regiment, 200th Anniv. — A1277

**2012, Oct. 13**    Perf. 13¾x13½
2666 A1277 3p multi    1.90 1.60

Christmas — A1278

**2012, Nov. 17**    Perf. 13½x13¾
2667 A1278 3p multi    1.90 1.60

### Miniature Sheet

Bats A1279

No. 2668: a, Sturnira lilium in flight. b, Sturnira lilium hanging and close-up of head. c, Histiotus laephotis. d, Histiotus montanus. e, Chrotopterus auritus in flight. f, Head of Chrotopterus auritus. g, Head of Noctilio leporinus. h, Noctilio leporinus in flight.

**2012, Dec. 22**    Perf. 13¾x13½
2668 A1279 3p Sheet of 8, #a-h    15.00 13.00

Battle of Salta, 200th Anniv. A1280

**2013, Feb. 23**    Perf. 14x13½
2669 A1280 3.50p multi    2.25 1.90

### Archaeological Artifacts Type of 2000

Designs: 30p, Ceremonial hatchet, Tehuelche culture. 40p, Basket with handle, Selk'nam culture. 50p, Basket with handle and lid, Wichi culture.

**Perf. 13½x13¾ Syncopated**
**2013, Mar. 1**
2670 A973 30p multi    22.00 22.00
2671 A973 40p multi    22.00 22.00
2672 A973 50p multi    22.00 22.00
Nos. 2670-2672 (3)    66.00 66.00

General Constituent Assembly of 1813, 200th Anniv. — A1281

**2013, Mar. 9**    Perf. 13½x13¾
2673 A1281 3.50p multi    2.25 2.00

Festivals A1282

Designs: No. 2674, 3.50p, National Folklore Festival, Cosquín. No. 2675, 3.50p, National Trout Festival, Junín de los Andes. No. 2676, 3.50p, National Lemon Festival, Tafí Viejo, vert. No. 2677, 3.50p, National Petroleum Festival, Comodoro Rivadavia, vert.

**Perf. 13¾x13½, 13½x13¾**
**2013, Mar. 23**
2674-2677 A1282 Set of 4    8.00 7.00

### Landmarks Type of 2004

Designs: 3.50p, Cancha de Bochas, Ischigualasto National Park. 30p, Hill of Seven Colors, Jujuy.

**Perf. 13¾x13½ Syncopated**
**2013, Mar.**
2678 A1063a 3.50p multi    1.75 1.75
2679 A1063a 30p multi    15.50 15.00

### Souvenir Sheet

Partido de Esteban Echeverría Area of Buenos Aires, Cent. — A1283

No. 2680: a, Door on building built in 1789. b, Plaza and flags, horiz.

**2013, Apr. 13**    Perf. 14
2680 A1283 Sheet of 2    4.75 4.25
   a.-b.    5p Either single    2.25 2.10

National University of Córdoba, 400th Anniv. — A1284

**2013, Apr. 27**    Perf. 14x13½
2681 A1284 3.50p multi    2.00 1.75

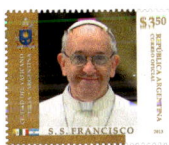

Election of Pope Francis A1285

No. 2682 — Arms of Pope Francis and: a, Pope Francis, flags of Vatican City, Italy and Argentina. b, Pope Francis in profile, flags of Vatican City and Argentina. c, Pope Francis waving, flags of Vatican City and Argentina. d, Pope Francis holding cross, flags of Vatican City and Argentina.

**2013, May 2**    Perf. 13¾x13½
2682    Vert. strip of 4    16.00 15.00
   a.-b.    A1285 3.50p Either single    1.50 1.50
   c.    A1285 10p multi    4.25 4.25
   d.    A1285 14p multi    6.00 6.00

See Italy No. 3179, Vatican City Nos. 1523-1526.

African Union, 50th Anniv. — A1286

**2013, June 1**    Litho.    Perf. 13½x13¾
2683 A1286 4p multi    1.75 1.50

Villa Carlos Paz, Cent. — A1287

**2013, July 27**    Litho.    Perf. 13¾x13½
2684 A1287 4p multi    1.75 1.50

### Souvenir Sheet

125th Session of the International Olympic Committee, Buenos Aires — A1288

No. 2685: a, Runners, Pierre de Coubertin (1863-1937), founder of Intl. Olympic Committee (60x30mm). b, Gymnast, flag of Argentina, Floralis Generica, sculpture by Eduardo Catalano (60x40mm).

**2013, Sept. 14**    Litho.    Perf. 14
2685 A1288 5p Sheet of 2, #a-b    4.50 4.00

Birds — A1289

Designs: No. 2686, 4p, Furnarius rufus. No. 2687, 4p, Podiceps gallardoi. No. 2688, 4p, Campephilus magellanicus, vert. No. 2689, 4p, Gubernatrix cristata, vert.

**Perf. 13¾x13½, 13½x13¾**
**2013, Oct. 19**    Litho.
2686-2689 A1289 Set of 4    7.50 6.50

A1290

A1291

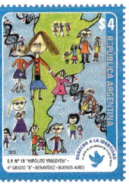

A1292

# ARGENTINA

Winning Designs in "Right to Identity" Children's Art Contest — A1293

**2013, Oct. 22    Litho.    Perf. 13¾x13½**
2690  A1290  4p multi         1.60  1.40
2691  A1291  4p multi         1.60  1.40
**Perf. 13½x13¾**
2692  A1292  4p multi         1.60  1.40
2693  A1293  4p multi         1.60  1.40
  Nos. 2690-2693 (4)          6.40  5.60

Sergeant Juan Bautista Cabral (c. 1789-1813), Hero in Battle of San Lorenzo — A1294

San Martín Regiment of Mounted Grenadiers in Battle of San Lorenzo — A1295

**2013, Nov. 9    Litho.    Perf. 13½x13¾**
2694  A1294  4p multi         1.60  1.40
**Perf. 14x13½**
2695  A1295  4p multi         1.60  1.40
  Battle of San Lorenzo, 200th anniv.

Campaign Against Discrimination — A1296

No. 2696 — Stylized people with joined hands and background color of: a, 4p, White. b, 13p, Black.

**2013, Nov. 9    Litho.    Perf. 13½x13¾**
2696  A1296  Horiz. pair, #a-b    6.25  5.75
  America Issue.

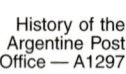 

History of the Argentine Post Office — A1297

No. 2697: a, Queen Juana of Castile, coat of arms, postal runner, map of Peru (opening of first post office in Lima, Peru, 1514) (30x30mm). b, Manuel Belgrano, Mariano Moreno, Cabildo, Buenos Aires (Post Office of the May Revolution, 1810) (30x40mm). c, President Juan Perón, and his wife, Eva (creation of Post Office and Telecommunications Secretariat, 1949) (30x40mm). d, Mail box, postal workers, flag of Argentina (renationalization of Postal Service, 10th anniv., 2013) (30x40mm). e, Pres. Nelson Kirchner, people with flags, mail boxes (renationalization of Postal Service, 2003) (63mm diameter).

**Litho., Litho. With Foil Application (10p)**
**2013, Nov. 19         Perf. 14**
2697  Miniature sheet of 5    11.00  9.75
  a.-d. A1297 5p Any single    1.75  1.60
  e.    A1297 10p multi        3.50  3.25

## Souvenir Sheet

Brasiliana 2013 Intl. Philatelic Exhibition, Rio de Janeiro — A1298

No. 2698: a, 4p, Dolichandra unguis-cati. b, 13p, Alouatta guariba, vert.

**2013, Nov. 23    Litho.    Perf. 14**
2698  A1298  Sheet of 2, #a-b    6.00  5.50

Argentine National Anthem, 200th Anniv. — A1299

**Perf. 13½x13¾**
**2013, Nov. 30         Litho.**
2699  A1299  4p multi          1.50  1.25

Christmas — A1300

**Perf. 13½x13¾**
**2013, Nov. 30         Litho.**
2700  A1300  4p multi          1.50  1.25

New Laws, Policies, and Regulations Affecting Argentina Society — A1301

Designs; 25c, New national idenification cards (resolution 1800/09). 50c, Marriage equality (law 26,618). 1p, Soccer balls (free television broadcasts of local soccer games). 2p, Airplane, oil well, envelope and mail box (nationalization of industries). 5p, Flasks and chemical symbols (law 26,421 establishing program to support Network of Argentinian Researchers and Scientists Abroad). 10p, Family, hands, roof (establishment of Pro.Cre.Ar. loan program). 30p, End of Impunity laws and reopening of criminal trials of Argentina's military dictatorship (law 25,779). 40p, Mandatory open primary elections with obligatory voting. 50p, Open digital television.

**Perf. 13½x13¾ Syncopated**
**2014, Jan. 20         Litho.**
2701  A1301  25c multi      .35  .35
2702  A1301  50c multi      .35  .35
2703  A1301  1p multi       .35  .35
2704  A1301  2p multi       .55  .55
2705  A1301  5p multi      1.40  .90
2706  A1301  10p multi     2.75 1.90
2707  A1301  30p multi     8.50 5.75
2708  A1301  40p multi    11.00 7.50
2709  A1301  50p multi    14.00 9.00
  Nos. 2701-2709 (9)       39.25 26.65

New Laws, Policies and Regulations Affecting Argentina Society — A1302

Designs: 25c, Nationalization of pension funds (law 26,425). 50c, Argentina Connected national telecommunications plan. 1p, Argentina-Bolivia pipeline integration. 2p, Latin American integration (Union of South American Nations). 3p, Creation of universities. 4p, Law regulating audiovisual communication services (law 26,522). 5p, Argentina Works Program. 6p, National Assisted Fertilization Act (law 26,862). 10p, National child allowance decrees (Decree 1602/09). 30p, Suffrage for 16-year-olds (law 26,774). 50p, Restructuring of national debt.

**Perf. 13½x13¾ Syncopated**
**2014         Litho.**
2710  A1302  25c multi      .35  .25
2711  A1302  50c multi      .35  .25
2712  A1302  1p multi       .35  .25
2713  A1302  2p multi       .55  .30
2714  A1302  3p multi       .80  .40
2715  A1302  4p multi      1.10  .50
2716  A1302  5p multi      1.40  .60
2717  A1302  6p multi      1.60  .75
2718  A1302  10p multi     2.75 1.25
2719  A1302  30p multi     8.00 3.75
2719A A1302  50p multi    13.00 12.00
  Nos. 2710-2719A (11)     30.25 20.30
  Issued: No. 2710-2719, 1/20; 50p, 8/25.

Jorge A. Newbery (1875-1914), Pilot, Airplane and Hot Air Balloon A1303

**2014, Mar. 5  Litho.  Perf. 13¾x13½**
2720  A1303  4.50p multi       1.50  1.25

Hugo Chávez (1954-2013), President of Venezuela A1304

Chávez: No. 2721, 10p, Waving, wearing presidential sash. No. 2722, 10p, Holding map of South America.

**2014, Mar. 5  Litho.  Perf. 13¾x13½**
2721-2722  A1304  Set of 2    5.75  5.25
  America Issue.

Argentine Presence in the Antarctic, 110th Anniv. — A1305

No. 2724 — Latin American Antarctic Progam Administrators emblem and: a, Scientific researcher and penguin (30x60mm). b, Plesiosaurs (60x30mm).

**Perf. 13¾x13½**
**2014, Mar. 25         Litho.**
2723  A1305  4.50p shown      1.50  1.25

### Souvenir Sheet
**Perf. 14**
2724  Sheet of 2              3.25  3.00
  a.-b. A1305 6p Either single  1.50  1.50

25th reunion of Latin American Antarctic Program Administrators, Buenos Aires (No. 2724).

Flora and Fauna of Iguazu Falls Area — A1306

No. 2725: a, Doxocopa linda mileta (40x40mm). b, Billbergia zebrina (30x40mm). c, Iguazu Falls and Toco toucan (70x40mm). d, Iguazu Falls (90x30mm).

**Litho. & Silk-Screened**
**2014, Apr. 14         Perf. 14**
2725  Miniature sheet of 4   9.75  9.00
  a.-b. A1306 8p Either single  2.00  2.00
  c.-d. A1306 10p Either single 2.50  2.50

## Souvenir Sheet

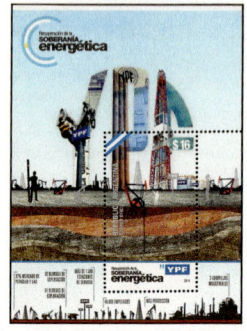

Renationalization of YPF Energy Company — A1307

**2014, May 5    Litho.    Perf. 14**
2726  A1307  16p multi        4.25  4.00

Battle of Montevideo, 200th Anniv. — A1308

**2014, May 19   Litho.   Perf. 14x13½**
2727  A1308  4.50p multi      1.40  1.10

National University of Tucuman, Cent. — A1309

**2014, May 26   Litho.   Perf. 14x13½**
2728  A1309  4.50p multi      1.40  1.10

2014 World Cup Soccer Championships, Brazil — A1310

No. 2729 — Shirts and schedules of Group F teams: a, Argentina. b, Bosnia & Herzegovina. c, Iran. d, Nigeria.

**2014, May 12   Litho.   Perf. 13½x13¾**
2729  Horiz. strip of 4      33.00 32.00
  a.-d. A1310 10p Any single  8.00  7.50

No. 2729 was quickly withdrawn from sale.

Myths and Legends — A1311

Designs: No. 2733, 10p, La Flor del Ceibo (the Ceibo flower). No. 2734, 10p, El Viento Zonda (the Zonda wind).

**Perf. 13½x13¾**
**2014, June 30         Litho.**
2733-2734  A1311  Set of 2    5.50  5.00
  America Issue.

# ARGENTINA

El Enterriano, by Eleodoro Ergasto Marenco (1914-96) — A1312

**2014, July 14 Litho. Perf. 13½x13¾**
2735 A1312 5p multi 1.50 1.25

Commercial Aircraft — A1313

Designs: No. 2736, 5p, Comet IV. No. 2737, 5p, Boeing 747-200. No. 2738, 5p, Boeing 737-800NG. No. 2739, 5p, Airbus 340-300.

**2014, July 21 Litho. Perf. 14x13½**
2736-2739 A1313 Set of 4 6.00 5.00

### Souvenir Sheet

Control of Aerolíneas Argentinas by Argentine Government, 6th Anniv. — A1314

### Litho. & Silk-Screened
**2014, July 21 Perf. 14**
2740 A1314 20p multi 5.25 5.00

### Souvenir Sheet

PhilaKorea 2014 Intl. Philatelic Exhibition, Seoul — A1315

No. 2741: a, Bird in flight (29mm diameter). b, Three birds (38mm diameter).

### Litho. & Silk-Screened With Foil Application
**2014, Aug. 11 Perf.**
2741 A1315 15p Sheet of 2, #a-b 7.50 7.25

Luis Alberto Spinetta (1950-2012), Rock Musician — A1316

**Perf. 13½x13¾**
**2014, Sept. 22 Litho.**
2742 A1316 10p multi 2.60 2.40

Monument to the Army of the Andes, Cent. — A1317

**Perf. 13½x13¾**
**2014, Sept. 25 Litho.**
2743 A1317 5p multi 1.50 1.25

Festivals — A1318

Designs: No. 2744, 5p, Cuevas de las Manos Festival, Perito Moreno. No. 2745, 5p, National Mate Festival, Paraná. No. 2746, 5p, 70th National Agriculture Festival, Esperanza. No. 2747, 5p, National Steam Train Festival, El Maitén.

**Perf. 13½x13¾**
**2014, Sept. 29 Litho.**
2744-2747 A1318 Set of 4 5.75 4.75

### Souvenir Sheet

1813 Coins of the United Provinces of the River Plate — A1319

No. 2748: a, Gold 8-escudo and silver 8-real coins. b, Silver coins, horiz.

**2014, Oct. 14 Litho. Perf. 14**
2748 A1319 6p Sheet of 2, #a-b 3.50 3.00

Julio Cortázar (1914-84), Writer — A1320

Prize-winning art in Cortázar stamp design contest by: No. 2749, 5p, Gastón Martino. No. 2750, 5p, José Rivadulla. No. 2751, 5p, Lucía Valentina Piuzzi, vert. No. 2752, 5p, Ana Gauna, vert.

**Perf. 13¾x13½, 13½x13¾**
**2014, Oct. 20 Litho.**
2749-2752 A1320 Set of 4 5.75 4.75

Non-Direct Blood Transfusions by Dr. Luis Agote, Cent. — A1321

**2014, Nov. 10 Litho. Perf. 14x13½**
2753 A1321 5p multi 1.50 1.25

Nativity, by Raúl Soldi (1905-94) — A1322

**Perf. 13½x13¾**
**2014, Nov. 21 Litho.**
2754 A1322 10p multi 2.60 2.40

Christmas. See Vatican City No. 1581.

Movie Stars — A1323

Designs: No. 2755, 5p, Tita Merello (1904-2002), actress. No. 2756, 5p, Alfredo Alcón (1930-2014), actor.

**Perf. 13½x13¾**
**2014, Nov. 25 Litho.**
2755-2756 A1323 Set of 2 2.90 2.40

Mar del Plata Intl. Film Festival, 60th anniv.

Nelson Mandela (1918-2013), President of South Africa — A1324

**Perf. 13¾x13½**
**2014, Dec. 15 Litho.**
2757 A1324 10p multi 2.60 2.40

Antarctopelta Oliveroi A1325

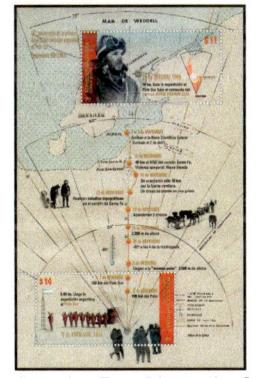

First Argentine Expedition to the South Pole, 50th Anniv. — A1326

No. 2759: a, 11p, Map and Col. Jorge Edgard Leal, expedition leader. b, 14p, Expedition members saluting flag of Argentina.

**2015, Mar. 9 Litho. Perf. 13¾x13½**
2758 A1325 6p multi 1.60 1.40

### Souvenir Sheet
**Perf. 14**
2759 A1326 Sheet of 2, #a-b 6.00 5.75

Argentine exploration and science projects in Antarctica.

Festivals — A1327

Designs: No. 2760, 6p, National Festival of the Longest Night, Ushuaia. No. 2761, 6p, National Drum Festival, Frías. No. 2762, 6p, National Chocolate Festival, Bariloche. No. 2763, 6p, National Cotton Festival, Presidencia Roque Sáenz Peña.

**2015, Apr. 27 Litho. Perf. 13½x13¾**
2760-2763 A1327 Set of 4 6.50 5.50

### Miniature Sheet

Trees A1328

No. 2764: a, Handroanthus impetiginosus. b, Araucaria araucana. c, Salix humboldtiana. d, Cercidium praecox.

**2015, Apr. 27 Litho. Perf. 13½x13¾**
2764 A1328 6p Sheet of 4, #a-d 6.50 5.50

### Souvenir Sheet

Exterior of Néstor Kirchner Cultural Center, Buenos Aires A1329

**2015, May 26 Litho. Perf. 14**
2765 A1329 20p multi + 6 labels 4.75 4.50

Free Peoples Congress, 200th Anniv. — A1330

**Perf. 13½x13¾**
**2015, June 29 Litho.**
2766 A1330 10p multi 2.50 2.25

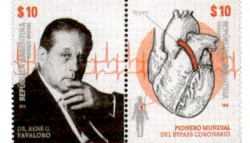

A1331

No. 2767: a, Dr. René G. Favaloro (1923-2000), cardiac surgeon. b, Heart with bypass pioneered by Dr. Favaloro.

**2015, July 13 Litho. Perf. 13½x13¾**
2767 A1331 10p Horiz. pair, #a-b 5.00 4.50

International Telecommunication Union, 150th Anniv. — A1332

**2015, Aug. 21 Litho. Perf. 14x13½**
2768 A1332 10p multi 2.50 2.25

United Nations, 70th Anniv. — A1333

**Perf. 13¾x13½**
**2015, Aug. 31 Litho.**
2769 A1333 10p multi 2.50 2.25

# ARGENTINA

### Souvenir Sheet

Interior of Nestor Kirchner Cultural Center, Buenos Aires — A1334

**2015, Sept. 14**  Litho.  Perf. 14
2770  A1334  20p multi + 9 labels  4.50  4.25

### Miniature Sheet

Birds — A1335

No. 2771: a, Ramphastos dicolorus. b, Ramphastos toco. c, Pteroglossus bailloni. d, Selenidera maculirostris.

Perf. 13¾x13½
**2015, Sept. 22**  Litho.
2771  A1335  7p Sheet of 4, #a-d  7.00  6.00

### Miniature Sheet

Mammals — A1336

No. 2772: a, Lama pacos. b, Lama guanicoe. c, Vicugna vicugna. d, Lama glama.

Perf. 13¾x13½
**2015, Sept. 22**  Litho.
2772  A1336  7p Sheet of 4, #a-d  7.00  6.00

A1337

A1338

A1339

A1340

Gustavo Cerati (1959-2014), Rock Musician — A1341

**2015, Oct. 9**  Litho.  Perf. 13¾x13½
2773  A1337  7p multi  1.75  1.50
2774  Horiz. strip of 4  9.50  8.50
  a. A1338 10p multi  2.10  2.10
  b. A1339 10p multi  2.10  2.10
  c. A1340 10p multi  2.10  2.10
  d. A1341 10p multi  2.10  2.10

### Souvenir Sheet

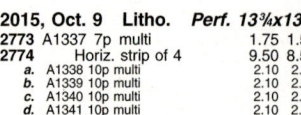

Ciudad Evita A1342

No. 2775: a, Man and house. b, Apartment complex.

Litho. (Sheet Margin Litho. & Embossed)
**2015, Oct. 13**  Perf. 14
2775  A1342  25p Sheet of 2, #a-b  11.00  10.50

Christmas — A1343

**2015, Nov. 2**  Litho.  Perf. 13½x13¾
2776  A1343  10p multi  2.40  2.10

### Souvenir Sheet

Pres. Juan D. Perón (1895-1974) — A1344

**2015, Nov. 17**  Litho.  Perf. 14
2777  A1344  29p multi  6.25  6.00

2015 Inauguration of Pres. Mauricio Macri — A1345

**2016, May 9**  Litho.  Perf. 13½x14
2778  A1345  8p multi  1.75  1.25

Campaign Against Human Trafficking — A1346

No. 2779 — Inscription starting with: a, "Yo le digo. . ." b, "Explotación. . ."

**2016, May 23**  Litho.  Perf. 13½x13¾
2779  A1346  8p Horiz. pair, #a-b  3.25  2.75
America Issue.

Argentine Naval Aviation, Cent. — A1347

**2016, June 6**  Litho.  Perf. 14x13½
2780  A1347  10p multi  2.10  1.75

Rubén Darío (1867-1916), Poet — A1348

Perf. 13¾x13½
**2016, June 10**  Litho.
2781  A1348  20p multi  4.00  3.50

Independence, 200th Anniv. — A1349

Perf. 13½x13¾ Syncopated
**2016, June 27**  Litho.
2782  A1349  10p multi  2.10  1.75

Open Cabildo of Buenos Aires of May 25, 1810 A1350

Battle of Tucumán and Members of the Second Triumvirate, 1812 — A1351

Argentine Declaration of Independence, 200th Anniv. — A1352

**2016, July 7**  Litho.  Perf. 14
2783  Sheet of 3  7.00  6.50
  a. A1350 10p multi  2.00  1.90
  b. A1351 10p multi  2.00  1.90
  c. A1352 10p multi  2.00  1.90
Road to Argentine Independence.

A1353

Coats of Arms — A1354

No. 2784 — Arms of: a, Argentina. b, Corrientes Province. c, Chaco Province. d, Formosa Province. e, Misiones Province. f, Catamarca Province. g, Jujuy Province. h, La Rioja Province. i, Salta Province. j, Santiago del Estero Province. k, Tucumán Province. l, Mendoza Province. m, San Juan Province. n, San Luis Province. o, Autonomous City of Buenos Aires. p, Buenos Aires Province. q, Córdoba Province. r, Entre Ríos Province. s, La Pampa Province. t, Santa Fe Province. u, Chubut Province. v, Neuquén Province. w, Río Negro Province. x, Santa Cruz Province. y, Tierra del Fuego, Antarctica and Southern Atlantic Islands Province.

**2016, July 7**  Litho.  Perf. 14
2784  Sheet of 25  50.00  45.00
  a. A1353 10p multi  2.00  2.00
  b.-y. A1354 10p Any single  2.00  2.00
  z. Booklet pane of 25, #2784a-2784y  —  —
  Complete booklet, #2784z

### Souvenir Sheet

July 9, 1816, Bas-relief by Lola Mora — A1355

No. 2785: a, Deputies at Congress of Tucumán, facing right. b, Three deputies, facing left, behind table.

**2016, July 7**  Litho.  Perf. 14
2785  A1355  10p Sheet of 2, #a-b, + label  4.25  3.50

Fruits — A1356

Designs: 1p, Prunus persica. 2p, Malus domestica. 5p, Citrus limon. 8p, Prunus salicina. 10p, Prunus avium. 30p, Vitis vinifera. 35p, Vaccinum spp. 40p, Pyrus communis. 50p, Citrus sinensis. 100p, Citrullus lanatus.

Perf. 13½x13¾ Syncopated
2016-19  Litho.
2786  A1356  1p multi  .30  .30
2787  A1356  2p multi  .30  .30
2788  A1356  5p multi  .85  .85
2789  A1356  8p multi  1.35  1.25
2790  A1356  10p multi  1.75  1.60
2791  A1356  30p multi  5.00  4.75
2791A A1356  35p sil & multi  2.25  2.10
2792  A1356  40p multi  7.00  6.50
2793  A1356  50p multi  8.25  8.00
2794  A1356  100p multi  16.50  16.00
  Nos. 2786-2794 (10)  43.55  41.65

Issued: 1p, 2p, 5p, 7/22; 8p, 10p, 30p, 100p, 8/4; 40p, 50p, 7/26; 35p, 2019.

Vegetables — A1357

Designs: 1p, Daucus carota. 2p, Cynara cardunculus. 3p, Zea mays. 4p, Lycopersicum esculentum. 5p, Asparagus officinalis. 8p, Solanum melongena. 10p, Solanum tuberosum. 30p, Capsicum annuum. 35p, Brasica oleracea var. Itálica. 50p, Cucurbita maxima. 100p, Allium cepa.

*Perf. 13½x13¾ Syncopated*

**2016-19** **Litho.**

| | | | | | |
|---|---|---|---|---|---|
| **2795** | A1357 | 1p | multi | .35 | .30 |
| **2796** | A1357 | 2p | multi | .35 | .30 |
| **2797** | A1357 | 3p | multi | .50 | .45 |
| **2798** | A1357 | 4p | multi | .70 | .65 |
| **2799** | A1357 | 5p | multi | .90 | .85 |
| **2800** | A1357 | 8p | multi | 1.50 | 1.25 |
| **2801** | A1357 | 10p | multi | 1.80 | 1.60 |
| **2802** | A1357 | 30p | multi | 5.25 | 4.75 |
| **2802A** | A1357 | 35p | sil & multi | 2.25 | 2.10 |
| **2803** | A1357 | 50p | multi | 8.75 | 8.25 |
| **2804** | A1357 | 100p | multi | 17.50 | 16.00 |
| | *Nos. 2795-2804 (11)* | | | 39.85 | 36.50 |

Issued: 1p, 4p, 8p, 50p, 100p, 8/4; 2p, 3p, 7/22; 5p, 10p, 30p, 7/26; 35p, 2019.

Miniature Sheet

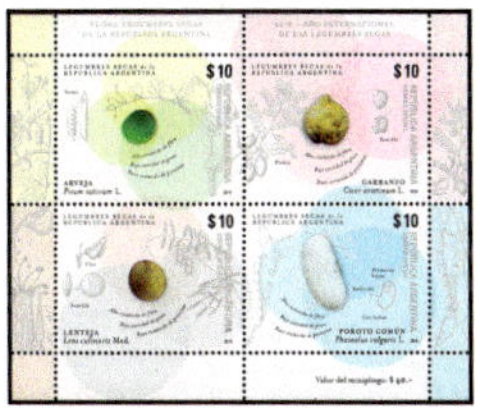


International Year of Pulses — A1358

No. 2805: a, Pisum sativum. b, Cicer arietinum. c, Lens culinaris. d, Phaseolus vulgaris.

*Perf. 13¾x13½*

**2016, Aug. 16** **Litho.**

**2805** A1358 10p Sheet of 4, #a-d 7.25 6.25

Miniature Sheet

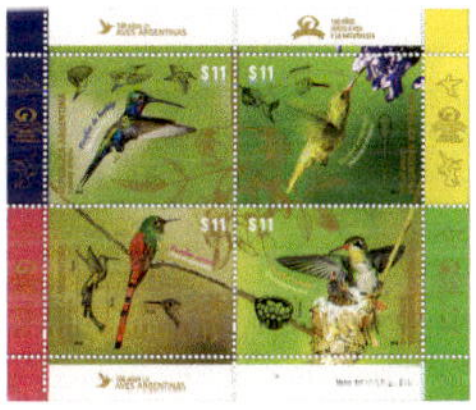

Aves Argentina, Cent. — A1359

No. 2806: a, Heliomaster furcifer. b, Hylocharis chrysura. c, Sappho sparganura. d, Chlorostilbon lucidus.

*Perf. 13¾x13½*

**2016, Sept. 19** **Litho.**

**2806** A1359 11p Sheet of 4, #a-d 8.00 7.00

Souvenir Sheet

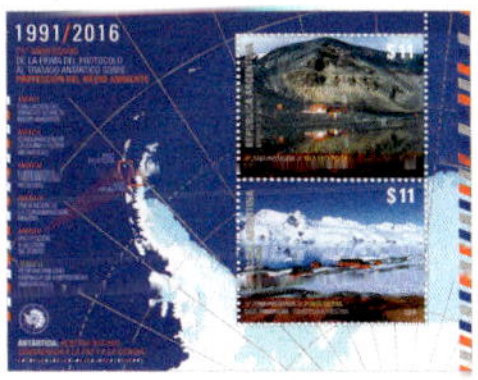


Signing of the Protocol to the Antarctic Treaty on Environmental Protection, 25th Anniv. — A1360

No. 2807: a, Base Decepción. b, Base Primavera.

**2016, Oct. 4** **Litho.** ***Perf. 14***

**2807** A1360 11p Sheet of 2, #a-b 4.00 3.50

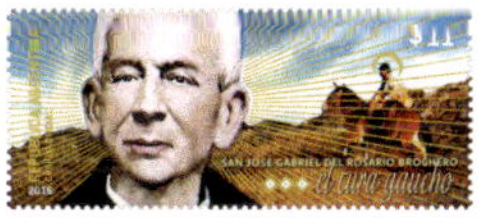

Canonization of St. José Gabriel del Rosario Brochero (1840-1914) — A1361

**2016, Oct. 17** **Litho.** ***Perf. 14x13½***

**2808** A1361 11p gold & multi 2.00 1.60

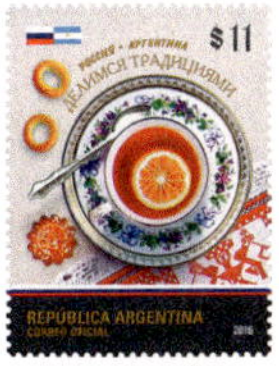


Russian Tea and Tea Service A1362

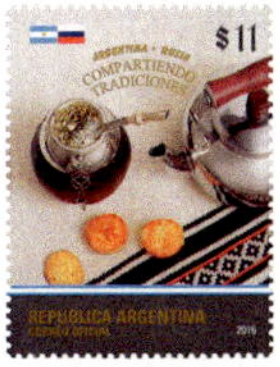


Argentinian Mate and Mate Service A1363

*Perf. 13½x13¾*

**2016, Nov. 14** **Litho.**

| | | | | | |
|---|---|---|---|---|---|
| **2809** | A1362 | 11p | gold & multi | 6.25 | 6.00 |
| **2810** | A1363 | 11p | gold & multi | 6.25 | 6.00 |

See Russia No. 7784.

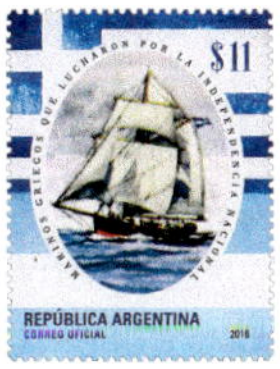


Sloop Nuestra Señora del Carmen, Flags of Greece and Argentina — A1364

**2016, Dec. 5** **Litho.** ***Perf. 13½x13¾***

**2811** A1364 11p multi 2.00 1.60

Remembrance of Greek soldiers who fought for independence for Argentina.

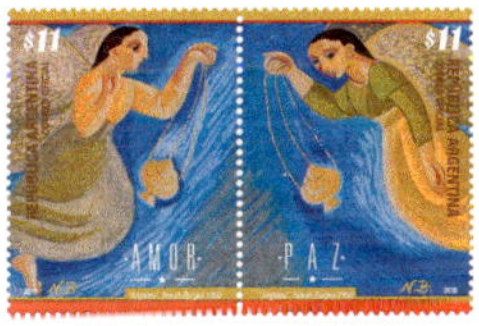


Christmas — A1365

No. 2812 — Angels, by Norah Borges: a, Angel facing right. b, Angel facing left.

*Perf. 13½x13¾*

**2016, Dec. 13** **Litho.**

**2812** A1365 11p Horiz. pair, #a-b 4.00 3.50

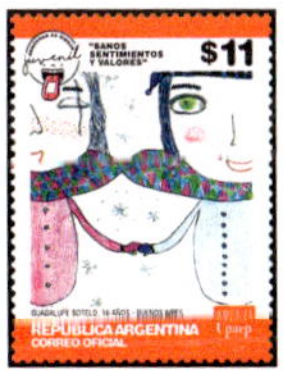


Winning Designs in Children's "Healthy Feelings and Values" Art Contest — A1366

Art by: No. 2813, 11p, Guadalupe Sotelo. No. 2814, 11p, Victoria Figueroa Fernández. No. 2815, 11p, Morena Gianella Oliva, horiz.

*Perf. 13½x13¾, 13¾x13½*

**2016, Dec. 19** **Litho.**

**2813-2815** A1366 Set of 3 6.00 5.25

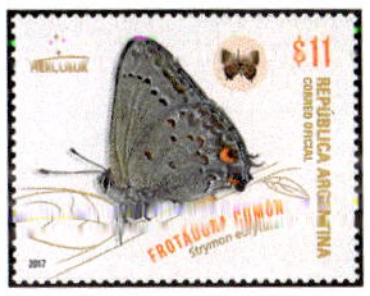


Butterflies A1367

Designs: 11p, Strymon eurytulus. 55p, Morpho epistrophus argentinus.

**2017, Jan. 23** **Litho.** ***Perf. 13¾x13½***

**2816-2817** A1367 Set of 2 10.50 10.00

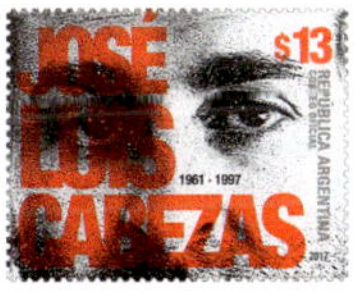


José Luis Cabezas (1961-97), Murdered Photojournalist A1368

**2017, May 9** **Litho.** ***Perf. 13¾x13½***

**2818** A1368 13p multi 2.40 2.10

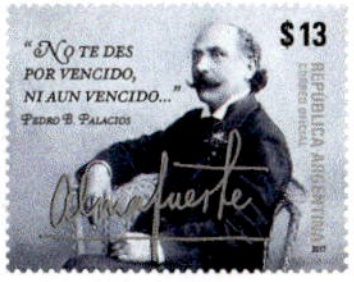


Pedro Bonifacio Palacios (1854-1917), Poet — A1369

**2017, May 15** **Litho.** ***Perf. 13¾x13½***

**2819** A1369 13p multi 2.40 2.10

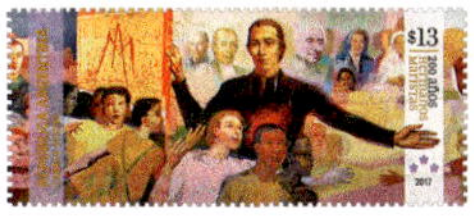


Marist Brothers, 200th Anniv. A1370

**2017, May 22** **Litho.** ***Perf. 14x13½***

**2820** A1370 13p multi 2.40 2.10

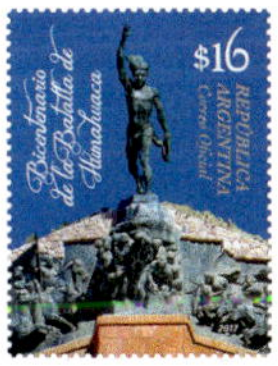


Battle of Humahuaca, 200th Anniv. — A1371

*Perf. 13½x13¾*

**2017, June 26** **Litho.**

**2821** A1371 16p multi 2.75 2.50

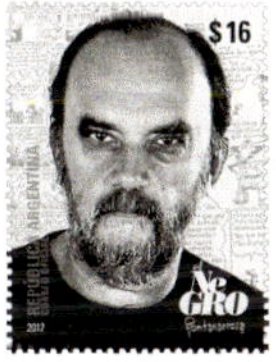


Roberto Fontanarrosa (1944-2007), Cartoonist — A1372

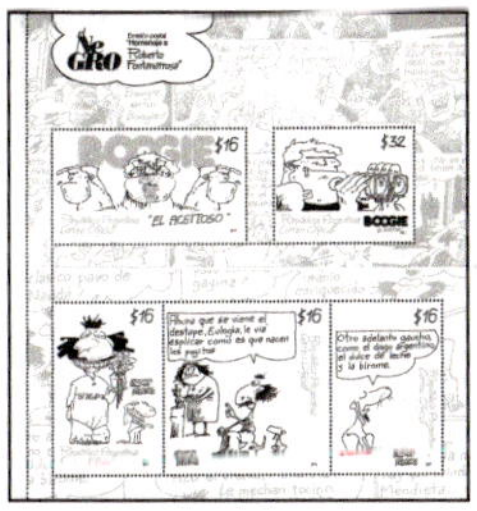


A1373

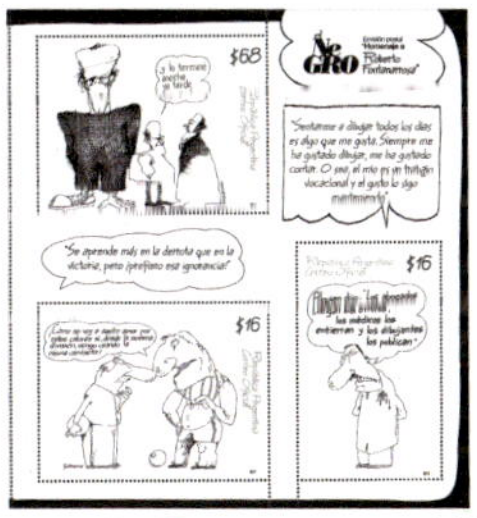


Cartoons by Fontanarrosa — A1374

No. 2823: a, Front and profile views of Boogie (70x40mm). b, Dog with Inodoro Pereyra holding flowers (40x60mm). c, Inodoro Pereyra talking with Eulogia (60x60mm). d, Dog of Inodoro Pereyra speaking (40x60mm). e, Boogie holding binoculars (50x40mm).

No. 2824: a, Man holding ball talking to soccer player (80x60mm). b, Man with pens in shirt pocket talking (50x80mm). c, Creator of Frankenstein monster talking to another man (80x60mm).

**2017, July 31** **Litho.** ***Perf. 13½x13¾***

**2822** A1372 16p multi 2.90 2.50

**Booklet Stamps**

***Perf. 14***

| | | | | | |
|---|---|---|---|---|---|
| **2823** | A1373 | Booklet pane of 5 | | 21.00 | — |
| *a.-d.* | | 16p Any single | | 3.50 | 3.50 |
| *e.* | | 32p black & silver | | 6.75 | 6.75 |
| **2824** | A1374 | Booklet pane of 3 | | 23.00 | — |
| *a.-b.* | | 16p Either single | | 3.50 | 3.50 |
| *c.* | | 68p black & silver | | 15.00 | 15.00 |
| | | Complete booklet | | 44.00 | |

Complete booklet contains Nos. 2823, 2824 and No. 2822 in a stamp mount and four post cards. It sold for 250p.

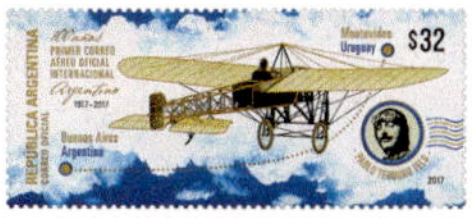


First Air Mail Flight from Buenos Aires to Montevideo, Uruguay, Cent. — A1375

**2017, Oct. 2** **Litho.** ***Perf. 14x13½***

**2825** A1375 32p multi 4.75 4.50

Souvenir Sheet

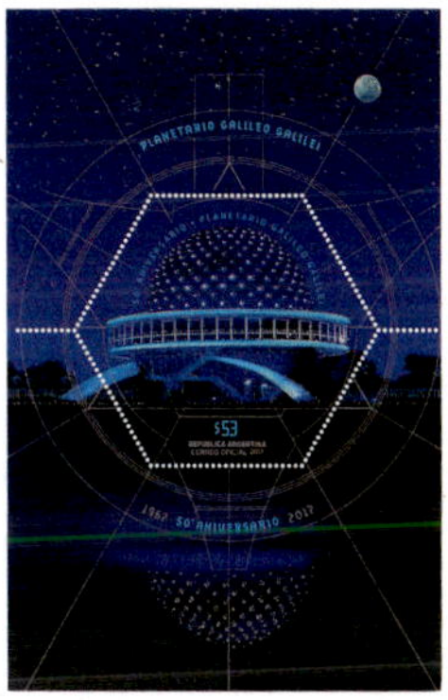


Galileo Galilei Planetarium, Buenos Aires, 50th Anniv. — A1376

**Litho. & Silk-Screened**

**2017, Oct. 31** ***Perf. 14***

**2826** A1376 53p multi 7.75 7.50

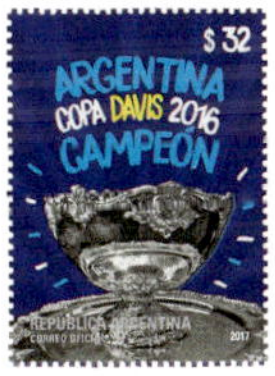


Argentina Men's Tennis Team, Winners of 2016 Davis Cup — A1377

Designs: 32p, Davis Cup. 53p, Davis Cup held by player's hands, horiz.

**2017, Nov. 6** **Litho.** ***Perf. 13½x13¾***

**2827** A1377 32p multi 4.75 4.50

**Souvenir Sheet**

***Perf. 14***

**2828** A1377 53p multi 7.75 7.50

No. 2828 contains one 40x30mm stamp.

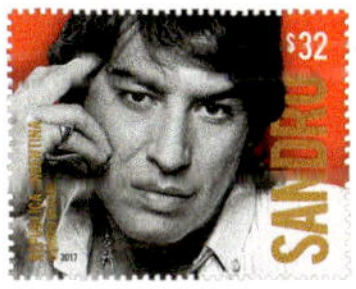


Sandro (Roberto Sánchez-Ocampo) (1945-2010), Singer — A1378

No. 2830: a, Hands of Sandro and guitar (70x40mm). b, Head of Sandro (40x50mm).

*Perf. 13¾x13½*

**2017, Nov. 21** **Litho.**

**2829** A1378 32p multi 4.75 4.50

**Souvenir Sheet**

**Litho. & Silk-Screened**

***Perf. 14***

| | | | | |
|---|---|---|---|---|
| **2830** | A1378 | Sheet of 2 | 12.50 | 12.00 |
| *a.* | | 32p multi | 4.50 | 4.50 |
| *b.* | | 53p multi | 9.50 | 7.50 |

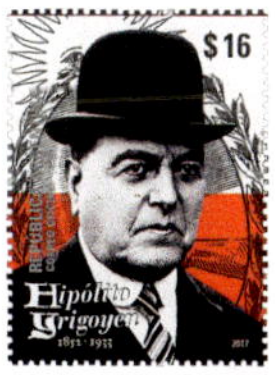


Pres. Hipólito Yrigoyen (1852-1933) A1379

*Perf. 13½x13¾*

**2017, Dec. 11** **Litho.**

**2831** A1379 16p multi 2.50 2.25

# ARGENTINA

A1380

A1381

Cartoons by Quino — A1382

No. 2833: a, Girl mailing letter (40x60mm). b, Girl walking (30x50mm).

**2017, Dec. 11**  Litho.  Perf. 14x13½
2832  A1380  32p multi  4.75  4.50

### Booklet Stamps
2833  A1381  Booklet pane of 2  13.00  —
  a.  32p black & gold  5.00  5.00
  b.  53p black & gold  7.25  7.25
2834  A1382  85p Booklet pane of 1  13.00  —
Complete booklet, #2833-2834  26.00
Christmas.

### Souvenir Sheet

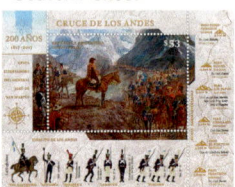
Crossing of the Andes of San Martín's Army, 200th Anniv. A1383

**2017, Dec. 26**  Litho.  Perf. 14
2835  A1383  53p multi  7.75  7.50

### Souvenir Sheet

Renewable Energy — A1384

No. 2836: a, Solar-powered building, biofuel plant, bicycle and automobile at fuel pump. b, Dam and wind generators.

**2018, Jan. 15**  Litho.  Perf. 14
2836  A1384  16p Sheet of 2, #a-b  5.00  4.50

### Souvenir Sheet

Astor Piazzolla (1921-92), Tango Composer — A1385

No. 2837: a, 45p, Piazzolla's hand on bandoneon keys. b, 75p, Piazzolla playing bandoneon.

**2018, May 8**  Litho.  Perf. 14
2837  A1385  Sheet of 2, #a-b  10.00  9.75

### Souvenir Sheet

Map of Continental Shelf Off Argentina and Antarctica — A1386

**2018, Sept. 10**  Litho.  Perf. 14
2838  A1386  120p sil & multi  8.50  8.25

National Gendarmerie, 80th Anniv. — A1387

Perf. 13½x13¾
**2018, Dec. 12**  Litho.
2839  A1387  50p multi  3.75  3.50

**Nos. 2125, 2190, 2217, 2248, 2275 and 2410-2412 Surcharged in Silver and Black**

### Methods and Perfs. As Before
**2018**
2840  A1123  2p on 75c #2411  .55  .55
2841  A973  5p on 10c #2125  1.50  1.50
2842  A1123  10p on 75c #2410  2.90  2.90
2843  A979a  25p on 10c #2217  7.00  7.00
2844  A1123  40p on 75c #2412  11.50  11.50

### Blocks of 8
2845  A1036  25p on 75c #2248  55.00  55.00
  a.-h.  Any single  7.00  7.00
2846  A1050  50p on 75c #2276  115.00  115.00
  a.-h.  Any single  14.50  14.50
2847  A1013  100p on 75c #2190  230.00  230.00
  a.-h.  Any single  29.00  29.00
Nos. 2840-2847 (8)  423.45  423.45
Placement of surcharge varies.

**Nos. 2076-2077, 2129, 2232, 2337, 2339, 2340, 2398-2401, and 2414-2415 Surcharged in Silver and Black With Added "UP" Inscription**

### Methods and Perfs. As Before
**2018**
2848  A1029  1p on 75c #2232  .40  .40
2849  A973  2p on 75c #2129  .55  .55
2850  A1116  10p on 75c #2398  2.90  2.90
2851  A1116  10p on 75c #2399  2.90  2.90
2852  A1116  10p on 75c #2400  2.90  2.90
2853  A1116  10p on 75c #2401  2.90  2.90
2853A  A943  30p on 75c #2076  9.50  9.50
2854  A943  30p on 75c #2077  8.50  8.50
2855  A1086  30p on 75c #2337  8.50  8.50
2856  A1086  30p on 75c #2339  8.50  8.50
2857  A1086  30p on 75c #2340  8.50  8.50
2858  A1125  100p on 75c #2414  29.00  29.00
2859  A1125  100p on 75c #2415  29.00  29.00
Nos. 2848-2859 (13)  114.05  114.05
Placement of surcharge varies.

A1388

Landmarks and Wildlife of Tierra del Fuego, Antarctica and South Atlantic Islands A1389

Designs: No. 2860, Les Eclaireurs Lighthouse. No. 2861, Pygoscelis papua. No. 2862, Brown Base. No. 2863, Hydrurga leptonyx.

**2019, Jan. 28**  Litho.  Perf. 13¾x13½
2860  A1388  170p multi  14.50  14.50
2861  A1388  180p multi  15.50  15.50

### Inscribed "UP" at Lower Left
2862  A1389  170p multi  14.50  14.50
2863  A1389  180p multi  15.50  15.50
Nos. 2860-2863 (4)  60.00  60.00

Eighth International Congress of the Spanish Language, Córdoba, Argentina — A1390

No. 2864: a, 35p, Spanish language books making "ñ". b, 145p, Jorge Luis Borges (1899-1986), writer.

Perf. 13½x13¾
**2019, Mar. 25**  Litho.
2864  A1390  Horiz. pair, #a-b  14.50  14.00

### Souvenir Sheet

Icebreaker A.R.A. Almirante Irízar — A1391

No. 2865: a, 40p, Icebreaker and raft (40x30mm). b, 160p, Icebreaker (40x50mm).

**2019, Apr. 29**  Litho. & Silk-Screened  Perf. 13¾
2865  A1391  Sheet of 2, #a-b  16.00  16.00

### Souvenir Sheet
Marambio Base, Antarctica, 50th Anniv. — A1392

No. 2866: a, 40p, Construction of Marambio Base in 1969, DHC-2 Beaver, Fokker F-27. b, 160p, Hercules C-130 and DHC-6 Twin Otter over Marambio Base.

**2019, Apr. 29**  Litho. & Silk-Screened  Perf. 14
2866  A1392  Sheet of 2, #a-b  16.00  16.00

Diplomatic Relations Between Argentina and Israel, 70th Anniv. — A1393

**2019, May 27**  Litho.  Perf. 13½x13¾
2867  A1393  100p gold & multi  8.00  7.50

New Year 2019 (Year of the Pig) A1394

**2019, May 27**  Litho. & Embossed  Perf.
2868  A1394  200p gold & multi  16.00  15.00

A1395

National Parks — A1396

Designs: No. 2869, Calilegua National Park. No. 2870, Los Cardones National Park. No. 2871, Río Pilcomayo National Park. No. 2872, El Palmar National Park. No. 2873, Ciervo de los Pantanos National Park. No. 2874, Talampaya National Park. No. 2875, Quebrada del Condorito National Park. No. 2876, Tierra del Fuego National Park. No. 2877, Iguazú National Park. No. 2878, Patagonia National Park. No. 2879, Nahuel Huapi National Park. No. 2880, Perito Moreno National Park. No. 2880A, Lihué Calel National Park. No. 2880B, Jaramillo Petrified Forest National Park.
No. 2881, Campos del Tuyú National Park. No. 2882, Aconquija National Park. No. 2883, El Impenetrable National Park. No. 2884, Sierra de las Quijadas National Park. No. 2885, El Rey National Park. No. 2886, El Leoncito National Park. No. 2887, Pre-Delta National Park. No. 2888, Los Glaciares National Park. No. 2889, Lanín National Park. No. 2889A, Monte León National Park. No. 2889B, Los Alerces National Park. No. 2889C, Iberá National Park. No. 2889D, Laguna Blanca National Park.

Perf. 13¾x13½ Syncopated
**2019-23**  Litho.
2869  A1395  1p multi  .40  .35
2870  A1395  2p multi  .40  .35
2871  A1395  5p multi  .40  .35
2872  A1395  10p multi  .85  .80
2873  A1395  20p multi  1.60  1.50
2874  A1395  30p multi  2.40  2.25
2875  A1395  40p multi  3.25  3.00
2876  A1395  50p multi  4.00  3.75
2877  A1395  100p multi  8.00  7.75
2878  A1395  200p multi  16.00  15.50
2879  A1395  300p multi  24.00  23.00
2880  A1395  400p multi  32.00  30.00
2880A  A1395  500p multi ('22)  8.50  8.50
2880B  A1395  1000p multi ('23)  7.75  7.75
Nos. 2869-2880B (14)  109.55  104.85

### Inscribed "UP" at Lower Left
2881  A1396  1p multi  .40  .35
2882  A1396  2p multi  .40  .35
2883  A1396  5p multi  .40  .35
2884  A1396  10p multi  .85  .80
2885  A1396  20p multi  1.60  1.50
2886  A1396  40p multi  3.25  3.00
2887  A1396  50p multi  4.00  3.75
2888  A1396  100p multi  8.00  7.50
2889  A1396  200p multi  16.00  15.50
2889A  A1396  300p multi  24.00  23.00
2889B  A1396  400p multi  32.00  30.00

# ARGENTINA 635

| | | | | |
|---|---|---|---|---|
| 2889C | A1396 500p multi ('22) | 8.50 | 8.50 | |
| 2889D | A1396 1000pmulti ('23) | 7.75 | 7.75 | |
| | Nos. 2881-2889D (13) | | 107.15 | 102.35 |

Issued: Nos. 2880A, 2889C, 5/15/22; Nos.2880B, 2889D, June 2023; others, 6/7/19. See Nos. 2913-2924.

Buses — A1397

Designs: No. 2890, 50p, Chevrolet bus used on Line 45, 1942. No. 2891, 50p, Mercedes-Benz 312 bus used on Line 159, 1961.

**2019, July 29**    Litho.    Perf. 13¾x13½
2890-2891   A1397   Set of 2   8.25   7.50

A1398

Carlos Gardel (1890-1935), Tango Singer — A1399

**Perf. 13½x13¾**
**2019, Aug. 27**    Litho.
2892   A1398   100p gold & multi   6.00   5.50

**Souvenir Sheet**
**Perf. 14**
2893   A1399   225p gold & multi   13.00   12.50

Angel Villoldo (1861-1919), Tango Musician A1400

Street Lamp and Tango Dancers A1401

Tango Ocore and Don Filatango, Mascot of 2019 International Philatelic Exhibition, Buenos Aires — A1402

Statue of Carlos Gardel (1890-1935), Tango Singer — A1403

Sign From Boedo Neighborhood, Buenos Aires — A1404

---

**Perf. 13¾x13½**
**2019, Aug. 28**    Litho.
2894   Booklet pane of 5   15.00   14.00
   a.   A1400 50p gold & multi   2.50   2.25
   b.   A1401 50p gold & multi   2.50   2.25
   c.   A1402 50p gold & multi   2.50   2.25
   d.   A1403 50p gold & multi   2.50   2.25
   e.   A1404 50p gold & multi   2.50   2.25
   Complete booklet, #2894   15.00   14.00

Tango seritage of Barracas, Caminito, San Telmo, Downtown and Boedo neighborhoods of Buenos Aires.

Mohandas K. Gandhi (1869-1948), Indian Nationalist Leader A1405

**Perf. 13¾x13½**
**2019, Sept. 30**    Litho.
2895   A1405 235p multi   13.00   13.00

**Souvenir Sheet**

Solo 1925-28 Buenos Aires-Washington D.C. Journey of A. F. Tschiffely (1895-1954) With Horses Mancha and Gato — A1406

**2019, Oct. 7**    Litho.    Perf. 13¾x14
2896   A1406 180p multi   8.50   8.00

Southern Fuegian Railway (Train at the End of the World), Ushuaia A1407

Various trains: 195p, 225p, 235p.

**2019, Oct. 15**    Litho.    Perf. 13¾x13½
2897-2899   A1407   Set of 3   30.00   30.00

Estudiantes de la Plata Soccer Team, Winners of 1968 Intercontinental Cup — A1408

**2019, Nov. 11**    Litho.    Perf. 13½x14
2900   A1408 125p multi   6.00   6.00

---

**Souvenir Sheet**

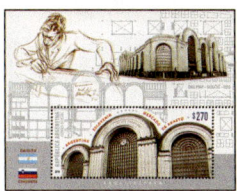

Mercado de Abasto, Buenos Aires, Designed by Viktor Sulcic (1895-1973) — A1409

**2019, Nov. 25**    Litho.    Perf. 14
2901   A1409 270p multi   12.50   12.50

Joint Issue between Argentina and Slovenia. See Slovenia No. 1365.

Loss of ARA San Juan Submarine, 2nd Anniv. — A1410

**2019, Nov. 15**    Litho.    Perf. 14x13½
2902   A1410 35p multi   1.75   1.50

La Nacion Newspaper, 150th Anniv. — A1411

**2019, Dec. 4**    Litho.    Perf. 14x13½
2903   A1411 80p multi   3.75   3.50

Christmas A1412

**2019, Dec. 9**    Litho.    Perf. 13¾x13½
2904   A1412 80p multi   3.75   3.50

A gritty substance covers parts of the vignette of No. 2904. Values are for stamps with surrounding selvage.

Transmission of Presidential Power — A1413

**2020, Oct. 8**    Litho.    Perf. 13½x13
2905   A1413 55p multi   1.60   1.40

---

**Souvenir Sheet**

Gen. Manuel Belgrano (1770-1820) — A1414

**2020, Oct. 12**    Litho.    Perf. 14
2906   A1414 125p multi   3.50   3.25

Ludwig van Beethoven (1770-1827), Composer — A1415

**2020, Oct. 26**    Litho.    Perf. 13½x13¾
2907   A1415 90p multi   2.60   2.40

New Year 2020 (Year of the Rat) — A1416

No. 2908: a, Rats, horse, dog, rooster, and dragon. b, Rats, pig and monkey. c, Rats, rabbit and snake. d, Rats, tiger and goat. e, Rats with red envelopes.
320p, Rat.

**2020, Nov. 2**    Litho.    Perf. 13¾x13½
2908   Booklet pane of 5   8.50   —
   a.-e.   A1416 55p Any single   1.60   1.60

**Souvenir Sheet**
**Litho. With Foil Application**
**Perf.**
2909   A1416 320p gold & multi   10.50   10.50

No. 2909 contains one 63mm diameter stamp.

**Souvenir Sheet**

First Raising of Argentine Flag in the Falkland Islands, 200th Anniv. — A1417

**2020, Nov. 6**    Litho.    Perf. 14
2910   A1417 90p multi   2.25   2.25

# ARGENTINA

### Souvenir Sheet

Apparition of the Virgin Mary in Catamarca Valley, 400th Anniv. — A1418

**2020, Nov. 30**    Litho.    *Perf. 14*
2911   A1418   90p multi     2.50   2.25

### Souvenir Sheet

Chrismas — A1419

No. 2912 — Details from Nativity Tympanum, by Gabriel Cercato: a, Angel in sky. b, Nativity scene.

**2020, Dec. 9**    Litho.    *Perf. 14*
2912   A1419   55p Sheet of 2, #a-b   2.75   2.60

**National Parks Type of 2019 With Microprinted "CORREOARGENTINO" and Denomination Above Large Denomination at Lower Right**

Designs: No. 2913, Calilegua National Park. No. 2914, Los Cardones National Park. No. 2915, Río Pilcomayo National Park. No. 2916, El Palmar National Park. No. 2917, Ciervo de los Pantanos National Park. No. 2918, Talampaya National Park. No. 2919, Quebrada del Condorito National Park. No. 2920, Tierra del Fuego National Park. No. 2921, Iguazú National Park. No. 2922, Patagonia National Park. No. 2923, Nahuel Huapi National Park. No. 2924, Perito Moreno National Park.

*Perf. 13¾x13½ Syncopated*
| 2020 ? | | | Litho. | |
|---|---|---|---|---|
| 2913 | A1395 | 1p multi | .30 | .25 |
| 2914 | A1395 | 2p multi | .30 | .25 |
| 2915 | A1395 | 5p multi | .30 | .25 |
| 2916 | A1395 | 10p multi | .30 | .25 |
| 2917 | A1395 | 20p multi | .60 | .55 |
| 2918 | A1395 | 30p multi | .85 | .75 |
| 2919 | A1395 | 40p multi | 1.20 | 1.10 |
| 2920 | A1395 | 50p multi | 1.50 | 1.40 |
| 2921 | A1395 | 100p multi | 2.90 | 2.60 |
| 2922 | A1395 | 200p multi | 5.75 | 5.25 |
| 2923 | A1395 | 300p multi | 8.75 | 8.00 |
| 2924 | A1395 | 400p multi | 11.50 | 10.50 |
| | Nos. 2913-2924 (12) | | 34.25 | 31.15 |

**UP National Parks Type of 2019 With Microprinted "CORREOARGENTINO" and Denomination Above Large Denomination at Lower Right**

Designs: No. 2925, El Impenetrable National Park. No. 2926, Sierra de las Quijadas National Park. No. 2927, El Rey National Park. No. 2928, El Leoncito National Park. No. 2929, Pre-Delta National Park. No. 2930, Los Glaciares National Park. No. 2931, Lanín National Park. No. 2932, Monte León National Park. No. 2933, Los Alerces National Park.

*Perf. 13¼x13½ Syncopated*
| 2020 ? | | | Litho. | |
|---|---|---|---|---|
| 2925 | A1396 | 5p sil & multi | .35 | .30 |
| 2926 | A1396 | 10p sil & multi | .35 | .30 |
| 2927 | A1396 | 20p sil & multi | .65 | .60 |
| 2928 | A1396 | 40p sil & multi | 1.30 | 1.10 |
| 2929 | A1396 | 50p sil & multi | 1.75 | 1.50 |
| 2930 | A1396 | 100p sil & multi | 3.25 | 3.00 |
| 2931 | A1396 | 200p sil & multi | 6.50 | 6.00 |
| 2932 | A1396 | 300p sil & multi | 9.75 | 9.00 |
| 2933 | A1396 | 400p sil & multi | 13.00 | 12.00 |
| | Nos. 2925-2933 (9) | | 36.90 | 33.80 |

Adrienne Bolland (1895-1975), First Woman to Fly From Argentina to Chile Over Andes Mountains — A1420

**2021, Apr. 5**    Litho.    *Perf. 14x13½*
2934   A1420   65p gold & multi   1.75   1.50
Bolland's trans-Andean flight, cent.

Federal Police, 200th Anniv. — A1421

**2021, Apr. 19**    Litho.    *Perf. 13¾x13½*
2935   A1421   105p gold & multi   2.50   2.25

Myrmecophaga Tridactyla — A1422

Various depictions of giant anteater with denomination at: No. 2936, 70p, UL. No. 2937, 70p, UR.

**2021, May 30**    Litho.    *Perf. 14x13½*
2936-2937   A1422   Set of 2   3.50   3.00

National Parks A1423

Designs: No. 2938, 70p, El Impenetrable National Park. No. 2939, 70p, Los Alerces National Park.

**2021, June 7**    Litho.    *Perf. 14x13½*
2938-2939   A1423   Set of 2   3.50   3.00
America issue.

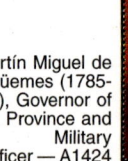

Martín Miguel de Güemes (1785-1821), Governor of Salta Province and Military Officer — A1424

*Perf. 13½x13¾*
**2021, June 17**    Litho.
2940   A1424   70p gold & multi   1.75   1.50

Ernesto Sabato (1911-2011), Writer — A1425

*Perf. 13¾x13½*
**2021, June 24**    Litho.
2941   A1425   110p sil & multi   2.60   2.40

City of Río Grande, Cent. — A1426

**2021, July 12**    Litho.    *Perf. 13¾x13½*
2942   A1426   70p sil & multi   1.75   1.50

Farm A1427      Lighthouse A1428

Ships in Harbor A1429     Railroad Station A1430

Cathedral A1431     YPF Oil Refinery A1432

School and Playground A1433     Provincial Government House, La Plata A1434

**2021, July 26**    Litho.    *Perf. 14*
| 2943 | | Sheet of 8 + 3 labels | 14.00 | 12.00 |
|---|---|---|---|---|
| a. | A1427 | 70p sil & multi | 1.75 | 1.50 |
| b. | A1428 | 70p sil & multi | 1.75 | 1.50 |
| c. | A1429 | 70p sil & multi | 1.75 | 1.50 |
| d. | A1430 | 70p sil & multi | 1.75 | 1.50 |
| e. | A1431 | 70p sil & multi | 1.75 | 1.50 |
| f. | A1432 | 70p sil & multi | 1.75 | 1.50 |
| g. | A1433 | 70p sil & multi | 1.75 | 1.50 |
| h. | A1434 | 70p sil & multi | 1.75 | 1.50 |

Buenos Aires Province, 200th anniv.

University of Buenos Aires, 200th Anniv. A1435

**2021, Aug. 12**    Litho.    *Perf. 14*
2944   A1435   200p gold   4.50   4.25
Values are for stamps with surrounding selvage.

Diplomatic Relations Between Argentina and Bulgaria, 90th Anniv. — A1436

Flags of Argentina and Bulgaria and: No. 2945, 220p, Erythrina crista-galli. No. 2946, 220p, Rosa x damascena.

**2021, Aug. 30**    Litho.    *Perf. 13½*
2945-2946   A1436   Set of 2   9.50   9.00
See Bulgaria No.

Beatification of Mamerto Esquiú (1826-83), Bishop of Córdoba — A1437

**2021, Sept. 6**    Litho.    *Perf. 13½*
2947   A1437   140p gold & multi   2.50   2.00

Appointment of Bruno Ramírez as First Argentinian Postman, 250th Anniv. — A1438

**2021, Sept. 14**    Litho.    *Perf. 14x13¾*
2948   A1438   140p multi   3.00   3.00

### Souvenir Sheet

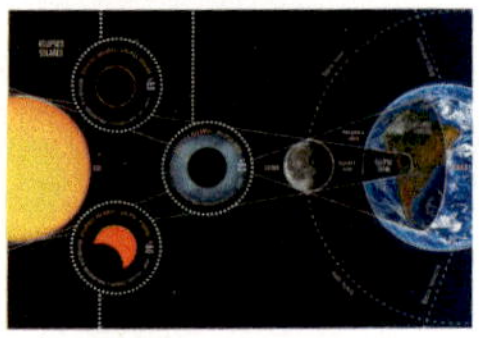

Solar Eclipses A1439

No. 2949: a, Annular eclipse. b, Total eclipse. c, Partial eclipse.

**Litho. & Silk-Screened**
**2021, Oct. 25**    *Perf.*
2949   A1439   80p Sheet of 3, #a-c   5.00   5.00

María Elena Walsh (1930-2011), Writer and Musician — A1440

**2021, Nov. 23**    Litho.    *Perf. 13½*
2950   A1440   140p gold & multi   2.75   2.75

### Souvenir Sheet

Mercosur, 30th Anniv. — A1441

**2021, Dec. 17**    Litho.    *Perf. 14*
2951   A1441   140p sil & multi   2.75   2.75

# ARGENTINA

### Souvenir Sheet

Christmas — A1442

**2021, Dec. 22** Litho. Perf. 14
2952 A1442 140p gold & multi 2.75 2.75

Buenos Aires Provincial Police, 200th Anniv. — A1443

**2021, Dec. 23** Litho. Perf. 13½
2953 A1443 140p gold & multi 2.75 2.75

A1444

New Year 2021 (Year of the Ox) A1445

No. 2954: a, Black ox. b, White ox with two calves. c, Black ox, white ox, two calves, three oxen in background, rooster and corn. d, Black ox, white ox, three oxen in background, snake. 380p, Head of ox.

**2022, Jan. 10** Litho. Perf. 13½
2954 Booklet pane of 4 + central label 7.00 —
a.-d. A1444 90p Any single 1.75 1.75
Complete booklet, #2954 7.00

### Souvenir Sheet
Litho. With Foil Application
Perf.

2955 A1445 380p gold & multi 7.25 7.25
Dated 2021.

Diplomatic Relations Between Argentina and People's Republic of China, 50th Anniv. — A1446

**2022, Feb. 21** Litho. Perf. 13½
2956 A1446 160p gold & multi 3.00 3.00

Beach and Map of the Falkland Islands A1447

**2022, Apr. 4** Litho. Perf. 14x13½
2957 A1447 100p sil & multi 1.75 1.75
Falkland Islands War, 40th anniv.

2022 Census A1448

**2022, May 2** Litho. Perf. 14x13½
2958 A1448 100p sil & multi 1.75 1.75

St. Luigi Orione (1872-1940) A1449

**2022, May 16** Litho. Perf. 14
2959 A1449 150p gold & multi 2.50 2.50
No. 2959 was printed in sheets of 4. See Italy No. 3837, Vatican City No. 1794.

Insects A1450

Designs: No. 2960, 100p, Xylocopa augusti. No. 2961, 100p, Dinoponera grandis.

**2022, May 23** Litho. Perf. 13½
2960-2961 A1450 Set of 2 3.50 3.50

150th Anniv. of Publication of *El Gaucho Martín Fierro*, Poem by José Hernández (1834-86) — A1451

**2022, July 14** Litho. Perf. 13½x13¾
2962 A1451 110p gold & multi 1.75 1.75

### Miniature Sheet

Argentina in the Antarctic — A1452

No. 2963 — Flag of Argentina and: a, Researchers hiking in Antarctica. b, Pygoscelis antarcticus. c, Ice floating near coast of Antarctica. d, Helicopter lifting cargo from A.R.A. Almirante Irízar.

**2022, Aug. 16** Litho. Perf. 13½
2963 A1452 Sheet of 4 11.50 11.50
a.-b. 130p Either single 1.90 1.90
c. 230p multi 3.25 3.25
d. 310p multi 4.25 4.25

Colocolo Opossum A1453

Hummingbird A1454

Rufous Hornero A1455

King Vulture A1456

South Andean Huemul A1457

Perf. 13¾x13½
**2022, Aug. 27** Litho.
2964 Horiz. strip of 5 12.50 12.50
a. A1453 130p multi 1.90 1.90
b. A1454 130p multi 1.90 1.90
c. A1455 130p multi 1.90 1.90
d. A1456 230p multi 3.25 3.25
e. A1457 230p multi 3.25 3.25
Children's drawings of animals native to Argentina. Garrahan Pediatric Hospital, 35th anniv.

Eva Perón (1919-52), First Lady of Argentina — A1458

**2022, Sept. 5** Litho. Perf. 13½x13¾
2965 A1458 400p multi 5.50 5.50

### Miniature Sheet

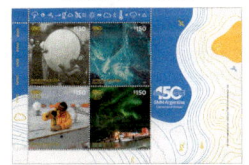

National Meteorological Service, 150th Anniv. — A1459

No. 2966: a, Meteorologists launching weather balloon, 1939. b, Satellite image of clouds over Argentina, 1984. c, Meteorologist adjusting equipment at Camp Marimbo, Antarctica. d, Aurora Australis over Belgrano II Base, Antarctica.

**2022, Oct. 4** Litho. Perf. 14
2966 A1459 150p Sheet of 4, #a-d 7.75 7.75

World Post Day — A1460

**2022, Oct. 11** Litho. Perf. 13½x13¾
2967 A1460 150p multi 1.90 1.90

Diplomatic Relations Between Argentina and South Korea, 60th Anniv. — A1461

**2022, Oct. 14** Litho. Perf. 14x13½
2968 A1461 890p multi 11.50 11.50

Berta Singerman (1901-98), Singer and Actress — A1462

**2022, Oct. 26** Litho. Perf. 14x13½
2969 A1462 150p multi 1.90 1.90
See Mexico No. 3272.

A1463

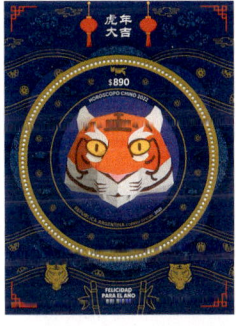

New Year 2022 (Year of the Tiger) A1464

No. 2970: a, Tiger looking right, legs not visible. b, Tiger standing, legs visible. c, Tiger in water, legs not visible. d, Tiger sitting, tail in foreground. 890p, Head of tiger.

**2022, Nov. 7** Litho. Perf 13½
2970 Booklet pane of 4 + central label 12.50 —
a.-b. A1463 150p Either single 1.90 1.90
c.-d. A1463 350p Either single 4.25 4.25
Complete booklet, #2970 12.50

### Souvenir Sheet
Perf.
2971 A1464 890p multi 11.00 11.00

Kama-sutra II, Xerograph by León Ferrari (1920-2013) A1465

Untitled Work by Ferrari A1466

**2022, Nov. 8** Litho. Perf. 13½
2972 A1465 150p multi 1.90 1.90
2973 A1466 150p multi 1.90 1.90
America issue.

Return to Argentina from Exile in Spain of Pres. Juan Perón (1895-1974), 50th Anniv. — A1467

**2022, Nov. 17** Litho. Perf. 14
2974 A1467 400p multi 4.75 4.75
See Spain No. 4633.

A1468

# ARGENTINA

A1469

A1470

Old Patagonian Express Narrow-
Gauge Railway, Cent. — A1471

| 2022, Nov. 22 | Litho. | Perf. 14x13½ |
|---|---|---|
| 2975 | Horiz. strip of 4 | 13.00 13.00 |
| a. | A1468 260p multi | 3.25 3.25 |
| b. | A1469 260p multi | 3.25 3.25 |
| c. | A1470 260p multi | 3.25 3.25 |
| d. | A1471 260p multi | 3.25 3.25 |
| e. | Booklet pane of 4, #2975a-2975d | 13.00 |
| | Complete booklet, #2975e | 13.00 |

**Archaeological Artifacts Type of 2000**

*Perf. 13½x13¾ Syncopated*

2009     Litho.

Birds of Argentina and
Poland — A1472

No. 2976: a, Furnarius rufus. b, Lophophanes cristatus.

| 2022, Nov. 25 | Litho. | Perf. 13½ |
|---|---|---|
| 2976 | A1472 Horiz. pair, #a-b | 12.50 12.50 |
| a. | 150p multi | 1.90 1.90 |
| b. | 870p multi | 10.50 10.50 |

See Poland No. 4643.

**Souvenir Sheet**

Yacimientos Petrolíferos Fiscales
Energy Company, Cent. — A1473

| 2022, Dec. 7 | Litho. | Perf. 14 |
|---|---|---|
| 2977 | A1473 260p multi | 3.00 3.00 |

Christmas
A1474

*Perf. 13¾x13½*

| 2022, Dec. 16 | | Litho. |
|---|---|---|
| 2978 | A1474 170p multi | 1.90 1.90 |

A1475

Ushuaia Tourist
Attractions
A1476

Designs: No. 2979, Waterfall, Tierra del Fuego National Park. No. 2980, Phrygilus

patagonicus. No. 2981, Port of Ushuaia. No. 2982, Les Eclaireurs Lighthouse.

| 2023, Jan. 6 | Litho. | Perf. 13¾x13½ |
|---|---|---|
| 2979 | A1475 1000p multi | 11.00 11.00 |
| 2980 | A1475 1020p multi | 11.00 11.00 |

**Inscribed "UP"**

| 2981 | A1476 1000p multi | 11.00 11.00 |
|---|---|---|
| 2982 | A1476 1020p multi | 11.00 11.00 |
| | Nos. 2979-2982 (4) | 44.00 44.00 |

**Miniature Sheet**

Cacti
A1477

No. 2983: a, Stetsonia coryne. b, Close-up of Stetsonia coryne flower. c, Trichocereus terscheckii. d, Close-up of Trichocereus terscheckii flowers. e, Gymnocalycium monvillei. f, Close-up of Gymnocalycium monvillei flower. g, Opuntia quimilo. h, Close-up of Opuntia quimilo flowers.

| 2023, Apr. 24 | Litho. | Perf. 13½ |
|---|---|---|
| 2983 | A1477 240p Sheet of 8, #a-h | 17.50 17.50 |

A1478

New Year 2023 (Year of the Rabbit)
A1479

No. 2984: a, Rabbit holding carrot in carrot patch. b, Four rabbits. c, Rabbit running in carrot patch. d, Five rabbits. 1460p, Rabbit, diff.

| 2023, May 15 | Litho. | Perf. 13½ |
|---|---|---|
| 2984 | Booklet pane of 4 + central label | 11.50 — |
| a.-b. | A1478 240p Either single | 2.00 2.00 |
| c.-d. | A1478 430p Either single | 3.75 3.75 |
| | Complete booklet, #2984 | 11.50 |

**Souvenir Sheet**

*Perf.*

| 2985 | A1479 1460p multi | 12.50 12.50 |
|---|---|---|

The rabbit in the design of No. 2985 is covered with fuzz.

Julieta Lanteri (1873-1932), Physician and Women's Rights Activist — A1480

| 2023, May 29 | Litho. | Perf. 14x13½ |
|---|---|---|
| 2986 | A1480 240p multi | 2.00 2.00 |

René Favaloro (1923-2000), Cardiac Surgeon — A1482

| 2023, July 12 | Litho. | Perf. 13½ |
|---|---|---|
| 2988 | A1482 240p multi | 1.75 1.75 |

## SEMI-POSTAL STAMPS

Samuel F. B. Morse
SP1

Globe
SP2

Landing of Columbus — SP5

Designs: 10c+5c, Alexander Graham Bell. 25c+15c, Rowland Hill.

**Wmk. RA in Sun (90)**

| 1944, Jan. 5 | Litho. | Perf. 13 |
|---|---|---|
| B1 | SP1 3c +2c lt vio & sl bl | 1.00 1.50 |
| B2 | SP2 5c +5c dl red & sl bl | .80 .50 |
| B3 | SP1 10c +5c org & slate bl | 1.50 .50 |
| B4 | SP1 25c +15c red brn & sl slate | 2.25 1.10 |
| B5 | SP5 1p +50c lt grn & sl bl | 9.50 10.00 |
| | Nos. B1-B5 (5) | 15.05 13.60 |

The surtax was for the Postal Employees Benefit Association.

Map of Argentina — SP6

| 1944, Feb. 17 | Wmk. 90 | Perf. 13 |
|---|---|---|
| B6 | SP6 5c +10c ol yel & slate | 1.10 .50 |
| B7 | SP6 5c +50c vio brn & slate | 5.00 1.50 |
| B8 | SP6 5c +1p dl org & slate | 13.50 7.00 |
| B9 | SP6 5c +20p dp bl & slate | 30.00 30.00 |
| | Nos. B6-B9 (4) | 49.60 39.00 |

The surtax was for the victims of the San Juan earthquake.

**Souvenir Sheets**

National Anthem and Flag
SP7

| 1944, July 17 | | Imperf. |
|---|---|---|
| B10 | SP7 5c +1p vio brn & lt bl | 9.00 5.00 |
| B11 | SP7 5c +50p bl blk & lt bl | 450.00 275.00 |

Surtax for the needy in the provinces of La Rioja and Catamarca.

> **Catalogue values for unused stamps in this section, from this point to the end of the section, are for Never Hinged items.**

Stamp Designing — SP8

| 1950, Aug. 26 | Photo. | Perf. 13½ |
|---|---|---|
| B12 | SP8 10c +10c violet | .30 .25 |
| | Nos. B12,CB1-CB5 (6) | 22.20 15.40 |

Argentine Intl. Philatelic Exhibition, 1950.

Poliomyelitis Victim — SP9

| 1956, Apr. 14 | | Perf. 13½x13 |
|---|---|---|
| B13 | SP9 20c +30c slate | .60 .35 |

The surtax was for the poliomyelitis fund. Head in design is from Correggio's "Antiope," Louvre.

Stamp of 1858 and Mail Coach on Raft — SP10

Designs: 2.40p+1.20p, Album, magnifying glass and stamp of 1858. 4.40p+2.20p, Government seat of Confederation, Parana.

| 1958, Mar. 29 | Litho. | Perf. 13½ |
|---|---|---|
| B14 | SP10 40c +20c brt grn & dl pur | .70 .50 |
| B15 | SP10 2.40p +1.20p ol gray & bl | .70 .50 |
| B16 | SP10 4.40p +2.20p lt bl & dp claret | .70 .50 |
| | Nos. B14-B16,CB8-CB12 (8) | 8.65 5.50 |

Surtax for Intl. Centennial Philatelic Exhibition, Paraná, Entre Rios, Apr. 19-27. Nos. B14-B16 exist imperf. Value, set of pairs, $200.

View of Flooded Land — SP11

| 1958, Oct. 4 | Photo. | Perf. 13½ |
|---|---|---|
| B17 | SP11 40c +20c brown | .35 .25 |
| | Nos. B17,CB13-CB14 (3) | 2.30 1.30 |

The surtax was for flood victims in the Buenos Aires district. Exists imperf. Value, pair $37.50.

Child Receiving Blood — SP12

| 1958, Dec. 20 | Litho. | Wmk. 90 |
|---|---|---|
| B18 | SP12 1p +50c blk & rose red | .75 .25 |

The surtax went to the Anti-Leukemia Foundation. Exists imperf. Value, pair $25.

# ARGENTINA 639

Runner — SP13

Designs: 50c+20c, Basketball players, vert. 1p+50c, Boxers, vert.

**1959, Sept. 5**  Perf. 13½
B19 SP13 20c +10c emer & blk  .40  .25
B20 SP13 50c +20c yel & blk  .40  .25
a. Torch missing  200.00  200.00
B21 SP13 1p +50c mar & blk  .40  .25
a. Torch missing  150.00  150.00
Nos. B19-B21,CB15-CB16 (5)  2.90  1.70

3rd Pan American Games, Chicago, Aug. 27-Sept. 7, 1959. See Nos. CB15-CB16.

Condor — SP14

Fork-tailed Flycatchers — SP14a

Magellanic Woodpecker — SP14b

**1960, Feb. 6**
B22 SP14 20c +10c dk bl  .65  .35
B23 SP14a 50c +20c dp vio bl  .65  .35
B24 SP14b 1p +50c brn & buff  .65  .35
Nos. B22-B24,CB17-CB18 (5)  3.45  1.75

The surtax was for child welfare work. See Nos. B30, CB17-CB18, CB29.

### Souvenir Sheet

Uprooted Oak Emblem SP15

**1960, Apr. 7**  Wmk. 90  Imperf.
B25 SP15 Sheet of 2  1.65  1.40
a. 1p + 50c bister & carmine  .60  .50
b. 4.20p + 2.10p app grn & dp clar  .60  .50

WRY, July 1, 1959-June 30, 1960. The surtax was for aid to refugees.

Jacaranda — SP16

Flowers: 1p+1p, Passionflower. 3p+3p, Orchid. 5p+5p, Tabebuia.

**1960, Dec. 3**  Photo.  Perf. 13½
B26 SP16 50c +50c deep blue  .35  .25
B27 SP16 1p +1p bluish grn  .35  .25
B28 SP16 3p +3p henna brn  .85  .35
B29 SP16 5p +5p dark brn  1.40  .60
Nos. B26-B29 (4)  2.95  1.45

"TEMEX 61" (Intl. Thematic Exposition). For overprints see Nos. B31-B34.

### Type of 1960

Bird: 4.20p+2.10p, Blue-eyed shag.

**1961, Feb. 25**  Wmk. 90  Perf. 13½
B30 SP14 4.20p +2.10p chest brn  .95  .35

Surtax for child welfare work. See No. CB29.

Nos. B26-B29 Ovptd. in Black, Brown, Blue or Red

**1961, Apr. 15**
B31 SP16 50c +50c deep blue  .50  .25
B32 SP16 1p +1p bluish grn (Brn)  .50  .25
B33 SP16 3p +3p hen brn (Bl)  .95  .25
B34 SP16 5p +5p dk brn (R)  1.30  .40
Nos. B31-B34 (4)  3.25  1.15

Day of the Americas, Apr. 14.

Cathedral, Cordoba SP17

Stamp of 1862 SP18

Design: 10p+10p, Cathedral, Buenos Aires.

 Perf. 13½
**1961, Oct. 21**  Wmk. 90  Photo.
B35 SP17 2p +2p rose claret  .35  .25
B36 SP18 3p +3p green  .50  .25
B37 SP17 10p +10p brt blue  1.10  .60
a. Souvenir sheet of 3  3.00  2.00
Nos. B35-B37 (3)  1.95  1.10

1962 International Stamp Exhibition. No. B37a contains three imperf. stamps similar to Nos. B35-B37 in dark blue.

Flight into Egypt, by Ana Maria Moncalvo — SP19

**1961, Dec. 16**  Litho.
B38 SP19 2p +1p lilac & blk brn  .40  .35
B39 SP19 10p +5p lt & dp clar  .80  .35

The surtax was for child welfare.

Mimus Saturninus Modulator — SP20

Design: 12p+6p, Zonotrichia capensis hypoleuca.

**1962, Dec. 29**  Perf. 13½
B40 SP20 4p +2p bis, brn & bl grn  1.30  .65
B41 SP20 12p +6p gray, yel, grn & brn  2.00  1.25

The surtax was for child welfare. See Nos. B44, B47, B48-B50, CB32, CB35-CB36.

Soccer — SP21

No. B43, Horsemanship.

**1963, May 18**  Perf. 13½
B42 SP21 4p +2p multi  .40  .25
B43 SP21 12p +6p multi  .70  .35
a. Dark carmine (jacket) omitted  15.00
Nos. B42-B43,CB31 (3)  2.30  1.10

4th Pan American Games, Sao Paulo. See No. CB31.

### Bird Type of 1962

4p +2p, Pyrocephalus rubineus rubineus.

**1963, Dec. 21**  Litho.
B44 SP20 4p +2p multi  .95  .30

The surtax was for child welfare. See No. CB32.

Fencers — SP22

4p+2p, National Stadium, Tokyo, horiz.

**1964, July 18**  Wmk. 90  Perf. 13½
B45 SP22 4p +2p red, ocher & brn  .35  .35
B46 SP22 12p +6p bl grn & blk  .50  .35
Nos. B45-B46,CB33 (3)  2.25  1.40

18th Olympic Games, Tokyo, Oct. 10-25, 1964. See No. CB33.

### Bird Type of 1962

4p +2p, Cardinal paroaria coronata.

**1964, Dec. 23**  Litho.
B47 SP20 4p +2p multi  1.10  .35

The surtax was for child welfare. See No. CB35.

SP22a

Designs: 8p+4p, Belonopterus cayennensis lampronotus. 10p+5p, Amblyramphus holosericeus, horiz. 20p+10p, Chloroceryle amazona.

**1966-67**  Perf. 13½
B48 SP22a 8p +4p blk, ol, brt grn & red  1.05  .35
B49 SP22a 10p +5p blk, bl, org & grn  1.05  .55
B50 SP22a 20p +10p blk, yel, bl & pink  .50  .35
Nos. B48-B50,CB36,CB38-CB39 (6)  6.10  3.50

The surtax was for child welfare. Issue dates: 8p+4p, Mar. 26, 1966. 10p+5p, Jan. 14, 1967. 20p+10p, Dec. 23, 1967.

Grandmother's Birthday, by Patricia Lynch; Lions Emblem — SP23

 Perf. 12½x13½
**1968, Dec. 14**  Litho.  Wmk. 90
B51 SP23 40p + 20p multi  .70  .40

1st Lions Intl. Benevolent Phil. Exhib. Surtax for the Children's Hospital Benevolent Fund.

White-faced Tree Duck — SP24

**1969, Sept. 20**  Wmk. 365  Perf. 13½
B52 SP24 20p + 10p multi  .70  .35

Surtax for child welfare. See No. CB40.

Slender-tailed Woodstar (Hummingbird) SP25

**1970, May 9**  Wmk. 365  Perf. 13½
B53 SP25 20c + 10c multi  .65  .40

The surtax was for child welfare. See Nos. CB41, B56-B59, B62-B63.

Dolphinfish — SP26

**1971, Feb. 20**  Unwmk.  Perf. 12½
Size: 75x15mm
B54 SP26 20c + 10c multi  .75  .45

Surtax for child welfare. See No. CB42.

Children with Stamps, by Mariette Lydis — SP27

**1971, Dec. 18**  Litho.  Perf. 13½
B55 SP27 1p + 50p multi  .75  .35

2nd Lions Intl. Solidarity Stamp Exhib.

### Bird Type of 1970

Birds: 25c+10c, Saffron finch. 65c+30c, Rufous-bellied thrush, horiz.

**1972, May 6**  Unwmk.  Perf. 13½
B56 SP25 25c + 10c multi  .50  .35
B57 SP25 65c + 30c multi  .75  .35

Surtax was for child welfare.

### Bird Type of 1970

Birds: 50c+25c, Southern screamer (chaja). 90c+45c, Saffron-cowled blackbird, horiz.

**1973, Apr. 28**
B58 SP25 50c + 25c multi  .75  .35
B59 SP25 90c + 45c multi  .95  .55

Surtax was for child welfare.

### Painting Type of Regular Issue

Designs: 15c+15c, Still Life, by Alfredo Gultero, horiz. 90c+90c, Nude, by Miguel C. Victorica, horiz.

**1973, Aug. 28**  Litho.  Perf. 13½
B60 A472 15c + 15c multi  .50  .35
B61 A472 90c + 90c multi  1.50  1.00

### Bird Type of 1970

Birds: 70c+30c, Blue seed-eater. 1.20p+60c, Hooded siskin.

**1974, May 11**  Litho.  Perf. 13½
B62 SP25 70c + 30c multi  .85  .35
B63 SP25 1.20p + 60c multi  1.25  .50

Surtax was for child welfare.

### Painting Type of 1974

Design: 70c+30c, The Lama, by Juan Batlle Planas.

**1974, May 11**  Litho.  Perf. 13½
B64 A477 70c + 30c multi  .45  .35

PRENFIL-74 UPU, Intl. Exhib. of Phil. Periodicals, Buenos Aires, Oct. 1-12.

Plushcrested Jay — SP28

Designs: 13p+6.50p, Golden-collared macaw. 20p+10p, Begonia. 40p+20p, Teasel.

**1976, June 12 Litho. *Perf. 13½***

| | | | |
|---|---|---|---|
| **B65** | SP28 7p + 3.50p multi | .75 | .35 |
| **B66** | SP28 13p + 6.50p multi | .90 | .35 |
| **B67** | SP28 20p + 10p multi | 1.10 | .40 |
| **B68** | SP28 40p + 20p multi | 1.50 | .60 |
| | *Nos. B65-B68 (4)* | 4.25 | 1.70 |

Argentine philately.

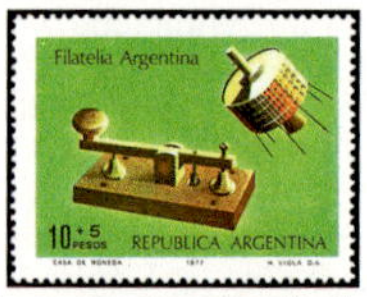


Telegraph, Communications Satellite — SP29

Designs: 20p+10p, Old and new mail trucks. 60p+30p, Old, new packet boats. 70p+35p, Biplane and jet.

**1977, July 16 Litho. *Perf. 13½***

| | | | |
|---|---|---|---|
| **B69** | SP29 10p + 5p multi | .40 | .35 |
| **B70** | SP29 20p + 10p multi | .80 | .60 |
| **B71** | SP29 60p + 30p multi | 1.60 | .85 |
| **B72** | SP29 70p + 35p multi | 1.80 | .90 |
| | *Nos. B69-B72 (4)* | 4.60 | 2.70 |

Surtax was for Argentine philately.
No. B70 exists with wmk. 365.

### Church of St. Francis Type, 1977

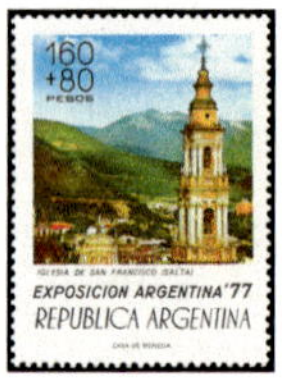


Inscribed "EXPOSICION ARGENTINA '77"

**1977, Aug. 27**

| | | | |
|---|---|---|---|
| **B73** | A515 160p + 80p multi | 2.50 | 2.00 |

Surtax was for Argentina '77 Philatelic Exhibition. Issued in sheets of 4. Value $13.

### No. B73 Overprinted with Soccer Cup Emblem

**1978, Feb. 4 Litho. *Perf. 13½***

| | | | |
|---|---|---|---|
| **B74** | A515 160p + 80p multi | 4.75 | 4.25 |
| *a.* | Souvenir sheet of 4 | 23.50 | 20.00 |

11th World Cup Soccer Championship, Argentina, June 1-25.

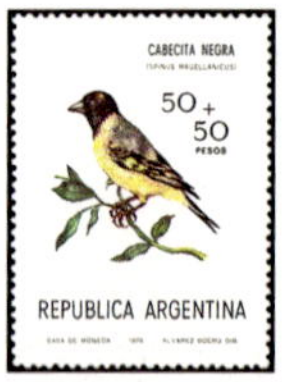


Spinus Magellanicus SP30

Birds: No. B76, Variable seedeater. No. B77, Yellow thrush. No. B78, Pyrocephalus rubineus. No. B79, Great kiskadee.

**1978, Aug. 5 Litho. *Perf. 13½***

| | | | |
|---|---|---|---|
| **B75** | SP30 50p + 50p multi | 1.75 | 1.00 |
| **B76** | SP30 100p + 100p multi | 1.75 | 1.00 |
| **B77** | SP30 150p + 150p multi | 2.75 | 1.50 |
| **B78** | SP30 200p + 200p multi | 2.75 | 1.75 |
| **B79** | SP30 500p + 500p multi | 4.75 | 3.50 |
| | *Nos. B75-B79 (5)* | 13.75 | 8.75 |

ARGENTINA '78, Inter-American Philatelic Exhibition, Buenos Aires, Oct. 27-Nov. 5. Nos. B75-B79 issued in sheets of 4 with marginal inscriptions commemorating Exhibition and 1978 Soccer Championship. Value, set $62.50.

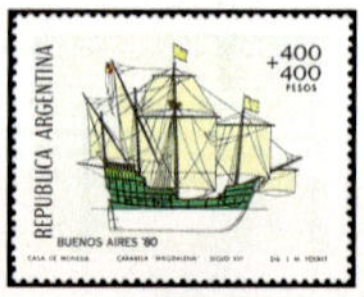


Caravel "Magdalena," 16th Century SP31

Sailing Ships: 500+500p, 3 master "Rio de la Plata," 17th cent. 600+600p, Corvette "Descubierta," 18th cent. 1500+1500p, Naval Academy yacht "A.R.A. Fortuna," 1979.

**1979, Sept. 8 Litho. *Perf. 13½***

| | | | |
|---|---|---|---|
| **B80** | SP31 400p +400p multi | 3.75 | 2.25 |
| **B81** | SP31 500p +500p multi | 4.50 | 2.50 |
| **B82** | SP31 600p +600p multi | 6.50 | 3.25 |
| **B83** | SP31 1500p +1500p multi | 15.00 | 8.00 |
| | *Nos. B80-B83 (4)* | 29.75 | 16.00 |

Buenos Aires '80, Intl. Philatelic Exhibition, 10/24-11/2/80. Issued in sheets of 4. Value, set $130.

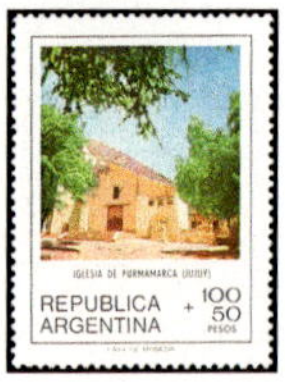


Purmamarca Church — SP32

Churches: 200p + 100p, Molinos. 300p + 150p, Animana. 400p + 200p, San Jose de Lules.

**1979, Nov. 3 Litho. *Perf. 13½***

| | | | |
|---|---|---|---|
| **B84** | SP32 100p + 50p multi | .50 | .35 |
| **B85** | SP32 200p + 100p multi | .75 | .35 |
| **B86** | SP32 300p + 150p multi | 1.05 | .35 |
| **B87** | SP32 400p + 200p multi | 1.50 | .50 |
| | *Nos. B84-B87 (4)* | 3.80 | 1.55 |

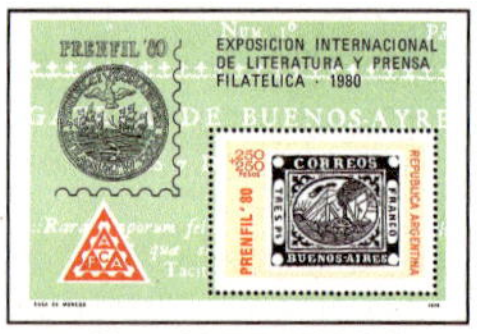


Buenos Aires No. 3, Exhibition and Society Emblems — SP33

Argentine Stamps: 750p+750p, type A580. 1000p+1000p, No. 91. 2000p+2000p, type A588.

**1979, Dec. 15 Litho. *Perf. 13½***

| | | | |
|---|---|---|---|
| **B88** | SP33 250p + 250p | 2.10 | 1.25 |
| **B89** | SP33 750p + 750p | 3.60 | 2.25 |
| **B90** | SP33 1000p + 1000p | 10.50 | 6.00 |
| **B91** | SP33 2000p + 2000p | 9.00 | 6.00 |
| | *Nos. B88-B91 (4)* | 25.20 | 15.50 |

PRENFIL '80, Intl. Philatelic Literature and Publications Exhib., Buenos Aires, Nov. 7-16, 1980.

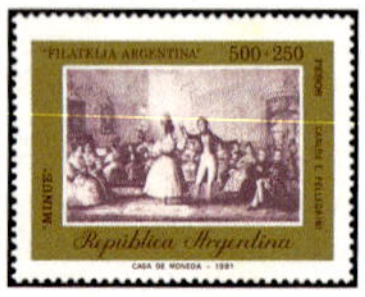


Minuet, by Carlos E. Pellegrini SP34

Paintings: 700p+350p, Media Cana, by Carlos Morel. 800p+400p, Cielito, by Pellegrini. 1000p+500p, El Gato, by Juan Leon Palliere.

**1981, July 11 Litho. *Perf. 13½***

| | | | |
|---|---|---|---|
| **B92** | SP34 500p + 250p multi | .95 | .45 |
| **B93** | SP34 700p + 350p multi | 1.50 | .80 |
| **B94** | SP34 800p + 400p multi | 1.50 | 1.00 |
| **B95** | SP34 1000p + 500p multi | 1.90 | 1.40 |
| | *Nos. B92-B95 (4)* | 5.85 | 3.65 |

Espamer '81 Intl. Stamp Exhib. (Americas, Spain, Portugal), Buenos Aires, Nov. 13-22.

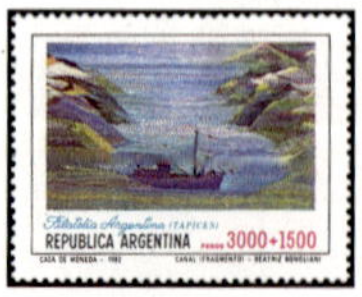


Canal, by Beatrix Bongliani (b. 1933) — SP35

Tapestries: 1000p+500p, Shadows, by Silvia Sieburger, vert. 2000p+1000p, Interpretation of a Rectangle, by Silke R. de Haupt, vert. 4000p+2000p, Tilcara, by Tana Sachs.

**1982, July 31 Litho. *Perf. 13½***

| | | | |
|---|---|---|---|
| **B96** | SP35 1000p + 500p multi | .65 | .40 |
| **B97** | SP35 2000p + 1000p multi | .85 | .50 |
| **B98** | SP35 3000p + 1500p multi | 1.00 | .60 |
| **B99** | SP35 4000p + 2000p multi | 1.20 | .70 |
| | *Nos. B96-B99 (4)* | 3.70 | 2.20 |

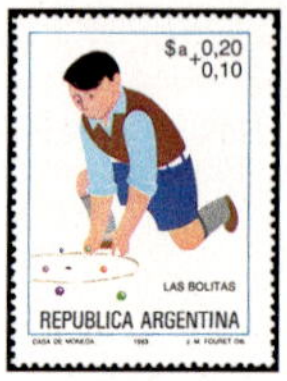


Boy Playing Marbles — SP36

No. B101, Jumping rope. No. B102, Hopscotch. No. B103, Flying kites. No. B104, Spinning top.

**1983, July 2 Litho. *Perf. 13½***

| | | | |
|---|---|---|---|
| **B100** | SP36 20c + 10c shown | .50 | .35 |
| **B101** | SP36 30c + 15c multi | .55 | .30 |
| **B102** | SP36 50c + 25c multi | 1.10 | .60 |
| **B103** | SP36 1p + 50c multi | 1.50 | .70 |
| **B104** | SP36 2p + 1p multi | 2.00 | 1.00 |
| | *Nos. B100-B104 (5)* | 5.65 | 2.95 |

Surtax was for natl. philatelic associations.
See Nos. B106-B110.

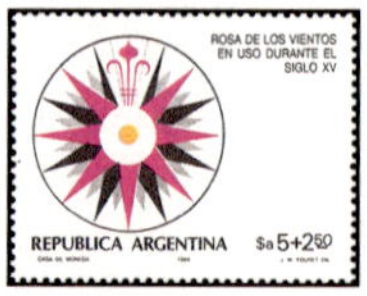


Compass, 15th Cent. — SP37

ARGENTINA '85 Intl. Stamp Show: b, Arms of Spain, Argentina. c, Columbus' arms. d-f, Columbus' arrival at San Salvador Island. Nos. B105d-B105f in continuous design; ships shown on singles range in size, left to right, from small to large. Surtax was for exhibition.

**1984, Apr. 28 Litho. *Perf. 13½***

| | | | |
|---|---|---|---|
| **B105** | Block of 6 | 6.00 | 4.50 |
| *a.-f.* | SP37 5p + 2.50p, any single | .80 | .45 |

### Children's Game Type of 1983

No. B106, Blind Man's Buff. No. B107, The Loop. No. B108, Leap Frog. No. B109, Rolling the loop. No. B110, Ball Mold.

**1984, July 7 Litho. *Perf. 13½***

| | | | |
|---|---|---|---|
| **B106** | SP36 2p + 1p multi | .60 | .25 |
| **B107** | SP36 3p + 1.50p multi | .60 | .30 |
| **B108** | SP36 4p + 2p multi | .90 | .40 |
| **B109** | SP36 5p + 2.50p multi | .90 | .40 |
| **B110** | SP36 6p + 3p multi | 1.25 | .60 |
| | *Nos. B106-B110 (5)* | 4.25 | 1.95 |

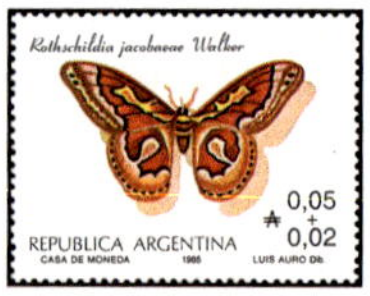


Butterflies SP38

No. B111, Rothschildia jacobaeae. No. B112, Heliconius erato phyllis. No. B113, Precis evarete hilaris. No. B114, Cyanopepla pretiosa. No. B115, Papilio androgeus.

**1985, Nov. 9 Litho. *Perf. 13½***

| | | | |
|---|---|---|---|
| **B111** | SP38 5c + 2c multi | 1.25 | .35 |
| **B112** | SP38 10c + 5c multi | 1.25 | .60 |
| **B113** | SP38 20c + 10c multi | 1.75 | .75 |
| **B114** | SP38 25c + 13c multi | 2.75 | 1.50 |
| **B115** | SP38 40c + 20c multi | 3.50 | 2.25 |
| | *Nos. B111-B115 (5)* | 10.50 | 5.45 |

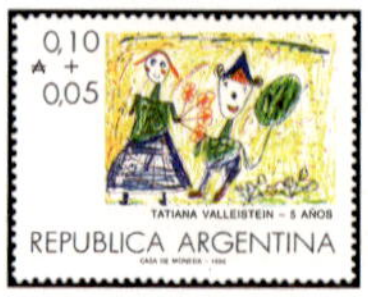


Children's Drawings SP39

No. B116, N. Pastor, vert. No. B117, T. Valleistein. No. B118, J.M. Flores, vert. No. B119, M.E. Pezzuto. No. B120, E. Diehl.

**1986, Aug. 30 Litho.**

| | | | |
|---|---|---|---|
| **B116** | SP39 5c + 2c multi | .35 | .25 |
| **B117** | SP39 10c + 5c multi | .50 | .35 |
| **B118** | SP39 20c + 10c multi | .85 | .60 |
| **B119** | SP39 25c + 13c multi | 1.20 | .85 |
| **B120** | SP39 40c + 20c multi | 1.75 | 1.25 |
| | *Nos. B116-B120 (5)* | 4.65 | 3.30 |

Surtax for natl. philatelic associations.

Miniature Sheets

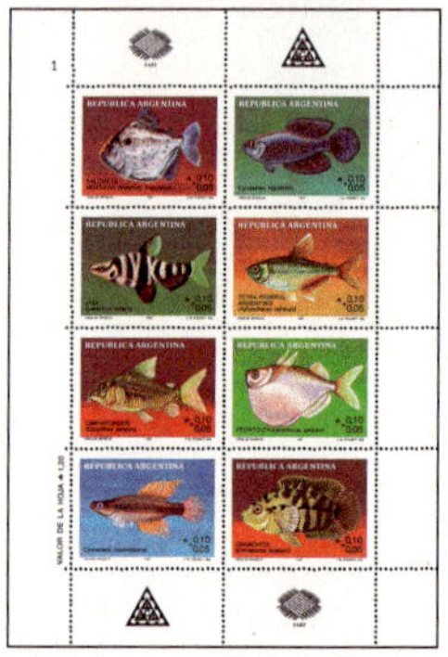

Fresh-water Fish — SP40

No. B121: a, Metynnis maculatus. b, Cynolebias nigripinnis. c, Leporinus solarii. d, Aphyocharax rathbuni. e, Corydoras aeneus. f, Thoracocharax securis. g, Cynolebias melanotaenia. h, Cichlasoma facetum.

No. B122: a, Tetragonopterus argenteus. b, Hemigrammus caudovittatus. c, Astyanax bimaculatus. d, Gymnocorymbus ternetzi. e, Hoplias malabaricus. f, Aphyocharax rubripinnis. g, Apistogramma agassizi. h, Pyrrhulina rachoviana.

**1987, June 27**

| | | | |
|---|---|---|---|
| **B121** | SP40 Sheet of 8 | 5.00 | 5.00 |
| *a.-h.* | 10c +5c, any single | .35 | .35 |
| **B122** | SP40 Sheet of 8 | 9.00 | 9.00 |
| *a.-h.* | 20c +10c, any single | .55 | .55 |

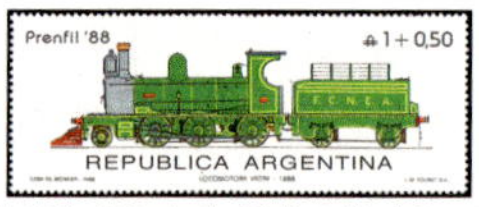


PRENFIL '88, Intl. Philatelic Literature and Media Exhibition, Buenos Aires, Nov. 25-Dec. 2 — SP41

Locomotives and railroad car: No. B123, Yatay locomotive, 1888. No. B124, FCCA electric passenger car, 1914. No. B125, B-15 locomotive, 1942. No. B126, GT-22 No. 200 locomotive, 1988.

**1988, June 4 Litho. *Perf. 13½***

| | | | |
|---|---|---|---|
| **B123** | SP41 1a +50c multi | 1.50 | .60 |
| **B124** | SP41 1a +50c multi | 1.50 | .60 |
| **B125** | SP41 1a +50c multi | 1.50 | .60 |
| **B126** | SP41 1a +50c multi | 1.50 | .60 |
| | *Nos. B123-B126 (4)* | 6.00 | 2.40 |

Nos. B123-B125 each issued in sheets of 4. Value, set $16.

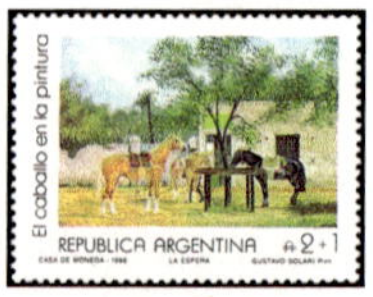


Horses — SP42

Paintings: No. B127, *The Waiting*, by Gustavo Solari. No. B128, *Mare and Foal*, by E. Castro. No. B129, *Saint Isidor*, by Castro. No. B130, *At Lagoon's Edge*, by F. Romero Carranza. No. B131, *Under the Tail*, by Castro.

**1988, Oct. 29 Litho. *Perf. 13½***

| | | | |
|---|---|---|---|
| **B127** | SP42 2a +1a multi | 2.00 | .60 |
| **B128** | SP42 2a +1a multi | 2.00 | .60 |
| **B129** | SP42 2a +1a multi | 2.00 | .60 |
| **B130** | SP42 2a +1a multi | 2.00 | .60 |
| **B131** | SP42 2a +1a multi | 2.00 | .60 |
| | *Nos. B127-B131 (5)* | 10.00 | 3.00 |

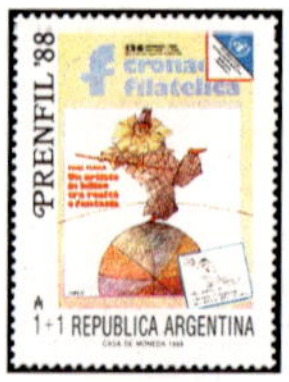


PRENFIL '88 — SP43

Covers of philatelic magazines: No. B132, *Cronaca Filatelica*, Italy. No. B133, *CO-FI*, Brazil. No. B134, *References de la Poste*, France. No. B135, *Postas Argentinas*.

# ARGENTINA

**1988, Nov. 26**   Litho.   **Perf. 13½**
| | | | |
|---|---|---|---|
| B132 | SP43 1a +1a multi | 1.25 | .40 |
| B133 | SP43 1a +1a multi | 1.25 | .40 |
| B134 | SP43 1a +1a multi | 1.25 | .40 |
| B135 | SP43 2a +2a multi | 1.25 | .40 |
| | Nos. B132-B135 (4) | 5.00 | 1.60 |

Nos. B132-B135 printed in sheets of 4. Value, set $14.

### Souvenir Sheet

ARBRAPEX '88 — SP44

Designs: No. B136a, *Candel Delivery at San Ignacio*, by Leonie Matthis, Cornelio Saavedra Museum, Buenos Aires. No. B136b, *Immaculate Conception*, a statue in the Isaac Fernandez Blanco Museum, Buenos Aires.

**1988, Nov. 26**     **Perf. 12**
| | | | |
|---|---|---|---|
| B136 | SP44 Sheet of 2 | 3.50 | 3.50 |
| a. | 2a +2a multi | 1.00 | .75 |
| b. | 3a +3a multi | 1.75 | 1.25 |

Fish — SP45

Designs: No. B137, *Diplomystes viedmensis*. No. B138, *Haplochiton taeniatus*. No. B139, *Percichthys trucha*. No. B140, *Galaxias platei*. No. B141, *Salmo fario*.

**1989, June 24**   Litho.   **Perf. 13½**
| | | | |
|---|---|---|---|
| B137 | SP45 10a +5a multi | 1.15 | .40 |
| B138 | SP45 10a +5a multi | 1.15 | .40 |
| B139 | SP45 10a +5a multi | 1.15 | .40 |
| B140 | SP45 10a +5a multi | 1.15 | .40 |
| B141 | SP45 10a +5a multi | 1.15 | .40 |
| | Nos. B137-B141 (5) | 5.75 | 2.00 |

Nos. B137-B141 printed in sheets of 4. Value, set $15.

Discovery of America 500th Anniv. (in 1992) and ESPAMER '90 — SP46

Documents and chronicles: No. B142, Columbus's coat of arms, *Book of Privileges* title page. No. B143, Illustration from *New Chronicle and Good Government*, by Guaman Poma de Ayala. No. B144, Illustration from *Discovery and Conquest of Peru*, by Pedro de Cieza de Leon. No. B145, Illustration from *Travel to the River Plate*, by Ulrico Schmidl.

**1989, Sept. 16**   Litho.   **Perf. 13½**
Yellow, Rose Violet & Black
| | | | |
|---|---|---|---|
| B142 | SP46 100a +50a | 2.25 | .85 |
| B143 | SP46 150a +50a | 2.25 | .85 |
| B144 | SP46 200a +100a | 2.25 | .85 |
| B145 | SP46 250a +100a | 2.25 | .85 |
| | Nos. B142-B145 (4) | 9.00 | 3.40 |

Nos. B142-B145 printed in sheets of 4. Value, set $17.

Insects — SP47

Designs: No. B146, *Podisus nigrispinus*. No. B147, *Adalia bipunctata*. No. B148, *Nabis punctipennis*. No. B149, *Hippodamia convergens*. No. B150, *Calleida suturalis*.

**1990, June 30**   Litho.   **Perf. 13½**
| | | | |
|---|---|---|---|
| B146 | SP47 1000a +500a multi | 1.40 | .95 |
| B147 | SP47 1000a +500a multi | 1.40 | .95 |
| B148 | SP47 1000a +500a multi | 1.40 | .95 |
| B149 | SP47 1000a +500a multi | 1.40 | .95 |
| B150 | SP47 1000a +500a multi | 1.40 | .95 |
| | Nos. B146-B150 (5) | 7.00 | 4.75 |

Nos. B146-B150 printed in sheets of 4. Value, set $24.

### Souvenir Sheet

First Natl. Exposition of Aerophilately — SP48

a, Lieut. Marcos A. Zar, Macchi seaplane. b, Capt. Antonio Parodi, Ansaldo SVA biplane.

**1990, July 14**   Litho.   **Perf. 12**
| | | | |
|---|---|---|---|
| B151 | SP48 Sheet of 2 | 10.00 | 6.50 |
| a. | 2000a +2000a multi | 3.00 | 2.50 |
| b. | 3000a +3000a multi | 3.00 | 2.50 |

### Souvenir Sheet

1992 Summer Olympics, Barcelona — SP49

Designs: a, Shot put. b, High jump. c, Hurdles. d, Pole vault.

**1990, Dec. 15**   Litho.   **Perf. 13½**
| | | | |
|---|---|---|---|
| B152 | SP49 Sheet of 4 | 12.00 | 12.00 |
| a.-d. | 2000a +2000a multi | 2.50 | 2.50 |

Espamer '91 Philatelic Exhibition. See No. B155.

### Souvenir Sheet

Discovery of America, 500th Anniv. (in 1992) — SP50

Voyage of Alesandro Malaspina, 1789-1794: a, Sailing ship. b, Malaspina. c, Indian, hut. d, Indian, horse, artist drawing.

**1990, Oct. 13**   Litho.   **Perf. 13½**
| | | | |
|---|---|---|---|
| B153 | SP50 Sheet of 4 | 13.00 | 12.00 |
| a.-d. | 2000a +1000a, any single | 2.00 | 2.00 |

Espamer '91, Buenos Aires.

### Souvenir Sheet

Race Cars and Drivers SP51

Designs: a, Juan Manuel Fangio. b, Juan Manuel Bordeu. c, Carlos Alberto Reutemann. d, Oscar and Juan Galvez.

**1991**   Litho.   **Perf. 13½**
| | | | |
|---|---|---|---|
| B154 | SP51 Sheet of 4 | 7.50 | 6.50 |
| a.-d. | 2500a +2500a, any single | 1.50 | 1.40 |

Espamer '91.

### 1992 Summer Olympics Type of 1990
### Souvenir Sheet

Women's gymnastics routines: a, Floor exercise. b, Uneven parallel bars. c, Balance beam. d, Rhythmic gymnastics.

**1991, June 29**   Litho.   **Perf. 13½**
| | | | |
|---|---|---|---|
| B155 | SP49 Sheet of 4 | 7.50 | 6.50 |
| a.-d. | 2500a +2500a, any single | 1.50 | 1.25 |

Espamer '91.

Iberoprenfil '92 — SP52

Designs: No. B156, Castor missile. No. B157, Satellite LUSAT 1.

**1991, Dec. 28**   Litho.   **Perf. 13½**
| | | | |
|---|---|---|---|
| B156 | SP52 4000a +4000a multi | 3.25 | 3.25 |
| B157 | SP52 4000a +4000a multi | 3.25 | 3.25 |

Dinosaurs — SP53

No. B158, Carnotaurus. No. B159, Amargasaurus.

**1992, May 2**   Litho.   **Perf. 13½**
| | | | |
|---|---|---|---|
| B158 | SP53 38c +38c multi | 2.50 | 2.50 |
| B159 | SP53 38c +38c multi | 2.50 | 2.50 |
| a. | Pair, #B158-B159 | 6.00 | 6.00 |

Iberoprenfil '92, Buenos Aires — SP54

Paintings by Raul Soldi (b. 1905): No. B160, The Fiesta. No. B161, Church of St. Anne of Glew.

**1992, Sept. 5**   Litho.   **Perf. 13½**
| | | | |
|---|---|---|---|
| B160 | SP54 76c +76c multi | 4.00 | 3.25 |
| B161 | SP54 76c +76c multi | 4.00 | 3.25 |

Parafil '92 — SP55

**1992, Nov. 21**   Litho.   **Perf. 13½**
| | | | |
|---|---|---|---|
| B162 | SP55 76c +76c multi | 4.00 | 3.25 |

2nd Argentine-Paraguayan Philatelic Exhibition, Buenos Aires.

### Souvenir Sheet

Birds — SP56

a, *Egretta thula*. b, *Amblyramphus holosericeus*. c, *Paroaria coronata*. d, *Chloroceryle amazona*.

**1993, July 17**   Litho.   **Perf. 13½**
| | | | |
|---|---|---|---|
| B163 | SP56 38c +38c Sheet of 4 | 9.00 | 9.00 |

### Souvenir Sheet

Latin American Air Post Philatelic Exhibition — SP57

Designs: a, 25c+25c, Antoine de Saint-Exupery (1940-44), pilot, author. b, 75c+75c, "The Little Prince," vert.

**1995, June 3**   Litho.   **Perf. 12**
| | | | |
|---|---|---|---|
| B164 | SP57 Sheet of 2, #a.-b. | 8.00 | 7.50 |

For overprint see No. B180.

### Souvenir Sheet

Exploration of Antarctica — SP58

75c+25c, Transport ship ARA Bahia Aguirre. 1.25p+75c, Argentine Air Force Hercules C-130.

**1995, July 8**
| | | | |
|---|---|---|---|
| B165 | SP58 Sheet of 2, #a.-b. | 9.50 | 9.00 |

Aerofila '96 — SP59

Historic airplanes, pilots: No. B166, "Plus ultra," Ramón Franco Bahamonde (1896-1938). No. B167, 14 Bis, Alberto Santos-Dumont (1873-1932). No. B168, Spirit of St. Louis, Charles A. Lindbergh (1902-1974). No. B169, Buenos Aires, Eduardo A. Olivero (1896-1966).

**1996, July 13**   Litho.   **Perf. 13½**
| | | | |
|---|---|---|---|
| B166 | SP60 25c +25c multi | 1.75 | 1.20 |
| B167 | SP59 25c +25c multi | 1.75 | 1.20 |
| B168 | SP59 50c +50c multi | 3.25 | 2.40 |
| B169 | SP59 50c +50c multi | 3.25 | 2.40 |
| | Nos. B166-B169 (4) | 10.00 | 7.20 |

Ceramic Murals from Buenos Aires Subway SP60

**1996, Sept. 21**   Litho.   **Perf. 13½**
| | | | |
|---|---|---|---|
| B170 | SP60 1p +50c Dragon | 4.50 | 3.75 |
| B171 | SP60 1.50p +1p Bird | 7.00 | 5.50 |

MEVIFIL '97, 1st Intl. Exhibition of Audio-Visual and Philatelic Information Media — SP61

Designs: No. B172, France Type A1. No. B173, Spain Type A3. No. B174, Argentina Type A4. No. B175, Buenos Aires Type A1.

**1997, May 10**   Litho.   **Perf. 13½**
| | | | |
|---|---|---|---|
| B172 | SP61 50c +50c multi | 2.50 | 2.25 |
| B173 | SP61 50c +50c multi | 2.50 | 2.25 |
| B174 | SP61 50c +50c multi | 2.50 | 2.25 |
| B175 | SP61 50c +50c multi | 2.50 | 2.25 |
| a. | Block of 4, #B172-B175 | 11.50 | 11.50 |

Issued in sheets of 16 stamps + 4 labels.

# ARGENTINA

Trains — SP62

Designs: No. B176, Las Nubes (Train to the Clouds), Salta. No. B177, Historical train, Buenos Aires. No. B178, Old Patagonian Express, Rio Negro-Chubut. No. B179, Southern Fueguino Railway, Tierra Del Fuego.

**1997, Sept. 6**   Litho.   *Perf. 13*
| | | | | |
|---|---|---|---|---|
| B176 | SP62 | 50c +50c multi | 4.00 | 3.25 |
| B177 | SP62 | 50c +50c multi | 4.00 | 3.25 |
| B178 | SP62 | 50c +50c multi | 4.00 | 3.25 |
| B179 | SP62 | 50c +50c multi | 4.00 | 3.25 |
| | Nos. B176-B179 (4) | | 16.00 | 13.00 |

### No. B164 Overprinted in Red Violet

**1997, Sept. 27**   Litho.   *Perf. 12*
B180   SP57   Sheet of 2    8.00   7.50

Cartography — SP63

Maps of the Buenos Aires area from: 25c+25c, 1546. No. B182, 17th century. No. B183, 1910. 75c+75c, 1999.

*Perf. 13¾x13½*

**1999, Nov. 20**   Litho.
| | | | | |
|---|---|---|---|---|
| B181 | SP63 | 25c + 25c multi | 1.00 | 1.00 |
| B182 | SP63 | 50c + 50c multi | 2.00 | 2.00 |
| B183 | SP63 | 50c + 50c multi | 2.00 | 2.00 |
| B184 | SP63 | 75c + 75c multi | 3.00 | 3.00 |
| a. | Block of 4, #B181-B184 | | 14.00 | 14.00 |

Methods of Transportation — SP64

No. B185: a, Bicycle. b, Graf Zeppelin. c, Train. d, Trolley.

**2000, Oct. 21**   Litho.   *Perf. 14x13½*
| | | | | |
|---|---|---|---|---|
| B185 | SP64 | Block of 4 | 12.00 | 11.00 |
| a. | 25c +25c multi | | 1.25 | 1.20 |
| b.-c. | 50c +50c Any single | | 2.50 | 2.40 |
| d. | 75c +75c multi | | 3.75 | 3.50 |

Cetaceans — SP65

No. B186: a, Burmeister's porpoise (Mariposa espinosa). b, River Plate dolphin. c, Minke whale. d, Humpback whale (Yubarta).

**2001, Sept. 15**   Litho.   *Perf. 14x13½*
| | | | | |
|---|---|---|---|---|
| B186 | Block of 4 | | 16.00 | 15.00 |
| a. | SP65 25c +25c multi | | 1.10 | 1.10 |
| b.-c. | SP65 50c +50c Any single | | 2.25 | 2.25 |
| d. | SP65 75c +75c multi | | 3.25 | 3.25 |

Reptiles — SP66

No. B187: a, Boa constrictor occidentalis. b, Caiman yacare. c, Tupinambis merianae. d, Chelonoidis carbonaria.

**2002, Aug. 24**   Litho.   *Perf. 14x13½*
| | | | | |
|---|---|---|---|---|
| B187 | Block of 4 | | 10.00 | 9.00 |
| a. | SP66 25c +25c multi | | .80 | .80 |
| b.-c. | SP66 50c +50c Either single | | 1.35 | 1.35 |
| d. | SP66 75c +75c multi | | 2.25 | 2.25 |

Bicycles — SP67

No. B188: a, Velocipede, 1855, Cycling Club champions, 1902. b, Velocipede, 1867, postman with delivery tricycle. c, Coventry Eagle touring bicycle, 1949, cyclists in park. d, Racing bicycle, 1960s, Palermo Velodrome, 1902.

**2003, Aug. 9**   Litho.   *Perf. 14x13¾*
| | | | | |
|---|---|---|---|---|
| B188 | Block of 4 | | 6.50 | 5.50 |
| a. | SP67 25c+25c multi | | .70 | .70 |
| b.-c. | SP67 50c+50c Either single | | 1.20 | 1.20 |
| d. | SP67 75c+75c multi | | 1.75 | 1.75 |

Ships — SP68

No. B189: a, A. R. A. Villarino. b, A. R. A. Pampa. c, A. R. A. Bahia Thetis. d, A. R. A. Cabo de Hornos.

**2004, Aug. 21**   Litho.   *Perf. 14x13½*
| | | | | |
|---|---|---|---|---|
| B189 | Block of 4 | | 6.50 | 5.25 |
| a. | SP68 25c +25c multi | | .55 | .55 |
| b.-c. | SP68 50c +50c either single | | .85 | .85 |
| d. | SP68 75c +75c multi | | 1.40 | 1.40 |

Merchant Ships — SP69

No. B190: a, Río de la Plata. b, Libertad. c, Campo Durán. d, Isla Soledad.

**2005, Sept. 24**   Litho.   *Perf. 14x13½*
| | | | | |
|---|---|---|---|---|
| B190 | Block of 4 | | 6.50 | 5.25 |
| a. | SP69 25c +25c multi | | .55 | .55 |
| b.-c. | SP69 50c +50c either single | | .85 | .85 |
| d. | SP69 75c +75c multi | | 1.40 | 1.40 |

River Boats — SP70

No. B191: a, Ciudad de Buenos Aires. b, Lambaré. c, Madrid. d, Rawson.

**2006, Aug. 19**   Litho.   *Perf. 14x13½*
| | | | | |
|---|---|---|---|---|
| B191 | Block of 4 | | 6.50 | 5.25 |
| a. | SP70 25c +25c multi | | .55 | .55 |
| b.-c. | SP70 50c +50c either single | | .85 | .85 |
| d. | SP70 75c +75c multi | | 1.40 | 1.40 |

Scouting, Cent. — SP71

No. B192: a, Scouts at campfire. b, Scout saluting near tent. c, Scout saluting, Scout with patrol flag. d, Scouts pulling rope.

**2007, July 28**   Litho.   *Perf. 13½x14*
| | | | | |
|---|---|---|---|---|
| B192 | Horiz. strip of 4 | | 6.50 | 5.00 |
| a. | SP71 25c +25c multi | | .40 | .40 |
| b. | SP71 50c +50c multi | | .80 | .80 |
| c. | SP71 75c +75c multi | | 1.10 | 1.10 |
| d. | SP71 1p +1p multi | | 1.40 | 1.40 |

Shells — SP72

Designs: 25c+25c, Calliostoma militaris. 50c+50c, Epitonium fabrizioi. 75c+75c, Odontocymbiola magellanica. 1p+1p, Trophon geversianus.

*Perf. 13½x13¾*

**2008, Aug. 23**   Litho.
B193-B196   SP72   Set of 4    5.00   4.00

Astronomical Observatories — SP73

Designs: No. B197, 50c+50c, Radio telescope, Argentine Institute of Radioastronomy. No. B198, 50c+50c, Telescope, La Plata Astronomical Observatory. No. B199, 1p+1p, El Lioncito Astronomical Complex. No. B200, 1p+1p, Telescope, Félix Aguilar Astronomical Observatory.

**2009, Aug. 22**   Litho.   *Perf. 14x13½*
B197-B200   SP73   Set of 4    5.50   4.50

Girl Guides and Girl Scouts, Cent. — SP74

Designs: No. B201, 75c+75c, Girl Scout salute. No. B202, 75c+75c, Hands of five Girl Scouts joined. No. B203, 1p+1p, Hands of Girl Scouts joined, campfire. No. B204, 1p+1p, Hand on shoulder of Girl Scout.

**2010, Aug. 21**   Litho.   *Perf. 13½x14*
B201-B204   SP74   Set of 4    5.50   4.50

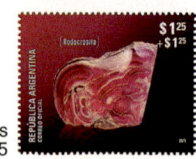

Minerals — SP75

Designs: No. B205, 1.25p+1.25p, Rhodochrosite (rodocrisita). No. B206, 1.25p+1.25p, Sulphur (azufre). No. B207, 1.25p+1.25p, Pyrite (pirita). No. B208, 1.25p+1.25p, Quartz (cuarzo).

**2011, Aug. 20**   *Perf. 13¾x13½*
B205-B208   SP75   Set of 4    7.00   6.50

### Minerals Type of 2011

Designs: No. B209, 1.50p+1.50p, Agate (agata). No. B210, 1.50p+1.50p, Amethyst (amatista). No. B211, 1.50p+1.50p, Fluorite (fluorita). No. B212, 1.50p+1.50p, Malachite (malaquita).

**2012, Aug. 25**
B209-B212   SP75   Set of 4    7.50   6.50

Extreme Sports — SP76

Designs: No. B213, 2p+2p, Skiing. No. B214, 2p+2p, Skateboarding. No. B215, 2p+2p, BMX cycling. No. B216, 2p+2p, Surfing.

**2013, Dec. 21**   Litho.   *Perf. 14x13½*
B213-B216   SP76   Set of 4    6.00   5.00

Volcanoes — SP77

Designs: No. B217, 5p+5p, Payú Liso. No. B218, 5p+5p, Llullaillaco. No. B219, 5p+5p, Lanín. No. B220, 5p+5p, Maipo.

*Perf. 13¾x13½*

**2014, Aug. 19**   Litho.
B217-B220   SP77   Set of 4    10.50   9.50

Clocks and Sundials — SP78

Designs: No. B221, 7p+7p, Los Colosos de Siemens Clock, Buenos Aires. No. B222, 7p+7p, Palacio Fuentes Clock Tower, Rosario. No. B223, 7p+7p, Jesuit Estate Sundial, Alta Gracia. No. B224, 7p+7p, Miroglio Brothers Clock, Buenos Aires.

**2015, Dec. 4**   Litho.   *Perf. 13½x13¾*
B221-B224   SP78   Set of 4    12.50   11.50

Railroad Mail Cars SP79

No. B225: a, Mail car with open door. b, Diagram of interior of mail car. c, Postal workers in mail car and on ground transfering mail. d, Mail car with closed doors.

**2016, Aug. 22**   Litho.   *Perf. 14x13½*
B225   SP79   10p+10p   Block of 4, #a-d    13.50   11.00

Ponchos — SP80

Designs: No. B226, 16p+16p, 60-stripe poncho, Litoral region. No. B227, 16p+16p, Cayupán poncho, La Pampa Province. No. B228, 16p+16p, Andino poncho, Catamarca Province. No. B229, 16p+16p, Pilagá poncho, Chaco Province.

*Perf. 13½x13¾*

**2017, Aug. 23**   Litho.
B226-B229   SP80   Set of 4    21.00   18.00

Map of Corrientes Province, Mesenger on Horseback, Postman, and Truck — SP81

Post Office Palace, Buenos Aires, and Tile SP82

**2018, Dec. 26**   Litho.   *Perf. 14x13½*
| | | | | |
|---|---|---|---|---|
| B230 | SP81 | 30p+15p sil & multi | 3.25 | 2.75 |
| B231 | SP82 | 30p+15p sil & multi | 3.25 | 2.75 |

Mail delivery in Corrientes area, 270th anniv., and Post Office Palace, 90th anniv.

Tango — SP83

Designs: No. B232, 50p+25p, Tango dancers. No. B233, 50p+25p, Bandoneon player.

*Perf. 13½x13¾*

**2019, Aug. 26** **Litho.**
**B232-B233** SP83 Set of 2 9.00 7.50

Horses SP84

"Turf" at: No. B234, 165p+55p, Right, horse and rider and their shadow. No. B235, 165p+55p, Left, horse race.

**2022, Dec. 19** **Litho.** ***Perf. 14x13½***
**B234-B235** SP84 Set of 2 5.00 5.00

## AIR POST STAMPS

Airplane Circles the Globe AP1

Eagle AP2

Wings Cross the Sea — AP3

Condor on Mountain Crag — AP4

Perforations of Nos. C1-C37 vary from clean-cut to rough and uneven, with many skipped perfs.

*Perf. 13x13½, 13½x13*

**1928, Mar. 1** **Litho.** **Wmk. 90**
**C1** AP1 5c lt red 1.50 .60
**C2** AP1 10c Prus blue 2.50 1.10
**C3** AP1 15c lt brown 2.50 1.00
**C4** AP1 18c lilac gray 4.00 3.00
*a.* 18c brown lilac 4.50 3.00
*b.* Double impression 375.00
**C5** AP2 20c ultra 3.00 1.00
**C6** AP2 24c deep blue 5.00 3.00
**C7** AP3 25c brt violet 5.00 1.60
**C8** AP3 30c rose red 6.00 1.25
**C9** AP4 35c rose 5.00 1.10
**C10** AP1 36c bister brn 3.00 1.60
**C11** AP4 50c gray black 5.00 .75
**C12** AP2 54c chocolate 5.00 2.25
**C13** AP2 72c yellow grn 6.00 2.25
*a.* Double impression 350.00
**C14** AP3 90c dk brown 11.00 2.00
**C15** AP3 1p slate bl & red 13.00 .90
**C16** AP3 1.08p rose & dk bl 18.00 5.00
**C17** AP4 1.26p dull vio & grn 25.00 10.00
**C18** AP4 1.80p blue & lil rose 25.00 10.00
**C19** AP4 3.60p gray & blue 50.00 22.00
*Nos. C1-C19 (19)* 195.50 70.40

The watermark on No. C4a is larger than on the other stamps of this set, measuring 10mm across Sun.

### Zeppelin First Flight

Air Post Stamps of 1928 Overprinted in Blue

**1930, May**
**C20** AP2 20c ultra 10.00 5.00
*a.* Inverted overprint 500.00
**C21** AP4 50c gray black 20.00 10.00
*a.* Inverted overprint 500.00
**C22** AP3 1p slate bl & red 25.00 12.50
*a.* Inverted overprint 850.00
**C23** AP4 1.80p blue & lil rose 70.00 30.00
**C24** AP4 3.60p gray & blue 200.00 90.00
*Nos. C20-C24 (5)* 325.00 147.50

### Overprinted in Green

**C25** AP2 20c ultra 13.00 8.00
**C26** AP4 50c gray black 15.00 10.00
**C27** AP3 90c dark brown 13.00 8.00
**C28** AP3 1p slate bl & red 25.00 15.00
**C29** AP4 1.80p blue & lil rose 700.00 500.00
*a.* Thick paper 1,000.
*Nos. C25-C29 (5)* 766.00 541.00

### Air Post Stamps of 1928 Overprinted in Red or Blue

On AP1-AP2

On AP3-AP4

**1931**
**C30** AP1 18c lilac gray 2.00 1.50
**C31** AP2 72c yellow green 14.00 10.50
**C32** AP3 90c dark brown 14.00 10.50
**C33** AP4 1.80p bl & lil rose (Bl) 30.00 22.50
**C34** AP4 3.60p gray & blue 57.50 40.00
*Nos. C30-C34 (5)* 117.50 85.00

1st anniv. of the Revolution of 1930.

### Zeppelin Issue

Nos. C1, C4, C4a, C14 Overprinted in Blue or Red

On AP1

On AP3

**1932, Aug. 4**
**C35** AP1 5c lt red (Bl) 3.00 2.00
**C36** AP1 18c lilac gray (R) 12.50 9.00
*a.* 18c brown lilac (R) 100.00 60.00
**C37** AP3 90c dark brown (R) 32.50 26.00
*Nos. C35-C37 (3)* 48.00 37.00

Plane and Letter AP5

Mercury AP6

Plane in Flight — AP7

*Perf. 13½x13, 13x13½*

**1940, Oct. 23** **Photo.** **Wmk. 90**
**C38** AP5 30c deep orange 12.00 .40
**C39** AP6 50c dark brown 12.00 .40
**C40** AP5 1p carmine 5.00 .25
**C41** AP7 1.25p deep green 2.00 .25
**C42** AP5 2.50p bright blue 4.00 .60
*Nos. C38-C42 (5)* 35.00 1.90

Plane and Letter AP8

Mercury and Plane AP9

*Perf. 13½x13, 13x13½*

**1942, Oct. 6** **Litho.** **Wmk. 90**
**C43** AP8 30c orange .35 .35
**C44** AP9 50c dull brn & buff .65 .35

No. C43 exists imperf. Value, pair $20.

See Nos. C49-C52, C57, C61.

Plane over Iguaçu Falls AP10

Plane over the Andes AP11

*Perf. 13½x13*

**1946, June 10** **Unwmk.**
**C45** AP10 15c dull red brn .35 .35
**C46** AP11 25c gray green .35 .35

See Nos. C53-C54.

Allegory of Flight AP12

Astrolabe AP13

*Perf. 13½x13, 13x13½*

**1946, Sept. 25** **Litho.** **Unwmk.**

**Surface-Tinted Paper**

**C47** AP12 15c sl grn, *pale grn* .55 .35
**C48** AP13 60c vio brn, *ocher* .55 .35

### Types of 1942

**1946-48** **Unwmk.** ***Perf. 13½x13***
**C49** AP8 30c orange 1.40 .25
**C50** AP9 50c dull brn & buff 2.50 .25
**C51** AP8 1p carmine ('47) 1.25 .25
**C52** AP8 2.50p brt blue ('48) 5.50 .75
*Nos. C49-C52 (4)* 10.65 1.50

No. C51 exists imperf. Value, pair $30.

### Types of 1946

**1948** **Wmk. 90**
**C53** AP10 15c dull red brn .35 .35
**C54** AP11 25c gray green .35 .35

Atlas (National Museum, Naples) AP14

Map of Argentine Republic, Globe and Caliper AP15

*Perf. 13½x13, 13x13½*

**1948-49** **Photo.** **Wmk. 288**
**C55** AP14 45c dk brown ('49) .40 .25
**C56** AP15 70c dark green .70 .40

4th Pan-American Reunion of Cartographers, Buenos Aires, Oct.-Nov., 1948.

### Mercury Type of 1942

**1949** **Litho.** ***Perf. 13x13½***
**C57** AP9 50c dull brn & buff .40 .35

Marksmanship Trophy — AP16

**1949, Nov. 4** **Photo.**
**C58** AP16 75c brown .75 .35

World Rifle Championship, 1949.

**Catalogue values for unused stamps in this section, from this point to the end of the section, are for Never Hinged items.**

Douglas DC-3 and Condor — AP17

*Perf. 13x13½*

**1951, June 20** **Wmk. 90**
**C59** AP17 20c dk olive grn .75 .35

10th anniversary of the State air lines.

Douglas DC-6 and Condor — AP18

**1951, Oct. 17** ***Perf. 13½***
**C60** AP18 20c blue .75 .35

End of Argentine 5-year Plan.

### Plane-Letter Type of 1942

**1951** **Litho.** ***Perf. 13½x13***
**C61** AP8 1p carmine .65 .35

No. C61 exists imperf. Value, pair $20.

Jesus by Leonardo da Vinci (detail, "Virgin of the Rocks") — AP19

*Perf. 13½x13*

**1956, Sept. 29** **Photo.** **Wmk. 90**
**C62** AP19 1p dull purple 1.00 .35

Issued to express the gratitude of the children of Argentina to the people of the world for their help against poliomyelitis.

Battle of Montevideo AP20

Leonardo Rosales and Tomas Espora AP21

Guillermo Brown — AP22

**1957, Mar. 2** ***Perf. 13½***
**C63** AP20 60c blue gray .50 .35
**C64** AP21 1p brt pink .60 .35
**C65** AP22 2p brown .60 .35
*Nos. C63-C65 (3)* 1.70 1.05

Cent. of the death of Admiral Guillermo Brown, founder of the Argentine navy.

Map of Americas & Arms of Buenos Aires — AP23

**1957, Aug. 16**
**C66** AP23 2p rose violet .75 .35

Issued to publicize the Inter-American Economic Conference in Buenos Aires.

# 644 ARGENTINA

Modern locomotive — AP24

**1957, Aug. 31  Wmk. 90  Perf. 13½**
C67  AP24  60c gray  .70  .35
Centenary of Argentine railroads.

AP25

No. C68, Globe, Flag, Compass Rose. No. C69, Key.

**1957, Sept. 14**
C68  AP25  1p multi  .50  .35
C69  AP25  2p multi  .70  .35
1957 International Congress for Tourism.

Birds Carrying Letters — AP26

**1957, Nov. 6**
C70  AP26  1p bright blue  .60  .35
Issued for Letter Writing Week, Oct. 6-12.

Early Plane — AP27

**1958, May 31  Perf. 13½**
C71  AP27  2p maroon  .60  .35
50th anniv. of the Argentine Aviation Club.

**Stamp Anniv. Type**

Designs: 80c, Stamp of Buenos Aires and view of the Plaza de la Aduana. 1p, Stamp of 1858 and "The Post of Santa Fe."

**1958  Litho.  Perf. 13½**
C72  A270  80c pale bis & sl bl  .55  .35
C73  A270  1p red org & dk bl  .55  .35
Cent. of the 1st postage stamps of Buenos Aires & the Argentine Confederation.
Issue dates: 80c, Oct. 18; 1p, Aug. 23.

Comet Jet over World Map — AP29

**1959, May 16  Perf. 13½**
C74  AP29  5p black & olive  .65  .35
Inauguration of jet flights by Argentine Airlines.

**Type of Regular Issue, 1960**

"Cabildo" and: 1.80p, Mariano Moreno. 5p, Manuel Belgrano and Juan Jose Castelli.

**Perf. 13½**
**1960, May 28  Wmk. 90  Photo.**
C75  A287  1.80p red brown  .50  .35
  a.  Souvenir sheet of 3  1.40  .95
C76  A287  5p buff & purple  .70  .35
  a.  Souvenir sheet of 3  2.00  1.50
Souvenir sheets are imperf. No. C75a contains one No. C75 and 1p and 2p resembling Nos. 713-714; stamps in reddish brown. No. C76a contains one No. C76 and 4.20p and 10.70p resembling Nos. 715-716; stamps are in green.

Symbolic of New Provinces — AP30

**1960, July 8  Litho.**
C77  AP30  1.80p dp car & blue  .60  .35
Elevation of the territories of Chubut, Formosa, Neuquen, Rio Negro and Santa Cruz to provinces.

**Type of Regular Issue, 1960**
**1960, Oct. 1  Photo.  Perf. 13½**
C78  A291  1.80p rose lilac  .75  .35
C79  A291  10.70p brt grnsh blue  1.00  .35

UNESCO Emblem — AP31

**1962, July 14  Litho.**
C80  AP31  13p ocher & brown  .85  .35
15th anniv. of UNESCO.

Mail Coach — AP32

**1962, Oct. 6  Wmk. 90  Perf. 13½**
C81  AP32  5.60p gray brn & blk  1.00  .35
Mailman's Day, Sept. 14, 1962.

**No. 695 and Type of 1959 Surcharged in Green**

**1962, Oct. 31  Photo.**
C82  A277  5.60p on 5p brown  .60  .35
C83  A277  18p on 5p brn, grnsh  1.40  .35

UPAE Emblem — AP33

**1962, Nov. 24  Photo.  Perf. 13½**
C84  AP33  5.60p dark blue  .65  .35
50th anniv. of the founding of the Postal Union of the Americas and Spain, UPAE.

Skylark — AP34

Design: 11p, Super Albatros.

**1963, Feb. 9  Litho.**
C85  AP34  5.60p blue & black  .45  .35
C86  AP34  11p blue, blk & red  .75  .35
9th World Gliding Championships.

Symbolic Plane — AP35

**1963-65  Wmk. 90  Perf. 13½**
C87  AP35  5.60p dk pur, car & brt grn  .55  .25
C88  AP35  7p black & bis ('64)  .75  .25
C88A  AP35  7p black & bis ('65)  8.00  1.00
C89  AP35  11p blk, dk pur & grn  .80  .25
C90  AP35  18p dk pur, red & vio bl  1.75  .35
C91  AP35  21p brown, red & gray  2.40  .40
Nos. C87-C91 (6)  14.25  2.50
"Argentina" reads down on No. C88, up on No. C88A. See Nos. C101-C104, C108-C111, C123-C126, C135-C141. For overprint and surcharges see Nos. C96, C146-C150.

**Type of Regular Issue, 1964**

Map of Falkland Islands (Islas Malvinas).

**1964, Feb. 22  Perf. 13½**
Size: 33x22mm
C92  A327  18p lt & dk bl & ol grn  3.00  .75

UPU Monument, Bern, and UN Emblem — AP36

**1964, May 23  Engr.  Perf. 13½**
C93  AP36  18p red & dk brown  .85  .35
15th UPU Cong., Vienna, Austria, 5-6/64.

Discovery of America, Florentine Woodcut — AP37

**1964, Oct. 10  Litho.**
C94  AP37  13p tan & black  1.10  .35
Day of the Race, Columbus Day.

Lt. Matienzo Base, Antarctica — AP38

**1965, Feb. 27  Photo.  Perf. 13½**
C95  AP38  11p salmon pink  .75  .35
Issued to publicize the national territory of Tierra del Fuego, Antarctic and South Atlantic Isles.

**No. C88A Overprinted in Silver**

**1965, Mar. 17  Litho.**
C96  AP35  7p black & bister  .60  .35
1st Rio de la Plata Stamp Show, sponsored jointly by the Argentine and Uruguayan Philatelic Associations, Montevideo, Mar. 19-28.

ITU Emblem — AP39

**1965, May 11  Wmk. 90  Perf. 13½**
C97  AP39  18p slate, blk & red  .65  .35
Centenary of the ITU.

Ascending Rocket — AP40

Design: 50p, Earth with trajectories and magnetic field, horiz.

**1965, May 29  Photo.  Perf. 13½**
C98  AP40  18p red org  .90  .30
C99  AP40  50p ultra  1.60  .55
6th Symposium on Space Research, held in Buenos Aires, and to honor the Natl. Commission of Space Research.

**Type of 1963-65 Inscribed "Republica Argentina"**

**1965, Oct. 13  Litho.  Wmk. 90**
C101  AP35  12p dk car rose & brn  1.50  .25
C102  AP35  15p vio blue & dk red  1.60  .50
C103  AP35  27.50p dk bl grn & gray  2.75  1.00
C104  AP35  30.50p dk brown & dk bl  3.25  1.50
Nos. C101-C104 (4)  9.10  3.25

Argentine Antarctica Map and Centaur Rocket — AP41

**1966, Feb. 19  Perf. 13½**
C105  AP41  27.50p bl, blk & dp org  1.40  .85
Launchings of sounding balloons and of a Gamma Centaur rocket in Antarctica during February, 1965.

Sea Gull and Southern Cross — AP42

**1966, May 14  Perf. 13½**
C106  AP42  12p Prus blue, blk & red  .65  .35
50th anniv. of the Naval Aviation School.

Blériot Plane Flown by Fels, 1917 — AP43

**1967, Sept. 2  Litho.  Perf. 13½**
C107  AP43  26p olive, bl & blk  .60  .35
Flight by Theodore Fels from Buenos Aires to Montevideo, Sept. 2, 1917, allegedly the 1st intl. airmail flight.

**Type of 1963-65 Inscribed "Republica Argentina" Reading Down**

**1967, Dec. 20  Perf. 13½**
C108  AP35  26p brown  .65  .25
C109  AP35  40p violet  5.75  .30
C110  AP35  68p blue green  3.75  .45
C111  AP35  78p ultra  1.60  .45
Nos. C108-C111 (4)  11.75  1.60

# ARGENTINA

Vito Dumas and Ketch "Legh II" — AP44

**1968, July 27**    Litho.    Wmk. 90
C112 AP44 68p bl, blk, red & vio bl    .90   .40

Issued to commemorate Vito Dumas's one-man voyage around the world in 1943.

### Type of Regular Issue and

Assembly Emblem AP45

40p, Globe and map of South America.

**1968, Oct. 19**    Litho.    Perf. 13½
C113 A395 40p brt pink, lt bl & blk    1.00   .30
C114 AP45 68p bl, lt bl, gold & blk    1.60   .55

4th Plenary Assembly of the Intl. Telegraph and Telephone Consultative Committee, Mar del Plata, Sept. 23-Oct. 25.

Radar Antenna, Balcarce Station — AP46

       Perf. 13½
**1969, Aug. 23**   Wmk. 90   Photo.
C115 AP46 40p blue gray    .95   .35

Communications by satellite through Intl. Telecommunications Consortium (INTELSAT).

Atucha Nuclear Center — AP47

**1969, Dec. 13**    Litho.    Wmk. 365
C116 AP47 26p blue & multi    2.50   .80

Completion of Atucha Nuclear Center.

### Type of 1963-65 Inscribed "Republica Argentina" Reading Down

**1969-71**        Perf. 13½
C123 AP35 40p violet    6.25   .40
C124 AP35 68p dk blue grn ('70)    2.25   .60
      Unwmk.
C125 AP35 26p yellow brn ('71)    .40   .35
C126 AP35 40p violet ('71)    3.25   .40
   Nos. C123-C126 (4)    12.15   1.75

Old Fire Engine and Fire Brigade Emblem AP48

**1970, Aug. 8**    Litho.    Unwmk.
C128 AP48 40c green & multi    1.75   .35

Centenary of the Fire Brigade.

Education Year Emblem — AP49

**1970, Aug. 29**       Perf. 13½
C129 AP49 68c blue & blk    1.00   .35

Issued for International Education Year.

Fleet Leaving Valparaiso, by Antonio Abel — AP50

**1970, Oct. 17**    Litho.    Perf. 13½
C130 AP50 26c multicolored    1.25   .35

150th anniv. of the departure for Peru of the liberation fleet from Valparaiso, Chile.

Sumampa Chapel — AP51

**1970, Nov. 7**        Photo.
C131 AP51 40c multicolored    1.25   .40

Bishopric of Tucuman, 400th anniversary.

Buenos Aires Planetarium AP52

**1970, Nov. 28**    Litho.    Perf. 13½
C132 AP52 40c multicolored    1.00   .35

Jorge Newbery and Morane Saulnier Plane — AP53

**1970, Dec. 19**
C133 AP53 26c bl, blk, yel & grn    .70   .35

24th Aeronautics and Space Week.

### Industries Type of Regular Issue

Design: 31c, Refinery.

**1971, Oct. 16**    Litho.    Perf. 13½
C134 A445 31c red, blk & yel    1.00   .35

### Type of 1963-65 Inscribed "Republica Argentina" Reading Down

**1971-74**        Unwmk
C135 AP35 45c brown    4.00   .35
C136 AP35 68c red    .55   .35
C137 AP35 70c vio blue ('73)    3.00   .50
C138 AP35 90c emerald ('73)    3.00   .50
C139 AP35 1.70p blue ('74)    .70   .25
C140 AP35 1.95p emerald ('74)    .70   .25
C141 AP35 2.65p dp claret ('74)    .70   .25
   Nos. C135-C141 (7)    12.65   2.45

Fluorescent paper was used for Nos. C135-C136, C138-C141. The 70c was issued on both papers. Value, 70c on fluorescent paper $5.50

Don Quixote, Drawing by Ignacio Zuloaga — AP54

**1975, Apr. 26**    Photo.    Perf. 13½
C145 AP54 2.75p yellow, blk & red    .85   .35

Day of the Race and for Espana 75 Intl. Philatelic Exhibition, Madrid, Apr. 4-13.

No. C87 Surcharged

**1975, Sept. 15**    Litho.    Wmk. 90
C146 AP35 9.20p on 5.60p    .95   .35
C147 AP35 19.70p on 5.60p    1.40   .35
C148 AP35 100p on 5.60p    6.00   2.25
   Nos. C146-C148 (3)    8.35   3.05

No. C87 Surcharged

**1975, Oct. 15**
C149 AP35 9.20p on 5.60p    1.1   .35
C150 AP35 19.70p on 5.60p    1.75   .60

Argentine State Airline, 50th Anniv. — AP55

No. C151, Junkers JU52-3M. No. C152, Grumman SA-16. No. C153, Fokker F-27. No. C154, Fokker F-28.

**1990, Sept. 15**    Litho.    Perf. 13½
C151 AP55 2500a multi    1.80   .90
C152 AP55 2500a multi    1.80   .90
C153 AP55 2500a multi    1.80   .90
C154 AP55 2500a multi    1.80   .90
   Nos. C151-C154 (4)    7.20   3.60

---

## AIR POST SEMI-POSTAL STAMPS

> Catalogue values for unused stamps in this section are for Never Hinged items.

### Philatelic Exhibition Type

Designs: No. CB1, Stamp engraving. No. CB2, Proofing stamp die. No. CB3, Sheet of stamps. No. CB4, The letter. No. CB5, Gen. San Martin.

       Perf. 13½
**1950, Aug. 26**   Wmk. 90   Photo.
CB1 SP8 45c + 45c vio bl    .35   .25
CB2 SP8 70c + 70c dk brn    .65   .40
   a. Souv. sheet of 3, #B12, CB1, CB2, imperf.    5.00   3.00
CB3 SP8 1p + 1p cerise    1.40   1.25
CB4 SP8 2.50p + 2.50p ol gray    9.00   6.00
CB5 SP8 5p + 5p dull grn    10.50   7.25
   Nos. CB1-CB5 (5)    21.90   15.15

Argentine Intl. Philatelic Exhib., 1950.

Pieta by Michelangelo SPAP2

**1951, Dec. 22**       Perf. 13½x13
CB6 SPAP2 2.45p + 7.55p grnsh blk    23.00   14.00

Surtax as for the Eva Peron Foundation.

Flower and Child's Head — SPAP3

**1958, Mar. 15**       Perf. 13½
CB7 SPAP3 1p +50c deep claret    .60   .35

Surtax for National Council for Children.

Stamp of 1858 — SPAP4

**1958, Mar. 29**    Litho.    Wmk. 90
CB8 SPAP4 1p + 50c gray ol & bl    .65   .35
CB9 SPAP4 2p + 1p rose lilac & vio    .80   .45
CB10 SPAP4 3p + 1.50p green & brown    .85   .55
CB11 SPAP4 5p + 2.50p gray ol & car rose    1.50   .90
CB12 SPAP4 10p + 5p gray ol & brn    2.75   1.75
   Nos. CB8-CB12 (5)    6.55   4.00

The surtax was for the Intl. Centennial Philatelic Exhibition, Buenos Aires, Apr. 19-27.

### Type of Semi-Postal Issue, 1958

Designs: 1p+50c, Flooded area. 5p+2.50p, House and truck under water.

**1958, Oct. 4**    Photo.    Perf. 13½
CB13 SP11 1p + 50c dull purple    .45   .25
CB14 SP11 5p + 2.50p grnsh blue    1.50   .80

The surtax was for victims of a flood in the Buenos Aires district.

### Type of Semi-Postal Issue

**1959, Sept. 5**    Litho.    Perf. 13½
CB15 SP13 2p + 1p Rowing    .70   .35
   a. Torch missing    170.00   170.00
CB16 SP13 3p + 1.50p Woman diver    1.00   .60
   a. Torch missing    170.00   170.00

### Bird Type of Semi-Postal Issue

2p+1p, Rufous tinamou. 3p+1.50p, Rhea.

**1960, Feb. 6**       Perf. 13½
CB17 SP14 2p + 1p rose car & sal    .70   .35
CB18 SP14 3p + 1.50p slate green    .80   .35

The surtax was for child welfare work. See No. CB29.

Buenos Aires Market Place, 1810 — SPAP5

6p+3p, Oxcart water carrier. 10.70p+5.00p, Settlers landing. 20p+10p, The Fort.

**1960, Aug. 20**    Photo.    Wmk. 90
CB19 SPAP5 2 + 1p rose brown    .35   .30
CB20 SPAP5 0 + 3p gray    .45   .30
CB21 SPAP5 10.70 + 5.30p blue    .80   .50
CB22 SPAP5 20 + 10p bluish grn    1.20   .85
   Nos. CB19-CB22 (4)    2.80   1.95

Inter-American Philatelic Exhibition EFIMAYO 1960, Buenos Aires, Oct. 12-24, held to for the sesquicentennial of the May Revolution of 1810.

No. CB22 exists imperf. Value, pair $40.
For overprints see Nos. CB25-CB28.

Seibo, National Flower — SPAP6

#CB24, Copihue, Chile's national flower.

**1960, Sept. 10** *Perf. 13½*

**CB23** SPAP6 6 + 3p lilac rose .70 .30
**CB24** SPAP6 10.70 + 5.30p ver 1.00 .40

The surtax was for earthquake victims in Chile. Nos. CB23-CB24 exist imperf. Value, each pair $40.

Nos. CB19-CB22 Overprinted

**1960, Oct. 8**

**CB25** SPAP5 2 + 1p rose brown .35 .30
**CB26** SPAP5 6 + 3p gray .45 .30
**CB27** SPAP5 10.70 + 5.30p blue .75 .40
**CB28** SPAP5 20 + 10p bluish green 1.50 .75
*Nos. CB25-CB28 (4)* 3.05 1.75

United Nations Day, Oct. 24, 1960.

### Type of Semi-Postal Issue, 1960

Design: Emperor penguins.

**1961, Feb. 25 Photo. Wmk. 90**

**CB29** SP14 1.80p + 90c gray .60 .35

The surtax was for child welfare work. Exists imperf. Value, pair $50.

Stamp of 1862 — SPAP7

**1962, May 19 Litho.**

**CB30** SPAP7 6.50p + 6.50p Prus bl & grnsh bl .95 .65

Opening of the "Argentina 62" Philatelic Exhibition, Buenos Aires, May 19-29. Exists imperf. Value, pair $40.

### Type of Semi-Postal Issue, 1963

**1963, May 18 Wmk. 90** *Perf. 13½*

**CB31** SP21 11p + 5p Bicycling 1.20 .50

Exists imperf. Value, pair $40.

### Type of Semi-Postal Issue, 1962

Design: Pitangus sulphuratus bolivianus.

**1963, Dec. 21** *Perf. 13½*

**CB32** SP20 11p + 5p multi 1.25 .60

The surtax was for child welfare.

### Type of Semi-Postal Issue, 1964

**1964, July 18 Litho.**

**CB33** SP22 11p + 5p Sailboat 1.40 .70

Exists imperf. Value, pair $50.

Crutch, Olympic Torch and Rings — SPAP8

**1964, Sept. 19 Litho.** *Perf. 13½*

**CB34** SPAP8 18p + 9p bluish grn, blk, red & yel .85 .60

13th "Olympic" games for the handicapped, Tokyo, 1964. Exists imperf. Value, pair $50.

### Bird Type of Semi-Postal Issue, 1962

Design: Iridoprocne leucopyga.

**1964, Dec. 23 Litho. Wmk. 90**

**CB35** SP20 18p + 9p multi 1.25 .85

The surtax was for child welfare.

Furnarius Rufus Rufus — SP22a

**1966, Mar. 26** *Perf. 13½*

**CB36** SP22a 27.50p + 12.50p bl, ocher, yel & grn 1.10 .85

The surtax was for child welfare.

Coat of Arms SPAP9

**1966, June 25 Litho.** *Perf. 13½*

**CB37** SPAP9 10p + 10p multi 2.00 1.40

ARGENTINA '66 Philatelic Exhibition held in connection with the sesquicentennial celebration of the Declaration of Independence, Buenos Aires, July 16-23. The surtax was for the Exhibition. Issued in sheets of 4.

Designs: 15p+7p, Thraupis bonariensis. 26p+13p, Ramphastos toco.

**1967 Litho. Wmk. 90**

**CB38** SP22a 15p + 7p blk, bl, grn & yel 1.75 1.00
**CB39** SP22a 26p + 13p blk, org, yel & bl .65 .40

The surtax was for child welfare.
Issued: 15p+7p, Jan. 14; 26p+13p, Dec. 23.

### Bird Type of Semi-Postal Issue, 1969

Design: Ceophloeus lineatus.

**1969, Sept. 20 Wmk. 365** *Perf. 13½*

**CB40** SP24 26p + 13p multi 1.05 .40

The surtax was for child welfare.

### Bird Type of Semi-Postal Issue, 1970

Design: Phoenicopterus ruber chilensis.

**1970, May 9 Litho. Wmk. 365**

**CB41** SP25 40c + 20c multi 1.05 .40

The surtax was for child welfare.

### Fish Type of Semi-Postal Issue, 1971

Design: Odostethes platensis.

**1971, Feb. 20 Unwmk.** *Perf. 12½*
**Size: 75x15mm**

**CB42** SP26 40c + 20c multi .75 .40

The surtax was for child welfare.

## OFFICIAL STAMPS

Regular Issues Overprinted in Black — a

**1884-87 Unwmk.** *Perf. 12, 14*

**O1** A29 ½c brown *40.00* *25.00*
**O2** A23 1c red 15.00 10.00
*b.* Perf. 12 100.00 80.00
**O3** A29 1c red 1.00 .85
*b.* Double overprint 100.00 100.00
**O4** A20 2c green 1.00 .50
*b.* Double overprint 120.00 120.00
**O5** A11 4c brown 1.00 .50
**O6** A7 8c lake 1.00 1.00
**O7** A8 10c green 100.00 50.00
**O8** A23 12c ultra (#45) 10.00 5.00
*a.* Perf. 14 1,000. 250.00
**O9** A29 12c grnsh blue 1.50 1.00
**O10** A19 24c blue 2.00 1.50
**O11** A21 25c lake 40.00 30.00
**O12** A12 30c orange 80.00 70.00
**O13** A13 60c black 50.00 40.00
**O14** A14 90c blue 40.00 30.00
*b.* Double overprint 120.00 120.00
*Nos. O1-O14 (14)* 382.50 265.35

### Inverted Overprint

*O1a* A29 ½c 30.00 20.00
*O2a* A23 1c Perf. 14 100.00 80.00
*c.* Perf. 12 75.00 —
*O3a* A29 1c 3.00 3.00
*O4a* A20 2c 120.00 100.00
*O5a* A11 4c 60.00 50.00
*O6a* A7 8c (Inverted overprint on reverse) *500.00* —
*O8b* A23 12c Perf. 12 20.00 —
*O9a* A29 12c 300.00 250.00
*O10a* A19 24c 10.00 5.00
*O13a* A13 60c 150.00 120.00
*O14a* A14 90c 120.00 120.00

**1884** ***Rouletted***

**O15** A17 16c green 3.00 2.00
*a.* Double overprint 25.00 —
*b.* Inverted overprint 300.00
**O16** A18 20c blue 15.00 12.00
*a.* Inverted overprint 120.00 80.00
**O17** A19 24c blue 2.50 1.50
*a.* Inverted overprint 8.00 5.00
*b.* Double ovpt., one inverted 250.00 —
*Nos. O15-O17 (3)* 20.50 15.50

### Overprinted Diagonally in Red

**1885** *Perf. 12*

**O18** A20 2c green 5.00 4.00
*a.* Inverted overprint 100.00
**O19** A11 4c brown 3.00 2.00
*a.* Inverted overprint 100.00 —
*b.* Double overprint 100.00 100.00
**O20** A13 60c black 50.00 40.00
**O21** A14 90c blue 450.00 275.00

**1885** ***Rouletted***

**O22** A19 24c blue 40.00 20.00

On all of these stamps, the overprint is found reading both upwards and downwards.
Counterfeits exist of No. O21 overprint and others.

Regular Issues Handstamped Horizontally in Black — b

**1884** *Perf. 12, 14*

**O23** A23 1c red 100.00 50.00
*a.* Perf. 12 400.00 300.00
**O24** A20 2c green, diagonal overprint 60.00 40.00
*a.* Horizontal overprint 450.00 300.00
**O25** A11 4c brown 25.00 20.00
**O26** A7 8c lake 25.00 20.00
**O27** A23 12c ultra 60.00 50.00

### Overprinted Diagonally

**O28** A19 24c bl, rouletted 50.00 35.00
**O29** A13 60c black 30.00 15.00

Counterfeit overprints exist.

Liberty Head — O1

*Perf. 11½, 12 and Compound*

**1901, Dec. 1 Engr.**

**O31** O1 1c gray .50 .25
*b.* Vert. pair, imperf. horiz. 80.00
*c.* Horiz. pair, imperf. vert. 100.00
**O32** O1 2c orange brown .50 .25
**O33** O1 5c red .50 .25
*b.* Vert. pair, imperf. horiz. 100.00
**O34** O1 10c dark green 1.00 .25
**O35** O1 30c dark blue 8.00 3.00
**O36** O1 50c orange 4.00 2.00
*Nos. O31-O36 (6)* 14.50 6.00

### Imperf, Pairs

*O31a* O1 1c 80.00
*O32a* O1 2c 80.00
*O33a* O1 5c 100.00
*O34a* O1 10c 80.00
*O35a* O1 30c 100.00
*O36a* O1 50c 150.00

Regular Stamps of 1935-51 Overprinted in Black — c

*Perf. 13x13½, 13½x13, 13*

**1938-54 Wmk. RA in Sun (90)**

**O37** A129 1c buff ('40) .75 .35
**O38** A130 2c dk brn ('40) .75 .35
**O39** A132 3c grn ('39) 1.75 .75
**O40** A132 3c lt gray ('39) .75 .35
**O41** A134 5c yel brn .75 .35
**O42** A195 5c car ('53) .90 .35
**O43** A137 10c carmine .60 .25
**O44** A137 10c brn ('39) 1.50 .35
**O45** A140 15c lt gray bl, type II ('47) .90 .35
**O46** A139 15c slate blue 1.50 .35
**O47** A139 15c pale ultra ('39) .90 .35
**O48** A139 20c blue ('53) 1.75 .75
**O49** A141 25c carmine .75 .35
*a.* Overprint 11mm 1.50 .35
**O49B** A143 40c dk violet 3.75 1.20
**O50** A144 50c red & org .75 .35
*a.* Overprint 11mm .75 .35
**O51** A146 1p brn blk & lt bl ('40) .90 .35
*a.* Overprint 11mm 13.50 .75
**O52** A224 1p choc & lt bl ('51) 3.00 .35
*a.* Overprint 11mm 2.25 .35
**O53** A147 2p brn lake & dk ultra (ovpt. 11mm) ('54) 3.00 .75
*Nos. O37-O53 (18)* 24.95 8.25

### Overprinted in Black on Stamps and Types of 1945-47

*Perf. 13x13½, 13½x13*

**1945-46 Unwmk.**

**O54** A130 2c sepia 6.00 5.00
**O55** A134 3c lt gray 4.00 4.00
**O56** A134 5c yel brn .60 .25
**O57** A195 5c dp car .50 .25
**O58** A137 10c brown 1.00 .25
*a.* Double overprint
**O59** A140 15c lt gray bl, type II .70 .25
**O61** A141 25c dull rose .50 .25
**O62** A144 50c red & org 1.00 .25
**O63** A146 1p brn blk & lt bl 1.00 .25
**O64** A147 2p brn lake & bl .60 .25
**O65** A148 5p ind & ol grn .80 .25
**O66** A149 10p dp cl & int blk 1.25 .50
**O67** A150 20p bl grn & brn 2.50 2.00
*Nos. O54-O67 (13)* 20.45 13.75

### Overprinted in Black on Stamps and Types of 1942-50

*Perf. 13, 13x13½*

**1944-51 Wmk. 288**

**O73** A132 3c lt gray 6.00 2.00
**O74** A134 5c yellow brown 2.00 .50
**O75** A137 10c red brown .60 .25
**O76** A140 15c lt gray bl, type II 1.00 .25
**O77** A144 50c red & org (overprint 11 mm) 8.00 2.00
**O78** A146 1p brn blk & lt bl (overprint 11mm) 10.00 5.00
*Nos. O73-O78 (6)* 27.60 10.00

**Catalogue values for unused stamps in this section, from this point to the end of the section, are for Never Hinged items.**

Nos. 600-606 Overprinted in Black — d

**1953 Wmk. 90** *Perf. 13*

**O79** A228 5c gray .50 .25
**O80** A228 10c rose lilac .50 .25
**O81** A228 20c rose pink .50 .25
**O82** A228 25c dull green .50 .25
**O83** A228 40c dull violet .50 .25
**O84** A228 45c deep blue .60 .25
**O85** A228 50c dull brown .50 .25

Nos. 611-617 Overprinted in Blue — e

*Perf. 13x13½, 13½x13*

O86 A229 1p dk brown .50 .25
O87 A229 1.50p dp green .60 .25
O88 A229 2p brt carmine .60 .25
O89 A229 3p indigo .60 .35

**Size: 30x40mm**

O90 A229 5p red brown 1.25 .80
O91 A228 10p red 10.00 7.00
O92 A229 20p green 100.00 90.00
*Nos. O79-O92 (14)* 117.15 100.65

No. 612 Overprinted in Blue — f

O93 A229 1.50p dp grn 3.00 1.50

**Regular Issues of 1954-59 Variously Overprinted in Black or Blue**

g

h

*Perf. 13½, 13x13½, 13½x13*

**1955-61 Litho. Wmk. 90**

O94 A237(c) 20c red (#629) .50 .25
O95 A237(d) 20c red (#629) .50 .25
O96 A237(d) 40c red, ovpt. 15mm (#630) .50 .25

**Engr.**

O97 A239(g) 50c bl (#632) .50 .25

**Photo.**

O98 A239(h) 1p brn (#635) .50 .25
O99 A239(e) 1p brn (Bl, #635) .50 .25
O100 A239(e) 1p brn (Dk, #635) .50 .25

**Engr.**

O101 A239(h) 3p vio brn (#638) .50 .25
O102 A240(h) 5p gray grn (#639) 1.00 .40
O103 A240(e) 10p yel grn (#640) 1.50 .50
O104 A240(f) 20p dl vio (#641) 3.00 2.00
O105 A240(h) 20p dl vio (#641) 1.50 .80
*a.* Perf 13½ (#641a) 2.00 1.00
O106 A241(e) 50p ultra & ind (#642) 3.00 1.50
*Nos. O94-O106 (13)* 14.00 7.20

The overprints on Nos. O99-O100 & O103-O104 are horizontal; that on No. O106 is vertical. On No. O106 overprint measures 23mm.

Issued: No. O102, 1957; Nos. O97, O101, O103, O105, 1958; Nos. O98-O99, O104, 1959; No. O100, 1960; No. O106, 1961.

**No. 659 Overprinted Type "d"**

**1957 Wmk. 90 Litho.** *Perf. 13*

O108 A133 20c dl pur (ovpt. 15mm) .50 .25

**Nos. 666, 658 and 663 Variously Overprinted**

**1957 Photo.** *Perf. 13x13½, 13½*

O109 A261(g) 2p claret .50 .25
O110 A254(e) 2.40p brown .50 .30
O111 A258(c) 4.40p grnsh gray .50 .25
*Nos. O109-O111 (3)* 1.50 .80

**Nos. 668, 685-687, 690-691, 693-705, 742, 742C and Types of 1959-65 Overprinted in Black, Blue or Red Types "e," "g," or**

i

j

k

m

n

**Lithographed; Photogravure**

**1960-68** *Perf. 13x13½, 13½*

O112 A128(g) 5c buff (vert. ovpt.) .50 .25
O113 A275(j) 10c sl grn .50 .30
O114 A275(j) 20c dl red brn 1.00 .80
O115 A275(i) 50c bister .50 .25
O116 A278(k) 1p brn .60 .30
O117 A278(j) 1p brn, photo. (vert. ovpt.) 2.00 .25
O117A A278(j) 1p brn, litho., (down) 10.00 2.00
O118 A276(j) 2p rose red .50 .25
O119 A312(m) 2p dp grn 1.00 .25
O120 A312(j) 2p brt grn (up) 2.00 .30
O121 A312(j) 2p grn litho. (down) 2.00 1.00
O122 A277(e) 3p dk bl (horiz.) .50 .25
O123 A277(j) 3p dk blue 30.00 10.00
O124 A276(j) 4p red, litho. .50 .25
O125 A312(j) 4p rose red, litho. (down) 1.00 .25
O126 A277(e) 5p brn (Bl) (horiz.) .80 .30
O127 A277(e) 5p brn (Bk) (horiz.) .60 .25
O128 A277(j) 6p sepia 1.00 .25
O130 A276(j) 8p red .50 .25
O131 A278(i) 10p lt red brn .60 .25
O132 A276(j) 10p vermilion 1.00 .25
O133 A278(j) 10p brn car (up) 4.00 1.00
O133A A278(j) 10p brn car (down) 90.00 30.00
O134 A278(m) 12p dk brn vio (horiz.) .50 .25
O135 A278(k) 20p Prus grn .60 .30
O136 A278(j) 20p Prus grn (up) .60 .25
O137 A276(j) 20p red, litho. .60 .30
O138 A276(m) 20p red, litho. (horiz.) .80 .30
O139 A278(j) 23p grn (vert. ovpt.) 1.50 .50
O140 A278(j) 25p dp vio, photo. (R) (up) 2.50 .80
O141 A278(j) 25p pur, litho. (R) (down) 2.50 1.00
O142 A241(n) 50p dk blue 6.00 3.00
O143 A279(m) 100p bl (horiz. ovpt.) 4.00 2.00
O144 A279(m) 100p blue (up) 4.00 1.00
O145 A280(m) 300p dp violet (horiz.) 12.00 8.00
*Nos. O112-O133,O134-O145 (34)* 96.70 36.95

The "m" overprint measures 15½mm on 2p; 14½mm on 12p, 100p and 300p; 13mm on 20p.

Issued: Nos. O122, O127, O135, 1961; Nos. O112-O114, O116, O118, 1962; No. O124, 1963; Nos. O119, O134, O143, 1964; Nos. O117, O125, O130, O139, O144, 1965; Nos. O120, O128, O132-O133, O136, O140, O142, O145, 1966; Nos. O121, O129, O137-O138, O141, 1967; No. O117A, 1968.

**Nos. 699, 823-825, 827-829, and Type of 1962 Overprinted in Black or Red Types "j," "m," or "o"**

o

**Inscribed: "Republica Argentina"**

**Litho., Photo., Engr.**

**1964-67 Wmk. 90** *Perf. 13½*

O149 A312(j) 6p rose red (down) 2.00 1.00
O153 A238a(m) 22p ultra 1.25 .50
O154 A238a(j) 43p dk car rose (down) 3.00 1.00
O155 A238a(j) 45p brn, photo. (up) 3.00 1.00
O156 A238a(j) 45p brn, litho. (up) 10.00 8.00
O157 A241(j) 50p dk bl (up) (R) 8.00 1.50
O158 A366(j) 90p ol bis (up) 10.00 8.00
O162 A495(o) 500p yel grn 25.00 20.00
*Nos. O149-O162 (8)* 62.25 41.00

Issued: No. O153, 1964; No. O155, 1966; Nos. O149, O156-O162, 1967.

**Type of 1959-67 Ovptd. Type "j"**

**1960 Litho. Wmk. 365** *Perf. 13½*

O163 A276 20p vermilion 1.00 .80

**Beginning with No. 2001, many Argentine stamps are inscribed "Correo Official," but are not official stamps.**

---

**OFFICIAL DEPARTMENT STAMPS**

**Regular Issues of 1911-38 Overprinted in Black**

**Ministry of Agriculture**

No. OD1

**1913 Type I** *Perf. 13½x12½*

OD1 A88 2c choc (#181) .50 .50
OD2 A88 1c ocher (#190) .50 .50
OD3 A88 2c choc (#191) 1.00 1.00
OD4 A88 5c red (#194) 1.00 .50
*a.* Perf. 13½ (#194a) 4.00 7.50
OD5 A88 12c dp bl (#196) 10.00 .50
*a.* Perf. 13½ (#196a) 10.00 1.00
*Nos. OD2-OD5 (4)* 12.50 2.50

**1915**

OD6 A88 1c ocher (#208) 1.50 1.00
OD7 A88 2c chocolate (#209) 1.00 .50
OD8 A88 5c red (#212) 2.00 1.00
*Nos. OD6-OD8 (3)* 4.50 2.50

No. OD9

**1916** *Perf. 13½*

OD9 A91 5c red (#220) 1.00 .50

No. OD11

No. OD15

**1918**

OD10 A94 12c blue (#238) 3.00 .50
OD11 A93 1c buff (#249) .50 .50
OD12 A93 2c brown (#250) .50 .50
OD13 A93 5c red (#253) .50 .50
OD14 A94 12c blue (#255) .50 .50
OD15 A94 20c ultra (#256) .50 .50
*Nos. OD10-OD15 (6)* 5.50 3.00

**1920** *Perf. 13½, 13½x12½ (OD16)*

OD16 A93 1c buff (#265) 2.00 1.25
OD17 A93 2c brown (#266A) 8.00 2.00
OD18 A93 5c red (#269A) .70 .50
*a.* Perf. 13½x12½ (#269) 1.40 .50
*Nos. OD16-OD18 (3)* 10.70 3.75

**1922** *Perf. 13½*

OD19 A94 12c blue (#311) 4.00 2.00
OD20 A94 20c ultra (#312) 100.00

No. OD23

**1923** *Perf. 13½x12½*

OD21 A104 1c buff (#324) 2.00 1.00
*a.* Perf. 13½ (#324A) 10.00 10.00
OD22 A104 2c dk brn (#325) .50 .50
OD23 A104 5c red (#328) .50 .50
*a.* Perf. 13½ (#328A) 2.00 .50
OD24 A104 12c deep blue (#330) .80 .50
OD25 A104 20c ultra (#331) .80 .50
*a.* Perf. 13½ (#331A) 12.00 8.00
*Nos. OD21-OD25 (5)* 4.60 3.00

**1924**

OD26 A104 1c buff (#341) .50 .50
*a.* Inverted ovpt. 20.00 15.00
OD27 A104 2c dk brn (#342) .50 .50
OD29 A104 5c red (#345) .50 .50
OD30 A104 10c dl grn (#346) 1.00 .50
OD31 A104 12c dp bl (#347) .50 .50
OD32 A104 20c dp bl (#348) .50 .50
*a.* Inverted ovpt 80.00 60.00
*Nos. OD26-OD32 (6)* 3.50 3.00

No. OD34

**1926**

OD34 A110 12c deep blue (#360) .50 .50

No. OD28B

**Type II**

**1931-36** *Perf. 13x13½, 13½x13*

OD27B A104 2c dk brn (#342) 10.00 6.00
OD28B A104 3c green (#343) .50 .50
OD29B A104 5c red (#345) .50 .50
OD30B A104 10c dl grn (#346) .50 .50
*c.* Typo (coil) (#346a) 1.00 1.00
OD32B A104 20c ultra (#348) 1.00 .50
*c.* Typo (coil) (#348a) 1.00 .50
OD33B A104 30c claret (#351) .50 .50
*c.* Typo (coil) (#351a) 1.00 .50

648 ARGENTINA

No. OD46

**1936-38** **Litho.**
OD35 A129 1c buff (#419) .50 .50
OD36 A130 2c dk brn (#420) .50 .50
OD37 A132 3c green (#422) 1.00 .50
OD38 A134 5c yel brn (#427) 1.00 .50
OD40 A139 15c lt gray bl (#436) 5.00 1.00
OD41 A140 20c lt ultra (#437) 6.00 .50
OD42 A140 20c lt ultra (#438) .80 .50
OD43 A141 25c car & pink (#441), perf. 13x13½ .50 .50
OD44 A142 30c org brn & yel brown (#442) .50 .50
OD45 A145 1p brn blk & Lt bl (#445) 10.00 4.00
OD46 A146 1p brn blk & lt bl (#446) 3.00 1.00
*Nos. OD35-OD46 (11)* 28.80 10.00

**Typo.** ***Perf. 13½***
OD38A A134 5c yel brn (#427) 1.00 .50
OD39A A137 10c carmine (#430) 1.00 .50
*b.* Perf. 13½x13 (#430a) 1.00 .50

### Ministry of War

No. OD47

**1913** **Type I** ***Perf. 13½x12½***
OD47 A88 2c choc (#181) 2.50 .50
OD48 A88 1c ocher (#190) .50 .50
OD49 A88 2c choc (#191) 8.00 .50
*a.* Perf. 13½ (#191a) 20.00 20.00
OD50 A88 5c red (#194) 1.00 .50
*a.* Inverted ovpt. 50.00 —
OD51 A88 12c dp bl (#196) .50 .50
*a.* Perf. 13½ (#196a) 10.00 6.00
*Nos. OD48-OD51 (4)* 10.00 2.00

**1915**
OD52 A88 1c ocher (#208) 60.00 12.00
OD53 A88 2c chocolate (#209) 4.00 .50
OD54 A88 5c red (#212) 8.00 .50
*Nos. OD52-OD54 (3)* 72.00 13.00

**1916** ***Perf. 13½***
OD55 A91 5c red (#220) 3.00 1.00
OD56 A92 12c blue (#222) 6.00 1.00

**1918**
OD57 A93 1c buff (#232) 2.00 .50
*a.* Perf. 13½x12½ (#232B) 10.00 6.00
OD58 A93 2c brown (#233) 24.00 1.50
*a.* Perf. 13½x12½ (#233B) 3.00 .50
OD59 A93 5c red (#236B) (Perf. 13½x12½) 1.50 .50
OD60 A94 12c blue (#238) 4.00 1.50
*Nos. OD57-OD60 (4)* 31.50 4.00

**1918**
OD61 A93 1c buff (#249) 3.00 1.00
*a.* Perf. 13½x12½ (#249B) 6.00 5.00
OD62 A93 2c brown (#250) .50 .50
*a.* Perf. 13½x12½ (#250B) 1.00 .50
OD63 A93 5c red (#253) 2.00 1.00
*a.* Perf. 13½x12½ (#253B) .50 .50
OD64 A94 12c blue (#255) 1.50 .50
OD65 A94 20c ultra (#256) 8.00 1.25
*Nos. OD61-OD65 (5)* 15.00 4.25

**1920**
OD66 A93 2c brown (#266A) 12.00 6.00
*a.* Perf. 13½x12½ (#266) 1.00 .50
OD67 A93 5c red (#269A) 10.00 6.00
*a.* Perf. 13½x12½ (#269) 10.00 6.00
OD68 A94 12c blue (#271) 2.00 .30
*Nos. OD66-OD68 (3)* 24.00 12.30

**1921**
OD69 A94 12c blue (#299) 18.00 5.00

No. OD72

**1922**
OD70 A93 1c buff (#305) 5.00 .60
OD71 A93 2c brown (13½x12½) (#306B) 10.00 2.00
OD72 A103 5c red (#309) 5.00 1.00
OD73 A94 20c ultra (#312) 2.00 .50
*Nos. OD70-OD73 (4)* 22.00 4.10

***Perf. 13½x12½***
OD74 A93 2c brown (#318A) 10.00 2.00

**1923** ***Perf. 13½x12½***
OD75 A104 1c buff (#324) 1.50 .50
*a.* Inverted ovpt. *20.00 18.00*
*b.* Perf. 13½ (#324A) 45.00 24.00
OD76 A104 2c dk brn (#325) .50 .50
*a.* Perf. 13½ (#325A) 2.00 .50
OD77 A104 5c red (#328) 1.00 .50
*a.* Inverted ovpt. *20.00 18.00*
*b.* Perf. 13½ (#328A) 4.00 4.00
OD78 A104 12c dp bl (#330) 2.00 .50
OD79 A104 20c ultra (#331) 6.00 .50
*a.* Perf. 13½ (#331A) 6.00 1.00
*b.* As "a.," inverted ovpt. *20.00 18.00*
*Nos. OD75-OD79 (5)* 11.00 2.50

**1924**
OD80 A104 1c buff (#341) 10.00 3.00
OD81 A104 2c dk brn (#342) 1.00 .50
OD82 A104 3c green (#343) 2.00 .50
OD83 A104 5c red (#345) .50 .50
OD84 A104 10c dl grn (#346) 6.00 .50
OD85 A104 20c ultra (#348) .50 .50
OD86 A104 30c claret (#351) 10.00 1.00
OD87 A105 1p blue & red (#353) 10.00 2.00
*Nos. OD80-OD87 (8)* 40.00 8.50

No. OD88

**1926**
OD88 A109 5c red (#359) 3.00 .50

No. OD82B

### Type II

**1931-36** ***Perf. 13½x12½, 13 (OD87B)***
OD82B A104 3c green (#343) 6.00 1.00
OD83B A104 5c red (#345) 1.25 .50
*c.* Inverted ovpt. — *60.00*
OD84B A104 10c dl grn (#346) 1.00 .50
*c.* Typo (coil) (346a) 5.00 1.00
OD85B A104 20c ultra (#348) 1.00 .50
*c.* Typo (coil) (#348a) 12.00 .50
OD86B A104 30c claret (#351) 1.50 .50
*c.* Typo (coil) (#351a) 2.00 .50
OD87B A105 1p blue & red (#353) 10.00 2.00
*Nos. OD82B-OD87B (6)* 20.75 5.00

No. OD90

**1936-38** **Litho.**
OD89 A129 1c buff (#419) .50 .50
OD90 A130 2c dk brn (#420) .50 .50
OD91 A132 3c green (#422) 1.00 .50
OD92 A134 5c yel brn (#427) .50 .50
OD93 A137 10c car (#430) .50 .50
OD94 A139 15c slate bl (#434) 1.60 .50
OD95 A140 20c lt ultra (#437) 14.00 .50
OD96 A140 20c lt ultra (#438) 1.00 .50
OD97 A141 25c car & pink (#441) .50 .50
OD98 A142 30c org brn & yel brown (#442) .50 .50
OD99 A144 50c red & org (#444) 1.50 .50
OD100 A145 1p brn blk & lt bl (#445) 4.00 2.00
OD101 A146 1p brn blk & lt bl (#446) 2.00 1.00
*Nos. OD89-OD101 (13)* 28.10 8.50

**Typo.** ***Perf. 13½***
OD92B A134 5c yel brn (#427) .50 .50
*c.* Inverted ovpt. 20.00 15.00
OD93B A137 10c car (#430) 1.00 .50
*c.* Inverted ovpt. 50.00 35.00
*d.* Perf. 13½x13 (#430a) 2.00 1.00

### Ministry of Finance

No. OD102

**1913** **Type I** ***Perf. 13½x12½***
OD102 A88 2c choc (#181) .50 .50
OD103 A88 1c ocher (#190) .50 .50
OD104 A88 2c choc (#191) .50 .50
OD105 A88 5c red (#194) .50 .50
OD106 A88 12c dp bl (#196) .50 .50
*a.* Perf. 13½ (#196a) 180.00 35.00
*Nos. OD103-OD106 (4)* 2.00 2.00

**1915**
OD107 A88 2c choc (#209) .50 .50
OD108 A88 5c red (#212) .50 .50

**1916** ***Perf. 13½***
OD109 A91 5c red (#220) .70 .60

**1917**
OD110 A93 2c brown (#233) .50 .50
OD111 A93 5c red (#236) 8.00 1.00
OD112 A94 12c blue (#238) .50 .50
*Nos. OD110-OD112 (3)* 9.00 2.00

**1918**
OD113 A93 2c brown (#250) *100.00*
OD114 A93 5c red (#253) .70 .50
*a.* Perf. 13½x12½ (#253B) 4.00 .50
OD115 A94 12c blue (#255) .70 .50
OD116 A94 20c ultra (#256) 2.00 1.00
*Nos. OD113-OD116 (4)* 3.40 102.00

**1920**
OD117 A93 1c buff (#265) 6.00 3.00
OD118 A93 2c brown (#266) 9.00 5.00
OD119 A93 5c #269 20.00 12.00
*a.* Perf. 13½ (#269A) 12.00 1.00
OD120 A94 12c blue (#271) (perf. 13½) 3.00 1.00
*Nos. OD117-OD120 (4)* 38.00 21.00

**1922**
OD121 A94 20c ultra (#312) 60.00 15.00

**1923** ***Perf. 13½x12½, 13½***
OD122 A104 1c buff (#324) *20.00 10.00*
*a.* Perf. 13½ (#324A) 10.00 6.00
OD123 A104 2c dk brn (#325) .50 .50
*a.* Perf. 13½ (#325A) — 12.00
OD124 A104 5c red (#328) .50 .50
*a.* Inverted ovpt. — *35.00*
*b.* Perf. 13½ (#328A) 2.00 1.00
OD125 A104 12c dp bl (#330) .70 .50
*a.* Perf. 13½ (#330A) 5.00 1.00
OD126 A104 20c ultra (#331) .50 .50
*a.* Perf. 13½ (#331A) 10.00 4.00
*Nos. OD122-OD126 (5)* 22.20 12.00

**1924** ***Perf. 13½x12½***
OD127 A104 2c dk brn (#342) 250.00 250.00
OD128 A104 5c red (#345) 2.00 .50
OD130 A104 12c dp bl (#347) 80.00 35.00
OD131 A104 20c ultra (#348) .50 .50
*Nos. OD127-OD131 (4)* 332.50 286.00

**1926**
OD134 A110 12c dp bl (#360) 60.00 25.00

No. OD129B

No. OD133B

**1931-36** **Type II**
OD127B A104 3c green (#343) 60.00 30.00
OD129B A104 10c dl grn (#346) .50 .50
*c.* Typo (coil) (#346a) 1.25 .50
OD131B A104 20c ultra (#348) 2.00 .50
*c.* Typo (coil) (#348a) 1.00 .50
OD132B A104 30c claret (#351) 1.00 .50
*c.* Typo (coil) (#351a) 3.00 .50

***Perf. 13***
OD133B A105 1p blue & red (#353) 2.00 1.00
*Nos. OD127B-OD133B (5)* 65.50 32.50

No. OD135

**1936-38** **Litho.** ***Perf. 13½x13***
OD135 A129 1c buff (#419) .50 .50
OD136 A130 2c dk brn (#420) .50 .50
OD137 A132 3c green (#422) 1.50 1.00
OD138 A134 5c yel brn (#427d) .50 .50
OD139 A137 10c car (#430) .50 .50
OD140 A139 15c slate blue (#434) ('36) 6.00 1.60
*a.* Inverted ovpt. — 80.00
OD141 A140 20c lt ultra (#437) 5.00 .50
OD142 A140 20c lt ultra (#438) .50 .50
OD143 A142 30c org brn & yel brown (#442) .50 .50
OD144 A145 1p brn blk & lt bl (#445) 10.00 3.00
OD145 A146 1p brn blk & lt bl (#446) 1.20 .80
*Nos. OD135-OD145 (11)* 26.70 9.90

**Typo.**
OD138A A134 5c yel brn (#427) .50 .50
*b.* Inverted ovpt. *50.00 50.00*
OD139A A137 10c car (#430) 2.00 .50
*b.* Perf. 13½x13 (#430a) 40.00 1.00

### Ministry of the Interior

No. OD169

**1913** **Type I** ***Perf. 13½x12½***
OD146 A88 2c choc (#181) 2.00 .50
OD147 A88 1c ocher (#190) .50 .50
OD148 A88 2c choc (#191) 5.00 2.00
OD149 A88 5c red (#194) 3.00 .50
OD150 A88 12c dp bl (#196) 2.50 .50
*a.* Perf. 13½ (#196a) 10.00 3.00
*Nos. OD146-OD150 (5)* 13.00 4.00

**1915**
OD151 A88 2c chocolate (#209) 4.00 1.20
OD152 A88 5c red (#212) 4.00 1.20

**1916** ***Perf. 13½***
OD153 A91 5c red (#220) 4.00 1.60

**1918**
OD154 A93 5c red (#236B) 10.00 1.00
OD155 A93 2c brown (#250) .50 .50
OD156 A93 5c red (#253) .70 .50
*a.* Perf. 13½x12½ (#253B) 2.00 .50
*Nos. OD154-OD156 (3)* 11.20 2.00

**1920**
OD157 A93 1c buff (13½x12½) (#265) *10.00 3.00*
OD158 A93 5c red (#269) 10.00 2.00

**1922** ***Perf. 13½***
OD160 A103 5c red (#309) 20.00 8.00
OD161 A94 12c blue (#311) 5.00 1.00
OD162 A94 20c ultra (#312) *2.00 2.00*
*Nos. OD160-OD162 (3)* 27.00 11.00

**1923** ***Perf. 13½x12½***
OD163 A104 1c buff (#324) 6.00 1.00
*a.* Perf. 13½ (#324A) 4.00 2.00
OD164 A104 2c dark brown (#325) .50 .50
*a.* Perf. 13½ (#325A) 50.00 30.00
OD165 A104 5c red (#328) 1.20 .50
*a.* Perf. 13½ (#328A) 10.00 1.00
OD166 A104 12c deep blue (#330) 12.00 4.00
*a.* Perf. 13½ (#330A) 45.00 20.00
OD167 A104 20c ultra (#331) 20.00 2.00
*a.* Perf. 13½ (#331A) 20.00 10.00
*Nos. OD163-OD167 (5)* 39.70 8.00

**1924**
OD168 A104 1c buff (#341) .50 .50
OD169 A104 2c dk brn (#342) 1.00 .50
OD170 A104 3c green (#343) 8.00 2.00
OD171 A104 5c red (#345) 1.00 .50
OD173 A104 12c dp bl (#347) 1.00 .50
OD174 A104 20c ultra (#348) 20.00 8.00
*Nos. OD168-OD174 (6)* 31.50 12.00

No. OD172B

### Type II

**1931-36** ***Perf. 13½x12½***
OD170B A104 3c green (#343) 2.00 2.00
OD171B A104 5c red (#345) .75 .50

ARGENTINA 649

OD172B A104 10c dull green (#346) 1.00 .50
c. Typo (coil) (#346a) .50 .50
OD174B A104 20c ultra (#348) 2.00 1.00
c. Typo (coil) (#348a) 2.00 1.00
OD175B A104 30c claret (#351) 6.00 1.00
c. Typo (coil) (#351a) 16.00 5.00
*Nos. OD170B-OD175B (5)* 11.75 5.00

No. OD182A

**1936-38 Litho. *Perf. 13½x13***

OD176 A129 1c buff (#419) .50 .50
OD177 A130 2c dk brn (#420) .50 .50
OD178 A132 3c green (#422) 1.00 .50
OD178A A134 5c yel brn (#427d) .50 .50
OD180 A139 15c slate bl (#434) ('36) 1.40 .50
OD181 A140 20c lt ultra (#437) 6.00 1.00
OD182 A140 20c lt ultra (#438) 1.00 .50
OD182A A142 30c org brn & yel brown (#442) .50 .50
OD182B A145 1p brn blk & lt blue (#445) 10.00 6.00
OD182C A146 1p brn blk & lt bl (#446) ('37) 1.25 .50
*Nos. OD176-OD182C (10)* 22.65 11.00

**Typo. *Perf. 13½***

OD178D A134 5c yel brn (#427) 1.25 .50
e. Inverted ovpt. 75.00
OD179D A137 10c car (#430) 1.60 .50
e. Perf. 13½x13 (#430a) 1.25 .75

## Ministry of Justice and Instruction

No. OD184

**1913 Type I *Perf. 13½x12½***

OD183 A88 2c choc (#181) 6.00 2.00
OD184 A88 1c ocher (#190) 8.00 1.00
OD185 A88 2c choc (#191) 6.00 1.00
a. Perf. 13½ (#191a) — 30.00
OD186 A88 5c red (#194) 2.00 .50
OD187 A88 12c dp bl (#196) 3.00 .50
*Nos. OD184-OD187 (4)* 19.00 3.00

**1915**

OD188 A88 1c ocher (#208) 2.00 1.00
OD189 A88 2c chocolate (#209) 2.00 .50
OD190 A88 5c red (#212) 6.00 .80
*Nos. OD188-OD190 (3)* 10.00 2.30

**1916 *Perf. 13½***

OD191 A91 5c red (#220) 3.00 .50
OD192 A92 12c blue (#222) 4.00 1.60

**1918**

OD193 A93 1c buff (#232) 3.00 1.00
a. Perf. 13½x12½ (#232B) 2.00 1.00
OD194 A93 2c brown (#233) 8.00 8.00
a. Perf. 13½x12½ (#233B) 4.00 1.00
OD195 A93 5c red (#236) 20.00 2.00
a. Perf. 13½x12½ (#236B) 10.00 1.00
OD196 A94 12c blue (#238) 90.00 20.00
*Nos. OD193-OD196 (4)* 121.00 31.00

OD197 A93 1c buff (#249) .60 .50
a. Perf. 13½x12½ (#249B) 200.00 14.00
OD198 A93 2c brown (#250) .50 .50
a. Perf. 13½x12½ (#250B) 1.00 .50
OD199 A93 5c red (#253) .50 .50
a. Perf. 13½x12½ (#253B) 1.00 .50
OD200 A94 12c blue (#255) .50 .50
OD201 A94 20c ultra (#256) 2.00 1.00
*Nos. OD197-OD201 (5)* 4.10 3.00

**1920 *Perf. 13½x12½***

OD202 A93 1c buff (#265) 1.50 1.00
OD203 A93 2c brown (#266) 1.00 .50
OD204 A93 5c red (#269) 1.00 .50
a. Perf. 13½ (#269A) 16.00 8.00
OD205 A94 12c blue (perf. 13½) (#271) 2.00 1.00
*Nos. OD202-OD205 (4)* 5.50 3.00

**1922 *Perf. 13½***

OD206 A93 1c buff (#305) 6.00 2.00
a. Perf. 13½x12½ (#305B) 1.50 .50
OD207 A93 2c brown, (perf. 13½x12½) (#306B) 8.00 2.00
OD208 A103 5c red (#309) 1.50 .50
a. Perf. 13½x12½ (#309B) 1.00 .50
OD209 A94 12c blue (#311) 50.00 16.00
OD210 A94 20c ultra (#312) 8.00 1.25
*Nos. OD206-OD210 (5)* 73.50 21.75

**1922 *Perf. 13½x12½***

OD211 A93 2c brown (#318A) 7.00 2.00

**1923**

OD212 A104 1c buff (#324) 1.25 .50
a. Perf. 13½ (#324A) 2.50 1.00
OD213 A104 2c dk brn (#325) .50 .50
a. Perf. 13½ (#325A) 2.00 1.00
b. As "a," inverted ovpt. 25.00 20.00
OD214 A104 5c red (#328) .50 .50
a. Perf. 13½ (#328A) 2.00 1.00
OD215 A104 12c dp bl (#330) .50 .50
OD216 A104 20c ultra (#331) 1.00 .50
a. Perf. 13½ (#331A) 2.00 1.00
*Nos. OD212-OD216 (5)* 3.75 2.50

**1924**

OD218 A104 1c buff (#341) .50 .50
OD219 A104 2c dk brn (#342) .50 .50
OD220 A104 3c green (#343) .60 .50
OD221 A104 5c red (#345) 2.00 2.00
OD222 A104 10c dl grn (#346) 5.00 2.00
OD223 A104 12c dp bl (#347) .50 .50
OD224 A104 20c ultra (#348) .50 .50
*Nos. OD218-OD224 (7)* 9.60 6.50

**1926**

OD227 A109 5c red (#359) .50 .50
a. Inverted ovpt. 35.00 30.00
OD228 A110 12c dp bl (#360) 1.00 .50

No. OD217B

**Type II**

**1931-36 *Perf. 13½x12½, 13***

OD217B A104 ½c red vio (#340) 10.00 6.00
OD218B A104 1c buff (#341) 1.00 1.00
OD220B A104 3c green (#343) .50 .50
c. Typo (coil) (#343b) .50 .50
OD221B A104 5c red (#345) 2.00 2.00
OD222B A104 10c dl grn (#346) .80 .50
c. Typo (coil) (#346a) 1.00 1.00
OD223B A104 12c dp bl (#347) 6.00 .60
OD224B A104 20c ultra (#348) .50 .50
c. Typo (coil) (#348a) .50 .50
OD225B A104 30c claret (#351) .50 .50
c. Typo (coil) (#351a) 2.50 1.00
OD226B A105 1p blue & red (Perf. 13½) (#353) 2.00 1.25
*Nos. OD217B-OD226B (9)* 23.30 12.85

No. OD229

**1936-38 *Perf. 13½x13***

OD229 A129 1c buff (#419) .50 .50
OD230 A130 2c dk brn (#420) .50 .50
OD231 A132 3c green (#422) .50 .50
OD232 A134 5c yel brn (#427d) .50 .50
OD234 A139 15c slate bl (#434) 2.00 1.00
OD234A A140 20c lt ultra (#437) .50 .50
OD234B A140 20c lt ultra (#438) .60 .50
OD234C A141 25c car & pink (#441) .50 .50
OD234D A142 30c org brn & yel brn (#442) 1.00 .50
OD234E A145 1p brn blk & lt bl (#445) 6.00 3.00
OD234F A146 1p brn blk & lt bl (#446) 6.00 2.00
*Nos. OD229-OD234F (11)* 18.60 10.00

**Typo. *Perf. 13½***

OD232A A134 5c yel brn (#427) .50 .50
OD233 A137 10c car (#430) .50 .50
a. Perf. 13½x13 (#430a) 2.00 .50

## Ministry of Marine

No. OD236

**1913 Type I *Perf. 13½x12½***

OD235 A88 2c choc (#181) 1.25 .50
a. Perf. 13½ (#181a) 150.00 75.00
OD236 A88 1c ocher (#190) .50 .50
OD237 A88 2c choc (#191) 24.00 .50
OD238 A88 5c red (#194) 3.00 .50
a. Perf. 13½ (#194a) 80.00 16.00
OD239 A88 12c dp bl (#196) .60 .50
*Nos. OD236-OD239 (4)* 28.10 2.00

**1915**

OD240 A88 2c chocolate (#209) 6.00 .50
OD241 A88 5c red (#212) 6.00 .50

**1918**

OD242 A93 1c buff (#232) .70 .50
OD243 A93 2c brown (#233) .70 .50
OD244 A93 5c red (#236) 1.40 .50
a. Perf. 13½ (#236B) 4.00 1.00
*Nos. OD242-OD244 (3)* 2.80 1.50

**1920 *Perf. 13½***

OD245 A93 1c buff (#249) .50 .50
OD246 A93 2c brown (#250) .70 .50
a. Perf. 13½x12½ (#250) 6.00 2.00
OD247 A93 5c red (#253) 7.00 .50
a. Perf. 13½x12½ (#253B) .60 .50
OD248 A94 12c blue (#255) 2.50 .60
OD249 A94 20c ultra (#256) 16.00 3.00
*Nos. OD245-OD249 (5)* 26.70 5.10

**1920**

OD250 A93 1c buff (#265A) (perf. 13½x12½) .50 .50
OD251 A93 2c brown (#266A) .70 .50
a. Perf. 13½x12½ (#266) .80 .50
OD252 A93 5c red (#269A) .80 .50
*Nos. OD250-OD252 (3)* 2.00 1.50

**1922**

OD253 A103 5c red (#309) 10.00 2.00
a. Perf. 13½x12½ (#309B) 3.00 .60
OD254 A94 12c blue (#311) 60.00 20.00
OD255 A94 20c ultra (#312) 90.00 16.00
*Nos. OD253-OD255 (3)* 160.00 38.00

**1923 *Perf. 13½x12½***

OD256 A104 1c buff (#324) .50 .50
a. Perf. 13½ (#324A) 150.00 60.00
OD257 A104 2c dk brn (#325) 2.00 .50
a. Inverted overprint — 75.00
b. Perf. 13½ (#325A) 24.00 2.00
OD258 A104 5c red (#328) 5.00 .50
a. Inverted overprint — 75.00
b. Perf. 13½ (#328A) 30.00 5.00
c. As "b," inverted overprint — 75.00
OD259 A104 12c deep blue (#330) 2.50 .50
a. Perf. 13½ (#330A) 36.00 4.00
OD260 A104 20c ultra (#331) 3.00 .50
a. Perf. 13½ (#331A) 16.00 2.00
*Nos. OD256-OD260 (5)* 13.00 2.50

**1924**

OD261 A104 1c buff (#341) 10.00 2.50
OD262 A104 2c dk brn (#342) .50 1.00
OD264 A104 5c red (#345) .50 .50
OD266 A104 20c ultra (#348) 16.00 .50
*Nos. OD261-OD266 (4)* 27.00 4.50

**1926**

OD269 A109 5c red (#359) .50 .25

No. OD264B

**Type II**

**1931-36 *Perf. 13½x12½, 13***

OD263B A104 3c grn (#343) 20.00 1.60
OD264B A104 5c red (#345) 3.00 .50
OD265B A104 10c dl grn (#346) 10.00 2.00
c. Typo (coil) (#346a) 2.00 .50
OD266B A104 20c ultra (#348) 20.00 2.00
c. Typo (coil) (#348a) 10.00 1.00
OD267B A104 30c claret (#351) 8.00 1.60
OD268B A105 1p blue & red (Perf. 13½) (#353) 120.00 60.00

No. OD270

**1936-38 *Perf. 13½x13***

OD270 A129 1c buff (#419) 1.00 .50
OD271 A130 2c dk brn (#420) .50 .50
OD272 A132 3c green (#422) 1.00 1.00
OD273 A134 5c yel brn (#427d) .50 .50
OD275 A139 15c slate bl (#434) ('36) 2.50 .60
OD276 A140 20c lt ultra (#437) 4.00 1.00
OD277 A140 20c lt ultra (#438) 2.00 .50
OD278 A142 30c org brn & yel brn (#442) ('36) 1.50 .50
OD279 A145 1p brn blk & lt bl (#445) ('36) 24.00 16.00
OD280 A146 1p brn blk & lt bl (#446) ('37) 16.00 4.00
*Nos. OD270-OD280 (10)* 53.00 25.10

**Typo. *Perf. 13½***

OD273A A134 5c yel brn (#427) 1.00 .60
b. Inverted overprint 25.00 25.00
OD274A A137 10c car (#430) 4.00 .50
b. Perf. 13½x13 (#430a) 1.50 .75

## Ministry of Public Works

No. OD281

**1913 Type I *Perf. 13½x12½***

OD281 A88 2c choc (#181) 4.00 .50
a. Perf. 13½ (#181a) 20.00 4.00
OD282 A88 1c ocher (#190) 2.00 .50
OD283 A88 5c red (#194) 3.00 .50
OD284 A88 12c dp bl (#196) 20.00 8.00
a. Perf. 13½ (#196a) 15.00 6.00
*Nos. OD282-OD284 (3)* 25.00 9.00

**1916 *Perf. 13½***

OD285 A91 5c red (#220) 70.00 20.00

**1918 *Perf. 13½x12½***

OD286 A93 2c brown (#233) *30.00 20.00*
OD287 A93 5c red (#236) *18.00 9.00*

**1920 *Perf. 13½***

OD288 A93 2c brown (#266) *35.00 8.00*
OD289 A93 5c red (#269) *20.00 2.00*
OD290 A94 12c blue (#271) *50.00 20.00*
*Nos. OD288-OD290 (3)* 105.00 30.00

**1923 *Perf. 13½x12½***

OD291 A104 1c buff (#324) .60 .50
a. Perf. 13½ (#324A) 40.00 *15.00*
OD292 A104 2c dk brn (#325) .50 .50
a. Perf. 13½ (#325A) 2.00 2.00
OD293 A104 5c red (#328) 4.00 1.00
a. Perf. 13½ (#328A) 6.00 2.00
OD294 A104 12c dp bl (#330) 4.00 2.00
a. Perf. 13½ (#330A) 4.00 1.00
OD295 A104 20c ultra (#331 4.00 .60
a. Perf. 13½ (#331A) 16.00 1.25
*Nos. OD291-OD295 (5)* 13.10 4.60

**1924**

OD296 A104 1c buff (#341) .50 .50
OD297 A104 2c dk brn (#342) .50 .50
OD299 A104 5c red (#345) .50 .50
OD301 A104 12c dp bl (#347) 60.00 20.00
OD302 A104 20c ultra (#348) .50 .50
*Nos. OD296-OD302 (5)* 62.00 22.00

**1926**

OD305 A109 5c red (#359) .60 .25

No. OD299B

**Type II**

**1931-36 *Perf. 13½x12½, 13***

OD298B A104 3c grn (#343) .50 .50
c. Typo (coil) (#343b) — 40.00
OD299B A104 5c red (#345) .60 .50
OD300B A104 10c dl grn (#346) .60 .50
c. Typo (coil) (#346a) 4.00 .50
OD301B A104 20c ultra typo (coil) (#348b) *50.00 10.00*

# ARGENTINA

| OD303B | A104 | 30c claret (#351) | 1.80 | .50 |
| OD304B | A105 | 1p blue & red (13½) (#353) | 200.00 | — |
| Nos. OD298B-OD304B (6) | | | 253.50 | 12.00 |

No. OD307

### 1936-38     Perf. 13½x13
| OD306 | A129 | 1c buff (#419) | .50 | .50 |
| OD307 | A130 | 2c dk brn (#420) | .60 | .50 |
| OD308 | A132 | 3c green (#422) | 2.00 | .50 |
| OD309 | A134 | 5c yel brn (#427d) | 1.00 | .50 |
| OD311 | A139 | 15c slate bl (#434) | 3.00 | 1.00 |
| OD312 | A140 | 20c lt ultra (#437) | 6.00 | .50 |
| OD313 | A140 | 20c lt ultra (#438) | 1.00 | .50 |
| OD314 | A142 | 30c org brn & yel brn (#442) ('36) | .60 | .50 |
| OD315 | A144 | 50c red & org (#444) ('36) | 5.00 | 5.00 |
| OD316 | A145 | 1p brn blk & lt bl (#445) ('36) | 10.00 | 6.00 |
| OD317 | A146 | 1p brn blk & lt bl (#446) ('37) | 2.00 | 1.00 |
| Nos. OD306-OD317 (11) | | | 31.70 | 16.50 |

### Typo.     Perf. 13½
| OD309A | A134 | 5c yel brn (#427) | 1.25 | .50 |
| b. | | Inverted overprint | — | 75.00 |
| OD310 | A137 | 10c car (#430) | 4.00 | .50 |
| a. | | Perf. 13½x13 (#430a) | 2.00 | .50 |

### Ministry of Foreign Affairs and Religion

No. OD318

### 1913    Type I    Perf. 13½x12½
| OD318 | A88 | 2c choc (#181) | 90.00 | 20.00 |
| OD319 | A88 | 1c ocher (#190) | .50 | .50 |
| OD320 | A88 | 2c choc (#191) | .50 | .50 |
| OD321 | A88 | 5c red (#194) | 3.00 | 1.00 |
| OD322 | A88 | 12c dp bl (#196) | 1.25 | .50 |
| a. | | Perf. 13½ (#196a) | 100.00 | 40.00 |
| Nos. OD319-OD322 (4) | | | 5.25 | 2.50 |

### 1915
| OD323 | A88 | 5c red (#212) | 3.00 | 1.75 |

### 1916     Perf. 13½
| OD324 | A91 | 5c red (#220) | 2.50 | .50 |

### 1918
| OD325 | A94 | 20c ultra (#256) | 20.00 | 8.00 |

### 1922
| OD326 | A93 | 1c buff, perf. 13½x12½ (#265) | 3.00 | 1.00 |
| OD327 | A93 | 5c red (#269) | 1.25 | .60 |

### 1922-23     Perf. 13½x12½
| OD328 | A93 | 2c brn (#306B) | 80.00 | 30.00 |
| OD329 | A103 | 5c red (#309B) | 100.00 | |

### Perf. 13½
| OD330 | A93 | 12c blue (#311) | 100.00 | |
| OD330A | A94 | 20c ultra (#312) | 100.00 | |

No. OD346

### 1923     Perf. 13½x12½
| OD331 | A104 | 1c buff (#324) | .60 | .50 |
| a. | | Perf. 13½ (#324A) | 25.00 | 10.00 |
| OD332 | A104 | 2c dk brn (#325) | 1.00 | .60 |
| a. | | Perf. 13½ (#325A) | 25.00 | 16.00 |
| OD333 | A104 | 5c red (#328) | .50 | .50 |
| a. | | Perf. 13½ (#328A) | 6.00 | 2.00 |
| OD334 | A104 | 12c dp bl (#330) | .50 | .50 |
| a. | | Perf. 13½ (#330A) | 5.00 | 2.00 |
| OD335 | A104 | 20c ultra (#331) | .50 | .50 |
| Nos. OD331-OD335 (5) | | | 3.10 | 2.60 |

### 1924
| OD337 | A104 | 1c buff (#341) | .60 | .50 |
| OD338 | A104 | 2c dk brn (#342) | .50 | .50 |
| OD339 | A104 | 3c green (#343) | .50 | .50 |
| OD340 | A104 | 5c red (#345) | .50 | .50 |
| OD341 | A104 | 10c dl grn (#346) | 8.00 | 1.00 |
| OD342 | A104 | 12c dp bl (#347) | .60 | .60 |
| OD343 | A104 | 20c ultra (#348) | .60 | .50 |
| OD344 | A104 | 30c claret (#351) | 4.00 | 2.00 |
| Nos. OD337-OD344 (8) | | | 15.30 | 6.00 |

### 1926
| OD346 | A110 | 12c dp bl (#360) | .50 | .60 |

### Type II

No. OD344B

### 1931-36     Perf. 13½x12½, 13½
| OD336B | A104 | ½c red vio (#340) | 10.00 | 5.00 |
| OD341B | A104 | 10c dl grn (#346) | 1.25 | .60 |
| OD343B | A104 | 20c ultra (typo, coil) (#348a) | .60 | .60 |
| OD344B | A104 | 30c claret (typo, coil) (#351a) | .60 | .60 |
| OD345B | A105 | 1p blue & red, perf. 13½ (#353) | 1.50 | 1.00 |
| Nos. OD336B-OD345B (5) | | | 13.95 | 7.80 |

No. OD347

### 1935-37    Typo.    Perf. 13x13½
| OD347 | A129 | 1c buff (#419) | .50 | .50 |
| OD348 | A130 | 2c dk brn (#420) | .50 | .50 |
| OD349 | A132 | 3c green (#422) | .50 | .50 |
| OD350 | A134 | 5c yel brn (#427d) | .50 | .50 |
| OD352 | A139 | 15c slate bl (#434) | .70 | .50 |
| OD353 | A140 | 20c lt ultra (#437) | 3.00 | .50 |
| OD354 | A140 | 20c lt ultra (#438) | .50 | .50 |
| OD355 | A142 | 30c org brn & yel brn (#442) | .50 | .50 |
| OD356 | A145 | 1p brn blk & lt bl (#445) | 20.00 | 10.00 |
| OD357 | A146 | 1p brn blk & lt bl (#446) | 1.50 | 1.00 |
| Nos. OD347-OD357 (10) | | | 28.20 | 15.00 |

### Typo.     Perf. 13½
| OD350B | A134 | 5c yel brn (#427) | .60 | .50 |
| OD351B | A137 | 10c car (#430) | .50 | .50 |
| c. | | Perf. 13½x13 (#430a) | 4.00 | .50 |

### PARCEL POST STAMPS

PP1

Postal Service Headquarters, Buenos Aires — PP2

### 2001    Litho.    Serpentine Die Cut 11 Self-Adhesive
| Q1 | PP1 | 1p red & black | 20.00 | 20.00 |

### Die Cut
| Q1A | PP1 | 1p red & black | 40.00 | 20.00 |
| Q2 | PP2 | 7p blue & black | 27.50 | 20.00 |
| Q3 | PP2 | 11p brown & black | 40.00 | 30.00 |
| Nos. Q1-Q3 (3) | | | 87.50 | 70.00 |

Nos. Q1-Q3 were sold only at Unidas Postal outlets. No. Q3 is inscribed "Caja Envio 2."

Stamps of Type PP2 lacking "U.P." in denominations of 7p, 11p, 16p, and 23p were issued in 1999, but were applied by postal workers to packages brought to post offices by customers with large mailings (Grandes Clientes). These stamps were not to be given to any customers purchasing them. Value, set unused $160.

The same sale and use restrictions applied to four other non-denominated stamps for use by "Grandes Clientes," which are inscribed "Caja Normalizada," have blue, brown-violet, gray-green, and ocher frames, and were issued in 1995. Value, set unused $550.

Nos. Q2 and Q3, though inscribed "Grandes Clientes," apparently were available for purchase by any customers, at Unidas Postal outlets.

---

## BUENOS AIRES

The central point of the Argentine struggle for independence. At intervals Buenos Aires maintained an independent government but after 1862 became a province of the Argentine Republic.

8 Reales = 1 Peso

> Values of Buenos Aires Nos. 1-8 vary according to condition. Quotations are for fine examples. Very fine to superb specimens sell at much higher prices, and inferior or poor stamps sell at reduced values, depending on the condition of the individual specimen.
> Nos. 1-8 are normally found without gum, and the values below are for such items. Examples with original gum sell for higher prices.

Steamship — A1

### 1858    Unwmk.    Typo.    Imperf.
| 1 | A1 | 1 (in) pesos lt brn | 500.00 | 300. |
| a. | | Double impression | | 700. |
| 2 | A1 | 2 (dos) pesos blue | 300.00 | 150. |
| b. | | Diag. half used as 1p on cover | | 7,500. |
| 3 | A1 | 3 (tres) pesos grn | 1,500. | 950. |
| a. | | 3p dark green | 2,000. | 1,500. |
| 4 | A1 | 4 (cuatro) pesos ver | 5,000. | 4,500. |
| a. | | Half used as 2p on cover | | 25,000. |
| b. | | 4p chestnut brown (error) | 30,000. | 40,000. |
| 5 | A1 | 5 (cinco) pesos org | 5,000. | 3,000. |
| a. | | 5p ocher | 5,000. | 3,000. |
| b. | | 5p olive yellow | 5,000. | 3,000. |

Issued: Nos. 2-5, Apr. 29; No. 1, Oct. 26.

### 1858, Oct. 26
| 6 | A1 | 4 (cuatro) reales brown | 350.00 | 300. |
| a. | | 4r gray brown | 400.00 | 300. |
| b. | | 4r chestnut | 350.00 | 300. |

### 1859, Jan. 1
| 7 | A1 | 1 (in) pesos blue | 200. | 200. |
| a. | | 1p indigo | 300. | 150. |
| b. | | Impression on reverse of stamp in blue | 28,500. | |
| c. | | Double impression | 2,800. | 700. |
| d. | | Vert. tête-bêche pair | | 675,000. |
| e. | | Horiz. tête-bêche pair | — | |
| f. | | Half used as 4r on cover | | 7,500. |
| 8 | A1 | 1 (to) pesos blue | 600. | 450. |

No. 7e is valued with faults.

Nos. 1, 2, 3 and 7 have been reprinted on very thick, hand-made paper. The same four stamps and No. 8 have been reprinted on thin, hard, white wove paper.

Counterfeits of Nos. 1-8 are plentiful.

Liberty Head — A2

### 1859, Sept. 3
| 9 | A2 | 4r green, *bluish* | 400.00 | 200.00 |
| 10 | A2 | 1p blue, fine impression | 40.00 | 25.00 |
| d. | | Double impression | 600.00 | 400.00 |
| e. | | Partial double impression | 325.00 | 175.00 |
| 11 | A2 | 2p vermilion, fine impression | 500.00 | 200.00 |
| a. | | 2p red, blurred impression | 375.00 | 125.00 |
| b. | | Vert. half used as 1p on cover | | 4,000. |

Both fine and blurred impressions of these stamps may be found. They have generally been called Paris and Local prints, respectively, but the opinion now obtains that the differences are due to the impression and that they do not represent separate issues. Values are for fine impressions. Rough or blurred impressions sell for less.

Many shades exist of Nos. 1-11.

### 1862, Oct. 4
| 12 | A2 | 1p rose | 350.00 | 150.00 |
| 13 | A2 | 2p blue | 350.00 | 90.00 |

All three values have been reprinted in black, brownish black, blue and red brown on thin hard white paper. The 4r has also been reprinted in green on bluish paper.

Values are for fine impressions. Rough or blurred impressions sell for less.

No. 13 exists with papermaker's wmk.

---

## CORDOBA

A province in the central part of the Argentine Republic.

100 Centavos = 1 Peso

Arms of Cordoba — A1

### 1858, Oct. 28    Unwmk.    Litho.    Imperf.    Laid Paper
| 1 | A1 | 5c blue | | 150. |
| 2 | A1 | 10c black | | 3,000. |

Cordoba stamps were printed on laid paper, but stamps from edges of the sheets sometimes do not show any laid lines and appear to be on wove paper. Counterfeits are plentiful.

---

## CORRIENTES

The northeast province of the Argentine Republic.

1 Real M(oneda) C(orriente) = 12½ Centavos M.C. = 50 Centavos
100 Centavos Fuertes = 1 Peso Fuerte

Nos. 1-2 were issued without gum. Nos. 3-8 were issued both with and without gum (values the same).

Ceres — A1

### 1856, Aug. 21    Unwmk.    Typo.    Imperf.
| 1 | A1 | 1r black, *blue* | 100.00 | 40.00 |

No. 1 used is valued with pen cancellation.

### Pen Stroke Through "Un Real"
### 1860, Feb. 8
| 2 | A1 | (3c) black, *blue* | 600.00 | 120.00 |

No. 2 used is valued with pen cancellation.

Ceres — A2

### 1860-80
| 3 | A2 | (3c) black, *blue* | 9.50 | 30.00 |
| 4 | A2 | (2c) blk, *yel grn* ('64) | 50.00 | 100.00 |
| a. | | (2c) black, *blue green* | 92.50 | 150.00 |

ARGENTINA — ARMENIA 651

5 A2 (2c) blk, *yel* ('67) 7.50 *19.00*
6 A2 (3c) blk, *dk bl* ('71) 3.00 *19.00*
7 A2 (3c) blk, *rose red* ('76) 150.00 70.00
*a.* (3c) black, *lil rose* ('75) 200.00 100.00
8 A2 (3c) blk, *dk rose* ('79) 8.00 *35.00*
*a.* (3c) black, *red vio* ('77) 75.00 50.00
*Nos. 3-8 (6)* 228.00 273.00

Pen canceled examples of Nos. 3-8 that do not indicate the town of origin sell for much less.

Printed from settings of 8 varieties, 3 or 4 impressions constituting a sheet. Some impressions were printed inverted and tete beche pairs may be cut from adjacent impressions.

From Jan. 1 to Feb. 24, 1864, No. 4 was used as a 5 centavos stamp but examples so used can only be distinguished when they bear dated cancellations.

*The reprints show numerous spots and small defects which are not found on the originals. They are printed on gray blue, dull blue, gray green, dull orange and light magenta papers.*

## ARMENIA

är-ˈmē-nē-ə

LOCATION — South of Russia bounded by Georgia, Azerbaijan, Iran and Turkey
GOVT. — Republic
AREA — 11,490 sq. mi.
POP. — 2,960,000 (2020 est.)
CAPITAL — Yerevan

With Azerbaijan and Georgia, Armenia made up the Transcaucasian Federation of Soviet Republics.

Stamps of Armenia were replaced in 1923 by those of Transcaucasian Federated Republics.

With the breakup of the Soviet Union on Dec. 26, 1991, Armenia and ten former Soviet republics established the Commonwealth of Independent States.

100 Kopecks = 1 Ruble
100 Luma = 1 Dram (1993)

**Catalogue values for unused stamps in this country are for Never Hinged items, beginning with Scott 430 in the regular postage section.**

Counterfeits abound of all Armenian stamps through Scott 390, both of the basic stamps and of overprinted and surcharged stamps.

**Watermark**

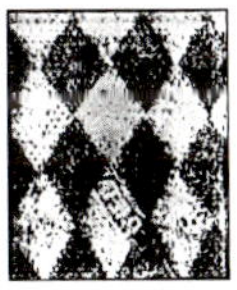

Wmk. 171 — Diamonds

Perforations
Perforations are the same as the basic Russian stamps.

**National Republic**
Russian Stamps of 1902-19 Handstamped

At least thirteen types exist of both framed and unframed overprints ("a" and "c"). The device is the Armenian "H," initial of Hayasdan (Armenia). Inverted and double overprints are found.

Surcharged

Type I — Without periods (two types).
Type II — Periods after 1st "K" and "60."

**Black Surcharge**

**1919 Unwmk. *Perf. 14x14½***
1 A14 60k on 1k orange (II) 2.00 5.00
*a.* Imperf. (I) 1.50 5.00
*b.* Imperf. (II) 2.00 3.00

**Violet Surcharge**
2 A14 60k on 1k orange (II) 5.00 5.00

Handstamped in Violet a

6 A15 4k carmine 5.00 7.00
7 A14 5k claret, imperf. 5.00 7.00
*a.* Perf. 10.00 10.00
9 A14 10k on 7k lt blue 10.00 15.00
10 A11 15k red brn & bl 5.00 7.00
11 A8 20k blue & car 5.00 7.00
13 A11 35k red brn & grn 5.00 7.00
14 A8 50k violet & green 5.00 7.00
15 A14 60k on 1k orange (II) 5.00 7.00
*a.* Imperf. (I) 10.00 10.00
*b.* Imperf. (II) 15.00 15.00
18 A13 5r dk bl, grn & pale bl 20.00 25.00
*a.* Imperf. 20.00 30.00
19 A12 7r dk green & pink 35.00 40.00
20 A13 10r scar, yel & gray 50.00 40.00

**Handstamped in Black**
31 A14 2k green, imperf. 4.00 4.00
*a.* Perf. 10.00 10.00
32 A14 3k red, imperf. 3.00 3.00
*a.* Perf. 10.00 10.00
33 A15 4k carmine 10.00 10.00
*a.* Imperf. 15.00 15.00
34 A14 5k claret 1.00 1.00
*a.* Imperf. 15.00 15.00
36 A15 10k dark blue 2.00 2.00
37 A14 10k on 7k lt blue 1.00 *4.00*
38 A11 15k red brn & bl 4.00 *7.50*
*a.* Imperf. 8.00 *15.00*
39 A8 20k blue & car 2.00 *5.00*
40 A11 25k green & gray vio 2.00 *5.00*
41 A11 35k red brn & grn 2.00 *4.00*
42 A8 50k violet & green 3.00 *5.00*
43 A14 60k on 1k orange (II) 5.00 5.00
43A A11 70k brown & org 3.00 3.00
*b.* Imperf. 2.00 *4.00*
44 A9 1r pale brn, dk brn & org 3.00 *5.00*
*a.* Imperf. 8.00 8.00
45 A12 3½r mar & lt grn, imperf. 3.00 *5.00*
*a.* Perf. 10.00 10.00
46 A13 5r dk bl, grn & pale bl 8.00 10.00
*a.* Imperf. 12.00 15.00
47 A12 7r dk green & pink 6.50 6.50
48 A13 10r scar, yel & gray 30.00 *50.00*

Handstamped in Violet c

**Wove Paper**

**Unwmk. *Perf.***
62 A14 2k green, imperf. 10.00 10.00
*a.* Perf. 15.00 15.00
63 A14 3k red, imperf. 2.50 2.50
*a.* Perf. 15.00 15.00
64 A15 4k carmine 10.00 10.00
65 A14 5k claret 5.00 5.00
*a.* Imperf. 15.00 15.00
67 A15 10k dark blue 5.00 *10.00*
68 A14 10k on 7k lt bl 3.50 3.50
69 A11 15k red brn & bl 5.00 *10.00*
70 A8 20k blue & car 3.00 *6.00*
71 A11 25k grn & gray vio 25.00 *15.00*
72 A11 35k red brn & grn 15.00 *20.00*
73 A8 50k violet & grn 5.00 *10.00*
74 A14 60k on 1k org (II) 10.00 *12.00*
*a.* Imperf. (I) 10.00 *12.00*
*b.* Imperf. (II) 10.00 *12.00*
75 A9 1r pale brn, dk brn & org 12.50 12.50
*a.* Imperf. 10.00 *12.00*
76 A12 3½r mar & lt grn, imperf. 6.00 6.00
*a.* Perf. 10.00 10.00
77 A13 5r dk bl, grn & pale bl, imperf. 12.50 12.50
*a.* Perf. 8.00 8.00
78 A12 7r dk green & pink 30.00 30.00
79 A13 10r scar, yel & gray 50.00 50.00

***Imperf***
85 A11 70k brown & org 25.00 25.00

Handstamped in Black

***Perf.***
90 A14 1k orange 10.00 10.00
*a.* Imperf. 10.00 10.00
91 A14 2k green, imperf. 1.00 *3.00*
*a.* Perf. 8.00 *10.00*
92 A14 3k red, imperf. 8.00 *10.00*
*a.* Perf. 1.00 *2.00*
93 A15 4k carmine 3.00 3.00
94 A14 5k claret 1.00 2.00
*a.* Imperf. 2.00 *5.00*
95 A14 7k light blue 5.00 *8.00*
96 A15 10k dark blue 10.00 *10.00*
97 A14 10k on 7k lt bl 10.00 *5.00*
98 A11 15k red brn & bl 2.00 *5.00*
99 A8 20k blue & car 5.00 *7.00*
100 A11 25k grn & gray vio 2.00 *5.00*
101 A11 35k red brn & grn 3.00 *5.00*
102 A8 50k violet & grn 2.00 *5.00*
102A A14 60k on 1k org, imperf. (I) 20.00 *30.00*
*b.* Imperf. (II) 4.00 *6.00*
*c.* Perf. (II) 8.00 8.00
103 A9 1r pale brn, dk brn & org 2.00 *5.00*
*a.* Imperf. 2.00 *5.00*
104 A12 3½r maroon & lt grn 5.00 *8.00*
*a.* Imperf. 5.00 8.00
105 A13 5r dk bl, grn & pale bl 7.00 9.00
*a.* Imperf. 8.00 12.00
106 A12 7r dk green & pink 15.00 *15.00*
107 A13 10r scar, yel & gray 25.00 *50.00*

***Imperf***
113 A11 70k brown & org 2.50 *4.00*

**Handstamped in Violet or Black**

Violet Surcharge, Type f

**1920 *Perf.***
120 A14 3r on 3k red, imperf. 10.00 15.00
*a.* Perf. 10.00 15.00
121 A14 5r on 3k red 10.00 10.00
122 A15 5r on 4k car 10.00 *12.00*
123 A14 5r on 5k claret, imperf. 5.00 *12.00*
*a.* Perf. 12.00 *20.00*
124 A15 5r on 10k dk blue 20.00 *30.00*
125 A14 5r on 10k on 7k lt bl 20.00 *30.00*
126 A8 5r on 20k bl & car 10.00 *15.00*

***Imperf***
127 A14 5r on 2k green 12.00 12.00
128 A11 5r on 35k red brn & grn 12.00 12.00

Black Surcharge, Type f or Type g (#130)

***Perf.***
130 A14 1r on 1k orange 10.00 12.00
*a.* Imperf. 15.00 15.00
131 A14 3r on 3k red 8.00 8.00
*a.* Imperf. 2.00 5.00
132 A15 3r on 4k carmine 25.00 25.00
133 A14 5r on 2k grn, imperf. 2.00 *3.00*
*a.* Perf. 5.00 5.00
134 A14 5r on 3k red 12.00 12.00
*a.* Imperf. 5.00 5.00
135 A15 5r on 4k carmine 4.00 *10.00*
*a.* Imperf. 10.00 10.00
136 A14 5r on 5k claret 3.00 *4.00*
*a.* Imperf. 1.00 *2.00*
137 A14 5r on 7k lt blue 3.00 *4.00*
138 A15 5r on 10k dk blue 2.00 *4.00*
139 A14 5r on 10k on 7k lt bl 2.00 *5.00*
140 A11 5r on 14k bl & rose 2.50 2.50
141 A11 5r on 15k red brn & blue 1.00 3.00
*a.* Imperf. 3.00 6.00
142 A8 5r on 20k bl & car 1.00 *3.00*
*a.* Imperf. 50.00 50.00
143 A11 5r on 20k on 14k bl & rose 75.00 *100.00*
144 A11 5r on 25k grn & gray vio 10.00 *15.00*

Black Surcharge, Type g or Type f (#148A, 151)

145 A14 10r on 1k org, imperf. 1.10 1.10
*a.* Perf. *125.00* *125.00*
146 A14 10r on 3k red *175.00* *175.00*
147 A14 10r on 5k claret 18.00 18.00
*a.* Imperf. 15.00
148 A8 10r on 20k bl & car 15.00 15.00
148A A11 10r on 25k grn & gray vio 10.00 10.00
149 A11 10r on 25k grn & gray vio 5.00 *6.00*
*a.* Imperf. 10.00 *20.00*
150 A11 10r on 35k red brn & grn 2.00 2.00
151 A8 10r on 50k brn vio & grn 50.00 50.00
152 A8 10r on 50k brn vio & grn 2.00 *3.00*
152A A11 10r on 70k brn & org, imperf. 5.00 5.00
*b.* Perf. *5.00* *5.00*
152C A8 25r on 20k bl & car 8.00 *10.00*
153 A11 25r on 25k grn & gray vio 5.00 5.00
154 A11 25r on 35k red brn & grn 20.00 *25.00*
*a.* Imperf. 4.00 4.00
155 A8 25r on 50k vio & grn 5.00 *8.00*
*a.* Imperf. 6.00 *8.00*
156 A11 25r on 70k brn & org 8.00 8.00
*a.* Imperf. 5.00 5.00
157 A9 50r on 1r pale brn, dk brn & org, imperf. 2.00 2.00
*a.* Perf. 20.00 *25.00*
158 A13 50r on 5r dk bl, grn & lt bl 45.00 45.00
*a.* Imperf. 50.00 50.00
159 A12 100r on 3½r mar & lt grn 15.00 *18.00*
*a.* Imperf. 10.00 10.00
160 A13 100r on 5r dk bl, grn & pale bl 15.00 20.00
*a.* Imperf. 75.00 75.00
161 A12 100r on 7r dk grn & pink 35.00 35.00
*a.* Imperf. 42.00 42.00
162 A13 100r on 10r scar, yel & gray 15.00 20.00

**Wmk. Wavy Lines (168)**
***Perf. 11½***
**Vertically Laid Paper**
163 A12 100r on 3½r blk & gray *150.00* *150.00*
164 A12 100r on 7r blk & yel *150.00* *150.00*

No. 168

**1920 Unwmk. *Imperf.***
**Wove Paper**
166 A14 (g) 1r on 60k on 1k org (I) 12.00 14.50
168 A14 (f) 5r on 1k orange 12.00 12.00
173 A11 (f) 5r on 35k red brn & grn 15.00 15.00
177 A11 (g) 50r on 70k brn & org 5.00 10.00
179 A12 (g) 50r on 3½r mar & lt grn 20.00 20.00
181 A9 (g) 100r on 1r pale brn, dk brn & org 25.00 25.00

**Romanov Issues**
Surcharged Types g or f (#185-187, 190) on Stamps of 1913

No. 187

No. 187C

**1920 *Perf. 13½***
184 A16 1r on 1k brn org 200.00 200.00
185 A18 3r on 3k rose red 75.00 75.00
186 A19 5r on 4k dull red 15.00 15.00
187 A22 5r on 14k blue grn 40.00 40.00
187A A19 10r on 4k dull red 40.00
187B A26 10r on 35k gray vio & dk grn 100.00
187C A19 25r on 4k dull red 100.00 100.00
188 A26 25r on 35k gray vio & dk grn *100.00* *100.00*
189 A28 25r on 70k yel grn & brn *100.00* *100.00*
190 A31 50r on 3r dk vio — —
190A A16 100r on 1k brn org 125.00 125.00
190B A17 100r on 2k green 125.00 125.00
191 A30 100r on 2r brown 125.00 125.00
192 A31 100r on 3r dk vio 100.00 100.00

On Stamps of 1915, Type g

### Thin Cardboard
### Inscriptions on Back
***Perf. 12***

| | | | | |
|---|---|---|---|---|
| 193 | A21 | 100r on 10k blue | 20.00 | |
| 194 | A23 | 100r on 15k brn | 20.00 | |
| 195 | A24 | 100r on 20k ol grn | 18.00 | |

On Stamps of 1916, Type f

***Perf. 13½***

| | | | | |
|---|---|---|---|---|
| 196 | A20 | 5r on 10k on 7k brown | 8.00 | 8.00 |
| 197 | A22 | 5r on 20k on 14k bl grn | 25.00 | 35.00 |

Surcharged Types f or g (#204-205A, 207-207C, 210-211) over Type c

### Type c in Violet
***Perf.***

| | | | | |
|---|---|---|---|---|
| 200 | A15 | 5r on 4k car | 50.00 | 55.00 |
| 201 | A15 | 5r on 10k dk bl | 50.00 | 50.00 |
| 202 | A11 | 5r on 15k red brn & bl | 50.00 | 50.00 |
| 203 | A8 | 5r on 20k blue & car | 50.00 | 50.00 |
| 204 | A11 | 10r on 25k grn & gray vio | 50.00 | 50.00 |
| 205 | A11 | 10r on 35k red brn & grn | 55.00 | 55.00 |
| 205A | A8 | 10r on 50k brn vio & grn | — | — |
| 206 | A8 | 25r on 50k brn vio & grn | 150.00 | 150.00 |
| 207 | A9 | 50r on 1r pale brn, dk brn & org, imperf. | 50.00 | 50.00 |
| a. | | Perf. | 50.00 | 50.00 |
| 207B | A12 | 100r on 3½r mar & lt grn | 100.00 | 100.00 |
| 207C | A12 | 100r on 7r dk grn & pink | 100.00 | 100.00 |

***Imperf***

| | | | | |
|---|---|---|---|---|
| 208 | A14 | 5r on 2k green | 50.00 | 50.00 |
| 209 | A14 | 5r on 5k claret | 50.00 | 50.00 |
| 210 | A11 | 25r on 70k brn & org | 75.00 | 75.00 |
| 211 | A13 | 100r on 5r dk bl, grn & pale bl | 100.00 | 110.00 |

Surcharged Types g or f (212-213, 215, 219-219A, 221-222) over Type c

### Type c in Black
***Perf.***

| | | | | |
|---|---|---|---|---|
| 212 | A14 | 5r on 7k lt bl | 150.00 | 150.00 |
| 213 | A14 | 5r on 10k on 7k lt bl | 75.00 | 75.00 |
| 214 | A11 | 5r on 15k red brn & bl | 50.00 | 60.00 |
| 215 | A8 | 5r on 20k blue & car | 50.00 | 50.00 |
| 215A | A11 | 10r on 5r on 25k grn & gray vio | 50.00 | 50.00 |
| 216 | A11 | 10r on 35k red brn & grn | 50.00 | 60.00 |
| 217 | A8 | 10r on 50k brn vio & grn | 50.00 | 50.00 |
| 217A | A9 | 50r on 1r pale brn, dk brn & org | 50.00 | 75.00 |
| b. | | Imperf. | 35.00 | 50.00 |
| 217C | A12 | 100r on 3½r mar & lt grn | 35.00 | 40.00 |
| 218 | A13 | 100r on 5r dk bl, grn & pale bl | 35.00 | 40.00 |
| a. | | Imperf. | 35.00 | 45.00 |
| 219 | A12 | 100r on 7r dk grn & pink | 50.00 | 50.00 |
| 219A | A13 | 100r on 10r scar, yel & gray | 45.00 | 55.00 |

***Imperf***

| | | | | |
|---|---|---|---|---|
| 220 | A14 | 1r on 60k on 1k org (I) | 50.00 | 50.00 |
| 221 | A14 | 5r on 2k green | 20.00 | 20.00 |
| 222 | A14 | 5r on 5k claret | 50.00 | 50.00 |
| 223 | A11 | 10r on 70k brn & org | 50.00 | 50.00 |
| 224 | A11 | 25r on 70k brn & org | 50.00 | 50.00 |

Surcharged Types g or f (#233) over Type a

### Type a in Violet
***Imperf***

| | | | | |
|---|---|---|---|---|
| 231 | A9 | 50r on 1r pale brn, dk brn & org | 150.00 | 175.00 |
| 232 | A13 | 100r on 5r dk bl, grn & pale bl | 150.00 | 160.00 |

Type a in Black

***Perf.***

| | | | | |
|---|---|---|---|---|
| 233 | A8 | 5r on 20k blue & car | 45.00 | 45.00 |
| 233A | A11 | 10r on 25k grn & gray vio | 35.00 | 35.00 |
| 234 | A11 | 10r on 35k red brn & grn | 185.00 | 185.00 |
| 235 | A12 | 100r on 3½r mar & lt grn | — | — |
| a. | | Imperf. | — | — |

***Imperf***

| | | | | |
|---|---|---|---|---|
| 237 | A14 | 5r on 2k green | 150.00 | 150.00 |
| 237A | A11 | 10r on 70k brn & org | — | — |

Surcharged Type a and New Value

### Type a in Violet
***Perf.***

| | | | | |
|---|---|---|---|---|
| 238 | A11 | 10r on 15k red brn & blue | 30.00 | 30.00 |

### Type a in Black

| | | | | |
|---|---|---|---|---|
| 239 | A8 | 5r on 20k blue & car | — | — |
| 239A | A8 | 10r on 20k blue & car | 20.00 | 20.00 |
| 239B | A8 | 10r on 50k brn red & grn | 30.00 | 40.00 |

***Imperf***

| | | | | |
|---|---|---|---|---|
| 240 | A12 | 100r on 3½r mar & lt grn | 50.00 | 60.00 |

Surcharged Type c and New Value

### Type c in Black

**1920** ***Perf.***

| | | | | |
|---|---|---|---|---|
| 241 | A15 | 5r on 4k red | — | — |
| 242 | A11 | 5r on 15k red brn & bl | — | — |
| 243 | A8 | 10r on 20k blue & car | 50.00 | 50.00 |
| 243A | A11 | 10r on 25k grn & gray vio | 50.00 | 50.00 |
| 244 | A11 | 10r on 35k red brn & grn | 50.00 | 50.00 |
| a. | | With additional srch. "5r" | 100.00 | 100.00 |
| 245 | A12 | 100r on 3½r mar & lt grn | — | — |

No. 248

***Imperf***

| | | | | |
|---|---|---|---|---|
| 247 | A14 | 3r on 3k red | 32.50 | 32.50 |
| 248 | A14 | 5r on 2k green | 30.00 | 30.00 |
| 249 | A9 | 50r on 1r pale brn, dk brn & org | 35.00 | 35.00 |

Type c in Violet

| | | | | |
|---|---|---|---|---|
| 249A | A14 | 5r on 2k green | — | — |

### Russia AR1-AR3 Surcharged

A1

A2

A3

***Perf. 14½x15***
**Wmk. 171**

| | | | | |
|---|---|---|---|---|
| 250 | A1 | 60k on 1k red & buff | 75.00 | 75.00 |
| 251 | A2 | 1r on 1k red & buff | 75.00 | 75.00 |
| 252 | A3 | 5r on 5k green & buff | 75.00 | 75.00 |
| 253 | A3 | 5r on 10k brn & buff | 75.00 | 75.00 |

Russian Semi-Postal Stamps of 1914-18 Srchd. with Armenian Monogram & New Values

### On Stamps of 1914

**Unwmk.** ***Perf.***

| | | | | |
|---|---|---|---|---|
| 255 | SP5 | 25r on 1k red brn & dk grn, *straw* | 75.00 | 75.00 |
| 256 | SP5 | 25r on 3k mar & gray grn, *pink* | 75.00 | 75.00 |
| 257 | SP5 | 50r on 7 dk brn & dk grn, *buff* | 125.00 | 150.00 |
| 258 | SP5 | 100r on 1k red brn & dk grn, *straw* | 100.00 | 100.00 |
| 259 | SP5 | 100r on 3k mar & gray grn, *pink* | 100.00 | 100.00 |
| 260 | SP5 | 100r on 7k dk brn & dk grn, *buff* | 100.00 | 100.00 |

No. 261

### On Stamps of 1915-19

| | | | | |
|---|---|---|---|---|
| 261 | SP5 | 25r on 1k org brn & gray | 125.00 | 125.00 |
| 262 | SP5 | 25r on 3k car & gray | 85.00 | 85.00 |
| 263 | SP5 | 50r on 10k dk bl & brn | 50.00 | 50.00 |
| 264 | SP5 | 100r on 1k org brn & gray | 100.00 | 100.00 |
| 265 | SP5 | 100r on 10k dk bl & brn | 125.00 | 125.00 |

These surcharged semi-postal stamps were used for ordinary postage.

A set of 10 stamps in the above designs was prepared in 1920, but not issued for postal use, though some were used fiscally. Value of set, $30. Reprints abound.

### Soviet Socialist Republic

Hammer and Sickle — A7

Mythological Monster — A8

Symbols of Soviet Republics on Designs from old Armenian Manuscripts A9

Ruined City of Ani A10

Mythological Monster — A11

Armenian Soldier — A12

Mythological Monster A13

Soviet Symbols, Armenian Designs A14

Mt. Alagöz and Plain of Shirak — A15

Fisherman on River Aras — A16

Post Office in Erevan and Mt. Ararat — A17

Ruin in City of Ani — A18

Street in Erevan A19

Lake Sevan and Sevan Monastery A20

Mythological Subject from old Armenian Monument A21

# ARMENIA

Mt. Ararat — A22

| 1921 | | Unwmk. | Perf. 11½ | |
|---|---|---|---|---|
| 278 | A7 | 1r gray green | 1.00 | |
| 279 | A8 | 2r slate gray | 1.00 | |
| 280 | A9 | 3r carmine | 1.00 | |
| 281 | A10 | 5r dark brown | 1.00 | |
| 282 | A11 | 25r gray | 1.00 | 5.00 |
| 283 | A12 | 50r red | 1.00 | |
| 284 | A13 | 100r orange | 1.00 | |
| 285 | A14 | 250r dark blue | 1.00 | |
| 286 | A15 | 500r brown vio | 1.00 | |
| 287 | A16 | 1,000r sea green | 1.00 | |
| 288 | A17 | 2,000r bister | 1.00 | |
| 289 | A18 | 5,000r dark brown | 1.00 | |
| 290 | A19 | 10,000r dull red | 1.00 | |
| 291 | A20 | 15,000r slate blue | 75.00 | |
| 292 | A21 | 20,000r lake | 2.00 | |
| 293 | A22 | 25,000r gray blue | 6.00 | |
| 294 | A22 | 25,000r brown olive | 10.00 | |
| | | Nos. 278-294 (17) | 106.00 | |

| | | Imperf. | | |
|---|---|---|---|---|
| 278a | A7 | 1r | 12.00 | |
| 279a | A8 | 2r | 1.00 | |
| 280a | A9 | 3r | 1.00 | |
| 281a | A10 | 5r | 1.00 | |
| 282a | A11 | 25r | 1.00 | 5.00 |
| 283a | A12 | 50r | 45.00 | |
| 284a | A13 | 100r | 1.00 | |
| 285a | A14 | 250r | 1.00 | |
| 286a | A15 | 500r | 1.00 | |
| 287a | A16 | 1,000r | 1.00 | |
| 288a | A17 | 2,000r | 1.00 | |
| 289a | A18 | 5,000r | 1.00 | |
| 290a | A19 | 10,000r | 1.00 | |
| 291a | A20 | 15,000r | 90.00 | |
| 292a | A21 | 20,000r | 2.00 | |
| 293a | A22 | 25,000r | 5.00 | |
| 294a | A22 | 25,000r | 5.00 | |
| | | Nos. 278a-294a (17) | 170.00 | 5.00 |

Except the 25r, Nos. 278-294 were not regularly issued and used. Most examples of Nos. 278-294a on the market are forgeries. Values are for genuine stamps.
For surcharges see Nos. 347-390.

Russian Stamps of 1909-17 Surcharged

## Lozenges of Varnish on Face

| 1921, Aug. | | Wove Paper | Perf. 13½ |
|---|---|---|---|
| 295 | A9 | 5,000r on 1r | 25.00 |
| 296 | A12 | 5,000r on 3½r | 25.00 |
| 297 | A13 | 5,000r on 5r | 25.00 |
| 298 | A12 | 5,000r on 7r | 25.00 |
| 299 | A13 | 5,000r on 10r | 25.00 |
| | | Nos. 295-299 (5) | 125.00 |

Nos. 295-299 were not officially issued. Counterfeits abound.

A23

Mt. Ararat & Soviet Star — A24

Soviet Symbols A25

Peasant A27

Crane A26

Harpy A28

Peasant Sowing A29

Soviet Symbols A30

Forging — A31

Plowing — A32

| 1922 | | | Perf. 11½ | |
|---|---|---|---|---|
| 300 | A23 | 50r green & red | .85 | |
| 301 | A24 | 300r slate bl & buff | 1.00 | |
| 302 | A25 | 400r blue & pink | 1.00 | |
| 303 | A26 | 500r vio & pale lil | 1.00 | |
| 304 | A27 | 1,000r dull bl & pale bl | 1.00 | |
| 305 | A28 | 2,000r black & gray | 1.25 | |
| 306 | A29 | 3,000r black & red | 1.25 | |
| 307 | A30 | 4,000r black & lt brn | 1.25 | |
| 308 | A31 | 5,000r blk & dull red | 1.25 | |
| 309 | A32 | 10,000r black & pale rose | 1.25 | |
| a. | | Tête-bêche pair | 100.00 | |
| | | Nos. 300-309 (10) | 11.10 | |

Nos. 300-309 were not issued without surcharge.
Stamps of types A23 to A32, printed in other colors than Nos. 300 to 309, are essays.

Nos. 300-309 with Hstmpd. Srch. in Rose, Violet or Black

| 1922 | | | | |
|---|---|---|---|---|
| 310 | | 10,000 on 50r (R) | 90.00 | 125.00 |
| 311 | | 10,000 on 50r (V) | 100.00 | 50.00 |
| 312 | | 10,000 on 50r | 25.00 | 25.00 |
| 313 | | 15,000 on 300r (R) | 120.00 | 150.00 |
| 314 | | 15,000 on 300r (V) | 100.00 | 75.00 |
| 315 | | 15,000 on 300r | 25.00 | |
| 316 | | 25,000 on 400r (R) | 75.00 | 60.00 |
| 317 | | 25,000 on 400r | 25.00 | 35.00 |
| 318 | | 30,000 on 500r (R) | 120.00 | 120.00 |
| 319 | | 30,000 on 500r (V) | 50.00 | 60.00 |
| 320 | | 30,000 on 500r | 25.00 | 35.00 |
| 321 | | 50,000 on 1,000r (R) | 250.00 | 250.00 |
| 322 | | 50,000 on 1,000r (V) | 200.00 | 100.00 |
| 323 | | 50,000 on 1,000r | 25.00 | 25.00 |
| 324 | | 75,000 on 3,000r | 25.00 | 35.00 |
| 325 | | 100,000 on 2,000r (R) | 250.00 | 250.00 |
| 326 | | 100,000 on 2,000r (V) | 100.00 | 50.00 |
| 327 | | 100,000 on 2,000r | 25.00 | 25.00 |
| 328 | | 200,000 on 4,000r (V) | 35.00 | 35.00 |
| 329 | | 200,000 on 4,000r | 20.00 | 20.00 |
| 330 | | 300,000 on 5,000r (V) | 50.00 | 60.00 |
| 331 | | 300,000 on 5,000r | 20.00 | 20.00 |
| 332 | | 500,000 on 10,000r (V) | 100.00 | 100.00 |
| 333 | | 500,000 on 10,000r | 10.00 | 10.00 |
| | | Nos. 310-333 (24) | 1,865. | 1,750. |

Forgeries exist.

Goose A33

Armenian Woman at Well A35

Armenian Village Scene — A34

Mt. Ararat — A36

Mt. Ararat — A37

### New Values in Gold Kopecks, Handstamped Surcharge in Black

| 1922 | | | Imperf. | |
|---|---|---|---|---|
| 334 | A33 | 1(k) on 250r rose | 25.00 | 35.00 |
| 335 | A33 | 1(k) on 250r gray | 25.00 | 35.00 |
| 336 | A34 | 2(k) on 500r rose | 25.00 | 35.00 |
| 337 | A34 | 3(k) on 500r gray | 25.00 | 35.00 |
| 338 | A35 | 4(k) on 1,000r rose | 25.00 | 35.00 |
| 339 | A35 | 4(k) on 1,000r gray | 25.00 | 35.00 |
| 340 | A36 | 5(k) on 1,000r rose | 25.00 | 35.00 |
| 341 | A36 | 10(k) on 1,000r rose | 25.00 | 35.00 |
| 342 | A37 | 15(k) on 5,000r rose | 47.50 | 52.50 |
| 343 | A37 | 20(k) on 5,000r gray | 25.00 | 35.00 |
| | | Nos. 334-343 (10) | 272.50 | 367.50 |

Nos. 334-343 were issued for postal tax purposes.
Nos. 334-343 exist without surcharge but are not known to have been issued in that condition. Counterfeits exist of both sets.

### Regular Issue of 1921 Handstamped with New Values in Black or Red Short, Thick Numerals

| 1922 | | | Imperf. | |
|---|---|---|---|---|
| 347 | A8 | 2(k) on 2r (R) | 500.00 | 400.00 |
| 350 | A11 | 4(k) on 25r (R) | 125.00 | 125.00 |
| 353 | A13 | 10(k) on 100r (R) | 24.00 | 24.00 |
| 354 | A14 | 15(k) on 250r | 5.00 | 5.00 |
| 355 | A15 | 20(k) on 500r | 15.00 | 15.00 |
| a. | | With "k" written in red | 12.00 | 12.00 |
| 357 | A22 | 50(k) on 25,000r bl (R) | 500.00 | 500.00 |
| 358 | A22 | 50(k) on 25,000r brn ol (R) | 600.00 | 500.00 |
| 359 | A22 | 50(k) on 25,000r brn ol | — | — |
| | | Nos. 347-358 (7) | 1,769. | 1,569. |

| | | Perf. 11½ | | |
|---|---|---|---|---|
| 360 | A7 | 1(k) on 1r, imperf. | 100.00 | 75.00 |
| a. | | Perf. | 50.00 | 50.00 |
| 361 | A7 | 1(k) on 1r (R) | 45.00 | 45.00 |
| a. | | Imperf. | 45.00 | 75.00 |
| 362 | A8 | 2(k) on 2r, imperf. | 47.50 | 60.00 |
| a. | | Perf. | 50.00 | 50.00 |
| 363 | A15 | 2(k) on 500r | 150.00 | 150.00 |
| a. | | Perf. | 100.00 | 100.00 |
| 364 | A15 | 2(k) on 500r (R) | 200.00 | 200.00 |
| 365 | A11 | 4(k) on 25r, imperf. | 30.00 | .75 |
| a. | | Perf. | 40.00 | 50.00 |
| 366 | A12 | 5(k) on 50r, imperf. | 24.00 | 36.00 |
| a. | | Perf. | 100.00 | 100.00 |
| 367 | A13 | 10(k) on 100r | 20.00 | 25.00 |
| a. | | Imperf. | 50.00 | 60.00 |
| 368 | A21 | 35(k) on 20,000r, imperf. | 50.00 | 100.00 |
| a. | | With "k" written in violet | 150.00 | 125.00 |
| b. | | Perf. | 150.00 | 100.00 |
| c. | | As "a," perf. | 90.00 | 100.00 |
| d. | | With "kop" written in violet, imperf. | | |
| | | Nos. 360-368 (9) | 666.50 | 691.75 |

### Manuscript Surcharge in Red
Perf. 11½

| 371 | A14 | 1k on 250r dk bl | 100.00 | 60.00 |

### Handstamped in Black or Red Tall, Thin Numerals

No. 381

| | | Imperf. | | |
|---|---|---|---|---|
| 377 | A11 | 4(k) on 25r (R) | 200.00 | 125.00 |
| 379 | A13 | 10(k) on 100r | 90.00 | 100.00 |
| 380 | A15 | 20(k) on 500r | 7.25 | 7.25 |
| 381 | A22 | 50k on 25,000r bl | 50.00 | 90.00 |
| a. | | Surcharged "50" only | 60.00 | 60.00 |
| 382 | A22 | 50k on 25,000r bl (R) | 14.50 | 14.50 |
| 382A | A22 | 50k on 25,000r brn ol | 29.00 | 29.00 |
| 382B | A22 | 50k on 25,000r brn ol (R) | 750.00 | 750.00 |
| | | Nos. 377-382A (6) | 390.75 | 365.75 |

On Nos. 381, 382 and 382A the letter "k" forms part of the surcharge.

| | | Perf. 11½ | | |
|---|---|---|---|---|
| 383 | A7 | 1(k) on 1r (R) | 40.00 | 40.00 |
| a. | | Imperf. | 100.00 | |
| 384 | A14 | 1(k) on 250r | 100.00 | 100.00 |
| 385 | A15 | 2(k) on 500r | 150.00 | 150.00 |
| a. | | Imperf. | 150.00 | 150.00 |
| 386 | A15 | 2(k) on 500r (R) | 24.00 | 24.00 |
| 387 | A9 | 3(k) on 3r | 40.00 | 50.00 |
| a. | | Imperf. | 40.00 | 50.00 |
| 388 | A21 | 3(k) on 20,000r, imperf. | 150.00 | 150.00 |
| a. | | Perf. | 150.00 | 150.00 |
| 389 | A11 | 4(k) on 25r | 100.00 | 100.00 |
| a. | | Imperf. | 120.00 | 120.00 |
| 390 | A12 | 5(k) on 50r, imperf. | 45.00 | 50.00 |
| a. | | Perf. | 50.00 | 75.00 |
| | | Nos. 383-390 (8) | 649.00 | 664.00 |

**Catalogue values for unused stamps in this section, from this point to the end of the section, are for Never Hinged items.**

Mt. Ararat — A45

| 1992, May 28 | | Litho. | Perf. 14 | |
|---|---|---|---|---|
| 430 | A45 | Strip of 3, #a.-c. | 3.50 | 3.50 |

a, 20k. b, 2r. c, 5r.

**Souvenir Sheet**

| 431 | A45 | 7r Eagle & Mt. Ararat | 45.00 | 45.00 |

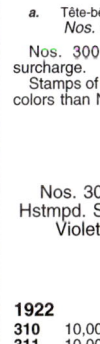

AT & T Communications System in Armenia — A45a

| 1992, July 1 | | Litho. | Perf. 13x13½ |
|---|---|---|---|
| 431A | A45a | 50k multicolored | 4.50 4.50 |

A46

1992 Summer Olympics, Barcelona: a, 40k, Ancient Greek wrestlers. b, 3.60r, Boxing. c, 5r, Weight lifting. d, 12r, Gymnastics.

| 1992, July 25 | | Litho. | Perf. 14 | |
|---|---|---|---|---|
| 432 | A46 | Strip of 4, #a.-d. | 3.50 | 3.50 |

A47

# ARMENIA

20k, Natl. flag. 1r, Goddess Waroubini, Orgov radio telescope. 2r, Yerevan Airport. No. 436, Goddess Anahit. No. 437, Runic message, 7th cent B.C. 5r, UPU emblem. 20r, Silver cup.

**1992-93   Litho.   Perf. 14½, 15x14½**

| 433 | A47 | 20k multicolored | .30 | .30 |
|---|---|---|---|---|
| 434 | A47 | 1r gray green | .30 | .30 |
| 435 | A47 | 2r blue | .40 | .40 |
| 436 | A47 | 3r brown | .60 | .60 |
| 437 | A47 | 3r bronze | .30 | .30 |
| 438 | A47 | 5r brown black | .90 | .90 |
| 439 | A47 | 20r gray | .70 | .70 |
|  |  | Nos. 433-439 (7) | 3.50 | 3.50 |

No. 435 is airmail. See Nos. 464-471, 521-524.

Issued: No. 436, 20k, 2r, 5r, 8/25/92; others, 5/12/93.

Religious Artifacts — A50

David of Sassoun, by Hakop Kojoian A50a

40k, Marker. 80k, Gospel page. 3.60r, Bas-relief, 13th cent. 5r, Icon of the Madonna.

**1993, May 23   Litho.   Perf. 14**

| 448 | A50 | 40k multicolored | .25 | .25 |
| 449 | A50 | 80k multicolored | .30 | .30 |
| 450 | A50 | 3.60r multicolored | .90 | .90 |
| 451 | A50 | 5r multicolored | 1.75 | 1.75 |
|  |  | Nos. 448-451 (4) | 3.20 | 3.20 |

**Souvenir Sheet**
**Perf. 14x13½**

| 451A | A50a | 12r multicolored | 8.00 | 8.00 |

Scenic Views A51

Designs: 40k, Garni Canyon, vert. 80k, Shaki Waterfall, Zangezur, vert. 3.60r, Arpa River Canyon, vert. 5r, Lake Sevan. 12r, Mount Aragats.

**1993, May 24   Perf. 14**

| 452 | A51 | 40k multicolored | .25 | .25 |
| 453 | A51 | 80k multicolored | .25 | .25 |
| 454 | A51 | 3.60r multicolored | .50 | .50 |
| 455 | A51 | 5r multicolored | .70 | .70 |
| 456 | A51 | 12r multicolored | 1.75 | 1.75 |
|  |  | Nos. 452-456 (5) | 3.45 | 3.45 |

Yerevan '93 — A52

**1993, May 25   Perf. 14½**

| 457 | A52 | 10r multicolored | .85 | .85 |
| a. |  | Min. sheet of 6 + 2 labels | 5.50 | 5.50 |

For surcharges see Nos. 485-486.

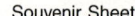
Souvenir Sheet

Noah's Descent from Mt. Ararat, by Hovhannes Aivazovsky — A52a

**1993, Aug. 4   Litho.   Perf. 14½**

| 458 | A52a | 7r multicolored | 4.00 | 4.00 |

Religious Relics, Echmiadzin — A53

Designs: 3r, Wooden panel, descent from cross, 9th cent. 5r, Gilded silver reliquary for Holy Cross of Khotakerats, 12r, Cross depicting right hand of St. Karapet, 14th cent. 30r, Reliquary for arm of St. Thaddeus the Apostle, 17th cent. 50r, Gilded silver vessel for consecrated ointment, 1815.

**1994, Aug. 4   Litho.   Perf. 14x14½**

| 459 | A53 | 3d multicolored | .25 | .25 |
| 460 | A53 | 5d multicolored | .25 | .25 |
| 461 | A53 | 12d multicolored | .65 | .65 |
| 462 | A53 | 30d multicolored | 1.25 | 1.25 |
| 463 | A53 | 50d multicolored | 2.00 | 2.00 |
|  |  | Nos. 459-463 (5) | 4.40 | 4.40 |

**Artifacts and Landmarks Type of 1993**

Gods of Van (Urartu): 10 l, Shivini, god of the sun. 50 l, Tayshaba, god of elements. 10d, Khaldi, supreme god.

25d, Natl. arms.

**1994, Aug. 4   Perf. 14½**

| 464 | A47 | 10 l black & brown | .25 | .25 |
| 465 | A47 | 50 l black & red brown | .25 | .25 |
| 469 | A47 | 10d black & gray | .85 | .85 |
| 471 | A47 | 25d red & bister | 2.00 | 2.00 |
|  |  | Nos. 464-471 (4) | 3.35 | 3.35 |

A54

**1994, Dec. 31   Litho.   Perf. 14½x14**

| 479 | A54 | 16d No. 1a | 1.10 | 1.10 |

First Armenian postage stamp, 75th anniv.

Early Printing Press — A54a

**1994, Dec. 30   Litho.   Perf. 14x14½**

| 480 | A54a | 30d multicolored | .60 | .60 |

First Armenian periodical, 200th anniv.

Natl. Arms, Stadium — A54b

**1994, Dec. 30   Litho.   Perf. 14x14½**

| 481 | A54b | 30d multicolored | .80 | .80 |

Natl. Olympic Committee.

Olympic Rings — A54c

**1994, Dec. 30   Litho.   Perf. 14x14½**

| 482 | A54c | 40d multicolored | 1.00 | 1.00 |

Intl. Olympic Committee, Cent.

A54d

**1994, Dec. 31   Litho.   Perf. 14x14½**

| 483 | A54d | 50d multi + label | 1.00 | 1.00 |

Ervand Otian (1869-1926)

A54e

**1994, Dec. 31   Litho.   Perf. 14½x14**

| 484 | A54e | 50d multi + label | 1.00 | 1.00 |

Levon Shant (1869-1951).

**No. 457 Surcharged in Blue or Red Brown**

a                          b

**1994, Sept. 10   Litho.   Perf. 14**

| 485 | A52(a) | 40d on 10r (Bl) | 5.50 | 5.50 |
| 486 | A52(b) | 40d on 10r (RB) | 5.50 | 5.50 |

Yerevan '94.

A55

Christianity in Armenia: 60d, Cross, 10th-11th cent. No. 488, Kings Abgar & Trdat, 1836. No. 489, St. Bartholomew, St. Thaddeus. 80d, St. Gregory, the Illuminator. 90d, Baptism of the Armenian people, 1892. 400d, Plan of Echmiadzin, c. 1660, engr. by Jakob Peeters.

**1995, Apr. 3   Litho.   Perf. 14x15**

| 487 | A55 | 60d multicolored | .65 | .65 |
| 488 | A55 | 70d multicolored | .65 | .65 |
| 489 | A55 | 70d multicolored | .65 | .65 |
| 490 | A55 | 80d multicolored | 1.00 | 1.00 |
| 491 | A55 | 90d multicolored | 1.10 | 1.10 |
|  |  | Nos. 487-491 (5) | 4.05 | 4.05 |

**Souvenir Sheet**

| 492 | A55 | 400d multicolored | 5.50 | 5.50 |

Nos. 488-489 are 45x44mm.

A56

**1995, Apr. 3**

| 493 | A56 | 150d gray & black | 1.60 | 1.60 |

Vazgen I (1908-94), Catholikos of All Armenians.

Armenia Fund — A57

**1995, Apr. 27   Perf. 15x14**

| 494 | A57 | 90d multicolored | 1.00 | 1.00 |

UN, 50th Anniv. — A58

**1995, Apr. 28**

| 495 | A58 | 90d multicolored | 1.00 | 1.00 |

Cultural Artifacts — A59

Designs: 30d, Black polished pottery, 14th-13th cent. B.C. 60d, Silver cup, 5th cent. B.C. 130d, Gohar carpet, 1700 A.D.

**1995, Apr. 27   Perf. 15x14**

| 496 | A59 | 30d multicolored | .35 | .35 |
| 497 | A59 | 60d multicolored | .65 | .65 |
| 498 | A59 | 130d multicolored | 1.50 | 1.50 |
|  |  | Nos. 496-498 (3) | 2.50 | 2.50 |

Birds — A60

**1995, Apr. 27   Perf. 14**

| 499 | A60 | 40d Milvus milvus | .85 | .85 |
| 500 | A60 | 60d Aquila chrysaetos | 1.25 | 1.25 |

End of World War II, 50th Anniv. — A61

Designs: No. 501, P. Kitsook, 408th Armenian Rifle Division. No. 502, A. Sargissin, N. Safarian, 89th Taman Armenian Triple Order-Bearer Division. No. 503, B. Chernikov, N. Tavartkeladze, V. Penkovsky, 76th Armenian Alpine Rifle Red Banner (51st Guards) Division. No. 504, S. Zakian, H. Babayan, I. Lyudnikov, 390th Armenian Rifle Division. No. 505, A. Vasillian, M. Dobrovolsky, Y. Grechany, G. Sorokin, 409th Armenian Rifle Division.

No. 506, vert.: a, Marshal Hovhannes Baghramian. b, Adm. Hovhannes Issakov. c, Marshal Hamazasp Babajanian. d, Marshal Sergey Khoudyakov.

No. 507: Return of the Hero, by Mariam Aslamazian.

**1995, Sept. 30   Litho.   Perf. 15x14**

| 501 | A61 | 60d multicolored | .60 | .60 |
| 502 | A61 | 60d multicolored | .60 | .60 |
| 503 | A61 | 60d multicolored | .60 | .60 |
| 504 | A61 | 60d multicolored | .60 | .60 |
| 505 | A61 | 60d multicolored | .60 | .60 |
|  |  | Nos. 501-505 (5) | 3.00 | 3.00 |

**Miniature Sheet**
**Perf. 15x14½**

| 506 | A61 | 60d Sheet of 4, #a.-d. | 3.25 | 3.25 |

# ARMENIA

### Souvenir Sheet
*Perf. 15x14*
507 A61 300d multicolored    4.00  4.00

Authors — A62

Designs: No. 508, Ghevond Alishan (1820-1901). No. 509, Gregor Artsruni (1845-92), vert. No. 510, Franz Werfel (1890-1945), vert.

**1995, Oct. 5    Litho.    Perf. 15x14**
508 A62 90d blue & black      .85  .85
509 A62 90d cream, blk, gold  .85  .85
510 A62 90d blue & maroon     .85  .85
  Nos. 508-510 (3)           2.55 2.55
Nos. 508-510 issued with se-tenant label.

A64

Prehistoric artifacts: 40d, Four-wheeled carriages, 15th cent. BC. 60d, Bronze model of geocentric solar system, 11-10th cent. BC, vert. 90d, Tombstone, Red Tufa, 7-6th cent. BC, vert.

**1995, Dec. 5    Perf. 14½x15, 15x14½**
512 A64 40d multicolored      .40  .40
513 A64 60d multicolored      .60  .60
514 A64 90d multicolored      .80  .80
  Nos. 512-514 (3)           1.80 1.80

A65

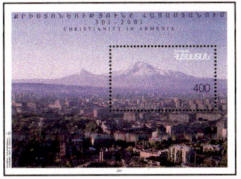

Christianity in Armenia — A66

Views of Yerevan: 60d, Brandy distillery, wine cellars. 80d, Abovian Street. 90d, Sports and concert complex. 100d, Baghramian Avenue. 120d, Republic Square.
400d, Panoramic photograph of Yerevan.

**1995, Dec. 5    Perf. 15x14**
515 A65 60d salmon & black    .50  .50
516 A65 80d pale org & blk    .60  .60
517 A65 90d buff & black      .70  .70
  **Size: 61x24mm**
518 A65 100d pale yel bis & blk  .80  .80
519 A65 120d dull org & blk   1.00 1.00
  Nos. 515-519 (5)           3.60 3.60

### Souvenir Sheet
520 A66 400d multicolored    4.25 4.25

No. 464 Surcharged in Green, Red, Blue Violet, or Red Brown

**1996, Mar. 30    Litho.    Perf. 14½**
521 A47 40d on 10l (G)       1.75 1.75
522 A47 100d on 10l (R)      3.50 3.50
523 A47 150d on 10l (BV)     5.00 5.00
524 A47 200d on 10l (RB)     7.00 7.00
  Nos. 521-524 (4)          17.25 17.25

Alexsandre Griboyedov (1795-1829), Writer — A67

**1996, Apr. 24    Litho.    Perf. 14x14½**
525 A67 90d multi + label     .90  .90

Khrimian Hayrik (1820-1907), Catholicos of All Armenians — A68

**1996, Apr. 30    Perf. 14½x14**
526 A68 90d brown & blue      .90  .90
No. 526 is printed se-tenant with label.

Admiral Lazar Serbryakov (1795-1862) — A69

**1996, Apr. 30**
527 A69 90d multi + label     .90  .90

Armenian Red Cross, 75th Anniv. — A70

**1996, May 4    Perf. 14x14½**
528 A70 60d multicolored      .60  .60

Motion Pictures, Cent. — A71

**1996, May 4    Perf. 14½x14**
529 A71 60d multicolored      .60  .60
No. 529 exists imperf. Value $45.

Endangered Fauna — A72

**1996, May 3    Perf. 14**
530 A72 40d Carpa aegagrus    .70  .70
531 A72 60d Panthera pardus  1.10 1.10

1996 Summer Olympics, Atlanta — A73

Designs: a, 40d, Cyclist. b, 60d, Athletic event. c, 90d, Wrestling.

**1996, July 25**
532 A73  Strip of 3, #a.-c.  1.90 1.90

Modern Olympic Games, Cent. — A74

**1996, July 25    Perf. 14x14½**
533 A74 60d multicolored      .80  .80

Fridtjof Nansen (1861-1930), Arctic Explorer A75

**1996, May 20    Litho.    Perf. 14x14½**
534 A75 90d multicolored     1.00 1.00

32nd Chess Olympiad, Yerevan — A76

Designs: No. 535, Petrosian-Botvinnik, World Championship match, Moscow, 1963. No. 536, Kasparov-Karpov, World Championship Match, Leningrad, 1986. No. 537, G. Kasparian, first prize winner, Contest of the Shakhmati v SSSR magazine, 1939. No. 538, 32nd Chess Olympiad, Yerevan.

**1996, Sept. 15    Litho.    Perf. 14**
535 A76 40d multicolored      .70  .70
536 A76 40d multicolored      .70  .55
537 A76 40d multicolored      .70  .70
538 A76 40d multicolored      .70  .70
  a.  Booklet pane, #535-538 3.00
      Complete booklet, 2 #538a 7.50
  Nos. 535-538 (4)           2.80 2.65
No. 538a issued 9/24.
Nos. 535-538 also exist imperf. Value $30.

Tigran Petrosian, World Chess Champion, Chess House, Yerevan — A77

**1996, Sept. 20    Perf. 14x15**
539 A77 90d multicolored      .75  .75
No. 539 also exists imperf. Value $20.

Capra Aegagrus — A78

World Wildlife Fund: 70d, Two running. 100d, One standing. 130d, One holding head down. 350d, Two facing forward.

**1996, Oct. 20    Litho.    Perf. 14½x14**
540 A78 70d multicolored      .40  .40
541 A78 100d multicolored     .50  .50
542 A78 130d multicolored     .70  .70
543 A78 350d multicolored    1.75 1.75
  a.  Block of 4, #540-543   3.50 3.50
  b.  Booklet pane, 2 #543a 10.00 10.00
      Complete booklet, #543b 12.00 12.00
Issued in sheets of 16 stamps.

Christianity in Armenia, 1700th Anniv. — A79

Armenian churches: No. 544, St. Catherine Church, St. Petersburg, 1780. No. 545, Church of the Holy Mother, Kishinev, 1803. No. 546, Church of the Holy Mother, Samarkand, 1903. No. 547, Armenian Church, Lvov, 1370. No. 548, St. Hripsime Church, Yalta, 1913.
500d, Church of St. Gevorg of Etchmiadzin, Tbilisi, 1805.

**1997, Mar. 19    Litho.    Perf. 14x15**
544 A79 100d multicolored     .85  .85
545 A79 100d multicolored     .85  .85
546 A79 100d multicolored     .85  .85
547 A79 100d multicolored     .85  .85
548 A79 100d multicolored     .85  .85
  Nos. 544-548 (5)           4.25 4.25

### Souvenir Sheet
549 A79 500d multicolored    3.50 3.50

First Armenian Printing Press, Etchmiadzin, 225th Anniv. — A80

**1997, Mar. 26    Litho.    Perf. 15x14**
550 A80 70d multicolored     1.00 1.00

Armenian Entertainers A81

Designs: No. 551, Folk singer, Jivani (1846-1909). No. 552, Arno Babajanian (1921-83), composer, vert.

**1997, Mar. 26    Perf. 15x14, 14x15**
551 A81 90d multicolored      .60  .60
552 A81 90d multicolored      .60  .60

Paintings from Natl. Gallery of Armenia — A82

Designs: No. 553, "One of my Dreams," by Eghishe Tadevossian. No. 554, "Countryside," by Gevorg Bashinjaghian. No. 555, "Portrait of Natalia Tehumian," by Hakob Hovnatanian. No. 556, "Salomé," by Vardges Sureniants.

**1997, May 28    Litho.    Perf. 15x14**
553 A82 150d multi           1.00 1.00
554 A82 150d multi           1.00 1.00
555 A82 150d multi, vert.    1.00 1.00
556 A82 150d multi, vert.    1.00 1.00
  Nos. 553-556 (4)           4.00 4.00
See Nos. 573-575.

Rouben Mamulian (1897-1987), Motion Picture Director — A83

**1997, Oct. 8    Litho.    Perf. 15x14**
557 A83 150d multicolored    1.00 1.00

Moscow '97, World Philatelic Exhibition — A84

170d, St. Basil's Cathedral.

**1997, Oct. 17    Perf. 14x15**
558 A84 170d multicolored    1.25 1.25

Eghishe Charents (1897-1937), Poet — A85

**1997, Oct. 19    Perf. 15x14**
559 A85 150d multicolored    1.00 1.00

A86

Europa (Stories and Legends): 170d, Hayk, the Progenitor of the Armenians. 250d, Vahagn, the Dragon Slayer.

**1997, Oct. 18    Perf. 14x15**
560 A86 170d multicolored    2.00 1.75
561 A86 250d multicolored    4.50 2.00

# ARMENIA

A87

40d, Iris lycotis. 170d, Iris elegantissima.

**1997, Dec. 19**    Litho.    *Perf. 14*
562 A87 40d multicolored .30 .30
563 A87 170d multicolored 1.20 1.20

Religious Buildings — A88

Designs: No. 564, San Lazzaro, the Mekhitarian Congregation, Venice. No. 565, St. Gregory the Illuminator Cathedral, Anthelias. No. 566, St. Khach Armenian Church, Rostov upon Don. No. 567, St. James Monastery, Jerusalem. No. 568, Nercissian School, Tbilisi.
500d, Lazarian Seminary, Moscow.

**1997, Dec. 22**    *Perf. 15x14, 14x15*
564 A88 100d multi, horiz. .70 .70
565 A88 100d multi .70 .70
566 A88 100d multi .70 .70
567 A88 100d multi, horiz. .70 .70
   Size: 60x21mm
568 A88 100d multi .70 .70
   Nos. 564-568 (5) 3.50 3.50
 **Souvenir Sheet**
569 A88 500d multicolored 3.00 3.00
Christianity in Armenia, 1700th anniv. (in 2001).

Christmas — A89

**1997, Dec. 26**    *Perf. 14x15*
570 A89 40d multicolored .80 .80

Diana, Princess of Wales (1961-97) — A90

**1998, Apr. 8**    Litho.    *Perf. 15x14*
571 A90 250d multicolored 1.50 1.50
No. 571 was issued in sheets of 5 + label.

Karabakh Movement, 10th Anniv. — A91

**1998, Feb. 20**    Litho.    *Perf. 13½x14*
572 A91 250d multicolored 2.25 2.25

**Paintings from Natl. Gallery of Armenia Type of 1997**

Designs: No. 573, "Tartar Women's Dance," by Alexander Bazhbeouk-Melikian. No. 574, "Family. Generations," by Yervand Kochar. No. 575, "Spring in Our Yard," by Haroutiun Kalents.

**1998, Feb. 21**    *Perf. 15x14, 14x15*
573 A82 150d multi 1.50 1.50
574 A82 150d multi, vert. 1.50 1.50
575 A82 150d multi, vert. 1.50 1.50
   Nos. 573-575 (3) 4.50 4.50

1998 World Cup Soccer Championships, France — A92

**1998, June 10**    Litho.    *Perf. 14x15*
576 A92 250d multicolored 2.25 2.25
No. 576 was issued in sheets of 10 and sheets of 8 + 2 labels. Value, sheet of 8 + 2 labels $20. Same, imperf $125.

National Holidays and Festivals — A93

Europa: 170d, Couple jumping over fire, Trndez. 250d, Girls taking part in traditional ceremony, Ascension Day.

**1998, June 24**    Litho.    *Perf. 15x14*
577 A93 170d multicolored 1.25 1.00
578 A93 250d multicolored 2.25 2.00

Butterflies — A94

**1998, June 26**    *Perf. 14*
579 A94 170d Papilio alexanor 1.00 1.00
580 A94 250d Rethera komarovi 1.50 1.50

National Costumes — A95

**1998, July 16**    Litho.    *Perf. 14x13½*
581 A95 170d Ayrarat 1.25 1.25
582 A95 250d Vaspurakan 1.75 1.75
 See Nos. 591-592.

Christianity in Armenia, 1700th Anniv. (in 2001) — A96

Churches: a, St. Forty Children's, 1958, Milan. b, St. Sargis, London, 1923. c, St. Vardan Cathedral, 1968, New York. d, St. Hovannes Cathedral, 1902, Paris. e, St. Gregory the Illuminator Cathedral, 1938, Buenos Aires.

**1998, Sept. 25**    Litho.    *Perf. 11½*
583 A96 100d Sheet of 5, #a.-e. 3.00 3.00

Memorial to Armenian Earthquake Victims — A97

**1998, Sept. 26**    *Perf. 15x14*
584 A97 250d multicolored 2.25 2.25
No. 584 was issued in sheets of 10 and sheets of 8 + 2 labels. Value, sheet of 8 + 2 labels $35.

Minerals — A98

**1998, Oct. 23**
585 A98 170d Pyrite 1.25 1.25
586 A98 250d Agate 1.75 1.75
 See Nos. 616-617.

Valery Bryusov (1873-1924), Writer — A99

**1998, Dec. 1**    *Perf. 14x15*
587 A99 90d multicolored 1.10 1.10

**Souvenir Sheet**

Sergei Parajanov, Film Director, 75th Birth Anniv. — A100

**1999, Apr. 19**    Litho.    *Perf. 14x14¾*
588 A100 500d multicolored 3.50 3.50
 a.   IBRA 99 emblem in margin 4.00 4.00

State Reserves — A101

**1999, Apr. 22**    *Perf. 14¾x14¼*
589 A101 170d Khosrov 1.00 1.00
590 A101 250d Kilijan 1.50 1.50
 Europa.

**National Costumes Type of 1998**

**1999, Apr. 20**    Litho.    *Perf. 14x13½*
591 A95 170d Karin 1.25 1.25
592 A95 250d Zangezour 2.00 2.00

Council of Europe, 50th Anniv. — A102

**1999, June 12**
593 A102 170d multicolored 1.75 1.75

Cilician Ships — A103

**1999, Aug. 12**    Litho.    *Perf. 14¾x14*
594 A103 170d orange & blue 1.25 1.25
595 A103 250d red & white 2.00 2.00
**With PhilexFrance 99 Emblem at LR**
596 A103 250d red & white 2.25 2.25
   Nos. 594-596 (3) 5.50 5.50

Domesticated Animals — A104

**1999, Aug. 19**    *Perf. 13¼x13¾*
597 A104 170d Armenian gampr dog 1.25 1.25
598 A104 250d Van cat 2.00 2.00
**With China 1999 World Philatelic Exhibition Emblem at LR**
599 A104 250d Van cat 2.50 2.50
   Nos. 597-599 (3) 5.75 5.75

**Souvenir Sheet**

First Pan-Armenian Games — A105

**1999, Aug. 28**    *Perf. 14¾x14*
600 A105 250d multicolored 3.00 3.00

**Souvenir Sheet**

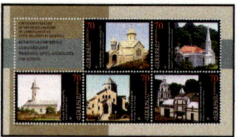
Christianity in Armenia, 1700th Anniv. (in 2001) — A106

Churches: a, St. Gregory the Illuminator, Cairo. b, St. Gregory the Illuminator, Singapore. c, St. Khach, Suceava, Romania. d, St. Savior, Worcester, Mass. e, Church of the Holy Mother, Madras, India.

**1999, Aug.**    Litho.    *Perf. 13¼x13¾*
601 A106 70d Sheet of 5, #a.-e. + label 7.50 7.50

UPU, 125th Anniv. — A107

**1999, Oct.**    *Perf. 14¾x14¼*
602 A107 270d multicolored 2.25 2.25

Politicians Assassinated Oct. 27, 1999 — A108

Designs: No. 603, Parliament Speaker Karen Demirchyan, Parliament building. No. 604, Prime Minister Vazgen Sargsyan, troops. 540d, Demirchyan, Sargsyan, Yuri Bakhshyan, Ruben Miroyan, Henrik Abrahamyan, Armenak Armenakyan, Leonard Petrossyan and Mikael Kotanyan.

   *Perf. 14¾x14¼*
**2000, Feb. 21**    Litho.
603 A108 250d multi 2.50 2.00
604 A108 250d multi 2.50 2.00
 a.   Sheet, 5 each #603-604 65.00 65.00
   *Imperf*
   Size: 60x44mm
605 A108 540d multi 5.00 5.00

Fish — A109

Designs: 50d, Salmo ischchan. 270d, Barbus goktschaicus.

**2000, May 23**    Litho.    *Perf. 13¼x13¾*
606 A109 50d multi 1.00 1.00
607 A109 270d multi 2.00 2.00

Fairy Tales — A110

70d, The Liar Hunter. 130d, The King and the Peddler.

**2000, May 25**    *Perf. 14¾x14¼*
608 A110 70d multicolored .65 .65
609 A110 130d multicolored 1.25 1.25

# ARMENIA 657

### Europa, 2000
### Common Design Type

**2000, June 19**    *Perf. 14¼x14¾*
610 CD17 40d multi .75 .75
611 CD17 500d multi 4.00 4.00

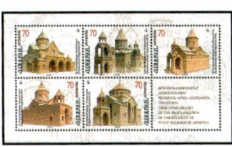

Christianity as State Religion, 1700th Anniv. — A111

No. 612: a, St. Gayane Church, Vagharshapat. b, Etchmiadzin Cathedral, Vagharshapat. c, Church of the Holy Mother, Khor Virap. d, St. Shoghakat Church, Vagharshapat. e, St. Hripsime Church, Vagharshapat.

**2000, July 10**   *Litho.*   *Perf. 13¼x13¾*
612 A111 70d Sheet of 5, #a-e, + label 4.00 4.00

2000 Summer Olympics, Sydney — A112

Designs: 10d, Basketball. 30d, Tennis. 500d, Weight lifting.

**2000, July 11**    *Perf. 13½x13¾*
613-615 A112 Set of 3 5.00 5.00

### Mineral Type of 1998

Designs: 170d, Quartz. 250d, Molybdenite.

**2000, Sept. 4**    *Perf. 14¾x14*
616-617 A98 Set of 2 3.25 3.25

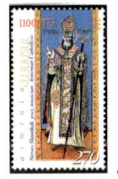

A113

**2000, Sept. 11**    *Perf. 14x14¾*
618 A113 270d multi 2.00 2.00

Nerses Shnorhali (1100-73), poet and musician.

Christmas — A114

**2000, Sept. 15**
619 A114 170d multi 1.40 1.40

Avetik Issahakian (1875-1957), Poet — A115

**2000, Sept. 17**    *Perf. 14¾x14*
620 A115 130d multi .90 .90

Musical Instruments — A116

Designs: 170d, Dhol. 250d, Duduk.

**2000, Dec. 22**   *Litho.*   *Perf. 14x13¼*
621-622 A116 Set of 2 3.50 3.50

---

Famous Armenians — A117

No. 623: a, Viktor Hambartsoumian (1908-96), cosmologist. b, Abraham Alikhanov (1904-70), physicist. c, Andranik Iossifian (1905-93), engineer. d, Sargis Saltikov (1905-83), metallurgist. e, Samuel Kochariants (1909-87), nuclear weapons scientist. f, Atrem Mikoyan (1905-70), aircraft designer. g, Norayr Sissakian (1907-66), biologist. h, Ivan Knunyants (1906-90), chemist. i, Nikoghayos Yenikolopian (1924-93), chemist.

No. 624: a, Nikoghayos Adonts (1871-1942), historian. b, Manouk Abeghian (1865-1944), grammarian. c, Hovhannes Toumanian (1869-1923), poet. d, Hrachya Ajarian (1876-1953), linguist. e, Gevorg Emin (1918-98), writer. f, Yervand Lalayan (1864-1931), anthropologist. g, Daniel Varoujan (1884-1915), poet. h, Paruyr Sevak (1924-71), writer. i, William Saroyan (1908-81), writer.

No. 625: a, Hamo Beknazarian (1892-1965), actor. b, Alexandre Tamanian (1878-1936), architect. c, Vahram Papazian (1888-1968), actor. d, Vassil Tahirov (1859-1938), viticulturist. e, Leonid Yengibarov (1935-72), mime. f, Haykanoush Danielian (1893-1958), singer. g, Sergo Hambartsoumian (1910-83) "Strongest man on Earth". h, Hrant Shahinian (1923-96), gymnast. i, Toros Toramanian (1864-1934), architectural historian.

No. 626: a, Komitas (1869-1935), composer. b, Aram Khachatourian (1903-78), composer. c, Martiros Sarian (1880-1972), artist. d, Avet Terterian (1929-94), composer. e, Alexandre Spendiarian (1871-1928), composer. f, Arshile Gorky (1904-48), artist. g, Minas Avetisian (1928-75), artist. h, Levon Orbeli (1882-1958), physiologist. i, Hripsimeh Simonian (1916-98), artist.

**2000, Dec. 23**    *Perf. 14¾x14¼*
623 Booklet pane of 9 8.75 8.75
 a.-i. A117 110d Any single .90 .90
624 Booklet pane of 9 8.75 8.75
 a.-i. A117 110d Any single .90 .90
625 Booklet pane of 9 8.75 8.75
 a.-i. A117 110d Any single .90 .90
626 Booklet pane of 9 8.75 8.75
 a.-i. A117 110d Any single .90 .90
 Booklet, #623-626 45.00

### Souvenir Sheet

Battle of Avarayr, 1550th Anniv. — A118

No. 627: a, 170d, St. Vardan Mamikonian (388-451). b, 270d, Battle of Avarayr, 451.

**2001, June 7**   *Litho.*   *Perf. 14x14¾*
627 A118 Sheet of 2, #a-b 5.00 5.00

Record of Lamentations, by St. Grigor Narekatzi, 1000th Anniv. — A119

**2001, June 8**   *Litho.*   *Perf. 14¾x14*
628 A119 25d multi 2.00 2.00

Europa — A120

Designs: 50d, Lake Sevan. 500d, Spandarian Reservoir.

**2001, June 9**
629-630 A120 Set of 2 5.75 5.75

Armenian Admission to Council of Europe — A121

**2001, June 11**
631 A121 240d multi 2.25 2.25

---

Worldwide Fund for Nature (WWF) — A122

Sciurus persicus: a, 40d, On branch. b, 50d, Eating. c, 80d, Close-up. d, 120d, Digging.

   *Perf. 13¼x13¾*
**2001, Aug. 25**    *Litho.*
632 A122 Block of 4, #a-d 4.00 4.00

### Souvenir Sheet

Second Pan-Armenian Games — A123

**2001, Aug. 18**   *Litho.*   *Perf. 14¾x14*
633 A123 300d multi 4.00 4.00

### Souvenir Sheet

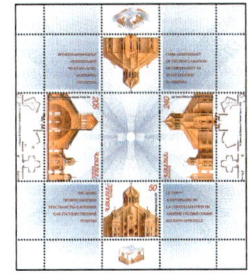

Christianity in Armenia, 1700th Anniv. — A124

Views of St. Gregory the Illuminator Cathedral, Yerevan: a, 50d, Front. b, 205d, Side (45x30mm). c, 240d, Side, diff. (45x30mm).

   *Perf. 13¾x13¼, 13¼x13¾*
**2001, Aug. 27**
634 A124 Sheet of 3, #a-c, + 6 labels 7.00 7.00
 d. As No. 634, with brown inscriptions in margins 65.00 65.00

Marginal inscriptions on No. 634d read "INTERNATIONAL / PHILATELIC EXHIBITION / ARMENIA '01/ 10-16 September, 2001, Yerevan," in English, Armenian, Russian and French. Souvenir sheet can be formed into a box which shows cathedral from various angles.

Ivan Lazarev (1735-1801) and Institute of Eastern Languages, Moscow — A125

**2001, Sept. 26**   *Litho.*   *Perf. 14¾x14*
635 A125 300d multi 8.00 8.00

See Russia No. 6665.

Native Costumes — A126

---

Man and woman from: 50d, Javakhch. 250r, Artzakh.

**2001, Sept. 27**    *Perf. 14x13½*
636-637 A126 Set of 2 3.00 3.00

6th World Wushu Championships A127

**2001, Oct. 3**    *Perf. 13¼x13¾*
638 A127 180d black 2.75 2.75

Year of Dialogue Among Civilizations — A128

**2001, Oct. 9**    *Perf. 14x14¾*
639 A128 275d multi 6.00 6.00

Commonwealth of Independent States, 10th Anniv. — A129

**2001, Nov. 29**
640 A129 205d multi 2.25 2.25

European Year of Languages A130

**2001, Dec. 21**    *Perf. 14¾x14*
641 A130 350d multi 5.00 5.00

Independence, 10th Anniv. — A131

**2001, Dec. 22**
642 A131 300d multi 2.75 2.75

Transportation A132

Designs: 180d, Cart. 205d, Phaeton.

**2001, Dec. 24**    *Perf. 13½x14*
643-644 A132 Set of 2 3.75 3.75

Medicinal Plants — A133

Designs: 85d, Hypericum perforatum. 205d, Thymus serpyllum.

**2001, Dec. 25**    *Perf. 13¼x13¾*
645-646 A133 Set of 2 3.00 3.00

Eagle — A134

**2002, Mar. 28**   *Litho.*   *Perf. 14¾x14*
647 A134 10d brown .30 .30
648 A134 25d green .50 .30
649 A134 50d dk blue 1.00 .60
 Nos. 647-649 (3) 1.80 1.20

See Nos. 674-676.

# ARMENIA

 Industries — A135

Designs: 120d, Calendar belt, 2nd cent. B.C., copper smelter. 350d, Containers, 7th cent. B.C., hops, barley, beer kettles.

**2002, Apr. 26**
650-651  A135  Set of 2          6.50 6.50

 National Gallery Artworks — A136

Designs: No. 652, 200d, Lily, by Edgar Chahine. No. 653, 200d, Salomé, sculpture by Hakob Gurjian.

**2002, Apr. 29**           **Perf. 14x14¾**
652-653  A136  Set of 2          3.50 3.50

 2002 World Cup Soccer Championships, Japan and Korea — A137

**2002, May 2**           **Perf. 14¾x14**
654  A137  350d multi          2.75 2.75

Souvenir Sheet

 Hovsep Pushman (1877-1906), Artist — A138

**2002, May 9**
655  A138  650d multi          5.00 5.00

 Hovhannes Tevossian (1902-58), Engineer — A139

**2002, May 14**
656  A139  350d multi          2.75 2.75

 Europa — A140

Designs: 70d, Magician's hat. 500d, Clown.

**2002, July 30**  Litho.  **Perf. 14x14¾**
657-658  A140  Set of 2          4.00 4.00

 Artemy Aivazian, Composer, Cent. of Birth — A141

**2002, July 31**           **Perf. 14¾x14**
659  A141  600d multi          4.75 4.75

Souvenir Sheet

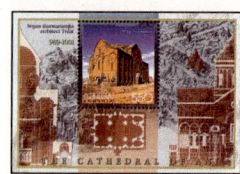 Cathedral of Ani, 1000th Anniv. (in 2001) — A142

           **Perf. 13¼x13¾**
**2002, Sept. 24**           Litho.
660  A142  550d multi          4.50 4.50

 Intl. Year of Mountains — A143

**2002-03**           **Perf. 14¾x14**
661  A143  350d multi          3.00 3.00
661a    Booklet pane of 3      9.00 9.00
Issued: No. 661, 9/26/02. No. 661a, 2003.

 Reptiles — A144

Designs: 170d, Lacerta armeniaca. 220d, Vipera raddei.

**2002-03**           **Perf. 13¼x13¾**
662-663  A144  Set of 2         3.50 3.50
663a    Booklet pane, 2 each #662-663  7.00 7.00
Issued: Nos. 662-663, 9/27/02. No. 663a, 2003.

 Women for Peace — A145

**2002, Dec. 20**  Litho.  **Perf. 14¾x14**
664  A145  220d multi          2.00 2.00

 Alexandrapol — Yeravan Railway, Cent. — A146

**2002, Dec. 21**
665  A146  350d multi          3.25 3.25

 Flowers — A147

Designs: 150d, Galanthus artjuschenkoae. 200d, Merendera mirzoevae.

**2002, Dec. 23**           **Perf. 13¼x13¾**
666-667  A147  Set of 2         3.00 3.00
667a    Booklet pane, 2 each #666-667   6.00 —
        Complete booklet, #661a, 663a, 667a        22.00
Issued: No. 667a, 2003.

 Space Research — A148

Designs: 120d, Cosmic ray research. 220d, Orion 1 and Orion 2 space observatories.

**2002, Dec. 24**           **Perf. 14¾x14**
668-669  A148  Set of 2         3.00 3.00

 Europa — A149

Poster art: 170d, Handle With Care!, by Artak Bagdassaryan. 250d, Armenia, Our Home, by Karen Koyojan.

           **Perf. 13½x13¼**
**2003, June 24**           Litho.
670-671  A149  Set of 2         4.50 4.50
671a    Booklet pane, 4 each #670-671      19.00 19.00
No. 671a was sold with booklet cover, but was unattached to it.

 Aram Khatchaturian (1903-78), Composer — A150

           **Perf. 13½x13¼**
**2003, June 25**           Litho.
672  A150  350d multi          3.00 3.00

 Larus Armenicus — A151

**2003, June 26**           **Perf. 12½**
673  A151  220d multi          1.75 1.75

**Eagle Type of 2002**
           **Perf. 13¼x13½**
**2003, Sept. 23**           Litho.
674  A134  70d red             .70  .70
675  A134  300d dk blue       2.50 2.50
676  A134  500d bister brn    5.00 5.00
   Nos. 674-676 (3)           8.20 8.20

Souvenir Sheet

 Transport Corridor Europe — Caucausus — Asia (TRACECA), 10th Anniv. — A152

**2003, Oct. 9**           **Perf. 13**
677  A152  480d multi          6.50 6.50

 First Armenian Postal Dispatch, 175th Anniv. — A153

**2003, Nov. 24**           **Perf. 13¼x13½**
678  A153  70d multi           .75  .75

 Introduction of Dram Currency, 10th Anniv. — A154

**2003, Nov. 25**
679  A154  170d multi          1.50 1.50

 A155

**2003, Nov. 25**           **Perf. 13½x13¼**
680  A155  350d multi          3.50 3.50
Siamanto (1878-1915), poet.

 A156

**2003, Nov. 27**
681  A156  200d multi          2.00 2.00
Vahan Tekeyan (1878-1945), poet.

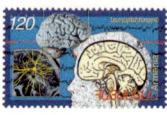 Neurophysiology A157

**2003, Nov. 28**           **Perf. 13¼x13½**
682  A157  120d multi          1.25 1.25

Souvenir Sheet

 Third Pan-Armenian Games, Yerevan — A158

**2003, Nov. 28**
683  A158  350d multi          4.00 4.00

Souvenir Sheet

 The Baptism, Miniature From Gospel of Ejmiatsin A159

**2003, Nov. 28**           **Perf. 13½x13¼**
684  A159  550d multi          6.00 6.00

 A160

Paintings in Museum of Russian Art: 200d, Still Life, by Alexander Shevchenko. 220d, In a Restaurant, by Konstantin Roudakov.

**2004, Sept. 6**  Litho.  **Perf. 13½x13¼**
685-686  A160  Set of 2         4.00 4.00

# ARMENIA

A161

**2004, Sept. 9**
687 A161 350d multi 3.50 3.50
FIFA (Fédération Internationale de Football Association), Cent.

Grapes — A162

Grape color: 170d, Yellow. 220d, Purple.
**2004, Sept. 8** Perf. 12½
688-689 A162 Set of 2 4.00 4.00

Souvenir Sheet
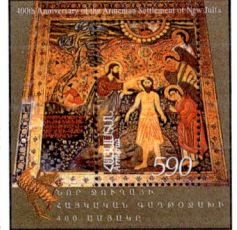
Armenian Settlement of New Julfa, 400th Anniv. A163

**2004, Sept. 9** Perf. 13
690 A163 590d multi 6.00 6.00

Animated Films — A164

Designs: 70d, Cat and Dog, 1937. 120d, Foxbook, 1975.
**2004, Sept. 10** Perf. 13¼x13½
691-692 A164 Set of 2 2.00 2.00

Aramayis Yerzinkyan (1879-1931), Statesman — A165

**2004, Sept. 11** Perf. 13½x13¼
693 A165 220d multi 2.50 2.50

Karabakh Horse — A166

**2005, Feb. 14** Litho. Perf. 12½
694 A166 350d multi 3.50 3.50
Dated 2004.

2004 Summer Olympics, Athens — A167

Hand: 70d, With Olympic Rings. 170d, As runner. 350d, As pistol.
**2005, Feb. 14**
695-697 A167 Set of 3 9.00 9.00
Dated 2004.

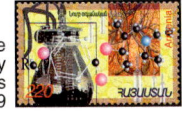
Intl. Day Against Desertification — A168

**2005, Feb. 21** Perf. 13½x13¼
698 A168 360d multi 3.50 3.50
Dated 2004.

Heart, Molecule and Chemistry Apparatus A169

**2005, Feb. 22**
699 A169 220d multi 2.25 2.25
Dated 2004.

Michael Nalbandian (1829-66), Writer — A170

**2005, Feb. 23**
700 A170 220d multi 2.25 2.25
Dated 2004.

Mouratsan (1854-1908), Writer — A171

**2005, Feb. 24**
701 A171 350d multi 3.50 3.50
Dated 2004.

Tigran Petrosian (1929-84), Chess Champion A172

**2005, Feb. 25**
702 A172 220d multi 3.00 3.00

Europa
A173 A174
**2005, Mar. 16** Perf. 13½x13¼
703 A173 70d multi 1.50 1.50
704 A174 350d multi 2.50 2.50
Dated 2004.

Souvenir Sheet

Goshavank Monastery — A175

**2005, Mar. 17** Perf. 12½
705 A175 480d multi 5.00 5.00
Dated 2004.

Armen Tigranian (1879-1950), Composer A176

**2005, Mar. 18** Perf. 13¼x13½
706 A176 220d multi 2.25 2.25
Dated 2004.

A177

**2005, Apr. 21** Perf. 13½x13¼
707 A177 350d multi 3.25 3.25
Armenian genocide, 90th anniv.

A178

**2005, Apr. 29**
708 A178 350d multi 4.00 4.00
End of World War II, 60th anniv.
No. 708 was issued in sheets of 10 and sheets of 8 + 2 labels. Value, sheet of 8 + 2 labels $425.

Anushavan Arzumanian (1904-65), Educator A179

**2005, May 2** Perf. 13¼x13½
709 A179 220d multi 2.00 2.00
Dated 2004.

Paintings by Martiros Sarian (1880-1972)
A180 A181
**2005, May 10** Perf. 13½x13¼
710 A180 170d Self-portrait 1.75 1.75
711 A181 200d Mount Aragats 2.00 2.00

Mother's Day — A182

**2005, Oct. 4** Litho. Perf. 13¼x13½
712 A182 350d multi 3.25 3.25

A183

Europa: 70d, Bread. 350d, Porridge.
**2005, Oct. 4** Perf. 13½x13¼
713-714 A183 Set of 2 4.00 4.00
714a Booklet pane, 4 each #713-714 16.00 —
No. 714a was sold with booklet cover, but unattached to it.

A184

**2005, Oct. 5**
715 A184 70d multi .75 .75
Armenian alphabet, 1600th anniv.

A185

**2005, Oct. 5**
716 A185 70d multi .75 .75
Vardan Ajemian (1905-77), theater director.

A186

**2005, Oct. 5**
717 A186 170d multi 1.75 1.75
Anania Shirakatsi (605-85), scientist.

Mher Mkrtchian (1930-93), Actor — A187

**2005, Oct. 6** Perf. 13¼x13½
718 A187 120d multi 1.10 1.10

Artem Mikoyan (1905-70), Aircraft Designer, and MiG Fighters — A188

**2005, Oct. 6**
719 A188 350d multi 3.25 3.25

# ARMENIA

Rugs — A189

Rugs from: 60d, 19th cent. 350d, 1904. 480d, 18th cent.

**2005, Oct. 6**     Perf. 13½x13¼
720-721 A189   Set of 2    3.50 3.50
**Souvenir Sheet**
722 A189 480d multi    4.50 4.50
No. 722 contains one 28x42mm stamp.

Armenia Year in Russia — A190

**2006, Jan. 22**   Litho.   Perf. 11¼
723 A190 350d multi    4.50 4.50
See Russia No. 6938.

Alexander Melik-Pashaev (1905-64), Conductor — A191

**2006, Mar. 27**    Perf. 13¼x13½
724 A191 70d multi    .90 .90
Dated 2005.

St. Mary's Russian Orthodox Cathedral, Yerevan — A192

**2006, Mar. 27**
725 A192 170d multi    2.00 2.00
Dated 2005.

Vakhtang Ananyan (1805-80), Writer — A193

**2006, Mar. 27**
726 A193 170d multi    2.00 2.00
Dated 2005.

Raphael Patkanian (1830-92), Writer — A194

**2006, Mar. 27**    Perf. 13½x13¼
727 A194 220d multi    2.25 2.25
Dated 2005.

2006 Winter Olympics, Turin — A195

Mountains and: 120d, 2006 Winter Olympics emblem. 170d, Emblem, map of Italy on snowboard.

**2006, Mar. 27**    Perf. 12½x12¾
728-729 A195   Set of 2    3.25 3.25
729a   Miniature sheet, 5 each #728-729    30.00 30.00
Dated 2005.

Spiridon Melikian (1880-1933), Musician — A196

**2006, Mar. 28**    Perf. 13½x13¼
730 A196 350d multi    3.50 3.50
Dated 2005.

**Souvenir Sheet**

Miniature Art Depicting Nativity and Adoration of the Magi — A197

**2006, Mar. 28**    Perf. 13¼x13½
731 A197 480d multi    5.50 5.50
Dated 2005.

Native Costumes — A198

Costumes from: 170d, Sassoun. 200d, Shatakhk.

**2006, Mar. 28**    Perf. 13½x13¼
732-733 A198   Set of 2    3.50 3.50
Dated 2005.

Insects — A199

Designs: 170d, Porphyrophora hamelii. 350d, Procerus scabrosus fallettianus.

**2006, Mar. 28**    Perf. 12¾x12½
734-735 A199   Set of 2    5.00 5.00
Dated 2005.

Europa Stamps, 50th Anniv. — A200

Designs: Nos. 736, 740a, 70d, Orange panel and "C." Nos. 737, 740b, 70d, Blue panel and "E." Nos. 738, 740c, 70d, Red panel and "P." Nos. 739, 740d, 70d, Green panel and "T."

**2006, Mar. 28**    Perf. 12¾x12½
**Stamps With "Europa 1956-2006" Inscription**
736-739 A200   Set of 4    3.50 3.50
**Souvenir Sheet**
**Stamps Without "Europa 1956-2006" Inscription**
740 A200 70d Sheet of 4, #a-d    3.50 3.50
Dated 2005.

**Souvenir Sheet**

Independence, 15th Anniv. — A201

**2006, Sept. 19**   Litho.   Perf. 12¾
741 A201 480d multi    5.00 5.00

World Peace — A202

**2006, Oct. 16**    Perf. 13½x13¼
742 A202 50d multi    .50 .50

**Souvenir Sheet**

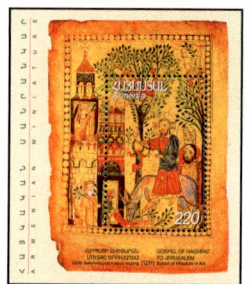

Gospel of Haghpat to Jerusalem — A203

**2006, Oct. 16**
743 A203 220d multi    2.50 2.50

2006 World Cup Soccer Championships, Germany — A204

**2006, Oct. 17**    Perf. 13¼x13½
744 A204 350d multi    3.75 3.75

Europa — A205

Designs: 200d, Gears and clock hands. 350d, Keys.

**2006, Oct. 17**
745-746 A205   Set of 2    4.50 4.50

Sergei Merkyurov (1881-1952), Sculptor — A206

**2006, Oct. 18**
747 A206 230d multi    2.25 2.25

**Souvenir Sheet**

Armenian General Benevolent Union, Cent. — A207

No. 748: a, Boghos Nubar (1851-1930). b, Signed document. c, Alex Manoogian (1901-96).

**2006, Oct. 18**    Perf. 13½x13¼
748 A207 120d Sheet of 3, #a-c    3.75 3.75

On Nov. 30, 2006, the Armenian Postal Service was sold to a Dutch-owned firm, HayPost CJSC, affiliated with the Netherlands Postal Corporation. The items illustrated below were released in early 2007 by the stamp producer for the Armenian Postal Service prior to this sale, but as of December 2007, were never put on sale at any HayPost CJSC post office and were not valid for postage. HayPost CJSC acquired the remaining stock of these items from the producer and is negotiating with the Armenian government to place these items on sale and make the items valid for postage. All valid postage stamps from 2007, starting with No. 749 below are inscribed "Post." The items illustrated below do not have this inscription.

# ARMENIA 661

 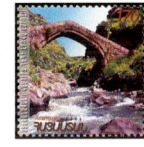

Smile of Reims, France — A208        Nativity, 15th Cent. Miniature, Armenia — A209

**2007, May 22    Litho.    Perf. 13¼x13**
749  A208  70d multi                      1.50  1.50
750  A209  350d multi                     7.50  7.50
See France Nos. 3335-3336.

Apricot — A210

**2007, July 6    Perf. 13¼x13¾**
751  A210  350d multi                     4.00  4.00

King Tigran the Great (c. 140-55 B.C.) — A211

**2007, July 19    Perf. 14¾x14**
Background Color
752  A211  50d red                        1.50  .50
753  A211  60d olive green                1.75  .60
754  A211  70d green                      2.10  .75
755  A211  120d blue                      3.50  1.20
Nos. 752-755 (4)                          8.85  3.05
See Nos. 780-783. Compare with types A240, A256, A271-A272.

Europa — A212

**2007, Sept. 12**
756  A212  350d multi                     4.00  4.00

Scouting, cent.

Gusan Sheram (1857-1938), Composer — A213

**2007, Sept. 13    Perf. 14x14¾**
757  A213  280d multi                     3.00  2.50

Margar Sedrakyan (1907-73), Cognac Producer — A214

**2007, Sept. 14    Perf. 14¾x14**
758  A214  170d multi                     2.00  1.50

Souvenir Sheet

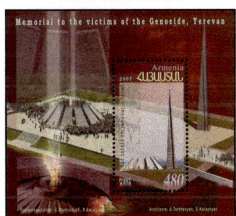

Genocide Memorial, Tsitsernakaberd — A215

**2007, Oct. 9    Perf. 14x14¾**
759  A215  480d multi                     5.00  3.50

Children's Art — A216

**2007, Oct. 24    Perf. 14¾x14**
760  A216  35d multi                      .65   .65

Rural Landscape, by Gevorg Bashinjaghyan (1857-1925) — A217

Kazbek, by Bashinjaghyan — A218

**2007, Oct. 24    Litho.**
761  A217  160d multi                     1.50  1.25
762  A218  220d multi                     2.25  1.75

Souvenir Sheet

Fourth Pan-Armenian Games, Yerevan — A219

**2007, Oct. 25    Perf. 14x14¾**
763  A219  360d multi                     3.50  3.00

Jean Garzou (1907-2000), Painter A220        Seda, by Garzou A221

**2007, Oct. 25    Perf. 14¾x14**
764  A220  180d multi                     1.75  1.40
765  A221  220d multi                     2.25  1.60

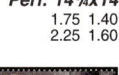

Norayr Sisakyan (1907-66), Biochemist A222

**2007, Oct. 26    Perf. 14¾x14**
766  A222  120d multi                     1.25  .90

Kamancha — A223

**2007, Oct. 27    Perf. 14x14¾**
767  A223  110d multi                     1.20  .90

Birds — A224

Designs: 120d, Pelecanus crispus. 200d, Aegypius monachus.

**2007, Oct. 27    Perf. 13¼x13¾**
768-769  A224  Set of 2                   4.00  3.00

Matenadaran Ancient Book Depository A225

**2007, Oct. 29    Perf. 14¾x14**
770  A225  200d multi                     2.00  1.75

Bagrat Nalbandyan (1902-90), Communications Administrator A226

**2007, Oct. 29    Litho.**
771  A226  230d multi                     2.50  1.75

# ARMENIA

N. Baghdasaryan (1907-88), Photojournalist — A227

**2007, Oct. 31**    *Perf. 14x14¾*
772   A227   200d multi    2.00   1.75

Intl. Solar Year — A228

**2007, Nov. 7**    *Perf. 14¾x14*
773   A228   170d multi    1.75   1.25

Busts of Goddesses — A229

Designs: 70d, Greek Goddess Aphrodite. 350d, Armenian Goddess Anahit.

**2007, Dec. 14**   Litho.   *Perf. 14x11½*
774-775   A229   Set of 2    5.00   5.00
See Greece Nos. 2328-2329.

2008 Summer Olympics, Beijing — A230

    *Perf. 13¼x13¾*
**2008, June 11**    Litho.
776   A230   350d multi    3.50   3.50

Wood Carving — A231

**2008, June 17**    *Perf. 14x14¾*
777   A231   120d multi    1.25   1.25

Europa — A232

**2008, June 18**    *Perf. 14¾x14*
778   A232   350d multi    3.50   3.50

Alexander Shirvanzade (1858-1935), Writer — A233

**2008, June 19**    *Perf. 14x14¾*
779   A233   280d multi    2.50   2.50

**King Tigran the Great Type of 2007**
**2008, June 20**    *Perf. 14¾x14*
       **Background Color**
780   A211   10d bright blue    .25   .25
781   A211   20d orange brn    .30   .25
782   A211   50d rose lilac    .60   .40
783   A211   1100d purple    9.00   9.00
    Nos. 780-783 (4)    10.15   9.90

Flowers — A234

Designs: 120d, Anemone fasciculata. 280d, Scabiosa caucasica.

**2008, Oct. 9**   Litho.   *Perf. 13¼x14*
784-785   A234   Set of 2    4.00   4.00

Yerevan State University of Architecture and Construction, 75th Anniv. — A235

**2008, Oct. 28**    *Perf. 14¾x14*
786   A235   220d multi    2.25   2.25

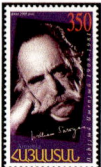

William Saroyan (1908-81), Writer — A236

**2008, Oct. 29**    *Perf. 14x14¾*
787   A236   350d multi    3.50   3.50

Victor Hambardzumyan (1908-96), Astrophysicist — A237

**2008, Oct. 20**    *Perf. 14¾x14*
788   A237   120d multi    1.50   1.50

Famous Men A238

No. 789: a, Peyo Yavorov (1878-1914), Bulgarian poet. b, Andranik Ozanian (1865-1927), Armenian general who participated in Balkan Wars.

**2008, Nov. 10**    *Perf. 13*
789    Horiz. pair    4.00   4.00
   a.   A238   70d multi    .60   .60
   b.   A238   350d multi    3.40   3.40
See Bulgaria No. 4492.

Dances — A239

Designs: 70d, Malambo sureño dancer, Argentina. 350d, Hoy-nazan dancers, Armenia.

**2009, Apr. 4**    *Perf. 12½x12¾*
790-791   A239   Set of 2    3.75   3.75
See Argentina Nos. 2512-2513.

King Tigran the Great (c. 140-55 B.C.) — A240

**2009, Apr. 8**    *Perf. 13¼*
     **Granite Paper**
     **Background Color**
792   A240   10d olive green    .25   .25
793   A240   25d yel bister    .25   .25
794   A240   50d cerise    .45   .45
795   A240   70d brown    .65   .65
796   A240   120d purple    1.10   1.10
797   A240   220d dark blue    2.10   2.10
798   A240   280d dk bl violet    2.60   2.60
799   A240   350d plum    3.25   3.25
    Nos. 792-799 (8)    10.65   10.65
Numerals are in a different font than on Type A211. Compare with types A256, A271-A272.

Van, Ancient Armenian Capital — A241

**2009, Apr. 29**    *Perf. 14¾x14*
800   A241   220d multi    1.75   1.75

Europa — A242

**2009, July 1**    *Perf. 13¼x13¾*
801   A242   350d multi    2.75   2.75
Intl. Year of Astronomy.

38th Chess Olympiad, Dresden, Germany — A243

Designs: 70d, Chess board, Armenian players holding flag. 280d, Chess pieces, Armenian flag.

**2009, July 29**    *Perf. 13¾x13¼*
802-803   A243   Set of 2    3.50   3.50
  803a    Miniature sheet of 10, 5 each #802-803    30.00   30.00

European Court of Human Rights, 50th Anniv. — A244

     *Perf. 12¾x13¼*
**2009, Nov. 13**    Litho.
804   A244   70d multi    15.00   15.00

Council of Europe, 60th Anniv. — A245

**2009, Nov. 13**    *Perf. 13¼x12¾*
805   A245   280d multi    15.00   15.00

Louis Braille (1809-52), Educator of the Blind — A246

**2009, Nov. 24**   Litho.   *Perf. 14¾x14*
806   A246   110d multi    1.25   1.10
No. 806 was issued in sheets of 10 and sheets of 8 + 2 labels. Value, sheet of 8 + 2 labels $12.

Daniel Varuzhan (1884-1915), Poet — A247

**2009, Dec. 8**    *Perf. 13¼x12¾*
807   A247   230d multi    2.25   2.25

**Souvenir Sheet**

Davit of Sasun Monument, Yerevan, 50th Anniv. — A248

**2009, Dec. 11**    *Perf. 14*
808   A248   360d multi    3.75   3.75

**Souvenir Sheet**

Olympic Champions — A249

No. 809: a, 70d, Hrant Shahinyan, gymnastics, 1952. b, 120d, Igor Novikov, pentathlon, 1956, 1964. c, 160d, Albert Azaryan, gymnastics, 1956, 1960.

**2009, Dec. 11**    Litho.
809   A249   Sheet of 3, #a-c    4.00   3.50

Khachatur Abovyan (1809-48), Writer — A250

**2009, Dec. 15**    *Perf. 12¾x13¼*
810   A250   170d multi    1.75   1.75

Animals — A251

Designs: 120d, Lutra lutra meridionalis. 160d, Ursus arctos syriacus.

**2009, Dec. 16**    *Perf. 14*
811-812   A251   Set of 2    3.00   2.75
  812a    Miniature sheet of 10, 5 each #811-812    15.00   15.00

Paintings in the National Gallery — A252

Designs: No. 813, 200d, Autumn. A Corner in Yerevan, by Sedrak Arakelyan. No. 814, 200d, Panna Paskevich, by Georgi Yakulov.

     *Perf. 13¼x12¾*
**2009, Dec. 16**    Litho.
813-814   A252   Set of 2    4.00   4.00

Vagharshapat Churches on UNESCO World Heritage List — A253

No. 815: a, Zvarnots Church. b, St. Hripsime Church. c, Mother See of Holy Etchmiadzin Church. d, St. Gayane Church.

**2009, Dec. 18**    *Perf. 14*
815   A253   70d Sheet of 4, #a-d    6.00   5.00

# ARMENIA

Christmas — A254

Madonna and Child with: 280d, Country name in white. 650d, Country name in black.

Perf. 13½x13¾
**2009, Dec. 18** Litho.
816 A254 280d multi  2.75  2.75
No. 816 was issued in sheets of 9 and sheets of 6 + 3 labels.

### Souvenir Sheet
Perf. 14
817 A254 650d multi  5.75  5.75
No. 817 contains one 30x60mm stamp.

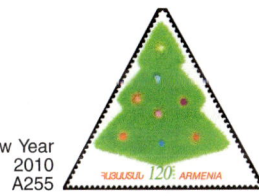

New Year 2010 — A255

Litho. with Flocking
**2009, Dec. 18** Perf. 14
818 A255 120d multi  7.50  7.50

King Tigran the Great (c. 140-55 B.C.) — A256

**2010, Jan. 29** Litho. Perf. 13x13¼
### Background Color
819 A256 10d cerise  .25  .25
820 A256 25d dark blue  .25  .25
821 A256 50d yel bister  .50  .50
822 A256 70d vermilion  .65  .65
823 A256 100d brown  .85  .85
824 A256 120d maroon  1.00  1.00
825 A256 200d gray  1.75  1.75
826 A256 220d purple  2.00  2.00
827 A256 280d red brown  2.50  2.50
828 A256 650d yel green  6.00  6.00
Nos. 819-828 (10)  15.75  15.75

### Self-Adhesive
Serpentine Die Cut 11¼
829 A256 10d cerise  .25  .25
830 A256 25d dark blue  .25  .25
831 A256 50d yel bister  .50  .50
832 A256 70d vermilion  .65  .65
833 A256 100d brown  .85  .85
834 A256 120d maroon  1.00  1.00
835 A256 200d gray  1.75  1.75
836 A256 220d purple  2.00  2.00
837 A256 280d red brown  2.50  2.50
838 A256 650d yel green  6.00  6.00
Nos. 829-838 (10)  15.75  15.75

Type A256 has no lettering below king's neck. The country name is smaller than that found on types A211 and A240. Compare with types A271-A272.

Henrik Kasparyan (1910-95), Chess Player — A257

**2010, Feb. 27** Perf. 14
839 A257 870d multi  8.00  8.00

Victory in World War II, 65th Anniv. — A258

**2010, May 6** Perf. 13¼x12¾
840 A258 350d multi  2.75  2.75

Cemetery for Russian Officers, Gyumri — A259

**2010, Aug. 20** Litho. Perf. 13¼x13
### Background Color
841 A259 350d light blue  2.75  2.75
### Souvenir Sheet
842 A259 650d maroon  5.75  5.75

Mt. Ararat A260     Flag of Armenia A261

**2010, Sept. 21** Perf. 12½x13
843 A260 350d multi  2.75  2.75
Perf. 13¼
844 A261 650d multi  5.00  5.00
Independence Day.

Yerevan and Mt. Ararat A262

Armenian Pavilion at Expo 2010, Shanghai — A263

**2010, Sept. 22** Perf. 14
845 A262 280d multi  2.25  2.25
Perf. 12½x13
846 A263 280d multi  2.25  2.25
Expo 2010, Shanghai.

Europa A264

**2010, Oct. 8** Perf. 13¼
847 A264 350d multi  2.75  2.75

2010 Youth Olympics, Singapore — A265

**2010, Nov. 26** Perf. 12½x13
848 A265 870d multi  7.50  7.50

2010 World Cup Soccer Championships, South Africa — A266

**2010, Nov. 26** Litho.
849 A266 1100d multi  10.00  10.00

### Souvenir Sheet
Olympic Champions — A267

**2010, Nov. 26** Perf. 13¼
850 A267 160d Sheet of 3, #a-c  4.50  4.50
No. 850: a, Vladimir Yengibaryan, boxing gold medalist, 1956. b, Faina Melnik, discus gold medalist, 1972. c, Yuri Vardanyan, weight lifting gold medalist, 1980.

### Souvenir Sheet

2010 Winter Olympics, Vancouver — A268

No. 851 — Skiers and 2010 Winter Olympics emblem at: a, 350d, Upper left. b, 500d, Center. c, 500d, Upper right.

**2010, Nov. 26**
851 A268 Sheet of 3, #a-c  13.00  13.00

Arakel Babakhanyan (1860-1932), Historian — A269

**2010, Dec. 27** Perf. 12½x13
852 A269 220d multi  2.00  2.00

Raffi (Hakob Melik Hakobyan) (1835-88), Writer — A270

**2010, Dec. 27** Perf. 13x12½
853 A270 220d multi  2.00  2.00

King Tigran the Great (c. 140-55 B.C.)
A271    A272

**2011, Feb. 1** Litho. Perf. 13¼
### Granite Paper
### Background Color
854 A271 10d dark blue  .25  .25
855 A272 35d gray brn  .30  .30
856 A272 50d green  .35  .35
857 A272 70d blue green  .55  .55
858 A272 120d org brown  .90  .90
859 A272 160d maroon  1.25  1.25
860 A272 220d dark red  1.75  1.75
861 A272 280d purple  2.10  2.10
862 A272 350d bister  2.75  2.75
863 A272 1100d dk brown  8.50  8.50
Nos. 854-863 (10)  18.70  18.70
Nos. 854-863 lack the word "Post." Compare with Types A211, A240 and A256.

Ruben Sevak (1885-1915), Writer — A273

**2011, Feb. 2** Perf. 13¼
864 A273 280d multi  2.50  2.50
Dated 2010.

A274

**2011, Feb. 2** Perf. 13¼
865 A274 280d multi  2.50  2.50
Vahan Teryan (1885-1920), writer. Dated 2010.

A275

Paintings in National Gallery: No. 866, 450d, Portrait of Actress Khmara, by Haroutyun Kalents. No. 867, 450d, Catholicos Mkrtich Khrimyan, by Vardghes Sourenyants.

**2011, Feb. 2** Perf. 13x12½
866-867 A275 Set of 2  7.50  7.50
Dated 2010.

### Souvenir Sheet

Pepo, First Armenian Film With Sound, 75th Anniv. (in 2010) — A276

No. 868: a, 170d, Actors Avet Avetisyan and Davit Malyan. b, 200d, Actor Hrachya Nercissyan. c, 500d, Actress Tatiana Makhmuryan.

**2011, Feb. 2** Perf. 13¼
868 A276 Sheet of 3, #a-c  7.50  7.50
Dated 2010.

Leonid Yenigbarov (1935-72), Circus Clown — A277

**2011, Feb. 2** Litho. Perf. 13x12½
869 A277 220d multi  2.00  2.00

Flora — A278

Designs: No. 870, 280d, Fritillaria armena. No. 871, 280d, Sambucus tigranii.

**2011, Feb. 2** Perf. 13¼
870-871 A278 Set of 2  5.00  5.00

# 664 ARMENIA

### Souvenir Sheet

Easter — A279

| 2011, Apr. 15 | Litho. | Perf. 12½x13 |
|---|---|---|
| 872 A279 1100d multi | | 9.00 9.00 |

Andranik Iossifian (1905-93), Designer of Meteorological Satellites — A280

First Man in Space, 50th Anniv. — A281

| 2011, Apr. 18 | | Perf. 13x12½ |
|---|---|---|
| 873 A280 200d multi | | 1.50 1.50 |
| | | Perf. 12½x13 |
| 874 A281 350d multi | | 3.00 3.00 |

Capitals of Belarus and Armenia — A282

No. 875 — Buildings and arms of: a, Minsk, Belarus. b, Yerevan, Armenia.

| 2011, June 1 | Litho. | Perf. 13 |
|---|---|---|
| 875 A282 200d Horiz. pair, #a-b | | 3.50 3.50 |

See Belarus No. 771.

### Souvenir Sheet

Communications Regional Commonwealth, 20th Anniv. — A283

| 2011, June 1 | | |
|---|---|---|
| 876 A283 200d multi | | 1.75 1.75 |

Writers — A284

Designs: 120d, Hovhannes Tumanian (1869-1923). 230d, Valery Bryusov (1873-1924).

| 2011, June 1 | | Perf. 12¾ |
|---|---|---|
| 877-878 A284 Set of 2 | | 3.00 3.00 |
| 878a Vert. pair, #877-878 | | 3.00 3.00 |

Nos. 877-878 each were printed in sheets of 9 + label. No. 878a was printed in sheets containing five pairs.
See Russia Nos. 7273-7274.

### Souvenir Sheet

Fifth Pan-Armenian Games — A285

| 2011, Aug. 20 | | |
|---|---|---|
| 879 A285 380d multi | | 3.50 3.50 |

Birds — A286

Designs: 230d, Luscinia svecica. 330d, Parus major.

| 2011, Sept. 5 | | Perf. 13¼ |
|---|---|---|
| 880 A286 230d multi | | 2.00 2.00 |
| 881 A286 330d multi | | 3.00 3.00 |
| a. Horiz. pair, #880-881 | | 5.00 5.00 |

Independence of Nagorno Karabakh From Azerbaijan, 20th Anniv. — A287

| 2011, Sept. 13 | | Perf. 13x13¼ |
|---|---|---|
| 882 A287 330d multi | | 3.00 3.00 |

Independence of Armenia, 20th Anniv. — A288

| 2011, Sept. 13 | | |
|---|---|---|
| 883 A288 380d multi | | 3.25 3.25 |

A289

Design: Fridtjof Nansen (1861-1930), Polar Explorer, Diplomat Assisting in Alleviating Armenian Refugee Crisis.

| 2011, Nov. 9 | | Perf. 13½ |
|---|---|---|
| 884 A289 350d olive bister | | 3.00 3.00 |

Commonwealth of Independent States, 20th Anniv. — A290

| 2011, Dec. 1 | | Perf. 13x12½ |
|---|---|---|
| 885 A290 280d multi | | 2.50 2.50 |

### Souvenir Sheet

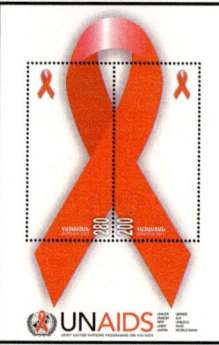

Joint United Nations Program on AIDS — A291

No. 886 — AIDS ribbons: a, 200d. b, 280d.

| 2011, Dec. 1 | | Perf. 13¼ |
|---|---|---|
| 886 A291 Sheet of 2, #a-b | | 4.25 4.25 |

2011 Junior Eurovision Song Contest, Yerevan — A292

| 2011, Dec. 3 | | Perf. 13¼x13 |
|---|---|---|
| 887 A292 230d multi | | 2.00 2.00 |
| a. Souvenir sheet of 4 | | 8.50 8.50 |

No. 887 was printed in sheets of 8.

Europa — A293

Photographs of forest in Dilijan Reserve with denominations at: No. 888, 350d, LL. No. 889, 350d, LR.

| 2011, Dec. 14 | | Perf. 12½x13 |
|---|---|---|
| 888-889 A293 Set of 2 | | 5.00 5.00 |

Intl. Year of Forests.

Grigor Zohrap (1861-1915), Lawyer and Writer — A294

| 2011, Dec. 23 | | Perf. 13¼x13 |
|---|---|---|
| 890 A294 170d multi | | 1.50 1.50 |

Children — A295

No. 891: a, 100d, Girl holding grapes and bird, flag of Armenia. b, 120d, Boy holding wheat stalks, flag of Nagorno Karabakh.

| 2011, Dec. 27 | | Litho. |
|---|---|---|
| 891 A295 Horiz. pair, #a-b | | 2.00 2.00 |

Youth philately. No. 891 was printed in sheets containing two pairs.

### Souvenir Sheet

UNESCO World Heritage Sites — A296

No. 892: a, 230d, Sanahin Monastery. b, 330d, Haghpat Monastery.

| 2011, Dec. 27 | | Perf. 13¼x13 |
|---|---|---|
| 892 A296 Sheet of 2, #a-b | | 5.00 5.00 |

Christmas and New Year's Day — A297

| 2011, Dec. 27 | | Perf. 13¼ |
|---|---|---|
| 893 A297 220d multi | | 2.00 2.00 |

Armenian Army, 20th Anniv. — A298

Army coat of arms and: 200d, Soldiers, tank, military vehicle, airplanes. 280d, Armenian flag.

| 2012, Feb. 9 | | Perf. 13¼x13 |
|---|---|---|
| 894-895 A298 Set of 2 | | 3.75 3.75 |

Admission to United Nations, 20th Anniv. — A299

| 2012, Mar. 23 | Litho. | Perf. 13x13¼ |
|---|---|---|
| 896 A299 350d multi | | 3.00 3.00 |

### Souvenir Sheet

Yerevan, World Book Capital — A300

| 2012, Apr. 22 | | |
|---|---|---|
| 897 A300 560d multi | | 5.00 5.00 |

Garegin Nzhdeh (1886-1955), Statesman — A301

| 2012, May 3 | | Perf. 13¼ |
|---|---|---|
| 898 A301 200d multi | | 1.75 1.75 |

Misak Metsarents (1886-1908), Poet — A302

| 2012, May 3 | | Perf. 13¼x13 |
|---|---|---|
| 899 A302 280d black | | 2.50 2.50 |

Armenian Alphabet — A303

First seven letters of Armenian alphabet in capital and lower-case.

| 2012, May 14 | | Perf. 13x13¼ |
|---|---|---|
| | Color of Panel at Left | |
| 900 A303 10d dull rose | | .30 .30 |
| 901 A303 25d yel green | | .30 .30 |
| 902 A303 50d gray blue | | .50 .50 |

**903** A303 70d dull blue .55 .55
**904** A303 100d greenish gray .85 .85
**905** A303 120d dull blue 1.10 1.10
**906** A303 280d lilac rose 2.25 2.25
*Nos. 900-906 (7)* 5.85 5.85

See Nos. 940-946, 983-989, 1066-1072, 1100-1104, 1110-1113, 1140-1142.

Khachkars — A304

Khachkar: 200d, By Master Poghos, Goshavank, 1291. 280d, Arinj, 13th cent.

**2012, June 14** ***Perf. 13¼***
**907-908** A304 Set of 2 3.75 3.75

Souvenir Sheet

Armenian Olympic Gold Medalists — A305

No. 909: a, Eduard Azaryan. b, Levon Julfalakyan. c, Hoksen Mirzoyan.

**2012, June 15**
**909** A305 160d Sheet of 3, #a-c 4.00 4.00

Souvenir Sheet

Mesrop Mashtots (361-440), Monk — A306

**2012, June 19** ***Perf. 14½x14¼***
**910** A306 560d multi 4.50 4.50

Hagigadar Monastery A307

**2012, Aug. 11** ***Perf. 13¼***
**911** A307 380d multi 3.00 3.00
*a.* Souvenir sheet of 2 + 2 labels 6.00 6.00

See Romania No. 5383.

Armenian Membership in Organization for Security and Cooperation in Europe, 20th Anniv. — A308

**2012, Sept. 7** ***Perf. 13x13¼***
**912** A308 330d multi 2.50 2.50

Ancient Artashat, Capital of Kingdom of Armenia, 185 B.C.-120 A.D. — A309

**2012, Oct. 30**
**913** A309 220d multi 1.75 1.75

Mount Ararat and Alexander Misnikyan (1886-1925), Bolshevik Leader — A310

**2012, Oct. 30**
**914** A310 230d multi 1.75 1.75

Samvel Kocharyants (1909-93), Nuclear Physicist — A311

**2012, Nov. 30** ***Perf. 14x13½***
**915** A311 350d multi 2.75 2.75

2012 Summer Olympics, London — A312

**2012, Nov. 30** ***Perf. 13¼***
**916** Horiz. strip of 3 5.00 5.00
*a.* A312 170d Boxing 1.25 1.25
*b.* A312 200d Weight lifting 1.40 1.40
*c.* A312 230d Wrestling 1.75 1.75

Miniature Sheet

Armenian Olympic Gold Medalists — A313

No. 917: a, Hrachya Petikyan, shooting, 1992. b, Israyel Militosyan, weight lifting, 1992. c, Mnatsakan Iskandaryan, boxing, 1992. d, Armen Nazaryan, boxing, 1996.

**2012, Nov. 30**
**917** A313 120d Sheet of 4, #a-d 4.00 4.00

Perch Proshyan (1837-1907), Writer — A314

**2012, Dec. 4** **Litho.**
**918** A314 170d multi 1.40 1.40

Lusine Zakaryan (1937-92), Opera Singer — A315

**2012, Dec. 4** ***Perf. 13x13¼***
**919** A315 220d multi 1.75 1.75

Religious Treasures of Etchmiadzin — A316

No. 920: a, 200d, Reliquary of Geghard, 1687. b, 220d, Cross with relic, 1746. c, 450d, Reliquary, Argadsz, St. Nshan, 13th cent.

**2012, Dec. 4** ***Perf. 13¼x13***
**920** A316 Horiz. strip of 3, #a-c 7.00 7.00

Ashot Hovhannisyan (1887-1977), First Secretary of Armenian Communist Party — A317

**2012, Dec. 5** ***Perf. 13x13¼***
**921** A317 170d black 1.75 1.75

A318

**2012, Dec. 5** ***Perf. 13¼x13***
**922** A318 280d multi 2.00 2.00

Hovsep Orbeli (1887-1961), President of Armenian Academy of Arts and Sciences.

A319

**2012, Dec. 5**
**923** A319 280d multi 2.00 2.00

Hayk Bzhishkyants (1887-1937), military leader.

Tigran Tchoukhadjian (1837-98), Composer — A320

**2012, Dec. 6** **Litho.**
**924** A320 330d multi 2.50 2.50

Hayastan All-Armenian Fund, 20th Anniv. — A321

**2012, Dec. 12** ***Perf. 13x13¼***
**925** A321 380d multi 3.00 3.00

Collective Security Treaty Organization, 20th Anniv. — A322

**2012, Dec. 17** ***Perf. 13¼x13***
**926** A322 230d multi 1.75 1.75

Tadevos Minasyants (1912-82), Minister of Communications A323

**2012, Dec. 27** ***Perf. 13x13¼***
**927** A323 170d multi 1.25 1.25

Tatev Monastery — A324

**2012, Dec. 27** **Litho.**
**928** A324 350d multi 2.50 2.50
*a.* Sheet of 4 + 2 labels 10.00 10.00

Europa.

Paintings in National Gallery of Armenia — A325

Designs: 220d, Dacha, by Marc Chagall. 280d, Self-portrait, by Rudolf Khachatryan.

**2012, Dec. 27** ***Perf. 13¼x13***
**929-930** A325 Set of 2 4.00 4.00

Souvenir Sheet

Sayat-Nova (1712-95), Musician — A326

**2012, Dec. 27**
**931** A326 560d multi 4.25 4.25

Children's Art — A327

Designs: 100d, Trees. 120d, Soccer player.

**2012, Dec. 28** ***Perf. 13¾***
**932-933** A327 Set of 2 1.60 1.60

Mammals — A328

Designs: 230d, Allactaga elater. 330d, Ovis orientalis gmelinii.

**2012, Dec. 28** ***Perf. 12½***
**934** A328 230d multi 1.50 1.50
**935** A328 330d multi 2.25 2.25
*a.* Horiz. pair, #934-935 4.00 4.00

Christmas and New Year's Day — A329

**2012, Dec. 28** ***Perf. 13x13¼***
**936** A329 220d multi 1.60 1.60

St. Sargis's Day — A330

**2013, Jan. 29** ***Perf. 13¼x13***
**937** A330 280d multi 2.25 2.25

# ARMENIA

### Souvenir Sheet

Churches — A331

No. 938: a, 160d, Holy Trinity Church, Yerevan. b, 200d, Church of Holy Archangels, St. Etchmiadzin. c, 200d, Church of St. Hakob of Msbin, Gyumri.

| 2013, Apr. 4 | | | Perf. 13¼ | |
|---|---|---|---|---|
| 938 | A331 | Sheet of 3, #a-c | 4.00 | 4.00 |

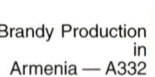

**Brandy Production in Armenia — A332**

| 2013, June 18 | | Perf. 13x13¼ | |
|---|---|---|---|
| 939 | A332 300d multi | 2.25 | 2.25 |

No. 939 was printed in sheets of 8 + 2 labels.

### Armenian Alphabet Type of 2012
Second group of seven letters of Armenian alphabet in capital and lower-case.

| 2013, July 30 | | Perf. 13x13¼ | |
|---|---|---|---|
| **Color of Panel at Left** | | | |
| 940 | A303 10d olive bister | .25 | .25 |
| 941 | A303 35d salmon rose | .25 | .25 |
| 942 | A303 50d green | .40 | .40 |
| 943 | A303 60d blue | .45 | .45 |
| 944 | A303 70d rose | .55 | .55 |
| 945 | A303 100d greenish blue | .75 | .75 |
| 946 | A303 120d gray blue | .95 | .95 |
| | Nos. 940-946 (7) | 3.60 | 3.60 |

**Europa — A333**

| 2013, Aug. 15 | | Litho. | |
|---|---|---|---|
| 947 | A333 350d multi | 2.75 | 2.75 |
| a. | Souvenir sheet of 4 | 11.00 | 11.00 |

**Johannes Lepsius (1858-1926), Documenter of Armenian Genocide A334**

**James Bryce (1838-1922), Documenter of Armenian Genocide A335**

| 2013, Aug. 16 | | Perf. 13x13¼ | |
|---|---|---|---|
| 948 | A334 280d multi | 2.00 | 2.00 |
| | | Perf. 13¼x13 | |
| 949 | A335 330d multi | 2.50 | 2.50 |

Armenian Genocide, cent. (in 2015).

### Souvenir Sheet

**Church of St. Grigor, Kecharis Monastery, Tsakhkadsor — A336**

| 2013, Aug. 24 | Litho. | Perf. 13¼x13 | |
|---|---|---|---|
| 950 | A336 480d multi | 4.00 | 4.00 |

### Souvenir Sheet
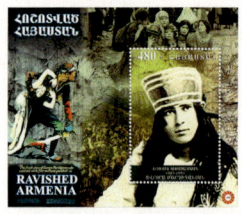
**Aurora Mardiganian (1901-94), Writer of Memoir "Ravished Armenia" — A337**

| | | Perf. 14¼x14½ | |
|---|---|---|---|
| 2013, Sept. 24 | | Litho. | |
| 951 | A337 480d multi | 4.00 | 4.00 |

### Souvenir Sheet

**Diplomatic Relations Between Armenia and Belarus, 20th Anniv. — A338**

| 2013, Oct. 24 | Litho. | Perf. 13 | |
|---|---|---|---|
| 952 | A338 650d multi | 5.00 | 5.00 |

See Belarus No. 879.

**Anton Kochinyan (1913-90), Politician — A339**

| 2013, Oct. 25 | Litho. | Perf. 13x13¼ | |
|---|---|---|---|
| 953 | A339 230d multi | 1.75 | 1.75 |

**Chess A340**

**A341**

No. 954: a, 200d, Chess pieces and board, stylized globe. b, 280d, Chessboard with rook in background.
No. 955 — Half of trophy, globe, chess pieces and chess board with: a, 200d, Black squares. b, 280d, White squares.

| 2013, Nov. 6 | Litho. | Perf. 13¼ | |
|---|---|---|---|
| 954 | A340 Horiz. pair, #a-b | 4.00 | 4.00 |
| c. | Souvenir sheet of 4, 2 each #954a-954b | 8.00 | 8.00 |
| d. | Souvenir sheet of 8, 4 each #954a-954b, + 8 labels | 17.00 | 17.00 |
| 955 | A341 Horiz. pair, #a-b | 4.00 | 4.00 |
| c. | Souvenir sheet of 4, 2 each #955a-955b | 8.00 | 8.00 |
| d. | Souvenir sheet of 8, 4 each #955a-955b, + 8 labels | 17.00 | 17.00 |

Armenia as World Chess Team Champion (No. 954); Armenia as 3-time Chess Olympiad champion (No. 955).

### Souvenir Sheet

**Church of St. Hovhannes, Gandzasar Monastery — A342**

| 2013, Nov. 8 | Litho. | Perf. 14¼x14½ | |
|---|---|---|---|
| 956 | A342 560d multi | 4.50 | 4.50 |

**Gyumri, Cultural Capital of Commonwealth of Independent States — A343**

| 2013, Nov. 11 | Litho. | Perf. 13x13¼ | |
|---|---|---|---|
| 957 | A343 560d multi + 2 flanking labels | 4.50 | 4.50 |

**Award of the President of Armenia A344**

No. 958 — Medal depicting: a, 180d, Eagle. b, 220d, Coat of arms.

| 2013, Nov. 15 | Litho. | Perf. 13¼x13 | |
|---|---|---|---|
| 958 | A344 Horiz. pair, #a-b | 3.25 | 3.25 |

**Ancient Capitals of Armenia — A345**

Designs: 160d, Armavir. 170d, Yervandashat.

| 2013, Nov. 19 | Litho. | Perf. 13x13¼ | |
|---|---|---|---|
| 959-960 | A345 Set of 2 | 2.50 | 2.50 |

**Beniamin Markarian (1913-85), Astrophysicist A346**

| 2013, Nov. 21 | Litho. | Perf. 13x13¼ | |
|---|---|---|---|
| 961 | A346 170d multi | 1.25 | 1.25 |

**Armenian Chairmanship of Council of Europe in 2013 — A347**

| 2013, Nov. 25 | Litho. | Perf. 13¼x13 | |
|---|---|---|---|
| 962 | A347 380d multi | 3.00 | 3.00 |

**Paintings — A348**

Designs: 230d, Family, by Ara Bekarian. 330d, Portrait of the Painter's Mother, by Stepan Aghajanian.

| 2013, Nov. 25 | Litho. | Perf. 13¼x13 | |
|---|---|---|---|
| 963-964 | A348 Set of 2 | 4.50 | 4.50 |

**Mushrooms — A349**

Designs: 230d, Macrolepiota rhacodes. 330d, Boletus edulis.

| 2013, Nov. 25 | Litho. | Perf. 12½ | |
|---|---|---|---|
| 965 | A349 230d multi | 1.75 | 1.75 |
| 966 | A349 330d multi | 2.75 | 2.75 |
| a. | Horiz. pair, #965-966 | 4.50 | 4.50 |

Nos. 965-966 each were printed in sheets of 8 + 2 labels. No. 966a was printed in a sheet containing 5 pairs.

**Hakop Kojoian (1883-1959), Painter A350**

**Armenian Herald, by Kojoian A351**

| 2013, Nov. 27 | Litho. | Perf. 13¼x13 | |
|---|---|---|---|
| 967 | A350 240d multi | 1.75 | 1.75 |
| 968 | A351 240d multi | 1.75 | 1.75 |
| a. | Horiz. pair, #967-968 | 3.50 | 3.50 |

Nos. 967-968 each were printed in sheets of 8. No. 968a was printed in sheets containing 4 pairs.

**Dram Currency, 20th Anniv. — A352**

| 2013, Nov. 29 | Litho. | Perf. 13x13¼ | |
|---|---|---|---|
| 969 | A352 380d multi | 3.00 | 3.00 |

### Souvenir Sheet

**2014 Winter Olympics, Sochi, Russia — A353**

No. 970: a, 350d, Cross-country skiing. b, 1100d, Alpine skiing.

| 2013, Dec. 2 | Litho. | Perf. 13¼ | |
|---|---|---|---|
| 970 | A353 Sheet of 2, #a-b | 11.00 | 11.00 |

**Lord Byron (1788-1824), Poet and Compiler of Armenian-English Dictionary — A354**

| 2013, Dec. 5 | Litho. | Perf. 12½ | |
|---|---|---|---|
| 971 | A354 350d multi | 2.75 | 2.75 |

**Telephones in Armenia, Cent. — A355**

| 2013, Dec. 10 | Litho. | Perf. 13x13¼ | |
|---|---|---|---|
| 972 | A355 170d multi | 1.40 | 1.40 |

**Vahran Papazian (1888-1968), Actor — A356**

| 2013, Dec. 16 | Litho. | Perf. 13x13¼ | |
|---|---|---|---|
| 973 | A356 230d multi | 1.75 | 1.75 |

**Chess — A357**

Designs: 100d, Chess pieces and boards. 120d, Chess pieces and board.

| 2013, Dec. 16 | Litho. | Perf. 13x13¼ | |
|---|---|---|---|
| 974-975 | A357 Set of 2 | 1.75 | 1.75 |

# ARMENIA

### Souvenir Sheet

Civil Aviation in Armenia, 80th Anniv. — A358

**2013, Dec. 16**    Litho.    Perf. 13¾
976   A358   500d multi      4.00   4.00

New Year 2014 — A359

**2013, Dec. 16**    Litho.    Perf. 13x13¼
977   A359   220d multi      1.75   1.75

Wine Production in Armenia — A360

**2013, Dec. 28**    Litho.    Perf. 13x13¼
978   A360   330d multi + label    2.50   2.50

No. 978 was printed in sheets of 4 + 4 labels. Two different labels were made available on separate sheets.

Armenian Kingdom of Cilicia — A361

Designs: 120d, King Levon III, ruler from 1270-89. 240d, Queen Keran, wife of King Levon III.

**2013, Dec. 28**    Litho.    Perf. 13x13¼
979-980   A361   Set of 2    2.75   2.75
980a    Horiz. pair, #979-980   3.00   3.00

Nos. 979-980 each were printed in sheets of 10. No. 980a was printed in sheets containing two pairs.

### Souvenir Sheet

Artsakh Movement (Campaign to Transfer Jurisdiction of Nagorno-Karabakh to Armenia), 25th Anniv. — A362

**2013, Dec. 28**    Litho.    Perf. 13x13¼
981   A362   400d multi      3.00   3.00

### Souvenir Sheet

Archaeological Items Found in Areni-1 Cave — A363

No. 982: a, 160d, Matting, c. 3500 B.C. b, 220d, Shoe, c. 3500 B.C.

**2013, Dec. 28**    Litho.    Perf. 13¼x13
982   A363   Sheet of 2, #a-b   3.00   3.00

**Armenian Alphabet Type of 2012**

Third group of seven letters of Armenian alphabet in capital and lower-case.

**2014, May 8**    Litho.    Perf. 13x13¼
**Color of Panel at Left**
983   A303   70d dull bl green    .60   .60
984   A303   120d rose lilac   1.00   1.00
985   A303   170d lilac    1.40   1.40
986   A303   220d gray green   1.75   1.75
987   A303   230d green blue   1.90   1.90
988   A303   280d blue   2.25   2.25
989   A303   380d rose   3.25   3.25
   Nos. 983-989 (7)   12.15   12.15

Intelligence Officers — A364

No. 990: a, Yakov Davtian (1888-1938). b, Ivan Agayants (1911-68). c, Haik Ovakimian (1898-1967). d, Ashot Akopian (1915-81). 350d, Gevork Vartanian (1924-2012).

**2014, May 20**    Litho.    Perf. 13x13¼
990   A364   230d Sheet of 4, #a-d   7.00   7.00

### Souvenir Sheet
Perf. 13¼x13½
991   A364   350d multi    3.00   3.00

No. 991 contains one 15x28mm stamp.

Europa — A365

Musical instruments: No. 992, 350d, Pku. No. 993, 350d, Zurna.

**2014, May 23**    Litho.    Perf. 13x13¼
992-993   A365   Set of 2   5.00   5.00

2014 World Cup Soccer Championships, Brazil — A366

**2014, June 27**    Litho.    Perf. 13x13¼
994   A366   380d multi   3.00   3.00

Armenian Kingdom of Cilicia — A367

Map and: No. 995, 240d, Ruins, Ayas. No. 996, 240d, Anamur Fortress. No. 997, 240d, Korikos Fortress.

**2014, July 4**    Litho.    Perf. 13x13¼
995-997   A367   Set of 3   5.00   5.00
997a    Souvenir sheet of 6, 2 each #995-997   10.00   10.00

John Kirakossian (1929-85), Historian — A368

**2014, July 29**    Litho.    Perf. 13x13¼
998   A368   330d multi   2.75   2.75

Armenian Genocide Monuments — A369

Monument in: No. 999, 280d, Boston, Massachusetts. No. 1000, 280d, Montevideo, Uruguay, horiz. 380d, Paris, France.

Perf. 13¼x13, 13x13¼
**2014, July 29**    Litho.
999-1001   A369   Set of 3   7.00   7.00

### Souvenir Sheet

Danish Mothers of Armenian Orphans — A370

No. 1002 — Medal and: a, Karen Jeppe (1875-1935). b, Maria Jacobsen (1882-1960).

**2014, July 29**    Litho.    Perf. 13¼x13
1002   A370   200d Sheet of 2, #a-b   3.00   3.00

Famous Men — A371

Building and: No. 1003, 280d, Toros Toramanian (1864-1934), architect. No. 1004, 280d, Nikolay Marr (1864-1934), archaeologist, linguist and architect.

**2014, Aug. 13**    Litho.    Perf. 13x13¼
1003-1004   A371   Set of 2   4.50   4.50

Hounan Avetissian (1914-43), Military Hero — A372

**2014, Aug. 15**    Litho.    Perf. 13¼x13
1005   A372   170d multi   1.25   1.25

Ancient Capitals of Armenia — A373

Designs: No. 1006, 240d, Dvin. No. 1007, 240d, Tigranakert.

**2014, Aug. 21**    Litho.    Perf. 13x13¼
1006-1007   A373   Set of 2   3.50   3.50

Hamo Sahian (1914-93), Poet — A374

Stepan Zorian (1889-1967), Writer — A375

**2014, Sept. 5**    Litho.    Perf. 13x13¼
1008   A374   220d multi   1.50   1.50
1009   A375   230d multi   1.75   1.75

Flora and Fauna — A376

Designs: 230d, Dianthus gabrielianae. 330d, Upupa epops.

**2014, Sept. 23**    Litho.    Perf. 12¾
1010-1011   A376   Set of 2   4.00   4.00

### Souvenir Sheet

Voskan Yerevantsi (1614-74), Book Publisher — A377

Perf. 13¼x13½
**2014, Sept. 26**    Litho.
1012   A377   650d multi   5.00   5.00

### Souvenir Sheet

World War I, Cont. A378

**2014, Sept. 29**    Litho.    Perf. 13¼x13
1013   A378   480d multi   3.50   3.50

Cross Stones (Khachkars) — A379

Designs: No. 1014, 240d, Holy Redeemer khachkar, Urtz, 1279. No. 1015, 240d, Mastara khachkar, 13th cent.

**2014, Dec. 12**    Litho.    Perf. 13¼
1014-1015   A379   Set of 2   3.50   3.50

### Souvenir Sheet

Holy Transfiguration Cathedral, Moscow — A380

**2014, Dec. 12**    Litho.    Perf. 13¼x13
1016   A380   870d multi   6.00   6.00

Skier — A381

**2014, Dec. 15**    Litho.    Perf. 13¼
1017   A381   350d multi   2.25   2.25

Dzitoghtyans House Museum, Gyumri — A383

No. 1019: a, Building exterior. b, Dining room.

**2014, Dec. 30 Litho. *Perf. 13x13¼***
**1019** A383 280d Horiz. pair, #a-b 3.50 3.50

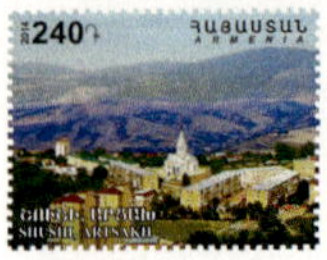
Shushi — A384

**2014, Dec. 30 Litho. *Perf. 13x13¼***
**1020** A384 240d multi 1.75 1.75

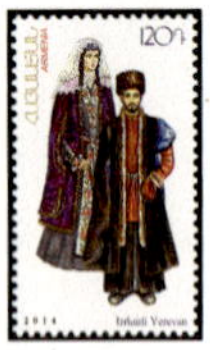
Traditional Costumes — A385

Designs: 120d, Man and woman from Yerevan. 230d, Man, woman and child from Gyumri.

**2014, Dec. 30 Litho. *Perf. 13¼x13***
**1021-1022** A385 Set of 2 2.75 2.75

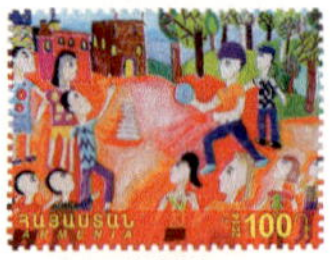
A386

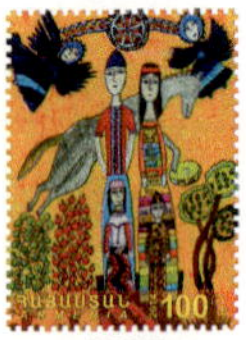
A387

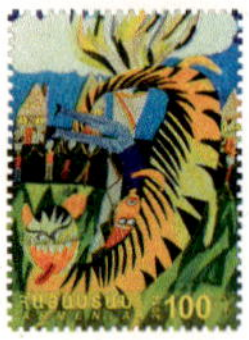
Children's Art — A388

**2014, Dec. 30 Litho. *Perf. 13x13¼***
**1023** A386 100d multi .75 .75

***Perf. 13¼x13***
**1024** A387 100d multi .75 .75
**1025** A388 100d multi .75 .75
*Nos. 1023-1025 (3)* 2.25 2.25

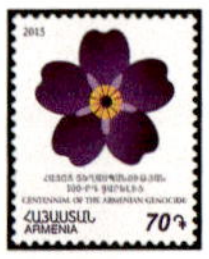
Forget-me-not — A389

**2015, Jan. 29 Litho. *Perf. 13¼x13***
**Background Color**

| | | | |
|---|---|---|---|
| **1026** | A389 70d white | .45 | .45 |
| **1027** | A389 120d pale yellow | .80 | .80 |
| **1028** | A389 240d pale peach | 1.50 | 1.50 |
| **1029** | A389 280d pale green | 1.75 | 1.75 |
| **1030** | A389 330d light blue | 2.25 | 2.25 |
| **1031** | A389 350d dull mauve | 2.40 | 2.40 |
| *a.* | Souvenir sheet of 1 | 2.40 | 2.40 |
| **1032** | A389 870d pale red vio | 5.75 | 5.75 |
| *a.* | Souvenir sheet of 1 | 5.75 | 5.75 |
| *b.* | Sheet of 14, 2 each #1026-1032 + central label | 30.00 | 30.00 |
| | *Nos. 1026-1032 (7)* | 14.90 | 14.90 |

Armenian Genocide, cent. Nos. 1026-1032 were each printed in sheets of 14 + central label. See Nos. 1048-1050.

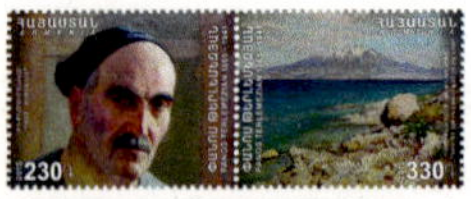
Paintings by Panos Terlemezian (1865-1941) — A390

No. 1033: a, 230d, Self-portrait. b, 330d, Mount Sipan from Ktuts Island.

**2015, Mar. 3 Litho. *Perf. 13x13¼***
**1033** A390 Horiz. pair, #a-b 4.50 4.50

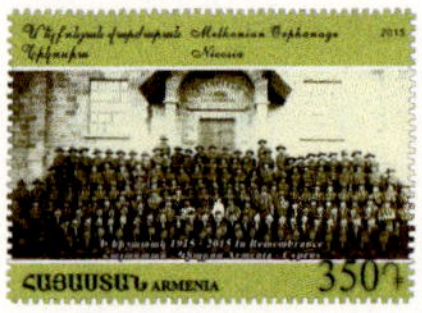
Melkonian Orphanage, Nicosia, Cyprus
A391

**2015, Apr. 2 Litho. *Perf. 14½x14¼***
**1034** A391 350d multi 3.00 3.00

See Cyprus No. 1232.

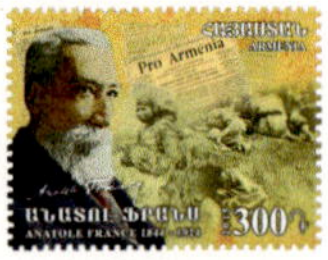
Anatole France (1844-1924), Writer — A392

**2015, Apr. 23 Litho. *Perf. 13x13¼***
**1035** A392 300d multi 2.50 2.50

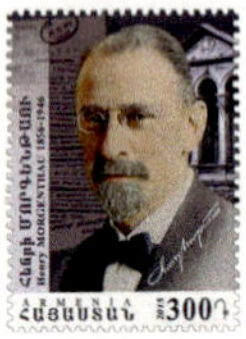
Henry Morgenthau, Sr. (1856-1946), U.S. Ambassador to the Ottoman Empire — A393

**2015, Apr. 23 Litho. *Perf. 13¼x13***
**1036** A393 300d multi 2.50 2.50

Souvenir Sheet

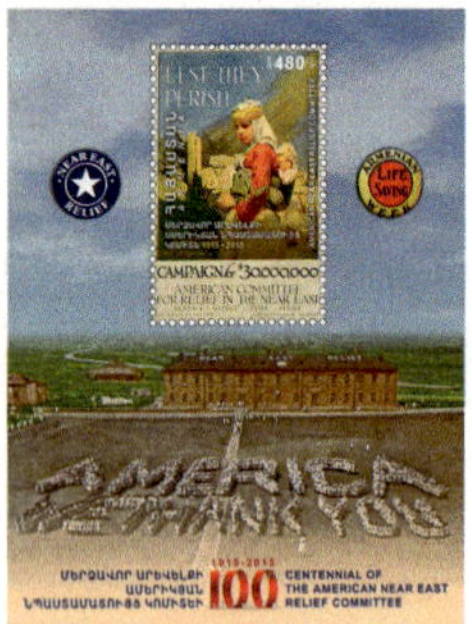
American Committee for Relief in the Near East, Cent. — A394

**2015, May 6 Litho. *Perf. 13***
**1037** A394 480d multi 3.75 3.75

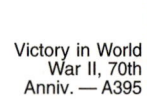

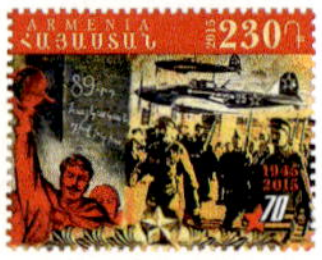
Victory in World War II, 70th Anniv. — A395

**2015, May 8 Litho. *Perf. 13x13¼***
**1038** A395 230d multi 2.00 2.00

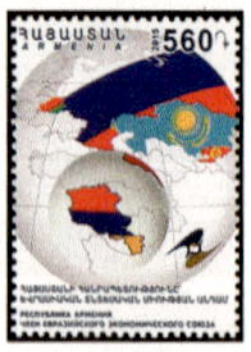
Eurasian Economic Union — A396

**2015, May 12 Litho. *Perf. 13¼x13***
**1039** A396 560d multi 4.50 4.50

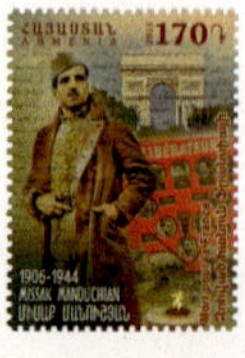
Missak Manouchian (1906-44), Poet — A397

**2015, May 26 Litho. *Perf. 13¼x13***
**1040** A397 170d multi 1.40 1.40

Souvenir Sheet

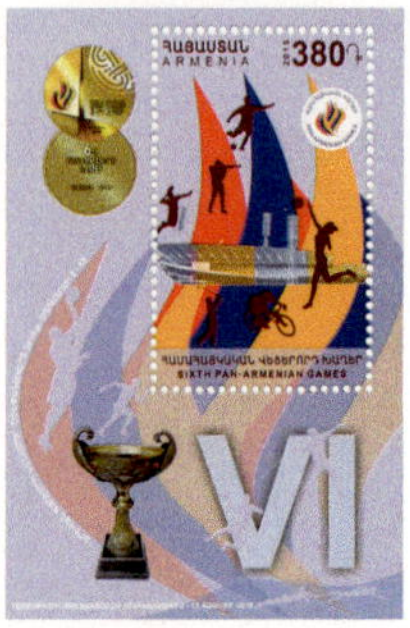
Sixth Pan-Armenian Games — A398

**2015, Aug. 5 Litho. *Perf. 13½x13¼***
**1041** A398 380d multi 3.25 3.25

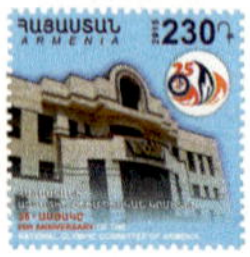
Armenian Olympic Committee, 25th Anniv. — A399

**2015, Sept. 29 Litho. *Perf. 13¼***
**1042** A399 230d multi 1.90 1.90

Souvenir Sheet

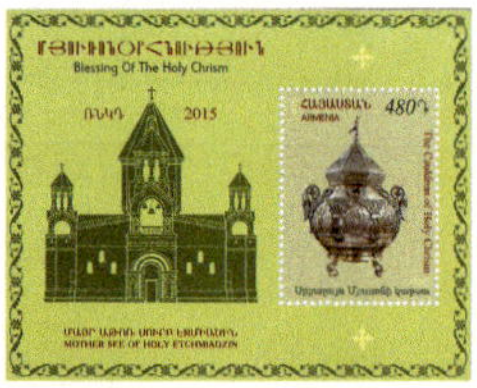
Blessing of the Holy Chrism
A400

**2015, Sept. 29 Litho. *Perf. 13¼x13***
**1043** A400 480d multi 3.75 3.75

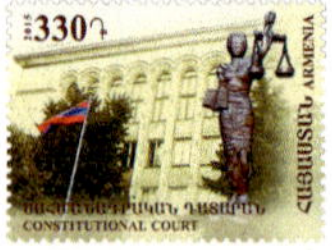
Constitutional Court, 20th Anniv. — A401

**2015, Oct. 8 Litho. *Perf. 13x13¼***
**1044** A401 330d multi 2.50 2.50

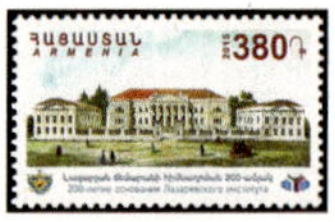
Lazarev Institute, Moscow, 200th Anniv. — A402

**2015, Oct. 23 Litho. *Perf. 13x13¼***
**1045** A402 380d multi 3.00 3.00

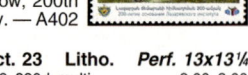

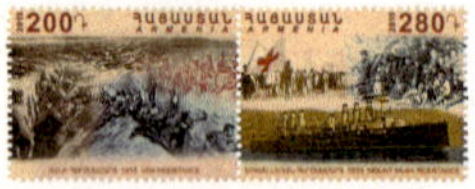
Resistance to the Armenian Genocide — A403

No. 1046: a, 200d, Resistance in Van, Turkey. b, 280d, Resistance at Mount Musa.

**2015, Oct. 29 Litho. *Perf. 13x13¼***
**1046** A403 Horiz. pair, #a-b 3.75 3.75

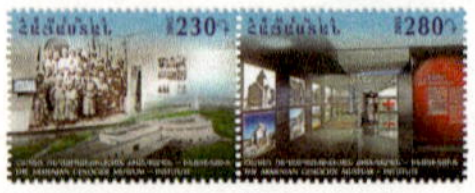
Armenian Genocide Museum and Institute, Yerevan — A404

No. 1047: a, 230d, Museum exterior and displays. b, 280d, Museum interior.

**2015, Nov. 21 Litho. *Perf. 13x13¼***
**1047** A404 Horiz. pair, #a-b 4.25 4.25

**Forget-me-not Type of 2015**

**2015, Dec. 24 Litho. *Perf. 13¼x13***
**Background Color**

| | | | |
|---|---|---|---|
| **1048** | A389 40d yellow | .35 | .35 |
| **1049** | A389 50d light blue | .40 | .40 |
| **1050** | A389 60d pink | .50 | .50 |
| | *Nos. 1048-1050 (3)* | 1.25 | 1.25 |

Nos. 1048-1050 were each printed in sheets of 14 + central label.

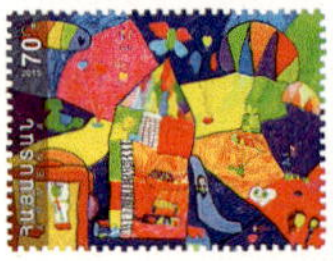
A405

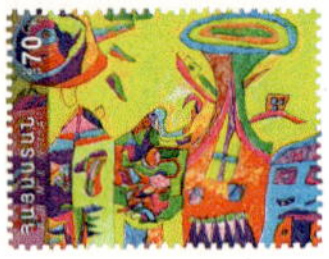
Children's Art — A406

**2015, Dec. 24 Litho. *Perf. 13x13¼***
**1051** A405 70d multi .70 .70
**1052** A406 70d multi .70 .70

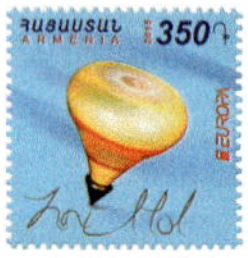
Top — A407

**2015, Dec. 28 Litho. *Perf. 13¼***
**1053** A407 350d multi 3.00 3.00

Europa.

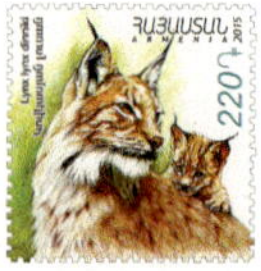
Flora and Fauna — A408

Designs: 220d, Lynx lynx dinniki. 280d, Sorbus hajastana.

**2015, Dec. 28 Litho. *Perf. 12¾***
**1054-1055** A408 Set of 2 4.00 4.00

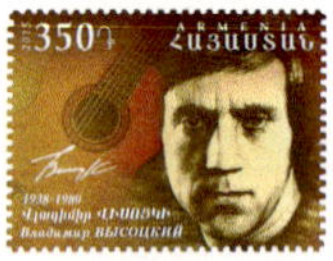
Vladimir Vysotsky (1938-80), Singer — A409

**2015, Dec. 30 Litho. *Perf. 13x13¼***
**1056** A409 350d multi 2.75 2.75

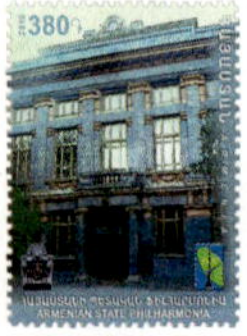
Armenian State Philharmonia, Yerevan — A410

**2015, Dec. 30 Litho. *Perf. 13¼x13***
**1057** A410 380d multi 3.00 3.00

Souvenir Sheet

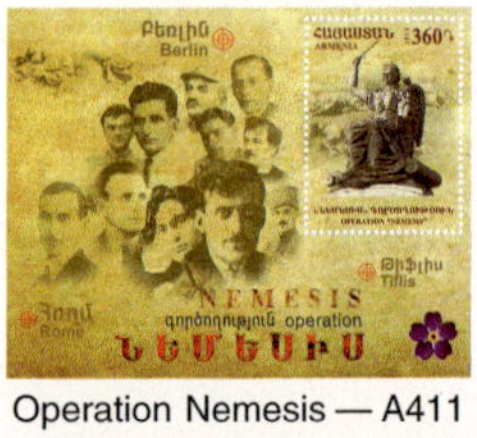
Operation Nemesis — A411

**2015, Dec. 30 Litho. *Perf. 13¼x13***
**1058** A411 360d multi 2.75 2.75

Operation Nemesis was a series of assassinations of people responsible for the Armenian Genocide.

# ARMENIA

### Souvenir Sheets

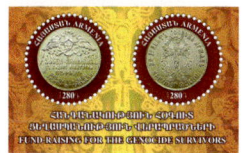

Medals and Orders for Fund-raising for Genocide Survivors — A413

No. 1059 — Order inscribed: a, Armenia. b, Servia, Syria, Armenia.
No. 1060 — Medal depicting: a, Two-headed bird. b, Cross.

**2015, Dec. 30   Litho.   Perf. 13¼**
1059  A412  280d Sheet of 2, #a-b   4.25  4.25
   **Perf.**
1060  A413  280d Sheet of 2, #a-b   4.25  4.25

### Souvenir Sheet

2016 Posteurop Plenary Assembly, Yerevan — A414

**2016, Apr. 20   Litho.   Perf. 13¼**
1061  A414  870d multi   6.50  6.50

### Souvenir Sheet

2016 World Stamp Show, New York A415

**2016, May 29   Litho.   Perf.**
1062  A415  650d multi   5.00  5.00

### Souvenir Sheet

2016 Summer Olympics, Rio de Janeiro — A416

**2016, May 29   Litho.   Perf. 13¼**
1063  A416  650d multi   5.00  5.00

Visit to Armenia of Pope Francis A417

No. 1064: a, 170d, Pope Francis and Yerevan. b, 230d, Pope Francis, cupola of St. Peter's Basilica. c, 380d, Pope Francis, statue of St. Gregory the Illuminator. d, 480d, Pope Francis, Etchmiadzin Cathedral.
870d, Pope Francis, St. Peter's Basilica, Etchmiadzin Cathedral, horiz.

**2016, June 24   Litho.   Perf. 13¼**
1064  A417  Sheet of 4, #a-d, + label   12.00  12.00
   **Souvenir Sheet**
   **Perf. 13¾x14**
1065  A417  870d multi   7.50  7.50
No. 1065 contains one 45x33mm stamp.

### Armenian Alphabet Type of 2012

Fourth group of seven letters of Armenian alphabet in capital and lower-case.

**2016, July 7   Litho.   Perf. 13x13¼**
**Color of Panel at Left**
1066  A303  70d salmon pink   .50  .50
1067  A303  120d apple green   .90  .90
1068  A303  170d red lilac   1.25  1.25
1069  A303  230d bister   1.75  1.75
1070  A303  280d olive   2.10  2.10
1071  A303  330d lt red brown   2.50  2.50
1072  A303  380d gray blue   3.00  3.00
   Nos. 1066-1072 (7)   12.00  12.00

2016 European Soccer Championships, France — A418

**2016, July 15   Litho.   Perf. 13x13¼**
1073  A418  500d multi   4.25  4.25

  A419

Independence, 25th Anniv. — A420

**2016, Sept. 21   Litho.   Perf. 13x13¼**
1074  A419  200d multi   1.60  1.60
   **Perf. 13¼x13**
1075  A420  300d multi   2.50  2.50

Tatevik Sazandarian (1916-99), Opera Singer — A421

**2016, Oct. 4   Litho.   Perf. 13¼x13**
1076  A421  230d multi   2.00  2.00

Arshak Fetvadjian (1866-1947), Painter — A422

No. 1077: a, 170d, Fetvadjian. b, 230d, Woman Playing the Mandolin, by Fetvadjian.

**2016, Oct. 7   Litho.   Perf. 13¼x13**
1077  A422  Pair, #a-b   3.25  3.25

Srbuhi Tyusab (1841-1901), Writer — A423

**2016, Oct. 20   Litho.   Perf. 13x13¼**
1078  A423  230d multi   1.75  1.75

### Souvenir Sheet

First Bible Printed in Armenian, 350th Anniv. — A424

**2016, Nov. 13   Litho.   Perf. 13¼x13**
1079  A424  560d multi   4.50  4.50

Sergey Paradjanov Museum, Yerevan — A425

**2016, Nov. 18   Litho.   Perf. 13¼**
1080    Horiz. pair   5.50  5.50
   a. A425  300d Museum exterior   2.50  2.50
   b. A425  380d Museum interior   3.00  3.00

Telbats Koubati  A426

**2016, Nov. 28   Litho.   Perf. 13¼x13**
1081  A426  170d multi   1.40  1.40

Europa A427

No. 1082: a, Dead and living trees. b, City, bicyclist, wind generators.

**2016, Dec. 1   Litho.   Perf. 13x13¼**
1082  A427  350d Pair, #a-b   5.25  5.25
   Think Green Issue.

### Souvenir Sheet

Argentine Boca Juniors Soccer Team, 1977, 2000 and 2003 Intercontinental Soccer Cup Champions — A428

**2016, Dec. 12   Litho.   Perf. 14**
1083  A428  500d multi   4.50  4.50

Ancient Capitals of Armenia — A429

Designs: 230d, Bagara, 2nd cent. B.C. 330d, Vagharshapat, 2nd cent. A.D.

**2016, Dec. 15   Litho.   Perf. 13x13¼**
1084-1085  A429  Set of 2   4.50  4.50

Armenia on Ancient Maps — A430

Designs: 300d, Babylonian map of the world, 6th cent. B.C. 330d, Map of Ptolemy's Greater Armenia, 2nd cent. A.D.

**2016, Dec. 15   Litho.   Perf. 13x13¼**
1086-1087  A430  Set of 2   5.00  5.00

Commonwealth of Independent States, 25th Anniv. — A431

**2016, Dec. 21   Litho.   Perf. 13¼x13**
1088  A431  380d multi   3.00  3.00

Stylized Animals — A432

Designs: No. 1089, 100d, Armenian gull. No. 1090, 100d, Van cat. No. 1091, 100d, Armenian mouflon.

**2016, Dec. 26   Litho.   Perf. 13¼x13**
1089-1091  A432  Set of 3   2.50  2.50

Children's Philately.

Birds — A433

Designs: 230d, Neophron percnopterus. 280d, Falco tinnunculus.

**2016, Dec. 29   Litho.   Perf. 12½**
1092-1093  A433  Set of 2   4.00  4.00

Flowers — A434

Designs: 230d, Tulipa sylvestris. 330d, Orchis tridentata.

**2016, Dec. 29   Litho.   Perf. 12½**
1094-1095  A434  Set of 2   1.60  1.60

Anna Hedwig Büll (1887-1981), Missionary Who Rescued Orphans From Armenian Genocide — A435

**2016, Dec. 30   Litho.   Perf. 13¼x13**
1096  A435  280d multi   2.10  2.10

# ARMENIA

Armenian Army, 25th Anniv. — A436

No. 1097 — Emblem and: a, Soldiers, tanks, trucks and flag. b, Soldiers and flags.

**2017, Jan. 27**   Litho.   Perf. 13x13¼
1097   A436   280d Pair, #a-b   4.25   4.25
No. 1097 was printed in sheets containing two pairs.

Alexander Mantashian (1842-1911), Industrialist and Philanthropist A437

**2017, Mar. 3**   Litho.   Perf. 14
1098   A437   380d multi   3.25   3.25

### Souvenir Sheet

Artur Aleksanyan, 2016 Olympic Greco-Roman Wrestling Gold Medalist — A438

**2017, May 30**   Litho.   Perf.
1099   A438   480d multi   4.00   4.00

### Armenian Alphabet Type of 2012

29th-32nd letters of Armenian alphabet in capital and lower-case.

**2017, June 2**   Litho.   Perf. 13x13¼
Color of Panel at Left
1100   A303   10d gray blue   .25   .25
1101   A303   50d olive green   .40   .40
1102   A303   70d dull rose   .55   .55
1103   A303   100d dull purple   .80   .80
Nos. 1100-1103 (4)   2.00   2.00

First Postage Stamps of Republic of Armenia, 25th Anniv. — A439

**2017, June 15**   Litho.   Perf. 12½
1104   A439   100d multi   .90   .90

Amberd Castle A440

**2017, July 10**   Litho.   Perf. 14
1105   A440   350d multi   3.00   3.00
Europa.

Hamo Beknazarian (1891-1965), Film Director and Actor — A441

**2017, July 13**   Litho.   Perf. 14
1106   A441   170d multi   1.50   1.50

Paintings by Gabriel Gyurjian (1892-1987) A442

Designs: 170d, Nork. 230d, Dsegh. Sunrise, and Gyurjian.

**2017, July 20**   Litho.   Perf. 13x13¼
1107-1108   A442   Set of 2   3.25   3.25

Helix Nebula — A443

**2017, July 27**   Litho.   Perf. 13x13¼
1109   A443   280d multi   2.25   2.25
Regional Astronomical Center. No. 1109 was printed in sheets of 8 + central label.

### Armenian Alphabet Type of 2012

Last group of four letters of Armenian alphabet in capital and lower-case.

**2017, Aug. 23**   Litho.   Perf. 13x13¼
Color of Panel at Left
1110   A303   230d brn rose   1.90   1.90
1111   A303   280d gray lilac   2.40   2.40
1112   A303   330d yellow brown   2.75   2.75
1113   A303   380d dl blue grn   3.25   3.25
Nos. 1110-1113 (4)   10.30   10.30

Independence, 25th Anniv. — A444

No. 1114: a, 200d, National colors of flags and Government House. b, 300d, Nation colors of flag & new building for various governmental ministries.

**2017, Oct. 9**   Litho.   Perf. 13x13¼
1114   A444   Horiz. pair, #a-b   4.25   4.25

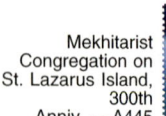

Mekhitarist Congregation on St. Lazarus Island, 300th Anniv. — A445

**2017, Oct. 23**   Litho.   Perf. 13x13¼
1115   A445   230d multi   1.90   1.90

### Souvenir Sheet

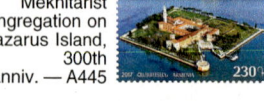

Houses of Worship A446

No. 1116: a, 300d, Blue Mosque, Yerevan. b, 350d, Holy Savior Cathedral, Isfahan, Iran.

**2017, Oct. 25**   Litho.   Perf. 13¾x14
1116   A446   Sheet of 2, #a-b   5.50   5.50
Joint issue between Armenia and Iran. See Iran No. 3178.

### Miniature Sheet

Paintings by Ivan Aivazovsky (1817-1900) — A447

No. 1117: a, 170d, Self-portrait, 1874 (29x35mm). b, 220d, Noah's Descent from Mt. Ararat, 1889 (43x25mm). c, 230d, Bayron's Visit to the Mekhitarists on the Island of St. Lazarus, 1899 (43x25mm). d, 380d, Seascape. Mediterranean Seashore, 1892 (43x25mm). e, 450d, The Ninth Wave, 1850 (43x25mm).

Perf. 14x13¾ (170d), 14
**2017, Nov. 7**   Litho.
1117   A447   Sheet of 5, #a-e   12.00   12.00

### Souvenir Sheet

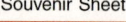

Diplomatic Relations Between Armenia and Russia, 25th Anniv. — A448

No. 1118 — Coat of arms of: a, Armenia ("25" at LL). b, Russia ("25" at LR).

**2017, Nov. 21**   Litho.   Perf. 13½
1118   A448   280d Sheet of 2, #a-b   4.75   4.75

Flag of Armenia and Emblem of Collective Security Treaty Organization A449

**2017, Nov. 30**   Litho.   Perf. 13x13¼
1119   A449   230d multi   1.90   1.90
Collective Security Treaty, 25th anniv., Collective Security Treaty Organization, 15th anniv.

Sergey Aganov (1917-96), Soviet Marshal — A450

**2017, Dec. 17**   Litho.   Perf. 13¼x13
1120   A450   160d multi   1.40   1.40

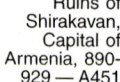

Ruins of Shirakavan, Capital of Armenia, 890-929 — A451

Map of Kars, Capital of Armenia, 929-61 — A452

**2017, Dec. 12**   Litho.   Perf. 13x13¼
1121   A451   160d multi   1.40   1.40
1122   A452   160d multi   1.40   1.40

Kirk Kerkorian (1917-2015), Businessman and Philanthropist — A453

**2017, Dec. 14**   Litho.   Perf. 13¼x13
1123   A453   380d multi   3.25   3.25

Kutahya Ceramics, 19th Cent. — A454

**2017, Dec. 18**   Litho.   Perf. 13x13¼
1124   A454   170d multi   1.50   1.50

Holy Martyrs of the Armenian Genocide — A455

**2017, Dec. 18**   Litho.   Perf. 13½
1125   A455   450d multi   3.75   3.75
No. 1125 was printed in sheets of 8 + 4 labels.

Yuri Oganessian, Nuclear Physicist Source of Name of Element 118, Oganesson A456

**2017, Dec. 28**   Litho.   Perf. 14
1126   A456   70d multi   .70   .70

Ghazanchetsots Cathedral, Shushi — A457

**2017, Dec. 28**   Litho.   Perf. 13x13¼
1127   A457   230d multi   1.90   1.90
Liberation of Shushi, 25th anniv.

Kevork V (1847-1930), Catholicos of Armenian Apostolic Church — A458

**2017, Dec. 28**   Litho.   Perf. 13¼x13
1128   A458   280d multi   2.40   2.40

Dinosaurs A459

Designs: 230d, Pterosaur. 280d, Tyrannosaurus.

**2017, Dec. 28**   Litho.   Perf. 13x13¼
1129-1130   A459   Set of 2   4.50   4.50

Christmas — A460

**2017, Dec. 28**   Litho.   Perf. 13¼x13
1131   A460   220d multi   1.90   1.90
When you turn stamp upside down you see a Christmas tree.

Flora and Fauna — A461

Designs: 230d, Ixiolirion montanum. 330d, Mustela nivalis.

**2017, Dec. 29**   Litho.   Perf. 12½
1132-1133   A461   Set of 2   4.75   4.75

# ARMENIA 671

### Souvenir Sheet

Dragon Stones A462

No. 1134: a, 160d, 360-centimeter tall dragon stone. b, 220d, 375-centimeter tall dragon stone.

**2017, Dec. 29**    Litho.    Perf. 14
1134   A462   Sheet of 2, #a-b    3.25   3.25

### Souvenir Sheet

World Cup and Flag of Brazil A463

**2017, Dec. 29**    Litho.    Perf. 13½
1135   A463   480d multi    4.00   4.00
Brazil, five-time World Cup Champion.

### Souvenir Sheet

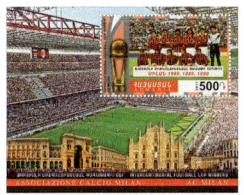

Intercontinental Cup and A. C. Milan Soccer Players — A464

**2017, Dec. 29**    Litho.    Perf. 14
1136   A464   500d multi    4.25   4.25
A. C. Milan, three-time Intercontinental Cup Champion.

### Souvenir Sheet

St. Grigor Narekatsi (951-1003), Poet — A465

**2017, Dec. 29**    Litho.    Perf. 13x13¼
1137   A465   870d multi    7.50   7.50

### Souvenir Sheet

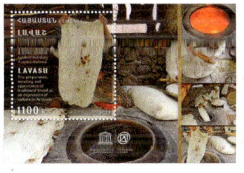

Lavash Bread A466

**2017, Dec. 29**    Litho.    Perf. 13½
1138   A466   1100d multi    9.25   9.25

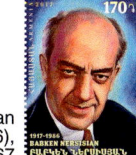

Babken Nersisian (1917-86), Actor — A467

**2018, Apr. 4**    Litho.    Perf. 14
1139   A467   170d multi    1.50   1.50

### Armenian Alphabet Type of 2012
33rd-35th letters in the Armenian alphabet.

**2018, Apr. 5**    Litho.    Perf. 13x13¼
Color of Panel at Left
1140   A303   70d ochre    .60   .60
1141   A303   230d gray green    2.00   2.00
1142   A303   330d gray olive    2.75   2.75
   Nos. 1140-1142 (3)    5.35   5.35

2018 Winter Olympics, Pyeongchang, South Korea — A468

**2018, June 6**    Litho.    Perf. 13½
1143   A468   380d multi    3.25   3.25

Office of the Prosecutor, Cent. — A469

**2018, July 1**    Litho.    Perf. 13¾x14
1144   A469   330d multi    3.00   3.00

2018 World Cup Soccer Championships, Russia — A470

**2018, July 25**    Litho.    Perf. 13x13¼
1145   A470   450d multi    4.00   4.00

Armenian General Athletic Union Scouts, Cent. A471

**2018, July 26**    Litho.    Perf. 14
1146   A471   330d multi    2.75   2.75

Goris, Cultural Capital of the Commonwealth of Independent States — A472

**2018, July 27**    Litho.    Perf. 13½
1147   A472   330d multi    2.75   2.75

Dances A473

No. 1148: a, Hov Arek dancers, Armenia. b, Manipuri dancers, India.

**2018, Aug. 29**    Litho.    Perf. 13x13¼
1148   A473   280d Horiz. pair, #a-b    4.75   4.75
See India Nos. 3053-3054.

Armenian Security Bodies, Cent. — A474

**2018, Sept. 24**    Litho.    Perf. 13x13¼
1149   A474   170d multi    1.50   1.50

Natural Bridge, Tsakkar — A475

**2018, Oct. 2**    Litho.    Perf. 13x13¼
1150   A475   350d multi    3.00   3.00
Europa.

### Souvenir Sheet

First Republic of Armenia, Cent. A476

**2018, Oct. 4**    Litho.    Perf. 13¼
1151   A476   480d multi    4.25   4.25

### Souvenir Sheet

17th Francophone Summit, Yerevan — A477

**2018, Oct. 8**    Litho.    Perf. 14
1152   A477   870d multi    7.50   7.50

### Souvenir Sheet

Charles Aznavour (1924-2018), Singer — A478

**2018, Oct. 11**    Litho.    Perf. 13½
1153   A478   870d multi    7.50   7.50

National Police, Cent. — A479

**2018, Oct. 31**    Litho.    Perf. 13x13¼
1154   A479   120d multi    1.10   1.10

Paintings by Hovhannes Zardaryan (1918-92) — A480

Designs: 170d, Spring. 230d, Winter Landscape, and Zardaryan

**2018, Nov. 6**    Litho.    Perf. 13x13¼
1155-1156   A480   Set of 2    3.50   3.50

Shikahogh Reserve A481

**2018, Nov. 8**    Litho.    Perf. 14
1157   A481   230d multi    1.90   1.90

A482

**2018, Nov. 22**    Litho.    Perf. 13x13¼
1158   A482   100d multi    .85   .85
Jamanak, Armenian Language Daily Newspaper of Istanbul, Turkey, 110th anniv.

Dram Currency, 25th Anniv. — A483

**2018, Nov. 22**    Litho.    Perf. 13¾
1159   A483   230d multi    1.90   1.90
Values are for stamps with surrounding selvage.

### Miniature Sheet

Yerevan, 2800th Anniv. A484

No. 1160: a, 220d, Erebuni Fortress excavations. b, 230d, Buildings on Amiryan Street, 1920. c, 350d, Yerevan Railroad Station. d, 650d, Alexander Spendidaryan National Academic Theater of Opera and Ballet.

**2018, Nov. 29**    Litho.    Perf. 13¼
1160   A484   Sheet of 4, #a-d    12.00   12.00

State Award for Global Contribution in Information Technology Sphere — A485

No. 1161: a, 160d, Medal. b, 170d, Trophy.

**2018, Nov. 30**    Litho.    Perf. 13¼x13
1161   A485   Horiz. pair, #a-b    2.75   2.75

Spitak Earthquake, 30th Anniv. — A486

**2018, Dec. 7**    Litho.    Perf. 13x13¼
1162   A486   230d multi    1.90   1.90

George VI (1868-1954), Catholicos of All Armenians — A487

**2018, Dec. 10**    Litho.    Perf. 13¼x13
1163   A487   230d multi    1.90   1.90

Prehistoric Animals — A488

# ARMENIA

Designs: 220d, Argentinosaurus. 280d, Tapejara.

| 2018, Dec. 14 | Litho. | Perf. 13x13¼ |
|---|---|---|
| 1164-1165 A488 Set of 2 | | 4.25 4.25 |

Flora and Fauna — A489

Designs: 230d, Punica granatum. 330d, Capoeta capoeta sevangi.

| 2018, Dec. 19 | Litho. | Perf. 12½ |
|---|---|---|
| 1166-1167 A489 Set of 2 | | 4.75 4.75 |

Armenpress (Armenian News Service), Cent. — A490

| 2018, Dec. 21 | Litho. | Perf. 13x13¼ |
|---|---|---|
| 1168 A490 120d multi | | 1.10 1.10 |

Hakob Paronian (1843-91) — A491

| 2018, Dec. 28 | Litho. | Perf. 13¼x13 |
|---|---|---|
| 1169 A491 230d multi | | 1.90 1.90 |

ErAZ 762 — A492

| 2018, Dec. 28 | Litho. | Perf. 13x13¼ |
|---|---|---|
| 1170 A492 380d multi | | 3.25 3.25 |

Anahit A493

Found Dream A494

| 2018, Dec. 28 | Litho. | Perf. 13¼x13 |
|---|---|---|
| 1171 A493 100d multi | | .85 .85 |
| | Perf. 12½ | |
| 1172 A494 230d multi | | 1.90 1.90 |

Armenian animated films.

Intercontinental Soccer Cup and Nacional Soccer Players of Uruguay — A495

| 2018, Dec. 28 | Litho. | Perf. 14 |
|---|---|---|
| 1173 A495 500d multi | | 4.25 4.25 |

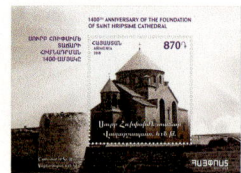

Saint Hripsime Cathedral, Vagharshapat, 1400th Anniv. — A496

| 2018, Dec. 28 | Litho. | Perf. 13½ |
|---|---|---|
| 1174 A496 870d multi | | 7.50 7.50 |

Christmas and New Year — A497

| 2018, Dec. 28 | Litho. | Perf. 12½ |
|---|---|---|
| 1175 A497 220d multi | | 1.90 1.90 |

New Year 2019 (Year of the Pig) — A498

| 2018, Dec. 28 | Litho. | Perf. 13x13¼ |
|---|---|---|
| 1176 A498 330d multi | | 2.75 2.75 |

Silva Kaputikyan (1919-2006), Poet — A499

| 2019, Jan. 22 | Litho. | Perf. 13¼x13 |
|---|---|---|
| 1177 A499 120d multi | | 1.10 1.10 |

8th Century B.C. Seals of the Kingdom of Ararat — A500

Various seals.

| 2019, Feb. 6 | Litho. | Perf. 13x13¼ |
|---|---|---|
| 1178 A500 70d multi | | .60 .60 |
| 1179 A500 120d multi | | 1.00 1.00 |
| 1180 A500 230d multi | | 1.90 1.90 |
| 1181 A500 330d multi | | 2.75 2.75 |
| Nos. 1178-1181 (4) | | 6.25 6.25 |

Souvenir Sheet

Hovhannes Toumanian (1869-1923), Poet — A501

| 2019, Feb. 18 | Litho. | Perf. 13 |
|---|---|---|
| 1182 A501 1100d multi | | 9.25 9.25 |

Calouste Sarkis Gulbenkian (1869-1955), Businessman and Philanthropist — A502

No. 1183 — Gulbenkian and: a, 230d, Jeweled peacock. b, 330d, Ceramic bowl, 18th cent.

| 2019, Mar. 26 | Litho. | Perf. 13x13¼ |
|---|---|---|
| 1183 A502 Horiz. pair, #a-b | | 4.75 4.75 |

Joint Issue between Armenia & Portugal. See Portugal Nos. 4109-4110.

Mammuthus Trogontherii — A503

| 2019, Mar. 27 | Litho. | Perf. 13x13¼ |
|---|---|---|
| 1184 A503 230d multi | | 1.90 1.90 |

Firefighters and Fire Truck — A504

| 2019, May 6 | Litho. | Perf. 13x13¼ |
|---|---|---|
| 1185 A504 330d multi | | 2.75 2.75 |

Historic Capitals of Armenia — A505

Designs: 160d, Map of Ani, 10th cent. capital, Ani Cathedral and bowl. 170d, Aerial view and map of Yerevan, 20th cent. capital, and bowl.

| 2019, May 16 | Litho. | Perf. 13x13¼ |
|---|---|---|
| 1186-1187 A505 Set of 2 | | 2.75 2.75 |

Hirundo Rustica — A506

| 2019, May 21 | Litho. | Perf. 13¼x13 |
|---|---|---|
| 1188 A506 350d multi | | 2.50 2.50 |

Europa.

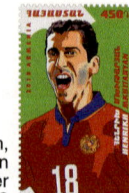

Mohandas K. Gandhi (1869-1948), Indian Nationalist Leader — A507

| 2019, May 23 | Litho. | Perf. 13¼x13 |
|---|---|---|
| 1189 A507 650d multi | | 5.50 5.50 |

Henrikh Mkhitaryan, Captain of Armenian National Soccer Team — A508

| 2019, June 4 | Litho. | Perf. 13½x12¾ |
|---|---|---|
| 1190 A508 450d multi | | 4.00 4.00 |

Yerevan State University, Cent. — A509

| 2019, June 27 | Litho. | Perf. 13x13¼ |
|---|---|---|
| 1191 A509 220d multi | | 1.90 1.90 |

Emblem of Eurasian Economic Union and Flags of Members as Puzzle Pieces — A510

| 2019, Aug. 9 | Litho. | Perf. 13½ |
|---|---|---|
| 1192 A510 330d multi | | 2.75 2.75 |

Souvenir Sheet

7th Pan-Armenian Games — A511

| 2019, Aug. 20 | Litho. | Perf. 13¼ |
|---|---|---|
| 1193 A511 870d multi | | 7.50 7.50 |

Etchmiadzin Cathedral, Vagharshapat A512

| 2019, Sept. 18 | Litho. | Perf. 13x13¼ |
|---|---|---|
| 1194 A512 220d multi | | 1.00 1.00 |

Aram Khachaturian (1903-78), Composer A513

| 2019, Sept. 27 | Litho. | Perf. 13x13¼ |
|---|---|---|
| 1195 A513 380d multi | | 1.75 1.75 |

Gevorg Emin (1919-98), Writer — A514

| 2019, Sept. 30 | Litho. | Perf. 13¼x13 |
|---|---|---|
| 1196 A514 120d multi | | .55 .55 |

History Museum of Armenia — A515

| 2019, Sept. 30 | Litho. | Perf. 13x13¼ |
|---|---|---|
| 1197 A515 220d multi | | 1.00 1.00 |

Souvenir Sheet

2019 World Congress on Information Technology, Yerevan — A516

| 2019, Oct. 7 | Litho. | Perf. 13¼ |
|---|---|---|
| 1198 A516 650d multi | | 4.00 4.00 |

# ARMENIA

First Armenian Postage Stamps, Cent. — A517

**2019, Nov. 11**    Litho.    Perf. 13x13¼
1199   A517   230d multi     1.10   1.10

Fauna — A518

Designs: 230d, Alcedo atthis. 330d, Panthera pardus ciscaucasica.

**2019, Nov. 12**    Litho.    Perf. 12½
1200-1201   A518   Set of 2    2.50   2.50

A519     A520
Chalcedony Seal    Jet Seal

**2019, Nov. 27**    Litho.    Perf. 13x13¼
1202   A519   10d multi     .30   .30
1203   A520   50d multi     .40   .40

### Souvenir Sheet

Komitas (1869-1935), Priest and Composer — A521

**2019, Dec. 1**    Litho.    Perf. 13¼x13
1204   A521   1100d multi    7.00   7.00

Hrachya Hovhannissian (1919-97), Poet — A522

**2019, Dec. 11**    Litho.    Perf. 13¼
1205   A522   120d multi    .55   .55

Admiral Ivan Isakov (1894-1967) — A523

**2019, Dec. 24**    Litho.    Perf. 13¼x13
1206   A523   120d multi    .75   .75

*Daredevils of Sassoun* Cartoon Character — A524

**2019, Dec. 24**    Litho.    Perf. 13x13¼
1207   A524   120d multi    .75   .75

### Souvenir Sheet

Peñarol Soccer Team, Winners of 1961, 1966 and 1982 Intercontinental Cup — A525

**2019, Dec. 24**    Litho.    Perf. 14
1208   A525   500d multi    3.25   3.25

Airplane and Mount Ararat A526

**2019, Dec. 26**    Litho.    Perf. 14
1209   A526   220d multi    1.40   1.40

Snowman Heads — A527

**2019, Dec. 26**    Litho.    Perf. 13¼
1210   A527   220d multi    1.40   1.40
Christmas and New Year's Day.

New Year 2020 (Year of the Rat) — A528

**2019, Dec. 26**    Litho.    Perf. 13¼x13
1211   A528   230d multi    1.40   1.40

7th Century B.C. Bronze Van Kingdom Throne Decoration — A529

**2020, May 26**    Litho.    Perf. 13x13¼
**Background Color**
1212   A529   10d orange     .35   .35
1213   A529   50d greenish blue   .35   .35
1214   A529   70d rose pink   .40   .40
1215   A529   100d yellow green   .60   .60
1216   A529   120d light blue    .75   .75
1217   A529   230d vermilion   1.50   1.50
1218   A529   330d plum    2.00   2.00
   Nos. 1212-1218 (7)    5.95   5.95
See Nos. 1236-1237.

Prehistoric Animals — A530

Designs: 230d, Basilosaurus. 280d, Diplodocus.

**2020, June 16**    Litho.    Perf. 13x13¼
1219-1220   A530   Set of 2    6.00   6.00

Bullet-riddled Wall With Armenian Inscription A531

**2020, June 26**    Litho.    Perf. 13x13¼
1221   A531   280d multi    2.00   2.00
End of World War II, 75th anniv.

Horse-drawn Mail Wagon in Gyumri — A532

**2020, July 3**    Litho.    Perf. 13x13¼
1222   A532   350d multi    2.25   2.25
Ancient Postal Routes.
Europa.

### Souvenir Sheet

Napoleon Bonaparte (1769-1821), Emperor of France — A533

**2020, July 10**    Litho.    Perf. 13¼x13
1223   A533   650d multi    3.00   3.00

Paintings by Jean Jansem (1920-2013) — A534

Designs: 280d, Self-portrait. 330d, Man, Woman and Child.

**2020, July 20**    Litho.    Perf. 13¼x13
1224-1225   A534   Set of 2    2.75   2.75

### Souvenir Sheet

Henri Verneuil (1920-2002), Film Director — A535

**2020, Sept. 1**    Litho.    Perf.
1226   A535   1100d multi    7.00   7.00

Sergo Hambardzumyan (1910-83), Weight Lifter — A536

**2020, Sept. 9**    Litho.    Perf. 13¼x13
1227   A536   120d multi    .80   .80

Alexander Harutyunyan (1920-2012), Composer — A537

**2020, Sept. 11**    Litho.    Perf. 13¼
1228   A537   220d multi    1.20   1.20

Church of St. Gregory the Illuminator, Singapore A538

**2020, Sept. 17**    Litho.    Perf. 13x13¼
1229   A538   120d multi    .80   .80

Paintings by Yeghishe Tadevossian (1870-1936) — A539

Designs: 230d, Self-portrait. 330d, Canal and Gondola, horiz.

   Perf. 13¼x13, 13x13¼
**2020, Nov. 11**    Litho.
1230-1231   A539   Set of 2    2.90   2.90

New Year 2021 (Year of the Ox) — A540

**2020, Nov. 13**    Litho.    Perf. 13¼
1232   A540   330d multi    1.75   1.75

Diana Apcar (1859-1937), Writer and Honorary Consul to Japan — A541

**2020, Nov. 23**    Litho.    Perf. 13¼x13
1233   A541   120d multi    .60   .60

Atabek Khnkoyan (1870-1935), Children's Book Writer — A542

**2020, Nov. 25**    Litho.    Perf. 13x13¼
1234   A542   120d multi    .80   .80

Lazar Sarian (1920-98), Composer — A543

**2020, Nov. 27**    Litho.    Perf. 13¼x13
1235   A543   120d multi    .60   .60

**Van Kingdom Throne Decoration Type of 2020**

**2020, Dec. 11**    Litho.    Perf. 13x13¼
**Background Color**
1236   A529   220d claret    1.20   1.20
1237   A529   280d blue    1.40   1.40

Cartoon, "In Blue Sea, In White Foam" — A544

**2020, Dec. 24**    Litho.    Perf. 13x13¼
1238   A544   120d multi    .60   .60

Bicycle — A545

**2020, Dec. 24**    Litho.    Perf. 13x13¼
1239   A545   220d multi    1.10   1.10

# ARMENIA

### Miniature Sheet

Paintings by Arshile Gorky (1904-48) — A546

No. 1240: a, 220d, Untitled, 1944 (29x35mm). b, 230d, Abstraction, 1936 (35x35mm). c, 350d, Landscape-Table, 1945 (35x35mm). d, 650d, Untitled, 1941 (30x40mm).

*Perf. 14x13¾ (220d), 13¼ (230d, 350d), 13¼x13 (650d)*
**2020, Dec. 25** Litho.
1240 A546 Sheet of 4, #a-d 8.00 8.00

Ophrys Apifera A547 — Tomares Romanovi A548

**2020, Dec. 28** Litho. *Perf. 12½*
1241 A547 230d multi 1.25 1.25
1242 A548 330d multi 1.75 1.75

### Souvenir Sheet

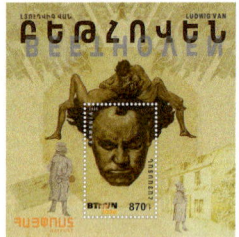

Ludwig van Beethoven (1770-1827), Composer — A549

**2020, Dec. 28** Litho. *Perf. 13*
1243 A549 870d multi 5.00 5.00

Hrachya Nersisian (1895-1961), Actor — A550

**2020, Dec. 29** Litho. *Perf. 13¼x13*
1244 A550 330d multi 2.00 2.00

Christmas and New Year's Day — A551

**2020, Dec. 29** Litho. *Perf. 13x13¼*
1245 A551 240d multi 1.50 1.50

### Souvenir Sheet

Printing House of Holy Etchmiadzin, 250th Anniv. — A552

**2021, Apr. 16** Litho. *Perf. 13x13¼*
1246 A552 400d multi 2.50 2.50

Tribute to Healthcare Workers in the COVID-19 Pandemic — A553

Background color: 220d, Dark blue. 230d, Orange. 280d, Red. 300d, Violet.

**2021, Apr. 16** Litho. *Perf. 13½*
1247-1250 A553 Set of 4 6.00 6.00
1250a Sheet of 8, 2 each #1247-1250 12.00 12.00

Steam Locomotive A554

**2021, Apr. 19** Litho. *Perf. 13x13¼*
1251 A554 190d multi 1.10 1.10

Cartoon, "Kikos" — A555

**2021, Apr. 21** Litho. *Perf. 13x13¼*
1252 A555 190d multi 1.10 1.10

Armenian College and Philanthropic Academy of Kolkata, 200th Anniv. — A556

**2021, Apr. 26** Litho. *Perf. 13¼*
1253 A556 160d multi 1.00 1.00

Bodil Biorn (1871-1960), Missionary and Founder of Orphanage in Alexandropol — A557

**2021, May 5** Litho. *Perf. 13½x13*
1254 A557 230d multi 1.40 1.40

Prehistoric Animals — A558

Designs: 230d, Titanoboa. 280d, Velociraptor.

**2021, May 6** Litho. *Perf. 13x13½*
1255-1256 A558 Set of 2 3.00 3.00

Aquila Chrysaetos A559

**2021, May 7** Litho. *Perf. 13x13½*
1257 A559 350d multi 2.25 2.25
Europa.

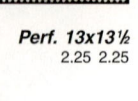

Ghapama (Stuffed Pumpkin) — A560

**2021, May 17** Litho. *Perf. 13½*
1258 A560 300d multi 1.75 1.75

Regional Communications Commonwealth, 30th Anniv. — A561

**2021, May 31** Litho. *Perf. 13x13½*
1259 A561 290d multi 1.60 1.60

Characters From Cartoon *Lazy Huri* — A562

**2021, June 1** Litho. *Perf. 13½x14*
1260 A562 70d multi .55 .55

2020 European Soccer Championships A563

**2021, June 3** Litho. *Perf. 13x13½*
1261 A563 290d multi 1.60 1.60
The 2020 European Soccer Championships were postponed until 2021 because of the COVID-19 pandemic.

2020 Summer Olympics, Tokyo — A564

**2021, June 4** Litho. *Perf. 13x13½*
1262 A564 500d multi 3.00 3.00
The 2020 Summer Olympics were postponed until 2021 because of the COVID-19 pandemic.

7th Century B.C. Bronze Van Kingdom Throne Decoration — A565

**2021** Litho. *Perf. 13x13¼*
**Background Color**
1263 A565 10d scarlet .30 .30
1264 A565 20d Turq blue .30 .30
1265 A565 50d ol gray .30 .30
1266 A565 70d pink .40 .40
1267 A565 100d brt green .60 .60
1268 A565 230d brn pur 1.40 1.40
1269 A565 290d dull blue 1.75 1.75
1270 A565 400d org red 2.50 2.50
1271 A565 450d dark blue gray 2.10 2.10
1272 A565 1000d bister yel 6.00 6.00
1273 A565 1600d bluish violet 9.50 9.50
Nos. 1263-1273 (11) 25.15 25.15

Issued: 10d, 20d, 50d, 70d, 100d, 230d, 290d, 1000d, 1600d, 6/7; 400d, 8/4; 450d, 12/15.

### Souvenir Sheet

Alexander Spendiaryan (1871-1928), Composer — A566

**2021, June 14** Litho. *Perf. 13½*
1274 A566 890d multi 5.00 5.00

Pghndzahank Fortress and Akhtala Monastery, Akhtala A567

**2021, June 16** Litho. *Perf. 14*
1275 A567 470d multi 3.00 3.00

Edward Mirzoyan (1921-2012), Composer A568

**2021, June 18** Litho. *Perf. 13x13½*
1276 A568 230d multi 1.25 1.25

### Souvenir Sheet

Arno Babajanyan (1921-83), Composer — A569

**2021, July 30** Litho. *Perf. 13¼x13*
1277 A569 1000d gold & multi 6.25 6.25

Clara Barton (1821-1912), Nurse and Founder of American Red Cross — A570

**2021, Aug. 26** Litho. *Perf. 13*
1278 A570 230d multi 1.25 1.25

Tourist Sites — A571

Designs: 230d, Lsake Sevan and Hayravank Monastery. 410d, Zorats Karer megaliths. 470d, Mermaid's Hair Waterfall. 710d, Temple of Garni.

**2021, Aug. 26** Litho. *Perf. 13½*
1279-1282 A571 Set of 4 11.00 11.00
1282a Souvenir sheet of 8, 2 each #1279-1282 22.00 22.00

Souvenir Sheet

Salome, Painting by Vardges Surenyants (1860-1921) — A572

**2021, Sept. 13 Litho. *Perf. 14½***
**1283** A572 890d multi 5.25 5.25

National Gallery of Armenia, cent.

Souvenir Sheet

Bombing of Ghazanchetsots Holy Savior Cathedral, 1st Anniv. — A573

No. 1284 — Cathedral: a, 940d, Before bombing. b, 950d, After bombing.

**2021, Sept. 14 Litho. *Perf. 13x13½***
**1284** A573 Sheet of 2, #a-b 11.00 11.00

Independence, 30th Anniv. — A574

***Serpentine Die Cut 13½x14***
**2021, Sept. 21 Litho.**
**On Plastic Film**
**Self-Adhesive**
**1285** A574 890d multi 5.25 5.25

Alexander Kemurdzhian (1921-2003), Designer of Lunokhod Lunar Rover — A575

**2021, Oct. 17 Litho. *Perf. 13x13¼***
**1286** A575 200d multi 1.25 1.25

Komitas State Conservatory, Yerevan, Cent. — A576

**2021, Oct. 20 Litho. *Perf. 13x13¼***
**1287** A576 290d multi 1.40 1.40

Souvenir Sheets

A577

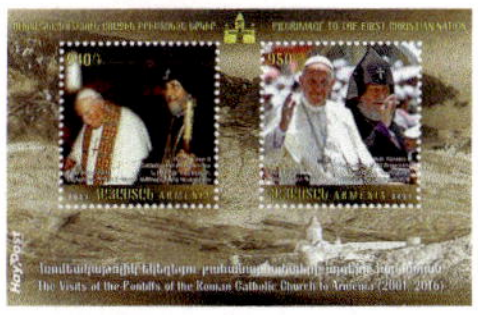

Papal Visits to Armenia A578

No. 1288: a, Pope John Paul II. b, Pope Francis.

No. 1289 — Catholicos Karekin II with: a, 940d, Pope John Paul II. b, 950d, Pope Francis.

**2021, Oct. 27 Litho. *Perf. 13¼***
**1288** A577 630d Sheet of 2, #a-b 6.00 6.00
**1289** A578 Sheet of 2, #a-b 9.00 9.00

2001 visit of Pope John Paul II and 2016 visit of Pope Francis.

Havasi (Armenak Markosyan) (1896-1978), Folk Singer — A579

**2021, Dec. 14 Litho. *Perf. 14***
**1290** A579 290d multi 1.75 1.75

Communist Party of China, Cent. — A580

**2021, Dec. 23 Litho. *Perf. 13¼x13***
**1291** A580 390d multi 2.25 2.25

New Year 2022 (Year of the Tiger) — A581

**Litho. With Foil Application**
**2021, Dec. 23 *Perf. 13¾***
**1292** A581 500d gold & multi 2.50 2.50

Values are for stamps with surrounding selvage.

Flora and Fauna — A582

Designs: 230d, Hemiechinus auritus. 290d, Ommatotriton ophryticus. 400d, Iris lineolata. 450d, Nymphaea alba.

***Perf. 13¼x13¾***
**2021, Dec. 24 Litho.**
**1293-1296** A582 Set of 4 8.50 8.50
*1296a* Sheet of 8, 2 each #1293-1296 17.00 17.00

Souvenir Sheet

Christmas and New Year's Day — A583

**2021, Dec. 24 Litho. *Perf.***
**1297** A583 890d multi 4.25 4.25

Yerevan Television Tower of Public Television Company of Armenia — A584

**2021, Dec. 27 Litho. *Perf. 13¼x13***
**1298** A584 400d multi 2.50 2.50

Diplomatic Relations Between Armenia and Egypt, 30th Anniv. — A585

**2022, Mar. 22 Litho. *Perf. 13½***
**1299** A585 400d multi 2.50 2.50

8th-7th Cent. B.C. Van Kingdom Bronze Winged Figurine — A586

**2022, Mar. 28 Litho. *Perf. 13x13¼***
**Background Color**

| | | | | | |
|---|---|---|---|---|---|
| **1300** | A586 | 10d | orange | .70 | .45 |
| **1301** | A586 | 20d | sage green | .70 | .45 |
| **1302** | A586 | 50d | rose lilac | .70 | .45 |
| **1303** | A586 | 70d | blue | .70 | .45 |
| **1304** | A586 | 100d | cerise | .70 | .45 |
| **1305** | A586 | 230d | Prussian green | 1.40 | .90 |
| **1306** | A586 | 290d | pink | 2.00 | 1.20 |
| **1307** | A586 | 400d | light blue | 2.60 | 1.60 |
| **1308** | A586 | 450d | black | 3.00 | 1.90 |
| **1309** | A586 | 1000d | purple brown | 6.75 | 4.00 |
| **1310** | A586 | 1600d | deep violet | 10.00 | 6.50 |
| | *Nos. 1300-1310 (11)* | | | 29.25 | 18.35 |

See Nos. 1331-1332.

Yeghishe Charents (1897-1937), Poet — A587

**2022, Apr. 4 Litho. *Perf. 13¼x13***
**1311** A587 400d multi 3.00 3.00

Paintings by Lavinia Bazhbeuk-Melikyan (1922-2005) — A588

Designs: 280d, Self-portrait with Zhilinskaya, 1965. 410d, Cacti, 1964.

**2022, Apr. 7 Litho. *Perf. 13¼x13***
**1312-1313** A588 Set of 2 5.00 5.00

Prehistoric Animals — A589

Designs: 220d, Triceratops. 280d, Liopleurodon.

**2022, Apr. 8 Litho. *Perf. 13x13¼***
**1314-1315** A589 Set of 2 2.75 2.75

Tram — A590

**2022, Apr. 11 Litho. *Perf. 13½***
**1316** A590 170d multi 1.00 1.00

Armenian Army, 30th Anniv. — A591

**Litho. & Embossed With Foil Application**
**2022, Apr. 13 *Perf. 13¼x13***
**1317** A591 500d sil & multi 3.50 3.50

2022 Winter Olympics, Beijing — A592

**Litho. With Foil Application**
**2022, Apr. 14 *Perf. 13½***
**1318** A592 330d multi 2.40 2.40

Sergey Hambardzumyan (1922-2018), Rector of Yerevan State University — A593

**2022, Apr. 21 Litho. *Perf. 13x13¼***
**1319** A593 220d multi 1.60 1.60

Astghik, Goddess of Love — A594

**2022, May 26 Litho. *Perf. 13½***
**1320** A594 350d multi 2.60 2.60

Europa.

Ignacy Lukasiewicz (1822-82), Inventor of Paraffin Lamp — A595

**2022, May 31 Litho. *Perf. 13½x13***
**1321** A595 160d multi 1.00 1.00

Tserents (Hovsep Shishmanian) (1822-88), Writer — A596

**2022, June 1 Litho. *Perf. 13x13½***
**1322** A596 290d multi 1.75 1.75

Souvenir Sheet

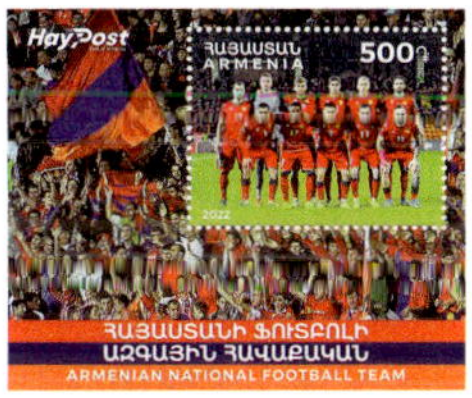

Armenian National Soccer Team — A597

**2022, June 2 Litho. *Perf. 13x13½***
**1323** A597 500d multi 3.00 3.00

A598

# ARMENIA

Design: Winning design in children's stamp design contest with theme of "The Future We Want."

**2022, June 7**    Litho.    *Perf. 13x13½*
1324   A598   290d multi      2.25   2.25

United Nations in Armenia, 30th anniv.

Armenian Presidency of Collective Security Treaty Organization A599

**2022, June 9**    Litho.    *Perf. 13½*
1325   A599   380d multi      3.00   3.00

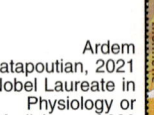

Ardem Patapoutian, 2021 Nobel Laureate in Physiology or Medicine — A600

**2022, June 14**    Litho.    *Perf. 13½*
1326   A600   350d multi      4.25   4.25

Khachatur Abovyan Armenian State Pedagogical University, Cent. — A601

**2022, June 20**    Litho.    *Perf. 13½x13*
1327   A601   590d multi      5.00   5.00

Davit Bek Monument, Kapan — A602

**2022, July 22**    Litho.    *Perf. 13½*
1328   A602   380d multi      2.50   2.50

Syunik Rebellion, 300th anniv.

Archag Tchobanian (1872-1954), Writer — A603

**2022, July 25**    Litho.    *Perf. 13¼x13*
1329   A603   320d multi      2.10   2.10

Holy Resurrection Church, Dhaka, Bangladesh A604

**2022, July 25**    Litho.    *Perf. 13x13½*
1330   A604   320d multi      2.60   2.60

**Bronze Winged Figure Type of 2022**

**Background Color**

**2022, July 26**    Litho.    *Perf. 13x13¼*
1331   A586   320d red      2.75   2.75
1332   A586   380d violet      3.00   3.00

Vahagn Davtyan (1922-96), Poet — A605

**2022, July 27**    Litho.    *Perf. 13½x13*
1333   A605   320d multi      2.75   2.75

**Souvenir Sheet**

St. John the Baptist Church, Shushi A606

No. 1334 — St. John the Baptist Church: a, 940d, Before aerial bombing by Azerbaijan forces. b, 950d, After aerial bombing.

**2022, July 27**    Litho.    *Perf. 13x13½*
1334   A606   Sheet of 2, #a-b    15.00   15.00

Grigor Gurzadyan (1922-2014), Astrophysicist, and Planetary Nebula — A607

**2022, July 28**    Litho.    *Perf. 13x13½*
1335   A607   380d multi      2.50   2.50

**Souvenir Sheet**

Scene From 1975 Motion Picture *A Bride From the North* A608

**2022, July 28**    Litho.    *Perf. 13x13½*
1336   A608   800d multi      5.00   5.00

Scene From 1972 Cartoon *Vin the Penguin* — A609

**2022, July 29**    Litho.    *Perf. 13x13½*
1337   A609   200d multi      1.60   1.60

Eurasian Economic Commission, 10th Anniv. — A610

**2022, Aug. 25**    Litho.    *Perf. 13½*
1338   A610   160d multi      1.10   1.10

Churches — A611

No. 1339: a, Armenian Apostolic Church of Saint Catherine, St. Petersburg, Russia (lt. blue panel). b, Russian Orthodox Church of St. Michael the Archangel, Gyumri, Armenia (reddish purple panel).

**2022, Aug. 30**    Litho.    *Perf. 13½*
1339   A611   500d Pair, #a-b    8.00   8.00

See Russia No. 8401.

Flora and Fauna — A612

Designs: 320d, Lilium armenum. 380d, Astrantia maxima. 500d, Otocolobus manul. 560d, Tichodroma muraria.

**2022, Sept. 7**    Litho.    *Perf. 13½*
1340-1343   A612   Set of 4    15.00   15.00
1343a    Souvenir sheet of 8, 2 each #1340-1343    30.00   30.00

**Souvenir Sheet**

2022 Men's European Boxing Championships, Yerevan — A613

**2022, Sept. 8**    Litho.    *Perf. 13¼x14*
1344   A613   800d multi      7.00   7.00

**Souvenir Sheet**

Sixth Starmus International Festival, Yerevan — A614

**2022, Sept. 8**    Litho.    *Perf. 13x13½*
1345   A614   500d multi      3.25   3.25

Tourist Sites — A615

Designs: 320d, Geghad Monastic Complex, Kotayk Region. 380d, Lake Sev, Syunik Region. 500d, Trchkan Waterfall, Shirak Region. 560d, Mount Aragats.

**2022, Sept. 12**    Litho.    *Perf. 13½*
1346-1349   A615   Set of 4    15.00   15.00
1349a    Souvenir sheet of 8, 2 each #1346-1349    30.00   30.00

Ohan Duryan (1922-2011), Conductor and Composer A616

**2022, Sept. 13**    Litho.    *Perf. 13x13½*
1350   A616   230d multi      1.90   1.90

2022 World Cup Soccer Championships, Qatar — A617

**2022, Sept. 13**    Litho.    *Perf. 13x13¼*
1351   A617   500d multi      4.25   4.25

Stepanavan "Sochut" Dendropark (Arboretum) A618

**2022, Sept. 14**    Litho.    *Perf. 13x13¼*
1352   A618   380d multi      3.25   3.25

Ghalinjakar Fortress, Berdavan — A619

**2022, Sept. 15**    Litho.    *Perf. 13½*
1353   A619   380d multi      3.25   3.25

Gata — A620

**2022, Sept. 16**    Litho.    *Perf. 13½x13*
1354   A620   380d multi      3.25   3.25

Yuri Yerznkyan (1922-96), Film Actor and Director — A621

**2022, Oct. 2**    Litho.    *Perf. 13x13¼*
1355   A621   320d multi      2.75   2.75

Rouben Mamoulian (1897-1987), Film Director — A622

**2022, Nov. 29**    Litho.    *Perf. 13½*
1356   A622   400d multi      3.25   3.25

Hovhannes Baghramyan (1897-1982), Marshal of the Soviet Union — A623

**2022, Nov. 30**    Litho.    *Perf. 13¼x13*
1357   A623   500d multi      4.25   4.25

2022 Junior Eurovision Song Contest, Yerevan — A624

**2022, Dec. 2**    Litho.    *Perf. 13x13¼*
1358   A624   400d multi      3.50   3.50

Carpet — A625

**2022, Dec. 19**    Embroidered    *Imperf.*
**Self-Adhesive**
1359   A625   3000d multi      21.00   21.00

# ARMENIA

New Year 2023 (Year of the Rabbit) — A626

**Litho. With Foil Application**
2022, Dec. 21     Perf. 13½
1360   A626   500d multi     4.25   4.25

Values are for stamps with surrounding selvage.

Christmas and New Year's Day — A627

**Litho. With Glitter Affixed**
2022, Dec. 22     Perf. 13¼x13
1361   A627   400d multi     3.00   3.00

Governmental Buildings in Yerevan — A628

Designs: No. 1362, 500d, Residence of the President of the Republic of Armenia, 1951. No. 1363, 500d, National Assembly Building, 1950. No. 1364, 500d, Building of the Government of the Republic of Armenia, 1926-39.

2022, Dec. 23     Litho.     Perf. 13½
1362-1364   A628   Set of 3     12.50   12.50

Religious Buildings — A629

Designs: No. 1365, Church of St. George, Nitrianska Blatnica, Slovakia. No. 1366, Tatev Monastery, Tatev, Armenia.

2023, Feb. 28     Litho.     Perf. 13x13¼
1365   A629   400d multi     3.00   3.00
1366   A629   400d multi     3.00   3.00

See Slovakia Nos.

A630

Ana Aslan (1897-1988), Gerontologist A631

2023, Apr. 3     Litho.     Perf. 13¼x13½
1367   A630   400d multi     3.00   3.00
1368   A631   400d multi     3.00   3.00

See Romania Nos.

7th Century B.C. Bronze Van Kingdom Throne Decoration — A632

2023, Apr. 12     Litho.     Perf. 13x13¼
**Background Color**
1369   A632   10d   white     .40   .30
1370   A632   20d   orange     .40   .30
1371   A632   50d   yel orange     .40   .30
1372   A632   100d   yel green     .80   .60
1373   A632   320d   purple     2.50   1.90

1374   A632   380d   dark red     2.90   2.25
1375   A632   400d   blue gray     2.90   2.25
1376   A632   1000d   olive green     7.50   5.75
1377   A632   1600d   blue     12.00   9.25
     Nos. 1369-1377 (9)     29.80   22.90

Yerevan Metro Train and Route Map — A633

2023, May 5     Litho.     Perf. 13x13¼
1378   A633   320d multi     2.10   2.10

Pasuts Tolma — A634

2023, May 10     Litho.     Perf. 13½
1379   A634   380d multi     2.50   2.50

Nikol Aghbalyan (1873-1947), Writer and Minister of Education — A635

2023, May 11     Litho.     Perf. 13½
1380   A635   320d multi     2.10   2.10

Karp Khachvankyan (1923-98), Actor and Director — A636

2023, May 12     Litho.     Perf. 13½
1381   A636   320d multi     2.10   2.10

Hrachya Ghaplanyan (1923-88), Actor and Founder of Yerevan Dramatic Theater — A637

2023, May 15     Litho.     Perf. 13½
1382   A637   320d multi     2.10   2.10

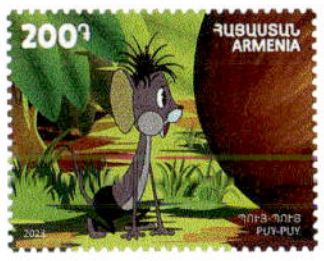

Puy-Puy, 1971 Animated Film — A638

2023, May 17     Litho.     Perf. 13x13¼
1383   A638   200d multi     1.50   1.50

1968 Motion Picture *Saroyan Brothers* A639

2023, June 8     Litho.     Perf. 13x13¼
1384   A639   800d multi     6.00   6.00

---

## SEMI-POSTAL STAMPS

International Children's Day — SP1

2008, June 1     Litho.     Perf. 14¾x14
B1   SP1   70d +30d multi + label     1.00   1.00

Surtax (on sheet margin) was for UNICEF.

Marguerite Barankitse, Burundian Humanitarian Awarded 2016 Aurora Prize — SP2

2017, May 26     Litho.     Perf. 12¾x13¼
B2   SP2   350d +150d multi + label     4.00   4.00

No. B2 was printed in sheets of 3 + 3 labels. The label is on either side of the stamp.

SP3

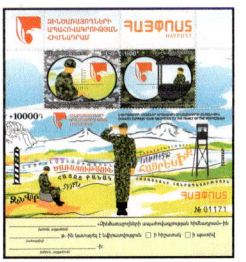

Insurance Foundation for Servicemen — SP4

No. B4 — Emblem of Insurance Foundation for Servicemen and: a, 350d, Soldier writing. b, 1100d, Soldier in watch tower.

2017, Sept. 18     Litho.     Perf. 13x13¼
B3   SP3   350d +150d multi + label     4.25   4.25
**Souvenir Sheet**
B4   SP4   Sheet of 2, #a-b     90.00   90.00

No. B4 was sold with a 10,000d surtax.

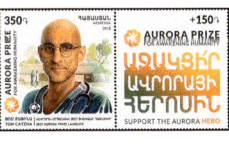

SP5

Design: Dr. Tom Catena, recipient of 2017 Aurora prize.

2018, June 4     Litho.     Perf. 14
B5   SP5   350d +150d multi + label     4.25   4.25

Kyaw Hla Aung, Recipient of 2018 Aurora Prize SP6

2019, Oct. 16     Litho.     Perf. 14
B6   SP6   350d +150d multi + label     3.25   3.25

No. B6 was printed in sheets of 3 + 3 labels. The label is on either side of the stamp.

Historical and Cultural Landmarks — SP7

Designs: 240d+120d, Agarakadzor Bridge. 300d+120d, Monastery of Marmashen. 350d+120d, Yererouyk Basilica.

2020, Nov. 30     Litho.     Perf. 13x13¼
B7   SP7   240d +120d multi + label     1.75   1.75
B8   SP7   330d +120d multi + label     2.25   2.25
B9   SP7   350d +120d multi + label     2.25   2.25
     Nos. B7-B9 (3)     6.25   6.25

Surtax for preservation of historical and cultural monuments of Armenia.

Mirza Dinnayi, Recipient of 2019 Aurora Prize SP8

2020, Dec. 5     Litho.     Perf. 14
B10   SP8   350d +150d multi + label     2.40   2.40

No. B10 was printed in sheets of 6 + 6 labels. The label is on either side of the stamp.

Sculptures — SP9

Designs: 120d+500d, Monument to David of Sassoun. 220d+500d, Mountain Dance Sculpture Group. 230d+500d, Monument to Leonid Yengibaryan (1935-72), circus clown. 280d+500d, Monument to Komitas (1869-1935), priest and composer. 300d+500d, Monument to Martiros Sarian (1880-1972), painter. 380d+500d, Monument to Arno Babajanyan (1921-83), composer. 500d+500d, Monument to Mesrop Mashtots (362-440), inventor of Armenian alphabet.

2020, Dec. 22     Litho.     Perf. 13¼
B11   SP9   120d +500d multi + label     3.25   3.25
B12   SP9   220d +500d multi + label     3.75   3.75
B13   SP9   230d +500d multi + label     3.75   3.75
B14   SP9   280d +500d multi + label     4.25   4.25
B15   SP9   330d +500d multi + label     4.50   4.50
B16   SP9   380d +500d multi + label     4.75   4.75
B17   SP9   500d +500d multi + label     5.25   5.25
    a.   Souvenir sheet of 7, #B11-B17 (without attached +500d labels) + 5000d label     37.50   37.50
     Nos. B11-B17 (7)     29.50   29.50

Historical and Cultural Landmarks — SP10

Designs: 230d+120d, Saints Peter and Paul Church, Aghjots Monastery. 290d+120d, Gandzasar Monastery. 330d+120d, Amaras Monastery.

2021, July 20     Litho.     Perf. 13x13¼
B18   SP10   230d +120d multi + label     2.10   2.10
B19   SP10   290d +120d multi + label     2.40   2.40

# ARMENIA — ARUBA

B20 SP10 330d +120d multi + label 2.75 2.75
Nos. B18-B20 (3) 7.25 7.25

Surtax for preservation of historical and cultural monuments of Armenia.

Fartuun Adan and Ilwad Elman, Recipients of 2020 Aurora Prize — SP11

**2021, Dec. 8   Litho.   Perf. 14**
B21 SP11 350d +150d multi + label 3.00 3.00

No. B21 was printed in sheets of 6 + 6 labels. The label is on either side of the stamp.

Soldiers SP12

**2021, Dec. 13   Litho.   Perf. 13½**
B22 SP12 290d +110d multi + label 2.50 2.50

Surtax for Insurance Foundation for Servicemen.

Historical and Cultural Landmarks — SP13

Designs: 230d+120d, Aghdzk Royal Tomb. 340d+120d, Khoranashat Monastic Complex. 350d+120d, Srvegh Monastery.

**2022, June 6   Litho.   Perf. 13x13¼**
B23 SP13 230d +120d multi + label 2.75 2.75
B24 SP13 340d +120d multi + label 3.50 3.50
B25 SP13 350d +120d multi + label 3.50 3.50
Nos. B23-B25 (3) 9.75 9.75

Surtax for preservation of historical and cultural monuments of Armenia.

Julienne Lusenge, Recipeint of 2021 Aurora Prize SP14

**2022, Oct. 31   Litho.   Perf. 14**
B26 SP14 350d +150d multi + label 3.00 3.00

No. B26 was printed in sheets of 6 + 6 labels. The label is on either side of the stamp.

Union of Philatelists and Numismatists, Cent. — SP15

**Perf. 13¼x13½**
**2022, Nov. 14   Litho.**
B27 SP15 380d +120d multi + label 4.25 4.25

No. B27 was printed in sheets of 6 + 6 labels. The label is on either side of the stamp.

Soldiers SP16

**2022, Nov. 30   Litho.   Perf. 13½**
B28 SP16 380d +120d multi + label 4.25 4.25

Surtax for Insurance Foundation for Servicemen. No. B28 was printed in sheets of 8 + 8 labels. The label is on either side of the stamp.

## AIR POST STAMPS

AP1

Design: 90d, Artiom Katsian (1886-1943), world record holding pilot on range and altitude in 1909.

**1995, Dec. 5   Litho.   Perf. 14x15**
C1 AP1 90d multicolored .75 .75

AP2

**1996, Apr. 30   Litho.   Perf. 14x14½**
C2 AP2 90d multicolored .90 .90

Nelson Stepanian (1913-44), WWII fighter ace.

## ARUBA
ə-'rü-bə

LOCATION — West Indies, north of Venezuela
AREA — 78 sq. mi.
POP. — 67,014
CAPITAL — Oranjestad

On Jan. 1, 1986 Aruba, formerly part of Netherlands Antilles, achieved a separate status within the Kingdom of the Netherlands.

100 Cents = 1 Gulden

Catalogue values for all unused stamps in this country are for Never Hinged items.

Used values are for CTO or stamps removed from first day covers. Postally used examples sell for more.

Traditional House — A1

**Perf. 14x13**
**1986-87   Litho.   Unwmk.**
| 1 | A1 | 5c shown | .40 | .25 |
| 2 | A1 | 15c King William III Tower | .90 | .40 |
| 3 | A1 | 20c Loading crane | .65 | .30 |
| 4 | A1 | 25c Lighthouse | 1.20 | .40 |
| 5 | A1 | 30c Snake | .80 | .65 |
| 6 | A1 | 35c Owl | 1.20 | .65 |
| 7 | A1 | 45c Shell | 1.00 | .65 |
| 8 | A1 | 55c Frog | 1.20 | .65 |
| 9 | A1 | 60c Water skier | 1.20 | .80 |
| 10 | A1 | 65c Net fishing | 1.15 | 1.00 |
| 11 | A1 | 75c Music box | 1.50 | 1.10 |
| 12 | A1 | 85c Pre-Columbian bisque pot | 1.50 | .80 |
| 13 | A1 | 90c Bulb cactus | 1.60 | 1.10 |
| 14 | A1 | 100c Grain | 1.60 | 1.10 |
| 15 | A1 | 150c Watapana tree | 2.40 | 1.60 |
| 16 | A1 | 250c Aloe plant | 3.25 | 3.25 |
| | | Nos. 1-16 (16) | 21.55 | 14.70 |

Issued: 5c, 30c, 60c, 150c, 1/1; 15c, 35c, 65c, 250c, 2/5; 20c, 45c, 75c, 100c, 4/7/87; 25c, 55c, 85c, 90c, 7/17/87.

Independence — A2

25c, Map. 45c, Coat of arms, vert. 55c, Natl. anthem, vert. 100c, Flag.

**1986, Jan. 1   Perf. 14x13, 13x14**
| 18 | A2 | 25c multicolored | 1.75 | .60 |
| 19 | A2 | 45c multicolored | 1.75 | 1.15 |
| 20 | A2 | 55c multicolored | 1.75 | 1.75 |
| 21 | A2 | 100c multicolored | 2.25 | 2.25 |
| | | Nos. 18-21 (4) | 7.50 | 5.75 |

Intl. Peace Year — A3

**1986, Aug. 29   Litho.   Perf. 14x13**
| 22 | A3 | 60c shown | 2.00 | 1.25 |
| 23 | A3 | 100c Barbed wire | 3.50 | 2.00 |

Princess Juliana and Prince Bernhard, 50th Wedding Anniv. — A4

**1987, Jan. 7   Photo.   Perf. 13x14**
| 24 | A4 | 135c multicolored | 3.50 | 2.75 |

State Visit of Queen Beatrix and Prince Claus of the Netherlands — A5

60c, Prince William-Alexander.

**1987, Feb. 16   Litho.   Perf. 14x13**
| 25 | A5 | 55c shown | 1.75 | 1.20 |
| 26 | A5 | 60c multicolored | 1.75 | 1.20 |

Tourism — A6

**1987, June 5   Litho.**
| 27 | A6 | 60c Beach and sea | 1.75 | 1.50 |
| 28 | A6 | 100c Rock and cacti | 2.50 | 2.00 |

Aloe Vera Plant — A7

**1988, Jan. 27   Litho.   Perf. 13x14**
| 29 | A7 | 45c Field | 1.90 | 1.00 |
| 30 | A7 | 60c Plant | 2.00 | 1.25 |
| 31 | A7 | 100c Harvest | 2.40 | 1.50 |
| | | Nos. 29-31 (3) | 6.30 | 3.75 |

Coins — A8

**1988, Mar. 16   Litho.   Perf. 13x14**
| 32 | A8 | 25c 25-cent | 1.40 | .50 |
| 33 | A8 | 55c 50-cent | 1.75 | 1.00 |
| 34 | A8 | 65c 5 and 10-cent | 2.10 | 1.35 |
| 35 | A8 | 150c 1-florin | 3.25 | 1.40 |
| | | Nos. 32-35 (4) | 8.50 | 5.25 |

Love Issue — A9

135c, Seashells, coastal scenery.

**1988, May 4**
| 36 | A9 | 70c shown | 1.75 | 1.00 |
| 37 | A9 | 135c multicolored | 2.25 | 2.00 |

A10

**1988, Aug. 24**
| 38 | A10 | 35c shown | 1.50 | .90 |
| 39 | A10 | 100c Emblems | 2.50 | 1.60 |

Aruba, the 162nd member of the Intl. Olympic Committee (35c), 1988 Summer Olympics, Seoul (100c).

Carnival — A11

**1989, Jan. 5   Perf. 14x13**
| 40 | A11 | 45c Two children | 2.00 | 1.00 |
| 41 | A11 | 60c Girl | 2.00 | 1.00 |
| 42 | A11 | 100c Entertainer | 2.50 | 1.50 |
| | | Nos. 40-42 (3) | 6.50 | 3.50 |

Maripampun, Omphalophalmum Rubrum — A12

**1989, Mar. 16   Litho.   Perf. 14x13**
| 43 | A12 | 35c Leaves | 1.50 | .75 |
| 44 | A12 | 55c Pods | 1.50 | 1.00 |
| 45 | A12 | 200c Blossom | 4.00 | 3.00 |
| | | Nos. 43-45 (3) | 7.00 | 4.75 |

New Year 1990 — A13

Dande band members playing instruments or singing: 25c, Violin, tambor, cuatro, marimba. 70c, Lead singer, guitar. 150c, Accordion, urri, guitar.

**1989, Nov. 16   Litho.   Perf. 13x14**
| 46 | A13 | 25c multicolored | 1.00 | .50 |
| 47 | A13 | 70c multicolored | 1.40 | 1.00 |
| 48 | A13 | 150c multicolored | 2.60 | 2.00 |
| | | Nos. 46-48 (3) | 5.00 | 3.50 |

UPU — A14

**1989, June 8   Litho.   Perf. 13x14**
| 49 | A14 | 250c multicolored | 6.00 | 3.75 |

Crotalus durissus unicolor — A15

# ARUBA

**1989, Aug. 24**     *Perf. 14x13*
50 A15 45c shown     1.50 .75
51 A15 55c multi, diff.     1.75 1.00
52 A15 60c multi, diff.     1.75 1.00
    Nos. 50-52 (3)     5.00 2.75

Snake species in danger of extinction.

Man Living in Harmony with Nature — A16

**1990, Feb. 7**     *Perf. 13x14, 14x13*
53 A16 45c The land     1.50 1.00
54 A16 55c shown     1.75 1.00
55 A16 100c The sea     3.00 2.00
    Nos. 53-55 (3)     6.25 4.00

Environmental protection. Nos. 53, 55 horiz.

Marine Life — A17

Designs: 60c, Giant caribbean anemone, Pederson's cleaning shrimp. 70c, Queen angelfish, red and orange coral. 100c, Banded coral shrimp, fire sponge, yellow boring sponge.

**1990, Apr. 4**     *Litho.*     *Perf. 14x13*
56 A17 60c multicolored     1.60 1.00
57 A17 70c multicolored     2.10 1.50
58 A17 100c multicolored     3.00 2.50
    Nos. 56-58 (3)     6.70 5.00

A18

200c, Character trademark.

**1990, May 30**     *Litho.*     *Perf. 13x14*
59 A18 35c multicolored     1.50 1.00
60 A18 200c multicolored     4.50 3.25

World Cup Soccer Championships, Italy.

A19

**1990, Sept. 12**
61 A19 45c Tools     1.40 1.00
62 A19 60c Stone figure     1.60 1.00
63 A19 100c Jar     2.75 1.50
    Nos. 61-63 (3)     5.75 3.50

Archeological discoveries.

Landscapes — A20

**1991, Jan. 31**     *Litho.*     *Perf. 14x13*
64 A20 55c Seashore     1.25 1.00
65 A20 65c Desert     1.50 1.30
66 A20 100c Cactus, ocean view     2.25 2.00
    Nos. 64-66 (3)     5.00 4.30

Working Women — A21

Designs: 35c, Taking care of others. 70c, Housewife. 100c, Women in society.

**1991, Mar. 28**     *Litho.*     *Perf. 13x14*
67 A21 35c multicolored     1.00 .50
68 A21 70c multicolored     1.50 1.25
69 A21 100c multicolored     2.00 1.75
    Nos. 67-69 (3)     4.50 3.50

Style of inscriptions varies.

Medicinal Plants — A22

65c, Ocimum sanctum. 75c, Jatropha gossypifolia. 95c, Croton flavens.

**1991, May 29**
70 A22 65c multicolored     1.50 1.00
71 A22 75c multicolored     1.75 1.25
72 A22 95c multicolored     2.00 1.50
    Nos. 70-72 (3)     5.25 3.75

A23

Aruban Handicrafts: 35c, Fish net, wood float, wooden needle. 250c, Straw hat, hat block.

**1991, July 31**     *Litho.*     *Perf. 13x14*
73 A23 35c lt bl, dk bl & blk     1.00 .75
74 A23 250c pink, lil rose & blk     4.25 3.50

A24

35c, Toucan. 70c, People shaking hands. 100c, Windmill.

**1991, Nov. 29**     *Litho.*     *Perf. 13x14*
75 A24 35c multicolored     1.00 1.00
76 A24 70c multicolored     1.50 1.00
77 A24 100c multicolored     2.50 2.00
    Nos. 75-77 (3)     5.00 4.00

Welcome to Aruba.

Aruba Postal Service, Cent. — A25

60c, Government decree, 1892, vert. 75c, First post office. 80c, Current post office.

*Perf. 13x14, 14x13*
**1992, Jan. 31**     *Litho.*
78 A25 60c multicolored     1.25 1.00
79 A25 75c multicolored     1.50 1.00
80 A25 80c multicolored     2.00 1.50
    Nos. 78-80 (3)     4.75 3.50

Equality Day — A26

No. 81, People of five races. No. 82, Woman, man, scales.

**1992, Mar. 25**     *Litho.*     *Perf. 14x13*
81 A26 100c multicolored     2.00 1.50
82 A26 100c multicolored     2.00 1.50

Discovery of America, 500th Anniv. — A27

**1992, July 30**     *Litho.*     *Perf. 13x14*
83 A27 30c Columbus     1.50 .50
84 A27 40c Sailing ship     1.50 .75
85 A27 50c Natives, map     1.50 1.00
    Nos. 83-85 (3)     4.50 2.25

Natural Bridges in Aruba — A28

Designs: 70c, Seroe Colorado Bridge, south coast. 80c, Natural Bridge, north coast.

**1992, Nov. 30**     *Litho.*     *Perf. 14x13*
86 A28 70c multicolored     1.50 1.00
87 A28 80c multicolored     1.75 1.00

Express Mail Service — A29

**1993, Jan. 29**     *Litho.*     *Perf. 13x14*
88 A29 200c multicolored     4.50 3.25

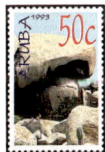

A30

Various rock formations found in Districts of Ayo and Casibari.

**1993, Mar. 31**     *Litho.*     *Perf. 13x14*
89 A30 50c multicolored     1.00 1.00
90 A30 60c multicolored     1.25 1.00
91 A30 100c multicolored     2.00 1.75
    Nos. 89-91 (3)     4.25 3.75

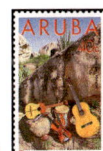

Folklore — A31

40c, String instruments, drum. 70c, Traditional music & games. 80c, Dera Gai song lyrics.

**1993, May 28**     *Litho.*     *Perf. 13x14*
92 A31 40c multicolored     1.20 1.00
93 A31 70c multicolored     1.30 1.00
94 A31 80c multicolored     1.50 1.50
    Nos. 92-94 (3)     4.00 3.50

Sailing Sports — A32

**1993, July 30**     *Litho.*     *Perf. 13x14*
95 A32 50c Sailboating     1.15 1.00
96 A32 65c Land sailing     1.35 1.00
97 A32 75c Wind surfing     1.50 1.25
    Nos. 95-97 (3)     4.00 3.25

Iguana — A33

*Perf. 14x13, 13x14*
**1993, Sept. 1**     *Litho.*
98 A33 35c Young     1.50 1.00
99 A33 60c Almost grown     1.65 1.25
100 A33 100c Mature, vert.     2.25 2.00
    Nos. 98-100 (3)     5.40 4.25

Burrowing Owl — A34

5c, Two adults. 10c, Two adults, young. 35c, Adult with prey, vert. 40c, Adult, vert.

*Perf. 14x13, 13x14*
**1994, Jan. 28**     *Litho.*
101 A34 5c multicolored     1.75 .50
102 A34 10c multicolored     1.75 .75
103 A34 35c multicolored     2.25 1.00
104 A34 40c multicolored     2.25 1.50
    Nos. 101-104 (4)     8.00 3.75

World Wildlife Fund.

A35

Intl. Olympic Committee, Cent.: 90c, Baron Pierre de Coubertin (1863-1937), founder of modern Olympics.

**1994, Mar. 29**     *Litho.*     *Perf. 13x14*
105 A35 50c multicolored     1.25 1.00
106 A35 90c multicolored     1.75 1.40

A36

150c, Mascot, soccer ball.

**1994, July 7**     *Litho.*     *Perf. 13x14*
107 A36 65c shown     1.50 1.25
108 A36 150c multicolored     3.00 2.50

1994 World Cup Soccer Championships, US.

Wild Fruit — A37

Designs: 40c, Malpighia punicifolia. 70c, Cordia sebestena. 85c, Pithecellobium unguis-cati. 150c, Coccoloba uvifera.

**1994, Sept. 28**     *Litho.*     *Perf. 13x14*
109 A37 40c multicolored     1.10 1.00
110 A37 70c multicolored     1.50 1.00
111 A37 85c multicolored     1.00 1.50
112 A37 150c multicolored     3.25 2.50
    Nos. 109-112 (4)     7.75 6.00

Architectural Landmarks — A38

Designs: 35c, Government building, 1888. 60c, Ecury residence, 1929, vert. 100c, Protestant Church, 1846, vert.

**1995, Jan. 27**     *Litho.*     *Perf. 14x13*
113 A38 35c multicolored     .90 .80
    *Perf. 13x14*
114 A38 60c multicolored     1.50 1.00
115 A38 100c multicolored     2.10 1.90
    Nos. 113-115 (3)     4.50 3.70

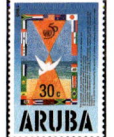

UN, 50th Anniv. — A39

Designs: 30c, Flags, sea, UN emblem, dove, text from UN charter. 200c, World with flags, doves, UN emblem.

**1995, Mar. 29 Litho. *Perf. 13x14***

**116** A39 30c multicolored 1.25 .75
**117** A39 200c multicolored 3.75 3.25

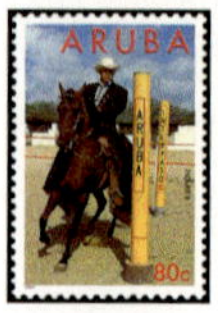


Interpaso Horses — A40

Designs: 25c, 10-time champion Casanova II, ribbons, horiz. 75c, Paso Fino, horiz. 80c, Horse doing figure 8. 90c, Girl on horse.

**1995, May 26 *Perf. 14x13, 13x14***

**118** A40 25c multicolored .90 .50
**119** A40 75c multicolored 1.60 1.25
**120** A40 80c multicolored 1.60 1.50
**121** A40 90c multicolored 1.90 1.50
*Nos. 118-121 (4)* 6.00 4.75

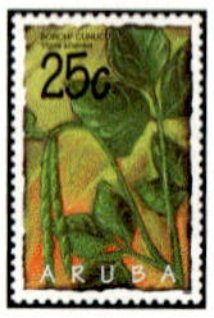


Vegetables — A41

25c, Vigna sinensis. 50c, Cucumis anguria. 70c, Hibiscus esculentus. 85c, Cucurbita moschata.

**1995, July 28 Litho. *Perf. 13x14***

**122** A41 25c multicolored .85 .50
**123** A41 50c multicolored 1.40 1.00
**124** A41 70c multicolored 1.50 1.25
**125** A41 85c multicolored 1.75 1.50
*Nos. 122-125 (4)* 5.50 4.25

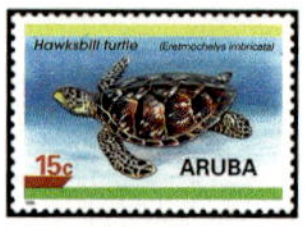


Turtles — A42

**1995, Sept. 27 Litho. *Perf. 14x13***

**126** A42 15c Hawksbill 1.75 .55
**127** A42 50c Green 2.25 1.00
**128** A42 95c Loggerhead 2.40 1.50
**129** A42 100c Leatherback 2.75 1.50
*Nos. 126-129 (4)* 9.15 4.55

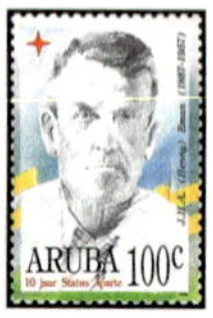


Separate Status, 10th Anniv. — A43

Statesmen and politicians: No. 130, Jan Hendrik Albert Eman (1887-1957). No. 131, Juan Enrique Irausquin (1904-62). No. 132, Cornelis Albert Eman (1916-67). No. 133, Gilberto Francois Croes (1938-86).

**1996, Jan. 1 Litho. *Perf. 13x14***

**130** A43 100c multicolored 1.90 1.50
**131** A43 100c multicolored 1.90 1.50
**132** A43 100c multicolored 1.90 1.50
**133** A43 100c multicolored 1.90 1.50
*Nos. 130-133 (4)* 7.60 6.00

The 1986 date on No. 133 is in error.

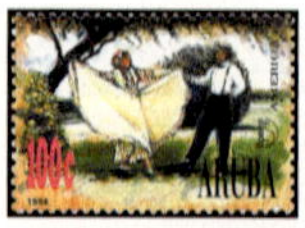


America Issue — A44

National dresswear: 65c, Woman wearing long, full dress, apron, vert. 70c, Man wearing hat, bow tie, white shirt, black pants, vert. 100c, Couple dancing.

***Perf. 13x14, 14x13***

**1996, Mar. 25 Litho.**

**134** A44 65c multicolored 2.25 1.00
**135** A44 70c multicolored 2.25 1.00
**136** A44 100c multicolored 3.00 1.50
*Nos. 134-136 (3)* 7.50 3.50

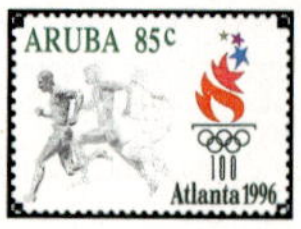


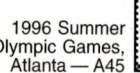

1996 Summer Olympic Games, Atlanta — A45

**1996, May 28 Litho. *Perf. 14x13***

**137** A45 85c Runners 2.00 1.25
**138** A45 130c Cyclist 2.50 2.25

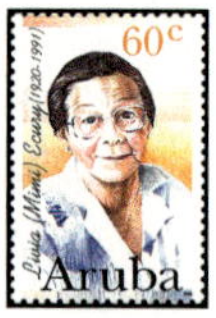


A46

Famous Women: No. 139, Livia (Mimi) Ecury (1920-91), nurse. No. 140, Lolita Euson (1914-94), poet. No. 141, Laura Wernet-Paskel (1911-62), teacher.

**1996, Sept. 27 Litho. *Perf. 13x14***

**139** A46 60c multicolored 1.50 1.50
**140** A46 60c multicolored 1.50 1.50
**141** A46 60c multicolored 1.50 1.50
*Nos. 139-141 (3)* 4.50 4.50

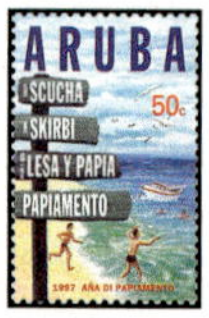


A47

Year of Papiamento 1997: 50c, Sign promoting use of Papiamento language, children playing on beach, people in water, boat. 140c, "Papiamento," sunrise.

**1997, Jan. 23 Litho. *Perf. 13x14***

**142** A47 50c multicolored 1.00 1.00
**143** A47 140c multicolored 2.50 2.50

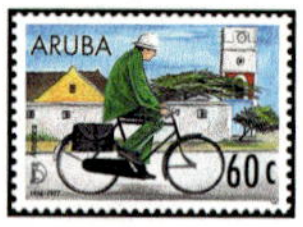


Mailman on Bicycle, 1936-57 — A48

America issue: 70c, Mailman handing mail to woman, jeep, 1957-88. 80c, Mailman on motor scooter placing mail in mailbox, 1995.

**1997, Mar. 27 Litho. *Perf. 14x13***

**144** A48 60c multicolored 2.75 1.50
**145** A48 70c multicolored 2.75 1.50
**146** A48 80c multicolored 2.75 1.50
*Nos. 144-146 (3)* 8.25 4.50

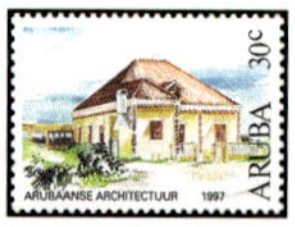


Aruban Architectrue — A49

30c, Decorated cunucu house. 65c, Steps with "popchi's." 100c, Arends's Building, vert.

**1997, May 22 Litho. *Perf. 14x13***

**147** A49 30c multicolored .90 .75
**148** A49 65c multicolored 1.75 1.25

***Perf. 13x14***

**149** A49 100c multicolored 2.00 1.75
*Nos. 147-149 (3)* 4.65 3.75

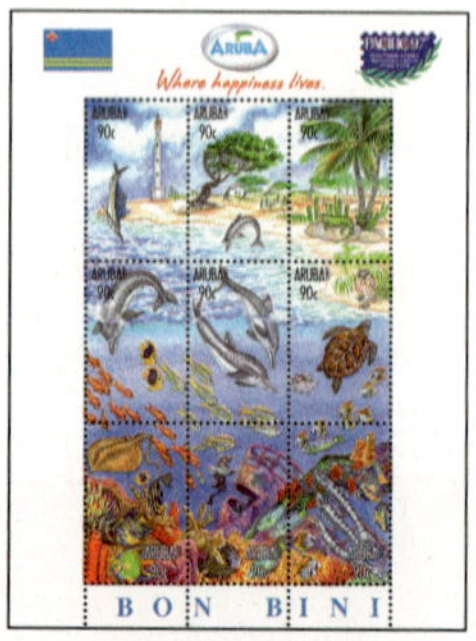


Marine Life — A50

Designs: a, Marlin jumping out of water, lighthouse. b, Dolphin jumping out of water, trees, plants on beach. c, Iguana on rock, beach. d, Dolphin, fish. e, Two dolphins, fish. f, Fish, turtles, owl on beach. g, Various fish among coral. h, Diver, shipwreck, fish, coral. i, Various fish.

**1997, May 29 Litho. *Perf. 12½x13***

**150** A50 90c Sheet of 9, #a.-i. 27.50 27.50

PACIFIC 97.

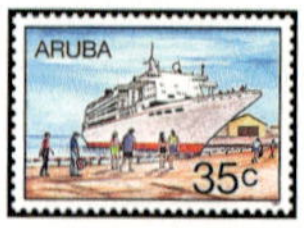


Cruise Tourism — A51

Designs: 35c, Ship at pier, tourists walking toward ship. 50c, Ship with gangway lowered, tourists. 150c, Ship out to sea, small boat.

**1997, July 24 Litho. *Perf. 14x13***

**151** A51 35c multicolored 1.25 .85
**152** A51 50c multicolored 1.50 1.10
**153** A51 150c multicolored 3.00 2.50
*Nos. 151-153 (3)* 5.75 4.45

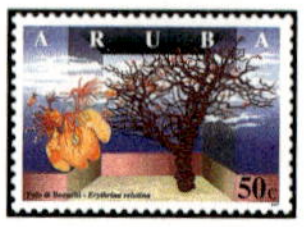


Aruban Wild Flowers — A52

50c, Erythrina velutina. 60c, Cordia dentata. 70c, Tabebuia billbergii. 130c, Guaiacum officinale.

**1997, Sept. 25**

**154** A52 50c multicolored 1.50 1.00
**155** A52 60c multicolored 1.75 1.25
**156** A52 70c multicolored 2.00 1.25
**157** A52 130c multicolored 2.75 2.00
*Nos. 154-157 (4)* 8.00 5.50

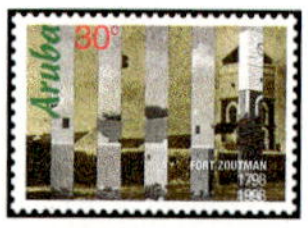


Fort Zoutman, Bicent. — A53

**1998, Jan. 13 Litho. *Perf. 14x13***

**158** A53 30c sepia & multi 1.00 .75
**159** A53 250c gray & multi 4.25 3.75

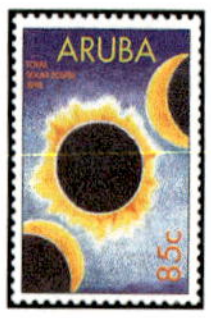


Total Solar Eclipse, 1998 — A54

100c, Map, track of eclipse.

**1998, Feb. 26 Litho. *Perf. 13x14***

**160** A54 85c shown 2.25 1.50
**161** A54 100c multicolored 2.75 1.60

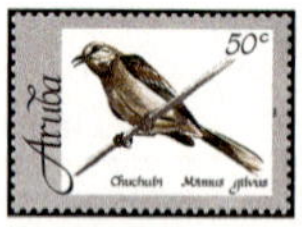


Native Birds — A55

50c, Mimus gilvus. 60c, Falco sparverius. 70c, Icterus icterus. 150c, Coereba flaveola.

***Perf. 14x13, 13x14***

**1998, July 10 Litho.**

**162** A55 50c multi 1.80 1.00
**163** A55 60c multi, vert. 2.00 1.25
**164** A55 70c multi, vert. 2.25 1.25
**165** A55 150c multi 3.25 2.75
*Nos. 162-165 (4)* 9.30 6.25

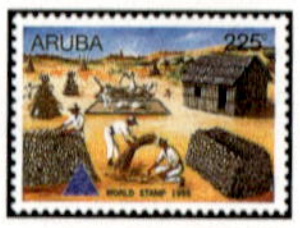


World Stamp 1998 — A56

**1998, Sept. 8 Litho. *Perf. 14x13***

**166** A56 225c multicolored 5.50 4.25

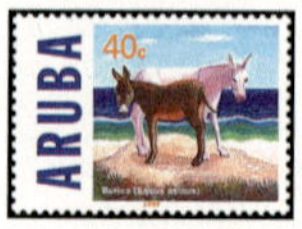


Endangered Animals — A57

Equus asinus: 40c, Two standing on hill. 65c, Three standing, rocks, cacti, tree. 100c, Adult, foal standing among rocks, cacti.

**1999, June 21 Litho. *Perf. 14x13***

**167** A57 40c multicolored 1.40 .75
**168** A57 65c multicolored 1.60 1.25
**169** A57 100c multicolored 2.40 2.00
*Nos. 167-169 (3)* 5.40 4.00

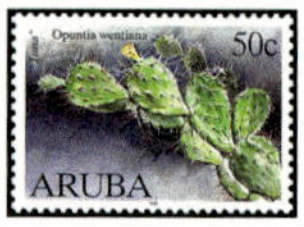


Cacti — A58

Designs: 50c, Opuntia wentiana. 60c, Lemaireocereus griseus. 70c, Cephalocereus lanuginosus. 75c, Cephalocereus lanuginosus (in bloom).

**1999, Mar. 31 Litho. *Perf. 14x13***

**170** A58 50c multicolored 1.50 1.00
**171** A58 60c multicolored 1.75 1.25
**172** A58 70c multicolored 1.75 1.25
**173** A58 75c multicolored 2.00 1.50
*Nos. 170-173 (4)* 7.00 5.00

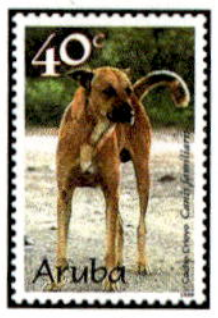


Dogs — A59

Various dogs, background: 40c, Trees. 60c, Cactus, aloe plant, rocks. 80c, Tree, sea. 165c, Sky, clouds.

**1999, May 31 Litho. *Perf. 13x14***

**174** A59 40c multicolored 1.50 1.00
**175** A59 60c multicolored 1.75 1.25
**176** A59 80c multicolored 2.00 1.50
**177** A59 165c multicolored 3.25 2.75
*Nos. 174-177 (4)* 8.50 6.50

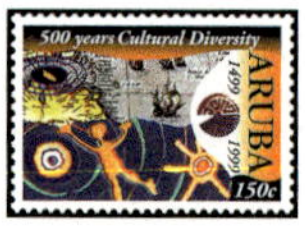


Discovery of Aruba, 500th Anniv. — A60

**1999, Aug. 9 Litho. *Perf. 14x13***

**178** A60 150c shown 2.75 2.25
**179** A60 175c Abstract paintings 3.25 2.75
 a. Souvenir sheet, #178-179 7.00 6.00

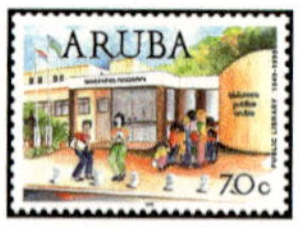


Natl. Library, 50th Anniv. — A61

**1999, Aug. 20**

**180** A61 70c shown 1.50 1.50
**181** A61 100c Original building 2.25 2.00

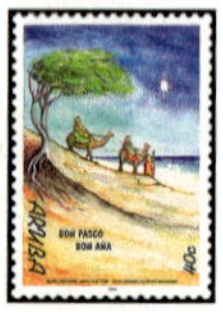


Christmas — A62

**Coil Stamps**

***Die Cut Perf. 13x13½***

**1999, Dec. 1 Self-Adhesive Litho.**

**182** A62 40c Magi on shore 1.80 1.00
**183** A62 70c Magi in desert 2.25 1.25
**184** A62 100c Holy Family 2.75 1.75
*Nos. 182-184 (3)* 6.80 4.00

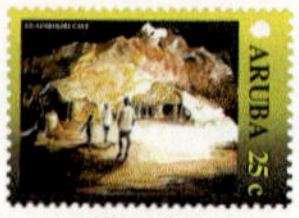


Tourist Attractions A62a

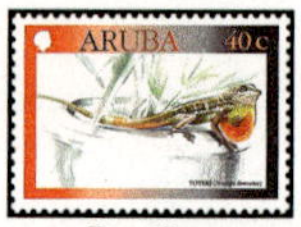


Reptiles A63

Tourist Attractions: 25c, Guadirikiri Cave. 55c, Cactus landscape. 85c, Hooiberg. 50c, Conchi. Reptiles: 40c, Norops lineatus. 60c, Iguana iguana, vert. 75c, Leptodeira annulata, vert. 150c, Cnemidophorus murinus.

**2000 Litho.** ***Perf. 14x13, 13x14***

| | | | | |
|---|---|---|---|---|
| **185** | A62a | 25c multi | 1.00 | .50 |
| **186** | A63 | 40c multi | 1.25 | .75 |
| **187** | A62a | 55c multi | 1.40 | 1.00 |
| **188** | A63 | 60c multi | 1.40 | 1.25 |
| **189** | A63 | 75c multi | 1.60 | 1.25 |
| **190** | A62a | 85c multi | 1.75 | 1.50 |
| **191** | A63 | 150c multi | 3.25 | 2.25 |
| **192** | A62a | 500c multi | 8.50 | 7.25 |
| | | *Nos. 185-192 (8)* | 20.15 | 15.75 |

Issued: 40c, 60c, 75c, 150c, 1/31; 25c, 55c, 85c, 500c, 6/5.

See Nos. 197-204.

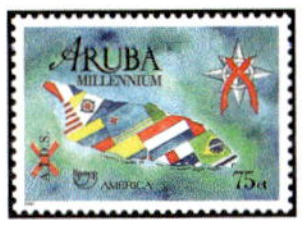
America Issue, Campaign Against AIDS — A64

175c, Ribbon on globe, vert.

***Perf. 14x13, 13x14***

**2000, Mar. 2 Litho.**

| | | | | |
|---|---|---|---|---|
| **193** | A64 | 75c Flags | 2.00 | 2.00 |
| **194** | A64 | 175c multicolored | 4.00 | 4.00 |

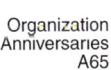

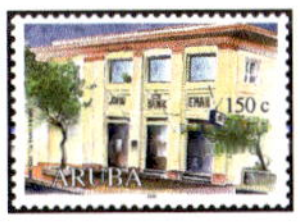
Organization Anniversaries A65

Designs: 150c, Aruba Bank N.V., 75th anniv. 165c, Alto Vista Church, 250th anniv.

**2000, Apr. 20 Litho.** ***Perf. 14x13***

| | | | | |
|---|---|---|---|---|
| **195** | A65 | 150c multi | 3.00 | 2.50 |
| **196** | A65 | 165c multi | 3.25 | 2.75 |

**Type of 2000**

Animals: 5c, Cat. 15c, Shells. 30c, Tortoise. 35c, Mud house, vert. 50c, Rabbit. 100c, Balashi gold smelter, vert. 200c, Parakeet. 250c, Rock crystals.

***Perf. 14x13, 13x14 (#200, 202)***

**2001 Litho.**

| | | | | |
|---|---|---|---|---|
| **197** | A63 | 5c multi | 1.10 | .50 |
| **198** | A62a | 15c multi | .50 | .40 |
| **199** | A63 | 30c multi | 1.75 | 1.00 |
| **200** | A62a | 35c multi | 1.00 | .95 |
| **201** | A63 | 50c multi | 1.75 | 1.00 |
| **202** | A62a | 100c multi | 2.50 | 2.10 |
| **203** | A63 | 200c multi | 4.50 | 4.00 |
| **204** | A62a | 250c multi | 5.25 | 4.75 |
| | | *Nos. 197-204 (8)* | 18.35 | 14.70 |

Issued: 5c, 30c, 50c, 200c, 1/31. 15c, 35c, 100c, 250c, 8/6.

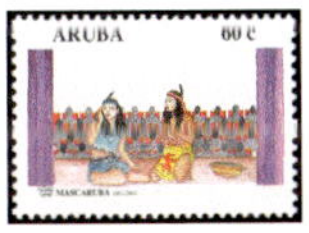
Mascaruba, 40th Anniv. — A66

Actors on stage and audience in: 60c: Background. 150c, Foreground.

**2001, Mar. 26 Litho.** ***Perf. 14x13***

**205-206** A66 Set of 2 4.50 4.00

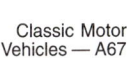

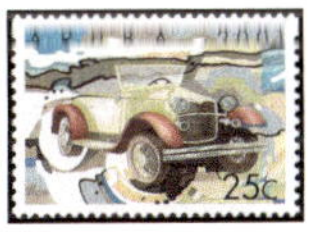
Classic Motor Vehicles — A67

Designs: 25c, 1930 Ford Crown Victoria Leatherback. 40c, 1933 Citroen Commerciale. 70c, 1948 Plymouth pickup truck. 75c, 1959 Ford Edsel.

**2001, May 31**

**207-210** A67 Set of 4 8.00 5.75

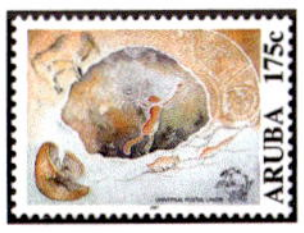
Year of Dialogue Among Civilizations — A68

**2001, Oct. 9 Litho.** ***Perf. 14x13***

**211** A68 175c multi 4.00 3.25

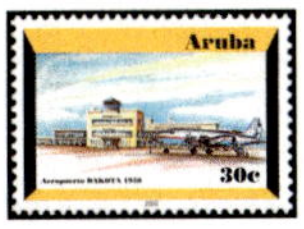
Airport Views — A69

Designs: 30c, Dakota Airport, 1950. 75c, Queen Beatrix Airport, 1972. 175c, Queen Beatrix Airport, 2000.

**2002, Jan. 31 Litho.** ***Perf. 14x13***

**212-214** A69 Set of 3 6.25 5.00

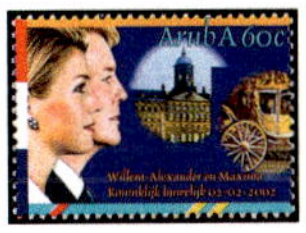
Royal Wedding — A70

Prince Willem-Alexander, Maxima Zorreguieta and: 60c, Royal palace, golden coach. 300c, Bourse of Berlage, New Church.

**2002, Feb. 2**

**215-216** A70 Set of 2 6.50 6.25

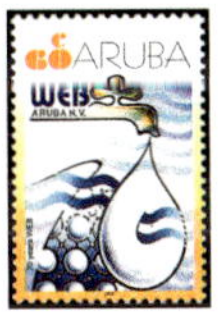
Water and Energy Company, 70th Anniv. — A71

Designs: 60c, Faucet and water drop, vert. 85c, Pipeline. 165c, Meter and meter-reading equipment, vert.

***Perf. 13x14, 14x13***

**2002, June 3 Litho.**

**217-219** A71 Set of 3 6.50 6.25

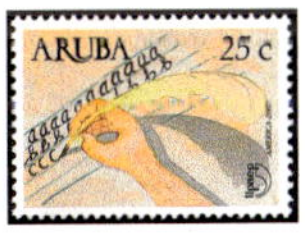
America Issue — Youth, Education and Literacy — A72

Designs: 25c, Hand writing letters with quill pen. 100c, Child looking over wall of letters.

**2002, July 15 Litho.** ***Perf. 14x12¾***

**220-221** A72 Set of 2 3.75 2.75

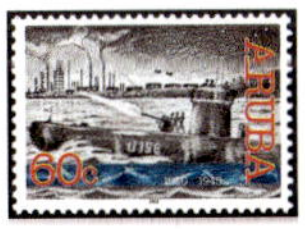
Aruba in World War II — A73

Designs: 60c, Attack on Lago Oil Refinery by German U-boat U-156. 75c, Torpedoing of ships by U-156. 150c, Statue of "Boy" Ecury, Aruban resistance fighter, Aruban militiaman, vert.

***Perf. 14x13, 13x14***

**2002, Sept. 9 Litho.**

**222-224** A73 Set of 3 8.00 5.50

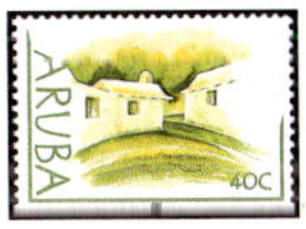
Mud Houses — A74

Various houses with frame color of: 40c, Yellow green. 60c, Blue green. 75c, Red.

**2003, Jan. 31 Litho.** ***Perf. 14x13***

**225-227** A74 Set of 3 3.75 3.00

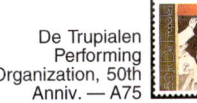

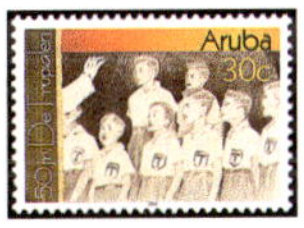
De Trupialen Performing Organization, 50th Anniv. — A75

Designs: 30c, Trupialen Boys' Choir. 50c, Play handbills. 100c, Emblems.

**2003, Mar. 31 Litho.** ***Perf. 14x13***

**228-230** A75 Set of 3 3.75 3.00

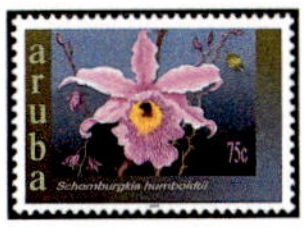
Orchids — A76

Designs: 75c, Schomburgkia humboldtii. 500c, Brassavola nodosa.

**2003, May 30 Litho.** ***Perf. 14x13***

**231-232** A76 Set of 2 11.00 11.00

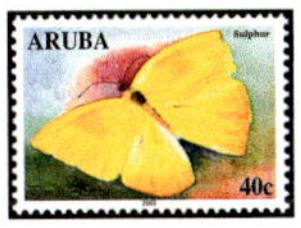
Butterflies — A77

Designs: 40c, Orange-barred sulphur. 75c, Monarch. 85c, Hairstreak. 175c, Gulf fritillary.

**2003, July 31**

**233-236** A77 Set of 4 8.75 7.00

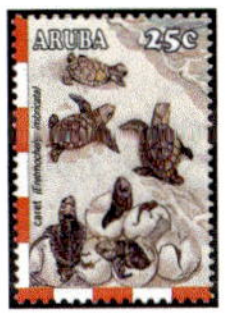
Endangered Animals — A78

Turtles: 25c, Eretmochelys imbricata, vert. 60c, Dermochelys coriacea. 75c, Chelonia mydas, vert. 150c, Caretta caretta.

***Perf. 13x14, 14x13***

**2003, Sept. 30 Litho.**

**237-240** A78 Set of 4 7.50 6.00

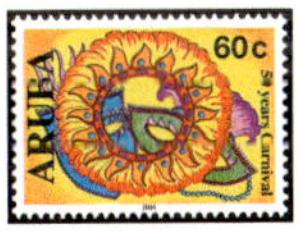
Carnival, 50th Anniv. — A79

Designs: 60c, Masks. 75c, Carnival Queen, vert. 150c, Aruba flag, Carnival participants.

***Perf. 14x13, 13x14***

**2004, Jan. 30 Litho.**

**241-243** A79 Set of 3 4.50 4.50

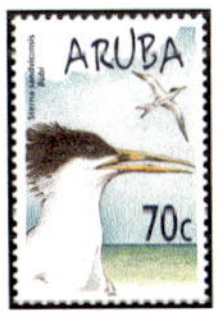
Birds — A80

Designs: 70c, Sterna sandvicensis. 75c, Pelecanus occidentalis. 80c, Fregata magnificens. 90c, Larus atricilla.

**2004, Mar. 31** ***Perf. 13x14***

**244-247** A80 Set of 4 7.00 5.00

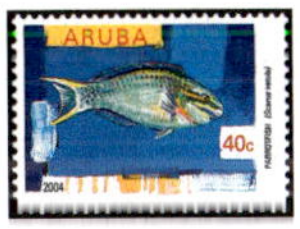
Fish — A81

Designs: 40c, Parrotfish. 60c, Queen angelfish. 75c, Squirrelfish. 100c, Smallmouth grunt.

**2004, May 31 Litho.** ***Perf. 14x13***

**248-251** A81 Set of 4 6.50 5.00

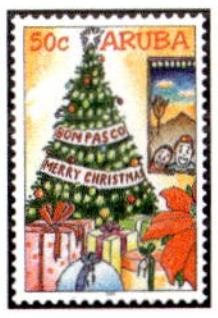
Christmas and New Year's Day — A82

Designs: 50c, Children, Christmas tree, gifts. 85c, Choir, stained glass window, candle, gifts. 125c, Fireworks display.

**2004, Dec. 1 Litho.** ***Perf. 13x14***

**252-254** A82 Set of 3 4.00 4.00

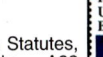

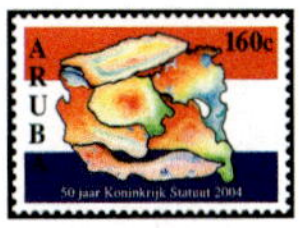
Kingdom Statutes, 50th Anniv. — A83

Designs: 160c, Collage of Netherlands Antilles islands. 165c, Kingdom Statute Monument.

**2004, Dec. 15** ***Perf. 14x13***

**255-256** A83 Set of 2 4.50 4.50

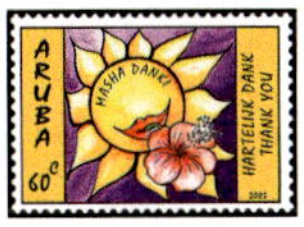
Greetings — A84

Designs: 60c, Sun, flower (Thank you). 75c, Cacti and rabbits (Love). 135c, Fish (Get well soon). 215c, Balloons and flag (Congratulations).

**2005, Jan. 31 Litho.** ***Perf. 14x13***

**257-260** A84 Set of 4 7.25 7.25

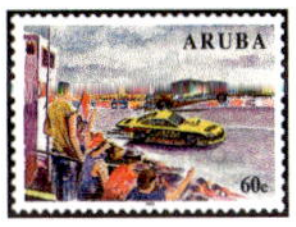
Drag Racing — A85

Drag racers: 60c, One car going airborne. 85c, One car with chute deployed. 185c, Cars at start line.

**2005, Mar. 16**

**261-263** A85 Set of 3 5.50 5.00

**Souvenir Sheet**

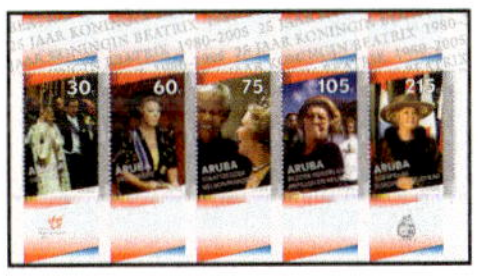
Reign of Queen Beatrix, 25th Anniv. A86

No. 264: a, 30c, At coronation, 1980. b, 60c, Making speech, 1991. c, 75c, With Nelson Mandela, 1999. d, 105c, Visiting Aruba and the Netherlands Antilles, 1999. e, 215c, Speaking before European Parliament, 2004.

**2005, Apr. 30 Litho.** ***Perf. 13¼x13¾***

**264** A86 Sheet of 5, #a-e 7.50 7.50

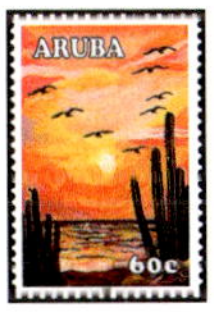
Sunsets — A87

Designs: 60c, Birds and cacti. 100c, Palm tree. 205c, Pelicans and pilings.

**2005, May 31** ***Perf. 13x14***

**265-267** A87 Set of 3 5.75 5.75

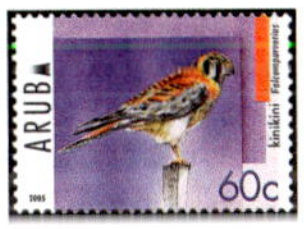
Birds of Prey — A88

Designs: 60c, Falco sparverius. 75c, Athene cunicularia. 135c, Pandion haliaetus. 200c, Polyborus plancus.

**2005, July 29 Litho.** ***Perf. 14x13***

**268-271** A88 Set of 4 8.75 8.75

*271a* Souvenir sheet, #268-271 8.75 8.75

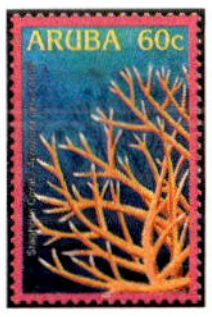
A89

# ARUBA

Corals: 60c, Staghorn coral. 75c, Blade fire coral. 100c, Deepwater sea fan. 215c, Smooth brain coral.

| 2005, Sept. 30 | Litho. | Perf. 13x14 |
|---|---|---|
| 272-275 A89 | Set of 4 | 7.00 7.00 |

A90

Children and philately: 75c, Girl, stamps. 85c, Boy with magnifying glass and stamp album. 125c, Boy with tongs and stock book.

| 2005, Oct. 31 | | |
|---|---|---|
| 276-278 A90 | Set of 3 | 4.75 4.75 |

Paintings — A91

Designs: 60c, House at Savaneta, by Jean Georges Pandellis. 75c, Haf di Rei, by Mateo Hayde. 185c, Landscape, by Julie Q. Oduber.

| 2006, Feb. 6 | Litho. | Perf. 14x13 |
|---|---|---|
| 279-281 A91 | Set of 3 | 5.50 5.50 |

Aruba YMCA, 50th Anniv. — A92

Designs: 75c, YMCA emblem. 205c, Children in playground, horiz.

Perf. 13x14, 14x13

| 2006, Apr. 3 | | Litho. |
|---|---|---|
| 282-283 A92 | Set of 2 | 4.50 4.50 |

Souvenir Sheet

Washington 2006 World Philatelic Exhibition — A93

No. 284 — Exhibition emblem and: a, Natural Bridge, head of iguana, tree and cactus. b, Cacti, tail of iguana, sailboat, vert.

| 2006, May 27 | Litho. | Perf. 12¾ |
|---|---|---|
| 284 A93 | 500c Sheet of 2, #a-b | 13.50 13.50 |

2006 World Cup Soccer Championships, Germany — A94

Designs: 75c, Children's drawing of goalie. 215c, Goalie's gloves and ball.

| 2006, June 5 | Litho. | Perf. 14x13 |
|---|---|---|
| 285-286 A94 | Set of 2 | 4.50 4.50 |

Hi-Winds Windsurfing Regatta, 20th Anniv. — A95

Designs: 60c, Hotel, windsurfers, kitesurfer, and fishing boats. 100c, Kitesurfers, windsurfer and flag in water. 125c, Windsurfers.

| 2006, July 3 | Litho. | Perf. 14x13 |
|---|---|---|
| 287-289 A95 | Set of 3 | 4.00 4.00 |

Fire Prevention — A96

Designs: 60c, Fire prevention, safety and extinguishing strategies. 100c, Firemen at house fire. 205c, Fire trucks.

| 2006, Sept. 29 | Litho. | Perf. 14x13 |
|---|---|---|
| 290-292 A96 | Set of 3 | 5.75 5.75 |

Arikok National Park — A97

Designs: 75c, Cas di Torto, goat and garden, Cunucu Arikok. 100c, View of Miralamar, vert. 200c, Dunes of Boca Prins.

| 2006, Oct. 31 | Litho. | Perf. 14x13 |
|---|---|---|
| 293-295 A97 | Set of 3 | 5.25 5.25 |

Souvenir Sheet

New Year 2007 (Year of the Pig) A98

No. 296: a, 205c, Pig. b, 215c, Dragon, vert.

| 2007, Feb. 15 | Litho. | Perf. 12¾ |
|---|---|---|
| 296 A98 | Sheet of 2, #a-b | 6.50 6.50 |

Casa Cuna Children's Home Foundation, 50th Anniv. — A99

Designs: 50c, Original Casa Cuna building, Luciana Maria Koolman. 125c, Children in hands. 150c, New Casa Cuna building.

| 2007, Apr. 4 | | Perf. 14x13 |
|---|---|---|
| 297-299 A99 | Set of 3 | 4.50 4.50 |

Museums in Oranjestad — A100

Designs: 70c, Museum of Antiquities. 85c, Numismatic Museum. 100c, Archaeological Museum. 135c, Historical Museum.

| 2007, July 2 | Litho. | Perf. 14x13 |
|---|---|---|
| 300-303 A100 | Set of 4 | 5.00 5.00 |

Souvenir Sheet

Wrecks and Reefs A101

No. 304: a, 200c, Pipeline system of wrecked oil tanker Pedernalis. b, 300c, Convair 400 airplane near Sonesta Island. c, 500c, Sea turtle, wreck of freighter Jane. d, 500c, Fish, wreck of freighter Antilla.

| 2007, Sept. 3 | Litho. | Perf. 14x13 |
|---|---|---|
| 304 A101 | Sheet of 4, #a-d | 17.00 17.00 |

Christmas and New Year's Day — A102

Designs: 70c, Infant and mother. 100c, Girl with toys and gift box. 150c, Boy at New Year's celebration.

| 2007, Oct. 17 | | |
|---|---|---|
| 305-307 A102 | Set of 3 | 4.00 4.00 |

Heineken Aruba Catamaran Regatta — A103

Designs: 40c, Catamarans on beach. 80c, Catamarans racing near race buoy. 125c, Competitor leaning off side of catamaran. 130c, Row of catamarans in race.

| 2007, Nov. 8 | | |
|---|---|---|
| 308-311 A103 | Set of 4 | 4.75 4.75 |

Alto Vista Church — A103a

| 2007-09 | Litho. | Perf. 14x13 |
|---|---|---|

Frame Color

| 311A | A103a | 5c pink | 1.00 | 1.00 |
| 311B | A103a | 10c blue | 1.00 | 1.00 |
| 311C | A103a | 25c lt bl grn | 1.00 | 1.00 |
| 311D | A103a | 50c yel green | 1.00 | 1.00 |
| 311E | A103a | 85c green | 1.00 | 1.00 |
| 311F | A103a | 90c lt grnsh bl | 1.00 | 1.00 |
| 311G | A103a | 100c salmon | 1.00 | 1.00 |
| 311H | A103a | 125c violet | 1.50 | 1.50 |
| 311I | A103a | 130c lt blue | 1.50 | 1.50 |
| 311J | A103a | 135c beige | 1.50 | 1.50 |
| 311K | A103a | 140c violet | 1.50 | 1.50 |
| 311L | A103a | 200c dull org | 2.00 | 2.00 |
| 311M | A103a | 215c gray | 2.50 | 2.50 |
| 311N | A103a | 220c gray | 2.50 | 2.50 |
| | | Nos. 311A-311N (14) | 17.45 | 17.45 |

Issued: 5c, 50c, 85c, 100c, 200c, 7/30/07; 135c, 9/3/08; 90c, 130c, 140c, 220c, 3/9/09. Others, 2007.

Most sets between Nos. 312-465 were printed in sheets containing two sets separated by a row of pictorial tabs. Sets with these tabs command a small premium.

Queen Beatrix, 70th Birthday — A104

Queen Beatrix: 75c, As one-year old with Dutch dignitaries. 125c, With Prince Claus and newborn Crown Prince Willem Alexander. 250c, In royal robes on day of accession to throne. 300c, With family of Crown Prince Willem Alexander.

| 2008, Jan. 31 | | Perf. 13x14 |
|---|---|---|
| 312-315 A104 | Set of 4 | 9.00 9.00 |

Aruban Cultural Year — A105

Designs: 80c, Carnival participants. 130c, Organ grinders. 205c, Dera Gai celebration. 275c, Dande musicians visiting home.

| 2008, Mar. 18 | Litho. | Perf. 14x13 |
|---|---|---|
| 316-319 A105 | Set of 4 | 7.50 7.50 |

2008 Summer Olympics, Beijing — A106

Designs: 50c, Running. 75c, Synchronized swimming. 100c, Men's rings, vert. 125c, Judo.

| 2008, Apr. 1 | Perf. 14x13, 13x14 |
|---|---|
| 320-323 A106 | Set of 4 | 4.75 4.75 |

Athene Cunicularia Arubensis — A107

Aruban burrowing owl: 100c, Entire bird. 150c, Two birds, horiz. 350c, Head of bird.

Perf. 13x14, 14x13

| 2008, June 2 | | Litho. |
|---|---|---|
| 324-326 A107 | Set of 3 | 7.50 7.50 |

Harley-Davidson Motorcycles A108

Designs: 175c, FRX Super Glide Big Boy. 225c, Knucklehead. 305c, Roadking.

| 2008, July 4 | Litho. | Perf. 14x13 |
|---|---|---|
| 327-329 A108 | Set of 3 | 8.00 8.00 |

Aruban Culture — A109

Designs: No. 330, Poem by Federico Oduber. No. 331, 240c, Watapana Magazine covers, vert. No. 332, Henry Habibe and poem by Habibe, vert.

| 2008, July 8 | Litho. | Perf. 13¾ |
|---|---|---|
| 330 A109 | 240c multi | 6.75 6.75 |
| 331 A109 | 240c multi | 6.75 6.75 |
| 332 A109 | 240c multi | 6.75 6.75 |
| a. | Souvenir sheet of 5, #330-332, Netherlands #1311, Netherlands Antilles #1187, + etiquette | 23.00 23.00 |
| | Nos. 330-332 (3) | 20.25 20.25 |

No. 332a sold for 10g. No. 330 also was available on Netherlands Nos. 1313a and 1313b and Netherlands Antilles No. 1189a.

Flowers A110

No. 333: a, 100c, Calatropis procera. b, 215c, Passiflora foetida.
No. 334: a, 185c, Thespesia populnea. b, 200c, Cryptostegia grandiflora.

| 2008, Aug. 8 | Litho. | Perf. 13½ |
|---|---|---|
| 333 A110 | Pair, #a-b | 3.50 3.50 |
| 334 A110 | Pair, #a-b | 4.50 4.50 |

Drawings by Rembrandt (1606-69) — A111

Designs: 350c, Self-portrait, 1652. 425c, Self-portrait, 1630. 500c, Beggars at door, 1648.

| 2008, Sept. 30 | Litho. | Perf. 13x14 |
|---|---|---|
| 335-337 A111 | Set of 3 | 14.00 14.00 |

Aruba in the Past — A112

# ARUBA

Designs: 100c, Carting of potable water. 200c, Clay houses. 215c, Processing of aloe resin.

| 2008, Nov. 3 | Litho. | Perf. 14x13 |
|---|---|---|
| 338-340 A112 | Set of 3 | 5.75 5.75 |

Louis Braille (1809-52), Educator of the Blind — A113

Designs: 200c, Braille. 215c, Walking stick for the blind.

| 2009, Jan. 5 | Litho. | Perf. 13x14 |
|---|---|---|
| 341-342 A113 | Set of 2 | 5.50 5.50 |

### Miniature Sheet

Carnival, 55th Anniv. A114

No. 343: a, 75c, Miss Carnival on float. b, 100c, Clown on float. c, 175c, Float with "55" and champagne bottle. d, 225c, Carnival dancers.

| 2009, Feb. 6 | Litho. | Perf. 13¼x13¾ |
|---|---|---|
| 343 A114 | Sheet of 4, #a-d | 8.50 8.50 |

Caves — A115

Designs: 175c, Tunnel of Love Cave. 200c, Fountain Cave. 225c, Guadirikiri Cave.

| 2009, Apr. 1 | | Perf. 14x13 |
|---|---|---|
| 344-346 A115 | Set of 3 | 6.75 6.75 |

### Souvenir Sheet

Global Warming A116

No. 347: a, 200c, Hurricane over map of Caribbean. b, 250c, Map of polar regions, mountains, parched earth. c, 250c, Pollution from industry and vehicles. d, 300c, Fluorescent light bulb, recycling symbols, windmill.

| 2009, June 2 | | |
|---|---|---|
| 347 A116 | Sheet of 4, #a-d | 12.00 12.00 |

### Souvenir Sheet

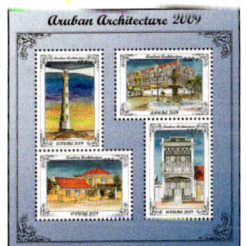

Architecture — A117

No. 348: a, 175c, California Lighthouse. b, 250c, Plaza Daniel Leo, horiz. c, 275c, Henriquez Building, horiz. d, 325c, Ecury Complex main building.

| 2009, July 3 | | Perf. 12¾ |
|---|---|---|
| 348 A117 | Sheet of 4, #a-d | 11.50 11.50 |

National Library, 60th Anniv. — A118

Book reader: 185c, Girl. 300c, Woman.

| 2009, Aug. 20 | Litho. | Perf. 13x14 |
|---|---|---|
| 349-350 A118 | Set of 2 | 5.75 5.75 |
| 350a | Vert. pair, #349-350 | 5.75 5.75 |

Dolphins — A119

Designs: 125c, Stenella frontalis. 200c, Steno bredanensis. 300c, Two Stenella frontalis. 325c, Group of Steno bredanensis at surface.

| 2009, Sept. 30 | | Perf. 14x13 |
|---|---|---|
| 351-354 A119 | Set of 4 | 14.00 14.00 |

Christmas — A120

Designs: 75c Madonna and Child. 120c, Angel and stars. 125c, Hands, globe, stars, "2009." 210c, Shepherds and sheep.

| 2009, Oct. 19 | | |
|---|---|---|
| 355-358 A120 | Set of 4 | 6.00 6.00 |

### Miniature Sheet

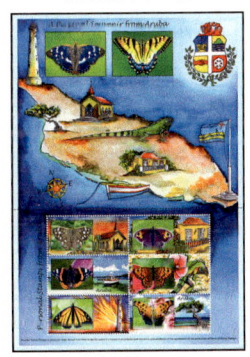

Personalized Stamps — A120a

No. 358A: b, Church. c, House. d, Boat. e, Lizard and flower. f, Lighthouse. g, Tree.

| 2009, Dec. 18 | Litho. | Perf. 13¼x14 |
|---|---|---|
| 358A A120a (295c) | Sheet of 6, #b-g | 22.00 22.00 |

No. 358A sold for 1770c or $20 in U.S. currency. Stamps could be personalized. Butterfly images shown are generic.

Recycling — A121

Various works of art from recycled materials: 90c, Island landscape. 180c, Post office, tree, and animal. 325c, Fish.

| 2010, Jan. 22 | Litho. | Perf. 13¼ |
|---|---|---|
| 359-361 A121 | Set of 3 | 6.75 6.75 |

Historic Airplanes A122

No. 362: a, 250c, Seaplane. b, 500c, Seaplane and lighthouse.

| 2010, Mar. 26 | | Perf. 13¼x13 |
|---|---|---|
| 362 A122 | Horiz. pair, #a-b | 8.50 8.50 |

Scouting in Aruba, 10th Anniv. A123

No. 363: a, 85c, Scouts observing nature. b, 95c, Scouts building fire. c, 135c, Scout near tent. d, 180c, Scouts playing drums.

| 2010, Apr. 1 | | Litho. |
|---|---|---|
| 363 A123 | Block of 4, #a-d | 6.50 6.50 |

End of World War II, 65th Anniv. — A124

No. 364: a, 140c, Large cannon. b, 200c, Beached torpedo. 275c, Equipment and ramp.

| 2010, May 4 | Litho. | Perf. 13¼x13 |
|---|---|---|
| 364 A124 | Vert. strip of 3, #a-c | 7.50 7.50 |

Parrots A125

No. 365 — Various parrots: a, 85c. b, 90c. c, 180c.

| 2010, June 2 | | Perf. 13x13¼ |
|---|---|---|
| 365 A125 | Horiz. strip of 3, #a-c | 5.00 5.00 |

Paintings by Vincent Van Gogh A126

No. 366: a, 200c, Self portrait with Gray Felt Hat. b, 250c, Still Life. Vase with Fifteen Sunflowers. c, 305c, Starry Night. d, 500c, Wheat Field with Crows.

| 2010, July 29 | | Perf. 13¼x13 |
|---|---|---|
| 366 A126 | Block of 4, #a-d | 15.00 15.00 |

Rum Shops — A127

No. 367: a, 100c, Escoville Rum Shop. b, 200c, Aruba Rum Shop. c, 255c, Caribbean Store.

| 2010, Sept. 13 | | |
|---|---|---|
| 367 A127 | Vert. strip of 3, #a-c | 7.50 7.50 |

Flowers — A128

No. 368: a, Caesalpinia pulcherrima. b, Dipladenia sanderi. c, Hibiscus. d, Adenium obesum. e, Bougainvillea. f, Ixora. g, Eichhornia crassipes. h, Passiflora caerulea. i, Allamanda cathartica. j, Nerium oleander.

| 2010, Sept. 29 | | Perf. 14 |
|---|---|---|
| 368 | Block of 10 | 23.00 23.00 |
| a.-j. | A128 200c Any single | 2.25 2.25 |

Houses of Worship A129

No. 369: a, 85c, Synagogue. b, 90c, Church. c, 135c, Church, diff. d, 240c, Church interior.

| 2010, Oct. 28 | | Perf. 13x13¼ |
|---|---|---|
| 369 A129 | Block of 4, #a-d | 6.75 6.75 |

Birds — A130

No. 370: a, Falco sparverius. b, Icterus icterus. c, Mimus gilvus. d, Egretta alba. e, Aratinga pertinax. f, Pelecanus occidentalis. g, Athene cunicularia arubensis. h, Coerba flaveola. i, Polyborus plancus. j, Colibri thalassinus.

| 2010, Nov. 17 | Litho. | Perf. 14 |
|---|---|---|
| 370 | Block of 10 | 23.00 23.00 |
| a.-j. | A130 200c Any single | 2.25 2.25 |

Briareus Caribbean Reef Octopus — A131

No. 371 — Various depictions of octopus: a, 100c. b, 175c. c, 255c. d, 300c.

| 2010, Nov. 30 | | Perf. 13¼x13 |
|---|---|---|
| 371 A131 | Block of 4, #a-d | 10.00 10.00 |

Butterflies — A132

No. 372: a, Zuleika. b, Blue morpho. c, Monarch. d, White peacock. e, Sulphur. f, Zebra. g, Malachito. h, Owl. i, Postman. j, Gulf fritillary.

| 2010, Dec. 22 | | Perf. 14 |
|---|---|---|
| 372 | Block of 10 | 23.00 23.00 |
| a.-j. | A132 200c Any single | 2.25 2.25 |

# ARUBA

Separate Political Status, 25th Anniv. A133

No. 373 — Curved lines and: a, 200c, Star. b, 300c, "Status Aparte." c, 300c, F. B. Tromp, first governor of Aruba, and J. H. A. Eman, first prime minister of Aruba, country name in white at UL. d, 400c, A. J. Booi, first president of Parliament, and G. F. Croes, political party leader, country name in red at LR.

**2011, Jan. 1**
373  A133   Block of 4, #a-d        14.00 14.00

Flowers — A134

No. 374: a, Catharanthus roseus. b, Echinopsis lageniformis. c, Allamanda cathartica. d, Cordia sebestena. e, Ipomoea pes-caprae. f, Hibiscus rosa-sinensis. g, Cassia fistula. h, Bougainvillea glabra. i, Delonix regia. j, Nerium oleander.

**2011, Feb. 16**                    **Perf. 14**
374       Block of 10               19.00 19.00
  a.-j.   A134 160c Any single       1.90  1.90

America Issue — A135

No. 375 — Hands with flags of: a, 200c, Portugal, United States, Cuba and Brazil. b, 250c, Honduras, Canada, Colombia and Chile. c, 350c, United States, Brazil, Aruba and Panama. d, 400c, Suriname, Colombia, Chile and Spain.
No. 376: a, Like No. 375a. b, Like No. 375b. c, Like No. 375c. d, Like No. 375d.

**2011, Mar. 23**
375       Vert. strip of 4          13.50 13.50
  a.  A135 200c multi                2.25  2.25
  b.  A135 250c multi                2.75  2.75
  c.  A135 350c multi                4.00  4.00
  d.  A135 400c multi                4.50  4.50

**Miniature Sheet**
376  A135 300c Sheet of 4, #a-d     13.50 13.50

Postal Union of the Americas, Spain and Portugal (UPAEP), cent.

Bank Notes — A136

No. 377: a, 1964 Indonesia 25 sen note. b, 1986 Bhutan 2 ngultrum note. c, 1949 Philippines 50 centavo note. d, 1987 Sudan 25 piastre note. e, 1976 Mozambique 100 escudo note. f, 1993 Haiti 25 gourde note. g, 1917 Göttingen 25 pfennig note. h, 1997 Turkey 250,000 lira note. i, 1977 Solomon Islands 10 dollar note. j, 1915 Lille 25 centime note. k, 1985 Egypt 25 piastre note. l, 1976 Albania 100 lek note.

**2011, Apr. 4**
377   A136   Block of 12            24.00 24.00
  a.-l.     167c Any single          2.00  2.00

Maastricht Paper Money Fair.

Peonies A137

No. 378 — Color of flowers: a, Dark red. b, Yellow. c, White. d, Pink. 350c, Pink peony.

**2011, May 11**   **Litho.**   **Perf. 14**
378  A137 110c Sheet of 4, #a-d    5.50 5.50
**Souvenir Sheet**
379  A137 350c multi               4.25 4.25

Fish — A138

No. 380: a, Holacanthus ciliaris. b, Chaetodon capistratus. c, Sparisoma viride. d, Pomacanthus paru. e, Balistes vetula. f, Lactophrys triqueter. g, Holocentrus rufus. h, Chaetodon striatus. i, Diodon holocanthus. j, Equetus punctatus.

**2011, June 15**
380       Block of 10              14.00 14.00
  a.-j.  A138 120c Any single       1.40  1.40

Chess — A139

No. 381 — Positions of chess pieces at end of 1956 match between Donald Byrne and winner Bobby Fischer: a, White queen on tan square. b, Black king on tan square. c, White knight on tan square. d, Black bishop on tan square. e, White pawn on tan square. f, Black bishop on green square. g, Black knight on tan square. h, Black rook on green square. i, White pawn on green square. j, White king on tan square. k, Black pawn on green square.

**2011, July 22**
381       Sheet of 15, #a-j, 5 #k +
          49 labels                 32.50 32.50
  a.-k.  A139 180c Any single        2.10  2.10

Mail Boxes of the World — A140

No. 382: a, Dark red rectangular pillar box. b, Orange red Estonian Post mail box. c, Yellow mail box. d, Blue USPS mail box. e, Yellow mail box inscribed "Postbriefkasten". f, Blue mail box with Cyrillic letters. g, Green pillar box with Chinese inscriptions. h, Red mail box inscribed "Brieven Drukwerken." i, Green mail box with two legs. j, Red hexagonal British pillar box.

**2011, Aug. 19**
382       Block of 10              17.50 17.50
  a.-j.  A140 150c Any single       1.75  1.75

Paintings by Jan Vermeer (1632-75) — A141

No. 383: a, Girl with a Red Hat (red frame). b, The Milkmaid (blue frame). c, The Lacemaker (brown frame). d, Girl with a Pearl Earring (red frame).

**2011, Sept. 21**  **Litho.**  **Perf. 14**
383       Vert. strip of 4         11.50 11.50
  a.    A141 200c multi             2.25  2.25
  b.-c. A141 250c Either single     2.75  2.75
  d.    A141 300c multi             3.50  3.50

Ships A142

No. 384 — Various tall ships with panel color of: a, 200c, Blue violet. b, 225c, Maroon, horiz. c, 250c, Blue violet, horiz. d, 250c, Maroon, horiz. e, 275c, Maroon, horiz. f, 300c, Blue violet.

**2011, Oct. 25**
384  A142   Block of 6, #a-f       17.50 17.50

Butterflies — A143

Designs: No. 385, 160c, Diaethria neglecta. No. 386, 160c, Lycaena cupreus lapidicola. No. 387, 160c, Pyrrhogyra edocla. No. 388, 160c, Anartia amathea amathea. No. 389, 160c, Anglais urticae. No. 390, 160c, Morpho aega. No. 391, 160c, Junonia coenia coenia (red violet background). No. 392, 160c, Junonia coenia coenia (dark purple background). No. 393, 160c, Dione juno juno. No. 394, 160c, Lycaena heteronea austin.

**2011, Dec. 1**
385-394  A143  Set of 10           18.50 18.50

Nos. 385-394 were printed in sheets containing two of each stamp + a central label.

Birds — A144

No. 395: a, Pithecophaga jeffreyi. b, Harpia harpyja. c, Morphnus guaianensis. d, Caracara plancus. e, Lophaetus occipitalis. f, Stephanoaetus coronatus. g, Haliaeetus leucocephalus. h, Vultur gryphus. i, Aquila chrysaetos. j, Falco sparverius.

**2012, Jan. 19**
395       Block of 10              17.50 17.50
  a.-j.  A144 150c Any single       1.75  1.75

Aruban Goats — A145

No. 396: a, Three goats on rocks. b, Two goats on rocks, horiz. c, Goat, horiz. d, Goat and cactus.

**2012, Feb. 21**
396       Strip of 4               11.00 11.00
  a.    A145 175c multi             2.00  2.00
  b.    A145 225c multi             2.50  2.50
  c.    A145 275c multi             3.00  3.00
  d.    A145 300c multi             3.50  3.50

2012 Summer Olympics, London A146

No. 397: a, Torch. b, Swimmer, horiz. c, Hurdler, horiz. d, "Olympia."

**2012, Apr. 27**
397  A146 500c Block of 4,
          #a-d                     22.50 22.50
  e.    Souvenir sheet of 4,
        #397a-397d                  22.50 22.50

Whales — A147

No. 398: a, Delphinapterus leucas. b, Kogia breviceps. c, Balaena mysticetus. d, Orcinus orca. e, Physeter macrocephalus. f, Balaenoptera musculus. g, Globicephala macrorhynchus. h, Mesoplodon europaeus. i, Balaenoptera edeni. j, Megaptera novaeangliae.

**2012, May 15**
398       Block of 10              14.00 14.00
  a.-j.  A147 120c Any single       1.40  1.40

Women's Dresses — A148

No. 399: a, 175c, Woman. b, 200c, Woman with Aruban flag. c, 200c, Two women dancing. d, 250c, Two women, diff.

**2012, June 21**
399   A148  Block of 4, #a-d        9.25  9.25

2012 Rembrandt Regatta — A149

No. 400 — Various sailboats: a, 150c, Horiz. b, 150c, Vert. c, 175c, Horiz. d, 175c, Vert. e, 200c, Horiz. f, 200c, Vert.

**2012, Aug. 7**
400  A149   Block of 6, #a-f       12.00 12.00

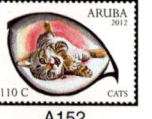 

Cats — A157

**2012, Sept. 20**
401  A150 110c multi                1.25  1.25
402  A151 110c multi                1.25  1.25
403  A152 110c multi                1.25  1.25
404  A153 110c multi                1.25  1.25
405  A154 110c multi                1.25  1.25
406  A155 110c multi                1.25  1.25
407  A156 110c multi                1.25  1.25
408  A157 110c multi                1.25  1.25
     Nos. 401-408 (8)              10.00 10.00

Nos. 401-408 were printed in sheets containing two of each stamp and two labels.

# ARUBA

Christmas and New Year's Day — A158

No. 409: a, 75c, Ornaments and tree. b, 120c, Gifts and Nativity manger. c, 125c, Candles. d, 210c, Fireworks and champagne flutes.

**2012, Oct. 18**
409  A158  Block of 4, #a-d  6.00  6.00

A159  A160

A161  A162
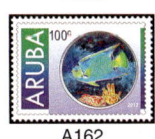
A163  A164

A165  A166

A167
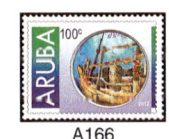

Underwater Exploration — A168

**2012, Nov. 15**
410  Block of 10  11.00  11.00
  a. A159 100c multi  1.10  1.10
  b. A160 100c multi  1.10  1.10
  c. A161 100c multi  1.10  1.10
  d. A162 100c multi  1.10  1.10
  e. A163 100c multi  1.10  1.10
  f. A164 100c multi  1.10  1.10
  g. A165 100c multi  1.10  1.10
  h. A166 100c multi  1.10  1.10
  i. A167 100c multi  1.10  1.10
  j. A168 100c multi  1.10  1.10

Orchids A169

No. 411: a, Laelia xanthina. b, Dendrobium. c, Dendrobium convolutum. d, Brassavola nodosa. e, Rossioglossum grande. f, Cattleya aclandiae. g, Cattleya. h, Epidendrum cinnabarinum. i, Phragmipedium cardinale. j, Phragmipedium. k, Phalaenopsis. l, Cattleya gaskelliana.

**2012, Dec. 20**
411  A169  200c  Block of 12, #a-l  27.00  27.00

Butterflies — A170

Designs: No. 412, 150c, Graphium sarpedon. No. 413, 150c, Danaus plexippus. No. 414, 150c, Danis danis. No. 415, 150c, Pseudacraea boisduvali. No. 416, 150c, Morpho peleides. No. 417, 150c, Scoptes alphaeus. No. 418, 150c, Jumonia oritya. No. 419, 150c, Palla ussheri. No. 420, 150c, Eryphanis polyxena. No. 421, 150c, Diaethria clymena. No. 422, 150c, Colias eurytheme. No. 423, 150c, Anthocharis cardamis.

**2013, Jan. 16**
412-423  A170  Set of 12  20.00  20.00

Nos. 412-423 were printed in sheets of 24 containing two of each stamp + a central label.

Wedding Dresses A171

No. 424: a, Brown and green dress. b, Blue gray strapless dress. c, Brown dress with white veil. d, Lilac dress with sash. e, White dress with black ribbon. f, Red dress with gray collar.

**2013, Feb. 28**
424  A171  200c  Block of 6, #a-f  13.50  13.50

Aruban Bank Notes — A172

No. 425: a, 10-florin banknote. b, 25-florin banknote. c, 50-florin banknote. d, 100-florin banknote. e, 500-florin banknote.

**2013, Apr. 5**
425  Horiz. strip of 5  11.50  11.50
  a.-e. A172 200c Any single  2.25  2.25

Printed in sheets containing two tete-beche strips.

A173  A174

A175  A176

Cruise Ships — A177

**2013, May 16**
426  Horiz. strip of 5  14.00  14.00
  a. A173 250c multi  2.75  2.75
  b. A174 250c multi  2.75  2.75
  c. A175 250c multi  2.75  2.75
  d. A176 250c multi  2.75  2.75
  e. A177 250c multi  2.75  2.75

No. 426 was printed in sheets containing two tete-beche strips.

Paintings by Frans Hals (c. 1582-1666) A179

Designs: Nos. 427a, 428a, Jester with a Lute. Nos. 427b, 428b, Singing Boy with a Flute.

**2013, June 17**
427  A178  500c  Horiz. pair, #a-b  11.50  11.50

**Souvenir Sheet**
428  A179  500c  Sheet of 2, #a-b  11.50  11.50

Birds A180

No. 429: a, Coereba flaveola. b, Aratinga pertinax arubensis. c, Anas bahamensis. d, Zonotrichia capensis. e, Colinus cristatus. f, Columbigallina passerina. g, Egretta thula. h, Icterus icterus. i, Mimus gilvus. j, Pelecanus occidentalis. k, Sterna eurygnatha. l, Athene cunicularia.

**2013, Aug. 1**
429  A180  167c  Block of 12, #a-l  22.50  22.50

Flowers — A181

No. 430: a, Passiflora. b, Canna. c, Bougainvillea. d, Aramyllis. e, Hibiscus. f, Ipomoea. g, Strelitzia. h, Lillium. i, Allamanda. j, Lantana.

**2013, Sept. 5**  Litho.  Perf. 14
400  Block of 10  22.50  22.50
  a.-j. A181 200c Any single  2.25  2.25

Printed in sheets containing two blocks that are tete-beche in relationship to each other.

Shells A182

No. 431: a, 200c, Tonna maculosa. b, 200c, Nerita versicolor. c, 250c, Tellina radiata. d, 275c, Cymatium caribbaeum. e, 275c, Oliva caribaeensis. f, 300c, Voluta musica.

**2013, Oct. 4**  Litho.  Perf. 14
431  A182  Block of 6, #a-f  17.00  17.00

Nature Photography A183

No. 432: a, Blenchi, by Eddie Thodé. b, Dos Playa, by Lara Kuiperi. c, Iris, by r. Kock. d, Barancanan di Ayo, by Stan Kuiperi. e, Respeta nos Naturalesa, by Joost Howard. f, Un Tesoro, by Bruce Harms. g, Serenidad, by Melissa Sweerts. h, Cactus Landscape, by Lara Kuiperi. i, Palo di Bonchi, by J. Dania. j, Tres Burico, by Lara Kuiperi.

**2013, Nov. 12**  Litho.  Perf. 14
432  Block of 10  14.00  14.00
  a.-j. A183 120c Any single  1.40  1.40

Wildlife — A184

No. 433: a, Agalychnis calidryas. b, Panthera onca with spotted fur. c, Ara macao. d, Ranitomega benedicta. e, Saimiri sciurous. f, Panthera onca with black fur. g, Ramphastos sulfuratus. h, Saguinus imperator.

**2013, Dec. 16**  Litho.  Perf. 14
433  Block of 8  16.00  16.00
  a.-h. A184 175c Any single  2.00  2.00

Paintings by Salvador Dalí (1904-89) — A185

No. 435: a, St. James of Compostela, 1957. b, Flores Surrealistas (Gala-Narciso), 1938. c, The Hallucinogenic Toreador, 1968-70. d, The Persistence of Memory, 1931, horiz. e, The Swallow's Tail, 1983, horiz. f, Elephants, 1948, horiz.

**2014, Jan. 17**  Litho.  Perf. 14
434  Block of 6  18.00  18.00
  a.-f. A185 258c Any single  3.00  3.00

Aruban Carnaval, 60th Anniv. — A186

No. 435: a, 300c, Woman with crown, vert. b, 300c, Woman with mask and feathered headdress, horiz. c, 325c, Woman with headdress, horiz. d, 325c, Woman with headdress and feathers, vert.

**2014, Feb. 13**  Litho.  Perf. 14
435  A186  Block of 4, #a-d  14.00  14.00

Automobiles A187

No. 436: a, Ford Thunderbird convertible. b, MG Midget convertible. c, Dodge Challenger. d, Ford Crown Victoria. e, Ford Mustang convertible. f, Chevrolet Corvette Sting Ray.

**2014, Mar. 14**  Litho.  Perf. 14
436  Block of 6  15.00  15.00
  a.-f. A187 225c Any single  2.50  2.50

Birds of Paradise — A188

No. 437: a, Paradisaea rudolphi. b, Lophorina superba, green background. c, Seleucidis melanoleuca. d, Paradisaea apoda,

# 686 ARUBA

e, Paradisaea minor. f, Lophorina superba, yellow background. g, Ptiloris victoriae. h, Cicinnurus regius. i, Cicinnurus respublica. j, Parotia carolae.

| 2014, Apr. 24 | Litho. | | Perf. 14 |
|---|---|---|---|
| 437 | Block of 10 | 27.50 | 27.50 |
| a.-j. | A188 250c Any single | 2.75 | 2.75 |

2014 World Cup Soccer Championships, Brazil — A189

No. 438 — World Cup trophy and: a, Player's foot approaching soccer ball. b, Two players attempting to head ball. c, Player making a diving kick. d, Player dribbling ball. e, Penalty kick. f, Soccer field.

| 2014, May 29 | Litho. | | Perf. 14 |
|---|---|---|---|
| 438 | A189 400c Block of 6, #a-f | 27.00 | 27.00 |

Astronomy — A190

No. 439: a, 350c, Twin planets in circle. b, 350c, Ringed planet. c, 375c, Venus. d, 375c, Star and planets.

| 2014, June 19 | Litho. | | Perf. 14 |
|---|---|---|---|
| 439 | A190 Block of 4, #a-d | 16.50 | 16.50 |

Miniature Sheets

Attacus Atlas A191

Papilio Cresphontes — A192

No. 440: a, Latin name of moth, "2014," part of wing. b, Head of moth. c, Tip of upper wing. d, Large country name, tip of wing. e, Abdomen of moth, bottom of wing. f, Bottom of wing.

No. 441: a, "2014," "cresphontes," part of wing. b, Parts of wings. c, Edge of top wing. d, Large country name, "Papilio," head of butterfly. e, Abdomen of butterfly. f, Bottom of wing.

| 2014, Aug. 21 | Litho. | | Perf. 14 |
|---|---|---|---|
| 440 | A191 200c Sheet of 6, #a-f | | 13.50 13.50 |
| 441 | A192 200c Sheet of 6, #a-f | | 13.50 13.50 |

Fruit A193

No. 442: a, Citrullus lanatus. b, Carica papaya. c, Mangifera indica. d, Annona muricata. e, Musa acuminata. f, Cucumis melo. g, Anacardium occidentale. h, Punica granatum.

| 2014, Sept. 26 | Litho. | | Perf. 14 |
|---|---|---|---|
| 442 | A193 175c Block of 8, #a-h | | 16.00 16.00 |

Christmas — A194

No. 443 — Ribbon with bow and: a, Bells. b, Gifts, candles, ornaments. c, Stars. d, Ornaments.

| 2014, Oct. 23 | Litho. | | Perf. 14 |
|---|---|---|---|
| 443 | Vert. strip of 4 | 6.50 | 6.50 |
| a. | A194 85c multi | .95 | .95 |
| b. | A194 130c multi | 1.50 | 1.50 |
| c. | A194 135c multi | 1.50 | 1.50 |
| d. | A194 220c multi | 2.50 | 2.50 |

Fishing Boats A195

No. 444: a, 250c, Six boats. b, 275c, Laly. c, 300c, Pikudito and other boats. d, 325c, Phasha and another boat.

| 2014, Nov. 19 | Litho. | | Perf. 14 |
|---|---|---|---|
| 444 | A195 Block of 4, #a-d | | 13.00 13.00 |

Dutch Royalty — A196

Designs: No. 445, 300c, King Willem-Alexander. No. 446, 300c, Queen Máxima. No. 447, 300c, King Willem-Alexander and Queen Máxima. No. 448, 300c, King Willem-Alexander, Queen Máxima, Queen Beatrix, Princess Catharina-Amalia, Princess Alexia and Princess Ariane. No. 449, 300c, King Willem-Alexander, Queen Máxima, Princess Catharina-Amalia, Princess Alexia and Princess Ariane waving.

| 2015, Jan. 30 | Litho. | | Perf. 14 |
|---|---|---|---|
| 445-449 | A196 Set of 5 | 17.00 | 17.00 |

Nos. 445-449 were printed in sheets of 10 containing two of each stamp + 2 labels.

Blue Flowers — A197

Designs: No. 450, 200c, Sisyrinchium angustifolium. No. 451, 200c, Lupinus lepidus. No. 452, 200c, Linum lewisii. No. 453, 200c, Amsonia tabernaemontana. No. 454, 200c, Ipomoea learii. No. 455, 200c, Guaiacum officinale. No. 456, 200c, Gentianopsis crinita. No. 457, 200c, Gentiana andrewsii. No. 458, 200c, Campanulastrum americanum. No. 459, 200c, Campanula rotundifolia.

| 2015, Feb. 26 | Litho. | | Perf. 14 |
|---|---|---|---|
| 450-459 | A197 Set of 10 | 22.50 | 22.50 |

Nos. 450-459 were printed in sheets of 20 containing two of each stamp + a central label.

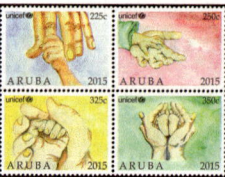

UNICEF A198

No. 460: a, 225c, Child holding finger of adult. b, 250c, Child's hand on adult's hand. c, 325c, Adult hand holding child's hand. d, 350c, Adult's hands holding child's feet.

| 2015, Mar. 25 | Litho. | | Perf. 14 |
|---|---|---|---|
| 460 | A198 Block of 4, #a-d | | 13.00 13.00 |

Paintings by Sandro Botticelli (c. 1445-1510) — A199

Paintings or Details: No. 461, The Birth of Venus (De geboorte van Venus). No. 462, The Madonna of the Book (Madonna del Libro). No. 463, Allegorical Portrait of a Woman, Possibly Simonetta Vespucci (Simonetta Vespucci als Maria Lactans). No. 464, The Annunciation (De Blijde Boodschap). No. 465, Madonna of the Magnificat (Madonna del Magnificat).

| 2015, Mar. 27 | Litho. | | Perf. 14 |
|---|---|---|---|
| 461 | A199 275c multi | 3.25 | 3.25 |
| 462 | A199 275c multi | 3.25 | 3.25 |
| 463 | A199 275c multi | 3.25 | 3.25 |
| 464 | A199 275c multi | 3.25 | 3.25 |
| 465 | A199 275c multi | 3.25 | 3.25 |
| a. | Block of 5, #461-465, + label | 16.50 | 16.50 |
| | Nos. 461-465 (5) | 16.25 | 16.25 |

Nos. 461-465 were printed in sheets of 10 containing two of each stamp + 2 labels.

Butterflies — A200

No. 466: a, Colias hyale. b, Carcharodus lavatherae. c, Anthocharis cardamines. d, Carcharodus flocciferus. e, Colias palaeno. f, Euchloe ausonia. g, Gonepteryx cleopatra. h, Heteropterus morpheus. i, Ochlodes venatus. j, Pyrgus fritillarius.

| 2015, June 30 | Litho. | | Perf. 14 |
|---|---|---|---|
| 466 | A200 220c Block of 10, #a-j | | 24.50 24.50 |

Cave Art — A201

No. 467: a, 350c, Black spirals in circle. b, 350c, Anthromorphic figure with curved arms and legs. c, 375c, Circles connected by lines. d, 375c, Oval with curved lines and dots.

| 2015, July 31 | Litho. | | Perf. 14 |
|---|---|---|---|
| 467 | A201 Block of 4, #a-d | | 16.50 16.50 |

Struthio Camelus A202

No. 468: a, Juvenile facing right, both feet on ground. b, Chick facing right, one foot raised. c, Adult facing left, bending with neck curved. d, Adult facing left with head up. e, Two chicks. f, Head of chick. g, Head of adult. h, Adult facing right. i, Head of adult near chick. j, Adult and juvenile.

| 2015, Aug. 28 | Litho. | | Perf. 14 |
|---|---|---|---|
| 468 | A202 225c Block of 10, #a-j | | 25.00 25.00 |

Beaches A203

No. 469 — Various beaches: a, 275c. b, 300c. c, 325c. d, 350c.

| 2015, Sept. 23 | Litho. | | Perf. 14 |
|---|---|---|---|
| 469 | A203 Block of 4, #a-d | | 14.00 14.00 |

Historic Buildings A204

No. 470: a, Old Hotel Colombia (red and white building with damaged wall). b, Quinta del Carmen. c, Eloy Arends Building (City Hall) (green and white building). d, Henriquez House (yellow building with red roof and stairway to second floor). e, Wild Family House (red and white building adjacent to parking lot). f, Former Aruba Bank Building (yellow building with red roof, cactus at right). g, Willem III Tower, Fort Zoutman (red and white tower), vert. h, San Nicolas Watertower (brown and yellow tower), vert.

| 2015, Oct. 16 | Litho. | | Perf. 14 |
|---|---|---|---|
| 470 | A204 175c Block of 8, #a-h | | 16.00 16.00 |

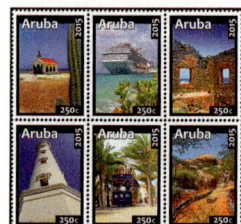

Tourist Attractions — A205

# ARUBA

No. 471: a, Alto Vista Chapel. b, Cruise liner. c, Bushiribana Gold Mill ruins. d, California Lighthouse. e, Double-decker streetcar. f, Rock formations

**2015, Nov. 13    Litho.    Perf. 14**
471   A205   250c Block of 6, #a-f    17.00   17.00

Fish — A206

Designs: 90c, Black beauty. 130c, Bluehead wrasse. 205c, Longfin damselfish. 220c, Blue Caribbean tang. 320c, Blackbar soldierfish.

**Perf. 13¼x12¾**
**2016, Feb. 29    Litho.**
472-476   A206   Set of 5    11.00   11.00

National Symbols — A207

Aruban: No. 477, 500c, Coat of arms. No. 478, 500c, Flag. No. 479, 500c, National anthem.

**Perf. 12¾x13¼**
**2016, Mar. 16    Litho.**
477-479   A207   Set of 3    17.00   17.00
479a    Souvenir sheet of 3, #477-479    17.00   17.00

Burrowing Owls — A208

Designs: 140c, Two owls. 200c, One owl. 320c, Three owls. 65c, Owl in flight.

**Perf. 13¼x12¾**
**2016, Mar. 31    Litho.**
480-483   A208   Set of 4    15.00   15.00

Butterflies — A209

Designs: 85c, Graphium weiskei. 90c, Papilio glaucus. 100c, Jacoona amrita. 130c, Agrias claudina. 135c, Eunica eurota. 220c, Papilio palinurus. 320c, Arginnis paphia. 420c, Aglais io.

**2016, Apr. 29    Litho.    Perf. 12¾x13¼**
484-491   A209   Set of 8    17.00   17.00

Medicinal Plants — A210

Designs: 100c, Aloe vera. 130c, Moringa olifera. 220c, Jatropha gossypiifolia. 250c, Lippia alba. 320c, Croton flavens.

**2016, May 31    Litho.    Perf. 12¾x13¼**
492-496   A210   Set of 5    11.50   11.50

2016 Summer Olympics, Rio de Janeiro — A211

Designs: 100c, Synchronized swimming. 130c, Swimming. 220c, Sailing. 500c, Abstract design.

**Perf. 13¼x12¾**
**2016, June 30    Litho.**
497-500   A211   Set of 4    11.00   11.00

Vegetables — A212

Designs: 90c, Phaseolus vulgaris. 130c, Capsicum annuum. 205c, Cucumis savitus. 220c, Solanum melongena. 320c, Hibiscus esculentus.

**2016, July 29    Litho.    Perf. 12¾x13¼**
501-505   A212   Set of 5    11.00   11.00

Birds — A213

Designs: 50c, Tricolored herons. 85c, Snowy egrets. 90c, Roseate spoonbills. 100c, Blue-winged teals. 130c, Scarlet ibises. 220c, Black skimmers. 250c, Ruby-topaz hummingbird. 325c, Whistling heron.

**Perf. 13¼x12¾**
**2016, Aug. 31    Litho.**
506-513   A213   Set of 8    14.00   14.00

Insects — A214

Designs: 50c, Odonata anisoptera. 90c, Blattaria periplaneta. 100c, Formicidae solenopsis. 130c, Tettigonia viridissima. 200c, Apis mollifera. 220c, Musca domestica. 275c, Vespula vulgaris. 320c, Psaltoda moerens.

**Perf. 13¼x12¾**
**2016, Sept. 30    Litho.**
514-521   A214   Set of 8    15.50   15.50

Musical Instruments — A215

G clef and: 100c, Bongo drums. 140c, Güiro (raspa). 205c, Accordion. 220c, Marimba. 500c, Steelpan drum.

**2016, Oct. 31    Litho.    Perf. 13¼x12¾**
522-526   A215   Set of 5    13.00   13.00

Antiques — A216

Designs: 90c, Sewing machine, coffee mill, oil lamp, sadiron. 130c, Sewing machine. 205c, Sadiron. 250c, Phonograph. 325c, Coffee mill and sadiron.

**Perf. 13¼x12¾**
**2016, Nov. 30    Litho.**
527-531   A216   Set of 5    11.50   11.50

Souvenir Sheet

New Year 2017 (Year of the Rooster) A217

No. 532: a, 200c, Rooster. b, 420c, Dragon.

**2017, Feb. 28    Litho.    Perf. 14x13¼**
532   A217   Sheet of 2, #a-b    7.00   7.00

Miniature Sheet

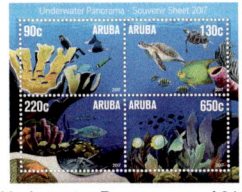

Underwater Panorama — A218

No. 533: a, 90c, Diver, rays, fish, coral. b, 130c, Sea turtles, fish, tube worm. c, 220c, Fish, coral, starfish. d, 650c, Fish and seaweed.

**Perf. 13¾x12¾**
**2017, Mar. 31    Litho.**
533   A218   Sheet of 4, #a-d    12.50   12.50

Houses — A219

Various houses: 85c, 90c, 100c, 130c, 140c, 200c, 220c, 320c.

**2017, Apr. 28    Litho.    Perf. 13¼x12¾**
534-541   A219   Set of 8    14.50   14.50

Sports — A220

Designs: 50c, Cycling. 85c, Baseball. 90c, Cross-country biking. 100c, Basketball. 130c, Soccer. 220c, Go-karting. 305c, Skateboarding. 390c, Tennis.

**2017, May 31    Litho.    Perf. 13¼x12¾**
542-549   A220   Set of 8    15.50   15.50

Birds — A221

Designs: 85c, Black-crowned night heron. 90c, Purple gallinule. 100c, Saffron finch. 130c, Yellow oriole. 200c, Amazon kingfisher. 220c, American flamingo. 250c, Least bittern. 305c, Yellow-billed cuckoo.

**Perf. 12¾x13¼**
**2017, June 30    Litho.**
550-557   A221   Set of 8    15.50   15.50

Postal Services in Aruba, 125th Anniv. — A222

Designs: 90c, Post office, man with wheelbarrow. 130c, Post office. 320c, Mailman on bicycle making delivery. 390c, Motorcyclist and Central Post Office.

**2017, July 31    Litho.    Perf. 13¼x12¾**
558-561   A222   Set of 4    10.50   10.50

Communication Devices — A223

Designs: 90c, Radio. 130c, Television, horiz. 220c, Telegraph, horiz. 305c, Typewriter, horiz. 420c, Telephone, horiz.

**Perf. 12¾x13¼, 13¼x12¾**
**2017, Aug. 31    Litho.**
562-566   A223   Set of 5    13.00   13.00

Tourist Attractions — A224

Designs: 65c, Anchor and donkey, Seroe Colorado. 90c, Lizard, Hooiberg. 100c, Ayo rock formation. 130c, Windsurfer near shipwreck. 200c, California Lighthouse. 220c, Fisherman and fishing boat. 300c, Fisherman casting net. 320c, Arikok National Park.

**Perf. 13¼x12¾**
**2017, Sept. 29    Litho.**
567-574   A224   Set of 8    16.00   16.00

Flowers — A225

Designs: 50c, Plumeria rubra. 90c, Erythrania velutina. 130c, Opuntia wentiana, horiz. 135c, Passiflora foetidal, horiz. 200c, Antigonon leptopus, horiz. 220c, Ixora coccinea, horiz. 305c, Calotropis procera. 320c, Acacia tortuosa.

**Perf. 12¾x13¼, 13¼x12¾**
**2017, Oct. 31    Litho.**
575-582   A225   Set of 8    16.50   16.50

Christmas — A226

Designs: 90c, Christmas ornaments and palm trees. 130c, Stocking cap on lighthouse. 220c, Candles, poinsettias, heart. 320c, Christmas gifts and beach umbrella.

**Perf. 12¾x13¼**
**2017, Nov. 30    Litho.**
583-586   A226   Set of 4    8.50   8.50

A227       A228

A229       Personalized Stamps — A230

**2018, Apr. 24    Litho.    Perf. 13¼x14**
587   A227   130c multi    1.50   1.50
588   A228   130c multi    1.50   1.50
589   A229   130c multi    1.50   1.50
590   A230   130c multi    1.50   1.50
   Nos. 587-590 (4)    6.00   6.00

Vignette portions of Nos. 587-590 could be personalized. The vignettes shown for types A227-A230 are generic images.

2018 World Cup Soccer Championships, Russia — A231

Designs: 130c, Two soccer players. 220c, Goalie making save.

**2018, June 15    Litho.    Perf. 13¼x13**
591-592   A231   Set of 2    4.00   4.00

# ARUBA

Greetings — A232

Designs: 85c, Birthday cake (Happy Birthday). 90c, Hands holding apple (Get Well), vert. 100c, Heart and hands (Valentine), vert. 130c, Orchid (Condolences). 230c, Flowers and hands (Thank You), vert. 650c, Hand and champagne bottle (Congratulations), vert.

*Perf. 13¼x12¾, 12¾x13¼*
**2018, July 31** Litho.
593-598 A232 Set of 6    14.50 14.50

Aspects of Aruban Culture — A233

Designs: 90c, Dancers (Celebrations). 130c, Aloe hanging from doorway (Traditions). 220c, Woman in dress (Folklorico Dress). 420c, Fish on plate (Typical food).

*Perf. 13¼x12¾*
**2018, Aug. 31** Litho.
599-602 A233 Set of 4    9.75 9.75

Water Sports — A234

Designs: 90c, Windsurfing. 130c, Surfing. 135c, Kitesurfing. 200c, Kayaking. 220c, Bodyboarding. 320c, Parasailing.

*Perf. 13¼x12¾*
**2018, Sept. 28** Litho.
603-608 A234 Set of 6    12.50 12.50

Pets — A235

Designs: 90c, Cats. 100c, Dog. 130c, Rabbit. 135c, Fish. 220c, Turtle. 500c, Parrots.

**2018, Oct. 31** Litho. *Perf. 13¼x12¾*
609-614 A235 Set of 6    13.00 13.00

Sustainable Energy — A236

Designs: 90c, Wind generators. 100c, Electric car. 130c, Solar panel, vert. 220c, Electric tram, vert. 320c, Bicycle.

*Perf. 13¼x12¾, 12¾x13¼*
**2018, Nov. 30** Litho.
615-619 A236 Set of 5    9.75 9.75

65th Aruba Carnaval — A237

Designs: 90c, Musicians and dancers. 130c, Singer in uniform, vert. 220c, Dancer, vert. 420c, Three dancers.

*Perf. 13¼x12¾, 12¾x13¼*
**2019, Mar. 1** Litho.
620-623 A237 Set of 4    9.75 9.75

Children at Play — A238

Designs: 90c, Girl jumping rope, girls in sack race. 100c, Girls with hula hoops, boy playing hop scotch. 130c, Boys rolling hoops and tires. 320c, Boys with top and yo-yo.

**2019, Apr. 28** Litho. *Perf. 12¾x13¼*
624-627 A238 Set of 4    7.25 7.25

Sports Stars — A239

Designs: No. 628, 220c, Sarah-Quita Offringa, windsurfer. No. 629, 220c, Xander Bogaerts, baseball player. No. 630, 220c, Shanayah Howell, bicycle motocross. No. 631, 220c, Chiara Petrocchi, taekwondo.

*Perf. 13¼x12¾*
**2019, June 28** Litho.
628-631 A239 Set of 4    10.00 10.00
631a    Souvenir sheet of 4, #628-631    10.00 10.00

Medicinal Plants — A240

Designs: 90c, Origanum vulgare. 130c, Mentha spicata, vert. 220c, Senna alexandrina, vert. 500c, Cymbopogon.

*Perf. 13¼x12¾, 12¾x13¼*
**2019, Aug. 30** Litho.
632-635 A240 Set of 4    10.50 10.50

Birds and Their Feathers — A241

Designs: 90c, Falco sparverius. 120c, Athene cunicularia arubensis. 130c, Falco peregrinus. 320c, Caracara cheriway.

**2019, Oct. 31** Litho. *Perf. 13¼x12¾*
636-639 A241 Set of 4    7.50 7.50

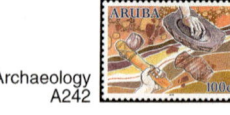

Archaeology A242

Designs: 100c, Ancient hatchet, potsherd, mortar and pestle. 130c, Archaeologists uncovering artifacts, vert. 220c, Ancinet shell in cross-section, creation of necklace, vert. 320c, Archaeologist unearthing skull, cross-section of burial urn.

*Perf. 13¼x12¾, 12¾x13¼*
**2019, Dec. 9** Litho.
640-643 A242 Set of 4    8.75 8.75

Earth Day, 50th Anniv. — A243

Designs: 100c, Hand holding Earth Day 50th anniversary emblem. 130c, Hands holding globe and recycling emblem, horiz. 220c, Hands holding seedling, horiz. 320c, Hands holding globe.

*Perf. 12¾x13¼, 13¼x12¾*
**2020, Apr. 22** Litho.
644-647 A243 Set of 4    8.75 8.75

Butterflies — A244

Designs: 90c, Battus polydamas. 130c, Hypna clytemnestra. 220c, Pachliopta aristolochiae. 420c, Papilio rumanzovia.

**2020, May 29** Litho. *Perf. 12¾x13¼*
648-651 A244 Set of 4    9.75 9.75

America Issue — A245

Designs: 90c, Building and palm trees. 130c, Yellow building with red roof. 220c, Nicholaas Store. 420c, Green building with date at top.

**2020, July 31** Litho. *Perf. 13¼x12¾*
652-655 A245 Set of 4    9.75 9.75

Medical Afflictions — A246

Designs: 90c, Alzheimer's disease. 130c, Cancer, vert. 220c, Diabetes, vert. 320c, Stroke.

*Perf. 13¼x12¾, 12¾x13¼*
**2020, Sept. 21** Litho.
656-659 A246 Set of 4    8.50 8.50

Martial Arts — A247

Inscriptions: 100c, Capoeira. 130c, Karate, vert. 220c, Greek wrestling, vert. 320c, Chinese martial art.

*Perf. 13¼x12¾, 12¾x13¼*
**2020, Oct. 30** Litho.
660-663 A247 Set of 4    8.75 8.75

Wagons Used in Phosphate Mining — A248

Designs: 90c, Locomotive pulling wagon. 130c, Wagon near miners. 220c, Miners pushing wagon. 420c, Locomotive pulling wagons.

*Perf. 13¼x12¾*
**2020, Nov. 30** Litho.
664-667 A248 Set of 4    8.50 8.50

## Souvenir Sheet

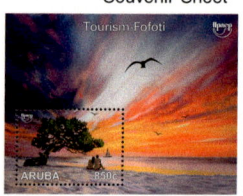

Fofoti Tree A249

**2021, Oct. 14** Litho. *Perf. 13¼x12¾*
668 A249 850c multi    9.50 9.50

America issue.

Agriculture — A250

Designs: 90c, Hands placing plant in ground, butterfly. 220c, Hand watering tomato plants. 320c, Coconut tree and watermelons. 420c, Woman picking fruit from tree.

**2021, Nov. 16** Litho. *Perf. 13¼x14*
669-672 A250 Set of 4    12.00 12.00

Fishing — A251

Designs: 100c, Fisherman casting net. 130c, Traditional fishing boat. 420c, Rock fishing. 500c, Deep sea fishing.

**2021, Dec. 3** Litho. *Perf. 14x13¼*
673-676 A251 Set of 4    13.00 13.00

Orchids — A252

Designs: 140c, Spathoglottis Big Red Fancy. 200c, Dendrobium nobile. 320c, Vanda Tessellate Blue. 650c, Cattleya habenaria rhodocheila.

**2022, Mar. 28** Litho. *Perf. 13¼x14*
677-680 A252 Set of 4    15.00 15.00

Flamingos — A253

Designs: 220c, Flamingo facing forward. 320c, Flamingo with head and wings extended. 420c, Flamingo in flight. 500c, Seven flamingos.

**2022, Apr. 29** Litho. *Perf. 13¼x13½*
681-684 A253 Set of 4    16.50 16.50

## Miniature Sheet

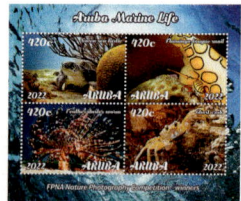

Winning Pictures in Marine Life Photography Contest — A254

No. 685: a, Green sea turtle. b, Flamingo tongue snail. c, Feather duster worm. d, Ghost crab.

**2022, June 8** Litho. *Perf. 13¼x13½*
685 A254 420c Sheet of 4, #a-d    19.00 19.00

## Souvenir Sheet

Aruba Postal Service, 130th Anniv. A255

No. 686 — Postal worker, letters and: a, Motorcycle, car, parcels, mailbox with open door. b, Bicycle, ship, car, and airplane. c, Bicycle and pillar box.

**2022, Aug. 1** Litho. *Perf. 14x13¾*
686 A255 220c Sheet of 3, #a-c    7.50 7.50

Children's Art — A256

Designs: No. 687, 220c, Family and two dogs. No. 688, 220c, Girl walking dog. No. 689, 220c, Boy washing dog. No. 690, 220c, Boy throwing stick for dog to fetch.

**2022, Oct. 4** Litho. *Perf. 14x13¼*
687-690 A256 Set of 4    10.00 10.00

# ARUBA

Tourist Attractions
A257

Designs: 130c, California Lighthouse. 220c, Casibari Rocks. 320c, Hooiberg. 420c, Natural Bridge.

| 2022, Nov. 1 | Litho. | Perf. 14x13¼ |
|---|---|---|
| 691-694 A257 | Set of 4 | 12.50 12.50 |

### Souvenir Sheet

New Year 2023 (Year of the Rabbit)
A258

No. 695: a, 220c, Rabbit, sun and cloud. b, 320c, Rabbit starting to leap. c, 520c, Rabbit leaping.

| 2023, Jan. 22 | Litho. | Perf. 13 |
|---|---|---|
| 695 A258 | Sheet of 3, #a-c | 12.00 12.00 |

Papiamento as an Official Language of Aruba, 20th Anniv. — A259

Aruban flora with English words and their Papiamento equivalent: 90c, "Thank you." 130c, "Welcome," horiz. 320c, "My beloved island," horiz. 420c, "Sweetheart."

| | Perf. 13¼x13, 13x13¼ | Litho. |
|---|---|---|
| 2023, May 21 | | |
| 696-699 A259 | Set of 4 | 11.00 11.00 |

## SEMI-POSTAL STAMPS

Surtax for child welfare organizations unless otherwise stated.

Solidarity — SP1

| 1986, May 7 | Litho. | Perf. 14x13 |
|---|---|---|
| B1 | SP1 30c + 10c shown | 1.75 1.00 |
| B2 | SP1 35c + 15c Three ropes | 1.75 1.00 |
| B3 | SP1 60c + 25c One rope | 2.50 1.60 |
| | Nos. B1-B3 (3) | 6.00 3.50 |

Surtax for social and cultural projects.

Child Welfare — SP2

No. B4, Boy, caterpillar. No. B5, Boy, cocoon. No. B6, Girl, butterfly.

| 1986, Oct. 29 | Litho. | Perf. 14x13 |
|---|---|---|
| B4 | SP2 45c + 20c multi | 2.75 1.00 |
| B5 | SP2 70c + 25c multi | 2.75 1.75 |
| B6 | SP2 100c + 10c multi | 3.50 2.25 |
| | Nos. B4-B6 (3) | 9.00 5.00 |

Christmas (Child Welfare) — SP3

No. B7, Boy on beach. No. B8, Drawing Christmas tree. No. B9, Child, creche figures.

| 1987, Oct. 27 | Litho. | Perf. 14x13 |
|---|---|---|
| B7 | SP3 25c +10c multi | 1.50 .75 |
| B8 | SP3 45c +20c multi | 2.00 1.00 |
| B9 | SP3 70c +30c multi | 2.75 1.50 |
| | Nos. B7-B9 (3) | 6.25 3.25 |

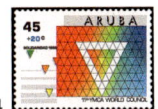

Solidarity — SP4

YMCA emblem in various geometric designs.

| 1988, Aug. 3 | Litho. | Perf. 14x13 |
|---|---|---|
| B10 | SP4 45c +20c shown | 2.00 1.00 |
| B11 | SP4 60c +25c multi, diff. | 2.00 1.50 |
| B12 | SP4 100c +50c multi, diff. | 2.50 2.00 |
| | Nos. B10-B12 (3) | 6.50 4.50 |

11th YMCA world council.
Surtax for social and cultural projects.

Children's Toys (Child Welfare) — SP5

| 1988, Oct. 26 | | Perf. 13x14 |
|---|---|---|
| B13 | SP5 45c +20c Jacks | 2.25 1.00 |
| B14 | SP5 70c +30c Top | 2.25 1.50 |
| B15 | SP5 100c +50c Kite | 3.00 2.00 |
| | Nos. B13-B15 (3) | 7.50 4.50 |

Child Welfare — SP6

No. B16, Baby spoon. No. B17, Chasing a ball. No. B18, Adult & child holding hands.

| 1989, Oct. 26 | | Perf. 14x13 |
|---|---|---|
| B16 | SP6 45c +20c multi | 2.00 1.00 |
| B17 | SP6 60c +30c multi | 2.25 1.25 |
| B18 | SP6 100c +50c multi | 3.00 2.00 |
| | Nos. B16-B18 (3) | 7.25 4.25 |

Solidarity — SP7

No. B20, Family, house.

| 1990, July 25 | | |
|---|---|---|
| B19 | SP7 55c +25c shown | 2.00 1.50 |
| B20 | SP7 100c +50c multi | 3.50 2.50 |

Surtax for social and cultural projects.

Child Welfare — SP8

Christmas song: No. B21, Wind surfboards. No. B23, Kites, lizard.

| 1990, Oct. 24 | Litho. | Perf. 13x14 |
|---|---|---|
| B21 | SP8 45c +20c multi | 1.50 1.00 |
| B22 | SP8 60c +30c shown | 2.00 1.25 |
| B23 | SP8 100c +50c multi | 3.00 2.00 |
| | Nos. B21-B23 (3) | 6.50 4.50 |

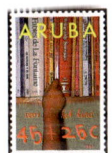

Child Welfare — SP9

Literacy: 45c+25c, Discovery of reading. 60c+35c, Pointing to letter. 100c+50c, Child reading.

| 1991, Oct. 25 | Litho. | Perf. 13x14 |
|---|---|---|
| B24 | SP9 45c +25c multi | 1.50 1.25 |
| B25 | SP9 60c +35c multi | 2.00 1.40 |
| B26 | SP9 100c +50c multi | 3.00 2.25 |
| | Nos. B24-B26 (3) | 6.50 4.90 |

Solidarity — SP10

55c+30c, Girl scouts, flag & emblem. 100c+50c, Hand holding cancer fund emblem, people.

| 1992, May 27 | Litho. | Perf. 14x13 |
|---|---|---|
| B27 | SP10 55c +30c multi | 2.00 1.50 |
| B28 | SP10 100c +50c multi | 3.50 2.25 |

Surtax for social and cultural projects.

Postal Services of Aruba, Cent. (Child Welfare) — SP11

Designs: 50c+30c, Heart. 70c+35c, Airplane, letters. 100c+55c, Pigeon with letter in beak, vert.

| 1992, Oct. 30 | Litho. | Perf. 14x13 |
|---|---|---|
| B29 | SP11 50c +30c multi | 1.90 1.25 |
| B30 | SP11 70c +35c multi | 2.10 1.40 |
| | | Perf. 13x14 |
| B31 | SP11 100c +50c multi | 3.00 2.25 |
| | Nos. B29-B31 (3) | 7.00 4.90 |

Youth Foreign Study Programs (Child Welfare) — SP12

Abstract designs of: 50c+30c, Landscapes. 75c+40c, Young man, scenes of other countries, vert. 100c+50c, Integrating cultures.

| 1993, Oct. 27 | Perf. 14x13, 13x14 |
|---|---|
| B32 SP12 50c +30c multi | 1.50 1.25 |
| B33 SP12 75c +40c multi | 2.00 1.90 |
| B34 SP12 100c +50c multi | 2.50 2.25 |
| Nos. B32-B34 (3) | 6.00 5.40 |

Solidarity — SP13

Intl. Year of the Family: 50c+35c, Family seated, reading, studying. 100c+50c, Family playing in front of house.

| 1994, May 30 | Litho. | Perf. 14x13 |
|---|---|---|
| B35 | SP13 50c +35c multi | 1.50 1.25 |
| B36 | SP13 100c +50c multi | 2.75 2.50 |

Surtax for social and cultural projects.

Child Welfare — SP14

Designs: 50c+30c, Children on anchor with umbrella. 80c+35c, Children inside Sun. 100c+50c, Child riding owl.

| 1994, Oct. 27 | Litho. | Perf. 14x13 |
|---|---|---|
| B37 | SP14 50c +30c multi | 2.00 1.50 |
| B38 | SP14 80c +35c multi | 2.40 2.00 |
| B39 | SP14 100c +50c multi | 2.50 2.50 |
| | Nos. B37-B39 (3) | 6.90 6.00 |

Child Welfare — SP15

Children's drawings. 50c+25c, Children with balloons, house. 70c+35c, Three people with picnic basket on sunny day. 100c+50c, People gardening on sunny day.

Solidarity — SP16

| 1995, Oct. 26 | Litho. | Perf. 13x14 |
|---|---|---|
| B40 | SP15 50c +25c multi | 1.75 1.25 |
| B41 | SP15 70c +35c multi | 2.25 1.75 |
| B42 | SP15 100c +50c multi | 3.00 2.50 |
| | Nos. B40-B42 (3) | 7.00 5.50 |

El Sol Naciente Lodge, 75th Anniv.: 60c+30c, Masonic emblems. 100c+ 50c, Columns, terrestrial and celestial globes.

| 1996, July 26 | Litho. | Perf. 13x14 |
|---|---|---|
| B43 | SP16 60c +30c multi | 2.50 1.50 |
| B44 | SP16 100c +50c multi | 3.50 2.50 |

Surtax for social and cultural projects (Solidarity)

Child Welfare — SP17

Cartoons: 50c+25c, Mother, baby rabbit waiting at school bus stop. 70c+35c, Mother, baby owl, outside school. 100c+50c, Children flying kite.

| 1996, Oct. 24 | Litho. | Perf. 14x13 |
|---|---|---|
| B45 | SP17 50c +25c multi | 1.75 1.25 |
| B46 | SP17 70c +35c multi | 2.25 1.75 |
| B47 | SP17 100c +50c multi | 2.50 2.40 |
| | Nos. B45-B47 (3) | 6.50 5.40 |

Child Welfare — SP18

Designs: 50c+25c, Girl sitting among aloe plants. 70c+35c, Boy, butterfly, cactus, vert. 100c+50c, Girl swimming under water, fish, coral.

| | Perf. 14x13, 13x14 |
|---|---|
| 1997, Oct. 23 | Litho. |
| B48 SP18 50c +25c multi | 1.50 1.25 |
| B49 SP18 70c +35c multi | 2.50 2.00 |
| B50 SP18 100c +50c multi | 2.50 2.50 |
| Nos. B48-B50 (3) | 6.50 5.75 |

Solidarity — SP19

Service Organizations: 60c+30c, Globe, emblem of Lions Intl., wheelchair balanced on map of Aruba. 100c+50c, Child reading book, emblem of Rotary Intl., woman in rocking chair.

| 1998, May 29 | Litho. | Perf. 14x13 |
|---|---|---|
| B51 | SP19 60c +30c multi | 2.50 1.50 |
| B52 | SP19 100c +50c multi | 3.50 2.75 |

Surtax for social and cultural projects.

Child Welfare — SP20

50c+25c, Girl performing traditional ribbon dance. 80c+40c, Boy playing a cuarta. 100c+50c, Two boys playing basketball.

| 1998, Oct. 22 | Litho. | Perf. 13x14 |
|---|---|---|
| B53 | SP20 50c +25c multi | 1.75 1.25 |
| B54 | SP20 80c +40c multi | 2.50 2.25 |
| B55 | SP20 100c +50c multi | 3.00 2.50 |
| | Nos. B53-B55 (3) | 7.25 6.00 |

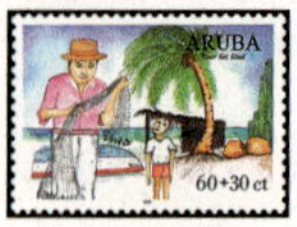
ARUBA
60+30 ct

Child Welfare — SP21

Designs: 60c+30c, Child on beach with man with fishing net. 80c+40c, Adult reading to children. 100c+50c, Mother, child, vert.

*Perf. 14x13, 13x14*

**1999, Oct. 21** **Litho.**

| | | | |
|---|---|---|---|
| **B56** | SP21 60c +30c multi | 1.75 | 1.50 |
| **B57** | SP21 80c +40c multi | 2.50 | 2.00 |
| **B58** | SP21 100c +50c multi | 3.00 | 2.50 |
| | *Nos. B56-B58 (3)* | 7.25 | 6.00 |

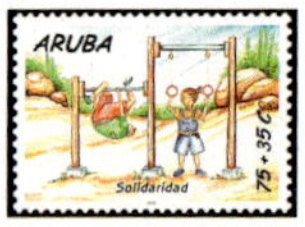
ARUBA
75+35c

Solidarity — SP22

75c+35c, Children on playground equipment. 100c+50c, Children playing in sand.

**2000, Aug. 28** **Litho.** ***Perf. 14x13***

| | | | |
|---|---|---|---|
| **B59-B60** | SP22 Set of 2 | 5.75 | 4.25 |

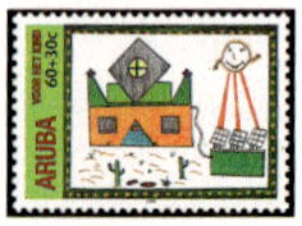
ARUBA
60+30c

Child Welfare — SP23

Children's art: 60c+30c, House with solar collectors. 80c+40c, House, girl, garbage can. 100c+50c, Flying automobiles.

**2000, Oct. 26**

| | | | |
|---|---|---|---|
| **B61-B63** | SP23 Set of 3 | 8.00 | 6.00 |

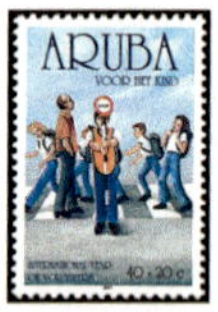
ARUBA

Child Welfare — SP24

Intl. Volunteers Year: 40c+20c, Children at crosswalk. 60c+30c, Boys walking dog. 100c+50c, Children depositing trash in can at beach.

**2001, Oct. 31** **Litho.** ***Perf. 13x14***

| | | | |
|---|---|---|---|
| **B64-B66** | SP24 Set of 3 | 7.00 | 5.75 |

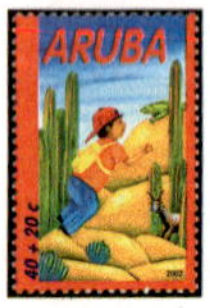
ARUBA
40 + 20c

Child Welfare — SP25

Designs: 40c+20c, Boy, iguana and goat. 60c+30c, Girl, hawksbill turtle, red crab, horiz. 100c+50c, Boy, pelicans, parakeet, conch shell.

*Perf. 13x14, 14x13*

**2002, Oct. 31** **Litho.**

| | | | |
|---|---|---|---|
| **B67-B69** | SP25 Set of 3 | 7.00 | 5.75 |

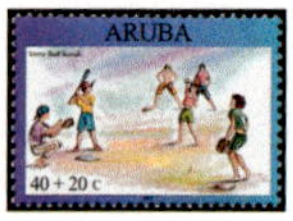
ARUBA
40 + 20 c

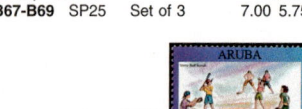

Child Welfare — SP26

Children playing: 40c+20c, Baseball. 60c+30c, Volleyball. 100c+50c, Soccer.

**2003, Oct. 31** **Litho.** ***Perf. 14x13***

| | | | |
|---|---|---|---|
| **B70-B72** | SP26 Set of 3 | 6.00 | 6.00 |

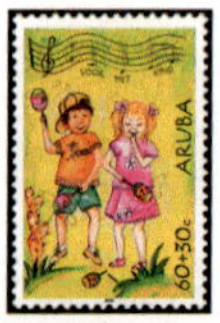
ARUBA
60+30c

Children's Welfare — SP27

Children playing: 60c+30c, Maracas. 85c+40c, Steel drum. 100c+50c, Tambourine, wiri.

**2004, Oct. 29** **Litho.** ***Perf. 13x14***

| | | | |
|---|---|---|---|
| **B73-B75** | SP27 Set of 3 | 5.50 | 5.00 |

## ASCENSION

ə-ˈsen͜t-shən

LOCATION — An island in the South Atlantic Ocean, 900 miles from Liberia

GOVT. — A part of the British Crown Colony of St. Helena

AREA — 34 sq. mi.

POP. — 806 (2016)

In 1922 Ascension was placed under the administration of the Colonial Office and annexed to the British Crown Colony of St. Helena. The only post office is at Georgetown.

12 Pence = 1 Shilling
20 Shillings = 1 Pound
100 Pence = 1 Pound (1971)

**Catalogue values for unused stamps in this country are for Never Hinged items, beginning with Scott 50.**

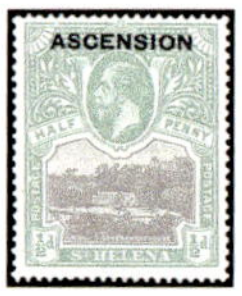
ASCENSION

Stamps and Types of St. Helena, 1912-22 Overprinted in Black or Red

**1922** **Wmk. 4** ***Perf. 14***

| | | | |
|---|---|---|---|
| **1** | A9 ½p green & blk | 8.00 | *29.00* |
| **2** | A10 1p green | 8.00 | *29.00* |
| **3** | A101 ½p rose red | 21.00 | *60.00* |
| **4** | A9 2p gray & blk | 21.00 | 16.00 |
| **5** | A9 3p ultra | 16.00 | *29.00* |
| **6** | A10 8p dl vio & blk | 34.00 | *62.50* |
| **7** | A10 2sh ultra & blk, *blue* | 120.00 | *150.00* |
| **8** | A10 3sh vio & blk | 175.00 | *200.00* |

**Wmk. 3**

| | | | |
|---|---|---|---|
| **9** | A9 1sh blk, *gray grn* (R) | 35.00 | *60.00* |
| | *Nos. 1-9 (9)* | 438.00 | *635.50* |
| | Set, never hinged | 675.00 | |

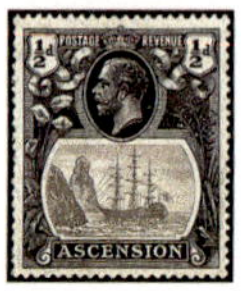
ASCENSION

Seal of Colony — A3

**1924-33** **Typo.** **Wmk. 4** ***Perf. 14***

**Chalky Paper**

| | | | |
|---|---|---|---|
| **10** | A3 ½p black & gray | 6.75 | *19.00* |
| **11** | A3 1p green & blk | 7.00 | *17.00* |
| **12** | A3 1½p rose red | 10.00 | *50.00* |
| **13** | A3 2p bluish gray & gray | 25.00 | 13.00 |
| **14** | A3 3p ultra | 10.00 | *19.00* |
| **15** | A3 4p blk & gray, *yel* | 60.00 | *100.00* |
| **16** | A3 5p ol & lil ('27) | 24.00 | *29.00* |
| **17** | A3 6p rose lil & gray | 62.50 | *125.00* |
| **18** | A3 8p violet & gray | 21.00 | *52.50* |
| **19** | A3 1sh brown & gray | 25.00 | *62.50* |
| **20** | A3 2sh ultra & gray, *blue* | 75.00 | *115.00* |
| **21** | A3 3sh blk & gray, *blue* | 110.00 | *110.00* |
| | *Nos. 10-21 (12)* | 436.25 | *712.00* |
| | Set, never hinged | 675.00 | |

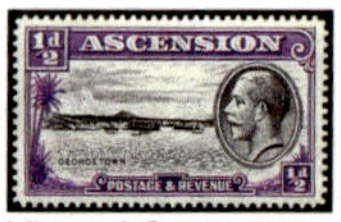
ASCENSION

View of Georgetown A4

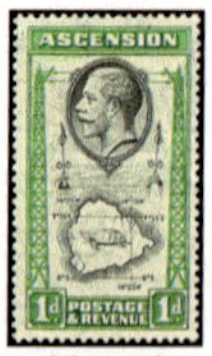
ASCENSION

Map of Ascension A5

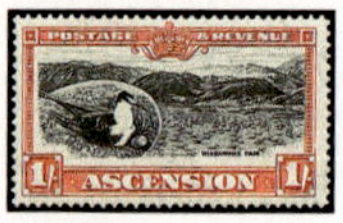
ASCENSION

Sooty Tern Breeding Colony — A9

Designs: 1½p, Pier at Georgetown. 3p, Long Beach. 5p, Three Sisters. 5sh, Green Mountain.

**1934, July 2** **Engr.**

| | | | |
|---|---|---|---|
| **23** | A4 ½p violet & blk | 1.10 | 1.00 |
| **24** | A5 1p lt grn & blk | 2.25 | 1.60 |
| **25** | A4 1½p red & black | 2.25 | *2.75* |
| **26** | A5 2p org & black | 2.25 | *3.00* |
| **27** | A4 3p ultra & blk | 2.75 | 1.90 |
| **28** | A4 5p blue & black | 2.75 | *4.00* |
| **29** | A5 8p dk brn & blk | 5.25 | *6.75* |
| **30** | A9 1sh car & blk | 22.50 | 12.00 |
| **31** | A5 2sh6p violet & blk | 57.50 | 50.00 |
| **32** | A4 5sh brown & blk | 62.50 | *70.00* |
| | *Nos. 23-32 (10)* | 161.10 | *153.00* |
| | Set, never hinged | 240.00 | |

Common Design Types pictured following the introduction.

**Silver Jubilee Issue**

Common Design Type

**1935, May 6** ***Perf. 11x12***

| | | | |
|---|---|---|---|
| **33** | CD301 1½p car & dk blue | 3.50 | *15.00* |
| **34** | CD301 2p blk & ultra | 10.00 | *37.50* |
| **35** | CD301 5p ind & grn | 22.50 | *32.50* |
| **36** | CD301 1sh brn vio & indigo | 22.50 | *42.50* |
| | *Nos. 33-36 (4)* | 58.50 | *127.50* |
| | Set, never hinged | 100.00 | |

25th anniv. of the reign of King George V.

**Coronation Issue**

Common Design Type

**1937, May 19** ***Perf. 13½x14***

| | | | |
|---|---|---|---|
| **37** | CD302 1p deep green | .75 | *1.50* |
| **38** | CD302 2p deep orange | 1.00 | .65 |
| **39** | CD302 3p bright ultra | 1.00 | .60 |
| | *Nos. 37-39 (3)* | 2.75 | *2.75* |
| | Set, never hinged | 3.50 | |

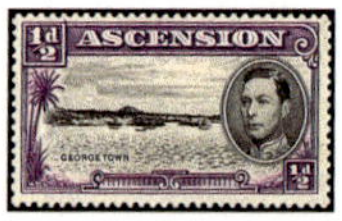
ASCENSION

Georgetown A11

Designs: No. 41, 41A, 2p, 4p, Green Mountain. No. 41D, 6p, 10sh, Three Sisters. 1½p, 2sh6p, Pier at Georgetown. 3p, 5sh, Long Beach.

***Perf. 13, 13½ (#41, 44, 45), 14 (#43C)***

**1938-53** **Center in Black**

| | | | |
|---|---|---|---|
| **40** | A11 ½p violet ('44) | .80 | *4.00* |
| | Never hinged | 1.50 | |
| ***a.*** | Perf. 13½ | 4.00 | *4.00* |
| | Never hinged | 8.00 | |
| **41** | A11 1p green | 30.00 | 13.50 |
| | Never hinged | 45.00 | |
| **41A** | A11 1p org yel ('42) | .25 | *.60* |
| | Never hinged | .45 | |
| ***b.*** | Perf. 14 ('49) | .40 | *16.00* |
| | Never hinged | .70 | |
| ***c.*** | Perf. 13½ | 8.00 | *9.00* |
| | Never hinged | 14.50 | |
| **41D** | A11 1p green ('49) | .35 | *1.50* |
| | Never hinged | .60 | |
| **42** | A11 1½p red ('44) | .65 | *.80* |
| | Never hinged | 1.00 | |
| ***a.*** | Perf. 14 ('49) | 1.90 | *13.50* |
| | Never hinged | 3.75 | |
| ***b.*** | Perf. 13½ | 5.75 | 1.40 |
| | Never hinged | 9.00 | |
| **42C** | A11 1½p lilac rose ('53) | .30 | *6.50* |
| | Never hinged | .55 | |
| ***d.*** | Perf. 14 ('49) | 1.35 | *1.10* |
| | Never hinged | 2.25 | |
| ***e.*** | 1½p carmine, perf 14 | 6.50 | 6.50 |
| | Never hinged | 12.00 | |
| **43** | A11 2p orange ('44) | .50 | .40 |
| | Never hinged | .80 | |
| ***a.*** | Perf. 14 ('49) | 2.25 | *37.50* |
| | Never hinged | 3.50 | |
| ***b.*** | Perf. 13½ | 5.75 | 1.00 |
| | Never hinged | 9.50 | |
| **43C** | A11 2p red ('49) | .90 | *1.90* |
| | Never hinged | 1.50 | |
| **44** | A11 3p ultra | 65.00 | 30.00 |
| | Never hinged | 110.00 | |
| **44A** | A11 3p black ('44) | .35 | *1.00* |
| | Never hinged | .70 | |
| ***c.*** | Perf. 13½ ('40) | 13.50 | 4.00 |
| | Never hinged | 21.00 | |
| **44B** | A11 4p ultra ('44) | 3.00 | 3.00 |
| | Never hinged | 5.25 | |
| ***d.*** | Perf. 13½ | 10.00 | 3.75 |
| | Never hinged | 17.50 | |
| **45** | A11 6p gray blue | 7.25 | 2.50 |
| | Never hinged | 13.00 | |
| ***a.*** | Perf. 13 ('44) | 7.50 | 7.50 |
| | Never hinged | 12.50 | |
| **46** | A11 1sh dk brn ('44) | 3.50 | 2.00 |
| | Never hinged | 5.00 | |
| ***a.*** | Perf. 13½ | 13.00 | 3.00 |
| | Never hinged | 22.50 | |
| **47** | A11 2sh6p car ('44) | 20.00 | *37.50* |
| | Never hinged | 30.00 | |
| ***a.*** | Perf. 13½ | 30.00 | 12.00 |
| | Never hinged | 47.50 | |
| ***b.*** | Frame printed doubly, one albino | *3,750.* | *5,000.* |
| | Never hinged | *5,250.* | |
| **48** | A11 5sh yel brn ('44) | 25.00 | 45.00 |
| | Never hinged | 40.00 | |
| ***a.*** | Perf. 13½ | 62.50 | 12.00 |
| | Never hinged | 100.00 | |
| **49** | A11 10sh red vio ('44) | 45.00 | *62.50* |
| | Never hinged | 62.50 | |
| ***a.*** | Perf. 13½ | 65.00 | 50.00 |
| | Never hinged | 120.00 | |
| ***b.*** | 10sh brt aniline red pur, perf 13 | 65.00 | 50.00 |
| | Never hinged | 125.00 | |
| | *Nos. 40-49 (16)* | 202.85 | *212.70* |
| | Set, never hinged | 315.00 | |

**Catalogue values for unused stamps in this section, from this point to the end of the section, are for Never Hinged items.**

**Peace Issue**

Common Design Type

*Perf. 13½x14*

**1946, Oct. 21** **Engr.** **Wmk. 4**

| | | | |
|---|---|---|---|
| **50** | CD303 2p deep orange | .40 | *1.00* |
| **51** | CD303 4p deep blue | .40 | *1.00* |

**Silver Wedding Issue**

Common Design Types

**1948, Oct. 20** **Photo.** ***Perf. 14x14½***

| | | | |
|---|---|---|---|
| **52** | CD304 3p black | .55 | .45 |

**Engraved; Name Typographed**

*Perf. 11½x11*

| | | | |
|---|---|---|---|
| **53** | CD305 10sh red violet | 55.00 | 50.00 |

The stamps formerly listed as Nos. 54-56 have been merged into the rest of the George VI definitive series as Nos. 41//43C.

**UPU Issue**

Common Design Types

**Engr.; Name Typo. on Nos. 58, 59**

**1949, Oct. 10** ***Perf. 13½, 11x11½***

| | | | |
|---|---|---|---|
| **57** | CD306 3p rose carmine | 1.25 | *2.00* |
| **58** | CD307 4p indigo | 4.25 | 1.50 |
| **59** | CD308 6p olive | 1.60 | 3.50 |
| **60** | CD309 1sh slate | 4.00 | 2.00 |
| | *Nos. 57-60 (4)* | 11.10 | 9.00 |

**Coronation Issue**

Common Design Type

**1953, June 2** **Engr.** ***Perf. 13½x13***

| | | | |
|---|---|---|---|
| **61** | CD312 3p gray & black | 1.25 | *2.75* |

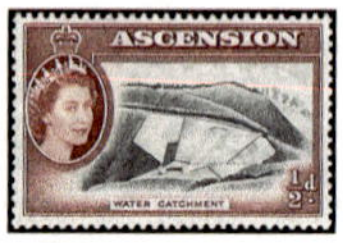
ASCENSION

Reservoir — A16

Designs: 1p, Map of Ascension. 1½p, Georgetown. 2p, Map showing Ascension between South America and Africa and cable lines. 2½p, Mountain road. 3p, Yellow-billed tropic bird. 4p, Longfinned tuna. 6p, Waves. 7p, Young green turtles. 1sh, Land crab. 2sh6p, Sooty tern (wideawake). 5sh, Perfect Crater. 10sh, View from Northwest.

**1956, Nov. 19** **Wmk. 4** ***Perf. 13***

**Center in Black**

| | | | |
|---|---|---|---|
| **62** | A16 ½p brown | .25 | .50 |
| **63** | A16 1p lilac rose | 2.75 | 2.50 |
| **64** | A16 1½p orange | .85 | 1.10 |
| **65** | A16 2p carmine | 3.00 | *3.25* |
| **66** | A16 2½p org brown | 1.50 | *3.25* |
| **67** | A16 3p blue | 3.75 | 1.10 |
| **68** | A16 4p turq blue | 1.25 | *1.75* |
| **69** | A16 6p dark blue | 1.25 | *2.50* |
| **70** | A16 7p olive | 2.50 | 1.75 |
| **71** | A16 1sh scarlet | 1.10 | *1.60* |
| **72** | A16 2sh6p brown violet | 30.00 | 9.00 |
| **73** | A16 5sh bright green | 40.00 | 19.00 |
| **74** | A16 10sh purple | 55.00 | 40.00 |
| | *Nos. 62-74 (13)* | 143.20 | 87.30 |

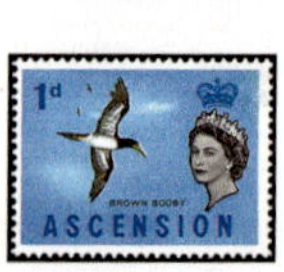
ASCENSION

Brown Booby — A17

Birds: 1½p, Black tern. 2p, Fairy tern. 3p, Red-billed tropic bird in flight. 4½p, Brown noddy. 6p, Sooty tern. 7p, Frigate bird. 10p,

Blue-faced booby. 1sh, Yellow-billed tropic bird. 1sh6p, Red-billed tropic bird. 2sh6p, Madeiran storm petrel. 5sh, Red-footed booby (brown phase). 10sh, Frigate birds. £1, Red-footed booby (white phase).

*Perf. 14x14½*

**1963, May 23 Photo. Wmk. 314**

| | | | | |
|---|---|---|---|---|
| 75 | A17 | 1p multicolored | 1.15 | .30 |
| 76 | A17 | 1½p multicolored | 1.75 | 1.00 |
| *b.* | | Blue omitted | 130.00 | |
| 77 | A17 | 2p multicolored | 1.40 | .30 |
| 78 | A17 | 3p multicolored | 1.50 | .30 |
| 79 | A17 | 4½p multicolored | 1.50 | .30 |
| 80 | A17 | 6p multicolored | 1.40 | .30 |
| 81 | A17 | 7p multicolored | 1.40 | .30 |
| 82 | A17 | 10p multicolored | 1.40 | .30 |
| 83 | A17 | 1sh multicolored | 1.40 | .30 |
| 84 | A17 | 1sh6p multicolored | 4.50 | 2.25 |
| | | Complete booklet, 4 each #75, 76, 77, 78, 80 and 84, in blocks of 4 | 90.00 | |
| 85 | A17 | 2sh6p multicolored | 8.00 | *12.00* |
| 86 | A17 | 5sh multicolored | 8.00 | *12.00* |
| 87 | A17 | 10sh multicolored | 14.50 | *14.00* |
| 88 | A17 | £1 multicolored | 22.00 | *16.00* |
| | | *Nos. 75-88 (14)* | 69.90 | *59.65* |

**Freedom from Hunger Issue**

Common Design Type

**1963, June 4 Wmk. 314**

| | | | | |
|---|---|---|---|---|
| 89 | CD314 | 1sh6p car rose | 1.00 | .50 |

**Red Cross Centenary Issue**

Common Design Type

**1963, Sept. 2 Litho. *Perf. 13***

| | | | | |
|---|---|---|---|---|
| 90 | CD315 | 3p black & red | 2.50 | 1.10 |
| 91 | CD315 | 1sh6p ultra & red | 4.25 | 2.25 |

**ITU Issue**

Common Design Type

*Perf. 11x11½*

**1965, May 17 Litho. Wmk. 314**

| | | | | |
|---|---|---|---|---|
| 92 | CD317 | 3p mag & violet | .50 | .40 |
| 93 | CD317 | 6p grnsh bl & brn org | 1.40 | .90 |

**Intl. Cooperation Year Issue**

Common Design Type

**1965, Oct. 25 Wmk. 314 *Perf. 14½***

| | | | | |
|---|---|---|---|---|
| 94 | CD318 | 1p bl grn & claret | .40 | .50 |
| 95 | CD318 | 6p lt vio & green | .90 | .90 |

**Churchill Memorial Issue**

Common Design Type

**1966, Jan. 24 Photo. *Perf. 14***

**Design in Black, Gold and Carmine Rose**

| | | | | |
|---|---|---|---|---|
| 96 | CD319 | 1p bright blue | .50 | .50 |
| 97 | CD319 | 3p green | 1.75 | .90 |
| 98 | CD319 | 6p brown | 2.25 | 1.50 |
| 99 | CD319 | 1sh6p violet | 5.50 | 3.50 |
| | | *Nos. 96-99 (4)* | 10.00 | 6.40 |

**World Cup Soccer Issue**

Common Design Type

**1966, July 1 Litho. *Perf. 14***

| | | | | |
|---|---|---|---|---|
| 100 | CD321 | 3p multicolored | 1.00 | .75 |
| 101 | CD321 | 6p multicolored | 1.50 | 1.25 |

**WHO Headquarters Issue**

Common Design Type

**1966, Sept. 20 Litho. *Perf. 14***

| | | | | |
|---|---|---|---|---|
| 102 | CD322 | 3p multicolored | 2.10 | 1.10 |
| 103 | CD322 | 1sh6p multicolored | 4.50 | 2.25 |

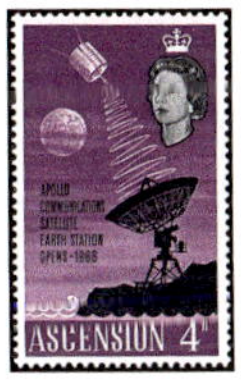

Apollo Satellite Station, Ascension — A18

**Wmk. 314**

**1966, Nov. 7 Photo. *Perf. 14***

| | | | | |
|---|---|---|---|---|
| 104 | A18 | 4p purple & black | .25 | .25 |
| 105 | A18 | 8p blue grn & blk | .25 | .25 |
| 106 | A18 | 1sh3p brn ol & blk | .25 | .25 |
| 107 | A18 | 2sh6p brt grnsh blue & black | .25 | .25 |
| | | *Nos. 104-107 (4)* | 1.00 | 1.00 |

Opening of the Apollo communications satellite-earth station, part of the US Apollo program.

**UNESCO Anniversary Issue**

Common Design Type

**1967, Jan. 3 Litho. *Perf. 14***

| | | | | |
|---|---|---|---|---|
| 108 | CD323 | 3p "Education" | 2.50 | 1.40 |
| 109 | CD323 | 6p "Science" | 3.50 | 1.90 |
| 110 | CD323 | 1sh6p "Culture" | 5.00 | 2.50 |
| | | *Nos. 108-110 (3)* | 11.00 | 5.80 |

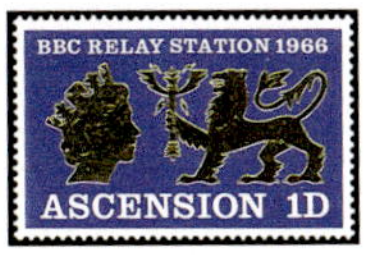

BBC Emblem — A19

**Photo.; Gold Impressed**

**1967, Dec. 1 Wmk. 314 *Perf. 14½***

| | | | | |
|---|---|---|---|---|
| 111 | A19 | 1p ultra & gold | .25 | .25 |
| 112 | A19 | 3p dk green & gold | .25 | .25 |
| 113 | A19 | 6p brt purple & gold | .25 | .25 |
| 114 | A19 | 1sh6p brt red & gold | .25 | .25 |
| | | *Nos. 111-114 (4)* | 1.00 | 1.00 |

Opening of the British Broadcasting Company's South Atlantic Relay Station on Ascension Island.

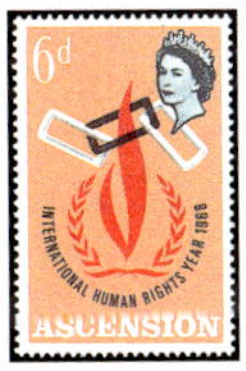

Human Rights Flame and Chain — A20

*Perf. 14½x14*

**1968, July 8 Litho. Wmk. 314**

| | | | | |
|---|---|---|---|---|
| 115 | A20 | 6p org, car & blk | .25 | .25 |
| 116 | A20 | 1sh6p gray, mag & blk | .30 | .30 |
| 117 | A20 | 2sh6p brt grn, plum & blk | .30 | .30 |
| | | *Nos. 115-117 (3)* | .85 | .85 |

International Human Rights Year.

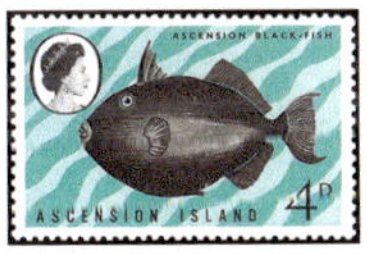

Blackfish — A21

Fish: No. 119, Sailfish. 6p, Oldwife. 8p, Leather jackets. 1sh6p, Yellowtails. 1sh9p, Tuna. 2sh3p, Mako sharks. 2sh11p, Rock hind (jack).

*Perf. 13x12½*

**1968-69 Wmk. 314 Litho.**

| | | | | |
|---|---|---|---|---|
| 118 | A21 | 4p brt grnsh bl & blk | .30 | .25 |
| 119 | A21 | 4p red & multi | .35 | .35 |
| 120 | A21 | 6p yel olive & multi | .40 | .40 |
| 121 | A21 | 8p brt rose lil & multi | .60 | .45 |
| 122 | A21 | 1sh6p brown & multi | 1.50 | *2.00* |
| 123 | A21 | 1sh9p emer & multi | 1.00 | .95 |
| 124 | A21 | 2sh3p ocher & multi | 1.50 | 1.25 |
| 125 | A21 | 2sh11p dp org & multi | 3.00 | 2.75 |
| | | *Nos. 118-125 (8)* | 8.65 | 8.40 |

Issue dates: No. 119, 6p, 1sh6p, 2sh11p, Mar. 3, 1969; others, Oct. 23, 1968.

See Nos. 130-133.

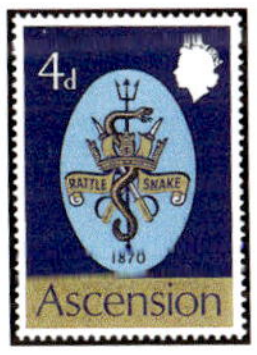

Arms of R.N.S. Rattlesnake — A22

Coats of Arms of Royal Naval Ships: 9p, Weston. 1sh9p, Undaunted. 2sh3p, Eagle.

*Perf. 14x14½*

**1969, Oct. 1 Photo. Wmk. 314**

| | | | | |
|---|---|---|---|---|
| 126 | A22 | 4p multicolored | .65 | .50 |
| 127 | A22 | 9p multicolored | .75 | .60 |
| 128 | A22 | 1sh9p multicolored | 1.25 | .75 |
| 129 | A22 | 2sh3p multicolored | 1.40 | .85 |
| *a.* | | Min. sheet of 4, #126-129 | 8.50 | 8.50 |
| | | *Nos. 126-129 (4)* | 4.05 | 2.70 |

See Nos. 134-137, 152-159, 166-169.

**Fish Type of 1968**

Deep-sea fish: 4p, Wahoo. 9p, Coalfish. 1sh9p, Dolphinfishes. 2sh3p, Soldierfish.

**1970, Apr. 6 Litho. *Perf. 14***

| | | | | |
|---|---|---|---|---|
| 130 | A21 | 4p bluish grn & multi | 4.00 | 2.75 |
| 131 | A21 | 9p org & multi | 3.00 | 2.75 |
| 132 | A21 | 1sh9p ultra & multi | 5.00 | 3.50 |
| 133 | A21 | 2sh3p gray & multi | 5.00 | 3.50 |
| | | *Nos. 130-133 (4)* | 17.00 | 12.50 |

**Naval Arms Type of 1969**

4p, Penelope. 9p, Carlisle. 1sh6p, Amphion. 2sh6p, Magpie.

*Perf. 12½x12*

**1970, Sept. 7 Photo. Wmk. 314**

| | | | | |
|---|---|---|---|---|
| 134 | A22 | 4p ultra, gold & blk | 1.25 | .30 |
| 135 | A22 | 9p lt bl, blk, gold & red | 1.50 | .55 |
| 136 | A22 | 1sh6p grnsh bl, gold & blk | 1.60 | 1.50 |
| 137 | A22 | 2sh6p lt grnsh bl, gold & blk | 2.25 | 2.10 |
| *a.* | | Miniature sheet of 4, #134-137 | 12.00 | *14.00* |
| | | *Nos. 134-137 (4)* | 6.60 | 4.45 |

**Decimal Currency Issue**

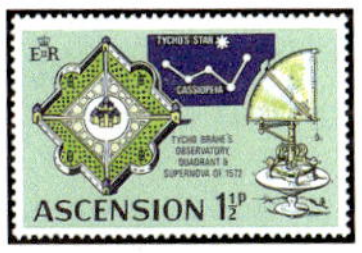

Tycho Brahe's Observatory, Quadrant and Supernova, 1572 — A23

Man into Space: ½p, Chinese rocket, 1232, vert. 1p, Medieval Arab astronomers, vert. 2p, Galileo, his telescope and drawing of moon, 1609. 2½p, Isaac Newton, telescope and apple. 3½p, Harrison's chronometer and ship, 1735. 4½p, First American manned orbital flight (Project Mercury, 1962, vert.). 5p, Reflector of Palomar telescope and ring nebula in Lyra, Messier 57. 7½p, Jodrell Bank telescope. 10p, Mariner 7, 1969, and telescopic view of Mars. 12½p, Sputnik 2 and dog Laika, 1957. 25p, Astronaut walking in space, 1965 (Gemini 4; vert.). 50p, US astronauts and moon landing module, 1969. £1, Future space research station.

**1971, Feb. 15 Litho. *Perf. 14½***

| | | | | |
|---|---|---|---|---|
| 138 | A23 | ½p multicolored | .25 | .25 |
| 139 | A23 | 1p multicolored | .25 | .25 |
| 140 | A23 | 1½p multicolored | .30 | .30 |
| 141 | A23 | 2p multicolored | .35 | .35 |
| 142 | A23 | 2½p multicolored | 1.10 | .90 |
| 143 | A23 | 3½p multicolored | 2.25 | .90 |
| | | Complete booklet, 4 each #138-143 | 30.00 | |
| 144 | A23 | 4½p multicolored | 1.50 | .95 |
| 145 | A23 | 5p multicolored | 1.25 | .90 |
| 146 | A23 | 7½p multicolored | 3.50 | 2.00 |
| 147 | A23 | 10p multicolored | 3.50 | 3.25 |
| 148 | A23 | 12½p multicolored | 4.50 | 3.50 |
| 149 | A23 | 25p multicolored | 5.50 | 3.25 |
| 150 | A23 | 50p multicolored | 4.50 | 3.75 |
| 151 | A23 | £1 multicolored | 4.50 | 4.50 |
| | | *Nos. 138-151 (14)* | 33.25 | 25.05 |

For overprints see Nos. 189-191.

Booklet also exists with a date of 5/71 on the back cover. Value, $45.

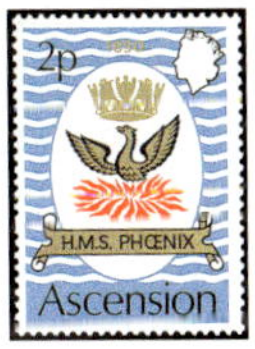

Arms of H.M.S. Phoenix — A24

Coats of Arms of Royal Naval Ships: 4p, Milford. 9p, Pelican. 15p, Oberon.

**1971, Nov. 15 Photo. *Perf. 13½x13***

| | | | | |
|---|---|---|---|---|
| 152 | A24 | 2p gold & multi | 1.00 | .25 |
| 153 | A24 | 4p gold & multi | 1.10 | .45 |
| 154 | A24 | 9p gold & multi | 1.50 | 1.10 |
| 155 | A24 | 15p gold & multi | 1.60 | *2.25* |
| *a.* | | Souvenir sheet of 4, #152-155 | 7.50 | *10.00* |
| | | *Nos. 152-155 (4)* | 5.20 | *4.05* |

**Naval Arms Type of 1969**

1½p, Lowestoft. 3p, Auckland. 6p, Nigeria. 17½p, Bermuda.

**1972, May 22 Litho. *Perf. 14x14½***

| | | | | |
|---|---|---|---|---|
| 156 | A22 | 1½p bl, gold & blk | .85 | .65 |
| 157 | A22 | 3p grnsh bl, gold & blk | .95 | .70 |
| 158 | A22 | 6p grn, gold, blk & bl | 1.00 | 1.00 |
| 159 | A22 | 17½p lil, gold, blk & red | 1.50 | *2.25* |
| *a.* | | Miniature sheet of 4, #156-159 | 4.25 | *6.50* |
| | | *Nos. 156-159 (4)* | 4.30 | *4.60* |

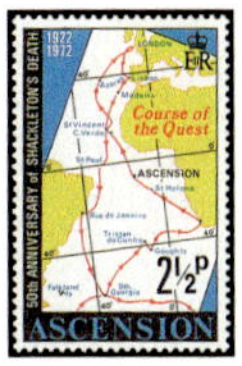

Course of Quest — A25

Designs: 4p, Shackleton and "Quest", horiz. 7½p, Shackleton's cabin and Quest in pack ice, horiz. 11p, Shackleton statue, London, and memorial cairn, South Georgia.

**1972, Aug. 2 *Perf. 14***

| | | | | |
|---|---|---|---|---|
| 160 | A25 | 2½p multicolored | .55 | .50 |
| 161 | A25 | 4p multicolored | .60 | .65 |
| 162 | A25 | 7½p multicolored | .60 | .70 |
| 163 | A25 | 11p multicolored | .75 | .90 |
| *a.* | | Souvenir sheet of 4, #160-163 | 3.00 | *5.00* |
| | | *Nos. 160-163 (4)* | 2.50 | 2.75 |

Sir Ernest Henry Shackleton (1874-1922), explorer of Antarctica.

**Silver Wedding Issue, 1972**

Common Design Type

Design: Queen Elizabeth II, Prince Philip, land crab and shark.

**1972, Nov. 20 Photo. *Perf. 14x14½***

| | | | | |
|---|---|---|---|---|
| 164 | CD324 | 2p violet & multi | .25 | .25 |
| 165 | CD324 | 16p car rose & multi | .45 | .45 |

**Naval Arms Type of 1969**

2p, Birmingham. 4p, Cardiff. 9p, Penzance. 13p, Rochester.

**1973, May 28 Litho. Wmk. 314**

| | | | | |
|---|---|---|---|---|
| 166 | A22 | 2p blue & multi | 2.25 | 1.40 |
| 167 | A22 | 4p yel grn & multi | 2.75 | 1.40 |
| 168 | A22 | 9p lt blue & multi | 3.25 | 1.60 |
| 169 | A22 | 13p violet & multi | 3.75 | 1.60 |
| *a.* | | Min. sheet of 4, #166-169 | 24.00 | 15.00 |
| | | *Nos. 166-169 (4)* | 12.00 | 6.00 |

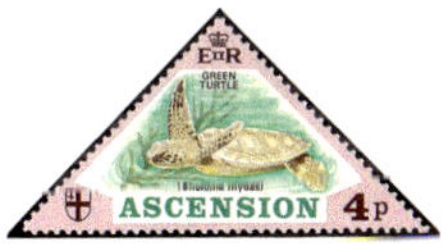

Turtles — A26

**1973, Aug. 28 *Perf. 13½***

| | | | | |
|---|---|---|---|---|
| 170 | A26 | 4p Green | 2.50 | 1.10 |
| 171 | A26 | 9p Loggerhead | 3.25 | 2.25 |
| 172 | A26 | 12p Hawksbill | 4.50 | 3.50 |
| | | *Nos. 170-172 (3)* | 10.25 | 6.85 |

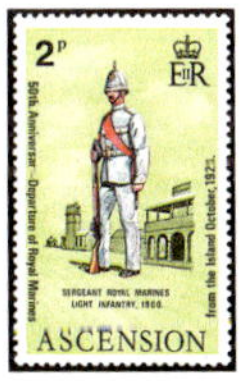

Light Infanty Marine Sergeant, 1900 — A27

Uniforms (Royal Marines): 6p, Private, 1816. 12p, Officer, Light Infantry, 1880. 20p, Color Sergeant, Artillery, 1910.

**1973, Oct. 31 *Perf. 14½***

| | | | | |
|---|---|---|---|---|
| 173 | A27 | 2p multicolored | 1.75 | 1.50 |
| 174 | A27 | 6p lt green & multi | 2.75 | 1.90 |
| 175 | A27 | 12p lt blue & multi | 3.00 | 2.75 |
| 176 | A27 | 20p lt lilac & multi | 3.50 | 3.00 |
| | | *Nos. 173-176 (4)* | 11.00 | 9.15 |

Departure of the Royal Marines from Ascension, 50th anniv.

**Princess Anne's Wedding Issue**

Common Design Type

**1973, Nov. 14 *Perf. 14***

| | | | | |
|---|---|---|---|---|
| 177 | CD325 | 2p ocher & multi | .25 | .25 |
| 178 | CD325 | 18p multicolored | .35 | .35 |

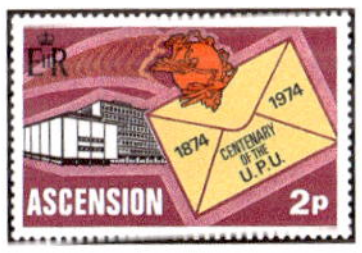

Letter and UPU Emblem — A29

UPU Cent.: 9p, Emblem and Mercury.

**Wmk. 314**

**1974, Mar. 27 Litho. *Perf. 14½***

| | | | | |
|---|---|---|---|---|
| 179 | A29 | 2p multicolored | .25 | .25 |
| 180 | A29 | 9p vio blue & multi | .40 | .40 |

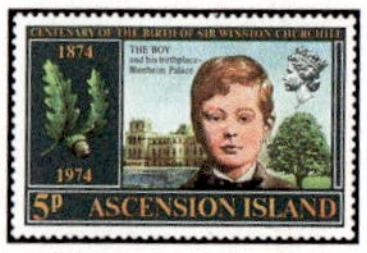


Young Churchill and Blenheim Palace — A30

25p, Churchill and UN Headquarters, NYC.

**1974, Nov. 30 Litho. Unwmk.**

| | | | | |
|---|---|---|---|---|
| **181** | A30 | 5p slate grn & multi | .25 | .25 |
| **182** | A30 | 25p purple & multi | .70 | .70 |
| *a.* | | Souvenir sheet of 2, #181-182 | 1.75 | *2.50* |

Sir Winston Churchill (1874-1965).

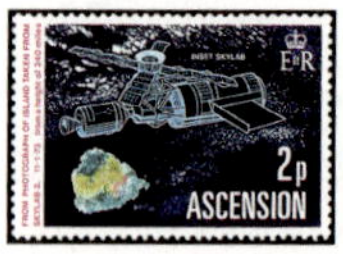


Skylab over Photograph of Ascension Taken by Skylab 3 — A31

Skylab Space Station: 18p, Command module and photo of Ascension from Skylab 4.

**1975, Mar. 20 Wmk. 314 *Perf. 14½***

| | | | | |
|---|---|---|---|---|
| **183** | A31 | 2p multicolored | .25 | .25 |
| **184** | A31 | 18p multicolored | .70 | .70 |

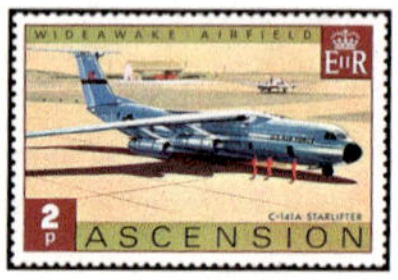


US Air Force C-141A Starlifter A32

Aircraft: 5p, Royal Air Force C-130 Hercules. 9p, Vickers VC-10. 24p, U.S. Air Force C-5A Galaxy.

***Perf. 13½x14***

**1975, June 19 Litho. Wmk. 314**

| | | | | |
|---|---|---|---|---|
| **185** | A32 | 2p multicolored | 1.00 | .60 |
| **186** | A32 | 5p multicolored | 1.50 | .75 |
| **187** | A32 | 9p multicolored | 1.50 | 1.50 |
| **188** | A32 | 24p multicolored | 2.50 | 2.50 |
| *a.* | | Souvenir sheet of 4, #185-188 | 17.00 | 17.50 |
| | | *Nos. 185-188 (4)* | 6.50 | 5.35 |

Wideawake Airfield, Ascension Island.

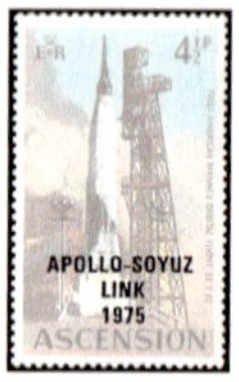


Nos. 144, 148-149 Overprinted

**1975, Aug. 18 Litho. *Perf. 14½***

| | | | | |
|---|---|---|---|---|
| **189** | A23 | 4½p multicolored | .25 | .25 |
| **190** | A23 | 12½p multicolored | .35 | .35 |
| **191** | A23 | 25p multicolored | .50 | .50 |
| | | *Nos. 189-191 (3)* | 1.10 | 1.10 |

Apollo Soyuz space test project (Russo-American cooperation), launching July 15; link-up, July 17.

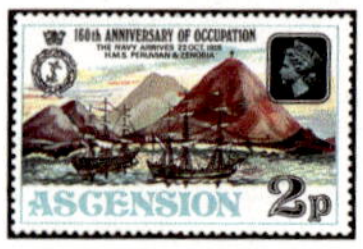


HMS Peruvian and Zenobia Arriving Oct. 22, 1815 — A33

Designs: 5p, Water Supply, Dampiers Drip. 9p, First Landing, Oct. 1815. 15p, The Garden on Green Mountain. All designs after paintings by Isobel McManus.

**1975, Oct. 22 Wmk. 373 *Perf. 14½***

| | | | | |
|---|---|---|---|---|
| **192** | A33 | 2p lt blue & multi | .25 | .25 |
| **193** | A33 | 5p lt blue & multi | .25 | .25 |
| **194** | A33 | 9p red & multi | .35 | .35 |
| **195** | A33 | 15p red & multi | .65 | .65 |
| | | *Nos. 192-195 (4)* | 1.50 | 1.50 |

British occupation, 160th anniv.

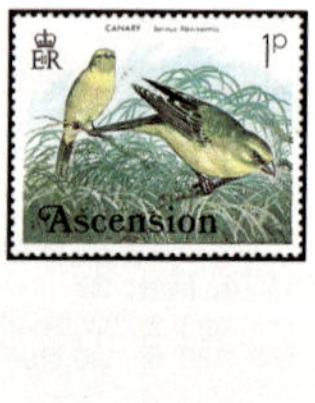


Canaries — A34

2p, Fairy tern, vert. 3p, Waxbills. 4p, Black noddy. 5p, Brown noddy. 6p, Common mynah. 7p, Madeira storm petrels. 8p, Sooty terns. 9p, White booby. 10p, Red-footed booby. 15p, Red-throated francolin. 18p, Brown booby. 25p, Red-billed bo'sun bird. 50p, Yellow-billed bo'sun bird. £1, Ascension frigatebird. £2, Boatswain Island Bird Sanctuary and birds.

***Perf. 14x14½, 14½x14***

**1976, Apr. 26 Litho. Wmk. 373**

**Size: 35x27mm, 27x35mm**

| | | | | |
|---|---|---|---|---|
| **196** | A34 | 1p multi | .50 | *1.75* |
| **197** | A34 | 2p multi | .55 | *1.75* |
| **198** | A34 | 3p multi | .55 | *1.75* |
| **199** | A34 | 4p multi, vert. | .60 | *1.75* |
| **200** | A34 | 5p multi | .75 | *1.75* |
| **201** | A34 | 6p multi | .75 | *1.75* |
| **202** | A34 | 7p multi, vert. | .75 | *1.75* |
| **203** | A34 | 8p multi | .75 | *1.75* |
| **204** | A34 | 9p multi, vert. | .75 | *1.75* |
| **205** | A34 | 10p multi | .75 | *1.75* |
| **206** | A34 | 15p multi, vert. | 1.50 | *1.75* |
| **207** | A34 | 18p multi, vert. | 1.50 | *1.75* |
| **208** | A34 | 25p multi | 1.60 | *1.75* |
| **209** | A34 | 50p multi | 2.25 | *2.75* |
| **210** | A34 | £1 multi, vert. | 2.75 | *3.25* |

***Perf. 13½***

**Size: 46x33mm**

| | | | | |
|---|---|---|---|---|
| **211** | A34 | £2 multicolored | 5.50 | 5.00 |
| | | *Nos. 196-211 (16)* | 21.80 | 33.75 |

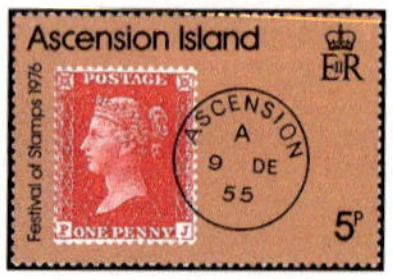


Great Britain Type A1 with Ascension Cancel — A35

9p, Ascension No. 1, vert. 25p, Freighter Southampton Castle.

**1976, May 4 *Perf. 13½x14, 14x13½***

| | | | | |
|---|---|---|---|---|
| **212** | A35 | 5p lt brn, car & blk | .25 | .25 |
| **213** | A35 | 9p gray grn, grn & blk | .25 | .25 |
| **214** | A35 | 25p blue & multi | .50 | .50 |
| | | *Nos. 212-214 (3)* | 1.00 | 1.00 |

Festival of Stamps 1976. See Tristan da Cunha No. 208a for souvenir sheet that contains one each of Ascension No. 214, St. Helena No. 297, and Tristan da Cunha No. 208.

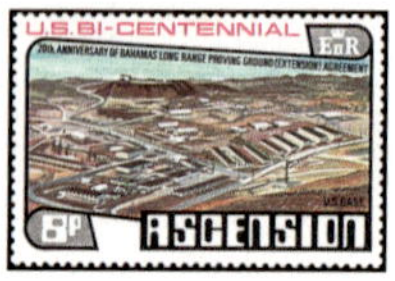


US Base — A36

Designs: 9p, NASA Station, Devil's Ashpit. 25p, Viking satellite landing on Mars.

**Wmk. 373**

**1976, July 4 Litho. *Perf. 13½***

| | | | | |
|---|---|---|---|---|
| **215** | A36 | 8p black & multi | .30 | .30 |
| **216** | A36 | 9p black & multi | .40 | .40 |
| **217** | A36 | 25p black & multi | .80 | *1.00* |
| | | *Nos. 215-217 (3)* | 1.50 | 1.70 |

American Bicentennial. No. 215 also for the 20th anniv. of Bahamas Long Range Proving Ground (extension) Agreement.

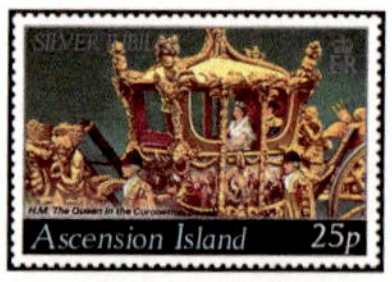


Queen in Coronation Coach — A37

Designs: 8p, Prince Philip on Ascension Island, 1957, vert. 12p, Queen leaving Buckingham Palace in coronation coach.

***Perf. 14x13½, 13½x14***

**1977, Feb. 7 Litho. Wmk. 373**

| | | | | |
|---|---|---|---|---|
| **218** | A37 | 8p multicolored | .25 | .25 |
| **219** | A37 | 12p multicolored | .25 | .25 |
| **220** | A37 | 25p multicolored | .30 | *.40* |
| | | *Nos. 218-220 (3)* | .80 | .90 |

Reign of Queen Elizabeth II, 25th anniv.

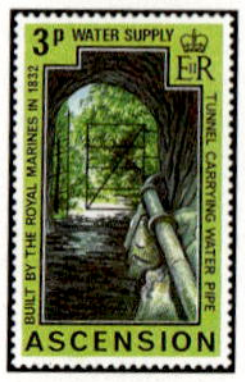


Water Pipe in Tunnel — A38

5p, Breakneck Valley wells. 12p, Break tank in pipe line, horiz. 25p, Dam & reservoir, horiz.

**1977, June 27 Litho. *Perf. 14½***

| | | | | |
|---|---|---|---|---|
| **221** | A38 | 3p multicolored | .25 | .25 |
| **222** | A38 | 5p multicolored | .25 | .25 |
| **223** | A38 | 12p multicolored | .30 | .30 |
| **224** | A38 | 25p multicolored | .50 | *.60* |
| | | *Nos. 221-224 (4)* | 1.30 | 1.40 |

Water supplies constructed by Royal Marines, 1832 and 1881.

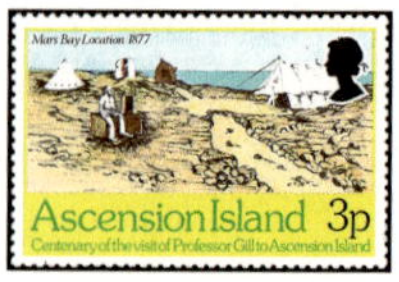


Mars Bay Site, 1877 — A39

Designs: 8p, Mars Bay and instrument sites. 12p, Prof. and Mrs. Gill before their tent. 25p, Map of Ascension.

***Perf. 13½x14***

**1977, Oct. 3 Litho. Wmk. 373**

| | | | | |
|---|---|---|---|---|
| **225** | A39 | 3p multicolored | .25 | .25 |
| **226** | A39 | 8p multicolored | .25 | .25 |
| **227** | A39 | 12p multicolored | .30 | *.40* |
| **228** | A39 | 25p multicolored | .60 | *.70* |
| | | *Nos. 225-228 (4)* | 1.40 | 1.60 |

Centenary of visit of Prof. David Gill (1843-1914), astronomer, to Ascension.

**Elizabeth II Coronation Anniversary Issue**

**Souvenir Sheet**

Common Design Types

**Unwmk.**

**1978, May 21 Litho. *Perf. 15***

| | | | | |
|---|---|---|---|---|
| **229** | | Sheet of 6 | 2.00 | 2.00 |
| *a.* | | CD326 25p Lion of England | .30 | .30 |
| *b.* | | CD327 25p Elizabeth II | .30 | .30 |
| *c.* | | CD328 25p Green turtle | .30 | .30 |

No. 229 contains 2 se-tenant strips of Nos. 229a-229c, separated by horizontal gutter with commemorative and descriptive inscriptions and showing central part of coronation procession with coach.

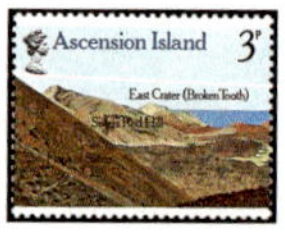


East Crater (Broken Tooth) — A40

Volcanoes: 5p, Hollands Crater (Hollow Tooth). 12p, Bears Back. 15p, Green Mountain. 25p, Two Boats village.

**1978, Sept. 4 Litho. *Perf. 14½***

| | | | | |
|---|---|---|---|---|
| **230** | A40 | 3p multicolored | .25 | .25 |
| **231** | A40 | 5p multicolored | .25 | .25 |
| **232** | A40 | 12p multicolored | .30 | .30 |
| **233** | A40 | 15p multicolored | .40 | .40 |
| **234** | A40 | 25p multicolored | .65 | .65 |
| *a.* | | Souvenir sheet, 2 each #230-234 | 3.00 | *4.75* |
| *b.* | | Strip of 5, #230-234 | 2.00 | 2.00 |

No. 234b shows panoramic view of volcanic terrain.

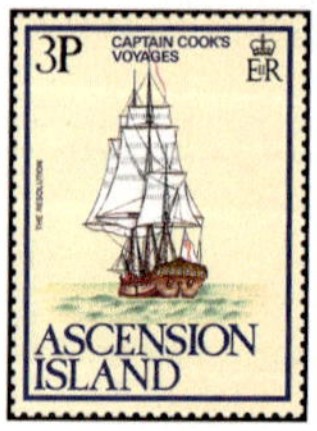


Resolution — A41

Capt. Cook's voyages: 8p, Cook's chronometer. 12p, Green turtle. 25p, Cook after Flaxman/Wedgwood medallion.

**Litho.; Litho. & Embossed. (25p)**

**1979, Jan. 8 *Perf. 11***

| | | | | |
|---|---|---|---|---|
| **235** | A41 | 3p multicolored | .25 | .25 |
| **236** | A41 | 8p multicolored | .30 | .30 |
| **237** | A41 | 12p multicolored | .55 | .55 |
| **238** | A41 | 25p multicolored | .75 | *.85* |
| | | *Nos. 235-238 (4)* | 1.85 | 1.95 |

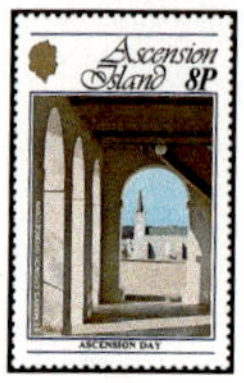


St. Mary's Church, Georgetown — A42

Designs: 12p, Old map of Ascension Island. 50p, Ascension, by Rembrandt.

**Wmk. 373**

**1979, May 24 Litho. *Perf. 14½***

| | | | | |
|---|---|---|---|---|
| **239** | A42 | 8p multicolored | .25 | .25 |
| **240** | A42 | 12p multicolored | .25 | .25 |
| **241** | A42 | 50p multicolored | .40 | *.50* |
| | | *Nos. 239-241 (3)* | .90 | 1.00 |

Ascension Day.

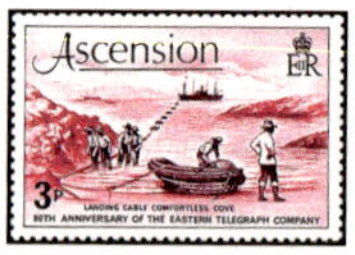


Landing Cable at Comfortless Cove — A43

Eastern Telegraph Co., 80th anniv.: 8p, Cable Ship Anglia. 12p, Map showing cables across the Atlantic, vert. 15p, Cable-laying ship. 25p, Cable and earth station.

**1979, Sept. 15**

| | | | | |
|---|---|---|---|---|
| **242** | A43 | 3p rose car & black | .25 | .25 |
| **243** | A43 | 8p dk yel grn & black | .25 | .25 |
| **244** | A43 | 12p yel bister & black | .30 | .30 |
| **245** | A43 | 15p violet & black | .40 | .40 |
| **246** | A43 | 25p deep org & black | .50 | .50 |
| | | *Nos. 242-246 (5)* | 1.70 | 1.70 |

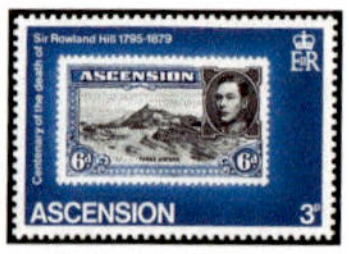


Ascension No. 45 — A44

**1979, Dec. 17 Wmk. 373 *Perf. 14***

| | | | | |
|---|---|---|---|---|
| **247** | A44 | 3p shown | .25 | .25 |
| **248** | A44 | 8p No. 73 | .25 | .25 |
| **249** | A44 | 12p No. 14, vert. | .25 | .25 |
| **250** | A44 | 50p Hill portrait, vert. | .45 | *.65* |
| | | *Nos. 247-250 (4)* | 1.20 | 1.40 |

Sir Rowland Hill (1795-1879), originator of penny postage.

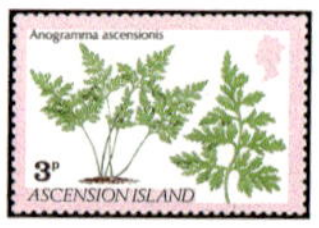


Anogramma Ascensionis — A45

6p, Xiphopteris ascensionense. 8p, Sporobolus caespitosus. 12p, Sporobolus durus, vert. 18p, Dryopteris ascensionis, vert. 24p, Marattia purpurascens, vert.

**1980, Feb. 18 Litho. *Perf. 14½***

| | | | | |
|---|---|---|---|---|
| **251** | A45 | 3p shown | .25 | .25 |
| **252** | A45 | 6p multicolored | .25 | .25 |
| **253** | A45 | 8p multicolored | .25 | .25 |
| **254** | A45 | 12p multicolored | .25 | .25 |
| **255** | A45 | 18p multicolored | .25 | .40 |
| **256** | A45 | 24p multicolored | .30 | .55 |
| | | *Nos. 251-256 (6)* | 1.55 | 1.95 |

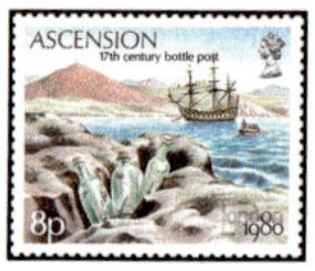


17th Century Bottle Post, London 1980 Emblem — A46

12p, 36-gun frigate, 19th century. 15p, "Garth Castle," 1863. 50p, "St. Helena," Lockheed C141.

**1980, May 1 Wmk. 373 *Perf. 14***

| | | | | |
|---|---|---|---|---|
| **257** | A46 | 8p shown | .25 | .25 |
| **258** | A46 | 12p multicolored | .30 | .30 |
| **259** | A46 | 15p multicolored | .35 | .35 |

**260** A46 50p multicolored .75 .75
*a.* Souvenir sheet of 4, #257-260 1.75 *2.25*
*Nos. 257-260 (4)* 1.65 1.65

London 1980 Intl. Stamp Exhib., May 6-14.

### Queen Mother Elizabeth Birthday
Common Design Type

**1980, Aug. 11 Litho. *Perf. 14***
**261** CD330 15p multicolored .40 .40

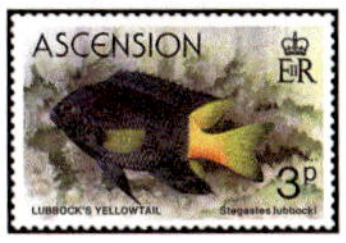

Lubbock's Yellowtail — A47

10p, Resplendent angelfish. 25p, Hedgehog butterflyfish. 40p, Marmalade razorfish.

**1980, Sept. 15 Litho. *Perf. 13½x14***
**262** A47 3p shown .40 .40
**263** A47 10p multicolored .50 .50
**264** A47 25p multicolored 1.00 .90
**265** A47 40p multicolored 1.25 *1.50*
*Nos. 262-265 (4)* 3.15 *3.30*

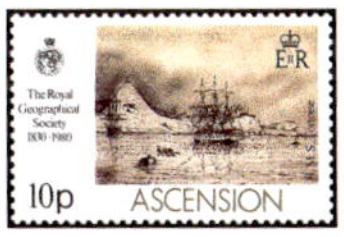

Tortoisen, by Thomas Maxon — A48

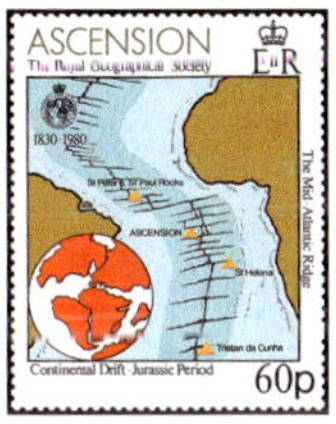

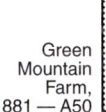

Map of South Atlantic Ridge and Contintental Drift — A49

15p, Wideawake Fair, by Linton Palmer, 1866.

**1980, Nov. 17 *Perf. 13½, 14 (60p)***
**266** A48 10p multicolored .25 *.40*
**267** A48 15p multicolored .30 *.45*
**268** A49 60p multicolored .90 *1.25*
*Nos. 266-268 (3)* 1.45 *2.10*

Royal Geographical Soc., 50th anniv.

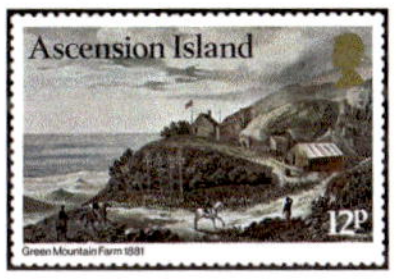

Green Mountain Farm, 1881 — A50

Designs: 15p, Two Boats, 1881. 20p, Green Mountain and Two Boats farms, 1981. 30p, Green Mountain Farm, 1981.

**1981, Feb. 15 Litho. *Perf. 14***
**269** A50 12p multicolored .25 .25
**270** A50 15p multicolored .30 .30
**271** A50 20p multicolored .30 *.35*
**272** A50 30p multicolored .40 *.50*
*Nos. 269-272 (4)* 1.25 1.40

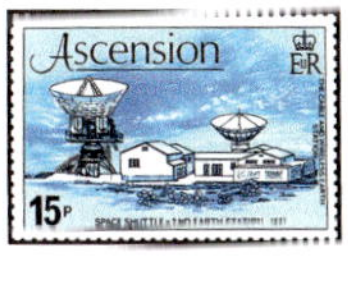

Cable and Wireless Earth Station — A51

**1981, Apr. 27 Litho. *Perf. 14***
**273** Sheet of 10 4.00 4.00
*a.* A51 15p multicolored .40 .40

Flight of Columbia space shuttle. Gutter contains story of Ascension and space shuttle; margin shows craft and dish antenna.

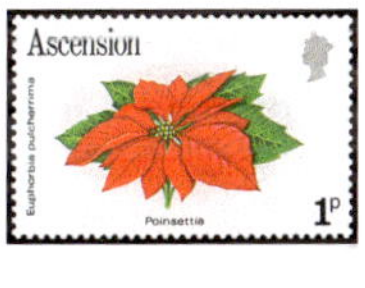

Poinsettia A52

2p, Clusterd wax flower. 3p, Kolanchoe, vert. 4p, Yellow pops. 5p, Camel's foot creeper. 8p, White oleander. 10p, Ascension lily, vert. 12p, Coral plant, vert. 15p, Yellow allamanda. 20p, Ascention euphorbia. 30p, Flame of the forest, vert. 40p, Bougainvillea. 50p, Solanum. £1, Ladies petticoat. £2, Red hibiscus.

**1981, May 11 Wmk. 373 *Perf. 13½***
**274** A52 1p shown .90 1.10
**275** A52 2p multicolored .70 1.10
**276** A52 3p multicolored .70 1.10
**277** A52 4p multicolored .90 1.10
**278** A52 5p multicolored .90 1.10
**279** A52 8p multicolored .90 1.10
**280** A52 10p multicolored .65 .95
**281** A52 12p multicolored 1.75 1.10
**282** A52 15p multicolored .75 .95
Complete booklet, 4 ea. #275, 276, 280 and 282, in blocks of 4 15.00
**283** A52 20p multicolored 1.10 .95
**284** A52 30p multicolored 1.35 1.60
**285** A52 40p multicolored 1.35 *3.00*

**Size: 42x53mm**

**286** A52 50p multicolored 1.40 *3.25*
**287** A52 £1 multicolored 2.10 *4.00*
**288** A52 £2 multicolored 3.25 *6.00*
*Nos. 274-288 (15)* 18.70 28.40

**1982, Aug. 27 Inscribed "1982"**
*275a* A52 2p Clustererd wax flower .60 1.25
*276a* A52 3p Kolanchoe, vert. .60 1.25
*280a* A52 10p Ascension lily, vert. .55 .75
*282a* A52 15p Yellow allamanda .60 .75
*283a* A52 20p Ascention euphorbia 1.10 .75
*287a* A52 £1 Ladies petticoat 1.75 *2.75*
*Nos. 275a-287a (6)* 5.20 7.50

For overprints see Nos. 321-322.

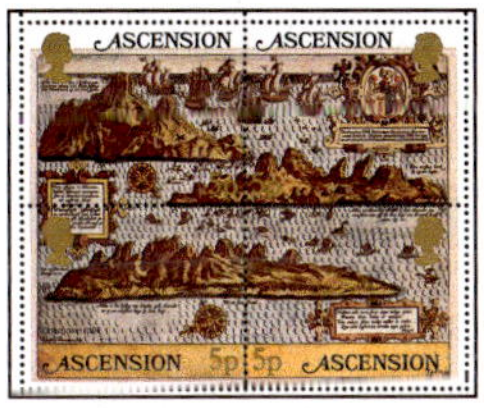

Linschoten's Map of Ascension, 1599. — A53

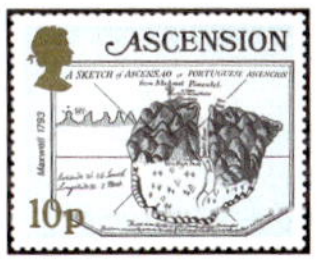

Maxwell's Map of Ascension, 1793 — A54

Old maps of Ascension: 12p, Maxwell, 1793, diff. 15p, Eckberg & Chapman, 1811. 40p, Campbell, 1819.

**1981, May 22 *Perf. 14½***
**289** A53 Sheet of 4 .60 .60
*a.-d.* 5p any single .25 .25
**290** A54 10p shown .25 .25
**291** A54 12p multicolored .30 .30
**292** A54 15p multicolored .35 .35
**293** A54 40p multicolored .65 .65
*Nos. 289-293 (5)* 2.15 2.15

### Royal Wedding Issue
Common Design Type

**1981, July 22 Wmk. 373 *Perf. 14***
**294** CD331 10p Bouquet .25 .25
**295** CD331 15p Charles .25 .25
**296** CD331 50p Couple .50 .50
*Nos. 294-296 (3)* 1.00 1.00

Nos. 294-296 each se-tenant with label.

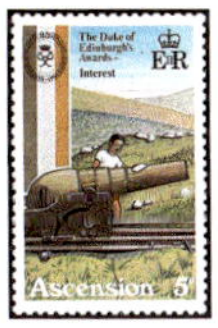

Man Shining Cannon — A55

**1981, Sept. 14 Litho. *Perf. 14***
**297** A55 5p shown .25 .25
**298** A55 10p Mountain climbing .25 .25
**299** A55 15p First aid treatment .25 .25
**300** A55 40p Duke of Edinburgh .35 .35
*Nos. 297-300 (4)* 1.10 1.10

Duke of Edinburgh's Awards, 25th anniv.

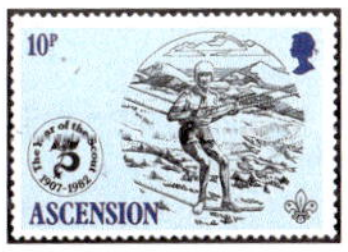

Scouting Year — A56

10p, Parallel rope walking. 15p, 1st Ascension scout flag. 25p, Radio operators. 40p, Baden-Powell.

**1982, Feb. 22 Litho. *Perf. 14***
**301** A56 10p multicolored .25 *.35*
**302** A56 15p multicolored .35 *.50*
**303** A56 25p multicolored .50 *.65*
**304** A56 40p multicolored .65 *.95*
*a.* Souvenir sheet of 4 1.60 *2.25*
*Nos. 301-304 (4)* 1.75 *2.45*

No. 304a contains stamps in designs of Nos. 301-304 (30x30mm, perf. 14½, diamond-shape).

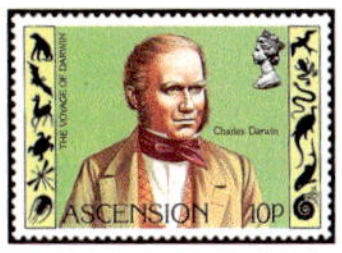

Sesquicentennial of Charles Darwin's Visit — A57

**1982, Apr. 19**
**305** A57 10p Portrait .30 *.40*
**306** A57 12p Pistols .35 *.50*
**307** A57 15p Rock crab .45 *.55*
**308** A57 40p Beagle .85 *.95*
*Nos. 305-308 (4)* 1.95 *2.40*

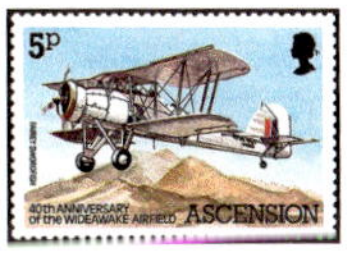

40th Anniv. of Wideawake Airfield — A58

5p, Fairey Swordfish. 10p, North American B25C Mitchell. 15p, Boeing EC-135N Aria. 50p, Lockheed Hercules.

**1982, June 15 Litho. *Perf. 14***
**309** A58 5p multicolored .85 .85
**310** A58 10p multicolored 1.00 1.00
Complete booklet, 4 ea. #309 and 310, in blocks of 4 7.75
**311** A58 15p multicolored 1.25 1.25
**312** A58 50p multicolored 2.00 2.00
*Nos. 309-312 (4)* 5.10 5.10

The cover of the booklet containing Nos. 309 and 310 exists with both brown and blue inscriptions. Same value.

### Princess Diana Issue
Common Design Type

***Perf. 14½x14***

**1982, July 1 Wmk. 373**
**313** CD333 12p Arms .55 .55
**314** CD333 15p Diana .55 .55
**315** CD333 25p Wedding .90 .90
**316** CD333 50p Portrait 1.50 1.50
*Nos. 313-316 (4)* 3.50 3.50

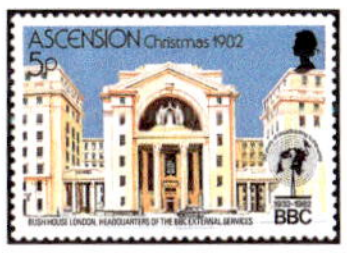

Christmas and 50th Anniv. of BBC Overseas Broadcasting A59

Anniv. Emblem and: 5p, Bush House (London headquarters). 10p, Atlantic relay station. 25p, Lord Reith, first director general. 40p, King George V delivering Christmas address, 1932.

**1982, Dec. 20 Litho. *Perf. 14***
**317** A59 5p multicolored .25 .25
**318** A59 10p multicolored .25 .25
**319** A59 25p multicolored .60 .60
**320** A59 40p multicolored .90 .90
*Nos. 317-320 (4)* 2.00 2.00

### Nos. 282a-283a Overprinted

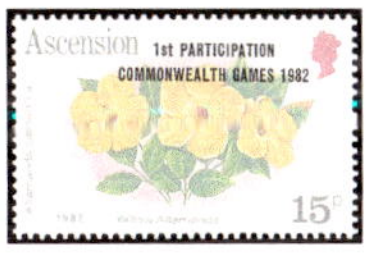


**1982 Litho. *Perf. 13½***
**321** A52 15p multicolored .30 .30
**322** A52 20p multicolored .40 .40

12th Commonwealth Games, Brisbane, Australia, Sept. 30-Oct. 9.

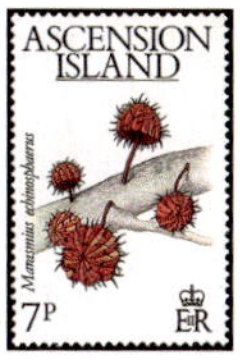

A60

7p, Marasmius echinosphaerus. 12p, Chlorophyllum molybdites. 15p, Leucocoprinus cepaestipes. 20p, Lycoperdon marginatum. 50p, Marasmiellus distantifolius.

**1983, Mar. 1 *Perf. 14***
**323** A60 7p multicolored .60 .30
**324** A60 12p multicolored .90 .50
**325** A60 15p multicolored 1.00 .60
**326** A60 20p multicolored 1.25 .70
**327** A60 50p multicolored 1.60 *1.75*
*Nos. 323-327 (5)* 5.35 *3.85*

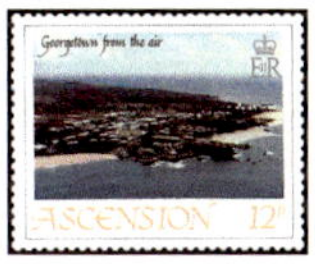

View of Georgetown — A61

15p, Farm, Green Mountain. 20p, Boatswain Bird Island. 60p, Telemetry Hill.

**1983, May 12 Litho. *Perf. 14***
**328** A61 12p shown .25 .25
**329** A61 15p multicolored .25 .25
**330** A61 20p multicolored .35 .35
**331** A61 60p multicolored .80 .80
*Nos. 328-331 (4)* 1.65 1.65

See Nos. 359-362.

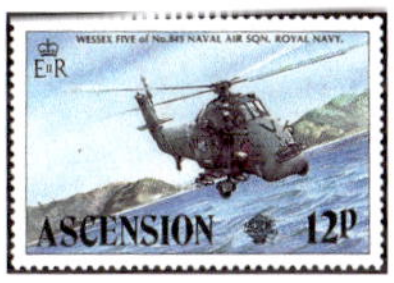

Manned Flight Bicentenary A62

Military Aircraft: 12p, Wessex Five helicopter. 15p, Vulcan B2. 20p, Nimrod MR2P, 60p, Victor K2.

**1983, Aug. 1 Wmk. 373 *Perf. 14***
**332** A62 12p multicolored .75 .75
**333** A62 15p multicolored .85 .85
**334** A62 20p multicolored .80 .80
**335** A62 60p multicolored 1.40 1.40
*Nos. 332-335 (4)* 3.80 3.80

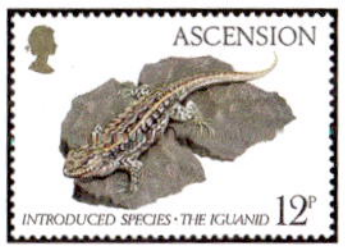

Introduced Species — A63

**1983, Sept. Litho. Wmk. 373**
**336** A63 12p Iguanid .40 .40
**337** A63 15p Rabbit .50 .50
**338** A63 20p Cat .60 .60
**339** A63 60p Donkey 1.25 1.25
*Nos. 336-339 (4)* 2.75 2.75

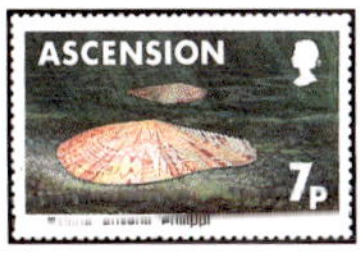

Tellina Antonii Philippi — A64

12p, Nodipecten nodosus. 15p, Cypraea lurida oceanica. 20p, Nerita ascensionis gmelin. 50p, Micromelo undatus.

**1983, Nov. 28 Litho. *Perf. 14½***
**340** A64 7p shown .25 .25
**341** A64 12p multicolored .30 .30
**342** A64 15p multicolored .40 .40
**343** A64 20p multicolored .50 .50
**344** A64 50p multicolored 1.10 1.10
*Nos. 340-344 (5)* 2.55 2.55

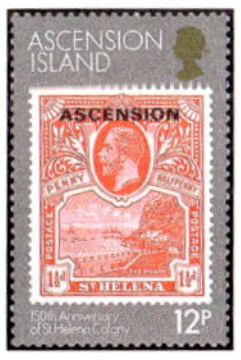

St. Helena Colony, 150th Anniv. — A65

Designs: First issue inscribed Ascension instead of overprinted.

**1984, Jan. 10 Litho. *Perf. 14***

**345** A65 12p No. 3 .25 *.40*
**346** A65 15p No. 4 .35 *.45*
**347** A65 20p No. 6 .45 *.55*
**348** A65 60p No. 9 1.00 *1.25*
*Nos. 345-348 (4)* 2.05 *2.65*

Souvenir Sheet

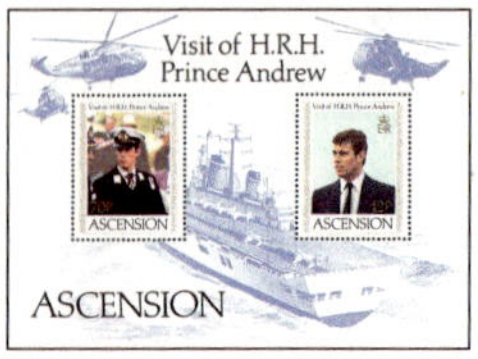


Visit of Prince Andrew A66

**1984, Apr. 10 *Perf. 14½x14***

**349** A66 Sheet of 2 1.50 1.50
*a.* 12p Andrew .25 .25
*b.* 70p In naval uniform 1.10 1.10

**Lloyd's List Issue**
Common Design Type

12p, Naval semaphore. 15p, "Southampton Castle". 20p, Pier Head. 70p, Dane.

**1984, May 28**

**351** CD335 12p multicolored .45 .25
**352** CD335 15p multicolored .55 .35
**353** CD335 20p multicolored .65 .45
**354** CD335 70p multicolored 1.25 *1.50*
*Nos. 351-354 (4)* 2.90 2.55

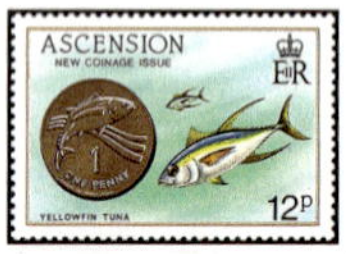

1984 Coins and Wildlife — A67

12p, One penny, yellowfin tuna. 15p, Two pence, donkeys. 20p, Fifty pence, green turtle. 70p, One pound, sooty terns.

**1984, June *Perf. 14***

**355** A67 12p multicolored .70 .70
**356** A67 15p multicolored .90 .90
**357** A67 20p multicolored .90 .90
**358** A67 70p multicolored 1.50 *2.00*
*Nos. 355-358 (4)* 4.00 4.50

**View Type of 1983**

12p, Devil's Riding School. 15p, St. Mary's Church. 20p, Two Boats Village. 70p, Ascension Island.

**1984, Oct. Litho. Wmk. 373**

**359** A61 12p multicolored .25 .25
**360** A61 15p multicolored .30 .30
**361** A61 20p multicolored .45 .45
**362** A61 70p multicolored 1.25 1.25
*Nos. 359-362 (4)* 2.25 2.25

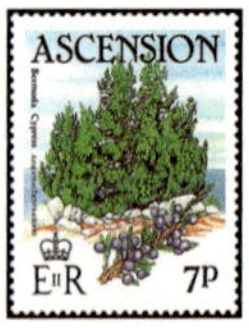

Trees — A68

7p, Bermuda cypress. 12p, Norfolk Island pine. 15p, Screwpine. 20p, Eucalyptus. 65p, Spore tree.

**1985, Mar. 8 Litho. *Perf. 14½x14***

**363** A68 7p multicolored .55 .45
**364** A68 12p multicolored .60 .50
**365** A68 15p multicolored .70 .65
**366** A68 20p multicolored .75 .75
**367** A68 65p multicolored 1.90 1.90
*Nos. 363-367 (5)* 4.50 4.25

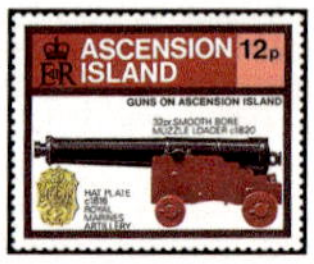

Military Firearms — A69

Large guns and insignia: 12p, Thirty-two pounder small bore muzzle loader, c. 1820; Royal Marines hat plate, c. 1816. 15p, Seven-inch rifled muzzle loader, c. 1866; royal cipher. 20p, Seven-pounder rifled muzzle loader, c. 1877; Royal Artillery badge. 70p, HMS Hood 5.5-inch gun; ship crest.

**1985, July 21 Wmk. 373 *Perf. 14½***

**368** A69 12p multicolored .55 .55
**369** A69 15p multicolored .80 .80
**370** A69 20p multicolored .80 .80
**371** A69 70p multicolored 2.00 *2.50*
*Nos. 368-371 (4)* 4.15 4.65

**Queen Mother 85th Birthday**
Common Design Type

12p, With Duke of York, Balmoral, 1924. 15p, With Princes Andrew and Edward. 20p, At Ascot. 70p, Christening of Prince Henry, Windsor Castle. 75p, Leaving the QEII, 1968.

***Perf. 14½x14***

**1985, June 7 Wmk. 384**

**372** CD336 12p multicolored .50 .50
**373** CD336 15p multicolored .50 .50
**374** CD336 20p multicolored .65 .65
**375** CD336 70p multicolored 1.50 1.50
*Nos. 372-375 (4)* 3.15 3.15

**Souvenir Sheet**

**376** CD336 75p multicolored 1.50 1.50

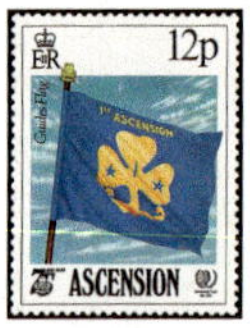

Intl. Youth Year, Girl Guides 75th Anniv. — A70

12p, Guides' banner. 15p, First aid. 20p, Camping. 70p, Lady Baden-Powell.

**1985, Oct. 4 Wmk. 373**

**377** A70 12p multicolored .60 .60
**378** A70 15p multicolored .65 .55
**379** A70 20p multicolored .75 .65
**380** A70 70p multicolored 2.00 *2.50*
*Nos. 377-380 (4)* 4.00 4.30

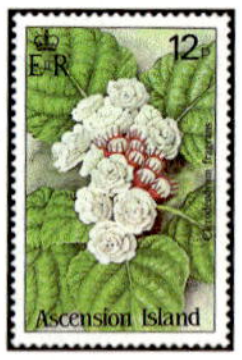

Wildflowers — A71

12p, Clerodendrum fragrans. 15p, Shell ginger. 20p, Cape daisy. 70p, Ginger lily.

**Wmk. 384**

**1985, Dec. 6 Litho. *Perf. 14***

**381** A71 12p multicolored .60 .60
**382** A71 15p multicolored .70 .70
**383** A71 20p multicolored .80 .80
**384** A71 70p multicolored 1.60 *2.25*
*Nos. 381-384 (4)* 3.70 4.35

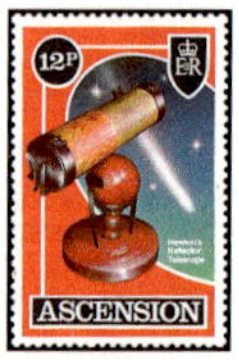

Halley's Comet — A72

Designs: 12p, Newton's reflector telescope. 15p, Edmond Halley, Old Greenwich Observatory. 20p, Short's Gregorian telescope, comet, 1759. 70p, ICE space probe, Ascension satellite tracking station.

**1986, Mar. 7**

**385** A72 12p multicolored .60 *.75*
**386** A72 15p multicolored .70 *.85*
**387** A72 20p multicolored .75 *.85*
**388** A72 70p multicolored 2.00 *2.75*
*Nos. 385-388 (4)* 4.05 *5.20*

**Queen Elizabeth II 60th Birthday**
Common Design Type

Designs: 7p, Infant photograph, 1926. 15p, 1st worldwide Christmas broadcast, 1952. 20p, Garter Ceremony, Windsor Castle, 1983. 35p, Royal Tour, New Zealand, 1981. £1, Visiting Crown Agents' offices, 1983.

**1986, Apr. 21 *Perf. 14x14½***

**389** CD337 7p scarlet, blk & sil .25 .25
**390** CD337 15p ultra, blk & sil .35 .35
**391** CD337 20p green & multi .45 .45
**392** CD337 35p violet & multi .50 .50
**393** CD337 £1 rose vio & multi 1.25 *1.75*
*Nos. 389-393 (5)* 2.80 3.30

For overprints see Nos. 431-435.

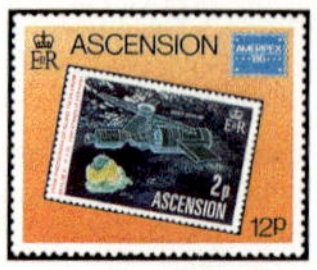

AMERIPEX '86 — A73

**1986, May 22 *Perf. 14½***

**394** A73 12p No. 183 .35 *.50*
**395** A73 15p No. 260 .50 *.60*
**396** A73 20p No. 215 .65 *.75*
**397** A73 70p No. 310 1.35 *2.00*
*Nos. 394-397 (4)* 2.85 *3.85*

**Souvenir Sheet**

**398** A73 75p Statue of Liberty, New York Harbor 3.50 3.50

Statue of Liberty, cent.

**Royal Wedding Issue, 1986**
Common Design Type

Designs: 15p, Couple kissing. 35p, Andrew in navy uniform, helicopter.

**Wmk. 384**

**1986, July 23 Litho. *Perf. 14***

**399** CD338 15p multicolored .50 .50
**400** CD338 35p multicolored 1.10 1.10

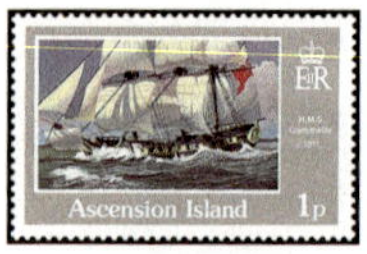

Ships — A74

1p, Ganymede, c. 1811. 2p, Kangaroo, c. 1811. 4p, Trinculo, c. 1811. 5p, Daring, c. 1811. 9p, Thais, c. 1811. 10p, Pheasant, 1819. 15p, Myrmidon, 1819. 18p, Atholl, 1825. 20p, Medina, 1830. 25p, Saracen, 1840. 30p, Hydra, c. 1845. 50p, Sealark, 1840. 70p, Rattlesnake, 1868. £1, Penelope, 1889. £2, Monarch, 1897.

**1986, Oct. 14 Wmk. 384 *Perf. 14½***

**401** A74 1p multicolored .90 *1.25*
**402** A74 2p multicolored 1.00 *1.25*
**403** A74 4p multicolored 1.00 *1.25*
**404** A74 5p multicolored 1.00 *1.25*
**405** A74 9p multicolored 1.10 *1.25*
**406** A74 10p multicolored 1.10 *1.25*
**407** A74 15p multicolored 1.25 *1.75*
**408** A74 18p multicolored 1.25 *1.75*
**409** A74 20p multicolored 1.25 *1.75*
**410** A74 25p multicolored 1.25 *2.00*
**411** A74 30p multicolored 1.25 *2.00*
**412** A74 50p multicolored 1.75 *2.75*
**413** A74 70p multicolored 2.50 *3.25*
**414** A74 £1 multicolored 3.50 *4.25*
**415** A74 £2 multicolored 6.50 *8.00*
*Nos. 401-415 (15)* 26.60 *35.00*

For surcharges see Nos. 502-504.

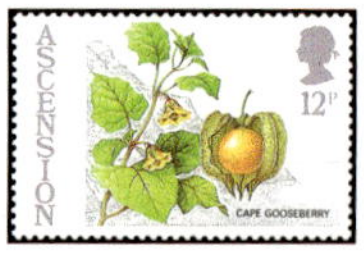

Edible Bush Fruits — A75

**1987, Jan. 29 *Perf. 14***

**416** A75 12p Cape gooseberry .90 .90
**417** A75 15p Prickly pear 1.00 1.00
**418** A75 20p Guava 1.10 1.10
**419** A75 70p Loquat 2.00 *2.50*
*Nos. 416-419 (4)* 5.00 5.50

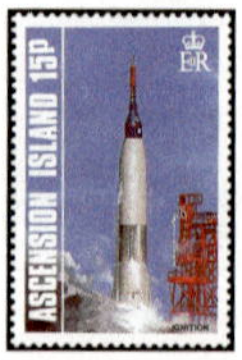

1st American Manned Orbital Space Flight, 25th Anniv. — A76

15p, Ignition. 18p, Lift-off. 25p, Reentry. £1, Splashdown.
70p, Friendship 7 capsule.

**1987, Mar. 30**

**420** A76 15p multicolored .85 .85
**421** A76 18p multicolored .95 .95
**422** A76 25p multicolored 1.25 1.25
**423** A76 £1 multicolored 3.50 3.50
*Nos. 420-423 (4)* 6.55 6.55

**Souvenir Sheet**

**424** A76 70p multicolored 2.50 2.50

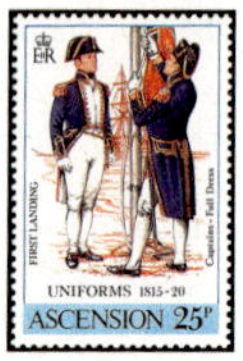

Military Uniforms, 1815-20 — A77

Designs: a, Captains in full dress, 1st landing on Ascenion. b, Surgeon and sailors at campsite. c, Seaman returning from Dampier's Drip with water supply. d, Midshipman at lookout post. e, Commander and surveyor.

**1987, June 29**

**425** Strip of 5 4.00 4.00
*a.-e.* A77 25p multicolored .70 .70

See Nos. 458, 482, 507.

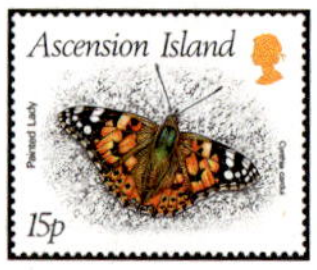

Butterflies — A78

**1987, Aug. 10 *Perf. 14½***

**426** A78 15p Painted lady 1.10 1.10
**427** A78 18p Monarch 1.10 1.10
**428** A78 25p Diadem 1.50 1.50
**429** A78 £1 Long-tailed blue 4.00 4.00
*Nos. 426-429 (4)* 7.70 7.70

See Nos. 436-439, 459-462.

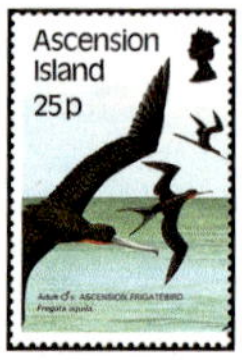

Birds — A79

Designs: a, Ascension frigatebirds (males). b, Brown booby, frigatebird, white boobies. c, Frigatebird, white booby. d, Ascension frigatebirds (females). e, Adult frigatebird feeding young.

**1987, Oct. 8 Wmk. 373 *Perf. 14***

**430** Strip of 5 11.00 11.00
*a.-e.* A79 25p any single 2.00 2.00

No. 430 has continuous design.
See No. 453.

**Nos. 389-393 Ovptd. "40TH WEDDING ANNIVERSARY" in Silver**

***Perf. 14x14½***

**1987, Dec. 9 Litho. Wmk. 384**

**431** CD337 7p scar, blk & sil .25 .25
**432** CD337 15p ultra, blk & sil .30 .30
**433** CD337 20p green & multi .50 .50
**434** CD337 35p violet & multi .75 .75
**435** CD337 £1 rose vio & multi 1.50 1.50
*Nos. 431-435 (5)* 3.30 3.30

40th wedding anniv. of Queen Elizabeth II and Prince Philip.

**Insects Type of 1987**

15p, Field cricket. 18p, Bush cricket. 25p, Ladybug. £1, Burnished brass moth.

**1988, Jan. 18 *Perf. 14½***

**436** A78 15p multicolored .80 .80
**437** A78 18p multicolored .90 .90
**438** A78 25p multicolored 1.25 1.25
**439** A78 £1 multicolored 4.25 4.25
*Nos. 436-439 (4)* 7.20 7.20

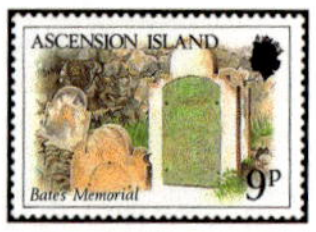

A80

Capt. William Bate (d. 1838), 1st Garrison Commander and Colonial Founder of Ascension: 9p, Bate's Memorial, St. Mary's Church. 15p, Commodore's Cottage, Cross Hill. 18p, North East or Bate's Cottage, 1833. 25p, Landmarks on map. 70p, Bate and 3 soldiers.

**1988, Apr. 14 Litho. *Perf. 14***

**440** A80 9p multicolored .30 .30
**441** A80 15p multicolored .50 .50
**442** A80 18p multicolored .60 .60

**443** A80 25p multicolored .85 .85
**444** A80 70p multicolored 2.00 2.00
*Nos. 440-444 (5)* 4.25 4.25

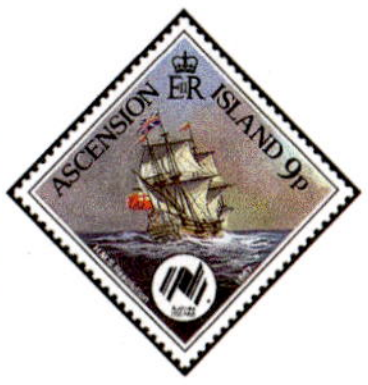

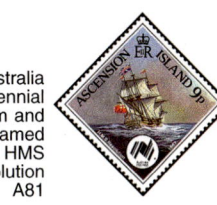

Australia Bicentennial Emblem and Ships Named HMS Resolution A81

9p, 3-Masted squarerigger, 1667. 18p, 3-Masted squarerigger, 1772. 25p, Navy cruiser, 1892. 65p, Battleship, 1916.

**1988, June 23 Litho. *Perf. 14***
**445** A81 9p multicolored 1.25 .50
**446** A81 18p multicolored 1.75 .80
**447** A81 25p multicolored 2.00 1.00
**448** A81 65p multicolored 3.00 2.00
*Nos. 445-448 (4)* 8.00 4.30

Australia bicentennial.

### Nos. 445-448 Overprinted

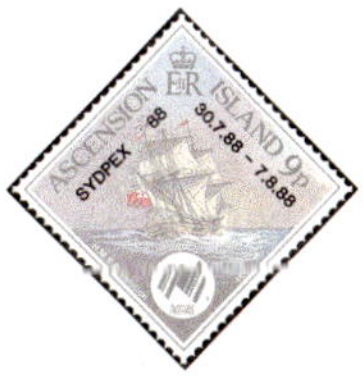

**Wmk. 384**

**1988, July 30 Litho. *Perf. 14***
**449** A81 9p multicolored .75 .55
**450** A81 18p multicolored 1.25 .90
**451** A81 25p multicolored 1.25 .95
**452** A81 65p multicolored 2.50 2.50
*Nos. 449-452 (4)* 5.75 4.90

SYDPEX '88, July 30-Aug. 7.

### Bird Type of 1987

Behaviors of the wideawake tern, Sterna fuscata: a, Two adults, flock overhead. b, Nesting (two birds). c, Nesting (three birds). d, Adult and young. e, Tern flapping its wings.

**1988, Aug. 15 *Perf. 14***
**453** Strip of 5 10.00 10.00
*a.-e.* A79 25p any single 1.90 1.90

No. 453 has continuous design.

### Lloyds of London, 300th Anniv.
Common Design Type

8p, Lloyd's Coffee House, Tower Street, 1688. 18p, Cable ship Alert, horiz. 25p, Satellite recovery in space, horiz. 65p, Ship Good Hope Castle on fire off Ascension, 1973.

**Wmk. 373**

**1988, Oct. 17 Litho. *Perf. 14***
**454** CD341 8p multicolored .40 .40
**455** CD341 18p multicolored .85 .85
**456** CD341 25p multicolored 1.25 1.25
**457** CD341 65p multicolored 2.50 2.50
*Nos. 454-457 (4)* 5.00 5.00

### Military Uniforms Type of 1987

Uniforms of the Royal Marines: a, Marines arrive in Ascension (marines), 1821. b, Semaphore station (officer, marine), 1829. c, Octagonal tank (sergeant), 1831. d, Water pipe tunnel (officers), 1833. e, Constructing barracks (officer), 1834.

**1988, Nov. 21**
**458** Strip of 5 8.50 8.50
*a.-e.* A77 25p multicolored 1.50 1.50

### Insect Type of 1987
**Wmk. 384**

**1989, Jan. 16 Litho. *Perf. 14½***
**459** A78 15p Plume moth 1.25 .80
**460** A78 18p Green bottle 1.25 .90
**461** A78 25p Weevil 1.00 .90
**462** A78 £1 Paper wasp 5.00 3.25
*Nos. 459-462 (4)* 8.50 5.85

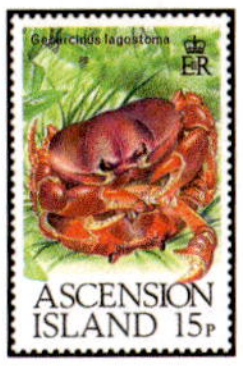

Land Crabs, Gecarcinus Lagostoma — A82

**1989, Apr. 17**
**463** A82 15p multicolored .75 .75
**464** A82 18p multi, diff. .80 .80
**465** A82 25p multi, diff. 1.25 1.25
**466** A82 £1 multi, diff. 4.00 4.00
*Nos. 463-466 (4)* 6.80 6.80

**Background designs continuous**
**467** A82 15p multicolored .55 .55
**467A** A82 18p multi, diff. .75 .75
**467B** A82 25p multi, diff. .95 .95
**467C** A82 £1 multi, diff. 4.00 4.00
*d.* Souvenir sheet of 4, #467-467C 7.50 7.50

### Moon Landing, 20th Anniv.
Common Design Type

Apollo 7: 15p, Tracking Station, Ascension Is. 18p, Launch, Cape Kennedy. 25p, Mission emblem. 70p, Expended Saturn IVB stage. £1, Lunar landing profile for the Apollo 11 mission.

**1989, July 20 *Perf. 14x13½***
**Size of Nos. 469-470: 29x29mm**
**468** CD342 15p multicolored .90 .65
**469** CD342 18p multicolored 1.00 .75
**470** CD342 25p multicolored 1.25 .95
**471** CD342 70p multicolored 2.25 2.25
*Nos. 468-471 (4)* 5.40 4.60

**Souvenir Sheet**
**472** CD342 £1 multicolored 4.00 4.00

Souvenir Sheet

A83

**1989, July 7 *Perf. 14x13½***
**473** A83 75p Emblems, No. 60 4.25 4.25

Miniature Sheet

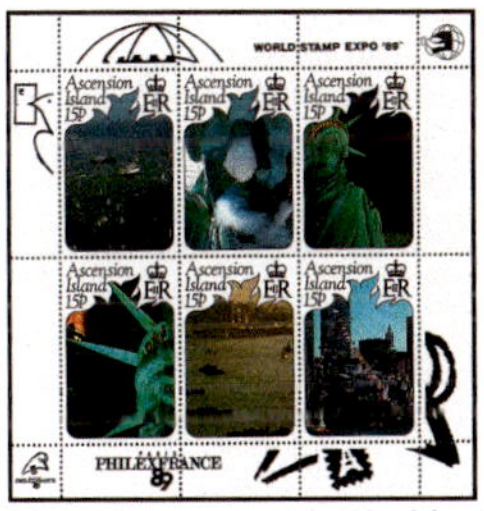

World Stamp Expo '89, Washington, DC, and PHILEXFRANCE '89, Paris — A84

The Statue of Liberty and scenes from the centenary celebrations, 1986: a, Operation Sail. b, Face. c, Upper body. d, Three crown points. e, Ships in harbor, view of lower Manhattan. f, Ship in port, New York City.

**1989, Aug. 21 Wmk. 373**
**474** A84 Sheet of 6 5.00 5.00
*a.-f.* 15p any single .70 .70

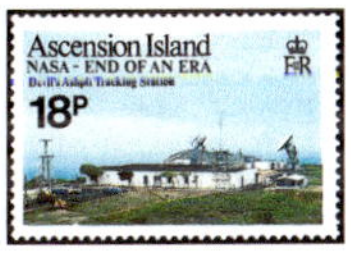

Devil's Ashpit Tracking Station — A85

**1989, Sept. 30 Wmk. 384 *Perf. 14***
**475** Sheet, 5 each #a.-b. 10.50 10.50
*a.* A85 18p shown .70 .70
*b.* A85 25p US space shuttle launch 1.10 1.10

Termination of NASA tracking operations, begun in 1965, at the station.

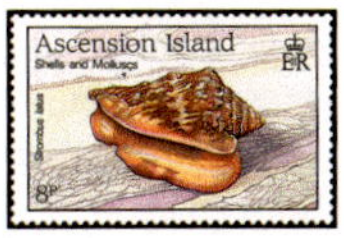

Shells and Mollusks — A86

Designs: 8p, Strombus latus. 18p, Tonna galea. 25p, Harpa doris. £1, Charonia variegata.

**Wmk. 384**

**1989, Nov. 6 Litho. *Perf. 14***
**476** A86 8p multicolored .70 .45
**477** A86 18p multicolored 1.25 .65
**478** A86 25p multicolored 1.75 .90
**479** A86 £1 multicolored 4.25 3.50
*Nos. 476-479 (4)* 7.95 5.50

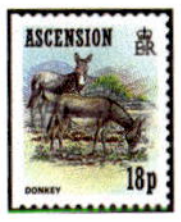

Donkeys — A87

***Perf. 14 on 3 Sides***

**1989, Nov. 17 Litho. Wmk. 384**
**Booklet Stamps**
**480** A87 18p shown *1.50 1.60*
*a.* Booklet pane of 6 *9.50*
**481** A87 25p Green turtle *2.00 1.60*
*a.* Booklet pane of 4 *8.00*

No. 480a sold for £1.

### Military Type of 1987

Royal Navy equipment, c. 1815-1820: a, Seaman's pistol, hat, cutlass. b, Midshipman's belt buckle, button, sword, hat. c, Surgeon's hat, sword, instrument chest. d, Captain's hat, telescope, sword. e, Admiral's epaulet, megaphone, hat, pocket.

**1990, Feb. 12 Litho. *Perf. 14***
**482** Strip of 5 6.50 6.50
*a.-e.* A77 25p any single 1.10 1.10

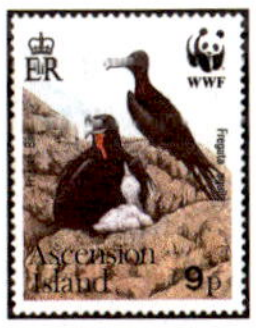

World Wildlife Fund — A88

Frigate birds *(Fregata aquila)*: 9p, Family group. 10p, Chick. 11p, Male in flight. 15p, Female and immature in flight.

***Perf. 14½x14***

**1990, Mar. 5 Litho. Wmk. 373**
**483** A88 9p multicolored *3.50 1.10*
**484** A88 10p multicolored *3.50 1.25*
**485** A88 11p multicolored *3.50 1.50*
**486** A88 15p multicolored *3.50 2.00*
*Nos. 483-486 (4) 14.00 5.85*

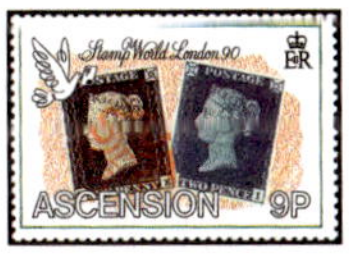

Great Britain Nos. 1-2 — A89

Exhibition emblem and: 18p, Early Ascension cancellations. 25p, Unloading mail at Wideawake Airfield. £1, Main P.O., Royal Mail van.

**1990, May 3 Litho. *Perf. 14***
**487** A89 9p shown .50 .50
**488** A89 18p multicolored .80 .80
**489** A89 25p multicolored 1.10 1.10
**490** A89 £1 multicolored 4.00 4.00
*Nos. 487-490 (4)* 6.40 6.40

Penny Black 150th anniv., Stamp World London '90.

### Queen Mother, 90th Birthday
Common Design Types

25p, Portrait, 1940. £1, King, Queen with soldiers.

**1990, Aug. 4 Wmk. 384 *Perf. 14x15***
**491** CD343 25p multi 1.25 1.25

***Perf. 14½***
**492** CD344 £1 multi 3.50 3.50

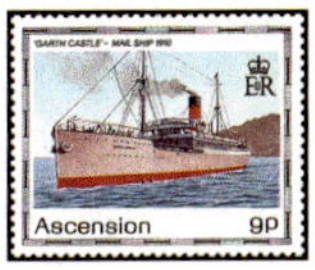

Garth Castle, 1910 — A90

Designs: 18p, RMS St. Helena, 1982. 25p, Launching new RMS St. Helena, 1989. 70p, Duke of York launching new RMS St. Helena. £1, New RMS St. Helena.

**Wmk. 373**

**1990, Sept. 13 Litho. *Perf. 14½***
**493** A90 9p multicolored 1.25 1.25
**494** A90 18p multicolored 1.60 1.60
**495** A90 25p multicolored 2.50 2.50
**496** A90 70p multicolored 4.25 4.25
*Nos. 493-496 (4)* 9.60 9.60

**Souvenir Sheet**
**497** A90 £1 multicolored 6.75 6.75

See St. Helena Nos. 535-539, Tristan da Cunha Nos. 482-486.

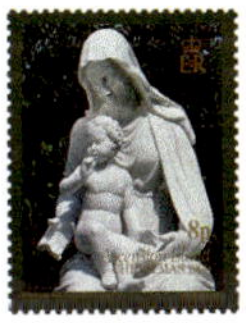

Christmas — A91

Sculpture (8p) and paintings of Madonna and Child by: 8p, Felici. 18p, Unknown artist. 25p, Gebhard. 65p, Gritti.

**1990, Oct. 24 *Perf. 14***
**498** A91 8p multicolored 1.00 .80
**499** A91 18p multicolored 1.75 1.40
**500** A91 25p multicolored 2.50 1.90
**501** A91 65p multicolored 4.00 4.00
*Nos. 498-501 (4)* 9.25 8.10

### Nos. 410, 412 & 414 Ovptd. in Silver "BRITISH FOR 175 YEARS"

**1991, Feb. 5 Wmk. 384 *Perf. 14½***
**502** A74 25p on #410 2.75 2.75
**503** A74 50p on #412 3.25 3.25
**504** A74 £1 on #414 4.50 4.50
*Nos. 502-504 (3)* 10.50 10.50

### Elizabeth & Philip, Birthdays
Common Design Types

**1991, June 18**
**505** CD345 25p multicolored 1.40 *1.60*
**506** CD346 25p multicolored 1.40 *1.60*
*a.* Pair, #505-506 + label 3.50 3.75

### Military Uniforms Type of 1987

Royal Marines Equipment 1821-1844: a, Officer's shako, epaulettes, belt plate, button. b, Officer's cap, sword, epaulettes, belt plate. c, Drum Major's shako with cords, staff. d, Sergeant's shako, chevrons, belt plate, canteen. e, Drummer's drum, sticks, shako.

**1991, Aug. 1 Wmk. 373 *Perf. 14***
**507** A77 25p Strip of 5, #a.-e. 9.50 9.50

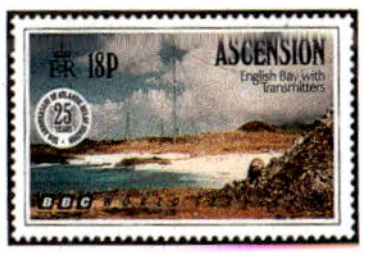

Atlantic Relay Station, 25th Anniv. — A92

15p, BBC Atlantic relay station. 18p, English Bay transmitters. 25p, Satellite receiving station. 70p, Antenna support tower.

**1991, Sept. 17 Wmk. 384 *Perf. 14½***
**508** A92 15p multi 1.40 1.40
**509** A92 18p multi 1.60 1.60
**510** A92 25p multi, vert. 2.00 2.00
**511** A92 70p multi, vert. 4.50 4.50
*Nos. 508-511 (4)* 9.50 9.50

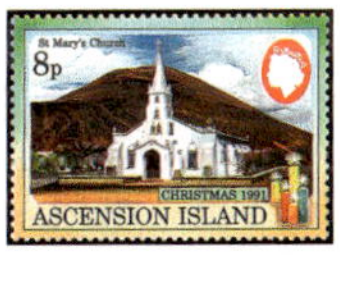

Christmas — A93

Designs: 8p, St. Mary's Church, exterior. 18p, St. Mary's Church, interior. 25p, Grotto of Our Lady of Ascension, exterior. 65p, Grotto of Our Lady of Ascension, interior.

**1991, Oct. 1** ***Perf. 14***

| | | | | |
|---|---|---|---|---|
| **512** | A93 | 8p multicolored | .85 | .70 |
| **513** | A93 | 18p multicolored | 1.50 | 1.25 |
| **514** | A93 | 25p multicolored | 2.00 | 1.50 |
| **515** | A93 | 65p multicolored | 3.75 | *4.50* |
| | | *Nos. 512-515 (4)* | 8.10 | 7.95 |

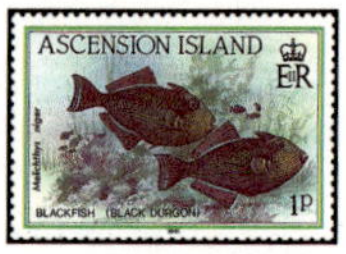

Fish — A94

1p, Blackfish. 2p, Five finger. 4p, Resplendent angelfish. 5p, Silver fish. 9p, Gurnard. 10p, Blue dad. 15p, Cunning fish. 18p, Grouper. 20p, Moray eel. 25p, Hardback soldierfish. 30p, Blue marlin. 50p, Wahoo. 70p, Yellowfin tuna. £1, Blue shark. £2.50, Bottlenose dolphin.

**Wmk. 373**

**1991, Dec. 10 Litho.** ***Perf. 14***

| | | | | |
|---|---|---|---|---|
| **516** | A94 | 1p multi | .70 | .70 |
| **517** | A94 | 2p multi | 1.00 | .75 |
| **518** | A94 | 4p multi | 1.10 | .95 |
| **519** | A94 | 5p multi | 1.10 | .95 |
| **520** | A94 | 9p multi | 1.50 | 1.10 |
| **521** | A94 | 10p multi | 1.50 | 1.10 |
| **522** | A94 | 15p multi | 2.00 | 1.10 |
| **523** | A94 | 18p multi | 2.00 | 1.25 |
| **524** | A94 | 20p multi | 2.00 | 1.50 |
| **525** | A94 | 25p multi | 2.00 | 1.60 |
| **526** | A94 | 30p multi | 2.00 | 1.75 |
| **527** | A94 | 50p multi | 2.50 | 2.50 |
| **528** | A94 | 70p multi | 3.25 | 3.25 |
| **529** | A94 | £1 multi | 3.75 | 3.75 |
| **530** | A94 | £2.50 multi | 7.50 | 7.50 |
| | | *Nos. 516-530 (15)* | 33.90 | 29.75 |

### Queen Elizabeth II's Accession to the Throne, 40th Anniv.

Common Design Type

**Wmk. 373**

**1992, Feb. 6 Litho.** ***Perf. 14***

| | | | | |
|---|---|---|---|---|
| **531** | CD349 | 9p multicolored | .45 | .45 |
| **532** | CD349 | 15p multicolored | .75 | .75 |
| **533** | CD349 | 18p multicolored | .90 | .90 |
| **534** | CD349 | 25p multicolored | 1.25 | 1.25 |
| **535** | CD349 | 70p multicolored | 2.75 | 2.75 |
| | | *Nos. 531-535 (5)* | 6.10 | 6.10 |

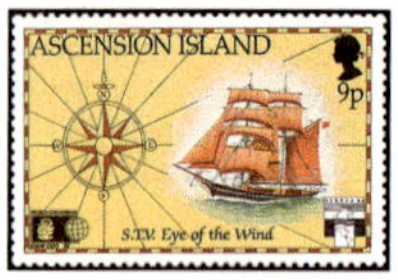

Discovery of America, 500th Anniv. — A95

9p, STV Eye of the Wind. 18p, STV Soren Larsen. 25p, Pinta, Santa Maria, & Nina. 70p, Columbus, Santa Maria.

**Wmk. 373**

**1992, Feb. 18 Litho.** ***Perf. 14***

| | | | | |
|---|---|---|---|---|
| **536** | A95 | 9p multicolored | 1.40 | .65 |
| **537** | A95 | 18p multicolored | 2.25 | .95 |
| **538** | A95 | 25p multicolored | 2.75 | 1.25 |
| **539** | A95 | 70p multicolored | 5.00 | 2.75 |
| | | *Nos. 536-539 (4)* | 11.40 | 5.60 |

World Columbian Stamp Expo '92, Chicago and Genoa '92 Intl. Philatelic Exhibitions.

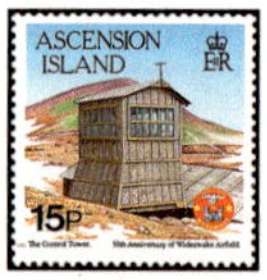

Wideawake Airfield, 50th Anniv. — A96

15p, Control tower. 18p, Nose hangar. 25p, Construction work. 70p, Laying fuel pipeline.

**Wmk. 373**

**1992, May 5 Litho.** ***Perf. 14***

| | | | | |
|---|---|---|---|---|
| **540** | A96 | 15p multicolored | .95 | .95 |
| **541** | A96 | 18p multicolored | 1.25 | 1.25 |
| **542** | A96 | 25p multicolored | 1.50 | 1.50 |
| **543** | A96 | 70p multicolored | 3.75 | 3.75 |
| | | *Nos. 540-543 (4)* | 7.45 | 7.45 |

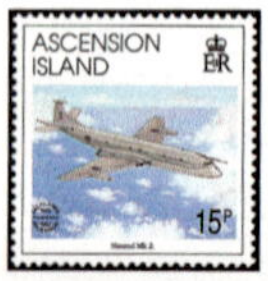

Ascension's Participation in Falkland Islands' Liberation, 10th Anniv. — A97

15p, Nimrod Mk.2. 18p, VC10. 25p, Wessex HU Mk.5 helicopter. 65p, Vulcan B2.

No. 548a, 15p + 3p like #544. b, 18p + 4p like #545. c, 25p + 5p like #546. d, 65p + 13p like #547.

**Wmk. 373**

**1992, June 12 Litho.** ***Perf. 14***

| | | | | |
|---|---|---|---|---|
| **544** | A97 | 15p multicolored | 1.25 | 1.10 |
| **545** | A97 | 18p multicolored | 1.25 | 1.10 |
| **546** | A97 | 25p multicolored | 1.90 | 1.50 |
| **547** | A97 | 65p multicolored | 3.00 | *4.25* |
| | | *Nos. 544-547 (4)* | 7.40 | 7.95 |

**Souvenir Sheet**

| | | | | |
|---|---|---|---|---|
| **548** | A97 | Sheet of 4, #a.-d. | 8.00 | 8.00 |

Surtax for Soldiers', Sailors,' and Airmen's Families Association.

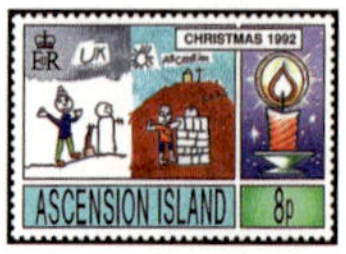

Christmas — A98

Children's drawings: 8p, Snowman, rocks, candle. 18p, Underwater Santa, Christmas tree. 25p, Hello, bells. 65p, Nativity Scene, angel.

**Wmk. 384**

**1992, Oct. 13 Litho.** ***Perf. 14***

| | | | | |
|---|---|---|---|---|
| **549** | A98 | 8p multicolored | 1.10 | .90 |
| **550** | A98 | 18p multicolored | 1.60 | 1.25 |
| **551** | A98 | 25p multicolored | 1.90 | 1.50 |
| **552** | A98 | 65p multicolored | 3.50 | 3.50 |
| | | *Nos. 549-552 (4)* | 8.10 | 7.15 |

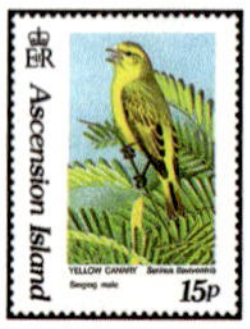

Yellow Canary — A99

15p, Singing male. 18p, Adult male, female. 25p, Young calling for food. 70p, Mixed flock.

**Wmk. 373**

**1993, Jan. 12 Litho.** ***Perf. 14½***

| | | | | |
|---|---|---|---|---|
| **553** | A99 | 15p multicolored | 1.25 | 1.25 |
| **554** | A99 | 18p multicolored | 1.40 | 1.40 |
| **555** | A99 | 25p multicolored | 1.75 | 1.75 |
| **556** | A99 | 70p multicolored | 4.00 | 4.00 |
| | | *Nos. 553-556 (4)* | 8.40 | 8.40 |

### Royal Air Force, 75th Anniv.

Common Design Type

Designs: 20p, Sopwith Snipe. No. 558, Supermarine Southampton. 30p, Avro Anson. 70p, Vickers Wellington 1C.

No. 561a, Westland Lysander. b, Gloster Meteor. c, DeHavilland Comet. d, British Aerospace Nimrod.

**Wmk. 373**

**1993, Apr. 1 Litho.** ***Perf. 14***

| | | | | |
|---|---|---|---|---|
| **557** | CD350 | 20p multicolored | 2.00 | 1.50 |
| **558** | CD350 | 25p multicolored | 2.00 | 1.50 |
| **559** | CD350 | 30p multicolored | 2.10 | 1.60 |
| **560** | CD350 | 70p multicolored | 3.75 | *4.25* |
| | | *Nos. 557-560 (4)* | 9.85 | 8.85 |

**Souvenir Sheet**

| | | | | |
|---|---|---|---|---|
| **561** | CD350 | 25p Sheet of 4, #a.-d. | 5.75 | 5.75 |

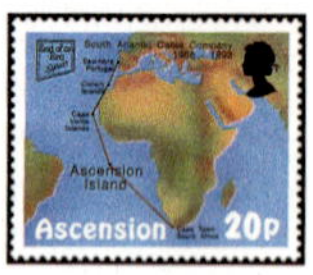

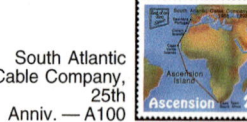

South Atlantic Cable Company, 25th Anniv. — A100

Designs: 20p, Map showing cable route. 25p, Cable ship laying cable. 30p, Map of Ascension. 70p, Cable ship off Ascension.

***Perf. 14x14½***

**1993, June 8 Litho. Wmk. 384**

| | | | | |
|---|---|---|---|---|
| **562** | A100 | 20p multicolored | 1.10 | 1.10 |
| **563** | A100 | 25p multicolored | 1.35 | 1.35 |
| **564** | A100 | 30p multicolored | 1.50 | 1.50 |
| **565** | A100 | 70p multicolored | 3.50 | 3.50 |
| | | *Nos. 562-565 (4)* | 7.45 | 7.45 |

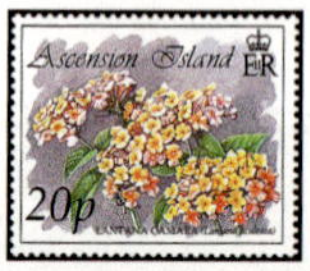

Flowers — A101

***Perf. 14x14½***

**1993, Aug. 3 Litho. Wmk. 384**

| | | | | |
|---|---|---|---|---|
| **566** | A101 | 20p Lantana camara | 1.50 | .75 |
| **567** | A101 | 25p Moonflower | 1.75 | .97 |
| **568** | A101 | 30p Hibiscus | 1.75 | 1.10 |
| **569** | A101 | 70p Frangipani | 4.00 | 3.50 |
| | | *Nos. 566-569 (4)* | 9.00 | 6.32 |

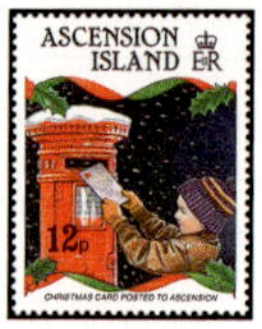

Christmas — A102

Designs: 12p, Child mailing Christmas card. 20p, Mail loaded onto Tristar. 25p, Plane in flight. 30p, Mail unloaded at Wideawake Airfield. 65p, Child reading card, Georgetown.

***Perf. 14½x14***

**1993, Oct. 19 Litho. Wmk. 373**

| | | | | |
|---|---|---|---|---|
| **570** | A102 | 12p multicolored | .75 | .40 |
| **571** | A102 | 20p multicolored | 1.25 | .45 |
| **572** | A102 | 25p multicolored | 1.40 | .50 |
| **573** | A102 | 30p multicolored | 2.25 | 2.25 |
| **574** | A102 | 65p multicolored | 2.75 | 2.75 |
| *a.* | | Souvenir sheet of 5, #570-574 | 11.00 | 11.00 |
| | | *Nos. 570-574 (5)* | 8.40 | 6.35 |

Stamps from No. 574a show a continuous design, while Nos. 570-574 have white borders on sides.

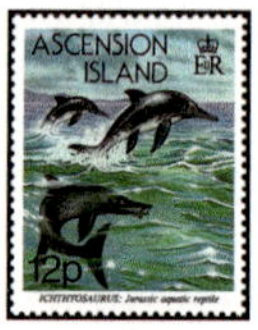

Prehistoric Aquatic Reptiles — A103

12p, Ichthyosaurus. 20p, Metriorhynchus. 25p, Mosasaurus. 30p, Elasmosaurus. 65p, Plesiosaurus.

**1994, Jan. 25 Wmk. 373** ***Perf. 14***

| | | | | |
|---|---|---|---|---|
| **575** | A103 | 12p multi | 1.00 | 1.00 |
| **576** | A103 | 20p multi | 1.25 | 1.25 |
| **577** | A103 | 25p multi | 1.50 | 1.50 |
| **578** | A103 | 30p multi | 1.50 | 1.50 |
| **579** | A103 | 65p multi | 2.75 | 2.75 |
| | | *Nos. 575-579 (5)* | 8.00 | 8.00 |

### Ovptd. with Hong Kong '94 Emblem

**1994, Feb. 18**

| | | | | |
|---|---|---|---|---|
| **580** | A103 | 12p on #575 | 1.00 | 1.00 |
| **581** | A103 | 20p on #576 | 1.60 | 1.60 |
| **582** | A103 | 25p on #577 | 1.60 | 1.60 |
| **583** | A103 | 30p on #578 | 1.75 | 1.75 |
| **584** | A103 | 65p on #579 | 3.00 | 3.00 |
| | | *Nos. 580-584 (5)* | 8.95 | 8.95 |

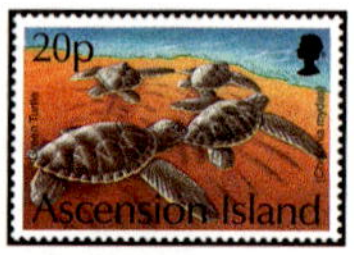

Green Turtle — A104

20p, Four on beach. 25p, Crawling in sand. No. 587, Crawling from sea. 65p, Swimming.

No. 589a, Side view, crawling from sea. b, Digging nest. c, Hatchlings heading to sea. d, Digging nest, diff.

**1994, Mar. 22**

| | | | | |
|---|---|---|---|---|
| **585** | A104 | 20p multicolored | 2.25 | 2.25 |
| **586** | A104 | 25p multicolored | 2.75 | 2.75 |
| **587** | A104 | 30p multicolored | 2.75 | 2.75 |
| **588** | A104 | 65p multicolored | 4.25 | *5.50* |
| | | *Nos. 585-588 (4)* | 12.00 | 13.25 |

**Souvenir Sheet**

| | | | | |
|---|---|---|---|---|
| **589** | A104 | 30p Sheet of 4, #a.-d. | 13.50 | 13.50 |

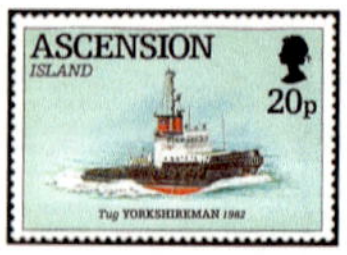

Civilian Ships — A105

Ships serving during Falkland Islands War, 1982: 20p, Tug Yorkshireman. 25p, Minesweeper support ship RMS St. Helena. 30p, Oil tanker British ESK. 65p, Cruise liner Uganda, hospital ship.

**1994, June 14**

| | | | | |
|---|---|---|---|---|
| **590** | A105 | 20p multicolored | 2.50 | 2.50 |
| **591** | A105 | 25p multicolored | 2.75 | 2.75 |
| **592** | A105 | 30p multicolored | 2.75 | 2.75 |
| **593** | A105 | 65p multicolored | 5.00 | 5.00 |
| | | *Nos. 590-593 (4)* | 13.00 | 13.00 |

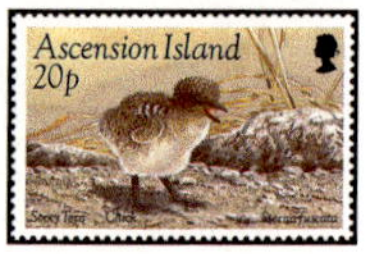

Sooty Tern — A106

**1994, Aug. 16**

| | | | | |
|---|---|---|---|---|
| **594** | A106 | 20p Chick | 1.40 | 1.40 |
| **595** | A106 | 25p Juvenile | 1.50 | 1.50 |
| **596** | A106 | 30p Brooding adult | 1.75 | 1.75 |
| **597** | A106 | 65p Displaying male | 2.75 | 2.75 |
| | | *Nos. 594-597 (4)* | 7.40 | 7.40 |

**Souvenir Sheet**

| | | | | |
|---|---|---|---|---|
| **598** | A106 | £1 Dread | 6.50 | 6.50 |

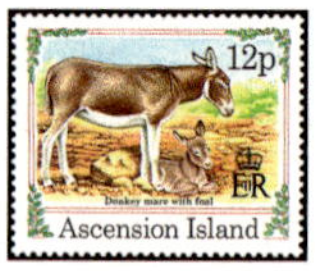

Christmas — A107

Donkeys: 12p, Mare with foal. 20p, Young adult. 25p, Foal. 30p, Adult, egrets. 65p, Adult.

**1994, Oct. 11** ***Perf. 14x14½***

| | | | | |
|---|---|---|---|---|
| **599** | A107 | 12p multicolored | 1.25 | 1.00 |
| **600** | A107 | 20p multicolored | 1.75 | 1.40 |
| **601** | A107 | 25p multicolored | 1.75 | 1.40 |
| **602** | A107 | 30p multicolored | 1.90 | 1.50 |
| **603** | A107 | 65p multicolored | 3.50 | *4.50* |
| | | *Nos. 599-603 (5)* | 10.15 | 9.80 |

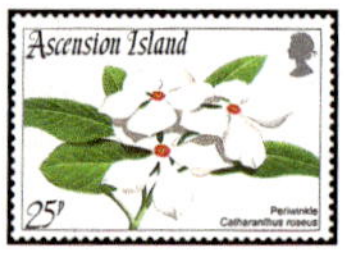

Flowers — A108

20p, Leonurus japonicus. 25p, Periwinkle. 30p, Four o'clock. 65p, Blood flower.

**1995, Jan. 10** ***Perf. 14***

| | | | | |
|---|---|---|---|---|
| **604** | A108 | 20p multi, vert. | 2.00 | 2.00 |
| **605** | A108 | 25p multi | 2.00 | 2.00 |
| **606** | A108 | 30p multi, vert. | 2.75 | 2.75 |
| **607** | A108 | 65p multi | 3.75 | 3.75 |
| | | *Nos. 604-607 (4)* | 10.50 | 10.50 |

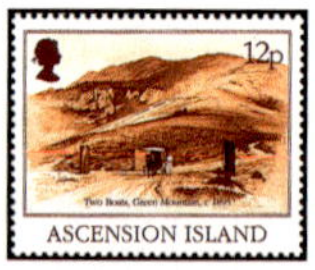

Island Scenes, c. 1895 — A109

Designs: 12p, Horse-drawn wagon, Two Boats, Green Mountain. 20p, Island stewards' store. 25p, Royal Navy headquarters, barracks. 30p, Police office. 65p, Pier head.

**1995, Mar. 7 Wmk. 384** ***Perf. 14½***

| | | | | |
|---|---|---|---|---|
| **608** | A109 | 12p sepia | .70 | .70 |
| **609** | A109 | 20p sepia | 1.00 | 1.00 |
| **610** | A109 | 25p sepia | 1.40 | 1.40 |
| **611** | A109 | 30p sepia | 2.50 | 2.50 |
| **612** | A109 | 65p sepia | 2.75 | 2.75 |
| | | *Nos. 608-612 (5)* | 8.35 | 8.35 |

### End of World War II, 50th Anniv.

Common Design Types

Designs: 20p, 5.5-inch guns taken from HMS Hood, 1941. 25p, Fairey Swordfish, first aircraft to land at Ascension. 30p, HMS Dorsetshire patrolling South Atlantic. 65p, HMS Devonshire patrolling South Atlantic.

£1, Reverse of War Medal, 1939-45.

**1995, May 8 Wmk. 373** ***Perf. 14***

| | | | | |
|---|---|---|---|---|
| **613** | CD351 | 20p multicolored | 2.25 | 2.25 |
| **614** | CD351 | 25p multicolored | 2.50 | 2.50 |
| **615** | CD351 | 30p multicolored | 3.00 | 3.00 |
| **616** | CD351 | 65p multicolored | 5.00 | 5.00 |
| | | *Nos. 613-616 (4)* | 12.75 | 12.75 |

**Souvenir Sheet**

| | | | | |
|---|---|---|---|---|
| **617** | CD352 | £1 multicolored | 8.75 | 8.75 |
| | | *Nos. 613-617 (5)* | 21.50 | 21.50 |

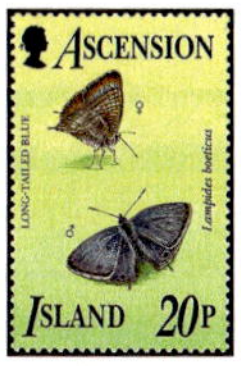


Butterflies — A110

20p, Long-tailed blue. 25p, Painted lady. 30p, Diadem. 65p, African monarch. £1, Red admiral.

**1995, Sept. 1** **Wmk. 384**

| | | | | | |
|---|---|---|---|---|---|
| 618 | A110 | 20p multi | | 1.90 | 1.90 |
| 619 | A110 | 25p multi | | 2.25 | 2.25 |
| 620 | A110 | 30p multi | | 2.25 | 2.25 |
| 621 | A110 | 65p multi | | 3.50 | 3.50 |
| | | *Nos. 618-621 (4)* | | 9.90 | 9.90 |

**Souvenir Sheet**

622 A110 £1 multi 8.50 8.50

Singapore '95 (No. 622).

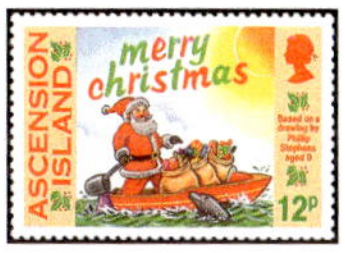


Christmas A111

Designs based on children's drawings: 12p, Santa on boat. 20p, Santa on wall. 25p, Santa in chimney. 30p, Santa on dolphin. 65p, South Atlantic run.

**1995, Oct. 10** **Wmk. 373**

| | | | | |
|---|---|---|---|---|
| 623 | A111 12p multicolored | | 1.25 | 1.25 |
| 624 | A111 20p multicolored | | 1.60 | 1.60 |
| 625 | A111 25p multicolored | | 1.75 | 1.75 |
| 626 | A111 30p multicolored | | 2.00 | 2.00 |
| 627 | A111 65p multicolored | | 3.50 | 3.50 |
| | *Nos. 623-627 (5)* | | 10.10 | 10.10 |

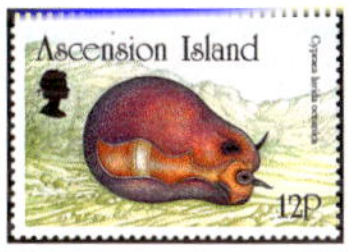


Mollusks — A112

12p, Cypraea lurida. 25p, Cypraea spurca. 30p, Harpa doris. 65p, Umbraculum umbraculum.

**Wmk. 384**

**1996, Jan. 10** **Litho.** ***Perf. 14***

| | | | |
|---|---|---|---|
| 628 | A112 12p multicolored | 2.50 | 2.50 |
| 629 | A112 25p multicolored | 3.00 | 3.00 |
| 630 | A112 30p multicolored | 3.25 | 3.25 |
| 631 | A112 65p multicolored | 4.00 | 4.00 |
| *a.* | Strip of 4, #628-631 | 14.00 | 14.00 |

**Queen Elizabeth II, 70th Birthday**

Common Design Type

Various portraits of Queen, scenes of Ascension:

20p, St. Marys Church. 25p, The Residency. 30p, Roman Catholic Grotto. 65p, The Exiles Club.

**Wmk. 384**

**1996, Apr. 22** **Litho.** ***Perf. 13½***

| | | | |
|---|---|---|---|
| 632 | CD354 20p multicolored | .80 | .80 |
| 633 | CD354 25p multicolored | .90 | .90 |
| 634 | CD354 30p multicolored | 1.10 | 1.10 |
| 635 | CD354 65p multicolored | 2.50 | 2.50 |
| | *Nos. 632-635 (4)* | 5.30 | 5.30 |

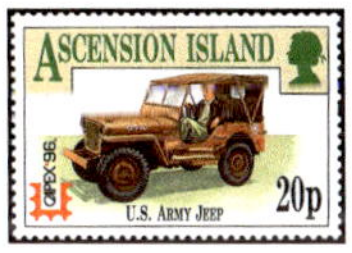


CAPEX '96 — A113

Island transport: 20p, US Army Jeep. 25p, 1924 Citroen 7.5HP two seater. 30p, 1930 Austin Ten-four Tourer. 65p, Series 1 Land Rover.

**Wmk. 384**

**1996, June 8** **Litho.** ***Perf. 14***

| | | | |
|---|---|---|---|
| 636 | A113 20p multicolored | 1.25 | 1.25 |
| 637 | A113 25p multicolored | 1.40 | 1.40 |
| 638 | A113 30p multicolored | 1.50 | 1.50 |
| 639 | A113 65p multicolored | 2.75 | 2.75 |
| | *Nos. 636-639 (4)* | 6.90 | 6.90 |

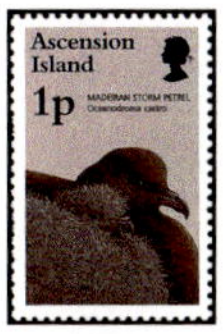


Birds and Their Young — A114

1p, Madeiran storm petrel. 2p, Red-billed tropicbird. 4p, Indian mynah. 5p, House sparrow. 7p, Common waxbill. 10p, White tern. 12p, Francolin. 15p, Brown noddy. 20p, Yellow canary. 25p, Black noddy. 30p, Red-footed booby. 40p, Yellow-billed tropicbird. 65p, Brown booby. £1, Masked booby. £2, Sooty tern. £3, Ascension frigate bird.

**Wmk. 373**

**1996, Aug. 12** **Litho.** ***Perf. 13***

| | | | |
|---|---|---|---|
| 640 | A114 1p multicolored | .25 | *1.00* |
| 641 | A114 2p multicolored | .25 | *1.00* |
| 642 | A114 4p multicolored | .25 | *1.00* |
| 643 | A114 5p multicolored | .25 | *1.00* |
| 644 | A114 7p multicolored | .25 | *1.00* |
| 645 | A114 10p multicolored | .35 | *1.25* |
| 646 | A114 12p multicolored | .40 | *1.50* |
| 647 | A114 15p multicolored | .50 | *1.50* |
| 648 | A114 20p multicolored | .75 | *1.50* |
| 649 | A114 25p multicolored | .90 | *1.50* |
| 650 | A114 30p multicolored | 1.10 | *1.50* |
| 651 | A114 40p multicolored | 1.50 | *2.00* |
| 652 | A114 65p multicolored | 2.50 | *3.25* |
| *a.* | Sheet of 1, perf. 14 | 4.50 | *4.50* |
| 653 | A114 £1 multicolored | 4.00 | *4.75* |
| *a.* | Souvenir sheet of 1 | 4.50 | 4.50 |
| 654 | A114 £2 multicolored | 8.25 | *9.00* |
| 655 | A114 £3 multicolored | 10.00 | *12.00* |
| | *Nos. 640-655 (16)* | 31.50 | *44.75* |

No. 652a for Hong Kong '97. Issued 2/3/97.

No. 653a for return of Hong Kong to China. Issued 7/1/97.

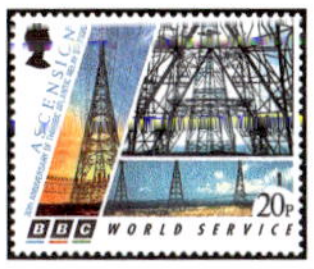


BBC Atlantic Relay Station, 30th Anniv. — A115

Various views of relay station: 20p, 25p, Towers. 30p, Towers, buildings. 65p, Satellite dish, towers, beach.

**1996, Sept. 9** **Wmk. 384** ***Perf. 14***

| | | | |
|---|---|---|---|
| 656 | A115 20p multicolored | .85 | .85 |
| 657 | A115 25p multicolored | 1.00 | 1.00 |
| 658 | A115 30p multicolored | 1.10 | 1.10 |
| 659 | A115 65p multicolored | 2.50 | 2.50 |
| | *Nos. 656-659 (4)* | 5.45 | 5.45 |

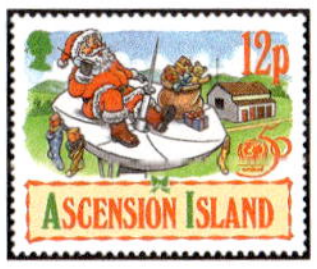


Christmas — A116

Santa Claus: 12p, On satellite dish. 20p, Playing golf. 25p, By beach. 30p, On RAF Tristar. 65p, Aboard RMS St. Helena.

***Perf. 14x14½***

**1996, Sept. 23** **Litho.** **Wmk. 373**

| | | | |
|---|---|---|---|
| 660 | A116 12p multicolored | .50 | .50 |
| 661 | A116 20p multicolored | .90 | .90 |
| 662 | A116 25p multicolored | .90 | .90 |
| 663 | A116 30p multicolored | 1.10 | 1.10 |
| 664 | A116 65p multicolored | 2.50 | 2.50 |
| | *Nos. 660-664 (5)* | 5.90 | 5.90 |

UNICEF, 50th anniv.

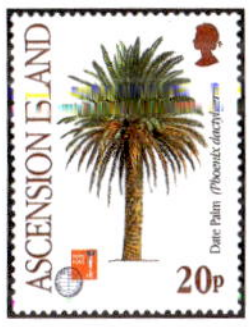


A117

20p, Date palm. 25p, Mauritius hemp. 30p, Norfolk Island pine. 65p, Dwarf palm.

**Wmk. 373**

**1997, Jan. 7** **Litho.** ***Perf. 14½***

| | | | |
|---|---|---|---|
| 665 | A117 20p multi | .80 | .80 |
| 666 | A117 25p multi | 1.00 | 1.00 |
| 667 | A117 30p multi | 1.15 | 1.15 |
| 668 | A117 65p multi | 2.25 | 2.25 |
| | *Nos. 665-668 (4)* | 5.20 | 5.20 |

Hong Kong '97.

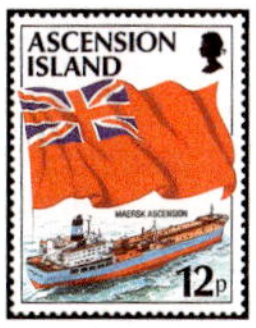


A118

Flag, ship or aircraft: 12p, Great Britain Red Ensign, tanker Maserk Ascension. 25p, RAF Ensign, Tristar. 30p, NASA emblem, Space Shuttle Atlantis. 65p, Royal Navy White Ensign, HMS Northumberland.

**Wmk. 373**

**1997, Apr. 1** **Litho.** ***Perf. 14½***

| | | | |
|---|---|---|---|
| 669 | A118 12p multicolored | 1.10 | 1.10 |
| 670 | A118 25p multicolored | 1.60 | 1.60 |
| 671 | A118 30p multicolored | 1.75 | 1.75 |
| 672 | A118 65p multicolored | 3.25 | 3.25 |
| | *Nos. 669-672 (4)* | 7.70 | 7.70 |

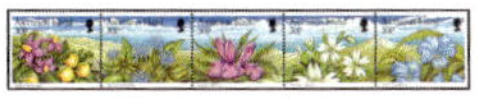

Herbs — A119

Designs: a, Solanum sodomaeum. b, Ageratum conyzoides. c, Leonurus sibricus. d, Cerastium vulgatum. e, Commelina diffusa.

***Perf. 14x14½***

**1997, June 7** **Litho.** **Wmk. 373**

673 A119 30p Strip of 5, #a.-e. 8.50 8.50

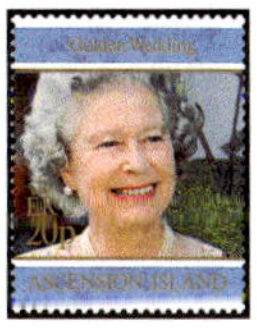

A120

Queen Elizabeth II and Prince Philip, 50th Wedding Anniv.: No. 674, Queen Elizabeth II. No. 675, Prince Philip playing polo. No. 676, Queen petting horse. No. 677, Prince Philip. No. 678, Prince Philip, Queen Elizabeth II. No. 679, Prince Harry, Prince William riding horses.

£1.50, Queen Elizabeth, Prince Philip riding in open carriage.

**Wmk. 384**

**1997, July 10** **Litho.** ***Perf. 13½***

| | | | |
|---|---|---|---|
| 674 | A120 20p multicolored | 1.50 | 1.50 |
| 675 | A120 20p multicolored | 1.50 | 1.50 |
| *a.* | Pair, #674-675 | 3.75 | 3.75 |
| 676 | A120 25p multicolored | 1.60 | 1.60 |
| 677 | A120 25p multicolored | 1.60 | 1.60 |
| *a.* | Pair, #676-677 | 4.00 | 4.00 |
| 678 | A120 30p multicolored | 1.75 | 1.75 |
| 679 | A120 30p multicolored | 1.75 | 1.75 |
| *a.* | Pair, #678-679 | 4.25 | 4.25 |
| | *Nos. 674-679 (6)* | 9.70 | 9.70 |

**Souvenir Sheet**

680 A120 £1.50 multicolored 7.75 7.75

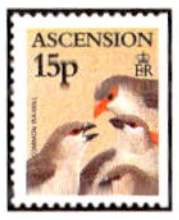


Birds — A121

**Booklet Stamps**

***Perf. 14 on 3 Sides***

**1997, Sept. 1** **Litho.** **Wmk. 373**

| | | | |
|---|---|---|---|
| 681 | A121 15p like #644 | 2.75 | 2.75 |
| 682 | A121 35p like #648 | 3.50 | 3.50 |
| *a.* | Booklet pane, 2 ea #681-682 | 12.50 | |
| | Complete booklet, #682a | 12.50 | |

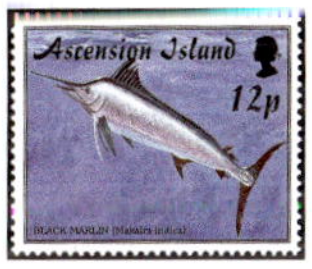


Game Fish — A122

12p, Black marlin. 20p, Atlantic sailfish. 25p, Swordfish. 30p, Wahoo. £1, Yellowfin tuna.

***Perf. 14x14½***

**1997, Sept. 3** **Litho.** **Wmk. 373**

| | | | |
|---|---|---|---|
| 683 | A122 12p multi | .90 | .90 |
| 684 | A122 20p multi | 1.40 | 1.40 |
| 685 | A122 25p multi | 1.50 | 1.50 |
| 686 | A122 30p multi | 1.60 | 1.60 |
| 687 | A122 £1 multi | 4.25 | 4.25 |
| | *Nos. 683-687 (5)* | 9.65 | 9.65 |

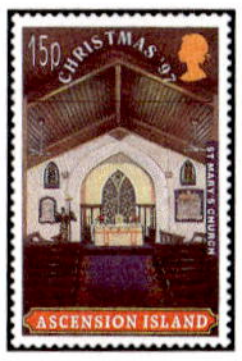


A123

St. Mary's Church (Christmas): 15p, Interior view. 35p, Stained glass window, Madonna and Child. 40p, Stained glass window, Falklands, 1982. 50p, Stained glass window.

**Wmk. 384**

**1997, Oct. 1** **Litho.** ***Perf. 14***

| | | | |
|---|---|---|---|
| 688 | A123 15p multicolored | .90 | .90 |
| 689 | A123 35p multicolored | 1.75 | 1.75 |
| 690 | A123 40p multicolored | 1.90 | 1.90 |
| 691 | A123 50p multicolored | 2.25 | 2.25 |
| | *Nos. 688-691 (4)* | 6.80 | 6.80 |

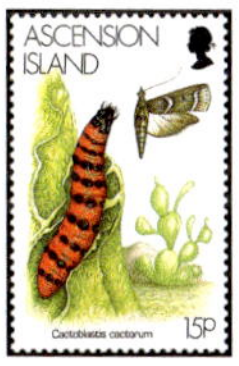


A124

Insects: 15p, Cactoblastis cactorum. 35p, Teleonemia scrupulosa. 40p, Neltumius arizonensis. 50p, Algarobius prosopis.

**Wmk. 373**

**1998, Feb. 10** **Litho.** ***Perf. 14***

| | | | |
|---|---|---|---|
| 692 | A124 15p multicolored | 1.60 | 1.60 |
| 693 | A124 35p multicolored | 2.10 | 2.10 |
| 694 | A124 40p multicolored | 2.75 | 2.75 |
| 695 | A124 50p multicolored | 2.75 | 2.75 |
| | *Nos. 692-695 (4)* | 9.20 | 9.20 |

**Diana, Princess of Wales (1961-97)**

Common Design Type

a, In polka-dotted dress. b, In yellow blouse. c, With longer hair style. d, Holding flowers.

***Perf. 14½x14***

**1998, Mar. 31** **Litho.** **Wmk. 373**

696 CD355 35p Sheet of 4, #a.-d. 5.25 5.25

No. 696 sold for £1.40 + 20p, with surtax from international sales being donated to the Princess Diana Memorial Fund and surtax from national sales being donated to designated local charity.

**Royal Air Force, 80th Anniv.**

Common Design Type of 1993 Re-inscribed

15p, Fairey Fawn. 35p, Vickers Vernon. 40p, Supermarine Spitfire F-22. 50p, Bristol Britannia C2.

No. 701: a, Blackburn Kangaroo. b, SE5a. c, Curtiss Kittyhawk III. d, Boeing Fortress II (B-17).

**Wmk. 384**

**1998, Apr. 1** **Litho.** ***Perf. 14***

| | | | |
|---|---|---|---|
| 697 | CD350 15p multicolored | 1.00 | 1.00 |
| 698 | CD350 35p multicolored | 2.10 | 2.10 |
| 699 | CD350 40p multicolored | 2.25 | 2.25 |
| 700 | CD350 50p multicolored | 2.75 | 2.75 |
| | *Nos. 697-700 (4)* | 8.10 | 8.10 |

**Souvenir Sheet**

701 CD350 50p Sheet of 4, #a.-d. 8.00 8.00

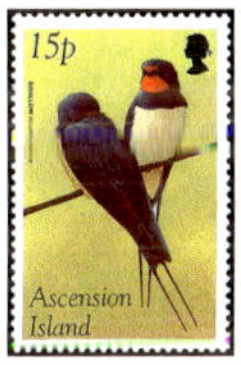


Birds — A125

**Wmk. 373**

**1998, June 15** **Litho.** ***Perf. 14***

| | | | |
|---|---|---|---|
| 702 | A125 15p Swallow | 1.25 | 1.25 |
| 703 | A125 25p House martin | 1.75 | 1.75 |
| 704 | A125 35p Cattle egret | 2.10 | 2.10 |
| 705 | A125 40p Swift | 2.10 | 2.10 |
| 706 | A125 50p Allen's gallinule | 2.25 | 2.25 |
| | *Nos. 702-706 (5)* | 9.45 | 9.45 |

# ASCENSION

Island Sports — A126

**Wmk. 373**
**1998, Aug. 17    Litho.    Perf. 14**
707  A126  15p Cricket             2.50   2.00
708  A126  35p Golf                3.25   2.50
709  A126  40p Soccer              2.50   2.50
710  A126  50p Trapshooting       2.50   2.50
         Nos. 707-710 (4)         10.75   9.50

Christmas — A127

Designs: 15p, Children's nativity play. 35p, Santa arriving on Ascension. 40p, Santa arriving at a party. 50p, Carol singers.

**Wmk. 373**
**1998, Oct. 1    Litho.    Perf. 14**
711  A127  15p multicolored       1.10   1.10
712  A127  35p multicolored       1.90   1.90
713  A127  40p multicolored       2.10   2.10
714  A127  50p multicolored       2.10   2.10
         Nos. 711-714 (4)          7.20   7.20

World War II Aircraft — A128

15p, Curtiss C-46 Commando. 35p, Douglas C-47 Dakota. 40p, Douglas C-54 Skymaster. 50p, Consolidated Liberator Mk.V. £1.50, Consolidated Liberator LB-30.

**Wmk. 373**
**1999, Jan. 20    Litho.    Perf. 14**
715  A128  15p multicolored       1.25   1.25
716  A128  35p multicolored       2.00   2.00
717  A128  40p multicolored       2.25   2.25
718  A128  50p multicolored       2.25   2.25
         Nos. 715-718 (4)          7.75   7.75
         **Souvenir Sheet**
719  A128  £1.50 multicolored    11.00  11.00
      Winston Churchill, 125th birth anniv.

Australia '99, World Stamp Expo — A129

Union Castle Mail Ships: 15p, SS Glengorm Castle. 35p, SS Gloucester Castle. 40p, SS Durham Castle. 50p, SS Garth Castle. £1, HMS Endeavour.

**Perf. 14½x14**
**1999, Mar. 5    Litho.    Wmk. 373**
720  A129  15p multicolored       1.25   1.25
721  A129  35p multicolored       2.25   2.25
722  A129  40p multicolored       2.40   2.40
723  A129  50p multicolored       2.40   2.40
         Nos. 720-723 (4)          8.30   8.30
         **Souvenir Sheet**
724  A129  £1 multicolored         6.75   6.75

World Wildlife Fund — A130

Fairy tern: No. 725, Two on branch. No. 726, One on branch. No. 727, Adult feeding chick. No. 728, Two in flight.

**Wmk. 384**
**1999, Apr. 27    Litho.    Perf. 14½**
725  A130  10p multicolored        .50    .45
726  A130  10p multicolored        .50    .45
727  A130  10p multicolored        .50    .45
728  A130  10p multicolored        .50    .45
  a.  Sheet of 16, 4 each #725-728 10.00 10.00
         Nos. 725-728 (4)          2.00   1.80

**Wedding of Prince Edward and Sophie Rhys-Jones**
**Common Design Type**
**Perf. 13¾x14**
**1999, June 19    Litho.    Wmk. 384**
729  CD356  50p Separate portraits  1.50  1.50
730  CD356  £1 Couple               3.00  3.00

**1st Manned Moon Landing, 30th Anniv.**
**Common Design Type**

Designs: 15p, Command and service modules. 35p, Moon from Apollo 11. 40p, Devil's Ashpit Tracking Station. 50p, Lunar module lifts off moon. £1.50, Looking at earth from moon.

**Perf. 14x13¾**
**1999, July 20    Litho.    Wmk. 384**
731  CD357  15p multicolored       1.25   1.25
732  CD357  35p multicolored       1.60   1.60
733  CD357  40p multicolored       1.60   1.60
734  CD357  50p multicolored       1.60   1.60
         Nos. 731-734 (4)          6.05   6.05
         **Souvenir Sheet**
         **Perf. 14**
735  CD357  £1.50 multicolored     6.75   6.75
No. 735 contains one 40mm circular stamp.

**Queen Mother's Century**
**Common Design Type**

Queen Mother: 15p, With King George VI, Winston Churchill. 35p, With Prince Charles. 40p, At Clarence House, 88th birthday. 50p, With drummers at Clarence House. £1.50, With Titanic.

**Wmk. 384**
**1999, Aug. 20    Litho.    Perf. 13½**
736  CD358  15p multicolored       1.25   1.25
737  CD358  35p multicolored       1.75   1.75
738  CD358  40p multicolored       2.00   2.00
739  CD358  50p multicolored       2.50   2.50
         Nos. 736-739 (4)          7.50   7.50
         **Souvenir Sheet**
740  CD358  £1.50 black            8.00   8.00

Christmas — A131

**Wmk. 384**
**1999, Oct. 6    Litho.    Perf. 13¾**
741  A131  15p 3 children          1.10   1.10
742  A131  35p 2 children, hats    2.10   2.10
743  A131  40p 2 children, bed     2.10   2.10
744  A131  50p 4 children          2.10   2.10
         Nos. 741-744 (4)          7.40   7.40

Cable and Wireless, Cent. — A132

**Perf. 13¼x13¾**
**1999, Dec. 13    Litho.    Wmk. 373**
745  A132  15p CS Anglia           1.75   1.75
746  A132  35p CS Cambria          2.50   2.50
747  A132  40p Map                 2.50   2.50
748  A132  50p CS Colonia          2.75   2.75
         Nos. 745-748 (4)          9.50   9.50
         **Souvenir Sheet**
749  A132  £1.50 CS Seine          8.00   8.00

Turtle Project — A133

15p, Young turtles. 35p, Turtle, trail at left. 40p, Turtle with tracking device on beach. 50p, Turtle with tracking device heading to sea.
No. 754: a, Turtle head, rock. b, Like 15p. c, Turtle on beach, sea. d, Turtle in surf.

**2000, Mar. 8    Litho.    Perf. 13¾**
750  A133  15p multi               1.10   1.10
751  A133  35p multi               1.90   1.90
752  A133  40p multi               1.90   1.90
753  A133  50p multi               2.10   2.10
         Nos. 750-753 (4)          7.00   7.00
         **Souvenir Sheet**
         **Perf. 14**
754  A133  25p Sheet of 4, #a-d   7.50   7.50
  e.  With Stamp Show 2000 emblem in margin  7.50  7.50
No. 754 contains four 40x26mm stamps.
No. 754e issued 5/8.

**Prince William, 18th Birthday**
**Common Design Type**

William: 10p, As baby laying on stomach and stuffed animal. 15p, As toddler, vert. 35p, Wearing suit and wearing cap, vert. 40p, Holding flowers, and in parka. 50p, In suit and in checked shirt.

**Perf. 13¾x14¼, 14¼x13¾**
**2000, June 21    Litho.    Wmk. 373**
**Stamps With White Border**
755  CD359  15p multi              1.00   1.00
756  CD359  35p multi              1.50   1.50
757  CD359  40p multi              2.25   2.25
758  CD359  50p multi              2.75   2.75
         Nos. 755-758 (4)          7.50   7.50
         **Souvenir Sheet**
         **Stamps Without White Border**
         **Perf. 14¼**
759      Sheet of 5                8.00   8.00
  a.  CD359  10p multi              .50    .50
  b.  CD359  15p multi              .75    .75
  c.  CD359  35p multi             1.50   1.50
  d.  CD359  40p multi             1.75   1.75
  e.  CD359  50p multi             2.25   2.25

Forts — A134

Designs: 15p, 1815 fortifications. 35p, Fort Thornton, 1817. 40p, Fort Hayes, 1860. 50p, Fort Bedford, 1940.

**Wmk. 373**
**2000, Aug. 14    Litho.    Perf. 14**
760-763  A134  Set of 4           9.00   9.00

Christmas A135

Carols: 15p, I Saw Three Ships. 25p, Silent Night. 40p, Away in a Manger. 90p, Hark, the Herald Angels Sing.

**2000, Oct. 16    Wmk. 384**
764-767  A135  Set of 4          12.50  12.50
         **Souvenir Sheet**

New Year 2001 (Year of the Snake) A136

Turtles: a, 25p, Green. b, 40p, Loggerhead.

**Wmk. 373**
**2001, Feb. 1    Litho.    Perf. 14½**
768  A136  Sheet of 2, #a-b       5.00   5.00
Hong Kong 2001 Stamp Exhibition.

Sinking of the Roebuck, Tercentenary — A137

Designs: 15p, Capt. William Dampier. 35p, Drawing of the Roebuck, horiz. 40p, Cave dwelling at Dampier's Drip, horiz. 50p, Map.

**2001, Feb. 25    Litho.    Perf. 14**
769-772  A137  Set of 4          11.00  11.00

Discovery of Ascension Island, 500th Anniv. — A138

Designs: 15p, Alfonso de Albuquerque. 35p, Portuguese caravel. 40p, Cantino map. 50p, Rear admiral Sir George Cockburn.

**Perf. 13¾x14¼**
**2001, Mar. 25    Litho.    Wmk. 384**
773-776  A138  Set of 4          10.50  10.50

The Age of Victoria — A139

Designs: 15p, Great Britain Type A1 with Ascension cancel, vert. 25p, Parade, 1901. 35p, HMS Phoebe. 40p, The Red Lion, 1863. 50p, Queen Victoria, vert. 65p, Sir Joseph Dalton Hooker, botanist, vert. £1.50, Queen Victoria's Funeral.

**Wmk. 373**
**2001, May 24    Litho.    Perf. 14**
777-782  A139  Set of 6          11.50  11.50
         **Souvenir Sheet**
783  A139  £1.50 multi            9.00   9.00
         **Souvenir Sheet**

Belgica 2001 Intl. Stamp Exhibition, Brussels — A140

Ascension tourist sites: a, 35p, Islander Hostel. b, 35p, The Residency. c, 40p, The Red Lion. d, 40p, Turtle Ponds.

**Wmk. 373**
**2001, June 9    Litho.    Perf. 14¼**
784  A140  Sheet of 4, #a-d      10.50  10.50

Birdlife International World Bird Festival — A141

Ascension frigate bird: 15p, On rock with wings outstretched. 35p, Chick, with mouth open. 40p, Pair in flight, horiz. 50p, Close-up of bird, horiz.

**Perf. 13¾x14¼, 14¼x13¾**
**2001, Oct. 1    Litho.    Wmk. 373**
785-788  A141  Set of 4           7.75   7.75
         **Souvenir Sheet**
789      Sheet, #785-788, 789a, perf. 14¼   8.00   8.00
  a.  A141  10p Two birds on rock  1.15   1.15

**Reign Of Queen Elizabeth II, 50th Anniv. Issue**
**Common Design Type**

Designs: Nos. 790, 794a, 15p, Princess Elizabeth with dog. Nos. 791, 794b, 35p, In 1978. Nos. 792, 794c, 40p, In 1946. Nos. 793,

# ASCENSION

794d, 50p, In 1998. No. 794e, 60p, 1955 portrait by Annigoni (38x50mm).

*Perf. 14¼x14½, 13¾ (#794e)*
**2002, Feb. 6    Litho.    Wmk. 373**
**With Gold Frames**
| 790 | CD360 | 15p multicolored | 1.10 | 1.10 |
| 791 | CD360 | 35p multicolored | 1.25 | 1.25 |
| 792 | CD360 | 40p multicolored | 1.75 | 1.75 |
| 793 | CD360 | 50p multicolored | 2.00 | 2.00 |
| | | Nos. 790-793 (4) | 6.10 | 6.10 |

**Souvenir Sheet**
**Without Gold Frames**
| 794 | CD360 | Sheet of 5, #a-e | 8.00 | 8.00 |

Falkland Islands War, 20th Anniv. — A142

Designs: 15p, Troops landing at English Bay. 35p, Weapons testing at Ascension. 40p, HMS Hermes and helicopter. 50p, Vulcan bomber at Wideawake Airfield.

**Wmk. 373**
**2002, June 14    Litho.    Perf. 14**
| 795-798 | A142 | Set of 4 | 6.00 | 6.00 |

**Queen Mother Elizabeth (1900-2002)**
Common Design Type

Designs: 35p, Wearing flowered bonnet (sepia photograph). 40p, Wearing pink hat. No. 801: a, 50p, Wearing hat (sepia photograph). b, £1, Wearing blue hat.

**Wmk. 373**
**2002, Aug. 5    Litho.    Perf. 14¼**
**With Purple Frames**
| 799 | CD361 | 35p multicolored | 1.10 | 1.10 |
| 800 | CD361 | 40p multicolored | 1.75 | 1.75 |

**Souvenir Sheet**
**Without Purple Frames**
*Perf. 14½x14¼*
| 801 | CD361 | Sheet of 2, #a-b | 6.00 | 6.00 |

Flowers and Local Scenes — A143

Designs: 10p, Vinca, Travellers palm. 15p, Mexican poppy, Broken Tooth. 20p, Ascension lily, St. Mary's Church. 25p, Goatweed, Boatswain Bird Island. 30p, Mauritius hemp, Cannon. 35p, Frangipani, Guest House. 40p, Ascension spurge, Wideawake tern. 50p, Lovechaste, Pier head. 65p, Yellowboy, Sisters Peak. 90p, Persian lilac, Two Boats School. £2, Wild currant, Green turtle. £5, Coral tree, Wideawake Airfield.

**Wmk. 373**
**2002, Aug. 28    Litho.    Perf. 14**
| 802 | A143 | 10p multi | .35 | .45 |
| 803 | A143 | 15p multi | .60 | .70 |
| 804 | A143 | 20p multi | .80 | .95 |
| 805 | A143 | 25p multi | 1.00 | 1.10 |
| 806 | A143 | 30p multi | 1.25 | 1.25 |
| 807 | A143 | 35p multi | 1.50 | 1.80 |
| 808 | A143 | 40p multi | 1.60 | 1.00 |
| 809 | A143 | 50p multi | 2.00 | 2.40 |
| 810 | A143 | 65p multi | 2.75 | 3.25 |
| 811 | A143 | 90p multi | 3.50 | 4.00 |
| 812 | A143 | £2 multi | 7.00 | 8.00 |
| 813 | A143 | £5 multi | 18.00 | 35.00 |
| | | Nos. 802-813 (12) | 40.35 | 60.80 |

Christmas — A144

Paintings: 15p, Ecce Ancilla Dominii, by Dante Gabriel Rossetti. 25p, The Holy Family and a Shepherd, by Titian, horiz. 35p, Christ Carrying the Cross, by Ambrogio Bergognone. 75p, Sketch for "The Ascension," by Benjamin West.

*Perf. 14x14¼, 14¼x14*
**2002, Oct. 9    Litho.    Wmk. 373**
| 814-817 | A144 | Set of 4 | 6.50 | 6.50 |

Ariane Downrange Tracking Station — A145

Designs: 35p, Ariane 4 on launchpad, vert. 40p, Map of downrange tracking stations. 65p, Automated Transfer vehicle in space. 90p, Ariane 5 launch, vert.

**2003, Jan. 13    Litho.    Perf. 14½**
| 818-821 | A145 | Set of 4 | 9.50 | 9.50 |
| 821a | | Souvenir sheet, #818-821 | 9.50 | 9.50 |

**Head of Queen Elizabeth II**
Common Design Type

**Wmk. 373**
**2003, June 2    Litho.    Perf. 13¾**
| 822 | CD362 | £3 multi | 12.50 | 12.50 |
| | | Nos. 822 (1) | 12.50 | 12.50 |

**Coronation of Queen Elizabeth II, 50th Anniv.**
Common Design Type

Designs: Nos. 823, 825a, 40p, Queen in carriage. Nos. 824, 825b, £1, Queen with crown at coronation.

*Perf. 14¼x14½*
**2003, June 2    Litho.    Wmk. 373**
**Vignettes Framed, Red Background**
| 823 | CD363 | 40p multicolored | 1.75 | 1.75 |
| 824 | CD363 | £1 multicolored | 4.50 | 4.50 |

**Souvenir Sheet**
**Vignettes Without Frame, Purple Panel**
| 825 | CD363 | Sheet of 2, #a-b | 6.25 | 6.25 |

**Prince William, 21st Birthday**
Common Design Type

No. 826: a, Color photograph at right. b, Color photograph at left.

**Wmk. 373**
**2003, June 21    Litho.    Perf. 14¼**
| 826 | | Horiz. pair | 7.25 | 7.25 |
| a.-b. | | CD364 75p Either single | 3.00 | 3.00 |

Powered Flight, Cent. A146

Designs: 15p, Bleriot XI. 20p, Vickers VC-10. 35p, BAe Harrier FRS Mk 1. 40p, Westland Sea King HAS Mk 4. 50p, Rockwell Space Shuttle. 90p, General Dynamics F-16. £1.50, Fairey Swordfish Mk II.

**Wmk. 373**
**2003, Aug. 12    Litho.    Perf. 14**
**Stamp + Label**
| 827-832 | A146 | Set of 6 | 11.00 | 11.00 |

**Souvenir Sheet**
| 833 | A146 | £1.50 multi | 8.00 | 8.00 |

Democracy, 1st Anniv., and Christmas A147

Dove and: 15p, Casting ballot. 25p, Island council session. 40p, Higher education. £1 Government headquarters.

**Wmk. 373**
**2003, Nov. 1    Litho.    Perf. 14**
| 834-837 | A147 | Set of 4 | 7.00 | 7.00 |

Birdlife International — A148

Masked booby: 15p, Adult and chick. 35p, Two adults, vert. 40p, Adult in flight. 50p, Adult with neck and wings extended. 90p, Adult.

*Perf. 14¼x13¾, 13¾x14¼*
**2004, Feb. 6    Litho.    Wmk. 373**
| 838-842 | A148 | Set of 5 | 10.00 | 10.00 |
| 842a | | Souvenir sheet, #838-842, perf. 14¼ | 10.00 | 10.00 |

Royal Horticultural Society, Bicent. — A149

Flora: 15p, Bougainvillea glabra (red flowers). 35p, Bougainvillea glabra (red violet flowers). 40p, Bougainvillea glabra (white flowers). 90p, Bougainvillea spectabilis. £1.50, Pteris adscensionis.

**Wmk. 373**
**2004, May 25    Litho.    Perf. 14**
| 843-846 | A149 | Set of 4 | 8.00 | 8.00 |

**Souvenir Sheet**
| 847 | A149 | £1.50 multi | 7.00 | 7.00 |

Fish — A150

Designs: 15p, Blue marlin underwater. 35p, Swordfish. 40p, Sailfish. 90p, White marlin. £1.50, Blue marlin breaching surface.

**Wmk. 373**
**2004, July 26    Litho.    Perf. 13¾**
| 848-851 | A150 | Set of 4 | 8.50 | 8.50 |

**Souvenir Sheet**
| 852 | A150 | £1.50 multi | 7.25 | 7.25 |

The Moon — A151

Designs: 15p, Lunar eclipse from Hummock Point. 25p, Lunar eclipse from Sister's Peak. 35p, Lunar eclipse from Daly's Craggs. £1.25, Moon and birds from Mars Bay.

**Wmk. 373**
**2004, Oct. 28    Litho.    Perf. 13½**
| 853-856 | A151 | Set of 4 | 8.50 | 8.50 |
| 856a | | Souvenir sheet of 1 | 6.00 | 6.00 |

Merchant Ships — A152

Designs: 15p, MV Ascension. 35p, RMS St. Helena. 40p, RMS Caronia. £1.25, MV Maersk Gannet.

**2004, Nov. 26    Perf. 13¼**
| 857-860 | A152 | Set of 4 | 9.50 | 9.50 |

Battle of Trafalgar, Bicent. A153

Designs: 15p, British carronade on sliding carriage. 25p, Royal Marine drummer boy, 1805, vert. 35p, HMS Britannia, vert. 40p, Horatio Nelson, by Jean Frances Rigaud. 50p, HMS Neptune and Santissima Trinidad. 90p, HMS Victory. No. 867, vert.: a, Horatio Nelson, by Lemuel Francis Abbott. b, HMS Ajax.

**Wmk. 373, Unwmkd. (#866)**
**2005, Apr. 29    Litho.    Perf. 13½**
| 861-866 | A153 | Set of 6 | 9.50 | 9.50 |

**Souvenir Sheet**
| 867 | A153 | £1 Sheet of 2, #a-b | 8.25 | 8.25 |

No. 866 has particles of wood from the HMS Victory embedded in the areas covered by a thermographic process that produces a shiny, raised effect.

Birdlife International A154

Birds: 15p, Fairy tern. 35p, White-tailed tropicbird. 40p, Brown booby. 50p, Brown noddy. £1.25, Red-billed tropicbird.

**Wmk. 373**
**2005, May 27    Litho.    Perf. 13¾**
| 868-872 | A154 | Set of 5 | 10.00 | 10.00 |
| 872a | | Souvenir sheet, #868-872 | 10.00 | 10.00 |

Tuna Fish — A155

Designs: 35p, Three yellowfin tunas. 40p, Skipjack tunas. 50p, Albacore tunas. £1.25, Bigeye tunas. £1.50, Yellowfin tuna jumping.

**Wmk. 373**
**2006, July 22    Litho.    Perf. 13¾**
| 873-876 | A155 | Set of 4 | 9.00 | 9.00 |

**Souvenir Sheet**
| 877 | A155 | £1.50 multi | 6.50 | 6.50 |

Pope John Paul II (1920-2005) — A156

**Wmk. 373**
**2005, Aug. 18    Litho.    Perf. 14**
| 878 | A156 | 40p multi | 2.00 | 2.00 |

Battle of Trafalgar, Bicent. — A157

Designs: 40p, HMS Victory. 65p, Ships in battle, horiz. 90p, Admiral Horatio Nelson.

*Perf. 13¼*
**2005, Oct. 21    Litho.    Unwmk.**
| 879-881 | A157 | Set of 3 | 9.50 | 9.50 |

Christmas — A158

Stories by Hans Christian Andersen (1805-75): 15p, The Little Fir Tree. 25p, The Mailcoach Passengers. 35p, The Little Match Girl. £1.25, The Snow Man.

**2005, Oct. 3    Wmk. 373    Perf. 14**
| 882-885 | A158 | Set of 4 | 8.50 | 8.50 |

Fish — A159

Designs: 20p, Black jack. 35p, Almaco jack. 50p, Horse-eye jack. £1, Rainbow runner. £1.50, Longfin crevalle jack.

## ASCENSION

**Wmk. 373**
**2006, Jan. 24**    Litho.    *Perf. 13¾*
886-889   A159   Set of 4    9.00   9.00
**Souvenir Sheet**
890   A159   £1.50 multi    6.25   6.25

Queen Elizabeth II, 80th Birthday — A160

"80" and Queen: 20p, As child. 40p, Wearing tiara. 50p, Wearing tiara, diff. £1.30, Wearing hat.
No. 895: a, Wearing tiara, diff. b, Without head covering.

**Wmk. 373**
**2006, Apr. 21**    Litho.    *Perf. 14¼*
891-894   A160   Set of 4    10.00   10.00
**Souvenir Sheet**
895   A160   £1 Sheet of 2, #a-b    8.75   8.75

 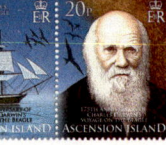

Anniversaries — A161

No. 896, 20p: a, HMS Beagle. b, Charles Darwin.
No. 897, 35p: a, SS Great Britain. b, Isambard Kingdom Brunel.
No. 898, 40p: a, Niña. b, Christopher Columbus.
No. 899, 50p: a, Map with lines of magnetic variation of the compass. b, Edmond Halley.

*Perf. 13x13¼*
**2006, July 24**    Litho.    Wmk. 373
**Horiz. Pairs, #a-b**
896-899   A161   Set of 4    13.00   13.00

Darwin's voyage on the Beagle, 175th anniv., birth of Brunel, 200th anniv., death of Columbus, 500th anniv., birth of Halley, 350th anniv.

Greetings A162

Designs: 15p, Long Beach (Greetings from Ascension). 25p, Sunset over lava flow (Merry Christmas). 35p, Dewpond (Seasons Greetings). £1.25, Boatswain Bird Island (Happy New Year).

**Wmk. 373**
**2006, Oct. 30**    Litho.    *Perf. 14¼*
900-903   A162   Set of 4    9.00   9.00

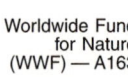

Worldwide Fund for Nature (WWF) — A163

Resplendent angelfish: 35p, Three fish. 40p, Seven fish. 50p, Three fish, diff. £1.25, Four fish.

*Perf. 13¾*
**2007, Mar. 23**    Litho.    Unwmk.
904-907   A163   Set of 4    9.00   9.00
907a    Sheet, 4 each #904-907    35.00   35.00

Falkland Islands War, 25th Anniv. — A164

Designs: Nos. 908, 913a, 35p, Handley Page Victor K Mk 2 tanker plane. Nos. 909, 912b, 40p, HMS Dumbarton Castle and Chinook helicopter. Nos. 910, 912c, 50p, HMS Fearless, landing craft and helicopters. Nos. 911, 913d, £1.25, Vulcan XM607 leaving Wideawake Airfield.
No. 912: a, RFA Tidespring refueling HMS Antrim. d, £1.25, Atlantic Conveyor and Harrier jet.
No. 913: b, 40p, Vickers VC 10 transport plane. c, 50p, Nimrod MR2 maritime reconnaisance plane.

**2007, May 25**    *Perf. 13¼x13*
**Stamps With White Frames**
908-911   A164   Set of 4    11.50   11.50
**Stamps Without White Frames**
912   A164   Sheet of 4, #a-d    12.00   12.00
913   A164   Sheet of 4, #a-d    12.00   12.00

Scouting, Cent. — A165

Lord Robert Baden-Powell blowing kudu horn and: 35p, Fleur-de-lis of scouts. 40p, Scouts rescuing turtle. 50p, Scouts on gun of HMS Hood. £1.25, Scouts on Land Rover.

**2007, July 9**    *Perf. 14*
914-917   A165   Set of 4    12.00   12.00

Mother Teresa (1910-97) and Princess Diana (1961-97) — A166

**2007, Aug. 31**
918   A166   50p multi    2.25   2.25

Wedding of Queen Elizabeth II and Prince Philip, 60th Anniv. A167

No. 919: a, 35p, Couple in 1947. b, 90p, Wedding program. c, £1.25, Couple in 2006.

**2007, Nov. 20**    Litho.    *Perf. 14¼*
919   A167   Horiz. strip of 3, #a-c    10.50   10.50

British Ornithological Union Expedition, 50th Anniv. — A168

No. 920, 15p: a, British Ornithological Union base. b, Drawing of extinct rail.
No. 921, 25p: a, Scientist recording sounds of Wideawake tern. b, Wideawake terns.
No. 922, 40p: a, Boatswainbird Island outpost. b, Masked booby.
No. 923, 50p: a, Scientist pushing dinghy in surf. b, Red-footed booby.

**2007, Dec. 10**    *Perf. 14¼*
**Horiz. Pairs, #a-b**
920-923   A168   Set of 4    12.00   12.00

Oviparous Creatures A169

Creature and eggs: 15p, Long-tailed blue butterfly. 20p, Ladybird beetle. 25p, Spiny lobster. 30p, Desert locust. 35p, Green turtle. 40p, Land crab. 50p, Red-footed booby. 65p, Coconut palm gecko. 90p, Common waxbill. £1, Yellowtail damselfish. £2.50, Madeiran storm petrel. £5, Red-necked francolin.

**2008, Feb. 5**    Litho.    *Perf. 14¼*
924   A169   15p multi    .55   .55
925   A169   20p multi    .75   .75
926   A169   25p multi    .90   .90
927   A169   30p multi    1.15   1.15
928   A169   35p multi    1.25   1.25
929   A169   40p multi    1.40   1.40
930   A169   50p multi    1.75   1.75
931   A169   65p multi    2.40   2.40
932   A169   90p multi    3.50   3.50
933   A169   £1 multi    3.75   3.75
934   A169   £2.50 multi    9.00   9.00
935   A169   £5 multi    18.00   18.00
    Nos. 924-935 (12)    44.40   44.40

Sharks — A170

Designs: 35p, Bluntnose sixgill shark. 40p, Scalloped hammerhead shark. 50p, Shortfin mako shark. £1.25, Whale shark. £1.50, Bigeye thresher shark.

**2008, Mar. 14**    Litho.    *Perf. 14*
936-939   A170   Set of 4    11.00   10.00
939a    Sheet of 16, 4 each #936-939    50.00   50.00
**Souvenir Sheet**
940   A170   £1.50 multi    6.25   6.25

National Aeronautical and Space Administration, 50th Anniv. — A171

Designs: No. 941, 35p, Bell X-1E airplane. No. 942, 35p, Apollo 11 Moon walk. 40p, Apollo 17 Lunar Rover. 50p, Space Shuttle Columbia. 65p, Hubble Space Telescope. 90p, International Space Station.

**2008, May 23**    Litho.    *Perf. 14*
941-946   A171   Set of 6    12.00   12.00

Royal Air Force, 90th Anniv. — A172

Airplanes: 15p, Sopwith 7F.1 Snipe. 35p, Vickers Wellington Mk 1C. 40p, Supermarine Spitfire Mk IX. 50p, Gloster Meteor F. IV. 65p, BAe Hawk. 90p, Typhoon F-2 Eurofighter.

**Unwmk.**
**2008, June 20**    Litho.    *Perf. 14*
947-952   A172   Set of 6    14.00   14.00

Botanists and Flowers — A173

Designs: 35p, Valerius Cordus (1515-44), and Cordia sebestena. 40p, Nehemiah Grew (1641-1712), and Grewia occidentalis. 50p, Charles Plumier (1646-1704), and Plumeria rubra. £2, Carl Peter Thunberg (1743-1828), and Thunbergia grandiflora.

**2008, Aug. 28**    Litho.    *Perf. 14*
953-956   A173   Set of 4    13.50   13.50

Christmas A174

Santa Claus: 15p, Holding microphone. 25p, With reindeer in surf. 50p, On inflatable lounger in water. £2, Piloting flying sleigh.

**2008, Nov. 22**
957-960   A174   Set of 4    11.00   11.00

Longest-Reigning British Monarchs — A175

Designs: 35p, King Henry III and Tower of London. 40p, King James I and Stirling Castle. 50p, King George III and Windsor Castle. 65p, Queen Victoria and Osborne House. £1.25, Queen Elizabeth II and Buckingham Palace.

**2008, Dec. 15**
961-965   A175   Set of 5    11.00   11.00

Marine Mammals A176

Designs: 35p, Bottlenose dolphins. 40p, Pantropical spotted dolphins. 50p, Sperm whale. £1.25, Gervais' beaked whales. £2, Humpback whale.

**2009, Mar. 23**    *Perf. 14x14¾*
966-969   A176   Set of 4    11.50   11.50
969a    Sheet, 4 each #966-969    40.00   40.00
**Souvenir Sheet**
970   A176   £2 multi    9.00   9.00

Naval Aviation, Cent. A177

No. 971, 35p: a, Flight Sub-lieutenant Rex Warneford and Victoria Cross. b, Moraine-Saulnier L destroys Zeppelin LZ-37.
No. 972, 35p: a, Squadron Commander Richard Bell Davies and Victoria Cross. b, Nieuport 10 taking off.
No. 973, 40p: a, Lieutenant Commander Eugene Esmonde and Victoria Cross. b, Fairey Swordfish attacking German warships.
No. 974, 50p: a, Lieutenant Robert Hampton Gray and Victoria Cross. b, Corsair bombing Japanese warships.

**2009, May 7**    *Perf. 14*
**Horiz. Pairs, #a-b**
971-974   A177   Set of 4    11.50   11.50

Botany — A178

Designs: No. 975, 35p, Raspberry. No. 976, 35p, Blue water lily. 40p, Prickly pear. 50p, Ascension lily. 65p, Yellowboy. 90p, Joseph Dalton Hooker (1817-1911), botanist.

**2009, Sept. 7**    *Perf. 14*
975-980   A178   Set of 6    11.00   11.00

Turtle Research and Conservation — A179

No. 981, 15p: a, Early turtle tracking and head of turtle. b, Dr. Archie Carr (1909-87) and map of Ascension.
No. 982, 35p: a, Turtle laying eggs and head of turtle. b, Turtle hatchlings and map of Ascension.
No. 983, 40p: a, Beach raking and head of turtle. b, Population monitoring and map of Ascension.
No. 984, 65p: a, Turtle rescue and head of turtle. b, Turtle rescue and map of Ascension.

**2009, Oct. 1**    *Perf. 13¾*
**Horiz. Pairs, #a-b**
981-984   A179   Set of 4    10.00   10.00

# ASCENSION

Charles Darwin (1809-82), Naturalist A180

Darwin and: 35p, Woodpecker finch. 40p, Marine iguanas. 50p, Galapagos tortoise. £2, Galapagos penguins.

**2009, Nov. 9**    **Unwmk.**    **Perf. 14**
985-988 A180    Set of 4    12.50   12.50

White-tailed Tropicbird A181

Designs: 35p, Bird in rock crevice. 40p, Bird on rock. 50p, Juvenile in flight. £1.25, Adult in flight.

**2009, Dec. 4**    **Litho.**    **Perf. 14**
989-992 A181    Set of 4    11.50   11.50
992a    Sheet, 4 each #989-992    47.50   47.50

Reef Fish — A182

Designs: 35p, Hardback soldier. 40p, Grouper. 50p, Five fingers. £1.25, Rock bullseye. £2, Softback soldier.

**2010, Mar. 19**    **Perf. 13¾**
993-996 A182    Set of 4    11.00   11.00
996a    Sheet, 4 each #993-996    47.50   47.50
**Souvenir Sheet**
997 A182    £2 multi    8.25   8.25

A183

Girl Guides, Cent. A184

Designs: 40p, Girl Guides wearing clown noses. 50p, Girl Guides and fish. 90p, Leader holding cake. £1.25, Girl Guide climbing rock. No. 1002: a, Olave Baden-Powell (1889-1977). b, Agnes Baden-Powell (1858-1945). c, Lord Robert Baden-Powell (1857-1941).

**2010, Apr. 10**    **Perf. 14**
998-1001 A183    Set of 4    11.50   11.50
**Souvenir Sheet**
1002 A184    £1 Sheet of 3, #a-c    11.50   11.50

**Miniature Sheet**

Battle of Britain, 70th Anniv. A185

No. 1003: a, Supermarine Spitfire R6803. b, Hawker Hurricane V7383. c, Supermarine Spitfire X4036. d, Hawker Hurricane R4175. e, Supermarine Spitfire R6885. f, Hawker Hurricane V6684. g, Supermarine Spitfire K9998. h, Hawker Hurricane R4118.

**2010, May 7**    **Perf. 14**
1003 A185 50p Sheet of 8 #a-h    15.00   15.00
London 2010 Festival of Stamps.

Yellow Canary — A186

Designs: 15p, Juvenile. 35p, Adult male on branch. 60p, Adult female. 90p, Adult male on ground.

**2010, Oct. 11**    **Perf. 13¾**
1004-1007 A186    Set of 4    8.25   8.25
1007a    Miniature sheet of 16, 4 each #1004-1007    36.00   36.00

Christmas A187

Designs: 15p, Christmas lunch. 40p, Christmas parade. 50p, Christingle. £1.25, Nativity play.

**2010, Nov. 17**    **Perf. 14**
1008-1011 A187    Set of 4    8.50   8.50

Rediscovery of the Parsley Fern — A188

Ascension National Park emblem and: 15p, HMS Erebus and HMS Terror approaching Ascension, 1843. 15p, Parsley fern. 35p, Parsley fern in situ. 40p, Parsley fern seedlings in pots. £1, Parsley fern cultivation at Kew Gardens.

**2011, Feb. 16**    **Perf. 13¾**
1012-1016 A188    Set of 5    7.00   7.00

Service of Queen Elizabeth II and Prince Philip A189

Designs: 15p, Queen Elizabeth II. 25p, Queen and Prince Philip. 35p, Queen and Prince Philip, diff. 40p, Queen and Prince Philip, diff. 60p, Queen and Prince Philip, diff. £1.25, Prince Philip. £2, Queen and Prince Philip, diff.

**2011, Mar. 23**    **Perf. 13¼**
1017-1022 A189    Set of 6    9.50   9.50
1022a    Sheet of 6, #1017-1022, + 3 labels    9.50   9.50
**Souvenir Sheet**
1023 A189    £2 multi    6.50   6.50

Royal Air Force Search and Rescue, 70th Anniv. A190

Emblem and Sea King helicopter: 35p, On airplane's cargo ramp. 40p, Flying near Ascension. 90p, Approaching HMS Dumbarton Castle. £1, Approaching HMS Spartan submarine.
£2.50, Sea King helicopter in flight.

**2011, May 19**
1024-1027 A190    Set of 4    8.25   8.25
**Souvenir Sheet**
1028 A190    £2.50 multi    7.75   7.75

**Miniature Sheet**

Peonies A191

No. 1029 — Peony color: a, Red. b, Gray lilac. c, Light orange. d, White.

**2011, June 22**    **Perf. 13¾**
1029 A191 50p Sheet of 4, #a-d    6.25   6.25

Wedding of Prince William and Catherine Middleton A192

Couple with Middleton: 35p, Wearing hat. 90p, Without hat. £1.25, Seated in coach in wedding dress.
£2, Couple standing on wedding day, vert.

**2011, July 20**    **Perf. 14**
1030-1032 A192    Set of 3    7.75   7.75
**Souvenir Sheet**
**Perf. 14¾x14**
1033 A192    £2 multi    6.25   6.25
No. 1033 contains one 29x45mm stamp.

Worldwide Fund for Nature (WWF) — A193

Phaethon aethereus: Nos. 1034, 1038a, 35p, Bird in rock crevice. Nos. 1035, 1038b, 40p, Two birds in flight. Nos. 1036, 1038c, 50p, Adult and juvenile in rock crevice. Nos. 1037, 1038d, £1.25, Bird in flight.

**2011, Aug. 31**
**Stamps With White Frames**
1034-1037 A193    Set of 4    7.50   7.50
**Stamps Without White Frames**
1038 A193    Strip of 4, #a-d    8.00   8.00
Nos. 1038a-1038d were printed in sheets of 16 stamps containing four strips.

Christmas — A194

Pantomimes: 15p, Mother Goose. 40p, Jack and the Beanstalk. 50p, Aladdin. £1.25, Cinderella.

**2011, Nov. 16**    **Perf. 14**
1039-1042 A194    Set of 4    6.75   6.75

Reign of Queen Elizabeth II, 60th Anniv. A195

Photographs of Queen Elizabeth II taken in: 15p, 2011. 25p, 1998. 35p, 1988. 40p, 1975. 60p, 1961. £1.25, 1953.
£2, 1977.

**2012, Feb. 6**    **Perf. 13¼**
1043-1048 A195    Set of 6    9.00   9.00
1048a    Sheet of 6, #1043-1048, + 3 labels    9.00   9.00
**Souvenir Sheet**
1049 A195    £2 multi    6.00   6.00

Reef Fish — A196

Designs: 35p, Trumpetfish. 40p, Peacock flounder. 90p, Queen triggerfish. £1, Scrawled filefish.
£2, Yellow goatfish.

**2012, Apr. 15**    **Litho.**    **Perf. 13¾**
1050-1053 A196    Set of 4    8.00   8.00
1053a    Sheet, 4 each #1050-1053    32.50   32.50
**Souvenir Sheet**
1054 A196    £2 multi    6.00   6.00

Sinking of the Titanic, Cent. — A197

Designs: 20p, The departure. 45p, The boat deck. 50p, The iceberg. £1, The sinking. £2, Abandoning ship.

**2012, Aug. 1**    **Perf. 14**
1055-1058 A197    Set of 4    6.50   6.50
**Souvenir Sheet**
1059 A197    £2 multi    6.00   6.00

Shackleton-Rowett Antarctic Expedition, 90th Anniv. — A198

No. 1060, 45p: a, Sir Ernest Shackleton (36x36mm). b, John Quiller Rowett (18x36mm). c, Frank Wild (36x36mm).
No. 1061, 50p: a, Quest leaving London (36x36mm). b, Quest at Ascension (18x36mm). c, Quest in ice (36x36mm).

**2012, Sept. 17**    **Perf. 13¼**
**Horiz. Strips of 3, #a-c**
1060-1061 A198    Set of 2    8.50   8.50

Christmas A199

Scenes from *A Christmas Carol*, by Charles Dickens: 25c, Ebenezer Scrooge passing Christmas carolers. 40p, Ghost visiting Scrooge. 50p, Scrooge carrying Tiny Tim, vert. £1.25, Scrooge watching boy deliver turkey, vert.

**2012, Nov. 15**    **Perf. 13¼x13½**
1062-1065 A199    Set of 4    7.25   7.25

**Miniature Sheet**

Wideawake Airfield, 70th Anniv. — A200

No. 1066: a, 45p, Wideawake tern. b, 50p, Douglas DC-3 Dakota. c, £1, Eurofighter Typhoon. d, £1.45, Masked booby.

**2012, Dec. 5**    **Perf. 13¼**
1066 A200    Sheet of 4, #a-d    13.00   13.00

# ASCENSION

Aircraft — A201

Designs: 15p, Fairey Swordfish. 20p, North American B-25 Mitchell. 25p, Lockheed C-130K Hercules. 30p, Hawker Siddeley Nimrod MR2. 40p, BAE Sea Harrier FRS1. 45p, Lockheed C-5 Galaxy. 50p, Douglas DC-3 Dakota. 65p, Avro Vulcan. 90p, McDonnell Douglas Phantom F-4. £1, Eurofighter Typhoon. £2.50, Lockheed C-121. £5, Shorts Belfast.

**2013, Jan. 15** — *Perf. 13¾*
| | | | | |
|---|---|---|---|---|
| 1067 | A201 | 15p multi | .50 | .50 |
| 1068 | A201 | 20p multi | .65 | .65 |
| 1069 | A201 | 25p multi | .80 | .80 |
| 1070 | A201 | 30p multi | .95 | .95 |
| 1071 | A201 | 40p multi | 1.25 | 1.25 |
| 1072 | A201 | 45p multi | 1.40 | 1.40 |
| 1073 | A201 | 50p multi | 1.60 | 1.60 |
| 1074 | A201 | 65p multi | 2.10 | 2.10 |
| 1075 | A201 | 90p multi | 3.00 | 3.00 |
| 1076 | A201 | £1 multi | 3.25 | 3.25 |
| 1077 | A201 | £2.50 multi | 8.00 | 8.00 |
| 1078 | A201 | £5 multi | 16.00 | 16.00 |
| Nos. 1067-1078 (12) | | | 39.50 | 39.50 |

Items Commemorating British Coronations A202

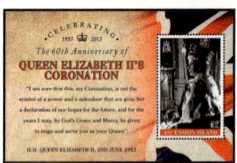

Coronation of Queen Elizabeth II, 60th Anniv. — A203

Various items commemorating the coronation of: 45p, Queen Victoria. 50p, King Edward VII. 70p, King George V. £1.10, King George VI. £1.25, Queen Elizabeth II.

**2013, Feb. 6** — *Perf. 14*
1079-1083  A202  Set of 5  12.00  12.00
**Souvenir Sheet**
*Perf. 14¾x14¼*
1084  A203  £2 multi  8.00  8.00

British Settlement of Ascension, Bicent. (in 2015) — A204

Imprisonment of Napoleon Bonaparte on Ascension: 45p, Joséphine Bonaparte at Malmaison, by François Pascal Simon. 50p, Bonaparte at the Bridge of Arcole, by Antoine-Jean Gros. 60p, Napoleon and his General Staff, by Jean-Léon Gérôme. £1.45, Napoleon as First Consul, detail of painting by Jean-Baptiste Isabey.

**2013, May 21** — *Perf. 13¾*
1085-1088  A204  Set of 4  11.00  11.00

Lady Margaret Thatcher (1925-2013), British Prime Minister — A205

Photographs of Thatcher: 45p, Giving "Victory" sign, 1976. 50p, In cockpit of Sea Harrier jet, 1982. 55p, Holding teacup during visit to Ascension, 1992. £1.45, At Order of the Garter ceremony, 1995.

**2013, June 14**
1089-1092  A205  Set of 4  11.00  11.00

Ascension Frigatebirds A206

Designs: 20p, Male and female. 45p, Male on egg. 50p, Chick. 60p, Female and chick. £1.10, Juvenile. £1.45, Male in flight.

**2013, Aug. 16** — *Perf. 13¼x13½*
1093-1098  A206  Set of 6  16.00  16.00

Shallow Marine Surveys Group — A207

Marine life: Nos. 1099, 1103a, 45p, Fire worm. Nos. 1100, 1103b, 50p, Black bar soldier fish. Nos. 1101, 1103c, 60p, Endemic white hawk fish. Nos. 1102, 1103d, £1.45, Atlantic blue tang.
No. 1104a, £1, Anemone, vert.

**2013, Aug. 29** — *Perf. 13¼x13½*
**Stamps With White Frames**
1099-1102  A207  Set of 4  11.00  11.00
**Stamps Without White Frames**
1103  A230  Strip of 4, #a-d  11.00  11.00
**Souvenir Sheet**
*Perf. 13½x13¼*
1104  A207  Sheet of 3 (see footnote)  11.00  11.00
  a.  A207 £1 multi  3.75  3.75

No. 1104 contains No. 1104a, Falkland Islands No. 1107a and South Georgia and South Sandwich Islands No. 485a. This sheet was sold in Ascension, Falkland Islands and South Georgia and South Sandwich Islands.

Churches A208

Stained-Glass Windows A209

Designs: 45p, Grotto of Our Lady Catholic Church. 50p, Window depicting Madonna and Child. 60p, St. Mary's Anglican Church. £1, Window depicting St. Michael.

**2013, Nov. 18** — *Litho.* — *Perf. 13¼*
**Stamps With White Frames**
1105  A208  45p multi  1.50  1.50
1106  A209  50p multi  1.75  1.75
1107  A208  60p multi  2.00  2.00
1108  A209  £1 multi  3.25  3.25
  Nos. 1105-1108 (4)  8.50  8.50
**Stamps Without White Frames**
1109  Horiz. strip of 4  8.50  8.50
  a. A208 45p multi  1.50  1.50
  b. A209 50p multi  1.75  1.75
  c. A208 60p multi  2.00  2.00
  d. A209 £1 multi  3.25  3.25
Christmas.

British Settlement of Ascension, Bicent. (in 2015) — A210

The Napoleonic Years: 50p, Engraving of Napoleon Bonaparte after signing of Treaty of Amiens, 1802. 55p, Napoleon I in Coronation Robes, by François Gérard. 60p, Lord Horatio Nelson, by Lemuel Francis Abbott. £1.60, Napoleon at Wagram, by Emile Jean-Horace Vernet.

**2014, Apr. 28** — *Litho.* — *Perf. 13¾*
1110-1113  A210  Set of 4  12.50  12.50

Royal Christenings — A211

Photograph from christening of: 50p, Queen Elizabeth II, 1926. 55p, Prince Charles, 1948. 60p, Prince William, 1982. £1.60, Prince George, 2013.

**2014, May 21** — *Litho.* — *Perf. 13x13¼*
1114-1117  A211  Set of 4  12.50  12.50

World War I, Cent. — A212

Various poppies: 50p, 55p, 60p, £1.60.

**2014, Aug. 4** — *Litho.* — *Perf. 14¾x14*
1118-1121  A212  Set of 4  12.50  12.50

Royal Marines, 350th Anniv. — A213

Designs: 20p, Duke of York and Albany's Maritime Regiment of Foot on man-of-war, 1664. 50p, Light Infantry and barracks on Ascension, 19th cent. 55p, Light Infantry at Gallipoli, 1915. 60p, Royal Marines Commandos at Eastney, 1970s. 65p, Royal Marines Band Service Bugler at Deal, 1996. £1, Royal Marines Commandos, 2014.

**2014, Oct. 28** — *Litho.* — *Perf. 14*
1122-1127  A213  Set of 6  12.50  12.50

Rosetta Mission — A214

Designs: 35p, Ariane 5 launching Rosetta. 55p, Rosetta spacecraft. 65p, Deploying Philae lander. £1.60, Descent of Philae. £3, Comet 67P/Churyumov-Gerasimenko.

**2014, Dec. 30** — *Litho.* — *Perf. 14*
1128-1131  A214  Set of 4  9.75  9.75
**Souvenir Sheet**
1132  A214  £3 multi  9.25  9.25

British Settlement of Ascension, Bicent. — A215

The Napoleonic Wars: 55p, Napoleon Bonaparte on the Borodino Heights, by Vasily V. Vereshchagin. 60p, Napoleon at Fontainebleau, by Paul Delaroche. 65p, Arthur Wellesley, 1st Duke of Wellington, by Thomas Lawrence. £1.60, Napoleon dictating his memoirs in exile.

**2015, Apr. 27** — *Litho.* — *Perf. 13¾*
1133-1136  A215  Set of 4  9.50  9.50

Magna Carta, 800th Anniv. — A216

Designs: 50p, King John examining Magna Carta. 55p, Ascension Government building.

60p, Magistrate's Court, Ascension. £1.60, Arms of Ascension, King John.

**2015, June 15** — *Litho.* — *Perf. 13*
1137-1140  A216  Set of 4  9.50  9.50

Queen Elizabeth II, Longest-Reigning British Monarch — A217

Queen Elizabeth II and events during her reign: 50p, Publications reporting on her coronation, 1953. 55p, First men on the Moon, 1969. 65p, Avro Vulcan (end of Cold War), 1991. £1.60, The Spirit of Chartwell in Diamond Jubilee celebration, 2012.

**2015, Sept. 9** — *Litho.* — *Perf. 14*
1141-1144  A217  Set of 4  9.00  9.00

British Settlement of Ascension, Bicent. — A218

200th anniversary emblem and: 35p, King George III. 50p, Flag of Ascension. 55p, Coat of arms of Ascension. £1.60, Queen Elizabeth II.

**2015, Oct. 22** — *Litho.* — *Perf. 14*
1145-1148  A218  Set of 4  8.50  8.50

William Dampier (1651-1715), Explorer — A219

Designs: 25p, Dampier. 35p, Dampier's ship, HMS Roebuck. £1, Sinking of HMS Roebuck at Ascension Island, 1701. £1.60, Diver and bell of HMS Roebuck.

**2015, Dec. 1** — *Litho.* — *Perf. 14*
1149-1152  A219  Set of 4  8.75  8.75

Worldwide Fund for Nature (WWF) — A220

Red-footed booby: 20p, Bird on rock. 50p, Adult and chick. 55p, Heads of brown and white morphs. £2, Juvenile.

*Perf. 13¼x13½*
**2016, Feb. 22** — *Litho.*
**Stamps With White Frames**
1153-1156  A220  Set of 4  8.75  8.75
**Stamps Without White Frames**
1157  Strip of 4  9.50  9.50
  a. A220 20p multi  .60  .60
  b. A220 50p multi  1.40  1.40
  c. A220 55p multi  1.60  1.60
  d. A220 £2 multi  5.75  5.75

Queen Elizabeth II, 90th Birthday — A221

Photograph of Queen Elizabeth II from: 50p, 1951. 55p, 1973. 65p, 1974. £1.60, 1995. £3, Queen Elizabeth II in 1961.

**2016, Apr. 21** — *Litho.* — *Perf. 14*
1158-1161  A221  Set of 4  8.75  8.75
**Souvenir Sheet**
1162  A221  £3 multi  8.00  8.00

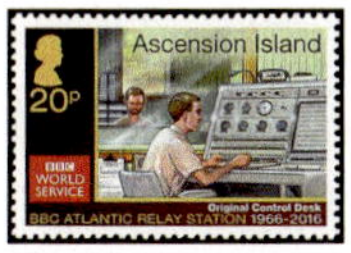


British Broadcasting Corporation Transmitting Station on Ascension, 50th Anniv. — A222

Designs: 20p, Original control desk. 25p, Klinka Klub and short wave antenna array towers, 1980s. 50p, Atlantic relay station, English Bay. 55p, Current transmitting station. 65p, BBC wind turbines, turtle. £1.60, Current transmitting station main office.

**2016, July 3 Litho. *Perf. 13½***
**1163-1168** A222 Set of 6 9.50 9.50

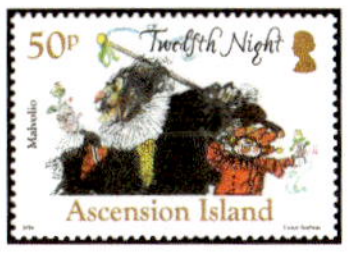


Scenes from Plays by William Shakespeare (1564-1616) A223

Designs: 50p, Twelfth Night. 55p, Henry V. 65p, Hamlet. £1.60, Romeo and Juliet.

**2016, Aug. 8 Litho. *Perf. 14***
**1169-1172** A223 Set of 4 7.75 7.75

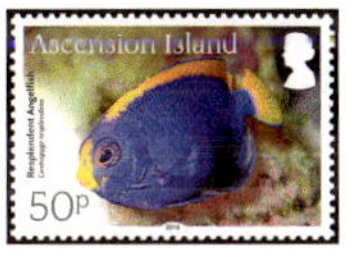


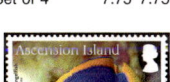

Fish — A224

Designs: 50p, Resplendent angelfish. 55p, White hawkfish. 65p, Ascension wrasse. £1.60, Yellowtail damselfish.

**2016, Oct. 17 Litho. *Perf. 13¼x13½***
**1173-1176** A224 Set of 4 7.25 7.25

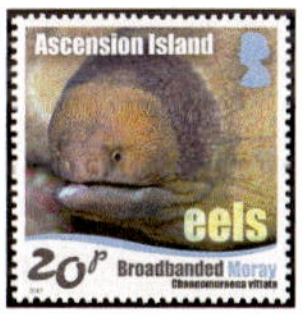


Eels — A225

Designs: 20p, Broadbanded moray eel. 35p, Whitespotted moray eel. 50p, Chain moray eel. 55p, Goldtail moray eel. 65p, Brown moray eel. £1.60, Spotted snake eel.

**2017, Apr. 12 Litho. *Perf. 13¼***
**1177-1182** A225 Set of 6 10.00 10.00

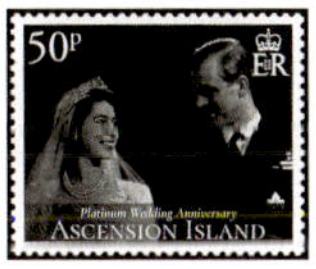


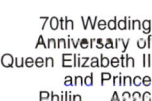

70th Wedding Anniversary of Queen Elizabeth II and Prince Philip — A226

Photographs of Queen Elizabeth II and Prince Philip from: 50p, 1947. 55p, 1963. 65p, 1982. £1.60, 2006.

**2017, Nov. 20 Litho. *Perf. 13x13¼***
**1183-1186** A226 Set of 4 8.00 8.00

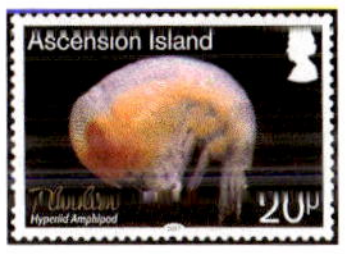


Plankton — A227

Designs: 20p, Hyperiid amphipod. 35p, Land crab zoea larva. 50p, Sapphirinid copepod. 55p, Stomatopod shrimp larva. 65p, Gastropod mollusc larva. £1.60, Polychaete worm larva.

**2017, Dec. 6 Litho. *Perf. 13¼x13½***
**1187-1192** A227 Set of 6 10.50 10.50

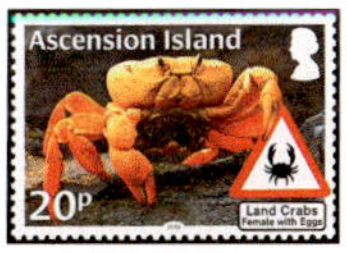


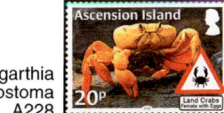

Johngarthia Lagostoma A228

Designs: 20p, Female crab with eggs. 35p, Crab in megalops phase. 50p, Juvenile crab. 55p, Crab feeding on moss. 65p, Crab in purple morph stage. £1.60, Crab in yellow morph stage.

**2018, Jan. 24 Litho. *Perf. 13½x13¾***
**1193-1198** A228 Set of 6 11.00 11.00

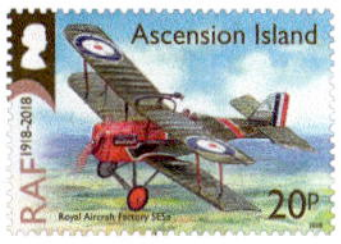


Royal Air Force, Cent. — A229

Designs: 20p, Royal Aircraft Factory SE5a. 35p, Hawker Hurricane. 50p, Avro Vulcan. £2, Tornado.

**2018, July 2 Litho. *Perf. 13¼x13½***
**1199-1202** A229 Set of 4 8.00 8.00

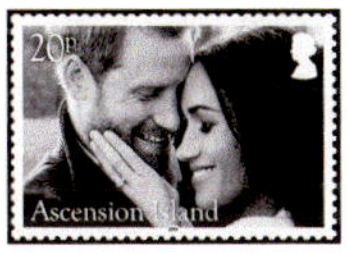


Wedding of Prince Harry and Meghan Markle — A230

Designs: 20p, Engagement photograph. 50p, Couple at dance performance. 55p, Couple at altar. £2, Couple in carriage.
£3, Couple leaving St. George's Chapel on wedding day, vert.

***Perf. 13¼x13½***
**2018, Aug. 14 Litho.**
**1203-1206** A230 Set of 4 8.50 8.50

**Souvenir Sheet**
***Perf. 13½x13¼***
**1207** A230 £3 multi 7.75 7.75

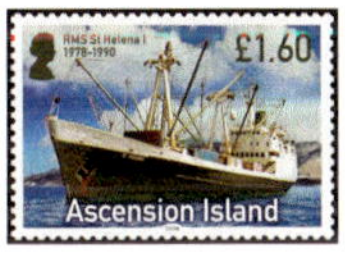


Ships — A231

Designs: £1.60, RMS St. Helena I, 1978-90. £2, RMS St. Helena II, 1990-2018.

**2018, Oct. 8 Litho. *Perf. 13¼x13¾***
**1208-1209** A231 Set of 2 9.25 9.25

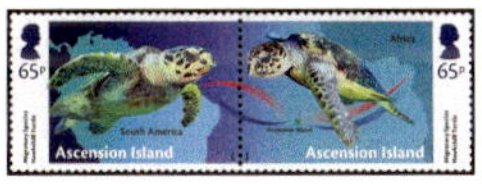


Migratory Turtles A232

No. 1210, 65p — Hawksbill turtle and map of: a, South America. b, Ascension Island and Africa.
No. 1211, £1 — Green turtle and map of: a, South America. b, Ascension Island and Africa.

**2018, Dec. 5 Litho. *Perf. 13¼x13½***
**Horiz. Pairs, #a-b**
**1210-1211** A232 Set of 2 8.50 8.50

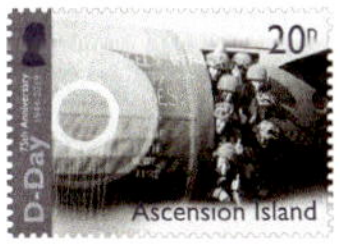


D-Day, 75th Anniv. — A233

Designs: 20p, Troops in door of glider. 35p, Third Infantry Division soldiers on French beach. 50p, Commandos coming ashore. £2, HMS Warspite shelling German batteries.

**2019, June 6 Litho. *Perf. 13¼x13½***
**1212-1215** A233 Set of 4 7.75 7.75

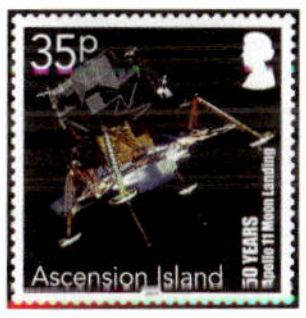


First Man on the Moon, 50th Anniv. — A234

Designs: 35p, Lunar Module in space. 55p, Astronaut on ladder of Lunar Module. £1, Astronaut on Moon. £1.60, Astronaut and United States flag on Moon.

**2019, Dec. 6 Litho. *Perf. 13¼***
**1216-1219** A234 Set of 4 9.25 9.25

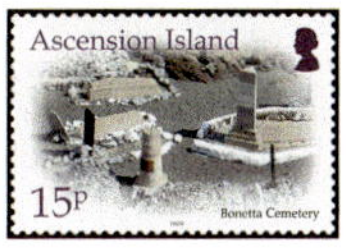


Island Scenes, Flora and Fauna — A235

Designs: 15p, Bonetta Cemetery. 20p, Ascension Island land crab. 25p, Red Lion Barracks, Green Mountain. 30p, Deadman's Beach. 40p, St. Mary's Church, Georgetown. 50p, Green sea turtle. 60p, Resplendent angelfish. 65p, Ascension donkeys. £1, Ascension lily. £1.30, Ascension Island frigatebirds. £2.50, Boatswainbird Island. £5, Wideawake tern.

***Perf. 13¼x13¾***
**2020, Dec. 22 Litho.**

| | | | | |
|---|---|---|---|---|
| **1220** | A235 | 15p multi | .40 | .40 |
| **1221** | A235 | 20p multi | .55 | .55 |
| **1222** | A235 | 25p multi | .70 | .70 |
| **1223** | A235 | 30p multi | .85 | .85 |
| **1224** | A235 | 40p multi | 1.10 | 1.10 |
| **1225** | A235 | 50p multi | 1.40 | 1.40 |
| **1226** | A235 | 60p multi | 1.60 | 1.60 |
| **1227** | A235 | 65p multi | 1.75 | 1.75 |
| **1228** | A235 | £1 multi | 2.75 | 2.75 |
| **1229** | A235 | £1.30 multi | 3.50 | 3.50 |
| **1230** | A235 | £2.50 multi | 6.75 | 6.75 |
| **1231** | A235 | £5 multi | 14.00 | 14.00 |
| | *Nos. 1220-1231 (12)* | | 35.35 | 35.35 |

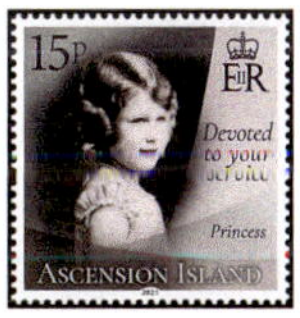


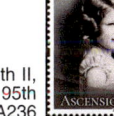

Queen Elizabeth II, 95th Birthday — A236

Designs: 15p, Princess Elizabeth, 1932. 20p, Queen Elizabeth II at her coronation. 35p, Queen Elizabeth II with Prince Philip. 65p, Queen Elizabeth II with her dog, 1952. £1, Queen Elizabeth II and Prince Philip, 2015. £1.60, Queen Elizabeth II, 2019.

**2021, Apr. 21 Litho. *Perf. 13¼***
**1232-1237** A236 Set of 6 11.00 11.00

See Isle of Man No. 2150a.

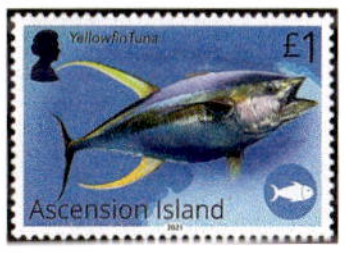


Blue Belt Program, 5th Anniv. — A237

Part of map of Ascension Island and: Nos. 1238, 1242a, £1, Yellowfin tuna. Nos. 1239, 1242b, £1, Masked booby. Nos. 1240, 1242c, £1, Green turtle. Nos. 1241, 1242d, £1, White-striped cleaner shrimp.

**2021, Nov. 9 Litho. *Perf. 13¼***
**Stamps With White Frames**
**1238-1241** A237 Set of 4 11.00 11.00

**Miniature Sheet**
**Stamps Without White Frames**
**1242** A237 £1 Sheet of 4, #a-d 11.00 11.00

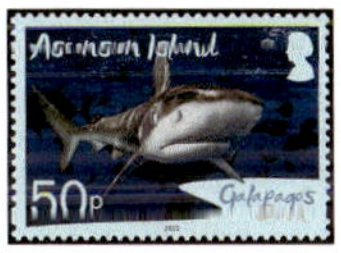


Galapagos Sharks — A238

Various photographs of Galapagos sharks: 50p, 55p, 65p, £1.60.
£3, Galapagos shark, diff.

**2022, Jan. 31 Litho. *Perf. 13¼x13½***
**1243-1246** A238 Set of 4 9.00 9.00

**Souvenir Sheet**
**1247** A238 £3 multi 8.25 8.25

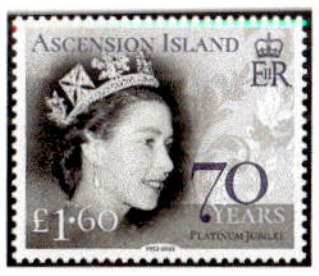


Reign of Queen Elizabeth II, 70th Anniv. — A239

Queen Elizabeth II wearing: £1.60, Crown. £2, Hat.
£3, Queen Elizabeth II, vert.

**2022, Apr. 14 Litho. *Perf. 13***
**1248-1249** A239 Set of 2 9.00 9.00

**Souvenir Sheet**
***Perf. 13x13¼***
**1250** A239 £3 multi 7.50 7.50

No. 1250 contains one 29x48mm stamp.

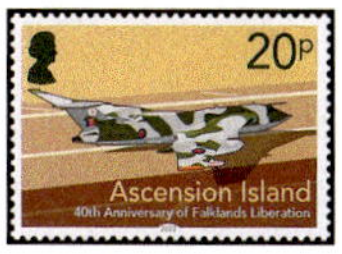


Liberation of the Falkland Islands, 40th Anniv. — A240

British military aircraft and ship used in the Falklands War: 20p, Victor refueling airplanes. 35p, RFA Sir Percivale. 50p, Chinook helicopter carrying cargo container. £3, Harrier GR 3 jet.

**2022, June 22 Litho. *Perf. 13½***
**1251-1254** A240 Set of 4 10.00 10.00

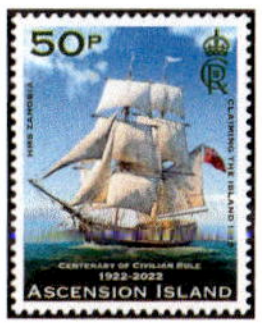


Civilian Rule in Ascension, Cent. — A241

Designs: 50p, HMS Zenobia. 55p, Robert Francis Peel (1874-1924), Governor of St. Helena, and first Governor of Ascension. 65p, King George V (1865-1936). £1.60, Flag of Ascension.

**2022, Dec. 19 Litho. *Perf. 13¼***
**1255-1258** A241 Set of 4 8.00 8.00

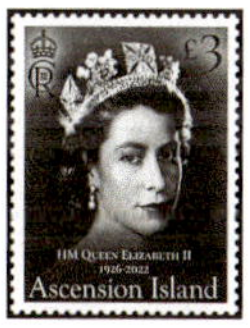


Queen Elizabeth II (1926-2022) — A242

Queen Elizabeth II: No. 1259, £3, Wearing crown, 1952. No. 1260, £3, Facing left, 2009.

**2023, Feb. 15 Litho. *Perf. 13x13¼***
**1259-1260** A242 Set of 2 14.50 14.50
*1260a* Souvenir sheet of 2, #1259-1260 14.50 14.50

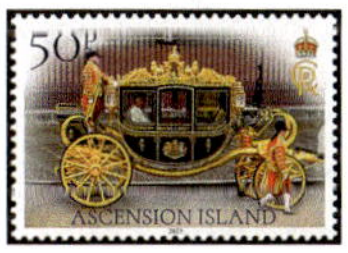


Coronation of King Charles III — A243

Designs: 50p, King Charles III and Queen Consort Camilla in Diamond Jubilee State Coach. 55p, Crowning of King Charles III. 65p, King Charles III and Queen Consort Camilla in Gold State Carriage after coronation. £1.60, King Charles III and Queen Consort Camilla waving.
£3, King Charles III holding scepter and orb, vert.

**2023, Sept. 7 Litho. *Perf. 13¼x13½***
**1261-1264** A243 Set of 4 8.25 8.25

**Souvenir Sheet**
***Perf. 13½x13¼***
**1265** A243 £3 multi 7.50 7.50

## AIR POST STAMPS

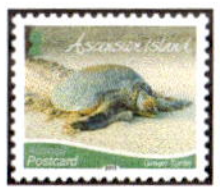

AP1

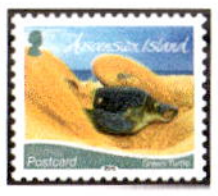

AP2

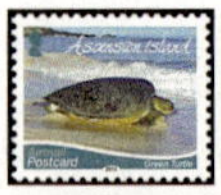
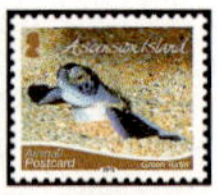

AP3 AP4

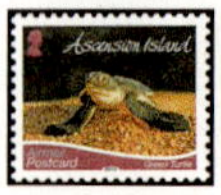
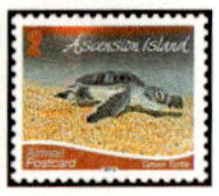

Green Turtles
AP5 AP6

**2015, Feb. 14 Litho. *Perf. 13¼***

**Stamps With White Frames**

| | | | |
|---|---|---|---|
| C1 | AP1 (50p) multi | 1.40 | 1.40 |
| *a.* | Dated "2019" | 1.40 | 1.40 |
| C2 | AP2 (50p) multi | 1.40 | 1.40 |
| *a.* | Dated "2019" | 1.40 | 1.40 |
| C3 | AP3 (50p) multi | 1.40 | 1.40 |
| *a.* | Dated "2019" | 1.40 | 1.40 |
| C4 | AP4 (50p) multi | 1.40 | 1.40 |
| *a.* | Dated "2019" | 1.40 | 1.40 |
| C5 | AP5 (50p) multi | 1.40 | 1.40 |
| *a.* | Dated "2019" | 1.40 | 1.40 |
| C6 | AP6 (50p) multi | 1.40 | 1.40 |
| *a.* | Dated "2019" | 1.40 | 1.40 |
| | *Nos. C1-C6 (6)* | 8.40 | 8.40 |

**Miniature Sheet**

**Stamps Without White Frames**

| | | | |
|---|---|---|---|
| C7 | Sheet of 6 | 8.50 | 8.50 |
| *a.* | AP1 (50p) multi | 1.40 | 1.40 |
| *b.* | AP2 (50p) multi | 1.40 | 1.40 |
| *c.* | AP3 (50p) multi | 1.40 | 1.40 |
| *d.* | AP4 (50p) multi | 1.40 | 1.40 |
| *e.* | AP5 (50p) multi | 1.40 | 1.40 |
| *f.* | AP6 (50p) multi | 1.40 | 1.40 |
| *g.* | Sheet of 6, #C7h-C7m, dated "2019" | 8.50 | 8.50 |
| *h.* | As #C7a, dated "2019" | 1.40 | 1.40 |
| *i.* | As #C7b, dated "2019" | 1.40 | 1.40 |
| *j.* | As #C7c, dated "2019" | 1.40 | 1.40 |
| *k.* | As #C7d, dated "2019" | 1.40 | 1.40 |
| *l.* | As #C7e, dated "2019" | 1.40 | 1.40 |
| *m.* | As #C7f, dated "2019" | 1.40 | 1.40 |

Issued: Nos. C1a-C6a, C7g, 12/12/19.

## POSTAGE DUE STAMPS

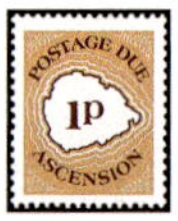

Outline Map of Ascension — D1

**1986 Litho. *Perf. 15x14***

| | | | | |
|---|---|---|---|---|
| J1 | D1 | 1p beige & brown | .25 | *.30* |
| J2 | D1 | 2p orange & brown | .25 | *.30* |
| J3 | D1 | 5p org ver & brn | .25 | *.30* |
| J4 | D1 | 7p violet & black | .25 | *.50* |
| J5 | D1 | 10p ultra & black | .45 | *.75* |
| J6 | D1 | 25p pale green & blk | .90 | *1.25* |
| | | *Nos. J1-J6 (6)* | 2.35 | *3.40* |

# AUSTRALIAN STATES

## NEW SOUTH WALES

ˈnü sauth ˈwā̦ə̦lz

LOCATION — Southeast coast of Australia in the South Pacific Ocean
GOVT. — British Crown Colony
AREA — 309,432 sq. mi.
POP. — 1,500,000 (estimated, 1900)
CAPITAL — Sydney

In 1901 New South Wales united with five other British colonies to form the Commonwealth of Australia. Stamps of Australia are now used.

12 Pence = 1 Shilling
20 Shillings = 1 Pound

### Watermarks

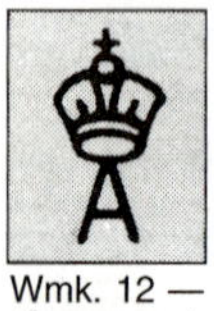

Wmk. 12 — Crown and Single-lined A

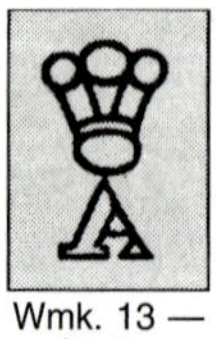

Wmk. 13 — Large Crown and Double-lined A

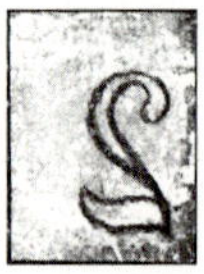

Wmk. 49 — Double-lined Numerals Corresponding with the Value

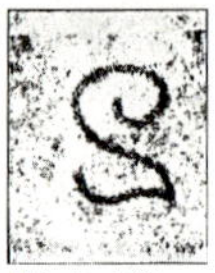

Wmk. 50 — Single-lined Numeral

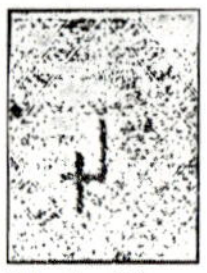

Wmk. 51 — Single-lined Numeral

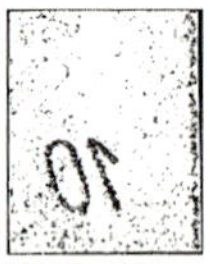

Wmk. 52 — Single-lined Numeral

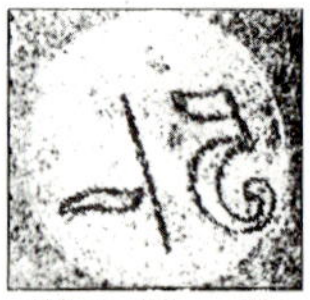

Wmk. 53 — 5/-

Wmk. 54 — Small Crown and NSW

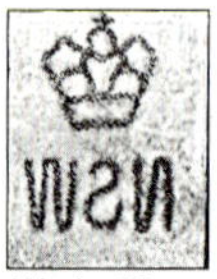

Wmk. 55 — Large Crown and NSW

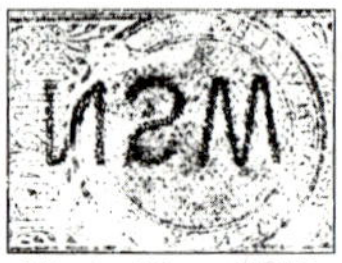

Wmk. 56 — NSW

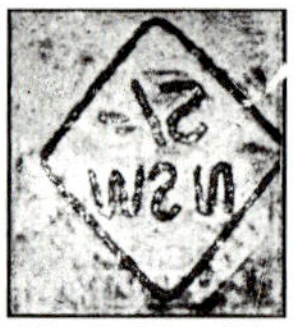

Wmk. 57 — 5/- NSW in Diamond

Wmk. 58 — 20/- NSW in Circle

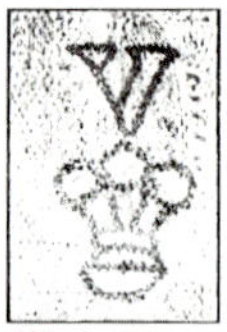

Wmk. 70 — V and Crown

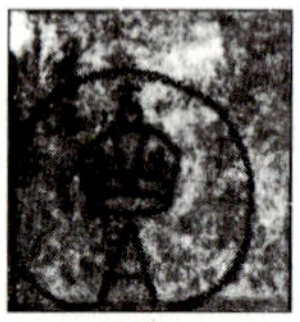

Wmk. 199 — Crown and A in Circle

Values for unused stamps are for examples with original gum as defined in the catalogue introduction except for Nos. 1-20 which are rarely found with gum and are valued without gum. Very fine examples of Nos. 35-100, F3-F5, J1-J10 and O1-O40 will have perforations touching the framelines or design on one or more sides due to the narrow spacing of the stamps on the plates and imperfect perforation methods. Stamps with perfs clear of the design on all four sides are scarce and will command higher prices.

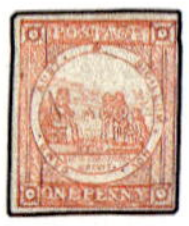

Seal of the Colony — A1

A1 has no clouds. A2 has clouds added to the design, except in pos. 15.

**1850 Unwmk. Engr. *Imperf.***

**Yellowish Wove Paper**

| | | | |
|---|---|---|---|
| 1 | A1 1p red, *yelsh wove* | 16,000. | 625.00 |
| *a.* | 1p brownish red | 17,250. | 650.00 |
| *c.* | 1p carmine | 17,250. | 650.00 |
| *d.* | 1p crimson lake | 17,250. | 650.00 |

**Bluish Wove Paper**

| | | | |
|---|---|---|---|
| *b.* | 1p red, *bluish wove* | 15,000. | 650.00 |
| *1e* | A1 1p lake | 16,000. | 650.00 |

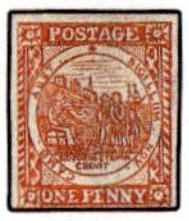

Seal of the Colony — A2

**Re-engraved, with Clouds**

**1850, Aug. Yellowish Wove Paper**

| | | | |
|---|---|---|---|
| 2 | A2 1p red, *yelsh wove* | 14,000. | 550.00 |
| *f.* | Hill unshaded | 18,500. | 850.00 |
| *g.* | No clouds | 18,500. | 850.00 |
| *h.* | No trees | 18,500. | 850.00 |
| *2i* | A2 1p vermilion | 13,750. | 675.00 |

**Bluish Wove Paper**

| | | | |
|---|---|---|---|
| *c.* | A3 1p carmine red, *bluish wove* | 13,250. | 750.00 |
| *j.* | Hill unshaded | 18,000. | 750.00 |
| *k.* | No clouds | 18,000. | 750.00 |
| *l.* | No trees | 18,000. | 750.00 |
| *2m* | A2 1p brownish lake | 13,500. | 750.00 |
| *2n* | A2 1p crimson lake | 13,500. | 750.00 |
| *2o* | A2 1p gooseberry red | 16,500. | 750.00 |

**Laid Paper**

| | | | |
|---|---|---|---|
| *b.* | A2 1p carmine red, *yellowish laid* | 18,000. | 800.00 |
| *p.* | Hill unshaded | — | 1,275. |
| *q.* | No clouds | — | 1,275. |
| *r.* | No trees | — | 1,275. |
| *e.* | 1p carmine red, *bluish laid* | | |
| *2s* | A2 1p vermilion, *bluish* | 19,000. | 600.00 |

Printed in panes of 25 (5x5). Twenty-five varieties.

Stamps from early impressions of the plate sell at considerably higher prices.

No. 1 was reproduced by the collotype process in a souvenir sheet distributed at the London International Stamp Exhibition 1950. The paper is white.

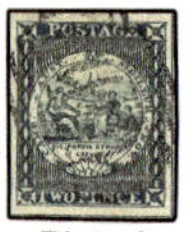

Plate I
A3

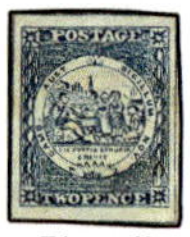

Plate II
A4

Plate I: Vertically lined background.

Plate I re-touched: Lines above and below "POSTAGE" and "TWO PENCE" deepened. Outlines of circular band around picture also deepened.

Plate II (First re-engraving of Plate I): Horizontally lined background; the bale on the left side is dated and there is a dot in the star in each corner.

Plate II retouched: Dots and dashes added in lower spandrels.

**Plate I**

**1850, Jan. 1 Early Impressions**

| | | | |
|---|---|---|---|
| *a.* | Early impression | 20,000. | 625.00 |
| *b.* | Double line on bale (Pos. 2/7) | | 1,250. |
| *3c* | A3 2p deep blue, *yelsh wove* | *18,000.* | 725.00 |

**Intermediate Impressions**

| | | | |
|---|---|---|---|
| *3d* | A3 2p gray blue, *yelsh wove* | 12,750. | 425.00 |
| *3e* | A3 2p deep blue, *yelsh wove* | 13,750. | 500.00 |

**Late (worn plate) Impressions**

| | | | |
|---|---|---|---|
| 3 | A3 2p blue, *yelsh wove* | 10,500. | 225.00 |
| *3f* | A3 2p deep blue, *yelsh wove* | 10,500. | 225.00 |

Printed in panes of 24 (12x2). Twenty-four varieties.

**Plate I, Retouched**

| | | | |
|---|---|---|---|
| 4 | A3 2p blue, *yelsh wove* | 12,750. | 360.00 |
| *4a* | A3 2p gray blue, *yelsh wove* | 13,750. | 450.00 |

Twelve varieties.

**Plate II**

**1850, Apr. Early Impressions**

| | | | |
|---|---|---|---|
| *h.* | Early impression | 16,500. | 350.00 |
| *j.* | "CREVIT" omitted (Pos. 2/1) | 22,500. | 1,000. |
| *k.* | Pick & shovel omitted (Pos. 1/10) | 22,000. | 625.00 |
| *l.* | No whip (Pos. 1/4, 1/8, 2/8) | — | 525.00 |
| *5m* | A3 2p bright blue, *bluish wove* | 16,500. | 350.00 |
| *5n* | A3 2p indigo blue, *yelsh wove* | 16,500. | 375.00 |
| *5o* | A3 2p lilac blue, *yelsh wove* | | *1,750.* |

**Late (worn plate) Impressions**

| | | | |
|---|---|---|---|
| 5 | A4 2p blue, *yelsh wove* | 10,500. | 175.00 |
| *a.* | 2p blue, *bluish wove* | 10,500. | 175.00 |
| *b.* | 2p 2p blue, *grayish wove* | 10,500. | 175.00 |
| *5p* | A4 2p prussian blue, *bluish wove* | 10,500. | 225.00 |
| *c.* | "CREVIT" omitted | 16,500. | 675.00 |
| *d.* | Pick and shovel omitted | — | 450.00 |
| *e.* | No whip | *14,750.* | 365.00 |

**Plate II, Retouched**

| | | | |
|---|---|---|---|
| 5F | A4 2p blue, *bluish wove* | 11,500. | 270.00 |
| *g.* | No whip | — | 425.00 |
| *i.* | "CREVIT" omitted | — | 585.00 |
| *5q* | A4 2p prussian blue, *bluish wove* | 11,500. | 360.00 |

Eleven varieties.

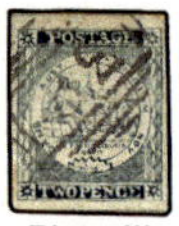

Plate III
A5

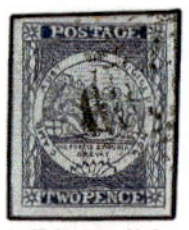

Plate IV
A6

Plate III (Second re-engraving of Plate I): The bale is not dated and, with the exception of Nos. 7, 10 and 12, it is single-lined. There are no dots in the stars.

Plate IV (Third re-engraving of Plate I): The bale is double-lined and there is a circle in the center of each star.

**1850-51 Wove Paper**

| | | | |
|---|---|---|---|
| 6 | A5 2p bl, *grayish wove* | 11,500. | 270.00 |
| *a.* | Fan with 6 segments | 14,500. | 585.00 |
| *b.* | Double-lined bale | — | 375.00 |
| *c.* | No whip | — | 425.00 |
| *6d* | A5 2p ultramarine | 11,500. | 270.00 |
| 7 | A6 2p blue, *bluish wove* ('51) | 12,500. | 225.00 |
| *b.* | 2p blue, *grayish wove* | 12,500. | 250.00 |
| *c.* | Fan with 6 segments (Pos. 2/8) | — | 375.00 |
| *d.* | No clouds (Pos. 2/10) | — | 375.00 |
| *e.* | Hill not shaded (Pos. 1/12) | — | 400.00 |
| *f.* | No waves (Pos. 1/9, 2/5) | — | *550.00* |
| *7g* | A6 2p 2p ultramarine | 12,500. | 270.00 |
| *7h* | A6 2p 2p prussian blue | 12,500. | 225.00 |

**Laid Paper**

| | | | |
|---|---|---|---|
| *7a* | A6 2p 2p ultra, *white laid* | 13,500. | 275.00 |
| *7i* | A6 2p prussian blue | 14,500. | 340.00 |
| *j.* | Fan with 6 segments (Pos. 2/8) | — | 450.00 |
| *k.* | No clouds (Pos. 2/10) | 17,500. | 450.00 |
| *l.* | Hill not shaded (Pos. 1/12) | | 450.00 |
| *m.* | No waves (Pos. 1/9, 2/5) | | 400.00 |
| *n.* | "PENOE" (Pos. 1/10, 2/12) | | 450.00 |

Twenty-four varieties.

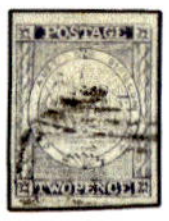

Plate V — A7

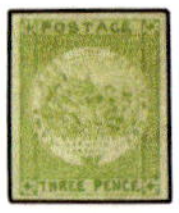

A8

Plate V (Fourth re-engraving of Plate I): There is a pearl in the fan-shaped ornament below the central design.

**1850-51 Wove Paper**

| | | | |
|---|---|---|---|
| 8 | A7 2p blue, *grayish wove* ('51) | 12,500. | 270.00 |
| *b.* | Fan with 6 segments (Pos. 2/8) | — | 450.00 |
| *c.* | Pick and shovel omitted (Pos. 2/5) | — | 475.00 |
| *8d* | A7 2p ultramarine | 12,500. | 270.00 |

**Laid Paper**

| | | | |
|---|---|---|---|
| *a.* | 2p ultra, *yellowish laid* | 15,500. | 450.00 |
| *e.* | Fan with 6 segments (Pos. 2/8) | — | 650.00 |
| *f.* | Pick and shovel omitted (Pos. 2/5) | — | 650.00 |

**Yellowish Wove Paper**

| | | | |
|---|---|---|---|
| *a.* | 3p green, *yellowish wove* | 12,500. | 350.00 |
| *9h* | A8 3p emerald green | 14,500. | 375.00 |
| *e.* | No whip | — | 550.00 |
| *f.* | "SIGIIIUM" for "SIGILLUM" (Pos. 5/3) | — | 725.00 |
| *9g* | A8 3p myrtle green | *23,500.* | *1,500.* |

**Bluish Wove Paper**

| | | | |
|---|---|---|---|
| 9 | A8 3p green, *bluish wove* | 12,500. | 325.00 |
| *9d* | A8 3p emerald green | 13,500. | 325.00 |
| *i.* | No whip (Pos. 4/3, 4/4) | — | 450.00 |
| *j.* | "SIGIIIUM" for "SIGILLUM" (Pos. 5/3) | — | 650.00 |

**Laid Paper**

| | | | |
|---|---|---|---|
| *b.* | 3p green, *yellowish laid* | 17,500. | 825.00 |
| *k.* | No whip (Pos. 4/3, 4/4) | — | *1,000.* |

AUSTRALIAN STATES — New South Wales 705

| | | | |
|---|---|---|---|
| *l.* | "SIGIIIUM" for "SIGILLUM" (Pos. 5/3) | — | *1,200.* |
| *c.* | 3p green, *bluish laid* | 17,500. | 825.00 |
| 9m A8 | 3p bright green, *yellowish laid* | *19,000.* | *900.00* |

Twenty-four varieties of No. 8, twenty-five of No. 9.

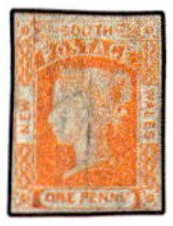

Queen Victoria — A9

TWO PENCE

Plate I — Background of wavy lines.

Plate II — Stars in corners.

Plate III (Plate I re-engraved) — Background of crossed lines.

**1851 Yellowish Wove Paper**

| | | | |
|---|---|---|---|
| **10** | A9 1p carmine | *4,500.* | 360.00 |
| *b.* | No leaves to right of "SOUTH" | *6,000.* | 900.00 |
| *c.* | Two leaves to right of "SOUTH" | *6,000.* | 1,000. |
| *d.* | "WALE" | *6,000.* | 1,000. |
| **11** | A9 2p ultra, Plate I | *2,250.* | 135.00 |

**1852 Bluish Laid Paper**

| | | | |
|---|---|---|---|
| **12** | A9 1p orange brown | 7,500. | 540.00 |
| *a.* | 1p claret | 7,500. | 525.00 |
| *b.* | As "a," no leaves to right of "SOUTH" | | 1,125. |
| *c.* | As "a," two leaves to right of "SOUTH" | | 1,250. |
| *d.* | As "a," "WALE" | | 1,250. |

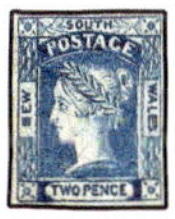

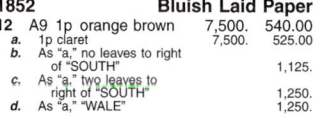

Queen Victoria — A10

SIX PENCE

Plate I — Background of fine lines.

Plate II (Plate I re-engraved) — Background of coarse lines.

**1852-55**

**Bluish or Grayish Wove Paper**

| | | | |
|---|---|---|---|
| **13** | A9 1p red | 2,250. | 180.00 |
| *a.* | 1p carmine | 2,250. | 180.00 |
| *b.* | 1p scarlet | 2,250. | 225.00 |
| *c.* | 1p brick red | 2,250. | 180.00 |
| *d.* | As "c," no leaves to right of "SOUTH" | 4,500. | 375.00 |
| *e.* | As "c," two leaves to right of "SOUTH" | | 500.00 |
| *f.* | As "c," "WALE" | | 500.00 |
| **14** | A9 2p blue, Plate I | 1,700. | 42.50 |
| *a.* | 2p ultramarine | 1,800. | 42.50 |
| *b.* | 2p slate | 1,750. | 42.50 |
| *c.* | 2p chalky blue | 1,750. | 42.50 |
| *d.* | 2p prussian blue | 1,250. | 42.50 |
| **15** | A10 2p blue, Plate II ('53) | 2,600. | 120.00 |
| *a.* | "WAEES" | *3,000.* | 525.00 |
| *b.* | 2p deep ultramarine | 2,600. | 150.00 |
| *c.* | 2p prussian blue | 2,600. | 135.00 |
| *d.* | As "c," "WAEES" | — | 550.00 |
| **16** | A9 2p blue, Plate III ('55) | 1,450. | 85.00 |
| *a.* | "WALES" partly covered with wavy lines | 5,500. | 325.00 |
| *b.* | 2p blue, *white paper* ('55) | 1,450. | 85.00 |
| *c.* | As "b," "WALES" partly covered with wavy lines | — | 300.00 |
| **17** | A9 3p green | 5,500. | 190.00 |
| *a.* | 3p emerald | *6,250.* | 270.00 |
| *b.* | As "a," "WACES" | — | *725.00* |
| *c.* | 3p deep green | 6,250. | 270.00 |
| *d.* | 3p yellow green | 6,250. | 250.00 |
| *e.* | As "d," "WACES" | — | 575.00 |
| *f.* | 3p blue green, *thick paper* | 6,250. | 300.00 |
| *g.* | As "f," "WACES" | | 825.00 |
| **18** | A9 6p brown, Plate I | 5,000. | 400.00 |
| *a.* | "WALLS" | *5,750.* | 1,250. |
| *b.* | 6p black brown | 5,000. | *1,250.* |
| *c.* | 6p yellow brown | 5,750. | 325.00 |
| *d.* | 6p chocolate brown | 5,250. | 325.00 |
| *e.* | 6p yellow brown, *white paper* | | *1,200.* |
| *f.* | As "e," *"WALLS" | | *2,700.* |
| **19** | A9 6p brown, Plate II | 5,750. | 375.00 |
| *a.* | 6p bister brown | 5,250. | 375.00 |
| **20** | A9 8p yellow ('53) | 19,000. | 1,000. |
| *a.* | 8p orange | 20,000. | 1,000. |
| *b.* | No leaves to right of "SOUTH" | — | *2,250.* |
| *c.* | No bow at back of head | — | *2,250.* |
| *d.* | No lines in spandrel | — | *1,350.* |

The plates of the 1, 2, 3 and 8p each contained 50 varieties and those of the 6p 25 varieties.

*The 2p, plate II, 6p, plate II, and 8p have been reprinted on grayish blue wove paper. The reprints of the 2p have the spandrels and background much worn. Most of the reprints of the 6p have no floreate ornaments to the right and left of "South." On all the values the wreath has been retouched.*

**Type of 1851 and**

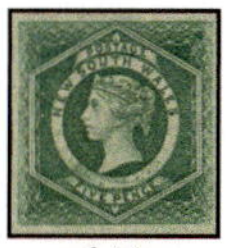

A11

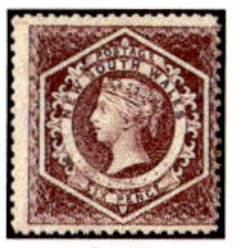

A12

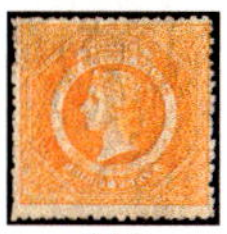

A13

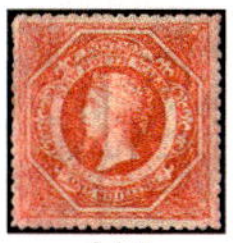

A14

**1854-55 Wmk. 49 *Imperf.***

| | | | |
|---|---|---|---|
| **23** | A9 1p orange | 575.00 | 52.50 |
| *a.* | No leaves to right of "SOUTH" | 1,100. | 180.00 |
| *b.* | Two leaves to right of "SOUTH" | 1,450. | 200.00 |
| *c.* | "WALE" | 1,450. | 200.00 |
| *d.* | 1d orange vermilion | 525.00 | 52.50 |
| **24** | A9 2p blue | 475.00 | 15.00 |
| *a.* | 2p ultramarine | 475.00 | 17.50 |
| *b.* | 2p Prussian blue | 475.00 | 17.50 |
| **25** | A9 3p green | 800.00 | 55.00 |
| *a.* | "WACES" | *2,150.* | 225.00 |
| *b.* | Watermarked "2" | *7,250.* | *2,000.* |

Value for No. 25b is for copy with the design cut into.

| | | | |
|---|---|---|---|
| **26** | A11 5p green | 1,600. | 725.00 |
| **27** | A12 6p sage green | 2,000. | 42.50 |
| **28** | A12 6p brown | 1,050. | 42.50 |
| *a.* | Watermarked "8" | *4,750.* | 160.00 |
| **29** | A12 6p gray | 750.00 | 85.00 |
| *a.* | 6p greenish gray | 1,950. | 75.00 |
| *b.* | 6p bluish gray | 1,950. | 85.00 |
| *c.* | 6p deep slate | 2,150. | 75.00 |
| *d.* | As "c," wmk sideways | | *1,250.* |
| *e.* | 6p fawn | 1,950. | 160.00 |
| *f.* | As "e," watermarked "8" | *4,750.* | 145.00 |
| *g.* | As "f," wmk sideways | | *540.00* |
| **30** | A13 8p orange ('55) | *25,000.* | 1,750. |
| *a.* | 8p yellow | *25,000.* | 1,575. |
| **31** | A14 1sh pale red brown | *5,250.* | 125.00 |
| *a.* | 1sh red | *5,000.* | 100.00 |
| *b.* | 1sh rose vermilion | *7,750.* | 100.00 |
| *c.* | As "b," watermarked "8" | *10,000.* | 225.00 |

See Nos. 38-42, 56, 58, 65, 67.

Nos. 38-42 exist with wide margins. Stamps with perforations trimmed are often offered as Nos. 26, 30, and 30a.

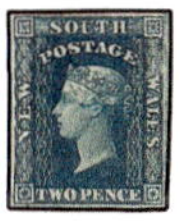

A15

**1856 *Imperf.***

| | | | |
|---|---|---|---|
| **32** | A15 1p red | 350.00 | 27.50 |
| *a.* | 1p orange red | 425.00 | 27.50 |
| *b.* | As "a," printed on both sides | *4,250.* | *2,500.* |
| *c.* | Watermarked "2" | | *9,500.* |
| *d.* | 1p carmine vermilion | 400.00 | 27.50 |
| **33** | A15 2p blue | 350.00 | 12.50 |
| *a.* | Watermarked "1" | | *9,500.* |
| *b.* | Watermarked "5" | 1,250. | 95.00 |
| *c.* | Watermarked "8" | | *8,250.* |
| *d.* | 2p dp turquoise blue | 375.00 | 15.00 |
| *e.* | 2p ultramarine | 350.00 | 15.00 |
| *f.* | 2p pale blue | 350.00 | 16.00 |
| **34** | A15 3p green | 2,000. | 125.00 |
| *a.* | 3p yellow green | 1,850. | 125.00 |
| *b.* | Watermarked "2" | | *5,000.* |
| *c.* | 3p bluish green ('56) | 1,950. | 125.00 |
| | *Nos. 32-34 (3)* | 2,700. | 165.00 |

The two known examples of No. 33c are in museums. Both are used.

*The 1p has been reprinted in orange on paper watermarked Small Crown and NSW, and the 2p in deep blue on paper watermarked single lined "2." These reprints are usually overprinted "SPECIMEN."*

See Nos. 34C-37, 54, 63, 90.

**1859 Litho.**

| | | | |
|---|---|---|---|
| **34C** | A15 2p light blue | — | 925.00 |
| | On cover | | *4,500.* |

**1860-63 Engr. Wmk. 49 *Perf. 13***

| | | | |
|---|---|---|---|
| **35** | A15 1p red | 175.00 | 25.00 |
| *a.* | 1p orange | 175.00 | 25.00 |
| *b.* | Perf. 12x13 | | *2,400.* |
| *c.* | Perf. 12 | 310.00 | 25.00 |
| **36** | A15 2p blue, perf. 12 | 275.00 | 16.00 |
| *a.* | Watermarked "1" | | *4,500.* |
| *c.* | Perf. 12x13 | *3,400.* | 425.00 |
| **37** | A15 3p blue green | 110.00 | 14.00 |
| *a.* | 3p yellow green | 125.00 | 11.00 |
| *b.* | 3p deep green | 125.00 | 10.00 |
| *c.* | Watermarked "6" | 250.00 | 16.00 |
| *d.* | Perf. 12 | 1,000. | 52.50 |
| **38** | A11 5p dark green | 110.00 | 27.50 |
| *a.* | 5p yellow green | 325.00 | 85.00 |
| *b.* | Perf. 12 | 475.00 | 125.00 |
| **39** | A12 6p brown, perf. 12 | 875.00 | 75.00 |
| *a.* | 6p gray, perf. 12 | 875.00 | 65.00 |
| **40** | A12 6p violet | 200.00 | 8.00 |
| *a.* | 6p aniline lilac | 1,500. | 160.00 |
| *b.* | Watermarked "5" | 850.00 | 30.00 |
| *c.* | Watermarked "12" | 800.00 | 25.00 |
| *e.* | Perf. 12 | 775.00 | 20.00 |
| *f.* | As "b," wmk sideways | | *1,250.* |
| **41** | A13 8p yellow | 575.00 | 50.00 |
| *a.* | 8p orange | 600.00 | 50.00 |
| *b.* | As "a," perf. 12 | *7,750.* | 1,450. |
| *c.* | 8p red orange | 575.00 | 65.00 |
| *d.* | As "c," perf 12 | *7,750.* | 1,450. |
| **42** | A14 1sh rose | 400.00 | 10.00 |
| *a.* | 1sh carmine | 390.00 | 10.00 |
| *b.* | As "a," perf. 12 | 400.00 | 30.00 |
| *c.* | 1sh crimson lake | 400.00 | 10.00 |
| *d.* | 1sh brownish red, perf 12 | 1,750. | 75.00 |
| *e.* | As "a," pair, imperf. between | | — |
| | *Nos. 35-42 (8)* | 2,720. | 225.50 |

**1864 Wmk. 50 *Perf. 13***

| | | | |
|---|---|---|---|
| **43** | A15 1p red | 135.00 | 67.50 |

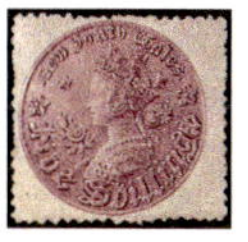

A16

**1861-80 Wmk. 53 *Perf. 13***

| | | | |
|---|---|---|---|
| **44** | A16 5sh dull violet | 365.00 | 60.00 |
| *a.* | 5sh purple | 410.00 | 85.00 |
| *b.* | 5sh dull violet, perf. 12 | 2,275. | 350.00 |
| *c.* | 5sh purple, perf. 12 | — | 90.00 |
| *d.* | 5sh purple, perf. 10 | 325.00 | 90.00 |
| *e.* | 5sh purple, perf. 12x10 | 450.00 | 90.00 |
| *f.* | 5sh royal purple, perf 13 ('72) | 000.00 | 77.50 |
| *g.* | 5sh deep rose lilac, perf 13 ('75) | 250.00 | 47.50 |
| *h.* | 5sh rose lilac, perf 10 ('83) | 300.00 | 60.00 |
| *i.* | 5sh purple, perf 10x12 ('85) | — | 225.00 |
| *j.* | 5sh reddish purple, perf 10 ('86) | 310.00 | 67.50 |
| *k.* | 5sh rose lilac, perf 11 ('88) | — | 150.00 |

See No. 101. For overprint see No. O11.

*Reprints are perf. 10 and overprinted "REPRINT" in black.*

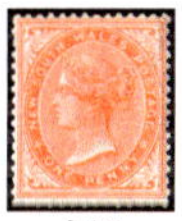

A17

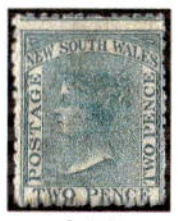

A18

**1862-65 Typo. Unwmk. *Perf. 13***

| | | | |
|---|---|---|---|
| **45** | A17 1p red ('65) | 225.00 | 47.50 |
| *a.* | Perf. 14 | 240.00 | 80.00 |
| *b.* | 1p brick red ('65) | 225.00 | 47.50 |
| **46** | A18 2p blue | 140.00 | 9.00 |
| *a.* | Perf. 14 | 240.00 | 95.00 |

**1863-64 Wmk. 50 *Perf. 13***

| | | | |
|---|---|---|---|
| **47** | A17 1p red | 85.00 | 11.00 |
| *a.* | Watermarked "2" | 270.00 | 37.50 |
| *b.* | 1p dark red brown | 325.00 | 50.00 |
| *c.* | 1p brick red | 85.00 | 12.00 |
| *d.* | 1p brick red, shiny surfaced paper ('65) | 335.00 | 175.00 |
| *e.* | Horiz. pair, imperf between | | *2,500.* |
| **48** | A18 2p blue | 65.00 | 3.50 |
| *a.* | Watermarked "1" | 260.00 | 6.50 |
| *b.* | 2p cobalt blue | 65.00 | 3.50 |
| *c.* | 2p Prussian blue | 67.50 | 4.00 |

**1862 Wmk. 49 *Perf. 13***

| | | | |
|---|---|---|---|
| **49** | A18 2p blue | 135.00 | 40.00 |
| *a.* | Watermarked "5" | 135.00 | 42.50 |
| *b.* | Perf. 12x13 | *675.00* | 250.00 |
| *c.* | Perf. 12 | 240.00 | 55.00 |

See Nos. 52-53, 61-62, 70-71.

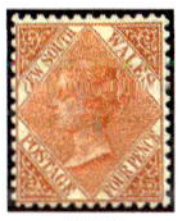

A19

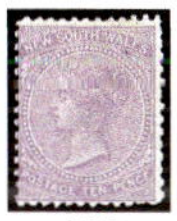

A20

**1867, Sept. Wmk. 51, 52 *Perf. 13***

| | | | |
|---|---|---|---|
| **50** | A19 4p red brown | *125.00* | 9.00 |
| *a.* | Imperf. | | |
| *b.* | 4p pale red brown | *125.00* | 9.00 |
| **51** | A20 10p lilac | 55.00 | 9.00 |
| | Ovptd. "SPECIMEN" | 30.00 | |
| *a.* | Imperf. | | |
| *b.* | Horiz. pair, imperf between | *3,250.* | |

See Nos. 55, 64, 91, 97, 117, 129.

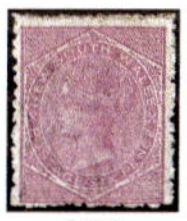

A21

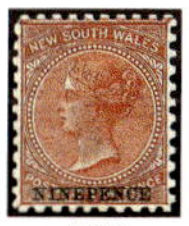

A22

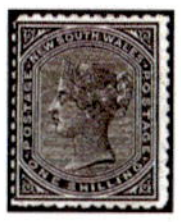

A23

**Typo.; Engr. (3p, 5p, 8p)**

**1871-84 Wmk. 54 *Perf. 13***

| | | | |
|---|---|---|---|
| **52** | A17 1p red | 42.50 | 3.75 |
| *a.* | Perf. 10 | 275.00 | 40.00 |
| *b.* | Perf. 13x10 | 36.00 | 3.25 |
| *c.* | Horiz. pair, imperf between | | *2,900.* |
| *d.* | 1p scarlet, perf. 10 | — | 190.00 |
| **53** | A18 2p blue | 47.50 | 2.00 |
| *a.* | Imperf. | | |
| *b.* | Horiz. pair, imperf vert. | | *3,250.* |
| *c.* | Perf. 10 | *275.00* | 27.50 |
| *d.* | Perf. 13x10 | 35.00 | 1.25 |
| *e.* | Perf. 12x13 | | |
| *f.* | 2p Prussian blue, perf. 11x12 | *275.00* | *40.00* |
| *g.* | As "f," perf. 10 | 145.00 | 22.50 |
| **54** | A15 3p green ('74) | 75.00 | 5.00 |
| *a.* | Perf. 11 | 180.00 | 115.00 |
| *b.* | Perf. 12 | — | *200.00* |
| *c.* | Perf. 10x12 | 160.00 | 50.00 |
| *d.* | Perf. 11x12 | 135.00 | 42.50 |
| *e.* | Perf. 10 | 95.00 | 12.00 |
| *f.* | 3p bright green, perf. 13x10 | 110.00 | 25.00 |
| *g.* | As "f," perf. 10 | 130.00 | 22.50 |
| **55** | A19 4p red brown ('77) | 120.00 | 17.50 |
| *a.* | Perf. 10 | 240.00 | 60.00 |
| *b.* | Perf. 13x10 | 135.00 | 7.50 |
| *c.* | Perf. 10x13 | 175.00 | 27.50 |
| **56** | A11 5p dk grn, perf. 10 ('84) | 42.50 | 45.00 |
| *a.* | Horiz. pair, imperf between | | 2,250. |
| *b.* | Perf. 12 | 275.00 | 110.00 |
| *c.* | Perf. 10x12 | 125.00 | 65.00 |
| *d.* | Perf. 10x13 | | |
| *e.* | 12x10 | 60.00 | 47.50 |
| **57** | A21 6p lilac ('72) | 105.00 | 2.50 |
| *a.* | Horiz. pair, imperf. between | — | *3,000.* |
| *b.* | Perf. 13x10 | 120.00 | 2.50 |
| *c.* | Perf. 10 | 125.00 | 2.50 |
| **58** | A13 8p yellow ('77) | 225.00 | 17.50 |
| *a.* | Imperf. | | |
| *b.* | Perf. 10 | 375.00 | 25.00 |
| *c.* | Perf. 13x10 | 250.00 | 24.00 |
| **59** | A22 9p on 10p red brown, perf. 12 (Bk) | 25.00 | 5.50 |
| *a.* | Double surcharge, blk & bl | *400.00* | |
| *b.* | Perf. 12x10 | *300.00* | *225.00* |
| *c.* | Perf. 10 | 17.50 | 12.50 |
| *d.* | Perf. 12x11 | 17.50 | 7.50 |
| *e.* | Perf. 11x12 | — | — |
| *f.* | Perf. 13 | 75.00 | 15.00 |
| *g.* | Perf. 11 | 62.50 | 12.50 |
| *h.* | Perf. 10x11 | 75.00 | 24.00 |
| **60** | A23 1sh black ('76) | 165.00 | 15.00 |
| *b.* | Perf. 13x10 | 210.00 | 17.50 |
| *c.* | Perf. 10 | 225.00 | 27.50 |
| *d.* | Perf. 11 | — | — |
| *e.* | Vert. pair, imperf between | | *3,000.* |
| *f.* | Pair, imperf | | *2,750.* |
| | *Nos. 52-60 (9)* | 847.50 | 113.75 |

The surcharge on No. 59 measures 15mm.

See Nos. 66, 68. For overprints see Nos. O1-O10.

**Typo.; Engr. (3p, 5p, 8p)**

**1882-91 Wmk. 55 *Perf. 11x12***

| | | | |
|---|---|---|---|
| **61** | A17 1p red | 11.00 | 1.50 |
| *a.* | Perf. 10 | 25.00 | 3.00 |
| *b.* | Perf. 10x13 | 125.00 | 9.50 |
| *c.* | Perf. 10x12 | 275.00 | 70.00 |
| *d.* | Perf. 12x11 | | 130.00 |
| *e.* | Perf. 10x11 | *500.00* | 130.00 |
| *f.* | Perf. 11 | | 160.00 |
| *g.* | Perf. 13 | 1,000. | 475.00 |
| *h.* | Perf. 13x10 | 72.50 | 3.00 |
| *i.* | Perf. 12x10 | — | 225.00 |
| *j.* | Perf. 11x10 | — | — |
| *k.* | Horiz. pair, imperf between | | *2,100.* |
| **62** | A18 2p blue | 12.50 | 1.00 |
| *a.* | Perf. 10 | 62.50 | 1.00 |
| *b.* | Perf. 13x10 | 160.00 | 7.50 |
| *c.* | Perf. 13 | 500.00 | 115.00 |
| *d.* | Perf. 12x10 | 425.00 | 100.00 |
| *e.* | Perf. 11 | | 100.00 |
| *f.* | Perf. 12x11 | 450.00 | 100.00 |
| *g.* | Perf. 11x10 | 500.00 | 160.00 |
| *h.* | Perf. 12 | | 250.00 |
| *i.* | Double impression | — | 800.00 |
| **63** | A15 3p green | 6.00 | 1.00 |
| *a.* | Imperf., pair | 500.00 | |
| *b.* | Vert. pair, imperf. btwn. | — | |
| *c.* | Horiz. pair, imperf. vert. | 750.00 | 675.00 |
| *d.* | Double impression | — | — |
| *e.* | Perf. 10 | 35.00 | 2.50 |
| *f.* | Perf. 11 | 10.00 | 1.00 |
| *g.* | Perf. 12 | 15.00 | 2.50 |
| *h.* | Perf. 12x11 | 7.25 | 1.00 |
| *i.* | Perf. 10x12 | 32.50 | 3.00 |
| *m.* | Perf. 10x11 | 40.00 | 3.25 |
| *n.* | Perf. 12x10 | 55.00 | 4.50 |
| *o.* | Wmk sideways | 65.00 | 12.50 |
| **64** | A19 4p red brown | 85.00 | 3.00 |
| *a.* | Perf. 10 | 125.00 | 5.50 |
| *b.* | Perf. 10x12 | 225.00 | 70.00 |
| *c.* | Perf. 12 | 325.00 | 190.00 |
| **65** | A11 5p dk blue green | 11.00 | 1.25 |
| *a.* | Imperf., pair | 500.00 | |
| *b.* | Perf. 11 | 12.00 | 1.25 |
| *c.* | Perf. 10 | 27.50 | 1.75 |
| *d.* | Perf. 12 | 27.50 | 1.75 |
| *e.* | Perf. 10x12 | 175.00 | 45.00 |
| *f.* | 5p green, perf. 12x11 | 12.00 | 1.25 |
| *g.* | 5p green, perf. 11x10 | 85.00 | 15.00 |
| *h.* | 5p green, perf. 12x10 | 90.00 | 10.00 |
| *i.* | 5p green, perf. 10x11 | 80.00 | 12.50 |

706 AUSTRALIAN STATES — New South Wales

*j.* 5p green, perf. 11 12.00 1.25
*k.* Wmk sideways 25.00 8.00
**66** A21 6p lilac, perf. 10 90.00 1.50
*a.* Horiz. pair, imperf. between *3,000.*
*b.* Perf. 10x12 110.00 8.00
*c.* Perf. 11x12 135.00 17.50
*d.* Perf. 12 135.00 10.00
*e.* Perf. 11x10 125.00 2.25
*f.* Perf. 11 135.00 7.75
*g.* Perf. 10x13 360.00
*h.* Perf. 12x11 110.00 2.50
*i.* Perf. 12x10 110.00 2.50
**67** A13 8p yellow, perf. 10 250.00 20.00
*a.* Perf. 11 250.00 25.00
*b.* Perf. 12 340.00 30.00
*c.* Perf. 10x12 310.00 27.50
**68** A23 1sh black 145.00 7.50
*a.* Perf. 10x13 — —
*b.* Perf. 10 150.00 7.50
*c.* Perf. 11 275.00 20.00
*d.* Perf. 10x12 — 290.00
*Nos. 61-68 (8)* 610.50 36.75

Nos. 63 and 65 exist with two types of watermark 55 — spacings of 1mm or 2mm between crown and NSW.

See No. 90. For surcharges and overprints see Nos. 92-94, O12-O19.

*The 1, 2, 4, 6, 8p and 1sh have been reprinted on paper watermarked Large Crown and NSW. The 1, 2, 4p and 1sh are perforated 11x12, the 6p is perforated 10 and the 8p 11. All are overprinted "REPRINT," the 1sh in red and the others in black.*

***Perf. 11x12***

**1886-87 Typo. Wmk. 56**

**Bluish Revenue Stamp Paper**

**70** A17 1p scarlet 22.00 10.00
*a.* Perf. 10 60.00 18.00
**71** A18 2p dark blue 45.00 8.00
*a.* Perf. 10 105.00 24.00
*b.* Imperf. *3,250.*

For overprint, see No. O20.

A24

***Perf. 12 (#73-75), 12x10 (#72, 75A) and Compound***

**1885-86 "POSTAGE" in Black**

**72** A24 5sh green & vio 850.00 150.00
*a.* Perf. 10 — —
*b.* Perf. 13 — —
**73** A24 10sh rose & vio 1,750. 275.00
*a.* Perf. 13 — —
**74** A24 £1 rose & vio *11,500. 4,750.*
*a.* Perf. 13 *8,250.*

**"POSTAGE" in Blue**

**Bluish Paper**

**75** A24 10sh rose & vio 325.00 75.00
*b.* Perf. 10 1,950. 250.00
*c.* Perf. 12x11 — —

**White Paper**

**75A** A24 £1 rose & vio 9,750. *4,750.*

For overprints, see Nos. O21-O23.

*The 5sh with black overprint and the £1 with blue overprint have been reprinted on paper watermarked NSW. They are perforated 12x10 and are overprinted "REPRINT" in black.*

**"POSTAGE" in Blue**

**1894 White Paper**

**76** A24 10sh rose & violet, perf 12 350.00 60.00
*a.* Double overprint
*b.* 10sh mauve & claret, perf 10 625.00 180.00
*c.* 10sh mauve & violet, perf 11 475.00 100.00
*d.* 10sh mauve & violet, perf 12x11 350.00 75.00

See No. 108B.

View of Sydney A25

Emu A26

Captain Cook A27

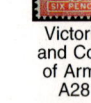

Victoria and Coat of Arms A28

Lyrebird A29

Kangaroo A30

**1888-89 Wmk. 55 *Perf. 11x12***

**77** A25 1p violet 15.00 1.00
*a.* Perf. 12 16.00 .50
*b.* Perf. 12x11½ 27.50 1.25
**78** A26 2p blue 22.00 .50
*a.* Imperf., pair 375.00 525.00
*b.* Perf. 12 22.00 .50
*c.* Perf. 12x11½ 22.00 .50
**79** A27 4p brown 30.00 5.50
*a.* Perf. 12x11½ 55.00 8.00
*b.* Perf. 12 55.00 5.00
*c.* Perf. 11 350.00 115.00
*d.* Imperf.
**80** A28 6p carmine rose 37.50 4.50
*a.* Perf. 12 40.00 10.50
*b.* Perf. 12x11½ 50.00 5.00
**81** A29 8p red violet 25.00 9.50
*a.* Perf. 12 25.00 9.50
*b.* Perf. 12x11½ 60.00 16.00
**82** A30 1sh maroon ('89) 55.00 2.50
*a.* Imperf., pair 1,450.
*b.* Perf. 12x11½ 57.50 3.00
*c.* Perf. 12 65.00 2.50
*d.* 1sh violet brown, perf 11x12 55.00 3.00
*e.* 1sh violet brown, perf 12x11½ 75.00 5.00
*f.* 1sh violet brown, perf 12 75.00 2.75
*Nos. 77-82 (6)* 184.50 23.50
Set, ovptd. "SPECIMEN" 210.00

First British settlement in Australia, cent.
For overprints see Nos. O24-O29.

**1888 Wmk. 56 *Perf. 11x12***

**83** A25 1p violet 45.00 8.00
**84** A26 2p blue 100.00 7.50

See Nos. 104B-106C, 113-115, 118, 125-127, 130.

Map of Australia A31

Governors Capt. Arthur Phillip (above) and Lord Carrington A32

**1888-89 Wmk. 53 *Perf. 10***

**85** A31 5sh violet ('89) 425.00 60.00
*a.* 5sh deep purple 400.00 55.00
**86** A32 20sh ultra 750.00 175.00

See Nos. 88, 120. For overprints see Nos. O30-O31.

**1890 Wmk. 57 *Perf. 10***

**87** A31 5sh violet 300.00 40.00
*a.* Perf. 11 375.00 50.00
*b.* Perf. 10x11 400.00 40.00
*c.* Perf. 12 450.00 60.00
*d.* 5sh mauve, perf 10 375.00 40.00
*e.* 5sh mauve, perf 11 375.00 50.00
*f.* Horiz. pair, imperf btwn. —

***Perf. 11x12, 12x11***

**Wmk. 58**

**88** A32 20sh ultra 400.00 90.00
*a.* Perf. 11 450.00 90.00
*b.* Perf. 12 475.00 160.00
*c.* 20sh cobalt blue, perf 10 525.00 170.00
*d.* As "c," perf 11 500.00 90.00
Nos. 87-88, ovptd. "SPECIMEN" 240.00

For overprints see Nos. O32-O33.

"Australia" — A33

**1890, Dec. 22 Wmk. 55 *Perf. 11x12***

**89** A33 2½p ultra 19.00 2.50
*a.* Perf. 12 25.00 4.00
*b.* Perf. 12x11½ 55.00 *50.00*
Overprinted "SPECIMEN" 35.00

For overprint see No. O35.

**Type of 1856**

**1891 Engr. Wmk. 52 *Perf. 10***

**90** A15 3p green 6.75 *50.00*
*a.* Double impression —
*b.* 3p light green 16.00 *62.50*

**Type of 1867**

**1893 Typo. *Perf. 11***

**91** A20 10p lilac 20.00 11.00
*a.* Perf. 10 22.50 13.00
*b.* Perf. 11x10 or 10x11 27.50 13.00
*c.* Perf. 12x11 160.00 17.00

**Types of 1862-84 Surcharged in Black**

a

b

**1891, Jan. 5 Wmk. 55 *Perf. 11x12***

**92** A17(a) ½p on 1p gray 10.50 *7.00*
*a.* Imperf. —
*b.* Surcharge omitted
*c.* Double surcharge *850.00*
**93** A21(b) 7½p on 6p brown 6.50 4.00
*a.* Perf. 10 5.50 11.00
*b.* Perf. 11 5.00 4.00
*c.* Perf. 12 15.00 5.00
*d.* Perf. 10x12 7.00 7.00

***Perf. 12x11½***

**94** A23(b) 12½p on 1sh red 10.50 8.00
*a.* Perf. 11x12 11.50 8.00
*b.* Perf. 10 11.50 8.50
*c.* Perf. 11 12.25 8.50
*d.* Perf. 12 14.00 8.00
*Nos. 92-94 (3)* 27.50 19.00
Nos. 92-94 overprinted "SPECIMEN" 90.00

For overprints see Nos. O34, O36-O37.

Victoria — A37

**1892-97 *Perf. 11x12***

**95** A37 ½p slate ('97) 5.00 .50
*a.* Perf. 12x11½ 5.00 .65
*b.* Perf. 12 5.00 .50
*c.* As #95, horiz. pair, imperf between *2,000.*
*d.* ½p gray, perf. 10 65.00 2.50
*e.* As "d," perf. 10x12 90.00 12.50
*f.* As "d," perf. 11 100.00 7.25
*g.* As "d," perf. 11x12 6.00 .50
As "g," overprinted "SPECIMEN" 25.00

See Nos. 102, 109, 121. For overprint see No. O38.

**Types of 1867-71**

**1897 *Perf. 11x12***

**96** A22 9p on 10p red brn (Bk) 20.00 25.00
*a.* 9p on 10p org brn (Bk) 20.00 25.00
*b.* Surcharge omitted
*c.* Double surcharge 325.00 450.00
*d.* Perf. 11 12.50 25.00
*e.* Perf. 12 13.00 25.00
**97** A20 10p violet 35.00 30.00
*a.* Perf. 12x11½ 12.00 25.00
*b.* Perf. 11 27.50 35.00
*c.* Perf. 12 24.00 32.50
Nos. 96-97, overprinted "SPECIMEN" 60.00

The surcharge on No. 96 measures 13½mm.
For overprints see Nos. O39-O40.

Seal A38

Victoria A39

A40

ONE PENNY:
Die I — The first pearl in the crown at the left is merged into the arch, the shading under the fleur-de-lis is indistinct, and the "s" of "WALES" is open.

Die II — The first pearl is circular, the vertical shading under the fleur-de-lis is clear, and the "s" of "WALES" not so open.

2½ PENCE:
Die I — There are 12 radiating lines in the star on the Queen's breast.

Die II — There are 16 radiating lines in the star. The eye is nearly full of color.

**1897 *Perf. 12***

**98** A38 1p rose red, II 5.00 .50
*a.* Die I, perf. 11x12 5.00 1.00
*b.* Imperf., pair *750.00*
*c.* Imperf. horiz., pair *850.00*
*d.* Die I, perf. 12x11½ 5.00 1.00
*e.* Die I, perf. 12 11.00 2.00
*f.* Die II, perf. 12x11½ 4.00 1.00
*g.* Die II, perf. 11x12 5.00 1.00
**99** A39 2p deep blue 17.50 1.50
*a.* Perf. 11x12 18.00 1.50
*b.* Perf. 12x11½ 9.00 1.50
**100** A40 2½p dp purple, II 42.50 2.50
*a.* Die I, perf. 12x11 30.00 2.50
*b.* Die I, perf. 11 32.50 4.00
*c.* Die I, perf. 11½x12 32.50 2.75
*d.* Die II, perf. 11x12 42.50 2.75
*e.* Die II, perf. 11½x12 32.50 2.75
*Nos. 98-100 (3)* 65.00 4.50
Nos. 98-100 overprinted "SPECIMEN" 75.00

Sixtieth year of Queen Victoria's reign.
See Nos. 103-104, 110-112, 122-124.

**Type of 1861**

**1897 Engr. Wmk. 53 *Perf. 11***

**101** A16 5sh red violet 60.00 16.00
*a.* Horiz. pair, imperf. btwn. *11,000.*
*b.* Perf. 11x12 or 12x11 60.00 24.00
*c.* Perf. 12 80.00 45.00

***Perf. 12x11½, 11½x12***

**1899, Oct. Typo. Wmk. 55**

HALF PENNY:
Die I — Narrow "H" in "HALF."

**102** A37 ½p blue green, I 4.00 1.50
*a.* Imperf., pair 250.00 *350.00*
**103** A39 2p ultra 5.75 1.00
*a.* Imperf., pair 325.00
**104** A40 2½p dk blue, II 9.00 1.75
*a.* Imperf., pair 350.00
**104B** A27 4p org brown 18.00 7.50
*c.* 4p red brown 35.00 17.00
*d.* As "c," imperf. pair 600.00
**105** A28 6p emerald 100.00 27.50
*a.* Imperf., pair 600.00
**106** A28 6p orange 50.00 5.00
*a.* 6p yellow 18.00 10.00
*b.* Imperf., pair 600.00
**106C** A29 8p magenta 47.50 6.00
*Nos. 102-106C (7)* 234.25 50.25

Lyrebird — A41

**1903 *Perf. 12x11½***

**107** A41 2sh6p blue green 55.00 22.50
Overprinted "SPECIMEN" 85.00

See Nos. 119, 131.

"Australia" — A42

**1903 Wmk. 70 *Perf. 12½***

**108** A42 9p org brn & ultra 20.00 3.50
Overprinted "SPECIMEN" 50.00
*a.* Perf. 11 *5,250. 1,850.*

See No. 128.

**Type of 1885-86**

**1904 Wmk. 56 *Perf. 12x11***

**"POSTAGE" in Blue**

**108B** A24 10sh brt rose & vio 425.00 90.00
*c.* Perf. 11 400.00 75.00
*d.* Perf. 14 375.00 85.00
*e.* 10sh aniline crimson & violet, perf 12 425.00 95.00
*f.* As "e," perf 12x11 325.00 55.00
*g.* 10sh claret & violet, chalky paper, perf 12x11 *475.00* 95.00

The watermark (NSW) of No. 108B is 20x7mm, with rounded angles in "N" and "W." On No. 75, the watermark is 21x7mm, with sharp angles in the "N" and "W."

HALF PENNY:
Die II — Wide "H" in "HALF."

***Perf. 11, 11x12½, 12x11½ and Compound***

**1905-06 — Wmk. 12**

| | | | | |
|---|---|---|---|---|
| **109** | A37 | ½p blue grn, II | 3.00 | 1.50 |
| *a.* | | ½p blue green, I | 4.50 | 1.00 |
| *b.* | | Booklet pane of 12 | — | |
| **110** | A38 | 1p car rose, II | 2.75 | .25 |
| *a.* | | Booklet pane of 6 | — | |
| *b.* | | Booklet pane of 12 | — | |
| **111** | A39 | 2p deep ultra | 2.25 | .40 |
| **112** | A40 | 2½p dk blue, II | 4.50 | 3.00 |
| **113** | A27 | 4p org brown | 10.50 | 4.50 |
| *a.* | | 4p red brown | 13.75 | 5.50 |
| **114** | A28 | 6p orange | 17.00 | 3.00 |
| *a.* | | 6p yellow | 19.00 | 4.50 |
| *b.* | | Perf. 11 | 350.00 | |
| **115** | A29 | 8p magenta | 27.50 | 8.00 |
| **117** | A20 | 10p violet | 16.25 | 6.00 |
| **118** | A30 | 1sh vio brown | 28.75 | 1.75 |
| **119** | A41 | 2sh6p blue green | 80.00 | 20.00 |

**Wmk. 199**

***Perf. 12x11 or 11x12***

| | | | | |
|---|---|---|---|---|
| **120** | A32 | 20sh ultra | 375.00 | 75.00 |
| *a.* | | Perf 12 | 400.00 | 90.00 |
| *b.* | | Perf 11 | 375.00 | 85.00 |
| | | *Nos. 109-115,117-120 (11)* | 567.50 | 123.40 |

**1906-07 — Wmk. 13**

| | | | | |
|---|---|---|---|---|
| **121** | A37 | ½p green, I | 5.00 | 7.50 |
| **122** | A38 | 1p rose, II | 27.00 | 5.00 |
| **123** | A39 | 2p ultra | 8.50 | 5.00 |
| **124** | A40 | 2½p blue, II | 70.00 | *130.00* |
| **125** | A27 | 4p org brown | 35.00 | 35.00 |
| **126** | A28 | 6p orange | 50.00 | 50.00 |
| *a.* | | 6p yellow | 50.00 | 50.00 |
| **127** | A29 | 8p red violet | 32.00 | 50.00 |
| **128** | A42 | 9p yel brn & ultra, perf. 12x12½ ('06) | 28.00 | 2.00 |
| *a.* | | Perf. 11 | 120.00 | 75.00 |
| *b.* | | 9p org brn & ultra, perf. 12x12½ | 19.00 | 2.00 |
| **129** | A20 | 10p violet | 35.00 | *60.00* |
| **130** | A30 | 1sh vio brown | 75.00 | 12.00 |
| *a.* | | Perf. 11 | — | 1,700. |
| **131** | A41 | 2sh6p blue green | 130.00 | 130.00 |
| | | *Nos. 121-131 (11)* | 495.50 | 486.50 |

Portions of some of the sheets on which the above are printed show the watermark "COMMONWEALTH OF AUSTRALIA." Stamps may also be found from portions of the sheet without watermark.

## SEMI-POSTAL STAMPS

SP1

Allegory of Charity — SP2

**1897, June — Wmk. 55 — *Perf. 11***

| | | | | |
|---|---|---|---|---|
| **B1** | SP1 | 1p (1sh) grn & brn | 50.00 | 50.00 |
| **B2** | SP2 | 2½p (2sh6p) rose, bl & gold | 250.00 | 240.00 |
| | | Nos. B1-B2 overprinted "SPECIMEN" | 300.00 | |

Diamond Jubilee of Queen Victoria.

The difference between the postal and face values of these stamps was donated to a fund for a home for consumptives.

## REGISTRATION STAMPS

Queen Victoria — R1

**Unwmk.**

**1856, Jan. 1 — Engr. — *Imperf.***

| | | | | |
|---|---|---|---|---|
| **F1** | R1 | (6p) orange & blue | *1,900.* | 250.00 |
| **F2** | R1 | (6p) red & blue | *2,000.* | 210.00 |
| *a.* | | Frame printed on back | *12,500.* | *5,250.* |

**1860 — *Perf. 12, 13***

| | | | | |
|---|---|---|---|---|
| **F3** | R1 | (6p) orange & blue | 1,150. | 80.00 |
| **F4** | R1 | (6p) red & blue | 1,200. | 85.00 |

Nos. F1 to F4 exist also on paper with papermaker's watermark in sheet.

**1863 — Wmk. 49**

| | | | | |
|---|---|---|---|---|
| **F5** | R1 | (6p) red & blue | 375.00 | 25.00 |
| *a.* | | (6p) red & Prussian blue | 375.00 | 27.50 |
| *b.* | | (6p) red & indigo | 475.00 | 35.00 |
| *c.* | | Double impression of frame | — | *850.00* |

Fifty varieties.

*Nos. F1-F2 were reprinted on thin white wove unwatermarked paper and on thick yellowish wove unwatermarked paper; the former are usually overprinted "SPECIMEN."*

*No. F4 was reprinted on thin white wove unwatermarked paper; perf. 10 and overprinted "REPRINT" in black.*

## POSTAGE DUE STAMPS

D1

***Perf. 10, 11, 11½, 12 and Compound***

**1891-92 — Typo. — Wmk. 55**

| | | | | |
|---|---|---|---|---|
| **J1** | D1 | ½p grn, perf 10 | 3.60 | 37.00 |
| *a.* | | Chalky paper | | |
| **J2** | D1 | 1p green | 35.00 | 4.00 |
| *a.* | | Perf 12 | 80.00 | 40.00 |
| *b.* | | Chalky paper | 30.00 | 4.50 |
| **J3** | D1 | 2p green | 24.00 | 4.00 |
| *a.* | | Perf 12x10 | 80.00 | 40.00 |
| *b.* | | Chalky paper | 27.00 | 6.50 |
| **J4** | D1 | 3p green | 65.00 | 14.00 |
| *b.* | | Chalky paper | 90.00 | 28.00 |
| **J5** | D1 | 4p green | 60.00 | 3.75 |
| *a.* | | Chalky paper | 60.00 | 13.00 |
| **J6** | D1 | 6p grn, perf 10 | 60.00 | 15.00 |
| **J7** | D1 | 8p grn, perf 10 | 125.00 | 27.00 |
| **J8** | D1 | 5sh grn, perf 10 | 300.00 | 60.00 |
| *a.* | | Perf 11 | 750.00 | 180.00 |
| *b.* | | Perf 11x12 | — | 375.00 |

***Perf. 12x10***

| | | | | |
|---|---|---|---|---|
| **J9** | D1 | 10sh green | 550.00 | — |
| *a.* | | Perf. 10 | 750.00 | 80.00 |
| **J10** | D1 | 20sh green | 650.00 | — |
| *a.* | | Perf. 10 | 850.00 | 125.00 |
| *b.* | | Perf. 12 | 1,500. | |
| | | *Nos. J1-J10 (10)* | 1,873. | 164.75 |

Used values for Nos. J8-J10 are for c-t-o stamps.

Nos. J1-J5 exist on both ordinary and chalky paper.

Used values for Nos. J8-J10 are for c-t-o stamps.

## OFFICIAL STAMPS

Regular Issues Overprinted in Black or Red

***Perf. 10, 11, 12, 13 and Compound***

**1879-80 — Wmk. 54**

| | | | | |
|---|---|---|---|---|
| **O1** | A17 | 1p red | 55.00 | 3.00 |
| *a.* | | Perf. 10 | 225.00 | 40.00 |
| *b.* | | Perf. 10x13 | 65.00 | 5.00 |
| **O2** | A18 | 2p blue | 55.00 | 2.75 |
| *a.* | | Perf. 11x12 | | 275.00 |
| *b.* | | Perf. 10 | 275.00 | 40.00 |
| **O3** | A15 | 3p green (R) | 1,000. | 375.00 |
| **O4** | A15 | 3p green | 200.00 | 32.50 |
| *a.* | | Watermarked "6" | — | 600.00 |
| *b.* | | Double overprint | — | *925.00* |
| *c.* | | 3p yel grn, perf 10 | 200.00 | 32.50 |
| *d.* | | 3p yel grn, perf 12 | 250.00 | 60.00 |
| **O5** | A19 | 4p red brown | 325.00 | 10.00 |
| *a.* | | Perf. 10x13 | 350.00 | 110.00 |
| **O6** | A11 | 5p dark green | 27.50 | 37.50 |
| **O7** | A21 | 6p lilac | 300.00 | 9.00 |
| *a.* | | Perf. 10 | 475.00 | 52.50 |
| *b.* | | Perf. 13x10 | 275.00 | 52.50 |
| **O8** | A13 | 8p yellow (R) | *1,500.* | *675.00* |
| **O9** | A13 | 8p yellow | — | 50.00 |
| *a.* | | Perf. 10 | 500.00 | 92.50 |
| **O10** | A23 | 1sh black (R) | 500.00 | 25.00 |
| *a.* | | Perf. 10 | — | 40.00 |
| *b.* | | Perf. 10x13 | — | 50.00 |
| *c.* | | Perf. 13x10 | — | 15.00 |

**1880 — Wmk. 53**

| | | | | |
|---|---|---|---|---|
| **O11** | A16 | 5sh lilac, perf. 11 | 475.00 | 100.00 |
| *a.* | | Double overprint | *4,500.* | *2,250.* |
| *b.* | | Perf. 10 | 600.00 | 125.00 |
| *c.* | | Perf. 12x10 | 775.00 | 130.00 |
| *d.* | | Perf. 13 | 875.00 | 110.00 |
| *e.* | | Perf. 10x12 | | — |

Two No. O14 overprint types: Type I, "O" and "S" 7mm apart. Type II, "O" and "S" 5.5mm apart.

**1881 — Wmk. 55**

| | | | | |
|---|---|---|---|---|
| **O12** | A17 | 1p red | 27.50 | 2.00 |
| *a.* | | Perf. 10x13 | | 140.00 |
| **O13** | A18 | 2p blue | 42.50 | 1.00 |
| *a.* | | Perf. 10x13 | 275.00 | 90.00 |
| **O14** | A15 | 3p green | 15.00 | 5.50 |
| *a.* | | Double overprint | | 675.00 |
| *b.* | | Perf. 12 | 225.00 | 110.00 |
| *c.* | | Perf. 11 | | |
| *d.* | | Type II ovpt | 40.00 | 15.00 |
| *e.* | | As "b," type II ovpt | 25.00 | 15.00 |
| *f.* | | Wmk sideways | 350.00 | 250.00 |
| **O15** | A19 | 4p red brown | 25.00 | 8.00 |
| *a.* | | Perf. 10x12 | 22.50 | 4.00 |
| *b.* | | Perf. 12 | 250.00 | 100.00 |
| **O16** | A11 | 5p dark green | 275.00 | *175.00* |
| *a.* | | Perf. 12 | 125.00 | 120.00 |
| *b.* | | Perf. 12x10 | — | — |
| *c.* | | Perf. 12x11 ('85) | 65.00 | 16.00 |
| **O17** | A21 | 6p lilac | 22.00 | 7.00 |
| *a.* | | Perf. 12 | | 45.00 |
| *b.* | | Perf. 11x12 | — | — |
| *c.* | | Perf. 12x11 ('85) | 90.00 | 20.00 |
| **O18** | A13 | 8p yellow | 27.50 | 12.50 |
| *a.* | | Double overprint | — | — |
| *b.* | | Perf. 12 | 175.00 | 45.00 |
| *c.* | | Perf. 11 ('85) | 27.50 | 29.00 |
| *d.* | | Perf. 10x12 or 12x10 ('85) | 26.00 | 11.00 |
| *e.* | | Triple overprint | — | — |
| **O19** | A23 | 1sh black (R) | 60.00 | *15.00* |
| *a.* | | Double overprint | | *500.00* |
| *b.* | | Perf. 10x13 | | 60.00 |
| *c.* | | Perf. 11x12, comb. | 30.00 | 8.00 |
| | | *Nos. O12-O19 (8)* | 494.50 | 226.00 |

Beware of other red overprints on watermark 55 stamps.

No. O14 exists with two overprint types: "O" and "S" 7mm and 5.5mm apart. For detailed listings, see the Scott Classic Specialized catalogue.

**1881 — Wmk. 56**

| | | | | |
|---|---|---|---|---|
| **O20** | A17 | 1p red | 105.00 | 9.00 |

**1887-90**

| | | | | |
|---|---|---|---|---|
| **O21** | A24 | 10sh on #75 | — | *3,500.* |
| **O22** | A24 | £1 on #75A | *38,000.* | *17,500.* |

No. 75 Overprinted

**1889**

| | | | | |
|---|---|---|---|---|
| **O23** | A24 | 10sh rose & vio | *5,750.* | *1,450.* |
| | | Overprinted "SPECIMEN" | 125.00 | |
| *a.* | | Perf. 10 | *7,500.* | *3,750.* |

Overprinted

**1888-89 — Wmk. 55**

| | | | | |
|---|---|---|---|---|
| **O24** | A25 | 1p violet | 6.50 | 2.00 |
| *a.* | | Overprinted "O" only | | |
| **O25** | A26 | 2p blue | 5.00 | .75 |
| **O26** | A27 | 4p red brown | 11.00 | 4.25 |
| **O27** | A28 | 6p carmine | 10.00 | 11.00 |
| **O28** | A29 | 8p red lilac | 27.50 | 12.00 |
| *a.* | | Perf 12 | 60.00 | 17.00 |
| **O29** | A30 | 1sh vio brown | 42.50 | 4.75 |
| *a.* | | Double overprint | | |
| *b.* | | 1sh purple brown, perf 12 | 45.00 | 7.00 |
| *c.* | | 1sh maroon, perf 11x12 ('90) | 45.00 | 4.00 |
| *d.* | | 1sh maroon, perf 12 | 45.00 | 4.50 |
| | | *Nos. O24-O29 (6)* | 102.50 | 34.75 |

**Wmk. 53**

| | | | | |
|---|---|---|---|---|
| **O30** | A31 | 5sh violet (R) | *2,100.* | *800.00* |
| **O31** | A32 | 20sh ultra | *20,000.* | *1,100.* |

**1890 — Wmk. 57**

| | | | | |
|---|---|---|---|---|
| **O32** | A31 | 5sh violet | *400.00* | 110.00 |
| *a.* | | 5sh, dull lilac, perf. 12 | 850.00 | 175.00 |
| *b.* | | 5sh lilac, perf 10 | 675.00 | 175.00 |

**Wmk. 58**

| | | | | |
|---|---|---|---|---|
| **O33** | A32 | 20sh ultra | *21,000.* | *1,150.* |
| | | O32b, O33 ovpted. "SPECIMEN" | 325.00 | |

Centenary of the founding of the Colony (Nos. O24-O33).

**1891 — Wmk. 55**

| | | | | |
|---|---|---|---|---|
| **O34** | A17(a) | ½p on 1p gray & black | 75.00 | 80.00 |
| *a.* | | Double overprint | 2,500. | |
| **O35** | A33 | 2½p ultra | 15.00 | 11.00 |
| **O36** | A21(b) | 7½p on 6p brn & black | 55.00 | 70.00 |
| **O37** | A23(b) | 12½p on 1sh red & black | 75.00 | *115.00* |

**1892**

| | | | | |
|---|---|---|---|---|
| **O38** | A37 | ½p gray, perf 11x12 | 6.00 | *20.00* |
| *a.* | | Perf 10 | 14.00 | *20.00* |
| *b.* | | Perf 12 | 13.00 | *13.00* |
| *c.* | | Perf 12x11½ | 35.00 | 18.00 |
| | | Overprinted "SPECIMEN" | 35.00 | |

**1894 — Wmk. 54**

| | | | | |
|---|---|---|---|---|
| **O39** | A22 | 9p on 10p red brn | 1,250. | 1,150. |
| | | Overprinted "SPECIMEN" | 85.00 | |

**Wmk. 52**

| | | | | |
|---|---|---|---|---|
| **O40** | A20 | 10p lilac, perf. 13 | 425.00 | *120.00* |
| *a.* | | Perf. 11x10 or 10x11 | 450.00 | *225.00* |
| *b.* | | Perf 10 | 450.00 | |
| *c.* | | Double overprint, one albino | 475.00 | |
| | | Overprinted "SPECIMEN" | 75.00 | |

*The official stamps became obsolete on Dec. 31, 1894. In Aug., 1895, sets of 32 varieties of "O.S." stamps, together with some envelopes and postal cards, were placed on sale at the Sydney post office at £2 per set.*

*These sets contained most of the varieties listed above and a few which are not known in the original issues. An obliteration consisting of the letters G.P.O. or N.S.W. in three concentric ovals was lightly applied to the center of each block of four stamps.*

*It is understood that the earlier stamps and many of the overprints were reprinted to make up these sets.*

# QUEENSLAND

'kwēnz-,land

LOCATION — Northeastern part of Australia
GOVT. — British Crown Colony
AREA — 670,500 sq. mi.
POP. — 498,129 (1901)
CAPITAL — Brisbane

Originally a part of New South Wales, Queensland was constituted a separate colony in 1859. It was one of the six British Colonies that united in 1901 to form the Commonwealth of Australia.

12 Pence = 1 Shilling
20 Shillings = 1 Pound

## MORETON BAY

Until 1860, Queensland, then known as Moreton Bay, utilized the postal service of New South Wales, and stamps of New South Wales were used until November 1, 1860. The New South Wales post offices in Queensland, with their opening dates and assigned cancellor numbers, were:

| Post Office | Opened |
|---|---|
| Brisbane | 1834 (#95) |
| Burnett's Inn (became Goodes Inn) | 1850 (#108) |
| Callandoon | 1850 (#74) |
| Condamine | 1856 (#151) |
| Dalby | 1854 (#133) |
| Drayton | 1846 (#85) |
| Gayndah | 1850 (#86) |
| Gladstone | 1854 (#131) |
| Goodes Inn | 1858 (#108) |
| Ipswich | 1846 (#87) |
| Maryborough | 1849 (#96) |
| Rockhampton | 1858 (#201) |
| Surat | 1852 (#110) |
| Taroom | 1856 (#152) |
| Toowoomba | 1858 (#214) |
| Warwick | 1848 (#81) |

708 AUSTRALIAN STATES — Queensland

Values for unused stamps are for examples with original gum as defined in the catalogue introduction. Very fine examples of Nos. 4-73, 84-125, 128-140, and F1-F3b will have perforations touching the design on at least one or more sides due to the narrow spacing of the stamps on the plates. Stamps with perfs clear of the design on all four sides are scarce and will command higher prices.

**Watermarks**

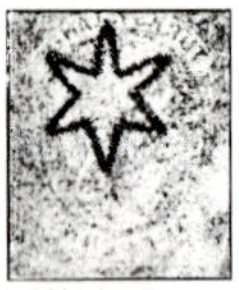
Wmk. 5 — Small Star

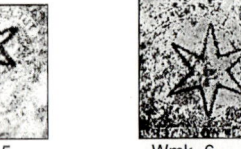

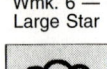

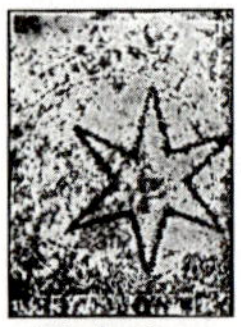
Wmk. 6 — Large Star

Wmk. 12 — Crown and Single-lined A

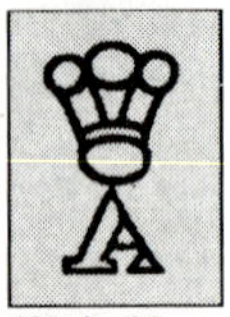
Wmk. 13 — Crown and Double-lined A

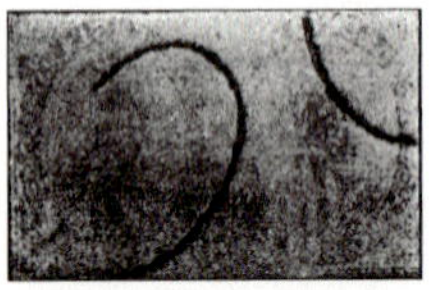
Wmk. 65 — "Queensland Postage Stamps" in Sheet in Script Capitals

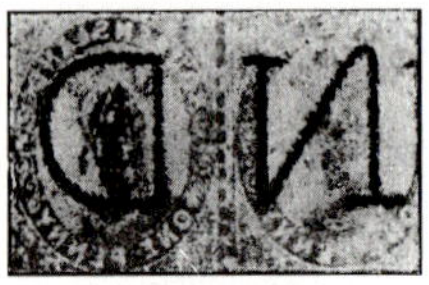
Wmk. 66

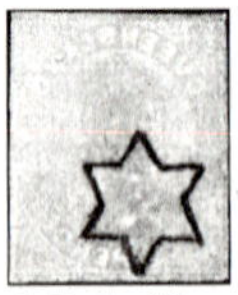
Wmks. 66 & 67 — "Queensland" in Large Single-lined Roman Capitals in the Sheet and Short-pointed Star to Each Stamp (Stars Vary Slightly in Size and Shape)

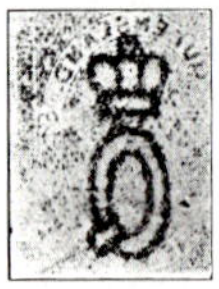
Wmk. 68 — Crown and Q

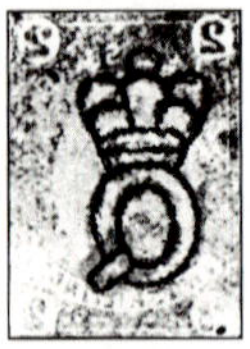
Wmk. 69 — Large Crown and Q

There are two varieties of the watermark 68, differing slightly in the position and shape of the crown and the tongue of the "Q."

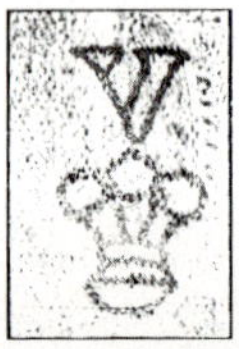
Wmk. 70 — V and Crown

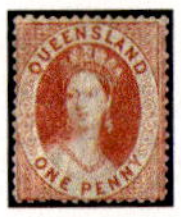
Queen Victoria — A1

**Wmk. 6**

**1860, Nov. 1 Engr. *Imperf.***

| | | | | |
|---|---|---|---|---|
| 1 | A1 | 1p deep rose | 6,600. | 775.00 |
| 2 | A1 | 2p deep blue | *18,500.* | *1,950.* |
| 3 | A1 | 6p deep green | *10,750.* | 825.00 |

***Clean-Cut Perf. 14 to 16***

| | | | | |
|---|---|---|---|---|
| 4 | A1 | 1p deep rose | 3,100. | 290.00 |
| 5 | A1 | 2p deep blue | 1,650. | 115.00 |
| *a.* | | Horiz. pair, imperf between | — | *5,500.* |
| 6 | A1 | 6p deep green | 1,850. | 75.00 |

***Clean-Cut Perf. 14 to 16***

**1860-61 Wmk. 5**

| | | | | |
|---|---|---|---|---|
| 6A | A1 | 2p blue | 1,150. | 105.00 |
| *b.* | | Horiz. pair, imperf. between | | 11,000. |
| 6D | A1 | 3p brown ('61) | 875.00 | 77.50 |
| 6E | A1 | 6p deep green | 1,550. | 77.50 |
| 6F | A1 | 1sh gray violet | 1,750. | 115.00 |

***Regular Perf. 14***

| | | | | |
|---|---|---|---|---|
| 6H | A1 | 1p rose | 475.00 | 57.50 |
| 6I | A1 | 2p deep blue | *1,100.* | 62.50 |

***Rough Perf. 14 to 16***

| | | | | |
|---|---|---|---|---|
| 7 | A1 | 1p deep rose | 115.00 | 47.50 |
| 8 | A1 | 2p blue | 350.00 | 27.50 |
| *a.* | | Horiz. pair, imperf between | *10,250.* | — |
| 9 | A1 | 3p brown ('61) | 90.00 | 30.00 |
| *a.* | | Horiz. pair, imperf. vert. | *10,250.* | — |
| 10 | A1 | 6p deep green | 675.00 | 27.50 |
| *a.* | | 6p yellow green | 775.00 | 27.50 |
| 11 | A1 | 1sh dull violet | 1,350. | 90.00 |

**Thick Yellowish Paper**

***Square Perf. 12½ to 13***

**1862-67 Unwmk.**

| | | | | |
|---|---|---|---|---|
| 12 | A1 | 1p Indian red | 525.00 | 70.00 |
| 13 | A1 | 1p orange ('63) | 120.00 | 16.00 |
| *a.* | | Perf. 13, round holes ('67) | 125.00 | 16.00 |
| *b.* | | Horiz. pair, imperf. between | | — |
| *c.* | | Imperf., pair | — | *2,600.* |
| 14 | A1 | 2p deep blue | 90.00 | 9.00 |
| *a.* | | 2p pale blue | 150.00 | 25.00 |
| *b.* | | Perf. 13, round holes ('67) | 90.00 | 9.00 |
| *c.* | | Imperf., pair | — | *2,500.* |
| *e.* | | Horiz. pair, imperf. between | | *15,000.* |
| *f.* | | Vert. pair, imperf. between | *5,750.* | |
| 15 | A1 | 3p brown ('63) | 125.00 | 42.50 |
| *a.* | | Imperf. | | |
| *b.* | | Perf. 13, round holes ('67) | 125.00 | 42.50 |
| 16 | A1 | 6p yellow grn ('63) | 190.00 | 11.00 |
| *a.* | | 6p green | 300.00 | 42.50 |
| *b.* | | Perf. 13, round holes ('67) | 195.00 | 13.50 |
| *c.* | | Imperf., pair | — | *2,600.* |
| *d.* | | Horiz. pair, imperf. between | — | *16,000.* |
| *e.* | | 6p apple green ('63) | 190.00 | 14.00 |
| 17 | A1 | 1sh gray ('63) | 400.00 | 22.50 |
| *b.* | | Imperf. horizontally | | |
| *c.* | | Horiz. pair, imperf. between | — | *17,000.* |
| *d.* | | Perf. 13, round holes ('67) | 400.00 | 24.00 |
| *e.* | | Vert. pair, imperf between | — | |

**White Wove Paper**

**1865 Wmk. 5 *Rough Perf. 13***

| | | | | |
|---|---|---|---|---|
| 18 | A1 | 1p orange | 125.00 | 57.50 |
| *a.* | | Horiz. pair, imperf. between | *6,250.* | |
| 19 | A1 | 2p light blue | 125.00 | 16.00 |
| *a.* | | Vert. pair, imperf. between | *8,500.* | |
| *b.* | | Half used as 1p on cover | | *4,250.* |
| *d.* | | 2p deep blue | 130.00 | 17.00 |
| 20 | A1 | 6p yellow green | 240.00 | 21.50 |
| *a.* | | 6p deep green | 290.00 | 21.50 |
| | | *Nos. 18-20 (3)* | 490.00 | 95.00 |

**1865 *Perf. 12½x13***

| | | | | |
|---|---|---|---|---|
| 18B | A1 | 1p orange vermilion | 165.00 | 77.50 |
| 19C | A1 | 2p blue | 280.00 | 77.50 |

***Perf. 13, Round Holes***

**1866 Wmk. 65**

| | | | | |
|---|---|---|---|---|
| 21 | A1 | 1p orange vermilion | 210.00 | 42.50 |
| 22 | A1 | 2p blue | 105.00 | 16.50 |
| *b.* | | Diagonal half used as 1p on cover | | — |

**1865 *Perf. 12½x13***

| | | | | |
|---|---|---|---|---|
| 21A | A1 | 1p orange vermilion | 290.00 | 72.50 |
| 22C | A1 | 2p blue | 290.00 | 72.50 |

**1866 Unwmk. Litho. *Perf. 13***

| | | | | |
|---|---|---|---|---|
| 23 | A1 | 4p lilac | 525.00 | 21.50 |
| *a.* | | 4p slate | 525.00 | 21.00 |
| | | Handstamped "SPECIMEN" | 65.00 | |
| 24 | A1 | 5sh pink | 1,350. | 135.00 |
| *a.* | | 5sh bright rose | 1,450. | 175.00 |
| | | Handstamped "SPECIMEN" | 80.00 | |
| *b.* | | Vert. pair, imperf between | | *8,750.* |

**Wmk. 66, 67**

**1868-74 Engr. *Perf. 13***

| | | | | |
|---|---|---|---|---|
| 25 | A1 | 1p orange ('71) | 100.00 | 7.00 |
| 26 | A1 | 2p blue | 77.50 | 3.25 |
| *a.* | | 2p pale blue | 82.50 | 5.75 |
| *b.* | | 2p bright blue | 87.50 | 2.50 |
| *c.* | | 2p greenish blue | 155.00 | 2.50 |
| *d.* | | 2p dark blue | 87.50 | 2.50 |
| 27 | A1 | 3p grnsh brn ('71) | 240.00 | 6.25 |
| *a.* | | 3p brown | 125.00 | 5.25 |
| *b.* | | 3p olive brown | 210.00 | 6.50 |
| 28 | A1 | 6p yel grn ('71) | 275.00 | 7.00 |
| *a.* | | 6p deep green | 325.00 | 16.50 |
| *b.* | | 6p green | 240.00 | 9.50 |
| 30 | A1 | 1sh grnsh gray ('72) | 950.00 | 47.50 |
| 31 | A1 | 1sh violet ('74) | 425.00 | 22.50 |
| *a.* | | 1sh brownish gray | 950.00 | 47.50 |

***Perf. 12***

| | | | | |
|---|---|---|---|---|
| 32 | A1 | 1p orange | 525.00 | 27.50 |
| 33 | A1 | 2p blue | *1,000.* | 72.50 |
| 34 | A1 | 3p brown | 775.00 | 215.00 |
| *a.* | | 3p greenish gray | — | 215.00 |
| 35 | A1 | 6p deep green | 1,850. | 47.50 |
| 36 | A1 | 1sh violet | 900.00 | 52.50 |

***Perf. 13x12***

| | | | | |
|---|---|---|---|---|
| 36A | A1 | 1p orange | | 195.00 |
| 37 | A1 | 2p blue | *1,675.* | 42.50 |
| 37A | A1 | 3p brown | | *350.00* |

*The reprints are perforated 13 and the colors differ slightly from those of the originals.*

**1868-75 Wmk. 68 *Perf. 13***

| | | | | |
|---|---|---|---|---|
| 38 | A1 | 1p orange | 115.00 | 5.75 |
| *a.* | | Imperf pair | 825.00 | |
| 39 | A1 | 1p rose ('74) | 95.00 | 15.00 |
| *a.* | | 1p deep rose red | 170.00 | 15.00 |
| 40 | A1 | 2p blue | 85.00 | 4.50 |
| *a.* | | Vert. pair, imperf between | | — |
| *b.* | | Imperf., pair | *600.00* | |
| *c.* | | 2p pale blue ('74) | 90.00 | 2.00 |
| 41 | A1 | 3p brown ('75) | 140.00 | 15.00 |
| 42 | A1 | 6p yel green ('69) | 200.00 | 6.00 |
| *a.* | | 6p apple green | 240.00 | 8.50 |
| *b.* | | 6p deep green | 210.00 | 8.50 |
| *c.* | | As "a," imperf pair | 725.00 | |
| 43 | A1 | 1sh violet ('75) | 425.00 | 67.50 |
| | | *Nos. 38-43 (6)* | *1,060.* | 113.75 |

**1876-78 *Perf. 12***

| | | | | |
|---|---|---|---|---|
| 44 | A1 | 1p orange | 77.50 | 6.00 |
| *a.* | | Imperf. | *450.00* | |
| *b.* | | 1p pale org vermilion | 87.50 | 6.00 |
| *c.* | | Vert. pair, imperf between | | — |
| 45 | A1 | 1p rose | 87.50 | 10.00 |
| *a.* | | 1p salmon | 125.00 | 12.50 |
| 46 | A1 | 2p blue | 75.00 | 1.75 |
| *a.* | | 2p pale blue | 135.00 | 14.00 |
| *b.* | | 2p deep blue | 75.00 | 2.00 |
| 47 | A1 | 3p brown | 125.00 | 9.00 |
| 48 | A1 | 6p yellow green | 275.00 | 4.25 |
| *a.* | | 6p apple green | 300.00 | 7.00 |
| *b.* | | 6p deep green | 275.00 | 9.50 |
| *c.* | | 6p green | 210.00 | 4.00 |
| 49 | A1 | 1sh violet | 110.00 | 8.50 |
| *m.* | | Vert. pair, imperf between | | — |
| *n.* | | 1sh purple | 275.00 | 5.00 |
| | | *Nos. 44-49 (6)* | 750.00 | 39.50 |

***Perf. 13x12***

| | | | | |
|---|---|---|---|---|
| 49B | A1 | 1p orange | | 145.00 |
| 49C | A1 | 2p blue | *1,450.* | 240.00 |
| 49D | A1 | 4p yellow | | 625.00 |
| 49E | A1 | 6p deep green | | 525.00 |

***Perf. 12½x13***

| | | | | |
|---|---|---|---|---|
| 49G | A1 | 1p org ver | | 575.00 |
| 49H | A1 | 2p deep blue | | 575.00 |
| 49J | A1 | 6p yellow green | | *1,350.* |

***Perf. 12½***

| | | | | |
|---|---|---|---|---|
| 49K | A1 | 2p deep blue | | *725.00* |

*The reprints are perforated 12 and are in paler colors than the originals.*

**1879 Unwmk. *Perf. 12***

| | | | | |
|---|---|---|---|---|
| 50 | A1 | 6p pale emerald | 475.00 | 30.00 |
| *a.* | | Horiz. pair, imperf. vert. | | *2,250.* |

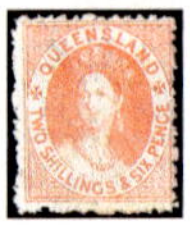
A2

**1875-81 Litho. Wmk. 68 *Perf. 13***

| | | | | |
|---|---|---|---|---|
| 50B | A1 | 4p yellow ('75) | *2,450.* | 115.00 |
| *a.* | | Handstamped "SPECIMEN" | 115.00 | |

***Perf. 12***

| | | | | |
|---|---|---|---|---|
| 51 | A1 | 4p buff ('76) | 1,750. | 50.00 |
| *a.* | | 4p yellow | 1,750. | 52.50 |
| 52 | A1 | 2sh pale blue ('81) | 170.00 | 57.50 |
| | | Fiscal cancellation | | 5.75 |
| *a.* | | 2sh deep blue | 200.00 | 57.50 |
| *b.* | | Imperf. | | — |
| *c.* | | 2sh blue | 165.00 | 57.50 |
| *d.* | | As "c" horiz. pair, imperf. vert. | *9,000.* | — |
| 53 | A2 | 2sh6p lt red ('81) | 375.00 | 75.00 |
| | | Fiscal cancellation | | 5.75 |
| *a.* | | 2sh6p bright scarlet | 375.00 | 77.50 |
| 54 | A1 | 5sh org brn ('81) | 575.00 | 115.00 |
| | | Fiscal cancellation | | 7.00 |
| *a.* | | 5sh fawn | 575.00 | 115.00 |
| 55 | A1 | 10sh brown ('81) | 975.00 | 190.00 |
| | | Fiscal cancellation | | 7.00 |
| *a.* | | Imperf., pair | *950.00* | |
| *b.* | | 10sh bister brown | 975.00 | 190.00 |
| 56 | A1 | 20sh rose ('81) | *2,600.* | *275.00* |
| | | Fiscal cancellation | | 7.00 |
| | | *Nos. 50B-56 (7)* | 8,895. | 877.50 |

Nos. 53-56, 62-64, 74-83 with pen (revenue) cancellations removed are often offered as unused.

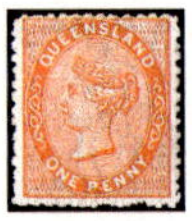
A3

**1879-81 Typo. Wmk. 68 *Perf. 12***

| | | | | |
|---|---|---|---|---|
| 57 | A3 | 1p rose red | 62.50 | 11.50 |
| *a.* | | 1p red orange | 67.50 | 12.00 |
| *b.* | | 1p brown orange | 87.50 | 9.00 |
| *c.* | | "QOEENSLAND" | *350.00* | *42.50* |
| *d.* | | Imperf. | | |
| *e.* | | Vert. pair, imperf. horiz. | | *750.00* |
| *f.* | | As "a" "QOGENSLAND" | 350.00 | 62.50 |
| *g.* | | As "b" "QOGENSLAND" | 650.00 | 62.50 |
| 58 | A3 | 2p gray blue | 90.00 | 3.25 |
| *a.* | | 2p deep ultra | 95.00 | 3.00 |
| *b.* | | Imperf. | — | |
| *c.* | | "PENGE" | 425.00 | 47.50 |
| *d.* | | "TW" joined | 90.00 | 1.75 |
| *e.* | | Vert. pair, imperf. horiz. | *1,000.* | |
| *f.* | | "QUEENSbAND" | *425.00* | *47.50* |
| *g.* | | As "a", "QUEENSbAND" | *425.00* | *47.50* |
| 59 | A3 | 4p orange yellow | 475.00 | 22.50 |
| *a.* | | Imperf. | — | |
| *b.* | | Horiz. pair, imperf. vert. | *12,750.* | — |
| 60 | A3 | 6p yellow green | 200.00 | 7.00 |
| *a.* | | Imperf. | — | |
| *b.* | | Horiz. pair, imperf. vert. | | — |
| *c.* | | 6p deep green | 190.00 | 7.50 |
| 61 | A3 | 1sh pale violet ('81) | 190.00 | 17.50 |
| *a.* | | 1sh deep violet | 200.00 | 11.50 |
| | | *Nos. 57-61 (5)* | 1,018. | 61.75 |

The stamps of type A3 were electrotyped from plates made up of groups of four types, differing in minor details. Two dies were used for the 1p and 2p, giving eight varieties for each of those values.

Nos. 59-60 exist imperf. vertically.

For surcharge see No. 65.

**Moiré on Back**

**1878-79 Unwmk.**

| | | | | |
|---|---|---|---|---|
| 62 | A3 | 1p brown org ('79) | 825.00 | 115.00 |
| *a.* | | "QOEENSLAND" | | *1,850.* |
| 63 | A3 | 2p deep ultra ('79) | 825.00 | 57.50 |
| *a.* | | "PENGE" | *4,400.* | 675.00 |
| 64 | A1 | 1sh red violet | 240.00 | 105.00 |
| | | Fiscal cancellation | | 5.00 |
| | | *Nos. 62-64 (3)* | 1,890. | 277.50 |

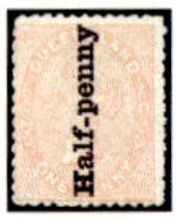

No. 57b Surcharged Vertically in Black

**1880 Wmk. 68**

| | | | | |
|---|---|---|---|---|
| 65 | A3 | ½p on 1p brn org | 425.00 | 240.00 |
| *a.* | | "QOEENSLAND" | *2,400.* | *1,250.* |

On No. 65, the surcharge reads from bottom to top. Stamps with surcharges reading downward are fakes.

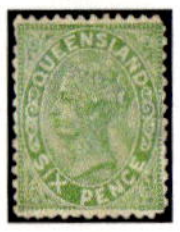
A4

**1882-83 Typo. *Perf. 12***

| | | | | |
|---|---|---|---|---|
| 66 | A4 | 1p pale red | 12.50 | 1.00 |
| *a.* | | 1p rose | 12.50 | 1.00 |
| *b.* | | Imperf. pair | — | |
| *c.* | | 1p deep vermilion | 12.50 | 1.00 |
| 67 | A4 | 2p gray blue | 25.00 | 1.00 |
| *a.* | | 2p deep ultra | 25.00 | 1.00 |
| *b.* | | Horiz. pair, imperf between | — | |
| 68 | A4 | 4p yellow ('83) | 55.00 | 3.50 |
| *a.* | | "PENGE" | *350.00* | 47.50 |
| *b.* | | Imperf., single | | — |

69 A4 6p yellow green 37.50 2.00
70 A4 1sh violet ('83) 57.50 13.50
*a.* 1sh lilac 30.00 8.00
*b.* 1sh deep purple 26.00 8.00
*c.* 1sh pale mauve 13.50 8.00
*Nos. 66-70 (5)* 187.50 21.00

There are eight minor varieties of the 1p, twelve of the 2p and four each of the other values. On the 1p there is a period after "PENNY." On all values the lines of shading on the neck extend from side to side.

Compare design A4 with A6, A10, A11, A15, A16.

**1883** ***Perf. 9½x12***
71 A4 1p rose 170.00 60.00
72 A4 2p gray blue 575.00 80.00
73 A4 1sh pale violet 300.00 75.00
*Nos. 71-73 (3)* 1,045. 215.00

Beware of faked perfs.

See Nos. 94, 95, 100.

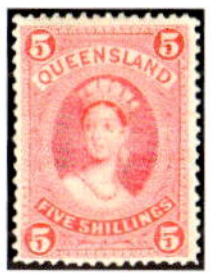
A5

**Wmk. 68 Twice Sideways**
**1882-85** **Engr.** ***Perf. 12***
**Thin Paper**
74 A5 2sh ultra 325.00 62.50
75 A5 2sh6p vermilion 140.00 26.00
76 A5 5sh car rose ('85) 140.00 26.50
77 A5 10sh brown 275.00 55.00
78 A5 £1 dk grn ('83) 575.00 130.00
*Nos. 74-78 (5)* 1,455. 300.00

The 2sh, 5sh and £1 exist imperf.

There are two varieties of the watermark on Nos. 74-78, as in the 1879-81 issue.

Stamps with revenue cancels sell for $3.25-6.50.

**1886** **Wmk. 69** ***Perf. 12***
**Thick Paper**
79 A5 2sh ultra 350.00 62.50
80 A5 2sh6p vermilion 60.00 26.00
81 A5 5sh car rose 60.00 40.00
82 A5 10sh dark brown 175.00 47.50
83 A5 £1 dark green 350.00 80.00
*Nos. 79-83 (5)* 995.00 266.00

High value stamps with cancellations removed are offered as unused.

Stamps with revenue cancels sell for $3.25-6.50.

See Nos. 126-127, 141-144.

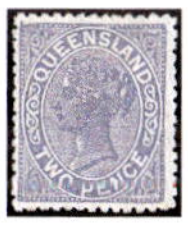
A6

**Redrawn**
**1887-89** **Typo.** **Wmk. 68** ***Perf. 12***
84 A6 1p orange 19.00 1.00
85 A6 2p gray blue 19.00 1.00
*a.* 2p deep ultra 25.00 1.00
*b.* Half used as 1p on cover —
86 A6 2sh red brown ('89) 85.00 80.00
*a.* 2sh pale brown 75.00 72.50

***Perf. 9½x12***
88 A6 2p deep ultra *450.00* 85.00
*Nos. 84-88 (4)* *573.00* 167.00

The 1p has no period after the value.

In the redrawn stamps the shading lines on the neck are not completed at the left, leaving an irregular white line along that side.

Variety "LA" joined exists on Nos. 84-86, 88, 90, 91, 93, 97, 98, 102.

On No. 88 beware of faked perfs.

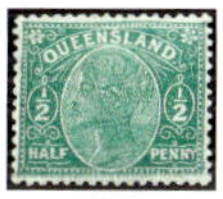
A7

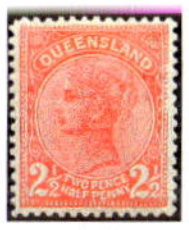
A8

**1890-92** ***Perf. 12½, 13***
89 A7 ½p green 16.00 2.00
*a.* ½p pale green 21.00 2.00
*b.* ½p deep blue green 0.00 2.00
90 A6 1p orange red 9.00 1.00
*a.* Imperf, pair 325.00 325.00
*b.* Double impression 675.00
91 A6 2p gray blue 10.00 .50
*a.* 2p pale blue 12.00 1.00
*b.* "FWO" for "TWO" 90.00 29.00
92 A8 2½p rose carmine 18.00 2.50
93 A6 3p brown ('92) 10.00 4.00
94 A4 4p orange 28.50 4.00
*a.* "PENGE" for "PENCE" 165.00 32.50
*b.* 4p orange yellow 32.00 7.50
*c.* As "b," "PENGE" for "PENCE" 180.00 45.00
*d.* 4p yellow 20.00 4.00
*e.* As "d," "PENGE" for "PENCE" 120.00 32.50
95 A4 6p green 12.00 2.00
96 A6 2sh red brown 50.00 52.50
*a.* 2sh pale brown 60.00 57.50
*Nos. 89-96 (8)* 153.50 68.50

The ½p and 3p exist imperf.

**1895** **Wmk. 69** ***Perf. 12½, 13***
**Thick Paper**
98 A6 1p orange 5.00 .50
*a.* 1p reddish vermilion 5.00 .50
99 A6 2p gray blue 7.00 .50
*b.* "FWO" for "TWO" 95.00 22.50

***Perf. 12***
100 A4 1sh pale violet 47.50 30.00
*Nos. 98-100 (3)* 59.50 31.00

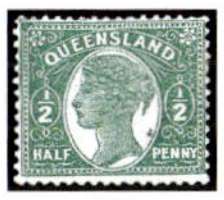
A9

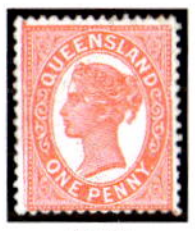
A10

**Moiré on Back**
**1895** **Unwmk.** ***Perf. 12½, 13***
101 A9 ½p green 11.00 8.00
*a.* Without moire 77.50
*b.* ½p deep green 11.00 8.00
102 A6 1p orange 2.50 2.50
*a.* "PE" missing 400.00 *80.00*
*b.* 1p reddish vermilion 2.50 3.00

**Wmk. 68**
103 A9 ½p green 3.50 2.00
*a.* ½p deep green 3.50 2.00
*b.* Printed on both sides 300.00
*c.* Double impression *2,000.* *2,000.*
104 A10 1p orange 4.00 .50
*a* 1p pale red 0.00 1.00
105 A10 2p gray blue 37.50 .50

**Wmk. 69**
**Thick Paper**
106 A9 ½p green, perf 12½ 3.00 6.50
*a.* Perf 13 3.00 6.50
*b.* Perf 12 47.50
*c.* 1p deep green, perf 12 47.50

**1895-96** **Unwmk.** **Thin Paper**
**Crown and Q Faintly Impressed**
107 A9 ½p green 2.50 6.50
108 A10 1p orange 3.50 2.50
108A A6 2p gray blue 14.00 *150.00*
*b.* "FWO" for "TWO" *175.00*

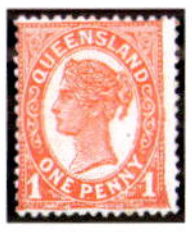
A11

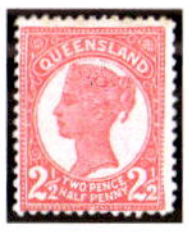
A12

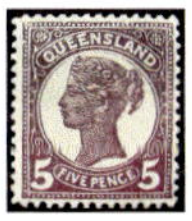
A13

**1895-96** **Wmk. 68**
109 A11 1p red 9.00 .75
110 A12 2½p rose 25.00 5.00
*a.* 2½p carmine 25.00 5.00
111 A13 5p violet brown 30.00 5.00
111A A11 6p yellow green *16,000.*

Only a few used examples of No. 111A are known, and readable cancels are from 1902. It is suggested that this otherwise unissued design was accidentally included in the plate of No. 120.

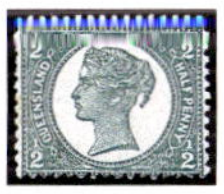
A14

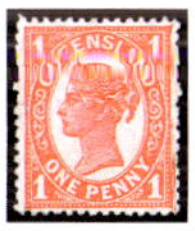
A15

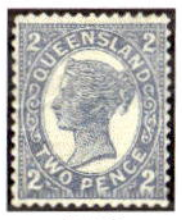
A16

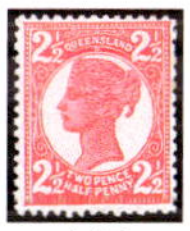
A17

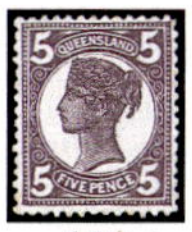
A18

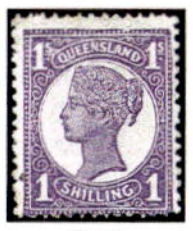
A19

TWO PENCE:

Type I — Point of bust does not touch frame.

Type II — First redrawing. The top of the crown, the chignon and the point of the bust touch the frame. The forehead is completely shaded.

Type III — Second redrawing. The top of crown does not touch the frame, though the chignon and the point of the bust do. The forehead and the bridge of the nose are not shaded.

**1897-1900** ***Perf. 12½, 13***
112 A14 ½p deep green 5.50 7.50
*a.* Perf. 12 145.00
113 A15 1p red 2.25 .40
*a.* Perf. 12 8.50 3.50
114 A16 2p gray blue (I) 9.00 .40
*a.* Perf. 12 725.00 7.00
115 A17 2½p rose 17.50 27.50
116 A17 2½p violet, *blue* 10.00 3.00
117 A15 3p brown 8.50 3.00
118 A15 4p bright yellow 14.00 3.00
119 A18 5p violet brown 9.50 3.00
120 A15 6p yellow green 8.00 3.25
121 A19 1sh lilac 15.00 3.50
*a.* 1sh light violet 15.00 3.50
122 A19 2sh turq blue 37.50 47.50
*Nos. 112-122 (11)* 136.75 102.05

See Nos. 130-140.

**1898** ***Serrated Roulette 13***
123 A15 1p scarlet 20.00 7.00
*a.* Serrated and perf. 13 10.00 6.00
*b.* Serrated in black 20.00 13.00
*c.* Serrated without color and in black 22.50 *26.00*
*d.* Same as "b," and perf. 13 80.00 *90.00*
*e.* Same as "c," and perf. 13 100.00 100.00

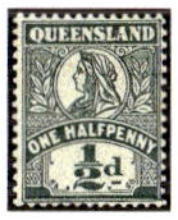
Victoria — A20

**1899** **Typo.** ***Perf. 12, 12½, 13***
124 A20 ½p blue green 3.50 2.50
*a.* ½p green, perf 12 120.00 65.00
*b.* ½p pale green 14.00 4.25

Unwatermarked stamps are proofs.

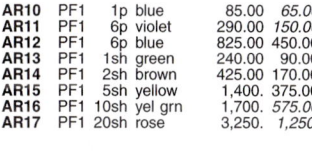

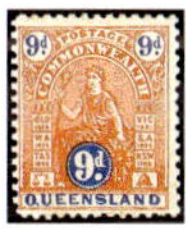
"Australia" — A21

NINE PENCE:

Type I — "QUEENSLAND" 18x1½mm.

Type II — "QUEENSLAND" 17½x1¼mm.

**1903** **Wmk. 70** ***Perf. 12½***
125 A21 9p org brn & ultra, II 60.00 7.50
*a.* Type I 45.00 7.50

See No. 128.

**Type of 1882**
**1903-06** **Wmk. 68** ***Perf. 12, 12½-13***
**Typographed, Perf. 12½-13 Irreg. ('03)**
125B A5 5sh rose 240.00 57.50
125C A5 £1 dark green *2,100.* *675.00*

**Lithographed, Perf. 12 ('05-'06)**
126 A5 5sh rose 180.00 95.00
127 A5 £1 dark green 575.00 125.00
*c.* Perf. 12½-13 Irreg. *1,150.* 165.00

**1907** **Typo.** **Wmk. 13** ***Perf. 12½***
128 A21 9p yel brn & ultra, I 24.00 4.50
*a.* Type II 80.00 7.00
*b.* Perf. 11, type II 5,500. 775.00

**1907** **Wmk. 68** ***Perf. 12½, 13***
129 A16 2p ultra, type II 12.00 5.50
129A A18 5p dark brown 17.50 6.50
*b.* 5p olive brown 17.50 4.75

**1907-09** **Wmk. 12**
130 A20 ½p deep green 2.25 *4.50*
131 A15 1p red 3.50 .30
*a.* Imperf., pair *450.00*
132 A16 2p ultra, II 40.00 3.50
133 A16 2p ultra, III 5.50 .30
134 A15 3p pale brown 27.50 2.50
135 A15 4p bright yellow 12.50 4.25
136 A15 4p gray black ('09) 27.50 6.50
137 A18 5p brown 42.50 22.00
*a.* 5p olive brown 24.00 25.00
138 A15 6p yellow green 22.50 4.00
139 A19 1sh violet 24.00 4.00
140 A19 2sh turquoise bl 40.00 47.50

**Wmk. 12 Sideways**
**Litho.**
141 A5 2sh6p dp org 45.00 45.00
*a.* 2sh6p dull orange ('10) 85.00 85.00
*b.* 2sh6p reddish orange ('12) 190.00 *210.00*
142 A5 5sh rose 90.00 60.00
*a.* 5sh deep rose ('10) 110.00 85.00
*b.* 5sh carmine red ('12) 275.00 *260.00*
143 A5 10sh dark brown 165.00 70.00
*a.* 10sh sepia ('12) 450.00 300.00
144 A5 £1 blue green 425.00 125.00
*a.* £1 dp blue green ('10) 575.00 325.00
*b.* £1 yellow green ('12) *1,850.* *1,350.*
*Nos. 130-144 (15)* 972.75 399.35

## POSTAL FISCAL STAMPS

Authorized for postal use from Jan. 1, 1880. Authorization withdrawn July 1, 1892.

Used values are for examples with postal cancellations used from Jan. 1, 1880 through June 30, 1892.

Beware of stamps with a pen cancellation removed and a fake postmark added.

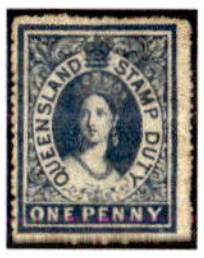
Queen Victoria — PF1

**1866-74** **Engr.** **Unwmk.** ***Perf. 13***
AR1 PF1 1p blue 150.00 27.50
AR2 PF1 6p violet 290.00 125.00
AR3 PF1 1sh green 250.00 85.00
AR4 PF1 2sh brown 425.00 210.00
AR5 PF1 2sh 6p red 525.00 170.00
AR6 PF1 5sh yellow 1,350. 425.00
AR7 PF1 6sh yellow *2,100.*
AR8 PF1 10sh yel grn 1,650. 575.00
AR9 PF1 20sh rose 3,250. *1,150.*

**Wmk. 68**
AR10 PF1 1p blue 85.00 *65.00*
AR11 PF1 6p violet 290.00 *150.00*
AR12 PF1 6p blue 825.00 450.00
AR13 PF1 1sh green 240.00 90.00
AR14 PF1 2sh brown 425.00 170.00
AR15 PF1 5sh yellow 1,400. 375.00
AR16 PF1 10sh yel grn 1,700. *575.00*
AR17 PF1 20sh rose 3,250. *1,250.*

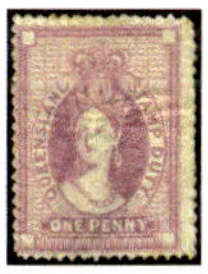
Queen Victoria — PF2

**1872-73** **Wmk. 69** ***Perf. 13***
AR18 PF2 1p lilac 75.00 25.00
AR19 PF2 6p brown 135.00 52.50
AR20 PF2 1sh green 170.00 55.00
AR21 PF2 2sh blue 275.00 75.00
AR22 PF2 2sh 6p ver 450.00 160.00
AR23 PF2 5sh org brn 575.00 240.00
AR24 PF2 10sh brown 1,150. *475.00*
AR25 PF2 20sh rose 2,850. *725.00*

***Perf. 12***
AR26 PF2 1p lilac 75.00 25.00
AR27 PF2 6p brown 135.00 50.00
AR28 PF2 2sh blue 275.00 75.00
AR29 PF2 2sh 6p ver 450.00 160.00
AR30 PF2 5sh org brn 575.00 240.00
AR31 PF2 10sh brown 1,150. *475.00*
AR32 PF2 20sh rose 3,000. *725.00*

**Unwmk.**
***Perf. 13***
AR33 PF2 1p lilac 85.00 25.00
AR34 PF2 6p lilac 140.00 52.50
AR35 PF2 6p brown 625.00 160.00
AR36 PF2 1sh green 210.00 52.50
AR37 PF2 2sh blue 350.00 *170.00*
AR38 PF2 2sh 6p ver 575.00 190.00
AR39 PF2 5sh org brn 775.00 240.00
AR40 PF2 10sh brown 1,375. 475.00
AR41 PF2 20sh rose 2,900. 725.00

***Perf. 12***
AR42 PF2 1p lilac 85.00 25.00
AR43 PF2 6p lilac 135.00 52.50
AR44 PF2 6p brown 625.00 165.00
AR45 PF2 1sh green 220.00 52.50
AR46 PF2 2sh blue 350.00 170.00
AR47 PF2 2sh 6p ver 575.00 190.00

**AR48** PF2 5sh org brn 800.00 240.00
**AR49** PF2 10sh brown 1,400. 475.00
**AR50** PF2 20sh rose 3,000. 750.00

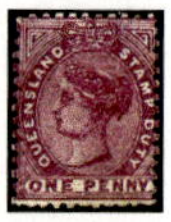

Queen Victoria — PF3

**1878-79 Engr. Unwmk. *Perf. 12***

**AR51** PF3 1p violet 100.00 19.50

**Wmk. 68**

**AR52** PF3 1p violet 150.00 75.00

### SEMI-POSTAL STAMPS

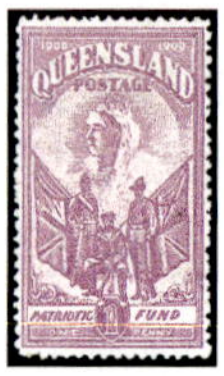

Queen Victoria, Colors and Bearers — SP1

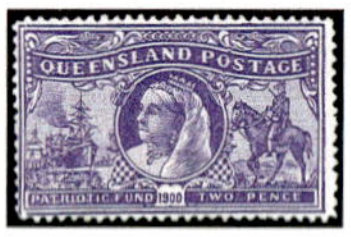

SP2

***Perf. 12, 12½***

**1900, June 19 Wmk. 68**

**B1** SP1 1p red lilac 160.00 110.00
On cover 250.00
**B2** SP2 2p deep violet 375.00 290.00
On cover 500.00
Nos. B1-B2 on one cover *750.00*

These stamps were sold at 1sh and 2sh respectively. The difference was applied to a patriotic fund in connection with the Boer War.

### REGISTRATION STAMPS

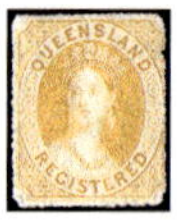

R1

***Clean-Cut Perf. 14 to 16***

**1861 Wmk. 5 Engr.**

**F1** R1 (6p) olive yellow 1,250. 100.00
*a.* Horiz. pair, imperf. vert. *13,000.*

***Rough Perf. 14 to 16***

**F2** R1 (6p) dull yellow 125.00 37.50

**1864 *Perf. 12½ to 13***

**F3** R1 (6p) golden yellow 190.00 40.00
*a.* Imperf.
*b.* Double impression *2,750.* —

*The reprints are watermarked with a small truncated star and perforated 12.*

## SOUTH AUSTRALIA

'sauth o-'strāl-yə

LOCATION — Central part of southern Australia
GOVT. — British Colony
AREA — 380,070 sq. mi.
POP. — 358,346 (1901)
CAPITAL — Adelaide

South Australia was one of the six British colonies that united in 1901 to form the Commonwealth of Australia.

12 Pence = 1 Shilling
20 Shillings = 1 Pound

Values for unused stamps are for examples with original gum as defined in the catalogue introduction.

Very fine examples of Nos. 10-60 and O1-O60 will have perforations slightly cutting into the framelines or design on one or more sides due to the narrow spacing of the stamps on the plates.

Stamps with perfs clear on all sides are scarce to rare and will command higher to substantially higher prices.

### Watermarks

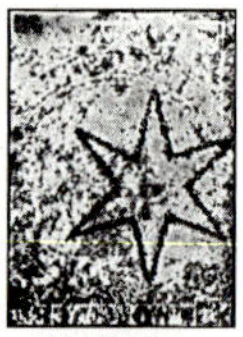

Wmk. 6 — Star with Long Narrow Points

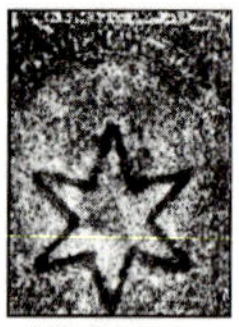

Wmk. 7 — Star with Short Broad Points

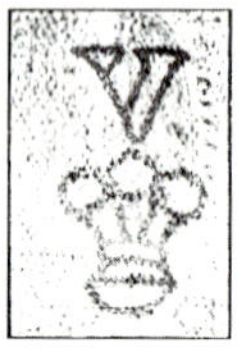

Wmk. 70 — Crown and V

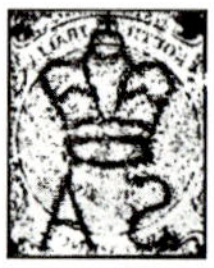

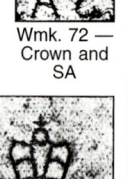

Wmk. 72 — Crown and SA

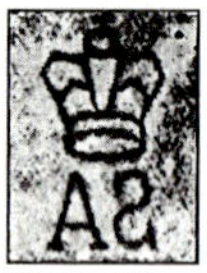

Wmk. 73 — Crown and SA, Letters Close

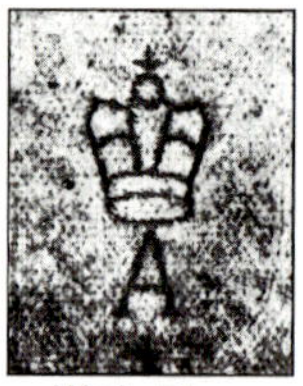

Wmk. 74 — Crown and Single-lined A

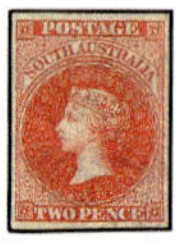

Queen Victoria — A1

**1855-56 Engr. Wmk. 6 *Imperf.***
**London Print**

**1** A1 1p dark green 12,500. 500.
**2** A1 2p dull carmine 850. 90.
**3** A1 6p deep blue 5,750. 180.
**4** A1 1sh violet ('56) *40,000.*

No. 4 was never put in use. Nos. 1 and 3 without watermark are proofs.

**1856-59 Local Print**

**5** A1 1p dp yel grn ('58) *10,000.* 625.00
*a.* 1p yellow green ('58) *9,000.* 750.00
**6** A1 2p blood red 3,500. 90.00
*a.* Printed on both sides *1,250.*
*b.* 2p orange red ('56) 2,600. 92.50
**7** A1 2p pale red ('57) 775. 55.00
*a.* Printed on both sides *850.00*
**8** A1 6p slate blue ('57) 4,750. 200.00
**9** A1 1sh orange ('57) 13,500. 475.00
*a.* Printed on both sides — —
*b.* 1sh red orange — 775.00

**1858-59 *Rouletted***

**10** A1 1p yel grn ('59) 700.00 70.00
*a.* Horiz. pair, imperf. between — —
*b.* 1p pale yellow green ('59) 700.00 75.00
**11** A1 2p pale red ('59) 140.00 22.50
*a.* Printed on both sides *750.00*
**12** A1 6p slate blue 500.00 40.00
**13** A1 1sh orange ('59) 1,125. 45.00
*c.* Printed on both sides *1,375.*

See Nos. 14-16, 19-20, 25-26, 28-29, 32, 35-36, 41-43, 47, 51-52, 69-70, 73, 113, 118. For overprints see Nos. O1-O2, O5, O7, O9, O11-O13, O17, O20, O27, O30, O32, O39-O40, O42, O52, O76, O85.

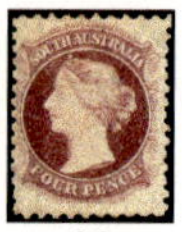

A2

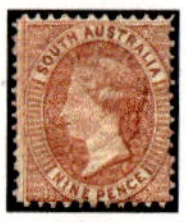

A3

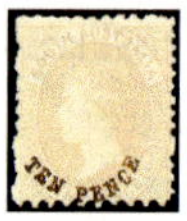

Surcharge on #22-24, 34, 49-50

**1860-69 *Rouletted***

**14** A1 1p dl bl grn 165.00 32.50
*a.* 1p deep green 600.00 85.00
*b.* 1p bright green 155.00 35.00
**15** A1 1p sage green 175.00 50.00
*a.* 1p deep yellow green ('69) 325.00
*b.* 1p pale sage green ('65) 150.00
**16** A1 2p ver ('62) 165.00 5.00
*a.* Horiz. pair, imperf. btwn. 4,000. 850.00
*b.* Rouletted and perf. all around *2,750.* *675.00*
*c.* 2p pale red 275.00 4.75
*d.* As "c," printed on both sides — 575.00
*e.* 2p bright vermilion ('64) 165.00 3.75
**18** A2 4p dull vio ('67) 185.00 50.00
**19** A1 6p grnsh bl ('63) 350.00 4.75
**20** A1 6p dull blue 425.00 7.50
*a.* 6p sky blue 300.00 7.75
*b.* 6p Prussian blue 1,500. 57.50
*c.* Horiz. pair, imperf btwn. 3,000. *3,250.*
*d.* 6p ultramarine 300.00 4.75
*e.* Horiz. pair, imperf. btwn. (#20f) — *2,750.*
*f.* 6p indigo blue — 75.00
*g.* Rouletted and perf. all around (#20f) *475.00*
*h.* 6p violet blue 500.00 8.00
*i.* 6p violet ultramarine ('68) 500.00 7.00
**21** A3 9p gray lilac ('69) 165.00 10.50
*a.* Double impression — —
*b.* Horiz. pair, imperf between 5,000.
*c.* Rouletted and perf. all around *2,900.* *250.00*
**22** A3 10p on 9p red org (Bl) ('66) 625.00 45.00
**23** A3 10p on 9p yel (Bl) ('67) 825.00 32.50
**24** A3 10p on 9p yel (Blk) ('69) 4,000. 75.00
*a.* Inverted surcharge — *7,500.*
*c.* Printed on both sides — *1,250.*
*d.* Rouletted x perf. 10 —
**24E** A1 1sh yellow ('61) 1,650. 35.00
*f.* Vert. pair, imperf. btwn. — 6,500.
**25** A1 1sh lake brn ('65) 325.00 13.50
*a.* Horiz. pair, imperf. btwn. — *2,750.*
**26** A1 1sh brown ('63) 425.00 32.50
*a.* 1sh chestnut ('64) 375.00 12.50
*b.* 1sh gray brown ('63) 450.00 35.00
**27** A2 2sh car ('67) 550.00 37.50
*a.* Vert. pair, imperf. btwn. *2,900.*

There are six varieties of the surcharge "TEN PENCE" in this and subsequent issues.

Nos. 16b, 20g, 21c, 28a, 32c, 33a are rouletted remainders that were later perforated.

See Nos. 31, 33, 46, 48, 53, 63, 68, 72, 74, 112, 113B, 119-120. For surcharges & overprints see Nos. 34, 44-45, 49-50, 59, 67, 71, O4, O6, O8, O10, O16-O19, O18, O21, O26, O28-O29, O31, O33, O36-O38, O41, O41B, O43, O53. Compare with design A6a.

**1867-72 *Perf. 11½ to 12½xRoulette***

**28** A1 1p blue green 625.00 65.00
*a.* Rouletted and perf. all around 750.00
**29** A1 1p grayish green ('70) 500.00 30.00
**29a** A1 1p bright green 450.00 25.00
*b.* 1p pale bright green ('67) 475.00 30.00
**31** A2 4p dull violet ('68) 3,500. 165.00
*a.* 4p purple ('69) — 135.00
**32** A1 6p Prus blue 1,150. 20.00
*a.* 6p sky blue 1,250. 20.00
*b.* Printed on both sides — —
*c.* Rouletted and perf. all around — *400.00*
*d.* 6p indigo blue ('69) 1,300. 27.50
*e.* As "d," rouletted and perf. all around — *525.00*
**33** A3 9p gray lilac ('72) — *275.00*
**34** A3 10p on 9p yel (Bl) ('68) 1,850. 37.50
*a.* Printed on both sides — *1,275.*
**35** A1 1sh chestnut ('68) 575.00 26.00
**36** A1 1sh lake brn ('69) 575.00 24.00
*a.* Rouletted and perf. all around — —

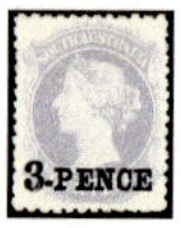

Nos. 44-45 Surcharged

***Perf. 10, 11½, 12½ and Compound***

**1867-74**

**41** A1 1p yel grn 190.00 20.00
**42** A1 1p blue green 200.00 20.00
*a.* Printed on both sides 1,050.
*b.* Horiz. pair, imperf between 3,200.
*c.* 1p pale bright green ('68) 400.00 65.00
*d.* 1p gray green ('68) 350.00 65.00
**43** A1 2p vermilion 1,400.
**44** A2 3p on 4p sky blue (Blk) ('70) 675.00 19.00
*a.* 3p on 4p ultra, black surcharge 190.00 8.75
*b.* Surcharge omitted *42,500.* *19,500.*
*c.* Double surcharge 3,750.
*d.* Surcharged on both sides 3,250.
*e.* Rouletted — *1,350.*
*f.* 3p on 4p Prussian blue ('71) *925.00*
**46** A2 4p dull violet 120.00 9.25
*a.* 4p dull purple ('68) 130.00 17.50
**47** A1 6p Prussian blue 425.00 8.00
*a.* 6p sky blue 750.00 12.50
*b.* Imperf. vert., pair —
*c.* Horiz. pair, imperf x perf 11½ *2,400.*
*d.* 6p indigo ('69) 425.00 19.00
**48** A3 9p red lilac ('72) 125.00 9.00
*a.* 9p violet 210.00 9.00
*b.* 9p red violet 210.00 9.50
*c.* Printed on both sides *925.00*
**49** A3 10p on 9p yel (Bl) ('68) *2,350.* 50.00
**50** A3 10p on 9p yel (Blk) ('69) 500.00 62.50
**51** A1 1sh dp brn 175.00 12.50
**52** A1 1sh red brown 190.00 12.50
*a.* 1sh chestnut 210.00 19.50
*b.* 1sh lake brown ('68) 240.00 17.50
**53** A2 2sh carmine 190.00 14.00
*a.* Printed on both sides 400.00
*b.* Horiz. pair, imperf. vert. —
*c.* 2sh pale rose pink ('69) 2,350. 185.00
*d.* 2sh deep rose pink ('69) — 125.00
*e.* 2sh carmine red ('69) 200.00 22.50

***Perf. 10***

**42e** A1 1p brt grn ('71) 350.00 24.00
**42f** A1 1p pale br grn ('70) 350.00 24.00
**42g** A1 1p gray green ('70) 400.00 27.50
**44g** A2 3p on 4p pale ultra (Blk) ('71) 675.00 22.00
**44h** A2 3p on 4p ultra (Blk) ('71) 190.00 10.50
**44i** A2 3p on 4p Pruss bl (Blk) ('71) *1,000.*
**45** A2 3p on 4p sl bl (Red) ('70) 1,700. 125.00
**46b** A2 4p dull lilac ('70) 240.00 12.50
**46c** A2 4p dull pur ('71) 210.00 12.50
**47e** A1 6p br blue ('70) 425.00 20.00
**47f** A1 6p indigo ('71) 625.00 18.50
**52c** A1 1sh chest ('71) 400.00 45.00

***Perf. 10x11½-12½, 11½-12½x10, or Compound***

**42h** A1 1p pale br grn 400.00 27.50
*i* Printed on both sides —
**42j** A1 1p deep green 240.00 11.50
**42k** A1 1p gray green 375.00 19.00
**44j** A2 3p on 4p ultra (Blk) 650.00 85.00
**46d** A2 4p dull lilac — 23.00
**46e** A2 4p slate lilac 240.00 22.50
**47g** A1 6p Prus blue 350.00 9.50
**47h** A1 6p br Pruss blue 375.00 12.00
**50a** A3 10p on 9p yel (Blk) ('69) 375.00 75.00
**52d** A1 1sh chestnut 450.00 85.00
**53f** A2 2sh carmine 400.00 75.00
**53g** A2 2sh rose pink — 240.00

See Nos. 67, O14, O28, O36.

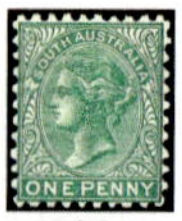

A6

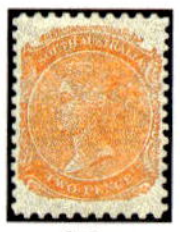

A6a

**1868 Typo. Wmk. 72** ***Rouletted***
**54** A6a 2p orange red 165.00 3.50
*a.* Imperf.
*b.* Printed on both sides 775.00
*c.* Horiz. pair, imperf. btwn. 1,750.
*d.* 2p deep brick red 175.00 7.50

**1869** ***Perf. 11½ to 12½xRoulette***
**55** A6a 2p orange red *180.00*

**1870** ***Perf. 10xRoulette***
**56** A6a 2p orange red 575.00 42.50

***Perf. 10, 11½, 12½ and Compound***
**1868-75**
**57** A6 1p bl grn ('75) 110.00 8.00
**58** A6a 2p orange red 27.50 1.25
*a.* Printed on both sides 425.00
*b.* Horiz. pair, imperf. vert.

**Engr.**
**59** A3 10p on 9p yel (Bl) *1,650.*

**1869 Typo. Wmk. 6** ***Rouletted***
**60** A6a 2p orange red 190.00 27.50
*a.* Imperf.
*b.* Printed on both sides

***Perf. 11½ to 12½xRoulette***
**61** A6a 2p orange red *2,100.* 125.00

***Perf. 11½ to 12½***
**61B** A6a 2p orange red — *1,250.*

See Nos. 62, 64-66, 97-98, 105-106, 115-116, 133-134, 145-146. For surcharges & overprints see Nos. 75, O3, O22-O25, O34-O35, O44-O47, O49, O55-O56, O62-O63, O68-O69, O74, O78-O79.

**1871 Wmk. 70** ***Perf. 10***
**62** A6a 2p orange red 200.00 50.00

**Engr.**
**63** A2 4p dull violet 5,750. 325.00
*a.* Printed on both sides *4,750.*

Examples of the 4p from edge of sheet sometimes lack watermark.

***Perf. 10, 11½, 12½ and Compound***
**1876-80 Typo. Wmk. 73**
**64** A6 1p green 45.00 1.50
**65** A6a 2p orange 57.50 1.00
**66** A6a 2p blood red ('80) 325.00 5.00
*Nos. 64-66 (3)* 427.50 7.50

See Nos. 97-98, 105-106, 115-116, 133-104, 145-140.

No. 71
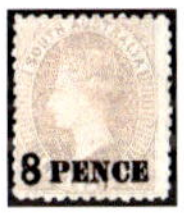


**1876-84 Engr. Wmk. 7**
**67** A2 3p on 4p ultra (Blk) 200.00 32.50
*a.* 3p on 4p deep blue 140.00 32.50
*b.* Double surcharge *1,950.*
**68** A2 4p reddish violet 100.00 6.00
*a.* 4p dull violet 100.00 7.50
*b.* 4p slate violet ('79) 175.00 16.00
**69** A1 6p deep blue 200.00 4.50
*a.* Horiz. pair, imperf. between —
*b.* Imperf.
*c.* 6p bright blue, perf 10 275.00 20.00
*d.* 6p Prussian blue, perf 10 250.00 25.00
**70** A1 6p pale ultra ('84) 160.00 3.00
**71** A3 8p on 9p bister brn 275.00 13.00
*a.* 8p on 9p yellow brown 290.00 11.00
*b.* 8p on 9p gray brown ('80) 240.00 7.00
*d.* Double surcharge 2,900.
*e.* Vert. pair, imperf between 5,000.
**72** A3 9p rose lilac 21.00 5.00
*a.* Printed on both sides 650.00
**73** A1 1sh red brown 100.00 3.25
*a.* 1sh brown 100.00 4.00
*b.* 1sh chocolate 27.50 4.00
*c.* As "b," horiz. pair, imperf. btwn. 475.00
*d.* 1sh sepia 29.00 6.75
*e.* As "d," vert. pair, imperf. btwn. 675.00
*f.* 1sh reddish lake brown, perf 10 575.00
**74** A2 2sh carmine 65.00 8.00
*a.* Horiz. pair, imperf. vert. *3,250.*
*b.* Imperf., pair

For overprint see No. O41.

Surcharged in Black
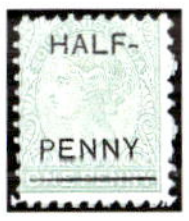


**1882 Wmk. 73** ***Perf. 10***
**75** A6 ½p on 1p green 15.00 15.00

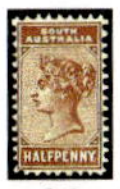

A9

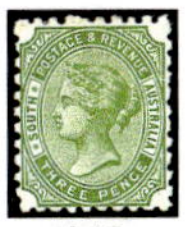
A10

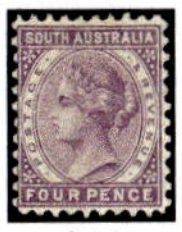

A11

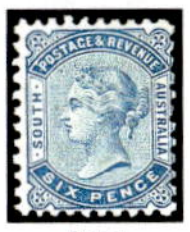

A12

***Perf. 10, 11½, 12½ and Compound***
**1883-93 Typo.**
**76** A9 ½p chocolate brown 20.00 2.00
*a.* ½p red brown ('89) 11.00 2.00
*b.* ½p bister brown 6.00 4.50
**78** A10 3p deep green ('93) 24.00 5.75
*a.* 3p olive green ('90) 27.50 5.75
*b.* 3p sage green ('86) 42.50 2.50
**79** A11 4p violet ('90) 62.50 2.75
*a.* 4p aniline violet ('93) 57.50 8.00
**80** A12 6p pale blue ('87) 77.50 3.50
*a.* 6p blue ('87) 62.50 1.50
*Nos. 76-80 (4)* 184.00 14.00

See Nos. 96, 100-101, 104, 108-109, 111. For surcharges & overprints see Nos. 94-95, 99, O48, O50-O51, O54, O57-O61, O64, O66-O67, O71, O73, O75, O81-O82.

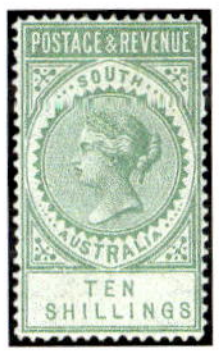

A13

**1886-96** ***Perf. 10, 11½ to 12½***
**81** A13 2sh6p violet 100.00 10.00
*a.* 2sh6p bright aniline violet 115.00 10.00
**82** A13 5sh rose 125.00 20.00
**83** A13 10sh green 275.00 75.00
**84** A13 15sh buff 950.00 275.00
**85** A13 £1 blue 525.00 180.00
**86** A13 £2 red brn 4,600. 550.00
**87** A13 50sh rose red 5,750. 675.00
**88** A13 £3 ol grn 6,750. 725.00
**89** A13 £4 lemon 11,500. 1,350.
**90** A13 £5 gray *11,500.*
**90A** A13 £5 brn ('96) *6,250.* 1,150.
**91** A13 £10 bronze *9,750.* *1,450.*
**92** A13 £15 silver *38,500.* 2,600.
**93** A13 £20 lilac *45,000.* 2,900.

***Perf. 10***
**81b** A13 2sh6p violet 145.00 17.50
**82a** A13 5sh rose 165.00 20.00
**83a** A13 10sh green 350.00 75.00
**84a** A13 15sh buff 900.00 375.00
**85a** A13 £1 blue 650.00 200.00
**86a** A13 £2 red brn 4,800. 575.00
**87a** A13 50sh rose red 6,250. 800.00
**88a** A13 £3 ol grn 7,250. 850.00
**89a** A13 £4 lemon 13,500. 525.00
**90b** A13 £5 gray *11,250.*
**91a** A13 £10 bronze *12,000.* *2,200.*
**92a** A13 £15 silver *40,000.*
**93a** A13 £20 lilac *50,000.*

For overprints see Nos. O83-O84.

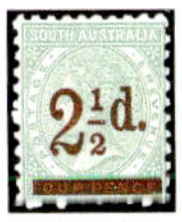

#94, 99

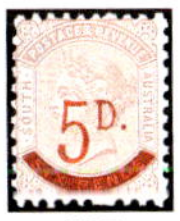

#95

***Perf. 10, 11½x12½ and Compound***
**1891 Brown Surcharge**
**94** A11 2½p on 4p green 8.00 3.00
*a.* "½" nearer the "2" 27.50 20.00
*b.* Pair, imperf. between *4,000.*
*c.* Fraction bar omitted 125.00 90.00

**Carmine Surcharge**
**95** A12 5p on 6p red brn 20.00 8.00
*a.* No period after "D" 175.00

See No. 99. For overprints see Nos. O48, O57, O59.

*Many stamps of the issues of 1855-91 have been reprinted; they are all on paper watermarked Crown and SA, letters wide apart, and are overprinted "REPRINT."*

**1893 Typo.** ***Perf. 15***
**96** A9 ½p brown 12.50 1.50
*a.* Horiz. pair, imperf. btwn 450.00
*b.* Pair, perf. 12 btwn; perf. 15 around 375.00 100.00
**97** A6 1p green 55.00 1.00
**98** A6a 2p orange 32.50 1.00
*a.* Vert. pair, imperf. between 1,000.
**99** A11 2½p on 4p green 65.00 3.00
*a.* "½" nearer the "2" 135.00 20.00
*b.* Fraction bar omitted
**100** A11 4p gray violet 55.00 4.50
**101** A12 6p blue 80.00 5.00
*Nos. 96-101 (6)* 300.00 16.00

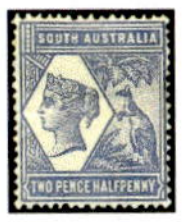

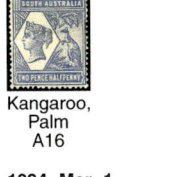

Kangaroo, Palm
A16

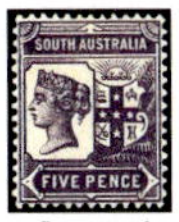

Coat of Arms
A17

**1894, Mar. 1**
**102** A16 2½p blue violet 20.00 2.00
**103** A17 5p dull violet 21.50 2.50

See Nos. 107, 110, 117, 135-136, 147, 151. For overprints see Nos. O65, O70, O72, O80.

**1895-97** ***Perf. 13***
**104** A9 ½p pale brown 5.50 1.00
**105** A6 1p green 12.50 1.00
*a.* Vert. pair, imperf. between
**106** A6a 2p orange 16.00 .50
**107** A16 2½p blue violet 10.00 2.00
**108** A10 3p ol grn ('97) 6.00 3.75
**109** A11 4p bright violet 6.50 1.00
**110** A17 5p dull violet 12.00 2.00
**111** A12 6p blue 12.00 1.50
*a.* 6p pale blue ('96) 12.50 1.50
*Nos. 104-111 (8)* 80.50 12.75

Some authorities regard the so-called redrawn 1p stamps with thicker lettering (said to have been issued in 1897) as impressions from a new or cleaned plate.

***Perf. 11½, 12½, Clean-Cut, Compound***
**1896 Engr. Wmk. 7**
**112** A3 9p lilac rose 20.00 5.75
**113** A1 1sh dark brown 27.50 5.00
*a.* Horiz. pair, imperf. vert. 475.00
*c.* Vert. pair, imperf. btwn. 675.00
**113B** A2 2sh carmine 42.50 8.00
*Nos. 112-113B (3)* 90.00 18.75

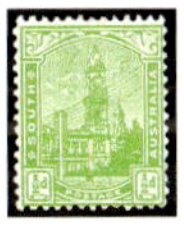
Adelaide Post Office — A18

**1899 Typo. Wmk. 73** ***Perf. 13***
**114** A18 ½p yellow green 8.00 1.50
**115** A6 1p carmine 10.00 1.50
*a.* 1p scarlet 9.00 1.50
**116** A6a 2p purple 7.50 .50
**117** A16 2½p dark blue 11.00 2.00
*Nos. 114-117 (4)* 36.50 5.50

See Nos. 132, 144. For overprint see No. O77.

***Perf. 11½, 12½***
**1901 Engr. Wmk. 72**
**118** A1 1sh dark brown 24.00 17.50
*a.* 1sh red brown 27.50 40.00
*b.* Horiz. pair, imperf. vert.
**119** A2 2sh carmine 27.50 13.50

**1902**
**120** A3 9p magenta 21.00 25.00

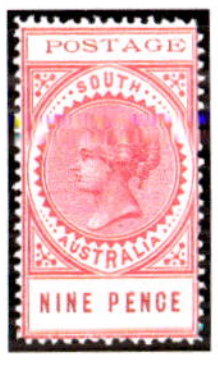

A19

The measurements given in parentheses are the length of the value inscription in the bottom panel.

***Perf. 11½, 12½ and Compound***
**1902-03 Typo. Wmk. 73**
**121** A19 3p olive grn 20.00 3.00
*a.* 3p olive grn (20mm), perf 12 32.50 3.75
*b.* Wmk sideways *1,850.*
**122** A19 4p red org 42.50 5.00
*a.* 4p red org (17.5-18mm), perf 12 25.00 3.00
**123** A19 6p blue grn 15.00 3.75
*a.* 6p blue grn (15mm), perf 12 27.50 20.00
**124** A19 8p ultra (value 19mm long) 9.00 20.00
**124A** A19 8p ultra (value 16½mm long) ('03) 12.50 17.50
*b.* "EIGNT" 2,600. *3,250.*
**125** A19 9p claret 19.00 15.00
*a.* Vert. pair, imperf. between 3,000.
*b.* Horiz. pair, imperf. between
*c.* 9p claret, perf 12 135.00 37.50
**126** A19 10p org buff 18.00 20.00
**127** A19 1sh brn ('03) 27.50 9.00
*a.* Horiz. pair, imperf. btwn.
*b.* Vert. pair, imperf. btwn. 2,900.
*c.* "Postage" and denomination in red brown *1,100.* *1,000.*
**128** A19 2sh6p purple 45.00 15.00
*a.* 2sh6p pale violet 90.00 50.00
**129** A19 5sh rose 135.00 80.00
**130** A19 10sh grn ('03) 225.00 100.00
**131** A19 £1 blue 525.00 275.00
*Nos. 121-131 (12)* 1,094. 563.25

**1904** ***Perf. 12x11½***
**132** A18 ½p yellow green 8.50 3.00
**133** A6 1p rose 8.75 1.00
**134** A6a 2p purple 15.00 1.00
**135** A16 2½p dark blue 16.00 6.50
**136** A17 5p dull violet 22.50 3.00
*Nos. 132-136 (5)* 70.75 14.50

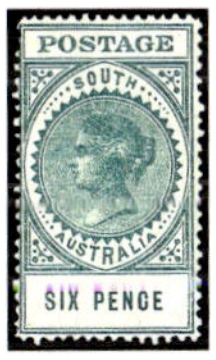

A20

**1904-08** ***Perf. 12 and 12x11½***
**137** A20 6p blue grn 42.50 3.00
*a.* Vert. pair, imperf. between *5,000.*
**138** A20 8p ultra ('06) 20.00 9.00
**139** A20 9p claret ('09) 11.00 4.25
**139A** A20 10p org buff ('07) 18.00 25.00
*b.* Vert. pair, imperf. between 4,500.
*c.* Horiz. pair, imperf. between 3,500. 3,500.
**140** A20 1sh brown 30.00 4.00
*a.* Vert. pair, imperf between 3,000.
*b.* Horiz. pair, imperf between 3,250.
**141** A20 2sh6p pur ('05) 75.00 32.50
**142** A20 5sh scarlet 85.00 50.00
*a.* 5sh pale rose, Perf 12½, small holes ('10) 140.00 75.00
**142B** A20 10sh grn ('08) 200.00 *150.00*
**143** A20 £1 dp blue 250.00 150.00
*a.* Perf 12½, small holes ('10) 350.00 175.00
*Nos. 137-143 (9)* 731.50 427.75

See Nos. 148-150, 152-157.

**1906-12 Wmk. 74**
**144** A18 ½p green 18.00 1.20
**145** A6 1p carmine 7.50 .25
**146** A6a 2p purple 8.00 1.25
*a.* Horiz. pair, imperf. between 2,500.
**147** A16 2½p dk blue ('11) 9.00 15.00
**148** A20 3p ol grn (value 19mm long) 15.00 5.00
*a.* Horiz. pair, imperf. between *5,750.*
**149** A20 3p ol grn (value 17mm long) ('09) 17.50 12.00
**150** A20 4p red org 25.00 9.00
**151** A17 5p dl vio ('08) 30.00 6.75
**152** A20 6p bl grn ('07) 7.50 11.00
*a.* Vert. pair, imperf. between 2,500. 2,750.
**153** A20 8p ultra ('09) 12.00 *24.00*
**154** A20 9p claret 22.50 5.00
*a.* Vert. pair, imperf. between 2,250.
*b.* Horiz. pair, imperf. between *5,000.*
**155** A20 1sh brown 12.50 5.50
*a.* Horiz. pair, imperf. between *3,750.*
*b.* Vert. pair, imperf. between 3,750.

| | | | | |
|---|---|---|---|---|
| 156 | A20 | 2sh6p pur ('09) | 80.00 | 32.50 |
| a. | | 2sh6p pale violet, perf 12 ('10) | 80.00 | 37.50 |
| b. | | 2sh6p pale violet, perf 12½ ('12) | 125.00 | 125.00 |
| 157 | A20 | 5sh lt red ('12) | 145.00 | 145.00 |
| | | *Nos. 144-157 (14)* | 409.50 | 273.45 |

## OFFICIAL STAMPS

### For Departments

### Regular Issues Overprinted in Red, Black or Blue:

A. (Architect), A. G. (Attorney General), A. O. (Audit Office), B. D. (Barracks Department), B. G. (Botanical Gardens), B. M. (Bench of Magistrates), C. (Customs), C. D. (Convict Department), C. L. (Crown Lands), C. O. (Commissariat Officer), C. S. (Chief Secretary), C. Sgn. (Colonial Surgeon), C. P. (Commissioner of Police), C. T. (Commissioner of Titles), D. B. (Destitute Board), D. R. (Deed Registry), E. (Engineer), E. B. (Education Board),

G. P. (Government Printer), G. S. (Government Storekeeper), G. T. (Goolwa Tramway), G. F. (Gold Fields), H. (Hospital), H. A. (House of Assembly), I. A. (Immigration Agent), I. E. (Intestate Estates), I. S. (Inspector of Sheep), L. A. (Lunatic Asylum), L. C. (Legislative Council), L. L. (Legislative Library), L. T. (Land Titles), M. (Military), M. B. (Marine Board), M. R. (Manager of Railways), M. R. G. (Main Roads Gambierton), N. T. (Northern Territory),

O. A. (Official Assignee), P. (Police), P. A. (Protector of Aborigines), P. O. (Post Office), P. S. (Private Secretary), P. W. (Public Works), R. B. (Road Board), R. G. (Registrar General of Births, &c.), S. (Sheriff), S. C. (Supreme Court), S.G. (Surveyor General), S. M. (Stipendiary Magistrate), S. T. (Superintendent of Telegraph), T. (Treasurer), T. R. (Titles Registry), V. (Volunteers), V. A. (Valuator), V. N. (Vaccination), W. (Waterworks).

**1868-74 Wmk. 6 *Rouletted***

| | | | | |
|---|---|---|---|---|
| O1 | A1 | 1p green | | *350.00* |
| O2 | A1 | 2p pale red | | *275.00* |
| O3 | A6a | 2p vermilion | | *150.00* |
| O4 | A2 | 4p dull violet | | *300.00* |
| O5 | A1 | 6p slate blue | | *300.00* |
| O6 | A3 | 9p gray lilac | | *500.00* |
| O7 | A1 | 1sh brown | | *300.00* |
| O8 | A2 | 2sh carmine | | *275.00* |

***Perf. 11½ to 12½ x Roulette***

| | | | | |
|---|---|---|---|---|
| O9 | A1 | 1p green | | *275.00* |
| O10 | A2 | 4p dull violet | | *850.00* |
| O11 | A1 | 6p blue | | *210.00* |
| O12 | A1 | 1sh brown | | *200.00* |

***Perf. 10, 11½, 12½ and Compound***

| | | | | |
|---|---|---|---|---|
| O13 | A1 | 1p green | | *150.00* |
| O14 | A2 | 3p on 4p sl bl (Red) | | *750.00* |
| O15 | A2 | 3p on 4p sl bl (Blk) | | *275.00* |
| O16 | A2 | 4p dull violet | | *250.00* |
| O17 | A1 | 6p deep blue | | *275.00* |
| O18 | A3 | 9p violet | | *500.00* |
| O19 | A3 | 10p on 9p yel (Blk) | | *500.00* |
| O20 | A1 | 1sh brown | *175.00* | *175.00* |
| O21 | A2 | 2sh carmine | | *125.00* |

***Rouletted***

**Wmk. 72**

| | | | | |
|---|---|---|---|---|
| O22 | A6a | 2p orange | | *135.00* |

***Perf. 11 ½ x Roulette***

| | | | | |
|---|---|---|---|---|
| O23 | A6a | 2p orange | | *175.00* |
| a. | | Perf 10 x Roulette | | *300.00* |

***Perf. 10, 11½, 12½ and Compound***

| | | | | |
|---|---|---|---|---|
| O24 | A6a | 2p orange | | *50.00* |

**Wmk. 70**

***Perf. 10***

| | | | | |
|---|---|---|---|---|
| O25 | A6a | 2p orange | | *125.00* |
| O26 | A2 | 4p dull violet | | *275.00* |

### For General Use

Overprinted in Black 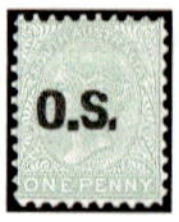

***Perf. 10, 11½, 12½ and Compound***

**1874 Wmk. 6**

| | | | | |
|---|---|---|---|---|
| O27 | A1 | 1p green | — | *500.00* |
| a. | | 1p dp yel green, perf 11½-12½x10 | 3,500. | *400.00* |
| b. | | As "a," printed on both sides | | 1,275. |
| O28 | A2 | 3p on 4p ultra | 9,000. | *3,500.* |
| a. | | No period after "S" | | *4,250.* |
| O29 | A2 | 4p dull violet | 90.00 | 9.50 |
| a. | | Inverted overprint | | |
| b. | | No period after "S" | | 85.00 |
| c. | | Perf. 11½-12½x10 | 3,000. | 600.00 |
| O30 | A1 | 6p deep blue | 275.00 | 9.50 |
| a. | | No period after "S" | | 125.00 |
| b. | | 6p Prussian blue, perf 11½-12½x10 | 200.00 | 12.50 |
| O31 | A3 | 9p violet | *4,500.* | *2,000.* |
| a. | | No period after "S" | *5,000.* | *2,500.* |
| O32 | A1 | 1sh red brown | 115.00 | 14.00 |
| a. | | Double overprint | | 350.00 |
| b. | | No period after "S" | 400.00 | 90.00 |
| O33 | A2 | 2sh carmine | 375.00 | 32.50 |
| a. | | Double overprint | | |
| b. | | No period after "S" | | 165.00 |
| c. | | 2sh carmine, perf 11½-12½x10 | | 160.00 |

**1874-75 Wmk. 72**

| | | | | |
|---|---|---|---|---|
| O34 | A6 | 1p blue green | 240.00 | 47.50 |
| a. | | Inverted overprint | | |
| O35 | A6a | 2p orange | 65.00 | 9.50 |

**1876-86 Wmk. 7**

| | | | | |
|---|---|---|---|---|
| O37 | A2 | 4p dull violet | 75.00 | 5.00 |
| O38 | A2 | 4p reddish vio | 75.00 | 3.00 |
| a. | | Double overprint | | |
| b. | | Inverted overprint | 1,000. | 350.00 |
| c. | | Dbl. ovpt., one inverted | | |
| O39 | A1 | 6p dark blue | 165.00 | 6.00 |
| a. | | Double overprint | | 225.00 |
| b. | | Inverted overprint | 1,500. | |
| O40 | A1 | 6p ultramarine | 150.00 | 5.50 |
| a. | | Double overprint | | |
| b. | | Inverted overprint | | |
| O41 | A1 | 8p on 9p yel brn | 6,500. | 3,500. |
| a. | | Double overprint | 7,750. | |
| O41B | A3 | 9p violet | *9,500.* | |
| O42 | A1 | 1sh red brown | 55.00 | 9.00 |
| a. | | Inverted overprint | 1,000. | 300.00 |
| b. | | Double overprint | | |
| O43 | A2 | 2sh carmine | 325.00 | 9.00 |
| a. | | Double overprint | — | 400.00 |
| b. | | Inverted overprint | — | 425.00 |
| c. | | No period after "S" | — | 100.00 |

**1880-91 Wmk. 73**

| | | | | |
|---|---|---|---|---|
| O44 | A6 | 1p blue green | 35.00 | 1.75 |
| a. | | Inverted overprint | | 140.00 |
| b. | | Double overprint | 275.00 | 140.00 |
| c. | | Dbl. ovpt., one inverted | | *750.00* |
| O45 | A6 | 1p yellow green | 55.00 | 1.00 |
| O46 | A6a | 2p orange | 18.00 | 1.00 |
| a. | | Inverted overprint | | 85.00 |
| b. | | Double overprint | 275.00 | 150.00 |
| c. | | Overprinted sideways | | |
| d. | | Dbl. ovpt., one inverted | | |
| e. | | Dbl. ovpt., both inverted | — | 425.00 |
| O47 | A6a | 2p blood red | 110.00 | 35.00 |
| O48 | A11 | 2½p on 4p green | 130.00 | 14.00 |
| a. | | "½" nearer the "2" | — | 55.00 |
| b. | | Double overprint | | |
| c. | | Pair, one without ovpt. | | 4,750. |
| | | *Nos. O44-O48 (5)* | 348.00 | 52.75 |

**1882-90 *Perf. 10***

| | | | | |
|---|---|---|---|---|
| O49 | A6 | ½p on 1p green | 130.00 | 25.00 |
| a. | | Inverted overprint | | |
| O50 | A11 | 4p violet | 140.00 | 13.00 |
| O51 | A12 | 6p blue | 60.00 | 1.50 |
| a. | | Double overprint | | |
| b. | | No period after "S" | | |
| | | *Nos. O49-O51 (3)* | 330.00 | 39.50 |

Overprinted in Black 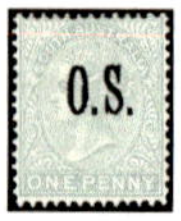

***Perf. 10, 11½, 12½ and Compound***

**1891 Wmk. 7**

| | | | | |
|---|---|---|---|---|
| O52 | A1 | 1sh red brown | 80.00 | 5.50 |
| a. | | No period after "S" | — | 100.00 |
| b. | | 1sh lake brown, perf 11½-12½ | 90.00 | 10.00 |
| c. | | 1sh Van Dyke brown | 160.00 | 10.00 |
| O53 | A2 | 2sh carmine | 90.00 | 10.00 |
| a. | | Double overprint | | |
| b. | | No period after "S" | *550.00* | |

**1891-95 Wmk. 73**

| | | | | |
|---|---|---|---|---|
| O54 | A9 | ½p brown | 50.00 | 7.50 |
| a. | | No period after "S" | 175.00 | 55.00 |
| O55 | A6 | 1p blue green | 70.00 | 2.00 |
| a. | | Double overprint | 275.00 | 100.00 |
| b. | | No period after "S" | 125.00 | 15.00 |
| O56 | A6a | 2p orange | 30.00 | .50 |
| a. | | No period after "S" | — | 45.00 |
| O57 | A11 | 2½p on 4p green | 45.00 | 35.00 |
| a. | | "½" nearer the "2" | 120.00 | 60.00 |
| b. | | Inverted overprint | 575.00 | |
| O58 | A11 | 4p violet | 70.00 | 5.00 |
| a. | | Double overprint | — | |
| O59 | A12 | 5p on 6p red brn | 50.00 | 18.00 |
| O60 | A12 | 6p blue | 45.00 | 2.50 |
| a. | | Double overprint | — | |
| b. | | No period after "S" | — | |
| | | *Nos. O54-O60 (7)* | 360.00 | 70.50 |

**1893 *Perf. 15***

| | | | | |
|---|---|---|---|---|
| O61 | A9 | ½p brown | 80.00 | 22.50 |
| O62 | A6 | 1p green | 10.00 | 1.25 |
| O63 | A6a | 2p orange | 32.50 | .60 |
| a. | | Inverted overprint | 30.00 | 80.00 |
| b. | | Double overprint | | 110.00 |
| O64 | A11 | 4p gray violet | 100.00 | 7.00 |
| a. | | Double overprint | 550.00 | 180.00 |
| O65 | A17 | 5p dull violet | 130.00 | 25.00 |
| O66 | A12 | 6p blue | 65.00 | 4.00 |
| | | *Nos. O61-O66 (6)* | 417.50 | 60.35 |

**1896 *Perf. 13***

| | | | | |
|---|---|---|---|---|
| O67 | A9 | ½p brown | 65.00 | 5.75 |
| a. | | Triple overprint | *500.00* | |
| O68 | A6 | 1p green | 45.00 | 1.50 |
| a. | | No period after "S" | 200.00 | 14.00 |
| O69 | A6a | 2p orange | 55.00 | .50 |
| a. | | No period after "S" | 180.00 | 10.00 |
| O70 | A16 | 2½p blue violet | 120.00 | 9.00 |
| a. | | No period after "S" | | 80.00 |
| O71 | A11 | 4p brt violet | 130.00 | 3.00 |
| a. | | Double overprint | *750.00* | 150.00 |
| b. | | No period after "S" | 375.00 | 55.00 |
| O72 | A17 | 5p dull violet | 130.00 | 32.50 |
| a. | | No period after "S" | 500.00 | |
| O73 | A12 | 6p blue | 70.00 | 3.00 |
| a. | | No period after "S" | 275.00 | 80.00 |
| | | *Nos. O67-O73 (7)* | 615.00 | 55.25 |

On No. O67a, one overprint is upright, two sideways.

### Same Overprint in Dark Blue

**1891-95 *Perf. 10***

| | | | | |
|---|---|---|---|---|
| O74 | A6 | 1p green | 250.00 | 5.00 |
| O75 | A12 | 6p blue | — | |

### Black Overprint

***Perf. 11½, 12½, Clean-Cut***

**1897 Wmk. 7**

| | | | | |
|---|---|---|---|---|
| O76 | A1 | 1sh brown | 75.00 | 5.50 |
| a. | | Double overprint | — | *550.00* |
| b. | | No period after "S" | | 375.00 |

Overprinted in Black 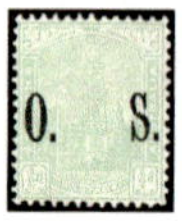

**1900 Wmk. 73 *Perf. 13***

| | | | | |
|---|---|---|---|---|
| O77 | A18 | ½p yellow green | 25.00 | 10.00 |
| a. | | Inverted overprint | 200.00 | |
| b. | | No period after "S" | 100.00 | |
| c. | | As "b," inverted overprint | — | |
| O78 | A6 | 1p carmine rose | 30.00 | 1.60 |
| a. | | Inverted overprint | 200.00 | 125.00 |
| b. | | Double overprint | | 650.00 |
| c. | | No period after "S" | 125.00 | 22.50 |
| O79 | A6a | 2p purple | 40.00 | 1.00 |
| a. | | Inverted ovpt. | 200.00 | 90.00 |
| b. | | No period after "S" | 110.00 | 20.00 |
| O80 | A16 | 2½p dark blue | 85.00 | 20.00 |
| a. | | Inverted overprint | *600.00* | 225.00 |
| b. | | No period after "S" | 325.00 | 110.00 |
| O81 | A11 | 4p violet | 85.00 | 6.00 |
| a. | | Inverted overprint | *650.00* | |
| b. | | No period after "S" | 275.00 | 85.00 |
| O82 | A12 | 6p blue | 50.00 | 5.50 |
| a. | | No period after "S" | 180.00 | 90.00 |
| | | *Nos. O77-O82 (6)* | 315.00 | 44.10 |

**1901 *Perf. 10***

| | | | | |
|---|---|---|---|---|
| O83 | A13 | 2sh6p violet | *8,750.* | *6,500.* |
| O84 | A13 | 5sh rose | *9,000.* | *7,500.* |

On Nos. O77-O82 the letters "O.S." are 11½mm apart; on Nos. O83-O84, 14½mm apart.

Overprinted in Black 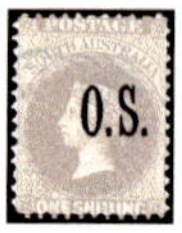

**1903 Wmk. 72 *Perf. 11½, 12½***

| | | | | |
|---|---|---|---|---|
| O85 | A1 | 1sh red brown | 110.00 | 50.00 |

## TASMANIA

taz-ˈmā-nē-ə

LOCATION — An island off the southeastern coast of Australia
GOVT. — British Colony
AREA — 26,215 sq. mi.
POP. — 172,475 (1901)
CAPITAL — Hobart

Tasmania was one of the six British colonies that united in 1901 to form the Commonwealth of Australia. The island was originally named Van Diemen's Land by its discoverer, Abel Tasman, the present name having been adopted in 1853. Stamps of Australia are now used.

12 Pence = 1 Shilling
20 Shillings = 1 Pound

### Watermarks

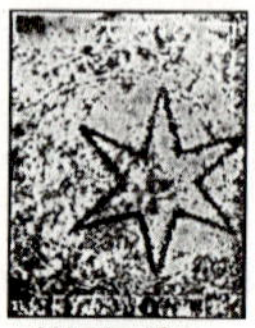
Wmk. 6 — Large Star

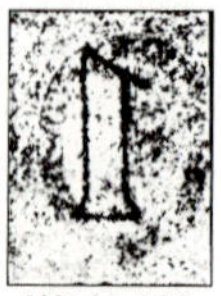
Wmk. 139 Double-lined Numeral

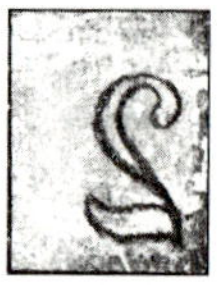
Wmk. 49 Double-lined Numeral

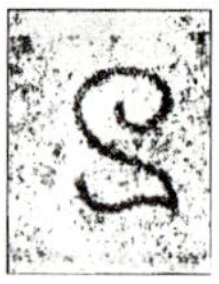
Wmk. 50 Single-lined "2"

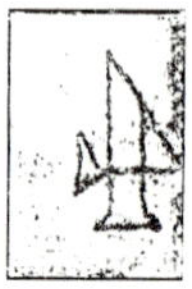
Wmk. 75 Double-lined Numeral

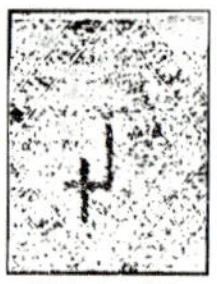
Wmk. 51 Single-lined "4"

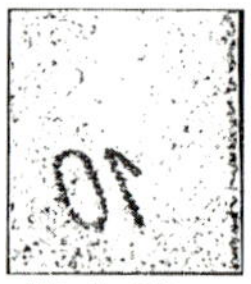
Wmk. 52 — Single-lined "10"

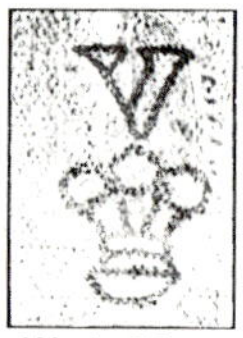
Wmk. 70 — V and Crown

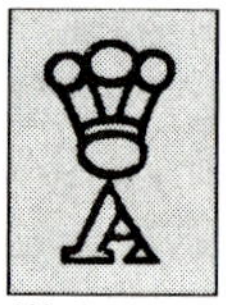
Wmk. 13 — Crown & Double-lined A

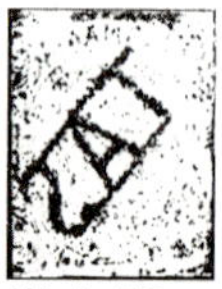
Wmk. 76 — TAS

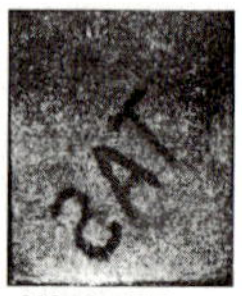
Wmk. 77 — TAS

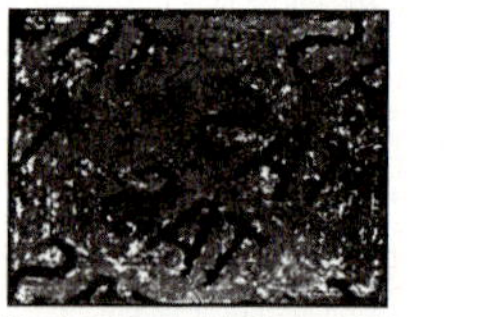
Wmk. 78 — Multiple TAS

Values for unused stamps are for examples with original gum as defined in the catalogue introduction except for Nos. 1-2b and 10 which are valued without gum as few examples exist with any remaining original gum. Very fine examples of Nos. 17-75a will have perforations touching the design on one or more sides due to the narrow spacing of the stamps on the plates. Stamps with perfs clear of the design on all four sides are scarce and command higher prices.

AUSTRALIAN STATES — Tasmania 713

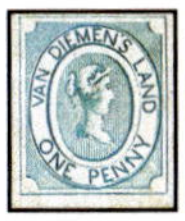
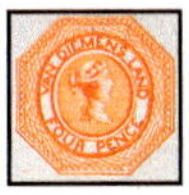

Queen Victoria
A1 A2

**Unwmk.**

**1853, Nov. 1 Engr. *Imperf.***

| No. | Type | Description | Unused | Used |
|---|---|---|---|---|
| 1 | A1 | 1p blue, fine impression, soft paper | 13,000. | 1,600. |
| 1a | A1 | 1p blue, blurred impression, hard paper | 12,000. | 1,350. |
| 2 | A2 | 4p red orange | 7,500. | 550.00 |
| a. | | 4p yellow orange | 7,000. | 425.00 |
| | | Cut to shape | | 25.00 |
| b. | | 4p orange, blurred impression ('55) | 7,000. | 425.00 |
| | | Cut to shape | | 25.00 |

Twenty-four varieties of each.

The 4p on vertically laid paper is believed to be a proof. Value, unused, $7,500.

*The reprints are made from defaced plates and show marks across the face of each stamp. They are on thin and thick, unwatermarked paper and thin cardboard; only the first are perforated. Nearly all the reprints of Tasmania may be found with and without the overprint "REPRINT."*

Nos. 1-47A with pen or revenue cancellations sell for a small fraction of the price of postally used examples. Stamps are found with pen cancellation removed.

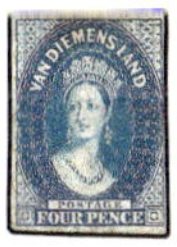

Queen Victoria — A3

**1855 Wmk. 6 Wove Paper**

| No. | Type | Description | Unused | Used |
|---|---|---|---|---|
| 4 | A3 | 1p dark carmine | 10,500. | 1,000. |
| 5 | A3 | 2p green | 5,750. | 500.00 |
| a. | | 2p deep green | 5,750. | 600.00 |
| 6 | A3 | 4p deep blue | 5,000. | 145.00 |
| a. | | 4p blue | 5,000. | 145.00 |

**1856-57 Unwmk.**

| No. | Type | Description | Unused | Used |
|---|---|---|---|---|
| 7 | A3 | 1p pale red | 13,500. | 700.00 |
| 8 | A3 | 2p emerald ('57) | 16,500. | 1,000. |
| 9 | A3 | 4p blue ('57) | 3,500. | 140.00 |
| a. | | 4p deep blue ('57) | 3,500. | 140.00 |
| b. | | 4p pale blue ('57) | — | 180.00 |

**1856 Pelure Paper**

| No. | Type | Description | Unused | Used |
|---|---|---|---|---|
| 10 | A3 | 1p brown red | 10,000. | 800.00 |

**1857-69 Wmk. 49, 75, 139**

| No. | Type | Description | Unused | Used |
|---|---|---|---|---|
| 11 | A3 | 1p carmine ('67) | 375.00 | 32.50 |
| a. | | 1p orange red ('65) | 400.00 | 40.00 |
| b. | | 1p brown red | 650.00 | 42.50 |
| c. | | Double impression | 650.00 | 300.00 |
| d. | | 1p brick red ('63) | 500.00 | 42.50 |
| e. | | Wmk. 50 (error) ('69) | | — |
| 12 | A3 | 2p sage green ('60) | 450.00 | 95.00 |
| a. | | 2p yellow green | 1,200. | 125.00 |
| b. | | 2p green | — | 67.50 |
| c. | | 2p dull emerald green | | 150.00 |
| d. | | As "b," double impression | | 325.00 |
| 13 | A3 | 4p pale blue | 500.00 | 30.00 |
| a. | | 4p blue | 425.00 | 32.50 |
| b. | | Printed on both sides | | — |
| c. | | 4p deep blue | — | 95.00 |
| d. | | As "a," double impression | | 275.00 |
| e. | | As "c," double impression | | 315.00 |
| g. | | 4p cobalt blue | — | 95.00 |
| | | *Nos. 11-13 (3)* | 1,325. | 157.50 |

See Nos. 17-19, 23-25, 29-31, 35-37, 39-41, 45-47A.

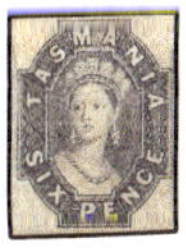
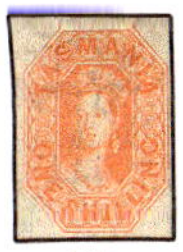

A4 A4a

**1858-67**

| No. | Type | Description | Unused | Used |
|---|---|---|---|---|
| 14 | A4 | 6p gray lilac ('63) | 950.00 | 95.00 |
| a. | | 6p red violet ('67) | 1,400. | 200.00 |
| b. | | Double impression ('63) | | 450.00 |
| c. | | 6p dull lilac | 1,500. | 100.00 |
| 15 | A4 | 6p blue gray ('65) | 1,150. | 150.00 |
| 16 | A4a | 1sh vermilion | *825.00* | 90.00 |
| | | *Nos. 14-16 (3)* | 2,925. | 335.00 |

No. 15 watermarked large star was not regularly issued.

Issued: No. 14c, 16, 1/58; No. 14, 4/63; No. 15, 2/65; No. 14a, 4/67.

**1864 *Rouletted***

| No. | Type | Description | Unused | Used |
|---|---|---|---|---|
| 17 | A3 | 1p carmine | *950.00* | 325.00 |
| a. | | 1p brick red | — | 500.00 |
| 18 | A3 | 2p yellow grn | — | 1,250. |
| 19 | A3 | 4p blue | — | 475.00 |
| 21 | A4 | 6p gray lilac | — | 525.00 |
| 22 | A4a | 1sh vermilion | — | 1,350. |

Values for Nos. 17-22 are for stamps showing rouletting on two or three sides. Examples with full roulettes on all four sides are rare.

**1864-69 *Perf. 10***

| No. | Type | Description | Unused | Used |
|---|---|---|---|---|
| 23 | A3 | 1p brick red | 210.00 | 70.00 |
| a. | | 1p carmine | 160.00 | 60.00 |
| b. | | 1p orange red | 200.00 | 60.00 |
| c. | | As "b," double impression | | — |
| 24 | A3 | 2p yellow green | 900.00 | 200.00 |
| a. | | 2p sage green | 850.00 | 240.00 |
| 25 | A3 | 4p blue | 450.00 | 22.50 |
| a. | | Double impression | | 240.00 |
| 26 | A4 | 6p lilac | 650.00 | 30.00 |
| a. | | 6p red lilac | 850.00 | 110.00 |
| 27 | A4 | 6p slate blue | 900.00 | 110.00 |
| 28 | A4a | 1sh vermilion | 700.00 | 65.00 |
| a. | | Horiz. pair, imperf. vert. | | |
| | | *Nos. 23-28 (6)* | 3,810. | 497.50 |

**1864-91 *Perf. 12, 12½***

| No. | Type | Description | Unused | Used |
|---|---|---|---|---|
| 29 | A3 | 1p carmine | 140.00 | 25.00 |
| a. | | 1p orange red | 175.00 | *40.00* |
| b. | | 1p brick red | 140.00 | 62.50 |
| c. | | Double impression | | — |
| d. | | Wmkd. "2" | | *3,000.* |
| | | As "d," pen cancel | | 325.00 |
| 30 | A3 | 2p yellow green | 650.00 | 110.00 |
| 31 | A3 | 4p blue | 400.00 | 26.00 |
| a. | | 4p deep blue | 400.00 | 25.00 |
| b. | | 4p cobalt blue | — | 65.00 |
| 32 | A4 | 6p red lilac | 200.00 | 47.50 |
| a. | | Horiz. pair, imperf between | | — |
| b. | | Vert. pair, imperf between | | — |
| c. | | 6p violet | 500.00 | 32.50 |
| d. | | As "c," Vert. pair, imperf between | | — |
| e. | | 6p purple ('84) | 175.00 | 22.50 |
| f. | | Horiz. pair, imperf between | *2,900.* | — |
| g. | | 6p dull claret ('91) | 52.50 | 15.00 |
| 34 | A4a | 1sh vermilion | 500.00 | 75.00 |
| a. | | Double impression | — | 200.00 |
| b. | | Horiz. pair, imperf. between | | *3,500.* |

***Perf. 10x12***

| No. | Type | Description | Unused | Used |
|---|---|---|---|---|
| *29e* | A3 | 1p carmine | *3,250.* | |
| *31c* | A3 | 4p blue | | *2,750.* |

***Perf. 12½***

| No. | Type | Description | Unused | Used |
|---|---|---|---|---|
| *29f* | A3 | 1p carmine | 120.00 | 27.50 |
| *29g* | A3 | 1p orange red | 190.00 | 52.50 |
| *29h* | A3 | 1p brick red | 175.00 | 52.50 |
| *30a* | A3 | 2p yellow green | 850.00 | 180.00 |
| *30b* | A3 | 2p sage green | 750.00 | 190.00 |
| *31d* | A3 | 4p blue | 500.00 | 57.50 |
| *31e* | A3 | 4p bright blue | 500.00 | 60.00 |
| *32h* | A4 | 6p purple | 900.00 | 145.00 |
| *32i* | A4 | 6p slate violet | 650.00 | 67.50 |
| 33 | A4 | 6p slate blue | 850.00 | 110.00 |
| *34c* | A4a | 1sh vermilion | 800.00 | 140.00 |

***Perf. 11½***

| No. | Type | Description | Unused | Used |
|---|---|---|---|---|
| *32j* | A4 | 6p dull lilac | 300.00 | 25.00 |
| *32k* | A4 | 6p lilac | 275.00 | 25.00 |
| l. | | Pair, imperf between | | 1,750. |
| *32m* | A4 | 6p dp slate lil ('75) | 275.00 | 25.00 |
| n. | | Imperf, pair | — | 1,400. |
| *32o* | A4 | 6p brt vio ('78) | 300.00 | 37.50 |
| p. | | Double impression | | 160.00 |
| q. | | Horiz. pair, imperf between | *4,750.* | |
| *32r* | A4 | 6p dl reddish lil ('79) | 200.00 | 45.00 |
| *34d* | A4a | 1sh dl ver ('73) | 375.00 | 70.00 |
| e. | | Horiz. pair, imperf between | | |
| *34f* | A4a | 1sh brnsh ver ('73) | 375.00 | 70.00 |

*The reprints are on unwatermarked paper, perforated 11½, and on thin cardboard, imperforate and perforated.*

***Perf. Pin-perf. 5½ to 9½, 13½ to 14½***

**1867**

| No. | Type | Description | Unused | Used |
|---|---|---|---|---|
| 35 | A3 | 1p carmine | 1,250. | 400.00 |
| 36 | A3 | 2p yel grn | | 975.00 |
| 37 | A3 | 4p blue | | 650.00 |
| 38 | A4 | 6p gray | | 650.00 |
| 38A | A4 | 6p red lilac | | 1,500. |
| 38B | A4a | 1sh vermilion | | |

***Pin-perf. 13½ to 14½***

| No. | Type | Description | Unused | Used |
|---|---|---|---|---|
| *35a* | A3 | 1p brick red | | 800.00 |
| *35b* | A3 | 1p dull vermilion | | 800.00 |
| *35c* | A3 | 1p carmine | | |
| 36a | A3 | 2p yel grn | | 1,500. |
| 37a | A3 | 4p pale blue | | 700.00 |
| 38Ac | A4 | 6p gray violet | | 2,750. |
| 38Bd | A4a | 1sh vermilion | | — |

***Oblique Roulette 14-15***

| No. | Type | Description | Unused | Used |
|---|---|---|---|---|
| 39 | A3 | 1p carmine | | 1,200. |
| a. | | 1p brick red | | 1,200. |
| b. | | 1p dull vermilion | | 1,250. |
| 40 | A3 | 2p yel grn | | 1,600. |
| 41 | A3 | 4p blue | | 1,250. |
| 42 | A4 | 6p gray | | 2,400. |
| 43 | A4 | 6p red lilac | | — |
| 44 | A4a | 1sh vermilion | | 2,900. |

***Oblique Roulette 10-10½***

| No. | Type | Description | Unused | Used |
|---|---|---|---|---|
| *39c* | A3 | 1p carmine | *3,000.* | 800.00 |
| *39d* | A3 | 1p brick red | | 1,000. |
| *40a* | A3 | 2p yellow green | | 1,500. |
| *41a* | A3 | 4p blue | | 1,100. |
| 43a | A4 | 6p gray lilac | | 2,400. |

***Oblique Roulette Imperf 10-10½***

| No. | Type | Description | Unused | Used |
|---|---|---|---|---|
| *41b* | A3 | 4p blue | | 1,100. |

**1868 *Serrate Perf. 19***

| No. | Type | Description | Unused | Used |
|---|---|---|---|---|
| 45 | A3 | 1p carmine | 1,000. | 300.00 |
| 46 | A3 | 2p yellow green | | 1,100. |
| 47 | A3 | 4p blue | *2,100.* | 300.00 |
| 47A | A3 | 6p purple | — | 1,250. |
| 47B | A3 | 1sh vermilion | | — |

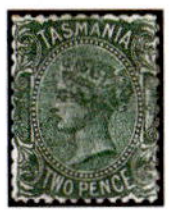

Queen Victoria — A5

**1870-71 Typo. Wmk. 50 *Perf. 11½***

| No. | Type | Description | Unused | Used |
|---|---|---|---|---|
| 48 | A5 | 2p blue green | 200.00 | 12.50 |
| a. | | Double impression | 5,500. | 2,000. |
| b. | | Perf. 12 | 210.00 | 12.50 |
| c. | | 2p green | 325.00 | 20.00 |
| d. | | As "c," perf. 12 | 200.00 | 11.00 |
| e. | | As "d," imperf, pair | | — |

See Nos. 49-75, 98, 108-109.

**Wmk. 51 *Perf. 12***

| No. | Type | Description | Unused | Used |
|---|---|---|---|---|
| 49 | A5 | 1p rose ('71) | 150.00 | 67.50 |
| a. | | Imperf., pair | 1,300. | 1,200. |
| 50 | A5 | 4p blue | 1,350. | 525.00 |

**Wmk. 52**

| No. | Type | Description | Unused | Used |
|---|---|---|---|---|
| 51 | A5 | 1p rose | 130.00 | 24.00 |
| a. | | Imperf. pair | 1,350. | 1,350. |
| c. | | Perf. 11½ | 1,350. | |
| 52 | A5 | 10p black | 27.50 | 52.50 |
| a. | | Imperf. pair | 750.00 | |
| b. | | Perf. 11½ | 52.50 | 52.50 |

*The reprints are on unwatermarked paper. The 4p has also been reprinted on thin cardboard, imperf and perf.*

**1871-76 Wmk. 76 *Perf. 11½***

| No. | Type | Description | Unused | Used |
|---|---|---|---|---|
| 53 | A5 | 1p rose | 18.00 | 2.50 |
| a. | | Imperf. | | |
| c. | | Perf. 12 | 155.00 | 35.00 |
| d. | | 1p carmine | 25.00 | 3.50 |
| e. | | 1p pink | 25.00 | 4.00 |
| f. | | As "d," perf. 12 | 170.00 | 40.00 |
| g. | | As "e," perf. 12 | 170.00 | 14.00 |
| 53B | A5 | 1p ver ('73) | 300.00 | 80.00 |
| 54 | A5 | 2p dp grn ('72) | 80.00 | 2.75 |
| a. | | 2p yellow green | 275.00 | 5.00 |
| b. | | 2p blue green | 57.50 | 2.75 |
| c. | | Imperf. pair | | 1,750. |
| d. | | 2p green, perf. 12 | 700.00 | 150.00 |
| e. | | Double impression | | |
| 55 | A5 | 3p brown | 80.00 | 5.00 |
| a. | | 3p purple brown | 80.00 | 5.00 |
| b. | | As "a," imperf. pair | | 1,150. |
| c. | | 3p brownish purple | 70.00 | 5.00 |
| 56 | A5 | 3p red brn ('71) | 90.00 | 5.00 |
| a. | | 3p indian red | 75.00 | 5.00 |
| b. | | Imperf. pair | 140.00 | |
| c. | | Vert. pair, imperf. horiz. | | |
| d. | | Perf. 12 | 145.00 | 24.00 |
| e. | | 3p deep red brown, perf. 12 | 145.00 | 24.00 |
| f. | | As "e," pair, imperf. between | | |
| 57 | A5 | 4p dull yel ('76) | 175.00 | 60.00 |
| a. | | Perf. 12 | 375.00 | 27.50 |
| b. | | 4p ocher | 100.00 | 10.00 |
| c. | | 4p buff | 85.00 | 12.00 |
| 58 | A5 | 9p blue | 32.50 | 9.00 |
| a. | | Imperf. pair | 575.00 | |
| b. | | Perf. 12 | 00.00 | 52.50 |
| c. | | Double impression | | *3,500.* |
| 59 | A5 | 5sh bright violet | 375.00 | 85.00 |
| a. | | Imperf. | | |
| b. | | Horiz. pair, imperf. vert. | | |
| c. | | Perf. 12 | 600.00 | 475.00 |
| d. | | 5sh purple | 375.00 | 85.00 |
| e. | | 5sh purple, perf. 12 | 575.00 | |
| | | Pen cancel | | 11.00 |
| | | *Nos. 53-59 (8)* | 1,151. | 249.25 |

*The reprints are on unwatermarked paper, the 5sh has also been reprinted on thin cardboard; all are perforated.*

**1878 Wmk. 77 *Perf. 14***

| No. | Type | Description | Unused | Used |
|---|---|---|---|---|
| 60 | A5 | 1p rose | 12.00 | 1.25 |
| 61 | A5 | 2p deep green | 12.00 | 1.25 |
| 62 | A5 | 8p violet brown | 15.00 | 10.00 |
| | | *Nos. 60-62 (3)* | 39.00 | 12.50 |

*The 8p has been reprinted on thin unwatermarked paper, perforated 11½.*

**1880-83 *Perf. 12, 11½***

| No. | Type | Description | Unused | Used |
|---|---|---|---|---|
| 63 | A5 | 3p indian red, perf. 12 | 10.00 | 9.00 |
| a. | | Imperf. pair | 475.00 | |
| b. | | Horiz. pair, imperf. between | *2,500.* | |
| c. | | Perf. 11½ | 25.00 | 5.50 |
| 64 | A5 | 4p lem, perf. 11½ ('83) | 85.00 | 20.00 |
| a. | | 4p olive yellow, perf. 11½ | 160.00 | 30.00 |
| b. | | Printed on both sides | *1,600.* | |
| c. | | Imperf. | | |
| d. | | 4p deep yellow, perf. 12 | 150.00 | 32.50 |

Type of 1871 Surcharged in Black

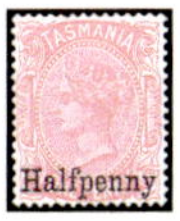

**1889 *Perf. 14***

| No. | Type | Description | Unused | Used |
|---|---|---|---|---|
| 65 | A5 | ½p on 1p carmine | 11.00 | *25.00* |
| a. | | "al" sideways in surcharge | *2,400.* | *2,100.* |

*No. 65 has been reprinted on thin cardboard, perforated 12, with the surcharge "Halfpenny" 19mm long.*

**1889-96 *Perf. 11½***

| No. | Type | Description | Unused | Used |
|---|---|---|---|---|
| 66 | A5 | ½p red orange | 3.25 | 3.50 |
| a. | | ½p yellow orange | 3.25 | 3.50 |
| b. | | Perf. 12 | 6.00 | *7.50* |
| 67 | A5 | 1p dull red | 17.50 | 3.50 |
| a. | | 1p vermilion | 14.00 | 3.00 |
| 68 | A5 | 1p car, perf. 12 | 8.25 | 3.25 |
| a. | | 1p pink, perf. 12 | 45.00 | 20.00 |
| b. | | 1p salmon rose, perf. 12 | 42.50 | 15.00 |
| c. | | Imperf. pair | 400.00 | *375.00* |

***Perf. 12***

| No. | Type | Description | Unused | Used |
|---|---|---|---|---|
| 69 | A5 | 4p bister ('96) | 16.00 | 7.50 |
| 70 | A5 | 9p chalky bl ('96) | 10.00 | 3.50 |
| | | *Nos. 66-70 (5)* | 55.00 | 21.25 |

**1891 Wmk. 76 *Perf. 11½***

| No. | Type | Description | Unused | Used |
|---|---|---|---|---|
| 71 | A5 | ½p orange | 80.00 | 60.00 |
| a. | | ½p brown orange | 60.00 | 55.00 |
| b. | | Imperf. pair | 325.00 | |
| c. | | Perf. 12 | 70.00 | 55.00 |
| 72 | A5 | 1p salmon rose | 25.00 | 11.00 |
| a. | | 1p carmine, perf. 12 | 50.00 | 50.00 |
| 73 | A5 | 4p ol bis, perf. 12 | 25.00 | 40.00 |
| | | *Nos. 71-73 (3)* | 130.00 | 111.00 |

See Nos. 98, 108-109.

Surcharged in Black

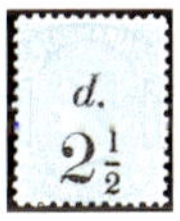

**1891 Wmk. 77 *Perf. 11½***

**Surcharge 14mm High**

| No. | Type | Description | Unused | Used |
|---|---|---|---|---|
| 74 | A5 | 2½p on 9p lt blue | 24.00 | 4.50 |
| a. | | Dbl. surcharge, one invtd. | 800.00 | *900.00* |
| b. | | Imperf. pair | — | |

***Perf. 12***

**Surcharge 15mm High**

| No. | Type | Description | Unused | Used |
|---|---|---|---|---|
| 75 | A5 | 2½p on 9p lt blue | 5.50 | 4.00 |
| a. | | Surcharged in blue | | |

*No. 74 has been reprinted on thin unwatermarked paper, imperforate. There is also a reprint on thin cardboard, in deep ultramarine, with surcharge 16½mm high, and perforated 12.*

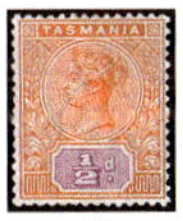
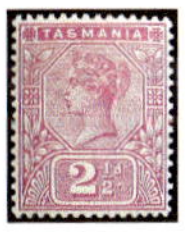

A8 A9

**1892-99 Typo. *Perf. 14***

| No. | Type | Description | Unused | Used |
|---|---|---|---|---|
| 76 | A8 | ½p orange & vio | 3.00 | 1.50 |
| 77 | A9 | 2½p magenta | 3.00 | 2.00 |
| 78 | A8 | 5p pale bl & brn | 9.00 | 4.00 |
| 79 | A8 | 6p blue vio & blk | 17.50 | 5.00 |
| 80 | A8 | 10p red brn & grn ('99) | 12.50 | 15.00 |
| 81 | A8 | 1sh rose & green | 13.00 | 3.50 |
| 82 | A8 | 2sh6p brown & blue | 40.00 | 42.50 |
| 83 | A8 | 5sh brn vio & red | 100.00 | 30.00 |
| 84 | A8 | 10sh brt vio & brn | 225.00 | 125.00 |
| 85 | A8 | £1 green & yel | 600.00 | 550.00 |
| | | *Nos. 76-85 (10)* | 1,023. | 778.50 |

No. 80 shows the numeral on white tablet.

See Nos. 99, 110-111.

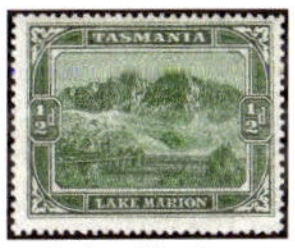
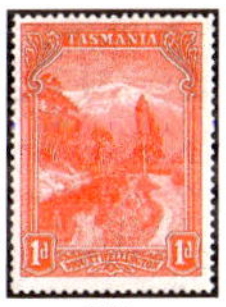

Lake Marion A10

Mt. Wellington A11

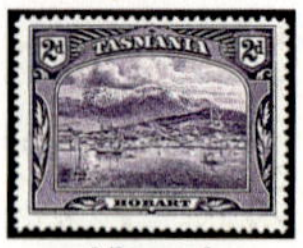


View of Hobart — A12

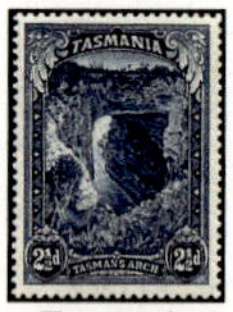


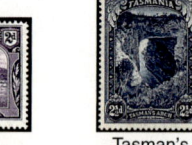

Tasman's Arch — A13

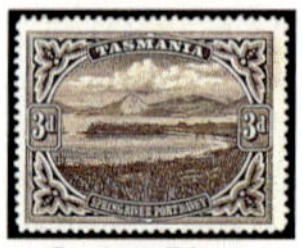


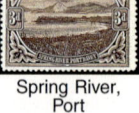

Spring River, Port Davey — A14

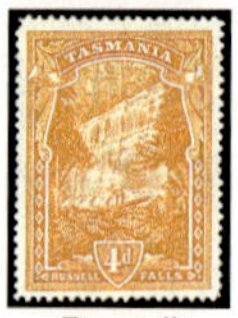


Russell Falls — A15

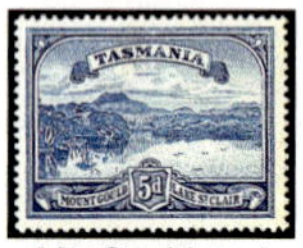


Mt. Gould and Lake St. Clair — A16

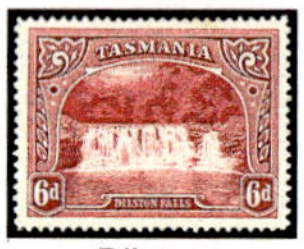


Dilston Falls — A17

**1899-1900 Engr. Wmk. 78 *Perf. 14***

| | | | | |
|---|---|---|---|---|
| **86** | A10 | ½p dark green | 10.00 | 7.00 |
| **87** | A11 | 1p carmine | 7.00 | 2.00 |
| **88** | A12 | 2p violet | 29.00 | 2.00 |
| **89** | A13 | 2½p dark blue | 27.50 | 4.00 |
| **90** | A14 | 3p dark brown | 25.00 | 6.50 |
| **91** | A15 | 4p ocher | 30.00 | 10.00 |
| **92** | A16 | 5p ultramarine | 50.00 | 12.50 |
| **93** | A17 | 6p lake | 35.00 | 45.00 |
| | | *Nos. 86-93 (8)* | 213.50 | 89.00 |

See Nos. 94-97, 102-107, 114-117.

***Perf. 11, 12½, 11x12½***

**1902-03 Litho., Typo. Wmk. 70**

| | | | | |
|---|---|---|---|---|
| **94** | A10 | ½p green | 6.50 | 1.75 |
| **95** | A11 | 1p carmine | 22.50 | 2.00 |
| **96** | A11 | 1p dull red | 22.50 | 5.00 |
| **97** | A12 | 2p violet | 16.00 | .80 |
| **98** | A5 | 9p blue | 25.00 | 4.00 |
| *a.* | | 9p ultramarine | 450.00 | |
| *b.* | | 9p indigo | 240.00 | |
| *c.* | | Perf. 11 | 9.00 | 20.00 |
| *d.* | | Perf 12½, wmkd. sideways | 40.00 | 17.00 |
| **99** | A8 | 1sh rose & green | 55.00 | 10.50 |
| *a.* | | Perf. 11 | 100.00 | 85.00 |
| | | *Nos. 94-99 (6)* | 147.50 | 24.05 |

Nos. 94, 97 are litho., Nos. 96, 98-99 typo. No. 95 was printed both ways.

No. 78 Surcharged in Black

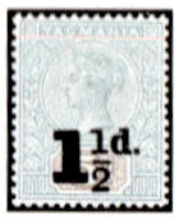


**1904 Wmk. 77 *Perf. 14***

| | | | | |
|---|---|---|---|---|
| **100** | A8 | 1½p on 5p blue & brn | 2.75 | 2.75 |

***Perf. 11, 12, 12½ and Compound***

**1905-08 Typo. Wmk. 13**

| | | | | |
|---|---|---|---|---|
| **102** | A10 | ½p dull green | 3.50 | 1.40 |
| *a.* | | Booklet pane of 12 | | |
| *b.* | | Perf. 11 | 3.50 | .80 |
| *c.* | | Compound perf. 12½, 11 | 140.00 | 35.00 |
| *d.* | | Compound perf. 11, 12 | 350.00 | |
| **103** | A11 | 1p carmine | 9.00 | .60 |
| *a.* | | Booklet pane of 18 | | |
| *b.* | | Perf. 11 | 8.00 | .35 |
| *c.* | | Compound perf. 12½, 11 | 6.00 | 7.50 |
| *d.* | | Compound perf. 12½, 12 | 195.00 | 70.00 |
| *e.* | | Compound perf. 11, 12 | 215.00 | 70.00 |
| **104** | A12 | 2p violet | 21.00 | 2.00 |
| *a.* | | Booklet pane of 18 | | |
| *b.* | | Perf. 11 | 7.50 | .35 |
| *c.* | | Compound perf. 12½, 11 | 45.00 | 20.00 |
| *d.* | | Compound perf. 12½, 12 | 490.00 | 150.00 |
| *e.* | | Compound perf. 11, 12 | 300.00 | 120.00 |
| **105** | A14 | 3p dark brown | 16.00 | 6.00 |
| *a.* | | Perf. 11 | 37.50 | 50.00 |
| *b.* | | Compound perf. 12½, 11 | 300.00 | 300.00 |
| **106** | A15 | 4p ocher | 25.00 | 5.00 |
| *a.* | | Perf. 11 | 70.00 | 24.00 |
| **107** | A17 | 6p lake | 85.00 | 10.00 |
| *a.* | | Perf. 11 | 105.00 | 10.00 |
| *b.* | | Compound perf. 12½, 11 | 540.00 | 540.00 |
| **108** | A5 | 8p violet brown | 22.50 | 9.00 |
| *a.* | | Perf. 11 | 23.00 | 9.00 |
| **109** | A5 | 9p blue | 9.00 | 8.00 |
| *a.* | | Perf. 11 | 9.00 | 12.00 |
| *b.* | | Compound perf. 12½, 11 | 130.00 | |
| *c.* | | Compound perf. 12½, 12 | 460.00 | |
| *d.* | | Compound perf. 11, 12 | 600.00 | |
| **110** | A8 | 1sh rose & green | 15.00 | 10.00 |
| *a.* | | Perf. 11 | 32.50 | 55.00 |
| *b.* | | Compound perf. 12½, 11 | 25.00 | 60.00 |
| *c.* | | Compound perf. 12½, 12 | 300.00 | |
| **111** | A8 | 10sh brt vio & brn | 325.00 | *350.00* |
| *a.* | | Perf. 11 | 475.00 | 475.00 |
| *b.* | | Compound perf. 12½, 12 | 515.00 | 515.00 |
| | | *Nos. 102-111 (10)* | 531.00 | 402.00 |

Nos. 104-107 also printed litho.

**1911 Redrawn**

| | | | | |
|---|---|---|---|---|
| **114** | A12 | 2p bright violet | 22.50 | 7.50 |
| *a.* | | Perf. 11 | 10.00 | 6.00 |
| *b.* | | Compound perf. 11, 12½ | 140.00 | 45.00 |
| *c.* | | Compound perf. 12, 12½ | 575.00 | |
| **115** | A15 | 4p dull yellow | 72.50 | 72.50 |
| *a.* | | Perf. 11 | 70.00 | 35.00 |
| **116** | A17 | 6p lake | 30.00 | *55.00* |
| *a.* | | Perf. 11 | 30.00 | 75.00 |
| *b.* | | Compound perf. 11, 12½ | 500.00 | |
| | | *Nos. 114-116 (3)* | 125.00 | 135.00 |

The redrawn 2p measures 33½x25mm instead of 32½x24½mm. There are many slight changes in the clouds and other parts of the design.

The 4p is much lighter, especially the waterfall and trees above it. This appears to be a new or cleaned plate rather than a redrawn one.

In the redrawn 6p there are more colored lines in the waterfall and the river and more white dots in the trees.

No. 114 Surcharged in Red

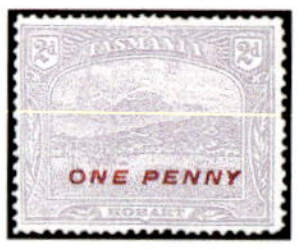


**1912**

| | | | | |
|---|---|---|---|---|
| **117** | A12 | 1p on 2p brt vio | 2.25 | 2.25 |
| *a.* | | Perf. 11 | 3.50 | 5.00 |
| *b.* | | Compound perf. 12½ 11 | 300.00 | *325.00* |

## POSTAL FISCAL STAMPS

Authorized for postal use by Act of November 1, 1882. Authorization withdrawn Nov. 30, 1900.

Used values are for examples with postal cancellations used from Nov. 1, 1882 through Nov. 30, 1900.

Beware of stamps with a pen cancellation removed, often regummed or with a fake postmark added.

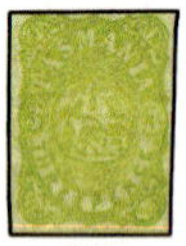

PF1

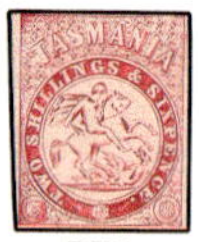

PF2

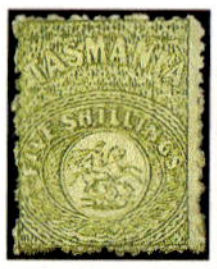

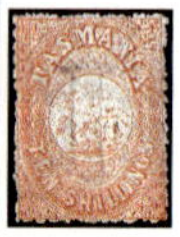

St. George and the Dragon
PF3 PF4

**1863-80 Engr. Wmk. 139 *Imperf.***

| | | | | |
|---|---|---|---|---|
| **AR1** | PF1 | 3p green | *800.00* | *300.00* |
| **AR2** | PF2 | 2sh 6p car | *800.00* | *300.00* |
| **AR3** | PF3 | 5sh green | *1,000.* | *450.00* |
| **AR4** | PF3 | 5sh brown | *1,500.* | *800.00* |
| **AR5** | PF4 | 10sh sal ('80) | *1,500.* | *800.00* |
| *a.* | | 10sh orange | *1,800.* | *800.00* |

For overprint see No. AR32.

***Perf. 10***

| | | | | |
|---|---|---|---|---|
| **AR6** | PF1 | 3p green | *550.00* | *225.00* |
| **AR7** | PF2 | 2sh 6p car | *450.00* | |
| **AR8** | PF3 | 5sh brown | *650.00* | |
| **AR9** | PF4 | 10sh orange | *600.00* | |

***Perf. 12***

| | | | | |
|---|---|---|---|---|
| **AR10** | PF1 | 3p green | *225.00* | *375.00* |
| **AR11** | PF2 | 2sh 6p car | *350.00* | *200.00* |
| **AR12** | PF3 | 5sh green | *500.00* | *225.00* |
| **AR13** | PF3 | 5sh brown | *650.00* | |
| **AR14** | PF4 | 10sh orange | *600.00* | *300.00* |

***Perf. 12½***

| | | | | |
|---|---|---|---|---|
| **AR15** | PF1 | 3p green | *650.00* | |
| **AR16** | PF2 | 2sh 6p car | *600.00* | |
| **AR17** | PF3 | 5sh brown | *900.00* | |
| **AR18** | PF4 | 10sh orange | *750.00* | |

***Perf. 11½***

| | | | | |
|---|---|---|---|---|
| **AR19** | PF1 | 3p green | *800.00* | |
| **AR20** | PF2 | 2sh 6p car | *400.00* | *200.00* |
| **AR21** | PF3 | 5sh green | *500.00* | *200.00* |
| **AR22** | PF4 | 10sh salmon | *600.00* | *350.00* |
| *a.* | | 10sh orange | *300.00* | *140.00* |

**Wmk. 77**

***Perf. 12***

| | | | | |
|---|---|---|---|---|
| **AR23** | PF2 | 2sh 6p car | 160.00 | 90.00 |
| *a.* | | Horiz. pair, imperf. btwn. | 2,500. | |

For overprint see No. AR33.

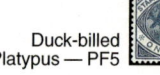

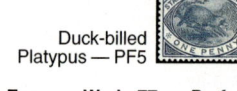

Duck-billed Platypus — PF5

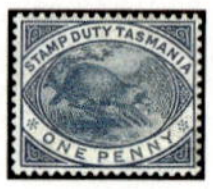


**1880 Engr. Wmk. 77 *Perf. 14***

| | | | | |
|---|---|---|---|---|
| **AR24** | PF5 | 1p slate | 60.00 | 12.00 |
| **AR25** | PF5 | 3p brown | 32.50 | 5.50 |
| **AR26** | PF5 | 6p lilac | 110.00 | 2.75 |
| **AR27** | PF5 | 1sh rose | 175.00 | 32.50 |

For overprints see Nos. AR28-AR31.

**Nos. AR24-AR27, AR2, AR23, 85 Overprinted "REVENUE"**

**1900, Nov. 15**

| | | | | |
|---|---|---|---|---|
| **AR28** | PF5 | 1p slate | 30.00 | 35.00 |
| **AR29** | PF5 | 3p brown | 42.50 | *40.00* |
| **AR30** | PF5 | 6p lilac | *125.00* | |
| **AR31** | PF5 | 1sh rose | *400.00* | 350.00 |
| **AR32** | PF2 | 2sh 6p car (#AR2) | *550.00* | 550.00 |
| **AR33** | PF2 | 2sh 6p car (#AR23) | *450.00* | |
| **AR34** | PF4 | 10sh orange | 850.00 | 800.00 |
| **AR35** | A8 | £1 grn & yel (#85) | 300.00 | *250.00* |

Nos. AR28-AR35 were not supposed to be postally used. Because of imprecise terminology, postal use was tolerated until all postal use of revenues ceased on Nov. 30, 1900.

Other denominations and watermarks were overprinted after postal use was no longer allowed.

# VICTORIA

vik-ˈtōr-ē-ə

LOCATION — In the extreme southeastern part of Australia
GOVT. — British Colony
AREA — 87,884 sq. mi.
POP. — 1,201,341 (1901)
CAPITAL — Melbourne

Victoria was one of the six former British colonies which united on Jan. 1, 1901, to form the Commonwealth of Australia.

12 Pence = 1 Shilling
20 Shillings = 1 Pound

Unused values for Nos. 1-16 are for stamps without gum as these stamps are seldom found with original gum. Otherwise, unused values are for stamps with original gum as defined in the catalogue introduction.

Very fine examples of all rouletted, perforated and serrate perforated stamps from Nos. 9-109 and F2 will have roulettes, perforations or serrate perforations touching the design. Examples clear on four sides range from scarce to rare and will command higher prices.

**Watermarks**

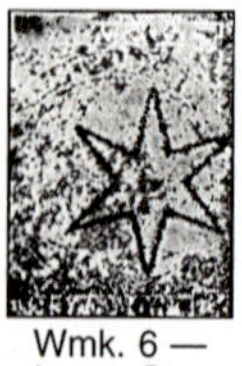

Wmk. 6 — Large Star

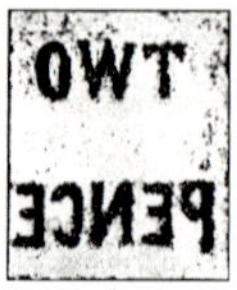

Wmk. 80

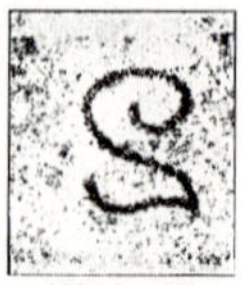

Wmk. 50

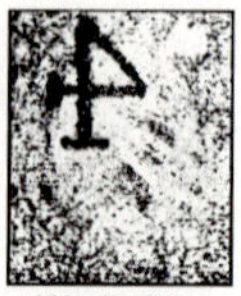

Wmk. 80a

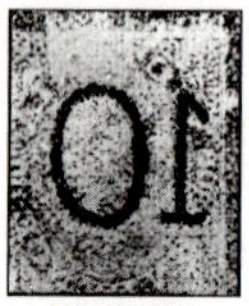

Wmk. 81

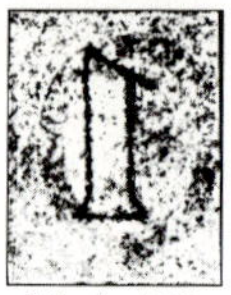

Wmk. 139

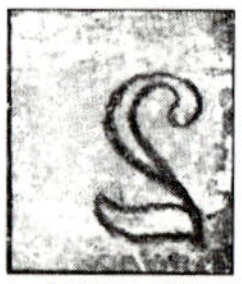

Wmk. 49

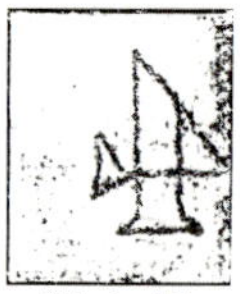

Wmk. 75

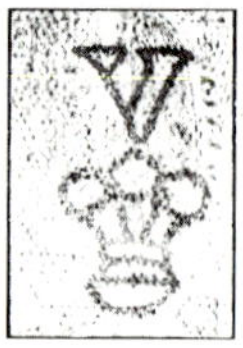

Wmk. 70 — V and Crown

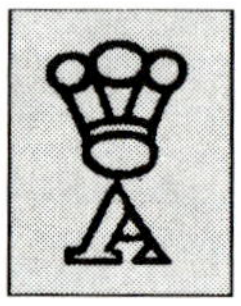

Wmk. 13 — Crown & Double-lined A

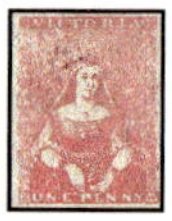

Queen Victoria — A1

**A1 TYPES**

1p:

Type I — "VICTORIA" very close to top of design, with very thin line of color between "VICTORIA" and frameline.

Type II — Thicker line of color between "VICTORIA" and frameline at top.

2p:

Type I — Border, two sets of nine wavy lines crisscrossing. Background, 22 groups of wavy triple lines below "VICTORIA."

Type II — Border, same. Background, 15 groups of wavy triple lines below "VICTORIA."

Type III — Border, two sets of five wavy lines crisscrossing. Background, same as type II.

3p:

Type I — Orb poorly defined, with white area at right and thicker at left. Central band of orb does not protrude at left.

Type II — Orb clearly defined, with white outlines at left and right. Central band of orb protrudes at left.

**1850 Litho. Unwmk. *Imperf.***

| | | | | |
|---|---|---|---|---|
| **1** | A1 | 1p dull red, II | 4,000. | 225.00 |
| *a.* | | 1p dull org ver, II | 5,500. | 750.00 |
| *b.* | | 1p brownish red, II ('51) | 1,500. | 210.00 |
| *c.* | | 1p dull brown, I | *19,000.* | 2,500. |
| *d.* | | 1p orange vermilion, I | *30,000.* | 5,500. |
| *e.* | | 1p orange brown, I | | 2,100. |
| **2** | A1 | 1p rose, II | *3,500.* | 200.00 |
| *a.* | | 1p pink, II | *1,750.* | 190.00 |
| *b.* | | 1p reddish brown, II ('51) | *5,500.* | 190.00 |
| **3** | A1 | 3p blue, I | *6,500.* | 450.00 |
| *a.* | | 3p light blue, II ('52) | *2,250.* | 110.00 |
| *b.* | | 3p bright blue, I | 7,500. | 625.00 |
| **4** | A1 | 3p indigo, II | *3,000.* | 100.00 |
| *a.* | | 3p pale grnsh blue, II ('52) | *3,500.* | 210.00 |
| | | *Nos. 1-4 (4)* | 17,000. | 975.00 |

Nos. 1-4 exist with and without frame line.

| | | | | |
|---|---|---|---|---|
| **5** | A1 | 2p lilac, I | *7,500.* | 550.00 |
| *a.* | | 2p brn lilac, I | *7,000.* | 550.00 |
| *b.* | | 2p orange brown, I | | *2,500.* |
| **6** | A1 | 2p brn lilac, II | 2,500. | 250.00 |
| *a.* | | 2p gray lilac, II | *6,000.* | 200.00 |
| **7** | A1 | 2p brn lilac, III | *7,250.* | 200.00 |
| *a.* | | 2p gray lilac, III | *11,000.* | 500.00 |
| *b.* | | Value omitted, III | | *17,500.* |
| **8** | A1 | 2p yel brn, III | 3,000. | 200.00 |

AUSTRALIAN STATES — Victoria 715

***Rouletted 7***

9 A1 1p vermilion — *3,350.*
10 A1 3p blue 2,500. 250.00
*a.* 3p deep blue *2,500.* 300.00

***Perf. 12***

12 A1 3p blue *2,000.* 175.00
*a.* 3p deep blue *2,000.* 175.00

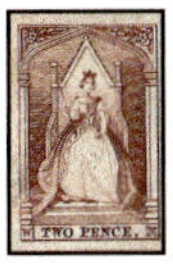

Victoria on Throne — A2

**1852 Engr. *Imperf.***

14 A2 2p reddish brn 900.00 35.00
*a.* 2p chestnut 150.00
*b.* 2p purple brown 1,000. 30.00

No. 14 was reprinted on paper with watermark 70, imperf. & perf. 12½, overprinted "REPRINT."

**1854 Litho.**

15 A2 2p gray brown 1,200. 45.00
*a.* 2p purple black 45.00
16 A2 2p brown lilac 300.00 40.00
*a.* 2p red lilac — 37.50
*b.* As "a," "TVO" for "TWO" *10,000.* 1,500.

Fifty varieties.

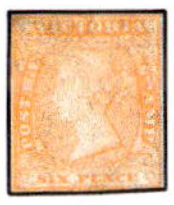

A3

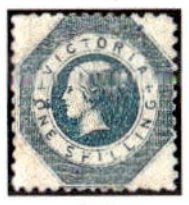

A4

**1854-58 Typo.**

17 A3 6p yellow orange 750.00 20.00
*a.* 6p dull orange 750.00 20.00
*b.* 6p reddish brown 1,250. 75.00

See Nos. 19-20, 22-24A, 26-28.

**Lithographed**

18 A4 1sh blue 450.00 17.50
*a.* 1sh greenish blue 450.00 14.00
*b.* 1sh indigo blue — 50.00

See Nos. 21, 25.

**Typographed**

19 A3 2sh green 3,000. 250.00

**1857-58 *Rouletted 7, 9½***

20 A3 6p orange — 87.50
*a.* 6p yellow orange — 100.00
*b.* 6p reddish brown — 115.00

**Lithographed**

21 A4 1sh blue — 160.00
*a.* 1sh greenish blue — 160.00

**Typographed**

22 A3 2sh green ('58) *7,000.* 675.00

***Small Serrate Perf. 19***

23 A3 6p orange — 125.00

***Large Serpentine Perf. 10½***

24 A3 6p orange — 125.00

***Serrate x Serpentine Perf.***

24A A3 6p orange — 200.00

**1859 Litho. *Perf. 12***

25 A4 1sh blue 250.00 25.00
*a.* 1sh greenish blue 275.00 27.50
*b.* 1sh indigo blue 52.50

**Typographed**

26 A3 2sh green 525.00 70.00

**1861 Wmk. "SIX PENCE" (80)**

27 A3 6p black 300.00 80.00

**Wmk. Single-lined "2" (50)**

**1864 *Perf. 12, 13***

28 A3 2sh blue, *green* 350.00 13.00

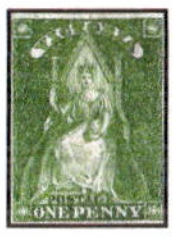

A5

**Wmk. Large Star (6)**

**1856, Oct. Engr. *Imperf.***

29 A5 1p green 250.00 42.50

**1858 *Rouletted 5½-6½***

30 A5 6p blue 350.00 28.00
*a.* 6p light blue 450.00 45.00

Nos. 29 and 30 have been reprinted on paper watermarked V and Crown. They are imperforate and overprinted "REPRINT."

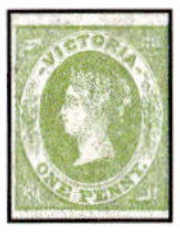

A6

**1857-61 Typo. *Imperf.***

**Wove Paper**

31 A6 1p yellow green 175.00 25.00
*a.* Printed on both sides *2,750.*
*b.* 1p deep green 230.00 47.50
32 A6 4p vermilion 450.00 15.00
*a.* Printed on both sides *2,750.*
*b.* 4p brownish vermilion 425.00 15.00
33 A6 4p rose 375.00 15.00
*a.* 4p dull red 260.00 12.00

***Rouletted 7 to 9½***

34 A6 1p yellow green 625.00 140.00
35 A6 4p rose — 57.50
*a.* 4p vermilion 160.00
*b.* 4p dull red 60.00
35A A6 4p vermilion 575.00

***Perf. 12***

36 A6 1p yellow green — 500.00

**Unwmk. *Imperf.***

37 A6 1p blue green 425.00 22.50
*a.* 1p emerald green 22.50
38 A6 2p lilac 400.00 21.00
*a.* 2p gray lilac 400.00 20.00
39 A6 4p rose *575.00* 47.50
*a.* 4p rose pink 575.00 42.50
*b.* 4p reddish pink 47.50

Examples of No. 39 printed in dull carmine on thin paper are regarded as printer's waste and of little value. They are also found printed on both sides.

***Rouletted 7 to 9½***

40 A6 1p emerald green 575.00 37.50
*a.* 1p pale emerald 525.00 35.00
41 A6 2p lilac 1,150. 725.00
42 A6 4p rose pink 400.00 11.50
*a.* Vert. pair, imperf. btwn. *750.00*
*b.* 4p reddish pink 20.00
*c.* 4p bright rose 400.00 11.50

***Perf. 12***

43 A6 1p blue green 225.00 20.00
*a.* 1p yellow green 325.00 24.00
*b.* Horiz. pair, imperf. btwn. —
*c.* As "a," on thin, glazed "Bordeaux" paper 240.00
44 A6 2p lilac 450.00
*a.* 2p gray lilac 400.00
45 A6 4p rose 300.00 8.00
*b.* Vert. pair, imperf. btwn. —

***Rouletted 5½-6½***

45C A6 4p dull rose 1,250.

***Serrate Rouletted 19***

45A A6 2p lilac 1,100. 600.00

**Laid Paper**

***Imperf***

46 A6 4p rose 825.00 35.00

***Rouletted 5 to 7***

47 A6 2p violet 275.00 10.50
*a.* 2p brown lilac 225.00 15.00
*b.* 2p dark lilac 300.00 25.00
48 A6 4p rose 250.00 7.25
*a.* 4p pale dull red, vertically laid paper 260.00 7.25
*b.* 4p pale dull red, horizontally laid paper *1,250.*
*c.* 4p dull rose red 225.00 6.25

***Serrate Rouletted 19***

48D A6 4p rose red *825.00*

***Perf. 12***

49 A6 1p green 300.00 25.00
*a.* Laid lines close together 35.00
50 A6 4p rose 200.00 15.00
*a.* Laid lines close together 13.00

**Wove Paper**

**1860 Wmk. Value in Words (80)**

51 A6 1p pale yellowish green 130.00 10.50
*a.* Wmk. "FOUR PENCE" (error) *9,750.*
*b.* 1p yellow green 125.00 7.25
52 A6 2p gray lilac 200.00 10.00
*a.* 2p brown lilac ('61) — 60.00
*b.* 2p bluish slate ('61) 200.00 9.50
*c.* 2p slate gray ('62) 9.50
*d.* 2p bluish gray ('63) 230.00 35.00

**Wmk. "THREE PENCE" (80)**

53 A6 2p bluish gray ('63) 225.00 25.00
*a.* 2p gray lilac ('62) 325.00 22.50

**Single-lined "2" (50)**

54 A6 2p lilac 300.00 18.00
*a.* 2p gray lilac 275.00 22.50
*b.* 2p brown lilac 225.00 21.00
*c.* As "a," wmkd. single-lined "6" *7,750.*
*d.* 2p gray violet ('63) 220.00 20.00
*e.* 2p slate ('63) 290.00 35.00

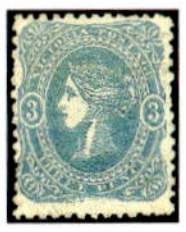

A7

**1860 Unwmk. Laid Paper**

56 A7 3p deep blue 650.00 77.50

**Wmk. Value in Words (80)**

***Perf. 11½ to 12***

**1860-64 Wove Paper**

57 A7 3p blue ('63) 350.00 7.00
*a.* "TRREE" instead of "THREE" in watermark 750.00
*b.* 3p pale blue ('61) 350.00 8.00
*c.* 3p bright blue ('61) 350.00 10.00
*d.* 3p deep blue ('64) 350.00 7.00
58 A7 3p claret 425.00 32.50
*a.* Perf. 13 450.00 35.00
59 A7 4p rose 200.00 5.00
*a.* 4p rose pink 10.00
*b.* 4p rose red 200.00 5.00
*c.* 4p rose carmine 10.00
60 A7 6p orange *8,500.* 400.00
61 A7 6p black 500.00 10.50
*a.* 6p gray black 500.00 10.50

**Wmk. "FIVE SHILLINGS" (80)**

62 A7 4p rose *3,750.* 25.00

**Wmk. Single-lined "4" (80a)**

**1863 *Imperf.***

63 A7 4p rose — *80.00*

***Rouletted***

64 A7 4p rose *2,500.* 275.00

***Perf. 11½ to 12***

65 A7 4p rose 180.00 10.50

**1863 Unwmk. *Perf. 12***

66 A7 4p rose 625.00 50.00
*a.* 4p rose pink, thin glazed "Bordeaux" paper 50.00
*b.* 4p rose, thick coarse paper 625.00 50.00

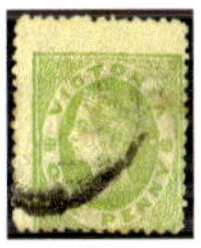

A8

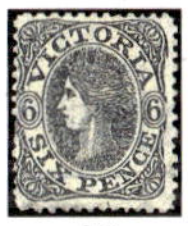

A9

**1861-63 Wmk. 80 *Perf. 11½ to 12***

67 A8 1p green 190.00 27.50
*a.* 1p olive green 30.00
68 A9 6p black 275.00 24.00
*a.* 6p gray black 275.00 25.00
*b.* 6p jet black 300.00 27.50

**Wmk. Double-lined "1" (139)**

69 A8 1p green 300.00 30.00
*a.* 1p dull green — 30.00
*b.* Horiz. pair, imperf between —

**Wmk. Single-lined Figures (50)**

70 A8 1p green 160.00 22.50
*a.* 1p apple green 100.00 21.00
*b.* 1p olive green 160.00 30.00
71 A9 6p gray black 200.00 8.00
*a.* 6p jet black — 10.00
*b.* 6p jet black, perf 13 250.00 10.00
*c.* 6p gray black, perf 13 200.00 8.00

The 1p and 6p of 1861-63 are known on paper without watermark but were probably impressions on the margins of watermarked sheets.

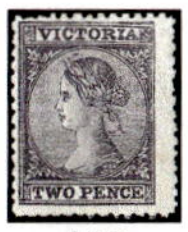

A10

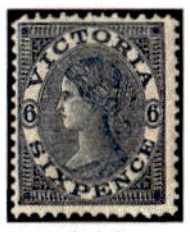

A11

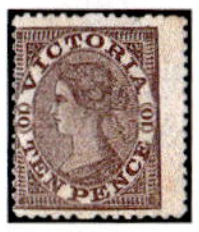

A12

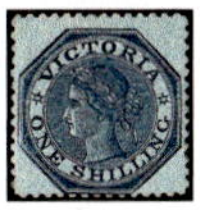

A13

**Wmk. Single-lined Figures (50, 80a, 81)**

**1863-67 *Perf. 11½ to 13***

74 A10 1p green 120.00 9.00
*a.* Double impression 1,500.
75 A10 2p gray lilac 140.00 10.00
*a.* 2p violet 160.00 15.00
76 A10 4p rose 190.00 4.00
*a.* Double impression 1,500.
77 A11 6p blue 150.00 5.00
78 A10 8p orange 900.00 140.00
79 A12 10p brn, *rose* 350.00 8.00
80 A13 1sh blue, *blue* 200.00 5.00
*Nos. 74-80 (7)* 2,050. 181.00

See Nos. 81-82, 84-96, 99-101, 108-112, 115-119, 124-126, 144, 188. Compare type A11 with type A54.

A14

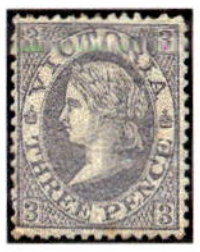

**Wmk. Double-lined "1" (139)**

81 A10 1p green 125.00 7.00
82 A10 2p gray lilac 325.00 10.50
83 A14 3p lilac 325.00 100.00
84 A11 6p blue 115.00 9.50
*Nos. 81-84 (4)* 890.00 127.00

See Nos. 97, 113, 114, 155, 186. Compare type A14 with type A51.

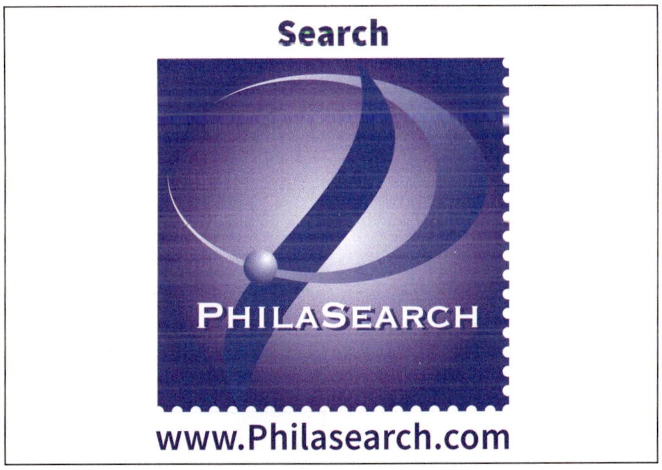

716 AUSTRALIAN STATES — Victoria

**Wmk. Double-lined "2" (49)**

| | | | | |
|---|---|---|---|---|
| 85 | A11 | 6p blue | *4,250.* | |

**Wmk. Single-lined "4" (80a)**

| | | | | |
|---|---|---|---|---|
| 86 | A10 | 1p green | 200.00 | 30.00 |
| 87 | A10 | 2p gray lilac | 250.00 | 10.50 |
| 88 | A11 | 6p blue | *2,750.* | |

**Wmk. Double-lined "4" (75)**

| | | | | |
|---|---|---|---|---|
| 89 | A10 | 1p green | 2,500. | 160.00 |
| 90 | A10 | 2p gray lilac | 250.00 | 8.00 |
| 91 | A10 | 4p rose | 300.00 | 9.50 |
| 92 | A11 | 6p blue | 325.00 | 35.00 |

**Wmk. Single-lined "6" (50)**

| | | | | |
|---|---|---|---|---|
| 93 | A10 | 1p green | 325.00 | 42.50 |
| 94 | A10 | 2p gray lilac | 350.00 | 11.50 |

**Wmk. Single-lined "8" (50)**

| | | | | |
|---|---|---|---|---|
| 95 | A10 | 1p green | 300.00 | 27.50 |
| 96 | A10 | 2p gray lilac | 325.00 | 10.50 |
| 97 | A14 | 3p lilac | 250.00 | 57.50 |
| 99 | A12 | 10p slate | 1,000. | 200.00 |

**Wmk. "SIX PENCE" (80)**

| | | | | |
|---|---|---|---|---|
| 100 | A10 | 1p green | 1,150. | 57.50 |
| 100A | A10 | 2p slate gray | | *16,000.* |
| 101 | A11 | 6p blue | 800.00 | 42.50 |
| *a.* | | 6p indigo blue | — | 42.50 |

All values of the 1864-67 series except the 3p and 8p are known on unwatermarked paper. They are probably varieties from watermarked sheets which have been so placed on the printing press that some of the stamps escaped the watermark.

One example of the 2p gray lilac, type A10, is reported to exist with only "PENCE" of watermark 80 showing. Some believe this is part of the "SIX PENCE" watermark.

**1870 Wmk. "THREE PENCE" (80)**

| | | | | |
|---|---|---|---|---|
| 108 | A11 | 6p blue | 525.00 | 37.50 |

**Wmk. "FOUR PENCE" (80)**

| | | | | |
|---|---|---|---|---|
| 109 | A11 | 6p blue | 800.00 | 55.00 |

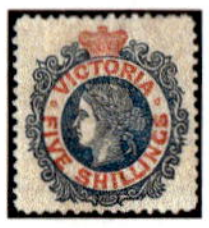
A15

**1867-78 Wmk. (70) *Perf. 11½ to 13***

| | | | | |
|---|---|---|---|---|
| 110 | A10 | 1p green | 125.00 | 4.50 |
| *a.* | | 1p bright olive green | 190.00 | 25.00 |
| 111 | A10 | 2p lilac | 120.00 | 4.00 |
| *a.* | | 2p gray lilac | 150.00 | 6.50 |
| 112 | A10 | 2p lilac, *lilac* | 140.00 | 7.00 |
| 113 | A14 | 3p red lilac | 550.00 | 60.00 |
| *a.* | | 3p lilac | 550.00 | 60.00 |
| 114 | A14 | 3p orange | 185.00 | 12.00 |
| *a.* | | 3p yellow | 100.00 | 20.00 |
| *b.* | | 3p org brn, glazed paper ('78) | 75.00 | 35.00 |
| 115 | A10 | 4p rose | 150.00 | 9.00 |
| *a.* | | 4p dl rose, glazed paper ('79) | 150.00 | 7.00 |
| *b.* | | Wmk sideways | | 80.00 |
| 116 | A11 | 6p blue | 100.00 | 7.00 |
| 117 | A11 | 6p ultra | 120.00 | 9.00 |
| *a.* | | 6p lilac blue | 130.00 | 17.50 |
| *b.* | | 6p light Prussian blue ('75) | 160.00 | 9.00 |
| 118 | A10 | 8p brn, *rose* | 140.00 | 9.00 |
| *a.* | | 8p choc, *pink* ('78) | 300.00 | 11.50 |
| *b.* | | Perf. 13x12 | | *350.00* |
| 119 | A13 | 1sh bl, *blue* | 300.00 | 25.00 |
| 120 | A15 | 5sh bl, *yel* | 4,500. | 500.00 |
| 121 | A15 | 5sh bl & rose | 700.00 | 25.00 |
| *a.* | | Without blue line under crown | 700.00 | 30.00 |
| *b.* | | 5sh ind bl & car | 850.00 | 60.00 |
| 122 | A15 | 5sh ultra & rose | 750.00 | 30.00 |

See Nos. 126, 144, 188. For surcharge see No. 124.

For additional stamps of type A15, see No. 191. Compare type A15 with type A58.

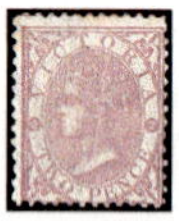
A16

**1870 *Perf. 13***

| | | | | |
|---|---|---|---|---|
| 123 | A16 | 2p lilac | 115.00 | 4.00 |
| *a.* | | Perf. 12 | 125.00 | 3.50 |

No. 110 Surcharged in Red

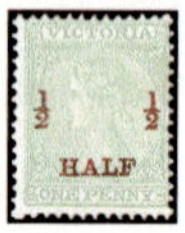

**1873, July 19 *Perf. 13, 12***

| | | | | |
|---|---|---|---|---|
| 124 | A10 | ½p on 1p green | 100.00 | 24.00 |
| *a.* | | Perf. 12 | 125.00 | 24.00 |

No. 79 Surcharged in Blue

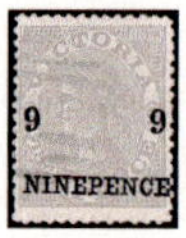

**1871 Wmk. Single-lined "10" (81)**

| | | | | |
|---|---|---|---|---|
| 125 | A12 | 9p on 10p brn, *rose* | 950.00 | 20.00 |
| *a.* | | Double surcharge | | *3,500.* |

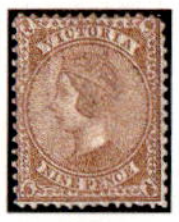
A19

**1873-78 Typo.**

| | | | | |
|---|---|---|---|---|
| 126 | A10 | 8p brown, *rose* ('78) | 250.00 | 6.50 |
| 127 | A19 | 9p brown, *rose* | 225.00 | 50.00 |

For additional stamps of type A19, see Nos. 128-129, 174-175. Compare type A19 with type A55.

**1875 Wmk. V and Crown (70)**

| | | | | |
|---|---|---|---|---|
| 128 | A19 | 9p brown, *rose* | 225.00 | 50.00 |

No. 128 Surcharged in Blue

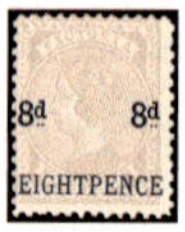

**1876**

| | | | | |
|---|---|---|---|---|
| 129 | A19 | 8p on 9p brn, *rose* | 700.00 | 40.00 |

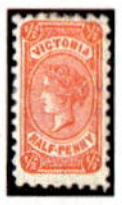
A21

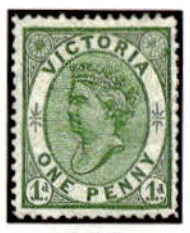
A22

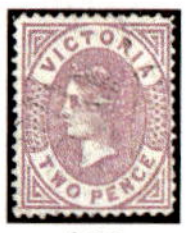
A23

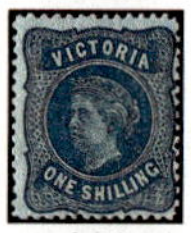
A24

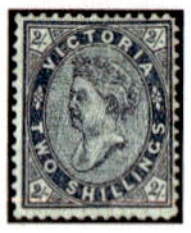
A25

**1873-81 *Perf. 13, 12***

| | | | | |
|---|---|---|---|---|
| 130 | A21 | ½p rose ('74) | 40.00 | 3.50 |
| *a.* | | ½p pink, glazed paper ('80) | 37.50 | 3.50 |
| *b.* | | ½p lil rose ('74) | 40.00 | 3.50 |
| 131 | A21 | ½p rose, *rose* ('78) | 100.00 | 55.00 |
| 132 | A22 | 1p grn ('75) | 80.00 | 2.75 |
| *a.* | | 1p yel grn, glazed paper | 90.00 | 2.50 |
| 133 | A22 | 1p grn, *gray* ('78) | 300.00 | 85.00 |
| 134 | A22 | 1p grn, *yel* ('78) | 175.00 | 45.00 |
| 135 | A23 | 2p violet | 100.00 | 1.30 |
| *a.* | | 2p pale mv ('80) | 100.00 | 1.25 |
| *b.* | | 2p pale mv, glazed paper ('79) | 100.00 | 1.60 |
| 136 | A23 | 2p vio, *grnsh* ('78) | 400.00 | 55.00 |
| 137 | A23 | 2p vio, *buff* ('78) | 375.00 | 55.00 |
| 137A | A23 | 2p vio, *lil* ('78) | — | *1,500.* |
| 138 | A24 | 1sh bl, *bl* ('76) | 175.00 | 5.00 |
| *a.* | | 1sh brt bl, *bl*, glazed paper ('83) | 200.00 | 6.00 |
| 139 | A25 | 2sh bl, *grn* ('81) | 325.00 | 25.00 |
| *a.* | | 2sh ultra, *grnsh*, glazed paper ('84) | | 45.00 |
| *b.* | | Wmk sideways | 325.00 | 25.00 |

See Nos. 140, 156A-158, 184, 189-190. Compare design A21 with design A46, A24 with A56, A25 with A57.

**1878 Double-lined Outer Oval**

| | | | | |
|---|---|---|---|---|
| 140 | A23 | 2p violet | 100.00 | 1.50 |
| *b.* | | Vert. pair, lower stamp imperf horiz. | | *3,500.* |

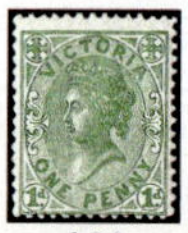
A26

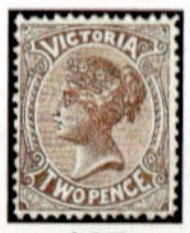
A27

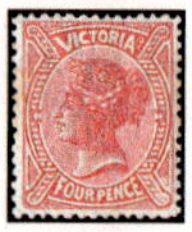
A28

**1880-84 *Perf. 12½***

| | | | | |
|---|---|---|---|---|
| 141 | A26 | 1p green ('84) | 200.00 | 30.00 |
| 142 | A27 | 2p brown | 85.00 | 4.50 |
| 143 | A27 | 2p lilac | 85.00 | 6.00 |
| 144 | A10 | 4p car rose | 125.00 | 10.00 |
| *a.* | | 4p lilac rose | 125.00 | 10.00 |
| 145 | A28 | 4p car rose ('81) | 125.00 | 10.00 |
| *a.* | | 4p pink ('82) | 125.00 | 9.50 |
| | | *Nos. 141-145 (5)* | 620.00 | 60.50 |

See Nos. 156, 185, 187. Compare design A26 with design A47, A27 with A49, A28 with A52.

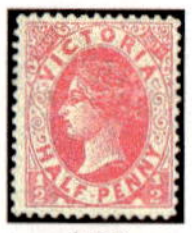
A29

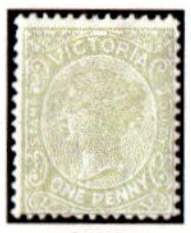
A30

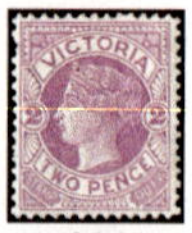
A31

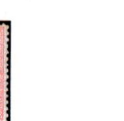

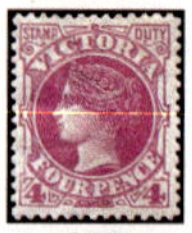
A32

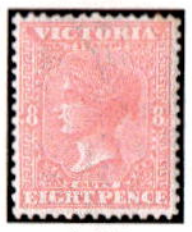
A33

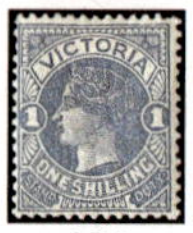
A34

**1884-86**

| | | | | |
|---|---|---|---|---|
| 146 | A29 | ½p rose | 35.00 | 3.50 |
| *a.* | | ½p salmon ('85) | 42.50 | 4.50 |
| 147 | A30 | 1p green | 35.00 | 4.50 |
| *a.* | | 1p pea green | 35.00 | 4.50 |
| 148 | A31 | 2p violet | 65.00 | 3.50 |
| *a.* | | 2p lilac rose | 75.00 | 3.50 |
| 149 | A30 | 3p bister | 70.00 | 5.00 |
| *a.* | | 3p ocher | 14.00 | 2.50 |
| 150 | A32 | 4p magenta | 125.00 | 8.50 |
| *a.* | | 4p violet (error) | *12,500.* | *1,750.* |
| 151 | A30 | 6p bright blue ('85) | 150.00 | 12.00 |
| *a.* | | 6p ultramarine ('85) | 190.00 | 14.00 |
| *b.* | | 6p gray blue ('85) | 150.00 | 5.00 |
| 152 | A33 | 8p rose, *rose* | 35.00 | 17.50 |
| 153 | A34 | 1sh blue, *yel* | 190.00 | 22.50 |
| 154 | A33 | 2sh olive, *grn* | 160.00 | 6.50 |
| | | *Nos. 146-154 (9)* | 865.00 | 83.50 |

See Nos. 177-178, 192A. Compare designs A31-A32 with designs A37-A38.

Nos. 114, 145, 138-139 Ovptd. Vertically in Blue or Black

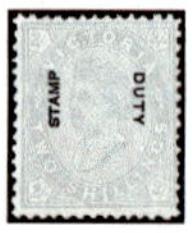

**1885**

| | | | | |
|---|---|---|---|---|
| 155 | A14 | 3p orange (Bl) | 75.00 | 60.00 |
| 156 | A28 | 4p car rose (Bl) | 65.00 | 85.00 |
| 156A | A24 | 1sh bl, *bl* (Bl) | 6,000. | *2,500.* |
| | | Revenue cancel | | *400.00* |
| 157 | A24 | 1sh bl, *bl* (Bk) | 140.00 | 60.00 |
| 158 | A25 | 2sh bl, *grn* (Bk) | 190.00 | 20.00 |
| *a.* | | Wmk sideways | 210.00 | 27.50 |
| | | *Nos. 155-156,157-158 (4)* | 470.00 | 225.00 |

Reprints of 4p and 1sh have brighter colors than originals. They lack the overprint "REPRINT."

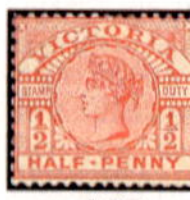
A35

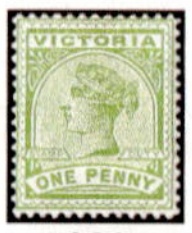
A36

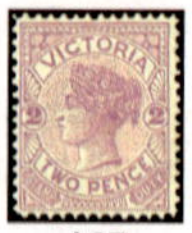
A37

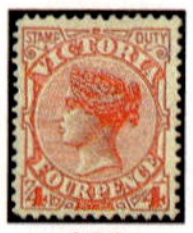
A38

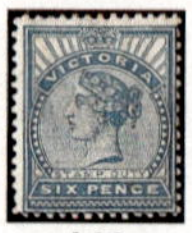
A39

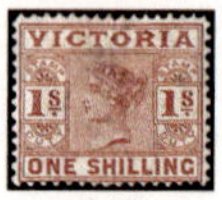
A40

**1886-87 *Perf. 12½***

| | | | | |
|---|---|---|---|---|
| 159 | A35 | ½p lilac | 50.00 | 14.00 |
| 160 | A35 | ½p rose | 17.50 | 1.40 |
| 160A | A35 | ½p scarlet | 15.00 | 1.50 |
| 161 | A36 | 1p green | 25.00 | 4.00 |
| 162 | A37 | 2p violet | 15.00 | 1.00 |
| *a.* | | 2p red lilac | 15.00 | 1.00 |
| *b.* | | Imperf. | | *1,100.* |
| 163 | A38 | 4p red | 27.50 | 1.50 |
| 164 | A39 | 6p blue | 50.00 | 1.25 |
| 165 | A39 | 6p ultra | 55.00 | 1.10 |
| 166 | A40 | 1sh lilac brown | 125.00 | 60.00 |
| | | *Nos. 159-166 (9)* | 380.00 | 85.75 |

See No. 180.

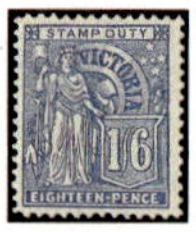
A41

**1889**

| | | | | |
|---|---|---|---|---|
| 167 | A41 | 1sh6p blue | 190.00 | 85.00 |
| 168 | A41 | 1sh6p orange | 45.00 | 15.00 |

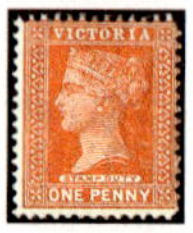
A42

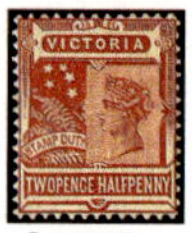
Southern Cross
A43

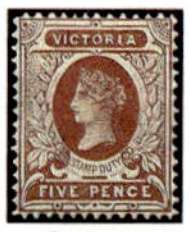
Queen Victoria
A44

**1890-95 *Perf. 12½***

| | | | | |
|---|---|---|---|---|
| 169 | A42 | 1p org brn | 37.50 | 1.50 |
| *a.* | | 1p chocolate brown | 37.50 | 1.50 |
| 170 | A42 | 1p yel brn | 37.50 | 1.00 |
| 171 | A42 | 1p brn org, *pink* ('91) | 37.50 | 1.00 |
| 172 | A43 | 2½p brn red, *yel* | 30.00 | 1.00 |
| 173 | A44 | 5p choc ('91) | 42.50 | 4.00 |
| 174 | A19 | 9p green ('92) | 32.50 | 16.00 |
| 175 | A19 | 9p rose red | 75.00 | 27.50 |
| *a.* | | 9p rose ('95) | 75.00 | 30.00 |
| 176 | A40 | 1sh deep claret | 60.00 | 4.00 |
| *a.* | | 1sh red brown | 60.00 | 8.50 |
| *b.* | | 1sh maroon | 100.00 | 7.00 |
| 177 | A33 | 2sh yel grn | 37.50 | 95.00 |
| 178 | A33 | 2sh emerald | 25.00 | 37.50 |
| | | *Nos. 169-178 (10)* | 415.00 | 188.50 |

In 1891 many stamps of the early issues were reprinted. They are on paper watermarked V and Crown, perforated 12, 12½, and overprinted "REPRINT."

See Nos. 181, 183, 192. Compare type A43 with type A50, A44 with A53.

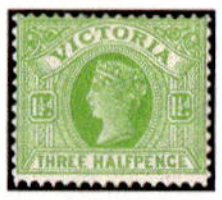
A45

**1897**

| | | | | |
|---|---|---|---|---|
| 179 | A45 | 1½p yellow green | 3.25 | *9.50* |

See No. 182. Compare type A45 with type A48.

**1899**

| | | | | |
|---|---|---|---|---|
| 180 | A35 | ½p emerald | 5.50 | 4.50 |
| 181 | A42 | 1p brt rose | 20.00 | 1.00 |
| 182 | A45 | 1½p red, *yel* | 5.00 | 8.50 |
| 183 | A43 | 2½p dark blue | 55.00 | 3.50 |
| | | *Nos. 180-183 (4)* | 85.50 | 17.50 |

**1901**

| | | | | |
|---|---|---|---|---|
| 184 | A21 | ½p blue green | 3.00 | 4.50 |
| *a.* | | "VICTCRIA" | 45.00 | 70.00 |
| 185 | A27 | 2p violet | 17.50 | 6.00 |
| 186 | A14 | 3p brown org | 16.00 | 6.00 |
| 187 | A28 | 4p bister | 27.50 | 37.50 |
| 188 | A11 | 6p emerald | 14.00 | 20.00 |
| 189 | A24 | 1sh orange yel | 87.50 | 50.00 |
| 190 | A25 | 2sh blue, *rose* | 45.00 | 80.00 |
| 191 | A15 | 5sh rose red & bl | 60.00 | 85.00 |
| | | *Nos. 184-191 (8)* | 270.50 | 289.00 |

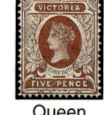

# AUSTRALIAN STATES — Victoria

## 1901

| | | | | |
|---|---|---|---|---|
| 192 | A42 | 1p olive green | 14.00 | 4.50 |
| 192A | A30 | 3p sage green | 42.50 | 24.00 |

Nos. 192-192A were available for postal use until June 30, 1901, and thereafter restricted to revenue use.

A46
A47 
A48 
A49 
A50 
A51 
A52 
A53 
A54 
A55 
A56 
A57 
A58 

### 1901    Perf. 11, 12½ and Compound

| | | | | |
|---|---|---|---|---|
| 193 | A46 | ½p blue green | 7.50 | 1.00 |
| 194 | A47 | 1p rose red | 7.50 | .50 |
| a. | | 1p rose | 22.50 | 1.75 |
| b. | | Wmk sideways | 10.00 | 5.00 |
| 195 | A48 | 1½p red, *yellow* | 3.75 | 1.25 |
| a. | | Perf. 11 | 175.00 | 110.00 |
| 196 | A49 | 2p violet | 27.50 | 2.00 |
| 197 | A50 | 2½p blue | 15.00 | 1.10 |
| 198 | A51 | 3p brown org | 12.50 | 2.75 |
| a. | | Wmk sideways | 22.50 | 42.50 |
| 199 | A52 | 4p bister | 10.50 | 1.25 |
| 200 | A53 | 5p chocolate | 17.50 | 1.10 |
| 201 | A54 | 6p emerald | 15.00 | 1.10 |
| 202 | A55 | 9p rose | 32.50 | 5.00 |
| a. | | Wmk sideways | 55.00 | 37.50 |
| 203 | A56 | 1sh org yel | 37.50 | 4.50 |
| 204 | A57 | 2sh blue, *rose* | 32.50 | 2.25 |
| 205 | A58 | 5sh rose red & bl | 65.00 | 30.00 |
| a. | | 5sh carmine & blue | 75.00 | 30.00 |
| | | Nos. 193-205 (13) | 284.25 | 53.80 |

See Nos. 209-229, 232.

King Edward VII
A59
A60

### 1905-10   Perf. 11, 12x12½, 12½, 12½x11   Wmk. 13

| | | | | |
|---|---|---|---|---|
| 218 | A46 | ½p blue green | 4.75 | 1.75 |
| 219 | A47 | 1p rose red | .45 | .45 |
| a. | | 1p carmine rose | 13.50 | 3.50 |
| b. | | Wmk sideways | 15.00 | 10.00 |
| 220 | A49 | 2p violet | 6.50 | 1.75 |
| a. | | 2p purple | 12.50 | .90 |
| 221 | A50 | 2½p blue | 5.75 | 1.75 |
| 222 | A51 | 3p brown org | 22.50 | 1.50 |
| a. | | 3p dull yellow | 22.50 | 4.50 |
| 223 | A52 | 4p bister | 10.00 | 1.25 |
| 224 | A53 | 5p chocolate | 10.00 | 11.00 |
| 225 | A54 | 6p emerald | 20.00 | 1.25 |
| 226 | A55 | 9p orange brown | 42.50 | 12.50 |
| a. | | 9p brown rose | 50.00 | 14.00 |
| 227 | A55 | 9p car rose | 15.00 | 3.50 |
| 228 | A56 | 1sh yellow ('08) | 17.50 | 2.25 |
| 229 | A58 | 5sh orange red & ultra | 90.00 | 30.00 |
| a. | | 5sh rose red & ultra | 100.00 | 50.00 |
| 230 | A59 | £1 pale red ('07) | 375.00 | 150.00 |
| a. | | £1 rose ('10) | 375.00 | 150.00 |
| 231 | A60 | £2 dull blue | 1,400. | 650.00 |
| | | Nos. 218-229 (12) | 244.95 | 68.95 |

### No. 220 Surcharged in Red

### 1912, July 1

| | | | | |
|---|---|---|---|---|
| 232 | A49 | 1p on 2p violet | 1.75 | 1.25 |

## POSTAL-FISCAL STAMPS

On Jan. 1, 1884, all postage and fiscal stamps were made available for either purpose. Fiscal stamps became invalid after June 30, 1901.

Used values are for examples with postal cancellations used from Jan. 1, 1884 through June 30, 1901.

Beware of stamps with a pen cancellation removed, often regummed or with a fake postmark added.

Stamps inscribed "Stamp Duty" that were issued primarily in postal rates in the normal postage stamp size are listed in the postage section (Nos. 146-170, 180-183, 192-192A). The stamps meeting primarily fiscal rates and in the larger fiscal stamp size, are listed here in the Postal-Fiscal section.

### Stamps Inscribed "Stamp Statute"

Victoria — PF1
PF1a (AR3) 
PF1b (AR5) 
PF1c (AR6) 
Coat of Arms — PF2 
PF3 

### Wmk. V and Crown (70)

### 1870-83    Typo.    Perf. 13

| | | | | |
|---|---|---|---|---|
| AR1 | PF1a | 1p green | 160.00 | 75.00 |
| | | Revenue cancel | | 7.25 |
| | | Perf. 12½ | 225.00 | 120.00 |
| AR2 | PF1 | 3p lilac | 2,100. | 600.00 |
| | | Revenue cancel | | 140.00 |
| AR3 | PF1a | 4p red | 1,500. | 550.00 |
| | | Revenue cancel | | 125.00 |
| AR4 | PF1a | 6p blue | 250.00 | 50.00 |
| | | Revenue cancel | | 14.00 |
| a. | | Perf. 12 | 225.00 | 42.50 |
| | | Revenue cancel | | 10.50 |
| AR5 | PF1b | 1sh blue, *blue* | 225.00 | 50.00 |
| | | Revenue cancel | | 14.00 |
| a. | | Perf. 12 | 250.00 | 55.00 |
| | | Revenue cancel | | 17.50 |
| b. | | Perf. 12½ | — | 90.00 |
| | | Revenue cancel | | 14.00 |
| c. | | Wmk. 50, perf. 13 | 290.00 | 50.00 |
| | | Revenue cancel | | 11.50 |
| d. | | Wmk. 50, perf. 12 | 325.00 | 60.00 |
| | | Revenue cancel | | 13.00 |
| AR6 | PF1c | 2sh blue, *grn* | 450.00 | 130.00 |
| | | Revenue cancel | | 30.00 |
| a. | | Perf. 12 | 450.00 | — |
| | | Revenue cancel | | 35.00 |
| b. | | Wmk. 50, perf. 13 | 375.00 | 125.00 |
| | | Revenue cancel | | 17.50 |
| c. | | Wmk. 50, perf. 12 | 375.00 | 125.00 |
| | | Revenue cancel | | 21.00 |
| AR7 | PF2 | 2sh6p org, *yel* | — | 350.00 |
| | | Revenue cancel | | 72.50 |
| a. | | Perf. 12 | 650.00 | 260.00 |
| | | Revenue cancel | | 72.50 |
| b. | | Perf. 12½ | — | 350.00 |
| | | Revenue cancel | | 87.50 |
| AR8 | PF1a | 5sh blue, *yel* | 825.00 | 140.00 |
| | | Revenue cancel | | 72.50 |
| a. | | Perf. 12 | 825.00 | — |
| b. | | Perf. 12½ | 825.00 | 140.00 |
| | | Revenue cancel | | 160.00 |
| | | Revenue cancel | 900.00 | |
| AR9 | PF1a | 10sh brn, *rose* | 3,250. | 500.00 |
| | | Revenue cancel | | 90.00 |
| a. | | Perf. 12 | 3,250. | 500.00 |
| b. | | Wmk. 50, perf. 13 | 3,250. | 500.00 |
| | | Revenue cancel | | 75.00 |
| c. | | Wmk. 50, perf. 12 | | |
| AR10 | PF1a | £1 lil, *yel* | 1,500. | 500.00 |
| | | Revenue cancel | | 90.00 |
| a. | | Perf. 12 | 4,500. | 500.00 |
| | | Revenue cancel | | 90.00 |
| b. | | Perf. 12½ | 4,500. | 500.00 |
| | | Revenue cancel | | 90.00 |
| AR11 | PF3 | £5 blk, *grn* | 22,500. | |
| | | Revenue cancel | | 135.00 |
| a. | | Perf. 12 | — | |
| b. | | Perf. 12½ | 22,500. | |
| | | Revenue cancel | | 450.00 |

Nos. AR1-AR12 distributed for postal use from Jan. 1, 1884 through Apr. 23, 1884.

### No. AR1 Surcharged "½d/HALF"

### 1879-96

| | | | | |
|---|---|---|---|---|
| AR12 | PF1 | ½p on 1p grn | 140.00 | 125.00 |
| | | Revenue cancel | | 42.50 |

### Stamps Inscribed "Stamp Duty"

PF4
PF5 
PF6 
PF7 
PF8 
PF9 
PF10 
PF11 
PF12 
PF13
PF14 
PF15
PF16 
PF17
PF18 
PF19
PF20 
PF21
PF22 
PF23
PF24 
PF25
PF26 
PF27
PF28 

### Wmk. V and Crown (70)

### 1879-96    Litho.    Perf. 13

| | | | | |
|---|---|---|---|---|
| AR13 | PF4 | 1p green | 175.00 | 65.00 |
| | | Revenue cancel | | 14.00 |
| a. | | Perf. 12 | 175.00 | 60.00 |
| | | Revenue cancel | | 14.00 |
| b. | | Perf. 12½ | — | 14.00 |

| | | | | |
|---|---|---|---|---|
| **AR14** | PF8 | 1sh 6p pink | 425.00 | 70.00 |
| | | Revenue cancel | | 21.00 |
| *a.* | | Perf. 12 | 425.00 | 80.00 |
| | | Revenue cancel | | 26.00 |
| *b.* | | Perf. 12½ | 425.00 | — |
| **AR15** | PF11 | 3sh vio, *blue* | 1,000. | 100.00 |
| | | Revenue cancel | | 21.00 |
| *a.* | | Perf. 12 | 1,000. | 100.00 |
| | | Revenue cancel | | 21.00 |
| *b.* | | Perf. 12½ | — | — |
| **AR16** | PF12 | 4sh orange | 175.00 | 24.00 |
| | | Revenue cancel | | 11.00 |
| *a.* | | Perf. 12 | 175.00 | 24.00 |
| | | Revenue cancel | | 11.00 |
| *b.* | | Perf. 12½ | — | — |
| **AR17** | PF14 | 6sh green | 575.00 | 75.00 |
| | | Revenue cancel | | 12.50 |
| *a.* | | Perf. 12½ | — | — |
| **AR18** | PF15 | 10sh brn, *pink* | 2,750. | 140.00 |
| | | Revenue cancel | | 62.50 |
| *a.* | | Perf. 12 | — | — |
| *b.* | | Perf. 12½ | — | — |
| **AR19** | PF16 | 15sh lilac | 11,000. | 650.00 |
| | | Revenue cancel | | 125.00 |
| **AR20** | PF17 | £1 orange | 1,250. | 125.00 |
| | | Revenue cancel | | 25.00 |
| *a.* | | Perf. 12½ | 1,250. | 125.00 |
| **AR21** | PF18 | £1 5sh pink | 7,500. | 600.00 |
| | | Revenue cancel | | 125.00 |
| **AR22** | PF19 | £1 10sh olive | 8,500 | 400.00 |
| | | Revenue cancel | | 75.00 |
| **AR23** | PF20 | 35sh lilac | *18,000.* | |
| | | Revenue cancel | | 350.00 |
| **AR24** | PF21 | £2 blue | — | 250.00 |
| | | Revenue cancel | | 37.50 |
| **AR25** | PF22 | 45sh violet | 13,000. | 550.00 |
| | | Revenue cancel | | 92.50 |
| **AR26** | PF23 | £5 rose | 18,000. | 1,800. |
| | | Revenue cancel | | 125.00 |
| **AR27** | PF24 | £6 blue, *pink* | — | — |
| | | Revenue cancel | | 175.00 |
| **AR28** | PF25 | £7 vio, *blue* | — | — |
| | | Revenue cancel | | 175.00 |
| **AR29** | PF26 | £8 scar, *yel* | — | — |
| | | Revenue cancel | | 200.00 |
| **AR30** | PF27 | £9 grn, *grn* | — | — |
| | | Revenue cancel | | 200.00 |

**Typo.**

| | | | | |
|---|---|---|---|---|
| **AR31** | PF4 | 1p green | 150.00 | 65.00 |
| | | Revenue cancel | | 8.75 |
| *a.* | | Perf. 12 | 150.00 | 65.00 |
| | | Revenue cancel | | 8.75 |
| *b.* | | Perf. 12½ | 150.00 | — |
| **AR32** | PF5 | 1p brown | 80.00 | 15.00 |
| | | Revenue cancel | | 1.40 |
| *a.* | | Perf. 12 | 80.00 | 16.00 |
| | | Revenue cancel | | 1.40 |
| *b.* | | Perf. 12½ | — | — |
| **AR33** | PF6 | 6p blue | 225.00 | 45.00 |
| | | Revenue cancel | | 5.75 |
| *a.* | | Perf. 12 | 225.00 | 55.00 |
| | | Revenue cancel | | 5.75 |
| *b.* | | Perf. 12½ | — | — |
| **AR34** | PF7 | 1sh blue, *blue* | 290.00 | 8.00 |
| | | Revenue cancel | | 5.75 |
| *a.* | | Perf. 12 | 290.00 | 13.00 |
| | | Revenue cancel | | 5.75 |
| *b.* | | Perf. 12½ | 290.00 | 9.00 |
| | | Revenue cancel | | 5.75 |
| **AR35** | PF7 | 1sh blue, *yel*, perf 12½ | 350.00 | 35.00 |
| | | Revenue cancel | | 17.50 |
| **AR36** | PF8 | 1sh 6p pink | 325.00 | 40.00 |
| | | Revenue cancel | | 17.50 |
| **AR37** | PF9 | 2sh blue, *grn* | 500.00 | 40.00 |
| | | Revenue cancel | | 13.00 |
| *a.* | | Perf. 12 | — | 50.00 |
| | | Revenue cancel | | 13.00 |
| *b.* | | Perf. 12½ | 500.00 | 50.00 |
| | | Revenue cancel | | 13.00 |
| **AR38** | PF10 | 2sh 6p org, perf 12½ | 240.00 | 40.00 |
| *a.* | | 2sh6p yellow ('85) | 160.00 | 17.50 |
| *b.* | | 2sh6p lemon yellow ('92) | 160.00 | 25.00 |
| | | Revenue cancel | | 5.75 |
| **AR39** | PF11 | 3sh maroon, *bl*, perf 12½ | 950.00 | 90.00 |
| | | Revenue cancel | | 14.00 |
| **AR40** | PF11 | 3sh bister | 160.00 | 17.50 |
| | | Revenue cancel | | 21.00 |
| **AR41** | PF12 | 4sh org, perf 12½ | 160.00 | 17.50 |
| | | Revenue cancel | | 7.25 |
| **AR42** | PF13 | 5sh claret, *yel* | 140.00 | 8.00 |
| | | Revenue cancel | | 5.75 |
| *a.* | | Perf. 12 | 160.00 | 20.00 |
| | | Revenue cancel | | 5.75 |
| *b.* | | Perf. 12½ | 190.00 | 22.50 |
| | | Revenue cancel | | 5.75 |
| **AR43** | PF13 | 5sh car rose | 140.00 | 20.00 |
| | | Revenue cancel | | 7.25 |
| **AR44** | PF14 | 6sh green | 375.00 | 70.00 |
| | | Revenue cancel | | 16.00 |
| **AR45** | PF15 | 10sh brn, *pink* | — | 140.00 |
| | | Revenue cancel | | 57.50 |
| *a.* | | Perf. 12 | — | — |
| *b.* | | Perf. 12½ | — | — |
| **AR46** | PF15 | 10sh green | 1,500. | 75.00 |
| | | Revenue cancel | | 20.00 |
| **AR47** | PF16 | 15sh brown | 2,600. | 110.00 |
| | | Revenue cancel | | 42.50 |
| **AR48** | PF17 | £1 org, *yel*, perf 12½ | 1,400. | 75.00 |
| | | Revenue cancel | | 25.00 |
| *a.* | | Perf. 12 | 1,500. | 90.00 |
| | | Revenue cancel | | 30.00 |
| **AR49** | PF18 | £1 5sh pink | 7,500. | 210.00 |
| | | Revenue cancel | | 75.00 |
| **AR50** | PF19 | £1 10sh olive | 7,500. | 190.00 |
| | | Revenue cancel | | 50.00 |
| **AR51** | PF21 | £2 blue | 2,750. | 140.00 |
| | | Revenue cancel | | 27.50 |
| *a.* | | Perf. 12 | — | 200.00 |
| | | Revenue cancel | | 27.50 |
| **AR52** | PF22 | 45sh gray lil | 14,000. | 240.00 |
| | | Revenue cancel | | 62.50 |
| **AR53** | PF23 | £5 rose, perf. 12 | — | 1,750. |
| | | Revenue cancel | | 105.00 |
| *a.* | | perf. 12½ | — | 1,800. |
| | | Revenue cancel | | 150.00 |
| **AR54** | PF28 | £10 lilac | 19,000. | 300.00 |
| | | Revenue cancel | | 62.50 |
| *a.* | | Perf. 12 | 19,000. | 475.00 |
| | | Revenue cancel | | 62.50 |

Nos. AR49-AR52, AR54, used, are valued cto.

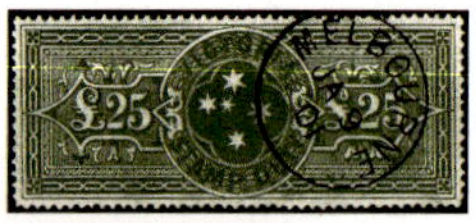
PF29

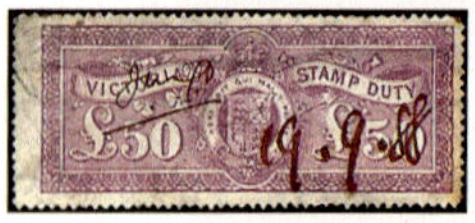
PF30

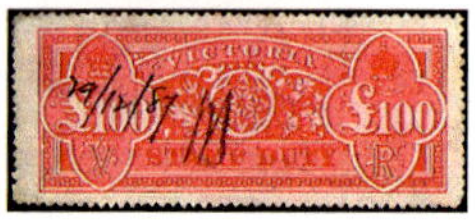
PF31

**Wmk. V and Crown (70)**

**1879-1900 Engr. *Perf. 12½***

| | | | | |
|---|---|---|---|---|
| **AR55** | PF29 | £25 green | *65,000.* | 1,500. |
| | | Revenue cancel | | 110.00 |
| *a.* | | Perf. 13 | | — |
| *b.* | | Perf. 12 | | — |
| **AR56** | PF30 | £50 violet | *75,000.* | 1,500. |
| | | Revenue cancel | | 125.00 |
| *a.* | | Perf. 13 | | — |
| **AR57** | PF31 | £100 red | — | — |
| | | Revenue cancel | | 225.00 |
| *a.* | | Perf. 13 | | — |
| *b.* | | Perf. 12 | | — |
| | | Revenue cancel | | 225.00 |

**Typo.**

| | | | | |
|---|---|---|---|---|
| **AR58** | PF29 | £25 green | — | 525.00 |
| *a.* | | Lithographed | | — |
| | | Revenue cancel | | 100.00 |
| **AR59** | PF30 | £50 violet | — | 700.00 |
| *a.* | | Lithographed | | — |
| | | Revenue cancel | | 140.00 |
| **AR60** | PF31 | £100 red | — | 1,200. |
| *a.* | | Lithographed | | — |
| | | Revenue cancel | | 225.00 |

Nos. AR55-AR60, used, are valued cto.

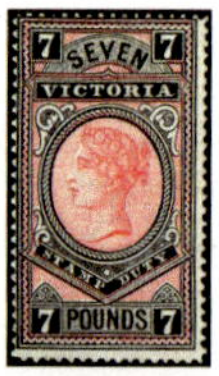
PF32

**1887-90 Typo.**

| | | | | |
|---|---|---|---|---|
| **AR61** | PF32 | £5 cl & ultra | *17,000.* | 210.00 |
| | | Revenue cancel | | 82.50 |
| **AR62** | PF32 | £6 blue & yel | *17,500.* | 240.00 |
| | | Revenue cancel | | 90.00 |
| **AR63** | PF32 | £7 blk & red | *20,000.* | 300.00 |
| | | Revenue cancel | | 110.00 |
| **AR64** | PF32 | £8 org & lil | *20,000.* | 325.00 |
| | | Revenue cancel | | 110.00 |
| **AR65** | PF32 | £9 red & green | *21,000.* | 350.00 |
| | | Revenue cancel | | 135.00 |

Nos. AR61-AR65, used, are valued cto.

## SEMI-POSTAL STAMPS

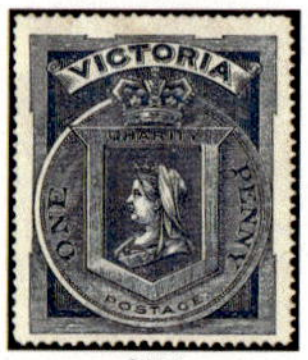
SP1

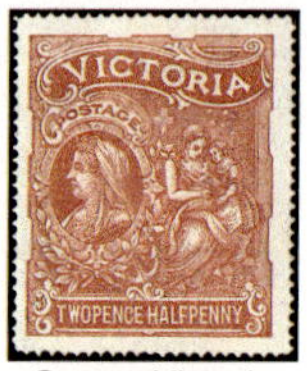
Queen Victoria and Figure of Charity — SP2

**Wmk. V and Crown (70)**

**1897, Oct. Typo. *Perf. 12½***

| | | | | |
|---|---|---|---|---|
| **B1** | SP1 | 1p deep blue | 27.50 | 27.50 |
| **B2** | SP2 | 2½p red brown | 140.00 | 110.00 |

These stamps were sold at 1sh and 2sh6p respectively. The premium was given to a charitable institution.

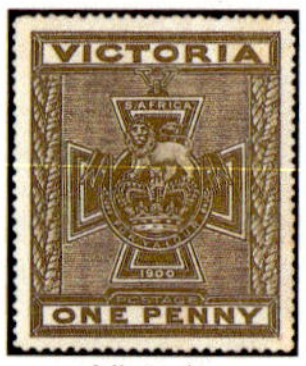
Victoria Cross — SP3

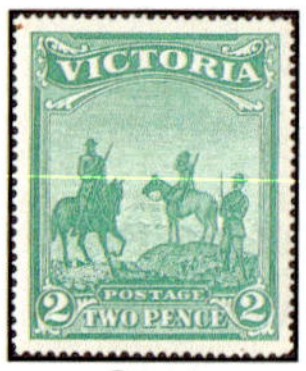
Scout Reporting — SP4

**1900**

| | | | | |
|---|---|---|---|---|
| **B3** | SP3 | 1p brown olive | 175.00 | 110.00 |
| **B4** | SP4 | 2p emerald | 325.00 | 250.00 |

These stamps were sold at 1sh and 2sh respectively. The premium was given to a patriotic fund in connection with the South African War.

## REGISTRATION STAMPS

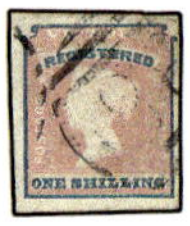
R1

**Unwmk.**

**1854, Dec. 1 Typo. *Imperf.***

| | | | | |
|---|---|---|---|---|
| **F1** | R1 | 1sh rose & blue | 5,250. | 225.00 |

**1857 *Rouletted 7***

| | | | | |
|---|---|---|---|---|
| **F2** | R1 | 1sh rose & blue | 12,500. | 425.00 |

## LATE FEE STAMP

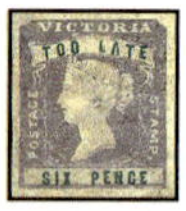
LF1

**Unwmk.**

**1855, Jan. 1 Typo. *Imperf.***

| | | | | |
|---|---|---|---|---|
| **I1** | LF1 | 6p lilac & green | 3,750. | 275.00 |

## POSTAGE DUE STAMPS

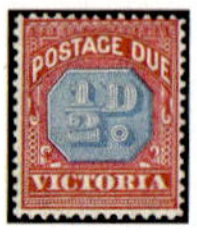
D1

**Wmk. V and Crown (70)**

**1890 Typo. *Perf. 12½***

| | | | | |
|---|---|---|---|---|
| **J1** | D1 | ½p claret & blue | 12.00 | 9.00 |
| **J2** | D1 | 1p claret & blue | 10.00 | 2.60 |
| **J3** | D1 | 2p claret & blue | 18.00 | 2.50 |
| **J4** | D1 | 4p claret & blue | 37.50 | 7.50 |
| **J5** | D1 | 5p claret & blue | 26.00 | 5.50 |
| **J6** | D1 | 6p claret & blue | 30.00 | 12.00 |
| **J7** | D1 | 10p claret & blue | 80.00 | 60.00 |
| **J8** | D1 | 1sh claret & blue | 60.00 | 12.00 |
| **J9** | D1 | 2sh claret & blue | 160.00 | 75.00 |
| **J10** | D1 | 5sh claret & blue | 225.00 | 120.00 |
| | | *Nos. J1-J10 (10)* | 658.50 | 306.10 |

**1891-94**

| | | | | |
|---|---|---|---|---|
| **J11** | D1 | ½p lake & blue | 10.00 | 7.50 |
| **J12** | D1 | 1p brn red & blue ('93) | 22.50 | 2.75 |
| **J13** | D1 | 2p brn red & blue ('93) | 30.00 | 2.75 |
| **J14** | D1 | 4p lake & blue ('94) | 40.00 | 12.50 |
| | | *Nos. J11-J14 (4)* | 102.50 | 25.50 |

**1894-96**

| | | | | |
|---|---|---|---|---|
| **J15** | D1 | ½p bl grn & rose | 12.50 | 3.00 |
| **J16** | D1 | 1p bl grn & rose | 17.50 | 2.25 |
| **J17** | D1 | 2p bl grn & rose | 32.50 | 3.50 |
| **J18** | D1 | 4p bl grn & rose | 15.00 | 1.75 |
| **J19** | D1 | 5p bl grn & rose | 50.00 | 42.50 |
| **J20** | D1 | 6p bl grn & rose | 27.50 | 27.50 |
| **J21** | D1 | 10p bl grn & rose | 60.00 | 12.00 |
| **J22** | D1 | 1sh bl grn & rose | 32.50 | 3.75 |
| **J23** | D1 | 2sh yel grn & rose | 100.00 | 27.50 |
| **J24** | D1 | 5sh yel grn & rose | 150.00 | 45.00 |
| | | *Nos. J15-J24 (10)* | 497.50 | 168.75 |

**1897-99**

| | | | | |
|---|---|---|---|---|
| **J15a** | D1 | ½p yel grn & pale scar | 7.00 | 4.50 |
| **J16a** | D1 | 1p yel grn & pale scar | 8.00 | 3.00 |
| **J17a** | D1 | 2p yel grn & pale scar | 30.00 | 1.75 |
| **J18a** | D1 | 4p yel grn & pale scar | 12.50 | 3.00 |
| **J19a** | D1 | 5p yel grn & pale scar | 22.50 | *27.50* |
| **J20a** | D1 | 6p yel grn & pale scar | 16.00 | 9.00 |
| | | *Nos. J15a-J20a (6)* | 96.00 | 48.75 |

**1905-09 Wmk. 13**

| | | | | |
|---|---|---|---|---|
| **J25** | D1 | ½p yel grn & rose | 7.00 | *15.00* |
| *a.* | | ½p pale green & pink | 32.50 | 25.00 |
| **J26** | D1 | 1p yel grn & rose | 7.50 | 3.00 |
| *a.* | | 1p pale green & pink | 75.00 | 11.50 |
| **J27** | D1 | 2p yel grn & rose | 55.00 | 7.00 |
| **J28** | D1 | 4p yel grn & rose | 27.50 | 30.00 |
| | | *Nos. J25-J28 (4)* | 97.00 | 55.00 |

A 5p with wmk. 13 exists but was not issued.

# WESTERN AUSTRALIA

ˈwes-tərn o-ˈstrāl-yə

LOCATION — Western part of Australia, occupying about a third of that continent
GOVT. — British Colony
AREA — 975,920 sq. mi.
POP. — 184,124 (1901)
CAPITAL — Perth

Western Australia was one of the six British colonies that united on January 1, 1901, to form the Commonwealth of Australia.

12 Pence = 1 Shilling
20 Shillings = 1 Pound

Unused values for Nos. 1-10 are for stamps without gum as these stamps are seldom found with original gum. Otherwise, unused values are for stamps with original gum as defined in the catalogue introduction.

Very fine examples of all rouletted and perforated stamps from Nos. 6-34 have roulettes or perforations touching the design. Examples clear on all four sides range from scarce to rare and will command higher prices.

**Watermarks**

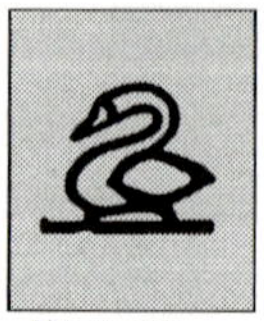
Wmk. 82 — Swan

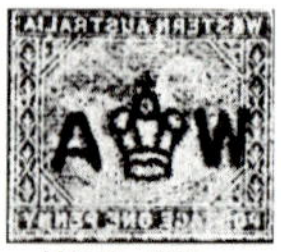
Wmk. 83 — Crown and W A

AUSTRALIAN STATES — Western Australia 719

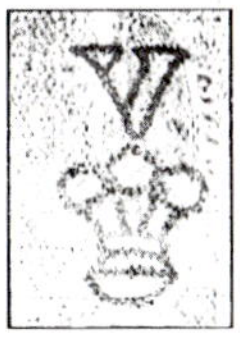

Wmk. 70 — V and Crown

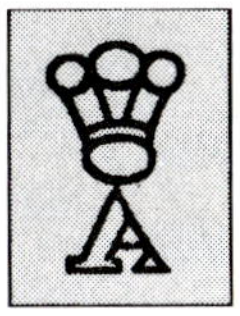

Wmk. 13 — Crown & Double-lined A

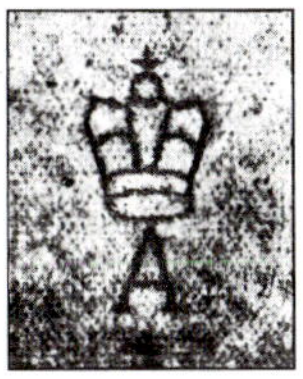

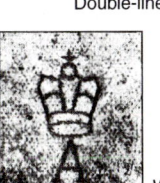

Wmk. 74 — Crown and Single-lined A

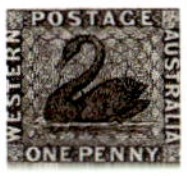 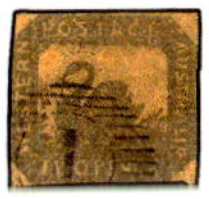

Swan

A1 A2

**1854-57 Engr. Wmk. 82** ***Imperf.***

1 A1 1p black 1,700. 350.

**Litho.**

2 A2 2p brown, *red* ('57) 9,500. 600.
*a.* 2p brown, *deep red* ('57) 9,500. 900.
*b.* Printed on both sides 12,000. 900.

See Nos. 4, 6-7, 9, 14-39, 44-52, 54, 59-61. For surcharges see Nos. 41, 55-56.

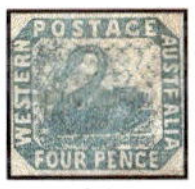 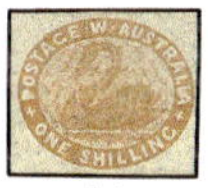

A3 A4

3 A3 4p blue 400. 225.
*a.* Frame inverted *200,000.*
As "a," cut to shape *27,500.*
*b.* 4p slate blue 4,500. 1,400.
4 A2 6p bronze ('57) *15,000.* 700.
5 A4 1sh pale brown 550. 350.
*a.* 1sh dark brown 700. 450.
*b.* 1sh dark red brown 2,250. 1,100.
*c.* 1sh pale red brown 26,500. 5,000.

**Engraved**

***Rouletted***

6 A1 1p black 5,500. 750.

**Lithographed**

7 A2 2p brn, *red* ('57) *15,000.* 2,000.
*a.* Printed on both sides 2,300.
8 A3 4p blue — 800.
9 A2 6p bronze ('57) *22,500.* 2,500.
10 A4 1sh brown 8,000. 1,250.

The 1p, 2p, 4p and 6p are known with pin-perforation but this is believed to be unofficial. No. 7a is only recorded used and with pin perforations.

**1860 Engr.** ***Imperf.***

14 A1 2p vermilion 160.00 90.00
*a.* 2p pale orange 140.00 90.00
15 A1 4p blue 350. *2,500.*
16 A1 6p dull green 3,250. 425.00

***Rouletted***

17 A1 2p vermilion 950.00 275.00
*a.* 2p pale orange 900.00 300.00
18 A1 4p deep blue 6,500. —
19 A1 6p dull green 6,500. 750.00

**1861** ***Clean-Cut Perf. 14 to 16***

20 A1 1p rose 750.00 150.00
*a.* Imperf.
21 A1 2p blue 240.00 45.00
*a.* Imperf., pair
*b.* Horiz. pair, imperf. vert.
22 A1 4p vermilion 2,000. *2,250.*
*a.* Imperf.
23 A1 6p purple brn 1,200. 120.00
*a.* Imperf.
24 A1 1sh green 2,250. 275.00
*a.* Imperf.

***Rough Perf. 14 to 16***

24B A1 1p rose 375.00 55.00
24C A1 6p pur brn, *bluish* 5,000. 525.00
24D A1 1sh deep green 5,500. 400.00

***Perf. 14***

25 A1 1p rose 400.00 70.00
25A A1 2p blue 180.00 50.00
25B A1 4p vermilion 500.00 200.00

**Unwmk.** ***Perf. 13***

26 A1 1p lake 85.00 6.00
28 A1 6p violet 375.00 55.00

**1865-79 Wmk. 1** ***Perf. 12½***

29 A1 1p bister 95.00 11.00
30 A1 1p yel ocher 125.00 17.50
31 A1 2p yellow 125.00 9.00
*a.* 2p lilac (error) ('79) *22,500.* *17,500.*
*b.* 2p chrome yellow 110.00 8.00
32 A1 4p carmine 160.00 8.00
*a.* Double impression *32,500.*
33 A1 6p violet 190.00 6.50
*a.* 6p lilac 325.00 7.00
*b.* 6p red lilac 300.00 7.00
*c.* Double impression *24,000.*
34 A1 1sh brt grn 300.00 22.50
Handstamped "SPECIMEN" 225.00
*a.* 1sh sage green 500.00 40.00
*Nos. 29-34 (6)* 995.00 74.50

**1872-78** ***Perf. 14***

35 A1 1p bister 180.00 6.00
36 A1 1p yellow ocher 115.00 3.00
37 A1 2p yellow 125.00 2.00
38 A1 4p carmine 700.00 130.00
39 A1 6p lilac 240.00 4.50
*Nos. 35-39 (5)* 1,360. 145.50

A5 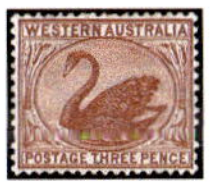

**1872 Typo.**

40 A5 3p red brown 65.00 6.00
*a.* 3p brown 65.00 8.50
Handstamped "SPECIMEN" 150.00

See Nos. 53, 92. For surcharges see Nos. 57, 69-72A.

No. 31 Surcharged in Green

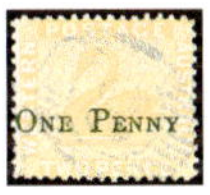


**1875 Engr.** ***Perf. 12½***

41 A1 1p on 2p yellow 850.00 60.00
*a.* Pair, one without surcharge
*b.* "O" of "ONE" omitted
*c.* Triple surcharge *7,500.*

Forged surcharges exist.

**1882 Wmk. 2** ***Perf. 12***

44 A1 1p ocher yellow 110.00 6.50
46 A1 2p yellow 175.00 6.00
47 A1 4p carmine 300.00 60.00
48 A1 6p pale violet 575.00 60.00
*Nos. 44-48 (4)* 1,160. 132.50

**1882** ***Perf. 14***

49 A1 1p ocher yellow 35.00 2.25
50 A1 2p yellow 45.00 2.25
51 A1 4p carmine 200.00 17.50
52 A1 6p pale violet 150.00 3.50
*a.* 6p violet 150.00 4.50
Handstamped "SPECIMEN" 160.00

**Typographed**

53 A5 3p red brown 11.00 4.50
*a.* 3p brown 19.00 4.50
*Nos. 49-53 (5)* 441.00 30.00

**1883 Engr.** ***Perf. 12x14***

54 A1 1p ocher yellow 3,000. 300.00

Nos. 44 and 49 Surcharged in Red

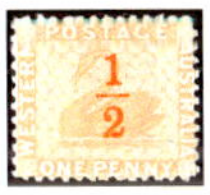

**1884** ***Perf. 12***

55 A1 ½p on 1p ocher yel 18.00 *32.50*

***Perf. 14***

56 A1 ½p on 1p ocher yel 32.50 *50.00*
*a.* Thin fraction bar 120.00 175.00

No. 40 Surcharged in Green

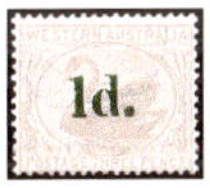


**1885 Typo. Wmk. 1**

57 A5 1p on 3p red brown 90.00 40.00
*a.* 1p on 3p brown 100.00 40.00
*b.* "1" with straight top 190.00 75.00
*c.* As "a," "1" with straight top 210.00 75.00

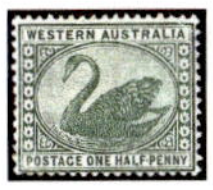 A8

**Wmk. Crown and C A (2)**

**1885 Typo.** ***Perf. 14***

58 A8 ½p green 6.00 1.25

See No. 89.

**1888 Engr.**

59 A1 1p rose 37.50 4.50
60 A1 2p slate 90.00 2.00
61 A1 4p red brown 90.00 37.50
*Nos. 59-61 (3)* 217.50 44.00

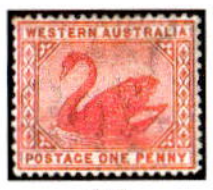 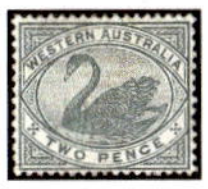

A9 A10

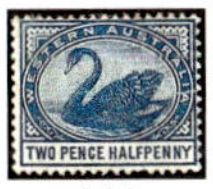 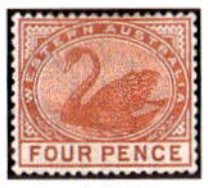

A11 A12

**1890-93 Typo.**

62 A9 1p carmine rose 55.00 1.25
63 A10 2p slate 37.50 4.50
64 A11 2½p blue 32.50 2.50
65 A12 4p orange brown 20.00 2.75
66 A12 5p bister 21.00 4.50
67 A12 6p violet 24.00 2.25
68 A12 1sh olive green 55.00 6.00
*Nos. 62-68 (7)* 245.00 23.75

See Nos. 73-74, 76, 80, 90, 94.

Nos. 40 and 53a Surcharged in Green

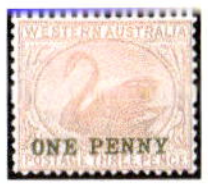


**1893 Wmk. Crown and C C (1)**

69 A5 1p on 3p red brown 20.00 11.00
*a.* 1p on 3p brown 20.00 11.00
*b.* Double surcharge *2,100.*

**Wmkd. Crown and C A (2)**

70 A5 1p on 3p brown 90.00 19.00

Nos. 40a and 53a Surcharged in Green

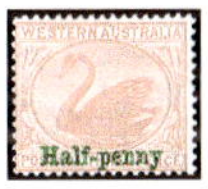


**1895 Wmk. Crown and C C (1)**

71 A5 ½p on 3p brown 13.00 *45.00*
*a.* Double surcharge *1,750.*

No. 72 Surcharged in Green and Red

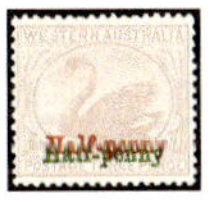

72 A5 ½p on 3p brown 120.00 *350.00*

**Wmk. Crown and C A (2)**

72A A5 ½p on 3p brown 90.00 *200.00*

After the supply of paper watermarked Crown and C C was exhausted, No. 72A was printed. Ostensibly this was to provide samples for Postal Union distribution, but a supply for philatelic demands was also made.

**Types of 1890-93 and**

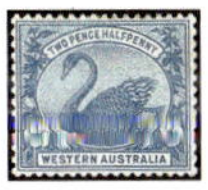

A15

**1899-1901 Typo. Wmk. 83**

73 A9 1p carmine rose 12.50 .30
74 A10 2p yellow 40.00 3.50
75 A15 2½p blue ('01) 21.00 1.25
*Nos. 73-75 (3)* 73.50 5.05

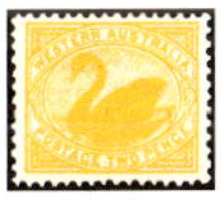 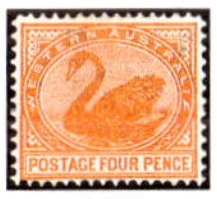

A16 A17

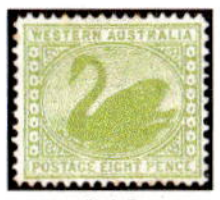 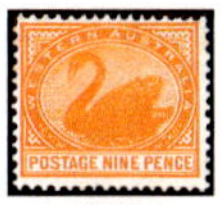

A18 A19

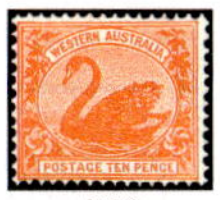 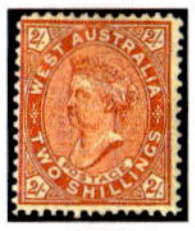

A20 A21

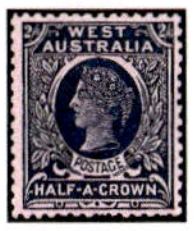 A22

Southern Cross — A23 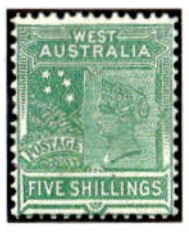

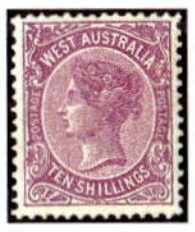 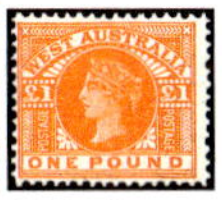

Queen Victoria

A24 A25

***Perf. 12½, 12x12½***

**1902-05 Wmk. 70**

76 A9 1p car rose 30.00 1.00
*a.* 1p salmon —
*b.* Perf. 11 400.00 50.00
*c.* Perf. 12½x11 1,350. 675.00
77 A16 2p yellow 30.00 5.00
*a.* Perf. 11 450.00 65.00
*b.* Perf. 12½x11 *1,900.* *1,100.*
79 A17 4p org brn 450.00 4.50
*a.* Perf. 11 1,400. 450.00
80 A12 5p ol bis, perf 12½ ('05) 160.00 100.00
*a.* Perf. 11 55.00 *80.00*
81 A18 8p pale yel grn 22.50 4.75
82 A19 9p orange 55.00 40.00
*b.* Perf. 11 180.00 *180.00*
83 A20 10p red 35.00 12.00
84 A21 2sh org red, *yel* ('06) 60.00 13.00
*a.* Perf. 11 450.00 225.00
*b.* 2sh orange brown, *yel* ('11) 50.00 32.50
*c.* 2sh bright red, *yel* 90.00 50.00
*d.* As "c," perf. 11 325.00 200.00
85 A22 2sh6p dk bl, *rose* 60.00 25.00
86 A23 5sh blue green 90.00 50.00
87 A24 10sh violet 190.00 110.00
*a.* 10sh bright purple 950.00 450.00
88 A25 £1 brown org 450.00 210.00
*a.* £1 orange 750.00 350.00
*Nos. 76-88 (12)* 1,633. 575.25

***Perf. 12½, 12x12½***

**1905-12 Wmk. 13**

89 A8 ½p dp grn ('10) 5.00 *9.00*
*a.* Perf 11 *3,000.*
90 A9 1p rose 25.00 4.00
*e.* Perf. 11 55.00 35.00
*f.* Perf. 12½x11 *1,250.* 500.00
91 A16 2p yellow 9.00 2.25
*a.* Perf. 11 55.00 50.00
*b.* Perf. 12½x11 *1,250.* 550.00
92 A5 3p brown 65.00 6.00
*a.* Perf. 11 25.00 19.00
*b.* Perf. 12½x11 1,500. 1,500.
93 A17 4p orange brn 50.00 20.00
*a.* 4p bister brown 60.00 20.00
*b.* Perf. 11 1,250. 290.00
94 A12 5p olive bis 40.00 32.50
*a.* Perf. 11, pale olive bister 60.00 12.00
*b.* Perf. 11, olive green 30.00 22.50
95 A18 8p pale yel grn ('12) 25.00 *82.50*
96 A19 9p orange 37.50 6.50
*b.* Perf. 11 200.00 *200.00*
97 A20 10p red orange 25.00 30.00
98 A23 5s blue green 200.00 150.00
*Nos. 89-98 (10)* 481.50 342.75

For surcharge see No. 103.

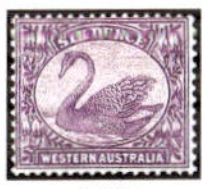 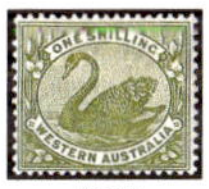

A26 A27

**1906-07 Wmk. 83** ***Perf. 14***

99 A26 6p bright violet 55.00 5.00
100 A27 1sh olive green 60.00 7.00

**1912 Wmk. 74 *Perf. 11½x12***

| | | | | |
|---|---|---|---|---|
| 101 | A26 | 6p bright violet | 21.00 | 19.00 |
| 102 | A27 | 1sh gray green | 35.00 | 50.00 |
| *a.* | | Perf. 12½ | | *2,750.* |

No. 91 Surcharged

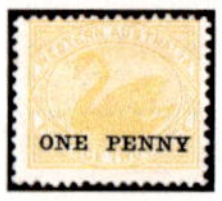


**1912 Wmk. 13 *Perf. 12½***

| | | | | |
|---|---|---|---|---|
| 103 | A16 | 1p on 2p yellow | 4.25 | *4.25* |
| *a.* | | Perf compound 12½x11 | *750.00* | *450.00* |

Stamps of Western Australia were replaced by those of Australia.

### POSTAL-FISCAL STAMPS

Postal use of the 1p telegraph stamp was authorized beginning Oct. 25, 1886.

Used values are for examples with postal cancellations.

Beware of stamps with a pen cancellation removed and a fake postmark added.

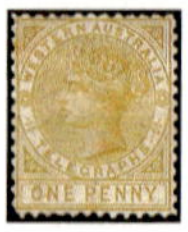

PF1

**1886 Wmk. 1 *Perf. 14***

| | | | | |
|---|---|---|---|---|
| AR1 | PF1 | 1p bister | 110.00 | 25.00 |

***Perf. 12½***

| | | | | |
|---|---|---|---|---|
| AR2 | PF1 | 1p bister | 110.00 | 25.00 |

Authorized for postal use by the Post and Telegraph Act of Sept. 5, 1893 were the current revenue stamps through the 1sh value.

Beware of stamps with a pen cancellation removed and a fake postmark added.

Because the Act specified current stamps, postally used examples from the provisional issue of of 1881 are not included here.

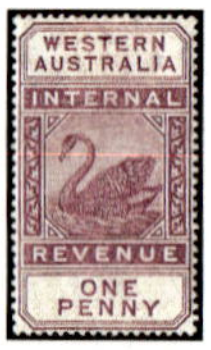


PF2

**1882 Wmk. 2 *Perf. 14***

| | | | | |
|---|---|---|---|---|
| AR3 | PF2 | 1p purple | 35.00 | 9.00 |
| AR4 | PF2 | 2p purple | 350.00 | 90.00 |
| AR5 | PF2 | 3p purple | 125.00 | 10.00 |
| AR6 | PF2 | 6p purple | 190.00 | 17.50 |
| AR7 | PF2 | 1sh purple | 350.00 | 40.00 |

The 6p is known postally used but was not authorized.

**Wmk. 83**

| | | | | |
|---|---|---|---|---|
| AR8 | PF2 | 1p purple | 42.50 | 10.00 |
| AR9 | PF2 | 3p purple | 125.00 | 11.00 |
| AR10 | PF2 | 6p purple | 175.00 | 15.00 |
| AR11 | PF2 | 1sh purple | 350.00 | 50.00 |

Nos. AR7, AR11 have a rectangular outer frame and a circular frame around the swan.

Higher values are known with postal cancels, some postally used, but these were not authorized.

## AUSTRALIA

o-'strāl-yə

LOCATION — Oceania, south of Indonesia, bounded on the west by the Indian Ocean

GOVT. — Self-governing dominion of the British Commonwealth

AREA — 2,967,909 sq. mi.

POP. — 25,500,000 (2020 est.)

CAPITAL — Canberra

Australia includes the former British colonies of New South Wales, Victoria, Queensland, South Australia, Western Australia and Tasmania.

12 Pence = 1 Shilling
20 Shillings = 1 Pound
100 Cents = 1 Dollar (1966)

**Catalogue values for unused stamps in this country are for Never Hinged items, beginning with Scott 197 in the regular postage section, Scott B1 in the semi-postal section, Scott C6 in the air post section, Scott J71 in the postage due section, and all of the Australian Antarctic Territory.**

### Watermarks

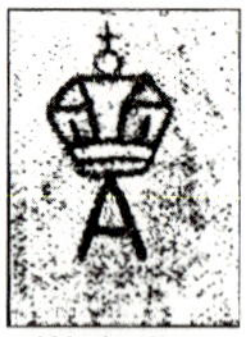

Wmk. 8 — Wide Crown and Wide A

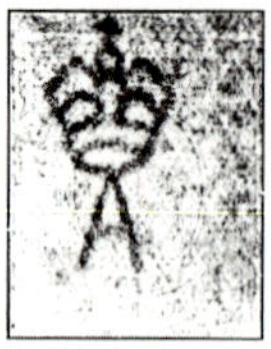

Wmk. 9 — Wide Crown and Narrow A

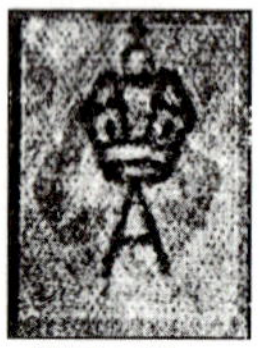

Wmk. 10 — Narrow Crown and Narrow A

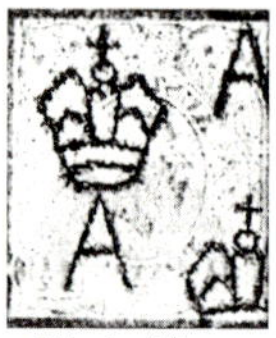

Wmk. 11 — Multiple Crown and A

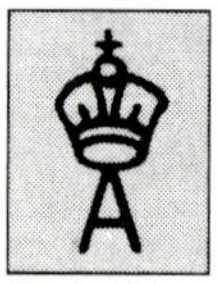

Wmk. 12 — Crown and Single-lined A

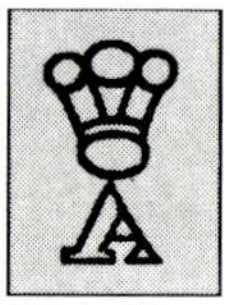

Wmk. 13 — Large Crown and Double-lined A

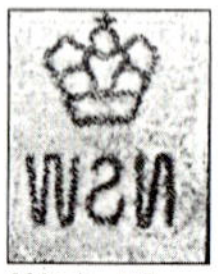

Wmk. 55 — Large Crown and NSW

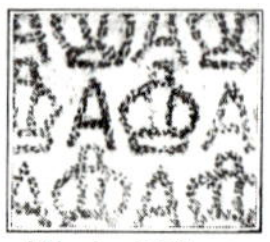

Wmk. 203 — Small Crown and A Multiple

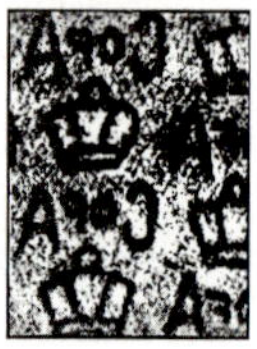

Wmk. 228 — Small Crown and C of A Multiple

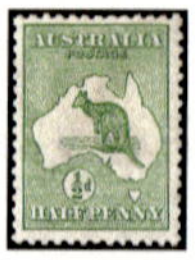


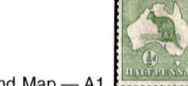

Kangaroo and Map — A1

Die I — The inside frameline has a break at left, even with the top of the letters of the denomination.

Die II — The frameline does not show a break (repaired die).

Die III — The left inside frameline shows a break opposite the face of the kangaroo.

Die IV — As Die III, with a break in the top outside frameline above the "ST" of "AUSTRALIA." The upper right inside frameline has an incomplete corner.

Dies are only indicated when there are more than one for any denomination.

**1913 Typo. Wmk. 8 *Perf. 11½, 12***

| | | | | |
|---|---|---|---|---|
| 1 | A1 | ½p green | 11.50 | 7.50 |
| | | Never hinged | 17.00 | |
| 2 | A1 | 1p car (I) | 17.50 | 1.75 |
| | | Never hinged | 24.00 | |
| *h.* | | 1p carmine (III) | 24.00 | 2.25 |
| | | Never hinged | 40.00 | |
| 3 | A1 | 2p gray | 70.00 | 10.00 |
| | | Never hinged | 140.00 | |
| 4 | A1 | 2½p dark blue | 70.00 | 25.00 |
| | | Never hinged | 140.00 | |
| 5 | A1 | 3p ol bis, die I | 140.00 | 17.50 |
| | | Never hinged | 280.00 | |
| *a.* | | Die II | 450.00 | 85.00 |
| | | Never hinged | *725.00* | |
| 6 | A1 | 4p orange | 150.00 | 40.00 |
| | | Never hinged | *300.00* | |
| 7 | A1 | 5p org brn | 135.00 | 50.00 |
| | | Never hinged | 270.00 | |
| 8 | A1 | 6p ultra (II) | 125.00 | 30.00 |
| | | Never hinged | *250.00* | |
| *b.* | | As #8, (III) | *4,650.* | *1,625.* |
| 9 | A1 | 9p purple | 140.00 | 37.50 |
| | | Never hinged | 280.00 | |
| 10 | A1 | 1sh blue green | 130.00 | 22.50 |
| | | Never hinged | 260.00 | |
| 11 | A1 | 2sh brown | 300.00 | 140.00 |
| | | Never hinged | 575.00 | |
| 12 | A1 | 5sh yel & gray | 550.00 | 260.00 |
| | | Never hinged | 1,100. | |
| 13 | A1 | 10sh pink & gray | 1,600. | 800.00 |
| | | Never hinged | *3,500.* | |
| 14 | A1 | £1 ultra & brn | 3,250. | 2,400. |
| | | Never hinged | *6,500.* | |
| 15 | A1 | £2 dp rose & blk | *6,000.* | *3,400.* |
| | | Never hinged | *12,000.* | |
| | | *Nos. 1-12 (12)* | 1,839. | 641.75 |

On No. 4, "2½d" is colorless in solid blue background.

See Nos. 38-59, 96-102, 121-129, 206.

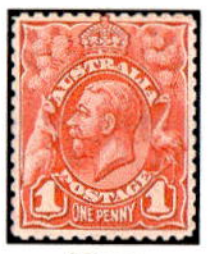


King George V
A2

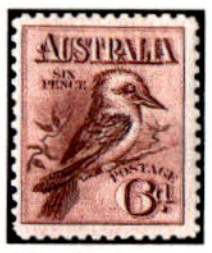


Kookaburra (Kingfisher)
A3

**1913-14 Unwmk. Engr. *Perf. 11***

| | | | | |
|---|---|---|---|---|
| 17 | A2 | 1p carmine | 5.25 | *6.50* |
| | | Never hinged | 8.00 | |
| *a.* | | Vert. pair, imperf. between | *2,750.* | |
| *b.* | | Horiz. pair, imperf. between | *4,250.* | |
| 18 | A3 | 6p lake brown ('14) | 100.00 | 62.50 |
| | | Never hinged | 160.00 | |

See No. 95.

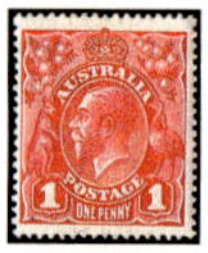


A4

ONE PENNY

Die I — Normal die, having outside the oval band with "AUSTRALIA" a white line and a heavy colored line.

Die Ia — As die I with a small white spur below the right serif at foot of the "1" in left tablet.

Die II — A heavy colored line between two white lines back of the emu's neck. A white scratch crossing the vertical shading lines at the lowest point of the bust.

TWO PENCE

Die I — The numeral "2" is thin. The upper curve is 1mm. across and a very thin line connects it with the foot of the figure.

Die II — The "2" is thicker than in die I. The top curve is 1½mm across and a strong white line connects it with the foot of the figure. There are thin vertical lines across the ends of the groups of short horizontal lines at each side of "TWO PENCE."

THREE PENCE

Die I — The ends of the thin horizontal lines in the background run into the solid color of the various parts of the design. The numerals are thin and the letters of "THREE PENCE" are thin and irregular.

Die II — The oval about the portrait, the shields with the numerals, etc., are outlined by thin white lines which separate them from the horizontal background lines. The numerals are thick and the letters of "THREE PENCE" are heavy and regular.

FIVE PENCE

Die I — The top of the flag of the "5" is slightly curved.

Die II — The top of the flag of the "5" is flat. There are thin white vertical lines across the ends of the short horizontal lines at each side of "FIVE PENCE."

**1914-24 Typo. Wmk. 9 *Perf. 14***

| | | | | |
|---|---|---|---|---|
| 19 | A4 | ½p emer ('15) | 3.75 | 1.60 |
| | | Never hinged | 7.50 | |
| *a.* | | Thin "½" at right | *18,000.* | *9,000.* |
| 20 | A4 | ½p org ('23) | 4.50 | 3.50 |
| | | Never hinged | 7.00 | |
| 21 | A4 | 1p red (I) | 20.00 | 1.75 |
| | | Never hinged | 30.00 | |
| *a.* | | 1p carmine rose (I) | 37.50 | 6.00 |
| | | Never hinged | 45.00 | |
| *b.* | | 1p red (Ia) | 500.00 | 9.00 |
| | | Never hinged | 1,000. | |
| *c.* | | 1p carmine (II) ('18) | 80.00 | 10.00 |
| | | Never hinged | 160.00 | |
| *d.* | | 1p scar (I), rough paper | 22.50 | 6.00 |
| *e.* | | 1p rose red (Ia), rough paper | 600.00 | 22.50 |
| *f.* | | 1p brt rose (Ia), rough paper | 1,275. | 150.00 |
| 22 | A4 | 1p vio (I) ('22) | 7.00 | 1.60 |
| | | Never hinged | 11.50 | |
| *a.* | | 1p red violet | 9.50 | 4.75 |
| | | Never hinged | 14.00 | |
| 23 | A4 | 1p grn (I) ('24) | 5.25 | 2.25 |
| | | Never hinged | 9.50 | |
| 24 | A4 | 1½p choc ('18) | 8.50 | 2.00 |
| | | Never hinged | 12.50 | |
| *a.* | | 1½p red brown | 13.00 | 2.25 |
| | | Never hinged | 18.00 | |
| *b.* | | 1½p black brown | 7.25 | 2.25 |
| | | Never hinged | 11.50 | |
| 25 | A4 | 1½p emer ('23) | 6.75 | 2.50 |
| | | Never hinged | 12.50 | |
| *a.* | | Rough paper | 350.00 | 145.00 |
| 26 | A4 | 1½p scar ('24) | 3.75 | 1.10 |
| | | Never hinged | 7.00 | |
| 27 | A4 | 2p brn org (I) ('20) | 16.00 | 2.75 |
| | | Never hinged | 30.00 | |
| *a.* | | 2p orange (I) ('20) | 16.00 | 2.25 |
| | | Never hinged | 30.00 | |
| *b.* | | Booklet pane of 6 | — | |
| 28 | A4 | 2p red (I) ('22) | 16.00 | 2.75 |
| | | Never hinged | 30.00 | |
| 29 | A4 | 2p red brn (I) ('24) | 20.00 | 11.00 |
| | | Never hinged | 35.00 | |
| 30 | A4 | 3p ultra (I) ('24) | 29.00 | 7.00 |
| | | Never hinged | 57.50 | |
| 31 | A4 | 4p org ('15) | 40.00 | 5.50 |
| | | Never hinged | 80.00 | |
| *a.* | | 4p yellow | 125.00 | 17.00 |
| | | Never hinged | 300.00 | |
| 32 | A4 | 4p violet ('21) | 20.00 | 16.00 |
| | | Never hinged | 30.00 | |
| 33 | A4 | 4p lt ultra ('22) | 60.00 | 12.00 |
| | | Never hinged | 100.00 | |
| 34 | A4 | 4p ol bis ('24) | 32.50 | 12.00 |
| | | Never hinged | 60.00 | |
| 35 | A4 | 4½p violet ('24) | 25.00 | 6.00 |
| | | Never hinged | 50.00 | |
| 36 | A4 | 5p org brn (I) ('15) | 42.50 | 6.50 |
| | | Never hinged | 85.00 | |
| 37 | A4 | 1sh4p lt blue ('20) | 100.00 | 30.00 |
| | | Never hinged | 180.00 | |
| | | *Nos. 19-37 (19)* | 460.50 | 127.80 |

See Nos. 60-76, 113-120, 124.

**1915 *Perf. 11½, 12***

| | | | | |
|---|---|---|---|---|
| 38 | A1 | 2p gray | 90.00 | 16.00 |
| | | Never hinged | 180.00 | |
| 39 | A1 | 2½p dark blue | 80.00 | 32.50 |
| | | Never hinged | 140.00 | |
| 40 | A1 | 6p ultra (II) | 170.00 | 25.00 |
| | | Never hinged | 325.00 | |
| *a.* | | Die III | *6,250.* | *2,500.* |
| 41 | A1 | 9p violet | 170.00 | 52.50 |
| | | Never hinged | 450.00 | |
| 42 | A1 | 1sh blue green | 160.00 | 30.00 |
| | | Never hinged | 360.00 | |
| 43 | A1 | 2sh brown | 600.00 | 110.00 |
| | | Never hinged | 1,500. | |
| 44 | A1 | 5sh yellow & gray | 850.00 | 300.00 |
| | | Never hinged | 2,250. | |
| | | *Nos. 38-44 (7)* | 2,120. | 566.00 |

**1915-24 Wmk. 10**

| | | | | |
|---|---|---|---|---|
| 45 | A1 | 2p gray (I) | 42.50 | 7.50 |
| | | Never hinged | 62.50 | |
| *a.* | | Die II, shiny paper | 45.00 | 17.50 |
| | | Never hinged | 67.50 | |
| 46 | A1 | 2½p dark blue | 25.00 | 10.00 |
| | | Never hinged | 40.00 | |
| *a.* | | "1" of fraction omitted | *47,500.* | *30,000.* |
| 47 | A1 | 3p ol bis (I) | 35.00 | 8.50 |
| | | Never hinged | 60.00 | |
| *a.* | | Die II | 190.00 | 52.50 |
| | | Never hinged | 325.00 | |
| *b.* | | 3p lt olive (IV) | 52.50 | 13.00 |
| | | Never hinged | 92.50 | |
| 48 | A1 | 6p ultra (II) | 100.00 | 8.75 |
| | | Never hinged | 190.00 | |
| *a.* | | 6p chalky blue (III) | 100.00 | 22.50 |
| | | Never hinged | 190.00 | |
| *c.* | | 6p ultra (IV) | 100.00 | 19.00 |
| | | Never hinged | 180.00 | |
| 49 | A1 | 6p yel brn (IV, '23) | 25.00 | 3.75 |
| | | Never hinged | 45.00 | |
| 50 | A1 | 9p violet (IV) | 70.00 | 16.00 |
| | | Never hinged | 140.00 | |
| *a.* | | 9p lilac (II) | 60.00 | 11.00 |
| | | Never hinged | 120.00 | |
| 51 | A1 | 1sh blue grn (II, '16) | 55.00 | 7.00 |
| | | Never hinged | 110.00 | |
| *b.* | | Die IV | 65.00 | 3.50 |

52 A1 2sh brn ('16) 240.00 15.00
Never hinged 500.00
53 A1 2sh vio brn (II, '24) 70.00 30.00
Never hinged 160.00
54 A1 5sh yel & gray ('18) 240.00 100.00
Never hinged 480.00
55 A1 10sh brt pink & gray ('17) 650.00 300.00
Never hinged 1,350.
56 A1 £1 ultra & brn org ('16) 3,000. 1,750.
Never hinged 6,500.
a. £1 ultra & brn ('16) 3,000. 1,750.
Never hinged 6,500.
57 A1 £1 gray (IV, '24) 800.00 350.00
Never hinged 1,750.
58 A1 £2 dp rose & blk ('19) 5,500. 3,250.
Never hinged 12,500.
59 A1 £2 rose & vio brn ('24) 4,250. 2,500.
Never hinged 11,000.
*Nos. 45-54 (10)* 902.50 206.50

### *Perf. 14, 14½, 14½x14*

**1918-23** **Wmk. 11**

60 A4 ½p emerald 7.25 2.50
Never hinged 12.50
a. Thin "½" at right 100.00 125.00
61 A4 1p rose (I) 26.00 17.00
Never hinged 45.00
62 A4 1p dl grn (I) ('24) 13.00 9.25
Never hinged 24.00
63 A4 1½p choc ('19) 11.00 2.25
Never hinged 17.50
a. 1½p red brown ('19) 11.50 4.00
Never hinged 23.00
*Nos. 60-63 (4)* 57.25 31.00

**1924** **Unwmk.** ***Perf. 14***

64 A4 1p green (I) 6.50 9.50
Never hinged 12.50
65 A4 1½p carmine 22.50 8.00
Never hinged 45.00

### *Perf. 14, 13½x12½*

**1926-30** **Wmk. 203**

66 A4 ½p orange 3.60 2.00
Never hinged 7.00
a. Perf. 14 ('27) 6.75 7.25
Never hinged 11.00
67 A4 1p green (I) 4.25 1.00
Never hinged 8.00
a. 1p green (Ia) 50.00 70.00
Never hinged 75.00
b. Perf. 14 4.25 1.75
Never hinged 8.25
68 A4 1½p rose red ('27) 4.00 1.75
Never hinged 8.00
c. Perf. 14 ('26) 11.00 2.25
Never hinged 21.00
69 A4 1½p red brn ('30) 5.50 5.50
Never hinged 9.75
70 A4 2p red brn (II, '28) 14.50 8.00
Never hinged 29.00
a. Perf. 14 (I, '27) 40.00 40.00
Never hinged 75.00
71 A4 2p red (II) ('30) 9.00 .90
Never hinged 20.00
a. Tête bêche pair 175,000.
c. Unwmkd. (II) ('31) 1,350. 2,400.
72 A4 3p ultra (II) ('29) 30.00 5.00
Never hinged 52.50
a. 3p ultra (I) 62.50 20.00
Never hinged 125.00
b. Perf. 14 40.00 10.00
Never hinged 72.50
73 A4 4p ol bis ('29) 27.50 3.50
Never hinged 50.00
a. Perf. 14 ('28) 62.50 40.00
Never hinged 125.00
74 A4 4½p dk vio ('27) 22.50 5.25
Never hinged 40.00
a. Perf. 13½x12½ ('28) 75.00 29.00
Never hinged 135.00
75 A4 5p brn buff (II) ('30) 40.00 7.00
Never hinged 75.00
76 A4 1sh4p pale turq bl ('28) 110.00 27.50
Never hinged 225.00
a. Perf. 14 ('27) 125.00 70.00
Never hinged 275.00
*Nos. 66-76 (11)* 270.75 67.40

For surcharges & overprints see Nos. 106-107, O3-O4.

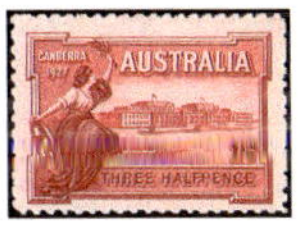


Parliament House, Canberra — A5

**Unwmk.**

**1927, May 9** **Engr.** ***Perf. 11***

94 A5 1½p brown red .60 .55
Never hinged 1.10
a. Vert. pair, imperf. btwn. 4,750. 4,250.
b. Horiz. pair, imperf. btwn. 10,000. 10,000.

Opening of Parliament House at Canberra.

### Melbourne Exhibition Issue

Kookaburra Type of 1914

**1928, Oct. 29**

95 A3 3p deep blue 5.00 7.25
Never hinged 7.25
a. Pane of 4 175.00 225.00
Never hinged 260.00

No. 95a was issued at the Melbourne Intl. Phil. Exhib. No marginal inscription. Printed in sheets of 60 stamps (15 panes). No. 95a exists imperf. Value, $300,000.

No. 95 was printed in sheets of 120 and issued Nov. 2 throughout Australia.

### Kangaroo-Map Type of 1913

*Perf. 11½, 12*

**1929-30** **Wmk. 203** **Typo.**

96 A1 6p brown 32.50 11.00
Never hinged 57.50
97 A1 9p violet 35.00 25.00
Never hinged 80.00
98 A1 1sh blue green 45.00 12.50
Never hinged 90.00
99 A1 2sh red brown 75.00 17.00
Never hinged 200.00
100 A1 5sh yel & gray 240.00 100.00
Never hinged 500.00
101 A1 10sh pink & gray 500.00 475.00
Never hinged 1,000.
102 A1 £2 dl red & blk ('30) 4,000. 800.00
Never hinged 8,000.
*Nos. 96-102 (7)* 4,928. 1,441.

For overprint see No. O5.

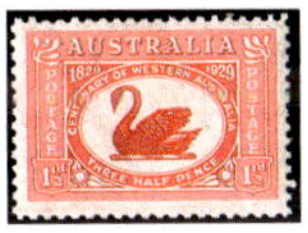


Black Swan — A6

**Unwmk.**

**1929, Sept. 28** **Engr.** ***Perf. 11***

103 A6 1½p dull red 2.00 2.00
Never hinged 3.25

Centenary of Western Australia.

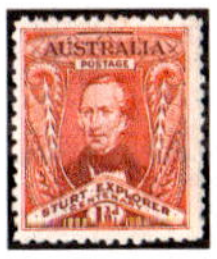


Capt. Charles Sturt — A7

**1930, June 2**

104 A7 1½p dark red 1.25 1.25
Never hinged 2.50
105 A7 3p dark blue 8.00 10.00
Never hinged 11.00

Capt. Charles Sturt's exploration of the Murray River, cent.

Nos. 68 and 74a surcharged

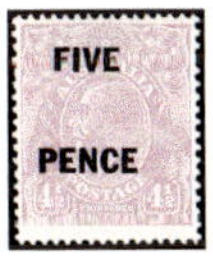


**1930** **Wmk. 203** ***Perf. 13½x12½***

106 A4 2p on 1½p rose red 2.50 1.25
Never hinged 4.00
107 A4 5p on 4½p dark violet 14.00 15.00
Never hinged 21.00

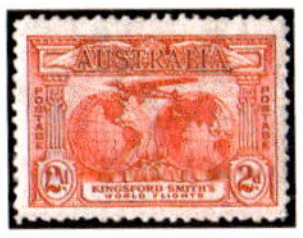


"Southern Cross" over Hemispheres — A8

### *Perf. 11, 11½*

**1931, Mar. 19** **Unwmk.**

111 A8 2p dull red 2.00 1.25
Never hinged 3.00
112 A8 3p blue 7.25 6.25
Never hinged 12.50
*Nos. 111-112,C2 (3)* 17.25 15.50

Trans-oceanic flights (1928-1930) of Sir Charles Edward Kingsford-Smith (1897-1935).

See No. C3 for similar design. For overprints see Nos. CO1, O1-O2.

### Types of 1913-23 Issues

*Perf. 13½x12½*

**1931-36** **Typo.** **Wmk. 228**

113 A4 ½p org ('32) 9.50 6.75
Never hinged 13.50
114 A4 1p green (I) 3.00 .40
Never hinged 5.00
115 A4 1½p red brn ('36) 8.00 13.50
Never hinged 12.50
116 A4 2p red (II) 2.50 .30
Never hinged 4.50
117 A4 3p ultra (II) ('32) 22.50 2.00
Never hinged 45.00
118 A4 4p ol bis ('33) 22.50 2.00
Never hinged 45.00
120 A4 5p brn buff (II) ('32) 22.50 1.00
Never hinged 35.00

### *Perf. 11½, 12; 13½x12½ (1sh4p)*

121 A1 6p yel brn ('36) 35.00 37.50
Never hinged 55.00
122 A1 9p violet ('32) 40.00 3.00
Never hinged 65.00
124 A4 1sh4p lt blue ('32) 60.00 9.00
Never hinged 145.00
125 A1 2sh red brn ('35) 10.00 2.75
Never hinged 20.00
126 A1 5sh yel & gray ('32) 175.00 20.00
Never hinged 400.00
127 A1 10sh pink & gray ('32) 400.00 200.00
Never hinged 1,000.
128 A1 £1 gray ('35) 700.00 275.00
Never hinged 1,400.
129 A1 £2 dl rose & blk ('34) 4,000. 800.00
Never hinged 9,250.
*Nos. 113-129 (15)* 5,511. 1,373.

For redrawn 2sh see No. 206. For overprints see Nos. O6-O11.

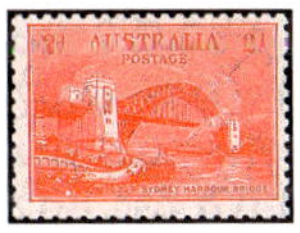


Sydney Harbor Bridge — A9

**Unwmk.**

**1932, Mar. 14** **Engr.** ***Perf. 11***

130 A9 2p red 2.00 1.60
Never hinged 5.00
131 A9 3p blue 5.00 4.00
Never hinged 10.00
132 A9 5sh gray green 460.00 275.00
Never hinged 1,300.

**Wmk. 228**

***Perf. 10½***

**Typo.**

133 A9 2p red 2.50 2.25
Never hinged 5.00

Opening of the Sydney Harbor Bridge on Mar. 19, 1932.

Value for 5sh, used, is for CTO examples.

For overprints see Nos. O12-O13.

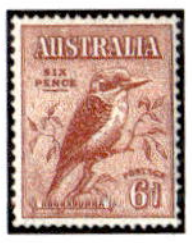


Kookaburra — A14

**1932, June 1** ***Perf. 13½x12½***

139 A14 6p light brown 15.00 1.25
Never hinged 27.50

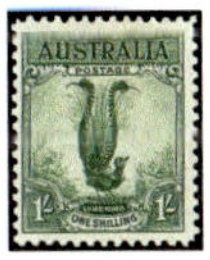


Male Lyrebird — A16

**1932, Feb. 15** **Unwmk.** ***Perf. 11***

**Size: 21½x25mm**

141 A16 1sh dark green 35.00 4.50
Never hinged 90.00

See No. 175, 300. For overprint see No. O14.

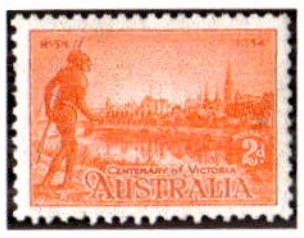


Yarra Yarra Tribesman, Yarra River and View of Melbourne — A17

**Wmk. 228**

**1934, July 2** **Engr.** ***Perf. 10½***

142 A17 2p vermilion 3.75 1.75
Never hinged 6.50
a. Perf. 11½ 5.00 4.50
Never hinged 10.00
143 A17 3p blue 4.50 4.00
Never hinged 10.00
a. Perf. 11½ 5.00 5.00
Never hinged 9.00
144 A17 1sh black 52.50 27.50
Never hinged 110.00
a. Perf. 11½ 62.50 35.00
Never hinged 120.00
*Nos. 142-144 (3)* 60.75 33.25

Centenary of Victoria.

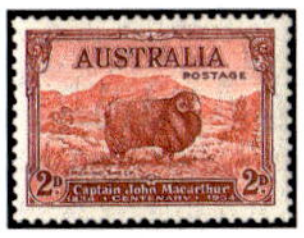


Merino Sheep — A18

**1934, Nov. 1** ***Perf. 11½***

147 A18 2p copper red 3.00 1.50
Never hinged 7.00
a. Die II 16.00 7.25
Never hinged 32.00
148 A18 3p dark blue 12.00 12.00
Never hinged 20.00
149 A18 9p dark violet 40.00 35.00
Never hinged 75.00
*Nos. 147-149 (3)* 55.00 48.50

Capt. John Macarthur (1767-1834), "father of the New South Wales woolen industry."

Two dies of 2p: I, shading on hill in background uneven from light to dark. II, shading is uniformly dark.

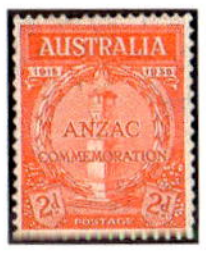


Cenotaph in Whitehall, London — A19

**1935, Mar. 18** ***Perf. 13½x12½***

150 A19 2p red 1.50 .50
Never hinged 3.00

***Perf. 11***

151 A19 1sh black 42.50 40.00
Never hinged 86.00

Anzacs' landing at Gallipoli, 20th anniv.

The 1sh perf 13½x12½ is a plate proof. Value, unused $2,250, mint never hinged $3,500.

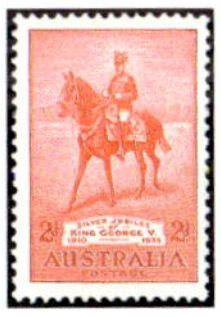


George V on His Charger "Anzac" — A20

**1935, May 2** ***Perf. 11½***

152 A20 2p red 2.00 .35
Never hinged 4.00
153 A20 3p blue 5.00 5.00
Never hinged 10.00
154 A20 2sh violet 42.50 40.00
Never hinged 85.00
*Nos. 152-154 (3)* 49.50 45.35

25th anniv. of the reign of King George V.

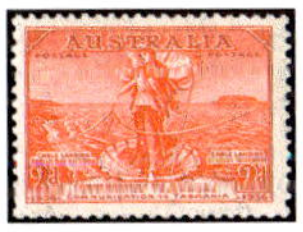


Amphitrite Joining Cables between Australia and Tasmania — A21

**1936, Apr. 1**

157 A21 2p red 1.00 .60
Never hinged 2.75
158 A21 3p dark blue 4.00 3.75
Never hinged 6.50

Australia/Tasmania telephone link.

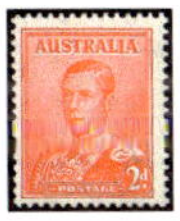


Edward VIII

A unique block of six unissued 2-penny King Edward VIII stamps realized the equivalent of U.S. $387,000 when it was sold at a London auction in 2014. A single stamp was separated from the block and sold at a Melbourne auction in 2015 for the equivalent of U.S. $123,600.

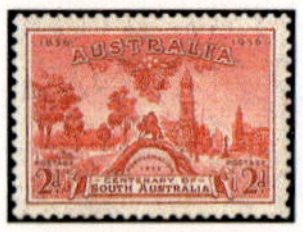

Proclamation Tree and View of Adelaide, 1936 — A22

**1936, Aug. 3**

| | | | | |
|---|---|---|---|---|
| 159 | A22 | 2p red | 1.00 | .60 |
| | | Never hinged | 2.40 | |
| 160 | A22 | 3p dark blue | 4.00 | 3.75 |
| | | Never hinged | 6.50 | |
| 161 | A22 | 1sh green | 14.00 | 11.00 |
| | | Never hinged | 27.50 | |
| | | *Nos. 159-161 (3)* | 19.00 | 15.35 |

Centenary of South Australia.

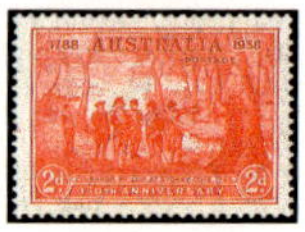

Gov. Arthur Phillip at Sydney Cove — A23

**1937, Oct. 1** ***Perf. 13x13½***

| | | | | |
|---|---|---|---|---|
| 163 | A23 | 2p red | 1.50 | .80 |
| | | Never hinged | 3.00 | |
| 164 | A23 | 3p ultra | 3.75 | 3.25 |
| | | Never hinged | 6.50 | |
| 165 | A23 | 9p violet | 14.00 | 12.00 |
| | | Never hinged | 25.00 | |
| | | *Nos. 163-165 (3)* | 19.25 | 16.05 |

150th anniversary of New South Wales.

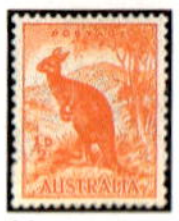

Kangaroo A24

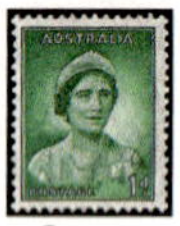

Queen Elizabeth A25

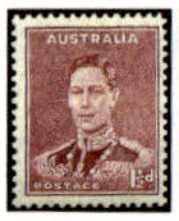

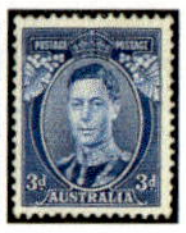

King George VI A26 A27

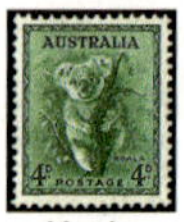

Koala A28

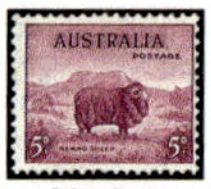

Merino Sheep A29

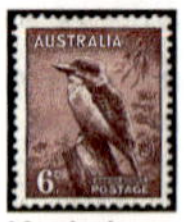

Kookaburra (Kingfisher) A30

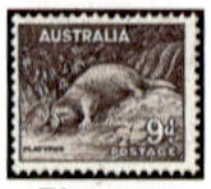

Platypus A31

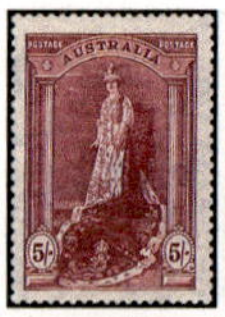

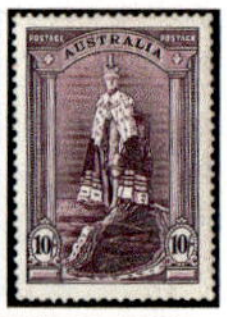

Queen Elizabeth and King George VI in Coronation Robes A32 A33

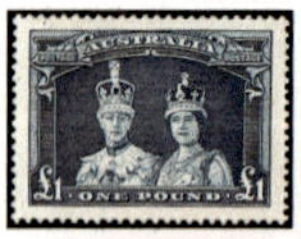

King George VI and Queen Elizabeth — A34

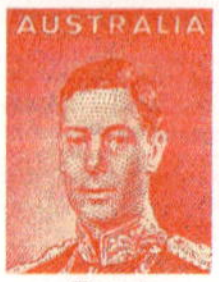

Type I

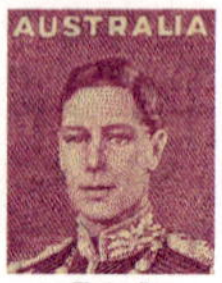

Type II

Two Types of A25 and A26:

Type I — Highlighted background. Lines around letters of Australia Postage and numerals of value.

Type II — Background of heavy diagonal lines without the highlighted effect. No lines around letters and numerals.

***Perf. 13½x14, 14x13½***

**1937-46 Engr. Wmk. 228**

| | | | | |
|---|---|---|---|---|
| 166 | A24 | ½p org, perf. 15x14 ('42) | .85 | .70 |
| | | Never hinged | 1.90 | |
| *a.* | | Perf. 13½x14 ('38) | 1.40 | .60 |
| | | Never hinged | 3.00 | |
| 167 | A25 | 1p emerald (I) | 1.10 | 1.00 |
| | | Never hinged | 2.25 | |
| 168 | A26 | 1½p dull red brn (II) | 4.00 | 3.50 |
| | | Never hinged | 7.00 | |
| *a.* | | Perf. 15x14 ('41) | 4.75 | 5.00 |
| | | Never hinged | 8.00 | |
| 169 | A26 | 2p scarlet (I) | 2.00 | .80 |
| | | Never hinged | 2.25 | |
| 170 | A27 | 3p ultramarine | 37.50 | 5.00 |
| | | Never hinged | 65.00 | |
| *a.* | | 3p dp ultra, thin paper ('38) | 30.00 | 5.00 |
| | | Never hinged | 55.00 | |
| 171 | A28 | 4p grn, perf. 15x14 ('42) | 1.00 | .30 |
| | | Never hinged | 2.00 | |
| *a.* | | Perf. 13½x14 ('38) | 3.25 | 2.50 |
| | | Never hinged | 9.00 | |
| 172 | A29 | 5p pale rose vio, perf. 14x15 ('46) | 1.00 | .80 |
| | | Never hinged | 2.00 | |
| *a.* | | Perf. 14x13½ ('38) | 3.00 | 2.50 |
| | | Never hinged | 4.75 | |
| 173 | A30 | 6p vio brn, perf. 15x14 ('42) | 1.00 | .30 |
| | | Never hinged | 2.00 | |
| *a.* | | Perf. 13½x14 | 12.50 | 2.40 |
| | | Never hinged | 25.00 | |
| *b.* | | 6p chocolate, perf. 15x14 | 1.40 | .55 |
| | | Never hinged | 2.25 | |
| 174 | A31 | 9p sep, perf. 14x15 ('43) | 2.00 | .45 |
| | | Never hinged | 3.00 | |
| *a.* | | Perf. 14x13½ ('38) | 4.50 | 2.40 |
| | | Never hinged | 9.00 | |
| 175 | A16 | 1sh gray grn, perf. 15x14 ('41) | 1.40 | .40 |
| | | Never hinged | 2.40 | |
| *a.* | | Perf. 13½x14 | 27.50 | 3.00 |
| | | Never hinged | 72.50 | |
| 176 | A27 | 1sh4p mag ('38) | 1.60 | *1.60* |
| | | Never hinged | 3.50 | |

***Perf. 13½***

| | | | | |
|---|---|---|---|---|
| 177 | A32 | 5sh dl red brn ('38) | 9.75 | 4.75 |
| | | Never hinged | 20.00 | |
| 178 | A33 | 10sh dl gray vio ('38) | 28.00 | 20.00 |
| | | Never hinged | 40.00 | |
| 179 | A34 | £1 bl gray ('38) | 70.00 | 42.50 |
| | | Never hinged | 115.00 | |
| | | *Nos. 166-179 (14)* | 161.20 | 82.10 |

No. 175 measures 17½x21½mm.

See Nos.223A, 293, 295, 298, 300. For surch. & overprints see Nos. 190, M1, M4-M5, M7.

**1938-42** ***Perf. 15x14***

| | | | | |
|---|---|---|---|---|
| 180 | A25 | 1p emerald (II) | 1.00 | .70 |
| 181 | A25 | 1p dl red brn (II) ('41) | .70 | .60 |
| 181B | A26 | 1½p bl grn (II) ('41) | .70 | *.80* |
| 182 | A26 | 2p scarlet (II) | 1.00 | .30 |
| 182B | A26 | 2p red vio (II) ('41) | .40 | .30 |
| 183 | A27 | 3p dk ultra ('40) | 29.00 | 3.00 |
| | | Never hinged | 57.50 | |
| 183A | A27 | 3p dk vio brn ('42) | .40 | .30 |
| | | *Nos. 180-183A (7)* | 33.20 | 6.00 |
| | | Set, never hinged | 72.50 | |

No. 183 differs from Nos. 170-170a in the shading lines on the king's left eyebrow which go downward, left to right, instead of the reverse. Also, more of the left epaulette shows.

For surcharges & ovpt. see Nos. 188-189, M3.

Coil Perforation

A special perforation was applied to stamps intended for use in coils to make separation easier. It consists of small and large holes (2 small, 10 large, 2 small) on the stamps' narrow side. Some of the stamps so perforated were sold in sheets.

This coil perforation may be found on Nos. 166, 181, 182, 182B, 193, 215, 223A, 231, 257, 315-316, 319, 319a and others.

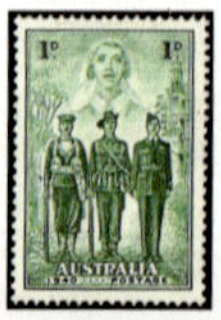

Nurse, Sailor, Soldier and Aviator — A35

***Perf. 13½x13***

**1940, July 15 Engr. Wmk. 228**

| | | | | |
|---|---|---|---|---|
| 184 | A35 | 1p green | 1.50 | *1.50* |
| | | Never hinged | 3.00 | |
| 185 | A35 | 2p red | 1.60 | *1.50* |
| | | Never hinged | 3.25 | |
| 186 | A35 | 3p ultra | 5.00 | *7.00* |
| | | Never hinged | 10.00 | |
| 187 | A35 | 6p chocolate | 15.00 | *13.00* |
| | | Never hinged | 30.00 | |
| | | *Nos. 184-187 (4)* | 23.10 | 23.00 |

Australia's participation in WWII.

No. 182 Surcharged in Blue

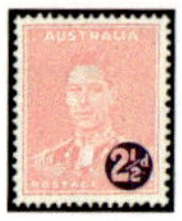

**1941, Dec. 10** ***Perf. 15x14***

| | | | | |
|---|---|---|---|---|
| 188 | A26 | 2½p on 2p red | .80 | *.80* |
| | | Never hinged | 1.50 | |

No. 183 Surcharged in Black and Yellow

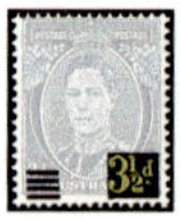

| | | | | |
|---|---|---|---|---|
| 189 | A27 | 3½p on 3p dk ultra | .90 | *.90* |
| | | Never hinged | 1.75 | |

No. 172a Surcharged in Purple

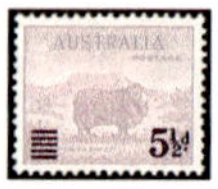

***Perf. 14x13½***

| | | | | |
|---|---|---|---|---|
| 190 | A29 | 5½p on 5p pale rose vio | 3.25 | *3.25* |
| | | Never hinged | 5.25 | |
| | | *Nos. 188-190 (3)* | 4.95 | 4.95 |

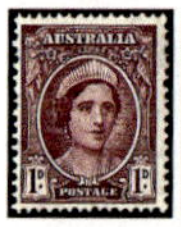

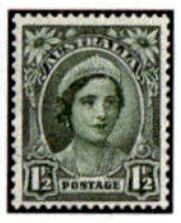

Queen Elizabeth A36 A37

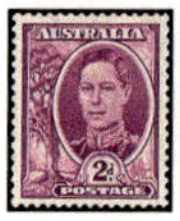

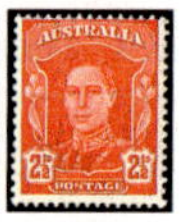

King George VI A38 A39

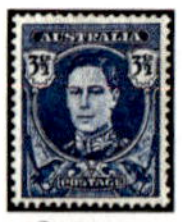

George VI and Blue Wrens A40

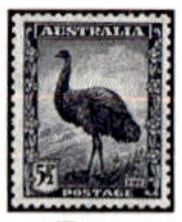

Emu A41

**1942-44 Engr.** ***Perf. 15x14***

| | | | | |
|---|---|---|---|---|
| 191 | A36 | 1p brown vio ('43) | .45 | .25 |
| 192 | A37 | 1½p green | .70 | .25 |
| 193 | A38 | 2p lt rose vio ('44) | .70 | .25 |
| 194 | A39 | 2½p red | .70 | .30 |
| 195 | A40 | 3½p ultramarine | .90 | .70 |
| 196 | A41 | 5½p indigo | 1.25 | 1.00 |
| | | *Nos. 191-196 (6)* | 4.70 | 2.75 |
| | | Set, never hinged | 8.00 | |

See Nos. 224-225. For overprint see No. M2.

**Catalogue values for unused stamps in this section, from this point to the end of the section, are for Never Hinged items.**

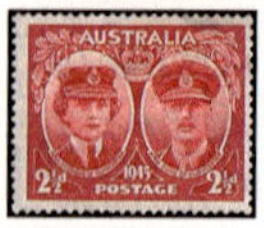

Duke and Duchess of Gloucester — A42

**1945, Feb. 19 Engr.** ***Perf. 14½***

| | | | | |
|---|---|---|---|---|
| 197 | A42 | 2½p brown red | .30 | .25 |
| 198 | A42 | 3½p bright ultra | .45 | *.50* |
| 199 | A42 | 5½p indigo | .55 | *.50* |
| | | *Nos. 197-199 (3)* | 1.30 | *1.25* |

Inauguration of the Duke of Gloucester as Governor General.

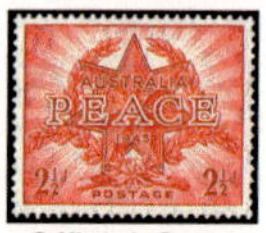

Official Crest and Inscriptions A43

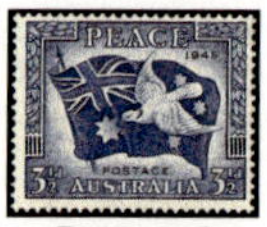

Dove and Australian Flag A44

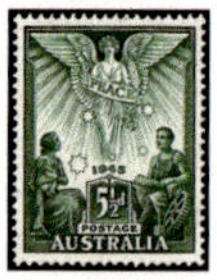

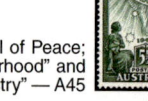

Angel of Peace; "Motherhood" and "Industry" — A45

**1946, Feb. 18 Wmk. 228** ***Perf. 14½***

| | | | | |
|---|---|---|---|---|
| 200 | A43 | 2½p carmine | .25 | .25 |
| 201 | A44 | 3½p deep ultra | .65 | *.50* |
| 202 | A45 | 5½p deep yellow green | .70 | *.50* |
| | | *Nos. 200-202 (3)* | 1.60 | *1.25* |

End of WWII. See Nos. 1456-1458.

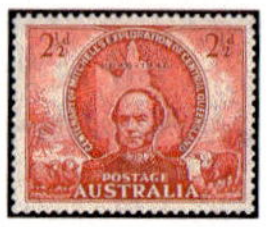

Sir Thomas Mitchell and Map of Queensland — A46

**1946, Oct. 14**

| | | | | |
|---|---|---|---|---|
| 203 | A46 | 2½p dark carmine | .25 | .25 |
| 204 | A46 | 3½p deep ultra | .50 | .40 |
| 205 | A46 | 1sh olive green | .50 | .40 |
| | | *Nos. 203-205 (3)* | 1.25 | 1.05 |

Sir Thomas Mitchell's exploration of central Queensland, cent.

**Kangaroo-Map Type of 1913 Redrawn**

**1945, Dec. Typo.** ***Perf. 11½***

| | | | | |
|---|---|---|---|---|
| 206 | A1 | 2sh dk red brown | 5.50 | 5.50 |

The R and A of AUSTRALIA are separated at the base and there is a single line between the value tablet and "Two Shillings." On No. 125 the tail of the R touches the A, while two lines appear between value tablet and "Two Shillings." There are many other minor differences in the design.

For overprint see No. M6.

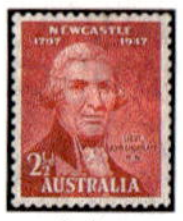

John Shortland A47

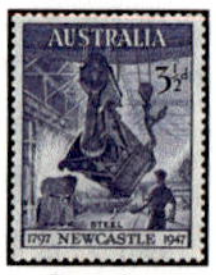

Pouring Steel A48

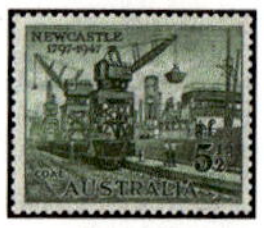

Loading Coal — A49

**1947, Sept. Engr.** ***Perf. 14½x14***

| | | | | |
|---|---|---|---|---|
| 207 | A47 | 2½p brown red | .35 | .25 |

***Perf. 14½***

| | | | | |
|---|---|---|---|---|
| 208 | A48 | 3½p deep blue | .65 | *.65* |
| 209 | A49 | 5½p deep green | .65 | *.40* |
| | | *Nos. 207-209 (3)* | 1.65 | 1.30 |

150th anniv. of the discovery of the Hunter River estuary, site of Newcastle by Lieut. John Shortland. By error the 2½p shows his father, Capt. John Shortland.

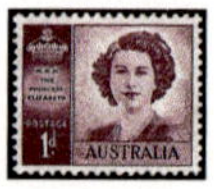

Princess Elizabeth — A50

# AUSTRALIA

**Perf. 14x14½**
**1947, Nov. 20**     **Wmk. 228**
210 A50 1p brown violet .40 .40
See Nos. 215 and 1595.

Hereford Bull A51

Crocodile A52

**1948, Feb. 16**     **Perf. 14½**
211 A51 1sh3p violet brown 2.50 1.25
212 A52 2sh chocolate 2.50 1.00
See No. 302.

William J. Farrer — A53

Design: No. 214, Ferdinand von Mueller.

**1948**     **Perf. 14½x14**
213 A53 2½p red .50 .25
214 A53 2½p dark red .45 .25

William J. Farrer (1845-1906), wheat researcher, and Ferdinand von Mueller (1825-1896), German born botanist.
Issue dates: No. 213, July 12. No. 214, Sept. 13.

### Elizabeth Type of 1947
**1948, Aug.**   **Unwmk.**   **Perf. 14x14½**
215 A50 1p brown violet .10 .25
See Nos. 210 and 1595.

Scout in Uniform — A55

**1948, Nov. 15**   **Engr.**   **Wmk. 228**
216 A55 2½p brown red .15 .25

Pan-Pacific Scout Jamboree, Victoria, Dec. 29, 1948 to Jan. 9, 1949. See No. 249.

Arms of Australia — A56

**1949-50**   **Wmk. 228**   **Perf. 14x13½**
218 A56 5sh dark red 4.50 1.25
219 A56 10sh red violet 29.00 2.00
220 A56 £1 deep blue 45.00 8.50
221 A56 £2 green ('50) 175.00 26.00
Nos. 218-221 (4) 253.50 37.75

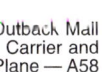
Henry Hertzborg Lawson (1867-1922), Author and Poet — A57

**Perf. 14½x14**
**1949, June 17**     **Unwmk.**
222 A57 2½p rose brown .50 .25

Outback Mail Carrier and Plane — A58

**1949, Oct. 10**
223 A58 3½p violet blue .40 .40
UPU, 75th anniv.

### Types of 1938, 1942-44 and

Aborigine — A59

**1948-50**   **Unwmk.**   **Perf. 14½x14**
223A A24 ½p orange ('49) .45 .25
224 A37 1½p green ('49) .35 .45
225 A38 2p lt rose violet 1.00 .55
**Wmk. 228**
226 A59 8½p dark brown ('50) .40 .40
Nos. 223A-226 (4) 2.20 1.65

Issued: 2p, Dec.; ½p, Sept.; 1½p, 8/29; 8½p, 8/14.
See Nos. 248, 303.

John Forrest — A60

**1949, Nov. 28**     **Wmk. 228**
227 A60 2½p brown red .40 .25

Forrest (1847-1918), explorer & statesman.

New South Wales A61

Victoria A62

First stamp designs.

**Perf. 14½x14**
**1950, Sept. 27**     **Unwmk.**
228 A61 2½p rose brown .40 .25
229 A62 2½p rose brown .40 .25
a. Pair, #228-229 1.60 1.25

Cent. of Australian adhesive postage stamps. Issued in sheets of 160 stamps containing alternate copies of Nos. 228 and 229.

Elizabeth A63

George VI A64

**1950-51**   **Engr.**   **Unwmk.**
230 A63 1½p deep green .80 .75
231 A63 2p yellow grn ('51) .30 .25
232 A64 2½p violet brn ('51) .30 .45
233 A64 3p dull green ('51) .35 .25
Nos. 230-233 (4) 1.75 1.70

Issued: 1½p, 6/19; 2p, 3/28; 2½p, 5/23; 3p, 11/14.

A65

A66

**1950-52**     **Wmk. 228**
234 A64 2½p red .25 .25
235 A64 3p red ('51) .35 .35
236 A65 3½p red brown ('51) .25 .25
237 A65 4½p scarlet ('52) .45 .45
238 A65 6½p choc ('52) .35 .35
238A A65 6½p blue green ('52) .45 .25
239 A66 7½p deep blue ('51) .50 .50
Nos. 234-239 (7) 2.70 2.40

Issued: 2½p, 4/12; 3p, 2/28; 7½p, 10/31; 3½p, 11/20; 4½p, No. 238, 2/20; No. 238A, 4/9.

A67

Founding of the Commonwealth of Australia, 50th Anniv. — A68

Designs: No. 240, Sir Edmund Barton. No. 241, Sir Henry Parkes, bearded. 5½p, Duke of York opening first Federal Parliament. 1sh6p, Parliament House, Canberra.

**Perf. 14½x14**
**1951, May 1**   **Engr.**   **Unwmk.**
240 A67 3p carmine 1.00 .25
241 A67 3p carmine 1.00 .25
a. Pair, #240, 241 2.00 2.00
242 A68 5½p deep blue 1.20 1.50
243 A68 1sh6p red brown 1.60 1.40
Nos. 240-243 (4) 4.80 3.40

Edward Hammond Hargraves — A69

Design: No. 245, Charles Joseph Latrobe (1801-1875), first governor of Victoria.

**1951, July 2**
244 A69 3p rose brown .80 .25
245 A69 3p rose brown .80 .25
a. Pair, #244, 245 2.00 1.60

Discovery of gold in Australia, cent. (No. 244); Establishment of representative government in Victoria, cent. (No. 245). Sheets contain alternate rows of Nos. 244 and 245.

King George VI — A70

**1952, Mar. 19**   **Wmk. 228**   **Perf. 14½**
247 A70 1sh½p slate blue 2.50 .85

### Aborigine Type of 1950 Redrawn
**Size: 20½x25mm**
248 A59 2sh6p dark brown 5.75 1.25

Portrait as on A59; lettering altered and value repeated at lower left. See No. 303.

### Scout Type of 1948
**Dated "1952-53"**
**Perf. 14x14½**
**1952, Nov. 19**     **Wmk. 228**
249 A55 3½p red brown .45 .25

Pan-Pacific Scout Jamboree, Greystanes, Dec. 30, 1952, to Jan. 9, 1953.

Modern Dairy, Butter Production — A71

**Perf. 14½**
**1953, Feb. 11**   **Unwmk.**   **Typo.**
250 A71 3p shown .90 .40
251 A71 3p Wheat .90 .40
252 A71 3p Beef .90 .40
a. Strip of 3, #250-252 8.00 8.00
253 A71 3½p shown .90 .40
254 A71 3½p Wheat .90 .40
255 A71 3½p Beef .90 .40
a. Strip of 3, #253-255 7.50 7.50
Nos. 250-255 (6) 5.40 2.40

Both the 3p and 3½p were printed in panes of 50 stamps: 17 Butter, 17 Wheat and 16 Beef. The stamps were issued to encourage food production.

Queen Elizabeth II — A72

**Perf. 14½x14**
**1953-54**     **Unwmk.**   **Engr.**
256 A72 1p purple .30 .30
256A A72 2½p deep blue ('54) .45 .30
257 A72 3p dark green .45 .25
**Wmk. 228**
258 A72 3½p dark red .55 .45
258B A72 6½p orange ('54) 1.50 .75
Nos. 256-258B (5) 3.25 2.05

Issued: 3½p, 4/21; 3p, 6/17; 1p, 8/19; 2½p, 6½p, 6/23.
See Nos. 292, 296.

### Coronation Issue

Queen Elizabeth II A73

**1953, May 25**     **Unwmk.**
259 A73 3½p rose red .60 .25
260 A73 7½p violet 1.00 1.00
261 A73 2sh dull green 2.00 1.50
Nos. 259-261 (3) 3.60 2.75

Boy and Girl with Calf — A74

**1953, Sept. 3**     **Perf. 14½**
262 A74 3½p dp green & red brn .50 .25

Official establishment of Young Farmers' Clubs, 25th anniv.

Lieut. Gov. David Collins A75

Sullivan Cove, Hobart A76

Design: No. 264, Lieut. Gov. William Paterson (facing left).

**1953, Sept. 23**     **Perf. 14½x14**
263 A75 3½p red brown .45 .25
264 A75 3½p red brown .60 .25
a. Pair, #263-264 1.60 1.60
265 A76 2sh green 4.00 2.50
Nos. 263-265 (3) 5.05 3.00

Settlement in Tasmania, 150th anniv. Sheets contain alternate rows of Nos. 263 and 264.

Tasmania Stamp of 1853 — A77

**1953, Nov. 11**     **Perf. 14½**
266 A77 3p red .40 .40

Tasmania's first postage stamps, cent.

Elizabeth II and Duke of Edinburgh — A78

Elizabeth II — A79

**1954, Feb. 2**     **Perf. 14½x14, 14x14½**
267 A78 3½p rose red .35 .25
268 A79 7½p purple .80 .80
269 A78 2sh green 1.60 1.00
Nos. 267-269 (3) 2.75 2.05

Visit of Queen Elizabeth II and the Duke of Edinburgh, 1954.

# AUSTRALIA

Telegraph Pole and Key — A80

**1954, Apr. 7**    **Engr.**    **Perf. 14**
270 A80 3½p dark red    .45 .25
Inauguration of the telegraph in Australia, cent.

Red Cross and Globe — A81

**1954, June 9**    **Perf. 14½x14**
271 A81 3½p deep blue & red    .40 .25
Australian Red Cross Society.

Swan — A82

**1954, Aug. 2**    **Unwmk.**    **Perf. 14½**
274 A82 3½p black    .40 .25
Western Australia's first postage stamp, cent.

Diesel and Early Steam Locomotives A83

**1954, Sept. 13**    **Perf. 14x14½**
275 A83 3½p red brown    .45 .25
Centenary of Australian railroads.

Antarctic Flora and Fauna and Map — A84

**1954, Nov. 17**    **Perf. 14**
276 A84 3½p black    .40 .25
Australia's interest in the Antarctic continent.

Olympic Circles and Arms of Melbourne — A85

**1954, Dec. 1**
277 A85 2sh dark blue    5.75 3.25
16th Olympic Games to be held in Melbourne Nov.-Dec. 1956. See No. 286.

Globe, Flags and Rotary Emblem — A86

**1955, Feb. 23**    **Perf. 14x14½**
278 A86 3½p carmine    .40 .25
Rotary International, 50th anniv.

Elizabeth II — A87

**1955, Mar. 9**    **Wmk. 228**    **Perf. 14½**
279 A87 1sh ½p dk gray blue    3.25 1.00
See No. 301.

Top of US Monument, Canberra — A88

**1955, May 4**    **Unwmk.**    **Perf. 14x14½**
280 A88 3½p deep ultra    .50 .25
Friendship between Australia and the US.

Cobb and Company Mail Coach — A89

**1955, July 6**    **Perf. 14½x14**
281 A89 3½p dark brown    .50 .25
282 A89 2sh brown    2.25 2.25
Pioneers of Australia's coaching era.

World Map, YMCA Emblem — A90

**Engr. and Typo.**
**1955, Aug. 10**    **Perf. 14**
283 A90 3½p Prus green & red    .40 .25
   a. Red omitted    25,000.
Centenary of YMCA.

Florence Nightingale and Modern Nurse — A91

**1955, Sept. 21**    **Engr.**    **Perf. 14x14½**
284 A91 3½p red violet    .40 .25
Centenary of Florence Nightingale's work in the Crimea and of the founding of modern nursing.

Queen Victoria — A92

**1955, Oct. 17**    **Perf. 14½**
285 A92 3½p green    .40 .25
South Australia's first postage stamps, cent.

**Olympic Type of 1954**
**1955, Nov. 30**    **Unwmk.**    **Perf. 14**
286 A85 2sh deep green    3.25 2.40
16th Olympic Games at Melbourne, Nov. 22-Dec. 8, 1956.

Queen Victoria, Queen Elizabeth II and Badges of Victoria, New South Wales and Tasmania — A93

**1956, Sept. 26**    **Perf. 14½x14**
287 A93 3½p brown carmine    .40 .25
Centenary of responsible government in Victoria, New South Wales and Tasmania.

Melbourne Coat of Arms A94

Southern Cross, Olympic Torch A95

Collins Street, Melbourne — A96

Design: 2sh, Melbourne across Yarra River.

**1956, Oct. 31**    **Engr.**    **Perf. 14½, 14**
288 A94 4p dark carmine    .50 .25
289 A95 7½p ultramarine    .75 1.00
**Photo.**
**Perf. 14x14½**
290 A96 1sh multicolored    .95 .50
**Perf. 12x11½**
**Granite Paper**
291 A96 2sh multicolored    1.60 1.25
   Nos. 288-291 (4)    3.80 3.00
16th Olympic Games, Melbourne, 11/22-12/8.
A lithographed souvenir sheet incorporating reproductions of Nos. 288-291 in reduced size was of private origin and not postally valid.

**Types of 1938-55 and**

Queen Elizabeth II — A97

**Perf. 14½x14, 14x15, 15x14, 14½**
| 1956-57 | Engr. | Unwmk. | | |
|---|---|---|---|---|
| 292 | A72 | 3½p dark red | 1.40 | .55 |
| 293 | A28 | 4p green | 2.00 | .45 |
| 294 | A97 | 4p claret ('57) | .45 | .25 |
| a. | | Booklet pane of 6 ('57) | 12.50 | |
| 295 | A30 | 6p brown violet | 3.50 | .55 |
| 296 | A72 | 6½p orange | 3.50 | .25 |
| 297 | A97 | 7½p violet ('57) | 1.60 | .55 |
| 298 | A31 | 9p sepia | 17.00 | 2.00 |
| 299 | A97 | 10p gray blue ('57) | 1.25 | .55 |
| 300 | A16 | 1sh gray green | 7.25 | 1.10 |
| 301 | A87 | 1sh7p redsh brn ('57) | 5.25 | .70 |
| 302 | A52 | 2sh chocolate | 14.00 | 1.10 |
| 303 | A59 | 2sh6p brown ('57) | 10.50 | 1.10 |
| | | Nos. 292-303 (12) | 67.70 | 9.15 |

No. 300 measures 17½x21½mm. No. 303 measures 20½x25mm and is the redrawn type of 1952.
Issued: 3½p, 7/2; 2sh, 7/21; No. 293, 6p, 8/18; 6½p, Sept. 9p, 1sh, 12/13; 2sh6p, 1/30; 10p, 3/6; No. 294, 1sh7p, 3/13; 7½p, 11/13.

South Australia Coat of Arms — A99

**1957, Apr. 17**    **Unwmk.**    **Perf. 14½**
304 A99 4p brown red    .40 .25
Centenary of responsible government in South Australia.
No. 304 exists in two types on alternate rows of the sheet. Type I — The scroll just passes through the hyphen between the dates. Type II — The scroll passing through the hyphen between "1857-1957" is longer. Both types are of equal value.

Caduceus and Map of Australia — A100

**1957, Aug. 21**    **Perf. 14½x14**
305 A100 7p violet blue    .60 .30
Royal Flying Doctor Service of Australia.

Star of Bethlehem and Praying Child — A101

**1957, Nov. 6**    **Engr.**
306 A101 3½p dull rose    .35 .25
307 A101 4p pale purple    .35 .25
Christmas.

Canberra War Memorial, Sailor and Airman — A102

Design: No. 309, As No. 308 with soldier and service woman. Printed in alternate rows in sheet.

**1958, Feb. 10**    **Unwmk.**
308 A102 5½p brown carmine    1.60 .70
309 A102 5½p brown carmine    1.60 .70
   a. Pair, #308-309    4.00 3.50

Sir Charles Kingsford-Smith and "Southern Cross" — A103

**1958, Aug. 27**    **Perf. 14x14½**
310 A103 8p brt violet blue    1.25 1.00
1st air crossing of the Tasman Sea, 30th anniv. See New Zealand No. 321.

Broken Hill Mine — A104

**1958, Sept. 10**    **Perf. 14½x14**
311 A104 4p brown    .40 .25
Broken Hill mining field, 75th anniv.

Nativity — A105

**1958, Nov. 5**    **Perf. 14½x15**
312 A105 3½p dark red    .30 .25
313 A105 4p dark purple    .30 .25
Christmas.

A106

A107

A108     A109

A110

# AUSTRALIA

Platypus
A111

Tasmanian
Tiger
A112

Flannel
Flower
A113

Aboriginal
Stockman Cutting
Out a Steer
A114

Die I

Die II

Designs: 3p, Queen Elizabeth II facing right. 6p, Banded anteater. 8p, Tiger cat. 9p, Kangaroos. 11p, Rabbit bandicoot. 1sh6p, Christmas bells (flower). 2sh3p, Wattle (flower). 2sh5p, Banksia (flower). 3sh, Waratah (flower).

FIVE PENCE
Die I — Four short lines inside "5" at right of ball; six short lines left of ball; full length line above ball is seventh from bottom. Odd numbered horizontal rows in each sheet are in Die I.
Die II — Five short lines inside "5" at right of ball; seven at left; full length line above ball is eighth from bottom. Even numbered horizontal rows in each sheet are in Die II.

*Perf. 14½x14, 14x14½, 14½*

| 1959-64 | | Engr. | Unwmk. | |
|---|---|---|---|---|
| 314 | A106 | 1p dull violet | .25 | .25 |
| 315 | A107 | 2p red brn ('62) | .40 | .35 |
| 316 | A108 | 3p bluish green | .35 | .25 |
| 317 | A108 | 3½p dark green | .25 | .25 |
| 318 | A109 | 4p carmine | 1.00 | .25 |
| a. | | Booklet pane of 6 | 29.00 | |
| 319 | A110 | 5p dark blue (I) | 1.00 | .25 |
| a. | | 5p dark blue (II) | 1.00 | .25 |
| b. | | Booklet pane of 6 ('60) | 17.00 | |
| 320 | A111 | 6p chocolate | 1.50 | .25 |
| 321 | A111 | 8p red brn ('60) | 1.50 | .25 |
| 322 | A111 | 9p brown black | 1.90 | .75 |
| 323 | A111 | 11p dk blue ('61) | 1.90 | .25 |
| 324 | A111 | 1sh slate green | 4.50 | .70 |
| 325 | A112 | 1sh2p dk purple ('62) | 1.90 | .35 |
| 326 | A113 | 1sh6p red, yel ('60) | 3.00 | 1.20 |
| 327 | A113 | 2sh dark blue | 2.00 | .25 |
| 328 | A113 | 2sh3p green, yel | 2.25 | .25 |
| 328A | A113 | 2sh3p yel grn ('64) | 6.00 | 3.25 |
| 329 | A113 | 2sh5p brn, yel ('60) | 7.50 | 1.10 |
| 330 | A113 | 3sh crimson | 3.25 | .45 |
| | | **Wmk. 228** | | |
| 331 | A114 | 5sh red brown, cream | 24.00 | 2.25 |
| a. | | red brown, white ('64) | 120.00 | 12.00 |
| | | Nos. 314-331 (19) | 64.45 | 12.90 |

Issued: 1p, 4p, 2/2; 3½p, 3/18; 2sh, 4/8; 3p, 5/20; 3sh, 7/15; 1sh, No. 328, 9/9; 5p, 10/1; 9p, 10/21; 1sh6p, 2/3/60; 2sh5p, 3/16/60; 8p, 5/11/60; 6p, 9/30/60; 11p, 5/3/61; 5sh, 7/26/61; 2p, 1sh2p, 3/21/62; No. 328A, 10/28/64.

**Luminescent Printings**

Paper with an orange red phosphorescence (surface coating), was used for some printings of the Colombo Plan 1sh, No. 340, the Churchill 5p, No. 389, and several regular postage stamps. These include 2p, 3p, 6p, 8p, 9p, 11p, 1sh2p, 1sh6p and 2sh3p (Nos. 315, 316, 365, 367, 321, 368, 323, 325, 369, 328A).

Stamps printed only on phosphorescent paper include the Monash 5p, Hargrave 5p, ICY 2sh3p and Christmas 5p (Nos. 388, 390-393) and succeeding commemoratives; the 2sh, 2sh6p and 3sh regular birds (Nos. 370, 372, 373); and most of the regular series in decimal currency.

Ink with a phosphorescent content was used in printing the 5p red, No. 366, almost all of the 5p red booklets, No. 366a, most of the decimal 4c regular, No. 397, and its booklet pane, No. 397a, and all of No. 398.

Postmaster Isaac
Nichols Boarding
Vessel to Receive
Mail — A115

**1959, Apr. 22** *Perf. 14½x14*
332 A115 4p dark gray blue .40 .25
First post office, Sydney, 150th anniv.

Parliament House,
Brisbane, and
Queensland
Arms — A116

**1959, June 5** *Perf. 14x14½*
333 A116 4p dk green & violet .40 .25
Cent. of Queensland self-government.

Approach of the
Magi — A117

**1959, Nov. 4** *Perf. 15x14½*
334 A117 5p purple .40 .25
Christmas.

Girl Guide and
Lord Baden-Powell
A118

**1960, Aug. 18** *Perf. 14½x14*
335 A118 5p dark blue .45 .25
50th anniversary of the Girl Guides.

The Overlanders by Sir
Daryl Lindsay — A119

**1960, Sept. 21** *Perf. 14½*
336 A119 5p lilac rose .40 .25
Exploration of Australia's Northern Territory, cent.
No. 336 exists in two types. Type I: Top edge of the mane is broken and right ear is not closed. Type II: Mane is smooth and the lines in the ear are closed.

Melbourne Cup and
Archer, 1861
Winner — A120

**1960, Oct. 12** *Unwmk.*
337 A120 5p sepia .40 .25
Centenary of the Melbourne Cup.

Queen Victoria — A121

**1960, Nov. 2** *Engr.* *Perf. 14½*
338 A121 5p dark green .40 .25
Centenary of the first Queensland stamps.

Open Bible and
Candle — A122

**1960, Nov. 9** *Unwmk.*
339 A122 5p maroon .40 .25
Christmas; beginning of 350th anniv. year of the publication of the King James translation of the Bible.

Colombo Plan
Emblem — A123

**1961, June 30** *Perf. 14x14½*
340 A123 1sh red brown 1.60 .30
Colombo Plan for the peaceful development of South East Asia countries, 10th anniv.

Dame Nellie Melba, by
Sir Bertram
Mackennal — A124

**1961, Sept. 20** *Perf. 14½*
341 A124 5p deep blue .45 .30
Dame Nellie Melba, singer, birth cent.

Page from Book of
Hours, 15th
Century — A125

**1961, Nov. 8** *Perf. 14½x14*
342 A125 5p reddish brown .40 .25
Christmas; end of the 350th anniv. year of the publication of the King James translation of the Bible.

John McDouall
Stuart — A126

**1962, July 25** *Unwmk.* *Perf. 14½*
345 A126 5p carmine .40 .25
First south-north crossing of Australia by John McDouall Stuart, cent.

Nurse and Rev.
Flynn's Grave — A127

**1962, Sept. 5** *Photo.* *Perf. 13½*
346 A127 5p multicolored .50 .30
a. Red omitted 450.00
Australian Inland Mission founded by Rev. John Flynn, 50th anniv.

Woman and
Globe — A128

**1962, Sept. 26** *Engr.* *Perf. 14x14½*
347 A128 5p dark green .40 .25
World Conf. of the Associated Country Women of the World, Melbourne, Oct. 2-12.

Madonna and
Child — A129

**1962, Oct. 17** *Perf. 14½*
348 A129 5p deep violet .40 .25
Christmas.

View of Perth and     Arms of
Kangaroo             Perth — A131
Paw — A130

**1962, Nov. 1** *Photo.* *Perf. 14*
349 A130 5p multicolored .75 .25
a. Red omitted 5,500.
*Perf. 14½x14*
350 A131 2sh3p emer, blk, red & ultra 4.00 3.50
British Empire and Commonwealth Games, Perth, Nov. 22-Dec. 1.
Perf 14x14¾ examples of Nos. 349-350 are from a booklet pane issued for the 2006 Commonwealth Games. These stamps were not valid for postage.

Elizabeth II     Elizabeth II
A132             and Prince
                 Philip
                 A133

**1963, Feb. 18** *Engr.* *Perf. 14½*
351 A132 5p dark green .50 .25
352 A133 2sh3 red brown 4.00 3.00
Visit of Elizabeth II and Prince Philip.
Perf 14 ½x14 lithographed examples of Nos. 351-352 come from the booklet footnoted under No. 2507. These stamps were not valid for postage.

Walter Burley
Griffin and Arms of
Canberra — A134

**1963, Mar. 8** *Unwmk.* *Perf. 14½x14*
353 A134 5p dark green .40 .25
50th anniv. of Canberra; Walter Burley Griffin, American architect, who laid out plan for Canberra.

## AUSTRALIA

Red Cross Centenary Emblem — A135

**1963, May 8  Photo.  Perf. 13½x13**
354  A135  5p dk blue, red & gray   .50   .25
Centenary of the International Red Cross.

Explorers Blaxland, Lawson and Wentworth Looking West from Mt. York — A136

**1963, May 28  Engr.  Perf. 14½x14**
355  A136  5p dark blue   .40   .25
1st crossing of the Blue Mts., 150th anniv.

Globe, Ship, Plane and Map of Australia — A137

**1963, Aug. 28  Unwmk.**
356  A137  5p red   .40   .25
Importance of exports to Australian economy.

Elizabeth II A138

Black-backed Magpie and Eucalyptus A139

Abel Tasman and Ship A144

George Bass, Whaleboat A145

Designs: 6p, Yellow-tailed thornbill, horiz. 1sh6p, Galah on tree stump. 2sh, Golden whistler. 2sh5p, Blue wren and bracken fern. 2sh6p, Scarlet robin, horiz. 3sh, Straw-necked ibis. 5sh, William Dampier and "Roebuck" sailing ship. 7sh6p, Capt. James Cook. 10sh, Matthew Flinders and three-master "Investigator." £2, Admiral Philip Parker King.

**Perf. 15x14**
**1963-65  Unwmk.  Engr.**
365  A138  5p green   .90   .25
  a. Booklet pane of 6 ('64)   35.00
  b. Pair, imperf. btwn.   2.75   2.00
366  A138  5p red   .90   .25
  a. Booklet pane of 6   45.00

**Photo.**
**Perf. 13½**
367  A139  6p multi   1.10   .35
  a. Vert. pair, imperf. btwn.
368  A139  9p multi   2.00   1.75
369  A139  1sh6p multi   1.75   1.40
370  A139  2sh multi   2.25   .55
371  A139  2sh5p multi   5.75   3.25
372  A139  2sh6p multi   4.75   3.00
  a. Red omitted   12,000.  12,000.
373  A139  3sh multi   3.25   2.00

**Engr.**
**Perf. 14½x14, 14½x15**
374  A144  4sh violet blue   3.75   .95

**Wmk. 228**
375  A145  5sh red brown   5.25   2.50
376  A144  7sh6p olive green   18.00   13.00
377  A144  10sh deep claret   32.50   8.00
378  A145  £1 purple   65.00   30.00
379  A145  £2 brn blk   97.50   80.00
Nos. 365-379 (15)   244.65   147.25

No. 365a was printed in sheets of 288 which were sold intact by the Philatelic Bureau. These sheets have been broken to obtain pairs and blocks which are imperf. between (see No. 365b).

Issued: No. 365, 4sh, 10/9/63; 10sh, £1, 2/26/64; 9p, 1sh6p, 2sh5p, 3/11/64; 6p, 8/19/64; 7sh6p, £2, 8/26/64; 5sh, 11/25/64; 2sh, 2sh6p, 3sh, 4/21/65; No. 366, 6/30/65. See Nos. 400-401, 406-417, 1727-1728.

Star of Bethlehem — A146

**1963, Oct. 25  Unwmk.  Perf. 14½**
380  A146  5p blue   .40   .25
Christmas.

Cable Around World and Under Sea — A147

**1963, Dec. 3  Photo.  Perf. 13½**
381  A147  2sh3p gray, ver, blk & blue   4.50   3.50
Opening of the Commonwealth Pacific (telephone) cable service (COMPAC). See New Zealand No. 364.

Bleriot 60 Plane, 1914 — A148

**1964, July 1  Engr.  Perf. 14½x14**
382  A148  5p olive green   .50   .25
383  A148  2sh3p red   3.25   3.25
50th anniv. of the first air mail flight in Australia; Maurice Guillaux, aviator.

Child Looking at Nativity Scene — A149

**1964, Oct. 21  Photo.  Perf. 13½**
384  A149  5p bl, blk, red & buff   .40   .25
  a. Red omitted   6,250.   2,750.
  b. Black omitted   2,750.
  c. Buff omitted   3,500.
Christmas.

No. 384a used is valued on cover. The red ink can be removed from No. 384 by bleaching.

"Simpson and His Donkey" by Wallace Anderson — A150

**1965, Apr. 14  Engr.  Perf. 14x14½**
385  A150  5p olive bister   .50   .25
386  A150  8p dark blue   .90   .80
387  A150  2sh3p rose claret   2.80   3.00
Nos. 385-387 (3)   4.20   4.05

50th anniv. of the landing of the Australian and New Zealand Army Corps (ANZAC) at Gallipoli, Turkey, Apr. 25, 1915. Private John Simpson Kirkpatrick saved the lives of many wounded soldiers. The statue erected in his honor stands in front of Melbourne's Shrine of Remembrance.

Radio Mast and Satellite Orbiting Earth — A151

**1965, May 10  Photo.  Perf. 13½**
388  A151  5p multicolored   .65   .25
  a. Gray omitted   5,000.   5,000.
ITU, cent.

Winston Churchill — A152

**1965, May 24**
389  A152  5p lt bl, pale gray, dk gray & blk   .40   .25
  a. Pale gray omitted (white face)   5,500.
  b. Dark gray ("Australia") omitted   7,500.

Sir Winston Spencer Churchill (1874-1965), statesman and WWII leader.
Two examples of No. 389b recorded, one damaged. Value is for sound example.
See New Zealand No. 371.

John Monash and Transmission Tower — A153

**1965, June 23  Photo.  Perf. 13½**
390  A153  5p red, yel, blk & lt brn   .40   .25

Birth cent. of General Sir John Monash (1865-1931), soldier, Vice-Chancellor of University of Melbourne and chairman of the Victoria state electricity commission.

Lawrence Hargrave and Sketch for 1902 Seaplane — A154

**1965, Aug. 4  Unwmk.  Perf. 13½**
391  A154  5p multicolored   .40   .25
  a. Purple (5d) omitted   600.00   600.00

50th anniv. of the death of Lawrence Hargrave (1850-1915), aviation pioneer.

ICY Emblem — A155

**1965, Sept. 1  Photo.  Perf. 13½**
392  A155  2sh3p lt blue & green   3.25   3.00
International Cooperation Year.

Nativity — A156

**1965, Oct. 20  Unwmk.  Perf. 13½**
393  A156  5p multicolored   .40   .25
  a. Gold omitted   5,500.
  b. Ultramarine omitted   1,000.
  c. Brown omitted (white faces)   5,000.
Christmas.

**Types of 1963-65 and**

Elizabeth II A157

Humbug Fish A158

Designs: No. 400, Yellow-tailed thornbill, horiz. 6c, blue-faced honeyeater, horiz. 8c, Coral fish. 9c, Hermit crab. 10c Anemone fish. 13c, Red-necked avocet. 15c, Galah on tree stump. 20c, Golden whistler. 24c Azure kingfisher, horiz. 25c, Scarlet robin, horiz. 30c Straw-necked ibis. 40c Abel Tasman and ship. 50c, William Dampier and "Roebuck" sailing ship. 75c, Capt. James Cook. $1, Matthew Flinders and three-master "Investigator." $2, George Bass and whaleboat. $4, Admiral Philip Parker King.

**Perf. 14½x14 (A157); 13½ (A158, A139)**
**Engr. (A157), Photo. (A158, A139)**
**1966-71**
394  A157  1c red brown   .45   .25
395  A157  2c olive green   .75   .25
396  A157  3c Prus green   .75   .25
397  A157  4c red   .30   .25
  a. Booklet pane of 5 + label   35.00
398  A157  5c on 4c red ('67)   .40   .25
  a. Booklet pane of 5 + label ('67)   7.00
399  A157  5c dk blue ('67)   .75   .25
  a. Booklet pane of 5 + label   12.50
400  A139  5c lt grn, blk, brn & yel   .55   .25
  a. Brown omitted   3,500.   —
401  A139  6c gray, blk, lem & bl   .80   .35
  b. Blue omitted   2,500.
401A  A157  6c orange ('70)   .50   .25
402  A157  7c brn, ver, gray   1.25   .25
402A  A157  7c dp rose lilac ('71)   .75   .40
403  A158  8c multicolored   1.25   .40
404  A158  9c multicolored   1.25   .35
405  A158  10c lt brn, blk, org & bl   1.25   .25
  a. Orange omitted   4,250.
  b. Blue omitted   3,000.   2,000.
406  A139  13c lt bl grn, blk, gray & red   2.25   .40
  a. Red omitted   2,250.
  b. Gray omitted   2,100.
407  A139  15c lt grn, blk, gray & rose   2.25   .90
  a. Rose omitted   4,500.
  b. Gray omitted   2,750.   750.00
408  A139  20c pink, blk, yel & gray   5.25   .30
  a. Yellow omitted   2,900.
  b. Gray omitted   750.00
409  A139  24c tan, blk, vio bl & org   1.10   1.10
410  A139  25c gray, grn, blk & red   4.00   .55
  a. Red omitted   5,750.
411  A139  30c lt grn, buff, blk & red   16.00   .85
  a. Red omitted   3,000.

**Engr.**
**Perf. 14½x14, 14½x15**
412  A144  40c violet blue   12.00   .25
413  A145  50c brown red   16.00   .25
414  A144  75c olive green   2.00   1.40
415  A144  $1 deep claret   3.25   .45
  a. Perf 15x14   125.00   32.50
416  A145  $2 purple   8.00   2.25
417  A145  $4 sepia   8.00   5.00
Nos. 394-417 (26)   91.10   17.70

No. 398 issued in booklets only.
Booklet panes of 10 of No. 399, and of 5 No. 400, are torn from sheets. They were issued for the use of "Australian Defence Forces," as the covers read, in Viet Nam.
Issued: Nos. 398, 399, 9/29/67; No. 401A, 9/28/70; No. 402A, 10/1/71; No. 415a, 1973; others, 2/14/66.

**Coil Stamps**
**1966-67  Photo.  Perf. 15 Horiz.**
418  A157  3c emerald, blk & buff   .60   .50
419  A157  4c org red, blk & buff   .70   .50
420  A157  5c blue, black & buff   .85   .25
Nos. 418-420 (3)   2.15   1.25
Issued: 5c, 9/29/67; others, 2/14/66.

Rescue — A159

**1966, July 6  Photo.  Perf. 13½**
421  A159  4c blue, ultra & black   .30   .25
Royal Life Saving Society, 75th anniv.

Adoration of the Shepherds — A160

**1966, Oct. 19  Photo.  Perf. 13½**
422  A160  4c olive & black   .30   .25
  a. Olive omitted   7,250.
Christmas.

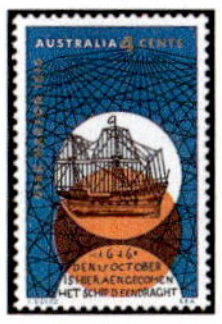

Dutch Sailing Ship, 17th Century — A161

**1966, Oct. 24 Photo. *Perf. 13½***

**423** A161 4c bl, blk, dp org & gold .30 .25
- *a.* Deep orange omitted *6,000.*
- *b.* Gold omitted *2,000.*

350th anniv. of Dirk Hartog's discovery of the Australian west coast, and his landing on the island named after him.

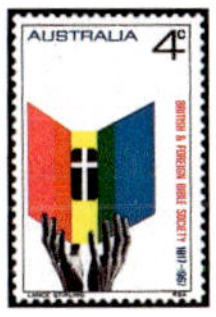

Hands Reaching for Bible — A162

**1967, Mar. 7 Photo. *Perf. 13½***

**424** A162 4c multicolored .30 .25

British and Foreign Bible Soc., 150th anniv.

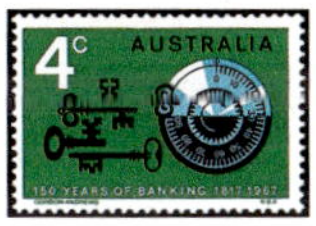

Combination Lock and Antique Keys — A163

**1967, Apr. 5 Photo. *Perf. 13½***

**425** A163 4c emerald, blk & lt blue .30 .25

150th anniv. of banking in Australia (Bank of New South Wales).

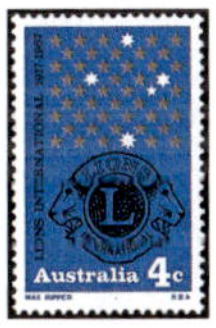

Lions Intl., 50th Anniv. — A164

**1967, June 7 Photo. *Perf. 13½***

**426** A164 4c ultra, black & gold .30 .25

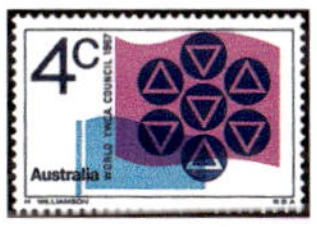

YWCA Emblems and Flags — A165

**1967, Aug. 21 Photo. *Perf. 13½***

**427** A165 4c dk blue, lt bl & lilac .30 .25

World Council Meeting of the YWCA, Monash University, Victoria, Aug. 14-Sept. 1.

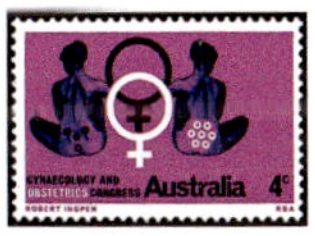

A166

Design: Seated women symbolizing obstetrics and gynecology, female symbol.

**1967, Sept. 20 Photo. *Perf. 13½***

**428** A166 4c lilac, dk blue & blk .30 .25

5th World Congress of Gynecology and Obstetrics, Sydney, Sept. 23-30.

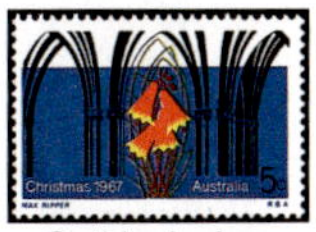

Gothic Arches and Christmas Bell Flower A167

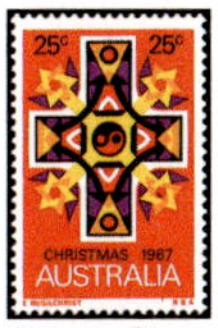

Cross, Stars of David and Yin Yang Forming Mandala A168

**1967 Photo. *Perf. 13½***

**429** A167 5c multicolored .30 .25
**430** A168 25c multicolored 2.25 2.00

Christmas.
Issue dates: 5c, Oct. 18; 25c, Nov. 27.

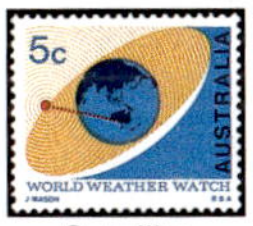

Satellite Orbiting Earth A169

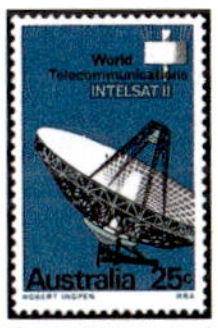

Satellite and Antenna, Moree, N.S.W. A170

Design: 20c, World weather map connecting Washington, Moscow and Melbourne, and computer and teleprinter tape spools.

**1968, Mar. 20 Photo. *Perf. 13½***

**431** A169 5c dull yel, red, bl & dk blue .90 .50
**432** A169 20c blue, blk & red 2.50 2.40
- *a.* Red omitted *3,000.*

**433** A170 25c Prus blue, blk & lt green 4.00 4.00
*Nos. 431-433 (3)* 7.40 6.90

Use of satellites for weather observations and communications.

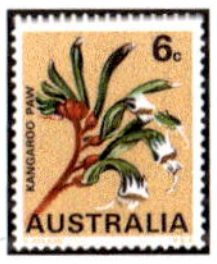

Kangaroo Paw, Western Australia — A171

State Flowers: 13c, Pink heath, Victoria. 15c, Tasmanian blue gum, Tasmania. 20c, Sturt's desert pea, South Australia. 25c, Cooktown orchid, Queensland. 30c, Waratah, New South Wales.

**1968, July 10 Photo. *Perf. 13½***
**Flowers in Natural Colors**

**434** A171 6c multicolored .55 .50
**435** A171 13c multicolored .65 .55
**436** A171 15c multicolored 2.25 .45
**437** A171 20c multicolored 5.00 .75
**438** A171 25c multicolored 4.75 .75
**439** A171 30c multicolored 1.25 .25
- *a.* Green omitted *3,750.*

*Nos. 434-439 (6)* 14.45 3.25

A 1971 reprinting of No. 439 shows more areas of white in the pink petals. This is scarcer than the first printing. Value, $4.75.

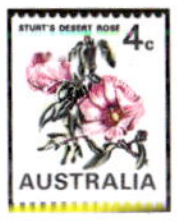

Sturt's Desert Rose, Northern Territory — A171a

Designs: 5c, Golden wattle, national flower. 7c, 10c, Sturt's desert pea.

**Coil Stamps**

**1970-75 *Perf. 14½ Horiz.***

**439A** A171a 2c dk grn & multi .25 .25
- *i.* Lettering and value bolder .25 .25

**439B** A171a 4c gray & multi .70 .45
**439C** A171a 5c gray & multi .25 .25
**439D** A171a 6c gray & multi 1.40 .55
- *h.* Green omitted *2,250.*

**439E** A171a 7c blk, red & grn .40 .25
- *f.* Green omitted 110.00

**439G** A171a 10c blk, red & grn .35 .25
*Nos. 439A-439G (6)* 3.35 2.00

Issued: 4c, 5c, 4/27; 6c, 10/28; 2c, 7c, 10/1/71; 10c, 1/15/75; No. 439Ai, 11/73.

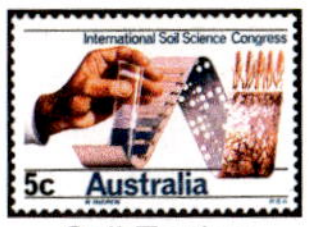

Soil Testing Through Chemistry & by Computer A172

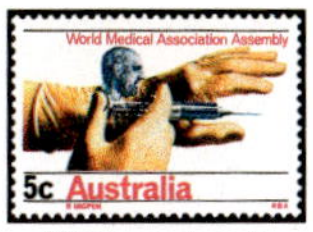

Hippocrates & Hands Holding Hypodermic A173

**1968, Aug. 6 Photo. *Perf. 13½***

**440** A172 5c multicolored .30 .25
**441** A173 5c multicolored .30 .25

9th Intl. Congress of Soil Science, University of Adelaide, Aug. 6-16 (No. 440); General Assembly of World Medical Associations, Sydney, Aug. 6-9 (No. 441). Nos. 440-441 printed in sheets of 100 in two separate panes of 50 connected by a gutter. Each sheet contains 10 gutter pairs.

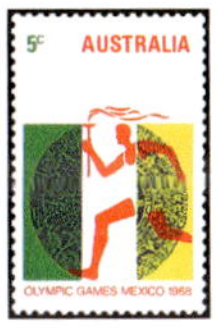

Runner and Aztec Calendar Stone — A174

Design: 25c, Aztec calendar stone and Mexican flag, horiz.

**1968, Oct. 2**

**442** A174 5c multicolored .55 .25
**443** A174 25c multicolored 2.00 1.75
- *a.* Green omitted *3,500.*

19th Olympic Games, Mexico City, Oct. 12-27. Nos. 442-443 printed in sheets of 100 in two separate panes of 50 connected by a gutter. Each sheet contains 10 gutter pairs.

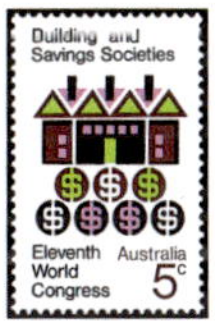

Symbolic House and Money — A175

**1968, Oct. 16**

**444** A175 5c multicolored .35 .35

11th Triennial Congress of the Intl. Union of Building Societies and Savings Associations, Sydney, Oct. 20-27.

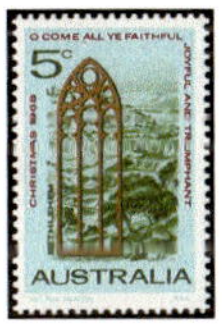

View of Bethlehem and Church Window — A176

**1968, Oct. 23 Photo. *Perf. 13½***

**445** A176 5c lt bl, red, grn & gold .30 .25
- *a.* Red omitted *3,500.* *2,000.*
- *b.* Gold omitted *850.00* *500.00*

Christmas.

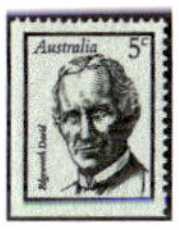

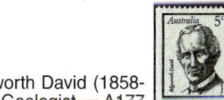

Edgeworth David (1858-1934), Geologist — A177

Famous Australians: No. 447, Caroline Chisholm (1808-77), social worker, reformer. No. 448, Albert Namatjira (1902-59), aborigine, artist. No. 449, Andrew Barton (Banjo) Paterson (1864-1941), poet, writer.

**1968, Nov. 6 Engr. *Perf. 15x14***

**446** A177 5c green, *greenish* 1.20 .35
- *a.* Booklet pane of 5 + label 6.50

**447** A177 5c purple, *pink* 1.20 .35
- *a.* Booklet pane of 5 + label 6.50

**448** A177 5c dark brown, *buff* 1.20 .35
- *a.* Booklet pane of 5 + label 6.50

**449** A177 5c indigo, *lt blue* 1.20 .35
- *a.* Booklet pane of 5 + label 6.50

*Nos. 446-449 (4)* 4.80 1.40

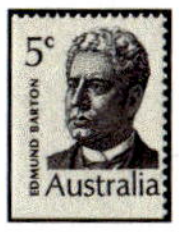

Sir Edmund Barton (1849-1920) — A178

Prime Ministers: No. 451, Alfred Deakin (1856-1919). No. 452, John C. Watson (1867-1941). No. 453, Sir George H. Reid (1845-1918).

**1969, Oct. 22 Engr. *Perf. 15x14***

**450** A178 5c indigo, *greenish* 1.20 .35
- *a.* Booklet pane of 5 + label 6.50

**451** A178 5c indigo, *greenish* 1.20 .35
- *a.* Booklet pane of 5 + label 6.50

**452** A178 5c indigo, *greenish* 1.20 .35
- *a.* Booklet pane of 5 + label 6.50

**453** A178 5c indigo, *greenish* 1.20 .35
- *a.* Booklet pane of 5 + label 6.50

*Nos. 450-453 (4)* 4.80 1.40

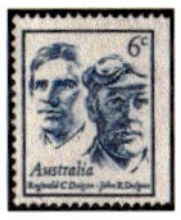

Reginald C. and John R. Duigan, Aviators — A179

Famous Australians: No. 455, Lachlan Macquarie (1761-1824), Governor of New South Wales. No. 456, Adam Lindsay Gordon (1833-70), poet. No. 457, Edward John Eyre (1815-1901), explorer.

**1970, Nov. 16 Engr. *Perf. 15x14***

**454** A179 6c dark blue 1.20 .50
- *a.* Booklet pane of 5 + label 6.50

**455** A179 6c dk brn, *salmon* 1.20 .50
- *a.* Booklet pane of 5 + label 6.50

**456** A179 6c magenta, *brt pink* 1.20 .50
- *a.* Booklet pane of 5 + label 6.50

**457** A179 6c brown red, *salmon* 1.20 .50
- *a.* Booklet pane of 5 + label 6.50

*Nos. 454-457 (4)* 4.80 2.00

Nos. 446-457 were issued in booklet panes only; all stamps have 1 or 2 straight edges.

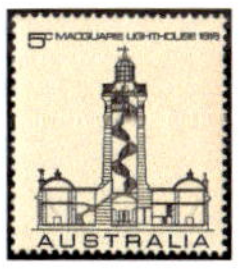

Macquarie Lighthouse — A180

**1968, Nov. 27 Engr. *Perf. 14½x13½***

**458** A180 5c indigo, *buff* .45 .50

Macquarie Lighthouse, Outer South Head, Sydney, 150th anniv.

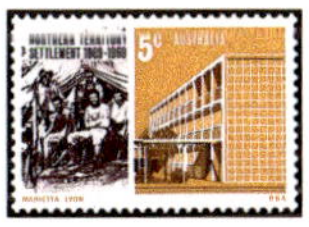

Surveyor George W. Goyder and Assistants, 1869; Building in Darwin, 1969 — A181

**1969, Feb. 5 Photo. *Perf. 13½***

**459** A181 5c black brn & dull yel .30 .25

First permanent settlement of the Northern Territory of Australia, cent.

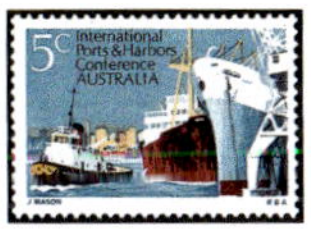

Melbourne Harbor Scene — A182

**1969, Feb. 26 Photo. *Perf. 13½***

**460** A182 5c dull blue & multi .30 .25

6th Biennial Conference of the Intl. Assoc. of Ports and Harbors, Melbourne, March 3-8.

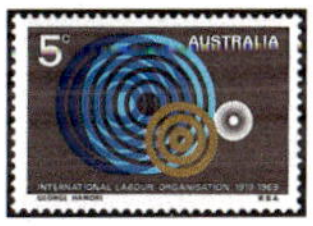

Overlapping Circles — A183

**1969, June 5 Photo. *Perf. 13½***

**461** A183 5c gray, vio bl, bl & gold .30 .25
- *a.* Gold omitted *3,000.*

ILO, 50th anniv.

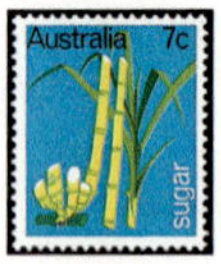
Sugar Cane — A184

Primary industries: 15c, Eucalyptus (timber). 20c, Wheat. 25c, Ram, ewe, lamb (wool).

**1969, Sept. 17** *Perf. 13½x13*
**462** A184 7c blue & multi 1.60 1.00
**463** A184 15c emerald & multi 4.75 3.00
*a.* Black omitted *1,750.* —
**464** A184 20c org brn & multi 2.40 1.20
**465** A184 25c gray, black & yel 3.25 1.20
*Nos. 462-465 (4)* 12.00 6.40

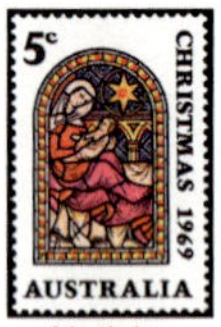
Nativity
A185

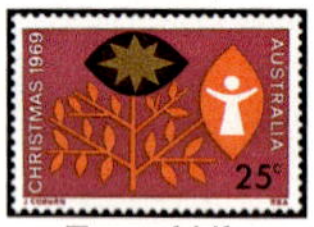
Tree of Life
A186

*Perf. 13½x13, 13x13½*
**1969, Oct. 15** **Photo.**
**466** A185 5c multicolored .40 .25
*a.* Yellow omitted *1,800.*
*b.* Magenta omitted *1,800.*
**467** A186 25c multicolored 3.00 2.75

Christmas.

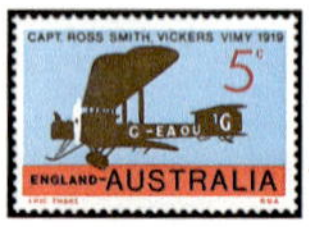
Vickers Vimy Flown by Ross Smith, England to Australia — A187

Designs: No. 469, B.E. 2E plane, automobile, spectators. No. 470, Ford truck, surveyors Lieuts. Hudson Fysh & P.J. McGinness.

**1969, Nov. 12** *Perf. 13x13½*
**468** A187 5c bl, blk, cop red & ol .75 .35
**469** A187 5c bl, blk, cop red & ol .75 .35
**470** A187 5c cop red, black & ol .75 .35
*a.* Strip of 3, #468-470 3.75 3.50
*Nos. 468-470 (3)* 2.25 1.05

1st England to Australia flight by Capt. Ross Smith & Lieut. Keith Smith, 50th anniv.
No. 470a has various combinations possible.

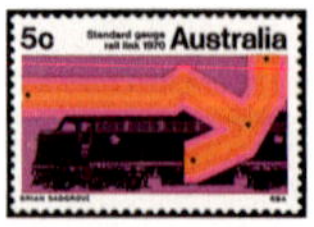
A188

Design: Diesel locomotive and new track linking Melbourne, Sydney and Brisbane with Perth.

**1970, Feb. 11 Photo.** *Perf. 13x13½*
**471** A188 5c multicolored .35 .25

Completion of the standard gauge railroad between Sydney and Perth.

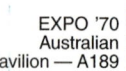

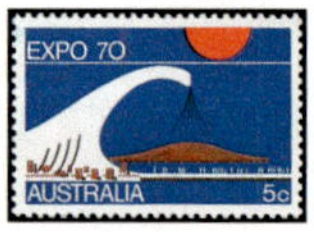
EXPO '70 Australian Pavilion — A189

Design: 20c, Southern Cross and Japanese inscription: "From the country of the south with warm feeling."

**1970, Mar. 16 Photo.** *Perf. 13x13½*
**472** A189 5c bl, blk, red & brnz .30 .25
**473** A189 20c red & black .75 .45

EXPO '70 Intl. Exhib., Osaka, Japan, Mar. 15-Sept. 13.

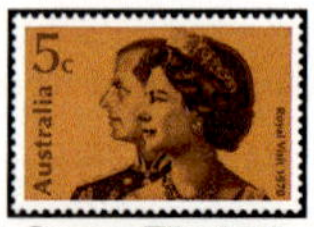
Queen Elizabeth II and Prince Philip — A190

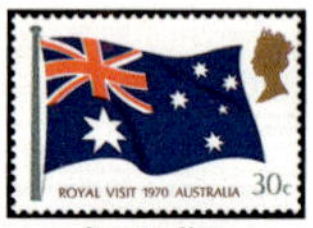
Australian Flag — A191

**1970, Mar. 31**
**474** A190 5c yel bister & black .50 .30
**475** A191 30c vio blue & multi 2.25 1.50

Visit of Queen Elizabeth II, Prince Philip and Princess Anne to Australia.

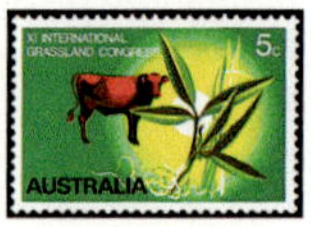
Steer, Alfalfa and Native Spear Grass — A192

**1970, Apr. 13 Photo.** *Perf. 13x13½*
**476** A192 5c emerald & multi .30 .35

11th Intl. Grasslands Congress, Surfers Paradise, Queensland, Apr. 13-23.

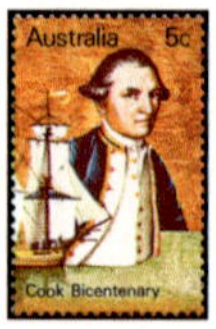
Capt. James Cook and "Endeavour" — A193

Designs: No. 478, Sextant, "Endeavour." No. 479, "Endeavour," landing party, kangaroo. No. 480, Daniel Charles Solander, Sir Joseph Banks, Cook, map, botanical drawing. No. 481, Cook taking possession with Union Jack; "Endeavour," coral. 30c, Cook, "Endeavour," sextant, kangaroo, aborigines.

**1970, Apr. 20** *Perf. 13½x13*
**Size: 24x35½mm**
**477** A193 5c org brn & multi .35 .25
**478** A193 5c org brn & multi .35 .25
**479** A193 5c org brn & multi .35 .25
**480** A193 5c org brn & multi .35 .25
**481** A193 5c org brn & multi .35 .25
*a.* Strip of 5, #477-481 2.40 2.40
**Size: 62x29mm**
**482** A193 30c org brn & multi 2.40 2.25
*a.* Souv. sheet, #477-482, imperf 16.00 12.00
*Nos. 477-482 (6)* 4.15 3.50

Cook's discovery and exploration of the eastern coast of Australia, 200th anniv.
No. 481a has continuous design.
No. 482a with brown marginal overprint "Souvenir Sheet ANPEX 1970. . ." is of private origin. Value $27.50.

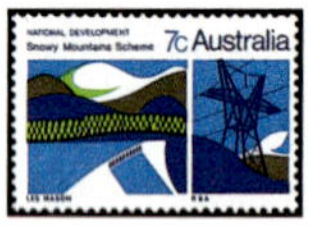
Snowy Mountains Hydroelectric Project — A194

Designs: 8c, Ord River hydroelectric project (dam, cotton plant and boll). 9c, Bauxite and aluminum production (mine, conveyor belt and aluminum window frame). 10c, Oil and natural gas (off-shore drilling rig and pipelines).

**1970, Aug. 31 Photo.** *Perf. 13x13½*
**483** A194 7c multicolored 1.20 .40
**484** A194 8c multicolored .25 .25
**485** A194 9c multicolored .50 .25
**486** A194 10c multicolored .60 .30
*Nos. 483-486 (4)* 2.55 1.20

Australian economic development.

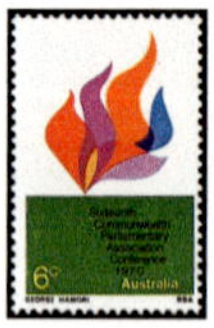
Flame Symbolizing Democracy and Freedom of Speech — A195

**1970, Oct. 2 Photo.** *Perf. 13½x13*
**487** A195 6c green & multi .30 .25

16th Commonwealth Parliamentary Assoc. Conference, Canberra, Oct. 2-9.

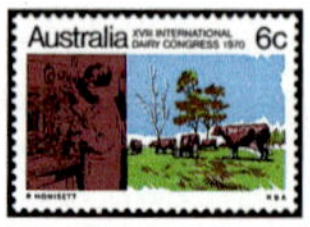
Herd of Illawarra Shorthorns and Laboratory — A196

**1970, Oct. 7** *Perf. 13x13½*
**488** A196 6c multicolored .30 .25

18th Intl. Dairy Cong., Sydney, Oct. 12-16.

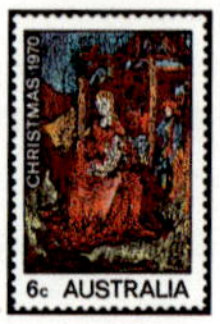
Madonna and Child, by William Beasley — A197

**1970, Oct. 14** *Perf. 13½x13*
**489** A197 6c multicolored .30 .25

Christmas.

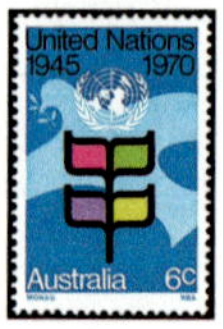
UN Emblem, Dove and Symbols — A198

**1970, Oct. 19**
**490** A198 6c blue & multi .30 .25

25th anniversary of the United Nations.

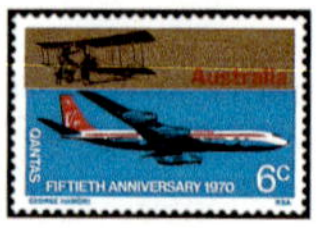
Qantas Boeing 707, and Avro 504 — A199

30c, Sunbeam Dyak powered Avro 504 on ground and Qantas Boeing 707 in the air.

**1970, Nov. 2** *Perf. 13x13½*
**491** A199 6c multicolored .40 .25
**492** A199 30c multicolored 1.25 1.25

Qantas, Australian overseas airlines, 50th anniv.

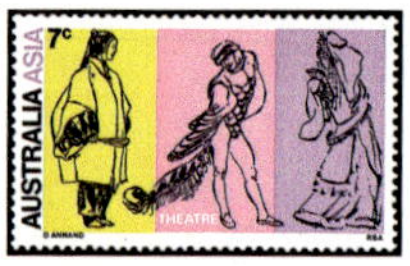
Japanese Noh Actor, Australian Dancer and Chinese Opera Character A200

15c, Chinese pipe, trumpet, Australian aboriginal didgeridoo, Thai fiddle, Indian double oboe, Tibetan drums. 20c, Red Sea dhow, Chinese junk, Australian lifeguard's surfboat, Malaysian & South Indian river boats.

**1971, Jan. 6 Photo.** *Perf. 13½x13*
**493** A200 7c multicolored 1.20 *.55*
**494** A200 15c multicolored 1.60 *1.25*
**495** A200 20c multicolored 1.45 *.70*
*Nos. 493-495 (3)* 4.25 2.50

Link between Australia and Asia; 28th Intl. Congress of Orientalists, Canberra, Jan. 6-12.

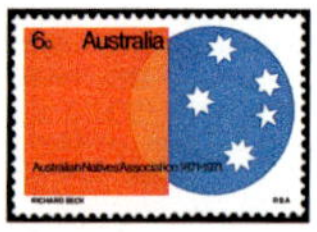
Southern Cross — A201

**1971, Apr. 21 Photo.** *Perf. 13x13½*
**496** A201 6c multicolored .30 .25

Australian Natives Assoc., cent.

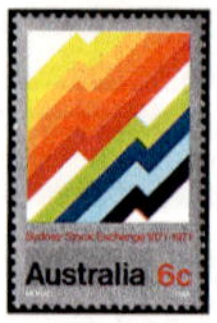
Symbolic Market Graphs — A202

**1971, May 5** *Perf. 13½x13*
**497** A202 6c silver & multi .30 .25

Centenary of Sydney Stock Exchange.

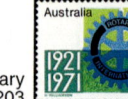

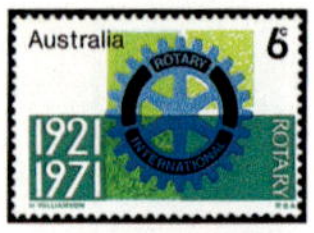
Rotary Emblem — A203

**1971, May 17** *Perf. 13x13½*
**498** A203 6c multicolored .30 .25

First Intl. Rotary Convention held in Australia, Sydney, May 16-20.

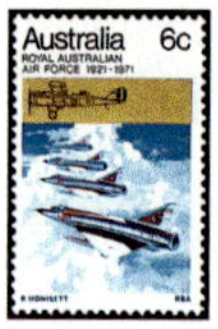
DH-9A, Australian Mirage Jet Fighters — A204

**1971, June 9** *Perf. 13½x13*
**499** A204 6c multicolored .55 .25

Royal Australian Air Force, 50th anniv.

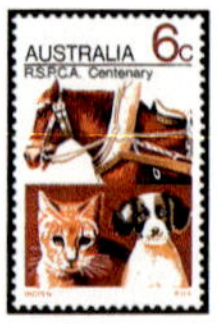
RSPCA Centenary — A205

Designs: 12c, Man and lamb (animal science). 18c, Kangaroo (fauna conservation). 24c, Seeing eye dog (animals' aid to man).

**1971, July 5 Photo.** *Perf. 13½x13*
**500** A205 6c blk, brown & org .25 .25
**501** A205 12c blk, dk grn & yel .45 .25
**502** A205 18c brown & multi .65 .35
*a.* Litho., perf. 14¾x14, dated "2013" (#1003b) .45 .45
**503** A205 24c blue & multi 1.20 .70
*Nos. 500-503 (4)* 2.55 1.55

Royal Society for Prevention of Cruelty to Animals in Australia, cent.
Issued: No. 502a, 5/10/2013.

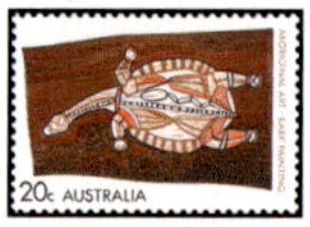
Longnecked Tortoise, Painted on Bark — A206

Aboriginal Art: 25c, Mourners' body paintings, Warramunga tribe. 30c, Cave painting, Western Arnhem Land, vert. 35c, Graveposts, Bathurst and Melville Islands, vert.

*Perf. 13x13½, 13½x13*
**1971, Sept. 29**
**504** A206 20c multicolored .45 .30
**505** A206 25c multicolored .45 .45
**506** A206 30c multicolored 1.50 .45
**507** A206 35c multicolored .55 .45
*Nos. 504-507 (4)* 2.95 1.65

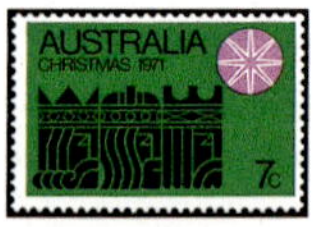
Three Kings and Star — A207

**1971, Oct. 13 Photo.** *Perf. 13½x13*
**508** Block of 7 45.00 35.00
*a.* A207 7c brt grn, dk bl (Kings) & lil 12.00 1.50
*b.* A207 7c lil, red brn, grn & dk bl 3.25 .70
*c.* A207 7c red brown & lilac 4.00 .80
*d.* A207 7c lilac, red brn & brt grn 3.25 .70
*e.* A207 7c red brown & dark blue 3.25 .70
*f.* A207 7c lilac, green & dk blue 15.00 3.00
*g.* A207 7c brt grn, dk bl & lilac (Kings) 3.25 .70

Christmas. Nos. 508a-508g printed se-tenant in sheets of 50. Each sheet contains 2 green crosses formed by 4 No. 508g and three No. 508a.

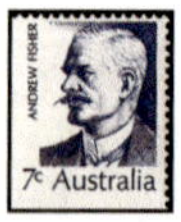
Andrew Fisher (1862-1928) — A208

Prime Ministers: No. 515, Joseph Cook (1860-1947). No. 516, William Morris Hughes (1864-1952). No. 517, Stanley Melbourne Bruce (1883-1967).

**1972, Mar. 8 Engr. *Perf. 15x14***

| | | | | |
|---|---|---|---|---|
| **514** | A208 | 7c dark blue | .70 | .40 |
| *a.* | | Booklet pane of 5 + label | 3.50 | |
| **515** | A208 | 7c dark red | .70 | .40 |
| *a.* | | Booklet pane of 5 + label | 3.50 | |
| **516** | A208 | 7c dark blue | .70 | .40 |
| *a.* | | Booklet pane of 5 + label | 3.50 | |
| **517** | A208 | 7c dark red | .70 | .40 |
| *a.* | | Booklet pane of 5 + label | 3.50 | |
| | | *Nos. 514-517 (4)* | 2.80 | 1.60 |

Nos. 514-517 were issued in booklets only; all stamps have one or two straight edges.

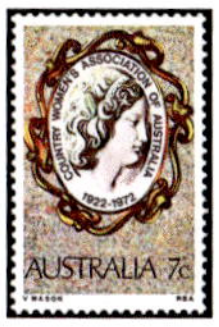
Cameo Brooch — A209

**1972, Apr. 18 Photo. *Perf. 13½***

| | | | | |
|---|---|---|---|---|
| **518** | A209 | 7c multicolored | .35 | .25 |

Country Women's Assoc., 50th anniv.

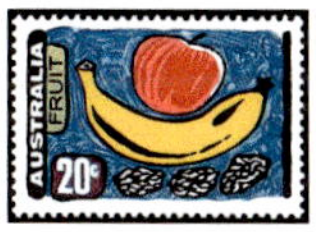
Apple and Banana — A210

**1972, June 14**

| | | | | |
|---|---|---|---|---|
| **519** | A210 | 20c shown | 2.40 | 1.50 |
| **520** | A210 | 25c Rice | 2.40 | 1.75 |
| **521** | A210 | 30c Fish | 1.75 | 1.75 |
| **522** | A210 | 35c Cattle | 4.00 | 3.00 |
| | | *Nos. 519-522 (4)* | 10.55 | 8.00 |

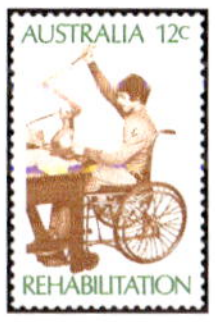
Worker in Sheltered Workshop — A211

18c, Amputee assembling electrical circuit. 24c, Boy wearing Toronto splint, playing ball.

**1972, Aug. 2 *Perf. 13½x13***

| | | | | |
|---|---|---|---|---|
| **523** | A211 | 12c grn & brn | .30 | .25 |
| **524** | A211 | 18c org & ol, horiz. | 1.25 | .60 |
| **525** | A211 | 24c brn & ultra | .50 | .25 |
| | | *Nos. 523-525 (3)* | 2.05 | 1.10 |

Rehabilitation of the handicapped.

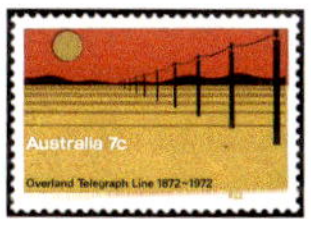
Overland Telegraph Line — A212

**1972, Aug. 22 Photo. *Perf. 13x13½***

| | | | | |
|---|---|---|---|---|
| **526** | A212 | 7c dk red, blk & lemon | .30 | .30 |

Centenary of overland telegraph line.

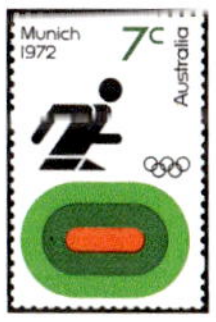
Athlete, Olympic Rings — A213

**1972, Aug. 28 *Perf. 13½x13***

| | | | | |
|---|---|---|---|---|
| **527** | A213 | 7c shown | .45 | .45 |
| **528** | A213 | 7c Swimming | .45 | .45 |
| **529** | A213 | 7c Rowing | .45 | .45 |
| **530** | A213 | 35c Equestrian | 3.25 | 2.75 |
| | | *Nos. 527-530 (4)* | 4.60 | 4.10 |

20th Olympic Games, Munich, 8/26-9/11.

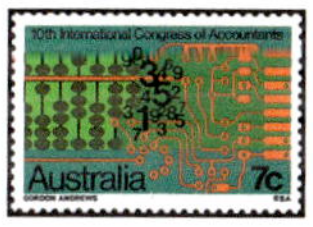
Abacus, Numerals, Computer Circuits — A214

**1972, Oct. 16 Photo. *Perf. 13x13½***

| | | | | |
|---|---|---|---|---|
| **531** | A214 | 7c multicolored | .30 | .30 |

10th Intl. Congress of Accountants.

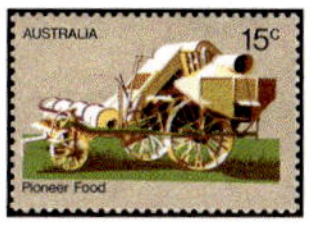
19th Cent. Combine Harvester — A215

5c, Pioneer family, vert. 10c, Water pump, vert. 40c, Pioneer house. 50c, Cobb & Co. coach. 60c, Early Morse key, vert. 80c, Paddle-wheel steamer.

***Perf. 13½x13, 13x13½***

**1972, Nov. 15 Photo.**

| | | | | |
|---|---|---|---|---|
| **532** | A215 | 5c multicolored | .25 | .25 |
| **533** | A215 | 10c multicolored | .35 | .25 |
| **534** | A215 | 15c shown | .30 | .25 |
| **535** | A215 | 40c multicolored | .60 | .25 |
| **536** | A215 | 50c multicolored | 1.00 | .25 |
| **537** | A215 | 60c multicolored | .90 | .55 |
| **538** | A215 | 80c multicolored | 1.25 | .65 |
| | | *Nos. 532-538 (7)* | 4.65 | 2.45 |

Australian pioneer life.

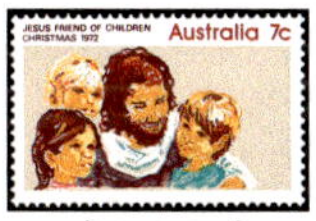
Jesus and Children A216

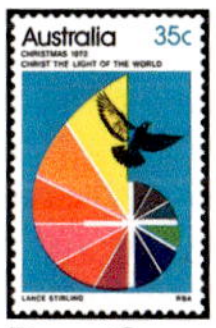
Dove, Cross and "Darkness into Light" A217

***Perf. 14½x14, 13½x13***

**1972, Nov. 29**

| | | | | |
|---|---|---|---|---|
| **539** | A216 | 7c tan & multi | .35 | .25 |
| **540** | A217 | 35c blue & multi | 8.00 | 6.50 |

Christmas.

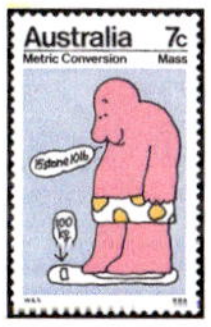
Metric Conversion, Mass — A218

Metric conversion: No. 542, Temperature, horiz. No. 543, Length. No. 544, Volume.

**1973, Mar. 7 Photo. *Perf. 14x14½***

| | | | | |
|---|---|---|---|---|
| **541** | A218 | 7c pale vio & multi | .60 | .40 |
| **542** | A218 | 7c yellow & multi | .60 | .40 |
| **543** | A218 | 7c yel green & multi | .60 | .40 |
| **544** | A218 | 7c brt rose & multi | .60 | .40 |
| | | *Nos. 541-544 (4)* | 2.40 | 1.60 |

Conversion to metric system.

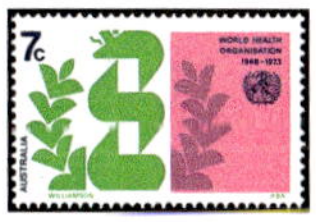
Stylized Caduceus and Laurel — A219

**1973, Apr. 4 Photo. *Perf. 14½x14***

| | | | | |
|---|---|---|---|---|
| **545** | A219 | 7c dk bl, emer & lil rose | .40 | .30 |

WHO, 25th anniv.

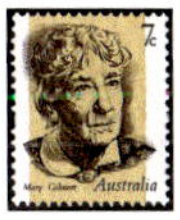
Dame Mary Gilmore, Writer — A220

Famous Australians: No. 547, William Charles Wentworth, explorer. No. 548, Sir Isaac Isaacs, lawyer, 1st Australian-born Governor-General. No. 549, Marcus Clarke, writer.

**Engr. & Litho.**

**1973, May 16 *Perf. 15x14***

| | | | | |
|---|---|---|---|---|
| **546** | A220 | 7c bister & black | .80 | .30 |
| **547** | A220 | 7c bister & black | .80 | .30 |
| **548** | A220 | 7c black & violet | .80 | .30 |
| **549** | A220 | 7c black & violet | .80 | .30 |
| *a.* | | Block of 4, #546-549 | 4.00 | 4.00 |

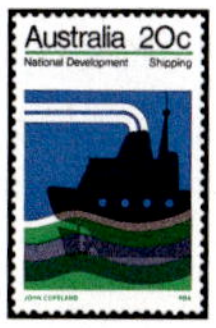
Shipping Industry — A221

Designs: 25c, Iron ore and steel. 30c, Truck convoy (beef road). 35c, Aerial mapping.

**1973, June 6 Photo. *Perf. 13½x13***

| | | | | |
|---|---|---|---|---|
| **550** | A221 | 20c ultra & multi | 1.75 | 1.40 |
| **551** | A221 | 25c red & multi | 1.50 | 1.40 |
| **552** | A221 | 30c ol brn & multi | 3.00 | 1.75 |
| **553** | A221 | 35c olive & multi | 2.00 | 1.75 |
| | | *Nos. 550-553 (4)* | 8.25 | 6.30 |

Australian economic development.

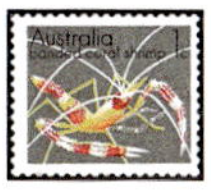
Banded Coral Shrimp — A222

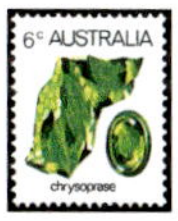
Chrysoprase A223

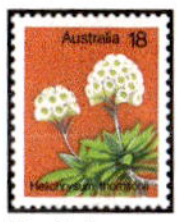
Helichrysum Thomsonii A223a

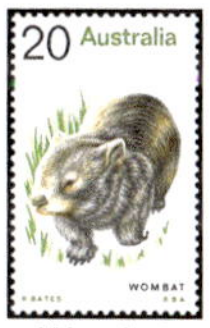
Wombat A224

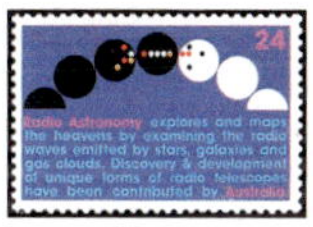
Radio Astronomy — A225

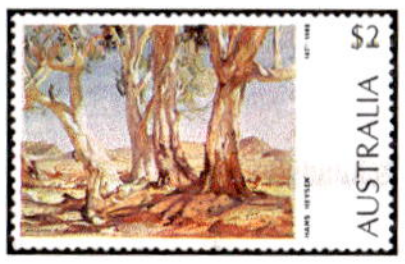
Red Gums of the Far North, by Hans Heysen A226

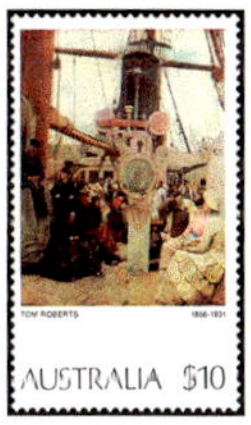
Coming South (Immigranto), by Tom Roberts — A226a

2c, Fiddler crab. 3c, Coral crab. 4c, Mauve stinger. 7c, Agate. 8c, Opal. 9c, Rhodonite. 10c, Star sapphire. 11c, Atomic absorption spectrophotometry. 25c, Spiny anteater. 30c, Brushtail possum. 33c, Immunology. 45c, Callistemon teretifolius, horiz. 48c, Oceanography. 75c, Feather-tailed glider.

Paintings: $1, Sergeant of Light Horse, by George Lambert. No. 575, On the Wallaby Track. $4, Shearing the Rams, by Tom Roberts. No. 577, McMahon's Point, by Arthur Streeton. No. 578, Mentone.

***Perf. 14x15, 15x14 (A222, A223, A223a); Perf. 14x14½ (A224); Perf. 13x13½ (A225, A226, $1)***

**1973-84 Photo.**

| | | | | |
|---|---|---|---|---|
| **554** | A222 | 1c shown | .25 | .25 |
| **555** | A222 | 2c multi | .25 | .25 |
| **556** | A222 | 3c multi | .25 | .25 |
| **557** | A222 | 4c multi | .25 | .25 |
| **558** | A223 | 6c shown | .25 | .25 |
| **559** | A223 | 7c multi | .30 | .25 |
| **560** | A223 | 8c multi | .30 | .25 |
| **561** | A223 | 9c multi | .30 | .25 |
| **562** | A223 | 10c multi ('74) | .35 | .25 |
| **563** | A225 | 11c multi ('75) | .65 | .30 |
| **564** | A223a | 18c shown ('75) | .60 | .25 |
| **565** | A224 | 20c shown ('74) | .45 | .25 |
| **566** | A225 | 24c shown ('75) | 1.00 | .45 |
| **567** | A224 | 25c multi ('74) | 1.25 | .60 |
| **568** | A224 | 30c multi ('74) | .65 | .25 |
| **569** | A225 | 33c multi ('75) | 1.00 | .80 |
| **570** | A223a | 45c multi ('75) | .80 | .35 |
| **571** | A225 | 48c multi ('75) | 1.25 | 1.00 |
| **572** | A224 | 75c multi ('74) | 1.25 | .60 |
| **573** | A226a | $1 multi ('74) | 1.60 | .40 |
| **574** | A226 | $2 shown ('74) | 3.25 | .75 |
| **575** | A226 | $2 multi ('81) | 3.25 | .75 |
| **576** | A226 | $4 multi ('74) | 6.00 | 2.75 |

**Litho.**

***Perf. 14½***

| | | | | |
|---|---|---|---|---|
| **577** | A226a | $5 multi ('79) | 8.00 | 2.75 |
| **578** | A226 | $5 multi ('84) | 7.50 | 3.50 |
| **579** | A226a | $10 shown ('77) | 16.00 | 4.00 |
| | | *Nos. 554-579 (26)* | 57.00 | 22.00 |

Issued: 1c-9c, 7/11; 20c, 25c, 30c, 75c, 2/13; $1, No. 574, $4, 4/24; 10c, 10/16; 11c, 24c, 33c, 48c, 5/14; 18c, 45c, 8/27; $10, 10/19; No. 577, 3/14; No. 575, 6/17; No. 578, 4/4.

No. 560 Surcharged in Red 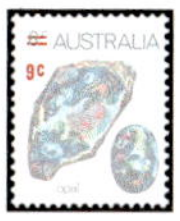

***Perf. 15x14***

| | | | | |
|---|---|---|---|---|
| **580** | A223 | 9c on 8c multi ('74) | .30 | .35 |

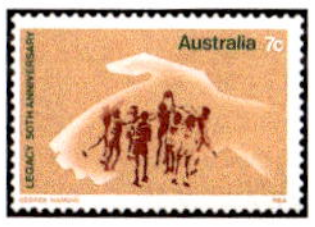
Hand Protecting Playing Children — A227

**1973, Sept. 5 Photo. *Perf. 13x13½***

| | | | | |
|---|---|---|---|---|
| **581** | A227 | 7c bis brn, grn & plum | .30 | .25 |

50th anniv. of Legacy, an ex-servicemen's organization concerned with the welfare of widows and children of servicemen.

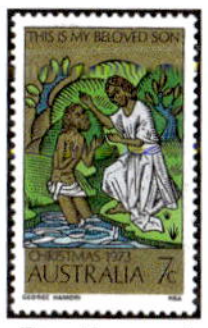
Baptism of Christ A228

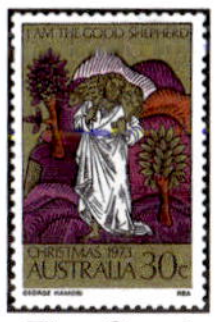
The Good Shepherd A229

**1973, Oct. 3 *Perf. 14x14½***

| | | | | |
|---|---|---|---|---|
| **582** | A228 | 7c gold & multi | .30 | .25 |
| *a.* | | Perf. 14x15 | 3.00 | .75 |

***Perf. 13½***

| | | | | |
|---|---|---|---|---|
| **583** | A229 | 30c gold & multi | 2.25 | 2.25 |

Christmas.

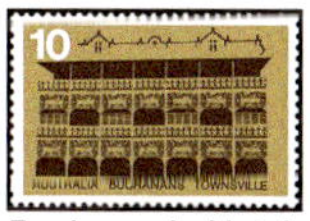
Buchanan's Hotel, Townsville A230

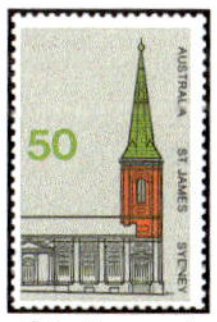
St. James' Church, Sydney A231

Designs: 7c, Opera House, Sydney. 40c, Como House, Melbourne.

**1973, Oct. 17 Photo. *Perf. 14½x14***

| | | | | |
|---|---|---|---|---|
| **584** | A230 | 7c lt blue & ultra | .35 | .25 |
| *a.* | | Perf. 15x14 | 4.50 | .90 |
| **585** | A230 | 10c bister & black | .50 | .35 |

***Perf. 13x13½, 13½x13***

| | | | | |
|---|---|---|---|---|
| **586** | A230 | 40c dl pink, gray & blk | .65 | .75 |
| **587** | A231 | 50c gray & multi | 1.60 | 1.25 |
| | | *Nos. 584-587 (4)* | 3.10 | 2.60 |

Australian architecture; opening of the Sydney Opera House, Oct. 14, 1973 (No. 584).

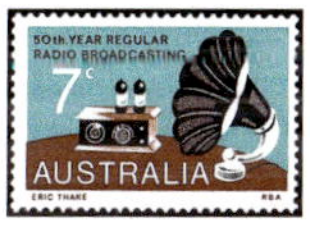
Radio and Gramophone Speaker — A232

**1973, Nov. 21 Photo. *Perf. 13½x13***

| | | | | |
|---|---|---|---|---|
| **588** | A232 | 7c dull blue, blk & brn | .35 | .25 |

Broadcasting in Australia, 50th anniv.

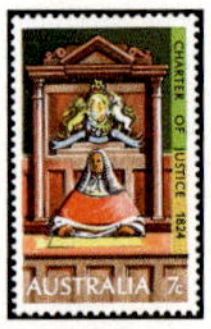

Supreme Court Judge on Bench — A233

**1974, May 15 Photo. *Perf. 14x14½***

**589** A233 7c multicolored .35 .25

150th anniv. of the proclamation of the Charter of Justice in New South Wales and Van Diemen's Land (Australia's Third Charter).

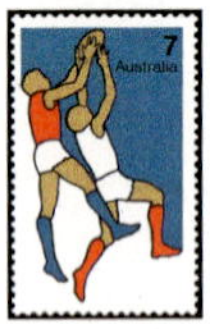

Australian Football — A234

**1974, July 24 Photo. *Perf. 14x14½***

**590** A234 7c shown .35 .25
**591** A234 7c Cricket .35 .25
*a.* Booklet pane of 1, litho., perf. 14¾x14, dated "2007" .25 —
**592** A234 7c Golf .35 .25
**593** A234 7c Surfing .35 .25
**594** A234 7c Tennis .35 .25
**595** A234 7c Bowls, horiz. .35 .25
**596** A234 7c Rugby, horiz. .35 .25
*Nos. 590-596 (7)* 2.45 1.75

No. 591a issued 11/14/2007.

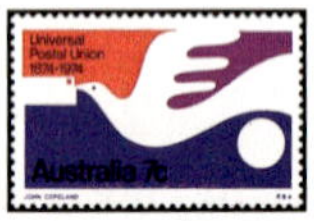

Carrier Pigeon — A235

Designs: 30c, Carrier pigeons, vert.

**1974, Oct. 9 Photo. *Perf. 14½x14***

**597** A235 7c multicolored .60 .25
*a.* Perf. 15x14 .60 .35

***Perf. 13½x13***

**598** A235 30c multicolored 1.60 1.20

UPU, cent. A booklet containing a strip of 5 each of Nos. 597-598 was produced and sold for $4 Australian by the National Stamp Week Promotion Council with government approval.

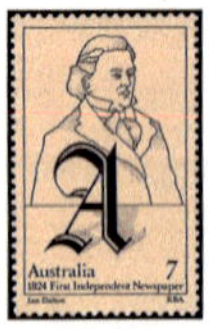

William Charles Wentworth — A236

**Typo. & Litho.**

**1974, Oct. 9 *Perf. 14x15***

**599** A236 7c bister & black .40 .25
*a.* Perf. 14x14½ 1.60 .40

Sesquicentennial of 1st Australian independent newspaper. W. C. Wentworth and Dr. Robert Wardell were the editors and the "A" is type from masthead of "The Australian."

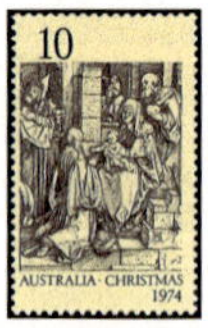

Adoration of the Kings, by Dürer — A237

Christmas: 35c, Flight into Egypt, by Albrecht Dürer.

**1974, Nov. 13 Engr. *Perf. 14x14½***

**600** A237 10c buff & black .40 .25
**601** A237 35c buff & black .90 .90

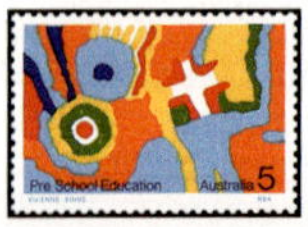

Pre-school Education — A238

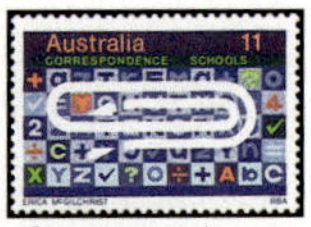

Correspondence Schools — A239

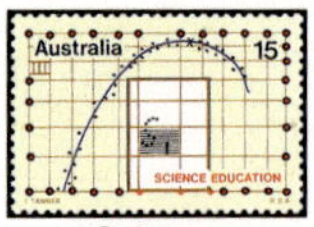

Science Education — A240

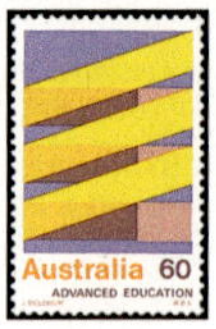

Advanced Education — A241

***Perf. 13x13½, 13½x13***

**1974, Nov. 20 Photo.**

**602** A238 5c multicolored .60 .25
**603** A239 11c multicolored .60 .25
**604** A240 15c multicolored .60 .40
**605** A241 60c multicolored 1.60 1.20
*Nos. 602-605 (4)* 3.40 2.10

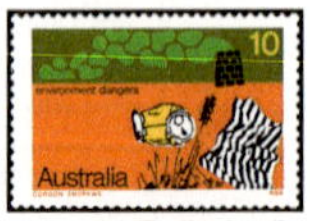

"Avoid Pollution" A242

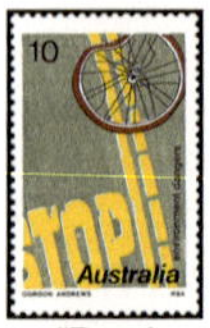

"Road Safety" A243

Design: No. 607, "Avoid bush fires."

**1975, Jan. 29 Photo. *Perf. 14½x14***

**606** A242 10c multicolored .55 .45
*a.* Perf. 15x14 9.50 5.00
**607** A242 10c multicolored .55 .45
*a.* Perf. 15x14 1.50 1.10

***Perf. 14x14½***

**608** A243 10c multicolored .55 .45
*Nos. 606-608 (3)* 1.65 1.35

Environmental dangers.

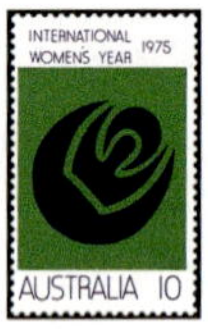

Symbols of Womanhood, Sun, Moon — A244

**1975, Mar. 12 Photo. *Perf. 14x14½***

**609** A244 10c dk vio blue & grn .35 .25

International Women's Year.

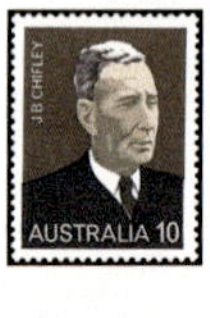

Joseph B. Chifley (1885-1951) — A245

No. 611, John Curtin, 1885-1945. No. 612, Arthur W. Fadden, 1895-1973. No. 613, Joseph A. Lyons, 1879-1939. No. 614, Earle Page, 1880-1963. No. 615, John H. Scullin, 1876-1953.

**1975, Mar. 26**

**610** A245 10c shown .35 .25
**611** A245 10c multicolored .35 .25
**612** A245 10c multicolored .35 .25
**613** A245 10c multicolored .35 .25
**614** A245 10c multicolored .35 .25
**615** A245 10c multicolored .35 .25
*Nos. 610-615 (6)* 2.10 1.50

Australian Prime Ministers.

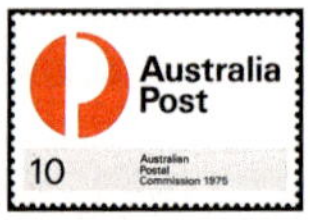

Australian Postal Commission A246

Design: No. 617, Australian Telecommunications Commission.

**1975, July 1 Photo. *Perf. 14½x14***

**616** A246 10c red, black & gray .65 .45
*a.* Perf. 15x14 .85 .45
**617** A246 10c yel, black & gray .65 .45
*a.* Pair, #616-617 1.60 1.25
*b.* Perf. 15x14 .85 .45
*c.* Pair, #616a, 617b 3.50 3.50

Formation of Australian Postal and Telecommunications Commissions. Printed checkerwise.

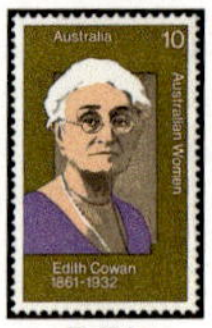

Edith Cowan, Judge and Legislator A247

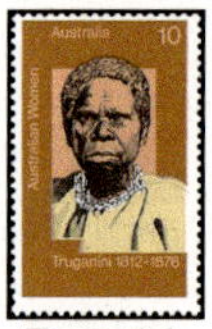

Truganini, Last Tasmanian Aborigine A248

Portraits: No. 619, Louisa Lawson (1848-1920), journalist. No. 620, Ethel Florence (Henry Handel) Richardson (1870-1946), novelist. No. 621, Catherine Spence (1825-1910), teacher, journalist, voting reformer. No. 622, Emma Constance Stone (1856-1902), first Australian woman physician.

**1975, Aug. 6 Photo. *Perf. 14x14½***

**618** A247 10c olive grn & multi .60 .30
*a.* Perf. 14x15 .60 .30
**619** A247 10c yel bister & multi .60 .30
*a.* Perf. 14x15 .60 .30
**620** A248 10c olive & multi .60 .30
*a.* Perf. 14x15 .60 .30
**621** A248 10c gray & multi .60 .30
*a.* Perf. 14x15 .60 .30
**622** A247 10c violet & multi .60 .30
*a.* Perf. 14x15 .60 .30
**623** A248 10c brown & multi .60 .30
*a.* Perf. 14x15 .60 .30
*Nos. 618-623 (6)* 3.60 1.80

Famous Australian women.

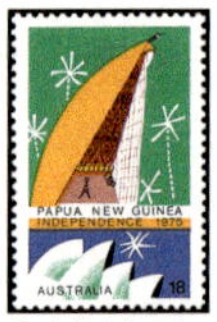

Spirit House (PNG) and Sydney Opera House A249

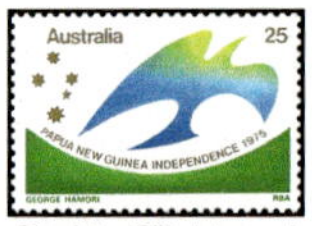

Bird in Flight and Southern Cross A250

**1975, Sept. 16 Photo. *Perf. 13½***

**624** A249 18c multicolored .45 .25
**625** A250 25c multicolored .80 .65

Papua New Guinea independence, Sept. 16, 1975.

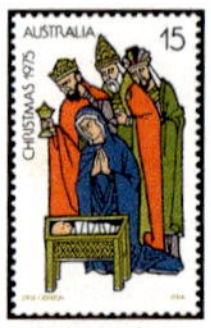

Adoration of the Kings A251

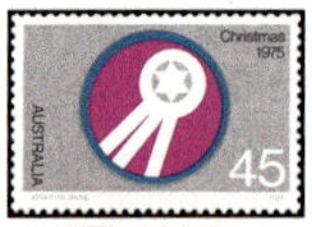

"The Light Shineth in the Darkness" A252

**1975, Oct. 29 Photo. *Perf. 14½x14***

**626** A251 15c multicolored .40 .25
**627** A252 45c silver & multi 1.60 1.50

Christmas.

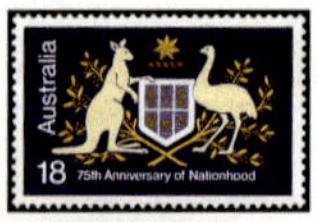

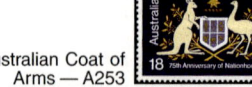

Australian Coat of Arms — A253

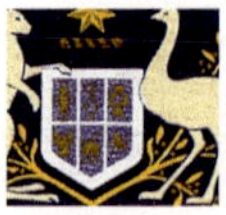

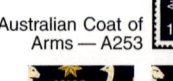

Type I

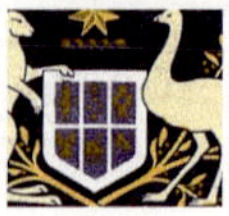

Type II

Type I — Kangaroo: eye is dot, right paw has 1 toe, left foot has 1 toe. Emu: feet have 1 toe.

Type II — Kangaroo: eye is line, right paw has 3 toes, left foot has 2 toes. Emu: feet have 2 toes.

Other differences exist.

**1976, Jan. 5 Photo. *Perf. 14½x14***

**628** A253 18c multicolored, type I .40 .25
*a.* Type II .95 .40

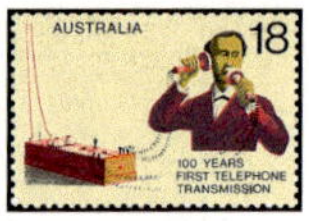

"Williams' Coffin" Telephone, 1878 — A254

**1976, Mar. 10 Photo. *Perf. 13½***

**629** A254 18c buff & multi .40 .30

Centenary of first telephone call by Alexander Graham Bell, Mar. 10, 1876.

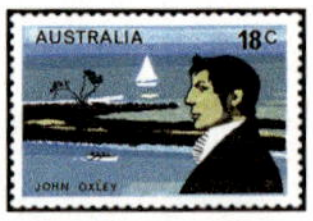

John Oxley — A255

Australian explorers: No. 631, Hamilton Hume and William Hovell. No. 632, John Forrest. No. 633, Ernest Giles. No. 634, Peter Warburton. No. 635, William Gosse.

**1976, June 9 Photo. *Perf. 13½***

**630** A255 18c shown .35 .25
**631** A255 18c multicolored .35 .25
**632** A255 18c multicolored .35 .25
**633** A255 18c multicolored .35 .25
**634** A255 18c multicolored .35 .25
**635** A255 18c multicolored .35 .25
*Nos. 630-635 (6)* 2.10 1.50

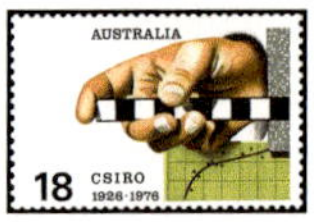

Survey Rule, Graph, Punched Tape — A256

**1976, June 15 *Perf. 15x14***

**636** A256 18c multicolored .40 .25

Commonwealth Scientific and Industrial Research Organization, 50th anniv.

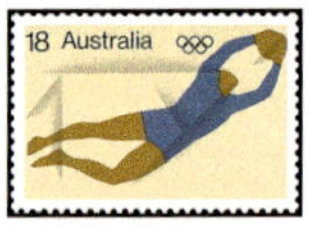

Soccer Goalkeeper A257

Olympic Rings and: No. 638, Woman gymnast, vert. 25c, Woman diver, vert. 40c, Bicycling.

***Perf. 13x13½, 13½x13***

**1976, July 14 Photo.**

**637** A257 18c multicolored .30 .25
**638** A257 18c multicolored .30 .25
**639** A257 25c multicolored .40 .40
**640** A257 40c multicolored .60 .50
*Nos. 637-640 (4)* 1.60 1.40

21st Olympic Games, Montreal, Canada, July 17-Aug. 1.

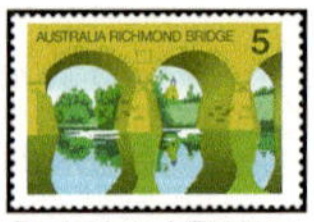

Richmond Bridge, Tasmania A258

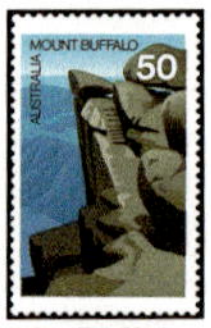

Mt. Buffalo, Victoria A259

Designs: 25c, Broken Bay, New South Wales. 35c, Wittenoom Gorge, Western Australia. 70c, Barrier Reef, Queensland. 85c, Ayers Rock, Northern Territory.

***Perf. 14½x14, 14x14½***

**1976, Aug. 25 Photo.**

**641** A258 5c multicolored .30 .25
**642** A258 25c multicolored .45 .25
**643** A258 35c multicolored .50 .30
**644** A259 50c multicolored .70 .30
**645** A258 70c multicolored 1.00 .40
**646** A258 85c multicolored 1.10 .70
*Nos. 641-646 (6)* 4.05 2.20

# AUSTRALIA

Blamire Young and Australia No. 59 — A260

**1976, Sept. 27 Photo. Perf. 13½**
647 A260 18c apple grn & multi .40 .25

**Miniature Sheet**
648 Sheet of 4 1.60 1.60
 a. A260 18c yellow & dark brown .40 .40
 b. A260 18c rose, dk brown & yel .40 .40
 c. A260 18c bl, dk brn, rose & yel .40 .40

Natl. Stamp Week, Sept. 27-Oct. 3. Blamire Young (1862-1935), designer of Australia's 1st issue. No. 648 shows different stages of 4-color printing. The 4th stamp in sheet is identical with No. 647.

Virgin and Child, after Simone Cantarini — A261

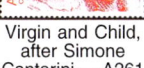

Holly, Toy Koala, Christmas Tree and Decoration, Partridge — A262

**1976, Nov. 1 Photo. Perf. 14½x14**
649 A261 15c blt car & lt blue .40 .25

**Perf. 13½**
650 A262 45c multicolored .80 .80

Christmas.

John Gould (1804-1881) Ornithologist — A263

Famous Australians: No. 652, Thomas Laby (1880-1946), nuclear scientist. No. 653, Sir Baldwin Spencer (1860-1929), anthropologist (aborigines). No. 654, Griffith Taylor (1880-1963), geographer and antarctic explorer.

**1976, Nov. 10 Perf. 15x14**
651 A263 18c shown .35 .25
652 A263 18c Laby .35 .25
653 A263 18c Spencer .35 .25
654 A263 18c Taylor .35 .25
 Nos. 651-654 (4) 1.40 1.00

Violinists — A264

**1977, Jan. 19 Photo. Perf. 14x14½**
655 A264 20c shown .30 .25
656 A264 30c Dramatic scene .35 .25
657 A264 40c Dancer .45 .30
658 A264 60c Opera singer .90 .40
 Nos. 655-658 (4) 2.00 1.20

Performing arts in Australia.

Elizabeth II — A265

Design: 45c, Elizabeth II and Prince Philip.

**1977, Feb. 2 Perf. 14x14½**
659 A265 18c multicolored .40 .30
660 A265 45c multicolored .75 .75

Reign of Queen Elizabeth II, 25th anniv. Perf 14½x14 examples of Nos. 659-660 are from a booklet pane containing 2 of each stamp, found in the booklet footnoted under No. 2507.

Wicket Keeper, Slip Fieldsman — A266

Cricket match, 19th century: No. 662, Umpire and batsman. No. 663, Two fieldsmen. No. 664, Batsman and umpire. No. 665, Bowler and fieldsman. 45c, Batsman facing bowler.

**1977, Mar. 9 Photo. Perf. 13½**
661 A266 18c gray & multi .45 .45
 a. Litho., perf. 14¾x14, dated "2007" .55 .55
662 A266 18c gray & multi .45 .45
 a. Litho., perf. 14¾x14, dated "2007" .55 .55
663 A266 18c gray & multi .45 .45
 a. Litho., perf. 14¾x14, dated "2007" .55 .55
664 A266 18c gray & multi .45 .45
 a. Litho., perf. 14¾x14, dated "2007" .55 .55
665 A266 18c gray & multi .45 .45
 a. Strip of 5, #661-665 3.00 3.00
 b. Litho., perf. 14¾x14, dated "2007" .55 .55
666 A266 45c gray & multi 1.00 1.00
 a. Litho., imperf., dated "2007" 1.25 1.25
 b. Booklet pane of 6, #661a, 662a, 663a, 664a, 665b, 666a 4.00
 Nos. 661-666 (6) 3.25 3.25

Nos. 661a, 662a, 663a, 664a, 665b, 666a, 666b issued 11/14/2007.

Parliament House, Canberra — A267

**1977, Apr. 13 Perf. 14½x14**
667 A267 18c multicolored .40 .25

Parliament House, Canberra, 50th anniv.

Trade Union Workers — A268

**1977, May 9 Photo. Perf. 13**
668 A268 18c multicolored .40 .25

Australian Council of Trade Unions (ACTU), 50th anniv.

Surfing Santa A269

Virgin and Child A270

**1977, Oct. 31 Photo. Perf 14x14½**
669 A269 15c multicolored .40 .25

**Perf. 13½x13**
670 A270 45c multicolored .75 .75

Christmas.

Australian Flag — A271

**1978, Jan. 26 Photo. Perf. 13x13½**
671 A271 18c multicolored .40 .30

Australia Day, 190th anniversary of first permanent settlement in New South Wales.

Harry Hawker and Sopwith "Camel" — A272

Australian Aviators and their Planes: No. 673, Bert Hinkler and Avro Avian. No. 674, Charles Kingsford-Smith and Fokker "Southern Cross." No. 675, Charles Ulm and "Southern Cross."

**1978, Apr. 19 Litho. Perf. 15½**
672 A272 18c ultra & multi .40 .30
673 A272 18c blue & multi .40 .30
674 A272 18c orange & multi .40 .30
675 A272 18c yellow & multi .40 .30
 a. Souv. sheet, 2 each #674-675, imperf. 2.25 2.00
 Nos. 672-675 (4) 1.60 1.20

No. 675a for 50th anniv. of first Trans-Pacific flight from Oakland, Cal., to Brisbane.

Beechcraft Baron Landing — A273

**1978, May 15 Photo. Perf. 13½**
676 A273 18c multicolored .40 .30

Royal Flying Doctor Service, 50th anniv.

Illawarra Flame Tree — A274

Australian trees: 25c, Ghost gum. 40c, Grass tree. 45c, Cootamundra wattle.

**1978, June 1**
677 A274 18c multicolored .25 .25
678 A274 25c multicolored .50 .50
679 A274 40c multicolored .65 .65
680 A274 45c multicolored .70 .70
 Nos. 677-680 (4) 2.10 2.10

Sturt's Desert Rose, Map of Australia — A275

**1978, June 19 Litho. Perf. 15½**
681 A275 18c multicolored .40 .25

Establishment of Government of the Northern Territory.

Hooded Dotterel — A276

Australian birds: 20c, Little grebe. 25c, Spur-wing Plover. 30c, Pied oystercatcher. 55c, Lotus bird.

**1978 Photo. Perf. 13½**
682 A276 5c multicolored .25 .25
683 A276 20c multicolored .40 .25
684 A276 25c multicolored .45 .25
685 A276 30c multicolored .70 .35
686 A276 55c multicolored .90 .60
 Nos. 682-686 (5) 2.70 1.70

Issued: Nos. 683, 686, July 3; others, July 17. See Nos. 713-718, 732-739, 768.

Australia No. 95 on Album Page — A277

**1978, Sept. 25 Litho. Perf. 15½**
687 A277 20c multicolored .40 .25
 a. Miniature sheet of 4 1.60 1.60

National Stamp Week; 50th anniv. of Melbourne Intl. Phil. Exhib., Oct. 1928.

Virgin and Child, by Simon Marmion — A278

Paintings from National Gallery, Victoria: 15c, Virgin and Child, after Van Eyck. 55c, Holy Family, by Perino del Vaga.

**1978 Perf. 15**
688 A278 15c multicolored .40 .25
689 A278 25c multicolored .55 .55
690 A278 55c multicolored 1.00 .80
 Nos. 688-690 (3) 1.95 1.60

Christmas. Issued: 25c, 10/3; others, 11/1.

Tulloch — A279

Race horses: 35c, Bernborough, vert. 50c, Phar Lap, vert. 55c, Peter Pan.

**Perf. 15x14, 14x15**
**1978, Oct. 18 Photo.**
691 A279 20c multicolored .40 .30
692 A279 35c multicolored .60 .40
693 A279 50c multicolored .80 .80
694 A279 55c multicolored 1.00 .90
 Nos. 691-694 (4) 2.80 2.40

Australian horse racing.

Flag Raising at Sydney Cove — A280

**1979, Jan. 26 Litho. Perf. 15½**
695 A280 20c multicolored .40 .30

Australia Day, Jan. 26.

Passenger Steamer Canberra — A281

Ferries and Murray River Steamers: 35c, M.V. Lady Denman. 50c, P.S. Murray River Queen. 55c, Hydrofoil Curl Curl.

**Perf. 13½, 15x14 (20c)**
**1979, Feb. 14 Photo.**
696 A281 20c multicolored .40 .30
697 A281 35c multicolored .60 .40
698 A281 50c multicolored .80 .80
699 A281 55c multicolored .90 .90
 Nos. 696-699 (4) 2.70 2.40

Port Campbell — A282

Designs: Australian National Parks.

**1979, Apr. 9 Litho. Perf. 15½**
700 A282 20c shown .35 .35
701 A282 20c Uluru .35 .35
702 A282 20c Royal .35 .35
703 A282 20c Flinders Ranges .35 .35
704 A282 20c Nambung .35 .35
 a. Strip of 5, #700-704 2.00 2.00
705 A282 20c Girraween, vert. .35 .35
706 A282 20c Mount Field, vert. .35 .35
 a. Pair, #705-706 .75 .75
 Nos. 700-706 (7) 2.45 2.45

Double Fairlie — A283

Australian steam locomotives: 35c, Puffing Billy. 50c, Pichi Richi. 55c, Zig Zag.

***Perf. 13½, 15x14 (20c)***

**1979, May 16** **Photo.**

**707** A283 20c multicolored .40 .30
**708** A283 35c multicolored .75 .40
**709** A283 50c multicolored .90 .80
**710** A283 55c multicolored .95 .80
*Nos. 707-710 (4)* 3.00 2.30

"Black Swan" — A284

**1979, June 6** **Photo.** ***Perf. 13½***

**711** A284 20c multicolored .40 .25

150th anniversary of Western Australia.

Children Playing, IYC Emblem — A285

**1979, Aug. 13** **Litho.** ***Perf. 13½x13***

**712** A285 20c multicolored .40 .25

International Year of the Child.

**Bird Type of 1978**

Australian birds: 1c, Zebra finch. 2c, Crimson finch. 15c, Forest kingfisher, vert. 20c, Eastern yellow robin. 40c, Lovely wren, vert. 50c, Flame robin, vert.

**1979, Sept. 17** **Photo.** ***Perf. 13½***

**713** A276 1c multicolored .25 .25
**714** A276 2c multicolored .25 .25
**715** A276 15c multicolored .35 .25
**716** A276 20c multicolored .45 .25
**717** A276 40c multicolored .75 .35
**718** A276 50c multicolored 1.00 .40
*Nos. 713-718 (6)* 3.05 1.75

Christmas Letters, Flag-wrapped Parcels — A286

Christmas: 15c, Nativity, icon. 55c, Madonna and Child, by Buglioni.

**1979** **Litho.** ***Perf. 13***

**719** A286 15c multicolored .35 .25
**720** A286 25c multicolored .45 .30
**721** A286 55c multicolored 1.00 .90
*Nos. 719-721 (3)* 1.80 1.45

Issue dates: 25c, Sept. 24. Others, Nov. 1.

Trout Fishing — A287

Sport fishing: 35c, Angler. 50c, Black marlin fishing. 55c, Surf fishing.

**1979, Oct. 24** **Photo.** ***Perf. 14x14½***

**722** A287 20c multicolored .35 .30
**723** A287 35c multicolored .50 .35
**724** A287 50c multicolored .80 .65
**725** A287 55c multicolored 1.20 .80
*Nos. 722-725 (4)* 2.85 2.10

Matthew Flinders, Map of Australia — A288

**1980, Jan. 23** **Litho.** ***Perf. 13½***

**726** A288 20c multicolored .40 .25

Australia Day, Jan. 28.

Dingo — A289

**1980, Feb. 20** **Litho.** ***Perf. 13½x13***

**727** A289 20c shown .35 .25
**728** A289 25c Border collie .45 .45
**729** A289 35c Australian terrier .55 .50
**730** A289 50c Australian cattle dog .75 .70
**731** A289 55c Australian kelpie .85 .80
*Nos. 727-731 (5)* 2.95 2.70

**Bird Type of 1978**

10c, Golden-shoulder parrot, vert. 22c, White-tailed kingfisher, vert. 28c, Rainbow bird, vert. 35c, Regent bower bird, vert. 45c, Masked woodswallow. 60c, King parrot, vert. 80c, Rainbow pitta. $1, Western magpie, vert.

***Perf. 13x12½ (10c, 28c, 35c, 60c, $1), 14x15 (22c), 12½x13 (45c, 80c)***

**1980** **Litho., Photo. (22c)**

**732** A276 10c multicolored .30 .25
*a.* Perf. 14½x14 1.75 .60
**733** A276 22c multicolored .40 .30
**734** A276 28c multicolored .60 .45
**735** A276 35c multicolored .70 .45
**736** A276 45c multicolored .95 .60
*a.* Perf. 14x14½ 3.50 2.00
**737** A276 60c multicolored 1.25 .60
**738** A276 80c multicolored 1.60 1.00
**739** A276 $1 multicolored 2.00 .45
*Nos. 732-739 (8)* 7.80 4.10

Issued: Nos. 733, 734, 737, 3/31; others, 7/1.

Queen Elizabeth II, 54th Birthday — A290

**1980, Apr. 21** **Litho.** ***Perf. 13x13½***

**740** A290 22c multicolored .35 .25

Wanderer — A291

**1980, May 7** **Litho.** ***Perf. 13x13½***

**741** Strip of 5 2.00 2.00
*a.* A291 22c shown .35 .35
*b.* A291 22c Stealing sheep .35 .35
*c.* A291 22c Squatter on horseback .35 .35
*d.* A291 22c Three troopers .35 .35
*e.* A291 22c Wanderer's ghost .35 .35

"Waltzing Matilda", poem by Andrew Barton Patterson (1864-1941). No. 741 in continuous design.

High Court Building, Canberra — A292

**1980, May 19**

**742** A292 22c multicolored .40 .25

Opening of High Court of Australia Building, Canberra, May 26.

Salvation Army Officers — A294

No. 748, St. Vincent de Paul Society, vert. No. 749, Meals on Wheels, vert. No. 750, "Life. Be in it." (Joggers, bicyclists).

***Perf. 13x13½, 13½x13***

**1980, Aug. 11**

**747** A294 22c shown .40 .30
**748** A294 22c multicolored .40 .30
**749** A294 22c multicolored .40 .30
**750** A294 22c multicolored .40 .30
*Nos. 747-750 (4)* 1.60 1.20

Mailman c. 1900 — A295

**1980, Sept. 29** **Litho.** ***Perf. 13x13½***

**751** A295 22c Mailbox .40 .25
**752** A295 22c shown .40 .25
**753** A295 22c Mail truck .40 .25
**754** A295 22c Mailman, mailbox .40 .25
**755** A295 22c Mailman, diff. .40 .25
*a.* Souvenir sheet of 3 1.50 1.50
*b.* Strip of 5, #751-755 2.00 2.00
*Nos. 751-755 (5)* 2.00 1.25

Natl. Stamp Week, Sept. 29-Oct. 5. Nos. 755a contains stamps similar to #751, 753, 755.

No. 755a overprinted "SYDPEX 80" was privately produced.

Holy Family, by Prospero Fontana — A296

Christmas: 15c, Virgin Enthroned, by Justin O'Brien. 60c, Virgin and Child, by Michael Zuern the Younger, 1680.

**1980** ***Perf. 13x13½***

**756** A296 15c multicolored .30 .25
**757** A296 28c multicolored .55 .45
**758** A296 60c multicolored .90 .65
*Nos. 756-758 (3)* 1.75 1.35

Issued: 15c, 60c, Nov. 3; 28c, Oct. 1.

CA-6 Wackett Trainer, 1941 — A297

Designs: Australian military training planes.

**1980, Nov. 19** ***Perf. 13½x14***

**759** A297 22c shown .40 .30
**760** A297 40c Winjeel, 1955 .65 .40
**761** A297 45c Boomerang, 1944 .75 .50
**762** A297 60c Nomad, 1975 .95 .80
*Nos. 759-762 (4)* 2.75 2.00

**Bird Type of 1978**

**1980, Nov. 17** **Litho.** ***Perf. 13½***

**768** A276 18c Spotted catbird, vert. .50 .25

Flag on Map of Australia — A298

**1981, Jan. 21** ***Perf. 13½x13***

**771** A298 22c multicolored .40 .25

Australia Day, Jan. 21.

Jockey Darby Munro (1913-1966), by Tony Rafty — A299

Australian sportsmen (Caricatures by Tony Rafty): 35c, Victor Trumper (1877-1915), cricket batsman. 55c, Norman Brookes (1877-1968), tennis player. 60c, Walter Lindrum (1898-1960), billiards player.

**1981, Feb. 18** ***Perf. 14x13½***

**772** A299 22c multicolored .40 .25
**773** A299 35c multicolored .65 .60
*a.* Booklet pane of 1, perf. 14¾x14, dated "2007" 1.10 —
**774** A299 55c multicolored 1.00 .90
**775** A299 60c multicolored 1.10 1.00
*Nos. 772-775 (4)* 3.15 2.75

No. 773a issued 11/14/2007.

Australia No. C2 and Cover — A300

22c, Australia No. C2, vert.

***Perf. 13x13½, 13½x13***

**1981, Mar. 25** **Litho.**

**776** A300 22c multicolored .45 .45
**777** A300 60c shown 1.10 .80

Australia-United Kingdom official airmail service, 50th anniv.

Map of Australia, APEX Emblem — A301

**1981, Apr. 6** **Photo.** ***Perf. 13x13½***

**778** A301 22c multicolored .40 .25

50th anniv. of APEX (young men's service club).

Queen Elizabeth's Personal Flag of Australia — A302

**1981, Apr. 21** **Litho.** ***Perf. 13***

**779** A302 22c multicolored .40 .25

Queen Elizabeth II, 55th birthday.

Perf 14x14¾ examples in a booklet pane of 4 come from the booklet footnoted under No. 2507.

License Inspected, Forrest Creek, by S.T. Gill — A303

Gold Rush Era (Sketches by S.T. Gill): No. 781, Puddling. No. 782, Quality of Washing Stuff. No. 783, Diggers on Route to Deposit Gold.

**1981, May 20** ***Perf. 13x13½***

**780** A303 22c multicolored .40 .30
**781** A303 22c multicolored .40 .30
**782** A303 22c multicolored .40 .30
**783** A303 22c multicolored .40 .30
*Nos. 780-783 (4)* 1.60 1.20

Lace Monitor — A303a

Tasmanian Tiger — A304

Two Types of A304:

Type I — Indistinct line at right of ear, stripes even with base of tail.

Type II — Heavy line at right of ear, stripes longer.

3c, Corroboree frog. 5c, Queensland hairy-nosed wombat, vert. 15c, Eastern snake-necked tortoise. 25c, Greater bilby, vert. 27c, Blue Mountains tree frog. 30c, Bridled nail-tailed wallaby, vert. 40c, Smooth knob-tailed gecko. 50c, Leadbeater's opossum. 55c, Stick-nest rat, vert. 65c, Yellow-faced whip snake. 70c, Crucifix toad. 75c, Eastern water dragon. 85c, Centralian blue-tongued lizard. 90c, Freshwater crocodile. 95c, Thorny devil.

**1981-83** **Litho.**

**784** A303a 1c shown .25 .25
**785** A303a 3c multicolored .40 .25
**786** A304 5c multicolored .35 .35
*b.* Imperf., dated "2007" .25 .25

**787** A303a 15c multicolored .40 .25
**788** A304 24c Type I, photo. & litho. .50 .40
*a.* Shown, type II, litho. .70 .40
*b.* Imperf., dated "2007" .50 .50
**789** A304 25c multicolored .65 .45
*b.* Imperf., dated "2007" .60 .60
**790** A303a 27c multicolored .60 .25
**791** A304 30c multicolored .90 .60
*a.* Imperf., dated "2007" .70 .70
**792** A303a 40c multicolored .85 .45
**793** A304 50c multicolored 1.10 .70
*b.* Imperf., dated "2007" 1.10 1.10
*c.* Booklet pane, 2 each #788b, 793b 3.50 —
**794** A304 55c multicolored 1.10 .70
*a.* Imperf., dated "2007" 1.25 1.25
*b.* Booklet pane, #786b, 789b, 791a, 794a 2.75 —
**795** A303a 65c multicolored 1.40 .70
**796** A303a 70c multicolored 1.40 .75
**797** A303a 75c multicolored 1.60 .75
**798** A303a 85c multicolored 1.75 1.00
**799** A303a 90c multicolored 1.90 .95
**800** A303a 95c multicolored 2.00 1.00
*Nos. 784-800 (17)* 17.15 9.80

Perfs: 1c, 70c, 85c, 95c, 13½; 3c, 15c, 27c, 40c, 50c, 65c, 75c, 90c, 12½x13; 5c, 25c, 30c, 55c, 13x12½; 24c, 13x13½.

Issued: 24c, 7/1/81; 5c, 25c, 30c, 50c, 55c, 7/15/81; 3c, 27c, 65c, 75c, 4/19/82; 15c, 40c, 90c, 6/16/82. 1c, 70c, 85c, 95c, 2/2/83.

Nos. 786b, 788b, 789b, 791a, 793b. 793c, 794a, 794b issued 6/26/07. No. 788b has wider spacing between text lines than on the original stamps.

**1982-84** ***Perf. 14x14½, 14½x14***

*785a* A303a 3c ('84) .70 .45
*786a* A304 5c ('84) 1.40 .50
*787a* A303a 15c ('84) 1.25 .60
*789a* A304 25c ('83) 1.40 .60
*790a* A303a 27c 1.10 .20
*792a* A303a 40c ('84) 3.00 1.10
*793a* A304 50c ('83) 2.25 1.10
*795a* A303a 65c ('84) 2.25 1.40
*797a* A303a 75c ('84) 2.60 1.40
*Nos. 785a-797a (9)* 15.95 7.45

Prince Charles and Lady Diana — A305

**1981, July 29** **Litho.** ***Perf. 13***
**804** A305 24c multicolored .45 .25
**805** A305 60c multicolored 1.25 *1.25*

Royal Wedding.

Fungi — A306

24c, Cortinarius cinnabarinus. 35c, Coprinus comatus. 55c, Armillaria luteobubalina. 60c, Cortinarius austro-venetus.

**1981, Aug. 19** **Litho.** ***Perf. 13***
**806** A306 24c multicolored .55 .40
**807** A306 35c multicolored .70 .70
**808** A306 55c multicolored 1.00 .80
**809** A306 60c multicolored 1.00 1.00
*Nos. 806-809 (4)* 3.25 2.90

Intl. Year of the Disabled — A307

**1981, Sept. 16** ***Perf. 14x13½***
**810** A307 24c multicolored .45 .30

Christmas Bush for His Adorning — A308

Christmas (Carols by William James and John Wheeler): 30c, The Silver Stars are in the Sky. 60c, Noeltime.

**1981** **Litho.** ***Perf. 13x13½***
**811** A308 18c multicolored .35 .25
**812** A308 30c multicolored .60 .60
**813** A308 60c multicolored 1.00 1.00
*Nos. 811-813 (3)* 1.95 1.85

Issue dates: 30c, Sept. 28; others, Nov. 2.

Globe — A309

**1981, Sept. 30**
**814** A309 24c multicolored .55 .40
**815** A309 60c multicolored 1.00 .95

Commonwealth Heads of Government Meeting, Melbourne, Sept. 30-Oct. 7.

Yacht — A310

24c, Ocean racer. 35c, Lightweight sharpie. 55c, 12-Meter. 60c, Sabot.

**1981, Oct. 14** **Litho.** ***Perf. 13x13½***
**816** A310 24c multicolored .45 .30
**817** A310 35c multicolored .60 .50
**818** A310 55c multicolored .85 .80
**819** A310 60c multicolored 1.00 .85
*Nos. 816-819 (4)* 2.90 2.45

Australia Day, Jan. 26 — A311

**1982, Jan. 20** **Litho.** ***Perf. 13x13½***
**820** A311 24c multicolored .45 .30

Sperm Whale — A312

35c, Southern right whale, vert. 55c, Blue whale, vert. 60c, Humpback whale.

**1982, Feb. 17** ***Perf. 13x13½, 13½x13***
**821** A312 24c shown .50 .40
**822** A312 35c multicolored .75 .70
**823** A312 55c multicolored 1.00 1.00
**824** A312 60c multicolored 1.20 1.10
*Nos. 821-824 (4)* 3.45 3.20

A trial printing of No. 824 exists with a greenish blue background and no white streaks at the UL. A small number of these stamps were sold by mistake.

Elizabeth II, 56th Birthday — A313

**1982, Apr. 21** ***Perf. 13½***
**825** A313 27c multicolored .50 .40

Roses — A314

27c, Marjorie Atherton. 40c, Imp. 65c, Minnie Watson. 75c, Satellite.

**1982, May 19** ***Perf. 13x13½***
**826** A314 27c multicolored .50 .30
**827** A314 40c multicolored .60 .60
**828** A314 65c multicolored 1.00 1.00
**829** A314 75c multicolored 1.20 1.10
*Nos. 826-829 (4)* 3.30 3.00

50th Anniv. of Australian Broadcasting Commission A315

No. 830, Announcer, microphone. No. 831, Emblem.

**1982, June 16** ***Perf. 13½x13***
**830** A315 27c multicolored .45 .35
**831** A315 27c multicolored .45 .35
*a.* Pair, #830-831 1.60 1.30

Nos. 830-831 se-tenant in continuous design.

Alice Springs Post Office, 1872 — A316

No. 833, Kingston, 1869. No. 834, York, 1893. No. 835, Flemington, 1890, vert. No. 836, Forbes, 1881, vert. No. 837, Launceston, 1889, vert. No. 838, Rockhampton, 1892, vert.

**1982, Aug. 4** ***Perf. 13½x14, 14x13½***
**832** A316 27c shown .40 .30
**833** A316 27c multicolored .40 .30
**834** A316 27c multicolored .40 .30
**835** A316 27c multicolored .40 .30
**836** A316 27c multicolored .40 .30
**837** A316 27c multicolored .40 .30
**838** A316 27c multicolored .40 .30
*Nos. 832-838 (7)* 2.80 2.10

Christmas — A317

1st Australian Christmas cards, 1881. 21c, horiz.

**1982** **Litho.** ***Perf. 14½***
**839** A317 21c multicolored .35 .25
**840** A317 35c multicolored .60 .35
**841** A317 75c multicolored 1.20 1.00
*Nos. 839-841 (3)* 2.15 1.60

Issue dates: 35c, Sept. 15; others, Nov. 1.

12th Commonwealth Games, Brisbane, Sept. 30-Oct. 9 — A318

**1982, Sept. 22** **Litho.** ***Perf. 14x14½***
**842** A318 27c Archery .50 .25
**843** A318 27c Boxing .50 .25
**844** A318 27c Weightlifting .50 .25
*a.* Souvenir sheet of 3, #842-844 1.75 1.75
**845** A318 75c Pole vault 1.25 1.25
*a.* Booklet pane of 4, #842-845, perf. 14x14¾ ('06) 3.00 —
*Nos. 842-845 (4)* 2.75 2.00

Nos. 842-842 are perf 14½. No. 844a is perf 13½x13.

No. 845a issued 3/1/2006.

Natl. Stamp Week — A319

**1982, Sept. 27** ***Perf. 13x13½***
**846** A319 27c No. 132 .50 .30

A320

Design: Gurgurr (Moon Spirit), Bark Painting by Yirawala Gunwinggu Tribe.

**1982, Oct. 12** ***Perf. 14½***
**847** A320 27c multicolored .50 .30

Opening of Natl. Gallery, Canberra.

A321

Various eucalypts (gum trees): 1c, Pink-flowered marri. 2c, Gungurru. 3c, Red-flowering gum. 10c, Tasmanian blue gum. 27c, Forrest's marlock.

***Perf. 12½x13½***

**1982, Nov. 17** **Photo.**
**848** A321 1c multicolored .25 .25
**849** A321 2c multicolored .25 .25
**850** A321 3c multicolored .65 *.35*
**851** A321 10c multicolored .65 *.40*
**852** A321 27c multicolored .65 .40
*a.* Bklt. pane, #850-851, 2 #848-849, 3 #852 + label 4.00
*b.* Bklt. pane, 2 ea #848-849, 852 2.00
*Nos. 848-852 (5)* 2.45 1.65

Nos. 848-852 issued in booklets only.

Mimi Spirits Singing and Dancing, by David Milaybuma — A322

Aboriginal Bark Paintings: Music and dance of the Mimi Spirits, Gunwinggu Tribe. 40c, Lofty Nabardayal. 65c, Jimmy Galareya. 75c, Dick Nguleingulei Murrumurru.

**1982, Nov. 17** **Litho.** ***Perf. 13½x14***
**853** A322 27c shown .50 .30
**854** A322 40c multicolored .60 .40
**855** A322 65c multicolored 1.00 .80
**856** A322 75c multicolored 1.25 .90
*Nos. 853-856 (4)* 3.35 2.40

Historic Fire Engines — A323

27c, Shand Mason Steam, 1891. 40c, Hotchkiss, 1914. 65c, Ahrens-Fox PS2, 1929. 75c, Merryweather Manual, 1851.

**1983, Jan. 12** ***Perf. 13½x14***
**857** A323 27c multicolored .50 .30
**858** A323 40c multicolored .75 .50
**859** A323 65c multicolored 1.00 .80
**860** A323 75c multicolored 1.20 1.20
*Nos. 857-860 (4)* 3.45 2.80

Australia Day — A324

**1983, Jan. 26** **Litho.** ***Perf. 14½***
**861** A324 27c Sirius .45 .30
**862** A324 27c Supply .45 .30
*a.* Pair, #861-862 1.10 1.10

A325

**1983, Feb. 2** ***Perf. 14x13½***
**863** A325 27c multicolored .50 .30
*863a* Perf. 14¾x14, dated "2013" (#1003b) .70 .70

Australia-New Zealand Closer Economic Relationship agreement (ANZCER).
Issued: No. 863a, 5/10/2013.

A326

No. 864, Equality, dignity. No. 865, Social justice, cooperation. No. 866, Liberty, freedom. No. 867, Peace, harmony.

**1983, Mar. 9 Litho. *Perf. 14½***

| | | | |
|---|---|---|---|
| **864** | A326 27c multicolored | .45 | .30 |
| **865** | A326 27c multicolored | .45 | .30 |
| **866** | A326 27c multicolored | .45 | .30 |
| **867** | A326 75c multicolored | 1.20 | 1.00 |
| | *Nos. 864-867 (4)* | 2.55 | 1.90 |

Commonwealth day.

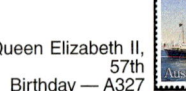

Queen Elizabeth II, 57th Birthday — A327

**1983, Apr. 20 *Perf. 14½***

| | | | |
|---|---|---|---|
| **868** | A327 27c Britannia | .45 | .35 |

World Communications Year — A328

**1983, May 18 Litho. *Perf. 13½x14***

| | | | |
|---|---|---|---|
| **869** | A328 27c multicolored | .45 | .35 |

50th Anniv. of Australian Jaycees Youth Organization A329

**1983, June 8**

| | | | |
|---|---|---|---|
| **870** | A329 27c multicolored | .45 | .35 |

St. John Ambulance Cent. — A330

**1983, June 8 *Perf. 13½x14***

| | | | |
|---|---|---|---|
| **871** | A330 27c multicolored | .45 | .35 |

Regent Skipper — A331

10c, Cairn's birdwing. 20c, Macleay's swallowtail. 27c, Ulysses. 30c, Chlorinda hairstreak. 35c, Blue tiger. 45c, Big greasy. 60c, Wood white. 80c, Amaryllis azure. $1, Sword grass brown.

**1983 *Perf. 13½, 14½x14 (30c)***

| | | | |
|---|---|---|---|
| **872** | A331 4c shown | .60 | .40 |
| **873** | A331 10c multicolored | .60 | .40 |
| **874** | A331 20c multicolored | .45 | .25 |
| **875** | A331 27c multicolored | .65 | .25 |
| **875A** | A331 30c multicolored | .80 | .25 |
| **876** | A331 35c multicolored | .80 | .35 |
| **877** | A331 45c multicolored | 1.00 | .45 |
| **878** | A331 60c multicolored | 1.20 | .55 |
| **879** | A331 80c multicolored | 1.40 | .80 |
| **880** | A331 $1 multicolored | 2.25 | 1.00 |
| | *Nos. 872-880 (10)* | 9.75 | 4.70 |

Issue dates: 30c, Oct. 24; others, June 15.

The Sentimental Bloke, by C.J. Dennis, 1909 — A332

Folktale scenes: a, The bloke. b, Doreen-the intro. c, The stror at coot. d, Hitched. e, The mooch of life.

**1983, Aug. 3 *Perf. 14½***

| | | | |
|---|---|---|---|
| **881** | Strip of 5 | 2.50 | 2.50 |
| *a.-e.* | A332 27c multi, any single | .45 | .40 |

Kookaburra Bird Wearing Santa Hat — A333

24c, Nativity. 85c, Holiday beach scene.

**1983 Litho. *Perf. 13½x14***

| | | | |
|---|---|---|---|
| **882** | A333 24c multicolored | .40 | .30 |
| **883** | A333 35c multicolored | .60 | .35 |
| **884** | A333 85c multicolored | 1.30 | .90 |
| | *Nos. 882-884 (3)* | 2.30 | 1.55 |

Christmas. Issued: No. 883, 9/14; Nos. 882, 884, 11/2.

Inland Explorers — A334

Clay sculptures by Dianne Quinn: No. 885, Ludwig Leichhardt (1813-48). No. 886, William John Wills (1834-61), Robert O'Hara Burke (1821-61). No. 887, Paul Edmund de Strzelecki (1797-1873). No. 888, Alexander Forrest (1849-1901).

**1983, Sept. 26 *Perf. 14½***

| | | | |
|---|---|---|---|
| **885** | A334 30c multicolored | .50 | .35 |
| **886** | A334 30c multicolored | .50 | .35 |
| **887** | A334 30c multicolored | .50 | .35 |
| **888** | A334 30c multicolored | .50 | .35 |
| | *Nos. 885-888 (4)* | 2.00 | 1.40 |

Australia Day — A335

**1984, Jan. 26 Litho. *Perf. 13½x14***

| | | | |
|---|---|---|---|
| **889** | A335 30c Cooks' Cottage | .45 | .30 |

50th Anniv. of Official Air Mail Service A336

Pilot Charles Ulm (1898-1934); his plane, "Faith in Australia," and different flight covers: No. 890, Australia-New Zealand. No. 891, Australia-Papua New Guinea.

**1984, Feb. 22 Litho. *Perf. 13½***

| | | | |
|---|---|---|---|
| **890** | A336 45c multicolored | .75 | *.75* |
| **891** | A336 45c multicolored | .75 | *.75* |
| *a.* | Pair, #890-891 | 2.25 | *2.25* |

Thomson, 1898 — A337

Australian-made vintage cars: b, Tarrant, 1906. c, Australian Six, 1919. d, Summit, 1923. e, Chic, 1924.

**1984, Mar. 14 *Perf. 14½***

| | | | |
|---|---|---|---|
| **892** | Strip of 5 | 2.40 | 2.40 |
| *a.-e.* | A337 30c any single | .45 | .35 |

Queen Elizabeth II, 58th Birthday — A338

**1984, Apr. 18 *Perf. 14½***

| | | | |
|---|---|---|---|
| **893** | A338 30c multicolored | .45 | .30 |

Clipper Ships — A339

30c, Cutty Sark, 1869, vert. 45c, Orient, 1853. 75c, Sobraon, 1866. 85c, Thermopylae, 1868, vert.

**1984, May 23 *Perf. 14x13½, 13½x14***

| | | | |
|---|---|---|---|
| **894** | A339 30c multicolored | .45 | .35 |
| **895** | A339 45c multicolored | .80 | .80 |
| **896** | A339 75c multicolored | 1.25 | 1.00 |
| **897** | A339 85c multicolored | 1.40 | 1.25 |
| | *Nos. 894-897 (4)* | 3.90 | 3.40 |

Freestyle Skiing — A340

No. 899, Slalom, horiz. No. 900, Cross-country, horiz. No. 901, Downhill.

**1984, June 6 Litho. *Perf. 14½***

| | | | |
|---|---|---|---|
| **898** | A340 30c shown | .50 | .35 |
| **899** | A340 30c multicolored | .50 | .35 |
| **900** | A340 30c multicolored | .50 | .35 |
| **901** | A340 30c multicolored | .50 | .35 |
| | *Nos. 898-901 (4)* | 2.00 | 1.40 |

Coral Hopper — A341

3c, Jimble. 5c, Tasseled anglerfish. 10c, Stonefish. 20c, Red handfish. 25c, Orange-tipped cowrie. 30c, Choat's wrasse. 33c, Leafy sea dragon. 40c, Red velvet fish. 45c, Textile cone shell. 50c, Blue-lined surgeonfish. 55c, Bennett's nudibranch. 60c, Lionfish. 65c, Stingray. 70c, Blue-ringed octopus. 80c, Pineapple fish. 85c, Regal angelfish. 90c, Crab-eyed goby. $1, Crown of thorns starfish.

***Perf. 13½, 14x14½ (30c, 33c)***

**1984-86 Litho.**

| | | | |
|---|---|---|---|
| **902** | A341 2c shown | .25 | .25 |
| **903** | A341 3c multicolored | .25 | .25 |
| **904** | A341 5c multicolored | .40 | .40 |
| **905** | A341 10c multicolored | .25 | .25 |
| **906** | A341 20c multicolored | .40 | .35 |
| **907** | A341 25c multicolored | .40 | .35 |
| **908** | A341 30c multicolored | .65 | .25 |
| **909** | A341 33c multicolored | .80 | .25 |
| **910** | A341 40c multicolored | .80 | .35 |
| **911** | A341 45c multicolored | .80 | .35 |
| **912** | A341 50c multicolored | 1.00 | .40 |
| **913** | A341 55c multicolored | 1.10 | .80 |
| **914** | A341 60c multicolored | 1.00 | .80 |
| **915** | A341 65c multicolored | 1.05 | .80 |
| **916** | A341 70c multicolored | 1.15 | 1.00 |
| **917** | A341 80c multicolored | 1.50 | 1.00 |
| **918** | A341 85c multicolored | 1.60 | 1.00 |
| **919** | A341 90c multicolored | 1.40 | 1.00 |
| **920** | A341 $1 multicolored | 1.60 | 1.10 |
| | *Nos. 902-920 (19)* | 16.40 | 10.95 |

Issued: 2c, 25c, 30c, 50c, 55c, 85c, 6/18; 33c, 1/20/85; 5c, 20c, 40c, 80c, 90c, 6/12/85; 3c, 10c, 45c, 60c, 65c, 70c, $1, 6/11/86.

1984 Summer Olympics — A342

Event stages: No. 922, Start (facing down). No. 923, Competing (facing right). No. 924, Finish, vert.

***Perf. 13½x14, 14x13½***

**1984, July 25 Litho.**

| | | | |
|---|---|---|---|
| **922** | A342 30c multicolored | .60 | .35 |
| **923** | A342 30c multicolored | .60 | .35 |
| **924** | A342 30c multicolored | .60 | .35 |
| | *Nos. 922-924 (3)* | 1.80 | 1.05 |

Ausipex '84 — A343

Designs: No. 926: a, Victoria #3. b, New South Wales #1. c, Tasmania #1. d, South Australia #1. e, Western Australia #1. f, Queensland #3.

**1984 Litho. *Perf. 14½***

| | | | |
|---|---|---|---|
| **925** | A343 30c No. 2 | .50 | .35 |

**Souvenir Sheet**

| | | | |
|---|---|---|---|
| **926** | Sheet of 7 | 4.00 | *4.75* |
| *a.-f.* | A343 30c any single | .50 | .40 |

No. 926 contains Nos. 925, 926a-926f. Issued: No. 925, Aug. 22; No. 926, Sept. 21.

Christmas — A344

24c, Angel and Child. 30c, Veiled Virgin and Child. 40c, Angel. 50c, Three Kings. 85c, Madonna and Child.

**1984 Litho. *Perf. 14x13½***

| | | | |
|---|---|---|---|
| **927** | A344 24c multicolored | .40 | .25 |
| **928** | A344 30c multicolored | .45 | .30 |
| **929** | A344 40c multicolored | .60 | .65 |
| **930** | A344 50c multicolored | .80 | .60 |
| **931** | A344 85c multicolored | 1.40 | 1.25 |
| | *Nos. 927-931 (5)* | 3.65 | 3.05 |

Stained-glass windows. Issue dates: 40c, Sept. 17; others, Oct. 30.

European Settlement Bicentenary — A345

Design: No. 932, Bicentennial Emblem.

Rock paintings: No. 933, Stick figures, Cobar Region, New South Wales. No. 934, Bunjil's Cave, Grampians, Western Victoria. No. 935, Quinkan Gallery, Cape York, Queensland. No. 936, Wandjina Spirit and Snake Babies, Gibb River, Western Australia. No. 937, Rock Python, Western Australia. No. 938, Silver Barramundi, Kakadu Natl. Park, Northern Territory. 85c, Rock Possum, Kakadu Natl. Park.

**1984, Nov. 7 Litho. *Perf. 14½***

| | | | |
|---|---|---|---|
| **932** | A345 30c multicolored | .55 | .30 |
| **933** | A345 30c multicolored | .55 | .30 |
| **934** | A345 30c multicolored | .55 | .30 |
| **935** | A345 30c multicolored | .55 | .30 |
| **936** | A345 30c multicolored | .55 | .30 |
| **937** | A345 30c multicolored | .55 | .30 |
| **938** | A345 30c multicolored | .55 | .30 |
| **939** | A345 85c multicolored | 1.75 | *1.90* |
| | *Nos. 932-939 (8)* | 5.60 | 4.00 |

Settlement of Victoria Sesquicentenary — A346

No. 940, Helmeted honeyeater. No. 941, Leadbeater's possum.

**1984, Nov. 19**

| | | | |
|---|---|---|---|
| **940** | A346 30c multicolored | .50 | .40 |
| **941** | A346 30c multicolored | .50 | .40 |
| *a.* | Pair, #940-941 | 1.25 | 1.25 |

Australia Day — A347

No. 942, Musgrave Ranges, by Sidney Nolan. No. 943, The Walls of China, by Russell Drysdale.

**1985, Jan. 25 Litho.**

| | | | |
|---|---|---|---|
| **942** | 30c multicolored | .55 | .35 |
| *a.* | Pair, #942 tete-beche | 2.50 | 2.50 |

# AUSTRALIA

| 943 | | 30c multicolored | .55 | .35 |
|---|---|---|---|---|
| a. | | A347 Pair, #942-943 | 1.50 | 1.40 |
| b. | | Pair, #943 tete-beche | 2.50 | 2.50 |

Intl. Youth Year — A348

**1985, Feb. 13    Litho.    Perf. 14x13½**
944  A348  30c multicolored    .55  .35

Royal Victorian Volunteer Artillery — A349

Colonial military uniforms: b, Western Australian Pinjarrah Cavalry. c, New South Wales Lancers. d, New South Wales Contingent to the Sudan. e, Victorian Mounted Rifles.

**1985, Feb. 25    Perf. 14½**
945  Strip of 5    2.50  2.40
a.-e.  A349 33c any single    .50  .30

District Nursing Service Centenary — A350

**1985, Mar. 13**
946  A350  33c multicolored    .60  .35

Australian Cockatoo A351

**Perf. 14 Horiz. on 1 or 2 sides**
**1985, Mar. 13**
947  A351  1c apple grn, yel & buff    1.40  1.25
948  A351  33c apple grn, yel & lt grnsh blue    1.40  .75
a.  Bklt. pane, 1 #947, 3 #948    6.50

Issued in booklets only.

A352

No. 949, Abel Tasman, explorer. No. 950, The Eendracht. No. 951, William Dampier. No. 952, Globe and hand.

**1985, Apr. 10    Perf. 13**
949  A352  33c multicolored    .60  .40
950  A352  33c multicolored    .60  .40
951  A352  33c multicolored    .60  .40
952  A352  90c multicolored    1.90  1.90
a.  Souvenir sheet of 4 #949-952    5.00  5.00
Nos. 949-952 (4)    3.70  3.10

Queen Elizabeth II, 59th Birthday — A353

33c, Queen's Badge, Order of Australia.

**1985, Apr. 22    Perf. 14x13½**
953  A353  33c multicolored    .50  .35
a.  Perf. 14¾x14, dated "2013" (#1003b)    .85  .85
Issued: No. 953a, 5/10/2013.

A354

**1985, May 15    Litho.    Perf. 14x13**
954  A354  33c Soil    .50  .25
955  A354  50c Air    1.00  .75
956  A354  80c Water    1.20  1.00
957  A354  90c Energy    1.40  1.25
Nos. 954-957 (4)    4.10  3.25

Environmental conservation.

A356

Illustrations from classic children's books: a, Elves & Fairies, by Annie Rentoul. b, The Magic Pudding, text and illustrations by Norman Lindsay. c, Ginger Meggs, by James Charles Bancks. d, Blinky Bill, by Dorothy Wall. e, Snugglepot and Cuddlepie, by May Gibbs.

**1985, July 17    Litho.    Perf. 14½**
960  A356  Strip of 5    3.25  3.00
a.-e.  33c any single    .50  .35

Electronic Mail — A357

**1985, Sept. 18    Litho.**
961  A357  33c multicolored    .55  .30

Christmas — A358

Angel in a ship, detail from a drawing by Albrecht Durer (1471-1528).

**1985, Sept. 18    Litho.**
962  A358  45c multicolored    .80  .35

See Nos. 967-970.

Coastal Shipwrecks — A359

Salvaged antiquities: 33c, Astrolabe from Batavia, 1629. 50c, German beardman (Bellarmine) jug from Vergulde Draeck, 1656. 90c, Wooden bobbins from Batavia, and scissors from Zeewijk, 1727. $1, Silver buckle from Zeewijk.

**1985, Oct. 2    Litho.    Perf. 13**
963  A359  33c multicolored    .65  .25
964  A359  50c multicolored    1.00  .95
965  A359  90c multicolored    1.90  1.75
966  A359  $1 multicolored    2.40  2.00
Nos. 963-966 (1)    5.95  4.95

**Christmas Type of 1985**
Illustrations by Scott Hartshorne.

**1985, Nov. 1    Litho.    Perf. 14**
967  A358  27c Angel with trumpet    .50  .25
968  A358  33c Angel with bells    .60  .35
969  A358  55c Angel with star    1.00  .80
970  A358  90c Angel with ornament    1.40  1.40
Nos. 967-970 (4)    3.50  2.80

Australia Day — A360

**1986, Jan. 24    Litho.    Perf. 14½**
971  A360  33c Aboriginal painting    .55  .35

AUSSAT — A361

Various communications satellites.

**1986, Jan. 24**
972  A361  33c multicolored    .65  .30
973  A361  80c multicolored    1.25  1.25

South Australia, Sesquicent. — A362

No. 974, Sailing ship Buffalo. No. 975, City Sign, sculpture by O.H. Hajek.

**1986, Feb. 12    Perf. 13½x14**
974  A362  33c multicolored    .50  .40
975  A362  33c multicolored    .50  .40
a.  Pair, #974-975    1.10  1.40

Cook's New Holland Expedition — A363

No. 976, Hibiscus merankensis. No. 977, Banksia serrata. No. 978, Dillenia alata. No. 979, Corria reflexa. No. 980, Parkinson. No. 981, Banks.

**1986, Mar. 12    Perf. 13**
976  A363  33c multicolored    .65  .35
977  A363  33c multicolored    .65  .35
978  A363  50c multicolored    1.10  1.25
979  A363  80c multicolored    1.60  1.40
980  A363  90c multicolored    1.75  1.75
981  A363  90c multicolored    1.75  1.75
Nos. 976-981 (6)    7.50  6.85

Australian bicentennial. Sydney Parkinson (d. 1775), artist. Sir Joseph Banks (1743-1820), naturalist.

Halley's Comet — A364

33c, Radio telescope, trajectory diagram.

**1986, Apr. 9    Perf. 14x13½**
982  A364  33c multicolored    .60  .40

Elizabeth II, 60th Birthday — A365

**1986, Apr. 21    Perf. 14½**
983  A365  33c multicolored    .60  .40

Horses — A366

33c, Brumbies. 80c, Stock horse mustering. 90c, Show-jumping. $1, Australian pony.

**1986, May 21**
984  A366  33c multicolored    .60  .30
985  A366  80c multicolored    1.40  1.25
986  A366  90c multicolored    1.60  1.40
987  A366  $1 multicolored    2.00  1.60
Nos. 984-987 (4)    5.60  4.55

Click Go the Shears, Folk Song — A366a

Lines from the song: b, Old shearer stands. c, Ringer looks around. d, Boss of the board. e, Tar-boy is there. f, Shearing is all over.

**1986, July 21    Litho.    Perf. 14½**
987A  Strip of 5    3.00  3.00
b.-f.  A366a 33c, any single    .50  .40

Amalgamated Shearers' Union, predecessor of the Australian Workers' Union, cent.

Australia Bicentennial — A367

Settling of Botany Bay penal colony: No. 988, King George III, c. 1767, by A. Ramsay. No. 989, Lord Sydney, secretary of state, 1783-1780, by Gilbert Stuart. No. 990, Capt. Arthur Phillip, 1st penal colony governor, by F. Wheatley, 1786. $1, Capt. John Hunter, governor, 1795-1800, by W. B. Bennett, 1815.

**1986, Aug. 6    Litho.    Perf. 13**
988  A367  33c multicolored    .80  .45
989  A367  33c multicolored    .80  .45
990  A367  33c multicolored    .80  .45
991  A367  $1 multicolored    2.25  2.25
Nos. 988-991 (4)    4.65  3.60

Wildlife — A368

Designs: a, Red kangaroo. b, Emu. c, Koala. d, Kookaburra. e, Platypus.

**1986, Aug. 13    Perf. 14½x14**
992  Strip of 5    3.50  3.50
a.-e.  A368 36c any single    .70  .60

Alpine Wildflowers — A369

3c, Royal bluebell. 5c, Alpine marsh marigold. 25c, Mount Buffalo sunray. 36c, Silver snow daisy.

**Rouletted 9½ Vert. on 1 or 2 sides**
**1986, Aug. 25    Booklet Stamps**
993  A369  3c multicolored    1.10  1.25
994  A369  5c multicolored    1.60  1.60
995  A369  25c multicolored    1.60  1.60
996  A369  36c multicolored    1.00  .80
a.  Bklt. pane, #993, #994, 2 #996    5.00
b.  Bklt. pane, #993, #995, 2 #996    5.25
Nos. 993-996 (4)    5.30  5.25

Orchids — A370

36c, Elythranthera emarginata. 55c, Dendrobium nindii. 90c, Caleana major. $1, Thelymitra variegata.

**1986, Sept. 18** *Perf. 14½*

**997** A370 36c multicolored .60 .25
**998** A370 55c multicolored .90 .90
**999** A370 90c multicolored 1.75 1.75
**1000** A370 $1 multicolored 2.00 2.00
*Nos. 997-1000 (4)* 5.25 4.90

America's Cup Triumph '83 — A371

No. 1001, Australia II crossing finish line. No. 1002, Trophy. No. 1003, Boxing kangaroo.

**1986, Sept. 26** *Perf. 14x13½*

**1001** A371 36c multicolored .60 .40
**1002** A371 36c multicolored .60 .40
**1003** A371 36c multicolored .60 .40
*a.* Perf. 14¾x14, dated "2013" (#1003b) .95 .95
*b.* Booklet pane of 4, #502a, 863a, 953a, 1003a 3.50 —
*Nos. 1001-1003 (3)* 1.80 1.20

Issued: Nos. 1003a, 1003b, 5/10/2013. No. 1003b was issued in a booklet also containing Nos. 1284b, 3534d and 3918.

Intl. Peace Year — A372

**1986, Oct. 22** **Litho.** *Perf. 14x13½*

**1004** A372 36c multicolored .55 .35

Christmas — A373

Kindergarten nativity play: No. 1005, Holy Family, vert. No. 1006, Three Kings, vert. No. 1007, Angels. No. 1008a, Angels, peasants. No. 1008b, Holy Family, angels, vert. No. 1008c, Shepherd, angels, vert. No. 1008d, Three Kings. No. 1008e, Shepherds.

**1986, Nov. 3** **Litho.**

**1005** A373 30c multicolored .60 .35
*a.* Perf 14x13½ 1.25 1.25
**1006** A373 36c multicolored .60 .40
**1007** A373 60c multicolored 1.10 1.10
*Nos. 1005-1007 (3)* 2.30 1.85

**Souvenir Sheet**

**1008** Sheet of 5 2.75 2.75
*a.-e.* A373 30c any single .55 .45

Perfs: Nos. 1005-1006, 1008c, 15x14½; Nos. 1007, 1008a 1008e, 14½x15.
No. 1008b, 15x14½x15x15; No. 1008d, 14½x15x14½x14½.

Australia Day — A374

No. 1009, Flag, circuit board. No. 1010, Made in Australia campaign emblem.

**1987, Jan. 23** **Litho.** *Perf. 13½x14*

**1009** A374 36c multicolored .60 .40
**1010** A374 36c multicolored .60 .40

America's Cup — A375

Views of yachts racing.

**1987, Jan. 28** *Perf. 15x14½*

**1011** A375 36c multicolored .60 .30
**1012** A375 55c multicolored 1.00 *1.10*
**1013** A375 90c multicolored 1.60 *1.60*
**1014** A375 $1 multicolored 1.90 1.75
*Nos. 1011-1014 (4)* 5.10 4.75

Fruits — A376

36c, Melons, grapes. 65c, Tropical fruit. 90c, Pears, apples, oranges. $1, Berries, peaches.

**1987, Feb. 11** *Perf. 14x13½*

**1015** A376 36c multicolored .60 .30
**1016** A376 65c multicolored 1.00 1.00
**1017** A376 90c multicolored 1.40 1.40
**1018** A376 $1 multicolored 2.00 1.75
*Nos. 1015-1018 (4)* 5.00 4.45

Agricultural Shows — A377

**1987, Apr. 10** **Litho.** *Perf. 14x13½*

**1019** A377 36c Livestock .60 .30
**1020** A377 65c Produce 1.00 1.00
**1021** A377 90c Carnival 1.40 1.40
**1022** A377 $1 Farmers 2.00 2.00
*Nos. 1019-1022 (4)* 5.00 4.70

Queen Elizabeth II, 61st Birthday — A378

**1987, Apr. 21** *Perf. 13½x14*

**1023** A378 36c multicolored .60 .40

First Fleet Leaving England — A379

Continuous design: No. 1024a, Convicts awaiting transportation. b, Capt. Arthur Phillip, Mrs. Phillip, longboat on shore. c, Sailors relaxing and working. d, Longboats heading from and to fleet. 4e, Fleet in harbor.
No. 1025a, Longboat approaching Tenerife, The Canary Isls. b, Fishing in Tenerife Harbor. $1, Fleet, dolphins.

**1987** *Perf. 13*

**1024** Strip of 5 3.75 3.75
*a.-e.* A379 36c any single .70 .40
**1025** Pair 1.60 1.50
*a.-b.* A379 36c any single .70 .40
**1026** A379 $1 multicolored 2.25 2.00
*Nos. 1024-1026 (3)* 7.60 7.25

Australia bicent.; departure of the First Fleet, May 13, 1787; arrival at Tenerife, June 1787.
Issued: No. 1024, 5/13; Nos. 1025-1026, 6/3.

**1987, Aug. 6**

First Fleet arrives at Rio de Janeiro, Aug. 1787: a, Whale, storm in the Atlantic. b, Citrus grove. c, Market. d, Religious procession. e, Fireworks over harbor.

**1027** Strip of 5 3.75 3.75
*a.-e.* A379 37c any single .60 .40

No. 1027 has a continuous design.

**1987, Oct. 13**

First Fleet arrives at Cape of Good Hope, Oct. 1787: No. 1028a, British officer surveys livestock and supplies, Table Mountain. No. 1028b, Ships anchored in Table Bay. No. 1029, Fishermen pull in nets as the Fleet approaches the Cape.

**1028** Pair 1.75 1.75
*a.-b.* A379 37c any single .75 .40
**1029** A379 $1 multicolored 1.90 1.40

No. 1028 has a continuous design.

**1988, Jan. 26**

Arrival of the First Fleet, Sydney Cove, Jan. 1788: a, Five aborigines on shore. b, Four aborigines on shore. c, Kangaroos. d, White cranes. e, Flag raising.

**1030** Strip of 5 4.00 3.75
*a.-e.* A379 37c any single .60 .40

Printed se-tenant in a continuous design.

The Early Years: Sydney Cove and Parramatta Colonies — A380

Details from panorama "View of Sydney from the East Side of the Cove," 1808, painted by convict artist John Eyre to illustrate The Present Picture of New South Wales, published in London in 1811, and paintings in British and Australian museums: a, Government House, 1790, Sydney, by midshipman George Raper. b, Government Farm, Parramatta, 1791, attributed to the Port Jackson Painter. c, Parramatta Road, 1796, attributed to convict artist Thomas Watling. d, The Rocks and Sydney Cove, 1800, an aquatint engraving by Edward Dayes. e, Sydney Hospital, 1803, by George William Evans, an explorer and surveyor-general of New South Wales. Printed se-tenant in a continuous design.

**1988, Apr. 13** **Litho.** *Perf. 13*

**1031** Strip of 5 3.75 3.50
*a.-e.* A380 37c any single .60 .40

Australia Bicentennial.

The Man from Snowy River, 1890, Ballad by A.B. Paterson — A381

Excerpts: a, At the station. b, Mountain bred. c, Terrible descent. d, At their heels. e, Brought them back.

**1987, June 24** *Perf. 14x13½*

**1034** Strip of 5 4.00 4.00
*a.-e.* A381 36c any single .60 .40

Printed se-tenant in a continuous design.

Fauna — A382

Designs: a, Possum. b, Cockatoo. c, Wombat. d, Rosella. e, Echidna.

**1987, July 1** *Perf. 14½x14*

**1035** Strip of 5 3.75 3.75
*a.-e.* A382 37c any single .60 .40

Printed se-tenant in a continuous design.

Technology — A383

**1987, Aug. 19** *Perf. 14½*

**1036** A383 37c Bionic ear .60 .30
**1037** A383 53c Microchips 1.00 .60
**1038** A383 63c Robotics 1.25 1.00
**1039** A383 68c Zirconia ceramics 1.40 1.25
*Nos. 1036-1039 (4)* 4.25 3.15

Children — A384

37c, Crayfishing. 55c, Cat's cradle. 90c, Eating meat pies. $1, Playing with a joey.

**1987, Sept. 16**

**1040** A384 37c multicolored .60 .25
**1041** A384 55c multicolored 1.00 *1.10*
**1042** A384 90c multicolored 1.60 1.40
**1043** A384 $1 multicolored 2.10 1.60
*Nos. 1040-1043 (4)* 5.30 4.35

Christmas — A385

Carolers: a, Woman, two girls. b, Man, two girls. c, Four children. d, Man, two women, boy. e, Six youths. 37c, Three women, two men. Nos. 1044a-1044e are vert.

**1987, Nov. 2** **Litho.** *Perf. 14½*

**1044** Strip of 5 3.75 3.50
*a.-e.* A385 30c any single .60 .35

*Perf. 13½x14*

**1045** A385 37c multicolored .60 .40
**1046** A385 63c shown 1.50 1.00
*Nos. 1044-1046 (3)* 5.85 4.90

Carols by Candlelight, Christmas Eve, Sidney Myer Bowl, Melbourne.

Aboriginal Crafts — A386

Designs: 3c, Spearthrower, Western Australia. 15c, Shield, New South Wales. No. 1049, Basket, Queensland. No. 1050, Bowl, Central Australia. No. 1051, Belt, Northern Territory.

*Perf. 15½ Horiz.*

**1987, Oct. 13** **Photo.**

**1047** A386 3c multicolored 1.60 1.50
**1048** A386 15c multicolored 4.00 4.00
**1049** A386 37c multicolored 1.00 1.00
*a.* Bklt. pane, 2 ea #1047, 1049 5.75
**1050** A386 37c multicolored 1.00 1.00
**1051** A386 37c multicolored 1.00 1.00
*a.* Bklt. pane, #1048, 3 #1050, 2 #1051 9.00
*Nos. 1047-1051 (5)* 8.60 8.50

Issued only in booklets.

Caricature of Australian Koala and American Bald Eagle — A387

**1988, Jan. 26** *Perf. 13*

**1052** A387 37c multicolored .75 .40

Australia bicentennial. See No. 1086 and US No. 2370.

Living Together — A388

Cartoons: 1c, Religion. 2c, Industry. 3c, Local government. 4c, Trade unions. 5c, Parliament. 10c, Transportation. 15c, Sports. 20c, Commerce. 25c, Housing. 30c, Welfare. 37c, Postal services. 39c, Tourism. 40c, Recreation. 45c, Health. 50c, Mining. 53c, Primary industry. 55c, Education. 60c, Armed Forces. 63c, Police. 65c, Telecommunications. 68c, The media. 70c, Science and technology. 75c, Visual arts. 80c, Performing arts. 90c, Banking. 95c, Law. $1, Rescue and emergency services.

**1988** *Perf. 14*

**1053** A388 1c multi .25 .25
**1054** A388 2c multi .25 .25
**1055** A388 3c multi .25 .25
**1056** A388 4c multi .25 .25
**1057** A388 5c multi .30 .25
**1058** A388 10c multi .30 .25
**1059** A388 15c multi .40 .25
**1060** A388 20c multi .60 .25
**1061** A388 25c multi .60 .25
**1062** A388 30c multi .60 .25
**1063** A388 37c multi .75 .25
*a.* Booklet pane of 10 10.50
**1063B** A388 39c multi .80 .35
*c.* Booklet pane of 10 9.00
**1064** A388 40c multi .80 .45
**1065** A388 45c multi .90 .45
**1066** A388 50c multi 1.00 .50
**1067** A388 53c multi 1.60 1.00
**1068** A388 55c multi 1.30 .65
**1069** A388 60c multi 1.25 .80
**1070** A388 63c multi 2.00 1.60
**1071** A388 65c multi 1.60 .80
**1072** A388 68c multi 2.00 1.10
**1073** A388 70c multi 1.60 .80
**1074** A388 75c multi 1.60 .80

**1075** A388 80c multi 1.60 .80
**1076** A388 90c multi 1.90 1.00
**1077** A388 95c multi 2.00 1.10
**1078** A388 $1 multi 2.00 1.25
*Nos. 1053-1078 (27)* 28.50 16.20

Issued: 1c, 2c, 3c, 5c, 30c, 40c, 55c, 60c, 63c, 65c, 68c, 75c, 95c, 3/16; 39c, 9/28; others, 2/17.

Queen Elizabeth II, 62nd Birthday — A389

**1988, Apr. 21** ***Perf. 14½***
**1079** A389 37c multicolored 1.00 .50

EXPO '88, Brisbane, Apr. 30-Oct. 30 — A390

**1988, Apr. 29** ***Perf. 13***
**1080** A390 37c multicolored 1.00 .50

Opening of Parliament House, Canberra — A391

**1988, May 9** ***Perf. 14½***
**1081** A391 37c multicolored 1.00 .50

Australia Bicentennial — A392

Designs: No. 1082, Colonist, clipper ship. No. 1083, British and Australian parliaments, Queen Elizabeth II. No. 1084, Cricketer W.G. Grace. No. 1085, John Lennon (1940-1980), William Shakespeare (1564-1616) and Sydney Opera House. Nos. 1083a, 1085a have continuous design picturing flag of Australia.

**1988, June 21 Litho.** ***Perf. 13***
**1082** A392 37c multicolored .85 .40
**1083** A392 37c multicolored .85 .40
*a.* Pair, #1082-1083 2.00 1.60
**1084** A392 $1 multicolored 1.75 *1.40*
*a.* Booklet pane of 1, imperf., dated "2007" 3.25 —
**1085** A392 $1 multicolored 1.75 *1.40*
*a.* Pair, #1084-1085 4.00 4.00
*Nos. 1082-1085 (4)* 5.20 3.60

No. 1084a issued 11/14/2007.
See Great Britain Nos. 1222-1225.

### Caricature Type of 1988

Design: Caricature of an Australian koala and New Zealand kiwi.

**1988, June 21 Litho.** ***Perf. 13½***
**1086** A387 37c multicolored 1.00 .60

Australia bicentennial. See New Zealand No. 907.

"Dream" Lore on Art of the Desert — A393

Aboriginal paintings from Papunya Settlement in the Flinders University Art Museum: 37c, Bush Potato Country, by Turkey Tolsen Tjupurrula with by David Corby Tjapaltjarri. 55c, Courtship Rejected, by Limpi Puntungka Tjapangati. 90c, Medicine Story, anonymous. $1, Ancestor Dreaming, by Tim Leura Tjapaltjarri.

**1988, Aug. 1 Litho.** ***Perf. 13***
**1087** A393 37c multicolored .80 .40
**1088** A393 55c multicolored 1.25 1.00
**1089** A393 90c multicolored 2.00 2.00
**1090** A393 $1 multicolored 2.25 2.00
*Nos. 1087-1090 (4)* 6.30 5.40

1988 Summer Olympics, Seoul — A394

37c, Basketball. 65c, Running. $1, Rhythmic gymnastics.

**1988, Sept. 14** ***Perf. 14½***
**1091** A394 37c multicolored .80 .50
**1092** A394 65c multicolored 1.60 1.25
**1093** A394 $1 multicolored 2.00 2.00
*Nos. 1091-1093 (3)* 4.40 3.75

34th Commonwealth Parliamentary Conference, Canberra — A395

37c, Scepter and mace.

**1988, Sept. 19**
**1094** A395 37c multicolored .80 .40

Works in the Contemporary Decorative Arts Collection at the Natl. Gallery — A396

2c, "Australian Fetish," by Peter Tully. 5c, Vase by Colin Levy. 39c, Teapot by Frank Bauer.

***Roulette 9 Horiz.***

**1988, Sept. 28 Litho.**
**1095** A396 2c multicolored 3.75 *4.00*
**1096** A396 5c multicolored 4.00 *4.00*
**1097** A396 39c multicolored 1.60 .60
*a.* Bklt. pane of 3 (2c, 2 39c) 6.75
*b.* Bklt. pane of 6 (5c, 5 39c) 8.00
*Nos. 1095-1097 (3)* 9.35 8.60

Nos. 1095-1097 issued in booklets only.

Views — A397

**1988, Oct. 17 Photo.** ***Perf. 13***
**1098** A397 39c The Desert .80 .40
**1099** A397 55c The Top End 1.20 .80
**1100** A397 65c The Coast 1.60 1.20
**1101** A397 70c The Bush 1.00 1.00
*Nos. 1098-1101 (4)* 5.50 4.00

Christmas — A398

Children's design contest winning drawings: 32c, Nativity scene, by Danielle Hush, age 7. 39c, Koala wearing a Santa hat, by Kylie Courtney, age 6. 63c, Cockatoo wearing a Santa hat, by Benjamin Stevenson, age 10.

**1988, Oct. 31** ***Perf. 13½x13***
**1102** A398 32c multicolored .80 .30
**1103** A398 39c multicolored .80 .40
**1104** A398 63c multicolored 1.60 1.20
*Nos. 1102-1104 (3)* 3.20 1.90

Sir Henry Parkes (1815-1896), Advocate of the Federation of the Six Colonies — A399

**1989, Jan. 25 Litho.** ***Perf. 14x13½***
**1105** A399 39c multicolored .80 .40

Australia Day.

Sports — A400

**1989, Feb. 13** ***Perf. 14x14½***
**1106** A400 1c Bowls .30 .25
*a.* Perf. 13¼x13¾ ('90) .40 .35
**1107** A400 2c Bowling .25 .25
*a.* Perf. 13¼x13¾ ('91) .25 .25
**1108** A400 3c Football .35 .25
**1109** A400 39c Fishing 1.00 .35
*a.* Booklet pane of 10 12.00
*d.* Perf. 13¼x13¾ on sides ('90) 2.25 *3.00*
*e.* Booklet pane of 10, #1109d 22.50
**1109B** A400 41c Cycling .80 .25
*c.* Booklet pane of 10 8.00
**1110** A400 55c Kite-flying 1.10 .85
**1111** A400 70c Cricket 1.60 1.10
*a.* Imperf., dated "2007" (from booklet pane No. 1302b) 2.25 2.25
**1112** A400 $1.10 Golf 2.00 1.40

No. 1109d also exists perfed on 4 sides from sheets. These are scarcer. Value, unused or used $17.50.
No. 1111a issued 11/14/2007.

**1990-94**
**1114** A400 5c Kayaking, canoeing 1.00 1.00
*a.* Perf. 13¼x13¾ .35 .25
**1115** A400 10c Windsurfing 1.00 1.00
*a.* Perf. 13¼x13¾ .70 .70
**1116** A400 20c Tennis 1.00 .35
*a.* Perf. 13¼x13¾ 2.00 .35
**1117** A400 65c Rock climbing 2.60 1.00
*a.* Perf. 13¼x13¾ 3.50 1.40
**1118** A400 $1 Running 2.25 1.60
*a.* Perf. 13¼x13¾ 4.75 3.50

Issued: Nos. 1114a, 1115a, 1116a, 1117a, 1118, 1/17/90; No. 1118a, 1/91; Nos. 1115, 1117, 2/92; No. 1116, 7/93; No. 1114, 3/94.

The 1990 year date on the original printing of No. 1117 is in serif type. The date on the 4 koala reprint of 2005 is in san-serif type.

**1990, Aug. 27**
**1119** A400 43c Skateboarding .85 .60
*a.* Booklet pane of 10 8.50

***Perf. 13½***
**1120** A400 $1.20 Hang-gliding 2.00 1.10

**1991, Aug. 22** ***Perf. 14x14½***
**1121** A400 75c Netball 1.25 .80
**1122** A400 80c Squash 1.25 .80
**1123** A400 85c Diving 1.40 .80
**1124** A400 90c Soccer 1.60 .80
*Nos. 1106-1124 (19)* 23.60 14.55

For self-adhesive stamps see Nos. 1185-1186.

Botanical Gardens A401

Designs: $2, Nooroo, New South Wales. $5, Mawarra, Victoria. $10, Palm House, Adelaide Botanical Garden. $20, A View of the Artist's House and Garden in Mills Plains, Van Diemen's Land by John Glover.

**1989-90 Litho. & Engr.** ***Perf. 14***
**1132** A401 $2 multicolored 4.00 1.60
*a.* Perf. 13¼x13¾ ('91) 7.50 4.00
**1133** A401 $5 multicolored 8.00 2.40
*a.* Perf. 13¼x13¾ 20.00 9.25
**1134** A401 $10 multicolored 15.00 5.75

**Litho with Foil Application**

***Perf. 14½x14***
**1135** A401 $20 multicolored 30.00 14.00
*Nos. 1132-1135 (4)* 57.00 23.75

Issued: $10, 4/12; $2, $5, 9/13; $20, 8/15/90.

Sheep — A402

**1989, Feb. 27 Litho.** ***Perf. 13½x14***
**1136** A402 39c Merino .80 .40
**1137** A402 39c Poll Dorset .80 .40
**1138** A402 85c Polwarth 1.75 1.60
**1139** A402 $1 Corriedale 2.00 1.60
*Nos. 1136-1139 (4)* 5.35 4.00

World Sheep and Wool Congress, Tasmania, Feb. 27-Mar. 6.

Queen Elizabeth II, 63rd Birthday — A403

**1989, Apr. 21 Litho.** ***Perf. 14½***
**1140** A403 39c Statue by John Dowie 1.00 .30

Colonial Australia — A404

Pastoral Era: a, Immigrant ship in port, c. 1835. b, Pioneer's hut, wool bales in dray. c, Squatter's homestead. d, Shepherds. e, Explorers.

**1989, May 10**
**1141** A404 Strip of 5 5.00 4.75
*a.-e.* 39c any single .80 .40

Stars of Stage and Screen — A405

Performers and directors: 39c, Gladys Moncrieff and Roy Rene, the stage, 1920's. 85c, Charles Chauvel and Chips Rafferty, talking films. $1, Nellie Stewart and James Cassius Williamson, the stage, 1890's. $1.10, Lottie Lyell and Raymond Longford, silent films.

**1989, July 12 Litho.** ***Perf. 14½***
**1142** A405 39c multicolored .80 .25
*a.* Perf. 14x13½ 11.50 11.50
**1143** A405 85c multicolored 1.75 *1.60*
**1144** A405 $1 multicolored 2.10 1.50
**1145** A405 $1.10 multicolored 2.10 1.60
*Nos. 1142-1145 (4)* 6.75 4.95

Impressionist Paintings — A406

Paintings by Australian artists: No. 1146, *Impression for Golden Summer*, by Sir Arthur Streeton. No. 1147, *All on a Summer's Day*, by Charles Conder, vert. No. 1148, *Petit Dejeuner*, by Frederick McCubbin. No. 1149, *Impression*, by Tom Roberts.

***Perf. 13½x14, 14x13½***

**1989, Aug. 23 Litho.**
**1146** A406 41c shown .80 .40
**1147** A406 41c multicolored .80 .40
**1148** A406 41c multicolored .80 .40
**1149** A406 41c multicolored .80 .40
*Nos. 1146-1149 (4)* 3.20 1.60

The Urban Environment A407

## AUSTRALIA

**1989, Sept. 1   Litho.   Perf. 15½**
**Booklet Stamps**
| | | | | |
|---|---|---|---|---|
|1150|A407|41c Freeways|.80|.45|
|1151|A407|41c Architecture|.80|.45|
|1152|A407|41c Commuter train|.80|.45|
|a.|  |Bklt. pane, 2 ea #1150, 1152, 3 #1151|7.50| |
| | |Nos. 1150-1152 (3)|2.40|1.35|

No. 1152a sold for $3.

Australian Youth Hostels, 50th Anniv. — A408

**1989, Sept. 13   Perf. 14½**
| | | | | |
|---|---|---|---|---|
|1153|A408|41c multicolored|1.00|.40|

Street Cars — A409

Designs: No. 1154, Horse-drawn tram, Adelaide, 1878. No. 1155, Steam tram, Sydney, 1884. No. 1156, Cable car, Melbourne, 1886. No. 1157, Double-deck electric tram, Hobart, 1893. No. 1158, Combination electric tram, Brisbane, 1901.

**1989, Oct. 11   Litho.   Perf. 13½x14**
| | | | | |
|---|---|---|---|---|
|1154|A409|41c multicolored|.90|.40|
|1155|A409|41c multicolored|.90|.40|
|1156|A409|41c multicolored|.90|.40|
|a.|  |Perf. 14½ on 3 sides|3.25|3.25|
|b.|  |Booklet pane of 10, #1156a|32.50| |
|1157|A409|41c multicolored|.90|.40|
|1158|A409|41c multicolored|.90|.40|
| | |Nos. 1154-1158 (5)|4.50|2.00|

Purchase of booklet containing No. 1156b included STAMPSHOW '89 admission ticket and a Melbourne one-day transit pass. Sold for $8.

Christmas — A410

Illuminations: 36c, Annunciation, from the Nicholai Joseph Foucault Book of Hours, c. 1510-20. 41c, Annunciation to the Shepherds, from the Wharncliffe Hours, c. 1475. 80c, Adoration of the Magi, from Parisian Book of Hours, c. 1490-1500.

**1989, Nov. 1   Perf. 14x13½**
| | | | | |
|---|---|---|---|---|
|1159|A410|36c multicolored|.60|.40|
|a.|  |Booklet pane of 10|7.25| |

**Perf. 15x14½**
| | | | | |
|---|---|---|---|---|
|1160|A410|41c multicolored|.80|.40|
|1161|A410|80c multicolored|1.40|1.20|
| | |Nos. 1159-1161 (3)|2.80|2.00|

Radio Australia, 50th Anniv. — A411

**1989, Nov. 1   Perf. 14x13½**
| | | | | |
|---|---|---|---|---|
|1162|A411|41c multicolored|1.00|.40|

Australia Day — A412

**1990, Jan. 17   Litho.   Perf. 15x14½**
| | | | | |
|---|---|---|---|---|
|1163|A412|41c Golden wattle|1.00|.40|

Special Occasions — A413

**1990, Feb. 7   Perf. 14x13½**
| | | | | |
|---|---|---|---|---|
|1164|A413|41c Thinking of You|.80|.40|
|a.|  |Booklet pane of 10|8.00| |
|b.|  |Perf. 14½ on 3 sides|3.50|1.10|
|c.|  |Booklet pane of 10, #1164b|35.00| |

See No. 1193.

Women Practicing Medicine in Australia, Cent. — A414

**1990, Feb. 7   Perf. 14½x15**
| | | | | |
|---|---|---|---|---|
|1165|A414|41c Constance Stone|.80|.40|

Dr. Constance Stone, Australia's first woman doctor.

A415

Fauna of the High Country: 41c, Greater glider. 65c, Spotted-tailed quoll. 70c, Mountain pygmy-possum. 80c, Brush-tailed rock-wallaby.

**1990, Feb. 21   Perf. 14x13½**
| | | | | |
|---|---|---|---|---|
|1166|A415|41c multicolored|.80|.40|
|1167|A415|65c multicolored|1.40|1.20|
|1168|A415|70c multicolored|1.50|1.20|
|1169|A415|80c multicolored|1.60|1.40|
| | |Nos. 1166-1169 (4)|5.30|4.20|

A416

No. 1170, Quit smoking. No. 1171, Don't drink and drive. No. 1172, Eat right. No. 1173, Medical check-ups.

**1990, Mar. 14**
| | | | | |
|---|---|---|---|---|
|1170|A416|41c multicolored|.80|.40|
|1171|A416|41c multicolored|.80|.40|
|1172|A416|41c multicolored|.80|.40|
|1173|A416|41c multicolored|.80|.40|
| | |Nos. 1170-1173 (4)|3.20|1.60|

Community health.

A417

Scenes from WW II, 1940-41: No. 1174, Anzacs at the front. No. 1175, Women working in factories, aircraft at the ready. 65c, Veterans and memorial parade. $1, Helicopters picking up wounded, cemetery. $1.10, Anzacs reading mail from home, 5 women watching departure of 2 ships.

**1990-2005   Litho.   Perf. 14½**
| | | | | |
|---|---|---|---|---|
|1174|A417|41c shown|.80|.35|
|1175|A417|41c multicolored|.80|.35|
|1176|A417|65c multicolored|1.25|1.00|
|a.|  |Booklet pane of 2, perf. 14½x14 ('05)|9.75|—|
|1177|A417|$1 multicolored|1.75|1.40|
|1178|A417|$1.10 multicolored|2.10|1.60|
| | |Nos. 1174-1178 (5)|6.70|4.70|

Australia and New Zealand Army Corps (ANZAC).
Issued: Nos. 1174-1178, 4/12/90. No. 1176a, Apr. 2005.

A418

**1990, Apr. 19   Perf. 14½**
| | | | | |
|---|---|---|---|---|
|1179|A418|41c multicolored|1.00|.40|

Queen Elizabeth's 64th birthday.

Penny Black, 150th Anniv. — A419

Stamps on stamps: a, New South Wales #44. b, South Australia #4. c, Tasmania #2. d, Victoria #120. e, Queensland #111A. f, Western Australia #3a.

**1990, May 1   Perf. 13½x14**
| | | | | |
|---|---|---|---|---|
|1180| |Block of 6|5.25|4.75|
|a.-f.| |A419 41c any single|.80|.40|
|g.| |Souvenir sheet of 6|5.75|5.50|
|h.| |As "g," with Stamp World London '90 emblem ovpt. in silver in sheet margin|16.00|16.00|

No. 1180h issued 5/3.

The Gold Rush — A420

a, Off to the diggings. b, The diggings. c, Panning for gold. d, Commissioner's tent. e, Gold escort.

**1990, May 16   Perf. 13**
| | | | | |
|---|---|---|---|---|
|1181| |Strip of 5|3.75|3.75|
|a.-e.| |A420 41c any single|.80|.40|

Cooperation in Antarctic Research — A421

41c, Glaciology. $1.10, Krill (marine biology).

**1990, June 13   Litho.   Perf. 14½x14**
| | | | | |
|---|---|---|---|---|
|1182|A421|41c multi|.80|.40|
|1183|A421|$1.10 multi|1.75|1.10|
|a.| |Min. sheet of 2, #1182-1183|2.75|2.75|
|b.| |#1183a overprinted|8.00|8.00|

No. 1183 is overprinted in gold, in sheet margin only, for NZ 1990 International Stamp Exhibition, Auckland, Aug. 24-Sept. 2, 1990. See Russia Nos. 5902-5903.

Colonial Australia — A422

Boom Time: a, Land boom. b, Building boom. c, Investment boom. d, Retail boom. e, Factory boom.

**1990, July 12   Litho.   Perf. 13**
| | | | | |
|---|---|---|---|---|
|1184| |Strip of 5|4.50|4.50|
|a.-e.| |A422 41c any single|.80|.40|

**Sports Type of 1989**
**1990-91   Typo.   Die Cut Perf. 11½**
**Self-Adhesive**
| | | | | |
|---|---|---|---|---|
|1185|A400|41c Cycling|1.00|.75|
|1186|A400|43c Skateboarding|1.00|.25|
|a.| |Litho.| |1.25|

Blue background has large dots on No. 1186 and smaller dots on No. 1186a. No. 1186 is on waxed paper backing printed with 0 to 4 koalas. No. 1186a is on plain paper backing printed with one kangaroo.
Issued: 41c, 5/16; No. 1186, 8/27; No. 1186a, 1991.

Salmon Gums by Robert Juniper — A423

43c, The Blue Dress by Brian Dunlop.

**Perf. 15½ Vert.**
**1990, Sept. 3   Litho.**
**Booklet Stamps**
| | | | | |
|---|---|---|---|---|
|1191|A423|28c multicolored|2.00|1.25|
|a.| |Perf. 14½ vert.|2.00|1.50|
|1192|A423|43c multicolored|1.00|.85|
|a.| |Bklt. pane, #1191, 4 #1192|9.50| |
|b.| |Perf. 14½ vert.|1.20|.60|
|c.| |Bklt. pane, #1191a, 4 #1192b|5.00| |

**Thinking Of You Type**
**1990, Sept. 3   Perf. 14½**
| | | | | |
|---|---|---|---|---|
|1193|A413|43c multicolored|.85|.50|
|a.| |Booklet pane of 10|8.00| |

Christmas — A424

**1990, Oct. 31   Litho.   Perf. 14½**
| | | | | |
|---|---|---|---|---|
|1194|A424|38c Kookaburras|.75|.35|
|a.| |Booklet pane of 10|8.00| |
|1195|A424|43c Nativity, vert.|.80|.40|
|a.| |Perf. 14¾x14, additionally dated "2013" (#3534d)|1.25|1.25|
|1196|A424|80c Opossum|1.60|1.60|
| | |Nos. 1194-1196 (3)|3.15|2.35|

Issued: No. 1195a, 5/10/2013.

Local Government in Australia, 150th Anniv. — A425

43c, Town Hall, Adelaide.

**1990, Oct. 31**
| | | | | |
|---|---|---|---|---|
|1197|A425|43c multi|1.00|.40|

Flags — A426

43c, National flag. 90c, White ensign. $1, Air Force ensign. $1.20, Red ensign.

**1991, Jan. 10   Litho.   Perf. 14½**
| | | | | |
|---|---|---|---|---|
|1199|A426|43c multi|.80|.45|
|1200|A426|90c multi|1.40|1.40|
|1201|A426|$1 multi|1.75|1.40|
|1202|A426|$1.20 multi|2.10|1.60|
| | |Nos. 1199-1202 (4)|6.05|4.85|

Australia Day.

Water Birds — A427

No. 1203, Black swan. No. 1204, Black-necked stork, vert. No. 1205, Cape Barren goose, vert. No. 1206, Chestnut teal.

**1991, Feb. 14**
| | | | | |
|---|---|---|---|---|
|1203|A427|43c multicolored|.80|.40|
|1204|A427|43c multicolored|.80|.40|
|1205|A427|85c multicolored|2.00|1.50|
|1206|A427|$1 multicolored|1.75|1.60|
| | |Nos. 1203-1206 (4)|5.35|3.90|

Women's Wartime Services, 50th Anniv. — A428

50th Anniv: No. 1208, Siege of Tobruk. $1.20, Australian War Memorial, Canberra.

**1991-2005 Litho. *Perf. 14½***

**1207** A428 43c shown .80 .40
*a.* Booklet pane of 4, perf. 14x14½ ('05) *9.75* —
**1208** A428 43c multicolored .80 .40
**1209** A428 $1.20 multicolored 2.10 1.60
*Nos. 1207-1209 (3)* 3.70 2.40

Issued: Nos. 1207-1209, 3/14/91. No. 1207a, Apr. 2005.

Queen Elizabeth II's 65th Birthday — A429

**1991, Apr. 11 Litho. *Perf. 14½***

**1210** A429 43c multicolored 1.00 .80

Insects — A430

No. 1211, Hawk moth. No. 1212, Cotton harlequin bug. No. 1213, Leichhardt's grasshopper. No. 1214, Jewel beetle.

**1991, Apr. 11**

**1211** A430 43c multicolored .80 .40
**1212** A430 43c multicolored .80 .40
**1213** A430 80c multicolored 1.75 1.50
**1214** A430 $1 multicolored 1.75 1.60
*Nos. 1211-1214 (4)* 5.10 3.90

Australian Photography, 150th Anniv. — A431

Designs: No. 1215a, Bondi, by Max Dupain, 1939. No. 1215b, Gears for the Mining Industry, Vickers Huwolt Melbourne, by Wolfgang Sievers, 1967. 70c, Wheel of Youth, by Harold Cazneaux, 1929. $1.20, Teacup Ballet, by Olive Cotton, 1935.

**1991, May 13 Litho. *Perf. 14½***

**1215** Pair 2.00 1.60
*a.-b.* A431 43c any single .85 .40
**1216** A431 70c blk, olive & cl 1.50 1.25
**1217** A431 $1.20 blk, gray & Prus bl 2.00 1.60
*Nos. 1215-1217 (3)* 5.50 4.45

Golden Days of Radio — A432

No. 1218, Music & variety shows. No. 1219, Soap operas. No. 1220, Quiz shows. No. 1221, Children's stories.

**1991, June 13 Litho. *Perf. 14½***

**1218** A432 43c multicolored .80 .40
**1219** A432 43c multicolored .80 .40
**1220** A432 85c multicolored 1.25 1.60
**1221** A432 $1 multicolored 2.10 1.75
*Nos. 1218-1221 (4)* 4.95 4.15

Pets — A433

**1991, July 25 Litho. *Perf. 14½***

**1222** A433 43c Puppy .80 .40
**1223** A433 43c Kitten .80 .40
**1224** A433 70c Pony 1.50 1.25
**1225** A433 $1 Cockatoo 1.75 1.60
*Nos. 1222-1225 (4)* 4.85 3.65

George Vancouver (1757-1798) and Edward John Eyre (1815-1901), Explorers — A434

**1991, Sept. 26 Litho. *Perf. 14½***

**1226** A434 $1.05 multicolored 1.75 1.25
*a.* Souvenir sheet of 1 2.25 2.25
*b.* As "a," overprinted in gold 7.50 7.50

Vancouver's visit to Western Australia, 200th anniv. and Eyre's journey to Albany, Western Australia, 150th anniv.

No. 1226b overprinted in sheet margin with show emblem and: "PHILANIPPON / WORLD STAMP / EXHIBITION / TOKYO / 16-24 NOV 1991" followed by Japanese inscription.

Issued: No. 1226b, Nov. 16.

Australian Literature of the 1890's — A435

Designs: 43c, Seven Little Australians by Ethel Turner. 75c, On Our Selection by Steele Rudd. $1, Clancy of the Overflow by A.B. "Banjo" Paterson, vert. $1.20, The Drover's Wife by Henry Lawson, vert.

**1991, Oct. 10**

**1227** A435 43c multicolored .80 .40
**1228** A435 75c multicolored 1.10 1.00
**1229** A435 $1 multicolored 1.75 1.25
**1230** A435 $1.20 multicolored 2.10 1.40
*Nos. 1227-1230 (4)* 5.75 4.05

Christmas — A436

38c, Shepherd. 43c, Baby Jesus. 90c, Wise man, camel.

**1991, Nov. 1**

**1231** A436 38c multi .60 .30
*a.* Booklet pane of 20 12.50
**1232** A436 43c multi .65 .30
**1233** A436 90c multi 1.60 1.60
*Nos. 1231-1233 (3)* 2.85 2.20

Thinking of You — A437

**1992, Jan. 2 Litho. *Perf. 14½***

**1234** A437 45c Wildflowers .85 .30
*a.* Booklet pane of 10 8.75

Threatened Species — A438

Designs: Nos. 1235a, 1241, Parma wallaby. Nos. 1235b, 1242, Ghost bat. Nos. 1235c, 1243, Long-tailed dunnart. Nos. 1235d, 1244, Little pygmy possum. Nos. 1235e, 1245, Dusky hopping mouse. Nos. 1235f, 1246, Squirrel glider.

**1992, Jan. 2 Litho. *Perf. 14x14½***

**1235** Block of 6 5.25 5.25
*a.-f.* A438 45c any single .80 .40

**Die Cut**
***Perf. 11½***
**Self-Adhesive**
**Size: 31x22mm**

**1241** A438 45c multicolored 1.00 .40
*a.* Typo. 1.00 .40
**1242** A438 45c multicolored 1.00 .40
*a.* Typo. 1.00 .40
**1243** A438 45c multicolored 1.00 .40
*a.* Typo. 1.00 .40
**1244** A438 45c multicolored 1.00 .40
*a.* Typo. 1.00 .40
**1245** A438 45c multicolored 1.00 .40
*a.* Typo. 1.00 .40
**1246** A438 45c multicolored 1.00 .40
*a.* Typo. 1.00 .40
*b.* Bklt. pane, 2 each #1241-1244, 1 each #1245-1246 10.00
*c.* Pane of 5, #1242-1246 6.00
*d.* Strip of 6, #1241-1246 6.00
*e.* Strip of 6, #1241a-1246a 6.00
*f.* #1246c overprinted 6.00
*g.* As "f," no die cutting *210.00*
*Nos. 1241-1246 (6)* 6.00 2.40

Litho. stamps are sharper in appearance than typo. stamps, most notably on the black lettering. Nos. 1246b and 1246c have tagging bars which make the right portion of the stamps appear toned.

No. 1246f — overprinted in Gold on sheet margin of No. 1246c with emblem of "WORLD COLUMBIAN / STAMP EXPO '92 / MAY 22-31, 1992 - CHICAGO." Issued in May.

See Nos. 1271-1293.

Wetlands A439

20c, Noosa River, Queensland. 45c, Lake Eildon, Victoria.

***Perf. 14½ Horiz.***
**1992, Jan. 2 Litho.**
**Booklet Stamps**

**1247** A439 20c multi 1.20 .85
*a.* Perf. 14 horiz. 2.50 .85
**1248** A439 45c multi .80 .80
*a.* Bklt. pane, #1247, 4 #1248 5.50
Complete booklet, #1248a 5.50
*b.* Perf. 14 horiz. 2.00 .65
*c.* Bklt. pane, #1247a, 4 #1248b 6.50
Complete booklet, #1248c 6.50

Sailing Ships — A440

No. 1249, Young Endeavour. No. 1250, Britannia, vert. No. 1251, Akarana, vert. No. 1252, John Louis.

**1992, Jan. 15 Litho. *Perf. 14½***

**1249** A440 45c multi .80 .40
**1250** A440 45c multi .80 .40
**1251** A440 $1.05 multi 1.75 1.60
**1252** A440 $1.20 multi 2.10 1.60
*a.* Sheet of 4, #1249-1252 6.50 6.50
*b.* As "a," overprinted 6.50 9.25
*c.* As "a," overprinted 13.00 10.50
*Nos. 1249-1252 (4)* 5.45 4.00

Australia Day. Discovery of America, 500th anniv. (No. 1252a).

Overprint in gold on sheet margin of No. 1252b contains emblem and "WORLD COLUMBIAN / STAMP EXPO '92 / MAY 22-31, 1992-CHICAGO." No. 1252b issued in May.

Overprint in gold on sheet margin of No. 1252c contains emblem and "GENOVA '92 / 18-27 SEPTEMBER." No. 1252c issued in Sept.

Australian Battles, 1942 — A441

No. 1253, Bombing of Darwin. No. 1254, Milne Bay. No. 1255, Kokoda Trail. No. 1256, Coral Sea. No. 1257, El Alamein.

**1992-2005 Litho. *Perf. 14½***

**1253** A441 45c multi .80 .40
**1254** A441 75c multi 1.25 .80
**1255** A441 75c multi 1.25 .80
**1256** A441 $1.05 multi 1.75 1.25
*a.* Booklet pane, #1253-1256, perf. 14x14½ ('05) *11.00* —
**1257** A441 $1.20 multi 2.00 1.25
*Nos. 1253-1257 (5)* 7.05 4.50

No. 1256a issued Apr. 2005.

Intl. Space Year — A442

45c, Helix Nebula. $1.05, The Pleiades. $1.20, Spiral Galaxy NGC 2997.

**1992, Mar. 19**

**1258** A442 45c multi .80 .40
**1259** A442 $1.05 multi 1.60 1.25
**1260** A442 $1.20 multi 2.40 1.60
*a.* Sheet of 3, #1258-1260 5.00 5.00
*b.* As "a," overprinted 9.00 9.00
*Nos. 1258-1260 (3)* 4.80 3.25

Overprint on sheet margin of No. 1260b contains emblem of "WORLD COLUMBIAN / STAMP EXPO '92 / MAY 22-31, 1992-CHICAGO." No. 1260b issued in May.

Queen Elizabeth II, 66th Birthday — A443

**1992, Apr. 9 *Perf. 14x14½***

**1261** A443 45c Wmk. 228 & #258 .90 .25

Vineyard Regions — A444

Designs: No. 1262, Hunter Valley New South Wales. No. 1263, North Eastern Victoria. No. 1264, Barossa Valley South Australia. No. 1265, Coonawarra South Australia. No. 1266, Margaret River Western Australia.

**1992, Apr. 9**

**1262** A444 45c multicolored .80 .55
**1263** A444 45c multicolored .80 .55
**1264** A444 45c multicolored .80 .55
**1265** A444 45c multicolored .80 .55
**1266** A444 45c multicolored .80 .55
*Nos. 1262-1266 (5)* 4.00 2.75

Land Care — A445

a, Salt action. b, Farm planning. c, Erosion control. d, Tree planting. e, Dune care.

**1992, June 11 Litho. *Perf. 14½x14***

**1267** Strip of 5 4.25 4.00
*a.-e.* A445 45c Any single .80 .40

1992 Summer Olympics and Paralympics, Barcelona — A446

**1992, July 2 *Perf. 14½***

**1268** A446 45c Cycling 1.40 .70
**1269** A446 $1.20 Weight lifting 2.40 2.00
**1270** A446 $1.20 High jump 2.40 2.00
*Nos. 1268-1270 (3)* 6.20 4.70

**Threatened Species Type of 1992**

Designs: 30c, Saltwater crocodile. 35c, Echidna. 40c, Platypus. No. 1274, Kangaroo. No. 1275, Adult kangaroo with joey. No. 1276, Two adult kangaroos. No. 1277, Four koalas. No. 1278, Koala walking. No. 1279, Koala in tree. 50c, Koala. 60c, Common brushtail possum. 70c, Kookaburra. Nos. 1283, 1283A, Pelican. 90c, Eastern gray kangaroo. 95c, Common wombat. $1.20, Pink cockatoo. $1.35, Emu.

**1992-98 Litho. *Perf. 14x14½***

**1271** A438 30c multi .80 .40
**1272** A438 35c multi .70 .35
**1273** A438 40c multi .80 .30
**1274** A438 45c orange & multi .80 .25
*a.* Brown panel 6.00 5.00
*b.* Bright orange panel 4.00 3.50
*c.* Additionally dated "2013" (#1284b) 1.50 1.50
**1275** A438 45c orange & multi .80 .25
*a.* Brown panel 6.00 5.00
*b.* Bright orange panel 4.00 3.50
*c.* Additionally dated "2013" (#1284b) 1.50 1.50
**1276** A438 45c orange & multi .80 .25
*a.* Sheet of 3, #1274-1276 10.00 10.00
*b.* Brown panel 6.00 5.00
*c.* Bright orange panel 4.00 3.50
*d.* Additionally dated "2013" (#1284b) 1.50 1.50
**1277** A438 45c orange & multi .80 .25
*a.* Brown panel 6.00 5.00
*b.* Bright orange panel 4.00 3.50
**1278** A438 45c orange & multi .80 .25
*a.* Brown panel 6.00 5.00
*b.* Bright orange panel 4.00 3.50
**1279** A438 45c orange & multi .80 .25
*a.* Block of 6, #1274-1279 6.50 6.50
*b.* Souv. sheet, #1274-1279 20.00 20.00
*c.* Brown panel 6.00 5.00

*d.* Block, #1274a-1275a, 1276b, 1277a-1278a, 1279c 36.00 36.00
*e.* Bright orange panel 4.00 3.50
*f.* Block, #1274b-1275b, 1276c, 1277b-1278b, 1279e 24.00 24.00

On No. 1279a Australia and denomination are orange, "KANGAROO" is 9mm long, and date is 1½mm long. Date is 1mm long and "KANGAROO" 8mm long on Nos. 1279d and 1279f. No. 1279d comes from 2 Koala printing. No. 1279f comes from 3 Koala printing.

**1280** A438 50c multi .80 .35
**1281** A438 60c multi 1.00 .65
**1282** A438 70c multi 1.00 .50
*a.* "Australia 70c" in brn ('96) 2.75 2.50
**1283** A438 85c peach panel at bottom 1.60 .80
**1283A** A438 85c yellow panel at bottom 3.25 3.00
**1284** A438 90c multi 1.35 .80
*a.* Additionally dated "2013" (#1284b) 3.25 3.00
*b.* Booklet pane of 4, #1274c, 1275c, 1276d, 1284a 6.50 —
**1285** A438 95c multi 1.60 .80
**1286** A438 $1.20 multi 1.90 1.60
*a.* "Australia $1.20" in brown ('98) 3.75 3.25
**1287** A438 $1.35 multi 2.40 2.00
*Nos. 1271-1287 (18)* 22.00 13.05

PHILAKOREA '94 (No. 1279b).
"Australia" and denominations on Nos. 1282, 1286 are in orange.
No. 1276a inscribed in sheet margin with "CHINA '96 — 9th Asian International Exhibition" in Chinese and English and exhibition emblems.
No. 1282a comes from 3 Koala or 1 Kangaroo and 1 Koala printing. No. 1286a comes from 1 Kangaroo printing.
No. 1283A is from the three koala printing.
Issued: 35c, 50c, 60c, 95c, 8/13; 40c, 70c, 90c, $1.20, 8/12/93; 30c, 85c, $1.35, 3/10/94; 45c, 5/12/94; No. 1279b, 8/94; No. 1282a, 3/96; No. 1276a, 5/18/96; No. 1283A, 1997; No. 1286a, 12/98; Nos. 1274c, 1275c, 1276d, 1284a, 1284b, 5/10/13. No. 1284b was issued in a booklet also containing Nos. 1003b, 3534d and 3918.

***Die Cut Perf. 11***

**1994, May 12 Litho.**

**Self-Adhesive**

**1288** A438 45c like #1274 1.75 .75
**1289** A438 45c like #1275 1.75 .75
**1290** A438 45c like #1276 1.75 .75
**1291** A438 45c like #1277 1.75 .75
**1292** A438 45c like #1278 1.75 .75
**1293** A438 45c like #1279 1.75 .75
*a.* Bklt. pane, #1290, 1293, 2 each #1288-1289, 1291-1292 17.50
*b.* Strip of 6, #1288-1293 11.50
*Nos. 1288-1293 (6)* 10.50 4.50

***Serpentine Die Cut 11½***

**1995 Typo. Self-Adhesive**

**Coil Stamps**

**1294** A438 45c Like #1274 1.00 .40
**1294A** A438 45c Like #1275 1.00 .40
**1294B** A438 45c Like #1276 1.00 .40
**1294C** A438 45c Like #1277 1.00 .40
**1294D** A438 45c Like #1278 1.00 .40
**1295** A438 45c Like #1279 1.00 .40
*a.* Strip of 6, #1294, 1294A-1294D, 1295 8.00
*Nos. 1294-1295 (6)* 6.00 2.40

Nos. 1294-1295 come from the third through seventh Koala printings by Pemara.

Opening of Sydney Harbor Tunnel, August 29 — A447

Sydney Harbor Bridge and Tunnel: a, Left side. b, Right side.

**1992, Aug. 28 Litho. *Perf. 14½***

**1296** A447 45c Pair, #a.-b. 4.50 4.50
*c.* Pair, #d.-e., perf 15½ 4.00 4.00

Buildings in Western Australia Goldfield Towns — A448

Designs: No. 1297, Warden's Courthouse, Coolgardie. No. 1298, Post Office, Kalgoorlie. $1.05, York Hotel, Kalgoorlie. $1.20, Town Hall, Kalgoorlie.

**1992, Sept. 17 Litho. *Perf. 14x14½***

**1297** A448 45c multicolored .80 .40
**1298** A448 45c multicolored .80 .40
**1299** A448 $1.05 multicolored 1.60 1.60
**1300** A448 $1.20 multicolored 2.00 1.60
*Nos. 1297-1300 (4)* 5.20 4.00

Sheffield Shield Cricket Competition, Cent. — A449

Cricket match, 1890s: 45c, Bowler. $1.20, Batsman, wicket keeper.

**1992, Oct. 15 Litho. *Perf. 14½***

**1301** A449 45c multicolored .75 .40
*a.* Perf. 14¾x14, dated "2007" 1.40 1.40
**1302** A449 $1.20 multicolored 2.00 1.60
*a.* Perf. 14¾x14, dated "2007" 3.75 3.75
*b.* Booklet pane of 3, #1111a, 1301a, 1302a 7.50 —

Nos. 1301a, 1302a, 1302b issued 11/14/2007.

Christmas — A450

Designs: 40c, Children dressed as Mary and Joseph with baby carriage. 45c, Boy jumping from bed Christmas morning. $1, Boy and girl singing Christmas carol.

**1992, Oct. 30 Litho. *Perf. 14x14½***

**1303** A450 40c multicolored .75 .35
*a.* Booklet pane of 20 14.00
**1304** A450 45c multicolored .75 .35
**1305** A450 $1 multicolored 1.60 1.25
*Nos. 1303-1305 (3)* 3.10 1.95

Watercolor Paintings by Albert Namatjira — A451

Designs: No. 1306a, Ghost Gum, Central Australia. b, Across the Plain to Mount Giles.

**1993, Jan. 14 Litho. *Perf. 14x15***

**1306** A451 45c Pair, #a.-b. 1.90 1.90

Australia Day.

Dreamings — A452

Aboriginal paintings: 45c, Wild Onion Dreaming, by Pauline Nakamarra Woods. 75c, Yam Plants, by Jack Wunuwun, vert. 85c, Goose Egg Hunt, by George Milpurrurru, vert. $1, Kalumpiwarra-Ngulalintji, by Rover Thomas.

***Perf. 14x14½, 14½x14***

**1993, Feb. 4 Litho.**

**1307** A452 45c red & multi .80 .40
**1308** A452 75c org yel & multi 1.40 .80
**1309** A452 85c buff & multi 1.60 1.10
**1310** A452 $1 salmon & multi 1.75 1.50
*Nos. 1307-1310 (4)* 5.55 3.80

World Heritage Sites in Australia A453

**1993, Mar. 4 Litho. *Perf. 14½x14***

**1311** A453 45c Uluru (Ayers Rock) .80 .40
**1312** A453 85c Fraser Island 1.60 .80
**1313** A453 95c Shark Bay 1.90 1.00
**1314** A453 $2 Kakadu 3.25 2.00
*Nos. 1311-1314 (4)* 7.55 4.20

See Nos. 1485-1488.

World War II Ships — A454

45c, Cruiser HMAS Sydney II. 85c, Corvette HMAS Bathurst. $1.05, Destroyer HMAS Arunta. $1.20, Hospital Ship Centaur.

**1993-2005 Litho. *Perf. 14x14½***

**1315** A454 45c multicolored .80 .40
**1316** A454 85c multicolored 1.25 1.00
**1317** A454 $1.05 multicolored 1.60 1.60
*a.* Booklet pane, #1315, 1317 ('05) 11.75 —
**1318** A454 $1.20 multicolored 2.40 1.60
*Nos. 1315-1318 (4)* 6.05 4.60

Issued: Nos. 1315-1318, 4/7/93. No. 1317a, April 2005.

Queen Elizabeth II, 67th Birthday — A455

**1993, Apr. 7 *Perf. 14½x14***

**1319** A455 45c multicolored .90 .40

A456

Designs based on 19th cent. trade union banners: No. 1320, Baker, shoe maker. No. 1321, Stevedore, seamstresses. $1, Blacksmith, telephone operator, cook. $1.20, Carpenters.

**1993, May 7 Litho. *Perf. 14½x14***

**1320** A456 45c multicolored .90 .40
**1321** A456 45c multicolored .90 .40
**1322** A456 $1 multicolored 1.60 1.20
**1323** A456 $1.20 multicolored 2.40 1.60
*Nos. 1320-1323 (4)* 5.80 3.60

Working life in the 1890s.

Trains — A457

Designs: No. 1324, Centenary Special, Tasmania. No. 1325, Spirit of Progress. No. 1326, Western Endeavour. No. 1327, Silver City Comet. No. 1328, Kuranda Tourist Train. No. 1329, The Ghan.

**1993, June 1 *Perf. 14x14½***

**1324** A457 45c multicolored .80 .80
**1325** A457 45c multicolored .80 .80
**1326** A457 45c multicolored .80 .80
**1327** A457 45c multicolored .80 .80
**1328** A457 45c multicolored .80 .80
**1329** A457 45c multicolored .80 .80
*a.* Block of 6, #1324-1329 7.75 7.75
*Nos. 1324-1329 (6)* 4.80 4.80

***Die Cut Perf. 11½x12***

**Self-Adhesive**

**1330** A457 45c like No. 1324 1.60 .40
**1331** A457 45c like No. 1325 1.60 .40
**1332** A457 45c like No. 1326 1.60 .40
**1333** A457 45c like No. 1327 1.60 .40
**1334** A457 45c like No. 1328 1.60 .40
**1335** A457 45c like No. 1329 1.60 .40
*a.* Strip of 6, #1330-1335 10.50
*b.* Bklt. pane, #1332, 1335, 2 ea #1330-1331, 1333-1334 12.00
*Nos. 1330-1335 (6)* 9.60 2.40

Aboriginal Art — A458

Aboriginal paintings: 45c, Black Cockatoo Feather, by Fiona Foley, vert. 75c, Ngarrgooroon Country, by Hector Jandany. $1, Ngak Ngak, by Ginger Riley. $1.05, Untitled work, by Robert Cole, vert.

***Perf. 14½x14, 14x14½***

**1993, July 1 Litho.**

**1336** A458 45c henna brown & multi .80 .40
**1337** A458 75c brown & multi 1.25 .80
**1338** A458 $1 gray & multi 1.75 1.25
**1339** A458 $1.05 olive & multi 2.00 1.40
*Nos. 1336-1339 (4)* 5.80 3.85

Dame Enid Lyons, MP, and Sen. Dorothy Tangney — A459

No. 1340, Stylized globe, natl. arms, Inter-Parliamentary Conf. emblem.

**1993, Sept. 2 Litho. *Perf. 14½***

**1340** A459 45c multicolored .80 .80
**1341** A459 45c multicolored .80 .80
*a.* Pair, #1340-1341 2.25 2.00

90th Inter-Parliamentary Union Conference (No. 1340). First women in Australian Federal Parliament, 50th anniv. (No. 1341). Nos. 1340-1341 printed in panes of 25 with 16 #1340 and 9 #1341. Panes with 16 #1341 and 9 #1340 were issued Nov. 19, but were available only through Philatelic Agency.

A460

A461

Dinosaurs: Nos. 1342, 1348, Ornithocheirus. Nos. 1343, 1349, Leaellynasaura. No. 1344, Allosaurus. No. 1345, Timimus. No. 1346, Muttaburrasaurus. No. 1347, Minmi.

**1993, Oct. 1 *Perf. 14x14½, 14½x14***

**1342** A460 45c multi, horiz. .80 .40
**1343** A460 45c multi .80 .40
**1344** A461 45c multi .80 .40
**1345** A461 45c multi .80 .40

**Size: 30x50mm**

**1346** A461 75c multi 1.25 .80
**1347** A461 $1.05 multi horiz. 1.60 1.60
*a.* Souvenir sheet of 6, #1342-1347, perf. 14¼ 6.00 6.00
*b.* As "a," overprinted 10.00 10.00
*c.* As "a," overprinted 10.00 10.00
*Nos. 1342-1347 (6)* 6.05 4.00

**Self-Adhesive**

***Die Cut Perf. 11½***

**1348** A460 45c multi horiz. 2.10 .80
**1349** A460 45c multi 2.10 .80
*a.* Bklt. pane, 5 each #1348-1349 22.00

Overprint in gold on sheet margin of No. 1347b contains "BANGKOK 1993" show emblem and "WORLD PHILATELIC / EXHIBITION / BANGKOK 1-10 OCTOBER 1993."
Overprint in gold on sheet margin of No. 1347c contains dinosaur and "Sydney / STAMP & COIN / SHOW / 15-17 October 1993."

Christmas — A462

**1993, Nov. 1 Litho. *Perf. 14½x14***

**1354** A462 40c Goodwill .70 .40
*a.* Booklet pane of 20 14.00
**1355** A462 45c Joy .80 .40
**1356** A462 $1 Peace 1.60 1.20
*Nos. 1354-1356 (3)* 3.10 2.00

Australia Day — A463

Landscape paintings: 45c, Shoalhaven River Bank-Dawn, by Arthur Boyd. 85c, Wimmera (from Mt. Arapiles), by Sir Sidney Nolan. $1.05, Lagoon, Wimmera, by Nolan. $2, White

Cockatoos in Paddock with Flame Trees, by Boyd, vert.

***Perf. 14½x14, 14x14½***

**1994, Jan. 13** **Litho.**

**1357** A463 45c multicolored .80 .40
**1358** A463 85c multicolored 1.40 .80
**1359** A463 $1.05 multicolored 2.10 2.10
**1360** A463 $2 multicolored 4.00 2.40
*Nos. 1357-1360 (4)* 8.30 5.70

See Nos.1418-1421, 1476-1479, 1572-1574.

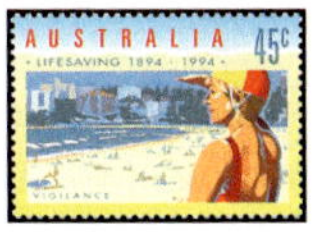

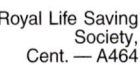

Royal Life Saving Society, Cent. — A464

**1994, Jan. 20** **Litho.** ***Perf. 14x14½***

**1361** A464 45c Vigilance .80 .40
**1362** A464 45c Education .80 .40
**1363** A464 95c Drill 1.60 1.20
**1364** A464 $1.20 Fitness 2.00 1.40
*Nos. 1361-1364 (4)* 5.20 3.40

***Die Cut Perf. 11½***

**Self-Adhesive**

**1365** A464 45c like #1361 1.60 .80
**1366** A464 45c like #1362 1.60 .80
*a.* Pair, #1365-1366 3.75
*b.* Booklet pane, 5 #1366a 19.00

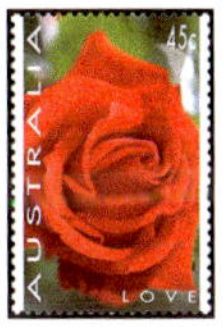

Thinking of You — A465

**1994, Feb. 3** **Litho.** ***Perf. 14½x14***

**1367** A465 45c Rose .90 .40
**1368** A465 45c Tulips .80 .40
**1369** A465 45c Poppies .80 .40
*a.* Pair, #1368-1369 2.00 1.75
*b.* Booklet pane, 5 #1369a 10.00
*Nos. 1367-1369 (3)* 2.50 1.20

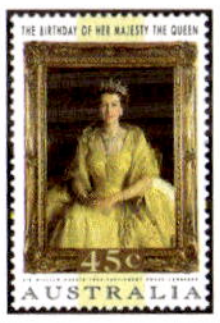

A466

**1994, Apr. 8** **Litho.** ***Perf. 14½***

**1370** A466 45c multicolored 1.25 .80

Queen Elizabeth II, 68th birthday.

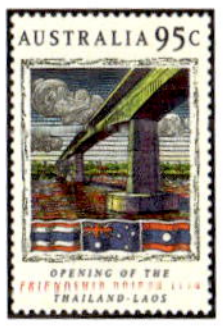

A467

**1994, Apr. 8** ***Perf. 14½x14***

**1371** A467 95c multicolored 1.90 1.60

Opening of Friendship Bridge, Thailand-Laos.

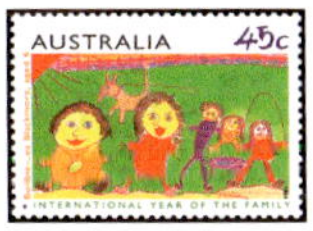

Intl. Year of the Family — A468

Children's paintings of their families: 45c, Bobbie Lea Blackmore. 75c, Kathryn Teoh. $1, Maree McCarthy.

**1994, Apr. 14** **Litho.** ***Perf. 14x14½***

**1372** A468 45c multicolored .80 .40
**1373** A468 75c multicolored 1.40 .80
**1374** A468 $1 multicolored 1.90 1.20
*Nos. 1372-1374 (3)* 4.10 2.40

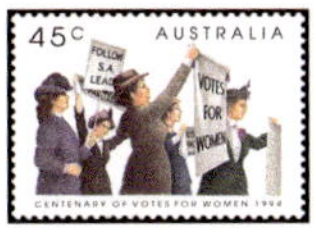

Australian Women's Right to Vote, Cent. — A469

**1994, June 9** **Litho.** ***Perf. 14x14½***

**1375** A469 45c multicolored 1.00 .55

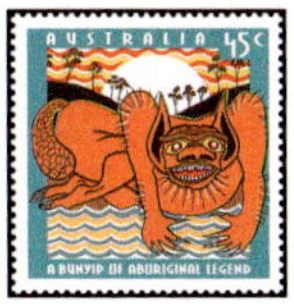

Bunyips Folklore Creatures — A470

Types of Bunyips: No. 1376, Aboriginal legend. No. 1377, Nature Spirit. 90c, Berkeley's Creek. $1.35, Natural history.

**1994, July 14** **Litho.** ***Perf. 14x14½***

**1376** A470 45c multicolored .80 .80
**1377** A470 45c multicolored .80 .80
*a.* Pair, #1376-1377 1.60 1.60
**1378** A470 90c multicolored 2.00 1.60
**1379** A470 $1.35 multicolored 2.40 2.40
*Nos. 1376-1379 (4)* 6.00 5.60

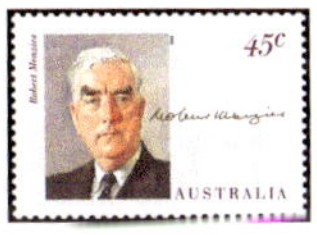

World War II Prime Ministers — A471

Designs: a, Robert Menzies. b, Arthur Fadden. c, John Curtin. d, Francis (Frank) Forde. e, Joseph Benedict (Ben) Chifley.

**1994-2005**

**1380** Strip of 5 6.00 6.00
*a.-e.* A471 45c any single .80 .80
*f.* Booklet pane, #1380a, 1380c ('05) *9.75* —

Issued: No. 1380, 8/11/94. No. 1380f, April 2005.

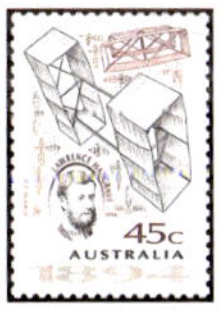

Aviation Pioneers — A472

Designs: No. 1381, Lawrence Hargrave, box kites. No. 1382, Ross and Keith Smith, Vickers Vimy. $1.35, Ivor McIntyre, Stanley Goble, Fairey IIID A10-3 seaplane. $1.80, Freda Thompson, DeHavilland Moth Major.

**1994, Aug. 29** **Engr.** ***Perf. 12***

**1381** A472 45c multicolored .80 .80
**1382** A472 45c multicolored .80 .80
**1383** A472 $1.35 multicolored 2.40 1.60
**1384** A472 $1.80 multicolored 3.00 2.40
*Nos. 1381-1384 (4)* 7.00 5.60

First England-Australia flight within 30-day time span (No. 1382). First aerial circumnavigation of Australia (No. 1383). First woman to fly solo from England-Australia (No. 1384).

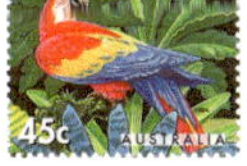

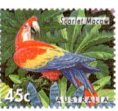

A473

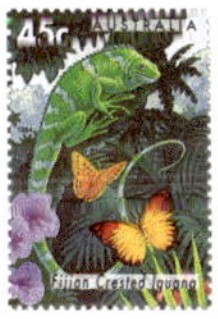

Australian Zoo Animals — A474

***Perf. 14x14½, 14½x14***

**1994, Sept. 28** **Litho.**

**1385** A473 45c Scarlet macaw .80 .80
**1386** A473 45c Cheetah, vert. .80 .80
**1387** A474 45c Fijian crested iguana .80 .80
**1388** A474 45c Orangutan .80 .80

**Size: 50x30mm**

***Perf. 14½x14***

**1389** A473 $1 Asian elephant 1.60 1.20
*a.* Souv. sheet of 5, #1385-1389, perf. 14½ 6.00 6.00
*b.* As "a," ovptd. 13.50 13.50
*c.* As "a," ovptd. 13.50 13.50
*d.* As "a," ovptd. 13.00 13.00
*e.* As "a," ovptd. 12.00 12.00
*Nos. 1385-1389 (5)* 4.80 4.40

**Self-Adhesive**

***Die Cut Perf. 11½***

**1390** A473 45c like #1385 3.00 .80
**1391** A473 45c like #1386 3.00 .80
*a.* Bklt. pane, 6 #1390, 4 #1391 25.00

Denomination is in LL corner on No. 1391.

Overprint in gold on sheet margin:

No. 1389b, show emblem and "Brisbane Stamp Show Zoos / October 21-23, 1994."

No. 1389c, show emblem and "SYDNEY / STAMP / AND / COIN / SHOW / 30/9/94 TO 2/10/94."

No. 1389d, show emblem and "Stampshow '94 Melbourne October 27-30 / National/State Centennial Exhibition 1894-1994."

No. 1389e, show emblem and "STAMP SHOW 94 / Fremantle Convention Centre / 5-6 November 1994."

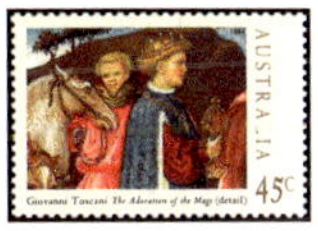

Christmas — A475

Details from Adoration of the Magi, by Giovanni Toscani: 40c, Madonna and Child, vert. 45c, One of Magi, horse and groom. $1, Joseph receiving frankincense from Magi. $1.80, Entire painting.

**1994, Oct. 31** **Litho.** ***Perf. 14½x14***

**1392** A475 40c multicolored .80 .35
*a.* Booklet pane of 20 16.00
Complete booklet, #1392a 16.00

***Perf. 14x14½***

**1393** A475 45c multicolored .80 .35
**1394** A475 $1 multicolored 1.60 1.25

**Size: 50x30mm**

**1395** A475 $1.80 multicolored 2.80 2.40
*Nos. 1392-1395 (4)* 6.00 4.35

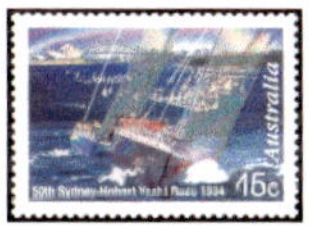

50th Sydney-Hobart Yacht Race — A476

Designs: a, Yachts bow-on, Sydney Opera House, Harbor Bridge. b, Two yachts abeam.

**1994, Oct. 31** ***Perf. 14½***

**1396** Pair 3.25 3.25
*a.-b.* A476 45c any single 1.10 .80

**Self-Adhesive**

***Die Cut Perf. 11½***

**1397** A476 45c like #1396a 3.00 .60
**1397A** A476 45c like #1396b 3.00 .60

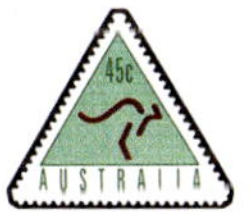

A477

**Self-Adhesive**
**Booklet Stamps**
**Background Color**

***Die Cut Perf. 17***

**1994, Nov. 2** **Litho.**

**1398** A477 45c bluish green 1.20 1.00
**1399** A477 45c blue 1.20 1.00
**1400** A477 45c purple 1.20 1.00
**1401** A477 45c yellow green 1.20 1.00
**1402** A477 45c pale yel green 1.20 1.00
**1403** A477 45c pale red brown 1.20 1.00
**1404** A477 45c rose 1.20 1.00
**1405** A477 45c orange yellow 1.20 1.00
*a.* Booklet pane of 20 24.00
*Nos. 1398-1405 (8)* 9.60 8.00

No. 1405a contains 3 each of Nos.1399, 1401, 1403, 1405 and 2 each of Nos. 1398, 1400, 1402, 1404. No. 1405a was sold in ATM machines, at the Natl. Philatelic Center, and Australian Philatelic Bureau.

Two printings differ slightly in shade and advertisement on back of pane.

---

Nos. 1406-1417 were deleted from the 2003 Standard catalogue. These self-adhesive stamps of design No. A438 have computer-generated denominations and exist with a large variety of different inscriptions for shows and other purposes.

---

**Australia Day Type of 1994**

Paintings: No. 1418, Back Verandah, by Russell Drysdale. No. 1419, Skull Springs Country, by Guy Grey-Smith. $1.05, Outcamp, by Robert Juniper. $1.20, Kite Flying, by Ian Fairweather.

**1995, Jan. 12** **Litho.** ***Perf. 15x14½***

**1418** A463 45c multicolored .80 .80
**1419** A463 45c multicolored .80 .80
**1420** A463 $1.05 multicolored 2.00 1.60
**1421** A463 $1.20 multicolored 2.40 1.60
*Nos. 1418-1421 (4)* 6.00 4.80

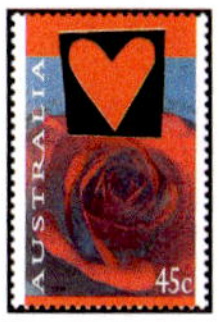

St. Valentine's Day — A478

Various designs: a, Red heart. b, Red & gold heart. c, Gold heart.

**1995, Feb. 6** **Litho.** ***Perf. 14½x14***

**1422** Strip of 3 2.75 2.40
*a.-c.* A478 45c any single .80 .40

See No. 1480.

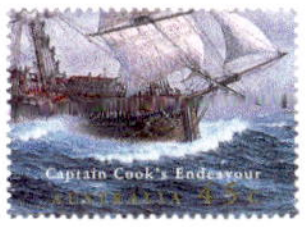

Endeavour — A479

No. 1423: a, Captain Cook's Endeavour. b, Replica.

**1995, Feb. 9** **Litho.** ***Perf. 14x14½***

**1423** Pair 2.75 2.75
*a.-b.* A479 45c any single .80 .80

**Booklet Stamps**

**Size: 44x26mm**

***Perf. 14 Horiz.***

**1424** A479 20c like #1423b 2.40 2.40
**1425** A479 45c like #1423a 2.40 2.40
*a.* Bklt. pane, #1424, 4 #1425 8.50 4.00
Complete booklet, #1425a 8.50

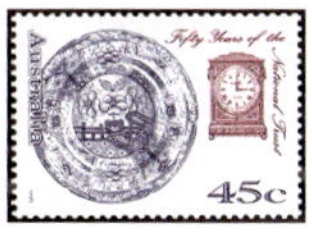

Natl. Trust, 50th Anniv. — A480

Designs: No. 1426a, Coalport plate, Regency style bracket clock. No. 1426b, 15th-16th cent. x-frame Italian style chair, 19th cent. Steiner doll. $1, Advance Australia teapot, neo-classical parian-ware statuette. $2, China urn, silver bowl.

**1995, Mar. 16** **Engr.** ***Perf. 14x14½***

**1426** Pair 2.00 1.00
*a.-b.* A480 45c any single .75 .40
**1427** A480 $1 red brn & bl 2.00 1.60
**1428** A480 $2 blue & green 3.00 2.00
*Nos. 1426-1428 (3)* 7.00 5.20

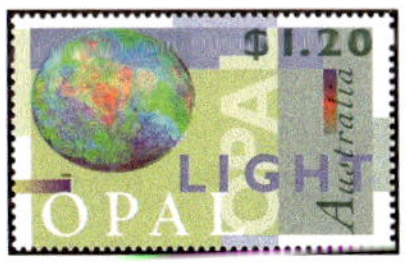

Opals A481

**1995, Apr. 5** **Litho.** ***Perf. 14½x14***

**1429** A481 $1.20 Light opal 2.00 1.60
**1430** A481 $2.50 Black opal 4.00 3.25

Nos. 1429-1430 each contain a holographic image. Soaking in water may affect the hologram.

See Nos. 1554-1555.

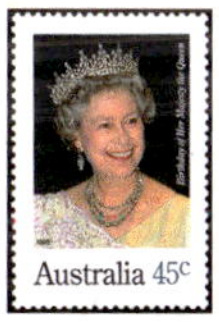

A482

**1995, Apr. 20** **Litho.** ***Perf. 14½***

**1431** A482 45c multicolored .80 .40

Queen Elizabeth II, 69th birthday.

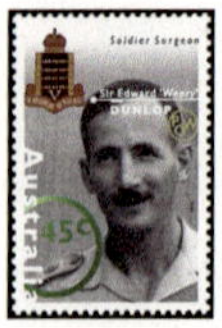
A483

Famous Australians from World War II — No. 1432, Sir Edward Dunlop. No. 1433, Mrs. Jessie Vasey. No. 1434, Tom Derrick. No. 1435, Rawdon Hume Middleton.

**1995, Apr. 20 Litho. *Perf. 14½x14***

1432 A483 45c multi 1.00 .80
1433 A483 45c multi 1.00 .80
1434 A483 45c multi 1.00 .80
1435 A483 45c multi 1.00 .80
*a.* Block of 4, #1432-1435 4.75 4.75
*Nos. 1432-1435 (4)* 4.00 3.20

**Self-Adhesive**

***Die Cut Perf. 11½***

1436 A483 45c like #1432 1.60 .80
1437 A483 45c like #1433 1.60 .80
1438 A483 45c like #1434 1.60 .80
1439 A483 45c like #1435 1.60 .80
*a.* Booklet pane, 4 #1436, 2 each #1437-1439 16.00
*b.* Strip of 4, #1436-1439 12.00
*Nos. 1436-1439 (4)* 6.40 3.20

See Nos. 1452-1455.

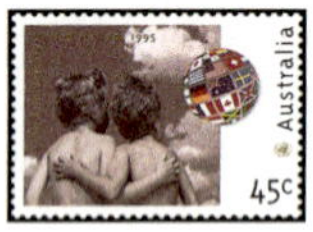
UN, 50th Anniv. — A484

**1995, May 11 Litho. *Perf. 14x14½***

1440 A484 45c + label, multi 1.10 .40
*a.* Block of 4 + 4 labels 5.75 5.25

No. 1440 was issued se-tenant with label in blocks of 4 + 4 labels in four designs. In alternating rows, labels appear on left or right side of stamp.

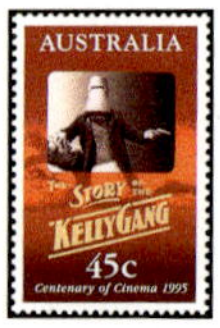
A485

Poster, scene from: No. 1441, The Story of the Kelly Gang, 1906. No. 1442, On Our Selection, 1932. No. 1443, Jedda, 1955. No. 1444, Picnic at Hanging Rock, 1970s. No. 1445, Strictly Ballroom, 1992.

**1995, June 8 Litho. *Perf. 14½x14***

1441 A485 45c multicolored .80 .80
1442 A485 45c multicolored .80 .80
1443 A485 45c multicolored .80 .80
1444 A485 45c multicolored .80 .80
1445 A485 45c multicolored .80 .80
*a.* Strip of 5, #1441-1445 5.75 5.75
*Nos. 1441-1445 (5)* 4.00 4.00

**Self-Adhesive**

***Die Cut Perf. 11½***

1446 A485 45c like #1441 .80 .80
1447 A485 45c like #1442 .80 .80
1448 A485 45c like #1443 .80 .80
1449 A485 45c like #1444 .80 .80
1450 A485 45c like #1445 .80 .80
*a.* Strip of 5, #1446-1450 20.00
*b.* Bklt. pane, 2 ea #1446-1450 16.00
*Nos. 1446-1450 (5)* 4.00 4.00

Motion Pictures, cent.

By its nature No. 1450b constitutes a complete booklet. The peelable backing serves as a booklet cover.

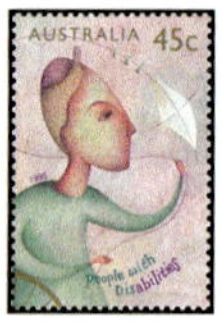
A486

People with Disabilities: No. 1451a, Person flying kite from wheelchair. b, Blind person playing violin, guide dog.

**1995, July 13 Litho. *Perf. 14½x14***

1451 Pair 2.25 2.25
*a.-b.* A486 45c any single .80 .40

**Famous Australians from World War II Type of 1995**

**1995-2005 Litho. *Perf. 14½x14***

1452 A483 45c Leon Goldsworthy .80 .80
*a.* Booklet pane, #1432, 1434, 1435, 1452 ('05) 9.75 —
1453 A483 45c Len Waters .80 .80
1454 A483 45c Ellen Savage .80 .80
*a.* Booklet pane, #1433, 1454 ('05) 10.75 —
1455 A483 45c Percy Collins .80 .80
*a.* Block of 4, #1452-1455 6.00 6.00
*Nos. 1452-1455 (4)* 3.20 3.20

Issued: Nos. 1452-1455, 8/10/95. Nos 1452a and 1454a, April 2005.

**Peace Types of 1946**

***Perf. 14x14½, 14½x14***

**1995, Aug. 10 Engr.**

1456 A43 45c red brown .95 .40
1457 A45 45c dark green .95 .40
1458 A44 $1.50 dark blue 2.75 2.00
*Nos. 1456-1458 (3)* 4.65 2.80

End of World War II, 50th anniv.

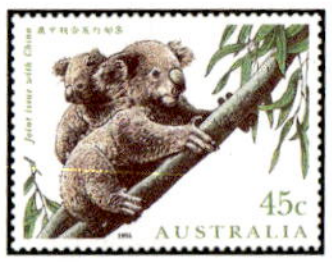
Wildlife — A487

Designs: a, Koalas. b, Pandas.

**1995, Sept. 1 Litho. *Perf. 14***

1459 Pair 2.25 2.25
*a.-b.* A487 45c any single .80 .80
*c.* Souv. sheet #1459a, perf. 11x11½ 2.25 2.25
*d.* Souv. sheet #1459b, perf. 11x11½ 2.50 2.50
*e.* #1459c Ovptd. in sheet margin 4.50 4.50
*f.* #1459d Ovptd. in sheet margin 4.50 4.50

Overprints read: No. 1459e: "AUSTRALIAN STAMP EXHIBITION." No. 1459f: "INTERNATIONAL STAMP & COIN EXPO. / BEIJING '95."

Issued: No. 1459f, 9/14/95.

See People's Republic of China Nos. 2597-2598.

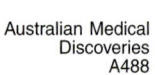

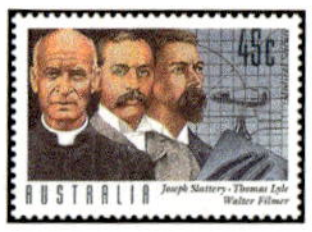
Australian Medical Discoveries A488

Designs: No. 1461a, Joseph Slattery, Thomas Lyle, Walter Filmer, x-ray pioneers. No. 1461b, Jean Macnamara, Macfarlane Burnet, viruses and immunology. No. 1461C, Fred Hollows, eye care, vert. $2.50, Howard Florey, co-discoverer of penicillin, vert.

**1995, Sept. 7 *Perf. 14x14½, 14½x14***

1461 Pair 2.40 1.60
*a.-b.* A488 45c any single .85 .80
1461C A488 45c multicolored 1.10 .75
1461D A488 $2.50 multicolored 4.00 4.00
*Nos. 1461-1461D (3)* 7.50 6.35

No. 1461D exists in sheetlets of 10.

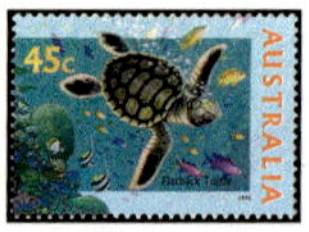
The World Down Under — A489

Designs: Nos. 1462a, 1465a, Flatback turtle. Nos. 1462b, 1465b, Flame angelfish, nudibranch. Nos. 1463a, 1465c, Potato cod, giant maori wrasse. Nos. 1463b, 1465d, Giant trevally. Nos. 1464a, 1465e, Black marlin. Nos. 1464b, 1465f, Mako & tiger sharks.

**1995, Oct. 3 Litho. *Perf. 14x14½***

1462 Pair 2.25 2.25
*a.-b.* A489 45c any single .80 .80
1463 Pair 2.25 2.25
*a.-b.* A489 45c any single .80 .80
1464 Pair 2.25 2.25
*a.-b.* A489 45c any single .80 .80
*Nos. 1462-1464 (3)* 6.75 6.75

**Miniature Sheet of 6**

1465 A489 45c #a.-f. 6.50 6.50
*g.* Ovptd. in sheet margin 9.00 9.00
*h.* Ovptd. in sheet margin 9.00 9.00
*i.* Ovptd. in sheet margin 9.00 9.00
*j.* Ovptd. in sheet margin 9.00 9.00
*k.* Ovptd. in sheet margin 9.00 9.00

Nos. 1462-1464 have pale blue border on three sides. No. 1465 is a continuous design and does not have the pale border. Fish on No. 1465 are printed with additional phosphor ink producing a glow-in-the-dark effect under ultraviolet light.

Overprints in gold in sheet margin of No. 1465 include show emblems and text:

No. 1465g: "ADELAIDE / STAMP AND / COLLECTIBLES / FAIR / 14/10/95 - / 15/10/95."

No. 1465h: "SYDNEY / CENTREPOINT 95 / STAMPSHOW."

No. 1465i: "Brisbane Stamp Show / 20-22 October 1995."

No. 1465j: "Melbourne Stamp & Coin Fair / 27-29 October 1995."

No. 1465k: "Swanpex WA / 28-29 October 1995."

**Booklet Stamps**

**Self-Adhesive**

***Die Cut Perf. 11½***

1466 A489 45c like #1462a 1.20 .40
1467 A489 45c like #1462b 1.20 .40
1468 A489 45c like #1463a 1.20 .40
1469 A489 45c like #1463b 1.20 .40
1470 A489 45c like #1464a 1.20 .40
1471 A489 45c like #1464b 1.60 .40
*a.* Booklet pane, #1470-1471, 2 each #1466-1469 14.00
*b.* Strip of 6, #1466-1471 14.00
*Nos. 1466-1471 (6)* 7.60 2.40

By its nature, No. 1471a constitutes a complete booklet. The peelable backing serves as a booklet cover.

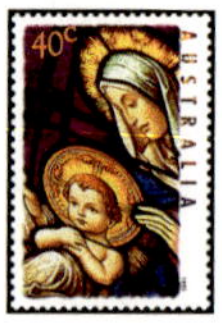
Christmas — A490

Stained glass windows, Our Lady Help of Christians Church, Melbourne: 40c, Madonna and Child. 45c, Angel carrying banner. $1, Three rejoicing angels.

**1995, Nov. 1 Litho. *Perf. 14½x14***

1472 A490 40c multicolored .80 .40
1473 A490 45c multicolored 1.25 .40
1474 A490 $1 multicolored 1.60 1.20
*Nos. 1472-1474 (3)* 3.65 2.00

**Booklet Stamp**

**Self-Adhesive**

***Die Cut Perf. 11½***

1475 A490 40c multicolored 1.25 .40
*a.* Booklet pane of 20 25.00

Madonna and Child on No. 1475 are printed with additional phosphor ink giving parts of the stamp a rough texture.

By its nature, No. 1475a constitutes a complete booklet. The peelable backing serves as a booklet cover, which also contains 20 labels. The complete booklet is also available with backing showing two different advertisements.

**Australia Day Type of 1994**

Paintings by Australian women: 45c, West Australian Banksia, by Margaret Preston, vert. 85c, The Babe is Wise, by Lina Bryans, vert. $1, The Bridge in Curve, by Grace Cossington Smith. $1.20, Beach Umbrellas, by Vida Lahey.

***Perf. 14x14½, 14½x14***

**1996, Jan. 16 Litho.**

1476 A463 45c multicolored 1.00 .35
1477 A463 85c multicolored 1.25 1.10
1478 A463 $1 multicolored 2.00 1.25
1479 A463 $1.20 multicolored 2.40 1.60
*a.* Block of 4, #1476-1479 8.00 6.50
*Nos. 1476-1479 (4)* 6.65 4.30

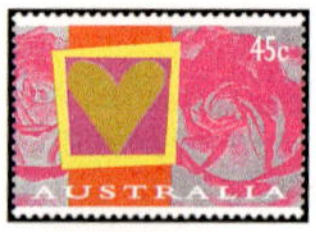
Heart and Roses — A491

**1996, Jan. 30 *Perf. 14x14½***

1480 A491 45c gold & multi 1.00 .40

See No. 1422.

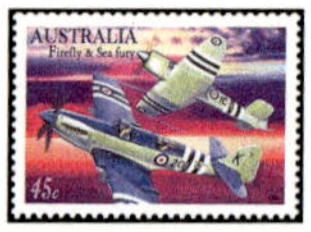
Military Aviation — A492

Airplanes: No. 1481, Firefly, Sea Fury. No. 1482, Beaufighter, Kittyhawk. No. 1483, Hornet. No. 1484, Kiowa.

**1996-2005 Litho. *Perf. 14x14½***

1481 A492 45c multicolored .80 .80
1482 A492 45c multicolored .80 .80
*a.* Booklet pane, #1481, 1482 ('05) 10.00 —
1483 A492 45c multicolored .80 .80
1484 A492 45c multicolored .80 .80
*a.* Block of 4, #1481-1484 4.00 4.00

Issued: 1481-1484, 2/26/96. No. 1482a, April 2005.

**Australian World Heritage Sites Type of 1993**

Designs: 45c, Tasmanian Wilderness. 75c, Willandra Lakes. 95c, Fossil Cave, Naracoorte. $1, Lord Howe Island.

**1996, Mar. 14 Litho. *Perf. 14½x14***

1485 A453 45c multicolored .75 .75
1486 A453 75c multicolored 1.25 1.25
1487 A453 95c multicolored 1.60 1.25
1488 A453 $1 multicolored 2.00 1.60
*a.* Booklet pane, #1311, 1314, 1485, 1488 ('06) 8.25 —
*Nos. 1485-1488 (4)* 5.60 4.85

No. 1488a issued 3/15/2006.

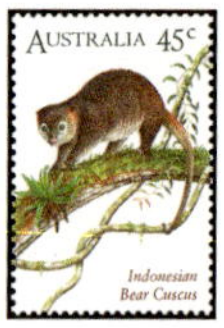
Indonesian Bear Cuscus — A493

No. 1489, Australian Spotted Cuscus.

**1996, Mar. 22**

1489 A493 45c multicolored .80 .80
1490 A493 45c multicolored .80 .80
*a.* Pair, Nos. 1489-1490 2.50 2.50
*b.* Souvenir sheet, No. 1490a 4.00 4.00
*c.* As "b," with World Philatelic Youth Exhibition emblem in sheet margin 9.25 9.25

No. 1490a has continuous design.

See Indonesia Nos. 1640-1642.

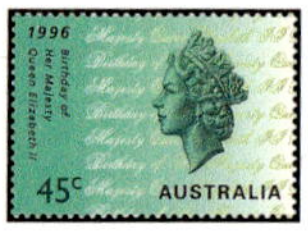
Queen Elizabeth II, 70th Birthday — A494

**Litho. & Engr.**

**1996, Apr. 11 *Perf. 14x14½***

1491 A494 45c multicolored 1.00 .40

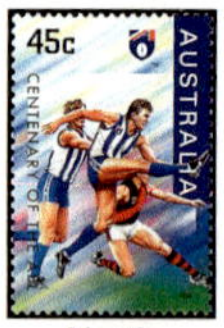
North Melbourne Kangaroos A495

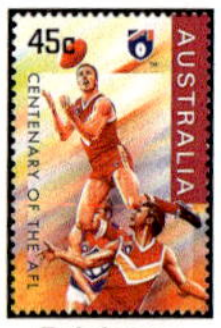
Brisbane Bears A496

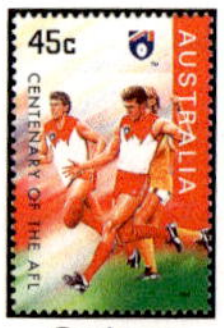
Sydney Swans A497

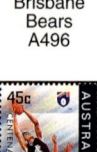

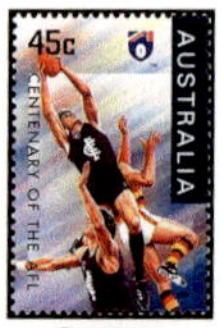
Carlton Blues A498

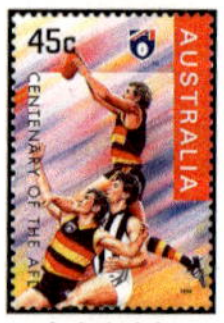
Adelaide Crows A499

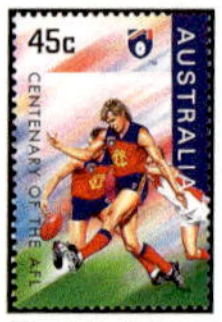
Fitzroy Lions A500

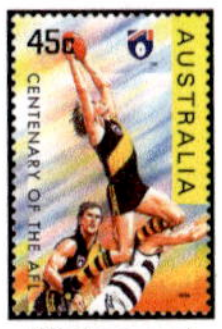
Richmond Tigers A501

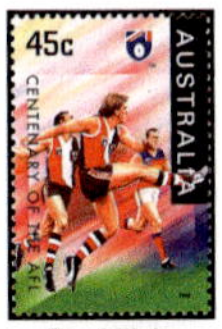
St. Kilda Saints A502

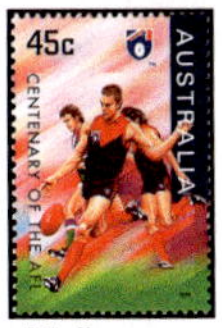
Melbourne Demons A503

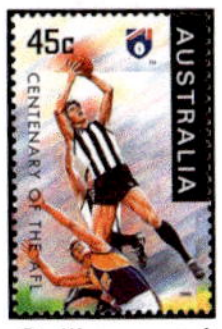
Collingwood Magpies A504

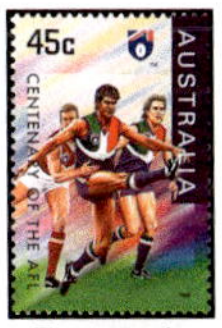
Fremantle Dockers A505

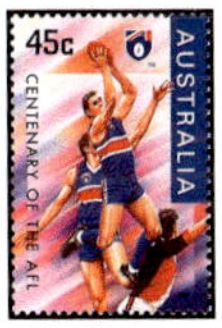
Footscray Bulldogs A506

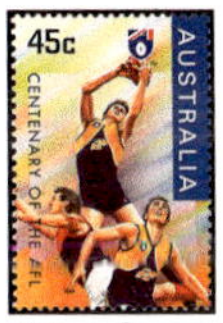
West Coast Eagles A507

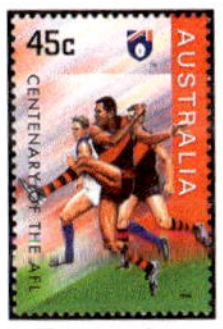
Essendon Bombers A508

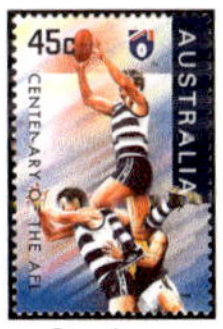
Geelong Cats A509

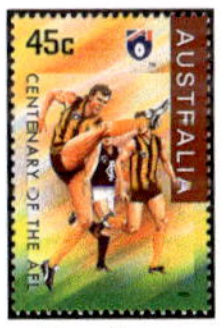
Hawthorn Hawks A510

**1996, Apr. 23 Litho. *Perf. 14½x14***

| | | | | |
|---|---|---|---|---|
| **1492** | A495 | 45c multicolored | .75 | .75 |
| **1493** | A496 | 45c multicolored | .75 | .75 |
| **1494** | A497 | 45c multicolored | .75 | .75 |
| **1495** | A498 | 45c multicolored | .75 | .75 |
| **1496** | A499 | 45c multicolored | .75 | .75 |
| **1497** | A500 | 45c multicolored | .75 | .75 |
| **1498** | A501 | 45c multicolored | .75 | .75 |
| **1499** | A502 | 45c multicolored | .75 | .75 |
| **1500** | A503 | 45c multicolored | .75 | .75 |
| **1501** | A504 | 45c multicolored | .75 | .75 |
| **1502** | A505 | 45c multicolored | .75 | .75 |
| **1503** | A506 | 45c multicolored | .75 | .75 |
| **1504** | A507 | 45c multicolored | .75 | .75 |
| **1505** | A508 | 45c multicolored | .75 | .75 |
| **1506** | A509 | 45c multicolored | .75 | .75 |
| **1507** | A510 | 45c multicolored | .75 | .75 |
| *a.* | | Min. sheet of 16, #1492-1507 | 15.00 | |
| | | *Nos. 1492-1507 (16)* | 12.00 | 12.00 |

**Booklet Stamps**

**Self-Adhesive**

***Serpentine Die Cut 11½***

| | | | | |
|---|---|---|---|---|
| **1508** | A495 | 45c multicolored | 1.00 | .40 |
| *a.* | | Booklet pane of 10 | 10.00 | |
| **1509** | A496 | 45c multicolored | 1.00 | .40 |
| *a.* | | Booklet pane of 10 | 10.00 | |
| **1510** | A497 | 45c multicolored | 1.00 | .40 |
| *a.* | | Booklet pane of 10 | 10.00 | |
| **1511** | A498 | 45c multicolored | 1.00 | .40 |
| *a.* | | Booklet pane of 10 | 10.00 | |
| **1512** | A499 | 45c multicolored | 1.00 | .40 |
| *a.* | | Booklet pane of 10 | 10.00 | |
| **1513** | A500 | 45c multicolored | 1.00 | .40 |
| *a.* | | Booklet pane of 10 | 10.00 | |
| **1514** | A501 | 45c multicolored | 1.00 | .40 |
| *a.* | | Booklet pane of 10 | 10.00 | |
| **1515** | A502 | 45c multicolored | 1.00 | .40 |
| *a.* | | Booklet pane of 10 | 10.00 | |
| **1516** | A503 | 45c multicolored | 1.00 | .40 |
| *a.* | | Booklet pane of 10 | 10.00 | |
| **1517** | A504 | 45c multicolored | 1.00 | .40 |
| *a.* | | Booklet pane of 10 | 10.00 | |
| **1518** | A505 | 45c multicolored | 1.00 | .40 |
| *a.* | | Booklet pane of 10 | 10.00 | |
| **1519** | A506 | 45c multicolored | 1.00 | .40 |
| *a.* | | Booklet pane of 10 | 10.00 | |
| **1520** | A507 | 45c multicolored | 1.00 | .40 |
| *a.* | | Booklet pane of 10 | 10.00 | |
| **1521** | A508 | 45c multicolored | 1.00 | .40 |
| *a.* | | Booklet pane of 10 | 10.00 | |
| **1522** | A509 | 45c multicolored | 1.00 | .40 |
| *a.* | | Booklet pane of 10 | 10.00 | |
| **1523** | A510 | 45c multicolored | 1.00 | .40 |
| *a.* | | Booklet pane of 10 | 10.00 | |
| | | *Nos. 1508-1523 (16)* | 16.00 | 6.40 |

By their nature, Nos. 1508a-1523a are complete booklets. The peelable paper backing serves as a booklet cover.

Australian Football League, cent.

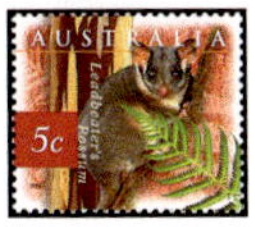
Flora and Fauna — A511

Designs: 5c, Leadbeater's possum. 10c, Powerful owl. 20c, Saltwater crocodile, Kangkong flower. 25c, Northern dwarf tree frog, red lily. No. 1528, Little kingfisher. No. 1529, Jacana. No. 1530, Jabiru. No. 1531, Brolga. $1, Big greasy butterfly, water lily. $2, Blackwood wattle. $5, Mountain ash, fern. $10, Kakadu Wetlands during lightning storm, great egret, red lily.

***Perf. 14x14½, 14½x14 (#1535)***

**1996-99 Litho.**

| | | | | |
|---|---|---|---|---|
| **1524** | A511 | 5c multi | .25 | .25 |
| **1525** | A511 | 10c multi | .30 | .25 |
| **1526** | A511 | 20c multi | .40 | .40 |
| **1527** | A511 | 25c multi | .55 | .40 |
| **1528** | A511 | 45c multi | .95 | .40 |
| **1529** | A511 | 45c multi | .95 | .40 |
| **1530** | A511 | 45c multi | .95 | .40 |
| **1531** | A511 | 45c multi | .95 | .40 |
| *a.* | | Block of 4, #1528-1531 | 4.50 | 4.00 |
| *b.* | | Souvenir sheet of 2, #1530-1531 | 7.50 | |
| **1532** | A511 | $1 multi | 2.10 | .65 |
| **1533** | A511 | $2 multi | 3.25 | 1.25 |

**Size: 30x50mm**

| | | | | |
|---|---|---|---|---|
| **1534** | A511 | $5 multi, vert. | 7.50 | 3.25 |

**Size: 50x30mm**

| | | | | |
|---|---|---|---|---|
| **1535** | A511 | $10 multi | 15.00 | 5.75 |
| *a.* | | Souvenir sheet of 1 | 18.00 | 18.00 |
| *b.* | | As "a," ovptd. in sheet margin | 30.00 | 30.00 |
| *c.* | | As "a," ovptd in sheet margin | 25.00 | 25.00 |
| *d.* | | As "a," ovptd in sheet margin | 29.00 | 21.00 |
| | | *Nos. 1524-1535 (12)* | 33.15 | 13.80 |

**Self-Adhesive**

***Serpentine Die Cut 11½, 11¼ (#1539i)***

| | | | | |
|---|---|---|---|---|
| **1536** | A511 | 45c like #1529 | 1.00 | .35 |
| **1537** | A511 | 45c like #1528 | 1.00 | .35 |
| **1538** | A511 | 45c like #1531 | 1.00 | .35 |
| **1539** | A511 | 45c like #1530 | 1.00 | .35 |
| *a.* | | Booklet pane, 3 ea #1536, #1538, 2 ea #1537, #1539 | 10.00 | |
| *b.* | | Strip of 4, #1536-1539 | 4.75 | |
| *h.* | | Sheet of 5, #1537-1539, 2 #1536 | 6.00 | |
| *i.* | | Booklet pane, 5 each #1536-1539 | 20.00 | |

***Serpentine Die Cut 12½x13***

| | | | | |
|---|---|---|---|---|
| **1539C** | A511 | 45c like #1529 | 1.50 | .55 |
| **1539D** | A511 | 45c like #1528 | 1.50 | .55 |
| **1539E** | A511 | 45c like #1531 | 1.50 | .55 |
| **1539F** | A511 | 45c like #1530 | 1.50 | .55 |
| *g.* | | Strip of 4, #1539C-1539F | 8.50 | |
| | | *Nos. 1536-1539F (8)* | 10.00 | 3.60 |

Nos. 1536-1539 are booklet stamps.

No. 1531b is inscribed in sheet margin with Shanghai '97 emblem and "International Stamp & Coin Exposition Shanghai '97" in Chinese and English.

No. 1535b is overprinted in silver in sheet margin with PACIFIC 97 emblem and "Australia Post Exhibition Sheet No. 4."

No. 1535c is overprinted in sheet margin for "Italia '98" in Milan.

No. 1535d is overprinted in copper in sheet margin with "PHILA NIPPON '01" and show emblem. Issued: No. 1535c, 8/1/01.

By its nature No. 1539a is a complete booklet. The peelable backing serves as a booklet cover.

Issued: 5c, 10c, $2, $5, 5/9/96; 20c, 25c, $1, $10, #1538a, 4/10/97; #1528-1531, 1536-1539, 6/2/97; #1531b, 11/17/97; #1539C-1539F, 11/13/99; No. 1539i, 9/1/98.

No. 1539i is a complete booklet.

See Nos. 1734-1746L, 1984-1995, 2060-2063, 2111-2114, 2159-2170, 2235-2238.

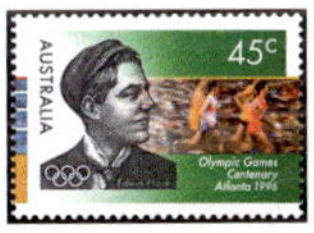
Modern Olympic Games, Cent. — A512

Designs: No. 1540, Edwin Flack, 1st Australian gold medalist, runners. No. 1541, Fanny Durack, 1st Australian woman gold medalist, swimmers. $1.05, Paralympics, Atlanta.

**Litho. & Engr.**

**1996, June 6 *Perf. 14x14½***

| | | | | |
|---|---|---|---|---|
| **1540** | A512 | 45c multicolored | .75 | .30 |
| **1541** | A512 | 45c multicolored | .75 | .30 |
| *a.* | | Pair, #1540-1541 | 2.25 | 1.75 |
| **1542** | A512 | $1.05 multicolored | 2.40 | 1.20 |
| | | *Nos. 1540-1542 (3)* | 3.90 | 1.80 |

Transfer of Olympic Flag from Atlanta to Sydney — A513

**1996, July 22 Litho.**

| | | | | |
|---|---|---|---|---|
| **1543** | A513 | 45c multicolored | 1.10 | .40 |

Issued in sheets of 10.

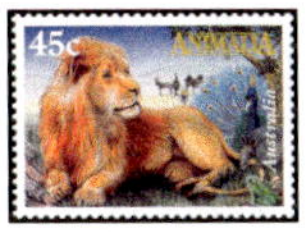
Children's Book Council, 50th Anniv. — A514

Covers from "Book of the Year" books: No. 1544, "Animalia." No. 1545, "Greetings from Sandy Beach." No. 1546, "Who Sank the Boat?" No. 1547, "John Brown, Rose and the Midnight Cat."

**1996, July 4 Litho. *Perf. 14x14½***

| | | | | |
|---|---|---|---|---|
| **1544** | A514 | 45c multicolored | 1.00 | 1.00 |
| **1545** | A514 | 45c multicolored | 1.00 | 1.00 |
| **1546** | A514 | 45c multicolored | 1.00 | 1.00 |
| **1547** | A514 | 45c multicolored | 1.00 | 1.00 |
| *a.* | | Block of 4, #1544-1547 | 4.50 | 4.50 |
| | | *Nos. 1544-1547 (4)* | 4.00 | 4.00 |

***Serpentine Die Cut 11½***

**Self-Adhesive**

| | | | | |
|---|---|---|---|---|
| **1548** | A514 | 45c like #1544 | 1.10 | .40 |
| **1549** | A514 | 45c like #1546 | 1.10 | .40 |
| **1550** | A514 | 45c like #1547 | 1.10 | .40 |
| **1551** | A514 | 45c like #1545 | 1.10 | .40 |
| *a.* | | Booklet pane, 4 #1548, 2 each #1549-1551 | 12.00 | |
| *b.* | | Strip of 4, #1548-1551 | 8.00 | |
| | | *Nos. 1548-1551 (4)* | 4.40 | 1.60 |

By its nature, No. 1551a is a complete booklet. The peelable paper backing serves as a booklet cover.

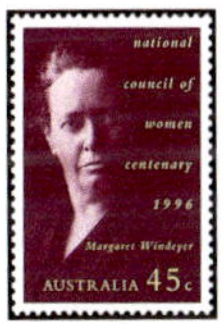
National Council of Women, Cent. — A515

Designs: 45c, Margaret Windeyer (1866-1939), honorary life president. $1, Rose Scott (1847-1925), founding executive member.

**1996, Aug. 8 Litho. *Perf. 14½x14***

| | | | | |
|---|---|---|---|---|
| **1552** | A515 | 45c claret & yellow | .80 | .30 |
| **1553** | A515 | $1 blue & yellow | 2.00 | 1.10 |

**Gems Type of 1995**

**1996, Sept. 5 Litho. *Perf. 14½x14***

| | | | | |
|---|---|---|---|---|
| **1554** | A481 | 45c Pearl | 1.60 | .30 |
| **1555** | A481 | $1.20 Diamond | 3.00 | 2.50 |

No. 1555 contains a round foil design. Soaking in water may affect the design.

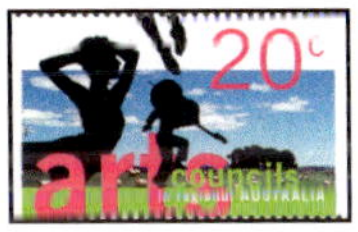
Arts Councils in Regional Australia A516

Silhouettes of performing artists, outdoor scene: 20c, Ballet dancer, violinist, field, bales, trees. 45c, Violinist, hand holding flower, dancer, tree in field.

***Perf. 14 Horiz.***

**1996, Sept. 12 Litho.**

**Booklet Stamps**

| | | | | |
|---|---|---|---|---|
| **1556** | A516 | 20c multicolored | 1.75 | 1.50 |
| **1557** | A516 | 45c multicolored | 1.50 | .60 |
| *a.* | | Bklt. pane, #1556, 4 #1557 | 5.75 | |
| | | Complete booklet, #1557a | 5.75 | |

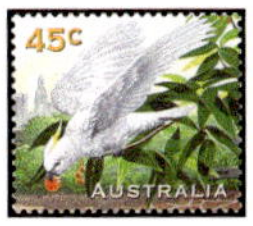
A517

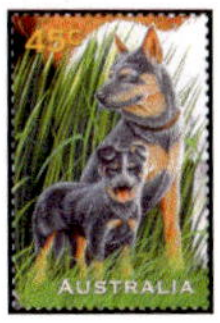
Pets — A518

**1996-97 *Perf. 14x14½, 14½x14***

| | | | | |
|---|---|---|---|---|
| **1558** | A517 | 45c Cockatoo | .75 | .75 |
| **1559** | A517 | 45c Ducks, vert. | .75 | .75 |
| **1560** | A517 | 45c Dog, cat, vert. | .75 | .40 |
| *a.* | | Pair, #1559-1560 | 2.00 | 2.00 |
| **1561** | A518 | 45c Dog, puppy | .75 | .75 |
| **1562** | A518 | 45c Kittens | .75 | .75 |
| *a.* | | Pair, #1561-1562 | 2.60 | 2.60 |

**Size: 30x50mm**

| | | | | |
|---|---|---|---|---|
| **1563** | A518 | 45c Pony mare, foal | .75 | .40 |
| *a.* | | Souvenir sheet, #1558-1563, perf. 14¼ | 6.00 | 6.00 |
| *b.* | | As "a," ovptd. | 8.00 | 8.00 |
| *c.* | | As "a," ovptd. | 8.00 | 8.00 |
| *d.* | | As "a," ovptd. | 8.00 | 8.00 |
| *e.* | | As "a," ovptd. | 8.00 | 8.00 |
| *f.* | | As "a," ovptd. | 8.00 | 8.00 |
| *g.* | | As "a," ovptd. | 8.00 | 8.00 |
| *h.* | | As "a," ovptd. | 8.00 | 8.00 |
| | | *Nos. 1558-1563 (6)* | 4.50 | 3.80 |

**Self-Adhesive**

***Serpentine Die Cut 11½***

| | | | | |
|---|---|---|---|---|
| **1564** | A518 | 45c like #1561 | 1.60 | .80 |
| **1565** | A518 | 45c like #1562 | 1.60 | .80 |
| *a.* | | Bklt. pane, 6 #1564, 4 #1565 | 15.00 | |

No. 1563a is a continuous design.

Overprints in gold on sheet margin: No. 1563b, show emblem and "10TH ASIAN INTERNATIONAL PHILATELIC EXHIBITION 1996" in Chinese and English. No. 1563c, pets emblem and, "ASDA CENTREPOINT '96 STAMP AND COIN SHOW / 5-7 October 1996." No. 1563d, pets emblem and "ST PETERS STAMP & COLLECTIBLE FAIR / 12-13 OCTOBER 1996." No. 1563e, pets emblem and "MELBOURNE '96 NATIONAL PHILATELIC EXHIBITION / 17-20 OCTOBER 1996." No. 1563f, pets emblem and "QUEENSLAND SPRING STAMP AND COIN SHOW / 25-27 OCTOBER 1996." No. 1563g, pets emblem and "SWANPEX '96 / 26-27 OCTOBER 1996." No. 1563h: Hong Kong '97 emblem and "11TH ASIAN INTERNATIONAL STAMP EXHIBITION / 12-16 FEBRUARY 1997."

By its nature, No. 1565a is a complete booklet. The peelable paper backing serves as a booklet cover.

Issued: Nos. 1558-1563, 1563a, 1564-1565, 10/1/96; Nos. 1563b-1563g, 10/3/96; No. 1563h, 2/12/97.

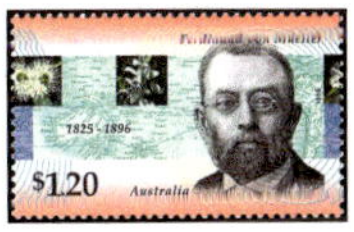
Baron Ferdinand von Mueller (1825-96), Botanist — A519

**1996, Oct. 9 *Perf. 14***

| | | | | |
|---|---|---|---|---|
| **1566** | A519 | $1.20 multicolored | 2.40 | 2.40 |

See Germany No. 1949.

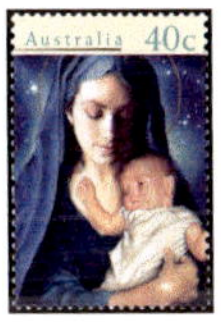
Christmas — A520

40c, Madonna and Child. 45c, Wise man. $1, Shepherd boy, lamb.

**1996, Nov. 1 *Perf. 14½x14***

| | | | | |
|---|---|---|---|---|
| **1567** | A520 | 40c multicolored | .80 | .35 |
| **1568** | A520 | 45c multicolored | .90 | .35 |
| **1569** | A520 | $1 multicolored | 1.60 | 1.25 |
| | | *Nos. 1567-1569 (3)* | 3.30 | 1.95 |

**Self-Adhesive**

***Serpentine Die Cut 12***

| | | | | |
|---|---|---|---|---|
| **1570** | A520 | 40c like #1567 | 2.00 | .40 |
| *a.* | | Booklet pane of 20 | 40.00 | |

By its nature, No. 1570a is a complete booklet. The peelable paper backing serves as a booklet cover.

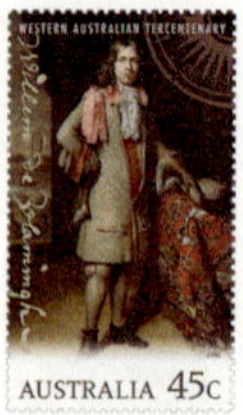


Exploration of Australian Coast & Christmas Island by Willem de Vlamingh, 300th Anniv. — A521

Portrait of a Dutch Navigator, by Jan Verkolje.

**1996, Nov. 1** ***Perf. 14x14½***

**1571** A521 45c multicolored .90 .30
*a.* Pair, #1571 & Christmas Is. #404 2.25 2.25

### Australia Day Type of 1994

Paintings: 85c, Landscape '74, by Fred Williams. 90c, The Balcony 2, by Brett Whiteley. $1.20, Fire Haze at Gerringong, by Lloyd Rees.

**1997, Jan. 16** **Litho.** ***Perf. 14½x14***

**1572** A463 85c multicolored 1.50 .75
**1573** A463 90c multicolored 1.60 1.25
**1574** A463 $1.20 multicolored 2.50 1.60
*Nos. 1572-1574 (3)* 5.60 3.60

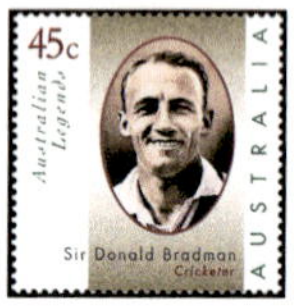


Sir Donald Bradman, Cricketer — A522

**1997, Jan. 23** **Litho.** ***Perf. 14¼***

**1575** A522 45c Portrait .80 .40
*a.* Without gold highlights, dated "2007" 1.40 1.40
**1576** A522 45c At bat .80 .40
*a.* Pair, No. 1575-1576 2.40 2.25
*b.* Booklet pane, #1575-1576 1.90 —
*c.* Without gold highlights, dated "2007" 1.40 1.40

No. 1576b issued 1/24/07. Nos. 1575a, 1576c issued 11/14/2007.
See Nos. 1634-1646, 1719-1722, 1800-1807, 1933-1936, 1941-1942, 2021-2030, 2125-2132, 2207-2210.

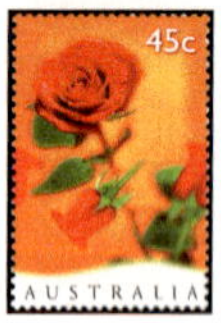


Greetings — A523

**1997, Jan. 29** ***Perf. 14½x14***

**1577** A523 45c Rose .80 .40

***Serpentine Die Cut 11½***

**Booklet Stamp**

**Self-Adhesive**

**1578** A523 45c like #1577 1.50 .30
*a.* Booklet pane of 10 15.00

By its nature, No. 1578a is a complete booklet. The peelable paper backing, which also contains 12 labels, serves as a booklet cover.

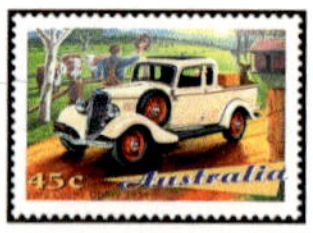

Classic Cars — A524

Automobiles: No. 1579, 1934 Ford Coupe Utility. No. 1580, 1948 GMH Holden 48-215 (FX). No. 1581, 1958 Austin Lancer. No. 1582, 1962 Chrysler Valiant R Series.

**1997, Feb. 27** **Litho.** ***Perf. 14x14½***

**1579** A524 45c multicolored .90 .90
*a.* Booklet pane of 4 3.75
**1580** A524 45c multicolored .90 .90
*a.* Booklet pane of 4 3.75
**1581** A524 45c multicolored .90 .90
*a.* Booklet pane of 4 3.75
**1582** A524 45c multicolored .90 .90
*a.* Booklet pane of 4 3.75
*b.* Block of 4, #1579-1582 4.50 4.50
Complete booklet, #1579a, 1580a, 1581a, 1582a 19.00
*Nos. 1579-1582 (4)* 3.60 3.60

Complete booklet contains 2 postal cards and 16 self-adhesive labels.

***Serpentine Die Cut 12***

**Booklet Stamps**

**Self-Adhesive**

**1583** A524 45c like #1579 1.25 .40
**1584** A524 45c like #1580 1.25 .40
**1585** A524 45c like #1581 1.25 .40
**1586** A524 45c like #1582 1.25 .40
*a.* Bklt. pane, 2 ea #1583, 1585, 3 ea #1584, 1586 12.50
*b.* Strip of 4, #1583-1586 12.50
*Nos. 1583-1586 (4)* 5.00 1.60

By its nature, No. 1586a is a complete booklet. The peelable backing serves as a booklet cover. The backing for No. 1586b is inscribed with a 3x8mm black vertical box and "SNP CAMBEC."

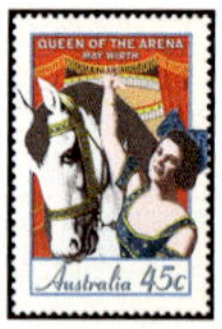


Circuses in Australia, 150th Anniv. — A525

Designs: No. 1591, Queen of the Arena, May Wirth (1894-1978). No. 1592, Wizard of the Wire, Con Colleano (1899-1973). No. 1593, Clowns. No. 1594, Tumblers.

**1997, Mar. 13** **Litho.** ***Perf. 14½x14***

**1591** A525 45c multicolored .80 .35
**1592** A525 45c multicolored .80 .35
**1593** A525 45c multicolored .80 .35
**1594** A525 45c multicolored .80 .35
*a.* Block of 4, #1591-1594 4.50 4.50
*Nos. 1591-1594 (4)* 3.20 1.40

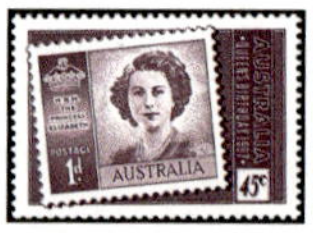


A526

**1997, Apr. 17** **Engr.** ***Perf. 14x14½***

**1595** A526 45c Design A50 1.00 .40

Queen Elizabeth II, 71st birthday, 50th wedding anniv.
See Nos. 210 and 215.

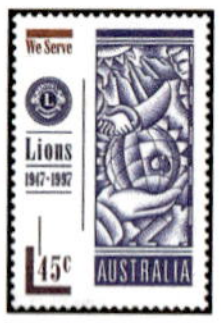


A527

**1997, Apr. 17** ***Perf. 14½x14***

**1596** A527 45c multicolored 1.00 .40

Lions Clubs of Australia, 50th anniv.

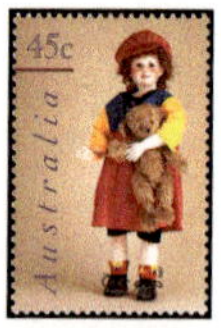


A528

Dolls and Teddy Bears: No. 1597, Doll wearing red hat. No. 1598, Bear standing. No. 1599, Doll wearing white dress holding teddy bear. No. 1600, Doll in brown outfit. No. 1601, Teddy bear seated.

**1997, May 8** **Litho.** ***Perf. 14½x14***

**1597** A528 45c multicolored .80 .80
**1598** A528 45c multicolored .80 .80
**1599** A528 45c multicolored .80 .80
**1600** A528 45c multicolored .80 .80
**1601** A528 45c multicolored .80 .80
*a.* Strip of 5, #1597-1601 5.50 5.50
*Nos. 1597-1601 (5)* 4.00 4.00

Nos. 1597-1601 were printed in sheets containing two strips of five. Some sheets exist overprinted in margin with picture of teddy bear and inscription "Brisbane Stamp & Coin Expo / 7-9 June 1997."

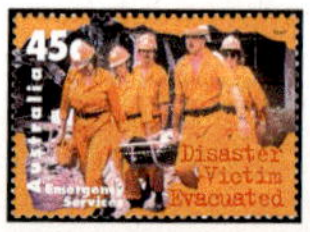


Emergency Services — A529

Designs: No. 1602, Disaster victim evacuated. No. 1603, Police rescue hiker. $1.05, Rapid response saves home. $1.20, Ambulance dash saves life.

**1997, July 10** **Litho.** ***Perf. 14x14½***

**1602** A529 45c multicolored .80 .80
**1603** A529 45c multicolored .80 .80
*a.* Pair, #1602-1603 2.00 1.60
**1604** A529 $1.05 multicolored 1.75 1.50
**1605** A529 $1.20 multicolored 2.40 1.60
*Nos. 1602-1605 (4)* 5.75 4.70

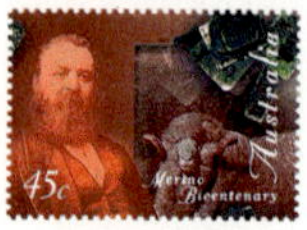


Arrival of Merino Sheep in Australia, Bicent. — A530

Designs: No. 1606, George Peppin, Junior (1827-76), breeder, Merino sheep. No. 1607, "Pepe" chair, uses of wool.

**1997, Aug. 7** **Litho.** ***Perf. 14x14½***

**1606** A530 45c multicolored .80 .40
**1607** A530 45c multicolored .80 .40
*a.* Pair, #1606-1607 2.00 2.00

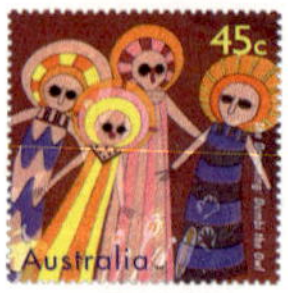


Scenes from "The Dreaming," Animated Stories for Children — A531

Designs: 45c, Dumbi the Owl. $1, The Two Willy-Willies. $1.20, How Brolga Became a Bird. $1.80, Tuggan-Tuggan.

**1997, Aug. 21** ***Perf. 14½***

**1608** A531 45c multicolored .80 .40
**1609** A531 $1 multicolored 1.75 1.25
**1610** A531 $1.20 multicolored 2.40 1.60
**1611** A531 $1.80 multicolored 3.25 2.00
*Nos. 1608-1611 (4)* 8.20 5.25

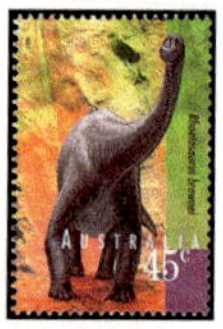


Prehistoric Animals — A532

Designs: No. 1612, Rhoetosaurus brownei. No. 1613, Mcnamaraspis kaprios. No. 1614, Ninjemys oweni. No. 1615, Paracyclotosaurus davidi. No. 1616, Woolungasaurus glendowerensis.

**1997, Sept. 4** **Litho.** ***Perf. 14½x14***

**1612** A532 45c multicolored .80 .40
**1613** A532 45c multicolored .80 .40
**1614** A532 45c multicolored .80 .40
**1615** A532 45c multicolored .80 .40
**1616** A532 45c multicolored .80 .40
*a.* Strip of 5, #1612-1616 6.50 5.00
*Nos. 1612-1616 (5)* 4.00 2.00

Printed in sheets of 10 stamps.

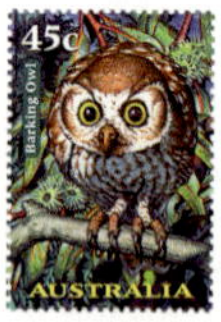


A533

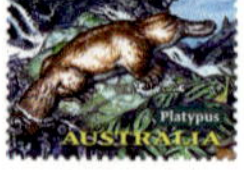


Nocturnal Animals — A534

No. 1617, Barking owl. No. 1618, Spotted-tailed quoll. No. 1619, Platypus. No. 1620, Brown antechinus. No. 1621, Dingo. No. 1622, Yellow-bellied glider.

***Perf. 14½x14, 14x14½***

**1997, Oct. 1** **Litho.**

**1617** A533 45c multicolored .80 .80
**1618** A533 45c multicolored .80 .80
*a.* Pair, #1617-1618 2.00 1.60
**1619** A534 45c multicolored .80 .80
**1620** A534 45c multicolored .80 .80
**1621** A534 45c multicolored .80 .80
*a.* Strip of 3, #1619-1621 3.25 3.25

**Size: 50x30mm**

**1622** A534 45c multicolored 1.40 .80
*a.* Souvenir sheet, #1617-1622, perf. 14¼ 6.00 6.00
*Nos. 1617-1622 (6)* 5.40 4.80

No. 1622a is printed with additional phosphor ink revealing a glow-in-the-dark spider and web under ultraviolet light.

**Size: 21x32mm**

***Serpentine Die Cut Perf. 11½***

**Self-Adhesive**

**1623** A533 45c like #1617 1.25 .40
**1624** A533 45c like #1618 1.25 .40
*a.* Booklet pane, 5 each #1623-1624 12.50
*b.* Pair, #1623-1624 4.00

By its nature No. 1624a is a complete booklet. The peelable paper backing serves as a booklet cover.

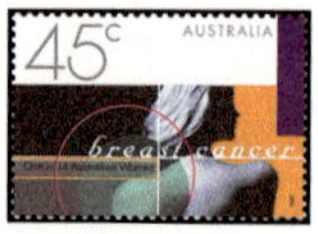


Breast Cancer Awareness — A535

**1997, Oct. 27** **Litho.** ***Perf. 14x14½***

**1625** A535 45c multicolored 1.00 .40

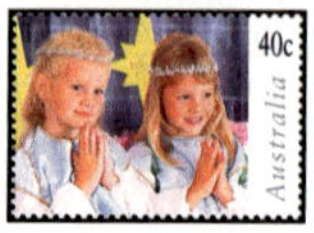


Christmas — A536

Children in Christmas Nativity pageant: 40c, Angels. 45c, Mary holding Baby Jesus. $1, Three Wise Men.

**1997, Nov. 3**

**1626** A536 40c multicolored .65 .35
**1627** A536 45c multicolored .75 .35
**1628** A536 $1 multicolored 1.60 1.25
*Nos. 1626-1628 (3)* 3.00 1.95

**Booklet Stamps**

**Serpentine Die Cut Perf. 11½**

**Self-Adhesive**

**1629** A536 40c multicolored .75 .40
*a.* Booklet pane of 20 15.00

By its nature No. 1629a is a complete booklet. The peelable paper backing serves as a booklet cover, which also contains 20 labels.

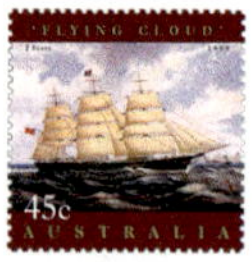


Maritime Heritage — A537

**1998, Jan. 15** **Litho.** ***Perf. 14½x14***

**1630** A537 45c Flying Cloud .80 .40
*a.* Pane of 10 9.00 9.00
**1631** A537 85c Marco Polo 1.25 .80
*a.* Sheet of 2, #1631 perf. 13½ & Canada #1779b *7.00 7.00*
**1632** A537 $1 Chusan 1.60 .80
**1633** A537 $1.20 Heather Belle 2.00 1.25
*Nos. 1630-1633 (4)* 5.65 3.25

Australia '99 (No. 1630a). World Stamp Expo. (No. 1631a).
See Canada No. 1779a.
Issued: No. 1630a, 6/17/98; No. 1631a, 3/19/99.

### Legends Type of 1997

Olympians: No. 1634: a, Betty Cuthbert. b, Cuthbert running. c, Herb Elliott. d, Elliott running. e, Dawn Fraser. f, Fraser swimming. g, Marjorie Jackson. h, Jackson running. i, Murray Rose. j, Rose swimming. k, Shirley Strickland. l, Strickland clearing hurdle.

**1998, Jan. 21** ***Perf. 14x14½***

**Size: 34x26mm**

**1634** Sheet of 12 14.00 14.00
*a.-l.* A522 45c any single .80 .80
*m.* Booklet pane, #1634a-1634d *5.50* —
*n.* Booklet pane, #1634e-1634h *5.50* —
*o.* Booklet pane, #1634i-1634l *5.50* —

### Booklet Stamps
### Self-Adhesive
### *Serpentine Die Cut 11½*
### Size: 34x25mm

**1635** A522 45c like #1634a 1.10 .40
**1636** A522 45c like #1634b 1.10 .40
**1637** A522 45c like #1634c 1.10 .40
**1638** A522 45c like #1634d 1.10 .40
**1639** A522 45c like #1634e 1.10 .40
**1640** A522 45c like #1634f 1.10 .40
**1641** A522 45c like #1634g 1.10 .40
**1642** A522 45c like #1634h 1.10 .40
**1643** A522 45c like #1634i 1.10 .40
**1644** A522 45c like #1634j 1.10 .40
**1645** A522 45c like #1634k 1.10 .40
**1646** A522 45c like #1634l 1.10 .40
*a.* Bklt. pane of 12, #1635-1646 20.00
*Nos. 1635-1646 (12)* 13.20 4.80

By its nature, No. 1646a is a complete booklet. The peelable backing serves as a booklet cover.

Nos. 1634m-1634o issued 1/24/07.

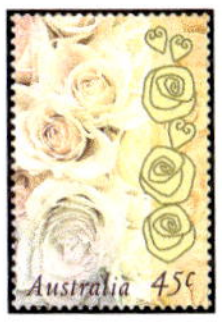

Greetings — A538

**1998, Feb. 12 Litho. *Perf. 14½x14***
**1647** A538 45c Champagne roses .90 .40

### Booklet Stamp
### Self-Adhesive
### *Serpentine Die Cut 11½*

**1648** A538 45c like #1647 .90 .65
*a.* Booklet pane of 10 11.00

By its nature No. 1648a is a complete booklet. The peelable paper backing, which contains 12 labels, serves as a booklet cover.

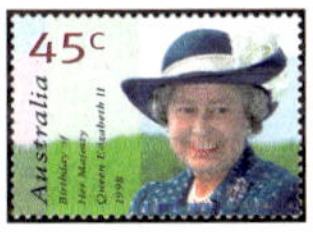

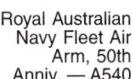

Queen Elizabeth II, 72nd Birthday — A539

**1998, Apr. 9 Litho. *Perf. 14x14½***
**1649** A539 45c multicolored 1.10 .65

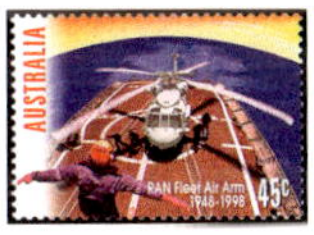

Royal Australian Navy Fleet Air Arm, 50th Anniv. — A540

**1998, Apr. 9**
**1650** A540 45c multicolored 1.10 .40

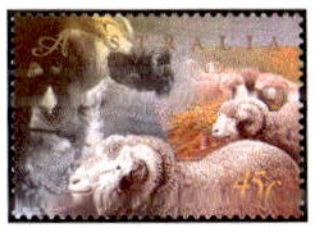

Farming in Australia — A541

Designs: No. 1651, Sheep for producing wool. No. 1652, Sheaves of wheat. No. 1653, Herding cattle on horseback. No. 1654, Harvesting sugar cane. No. 1655, Dairy cattle, man on motorcycle.

**1998, Apr. 21**
**1651** A541 45c multicolored .80 .40
**1652** A541 45c multicolored .80 .40
**1653** A541 45c multicolored .80 .40
**1654** A541 45c multicolored .80 .40
**1655** A541 45c multicolored .80 .40
*a.* Strip of 5, #1651-1655 4.75 4.75
*Nos. 1651-1655 (5)* 4.00 2.00

### Booklet Stamps
### Self-Adhesive
### *Serpentine Die Cut 11½*
### Size: 37x25mm

**1656** A541 45c like #1651 1.25 .40
**1657** A541 45c like #1652 1.25 .40
**1658** A541 45c like #1653 1.25 .40
**1659** A541 45c like #1654 1.25 .40
**1660** A541 45c like #1655 1.25 .40
*a.* Bklt. pane, 2 ea #1656-1660 16.00
*Nos. 1656-1660 (5)* 6.25 2.00

The peelable backing of No. 1660a serves as a booklet cover.

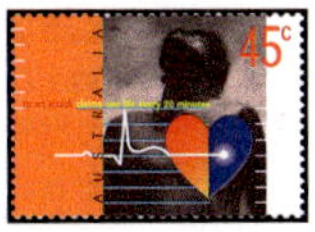

Heart Health — A542

**1998, May 4 Litho. *Perf. 14x14½***
**1661** A542 45c multicolored 1.10 .40

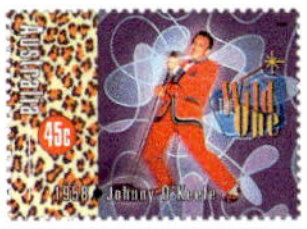

Rock and Roll in Australia — A543

a, "The Wild One," by Johnny O'Keefe, 1958. b, "Oh Yeah Uh Huh," by Col Joye and the Joye Boys, 1959. c, "He's My Blonde-headed Stompie Wompie Real Gone Surfer Boy," by Little Pattie, 1963. d, "Shakin' All Over," by Normie Rowe, 1965. e, "She's So Fine," by The Easybeats, 1965. f, "The Real Thing," by Russell Morris, 1969. g, "Turn Up Your Radio," by The Masters Apprentices, 1970. h, "Eagle Rock," by Daddy Cool, 1971. i, "Most People I Know Think That I'm Crazy," by Billy Thorpe & the Aztecs, 1972. j, "Horror Movie," by Skyhooks, 1974. k, "It's a Long Way to the Top," by AC/DC, 1975. l, "Howzat," by Sherbet, 1976.

**1998, May 26**
**1662** A543 Sheet of 12 12.00 12.00
*a.-l.* 45c any single .80 .80

### Coil Stamps
### Self-Adhesive
### *Serpentine Die Cut 11½*
### Size: 37x25mm

**1663** A543 45c like #1662a 1.10 .50
**1664** A543 45c like #1662b 1.10 .50
**1665** A543 45c like #1662c 1.10 .50
**1666** A543 45c like #1662d 1.10 .50
**1667** A543 45c like #1662e 1.10 .50
**1668** A543 45c like #1662f 1.10 .50
**1669** A543 45c like #1662g 1.10 .50
**1670** A543 45c like #1662h 1.10 .50
**1671** A543 45c like #1662i 1.10 .50
**1672** A543 45c like #1662j 1.10 .50
**1673** A543 45c like #1662k 1.10 .50
**1674** A543 45c like #1662l 1.10 .50
*a.* Strip of 12 + label 18.00
*Nos. 1663-1674 (12)* 13.20 6.00

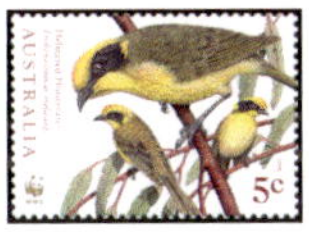

Endangered Birds — A544

World Wildlife Fund: No. 1675, Helmeted honeyeater. No. 1676, Orange-bellied parrot. No. 1677, Red-tailed black cockatoo. No. 1678, Gouldian finch.

**1998, June 25 *Perf. 14x14½***
**1675** A544 5c multicolored .40 .40
**1676** A544 5c multicolored .40 .40
*a.* Pair, #1675-1676 1.60 1.60
**1677** A544 45c multicolored .80 .80
**1678** A544 45c multicolored .80 .80
*a.* Pair, #1677-1678 2.10 2.10

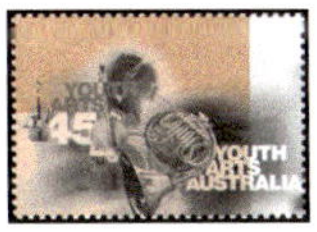

Performing and Visual Arts — A545

Young people: No. 1679, Playing French horn. No. 1680, Dancing.

**1998, July 16 Litho. *Perf. 14x14½***
**1679** A545 45c multicolored .80 .80
**1680** A545 45c multicolored .80 .80
*a.* Pair, #1679-1680 2.25 2.25

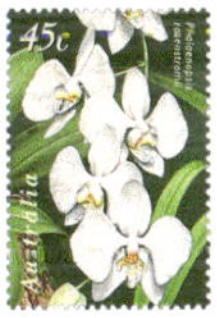

Orchids — A546

Designs: 45c, Phalaenopsis rosenstromii. 85c, Arundina graminifolia. $1, Grammatophyllum speciosum. $1.20, Dendrobium phalaenopsis.

**1998, Aug. 6 Litho. *Perf. 14½x14***
**1681** A546 45c multicolored .80 .40
**1682** A546 85c multicolored 1.30 .75
**1683** A546 $1 multicolored 1.60 1.00
**1684** A546 $1.20 multicolored 2.00 1.75
*a.* Souvenir sheet, #1681-1684 6.50 6.50
*Nos. 1681-1684 (4)* 5.70 3.90

See Singapore Nos. 858-861b.

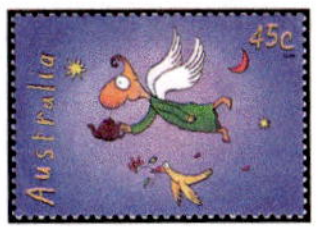

The Teapot of Truth, by Cartoonist Michael Leunig — A547

Designs: No. 1685, Angel carrying teapot, bird with flower. No. 1686, Birds perched on heart-shaped vine. No. 1687, Characters using their heads to pour tea into cup. $1, Stylized family. $1.20, Stylized teapot with face & legs.

**1998, Aug. 13 *Perf. 14x14½***
**1685** A547 45c multicolored 1.60 1.25
*a.* Booklet pane of 4 6.50
**1686** A547 45c multicolored 1.60 1.25
*a.* Booklet pane of 4 6.50
**1687** A547 45c multicolored 1.60 1.25
*a.* Booklet pane of 4 6.50

### Size: 30x25mm

**1688** A547 $1 multicolored 2.60 2.60
*a.* Booklet pane of 2 5.25
**1689** A547 $1.20 multicolored 3.25 3.25
*a.* Booklet pane of 2 6.25
Complete booklet, #1685a, 1686a, 1687a, 1688a, 1689a, 1 postal card & 16 self-adhesive labels 35.00
*Nos. 1685-1689 (5)* 10.65 9.60

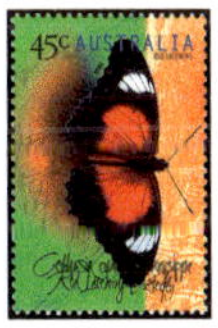

A548

Butterflies — No. 1690, Red lacewing. No. 1691, Dull oakblue. No. 1692, Meadow argus. No. 1693, Ulysses. No. 1694, Common red-eye.

**1998, Sept. 3 Litho. *Perf. 14½x14***
**1690** A548 45c multicolored .80 .80
**1691** A548 45c multicolored .80 .80
**1692** A548 45c multicolored .80 .80
**1693** A548 45c multicolored .80 .80
**1694** A548 45c multicolored .80 .80
*a.* Strip of 5, #1690-1694 5.50 5.25
*b.* Souv. sheet of 5, #1690-1694 7.00 7.00
*Nos. 1690-1694 (5)* 4.00 4.00

No. 1694b for China 1999 World Philatelic Exhibition. Issued 8/21/99.

### Self-Adhesive
### *Serpentine Die Cut 11½*

**1695** A548 45c like #1690 1.00 .40
**1696** A548 45c like #1691 1.00 .40
**1697** A548 45c like #1692 1.00 .40
**1698** A548 45c like #1693 1.00 .40
**1699** A548 45c like #1694 1.00 .40
*a.* Strip of 5, #1695-1699 8.75
*Nos. 1695-1699 (5)* 5.00 2.00

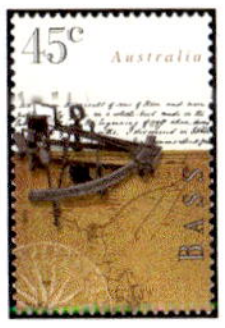

A549

Designs: No. 1700, Sextant, map of Bass Strait. No. 1701, Telescope, map of Van Diemen's Land (Tasmania).

**1998, Sept. 10 *Perf. 14½x14***
**1700** A549 45c multicolored 1.00 .40
**1701** A549 45c multicolored 1.00 .40
*a.* Pair, #1700-1701 2.40 2.25

Circumnavigation of Tasmania by George Bass (1771-c. 1803) and Matthew Flinders (1774-1814), bicent.

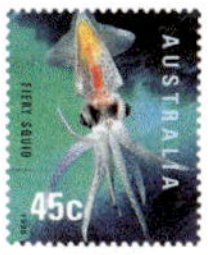

A550

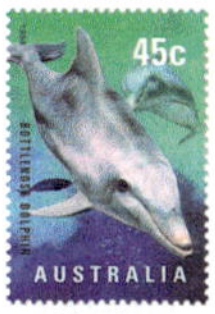

Marine Life — A551

Designs: No. 1702, Fiery squid. No. 1703, Manta ray. No. 1704, Bottlenose dolphin. No. 1705, Weedy seadragon. No. 1706, Southern right whale. No. 1707, White pointer shark.

### *Perf. 14½x14, 14x14½*

**1998, Oct. 1 Litho.**
**1702** A550 45c multi .80 .80
**1703** A550 45c multi, horiz. .80 .80
**1704** A551 45c multi .80 .80
**1705** A551 45c multi .80 .80
*a.* Pair, #1704-1705 2.25 2.25

### Size: 50x30mm

**1706** A551 45c multi, horiz. .80 .80
**1707** A551 45c multi .80 .80
*a.* Souvenir sheet, #1702-1707 6.00 5.75
*Nos. 1702-1707 (6)* 4.80 4.80

### Booklet Stamps
### Self-Adhesive
### *Serpentine Die Cut Perf. 11½*

**1708** A551 45c like #1704 1.10 .40
**1709** A551 45c like #1705 1.10 .40
*a.* Bklt. pane, 5 ea #1708-1709 11.00

No. 1709a is a complete booklet. The peelable paper backing serves as a booklet cover.

Nos. 1708-1709 also exist in coils, issued in rolls of 100 with surrounding selvage removed. Value, set of singles $4.50.

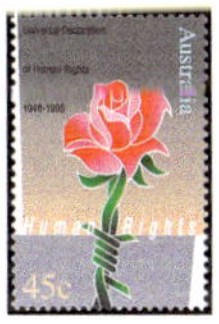

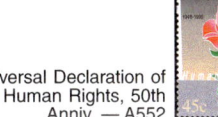

Universal Declaration of Human Rights, 50th Anniv. — A552

**1998, Oct. 22 Litho. *Perf. 14½x14***
**1712** A552 45c multicolored 1.10 .60

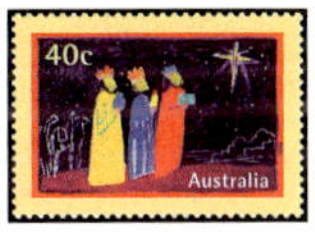

Christmas — A553

40c, Magi. 45c, Nativity. $1, Journey to Bethlehem.

**1998, Nov. 2 *Perf. 14x14½***
**1713** A553 40c multicolored .80 .55
**1714** A553 45c multicolored .90 .80
**1715** A553 $1 multicolored 2.00 2.00
*Nos. 1713-1715 (3)* 3.70 3.35

### Booklet Stamp
### Self-Adhesive
### *Serpentine Die Cut Perf. 11½*

**1716** A553 40c multicolored 1.10 .55
*a.* Booklet pane of 20 22.00

No. 1716a is a complete booklet.

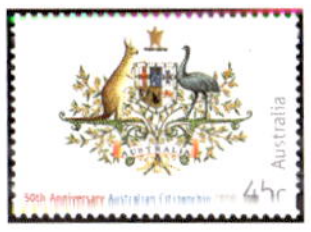

Nationality and Citizenship Act, 50th Anniv. A554

**1999, Jan. 14 Litho. *Perf. 14x14½***
**1717** A554 45c multicolored 1.10 .50

### *Die Cut Perf. 11¾*
### Self-Adhesive

**1718** A554 45c multicolored 1.10 .55

### Legends Type of 1997

Designs: Nos. 1719, 1721, Arthur Boyd, artist. Nos. 1720, 1722, "Nebuchadnezzar on Fire Falling over a Waterfall," by Boyd.

**1999, Jan. 22 Litho. *Perf. 14x14½***
**1719** A522 45c multicolored .80 .80
**1720** A522 45c multicolored .80 .80
*a.* Pair, #1719-1720 2.25 2.25
*b.* Booklet pane, #1719-1720 3.00 —

### Booklet Stamps
### Self-Adhesive
***Serpentine Die Cut Perf. 11½***

**1721** A522 45c multicolored 1.10 .55
**1722** A522 45c multicolored 1.10 .55
*a.* Bklt. pane, 5 ea #1721-1722 11.00

No. 1722a is a complete booklet.
No. 1720b issued 1/24/07.

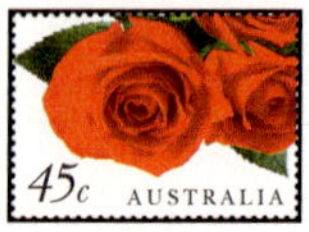
Love — A555

**1999, Feb. 4** ***Perf. 14x14½***
**1723** A555 45c Red roses .75 .65

### Booklet Stamp
### Self-adhesive
***Serpentine Die Cut Perf. 11½***

**1724** A555 45c like #1723 1.10 .55
*a.* Booklet pane of 10 11.00

No. 1724a is a complete booklet.

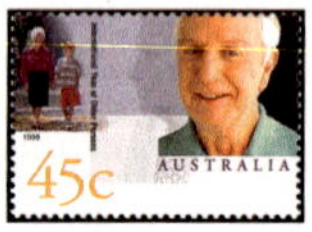
Intl. Year of Older Persons — A556

Designs: No. 1725, Woman walking with girl, man up close. No. 1726, Woman up close, man playing soccer with boy.

**1999, Feb. 11** ***Perf. 14x14½***
**1725** A556 45c multicolored .80 .40
**1726** A556 45c multicolored .80 .40
*a.* Pair, #1725-1726 1.60 2.25

### Early Navigators Type of 1963

No. 1727: a, like #374. b, like #376. c, like #377.
No. 1728: a, like #375. b, like #379. c, like #378.

***Perf. 14x14½, 14½x14***
**1999, Mar. 19** **Litho.**
**1727** Sheet of 3 5.25 5.00
*a.-c.* A144 45c any single 1.00 1.00
*d.* As #1727, imperf. 12.00 12.00
*e.* As #1727, perfin "A99" in sheet margin 45.00 45.00
**1728** Sheet of 3 5.25 5.00
*a.-c.* A145 45c any single 1.00 1.00
*d.* As #1728, imperf. 12.00 12.00
*e.* As #1728, perfin "A99" in sheet margin 45.00 45.00

Australia '99, World Stamp Expo.
Nos. 1727e-1728e were made from Nos. 1727d-1728d at Australia '99. Examples different perforations or with the perforating and "A99" inverted were intentionally misperfed personally by patrons of the show.

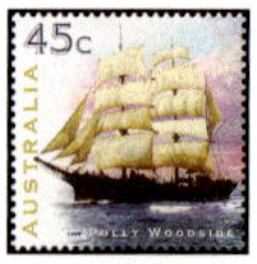
Sailing Ships — A557

**1999, Mar. 19** ***Perf. 14½x14***
**1729** A557 45c Polly Woodside .90 .55
*a.* Perf 14x14½ 3.00 3.00
*b.* Souvenir sheet of 2, #1729a, Ireland #1173a 6.00 6.00
**1730** A557 85c Alma Doepel 1.75 1.60
**1731** A557 $1 Enterprize 1.90 1.60
**1732** A557 $1.05 Lady Nelson 2.00 1.60
*Nos. 1729-1732 (4)* 6.55 5.35

Australia '99, World Stamp Expo (No. 1729a). See Ireland No. 1173.
No. 1729 was issued in sheets of 20 with a se-tenant label showing Australia '99 logo. Panes of 10 No. 1729 with labels were sold only at the show, where patrons could have their photos printed on the label.

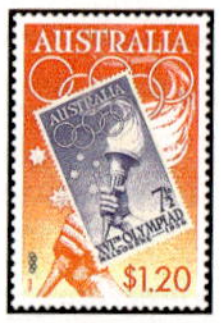
Olympic Torch — A558

**1999, Mar. 22**
**1733** A558 $1.20 #289 2.00 2.00

### Flora & Fauna Type of 1996

Flowers: Nos. 1734, 1742A, 1743, 1746B, 1746I, Correa reflexa. Nos. 1735, 1742B, 1744, 1746C, 1746J, Hibbertia scandens. Nos. 1736, 1742C, 1745, 1746D, 1746K, Ipomoea pes-caprae. Nos. 1737, 1742D, 1746, 1746E, 1746L, Wahlenbergia stricta.
70c, Humpback whales, zebra volute. No. 1739, Brahminy kite, checkerboard helmet shell. No. 1740, Fraser Island, chambered nautilus. $1.05, Loggerhead turtle, baler. $1.20, White-bellied sea eagle, Campbell's stromb.

**1999** **Litho.** ***Perf. 14x14½***
**1734** A511 45c multicolored .80 .40
**1735** A511 45c multicolored .80 .40
**1736** A511 45c multicolored .80 .40
**1737** A511 45c multicolored .80 .40
*a.* Block of 4, #1734-1737 3.75 3.75
**1738** A511 70c multicolored 1.40 1.40
**1739** A511 90c multicolored 1.60 1.25
**1740** A511 90c multicolored 1.60 1.25
*a.* Pair, #1739-1740 3.50 3.25
**1741** A511 $1.05 multicolored 2.10 1.90
**1742** A511 $1.20 multicolored 2.40 2.40
*Nos. 1734-1742 (9)* 12.30 9.80

### Booklet Stamps
***Serpentine Die Cut 11, 11¼ (#1742Df)***
### Self-Adhesive

**1742A** A511 45c like #1734 1.00 .40
**1742B** A511 45c like #1735 1.00 .40
**1742C** A511 45c like #1736 1.00 .40
**1742D** A511 45c like #1737 1.00 .40
*e.* Booklet pane, 3 each #1742A, 1742C, 2 each #1742B, 1742D 10.00
*f.* Booklet pane, 5 each #1742A-1742D 19.00

***Die Cut perf. 12½x12¾***
**1743** A511 45c like #1734 1.00 .40
**1744** A511 45c like #1735 1.00 .40
**1745** A511 45c like #1736 1.00 .40
**1746** A511 45c like #1737 1.00 .40
*a.* Booklet pane, 3 each #1743, 1745, 2 each #1744, #1746 10.00
*g.* Strip of 4, #1743-1746 4.50
*Nos. 1742A-1746 (8)* 8.00 3.20

Nos. 1742De, 1746a are complete booklets.

### Coil Stamps
***Serpentine Die Cut 11½***

**1746B** A511 45c like #1734 1.10 .40
**1746C** A511 45c like #1735 1.10 .40
**1746D** A511 45c like #1736 1.10 .40
**1746E** A511 45c like #1737 1.10 .40
*f.* Strip of 4, #1746B-1746E 5.25
*h.* Pane, #1746B, 1746D-1746E, 2 #1746C 5.75

***Serpentine Die Cut 13***
**1746I** A511 45c like #1734 1.10 .40
**1746J** A511 45c like #1735 1.10 .40
**1746K** A511 45c like #1736 1.10 .40
**1746L** A511 45c like #1737 1.10 .40
*m.* Strip of 4, #1746I-1746K 5.25
*Nos. 1746B-1746L (8)* 8.80 3.20

Issued: Nos. 1738-1742, 7/8; 1746B-1746E, 1746I-1746L, 4/8.
No. 1742Df is a complete booklet.

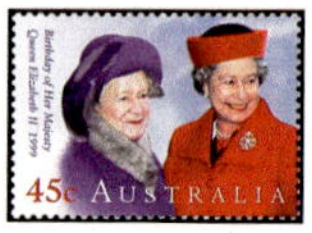
Queen Mother and Queen Elizabeth II — A559

**1999, Apr. 15** ***Perf. 14x14½***
**1747** A559 45c multicolored 1.00 .75

Queen Elizabeth II, 73rd birthday.

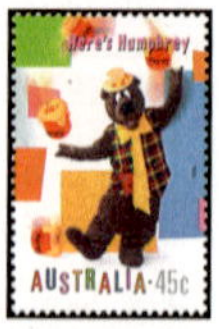
Children's Television Programs — A560

Designs: Nos. 1748, 1753, "Here's Humphrey." Nos. 1749, 1754, "Bananas in Pajamas." Nos. 1750, 1755, "Mr. Squiggle." Nos. 1751, 1756, Teddy bears from "Play School." Nos. 1752, 1757, Clock, dog, boy from "Play School."

**1999, May 6** **Litho.** ***Perf. 14½x14***
**1748** A560 45c multicolored 1.00 .75
**1749** A560 45c multicolored 1.00 .75
**1750** A560 45c multicolored 1.00 .75
**1751** A560 45c multicolored 1.00 .75
**1752** A560 45c multicolored 1.00 .75
*a.* Strip of 5, #1748-1752 5.75 5.75
*Nos. 1748-1752 (5)* 5.00 3.75

### Self-Adhesive
***Serpentine Die Cut 11½x11¼***

**1753** A560 45c like #1748 1.10 .40
**1754** A560 45c like #1749 1.10 .40
**1755** A560 45c like #1750 1.10 .40
**1756** A560 45c like #1751 1.10 .40
**1757** A560 45c like #1752 1.10 .40
*a.* Bklt. pane, 2 ea #1753-1757 18.00
*Nos. 1753-1757 (5)* 5.50 2.00

No. 1757a is a complete booklet.

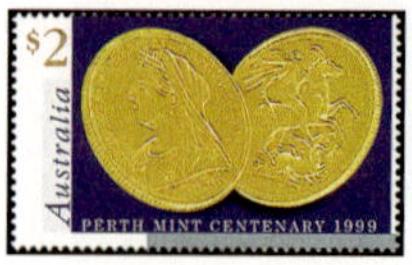
Perth Mint, Cent. A561

**1999, May 13** **Litho.** ***Perf. 14¼x14***
**1758** A561 $2 gold & multi 4.00 3.75

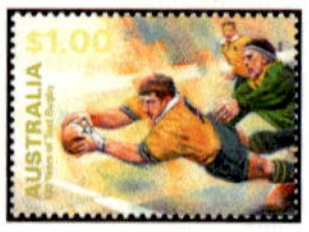
Test Rugby in Australia, Cent. — A562

Designs: Nos. 1759, 1763, Kicking ball, vert. Nos. 1760, 1764, Catching ball. $1, Diving with ball. $1.20, Being tackled.

**1999, June 8** **Litho.** ***Perf. 14½x14***
**1759** A562 45c multi 1.00 .75
**1760** A562 45c multi, vert. 1.00 .75
*a.* Pair, #1759-1760 2.25 2.25

***Perf. 14x14½***
**1761** A562 $1 multi 2.25 2.25
**1762** A562 $1.20 multi 2.50 2.50

***Serpentine Die Cut 11½***
### Self-Adhesive
### Coil Stamps

**1763** A562 45c like #1759 1.75 .60
**1764** A562 45c like #1760 1.75 .60
*a.* Pair, #1763-1764 3.50

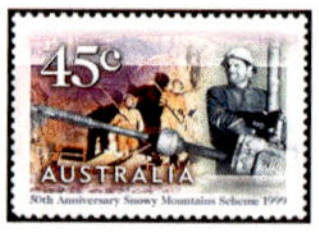
Snowy Mountains Hydroelectric Projects, 50th Anniv. — A563

Designs: No. 1765, Rock bolters at Tumut 2 Power Station Hall, driller at Tooma-Tumut Tunnel. No. 1766, English class for migrant workers at Cooma. No. 1767, Eucumbene Dam, Tumut 2 Tailwater Tunnel. No. 1768, Island Bend Dam, German carpenters.

**1999, Aug. 12** **Litho.** ***Perf. 14x14½***
**1765** A563 45c multicolored 1.00 .75
**1766** A563 45c multicolored 1.00 .75
**1767** A563 45c multicolored 1.00 .75
**1768** A563 45c multicolored 1.00 .75
*a.* Block of 4, #1765-1768 4.50 4.50
*Nos. 1765-1768 (4)* 4.00 3.00

### Self-Adhesive
### Coil Stamps
### Litho.
***Serpentine Die Cut 11¾***

**1769** A563 45c Like #1765 1.25 .40
**1770** A563 45c Like #1766 1.25 .40
**1771** A563 45c Like #1767 1.25 .40
**1772** A563 45c Like #1768 1.25 .40
*a.* Strip of 4, #1769-1772 6.00 5.25
*Nos. 1769-1772 (4)* 5.00 1.60

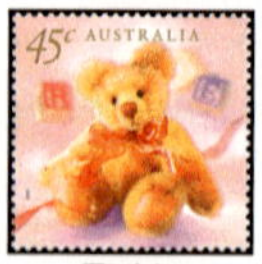
Teddy Bear — A564

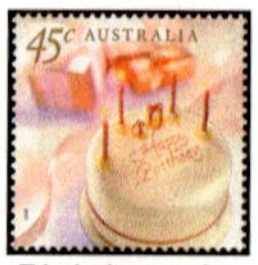
Birthday cake — A564a

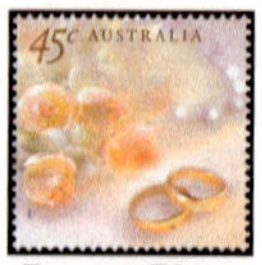
Roses, Rings — A564b

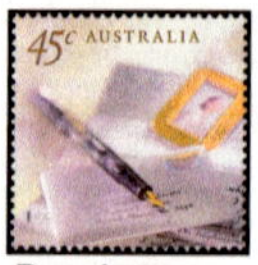
Pen, Letter — A564c

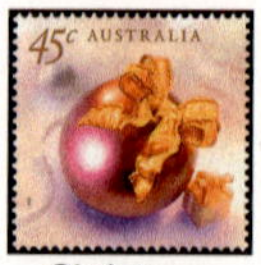
Christmas Ornament — A564d

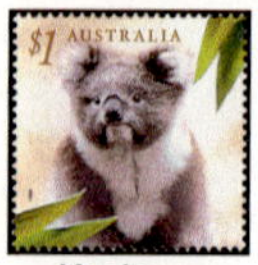
Koala — A564e

**1999-2003** **Litho.** ***Perf. 14½x14***
**1773** A564 45c multicolored .90 .65
**1774** A564a 45c multicolored .90 .65
**1775** A564b 45c multicolored .90 .65
*a.* Booklet pane of 4 + 4 labels ('02) 3.75 —
Booklet, 5 #1775a 27.50
**1776** A564c 45c multicolored .90 .65
**1777** A564d 45c multicolored .90 .75
*a.* Booklet pane of 4 + 4 labels 3.75 —
Complete booklet, 5 #1777a 27.50
**1778** A564e $1 multicolored 2.60 2.60
*Nos. 1773-1778 (6)* 7.10 5.95

Greetings.
Nos. 1773-1778 each were printed with a se-tenant label at right in sheets of 20. Size of label is 24mm wide on No. 1777, 19mm wide on No. 1775a, 17mm on others. Labels were inscribed with phrases appropriate to the stamp design, or blank, upon which Australia Post printed photographs, sent to them through special orders. No. 1775a and 1777a each come with five different margins, each of which is found in the respective booklet, which sold for $9.95.
Issued: Nos. 1773-1778, 9/1/99; No. 1775a, 3/12/02. No. 1777a, 10/31/03.
See No. 1926.
Compare with types A631, A633, A634.

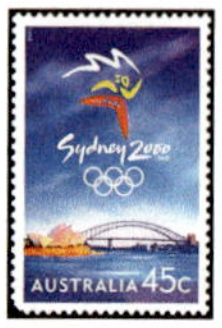
2000 Olympic Games, Sydney — A565

**1999, Sept. 14** **Litho.** ***Perf. 14½x14***
**1779** A565 45c multicolored 1.00 .75

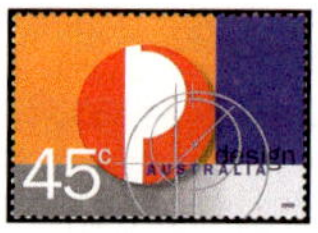
Sydney Design 99, Intl. Design Congress — A566

Designs: 45c, Australia Post emblem. 90c, Embryo chair. $1.35, Possum skin textile design. $1.50, Storey Hall, Royal Melbourne Institute of Technology.

**1999, Sept. 16** **Litho.** ***Perf. 14x14½***
**1780** A566 45c multicolored 1.25 .75
**1781** A566 90c multicolored 1.60 1.25
**1782** A566 $1.35 multicolored 2.40 2.00
**1783** A566 $1.50 multicolored 2.75 2.75
*Nos. 1780-1783 (4)* 8.00 6.75

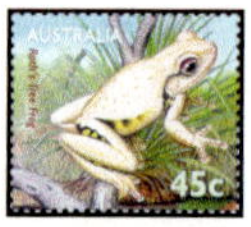
Pond Fauna — A567

Designs: Nos. 1784, 1790c, Roth's tree frog. Nos. 1785, 1790d, Dragonfly. Nos. 1786, 1790b, Sacred kingfisher. Nos. 1787, 1790f, Magnificent tree frog. Nos. 1788, 1790e, 1791, Northern dwarf tree frog. Nos. 1789, 1790a, 1792, Javelin frog.
No. 1793, Sacred kingfisher. No. 1794, Magnificent tree frog.

**1999, Oct. 1** **Litho.** ***Perf. 14x14½***
**1784** A567 45c multicolored .95 .80
**1785** A567 45c multicolored .95 .80
*a.* Pair, #1784-1785 2.25 2.25

### Size: 26x38mm
***Perf. 14½x14***

**1786** A567 45c multicolored .95 .80
**1787** A567 45c multicolored .95 .80
*a.* Pair, #1786-1787 2.25 2.25

### Size: 25x30mm

**1788** A567 50c multicolored 1.10 .90
**1789** A567 50c multicolored 1.10 .90
*a.* Pair, #1788-1789 2.40 2.40
*Nos. 1784-1789 (6)* 6.00 5.00

### Souvenir Sheet

*Perf. 14½*

| | | | | |
|---|---|---|---|---|
| **1790** | A567 | Sheet of 6, #a-f | 7.00 | 7.00 |
| *g.* | | Ovptd. in sheet margin for Bangkok 2000 Exhibition | 12.00 | 12.00 |
| *h.* | | Ovptd. in gold in sheet margin for Adelaide Stamp '99 Exhibition | 15.00 | 15.00 |

No. 1790d has foil impression on dragonfly's wings.

No. 1790 with overprints for Victorian and South Australian Philatelic Congresses in 1999 are unofficial.

No. 1790h was issued by Australia Post. Another, unofficial, overprint in black (with an orange and black sticker affixed) was applied to other souvenir sheets by the event organizers using the same logo.

### Self-Adhesive

*Serpentine Die Cut 11¼*

**Size: 25x30mm**

| | | | | |
|---|---|---|---|---|
| **1791** | A567 | 50c multicolored | 1.40 | .60 |
| **1792** | A567 | 50c multicolored | 1.40 | .60 |
| *a.* | | Bklt. pane, 5 ea #1791-1792 | 17.00 | |

Nos. 1791-1792 are booklet stamps. No. 1792a is a complete booklet.

*Die Cut Perf. 11¾*

**Size: 26x38mm**

| | | | | |
|---|---|---|---|---|
| **1793** | A567 | 45c multicolored | 1.25 | .60 |
| **1794** | A567 | 45c multicolored | 1.25 | .60 |
| *a.* | | Pair, #1793-1794 | 4.25 | 4.25 |

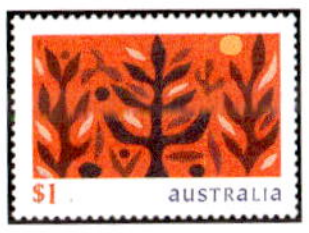

Christmas — A568

**1999, Nov. 1** *Perf. 14½x14*

| | | | | |
|---|---|---|---|---|
| **1795** | A568 | 40c Madonna and child, vert. | 1.00 | .75 |

*Perf. 14x14½*

| | | | | |
|---|---|---|---|---|
| **1796** | A568 | $1 Tree | 2.25 | 2.25 |

### Booklet Stamp
### Self-Adhesive

*Serpentine Die Cut 11¾*

| | | | | |
|---|---|---|---|---|
| **1797** | A568 | 40c Like #1795 | 1.00 | .40 |
| *a.* | | Booklet pane of 20 | 20.00 | |

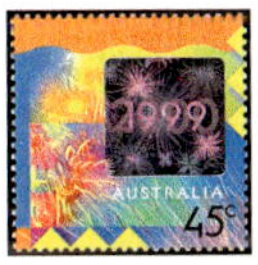

Celebrate 2000 — A569

**1999, Nov. 1** **Litho.** *Perf. 14½x14*

| | | | | |
|---|---|---|---|---|
| **1798** | A569 | 45c multicolored | 1.10 | .75 |

No. 1798 has a holographic image. Soaking in water may affect hologram.

Sheets of 10 exist with 10 labels inscribed "Celebrate 2000."

No. 1798 was also printed with a se-tenant label at right in sheets of 20. Labels were inscribed "Celebrate 2000" or blank, upon which Australia Post printed photographs, sent to them through special orders.

Sheets of 10 stamps plus 10 photo labels have been available at special events. These have the sheet selvage inscribed for each event. Most of these have been available only at the event and exist in very limited quantities.

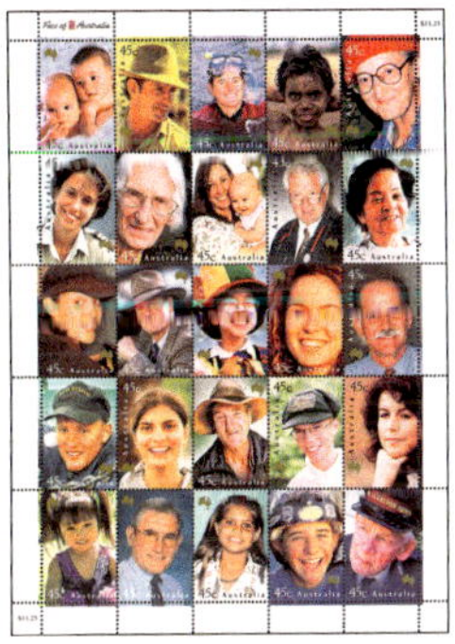

Faces of Australia A570

Ordinary people: a, Nicholle and Meghan Triandis, baby twins. b, David Willis, cattleman with hat. c, Natasha Bramley, with snorkel gear. d, Cyril Watson, Aboriginal boy. e, Mollie Dowdall, with red hat. f, Robin Dicks, in khaki uniform. g, Mary Simons, with gray hair. h, Peta and Samantha Nieuwerth, mother and daughter. i, Dr. John Matthews, with stethoscope. j, Edith Dizon-Fitzsimmons, with large earrings. k, Philippa Weir, with brown hat. l, John Thurgar, with suit, tie and hat. m, Miguel Alzona, with large, multicolored hat. n, Rachael Thomson, girl with wavy hair. o, Necip Akarsu, with mustache. p, Justin Allan, with HMAS Brisbane cap. q, Wadad Dennaoui, with checked blouse. r, Jack Laity, with hat and jacket. s, Kelsey Stubbin, with Australia cap. t, Gianna Rossi, with hand on chin. u, Paris Hansch, young girl. v, Donald George Whatham, in shirt and tie. w, Stacey Coull, Aboriginal girl in patterned blouse. x, Alex Payne, with bicycle helmet. y, John Lodge, with Salvation Army hat.

**2000, Jan. 1** **Litho.** *Perf. 14¾x13¾*

| | | | | |
|---|---|---|---|---|
| **1799** | A570 | Sheet of 25 | 24.00 | 24.00 |
| *a.-y.* | | 45c Any single | .95 | .80 |

### Legends Type of 1997

Aging veterans of World War I: Nos. 1800, 1804, Walter Parker. Nos. 1801, 1805, Roy Longmore. Nos. 1802, 1806, Alec Campbell. Nos. 1803, 1807, 1914-15 Star.

**2000, Jan. 21** **Litho.** *Perf. 14x14¾*

**Size: 34x26mm**

| | | | | |
|---|---|---|---|---|
| **1800** | A522 | 45c multi | .95 | .80 |
| **1801** | A522 | 45c multi | .95 | .80 |
| **1802** | A522 | 45c multi | .95 | .80 |
| **1803** | A522 | 45c multi | .95 | .80 |
| *a.* | | Block of 4, #1800-1803 | 4.00 | 3.60 |
| *b.* | | Booklet pane, #1800-1803 | *6.00* | — |
| | | *Nos. 1800-1803 (4)* | 3.80 | 3.20 |

### Self-Adhesive

*Die Cut Perf. 11¾*

| | | | | |
|---|---|---|---|---|
| **1804** | A522 | 45c multi | 1.00 | .75 |
| **1805** | A522 | 45c multi | 1.00 | .75 |
| **1806** | A522 | 45c multi | 1.00 | .75 |
| **1807** | A522 | 45c multi | 1.00 | .75 |
| *a.* | | Complete booklet, 2 each #1804-1806, 4 #1807 | 13.00 | |
| | | *Nos. 1804-1807 (4)* | 4.00 | 3.00 |

No. 1803b issued 1/24/07.

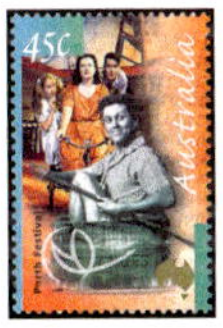

A571

Arts festivals.

**2000, Feb. 24** **Litho.** *Perf. 14¾x14*

| | | | | |
|---|---|---|---|---|
| **1808** | A571 | 45c Perth | .95 | .75 |
| **1809** | A571 | 45c Adelaide | .95 | .75 |
| **1810** | A571 | 45c Sydney | .95 | .75 |
| **1811** | A571 | 45c Melbourne | .95 | .75 |
| **1812** | A571 | 45c Brisbane | .95 | .75 |
| *a.* | | Strip of 5, #1808-1812 | 4.75 | 4.75 |
| | | *Nos. 1808-1812 (5)* | 4.75 | 3.75 |

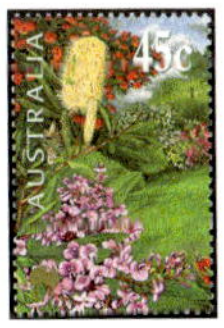

A572

Gardens: Nos. 1813, 1818, 1823, Coast banksia, false sarsaparilla, swamp bloodwood (denomination at UR). Nos. 1814, 1819, 1824, Swamp bottlebrush, Eastern spinebill (denomination at UL). Nos. 1815, 1820, 1825, Canna X generalis varieties (denomination at LL). Nos. 1816, 1821, 1826, Pond, roses, purple swamphen (denomination at UR). Nos. 1817, 1822, 1827, Pond, hibiscus, nerium oleander (denomination at UL).

**2000, Mar. 23** **Litho.** *Perf. 14¾x14*

| | | | | |
|---|---|---|---|---|
| **1813** | A572 | 45c multi | .95 | .95 |
| **1814** | A572 | 45c multi | .95 | .95 |
| **1815** | A572 | 45c multi | .95 | .95 |
| **1816** | A572 | 45c multi | .95 | .95 |
| **1817** | A572 | 45c multi | .95 | .95 |
| *a.* | | Horiz. strip, #1813-1817 | 4.75 | 4.75 |
| | | *Nos. 1813-1817 (5)* | 4.75 | 4.75 |

### Booklet Stamps
### Self-Adhesive

*Serpentine Die Cut 11½x11¼*

**Pale Green Frames**

| | | | | |
|---|---|---|---|---|
| **1818** | A572 | 45c multi | 1.10 | .75 |
| **1819** | A572 | 45c multi | 1.10 | .75 |
| **1820** | A572 | 45c multi | 1.10 | .75 |
| **1821** | A572 | 45c multi | 1.10 | .75 |
| **1822** | A572 | 45c multi | 1.10 | .75 |
| *a.* | | Booklet, 2 each #1818-1822 | 11.50 | |
| | | *Nos. 1818-1822 (5)* | 5.50 | 3.75 |

### Coil Stamps
### Self-Adhesive

*Serpentine Die Cut 11¾*

**Pale Green Frames**

| | | | | |
|---|---|---|---|---|
| **1823** | A572 | 45c multi | 1.25 | .75 |
| **1824** | A572 | 45c multi | 1.25 | .75 |
| **1825** | A572 | 45c multi | 1.25 | .75 |
| **1826** | A572 | 45c multi | 1.25 | .75 |
| **1827** | A572 | 45c multi | 1.25 | .75 |
| *a.* | | Strip of 5, #1823-1827 | 7.50 | |
| | | *Nos. 1823-1827 (5)* | 6.25 | 3.75 |

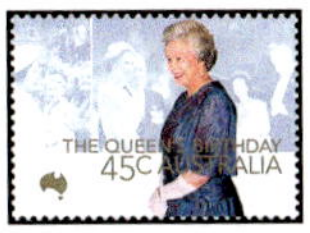

Queen Elizabeth II, 74th Birthday — A573

**2000, Apr. 13** **Litho.** *Perf. 14x14¾*

| | | | | |
|---|---|---|---|---|
| **1828** | A573 | 45c multi | 1.00 | .75 |

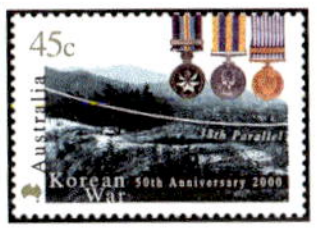

Korean War, 50th Anniv. — A574

**2000, Apr. 18**

| | | | | |
|---|---|---|---|---|
| **1829** | A574 | 45c multi | 1.00 | .75 |

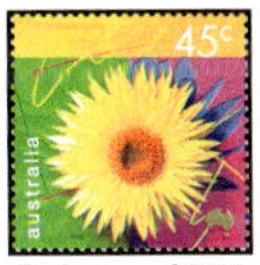

Daisy — A575

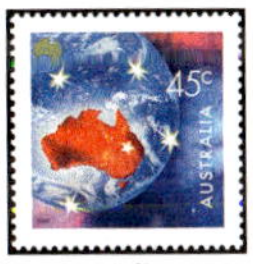

Australia on Globe, Southern Cross — A576

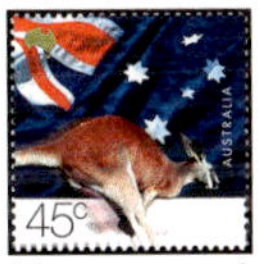

Kangaroo and Flag — A577

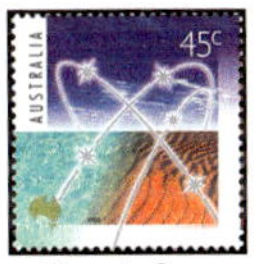

Sand, Sea and Sky — A578

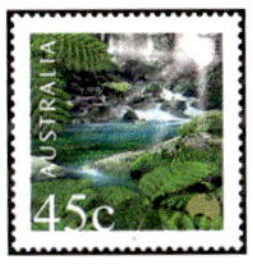

Rainforest — A579

**2000, May 11** *Perf. 14½x14*

| | | | | |
|---|---|---|---|---|
| **1830** | A575 | 45c multi + label | 1.20 | .75 |
| **1831** | A576 | 45c multi + label | 1.20 | .75 |
| **1832** | A577 | 45c multi + label | 1.20 | .75 |
| **1833** | A578 | 45c multi + label | 1.20 | .75 |
| **1834** | A579 | 45c multi + label | 1.20 | .75 |
| | | *Nos. 1830-1834 (5)* | 6.00 | 3.75 |

Nos. 1830-1834 each issued in sheets of 20 stamps and labels, with and without decorative selvage.

Sheets containing 10 No. 1831 with margins and ten labels that could be personalized were sold for $12, $2 of which was donated to volunteer organizations of the purchaser's choice. Volunteer organizations could purchase these sheets and offer them for resale in fundraising projects.

No. 1832 exists in a sheet of 10+10 labels that sold sold for $16. Sheet has decorative selvage and labels showing stock photo.

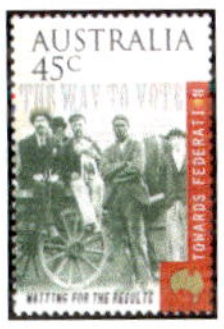

The Move Towards Federation — A580

Designs: No. 1835, Taking the vote. No. 1836, Waiting for the results. No. 1837, The fair new nation. No. 1838, Queen Victoria.

**2000, May 22** *Perf. 14¾x14*

| | | | | |
|---|---|---|---|---|
| **1835** | A580 | 45c multi | .90 | .75 |
| **1836** | A580 | 45c multi | .90 | .75 |
| *a.* | | Pair, #1835-1836 | 2.00 | 2.00 |

**Size: 30x50mm**

*Perf. 14x14½*

| | | | | |
|---|---|---|---|---|
| **1837** | A580 | $1.50 multi | 2.40 | 2.40 |
| **1838** | A580 | $1.50 multi | 2.40 | 2.40 |
| *a.* | | Pair, #1837-1838 | 5.00 | 5.00 |
| *b.* | | Souvenir sheet, #1836a, 1838a | 7.25 | 7.25 |
| *c.* | | As "b," with marginal inscription for The Stamp Show 2000, London | 14.00 | 14.00 |
| | | *Nos. 1835-1838 (4)* | 6.60 | 6.30 |

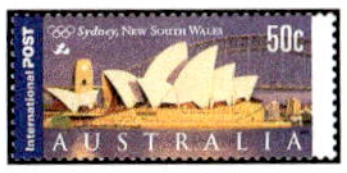

Tourist Attractions A581

Designs: 50c, Sydney Opera House. $1, Nandroya Falls. $1.50, Sydney Harbour Bridge. $2, Cradle Mountain. $3, The Pinnacles. $4.50, Flinders Ranges. $5, Twelve Apostles. $10, Devils Marbles.

**2000, June 20** **Litho.** *Perf. 14½x14*

| | | | | |
|---|---|---|---|---|
| **1839** | A581 | 50c multi | .80 | .75 |
| **1840** | A581 | $1 multi | 1.60 | 1.50 |
| **1841** | A581 | $1.50 multi | 2.40 | 2.25 |
| **1842** | A581 | $2 multi | 3.25 | 2.75 |
| **1843** | A581 | $3 multi | 4.75 | 4.50 |

**Size: 56x25mm**

*Perf. 14x14½*

| | | | | |
|---|---|---|---|---|
| **1844** | A581 | $4.50 multi | 7.25 | 6.75 |
| **1845** | A581 | $5 multi | 8.00 | 7.25 |
| **1846** | A581 | $10 multi | 16.00 | 14.40 |
| | | *Nos. 1839-1846 (8)* | 44.05 | 40.15 |

See Nos. 1925, 1979-1983, 2055-2059, 2077-2080, 2280-2283.

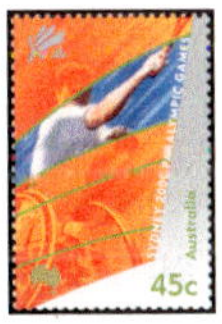

2000 Paralympics, Sydney — A582

Designs: Nos. 1847, 1855, Wheelchair tennis. Nos. 1848, 1856, Amputee running. Nos. 1849, 1853, Wheelchair basketball. Nos. 1850, 1852, Cycling for the visually impaired. Nos. 1851, 1854, Amputee shot put.

**2000, July 3** **Litho.** *Perf. 14¾x14*

| | | | | |
|---|---|---|---|---|
| **1847** | A582 | 45c multi | .75 | .75 |
| **1848** | A582 | 45c multi | .75 | .75 |
| *a.* | | Pair, #1847-1848 | 2.00 | 2.00 |
| **1849** | A582 | 49c multi | 1.00 | 1.00 |
| **1850** | A582 | 49c multi | 1.00 | 1.00 |
| **1851** | A582 | 49c multi | 1.00 | 1.00 |
| *a.* | | Strip of 3, #1849-1851 | 3.25 | 3.25 |
| | | *Nos. 1847-1851 (5)* | 4.50 | 4.50 |

### Booklet Stamps
### Self-Adhesive

*Die Cut Perf. 11½x11¾*

| | | | | |
|---|---|---|---|---|
| **1852** | A582 | 49c multi | 1.25 | .75 |
| **1853** | A582 | 49c multi | 1.25 | .75 |
| **1854** | A582 | 49c multi | 1.25 | .75 |
| *a.* | | Bklt., 4 ea #1852-1853, 2 #1854 | 14.50 | |

### Coil Stamps
### Self-Adhesive

*Serpentine Die Cut 11¾*

| | | | | |
|---|---|---|---|---|
| **1855** | A582 | 45c multi | 1.10 | .85 |
| **1856** | A582 | 45c multi | 1.10 | .85 |
| *a.* | | Pair, #1855-1856 | 3.00 | 3.00 |
| | | *Nos. 1852-1856 (5)* | 5.95 | 3.95 |

No. 1851 exists without Tasmania in the map of Australia at LL. Value $20.

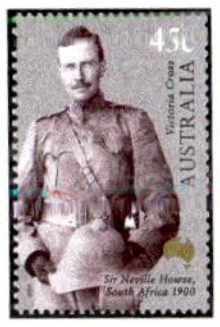

Australian Victoria Cross, Cent. — A583

Designs: No. 1857, Sir Neville Howse. No. 1858, Sir Arthur Roden Cutler. No. 1859, Victoria Cross. No. 1860, Edward Kenna. No. 1861, Keith Payne.

**2000, July 24** **Litho.** *Perf. 14¾x14*

| | | | | |
|---|---|---|---|---|
| **1857** | A583 | 45c multi | .95 | .75 |
| **1858** | A583 | 45c multi | .95 | .75 |
| **1859** | A583 | 45c multi | .95 | .75 |
| **1860** | A583 | 45c multi | .95 | .75 |
| **1861** | A583 | 45c multi | .95 | .75 |
| *a.* | | Horiz. strip of 5, #1857-1861 | 5.00 | 5.00 |
| | | *Nos. 1857-1861 (5)* | 4.75 | 3.75 |

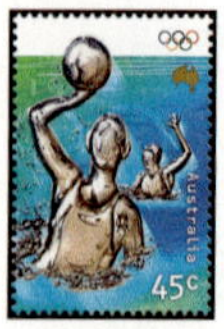

Olympic Sports — A584

Designs: Nos. 1862a, 1869, Water polo. Nos. 1862b, 1870, Women's field hockey. Nos. 1862c, 1863, Swimming. Nos. 1862d, 1865, Basketball. Nos. 1862e, 1866, Triathlon cycling. Nos. 1862f, 1871, Equestrian. Nos. 1862g, 1872, Tennis. Nos. 1862h, 1864, Rhythmic gymnastics. Nos. 1862i, 1867, Runner. Nos. 1862j, 1868, Rowing.

**2000, Aug. 17 Litho.** ***Perf. 14¾x14***

**1862** Sheet of 10 11.50 11.50
*a.-j.* A584 45c Any single .80 .80
*k.* As #1862, with inscription added in sheet margin 20.00 20.00

No. 1862k was issued 9/15/00 and has additional multicolored inscription in upper sheet margin reading "15-28 / September / 2000 / OLYMPHILEX 2000" and show emblem.

**Booklet Stamps**

**Self-Adhesive**

***Serpentine Die Cut 11½x11¼***

**1863** A584 45c multi 1.00 .70
**1864** A584 45c multi 1.00 .70
**1865** A584 45c multi 1.00 .70
**1866** A584 45c multi 1.00 .70
**1867** A584 45c multi 1.00 .70
**1868** A584 45c multi 1.00 .70
**1869** A584 45c multi 1.00 .70
**1870** A584 45c multi 1.00 .70
**1871** A584 45c multi 1.00 .70
**1872** A584 45c multi 1.00 .70
*a.* Booklet, #1863-1872 14.00
*Nos. 1863-1872 (10)* 10.00 7.00

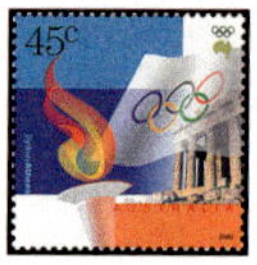

Sydney and Athens — A585

Olympic torch, flag and: 45c, Parthenon. $1.50, Sydney Opera House.

**2000, Sept. 15 Litho.** ***Perf. 14½x14***

**1873** A585 45c multi + label 1.00 .60
**1874** A585 $1.50 multi + label 2.40 2.40

Nos. 1873-1874 were issued in sheets of 20 stamps and 20 se-tenant labels. Labels were inscribed "Sydney Athens." These sheets could be ordered with personalized labels, as could sheets with a stock photo.

See Greece Nos. 1968-1969.

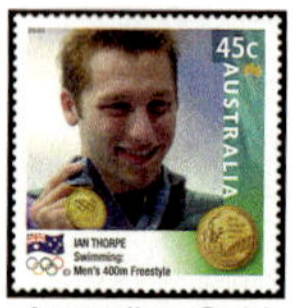

Australian Gold Medalists at 2000 Olympics A586

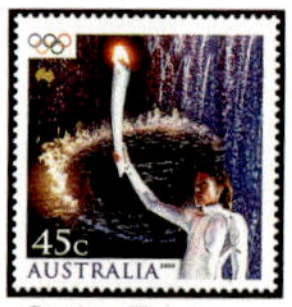

Cathy Freeman Lighting Olympic Flame A587

Medal Winners: Nos. 1875, 1891, Ian Thorpe. Nos. 1876, 1892, Men's 4x100-meter freestyle relay swimming team. Nos. 1877, 1893, Michael Diamond. Nos. 1878, 1894, Three day event equestrian team. Nos. 1879, 1895, Susie O'Neill. Nos. 1880, 1896, Men's 4x200-meter freestyle relay swimming team. Nos. 1881, 1897, Simon Fairweather. Nos. 1882, 1898, Brett Aitken, Scott McGrory. Nos. 1883, 1899, Grant Hackett. Nos. 1884, 1900, Women's water polo team. Nos. 1885, 1901, Natalie Cook, Kerri Pottharst. Nos. 1886, 1902, Cathy Freeman. Nos. 1887, 1903, Lauren Burns. Nos. 1888, 1904, Women's field hockey team. Nos. 1889, 1905, Jenny Armstrong, Belinda Stowell. Nos. 1890, 1906, Tom King, Mark Turnbull.

**2000 Digitally Printed** ***Perf. 14¼***

**1875** A586 45c multi 1.00 .80
**1876** A586 45c multi 1.00 .80
**1877** A586 45c multi 1.00 .80
**1878** A586 45c multi 1.00 .80
**1879** A586 45c multi 1.00 .80
**1880** A586 45c multi 1.00 .80
**1881** A586 45c multi 1.00 .80
**1882** A586 45c multi 1.00 .80
**1883** A586 45c multi 1.00 .80
**1884** A586 45c multi 1.00 .80
**1885** A586 45c multi 1.00 .80
**1886** A586 45c multi 1.00 .80
**1887** A586 45c multi 1.00 .80
**1888** A586 45c multi 1.00 .80
**1889** A586 45c multi 1.00 .80
**1890** A586 45c multi 1.00 .80

**Litho.**

**1891** A586 45c multi 1.10 1.10
**1892** A586 45c multi 1.10 1.10
**1893** A586 45c multi 1.10 1.10
**1894** A586 45c multi 1.10 1.10
**1895** A586 45c multi 1.10 1.10
**1896** A586 45c multi 1.10 1.10
**1897** A586 45c multi 1.10 1.10
**1898** A586 45c multi 1.10 1.10
**1899** A586 45c multi 1.10 1.10
**1900** A586 45c multi 1.10 1.10
**1901** A586 45c multi 1.10 1.10
**1902** A586 45c multi 1.10 1.10
**1903** A586 45c multi 1.10 1.10
**1904** A586 45c multi 1.10 1.10
**1905** A586 45c multi 1.10 1.10
**1906** A586 45c multi 1.10 1.10
**1907** A587 45c multi 1.60 1.60
*Nos. 1875-1907 (33)* 35.20 32.00

Issued: Nos. 1875-1876, 9/17; No. 1877, 9/18; Nos. 1891-1892, 9/19; Nos. 1878-1880, 1893, 9/20; No. 1881, 9/21; Nos. 1882, 1894-1896, 9/22; No. 1897, 9/23; Nos. 1883-1884, 1898, 9/24; Nos. 1885-1886, 1899-1900, 9/26; Nos. 1887, 1901-1902, 9/28; Nos. 1888, 1903, 9/30; Nos. 1889-1890, 10/1; No. 1904, 10/2; Nos. 1905-1906, 10/3; No. 1907, 10/10.

Nos. 1875-1890 have shinier appearance than Nos. 1891-1906. Olympic rings, flag stars and flag edge on Nos. 1875-1890 has a more ragged appearance than Nos. 1891-1906, which have crisp details.

Nos. 1875-1907 printed in sheets of 10. Sheets of Nos. 1875-1890 exist rouletted at either the right or left and have one of six red animal imprints in lower right margin representing where the sheets were made (Platypus, Sydney; Kookaburra, Canberra; Koala, Brisbane; Swan, Perth; Kangaroo, Adelaide; Opossum, Melbourne). Sheets of Nos. 1875-1890 were placed on sale at 67 outlets within 24 hours of the awarding of the medals to the athletes. Sheets of Nos. 1891-1906, which have a straight-edged right margin and a red Australia map imprint in lower right margin, gradually became available nationwide as stocks were printed and shipped.

A sheet containing Nos. 1891-1907 and 8 labels was available only in the Australia Post annual collection. Value, $50.

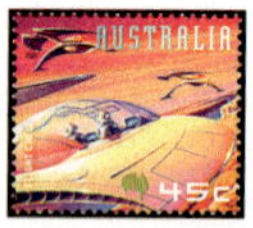

Space — A588

Designs: Nos. 1908, 1914a, Flight crew. Nos. 1909, 1914b, Robots, vert. Nos. 1910, 1914c, 1915, 1917, Astronaut, vert. Nos. 1911, 1914d, 1916, 1918, Terrain, vert. Nos. 1912, 1914e, Spacecraft. Nos. 1913, 1914f, Launch site, vert.

***Perf. 14x14½, 14½x14***

**2000, Oct. 3 Litho.**

**1908** A588 45c multi .95 .95
**1909** A588 45c multi .95 .95

**Size: 26x38mm**

**1910** A588 45c multi .95 .95
**1911** A588 45c multi .95 .95
*a.* Pair, #1910-1911 2.25 2.25

**Size: 50x30mm**

**1912** A588 45c multi .95 .95

**Size: 30x50mm**

**1913** A588 45c multi .95 .95
*Nos. 1908-1913 (6)* 5.70 5.70

**Souvenir Sheet**

**Litho. with Translucent Foil**

***Perf. 14½***

**1914** Sheet of 6 5.00 5.00
*a.-f.* A588 45c any single .80 .80
*g.* As #1914, ovptd. in margin in gold 14.00 14.00

**Booklet Stamps**

**Litho.**

**Self-Adhesive**

***Serpentine Die Cut 11½x11¼***

**1915** A588 45c multi 1.00 .60
**1916** A588 45c multi 1.00 .60
*a.* Booklet, 5 each #1915-1916 12.00

**Coil Stamps**

***Serpentine Die Cut 11½***

**1917** A588 45c multi 1.10 .60
**1918** A588 45c multi 1.10 .60
*a.* Pair, #1917-1918 2.50 2.00

Nos. 1915-1918 have pink and gray frames.

No 1914g overprinted with emblem of Hong Kong 2001 Stamp Exhibition. Issued 2/1/01.

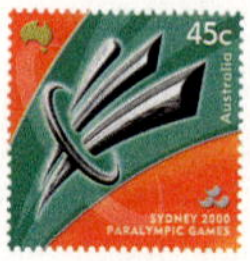

2000 Paralympics, Sydney — A589

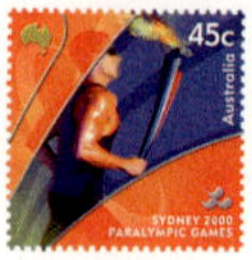

Designs: No. 1919, Paralympics emblem. No. 1920, Runner with torch.

**2000, Oct. 18 Litho.** ***Perf. 14½x14***

**1919** A589 45c multi + label 1.25 1.00
**1920** A589 45c multi + label 1.25 1.00

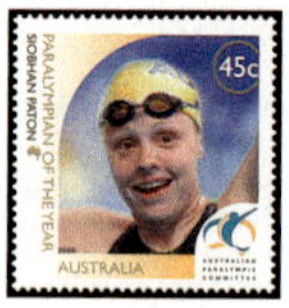

Siobhan Paton, Paralympian of the Year — A590

**2000, Oct. 31** ***Perf. 14¼***

**1921** A590 45c multi 1.00 .75

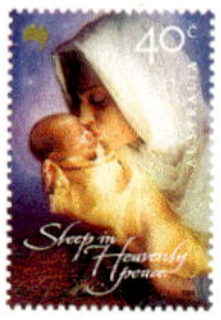

Christmas — A591

40c, Madonna and child. 45c, Manger.

**2000, Nov. 1 Litho.** ***Perf. 14½x14***

**1922** A591 40c multi .75 .50
**1923** A591 45c multi .75 .50
*a.* Souvenir sheet, #1922-1923 2.25 2.25

**Booklet Stamp**

***Serpentine Die Cut 11¾***

**1924** A591 40c multi .85 .70
*a.* Booklet of 20 + 20 stickers 17.25

**Tourist Attractions Type of 2000**

**2000, Nov. 1** ***Perf. 14½x14***

**1925** A581 80c Byron Bay 1.75 1.50

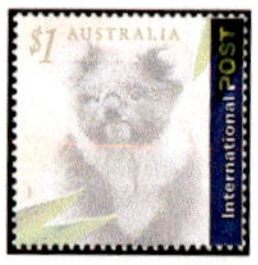

No. 1778 Digitally Overprinted in Dark Blue

**2001, Jan. Litho.** ***Perf. 14½x14***

**1926** A564 $1 multi + label *17.50 17.50*

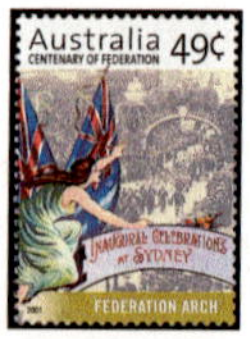

Federation of Australia, Cent. — A592

Designs: Nos. 1927, 1931, Federation Arch, Sydney. Nos. 1928, 1932, Sir Edmund Barton, first prime minister. No. 1929, National celebrations, horiz (50x30mm). No. 1930, State banquet (30x50mm).

***Perf. 14¾x14, 14x14¾***

**2001, Jan. 1 Litho.**

**1927** A592 49c multi 1.00 .80
**1928** A592 49c multi 1.00 .80
*a.* Pair, #1927-1928 3.00 2.50
**1929** A592 $2 multi 3.25 2.75
**1930** A592 $2 multi 3.25 2.75
*a.* Souvenir sheet, #1927-1930, perf. 14½ 10.00 10.00
*Nos. 1927-1930 (4)* 8.50 7.10

**Self-Adhesive**

**Booklet Stamps**

***Serpentine Die Cut 11½x11***

**1931** A592 49c multi 1.00 .30
*a.* Serpentine die cut 11½x11¾ — —
**1932** A592 49c multi 1.00 .30
*a.* Booklet, 5 each # 1931-1932 11.50

**Australian Legends Type of 1997**

Slim Dusty, musician: Nos. 1933, 1935, With guitar. Nos. 1934, 1936, Wearing blue shirt.

**2001, Jan. 25** ***Perf. 14x14¾***

**Size: 34x26mm**

**1933** A522 45c multi 1.10 1.00
**1934** A522 45c multi 1.10 1.00
*a.* Pair, #1933-1934 2.50 2.00
*b.* Booklet pane, #1933-1934 *3.00* —

**Self-Adhesive**

**Booklet Stamps**

***Serpentine Die Cut 11x11½***

**1935** A522 45c multi 1.10 .75
**1936** A522 45c multi 1.10 .75
*a.* Booklet, 5 each #1935-1936 11.50
*Nos. 1933-1936 (4)* 4.40 3.50

No. 1934b issued 1/24/07.

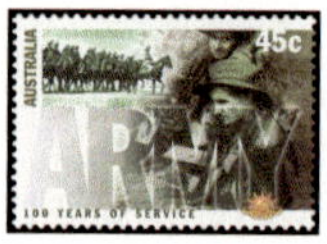

Australian Army, Cent. — A593

Rising Sun badge and: No. 1937, Light Horse Brigade, 1940, soldiers in New Guinea, 1943. No. 1938, Soldier in UN peacekeeping mission carrying Rwandan child, 1995, soldiers on commando officer selection course, 1997.

**2001-05** ***Perf. 14x14¾***

**1937** A593 45c multi 1.10 .75
**1938** A593 45c multi 1.10 .75
*a.* Pair, #1937-1938 2.50 2.00
*b.* Booklet pane, #1937-1938 *16.00* —
Complete booklet, #1176a, 1207a, 1256a, 1317a, 1380f, 1452a, 1454a, 1482a, 1938b 100.00

Issued: Nos. 1937-1938, 2/15/01. No. 1938b, 4/05. Complete booklet sold for $14.95.

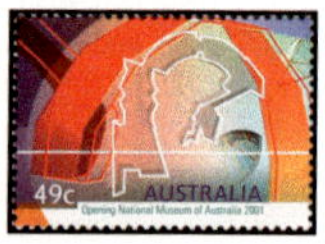

Opening of National Museum, Canberra — A594

Designs: No. 1939, Museum floor plan. No. 1940, Pangk (wallaby sculpture), by George MacNaught and Joe Ngallametta.

**2001, Mar. 8**

**1939** A594 49c multi 1.00 .85
*a.* Additionally dated "2013" (#1940c) 1.10 1.10
**1940** A594 49c multi 1.00 .85
*a.* Pair, #1939-1940 2.25 2.00
*b.* Additionally dated "2013" (#1940c) 1.10 1.10
*c.* Booklet pane of 2, #1939a, 1940b 2.25 —

Issued: Nos. 1939a, 1940b, 1940c, 3/5/13. No. 1938d was issued in booklet along with Nos. 2710c, 2869e, 3107c, 3349b and 3877a.

**Australian Legends Type of 1997**

Similar to Nos. 1575-1576, but with cropped designs and "1908-2001" inscription added.

**2001, Mar. 13** ***Perf. 14¼***

**1941** A522 45c Like #1575 1.00 .80
*a.* Without gold highlights, dated "2007" 1.40 1.40
**1942** A522 45c Like #1576 .80 .80
*a.* Pair, #1941-1942 2.25 2.00
*b.* Without gold highlights, dated "2007" 1.40 1.40

Nos. 1941a, 1942b issued 11/14/07.

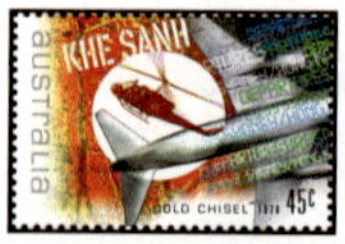

Rock Music — A595

Designs: Nos. 1943a, 1953, Khe Sanh, by Cold Chisel, 1978. Nos. 1943b, 1952, Down Under, by Men at Work, 1981. Nos. 1943c, 1951, Power and the Passion, by Midnight Oil, 1983. Nos. 1943d, 1950, Original Sin, by INXS. Nos. 1943e, 1949, You're the Voice, by John Farnham, 1986. Nos. 1943f, 1948, Don't Dream It's Over, by Crowded House, 1986. Nos. 1943g, 1947, Treaty, by Yothu Yindi, 1991. Nos. 1943h, 1946, Tomorrow, by Silverchair, 1994. Nos. 1943i, 1945, Confide in

Me, by Kylie Minogue, 1994. Nos. 1943j, 1944, Truly, Madly, Deeply, by Savage Garden, 1997.

**2001, Mar. 20 Litho. *Perf. 14x14¾***

**1943** Sheet of 10 10.00 10.00
*a.-j.* A595 45c Any single 1.00 .80

**Self-Adhesive**

***Serpentine Die Cut 11¼x11½***

**1944** A595 45c multi 1.00 .80
**1945** A595 45c multi 1.00 .80
**1946** A595 45c multi 1.00 .80
**1947** A595 45c multi 1.00 .80
**1948** A595 45c multi 1.00 .80
**1949** A595 45c multi 1.00 .80
**1950** A595 45c multi 1.00 .80
**1951** A595 45c multi 1.00 .80
**1952** A595 45c multi 1.00 .80
**1953** A595 45c multi 1.00 .80
*a.* Horiz. strip of 10, #1944-1953 14.50
*b.* Booklet, #1944-1953 10.00
*Nos. 1944-1953 (10)* 10.00 8.00

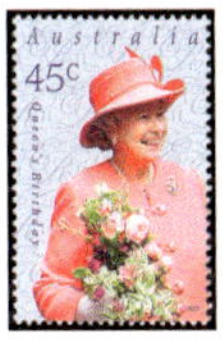
Queen Elizabeth II, 75th Birthday — A596

**2001, Apr. 12 Litho. *Perf. 14¾x14***

**1954** A596 45c multi 1.00 .75

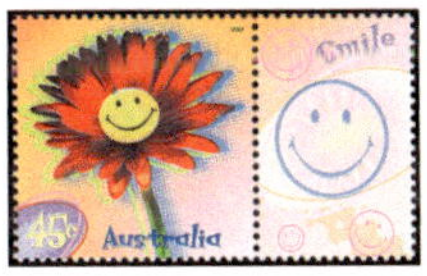
Flower A597

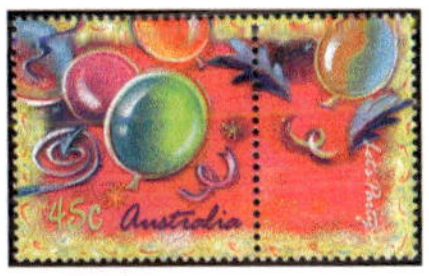
Balloons A598

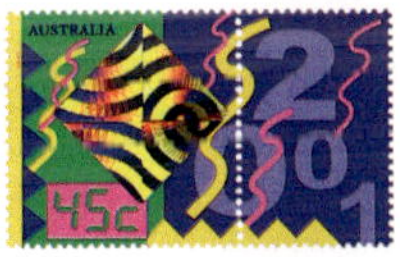
Streamers A599

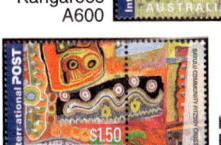

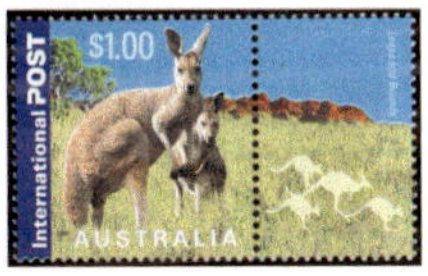
Kangaroos A600

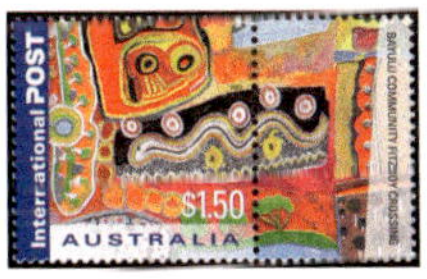
Bayulu Banner A601

**Litho., Litho with Hologram (#1957)**

**2001-03 *Perf. 14½x14***

**1955** A597 45c multi + label .80 .80
**1956** A598 45c multi + label .80 .80
**1957** A599 45c multi + label .80 .80
**1958** A600 $1 multi + label 2.00 1.60
*a.* Booklet pane of 4 + 4 labels 8.75 —
Complete booklet, 2 #1958a 22.00
**1959** A601 $1.50 multi + label 2.50 2.50
*Nos. 1955-1959 (5)* 6.90 6.50

Issued: Nos. 1955-1959, 4/24/01. No. 1958a, 10/31/03.

The complete booklet, which sold for $10.95, contains two panes of No. 1958a with different margins.

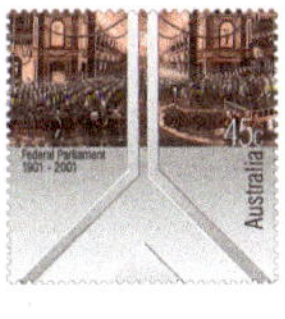
Federal Parliament, Cent. — A602

Designs: No. 1960, The Opening of the First Federal Parliament, 9 May 1901, by Charles Nuttall. No. 1961, Opening of the First Parliament of the Commonwealth of Australia by H.R.H. The Duke of Cornwall and York (Later King George V), May 9, 1901, by Tom Roberts.

**2001, May 3 Litho. *Perf. 14¼***

**1960** A602 45c multi 1.00 .65
*a.* Souvenir sheet of 1 2.00 2.00
**1961** A602 $2.45 multi 4.00 4.00
*a.* Souvenir sheet of 1 5.50 5.50

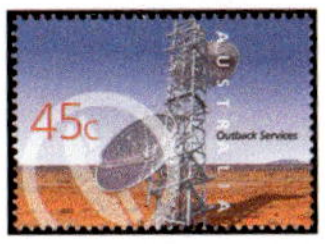
Outback Services — A603

Designs: Nos. 1962, 1967, 1972, Telecommunications. Nos. 1963, 1968, 1973, Transport. Nos. 1964, 1969, 1974, School of the Air. Nos. 1965, 1970, 1975, Postal service. Nos., 1966, 1971, 1976, Royal flying Doctor Service.

**2001, June 5 *Perf. 14x14½***

**1962** A603 45c multi 1.00 .75
**1963** A603 45c multi 1.00 .75
**1964** A603 45c multi 1.00 .75
**1965** A603 45c multi 1.00 .75
**1966** A603 45c multi 1.00 .75
*a.* Horiz. strip, #1962-1966 5.00 4.75
*Nos. 1962-1966 (5)* 5.00 3.75

**Self-Adhesive**

**Coil Stamps**

***Serpentine Die Cut 11¼***

**1967** A603 45c multi 1.25 .95
**1968** A603 45c multi 1.25 .95
**1969** A603 45c multi 1.25 .95
**1970** A603 45c multi 1.25 .95
**1971** A603 45c multi 1.25 .95
*a.* Horiz. strip, #1967-1971 8.00

**Booklet Stamps**

***Serpentine Die Cut 11¾***

**1972** A603 45c multi 1.00 .75
**1973** A603 45c multi 1.00 .75
**1974** A603 45c multi 1.00 .75
**1975** A603 45c multi 1.00 .75
**1976** A603 45c multi 1.00 .75
*a.* Booklet, 2 each #1972-1976 11.00
*Nos. 1967-1976 (10)* 11.25 8.50

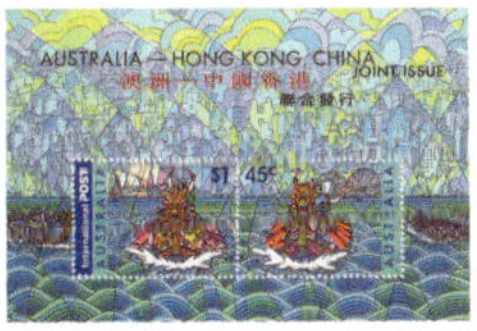

Dragon Boat Races — A604

Dragon boats and: 45c, Hong Kong Convention and Exhibition Center. $1, Sydney Opera House.

**2001, June 25 *Perf. 14x14½***

**1977** 45c multi 1.10 .85
**1978** $1 multi 2.25 2.25
*a.* A604 Souvenir sheet, #1977-1978 3.50 3.50

See Hong Kong Nos. 938-939.

**Tourist Attraction Type of 2000**

Designs: 50c, Blue Mountains. $1, Murrumbidgee River. $1.50, Port Douglas. $20, Uluru.

**Litho., Litho with Foil Application ($20)**

**2001, July 12 *Perf. 14½x14***

**1979** A581 50c multi 1.00 1.00
**1980** A581 $1 multi 2.00 2.00
**1981** A581 $1.50 multi 3.00 3.00

**Size: 56x25mm**

***Perf. 14x14½***

**1982** A581 $20 multi 24.00 24.00
*Nos. 1979-1982 (4)* 30.00 30.00

**Booklet Stamp**

**Self-Adhesive**

***Serpentine Die Cut 11¼x10½***

**1983** A581 50c multi 1.10 1.00
*a.* Booklet, 10 #1983 11.50

**Flora & Fauna Type of 1996**

Birds: Nos. 1984, 1988, 1992, Variegated fairy wren. Nos. 1985, 1989, 1993, Painted firetail. Nos. 1986, 1990, 1994, Crimson chat. Nos. 1987, 1991, 1995, Budgerigar.

**2001-02 Litho. *Perf. 14x14½***

**1984** A511 45c multi 1.00 .75
**1985** A511 45c multi 1.00 .75
**1986** A511 45c multi 1.00 .75
**1987** A511 45c multi 1.00 .75
*a.* Block of 4, #1984-1987 4.25 4.25
*Nos. 1984-1987 (4)* 4.00 3.00

**Self-Adhesive**

**Coil Stamps**

***Die Cut Perf. 12½x12¾***

**1988** A511 45c multi 1.25 .75
**1989** A511 45c multi 1.25 .75
**1990** A511 45c multi 1.25 .75
**1991** A511 45c multi 1.25 .75
*a.* Horiz. strip of 4, #1988-1991 5.25 5.25

**Booklet Stamps**

***Serpentine Die Cut 11¼***

**1992** A511 45c multi 1.25 .75
**1993** A511 45c multi 1.25 .75
**1994** A511 45c multi 1.25 .75
**1995** A511 45c multi 1.25 .75
*a.* Booklet pane, #1993, 1995 4.50
*b.* Booklet pane, #1992-1995, rouletted at bottom 7.50
Booklet, #1995a, 2 #1995b 12.00
*c.* Booklet pane, #1992-1995, rouletted at side 15.00
Booklet, 5 #1995c 85.00
*d.* Pane, #1992-1994, 2 #1995 9.50
*e.* Coil strip, #1992-1995 5.50
*f.* As "d," with Philakorea 2002 ovpt. in margin ('02) 15.00
*g.* As "d," with China 2002 Stamp & Coin Expo ovpt. in margin ('02) 15.00
*h.* As "d," with Hafnia '01 ovpt. in margin 27.50
*Nos. 1988-1995 (8)* 10.00 6.00

Issued: No. 1995f, 8/2/02; No. 1995g, 9/28/02. No. 1995h, 10/16/01. Rest of set, 8/9/01.

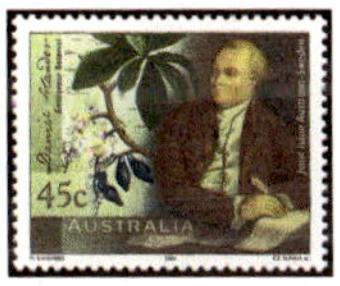
Daniel Solander (1733-82), Botanist on Endeavour A605

Designs: 45c, Barringtonia calyptrata and Solander. $1.50, Cochlospermum gillivraei and Endeavour.

***Perf. 12½x12¾***

**2001, Aug. 16 Litho. & Engr.**

**1996** A605 45c multi 1.25 .90
**1997** A605 $1.50 multi 3.25 3.25

See Sweden No. 2419.

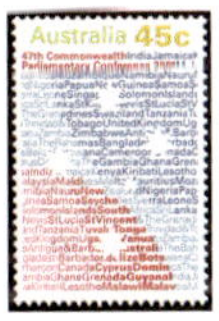
Commonwealth Heads of Government Meeting, Brisbane — A606

**2001, Sept. 4 Litho. *Perf. 14½x14***

**1998** A606 45c Southern Cross 1.00 .75
**1999** A606 45c Australia on globe 1.00 .75
*a.* Pair, #1998-1999 2.25 2.25

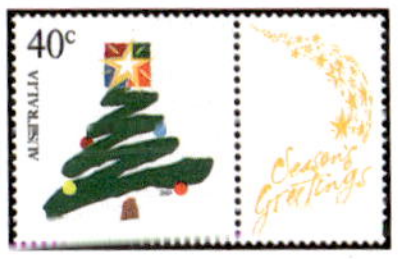
Christmas A607

**2001, Sept. 4 *Perf. 14½x14***

**Stamp + Label**

**2000** A607 40c Christmas tree .85 .70
**2001** A607 80c Star 1.60 1.60

Nos. 2000-2001 were each printed in sheets of 20 + 20 labels. The labels could be personalized.

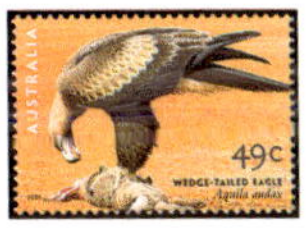
Birds of Prey — A608

Designs: No. 2002, Wedge-tailed eagle. No. 2003, Nankeen kestrel. No. 2004, Red goshawk, vert. No. 2005, Spotted harrier, vert.

***Perf. 14x14½, 14½x14***

**2001, Sept. 11**

**2002** A608 49c multi 1.00 .80
**2003** A608 49c multi 1.00 .80
*a.* Pair, #2002-2003 2.50 2.50
**2004** A608 98c multi 1.60 1.60
**2005** A608 98c multi 1.60 1.60
*a.* Pair, #2004-2005 4.00 2.50
*Nos. 2002-2005 (4)* 5.20 4.80

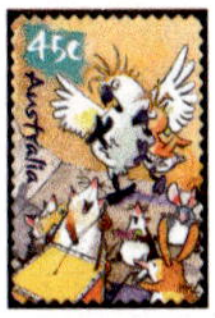
Caricatures of Australian Wildlife by Roland Harvey — A609

Designs: Nos. 2006, 2012, Bilby and antechinus musicians, dancing cockatoo. Nos. 2007, 2013, Koala with birthday cake. Nos. 2008, 2014, Ring-tailed possums with drinks and food. Nos. 2009, 2015, Bilbies, crocodile, emu, koala and gifts. Nos. 2010, 2016, Wombat and ladder. Nos. 2011, 2017, Wallabies, echidnas, platypus and ladder.

**2001, Oct. 2 *Perf. 14½x14***

**2006** A609 45c multi 1.00 .80
**2007** A609 45c multi 1.00 .80
**2008** A609 45c multi 1.00 .80
*a.* Horiz. strip of 3, #2006-2008 3.00 3.00
*b.* Souvenir sheet, #2006-2008 3.50 3.50
**2009** A609 45c multi 1.00 .80
**2010** A609 45c multi 1.00 .80
**2011** A609 45c multi 1.00 .80
*a.* Horiz. strip, #2009-2011 3.00 3.00
*b.* Souvenir sheet, #2009-2011 3.00 3.00
*Nos. 2006-2011 (6)* 6.00 4.80

**Self-Adhesive**

***Serpentine Die Cut 11½x11***

**2012** A609 45c multi 1.00 .80
**2013** A609 45c multi 1.00 .80
**2014** A609 45c multi 1.00 .80
**2015** A609 45c multi 1.00 .80
**2016** A609 45c multi 1.00 .80
**2017** A609 45c multi 1.00 .80
*a.* Coil strip, 2012-2017 7.50
*b.* Booklet, #2014-2015, 2 each #2012-2013, 2016-2017 12.00
*Nos. 2012-2017 (6)* 6.00 4.80

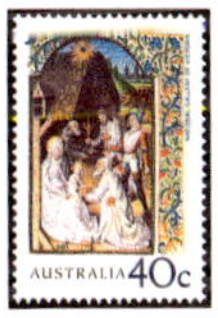
Christmas — A610

Illuminations from the Wharncliffe Hours, by Maitre Francois: 40c, Adoration of the Magi. 45c, Flight into Egypt.

**2001, Nov. 1 *Perf. 14½x14***

**2018** A610 40c multi 1.00 .60
**2019** A610 45c multi 1.25 .65

**Self-Adhesive**

***Serpentine Die Cut 11½x11¼***

**2020** A610 40c multi 1.10 .25
*a.* Booklet of 20 + 20 labels 22.00

**Australian Legends Type of 1997**

Medical researchers: Nos. 2021, 2026, Sir Gustav Nossal. Nos. 2022, 2027, Nancy Mills. No. 2023, 2028, Peter Doherty. Nos. 2024, 2029, Fiona Stanley. Nos. 2025, 2030, Donald Metcalf.

**2002, Jan. 23 Litho. *Perf. 14x14¾***

**Size: 34x26mm**

**2021** A522 45c multi .95 .75
**2022** A522 45c multi .95 .75
**2023** A522 45c multi .95 .75
**2024** A522 45c multi .95 .75
**2025** A522 45c multi .95 .75
*a.* Vert. strip, #2021-2025 5.00 5.00
*b.* Booklet pane, #2021-2025 8.00 8.00
*Nos. 2021-2025 (5)* 4.75 3.75

**Booklet Stamps**

**Self-Adhesive**

***Serpentine Die Cut 11x11½***

**2026** A522 45c multi 1.00 1.00
**2027** A522 45c multi 1.00 1.00
**2028** A522 45c multi 1.00 1.00
**2029** A522 45c multi 1.00 1.00
**2030** A522 45c multi 1.00 1.00
*a.* Booklet, 2 each #2026-2030 12.50
*Nos. 2026-2030 (5)* 5.00 5.00

No. 2025b issued 1/24/07.

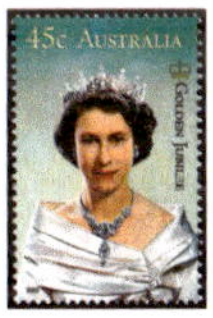
Reign of Queen Elizabeth II, 50th Anniv. — A611

Queen: 45c, As young woman. $2.45, In 2000.

**2002, Feb. 6** *Perf. 14¾x14*

| | | |
|---|---|---|
| **2031** A611 45c multi | .95 | .70 |
| **2032** A611 $2.45 multi | 5.00 | 5.00 |
| *a.* Souvenir sheet, #2031-2032 | 6.25 | 6.25 |

A booklet pane containing 2 each of Nos. 2031-2032 is found in the booklet footnoted under No. 2507.

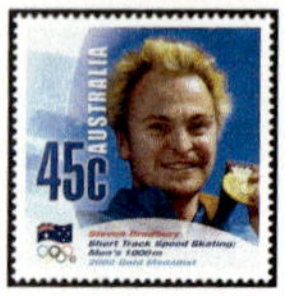

Gold Medalists at 2002 Winter Olympics, Salt Lake City — A612

Designs: No. 2033, Steven Bradbury. No. 2034, Alisa Camplin.

**2002** *Perf. 14¼*

| | | |
|---|---|---|
| **2033** A612 45c multi | 1.10 | 1.00 |
| **2034** A612 45c multi | 1.10 | 1.00 |

Issued: No. 2033, 2/20; No. 2034, 2/22.

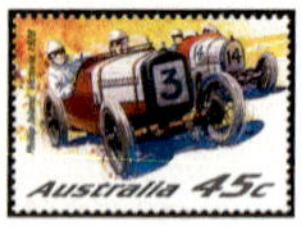

Race Cars — A613

Designs: Nos. 2035, 2041, Victoria Austin 7 and Bugatti Type 40, Phillip Island, Victoria, 1928. Nos. 2036, 2042, Jaguar Mark II, Mallala, South Australia, 1963. Nos. 2037, 2043, Repco-Brabham, Sandown, Victoria, 1966. Nos. 2038, 2044, Holden Torana XU1 and Ford Falcon XY GTHO, Bathurst, New South Wales, 1972. Nos. 2039, 2045, Williams FW07 Ford, Calder, Victoria, 1980. Nos. 2040, 2046, Benetton-Renault, Albert Park, Victoria, 2001.

**2002, Feb. 27** *Perf. 14x14¾*

| | | |
|---|---|---|
| **2035** A613 45c multi | 1.00 | .75 |
| **2036** A613 45c multi | 1.00 | .75 |
| **2037** A613 45c multi | 1.00 | .75 |
| **2038** A613 45c multi | 1.00 | .75 |
| **2039** A613 45c multi | 1.00 | .75 |
| **2040** A613 45c multi | 1.00 | .75 |
| *a.* Block of 6, #2035-2040 | 7.00 | 7.00 |
| *Nos. 2035-2040 (6)* | 6.00 | 4.50 |

**Self-Adhesive**

***Serpentine Die Cut 11¼x11½***

| | | |
|---|---|---|
| **2041** A613 45c multi | 1.00 | .80 |
| **2042** A613 45c multi | 1.00 | .80 |
| **2043** A613 45c multi | 1.00 | .80 |
| **2044** A613 45c multi | 1.00 | .80 |
| **2045** A613 45c multi | 1.00 | .80 |
| **2046** A613 45c multi | 1.00 | .80 |
| *a.* Coil strip, #2041-2046 | 9.00 | |
| *b.* Booklet, #2045-2046, 2 each #2041-2044 | 10.00 | |
| *Nos. 2041-2046 (6)* | 6.00 | 4.80 |

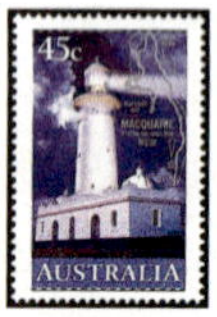

Lighthouses and Maps — A614

Designs: 45c, Macquarie, New South Wales. Nos. 2048, 2051, Troubridge Island, South Australia. Nos. 2049, 2052, Cape Naturaliste, Western Australia. $1.50, Cape Bruny, Tasmania.

**2002, Mar. 12** *Perf. 14½x14*

| | | |
|---|---|---|
| **2047** A614 45c multi | 1.40 | .60 |
| *a.* Booklet pane of 4 | 5.75 | — |
| **2048** A614 49c multi | 1.40 | .90 |
| *a.* Booklet pane of 2 | 2.75 | — |
| **2049** A614 49c multi | 1.40 | .90 |
| *a.* Horiz. pair, #2048-2049 | 2.75 | 2.00 |
| *b.* Booklet pane of 2 | 2.75 | — |
| **2050** A614 $1.50 multi | 2.25 | 2.00 |
| *a.* Booklet pane of 2 | 7.00 | — |
| *b.* Booklet pane, #2047-2050 | 7.75 | — |
| Booklet, #2047a, 2048a, 2049b, 2050a, 2050b | 25.75 | |

**Booklet Stamps**

**Self-Adhesive**

***Serpentine Die Cut 11¾***

| | | |
|---|---|---|
| **2051** A614 49c multi | 1.00 | .50 |
| **2052** A614 49c multi | 1.00 | .50 |
| *a.* Booklet, 5 each #2051-2052 | 13.50 | |
| *Nos. 2047-2052 (6)* | 8.45 | 5.40 |

Booklet containing Nos. 2047a-2050b sold for $9.95.

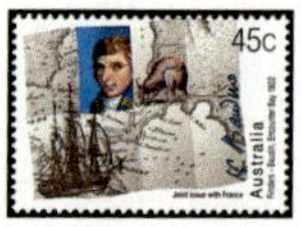

Encounter of Matthew Flinders and Nicolas Baudin, Bicent. — A615

Map, ship and: 45c, Baudin and kangaroo. $1.50, Flinders and Port Lincoln parrot.

**2002, Apr. 4** *Perf. 14x14¾*

| | | |
|---|---|---|
| **2053** A615 45c multi | 1.25 | .75 |
| **2054** A615 $1.50 multi | 2.50 | 2.10 |

See France Nos. 2882-2883.

**Tourist Attractions Type of 2000**

Designs: 50c, Walker Flat. $1, Mt. Roland. $1.50, Cape Leveque.

**2002, May 1** *Perf. 14½x14*

| | | |
|---|---|---|
| **2055** A581 50c multi | 1.10 | 1.00 |
| **2056** A581 $1 multi | 2.25 | 2.25 |
| **2057** A581 $1.50 multi | 3.25 | 3.25 |

**Booklet Stamps**

**Self-Adhesive**

***Serpentine Die Cut 11¼x10½***

| | | |
|---|---|---|
| **2058** A581 50c multi | 1.40 | .85 |
| **2059** A581 $1 multi | 2.25 | 2.00 |
| *a.* Booklet, 6 #2058, 4 #2059 | 18.00 | |
| *Nos. 2055-2059 (5)* | 10.25 | 9.35 |

**Flora & Fauna Type of 1996**

Designs: 50c, Desert star flower. $1, Bilby. $1.50, Thorny devil. $2, Great Sandy Desert.

**2002, June 4 Litho.** *Perf. 14x14½*

| | | |
|---|---|---|
| **2060** A511 50c multi | .75 | .55 |
| **2061** A511 $1 multi | 1.50 | 1.25 |
| **2062** A511 $1.50 multi | 2.25 | 1.75 |

***Perf. 14½x14***

**Size: 50x30mm**

| | | |
|---|---|---|
| **2063** A511 $2 multi | 3.00 | 2.40 |
| *Nos. 2060-2063 (4)* | 7.50 | 5.95 |

See Nos. 2112-2114 for self-adhesive versions of 50c stamp.

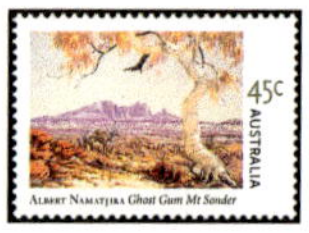

Paintings by Albert Namatjira (1902-59) — A616

Designs: Nos. 2064, 2068, Ghost Gum Mt. Sonder, MacDonnel Ranges. Nos. 2065, 2069, Mt. Hermannsburg. Nos. 2066, 2070, Glen Helen Country. Nos. 2067, 2071, Simpsons Gap.

**2002, July 2 Litho.** *Perf. 14x14¾*

| | | |
|---|---|---|
| **2064** A616 45c multi | .95 | .75 |
| *a.* Booklet pane of 4 | 4.00 | 4.00 |
| **2065** A616 45c multi | .95 | .75 |
| *a.* Booklet pane of 4 | 4.00 | 4.00 |
| **2066** A616 45c multi | .95 | .75 |
| *a.* Booklet pane of 4 | 4.00 | 4.00 |
| **2067** A616 45c multi | .95 | .75 |
| *a.* Block of 4, #2064-2067 | 4.25 | 3.75 |
| *b.* Souvenir sheet of 4, #2064-2067 | 4.25 | 3.75 |
| *c.* Booklet pane of 4 | 4.00 | 4.00 |
| *d.* Booklet pane, #2067b | 4.25 | 4.25 |
| Booklet, #2064a, 2065a, 2066a, 2067c, 2067d | 20.75 | |
| *Nos. 2064-2067 (4)* | 3.80 | 3.00 |

***Serpentine Die Cut 11x11½***

**Self-Adhesive**

| | | |
|---|---|---|
| **2068** A616 45c multi | 1.00 | .75 |
| **2069** A616 45c multi | 1.00 | .75 |
| **2070** A616 45c multi | 1.00 | .75 |
| **2071** A616 45c multi | 1.00 | .75 |
| *a.* Booklet pane of 10, 3 each #2068-2069, 2 each #2070-2071 | 10.00 | |
| *b.* Coil strip of 4, #2068-2071 | 4.50 | |
| *Nos. 2068-2071 (4)* | 4.00 | 3.00 |

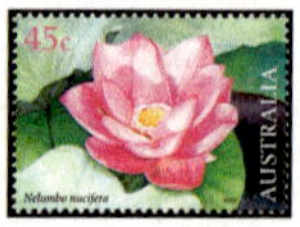

Australia — Thailand Diplomatic Relations, 50th Anniv. — A617

Designs: 45c, Nelumbo nucifera. $1, Nymphaea immutabilis.

**2002, Aug. 6 Litho.** *Perf. 14x14½*

| | | |
|---|---|---|
| **2072** A617 45c multi | 1.00 | .75 |
| **2073** A617 $1 multi | 2.25 | 2.00 |
| *a.* Souvenir sheet, #2072-2073 | 3.25 | 2.75 |
| *b.* As "a," overprinted in gold in margin | 8.50 | 8.50 |

Overprint on margin of No. 2073b has IFSDA and APTA emblems and text reading "50th Anniversary International Federation / of Stamp Dealers Associations."

See Thailand Nos. 2028-2029.

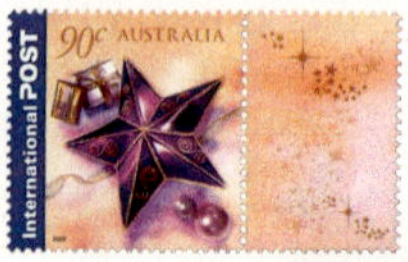

Christmas A618

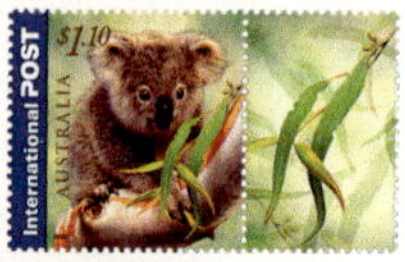

Koala A619

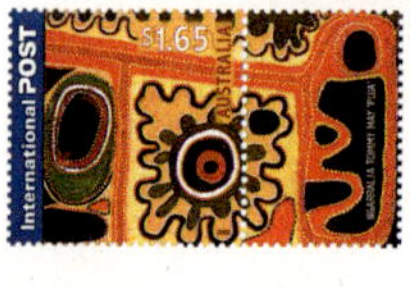

Puja, by Ngarralja Tommy May — A620

**2002** *Perf. 14¼x14*

| | | |
|---|---|---|
| **2074** A618 90c multi + label | 1.90 | 1.90 |
| **2075** A619 $1.10 multi + label | 2.25 | 2.25 |
| **2076** A620 $1.65 multi + label | 3.50 | 3.50 |
| *a.* Booklet pane of 4 + 4 labels | 13.75 | — |
| Complete booklet, 3 #2076a | 50.00 | |
| *Nos. 2074-2076 (3)* | 7.65 | 7.65 |

Issued: 2074-2076, 8/23. No. 2076a, 10/31.

Nos. 2074-2076 were each printed in sheets of 20 stamps + 20 labels. Labels on some sheets could be personalized for an additional fee.

The complete booklet, which sold for $20.75, contains three panes of No. 2076a with different margins.

**Tourist Attractions Type of 2000**

Designs: $1.10, Coonawarra. $1.65, Gariwerd-Grampians Natl. Park. $2.20, National Library. $3.30, Cape York.

**2002, Aug. 23 Litho.** *Perf. 14½x14*

| | | |
|---|---|---|
| **2077** A581 $1.10 multi | 2.25 | 2.25 |
| **2078** A581 $1.65 multi | 3.50 | 3.50 |
| **2079** A581 $2.20 multi | 4.50 | 4.50 |
| **2080** A581 $3.30 multi | 7.00 | 6.00 |
| *Nos. 2077-2080 (4)* | 17.25 | 16.25 |

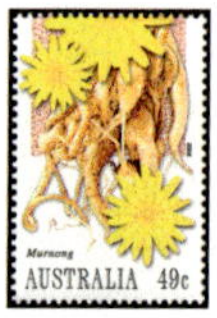

Aboriginal Food Plants — A621

Designs: Nos. 2081, 2088, Murnong. Nos. 2082, 2087, Acacia seeds. Nos. 2083, 2086, Quandong. Nos. 2084, 2090, Honey grevillea. Nos. 2085, 2089, Lilly-pilly.

**2002, Sept. 3 Litho.** *Perf. 14¾x14*

| | | |
|---|---|---|
| **2081** A621 49c multi | 1.00 | .75 |
| **2082** A621 49c multi | 1.00 | .75 |
| **2083** A621 49c multi | 1.00 | .75 |
| **2084** A621 49c multi | 1.00 | .75 |
| **2085** A621 49c multi | 1.00 | .75 |
| *a.* Horiz. strip of 5, #2081-2085 | 5.00 | 4.75 |
| *b.* Tete beche block of 10, 2 each # 2081-2085 | 10.00 | 11.50 |
| *Nos. 2081-2085 (5)* | 5.00 | 3.75 |

**Booklet Stamps**

**Self-Adhesive**

***Serpentine Die Cut 11¾***

| | | |
|---|---|---|
| **2086** A621 49c multi | 1.00 | .80 |
| **2087** A621 49c multi | 1.00 | .80 |
| **2088** A621 49c multi | 1.00 | .80 |
| **2089** A621 49c multi | 1.00 | .80 |
| **2090** A621 49c multi | 1.00 | .80 |
| *a.* Booklet pane, 2 each #2086-2090 | 11.00 | |
| *Nos. 2086-2090 (5)* | 5.00 | 4.00 |

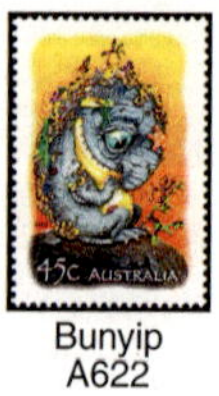

Bunyip A622

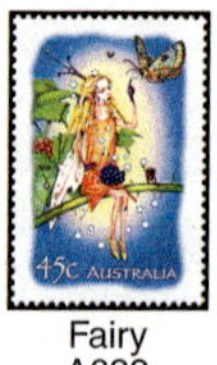

Fairy A623

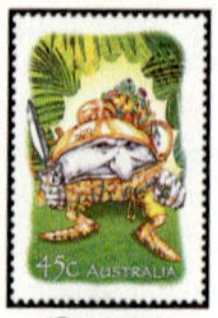

Gnome A624

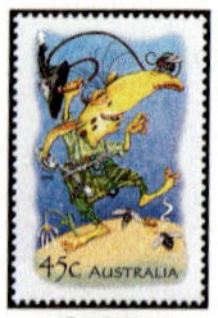

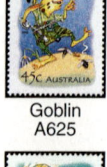

Goblin A625

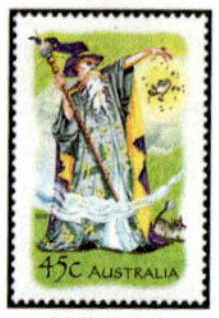

Wizard A626

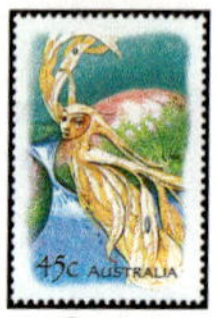

Sprite A627

**2002, Sept. 25** *Perf. 14¾x14*

| | | |
|---|---|---|
| **2091** A622 45c multi | 1.00 | .75 |
| **2092** A623 45c multi | 1.00 | .75 |
| **2093** A624 45c multi | 1.00 | .75 |
| *a.* Horiz. strip of 3, #2091-2093 | 3.00 | 3.00 |
| **2094** A625 45c multi | 1.00 | .75 |
| **2095** A626 45c multi | 1.00 | .75 |
| **2096** A627 45c multi | 1.00 | .75 |
| *a.* Horiz. strip of 3, #2094-2096 | 3.00 | 3.00 |
| *b.* Souvenir sheet, #2091-2096 | 6.50 | 6.50 |
| *Nos. 2091-2096 (6)* | 6.00 | 4.50 |

**Self-Adhesive**

***Serpentine Die Cut 11½x11***

| | | |
|---|---|---|
| **2097** A622 45c multi | 1.00 | .75 |
| **2098** A623 45c multi | 1.00 | .75 |
| **2099** A624 45c multi | 1.00 | .75 |
| **2100** A625 45c multi | 1.00 | .75 |
| **2101** A626 45c multi | 1.00 | .75 |
| **2102** A627 45c multi | 1.00 | .75 |
| *a.* Vert. coil strip of 6, #2097-2102 | 6.00 | |
| *b.* Booklet pane, #2097, 2102, 2 each #2098-2101 | 10.00 | |
| *Nos. 2097-2102 (6)* | 6.00 | 4.50 |

Characters from The Magic Rainforest, by John Marsden.

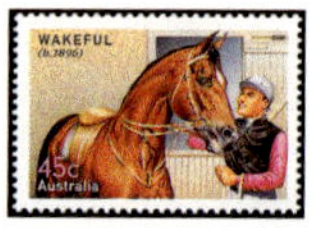

Race Horses — A628

**2002, Oct. 15 Litho.** *Perf. 14x14½*

| | | |
|---|---|---|
| **2103** A628 45c Wakeful | 1.00 | .75 |
| **2104** A628 45c Rising Fast | 1.00 | .75 |
| **2105** A628 45c Manikato | 1.00 | .75 |
| **2106** A628 45c Might and Power | 1.00 | .75 |
| **2107** A628 45c Sunline | 1.00 | .75 |
| *a.* Horiz. strip of 5, #2103-2107 | 5.25 | 5.25 |
| *Nos. 2103-2107 (5)* | 5.00 | 3.75 |

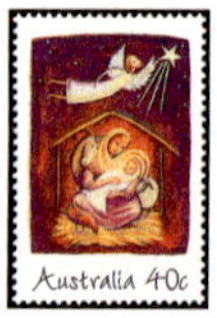

Christmas — A629

**2002, Nov. 1** *Perf. 14½x14*

| | | |
|---|---|---|
| **2108** A629 40c Nativity | 1.00 | .80 |
| **2109** A629 45c Magi | 1.00 | .70 |

**Self-Adhesive**

**Booklet Stamp**

***Serpentine Die Cut 11¼***

| | | |
|---|---|---|
| **2110** A629 40c Nativity | 1.00 | .70 |
| *a.* Booklet pane of 20 + 20 labels | 20.00 | |
| *Nos. 2108-2110 (3)* | 3.00 | 2.20 |

**Flora and Fauna Type of 1996**

Designs: 50c, Desert star flower. $1.45, Blue orchid.

**2003 Litho.** *Perf. 14x14½*

| | | |
|---|---|---|
| **2111** A511 $1.45 multi | 3.25 | 3.25 |

**Self-Adhesive**

**Coil Stamps**

***Serpentine Die Cut 11¼***

| | | |
|---|---|---|
| **2112** A511 50c multi | 1.00 | .50 |

***Serpentine Die Cut 12¾***

| | | |
|---|---|---|
| **2113** A511 50c multi | 1.00 | .50 |

### Booklet Stamp
***Serpentine Die Cut 11¼x11***

**2114** A511 50c multi 1.00 .50
*a.* Booklet pane of 10 10.00
*b.* Booklet pane of 20 22.50
*Nos. 2111-2114 (4)* 6.25 4.75

Issued: 50c, 1/7; $1.45, 2/11.

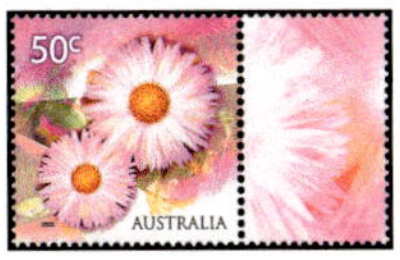

Flowers A630

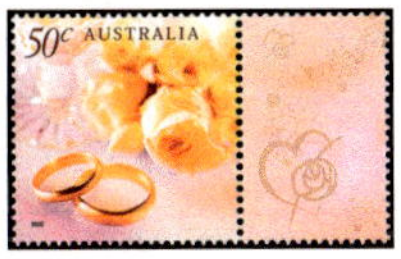

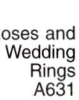

Roses and Wedding Rings A631

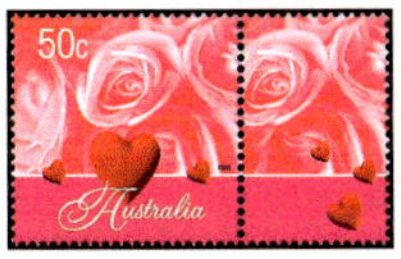

Roses and Hearts A632

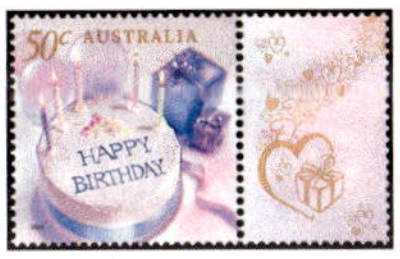

Birthday Cake, Balloons and Gifts — A633

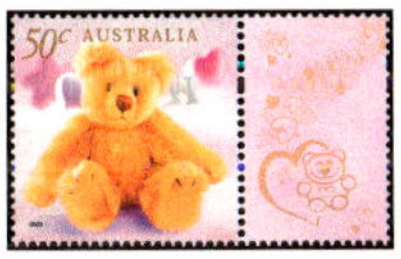

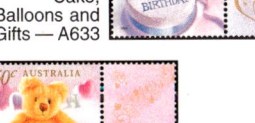

Teddy Bear — A634

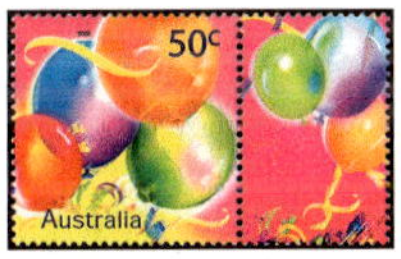

Balloons and Streamers A635

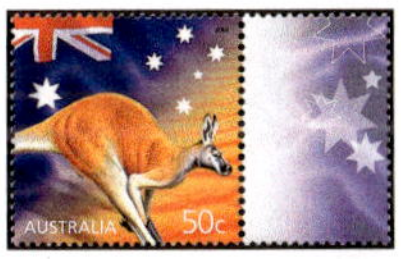

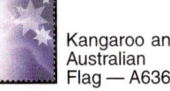

Kangaroo and Australian Flag — A636

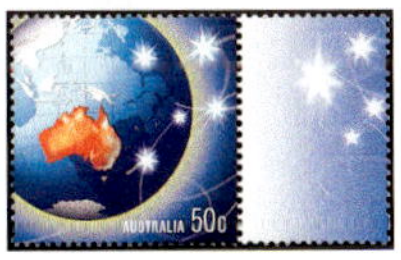

Australia on Globe A637

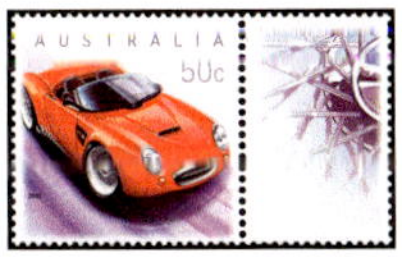

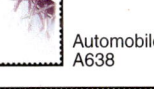

Automobile A638

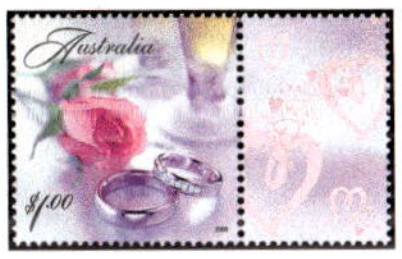

Rose and Wedding Rings A639

**2003** ***Perf. 14½x14***

**2115** A630 50c multi + label 1.50 .85
*a.* Booklet pane of 4 + 4 labels 6.00
Booklet, 5 #2115a 30.00
**2116** A631 50c multi + label 1.50 .85
*a.* Booklet pane of 4 + 4 labels 6.00
Booklet, 5 #2116a 30.00
**2117** A632 50c multi + label 1.50 .85
*a.* Booklet pane of 4 + 4 labels 6.00
Booklet, 5 #2117a 30.00
*b.* Strip of 3, #2115-2117, + 3 labels 4.50
**2118** A633 50c multi + label 1.50 .85
*a.* Booklet pane of 4 + 4 labels 6.00
Booklet, 5 #2118a 30.00
**2119** A634 50c multi + label 1.50 .85
*a.* Booklet pane of 4 + 4 labels 6.00 —
Complete booklet, 5 #2119a 30.00
**2120** A635 50c multi + label 1.50 .85
*a.* Booklet pane of 4 + 4 labels 6.00
Booklet, 5 #2120a 30.00
*b.* Strip of 3, #2118-2120, + 3 labels 3.50
**2121** A636 50c multi + label 1.50 .85
**2122** A637 50c multi + label 1.50 .85
*a.* Booklet pane of 4 + 4 labels 6.00 —
Complete booklet, 5 #2122a 30.00
**2123** A638 50c multi + label 1.50 .85
*a.* Strip of 3, #2121-2123, + 3 labels 4.50
**2124** A639 $1 multi + label 1.75 1.75
*a.* Booklet pane of 4 + 4 labels 7.00
Booklet, 5 #2124a 35.00
*Nos. 2115-2124 (10)* 15.25 9.40

Issued: No. 2119a, 10/31/03; No. 2122a, 3/16/04. Rest of set, 1/7/03.

Panes of 20 stamps containing the same design could have labels personalized. The personalized panes sold for a higher price.

Nos. 2115a, 2116a, 2117a, 2118a, 2119a, 2120a, 2122a and 2124a come in complete booklets, each containing 5 panes, each pane having different margins. Some panes are found in a number of different booklets.

### Australian Legends Type of 1997

Tennis players: Nos. 2125, 2129, Margaret Court with Wimbledon trophy. Nos. 2126, 2131, Court in action. Nos. 2127, 2130, Rod Laver with Wimbledon trophy. Nos. 2128, 2132, Laver in action.

**2003, Jan. 24** ***Perf. 14x14¾***
**Size: 34x26mm**

**2125** A522 50c multi 1.00 .70
**2126** A522 50c multi 1.00 .70
**2127** A522 50c multi 1.00 .70
**2128** A522 50c multi 1.00 .70
*a.* Block of 4, #2125-2128 5.25 4.75
*b.* Booklet pane, #2125-2128 *6.00* —
*Nos. 2125-2128 (4)* 4.00 2.80

**Self-Adhesive**
**Booklet Stamps**
***Serpentine Die Cut 11x11½***

**2129** A522 50c multi 1.00 .50
**2130** A522 50c multi 1.00 .50
**2131** A522 50c multi 1.00 .50
**2132** A522 50c multi 1.00 .50
*a.* Booklet pane, 3 each #2129-2130, 2 each #2131-2132 10.00
*Nos. 2129-2132 (4)* 4.00 2.00

No. 2128b issued 1/24/07.

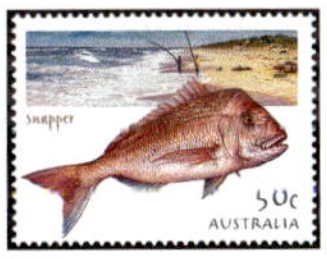

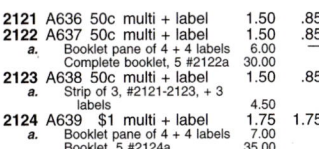

Fish — A640

**2003, Feb. 11** ***Perf. 14½x14***

**2133** A640 50c Snapper 1.00 .60
**2134** A640 50c Murray cod 1.00 .60
**2135** A640 50c Brown trout 1.00 .60
**2136** A640 50c Yellowfin tuna 1.00 .60
**2137** A640 50c Barramundi 1.00 .60
*a.* Horiz. strip of 5, #2133-2137 5.75 4.50
*Nos. 2133-2137 (5)* 5.00 3.00

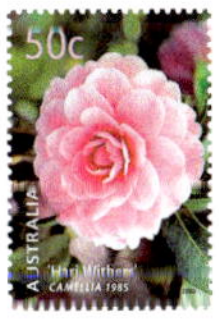

Australian Cultivars — A641

Designs: Nos. 2138, 2143, Hari Withers camellia. Nos. 2139, 2144, Victoria Gold rose. Nos. 2140, 2145, Superb grevillea. Nos. 2141, 2146, Bush Tango kangaroo paw. Nos. 2142, 2147, Midnight rhododendron.

**2003, Mar. 25** ***Perf. 14¾x14***

**2138** A641 50c multi .95 .70
**2139** A641 50c multi .95 .70
**2140** A641 50c multi .95 .70
**2141** A641 50c multi .95 .70
**2142** A641 50c multi .95 .70
*a.* Horiz. strip of 5, #2138-2142 5.75 5.00
*Nos. 2138-2142 (5)* 4.75 3.50

**Self-Adhesive**
***Serpentine Die Cut 11½x11¼***

**2143** A641 50c multi 1.00 .35
**2144** A641 50c multi 1.00 .35
**2145** A641 50c multi 1.00 .35
**2146** A641 50c multi 1.00 .35
**2147** A641 50c multi 1.00 .35
*a.* Coil strip of 5, #2143-2147 5.00
*b.* Booklet pane, 2 each #2143-2147 10.00
*Nos. 2143-2147 (5)* 5.00 1.75

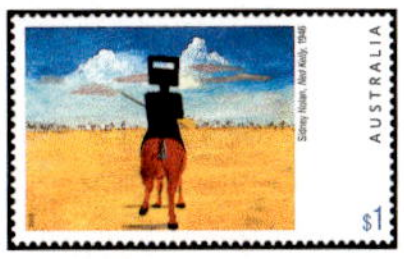

Paintings A642

Designs: No. 2148, Ned Kelly, by Sidney Nolan. No. 2149, Family Home, Suburban Exterior, by Howard Arkley. $1.45, Cord Drawn Long, Expectant, by Robert Jacks. $2.45, Girl, by Joy Hester.

**2003, May 6** **Litho.** ***Perf. 14½x14***

**2148** A642 $1 multi 1.75 1.50
**2149** A642 $1 multi 1.75 1.50
*a.* Horiz. pair, #2148-2149 3.50 3.25
**2150** A642 $1.45 multi 3.25 2.75
**2151** A642 $2.45 multi 4.75 4.00
*Nos. 2148-2151 (4)* 11.50 9.75

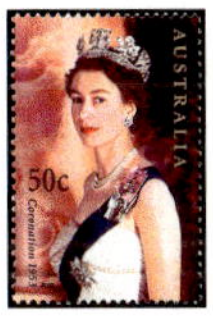

Coronation of Queen Elizabeth II, 50th Anniv. — A643

Designs: 50c, Queen Elizabeth II, 1953. $2.45, St. Edward's Crown.

**2003, June 2** **Litho.** ***Perf. 14¾x14***

**2152** A643 50c multi 1.00 1.00
**2153** A643 $2.45 multi 4.00 3.25
*a.* Souvenir sheet, #2152-2153 6.50 6.50

**Booklet Stamp**
**Self-Adhesive**
***Serpentine Die Cut 11½x11¼***

**2154** A643 50c multi .90 .40
*a.* Booklet pane of 10 9.00
*Nos. 2152-2154 (3)* 5.90 4.65

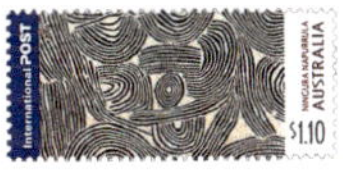

Papunya Tula Aboriginal Art — A644

Untitled works by: $1.10, Ningura Napurrula. $1.65, Naata Nungurrayi. $2.20, Graham Tjupurrula. $3.30, Dini Campbell Tjampitjinpa.

**2003, June 17** ***Perf. 14½x14***

**2155** A644 $1.10 multi 2.00 2.00
**2156** A644 $1.65 multi 3.00 3.00

**Size: 56x25mm**
***Perf. 14x14½***

**2157** A644 $2.20 multi 4.00 4.00
**2158** A644 $3.30 multi 5.75 5.75
*Nos. 2155-2158 (4)* 14.75 14.75

### Flora & Fauna Type of 1996

Designs: Nos. 2159, 2163, 2167, Orange-thighed tree frog. Nos. 2160, 2164, 2168, Green-spotted triangle butterfly. Nos. 2161, 2165, 2169, Striped possum. Nos. 2162, 2166, 2170, Yellow-bellied sunbird.

**2003, July 8** **Litho.** ***Perf. 14x14¼***

**2159** A511 50c multi .85 .40
**2160** A511 50c multi .85 .40
**2161** A511 50c multi .85 .40
**2162** A511 50c multi .85 .40
*a.* Block of 4, #2159-2162 3.75 3.75
*Nos. 2159-2162 (4)* 3.40 1.60

**Self-Adhesive**
***Serpentine Die Cut 11¼***

**2163** A511 50c multi 1.00 .40
**2164** A511 50c multi 1.00 .40
*a.* Booklet pane of 2, #2163-2164 2.25
**2165** A511 50c multi 1.00 .40
**2166** A511 50c multi 1.00 .40
*a.* Booklet pane of 4, #2163-2166, rouletted at bottom 4.50
Complete booklet, #2164a, 2 #2166a 10.25
*b.* Booklet pane of 4, #2163-2166, rouletted at side 4.50
Complete booklet, 5 #2166b 23.00
*c.* Coil strip of 4, #2163-2166 4.50

**Coil Stamps**
***Serpentine Die Cut 12¾***

**2167** A511 50c multi 1.10 .40
**2168** A511 50c multi 1.10 .40
**2169** A511 50c multi 1.10 .40
**2170** A511 50c multi 1.10 .40
*a.* Strip of 4, #2167-2170 5.25
*Nos. 2163-2170 (8)* 8.40 3.20

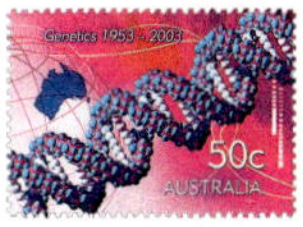

Genetics — A645

Map of Australia and: No. 2171, DNA molecule. No. 2172, Kangaroo chromosomes in cell division.

**2003, July 8** **Litho.** ***Perf. 14x14¾***

**2171** A645 50c red & multi 1.00 .80
**2172** A645 50c grn & multi 1.00 .80
*a.* Horiz. pair, #2171-2172 2.50 2.50

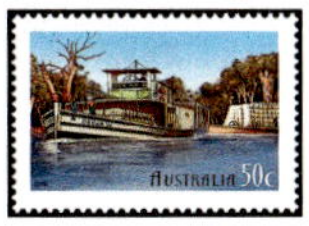

Murray River Shipping, 150th Anniv. — A646

Murray River vessels: Nos. 2173, 2178, Oscar W. Nos. 2174, 2179, Marion. Nos. 2175, 2180, Ruby. Nos. 2176, 2181, Pyap. Nos. 2177, 2182, Adelaide.

**2003, Aug. 5** **Litho.** ***Perf. 14x14¾***

**2173** A646 50c multi .90 .70
*a.* Booklet pane of 4 3.75 —
**2174** A646 50c multi .90 .70
*a.* Booklet pane of 4 3.75 —
**2175** A646 50c multi .90 .70
*a.* Booklet pane of 4 3.75 —
**2176** A646 50c multi .90 .70
*a.* Booklet pane of 4 3.75 —
**2177** A646 50c multi .90 .70
*a.* Booklet pane of 4 3.75 —
Complete booklet, #2173a-2177a 20.00
*b.* Horiz. strip of 5, #2173-2177 4.50 4.00
*Nos. 2173-2177 (5)* 4.50 3.50

**Self-Adhesive**
***Serpentine Die Cut 11¼x11½***

**2178** A646 50c multi 1.10 .45
**2179** A646 50c multi 1.10 .45
**2180** A646 50c multi 1.10 .45
**2181** A646 50c multi 1.10 .45
**2182** A646 50c multi 1.10 .45
*a.* Horiz. coil strip of 5, #2178-2182 5.75
*b.* Booklet pane, 2 each #2178-2182 11.00
*Nos. 2178-2182 (5)* 5.50 2.25

The booklet containing Nos. 2173a-2177a sold for $10.95.

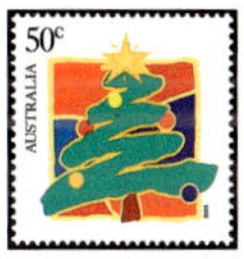

Christmas — A647

**2003, Aug. 5** **Litho.** ***Perf. 14½x14***

**2183** A647 50c Christmas tree .80 .60
*a.* Sheet of 20 + 20 labels 35.00
**2184** A647 90c Star 1.60 1.50
*a.* Sheet of 20 + 20 labels 50.00

Labels on Nos. 2183a and 2184a could be personalized. No. 2183a sold for $23 on day of issue; No. 2184a for $32.

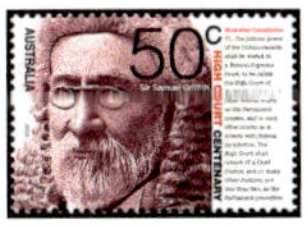

High Court of Australia, Cent. — A648

Designs: 50c, Sir Samuel Griffith (1845-1920), first Chief Justice, text from Constitution about High Court. $1.45, "Justice," names of significant cases.

**2003, Sept. 2** **Litho.** ***Perf. 14x14¾***

**2185** A648 50c multi .80 .80
**2186** A648 $1.45 multi 2.50 2.50
*a.* Souvenir sheet, #2185-2186 4.00 *4.25*

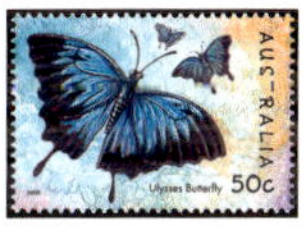

Insects — A649

Designs: Nos. 2187, 2198, Ulysses butterfly. Nos. 2188, 2197, Leichhardt's grasshopper. Nos. 2189, 2196, Vedalia ladybird. Nos. 2190, 2195, Green mantid and damselfly. Nos. 2191, 2194, Emperor gum moth caterpillar. Nos. 2192, 2193, Fiddler beetle.

**2003, Sept. 24** *Perf. 14x14¾*

2187 A649 50c multi .80 .60
2188 A649 50c multi .80 .60
2189 A649 50c multi .80 .60
*a.* Horiz. strip, #2187-2189 3.25 3.25
2190 A649 50c multi .80 .60
2191 A649 50c multi .80 .60
2192 A649 50c multi .80 .60
*a.* Horiz. strip, #2190-2192 3.25 3.25
*b.* Souvenir sheet, #2187-2192 5.75 5.75
*c.* As "b," with Bangkok 2003 emblem in margin in gold 8.00 8.00
*Nos. 2187-2192 (6)* 4.80 3.60

**Self-Adhesive**

***Serpentine Die Cut 11x11¼***

2193 A649 50c multi 1.00 .40
2194 A649 50c multi 1.00 .40
2195 A649 50c multi 1.00 .40
2196 A649 50c multi 1.00 .40
2197 A649 50c multi 1.00 .40
2198 A649 50c multi 1.00 .40
*a.* Horiz. coil strip, #2193-2198 6.75
*b.* Booklet pane, #2193-2194, 2 each #2195-2198 12.00
*Nos. 2193-2198 (6)* 6.00 2.40

No. 2193c issued 10/4.

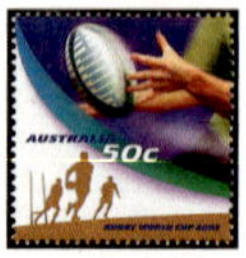

2003 Rugby World Cup — A650

Designs: 50c, Players running with ball, hands and ball. $1.10, Webb Ellis Cup, Telstra Stadium. $1.65, Player kicking at goal, ball in hand.

**2003, Oct. 8** **Litho.** *Perf. 14½x14*

2199 A650 50c multi 1.00 .85
*a.* Booklet pane of 3 3.50 —
2200 A650 $1.10 multi 2.25 2.25
*a.* Booklet pane of 3 7.00 —
2201 A650 $1.65 multi 3.25 3.25
*a.* Booklet pane of 3 10.50 —
Complete booklet, #2199a, 2200a, 2201a 24.00
*b.* Souvenir sheet, #2199-2201 7.00 7.00
*Nos. 2199-2201 (3)* 6.50 6.35

Booklet sold for $10.95.

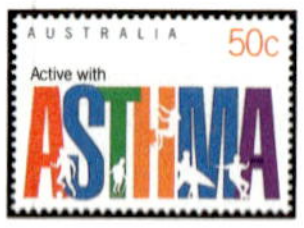

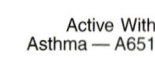

Active With Asthma — A651

**2003, Oct. 14** *Perf. 14x14½*

2202 A651 50c multi 1.00 .70

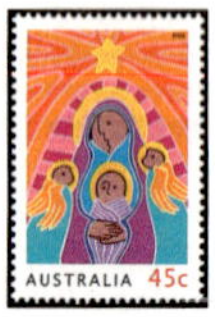

Christmas — A652

Designs: 45c, Madonna and Child with Angels. 50c, Three Wise Men. 90c, Angel Appearing to the Shepherds.

**2003, Oct. 31** *Perf. 14½x14*

2203 A652 45c multi .75 .80
2204 A652 50c multi .80 .80
2205 A652 90c multi 1.60 1.60

**Booklet Stamp**

**Self-Adhesive**

***Serpentine Die Cut 11½x11¼***

2206 A652 45c multi .95 .60
*a.* Booklet pane of 20 + 20 labels 20.00
*Nos. 2203-2206 (4)* 4.10 3.80

**Australian Legends Type of 1997**

Dame Joan Sutherland, opera singer: Nos. 2207, 2209, In costume. Nos. 2208, 2210, In black and red dress.

**2004, Jan. 23** **Litho.** *Perf. 14x14¾*

**Size: 37x26mm**

2207 A522 50c multi .90 .70
2208 A522 50c multi .90 .70
*a.* Horiz. pair, #2207-2208 2.00 2.00
*b.* Booklet pane, #2207-2208 *3.00* —

**Booklet Stamps**

**Self-Adhesive**

***Serpentine Die Cut 11x11½***

2209 A522 50c multi 1.00 .40
2210 A522 50c multi 1.00 .40
*a.* Booklet pane, 5 each #2209-2210 11.00
*Nos. 2207-2210 (4)* 3.80 2.20

No. 2208b issued 1/24/07.

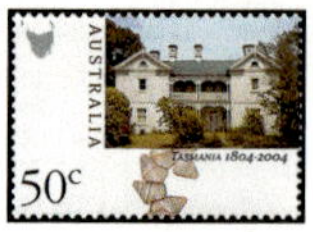

Settlement of Hobart Town, Tasmania, Bicent. — A653

Segment of shell necklace, map of Tasmania and: No. 2211, Cheshunt House, Deloraine. No. 2212, Complete shell necklace. No. 2213, Mount Wellington. No. 2214, Hobart Town from Kangaroo Point, by John Glover.

**2004, Feb. 3** **Litho.** *Perf. 14x14½*

2211 A653 50c multi 1.00 .70
2212 A653 50c multi 1.00 .70
*a.* Pair, #2211-2212 2.00 1.60
2213 A653 $1 multi 2.00 1.60
2214 A653 $1 multi 2.00 1.60
*a.* Pair, #2213-2214 4.00 3.50
*b.* Souvenir sheet, #2211-2214 6.25 6.25
*c.* As "b," ovptd. for Paris Exhib. 2004 *35.00* *35.00*
*d.* As "b," ovptd. for China 2005 exhibition *20.00* *20.00*
*Nos. 2211-2214 (4)* 6.00 4.60

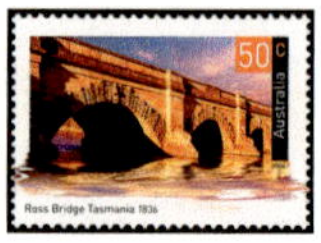

Historic Bridges — A654

Designs: Nos. 2215, 2220, Ross Bridge, Tasmania, 1836. Nos. 2216, 2221, Lockyer Creek Bridge, Queensland, 1911. Nos. 2217, 2222, Sydney Harbour Bridge, 1932. Nos. 2218, 2223, Birkenhead Bridge, Adelaide, 1940. Nos. 2219, 2224, Bolte Bridge, Melbourne, 1999.

**2004, Mar. 2** **Litho.** *Perf. 14x14½*

2215 A654 50c multi .90 .70
*a.* Booklet pane of 4 4.00 —
2216 A654 50c multi .90 .70
*a.* Booklet pane of 4 4.00 —
2217 A654 50c multi .90 .70
*a.* Booklet pane of 4 4.00 —
2218 A654 50c multi .90 .70
*a.* Booklet pane of 4 4.00 —
2219 A654 50c multi .90 .70
*a.* Booklet pane of 4 4.00 —
Complete booklet, #2215a, 2216a, 2217a, 2218a, 2219a 21.00
*b.* Horiz. strip of 5, #2215-2219 5.25 4.00
*c.* Booklet pane of 6 ('06) 6.25 —
*Nos. 2215-2219 (5)* 4.50 3.50

The complete booklet No. 2219a sold for $10.95.

No. 2219c issued 3/1/06.

**Self-Adhesive**

***Serpentine Die Cut 11x11½***

2220 A654 50c multi 1.40 .90
2221 A654 50c multi 1.40 .90
2222 A654 50c multi 1.40 .90
2223 A654 50c multi 1.40 .90
2224 A654 50c multi 1.40 .90
*a.* Horiz. coil strip of 5, #2220-2224 7.25
*b.* Booklet pane, 2 each #2220-2224 14.50
*Nos. 2220-2224 (5)* 7.00 4.50

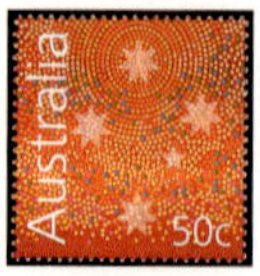

Southern Cross — A655

**2004-05** *Perf. 14½x14*

2225 A655 50c multi .90 .70
*a.* Booklet pane of 4 + 4 labels 4.25 —
Complete booklet, 5 #2225a 22.00

Issued: No. 2225, 3/16/04. No. 2225a, Jan. 2005. No. 2225a was issued in a variety of complete booklets, each containing 5 panes with different margins. Each complete booklet sold for $10.95.

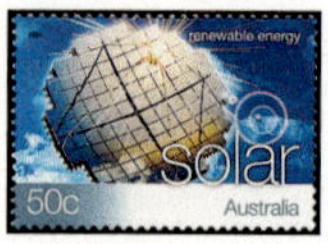

Renewable Energy — A656

Designs: Nos. 2226, 2230, Solar energy. Nos. 2227, 2231, Wind energy. Nos. 2228, 2232, Hydroelectric energy. Nos. 2229, 2233, Biomass energy.

**2004, Mar. 30** *Perf. 14x14½*

2226 A656 50c multi .90 .70
2227 A656 50c multi .90 .70
2228 A656 50c multi .90 .70
2229 A656 50c multi .90 .70
*a.* Block of 4, #2226-2229 3.75 3.75
*Nos. 2226-2229 (4)* 3.60 2.80

**Coil Stamps**

**Self-Adhesive**

***Serpentine Die Cut 11x11½***

2230 A656 50c multi 1.00 .50
2231 A656 50c multi 1.00 .50
2232 A656 50c multi 1.00 .50
2233 A656 50c multi 1.00 .50
*a.* Horiz. strip of 4, #2230-2233 4.25
*Nos. 2230-2233 (4)* 4.00 2.00

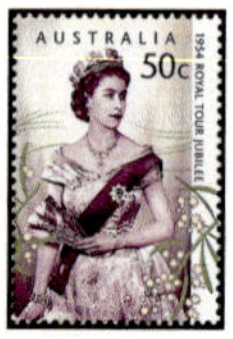

Royal Visit, 50th Anniv. — A657

**2004, Apr. 13** *Perf. 14½x14*

2234 A657 50c multi .90 .70
*a.* Booklet pane of 4 4.25 —
Complete booklet, 5 #2234a 22.00

The booklet, which contains five panes with different margins, sold for $10.95. Another booklet pane, with a different margin, is found in the booklet footnoted under No. 2507.

**Flora & Fauna Type of 1996**

Designs: 5c, Red lacewing butterfly. 10c, Blue-banded eggfly butterfly. 75c, Cruiser butterfly. $2, Butterflies, Daintree National Park rainforest.

**2004, May 4** **Litho.** *Perf. 14x14½*

2235 A511 5c multi .25 .25
2236 A511 10c multi .25 .25
2237 A511 75c multi 1.60 .95

**Size: 50x30mm**

***Perf. 14½x14***

2238 A511 $2 multi 3.50 3.00
*Nos. 2235-2238 (4)* 5.60 4.45

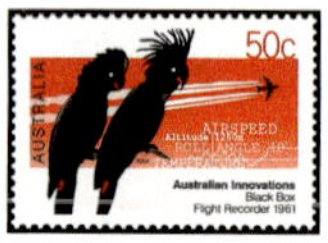

Australian Innovations A658

Designs: Nos. 2239, 2248, Black box flight recorder, 1961. Nos. 2240, 2247, Ultrasound imaging equipment, 1976. Nos. 2241, 2246, Racecam television sports coverage, 1979. Nos. 2242, 2245, Baby safety capsule, 1984. Nos. 2243, 2244, Polymer banknotes, 1988.

**2004, May 18** *Perf. 14x14½*

2239 A658 50c multi 1.00 .70
2240 A658 50c multi 1.00 .70
2241 A658 50c multi 1.00 .70
2242 A658 50c multi 1.00 .70
2243 A658 50c multi 1.00 .70
*a.* Horiz. strip, #2239-2243 5.00 5.00
*Nos. 2239-2243 (5)* 5.00 3.50

**Booklet Stamps**

**Self-Adhesive**

***Serpentine Die Cut 11x11½***

2244 A658 50c multi 1.10 .50
2245 A658 50c multi 1.10 .50
2246 A658 50c multi 1.10 .50
2247 A658 50c multi 1.10 .50
2248 A658 50c multi 1.10 .50
*a.* Booklet pane, 2 each #2244-2248 11.00
*Nos. 2244-2248 (5)* 5.50 2.50

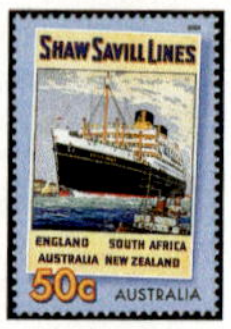

Passenger Ship Travel Posters — A659

Designs: 50c, Shaw Savill Lines. $1, Awatea, Union Steam Ship Co. $1.45, Orient Line. $2, Elder Dempster & Commonwealth Line.

**2004, June 1** **Litho.** *Perf. 14½x14*

2249 A659 50c multi 1.00 .70
2250 A659 $1 multi 1.60 1.25
2251 A659 $1.45 multi 2.40 1.75
2252 A659 $2 multi 3.25 2.40
*Nos. 2249-2252 (4)* 8.25 6.10

***Serpentine Die Cut 11½x11¼***

***Syncopated***

2252A A659 50c Like #2249, *2005* 5.00 2.50

**Booklet Stamp**

**Self-Adhesive**

***Serpentine Die Cut 11½x11¼***

2253 A659 50c multi 1.10 .50
*a.* Booklet pane of 10 11.00

Issued: Nos. 2249-2252, 2253, 6/1/04. No. 2252A, 2/22/05. No. 2252A issued in sheet of 10.

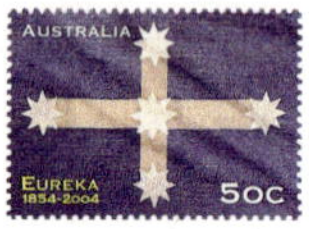

Eureka Stockade, 150th Anniv. — A660

Designs: 50c, Eureka flag. $2.45, Peter Lalor (1827-89), leader of rebellious gold diggers.

**2004, June 29** *Perf. 14x14½*

2254 A660 50c multi 1.00 .70
*a.* Booklet pane of 2 2.25 —
2255 A660 $2.45 multi 4.00 3.25
*a.* Booklet pane of 2 10.25 —
*b.* Booklet pane, #2254-2255 6.25
Complete booklet, #2255a, 2255b, 2 #2254a 25.00
*c.* Souvenir sheet, #2254-2255 5.75 5.75

No. 2255b has perfs that extend to the right margin. No. 2255c does not have perfs that extend through the margin. The margin is larger on No. 2255b than on No. 2255c. The complete booklet sold for $10.95.

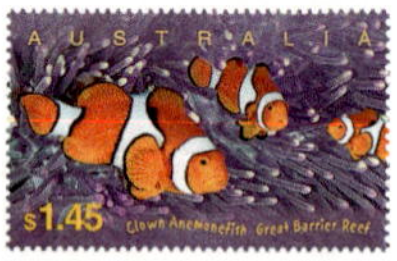

Tourist Attractions A661

Designs: No. 2256, Koala, Eastern Australia, vert. No. 2257, Little penguin, Phillip Island, vert. $1.45, Clown anemonefish, Great Barrier Reef. $2.45, Beach, Gold Coast.

***Perf. 14x14½, 14½x14***

**2004, July 13** **Litho.**

2256 A661 $1 multi 1.50 1.25
2257 A661 $1 multi 1.60 1.25
*a.* Horiz. pair, #2256-2257 4.50 4.50
2258 A661 $1.45 multi 3.00 2.00

**Litho. With Foil Application**

2259 A661 $2.45 multi 5.00 4.75
*Nos. 2256-2259 (4)* 11.10 9.25

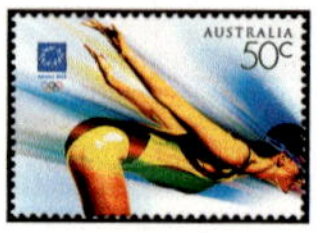

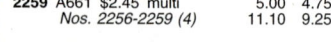

2004 Summer Olympics and Paralympics, Athens — A662

**2004, Aug. 3** **Litho.** *Perf. 14x14½*

2260 A662 50c Swimmer 1.00 .70
2261 A662 $1.65 Runner 2.75 2.75
2262 A662 $1.65 Cyclist 2.75 2.75
*Nos. 2260-2262 (3)* 6.50 6.20

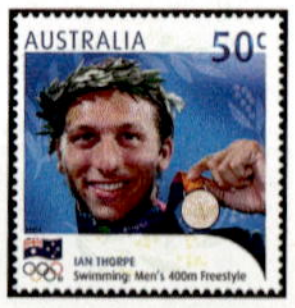

Gold Medalists at 2004 Summer Olympics, Athens — A663

Designs: No. 2263, Ian Thorpe, Men's swimming 400m freestyle. No. 2264, Women's 4x100m medley relay swimming team. No. 2265, Sara Carrigan, Women's cycling road race. No. 2266, Petria Thomas, Women's swimming 100m butterfly. No. 2267, Suzanne Balogh, Women's trap shooting. No. 2268, Ian Thorpe, Men's swimming 200m freestyle. No. 2269, Jodie Henry, Women's swimming 100m freestyle. No. 2270, Anna Meares, Women's cycling 500m time trial. No. 2271, James Tomkins and Drew Ginn, Men's rowing pairs. No. 2272, Grant Hackett, Men's swimming 1500m freestyle. No. 2273, Women's 4x100 freestyle relay swimming team. No. 2274, Chantelle Newbery, Women's diving 10m platform. No. 2275, Men's 4000m team pursuit cycling team. No. 2276, Ryan Bayley, Men's cycling individual sprint. No. 2277, Graeme Brown and Stuart O'Grady, Men's cycling Madison. No. 2278, Ryan Bayley, Men's cycling Keirin. No. 2279, Men's field hockey team.

**2004 Litho. *Perf. 14¼***

| | | | | |
|---|---|---|---|---|
| **2263** | A663 | 50c multi | 1.00 | .80 |
| **2264** | A663 | 50c multi | 1.00 | .80 |
| **2265** | A663 | 50c multi | 1.00 | .80 |
| **2266** | A663 | 50c multi | 1.00 | .80 |
| **2267** | A663 | 50c multi | 1.00 | .80 |
| **2268** | A663 | 50c multi | 1.00 | .80 |
| **2269** | A663 | 50c multi | 1.00 | .80 |
| **2270** | A663 | 50c multi | 1.00 | .80 |
| **2271** | A663 | 50c multi | 1.00 | .80 |
| **2272** | A663 | 50c multi | 1.00 | .80 |
| **2273** | A663 | 50c multi | 1.00 | .80 |
| **2274** | A663 | 50c multi | 1.00 | .80 |
| **2275** | A663 | 50c multi | 1.00 | .80 |
| **2276** | A663 | 50c multi | 1.00 | .80 |
| **2277** | A663 | 50c multi | 1.00 | .80 |
| **2278** | A663 | 50c multi | 1.00 | .80 |
| **2279** | A663 | 50c multi | 1.00 | .80 |
| | | *Nos. 2263-2279 (17)* | 17.00 | 13.60 |

Issued: Nos. 2263-2264, 8/16; Nos. 2265-2266, 8/17; Nos. 2267-2268, 8/18; Nos. 2269-2273, 8/23; No. 2274, 8/24; No. 2275, 8/25; No. 2276. 8/26; Nos. 2277-2278, 8/27; No. 2279, 8/30.

A sheet containing Nos. 2263-2279 was available only in the Australia Post annual collection. Value, $50.

### Tourist Attractions Type of 2000

Designs: $1.20, Entrance Beach, Broome, Western Australia. $1.80, Mt. William National Park, Tasmania. $2.40, Potato Point, Bodalla, New South Wales. $3.60, Point Gibbon, South Australia.

**2004, Sept. 6 *Perf. 14½x14***

| | | | | |
|---|---|---|---|---|
| **2280** | A581 | $1.20 multi | 2.40 | 1.75 |
| **2281** | A581 | $1.80 multi | 3.25 | 2.75 |
| **2282** | A581 | $2.40 multi | 4.00 | 4.00 |
| **2283** | A581 | $3.60 multi | 5.50 | 5.50 |
| | | *Nos. 2280-2283 (4)* | 15.15 | 14.00 |

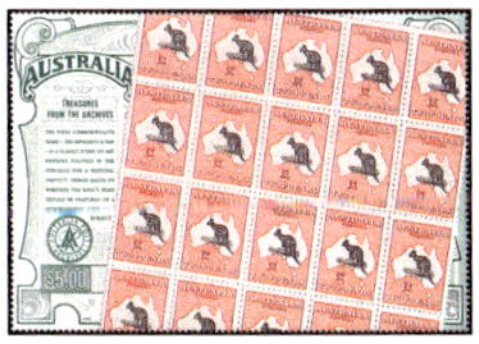

Block of £2 Kangaroo & Map Stamps from Australia Post Archives — A664

**2004, Sept. 7 *Perf. 14¼***

| | | | | |
|---|---|---|---|---|
| **2284** | A664 | $5 multi | 11.00 | 9.25 |

**Souvenir Sheet**

**Self-Adhesive**

***Serpentine Die Cut 11¼***

| | | | | |
|---|---|---|---|---|
| **2285** | A664 | $5 multi | 11.00 | 11.00 |

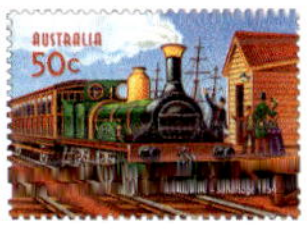


Australian Railways, 150th Anniv. — A665

Designs: Nos. 2286, 2291, Melbourne to Sandridge line, 1854. Nos. 2287, 2292, Sydney to Parramatta line, 1855. Nos. 2288, 2293, Helidon to Toowoomba line, 1867. Nos. 2289, 2294, Kalgoorlie to Port Augusta line, 1917. Nos. 2290, 2295, Alice Springs to Darwin line, 2004.

**2004, Sept. 7 *Perf. 14x14¾***

| | | | | |
|---|---|---|---|---|
| **2286** | A665 | 50c multi | .95 | .70 |
| *a.* | | Booklet pane of 4 | 4.25 | — |
| **2287** | A665 | 50c multi | .95 | .70 |
| *a.* | | Booklet pane of 4 | 4.25 | — |
| **2288** | A665 | 50c multi | .95 | .70 |
| *a.* | | Booklet pane of 4 | 4.25 | — |
| **2289** | A665 | 50c multi | .95 | .70 |
| *a.* | | Booklet pane of 4 | 4.25 | — |
| **2290** | A665 | 50c multi | .95 | .70 |
| *a.* | | Booklet pane of 4 | 4.25 | — |
| | | Complete booklet, #2286a-2290a | 22.00 | |
| *b.* | | Horiz. strip, #2286-2290 | 5.25 | 5.25 |
| | | *Nos. 2286-2290 (5)* | 4.75 | 3.50 |

Complete booklet of Nos. 2286a-2290a sold for $10.95.

**Self-Adhesive**

**With Designs Lightened at Stamp Edges**

***Serpentine Die Cut 11¼x11½***

| | | | | |
|---|---|---|---|---|
| **2291** | A665 | 50c multi | 1.00 | .60 |
| **2292** | A665 | 50c multi | 1.00 | .60 |
| **2293** | A665 | 50c multi | 1.00 | .60 |
| **2294** | A665 | 50c multi | 1.00 | .60 |
| **2295** | A665 | 50c multi | 1.00 | .60 |
| *a.* | | Horiz. coil strip, #2291-2295 | 5.50 | |
| *b.* | | Booklet pane, 2 each #2291-2295 | 11.00 | |
| | | *Nos. 2291-2295 (5)* | 5.00 | 3.00 |

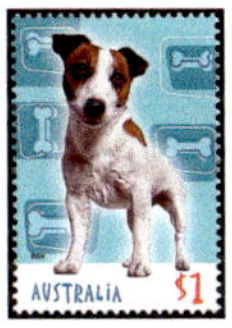


Cats and Dogs — A666

Designs: Nos. 2296, 2302, Cat (fish background). Nos. 2297, 2304, Cat (mouse background). Nos. 2298, 2301, Labrador retriever puppy (ball background). Nos. 2299, 2303, West Highland terriers (paw print background). $1, Jack Russell terrier (bone background).

**2004, Sept. 21 *Perf. 14¾x14***

| | | | | |
|---|---|---|---|---|
| **2296** | A666 | 50c multi | 1.00 | .70 |
| *a.* | | Booklet pane of 4 | 4.25 | — |
| **2297** | A666 | 50c multi | 1.00 | .70 |
| *a.* | | Horiz. pair, #2296-2297 | 2.25 | 1.60 |
| *b.* | | Booklet pane of 4 | 4.25 | — |
| *c.* | | Booklet pane, 2 each #2296-2297 | 4.50 | — |
| | | Complete booklet, #2296a, 2297b, 3 #2297c | 21.00 | |
| **2298** | A666 | 50c multi | 1.00 | .70 |
| *a.* | | Booklet pane of 4 | 4.25 | — |
| **2299** | A666 | 50c multi | 1.00 | .70 |
| *a.* | | Horiz. pair, #2298-2299 | 2.25 | 1.60 |
| *b.* | | Booklet pane of 4 | 4.25 | — |
| *c.* | | Booklet pane, 2 each #2298-2299 | 4.50 | — |
| **2300** | A666 | $1 multi | 2.00 | 1.60 |
| *a.* | | Booklet pane of 2 | 4.25 | — |
| | | Complete booklet, #2298a, 2299b, 2300a, 2 #2299c | 21.00 | |
| *b.* | | Souvenir sheet, #2296-2300 | 5.50 | 5.50 |
| | | *Nos. 2296-2300 (5)* | 6.00 | 4.40 |

The complete booklets each sold for $10.95. The Cat booklet contains three examples of No. 2297c, each with different margins and stamp arrangements. The Dog booklet contains two examples of No. 2299c with different margins and stamp arrangements.

**Self-Adhesive**

**Booklet Stamps**

***Serpentine Die Cut 11¼ Syncopated***

| | | | | |
|---|---|---|---|---|
| **2301** | A666 | 50c multi | .80 | .60 |
| **2302** | A666 | 50c multi | .80 | .60 |
| **2303** | A666 | 50c multi | .80 | .60 |
| *a.* | | Booklet pane, 3 #2301, 2 #2303 | 5.25 | |
| **2304** | A666 | 50c multi | .80 | .60 |
| *a.* | | Booklet pane, 3 each #2301-2302, 2 each #2303-2304 | 9.00 | |
| *b.* | | Booklet pane, 3 #2302, 2 #2304 | 5.25 | |
| **2305** | A666 | $1 multi | 2.25 | 1.25 |
| *a.* | | Booklet pane of 5 | 11.00 | |
| | | *Nos. 2301-2305 (5)* | 5.45 | 3.65 |

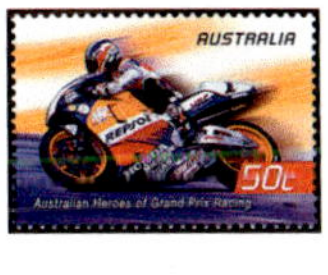


Grand Prix Motorcycle Racing — A667

Designs: Nos. 2306, 2311, Mick Doohan (motorcycle #1, red panel). Nos. 2307, 2312, Wayne Gardner (motorcycle #1, blue panel). Nos. 2308, 2313, Troy Bayliss (motorcycle #12, orange red panel). Nos. 2309, 2314, Daryl Beattie (motorcycle #4, green panel). Nos. 2310, 2315, Garry McCoy (motorcycle #8, yellow orange panel).

**2004, Oct. 12 Litho. *Perf. 14x14¾***

| | | | | |
|---|---|---|---|---|
| **2306** | A667 | 50c multi | .95 | .70 |
| **2307** | A667 | 50c multi | .95 | .70 |
| **2308** | A667 | 50c multi | .95 | .70 |
| **2309** | A667 | 50c multi | .95 | .70 |
| **2310** | A667 | 50c multi | .95 | .70 |
| *a.* | | Horiz. strip of 5, #2306-2310 | 5.25 | 4.00 |
| | | *Nos. 2306-2310 (5)* | 4.75 | 3.50 |

**Self-Adhesive**

***Serpentine Die Cut 11¼ Syncopated***

| | | | | |
|---|---|---|---|---|
| **2311** | A667 | 50c multi | 1.00 | .70 |
| **2312** | A667 | 50c multi | 1.00 | .70 |
| **2313** | A667 | 50c multi | 1.00 | .70 |
| **2314** | A667 | 50c multi | 1.00 | .70 |
| **2315** | A667 | 50c multi | 1.00 | .70 |
| *a.* | | Horiz. coil strip, #2311-2315 | 6.00 | |
| *b.* | | Booklet pane, 2 each #2311-2315 | 11.00 | |
| | | *Nos. 2311-2315 (5)* | 5.00 | 3.50 |

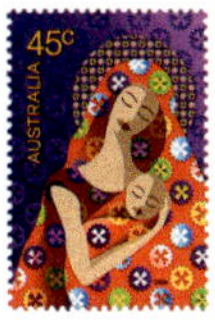


Christmas — A668

Designs: 45c, Madonna and Child. 50c, Shepherds. $1, Magi, horiz.

**2004, Nov. 1 *Perf. 14¾x14, 14x14¾***

| | | | | |
|---|---|---|---|---|
| **2316** | A668 | 45c multi | .80 | .65 |
| **2317** | A668 | 50c multi | .85 | .75 |
| **2318** | A668 | $1 multi | 1.60 | 1.60 |
| | | *Nos. 2316-2318 (3)* | 3.25 | 3.00 |

**Self-Adhesive**

**Booklet Stamps**

***Serpentine Die Cut 11¼ Syncopated***

| | | | | |
|---|---|---|---|---|
| **2319** | A668 | 45c multi | .95 | .85 |
| *a.* | | Booklet pane of 20 + 20 etiquettes | 20.00 | |
| **2320** | A668 | $1 multi | 2.00 | 1.60 |
| *a.* | | Booklet pane of 5 | 10.00 | |

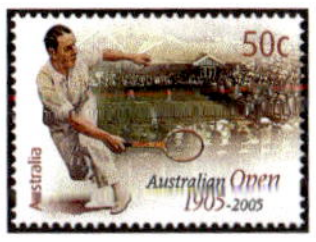


Australian Tennis Open, Cent. — A669

Designs: 50c, Male player, tennis court and stands, 1905. $1.80, Female player, tennis court and stands, 2005.

**2005, Jan. 11 Litho. *Perf. 14x14¾***

| | | | | |
|---|---|---|---|---|
| **2321** | A669 | 50c multi | 1.00 | .65 |
| *a.* | | Booklet pane of 2 | 2.25 | — |
| **2322** | A669 | $1.80 multi | 3.50 | 2.00 |
| *a.* | | Booklet pane of 2 | 8.50 | — |
| | | Complete booklet, 2 each #2321a, 2322a | 25.00 | |

The complete booklet contains two examples of Nos. 2321a and 2322a, each with different margins.

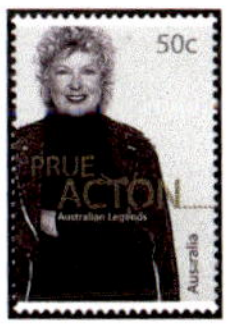


Australian Legends — Fashion Designers — A670

Designs: Nos. 2323, 2329, Prue Acton. Nos. 2324, 2330, Jenny Bannister. Nos. 2325, 2331, Collette Dinnigan. Nos. 2326, 2332, Akira Isogawa. Nos. 2327, 2333, Joe Saba. Nos. 2328, 2334, Carla Zampatti.

**2005, Jan. 21 *Perf. 14¾x14***

| | | | | |
|---|---|---|---|---|
| **2323** | A670 | 50c multi | .80 | .70 |
| **2324** | A670 | 50c multi | 1.00 | .70 |
| *a.* | | Horiz. pair, #2323-2324 | 1.75 | 1.60 |
| *b.* | | Booklet pane, #2323-2324 | 3.00 | — |
| **2325** | A670 | 50c multi | .80 | .70 |
| **2326** | A670 | 50c multi | .80 | .70 |
| *a.* | | Horiz. pair, #2325-2326 | 1.75 | 1.60 |
| *b.* | | Booklet pane, #2325-2326 | 3.00 | — |
| **2327** | A670 | 50c multi | .80 | .70 |
| **2328** | A670 | 50c multi | .80 | .70 |
| *a.* | | Horiz. pair, #2327-2328 | 1.75 | 1.60 |
| *b.* | | Booklet pane, #2327-2328 | 3.00 | — |
| | | *Nos. 2323-2328 (6)* | 5.00 | 4.20 |

**Self-Adhesive**

**Booklet Stamps**

***Serpentine Die Cut 11¼ Syncopated***

| | | | | |
|---|---|---|---|---|
| **2329** | A670 | 50c multi | .90 | .60 |
| **2330** | A670 | 50c multi | .90 | .60 |
| *a.* | | Booklet pane, 5 each #2329-2330 | 10.00 | |
| **2331** | A670 | 50c multi | .90 | .60 |
| **2332** | A670 | 50c multi | .90 | .60 |
| *a.* | | Booklet pane, 5 each #2331-2332 | 10.00 | |
| **2333** | A670 | 50c multi | .90 | .60 |
| **2334** | A670 | 50c multi | .90 | .60 |
| *a.* | | Booklet pane, 5 each #2333-2334 | 10.00 | |
| | | *Nos. 2329-2334 (6)* | 5.40 | 3.60 |

Nos. 2324b, 2326b, 2328b, 1/24/07.

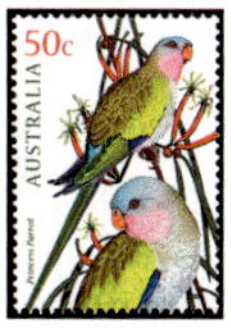


Parrots — A671

Designs: Nos. 2335, 2340, Princess parrot. Nos. 2336, 2344, Rainbow lorikeet. Nos. 2337, 2343, Green rosella. Nos. 2338, 2342, Red-capped parrot. Nos. 2339, 2341, Purple-crowned lorikeet.

**2005, Feb. 8 *Perf. 14¾x14***

| | | | | |
|---|---|---|---|---|
| **2335** | A671 | 50c multi | 1.00 | .70 |
| **2336** | A671 | 50c multi | 1.00 | .70 |
| **2337** | A671 | 50c multi | 1.00 | .70 |
| **2338** | A671 | 50c multi | 1.00 | .70 |
| **2339** | A671 | 50c multi | 1.00 | .70 |
| *a.* | | Horiz. strip of 5, #2335-2339 | 5.50 | 4.75 |
| | | *Nos. 2335-2339 (5)* | 5.00 | 3.50 |

A sheet containing Nos. 2335-2339 + 4 labels was available only with purchase of the "2005 Collection of Australian Stamps." Value $24.

**Self-Adhesive**

**Coil Stamps**

***Serpentine Die Cut 11¼ Syncopated***

| | | | | |
|---|---|---|---|---|
| **2340** | A671 | 50c multi | 1.10 | .60 |
| **2341** | A671 | 50c multi | 1.10 | .60 |
| **2342** | A671 | 50c multi | 1.10 | .60 |
| **2343** | A671 | 50c multi | 1.10 | .60 |
| **2344** | A671 | 50c multi | 1.10 | .60 |
| *a.* | | Vert. strip of 5, #2340-2344 | 6.00 | |
| | | *Nos. 2340-2344 (5)* | 5.50 | 3.00 |

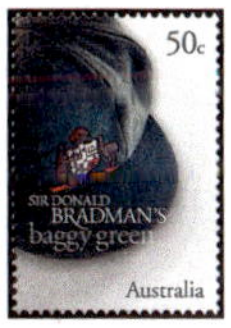


Sports Memorabilia — A672

Designs: No. 2345, Sir Donald Bradman's cricket cap. No. 2346, Lionel Rose's boxing gloves. No. 2347, Marjorie Jackson's running spikes. No. 2348, Racing silks of Phar Lap's jockeys.

**2005, Mar. 8 Litho. *Perf. 14¾x14***

| | | | | |
|---|---|---|---|---|
| **2345** | A672 | 50c multi | .90 | .70 |
| *a.* | | Booklet pane of 5, #1575a, 1576c, 1941a, 1942b, 2345 dated "2007" | 7.50 | — |
| **2346** | A672 | 50c multi | .90 | .70 |
| *a.* | | Horiz. pair, #2345-2346 | 2.25 | 2.00 |
| **2347** | A672 | $1 multi | 1.60 | 1.20 |
| **2348** | A672 | $1 multi | 1.60 | 1.20 |
| *a.* | | Horiz. pair, #2347-2348 | 4.50 | 4.50 |
| | | *Nos. 2345-2348 (4)* | 5.00 | 3.80 |

No. 2345a issued 11/14/2007.

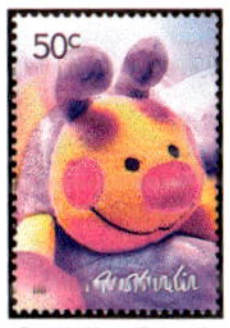


Child's Plush Toy A673

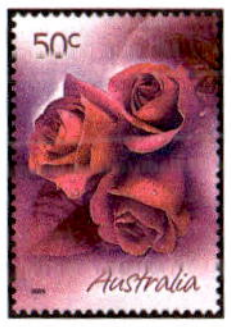


Red Roses A674

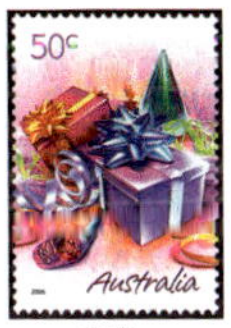


Gifts A675

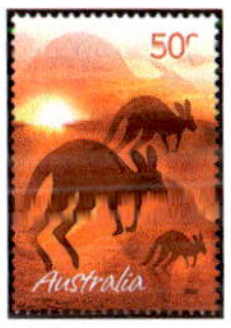


Kangaroos A676

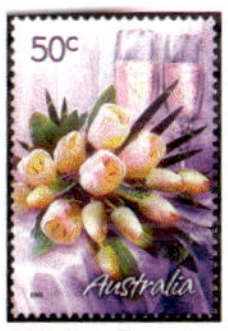


White Roses A677

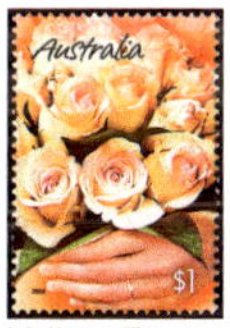


Yellow Roses and Woman's Hand A678

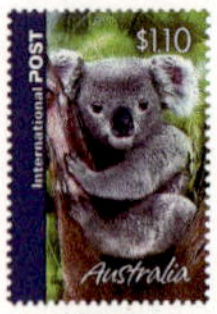

Koala
A679

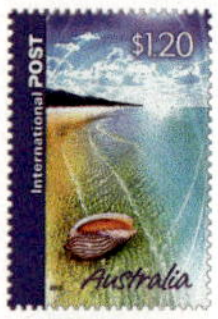

Shell on
Beach
A680

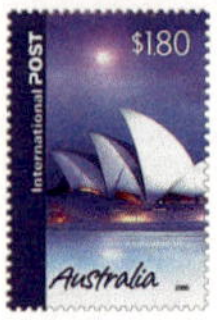

Sydney Opera
House — A681

**2005, Mar. 22** *Perf. 14¾x14*

**2349** A673 50c multi .90 .70
**2350** A674 50c multi .90 .70
**2351** A675 50c multi .90 .70
**2352** A676 50c multi .90 .70
*a.* Additionally dated "2013" (#3534d) 1.25 1.25
**2353** A677 50c multi .90 .70
*a.* Horiz. strip, #2349-2353 5.00 5.00
**2354** A678 $1 multi 1.60 1.60
**2355** A679 $1.10 multi 2.25 2.25
**2356** A680 $1.20 multi 2.40 2.40
**2357** A681 $1.80 multi 3.50 3.50
*Nos. 2349-2357 (9)* 14.25 13.25

Issued: No. 2352a, 5/10/2013.

**Booklet Stamps**
**Self-Adhesive**
***Serpentine Die Cut 11x11¼***
***Syncopated***

**2358** A673 50c multi 3.75 *3.25*
*a.* Booklet pane of 4 15.00
Complete booklet, 5 #2358a 75.00
**2359** A674 50c multi 3.75 *3.25*
*a.* Booklet pane of 4 15.00
Complete booklet, 5 #2359a 75.00
**2360** A675 50c multi 3.75 *3.25*
*a.* Booklet pane of 4 15.00
Complete booklet, 5 #2360a 75.00
**2361** A677 50c multi 3.75 *3.25*
*a.* Booklet pane of 4 15.00
Complete booklet, 5 #2361a 75.00
**2362** A678 $1 multi 6.25 *6.25*
*a.* Booklet pane of 4 25.00
Complete booklet, 5 #2362a 125.00
**2363** A679 $1.10 multi 6.50 *8.00*
*a.* Booklet pane of 4 26.00
Complete booklet, 2 #2363a 130.00
**2364** A680 $1.20 multi 7.00 *9.00*
*a.* Booklet pane of 2 14.00
**2365** A681 $1.80 multi 7.50 *13.00*
*a.* Booklet pane of 2 15.00
Complete booklet, 2 each #2364a, 2365a 30.00
*Nos. 2358-2365 (8)* 42.25 49.25

Each pane in the various complete booklets has a different margin. The complete booklets containing Nos. 2358-2361 each sold for $10.95, the complete booklet containing No. 2362 sold for $20.95, and the complete booklets containing Nos. 2363-2365 sold for $12.95.

See Nos. 2439-2447.

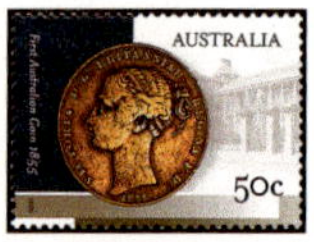

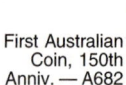

First Australian
Coin, 150th
Anniv. — A682

1855 One sovereign coin: Nos. 2366, 2368a, Obverse. Nos. 2367, 2368b, Reverse.

**2005, Apr. 21** **Litho.** *Perf. 14x14¾*

**2366** A682 50c multi 1.00 .75
**2367** A682 $2.45 multi 4.00 3.60
*a.* Booklet pane, #2366-2367 7.75 —

**Litho. & Embossed with Foil Application**

**2368** Sheet of 2 6.00 6.00
*a.* A682 50c multi .90 .90
*b.* A682 $2.45 multi 5.00 5.00

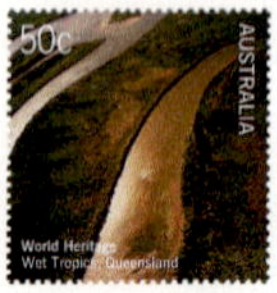

UNESCO World
Heritage Sites in
Australia and Great
Britain — A683

Designs: No. 2369, Wet Tropics of Queensland, Australia. No. 2370, Stonehenge, England. No. 2371, Greater Blue Mountains Area, New South Wales, Australia. No. 2372, Blenheim Castle, England. No. 2373, Purnululu National Park, Western Australia. No. 2374, Heart of Neolithic Orkney, Scotland. No. 2375, Ayers Rock, Uluru-Kata Tjuta National Park, Northern Territory, Australia. No. 2376, Hadrian's Wall, England.

**2005, Apr. 21** **Litho.** *Perf. 14¼*

**2369** A683 50c multi .95 .70
**2370** A683 50c multi .95 .70
*a.* Horiz. pair, #2369-2370 2.00 2.00
**2371** A683 50c multi 1.00 .70
**2372** A683 50c multi 1.00 .70
*a.* Horiz. pair, #2371-2372 2.00 2.00
**2373** A683 $1 multi 1.60 1.20
**2374** A683 $1 multi 1.60 1.20
*a.* Horiz. pair, #2373-2374 3.60 3.60
*b.* Booklet pane, #2369-2370, 2373-2374, + 4 labels 7.75 —
**2375** A683 $1.80 multi 3.75 3.25
**2376** A683 $1.80 multi 3.75 3.25
*a.* Horiz. pair, #2375-2376 7.50 7.50
*b.* Booklet pane, #2371-2372, 2375-2376, + 4 labels 11.50 —
*Nos. 2369-2376 (8)* 14.60 11.70

See Great Britain Nos. 2280-2287.

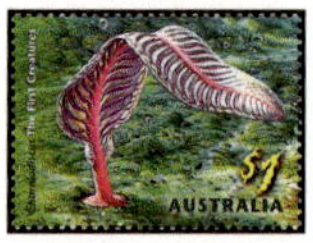

Creatures of the
Slime — A684

**2005, Apr. 21** *Perf. 14x14¾*

**2377** A684 50c Tribrachidium .90 .70
**2378** A684 50c Dickinsonia .90 .70
**2379** A684 50c Spriggina .90 .70
**2380** A684 50c Kimberella .90 .70
**2381** A684 50c Inaria .90 .70
*a.* Horiz. strip of 5, #2377-2381 5.00 4.75
**2382** A684 $1 Charnodiscus 1.75 1.60
*a.* Souvenir sheet, #2377-2382 7.50 7.50
*b.* Booklet pane, #2377-2382 9.00 —
*Nos. 2377-2382 (6)* 6.25 5.10

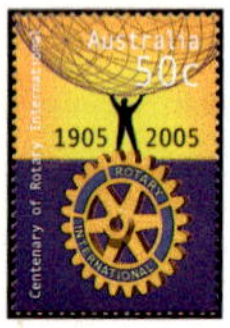

Rotary International,
Cent. — A685

**2005, Apr. 21** *Perf. 14¾x14*

**2383** A685 50c multi .90 .65
*a.* Imperf. 8.00 8.00

**Self-Adhesive**
***Serpentine Die Cut 11½x11¼***
***Syncopated***

**2384** A685 50c multi .90 .65
*a.* Booklet pane of 10 10.25
*b.* Booklet pane of 1 1.40 —
Complete booklet, #2367a, 2374b, 2376b, 2382b, 2384b 40.00

No. 2383a was sold at the Pacific Explorer Intl. Philatelic Exhibition 2005.

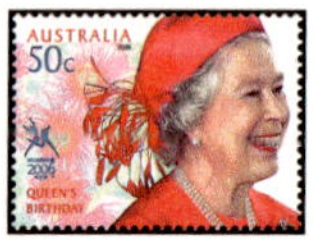

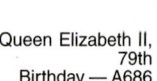

Queen Elizabeth II,
79th
Birthday — A686

**2005, May 10** *Perf. 14x14¾*

**2385** A686 50c multi 1.00 .70
*a.* Booklet pane of 4 4.00 —
Complete booklet, 5 #2385a 29.00

2006 Commonwealth Games, Melbourne. No. 2385a was issued in a booklet that sold for $10.95, with the 5 panes having different margins.

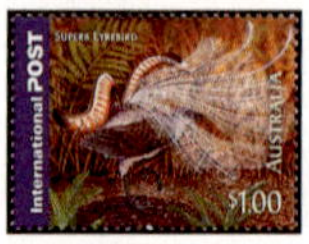

Bush
Wildlife — A687

No. 2386, Superb lyrebird. Nos. 2387, 2390, Laughing kookaburra. Nos. 2388, 2391, Koala. Nos. 2389, 2392, Red kangaroo.

**2005, June 7** *Perf. 14x14¾*

**2386** A687 $1 multi 1.75 1.20
**2387** A687 $1.10 multi 1.90 1.50
**2388** A687 $1.20 multi 2.10 1.60
**2389** A687 $1.80 multi 3.25 2.40
*Nos. 2386-2389 (4)* 9.00 6.70

***Serpentine Die Cut 11¼x11½***
***Syncopated***
**Self-Adhesive**
**Booklet Stamps**

**2390** A687 $1.10 multi 1.75 1.60
*a.* Booklet pane of 5 10.00
**2391** A687 $1.20 multi 2.40 2.25
*a.* Booklet pane of 5 12.00
**2392** A687 $1.80 Red kangaroo 3.25 3.25
*a.* Booklet pane of 5 17.00
*Nos. 2390-2392 (3)* 7.40 7.10

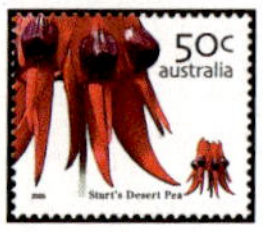

Wild Flowers — A688

Designs: Nos. 2393, 2397, 2401, Sturt's desert pea. Nos. 2394, 2398, 2402, Coarse-leaved mallee. Nos. 2395, 2399, 2403, Common fringe lily. Nos. 2396, 2400, 2404, Swamp daisy.

**2005, July 5** *Perf. 14x14½*

**2393** A688 50c multi 1.00 .40
**2394** A688 50c multi 1.00 .40
**2395** A688 50c multi 1.00 .40
**2396** A688 50c multi 1.00 .40
*a.* Horiz. strip of 4, #2393-2396 4.00 3.75
*Nos. 2393-2396 (4)* 4.00 1.60

**Self-Adhesive**
***Serpentine Die Cut 11¼x11***

**2397** A688 50c multi 1.25 .70
**2398** A688 50c multi 1.25 .70
**2399** A688 50c multi 1.25 .70
**2400** A688 50c multi 1.25 .70
*a.* Horiz. coil strip of 4, #2397-2400 5.00
*b.* Booklet pane of 10, 3 each #2397-2398, 2 each #2399-2400 11.00
*c.* Booklet pane of 20, 5 each #2397-2400 20.00
*d.* Booklet pane of 5, #2398-2400, 2 #2397 6.50

**Coil Stamps**
***Die Cut Perf. 12¾***

**2401** A688 50c multi 1.35 .70
**2402** A688 50c multi 1.35 .70
**2403** A688 50c multi 1.35 .70
**2404** A688 50c multi 1.35 .70
*a.* Horiz. coil strip of 4, #2401-2404 5.50
*Nos. 2397-2404 (8)* 10.40 5.60

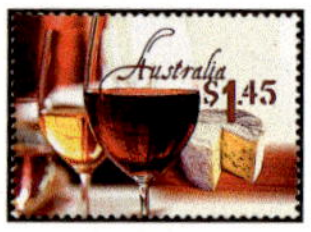

Australian
Wine — A689

Designs: Nos. 2405, 2410, Grapevine, vineyard. Nos. 2406, 2411, Grapes, grape leaves. No. 2407, Grape pickers, basket of grapes, wine bottle. No. 2408, Wine bottle, corkscrew, wine barrels. $1.45, Wine glasses, cheese.

**2005, July 19** *Perf. 14x14¾*

**2405** A689 50c multi .90 .70
**2406** A689 50c multi .90 .70
*a.* Horiz. pair, #2405-2406 2.00 1.60
*b.* Booklet pane, #2406a 2.25 —
*c.* Booklet pane, 2 #2406a 4.50 —
**2407** A689 $1 multi 1.60 1.25
**2408** A689 $1 multi 1.60 1.25
*a.* Horiz. pair, #2407-2408 3.75 2.75
*b.* Booklet pane, 2 #2408a 9.25 —
**2409** A689 $1.45 multi 2.75 2.40
*a.* Booklet pane of 2 6.25 —
Complete booklet, #2406b, 2406c, 2408b, 2409a 22.50
*Nos. 2405-2409 (5)* 7.75 6.30

**Booklet Stamps**
**Self-Adhesive**
***Serpentine Die Cut 11¼x11½***
***Syncopated***

**2410** A689 50c multi 1.00 .65
**2411** A689 50c multi 1.00 .65
*a.* Booklet pane, 5 each #2410-2411 11.00

Complete booklet sold for $10.95.

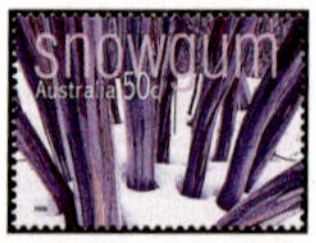

Trees — A690

Designs: Nos. 2412, 2417, Snowgum. Nos. 2413, 2418, Wollemi pine. Nos. 2414, 2419, Boab. Nos. 2415, 2420, Karri. Nos. 2416, 2421, Moreton Bay fig.

**2005, Aug. 8** *Perf. 14x14¾*

**2412** A690 50c multi 1.00 .70
**2413** A690 50c multi 1.00 .70
**2414** A690 50c multi 1.00 .70
**2415** A690 50c multi 1.00 .70
**2416** A690 50c multi 1.00 .70
*a.* Horiz. strip of 5, #2412-2416 5.00 4.00
*Nos. 2412-2416 (5)* 5.00 3.50

**Coil Stamps**
***Serpentine Die Cut 11¼x11½***
***Syncopated***

**2417** A690 50c multi 1.00 .70
**2418** A690 50c multi 1.00 .70
**2419** A690 50c multi 1.00 .70
**2420** A690 50c multi 1.00 .70
**2421** A690 50c multi 1.00 .70
*a.* Horiz. strip of 5, #2417-2421 6.00
*Nos. 2417-2421 (5)* 5.00 3.50

Nos. 2417-2421 have "frames" that are faded portions of the design.

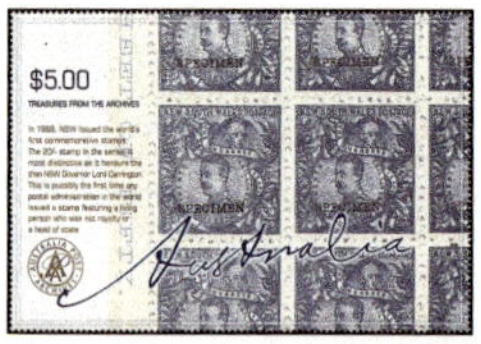

Portion of Specimen Pane of New South Wales No. 86 from Australia Post Archives — A691

**2005, Sept. 6** **Litho.** *Perf. 14¼*

**2422** A691 $5 multi 10.00 10.00

No. 2422 exists imperf.

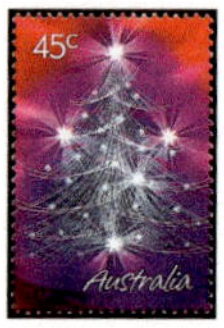

Southern Cross — A692

Southern Cross and: 45c, Christmas tree. 50c, Map of Oceania and East Asia.

**2005** *Perf. 14½x14*

**2423** A692 45c multi .90 .35
*a.* Booklet pane of 4 5.75 —
Complete booklet (see footnote) 24.00
**2424** A692 50c multi 1.00 .60

Issued: Nos. 2423, 2424, 9/6. No. 2423a, 11/1. No. 2423a exists with three different margins, each of which appear in a booklet also containing two examples of Christmas Island No. 452a. The complete booklet sold for $9.95.

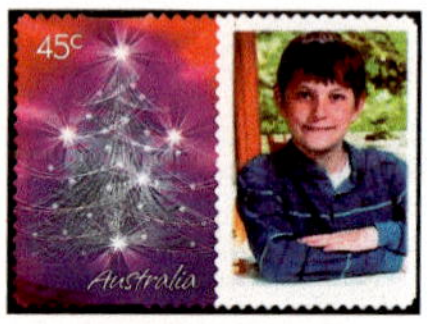

Southern Cross With Personalized Picture — A692a

***Serpentine Die Cut 11½x11¼***
***Syncopated***

**2005, Sept. 6** **Litho.**

**Self-Adhesive**

**2425** A692a 45c Like #2423 2.50 2.50
**2426** A692a 50c Like #2424 2.50 2.50

Nos. 2425-2426 were sold in sheets of 20 and have personalized pictures and a straight edge at right, and lack separations between the stamp and the picture. Sheets of 20 of No. 2425 sold for $22, and of No. 2426, $23.

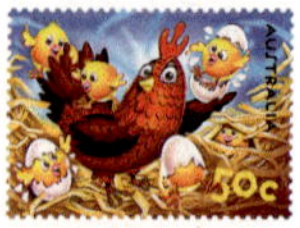

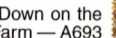

Down on the
Farm — A693

Designs: Nos. 2427, 2433, Hen and chicks. Nos. 2428, 2434, Lambs and insects. Nos. 2429, 2437, Goats and rabbit. Nos. 2430, 2435, Pigs and frog. Nos. 2431, 2436, Cow and bird. $1, Horse, dogs, birds, lizard.

AUSTRALIA 755

**2005, Oct. 4 Litho. *Perf. 14x14¾***

| | | | | |
|---|---|---|---|---|
| 2427 | A693 50c multi | | 1.00 | .70 |
| a. | Booklet pane of 1 | | 1.40 | — |
| 2428 | A693 50c multi | | 1.00 | .70 |
| a. | Booklet pane of 1 | | 1.40 | — |
| 2429 | A693 50c multi | | 1.00 | .70 |
| a. | Booklet pane of 1 | | 1.40 | — |
| 2430 | A693 50c multi | | 1.00 | .70 |
| a. | Booklet pane of 1 | | 1.40 | — |
| 2431 | A693 50c multi | | 1.00 | .70 |
| a. | Booklet pane of 1 | | 1.40 | — |
| b. | Horiz. strip of 5, #2427-2431 | | 5.00 | 4.00 |
| 2432 | A693 $1 multi | | 2.00 | 1.60 |
| a. | Booklet pane of 1 | | 2.75 | — |
| b. | Souvenir sheet, #2427-2432 | | 7.00 | 7.00 |
| c. | Booklet pane of 1 #2432b (120x190mm) | | 10.00 | — |
| | Complete booklet, #2427a-2432a, 2432c | | 20.00 | |
| | *Nos. 2427-2432 (6)* | | 7.00 | 5.10 |

The complete booklet containing Nos. 2427a-2432a and 2432c sold for $9.95.

### Booklet Stamps
### Self-Adhesive
***Serpentine Die Cut 11¼ Syncopated***

| | | | |
|---|---|---|---|
| 2433 | A693 50c multi | 1.00 | .70 |
| 2434 | A693 50c multi | 1.00 | .70 |
| 2435 | A693 50c multi | 1.00 | .70 |
| 2436 | A693 50c multi | 1.00 | .70 |
| 2437 | A693 50c multi | 1.00 | .70 |
| a. | Booklet pane of 5, #2433-2437 | 6.75 | — |
| b. | Booklet pane of 10, 2 each #2433-2437 | 10.00 | |
| c. | Booklet pane of 20, 4 each #2433-2437 | 20.00 | |
| 2438 | A693 $1 multi | 2.00 | 1.60 |
| a. | Booklet pane of 5 | 12.00 | — |
| | *Nos. 2433-2438 (6)* | 7.00 | 5.10 |

### Greetings Types of 2005 With Personalized Photo at Right Like Type A692a
***Serpentine Die Cut 11½x11¼ Syncopated***

**2005 Self-Adhesive**

| | | | |
|---|---|---|---|
| 2439 | A673 50c multi | 5.00 | 5.00 |
| 2440 | A674 50c multi | 5.00 | 5.00 |
| 2441 | A675 50c multi | 5.00 | 5.00 |
| 2442 | A676 50c multi | 5.00 | 5.00 |
| 2443 | A677 50c multi | 5.00 | 5.00 |
| 2444 | A678 $1 multi | 8.00 | 8.00 |
| 2445 | A679 $1.10 multi | 5.75 | 7.25 |
| 2446 | A680 $1.20 multi | 6.50 | 8.00 |
| 2447 | A681 $1.80 multi | 5.50 | 5.50 |
| | *Nos. 2439-2447 (9)* | 50.75 | 53.75 |

Nos. 2439-2447 were sold in sheets of 20 and have personalized pictures and a straight edge at right, and lack separations between the stamp and the picture. Sheets of 20 of Nos. 2439-2443 sold for $23 each, of No. 2444, $33.50, of No. 2445, $35, of No. 2446, $37, of No. 2447, $48.

Christmas — A694

Designs: Nos. 2448, 2450, Madonna and Child. Nos. 2449, 2451, Angel, horiz.

**2005, Nov. 1 Litho. *Perf. 14½x14***

| | | | |
|---|---|---|---|
| 2448 | A694 45c multi | .80 | .35 |

***Perf. 14x14½***

| | | | |
|---|---|---|---|
| 2449 | A694 $1 multi | 1.60 | 1.60 |

### Booklet Stamps
### Self-Adhesive
***Serpentine Die Cut 11½x11¼ Syncopated***

| | | | |
|---|---|---|---|
| 2450 | A694 45c multi | 1.00 | .75 |
| a. | Booklet pane of 20 | 20.00 | |

***Serpentine Die Cut 11¼x11½ Syncopated***

| | | | |
|---|---|---|---|
| 2451 | A694 $1 multi | 2.25 | 2.00 |
| a. | Booklet pane of 5 | 11.00 | |
| | *Nos. 2448-2451 (4)* | 5.65 | 4.70 |

Emblem of 2006 Commonwealth Games, Melbourne A695

Commonwealth Games Athletes A696

Highlights of Commonwealth Games — A697

Medalists at Commonwealth Games — A698

"Equality, Humanity, Destiny" A699

"Destiny, Equality, Humanity" A700

"Humanity, Destiny, Equality" A701

Designs: Nos. 2455, 2458, Runner crouching before race. $1.25, Cyclist. $1.85, Athlete holding ball.

No. 2459 — Sheet #1: a, Trolley car with wings. b, Fish sculpture. c, Cat and mouse puppets. d, Queen Elizabeth II. e, Opening ceremony crowd and fireworks.

No. 2460 — Sheet #2: a, Anna Meares. b, Equality, Humanity, destiny. c, Stephanie Rice swimming. d, Destiny, Equality, Humanity. e, Den Kersten.

No. 2461 — Sheet #3: a, Ryan Bayley holding flag. b, Adam Vella & Michael Diamond. c, Sean Finning. d, Deserie Baynes & Suzanne Balogh. e, Danni Miatke. f, Women's Artistic Gymnastics team. g, Kate Bates. h, Leisel Jones wearing swim cap and waving. i, David Moore & Daniel Repacholi.

No. 2462 — Sheet #4: a, Brad Kahlfeldt. b, Libby Lenton, lane marker in background. c, Josh Jefferis on pommel horse. d, Emma Snowsill.

No. 2463 — Sheet #5: a, Leisel Jones wearing sweatsuit. b, Ryan Bayley wearing cycling helmet. c, Matthew Cowdrey in water. d, Chloe Sims. e, Sophie Edington in water. f, Women's 4x200m freestyle swim team. g, Ben Turner.

No. 2464 — Sheet #6: a, Katie Mactier. b, Russell Mark & Craig Trembath. c, Jessicah Schipper in water. d, Kerryn McCann. e, Lalita Yauhleuskaya & Dina Aspandiyarova.

No. 2465 — Sheet #7: a, Lauryn Mark & Natalia Rahman. b, Jane Saville. c, Libby Lenton, pushing on lane marker. d, Nathan Deakes in 20km walk. e, Lisa McIntosh.

No. 2466 — Sheet #8: a, Leisel Jones with fist raised. b, Men's triples lawn bowling team. c, Sophie Edington holding medal. d, Matthew Cowdrey wearing sweatsuit. e, Brooke Krueger-Billett. f, Josh Jefferis kissing medal. g, Natalie Grinham. h, Women's 4x100m freestyle swim team. i, Joanna Fargus.

No. 2467 — Sheet #9: a, Alex Karapetyan. b, Jessicah Schipper wearing sweatsuit. c, Nathan O'Neill. d, Lalita Yauhleuskaya holding medal.

No. 2468 — Sheet #10: a, Hollie Dykes. b, Men's 4x100m medley swim team. c, Oenone Wood. d, Women's 4x100m medley swim team. e, Stephanie Rice with arm raised. f, Damian Istria. g, Deborah Lovely.

No. 2469 — Sheet #11: a, Chantelle Newbery & Loudy Tourky. b, John Steffensen. c, Bree Cole & Sharleen Stratton. d, Lyncey Armitage & Karen Murphy.

No. 2470 — Sheet #12: a, Heath Francis. b, Jana Pittman. c, Lalita Yauhleuskaya wearing sight. d, Scott Martin. e, Loudy Tourky. f, Women's basketball team. g, Chris Rae. h, Bruce Scott.

No. 2471 — Sheet #13: a, Nathan Deakes in 50km walk. b, Bronwyn Thompson. c, Robert Newbery & Mathew Helm. d, Steven Hooker. e, Stuart Rendell. f, Kelvin Kerkow. g, Men's basketball team.

No. 2472 — Sheet #14: a, Women's 4x400m relay team. b, Kym Howe. c, Women's field hockey team. d, Mathew Helm. e, Men's 4x400m relay team. f, Bradley Pitt. g, Jarrod Fletcher.

No. 2473 — Sheet #15: a, Natalie Bates. b, Natalie Grinham & Joe Kneipp. c, Men's field hockey team. d, Rachael Grinham & Natalie Grinham. e, Mathew Hayman.

No. 2474 — Sheet #16: a, Dancer on hoops. b, Women wearing hats. c, Dancer. d, Lit-up stadium and fireworks. e, Darkened stadium and fireworks.

No. 2475 — Sheet #17 — Kerryn McCann: a, Running, with opponents in background. b, Drinking from water bottle. c, Running past opponent, profile. d, Running on track with opponent. e, With hands over mouth. f, Collapsed on track. g, With both arms raised. h, Holding flag. i, Raising flower bouquet. j, Holding medal.

**2006 Litho. *Perf. 14¾x14***

| | | | |
|---|---|---|---|
| 2452 | A695 50c shown | .90 | .75 |
| a. | Sheet of 9 + 9 labels | 27.50 | — |
| b. | Booklet pane of 4 | 4.25 | — |

### Self-Adhesive (#2453-2454)
***Serpentine Die Cut 11¼ Syncopated***

| | | | |
|---|---|---|---|
| 2453 | A695 50c multi | .75 | .75 |
| a. | Booklet pane of 4 | 4.50 | |

### With Personalized Photo at Right Like Type A692a
### Booklet Stamp
***Serpentine Die Cut 11½x11¼ on 3 Sides, Syncopated***

| | | | |
|---|---|---|---|
| 2454 | A695 50c multi | 1.50 | 1.50 |
| a. | Booklet pane of 4 | 7.00 | |

***Perf. 14x14¾***

| | | | |
|---|---|---|---|
| 2455 | A696 50c shown | .80 | .60 |
| 2456 | A696 $1.25 multi | 2.00 | 2.00 |
| 2457 | A696 $1.85 multi | 2.75 | 2.75 |
| a. | Souvenir sheet, #2455-2457, 142x75mm sheet | 5.50 | 5.50 |
| b. | Booklet pane, #2455-2457, in 168x118mm pane | 7.75 | — |
| | Complete booklet, #1488a, 2457b, 2 each #2453a, 2454a, + 3 postal cards | 37.50 | |
| c. | Booklet pane, #2455-2457, in 156x103mm pane | 7.75 | — |
| | Complete booklet, #845a, 2219c, 2452b, 2457c | 22.00 | |
| | *Nos. 2455-2457 (3)* | 5.55 | 5.35 |

### Booklet Stamp
### Self-Adhesive
***Serpentine Die Cut 11¼ Syncopated***

| | | | |
|---|---|---|---|
| 2458 | A696 50c multi | .90 | .75 |
| a. | Booklet pane of 10 | 10.00 | |

### Miniature Sheets
***Perf. 14½x14***

| | | | |
|---|---|---|---|
| 2459 | Sheet of 5 | 7.25 | 15.00 |
| a.-e. | A697 50c any single | 1.40 | 3.00 |
| 2460 | Sheet of 5 | 7.25 | 11.00 |
| a. | A698 50c multi | 1.40 | 3.00 |
| b. | A699 50c multi | 1.40 | 1.00 |
| c. | A698 50c multi | 1.40 | 3.00 |
| d. | A700 50c multi | 1.40 | 1.00 |
| e. | A698 50c multi | 1.40 | 3.00 |
| 2461 | Sheet of 10, #2460b, 2461a-2461i | 14.50 | 28.00 |
| a.-i. | A698 50c any single | 1.40 | 3.00 |
| 2462 | Sheet of 5, #2460b, 2462a-2462d | 7.25 | 13.00 |
| a.-d. | A698 50c any single | 1.40 | 3.00 |
| 2463 | Sheet of 10, #2460b, 2460d, 2463a-2463h | 14.50 | 24.00 |
| a.-g. | A698 50c any single | 1.40 | 3.00 |
| h. | A701 50c multi | 1.40 | 1.00 |
| 2464 | Sheet of 5 | 7.25 | 15.00 |
| a.-e. | A698 50c any single | 1.40 | 3.00 |
| 2465 | Sheet of 5 | 7.25 | 15.00 |
| a.-e. | A698 50c any single | 1.40 | 3.00 |
| 2466 | Sheet of 10, #2460b, 2466a-2466i | 14.50 | 28.00 |
| a.-i. | A698 50c any single | 1.40 | 3.00 |
| 2467 | Sheet of 5, #2460b, 2467a-2467d | 7.25 | 13.00 |
| a.-d. | A698 50c any single | 1.40 | 3.00 |
| 2468 | Sheet of 10, #2460b, 2460d, 2463h, 2468a-2468g | 14.50 | 24.00 |
| a.-g. | A698 50c any single | 1.40 | 3.00 |
| 2469 | Sheet of 5, #2460b, 2469a-2469d | 7.25 | 13.00 |
| a.-d. | A698 50c any single | 1.40 | 3.00 |
| 2470 | Sheet of 10, #2460b, 2460d, 2470a-2470h | 14.50 | 26.00 |
| a.-h. | A698 50c any single | 1.40 | 3.00 |
| 2471 | Sheet of 10, #2460b, 2460d, 2463h, 2471a-2471g | 14.50 | 24.00 |
| a.-g. | A698 50c any single | 1.40 | 3.00 |
| 2472 | Sheet of 10, #2460b, 2460d, 2463h, 2472a-2472g | 14.50 | 24.00 |
| a.-g. | A698 50c any single | 1.40 | 3.00 |
| 2473 | Sheet of 5 | 7.25 | 15.00 |
| a.-e. | A698 50c any single | 1.40 | 3.00 |
| 2474 | Sheet of 5 | 7.25 | 15.00 |
| a.-e. | A697 50c any single | 1.40 | 3.00 |
| 2475 | Sheet of 10 | 14.50 | 30.00 |
| a.-j. | A697 50c any single | 1.40 | 3.00 |
| | *Nos. 2459-2475 (17)* | 181.25 | 333.00 |

Issued: Nos. 2452-2453, 1/12; Nos. 2454, 2457b, 3/15; Nos. 2452b, 2455-2458, 2457c, 3/1; No. 2459, 3/16; No. 2460, 3/17; No. 2461, 3/18; Nos. 2462, 2463, 3/19; No. 2464, 3/20; Nos. 2465, 2466, 3/21; Nos. 2467, 2468, 3/22; No. 2469, 3/23; No. 2470, 3/24; No. 2471, 3/25; No. 2472, 3/26; Nos. 2473, 2474, 3/27; No. 2475, 3/28.

No. 2452a sold for $15.95. Labels could be personalized.

Complete booklet containing No. 2454 sold for $19.95. Labels could be personalized.

Complete booklet containing No. 2457c sold for $10.95 and included a booklet pane with perf. 14x14¾ lithographed examples of Nos. 349-350 which were not valid for postage.

A booklet issued 2/1, containing #2452b, an imperf booklet pane of 4 #2452, a booklet pane of 2 #2453, a booklet pane of 1 #2453 and four 50c coins, sold for $24.95.

Dame Edna Everage in 2004 A702

Barry Humphries A703

Inscriptions: Nos. 2476, 2481, Mrs. Norm Everage, 1969. Nos. 2477, 2482, Mrs. Edna Everage, 1973. Nos. 2478, 2483, Dame Edna Everage, 1982.

**2006, Jan. 20 Litho. *Perf. 14½x14***

| | | | |
|---|---|---|---|
| 2476 | A702 50c multi | .80 | .70 |
| 2477 | A702 50c multi | .80 | .70 |
| 2478 | A702 50c multi | .80 | .70 |
| 2479 | A702 50c shown | .80 | .70 |
| 2480 | A703 50c shown | .80 | .70 |
| a. | Horiz. strip of 5, #2476-2480 | 4.75 | 4.00 |
| b. | Booklet pane, #2476-2480 | 5.25 | — |
| | Complete booklet | 45.00 | |
| | *Nos. 2476-2480 (5)* | 4.00 | 3.50 |

### Booklet Stamps
### Self-Adhesive
***Serpentine Die Cut 11¼ Syncopated***

| | | | |
|---|---|---|---|
| 2481 | A702 50c multi | .75 | .75 |
| 2482 | A702 50c multi | .75 | .75 |
| 2483 | A702 50c multi | .75 | .75 |
| a. | Booklet pane, 4 #2481, 3 each #2482-2483 | 9.00 | |
| 2484 | A702 50c multi | .75 | .75 |
| 2485 | A703 50c multi | .75 | .75 |
| a. | Booklet pane, 5 each #2484-2485 | 9.00 | |
| | *Nos. 2481-2485 (5)* | 3.75 | 3.75 |

Edna Everage, stage character played by Barry Humphries.

No. 2480b issued 1/24/07. Complete booklet, which sold for $22.95, contains Nos. 1576b, 1634m, 1634n, 1634o, 1720b, 1803b, 1934b, 2025b, 2128b, 2208b, 2324b, 2326b, 2328b, and 2480b.

Rose — A704

**2006, Jan. 27 Litho. *Perf. 14x14¾***

| | | | |
|---|---|---|---|
| 2486 | A704 50c multi | 1.00 | 1.00 |

### With White Border
### Self-Adhesive
### Litho. & Typo.
***Serpentine Die Cut 11¼ Syncopated***

| | | | |
|---|---|---|---|
| 2487 | A704 50c multi | 1.60 | 1.60 |

### Booklet Stamp
### Litho.

| | | | |
|---|---|---|---|
| 2488 | A704 50c multi | 1.00 | 1.00 |
| a. | Booklet pane of 10 | 10.00 | |

No. 2487 has a scratch-and-sniff area with a rose scent applied to the center of the rose, has a denomination composed of small black dots, and was printed in sheets of 10. No. 2488 lacks the scrach and sniff panel and has a solid gray denomination.

Flowers — A705

Designs: $1, Pincushion hakea. $2, Donkey orchid. $5, Mangles kangaroo paw. $10, Waratah.

**2006, Feb. 7 Litho. *Perf. 14x14½***

**2489** A705 $1 multi 2.00 1.40
**2490** A705 $2 multi 3.25 2.50

***Perf. 14½x14***

**Size:50x30mm**

**2491** A705 $5 multi 7.75 6.50
*a.* Souvenir sheet of 1 6.50 6.50
**2492** A705 $10 multi 15.50 13.00
*Nos. 2489-2492 (4)* 28.50 23.40

**Souvenir Sheet**

**Litho. & Embossed**

**2493** A705 $10 multi 20.00 20.00

Issued: No. 2491a, 9/30/22. 2022 Perth Stamp & Coin Show (No. 2491a).

Dale Begg-Smith, Men's Moguls Gold Medalist at 2006 Winter Olympics, Turin — A706

**2006, Feb. 15 Litho. *Perf. 14½***

**2494** A706 50c multi 2.75 2.00

Animals A707

Royal Exhibition Building, Melbourne A708

Designs: 2495, 5c, Platypus. 2496, 25c, Short-beaked echidna. No. 2497, $1.25, Common wombat. Nos. 2498, $1.25, Koala, vert. No. 2499, $1.85, Tasmanian devil. 2501, $2.50, Greater bilby. 2502, $3.70, Dingo.

**2006 *Perf. 14x14¾, 14¾x14***

**2495** A707 5c multi .25 .25
**2496** A707 25c multi .50 .35
**2497** A707 $1.25 multi 2.00 2.00
**2498** A707 $1.25 multi 2.50 2.50
*a.* Souvenir sheet of 1, with China 2006 emblem and Great Wall of China in sheet margin 2.25 2.25
*b.* As "a," with Sydney landmarks in sheet margin 2.25 2.25
**2499** A707 $1.85 multi 3.25 3.25
**2500** A708 $1.85 multi 3.75 3.75
**2501** A707 $2.50 multi 4.00 4.00
**2502** A707 $3.70 multi 6.50 6.50
*Nos. 2495-2502 (8)* 22.75 22.60

**Self-Adhesive**

**Booklet Stamps**

***Serpentine Die Cut 11¼ Syncopated***

**2503** A707 $1.25 multi 2.50 2.50
*a.* Booklet pane of 5 12.75
*b.* Booklet pane of 2 5.75
Complete booklet, 4 #2503b 23.00
*c.* As "a," with Washington 2000 Exhib. emblem added to lower right margin of bklt. pane 13.75
**2504** A708 $1.85 multi 3.75 3.75
*a.* Booklet pane of 5 19.00
*b.* Booklet pane of 2 7.50
Complete booklet, 4 #2504b 30.00

Issued: Nos. 2498, 2500, 2503, 2504, 5/2; No. 2503c, 5/27; others, 3/6.

Each of the four panes of Nos. 2503b and 2504b in the complete booklets have different margins. The complete booklet containing No. 2503b sold for $12.95; the booklet containing No. 2504b sold for $14.95.

Nos. 2498a-2498b issued 10/26.

See Nos. 2542-2543, 2674, 2676, 2678, 5010.

Queen Elizabeth II, 80th Birthday
A709 A710

**2006, Apr. 19 *Perf. 14¾x14***

**2505** A709 50c multi 1.00 1.00
*a.* Booklet pane of 2 2.00 —
*b.* Dated "2010" 2.00 1.00
**2506** A710 $2.45 multi 4.75 4.75
*a.* Booklet pane of 2 10.00 —
*b.* Booklet pane, #2505-2506, 153x104mm pane size 6.00 —
Complete booklet, #2506a, 2506b, 2 #2505a 20.00
*c.* Souvenir sheet, #2505-2506, 105x70mm sheet size 6.50 6.50

**Self-Adhesive**

**Booklet Stamp**

***Serpentine Die Cut 11¼ Syncopated***

**2507** A709 50c multi 1.00 .75
*a.* Booklet pane of 10 10.00

Complete booklet containing Nos. 2505-2506 sold for $10.95.

---

A booklet commemorating royal visits to Australia containing a booklet pane of 2 each of lithographed, perf. 14x14¾ example of Nos. 474-475, a booklet pane of 4 lithographed, perf. 14x14¾ examples of No. 779, a booklet pane of 2 each of lithographed perf. 14½x14 examples of Nos. 659-660, a booklet pane of 2 each Nos. 2031-2032, a booklet pane of No. 2234a with a different margin, a booklet pane of 2 each of perf. 14½x14 examples of Nos. 351-352 (not valid for postage), and a 50c coin was released in 2006. It sold for $15.95.

---

Lighthouses — A711

Designs: Nos. 2508, 2513, Point Lonsdale Lighthouse, Victoria. Nos. 2509, 2514, Cape Don Lighthouse, Northern Territory. Nos. 2510, 2515, Wollongong Head Lighthouse, New South Wales. Nos. 2511, 2516, Casuarina Point Lighthouse, Western Australia. Nos. 2512, 2517, Point Cartwright Lighthouse, Queensland.

**2006, May 2 *Perf. 14¾x14***

**2508** A711 50c multi .80 .70
**2509** A711 50c multi .80 .70
**2510** A711 50c multi .80 .70
*a.* Booklet pane, #2509, 2510, 2 #2508 4.25 —
*b.* Booklet pane, #2508, 2509, 2 #2510 4.25 —
**2511** A711 50c multi .80 .70
**2512** A711 50c multi .80 .70
*a.* Horiz. strip, #2508-2512 4.50 4.50
*b.* Booklet pane, #2511, 2512, 2 #2509 4.25 —
*c.* Booklet pane, #2510, 2512, 2 #2511 4.25 —
*d.* Booklet pane, #2508, 2511, 2 #2512 4.25 —
Complete booklet, #2510a, 2510b, 2512b, 2512c, 2512d 20.00
*Nos. 2508-2512 (5)* 4.00 3.50

**Coil Stamps**

**Self-Adhesive**

***Serpentine Die Cut 11¼ Syncopated***

**2513** A711 50c multi .75 .75
**2514** A711 50c multi .75 .75
**2515** A711 50c multi .75 .75
**2516** A711 50c multi .75 .75
**2517** A711 50c multi .75 .75
*a.* Vert. strip, #2513-2517 5.75

Complete booklet sold for $10.95.

2006 World Cup Soccer Championships, Germany — A712

Soccer player, 2006 World Cup emblem and word: Nos. 2518, 2522, "Play." Nos. 2519, 2523, "Goal." $1.25, "Save." $1.85, "Shot."

**2006, May 9 *Perf. 14x14¾***

**2518** A712 50c multi .80 .70
**2519** A712 50c multi .80 .70
*a.* Horiz. pair, #2518-2519 2.25 2.25
**2520** A712 $1.25 multi 1.90 1.75
**2521** A712 $1.85 multi 3.00 3.00
*a.* Souvenir sheet, #2518-2521 8.00 8.00
*b.* As "a," with 2006 Paris Exhib. ovpt. 9.25 9.25
*Nos. 2518-2521 (4)* 6.50 6.15

**Booklet Stamps**

**Self-Adhesive**

***Serpentine Die Cut 11¼ Syncopated***

**2522** A712 50c multi 1.00 .75
**2523** A712 50c multi 1.00 .75
*a.* Booklet pane, 5 each #2522-2523 11.00

No. 2521b issued 6/17.

Postie Kate — A713

Kate: Nos. 2524, 2529, Writing address on letter. Nos. 2525, 2530, On motorcycle, delivering letter. Nos. 2526, 2531, With van, delivering package. Nos. 2527, 2532, Riding motorcycle in rain. Nos. 2528, 2533, Waving.

**2006, June 1 Litho. *Perf. 14x14¾***

**2524** A713 50c multi .75 .60
*a.* Booklet pane of 1 1.75 —
**2525** A713 50c multi .75 .60
*a.* Booklet pane of 1 1.75 —
**2526** A713 50c multi .75 .60
*a.* Booklet pane of 1 1.75 —
**2527** A713 50c multi .75 .60
*a.* Booklet pane of 1 1.75 —
**2528** A713 50c multi .75 .60
*a.* Horiz. strip of 5, #2524-2528 4.00 3.60
*b.* Booklet pane of 1 1.75 —
*Nos. 2524-2528 (5)* 3.75 3.00

**Booklet Stamps**

**Self-Adhesive**

***Serpentine Die Cut 11¼ Syncopated***

**2529** A713 50c multi 1.00 .60
**2530** A713 50c multi 1.00 .60
**2531** A713 50c multi 1.00 .60
**2532** A713 50c multi 1.00 .60
**2533** A713 50c multi 1.00 .60
*a.* Booklet pane, 2 each #2529-2533 11.00
*b.* Booklet pane, 4 each #2529-2533 20.00
*c.* Booklet pane, #2529-2533 5.00
Complete booklet, #2524a, 2525a, 2526a, 2527a, 2528b, 2533c 20.00
*Nos. 2529-2533 (5)* 5.00 3.00

Complete booklet sold for $9.95.

Worldwide Fund for Nature (WWF) — A714

Designs: Nos. 2534, 2538, Humpback whale. Nos. 2535, 2539, Blue whale. $1.25, Fin whale. $1.85, Southern bottlenose whale.

**2006, June 6 *Perf. 14x14¾***

**2534** A714 50c multi .75 .60
**2535** A714 50c multi .75 .60
*a.* Horiz. pair, #2534-2535 2.00 2.00
**2536** A714 $1.25 multi 2.50 2.50
**2537** A714 $1.85 multi 3.00 3.00
*a.* Souvenir sheet, #2534-2537 6.00 5.25
*Nos. 2534-2537 (4)* 7.00 6.70

**Self-Adhesive**

***Serpentine Die Cut 11¼ Syncopated***

**Coil Stamps**

**2538** A714 50c multi 1.10 .95
**2539** A714 50c multi 1.10 .95
*a.* Horiz. pair, #2538-2539 2.25

**Booklet Stamps**

**2540** A714 $1.25 multi 6.50 6.50
*a.* Booklet pane of 5 32.50
**2541** A714 $1.85 multi 7.25 7.25
*a.* Booklet pane of 5 37.50
*Nos. 2538-2541 (4)* 15.95 15.65

**Types of 2006 With Personalized Photo at Right Like Type A692a**

Designs: $1.25, Koala. $1.85, Royal Exhibition Building.

***Serpentine Die Cut 11½x11¼ Syncopated***

**2006 Litho.**

**Self-Adhesive**

**2542** A707 $1.25 multi *8.00 8.00*
**2543** A708 $1.85 multi *12.00 12.00*

Nos. 2542-2543 were sold in sheets of 20 and have personalized pictures and a straight edge at right, and lack separations between the stamp and the pictures. Sheets of 20 of No. 2542 sold for $38, and of No. 2543, $49.

Extreme Sports — A715

Designs: 50c, Surfing. $1, Snowboarding. $1.45, Skateboarding. $2, Freestyle motocross.

**2006, July 18 Litho. *Perf. 14x14¾***

**2544** A715 50c multi .75 .70
**2545** A715 $1 multi 1.50 1.25
**2546** A715 $1.45 multi 2.50 2.50
**2547** A715 $2 multi 3.25 3.25
*Nos. 2544-2547 (4)* 8.00 7.70

Cars and Trucks — A716

Designs: Nos. 2548, 2553, 1917 Ford TT Truck. Nos. 2549, 2554, 1956 Holden FE. Nos. 2550, 2555, 1961 Morris 850. Nos. 2551, 2556, 1976 Holden Sandman HX. Nos. 2552, 2557, 1985 Toyota Land Cruiser FJ60.

**2006, Aug. 15 *Perf. 14x14¾***

**2548** A716 50c multi .75 .70
*a.* Booklet pane of 4 3.50 —
**2549** A716 50c multi .75 .70
*a.* Booklet pane of 4 3.50 —
**2550** A716 50c multi .75 .70
*a.* Booklet pane of 4 3.50 —
**2551** A716 50c multi .75 .70
*a.* Booklet pane of 4 3.50 —
**2552** A716 50c multi .75 .70
*a.* Booklet pane of 4 3.50 —
Complete booklet, #2548a-2552a 18.00
*b.* Horiz. strip of 5, #2548-2552 4.75 4.00
*Nos. 2548-2552 (5)* 3.75 3.50

**Booklet Stamps**

**Self-Adhesive**

***Serpentine Die Cut 11¼ Syncopated***

**2553** A716 50c multi .90 .70
*a.* Booklet pane of 10 11.00
*b.* Missing 2006 date
**2554** A716 50c multi .90 .70
*a.* Booklet pane of 10 11.00
**2555** A716 50c multi .90 .70
*a.* Booklet pane of 10 11.00
**2556** A716 50c multi .90 .70
*a.* Booklet pane of 10 11.00
**2557** A716 50c multi .90 .70
*a.* Booklet pane of 10 11.00
*b.* Booklet pane, 2 each #2553-2557 16.00
*Nos. 2553-2557 (5)* 4.50 3.50

Complete booklet containing Nos. 2548a-2552a sold for $10.95.

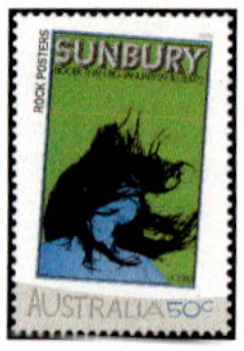


Rock Posters — A717

Designs: Nos. 2558a, 2559a, Sunbury Rock Festival, 1972. Nos. 2558b, 2559b, Magic Dirt Tour, 2002. Nos. 2558c, 2559c, The Masters Apprentices Parramatta concert, 1972. Nos. 2558d, 2559d, Goanna's Spirit of Place album, 1983. Nos. 2558e, 2559e, Angels, Sports and Paul Kelly and the Dots Latrobe concert, 1979. Nos. 2558f, 2559f, Midnight Oil, 1979. Nos. 2558g, 2559g, Big Day Out Festival, 2003. Nos. 2558h, 2559h, Apollo Bay Music Festival, 1999. Nos. 2558i, 2559i, Rolling Stones Australian Tour, 1973. Nos. 2558j, 2559j, Mental as Anything's Another Falcon Tour, 1990.

**2006, Sept. 12 Litho. *Perf. 14½x14***

**2558** Sheet of 10 16.00 16.00
*a.-j.* A717 50c Any single .95 .95
*k.* Booklet pane of 2 #2558a 2.25 —
*l.* Booklet pane of 2 #2558b 2.25 —
*m.* Booklet pane of 2 #2558c 2.25 —
*n.* Booklet pane of 2 #2558d 2.25 —
*o.* Booklet pane of 2 #2558e 2.25 —
*p.* Booklet pane of 2 #2558f 2.25 —
*q.* Booklet pane of 2 #2558g 2.25 —
*r.* Booklet pane of 2 #2558h 2.25 —
*s.* Booklet pane of 2 #2558i 2.25 —
*t.* Booklet pane of 2 #2558j 2.25 —
Complete booklet, #2558k-2558t 22.00

**Self-Adhesive**

***Serpentine Die Cut 11½x11¼ Syncopated***

2559 Booklet pane of 10 16.00
a.-j. A717 50c Any single 1.00 1.00

Complete booklet containing Nos. 2558k-2558t sold for $10.95.

Dangerous Australian Wildlife — A718

Designs: Nos. 2560, 2566, White shark. Nos. 2561, 2567, Eastern brown snake. Nos. 2562, 2568, Box jellyfish. Nos. 2563, 2569, Saltwater crocodile. Nos. 2564, 2570, Blue-ringed octopus. Nos. 2565, 2571, Yellow-bellied sea snake.

**2006, Oct. 3 Litho. *Perf. 14x14¾***

2560 A718 50c multi 1.00 .70
a. Booklet pane of 2 2.25 —
2561 A718 50c multi 1.00 .70
2562 A718 50c multi 1.00 .70
a. Booklet pane of 2 2.25 —
2563 A718 50c multi 1.00 .70
a. Booklet pane of 2 2.25 —
2564 A718 50c multi 1.00 .70
a. Horiz. strip of 5, #2560-2564 5.00 5.00
b. Booklet pane of 2 2.25 —
2565 A718 $1 multi 1.90 1.90
a. Booklet pane, 2 each #2561, 2565 6.50 —
b. Booklet pane, #2560-2565 (page 26) 7.50 —
c. Souvenir sheet, #2560-2565 7.75 7.75
Complete booklet, #2560a, 2562a, 2563a, 2564b, 2565a, 2565b 25.00
*Nos. 2560-2565 (6)* 6.90 5.40

**Self-Adhesive**

***Serpentine Die Cut 11 Syncopated***

2566 A718 50c multi 1.00 .70
2567 A718 50c multi 1.00 .70
2568 A718 50c multi 1.00 .70
2569 A718 50c multi 1.00 .70
2570 A718 50c multi 1.00 .70
a. Horiz. coil strip of 5, #2566-2570 5.75
b. Booklet pane, #2566-2570 7.00
2571 A718 $1 multi 1.75 1.75
a. Booklet pane of 5 9.00
*Nos. 2566-2571 (6)* 6.75 5.25

Complete booklet sold for $10.95. A souvenir sheet similar to No. 2565c containing partially perforated examples of Nos. 2560-2564 and a stamp that is assumed to be invalid depicting a red-back spider sold for $9.95. Value $25.

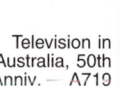

Television in Australia, 50th Anniv. — A719

Television shows: Nos. 2572, 2577, IMT (In Melbourne Tonight). Nos. 2573, 2578, Homicide. Nos. 2574, 2579, Dateline. Nos. 2575, 2580, Neighbours. Nos. 2576, 2581, Kath & Kim.

**2006, Oct. 24 Litho. *Perf. 14x14¾***

2572 A719 50c multi .75 .60
2573 A719 50c multi .75 .60
2574 A719 50c multi .75 .60
2575 A719 50c multi .75 .60
2576 A719 50c multi .75 .60
a. Horiz. strip of 5, #2572-2576 4.50 4.50
*Nos. 2572-2576 (5)* 3.75 3.00

**Self-Adhesive**

***Serpentine Die Cut 11¼x11½ Syncopated***

2577 A719 50c multi .90 .30
a. Booklet pane of 10 #2577 9.00
2578 A719 50c multi .90 .30
2579 A719 50c multi .90 .30
2580 A719 50c multi .90 .30
2581 A719 50c multi .90 .30
a. Booklet pane of 10 #2581 9.25
b. Booklet pane of 10, 2 each #2577-2581 9.25
c. Horiz. coil strip of 5, #2577-2581 5.25
*Nos. 2577-2581 (5)* 4.50 1.50

Melbourne Summer Olympics, 50th Anniv. — A720

1956 Melbourne Olympics emblem and: No. 2582, Australia #291, Olympic torch. No. 2583, View of Melbourne across Yarra River, 2006, Olympic torch. No. 2584, Australia #290, runners. No. 2585, Collins Street, Melbourne, 2006, runners.

**2006, Nov. 1 *Perf. 14¾x14***

2582 A720 50c multi .90 .70
2583 A720 50c multi .90 .70
a. Horiz. pair, #2582-2583 2.00 2.00
2584 A720 $1 multi 1.90 1.20
2585 A720 $1 multi 1.90 1.20
a. Horiz. pair, #2584-2585 4.80 2.75
*Nos. 2582-2585 (4)* 5.60 3.80

Christmas — A721

Designs: 45c, Madonna and Child. 50c, Magus with gift. $1.05, Shepherd and lamb.

**2006, Nov. 1 *Perf. 14¾x14***

2586 A721 45c multi .80 .40
2587 A721 50c multi .80 .50
2588 A721 $1.05 multi 1.60 1.60
*Nos. 2586-2588 (3)* 3.20 2.50

**Self-Adhesive**

**Booklet Stamps**

***Serpentine Die Cut 11½x11¼ Syncopated***

2589 A721 45c multi .80 .30
a. Booklet pane of 20 16.00
2590 A721 $1.05 multi 1.90 .30
a. Booklet pane of 5 9.25

Australian Victory in 2006 Ashes Cricket Match — A722

Designs: 50c, Players celebrating. $1.85, Players with Ashes Urn.

**2007, Jan. 16 Litho. *Perf. 14½x14***

2591 A722 50c multi .75 .65
a. Imperf. 2.00 2.00
2592 A722 $1.85 multi 2.75 2.40
a. Souvenir sheet, #2591-2592 4.50 4.50
b. Imperf. *15.00* *12.00*
c. Booklet pane of 2, #2591a, 2592b 7.50 —
Complete booklet, #591a, 666b, 773a, 1084a, 1302b, 2345a, 2592c 32.00

**Booklet Stamps**

**Self-Adhesive**

***Serpentine Die Cut 10¾x11¼ Syncopated***

2593 A722 50c multi 1.50 .75
a. Booklet pane of 5 7.50
2594 A722 $1.85 multi 5.00 2.50
a. Booklet pane of 5 25.00
*Nos. 2591-2594 (4)* 10.00 6.30

Nos. 2591a, 2592b, 2592c issued 11/14/07. Complete booklet sold for $14.95 and was not made available to foreign addresses.

Horse Racing Personalities — A723

Designs: Nos. 2595, 2607, Scobie Breasley, jockey, in silks. No. 2596, Breasley on horse. Nos. 2597, 2608, Bart Cummings, horse trainer, with binoculars. No. 2598, Cummings holding trophy. No. 2599, Roy Higgins, jockey, in silks. Nos. 2600, 2609, Higgins on horse. No. 2601, Bob Ingham, horse breeder. Nos. 2602, 2610, Ingham with horse. Nos. 2603, 2611, George Moore, jockey, in silks. No. 2604, Moore on horse. Nos. 2605, 2612, John Tapp, horse race announcer. No. 2606, Tapp with binoculars.

**2007, Jan. 24 *Perf. 14½x14***

2595 A723 50c multi .90 .75
2596 A723 50c multi .90 .75
2597 A723 50c multi .90 .75
2598 A723 50c multi .90 .75
a. Block of 4, #2595-2598 3.75 3.00
2599 A723 50c multi .90 .75
2600 A723 50c multi .90 .75
2601 A723 50c multi .90 .75
2602 A723 50c multi .90 .75
a. Block of 4, #2599-2602 3.75 3.00
2603 A723 50c multi .90 .75
2604 A723 50c multi .90 .75
2605 A723 50c multi .90 .75
2606 A723 50c multi .90 .75
a. Block of 4, #2603-2606 3.75 3.00
*Nos. 2595-2606 (12)* 10.80 9.00

**Booklet Stamps**

**Self-Adhesive**

***Serpentine Die Cut 11x11¼ Syncopated***

2607 A723 50c multi .90 .30
2608 A723 50c multi .90 .30
a. Booklet pane of 10, 5 each #2607-2608 9.25
2609 A723 50c multi .90 .30
2610 A723 50c multi .90 .30
a. Booklet pane of 10, 5 each #2609-2610 9.25
2611 A723 50c multi .90 .30
2612 A723 50c multi .90 .30
a. Booklet pane of 10, 5 each #2611-2612 9.25
*Nos. 2607-2612 (6)* 5.40 1.80

Flowers — A724

Designs: Nos. 2613, 2617, 2621, Tasmanian Christmas bell. Nos. 2614, 2618, 2622, Green spider flower. Nos. 2615, 2619, 2623, Sturt's desert rose. Nos. 2616, 2620, 2624, Phebalium whitei.

**2007, Feb. 13 Litho. *Perf. 14x14½***

2613 A724 50c multi .90 .40
2614 A724 50c multi .90 .40
2615 A724 50c multi .90 .40
2616 A724 50c multi .90 .40
a. Horiz. strip of 4, #2613-2616 3.75 3.00
*Nos. 2613-2616 (4)* 3.60 1.60

**Self-Adhesive**

***Serpentine Die Cut 11¼***

2617 A724 50c multi .90 .30
2618 A724 50c multi .90 .30
2619 A724 50c multi .90 .30
2620 A724 50c multi .90 .30
a. Horiz. coil strip of 4, #2617-2620 3.75
b. Booklet pane of 10, 3 each #2617-2618, 2 each #2619-2620 9.25
c. Booklet pane of 20, 5 each #2617-2620 18.50

**Coil Stamps**

***Die Cut Perf. 12¾***

2621 A724 50c multi .90 .30
2622 A724 50c multi .90 .30
2623 A724 50c multi .90 .30
2624 A724 50c multi .90 .30
a. Horiz. strip of 4, #2621-2624 3.75
*Nos. 2617-2624 (8)* 7.20 2.40

12th FINA World Swimming Championships, Melbourne — A725

**2007, Feb. 20 *Perf. 14½x14***

2625 A725 50c multi 1.00 1.00

**Coil Stamp**

**Self-Adhesive**

***Serpentine Die Cut 11¼ Syncopated***

2626 A725 50c multi 1.10 .30

Islands — A726

Designs: 10c, Maria Island, Tasmania. 30c, Rottnest Island, Western Australia. $1.30, Green Island, Queensland. $1.95, Fraser Island, Queensland. $2.60, Kangaroo Island, South Australia. $3.85, Lord Howe Island, New South Wales.

**2007, Mar. 5 *Perf. 14x14½***

2627 A726 10c multi .25 .25
2628 A726 30c multi .60 .30
2629 A726 $1.30 multi 2.25 1.60
2630 A726 $1.95 multi 3.50 2.40
2631 A726 $2.60 multi 4.50 2.25
2632 A726 $3.85 multi 7.00 3.50
*Nos. 2627-2632 (6)* 18.10 10.30

**Booklet Stamps**

**Self-Adhesive**

***Serpentine Die Cut 11¼ Syncopated***

2633 A726 $1.30 multi 2.25 .30
a. Booklet pane of 5 30.00
2634 A726 $1.95 multi 3.50 .30
a. Booklet pane of 5 40.00

Surf Life Saving Australia, Cent. — A727

Designs: Nos. 2635, 2639, Female lifeguard. Nos. 2636, 2640, Male lifeguards. $1, Surf boat crew. $2, Nippers (junior lifeguards). $2.45, Inflatable rescue boat and crew, vert. (30x50mm).

**2007, Mar. 6 Litho. *Perf. 14x14½***

2635 A727 50c multi .90 .90
a. Booklet pane of 1 1.25 —
2636 A727 50c multi .90 .90
a. Horiz. pair, #2635-2636 1.90 1.90
b. Booklet pane of 1 1.25 —
2637 A727 $1 multi 1.90 1.40
a. Booklet pane of 1 2.50 —
2638 A727 $2 multi 3.75 2.75
a. Booklet pane of 1 5.25 —
*Nos. 2635-2638 (4)* 7.45 5.95

**Self-Adhesive**

**Coil Stamps (#2639-2640)**

***Serpentine Die Cut 11¼ Syncopated***

2639 A727 50c multi .90 .30
2640 A727 50c multi .90 .30
a. Horiz. pair, #2639-2640 1.90

**Litho. With Three-Dimensional Plastic Affixed**

2641 A727 $2.45 multi 4.25 4.25
a. Souvenir sheet of 2 8.50
b. Booklet pane, as "a," with rouletting at left of pane 12.50
Complete booklet, #2635a, 2636b, 2637a, 2638a, 2641b 23.00

Complete booklet sold for $12.95. No. 2641a does not have rouletting at left side of sheet.

Signs of the Zodiac — A728

Designs: Nos. 2642, 2654, 2665B, Aries. Nos. 2643, 2655, 2665C, Taurus. Nos. 2644, 2656, 2665D, Gemini. Nos. 2645, 2657, 2665E, Cancer. Nos. 2646, 2658, 2665F, Leo. Nos. 2647, 2659, 2665G, Virgo. Nos. 2648, 2660, 2665H, Libra. Nos. 2649, 2661, 2665I, Scorpio. Nos. 2650, 2662, 2665J, Sagittarius. Nos. 2651, 2663, 2665K, Capricorn. Nos. 2652, 2664, 2665L, Aquarius. Nos. 2653, 2665, 2665M, Pisces.

**2007, Apr. 3 Litho. *Perf. 14½x14***

2642 A728 50c multi .95 .95
2643 A728 50c multi .95 .95
2644 A728 50c multi .95 .95
2645 A728 50c multi .95 .95
a. Block of 4, #2642-2645 4.00
2646 A728 50c multi .95 .95
2647 A728 50c multi .95 .95
2648 A728 50c multi .95 .95
2649 A728 50c multi .95 .95
a. Block of 4, #2646-2649 4.00
2650 A728 50c multi .95 .95
2651 A728 50c multi .95 .95
2652 A728 50c multi .95 .95
2653 A728 50c multi .95 .95
a. Block of 4, #2650-2653 4.00
*Nos. 2642-2653 (12)* 11.40 11.40

**Booklet Stamps**

**Self-Adhesive**

***Serpentine Die Cut 11¼ Syncopated***

2654 A728 50c multi 1.00 .30
a. Booklet pane of 10 10.50
2655 A728 50c multi 1.00 .30
a. Booklet pane of 10 10.50
2656 A728 50c multi 1.00 .30
a. Booklet pane of 10 10.50
2657 A728 50c multi 1.00 .30
a. Booklet pane of 10 10.50
2658 A728 50c multi 1.00 .30
a. Booklet pane of 10 10.50
2659 A728 50c multi 1.00 .30
a. Booklet pane of 10 10.50
2660 A728 50c multi 1.00 .30
a. Booklet pane of 10 10.50
2661 A728 50c multi 1.00 .30
a. Booklet pane of 10 10.50
2662 A728 50c multi 1.00 .30
a. Booklet pane of 10 10.50
2663 A728 50c multi 1.00 .30
a. Booklet pane of 10 10.50

**2664** A728 50c multi 1.00 .30
*a.* Booklet pane of 10 10.50
**2665** A728 50c multi 1.00 .30
*a.* Booklet pane of 10 10.50
*Nos. 2654-2665 (12)* 12.00 3.60

### With Personalized Photo at Right Like Type A692a
### *Serpentine Die Cut 11½x11¼ Syncopated*
### Self-Adhesive

**2665B** A728 50c multi 2.50 *2.50*
**2665C** A728 50c multi 2.50 *2.50*
**2665D** A728 50c multi 2.50 *2.50*
**2665E** A728 50c multi 2.50 *2.50*
**2665F** A728 50c multi 2.50 *2.50*
**2665G** A728 50c multi 2.50 *2.50*
**2665H** A728 50c multi 2.50 *2.50*
**2665I** A728 50c multi 2.50 *2.50*
**2665J** A728 50c multi 2.50 *2.50*
**2665K** A728 50c multi 2.50 *2.50*
**2665L** A728 50c multi 2.50 *2.50*
**2665M** A728 50c multi 2.50 *2.50*
*Nos. 2665B-2665M (12)* 30.00 *30.00*

Nos. 2665B-2665M were sold in sheets of 20 and have personalized pictures and a straight edge at right, and lack separations between the stamp and the pictures. Sheets of 20 of Nos. 2665B-2665M each sold for $23.

Travel Posters of the 1930s — A729

Designs: 50c, At the Beach, by Percy Trompf. $1, Fishing, by John Vickery. $2, Riding in the Country, by James Northfield. $2.45, Winter Sport, by Northfield.

**2007, Apr. 10** *Perf. 14½x14*

**2666** A729 50c multi .95 .75
**2667** A729 $1 multi 2.00 1.60
*a.* Booklet pane of 2, #2666-2667 3.25 —
**2668** A729 $2 multi 4.00 3.00
**2669** A729 $2.45 multi 5.00 3.75
*a.* Booklet pane of 4, #2666-2669 12.00 —
*b.* Booklet pane of 2, #2666, 2669 6.00 —
Complete booklet, #2667a, 2669a, 2669b 21.00
*Nos. 2666-2669 (4)* 11.95 9.10

Queen Elizabeth II, 81st Birthday — A730

**2007, Apr. 18** *Perf. 14x14½*

**2670** A730 50c multi .95 .75

Shipwrecks A731

Designs: 50c, Admella, 1859. $1, Loch Ard, 1878. $2, Dunbar, 1857.

**2007, May 1** **Litho.** *Perf. 14x14½*

**2671** A731 50c multi .95 .70
**2672** A731 $1 multi 2.00 1.60
**2673** A731 $2 multi 4.00 3.25
*Nos. 2671-2673 (3)* 6.95 5.55

### Animals Type of 2006 and

Sydney Harbour Bridge — A732

Design: $1.30, Yellow-footed rock wallaby, vert.

**2007** **Litho.** *Perf. 14½x14*

**2674** A707 $1.30 multi 2.50 2.50
**2675** A732 $1.95 multi 3.75 3.75
*a.* Imperf. x perf. 14 x imperf. x imperf. 3.75 3.75
*b.* Souvenir sheet, #2675, 2675a 7.50 7.50
*c.* Souvenir sheet, 2 #2675 7.75 7.75
*d.* As "b," with Sberatel Exhib., Prague ovpt. 9.75 9.75
*e.* As "c," with Bangkok 2007 Exhib. ovpt. 9.75 9.75

### Self-Adhesive
### Booklet Stamps
### *Serpentine Die Cut 11¼ Syncopated*

**2676** A707 $1.30 multi 3.25 3.25
*a.* Booklet pane of 2 6.25
Complete booklet, 4 #2676a 25.00
**2677** A732 $1.95 multi 4.00 4.00
*a.* Booklet pane of 1 4.00
*b.* Booklet pane of 2 8.00
Complete booklet, #2677a, 3 #2677b 29.00

### With Personalized Photo at Right Like Type A692a
### *Serpentine Die Cut 11½x11¼*

**2678** A707 $1.30 multi 4.50 4.50
**2679** A732 $1.95 multi 5.75 5.75

Issued: Nos. 2674-2679, 5/8; No. 2675b, 6/15. Complete booklet containing No. 2676 sold for $12.95. It contains four different examples of No. 2676a. The booklet containing No. 2677 sold for $14.95, and it contains three different examples of No. 2677b.

No. 2675c issued 6/15. Margin of No. 2675c is overprinted in gold with emblem for Sydney Philatelic Show.

Nos. 2678-2679 were sold in sheets of 20 and have personalized pictures and a straight edge at right, and lack separations between the stamp and the picture. A sheet of 20 of No. 2678 sold for $39; of No. 2679, $51.

Circus Performers — A733

Circus acts: Nos. 2680, 2685, 2690, Torch juggler. Nos. 2681, 2686, 2691, Contortionist. Nos. 2682, 2687, 2692, Trapeze artists. Nos. 2683, 2688, 2693, Acrobats. Nos. 2684, 2689, 2694, Human cannonball.

**2007, May 15** **Litho.** *Perf. 14½x14*

**2680** A733 50c multi .95 .95
**2681** A733 50c multi .95 .95
*a.* Booklet pane of 2 2.50 —
**2682** A733 50c multi .95 .95
*a.* Booklet pane of 2 2.50 —
**2683** A733 50c multi .95 .95
*a.* Booklet pane of 2 2.50 —
**2684** A733 50c multi .95 .95
*a.* Horiz. strip of 5, #2680-2684 5.00 5.00
*b.* Booklet pane, #2680-2684 6.25 —
*c.* Booklet pane, 2 each # 2680, 2684 5.25 —
*Nos. 2680-2684 (5)* 4.75 4.75

### Booklet Stamps
### Self-Adhesive
### *Serpentine Die Cut 11¼ Syncopated*

**2685** A733 50c multi 1.10 .40
**2686** A733 50c multi 1.10 .40
**2687** A733 50c multi 1.10 .40
**2688** A733 50c multi 1.10 .40
**2689** A733 50c multi 1.10 .40
*a.* Booklet pane, 2 each #2685-2689 11.50

### Litho. With Foil Application

**2690** A733 50c multi 1.40 1.40
**2691** A733 50c multi 1.40 1.40
**2692** A733 50c multi 1.40 1.40
**2693** A733 50c multi 1.40 1.40
**2694** A733 50c multi 1.40 1.40
*a.* Booklet pane, #2690-2694 7.25
Complete booklet, #2681a, 2682a, 2683a, 2684b, 2684c, 2694a 25.00
*Nos. 2685-2694 (10)* 12.50 9.00

Complete booklet sold for $12.95. Nos. 2690-2694 each have gold stars and a portion of stamp covered by varnish.

Tourist Attractions — A734

Designs: Nos. 2695, 2700, Big Guitar, Tamworth, New South Wales. Nos. 2696, 2701, Big Lobster, Kingston Southeast, South Australia. Nos. 2697, 2702, Big Banana, Coffs Harbour, New South Wales. Nos. 2698, 2703, Big Merino Sheep, Goulburn, New South Wales. Nos. 2699, 2704, Big Pineapple, Nambour, Queensland.

**2007, June 5** *Perf. 14½x14*

**2695** A734 50c multi .95 .95
**2696** A734 50c multi .95 .95
**2697** A734 50c multi .95 .95
**2698** A734 50c multi .95 .95
**2699** A734 50c multi .95 .95
*a.* Horiz. strip of 5, #2695-2699 5.00 5.00
*Nos. 2695-2699 (5)* 4.75 4.75

### Booklet Stamps
### Self-Adhesive
### *Serpentine Die Cut 11¼ Syncopated*

**2700** A734 50c multi 1.10 .40
**2701** A734 50c multi 1.10 .40
**2702** A734 50c multi 1.10 .40
**2703** A734 50c multi 1.10 .40
**2704** A734 50c multi 1.10 .40
*a.* Booklet pane, 2 each #2700-2704 11.50
*Nos. 2700-2704 (5)* 5.50 2.00

Endangered Animals — A735

Designs: No. 2705, Gray-headed flying fox. No. 2706, Mountain pygmy possum. $1.25, Flatback turtle, horiz. $1.30, Wandering albatross, horiz.

**2007, June 26** *Perf. 14½x14*

**2705** A735 50c multi .95 .70
*a.* Booklet pane of 2 #2705 2.25 —
**2706** A735 50c multi .95 .70
*a.* Horiz. pair, #2705-2706 2.00 1.40
*b.* Booklet pane of 2 #2706 2.25 —

### *Perf. 14x14½*

**2707** A735 $1.25 multi 2.40 1.90
*a.* Booklet pane of 2 5.75 —
**2708** A735 $1.30 multi 2.50 2.00
*a.* Booklet pane of 2 6.00 —
Complete booklet, #793c, 794b, 2705a, 2706b, 2707a, 2708a 23.00

Complete booklet sold for $10.95.

Modern Architecture A736

Designs: No. 2709, Former ICI House, Melbourne. No. 2710, Academy of Science, Canberra. $1, Council House, Perth. $2.45, Sydney Opera House.

**2007, July 10** *Perf. 14x14¾*

**2709** A736 50c multi .95 .70
**2710** A736 50c multi .95 .70
*a.* Horiz. pair, #2709-2710 2.00 1.40
*b,* Additionally dated "2013" (#2710c) 1.10 1.10
*c.* Booklet pane of 2 #2710b 2.25 —
**2711** A736 $1 multi 2.00 1.60
**2712** A736 $2.45 multi 5.00 3.75
*a.* Souvenir sheet, #2709-2712 9.00 9.00

Due to the arrangement of the stamps on No. 2712a, the left side of the top row of perfs on each of the stamps is perf. 14 and the right side of the top row is perf. 14¾.

No. 2712a exists imperf from a telephone drawing at a substantial premium over face value. Value for single souvenir sheet, $17.50.

Issued: Nos. 2710b, 2710c, 3/5/13. No. 2710c was issued in booklet along with Nos. 1940c, 2869e, 3107c, 3349b and 3877a.

Markets — A737

Designs: Nos. 2713, 2718, Queen Victoria Market, Melbourne. Nos. 2714, 2719, Rusty's Market, Cairns. Nos. 2715, 2720, Sydney Fish Market. Nos. 2716, 2721, Adelaide Central Market. Nos. 2717, 2722, Hume Murray Farmers Market, Albury Wodonga.

**2007, July 24** *Perf. 14½x14*

**2713** A737 50c multi .95 .95
**2714** A737 50c multi .95 .95
**2715** A737 50c multi .95 .95
**2716** A737 50c multi .95 .95
**2717** A737 50c multi .95 .95
*a.* Horiz. strip of 5, #2713-2717 5.00 5.00
*Nos. 2713-2717 (5)* 4.75 4.75

### Booklet Stamps
### Self-Adhesive
### *Serpentine Die Cut 11¼ Syncopated*

**2718** A737 50c multi 1.10 .40
*a.* Booklet pane of 10 11.50
**2719** A737 50c multi 1.10 .40
*a.* Booklet pane of 10 11.50
**2720** A737 50c multi 1.10 .40
*a.* Booklet pane of 10 11.50
**2721** A737 50c multi 1.10 .40
*a.* Booklet pane of 10 11.50
**2722** A737 50c multi 1.10 .40
*a.* Booklet pane of 10 11.50
*Nos. 2718-2722 (5)* 5.50 2.00

Asia-Pacific Economic Cooperation Forum, Sydney — A738

**2007, Aug. 28** *Perf. 14x14½*

**2723** A738 50c multi .95 .95

### Coil Stamp
### Self-Adhesive
### *Serpentine Die Cut 11¼x11½ Syncopated*

**2724** A738 50c multi .95 .30

Special Air Service, 50th Anniv. — A739

**2007, Sept. 4** *Perf. 14x14½*

**2725** A739 50c multi .95 .75

This stamp exists with "SAS" insignia embossed with gold foil. This was a restricted issue sold at far more than face value by the Philatelic Bureau.

Botanical Gardens — A740

Designs: Nos. 2726, 2731, Brisbane Botanic Gardens, Mt. Coot-tha. Nos. 2727, 2732, Kings Park and Botanic Gardens, Perth. Nos. 2728, 2733, Royal Botanic Gardens and Domain, Sydney. Nos. 2729, 2734, Royal Botanic Gardens, Melbourne. Nos. 2730, 2735, Botanic Gardens of Adelaide.

**2007, Sept. 12** *Perf. 14x14½*

**2726** A740 50c multi .95 .95
*a.* Booklet pane of 4 4.25 —
**2727** A740 50c multi .95 .95
*a.* Booklet pane of 4 4.25 —
**2728** A740 50c multi .95 .95
*a.* Booklet pane of 4 4.25 —
**2729** A740 50c multi .95 .95
*a.* Booklet pane of 4 4.25 —
**2730** A740 50c multi .95 .95
*a.* Booklet pane of 4 4.25 —
Complete booklet, #2726a-2730a 22.00
*b.* Horiz. strip of 5, #2726-2730 5.00 5.00
*Nos. 2726-2730 (5)* 4.75 4.75

### Self-Adhesive
### *Serpentine Die Cut 11¼x11½ Syncopated*

**2731** A740 50c multi .95 .30
**2732** A740 50c multi .95 .30
**2733** A740 50c multi .95 .30
**2734** A740 50c multi .95 .30
**2735** A740 50c multi .95 .30
*a.* Horiz. coil strip of 5, #2731-2735 5.00
*b.* Booklet pane of 20, 5 each #2731-2735, + 10 labels 19.50
*Nos. 2731-2735 (5)* 4.75 1.50

Complete booklet sold for $10.95.

Space Age, 50th Anniv. — A741

Designs: Nos. 2736, 2743, Sputnik, 1957. Nos. 2737, 2744, First space walk, 1965. Nos. 2738, 2745, First Moon walk, 1969. Nos. 2739, 2746, Voyager, 1977. Nos. 2740, 2747, International Space Station, 1998. Nos. 2741, 2742a, Hubble Space Telescope, 1990, horiz.

**2007, Oct. 2** **Litho.** *Perf. 14½x14*

**2736** A741 50c multi 1.00 1.00
*a.* Booklet pane of 2 2.40 —
**2737** A741 50c multi 1.00 1.00
*a.* Booklet pane of 2 2.40 —

**2738** A741 50c multi 1.00 1.00
*a.* Booklet pane of 2 2.40 —
**2739** A741 50c multi 1.00 1.00
*a.* Booklet pane of 2 2.40 —
**2740** A741 50c multi 1.00 1.00
*a.* Horiz. strip of 5, #2736-2740 5.25 5.25
*b.* Booklet pane of 2 2.40 —
*c.* Booklet pane of 5, #2736-2740 6.00 —
**2741** A741 $1 multi, 50x30mm 2.25 2.25
*a.* Booklet pane of 2 5.00 —
Complete booklet, #2736a, 2737a, 2738a, 2739a, 2740b, 2740c, 2741a 23.00
*Nos. 2736-2741 (6)* 7.25 7.25

### Souvenir Sheet

**2742** Sheet of 6, #2736-2740, 2742a 7.50 7.50
*a.* A741 $1 multi, 52x43mm 2.25 2.25

A souvenir sheet in the 50c denomination exists. It was sold in a restricted sale with a normal souvenir sheet and a coin at a price far in advance of face value.

### Self-Adhesive
### Booklet Stamps
### *Serpentine Die Cut 11¼ Syncopated*

**2743** A741 50c multi 1.00 .30
**2744** A741 50c multi 1.00 .30
**2745** A741 50c multi 1.00 .30
**2746** A741 50c multi 1.00 .30
**2747** A741 50c multi 1.00 .30
*a.* Coil strip of 5, #2743-2747 5.25
*b.* Booklet pane, 2 each #2743-2747 10.00
*Nos. 2743-2747 (5)* 5.00 1.50

Complete booklet sold for $10.95.

Trailer Campers — A742

People and trailer campers from: Nos. 2748, 2753, 1950s. Nos. 2749, 2754, 1960s. Nos. 2750, 2755, 1970s. Nos. 2751, 2756, 1980s. Nos. 2752, 2757, Today.

**2007, Oct. 16** *Perf. 14x14½*

**2748** A742 50c multi 1.10 1.10
*a.* Booklet pane of 4 5.00 —
**2749** A742 50c multi 1.10 1.10
*a.* Booklet pane, 2 each #2748-2749 5.00 —
**2750** A742 50c multi 1.10 1.10
*a.* Booklet pane of 4 5.00 —
**2751** A742 50c multi 1.10 1.10
*a.* Booklet pane, 2 each #2750-2751 5.00 —
**2752** A742 50c multi 1.10 1.10
*a.* Horiz. strip of 5, #2748-2752 5.50 5.50
*b.* Booklet pane of 4 5.00 —
Complete booklet, #2748a, 2749a, 2750a, 2751a, 2752b 25.00
*Nos. 2748-2752 (5)* 5.50 5.50

### Self-Adhesive
### Booklet Stamps
### *Serpentine Die Cut 11¼ Syncopated*

**2753** A742 50c multi 1.10 .30
*a.* Booklet pane of 10 11.00 —
**2754** A742 50c multi 1.10 .30
*a.* Booklet pane of 10 11.00 —
**2755** A742 50c multi 1.10 .30
*a.* Booklet pane of 10 11.00 —
**2756** A742 50c multi 1.10 .30
*a.* Booklet pane of 10 11.00 —
**2757** A742 50c multi 1.10 .30
*a.* Booklet pane of 10 11.00
*b.* Booklet pane, 2 each #2753-2757 11.00 —
*Nos. 2753-2757 (5)* 5.50 1.50

Complete booklet sold for $10.95.

Christmas — A743

Designs of past Australian Christmas stamps with original denominations removed: Nos. 2758, 2763, 2768, #669. Nos. 2759, 2764, 2769, #1195. Nos. 2760, 2765, #1567. Nos. 2761, 2766, #306, horiz. Nos. 2762, 2767, 2770, #931.

### *Perf. 14½x14, 14x14½*

**2007, Nov. 1** **Litho.**

**2758** A743 45c multi .95 .95
*a.* Booklet pane of 4 4.25 —
**2759** A743 45c multi .95 .95
*a.* Booklet pane of 4 4.25 —
**2760** A743 45c multi .95 .95
*a.* Horiz. pair, #2759-2760 2.00 2.00
*b.* Booklet pane of 4 4.25 —
**2761** A743 50c multi 1.10 1.10
*a.* Booklet pane of 2 2.25 —
**2762** A743 $1.10 multi 2.40 2.40
*a.* Booklet pane of 1 2.50 —
*Nos. 2758-2762 (5)* 6.35 6.35

### Self-Adhesive
### *Serpentine Die Cut 11¼ Syncopated*

**2763** A743 45c multi .95 .30
*a.* With varnish block over stamp vignette .95 .30
**2764** A743 45c multi .95 .30
*a.* Booklet pane of 20 20.00
**2765** A743 45c multi .95 .95
*a.* Booklet pane of 20 20.00
**2766** A743 50c multi 1.10 1.10
*a.* Booklet pane of 5 5.50
**2767** A743 $1.10 multi 2.40 2.40
*a.* Booklet pane of 5 12.00
*b.* Souvenir sheet, #2763-2767 6.50
*c.* Booklet pane, #2763-2767 7.00
Complete booklet, #2758a, 2759a, 2760b, 2761a, 2762a, 2767c 25.00
*Nos. 2763-2767 (5)* 6.35 5.05

Complete booklet sold for $10.95. Size of No. 2767b is 156x100mm. Size of No. 2767c is 156x104mm.

### With Personalized Photo at Right Like Type A692a
### *Serpentine Die Cut 11½x11¼ Syncopated*

**2768** A743 45c multi 2.40 2.40
**2769** A743 45c multi 2.40 2.40
**2770** A743 $1.10 multi 3.75 3.75
*Nos. 2768-2770 (3)* 8.55 8.55

Nos. 2768-2770 were sold in sheets of 20 and have personalized pictures and a straight edge at right, and lack separations between the stamp and the pictures. Sheets of 20 of Nos. 2768 and 2769 sold for $22, and of No. 2770, $35.

---

A booklet titled "Behind the Stamp," which contained four panes, sold for $19.95. The panes were in two designs, one containing Nos. 740, 1164, 1193, 1891 and a litho. reproduction of No. 277, the other containing Nos. 400, 616-617, 882, 1063 and a reproduction of No. 367. The stamps within both panes were dated "2007" and the panes were either perforated with a different gauge than the original stamps or imperforate.

---

Red Rose — A744

**2008, Jan. 15** **Litho.** *Perf. 14*

**2771** A744 50c multi 1.00 1.00

### Litho. With Foil Application
### *Serpentine Die Cut 11¼ Syncopated*
### Self-Adhesive

**2772** A744 50c multi 1.00 .30

### Booklet Stamp
### Litho.

**2773** A744 50c multi 1.10 .30
*a.* Booklet pane of 4 4.50
Complete booklet, 5 #2773a 22.50

### With Personalized Photo at Right Like Type A692a
### *Serpentine Die Cut 11½x11¼ Syncopated*

**2774** A744 50c multi 2.40 2.40

No. 2772 was printed in a sheet of 10 + 10 labels, having rose-scented scratch and sniff areas on the rose and the labels. No. 2773 lacks the scratch and sniff areas. The complete booklet, which sold for $10.95, contains five examples of No. 2773a, each with a different margin.

No. 2774 was sold in sheets of 20 for $23 and have personalized pictures and a straight edge at right, and lack separations between the stamp and the personalized photo.

Philanthropists — A745

Designs: Nos. 2775, 2782, Dame Elisabeth Murdoch. Nos. 2776, 2781, Victor and Loti Smogron. Nos. 2777, 2780, Lady Mary Fairfax. Nos. 2778, 2779, Frank Lowy.

**2008, Jan. 23** **Litho.** *Perf. 14¾x14*

**2775** A745 50c multi 1.25 1.25
**2776** A745 50c multi 1.25 1.25
**2777** A745 50c multi 1.25 1.25
**2778** A745 50c multi 1.25 1.25
*a.* Horiz. strip of 4, #2775-2778 5.00 5.00
*Nos. 2775-2778 (4)* 5.00 5.00

### Coil Stamps
### Self-Adhesive
### *Serpentine Die Cut 11¼ Syncopated*

**2779** A745 50c multi 1.00 .30
**2780** A745 50c multi 1.00 .30
**2781** A745 50c multi 1.00 .30
**2782** A745 50c multi 1.00 .30
*a.* Vert. strip of 4, #2779-2782 4.00
*Nos. 2779-2782 (4)* 4.00 1.20

Organ and Tissue Donation — A746

**2008, Feb. 5** *Perf. 14¾x14*

**2783** A746 50c multi 1.10 1.10

### Booklet Stamp
### Self-Adhesive
### *Serpentine Die Cut 11¼ Syncopated*

**2784** A746 50c multi 1.10 .30
*a.* Booklet pane of 10 11.00

Scouting in Australia, Cent. — A747

Australian Scouting emblem and: 50c, Four scouts near tent. $1.35, Scouts from various nations. $2, Lord Robert Baden-Powell.

**2008, Feb. 19** *Perf. 14*

**2785** A747 50c multi 1.10 1.10
**2786** A747 $1.35 multi 2.75 2.75
**2787** A747 $2 multi 4.25 4.25
*a.* Perf. 14x14½ 4.25 4.25
*b.* Souvenir sheet, 2 #2787a 8.50 8.50
*Nos. 2785-2787 (3)* 8.10 8.10

### Self-Adhesive
### *Serpentine Die Cut 11¼ Syncopated*
### Coil Stamp

**2788** A747 50c multi 1.10 .30

### Booklet Stamps

**2789** A747 $1.35 multi 2.75 1.40
*a.* Booklet pane of 5 14.50
**2790** A747 $2 multi 4.25 2.25
*a.* Booklet pane of 5 22.00
*Nos. 2788-2790 (3)* 8.10 3.95

Canberra Stamp Show (No. 2787b).

Gorges — A748

Designs: $1.35, Greco River Gorge, New South Wales. $2, Walpa Gorge, Northern Territory, horiz. $2.70, Katherine Gorge, Northern Territory, horiz. $4, Geikie Gorge, Western Australia, horiz.

**2008, Mar. 3** **Litho.** *Perf. 14*

**2791** A748 $1.35 multi 2.75 2.75
**2792** A748 $2 multi 4.25 4.25
**2793** A748 $2.70 multi 5.75 2.75
**2794** A748 $4 multi 8.50 4.25
*Nos. 2791-2794 (4)* 21.25 14.00

### Booklet Stamps (#2795-2796)
### Self-Adhesive
### *Serpentine Die Cut 11½x11¼ Syncopated*

**2795** A748 $1.35 multi 7.50 5.00
*a.* Booklet pane of 5 37.50
*b.* Booklet pane of 2 15.00 —
Complete booklet, 4 #2795b 68.00
**2796** A748 $2 multi 9.00 7.50
*a.* Booklet pane of 5 45.00
*b.* Booklet pane of 2 18.00 —
Complete booklet, 4 #2796b 72.00

### With Personalized Photo at Right Like Type A692a

**2797** A748 $1.35 multi *8.00 8.00*
**2798** A748 $2 multi *12.00 12.00*

Nos. 2797-2798 each were sold in sheets of 20 and have personalized pictures and a straight edge at right, and lack separations between the stamp and the personalized photo. Sheets of 20 of No. 2797 sold for $40, and of No. 2798, $52.

Complete booklet containing No. 2795b sold for $10.95, and containing No. 2796b, $16.95. Each booklet contains four panes with differing margins.

World Youth Day — A749

Various depictions of Pope Benedict XVI with "08" in: 50c, Light blue. $1.35, Pink. $2, Light green.

**2008, Mar. 4** *Perf. 14*

**2799** A749 50c multi 1.10 .85
**2800** A749 $1.35 multi 2.75 2.75
**2801** A749 $2 multi 4.25 4.25
*Nos. 2799-2801 (3)* 8.10 7.85

### Booklet Stamps (#2802-2803)
### Self-Adhesive
### *Serpentine Die Cut 11½x11¼ Syncopated*

**2802** A749 $1.35 multi 4.75 .40
*a.* Booklet pane of 5 22.50
**2803** A749 $2 multi 7.50 2.50
*a.* Booklet pane of 5 37.50

### With Personalized Photo at Right Like Type A692a

**2804** A749 50c multi 5.00 3.00
**2805** A749 $1.35 multi 8.00 8.00
**2806** A749 $2 multi 10.00 10.00
*Nos. 2804-2806 (3)* 23.00 21.00

Nos. 2804-2806 each were sold in sheets of 20 and have personalized pictures and a straight edge at right, and lack separations between the stamp and the personalized photo. Sheets of 20 of No. 2804 sold for $23, No. 2805, sold for $40, and No. 2806 sold for $52.

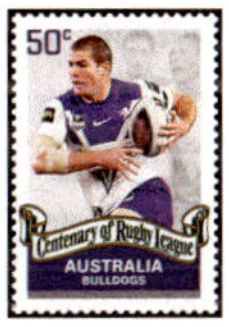

Rugby League, Cent. — A750

Players and teams: Nos. 2807, 2823, Andrew Ryan, Bulldogs. Nos. 2808, 2824, Scott Prince, Titans. Nos. 2809, 2825, Brett Kimmorley, Sharks. Nos. 2810, 2826, Danny Buderus, Knights. Nos. 2811, 2827, Johnathan Thurston, Cowboys. Nos. 2812, 2828, Darren Lockyer, Broncos. Nos. 2813, 2829, Matt Orford, Sea Eagles. Nos. 2814, 2830, Cameron Smith, Storm. Nos. 2815, 2831, Craig Fitzgibbon, Roosters. Nos. 2816, 2832, Alan Tongue, Raiders. Nos. 2817, 2833, Dean Widders, Rabbitohs. Nos. 2818, 2834, Tony Puletua, Panthers. Nos. 2819, 2835, Mark Gasnier, Dragons. Nos. 2820, 2836, Nathan Cayless, Eels. Nos. 2821, 2837, Robbie Farah, Wests Tigers. Nos. 2822, 2838, Steve Price, Warriors.

**2008, Mar. 24** *Perf. 14*

**2807** A750 50c multi 1.10 1.10
**2808** A750 50c multi 1.10 1.10
**2809** A750 50c multi 1.10 1.10
**2810** A750 50c multi 1.10 1.10
*a.* Block of 4, #2807-2810 4.50 4.50
**2811** A750 50c multi 1.10 1.10
**2812** A750 50c multi 1.10 1.10
**2813** A750 50c multi 1.10 1.10
**2814** A750 50c multi 1.10 1.10
*a.* Block of 4, #2811-2814 4.50 4.50
**2815** A750 50c multi 1.10 1.10
**2816** A750 50c multi 1.10 1.10
**2817** A750 50c multi 1.10 1.10
**2818** A750 50c multi 1.10 1.10
*a.* Block of 4, #2815-2818 4.50 4.50
**2819** A750 50c multi 1.10 1.10
**2820** A750 50c multi 1.10 1.10
**2821** A750 50c multi 1.10 1.10
**2822** A750 50c multi 1.10 1.10
*a.* Block of 4, #2819-2822 4.50 4.50
*Nos. 2807-2822 (16)* 17.60 17.60

### Booklet Stamps
### Self-Adhesive
***Serpentine Die Cut 11 Syncopated***

**2823** A750 50c multi 1.10 .30
*a.* Booklet pane of 10 11.00
**2824** A750 50c multi 1.10 .30
*a.* Booklet pane of 10 11.00
**2825** A750 50c multi 1.10 .30
*a.* Booklet pane of 10 11.00
**2826** A750 50c multi 1.10 .30
*a.* Booklet pane of 10 11.00
**2827** A750 50c multi 1.10 .30
*a.* Booklet pane of 10 11.00
**2828** A750 50c multi 1.10 .30
*a.* Booklet pane of 10 11.00
**2829** A750 50c multi 1.10 .30
*a.* Booklet pane of 10 11.00
**2830** A750 50c multi 1.10 .30
*a.* Booklet pane of 10 11.00
**2831** A750 50c multi 1.10 .30
*a.* Booklet pane of 10 11.00
**2832** A750 50c multi 1.10 .30
*a.* Booklet pane of 10 11.00
**2833** A750 50c multi 1.10 .30
*a.* Booklet pane of 10 11.00
**2834** A750 50c multi 1.10 .30
*a.* Booklet pane of 10 11.00
**2835** A750 50c multi 1.10 .30
*a.* Booklet pane of 10 11.00
**2836** A750 50c multi 1.10 .30
*a.* Booklet pane of 10 11.00
**2837** A750 50c multi 1.10 .30
*a.* Booklet pane of 10 11.00
**2838** A750 50c multi 1.10 .30
*a.* Booklet pane of 10 11.00
*b.* Booklet pane of 20, #2823-2829, 2831-2838, 5 #2830 22.00
*Nos. 2823-2838 (16)* 17.60 4.80

A booklet containing one Rugby League dollar coin, and panes containing Nos. 2810a, 2814a, 2818a, 2822a, and four No. 2814, each in perf. 14½x14, sold for $15.95.

Heavy Haulers — A751

Designs: Nos. 2839, 2844, 2849, Excavator. Nos. 2840, 2845, 2850, Dump truck. Nos. 2841, 2846, 2851, Road train. Nos. 2842, 2847, 2852, Locomotive and ore cars. Nos. 2843, 2848, 2853, Ore carrier MS Berge Stahl.

**2008, Apr. 1** ***Perf. 14***
### Without White Frames

**2839** A751 50c multi 1.10 1.10
**2840** A751 50c multi 1.10 1.10
**2841** A751 50c multi 1.10 1.10
**2842** A751 50c multi 1.10 1.10
**2843** A751 50c multi 1.10 1.10
*a.* Horiz. strip of 5, #2839-2843 5.50 5.50
*Nos. 2839-2843 (5)* 5.50 5.50

### Booklet Stamps
### Self-Adhesive
***Serpentine Die Cut 11 Syncopated***

**2844** A751 50c multi 1.10 .60
**2845** A751 50c multi 1.10 .60
**2846** A751 50c multi 1.10 .60
**2847** A751 50c multi 1.10 .60
**2848** A751 50c multi 1.10 .60
*a.* Booklet pane, 4 each #2844-2848 22.00

### Coil Stamps
### With White Frames

**2849** A751 50c multi 1.10 .60
**2850** A751 50c multi 1.10 .60
**2851** A751 50c multi 1.10 .60
**2852** A751 50c multi 1.10 .60
**2853** A751 50c multi 1.10 .60
*a.* Vert. strip of 5, #2849-2853 5.50
*Nos. 2844-2853 (10)* 11.00 6.00

ANZAC Day — A752

Designs: Nos. 2854, 2863, Veterans marching. Nos. 2855, 2862, Laying of wreaths at memorial. Nos. 2856, 2861, Buglers. Nos. 2857, 2860, Veteran holding child. Nos. 2858, 2859, Young people at Gallipoli.

**2008, Apr. 16** ***Perf. 14***

**2854** A752 50c multi 1.10 1.10
*a.* Perf. 14¾x14 1.10 1.10
*b.* Booklet pane, 4 #2854a 5.00 —
**2855** A752 50c multi 1.10 1.10
*a.* Perf. 14¾x14 1.10 1.10
*b.* Booklet pane, 4 #2855a 5.00 —
*c.* Souvenir sheet, 2 each #2854-2855, perf. 14 4.50 4.50
**2856** A752 50c multi 1.10 1.10
*a.* Perf. 14¾x14 1.10 1.10
*b.* Booklet pane, 4 #2856a 5.00 —
*c.* Souvenir sheet of 4 #2856a 4.50 4.50
*d.* Souvenir sheet, 2 each #2855-2856, perf. 14 4.50 4.50
**2857** A752 50c multi 1.10 1.10
*a.* Perf. 14¾x14 1.10 1.10
*b.* Booklet pane, 4 #2857a 5.00 —
**2858** A752 50c multi 1.10 1.10
*a.* Perf. 14¾x14 1.10 1.10
*b.* Booklet pane, 4 #2858a 5.00 —
Complete booklet, #2854b-2858b 25.00
*c.* Souvenir sheet, #2854a-2858a 5.50
*d.* Horiz. strip of 5, #2854-2858 5.50 5.50
*Nos. 2854-2858 (5)* 5.50 5.50

### Coil Stamps
### Self-Adhesive
***Serpentine Die Cut 11 Syncopated***

**2859** A752 50c multi 1.10 .60
**2860** A752 50c multi 1.10 .60
**2861** A752 50c multi 1.10 .60
**2862** A752 50c multi 1.10 .60
**2863** A752 50c multi 1.10 .60
*a.* Vert. strip of 5, #2859-2863 5.50
*Nos. 2859-2863 (5)* 5.50 3.00

Complete booklet sold for $10.95.
2008 World Stamp Championships, Israel (No. 2856c). Issued: No. 2855c, 11/3; No. 2856d, 11/5.

Queen's Birthday — A753

Designs: 50c, Queen Elizabeth II. $2, Order of Australia badge.

**2008, Apr. 18** ***Perf. 14***

**2864** A753 50c multi 1.10 .85
*a.* Perf. 14¾x14 1.10 .85
*b.* Dated "2010" 2.00 1.00
**2865** A753 $2 multi 4.25 2.25
*a.* Perf. 14¾x14 4.25 2.25
*b.* Souvenir sheet, #2864a, 2865a 5.50 5.50

First Hot-air Balloon Flight in Australia, 150th Anniv. — A754

Hot-air balloons over: Nos. 2866, 2870, Sydney Harbour Bridge and Sydney Opera House. Nos. 2867, 2871, Mount Feathertop, Victoria (red denomination). Nos. 2868, 2873, Western MacDonnell Ranges, Northern Territory (lilac denomination). Nos. 2869, 2872, Canberra.

**2008, May 6 Litho.** ***Perf. 14x14¾***

**2866** A754 50c multi 1.10 1.10
*a.* Booklet pane of 4 5.00 —
**2867** A754 50c multi 1.10 1.10
*a.* Booklet pane of 4 5.00 —
**2868** A754 50c multi 1.10 1.10
*a.* Booklet pane of 4 5.00 —
**2869** A754 50c multi 1.10 1.10
*a.* Booklet pane of 4 5.00 —
*b.* Booklet pane of 4, #2866-2869 5.00 —
Complete booklet, #2866a-2869a, 2869b 25.00
*c.* Horiz. strip of 4, #2866-2869 4.50 4.50
*d.* Additionally dated "2013" (#2869e) 1.10 1.10
*e.* Booklet pane of 2 #2869d 2.25 —
*Nos. 2866-2869 (4)* 4.40 4.40

Issued: Nos. 2869d, 2869e, 3/5/13. No. 2869e was issued in booklet along with Nos. 1940c, 2710c, 3107c, 3349b and 3877a.

### Booklet Stamps
### Self-Adhesive
***Serpentine Die Cut 11 Syncopated***

**2870** A754 50c multi 1.10 .30
**2871** A754 50c multi 1.10 .30
**2872** A754 50c multi 1.10 .30
**2873** A754 50c multi 1.10 .30
*a.* Booklet pane, 4 #2870, 2 each #2871-2873 11.00
*Nos. 2870-2873 (4)* 4.40 1.20

Complete booklet sold for $10.95.

Working Dogs — A755

Designs: Nos. 2874, 2879, German shepherd. Nos. 2875, 2880, Australian cattle dog. Nos. 2876, 2881, Beagle. Nos. 2877, 2882, Border collie. Nos. 2878, 2883, Labrador retriever.

**2008, June 10 Litho.** ***Perf. 14¾x14***

**2874** A755 50c multi 1.10 1.10
*a.* Booklet pane of 4 5.00 —
**2875** A755 50c multi 1.10 1.10
*a.* Booklet pane of 4 5.00 —
**2876** A755 50c multi 1.10 1.10
*a.* Booklet pane of 4 5.00 —
**2877** A755 50c multi 1.10 1.10
*a.* Booklet pane of 4 5.00 —
**2878** A755 50c multi 1.10 1.10
*a.* Booklet pane of 4 5.00 —
Complete booklet, #2874a-2878a 25.00
*b.* Horiz. strip of 5, #2874-2878 5.50 5.50
*Nos. 2874-2878 (5)* 5.50 5.50

### Booklet Stamps
### Self-Adhesive
***Serpentine Die Cut 11 Syncopated***

**2879** A755 50c multi 1.10 .30
*a.* Booklet pane of 10 + 5 stickers 11.00
**2880** A755 50c multi 1.10 .30
*a.* Booklet pane of 10 + 5 stickers 11.00
**2881** A755 50c multi 1.10 .30
*a.* Booklet pane of 10 + 5 stickers 11.00
**2882** A755 50c multi 1.10 .30
*a.* Booklet pane of 10 + 5 stickers 11.00
**2883** A755 50c multi 1.10 .30
*a.* Booklet pane of 10 + 5 stickers 11.00
*b.* Booklet pane of 10, 2 each #2879-2883, + 5 stickers 11.00
*Nos. 2879-2883 (5)* 5.50 1.50

Complete booklet sold for $10.95.

2008 Summer Olympics, Beijing — A756

**2008, June 24** ***Perf. 14¾x14***

**2884** A756 50c multi 1.10 1.10

### Coil Stamp
### Self-Adhesive
***Serpentine Die Cut 11 Syncopated***

**2885** A756 50c multi 1.10 .30

Ecology — A757

Slogans: Nos. 2886, 2890, Save water. Nos. 2887, 2891, Reduce waste. Nos. 2888, 2892, Travel smart. Nos. 2889, 2893, Save energy.

**2008, July 8 Litho.** ***Perf. 14x14¾***

**2886** A757 50c multi 1.10 1.10
**2887** A757 50c multi 1.10 1.10
**2888** A757 50c multi 1.10 1.10
**2889** A757 50c multi 1.10 1.10
*a.* Block of 4, #2886-2889 4.50 4.50
*Nos. 2886-2889 (4)* 4.40 4.40

### Self-Adhesive
***Serpentine Die Cut 11¼x11 Syncopated***

**2890** A757 50c multi 1.10 .30
*a.* Booklet pane of 2 2.25
**2891** A757 50c multi 1.10 .30
*a.* Booklet pane of 2 2.25
**2892** A757 50c multi 1.10 .30
*a.* Booklet pane of 2 2.25
**2893** A757 50c multi 1.10 .30
*a.* Booklet pane of 2 2.25
*b.* Booklet pane of 4, #2890-2893 4.50
*c.* Double-sided booklet pane of 8, 2 each #2890-2893 9.25
Complete booklet, #2890a, 2891a, 2892a, 2893a, 2893b, 2893c 24.00
*d.* Double-sided booklet of 20, 5 each #2890-2893 22.00
*e.* Horiz. coil strip of 4, #2890-2893 4.50
*Nos. 2890-2893 (4)* 4.40 1.20

Complete booklet sold for $10.95.

Quarantine Laws, Cent. — A758

**2008, July 15** ***Perf. 14¾x14***

**2894** A758 50c multi 1.10 1.10

### Coil Stamp
### Self-Adhesive
***Serpentine Die Cut 11x11¼ Syncopated***

**2895** A758 50c multi 1.10 .30

Australian Football, 150th Anniv. — A759

**2008, July 29** ***Perf. 14¾x14***

**2896** A759 50c multi 1.10 .85

2008 Summer Olympics, Beijing — A760

No. 2897, Basketball. Nos. 2898, 2900, Cycling. Nos. 2899, 2901, Rhythmic gymnastics.

**2008, Aug. 1**

**2897** A760 50c multi 1.10 .85
**2898** A760 $1.30 multi 2.75 2.75
**2899** A760 $1.35 multi 2.75 2.75
*Nos. 2897-2899 (3)* 6.60 6.35

### Litho.
***Serpentine Die Cut 11¼ Syncopated***
### Booklet Stamps
### Self-Adhesive

**2900** A760 $1.30 multi 2.75 .30
*a.* Booklet pane of 5 14.00
**2901** A760 $1.35 multi 2.75 .30
*a.* Booklet pane of 5 14.50

Scenes From World Youth Day — A761

Designs: No. 2902, Pilgrims at opening mass. No. 2903, Papal welcome. No. 2904, Stations of the Cross. No. 2905, Pilgrimage walk. No. 2906, Pope Benedict XVI at final mass.

**2008, July 24 Litho.** ***Perf. 14½x14***

**2902** A761 50c multi 2.00 *2.00*
**2903** A761 50c multi 2.00 *2.00*
**2904** A761 50c multi 2.00 *2.00*
**2905** A761 50c multi 2.00 *2.00*
**2906** A761 50c multi 2.00 *2.00*
*a.* Vert. strip of 5, #2902-2906 12.00 *12.00*
*Nos. 2902-2906 (5)* 10.00 10.00

Aircraft — A762

Designs: No. 2907, Bristol Tourer. No. 2908, Short S.30 Empire Flying Boat. No. 2909, Lockheed Super Constellation. $2, Airbus A380.

**2008, Aug. 5** ***Perf. 14***

**2907** A762 50c multi 1.00 .80
*a.* Perf. 14x14¾ 1.25 1.25
*b.* Booklet pane of 2, #2907a 2.50 —
**2908** A762 50c multi 1.00 .80
*a.* Perf. 14x14¾ 1.25 1.25
*b.* Booklet pane of 2, #2907a 2.50 —
**2909** A762 50c multi 1.00 .80
*a.* Perf. 14x14¾ 1.25 1.25
*b.* Booklet pane of 2, #2907a 2.50 —
*c.* Horiz. strip of 3, #2907-2909 3.00 2.40

| | | | |
|---|---|---|---|
| **2910** | A762 $2 multi | 4.00 | 2.00 |
| *a.* | Perf. 14x14¾ | 5.50 | 5.50 |
| *b.* | Booklet pane of 1, #2907a | 5.50 | — |
| *c.* | Booklet pane of 4, #2907a-2910a | 9.50 | — |
| | Complete booklet, #2907b, 2908b, 2909b, 2910b, 2910c | 23.00 | |
| *d.* | Souvenir sheet, 2 each #2868, 2910a | 9.50 | 9.50 |
| | *Nos. 2907-2910 (4)* | 7.00 | 4.40 |

**Booklet Stamp**

**Self-Adhesive**

***Serpentine Die Cut 11¼ Syncopated***

| | | | |
|---|---|---|---|
| **2911** | A762 $2 multi | 4.00 | 2.00 |
| *a.* | Booklet pane of 5 | 20.00 | |

Complete booklet sold for $10.95. Issued: No./ 2910d, 8/22. SunStamp 2008 Philatelic Exhibition, Brisbane (No. 2910d).

Gold Medalists at 2008 Summer Olympics, Beijing — A763

Designs: No. 2912, Stephanie Rice, Women's swimming 400m individual medley. No. 2913, Lisbeth Trickett, Women's swimming 100m butterfly. No. 2914, Leisel Jones, Women's swimming, 100m breaststroke. No. 2915, Stephanie Rice, Women's swimming 200m individual medley. No. 2916, Women's 4x200m freestyle relay swimming team. No. 2917, Drew Ginn and Duncan Free, Men's rowing pairs. No. 2918, David Crawshay and Scott Brennan, Men's rowing double sculls. No. 2919, Women's 4x100m medley relay swimming team. No. 2920, Emma Snowsill, Women's triathlon. No. 2921, Malcolm Page and Nathan Wilmot, Men's sailing 470 crew. No. 2922, Tessa Parkinson and Elise Rechichi, Women's sailing 470 crew. No. 2923, Ken Wallace, Men's single kayak 500m. No. 2924, Steven Hooker, Men's pole vault. No. 2925, Matthew Mitcham, Men's 10m platform diving.

**2008, Aug. Litho. *Perf. 14¼***

| | | | |
|---|---|---|---|
| **2912** | A763 50c multi | .95 | .75 |
| **2913** | A763 50c multi | .95 | .75 |
| **2914** | A763 50c multi | .95 | .75 |
| **2915** | A763 50c multi | .95 | .75 |
| **2916** | A763 50c multi | .95 | .75 |
| **2917** | A763 50c multi | .95 | .75 |
| **2918** | A763 50c multi | .95 | .75 |
| **2919** | A763 50c multi | .95 | .75 |
| **2920** | A763 50c multi | .95 | .75 |
| **2921** | A763 50c multi | .95 | .75 |
| **2922** | A763 50c multi | .95 | .75 |
| **2923** | A763 50c multi | .95 | .75 |
| **2924** | A763 50c multi | .95 | .75 |
| **2925** | A763 50c multi | .95 | .75 |
| | *Nos. 2912-2925 (14)* | 13.30 | 10.50 |

Issued: Nos. 2912, 8/11; No. 2913, 8/12; No. 2914, 8/13; No. 2915, 8/14; No. 2916, 8/15; Nos. 2917-2919, 8/18; Nos. 2920-2922, 8/19; Nos. 2923-2925, 8/25. Nos. 2912-2925 were printed in sheets of 10. Digitally printed versions of Nos. 2912-2925 were printed in Beijing in sheets of 10. The digitally printed stamps were only available in complete sets of 14 sheets to collectors in Australia who pre-ordered the sets, and purchasers at the Olympex Stamp Exhibition in China. The digitally printed stamps have a larger dot pattern, most evident in the background and the Olympic rings, and a browner cast to the orange background.

Waterfalls — A764

Designs: $1.40, Russell Falls, Tasmania. $2.05, Jim Jim Falls, Northern Territory. $2.80, Spa Pool, Hammersley Gorge, Western Australia. $4.10, Mackenzie Falls, Victoria.

**2008, Sept. 8 Litho. *Perf. 14¾x14***

| | | | |
|---|---|---|---|
| **2926** | A764 $1.40 multi | 2.50 | 2.50 |
| **2927** | A764 $2.05 multi | 3.75 | 3.75 |
| **2928** | A764 $2.80 multi | 5.25 | 2.50 |
| **2929** | A764 $4.10 multi | 7.50 | 3.75 |
| | *Nos. 2926-2929 (4)* | 19.00 | 12.50 |

**Booklet Stamps**

**Self-Adhesive**

***Serpentine Die Cut 11¼ Syncopated***

| | | | |
|---|---|---|---|
| **2930** | A764 $1.40 multi | 2.50 | .30 |
| *a.* | Booklet pane of 5 | 13.00 | |
| *b.* | Booklet pane of 2 | 5.50 | |
| | Complete booklet, 4 #2930b | 22.00 | |
| **2931** | A764 $2.05 multi | 3.75 | 1.90 |
| *a.* | Booklet pane of 5 | 19.00 | |
| *b.* | Booklet pane of 2 | 7.75 | |
| | Complete booklet, 4 #2931b | 30.00 | |

**With Personalized Photo at Right Like Type A692a**

***Serpentine Die Cut 11½x11¼ Syncopated***

**Self-Adhesive**

| | | | |
|---|---|---|---|
| **2932** | A764 $1.40 multi | 3.75 | 3.75 |
| **2933** | A764 $2.05 multi | 5.00 | 5.00 |

Complete booklet containing No. 2930 sold for $11.95; booklet containing No. 2931, $16.95. Margins for each pane in the complete booklets differ.

Nos. 2932-2933 each were sold in sheets of 20 and have personalized pictures and a straight edge at right, and lack separations between the stamp and the personalized photo. Sheets of 20 of No. 2932 sold for $41, and No. 2933 sold for $53.

Tourist Areas of Cities — A765

Designs: Nos. 2934, 2941, 2945, Luna Park, Melbourne. Nos. 2935, 2942, 2946, South Bank, Brisbane. Nos. 2936, 2943, 2947, The Rocks, Sydney. Nos. 2937, 2944, 2948, Fishermans Wharf, Fremantle. $1.10, Foreshore, Cairns. $1.65, Salamanca Place, Hobart. $2.75, Glenelg, Adelaide (50x30mm).

**2008, Sept. 8 Litho. *Perf. 14x14½***

| | | | |
|---|---|---|---|
| **2934** | A765 55c multi | .95 | .95 |
| **2935** | A765 55c multi | .95 | .95 |
| **2936** | A765 55c multi | .95 | .95 |
| **2937** | A765 55c multi | .95 | .95 |
| *a.* | Block of 4, #2934-2937 | 4.00 | 4.00 |
| *b.* | Sheet of 4, #2934-2937 | 4.00 | 4.00 |
| *c.* | Block of 4, #2934-2937, perf. 13½x14 | *18.00* | *18.00* |
| **2938** | A765 $1.10 multi | 2.00 | 1.60 |
| **2939** | A765 $1.65 multi | 3.00 | 2.25 |

***Perf. 14½x14***

| | | | |
|---|---|---|---|
| **2940** | A765 $2.75 multi | 5.00 | 2.40 |
| | *Nos. 2934-2940 (7)* | 13.80 | 10.05 |

**Self-Adhesive**

**Coil Stamps**

***Die Cut Perf. 12¾***

| | | | |
|---|---|---|---|
| **2941** | A765 55c multi | .95 | .30 |
| **2942** | A765 55c multi | .95 | .30 |
| **2943** | A765 55c multi | .95 | .30 |
| **2944** | A765 55c multi | .95 | .30 |
| *a.* | Horiz. strip of 4, #2941-2944 | 4.00 | |

**Booklet Stamps**

***Serpentine Die Cut 11¼***

| | | | |
|---|---|---|---|
| **2945** | A765 55c multi | .95 | .30 |
| *a.* | Booklet pane of 10 | 9.75 | |
| **2946** | A765 55c multi | .95 | .30 |
| *a.* | Booklet pane of 10 | 9.75 | |
| **2947** | A765 55c multi | .95 | .30 |
| *a.* | Booklet pane of 10 | 9.75 | |
| **2948** | A765 55c multi | .95 | .30 |
| *a.* | Booklet pane of 10 | 9.75 | |
| *b.* | Booklet pane of 20, 5 each #2945-2948 | 20.00 | |
| | *Nos. 2941-2948 (8)* | 7.60 | 2.40 |

Issued: No. 2937b, 5/14/09. Hong Kong 2009 Intl. Stamp Exhibition (No. 2937b).

Australia and Southern Cross A766

Balloons A767

Bird and Beach A768

Stylized Map A769

Sparklers A770

Flowers and Silver Wedding Rings A771

Gold Wedding Rings A772

Baby's Feet A773

Heart and Roses A774

Roses and Wedding Gown A775

**2008, Sept. 23 *Perf. 14½x14***

| | | | |
|---|---|---|---|
| **2949** | A766 55c multi | .95 | .95 |

***Perf. 14¾x14***

| | | | |
|---|---|---|---|
| **2950** | A767 55c multi | .95 | .95 |
| **2951** | A768 55c multi | .95 | .95 |
| **2952** | A769 55c multi | .95 | .95 |
| *a.* | Souvenir sheet of 2 + 2 labels, Chips Rafferty in margin | 4.25 | 4.25 |
| *b.* | As "a," Errol Flynn in margin | 4.25 | 4.25 |
| **2953** | A770 55c multi | .95 | .95 |
| *a.* | Block of 4, #2950-2953 | 4.00 | 4.00 |
| **2954** | A771 55c multi | .95 | .95 |
| **2955** | A772 55c multi | .95 | .95 |
| **2956** | A773 55c multi | .95 | .95 |
| **2957** | A774 55c multi | .95 | .95 |
| *a.* | Block of 4, #2954-2957 | 4.00 | 4.00 |
| **2958** | A775 $1.10 multi | 2.00 | 1.60 |
| | *Nos. 2949-2958 (10)* | 10.55 | 10.15 |

Nos. 2952a and 2952b were sold with Nos. 3009b and 3010d in a set for $12.95.

**Booklet Stamps**

**Self-Adhesive**

***Serpentine Die Cut 11¼ Syncopated***

| | | | |
|---|---|---|---|
| **2959** | A767 55c multi | 1.00 | .30 |
| *a.* | Booklet pane of 4 | 4.25 | |
| | Complete booklet, 5 #2959a | 22.00 | |
| *b.* | Booklet pane of 10 | 10.50 | |
| **2960** | A770 55c multi | 1.00 | .30 |
| *a.* | Booklet pane of 4 | 4.25 | |
| | Complete booklet, 5 #2960a | 22.00 | |
| *b.* | Booklet pane of 10 | 10.50 | |
| **2961** | A771 55c multi | 1.00 | .30 |
| *a.* | Booklet pane of 4 | 4.25 | |
| | Complete booklet, 5 #2961a | 22.00 | |
| **2962** | A772 55c multi | 1.00 | .30 |
| *a.* | Booklet pane of 4 | 4.25 | |
| | Complete booklet, 5 #2962a | 22.00 | |
| *b.* | Booklet pane of 10 | 10.50 | |
| **2963** | A773 55c multi | 1.00 | .30 |
| *a.* | Booklet pane of 4 | 4.25 | |
| | Complete booklet, 5 #2963a | 22.00 | |
| *b.* | Booklet pane of 10 | 10.50 | |
| **2964** | A774 55c multi | 1.00 | .30 |
| *a.* | Booklet pane of 4 | 4.25 | |
| | Complete booklet, 5 #2964a | 22.00 | |
| **2965** | A775 $1.10 multi | 2.00 | 2.00 |
| *a.* | Booklet pane of 4 | 8.00 | |
| | Complete booklet, 5 #2965a | 41.00 | |
| *b.* | Booklet pane of 10 | 20.00 | |
| | *Nos. 2959-2965 (7)* | 8.00 | 3.80 |

**With Personalized Photo at Right Like Type A692a**

***Serpentine Die Cut 11½x11¼ Syncopated***

**Self-Adhesive**

| | | | |
|---|---|---|---|
| **2966** | A767 55c multi | 2.25 | 2.25 |
| **2967** | A768 55c multi | 2.25 | 2.25 |
| **2968** | A769 55c multi | 2.25 | 2.25 |
| **2969** | A770 55c multi | 2.25 | 2.25 |
| **2970** | A771 55c multi | 2.25 | 2.25 |
| **2971** | A772 55c multi | 2.25 | 2.25 |
| **2972** | A773 55c multi | 2.25 | 2.25 |
| **2973** | A774 55c multi | 2.25 | 2.25 |
| **2974** | A775 $1.10 multi | 3.25 | 3.25 |
| | *Nos. 2966-2974 (9)* | 21.25 | 21.25 |

Issued: Nos. 2959b, 2960b, 2962b, 2963b, 2965b, 3/2/09.

Complete booklet containing No. 2965 sold for $22.95; booklets containing Nos. 2959-2964 each sold for $11.95. Each booklet contained panes with five different margins.

Nos. 2966-2974 each were sold in sheets of 20 and have personalized pictures and a straight edge at right, and lack separations between the stamp and the personalized photo. Sheets of 20 of Nos. 2966-2973 each sold for $24, and No. 2974 sold for $35.

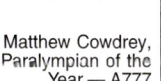

Large Extinct Animals — A776

Designs: Nos. 2975, 2981, Genyornis. Nos. 2976, 2982, Diprotodon. Nos. 2977, 2983, Thylacoleo. Nos. 2978, 2984, Thylacine. No. 2979, Megalania, horiz. (52x37mm). No. 2980, Procoptodon, horiz. (52x37mm).

**2008, Oct. 1 Litho. *Perf. 14½x14***

| | | | |
|---|---|---|---|
| **2975** | A776 55c multi | .95 | .95 |
| *a.* | Perf. 14 | .95 | .95 |
| *b.* | Booklet pane of 2 #2975 | 2.25 | — |
| **2976** | A776 55c multi | .95 | .95 |
| *a.* | Perf. 14 | .95 | .95 |
| *b.* | Booklet pane of 2 #2976 | 2.25 | — |
| **2977** | A776 55c multi | .95 | .95 |
| *a.* | Perf. 14 | .95 | .95 |
| *b.* | Booklet pane of 2 #2977 | 2.25 | — |
| **2978** | A776 55c multi | .95 | .95 |
| *a.* | Perf. 14 | .95 | .95 |
| *b.* | Horiz. strip of 4, #2975-2978 | 4.00 | 4.00 |
| *c.* | Booklet pane of 2 #2978 | 2.25 | — |
| *d.* | Booklet pane of 4, #2975-2978 | 4.25 | — |
| **2979** | A776 $1.10 multi | 2.00 | 1.60 |
| *a.* | Perf. 14 | .95 | .95 |
| *b.* | Booklet pane of 2 #2979 | 4.25 | — |
| **2980** | A776 $1.10 multi | 2.00 | 1.60 |
| *a.* | Perf. 14 | .95 | .95 |
| *b.* | Horiz. pair, #2979-2980 | 4.00 | 4.00 |
| *c.* | Souvenir sheet, #2975a-2980a | 8.00 | 8.00 |
| *d.* | Booklet pane of 2 #2980 | 4.25 | — |
| *e.* | Booklet pane of 2, #2979-2980 | 4.25 | — |
| | Complete booklet, #2975b, 2976b, 2977b, 2978c, 2978d, 2979b, 2980d, 2980e | 26.50 | |
| *f.* | As "c," overprinted with Beijing 2008 Stamp Exposition emblem in margin | 7.00 | 7.00 |
| | *Nos. 2975-2980 (6)* | 7.80 | 7.00 |

**Self-Adhesive**

***Serpentine Die Cut 11¼ Syncopated***

| | | | |
|---|---|---|---|
| **2981** | A776 55c multi | .95 | .30 |
| **2982** | A776 55c multi | .95 | .30 |
| **2983** | A776 55c multi | .95 | .30 |
| **2984** | A776 55c multi | .95 | .30 |
| *a.* | Vert. coil strip of 4, #2981-2984 | 4.00 | |
| *b.* | Booklet pane of 10, 3 each #2981-2982, 2 each #2983-2984 | 9.75 | |
| | *Nos. 2981-2984 (4)* | 3.80 | 1.20 |

Complete booklet sold for $13.95. Issued: No. 2980f, 10/24.

Matthew Cowdrey, Paralympian of the Year — A777

**2008, Oct. 24 Litho. *Perf. 14¼***

| | | | |
|---|---|---|---|
| **2985** | A777 55c multi | .85 | .70 |

Christmas

A778 A779

Star of Bethlehem and: Nos. 2987, 2992, 2995, Madonna and child. No. 2988, 2996, Angel. Nos. 2989, 2993, Magus.

**2008, Oct. 31 Litho. *Perf. 14¾x14***

| | | | |
|---|---|---|---|
| **2986** | A778 50c multi | .80 | .80 |
| **2987** | A779 50c multi | .80 | .80 |
| **2988** | A779 55c multi | .85 | .70 |
| **2989** | A779 $1.20 multi | 1.90 | 1.90 |
| | *Nos. 2986-2989 (4)* | 4.35 | 4.20 |

### Booklet Stamps
### Self-Adhesive
### Litho. & Typo.
***Serpentine Die Cut 11¼ Syncopated***

**2990** A778 50c multi .80 .30
*a.* Booklet pane of 10 8.00 —

### Litho.

**2991** A778 50c multi .80 .30
*a.* Booklet pane of 20 16.00
**2992** A779 50c multi .80 .30
*a.* Booklet pane of 20 16.00
**2993** A779 $1.20 multi 1.90 .30
*a.* Booklet pane of 5 9.25
*Nos. 2990-2993 (4)* 4.30 1.20

### With Personalized Photo at Right Like Type A692a
***Serpentine Die Cut 11½x11¼ Syncopated***
### Self-Adhesive

**2994** A778 50c multi 1.75 1.75
**2995** A779 50c multi 1.75 1.75
**2996** A779 55c multi 1.75 1.75
*Nos. 2994-2996 (3)* 5.25 5.25

Nos. 2994-2996 each were sold in sheets of 20 and have personalized pictures and a straight edge at right, and lack separations between the stamp and the personalized photo. Sheets of 20 of Nos. 2994-2995 each sold for $23, and No. 2996 sold for $24.

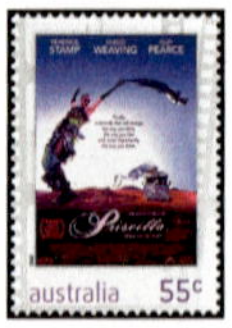

Posters for Popular Australian Films — A780

Poster for: Nos. 2997, 3002, The Adventures of Priscilla, Queen of the Desert. Nos. 2998, 3003, The Castle. Nos. 2999, 3004, Muriel's Wedding. Nos. 3000, 3005, Lantana. Nos. 3001, 3006, Gallipoli.

**2008, Nov. 3 Litho. *Perf. 14¾x14***

**2997** A780 55c multi .85 .85
**2998** A780 55c multi .85 .85
**2999** A780 55c multi .85 .85
**3000** A780 55c multi .85 .85
**3001** A780 55c multi .85 .85
*a.* Horiz. strip of 5, #2997-3001 4.25 4.25
*Nos. 2997-3001 (5)* 4.25 4.25

### Self-Adhesive
***Serpentine Die Cut 11¼ Syncopated***

**3002** A780 55c multi .85 .30
*a.* Booklet pane of 10 8.50
**3003** A780 55c multi .85 .30
*a.* Booklet pane of 10 8.50
**3004** A780 55c multi .85 .30
*a.* Booklet pane of 10 8.50
**3005** A780 55c multi .85 .30
*a.* Booklet pane of 10 8.50
**3006** A780 55c multi .85 .30
*a.* Booklet pane of 10 8.50
*b.* Booklet pane of 10, 2 each #3002-3006 8.50
*c.* Vert. coil strip of 5, #3002-3006 4.25
*d.* Souvenir sheet of 10, 1 ea #3002, 3004-3006, 6 #3003 11.00
*Nos. 3002-3006 (5)* 4.25 1.50

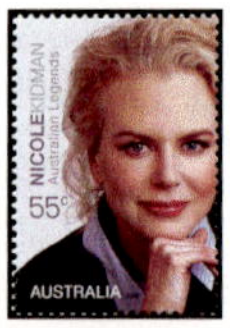

Academy Award-winning Actors and Actresses — A781

Designs: Nos. 3007, 3015, Nicole Kidman. Nos. 3008, 3016, Russell Crowe. Nos. 3009, 3018, Geoffrey Rush. Nos. 3010, 3017, Cate Blanchett. Nos. 3011, 3020, Crowe in *Gladiator.* Nos. 3012, 3019, Kidman in *Moulin Rouge!* Nos. 3013, 3021, Blanchett in *Elizabeth: The Golden Age.* Nos. 3014, 3022, Rush in *Shine.*

**2009, Jan. 22 Litho. *Perf. 14¾x14***

**3007** A781 55c multi .80 .80
*a.* Booklet pane of 4 4.25 —
**3008** A781 55c multi .80 .80
*a.* Booklet pane of 4 4.25 —
*b.* Sheet of 10 + 10 labels 14.00 14.00
**3009** A781 55c multi .80 .80
*a.* Booklet pane of 4 4.25 —
*b.* Souvenir sheet of 4 8.25 8.25
**3010** A781 55c multi .85 .85
*a.* Booklet pane of 4 4.25 —
*b.* Block of 4, #3007-3010 3.50 3.50
*c.* Booklet pane of 4, #3007-3010 4.25 —
*d.* Souvenir sheet of 4, #3007-3010 8.25 8.25
**3011** A781 55c multi .85 .85
*a.* Booklet pane of 4 4.25 —
*b.* Booklet pane of 4, 2 each #3008, 3011 4.25 —
Complete booklet, #3008a, 3010c, 3011a, 3011b 17.00
**3012** A781 55c multi .85 .85
*a.* Booklet pane of 4 4.25 —
*b.* Booklet pane of 4, 2 each #3007, 3012 4.25 —
Complete booklet, #3007a, 3010c, 3012a, 3012b 17.00
**3013** A781 55c multi .85 .85
*a.* Booklet pane of 4 4.25 —
*b.* Booklet pane of 4, 2 each #3010, 3013 4.25 —
Complete booklet, #3010a, 3010c, 3013a, 3013b 17.00
**3014** A781 55c multi .85 .85
*a.* Booklet pane of 4 4.25 —
*b.* Booklet pane of 4, 2 each #3009, 3014 4.25 —
Complete booklet, #3009a, 3010c, 3014a, 3014b 17.50
*c.* Block of 4, #3011-3014 3.50 3.50
*Nos. 3007-3014 (8)* 6.65 6.65

Issued: No. 3008b, 5/6/10. Two sheets of 3008b, each sheet having different labels, were sold together as a set for $13.50. Nos. 3009b and 3010d were sold with Nos. 2952a and 2952b in a set for $12.95.

### Self-Adhesive
### Booklet Stamps
***Serpentine Die Cut 11¼ Syncopated***

**3015** A781 55c multi .85 .30
**3016** A781 55c multi .85 .30
**3017** A781 55c multi .85 .30
**3018** A781 55c multi .85 .30
**3019** A781 55c multi .85 .30
*a.* Booklet pane of 10, 5 each #3015, 3019 8.50
**3020** A781 55c multi .85 .30
*a.* Booklet pane of 10, 5 each #3016, 3020 8.50
**3021** A781 55c multi .85 .30
*a.* Booklet pane of 10, 5 each #3017 3021 8.50
**3022** A781 55c multi .85 .30
*a.* Booklet pane of 20, 3 each #3015-3018, 2 each #3019-3022 17.00
*b.* Booklet pane of 10, 5 each #3019, 3022 8.50
*Nos. 3015-3022 (8)* 6.80 2.40

Each complete booklet sold for $10.95.

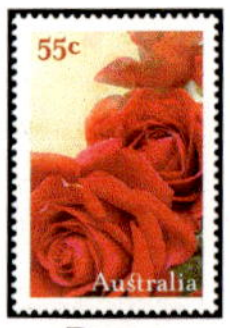

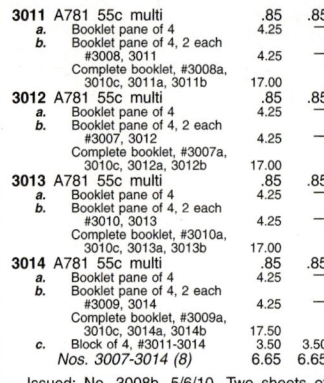

Roses A782

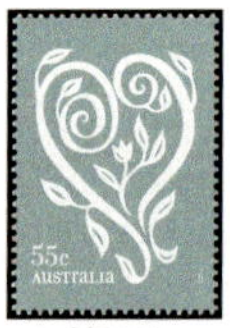

Heart A783

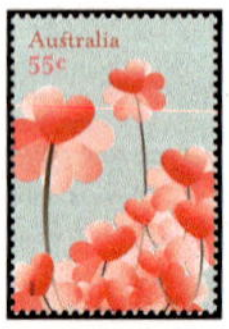

Flowers With Heart-Shaped Petals — A784

**2009, Feb. 3 Litho. *Perf. 14¾x14***

**3023** A782 55c multi .80 .80
**3024** A783 55c gray blue .80 .80
**3025** A784 55c multi .80 .80
*a.* Pair, #3024-3025 1.60 1.60
*Nos. 3023-3025 (3)* 2.40 2.40

### Booklet Stamps
### Self-Adhesive
***Serpentine Die Cut 11¼ Syncopated***

**3026** A782 55c multi .80 .80
*a.* Booklet pane of 10 8.00
**3027** A783 55c gray blue .80 .80
*a.* Booklet pane of 10 8.00
**3028** A784 55c multi .80 .80
*a.* Booklet pane of 10 8.00

### Litho. With Foil Application

**3029** A784 55c multi .80 .80

### Litho. With Flocking

**3030** A783 55c gray blue .80 .80
*a.* Booklet pane of 10, 2 each #3029-3030 8.00
*Nos. 3026-3030 (5)* 4.00 4.00

### With Personalized Photo at Right Like Type A692a
***Syncopated Die Cut 11½x11¼ Syncopated***
### Self-Adhesive

**3031** A782 55c multi 1.75 1.75
**3032** A783 55c multi 1.75 1.75
**3033** A784 55c multi 1.75 1.75
*Nos. 3031-3033 (3)* 5.25 5.25

Nos. 3031-3033 each were sold in sheets of 20 and have personalized pictures and a straight edge at right and lack separations between the stamp and the personalized photo. Sheets of 20 of each stamp sold for $24.

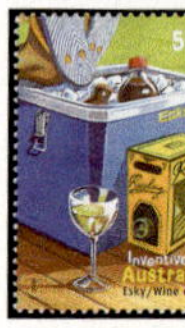

Australian Inventions — A785

Designs: Nos. 3034, 3039, Esky (insulated cooler), wine cask. Nos. 3035, 3040, Hills hoist (rotatable clothes line frame). Nos. 3036, 3041, Speedos (swim wear), zinc oxide cream. Nos. 3037, 3042, Ute (utility vehicle), B&D Roll-A-Door (garage door). Nos. 3038, 3043, Victa rotary lawnmower.

**2009, Feb. 19 Litho. *Perf. 14¾x14***

**3034** A785 55c multi .80 .80
*a.* Booklet pane of 4 4.00 —
*b.* As #3034, perf. 14 .80 .80
**3035** A785 55c multi .80 .80
*a.* Booklet pane of 4 4.00 —
*b.* As #3035, perf. 14 .80 .80
**3036** A785 55c multi .80 .80
*a.* Booklet pane of 4 4.00 —
*b.* As #3036, perf. 14 .80 .80
**3037** A785 55c multi .80 .80
*a.* Booklet pane of 4 4.00 —
*b.* As #3037, perf. 14 .80 .80
**3038** A785 55c multi .80 .80
*a.* Booklet pane of 4 4.00 —
Complete booklet, #3034a, 3035a, 3036a, 3037a, 3038a 19.50
*b.* As #3038, perf. 14 .80 .80
*c.* Souvenir sheet, #3034b-3038b 4.00 4.00
*d.* Horiz. strip of 5, #3034-3038 4.00 4.00
*Nos. 3034-3038 (5)* 4.00 4.00

### Self-Adhesive
***Serpentine Die Cut 11¼ Syncopated***

**3039** A785 55c multi .80 .30
**3040** A785 55c multi .80 .30
**3041** A785 55c multi .80 .30
**3042** A785 55c multi .80 .30
**3043** A785 55c multi .80 .30
*a.* Vert. coil strip of 5, #3039-3043 4.00
*b.* Booklet pane of 10, 2 each #3039-3043 8.00
*Nos. 3039-3043 (5)* 4.00 1.50

Complete booklet sold for $12.95.

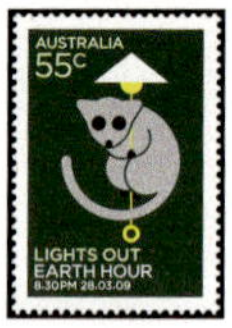

Earth Hour — A786

Animals and slogan: Nos. 3044, 3047, Lights out. No. 3045, 3048, Switch off. $2.05, Save energy.

**2009, Mar. 11 *Perf. 14¾x14***

**3044** A786 55c multi .90 .90
**3045** A786 55c multi .90 .90
*a.* Horiz. pair, #3044-3045 1.90 1.90
**3046** A786 $2.05 multi 3.50 3.50
*Nos. 3044-3046 (3)* 5.30 5.30

### Booklet Stamps
### Self-Adhesive
***Serpentine Die Cut 11¼ Syncopated***

**3047** A786 55c multi .90 .30
**3048** A786 55c multi .90 .30
*a.* Booklet pane of 20, 10 each #3047-3048 18.50

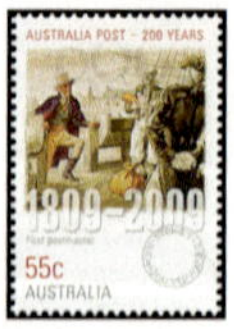

Australia Post, Bicent. — A787

Inscriptions: Nos. 3049a, 3050, First postmaster. Nos. 3049b, 3051, Early post office. Nos. 3049c, 3052, Early posting box. Nos. 3049d, 3053, News from home. Nos. 3049e, 3054, Early air mail. Nos. 3049f, 3055, Home delivery. Nos. 3049g, 3056, Post-war immigration. Nos. 3049h, 3057, Retail post shop. Nos. 3049i, 3058, Express post. Nos. 3049j, 3059, Part of every day.

**2009, Mar. 25 *Perf. 14¾x14***

**3049** Sheet of 10 9.25 9.25
*a.-j.* A787 55c Any single .90 .90
*k.* Booklet pane of 10, #3049a-3049j 11.00 —
*l.* As "k," imperf. 11.00
Complete booklet, #3049l, 2 #3049k 32.50

### Self-Adhesive
***Serpentine Die Cut 11¼ Syncopated***

**3050** A787 55c multi .90 .30
**3051** A787 55c multi .90 .30
**3052** A787 55c multi .90 .30
**3053** A787 55c multi .90 .30
**3054** A787 55c multi .90 .30
**3055** A787 55c multi .90 .30
**3056** A787 55c multi .90 .30
**3057** A787 55c multi .90 .30
**3058** A787 55c multi .90 .30
**3059** A787 55c multi .90 .30
*a.* Vert. coil strip of 10, #3050-3059 9.00
*b.* Booklet pane of 10, #3050-3059 9.00
*Nos. 3050-3059 (10)* 9.00 3.00

Complete booklet sold for $19.95. Compare with type A806.

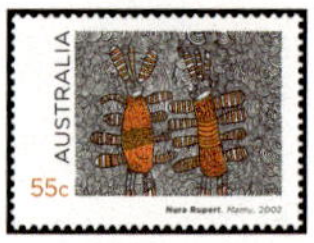

Aboriginal Art — A788

Designs: No. 3060, Mamu, by Nura Rupert. No. 3061, All the Jila, by Jan Billycan. No. 3062, Mina Mina, by Judy Napangardi Watson. $1.40, Untitled work from the Mission Series, by Elaine Russell. $2.05, Natjula, by Tjuruparu Watson.

**2009, Apr. 1 *Perf. 14x14¾***

**3060** A788 55c multi .90 .70
**3061** A788 55c multi .90 .70
**3062** A788 55c multi .90 .70
*a.* Horiz. strip of 3, #3060-3062 2.75 2.00
**3063** A788 $1.40 multi 2.25 1.10
**3064** A788 $2.05 multi 3.50 1.75
*Nos. 3060-3064 (5)* 8.45 4.95

### Self-Adhesive
### Booklet Stamps
***Serpentine Die Cut 11¼ Syncopated***

**3065** A788 $1.40 multi 2.25 1.10
*a.* Booklet pane of 5 11.50
**3066** A788 $2.05 multi 3.50 1.75
*a.* Booklet pane of 5 17.50

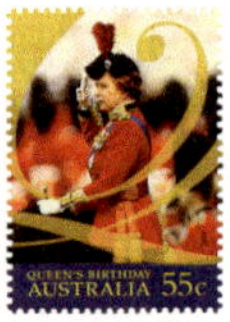

Queen's Birthday — A789

Queen Elizabeth II: 55c, In uniform. $2.05, Wearing green coat and hat.

**2009, Apr. 15 *Perf. 14¾x14***

**3067** A789 55c multi .90 .70
*a.* Booklet pane of 2 2.25 —
*b.* Dated "2010" 2.00 1.00
**3068** A789 $2.05 multi 3.50 1.75
*a.* Booklet pane of 2 8.50 —
*b.* Souvenir sheet of 2, #3067-3068 4.50 2.40
*c.* Booklet pane, #3068b 5.25 —
Complete booklet, #3068a, 3068c, 2 #3067a 18.50

Complete booklet sold for $10.95.

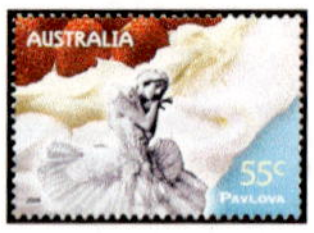

Eponymous Desserts — A790

Designs: Nos. 3069, 3073, Anna Pavlova and Pavlova. Nos. 3070, 3074, Dame Nellie Melba and Peach Melba. Nos. 3071, 3075, Baron and Lady Lamington and Lamingtons. Nos. 3072, 3076, ANZAC soldiers and ANZAC biscuits.

**2009, May 15 Litho. *Perf. 14x14¾***

**3069** A790 55c multi 1.00 1.00
*a.* Booklet pane of 4 5.25 —
**3070** A790 55c multi 1.00 1.00
*a.* Booklet pane of 4 5.25 —
**3071** A790 55c multi 1.00 1.00
*a.* Booklet pane of 4 5.25 —
**3072** A790 55c multi 1.00 1.00
*a.* Booklet pane of 4 5.25 —
Complete booklet, #3069a-3072a 20.75
*b.* Horiz. strip of 4, #3069-3072 4.25 4.25
*Nos. 3069-3072 (4)* 4.00 4.00

### Booklet Stamps
### Self-Adhesive
*Serpentine Die Cut 11¼ Syncopated*

| | | | |
|---|---|---|---|
| **3073** | A790 55c multi | 1.00 | .30 |
| **3074** | A790 55c multi | 1.00 | .30 |
| **3075** | A790 55c multi | 1.00 | .30 |
| **3076** | A790 55c multi | 1.00 | .30 |
| *a.* | Booklet pane of 10, 3 each #3073-3074, 2 each #3075-3076 | 11.00 | |
| | *Nos. 3073-3076 (4)* | 4.00 | 1.20 |

Complete booklet sold for $10.95.

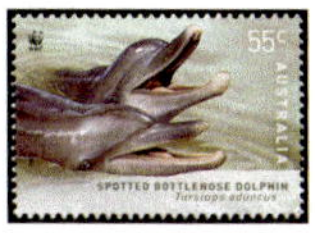

Worldwide Fund for Nature (WWF) — A791

Designs: 55c, Spotted bottlenose dolphins. $1.35, Hourglass dolphins. $1.40, Southern right whale dolphins. $2.05, Dusky dolphins.

**2009, May 26** *Perf. 14x14¾*

| | | | |
|---|---|---|---|
| **3077** | A791 55c multi | 1.00 | .80 |
| **3078** | A791 $1.35 multi | 2.50 | 2.50 |
| **3079** | A791 $1.40 multi | 2.50 | 2.50 |
| **3080** | A791 $2.05 multi | 3.75 | 3.75 |
| *a.* | Souvenir sheet, #3077-3080 | 10.00 | 10.00 |
| | *Nos. 3077-3080 (4)* | 9.75 | 9.55 |

### Booklet Stamps
### Self-Adhesive
*Serpentine Die Cut 11¼ Syncopated*

| | | | |
|---|---|---|---|
| **3081** | A791 $1.35 multi | 2.50 | 2.50 |
| *a.* | Booklet pane of 5 | 13.00 | |
| **3082** | A791 $1.40 multi | 2.50 | 2.50 |
| *a.* | Booklet pane of 5 | 13.00 | |
| **3083** | A791 $2.05 multi | 3.75 | 3.75 |
| *a.* | Booklet pane of 5 | 19.00 | |
| | *Nos. 3081-3083 (3)* | 8.75 | 8.75 |

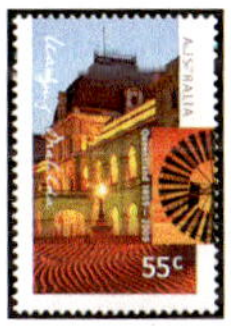

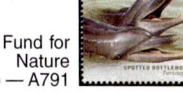

Queensland, 150th Anniv. — A792

Designs: 55c, Queensland Parliament, windmill. $2.75, Great Barrier Reef, red-eyed tree frog.

**2009, June 9 Litho.** *Perf. 14¾x14*

| | | | |
|---|---|---|---|
| **3084** | A792 55c multi | 1.00 | .80 |
| **3085** | A792 $2.75 multi | 5.25 | 4.00 |
| *a.* | Souvenir sheet, #3084-3085 | 6.25 | 6.25 |

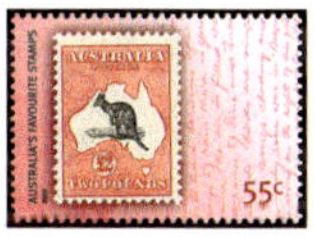

Australia's Favorite Stamps — A793

Designs: Nos. 3086, 3091, 3095B, Australia #15. Nos. 3087, 3092, Australia #132. Nos. 3088, 3093, Australia #200. Nos. 3089, 3094, Australia #226. Nos. 3090, 3095, Australia #18.

**2009, June 26 Litho.** *Perf. 14x14¾*

| | | | |
|---|---|---|---|
| **3086** | A793 55c multi | 1.00 | 1.00 |
| *a.* | Booklet pane of 4 | 4.50 | — |
| **3087** | A793 55c multi | 1.00 | 1.00 |
| *a.* | Booklet pane of 4 | 4.50 | — |
| **3088** | A793 55c multi | 1.00 | 1.00 |
| *a.* | Booklet pane of 4 | 4.50 | — |
| **3089** | A793 55c multi | 1.00 | 1.00 |
| *a.* | Booklet pane of 4 | 4.50 | — |
| **3090** | A793 55c multi | 1.00 | 1.00 |
| *a.* | Booklet pane of 4 | 4.50 | — |
| | Complete booklet, #3086a-3090a | 23.00 | |
| *b.* | Horiz. strip of 5, #3086-3090 | 5.25 | 5.25 |
| | *Nos. 3086-3090 (5)* | 5.00 | 5.00 |

### Self-Adhesive
*Serpentine Die Cut 11¼ Syncopated*

| | | | |
|---|---|---|---|
| **3091** | A793 55c multi | 1.00 | .30 |
| **3092** | A793 55c multi | 1.00 | .30 |
| **3093** | A793 55c multi | 1.00 | .30 |
| **3094** | A793 55c multi | 1.00 | .30 |
| **3095** | A793 55c multi | 1.00 | .30 |
| *a.* | Horiz. coil strip of 5, #3091-3095 | 5.25 | |
| | *Nos. 3091-3095 (5)* | 5.00 | 1.50 |

### Litho. & Embossed
*Serpentine Die Cut 11¼ Syncopated*
### Self-Adhesive

| | | | |
|---|---|---|---|
| **3095B** | A793 55c multi | 1.00 | .30 |
| *c.* | Sheet of 13, #3091-3095, 8 #3095B | 14.00 | |

The complete booklet sold for $12.95. Nos. 3091-3095 each were printed by two different printers. There is no noticeable difference between single coil stamps, but Pemara-printed stamps are slightly closer to each other on the strip compared to the McKellar Renown-printed stamps.

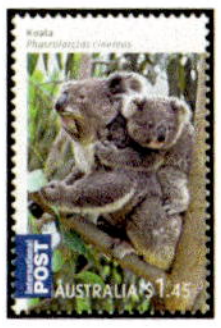

Marsupials and Their Young — A794

Designs: $1.45, Koalas. $2.10, Eastern gray kangaroos. $2.90, Brushtail possums, horiz. $4.20, Common wombats, horiz.

**2009, July 1** *Perf. 14¾x14*

| | | | |
|---|---|---|---|
| **3096** | A794 $1.45 multi | 2.75 | 2.75 |
| **3097** | A794 $2.10 multi | 4.00 | 4.00 |
| *a.* | Additionally dated "2013" (#3534d) | 5.50 | 5.50 |

*Perf. 14x14¾*

| | | | |
|---|---|---|---|
| **3098** | A794 $2.90 multi | 5.50 | 2.75 |
| **3099** | A794 $4.20 multi | 7.75 | 4.00 |
| | *Nos. 3096-3099 (4)* | 20.00 | 13.50 |

Issued: No. 3097a, 5/10/13.

### Booklet Stamps
### Self-Adhesive
*Serpentine Die Cut 11¼ Syncopated*

| | | | |
|---|---|---|---|
| **3100** | A794 $1.45 multi | 2.75 | 1.40 |
| *a.* | Booklet pane of 5 | 14.00 | |
| **3101** | A794 $2.10 multi | 4.00 | 2.00 |
| *a.* | Booklet pane of 5 | 20.00 | |

### With Personalized Photo at Right Like Type A692a
*Serpentine Die Cut 11¼ Syncopated*
### Self-Adhesive

| | | | |
|---|---|---|---|
| **3102** | A794 $1.45 multi | 4.00 | 4.00 |
| **3103** | A794 $2.10 multi | 5.25 | 5.25 |

Nos. 3102-3103 each were sold in sheets of 20 and have personalized pictures and a straight edge at right and lack separations between the stamp and the personalized photo. Sheets of 20 of No. 3102 sold for $42; No. 3103, for $54.

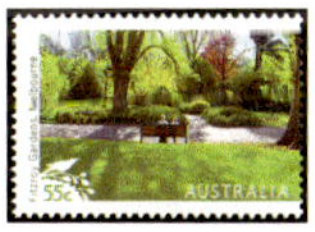

Parks and Gardens — A795

Designs: Nos. 3104, 3109, Fitzroy Gardens, Melbourne. Nos. 3105, 3110, Roma Street Parkland, Brisbane. Nos. 3106, 3111, St. David's Park, Hobart. Nos. 3107, 3112, Commonwealth Park, Canberra. Nos. 3108, 3113, Hyde Park, Sydney.

**2009, July 14 Litho.** *Perf. 14x14¾*

| | | | |
|---|---|---|---|
| **3104** | A795 55c multi | 1.10 | 1.10 |
| *a.* | Booklet pane of 4 | 5.25 | — |
| *b.* | Sheet of 4, #3072, 3086, 3090, 3104 | 4.25 | 4.25 |
| **3105** | A795 55c multi | 1.10 | 1.10 |
| *a.* | Booklet pane of 4 | 5.25 | — |
| **3106** | A795 55c multi | 1.10 | 1.10 |
| *a.* | Booklet pane of 4 | 5.25 | — |
| **3107** | A795 55c multi | 1.10 | 1.10 |
| *a.* | Booklet pane of 4 | 5.25 | — |
| *b.* | Additionally dated "2013" (#3107c) | 1.25 | 1.25 |
| *c.* | Booklet pane of 2 #3107b | 2.50 | — |
| **3108** | A795 55c multi | 1.10 | 1.10 |
| *a.* | Booklet pane of 4 | 5.25 | — |
| | Complete booklet, #3104a-3108a | 26.00 | |
| *b.* | Horiz. strip of 5, #3104-3108 | 5.50 | 5.50 |
| | *Nos. 3104-3108 (5)* | 5.50 | 5.50 |

Issued: Nos. 3107b, 3107c, 3/5/13. No. 3107c was issued in booklet along with Nos. 1940c, 2710c, 2869e, 3349b and 3877a.

### Coil Stamps
### Self-Adhesive
*Serpentine Die Cut 11¼ Syncopated*

| | | | |
|---|---|---|---|
| **3109** | A795 55c multi | 1.10 | .30 |
| **3110** | A795 55c multi | 1.10 | .30 |
| **3111** | A795 55c multi | 1.10 | .30 |
| **3112** | A795 55c multi | 1.10 | .30 |
| **3113** | A795 55c multi | 1.10 | .30 |
| *a.* | Horiz. strip of 5, #3109-3113 | 5.25 | |
| *b.* | Booklet pane of 10, 2 each #3109-3113 | 11.00 | |
| | *Nos. 3109-3113 (5)* | 5.50 | 1.50 |

The complete booklet sold for $12.95.
Issued: No. 3104b, 7/23. Melbourne Stamp Show 09 (No. 3104b).

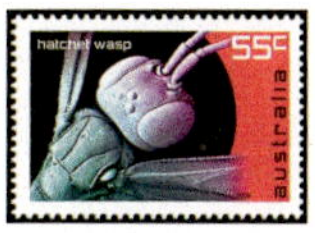

Insects and Spiders — A796

Designs: Nos. 3114, 3120a, 3121, Hatchet wasp. Nos. 3115, 3120b, 3122, Praying mantis. Nos. 3116, 3120c, 3123, Ground beetle. Nos. 3117, 3120d, 3124, Jumping spider. Nos. 3118, 3120e, 3125, Ant. $1.10, Weevil.

**2009, July 28 Litho.** *Perf. 14x14¾*

| | | | |
|---|---|---|---|
| **3114** | A796 55c multi | 1.10 | 1.10 |
| **3115** | A796 55c multi | 1.10 | 1.10 |
| **3116** | A796 55c multi | 1.10 | 1.10 |
| **3117** | A796 55c multi | 1.10 | 1.10 |
| **3118** | A796 55c multi | 1.10 | 1.10 |
| *b.* | Horiz. strip of 5, #3114-3118 | 5.25 | 5.25 |
| **3119** | A796 $1.10 multi | 2.25 | 1.60 |
| | *Nos. 3114-3119 (6)* | 7.75 | 7.10 |

### Miniature Sheet
### With Square of Thermochromic Ink Covering Magnification Squares

| | | | |
|---|---|---|---|
| **3120** | Sheet of 6 | 7.75 | 7.75 |
| *a.-e.* | A796 55c Any single | 1.10 | 1.10 |
| *f.* | A796 $1.10 multi | 2.25 | 2.25 |

### Coil Stamps
### Self-Adhesive
*Serpentine Die Cut 11¼ Syncopated*

| | | | |
|---|---|---|---|
| **3121** | A796 55c multi | 1.10 | .30 |
| **3122** | A796 55c multi | 1.10 | .30 |
| **3123** | A796 55c multi | 1.10 | .30 |
| **3124** | A796 55c multi | 1.10 | .30 |
| **3125** | A796 55c multi | 1.10 | .30 |
| *a.* | Horiz. strip of 5, #3121-3125 | 5.25 | |
| | *Nos. 3121-3125 (5)* | 5.50 | 1.50 |

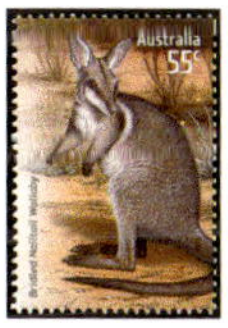

Endangered Wildlife — A797

Designs: Nos. 3126, 3132, Bridled nailtail wallaby. Nos. 3127, 3133, Norfolk Island green parrot. Nos. 3128, 3134, Subarctic fur seal. Nos. 3129, 3135, Christmas Island blue-tailed skink. Nos. 3130, 3136, Green turtle.

**2009, Aug. 4 Litho.** *Perf. 14¾x14*
### "Australia" Above Denomination

| | | | |
|---|---|---|---|
| **3126** | A797 55c multi | 1.10 | 1.10 |
| **3127** | A797 55c multi | 1.10 | 1.10 |
| **3128** | A797 55c multi | 1.10 | 1.10 |
| **3129** | A797 55c multi | 1.10 | 1.10 |
| **3130** | A797 55c multi | 1.10 | 1.10 |
| *a.* | Horiz. strip of 5, #3126-3130 | 5.50 | 5.50 |
| | *Nos. 3126-3130 (5)* | 5.50 | 5.50 |
| **3131** | A797 55c Sheet of 5, #3126, 3128-3130, Norfolk Island #980 | 5.50 | 5.50 |

### Booklet Stamps
### Self-Adhesive
*Serpentine Die Cut 11¼ Syncopated*

| | | | |
|---|---|---|---|
| **3132** | A797 55c multi | 1.10 | .30 |
| **3133** | A797 55c multi | 1.10 | .30 |
| **3134** | A797 55c multi | 1.10 | .30 |
| **3135** | A797 55c multi | 1.10 | .30 |
| **3136** | A797 55c multi | 1.10 | .30 |
| *a.* | Booklet pane of 20, 4 each #3132-3136 | 22.00 | |
| | *Nos. 3132-3136 (5)* | 5.50 | 1.50 |

Inscribed on the left side of Nos. 3128 and 3134 is "Australian Antarctic Territory"; on Nos. 3129 and 3135, "Christmas Island"; and on Nos. 3130 and 3136, "Cocos (Keeling) Islands." All recent stamps of the Australian possessions of Australian Antarctic Territory, Christmas Island and Cocos Islands are doubly-inscribed with "Australia" and the territory's name, and all stamps inscribed "Australia," "Australian Antarctic Territory," "Christmas Island," or "Cocos Islands," are valid for postage anywhere in those four areas. However, because Nos. 3128-3130 and 3134-3136 have the territorial inscriptions at the side rather than above the denomination like similar Norfolk Island stamps, Nos. 979-983, they will be listed here only and not in the listings for each of these territories. No. 3131 is identical to Norfolk Island No. 984. Norfolk Island No. 980 has "Norfolk Island" above the denomination, which differentiates it from Australia No. 3127.

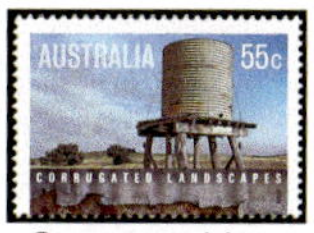

Corrugated Iron Water Tank, Fleurieu Peninsula, South Australia — A798

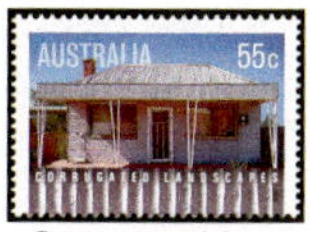

Corrugated Iron House, Broken Hill, New South Wales — A799

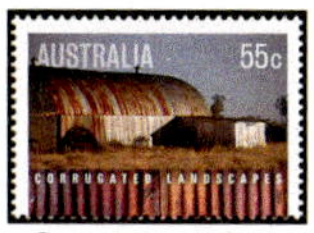

Corrugated Iron Shearing Shed, Bushy Park Cattle Station, Queensland A800

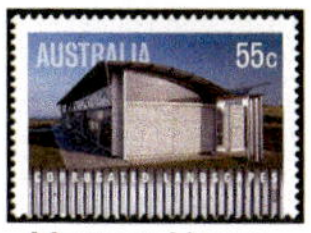

Magney House, Bingie Bingie Point, New South Wales A801

**2009, Aug. 11** *Perf. 14x14¾*

| | | | |
|---|---|---|---|
| **3137** | A798 55c multi | 1.10 | 1.10 |
| *a.* | Booklet pane of 4 | 5.25 | — |
| **3138** | A799 55c multi | 1.10 | 1.10 |
| *a.* | Booklet pane of 4 | 5.25 | — |
| **3139** | A800 55c multi | 1.10 | 1.10 |
| *a.* | Booklet pane of 4 | 5.25 | — |
| **3140** | A801 55c multi | 1.10 | 1.10 |
| *a.* | Booklet pane of 4 | 5.25 | — |
| | Complete booklet, #3137a-3140a | 22.00 | |
| *b.* | Horiz. strip of 4, #3137-3140 | 4.50 | 4.50 |
| | *Nos. 3137-3140 (4)* | 4.40 | 4.40 |

### Self-Adhesive
*Serpentine Die Cut 11¼ Syncopated*

| | | | |
|---|---|---|---|
| **3141** | A798 55c multi | 1.10 | .30 |
| **3142** | A799 55c multi | 1.10 | .30 |
| **3143** | A800 55c multi | 1.10 | .30 |
| **3144** | A801 55c multi | 1.10 | .30 |
| *a.* | Horiz. coil strip of 4, #3141-3144 | 4.50 | |
| *b.* | Booklet pane of 20, 5 each #3141-3144 | 22.00 | |
| | *Nos. 3141-3144 (4)* | 4.40 | 1.20 |

Complete booklet sold for $10.95.

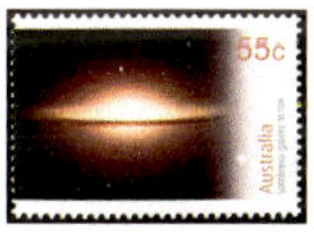

Intl. Year of Astronomy — A802

Designs: 55c, Sombrero Galaxy (M104). $1.45, Reflection Nebula (M78). $2.10, Spiral Galaxy (M83).

**2009, Aug. 25** *Perf. 14x14¾*

| | | | |
|---|---|---|---|
| **3145** | A802 55c multi | 1.10 | .85 |
| **3146** | A802 $1.45 multi | 2.75 | 2.25 |
| **3147** | A802 $2.10 multi | 4.00 | 3.00 |
| *a.* | Souvenir sheet, #3145-3147 | 8.00 | 6.00 |
| | *Nos. 3145-3147 (3)* | 7.85 | 6.10 |

No. 3147a exists imperf from a telephone drawing at a substantial premium over face value. Value for a single sheet, $22.

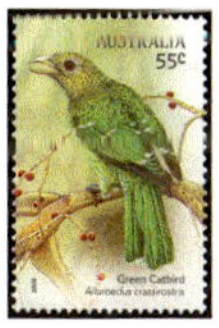

Birds — A803

Designs: 55c, Green catbird. $1.10, Noisy scrub-bird. $1.65, Mangrove golden whistler. $2.75, Scarlet honeyeater.

**2009, Sept. 9 Litho.** *Perf. 14¾x14*

| | | | |
|---|---|---|---|
| **3148** | A803 55c multi | 1.10 | 1.10 |
| *a.* | Additionally dated "2013" | 1.10 | 1.10 |
| **3149** | A803 $1.10 multi | 2.25 | 1.60 |
| *a.* | Booklet pane of 2, #3148-3149 | 4.25 | — |
| *b.* | Additionally dated "2013" | 2.10 | 2.10 |
| **3150** | A803 $1.65 multi | 3.50 | 2.50 |
| *a.* | Booklet pane of 2, #3149-3150 | 7.25 | — |
| *b.* | Booklet pane of 2, #3148, 3150 | 6.75 | — |
| *c.* | Additionally dated "2013" | 3.25 | 3.25 |
| **3151** | A803 $2.75 multi | 5.50 | 4.25 |
| *a.* | Booklet pane of 2, #3148, 3151 | 8.50 | — |
| | Complete booklet, #3149a, 3150a, 3150b, 3151a | 26.00 | |
| *b.* | Additionally dated "2013" | 5.50 | 5.50 |
| *c.* | Booklet pane of 4, #3148a, 3149b, 3150c, 3151d | 12.00 | — |
| | *Nos. 3148-3151 (4)* | 12.35 | 9.45 |

Issued: Nos. 3148a, 3149b, 3150c, 3151b, 3151c, 5/11/13. No. 3151c was issued in a booklet also containing Nos. 3376b, 3665b and 3925a.

### Self-Adhesive

***Serpentine Die Cut 11¼ Syncopated***

**3152** A803 55c multi .95 .25
*a.* Booklet pane of 20 19.00

Complete booklet sold for $12.95.

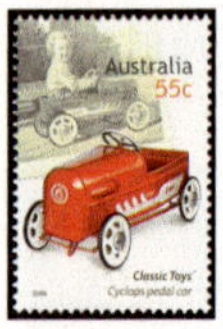


Toys — A804

Children and: Nos. 3153, 3158, Cyclops pedal car. Nos. 3154, 3159, Test Match board game. Nos. 3155, 3160, Barbie doll. Nos. 3156, 3161, Malvern Star Dragstar bicycle. Nos. 3157, 3162, Cabbage Patch Kids doll.

**2009, Sept. 25** ***Perf. 14¾x14***

**3153** A804 55c multi 1.10 1.10
*a.* Booklet pane of 4 5.25 —
**3154** A804 55c multi 1.10 1.10
*a.* Booklet pane of 4 5.25 —
**3155** A804 55c multi 1.10 1.10
*a.* Booklet pane of 4 5.25 —
*b.* Sheet of 10 #3155 + 10 labels 22.00 22.00
**3156** A804 55c multi 1.10 1.10
*a.* Booklet pane of 4 5.25 —
**3157** A804 55c multi 1.10 1.10
*a.* Booklet pane of 4 5.25 —
Complete booklet, #3153a, 3154a, 3155a, 3156a, 3157a 26.00
*b.* Horiz. strip of 5, #3153-3157 5.50 5.50
*Nos. 3153-3157 (5)* 5.50 5.50

No. 3155b sold for $10.95.

### Booklet Stamps
### Self-Adhesive

***Serpentine Die Cut 11¼ Syncopated***

**3158** A804 55c multi 1.10 .30
**3159** A804 55c multi 1.10 .30
**3160** A804 55c multi 1.10 .30
**3161** A804 55c multi 1.10 .30
**3162** A804 55c multi 1.10 .30
*a.* Booklet pane of 10, 2 each #3158-3162 11.00
*Nos. 3158-3162 (5)* 5.50 1.50

Complete booklet sold for $12.95.

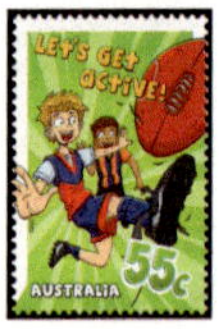


Children Playing Sports — A805

"Let's get active" and children playing: Nos. 3163, 3169, Australian rules football. Nos. 3164, 3170, Basketball. Nos. 3165, 3171, Soccer. Nos. 3166, 3172, Netball. Nos. 3167, 3173, Cricket. Nos. 3168, 3174, Tennis.

**2009, Oct. 6** ***Perf. 14¾x14***

**3163** A805 55c multi 1.10 1.10
**3164** A805 55c multi 1.10 1.10
**3165** A805 55c multi 1.10 1.10
**3166** A805 55c multi 1.10 1.10
**3167** A805 55c multi 1.10 1.10
**3168** A805 55c multi 1.10 1.10
*a.* Block of 6, #3163-3168 7.00 7.00
*b.* Souvenir sheet, #3163-3168 7.00 7.00
*Nos. 3163-3168 (6)* 6.60 6.60

### Booklet Stamps
### Self-Adhesive

***Serpentine Die Cut 11¼ Syncopated***

**3169** A805 55c multi 1.10 .30
*a.* Booklet pane of 10 11.50
**3170** A805 55c multi 1.10 .30
*a.* Booklet pane of 10 11.50
**3171** A805 55c multi 1.10 .30
*a.* Booklet pane of 10 11.50
**3172** A805 55c multi 1.10 .30
*a.* Booklet pane of 10 11.50
**3173** A805 55c multi 1.10 .30
*a.* Booklet pane of 10 11.50
**3174** A805 55c multi 1.10 .30
*a.* Booklet pane of 10 11.50
*b.* Booklet pane of 10, #3172, 3174, 2 each #3169-3171, 3173 11.50
*Nos. 3169-3174 (6)* 6.60 1.80

Miniature Sheet

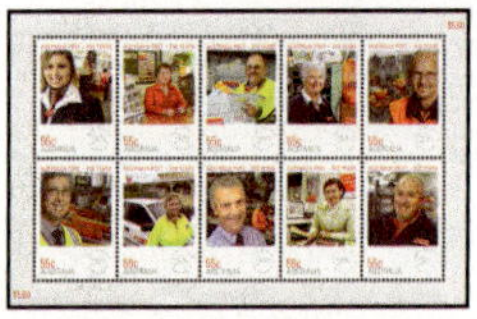

Australia Post Employees — A806

No. 3175: a, Patrica Crabb (with white blouse with red dots). b, Shirley Freeman (at counter, with brochures at left). c, Vinko Romank (lifting mail tubs). d, Valda Knott (sorting boxes in background). e, Gordon Morgan (motorcycle in background). f, Vongpradith Phongsavan (with conveyor belt in background). g, Norma Thomas (with contractor delivery automobile). h, John Marsh (with blue shirt and tie). i, Anne Brun (at desk, with computer keyboard at left). j, Russell Price (with beard).

**2009, Oct. 13** ***Perf. 14¾x14***

**3175** A806 Sheet of 10 11.50 8.50
*a.-j.* 55c Any single 1.10 .85

Australia Post, bicent. Compare with Type A787.

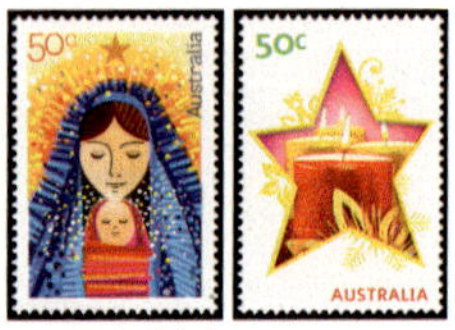


Christmas
A807 A808

Designs: Nos. 3176, 3183, Madonna and Child. Nos. 3177, 3184, 3190, 3195, Candles in star frame. Nos. 3178, 3185, 3191, 3196, Tree ornaments in Christmas tree frame. Nos. 3179, 3186, 3192, 3197, Gifts in stocking cap frame. Nos. 3180, 3187, 3193, 3198, Ornaments in bell frame. Nos. 3181, 3188, 3194, 3199, Candy canes in stocking frame. $1.25, Magi.

**2009, Nov. 2 Litho.** ***Perf. 14¾x14***

**3176** A807 50c multi 1.10 1.10
**3177** A808 50c multi 1.10 1.10
**3178** A808 50c multi 1.10 1.10
**3179** A808 50c multi 1.10 1.10
**3180** A808 50c multi 1.10 1.10
**3181** A808 50c multi 1.10 1.10
*a.* Horiz. strip of 5, #3177-3181 5.50 5.50
**3182** A807 $1.25 multi 2.75 2.75
*a.* Souvenir sheet of 2, #3176, 3182 4.00 4.00
*Nos. 3176-3182 (7)* 9.35 9.35

### Booklet Stamps (#3183-3194)
### Self-Adhesive

***Serpentine Die Cut 11¼ Syncopated***

**3183** A807 50c multi 1.10 .30
*a.* Booklet pane of 20 22.00
**3184** A808 50c multi 1.10 .30
**3185** A808 50c multi 1.10 .30
**3186** A808 50c multi 1.10 .30
**3187** A808 50c multi 1.10 .30
**3188** A808 50c multi 1.10 .30
*a.* Booklet pane of 10, 2 each #3184-3188 11.00
**3189** A807 $1.25 multi 2.75 .30
*a.* Booklet pane of 5 14.00

### Litho. With Foil Application
### Frames in Gold

**3190** A808 50c multi 1.10 .30
**3191** A808 50c multi 1.10 .30
**3192** A808 50c multi 1.10 .30
**3193** A808 50c multi 1.10 .30
**3194** A808 50c multi 1.10 .30
*a.* Booklet pane of 10, 2 each #3190-3194 11.00
*Nos. 3183-3194 (12)* 14.85 3.60

### With Personalized Photo at Right Like Type A692a

**3195** A808 50c multi 2.40 2.40
**3196** A808 50c multi 2.40 2.40
**3197** A808 50c multi 2.40 2.40
**3198** A808 50c multi 2.40 2.40
**3199** A808 50c multi 2.40 2.40
*Nos. 3195-3199 (5)* 12.00 12.00

Nos. 3195-3199 were sold in sheets of 20 containing 4 of each stamp, have personalized pictures and a straight edge at right and lack separations between the stamp and the personalized photo. Sheets of 20 of sold for $23.

No. 3197 exists without "Australia" and the denomination.

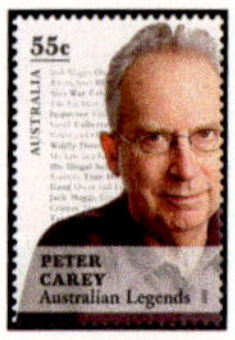


Authors — A809

Designs: Nos, 3200, 3212, Color photograph of Peter Carey. No. 3201, Black-and-white photograph of Carey. No. 3202, Black-and-white photograph of David Malouf. Nos. 3203, 3213, Color photograph of Malouf. Nos, 3204, 3214, Color photograph of Colleen McCullough. No. 3205, Black-and-white photograph of McCullough. No. 3206, Black-and-white photograph of Bryce Courtenay. Nos. 3207, 3215, Color photograph of Courtenay. Nos, 3208, 3216, Color photograph of Thomas Keneally. No. 3209, Black-and-white photograph of Keneally. No. 3210, Black-and-white photograph of Tim Winton. Nos. 3211, 3217, Color photograph of Winton.

**2010, Jan. 21 Litho.** ***Perf. 14¾x14***

**3200** A809 55c multi 1.10 1.10
**3201** A809 55c black & gray 1.10 1.10
**3202** A809 55c black & gray 1.10 1.10
**3203** A809 55c multi 1.10 1.10
*a.* Block of 4, #3200-3203 4.50 4.50
*b.* Booklet pane of 4, #3203-3203 8.50 —
*c.* As "b," with color separations of stamps 8.50 —
**3204** A809 55c multi 1.10 1.10
**3205** A809 55c black & gray 1.10 1.10
**3206** A809 55c black & gray 1.10 1.10
**3207** A809 55c multi 1.10 1.10
*a.* Block of 4, #3204-3207 4.50 4.50
*b.* Booklet pane of 4, #3204-3207 8.50 —
*c.* As "b," with color separations of stamps 8.50 —
**3208** A809 55c multi 1.10 1.10
**3209** A809 55c black & gray 1.10 1.10
**3210** A809 55c black & gray 1.10 1.10
**3211** A809 55c multi 1.10 1.10
*a.* Block of 4, #3208-3211 4.50 4.50
*b.* Booklet pane of 4, #3208-3211 8.50 —
*c.* As "b," with color separations of stamps 8.50 —
Complete booklet, #3203b, 3203c, 3207b, 3207c, 3211b, 3211c 52.00
*Nos. 3200-3211 (12)* 13.20 13.20

### Booklet Stamps
### Self-Adhesive

***Serpentine Die Cut 11¼ Syncopated***

**3212** A809 55c multi 1.10 .30
**3213** A809 55c multi 1.10 .30
**3214** A809 55c multi 1.10 .30
**3215** A809 55c multi 1.10 .30
**3216** A809 55c multi 1.10 .30
**3217** A809 55c multi 1.10 .30
*a.* Booklet pane of 20, 5 #3214, 3 each #3212-3213, 3215-3217 23.00
*Nos. 3212-3217 (6)* 6.60 1.80

Complete booklet sold for $24.95. Color separations were not valid for postage.

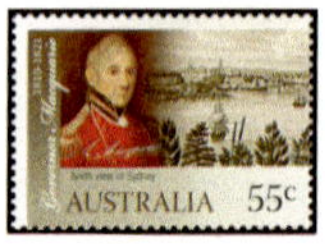


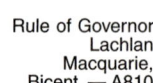

Rule of Governor Lachlan Macquarie, Bicent. — A810

Designs: No. 3218, Macquarie (1762-1824) and north view of Sydney. No. 3219, Port Jackson and Sydney Town. No. 3220, Parramatta Female Penitentiary. No. 3221, Governor's Sydney Stables.

**2010, Feb. 16** ***Perf. 14x14¾***

**3218** A810 55c multi 1.10 .85
*a.* Booklet pane of 4 5.75 —
**3219** A810 55c multi 1.10 .85
*a.* Booklet pane of 4 5.75 —
**3220** A810 55c multi 1.10 .85
*a.* Booklet pane of 4 5.75 —
**3221** A810 55c multi 1.10 .85
*a.* Booklet pane of 4 5.75 —
Complete booklet, #3218a-3221a 23.00
*b.* Block of 4, #3218-3221 4.50 3.50
*Nos. 3218-3221 (4)* 4.40 3.40

Complete booklet sold of $10.95.

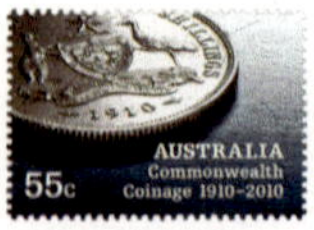


Coinage of the Australian Commonwealth, Cent. — A811

1910 two shilling coin: Nos. 3222, 3224a, Reverse depicting Australian coat of arms. Nos. 3223, 3224b, Obverse depicting King Edward VII.

**2010, Feb. 23 Litho.** ***Perf. 14x14¾***

**3222** A811 55c multi 1.10 .85
**3223** A811 $2.75 multi 5.75 2.75

### Souvenir Sheet
### Litho. & Embossed With Foil Application

**3224** Sheet of 2 7.00 3.75
*a.* A811 55c multi 1.10 .85
*b.* A811 $2.75 multi 5.75 2.75

No. 3224 exists imperf from a telephone drawing at a substantial premium over face value. Value for single souvenir sheet, $14.

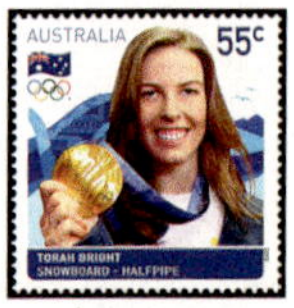


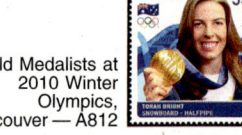

Gold Medalists at 2010 Winter Olympics, Vancouver — A812

Designs: No. 3225, Torah Bright, Snowboard halfpipe. No. 3226, Lydia Lassila, Freestyle skiing aerials.

**2010 Litho.** ***Perf. 14¼***

**3225** A812 55c multi 1.10 .85
**3226** A812 55c multi 1.10 .85

Issued: No. 3225, 2/25; No. 3226, 3/3.

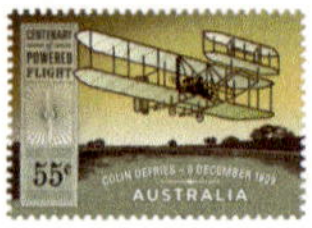


Powered Flight in Australia, Cent. (in 2009) — A813

Airplane of: 55c, Colin Defries. $1.45, John Duigan. $2.10, Harry Houdini.

**2010, Mar. 9** ***Perf. 14x14¾***

**3227** A813 55c multi 1.10 .85
**3228** A813 $1.45 multi 3.25 1.60
*a.* Souvenir sheet, #3218, 3223, 3227, 3228 11.00 11.00
*b.* Sheet of 4, 2 each #3227-3228 9.00 6.75
**3229** A813 $2.10 multi 4.50 2.25
*Nos. 3227-3229 (3)* 8.85 4.70

### Booklet Stamps
### Self-Adhesive

***Serpentine Die Cut 11¼ Syncopated***

**3230** A813 $1.45 multi 3.25 1.60
*a.* Booklet pane of 5 16.00
**3231** A813 $2.10 multi 4.50 2.25
*a.* Booklet pane of 5 23.00

2010 Canberra Stamp Show (No. 3228a). London 2010 Festival of Stamps (No. 3228b). Issued: No. 3228a, 3/12. No. 3228b, 5/8.

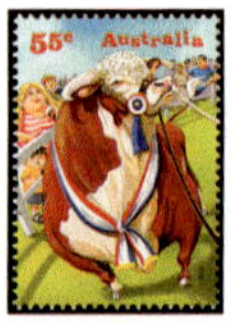


Agricultural Shows — A814

Designs: Nos. 3232, 3237, Prize bull. Nos. 3233, 3238, Cake decorating competition. Nos. 3234, 3239, Horse competition. Nos. 3235, 3240, Wood chopping competition. Nos. 3236, 3241, Dog show.

**2010, Mar. 23 Litho.** ***Perf. 14¾x14***

**3232** A814 55c multi 1.10 1.10
*a.* Booklet pane of 4 5.50 —
**3233** A814 55c multi 1.10 1.10
*a.* Booklet pane of 4 5.50 —
**3234** A814 55c multi 1.10 1.10
*a.* Booklet pane of 4 5.50 —
**3235** A814 55c multi 1.10 1.10
*a.* Booklet pane of 4 5.50 —
**3236** A814 55c multi 1.10 1.10
*a.* Booklet pane of 4 5.50 —
Complete booklet, #3232a-3236a 27.50
*b.* Horiz. strip of 5, #3232-3236 5.75 5.75
*c.* Souvenir sheet, #3232-3236 5.75 5.75
*Nos. 3232-3236 (5)* 5.50 5.50

### Booklet Stamps
### Self-Adhesive

***Serpentine Die Cut 11¼ Syncopated***

**3237** A814 55c multi 1.10 .30
**3238** A814 55c multi 1.10 .30
**3239** A814 55c multi 1.10 .30
**3240** A814 55c multi 1.10 .30
**3241** A814 55c multi 1.10 .30
*a.* Booklet pane of 10, 2 each #3237-3241 11.50 —
*Nos. 3237-3241 (5)* 5.50 1.50

Complete booklet sold for $12.95.

Queen's Birthday — A815

**2010, Apr. 6** *Perf. 14¾x14*

3242 A815 55c multi 1.25 1.25
*a.* Sheet of 4, #2505b, 2864b, 3067b, 3242 8.00 4.00

**Booklet Stamp**

**Self-Adhesive**

***Serpentine Die Cut 11¼ Syncopated***

3243 A815 55c multi 1.25 .30
*a.* Booklet pane of 10 12.75

Issued: No. 3242a, 5/8. London 2010 Festival of Stamps (No. 3242a).

Kokoda Campaign, 68th Anniv. — A816

Designs: Nos. 3244, 3249, Soldiers in battle. Nos. 3245, 3250, Injured Australian soldier, Papuan natives. Nos. 3246, 3251, Veterans of Kokoda Campaign, Papuan houses. Nos. 3247, 3252, Tourists at Kokoda. $1.45, Veterans at Kokoda Campaign Memorial, Isurava, Papua New Guinea.

**2010, Apr. 20** *Perf. 14¾x14*

3244 A816 55c multi 1.10 1.10
3245 A816 55c multi 1.10 1.10
*a.* Booklet pane of 4, 2 each #3244-3245 6.25
3246 A816 55c multi 1.10 1.10
3247 A816 55c multi 1.10 1.10
*a.* Booklet pane of 4 6.25 —
*b.* Horiz. strip of 4, #3244-3247 4.50 4.50
3248 A816 $1.45 multi 3.25 2.40
*a.* Booklet pane of 4, 2 each #3246, 3248 11.50
Complete booklet, #3245a, 3247a, 3248a 24.00
*b.* Souvenir sheet, #3244-3248 7.75 7.75
*Nos. 3244-3248 (5)* 7.65 6.80

**Self-Adhesive**

***Serpentine Die Cut 11¼ Syncopated***

3249 A816 55c multi 1.10 .30
3250 A816 55c multi 1.10 .30
3251 A816 55c multi 1.10 .30
3252 A816 55c multi 1.10 .30
*a.* Vert. coil strip of 4, #3249-3252 4.50
*b.* Booklet pane of 10, 2 each #3250, 3252, 3 each #3249, 3251 11.50
*Nos. 3249-3252 (4)* 4.40 1.20

Complete booklet sold for $10.95. See Papua New Guinea Nos. 1455-1456.

Queen Victoria ("Chalon Head" Portrait of Tasmania and Queensland Stamps) — A817

**2010, May 7** **Litho.** *Perf. 14x13½*

3253 A817 $5 multi 10.00 5.25
*a.* Souvenir sheet of 1 10.00 5.25
*b.* As "a," with London 2010 emblem in gold in sheet margin 8.25 8.25

No. 3253 has simulated toning. A souvenir sheet with a litho. and engraved stamp sold for $15.

Issued: No. 3253b, 5/8.

Railway Journeys — A818

Designs: Nos. 3254, 3258, The Ghan. Nos. 3255, 3259, West Coast Wilderness Railway, Tasmania. Nos. 3256, 3260, The Indian Pacific. $2.10, Kuranda Scenic Railway, Queensland (50x30mm).

**2010, May 7** *Perf. 14x14¾*

3254 A818 55c multi 1.10 1.10
3255 A818 55c multi 1.10 1.10
3256 A818 55c multi 1.10 1.10
*a.* Booklet pane of 4, #3254, 3255, 2 #3256 6.50 —
*b.* Booklet pane of 4, #3255, 3256, 2 #3254 6.50 —
*c.* Booklet pane of 4, #3254, 3256, 2 #3255 6.50 —

***Perf. 13½x14***

3257 A818 $2.10 multi 4.25 2.25
*a.* Booklet pane of 1 6.25 —
Complete booklet, #3256a-3256c, 3257a 26.50
*b.* Souvenir sheet of 1 4.25 2.25
*c.* As "b," with London 2010 emblem in gold in sheet margin 3.50 3.50
*Nos. 3254-3257 (4)* 7.55 5.55

**Self-Adhesive**

***Serpentine Die Cut 11¼ Syncopated***

3258 A818 55c multi 1.10 .30
3259 A818 55c multi 1.10 .30
3260 A818 55c multi 1.10 .30
*a.* Horiz. coil strip of 3, #3258-3260 3.50
*b.* Booklet pane of 20, 8 each #3258-3259, 4 #3260 23.00

***Serpentine Die Cut 11¼***

3261 A818 $2.10 multi 4.25 2.25
*a.* Booklet pane of 5 22.00
*Nos. 3258-3261 (4)* 7.55 3.15

No. 3257a has blue panels at the sides. Complete booklet sold for $12.95.

Issued: No. 3257c, 5/8.

Expo 2010, Shanghai — A819

Designs: No. 3262, Australian Pavilion. No. 3263, Australian kookaburra mascot, Peng Peng.

**2010, May 18** *Perf. 14¾x14*

3262 A819 55c multi 1.00 .80
3263 A819 55c multi 1.00 .80
*a.* Pair, #3262-3263 2.00 1.60

UNESCO World Heritage Sites in Australia — A820

Designs: Nos. 3264, 3268, Purnululu National Park. Nos. 3265, 3269, Kakadu National Park. No. 3266, Gondwana Rainforests, horiz. No. 3267, Tasmanian Wilderness, horiz.

**2010, May 25** *Perf. 14¾x14*

3264 A820 55c multi 1.00 1.00
3265 A820 55c multi 1.00 1.00
*a.* Horiz. pair, #3264-3265 2.00 2.00

***Perf. 14x14¾***

3266 A820 $1.10 multi 2.25 1.60
3267 A820 $1.10 multi 2.25 1.60
*a.* Horiz. pair, #3266-3267 4.50 3.25
*Nos. 3264-3267 (4)* 6.50 5.20

**Self-Adhesive**

***Serpentine Die Cut 11¼ Syncopated***

3268 A820 55c multi 1.00 1.00
3269 A820 55c multi 1.00 1.00
*a.* Vert. coil pair, #3268-3269 2.00
*b.* Booklet pane of 10, 5 each #3268-3269 10.00

Fish — A821

Designs: 5c, Coral rabbitfish. Nos. 3271, 3278, 3283, Clown triggerfish. Nos. 3272, 3279, 3284, Spotted sweetlips. Nos. 3273, 3280, 3285, Golden damsel. Nos. 3274, 3281, 3286, Regal angelfish. $1.20, Saddle butterflyfish. $1.80, Chevron butterflyfish. $3, Orangefin anemonefish.

**2010, June 21** **Litho.** *Perf. 14x14½*

3270 A821 5c multi .25 .25
3271 A821 60c multi 1.00 .25
3272 A821 60c multi 1.00 .25
*a.* Souvenir sheet, #3271, 3272, 2 #3270 2.40 2.40
3273 A821 60c multi 1.00 .25
3274 A821 60c multi 1.00 .25
*a.* Block or strip of 4, #3271-3274 4.00 1.00
3275 A821 $1.20 multi 2.00 1.00
3276 A821 $1.80 multi 3.00 1.50

***Perf. 14½x14***

**Size: 50x30mm (#3277)**

3277 A821 $3 multi 5.00 2.50
*Nos. 3270-3277 (8)* 14.25 6.25

**Coil Stamps**

**Self-Adhesive**

***Die Cut Perf. 12¾***

3278 A821 60c multi 1.00 .25
3279 A821 60c multi 1.00 .25
3280 A821 60c multi 1.00 .25
3281 A821 60c multi 1.00 .25
*a.* Horiz. strip of 4, #3278-3281 4.00

**Booklet Stamps**

***Serpentine Die Cut 11¼***

3282 A821 5c multi .25 .25
*a.* Booklet pane of 20 4.00
3283 A821 60c multi 1.00 .25
3284 A821 60c multi 1.00 .25
3285 A821 60c multi 1.00 .25
3286 A821 60c multi 1.00 .25
*a.* Booklet pane of 10, 3 each #3283-3284, 2 each #3285-3286 10.00
*b.* Booklet pane of 20, 5 each #3283-3286 20.00
*Nos. 3278-3286 (9)* 8.25 2.25

Issued: No. 3272a, 8/4/10. Bangkok 2010 Intl. Stamp Exhibition (No. 3272a).

Beaches — A822

Designs: $1.50, Bay of Fires, Tasmania. $2.20, Cape Tribulation, Queensland. $4.30, Hellfire Bay, Western Australia, horiz.

**2010, June 28** *Perf. 14¾x14*

3287 A822 $1.50 multi 2.50 1.25
3288 A822 $2.20 multi 3.75 1.90

**Size: 50x30mm (#3289)**

***Perf. 14½x14***

3289 A822 $4.30 multi 7.25 3.75
*Nos. 3287-3289 (3)* 13.50 6.90

**Booklet Stamps**

**Self-Adhesive**

***Serpentine Die Cut 11¼ Syncopated***

3290 A822 $1.50 multi 2.50 1.25
*a.* Booklet pane of 5 12.50
3291 A822 $2.20 multi 3.75 1.90
*a.* Booklet pane of 5 19.00

**With Personalized Photo at Right Like Type A692a**

***Serpentine Die Cut 11½x11¼ Syncopated***

3292 A822 $1.50 multi 3.75 3.75
3293 A822 $2.20 multi 4.75 4.75

Nos. 3292-3293 each were printed in sheets of 20 and have personalized pictures and a straight edge at right, and lack separations between the stamp and the personalized photo. Sheets of 20 of No. 3292 sold for $40, and No. 3293 sold for $56.

Adopted Dogs — A823

Designs: Nos. 3294, 3299, Piper. Nos. 3295, 3300, Jessie. Nos. 3296, 3301, Buckley. Nos. 3297, 3302, Daisy. Nos. 3298, 3303, Tigger.

**2010, June 29** *Perf. 14¾x14*

3294 A823 60c multi 1.00 1.00
3295 A823 60c multi 1.00 1.00
3296 A823 60c multi 1.00 1.00
3297 A823 60c multi 1.00 1.00
3298 A823 60c multi 1.00 1.00
*a.* Horiz. strip of 5, #3294-3298 5.00 5.00
*Nos. 3294-3298 (5)* 5.00 5.00

**Self-Adhesive**

***Serpentine Die Cut 11¼ Syncopated***

3299 A823 60c multi 1.00 .25
3300 A823 60c multi 1.00 .25
3301 A823 60c multi 1.00 .25
3302 A823 60c multi 1.00 .25
3303 A823 60c multi 1.00 .25
*a.* Vert. coil strip of 5, #3299-3303 5.00
*b.* Booklet pane of 10, 2 each #3299-3303 10.00
*Nos. 3299-3303 (5)* 5.00 1.25

No. 3303a was produced by two different printers, Pemara and McKellar Renown. The stamps have the printer's name on the backing paper, but are essentially identical to each other.

Emergency Services — A824

000 Emergency Services emblem and: Nos. 3304, 3308, "Stay Focused, Stay Relevant, Stay on Line." Nos. 3305, 3309, Police Helicopter. Nos. 3306, 3310, Fire. Nos. 3307, 3311, Ambulance Cross.

**2010, July 13** *Perf. 14¾x14*

3304 A824 60c multi 1.10 1.10
3305 A824 60c multi 1.10 1.10
3306 A824 60c multi 1.10 1.10
3307 A824 60c multi 1.10 1.10
*a.* Horiz. strip of 4, #3304-3307 4.40 4.40
*Nos. 3304-3307 (4)* 4.40 4.40

**Self-Adhesive**

***Serpentine Die Cut 11¼ Syncopated***

3308 A824 60c multi 1.10 .25
3309 A824 60c multi 1.10 .25
3310 A824 60c multi 1.10 .25
3311 A824 60c multi 1.10 .25
*a.* Vert. coil strip of 4, #3308-3311 4.40
*b.* Booklet pane of 20, 5 each #3308-3311 22.00
*Nos. 3308-3311 (4)* 4.40 1.00

Southern Cross — A825

**2010, July 19** *Perf. 14½x14*

3312 A825 60c Blue sky 1.10 1.10
*a.* Sheet of 20 + 20 labels 27.00 27.00
3313 A825 60c Purple & orange sky 1.10 1.10
*a.* Horiz. pair, #3312-3313 2.25 2.25
*b.* Sheet of 20 + 20 labels 27.00 27.00
*c.* Perf. 14x14½, + label at bottom 1.40 1.40

Nos. 3312a and 3313b each sold for $12.95 and have labels depicting various National Rugby League and Australian Football League team emblems that could not be personalized. No. 3313c was issued in sheet of 10 + 10 labels depicting race horse Black Caviar that were sold in groups of 2 sheets that sold for $12.95.

Balloons A826

Teddy Bear A827

Wattle A828

Flowers A829

Tulips A830

Roses A831

Flowers and Champagne Flutes
A832

Wedding Rings
A833

**2010, July 19** *Perf. 14¾x14*

**3314** A826 60c multi 1.10 1.10
**3315** A827 60c multi 1.10 1.10
**3316** A828 60c multi 1.10 1.10
*a.* Horiz. strip of 3, #3314-3316 3.30 3.30
**3317** A829 60c multi 1.10 1.10
**3318** A830 60c multi 1.10 1.10
**3319** A831 60c multi 1.10 1.10
**3320** A832 60c multi 1.10 1.10
*a.* Block of 4, #3317-3320 4.40 4.40
**3321** A833 $1.20 multi 2.25 2.25
*Nos. 3314-3321 (8)* 9.95 9.95

**Booklet Stamps**

**Self-Adhesive**

***Serpentine Die Cut 11¼ Syncopated***

**3322** A826 60c multi 1.10 .25
*a.* Booklet pane of 10 11.00
**3323** A827 60c multi 1.10 .25
*a.* Booklet pane of 10 11.00
**3324** A828 60c multi 1.10 .25
*a.* Booklet pane of 10 11.00
**3325** A830 60c multi 1.10 .25
*a.* Booklet pane of 10 11.00
**3326** A831 60c multi 1.10 .25
*a.* Booklet pane of 10 11.00
**3327** A833 $1.20 multi 2.25 1.10
*a.* Booklet pane of 10 22.50
*Nos. 3322-3327 (6)* 7.75 2.35

**With Personalized Photo at Right Like Type A692a**

***Serpentine Die Cut 11½x11¼ Syncopated***

**3328** A826 60c multi 2.25 2.25
**3329** A827 60c multi 2.25 2.25
**3330** A828 60c multi 2.25 2.25
**3331** A829 60c multi 2.25 2.25
**3332** A830 60c multi 2.25 2.25
**3333** A831 60c multi 2.25 2.25
**3334** A832 60c multi 2.25 2.25
**3335** A833 $1.20 multi 3.50 3.50
*Nos. 3328-3335 (8)* 19.25 19.25

Nos. 3328-3335 each were printed in sheets of 20 and have personalized pictures and a straight edge at right, and lack separations between the stamp and the personalized photo. Sheets of 20 of Nos. 3328-3334 each sold for $25, and No. 3335 sold for $37.

See No. 3401.

Australian Taxation Office, Cent. — A834

**2010, July 27 Litho.** *Perf. 14x14¾*

**3336** A834 60c multi 1.10 .85

Burke and Wills Expedition, 150th Anniv. — A835

Designs: Nos. 3337, 3341, Explorers Robert Burke (1820-61) and William J. Wills (1834-61). Nos. 3338, 3342, Burke and Wills on horses leaving Melbourne. No. 3339, Expedition members returning from Gulf of Carpenteria. No. 3340, Expedition members heading towards Mt. Hopeless.

**2010, Aug. 3 Litho.** *Perf. 14x14¾*

**3337** A835 60c multi 1.10 1.10
*a.* Booklet pane of 4 5.00 —
**3338** A835 60c multi 1.10 1.10
*a.* Horiz. pair, #3337-3338 2.20 2.20
*b.* Booklet pane of 4 5.00 —
**3339** A835 $1.20 multi 2.25 2.25
*a.* Booklet pane of 2 5.00 —
**3340** A835 $1.20 multi 2.25 2.25
*a.* Horiz. pair, #3339-3340 4.50 4.50
*b.* Booklet pane of 2 5.00 —
Complete booklet, #3337a, 3338b, 3339a, 3340b 20.00
*Nos. 3337-3340 (4)* 6.70 6.70

**Coil Stamps**

**Self-Adhesive**

***Serpentine Die Cut 11¼ Syncopated***

**3341** A835 60c multi 1.10 .25
**3342** A835 60c multi 1.10 .25
*a.* Horiz. pair, #3341-3342 2.20

Complete booklet sold for $10.95.

See Australian Antarctic Territory No. L149b.

Girl Guides, Cent. — A836

Emblem, early Girl Guides and: 60c, Girl Guide with helmet and climbing rope. $1.50, Girl Guides wearing hats. $2.20, Olave Baden-Powell.

**2010, Aug. 31 Litho.** *Perf. 14x14¾*

**3343** A836 60c multi 1.10 1.10
**3344** A836 $1.50 multi 2.75 2.75
**3345** A836 $2.20 multi 4.00 4.00
*Nos. 3343-3345 (3)* 7.85 7.85

**Self-Adhesive**

***Serpentine Die Cut 11¼ Syncopated***

**3346** A836 60c multi 1.10 .25
*a.* Booklet pane of 20 22.00

**Booklet Stamps**

**3347** A836 $1.50 multi 2.75 1.40
*a.* Booklet pane of 5 14.00
**3348** A836 $2.20 multi 4.00 2.00
*a.* Booklet pane of 5 20.00
*Nos. 3346-3348 (3)* 7.85 3.65

Dedication of National Service Memorial, Canberra — A837

**2010, Sept. 8 Litho.** *Perf. 14x14¾*

**3349** A837 60c multi 1.10 1.10
*a.* Additionally dated "2013" (#3349b) 1.25 1.25
*b.* Booklet pane of 4 #3349a 5.00 —

Issued: Nos. 3349a, 3349b, 3/5/13. No. 3349b was issued in booklet along with Nos. 1940b, 2710c, 2869e, 3107c and 3877a.

**Booklet Stamp**

**Self-Adhesive**

***Serpentine Die Cut 11¼ Syncopated***

**3350** A837 60c multi 1.10 .25
*a.* Booklet pane of 10 11.00

Long Weekend Vacations — A838

People on weekend vacations: Nos. 3351, 3356, Boating at beach, 1950s. Nos. 3352, 3357, Camping, 1960s. Nos. 3353, 3358, Surfing at beach, 1970s. Nos. 3354, 3359, Houseboating on river, 1980s. Nos. 3355, 3360, At winter resort, 1990s.

**2010, Sept. 22** *Perf. 14x14¾*

**3351** A838 60c multi 1.25 1.25
*a.* Booklet pane of 4 5.50 —
**3352** A838 60c multi 1.25 1.25
*a.* Booklet pane of 4 5.50 —
**3353** A838 60c multi 1.25 1.25
*a.* Booklet pane of 4 5.50 —
**3354** A838 60c multi 1.25 1.25
*a.* Booklet pane of 4 5.50 —
**3355** A838 60c multi 1.25 1.25
*a.* Booklet pane of 4 5.50 —
Complete booklet, #3351a-3355a 27.50
*b.* Horiz. strip of 5, #3351-3355 6.25 6.25
*Nos. 3351-3355 (5)* 6.25 6.25

**Self-Adhesive**

***Serpentine Die Cut 11¼ Syncopated***

**3356** A838 60c multi 1.25 .25
**3357** A838 60c multi 1.25 .25
**3358** A838 60c multi 1.25 .25
**3359** A838 60c multi 1.25 .25
**3360** A838 60c multi 1.25 .25
*a.* Horiz. coil strip of 5, #3356-3360 6.25
*b.* Booklet pane of 10, 2 each #3356-3360 12.50
*Nos. 3356-3360 (5)* 6.25 1.25

Complete booklet sold for $13.95.

Care for Wildlife — A839

Designs: Nos. 3361, 3367, Common wombat. Nos. 3362, 3368, Eastern gray kangaroo. Nos. 3363, 3369, Koala. Nos. 3364, 3370, Gray-headed flying fox. Nos. 3365, 3371, Southern boobook. $1.20, Ringtail possum.

**2010, Oct. 5 Litho.** *Perf. 14¾x14*

**Denomination Color**

**3361** A839 60c orange brown 1.25 1.25
**3362** A839 60c blue 1.25 1.25
**3363** A839 60c green 1.25 1.25
**3364** A839 60c red brown 1.25 1.25
**3365** A839 60c bister 1.25 1.25
*a.* Horiz. strip of 5, #3361-3365 6.25 6.25
**3366** A839 $1.20 red 2.40 1.75
*a.* Souvenir sheet of 6, #3361-3366 8.75 8.75
*Nos. 3361-3366 (6)* 8.65 8.00

**Self-Adhesive**

***Serpentine Die Cut 11¼ Syncopated***

**3367** A839 60c orange brown 1.25 .25
**3368** A839 60c blue 1.25 .25
**3369** A839 60c green 1.25 .25
**3370** A839 60c red brown 1.25 .25
**3371** A839 60c bister 1.25 .25
*a.* Vert. coil strip of 5, #3367-3371 6.25
*b.* Booklet pane of 10, 2 each #3367-3371 12.50
*Nos. 3367-3371 (5)* 6.25 1.25

Canonization of St. Mary MacKillop (1842-1909) — A840

**2010, Oct. 18** *Perf. 14¾x14*

**3372** A840 60c multi 1.25 .95

Kingfishers — A841

Designs: 60c, Red-backed kingfisher. $1.20, Sacred kingfisher. $1.80, Blue-winged kookaburra. $3, Yellow-billed kingfisher.

**2010, Oct. 26** *Perf. 14¾x14*

**3373** A841 60c multi 1.25 1.25
*a.* Additionally dated "2013" 1.25 1.25
**3374** A841 $1.20 multi 2.50 1.90
*a.* Additionally dated "2013" 2.40 2.40
**3375** A841 $1.80 multi 3.75 1.90
*a.* Additionally dated "2013" 3.50 3.50
**3376** A841 $3 multi 6.25 3.25
*a.* Additionally dated "2013" 5.75 5.75
*b.* Booklet pane of 4, #3373a, 3374a, 3375a, 3376a 13.00 —
*Nos. 3373-3376 (4)* 13.75 8.30

Issued: Nos. 3373a, 3374a, 3375a, 3376a, 3376b, 5/11/13. No. 3376b was issued in a booklet also containing Nos. 3151c, 3665b and 3925a.

**Self-Adhesive**

***Serpentine Die Cut 11¼ Syncopated***

**3377** A841 60c multi 1.25 .25
*a.* Booklet pane of 10 12.50

150th Running of the Melbourne Cup Horse Race — A842

Designs: No. 3378, Melbourne Cup. Nos. 3379, 3382, Carbine, 1890 winner, horiz. Nos. 3380, 3383, Phar Lap, 1930 winner, horiz. Nos. 3381, 3384, Saintly, 1996 winner, horiz.

**2010, Nov. 1 Litho.** *Perf. 14¾x14*

**3378** A842 60c multi 1.25 .95
*a.* Booklet pane of 4 7.25 —

***Perf. 14x14¾***

**3379** A842 60c multi 1.25 1.25
*a.* Booklet pane of 4 7.25 —
**3380** A842 60c multi 1.25 1.25
*a.* Booklet pane of 4 7.25 —
**3381** A842 60c multi 1.25 1.25
*a.* Booklet pane of 4 7.25 —
Complete booklet, #3378a, 3379a, 3380a, 3381a 29.00
*b.* Souvenir sheet, #3378-3381 5.00 5.00
*Nos. 3378-3381 (4)* 5.00 4.70

No. 3381b exists imperf from a telephone drawing at a substantial premium over face value. Value for single souvenir sheet, $15.

**Booklet Stamps**

**Self-Adhesive**

***Serpentine Die Cut 11¼ Syncopated***

**3382** A842 60c multi 1.25 .25
**3383** A842 60c multi 1.25 .25
**3384** A842 60c multi 1.25 .25
*a.* Booklet pane of 20, 7 each #3382-3383, 6 #3384 25.00
*Nos. 3382-3384 (3)* 3.75 75.00

Complete booklet sold for $13.95 and also included imperforate and gummed lithographed pages reproducing pairs of Nos. 337, 693, 694, 2104 and 2106 that were not valid for postage.

Christmas
A843 A844

Designs: Nos. 3385, 3390, 3393, 3396, Girl writing letter to Santa Claus. Nos. 3386, 3389, 3394, 3395, Santa Claus reading letter. Nos. 3387, 3391, Adoration of the Magi. $1.30, Adoration of the Shepherds.

**2010, Nov. 1 Litho.** *Perf. 14¾x14*

**3385** A843 55c multi 1.10 1.10
**3386** A843 55c multi 1.10 1.10
*a.* Horiz. pair, #3385-3386 2.25 2.25
**3387** A844 55c multi 1.10 1.10
**3388** A844 $1.30 multi 2.75 2.75
*Nos. 3385-3388 (4)* 6.05 6.05

**Booklet Stamps**

**Self-Adhesive**

***Serpentine Die Cut 11¼ Syncopated***

**3389** A843 55c multi 1.10 .25
**3390** A843 55c multi 1.10 .25
*a.* Booklet pane of 20, 10 each #3389-3390 22.00
**3391** A844 55c multi 1.10 .25
*a.* Booklet pane of 20 22.00
**3392** A844 $1.30 multi 2.75 1.40
*a.* Booklet pane of 5 14.00

**Litho. With Foil Application**

**3393** A843 55c multi 1.10 .25
*a.* Booklet pane of 10 11.00
**3394** A843 55c multi 1.10 .25
*a.* Booklet pane of 10 11.00
*Nos. 3389-3394 (6)* 8.25 2.65

**With Personalized Photo at Right Like Type A692a**

**Litho.**

**Self-Adhesive**

***Serpentine Die Cut 11½x11¼ Syncopated***

**3395** A843 55c multi 2.50 2.50
**3396** A843 55c multi 2.50 2.50

Nos. 3395-3396 were printed together in sheets of 20 (10 of each design), and have personalized pictures and a straight edge at right and lack separations between the stamp and the personalized photo. Sheets of 20 sold for $24.

**Champagne Flutes Type of 2010 and**

Roses
A845

Hearts and Flowers
A846

**2011, Jan. 18** *Perf. 14¾x14*

**3397** A845 60c multi 1.25 1.25
**3398** A846 60c multi 1.25 1.25
*a.* Horiz. pair, #3397-3398 2.50 2.50

**Booklet Stamps**
**Self-Adhesive**
***Serpentine Die Cut 11¼ Syncopated***

**3399** A845 60c multi 1.25 .25
*a.* Booklet pane of 12 12.50
**3400** A846 60c multi 1.25 .25
*a.* Booklet pane of 12 12.50
**3401** A832 60c multi 1.25 .60
*a.* Booklet pane of 12 12.50
*Nos. 3399-3401 (3)* 3.75 1.10

**With Personalized Photo at Right Like Type A692a**
***Serpentine Die Cut 11½x11¼ Syncopated***

**3402** A845 60c multi 2.50 2.50
**3403** A846 60c multi 2.50 2.50

Nos. 3395-3396 each were printed in sheets of 20 and have personalized pictures and a straight edge at right and lack separations between the stamp and the personalized photo. Sheets of 20 of Nos. 3402-3403 each sold for $25.
No. 3401 dated 2010.

Famous Women — A848

Designs: Nos. 3404, 3408, Eva Cox, feminist. Nos. 3405, 3409, Germaine Greer, writer on feminist topics. Nos. 3406, 3410, Elizabeth Evatt, jurist. Nos. 3407, 3411, Anne Summers, writer.

**2011, Jan. 20** *Perf. 14¾x14*

**3404** A848 60c multi 1.25 1.25
**3405** A848 60c multi 1.25 1.25
**3406** A848 60c multi 1.25 1.25
**3407** A848 60c multi 1.25 1.25
*a.* Horiz. strip of 4, #3404-3407 5.00 5.00
*Nos. 3404-3407 (4)* 5.00 5.00

**Booklet Stamps**
**Self-Adhesive**
***Serpentine Die Cut 11¼ Syncopated***

**3408** A848 60c multi 1.25 .25
**3409** A848 60c multi 1.25 .25
**3410** A848 60c multi 1.25 .25
**3411** A848 60c multi 1.25 .25
*a.* Booklet pane of 20, 5 each #3408-3411 25.00
*Nos. 3408-3411 (4)* 5.00 1.00

Intl. Women's Day, Cent. — A849

**2011, Feb. 15** *Perf. 14x14¾*

**3412** A849 60c multi 1.25 .95
*a.* Miniature sheet of 10 12.50 12.50

Military Aircraft — A850

Designs: Nos. 3413, 3417, F-111. Nos. 3414, 3418, F/A-18F. $1.20, Wedge Tail. $3, C-17.

**2011, Feb. 22** *Perf. 14x14¾*

**3413** A850 60c multi 1.25 1.25
**3414** A850 60c multi 1.25 1.25
**3415** A850 $1.20 multi 2.40 1.90
*a.* Souvenir sheet of 4, #3337, 3339, 3413, 3415 7.75 7.75
**3416** A850 $3 multi 6.00 4.50
*a.* Souvenir sheet of 4, #3413-3416 11.00 11.00
*Nos. 3413-3416 (4)* 10.90 8.90

**Booklet Stamps**
**Self-Adhesive**
***Serpentine Die Cut 11¼ Syncopated***

**3417** A850 60c multi 1.25 .25
**3418** A850 60c multi 1.25 .25
*a.* Booklet pane of 10, 5 each #3417-3418 12.50

Issued: No. 3415a, 3/31. Sydney Stamp Expo 2011 (No. 3415a).

Flowers — A851

Designs: Nos. 3419, 3424, Gerbera daisy. Nos. 3420, 3425, Jacarandas. Nos. 3421, 3426, Australian everlasting. Nos. 3422, 3427, Violet. Nos. 3423, 3428, Tulip.

**2011, Mar. 8** **Litho.** *Perf. 14¾x14*

**3419** A851 60c multi 1.25 1.25
*a.* Booklet pane of 4 5.25 —
**3420** A851 60c multi 1.25 1.25
*a.* Booklet pane of 4 5.25 —
**3421** A851 60c multi 1.25 1.25
*a.* Booklet pane of 4 5.25 —
**3422** A851 60c multi 1.25 1.25
*a.* Booklet pane of 4 5.25 —
**3423** A851 60c multi 1.25 1.25
*a.* Booklet pane of 4 5.25 —
Complete booklet, #3419a, 3420a, 3421a, 3422a, 3423a 27.00
*b.* Horiz. strip of 5, #3419-3423 6.25 6.25
*Nos. 3419-3423 (5)* 6.25 6.25

**Self-Adhesive**
***Serpentine Die Cut 11¼ Syncopated***

**3424** A851 60c multi 1.25 .25
**3425** A851 60c multi 1.25 .25
**3426** A851 60c multi 1.25 .25
**3427** A851 60c multi 1.25 .25
**3428** A851 60c multi 1.25 .25
*a.* Vert. coil strip of 5, #3424-3428 6.25
*b.* Booklet pane of 20, 4 each #3424-3428 25.00
*Nos. 3424-3428 (5)* 6.25 1.25

Complete booklet sold for $12.95.

Paintings of Flowers in National Gallery of Victoria — A852

Paintings: Nos. 3429, 3434, A Bunch of Flowers, by Nora Heysen. Nos. 3430, 3435, Camellias, by Arnold Shore. Nos. 3431, 3436, Fruit and Flowers, by Vida Lahey. Nos. 3432, 3437, Still Life, Zinnias, by Roy de Maistre. Nos. 3433, 3438, A Cottage Bunch, by Hans Heysen.

**2011, Mar. 22** *Perf. 14x14¾*

**3429** A852 60c multi 1.25 1.25
**3430** A852 60c multi 1.25 1.25
**3431** A852 60c multi 1.25 1.25
**3432** A852 60c multi 1.25 1.25
**3433** A852 60c multi 1.25 1.25
*a.* Horiz. strip of 5, #3429-3433 6.25 6.25
*Nos. 3429-3433 (5)* 6.25 6.25

**Self-Adhesive**
***Serpentine Die Cut 11¼ Syncopated***

**3434** A852 60c multi 1.25 .25
**3435** A852 60c multi 1.25 .25
**3436** A852 60c multi 1.25 .25
**3437** A852 60c multi 1.25 .25
**3438** A852 60c multi 1.25 .25
*a.* Horiz. coil strip of 5, #3434-3438 6.25
*b.* Booklet pane of 10, 2 each #3434-3438 12.50
*Nos. 3434-3438 (5)* 6.25 1.25

Lake Eyre — A853

Lake Eyre: 60c, In dry season. $1.55, With new growth. $2.25, Bird life. $3.10, In flood.

**2011, Apr. 4** *Perf. 14½x14*

**3439** A853 60c multi 1.25 .65
**3440** A853 $1.55 multi 3.25 3.25
**3441** A853 $2.25 multi 4.75 4.75
**3442** A853 $3.10 multi 6.50 3.25
*Nos. 3439-3442 (4)* 15.75 11.90

**Booklet Stamps**
**Self-Adhesive**
***Serpentine Die Cut 11¼***

**3443** A853 $1.55 multi 3.25 1.60
*a.* Booklet pane of 5 16.50
**3444** A853 $2.25 multi 4.75 2.40
*a.* Booklet pane of 5 24.00

A854

Portraits of Queen Elizabeth II by: 60c, Brian Dunlop, 1984. $2.25, Rolf Harris, 2005.

**2011, Apr. 5** *Perf. 14¾x14*

**3445** A854 60c multi 1.25 .65
**3446** A854 $2.25 multi 4.75 2.40
*a.* Souvenir sheet of 2, #3445-3446 6.00 6.00

Queen Elizabeth II, 85th birthday.

A855

Background color: 60c, Pale olive green. $2.25, White.

**2011, Apr. 12** *Perf. 14¾x14*

**3447** A855 60c multi 1.25 1.25
**3448** A855 $2.25 multi 4.75 2.40
*a.* Souvenir sheet of 2, #3447-3448 6.00 6.00

**Booklet Stamp**
**Self-Adhesive**
***Serpentine Die Cut 11¼ Syncopated***

**3449** A855 60c multi 1.25 .25
*a.* Booklet pane of 10 12.50

Wedding of Prince William and Catherine Middleton.

Wedding Photograph of Prince Willliam and Wife Catherine — A856

**2011, May 4** *Perf. 14¼*

**3450** A856 60c multi 1.25 1.25

**Booklet Stamp**
**Self-Adhesive**
***Serpentine Die Cut 11¼ Syncopated***

**3451** A856 60c multi 1.25 .25
*a.* Booklet pane of 10 12.50

Dame Nellie Melba (1861-1931), Operatic Soprano — A857

**2011, May 10** *Perf. 14¾x14*

**3452** A857 60c multi 1.25 1.25

**Booklet Stamp**
**Self-Adhesive**
***Serpentine Die Cut 11¼ Syncopated***

**3453** A857 60c multi 1.25 .25
*a.* Booklet pane of 20 25.00

Native Agricultural Products — A858

Designs: Nos. 3454, 3458, Eucalyptus oil. Nos. 3455, 3459, Australian honey. Nos. 3456, 3460, Macadamia nuts. Nos. 3457, 3461, Tea tree oil.

**2011, May 17** *Perf. 14x14¾*

**3454** A858 60c multi 1.25 1.25
**3455** A858 60c multi 1.25 1.25
**3456** A858 60c multi 1.25 1.25
**3457** A858 60c multi 1.25 1.25
*a.* Horiz. strip of 4, #3454-3457 5.00 5.00
*Nos. 3454-3457 (4)* 5.00 5.00

**Self-Adhesive**
***Serpentine Die Cut 11¼ Syncopated***

**3458** A858 60c multi 1.25 .25
**3459** A858 60c multi 1.25 .25
**3460** A858 60c multi 1.25 .25
**3461** A858 60c multi 1.25 .25
*a.* Horiz. coil strip of 4, #3458-3461 5.00
*b.* Booklet pane of 10, 4 #3458, 2 each #3459-3461 12.50
*Nos. 3458-3461 (4)* 5.00 1.00

Southern Cross With Sports Team Emblem A859

**Booklet Stamps**
**Self-Adhesive**
**Blue Sky**
**With Emblem of Australian Rules Football Team**
**Adelaide Crows**

***Serpentine Die Cut 10¾x11¼ Syncopated***

**2011, Apr. 12** **Litho.**

**3462** A859 60c Emblem at R 1.50 .75
**3463** A859 60c Emblem at L 1.50 .75
*a.* Booklet pane of 10, 5 each #3462-3463 15.00

**Carlton Blues**

**3464** A859 60c Emblem at R 1.50 .75
**3465** A859 60c Emblem at L 1.50 .75
*a.* Booklet pane of 10, 5 each #3464-3465 15.00

**Essendon Bombers**

**3466** A859 60c Emblem at R 1.50 .75
**3467** A859 60c Emblem at L 1.50 .75
*a.* Booklet pane of 10, 5 each #3466-3467 15.00

**Geelong Cats**

**3468** A859 60c Emblem at R 1.50 .75
**3469** A859 60c Emblem at L 1.50 .75
*a.* Booklet pane of 10, 5 each #3468-3469 15.00

**Gold Coast Suns**

**3470** A859 60c Emblem at R 1.50 .75
**3471** A859 60c Emblem at L 1.50 .75
*a.* Booklet pane of 10, 5 each #3470-3471 15.00

**North Melbourne Kangaroos**

**3472** A859 60c Emblem at R 1.50 .75
**3473** A859 60c Emblem at L 1.50 .75
*a.* Booklet pane of 10, 5 each #3472-3473 15.00

**Port Adelaide Power**

**3474** A859 60c Emblem at R 1.50 .75
**3475** A859 60c Emblem at L 1.50 .75
*a.* Booklet pane of 10, 5 each #3474-3475 15.00

**West Coast Eagles**

**3476** A859 60c Emblem at R 1.50 .75
**3477** A859 60c Emblem at L 1.50 .75
*a.* Booklet pane of 10, 5 each #3476-3477 15.00

**Western Bulldogs**

**3478** A859 60c Emblem at R 1.50 .75
**3479** A859 60c Emblem at L 1.50 .75
*a.* Booklet pane of 10, 5 each #3478-3479 15.00

**Purple & Orange Sky**
**Brisbane Lions**

**3480** A859 60c Emblem at R 1.50 .75
**3481** A859 60c Emblem at L 1.50 .75
*a.* Booklet pane of 10, 5 each #3480-3481 15.00

**Collingwood Magpies**

**3482** A859 60c Emblem at R 1.50 .75
**3483** A859 60c Emblem at L 1.50 .75
*a.* Booklet pane of 10, 5 each #3482-3483 15.00

**Fremantle Dockers**

**3484** A859 60c Emblem at R 1.50 .75
**3485** A859 60c Emblem at L 1.50 .75
*a.* Booklet pane of 10, 5 each #3484-3485 15.00

**Hawthorn Hawks**

**3486** A859 60c Emblem at R 1.50 .75
**3487** A859 60c Emblem at L 1.50 .75
*a.* Booklet pane of 10, 5 each #3486-3487 15.00

**Melbourne Demons**

**3488** A859 60c Emblem at R 1.50 .75
**3489** A859 60c Emblem at L 1.50 .75
*a.* Booklet pane of 10, 5 each #3488-3489 15.00

### Richmond Tigers

3490 A859 60c Emblem at R 1.50 .75
3491 A859 60c Emblem at L 1.50 .75
a. Booklet pane of 10, 5 each #3490-3491 15.00

### St. Kilda Saints

3492 A859 60c Emblem at R 1.50 .75
3493 A859 60c Emblem at L 1.50 .75
a. Booklet pane of 10, 5 each #3492-3493 15.00

### Sydney Swans

3494 A859 60c Emblem at R 1.50 .75
3495 A859 60c Emblem at L 1.50 .75
a. Booklet pane of 10, 5 each #3494-3495 15.00

### Blue Sky With National Rugby League Emblems

### North Queensland Cowboys

3496 A859 60c Emblem at R 1.50 .75
3497 A859 60c Emblem at L 1.50 .75
a. Booklet pane of 10, 5 each #3496-3497 15.00

### St. George Illawarra Dragons

3498 A859 60c Emblem at R 1.50 .75
3499 A859 60c Emblem at L 1.50 .75
a. Booklet pane of 10, 5 each #3498-3499 15.00

### Parramatta Eels

3500 A859 60c Emblem at R 1.50 .75
3501 A859 60c Emblem at L 1.50 .75
a. Booklet pane of 10, 5 each #3500-3501 15.00

### Newcastle Knights

3502 A859 60c Emblem at R 1.50 .75
3503 A859 60c Emblem at L 1.50 .75
a. Booklet pane of 10, 5 each #3502-3503 15.00

### Penrith Panthers

3504 A859 60c Emblem at R 1.50 .75
3505 A859 60c Emblem at L 1.50 .75
a. Booklet pane of 10, 5 each #3504-3505 15.00

### Canberra Raiders

3506 A859 60c Emblem at R 1.50 .75
3507 A859 60c Emblem at L 1.50 .75
a. Booklet pane of 10, 5 each #3506-3507 15.00

### Sydney Roosters

3508 A859 60c Emblem at R 1.50 .75
3509 A859 60c Emblem at L 1.50 .75
a. Booklet pane of 10, 5 each #3508-3509 15.00

### Cronulla Sutherland Sharks

3510 A859 60c Emblem at R 1.50 .75
3511 A859 60c Emblem at L 1.50 .75
a. Booklet pane of 10, 5 each #3510-3511 15.00

### Gold Coast Titans

3512 A859 60c Emblem at R 1.50 .75
3513 A859 60c Emblem at L 1.50 .75
a. Booklet pane of 10, 5 each #3512-3513 15.00

### Purple & Orange Sky Brisbane Broncos

3514 A859 60c Emblem at R 1.50 .75
3515 A859 60c Emblem at L 1.50 .75
a. Booklet pane of 10, 5 each #3514-3515 15.00

### Canterbury-Bankstown Bulldogs

3516 A859 60c Emblem at R 1.50 .75
3517 A859 60c Emblem at L 1.50 .75
a. Booklet pane of 10, 5 each #3516-3517 15.00

### South Sydney Rabbitohs

3518 A859 60c Emblem at R 1.50 .75
3519 A859 60c Emblem at L 1.50 .75
a. Booklet pane of 10, 5 each #3518-3519 15.00

### Manly Warringah Sea Eagles

3520 A859 60c Emblem at R 1.50 .75
3521 A859 60c Emblem at L 1.50 .75
a. Booklet pane of 10, 5 each #3520-3521 15.00

### Melbourne Storm

3522 A859 60c Emblem at R 1.50 .75
3523 A859 60c Emblem at L 1.50 .75
a. Booklet pane of 10, 5 each #3522-3523 15.00

### New Zealand Warriors

3524 A859 60c Emblem at R 1.50 .75
3525 A859 60c Emblem at L 1.50 .75
a. Booklet pane of 10, 5 each #3524-3525 15.00

### Wests Tigers

3526 A859 60c Emblem at R 1.50 .75
3527 A859 60c Emblem at L 1.50 .75
a. Booklet pane of 10, 5 each #3526-3527 15.00
*Nos. 3462-3527 (66)* 99.00 49.50

Each booklet, Nos. 3463a-3527a, sold for $6.95. Stamps with team emblem at right have straight edge at right, and stamps with team emblem at left have straight edge at left.

Australian Navy, Cent. — A860

Sailor and: Nos. 3528, 3530, HMAS Australia and biplane. Nos. 3529, 3531, HMAS Sydney and helicopter.

**2011, June 14** *Perf. 14x14¾*
3528 A860 60c multi 1.40 1.40
3529 A860 60c multi 1.40 1.40
a. Horiz. pair, #3528-3529 2.80 2.80

### Booklet Stamps Self-Adhesive

*Serpentine Die Cut 11¼ Syncopated*
3530 A860 60c multi 1.40 .25
3531 A860 60c multi 1.40 .25
a. Booklet pane of 20, 10 each #3530-3531 28.00

A861

Baby animals: 60c, Bilby. $1.60, Dingo. $1.65, Kangaroo. $2.35, Koala. $4.70, Sugar glider.

**2011, July 1 Litho.** *Perf. 14¾x14*
3532 A861 60c multi 1.40 1.10
3533 A861 $1.60 multi 3.50 1.75
a. Souvenir sheet of 1 3.50 3.50
3534 A861 $1.65 multi 3.50 3.50
a. Souvenir sheet of 2, #3533-3534 7.00 7.00
b. Souvenir sheet of 1 3.50 3.50
c. Additionally dated "2013" 4.25 4.25
d. Booklet pane of 4, #1195a, 2352a, 3097a, 3534c 12.50 —
3535 A861 $2.35 multi 5.00 5.00
a. Souvenir sheet of 2 9.75 9.75
3536 A861 $4.70 multi 10.00 5.00
*Nos. 3532-3536 (5)* 23.40 16.35

Issued: No. 3534a, 7/28; No. 3535a, 6/18/12. Nos. 3533a, 3534b, 11/11. PhilaNippon '11 World Stamp Exhibition, Yokohama (No. 3534a). 2012 World Stamp Championship, Indonesia (No. 3535a). China 2011 Intl. Stamp Exhibition, Wuxi (Nos. 3533a, 3534b). Nos. 3534c, 3534d, 5/10/13. No. 3534d was issued in a booklet also containing Nos. 1003b, 1284b, and 3918.

### Booklet Stamps Self-Adhesive

*Serpentine Die Cut 11¼ Syncopated*
3537 A861 $1.65 multi 3.50 1.75
a. Booklet pane of 5 17.50
3538 A861 $2.35 multi 5.00 2.50
a. Booklet pane of 5 25.00

### With Personalized Photo at Right Like Type A692a

*Serpentine Die Cut 11½x11¼ Syncopated*
3539 A861 $1.60 multi 4.75 4.75
3540 A861 $1.65 multi 5.00 5.00
3541 A861 $2.35 multi 11.50 11.50
*Nos. 3539-3541 (3)* 21.25 21.25

Nos. 3539-3541 each were printed in sheets of 20 and have personalized pictures and at straight edge at right, and lack separations between the stamp and the personalized photo. Sheets of 20 of No. 3539 sold for $45; No. 3540, $46; No. 3541, $106.

A862

**2011, July 5** *Perf. 14¾x14*
3542 A862 60c yellow & black 1.40 1.10

Amnesty International, 50th anniv.

Living Australian — A863

Photographs of Australian scenes: Nos. 3543, 3548, Boy and dog on beach. Nos. 3544, 3549, Children with flags painted on faces hugging. Nos. 3545, 3550, Reflection in sunglasses of sports fans in stadium. Nos. 3546, 3551, Aboriginal boy performing wedge tail eagle dance. Nos. 3547, 3552, Kangaroo resting on beach.

**2011, July 5** *Perf. 14x14¾*

### Denomination Color

3543 A863 60c orange 1.40 1.40
3544 A863 60c purple 1.40 1.40
3545 A863 60c green 1.40 1.40
3546 A863 60c red violet 1.40 1.40
3547 A863 60c blue 1.40 1.40
a. Horiz. strip of 5, #3543-3547 7.00 7.00

### Self-Adhesive

*Serpentine Die Cut 11¼ Syncopated*
3548 A863 60c orange 1.40 .25
3549 A863 60c purple 1.40 .25
3550 A863 60c green 1.40 .25
3551 A863 60c red violet 1.40 .25
3552 A863 60c blue 1.40 .25
a. Horiz. coil strip of 5, #3548-3552 7.00
b. Booklet pane of 10, 2 each #3548-3552 14.00
*Nos. 3548-3552 (5)* 7.00 1.25

Skiing — A864

Designs: 60c, Child learning to ski. $1.60, Snowboarder, horiz. $1.65, Downhill skier, horiz.

**2011, July 19** *Perf. 14¾x14*
3553 A864 60c multi 1.25 1.25

*Perf. 14x14¾*
3554 A864 $1.60 multi 3.50 3.50
3555 A864 $1.65 multi 3.50 3.50
*Nos. 3553-3555 (3)* 8.25 8.25

### Self-Adhesive Coil Stamp

*Serpentine Die Cut 11¼ Syncopated*
3556 A864 60c multi 1.25 .25

### Booklet Stamps

3557 A864 $1.60 multi 3.50 1.75
a. Booklet pane of 5 17.50
3558 A864 $1.65 multi 3.50 1.75
a. Booklet pane of 5 17.50
*Nos. 3556-3558 (3)* 8.25 3.75

Items Depicted on Australian States Stamps — A865

Designs: No. 3559, Kangaroo and lyrebird. No. 3560, Black swan and Southern Cross.

**2011, July 28** *Perf. 14x13½*
3559 A865 $2 pale grn & blue 4.25 2.10
3560 A865 $2 pink & blue 4.25 2.10
a. Pair, #3559-3560 8.50 4.25
b. Souvenir sheet of 2, #3559-3560 8.50 4.25

A limited edition of No. 3560b with a gold overprint in the sheet margin exists.

Worldwide Fund for Nature (WWF), 50th Anniv. — A866

Designs: No. 3561, Quokka. No. 3562, Southern elephant seal. No. 3563, Dugong. No. 3564, Christmas Island shrew.

**2011, Aug. 30 Litho.** *Perf. 14x14¾*
3561 A866 60c multi 1.25 .95
3562 A866 60c multi 1.25 .95
3563 A866 60c multi 1.25 .95
3564 A866 60c multi 1.25 .95
a. Block of 4, #3561-3564 5.00 4.00
b. Souvenir sheet of 4, #3561-3564, #3561 at UL 5.00 5.00
c. Souvenir sheet of 4, #3561-3564, #3562 at UL 5.00 5.00
d. Souvenir sheet of 4, #3561-3564, #3563 at UL 5.00 5.00
e. Souvenir sheet of 4, #3561-3564, #3564 at UL 5.00 5.00
*Nos. 3561-3564 (4)* 5.00 3.80

Along with the "Australia" inscription at left, inscribed at the bottom above the animal's name is "Australian Antarctic Territory" on No. 3562, "Cocos (Keeling) Islands" on No. 3563, and "Christmas Island" on No. 3564. All recent stamps of the Australian possessions of Australian Antarctic Territory, Cocos Islands and Christmas Island are doubly-inscribed with "Australia" and the possession's name, and all stamps inscribed "Australia," "Australian Antarctic Territory," "Cocos Islands," or "Christmas Island" are valid for postage anywhere in those four areas. As there was no attempt to make the stamps bearing the names of these possessions in this set available separately in those locations they will be listed here only and not in the listings for each of the possessions.

2011 Presidents Cup Golf Tournament, Melbourne — A867

Designs: Nos. 3565, 3570, Hand on golf club. Nos. 3566, 3569B, 3571, Presidents Cup. Nos. 3567, 3572, Golf shoes, glove and ball. $1.65, Golf club and ball. $2.35, Clubs in golf bag.

**2011, Sept. 27** *Perf. 14¾x14*
3565 A867 60c multi 1.25 1.25
3566 A867 60c multi 1.25 1.25
3567 A867 60c multi 1.25 1.25
a. Horiz. strip of 3, #3565-3567 3.75 3.75
3568 A867 $1.65 multi 3.25 3.25
3569 A867 $2.35 multi 4.75 4.75
a. Souvenir sheet of 5, #3565-3569 12.00 12.00
*Nos. 3565-3569 (5)* 11.75 11.75

### Litho. & Embossed With Foil Application

3569B A867 60c multi 1.25 1.25

No. 3569B was printed in sheets of 15 that sold for $9.45.

### Litho.

### Self-Adhesive

*Serpentine Die Cut 11¼ Syncopated*
3570 A867 60c multi 1.25 .25
3571 A867 60c multi 1.25 .25
3572 A867 60c multi 1.25 .25
a. Booklet pane of 10, 4 each # 3570-3571, 2 #3572 12.50
b. Vert. coil strip of 3, #3570-3572 3.75
3573 A867 $1.65 multi 3.25 1.60
a. Booklet pane of 5 16.50
3574 A867 $2.35 multi 4.75 2.40
a. Booklet pane of 5 24.00
*Nos. 3570-3574 (5)* 11.75 4.75

Mythical Creatures — A868

Designs: Nos. 3575, 3581, Fairy. Nos. 3576, 3582, Troll. Nos. 3577, 3583, Mermaid. Nos. 3578, 3584, Griffin. Nos. 3579, 3585, Unicorn. $1.20, Dragon.

**2011, Oct. 4 Litho.** *Perf. 14¾x14*
3575 A868 60c multi 1.25 1.25
3576 A868 60c multi 1.25 1.25
3577 A868 60c multi 1.25 1.25
3578 A868 60c multi 1.25 1.25
3579 A868 60c multi 1.25 1.25
a. Horiz. strip of 5, #3575-3579 6.25 6.25
3580 A868 $1.20 multi 2.40 1.90
a. Souvenir sheet of 6, #3575-3580 8.75 8.75
*Nos. 3575-3580 (6)* 8.65 8.15

**Booklet Stamps**
**Self-Adhesive**

*Serpentine Die Cut 11¼ Syncopated*

**3581** A868 60c multi 1.25 .25
**3582** A868 60c multi 1.25 .25
**3583** A868 60c multi 1.25 .25
**3584** A868 60c multi 1.25 .25
**3585** A868 60c multi 1.25 .25
*a.* Booklet pane of 10, 2 each #3581-3585 12.50
*b.* Booklet pane of 20, 4 each #3581-3585 25.00
*Nos. 3581-3585 (5)* 6.25 1.25

Commonwealth Heads of Government Meeting, Perth — A869

**2011, Oct. 18** *Perf. 14½x14*

**3586** A869 60c multi 1.25 .95

Diplomatic Relations Between Australia and South Korea, 50th Anniv. — A870

Designs: 60c, Korean woman playing haegeum. $1.65, Australian aborigine playing didgeridoo.

**2011, Oct. 31** *Perf. 13¼x13*

**3587** A870 60c multi 1.25 .95
**3588** A870 $1.65 multi 3.50 1.75

**Booklet Stamp**
**Self-Adhesive**

*Serpentine Die Cut 11¼ Syncopated*

**3589** A870 $1.65 multi 3.50 1.75
*a.* Booklet pane of 5 17.50

See South Korea No. 2373.

Christmas
A871 A872

Designs: Nos. 3590, 3595, Madonna and Child. Nos. 3591, 3596, 3599, 3601, Star on Christmas tree. Nos. 3592, 3597, 3600, 3602, Star and gift. 60c, Star and fruit tree branches. $1.50, Magi and camels, horiz.

**2011, Oct. 31** **Litho.** *Perf. 14¾x14*

**3590** A871 55c multi 1.10 1.10
**3591** A872 55c multi 1.10 1.10
**3592** A872 55c multi 1.10 1.10
*a.* Horiz. pair, #3591-3592 2.20 2.20
**3593** A872 60c multi 1.25 1.25

*Perf. 14x14¾*

**3594** A871 $1.50 multi 3.25 3.25
*Nos. 3590-3594 (5)* 7.80 7.80

**Booklet Stamps**
**Self-Adhesive**

*Serpentine Die Cut 11¼ Syncopated*

**3595** A871 55c multi 1.10 .25
*a.* Booklet pane of 20 + 20 etiquettes 22.00
**3596** A872 55c multi 1.10 .25
**3597** A872 55c multi 1.10 .25
*a.* Booklet pane of 20, 10 each #3596-3597 + 20 etiquettes 22.00
**3598** A871 $1.50 multi 3.25 1.60
*a.* Booklet pane of 5 16.50

**Litho. With Foil Application**

**3599** A872 55c multi 1.10 .25
*a.* Booklet pane of 10 11.00
**3600** A872 55c multi 1.10 .25
*a.* Booklet pane of 10 11.00
*Nos. 3595-3600 (6)* 8.75 2.85

**Litho.**
**With Personalized Photo at Right Like Type A692a**

*Serpentine Die Cut 11½x11¼ Syncopated*

**3601** A872 55c multi 2.50 2.50
**3602** A872 55c multi 2.50 2.50
**3603** A872 60c multi 2.60 2.60
*Nos. 3601-3603 (3)* 7.60 7.60

Nos. 3601-3603 each were printed in sheets of 20 and have personalized pictures and a straight edge at right, and lack separations between the stamp and the personalized photo. Sheets of 20 of Nos. 3601 and 3602 each sold for $24, for No. 3603, $25.

Remembrance Day — A873

Lines from "In Flanders Fields," poem by John McCrae, and: 60c, Poppy, bugler. $1.20, Two poppies, two soldiers.

**2011, Nov. 2** **Litho.** *Perf. 14x14¾*

**3604** A873 60c multi 1.25 1.25
**3605** A873 $1.20 multi 2.50 1.90
*a.* Souvenir sheet of 2, #3604-3605 3.75 3.25

**Self-Adhesive**

*Serpentine Die Cut 11¼ Syncopated*

**3606** A873 60c multi 1.25 .25
*a.* Booklet pane of 10 12.50

No. 3606 was issued in coils and booklets.

ANZUS Treaty, 60th Anniv. — A874

Design: Australian Lieutenant General Sydney F. Rowell, New Zealand Major General William Gentry, and U.S. Admiral Arthur Radford.

**2011, Nov. 16** *Perf. 14x14¾*

**3607** A874 60c multi 1.25 .95

Cupcake and Birthday Candle
A875

Teddy Bear
A876

Balloons and Streamers
A877

"Love" and Hearts
A878

Birds
A879

Rose
A880

**2012, Jan. 17** *Perf. 14¾x14*

**3608** A875 60c multi 1.25 1.25
**3609** A876 60c multi 1.25 1.25
**3610** A877 60c multi 1.25 1.25
**3611** A878 60c multi 1.25 1.25
**3612** A879 60c multi 1.25 1.25
*a.* Horiz. strip of 5, $3608-3612 6.25 6.25
**3613** A880 $1.20 multi 2.60 2.60
*Nos. 3608-3613 (6)* 8.85 8.85

**Booklet Stamps**
**Self-Adhesive**

*Serpentine Die Cut 11¼ Syncopated*

**3614** A875 60c multi 1.25 .25
*a.* Booklet pane of 10 + 5 stickers 12.50
**3615** A876 60c multi 1.25 .25
*a.* Booklet pane of 10 + 5 stickers 12.50
**3616** A877 60c multi 1.25 .25
*a.* Booklet pane of 10 + 5 stickers 12.50
**3617** A878 60c multi 1.25 .25
*a.* Booklet pane of 10 + 5 stickers 12.50
**3618** A879 60c multi 1.25 .25
*a.* Booklet pane of 10 + 5 stickers 12.50
**3619** A880 $1.20 multi 2.75 1.40
*a.* Booklet pane of 4 11.00
Complete booklet, 5 #3619a 55.00
*Nos. 3614-3619 (6)* 9.00 2.65

**With Personalized Photo at Right Like Type A692a**

*Serpentine Die Cut 11½x11¼ Syncopated*

**3620** A875 60c multi 2.75 2.75
**3621** A876 60c multi 2.75 2.75
**3622** A877 60c multi 2.75 2.75
**3623** A878 60c multi 2.75 2.75
**3624** A879 60c multi 2.75 2.75
**3625** A880 $1.20 multi 4.00 4.00
*Nos. 3620-3625 (6)* 17.75 17.75

Complete booklet sold for $24.95 and contains five booklet panes of No. 3619a, each with a different margin.

Nos. 3620-3625 each were printed in sheets of 20 and have personalized pictures and a straight edge at right, and lack separations between the stamp and the personalized photo. Sheets of 20 of Nos. 3620-3624 each sold for $25, for No. 3625, $37.

Athletes — A881

Designs: Nos. 3626, 3634, Ron Barassi, Australian Rules Football player. Nos. 3627, 3635, Gary Ablett, Jr., Australian Rules Football player. Nos. 3628, 3636, John Raper, Rugby League player. Nos. 3629, 3637, Billy Slater, Rugby League player. Nos. 3630, 3638, David Campese, Rugby Union player. Nos. 3631, 3639, David Pocock, Rugby Union player. Nos. 3632, 3640, Joe Marston, soccer player. Nos. 3633, 3641, Mark Schwarzer, soccer player.

**2012, Jan. 20** *Perf. 14¾x14*

**3626** A881 60c multi 1.25 1.25
*a.* Booklet pane of 4 5.50 —
**3627** A881 60c multi 1.25 1.25
*a.* Booklet pane of 4 5.50 —
**3628** A881 60c multi 1.25 1.25
*a.* Booklet pane of 4 5.50 —
**3629** A881 60c multi 1.25 1.25
*a.* Booklet pane of 4 5.50 —
**3630** A881 60c multi 1.25 1.25
*a.* Booklet pane of 4 5.50 —
**3631** A881 60c multi 1.25 1.25
*a.* Booklet pane of 4 5.50 —
**3632** A881 60c multi 1.25 1.25
*a.* Booklet pane of 4 5.50 —
**3633** A881 60c multi 1.25 1.25
*a.* Booklet pane of 4 5.50 —
Complete booklet, #3626a-3633a 44.00
*Nos. 3626-3633 (8)* 10.00 10.00

**Booklet Stamps**
**Self-Adhesive**

*Serpentine Die Cut 11¼ Syncopated*

**3634** A881 60c multi 1.25 .25
*a.* Booklet pane of 10 12.50
**3635** A881 60c multi 1.25 .25
*a.* Booklet pane of 10 12.50
**3636** A881 60c multi 1.25 .25
*a.* Booklet pane of 10 12.50
**3637** A881 60c multi 1.25 .25
*a.* Booklet pane of 10 12.50
**3638** A881 60c multi 1.25 .25
*a.* Booklet pane of 10 12.50
**3639** A881 60c multi 1.25 .25
*a.* Booklet pane of 10 12.50
**3640** A881 60c multi 1.25 .25
*a.* Booklet pane of 10 12.50
**3641** A881 60c multi 1.25 .25
*a.* Booklet pane of 10 12.50
*Nos. 3634-3641 (8)* 10.00 2.00

Complete booklet sold for $19.95.

Technological Changes Through the Years — A882

Designs: Nos. 3642, 3647, Woman on pay telephone, 4G phone. Nos. 3643, 3648, Man carrying ice to icebox, modern refrigerator. Nos. 3644, 3649, Family watching black-and-white television, flat-screen television. Nos. 3645, 3650, Man with vinyl records and record player, digital media player. Nos. 3646, 3651, Man reading paper road map, global positioning system.

**2012, Feb. 7** *Perf. 14x14¾*

**3642** A882 60c multi 1.40 1.40
**3643** A882 60c multi 1.40 1.40
**3644** A882 60c multi 1.40 1.40
**3645** A882 60c multi 1.40 1.40
**3646** A882 60c multi 1.40 1.40
*a.* Horiz. strip of 5, #3642-3646 7.00 7.00
*b.* Souvenir sheet of 5, #3642-3646 7.00 7.00

**Self-Adhesive**

*Serpentine Die Cut 11¼ Syncopated*

**3647** A882 60c multi 1.40 .25
**3648** A882 60c multi 1.40 .25
**3649** A882 60c multi 1.40 .25
**3650** A882 60c multi 1.40 .25
**3651** A882 60c multi 1.40 .25
*a.* Horiz. coil strip of 5, #3647-3651 7.00
*b.* Booklet pane of 10, 2 each #3647-3651 14.00
*Nos. 3647-3651 (5)* 7.00 1.25

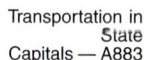

Transportation in State Capitals — A883

Designs: Nos. 3652, 3657, O-Bahn bus system, Adelaide. Nos. 3653, 3658, Ferry in Sydney Harbor. Nos. 3654, 3659, Train in Perth. Nos. 3655, 3660, St. Kilda-bound tram, Melbourne. Nos. 3656, 3661, North Sydney-bound double-decker train, Sydney.

**2012, Feb. 21** *Perf. 14x14¾*

**3652** A883 60c multi 1.40 1.40
*a.* Booklet pane of 4 5.75 —
**3653** A883 60c multi 1.40 1.40
*a.* Booklet pane of 4 5.75 —
**3654** A883 60c multi 1.40 1.40
*a.* Booklet pane of 4 5.75 —
**3655** A883 60c multi 1.40 1.40
*a.* Booklet pane of 4 5.75 —
**3656** A883 60c multi 1.40 1.40
*a.* Booklet pane of 4 5.75 —
Complete booklet, #3652a-3656a 29.00
*b.* Horiz. strip of 5, #3652-3656 7.00 7.00

**Booklet Stamps**
**Self-Adhesive**

*Serpentine Die Cut 11¼ Syncopated*

**3657** A883 60c multi 1.40 .25
**3658** A883 60c multi 1.40 .25
**3659** A883 60c multi 1.40 .25
**3660** A883 60c multi 1.40 .25
**3661** A883 60c multi 1.40 .25
*a.* Booklet pane of 20, 4 each #3657-3661 28.00
*Nos. 3657-3661 (5)* 7.00 1.25

Complete booklet sold for $12.95.

Ducks — A884

Designs: Nos. 3662, 3666, Radjah shelduck. Nos. 3663, 3667, Pink-eared duck. $1.65, Australian shelduck. $2.35, Plumed whistling duck.

**2012, Mar. 6** *Perf. 14x14¾*

**3662** A884 60c multi 1.25 1.25
*a.* Additionally dated "2013" 1.25 1.25
**3663** A884 60c multi 1.25 1.25
*a.* Additionally dated "2013" 1.25 1.25
**3664** A884 $1.65 multi 3.50 3.50
*a.* Additionally dated "2013" 3.25 3.25
**3665** A884 $2.35 multi 5.00 5.00
*a.* Additionally dated "2013" 4.50 4.50
*b.* Booklet pane of 4, #3662a, 3663a, 3664a, 3665a 10.50 —
*Nos. 3662-3665 (4)* 11.00 11.00

Issued: Nos. 3662a, 3663a, 3664a, 3665a, 3665b, 5/11/13. No. 3665b was issued in a booklet also containing Nos. 3151c, 3376b and 3925a.

**Self-Adhesive**

*Serpentine Die Cut 11¼ Syncopated*

**3666** A884 60c multi 1.25 .25
**3667** A884 60c multi 1.25 .25
*a.* Horiz. coil pair, #3666-3667 2.50
*b.* Booklet pane of 10, 5 each #3666-3667 25.00

**Booklet Stamps**

**3668** A884 $1.65 multi 3.50 1.75
*a.* Booklet pane of 5 17.50

**3669** A884 $2.35 multi 5.00 2.50
*a.* Booklet pane of 5 25.00
*Nos. 3666-3669 (4)* 11.00 4.75

Farm Products — A885

Designs: 10c, Dairy cows. 20c, Pineapples. $1, Wine grapes. $3, Sunflowers. $5, Apples.

**2012, Mar. 20** ***Perf. 14x14½***

**3670** A885 10c multi .25 .25
**3671** A885 20c multi .40 .25
*a.* As No. 3671, with part of design and 1mm wide white space separating designs at left side 1.10 1.10

**Size: 50x30mm**

***Perf. 14½x14***

**3672** A885 $1 multi 2.10 1.10
**3673** A885 $3 multi 6.25 3.25
**3674** A885 $5 multi 10.50 5.25
*Nos. 3670-3674 (5)* 19.50 10.10

No. 3671 has a white margin extending to the perforation tips at left. Four of the five stamps in the bottom row of the bottom pane in the sheet of 100 stamps (composed of two panes of 50) are No. 3671a.

See Nos. 3712-3723.

Compulsory Voting Enrollment, Cent. — A886

**2012, Mar. 27** **Litho.** ***Perf. 14¾x14***

**3675** A886 60c multi 1.25 .95

Reign of Queen Elizabeth II, 60th Anniv. — A887

Photograph of Queen Elizabeth II in: 60c, 1952. $2.35, 2012.

**2012, Apr. 3** ***Perf. 14¾x14***

**3676** A887 60c multi 1.25 .95
**3677** A887 $2.35 multi 5.00 5.00
*a.* Souvenir sheet of 2, #3676-3677 6.25 6.00

**Booklet Stamp**
**Self-Adhesive**

***Serpentine Die Cut 11¼ Syncopated***

**3678** A887 $2.35 multi 5.00 2.50
*a.* Booklet pane of 5 25.00

Medical Doctors — A888

Designs: Nos. 3679, 3684, Dr. Jane Stocks Greig (1872-1939), public health specialist. Nos. 3680, 3685, Dame Kate Campbell (1899-1986), pediatrician. Nos. 3681, 3686, Dr. Victor Chang (1936-91), cardiac surgeon. Nos. 3682, 3687, Dr. Fred Hollows (1929-93), ophthalmologist. Nos. 3683, 3688, Dr. Chris O'Brien (1952-2009), surgeon.

**2012, Apr. 10** ***Perf. 14¾x14***

**3679** A888 60c multi 1.25 1.25
**3680** A888 60c multi 1.25 1.25
**3681** A888 60c multi 1.25 1.25
**3682** A888 60c multi 1.25 1.25
**3683** A888 60c multi 1.25 1.25
*Nos. 3679-3683 (5)* 6.25 6.25

**Coil Stamps**
**Self-Adhesive**

***Serpentine Die Cut 11¼ Syncopated***

**3684** A888 60c multi 1.25 .25
**3685** A888 60c multi 1.25 .25
**3686** A888 60c multi 1.25 .25
**3687** A888 60c multi 1.25 .25
**3688** A888 60c multi 1.25 .25
*a.* Vert. coil strip of 5, #3684-3688 6.25
*Nos. 3684-3688 (5)* 6.25 1.25

Rising Sun Badge — A889

Rising Sun Badge in use from: Nos. 3689, 3694, 1902-04. Nos. 3690, 3695, 1904-49. Nos. 3691, 3696, 1954-69. Nos. 3692, 3697, 1969-91. Nos. 3693, 3698, 1991-present.

**2012, Apr. 17** ***Perf. 14x14¾***

**3689** A889 60c multi 1.25 1.25
**3690** A889 60c multi 1.25 1.25
**3691** A889 60c multi 1.25 1.25
**3692** A889 60c multi 1.25 1.25
**3693** A889 60c multi 1.25 1.25
*a.* Horiz. strip of 5, #3689-3693 6.25 6.25
*b.* Souvenir sheet of 5, #3689-3693 6.25 6.25

**Booklet Stamps**
**Self-Adhesive**

***Serpentine Die Cut 11¼ Syncopated***

**3694** A889 60c multi 1.25 .25
**3695** A889 60c multi 1.25 .25
**3696** A889 60c multi 1.25 .25
**3697** A889 60c multi 1.25 .25
**3698** A889 60c multi 1.25 .25
*a.* Booklet pane of 10, 2 each #3694-3698 12.50
*Nos. 3694-3698 (5)* 6.25 1.25

Limited editions exist of No. 3698a with a gold overprint in the margin, and a part-perforate sheet of seven stamps (five similar to Nos. 3689-3693, and two different $1 stamps).

Nudibranchs A890

Designs: Nos. 3699, 3705, Chromodoris westraliensis. Nos. 3700, 3706, Godiva sp. Nos. 3701, 3707, Flabellina rubrolineata. No. 3702, Phyllidia ocellata. No. 3703, Thorunna florens. $1.80, Nembrotha purpureolineata.

**2012, May 8** ***Perf. 14x14¾***

**3699** A890 60c multi 1.25 1.25
*a.* Booklet pane of 4 5.25 —
**3700** A890 60c multi 1.25 1.25
*a.* Booklet pane of 4 5.25 —
**3701** A890 60c multi 1.25 1.25
*a.* Booklet pane of 4 5.25 —
**3702** A890 $1.20 multi 2.40 1.90
**3703** A890 $1.20 multi 2.40 1.90
*a.* Booklet pane of 4, #3699-3702 6.50 —
**3704** A890 $1.80 multi 3.75 1.90
*a.* Booklet pane of 4, #3699-3701, 3704 7.75 —
Complete booklet, #3699a, 3700a, 3701a, 3703a, 3704a 30.00
*b.* Souvenir sheet of 6, #3699-3704 12.50 12.50
*Nos. 3699-3704 (6)* 12.30 9.45

**Booklet Stamps**
**Self-Adhesive**

***Serpentine Die Cut 11¼ Syncopated***

**3705** A890 60c multi 1.25 .25
**3706** A890 60c multi 1.25 .25
**3707** A890 60c multi 1.25 .25
*a.* Booklet pane of 20, 7 each #3705-3706, 6 #3707 25.00
*Nos. 3705-3707 (3)* 3.75 .75

Complete booklet sold for $14.95.

Australian Flag, Olympic Rings, London Tourist Attractions — A891

**2012, June 5** ***Perf. 14¾x14***

**3708** A891 60c multi 1.25 1.25

**Self-Adhesive**

***Serpentine Die Cut 11¼ Syncopated***

**3709** A891 60c multi 1.25 .25
*a.* Booklet pane of 10 12.50

2012 Summer Olympics, London.

Colonial Heritage — A892

Designs: No. 3710, Redrawn vignette of New South Wales #1. No. 3710, Redrawn vignette of Tasmania #88.

**2012, June 19** ***Perf. 14x14½***

**3710** A892 $2 yellow & blue 4.25 2.10
*a.* Perf. 14x13½ 4.25 2.10
**3711** A892 $2 lt blue & blue 4.25 2.10
*a.* Perf. 14x13½ 4.25 2.10
*b.* Horiz. pair, #3710-3711 8.50 4.25
*c.* Souvenir sheet of 2, #3710a, 3711a 8.50 4.25

**Farm Products Type of 2012**

Designs: Nos. 3712, 3716, 3720, Beef cattle. Nos. 3713, 3717, 3721, Oranges. Nos. 3714, 3718, 3722, Sugar. Nos. 3715, 3719, 3723, Wool.

**2012, June 26** **Litho.** ***Perf. 14x14½***

**3712** A885 60c multi 1.25 .25
**3713** A885 60c multi 1.25 .25
**3714** A885 60c multi 1.25 .25
**3715** A885 60c multi 1.25 .25
*a.* Block of 4, #3712-3715 5.00 2.50
*Nos. 3712-3715 (4)* 5.00 1.00

**Coil Stamps**
**Self-Adhesive**

***Serpentine Die Cut 12¾***

**3716** A885 60c multi 1.25 .25
**3717** A885 60c multi 1.25 .25
**3718** A885 60c multi 1.25 .25
**3719** A885 60c multi 1.25 .25
*a.* Horiz. strip of 4, #3716-3719 5.00

**Booklet Stamps**

***Serpentine Die Cut 11¼***

**3720** A885 60c multi 1.25 .25
**3721** A885 60c multi 1.25 .25
**3722** A885 60c multi 1.25 .25
**3723** A885 60c multi 1.25 .25
*a.* Booklet pane of 10, 2 each #3720, 3722-3723, 4 #3721 12.50
*b.* Booklet pane of 20, 5 each #3720-3723 25.00
*Nos. 3716-3723 (8)* 10.00 2.00

Inland Exploration A893

Designs: No. 3724, Explorers crossing Blue Mountains, 1813. No. 3725, Explorers William Lawson, William Charles Wentworth and Gregory Blaxland. No. 3726, Explorer John McDouall Stuart. No. 3727, Stuart Overland Crossing Expedition planting flag on Indian Ocean coast.

**2012, July 3** ***Perf. 14x14¾***

**3724** A893 60c multi 1.25 .95
**3725** A893 60c multi 1.25 .95
*a.* Horiz. pair, #3724-3725 2.50 1.90
**3726** A893 $1.20 multi 2.50 2.00
**3727** A893 $1.20 multi 2.50 2.00
*a.* Horiz. pair, #3726-3727 5.00 4.00
*b.* Souvenir sheet of 4, #3724-3727 7.50 6.00
*Nos. 3724-3727 (4)* 7.50 5.90

Sports of the Summer Olympics — A894

Designs: 60c, Swimming. $1.60, Pole vault. $2.30, Rowing.

**2012, July 17** ***Perf. 14x14¾***

**3728** A894 60c multi 1.25 1.25
**3729** A894 $1.60 multi 3.50 3.50
**3730** A894 $2.35 multi 5.00 5.00
*Nos. 3728-3730 (3)* 9.75 9.75

**Coil Stamp**
**Self-Adhesive**

***Serpentine Die Cut 11¼ Syncopated***

**3731** A894 60c multi 1.25 .25

**Booklet Stamps**

**3732** A894 $1.60 multi 3.50 1.75
*a.* Booklet pane of 5 17.50
**3733** A894 $2.35 multi 5.00 2.50
*a.* Booklet pane of 5 25.00
*Nos. 3731-3733 (3)* 9.75 4.50

Photographs of Everyday Life in Australia — A895

Designs: Nos. 3734, 3740, Little Wonders, by Ann Clark (children on beach). Nos. 3735, 3742, The Godfathers, by Chevelle Williams (sheep in pen). Nos. 3736, 3741, Is There a Letter for Me?, by Wanda Lach (row of mailboxes in rural area). Nos. 3737, 3743, Lunch on the Harbor, by Damian Madden (seagull with French fry in beak). Nos. 3738, 3739, Fuel Ask at the Store Across the Road, by Ronald Rockman (rural gas station).

**2012, July 24** ***Perf. 14x14¾***

**3734** A895 60c multi 1.25 1.25
**3735** A895 60c multi 1.25 1.25
**3736** A895 60c multi 1.25 1.25
**3737** A895 60c multi 1.25 1.25
**3738** A895 60c multi 1.25 1.25
*a.* Horiz. strip of 5, #3734-3738 6.25 6.25
*Nos. 3734-3738 (5)* 6.25 6.25

**Booklet Stamps**
**Self-Adhesive**

***Serpentine Die Cut 11¼ Syncopated***

**3739** A895 60c multi 1.25 .25
**3740** A895 60c multi 1.25 .25
**3741** A895 60c multi 1.25 .25
**3742** A895 60c multi 1.25 .25
**3743** A895 60c multi 1.25 .25
*a.* Booklet pane of 20, 4 each #3739-3742 25.00
*Nos. 3739-3743 (5)* 6.25 1.25

Souvenir Sheet

Emblem of Australia 2013 World Stamp Expo and Royal Exhibition Building, Melbourne — A896

**2012, June 18** **Litho.** ***Perf. 14¾x14***

**3744** A896 $1.85 multi 3.75 1.90

A limited edition of No. 3744 with a gold overprint in the sheet margin exists.

Australian Gold Medalists at 2012 Summer Olympics, London — A897

Designs: No. 3745, Women's 4x100 meter freestyle swimming relay team. No. 3746, Tom Slingsby, men's Laser class sailing. No. 3747, Anna Meares, women's sprint cycling. No. 3748, Iain Jensen and Nathan Outteridge, men's 49er class sailing. No. 3749, Sally Pearson, women's 100 meter hurdles. No. 3750, Men's 1000 meter kayak fours team. No. 3751, Mathew Belcher and Malcolm Page, men's 470 class sailing.

**2012** ***Perf. 14¼***

**3745** A897 60c multi 1.25 .95
**3746** A897 60c multi 1.25 .95
**3747** A897 60c multi 1.25 .95
**3748** A897 60c multi 1.25 .95
**3749** A897 60c multi 1.25 .95
**3750** A897 60c multi 1.25 .95
**3751** A897 60c multi 1.25 .95
*Nos. 3745-3751 (7)* 8.75 6.65

Nos. 3745-3751 each were printed in sheets of 10. Issued: No. 3745, 7/31; No. 3746, 8/9; No. 3747, 8/10; others, 8/13.

See No. 4506B.

Portraits of Autralian Nobel Prize Winners — A898

Portrait of: Nos. 3752, 3757, Sir Frank Macfarlane Burnet, by Clifton Pugh. Nos. 3753, 3758, Sir John Carew Eccles, by Judy Cassab. Nos. 3754, 3759, Patrick White, by Brett Whiteley. Nos. 3755, 3760, Sir Howard Walter Florey, by Allan Gwynne-Jones. Nos. 3756, 3761, William Lawrence Bragg, by Sir William Dargie.

**2012, Aug. 28 Litho. *Perf. 14¾x14***

**3752** A898 60c multi 1.25 1.25
**3753** A898 60c multi 1.25 1.25
**3754** A898 60c multi 1.25 1.25
**3755** A898 60c multi 1.25 1.25
**3756** A898 60c multi 1.25 1.25
*a.* Horiz. strip of 5, #3752-3756 6.25 6.25
*Nos. 3752-3756 (5)* 6.25 6.25

**Self-Adhesive**

***Serpentine Die Cut 11¼ Syncopated***

**3757** A898 60c multi 1.25 .25
**3758** A898 60c multi 1.25 .25
**3759** A898 60c multi 1.25 .25
**3760** A898 60c multi 1.25 .25
**3761** A898 60c multi 1.25 .25
*a.* Vert. coil strip of 5, #3757-3761 6.25
*b.* Booklet pane of 10, 2 each #3757-3761 12.50
*Nos. 3757-3761 (5)* 6.25 1.25

Road Trips — A899

Designs: Nos. 3762, 3769, Station wagon at Port Arthur, Tasmania. Nos. 3763, 3767, Volkswagen Bus at Great Barrier Reef, Queensland. Nos. 3764, 3768, Motorcyclists picnicking near Margaret River, Western Australia. $1.65, Station wagon at Phillip Island, Victoria. $2.35, Car at camel race, Alice Springs, Northern Territory.

**2012, Sept. 10 *Perf. 14¼***

**3762** A899 60c multi 1.25 1.25
**3763** A899 60c multi 1.25 1.25
**3764** A899 60c multi 1.25 1.25
*a.* Horiz. strip of 3, #3762-3764 3.75 3.75
**3765** A899 $1.65 multi 3.50 1.75
**3766** A899 $2.35 multi 4.75 2.40
*a.* Souvenir sheet of 5, #3762-3766 12.00 12.00
*Nos. 3762-3766 (5)* 12.00 7.90

**Booklet Stamps**
**Self-Adhesive**

***Serpentine Die Cut 11¼ Syncopated***

**3767** A899 60c multi 1.25 .25
**3768** A899 60c multi 1.25 .25
**3769** A899 60c multi 1.25 .25
*a.* Booklet pane of 10, 3 each #3767, 3769, 4 #3768 12.50
**3770** A899 $1.65 multi 3.50 1.75
*a.* Booklet pane of 5 17.50
**3771** A899 $2.35 multi 4.75 2.40
*a.* Booklet pane of 5 24.00
*Nos. 3767-3771 (5)* 12.00 4.90

Compare with type A933.

Wilderness Areas — A900

Designs: $1.65, Nullarbor Plain, Western Australia. $2.35, Daintree National Park, Queensland. $4.50, Cradle Mountain, Tasmania.

**2012, Sept. 25 *Perf. 14¾x14***

**3772** A900 $1.65 multi 3.50 1.75
**3773** A900 $2.35 multi 4.75 2.40
**3774** A900 $4.50 multi 9.25 4.75
*Nos. 3772-3774 (3)* 17.50 8.90

**Booklet Stamps**
**Self-Adhesive**

***Serpentine Die Cut 11¼ Syncopated***

**3775** A900 $1.65 multi 3.50 1.75
*a.* Booklet pane of 5 17.50
**3776** A900 $2.35 multi 4.75 2.40
*a.* Booklet pane of 5 24.00

Animals in Australian Zoos — A901

Designs: No. 3777, Sumatran tiger, Melbourne Zoo, Victoria. Nos. 3778, 3789, Wedge-tailed hawk, Healesville Sanctuary, Victoria. Nos. 3779, 3787. Sumatran orangutan, Perth Zoo, Western Australia. Nos. 3780, 3786, Giant panda, Adelaide Zoo, South Australia. Nos. 3781, 3785, Giraffe, Taronga Zoo, Sydney, New South Wales. Nos. 3782, 3788, Saltwater crocodile, Australia Zoo, Sunshine Coast, Queensland. Nos. 3783, 3784, Black rhinoceros, Taronga Western Plains Zoo, Dubbo, New South Wales.

**2012, Sept. 28 *Perf. 13¾x14***

**3777** A901 60c multi 1.25 .95

**Size: 37x26mm**

***Perf. 14x14¾***

**3778** A901 60c multi 1.25 1.25
**3779** A901 60c multi 1.25 1.25
**3780** A901 60c multi 1.25 1.25
**3781** A901 60c multi 1.25 1.25
**3782** A901 60c multi 1.25 1.25
**3783** A901 60c multi 1.25 1.25
*a.* Souvenir sheet of 7, #3777-3783 8.75 8.75
*Nos. 3777-3783 (7)* 8.75 8.45

**Self-Adhesive**

***Serpentine Die Cut 11¼ Syncopated***

**3784** A901 60c multi 1.25 .25
**3785** A901 60c multi 1.25 .25
**3786** A901 60c multi 1.25 .25
**3787** A901 60c multi 1.25 .25
**3788** A901 60c multi 1.25 .25
**3789** A901 60c multi 1.25 .25
*a.* Horiz. coil strip of 6, #3784-3789 7.50
*b.* Booklet pane of 20, 4 each #3784-3785, 3 each #3786-3789 25.00
*Nos. 3784-3789 (6)* 7.50 1.50

Auto Racing at Bathurst, 50th Anniv. — A902

Designs: Nos. 3790, 3794, Race car, country name in red. Nos. 3791, 3797, Mount Panorama Race Track, country name in yellow green. Nos. 3792, 3796, Race car, country name in blue. Nos. 3793, 3795, Race car, country name in yellow.

**2012, Oct. 2 *Perf. 14x14¾***

**3790** A902 60c multi 1.25 1.25
**3791** A902 60c multi 1.25 1.25
**3792** A902 60c multi 1.25 1.25
**3793** A902 60c multi 1.25 1.25
*a.* Block of 4, #3790-3793 5.00 5.00
*b.* Souvenir sheet of 4, #3790-3793 5.00 5.00
*Nos. 3790-3793 (4)* 5.00 5.00

**Booklet Stamps**
**Self-Adhesive**

***Serpentine Die Cut 11¼ Syncopated***

**3794** A902 60c multi 1.25 .25
**3795** A902 60c multi 1.25 .25
**3796** A902 60c multi 1.25 .25
**3797** A902 60c multi 1.25 .25
*a.* Booklet pane of 10, 2 each #3794-3796, 4 #3797 12.50
*Nos. 3794-3797 (4)* 5.00 1.00

Susie O'Neill, Swimmer — A903

O'Neill: No. 3798, Wearing black jacket. No. 3799, Swimming in pool.

**2012, Oct. 12 *Perf. 14¾x14***

**3798** A903 60c multi 1.25 .95
**3799** A903 60c multi 1.25 .95
*a.* Pair, #3798-3799 2.50 1.90

Australian Ballet, 50th Anniv. — A904

Designs: Nos. 3800, 3802, One dancer. Nos. 3801, 3803, Two dancers.

**2012, Oct. 16 *Perf. 14¾x14***

**3800** A904 60c multi 1.25 1.25
**3801** A904 60c multi 1.25 1.25
*a.* Pair, #3800-3801 2.50 2.50

**Coil Stamps**
**Self-Adhesive**

***Serpentine Die Cut 11¼ Syncopated***

**3802** A904 60c multi 1.25 .25
**3803** A904 60c multi 1.25 .25
*a.* Vert. pair, #3802-3803 2.50

Lawn Bowling — A905

Designs: 60c, Female bowlers. $1.20, Male bowlers.

**2012, Nov. 1 *Perf. 14x14¾***

**3804** A905 60c multi 1.25 .95
**3805** A905 $1.20 multi 2.50 1.90
*a.* Souvenir sheet of 2, #3804-3805 3.75 3.00

Christmas
A906 A907

Designs: Nos. 3806, 3811, Detail of Madonna and Child from Adoration of the Magi tapestry. Nos. 3807, 3812, 3815, 3817, Reindeer. Nos. 3808, 3813, 3816, 3818, Gifts. 60c, Bells. $1.60, Entire Adoration of the Magi tapestry (50x30mm), horiz.

**2012, Nov. 1 *Perf. 14¾x14***

**3806** A906 55c multi 1.25 1.25
**3807** A907 55c multi 1.25 1.25
**3808** A907 55c multi 1.25 1.25
**3809** A907 60c multi 1.25 .60

***Perf. 14½x14***

**3810** A906 $1.60 multi 3.50 1.75
*Nos. 3806-3810 (5)* 8.50 6.10

**Booklet Stamps**
**Self-Adhesive**

***Serpentine Die Cut 11¼ Syncopated***

**3811** A906 55c multi 1.25 .25
*a.* Booklet pane of 20 25.00
**3812** A907 55c multi 1.25 .25
**3813** A907 55c multi 1.25 .25
*a.* Booklet pane of 20, 10 each #3812-3813 25.00
**3814** A906 $1.60 multi 3.50 1.75
*a.* Booklet pane of 5 17.50

**Litho. With Foil Application**

**3815** A907 55c multi 1.25 .25
*a.* Booklet pane of 10 12.50

**Litho. & Embossed With Foil Application**

**3816** A907 55c multi 1.25 .25
*a.* Booklet pane of 10 12.50
*Nos. 3811-3816 (6)* 9.75 3.00

**With Personalized Photo at Right Like Type A692a**
**Litho.**

***Serpentine Die Cut 11½x11¼ Syncopated***

**3817** A907 55c multi 2.50 2.50
**3818** A907 55c multi 2.50 2.50

Nos. 3817-3818 each were printed in sheets of 20 and have personalized pictures and straight edge at right, and lack separations between the stamp an the personalized photo. Sheets of 20 of each stamp sold for $24.

Jacqueline Freney, Paralympian of the Year — A908

**2012, Nov. 9 *Perf. 14¼***

**3819** A908 60c multi 1.25 .95

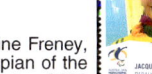

Musical Legends — A909

Designs: Nos. 3820, 3830, AC/DC (rock band). Nos. 3821, 3831, Cold Chisel (rock band). Nos. 3822, 3832, INXS (rock band). Nos. 3823, 3833, John Farnham (singer). Nos. 3824, 3834, Kylie Minogue (singer). Nos. 3825, 3835, Men At Work (rock band). Nos. 3826, 3836, Ian "Molly" Meldrum (record producer). Nos. 3827, 3837, Olivia Newton-John (singer). No. 3828, 3838, Paul Kelly (singer). Nos. 3829, 3839, The Seekers (rock band).

**2013, Jan. 18 *Perf. 14¾x14***

**3820** A909 60c multi 1.25 1.25
*a.* Booklet pane of 4 5.25 —
**3821** A909 60c multi 1.25 1.25
*a.* Booklet pane of 4 5.25 —
*b.* Horiz. pair, #3820-3821 2.50 2.50
**3822** A909 60c multi 1.25 1.25
*a.* Booklet pane of 4 5.25 —
**3823** A909 60c multi 1.25 1.25
*a.* Booklet pane of 4 5.25 —
**3824** A909 60c multi 1.25 1.25
*a.* Booklet pane of 4 5.25 —
**3825** A909 60c multi 1.25 1.25
*a.* Booklet pane of 4 5.25 —
**3826** A909 60c multi 1.25 1.25
*a.* Booklet pane of 4 5.25 —
*b.* Horiz. pair, #3824, 3826 2.50 2.50
**3827** A909 60c multi 1.25 1.25
*a.* Booklet pane of 4 5.25 —
*b.* Horiz. pair, #3823, 3827 2.50 2.50
**3828** A909 60c multi 1.25 1.25
*a.* Booklet pane of 4 5.25 —
*b.* Horiz. pair, #3822, 3828 2.50 2.50
**3829** A909 60c multi 1.25 1.25
*a.* Booklet pane of 4 5.25 —
*b.* Horiz. pair, #3825, 3829 2.50 2.50
Complete booklet, #3820a-3829a 52.50
*Nos. 3820-3829 (10)* 12.50 12.50

**Booklet Stamps**
**Self-Adhesive**

***Serpentine Die Cut 11¼ Syncopated***

**3830** A909 60c multi 1.25 .25
*a.* Booklet pane of 10 12.50
**3831** A909 60c multi 1.25 .25
*a.* Booklet pane of 10 12.50
**3832** A909 60c multi 1.25 .25
*a.* Booklet pane of 10 12.50
**3833** A909 60c multi 1.25 .25
*a.* Booklet pane of 10 12.50
**3834** A909 60c multi 1.25 .25
*a.* Booklet pane of 10 12.50
**3835** A909 60c multi 1.25 .25
*a.* Booklet pane of 10 12.50
**3836** A909 60c multi 1.25 .25
*a.* Booklet pane of 10 12.50
**3837** A909 60c multi 1.25 .25
*a.* Booklet pane of 10 12.50
**3838** A909 60c multi 1.25 .25
*a.* Booklet pane of 10 12.50
**3839** A909 60c multi 1.25 .25
*a.* Booklet pane of 10 12.50
*Nos. 3830-3839 (10)* 12.50 2.50

Complete booklet sold for $24.95.

Eucalyptus Leaves
A910

Map of Australia
A911

Rose Petal
A912

Orchid
A913

Gifts and Champagne Flutes — A914

**2013, Feb. 5 Litho. *Perf. 14¾x14***

**3840** A910 60c multi 1.25 1.25
**3841** A911 60c blue & multi 1.25 1.25
**3842** A911 60c org & multi 1.25 1.25
**3843** A912 60c multi 1.25 1.25
**3844** A913 60c multi 1.25 1.25
*a.* Horiz. strip of 5, #3840-3844 6.25 6.25
**3845** A914 $1.20 multi 2.50 2.50
*Nos. 3840-3845 (6)* 8.75 8.75

### Booklet Stamps
### Self-Adhesive

***Serpentine Die Cut 11¼ Syncopated***

**3846** A910 60c multi 1.25 .25
*a.* Booklet pane of 10 + 5 stickers 12.50
**3847** A911 60c blue & multi 1.25 .25
**3848** A911 60c org & multi 1.25 .25
*a.* Booklet pane of 10, 5 each #3847-3848, + 5 stickers 12.50
**3849** A912 60c multi 1.25 .25
*a.* Booklet pane of 10 + 5 stickers 12.50
**3850** A913 60c multi 1.25 .25
*a.* Booklet pane of 10 + 5 stickers 12.50
**3851** A914 $1.20 multi 2.50 1.25
*a.* Booklet pane of 10 + 5 stickers 25.00
*b.* Booklet pane of 4 10.50
Complete booklet, 5 #3851b 52.50
*Nos. 3846-3851 (6)* 8.75 2.50

Complete booklet sold for $24.95 and contains five examples of No. 3851b, each with a different image in pane margin.

### With Personalized Photo at Right Like Type A692a

***Serpentine Die Cut 11½x11¼ Syncopated***

**3852** A910 60c multi 2.60 2.60
**3853** A911 60c blue & multi 2.60 2.60
**3854** A911 60c org & multi 2.60 2.60
**3855** A912 60c multi 2.60 2.60
**3856** A913 60c multi 2.60 2.60
**3857** A914 $1.20 multi 3.75 3.75
*Nos. 3852-3857 (6)* 16.75 16.75

Nos, 3852-3857 each were printed in sheets of 20 and have personalized pictures and a straight edge at right and lack separations between the stamp and the personalized photo. Sheets of 20 of Nos. 3852-3856 sold for $25 each, No. 3857, $37.

Women and Surfboards A915

Surfer and Stylized Waves A916

Surfboards on Automobile Roof — A917

Surfer — A918

**2013, Feb. 12 Litho. *Perf. 14x14¾***

**3858** A915 60c multi 1.25 1.25
*a.* Booklet pane of 4 5.25 —
**3859** A916 60c multi 1.25 1.25
*a.* Booklet pane of 4 5.25 —
**3860** A917 60c multi 1.25 1.25
*a.* Booklet pane of 4 5.25 —
**3861** A918 60c multi 1.25 1.25
*a.* Booklet pane of 4 5.25 —
*b.* Booklet pane of 4, #3858-3861, #3859 in UL 5.25 —
Complete booklet, #3858a, 3859a, 3860a, 3861a, 3861b 26.50
*c.* Block of 4, #3851-3861 5.00 5.00
*d.* Souvenir sheet of 4, #3858-3861, #3858 in UL 5.00 5.00
*Nos. 3858-3861 (4)* 5.00 5.00

### Self-Adhesive

***Serpentine Die Cut 11¼ Syncopated***

**3862** A915 60c multi 1.25 .25
**3863** A916 60c multi 1.25 .25
**3864** A917 60c multi 1.25 .25
**3865** A918 60c multi 1.25 .25
*a.* Horiz. coil strip of 4, #3862-3865 5.00
*b.* Booklet pane of 10, 3 each #3862, 3865, 2 each #3863-3864 12.50
*Nos. 3862-3865 (4)* 5.00 1.00

Complete booklet sold for $12.95.

Dogs — A919

Designs: Nos. 3866, 3871, Miniature schnauzer. Nos. 3867, 3872, Miniature dachshund. Nos. 3868, 3873, Cavalier King Charles spaniel. Nos. 3869, 3874, Pug. Nos. 3870, 3875, Australian terrier.

**2013, Feb. 19 *Perf. 14¾x14***

**3866** A919 60c multi 1.25 1.25
**3867** A919 60c multi 1.25 1.25
**3868** A919 60c multi 1.25 1.25
**3869** A919 60c multi 1.25 1.25
**3870** A919 60c multi 1.25 1.25
*a.* Horiz. strip of 5, #3866-3870 6.25 6.25
*Nos. 3866-3870 (5)* 6.25 6.25

### Booklet Stamps
### Self-Adhesive

***Serpentine Die Cut 11¼ Syncopated***

**3871** A919 60c multi 1.25 .25
*a.* Booklet pane of 10 + 5 stickers 12.50
**3872** A919 60c multi 1.25 .25
*a.* Booklet pane of 10 + 5 stickers 12.50
**3873** A919 60c multi 1.25 .25
*a.* Booklet pane of 10 + 5 stickers 12.50
**3874** A919 60c multi 1.25 .25
*a.* Booklet pane of 10 + 5 stickers 12.50
**3875** A919 60c multi 1.25 .25
*a.* Booklet pane of 10 + 5 stickers 12.50
*Nos. 3871-3875 (5)* 6.25 1.25

Canberra, Cent. — A920

Map and: 60c, National Portrait Gallery. $2.35, Parliament House.

**2013, Mar. 5 *Perf. 14x14¾***

**3876** A920 60c multi 1.25 1.25
**3877** A920 $2.35 multi 4.75 2.40
*a.* Booklet pane of 4, 2 each #3876-3877 13.00 —
Complete booklet, #1940c, 2710c, 2869e, 3107c, 3349b, 3877a 27.50

### Self-Adhesive

***Serpentine Die Cut 11¼ Syncopated***

**3878** A920 60c multi 1.25 .25
*a.* Booklet pane of 20 25.00

Complete booklet sold for $12.95. No. 3878 was issued in coils and booklet panes.

Paintings in National Gallery of Australia — A921

Designs: Nos. 3879, 3884, Dandenong Ranges from 'Beleura,' by Eugene von Guérard. Nos. 3880, 3885, In the Flinders - Far North, by Hans Heysen. Nos. 3881, 3886, Land of the Golden Fleece, by Arthur Streetson. Nos. 3882, 3887, Mr. Robinson's House on the Derwent, Van Diemen's Land, by John Glover. Nos. 3883, 3888, Studley Park at Sunrise, by Nicholas Chevalier.

**2013, Mar. 19 *Perf. 14¾x14***

**3879** A921 60c multi 1.25 1.25
**3880** A921 60c multi 1.25 1.25
**3881** A921 60c multi 1.25 1.25
**3882** A921 60c multi 1.25 1.25
**3883** A921 60c multi 1.25 1.25
*a.* Horiz. strip of 5, #3879-3883 6.25 6.25
*Nos. 3879-3883 (5)* 6.25 6.25

### Booklet Stamps
### Self-Adhesive

***Serpentine Die Cut 11¼ Syncopated***

**3884** A921 60c multi 1.25 .25
**3885** A921 60c multi 1.25 .25
**3886** A921 60c multi 1.25 .25
**3887** A921 60c multi 1.25 .25
**3888** A921 60c multi 1.25 .25
*a.* Booklet pane of 10, 2 each #3884-3888 12.50
*Nos. 3884-3888 (5)* 6.25 1.25

Baby Animals — A922

Designs: $1.70, Kookaburra. $1.75, Wombat. $2.60, Echidna. $4.65, Platypus. $6.45, Possum.

**2013, Apr. 2 *Perf. 14¾x14***

**3889** A922 $1.70 multi 3.50 3.50
**3890** A922 $1.75 multi 3.75 3.75
**3891** A922 $2.60 multi 5.50 5.50
**3892** A922 $4.65 multi 9.75 7.50
**3893** A922 $6.45 multi 13.50 10.00
*Nos. 3889-3893 (5)* 36.00 30.25

### Booklet Stamps
### Self-Adhesive

***Serpentine Die Cut 11¼ Syncopated***

**3894** A922 $1.70 multi 3.50 1.75
*a.* Booklet pane of 5 17.50
**3895** A922 $1.75 multi 3.75 1.90
*a.* Booklet pane of 5 19.00
**3896** A922 $2.60 multi 5.50 2.75
*a.* Booklet pane of 5 27.50
*Nos. 3894-3896 (3)* 12.75 6.40

### With Personalized Photo at Right Like Type A692a

***Serpentine Die Cut 11½x11¼ Syncopated***

**3898** A922 $1.75 multi 5.00 5.00
**3899** A922 $2.60 multi 6.75 6.75

Nos, 3898-3899 each were printed in sheets of 20 and have personalized pictures and a straight edge at right and lack separations between the stamp and the personalized photo. Sheets of 20 of No. 3898 sold for $48, No. 3899, $65.

Coach — A923

Queen Elizabeth II — A924

**2013, Apr. 9 Litho. *Perf. 14¾x14***

**3900** A923 60c multi 1.25 .95
*a.* Booklet pane of 1 1.25 —
**3901** A924 $2.60 multi 5.50 5.50
*a.* Souvenir sheet of 2, #3900-3901 6.75 6.75
*b.* Booklet pane of 1 5.50 —
*c.* Booklet pane of 3 16.50 —
Complete booklet, #3901b, 2 each #3900a, 3901c, + 50c coin 41.00

Complete booklet sold for $19.95.

### Booklet Stamp
### Self-Adhesive

***Serpentine Die Cut 11¼ Syncopated***

**3902** A924 $2.60 multi 5.50 2.75
*a.* Booklet pane of 5 27.50

### Litho. & Embossed

***Perf. 14¾x14***

**3903** A923 60c multi 1.40 1.40

Coronation of Queen Elizabeth II, 60th anniv. Examples of No. 3901a with an overprint for the Australia 2013 World Stamp Expo were made given to the show organizers and sold only by them. No. 3903 was printed in sheets of 10 that sold for $6.45.

Botanical Gardens — A925

Designs: Nos. 3904, 3909, Royal Tasmanian Botanical Gardens, Hobart. Nos. 3905, 3910, Australian National Botanic Gardens, Canberra. Nos. 3906, 3911, Blue Mountains Botanic Garden, Mount Tomah, New South Wales. Nos. 3907, 3912, Darwin Botanic Gardens, Darwin, Northern Territory. No. 3908, 3913, Royal Botanic Gardens, Cranbourne, Victoria.

**2013, Apr. 23 Litho. *Perf. 14x14¾***

**3904** A925 60c multi 1.25 1.25
*a.* Booklet pane of 4 + 2 labels 5.50 —
**3905** A925 60c multi 1.25 1.25
*a.* Booklet pane of 4 + 2 labels 5.50 —
**3906** A925 60c multi 1.25 1.25
*a.* Booklet pane of 4 + 2 labels 5.50 —
**3907** A925 60c multi 1.25 1.25
*a.* Booklet pane of 4 + 2 labels 5.50 —
**3908** A925 60c multi 1.25 1.25
*a.* Booklet pane of 4 + 2 labels 5.50 —
Complete booklet, #3904a, 3905a, 3906a, 3907a, 3908a 27.50
*b.* Horiz. strip of 5, #3904-3908 6.25 6.25
*Nos. 3904-3908 (5)* 6.25 6.25

### Coil Stamps
### Self-Adhesive

***Serpentine Die Cut 11¼ Syncopated***

**3909** A925 60c multi 1.25 .25
**3910** A925 60c multi 1.25 .25
**3911** A925 60c multi 1.25 .25
**3912** A925 60c multi 1.25 .25
**3913** A925 60c multi 1.25 .25
*a.* Horiz. strip of 5, #3909-3913 6.25
*Nos. 3909-3913 (5)* 6.25 1.25

Complete booklet sold for $12.95. Examples of complete booklets with overprints for the Australia 2013 World Stamp Expo were made given to the show organizers and sold only by them.

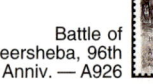

Battle of Beersheba, 96th Anniv. — A926

Designs: 60c, Statue of Australian Light Horseman, by Peter Corlett, Beersheva, Israel. $2.60, Australian Light Horsemen, photograph of battle re-enactment.

**2013, May 10 *Perf. 13x13½***

**3914** A926 60c multi 1.25 .95
**3915** A926 $2.60 multi 5.00 3.75

See Israel Nos. 1975-1976.

Black Caviar, Undefeated Racehorse — A927

**2013, May 10 *Perf. 14¾x14***

**3916** A927 60c multi 1.25 1.25

### Booklet Stamp
### Self-Adhesive

***Serpentine Die Cut 11¼ Syncopated***

**3917** A927 60c multi 1.25 .25
*a.* Booklet pane of 10 12.50

Stamps like No. 3916 but with a white frame were printed in limited-quantity sheets of 10 that were sold in special packages only at the Australia 2013 World Stamp Expo.

Stamps Depicting Kangaroos — A928

**2013, May 10 Litho. *Imperf.***

**3918** A928 $1.62 Booklet pane 3.50 —
Complete booklet, #1003b, 1284b, 3534d, 3918 25.00

No. 3918 contains imperforate examples of Nos. 992a, 1030c, 1063B and 2121, but these stamps were not valid for postage individually as cutouts from the entire booklet pane. Complete booklet sold for $12.95, and also contains a perforated booklet pane containing lithographed reproductions of Nos. 166 and 322 that is invalid for postage.

Kangaroo and Map Stamps, Cent. — A929

**2013, May 10 Litho. *Perf. 14¼x14***

**3919** A929 $10 red 19.00 9.50
*a.* Souvenir sheet of 1 19.00 9.50

A booklet containing an imperforate example of No. 3919 sold for $24.95.

First Commonwealth of Australia Banknotes, Cent. — A930

Designs: 60c, Scene from ceremony for numbering first banknote. $2.60, Arms of Australia.

**2013, May 11 Litho. *Perf. 14x13½***

**3920** A930 60c multi 1.25 .95
**3921** A930 $2.60 multi 5.00 3.75
*a.* Souvenir sheet of 2, #3920-3921 6.25 4.75

Examples of No. 3921a overprinted in the margin with the emblem of the 2013 Melbourne World Stamp Expo were sold by the exhibitions organizers for $15.

Pardalotes — A931

Designs: 60c, Forty-spotted pardalote. $1.20, Spotted pardalotes. $1.80, Red-browed pardalote. $3, Striated pardalote.

**2013, May 11 Litho. *Perf. 14x14¾***

**3922** A931 60c multi 1.25 1.25
**3923** A931 $1.20 multi 2.25 2.25
**3924** A931 $1.80 multi 3.50 2.60
**3925** A931 $3 multi 5.75 4.50
*a.* Booklet pane of 4, #3922-3925 13.00 —
Complete booklet, #3151c, 3070b, 3665b, 3925a 48.50
*Nos. 3922-3925 (4)* 12.75 10.60

**Coil Stamp**
**Self-Adhesive**
***Serpentine Die Cut 11¼ Syncopated***

**3926** A931 60c multi 1.25 .25

**Booklet Stamp**

**3927** A931 $1.20 multi 2.25 .50
*a.* Booklet pane of 5 11.50

Complete booklet sold for $24.95.

State Government Houses — A932

Government House of: Nos. 3928, 3932, South Australia. Nos. 3929, 3933, Western Australia. Nos. 3930, 3934, New South Wales. Nos. 3931, 3935, Tasmania.

**2013, June 11 Litho. *Perf. 14x14¾***

**3928** A932 60c multi 1.25 1.25
**3929** A932 60c multi 1.25 1.25
**3930** A932 60c multi 1.25 1.25
**3931** A932 60c multi 1.25 1.25
*a.* Block of 4, #3928-3931 5.00 5.00
*Nos. 3928-3931 (4)* 5.00 5.00

**Self-Adhesive**
***Serpentine Die Cut 11¼ Syncopated***

**3932** A932 60c multi 1.25 .25
**3933** A932 60c multi 1.25 .25
**3934** A932 60c multi 1.25 .25
**3935** A932 60c multi 1.25 .25
*a.* Horiz. coil strip of 4, #3932-3935 5.00
*b.* Booklet pane of 20, 5 each #3932-3935 25.00
*Nos. 3932-3935 (4)* 5.00 1.00

Road Trips — A933

Designs: Nos. 3936, 3942, Utility vehicle in Sydney. Nos. 3937, 3941, Station wagon in Melbourne. Nos, 3938, 3945, Car on roller coaster tracks, Gold Coast. Nos. 3939, 3943, Utility vehicle and camper in Adelalde. Nos. 3940, 3944, Car and camper in Canberra.

**2013, July 2 Litho. *Perf. 14¼***

**3936** A933 60c multi 1.10 1.10
**3937** A933 60c multi 1.10 1.10
**3938** A933 60c multi 1.10 1.10
**3939** A933 60c multi 1.10 1.10
**3940** A933 60c multi 1.10 1.10
*a.* Souvenir sheet of 5, #3936-3940 5.50 5.50
*Nos. 3936-3940 (5)* 5.50 5.50

**Booklet Stamps**
**Self-Adhesive**
***Serpentine Die Cut 11¼ Syncopated***

**3941** A933 60c multi 1.10 .25
**3942** A933 60c multi 1.10 .25
*a.* Booklet pane of 10, 5 each #3941-3942 11.00
**3943** A933 60c multi 1.10 .25
**3944** A933 60c multi 1.10 .25
**3945** A933 60c multi 1.10 .25
*a.* Booklet pane of 20, 7 each #3943, 3945, 6 #3944 22.00
*Nos. 3941-3945 (5)* 5.50 1.25

Aboriginal Leaders — A934

Designs: Nos. 3946, 3951, Shirley Smith (1921-98), justice and welfare advocate. Nos. 3947, 3952, Neville Bonner (1922-99), first Aboriginal member of Australian Parliament. Nos. 3948, 3953, Oodgeroo Noonuccal (1920-93), poet. Nos. 3949, 3954, Eddie "Koiki" Mabo (1936-92), plaintiff in historic Aboriginal land rights lawsuit. Nos. 3950, 3955, Charles Perkins (1936-2000), Secretary of the Department of Aboriginal Affairs.

**2013, July 9 Litho. *Perf. 14¾x14***

**3946** A934 60c multi 1.10 1.10
*a.* Booklet pane of 4 4.75 —
**3947** A934 60c multi 1.10 1.10
*a.* Booklet pane of 4 4.75 —
**3948** A934 60c multi 1.10 1.10
*a.* Booklet pane of 4 4.75 —
**3949** A934 60c multi 1.10 1.10
*a.* Booklet pane of 4 4.75 —
**3950** A934 60c multi 1.10 1.10
*a.* Booklet pane of 4 4.75 —
Complete booklet, #3946a, 3947a, 3948a, 3949a, 3950a 24.00
*b.* Horiz. strip of 5, #3946-3950 5.50 5.50
*Nos. 3946-3950 (5)* 5.50 5.50

**Coil Stamps**
**Self-Adhesive**
***Serpentine Die Cut 11¼ Syncopated***

**3951** A934 60c multi 1.10 .25
**3952** A934 60c multi 1.10 .25
**3953** A934 60c multi 1.10 .25
**3954** A934 60c multi 1.10 .25
**3955** A934 60c multi 1.10 .25
*a.* Vert. coil strip of 5, #3951-3955 5.50
*Nos. 3951-3955 (5)* 5.50 1.25

Complete booklet sold for $12.95.

Birth of Prince George of Cambridge — A935

**2013, July 22 Litho. *Perf. 14¼***

**3956** A935 60c multi 1.10 1.10

**Booklet Stamp**
**Self-Adhesive**
***Serpentine Die Cut 11¼ Syncopated***

**3957** A935 60c multi 1.10 .25
*a.* Booklet pane of 10 11.00

Headline News — A936

News stories of: Nos. 3958, 3962, August 15, 1945 (end of World War II). Nos. 3959, 3963, July 21, 1969 (first man on the Moon). Nos. 3960, 3964, December 25, 1974 (destruction of Darwin by Cyclone Tracy). Nos. 3961, 3965, September 27, 1983 (victory of Australia in America's Cup yacht races).

**2013, July 23 Litho. *Perf. 14¾x14***

**3958** A936 60c multi 1.10 1.10
**3959** A936 60c multi 1.10 1.10
**3960** A936 60c multi 1.10 1.10
**3961** A936 60c multi 1.10 1.10
*a.* Block of 4, #3958-3961 4.40 4.40
*b.* Souvenir sheet of 4, #3958-3961 4.40 4.40
*Nos. 3958-3961 (4)* 4.40 4.40

**Self-Adhesive**
***Serpentine Die Cut 11¼ Syncopated***

**3962** A936 60c multi 1.10 .25
**3963** A936 60c multi 1.10 .25
**3964** A936 60c multi 1.10 .25
**3965** A936 60c multi 1.10 .25
*a.* Vert. coil strip of 4, #3962-3965 4.40
*b.* Booklet pane of 20, 5 each #3962-3965 22.00
*Nos. 3962-3965 (4)* 4.40 1.00

Carnivorous Plants — A937

Designs: Nos. 3966, 3970, Cephalotus follicularis and ants. Nos. 3967, 3971, Drosera rupicola and fly. Nos. 3968, 3972, Drosera lowriei and butterfly. Nos. 3969, 3973, Nepenthes rowanae and frog.

**2013, Aug. 13 Litho. *Perf. 14¾x14***

**3966** A937 60c multi 1.10 1.10
**3967** A937 60c multi 1.10 1.10
**3968** A937 60c multi 1.10 1.10
**3969** A937 60c multi 1.10 1.10
*a.* Block of 4, #3966-3969 4.40 4.40
*Nos. 3966-3969 (4)* 4.40 4.40

**Booklet Stamps**
***Serpentine Die Cut 11¼ Syncopated***

**3970** A937 60c multi 1.10 .25
**3971** A937 60c multi 1.10 .25
**3972** A937 60c multi 1.10 .25
**3973** A937 60c multi 1.10 .25
*a.* Booklet pane of 10, 3 each #3970, 3972, 2 each #3971, 3973 11.00
*Nos. 3970-3973 (4)* 4.40 1.00

Coral Reefs A938

Designs: Nos. 3974, 3979, Underwater view of Ningaloo Reef, Western Australia. Nos. 3975, 3978, Underwater view of Great Barrier Reef, Queensland. Nos. 3976, 3981, Aerial veiw of Ningaloo Reef. Nos. 3977, 3980, Aerial view of Great Barrier Reef.

**2013, Aug. 20 Litho. *Perf. 14½x14***

**3974** A938 60c multi 1.10 1.10
*a.* Perf. 13½x14 1.10 1.10
**3975** A938 60c multi 1.10 1.10
*a.* Horiz. pair, #3974-3975 2.20 2.20
*b.* Perf. 13½x14 1.10 1.10
**3976** A938 $1.20 multi 2.25 2.25
*a.* Perf. 13½x14 2.25 2.25
**3977** A938 $1.20 multi 2.25 2.25
*a.* Horiz. pair, #3976-3977 4.50 4.50
*b.* Perf. 13½x14 2.25 2.25
*c.* Souvenir sheet of 4, #3974a, 3975b, 3976a, 3977b 6.75 6.75
*Nos. 3974-3977 (4)* 6.70 6.70

**Booklet Stamps**
**Self-Adhesive**
***Serpentine Die Cut 10½ Syncopated***

**3978** A938 60c multi 1.10 .25
**3979** A938 60c multi 1.10 .25
*a.* Booklet pane of 20, 10 each #3978-3979 22.00
**3980** A938 $1.20 multi 2.25 .50
**3981** A938 $1.20 multi 2.25 .50
*a.* Booklet pane of 5, 3 #3980, 2 #3981 11.50
*Nos. 3978-3981 (4)* 6.70 1.50

Poultry Breeds — A939

Designs: No. 3982, Australian Game hen and rooster. No. 3983, Australian Pit Game hen and chicks. Nos. 3984, 3985, Australorp hens (37x26mm).

**2013, Sept. 3 Litho. *Perf. 14x13½***

**3982** A939 60c multi 1.10 .85
*a.* Booklet pane of 4 4.75 —
**3983** A939 60c multi 1.10 .85
*a.* Booklet pane of 4 4.75 —
*b.* Booklet pane of 4, 2 each #3982-3983 4.75 —

***Perf. 14x14¾***

**3984** A939 60c multi 1.10 1.10
*a.* Booklet pane of 4 4.75 —
*b.* Souvenir sheet of 3, #3982-3984 3.30 3.30
Complete booklet, #3982a, 3983a, 3983b, 2 #3984a 24.00
*Nos. 3982-3984 (3)* 3.30 2.80

**Booklet Stamp**
**Self-Adhesive**
***Serpentine Die Cut 11¼ Syncopated***

**3985** A939 60c multi 1.10 .25
*a.* Booklet pane of 10 11.00

Complete booklet sold for $12.95 and contains two examples of No. 3984a having different margins.

Dinosaurs — A940

Designs: Nos. 3986, 3992, Koolasuchus. Nos. 3987, 3995, Serendipaceratops (20x37mm). No. 3988, Timimus (30x50mm). Nos. 3989, 3993, Diamantinasaurus, horiz. No. 3990, Qantassaurus, horiz. (50x30mm). Nos. 3991, 3994, Australovenator (26x37mm).

**2013, Sept. 24 Litho. *Perf. 14½x14***

**3986** A940 60c multi 1.25 1.25
*a.* Booklet pane of 4 5.00 —
*b.* Perf. 14½ 1.25 1.25

***Perf. 14¾x14***

**3987** A940 60c multi 1.25 1.25
*a.* Booklet pane of 4 5.00 —
*b.* Perf. 14½ 1.25 1.25

***Perf. 14x14½***

**3988** A940 60c multi 1.25 1.25
*a.* Perf. 14x13½ 1.25 1.25
*b.* Booklet pane of 2 #3988a 2.50 —
*c.* Perf. 14½ 1.25 1.25

***Perf. 14x14½***

**3989** A940 60c multi 1.25 1.25
*a.* Booklet pane of 4 5.00 —
*b.* Perf. 14½ 1.25 1.25

***Perf. 14½x14***

**3990** A940 60c multi 1.25 1.25
*a.* Perf. 13½x14 1.25 1.25
*b.* Booklet pane of 2 #3990a 2.50 —
*c.* Perf. 14½ 1.25 1.25

***Perf. 14¾x14***

**3991** A940 60c multi 1.25 1.25
*a.* Booklet pane of 4 5.00 —
Complete booklet, #3986a, 3987a, 3988b, 3989a, 3990b, 3991a 25.00
*b.* Perf. 14½ 1.25 1.25
*c.* Souvenir sheet of 6, #3986b, 3987b, 3988c, 3989b, 3990c, 3991b 7.50 7.50
*Nos. 3986-3991 (6)* 7.50 7.50

**Booklet Stamps**
**Self-Adhesive**
***Serpentine Die Cut 11¼***

**3992** A940 60c multi 1.25 .25
**3993** A940 60c multi 1.25 .25
*a.* Booklet pane of 10, 5 each #3992-3993 12.50

***Serpentine Die Cut 11¼ Syncopated***

**3994** A940 60c multi 1.25 .25
**3995** A940 60c multi 1.25 .25
*a.* Booklet pane of 20, 10 each #3994-3995 25.00
*Nos. 3992-3995 (4)* 5.00 1.00

Complete booklet sold for $12.95.

Historic Railroad Stations — A941

Station at: Nos. 3996, 4000, Maryborough, Victoria. Nos. 3997, 4001, Quorn, South Australia. Nos. 3998, 4002, Hay, New South Wales. Nos. 3999, 4003, Normanton, Queensland.

**2013, Oct. 8 Litho. *Perf. 14x14¾***

**3996** A941 60c multi 1.25 1.25
**3997** A941 60c multi 1.25 1.25
**3998** A941 60c multi 1.25 1.25
**3999** A941 60c multi 1.25 1.25
*a.* Block of 4, #3996-3999 5.00 5.00
*Nos. 3996-3999 (4)* 5.00 5.00

### Self-Adhesive

***Serpentine Die Cut 11¼ Syncopated***

**4000** A941 60c multi 1.25 .25
**4001** A941 60c multi 1.25 .25
**4002** A941 60c multi 1.25 .25
**4003** A941 60c multi 1.25 .25
*a.* Horiz. coil strip of 4, #4000-4003 5.00
*b.* Booklet pane of 10, 3 each #4000-4001, 2 each #4002-4003 12.50
*Nos. 4000-4003 (4)* 5.00 1.00

Ludwig Leichhardt (1813-48), Explorer of Outback Region — A942

**2013, Oct. 15 Litho.** ***Perf. 14¼***
**4004** A942 60c multi 1.25 .95

See Germany No. 2752.

Early Australian Coinage — A943

Designs: 60c, Holey dollar and dumps. $3, Holey dollars.

**2013, Oct. 22 Litho.** ***Perf. 14x14¾***
**4005** A943 60c multi 1.25 .95
**4006** A943 $3 multi 5.75 4.50

### Souvenir Sheet

### Litho. & Embossed With Foil Application

**4007** Sheet of 2 7.00 7.00
*a.* A943 60c multi 1.25 .95
*b.* A943 $3 multi 5.75 4.50

Christmas
A944 A945

Designs: Nos. 4008, 4014, Madonna and Child. Nos. 4009, 4015, 4019, Christmas tree. Nos. 4010, 4016, 4020, Gift. 60c, Candle. Nos. 4012, 4017, Bell. Nos. 4013, 4018, Adoration of the Shepherds.

**2013, Nov. 1 Litho.** ***Perf. 14¾x14***
**4008** A944 55c multi 1.10 1.10
**4009** A945 55c multi 1.10 1.10
**4010** A945 55c multi 1.10 1.10
*a.* Horiz. pair, #4009-4010 2.20 2.20
**4011** A945 60c multi 1.25 .95
**4012** A945 $1.70 multi 3.25 1.60
**4013** A944 $2.55 multi 4.75 2.40
*a.* Souvenir sheet of 2, #4008, 4013 6.00 6.00
*Nos. 4008-4013 (6)* 12.55 8.25

### Booklet Stamps Self-Adhesive

***Serpentine Die Cut 11¼ Syncopated***

**4014** A944 55c multi 1.10 .25
*a.* Booklet pane of 20 + 10 etiquettes 22.00
**4015** A945 55c multi 1.10 .25
**4016** A945 55c multi 1.10 .25
*a.* Booklet pane of 20, 10 each #4015-4016, + 10 etiquettes 22.00
**4017** A945 $1.70 multi 3.25 1.60
*a.* Booklet pane of 5 16.50
**4018** A944 $2.55 multi 4.75 2.40
*a.* Booklet pane of 5 24.00

### Litho. & Embossed With Foil Application

**4019** A945 55c multi 1.10 .25
*a.* Booklet pane of 10 11.00
**4020** A945 55c multi 1.10 .25
*a.* Booklet pane of 10 11.00
*Nos. 4014-4020 (7)* 13.50 5.25

Christening of Prince George of Cambridge — A946

Duke and Duchess of Cambridge with Prince George: 60c, White background. $2.60, Yellow background.

**2014, Jan. 7 Litho.** ***Perf. 14¾x14***
**4022** A946 60c multi 1.10 1.10
**4023** A946 $2.60 multi 4.75 4.75
*a.* Souvenir sheet of 2, #4022-4023 6.00 6.00

### Booklet Stamps Self-Adhesive

***Serpentine Die Cut 11¼ Syncopated***

**4024** A946 60c multi 1.10 .25
*a.* Booklet pane of 10 11.00
**4025** A946 $2.60 multi 4.75 2.40
*a.* Booklet pane of 5 24.00

Orchids — A947

Designs: Nos. 4026, 4030, Golden rock orchid. Nos. 4027, 4031, Bee orchid. Nos. 4028, 4032, Orange blossom orchid. Nos. 4029, 4033, Shirt orchid.

**2014, Jan. 14 Litho.** ***Perf. 14¾x14***
**4026** A947 60c multi 1.10 1.10
**4027** A947 60c multi 1.10 1.10
**4028** A947 60c multi 1.10 1.10
**4029** A947 60c multi 1.10 1.10
*a.* Horiz. strip of 4, #4026-4029 4.40 4.40
*Nos. 4026-4029 (4)* 4.40 4.40

### Booklet Stamps Self-Adhesive

***Serpentine Die Cut 11¼ Syncopated***

**4030** A947 60c multi 1.10 .25
**4031** A947 60c multi 1.10 .25
**4032** A947 60c multi 1.10 .25
**4033** A947 60c multi 1.10 .25
*a.* Booklet pane of 10, 2 each #4030, 4032, 3 each #4031, 4033 11.00
*b.* Booklet pane of 20, 5 each #4030-4033 22.00
*Nos. 4030-4033 (4)* 4.40 1.00

Cooking Celebrities — A948

Designs: Nos. 4034, 4039, Margaret Fulton. Nos. 4035, 4040, Maggie Beer. Nos. 4036, 4041, Stephanie Alexander. Nos. 4037, 4042, Neil Perry. Nos. 4038, 4043, Kylie Kwong.

**2014, Jan. 17 Litho.** ***Perf. 14¾x14***
**4034** A948 60c multi 1.10 1.10
*a.* Booklet pane of 4 5.25 —
**4035** A948 60c multi 1.10 1.10
*a.* Booklet pane of 4 5.25 —
**4036** A948 60c multi 1.10 1.10
*a.* Booklet pane of 4 5.25 —
**4037** A948 60c multi 1.10 1.10
*a.* Booklet pane of 4 5.25 —
**4038** A948 60c multi 1.10 1.10
*a.* Booklet pane of 4 5.25 —
Complete booklet, #4034a, 4035a, 4036a, 4037a, 4038a 22.00
*Nos. 4034-4038 (5)* 5.50 5.50

### Booklet Stamps Self-Adhesive

***Serpentine Die Cut 11¼ Syncopated***

**4039** A948 60c multi 1.10 .25
*a.* Booklet pane of 10 11.00
**4040** A948 60c multi 1.10 .25
*a.* Booklet pane of 10 11.00
**4041** A948 60c multi 1.10 .25
*a.* Booklet pane of 10 11.00
**4042** A948 60c multi 1.10 .25
*a.* Booklet pane of 10 11.00
**4043** A948 60c multi 1.10 .25
*a.* Booklet pane of 10 11.00
*Nos. 4039-4043 (5)* 5.50 1.25

Complete booklet sold for $14.95.

Victory of Australian Cricket Team in 2013-14 Ashes Test Matches A949

Designs: 60c, Ashes urn. $2.60, Australian cricket team.

**2014, Jan. 20 Litho.** ***Perf. 14¾x14***
**4044** A949 60c multi 1.10 .85
**4045** A949 $2.60 multi 4.75 4.75
*a.* Souvenir sheet of 2, #4044-4045 6.00 6.00

### Booklet Stamp Self-Adhesive

***Serpentine Die Cut 11½x11¼***

**4046** A949 $2.60 multi 4.75 2.40
*a.* Booklet pane of 5 24.00

Hearts A950 Rose A951

**2014, Feb. 4 Litho.** ***Perf. 14¾x14***
**4047** A950 60c multi 1.10 1.10
**4048** A951 60c multi 1.10 1.10
*a.* Pair, #4047-4048 2.20 2.20

### Booklet Stamps Self-Adhesive

***Serpentine Die Cut 11¼ Syncopated***

**4049** A950 60c multi 1.10 .25
*a.* Booklet pane of 10 11.00
**4050** A951 60c multi 1.10 .25
*a.* Booklet pane of 20 22.00

### With Personalized Photo at Right Like Type A692a

***Serpentine Die Cut 11½x11¼ Syncopated***

**4051** A950 60c multi 2.25 2.25
**4052** A951 60c multi 2.25 2.25

Nos, 4051-4052 each were printed in sheets of 20 and have personalized pictures and a straight edge at right and lack separations between the stamp and the personalized photo. Sheets of 20 of each stamp sold for $25.

National and State Floral Emblems — A952

Designs: Nos. 4053, 4060, 4064, Tasmanian blue gum (Tasmania). Nos. 4054, 4061, 4065, Waratah (New South Wales). Nos. 4055, 4062, 4066, Golden wattle (Australia). Nos. 4056, 4063, 4067, Common heath (Victoria). $1.40, Cooktown orchid (Queensland). $2.10, Kangaroo paw (Western Australia). $3.50, Sturt's desert pea (South Australia).

**2014, Mar. 24 Litho.** ***Perf. 14½x14***
**4053** A952 70c multi 1.40 1.40
**4054** A952 70c multi 1.40 1.40
**4055** A952 70c multi 1.40 1.40
**4056** A952 70c multi 1.40 1.40
*a.* Horiz. strip of 4, #4053-4056 5.60 5.60
**4057** A952 $1.40 multi 2.60 1.40
**4058** A952 $2.10 multi 4.00 2.00
**4059** A952 $3.50 multi 6.50 3.25
*Nos. 4053-4059 (7)* 18.70 12.25

### Coil Stamp Self-Adhesive

***Serpentine Die Cut 12¾***

**4060** A952 70c multi 1.40 .25
**4061** A952 70c multi 1.40 .25
**4062** A952 70c multi 1.40 .25
**4063** A952 70c multi 1.40 .25
*a.* Vert. strip of 4, #4060-4063 5.60

### Booklet Stamps

***Serpentine Die Cut 11¼***

**4064** A952 70c multi 1.40 .25
**4065** A952 70c multi 1.40 .25
**4066** A952 70c multi 1.40 .25
**4067** A952 70c multi 1.40 .25
*a.* Booklet pane of 10, 3 each #4064-4065, 2 each #4066-4067 14.00
*b.* Booklet pane of 20, 5 each #4064-4067 28.00
*Nos. 4060-4067 (8)* 11.20 2.00

Map of Australia on Beach A953

Kangaroo A954

***Serpentine Die Cut 11¼ Syncopated***
**2014, Mar. 24 Litho.**

### Booklet Stamps Self-Adhesive

**4068** A953 (70c) multi 1.40 .25
**4069** A954 (70c) multi 1.40 .25
*a.* Booklet pane of 5, 2#4068, 3 #4069 7.25

No. 4069a was made available to holders of Australia Post My Post Concession Account card and the general public. Pensioners, veterans, the disabled, and others typically on low or fixed incomes, could apply at their local post office to receive a Concession Account card. Those eligible to receive the card were sent a free example of No. 4069a, which was mailed with the card. Card holders, when showing the card at the post office and having the information recorded, could purchase up to ten No. 4069a every year for $3 (60c per stamp, lower than the 70c letter rate instituted on March 31). 10,000 examples of No. 4069a were made available to others through the philatelic bureau, but these were sold for $3.95 (79c per stamp). There are no differences between the stamps offered to card holders and the general public, aside from the selling price. Nos. 4068 and 4069 were valid only on letters, and could not be used on parcels or international mail.

Queen Elizabeth II, 88th Birthday — A955

Queen Elizabeth II facing: 70c, Left. $2.60, Right.

**2014, Apr. 8 Litho.** ***Perf. 14¾x14***
**4070** A955 70c multi 1.40 1.10
**4071** A955 $2.60 multi 5.00 2.50
*a.* Souvenir sheet of 2, #4070-4071 6.50 3.75

### Booklet Stamp Self-Adhesive

***Serpentine Die Cut 11¼ Syncopated***

**4072** A955 $2.60 multi 5.00 2.50
*a.* Booklet pane of 5 25.00

Map of Australia A956

Balloons and Streamers A957

Baby's Mobile A958

Fireworks A959

Rose A960

Stylized Flowers A961

Champagne Flutes A962

Wedding Rings and Roses A963

Wedding Rings — A964

**2014, Apr. 15 Litho. *Perf. 14¾x14***

**4073** A956 70c blue & multi 1.40 .70
**4074** A956 70c red & multi 1.40 .70
*a.* Horiz. pair, #4073-4074 2.80 1.40
**4075** A957 70c multi 1.40 1.40
**4076** A958 70c multi 1.40 1.40
**4077** A959 70c multi 1.40 1.40
**4078** A960 70c multi 1.40 1.40
**4079** A961 70c multi 1.40 1.40
**4080** A962 70c multi 1.40 1.40
**4081** A963 70c multi 1.40 1.40
**4082** A964 $1.40 multi 2.60 1.40
*Nos. 4073-4082 (10)* 15.20 12.60

**Booklet Stamps**
**Self-Adhesive**
***Serpentine Die Cut 11¼ Syncopated***

**4083** A957 70c multi 1.40 .25
*a.* Booklet pane of 10 14.00
**4084** A958 70c multi 1.40 .25
*a.* Booklet pane of 10 14.00
**4085** A959 70c multi 1.40 .25
*a.* Booklet pane of 10 14.00
**4086** A960 70c multi 1.40 .25
*a.* Booklet pane of 10 14.00
**4087** A961 70c multi 1.40 .25
*a.* Booklet pane of 10 14.00
**4088** A962 70c multi 1.40 .25
*a.* Booklet pane of 10 14.00
**4089** A963 70c multi 1.40 .25
*a.* Booklet pane of 10 14.00
**4090** A964 $1.40 multi 2.60 1.40
*a.* Booklet pane of 4 10.50
Complete booklet, 5 #4090a 52.50
*Nos. 4083-4090 (8)* 12.40 3.15

Complete booklet contains 5 examples of No. 4090a, each with different pane margins.

**With Personalized Photo at Right Like Type A692a**
***Serpentine Die Cut 11½x11¼ Syncopated***

**4091** A956 70c blue & multi 2.50 2.50
**4092** A957 70c multi 2.50 2.50
**4093** A958 70c multi 2.50 2.50
**4094** A959 70c multi 2.50 2.50
**4095** A960 70c multi 2.50 2.50
**4096** A961 70c multi 2.50 2.50
**4097** A962 70c multi 2.50 2.50
**4098** A963 70c multi 2.50 2.50
**4099** A964 $1.40 multi 3.75 3.75
*Nos. 4091-4099 (9)* 23.75 23.75

Nos. 4091-4099 each were printed in sheets of 20 and have personalized pictures and a straight edge at right and lack separations between the stamp and the personalized photo. Sheets of 20 of Nos. 4091-4098 sold for $27 each, No. 4099, $41.

World War I, Cent. — A965

Inscriptions: Nos. 4100, 4105, War Declared! Nos. 4101, 4106, Australians in Action. Nos. 4102, 4107, Troops Depart. Nos. 4103, 4108, Training, Mena Camp (Egypt). Nos. 4104, 4109, Our Boys.

**2014, Apr. 22 Litho. *Perf. 14¼***

**4100** A965 70c multi 1.40 1.40
**4101** A965 70c multi 1.40 1.40
**4102** A965 70c multi 1.40 1.40
**4103** A965 70c multi 1.40 1.40
**4104** A965 70c multi 1.40 1.40
*a.* Souvenir sheet of 5, #4100-4104 7.00 7.00
*Nos. 4100-4104 (5)* 7.00 7.00

**Booklet Stamps**
**Self-Adhesive**
***Serpentine Die Cut 11¼ Syncopated***

**4105** A965 70c multi 1.40 .25
**4106** A965 70c multi 1.40 .25
**4107** A965 70c multi 1.40 .25
**4108** A965 70c multi 1.40 .25
**4109** A965 70c multi 1.40 .25
*a.* Booklet pane of 10, 2 each #4105-4109 14.00
*Nos. 4105-4109 (5)* 7.00 1.25

Australian Red Cross, Cent. — A966

**2014, May 6 Litho. *Perf. 14x14¾***

**4110** A966 70c multi 1.40 1.40

**Coil Stamp**
**Self-Adhesive**
***Serpentine Die Cut 11¼ Syncopated***

**4111** A966 70c multi 1.40 .25

Poems by Andrew Barton "Banjo" Paterson (1864-1941) A967

Designs: Nos. 4112, 4116, Clancy of the Overflow. Nos. 4113, 4117, The Man from Snowy River. Nos. 4114, 4118, Waltzing Matilda. Nos. 4115, 4119, Mulga Bill's Bicycle.

**2014, May 13 Litho. *Perf. 14x14¾***

**4112** A967 70c multi 1.40 1.40
*a.* Booklet pane of 4 5.60 —
**4113** A967 70c multi 1.40 1.40
*a.* Booklet pane of 4 5.60 —
**4114** A967 70c multi 1.40 1.40
*a.* Booklet pane of 4 5.60 —
**4115** A967 70c multi 1.40 1.40
*a.* Block of 4, #4112-4115 5.60 5.60
*b.* Souvenir sheet of 4, #4112-4115 5.60 5.60
*c.* Booklet pane of 4 #4115 5.60 —
*d.* Booklet pane of 4, #4112-4115 5.60 —
Complete booklet, #4112a, 4113a, 4114a, 4115c, 2 #4115d 34.00
*Nos. 4112-4115 (4)* 5.60 5.60

**Self-Adhesive**
***Serpentine Die Cut 11¼ Syncopated***

**4116** A967 70c multi 1.40 .25
**4117** A967 70c multi 1.40 .25
**4118** A967 70c multi 1.40 .25
**4119** A967 70c multi 1.40 .25
*a.* Horiz. coil strip of 4, #4116-4119 5.60
*b.* Booklet pane of 10, 3 each #4116-4117, 2 each #4118-4119 14.00
*Nos. 4116-4119 (4)* 5.60 1.00

The complete booklet sold for $16.95. In the complete booklet, one of the two examples of No. 4115d has a booklet pane margin similar to No. 4115b.

G20 Summit, Brisbane — A968

**2014, June 3 Litho. *Perf. 14¾x14***

**4120** A968 70c multi 1.40 1.10

King George V Typographed Stamps, Cent. — A969

**2014, June 17 Litho. *Perf. 14½x14***

**4121** A969 70c red 1.40 1.10
*a.* Booklet pane of 4 5.60 —
**4122** A969 70c red brown 1.40 1.10
*a.* Booklet pane of 4 5.60 —
**4123** A969 70c purple 1.40 1.10
*a.* Booklet pane of 4 5.60 —
**4124** A969 70c green 1.40 1.10
*a.* Booklet pane of 4 5.60 —
*b.* Booklet pane of 4, #4121-4124 5.60 —
*c.* Booklet pane of 4, #4121-4124, imperf. 5.60 —
Complete booklet, #4121a, 4122a, 4123a, 4124a, 4124b, 4124c 34.00
*d.* Block or strip of 4, #4121-4124 5.60 4.40
*e.* Souvenir sheet of 4, #4121-4124 5.60 4.40
*f.* Sheet of 10, 4 #4121, 2 each #4122-4124 14.00 11.00

**Typo.**

**4125** A969 70c red 1.40 1.10
**4126** A969 70c purple 1.40 1.10
**4127** A969 70c green 1.40 1.10
**4128** A969 70c red brown 1.40 1.10
*a.* Horiz. strip of 4, #4125-4128 5.60 4.40
*b.* Sheet of 10, 4 #4125, 2 each #4126-4128 14.00 11.00
*Nos. 4121-4128 (8)* 11.20 8.80

Complete booklet sold for $16.95. Nos. 4124f and 4128b were sold together for $14.45.

First Air Mail in Australia, Cent. — A970

Designs: 70c, Spectators watching airplane in flight. $2.60, Maurice Guillaux piloting Bleriot XI airplane.

**2014, July 1 Litho. *Perf. 14¼***

**4129** A970 70c multi 1.40 1.10
*a.* Booklet pane of 4 5.75 —
**4130** A970 $2.60 multi 5.00 2.50
*a.* Booklet pane of 4 20.50 —
*b.* Booklet pane of 2, #4129-4130 6.50 —
Complete booklet, #4130a, 4130b, 2 #4129a 38.50
*c.* Souvenir sheet of 2, #4129-4130 6.50 —

Complete booklet sold for $19.95. The two examples of No. 4129a in the booklet have different pane margins.

Visit of Duke and Duchess of Cambridge and Prince George — A971

Designs: 70c, Duke and Duchess, Sydney Harbour Bridge. $2.60, Duke and Duchess, Prince George, and bilby.

**2014, July 8 Litho. *Perf. 14¼***

**4131** A971 70c multi 1.40 1.40
**4132** A971 $2.60 multi 5.00 5.00
*a.* Souvenir sheet of 2, #4131-4132 6.50 6.50

**Booklet Stamps**
**Self-Adhesive**
***Serpentine Die Cut 11¼ Syncopated***

**4133** A971 70c multi 1.40 .25
*a.* Booklet pane of 10 14.00
**4134** A971 $2.60 multi 5.00 2.50
*a.* Booklet pane of 5 25.00

Equestrian Events — A972

Designs: Nos. 4135, 4140, Pony Club. Nos. 4136, 4141, Polocrosse. Nos. 4137, 4142, Show jumping. Nos. 4138, 4143, Cross-country. Nos. 4139, 4144, Dressage.

**2014, July 15 Litho. *Perf. 14¾x14***

**4135** A972 70c multi 1.40 1.40
**4136** A972 70c multi 1.40 1.40
**4137** A972 70c multi 1.40 1.40
**4138** A972 70c multi 1.40 1.40
**4139** A972 70c multi 1.40 1.40
*Nos. 4135-4139 (5)* 7.00 7.00

**Self-Adhesive**
***Serpentine Die Cut 11¼ Syncopated***

**4140** A972 70c multi 1.40 .25
*a.* Booklet pane of 10 14.00
**4141** A972 70c multi 1.40 .25
*a.* Booklet pane of 10 14.00
**4142** A972 70c multi 1.40 .25
*a.* Booklet pane of 10 14.00
**4143** A972 70c multi 1.40 .25
*a.* Booklet pane of 10 14.00
**4144** A972 70c multi 1.40 .25
*a.* Booklet pane of 10 14.00
*b.* Vert. coil strip of 5, #4140-4144 7.00
*Nos. 4140-4144 (5)* 7.00 1.25

Norfolk Island Pine — A973

Norfolk Island Pine and: 70c, Cottesloe Beach, Western Australia. $1.40, Old Military Barracks, Kingston, Norfolk Island.

**2014, July 22 Litho. *Perf. 14x14¾***

**4145** A973 70c multi 1.40 1.10
**4146** A973 $1.40 multi 2.60 2.00

See Norfolk Island Nos. 1090-1091.

Australian Military Centenaries A974

Designs: Nos. 4147, 4149, Military aviation, cent. Nos. 4148, 4150, Submarines, cent.

**2014, Aug. 5 Litho. *Perf. 14x14¾***

**4147** A974 70c multi 1.40 1.40
**4148** A974 70c multi 1.40 1.40
*a.* Vert. pair, #4147-4148 2.80 2.80
*b.* Souvenir sheet of 2, #4147-4148 2.80 2.80

**Booklet Stamps**
**Self-Adhesive**
***Serpentine Die Cut 11¼ Syncopated***

**4149** A974 70c multi 1.40 .25
**4150** A974 70c multi 1.40 .25
*a.* Booklet pane of 20, 10 each #4149-4150 28.00

Mid-20th Century Advertisements — A975

Advertisement for: Nos. 4151, 4156, Phillip Island Tourism. Nos. 4152, 4157, Harper's Empire Self-Raising Flour. Nos. 4153, 4158, Trans-Australian Airways. Nos. 4154, 4159, Jacko Shoe Polish. Nos. 4155, 4160, Swallow & Ariell's Teddy Bear Biscuits.

**2014, Aug. 19 Litho. *Perf. 14¾x14***

**4151** A975 70c multi 1.40 1.40
**4152** A975 70c multi 1.40 1.40
**4153** A975 70c multi 1.40 1.40
**4154** A975 70c multi 1.40 1.40
**4155** A975 70c multi 1.40 1.40
*a.* Horiz. strip of 5, #4151-4155 7.00 7.00
*b.* Souvenir sheet of 5, #4151-4155 7.00 7.00
*Nos. 4151-4155 (5)* 7.00 7.00

**Coil Stamps**
**Self-Adhesive**
***Serpentine Die Cut 11¼ Syncopated***

**4156** A975 70c multi 1.40 .25
**4157** A975 70c multi 1.40 .25
**4158** A975 70c multi 1.40 .25
**4159** A975 70c multi 1.40 .25
**4160** A975 70c multi 1.40 .25
*a.* Vert. strip of 5, #4156-4160 7.00
*Nos. 4156-4160 (5)* 7.00 1.25

Aurora Australis (Southern Lights) — A976

Various photographs of auroras with denomination at: Nos. 4161, 4163, 4165, LL. Nos. 4162, 4164, 4166, LR.

**2014, Aug. 26 Litho. *Perf. 14x14¾***

**4161** A976 70c multi 1.40 1.40
**4162** A976 70c multi 1.40 1.40
*a.* Horiz. pair, #4161-4162 2.80 2.80
**4163** A976 $1.40 multi 2.60 2.00
**4164** A976 $1.40 multi 2.60 2.00
*a.* Horiz. pair, #4163-4164 5.20 4.00
*b.* Souvenir sheet of 4, #4161-4164 8.00 8.00
*Nos. 4161-4164 (4)* 8.00 6.80

**Booklet Stamps**
**Self-Adhesive**

**4165** A976 70c multi 1.40 .25
**4166** A976 70c multi 1.40 .25
*a.* Booklet pane of 10, 5 each #4165-4166 14.00

On No. 4164b, Nos. 4162a and 4164a are tete-beche in relationship to each other.

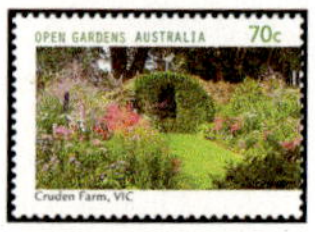


Gardens — A977

Designs: Nos. 4167, 4172, Cruden Farm, Victoria. Nos. 4168, 4173, Mendel Gardens, Western Australia. Nos. 4169, 4176, Niwajiri, South Australia. Nos. 4170, 4174, Walcott Gardens, Australian Capital Territory. Nos. 4171, 4175, Wychwood, Tasmania.

**2014, Sept. 2 Litho.** ***Perf. 14x14¾***

**4167** A977 70c multi 1.40 1.40
**4168** A977 70c multi 1.40 1.40
**4169** A977 70c multi 1.40 1.40
**4170** A977 70c multi 1.40 1.40
**4171** A977 70c multi 1.40 1.40
*a.* Horiz. strip of 5, #4167-4171 7.00 7.00
*Nos. 4167-4171 (5)* 7.00 7.00

**Booklet Stamps**
**Self-Adhesive**

***Serpentine Die Cut 11¼ Syncopated***

**4172** A977 70c multi 1.40 .25
**4173** A977 70c multi 1.40 .25
**4174** A977 70c multi 1.40 .25
**4175** A977 70c multi 1.40 .25
**4176** A977 70c multi 1.40 .25
*a.* Booklet pane of 20, 4 each #4172-4176 28.00
*Nos. 4172-4176 (5)* 7.00 1.25

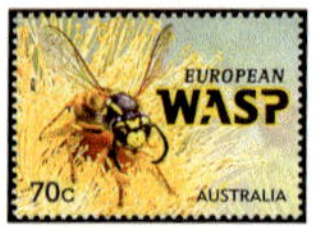


Venomous Creatures — A978

Designs: Nos. 4177, 4186, European wasp. Nos. 4178, 4185, Lionfish. Nos. 4179, 4183, Bull ant. Nos. 4180, 4187, Tiger snake. Nos. 4181, 4188, Stonefish. Nos. 4182, 4184, Stingray.

**2014, Sept. 23 Litho.** ***Perf. 14x14¾***

**4177** A978 70c multi 1.25 1.25
**4178** A978 70c multi 1.25 1.25
**4179** A978 70c multi 1.25 1.25
**4180** A978 70c multi 1.25 1.25
*a.* Souvenir sheet of 6, 2 each #4177, 4179, 4180, + 6 labels 7.75 7.75
**4181** A978 70c multi 1.25 1.25
**4182** A978 70c multi 1.25 1.25
*a.* Souvenir sheet of 6, #4177-4182 7.50 7.50
*b.* Souvenir sheet of 6, 2 each #4176, 4181, 4182, + 6 labels 7.75 7.75
*Nos. 4177-4182 (6)* 7.50 7.50

**Booklet Stamps**
**Self-Adhesive**

***Serpentine Die Cut 11¼ Syncopated***

**4183** A978 70c multi 1.25 .25
**4184** A978 70c multi 1.25 .25
**4185** A978 70c multi 1.25 .25
**4186** A978 70c multi 1.25 .25
**4187** A978 70c multi 1.25 .25
**4188** A978 70c multi 1.25 .25
*a.* Booklet pane of 10, #4185, 4188, 2 each #4183-4184, 4186-4187 12.50
*b.* Booklet pane of 20, 3 each #4183, 4185, 4187, 4188, 4 each #4184, 4186 25.00
*Nos. 4183-4188 (6)* 7.50 1.50

A souvenir sheet of six containing one each of Nos. 4177-4182 + six labels was sold with a die and game pieces that sold for $9.95. Nos. 4180a and 4182b sold together as a set in a folder for $8.85.

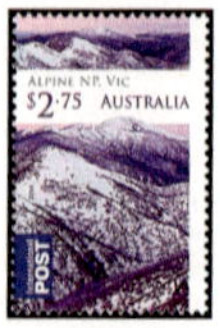


National Parks — A979

Designs: $2.75, Alpine National Park, Victoria. $5.35, Blue Mountains National Park, New South Wales. $7.40, Judbarra/Gregroy National Park, Northern Territory.

**2014, Oct. 1 Litho.** ***Perf. 14¾x14***

**4189** A979 $2.75 multi 5.00 2.50
**4190** A979 $5.35 multi 9.50 4.75
**4191** A979 $7.40 multi 13.00 6.50
*Nos. 4189-4191 (3)* 27.50 13.75

**Booklet Stamp**
**Self-Adhesive**

***Serpentine Die Cut 11¼ Syncopated***

**4192** A979 $2.75 multi 5.00 2.50
*a.* Booklet pane of 5 25.00

**National Parks Type of 2014 With Personalized Photo at Right Like Type A692a**

***Serpentine Die Cut 11½x11¼ Syncopated***

**2014, Oct. 1 Litho.**

**Self-Adhesive**

**4193** A979 $2.75 multi 6.00 6.00

No. 4193 was printed in sheets of 20 and has personalized picture and a straight edge at right and lack separations between the stamp and personalized photo. Sheets of 20 of No. 4193 sold for $68.

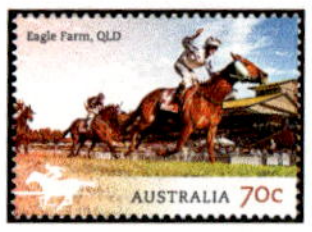


Horse Racing Tracks — A980

Designs: Nos. 4194, 4198, Eagle Farm, Queensland. Nos. 4195, 4199, Royal Randwick, New South Wales. Nos. 4196, 4200, Morphettville, South Australia. Nos. 4197, 4201, Flemington, Victoria.

**2014, Oct. 7 Litho.** ***Perf. 14x14¾***

**4194** A980 70c multi 1.25 1.25
**4195** A980 70c multi 1.25 1.25
**4196** A980 70c multi 1.25 1.25
**4197** A980 70c multi 1.25 1.25
*a.* Horiz. strip of 4, #4194-4197 5.00 5.00
*Nos. 4194-4197 (4)* 5.00 5.00

**Self-Adhesive**

***Serpentine Die Cut 11¼ Syncopated***

**4198** A980 70c multi 1.25 .25
**4199** A980 70c multi 1.25 .25
**4200** A980 70c multi 1.25 .25
**4201** A980 70c multi 1.25 .25
*a.* Horiz. coil strip of 4, #4198-4201 5.00
*b.* Booklet pane of 10, 3 each #4198-4199, 2 each #4200-4201 12.50
*Nos. 4198-4201 (4)* 5.00 1.00

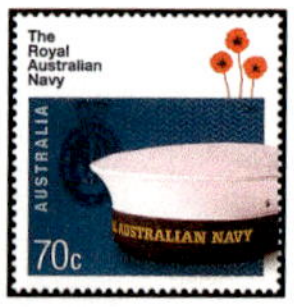


Australian Defense Force, Cent. — A981

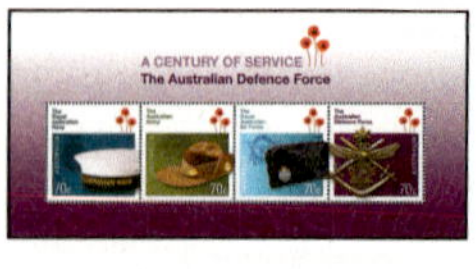


Poppies and: Nos. 4202, 4206, Cap of Royal Australian Navy. Nos. 4203, 4209, Hat of Australian Army. Nos. 4204, 4207, Cap of Royal Australian Air Force. Nos. 4205, 4208, Australian Defense Force badge.

**2014, Oct. 21 Litho.** ***Perf. 14¼***

**4202** A981 70c multi 1.25 1.25
**4203** A981 70c multi 1.25 1.25
**4204** A981 70c multi 1.25 1.25
**4205** A981 70c multi 1.25 1.25
*a.* Souvenir sheet of 4, #4202-4205 5.00 5.00
*Nos. 4202-4205 (4)* 5.00 5.00

**Booklet Stamps**
**Self-Adhesive**

***Serpentine Die Cut 11¼ Syncopated***

**4206** A981 70c multi 1.25 .25
**4207** A981 70c multi 1.25 .25
**4208** A981 70c multi 1.25 .25
**4209** A981 70c multi 1.25 .25
*a.* Booklet pane of 10, 2 each #4206, 4207, 4209, 4 #4208 12.50

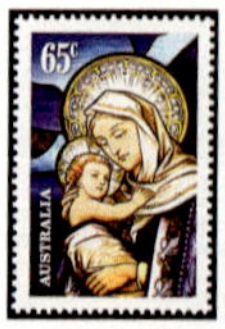


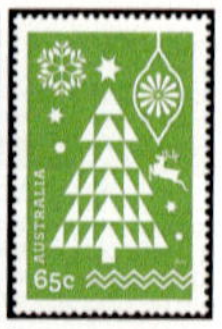


Christmas
A982 A983

Designs: Nos. 4210, 4216, Madonna and Child. Nos. 4211, 4217, 4221, Snowflake, ornament, Christmas tree, reindeer. Nos. 4212, 4218, 4222, Star, ornament, gift. 70c, Snowflake, ornament, holly leaves, dove, star. Nos. 4214, 4219, Snowflake and bells. Nos. 4215, 4220, Angels.

**2014, Oct. 31 Litho.** ***Perf. 14¾x14***

**4210** A982 65c multi 1.10 1.10
**4211** A983 65c green 1.10 1.10
**4212** A983 65c red 1.10 1.10
*a.* Horiz. pair, #4211-4212 2.20 2.20
**4213** A983 70c blue green 1.25 .95
**4214** A983 $1.70 pur & dk bl 3.00 1.50
**4215** A982 $2.55 multi 4.50 2.25
*a.* Souvenir sheet of 2, #4210, 4215 5.75 5.75
*Nos. 4210-4215 (6)* 12.05 8.00

**Self-Adhesive**
**Booklet Stamps**

***Serpentine Die Cut 11¼ Syncopated***

**4216** A982 65c multi 1.10 .25
*a.* Booklet pane of 20 + 20 etiquettes 22.00
**4217** A983 65c green 1.10 .25
**4218** A983 65c red 1.10 .25
*a.* Booklet pane of 20, 10 each #4217-4218, + 20 etiquettes 22.00
**4219** A983 $1.70 pur & dk bl 3.00 1.50
*a.* Booklet pane of 5 15.00
**4220** A982 $2.55 multi 4.50 2.25
*a.* Booklet pane of 5 22.50

**Litho. With Foil Application**

**4221** A983 65c green 1.10 .25
*a.* Booklet pane of 10 11.00
**4222** A983 65c red 1.10 .25
*a.* Booklet pane of 10 11.00
*Nos. 4216-4222 (7)* 13.00 5.00

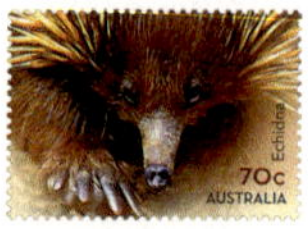


Marsupials — A984

Designs: Nos. 4225, 4234, Echidna. Nos. 4226, 4233, Common wombat. Nos. 4227, 4231, Eastern gray kangaroo. Nos. 4228, 4232, Koala. No. 4229, Numbat. No. 4230, Tasmanian devil.

**2015, Jan. 13 Litho.** ***Perf. 14x14¾***

**4225** A984 70c multi 1.10 1.10
**4226** A984 70c multi 1.10 1.10
**4227** A984 70c multi 1.10 1.10
**4228** A984 70c multi 1.10 1.10
*a.* Block of 4, #4225-4228 4.40 4.40
**4229** A984 $1.40 multi 2.25 1.75
**4230** A984 $1.40 multi 2.25 1.75
*a.* Vert. pair, #4229-4230 4.50 3.50
*b.* Souvenir sheet of 6, #4225-4230 9.00 9.00
*Nos. 4225-4230 (6)* 8.90 7.90

**Booklet Stamps**
**Self-Adhesive**

***Serpentine Die Cut 11¼ Syncopated***

**4231** A984 70c multi 1.10 .25
**4232** A984 70c multi 1.10 .25
**4233** A984 70c multi 1.10 .25
**4234** A984 70c multi 1.10 .25
*a.* Booklet pane of 10, 3 each #4231-4232, 2 each #4233-4234 11.00
*b.* Booklet pane of 20, 5 each #4231-4234 22.00
*Nos. 4231-4234 (4)* 4.40 1.00

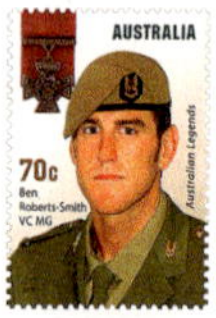


Victoria Cross Recipients — A985

Designs: Nos. 4235, 4240, Ben Roberts-Smith. Nos. 4236, 4241, Cameron Baird (1981-2013). Nos. 4237, 4242, Mark Donaldson. Nos. 4238, 4243, Dan Keighran. Nos. 4239, 4244, Keith Payne.

**2015, Jan. 22 Litho.** ***Perf. 14¾x14***

**4235** A985 70c multi 1.10 1.10
**4236** A985 70c multi 1.10 1.10
**4237** A985 70c multi 1.10 1.10
**4238** A985 70c multi 1.10 1.10
**4239** A985 70c multi 1.10 1.10
*a.* Souvenir sheet of 5, #4235-4239 5.50 5.50
*Nos. 4235-4239 (5)* 5.50 5.50

**Booklet Stamps**
**Self-Adhesive**

***Serpentine Die Cut 11¼ Syncopated***

**4240** A985 70c multi 1.10 .25
*a.* Booklet pane of 10 11.00
**4241** A985 70c multi 1.10 .25
*a.* Booklet pane of 10 11.00
**4242** A985 70c multi 1.10 .25
*a.* Booklet pane of 10 11.00
**4243** A985 70c multi 1.10 .25
*a.* Booklet pane of 10 11.00
**4244** A985 70c multi 1.10 .25
*a.* Booklet pane of 10 11.00
*Nos. 4240-4244 (5)* 5.50 1.25

Souvenir Sheet

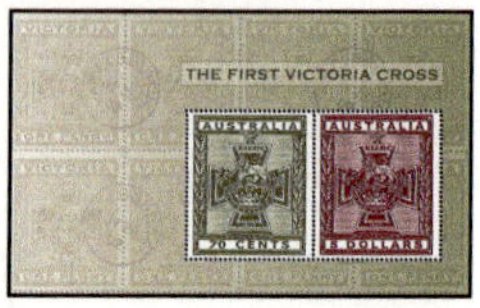


Victoria Cross A986

**2015, Jan. 22 Litho.** ***Perf. 14x14¾***

**4245** A986 Sheet of 2 9.00 9.00
*a.* 70c olive green 1.10 .85
*b.* $5 violet 7.75 5.75

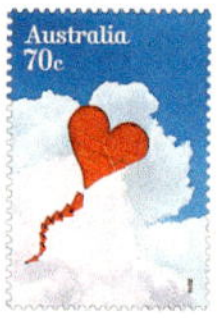


Heart-Shaped Items — A987

Designs: Nos. 4246, 4251, Kite. Nos. 4247, 4252, Airplane contrail. Nos. 4248, 4250, Hot-air balloon. Nos. 4249, 4253, Cloud.

**2015, Feb. 3 Litho.** ***Perf. 14¾x14***

**4246** A987 70c multi 1.10 1.10
**4247** A987 70c multi 1.10 1.10
**4248** A987 70c multi 1.10 1.10
**4249** A987 70c multi 1.10 1.10
*a.* Horiz. strip of 4, #4246-4249 4.40 4.40
*Nos. 4246-4249 (4)* 4.40 4.40

**Booklet Stamps**
**Self-Adhesive**

***Serpentine Die Cut 11¼ Syncopated***

**4250** A987 70c multi 1.10 .25
**4251** A987 70c multi 1.10 .25
**4252** A987 70c multi 1.10 .25
**4253** A987 70c multi 1.10 .25
*a.* Booklet pane of 20, 7 each #4250-4251, 3 each #4252-4253 22.00
*b.* Booklet pane of 10, 5 each #4252-4253 11.00
*Nos. 4250-4253 (4)* 4.40 1.00

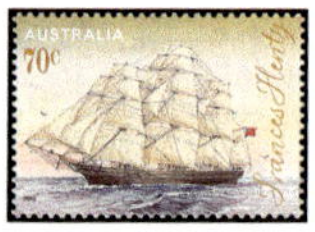


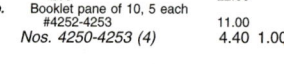

Clipper Ships — A988

Designs: No. 4254, Frances Henty. No. 4255, Phoenician. No. 4256, Arabian. No. 4257, Monkchester.

**2015, Feb. 17 Litho.** ***Perf. 14x14¾***

**4254** A988 70c multi 1.10 .85
**4255** A988 70c multi 1.10 .85
*a.* Horiz. pair, #4254-4255 2.20 1.70
**4256** A988 $1.40 multi 2.25 1.75
**4257** A988 $1.40 multi 2.25 1.75
*a.* Horiz. pair, #4256-4257 4.50 3.50
*Nos. 4254-4257 (4)* 6.70 5.20

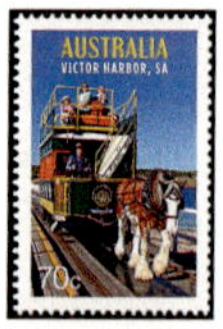


Tourist Attractions — A989

Designs: Nos. 4258, 4262, Horse-drawn tram, Victor Harbour, South Australia. Nos. 4259, 4263, Seaplane, Whitsunday Islands, Queensland. Nos. 4260, 4264, Steam train, Dandenong Ranges, Victoria. Nos. 4261, 4265, Cruise boat, Katherine Gorge, Northern Territory.

**2015, Mar. 3 Litho.** ***Perf. 14¾x14***

**4258** A989 70c multi 1.10 1.10
**4259** A989 70c multi 1.10 1.10
**4260** A989 70c multi 1.10 1.10
**4261** A989 70c multi 1.10 1.10
*a.* Horiz. strip of 4, #4258-4261 4.40 4.40
*Nos. 4258-4261 (4)* 4.40 4.40

**Self-Adhesive**

***Serpentine Die Cut 11¼ Syncopated***

**4262** A989 70c multi 1.10 .25
**4263** A989 70c multi 1.10 .25
**4264** A989 70c multi 1.10 .25
**4265** A989 70c multi 1.10 .25
*a.* Vert. coil strip of 4, #4262-4265 4.40
*b.* Booklet pane of 10, 3 each #4262, 4264, 2 each #4263, 4265 11.00
*Nos. 4262-4265 (4)* 4.40 1.00

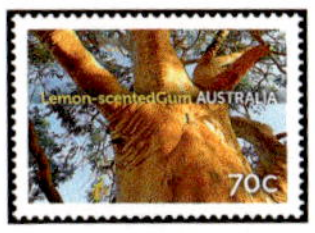


Trees — A990

Designs: 70c, Lemon-scented gum tree. $1.40, Queensland bottle tree. No. 4268, Green fig tree. No. 4269, Moonah tree.

**2015, Mar. 17 Litho. *Perf. 14x14¾***

**4266** A990 70c multi 1.10 .85
**4267** A990 $1.40 multi 2.25 1.75
**4268** A990 $2.10 multi 3.25 2.50
**4269** A990 $2.10 multi 3.25 2.50
*a.* Horiz. pair, #4268-4269 6.50 5.00
*b.* Souvenir sheet of 4, #4266-4269 10.00 10.00
*Nos. 4266-4269 (4)* 9.85 7.60

**Self-Adhesive**
**Printed on Wood Veneer**

***Serpentine Die Cut 11¼ Syncopated***

**4270** A990 70c multi 1.25 1.25

No. 4270 was printed in sheets of 10. The sheet was sold only in a package, together with a sheet of 10 of No. 4266. The package sold for $14.95.

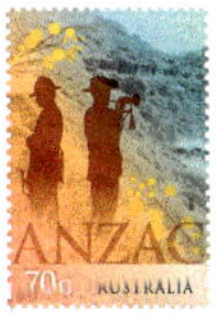


Australian and New Zealand Army Corps, Cent. — A991

Soldier and bugler with bugler facing: 70c, Right. $1.85, Left.

**2015, Apr. 7 Litho. *Perf. 14¾x14***

**4271** A991 70c multi 1.10 1.10
**4272** A991 $1.85 multi 3.00 3.00
*a.* Souvenir sheet of 2, #4271-4272 4.25 4.25

**Booklet Stamps**
**Self-Adhesive**

***Serpentine Die Cut 11¼ Syncopated***

**4273** A991 70c multi 1.10 .25
*a.* Booklet pane of 10 11.00
**4274** A991 $1.85 multi 3.00 1.50
*a.* Booklet pane of 5 15.00

See New Zealand Nos. 2584-2585.

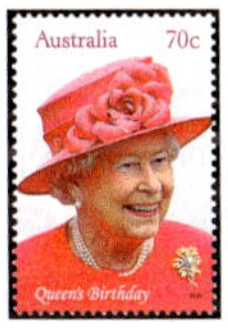


Queen Elizabeth II, 89th Birthday — A992

Hat color: 70c, Red. $2.75, Blue.

**2015, Apr. 7 Litho. *Perf. 14¾x14***

**4275** A992 70c multi 1.10 .85
*a.* Booklet pane of 4 4.75 —
**4276** A992 $2.75 multi 4.50 2.25
*a.* Souvenir sheet of 2, #4275-4276 5.75 5.75
*b.* Booklet pane of 2 9.00 —
*c.* Booklet pane of 2, #4275-4276 5.75 —
Complete booklet, #4276b, 4276c, 2 #4275a 24.50

**Booklet Stamp**
**Self-Adhesive**

***Serpentine Die Cut 11¼ Syncopated***

**4277** A992 $2.75 multi 4.50 2.25
*a.* Booklet pane of 5 22.50

Complete booklet sold for $14.95.

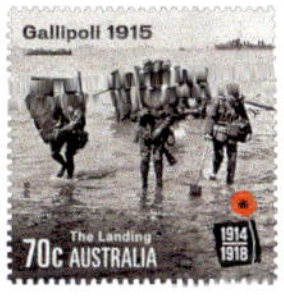


World War I, Cent. — A993

Australian soldiers involved in Gallipoli campaign: Nos. 4278, 4283, Landing at Gallipoli. Nos. 4279, 4284, Lance Corporal Albert Jacka and Victoria Cross. Nos. 4280, 4285, At Lone Pine. Nos. 4281, 4286, With donkey used for recovering wounded soldiers. Nos. 4282, 4287, Near cannon before evacuation.

**2015, Apr. 14 Litho. *Perf. 14¼***

**4278** A993 70c multi 1.10 1.10
*a.* Booklet pane of 4 4.75 —
**4279** A993 70c multi 1.10 1.10
*a.* Booklet pane of 4 4.75 —
**4280** A993 70c multi 1.10 1.10
*a.* Booklet pane of 4 4.75 —
**4281** A993 70c multi 1.10 1.10
*a.* Booklet pane of 4 4.75 —
**4282** A993 70c multi 1.10 1.10
*a.* Booklet pane of 4 4.75 —
Complete booklet, #4278a, 4279a, 4280a, 4281a, 4282a 24.00
*b.* Horiz. strip of 5, #4278-4282 5.50 5.50
*c.* Souvenir sheet of 5, #4278-4282 5.50 5.50
*Nos. 4278-4282 (5)* 5.50 5.50

**Booklet Stamps**
**Self-Adhesive**

***Serpentine Die Cut 11¼ Syncopated***

**4283** A993 70c multi 1.10 .25
**4284** A993 70c multi 1.10 .25
**4285** A993 70c multi 1.10 .25
**4286** A993 70c multi 1.10 .25
**4287** A993 70c multi 1.10 .25
*a.* Booklet pane of 10, 2 each #4283-4287 11.00
*Nos. 4283-4287 (5)* 5.50 1.25

Complete booklet sold for $14.95.

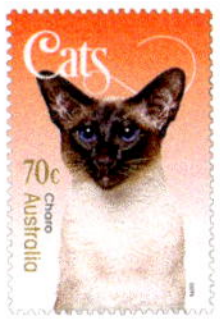


Cats — A994

Cats named: Nos. 4288, 4293, Charo. Nos. 4289, 4294, Bubu. Nos. 4290, 4295, Sweeie. Nos. 4291, 4296, Cato. Nos. 4292, 4297, Briony.

**2015, May 5 Litho. *Perf. 14¾x14***

**4288** A994 70c multi 1.10 1.10
**4289** A994 70c multi 1.10 1.10
**4290** A994 70c multi 1.10 1.10
**4291** A994 70c multi 1.10 1.10
**4292** A994 70c multi 1.10 1.10
*a.* Horiz. strip of 5, #4288-4292 5.50 5.50
*Nos. 4288-4292 (5)* 5.50 5.50

**Self-Adhesive**

***Serpentine Die Cut 11¼ Syncopated***

**4293** A994 70c multi 1.10 .25
*a.* Booklet pane of 10 11.00
**4294** A994 70c multi 1.10 .25
*a.* Booklet pane of 10 11.00
**4295** A994 70c multi 1.10 .25
*a.* Booklet pane of 10 11.00
**4296** A994 70c multi 1.10 .25
*a.* Booklet pane of 10 11.00
**4297** A994 70c multi 1.10 .25
*a.* Booklet pane of 10 11.00
*b.* Vert. coil strip of 5, #4293-4297 5.50
*Nos. 4293-4297 (5)* 5.50 1.25

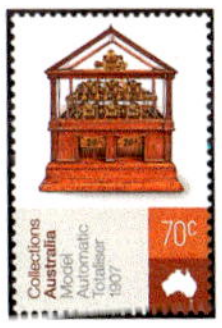


Items in Australian Museums — A995

Designs: Nos. 4298, 4303, 1907 Model automatic totalizer, from Museum of Applied Arts and Sciences, Sydney. Nos. 4299, 4302, Turtle sculpture by Ellarose Savage, Australian Museum, Sydney. Nos. 4300, 4305, Anchor of HMS Endeavour, National Museum of Australia, Canberra. Nos. 4301, 4304, Replica of "Welcome Stranger" gold nugget, Gold Museum, Sovereign Hill, Victoria.

**2015, May 19 Litho. *Perf. 14¾x14***

**4298** A995 70c multi 1.10 1.10
**4299** A995 70c multi 1.10 1.10
**4300** A995 70c multi 1.10 1.10
**4301** A995 70c multi 1.10 1.10
*a.* Block of 4, #4298-4301 4.40 4.40
*b.* Souvenir sheet of 4, #4298-4301 4.40 4.40
*Nos. 4298-4301 (4)* 4.40 4.40

**Coil Stamps**
**Self-Adhesive**

***Serpentine Die Cut 11¼ Syncopated***

**4302** A995 70c multi 1.10 .25
**4303** A995 70c multi 1.10 .25
**4304** A995 70c multi 1.10 .25
**4305** A995 70c multi 1.10 .25
*a.* Vert. strip of 4, #4302-4305 4.40
*Nos. 4302-4305 (4)* 4.40 1.00

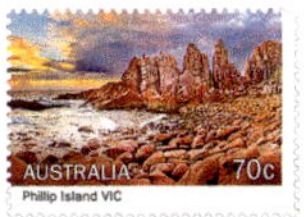


Islands — A996

Designs: Nos. 4306, 4310, Phillip Island, Victoria. Nos. 4307, 4311, Lady Musgrave Island, Queensland. $1.40, Bruny Island, Tasmania. $2.10, Buccaneer Archipelago, Western Australia.

**2015, June 2 Litho. *Perf. 14x14¾***

**4306** A996 70c multi 1.10 1.10
**4307** A996 70c multi 1.10 1.10
*a.* Horiz. pair, #4306-4307 2.20 2.20
**4308** A996 $1.40 multi 2.25 1.10
**4309** A996 $2.10 multi 3.25 1.60
*Nos. 4306-4309 (4)* 7.70 4.90

**Booklet Stamps**
**Self-Adhesive**

***Serpentine Die Cut 11¼ Syncopated***

**4310** A996 70c multi 1.10 .25
**4311** A996 70c multi 1.10 .25
*a.* Booklet pane of 10, 5 each #4310-4311 11.00

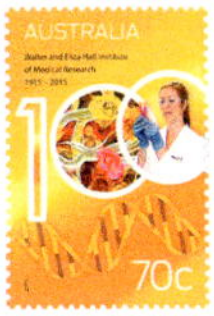


Walter and Eliza Hall Institute of Medical Research, Cent. — A997

**2015, June 30 Litho. *Perf. 14¾x14***

**4312** A997 70c multi 1.10 .85
*a.* Booklet pane of 4 4.50 —
Complete booklet, 5 #4312a 22.50

Complete booklet sold for $14.95.

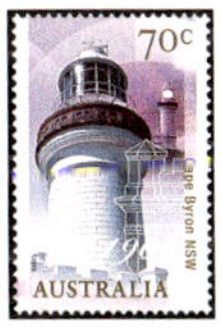


Lighthouses — A998

Designs: Nos. 4313, 4317, Cape Byron Lighthouse, New South Wales. Nos. 4314, 4318, Cape Leeuwin Lighthouse, Western Australia. Nos. 4315, 4319, North Reef Lighthouse, Queensland. Nos. 4316, 4320, Tasman Island Lighthouse, Tasmania.

**2015, July 7 Litho. *Perf. 14¾x14***

**4313** A998 70c multi 1.10 1.10
*a.* Booklet pane of 4 4.50 —
**4314** A998 70c multi 1.10 1.10
*a.* Booklet pane of 4 4.50 —
**4315** A998 70c multi 1.10 1.10
*a.* Booklet pane of 4 4.50 —
**4316** A998 70c multi 1.10 1.10
*a.* Booklet pane of 4 4.50 —
*b.* Booklet pane of 4, #4313-4316 4.50 —
Complete booklet, #4313a, 4314a, 4315a, 4316a, 4316b 22.50
*c.* Block of 4, #4313-4316 4.40 4.40
*Nos. 4313-4316 (4)* 4.40 4.40

**Self-Adhesive**

***Serpentine Die Cut 11¼ Syncopated***

**4317** A998 70c multi 1.10 .25
**4318** A998 70c multi 1.10 .25
**4319** A998 70c multi 1.10 .25
**4320** A998 70c multi 1.10 .25
*a.* Booklet pane of 20, 5 each #4317-4320 22.00
*b.* Vert. coil strip of 4, #4317-4320 4.40
*Nos. 4317-4320 (4)* 4.40 1.00

Complete booklet sold for $14.95.

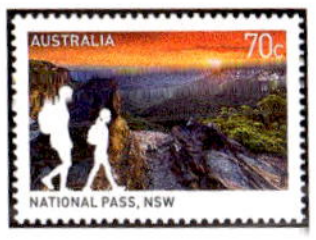


Hiking Trails — A999

Designs: Nos. 4321, 4326, National Pass Track, New South Wales. Nos. 4322, 4328, Cape to Cape Track, Western Australia. Nos. 4323, 4325, Larapinta Trail, Northern Territory. Nos. 4324, 4327, Overland Track, Tasmania.

**2015, July 14 Litho. *Perf. 14x14¾***

**4321** A999 70c multi 1.10 1.10
**4322** A999 70c multi 1.10 1.10
**4323** A999 70c multi 1.10 1.10
**4324** A999 70c multi 1.10 1.10
*a.* Horiz. strip of 4, #4321-4324 4.40 4.40
*b.* Souvenir sheet of 4, #4321-4324 4.40 4.40
*Nos. 4321-4324 (4)* 4.40 4.40

**Self-Adhesive**

***Serpentine Die Cut 11¼ Syncopated***

**4325** A999 70c multi 1.10 .25
**4326** A999 70c multi 1.10 .25
**4327** A999 70c multi 1.10 .25
**4328** A999 70c multi 1.10 .25
*a.* Booklet pane of 10, 3 each #4325, 4327, 2 each #4326, 4328 11.00
*b.* Horiz. coil strip of 4, #4325-4328 4.40
*Nos. 4325-4328 (4)* 4.40 1.00

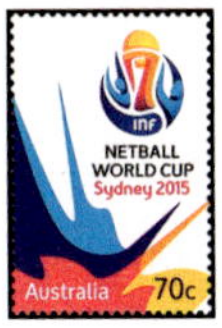


2015 Netball World Cup, Sydney — A1000

**2015, Aug. 8 Litho. *Perf. 14¾x14***

**4329** A1000 70c multi 1.10 .85

**Booklet Stamp**
**Self-Adhesive**

***Serpentine Die Cut 11¼ Syncopated***

**4330** A1000 70c multi 1.10 .25
*a.* Booklet pane of 20 20.00

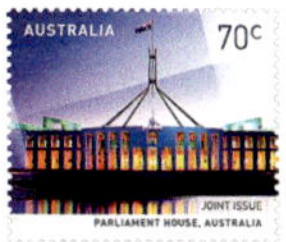


Houses of Parliament — A1001

Houses of Parliament in: 70c, Australia. $1.85, New Zealand. $1.95, Singapore.

**2015, Aug. 14 Litho. *Perf. 14¼***

**4331** A1001 70c multi 1.10 .85
**4332** A1001 $1.85 multi 2.75 1.40
**4333** A1001 $1.95 multi 3.00 1.50
*a.* Souvenir sheet of 3, #4331-4333 7.00 7.00
*Nos. 4331-4333 (3)* 6.85 3.75

Diplomatic relations of Singapore with Australia and New Zealand, 50th anniv.

See New Zealand No. 2600, Singapore Nos. 1743-1745.

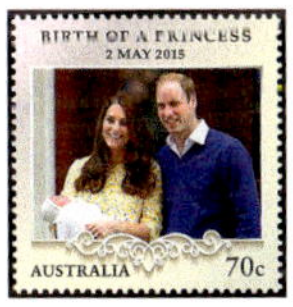


Birth of Princess Charlotte of Cambridge — A1002

**2015, Aug. 25 Litho. *Perf. 14¼***

**4334** A1002 70c multi 1.00 1.00

**Booklet Stamp**
**Self-Adhesive**

***Serpentine Die Cut 11¼ Syncopated***

**4335** A1002 70c multi 1.00 .25
*a.* Booklet pane of 10 10.00

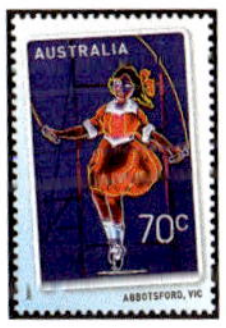


Neon Signs — A1003

Designs: Nos. 4336, 4339, Skipping Girl Vinegar sign, Abbotsford, Victoria, 1936. Nos. 4337, 4340, Pink Poodle Motel sign, Surfers Paradise, Queensland, 1967. $1.40, Dandy Pig sign for Gippsland Co-operative Bacon Curing Company, Dandenong, Victoria, 1950s.

**2015, Sept. 1 Litho. *Perf. 14¾x14***

**4336** A1003 70c multi 1.00 1.00
**4337** A1003 70c multi 1.00 1.00
**4338** A1003 $1.40 multi 2.00 1.50
*a.* Souvenir sheet of 3, #4336-4338 4.00 4.00
*Nos. 4336-4338 (3)* 4.00 3.50

**Self-Adhesive**

***Serpentine Die Cut 11¼ Syncopated***

**4339** A1003 70c multi 1.00 1.00
**4340** A1003 70c multi 1.00 1.00
*a.* Vert. coil pair, #4339-4340 2.00
*b.* Booklet pane of 10, 5 each #4339-4340 10.00

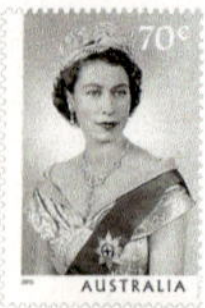

A1004

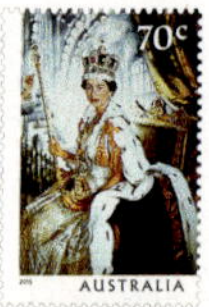

A1005

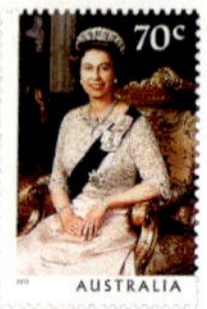

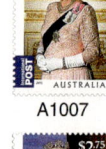

A1006

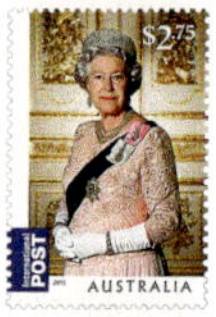

A1007

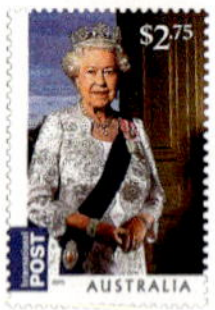

Queen Elizabeth II, Longest-Reigning British Monarch — A1008

**2015, Sept. 9 Litho. *Perf. 14¾x14***

**4341** A1004 70c black 1.00 .75
*a.* Booklet pane of 4 4.25 —
**4342** A1005 70c multi 1.00 .75
*a.* Booklet pane of 4 4.25 —
**4343** A1006 70c multi 1.00 .75
*a.* Booklet pane of 4 4.25 —
*b.* Horiz. strip of 3, #4341-4343 3.00 2.25
**4344** A1007 $2.75 multi 4.00 4.00
*a.* Booklet pane of 2 8.00 —
**4345** A1008 $2.75 multi 4.00 4.00
*a.* Booklet pane of 2 8.00 —
Complete booklet, #4341a, 4342a, 4343a, 4344a, 4345a 29.00
*b.* Horiz. pair, #4344-4345 8.00 8.00
*c.* Souvenir sheet of 5, #4341-4345 11.00 11.00
*Nos. 4341-4345 (5)* 11.00 10.25

**Booklet Stamps**
**Self-Adhesive**
***Serpentine Die Cut 11¼ Syncopated***

**4346** A1007 $2.75 multi 4.00 4.00
**4347** A1008 $2.75 multi 4.00 4.00
*a.* Booklet pane of 5, 2 #4346, 3 #4347 20.00

Complete booklet sold for $19.95.

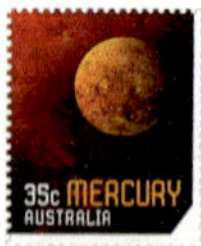

Planets — A1009

Designs: Nos. 4348, 4356a, Mercury. Nos. 4349, 4356b, Mars, horiz. Nos. 4350, 4356c, 4357, Earth. Nos. 4351, 4356d, 4358, Uranus. Nos. 4352, 4356e, 4359, Neptune, horiz. Nos. 4353, 4356f, 4360, Venus, horiz. Nos. 4354, 4356g, Jupiter. Nos. 4355, 4356h, Saturn, horiz.

**Litho., Litho. & Silk-Screened (#4356)**
**2015, Sept. 22 *Perf. 14½x14***
**Stamps With White Frames on Two Sides**

**4348** A1009 35c multi .50 .40

***Perf. 14x14½***

**4349** A1009 35c multi .50 .40
*a.* Pair, #4348-4349 1.00 .80

**Size: 26x38mm**
***Perf. 14¾x14***

**4350** A1009 70c multi 1.00 1.00
**4351** A1009 70c multi 1.00 1.00

**Size:36x28mm**
***Perf. 14x14¾***

**4352** A1009 70c multi 1.00 1.00
**4353** A1009 70c multi 1.00 1.00

**Size: 30x50mm**
***Perf. 14x14½***

**4354** A1009 70c multi 1.00 1.00

**Size: 50x30mm**
***Perf. 14½x14***

**4355** A1009 70c multi 1.00 1.00
*Nos. 4348-4355 (8)* 7.00 6.80

**Miniature Sheet**
**Stamps Without White Frames**
***Perf. 14½, 14x14½ (#4356e, 4356f)***

**4356** Sheet of 8 7.00 7.00
*a.* A1009 35c multi .50 .40
*b.* A1009 35c multi .50 .40
*c.* A1009 70c multi, 26x38mm 1.00 .75
*d.* A1009 70c multi, 26x38mm 1.00 .75
*e.* A1009 70c multi, 38x26mm 1.00 .75
*f.* A1009 70c multi, 38x26mm 1.00 .75
*g.* A1009 70c multi, 30x50mm 1.00 .75
*h.* A1009 70c multi, 50x30mm 1.00 .75

**Litho.**
***Serpentine Die Cut 11¼ Syncopated***
**Booklet Stamps**
**Self-Adhesive**
**Size: 26x38mm**
**Stamps With White Frames on Two Sides**

**4357** A1009 70c multi 1.00 .25
**4358** A1009 70c multi 1.00 .25
*a.* Booklet pane of 20, 10 each #4357-4358 20.00

**Size: 38x26mm**

**4359** A1009 70c multi 1.00 .25
**4360** A1009 70c multi 1.00 .25
*a.* Booklet pane of 10, 5 each #4359-4360 10.00
*Nos. 4357-4360 (4)* 4.00 1.00

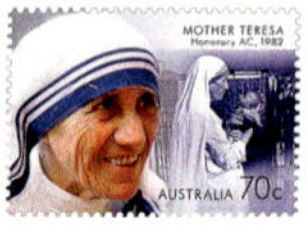

Humanitarians Honored by Australia — A1010

Designs: Nos. 4361, 4364, Mother Teresa (1910-97), Honorary Companion of the Order of Australia. Nos. 4362, 4365, Nelson Mandela (1918-2013), Honorary Companion of the Order of Australia. Nos. 4363, 4366, Raoul Wallenberg (1912-45), Honorary Citizen of Australia.

**2015, Oct. 5 Litho. *Perf. 14x14¾***

**4361** A1010 70c multi 1.00 1.00
**4362** A1010 70c multi 1.00 1.00
**4363** A1010 70c multi 1.00 1.00
*Nos. 4361-4363 (3)* 3.00 3.00

**Booklet Stamps**
**Self-Adhesive**
***Serpentine Die Cut 11¼ Syncopated***

**4364** A1010 70c multi 1.00 .25
*a.* Booklet pane of 10 10.00
**4365** A1010 70c multi 1.00 .25
*a.* Booklet pane of 10 10.00
**4366** A1010 70c multi 1.00 .25
*a.* Booklet pane of 10 10.00
*Nos. 4364-4366 (3)* 3.00 .75

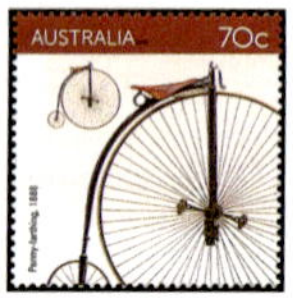

Bicycles — A1011

Designs: Nos. 4367, 4371, 1888 Basset & Co. penny-farthing. Nos. 4368, 4372, Sutherland ladies' safety bicycle, c. 1910. $1.85, Finlay Bros. men's sprung-frame saftey bicycle, 1930s. $2.75, Baum Cycles custom-made road bicycle, 2015.

**2015, Oct. 13 Litho. *Perf. 14¼***

**4367** A1011 70c multi 1.00 1.00
*a.* Booklet pane of 4 4.00 —
**4368** A1011 70c multi 1.00 1.00
*a.* Booklet pane of 4 4.00 —
*b.* Horiz. pair, #4367-4368 2.00 2.00
**4369** A1011 $1.85 multi 2.75 1.40
*a.* Booklet pane of 2 5.50 —
**4370** A1011 $2.75 multi 4.00 4.00
*a.* Booklet pane of 2 8.00 —
Complete booklet, #4367a, 4368a, 4369a, 4370a 21.50
*Nos. 4367-4370 (4)* 8.75 7.40

**Booklet Stamps**
**Self-Adhesive**
***Serpentine Die Cut 11¼ Syncopated***

**4371** A1011 70c multi 1.00 .25
**4372** A1011 70c multi 1.00 .25
*a.* Booklet pane of 20, 10 each #4371-4372 20.00
**4373** A1011 $2.75 multi 4.00 2.00
*a.* Booklet pane of 5 20.00
*Nos. 4371-4373 (3)* 6.00 2.50

Complete booklet sold for $14.95.

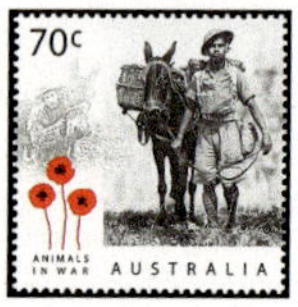

Animals in War — A1012

Poppies, soldiers and: Nos. 4374, 4379, Donkeys. Nos. 4375, 4380, Dogs. Nos. 4376, 4381, Horses. Nos. 4377, 4383, Pigeons. Nos. 4378, 4382, Camels.

**2015, Oct. 27 Litho. *Perf. 14¼***

**4374** A1012 70c multi 1.00 1.00
**4375** A1012 70c multi 1.00 1.00
**4376** A1012 70c multi 1.00 1.00
**4377** A1012 70c multi 1.00 1.00
**4378** A1012 70c multi 1.00 1.00
*a.* Souvenir sheet of 5, #4374-4378 5.00 5.00
*Nos. 4374-4378 (5)* 5.00 5.00

**Booklet Stamps**
**Self-Adhesive**
***Serpentine Die Cut 11¼ Syncopated***

**4379** A1012 70c multi 1.00 .25
**4380** A1012 70c multi 1.00 .25
**4381** A1012 70c multi 1.00 .25
**4382** A1012 70c multi 1.00 .25
**4383** A1012 70c multi 1.00 .25
*a.* Booklet pane of 10, 2 each #4379-4383 10.00
*Nos. 4379-4383 (5)* 5.00 1.25

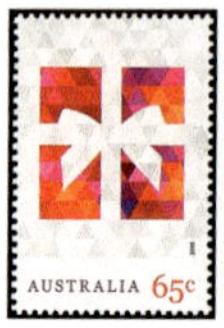

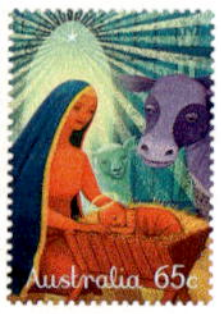

Christmas
A1013 A1014

Designs: Nos. 4384, 4389, 4394, Gift box with ribbon. Nos. 4385, 4390, 4395, Green doves. Nos. 4386, 4391, Nativity. Nos. 4387, 4392, Blue doves. Nos. 4388, 4393, Magi.

**2015, Oct. 30 Litho. *Perf. 14¾x14***

**4384** A1013 65c multi .95 .95
**4385** A1013 65c multi .95 .95
*a.* Horiz. pair, #4384-4385 1.90 1.90
**4386** A1014 65c multi .95 .95
**4387** A1013 $1.70 multi 2.50 2.50
**4388** A1014 $2.55 multi 3.75 3.75
*a.* Souvenir sheet of 2, #4386, 4388 4.75 4.75
*Nos. 4384-4388 (5)* 9.10 9.10

**Booklet Stamps**
**Self-Adhesive**
***Serpentine Die Cut 11¼ Syncopated***

**4389** A1013 65c multi .95 .25
**4390** A1013 65c multi .95 .25
*a.* Booklet pane of 20, 10 each #4389-4390 19.00
**4391** A1014 65c multi .95 .25
*a.* Booklet pane of 20 19.00
**4392** A1013 $1.70 multi 2.50 1.25
*a.* Booklet pane of 5 12.50
**4393** A1014 $2.55 multi 3.75 1.90
*a.* Booklet pane of 5 19.00

**Litho. & Silk-Screened**

**4394** A1013 65c multi .95 .25
*a.* Booklet pane of 10 9.50

**Litho. With Foil Application**

**4395** A1013 65c multi .95 .25
*a.* Booklet pane of 10 9.50
*Nos. 4389-4395 (7)* 11.00 4.40

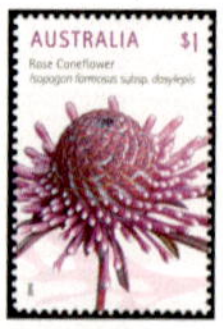

Wildflowers — A1015

Designs: Nos. 4398, 4402, 4405, Rose coneflower. Nos. 4399, 4403, 4406, Spiny mirbelia. Nos. 4400, 4404, 4407, Blue devil. $2, Golden rainbow.

**2015, Dec. 15 Litho. *Perf. 14¾x14***

**4398** A1015 $1 multi 1.50 1.50
**4399** A1015 $1 multi 1.50 1.50
**4400** A1015 $1 multi 1.50 1.50
*a.* Horiz. strip of 3, #4398-4400 4.50 4.50
**4401** A1015 $2 multi 3.00 1.50
*Nos. 4398-4401 (4)* 7.50 6.00

**Self-Adhesive**
***Serpentine Die Cut 11¼ Syncopated***

**4402** A1015 $1 multi 1.50 .25
**4403** A1015 $1 multi 1.50 .25
**4404** A1015 $1 multi 1.50 .25
*a.* Vert. coil strip of 3, #4402-4404 4.50
*b.* Booklet pane of 10, 4 #4402, 3 each #4403-4404 15.00
*c.* Booklet pane of 20, 8 #4402, 5 #4403, 7 #4404 30.00
*Nos. 4402-4404 (3)* 4.50 .75

**With Personalized Photo at Right Like Type A692a**
***Serpentine Die Cut 11½x11¼ Syncopated***
**Self-Adhesive**

**4405** A1015 $1 multi 2.40 2.40
**4406** A1015 $1 multi 2.40 2.40
**4407** A1015 $1 multi 2.40 2.40
**4408** A1015 $2 multi 4.00 4.00
*Nos. 4405-4408 (4)* 11.20 11.20

Nos. 4405-4408 were each printed in sheets of 20 and have personalized pictures and a straight edge at right and lack separations between the stamp and the personalized photo. Sheets of 20 of Nos. 4405-4407 sold for $33 each, No. 4408, $53.

See No. 4653.

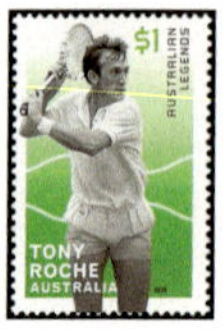

Tennis Players — A1016

Designs: Nos. 4409, 4412, Tony Roche. Nos. 4410, 4413, Fred Stolle. Nos. 4411a, 4414, Pat Cash. Nos. 4411b, 4415, Ashley Cooper. Nos. 4411c, 4416, Roy Emerson. Nos. 4411d, 4417, Neale Fraser. Nos. 4411e, 4418, Evonne Goolagong Cawley. Nos. 4411f, 4419, John Newcombe. Nos. 4411g, 4420, Patrick Rafter. Nos. 4411h, 4421, Ken Rosewall. Nos. 4411i, 4422, Frank Sedgman. Nos. 4411j, 4423, Lleyton Hewitt.

**2016, Jan. 21 Litho. *Perf. 14¾x14***

**4409** A1016 $1 multi 1.50 1.50
**4410** A1016 $1 multi 1.50 1.50
*a.* Vert. pair, #4409-4410 3.00 3.00
**4411** Sheet of 10 15.00 15.00
*a.-j.* A1016 $1 Any single 1.50 1.50

**Booklet Stamps**
**Self-Adhesive**
***Serpentine Die Cut 11¼ Syncopated***

**4412** A1016 $1 multi 1.50 .25
*a.* Booklet pane of 10 15.00
**4413** A1016 $1 multi 1.50 .25
*a.* Booklet pane of 10 15.00
**4414** A1016 $1 multi 1.50 .25
*a.* Booklet pane of 10 15.00
**4415** A1016 $1 multi 1.50 .25
*a.* Booklet pane of 10 15.00
**4416** A1016 $1 multi 1.50 .25
*a.* Booklet pane of 10 15.00
**4417** A1016 $1 multi 1.50 .25
*a.* Booklet pane of 10 15.00
**4418** A1016 $1 multi 1.50 .25
*a.* Booklet pane of 10 15.00
**4419** A1016 $1 multi 1.50 .25
*a.* Booklet pane of 10 15.00
**4420** A1016 $1 multi 1.50 .25
*a.* Booklet pane of 10 15.00
**4421** A1016 $1 multi 1.50 .25
*a.* Booklet pane of 10 15.00
**4422** A1016 $1 multi 1.50 .25
*a.* Booklet pane of 10 15.00
**4423** A1016 $1 multi 1.50 .25
*a.* Booklet pane of 10 15.00
*Nos. 4412-4423 (12)* 18.00 3.00

White Roses A1017

Champagne Flutes A1018

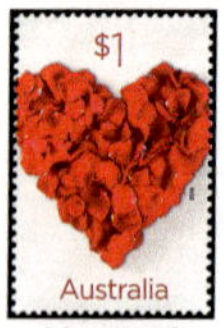

Heart of Red Roses A1019

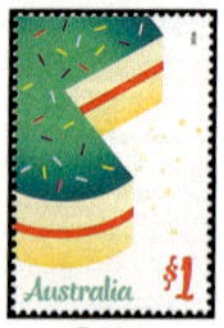

Cake A1020

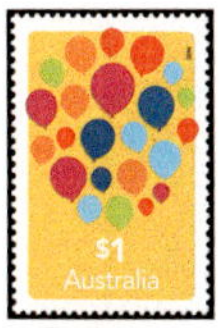
Balloons
A1021

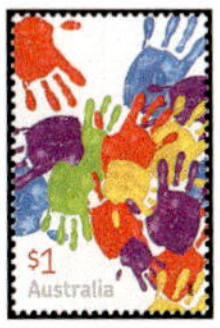
Handprints
A1022

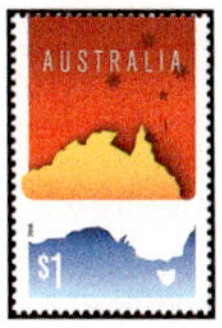
Map of
Australia
A1023

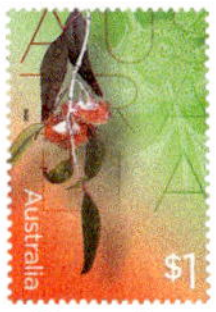
Flowering
Gum
A1024

Wattle
A1025

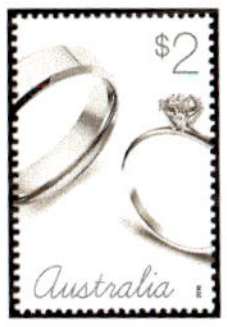
Engagement
and
Wedding
Rings
A1026

**2016, Jan. 25 Litho. *Perf. 14¾x14***

**4424** A1017 $1 multi 1.50 1.50
**4425** A1018 $1 multi 1.50 1.50
**4426** A1019 $1 multi 1.50 1.50
**4427** A1020 $1 multi 1.50 1.50
**4428** A1021 $1 multi 1.50 1.50
**4429** A1022 $1 multi 1.50 1.50
**4430** A1023 $1 multi 1.50 1.10
**4431** A1024 $1 multi 1.50 1.10
**4432** A1025 $1 multi 1.50 1.10
**4433** A1026 $2 multi 3.00 3.00
*Nos. 4424-4433 (10)* 16.50 15.30

**Booklet Stamps**
**Self-Adhesive**

***Serpentine Die Cut 11¼ Syncopated***

**4434** A1017 $1 multi 1.50 .25
*a.* Booklet pane of 10 + 5 stickers 15.00
**4435** A1018 $1 multi 1.50 .25
*a.* Booklet pane of 10 + 5 stickers 15.00
**4436** A1019 $1 multi 1.50 .25
*a.* Booklet pane of 10 + 5 stickers 15.00
**4437** A1020 $1 multi 1.50 .25
*a.* Booklet pane of 10 + 5 stickers 15.00
**4438** A1021 $1 multi 1.50 .25
*a.* Booklet pane of 10 + 5 stickers 15.00
**4439** A1022 $1 multi 1.50 .25
*a.* Booklet pane of 10 + 5 stickers 15.00
**4440** A1026 $2 multi 3.00 1.50
*a.* Booklet pane of 4 12.00
Complete booklet, 4 #4440a 48.00
*Nos. 4434-4440 (7)* 12.00 3.00

Complete booklet sold for $32.95 and contains four examples of No. 4440a, each with a different pane margin.

**With Personalized Photo at Right Like Type A692a**

***Serpentine Die Cut 11½x11¼ Syncopated***

**Self-Adhesive**

**4441** A1017 $1 multi 2.40 2.40
**4442** A1018 $1 multi 2.40 2.40
**4443** A1019 $1 multi 2.40 2.40
**4444** A1020 $1 multi 2.40 2.40
**4445** A1021 $1 multi 2.40 2.40
**4446** A1022 $1 multi 2.40 2.40
**4447** A1023 $1 multi 2.40 2.40
**4448** A1024 $1 multi 2.40 2.40
**4449** A1025 $1 multi 2.40 2.40
**4450** A1026 $2 multi 3.75 3.75
*Nos. 4441-4450 (10)* 25.35 25.35

Nos. 4441-4450 were each printed in sheets of 20 and have personalized pictures and a straight edge at right and lack separations between the stamp and the personalized photo. Sheets of 20 of Nos. 4441-4449 sold for $33 each, No. 4450, $53.

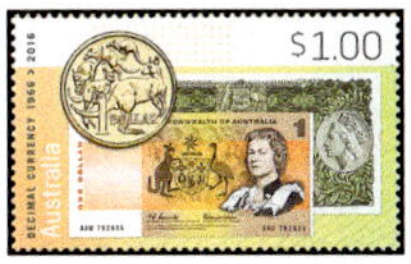
Australian One Pound Banknote, One Dollar Banknote and Coin
A1027

**2016, Feb. 9 Litho. *Perf. 14½x14***

**4451** A1027 $1 multi 1.50 1.10
*a.* Perf. 13½x14 1.50 1.10
*b.* Booklet pane of 4 #4451a 6.00 —
Complete booklet, 5 #4451b 30.00

Complete booklet sold for $20.95, and contained five examples of No. 4451b, each with different pane margins.

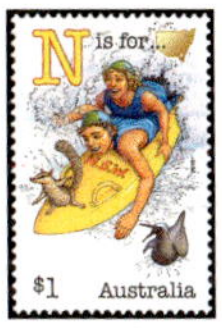
Items Starting With Same Letter — A1028

Designs: Nos. 4452, 4457, Numbat, nippers (junior lifeguards) on surfboard, New South Wales map. Nos. 4453, 4458, Quokka, quoll, queue sign, Quokkair plane, Queensland map. Nos. 4454, 4459, Surf, surfboard, sand castle, starfish, sausage, shark toy, shell, snail, South Australia map. Nos. 4455, 4460, Vegetables, Victa lawnmower, violins, Vegemite sandwich, Victoria map. Nos. 4456, 4461, Wombat, wattle, waratah, water hose, Western Australia Cricket Association bat and ball, Western Australia map.

**2016, Mar. 1 Litho. *Perf. 14¾x14***

**4452** A1028 $1 multi 1.50 1.50
**4453** A1028 $1 multi 1.50 1.50
**4454** A1028 $1 multi 1.50 1.50
**4455** A1028 $1 multi 1.50 1.50
**4456** A1028 $1 multi 1.50 1.50
*a.* Horiz. strip of 5, #4452-4456 7.50 7.50
*Nos. 4452-4456 (5)* 7.50 7.50

**Booklet Stamps**
**Self-Adhesive**

***Serpentine Die Cut 11¼ Syncopated***

**4457** A1028 $1 multi 1.50 .25
*a.* Booklet pane of 10 15.00
**4458** A1028 $1 multi 1.50 .25
*a.* Booklet pane of 10 15.00
**4459** A1028 $1 multi 1.50 .25
*a.* Booklet pane of 10 15.00
**4460** A1028 $1 multi 1.50 .25
*a.* Booklet pane of 10 15.00
**4461** A1028 $1 multi 1.50 .25
*a.* Booklet pane of 10 15.00
*Nos. 4457-4461 (5)* 7.50 1.25

See Nos. 4520-4529, 4697-4706, 4853-4862, 5027-5038.

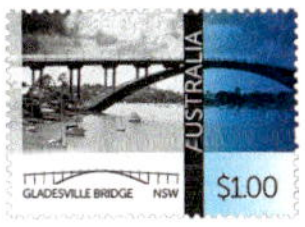
Bridges — A1029

Designs: Nos. 4462, 4465, Gladesville Bridge, New South Wales. Nos. 4463, 4467, Story Bridge, Queensland. Nos. 4464, 4466, Tasman Bridge, Tasmania.

**2016, Mar. 15 Litho. *Perf. 14x14¾***

**4462** A1029 $1 multi 1.60 1.60
**4463** A1029 $1 multi 1.60 1.60
**4464** A1029 $1 multi 1.60 1.60
*a.* Horiz. strip of 3, #4462-4464 4.80 4.80
*Nos. 4462-4464 (3)* 4.80 4.80

**Booklet Stamps**
**Self-Adhesive**

***Serpentine Die Cut 11¼ Syncopated***

**4465** A1029 $1 multi 1.60 .25
**4466** A1029 $1 multi 1.60 .25
**4467** A1029 $1 multi 1.60 .25
*a.* Booklet pane of 20, 7 each #4465-4466, 6 #4467 32.00
*Nos. 4465-4467 (3)* 4.80 .75

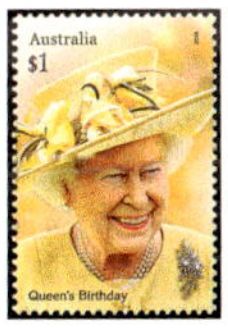
Queen Elizabeth II, 90th Birthday — A1030

Designs: $1, Queen Elizabeth II. $2.75, Golden wattle diamond brooch.

**2016, Apr. 5 Litho. *Perf. 14¾x14***

**4468** A1030 $1 multi 1.60 1.25
**4469** A1030 $2.75 multi 4.25 4.25
*a.* Souvenir sheet of 2, #4468-4469 6.00 6.00

**Booklet Stamp**
**Self-Adhesive**

***Serpentine Die Cut 11¼ Syncopated***

**4470** A1030 $2.75 multi 4.25 2.10
*a.* Booklet pane of 5 21.50

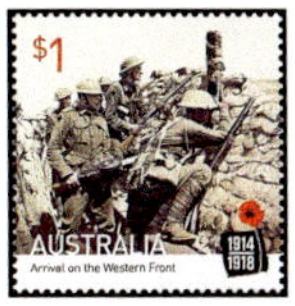
World War I, Cent. — A1031

Poppy and: Nos. 4471, 4476, Soldiers arriving on the Western Front. Nos. 4472, 4477, Somme Offensive. Nos. 4473, 4478, Referendum on conscription. Nos. 4474, 4479, Matron Grace Wilson of Australian Army Nursing Service, and Royal Red Cross, First Class. Nos. 4475, 4480, Soldier writing letter home.

**2016, Apr. 12 Litho. *Perf. 14¼***

**4471** A1031 $1 multi 1.60 1.60
**4472** A1031 $1 multi 1.60 1.60
**4473** A1031 $1 multi 1.60 1.60
**4474** A1031 $1 multi 1.60 1.60
*a.* Booklet pane of 4, #4471-4474 6.50 —
**4475** A1031 $1 multi 1.60 1.60
*a.* Booklet pane of 4, #4472-4475 6.50 —
*b.* Booklet pane of 4, #4471, 4473-4475 6.50 —
*c.* Booklet pane of 4, #4471-4472, 4474-4475 6.50 —
*d.* Booklet pane of 4, #4471-4473, 4475 6.50 —
Complete booklet, #4474a, 4475a, 4475b, 4475c, 4475d 32.50
*e.* Souvenir sheet of 5, #4471-4475 8.00 8.00
*Nos. 4471-4475 (5)* 8.00 8.00

**Booklet Stamps**
**Self-Adhesive**

***Serpentine Die Cut 11¼ Syncopated***

**4476** A1031 $1 multi 1.60 .25
**4477** A1031 $1 multi 1.60 .25
**4478** A1031 $1 multi 1.60 .25
**4479** A1031 $1 multi 1.60 .25
**4480** A1031 $1 multi 1.60 .25
*a.* Booklet pane of 10, 2 each #4476-4480 16.00
*Nos. 4476-4480 (5)* 8.00 1.25

Complete booklet sold for $20.95.

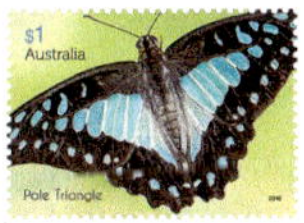
Butterflies — A1032

Designs: Nos. 4481, 4485, Pale triangle butterfly. Nos. 4482, 4487, Bordered rustic butterfly. Nos. 4483, 4486, Cairns birdwing butterfly. $2.75, Chequered swallowtail butterfly.

**2016, May 3 Litho. *Perf. 14x14¾***

**4481** A1032 $1 multi 1.50 1.50
**4482** A1032 $1 multi 1.50 1.50
**4483** A1032 $1 multi 1.50 1.50
**4484** A1032 $2.75 multi 4.00 4.00
*a.* Souvenir sheet of 4, #4481-4484 8.50 8.50
*Nos. 4481-4484 (4)* 8.50 8.50

**Self-Adhesive**

***Serpentine Die Cut 11¼ Syncopated***

**4485** A1032 $1 multi 1.50 .25
**4486** A1032 $1 multi 1.50 .25
**4487** A1032 $1 multi 1.50 .25
*a.* Horiz. coil strip of 3, #4485-4487 4.50
*b.* Booklet pane of 20, 7 each #4485, 4487, 6 #4486 30.00

**Booklet Stamp**

**4488** A1032 $2.75 multi 4.00 2.00
*a.* Booklet pane of 5 20.00
*Nos. 4485-4488 (4)* 8.50 2.75

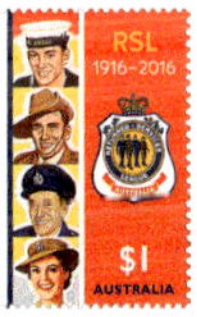
Returned and Services League of Australia, Cent. — A1033

**2016, May 31 Litho. *Perf. 14¾x14***

**4489** A1033 $1 multi 1.50 1.50

**Booklet Stamp**
**Self-Adhesive**

***Serpentine Die Cut 11¼ Syncopated***

**4490** A1033 $1 multi 1.50 .25
*a.* Booklet pane of 20 30.00

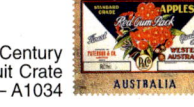

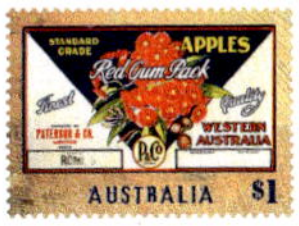
Early 20th Century Fruit Crate Labels — A1034

Labels for: Nos. 4491, 4495, Paterson & Co. "Red Gum Pack" Apples. Nos. 4492, 4496, The River's Pride Navel Oranges. Nos. 4493, 4497, L. H. Kile "Robin" Apples. Nos. 4494, 4498, W. H. Price Ltd. Special Ohanez Grapes.

**2016, June 7 Litho. *Perf. 14x14¾***

**4491** A1034 $1 multi 1.50 1.50
*a.* Booklet pane of 4 6.50 —
**4492** A1034 $1 multi 1.50 1.50
*a.* Booklet pane of 4 6.50 —
**4493** A1034 $1 multi 1.50 1.50
*a.* Booklet pane of 4 6.50 —
**4494** A1034 $1 multi 1.50 1.50
*a.* Booklet pane of 4 6.50 —
Complete booklet, #4491a, 4492a, 4493a, 4494a 26.00

**Self-Adhesive**

***Serpentine Die Cut 11¼ Syncopated***

**4495** A1034 $1 multi 1.50 .25
**4496** A1034 $1 multi 1.50 .25
**4497** A1034 $1 multi 1.50 .25
**4498** A1034 $1 multi 1.50 .25
*a.* Horiz. coil strip of 4, #4495-4498 6.00
*b.* Booklet pane of 10, 3 each #4496-4497, 2 each #4497-4498 15.00
*Nos. 4495-4100 (4)* 6.00 1.00

Complete booklet sold for $16.95.

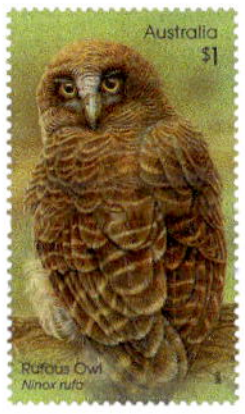
Owls — A1035

Designs: Nos. 4499, 4505, Rufous owl. Nos. 4500, 4503, Eastern grass owl. Nos. 4501, 4504, Sooty owl. Nos. 4502, 4506, Southern boobook owl.

**2016, July 5 Litho. *Perf. 14x13½***

**4499** A1035 $1 multi 1.50 1.50
*a.* Booklet pane of 2 3.25 —
**4500** A1035 $1 multi 1.50 1.50
*a.* Booklet pane of 2 3.25 —
*b.* Booklet pane of 2, #4499-4500 3.25 —
**4501** A1035 $1 multi 1.50 1.50
*a.* Booklet pane of 2 3.25 —
*b.* Booklet pane of 2, #4500-4501 3.25 —
**4502** A1035 $1 multi 1.50 1.50
*a.* Booklet pane of 2 3.25 —
*b.* Booklet pane of 2, #4501-4502 3.25 —
*c.* Booklet pane of 2, #4499, 4502 3.25 —
Complete booklet, #4499a, 4500a, 4500b, 4501a, 4501b, 4502a, 4502b, 4502c 26.00
*d.* Souvenir sheet of 4, #4499-4502 6.00 6.00
*Nos. 4499-4502 (4)* 6.00 6.00

**Booklet Stamps**
**Self-Adhesive**

***Serpentine Die Cut11¼x10¾ Syncopated***

**4503** A1035 $1 multi 1.50 .25
**4504** A1035 $1 multi 1.50 .25
**4505** A1035 $1 multi 1.50 .25
**4506** A1035 $1 multi 1.50 .25
*a.* Booklet pane of 10, 2 each #4503, 4506, 3 each #4504-4505 15.00

Complete booklet sold for $16.95.

**Olympic Gold Medalist Type of 2012**

Design: $1, Jared Tallent, men's 50-kilometer walk.

**2016, July 23 Litho. *Perf. 14½***

**4506B** A897 $1 multi 1.50 1.10

Tallent originally received a 2012 Olympic silver medal, but was awarded a gold medal in 2016 after Sergey Kirdyapkin was stripped of his medal for doping.

780　　　　　　　　　　　　　　　　　　　　　　　　　AUSTRALIA

*Play School* Children's Television Program, 50th Anniv. — A1036

Designs: $1, Jemima and Humpty. $2, Big Ted and Little Ted.

2016, July 26　Litho.　Perf. 14¾x14
4507　A1036　$1 multi　　　　1.50　1.50
4508　A1036　$2 multi　　　　3.00　2.25
  a.　Souvenir sheet of 2, #4507-4508　　　　　　　　4.50　4.50

**Booklet Stamp**
**Self-Adhesive**
*Serpentine Die Cut 11¼ Syncopated*
4509　A1036　$1 multi　　　　1.50　.25
  a.　Booklet pane of 10　15.00

**With Personalized Photo at Right Like Type A692a**
*Serpentine Die Cut 11½x11¼ Syncopated*
**Self-Adhesive**
4510　A1036　$1 multi　　　　2.50　2.50

No. 4510 was printed in a sheet of 20 and has personalized pictures and a straight edge at right and lack separations between the stamp and the personalized photo. Sheets of 20 sold for $33 each.

2016 Summer Olympics, Rio de Janeiro — A1037

2016, Aug. 2　Litho.　Perf. 14x14¾
4511　A1037　$1 multi　　　　1.50　1.10

Australian Gold Medalists at 2016 Summer Olympics, Rio de Janeiro — A1038

Designs: No. 4512, Mack Horton, men's 400-meter freestyle. No. 4513, Women's 4x100 meter freestyle relay team. No. 4514, Catherine Skinner, women's trap shooting. No. 4515, Women's rugby sevens team. No. 4516, Kyle Chalmers, men's 100-meter freestyle. No. 4517, Kimberley Brennan, women's single sculls. No. 4518, Tom Burton, men's Laser class sailing. No. 4519, Chloe Esposito, women's individual modern pentahlon.

2016　Litho.　Perf. 14¼
4512　A1038　$1 multi　　　　1.50　1.10
4513　A1038　$1 multi　　　　1.50　1.10
4514　A1038　$1 multi　　　　1.50　1.10
4515　A1038　$1 multi　　　　1.50　1.10
4516　A1038　$1 multi　　　　1.50　1.10
4517　A1038　$1 multi　　　　1.50　1.10
4518　A1038　$1 multi　　　　1.50　1.10
4519　A1038　$1 multi　　　　1.50　1.10
  Nos. 4512-4519 (8)　12.00　8.80

Nos. 4512-4519 were each printed in sheets of 10. Issued: Nos. 4512-4514, 8/8; No. 4515, 8/9; No. 4516, 8/11; No. 4517, 8/15; No. 4518, 8/17; No. 4519, 8/18.

**Items Starting With Same Letter Type of 2016**

Designs: Nos. 4520, 4525, Ant, Australian Rules Footballer players and ball, ANZAC memorial. Nos. 4521, 4526, Couple at campfire with Canberra map, crocodile, cockatoo. Nos. 4522, 4527, Lace monitor, lyrebird on lounge, Lamingtons on log. Nos. 4523, 4528, Rugby ball, refrigerator, rocket, reel, ruler, rope, Red Center poster. Nos. 4524, 4529, Tasmania map, Tasmanian devil, tradesman in tinnie (boat) with toolbelt.

2016, Aug. 16　Litho.　Perf. 14¾x14
4520　A1028　$1 multi　　　　1.50　1.50
4521　A1028　$1 multi　　　　1.50　1.50
4522　A1028　$1 multi　　　　1.50　1.50
4523　A1028　$1 multi　　　　1.50　1.50
4524　A1028　$1 multi　　　　1.50　1.50
  Nos. 4520-4524 (5)　　7.50　7.50

**Self-Adhesive**
*Serpentine Die Cut 11¼ Syncopated*
4525　A1028　$1 multi　　　　1.50　.25
  a.　Booklet pane of 10　15.00
4526　A1028　$1 multi　　　　1.50　.25
  a.　Booklet pane of 10　15.00

4527　A1028　$1 multi　　　　1.50　.25
  a.　Booklet pane of 10　15.00
4528　A1028　$1 multi　　　　1.50　.25
  a.　Booklet pane of 10　15.00
4529　A1028　$1 multi　　　　1.50　.25
  a.　Booklet pane of 10　15.00
  b.　Vert. coil strip of 5, #4525-4529　　　　　　　　7.50
  Nos. 4525-4529 (5)　7.50　1.25

Jewel Beetles — A1039

Designs: Nos. 4530, 4534, Stigmodera gratiosa. Nos. 4531, 4535, Castiarina klugii. No. 4532, Temognatha alternata. No. 4533, Julodimorpha bakewellii.

2016, Sept. 6　Litho.　Perf. 14¾x14
4530　A1039　$1 multi　　　　1.60　1.60
4531　A1039　$1 multi　　　　1.60　1.60
  a.　Horiz. pair, #4530-4531　3.20　3.20
4532　A1039　$2 multi　　　　3.25　2.40
4533　A1039　$2 multi　　　　3.25　2.40
  a.　Horiz. pair, #4532-4533　6.50　4.80
  Nos. 4530-4533 (4)　9.70　8.00

**Self-Adhesive**
*Serpentine Die Cut 11¼ Syncopated*
4534　A1039　$1 multi　　　　1.60　.25
4535　A1039　$1 multi　　　　1.60　.25
  a.　Vert. coil pair, #4534-4535　3.20
  b.　Booklet pane of 20, 10 each #4534-4535　　　　　32.00

Landing of Dirk Hartog in Western Australia, 400th Anniv. — A1040

2016, Sept. 13　Litho.　Perf. 14¾x14
4536　A1040　$2 multi　　　　3.25　2.40

A1041

Endangered Animals A1042

Designs: No. 4537, Orange-bellied parrots. No. 4538, Northern quolls. Nos. 4539, 4544, Snow leopards. Nos. 4540, 4545, Western swamp tortoise. Nos. 4541, 4546, Western lowland gorillas. Nos. 4542, 4547, Asian elephants. Nos. 4543, 4548, Southern corroboree frog.

2016, Sept. 20　Litho.　Perf. 14x14¾
4537　A1041　50c multi　　　　.80　.60
4538　A1041　50c multi　　　　.80　.60
  a.　Horiz. pair, #4537-4538　1.60　1.20
4539　A1041　$1 multi　　　　1.60　1.60
4540　A1041　$1 multi　　　　1.60　1.60
4541　A1041　$1 multi　　　　1.60　1.60
4542　A1041　$1 multi　　　　1.60　1.60
　　　Perf. 13¾x14
4543　A1042　$1 multi　　　　1.60　1.60
  a.　Souvenir sheet of 7, #4537-4543　　　　　　　　9.75　9.75
  Nos. 4537-4543 (7)　9.60　9.20

**Self-Adhesive**
*Serpentine Die Cut 11¼ Syncopated*
4544　A1041　$1 multi　　　　1.60　.25
4545　A1041　$1 multi　　　　1.60　.25
4546　A1041　$1 multi　　　　1.60　.25
4547　A1041　$1 multi　　　　1.60　.25
  a.　Horiz. coil strip of 4, #4544-4547　　　　　　　　6.40
  b.　Booklet pane of 20, 6 each #4544-4545, 4 each #4546, 4547　　　　32.00

**Booklet Stamp**
*Serpentine Die Cut 10¾x11 Syncopated*
4548　A1042　$1 multi　　　　1.60　.25
  a.　Booklet pane of 10　16.00
  Nos. 4544-4548 (5)　8.00　1.25

Taronga Zoo, cent. (Nos. 4543, 4548).

Monotremes — A1043

Designs: $2.10, Platypus. $2.95, Short-beaked echidna.

2016, Sept. 26　Litho.　Perf. 14¾x14
4549　A1043　$2.10 multi　　　3.25　3.25
4550　A1043　$2.95 multi　　　4.50　4.50
  a.　Souvenir sheet of 2, #4549-4550　　　　　　　　7.75　7.75

**Booklet Stamps**
**Self-Adhesive**
*Serpentine Die Cut 11¼ Syncopated*
4551　A1043　$2.10 multi　　　3.25　1.60
  a.　Booklet pane of 5　16.50
4552　A1043　$2.95 multi　　　4.50　2.25
  a.　Booklet pane of 5　22.50

**With Personalized Photo at Right Like Type A692a**
*Serpentine Die Cut 11½x11¼ Syncopated*
4553　A1043　$2.10 multi　　　4.25　4.25
4554　A1043　$2.95 multi　　　5.50　5.50

Nos. 4553-4554 were each printed in sheets of 20 and have personalized pictures and a straight edge at right and lack separations between the stamp and the personalized photo. Sheets of 20 of No. 4553 sold for $55 each, No. 4554, $72.

Australian Involvement in Viet Nam War — A1044

Poppies and inscription: Nos. 4555, 4560, In the field. Nos. 4556, 4561, Long Tan Cross. Nos. 4557, 4562, Aid and recreation. Nos. 4558, 4563, Opposition and withdrawal. Nos. 4559, 4564, Commemoration.

2016, Oct. 11　Litho.　Perf. 14¼
4555　A1044　$1 multi　　　　1.60　1.60
  a.　Booklet pane of 4　6.50　—
4556　A1044　$1 multi　　　　1.60　1.60
  a.　Booklet pane of 4　6.50　—
4557　A1044　$1 multi　　　　1.60　1.60
  a.　Booklet pane of 4　6.50　—
4558　A1044　$1 multi　　　　1.60　1.60
  a.　Booklet pane of 4　6.50　—
4559　A1044　$1 multi　　　　1.60　1.60
  a.　Complete booklet, #4555a, 4556a, 4557a, 4558a, 4559a　　　　　　32.50
  b.　Souvenir sheet of 5, #4555-4559　　　　　　　8.00　8.00
  Nos. 4555-4559 (5)　8.00　8.00

**Booklet Stamps**
**Self-Adhesive**
*Serpentine Die Cut 11¼ Syncopated*
4560　A1044　$1 multi　　　　1.60　.25
4561　A1044　$1 multi　　　　1.60　.25
4562　A1044　$1 multi　　　　1.60　.25
4563　A1044　$1 multi　　　　1.60　.25
4564　A1044　$1 multi　　　　1.60　.25
  a.　Booklet pane of 10, 2 each #4560-4564　　　　16.00
  Nos. 4560-4564 (5)　8.00　1.25

Complete booklet sold for $20.95.

Dylan Alcott, Paralympian of the Year — A1045

2016, Oct. 18　Litho.　Perf. 14¼
4565　A1045　$1 multi　　　　1.60　1.25

No. 4565 exists in sheets of 10.

Christmas
A1046　　　A1047

Designs: Nos. 4566, 4571, 4576, 4578, Star and "Goodwill." Nos. 4567, 4572, 4577, 4579, Gift and "Joy." Nos. 4568, 4573, 4580, Madonna and Child. Nos. 4569, 4574, 4581, Angel. Nos. 4570, 4575, Magi.

2016, Oct. 31　Litho.　Perf. 14¾x14
4566　A1046　65c multi　　　1.00　1.00
4567　A1046　65c multi　　　1.00　1.00
  a.　Horiz. pair, #4566-4567　2.00　2.00
4568　A1047　65c multi　　　1.00　1.00
4569　A1047　$1.70 multi　　2.60　2.60
4570　A1047　$2.55 multi　　4.00　4.00
  a.　Souvenir sheet of 3, #4568-4570　　　　　　　7.75　7.75
  Nos. 4566-4570 (5)　9.60　9.60

**Booklet Stamps**
**Self-Adhesive**
*Serpentine Die Cut 11¼ Syncopated*
4571　A1046　65c multi　　　1.00　.25
4572　A1047　65c multi　　　1.00　.25
  a.　Booklet pane of 20, 10 each #4971-4972, + 20 etiquettes　　　　　　　20.00
4573　A1047　65c multi　　　1.00　.25
  a.　Booklet pane of 20 + 20 etiquettes　　　　　20.00
4574　A1047　$1.70 multi　　2.60　1.40
  a.　Booklet pane of 5　13.00
4575　A1047　$2.55 multi　　4.00　2.00
  a.　Booklet pane of 5　20.00

**Litho. & Embossed With Foil Application**
4576　A1046　65c multi　　　1.00　.25
  a.　Booklet pane of 10　10.00
4577　A1046　65c multi　　　1.00　.25
  a.　Booklet pane of 10　10.00
  Nos. 4571-4577 (7)　11.60　4.65

**With Personalized Photo at Right Like Type A692a**
**Litho.**
*Serpentine Die Cut 11½x11¼ Syncopated*
4578　A1046　65c multi　　　2.00　2.00
4579　A1046　65c multi　　　2.00　2.00
4580　A1047　65c multi　　　2.00　2.00
4581　A1047　$1.70 multi　　3.50　3.50
  Nos. 4578-4581 (4)　9.50　9.50

Nos. 4578-4581 were each printed in sheets of 20 and have personalized pictures and a straight edge at right and lack separations between the stamp and the personalized photo. Sheets of 20 of No. 4578-4580 each sold for $26 each, No. 4581, $47.

Rose　　　　　Heart
A1048　　　　A1049

2017, Feb. 7　Litho.　Perf. 14¾x14
4582　A1048　$1 multi　　　1.60　1.60
4583　A1049　$1 multi　　　1.60　1.60

**Booklet Stamps**
**Self-Adhesive**
*Serpentine Die Cut 11¼ Syncopated*
4584　A1048　$1 multi　　　1.60　.25
  a.　Booklet pane of 10　16.00
4585　A1049　$1 multi　　　1.60　.25
  a.　Booklet pane of 10　16.00

**With Personalized Photo at Right Like Type A692a**
**Litho.**
*Serpentine Die Cut 11½x11¼ Syncopated*
**Self-Adhesive**
4586　A1048　$1 multi　　　2.60　2.60
4587　A1049　$1 multi　　　2.60　2.60

Nos. 4586-4587 were each printed in sheets of 20 and have personalized pictures and a straight edge at right and lack separations between the stamp and the personalized photo. Sheets of 20 of Nos. 4586-4587 sold for $33 each.

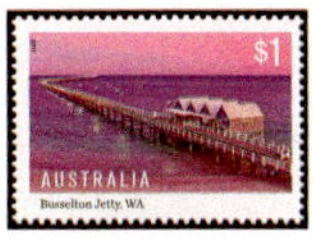

Jetties — A1050

Designs: Nos. 4588, 4592, Busselton Jetty, Western Australia. Nos. 4589, 4593, Tumby Bay Jetty, South Australia. $2.10, Shelley Beach Jetty, Victoria. $2.95, Kincumber Jetty, New South Wales.

**2017, Feb. 21 Litho. *Perf. 14x14¾***

**4588** A1050 $1 multi 1.60 1.60
**4589** A1050 $1 multi 1.60 1.60
*a.* Horiz. pair, #4588-4589 3.20 3.20
**4590** A1050 $2.10 multi 3.25 3.25
**4591** A1050 $2.95 multi 4.50 4.50
*Nos. 4588-4591 (4)* 10.95 10.95

**Self-Adhesive**

***Serpentine Die Cut 11¼ Syncopated***

**4592** A1050 $1 multi 1.60 1.60
**4593** A1050 $1 multi 1.60 1.60
*a.* Horiz. coil pair, #4592-4593 3.20
*b.* Booklet pane of 10, 5 each #4592-4593 16.00

**Booklet Stamps**

**4594** A1050 $2.10 multi 3.25 1.60
*a.* Booklet pane of 5 16.50
**4595** A1050 $2.95 multi 4.50 4.50
*a.* Booklet pane of 5 22.50
*Nos. 4592-4595 (4)* 10.95 9.30

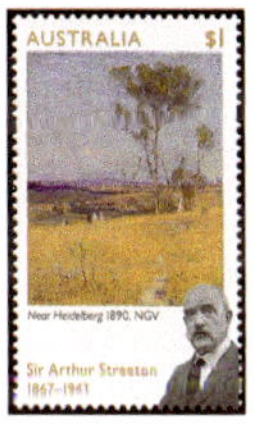

Paintings and Artists — A1051

Designs: No. 4596, Near Heidelberg, by Sir Arthur Streeton (1867-1943). No. 4597, Footballer, by Sir Sidney Nolan (1917-92).

**2017, Mar. 30 Litho. *Perf. 14x13½***

**4596** A1051 $1 multi 1.60 1.25
**4597** A1051 $1 multi 1.60 1.25
*a.* Horiz. pair, #4596-4597 3.20 2.50

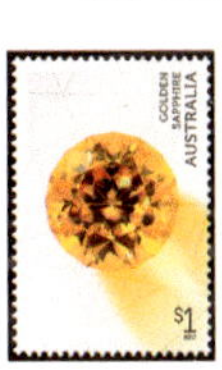

Gems — A1052

Designs: Nos. 4598, 4602, Golden sapphire. Nos. 4599, 4603, Rhodonite. No. 4600, Fluorite. No. 4601, Pink diamond.

**2017, Mar. 30 Litho. *Perf. 14¾x14***

**4598** A1052 $1 multi 1.60 1.60
*a.* Booklet pane of 4 6.50 —
**4599** A1052 $1 multi 1.60 1.60
*a.* Horiz. pair, #4598-4599 3.20 3.20
*b.* Booklet pane of 4 6.50 —
**4600** A1052 $2 multi 3.00 2.25
*a.* Booklet pane of 4 12.50 —
**4601** A1052 $2 multi 3.00 2.25
*a.* Horiz. pair, #4600-4601 6.00 4.50
*b.* Booklet pane of 4 12.50 —
*c.* Booklet pane of 4, #4598-4601 9.50 —
Complete booklet, #4598a, 4599b, 4600a, 4601b, 4601c 47.50
*d.* Souvenir sheet of 4, #4598-4601 9.25 7.75
*Nos. 4598-4601 (4)* 9.20 7.70

**Self-Adhesive**

***Serpentine Die Cut 11¼ Syncopated***

**4602** A1052 $1 multi 1.60 1.60
**4603** A1052 $1 multi 1.60 1.60
*a.* Vert. coil pair, #4602-4603 3.20
*b.* Booklet pane of 10, 5 each #4602-4603 16.00

Complete booklet sold for $30.95.

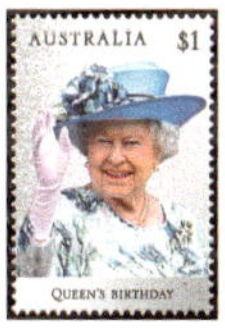

A1053

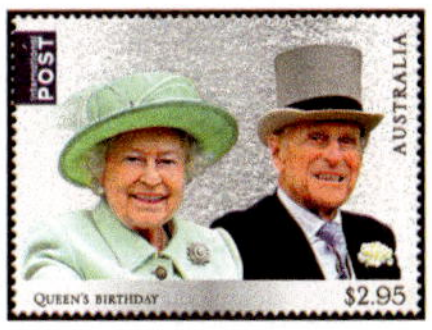

Queen Elizabeth II, 91st Birthday A1054

**2017, Apr. 4 Litho. *Perf. 14¾x14***

**4604** A1053 $1 multi 1.50 1.50
**4605** A1054 $2.95 multi 4.50 4.50
*a.* Souvenir sheet of 2, #4604-4605 6.00 6.00

**Booklet Stamps**
**Self-Adhesive**

***Serpentine Die Cut 11¼ Syncopated***

**4606** A1053 $1 multi 1.50 .25
*a.* Booklet pane of 10 15.00

***Serpentine Die Cut 11¼***

**4607** A1054 $2.95 multi 4.50 2.25
*a.* Booklet pane of 5 22.50

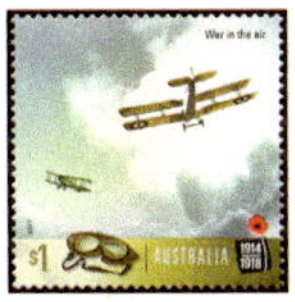

World War I, Cent. — A1055

Poppy and: Nos. 4608, 4613, War in the air. Nos. 4609, 4614, Third Battle of Ypres. Nos. 4610, 4616, Support for the troops. Nos. 4611, 4615, Sinai-Palestine campaign. Nos. 4612, 4617, War correspondent Charles Bean.

**2017, Apr. 18 Litho. *Perf. 14¼***

**4608** A1055 $1 multi 1.50 1.50
**4609** A1055 $1 multi 1.50 1.50
**4610** A1055 $1 multi 1.50 1.50
**4611** A1055 $1 multi 1.50 1.50
*a.* Booklet pane of 4, #4608-4611 6.50 —
**4612** A1055 $1 multi 1.50 1.50
*a.* Booklet pane of 4, #4608-4610, 4612 6.50 —
*b.* Booklet pane of 4, #4609-4612 6.50 —
*c.* Booklet pane of 4, #4608, 4610-4612 6.50 —
*d.* Booklet pane of 4, #4608-4609, 4611-4612 6.50 —
Complete booklet, #4611a, 4612a, 4612b, 4612c, 4612d 32.50
*e.* Souvenir sheet of 5, #4608-4612 7.50 7.50
*Nos. 4608-4612 (5)* 7.50 7.50

**Booklet Stamps**
**Self-Adhesive**

***Serpentine Die Cut 11¼ Syncopated***

**4613** A1055 $1 multi 1.50 .25
**4614** A1055 $1 multi 1.50 .25
**4615** A1055 $1 multi 1.50 .25
**4616** A1055 $1 multi 1.50 .25
**4617** A1055 $1 multi 1.50 .25
*a.* Booklet pane of 10, 2 each #4613-4617 15.00
*Nos. 4613-4617 (5)* 7.50 1.25

Complete booklet sold for $20.95.

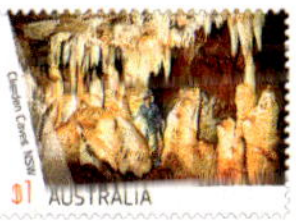

Caves — A1056

Designs: Nos. 4618, 4622, Cliefden Caves, New South Wales. Nos. 4619, 4623, Weebubbie Cave, Western Australia. $2, Undara Lava Tube, Queensland. $3, Kubla Khan Cave, Tasmania.

**2017, May 2 Litho. *Perf. 14x14¾***

**4618** A1056 $1 multi 1.50 1.50
**4619** A1056 $1 multi 1.50 1.50
*a.* Horiz. pair, #4618-4619 3.00 3.00
**4620** A1056 $2 multi 3.00 2.25
**4621** A1056 $3 multi 4.50 2.25
*Nos. 4618-4621 (4)* 10.50 7.50

**Self-Adhesive**

***Serpentine Die Cut 11¼ Syncopated***

**4622** A1056 $1 multi 1.50 .25
**4623** A1056 $1 multi 1.50 .25
*a.* Horiz. coil pair, #4622-4623 3.00
*b.* Booklet pane of 20, 10 each #4622-4623 30.00

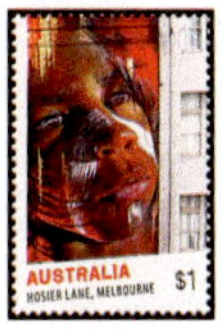

Street Art — A1057

Art: Nos. 4624, 4628, Indigenous Boy, by Adnate, Hosier Lane, Melbourne. Nos. 4625, 4631, Woman, by Vans the Omega, Railway Terrace, Adelaide. Nos. 4626, 4630, Forever Curious, by Rone and Phibs, Rutledge Lane, Melbourne. Nos. 4627, 4629, Shinka, by Fin DAC, Little Rundle Street, Adelaide.

**2017, May 16 Litho. *Perf. 14¾x14***

**4624** A1057 $1 multi 1.50 1.50
**4625** A1057 $1 multi 1.50 1.50
**4626** A1057 $1 multi 1.50 1.50
**4627** A1057 $1 multi 1.50 1.50
*a.* Souvenir sheet of 4, #4624-4627 6.00 6.00
*Nos. 4624-4627 (4)* 6.00 6.00

**Booklet Stamps**
**Self-Adhesive**

***Serpentine Die Cut 11¼ Syncopated***

**4628** A1057 $1 multi 1.50 .25
**4629** A1057 $1 multi 1.50 .25
**4630** A1057 $1 multi 1.50 .25
**4631** A1057 $1 multi 1.50 .25
*a.* Booklet pane of 10, 2 each #4628, 4631, 3 each #4629-4630 15.00
*Nos. 4628-4631 (4)* 6.00 1.00

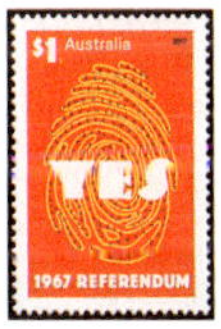

1907 Constitutional Amendment Referendum, 50th Anniv. — A1058

**2017, May 24 Litho. *Perf. 14¾x14***

**4632** A1058 $1 multi 1.50 1.10

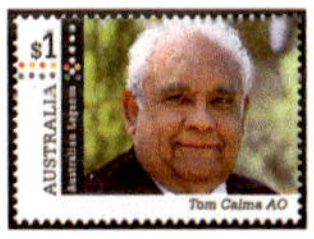

Distinguished Aborigines A1059

Designs: Nos. 4633, 4636, Tom Calma, University of Canberra Chancellor. Nos. 4634, 4637, Lowitja O'Donoghue, nurse, and first chairperson of Aboriginal and Torres Strait Islander Commission. Nos. 4635, 4638, Galarrwuy Yunupingu, Aboriginal land rights activist.

**2017, May 29 Litho. *Perf. 14x14¾***

**4633** A1059 $1 multi 1.50 1.50
**4634** A1059 $1 multi 1.50 1.50
**4635** A1059 $1 multi 1.50 1.50
*Nos. 4633-4635 (3)* 4.50 4.50

**Booklet Stamps**
**Self-Adhesive**

***Serpentine Die Cut 11¼ Syncopated***

**4636** A1059 $1 multi 1.50 .25
**4637** A1059 $1 multi 1.50 .25
**4638** A1059 $1 multi 1.50 .25
*a.* Booklet pane of 20, 7 each #4636-4637, 6 #4638 30.00
*Nos. 4636-4638 (3)* 4.50 .75

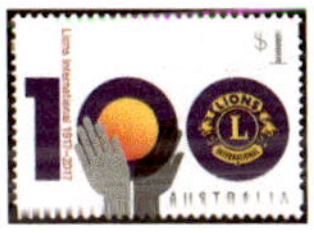

Lions Clubs International, Cent. — A1060

**2017, June 7 Litho. *Perf. 14x14¾***

**4639** A1060 $1 multi 1.60 1.60

**Booklet Stamp**
**Self-Adhesive**

***Serpentine Die Cut 11¼ Syncopated***

**4640** A1060 $1 multi 1.60 .25
*a.* Booklet pane of 20 32.00

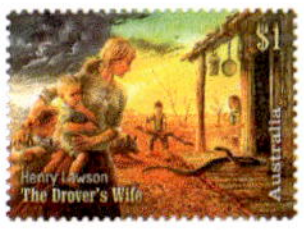

Scenes from Works Written by Henry Lawson (1867-1922) A1061

Scene from: $1, *The Drover's Wife.* $2.95, *Mitchell: A Character Sketch.*

**2017, June 13 Litho. *Perf. 14x14¾***

**4641** A1061 $1 multi 1.60 1.60
**4642** A1061 $2.95 multi 4.50 4.50
*a.* Souvenir sheet of 2, #4641-4642 6.25 6.25

**Booklet Stamps**
**Self-Adhesive**

***Serpentine Die Cut 11¼ Syncopated***

**4643** A1061 $1 multi 1.60 1.60
*a.* Booklet pane of 20 32.00
**4644** A1061 $2.95 multi 4.50 4.50
*a.* Booklet pane of 5 22.50

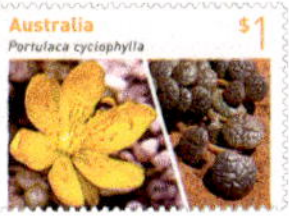

Succulent Plants — A1062

Designs: Nos. 4645, 4649, Portulaca cyclophylla. Nos. 4646, 4650, Tecticornia verrucosa. Nos. 4647, 4651, Calandrinia creethae. Nos. 4648, 4652, Gunniopsis quadrifida.

**2017, June 20 Litho. *Perf. 14x14¾***

**4645** A1062 $1 multi 1.60 1.60
**4646** A1062 $1 multi 1.60 1.60
**4647** A1062 $1 multi 1.60 1.60
**4648** A1062 $1 multi 1.60 1.60
*Nos. 4645-4648 (4)* 6.40 6.40

**Self-Adhesive**

***Serpentine Die Cut 11¼ Syncopated***

**4649** A1062 $1 multi 1.60 .25
**4650** A1062 $1 multi 1.60 .25
**4651** A1062 $1 multi 1.60 .25
**4652** A1062 $1 multi 1.60 .25
*a.* Horiz. coil strip of 4, #4649-4652 6.40
*b.* Booklet pane of 10, 3 each #4649-4650, 2 each #4651-4652 16.00
*Nos. 4649-4652 (4)* 6.40 1.00

**Wildflowers Type of 2015**

***Serpentine Die Cut 11¼ Syncopated***

**2017, July 4 Self-Adhesive Litho.**

**Booklet Stamp**

**4653** A1015 $2 Golden rainbow 3.25 1.60
*a.* Booklet pane of 5 16.50

Dated 2016.

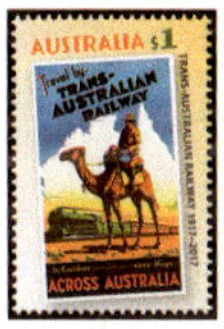
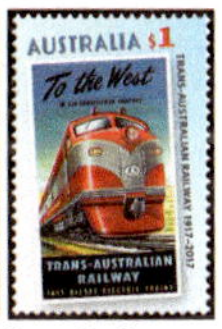

Trans-Australian Railway Travel Posters
A1063 A1064

**2017, July 4 Litho. *Perf. 14¾x14***

**4654** A1063 $1 multi 1.60 1.60
**4655** A1064 $1 multi 1.60 1.60
*a.* Souvenir sheet of 2, #4654-4655 3.25 3.25

**Booklet Stamps**
**Self-Adhesive**

***Serpentine Die Cut 11¼ Syncopated***

**4656** A1063 $1 multi 1.60 .25
**4657** A1064 $1 multi 1.60 .25
*a.* Booklet pane of 10, 5 each #4656-4657 16.00

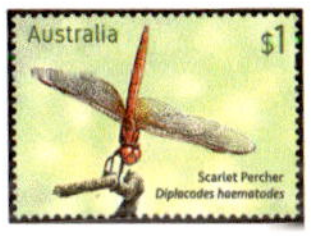

A1065

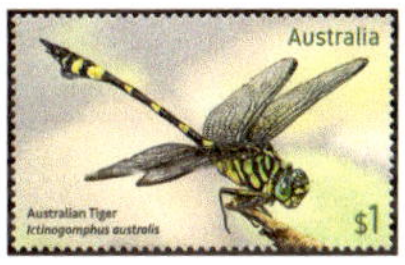

Dragonflies A1066

Designs: Nos. 4658, 4663, Scarlet percher. Nos. 4659, 4664, Arrowhead rockmaster. Nos. 4660, 4666, Australian tiger. Nos. 4661, 4667, Jewel flutterer. Nos. 4662, 4665, Beautiful petaltail.

**2017, Aug. 1 Litho. *Perf. 14x14¾***

**4658** A1065 $1 multi 1.60 1.60
*a.* Perf. 14x14¾x13¾x14¾ 1.60 1.60

**4659** A1065 $1 multi 1.60 1.60
*a.* Perf. 14x14¾x13¾x14¾ 1.60 1.60

***Perf. 13¾x14***

**4660** A1066 $1 multi 1.60 1.60
**4661** A1066 $1 multi 1.60 1.60
**4662** A1066 $1 multi 1.60 1.60
*a.* Souvenir sheet of 5, #4658a, 4659a, 4660-4662 8.00 8.00
*Nos. 4658-4662 (5)* 8.00 8.00

**Self-Adhesive**

***Serpentine Die Cut 11¼ Syncopated***

**4663** A1065 $1 multi 1.60 .25
**4664** A1065 $1 multi 1.60 .25
*a.* Horiz. coil pair, #4663-4664 3.20
*b.* Booklet pane of 20, 10 each #4663-4664 32.00

**Booklet Stamps**

***Serpentine Die Cut 10¾ Syncopated***

**4665** A1066 $1 multi 1.60 .25
**4666** A1066 $1 multi 1.60 .25
**4667** A1066 $1 multi 1.60 .25
*a.* Booklet pane of 10, 3 each #4665, 4667, 4 #4666 16.00
*Nos. 4663-4667 (5)* 8.00 1.25

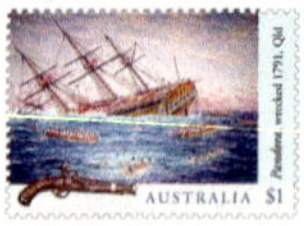

Shipwrecks A1067

Wreck of: Nos. 4668, 4671, HMS Pandora, 1791, and pistol. Nos. 4669, 4672, PS Clonmel, 1841, and decanter. Nos. 4670, 4673, Zuytdorp, 1712, and silver coin.

**2017, Aug. 29 Litho. *Perf. 14x14¾***

**4668** A1067 $1 multi 1.60 1.60
**4669** A1067 $1 multi 1.60 1.60
**4670** A1067 $1 multi 1.60 1.60
*a.* Booklet pane of 4, #4669, 4670, 2 #4668 6.75 —
*b.* Booklet pane of 4, #4668, 4670, 2 #4669 6.75 —
*c.* Booklet pane of 4, #4668, 4669, 2 #4670 (#4670 at UL and LR) 6.75 —
*d.* Booklet pane of 4, #4668, 4669, 2 #4670 (#4670 at UR and LL) 6.75 —
Complete booklet, #4670a, 4670c, 4670d, 2 #4670b 34.00
*Nos. 4668-4670 (3)* 4.80 4.80

**Self-Adhesive**

***Serpentine Die Cut 11¼ Syncopated***

**4671** A1067 $1 multi 1.60 .25
**4672** A1067 $1 multi 1.60 .25
**4673** A1067 $1 multi 1.60 .25
*a.* Horiz. coil strip of 3, #4671-4673 4.80
*b.* Booklet pane of 10, 4 #4671, 3 each #4672-4673 16.00
*Nos. 4671-4673 (3)* 4.80 .75

Complete booklet sold for $20.95. The pane margins differ on the two examples of No. 4670b in the complete booklet.

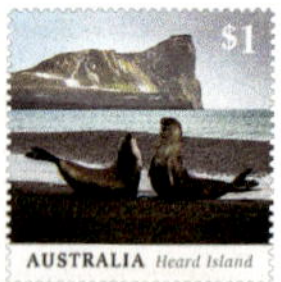

Heard Island — A1068

Designs: No. 4674, Southern elephant seals. No. 4675, Kerguelen cabbage. No. 4676, King penguins. No. 4677, Baudissin Glacier.

**2017, Sept. 5 Litho. *Perf. 14¼***

**4674** A1068 $1 multi 1.60 1.25
**4675** A1068 $1 multi 1.60 1.25
**4676** A1068 $1 multi 1.60 1.25
**4677** A1068 $1 multi 1.60 1.25
*a.* Souvenir sheet of 4, #4674-4677 6.50 5.00
*Nos. 4674-4677 (4)* 6.40 5.00

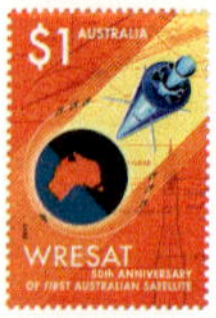

Launch of Weapons Research Satellite, 50th Anniv. — A1069

**2017, Sept. 12 Litho. *Perf. 14¾x14***

**4678** A1069 $1 multi 1.60 1.60

**Booklet Stamp**
**Self-Adhesive**

***Serpentine Die Cut 11¼ Syncopated***

**4679** A1069 $1 multi 1.60 .25
*a.* Booklet pane of 20 32.00

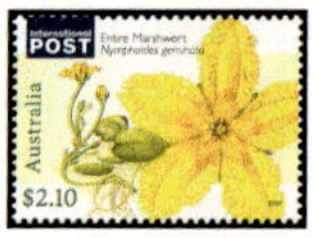

Water Plants — A1070

Designs: $2.10, Entire marshwort. $2.30, Giant waterlily. $3, Lotus lily.

**2017, Sept. 27 Litho. *Perf. 14x14¾***

**4680** A1070 $2.10 multi 3.25 3.25
**4681** A1070 $2.30 multi 3.75 3.75
**4682** A1070 $3 multi 4.75 4.75
*Nos. 4680-4682 (3)* 11.75 11.75

**Booklet Stamps**
**Self-Adhesive**

***Serpentine Die Cut 11¼ Syncopated***

**4683** A1070 $2.10 multi 3.25 1.60
*a.* Booklet pane of 5 16.50
**4684** A1070 $2.30 multi 3.75 1.90
*a.* Booklet pane of 5 19.00
**4685** A1070 $3 multi 4.75 2.40
*a.* Booklet pane of 5 24.00
*Nos. 4683-4685 (3)* 11.75 5.90

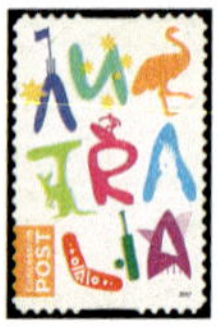

"Australia" — A1071

***Serpentine Die Cut 11¼ Syncopated***

**2017, Oct. 2 Self-Adhesive Litho.**

**Booklet Stamps**

**4686** A1071 ($1) multi 1.75 .25
*a.* Booklet pane of 5 8.75

No. 4686a was made available to holders of Australia Post My Post Concession Account card and the general public. Pensioners, veterans, the disabled, and others typically on low or fixed incomes, could apply at their local post office to receive a Concession Account card. Those eligible to receive the card were sent a free example of No. 4686a, which was mailed with the card. Card holders, when showing the card at the post office and having the information recorded, could purchase up to ten No. 4686a every year for $3 (60c per stamp, lower than the $1 letter rate). The examples of No. 4686a made available to the public through the philatelic bureau sold for $5.45 ($1.09 per stamp). There are no differences between the stamps offered to card holders and the general public, aside from the selling price. No. 4686 was valid only on domestic letters and could not be used on parcels or international mail.

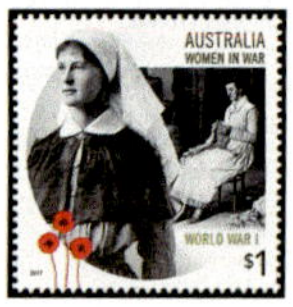

Women at War — A1072

Poppies and women in: Nos. 4687, 4692, World War I. Nos. 4688, 4693, World War II. Nos. 4689, 4694, Korea and Viet Nam. Nos. 4690, 4695, Afghanistan and Iraq. Nos. 4691, 4696, Peacekeeping.

**2017, Oct. 6 Litho. *Perf. 14¼***

**4687** A1072 $1 multi 1.60 1.60
**4688** A1072 $1 multi 1.60 1.60
**4689** A1072 $1 multi 1.60 1.60
**4690** A1072 $1 multi 1.60 1.60
**4691** A1072 $1 multi 1.60 1.60
*a.* Souvenir sheet of 5, #4687-4691 8.00 8.00
*Nos. 4687-4691 (5)* 8.00 8.00

**Booklet Stamps**
**Self-Adhesive**

***Serpentine Die Cut 11¼ Syncopated***

**4692** A1072 $1 multi 1.60 .25
**4693** A1072 $1 multi 1.60 .25
**4694** A1072 $1 multi 1.60 .25
**4695** A1072 $1 multi 1.60 .25
**4696** A1072 $1 multi 1.60 .25
*a.* Booklet pane of 10, 2 each #4692-4696 16.00
*Nos. 4692-4696 (5)* 8.00 1.25

**Items Starting With Same Letter Type of 2016**

Designs: Nos. 4697, 4702, Barramundi in billy on barbecue, blowflies, and budgie-smugglers (bathing suit). Nos. 4698, 4703, Galahs, gasket, gecko, gnome, man in gumboots, signs to Gladstone, Great Barrier Reef and Gulargambone. Nos. 4699, 4704, Jabiru, jillaroo, jam and jumbucks. No. 4700, 4705, Kangaroo, koala, kelpie. Nos. 4701, 4706, Ulysses butterfly, ute, uggs, umpire with ukulele, umbrella.

**2017, Oct. 17 Litho. *Perf. 14¾x14***

**4697** A1028 $1 multi 1.60 1.60
**4698** A1028 $1 multi 1.60 1.60
**4699** A1028 $1 multi 1.60 1.60
**4700** A1028 $1 multi 1.60 1.60
**4701** A1028 $1 multi 1.60 1.60
*Nos. 4697-4701 (5)* 8.00 8.00

**Self-Adhesive**

***Serpentine Die Cut 11¼ Syncopated***

**4702** A1028 $1 multi 1.60 .25
*a.* Booklet pane of 10 16.00
**4703** A1028 $1 multi 1.60 .25
*a.* Booklet pane of 10 16.00
**4704** A1028 $1 multi 1.60 .25
*a.* Booklet pane of 10 16.00
**4705** A1028 $1 multi 1.60 .25
*a.* Booklet pane of 10 16.00
**4706** A1028 $1 multi 1.60 .25
*a.* Booklet pane of 10 16.00
*b.* Vert. coil strip of 5, #4702-4706 8.00
*Nos. 4702-4706 (5)* 8.00 1.25

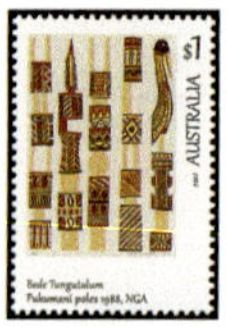

Aboriginal Art — A1073

Designs: Nos. 4707, 4711, Pukumani Poles, by Bede Tungutalum. Nos. 4708, 4712, Waterlili and Gaya, by Banduk Marika. No. 4709, Untitled, by Tungutalum. No. 4710, Guyamala, by Marika.

**2017, Oct. 24 Litho. *Perf. 14¾x14***

**4707** A1073 $1 multi 1.60 1.60
**4708** A1073 $1 multi 1.60 1.60
**4709** A1073 $2 multi 3.25 3.25
**4710** A1073 $2 multi 3.25 3.25
*Nos. 4707-4710 (4)* 9.70 9.70

**Booklet Stamps**
**Self-Adhesive**

***Serpentine Die Cut 11¼ Syncopated***

**4711** A1073 $1 multi 1.60 .25
**4712** A1073 $1 multi 1.60 .25
*a.* Booklet pane of 20, 10 each #4711-4712 32.00

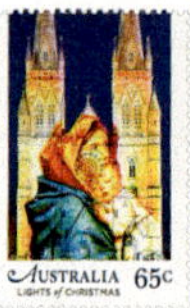

Christmas
A1074 A1075

Designs: Nos. 4713, 4718, Madonna and Child projected on St. Mary's Cathedral, Sydney. Nos. 4714, 4719, 4723, Christmas gift boxes. Nos. 4715, 4720, 4724, Star and Christmas tree. $2, Bells. $2.30, Small Cowper Madonna projected on St. Mary's Cathedral.

**2017, Nov. 1 Litho. *Perf. 14¾x14***

**4713** A1074 65c multi 1.00 1.00
**4714** A1075 65c multi 1.00 1.00
**4715** A1075 65c multi 1.00 1.00
*a.* Horiz. pair, #4714-4715 2.00 2.00
**4716** A1075 $2 multi 3.25 1.60
**4717** A1074 $2.30 multi 3.50 1.75
*a.* Souvenir sheet of 2, #4713, 4717 4.50 2.75
*Nos. 4713-4717 (5)* 9.75 6.35

**Booklet Stamps**
**Self-Adhesive**

***Serpentine Die Cut 11¼ Syncopated***

**4718** A1074 65c multi 1.00 .25
*a.* Booklet pane of 20 + 20 labels 20.00
**4719** A1075 65c multi 1.00 .25
**4720** A1075 65c multi 1.00 .25
*a.* Booklet pane of 20, 10 each #4719-4720 + 20 labels 20.00
**4721** A1075 $2 multi 3.25 1.60
*a.* Booklet pane of 5 16.50
**4722** A1074 $2.30 multi 3.50 1.75
*a.* Booklet pane of 5 17.50

**Litho. With Foil Application**

**4723** A1075 65c gold & multi 1.00 .25
*a.* Booklet pane of 10 10.00
**4724** A1075 65c gold & multi 1.00 .25
*a.* Booklet pane of 10 10.00
*Nos. 4718-4724 (7)* 11.75 4.60

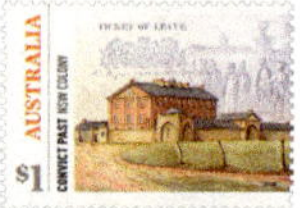

Australian Convict Heritage — A1076

Designs: Nos. 4730, 4733, Hyde Park Barracks, Sydney, New South Wales Colony, ticket of leave, and chain gang. Nos. 4731, 4734, Penitentiary, Van Diemen's Land, convict love token. $3, Convict Establishment (Fremantle Prison), Swan River Colony, article from newspaper about life on convict transport ships.

**2018, Jan. 16 Litho. *Perf. 14x14¾***

**4730** A1076 $1 multi 1.60 1.60
**4731** A1076 $1 multi 1.60 1.60
**4732** A1076 $3 multi 5.00 2.50
*Nos. 4730-4732 (3)* 8.20 5.70

**Self-Adhesive**

***Serpentine Die Cut 11¼ Syncopated***

**4733** A1076 $1 multi 1.60 .25
**4734** A1076 $1 multi 1.60 .25
*a.* Horiz. coil pair, #4733-4734 3.20
*b.* Booklet pane of 10, 5 each #4733-4734 16.00

**Booklet Stamp**

**4735** A1076 $3 multi 5.00 2.50
*a.* Booklet pane of 5 25.00
*Nos. 4733-4735 (3)* 8.20 3.00

Nos. 4732 & 4735 are inscribed: "International Post".

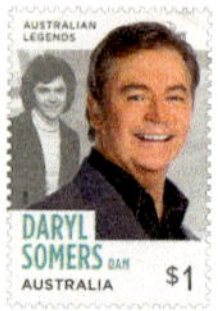

Television Personalities — A1077

Designs: Nos. 4736, 4741, Daryl Somers, television host. Nos. 4737, 4742, Denise Drysdale, singer and dancer. Nos. 4738, 4743, Bert Newton, television host. Nos. 4739, 4744, Kerri-Anne Kennerley, television host. Nos. 4740-4745, Ray Martin, television journalist.

**2018, Jan. 18 Litho. *Perf. 14¾x14***

**4736** A1077 $1 multi 1.60 1.60
**4737** A1077 $1 multi 1.60 1.60
**4738** A1077 $1 multi 1.60 1.60
**4739** A1077 $1 multi 1.60 1.60
**4740** A1077 $1 multi 1.60 1.60
*Nos. 4736-4740 (5)* 8.00 8.00

**Booklet Stamps**
**Self-Adhesive**

***Serpentine Die Cut 11¼ Syncopated***

**4741** A1077 $1 multi 1.60 .25
*a.* Booklet pane of 10 16.00
**4742** A1077 $1 multi 1.60 .25
*a.* Booklet pane of 10 16.00
**4743** A1077 $1 multi 1.60 .25
*a.* Booklet pane of 10 16.00
**4744** A1077 $1 multi 1.60 .25
*a.* Booklet pane of 10 16.00
**4745** A1077 $1 multi 1.60 .25
*a.* Booklet pane of 10 16.00
*Nos. 4741-4745 (5)* 8.00 1.25

Bird A1078

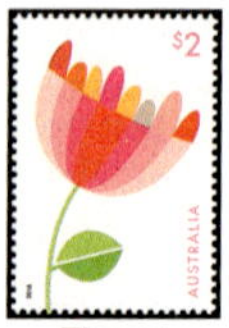

Flower A1079

**2018, Feb. 6 Litho. *Perf. 14¾x14***

**4746** A1078 $1 multi 1.60 1.60
**4747** A1079 $2 multi 3.25 1.60

**Booklet Stamp**
**Self-Adhesive**

***Serpentine Die Cut 11¼ Syncopated***

**4748** A1078 $1 multi 1.60 .25
*a.* Booklet pane of 10 16.00

**With Personalized Photo at Right Like Type A692a**

***Serpentine Die Cut 11½x11¼ Syncopated***

**4749** A1078 $1 multi 2.50 2.50
**4750** A1079 $1 multi 2.50 2.50

Nos. 4749-4750 were each printed in sheets of 20 and have personalized pictures and a straight edge at right and lack separations between the stamp and the personalized photo. Sheets of 20 of Nos. 4749-4750 sold for $33 each.

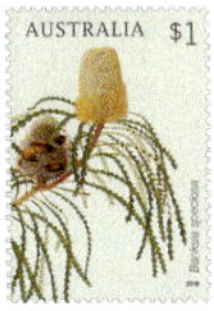


Banksia Flowers — A1080

Designs: Nos. 4751, 4755, 4759, Banksia speciosa. Nos. 4752, 4756, 4760, Banksia grossa. Nos. 4753, 4757, 4761, Baksia coccinea. Nos. 4754, 4758, 4762, Banksia cuneata.

**2018, Feb. 20 Litho. *Perf. 14¾x14***

**4751** A1080 $1 multi 1.60 1.60
**4752** A1080 $1 multi 1.60 1.60
**4753** A1080 $1 multi 1.60 1.60
**4754** A1080 $1 multi 1.60 1.60
*a.* Souvenir sheet of 4, #4751-4754 6.50 6.50
*Nos. 4751-4754 (4)* 6.40 6.40

**Booklet Stamps**
**Self-Adhesive**

***Serpentine Die Cut 11¼ Syncopated***

**4755** A1080 $1 multi 1.60 .25
**4756** A1080 $1 multi 1.60 .25
**4757** A1080 $1 multi 1.60 .25
**4758** A1080 $1 multi 1.60 .25
*a.* Booklet pane of 20, 5 each #4755-4758 32.00
*Nos. 4755-4758 (4)* 6.40 1.00

**With Personalized Photo at Right Like Type A692a**

***Serpentine Die Cut 11½x11¼ Syncopated***

**4759** A1080 $1 multi 2.50 2.50
**4760** A1080 $1 multi 2.50 2.50
**4761** A1080 $1 multi 2.50 2.50
**4762** A1080 $1 multi 2.50 2.50
*Nos. 4759-4762 (4)* 10.00 10.00

Nos. 4759-4762 were each printed in sheets of 20 and have personalized pictures and a straight edge at right and lack separations between the stamp and the personalized photo. Sheets of 20 of Nos. 4759-4762 sold for $33 each.

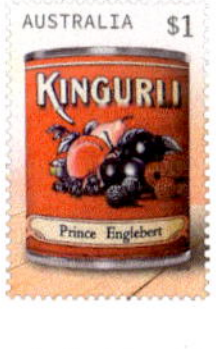


19th and 20th Century Jam Can Labels — A1081

Label for: Nos. 4763, 4767, Kingurli Prince Engelbert Plum Jam. Nos. 4764, 4768, Peacock's Apricot Jam. Nos. 4765, 4769, Melray Blackberry Jam. Nos. 4766, 4770, Alva Dark Plum Jam.

**2018, Mar. 6 Litho. *Perf. 14¾x14***

**4763** A1081 $1 multi 1.60 1.60
**4764** A1081 $1 multi 1.60 1.60
**4765** A1081 $1 multi 1.60 1.60
**4766** A1081 $1 multi 1.60 1.60
*Nos. 4763-4766 (4)* 6.40 6.40

**Booklet Stamps**
**Self-Adhesive**

***Serpentine Die Cut 11¼ Syncopated***

**4767** A1081 $1 multi 1.60 .25
*a.* Booklet pane of 10 16.00
**4768** A1081 $1 multi 1.60 .25
*a.* Booklet pane of 10 16.00
**4769** A1081 $1 multi 1.60 .25
*a.* Booklet pane of 10 16.00
**4770** A1081 $1 multi 1.60 .25
*a.* Booklet pane of 10 16.00
*Nos. 4767-4770 (4)* 6.40 1.00

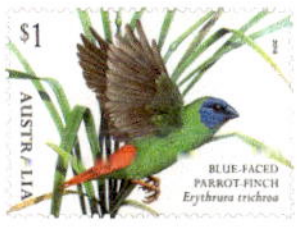


Finches — A1082

Designs: Nos. 4771, 4775, Blue-faced parrot-finch. Nos. 4772, 4776, Double-barred finches. Nos. 4773, 4777, Star finches. Nos. 4774, 4778, Zebra finches.

**2018, Mar. 16 Litho. *Perf. 14x14¾***

**4771** A1082 $1 multi 1.60 1.60
**4772** A1082 $1 multi 1.60 1.60
**4773** A1082 $1 multi 1.60 1.60
**4774** A1082 $1 multi 1.60 1.60
*Nos. 4771-4774 (4)* 6.40 6.40

**Self-Adhesive**

***Serpentine Die Cut 11¼ Syncopated***

**4775** A1082 $1 multi 1.60 .25
**4776** A1082 $1 multi 1.60 .25
**4777** A1082 $1 multi 1.60 .25
**4778** A1082 $1 multi 1.60 .25
*a.* Horiz. coil strip of 4, #4775-4778 6.40
*b.* Booklet pane of 10, 3 each #4775-4776, 2 each #4777-4778 16.00
*Nos. 4775-4778 (4)* 6.40 1.00

See Nos. 4811-4813.

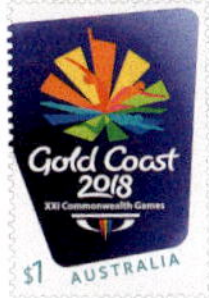


2018 Commonwealth Games, Gold Coast, Queensland — A1083

**2018, Mar. 20 Litho. *Perf. 14¾x14***

**4779** A1083 $1 multi 1.60 1.25

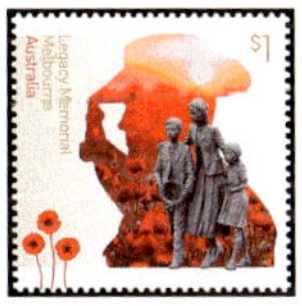


War Memorials — A1084

Poppies, silhouette of soldier and: Nos. 4780, 4788, Legacy Memorial, Melbourne. Nos. 4781, 4785, Avenue of Honor, Ballarat. Nos. 4782, 4786, Cobbers Statue, Fromelles, France. Nos. 4783, 4787, Cenotaph, Darwin. Nos. 4784, 4786, Tomb of the Unknown Australian Soldier, Canberra.

**2018, Apr. 10 Litho. *Perf. 14¼***

**4780** A1084 $1 multi 1.50 1.50
*a.* Booklet pane of 4 7.50 —
**4781** A1084 $1 multi 1.50 1.50
*a.* Booklet pane of 4 7.50 —
**4782** A1084 $1 multi 1.50 1.50
*a.* Booklet pane of 4 7.50 —
**4783** A1084 $1 multi 1.50 1.50
*a.* Booklet pane of 4 7.50 —
**4784** A1084 $1 multi 1.50 1.50
*a.* Booklet pane of 4 7.50 —
Complete booklet, #4780a, 4781a, 4782a, 4783a, 4784a 31.50
*b.* Souvenir sheet of 5, #4780-4784 7.50 7.50
*Nos. 4780-4784 (5)* 7.50 7.50

**Booklet Stamps**
**Self-Adhesive**

***Serpentine Die Cut 11¼ Syncopated***

**4785** A1084 $1 multi 1.50 .25
**4786** A1084 $1 multi 1.50 .25
**4787** A1084 $1 multi 1.50 .25
**4788** A1084 $1 multi 1.50 .25
**4789** A1084 $1 multi 1.50 .25
*a.* Booklet pane of 10, 2 each #4785-4789 15.00
*Nos. 4785-4789 (5)* 7.50 1.25

Complete booklet sold for $20.95.

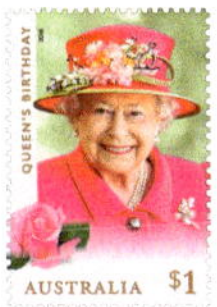


Queen Elizabeth II, 92nd Birthday — A1085

Queen Elizabeth II: $1, And Queen Elizabeth rose. $3, Holding bouquet of flowers.

**2018, Apr. 17 Litho. *Perf. 14¾x14***

**4790** A1085 $1 multi 1.50 1.50
**4791** A1085 $3 multi 4.50 2.25
*a.* Souvenir sheet of 2, #4790-4791 6.00 3.75

**Booklet Stamps**
**Self-Adhesive**

***Serpentine Die Cut 11¼ Syncopated***

**4792** A1085 $1 multi 1.50 .25
*a.* Booklet pane of 10 15.00
**4793** A1085 $3 multi 4.50 2.25
*a.* Booklet pane of 5 22.50

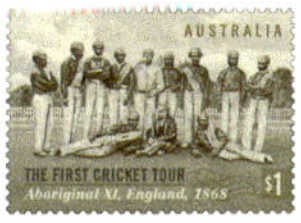


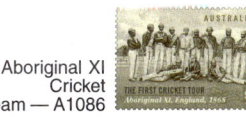

1868 Aboriginal XI Cricket Team — A1086

**2018, May 1 Litho. *Perf. 14x14¾***

**4794** A1086 $1 multi 1.50 1.10

First overseas tour of an Australian cricket team, 150th anniv.

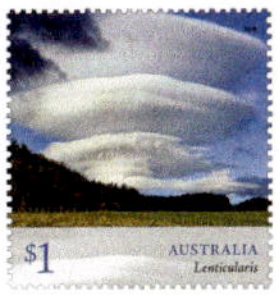


Clouds — A1087

Cloud type: Nos. 4795, 4799, Lenticularis. Nos. 4796, 4800, Mammatus. Nos. 4797, 4801, Cumulonimbus. Nos. 4798, 4802, Arcus.

**2018, May 1 Litho. *Perf. 14¼x14***

**4795** A1087 $1 multi 1.50 1.50
**4796** A1087 $1 multi 1.50 1.50
**4797** A1087 $1 multi 1.50 1.50
**4798** A1087 $1 multi 1.50 1.50
*a.* Souvenir sheet of 4, #4795-4798 6.00 6.00
*Nos. 4795-4798 (4)* 6.00 6.00

**Booklet Stamps**
**Self-Adhesive**

***Serpentine Die Cut 11¼ Syncopated***

**4799** A1087 $1 multi 1.50 .25
*a.* Booklet pane of 10 15.00
**4800** A1087 $1 multi 1.50 .25
*a.* Booklet pane of 10 15.00
**4801** A1087 $1 multi 1.50 .25
*a.* Booklet pane of 10 15.00
**4802** A1087 $1 multi 1.50 .25
*a.* Booklet pane of 10 15.00
*Nos. 4799-4802 (4)* 6.00 1.00

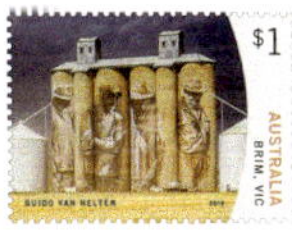


Silo Art — A1088

Silo from: Nos. 4803, 4807, Brim, Victoria. Nos. 4804, 4808, Ravensthorpe, Western Australia. Nos. 4805, 4809, Thallon, Queensland. Nos. 4806, 4810, Weethalle, New South Wales.

**2018, May 21 Litho. *Perf. 14x14¾***

**4803** A1088 $1 multi 1.50 1.50
**4804** A1088 $1 multi 1.50 1.50
*a.* Booklet pane of 4, 2 each #4803, 4804 6.25 —
**4805** A1088 $1 multi 1.50 1.50
*a.* Booklet pane of 4, 2 each #4803, 4805 6.25 —
**4806** A1088 $1 multi 1.50 1.50
*a.* Booklet pane of 4, #4803-4806 6.25 —
*b.* Booklet pane of 4, 2 each #4804, 4806 6.25 —
*c.* Booklet pane of 4, 2 each #4805, 4806 6.25 —
Complete booklet, #4804a, 4805a, 4806a, 4806b, 4806c 31.50
*d.* Souvenir sheet of 4, #4803-4806 6.00 6.00
*Nos. 4803-4806 (4)* 6.00 6.00

**Booklet Stamps**
**Self-Adhesive**

***Serpentine Die Cut 11¼ Syncopated***

**4807** A1088 $1 multi 1.50 .25
*a.* Booklet pane of 10 15.00
**4808** A1088 $1 multi 1.50 .25
*a.* Booklet pane of 10 15.00
**4809** A1088 $1 multi 1.50 .25
*a.* Booklet pane of 10 15.00
**4810** A1088 $1 multi 1.50 .25
*a.* Booklet pane of 10 15.00
*Nos. 4807-4810 (4)* 6.00 1.00

Complete booklet sold for $20.95.

**Finches Type of 2018**

Designs: No. 4811, Gouldian finches. No. 4812, Beautiful firetail. $2, Black-throated finches.

**2018, June 5 Litho. *Perf. 14x13¾***

**4811** A1082 $1 multi 1.50 1.10
**4812** A1082 $1 multi 1.50 1.10
**4813** A1082 $2 multi 3.00 2.25
*a.* Souvenir sheet of 3, #4811-4813 6.00 4.50
*Nos. 4811-4813 (3)* 6.00 4.45

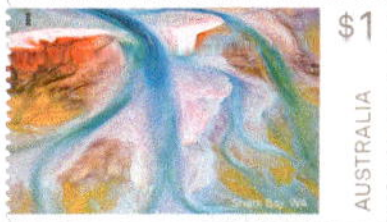


Art in Nature A1089

Aerial photographs of: Nos. 4814, 4818, Shark Bay, Western Australia. Nos. 4815, 4819, Lake MacDonnell, South Australia. Nos. 4816, 4820, Wyadup Rocks, Western Australia. Nos. 4817, 4821, Cape Capricorn, Queensland.

**2018, June 12 Litho. *Perf. 14½x14***

**4814** A1089 $1 multi 1.50 1.50
**4815** A1089 $1 multi 1.50 1.50
**4816** A1089 $1 multi 1.50 1.50
**4817** A1089 $1 multi 1.50 1.50
*a.* Souvenir sheet of 4, #4814-4817 6.00 6.00
*Nos. 4814-4817 (4)* 6.00 6.00

**Booklet Stamps**
**Self-Adhesive**

***Serpentine Die Cut 10¾x11 Syncopated***

**4818** A1089 $1 multi 1.50 .25
*a.* Booklet pane of 10 15.00
**4819** A1089 $1 multi 1.50 .25
*a.* Booklet pane of 10 15.00
**4820** A1089 $1 multi 1.50 .25
*a.* Booklet pane of 10 15.00
**4821** A1089 $1 multi 1.50 .25
*a.* Booklet pane of 10 15.00
*Nos. 4818-4821 (4)* 6.00 1.00

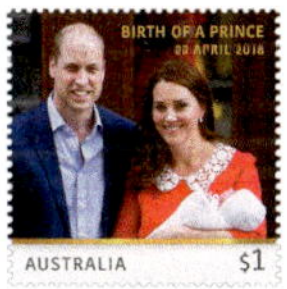


Birth of Prince Louis of Cambridge — A1090

**2018, July 3 Litho. *Perf. 14¼***

**4822** A1090 $1 multi 1.50 1.10

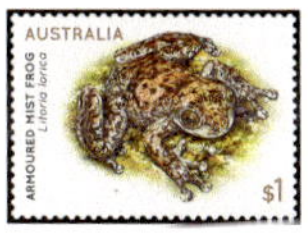


Frogs A1091

Designs: No. 4823, Armored mist frog. No. 4824, Australian lace-lid. No. 4825, Baw baw frog. No. 4826, Tasmanian tree frog.

**2018, July 10 Litho. *Perf. 14x14¾***

**4823** A1091 $1 multi 1.50 1.10
**4824** A1091 $1 multi 1.50 1.10
**4825** A1091 $1 multi 1.50 1.10
**4826** A1091 $1 multi 1.50 1.10
*a.* Souvenir sheet of 4, #4823-4826 6.00 4.50
*Nos. 4823-4826 (4)* 6.00 4.40

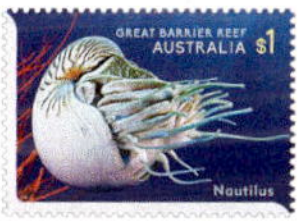


Reef Animals — A1092

Designs: Nos. 4827, 4832a, 4833, Nautilus. Nos. 4828, 4832b, 4834, Green sea turtle. Nos. 4829, 4832c, 4835, Olive sea snake. Nos. 4830, 4832d, 4836, Emperor angelfish. Nos. 4831, 4832e, Gray reef shark (50x30mm).

***Perf. 14x14¾, 14¼x14 (#4431, 4432e)***

**2018, Aug. 1 Litho.**

**Stamps With White Frames on Two Sides**

**4827** A1092 $1 multi 1.50 1.50
*a.* Booklet pane of 4 6.25 —
**4828** A1092 $1 multi 1.50 1.50
*a.* Booklet pane of 4 6.25 —
**4829** A1092 $1 multi 1.50 1.50
*a.* Booklet pane of 4 6.25 —
**4830** A1092 $1 multi 1.50 1.50
*a.* Booklet pane of 4 6.25 —
**4831** A1092 $2 multi 3.00 3.00
*a.* Booklet pane of 2 6.25 —
Complete booklet, #4827a, 4828a, 4829a, 4830a, 4831a 31.50
*Nos. 4827-4831 (5)* 9.00 9.00

**Souvenir Sheet**
**Stamps Without White Frames**

**4832** Sheet of 5 9.00 6.75
*a.-d.* A1092 $1 Any single 1.50 1.10
*e.* A1092 $2 multi 3.00 2.25

**Booklet Stamps**
**Self-Adhesive**
**Stamps With White Frames on Two Sides**

***Serpentine Die Cut 11¼ Syncopated***

**4833** A1092 $1 multi 1.50 .25
**4834** A1092 $1 multi 1.50 .25
**4835** A1092 $1 multi 1.50 .25
**4836** A1092 $1 multi 1.50 .25
*a.* Booklet pane of 10, 3 each #4833-4834, 2 each #4835-4836 15.00
*b.* Booklet pane of 20, 5 each #4833-4836 30.00
*Nos. 4833-4836 (4)* 6.00 1.00

Complete booklet sold for $20.95.

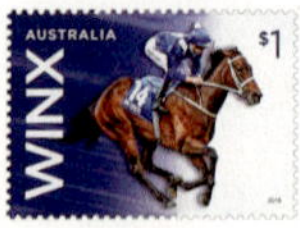


Winx, Winner of 27 Consecutive Stakes Races — A1093

**2018, Aug. 18 Litho. *Perf. 14x14¾***

**4837** A1093 $1 multi 1.50 1.50

**Booklet Stamp**
**Self-Adhesive**

***Serpentine Die Cut 11¼ Syncopated***

**4838** A1093 $1 multi 1.50 .25
*a.* Booklet pane of 10 15.00

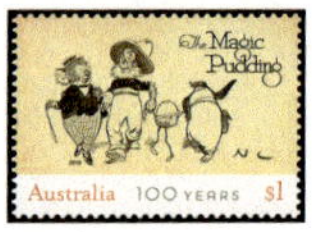


Illustrations From Children's Novels About the Australian Bush — A1094

Illustration from: No. 4839, *The Magic Pudding*, by Norman Lindsay. No. 4840, *Tales of Snugglepot and Cuddlepie: Their Adventures Wonderful*, by May Gibbs.

**2018, Aug. 21 Litho. *Perf. 14x14¾***

**4839** A1094 $1 multi 1.50 1.10
**4840** A1094 $1 multi 1.50 1.10
*a.* Souvenir sheet of 2, #4839-4840 3.00 2.25

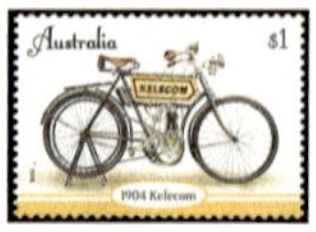


Motorcycles A1095

Designs: Nos. 4841, 4845, 4849, 1904 Kelecom. Nos. 4842, 4846, 4850, 1912 The Precision. Nos. 4843, 4847, 4851, 1919 Whiting V4. Nos. 4844, 4848, 4852, 1923 Invincible J.A.P.

**2018, Sept. 4 Litho. *Perf. 14x14¾***

**4841** A1095 $1 multi 1.50 1.50
*a.* Booklet pane of 4 6.00 —
**4842** A1095 $1 multi 1.50 1.50
*a.* Booklet pane of 4 6.00 —
**4843** A1095 $1 multi 1.50 1.50
*a.* Booklet pane of 4 6.00 —
**4844** A1095 $1 multi 1.50 1.50
*a.* Booklet pane of 4 6.00 —
*b.* Booklet pane of 4, #4841-4844 6.00 —
Complete booklet, #4841a, 4842a, 4843a, 4844a, 4844b 30.00
*Nos. 4841-4844 (4)* 6.00 6.00

**Booklet Stamps**
**Self-Adhesive**

***Serpentine Die Cut 11¼ Syncopated***

**4845** A1095 $1 multi 1.50 .25
*a.* Booklet pane of 10 15.00
**4846** A1095 $1 multi 1.50 .25
*a.* Booklet pane of 10 15.00
**4847** A1095 $1 multi 1.50 .25
*a.* Booklet pane of 10 15.00
**4848** A1095 $1 multi 1.50 .25
*a.* Booklet pane of 10 15.00
*Nos. 4845-4848 (4)* 6.00 1.00

**Typo.**
**Coil Stamps**

**4849** A1095 $1 multi 1.50 .25
**4850** A1095 $1 multi 1.50 .25
**4851** A1095 $1 multi 1.50 .25
**4852** A1095 $1 multi 1.50 .25
*a.* Horiz. strip of 4, #4849-4852 6.00
*Nos. 4849-4852 (4)* 6.00 1.00

Complete booklet sold for $20.95. Typographed coil stamps have larger dots in images than lithographed booklet stamps.

**Items Starting With Same Letter Type of 2016**

Designs: Nos. 4853, 4858, Emu, egg. echidna, Eureka flag. Nos. 4854, 4859, Organ, obelisk, oar, oven, octopus, owl, oil heater, oilskin coat, opal opera house. Nos. 4855, 4860, X-ray, xylophone, Xanthorrhea grass tree. XXXX beer, Xerox machine. Nos. 4856, 4861, Yacht, yo-yo, yowie, yabbies (crawfish). Nos. 4857, 4862, Zombie on zebra crossing (crosswalk), zoologist, zebra finches.

**2018, Sept. 18 Litho. *Perf. 14¾x14***

**4853** A1028 $1 multi 1.50 1.50
**4854** A1028 $1 multi 1.50 1.50
**4855** A1028 $1 multi 1.50 1.50
**4856** A1028 $1 multi 1.50 1.50
**4857** A1028 $1 multi 1.50 1.50
*Nos. 4853-4857 (5)* 7.50 7.50

**Booklet Stamps**
**Self-Adhesive**

***Serpentine Die Cut 11¼ Syncopated***

**4858** A1028 $1 multi 1.50 .25
*a.* Booklet pane of 10 15.00
**4859** A1028 $1 multi 1.50 .25
*a.* Booklet pane of 10 15.00
**4860** A1028 $1 multi 1.50 .25
*a.* Booklet pane of 10 15.00
**4861** A1028 $1 multi 1.50 .25
*a.* Booklet pane of 10 15.00
**4862** A1028 $1 multi 1.50 .25
*a.* Booklet pane of 10 15.00
*Nos. 4858-4862 (5)* 7.50 1.25

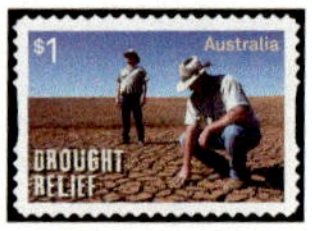


Farmers Inspecting Parched Land — A1095a

***Serpentine Die Cut 11¼ Syncopated***
**2018, Sept. 20 Litho.**

**Booklet Stamp**
**Self-Adhesive**

**4862B** A1095a $1 multi 1.50 .75
*c.* Booklet pane of 5 7.50

With the sale of each booklet pane of No. 4862Bc, Australia Post donated $2 to Rural Aid Limited to provide drought assistance to farms and communities.

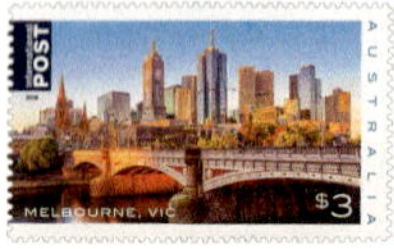


Australian Cities A1096

Designs: $3, Melbourne. $4.60, Adelaide. $7.50, Brisbane.

**2018, Sept. 25 Litho. *Perf. 14¼x14***

**4863** A1096 $3 multi 4.50 4.50
**4864** A1096 $4.60 multi 6.75 3.50
**4865** A1096 $7.50 multi 11.00 5.50
*Nos. 4863-4865 (3)* 22.25 13.50

**Booklet Stamp**
**Self-Adhesive**

***Serpentine Die Cut 10¾x11 Syncopated***

**4866** A1096 $3 multi 4.50 2.25
*a.* Booklet pane of 5 22.50

See Nos. 5011-5013.

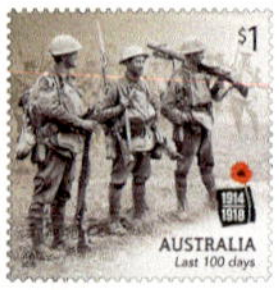


World War I, Cent. — A1097

Poppy and: Nos. 4867, 4872, Soldiers resting in last hundred days of war. Nos. 4868, 4873, Lieutenant General Sir John Monash (1865-1931). Nos. 4869, 4874, Armistice declaration. Nos. 4870, 4875, Australian women awaiting return of troops. Nos. 4871, 4876, Children honoring fallen soldiers at cemetery.

**2018, Oct. 2 Litho. *Perf. 14¼***

**4867** A1097 $1 multi 1.50 1.50
**4868** A1097 $1 multi 1.50 1.50
**4869** A1097 $1 multi 1.50 1.50
**4870** A1097 $1 multi 1.50 1.50
*a.* Booklet pane of 4, #4867-4870 6.00 —
**4871** A1097 $1 multi 1.50 1.50
*a.* Booklet pane of 4, #4868-4871 6.00 —
*b.* Booklet pane of 4, #4867, 4869-4871 6.00 —
*c.* Booklet pane of 4, #4867-4868, 4870-4871 6.00 —
*d.* Booklet pane of 4, #4867-4869, 4871 6.00 —
Complete booklet, #4870a, 4871a, 4871b, 4871c, 4871d 30.00
*e.* Souvenir sheet of 5, #4867-4871 7.50 7.50
*Nos. 4867-4871 (5)* 7.50 7.50

**Booklet Stamps**
**Self-Adhesive**

***Serpentine Die Cut 11¼ Syncopated***

**4872** A1097 $1 multi 1.50 .25
**4873** A1097 $1 multi 1.50 .25
**4874** A1097 $1 multi 1.50 .25
**4875** A1097 $1 multi 1.50 .25
**4876** A1097 $1 multi 1.50 .25
*a.* Booklet pane of 10, 2 each #4872-4876 15.00
*Nos. 4872-4876 (5)* 7.50 1.25

Complete booklet sold for $20.95.

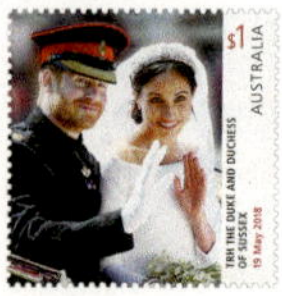


Wedding of Prince Harry and Meghan Markle — A1098

**2018, Oct. 2 Litho. *Perf. 14¼***

**4877** A1098 $1 multi 1.50 1.10

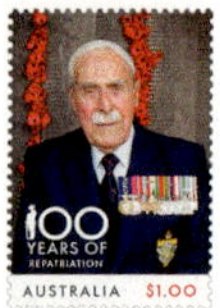


Veteran A1099

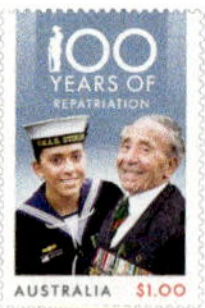


Two Veterans A1100

**2018, Oct. 23 Litho. *Perf. 14¾x14***

**4878** A1099 $1 multi 1.50 1.10
**4879** A1100 $1 multi 1.50 1.10
*a.* Pair, #4878-4879 3.00 2.25

Repatriation of veterans by Department of Veterans' Affairs, cent.

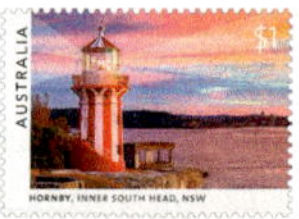


Lighthouses Near Sydney — A1101

Designs: Nos. 4880, 4883, Hornby Lighthouse. Nos. 4881, 4884, Robertsons Point Lighthouse. Nos. 4882, 4885, Macquarie Lighthouse.

**2018, Oct. 23 Litho. *Perf. 14x14¾***

**4880** A1101 $1 multi 1.50 1.50
**4881** A1101 $1 multi 1.50 1.50
**4882** A1101 $1 multi 1.50 1.50
*a.* Booklet pane of 4, #4881-4882, 2 #4880 6.00 —
*b.* Booklet pane of 4, #4880, 4882, 2 #4881 6.00 —
*c.* Booklet pane of 4, #4880-4881, 2 #4882 (#4480 at UR) 6.00 —
*d.* Booklet pane of 4, 2 each #4880-4881 6.00 —
*e.* Booklet pane of 4, #4880-4881, 2 #4882 (#4480 at UL) 6.00 —
Complete booklet, #4882a, 4882b, 4882c, 4882d, 4882e 30.00
*f.* Souvenir sheet of 3, #4880-4882 4.50 4.50
*Nos. 4880-4882 (3)* 4.50 4.50

**Self-Adhesive**

***Serpentine Die Cut 11¼ Syncopated***

**4883** A1101 $1 multi 1.50 .25
**4884** A1101 $1 multi 1.50 .25
**4885** A1101 $1 multi 1.50 .25
*a.* Horiz. coil strip of 3, #4883-4885 4.50
*b.* Booklet pane of 10, 4 #4883, 3 each #4884-4885 15.00
*Nos. 4883-4885 (3)* 4.50 .75

Complete booklet sold for $20.95.

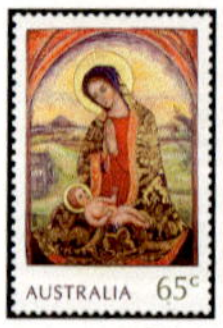


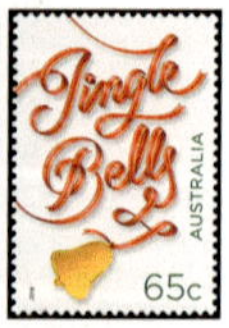


Christmas
A1102 A1103

Designs: Nos. 4886, 4891, Madonna and Child. Nos. 4887, 4892, 4896, "Jingle Bells" and bell. Nos. 4888, 4893, 4897, "Glad Tidings" and Christmas tree. $2, "Noel" and star. $2.30, Angels.

**2018, Nov. 1 Litho. *Perf. 14¾x14***

**4886** A1102 65c multi .95 .95
**4887** A1103 65c multi .95 .95
**4888** A1103 65c multi .95 .95
*a.* Horiz. pair, #4887-4888 1.90 1.90
**4889** A1103 $2 multi 3.00 3.00
**4890** A1102 $2.30 multi 3.50 3.50
*a.* Souvenir sheet of 2, #4886, 4890 4.50 4.50
*Nos. 4886-4890 (5)* 9.35 9.35

**Booklet Stamps**
**Self-Adhesive**

***Serpentine Die Cut 11¼ Syncopated***

**4891** A1102 65c multi .95 .25
*a.* Booklet pane of 20 + 20 etiquettes 19.00
**4892** A1103 65c multi .95 .25
**4893** A1103 65c multi .95 .25
*a.* Booklet pane of 20, 10 each #4892-4893, + 20 etiquettes 19.00
**4894** A1103 $2 multi 3.00 1.50
*a.* Booklet pane of 5 15.00
**4895** A1102 $2.30 multi 3.50 1.75
*a.* Booklet pane of 5 17.50

**Litho. With Foil Application**

**4896** A1103 65c multi .95 .25
*a.* Booklet pane of 10 + 10 etiquettes 9.50
**4897** A1103 65c multi .95 .25
*a.* Booklet pane of 10 + 10 etiquettes 9.50
*Nos. 4891-4897 (7)* 11.25 4.50

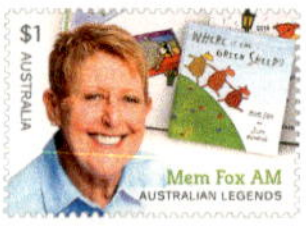


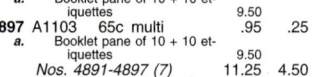

Writers of Children's Books and Their Works — A1104

Designs: Nos. 4903, 4908, Mem Fox, *Where is the Green Sheep?* Nos. 4904, 4909, Morris Gleitzman, *Once*. Nos. 4905, 4910, Leigh Hobbs, *Mr. Chicken Goes to Paris*. Nos. 4906, 4911, Alison Lester, *Magic Beach*. Nos. 4907, 4912, Shaun Tan, *The Lost Thing*.

**2019, Jan. 17 Litho. *Perf. 14x14¾***

**4903** A1104 $1 multi 1.50 1.50
**4904** A1104 $1 multi 1.50 1.50
**4905** A1104 $1 multi 1.50 1.50
**4906** A1104 $1 multi 1.50 1.50
**4907** A1104 $1 multi 1.50 1.50
*Nos. 4903-4907 (5)* 7.50 7.50

**Booklet Stamps**
**Self-Adhesive**

***Serpentine Die Cut 11¼ Syncopated***

**4908** A1104 $1 multi 1.50 .25
*a.* Booklet pane of 10 15.00
**4909** A1104 $1 multi 1.50 .25
*a.* Booklet pane of 10 15.00
**4910** A1104 $1 multi 1.50 .25
*a.* Booklet pane of 10 15.00
**4911** A1104 $1 multi 1.50 .25
*a.* Booklet pane of 10 15.00
**4912** A1104 $1 multi 1.50 .25
*a.* Booklet pane of 10 15.00
*Nos. 4908-4912 (5)* 7.50 1.25

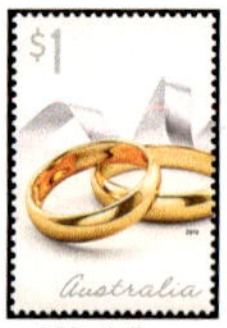


Wedding Rings A1105

Bird Carrying Flower A1106

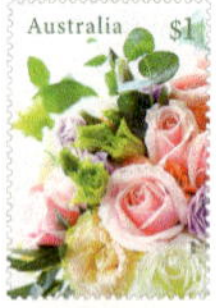


Roses A1107

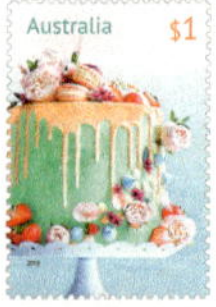


Decorated Cake A1108

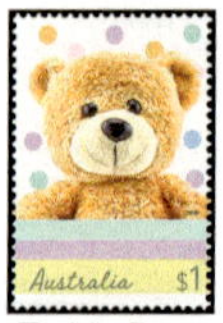


Teddy Bear A1109

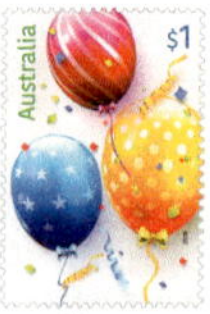


Party Balloons A1110

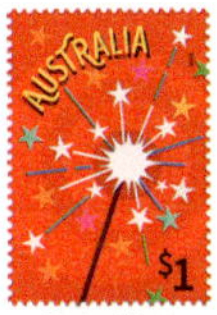

Sparkler
A1111

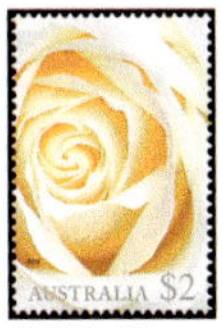

White Rose
A1112

**2019, Feb. 5 Litho. *Perf. 14¾x14***

**4913** A1105 $1 multi 1.50 1.50
**4914** A1106 $1 multi 1.50 1.50
**4915** A1107 $1 multi 1.50 1.50
**4916** A1108 $1 multi 1.50 1.50
**4917** A1109 $1 multi 1.50 1.50
**4918** A1110 $1 multi 1.50 1.50
**4919** A1111 $1 multi 1.50 1.50
**4920** A1112 $2 multi 3.00 3.00
*Nos. 4913-4920 (8)* 13.50 13.50

**Booklet Stamps**
**Self-Adhesive**

***Serpentine Die Cut 11¼ Syncopated***

**4921** A1105 $1 multi 1.50 .25
*a.* Booklet pane of 10 15.00
**4922** A1106 $1 multi 1.50 .25
*a.* Booklet pane of 10 15.00
**4923** A1107 $1 multi 1.50 .25
*a.* Booklet pane of 10 15.00
**4924** A1108 $1 multi 1.50 .25
*a.* Booklet pane of 10 15.00
**4925** A1109 $1 multi 1.50 .25
*a.* Booklet pane of 10 15.00
**4926** A1110 $1 multi 1.50 .25
*a.* Booklet pane of 10 15.00
**4927** A1111 $1 multi 1.50 .25
*a.* Booklet pane of 10 15.00
**4928** A1112 $2 multi 3.00 1.50
*a.* Booklet pane of 4 12.00
Complete booklet, 4 #4928a 48.00
*Nos. 4921-4928 (8)* 13.50 3.25

**With Personalized Photo at Right Like Type A692a**

***Serpentine Die Cut 11¼x11¼ Syncopated***

**4929** A1105 $1 multi 2.40 2.40
**4930** A1106 $1 multi 2.40 2.40
**4931** A1107 $1 multi 2.40 2.40
**4932** A1108 $1 multi 2.40 2.40
**4933** A1109 $1 multi 2.40 2.40
**4934** A1110 $1 multi 2.40 2.40
**4935** A1111 $1 multi 2.40 2.40

Complete booklet sold for $32.95 and contains four examples of No. 4928a with different pane margins.

An additional stamp was issued in this set. The editors would like to see any example of it.

Nos. 4929-4935 were each printed in sheets of 20 and have personalized pictures and a straight edge at right and lack separations between the stamp and the personalized photo. Sheets of 20 of Nos. 4929-4935 sold for $33 each.

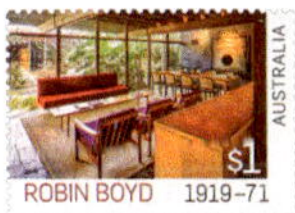

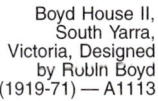

Boyd House II, South Yarra, Victoria, Designed by Robin Boyd (1919-71) — A1113

**2019, Feb. 12 Litho. *Perf. 14x14¾***

**4937** A1113 $1 multi 1.40 1.10

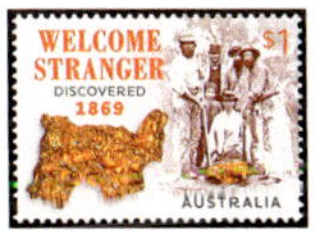

Discovery of Welcome Stranger Gold Nugget, 150th Anniv. — A1114

**2019, Feb. 26 Litho. *Perf. 14x14¾***

**4938** A1114 $1 multi 1.40 1.10

**Booklet Stamp**
**Self-Adhesive**

***Serpentine Die Cut 11¼ Syncopated***

**4939** A1114 $1 multi 1.40 .25
*a.* Booklet pane of 20 28.00

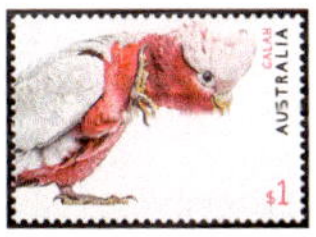

Australian Animals — A1115

Designs: Nos. 4940, 4944, Galah. Nos. 4941, 4945, Red kangaroo. Nos. 4942, 4946, Tasmanian devil. Nos. 4943, 4947, Blue-tongue lizard.

**2019, Mar. 5 Litho. *Perf. 14x14¾***

**4940** A1115 $1 multi 1.40 1.40
**4941** A1115 $1 multi 1.40 1.40
**4942** A1115 $1 multi 1.40 1.40
**4943** A1115 $1 multi 1.40 1.40
*Nos. 4940-4943 (4)* 5.60 5.60

**Self-Adhesive**

***Serpentine Die Cut 11¼ Syncopated***

**4944** A1115 $1 multi 1.40 .25
*a.* Booklet pane of 10 14.00
**4945** A1115 $1 multi 1.40 .25
*a.* Booklet pane of 10 14.00
**4946** A1115 $1 multi 1.40 .25
*a.* Booklet pane of 10 14.00
**4947** A1115 $1 multi 1.40 .25
*a.* Booklet pane of 10 14.00
*b.* Hoirz. coil strip of 4, #4944-4947 5.60
*Nos. 4944-4947 (4)* 5.60 1.00

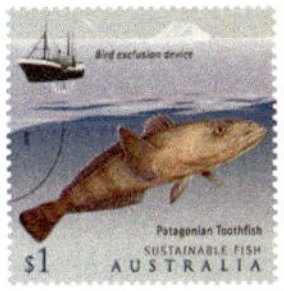

Sustainable Fish — A1116

Designs: Nos. 4948, 4951, Patagonian toothfish and fishing boat with bird exclusion device. Nos. 4949, 4952, Blue grenadier and fishing boat with seal excluder device. Nos. 4950, 4953, Tiger flathead and fishing boat with mesh net.

**2019, Mar. 14 Litho. *Perf. 14¼***

**4948** A1116 $1 multi 1.50 1.50
**4949** A1116 $1 multi 1.50 1.50
**4950** A1116 $1 multi 1.50 1.50
*a.* Souvenir sheet of 3, #4948-4950 4.50 4.50
*Nos. 4948-4950 (3)* 4.50 4.50

**Booklet Stamps**
**Self-Adhesive**

***Serpentine Die Cut 11¼ Syncopated***

**4951** A1116 $1 multi 1.50 .25
**4952** A1116 $1 multi 1.50 .25
**4953** A1116 $1 multi 1.50 .25
*a.* Booklet pane of 10, 4 #4951, 3 each #4952-4953 15.00
*Nos. 4951-4953 (3)* 4.50 .75

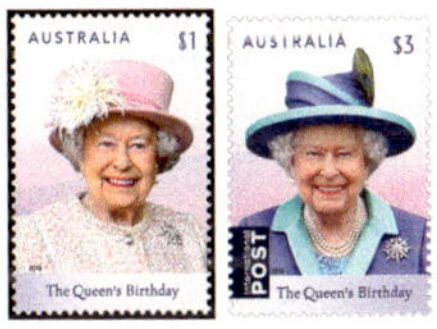

Queen Elizabeth II, 93rd Birthday
A1117 A1118

**2019, Apr. 9 Litho. *Perf. 14¾x14***

**4954** A1117 $1 multi 1.40 1.10
**4955** A1118 $3 multi 4.25 4.25
*a.* Souvenir sheet of 2, #4954-4955 5.75 5.75

**Booklet Stamp**
**Self-Adhesive**

***Serpentine Die Cut 11¼ Syncopated***

**4956** A1118 $3 multi 4.25 2.10
*a.* Booklet pane of 5 21.50

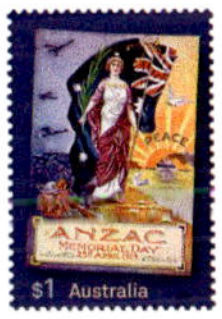

ANZAC Day — A1119

Cover of: $1, 1919 ANZAC Memorial Day souvenir program. $3, 1919 ANZAC Day souvenir program for Australian Depots in France.

**2019, Apr. 16 Litho. *Perf. 14¾x14***

**4957** A1119 $1 blue & multi 1.40 1.40
**4958** A1119 $3 red & multi 4.25 3.25
*a.* Souvenir sheet of 2, #4957-4958 5.75 5.75

**Booklet Stamp**
**Self-Adhesive**

***Serpentine Die Cut 11¼ Syncopated***

**4959** A1119 $1 blue & multi 1.40 .25
*a.* Booklet pane of 20 28.00

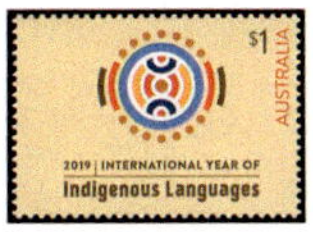

International Year of Indigenous Languages A1120

**2019, Apr. 30 Litho. *Perf. 14x14¾***

**4960** A1120 $1 multi 1.40 1.10

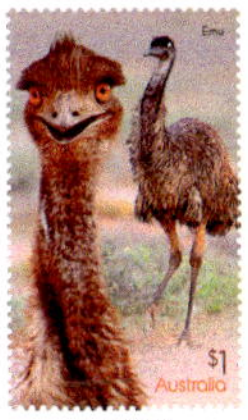

A1121

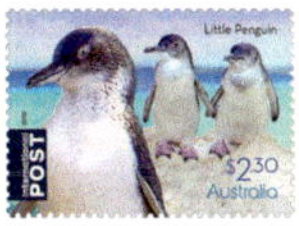

Flightless Birds — A1122

Designs: No. 4961, Emu. No. 4962, Southern cassowary. $2.30, Little penguin.

**2019, May 7 Litho. *Perf. 14x14½***

**4961** A1121 $1 multi 1.40 1.10
**4962** A1121 $1 multi 1.40 1.10

***Perf. 14x14¾***

**4963** A1122 $2.30 multi 3.25 3.25

**Booklet Stamp**
**Self-Adhesive**

***Serpentine Die Cut 11¼ Syncopated***

**4964** A1122 $2.30 multi 3.25 1.60
*a.* Booklet pane of 5 16.50

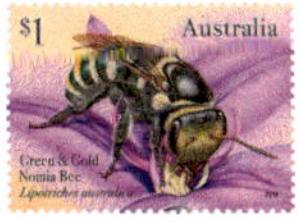

Native Bees — A1123

Designs: Nos. 4965, 4969, Green and gold nomia bee. Nos. 4966, 4970, Neon cuckoo bee. Nos. 4967, 4971, Wasp-mimic bee. Nos. 4968, 4972, Resin bee.

**2019, May 14 Litho. *Perf. 14x14¾***

**4965** A1123 $1 multi 1.40 1.40
**4966** A1123 $1 multi 1.40 1.40
**4967** A1123 $1 multi 1.40 1.40
**4968** A1123 $1 multi 1.40 1.40
*Nos. 4965-4968 (4)* 5.60 5.60

**Booklet Stamps**
**Self-Adhesive**

***Serpentine Die Cut 11¼ Syncopated***

**4969** A1123 $1 multi 1.40 .25
*a.* Booklet pane of 10 14.00
**4970** A1123 $1 multi 1.40 .25
*a.* Booklet pane of 10 14.00
**4971** A1123 $1 multi 1.40 .25
*a.* Booklet pane of 10 14.00
**4972** A1123 $1 multi 1.40 .25
*a.* Booklet pane of 10 14.00
*Nos. 4969-4972 (4)* 5.60 1.00

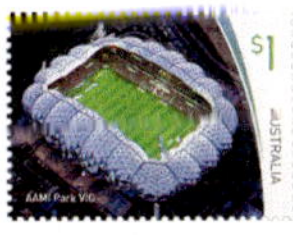

Sports Stadiums — A1124

Designs: Nos. 4973, 4977, AAMI Park, Melbourne. Nos. 4974, 4978, Optus Stadium, Perth. Nos. 4975, 4979, Sydney Cricket Ground. No. 4976, 4980, Melbourne Cricket Ground.

**2019, June 4 Litho. *Perf. 14x14¾***

**4973** A1124 $1 multi 1.40 1.40
**4974** A1124 $1 multi 1.40 1.40
**4975** A1124 $1 multi 1.40 1.40
**4976** A1124 $1 multi 1.40 1.40
*Nos. 4973-4976 (4)* 5.60 5.60

**Booklet Stamps**
**Self-Adhesive**

***Serpentine Die Cut 11¼ Syncopated***

**4977** A1124 $1 multi 1.40 .25
*a.* Booklet pane of 10 14.00
**4978** A1124 $1 multi 1.40 .25
*a.* Booklet pane of 10 14.00
**4979** A1124 $1 multi 1.40 .25
*a.* Booklet pane of 10 14.00
**4980** A1124 $1 multi 1.40 .25
*a.* Booklet pane of 10 14.00
*Nos. 4977-4980 (4)* 5.60 1.00

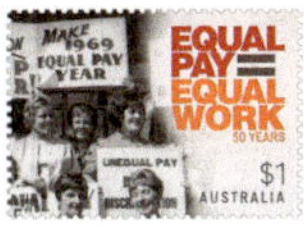

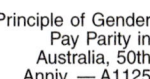

Principle of Gender Pay Parity in Australia, 50th Anniv. — A1125

**2019, June 18 Litho. *Perf. 14x14¾***

**4981** A1125 $1 multi 1.40 1.10

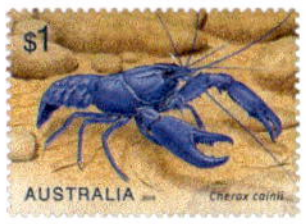

Crayfish — A1126

Designs: No. 4982, Cherax cainii. No. 4983, Astacopsis gouldi. No. 4984, Euastacus sulcatus.

**2019, July 2 Litho. *Perf. 14x14¾***

**4982** A1126 $1 multi 1.40 1.10
**4983** A1126 $1 multi 1.40 1.10
**4984** A1126 $1 multi 1.40 1.10
*Nos. 4982-4984 (3)* 4.20 3.30

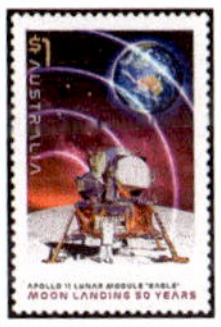

First Man on the Moon, 50th Anniv. — A1127

Designs: Nos. 4985, 4990, Apollo 11 Lunar Module "Eagle". Nos. 4986, 4991, Parkes Radio Telescope, Parkes, New South Wales. Nos. 4987, 4992, First Moon walk. Nos. 4988, 4993, Telecast of moon walk via Honeysuckle Creek Tracking Station, Australian Capital Territory.

**2019, July 16 Litho. *Perf. 14¾x14***

**4985** A1127 $1 multi 1.40 1.40
**4986** A1127 $1 multi 1.40 1.40
**4987** A1127 $1 multi 1.40 1.40
**4988** A1127 $1 multi 1.40 1.40
*Nos. 4985-4988 (4)* 5.60 5.60
**4989** Souvenir sheet of 4, #4985, 4987, 4989a, 4989b 5.60 5.60
*a.* A1127 $1 As #4986, Litho. with silver foil application 1.40 1.40
*b.* A1127 $1 As #4988, Litho. with silver foil application 1.40 1.40

**Self-Adhesive**

***Serpentine Die Cut 11¼ Syncopated***

**4990** A1127 $1 multi 1.40 .25
*a.* Booklet pane of 10 14.00
**4991** A1127 $1 multi 1.40 .25
*a.* Booklet pane of 10 14.00
**4992** A1127 $1 multi 1.40 .25
*a.* Booklet pane of 10 14.00
**4993** A1127 $1 multi 1.40 .25
*a.* Booklet pane of 10 14.00
*b.* Vert. coil strip of 4, #4990-4993 5.60
*Nos. 4990-4993 (4)* 5.60 1.00

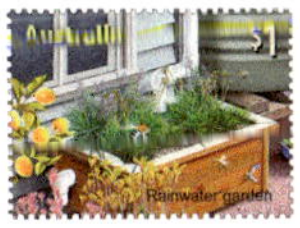

Gardening — A1128

Designs: Nos. 4994, 4999, Rainwater garden. Nos. 4995, 5000, Worm farm. Nos. 4996, 5001, Nest box. Nos. 4997, 5002, Pollinators. $2, Vegetable garden.

**2019, Aug. 1 Litho. *Perf. 14x14¾***

**4994** A1128 $1 multi 1.40 1.40
*a.* Booklet pane of 4 5.75
**4995** A1128 $1 multi 1.40 1.40
*a.* Booklet pane of 4 5.75 —
**4996** A1128 $1 multi 1.40 1.40
*a.* Booklet pane of 4 5.75 —

**Size: 50x30mm**

***Perf. 14½x14***

**4997** A1128 $1 multi 1.40 1.40
*a.* Booklet pane of 4 5.75 —
**4998** A1128 $2 multi 2.75 2.10
*a.* Booklet pane of 2 5.75 —
Complete booklet, #4994a, 4995a, 4996a, 4997a, 4998a 29.00
*b.* Souvenir sheet of 5, #4994-4998 8.50 7.75
*Nos. 4994-4998 (5)* 8.35 7.70

**Booklet Stamps**
**Self-Adhesive**
**Size: 38x26mm**

***Serpentine Die Cut 11¼ Syncopated***

**4999** A1128 $1 multi 1.40 .25
**5000** A1128 $1 multi 1.40 .25
**5001** A1128 $1 multi 1.40 .25
*a.* Booklet pane of 20, 6 each #4999, 5001, 7 #5000 28.00

**Size: 50x30mm**

***Serpentine Die Cut 10¾ Syncopated***

**5002** A1128 $1 multi 1.40 .25
*a.* Booklet pane of 10 14.00
*Nos. 4999-5002 (4)* 5.60 1.00

Complete booklet sold for $20.95.

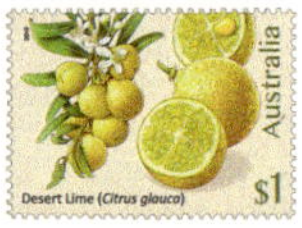


Bush Citrus — A1129

Designs: Nos. 5003, 5006, Desert lime. Nos. 5004, 5007, Finger lime. Nos. 5005, 5008, Lemon aspen.

**2019, Aug. 13 Litho. *Perf. 14x14¾***

**5003** A1129 $1 multi 1.40 1.40
**5004** A1129 $1 multi 1.40 1.40
**5005** A1129 $1 multi 1.40 1.40
*a.* Souvenir sheet of 3, #5003-5005 4.25 4.25
*Nos. 5003-5005 (3)* 4.20 4.20

**Coil Stamps**
**Self-Adhesive**

***Serpentine Die Cut 11¼ Syncopated***

**5006** A1129 $1 multi 1.40 .25
**5007** A1129 $1 multi 1.40 .25
**5008** A1129 $1 multi 1.40 .25
*a.* Horiz. coil strip of 3, #5006-5008 4.25
*Nos. 5006-5008 (3)* 4.20 .75

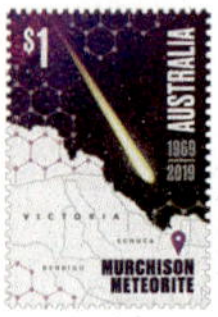


Fall to Earth of Murchison Meteorite, 50th Anniv. — A1130

**2019, Sept. 10 Litho. *Perf. 14¾x14***

**5009** A1130 $1 multi 1.40 1.10

**Animals Type of 2006**

Design: $2.50, Greater bilby.

***Serpentine Die Cut 11¼ Syncopated***
**2019, Sept. 23 Litho.**

**Booklet Stamp**
**Self-Adhesive**

**5010** A707 $2.50 multi 3.50 1.75
*a.* Booklet pane of 5 17.50

**Australian Cities Type of 2018**

Designs: $3.20, Sydney. $5, Perth.

**2019, Sept. 23 Litho. *Perf. 14¼x14***

**5011** A1096 $3.20 multi 4.25 4.25
**5012** A1096 $5 multi 6.75 3.00

**Booklet Stamp**
**Self-Adhesive**

***Serpentine Die Cut 10¾x11 Syncopated***

**5013** A1096 $3.20 multi 4.25 2.10
*a.* Booklet pane of 5 21.50

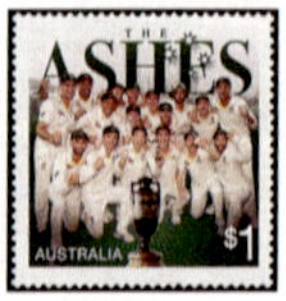


Australian Team for 2019 The Ashes Test Cricket Series With Trophy — A1131

**2019, Oct. 1 Litho. *Perf. 14¼***

**5014** A1131 $1 multi 1.40 1.10

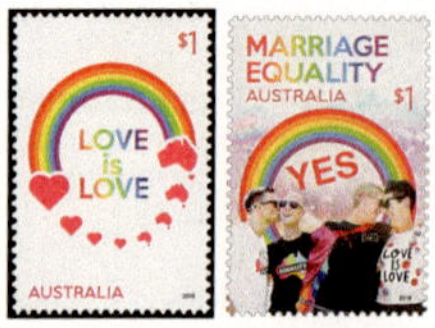


Marriage Equality
A1132 A1133

**2019, Oct. 1 Litho. *Perf. 14¾x14***

**5015** A1132 $1 multi 1.40 1.10
**5016** A1133 $1 multi 1.40 1.10

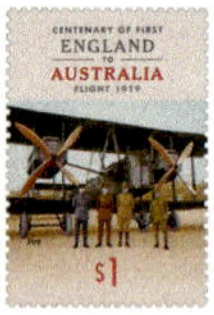


Vickers Vimy and Crew — A1134

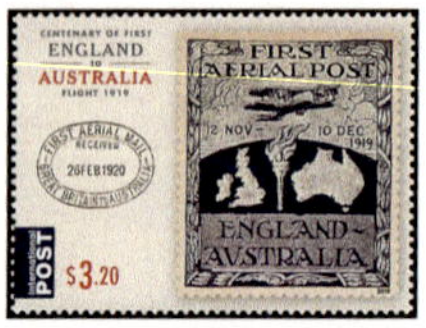


Label and Handstamp for First Great Britain to Australia Airmail Flight
A1135

**2019, Oct. 1 Litho. *Perf. 14¾x14***

**5017** A1134 $1 multi 1.40 1.40
*a.* Booklet pane of 4 5.75 —
**5018** A1135 $3.20 multi 4.25 4.25
*a.* Booklet pane of 2 9.25 —
Complete booklet, #5018a, 4 #5017a 32.50
*b.* Souvenir sheet of 2, #5017-5018 5.75 5.75

**Booklet Stamps**
**Self-Adhesive**

***Serpentine Die Cut 11¼ Syncopated***

**5019** A1134 $1 multi 1.40 .25
*a.* Booklet pane of 20 28.00 —

***Serpentine Die Cut 11¾x11½ Syncopated***

**5020** A1135 $3.20 multi 4.25 2.10
*a.* Booklet pane of 5 21.50 —

First Great Britain-Australia airmail flight, captained by Ross Smith, cent. Complete booklet contains four examples of No. 5017a, each with different pane margins, and sold for $23.95.

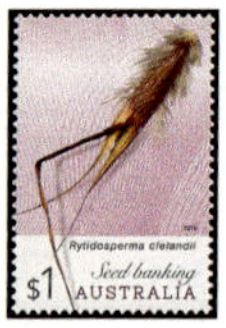


Seeds of Endangered Plant Species in Seed Banks — A1136

Designs: Nos. 5021, 5024, Rytidosperma clelandii. Nos. 5022, 5025, Epacris petrophila. Nos. 5023, 5026, Petrophile latericola.

**2019, Oct. 8 Litho. *Perf. 14¾x14***

**5021** A1136 $1 multi 1.40 1.40
**5022** A1136 $1 multi 1.40 1.40
**5023** A1136 $1 multi 1.40 1.40
*Nos. 5021-5023 (3)* 4.20 4.20

**Booklet Stamps**
**Self-Adhesive**

***Serpentine Die Cut 11¼ Syncopated***

**5024** A1136 $1 multi 1.40 .25
*a.* Booklet pane of 10 14.00
**5025** A1136 $1 multi 1.40 .25
*a.* Booklet pane of 10 14.00
**5026** A1136 $1 multi 1.40 .25
*a.* Booklet pane of 10 14.00
*Nos. 5024-5026 (3)* 4.20 .75

**Items Starting With Same Letter Type of 2016**

Designs: Nos. 5027, 5033, Dog, digger, Daily News, dentures, dunny (outhouse). Nos. 5028, 5034, Father, fish in fish creel, fishing pole and gear, child with football. Nos. 5029, 5035, Housewife hanging laundry on Hills Hoist, hibiscus. Nos. 5030, 5036, Ibis, ironing board, ironman triathlete holding iron. Nos. 5031, 5037, Mechanic feeding macadamia nuts to mud crab, milk carton, mallet. Nos. 5032, 5038, Platypus eating peach and pineapple pavlova, presents, possum, python, pelican, picket fence.

**2019, Oct. 22 Litho. *Perf. 14¾x14***

**5027** A1028 $1 multi 1.40 1.40
**5028** A1028 $1 multi 1.40 1.40
**5029** A1028 $1 multi 1.40 1.40
**5030** A1028 $1 multi 1.40 1.40
**5031** A1028 $1 multi 1.40 1.40
**5032** A1028 $1 multi 1.40 1.40
*a.* Souvenir sheet of 6, #5027-5032 8.50 8.50
*Nos. 5027-5032 (6)* 8.40 8.40

**Booklet Stamps**
**Self-Adhesive**

***Serpentine Die Cut 11¼ Syncopated***

**5033** A1028 $1 multi 1.40 .25
*a.* Booklet pane of 10 14.00
**5034** A1028 $1 multi 1.40 .25
*a.* Booklet pane of 10 14.00
**5035** A1028 $1 multi 1.40 .25
*a.* Booklet pane of 10 14.00
**5036** A1028 $1 multi 1.40 .25
*a.* Booklet pane of 10 14.00
**5037** A1028 $1 multi 1.40 .25
*a.* Booklet pane of 10 14.00
**5038** A1028 $1 multi 1.40 .25
*a.* Booklet pane of 10 14.00
*Nos. 5033-5038 (6)* 8.40 1.50

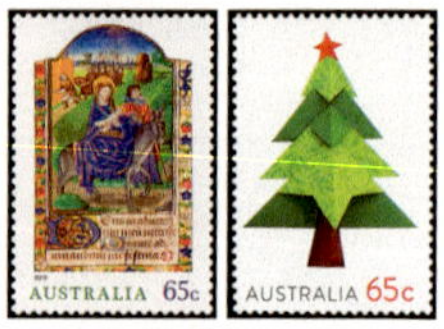


Christmas
A1137 A1138

Designs: Nos. 5039, 5044, 5051Flight into Egypt. Nos. 5040, 5046, 5049, 5052, Christmas tree. Nos. 5041, 5045, 5050, Star. Nos. 5042, 5047, 5053, Adoration of the Magi. Nos. 5043, 5048, 5054, Christmas gift.

**2019, Nov. 1 Litho. *Perf. 14¾x14***

**5039** A1137 65c multi .90 .90
**5040** A1138 65c multi .90 .90
**5041** A1138 65c multi .90 .90
*a.* Horiz. pair, #5040-5041 1.80 1.80
**5042** A1137 $2.20 multi 3.00 3.00
*a.* Souvenir sheet of 2, #5039, 5042 4.00 4.00
**5043** A1138 $2.20 multi 3.00 3.00
*Nos. 5039-5043 (5)* 8.70 8.70

**Booklet Stamps**
**Self-Adhesive**

***Serpentine Die Cut 11¼ Syncopated***

**5044** A1137 65c multi .90 .25
*a.* Booklet pane of 20 + 20 etiquettes 18.00
**5045** A1138 65c multi .90 .25
**5046** A1138 65c multi .90 .25
*a.* Booklet pane of 20, 10 each #5045-5046, + 20 etiquettes 18.00
**5047** A1137 $2.20 multi 3.00 1.50
*a.* Booklet pane of 5 15.00
**5048** A1138 $2.20 multi 3.00 1.50
*a.* Booklet pane of 5 15.00

**Litho. With Foil Application**

**5049** A1138 65c multi .90 .25
*a.* Booklet pane of 10 + 10 etiquettes 9.00
**5050** A1138 65c multi .90 .25
*a.* Booklet pane of 10 + 10 etiquettes 9.00
*Nos. 5044-5050 (7)* 10.50 4.25

**With Personalized Photo at Right Like Type A692a**
**Litho.**

***Serpentine Die Cut 11½x11¼ Syncopated***

**5051** A1137 65c multi 2.00 2.00
**5052** A1138 65c multi 2.00 2.00
**5053** A1137 $2.20 multi 6.75 6.75
**5054** A1138 $2.20 multi 6.75 6.75
*Nos. 5051-5054 (4)* 17.50 17.50

Nos. 5051-5054 were each printed in sheets of 20 and have personalized pictures and a straight edge at right and lack separations between the stamp and the personalized photo. Sheets of 20 of Nos. 5051-5052 sold for $26 each, and sheets of 20 of Nos. 5053-5054 sold for $57 each.

---

On Dec. 16, 2019, Australia Post began issuing self-adhesive personalizable stamps in nine different shapes (Australia, speech bubble, teddy bear, heart, present, star, house, curved frame and decorative frame), with each shape available initially with six different denominations (65c, $1.10, $2.20, $3.30, $5.50, and $2.20 for international use). These stamps could only be purchased in sheets of 20.

---

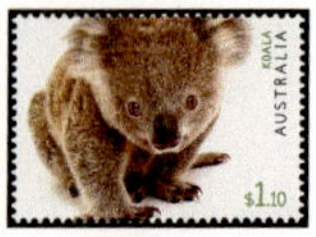


Marsupials
A1139

Designs: Nos. 5055, 5059, Koala. Nos. 5056, 5060, Wombat. $2.20, Echidna. $3.30, Sugar glider.

**2019, Dec. 16 Litho. *Perf. 14x14¾***

**5055** A1139 $1.10 multi 1.60 1.60
*a.* Souvenir sheet of 4 6.50 6.50
**5056** A1139 $1.10 multi 1.60 1.60
*a.* Souvenir sheet of 4 6.50 6.50
**5057** A1139 $2.20 multi 3.25 1.60
*a.* Souvenir sheet of 2 6.50 6.50
**5058** A1139 $3.30 multi 4.75 2.40
*a.* Souvenir sheet of 2 9.50 5.00
*Nos. 5055-5058 (4)* 11.20 7.20

**Self-Adhesive**

***Serpentine Die Cut 11¼ Syncopated***

**5059** A1139 $1.10 multi 1.60 .25
*a.* Booklet pane of 10 16.00
**5060** A1139 $1.10 multi 1.60 .25
*a.* Booklet pane of 20 32.00
*b.* Horiz. coil pair, #5059-5060 3.20

NZ 2020 Stamp Exhibition, Auckland, New Zealand (Nos. 5055a, 5056a, 5057a, 5058a). Issued: Nos. 5055a, 5056a, 5057a, 5058a, Mar. 2020. The NZ 2020 Stamp Exhibition was halted on Mar. 21, 2020 because of the COVID-19 pandemic.

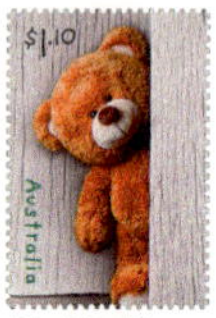


Teddy Bear
A1140

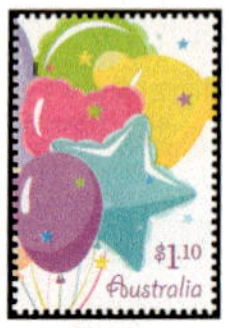


Party Balloons
A1141

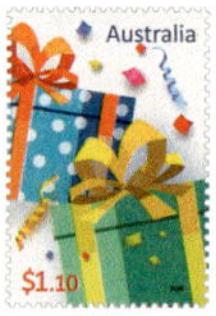


Gifts
A1142

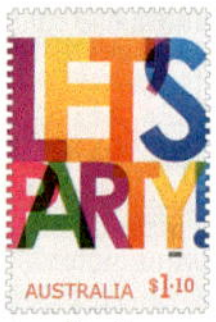


"Let's Party!"
A1143

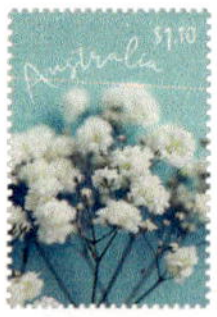


Flowers
A1144

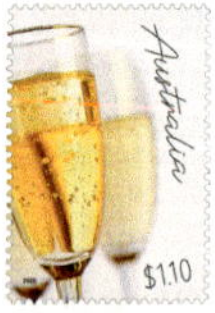


Champagne Flutes
A1145

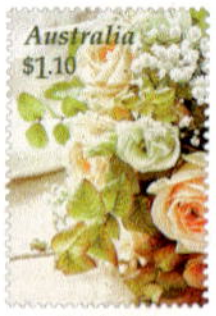


Bridal Bouquet
A1146

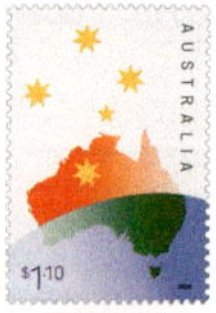


Map of Australia and Southern Cross Constellation
A1147

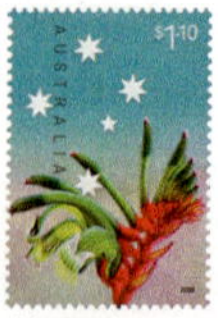


Kangaroo's Paw Flower and Southern Cross Constellation
A1148

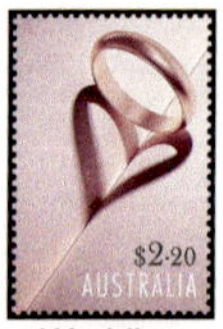


Wedding Ring
A1149

**2020, Jan. 2 Litho. *Perf. 14¾x14***

| | | | | | |
|---|---|---|---|---|---|
| **5061** | A1140 | $1.10 | multi | 1.60 | 1.60 |
| **5062** | A1141 | $1.10 | multi | 1.60 | 1.60 |
| **5063** | A1142 | $1.10 | multi | 1.60 | 1.60 |
| **5064** | A1143 | $1.10 | multi | 1.60 | 1.60 |
| **5065** | A1144 | $1.10 | multi | 1.60 | 1.60 |
| **5066** | A1145 | $1.10 | multi | 1.60 | 1.60 |
| **5067** | A1146 | $1.10 | multi | 1.60 | 1.60 |
| **5068** | A1147 | $1.10 | multi | 1.60 | 1.25 |
| **5069** | A1148 | $1.10 | multi | 1.60 | 1.25 |
| **5070** | A1149 | $2.20 | multi | 3.25 | 3.25 |
| *a.* | Souvenir sheet of 10, #5061-5070 | | | 18.00 | 18.00 |
| | *Nos. 5061-5070 (10)* | | | 17.65 | 16.95 |

**Booklet Stamps**
**Self-Adhesive**

***Serpentine Die Cut 11¼ Syncopated***

| | | | | | |
|---|---|---|---|---|---|
| **5071** | A1140 | $1.10 | multi | 1.60 | .25 |
| *a.* | Booklet pane of 10 + 5 stickers | | | 16.00 | |
| **5072** | A1141 | $1.10 | multi | 1.60 | .25 |
| *a.* | Booklet pane of 10 + 5 stickers | | | 16.00 | |
| **5073** | A1142 | $1.10 | multi | 1.60 | .25 |
| *a.* | Booklet pane of 10 + 5 stickers | | | 16.00 | |
| **5074** | A1143 | $1.10 | multi | 1.60 | .25 |
| *a.* | Booklet pane of 10 + 5 stickers | | | 16.00 | |
| **5075** | A1144 | $1.10 | multi | 1.60 | .25 |
| *a.* | Booklet pane of 10 + 5 stickers | | | 16.00 | |
| **5076** | A1145 | $1.10 | multi | 1.60 | .25 |
| *a.* | Booklet pane of 10 + 5 stickers | | | 16.00 | |
| **5077** | A1146 | $1.10 | multi | 1.60 | .25 |
| *a.* | Booklet pane of 10 + 5 stickers | | | 16.00 | |
| **5078** | A1149 | $2.20 | multi | 3.25 | 1.60 |
| *a.* | Booklet pane of 4 | | | 13.00 | |
| | Complete booklet, 4 #5078a | | | 52.00 | |
| | *Nos. 5071-5078 (8)* | | | 14.45 | 3.35 |

Complete booklet sold for $35.95 and the four panes in it have different pane margins.

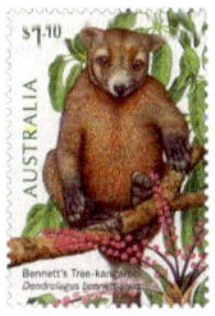

Tree-dwelling Mammals — A1150

Designs: No. 5089, Bennett's tree kangaroo. No. 5090, Spectacled flying fox. No. 5091, Lemuroid ringtail possum.

**2020, Jan. 21 Litho. *Perf. 14¾x14***

| | | | | | |
|---|---|---|---|---|---|
| **5089** | A1150 | $1.10 | multi | 1.50 | 1.10 |
| **5090** | A1150 | $1.10 | multi | 1.50 | 1.10 |
| **5091** | A1150 | $1.10 | multi | 1.50 | 1.10 |
| *a.* | Souvenir sheet of 3, #5089-5091 | | | 4.50 | 3.50 |
| | *Nos. 5089-5091 (3)* | | | 4.50 | 3.30 |

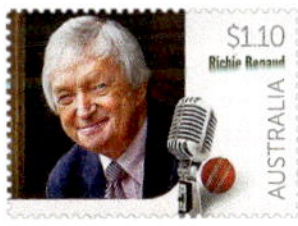

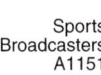

Sports Broadcasters A1151

Designs: No. 5092, Richie Benaud (1930-2015), cricket commentator. No. 5093, Reg Gasnier (1939-2014), rugby commentator. No. 5094, Les Murray (1945-2017), soccer commentator. $2.20, Lou Richards (1923-2017), Jack Dyer (1913-2003), and Bob Davis (1928-2011), Australia rules football commentators.

**2020, Feb. 4 Litho. *Perf. 14x14¾***

| | | | | | |
|---|---|---|---|---|---|
| **5092** | A1151 | $1.10 | multi | 1.50 | 1.10 |
| *a.* | Booklet pane of 4 | | | 6.00 | — |
| **5093** | A1151 | $1.10 | multi | 1.50 | 1.10 |
| *a.* | Booklet pane of 4 | | | 6.00 | — |
| **5094** | A1151 | $1.10 | multi | 1.50 | 1.10 |
| *a.* | Booklet pane of 4 | | | 6.00 | — |

**Size: 50x30mm**

***Perf. 14¼x14***

| | | | | | |
|---|---|---|---|---|---|
| **5095** | A1151 | $2.20 | multi | 3.00 | 2.25 |
| *a.* | Booklet pane of 2 | | | 6.00 | — |
| | Complete booklet, #5092a, 5093a, 5094a, 3 #5095a | | | 36.00 | |
| | *Nos. 5092-5095 (4)* | | | 7.50 | 5.55 |

Complete booklet sold for $26.95 and the three panes of No. 5095a in it have different pane margins.

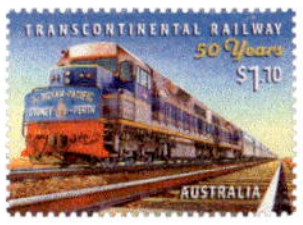

Completion of Standard Gauge Transcontinental Rail Line, 50th Anniv. — A1152

**2020, Feb. 11 Litho. *Perf. 14x14¾***

| | | | | | |
|---|---|---|---|---|---|
| **5096** | A1152 | $1.10 | multi | 1.50 | 1.50 |
| *a.* | Souvenir sheet of 4 | | | 6.00 | 6.00 |

**Booklet Stamp**
**Self-Adhesive**

***Serpentine Die Cut 11¼ Syncopated***

| | | | | | |
|---|---|---|---|---|---|
| **5097** | A1152 | $1.10 | multi | 1.50 | .25 |
| *a.* | Booklet pane of 20 | | | 30.00 | |

Canberra Stampshow 2020 (No. 5096a). Issued: No. 5096a, 3/13/20.

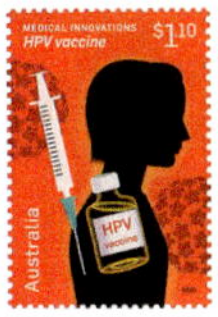

Medical Innovations — A1153

Designs: Nos. 5098, 5102, Human papillomavirus vaccine. Nos. 5099, 5103, Implanted cardiac pacemaker. Nos. 5100, 5104, Spray-on skin cells. $3.20, Medical use of penicillin.

**2020, Feb. 18 Litho. *Perf. 14¾x14***

| | | | | | |
|---|---|---|---|---|---|
| **5098** | A1153 | $1.10 | multi | 1.50 | 1.50 |
| **5099** | A1153 | $1.10 | multi | 1.50 | 1.50 |
| **5100** | A1153 | $1.10 | multi | 1.50 | 1.50 |
| **5101** | A1153 | $3.20 | multi | 4.25 | 4.25 |
| | *Nos. 5098-5101 (4)* | | | 8.75 | 8.75 |

**Booklet Stamps**
**Self-Adhesive**

***Serpentine Die Cut 11¼ Syncopated***

| | | | | | |
|---|---|---|---|---|---|
| **5102** | A1153 | $1.10 | multi | 1.50 | .25 |
| **5103** | A1153 | $1.10 | multi | 1.50 | .25 |
| **5104** | A1153 | $1.10 | multi | 1.50 | .25 |
| *a.* | Booklet pane of 20, 8 #5102, 7 #5103, 5 #5104 | | | 30.00 | |
| **5105** | A1153 | $3.20 | multi | 4.25 | 2.10 |
| *a.* | Booklet pane of 5 | | | 21.50 | |
| | *Nos. 5102-5105 (4)* | | | 8.75 | 2.85 |

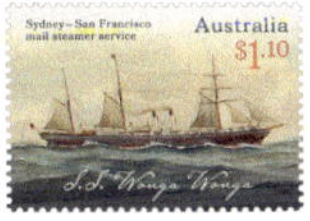

S.S. Wonga Wonga — A1154

**2020, Mar. 3 Litho. *Perf. 14x14¾***

| | | | | | |
|---|---|---|---|---|---|
| **5106** | A1154 | $1.10 | multi | 1.50 | 1.10 |

Mail steamer service between Sydney and San Francisco, 150th anniv.

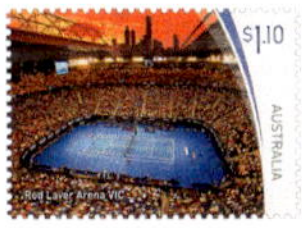

Sports Stadiums — A1155

Designs. Nos. 5107, 5111, Rod Laver Arena, Melbourne. Nos. 5108, 5112, Adelaide Oval, Adelaide. Nos. 5109, 5113, Anne Meares Velodrome, Brisbane. Nos. 5110, 5114, Sydney Olympic Park Aquatic Center, Sydney.

**2020, Mar. 24 Litho. *Perf. 14x14¾***

| | | | | | |
|---|---|---|---|---|---|
| **5107** | A1155 | $1.10 | multi | 1.40 | 1.40 |
| **5108** | A1155 | $1.10 | multi | 1.40 | 1.40 |
| **5109** | A1155 | $1.10 | multi | 1.40 | 1.40 |
| **5110** | A1155 | $1.10 | multi | 1.40 | 1.40 |
| | *Nos. 5107-5110 (4)* | | | 5.60 | 5.60 |

**Self-Adhesive**

***Serpentine Die Cut 11¼ Syncopated***

| | | | | | |
|---|---|---|---|---|---|
| **5111** | A1155 | $1.10 | multi | 1.40 | .25 |
| *a.* | Booklet pane of 10 | | | 14.00 | |
| **5112** | A1155 | $1.10 | multi | 1.40 | .25 |
| *a.* | Booklet pane of 10 | | | 14.00 | |
| **5113** | A1155 | $1.10 | multi | 1.40 | .25 |
| *a.* | Booklet pane of 10 | | | 14.00 | |
| **5114** | A1155 | $1.10 | multi | 1.40 | .25 |
| *a.* | Booklet pane of 10 | | | 14.00 | |
| *b.* | Horiz. coil strip of 4, #5111-5114 | | | 5.60 | |
| | *Nos. 5111-5114 (4)* | | | 5.60 | 1.00 |

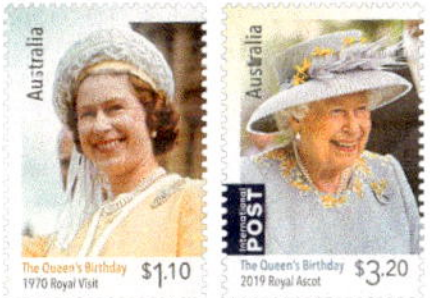

Queen Elizabeth II, 94th Birthday

A1156 A1157

**2020, Apr. 7 Litho. *Perf. 14¾x14***

| | | | | | |
|---|---|---|---|---|---|
| **5115** | A1156 | $1.10 | multi | 1.40 | 1.10 |
| **5116** | A1157 | $3.20 | multi | 4.25 | 4.25 |
| *a.* | Souvenir sheet of 2, #5115-5116 | | | 5.75 | 5.75 |

**Booklet Stamp**
**Self-Adhesive**

***Serpentine Die Cut 11¼ Syncopated***

| | | | | | |
|---|---|---|---|---|---|
| **5117** | A1157 | $3.20 | multi | 4.25 | 2.10 |
| *a.* | Booklet pane of 5 | | | 21.50 | |

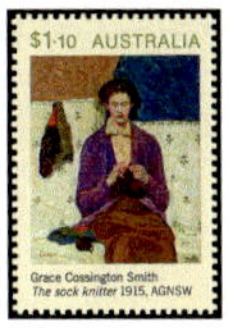

ANZAC Day — A1158

Paintings: Nos. 5118, 5122, The Sock Knitter, by Grace Cossington Smith (1892-1984). Nos. 5119, 5123, A Man, by Hilda Rix Nicholas (1884-1961). Nos. 5120, 5124, Group of VADS, by William Dargie (1912-2003). Nos. 5121, 5125, Bomber Crew, by Stella Bowen (1893-1947).

**2020, Apr. 14 Litho. *Perf. 14¾x14***

| | | | | | |
|---|---|---|---|---|---|
| **5118** | A1158 | $1.10 | multi | 1.40 | 1.40 |
| **5119** | A1158 | $1.10 | multi | 1.40 | 1.40 |
| **5120** | A1158 | $1.10 | multi | 1.40 | 1.40 |
| **5121** | A1158 | $1.10 | multi | 1.40 | 1.40 |
| *a.* | Souvenir sheet of 4, #5118-5121 | | | 5.75 | 5.75 |
| | *Nos. 5118-5121 (4)* | | | 5.60 | 5.60 |

**Coil Stamps**
**Self-Adhesive**

***Serpentine Die Cut 11¼ Syncopated***

| | | | | | |
|---|---|---|---|---|---|
| **5122** | A1158 | $1.10 | multi | 1.40 | .25 |
| **5123** | A1158 | $1.10 | multi | 1.40 | .25 |
| **5124** | A1158 | $1.10 | multi | 1.40 | .25 |
| **5125** | A1158 | $1.10 | multi | 1.40 | .25 |
| *a.* | Vert. coil strip of 4, #5122-5125 | | | 6.00 | |
| | *Nos. 5122-5125 (4)* | | | 5.60 | 1.00 |

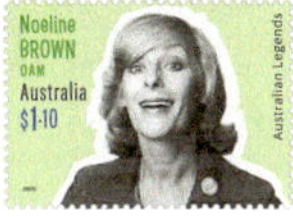

Comedians A1159

Designs: Nos. 5126, 5130, Noeline Brown. Nos. 5127, 5131, Adam Hills. Nos. 5128, 5132, Garry McDonald. Nos. 5129, 5133, Magda Szubanski.

**2020, Apr. 15 Litho. *Perf. 14x14¾***

| | | | | | |
|---|---|---|---|---|---|
| **5126** | A1159 | $1.10 | multi | 1.40 | 1.40 |
| **5127** | A1159 | $1.10 | multi | 1.40 | 1.40 |
| **5128** | A1159 | $1.10 | multi | 1.40 | 1.40 |
| **5129** | A1159 | $1.10 | multi | 1.40 | 1.40 |
| | *Nos. 5126-5129 (4)* | | | 5.60 | 5.60 |

**Booklet Stamps**
**Self-Adhesive**

***Serpentine Die Cut 11¼ Syncopated***

| | | | | | |
|---|---|---|---|---|---|
| **5130** | A1159 | $1.10 | multi | 1.40 | .25 |
| *a.* | Booklet pane of 10 | | | 14.00 | |
| **5131** | A1159 | $1.10 | multi | 1.40 | .25 |
| *a.* | Booklet pane of 10 | | | 14.00 | |
| **5132** | A1159 | $1.10 | multi | 1.40 | .25 |
| *a.* | Booklet pane of 10 | | | 14.00 | |
| **5133** | A1159 | $1.10 | multi | 1.40 | .25 |
| *a.* | Booklet pane of 10 | | | 14.00 | |
| | *Nos. 5130-5133 (4)* | | | 5.60 | 1.00 |

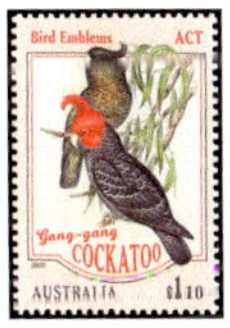

State and Territory Birds — A1160

Designs: Nos. 5134, 5140, Gang-gang cockatoo, Australian Capital Territory. Nos. 5135, 5141, Helmeted honeyeater, Victoria. Nos. 5136, 5142, Wedge-tailed eagle, Northern Territory. Nos. 5137, 5143, Laughing kookaburra, New South Wales. Nos. 5138, 5144, Brolga, Queensland. Nos. 5139, 5145, Black swan, Western Australia, horiz.

**2020, Apr. 21 Litho. *Perf. 14¾x14***

| | | | | | |
|---|---|---|---|---|---|
| **5134** | A1160 | $1.10 | multi | 1.40 | 1.40 |
| **5135** | A1160 | $1.10 | multi | 1.40 | 1.40 |
| **5136** | A1160 | $1.10 | multi | 1.40 | 1.40 |
| **5137** | A1160 | $1.10 | multi | 1.40 | 1.40 |
| **5138** | A1160 | $1.10 | multi | 1.40 | 1.40 |

***Perf. 14x14¾***

| | | | | | |
|---|---|---|---|---|---|
| **5139** | A1160 | $1.10 | multi | 1.40 | 1.40 |
| *a.* | Souvenir sheet of 4 #5139 | | | 5.75 | 5.75 |
| *b.* | Souvenir sheet of 4 with Perth 2022 Stamp and Coin Show emblem in sheet margin | | | 6.75 | 5.25 |
| | *Nos. 5134-5139 (6)* | | | 8.40 | 8.40 |

**Booklet Stamps**
**Self-Adhesive**

***Serpentine Die Cut 11¼ Syncopated***

| | | | | | |
|---|---|---|---|---|---|
| **5140** | A1160 | $1.10 | multi | 1.40 | .25 |
| *a.* | Booklet pane of 10 | | | 14.00 | |
| **5141** | A1160 | $1.10 | multi | 1.40 | .25 |
| *a.* | Booklet pane of 10 | | | 14.00 | |
| **5142** | A1160 | $1.10 | multi | 1.40 | .25 |
| *a.* | Booklet pane of 10 | | | 14.00 | |
| **5143** | A1160 | $1.10 | multi | 1.40 | .25 |
| *a.* | Booklet pane of 10 | | | 14.00 | |
| **5144** | A1160 | $1.10 | multi | 1.40 | .25 |
| *a.* | Booklet pane of 10 | | | 14.00 | |
| **5145** | A1160 | $1.10 | multi | 1.40 | .25 |
| *a.* | Booklet pane of 10 | | | 14.00 | |
| | *Nos. 5140-5145 (6)* | | | 8.40 | 1.50 |

Issued: No. 5139a, 9/19. No. 5139b, 3/4/22. 2020 Perth Stamp and Coin Show (No. 5139a). 2022 Perth Stamp and Coin Show (No. 5139b).

Miniature Sheet

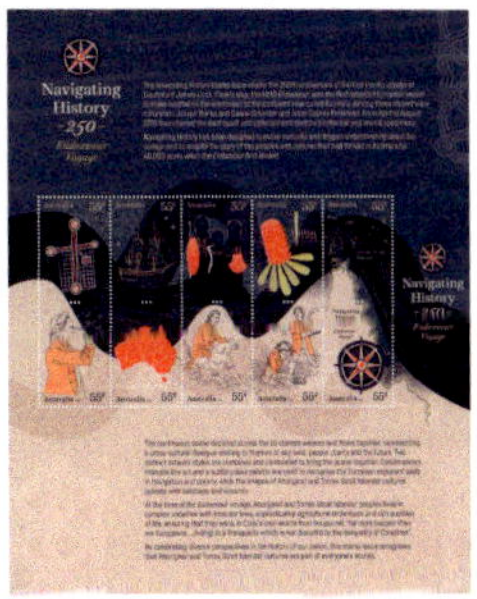

First Pacific Voyage of the HMS Endeavour, 250th Anniv. — A1161

Nos. 5146 and 5147: a, Southern Cross constellation. b, HMS Endeavour. c, Silhouettes of indigenous Australians. d, Flower and needle. e, Map of Australian coast and Torres Strait Islands. f, Lieutenant James Cook using sextant. g, Map of Australia. h, Expedition member oitting. i, Naturalists Joseph Banks and Daniel Solander. j, Compass rose.

***Perf. 14 Syncopated***

**2020, Apr. 29 Litho.**

| | | | | |
|---|---|---|---|---|
| **5146** | A1161 | Sheet of 10 | 7.00 | 7.00 |
| *a.-j.* | | 55c Any single | .70 | .70 |

**Booklet Stamps**
**Self-Adhesive**

***Serpentine Die Cut 11¾ Syncopated on 3 Sides***

| | | | | |
|---|---|---|---|---|
| **5147** | A1161 | Booklet pane of 10 | 7.00 | |
| *a.-j.* | | 55c Any single | .70 | .25 |

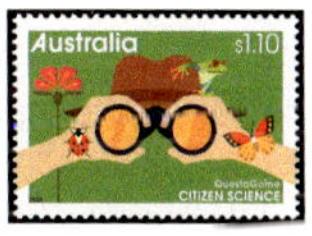

Citizen Science — A1162

Inscriptions: Nos. 5148, 5152, QuestaGame. Nos. 5149, 5153, Ngukurr Wi Stadi Bla Kantri (We study the country). Nos. 5150, 5154, Butterflies Australia. Nos. 5151, 5155, Zika Mozzie Seeker.

**2020, May 19 Litho. *Perf. 14x14¾***

| | | | | | |
|---|---|---|---|---|---|
| **5148** | A1162 | $1.10 | multi | 1.50 | 1.50 |
| **5149** | A1162 | $1.10 | multi | 1.50 | 1.50 |
| **5150** | A1162 | $1.10 | multi | 1.50 | 1.50 |
| **5151** | A1162 | $1.10 | multi | 1.50 | 1.50 |
| | *Nos. 5148-5151 (4)* | | | 6.00 | 6.00 |

**Booklet Stamps**
**Self-Adhesive**

***Serpentine Die Cut 11¼ Syncopated***

| | | | | | |
|---|---|---|---|---|---|
| **5152** | A1162 | $1.10 | multi | 1.50 | .25 |
| *a.* | Booklet pane of 10 | | | 15.00 | |
| **5153** | A1162 | $1.10 | multi | 1.50 | .25 |
| *a.* | Booklet pane of 10 | | | 15.00 | |
| **5154** | A1162 | $1.10 | multi | 1.50 | .25 |
| *a.* | Booklet pane of 10 | | | 15.00 | |
| **5155** | A1162 | $1.10 | multi | 1.50 | .25 |
| *a.* | Booklet pane of 10 | | | 15.00 | |
| | *Nos. 5152-5155 (4)* | | | 6.00 | 1.00 |

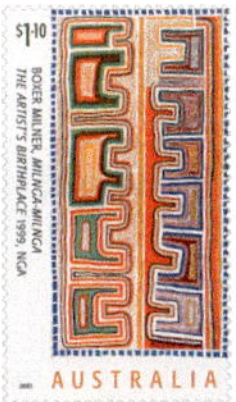

Art by Western Desert Aboriginals — A1163

Designs: No. 5156, Milnga-Milnga, The Artist's Birthplace, by Boxer Milner (c.1935-2009). No. 5157, Tingarri Mamultjulkulakutu, by Fred Ward Tjungurrayi. No. 5158, Untitled painting by Eubena Nampitjin (c. 1925-2013). $2.20, Kangaroo Dreaming, by Walter Tjampitjinpa (c. 1912-81).

**2020, June 9 Litho. *Perf. 14x14¼***

**5156** A1163 $1.10 multi 1.50 1.10
**5157** A1163 $1.10 multi 1.50 1.10
**5158** A1163 $1.10 multi 1.50 1.10
**5159** A1163 $2.20 multi 3.00 3.00
*Nos. 5156-5159 (4)* 7.50 6.30

**Booklet Stamp**
**Self-Adhesive**

***Serpentine Die Cut 11x10¾ Syncopated***

**5160** A1163 $2.20 multi 3.00 1.50
*a.* Booklet pane of 5 15.00

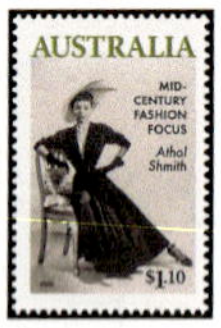


Fashion Photography — A1164

Photograph from: No. 5161, 1949, by Athol Shmith (1914-90). No. 5162, 1959, by Helmut Newton (1920-2004). No. 5163, 1960s, by Henry Talbot (1920-99). No. 5164, 1972, Bruno Benini (1925-2001).

**2020, June 16 Litho. *Perf. 14¾x14***

**5161** A1164 $1.10 multi 1.50 1.10
**5162** A1164 $1.10 multi 1.50 1.10
**5163** A1164 $1.10 multi 1.50 1.10
**5164** A1164 $1.10 multi 1.50 1.10
*a.* Souvenir sheet of 4, #5161-5164 6.00 4.50
*Nos. 5161-5164 (4)* 6.00 4.40

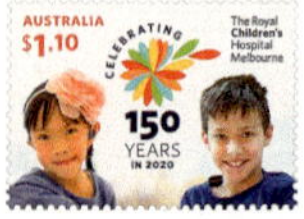


Royal Children's Hospital Melbourne, 150th Anniv. — A1165

**2020, July 7 Litho. *Perf. 14x14¾***

**5165** A1165 $1.10 multi 1.60 1.60

**Booklet Stamp**
**Self-Adhesive**

***Serpentine Die Cut 11¼ Syncopated***

**5166** A1165 $1.10 multi 1.60 .25
*a.* Booklet pane of 10 16.00

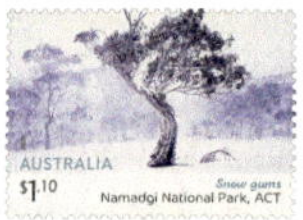


Australian Alps — A1166

Designs: Nos. 5167, 5170, Snow gum trees, Namadgi National Park, Australian Capital Territory. Nos. 5168, 5171, The Cathedral, Mount Buffalo National Park, Victoria. Nos. 5169, 5172, Swampy Plain River, Kosciuszko National Park, New South Wales.

**2020, July 21 Litho. *Perf. 14x14¾***

**5167** A1166 $1.10 multi 1.60 1.60
**5168** A1166 $1.10 multi 1.60 1.60
**5169** A1166 $1.10 multi 1.60 1.60
*a.* Souvenir sheet of 3, #5167-5169 4.80 4.80
*Nos. 5167-5169 (3)* 4.80 4.80

**Coil Stamps**
**Self-Adhesive**

***Serpentine Die Cut 11¼ Syncopated***

**5170** A1166 $1.10 multi 1.60 .25
**5171** A1166 $1.10 multi 1.60 .25
**5172** A1166 $1.10 multi 1.60 .25
*a.* Horiz. strip of 3, #5170-5172 4.80
*Nos. 5170-5172 (3)* 4.80 .75

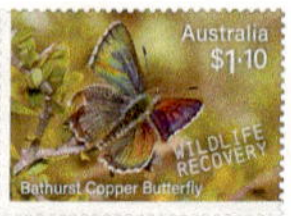


A1167

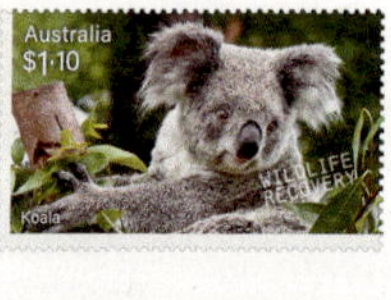


Wildlife Recovery A1168

Animals severly affected by loss of habitat in Australian bushfires: Nos. 5173, 5179, Bathurst copper butterfly. Nos. 5174, 5180, Davies' tree frog. Nos. 5175, 5181, Kangaroo Island dunnart. Nos. 5176, 5182, Regent honeyeater. Nos. 5177, 5183, Blue Mountains water skink. No. 5178, Koala.

**2020, Aug. 4 Litho. *Perf. 14x14¾***

**5173** A1167 $1.10 multi 1.60 1.60
**5174** A1167 $1.10 multi 1.60 1.60
**5175** A1167 $1.10 multi 1.60 1.60
**5176** A1167 $1.10 multi 1.60 1.60
**5177** A1167 $1.10 multi 1.60 1.60

***Perf. 14¼x14***

**5178** A1168 $1.10 multi 1.60 1.60
*a.* Souvenir sheet of 6, #5173-5178 9.75 9.75
*Nos. 5173-5178 (6)* 9.60 9.60

**Booklet Stamp**
**Self-Adhesive**

***Serpentine Die Cut 11¼ Syncopated***

**5179** A1167 $1.10 multi 1.60 .25
*a.* Booklet pane of 10 16.00
**5180** A1167 $1.10 multi 1.60 .25
*a.* Booklet pane of 10 16.00
**5181** A1167 $1.10 multi 1.60 .25
*a.* Booklet pane of 10 16.00
**5182** A1167 $1.10 multi 1.60 .25
*a.* Booklet pane of 10 16.00
**5183** A1167 $1.10 multi 1.60 .25
*a.* Booklet pane of 10 16.00
*Nos. 5179-5183 (5)* 8.00 1.25

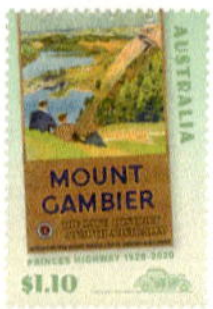


Princes Highway, Cent. — A1169

Automobile and travel poster for: No. 4184, Mount Gambier. No. 4185, Geelong. No. 4186, Melbourne. No. 4187, Sydney.

**2020, Aug. 11 Litho. *Perf. 14¾x14***

**5184** A1169 $1.10 multi 1.60 1.25
**5185** A1169 $1.10 multi 1.60 1.25
**5186** A1169 $1.10 multi 1.60 1.25
**5187** A1169 $1.10 multi 1.60 1.25
*Nos. 5184-5187 (4)* 6.40 5.00

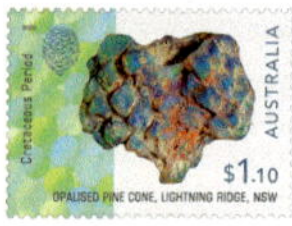


Opalized Fossils — A1170

Fossil of: Nos. 5188, 5194, Pine cone. Nos. 5189, 5193, Theropod tooth. Nos. 5190, 5192, Moon snail. Nos. 5191, 5195, Wood.

**2020, Aug. 17 Litho. *Perf. 14x14¾***

**5188** A1170 $1.10 multi 1.60 1.60
**5189** A1170 $1.10 multi 1.60 1.60
**5190** A1170 $1.10 multi 1.60 1.60
**5191** A1170 $1.10 multi 1.60 1.60
*a.* Souvenir sheet of 4, #5188-5191 6.50 6.50
*Nos. 5188-5191 (4)* 6.40 6.40

**Booklet Stamps**
**Self-Adhesive**

***Serpentine Die Cut 11¼ Syncopated***

**5192** A1170 $1.10 multi 1.60 .25
**5193** A1170 $1.10 multi 1.60 .25
**5194** A1170 $1.10 multi 1.60 .25
**5195** A1170 $1.10 multi 1.60 .25
*a.* Booklet pane of 10, 3 each #5192-5193, 2 each #5194-5195 16.00
*b.* Booklet pane of 20, 5 each #5192-5195 32.00
*Nos. 5192-5195 (4)* 6.40 1.00

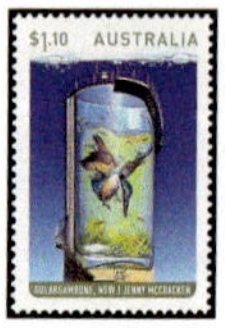


Art on Water Towers — A1171

Designs: Nos. 5196, 5200, Lucky Dip, by Jenny McCracken on Gulargambone, New South Wales water tower. Nos. 5197, 5201, Man's Face, by Guido van Helten on Winton, Victoria water tower. Nos. 5198, 5202, Eastern Bearded Dragon, by Apparition Media on Narrandera, New South Wales water tower. No. 5199, 5203, Man with Safety Helmet, by Vans the Omega, on Snowtown, South Australia water tower.

**2020, Sept. 7 Litho. *Perf. 14¾x14***

**5196** A1171 $1.10 multi 1.60 1.60
**5197** A1171 $1.10 multi 1.60 1.60
**5198** A1171 $1.10 multi 1.60 1.60
**5199** A1171 $1.10 multi 1.60 1.60
*a.* Souvenir sheet of 4, #5196-5199 6.50 6.50
*Nos. 5196-5199 (4)* 6.40 6.40

**Booklet Stamps**
**Self-Adhesive**

***Serpentine Die Cut 11¼ Syncopated***

**5200** A1171 $1.10 multi 1.60 .25
*a.* Booklet pane of 10 16.00
**5201** A1171 $1.10 multi 1.60 .25
*a.* Booklet pane of 10 16.00
**5202** A1171 $1.10 multi 1.60 .25
*a.* Booklet pane of 10 16.00
**5203** A1171 $1.10 multi 1.60 .25
*a.* Booklet pane of 10 16.00
*Nos. 5200-5203 (4)* 6.40 1.00

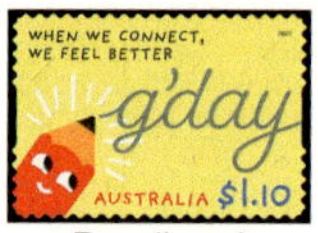


Pencil and "G'day" — A1172

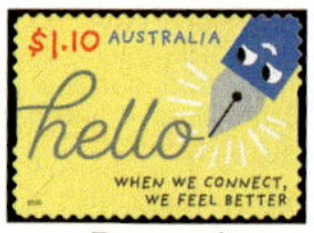


Pen and "Hello" — A1173

***Serpentine Die Cut 11¼ Syncopated***

**2020, Oct. 1 Litho.**

**Self-Adhesive**

**5204** A1172 $1.10 multi 1.60 .80
**5205** A1173 $1.10 multi 1.60 .80
*a.* Horiz. pair, #5204-5205 3.20

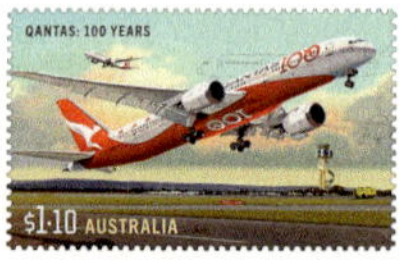


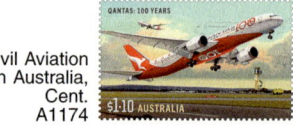

Civil Aviation in Australia, Cent. A1174

Designs: $1.10, Qantas Dreamliner at Sydney Airport. $2.20, Biplane and 1920 Act concerning civil aviation.

**2020, Oct. 6 Litho. *Perf. 14½x14***

**5206** A1174 $1.10 multi 1.60 1.60
**5207** A1174 $2.20 multi 3.25 2.40
*a.* Souvenir sheet of 2, #5206-5207 5.00 3.75

**Booklet Stamp**
**Self-Adhesive**

***Serpentine Die Cut 10¾ Syncopated***

**5208** A1174 $1.10 multi 1.60 .25
*a.* Booklet pane of 10 16.00

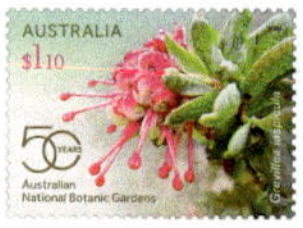


Australian National Botanic Gardens, Canberra, 50th Anniv. — A1175

Designs: Nos. 5209, 5211, 5213, Grevillea iaspicula. Nos. 5210, 5212, 5214, Banksia marginata.

**2020, Oct. 13 Litho. *Perf. 14x14¾***

**5209** A1175 $1.10 multi 1.60 1.60
**5210** A1175 $1.10 multi 1.60 1.60
*a.* Souvenir sheet of 2, #5209-5210 3.25 3.25

**Self-Adhesive**
**Country Name in Gray Green**
**Consistent Shading on "50"**

***Serpentine Die Cut 11¼ Syncopated***

**5211** A1175 $1.10 multi 1.60 .25
**5212** A1175 $1.10 multi 1.60 .25
*a.* Horiz. coil pair, #5211-5212 3.20
*b.* Booklet pane of 10, 5 each #5211-5212 16.00

**Digitally Printed**
**Booklet Stamps**
**Country Name in Green**
**Lighter Color on Edges of "50" Than in Center of Numbers**

**5213** A1175 $1.10 multi 1.60 .25
**5214** A1175 $1.10 multi 1.60 .25
*a.* Booklet pane of 10, 5 each #5213-5214 16.00

The covers and pictures at the bottoms of the opened booklet panes differ on Nos. 5212b and 5214a.

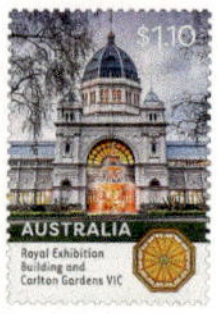


UNESCO World Heritage Sites in Australia — A1176

Designs: Nos. 5215, 5219, Royal Exhibition Building and Carlton Gardens, Melbourne, Victoria. Nos. 5216, 5220, Budj Bim Cultural Landscape, Victoria. Nos. 5217, 5221, Cascades Female Factory, Tasmania. Nos. 5218, 5222, Sydney Opera House, Sydney, New South Wales.

**2020, Oct. 20 Litho. *Perf. 14¾x14***

**5215** A1176 $1.10 multi 1.60 1.60
**5216** A1176 $1.10 multi 1.60 1.60
**5217** A1176 $1.10 multi 1.60 1.60
**5218** A1176 $1.10 multi 1.60 1.60
*Nos. 5215-5218 (4)* 6.40 6.40

**Booklet Stamps**
**Self-Adhesive**

***Serpentine Die Cut 11¼ Syncopated***

**5219** A1176 $1.10 multi 1.60 .25
*a.* Booklet pane of 10 16.00
**5220** A1176 $1.10 multi 1.60 .25
*a.* Booklet pane of 10 16.00
**5221** A1176 $1.10 multi 1.60 .25
*a.* Booklet pane of 10 16.00
**5222** A1176 $1.10 multi 1.60 .25
*a.* Booklet pane of 10 16.00
*Nos. 5219-5222 (4)* 6.40 1.00

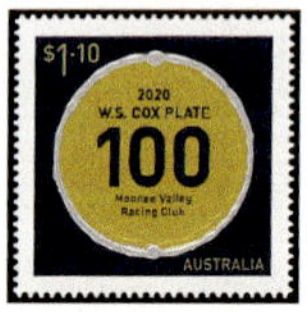


100th Running of the W. S. Cox Plate Horse Race — A1177

**Litho. & Embossed With Foil Application**

**2020, Oct. 22 *Perf. 14¼***

**5223** A1177 $1.10 dk blue & gold 1.60 1.25

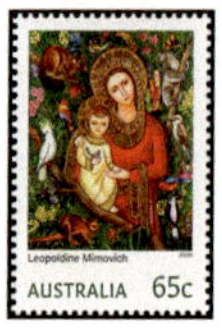


A1178

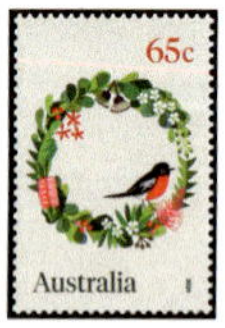


Christmas — A1179

Designs: Nos. 5224, 5229, Painting of Madonna and Child, by Leopoldine Mimovich (1920-2019). Nos. 5225, 5230, Christmas wreath. Nos. 5226, 5231, Christmas stocking with flowers. Nos. 5227, 5232, Painting of Holy Family, by Mimovich. Nos. 5228, 5233, Christmas ornament, flowers and holly.

**2020, Oct. 30 Litho. *Perf. 14¾x14***

**5224** A1178 65c multi .95 .95
**5225** A1179 65c multi .95 .95
**5226** A1179 65c multi .95 .95
*a.* Horiz. pair, #5225-5226 1.90 1.90
**5227** A1178 $2.20 multi 3.25 3.25
*a.* Souvenir sheet of 2, #5224, 5227 4.25 4.25
**5228** A1179 $2.20 multi 3.25 3.25
*Nos. 5224-5228 (5)* 9.35 9.35

**Booklet Stamps**
**Self-Adhesive**

***Serpentine Die Cut 11¼ Syncopated***

**5229** A1178 65c multi .95 .25
*a.* Booklet pane of 20 + 20 etiquettes 19.00
**5230** A1179 65c multi .95 .25
*a.* With glossier varnish .95 .25
*b.* Booklet pane of 10 #5230a + 10 etiquettes 9.50
**5231** A1179 65c multi .95 .25
*a.* Booklet pane of 20 10 each #5230-5231, + 20 etiquettes 19.00
*b.* With glossier varnish .95 .25
*c.* Booklet pane of 10 #5231b + 10 etiquettes 9.50
**5232** A1178 $2.20 multi 3.25 1.60
*a.* Booklet pane of 5 16.50
**5233** A1179 $2.20 multi 3.25 1.60
*a.* Booklet pane of 5 16.50
*Nos. 5229-5233 (5)* 9.35 3.95

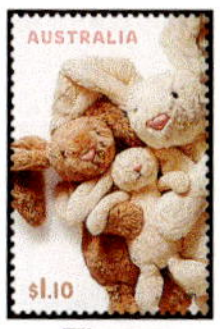
Three Stuffed Rabbit Dolls A1180

"Thank You" A1181

Bunch of Balloons A1182

Heart A1183

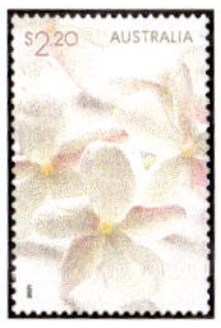
White Flowers — A1184

**2021, Jan. 25 Litho. *Perf. 14¾x14***

**5234** A1180 $1.10 multi 1.75 1.75
**5235** A1181 $1.10 multi 1.75 1.75
**5236** A1182 $1.10 multi 1.75 1.75
**5237** A1183 $1.10 multi 1.75 1.75
**5238** A1184 $2.20 multi 3.50 3.50
*a.* Souvenir sheet of 5, #5234-5238 10.50 10.50
*Nos. 5234-5238 (5)* 10.50 10.50

**Booklet Stamps**
**Self-Adhesive**

***Serpentine Die Cut 11¼ Syncopated***

**5239** A1180 $1.10 multi 1.75 .25
*a.* Booklet pane of 10 17.50
**5240** A1181 $1.10 multi 1.75 .25
*a.* Booklet pane of 10 17.50
**5241** A1182 $1.10 multi 1.75 .25
*a.* Booklet pane of 10 17.50
**5242** A1183 $1.10 multi 1.75 .25
*a.* Booklet pane of 10 17.50
**5243** A1184 $2.20 multi 3.50 1.75
*a.* Booklet pane of 4 14.00
Complete booklet, 4 #5243a 56.00
*Nos. 5239-5243 (5)* 10.50 2.75

Complete booklet sold for $35.95 and includes a pane of 20 stickers. Each booklet pane in complete booklet has a different booklet pane margin.

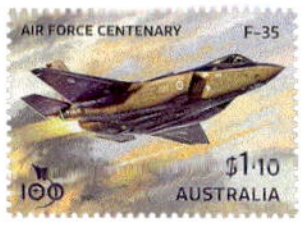
Royal Australian Air Force, Cent. — A1185

Designs: $1.10, F-35. $3.30, SE5A.

**2021, Feb. 9 Litho. *Perf. 14x14¾***

**5244** A1185 $1.10 multi 1.75 1.75
**5245** A1185 $3.30 multi 5.25 2.60
*a.* Souvenir sheet of 2, #5244-5245 7.00 4.50
*b.* Souvenir sheet of 2, #5244-5245, with Perth Stamp and Coin Show emblem in sheet margin 7.00 4.50

**Coil Stamp**
**Self-Adhesive**
**Inkjet Printed**

***Serpentine Die Cut 11¼ Syncopated***

**5246** A1185 $1.10 multi 1.75 .25

Issued: No. 5245b, 3/12. 2021 Perth Stamp and Coin Show (No. 5245b).

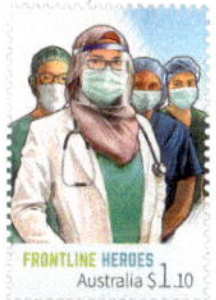
Medical Personnel A1186

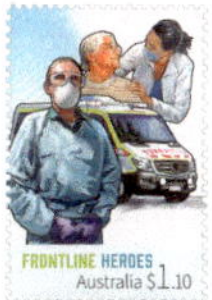
Ambulance Driver and Health Care Worker A1187

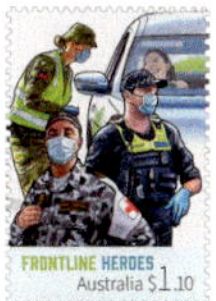
Police and Defense Force Personnel A1188

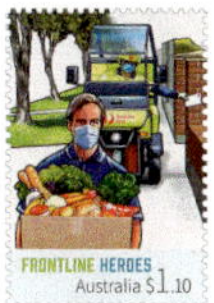
Postal Worker and Grocery Deliveryman A1189

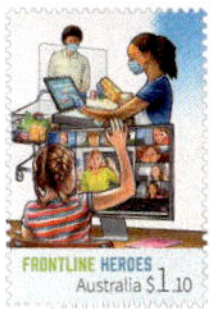
Store Cashier and Teacher on Computer — A1190

**2021, Feb. 16 Litho. *Perf. 14¾x14***

**5247** A1186 $1.10 multi 1.75 1.75
*a.* Souvenir sheet of 4 with 2022 Canberra Stampshow emblem in sheet margin 6.75 5.25
**5248** A1187 $1.10 multi 1.75 1.75
**5249** A1188 $1.10 multi 1.75 1.75
**5250** A1189 $1.10 multi 1.75 1.75
**5251** A1190 $1.10 multi 1.75 1.75
*a.* Horiz. strip of 5, #5247-5251 8.75 8.75
*b.* Souvenir sheet of 5, #5247-5251 8.75 8.75
*Nos. 5247-5251 (5)* 8.75 8.75

**Booklet Stamps**
**Self-Adhesive**

***Serpentine Die Cut 11¼ Syncopated***

**5252** A1186 $1.10 multi 1.75 .25
**5253** A1187 $1.10 multi 1.75 .25
**5254** A1188 $1.10 multi 1.75 .25
**5255** A1189 $1.10 multi 1.75 .25
**5256** A1190 $1.10 multi 1.75 .25
*a.* Booklet pane of 10, 2 each #5252-5256 17.50
*Nos. 5252-5256 (5)* 8.75 1.25

Frontline workers during the COVID-19 pandemic. Issued: No. 5247a, 3/18/22. 2022 Canberra Stampshow (No. 5247a).

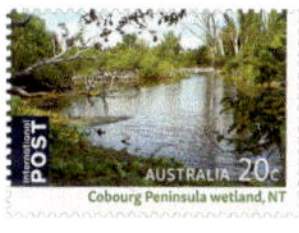
Ramsar Convention Wetlands — A1191

Designs: 20c, Cobourg Peninsula Wetland, Northern Territory. $2.70, Moreton Bay Wetland, Queensland. $3.40, Blue Lake Wetland, New South Wales. $3.50, Riverland Wetland, South Australia.

**2021, Feb. 22 Litho. *Perf. 14x14¾***

**5257** A1191 20c multi .35 .25
**5258** A1191 $2.70 multi 4.25 4.25
**5259** A1191 $3.40 multi 5.25 5.25
**5260** A1191 $3.50 multi 5.50 5.50
*Nos. 5257-5260 (4)* 15.35 15.25

**Booklet Stamps**
**Self-Adhesive**

***Serpentine Die Cut 11¼ Syncopated***

**5261** A1191 $2.70 multi 4.25 2.10
*a.* Booklet pane of 5 21.50
**5262** A1191 $3.40 multi 5.25 2.60
*a.* Booklet pane of 5 26.50
**5263** A1191 $3.50 multi 5.50 2.75
*a.* Booklet pane of 5 27.50
*Nos. 5261-5263 (3)* 15.00 7.45

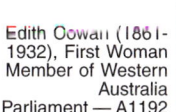

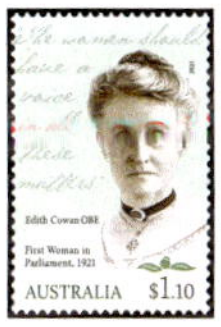
Edith Cowan (1861-1932), First Woman Member of Western Australia Parliament — A1192

**2021, Mar. 2 Litho. *Perf. 14¾x14***

**5264** A1192 $1.10 multi 1.75 1.30

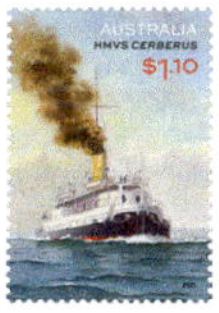
Arrival in Australia of HMVS Cerberus, 150th Anniv. — A1193

**2021, Mar. 22 Litho. *Perf. 14¾x14***

**5265** A1193 $1.10 multi 1.75 1.30

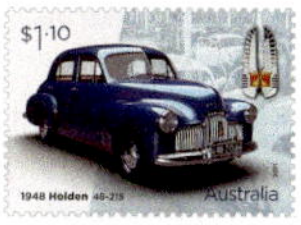
Holden Automobiles A1194

Designs: Nos. 5266, 5271, 1948 Holden 48-215. Nos. 5267, 5272, 1963 Holden EH Premier. Nos. 5268, 5273, 1968 Holden HK Monaro GTS 327. Nos. 5269, 5274, 1971 Holden HQ Kinswood Ute. Nos. 5270, 5275, 2006 Holden VE Commodore SS V.

**2021, Mar. 22 Litho. *Perf. 14x14¾***

**5266** A1194 $1.10 multi 1.75 1.75
**5267** A1194 $1.10 multi 1.75 1.75
**5268** A1194 $1.10 multi 1.75 1.75
**5269** A1194 $1.10 multi 1.75 1.75
**5270** A1194 $1.10 multi 1.75 1.75
*a.* Souvenir sheet of 5, #5266-5270 8.75 8.75
*Nos. 5266-5270 (5)* 8.75 8.75

**Booklet Stamps**
**Self-Adhesive**

***Serpentine Die Cut 11¼ Syncopated***

**5271** A1194 $1.10 multi 1.75 .25
*a.* Booklet pane of 10 17.50
**5272** A1194 $1.10 multi 1.75 .25
*a.* Booklet pane of 10 17.50
**5273** A1194 $1.10 multi 1.75 .25
*a.* Booklet pane of 10 17.50
**5274** A1194 $1.10 multi 1.75 .25
*a.* Booklet pane of 10 17.50
**5275** A1194 $1.10 multi 1.75 .25
*a.* Booklet pane of 10 17.50
*Nos. 5271-5275 (5)* 8.75 1.25

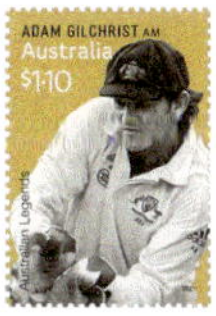
Cricket Players — A1195

Designs: Nos. 5276, 5282, Adam Gilchrist. Nos. 5277, 5283, Ricky Ponting. Nos. 5278, 5284, Ellyse Perry. Nos. 5279, 5285, Jason Gillespie. Nos. 5280, 5286, Allan Border. Nos. 5281, 5287, Dennis Lillee.

**2021, Mar. 26 Litho. *Perf. 14¾x14***

**5276** A1195 $1.10 multi 1.75 1.75
**5277** A1195 $1.10 multi 1.75 1.75
*a.* Horiz. pair, #5276-5277 3.50 3.50
**5278** A1195 $1.10 multi 1.75 1.75
**5279** A1195 $1.10 multi 1.75 1.75
*a.* Horiz. pair, #5278-5279 3.50 3.50
**5280** A1195 $1.10 multi 1.75 1.75
**5281** A1195 $1.10 multi 1.75 1.75
*a.* Horiz. pair, #5280-5281 3.50 3.50
*Nos. 5276-5281 (6)* 10.50 10.50

**Booklet Stamps**
**Self-Adhesive**

***Serpentine Die Cut 11¼ Syncopated***

**5282** A1195 $1.10 multi 1.75 .25
*a.* Booklet pane of 10 17.50
**5283** A1195 $1.10 multi 1.75 .25
*a.* Booklet pane of 10 17.50
**5284** A1195 $1.10 multi 1.75 .25
*a.* Booklet pane of 10 17.50
**5285** A1195 $1.10 multi 1.75 .25
*a.* Booklet pane of 10 17.50
**5286** A1195 $1.10 multi 1.75 .25
*a.* Booklet pane of 10 17.50
**5287** A1195 $1.10 multi 1.75 .25
*a.* Booklet pane of 10 17.50
*Nos. 5282-5287 (6)* 10.50 1.50

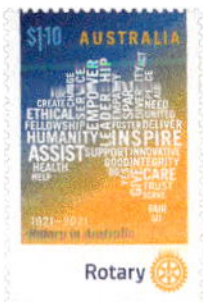
Rotary International in Australia, Cent. — A1196

**2021, Apr. 6 Litho. *Perf. 14¾x14***

**5288** A1196 $1.10 multi 1.75 1.30

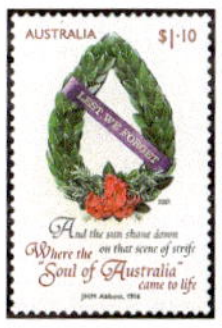
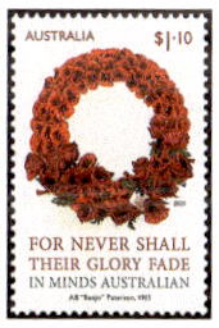
ANZAC Day Wreaths
A1197 A1198

**2021, Apr. 13 Litho. *Perf. 14¾x14***

**5289** A1197 $1.10 multi 1.75 1.75
**5290** A1198 $1.10 multi 1.75 1.75
*a.* Souvenir sheet of 2, #5289-5290 3.50 3.50

**Booklet Stamps**
**Self-Adhesive**

***Serpentine Die Cut 11¼ Syncopated***

**5291** A1197 $1.10 multi 1.75 .25
**5292** A1198 $1.10 multi 1.75 .25
*a.* Booklet pane of 20, 10 each #5291-5292 35.00

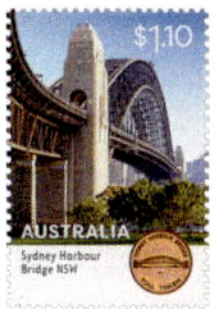
Landmarks on Australian National Heritage List — A1199

Designs: No. 5293, Sydney Harbour Bridge and toll token. No. 5294, Queen Victoria Market, Melbourne and various foodstuffs. No. 5295, Old Parliament House, Canberra and ceremonial mace.

**2021, May 10 Litho. *Perf. 14¾x14***

**5293** A1199 $1.10 multi 1.75 1.30
**5294** A1199 $1.10 multi 1.75 1.30
**5295** A1199 $1.10 multi 1.75 1.30
*Nos. 5293-5295 (3)* 5.25 3.90

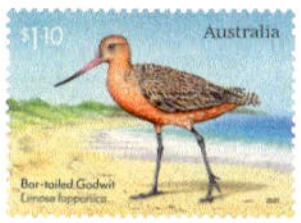
Migratory Shorebirds A1200

Designs: Nos. 5296, 5299, Bar-tailed godwit. Nos. 5297, 5300, Great knot. Nos. 5298, 5301, Eastern curlew.

**2021, May 18 Litho. *Perf. 14x14¾***

**5296** A1200 $1.10 multi 1.75 1.75
**5297** A1200 $1.10 multi 1.75 1.75
**5298** A1200 $1.10 multi 1.75 1.75
*a.* Souvenir sheet of 3, #5296-5298 5.25 5.25
*Nos. 5296-5298 (3)* 5.25 5.25

**Booklet Stamps**
**Self-Adhesive**

***Serpentine Die Cut 11¼ Syncopated***

**5299** A1200 $1.10 multi 1.75 .25
*a.* Booklet pane of 10 17.50
**5300** A1200 $1.10 multi 1.75 .25
*a.* Booklet pane of 10 17.50
**5301** A1200 $1.10 multi 1.75 .25
*a.* Booklet pane of 10 17.50
*Nos. 5299-5301 (3)* 5.25 .75

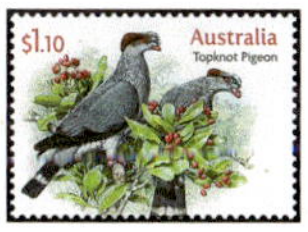
Pigeons and Doves — A1201

Designs: Nos. 5302, 5306, Topknot pigeons. Nos. 5303, 5307, Superb fruit-doves. Nos. 5304, 5308, White-headed pigeons. Nos. 5305, 5309, Squatter pigeons.

**2021, June 1 Litho. *Perf. 14x14¾***

**5302** A1201 $1.10 multi 1.75 1.75
**5303** A1201 $1.10 multi 1.75 1.75
**5304** A1201 $1.10 multi 1.75 1.75
**5305** A1201 $1.10 multi 1.75 1.75
*a.* Souvenir sheet of 4, #5302-5305 7.00 7.00
*Nos. 5302-5305 (4)* 7.00 7.00

**Coil Stamps**
**Self-Adhesive**

***Serpentine Die Cut 11¼ Syncopated***

**5306** A1201 $1.10 multi 1.75 .25
**5307** A1201 $1.10 multi 1.75 .25
**5308** A1201 $1.10 multi 1.75 .25
**5309** A1201 $1.10 multi 1.75 .25
*a.* Horiz. strip of 4, #5306-5309 7.00
*Nos. 5306-5309 (4)* 7.00 1.00

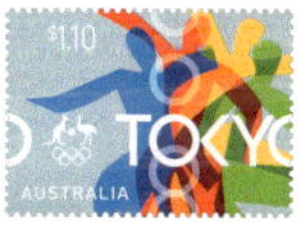
2020 Summer Olympics, Tokyo — A1202

**2021, July 6 Litho. *Perf. 14x14¾***

**5310** A1202 $1.10 multi 1.75 1.30

The 2020 Summer Olympics were postponed until 2021 because of the COVID-19 pandemic.

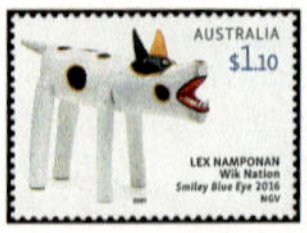


Contemporary Sculptures
A1203

Designs: No. 5311, 5315, Smiley Blue Eye, by Lex Namponan. Nos. 5312, 5316, Planet, by Inge King (1915-2016). Nos. 5313, 5317, Rigel, by Lenton Parr (1924-2003). Nos. 5314, 5318, Eel Trap, by Yvonne Koolmatrie.

**2021, July 6 Litho. *Perf. 14x14¾***

**5311** A1203 $1.10 multi 1.75 1.75
**5312** A1203 $1.10 multi 1.75 1.75
**5313** A1203 $1.10 multi 1.75 1.75
**5314** A1203 $1.10 multi 1.75 1.75
*a.* Souvenir sheet of 4, #5311-5314 7.00 7.00
*Nos. 5311-5314 (4)* 7.00 7.00

**Booklet Stamps**
**Self-Adhesive**

***Serpentine Die Cut 11¼ Syncopated***

**5315** A1203 $1.10 multi 1.75 .25
**5316** A1203 $1.10 multi 1.75 .25
**5317** A1203 $1.10 multi 1.75 .25
**5318** A1203 $1.10 multi 1.75 .25
*a.* Booklet pane of 10, 3 each #5315-5316, 2 each #5317-5318 17.50
*Nos. 5315-5318 (4)* 7.00 1.00

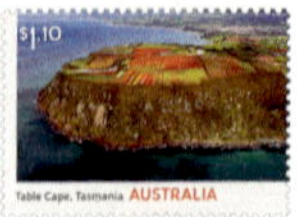


Extinct Volcanoes
A1204

Designs: Nos. 5319, 5323, Table Cape, Tasmania. Nos. 5320, 5324, Wollumbin Mount Warning, New South Wales. Nos. 5321, 5325, Mount Elephant, Victoria. Nos. 5322, 5326, Lord Howe Island, New South Wales.

**2021, July 13 Litho. *Perf. 14x14¾***

**5319** A1204 $1.10 multi 1.75 1.75
**5320** A1204 $1.10 multi 1.75 1.75
**5321** A1204 $1.10 multi 1.75 1.75
**5322** A1204 $1.10 multi 1.75 1.75
*Nos. 5319-5322 (4)* 7.00 7.00

**Self-Adhesive**

***Serpentine Die Cut 11¼ Syncopated***

**5323** A1204 $1.10 multi 1.75 .25
**5324** A1204 $1.10 multi 1.75 .25
**5325** A1204 $1.10 multi 1.75 .25
**5326** A1204 $1.10 multi 1.75 .25
*a.* Horiz. coil strip of 4, #5323-5326 7.00
*b.* Booklet pane of 20, 5 each #5323-5326 35.00
*Nos. 5323-5326 (4)* 7.00 1.00

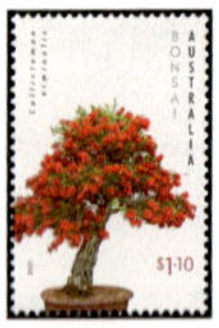


Native Bonsai Trees — A1205

Designs: No. 5327, Callistemon viminalis. No. 5328, Ficus rubiginosa. Nos. 5329, 5330, Melaleuca linariifolia.

**2021, July 27 Litho. *Perf. 14¾x14***

**5327** A1205 $1.10 multi 1.75 1.30
**5328** A1205 $1.10 multi 1.75 1.30
**5329** A1205 $2.70 multi 4.00 4.00
*a.* Souvenir sheet of 3, #5327-5329 7.50 6.75
*Nos. 5327-5329 (3)* 7.50 6.60

**Booklet Stamp**
**Self-Adhesive**

***Serpentine Die Cut 11¼ Syncopated***

**5330** A1205 $2.70 multi 4.00 2.00
*a.* Booklet pane of 5 20.00

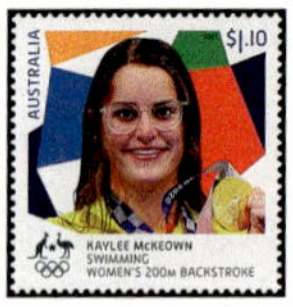


Australian Gold Medalists at the 2020 Summer Olympics, Tokyo — A1206

Designs: No. 5331, Kaylee McKeown, women's 200-meter backstroke. No. 5332, McKeown, women's 100-meter backstroke. No. 5333, Women's 4x100-meter freestyle relay team. No. 5334, Ariarne Titmus, women's 400-meter freestyle. No. 5335, Titmus, Women's 200-meter freestyle. No. 5336, Men's four-man rowing team. No. 5337, Women's four-woman rowing team. No. 5338, Zac Stubblety-Cook, men's 200-meter backstroke. No. 5339, Jessica Fox, women's canoe slalom. No. 5340, Logan Martin, men's BMX freestyle cycling. No. 5341, Matt Wearn, men's laser sailing. No. 5342, Emma McKeon, women's 50-meter freestyle. No. 5343, McKeon, women's 100-meter freestyle. No. 5344, Women's 4x100-meter medley relay team. No. 5345, Keegan Palmer, men's park skateboarding. No. 5346, Mathew Belcher and Will Ryan, men's 470 sailing. No. 5347, Tom Green and Jean van der Westhuyzen, men's 1000-meter 2-man canoe sprint.

**2021 Litho. *Perf. 14¼***

**5331** A1206 $1.10 multi 1.75 1.30
**5332** A1206 $1.10 multi 1.75 1.30
**5333** A1206 $1.10 multi 1.75 1.30
**5334** A1206 $1.10 multi 1.75 1.30
**5335** A1206 $1.10 multi 1.75 1.30
**5336** A1206 $1.10 multi 1.75 1.30
**5337** A1206 $1.10 multi 1.75 1.30
**5338** A1206 $1.10 multi 1.75 1.30
**5339** A1206 $1.10 multi 1.75 1.30
**5340** A1206 $1.10 multi 1.75 1.30
**5341** A1206 $1.10 multi 1.75 1.30
**5342** A1206 $1.10 multi 1.75 1.30
**5343** A1206 $1.10 multi 1.75 1.30
**5344** A1206 $1.10 multi 1.75 1.30
**5345** A1206 $1.10 multi 1.75 1.30
**5346** A1206 $1.10 multi 1.75 1.30
**5347** A1206 $1.10 multi 1.75 1.30
*Nos. 5331-5347 (17)* 29.75 22.10

Nos. 5331-5347 were each issued in sheets of 10. Issued: No. 5331, 7/27; Nos. 5332-5334, 7/28; Nos. 5335-5337, 7/29; Nos. 5338-5339, 7/30; Nos. 5340-5344, 8/2; Nos. 5345-5347, 8/6. The 2020 Summer Olympics were postponed until 2021 because of the COVID-19 pandemic.

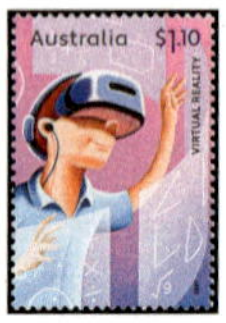


Science, Technology, Engineering, Arts and Mathematics Education — A1207

Designs: Nos. 5348, 5353, Virtual reality. Nos. 5349, 5354, Hydroponics. Nos. 5350, 5355, Space study. Nos. 5351, 5356, Robotics. Nos. 5352, 5357, Urban design.

**2021, Aug. 3 Litho. *Perf. 14¾x14***

**5348** A1207 $1.10 multi 1.75 1.75
**5349** A1207 $1.10 multi 1.75 1.75
**5350** A1207 $1.10 multi 1.75 1.75
**5351** A1207 $1.10 multi 1.75 1.75
**5352** A1207 $1.10 multi 1.75 1.75
*a.* Souvenir sheet of 5, #5348-5352 8.75 8.75
*Nos. 5348-5352 (5)* 8.75 8.75

**Booklet Stamps**
**Self-Adhesive**

***Serpentine Die Cut 11¼ Syncopated***

**5353** A1207 $1.10 multi 1.75 .25
**5354** A1207 $1.10 multi 1.75 .25
**5355** A1207 $1.10 multi 1.75 .25
**5356** A1207 $1.10 multi 1.75 .25
**5357** A1207 $1.10 multi 1.75 .25
*a.* Booklet pane of 10, 2 each #5353-5357 17.50
*Nos. 5353-5357 (5)* 8.75 1.25

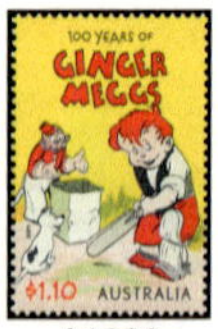


A1208

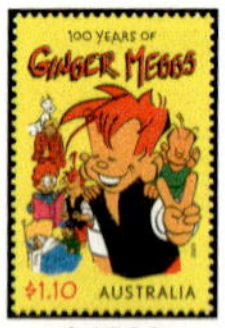


A1209

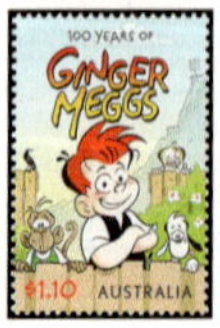


Ginger Meggs Comic Strips, Cent. — A1210

**2021, Sept. 7 Litho. *Perf. 14¾x14***

**5358** A1208 $1.10 multi 1.60 1.25
**5359** A1209 $1.10 multi 1.60 1.25
**5360** A1210 $1.10 multi 1.60 1.25
*a.* Souvenir sheet of 3, #5358-5360 4.80 3.75
*Nos. 5358-5360 (3)* 4.80 3.75

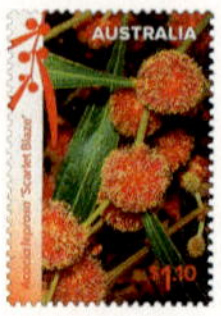


Wattle Blossoms — A1211

Designs: Nos. 5361, 5364, Acacia leprosa "Scarlet Blaze." Nos. 5362, 5365, Acacia purpureopetala. Nos. 5363, 5366, Acacia alata var. biglandulosa.

**2021, Sept. 14 Litho. *Perf. 14¾x14***

**5361** A1211 $1.10 multi 1.60 1.60
**5362** A1211 $1.10 multi 1.60 1.60
**5363** A1211 $1.10 multi 1.60 1.60
*a.* Souvenir sheet of 3, #5361-5363 4.80 4.80
*Nos. 5361-5363 (3)* 4.80 4.80

**Booklet Stamps**
**Self-Adhesive**

***Serpentine Die Cut 11¼ Syncopated***

**5364** A1211 $1.10 multi 1.60 .25
**5365** A1211 $1.10 multi 1.60 .25
**5366** A1211 $1.10 multi 1.60 .25
*a.* Booklet pane of 10, 4 #5364, 3 each #5365-5366 16.00
*Nos. 5364-5366 (3)* 4.80 .75

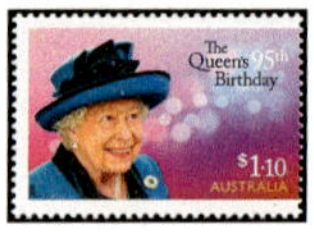


A1212

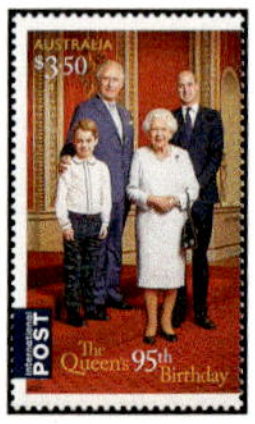


Queen Elizabeth II, 95th Birthday — A1213

**2021, Sept. 21 Litho. *Perf. 14x14¾***

**5367** A1212 $1.10 multi 1.60 1.25

***Perf. 14x14¼***

**5368** A1213 $3.50 multi 5.25 2.60
*a.* Souvenir sheet of 2, #5367-5368 7.00 4.00

**Booklet Stamp**
**Self-Adhesive**

***Serpentine Die Cut 11x10¾ Syncopated***

**5369** A1213 $3.50 multi 5.25 2.60
*a.* Booklet pane of 5 26.50

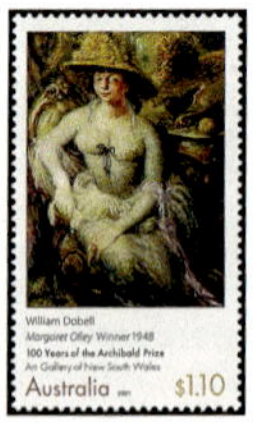


Archibald Prize, Cent. — A1214

Archibald Prize-winning portrait of: No. 5370, Margaret Olley, 1948 winner, by William Dobell (1899-1970). No. 5371, Albert Namatjira, 1956 winner, by William Dargie (1912-2003). No. 5372, Hugo Weaving, 2013 winner, by Del Kathryn Barton.

**2021, Sept. 28 Litho. *Perf. 14x14¼***

**5370** A1214 $1.10 multi 1.60 1.25
**5371** A1214 $1.10 multi 1.60 1.25
**5372** A1214 $1.10 multi 1.60 1.25
*Nos. 5370-5372 (3)* 4.80 3.75

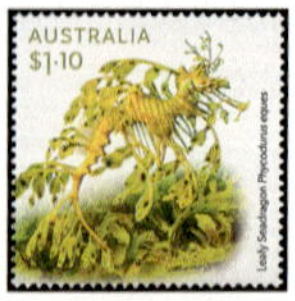


Animals Using Mimicry — A1215

Designs: No. 5373, Leafy seadragon. No. 5374, Tawny frogmouth. $2.20, Macleay's spectre.

**2021, Oct. 5 Litho. *Perf. 14¼***

**5373** A1215 $1.10 multi 1.75 1.30
**5374** A1215 $1.10 multi 1.75 1.30
**5375** A1215 $2.20 multi 3.50 1.75
*a.* Souvenir sheet of 3, #5373-5375 7.00 4.50
*Nos. 5373-5375 (3)* 7.00 4.35

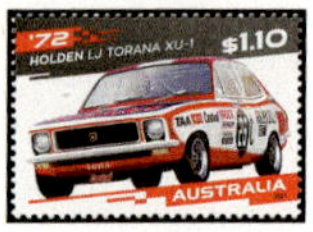


Retirement of Holden Automobiles Brand — A1216

Designs: Nos. 5376, 5381, 1972 Holden LJ Torana XU-1. Nos. 5377, 5382, 1993, Holden VP Commodore. Nos. 5378, 5383, 1996 Holden VR Commodore. Nos. 5379, 5384, 2001 Holden VX Commodore. Nos. 5380, 5385, 2020 Holden ZB Commodore.

**2021, Oct. 7 Litho. *Perf. 14x14¾***

**5376** A1216 $1.10 multi 1.75 1.75
**5377** A1216 $1.10 multi 1.75 1.75
**5378** A1216 $1.10 multi 1.75 1.75
**5379** A1216 $1.10 multi 1.75 1.75
**5380** A1216 $1.10 multi 1.75 1.75
*a.* Souvenir sheet of 5, #5376-5380 8.75 8.75
*Nos. 5376-5380 (5)* 8.75 8.75

**Booklet Stamps**
**Self-Adhesive**

***Serpentine Die Cut 11¼ Syncopated***

**5381** A1216 $1.10 multi 1.75 .25
*a.* Booklet pane of 10 17.50
**5382** A1216 $1.10 multi 1.75 .25
*a.* Booklet pane of 10 17.50
**5383** A1216 $1.10 multi 1.75 .25
*a.* Booklet pane of 10 17.50
**5384** A1216 $1.10 multi 1.75 .25
*a.* Booklet pane of 10 17.50
**5385** A1216 $1.10 multi 1.75 .25
*a.* Booklet pane of 10 17.50
*Nos. 5381-5385 (5)* 8.75 1.25

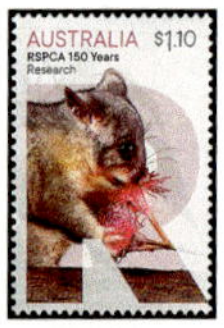


Royal Society for Prevention of Cruelty to Animals, 150th Anniv. — A1217

Designs: Nos. 5386, 5391, "R," marsupial and flower. Nos. 5387, 5392, "S," cat. Nos. 5388, 5393, "P," dog. Nos. 5389, 5394, "C," pig. Nos. 5390, 5395, "A," horse.

**2021, Oct. 19 Litho. *Perf. 14¾x14***

**5386** A1217 $1.10 multi 1.75 1.75
**5387** A1217 $1.10 multi 1.75 1.75
**5388** A1217 $1.10 multi 1.75 1.75
**5389** A1217 $1.10 multi 1.75 1.75
**5390** A1217 $1.10 multi 1.75 1.75
*a.* Souvenir sheet of 5, #5386-5390 8.75 8.75
*Nos. 5386-5390 (5)* 8.75 8.75

**Self-Adhesive**

***Serpentine Die Cut 11¼ Syncopated***

**5391** A1217 $1.10 multi 1.75 .25
*a.* Booklet pane of 10 17.50
**5392** A1217 $1.10 multi 1.75 .25
*a.* Booklet pane of 10 17.50
**5393** A1217 $1.10 multi 1.75 .25
*a.* Booklet pane of 10 17.50
**5394** A1217 $1.10 multi 1.75 .25
*a.* Booklet pane of 10 17.50
**5395** A1217 $1.10 multi 1.75 .25
*a.* Booklet pane of 10 17.50
*b.* Vert. coil strip of 5, #5391-5395 8.75
*Nos. 5391-5395 (5)* 8.75 1.25

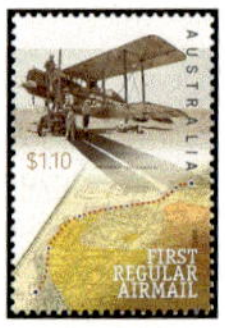


First Regular Airmail Flights, Cent. — A1218

**2021 Litho. *Perf. 14¾x14***

**5396** A1218 $1.10 multi 1.75 1.30
*a.* Souvenir sheet of 4 with text for Newcastle Stamp and Coin Expo 2022 in sheet margin 6.50 5.00
*b.* Souvenir sheet of 4, Perth Stamp & Coin show emblem in sheet margin 7.00 5.25

Issued: No. 5396, 10/22; No. 5396a, 5/27/22; No. 5396b, 10/29/21 . Newcastle Stamp and Coin Expo 2022 (No. 5396a).

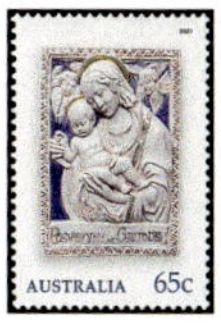

Christmas
A1219 A1220

Designs: Nos. 5397, 5402, Rectangular glazed terracotta plaque depicting Madonna and Child, by Della Robbia family of artists. Nos. 5398, 5404, 5407, Gingerbread cookie in shape of Christmas tree. Nos. 5399, 5403, 5408, Gingerbread cookie in shape of gift box with bow. Nos. 5400, 5405, Round glazed terracotta plaque depicting Madonna and Child, by Figli de Giuseppe Cantagalli. Nos. 5401, 5406, Gingerbread cookie in shape of star.

**2021, Nov. 1 Litho. *Perf. 14¾x14***

**5397** A1219 65c multi 1.00 1.00
**5398** A1220 65c multi 1.00 1.00
**5399** A1220 65c multi 1.00 1.00
*a.* Horiz. pair, #5398-5399 2.00 2.00
**5400** A1219 $2.40 multi 3.75 1.90
*a.* Souvenir sheet of 2, #5397-5400 4.75 3.00
**5401** A1220 $2.40 multi 3.75 1.90
*Nos. 5397-5401 (5)* 10.50 6.80

**Booklet Stamps**
**Self-Adhesive**

***Serpentine Die Cut 11¼ Syncopated***

**5402** A1219 65c multi 1.00 .25
*a.* Booklet pane of 20 + 20 etiquettes 20.00
**5403** A1220 65c multi 1.00 .25
**5404** A1220 65c multi 1.00 .25
*a.* Booklet pane of 20, 10 each #5403-5404 + 20 etiquettes 20.00
**5405** A1219 $2.40 multi 3.75 1.90
*a.* Booklet pane of 5 10.00
**5406** A1220 $2.40 multi 3.75 1.90
*a.* Booklet pane of 5 19.00

**Litho. With Foil Application**

**5407** A1220 65c multi 1.00 .25
*a.* Booklet pane of 10 + 10 etiquettes 10.00
**5408** A1220 65c multi 1.00 .25
*a.* Booklet pane of 10 + 10 etiquettes 10.00
*Nos. 5402-5408 (7)* 12.50 5.05

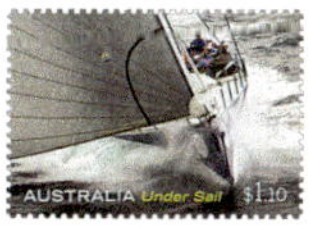

Boats Under Sail — A1221

Designs: No. 5409, Sailors competing in Sydney-Hobart Yacht Race. No. 5410, Sailors hanging off side of catamaran during the Australian Sailing Youth Championships. $2.20, Crew using trapeze to counterbalance wind on a 16-foot skiff.

**2022, Jan. 11 Litho. *Perf. 14x14¾***

**5409** A1221 $1.10 multi 1.60 1.25
**5410** A1221 $1.10 multi 1.60 1.25
**5411** A1221 $2.20 multi 3.25 2.50
*Nos. 5409-5411 (3)* 6.45 5.00

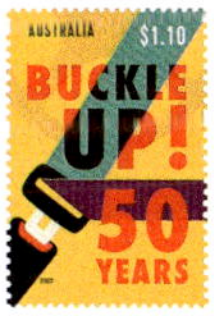

Legislation Requiring Use of Seat Belts, 50th Anniv. — A1222

**2022, Jan. 2 Litho. *Perf. 14¾x14***

**5412** A1222 $1.10 multi 1.60 1.60

**Coil Stamp**
**Self-Adhesive**

***Serpentine Die Cut 11¼ Syncopated***

**5413** A1222 $1.10 multi 1.60 .25

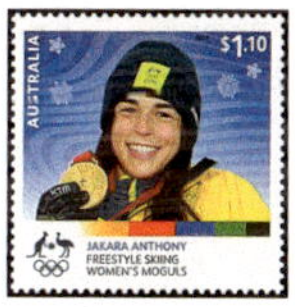

Jakara Anthony, Freestyle Skiing Gold Medalist at 2022 Winter Olympics — A1223

**2022, Feb. 8 Litho. *Perf. 14¼***

**5414** A1223 $1.10 multi 1.60 1.25

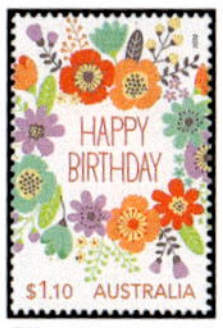

Flowers and "Happy Birthday" A1224

Rubber Duck A1225

Tic-Tac-Toe Game A1226

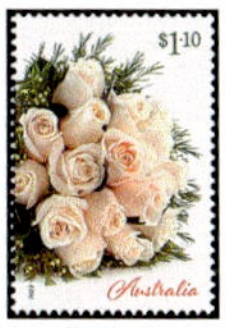

Roses A1227

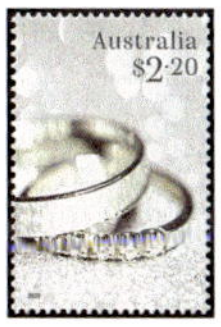

Wedding Rings — A1228

**2022, Feb. 8 Litho. *Perf. 14¾x14***

**5415** A1224 $1.10 multi 1.60 1.60
**5416** A1225 $1.10 multi 1.60 1.60
**5417** A1226 $1.10 multi 1.60 1.60
**5418** A1227 $1.10 multi 1.60 1.60
**5419** A1228 $2.20 multi 3.25 3.25
*a.* Souvenir sheet of 5, #5415-5419 10.00 10.00
*Nos. 5415-5419 (5)* 9.65 9.65

**Booklet Stamps**
**Self-Adhesive**

***Serpentine Die Cut 11¼ Syncopated***

**5420** A1224 $1.10 multi 1.60 .25
*a.* Booklet pane of 10 + 5 stickers 16.00
**5421** A1225 $1.10 multi 1.60 .25
*a.* Booklet pane of 10 + 5 stickers 16.00
**5422** A1226 $1.10 multi 1.60 .25
*a.* Booklet pane of 10 + 5 stickers 16.00
**5423** A1227 $1.10 multi 1.60 .25
*a.* Booklet pane of 10 + 5 stickers 16.00
**5424** A1228 $2.20 multi 3.25 .50
*a.* Booklet pane of 4 13.00
Complete booklet, 4 #5424a 52.00
*Nos. 5420-5424 (5)* 9.65 1.50

Complete booklet sold for $35.95 and contains four panes, each with different pane margins, and a pane of 20 stickers.

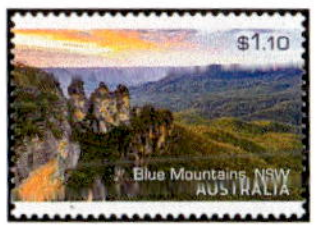

UNESCO World Heritage Sites In Australia — A1229

Designs: Nos. 5425, 5429, Blue Mountains, New South Wales. Nos. 5426, 5430, Flinders Ranges, South Australia. Nos. 5427, 5431, Ningaloo Coast, Western Australia. Nos. 5428, 5432, Gondwana Rainforests, New South Wales.

**2022, Feb. 22 Litho. *Perf. 14x14¾***

**5425** A1229 $1.10 multi 1.60 1.60
**5426** A1229 $1.10 multi 1.60 1.60
**5427** A1229 $1.10 multi 1.60 1.60
**5428** A1229 $1.10 multi 1.60 1.60
*Nos. 5425-5428 (4)* 6.40 6.40

**Booklet Stamps**
**Self-Adhesive**

***Serpentine Die Cut 11¼ Syncopated***

**5429** A1229 $1.10 multi 1.60 .25
**5430** A1229 $1.10 multi 1.60 .25
**5431** A1229 $1.10 multi 1.60 .25
**5432** A1229 $1.10 multi 1.60 .25
*a.* Booklet pane of 10, 3 each #5429-5430, 2 each #5431-5432 16.00
*Nos. 5429-5432 (4)* 6.40 1.00

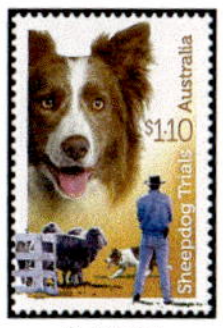

A1230

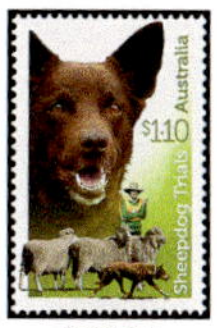

A1231

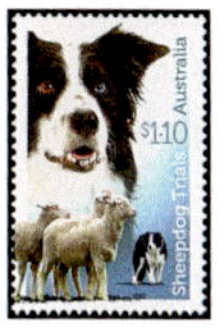

National Sheepdog Trials, 150th Anniv. — A1232

**2022, Mar. 8 Litho. *Perf. 14¾x14***

**5433** A1230 $1.10 multi 1.75 1.75
**5434** A1231 $1.10 multi 1.75 1.75
**5435** A1232 $1.10 multi 1.75 1.75
*a.* Souvenir sheet of 3, #5433-5435 5.25 5.25
*Nos. 5433-5435 (3)* 5.25 5.25

**Self-Adhesive**

***Serpentine Die Cut 11¼ Syncopated***

**5436** A1230 $1.10 multi 1.75 .25
*a.* Booklet pane of 10 17.50
**5437** A1231 $1.10 multi 1.75 .25
*a.* Booklet pane of 10 17.50
**5438** A1232 $1.10 multi 1.75 .25
*a.* Booklet pane of 10 17.50
*b.* Vert. coil strip of 3, #5436-5438 5.25
*Nos. 5436-5438 (3)* 5.25 .75

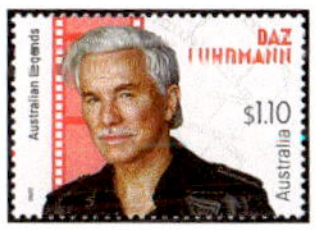

Australian Film Directors — A1233

Designs: Nos. 5439, 5444, Baz Luhrmann. Nos. 5440, 5445, Peter Weir. Nos. 5441, 5446, Warwick Thornton. Nos. 5442, 5447, Gillian Armstrong. Nos. 5443, 5448, George Miller.

**2022, Mar. 15 Litho. *Perf. 14x14¾***

**5439** A1233 $1.10 multi 1.75 1.75
**5440** A1233 $1.10 multi 1.75 1.75
**5441** A1233 $1.10 multi 1.75 1.75
**5442** A1233 $1.10 multi 1.75 1.75
**5443** A1233 $1.10 multi 1.75 1.75
*Nos. 5439-5443 (5)* 8.75 8.75

**Booklet Stamps**
**Self-Adhesive**

***Serpentine Die Cut 11¼ Syncopated***

**5444** A1233 $1.10 multi 1.75 .25
*a.* Booklet pane of 10 17.50
**5445** A1233 $1.10 multi 1.75 .25
*a.* Booklet pane of 10 17.50
**5446** A1233 $1.10 multi 1.75 .25
*a.* Booklet pane of 10 17.50
**5447** A1233 $1.10 multi 1.75 .25
*a.* Booklet pane of 10 17.50
**5448** A1233 $1.10 multi 1.75 .25
*a.* Booklet pane of 10 17.50
*Nos. 5444-5448 (5)* 8.75 1.25

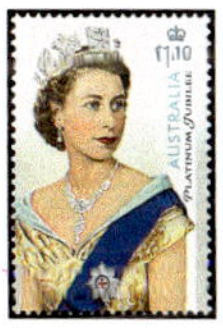
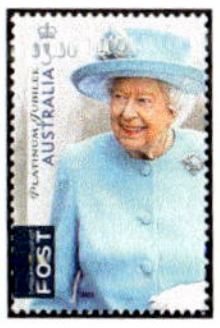

Reign of Queen Elizabeth II, 70th Anniv.
A1234 A1235

**2022, Apr. 5 Litho. *Perf. 14¾x14***

**5449** A1234 $1.10 multi 1.60 1.60
**5450** A1235 $3.50 multi 5.00 5.00
*a.* Souvenir sheet of 2, #5449-5450 6.75 6.75

**Booklet Stamps**
**Self-Adhesive**

***Serpentine Die Cut 11¼ Syncopated***

**5451** A1234 $1.10 multi 1.60 .25
*a.* Booklet pane of 10 16.00
**5452** A1235 $3.50 multi 5.00 2.50
*a.* Booklet pane of 5 25.00

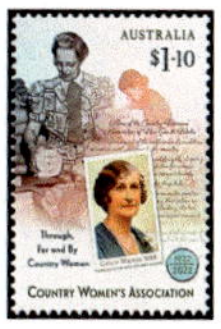

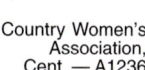

Country Women's Association, Cent. — A1236

**2022, Apr. 26 Litho. *Perf. 14¾x14***

**5453** A1236 $1.10 multi 1.60 1.25

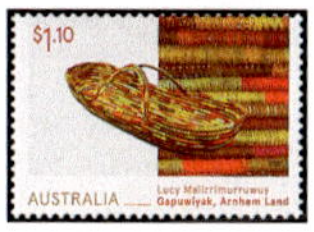

Aboriginal Fiber Art — A1237

Designs: Nos. 5454, 5457, Coiled baby basket, by Lucy Malirrimurruwuy. Nos. 5455, 5458, Conical basket, by Mary Djupuduwuy (1945-2005). Nos. 5456, 5459, Flat-bottomed basket, by Nancy Walinyinawuy (1940-2017).

**2022, May 3 Litho. *Perf. 14x14¾***

**5454** A1237 $1.10 multi 1.60 1.60
**5455** A1237 $1.10 multi 1.60 1.60
**5456** A1237 $1.10 multi 1.60 1.60
*Nos. 5454-5456 (3)* 4.80 4.00

**Booklet Stamps**
**Self-Adhesive**

***Serpentine Die Cut 11¼ Syncopated***

**5457** A1237 $1.10 multi 1.60 .25
*a.* Booklet pane of 10 16.00
**5458** A1237 $1.10 multi 1.60 .25
*a.* Booklet pane of 10 16.00
**5459** A1237 $1.10 multi 1.60 .25
*a.* Booklet pane of 10 16.00
*Nos. 5457-5459 (3)* 4.80 .75

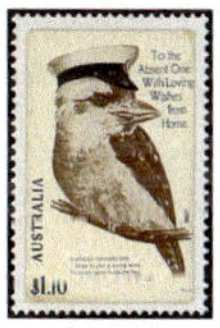

A1238

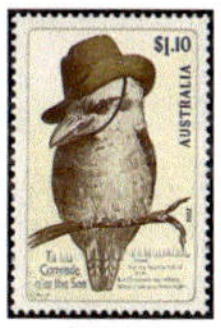

A1239

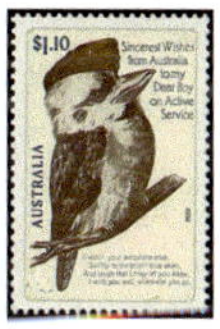

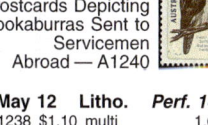

World War I Era Postcards Depicting Kookaburras Sent to Servicemen Abroad — A1240

**2022, May 12 Litho. *Perf. 14¾x14***

**5460** A1238 $1.10 multi 1.60 1.60
**5461** A1239 $1.10 multi 1.60 1.60
**5462** A1240 $1.10 multi 1.60 1.60
*a.* Souvenir sheet of 3, #5460-5462 4.80 4.80
*Nos. 5460-5462 (3)* 4.80 4.80

**Booklet Stamps**
**Self-Adhesive**

***Serpentine Die Cut 11¼ Syncopated***

**5463** A1238 $1.10 multi 1.60 .25
**5464** A1239 $1.10 multi 1.60 .25
**5465** A1240 $1.10 multi 1.60 .25
*a.* Booklet pane of 20, 7 each #5463-5464, 6 #5465 32.00
*Nos. 5463-5465 (3)* 4.80 .75

Anzac Day.

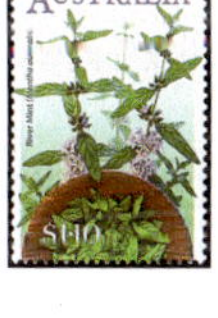

Bush Seasonings — A1241

Designs: No. 5466, River mint. No. 5467, Mountain pepper. No. 5468, Lemon myrtle.

**2022, May 24 Litho. *Perf. 14¾x14***

**5466** A1241 $1.10 multi 1.60 1.25
*a.* Tete-beche pair 3.20 2.50
*b.* Booklet pane of 4 6.75 —
*c.* Booklet pane of 4 (two tete-beche pairs) 6.75 —
**5467** A1241 $1.10 multi 1.60 1.25
*a.* Tete-beche pair 3.20 2.50
*b.* Booklet pane of 4 6.75 —
*c.* Booklet pane of 4 (two tete-beche pairs) 6.75 —
**5468** A1241 $2.20 multi 3.25 2.40
*a.* Tete-beche pair 6.50 4.80
*b.* Booklet pane of 4 13.50 —
*c.* Booklet pane of 4 (two tete-beche pairs) 13.50 —

Complete booklet, #5466b, 5466c, 5467b, 5467c, 5468b, 5468c 54.00
*d.* Souvenir sheet of 6, 2 each #5466-5468 (three tete-beche pairs) 13.00 13.00
*Nos. 5466-5468 (3)* 6.45 4.90

Complete booklet sold for $36.95.

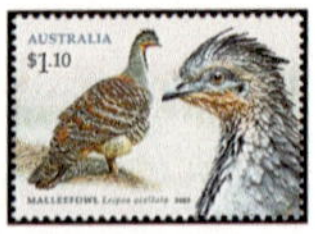

Megapodes A1242

Designs: Nos. 5469, 5472, Malleefowl. Nos. 5470, 5473, Australian brush-turkey. Nos. 5471, 7474, Orange-footed scrubfowl.

**2022, June 7 Litho. *Perf. 14x14¾***

**5469** A1242 $1.10 multi 1.60 1.60
**5470** A1242 $1.10 multi 1.60 1.60
**5471** A1242 $1.10 multi 1.60 1.60
*a.* Souvenir sheet of 3, #5469-5471 4.80 4.80
*Nos. 5469-5471 (3)* 4.80 4.80

**Booklet Stamps**
**Self-Adhesive**

***Serpentine Die Cut 11¼ Syncopated***

**5472** A1242 $1.10 multi 1.60 .25
*a.* Booklet pane of 10 16.00
**5473** A1242 $1.10 multi 1.60 .25
*a.* Booklet pane of 10 16.00
**5474** A1242 $1.10 multi 1.60 .25
*a.* Booklet pane of 10 16.00
*Nos. 5472-5474 (3)* 4.80 .75

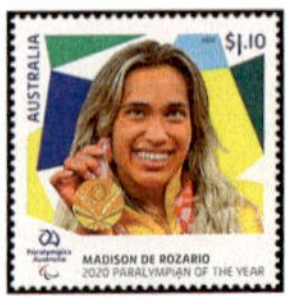

2020 and 2022 Paralympians of the Year — A1243

Designs: No. 5475, Madison de Rozario, 2020. No. 5476, Ben Tudhope, 2022.

**2022, June 10 Litho. *Perf. 14¼***

**5475** A1243 $1.10 multi 1.60 1.25
**5476** A1243 $1.10 multi 1.60 1.25

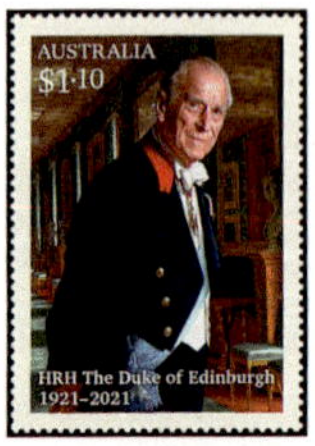


Prince Philip (1921-2021) A1244

**2022, June 14 Litho. *Perf. 14x14¾***

**Stamp With Cream Frame**

**5477** A1244 $1.10 multi 1.60 1.25

**Souvenir Sheet**
**Stamp Without Cream Frame**

**5478** A1244 $1.10 multi 1.60 1.25

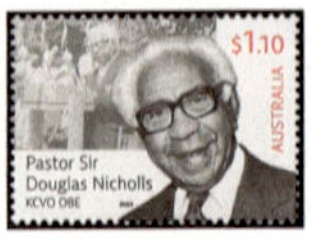

Sir Douglas Nicholls (1906-88), Pastor and Governor of South Australia — A1245

**2022, July 5 Litho. *Perf. 14x14¾***

**5479** A1245 $1.10 multi 1.60 1.25

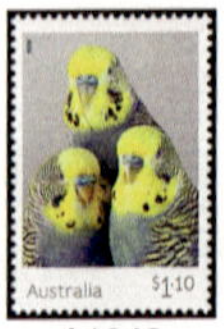

A1246

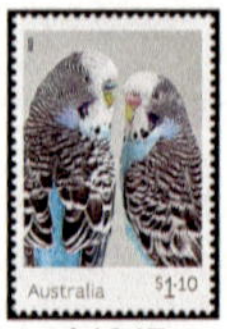

A1247

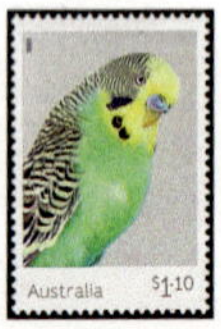

Budgerigars — A1248

**2022, July 11 Litho. *Perf. 14¾x14***

**5480** A1246 $1.10 multi 1.60 1.60
**5481** A1247 $1.10 multi 1.60 1.60
**5482** A1248 $1.10 multi 1.60 1.60
*a.* Souvenir sheet of 3, #5480-5482 4.80 4.80
*Nos. 5480-5482 (3)* 4.80 4.80

**Booklet Stamps**
**Self-Adhesive**

***Serpentine Die Cut 11¼ Syncopated***

**5483** A1246 $1.10 multi 1.60 .25
*a.* Booklet pane of 10 16.00
**5484** A1247 $1.10 multi 1.60 .25
*a.* Booklet pane of 10 16.00
**5485** A1248 $1.10 multi 1.60 .25
*a.* Booklet pane of 10 16.00
*Nos. 5483-5485 (3)* 4.80 .75

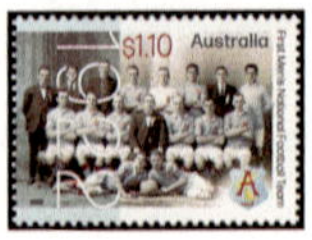

Australian Men's National Soccer Team, Cent. — A1249

Players from: No. 5486, 1922. No. 5487, 2022.

**2022, July 19 Litho. *Perf. 14x14¾***

**5486** A1249 $1.10 multi 1.60 1.25
**5487** A1249 $1.10 multi 1.60 1.25
*a.* Souvenir sheet of 2, #5486-5487 3.25 2.50

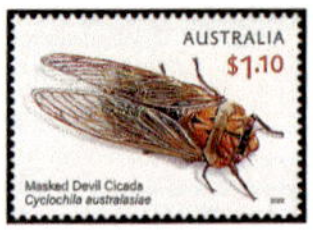

Cicadas — A1250

Designs: No. 5488, Masked devil cicada. No. 5489, Golden emperor cicada. No. 5490, Sandgrinder cicada.

**2022, Aug. 2 Litho. *Perf. 14x14¾***

**5488** A1250 $1.10 multi 1.50 1.10
**5489** A1250 $1.10 multi 1.50 1.10
**5490** A1250 $1.10 multi 1.50 1.10
*a.* Souvenir sheet of 3, #5488-5490 4.50 3.50
*Nos. 5488-5490 (3)* 4.50 3.30

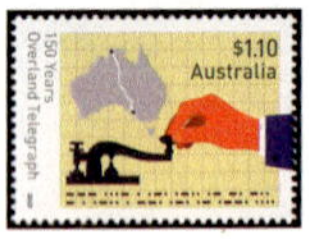

Adelaide-Darwin Overland Telegraph Line, 150th Anniv. — A1251

**2022, Aug. 23 Litho. *Perf. 14x14¾***

**5491** A1251 $1.10 multi 1.50 1.10

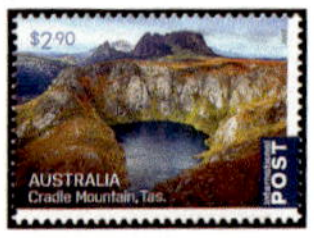

Aerial Views — A1252

Designs: $2.90, Cradle Mountain, Tasmania. $3.50, Kakadu National Park, Northern Territory. $3.70, Bungle Bungle Range, Western Australia. $4, Great Barrier Reef, Queensland.

**2022, Aug. 23 Litho. *Perf. 14x14¾***

**5492** A1252 $2.90 multi 4.00 4.00
**5493** A1252 $3.50 multi 4.75 4.75
**5494** A1252 $3.70 multi 5.00 5.00
**5495** A1252 $4 multi 5.50 2.75
*Nos. 5492-5495 (4)* 19.25 16.50

**Booklet Stamps**
**Self-Adhesive**

***Serpentine Die Cut 11¼ Syncopated***

**5496** A1252 $2.90 multi 4.00 2.00
*a.* Booklet pane of 5 20.00
**5497** A1252 $3.50 multi 4.75 2.40
*a.* Booklet pane of 5 24.00
**5498** A1252 $3.70 multi 5.00 2.50
*a.* Booklet pane of 5 25.00
*Nos. 5496-5498 (3)* 13.75 6.90

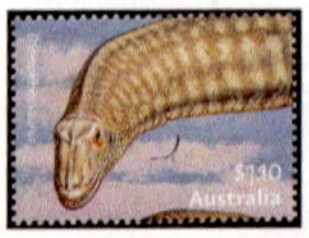

A1253

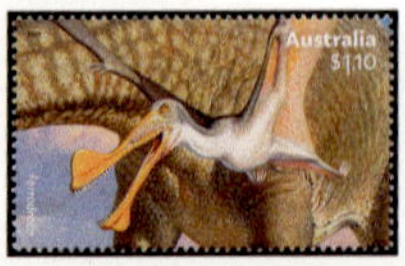

Dinosaurs A1254

Designs: Nos. 5499, 5504, Diamantinasaurus. Nos. 5500, 5505, Elaphrosaurine. Nos. 5501, 5506, Australovenator. Nos. 5502, 5507, Ferrodraco. Nos. 5503, 5508, Kunbarrasaurus.

**2022, Sept. 5 Litho. *Perf. 14x14¾***

**5499** A1253 $1.10 multi 1.50 1.50
**5500** A1253 $1.10 multi 1.50 1.50
**5501** A1253 $1.10 multi 1.50 1.50

***Perf. 14¼x14***

**5502** A1254 $1.10 multi 1.50 1.50
**5503** A1254 $1.10 multi 1.50 1.50
*a.* Souvenir sheet of 5, #5499-5503 7.50 7.50
*Nos. 5499-5503 (5)* 7.50 7.50

**Booklet Stamps**
**Self-Adhesive**

***Serpentine Die Cut 11¼ Syncopated***

**5504** A1253 $1.10 multi 1.50 .25
*a.* Booklet pane of 10 15.00
**5505** A1253 $1.10 multi 1.50 .25
*a.* Booklet pane of 10 15.00
**5506** A1253 $1.10 multi 1.50 .25
*a.* Booklet pane of 10 15.00

***Serpentine Die Cut 10¾x11 Syncopated***

**5507** A1254 $1.10 multi 1.50 .25
*a.* Booklet pane of 10 15.00
**5508** A1254 $1.10 multi 1.50 .25
*a.* Booklet pane of 10 15.00
*Nos. 5504-5508 (5)* 7.50 1.25

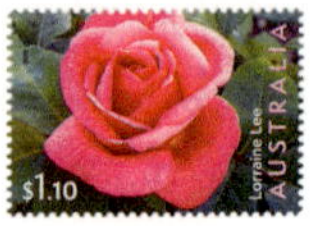

Rose Varieties — A1255

Designs: Nos. 5509, 5515, Lorraine Lee. Nos. 5510, 5514, Lady of Australia. Nos. 5511, 5516, Governor Marie Bashir. Nos. 5512, 5513, Dusky Moon.

**2022, Sept. 13 Litho. *Perf. 14x14¾***

**5509** A1255 $1.10 multi 1.50 1.50
**5510** A1255 $1.10 multi 1.50 1.50
**5511** A1255 $1.10 multi 1.50 1.50
**5512** A1255 $1.10 multi 1.50 1.50
*a.* Souvenir sheet of 4, #5509-5512 6.00 6.00
*b.* Souvenir sheet of 4, 2 each #5509, 5512 6.00 6.00
*c.* Souvenir sheet of 10, 5 each #5509, 5512 15.00 15.00
*Nos. 5509-5512 (4)* 6.00 6.00

**Booklet Stamps**
**Self-Adhesive**

***Serpentine Die Cut 11¼ Syncopated***

**5513** A1255 $1.10 multi 1.50 .25
**5514** A1255 $1.10 multi 1.50 .25
**5515** A1255 $1.10 multi 1.50 .25
**5516** A1255 $1.10 multi 1.50 .25
*a.* Booklet pane of 20, 5 each #5513-5516 30.00
*Nos. 5513-5516 (4)* 6.00 1.00

Nos. 5512b and 5512c were impregnated with a rose scent and were sold together in a folder for $15.85.

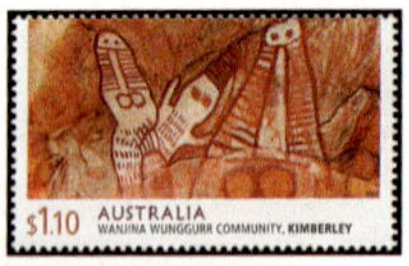

A1256

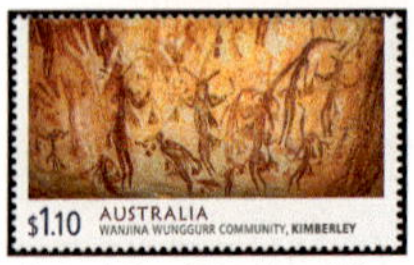

Rock Art of the Wanjina Wunggurr Community in the Kimberley Region A1257

**2022, Sept. 20 Litho. *Perf. 14¼x14***

**5517** A1256 $1.10 multi 1.50 1.10
**5518** A1257 $1.10 multi 1.50 1.10
*a.* Souvenir sheet of 2, #5517-5518 3.00 2.25

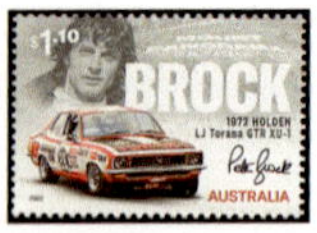

Peter Geoffrey Brock (1945-2006), Race Car Driver, and His Cars — A1258

Brock and: Nos. 5519, 5524, 1972 Holden LJ Torana GTR XU-1. Nos. 5520, 5525, 1979 Holden LX Torana SS A9X. Nos. 5521, 5526, 1980 Holden VC Commodore. Nos. 5522, 5527, 1984 Holden VK Commodore. Nos. 5523, 5528, 1987 Holden VL Commodore SS Group A.

**2022, Oct. 3 Litho. *Perf. 14x14¾***

**5519** A1258 $1.10 multi 1.50 1.50
*a.* Perf. 14 1.50 1.50
**5520** A1258 $1.10 multi 1.50 1.50
*a.* Perf. 14 1.50 1.50
**5521** A1258 $1.10 multi 1.50 1.50
*a.* Perf. 14 1.50 1.50
**5522** A1258 $1.10 multi 1.50 1.50
*a.* Perf. 14 1.50 1.50
**5523** A1258 $1.10 multi 1.50 1.50
*a.* Perf. 14 1.50 1.50
*b.* Souvenir sheet of 5, #5519a-5523a 7.50 7.50
*Nos. 5519-5523 (5)* 7.50 7.50

**Booklet Stamps**
**Self-Adhesive**

***Serpentine Die Cut 11¼ Syncopated***

**5524** A1258 $1.10 multi 1.50 .25
*a.* Booklet pane of 10 15.00
**5525** A1258 $1.10 multi 1.50 .25
*a.* Booklet pane of 10 15.00
**5526** A1258 $1.10 multi 1.50 .25
*a.* Booklet pane of 10 15.00
**5527** A1258 $1.10 multi 1.50 .25
*a.* Booklet pane of 10 15.00
**5528** A1258 $1.10 multi 1.50 .25
*a.* Booklet pane of 10 15.00
*Nos. 5524-5528 (5)* 7.50 1.25

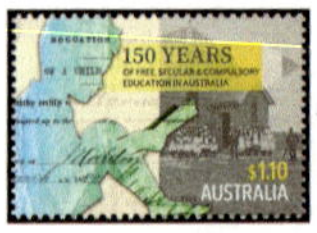

Free, Secular and Compulsory Education, 150th Anniv. — A1259

**2022, Oct. 11 Litho. *Perf. 14x14¾***

**5529** A1259 $1.10 multi 1.50 1.50

**Coil Stamp**
**Self-Adhesive**

***Serpentine Die Cut 11¼ Syncopated***

**5530** A1259 $1.10 multi 1.50 .25

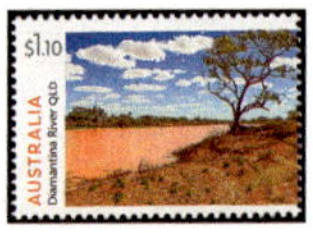

Rivers — A1260

Designs: No. 5531, Diamantina River, Queensland. No. 5532, Murrumbidgee River, Australian Capital Territory. No. 5533, Murray River, South Australia. No. 5534, Gordon River, Tasmania.

**2022, Oct. 25 Litho. *Perf. 14x14¾***

**5531** A1260 $1.10 multi 1.50 1.10
**5532** A1260 $1.10 multi 1.50 1.10
**5533** A1260 $1.10 multi 1.50 1.10
**5534** A1260 $1.10 multi 1.50 1.10
*Nos. 5531-5534 (4)* 6.00 4.40

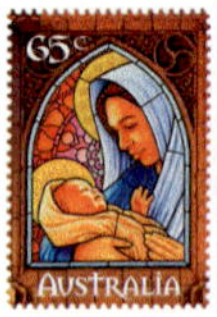

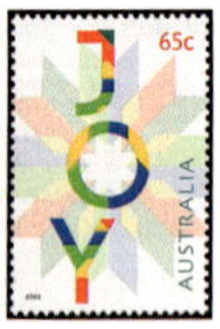

Christmas

A1261 A1262

Designs: Nos. 5535, 5540, Madonna and Child. Nos. 5536, 5541, 5545, "Joy." Nos. 5537, 5542, 5546, "Peace." Nos. 5538, 5543, Angel. Nos. 5539, 5544, "Noel."

**2022, Nov. 1 Litho. *Perf. 14¾x14***

**5535** A1261 65c multi .85 .85
**5536** A1262 65c multi .85 .85
**5537** A1262 65c multi .85 .85
*a.* Horiz. pair, #5536-5537 1.70 1.70
**5538** A1261 $2.60 multi 3.50 3.50
*a.* Souvenir sheet of 2, #5535, 5538 4.50 4.50
**5539** A1262 $2.60 multi 3.50 3.50
*Nos. 5535-5539 (5)* 9.55 9.55

**Booklet Stamps**
**Self-Adhesive**

***Serpentine Die Cut 11¼ Syncopated***

**5540** A1261 65c multi .85 .25
*a.* Booklet pane of 20 + 20 etiquettes 17.00
**5541** A1262 65c multi .85 .25
**5542** A1262 65c multi .85 .25
*a.* Booklet pane of 20, 10 each #5541-5542 + 20 etiquettes 17.00
**5543** A1261 $2.60 multi 3.50 1.75
*a.* Booklet pane of 5 17.50
**5544** A1262 $2.60 multi 3.50 1.75
*a.* Booklet pane of 5 17.50

**Litho. With Foil Application**

**5545** A1262 65c multi .85 .25
*a.* Booklet pane of 10 + 10 etiquettes 8.50

**5546** A1262 65c multi .85 .25
*a.* Booklet pane of 10 + 10 etiquettes 8.50
*Nos. 5540-5546 (7)* 11.25 4.75

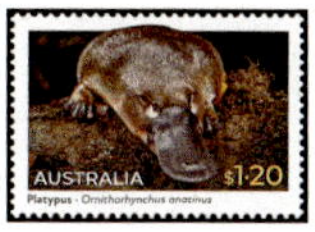

Native Mammals — A1263

Designs: Nos. 5547, 5551, Platypus. Nos. 5548, 5552, Eastern quoll. $2.40, Quokka. $3.60, Mountain pygmy possum.

**2022, Dec. 19 Litho. *Perf. 14x14¾***
**5547** A1263 $1.20 multi 1.60 1.60
**5548** A1263 $1.20 multi 1.60 1.60
**5549** A1263 $2.40 multi 3.25 2.40
**5550** A1263 $3.60 multi 5.00 3.75
*Nos. 5547-5550 (4)* 11.45 9.35

**Self-Adhesive**

***Serpentine Die Cut 11¼ Syncopated***
**5551** A1263 $1.20 multi 1.60 .30
**5552** A1263 $1.20 multi 1.60 .30
*a.* Horiz. coil pair, #5551-5552 3.20
*b.* Booklet pane of 10, 5 each #5551-5552 16.00
*c.* Booklet pane of 20, 10 each #5551-5552 32.00

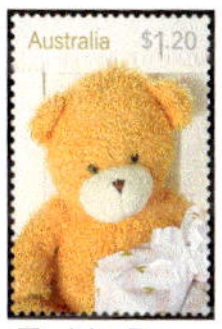
Teddy Bear A1264

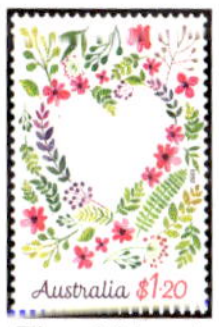
Floral Heart A1265

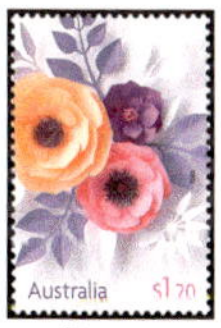
Paper Flowers A1266

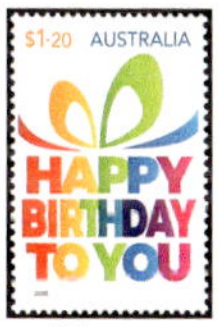

"Happy Birthday to You" A1267

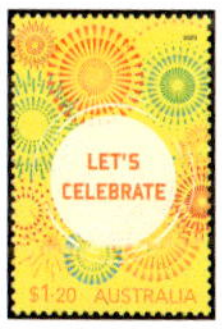

"Let's Celebrate" A1268

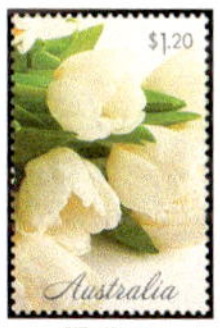
Tulips A1269

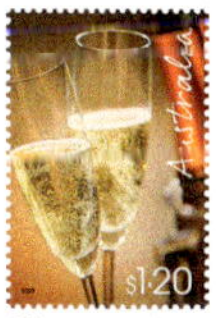
Champagne Flutes A1270

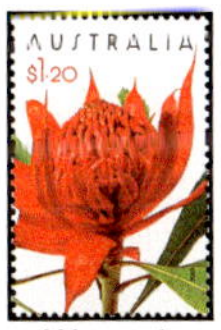

Waratah Flowers A1271

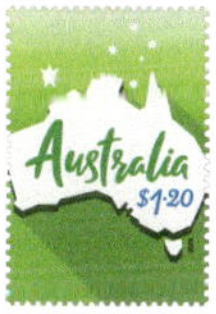

Map of Australia A1272

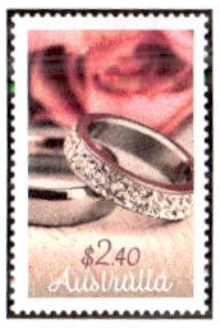

Wedding Rings A1273

**2023, Jan. 3 Litho. *Perf. 14¾x14***
**5553** A1264 $1.20 multi 1.60 1.60
**5554** A1265 $1.20 multi 1.60 1.60
**5555** A1266 $1.20 multi 1.60 1.60
**5556** A1267 $1.20 multi 1.60 1.60
**5557** A1268 $1.20 multi 1.60 1.60
**5558** A1269 $1.20 multi 1.60 1.60
**5559** A1270 $1.20 multi 1.60 1.60
**5560** A1271 $1.20 multi 1.60 1.60
**5561** A1272 $1.20 multi 1.60 1.25
**5562** A1273 $2.40 multi 3.25 2.50
*a.* Souvenir sheet of 10, #5553-5562 18.00 18.00
*Nos. 5553-5562 (10)* 17.65 16.55

**Booklet Stamps**
**Self-Adhesive**

***Serpentine Die Cut 11¼ Syncopated***
**5563** A1264 $1.20 multi 1.60 .30
*a.* Booklet pane of 10 16.00
**5564** A1265 $1.20 multi 1.60 .30
*a.* Booklet pane of 10 16.00
**5565** A1266 $1.20 multi 1.60 .30
*a.* Booklet pane of 10 16.00
**5566** A1267 $1.20 multi 1.60 .30
*a.* Booklet pane of 10 16.00
**5567** A1268 $1.20 multi 1.60 .30
*a.* Booklet pane of 10 16.00
**5568** A1269 $1.20 multi 1.60 .30
*a.* Booklet pane of 10 16.00
**5569** A1270 $1.20 multi 1.60 .30
*a.* Booklet pane of 10 16.00
**5570** A1271 $1.20 multi 1.60 .30
*a.* Booklet pane of 10 16.00
**5571** A1273 $2.40 multi 3.25 1.60
*a.* Booklet pane of 4 13.00
Complete booklet, 4 #5571a 52.50
*Nos. 5563-5571 (9)* 16.05 4.00

The complete booklet, which sold for $38.95, contains four panes of No. 5571a, each with different pane margins.

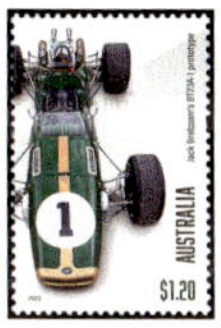

Items Used in Sporting Events by Famous Australian Athletes — A1274

Designs: Nos. 5572, 5576, BT23A-1 prototype race car of Jack Brabham (1926-2014). Nos. 5573, 5577, Dunlop tennis racket of Evonne Goolagong Cawley. Nos. 5574, 5578, Road bicycle of Hubert Opperman (1904-96). Nos. 5575, 5579, Racing wheelchair of Kurt Fearnley.

**2023, Feb. 7 Litho. *Perf. 14¾x14***
**5572** A1274 $1.20 multi 1.60 1.60
**5573** A1274 $1.20 multi 1.60 1.60
**5574** A1274 $1.20 multi 1.60 1.60
**5575** A1274 $1.20 multi 1.60 1.60
*a.* Souvenir sheet of 4, #5572-5575 6.50 6.50
*Nos. 5572-5575 (4)* 6.40 6.40

**Booklet Stamps**
**Self-Adhesive**

***Serpentine Die Cut 11¼ Syncopated***
**5576** A1274 $1.20 multi 1.60 .30
*a.* Booklet pane of 10 16.00
**5577** A1274 $1.20 multi 1.60 .30
*a.* Booklet pane of 10 16.00
**5578** A1274 $1.20 multi 1.60 .30
*a.* Booklet pane of 10 16.00
**5579** A1274 $1.20 multi 1.60 .30
*a.* Booklet pane of 10 16.00
*Nos. 5576-5579 (4)* 6.40 1.20

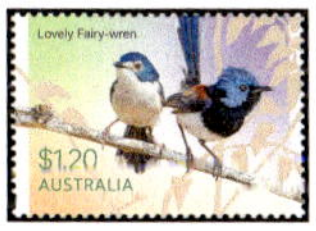

Fairy Wrens — A1275

Designs: Nos. 5580, 5584, Lovely fairy wren. Nos. 5581, 5585, Superb fairy wren. Nos. 5582, 5586, Red-backed fairy wren. Nos. 5583, 5587, Purple-crowned fairy wren.

**2023 Litho. *Perf. 14x14¾***
**5580** A1275 $1.20 multi 1.60 1.60
**5581** A1275 $1.20 multi 1.60 1.60
**5582** A1275 $1.20 multi 1.60 1.60
**5583** A1275 $1.20 multi 1.60 1.60
*a.* Souvenir sheet of 4, #5580-5583 6.50 6.50
*b.* As "a," with Perth Stamp and Coin Show emblem in sheet margin 6.50 6.50
*Nos. 5580-5583 (4)* 6.40 6.40

**Booklet Stamps**
**Self-Adhesive**

***Serpentine Die Cut 11¼ Syncopated***
**5584** A1275 $1.20 multi 1.60 .30
**5585** A1275 $1.20 multi 1.60 .30
**5586** A1275 $1.20 multi 1.60 .30
**5587** A1275 $1.20 multi 1.60 .30
*a.* Booklet pane of 20, 5 each #5584-5587 32.00
*Nos. 5584-5587 (4)* 6.40 1.20

Issued: No. 5583b, 3/24; others, 2/21.

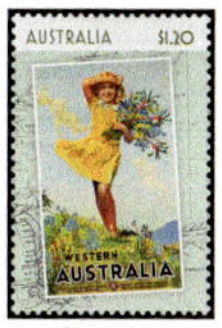

Poster Promoting Travel to Western Australia A1276

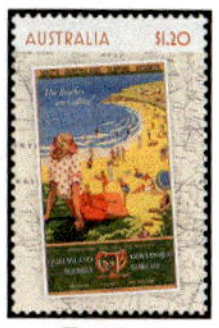

Poster Promoting Travel to Queensland A1277

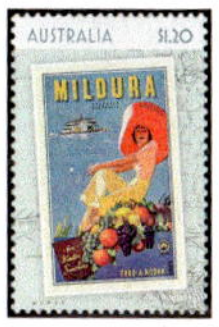

Poster Promoting Travel to Mildura, Victoria — A1278

**2023, Mar. 7 Litho. *Perf. 14¾x14***
**5588** A1276 $1.20 multi 1.60 1.60
**5589** A1277 $1.20 multi 1.60 1.60
**5590** A1278 $1.20 multi 1.60 1.60
*Nos. 5588-5590 (3)* 4.80 4.80

**Booklet Stamps**
**Self-Adhesive**

***Serpentine Die Cut 11¼ Syncopated***
**5591** A1276 $1.20 multi 1.60 .30
**5592** A1277 $1.20 multi 1.60 .30
**5593** A1278 $1.20 multi 1.60 .30
*a.* Booklet pane of 10, 4 #5591, 3 each #5592-5593 16.00
*Nos. 5591-5593 (3)* 4.80 .90

Travel posters of the 1930s.

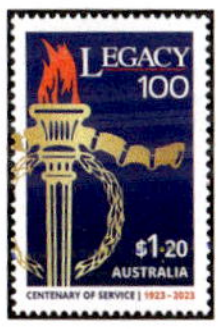

Legacy Australia, Cent. — A1279

**2023, Mar. 21 Litho. *Perf. 14¾x14***
**5594** A1279 $1.20 multi 1.60 1.60

**Coil Stamp**
**Self-Adhesive**

***Serpentine Die Cut 11¼ Syncopated***
**5595** A1279 $1.20 multi 1.60 .30

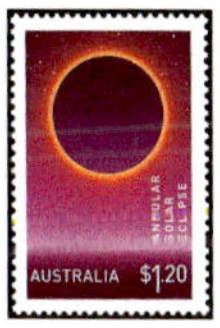

Solar Eclipses — A1280

Designs: Nos. 5596, 5599, Annular solar eclipse. Nos. 5597, 5600, Total solar eclipse. Nos. 5598, 5601, Partial solar eclipse.

**2023, Apr. 11 Litho. *Perf. 14¾x14***
**5596** A1280 $1.20 multi 1.60 1.60
**5597** A1280 $1.20 multi 1.60 1.60
**5598** A1280 $1.20 multi 1.60 1.60
*a.* Souvenir sheet of 3, #5596-5598 4.80 4.80
*Nos. 5596-5598 (3)* 4.80 4.80

**Booklet Stamps**
**Self-Adhesive**

***Serpentine Die Cut 11¼ Syncopated***
**5599** A1280 $1.20 multi 1.60 .30
**5600** A1280 $1.20 multi 1.60 .30
**5601** A1280 $1.20 multi 1.60 .30
*a.* Booklet pane of 10, 4 #5599, 3 each #5600-5601 16.00
*Nos. 5599-5601 (3)* 4.80 .90

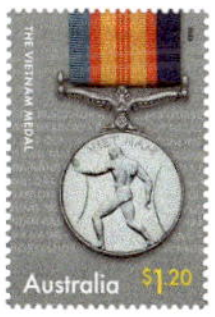

Australian Vietnam War Medals — A1282

Designs: $1.20, Vietnam Medal. $2.40, Vietnam Logistic and Support Medal.

**2023, Apr. 18 Litho. *Perf. 14¾x14***
**5602** A1282 $1.20 multi 1.60 1.60
**5603** A1282 $2.40 multi 3.25 2.40
*a.* Souvenir sheet of 2, #5602-5603 5.00 4.00

**Booklet Stamp**
**Self-Adhesive**

***Serpentine Die Cut 11¼ Syncopated***
**5604** A1282 $1.20 multi 1.60 1.60
*a.* Booklet pane of 20 32.00

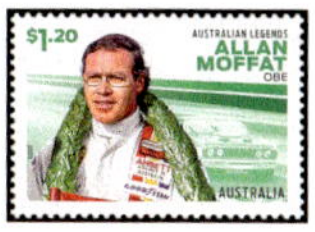

V8 Supercars Championship Race Car Drivers — A1283

Designs: Nos. 5605, 5609, Allan Moffat. Nos. 5606, 5610, Dick Johnson. Nos. 5607, 5611, Mark Skaife. Nos. 5608, 5612, Craig Lowndes.

**2023, Apr. 27 Litho. *Perf. 14x14¾***
**5605** A1283 $1.20 multi 1.60 1.60
**5606** A1283 $1.20 multi 1.60 1.60
**5607** A1283 $1.20 multi 1.60 1.60
**5608** A1283 $1.20 multi 1.60 1.60
*Nos. 5605-5608 (4)* 6.40 6.40

**Booklet Stamps**
**Self-Adhesive**
**5609** A1283 $1.20 multi 1.60 .30
*a.* Booklet pane of 10 16.00
**5610** A1283 $1.20 multi 1.60 .30
*a.* Booklet pane of 10 16.00
**5611** A1283 $1.20 multi 1.60 .30
*a.* Booklet pane of 10 16.00
**5612** A1283 $1.20 multi 1.60 .30
*a.* Booklet pane of 10 16.00
*Nos. 5609-5612 (4)* 6.40 1.20

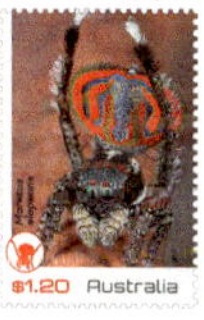

Peacock Spiders — A1284

Designs: Nos. 5613, 5616, Maratus elephans. Nos. 5614, 5617, Maratus purcellae. Nos. 5615, 5618, Maratus speciosus.

**2023, May 9 Litho. *Perf. 14¾x14***
**5613** A1284 $1.20 multi 1.60 1.60
**5614** A1284 $1.20 multi 1.60 1.60
**5615** A1284 $1.20 multi 1.60 1.60
*a.* Souvenir sheet of 3, #5613-5615 4.80 4.00
*Nos. 5613-5615 (3)* 4.80 4.80

**Booklet Stamps**
**Self-Adhesive**

***Serpentine Die Cut 11¼ Syncopated***
**5616** A1284 $1.20 multi 1.60 .30
**5617** A1284 $1.20 multi 1.60 .30
**5618** A1284 $1.20 multi 1.60 .30
*a.* Booklet pane of 10, 4 #5616, 3 each #5617-5618 16.00
*Nos. 5616-5618 (3)* 4.80 .90

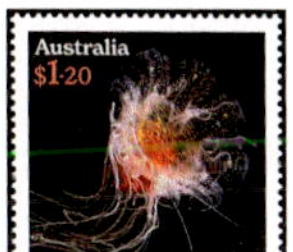

Jellyfish — A1285

Designs: Nos. 5619, 5623, Lion's mane jellyfish. Nos. 5620, 5624, Blue blubber jellyfish. Nos. 5621, 5625, Moon jellyfish. Nos. 5622, 5626, Bazinga jellyfish.

**2023, May 16 Litho. *Perf. 14¼***
**5619** A1285 $1.20 multi 1.60 1.60
**5620** A1285 $1.20 multi 1.60 1.60
**5621** A1285 $1.20 multi 1.60 1.60
**5622** A1285 $1.20 multi 1.60 1.60
*a.* Souvenir sheet of 4, #5619-5622 6.50 6.50
*Nos. 5619-5622 (4)* 6.40 6.40

**Booklet Stamps**
**Self-Adhesive**

***Serpentine Die Cut 11½ Syncopated***
**5623** A1285 $1.20 multi 1.60 .30
*a.* Booklet pane of 10 16.00
**5624** A1285 $1.20 multi 1.60 .30
*a.* Booklet pane of 10 16.00
**5625** A1285 $1.20 multi 1.60 .30
*a.* Booklet pane of 10 16.00
**5626** A1285 $1.20 multi 1.60 .30
*a.* Booklet pane of 10 16.00
*Nos. 5623-5626 (4)* 6.40 1.20

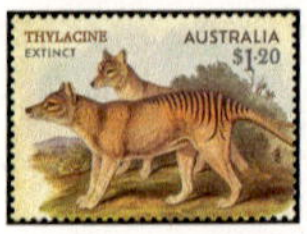

Extinct Mammals — A1286

Designs: Nos. 5627, 5630, Thylacines. Nos. 5628, 5631, Toolache wallabies. Nos. 5629, 5632, Long-tailed hopping mice.

**2023, June 1 Litho. *Perf. 14x14¾***

**5627** A1286 $1.20 multi 1.60 1.60
**5628** A1286 $1.20 multi 1.60 1.60
**5629** A1286 $1.20 multi 1.60 1.60
*a.* Souvenir sheet of 3, #5627-5629 4.80 4.80
*Nos. 5627-5629 (3)* 4.80 4.80

**Booklet Stamps**
**Self-Adhesive**

***Serpentine Die Cut 11¼ Syncopated***

**5630** A1286 $1.20 multi 1.60 .30
**5631** A1286 $1.20 multi 1.60 .30
**5632** A1286 $1.20 multi 1.60 .30
*a.* Booklet pane of 10, 4 #5630, 3 each #5631-5632 16.00
*Nos. 5630-5632 (3)* 4.80 .90

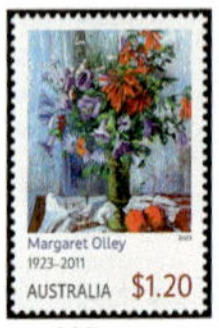

Winter Flowers, Painting by Margaret Olley (1923-2011) A1287

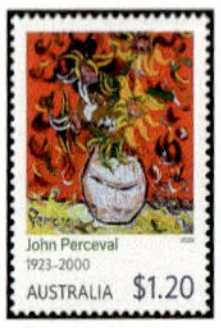

Sunflowers, Painting by John Perceval (1923-2000) A1288

**2023, June 6 Litho. *Perf. 14¾x14***

**5633** A1287 $1.20 multi 1.60 1.60
**5634** A1288 $1.20 multi 1.60 1.60

**Booklet Stamps**
**Self-Adhesive**

***Serpentine Die Cut 11¼ Syncopated***

**5635** A1287 $1.20 multi 1.60 .30
*a.* Booklet pane of 10 16.00
**5636** A1288 $1.20 multi 1.60 .30
*a.* Booklet pane of 10 16.00

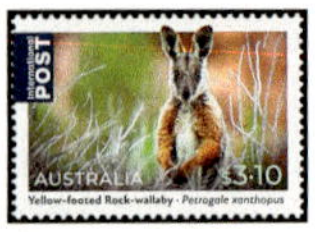

Native Mammals — A1289

Designs: $3.10, Yellow-footed rock wallaby. $3.90, Bilby. $4.30, Koala.

**2023, June 26 Litho. *Perf. 14x14¾***

**5637** A1289 $3.10 multi 4.25 4.25
**5638** A1289 $3.90 multi 5.25 5.25
**5639** A1289 $4.30 multi 5.75 4.50
*Nos. 5637-5639 (3)* 15.25 14.00

**Booklet Stamps**
**Self-Adhesive**

***Serpentine Die Cut 11¼ Syncopated***

**5640** A1289 $3.10 multi 4.25 2.10
*a.* Booklet pane of 5 21.50
**5641** A1289 $3.90 multi 5.25 2.60
*a.* Booklet pane of 5 26.50

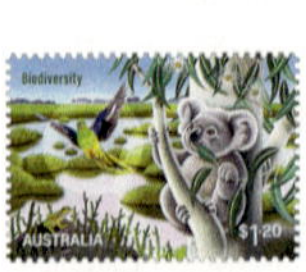

Sustainable Future — A1290

Inscriptions: Nos. 5642, 5645, Biodiversity. Nos. 5643, 5646, Indigenous land management. Nos. 5644, 5647, Renewable energy.

**2023, June 27 Litho. *Perf. 14x14¾***

**5642** A1290 $1.20 multi 1.60 1.60
**5643** A1290 $1.20 multi 1.60 1.60
**5644** A1290 $1.20 multi 1.60 1.60
*a.* Souvenir sheet of 3, #5642-5644 4.80 4.80
*Nos. 5642-5644 (3)* 4.80 4.80

**Self-Adhesive**

***Serpentine Die Cut 11¼ Syncopated***

**5645** A1290 $1.20 multi 1.60 .30
*a.* Booklet pane of 10 16.00
**5646** A1290 $1.20 multi 1.60 .30
*a.* Booklet pane of 10 16.00
**5647** A1290 $1.20 multi 1.60 .30
*a.* Booklet pane of 10 16.00
*b.* Horiz. coil strip of 3, #5645-5647 4.80
*Nos. 5645-5647 (3)* 4.80 .90

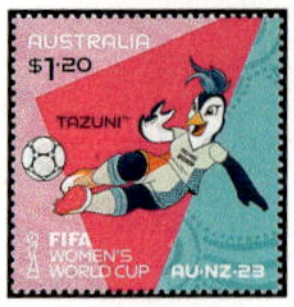

2022 Women's World Cup Soccer Championships, Australia and New Zealand — A1292

**2023, July 11 Litho. *Perf. 14¼***

**5649** A1292 $1.20 multi 1.60 1.25

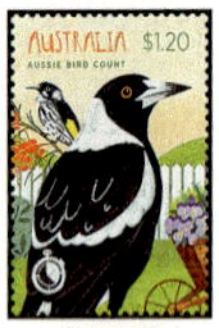

A1293

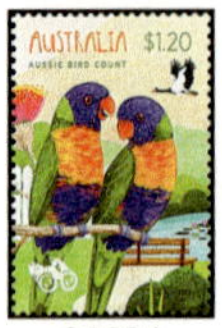

A1294

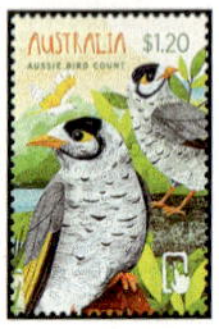

BirdLife Australia's Annual Bird Count — A1295

**2023, Aug. 15 Litho. *Perf. 14½x14***

**5650** A1293 $1.20 multi 1.60 1.25
**5651** A1294 $1.20 multi 1.60 1.25
**5652** A1295 $1.20 multi 1.60 1.25
*a.* Souvenir sheet of 3, #5650-5652 4.80 3.75
*Nos. 5650-5652 (3)* 4.80 3.75

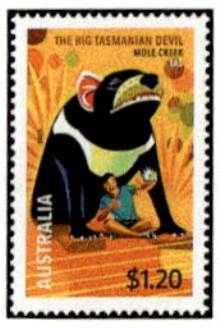

Large Australian Statues — A1296

Designs: Nos. 5653, 5658, Big Tasmanian Devil, Mole Creek, Tasmania. Nos. 5654, 5659, Big Swoop, Canberra, Australian Capital Territory. Nos. 5655, 5660, Giant Koala, Dadswells Bridge, Victoria. Nos. 5656, 5661, Giant Murray Cod, Swan Hill, Victoria. Nos. 5657, 5662, Big Jumping Crocodile, Wak Wak, Northern Territory.

**2023, Sept. 4 Litho. *Perf. 14¾x14***

**5653** A1296 $1.20 multi 1.60 1.60
**5654** A1296 $1.20 multi 1.60 1.60
**5655** A1296 $1.20 multi 1.60 1.60
**5656** A1296 $1.20 multi 1.60 1.60
**5657** A1296 $1.20 multi 1.60 1.60
*a.* Souvenir sheet of 5, #5653-5657 8.00 8.00
*Nos. 5653-5657 (5)* 8.00 8.00

**Booklet Stamps**
**Self-Adhesive**

***Serpentine Die Cut 11¼ Syncopated***

**5658** A1296 $1.20 multi 1.60 .30
*a.* Booklet pane of 10 16.00
**5659** A1296 $1.20 multi 1.60 .30
*a.* Booklet pane of 10 16.00
**5660** A1296 $1.20 multi 1.60 .30
*a.* Booklet pane of 10 16.00
**5661** A1296 $1.20 multi 1.60 .30
*a.* Booklet pane of 10 16.00
**5662** A1296 $1.20 multi 1.60 .30
*a.* Booklet pane of 10 16.00
*Nos. 5658-5662 (5)* 8.00 1.50

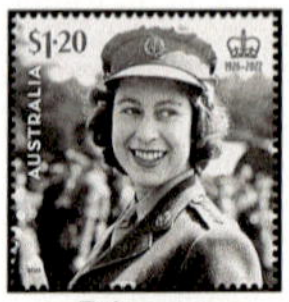

Princess Elizabeth in Junior Commander Uniform, 1945 — A1297

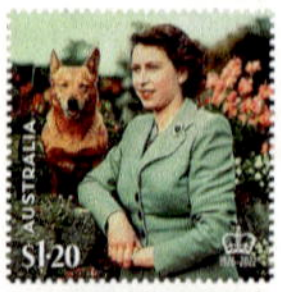

Queen Elizabeth II and Corgi, 1952 — A1298

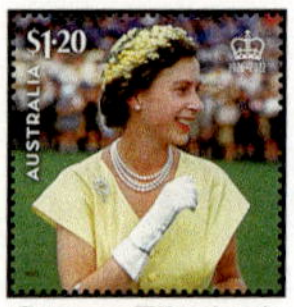

Queen Elizabeth II Visiting Australia, 1954 — A1299

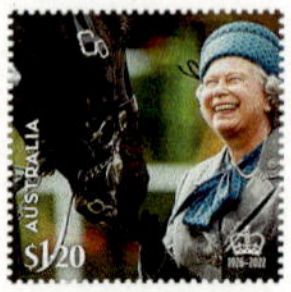

Queen Elizabeth II and Horse, 1997 — A1300

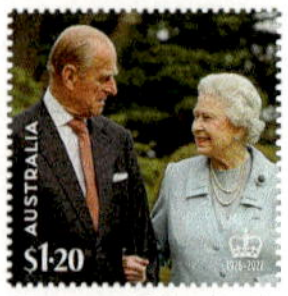

Queen Elizabeth II and Husband, Prince Philip, 2007 — A1301

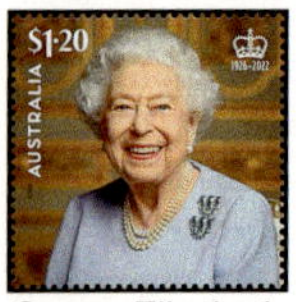

Queen Elizabeth II, 2022 — A1302

**2023, Sept. 19 Litho. *Perf. 14¼***

**5663** A1297 $1.20 multi 1.60 1.25
**5664** A1298 $1.20 multi 1.60 1.25
**5665** A1299 $1.20 multi 1.60 1.25
**5666** A1300 $1.20 multi 1.60 1.25
**5667** A1301 $1.20 multi 1.60 1.25
**5668** A1302 $1.20 multi 1.60 1.25
*a.* Souvenir sheet of 6, #5663-5668 9.75 7.50
*b.* Souvenir sheet of 4, #5664, 5665, 5666, 5668 6.50 6.50
*Nos. 5663-5668 (6)* 9.60 7.50

Queen Elizabeth II (1926-2022). Perth 2023 National Stamp Exhibition (No. 5668b). Issued: No. 5668b, 11/2.

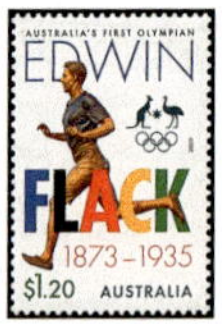

Edwin Flack (1873-1935), First Australia Olympic Gold Medalist, 1896 — A1303

**2023, Sept. 26 Litho. *Perf. 14¾x14***

**5669** A1303 $1.20 multi 1.60 1.25

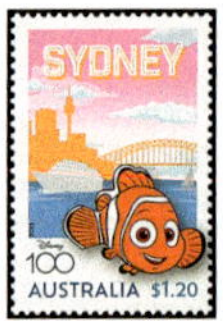

Walt Disney Company, Cent. — A1304

Characters from Disney animated films in Australia: Nos. 5670, 5674, Nemo in Sydney Harbor. Nos. 5671, 5675, Ariel at Great Barrier Reef. Nos. 5672, 5676, Mickey and Minnie Mouse on Great Ocean Road, Victoria. Nos. 5673, 5677, Kanga and Roo at the Red Center, Northern Territory.

**2023, Oct. 3 Litho. *Perf. 14¾x14***

**5670** A1304 $1.20 multi 1.60 1.60
**5671** A1304 $1.20 multi 1.60 1.60
**5672** A1304 $1.20 multi 1.60 1.60
**5673** A1304 $1.20 multi 1.60 1.60
*a.* Souvenir sheet of 4, #5670-5673 6.50 6.50
*Nos. 5670-5673 (4)* 6.40 6.40

**Booklet Stamps**
**Self-Adhesive**

***Serpentine Die Cut 11¼ Syncopated***

**5674** A1304 $1.20 multi 1.60 .30
**5675** A1304 $1.20 multi 1.60 .30
**5676** A1304 $1.20 multi 1.60 .30
**5677** A1304 $1.20 multi 1.60 .30
*a.* Booklet pane of 10, 3 each #5674-5675, 2 each #5676-5677 16.00
*Nos. 5674-5677 (4)* 6.40 1.20

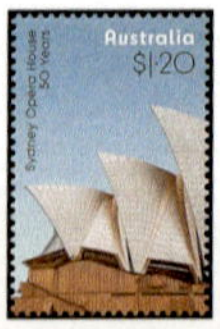

Sydney Opera House, 50th Anniv. — A1305

Designs: $1.20, West Elevation. $3, North Elevation.

**2023, Oct. 10 Litho. *Perf. 14***

**5678** A1305 $1.20 multi 1.60 1.60
*a.* Perf. 14¾x14 1.60 1.60
**5679** A1305 $3 multi 4.00 2.00
*a.* Perf. 14¾x14 4.00 2.00
*b.* Souvenir sheet of 2, #5678a-5679a 5.75 3.75

**Coil Stamp**
**Self-Adhesive**

***Serpentine Die Cut 11¼ Syncopated***

**5680** A1305 $1.20 multi 1.60 .30

**Booklet Stamp**

**5681** A1305 $3 multi 4.00 2.00
*a.* Booklet pane of 5 20.00

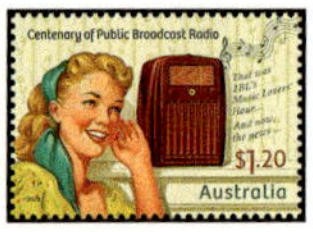

First Radio Broadcast in Australia, Cent. — A1306

**2023, Oct. 17 Litho. *Perf. 14***

**5682** A1306 $1.20 multi 1.60 1.25
*a.* Souvenir sheet of 4, #4115, 5501, 2 #5682 5.75 5.75

Perth 2023 National Stamp Exhibition (No. 5682a). Issued: No. 5682a, 11/2.

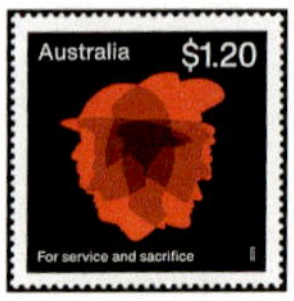

Remembrance Day Poppies — A1307

Color of poppy: Nos. 5683, 5686, Red. Nos. 5684, 5687, White. Nos. 5685, 5688, Purple.

**2023, Oct. 24 Litho. *Perf. 14¼***

**5683** A1307 $1.20 multi 1.60 1.60
**5684** A1307 $1.20 multi 1.60 1.60
**5685** A1307 $1.20 multi 1.60 1.60
*a.* Souvenir sheet of 3, #5683-5685 5.00 5.00
*Nos. 5683-5685 (3)* 4.80 4.80

**Booklet Stamps**
**Self-Adhesive**

***Serpentine Die Cut 11¼ Syncopated***

**5686** A1307 $1.20 multi 1.60 .30
*a.* Booklet pane of 10 16.00
**5687** A1307 $1.20 multi 1.60 .30
*a.* Booklet pane of 10 16.00
**5688** A1307 $1.20 multi 1.60 .30
*a.* Booklet pane of 10 16.00
*Nos. 5686-5688 (3)* 4.80 .90

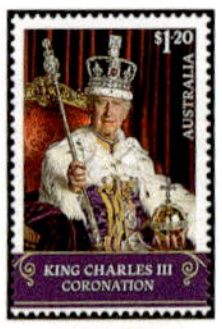

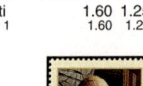

Coronation of King Charles III — A1308

**2023, Nov. 1 Litho. *Perf. 14¾x14***

**5689** A1308 $1.20 multi 1.60 1.25
*a.* Souvenir sheet of 1 1.60 1.25

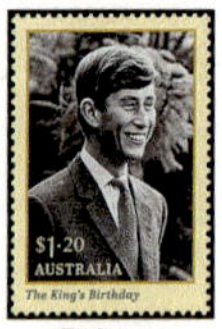

Prince Charles in 1966 A1309

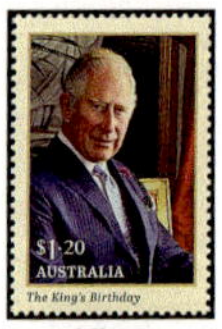

King Charles III A1310

**2023, Nov. 1 Litho. *Perf. 14¾x14***

**5690** A1309 $1.20 multi 1.60 1.25
**5691** A1310 $1.20 multi 1.60 1.25
*a.* Souvenir sheet of 2, #5690-5691 3.25 2.50

75th birthday of King Charles III. No. 5691a has foil application on sheet margin.

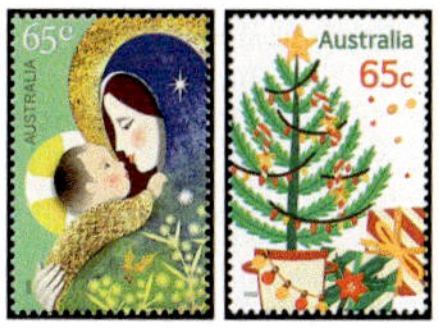

Christmas
A1311 A1312

Designs: Nos. 5692, 5697, Madonna and Child. Nos. 5693, 5698, 5702, Christmas tree and gifts. Nos. 5694, 5699, 5703, Letter to Santa Claus. Nos. 5695, 5700, Magi and camel. Nos. 5696, 5701, Christmas tree ornament.

**2023, Nov. 1 Litho. *Perf. 14x13¾***

| | | | | |
|---|---|---|---|---|
| **5692** | A1311 | 65c multi | .85 | .85 |
| *a.* | | Perf. 14¾x14 | .85 | .85 |
| **5693** | A1312 | 65c multi | .85 | .85 |
| **5694** | A1312 | 65c multi | .85 | .85 |
| *a.* | | Horiz. pair, #5693-5694 | 1.70 | 1.70 |
| **5695** | A1311 | $3 multi | 4.00 | 4.00 |
| *a.* | | Perf. 14¾x14 | 4.00 | 4.00 |
| *b.* | | Souvenir sheet of 2, #5692a, 5695a | 5.00 | 5.00 |
| **5696** | A1312 | $3 multi | 4.00 | 4.00 |
| | | *Nos. 5692-5696 (5)* | 10.55 | 10.55 |

**Booklet Stamps**
**Self-Adhesive**

***Serpentine Die Cut 11¼ Syncopated***

| | | | | |
|---|---|---|---|---|
| **5697** | A1311 | 65c multi | .85 | .30 |
| *a.* | | Booklet pane of 20 + 20 etiquettes | 17.00 | |
| **5698** | A1312 | 65c multi | .85 | .30 |
| **5699** | A1312 | 65c multi | .85 | .30 |
| *a.* | | Booklet pane of 20, 10 each #5698-5699 + 20 etiquettes | 17.00 | |
| **5700** | A1311 | $3 multi | 4.00 | 2.00 |
| *a.* | | Booklet pane of 5 | 20.00 | |
| **5701** | A1312 | $3 multi | 4.00 | 2.00 |
| *a.* | | Booklet pane of 5 | 20.00 | |

**Litho. With Foil Application**

| | | | | |
|---|---|---|---|---|
| **5702** | A1312 | 65c multi | .85 | .30 |
| *a.* | | Booklet pane of 10 + 10 etiquettes | 8.50 | |
| **5703** | A1312 | 65c multi | .85 | .30 |
| *a.* | | Booklet pane of 10 + 10 etiquettes | 8.50 | |
| | | *Nos. 5697-5703 (7)* | 12.25 | 5.50 |

## SEMI-POSTAL STAMPS

**Catalogue values in this section are for Never Hinged items.**

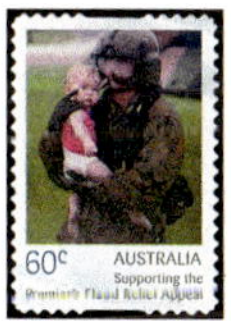

Queensland Flood Relief — SP1

Designs: No. B1, Rescuer holding baby. No. B2, Flooded buildings, ground-level view. No. B3, Rescuers taking pet from house. No. B4, Kangaroo stranded on island in flood. No. B5, Flooded buildings, aerial view.

***Serpentine Die Cut 11¼ Syncopated***
**2011, Jan. 27 Litho.**
**Self-Adhesive**

| | | | | |
|---|---|---|---|---|
| **B1** | SP1 | 60c+(20c) multi | 1.75 | 1.75 |
| **B2** | SP1 | 60c+(20c) multi | 1.75 | 1.75 |
| **B3** | SP1 | 60c+(20c) multi | 1.75 | 1.75 |
| **B4** | SP1 | 60c+(20c) multi | 1.75 | 1.75 |
| **B5** | SP1 | 60c+(20c) multi | 1.75 | 1.75 |
| *a.* | | Sheet of 10, 2 each #B1-B5 | 17.50 | |
| | | *Nos. B1-B5 (5)* | 8.75 | 8.75 |

Surtax for Premier's Flood Relief Appeal.

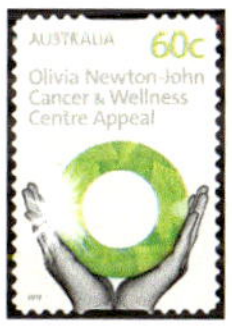

Leaves in Ring and Hands — SP2

**2012, June 26 Self-Adhesive**

| | | | | |
|---|---|---|---|---|
| **B6** | SP2 | 60c+(20c) multi | 1.75 | 1.75 |

Printed in sheets of 10. Surtax for Olivia Newton-John Cancer and Wellness Center.

## AIR POST STAMPS

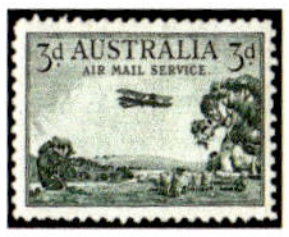

Airplane over Bush Lands — AP1

**Unwmk.**
**1929, May 20 Engr. *Perf. 11***

| | | | | |
|---|---|---|---|---|
| **C1** | AP1 | 3p deep green | 9.25 | 8.50 |
| | | Never hinged | 14.50 | |
| *a.* | | Booklet pane of 4 ('30) | 450.00 | |

**Kingsford-Smith Type of 1931**

**1931, Mar. 19**

| | | | | |
|---|---|---|---|---|
| **C2** | A8 | 6p gray violet | 8.00 | 8.00 |
| | | Never hinged | 11.50 | |

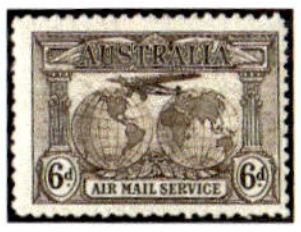

AP3

**1931, Nov. 4**

| | | | | |
|---|---|---|---|---|
| **C3** | AP3 | 6p olive brown | 17.00 | 14.00 |
| | | Never hinged | 35.00 | |

For overprint see No. CO1.

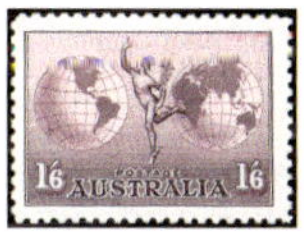

Mercury and Hemispheres AP4

**1934, Dec. 1 *Perf. 11***

| | | | | |
|---|---|---|---|---|
| **C4** | AP4 | 1sh6p violet brown | 40.00 | 8.00 |
| | | Never hinged | 97.50 | |

***Perf. 13½x14***
**1937, Oct. 22 Wmk. 228**

| | | | | |
|---|---|---|---|---|
| **C5** | AP4 | 1sh6p violet brown | 8.50 | 1.40 |
| | | Never hinged | 14.50 | |

**Catalogue values for unused stamps in this section, from this point to the end of the section, are for Never Hinged items.**

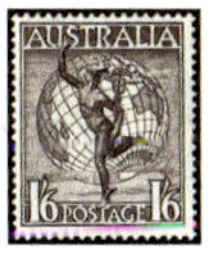

Mercury and Globe — AP5

**1949, Sept. 1 *Perf. 14½***

| | | | | |
|---|---|---|---|---|
| **C6** | AP5 | 1sh6p sepia | 2.25 | .80 |

**1956, Dec. 6 Unwmk.**

| | | | | |
|---|---|---|---|---|
| **C7** | AP5 | 1sh6p sepia | 18.50 | 1.10 |

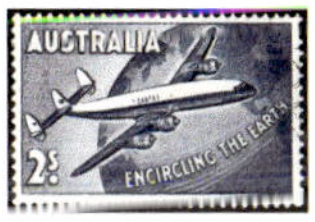

Super-Constellation over Globe — AP6

**1958, Jan. 6 *Perf. 14½x14***

| | | | | |
|---|---|---|---|---|
| **C8** | AP6 | 2sh dark violet blue | 2.75 | 2.25 |

Inauguration of Australian "Round the World" air service.

## AIR POST OFFICIAL STAMP

No. C3 Overprinted

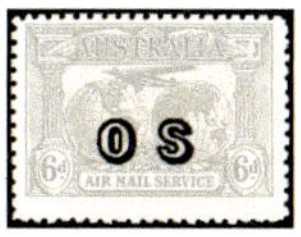

***Perf. 11, 11½***
**1931, Nov. 17 Unwmk.**

| | | | | |
|---|---|---|---|---|
| **CO1** | AP3 | 6p olive brown | 35.00 | *35.00* |
| | | Never hinged | 57.50 | |

Issued primarily for official use, but to prevent speculation, a quantity was issued for public distribution.

## POSTAGE DUE STAMPS

Very fine examples of Nos. J1-J38 will have perforations touching the design on one or more sides due to the narrow spacing of the stamps on the plates. Stamps with perfs clear of the design on all four sides are scarce and will command higher prices.

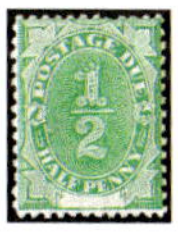

D1

**1902 Typo. Wmk. 55 *Perf. 11½, 12***

| | | | | |
|---|---|---|---|---|
| **J1** | D1 | ½p emerald | 5.75 | 7.00 |
| **J2** | D1 | 1p emerald | 27.00 | 14.00 |
| *a.* | | Perf. 11 | *2,650.* | *1,000.* |
| *b.* | | Perf. 11x11½ | 400.00 | 160.00 |
| **J3** | D1 | 2p emerald | 67.50 | 11.50 |
| *a.* | | Perf. 11x11½ | 525.00 | 190.00 |
| **J4** | D1 | 3p emerald | 52.50 | 32.50 |
| **J5** | D1 | 4p emerald | 52.50 | 15.00 |
| **J6** | D1 | 6p emerald | 62.50 | 12.50 |
| **J7** | D1 | 8p emerald | 105.00 | 90.00 |
| **J8** | D1 | 5sh emerald | 210.00 | 80.00 |
| | | *Nos. J1-J8 (8)* | 582.75 | 262.50 |

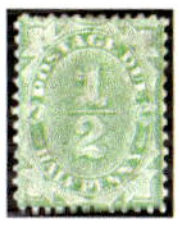

D2

***Perf. 11½, 12, Compound with 11***
**1902-04**

| | | | | |
|---|---|---|---|---|
| **J9** | D2 | ½p emerald | 22.00 | *18.00* |
| *a.* | | Perf. 11 | 575.00 | 325.00 |
| **J10** | D2 | 1p emerald, Perf 12x11 | 21.00 | 5.00 |
| *a.* | | Perf. 11 | 170.00 | 32.50 |
| *b.* | | Perf 11½ | 200.00 | 140.00 |
| *c.* | | Perf 11x11½ | 37.50 | 11.50 |
| **J11** | D2 | 2p emerald | 52.50 | 3.50 |
| *a.* | | Perf. 11 | 240.00 | 30.00 |
| *b.* | | Perf 12 | — | 180.00 |
| *c.* | | Perf 11x11½ | 120.00 | 37.50 |
| *d.* | | Perf 11x12 | 140.00 | 45.00 |
| **J12** | D2 | 3p emerald | 95.00 | 18.00 |
| *a.* | | Perf. 11 | 160.00 | 62.50 |
| *b.* | | Perf 12 | 375.00 | 110.00 |
| **J13** | D2 | 4p emerald | 80.00 | 27.50 |
| *a.* | | Perf. 11 | 275.00 | 75.00 |
| **J14** | D2 | 5p emerald | 70.00 | 25.00 |
| *a.* | | Perf. 11 | 400.00 | 57.50 |
| *b.* | | Perf 12 | 75.00 | 20.00 |
| **J15** | D2 | 6p emerald | 75.00 | 12.50 |
| *a.* | | Perf. 11 | 100.00 | 17.50 |
| **J16** | D2 | 8p emerald | 150.00 | 60.00 |
| **J17** | D2 | 10p emerald | 100.00 | 25.00 |
| *a.* | | Perf 12x11½ | 125.00 | 20.00 |
| **J18** | D2 | 1sh emerald | 85.00 | 20.00 |
| *a.* | | Perf. 11 | 500.00 | 45.00 |
| *b.* | | Perf 12x11½ | 120.00 | 30.00 |
| **J19** | D2 | 2sh emerald | 135.00 | 135.00 |
| *a.* | | Perf 11½, 12 | 200.00 | 200.00 |
| **J20** | D2 | 5sh emerald | 475.00 | 475.00 |
| *a.* | | Perf. 11 | 1,700. | 300.00 |

***Perf. 11***

| | | | | |
|---|---|---|---|---|
| **J21** | D2 | 10sh emerald | *2,250.* | *1,900.* |
| **J22** | D2 | 20sh emerald | *4,500.* | *2,750.* |
| | | *Nos. J9-J20 (12)* | 1,361. | 824.50 |

***Perf. 11½, 12 Compound with 11***
**1906 Wmk. 12**

| | | | | |
|---|---|---|---|---|
| **J23** | D2 | ½p emerald | 16.00 | 18.00 |
| **J24** | D2 | 1p emerald | 30.00 | 5.75 |
| *a.* | | Perf. 11 | *3,250.* | *1,150.* |
| **J25** | D2 | 2p emerald | 80.00 | 10.00 |
| **J26** | D2 | 3p emerald | 950.00 | 350.00 |
| **J27** | D2 | 4p emerald | 77.50 | 24.00 |
| *a.* | | Perf. 11 | *5,750.* | *3,500.* |
| **J28** | D2 | 6p emerald | 77.50 | 25.00 |
| | | *Nos. J23-J28 (6)* | 1,231. | 432.75 |

**1907 Wmk. 13 *Perf. 11½x11***

| | | | | |
|---|---|---|---|---|
| **J29** | D2 | ½p emerald | 37.50 | *80.00* |
| **J30** | D2 | 1p emerald | 150.00 | 80.00 |
| **J31** | D2 | 2p emerald | 300.00 | 175.00 |
| **J32** | D2 | 4p emerald | 300.00 | 165.00 |
| **J33** | D2 | 6p emerald | 350.00 | 250.00 |
| | | *Nos. J29-J33 (5)* | 1,138. | 750.00 |

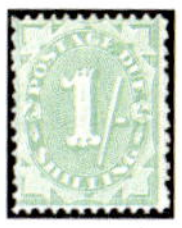

D3

***Perf. 11 (2sh, 10sh, 20sh), 11½x11 (1sh, 5sh)***
**1908-09 Wmk. 12**

| | | | | |
|---|---|---|---|---|
| **J34** | D3 | 1sh emer ('09) | 125.00 | 17.50 |
| **J35** | D3 | 2sh emerald | *1,050.* | *18,000.* |
| **J36** | D3 | 5sh emerald | 275.00 | 52.50 |
| **J37** | D3 | 10sh emerald | *2,750.* | *27,500.* |
| **J38** | D3 | 20sh emerald | *7,500.* | *52,500.* |

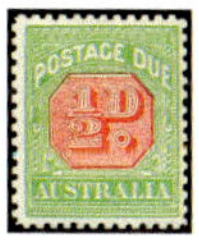

D4

**1909-23 Wmk. 13 *Perf. 12x12½***

| | | | | |
|---|---|---|---|---|
| **J39** | D4 | ½p grn & car | 32.00 | *45.00* |
| *a.* | | Perf 11, grn & rose ('14) | 20.00 | 17.00 |
| *b.* | | Perf 12½, grn & scar ('13) | 37.50 | 29.00 |
| *c.* | | Perf 14 ('19) | 20.00 | 10.00 |
| **J40** | D4 | 1p grn & car | 23.00 | 9.75 |
| *a.* | | Perf 11, yel grn & rose, thicker paper, thick yellowish gum | 4,000. | 1,500. |
| *b.* | | Perf 11, brt apple grn & rose, thin paper, thin white gum ('14) | 20.00 | 8.50 |
| *c.* | | Perf 14 ('14) | 70.00 | 17.00 |
| **J41** | D4 | 2p grn & car | 40.00 | 6.00 |
| *a.* | | Perf 11 | *35,000.* | *13,750.* |
| *b.* | | Perf 14 ('18) | 29.00 | 7.50 |
| **J42** | D4 | 3p grn & car | 35.00 | 14.50 |
| *a.* | | Perf 14, green & rose ('16) | 150.00 | 52.00 |
| **J43** | D4 | 4p grn & car | 24.00 | 11.50 |
| *a.* | | Perf 14 ('21) | 200.00 | 70.00 |
| **J44** | D4 | 6p grn & car | 30.00 | 4.50 |
| *a.* | | Perf 11 | *37,000.* | *25,000.* |
| **J45** | D4 | 1sh grn & car | 33.00 | 9.25 |
| *a.* | | Perf 14, yel grn & scarlet ('23) | 45.00 | 23.00 |
| **J46** | D4 | 2sh grn & car | 115.00 | 16.00 |
| **J47** | D4 | 5sh grn & car | 175.00 | 17.00 |
| **J48** | D4 | 10sh grn & car | 275.00 | 170.00 |
| *a.* | | Perf 14, yel grn & scarlet ('21) | 1,500. | |
| **J49** | D4 | £1 grn & car | 525.00 | 325.00 |
| *a.* | | Perf 14, yel grn & scar ('21) | 1,000. | |
| | | *Nos. J39-J49 (11)* | 1,307. | 628.50 |

Nos. J39-J48 and J40a, J41a, J44a are from the 1909 printings and have thicker paper and thick yellowish gum. The other listings are from the 1912-23 printings on thinner paper with thin white gum.

**1922-30 Wmk. 10 *Perf. 14, 11 (4p)***

| | | | | |
|---|---|---|---|---|
| **J50** | D4 | ½p grn & car ('23) | 9.25 | 7.50 |
| **J51** | D4 | 1p green & car | 7.50 | 2.25 |
| **J52** | D4 | 1½p grn & rose ('25) | 4.25 | 7.50 |
| **J53** | D4 | 2p green & car | 9.25 | 4.25 |
| **J54** | D4 | 3p green & car | 17.00 | 3.25 |
| **J55** | D4 | 4p grn & car ('30) | 17.00 | 8.00 |
| *a.* | | Perf 14 | 52.00 | 23.00 |
| **J56** | D4 | 6p green & car | 37.50 | 18.50 |
| | | *Nos. J50-J56 (7)* | 101.75 | 51.25 |
| | | Set, never hinged | 200.00 | |

**1931-36 Wmk. 228 *Perf. 11***

| | | | | |
|---|---|---|---|---|
| **J57** | D4 | ½p yel grn & rose ('34) | 23.00 | 23.00 |
| **J58** | D4 | 1p yel grn & rose ('32) | 9.00 | 2.25 |
| *a.* | | Perf 14 | 14.00 | 11.50 |
| **J59** | D4 | 2p yel grn & rose ('33) | 10.50 | 2.25 |
| *a.* | | Perf 14 | 11.50 | 11.50 |
| **J60** | D4 | 3p yel grn & rose ('36) | 140.00 | 115.00 |
| **J61** | D4 | 4p yel grn & rose ('34) | 29.00 | 4.50 |
| **J62** | D4 | 6p yel grn & rose ('36) | 550.00 | 500.00 |
| **J63** | D4 | 1sh yel grn & rose ('34) | 70.00 | 30.00 |
| | | *Nos. J57-J63 (7)* | 831.50 | 677.00 |
| | | Set, never hinged | 1,400. | |

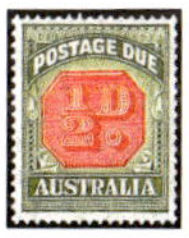

D5

**Engraved; Value Typo.**
**1938 *Perf. 14½x14***

| | | | | |
|---|---|---|---|---|
| **J64** | D5 | ½p green & car | 3.50 | *3.50* |
| **J65** | D5 | 1p green & car | 12.50 | 1.10 |
| **J66** | D5 | 2p green & car | 12.50 | 2.25 |
| **J67** | D5 | 3p green & car | 55.00 | 23.00 |
| **J68** | D5 | 4p green & car | 16.00 | 1.10 |

| | | | | |
|---|---|---|---|---|
| **J69** | D5 | 6p green & car | 100.00 | 45.00 |
| **J70** | D5 | 1sh green & car | 57.50 | 20.00 |
| | | *Nos. J64-J70 (7)* | 257.00 | 95.95 |
| | | Set, never hinged | 400.00 | |

**Catalogue values for unused stamps in this section, from this point to the end of the section, are for Never Hinged items.**

### Type of 1938
### Value Tablet Redrawn

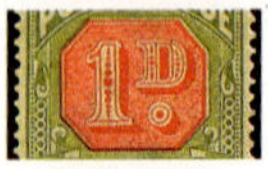

Original

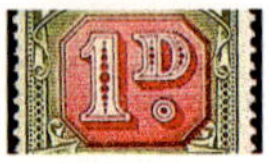

Redrawn

Pence denominations: "D" has melon-shaped center in redrawn tablet. The 1909-45 3p differs slightly, having no vertical white stroke half filling the right side of "D" center.

1sh. 1938: Numeral "1" narrow, with six background lines above.

1sh. 1947: Numeral broader, showing more white space around dotted central ornament. Three lines above.

**1946-57** **Wmk. 228**

| | | | | |
|---|---|---|---|---|
| **J71** | D5 | ½p grn & car ('56) | 7.00 | 5.75 |
| **J72** | D5 | 1p grn & car ('47) | 4.50 | 1.10 |
| **J73** | D5 | 2p green & car | 8.00 | 1.10 |
| **J74** | D5 | 3p green & car | 10.00 | 1.10 |
| **J75** | D5 | 4p grn & car ('52) | 14.00 | 1.40 |
| **J76** | D5 | 5p grn & car ('48) | 18.50 | 2.25 |
| **J77** | D5 | 6p grn & car ('47) | 18.50 | 2.90 |
| **J78** | D5 | 7p grn & car ('53) | 8.00 | 7.00 |
| **J79** | D5 | 8p grn & car ('57) | 26.00 | 23.00 |
| **J80** | D5 | 1sh grn & car ('47) | 29.00 | 4.50 |
| | | *Nos. J71-J80 (10)* | 143.50 | 50.10 |

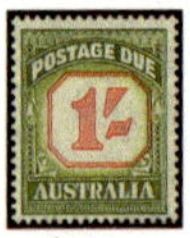


D5a

**1953-54**

### White Tablet, Carmine Numeral

| | | | | |
|---|---|---|---|---|
| **J81** | D5a | 1sh grn & car ('54) | 10.00 | 6.25 |
| **J82** | D5a | 2sh green & car | 16.00 | 14.50 |
| **J83** | D5a | 5sh green & car | 15.00 | 8.50 |
| | | *Nos. J81-J83 (3)* | 41.00 | 29.25 |

Issued: 2sh, 5sh, Aug. 26; 1sh, Feb. 17.

### Redrawn Type of 1947-57

Two Types of Some Pence Values:

Type I — Background lines touch numeral, "D" and period.

Type II — Lines do not touch numeral, etc.

Second engraving of 1sh has sharper and thicker lines.

The ½p type II has 7 dots under the "2."

The 8p type II has distinct lines in centers of "8" and between "8" and "D."

### Engr.; Value Typo.

**1958-60** **Unwmk.** ***Perf. 14½x14***

| | | | | |
|---|---|---|---|---|
| **J86** | D5 | ½p grn & car, II | 7.00 | 4.25 |
| *a.* | | Six dots under the "2" | 9.25 | 2.25 |
| **J87** | D5 | 1p grn & car, II | 5.75 | 1.10 |
| *a.* | | Type I | 5.75 | 2.25 |
| **J88** | D5 | 3p grn & car, II | 5.75 | 4.50 |
| **J89** | D5 | 4p grn & car, I | 11.50 | 10.00 |
| *a.* | | Type II ('59) | 9.25 | *9.25* |
| **J90** | D5 | 5p grn & car, I | 29.00 | 17.50 |
| *a.* | | Type II ('59) | 100.00 | 40.00 |
| **J91** | D5 | 6p grn & car, II | 10.00 | 5.25 |
| **J92** | D5 | 8p grn & car, II | 29.00 | *29.00* |
| *a.* | | Indistinct lines | 23.00 | 23.00 |
| **J93** | D5 | 10p grn & car, II | 17.00 | 6.25 |

### White Tablet, Carmine Numeral

| | | | | |
|---|---|---|---|---|
| **J94** | D5a | 1sh green & car | 29.00 | 7.00 |
| *a.* | | 2nd redrawing ('60) | 29.00 | 5.75 |
| **J95** | D5a | 2sh grn & car | 35.00 | 21.00 |
| | | *Nos. J86-J95 (10)* | 179.00 | 105.85 |

Issued: 1sh, 9/8/58; 10p, 12/9/59; 2sh, 3/8/60; 3p, 6p, 5/25/60; others, 2/27/58.

## MILITARY STAMPS

### Nos. 166, 191, 183A, 173, 175, 206 and 177 Overprinted in Black

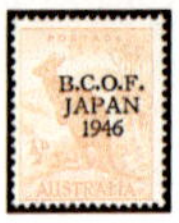


a

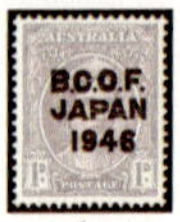


b

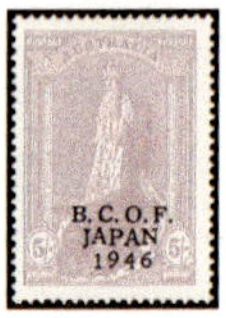


c

***Perf. 14½x14, 15x14, 11½, 13½x13***

**1946-47** **Wmk. 228**

| | | | | |
|---|---|---|---|---|
| **M1** | A24(a) | ½p orange | 3.50 | 3.50 |
| | | Never hinged | 5.75 | |
| **M2** | A36(b) | 1p brown vio | 3.50 | 3.50 |
| | | Never hinged | 5.75 | |
| *a.* | | Blue overprint | 115.00 | 77.50 |
| | | Never hinged | 140.00 | |
| **M3** | A27(b) | 3p dk vio brn | 3.50 | *3.50* |
| | | Never hinged | 5.75 | |
| *a.* | | Double overprint | *1,250.* | |
| **M4** | A30(a) | 6p brn violet | 12.00 | 11.50 |
| | | Never hinged | 18.00 | |
| **M5** | A16(a) | 1sh gray green | 12.00 | 11.50 |
| | | Never hinged | 18.00 | |
| **M6** | A1(c) | 2sh dk red brn | 35.00 | 45.00 |
| | | Never hinged | 70.00 | |
| **M7** | A32(c) | 5sh dl red brn | 140.00 | *200.00* |
| | | Never hinged | 250.00 | |
| | | *Nos. M1-M7 (7)* | 209.50 | 278.50 |

"B.C.O.F." stands for "British Commonwealth Occupation Force."

Issue dates: Nos. M1-M3, Oct. 11, 1946, Nos. M4-M7, May 8, 1947.

## OFFICIAL STAMPS

Overprinted Official stamps are comparatively more difficult to find well centered than the basic issues on which they are printed. This is because poorly centered sheets that had been discarded were purposely chosen to be overprinted to save money.

### Perforated Initials

**In 1913-31, postage stamps were perforated "OS" for federal official use. The Scott Standard Catalogues do not list officials with perforated initials, but listings for these Australian stamps will be found in the *Scott Classic Specialized Catalogue.***

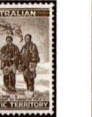

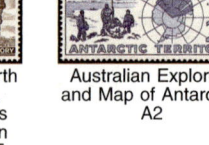

Overprinted

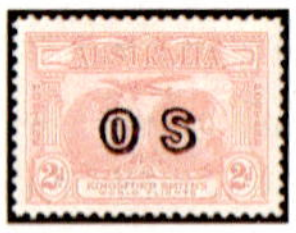


### On Regular Issue of 1931

**1931, May 4** **Unwmk.** ***Perf. 11, 11½***

| | | | | |
|---|---|---|---|---|
| **O1** | A8 | 2p dull red | 60.00 | 22.50 |
| **O2** | A8 | 3p blue | 225.00 | 35.00 |

These stamps were issued primarily for official use but to prevent speculation a quantity was issued for public distribution.

Used values are for CTO examples.

Counterfeit overprints exist.

### On Regular Issues of 1928-32

**1932** **Wmk. 203** ***Perf. 13½x12½***

| | | | | |
|---|---|---|---|---|
| **O3** | A4 | 2p red (II) | 25.00 | 13.00 |
| **O4** | A4 | 4p olive bister | 40.00 | 26.00 |

***Perf. 11½, 12***

| | | | | |
|---|---|---|---|---|
| **O5** | A1 | 6p brown | 97.50 | 90.00 |

**1932-33** **Wmk. 228** ***Perf. 13½x12½***

| | | | | |
|---|---|---|---|---|
| **O6** | A4 | ½p orange | 11.00 | 1.65 |
| *a.* | | Inverted overprint | *30,000.* | *21,000.* |
| **O7** | A4 | 1p green (I) | 6.00 | .50 |
| **O8** | A4 | 2p red (II) | 25.00 | .60 |
| *a.* | | Inverted overprint | | *47,500.* |
| **O9** | A4 | 3p ultra (II) ('33) | 10.00 | 5.00 |
| **O10** | A4 | 5p brown buff | 52.50 | 30.00 |

***Perf. 11½, 12***

| | | | | |
|---|---|---|---|---|
| **O11** | A1 | 6p yel brn | 42.50 | 22.50 |
| *a.* | | Inverted overprint | | *72,500.* |
| | | *Nos. O6-O11 (6)* | 147.00 | 60.25 |
| | | Set, never hinged | 275.00 | |

**1932** **Unwmk.** ***Perf. 11, 11½***

| | | | | |
|---|---|---|---|---|
| **O12** | A9 | 2p red | 7.25 | 6.00 |
| **O13** | A9 | 3p blue | 24.00 | 24.00 |
| **O14** | A16 | 1sh gray green | 72.50 | 52.50 |
| | | *Nos. O12-O14 (3)* | 103.75 | 82.50 |
| | | Set, never hinged | 160.00 | |

## AUSTRALIAN ANTARCTIC TERRITORY

**Catalogue values for all unused stamps in this section are for Never Hinged items.**

All stamps, except Nos. L1-L7, are also valid for postage in Australia.

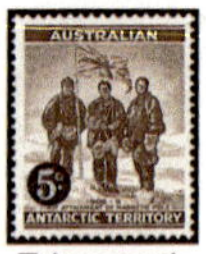


Edgeworth David, Douglas Mawson and A.F. McKay (1908-09 South Pole Expedition) A1

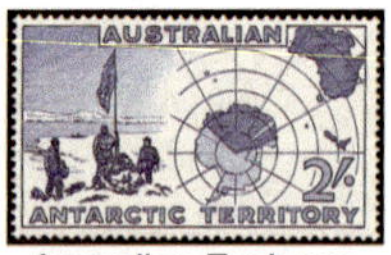


Australian Explorers and Map of Antarctica A2

Designs: 8p, Loading weasel (snow truck). 1sh, Dog team and iceberg, vert. 2sh3p, Emperor penguins and map, vert.

***Perf. 14½, 14½x14, 14x14½***

**1957-59** **Engr.** **Unwmk.**

| | | | | |
|---|---|---|---|---|
| **L1** | A1 | 5p brown | .65 | .30 |
| **L2** | A2 | 8p dark blue | 2.25 | 1.00 |
| **L3** | A2 | 1sh dark green | 2.75 | 1.75 |
| **L4** | A2 | 2sh ultra ('57) | 1.50 | .90 |
| **L5** | A2 | 2sh3p green | 7.50 | 3.50 |
| | | *Nos. L1-L5 (5)* | 14.65 | 7.45 |
| | | Set, hinged | 8.50 | |

Nos. L1 and L2 were printed as 4p and 7p stamps and surcharged typographically in black and dark blue before issuance.

Sizes of stamps: No. L2, 34x21mm; Nos. L3, L5, 21x34mm; No. L4, 43½x25½mm.

**1961, July 5** ***Perf. 14½***

| | | | | |
|---|---|---|---|---|
| **L6** | A1 | 5p dark blue | 1.00 | .45 |

The denomination on No. L6 is not within a typographed circle, but is part of the engraved design.

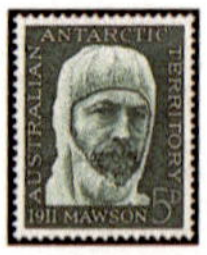


Sir Douglas Mawson — A3

**1961, Oct. 18**

| | | | | |
|---|---|---|---|---|
| **L7** | A3 | 5p dark green | .50 | .40 |

50th anniv. of the 1911-14 Australian Antarctic Expedition.

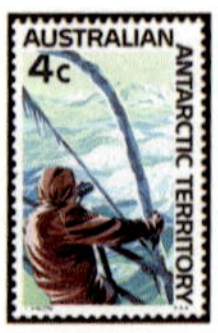


Lookout and Iceberg — A4

Designs: 1c, Aurora australis and camera dome. 2c, Banding penguins. 5c, Branding of elephant seals. 7c, Measuring snow strata. 10c, Wind gauges. 15c, Weather balloon. 20c, Helicopter. 25c, Radio operator. 50c, Ice compression tests. $1, "Mock sun" (parhelion) and dogs. 20c, 25c, 50c and $1 horizontal.

***Perf. 13½x13, 13x13½***

**1966-68** **Photo.** **Unwmk.**

| | | | | |
|---|---|---|---|---|
| **L8** | A4 | 1c multicolored | .50 | .30 |
| **L9** | A4 | 2c multicolored | .50 | *.75* |
| **L10** | A4 | 4c multicolored | .60 | .50 |
| **L11** | A4 | 5c multicolored | 1.40 | .50 |
| **L12** | A4 | 7c multicolored | .75 | .50 |
| **L13** | A4 | 10c multicolored | 1.00 | 1.00 |
| **L14** | A4 | 15c multicolored | 4.75 | 1.40 |
| **L15** | A4 | 20c multicolored | 8.00 | 2.75 |
| **L16** | A4 | 25c multicolored | 2.00 | 2.00 |
| **L17** | A4 | 50c multicolored | 5.00 | 4.00 |
| **L18** | A4 | $1 multicolored | 20.00 | 12.00 |
| | | *Nos. L8-L18 (11)* | 44.50 | 25.70 |
| | | Set, hinged | 34.00 | |

Issued: 5c, 9/25/68; others, 9/28/66.

Nos. L8-L18 are on phosphorescent helecon paper. Fluorescent orange is one of the colors used in printing the 10c, 15c, 20c and 50c.

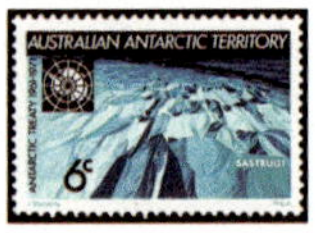


Sastrugi Snow Formation — A5

**1971, June 23** **Photo.** ***Perf. 13x13½***

| | | | | |
|---|---|---|---|---|
| **L19** | A5 | 6c shown | .85 | .65 |
| **L20** | A5 | 30c Pancake ice | 4.50 | *3.50* |

10th anniv. of the Antarctic Treaty pledging peaceful uses of and scientific cooperation in Antarctica.

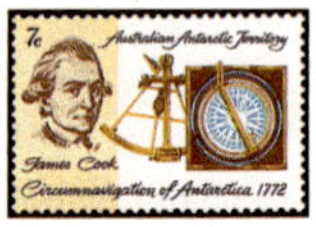


Capt. Cook, Sextant, Azimuth Compass — A6

Design: 35c, Chart of Cook's circumnavigation of Antarctica, and "Resolution."

**1972, Sept. 13** **Photo.** ***Perf. 13x13½***

| | | | | |
|---|---|---|---|---|
| **L21** | A6 | 7c bister & multi | 1.05 | .75 |
| **L22** | A6 | 35c buff & multi | 4.25 | 4.25 |

Bicentenary of Capt. James Cook's circumnavigation of Antarctica.

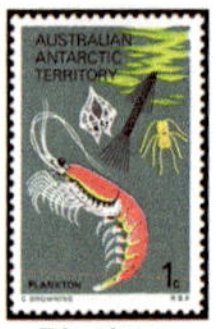


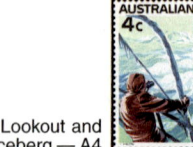

Plankton and Krill Shrimp A7

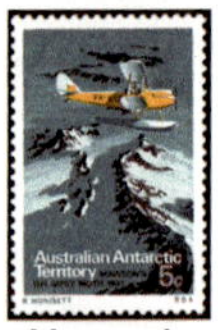


Mawson's D.H. Gipsy Moth, 1931 A8

Food Chain (Essential for Survival): 7c, Adelie penguin feeding on krill shrimp. 9c, Leopard seal pursuing fish, horiz. 10c, Killer whale hunting seals, horiz. 20c, Wandering albatross, horiz. $1, Sperm whale attacking giant squid.

Explorers' Aircraft: 8c, Rymill's DH Fox Moth returning to Barry Island. 25c, Hubert Wilkins Lockheed Vega, horiz. 30c, Lincoln Ellsworth's Northrop Gamma. 35c, Lars Christensen's Avro Avian and Framnes Mountains, horiz. 50c, Richard Byrd's Ford Tri-Motor dropping US flag over South Pole.

***Perf. 13½x13, 13x13½***

**1973, Aug. 15**

| | | | | |
|---|---|---|---|---|
| **L23** | A7 | 1c multicolored | .25 | .25 |
| **L24** | A8 | 5c multicolored | .25 | .25 |
| **L25** | A7 | 7c multicolored | 1.00 | .90 |
| **L26** | A8 | 8c multicolored | .25 | *.50* |
| **L27** | A7 | 9c multicolored | .25 | .25 |
| **L28** | A7 | 10c multicolored | 2.50 | 1.75 |
| **L29** | A7 | 20c multicolored | .70 | .60 |
| **L30** | A8 | 25c multicolored | .55 | .60 |
| **L31** | A8 | 30c multicolored | .55 | *.70* |
| **L32** | A8 | 35c multicolored | .55 | *.70* |
| **L33** | A8 | 50c multicolored | 1.00 | *.75* |
| **L34** | A7 | $1 multicolored | 1.75 | *2.00* |
| | | *Nos. L23-L34 (12)* | 9.60 | 9.25 |

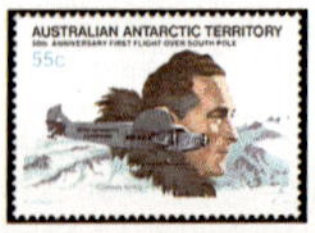


Adm. Byrd, Plane, Mountains — A9

Design: 20c, Adm. Byrd, Floyd Bennett tri-motored plane, map of Antarctica.

**1979, June 20 Litho. *Perf. 15½***

| | | | | |
|---|---|---|---|---|
| **L35** | A9 | 20c multicolored | .40 | *.60* |
| **L36** | A9 | 55c multicolored | .85 | *1.10* |

50th anniv. of first flight over South Pole by Richard Byrd (1888-1957).

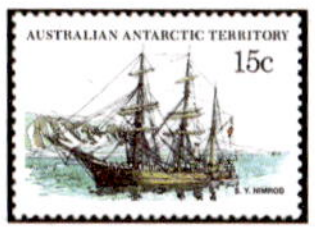


"S.Y. Nimrod" — A10

Designs: 1c, S.Y. Aurora. 2c, R.Y. Penola. 5c, M.V. Thala Dan. 10c, H.M.S. Challenger. No. L41, S.S. Morning. No. L42, S.Y. Nimrod, stern view. 20c, R.R.S. Discovery II. 22c, R.Y.S. Terra Nova. 25c, S.S. Endurance. 30c, S.S. Fram. 35c, M.S. Nella Dan. 40c, M.S. Kista Dan. 45c, L'Astrolabe. 50c, S.S. Norvegia. 55c, S.Y. Discovery. $1, H.M.S. Resolution.

2c, 5c, 22c, 25c, 40c, 55c, $1 are vertical.

***Perf. 13½x13, 13x13½***

**1979-81 Litho.**

| | | | | |
|---|---|---|---|---|
| **L37** | A10 | 1c multi | .25 | .25 |
| **L38** | A10 | 2c multi | .25 | .25 |
| **L39** | A10 | 5c multi | .25 | *.25* |
| **L40** | A10 | 10c multi | .30 | *.25* |
| **L41** | A10 | 15c multi | 1.15 | *2.60* |
| **L42** | A10 | 15c shown | .25 | *.30* |
| **L43** | A10 | 20c multi | .30 | *1.00* |
| **L44** | A10 | 22c multi | .50 | *.30* |
| **L45** | A10 | 25c multi | .50 | *.70* |
| **L46** | A10 | 30c multi | .50 | *1.30* |
| **L47** | A10 | 35c multi | .60 | *1.30* |
| **L48** | A10 | 40c multi | .80 | *1.30* |
| **L49** | A10 | 45c multi | .80 | *1.30* |
| **L50** | A10 | 50c multi | .80 | *1.00* |
| **L51** | A10 | 55c multi | 1.00 | *2.60* |
| **L52** | A10 | $1 multi | 2.00 | *3.25* |
| | | *Nos. L37-L52 (16)* | 10.25 | *17.95* |

Issued: 5c, 20c, 25c, 30c, 55c, 8/29; 1c, No. L41, 22c, 35c, $1, 5/21/80; 2c, 10c, No. L42, 40c, 45c, 50c, 9/9/81.

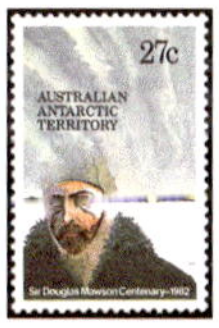


A11

**1982, May 5 Litho. *Perf. 14x13½***

| | | | | |
|---|---|---|---|---|
| **L53** | A11 | 27c Mawson, landscape | .35 | *.25* |
| **L54** | A11 | 75c Mawson, map | 1.00 | *1.40* |

Sir Douglas Mawson (1882-1958), explorer.

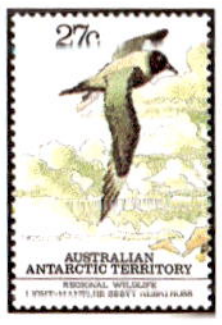


A12

Local Wildlife: a, Light-mantled sooty albatross. b, Macquarie Isld. shags. c, Elephant seals. d, Royal penguins. e, Antarctic prions.

**1983, Apr. 6 Litho. *Perf. 14½***

| | | | | |
|---|---|---|---|---|
| **L55** | | Strip of 5, multi | 3.50 | 3.50 |
| ***a.-e.*** | | A12 27c, any single | .70 | .50 |

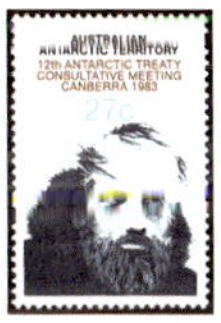


12th Antarctic Treaty Consultative Meeting, Canberra, Sept. 13-27 — A13

**1983, Sept. 7 Litho. *Perf. 14½***

| | | | | |
|---|---|---|---|---|
| **L56** | A13 | 27c multicolored | .45 | .50 |

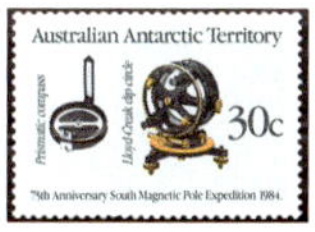


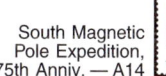

South Magnetic Pole Expedition, 75th Anniv. — A14

**1984, Jan. 16**

| | | | | |
|---|---|---|---|---|
| **L57** | A14 | 30c Prismatic compass | .50 | .50 |
| **L58** | A14 | 85c Aneroid barometer | 1.50 | *2.00* |

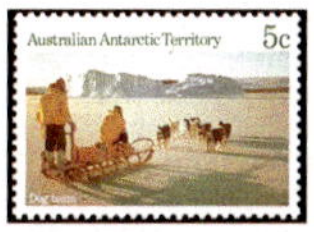


Dog Team, Mawson Station — A15

2c, Summer afternoon. 10c, Evening. 15c, Prince Charles Mts. 20c, Morning. 25c, Sea ice, iceberg. 30c, Mt. Coates. 33c, Iceberg Alley, Mawson. 36c, Winter evening. 45c, Brash ice, vert. 60c, Midwinter shadows. 75c, Coastline. 85c, Landing field. 90c, Pancake ice, vert. $1, Emperor penguins, Auster Rookery.

**1984-87 Litho. *Perf. 14½x15***

| | | | | |
|---|---|---|---|---|
| **L60** | A15 | 2c multi | .25 | .25 |
| **L61** | A15 | 5c shown | .25 | .25 |
| **L62** | A15 | 10c multi | .25 | .25 |
| **L63** | A15 | 15c multi | .30 | .25 |
| **L64** | A15 | 20c multi | .35 | .30 |
| **L65** | A15 | 25c multi | .40 | .35 |
| **L66** | A15 | 30c multi | .50 | .45 |
| **L67** | A15 | 33c multi | .55 | .45 |
| **L68** | A15 | 36c multi | .60 | .30 |
| **L69** | A15 | 45c multi | .75 | .65 |
| **L70** | A15 | 60c multi | 1.00 | .80 |
| **L71** | A15 | 75c multi | 1.25 | 1.10 |
| **L72** | A15 | 85c multi | 1.50 | 1.25 |
| **L73** | A15 | 90c multi | 1.50 | 1.25 |
| **L74** | A15 | $1 multi | 1.75 | 1.40 |
| | | *Nos. L60-L74 (15)* | 11.20 | 9.30 |

Issued: 5, 25, 30, 75, 85c, 7/18/84; 15, 33, 45, 90c, $1, 8/7/85; 2, 10, 20, 36, 60c, 3/11/87.

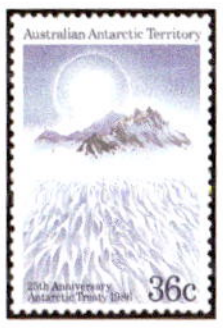


Antarctic Treaty, 25th Anniv. — A16

**1986, Sept. 17 Litho. *Perf. 14x13½***

| | | | | |
|---|---|---|---|---|
| **L75** | A16 | 36c multicolored | 1.00 | .85 |

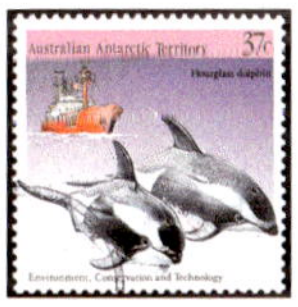


Environment, Conservation and Technology — A17

No. L76: a, Hour-glass dolphins and the *Nella Dan.* b, Emperor penguins and Davis Station. c, Crabeater seal and helicopters. d, Adelie penguins and snow-ice transport vehicle. e, Gray-headed albatross and photographer.

**1988, July 20 Litho. *Perf. 13***

| | | | | |
|---|---|---|---|---|
| **L76** | | Strip of 5 | 6.00 | 6.00 |
| ***a.-e.*** | | A17 37c any single | 1.05 | 1.05 |

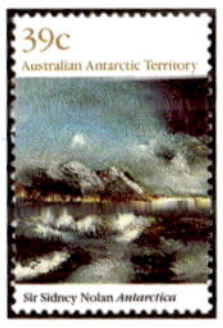


Paintings by Sir Sidney Nolan (b. 1917) — A18

No. L77, Antarctica. No. L78, Iceberg Alley. No. L79, Glacial Flow. No. L80, Frozen Sea.

**1989, June 14 Litho. *Perf. 14x13½***

| | | | | |
|---|---|---|---|---|
| **L77** | A18 | 39c multicolored | .90 | .60 |
| **L78** | A18 | 39c multicolored | .90 | .60 |
| **L79** | A18 | 60c multicolored | 1.50 | 1.50 |
| **L80** | A18 | 80c multicolored | 2.25 | 2.25 |
| | | *Nos. L77-L80 (4)* | 5.55 | 4.95 |

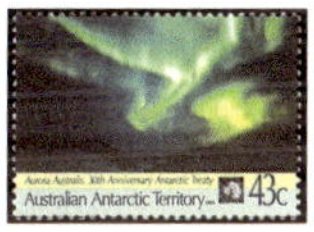


Aurora Australis — A19

Design: $1.20, Research ship Aurora Australis.

**1991, June 20 Litho. *Perf. 14½***

| | | | | |
|---|---|---|---|---|
| **L81** | A19 | 43c multicolored | .80 | .80 |
| **L82** | A19 | $1.20 multicolored | 2.25 | 1.50 |

Antarctic Treaty, 30th anniv. (No. L81).

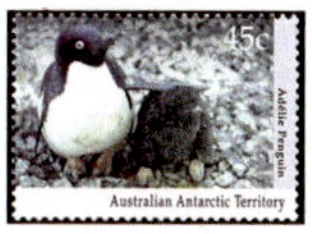


Regional Wildlife — A20

45c, Adelie penguin. 75c, Elephant seal. 85c, Northern giant petrel. 95c, Weddell seal. $1, Royal penguins. $1.20, Emperor penguin, vert. $1.40, Fur seals. $1.50, King penguins, vert.

***Perf. 14x14½, 14½x14***

**1992-93 Litho.**

| | | | | |
|---|---|---|---|---|
| **L83** | A20 | 45c multi | .75 | .65 |
| **L84** | A20 | 75c multi | 1.25 | 1.10 |
| **L85** | A20 | 85c multi | 1.50 | 1.40 |
| **L86** | A20 | 95c multi | 1.60 | 1.50 |
| **L86A** | A20 | $1 multi | 1.75 | 1.60 |
| **L87** | A20 | $1.20 multi | 1.90 | 1.75 |
| **L88** | A20 | $1.40 multi | 2.40 | 2.00 |
| **L89** | A20 | $1.50 multi | 2.60 | 2.25 |
| | | *Nos. L83-L89 (8)* | 13.75 | 12.25 |

Issued: $1, $1.40, $1.50, 1/14/93; others, 5/14/92.

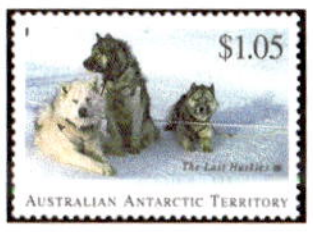


The Last Huskies — A21

45c, Dog up close, vert. 75c, Sled team. 85c, Dog seated, vert. $1.05, Three dogs.

**1994, Jan. 13 Litho. *Perf. 14½***

| | | | | |
|---|---|---|---|---|
| **L90** | A21 | 45c multi | 1.00 | .75 |
| **L91** | A21 | 75c multi | 1.50 | 1.50 |
| **L92** | A21 | 85c multi | 2.25 | 2.25 |
| **L93** | A21 | $1.05 multi | 2.50 | 2.50 |
| | | *Nos. L90-L93 (4)* | 7.25 | 7.00 |

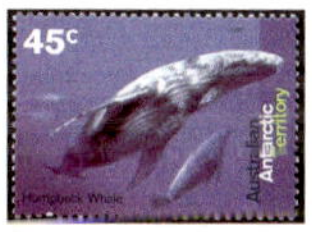


Whales & Dolphins — A22

**1995, June 15 Litho. *Perf. 14½***

| | | | | |
|---|---|---|---|---|
| **L94** | A22 | 45c Humpback whale | .95 | .85 |
| **L95** | A22 | 45c Hourglass dolphin, vert. | .95 | .85 |
| **L96** | A22 | 45c Minke whale, vert. | .95 | .85 |
| ***a.*** | | Pair, #L95-L96 | 2.25 | 2.25 |
| **L97** | A22 | $1 Killer whale | 2.50 | 2.50 |
| ***a.*** | | Souvenir sheet of 4, #L94-L97 | 7.75 | 7.75 |
| ***b.*** | | As "a," overprinted | *65.00* | *65.00* |
| ***c.*** | | As "a," overprinted | *40.00* | *40.00* |
| | | *Nos. L94-L97 (4)* | 5.35 | 5.05 |

No. L97b is overprinted in gold in sheet margin with Singapore '95 emblem and: "Australia Post Exhibition Sheet No. 2," and, in both Chinese and English, with "Singapore 95 World Stamp Exhibition."

No. L97c is overprinted in gold in sheet margin with exhibition emblem, "Australian Post Exhibition Sheet No. 3" and CAPEX '96 WORLD PHILATELIC EXHIBITION / EXPOSITION PHILATELIQUE MONDIALE.

Issued: No. L97b, 9/1/95; No. L97c, 6/15/96.

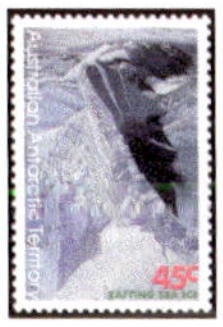


Landscapes, by Christian Clare Robertson — A23

Designs: No. L98, Rafting sea ice. No. L99, Shadow on the Plateau. $1, Ice cave. $1.20, Twelve Lake.

**1996, May 16 Litho. *Perf. 14½x14***

| | | | | |
|---|---|---|---|---|
| **L98** | A23 | 45c multicolored | 1.25 | .95 |
| **L99** | A23 | 45c multicolored | 1.25 | .95 |
| ***a.*** | | Pair, Nos. L98-L99 | 2.50 | 2.25 |
| **L100** | A23 | $1 multicolored | 2.25 | 2.50 |
| **L101** | A23 | $1.20 multicolored | 3.00 | 2.40 |
| | | *Nos. L98-L101 (4)* | 7.75 | 6.80 |

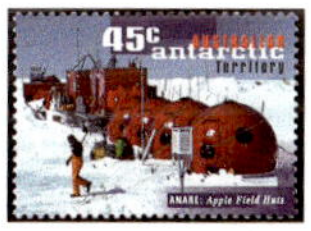


Australian Natl. Antarctic Research Expeditions, 50th Anniv. — A24

Designs: No. L102, Apple field huts. No. L103, Inside an apple hut. 95c, Summer surveying. $1.05, Sea ice research. $1.20, Remote field camp.

**1997, May 15 Litho. *Perf. 14x14½***

| | | | | |
|---|---|---|---|---|
| **L102** | A24 | 45c multicolored | 1.10 | .90 |
| **L103** | A24 | 45c multicolored | 1.10 | .90 |
| ***a.*** | | Pair, #L102-L103 | 2.25 | 2.25 |
| **L104** | A24 | 95c multicolored | 2.50 | 2.25 |
| **L105** | A24 | $1.05 multicolored | 2.10 | 2.40 |
| **L106** | A24 | $1.20 multicolored | 2.75 | 2.50 |
| | | *Nos. L102-L106 (5)* | 9.55 | 8.95 |

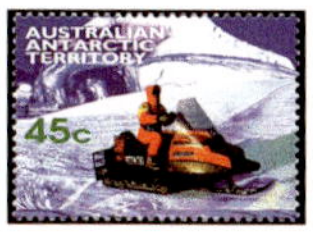


Modes of Transportation A25

Designs: No. L107, Snowmobile. No. L108, Ship, "Aurora Australis." $1, Helicopter airlifting a four-wheel drive ATV, vert. $2, Antarctic Hagglunds (rubber-tracked vehicles with fiberglass cabins), vert.

***Perf. 14x14½, 14½x14***

**1998, Mar. 5 Litho.**

| | | | | |
|---|---|---|---|---|
| **L107** | A25 | 45c multicolored | 1.00 | 1.00 |
| **L108** | A25 | 45c multicolored | 1.00 | 1.00 |
| ***a.*** | | Pair, #L107-L108 | 2.50 | 2.50 |
| **L109** | A25 | $1 multicolored | 2.50 | 3.00 |
| **L110** | A25 | $2 multicolored | 5.25 | 4.50 |
| | | *Nos. L107-L110 (4)* | 9.75 | 9.50 |

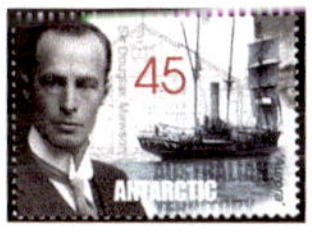


Preservation of Huts used During Mawson's Antarctic Expedition — A26

Designs: No. L111, Photograph of Mawson, sailing ship Aurora. No. L112, Photograph, "Home of the Blizzard," by Frank Hurley. 90c, Photograph, "Huskie Team," by Xavier Mertz. $1.35, Huts restoration.

**1999, May 13 Litho. *Perf. 14x14½***

| | | | | |
|---|---|---|---|---|
| **L111** | A26 | 45c multicolored | 1.00 | 1.00 |
| **L112** | A26 | 45c multicolored | 1.00 | 1.00 |
| ***a.*** | | Pair, #L111-L112 | 2.40 | 2.40 |
| **L113** | A26 | 90c multicolored | 2.75 | 3.00 |
| **L114** | A26 | $1.35 multicolored | 4.00 | 3.50 |
| | | *Nos. L111-L114 (4)* | 8.75 | 8.50 |

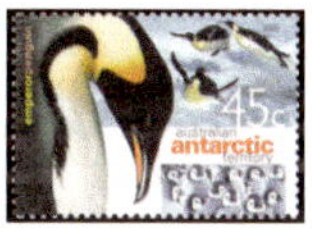


Penguins — A27

**2000, July 24 Litho. *Perf. 13¾x14½***

| | | | | |
|---|---|---|---|---|
| **L115** | A27 | 45c Emperor penguins | 1.25 | 1.25 |
| **L116** | A27 | 45c Adélie penguins | 1.25 | 1.25 |
| ***a.*** | | Pair, #L115-L116 | 4.75 | 4.75 |

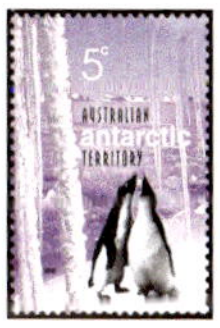


Australians in the Antarctic, Cent. — A28

No. L117: a, Penguins and icicles. b, Louis Bernacchi, physicist. c, Nimrod. d, Scientists at South Magnetic Pole. e, Griffith Taylor and Frank Debenham, geologists. f, First radio used in Antarctica. g, First flight over Antarctica. h, Sir Douglas Mawson, explorer. i, BANZARE (British, Australian and New Zealand Antarctic Research Expedition). j, Australia's claim to territory. k, Establishment of ANARE (Australian National Antarctic Research Expeditions). l, Transport. m, Aurora Australis. n, Climate research. o, Cold-weather clothing. p, Nella Dan. q, First women on Antarctica. r, Communications. s, Tourism. t, Satellite view of Antarctica.

**2001, May 17 Litho. *Perf. 14¾x14***

| | | | | |
|---|---|---|---|---|
| **L117** | | Sheet of 20 | 18.50 | 18.50 |
| ***a.-e.*** | | A28 5c Any single | .40 | .40 |
| ***f.-j.*** | | A28 10c Any single | .50 | .50 |
| ***k.-o.*** | | A28 25c Any single | .60 | .60 |
| ***p.-t.*** | | A28 45c Any single | .75 | .75 |

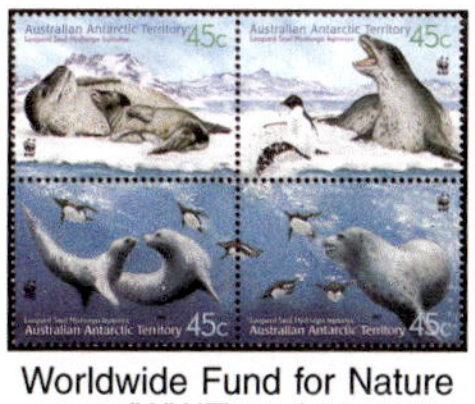


Worldwide Fund for Nature (WWF) — A29

No. L118: a, Leopard seal and pup on ice. b, Leopard seal and penguin on ice. c, Penguins, two leopard seals in water. d, Penguins, leopard seal in water.

**2001, Sept. 11 Litho. *Perf. 14x14½***

| | | | | |
|---|---|---|---|---|
| L118 | A29 | Block of 4 | 6.75 | 8.00 |
| *a.-d.* | | 45c Any single | 1.00 | 1.00 |

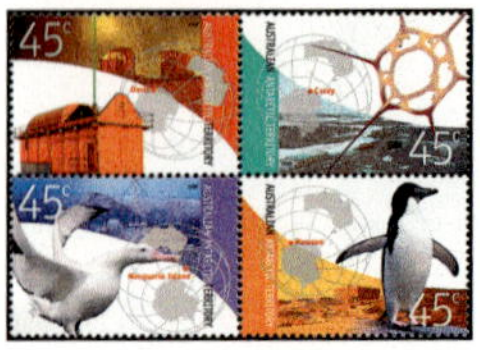

Antarctic Base Stations A30

Maps showing station locations and: a, Light Detection and Ranging Instrument, aurora australis, Davis Station. b, Diatom, Casey Station. c, Wandering albatross, Macquarie Island Station. d, Adèlie penguin, Mawson Station.

**2002, July 2 Litho. *Perf. 14x14¾***

| | | | | |
|---|---|---|---|---|
| L119 | A30 | Block of 4, #a-d | 7.00 | 7.00 |
| *a.-d.* | | 45c Any single | 1.00 | 1.00 |

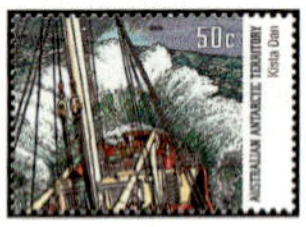

Ships — A31

Designs: No. L120, Kista Dan, No. L121, Magga Dan. $1, Thala Dan, vert. $1.45, Nella Dan, vert.

***Perf. 14x14½, 14½x14***

**2003, Apr. 29 Litho.**

| | | | | |
|---|---|---|---|---|
| L120 | A31 | 50c multi | 1.00 | 1.00 |
| L121 | A31 | 50c multi | 1.00 | 1.00 |
| *a.* | | Horiz. pair, #L120-L121 | 2.25 | 2.25 |
| L122 | A31 | $1 multi | 2.25 | 2.25 |
| L123 | A31 | $1.45 multi | 3.75 | 3.75 |
| | | *Nos. L120-L123 (4)* | 8.00 | 8.00 |

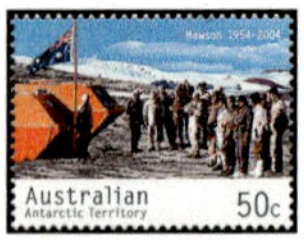

Mawson Station, 50th Anniv. — A32

Designs: No. L124, Naming ceremony, 1954. No. L125, Station buildings. $1, Barge and airplane. $1.45, Auster Emperor Penguin Rookery.

**2004, Feb. 13 Litho. *Perf. 14x14½***

| | | | | |
|---|---|---|---|---|
| L124 | A32 | 50c multi | 1.00 | 1.00 |
| L125 | A32 | 50c multi | 1.00 | 1.00 |
| *a.* | | Horiz. pair, #L124-L125 | 2.50 | 2.50 |
| L126 | A32 | $1 multi | 3.00 | 3.00 |
| L127 | A32 | $1.45 multi | 4.00 | 4.00 |
| | | *Nos. L124-L127 (4)* | 9.00 | 9.00 |

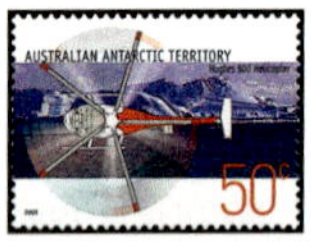

Aircraft — A33

Designs: No. L128, Hughes 500 helicopter. No. L129, De Havilland DHC-2 Beaver. $1, Pilatus PC-6 Porter. $1.45, Douglas DC-3/Dakota C-47.

**2005, Sept. 6 Litho. *Perf. 14x14½***

| | | | | |
|---|---|---|---|---|
| L128 | A33 | 50c multi | 1.00 | 1.00 |
| L129 | A33 | 50c multi | 1.00 | 1.00 |
| *a.* | | Horiz. pair, #L128-L129 | 2.25 | 2.25 |
| L130 | A33 | $1 multi | 2.75 | 2.75 |
| L131 | A33 | $1.45 multi | 4.50 | 4.50 |
| | | *Nos. L128-L131 (4)* | 9.25 | 9.25 |

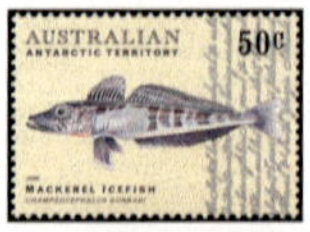

Fish — A34

Designs: No. L132, Mackerel icefish. No. L133, Lanternfish. No. L134, Eaton's skate. No. L135, Patagonian toothfish.

**2006, Aug. 1 Litho. *Perf. 14x14¾***

| | | | | |
|---|---|---|---|---|
| L132 | A34 | 50c multi | .90 | .90 |
| L133 | A34 | 50c multi | .90 | .90 |
| *a.* | | Horiz. pair, #L132-L133 | 2.50 | 2.50 |
| L134 | A34 | $1 multi | 2.00 | 2.00 |
| L135 | A34 | $1 multi | 2.00 | 2.00 |
| *a.* | | Horiz. pair, #L134-L135 | 5.00 | 5.00 |
| | | *Nos. L132-L135 (4)* | 5.80 | 5.80 |

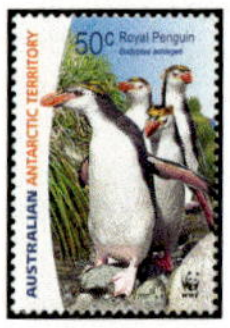

Worldwide Fund For Nature (WWF) — A35

Royal penguins: No. L136, Four marching. No. L137, Nesting. No. L138, Two contesting territory (denomination at bottom), horiz. No. L139, Two courting (denomination at left), horiz.

**2007, Aug. 7 Litho. *Perf. 14½x14***

| | | | | |
|---|---|---|---|---|
| L136 | A35 | 50c multi | 1.00 | 1.00 |
| L137 | A35 | 50c multi | 1.00 | 1.00 |
| *a.* | | Horiz. pair, #L136-L137 | 2.75 | 2.00 |

***Perf. 14x14½***

| | | | | |
|---|---|---|---|---|
| L138 | A35 | $1 multi | 1.50 | 1.50 |
| L139 | A35 | $1 multi | 1.50 | 1.50 |
| *a.* | | Vert. pair, #L138-L139 | 5.75 | 4.75 |
| | | *Nos. L136-L139 (4)* | 5.00 | 5.00 |

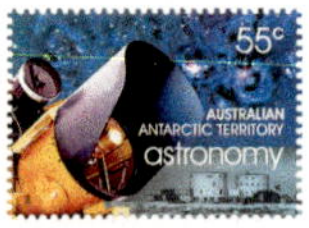

International Polar Year — A36

Designs: No. L140, Astronomy. No. L141, Glaciology. No. L142, Marine biology. No. L143, Oceanography.

**2008, Sept. 16 Litho. *Perf. 14x14½***

| | | | | |
|---|---|---|---|---|
| L140 | A36 | 55c multi | 1.00 | 1.00 |
| L141 | A36 | 55c multi | 1.00 | 1.00 |
| *a.* | | Vert. pair, #L140-L141 | 3.00 | 2.75 |
| L142 | A36 | $1.10 multi | 1.75 | 1.75 |
| L143 | A36 | $1.10 multi | 1.75 | 1.75 |
| *a.* | | Vert. pair, #L142-L143 | 6.00 | 6.00 |
| *b.* | | Souvenir sheet, #L140-L143 | 11.50 | 12.50 |
| | | *Nos. L140-L143 (4)* | 5.50 | 5.50 |

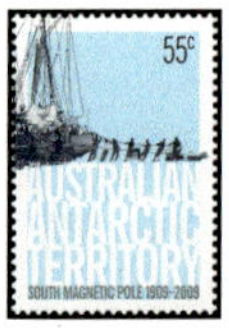

Discovery of South Magnetic Pole, Cent. — A37

Designs: No. L144, Crew unloading the Nimrod. No. L145, Crew depositing expedition provisions by automobile. No. L146, Men at Northern Party camp. No. L147, Alistair Mackay, Douglas Mawson,and Edgeworth David with flag at South Magnetic Pole.

**2009, Jan. 8 Litho. *Perf. 14½x14***

| | | | | |
|---|---|---|---|---|
| L144 | A37 | 55c lt bl & blk | 1.00 | .75 |
| L145 | A37 | 55c lt bl & multi | 1.00 | .75 |
| *a.* | | Horiz. pair, #L144-L145 | 2.40 | 2.60 |
| L146 | A37 | $1.10 lt bl & blk | 2.40 | 1.60 |
| L147 | A37 | $1.10 lt bl & blk | 2.40 | 1.60 |
| *a.* | | Horiz. pair, #L146-L147 | 5.00 | 5.00 |
| *b.* | | Souvenir sheet, #L144-L147 | 7.50 | 8.00 |
| | | *Nos. L144-L147 (4)* | 6.80 | 4.70 |

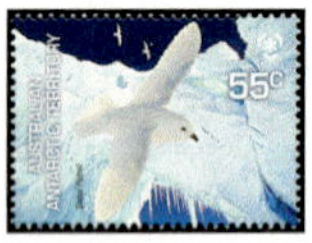

International Polar Year — A38

Designs: 55c, Snow petrel. $2.05, Jade iceberg.

**2009, Mar. 4 Litho. *Perf. 14x14¾***

| | | | | |
|---|---|---|---|---|
| L148 | A38 | 55c multi | 1.60 | 1.30 |
| L149 | A38 | $2.05 multi | 5.00 | 3.25 |
| *a.* | | Souvenir sheet, #L148-L149 | 8.00 | 4.50 |
| *b.* | | Sheet of 2, Australia #3337, Australian Antarctic Terr. #L149 | 10.00 | 10.00 |

Issued: No. L149b, 8/20/10. Stampex 2010, Adelaide (No. L149b).

For Endangered Wildlife stamps inscribed "Australian Antarctic Territory" see Australia Nos. 3128 and 3134.

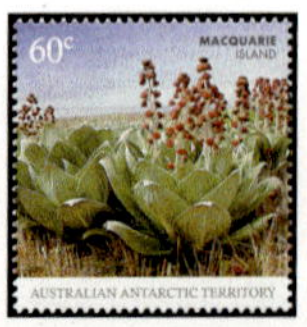

Macquarie Island — A39

Designs: No. L150, Pleurophyllum hookeri (flower). No. L151, Southern elephant seal. No. L152, Mawson Point Stacks (green terrain). No. L153, Caroline Cove (brown terrain).

**2010, Oct. 26 Litho. *Perf. 14¼***

| | | | | |
|---|---|---|---|---|
| L150 | A39 | 60c multi | 1.00 | 1.00 |
| L151 | A39 | 60c multi | 1.00 | 1.00 |
| *a.* | | Horiz. pair, #L150-L151 | 3.00 | 3.00 |
| L152 | A39 | $1.20 multi | 1.90 | 1.90 |
| L153 | A39 | $1.20 multi | 1.90 | 1.90 |
| *a.* | | Horiz. pair, #L152-L153 | 6.00 | 6.00 |
| *b.* | | Souvenir sheet, #L150-L153 | 12.00 | 12.00 |
| | | *Nos. L150-L153 (4)* | 5.80 | 5.80 |

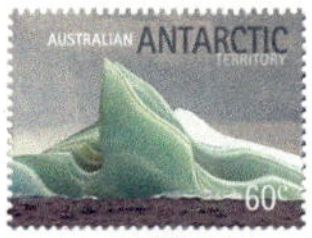

A40

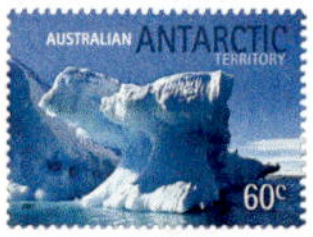

A41

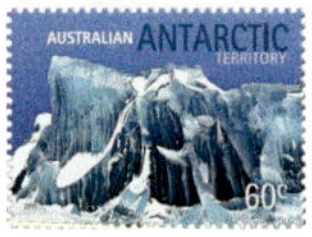

A42

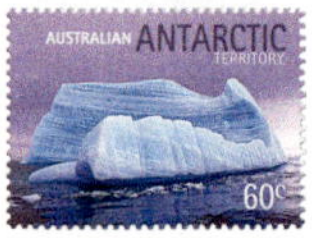

Icebergs — A43

**2011, June 7 Litho. *Perf. 14x14¾***

| | | | | |
|---|---|---|---|---|
| L154 | | Block of 4 | 5.00 | 5.00 |
| *a.* | | A40 60c multi | 1.00 | 1.00 |
| *b.* | | A41 60c multi | 1.00 | 1.00 |
| *c.* | | A42 60c multi | 1.00 | 1.00 |
| *d.* | | A43 60c multi | 1.00 | 1.00 |
| *e.* | | Souvenir sheet of 4, #L154a-L154d | 8.00 | 8.00 |

**Booklet Stamps**
**Self-Adhesive**
**Stamps With Grayed Frame**

***Serpentine Die Cut 11¼ Syncopated***

| | | | | |
|---|---|---|---|---|
| L155 | A40 | 60c multi | 1.00 | .30 |
| L156 | A41 | 60c multi | 1.00 | .30 |
| L157 | A42 | 60c multi | 1.00 | .30 |
| L158 | A43 | 60c multi | 1.00 | .30 |
| *a.* | | Booklet pane of 10, 3 each #L155-L156, 2 each #L157-L158 | 12.00 | |
| | | *Nos. L155-L158 (4)* | 4.00 | 1.20 |

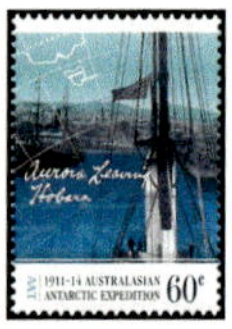

Australasian Antarctic Expedition, Cent. — A44

No. L159: a, Map and mast of SY Aurora. b, John King Davis (1884-1967), captain of the SY Aurora. c, SY Aurora and postmark. d, Expedition members landing at Macquarie Island. e, Birds on Macquarie Island.

**2011, Aug. 2 *Perf. 14¾x14***

| | | | | |
|---|---|---|---|---|
| L159 | | Horiz. strip of 5 | 7.00 | 7.25 |
| *a.-e.* | | A44 60c Any single | 1.00 | 1.00 |
| *f.* | | Souvenir sheet of 5, #L159a-L159e | 9.50 | 7.25 |

For WWF stamp inscribed "Australian Antarctic Territory" see Australia No. 3562.

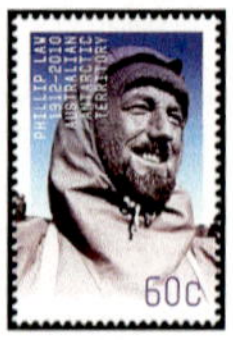

Dr. Philip Law (1912-2010), Polar Explorer — A45

Designs: 60c, Law. $1.20, Map of Antarctica, Law and helicopter at Arthurson Bluff. $1.80, Map of Antarctica, opening of Mawson Station.

**2012, Mar. 6 Litho. *Perf. 14¾x14***

| | | | | |
|---|---|---|---|---|
| L160 | A45 | 60c multi | 1.75 | 1.40 |
| L161 | A45 | $1.20 multi | 3.50 | 2.75 |
| L162 | A45 | $1.80 multi | 5.50 | 2.75 |
| *a.* | | Souvenir sheet of 3, #L160-L162 | 11.00 | 8.50 |
| | | *Nos. L160-L162 (3)* | 10.75 | 6.90 |

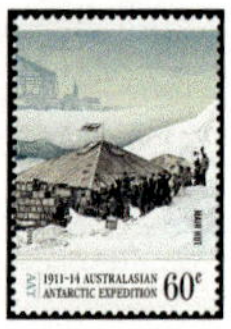

Australasian Antarctic Expedition, Cent. — A46

Designs: No. L163, Main hut. No. L164, Xavier Mertz and dogs. No. L165, Belgrave Ninnis and dogs. No. L166, Bow of SY Aurora, map of Cape Denison, penguins. No. L167, Stern of SY Aurora, expedition members carrying supplies from ship.

**2012, Sept. 4**

| | | | | |
|---|---|---|---|---|
| L163 | A46 | 60c multi | 1.00 | 1.00 |
| L164 | A46 | 60c multi | 1.00 | 1.00 |
| L165 | A46 | 60c multi | 1.00 | 1.00 |
| *a.* | | Horiz. strip of 3, #L163-L165 | 5.00 | 4.00 |
| L166 | A46 | $1.20 multi | 1.50 | 1.50 |
| L167 | A46 | $1.20 multi | 1.50 | 1.50 |
| *a.* | | Horiz. pair, #L166-L167 | 6.75 | 5.50 |
| *b.* | | Souvenir sheet of 5, #L163-L167 | 12.00 | 9.50 |
| | | *Nos. L163-L167 (5)* | 6.00 | 6.00 |

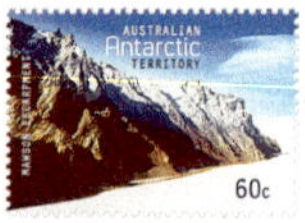

Mountains — A47

Designs: No. L168, Mt. Parsons. No. L169, Mawson Escarpment. $1.20, South Masson Range. $1.80, David Range.

**2013, Mar. 12 Litho. *Perf. 14x14¾***

| | | | | |
|---|---|---|---|---|
| L168 | A47 | 60c multi | .90 | .95 |
| L169 | A47 | 60c multi | .90 | .95 |
| *a.* | | Horiz. pair, #L168-L169 | 2.50 | 1.90 |
| L170 | A47 | $1.20 multi | 2.50 | 1.90 |
| L171 | A47 | $1.80 multi | 3.75 | 3.00 |
| *a.* | | Souvenir sheet of 4, #L168-L171 | 8.75 | 8.75 |
| | | *Nos. L168-L171 (4)* | 8.05 | 6.80 |

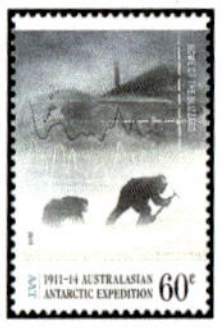

Australasian Antarctic Expedition, Cent. — A48

Designs: No. L172, Men walking in blizzard. No. L173, Man checking wind recorder. No. L174, Weddell seal, Cape petrels. No. L175, Wireless operator Walter Hannam. No. L176, Frank Wild, leader of Western Party of Expedition.

**2013, Sept. 10 *Perf. 14¾x14***

| | | | | |
|---|---|---|---|---|
| L172 | A48 | 60c multi | 1.10 | .85 |
| L173 | A48 | 60c multi | 1.10 | .85 |
| L174 | A48 | 60c multi | 1.10 | .85 |
| *a.* | | Horiz. strip of 3, #L172-L174 | 3.30 | 2.60 |
| L175 | A48 | $1.20 multi | 2.25 | 1.75 |
| L176 | A48 | $1.20 multi | 2.25 | 1.75 |
| *a.* | | Horiz. pair, #L175-L176 | 4.50 | 3.50 |
| *b.* | | Souvenir sheet of 5, #L172-L176 | 8.00 | 8.00 |
| | | *Nos. L172-L176 (5)* | 7.80 | 6.05 |

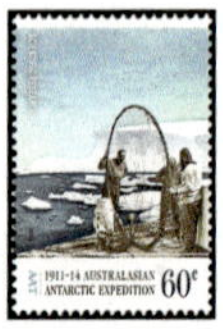

Australasian Antarctic Expedition, Cent. — A49

Designs: No. L177, Scientific researchers with large net. No. L178, Expedition members on SY Aurora. No. L179, Sir Douglas Mawson (1882-1958), expedition leader. No. L180, Mawson on motor launch, Cape Denison. No. L181, Frank Hurley with movie camera.

**2014, Feb. 18 Litho. *Perf. 14¾x14***

| | | | | |
|---|---|---|---|---|
| L177 | A49 | 60c multi | 1.10 | .85 |
| L178 | A49 | 60c multi | 1.10 | .85 |
| L179 | A49 | 60c multi | 1.10 | .85 |
| *a.* | | Horiz. strip of 3, #L177-L179 | 3.30 | 2.60 |
| L180 | A49 | $1.20 multi | 2.25 | 1.75 |
| L181 | A49 | $1.20 multi | 2.25 | 1.75 |
| *a.* | | Horiz. pair, #L180-L181 | 4.50 | 3.50 |
| *b.* | | Souvenir sheet of 5, #L177-L181 | 8.00 | 8.00 |
| | | *Nos. L177-L181 (5)* | 7.80 | 6.05 |

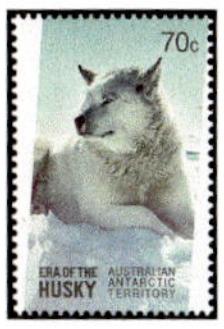


Husky — A50

Designs: Nos. L182, L186, Gray husky (shown). Nos. L183, L186, Brown husky. No. L184, Dog team with drivers in orange parkas, horiz. No. L185, Dog team with drivers in black parkas, horiz.

*Perf. 14¾x14, 14x14¾*

**2014, Sept. 9 Litho.**

| | | | | |
|---|---|---|---|---|
| **L182** | A50 | 70c multi | 1.25 | 1.25 |
| **L183** | A50 | 70c multi | 1.25 | 1.25 |
| *a.* | | Horiz. pair, #L182-L183 | 2.50 | 2.50 |
| **L184** | A50 | $1.40 multi | 2.50 | 2.00 |
| **L185** | A50 | $1.40 multi | 2.50 | 2.00 |
| *a.* | | Horiz. pair, #L184-L185 | 5.00 | 4.00 |
| *b.* | | Souvenir sheet of 4, #L182-L185 | 7.50 | 7.50 |
| | | *Nos. L182-L185 (4)* | 7.50 | 6.50 |

**Booklet Stamps Self-Adhesive**

***Serpentine Die Cut 11¼ Syncopated***

| | | | | |
|---|---|---|---|---|
| **L186** | A50 | 70c multi | 1.25 | .25 |
| **L187** | A50 | 70c multi | 1.25 | .25 |
| *a.* | | Booklet pane of 10, 5 each #L186-L187 | 12.50 | |

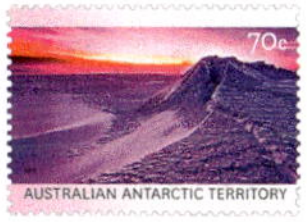


Antarctic Atmospheric Conditions — A51

Various Antarctic landscapes and atmospheric conditions with denomination at: No. L188, UR. No. L189, UL. No. L190, UR. No. L191, UL.

**2015, May 26 Litho. *Perf. 14x14¾***

| | | | | |
|---|---|---|---|---|
| **L188** | A51 | 70c multi | 1.10 | .85 |
| **L189** | A51 | 70c multi | 1.10 | .85 |
| *a.* | | Horiz. pair, #L188-L189 | 2.20 | 1.70 |
| **L190** | A51 | $1.40 multi | 2.25 | 1.75 |
| **L191** | A51 | $1.40 multi | 2.25 | 1.75 |
| *a.* | | Horiz. pair, #L190-L191 | 4.50 | 3.50 |
| *b.* | | Souvenir sheet of 4, #L188-L191 | 6.75 | 6.75 |
| | | *Nos. L188-L191 (4)* | 6.70 | 5.20 |

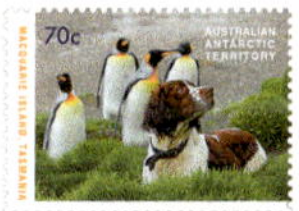

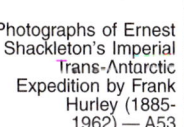

Dogs Involved in Macquarie Island Pest Eradication — A52

Dogs and: No. L192, Penguins. No. L193, Man with backpack. No. L194, Woman. No. L195, Man in winter coat.

**2015, Sept. 9 Litho. *Perf. 14x14¾***

| | | | | |
|---|---|---|---|---|
| **L192** | A52 | 70c multi | 1.00 | .75 |
| **L193** | A52 | 70c multi | 1.00 | .75 |
| *a.* | | Horiz. pair, #L192-L193 | 2.00 | 1.50 |
| **L194** | A52 | $1.40 multi | 2.00 | 1.50 |
| **L195** | A52 | $1.40 multi | 2.00 | 1.50 |
| *a.* | | Horiz. pair, #L194-L195 | 4.00 | 3.00 |
| *b.* | | Souvenir sheet of 4, #L192-L195 | 6.00 | 6.00 |
| | | *Nos. L192-L195 (4)* | 6.00 | 4.50 |

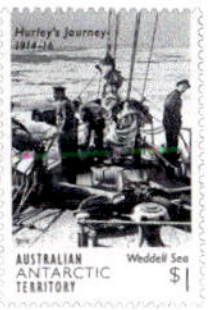

Photographs of Ernest Shackleton's Imperial Trans-Antarctic Expedition by Frank Hurley (1885-1962) — A53

Inscriptions: No. L196, Weddell Sea. No. L197, Ice-bound. No. L198, Ocean Camp. No. L199, Rescue Mission. $3, At Work.

**2016, June 21 Litho. *Perf. 14¾x14***

| | | | | |
|---|---|---|---|---|
| **L196** | A53 | $1 multi | 1.50 | 1.10 |
| **L197** | A53 | $1 multi | 1.50 | 1.10 |
| *a.* | | Horiz. pair, #L196-L197 | 3.00 | 2.25 |
| **L198** | A53 | $2 multi | 3.00 | 2.25 |
| **L199** | A53 | $2 multi | 3.00 | 2.25 |
| *a.* | | Horiz. pair, #L198-L199 | 6.00 | 4.50 |
| **L200** | A53 | $3 multi | 4.50 | 3.50 |
| *a.* | | Souvenir sheet of 5, #L196-L200 | 13.50 | 13.50 |
| | | *Nos. L196-L200 (5)* | 13.50 | 10.20 |

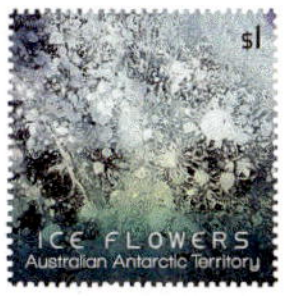


Ice Flowers (Frost Formations) — A54

Various ice flowers. Denomination at UR on Nos. L201, L203, L205a, L205c, L206, Denomination at UL on Nos. L202, L204, L205b, L205d, L207.

**Litho., Litho & Embossed With Foil Application (#L205)**

**2016, Sept. 20 *Perf. 14¼***

| | | | | |
|---|---|---|---|---|
| **L201** | A54 | $1 multi | 1.60 | 1.60 |
| **L202** | A54 | $1 multi | 1.60 | 1.60 |
| *a.* | | Horiz. pair, #L201-L202 | 3.20 | 3.20 |
| **L203** | A54 | $2 multi | 3.25 | 1.60 |
| **L204** | A54 | $3 multi | 4.75 | 2.40 |
| | | *Nos. L201-L204 (4)* | 11.20 | 7.20 |

**Miniature Sheet**

| | | | | |
|---|---|---|---|---|
| **L205** | | Sheet of 4 | 11.50 | 6.50 |
| *a.-b.* | | A54 $1 Either single | 1.60 | 1.25 |
| *c.* | | A54 $2 multi | 3.25 | 1.60 |
| *d.* | | A54 $3 multi | 4.75 | 2.40 |

**Booklet Stamps Self-Adhesive**

***Serpentine Die Cut 11¼ Syncopated***

| | | | | |
|---|---|---|---|---|
| **L206** | A54 | $1 multi | 1.60 | .25 |
| **L207** | A54 | $1 multi | 1.60 | .25 |
| *a* | | Booklet pane of 10, 5 each #L206-L207 | 16.00 | |

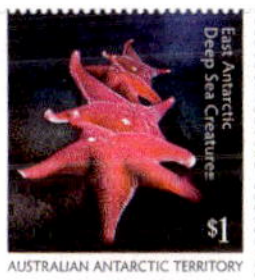


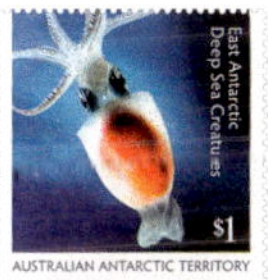


A55 A56

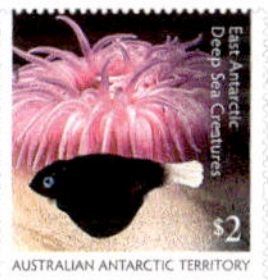


A57

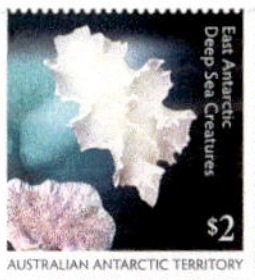


East Antarctic Deep Sea Creatures — A58

**2017, Mar. 7 Litho. *Perf. 14¼***

| | | | | |
|---|---|---|---|---|
| **L208** | A55 | $1 multi | 1.60 | 1.25 |
| **L209** | A56 | $1 multi | 1.60 | 1.25 |
| *a.* | | Horiz. pair, #L208-L209 | 3.20 | 2.50 |
| **L210** | A57 | $2 multi | 3.00 | 2.25 |
| **L211** | A58 | $2 multi | 3.00 | 2.25 |
| *a.* | | Horiz. pair, #L210-L211 | 6.00 | 4.50 |
| *b.* | | Souvenir sheet of 4, #L208-L211 | 9.25 | 7.00 |
| | | *Nos. L208-L211 (4)* | 9.20 | 7.00 |

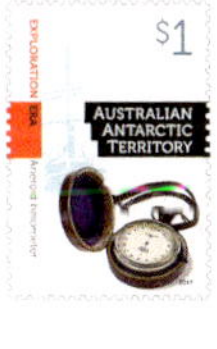


Cultural Heritage — A59

Designs: No. L212, Aneroid barometer and ship. No. L213, Proclamation of Sir Douglas Mawson and map of Antarctica. $2, Weasel M29 vehicle and mountains.

**2017, Sept. 19 Litho. *Perf. 14¾x14***

| | | | | |
|---|---|---|---|---|
| **L212** | A59 | $1 multi | 1.60 | 1.25 |
| **L213** | A59 | $1 multi | 1.60 | 1.25 |
| **L214** | A59 | $2 multi | 3.25 | 1.60 |
| *a.* | | Souvenir sheet of 3, #L212-L214 | 6.50 | 4.25 |
| | | *Nos. L212-L214 (3)* | 6.45 | 4.10 |

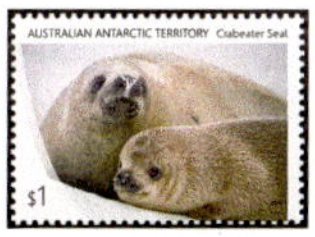


Crabeater Seals — A60

Designs: No. L215, Two seals. No. L216, Seal in water. No. L217, Two seals, diff. No. L218, One seal.

**2018, Mar. 27 Litho. *Perf. 14x14¾***

| | | | | |
|---|---|---|---|---|
| **L215** | A60 | $1 multi | 1.60 | 1.25 |
| **L216** | A60 | $1 multi | 1.60 | 1.25 |
| **L217** | A60 | $2 multi | 3.25 | 1.60 |
| **L218** | A60 | $2 multi | 3.25 | 1.60 |
| *a.* | | Souvenir sheet of 4, #L215-L218 | 9.75 | 5.75 |
| | | *Nos. L215-L218 (4)* | 9.70 | 5.70 |

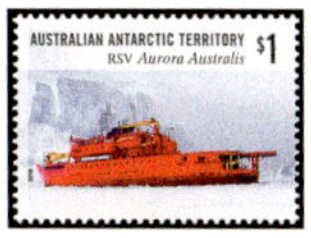


RSV Aurora Australis, 30th Anniv. — A61

Designs: No. L219, Ship in ice. No. L220, Ship and penguins. No. L221, Wave approaching ship. No. L222, Aerial view of ship in ice.

**2018, Sept. 25 Litho. *Perf. 14x14¾***

| | | | | |
|---|---|---|---|---|
| **L219** | A61 | $1 multi | 1.50 | 1.10 |
| **L220** | A61 | $1 multi | 1.50 | 1.10 |
| **L221** | A61 | $2 multi | 3.00 | 2.25 |
| **L222** | A61 | $2 multi | 3.00 | 2.25 |
| *a.* | | Souvenir sheet of 4, #L219-L222 | 9.00 | 6.75 |
| | | *Nos. L219-L222 (4)* | 9.00 | 6.70 |

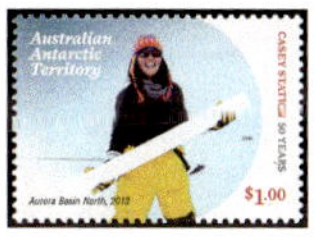


Carey Research Station, 50th Anniv. — A62

Designs: No. L223, Scientist holding equipment at Aurora Basin North, 2013. No. L224, Casey Repstat, 1971. No. L225, Tents at Aurora Basin North, 2013. No. L226, Casey Station, 2015.

**2019, Mar. 26 Litho. *Perf. 14x14¾***

| | | | | |
|---|---|---|---|---|
| **L223** | A62 | $1 multi | 1.50 | 1.10 |
| **L224** | A62 | $1 multi | 1.50 | 1.10 |
| **L225** | A62 | $2 multi | 3.00 | 2.25 |
| **L226** | A62 | $2 multi | 3.00 | 2.25 |
| *a.* | | Souvenir sheet of 4, #L223-L226 | 9.00 | 6.75 |
| | | *Nos. L223-L226 (4)* | 9.00 | 6.70 |

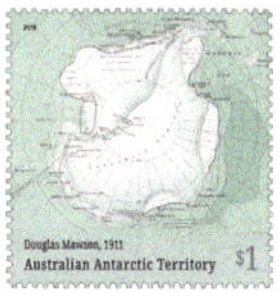


Mapping the Australian Antarctic Territory — A63

Maps by: No. L227, Douglas Mawson, 1911. No. L228, Department of the Interior, 1939. No. L229, Division of National Mapping, 1971. No. L230, Australian Antarctic Division, 1993.

**2019, Aug. 20 Litho. *Perf. 14¼***

| | | | | |
|---|---|---|---|---|
| **L227** | A63 | $1 multi | 1.40 | 1.10 |
| **L228** | A63 | $1 multi | 1.40 | 1.10 |
| **L229** | A63 | $2 multi | 2.75 | 2.10 |
| **L230** | A63 | $2 multi | 2.75 | 2.10 |
| *a.* | | Souvenir sheet of 4, #L227-L230 | 8.50 | 8.50 |
| | | *Nos. L227-L230 (4)* | 8.30 | 6.40 |

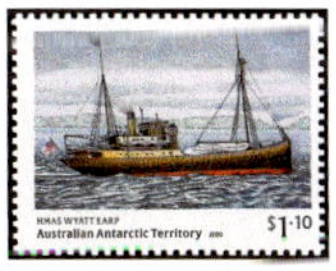


1948 HMAS Wyatt Earp Expedition — A64

Designs: No. L231, HMAS Wyatt Earp. No. L232, Royal Australian Air Force Vought Kingfisher. $3.30, HMAS Wyatt Earp and Royal Australian Air Force Vought Kingfisher.

*Perf. 12¼x13¼*

**2020, Mar. 31 Litho. & Engr.**

| | | | | |
|---|---|---|---|---|
| **L231** | A64 | $1.10 multi | 1.40 | 1.10 |
| **L232** | A64 | $1.10 multi | 1.40 | 1.10 |
| **L233** | A64 | $3.30 multi | 4.00 | 3.00 |
| *a.* | | Souvenir sheet of 3, #L231-L233 | 7.00 | 5.25 |
| | | *Nos. L231-L233 (3)* | 6.80 | 5.20 |

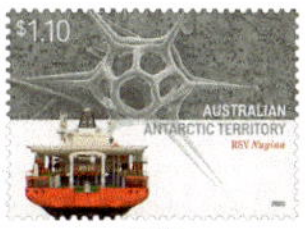


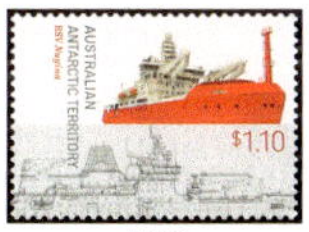


A65 A66

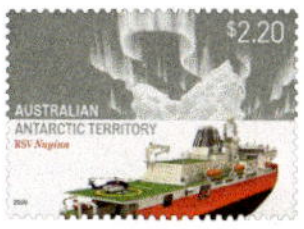


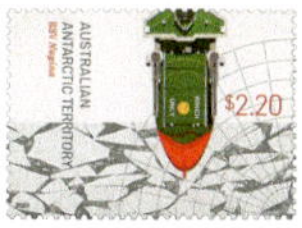


A67 Arrival of New Icebreaker RSV Nuyina — A68

**2020, Sept. 29 Litho. *Perf. 14x14¾***

| | | | | |
|---|---|---|---|---|
| **L234** | A65 | $1.10 multi | 1.60 | 1.25 |
| **L235** | A66 | $1.10 multi | 1.60 | 1.25 |
| **L236** | A67 | $2.20 multi | 3.25 | 2.40 |
| **L237** | A68 | $2.20 multi | 3.25 | 2.40 |
| *a.* | | Souvenir sheet of 4, #L234-L237 | 9.75 | 9.75 |
| | | *Nos. L234-L237 (4)* | 9.70 | 7.30 |

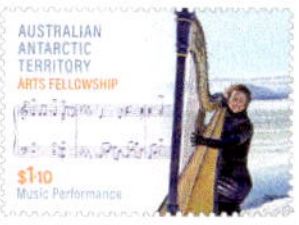


Australian Antarctic Arts Fellowship — A69

Designs: No. L238, Music performance. No. L239, Painting. No. L240, Sound recording. No. L241, Photography.

**2021, Mar. 16 Litho. *Perf. 14x14¾***

| | | | | |
|---|---|---|---|---|
| **L238** | A69 | $1.10 multi | 1.75 | 1.30 |
| **L239** | A69 | $1.10 multi | 1.75 | 1.30 |
| **L240** | A69 | $2.20 multi | 3.50 | 2.60 |
| **L241** | A69 | $2.20 multi | 3.50 | 2.60 |
| *a.* | | Souvenir sheet of 4, #L238-L241 | 10.50 | 8.00 |
| | | *Nos. L238-L241 (4)* | 10.50 | 7.80 |

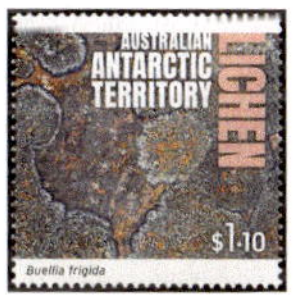


Lichens — A70

Designs: No. L242, Buellia frigida. No. L243, Xanthoria mawsonii. $2.20, Umbilicaria decussata. $3.30, Xanthoria elegans.

**2021, Oct. 5 Litho. *Perf. 14¼***

| | | | | |
|---|---|---|---|---|
| **L242** | A70 | $1.10 multi | 1.75 | 1.30 |
| **L243** | A70 | $1.10 multi | 1.75 | 1.30 |
| **L244** | A70 | $2.20 multi | 3.50 | 2.60 |
| **L245** | A70 | $3.30 multi | 5.00 | 3.75 |
| *a.* | | Souvenir sheet of 4, #L242-L245 | 12.00 | 9.00 |
| | | *Nos. L242-L245 (4)* | 12.00 | 8.95 |

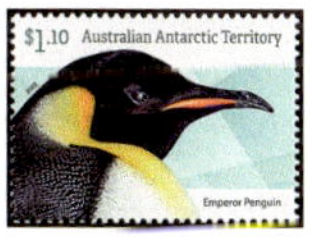


Penguins — A71

Designs: No. L246, Head of Emperor penguin. No. L247, Emperor penguins. No. L248, Head of Adélie penguin. No. L249, Adélie penguins.

**2022, Mar. 22 Litho. *Perf. 14x14¾***

| | | | | |
|---|---|---|---|---|
| **L246** | A71 | $1.10 multi | 1.75 | 1.30 |
| **L247** | A71 | $1.10 multi | 1.75 | 1.30 |
| **L248** | A71 | $2.20 multi | 3.25 | 2.50 |
| **L249** | A71 | $2.20 multi | 3.25 | 2.50 |
| *a.* | | Souvenir sheet of 4, #L246-L249 | 10.00 | 7.75 |
| | | *Nos. L246-L249 (4)* | 10.00 | 7.00 |

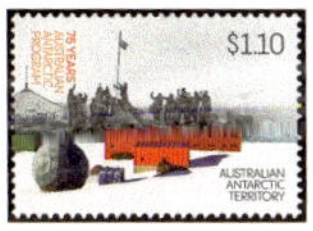


Australian Antarctic Program, 75th Anniv. — A72

Designs: No. L250, Flag raising cermony, building and equipment. No. L251, Australian National Antarctic Research Expedition team members, sled and flag, vehicle for Antarctic transportation, vert. No. L252, Researcher with microscope, researcher in snow, vert. No. L253, Airplanes.

*Perf. 14x14¾, 14¾x14*

**2022, Aug. 9 Litho.**

| | | | | |
|---|---|---|---|---|
| **L250** | A72 | $1.10 multi | 1.50 | 1.10 |
| **L251** | A72 | $1.10 multi | 1.50 | 1.10 |
| **L252** | A72 | $2.20 multi | 3.00 | 2.25 |
| **L253** | A72 | $2.20 multi | 3.00 | 2.25 |
| *a.* | | Souvenir sheet of 4, #L250-L253 | 9.00 | 6.75 |
| | | *Nos. L250-L253 (4)* | 9.00 | 6.70 |

## AUSTRALIA — Australian Antarctic Territory

Paintings of Antarctica by Sidney Nolan (1917-92) — A73

Paintings: No. L254, Volcanic Ridge. No. L255, Bird. No. L256, Antarctica. No. L257, Explorers.

**2023, Mar. 14   Litho.   Perf. 14¾x14**
| | | | | |
|---|---|---|---|---|
| L254 | A73 | $1.20 multi | 1.60 | 1.25 |
| L255 | A73 | $1.20 multi | 1.60 | 1.25 |
| L256 | A73 | $2.40 multi | 3.25 | 2.40 |
| L257 | A73 | $2.40 multi | 3.25 | 2.40 |
| a. | | Souvenir sheet of 4, #L254-L257 | 9.75 | 7.50 |
| | | Nos. L254-L257 (4) | 9.70 | 7.30 |

Circumnavigation of Antarctica, 250th Anniv. — A74

Designs: $1.20, Coordinates of the first crossing of the Antarctic Circle. No. L259, K1 chronometer. No. L260, HMS Resolution.

**2023, Aug. 22   Litho.   Perf. 14x14½**
| | | | | |
|---|---|---|---|---|
| L258 | A74 | $1.20 multi | 1.60 | 1.25 |
| L259 | A74 | $2.40 multi | 3.25 | 2.50 |
| L260 | A74 | $2.40 multi | 3.25 | 2.50 |
| a. | | Souvenir sheet of 3, #L258-L260 | 8.25 | 6.25 |
| | | Nos. L258-L260 (3) | 8.10 | 6.25 |

**NEW! 2023 NATIONAL MINUTEMAN MINKUS All American NOW AVAILABLE!**

A complete supplement of all U.S. listings assigned a major Scott number through 2023 in the Scott Standard Postage Stamp Catalogue and Scott New Listings Update, found in the Linn's Stamp News Monthly issue.

*Preorder your supplements today!*

| ITEM NO. | | RETAIL | AA |
|---|---|---|---|
| 100S023 | Scott US National 2023 Pages only | $28.99 | **$24.64** |
| 180S023 | Scott US Minuteman 2023 Pages only | $28.99 | **$24.64** |
| MAA123 | Minkus All-American Pt 1 for 2023 Pages only | $28.99 | **$24.64** |
| 100S023BB | Scott US National 2023 with Mount kit (black) | $71.99 | **$61.19** |
| 100S023BC | Scott US National 2023 with Mount kit (clear) | $71.99 | **$61.19** |
| 180S023BB | Scott US Minuteman 2023 with Mount kit (black) | $71.99 | **$61.19** |
| 180S023BC | Scott US Minuteman 2023 with Mount kit (clear) | $71.99 | **$61.19** |
| MAA123BB | Minkus All-American Pt 1 2023 with Mount kit (black) | $71.99 | **$61.19** |
| MAA123BC | Minkus All-American Pt 1 2023 with Mount kit (clear) | $71.99 | **$61.19** |

### ADD The Scott Mount Kit to your supplement pages and SAVE!

The U.S. mount kits are designed specifically for the Scott National, Minuteman, and Minkus All-American yearly supplement pages. These sturdy custom mounts are easy to use and take the guess work out of selecting the correct mount for your stamps. The U.S. mount packs are available in black or clear. Don't wait because we only offer a limited quantity.

**AmosAdvantage.com | 1-800-572-6885**

**ORDERING INFORMATION:** *AA prices apply to paid subscribers of Amos Media titles, or for orders placed online. Prices, terms and product availability subject to change. **SHIPPING & HANDLING:** U.S.: Orders total $0-$10.00 charged $4.99 shipping. U.S. Order total $10.01-$74.99 charged $9.99 shipping. Orders totaling $75+ will ship FREE! Taxes will apply in CA, OH, & IL. Canada: 20% of order total. Minimum charge $19.99 Maximum charge $200.00. Foreign orders are shipped via FedEx Intl. or USPS and billed actual freight.

# INDEX AND IDENTIFIER

All page numbers shown are those in this Volume 1A. Postage stamps that do not have English words on them are shown in the Illustrated Identifier.

|  |  |
|---|---|
| A & T ovptd. on French Colonies | 519 |
| Aberdeen, Miss. | 222 |
| Abingdon, Va. | 222 |
| Abu Dhabi | 311, Vol. 5A, Vol. 6B |
| Abyssinia (Ethiopia) | Vol. 2B |
| A.C.C.P., A.D.C.P. | Vol. 1B |
| A Certo ovptd. on stamps of Peru | Vol. 5A |
| Acores | Vol. 1B, Vol. 5B |
| Aden | 312 |
| AEF | Vol. 2B |
| Aegean Islands (Greek Occupation) | Vol. 3A |
| Aegean Islands (Italian Occupation) | Vol. 3B |
| Aeroport International de Kandahar (Afghanistan #679) | 327 |
| Afars and Issas | 314 |
| AFF EXCEP | Vol. 2B |
| Afghanistan, Afghan, Afghanes | 317 |
| AFR | Vol. 5B |
| Africa, British Offices | Vol. 3A |
| Africa, German East | Vol. 3A |
| Africa, German South-West | Vol. 3A |
| Africa, Italian Offices | Vol. 3B |
| Africa Occidental Espanola | Vol. 6A |
| Africa Orientale Italiana | Vol. 3B |
| Africa, Portuguese | Vol. 5B |
| Afrique Equatoriale Francaise | Vol. 2A, Vol. 2B, Vol. 4B, Vol. 6B |
| Afrique Francaise | Vol. 2B |
| Afrique Occidentale Francaise | Vol. 2B |
| Agion Oros Athoc (Greece) | Vol. 3A |
| Aguera, La | 346 |
| Aguinaldo | Vol. 5A |
| AHA (Confed. #44X1) | 226 |
| Aimeliik (Palau #686) | Vol. 5A |
| Airai (Palau #686) | Vol. 5A |
| Aitutaki | 346 |
| Ajman | 359, Vol. 6B |
| Aland Islands | Vol. 2B |
| Alaouites | 359 |
| Albania | 360 |
| Albania, Greek Occupation | Vol. 3A |
| Albania, Italian Offices | Vol. 3B |
| Albany, Ga. | 222 |
| Alderney | Vol. 3A |
| Aleppo | Vol. 6A |
| Alerta ovptd. on stamps of Peru | Vol. 5A |
| Alexandretta, Alexandrette | 408 |
| Alexandria, Alexandrie, French Offices | Vol. 2B |
| Alexandria, Va. | 1 |
| Alexandroupolis | Vol. 3A |
| Algeria, Algerie | 408 |
| Allemagne Duitschland | Vol. 3A |
| Allenstein | 451 |
| Allied Military Government (Austria) | Vol. 1B |
| Allied Military Gov. (Germany) | Vol. 3A |
| Allied Military Government (Italy) | Vol. 3B |
| Allied Military Government (Trieste) | Vol. 3B |
| Allied Occupation of Azerbaijan | Vol. 3B |
| Allied Occupation of Thrace | Vol. 6B |
| A L'Ocassion de la Journée Internationale de l'Alphabetisation (Afghan. #951) | 332 |
| Alsace | Vol. 2B |
| Alsace and Lorraine | Vol. 2B |
| Alwar | Vol. 3B |
| A M G | Vol. 1B, Vol. 3A, Vol. 3B |
| A.M.G./F.T.T. | Vol. 3B |
| A.M.G./V.G. | Vol. 3B |
| AM Post | Vol. 3A |
| Anatolia | Vol. 6B |
| Ancachs | Vol. 5A |
| Andalusian Provinces | Vol. 6A |
| Anderson Court House, S.C. | 222 |
| Andorra, Andorre | 451 |
| Andorra | 465 |
| Angaur (Palau #686) | Vol. 5A |
| Angola | 486 |
| Angra | 506 |
| Anguilla | 506, Vol. 5B |
| Anhwei | Vol. 2A |
| Anjouan | 519 |
| Anna surcharged on France | Vol. 2B |
| Anna surcharged on Great Britain | Vol. 5A |
| Anna, Annas | Vol. 3B |
| Annam | Vol. 3B |
| Annam and Tonkin | 519 |
| Annapolis, Md. | 1 |
| Ano do X Aniversario Comunidade dos Paises de Lingua Portuguesa (Angola 1298-1300) | 502 |
| Antigua | 519, Vol. 5B |
| Antigua & Barbuda | 526 |
| Antioquia | Vol. 2A |
| A.O. ovptd. on Congo | Vol. 3A |
| AOF on France | Vol. 2B |
| A.O.I. ovpt. on Italy | Vol. 3B |
| A Payer Te Betalen | Vol. 1B |
| A percevoir (see France, French colonies, postage due) | Vol. 2B, Vol. 3A |
| Apurimac | Vol. 5A |
| A R | Vol. 4B |
| A.R. ovptd. on stamps of Colombia | Vol. 5A |
| Arabie Saoudite | Vol. 6A |
| Arad | Vol. 3B |
| A receber (See Portuguese Colonies) | Vol. 5B |
| Arequipa | Vol. 5A |
| Argentina | 574 |
| Argyrokastron | Vol. 2B |
| Arica | Vol. 5A |
| Armenia | 651, Vol. 6B |
| Armenian stamps ovptd. or surcharged | Vol. 3A, Vol. 6B |
| Army of the North | Vol. 5B |
| Army of the Northwest | Vol. 5B |
| Aruba | 678 |
| Arwad | Vol. 5B |
| Ascension | 690 |
| Assistencia Nacionalaos Tuberculosos | Vol. 5B |
| Asturias Province | Vol. 6A |
| Athens, Ga. | 222 |
| Atlanta, Ga. | 222 |
| Aunus, ovptd. on Finland | Vol. 5B |
| Austin, Miss. | 222 |
| Austin, Tex. | 222 |
| Australia | 720 |
| Australia, Occupation of Japan | 796 |
| Australian Antarctic Territory | 796 |
| Australian States | 704 |
| Austria | Vol. 1B |
| Austria, Allied Military Govt. | Vol. 1B |
| Austria, Adm. of Liechtenstein | Vol. 4A |
| Austria, Lombardy-Venetia | Vol. 1B |
| Austria-Hungary | Vol. 1B |
| Austrian Occupation of Italy | Vol. 3B |
| Austrian Occupation of Montenegro | Vol. 4B |
| Austrian Occupation of Romania | Vol. 5B |
| Austrian Occupation of Serbia | Vol. 6A |
| Austrian Offices Abroad | Vol. 1B |
| Austrian stamps surcharged or overprinted | Vol. 1B, Vol. 3B, Vol. 5B, Vol. 6B |
| Autaugaville, Ala. | 222 |
| Autopakelli, Autoranti | Vol. 2B |
| Avisporto | Vol. 2B |
| Ayacucho | Vol. 5A |
| Aytonomoe | Vol. 2B |
| Azerbaijan, Azerbaycan, Azerbaycan, Azerbaidjan | Vol. 1B, Vol. 3B, Vol. 6B |
| Azirbayedjan | Vol. 3B |
| Azores | Vol. 1B, Vol. 5B |
| B | Vol. 1B, Vol. 5A, Vol. 6A |
| B ovptd. on Straits Settlements | Vol. 1B |
| Baden | Vol. 3A |
| Baghdad | Vol. 4B |
| Bahamas | Vol. 1B |
| Bahawalpur | Vol. 5A |
| Bahrain | Vol. 1B, Vol. 5A |
| Baja California | Vol. 4B |
| Bajar Porto | Vol. 3B |
| Baku | Vol. 1B |
| Balcony Falls, Va. | 222 |
| Baltimore, Md. | 1, 191 |
| Bamra | Vol. 3B |
| Banat, Bacska | Vol. 3B |
| Bangkok | Vol. 1B |
| Bangladesh | Vol. 1B |
| Bani ovptd. on Austria | Vol. 5B |
| Bani ovptd. on Hungary | Vol. 3B |
| Baranya | Vol. 3B |
| Barbados | Vol. 1B |
| Barbuda | Vol. 1B |
| Barcelona | Vol. 6A |
| Barnwell Court House, S.C. | 222 |
| Barranquilla | Vol. 2A |
| Barwani | Vol. 3B |
| Basel | Vol. 6A |
| Bashahr | Vol. 3B |
| Basque Provinces | Vol. 6A |
| Basutoland | Vol. 1B |
| Batavia | Vol. 5A |
| Baton Rouge, La. | 222 |
| Batum, Batym (British Occupation) | Vol. 1B |
| Bavaria | Vol. 3A |
| Bayar Porto | Vol. 3B |
| Bayer., Bayern | Vol. 3A |
| B.C.A. ovptd. on Rhodesia | Vol. 1B |
| B.C.M. | Vol. 4B |
| B.C.O.F. | 796 |
| Beaufort, S.C. | 222 |
| Beaumont, Tex. | 222 |
| Bechuanaland | Vol. 1B |
| Bechuanaland Protectorate | Vol. 1B |
| Beckmann's City Post | 191 |
| Behie | Vol. 6B |
| Belarus | Vol. 1B |
| Belgian (Belgisch) Congo | Vol. 1B |
| Belgian East Africa | Vol. 5B |
| Belgian Occ. of German East Africa | Vol. 3A |
| Belgian Occupation of Germany | Vol. 3A |
| Belgien | Vol. 1B |
| Belgium, Belgique, Belgie | Vol. 1B |
| Belgium (German Occupation) | Vol. 1B |
| Belize | Vol. 1B |
| Belize, Cayes of | Vol. 1B |
| Benadir | Vol. 6A |
| Bengasi | Vol. 3B |
| Beni | Vol. 1B |
| Benin | Vol. 1B |
| Benin, People's Republic of | Vol. 1B |
| Bequia | Vol. 5B |
| Bergedorf | Vol. 3A |
| Berlin | Vol. 3A |
| Berlin-Brandenburg | Vol. 3A |
| Bermuda | Vol. 1B |
| Besetztes Gebiet Nordfrankreich | Vol. 2B |
| Besieged ovptd. on Cape of Good Hope | Vol. 2A, Vol. 6B |
| Beyrouth, French Offices | Vol. 2B |
| Beyrouth, Russian Offices | Vol. 5D |
| B. Guiana | Vol. 1B |
| B. Hneipoe | Vol. 2B |
| Bhopal | Vol. 3B |
| Bhor | Vol. 3B |
| Bhutan | Vol. 1B |
| Biafra | Vol. 1B |
| Bijawar | Vol. 3B |
| B.I.O.T. ovptd. on Seychelles | Vol. 1B |
| Bishop's City Post | 191 |
| Blagoveshchensk | Vol. 2B |
| Bluefields | Vol. 5A |
| Bluffton, S.C. | 223 |
| B.M.A. Eritrea | Vol. 3A |
| B.M.A. Malaya | Vol. 6A |
| B.M.A. Somalia | Vol. 3A |
| B.M.A. Tripolitania | Vol. 3A |
| Bocas del Toro | Vol. 5A |
| Boer Occupation | Vol. 2A |
| Bogota | Vol. 2A |
| Bohemia and Moravia | Vol. 2B |
| Bohmen and Mahren | Vol. 2B |
| Boletta, Bollettino | Vol. 3B, Vol. 6A |
| Bolivar | Vol. 2A |
| Bolivia | Vol. 1B |
| Bollo | Vol. 3B |
| Bollo Postale | Vol. 6A |
| Bophuthatswana | Vol. 6A |
| Borneo | Vol. 5A |
| Boscawen, N.H. | 1 |
| Bosna i Hercegovina | Vol. 1B, Vol. 6B |
| Bosnia and Herzegovina | Vol. 1B, Vol. 6B |
| Bosnia, Muslim Gov. in Sarajevo | Vol. 1B |
| Bosnia, Croat Administration, Mostar | Vol. 1B |
| Bosnia, Serb Administration, Banja Luca | Vol. 1B |
| Bosnia stamps overprinted or surcharged | Vol. 1B, Vol. 3B, Vol. 6B |
| Bosnien Herzegowina | Vol. 1B |
| Boston, Mass. | 191 |
| Botswana | Vol. 1B |
| Boyaca | Vol. 2A |
| Brattleboro, Vt. | 1 |
| Braunschweig | Vol. 3A |
| Brazil, Brasil | Vol. 1B |
| Bremen | Vol. 3A |
| Bridgeville, Ala. | 223 |
| British Administration of Bahrain | Vol. 1B |
| British Antarctic Territory | Vol. 1B |
| British Bechuanaland | Vol. 1B |
| British Central Africa | Vol. 1B |
| British Colonies - Dies I & II | See table of contents |
| British Columbia & Vancouver Is. | Vol. 2A |
| British Consular Mail | Vol. 1B |
| British Dominion of Samoa | Vol. 5B |
| British East Africa | Vol. 1B |
| British Forces in Egypt | Vol. 2B |
| British Guiana | Vol. 1B |
| British Honduras | Vol. 1B |
| British Indian Ocean Territory | Vol. 1B |
| British Mandate of Jordan | Vol. 4A |
| British Levant | Vol. 3A |
| British New Guinea | Vol. 5A |
| British North Borneo | Vol. 5A |
| British Occupation (of Batum) | Vol. 1B |
| British Occupation of Bushire | Vol. 1B |
| British Occupation of Cameroun | Vol. 2A |
| British Occupation of Crete | Vol. 2A |
| British Occupation of Faroe Is. | Vol. 2B |
| British Occ. of German East Africa | Vol. 3A |
| British Occupation of Iraq | Vol. 3B, Vol. 4B |
| British Occupation of Mesopotamia | Vol. 4B |
| British Occ. of Orange River Colony | Vol. 5A |
| British Occupation overprint | Vol. 1B |
| British Occupation of Palestine | Vol. 5A |
| British Occupation of Persia | Vol. 1B |
| British Occupation of Togo | Vol. 6B |
| British Occ. of Transvaal | Vol. 6B |
| British Offices in Africa | Vol. 3A |
| British Offices in China | Vol. 3A |
| British Offices in Morocco | Vol. 3A |
| British Offices in Tangier | Vol. 3A |
| British Off. in the Turkish Empire | Vol. 3A |
| British Protectorate of Egypt | Vol. 2B |
| British Samoa | Vol. 5B |
| British Solomon Islands | Vol. 6A |
| British Somaliland (Somaliland Protectorate) | Vol. 6A |
| British South Africa (Rhodesia) | Vol. 5B |
| British stamps surcharged | Vol. 5A |
| British Vice-Consulate | Vol. 4B |
| British Virgin Islands | Vol. 6B |
| British Zone (Germany) | Vol. 3A |
| Brown & McGill's U.S.P.O. Despatch | 191 |
| Brunei | Vol. 1B |
| Brunei (Japanese Occupation) | Vol. 1B |
| Brunswick | Vol. 3A |
| Buchanan | 1, Vol. 4A |
| Buenos Aires | 650 |
| Bulgaria, Bulgarie | Vol. 1B |
| Bulgarian Occupation of Romania | Vol. 5B |
| Bulgarian stamps overprinted or surcharged | Vol. 3A, Vol. 5B, Vol. 6B |
| Bundi | Vol. 3B |
| Bundi stamps overprinted | Vol. 3B |
| Bureau International | Vol. 6A |
| Burgenland | Vol. 1B |
| Burgos | Vol. 6A |
| Burma | Vol. 1B |
| Burma (Japanese Occupation) | Vol. 1B |
| Burundi | Vol. 1B |
| Bushire | Vol. 1B |
| Bussahir | Vol. 3B |
| Buu-Chinh | Vol. 6B |
| Buu-Bien | Vol. 6B |
| Byelorussia | Vol. 1B |
| Cabo, Cabo Gracias a Dios | Vol. 5A |
| Cabo Juby, Jubi | Vol. 2A |
| Cabo Verde | Vol. 2A |
| Cadiz | Vol. 6A |
| Caicos | Vol. 6B |
| Calchi | Vol. 3B |
| Cali | Vol. 3B |
| Calino, Calimno | Vol. 3B |
| Callao | Vol. 5A |
| Camb. Aust. Sigillum Nov. | 704 |
| Cambodia, (Int. Com., India) | Vol. 3B |
| Cambodia, Cambodge | Vol. 2A, Vol. 3B |
| Camden, S.C. | 223 |
| Cameroons (U.K.T.T.) | Vol. 2A |
| Cameroun (Republique Federale) | Vol. 2A |
| Campeche | Vol. 4B |
| Canada | Vol. 2A |
| Canadian Provinces | Vol. 2A |
| Canal Zone | 232 |
| Canary Islands, Canarias | Vol. 6A |
| Candia | Vol. 2A |
| Canouan | Vol. 5B |
| Canton, French Offices | Vol. 2B |
| Canton, Miss. | 223 |
| Cape Juby | Vol. 2A |

802 INDEX AND IDENTIFIER


Cape of Good Hope .................... Vol. 2A
Cape of Good Hope stamps surchd. (see Griqualand West) ... Vol. 3A
Cape Verde ................................. Vol. 2A
Carchi ......................................... Vol. 3B
Caribbean Netherlands ............... Vol. 2A
Caribisch Nederland ................... Vol. 2A
Carinthia ...................... Vol. 1B, Vol. 6B
Carlist .......................................... Vol. 6A
Carolina City, N.C. ........................... 223
Caroline Islands .......................... Vol. 2A
Carpatho-Ukraine ........................ Vol. 2B
Carriacou & Petite Martinique ..... Vol. 3A
Carriers Stamps ............................... 191
Cartagena ..................................... Vol. 2A
Cartersville, Ga. ................................ 223
Carupano ..................................... Vol. 6B
Caso ............................................. Vol. 3B
Castellorizo, Castelrosso ............ Vol. 2A
Catalonia ..................................... Vol. 6A
Cauca ........................................... Vol. 2A
Cavalla (Greek) ............................ Vol. 3A
Cavalle, Cavalla (French) ............. Vol. 2B
Cayes of Belize ............................. Vol. 1B
Cayman Islands ............................ Vol. 2A
CCCP ........................................... Vol. 5B
C.CH. on French Colonies ............ Vol. 2A
C.E.F. ovptd. on Cameroun ......... Vol. 2A
C.E.F. ovptd. on India .................. Vol. 3B
Cefalonia ovptd. on Greece ......... Vol. 3B
Celebes ........................................ Vol. 5A
Cent, cents ... 221, Vol. 2B, Vol. 4B, Vol. 5A
Centenaire Algerie RF (France No. 255) ......................... Vol. 2B
Centenary-1st Postage Stamp (Pakistan #63-64) ....................... Vol. 5A
Centesimi overprinted on Austria or Bosnia ....................... Vol. 3B
Centesimi di corona ...... Vol. 1B, Vol. 2B
Centimes ...................................... Vol. 2B
Centimes ovptd. on Austria ......... Vol. 1B
Centimes ovptd. on Germany ..... Vol. 3A
Centimos (no country name) ....... Vol. 6A
Centimos ovptd. on France ......... Vol. 2B
Central Africa (Centrafricaine) ..... Vol. 2A
Central African Republic ............. Vol. 2A
Central China ............................... Vol. 2A
Central Lithuania .......................... Vol. 2A
Cephalonia ................................... Vol. 3B
Cerigo ........................... Vol. 3A, Vol. 3B
Cervantes ..................................... Vol. 6A
Ceska Republica .......................... Vol. 2B
Ceskoslovenska, Ceskoslovensko .......................... Vol. 2B
Ceylon .......................................... Vol. 2A
CF ................................................ Vol. 2B
CFA .............................................. Vol. 2B
C.G.H.S. ....................................... Vol. 6B
Ch ................................. Vol. 3B, Vol. 4A
Chachapoyas ................................ Vol. 5A
Chad ............................................. Vol. 2A
Chahar .......................................... Vol. 2A
Chala ............................................ Vol. 5A
Chamba ........................................ Vol. 3B
Channel Islands ............................ Vol. 3A
Chapel Hill, N.C. ............................... 223
Charkhari ...................................... Vol. 3B
Charleston, S.C. ............................... 223
Charlotte, N.C. .................................. 223
Charlottesville, Va. ............................ 223
Chateau de Beggen (Luxembourg #1466) ................... Vol. 4A
Chateau de Dommeldange (Luxembourg #1467) ................... Vol. 4A
Chattanooga, Tenn. .......................... 223
Chekiang ...................................... Vol. 2A
Chemins des Fer ........................... Vol. 2B
Cherifien Posts ............................. Vol. 2B
Chiapas ......................................... Vol. 4B
Chiclayo ........................................ Vol. 5A
Chiffre ........................... See France and French colonies, postage due
Chihuahua .................................... Vol. 4B
Chile ............................................. Vol. 2A
Chilean Occupation of Peru ......... Vol. 5A
Chimarra ....................................... Vol. 2B
China, Chinese .............................. Vol. 2A
China (Japanese Occupation) ..... Vol. 2A
China Expeditionary Force (India) .... Vol. 3B
China, British Offices ................... Vol. 3A
China, Formosa ............ Vol. 2A, Vol. 4A
China, French Offices .................. Vol. 2B
China, German Offices ................. Vol. 3A
China, Italian Offices ................... Vol. 3B
China, Japanese Offices .............. Vol. 4A
China, Northeastern Provinces ... Vol. 2A
China, Offices in Manchuria ........ Vol. 2A
China, Offices in Tibet ................. Vol. 2A
China, People's Republic ............ Vol. 2A
China, People's Republic Regional Issues ........................ Vol. 2A
China, People's Republic Hong Kong ................................ Vol. 3B
China, People's Republic Macao .... Vol. 4B
China, Republic of......................... Vol. 2A
China, Russian Offices ................ Vol. 5B
China, United States Offices ............ 177
Chine ............................................ Vol. 2B
Chios ............................................ Vol. 3A
Chita ............................................. Vol. 2B
Chosen .......................................... Vol. 4A
Christiansburg, Va. ........................... 223
Christmas Island ........................... Vol. 2A
Chungking .................................... Vol. 2B
C.I.H.S. ......................................... Vol. 6B
Cilicia, Cilicie .... Vol. 2A, Vol. 5A, Vol. 6A
Cincinnati, O. .................................... 191
Cinquan Tenaire ........................... Vol. 5A
Cirenaica ...................................... Vol. 2B
Ciskei ........................................... Vol. 6A
City Despatch Post ........................... 191
City Post ........................................... 191
Cleveland, O. .................................... 191
Cluj .............................................. Vol. 3B
c/m ............................................... Vol. 2B
C.M.T. ........................................... Vol. 6B
Coamo .................................. 247, Vol. 5B
Cochin .......................................... Vol. 3B
Cochin China ............................... Vol. 2A
Cochin, Travancore ...................... Vol. 3B
Co. Ci. ovptd. on Yugoslavia ...... Vol. 6B
Cocos Islands .............................. Vol. 2A
Colaparchee, Ga. .............................. 223
Colis Postaux ..... Vol. 1B, Vol. 2B, Vol. 3B
Colombia ...................... Vol. 2A, Vol. 5A
Colombian Dominion of Panama .... Vol. 5A
Colombian States ......................... Vol. 2A
Colon ............................................ Vol. 5A
Colonie (Coloniali) Italiane .......... Vol. 3B
Colonies de l'Empire Francaise .... Vol. 2B
Columbia, S.C. .................................. 223
Columbia, Tenn. ................................ 223
Columbus Archipelago ................ Vol. 2B
Columbus, Ga. .................................. 223
Comayagua .................................. Vol. 3B
Commando Brief .......................... Vol. 5A
Common Designs ..... See table of contents
Commissioning of Maryan Babangida (Nigeria #607) ........... Vol. 5A
Communicaciones ........................ Vol. 6A
Communist China ......................... Vol. 2A
Comores, Archipel des ............... Vol. 2A
Comoro Islands (Comores, Comorien) ..................... Vol. 2A, Vol. 4B
Compania Colombiana ............... Vol. 2A
Confederate States ........................... 221
Congo ........................... Vol. 1B, Vol. 2A
Congo Democratic Republic ...... Vol. 2A, Vol. 6B
Congo People's Republic (ex-French) ................................ Vol. 2A
Congo, Belgian (Belge) ............... Vol. 1B
Congo Francais ............................ Vol. 2B
Congo, Indian U.N. Force ........... Vol. 3B
Congo, Portuguese ...................... Vol. 5B
Congreso ...................................... Vol. 6A
Conseil de l'Europe ..................... Vol. 2B
Constantinople, Georgian Offices ... Vol. 3A
Constantinople, Polish Offices .... Vol. 5B
Constantinople, Italian Offices .... Vol. 3B
Constantinople, Romanian Offices ........................................ Vol. 5B
Constantinople, Russian Offices ... Vol. 5B
Constantinople, Turkey ............... Vol. 6B
Contribucao Industrial (Macao A14, P. Guinea WT1) .... Vol. 4B, Vol. 5B
Convention States (India) ........... Vol. 3B
Coo ............................................... Vol. 3B
Cook Islands ................................. Vol. 2A
Cook Islands, Niue ....................... Vol. 5A
Cordoba ........................................... 650
Corea, Coree ................................ Vol. 4A
Corfu ............................ Vol. 2A, Vol. 3B
Corona ......................... Vol. 1B, Vol. 2B
Correio, Correios e Telegraphos .... Vol. 5B
Correo Submarino ........................ Vol. 6A
Correo, Correos (no name) ............. 247, Vol. 2A, Vol. 5A, Vol. 6A
Corrientes ......................................... 650
Cos ............................................... Vol. 3B
Costa Atlantica ............................. Vol. 5A
Costa Rica .................................... Vol. 2A
Costantinopoli .............................. Vol. 3B
Cote d'Ivoire ................................ Vol. 3B
Cote des Somalis ......................... Vol. 6A
Council of Europe ......................... Vol. 2B
Cour Permanente de Justice Internationale ............................. Vol. 5A
Courtland, Ala. .................................. 223
Cpbnja .......................................... Vol. 6A
Cracow ......................................... Vol. 5B
Crete ............................ Vol. 2A, Vol. 3B
Crete, Austrian Offices ................ Vol. 1B
Crete, French Offices .................. Vol. 2B
Crete, Italian Offices .................... Vol. 3B
Crimea .......................... Vol. 5B, Vol. 6A
Croat Administration of Bosnia, Mostar ......................................... Vol. 1B
Croatia ......................................... Vol. 2A
Croatia-Slavonia .......................... Vol. 6B
Croissant Rouge Turc. ................ Vol. 6B
C.S.A. Postage ................................. 230
CTOT ........................................... Vol. 1B
Cuautla ........................................ Vol. 4B
Cuthbert, GA ..................................... 223
Cuba ................................... 236, Vol. 2A
Cuba stamps overprinted ........... Vol. 5B
Cuba, U.S. Administration .... 236, Vol. 2A
Cucuta ......................................... Vol. 2A
Cuernavaca .................................. Vol. 4B
Cundinamarca .............................. Vol. 2A
Curacao ......................... Vol. 2A, Vol. 5A
Cuzco ........................................... Vol. 5A
C.X.C. on Bosnia and Herzegovina ............................... Vol. 6B
Cyprus ......................................... Vol. 2B
Cyprus, Turkish Republic of Northern ..................................... Vol. 6B
Cyrenaica ......... Vol. 2B, Vol. 3A, Vol. 4A
Czechoslovakia ........................... Vol. 2B
Czechoslovak Legion Post .......... Vol. 2B
Czech Rep. .................................. Vol. 2B

**D ............................................... Vol. 3B**
Dahomey ....................... Vol. 1B, Vol. 2B
Dakar-Abidjan .............................. Vol. 2B
Dalmatia ....................................... Vol. 2B
Dalton, Ga. ....................................... 223
Danish West Indies ............ 237, Vol. 2B
Danmark ...................................... Vol. 2B
Dansk-Vestindien ............... 237, Vol. 2B
Dansk-Vestindiske .............. 237, Vol. 2B
Danville, Va. ..................................... 224
Danzig .......................................... Vol. 2B
Danzig, Polish Offices ................ Vol. 5B
Dardanelles .................................. Vol. 5B
Darlington C.H., S.C......................... 221
Datia (Duttia) ............................... Vol. 3B
D.B.L. ovptd. on Siberia and Russia ......................................... Vol. 2B
D.B.P. (Dalni Vostochini Respoublika) ............................ Vol. 2B
D. de A. ....................................... Vol. 2A
DDR ............................................. Vol. 3A
Debrecen ..................................... Vol. 3B
Deccan (Hyderabad) ................... Vol. 3B
Dedeagatch (Greek) .................... Vol. 3A
Dedeagh, Dedeagatch (French) ... Vol. 2B
Deficit ........................................... Vol. 5A
Demopolis, Ala. ................................ 224
Denikin ......................................... Vol. 6A
Denmark ...................................... Vol. 2B
Denmark stamps surcharged ...... Vol. 2B
Denver Issue, Mexico ................. Vol. 4B
Den Waisen ovptd. on Italy ......... Vol. 6B
Despatch (US 1LB, 5LB) .................. 191
Deutsch-Neu-Guinea .................. Vol. 3A
Deutsch-Ostafrika ....................... Vol. 3A
Deutsch-Sudwest Afrika ............. Vol. 3A
Deutsche Bundespost ................. Vol. 3A
Deutsche Demokratische Republik ..................................... Vol. 3A
Deutsche Nationalversammlung ... Vol. 3A
Deutsche Post ............................. Vol. 3A
Deutsche Post Berlin .................. Vol. 3A
Deutsche(s) Reich ....................... Vol. 3A
Deutsche Reich, Nr.21, Nr.16 ...... Vol. 3A
Deutschland ................................ Vol. 3A
Deutschosterreich ....................... Vol. 1B
Dhar ............................................. Vol. 3B
Diego-Suarez ............................... Vol. 2B
Diego-Suarez stamps surcharged ................................ Vol. 4B
Dienftmarke (Dienstmarke) .......... Vol. 3A
Dies I & II, British Colonies ...... See table of contents
Diligencia ..................................... Vol. 6B
Dinar ............................................ Vol. 6B
Dire-Dawa .................................... Vol. 2B
Dispatch (US 1LB) ............................ 191
Distrito ovptd. on Arequipa ......... Vol. 5A
DJ ovptd. on Obock ..................... Vol. 6A
Djibouti (Somali Coast) ... Vol. 2B, Vol. 6A
Dobruja District ........................... Vol. 5B
Dodecanese Islands ...... Vol. 3A, Vol. 3B
Dollar, ovptd. on Russia .............. Vol. 5B
Dominica ...................................... Vol. 2B
Dominican Republic, Dominicana ... Vol. 2B
Don Government ......................... Vol. 6A
Dorpat .......................................... Vol. 2B
Drzava SHS ................................. Vol. 6B
Dubai ............... Vol. 2B, Vol. 5A, Vol. 6B
Duck Stamps (Hunting Permit) ......... 217
Duitsch Oost Afrika overprinted on Congo ................................... Vol. 3A
Duke de la Torre Regency ........... Vol. 6A
Dulce et Decorum est Pro Patria Mori (Nepal O1) ............... Vol. 5A
Dungarpur .................................... Vol. 3B
Durazzo ........................................ Vol. 3B
Dutch Guiana (Surinam) ............. Vol. 6A
Dutch Indies ................................ Vol. 5A
Dutch New Guinea ...................... Vol. 5A
Duttia ........................................... Vol. 3B

**EA ..................................................... 411**
E.A.F. overprinted on stamps of Great Britain ........................... Vol. 3A
East Africa (British) ..................... Vol. 1B
East Africa (German) ................... Vol. 3A
East Africa (Italian) ..................... Vol. 3B
East Africa and Uganda Protectorates ................ Vol. 2B, Vol. 4A
East Africa Forces ....................... Vol. 3A
East China ................................... Vol. 2A
Eastern Rumelia .......................... Vol. 2B
Eastern Rumelia stamps overprinted ................................ Vol. 6B
Eastern Silesia ............................ Vol. 2B
Eastern Szechwan ....................... Vol. 2A
Eastern Thrace ............................ Vol. 6B
East India .................................... Vol. 3B
East Saxony ................................ Vol. 3A
East Timor ............................ 310, Vol. 6B
Eatonton, Ga. ................................... 224
Ecuador ....................................... Vol. 2B
E.E.F. ........................................... Vol. 5A
Eesti ............................................. Vol. 2B
Egeo ............................................. Vol. 3B
Egiziane (Egypt types A9-A10) .... Vol. 2B
Egypt, Egypte, Egyptiennes ....... Vol. 2B, Vol. 5A
Egypt, French Offices ................. Vol. 2B
Eire, Eireann (Ireland) ................. Vol. 3B
Ekaterinodar ................................ Vol. 6A
Elobey, Annobon and Corisco .... Vol. 2B
El Salvador .................................. Vol. 5B
Elsas, Elfas .................................. Vol. 2B
Elua Keneta ...................................... 238
Emory, Va. ........................................ 224
Empire, Franc, Francais .............. Vol. 2B
En ................................................. Vol. 4A
England ....................................... Vol. 3A
Epirus .......................................... Vol. 2B
Equateur (Ecuador #19-21) ......... Vol. 2B
Equatorial Guinea ....................... Vol. 2B
Eritrea .......................................... Vol. 2B
Eritrea (British Military Administration) ........................... Vol. 3A
Escuelas ...................................... Vol. 6B
Espana, Espanola ........................ Vol. 6A
Estado da India ............................ Vol. 5B
Est Africain Allemand overprinted on Congo ............... Vol. 3A
Estensi ......................................... Vol. 3B
Estero .......................................... Vol. 3B
Estland ......................... Vol. 2B, Vol. 5B
Estonia ......................... Vol. 2B, Vol. 5B
Etablissments Francais dans l'Inde ................................... Vol. 2B
Ethiopia, Etiopia, Ethiopie, Ethiopiennes ................ Vol. 2B, Vol. 3A
Eupen ........................................... Vol. 3A
Europe .......................................... Vol. 3A
Express Letter .............................. Vol. 2A

**15 August 1947 (Pakistan #23) ... Vol. 5A**
500 anos, viaje del descubrimiento de istmo (Panama #897) ............ Vol. 5A
F. A. F. L. ..................................... Vol. 6A
Falkland Dependencies ............... Vol. 2B
Falkland Islands .......................... Vol. 2B
Far Eastern Republic ................... Vol. 2B
Far Eastern Republic surcharged or ovptd. ..................................... Vol. 6A
Faridkot ........................................ Vol. 3B
Faroe Islands ............................... Vol. 2B
FCFA ovptd. on France ............... Vol. 2B
Federacion .................................. Vol. 6B
Federal Republic (Germany) ........ Vol. 3A
Federated Malay States .............. Vol. 4B
Fen, Fn. (Manchukuo) ................. Vol. 4B
Fernando Po, Fdo. Poo ............... Vol. 2B

INDEX AND IDENTIFIER 803


Feudatory States ........................ Vol. 3B
Fezzan, Fezzan-Ghadames ......... Vol. 4A
Fiera Campionaria Tripoli ........... Vol. 4A
Fiji .............................................. Vol. 2B
Fiji overprinted or surcharged ...... Vol. 5A
Filipinas, Filipas. ......................... Vol. 5A
Fincastle, Va. .................................. 224
Finland ....................................... Vol. 2B
Finnish Occupation of Karelia ..... Vol. 4A
Finnish Occupation of Russia .... Vol. 4A, Vol. 5B
Fiume ......................................... Vol. 2B
Fiume-Kupa Zone (Fiumano Kupa) ......................... Vol. 6B
Five Cents (Confed. #53X) ............. 227
Florida ....................................... Vol. 6B
F. M. ........................................... Vol. 2B
Foochow, Chinese ...................... Vol. 2A
Foochow, German ...................... Vol. 3A
Formosa ...................... Vol. 2A, Vol. 4A
Foroyar ...................................... Vol. 2B
Forsyth, Ga. .................................... 224
Fort Valley, Ga. ......................... 224, 230
Franc ........................................... Vol. 2B
Franc ovptd. on Austria .............. Vol. 1B
Franca ovptd. on stamps of Peru ... Vol. 5A
Francais, Francaise ...... See France and French colonies
France ........................................ Vol. 2B
France (German occupation) ...... Vol. 2B
France D'Outre Mer .................. Vol. 2B
Franco Bollo .............................. Vol. 3B
Franco Marke ............................. Vol. 3A
Franco Scrisorei ......................... Vol. 5B
Franklin, N.C. ................................... 224
Franqueo .................................... Vol. 5A
Franquicia .................................. Vol. 6A
Fraziersville, S.C. ........................... 224
Fredericksburg, Va. ........................ 224
Free ................................................ 191
Frei Durch Ablosung .................. Vol. 3A
Freimarke (No Country Name) ...... Vol. 3A
French Administration of Andorra .... 465
French Administration of Saar .... Vol. 5B
French Colonies ......................... Vol. 2B
French Colonies surcharged or overprinted .......... 519, Vol. 2B, Vol. 3A, Vol. 3B, Vol. 4B, Vol. 5A, Vol. 6A
French Commemoratives Index ... Vol. 2B
French Congo ............................. Vol. 2B
French Equatorial Africa ............ Vol. 2A, Vol. 2B, Vol. 4B, Vol. 6B
French Guiana ............................ Vol. 2B
French Guinea ............................ Vol. 2B
French India ............................... Vol. 2B
French Levant .............. Vol. 2B, Vol. 6A
French Mandate of Alaouites ........... 359
French Mandate of Lebanon ....... Vol. 4A
French Morocco .......................... Vol. 2B
French Occupation of Cameroun .... Vol. 2A
French Occupation of Castellorizo ................................ Vol. 2A
French Occupation of Crete ........ Vol. 2A
French Occupation of Germany .... Vol. 3A
French Occupation of Hungary ... Vol. 3B
French Occupation of Libya ........ Vol. 4A
French Occupation of Syria ........ Vol. 6A
French Occupation of Togo ........ Vol. 6B
French Oceania ......................... Vol. 2B
French Offices Abroad ............... Vol. 2B
French Offices in China .............. Vol. 2B
French Offices in Crete .............. Vol. 2B
French Offices in Egypt .............. Vol. 2B
French Offices in Madagascar .... Vol. 4B
French Offices in Morocco ........... Vol. 2B
French Offices in Tangier ........... Vol. 2B
French Offices in Turkish Empire ... Vol. 2B
French Offices in Turkish Empire surcharged ................................ Vol. 6A
French Offices in Zanzibar .......... Vol. 2B
French Polynesia ........................ Vol. 2B
French Saar ................................ Vol. 5B
French Southern and Antarctic Territories ................................ Vol. 2B
French stamps inscribed CFA ..... Vol. 2B
French stamps surcharged ........ Vol. 2B, Vol. 4B, Vol. 6A
French Sudan ............................. Vol. 2B
French West Africa ..................... Vol. 2B
French Zone (Germany) .............. Vol. 3A
Frimarke, Frmrk (No Country Name) ............. Vol. 2B, Vol. 5A, Vol. 6A
Fujeira ........................... Vol. 2B, Vol. 6B
Fukien ........................................ Vol. 2A
Funafuti ..................................... Vol. 6B
Funchal ...................................... Vol. 2B

**G or GW overprinted on Cape of Good Hope ................ Vol. 3A**
GAB on French Colonies ............ Vol. 3A
Gabon, Gabonaise ...................... Vol. 3A
Gainesville, Ala. ................................ 222
Galapagos Islands ...................... Vol. 2B
Galveston, Tex. ................................ 224
Gambia ....................................... Vol. 3A
Gaston, N.C. .................................... 224
Gaza ........................................... Vol. 3B
G & (et) D overprinted on French Colonies ....................... Vol. 3A
G.E.A. ovptd. ................ Vol. 3A, Vol. 6A
General Gouvernement (Poland) ... Vol. 5B
Geneva, Geneve ......................... Vol. 6A
Georgetown, S.C. ............................ 224
Georgia ......................... Vol. 3A, Vol. 6B
Georgia, Offices in Turkey .......... Vol. 3A
Georgienne, Republique ............ Vol. 3A
German Administration of Albania ... 363
German Administration of Danzig ... Vol. 2B
German Administration of Saar ... Vol. 5B
German Democratic Republic ..... Vol. 3A
German Dominion of Cameroun ... Vol. 2A
German Dominion of Caroline Islands ...................................... Vol. 2A
German Dominion of Mariana Is. .... Vol. 4B
German Dominion of Marshall Is. .... Vol. 4B
German Dominion of Samoa ....... Vol. 5B
German Dominion of Togo ......... Vol. 6B
German East Africa .................... Vol. 3A
German East Africa (Belgian occ.) ... Vol. 3A
German East Africa (British occ.) ..... Vol. 3A
German New Guinea .................. Vol. 3A
German New Guinea (New Britain) ............................. Vol. 5A
German Occupation of Belgium ... Vol. 1B
German Occupation of Estonia ... Vol. 2B
German Occupation of France .... Vol. 2B
German Occupation of Guernsey ... Vol. 3A
German Occupation of Ionian Is. .... Vol. 3B
German Occupation of Jersey ..... Vol. 3A
German Occupation of Latvia ..... Vol. 4A
German Occupation of Lithuania ..... Vol. 5B
German Occupation of Ljubljana .... Vol. 6B
German Occupation of Luxembourg ................................ Vol. 4A
German Occupation of Macedonia .................................. Vol. 4B
German Occupation of Montenegro ............................... Vol. 4B
German Occupation of Poland .... Vol. 5B
German Occupation of Romania .... Vol. 5B
German Occupation of Russia .... Vol. 5B
German Occupation of Serbia .... Vol. 6A
German Occupation of Ukraine .... Vol. 5B
German Occupation of Yugoslavia ................................. Vol. 6B
German Occupation of Zante ..... Vol. 3B
German Offices in China ............ Vol. 3A
German Offices in China surcharged ................................ Vol. 4A
German Offices in Morocco ........ Vol. 3A
German Offices in Turkish Empire .... Vol. 3A
German Protectorate of Bohemia and Moravia .............................. Vol. 2B
German South-West Africa ......... Vol. 3A
German stamps surchd. or ovptd. ...............Vol. 3A, Vol. 5B, Vol. 6A
German States ............................ Vol. 3A
Germany ..................................... Vol. 3A
Germany (Allied Military Govt.) .... Vol. 3A
Gerusalemme ............................. Vol. 3B
Ghadames .................................. Vol. 4A
Ghana ......................................... Vol. 3A
Gibraltar ...................................... Vol. 3A
Gilbert and Ellice Islands ............ Vol. 3A
Gilbert Islands ............................ Vol. 3A
Giumulzina District ..................... Vol. 6B
Gniezno ...................................... Vol. 5B
Gold Coast .................................. Vol. 3A
Golfo del Guinea ......................... Vol. 6A
Goliad, Tex. ...................................... 224
Gonzales, Tex. ................................. 225
Gorny Slask ................................ Vol. 6B
Government (U.S. 1LB) ..................... 191
Governo Militare Alleato ............. Vol. 3B
G.P.E. ovptd. on French Colonies ... Vol. 3A
Graham Land .............................. Vol. 2B
Granada ...................................... Vol. 6A
Granadine Confederation, Granadina ................................... Vol. 2A
Grand Comoro, Grande Comore ..... Vol. 3A
Grand Liban, Gd Liban ............... Vol. 4A
Great Britain (see also British) ..... Vol. 3A
Great Britain, Gaelic ovpt. ........... Vol. 3B
Great Britain, Offices in Africa ..... Vol. 3A
Great Britain, Offices in China .... Vol. 3A
Great Britain, Offices in Morocco Vol. 3A
Great Britain, Offices in Turkish Empire ............................. Vol. 3A
Greater Rajasthan Union ............. Vol. 3B
Greece ........................................ Vol. 3A
Greek Occupation of Albania, North Epirus, Dodecanese Islands ...................................... Vol. 3A
Greek Occupation of Epirus ........ Vol. 3A
Greek Occ. of the Aegean Islands .... Vol. 3A
Greek Occupation of Thrace ....... Vol. 6B
Greek Occupation of Turkey ...... Vol. 3A, Vol. 6B
Greek stamps overprinted .........Vol. 2B, Vol. 6B
Greenland ................................... Vol. 3A
Greensboro, Ala. .............................. 225
Greensboro, N.C. ............................ 225
Greenville .................................... Vol. 4A
Greenville, Ala. ................................ 225
Greenville, Tenn. .............................. 225
Greenville Court House, S.C. .......... 225
Greenwood Depot, Va. .................... 225
Grenada ...................................... Vol. 3A
Grenadines of Grenada .............. Vol. 3A
Grenadines of St. Vincent ........... Vol. 5B
Grenville ..................................... Vol. 4A
G.R.I. overprinted on German New Guinea .............................. Vol. 5A
G.R.I. overprinted on German Samoa ...................................... Vol. 5B
G.R.I. overprinted on Marshall Is. .... Vol. 5A
Griffin, Ga. ....................................... 225
Griqualand West ......................... Vol. 3A
Grodno District ........................... Vol. 4A
Gronland .................................... Vol. 3A
Grossdeutsches Reich (Germany #529) ..................... Vol. 3A
Groszy ........................................ Vol. 5B
Grove Hill, Ala. ................................. 225
Gruzija (Georgia) ......................... Vol. 3A
Guadalajara ................................. Vol. 4B
Guadeloupe ................................ Vol. 3A
Guam ............................................... 238
Guanacaste ................................. Vol. 2A
Guatemala ................................... Vol. 3A
Guayana ..................................... Vol. 6B
Guernsey .................................... Vol. 3A
Guernsey, German Occupation ... Vol. 3A
Guiana, British ............................ Vol. 1B
Guiana, Dutch ............................. Vol. 6A
Guiana, French ........................... Vol. 2B
Guine ............................ Vol. 3A, Vol. 5B
Guinea ........................... Vol. 3A, Vol. 6A
Guinea Ecuatorial ....................... Vol. 2B
Guinea, French ........................... Vol. 2B
Guinea, Portuguese .................... Vol. 5B
Guinea, Spanish .......................... Vol. 6A
Guinea-Bissau, Guine-Bissau ..... Vol. 3A
Guinee ........................... Vol. 2B, Vol. 3A
Guipuzcoa Province .................... Vol. 6A
Gultig 9, Armee ........................... Vol. 5B
Guyana ....................................... Vol. 3A
Guyane, Guy. Franc. .................. Vol. 2B
G.W. ovptd. on Cape of Good Hope ............................... Vol. 3A
Gwalior ....................................... Vol. 3B

**Habilitado-1/2 (Tlacotalpan #1) Vol. 4B**
Habilitado on Stamps of Cuba ....... 236, Vol. 2A, Vol. 5A
Habilitado on Telegrafos or revenues ...................... Vol. 5A, Vol. 6A
Hadhramaut ...................................... 314
Hainan Island .............................. Vol. 2A
Haiti ............................................ Vol. 3B
Hall, A. D. (Confed. #27XU1) ............ 224
Hallettsville, Tex. ............................. 225
Hamburg ...................................... Vol. 3A
Hamburgh, S.C. ............................... 225
Hamilton, Bermuda ..................... Vol. 1B
Hanover, Hannover ..................... Vol. 3A
Harar ........................................... Vol. 2B
Harper ......................................... Vol. 4A
Harrisburgh, Tex. ............................. 225
Hatay ........................................... Vol. 3B
Hatirasi (Turkey Design PT44) ..... Vol. 6B
Hatohobei (Palau #686) .............. Vol. 5A
Haute Silesie ............................... Vol. 6B
Haute Volta ................................. Vol. 1B
Haut Senegal-Niger .................... Vol. 6B
Hawaii, Hawaiian ............................. 238
H B A ovptd. on Russia .............. Vol. 6A
Hebrew inscriptions .................... Vol. 3B
H.E.H. The Nizam's (Hyderabad) ... Vol. 3B
Heilungkiang ............................... Vol. 2A
Hejaz ........................................... Vol. 6A
Hejaz-Nejd .................................. Vol. 6A
Hejaz overprinted .......... Vol. 4A, Vol. 6A
Helena, Tex. ...................................... 225
Heligoland, Helgoland ................ Vol. 3B
Hellas .......................................... Vol. 3A
Helsinki (Helsingfors) ................. Vol. 2B
Helvetia, Helvetica (Switzerland) ... Vol. 6A
Heraklion .................................... Vol. 2A
Herceg Bosna ............................. Vol. 1B
Herzegovina ................................ Vol. 1B
Herzogth ..................................... Vol. 3A
H.H. Nawabshah Jahanbegam ... Vol. 3B
H.I. Postage ...................................... 238
Hillsboro, N.C. ......................... 225, 230
Hoi Hao, French Offices ............. Vol. 2B
Holkar (Indore) ........................... Vol. 3B
Holland (Netherlands) ................. Vol. 5A
Hollandale, Tex. ............................... 225
Holstein ...................................... Vol. 3A
Honan ......................................... Vol. 2A
Honda ......................................... Vol. 2A
Honduras .................................... Vol. 3B
Honduras, British ....................... Vol. 1B
Hong Kong ................... Vol. 2A, Vol. 3B
Hong Kong (Japanese Occupation) ............................... Vol. 3B
Hong Kong Special Admin. Region ........................................ Vol. 3B
Hong Kong ovptd. China ........... Vol. 3A
Honour's (Hondur's) City ................. 191
Hopeh ......................................... Vol. 2A
Hopei .......................................... Vol. 2A
Horta ........................................... Vol. 3B
Houston, Tex. ................................... 225
Hrvatska ........... Vol. 1B, Vol. 2A, Vol. 6B
Hrzgl. .......................................... Vol. 3A
Huacho ....................................... Vol. 5A
Hunan ......................................... Vol. 2A
Hungary ........................ Vol. 1B, Vol. 3B
Hungary (French Occupation) ..... Vol. 3B
Hungary (Romanian Occupation) .... Vol. 3B
Hungary (Serbian Occupation) .... Vol. 3B
Huntsville, Tex. ................................. 225
Hupeh ......................................... Vol. 2A
Hyderabad (Deccan) .................. Vol. 3B

**I.B. (West Irian) ........................ Vol. 3B**
Icaria ........................................... Vol. 3A
ICC ovptd. on India .................... Vol. 3B
Iceland ........................................ Vol. 3B
Idar ............................................. Vol. 3B
I.E.F. ovptd. on India .................. Vol. 3B
I.E.F. 'D' ovptd. on Turkey .......... Vol. 4B
Ierusalem .................................... Vol. 5B
Ifni ............................................... Vol. 3B
Ile Rouad ..................................... Vol. 5B
Imperio Colonial Portugues ......... Vol. 5B
Imposto de Selo .......................... Vol. 5B
Impuesto (Impto) de Guerra ........ Vol. 6A
Inde. Fcaise ................................ Vol. 2B
Independence, Tex. ......................... 225
Index of U.S. Issues ........................ 160
India ............................. Vol. 3B, Vol. 5B
India, China Expeditionary Force .... Vol. 3B
India, Convention States ............. Vol. 3B
India, Feudatory States .............. Vol. 3B
India, French .............................. Vol. 2B
India, Portuguese ....................... Vol. 5B
India stamps overprinted ........... Vol. 3B, Vol. 4A, Vol. 5A
India, surcharge and crown ......... Vol. 6A
Indian Custodial Unit, Korea ....... Vol. 3B
Indian Expeditionary Force ......... Vol. 3B
Indian U.N. Force, Congo ........... Vol. 3B
Indian U.N. Force, Gaza ............. Vol. 3B
Indian Postal Administration of Bahrain ....................................... Vol. 1B
Indo-China, Indo-chine ................ Vol. 3B
Indo-China stamps surcharged ... Vol. 6B
Indo-China, Int. Commission ...... Vol. 3B
Indonesia ...................... Vol. 3B, Vol. 5A
Indore ......................................... Vol. 3B
Industrielle Kriegswirschaft ......... Vol. 6A
Inhambane .................................. Vol. 3B
Inini ............................................. Vol. 3B
Inland (Liberia #21) .................... Vol. 4A
Inner Mongolia (Meng Chiang) .... Vol. 2A
Insufficiently prepaid .................. Vol. 6B
Instrucao ..................................... Vol. 6B
Instruccion .................................. Vol. 6B
International Bureau of Education ... Vol. 6A
International Commission in Indo-China ................................ Vol. 3B
International Court of Justice ...... Vol. 5A
International Labor Bureau .......... Vol. 6A
International Olympic Committee .... Vol. 6A
International Refugee Organization ............................ Vol. 6A
International Telecommunication Union ........................................ Vol. 6A
Ionian Islands, IONIKON KPATOE ... Vol. 3B

804 INDEX AND IDENTIFIER

I.O.V.R. .......... Vol. 5B
Iran, Iraniennes .......... Vol. 3B
Iran (Bushire) .......... Vol. 1B
Iran, Turkish Occupation .......... Vol. 3B
Iran with Rs. 10 denomination (Pakistan #1101) .......... Vol. 5A
Iraq .......... Vol. 3B
Iraq (British Occupation) ..... Vol. 3B, Vol. 4B
Ireland .......... Vol. 3B
Ireland, Northern .......... Vol. 3A
Irian Barat .......... Vol. 3B
Isabella, Ga. .......... 226
Island .......... Vol. 3B
Isle of Man .......... Vol. 3A
Isole Italiane dell'Egeo .......... Vol. 3B
Isole Jonie .......... Vol. 3B
Israel .......... Vol. 3B
Istria .......... Vol. 6B
Itaca ovptd. on Greece .......... Vol. 3B
Ita-Karjala .......... Vol. 4A
Italia, Italiano, Italiane .......... Vol. 3B
Italian Colonies .......... Vol. 3B
Italian Dominion of Albania .......... 363
Italian Dominion of Castellorizo .... Vol. 2A
Italian East Africa .......... Vol. 3B
Italian Jubaland .......... Vol. 5A
Italian Occ. of Aegean Islands .... Vol. 3B
Italian Occupation of Austria ....... Vol. 1B
Italian Occupation of Corfu ......... Vol. 2A
Italian Occupation of Crete ......... Vol. 2A
Italian Occupation of Dalmatia .... Vol. 2B
Italian Occupation of Ethiopia ..... Vol. 2B
Italian Occupation of Fiume-Kupa .......... Vol. 6B
Italian Occupation of Ionian Islands .......... Vol. 3B
Italian Occupation of Ljubljana ... Vol. 6B
Italian Occupation of Montenegro ... Vol. 4B
Italian Occupation of Yugoslavia ... Vol. 6B
Italian Offices Abroad .......... Vol. 3B
Italian Offices in Africa .......... Vol. 3B
Italian Offices in Albania .......... Vol. 3B
Italian Offices in China .......... Vol. 3B
Italian Offices in Constantinople .... Vol. 3B
Italian Offices in Crete .......... Vol. 3B
Italian Offices in the Turkish Empire .......... Vol. 3B
Italian Social Republic .......... Vol. 3B
Italian Somaliland .......... Vol. 6A
Italian Somaliland (E.A.F.) .......... Vol. 3A
Italian stamps surcharged .......... Vol. 1B, Vol. 2B, Vol. 3B
Italian States .......... Vol. 3B
Italy (Allied Military Govt.) .......... Vol. 3B
Italy (Austrian Occupation) .......... Vol. 3B
Italy .......... Vol. 3B
Ithaca .......... Vol. 3B
Iuka, Miss. .......... 226
Ivory Coast .......... Vol. 3B

**J. ovptd. on stamps of Peru .... Vol. 5A**
Jackson, Miss. .......... 221, 226
Jacksonville, Ala. .......... 226
Jacksonville, Fla. .......... 226
Jaffa .......... Vol. 5B
Jaipur .......... Vol. 3B
Jamaica .......... Vol. 4A
Jamhuri .......... Vol. 6B
Jammu .......... Vol. 3B
Jammu and Kashmir .......... Vol. 3B
Janina .......... Vol. 3B
Japan, Japanese .......... Vol. 4A
Japan (Australian Occ.) .......... 796
Japan (Taiwan) .......... Vol. 2A, Vol. 4A
Japanese Offices Abroad .......... Vol. 4A
Japan Occupation of Brunei ....... Vol. 1B
Japan Occupation of Burma ....... Vol. 1B
Japan Occupation of China ........ Vol. 2A
Japan Occupation of Dutch Indies .......... Vol. 5A
Japan Occupation of Hong Kong ... Vol. 3B
Japan Occupation of Johore ...... Vol. 4B
Japan Occupation of Kedah ....... Vol. 4B
Japan Occupation of Kelantan .... Vol. 4B
Japan Occupation of Malacca .... Vol. 4B
Japan Occupation of Malaya ...... Vol. 4B
Japan Occupation of Negri Sembilan .......... Vol. 4B
Japan Occupation of Netherlands Indies .......... Vol. 5A
Japan Occupation of North Borneo .......... Vol. 5A
Japan Occupation of Pahang ..... Vol. 4B
Japan Occupation of Penang ..... Vol. 4B
Japan Occupation of Perak ........ Vol. 4B
Japan Occupation of Philippines .......... 245, Vol. 5A
Japan Occupation of Sarawak .... Vol. 6A
Japan Occupation of Selangor ... Vol. 4B
Japan Occupation of Sts. Settlements .......... Vol. 6A
Japan Occ. of Trengganu .......... Vol. 4B
Other Japanese Stamps Overprinted .... Vol. 1B, Vol. 2A, Vol. 4A, Vol. 5A
Jasdan .......... Vol. 3B
Java .......... Vol. 3B, Vol. 5A
Jedda .......... Vol. 6A
Jeend .......... Vol. 3B
Jehol .......... Vol. 2A
Jersey .......... Vol. 3A
Jersey, German Occupation ....... Vol. 3A
Jerusalem, Italian Offices .......... Vol. 3B
Jerusalem, Russian Offices ......... Vol. 5B
Jetersville, Va. .......... 226
Jhalawar .......... Vol. 3B
Jhind, Jind .......... Vol. 3B
Johore, Johor .......... Vol. 4B
Jonesboro, Tenn. .......... 226
J. P. Johnson (Confed. #66X1) ......... 228
Jordan .......... Vol. 4A
Jordan (Palestine Occ.) .......... Vol. 4A
Journaux .......... Vol. 2B
Juan Fernandez Islands (Chile) ... Vol. 2A
Jubile de l'Union Postale Universelle (Switzerland #98) .......... Vol. 6A
Jugoslavia, Jugoslavija .......... Vol. 6B
Junagarh .......... Vol. 3B

**K .......... 651**
KA3AKCTAH .......... Vol. 4A
Kabul .......... 317, 319
Kalaallit Nunaat, Kalatdlit Nunat .... Vol. 3A
Kamerun .......... Vol. 2A
Kampuchea .......... Vol. 2A
Kansu .......... Vol. 2A
Karelia, Karjala .......... Vol. 4A
Karema ovptd. on Belgian Congo ... Vol. 3A
Karki .......... Vol. 3B
Karolinen .......... Vol. 2A
Kashmir .......... Vol. 3B
Katanga .......... Vol. 4A
Kathiri State of Seiyun .......... 312
Kaunas .......... Vol. 4A, Vol. 5B
Kayangel (Palau #686) .......... Vol. 5A
Kazakhstan, Kazahstan, Kazakstan .......... Vol. 4A
Kedah .......... Vol. 4B
Keeling Islands .......... Vol. 2A
Kelantan .......... Vol. 4B
Kentta Postia .......... Vol. 2B
Kenya .......... Vol. 4A
Kenya and Uganda .......... Vol. 4A
Kenya, Uganda, Tanzania .......... Vol. 4A
Kenya, Uganda, Tanganyika ........ Vol. 4A
Kenya, Uganda, Tanganyika, Zanzibar .......... Vol. 4A
Kerassunde .......... Vol. 5B
Kermanshah .......... Vol. 3B
K.G.C.A. ovptd. on Yugoslavia .... Vol. 6B
K.G.L. .......... 237, Vol. 2B
Kharkiv .......... Vol. 6B
Khmer Republic .......... Vol. 2A
Khor Fakkan .......... Vol. 6A
Kiangsi .......... Vol. 2A
Kiangsu .......... Vol. 2A
Kiauchau, Kiautschou .......... Vol. 4A
Kibris .......... Vol. 6B
Kibris Cumhuriyeti (Cyprus #198-200) .......... Vol. 2B
Kigoma ovptd. on Belgian Congo ... Vol. 3A
Kilis .......... Vol. 6A
King Edward VII Land (New Zealand #121a) .......... Vol. 5A
Kingman's City Post .......... 191
Kingston, Ga. .......... 226
Kionga .......... Vol. 4A
Kirghizia .......... Vol. 4A
Kiribati .......... Vol. 4A
Kirin .......... Vol. 2A
Kishangarh, Kishengarh .......... Vol. 3B
Kithyra .......... Vol. 3A, Vol. 3B
K.K. Post Stempel (or Stampel) ... Vol. 1B
K.K.T.C. (Turk. Rep. N. Cyprus #RA1) .......... Vol. 6B
Klaipeda .......... Vol. 4B
Knoxville, Tenn. .......... 226
Kolomyia .......... Vol. 6B
Kolozsvar .......... Vol. 3B
Kon .... Vol. 1B, Vol. 2B, Vol. 4A, Vol. 5B, Vol. 6A
Kongeligt .......... Vol. 2B
Kop Koh .......... Vol. 2B
Korca, Korce (Albania) .......... 360
Korea .......... Vol. 4A
Korea, Democratic People's Republic .......... Vol. 4A
Korea (Japanese Offices) .......... Vol. 4A
Korea, Indian Custodial Unit ....... Vol. 3B
Korea, North .......... Vol. 4A
Korea, Soviet occupation .......... Vol. 4A
Korea, U.S. Military Govt. .......... Vol. 4A
Koritsa .......... Vol. 2B
Koror (Palau #686) .......... Vol. 5A
Korytsa (Albania #81) .......... 361
Kos .......... Vol. 3B
Kosova .......... Vol. 4A
Kosovo .......... 310, Vol. 4A
Kotah .......... Vol. 3B
Kouang Tcheou-Wan .......... Vol. 2B
KPHTH (Crete) .......... Vol. 2A
Kr., Kreuzer .......... Vol. 1B, Vol. 3B
Kraljevstvo, Kraljevina .......... Vol. 6B
K.S.A. .......... Vol. 6A
Kuban Government .......... Vol. 6A
K.U.K., K. und K. .......... Vol. 1B, Vol. 3B, Vol. 5B
Kunming .......... Vol. 2B
Kupa Zone .......... Vol. 6B
Kurdistan .......... Vol. 3B
Kurland, Kurzeme .......... Vol. 4A, Vol. 5B
Kurus .......... Vol. 6B
Kuwait, Koweit .......... Vol. 4A, Vol. 5A
Kwangchowan .......... Vol. 2B
Kwangsi .......... Vol. 2A
Kwangtung .......... Vol. 2A
Kweichow .......... Vol. 2A
K. Wurtt. Post .......... Vol. 3A
Kyiv .......... Vol. 6B
Kyrgyz Express Post .......... Vol. 4A
Kyrgyzstan .......... Vol. 4A

**La Aguera .......... 346**
Labuan .......... Vol. 4A
La Canea .......... Vol. 3B
Lady McLeod .......... Vol. 6B
La Georgie .......... Vol. 3A
Lagos .......... Vol. 4A
La Grange, Tex. .......... 226
Laibach .......... Vol. 6B
Lake City, Fla. .......... 226
Lanchow .......... Vol. 2A
Land Post .......... Vol. 3A
Lao, Laos .......... Vol. 4A
Laos (Int. Com., India) .......... Vol. 3B
L.A.R. .......... Vol. 4A
Las Bela .......... Vol. 3B
Latakia, Lattaquie .......... Vol. 4A
Latvia, Latvija .......... Vol. 4A, Vol. 5B
Laurens Court House, S.C. .......... 226
Lavaca .......... 228
League of Nations .......... Vol. 6A
Lebanon .......... Vol. 4A, Vol. 5A, Vol. 6A
Leeward Islands .......... Vol. 4A
Lefkas .......... Vol. 3A, Vol. 3B
Lei ovptd. on Austria .......... Vol. 5B
Lemnos .......... Vol. 3A
Lenoir, N.C. .......... 226
Lero, Leros .......... Vol. 3B
Lesbos .......... Vol. 3A
Lesotho .......... Vol. 4A
Lesser Sundas .......... Vol. 5A
Lettland, Lettonia .......... Vol. 4A
Letzebuerg .......... Vol. 4A
Levant, British .......... Vol. 3A
Levant, French .......... Vol. 2B, Vol. 6A
Levant, Italian .......... Vol. 3B
Levant, Polish .......... Vol. 5B
Levant, Romanian .......... Vol. 5B
Levant, Russian .......... Vol. 5B
Levant, Syrian (on Lebanon) ....... Vol. 6A
Lexington, Miss. .......... 226
Lexington, Va. .......... 226
Liaoning .......... Vol. 2A
Liban, Libanaise .......... Vol. 4A
Libau ovptd. on German .......... Vol. 4A
Liberia .......... Vol. 4A
Liberty, Va. .......... 226
Libya, Libia, Libye .......... Vol. 4A
Libyan Arab Republic .......... Vol. 4A
Liechtenstein .......... Vol. 4A
Lietuva, Lietuvos .......... Vol. 4A
Lifland .......... Vol. 5B
Ligne Aeriennes de la France Libre (Syria #MC5) .......... Vol. 6A
Lima .......... Vol. 5A
Limestone Springs, S.C. .......... 226
L'Inde .......... Vol. 2B
Linja-Autorahti Bussfrakt .......... Vol. 2B
Lipso, Lisso .......... Vol. 3B
Lithuania .......... Vol. 4A, Vol. 5B
Lithuania, Central .......... Vol. 2A
Lithuanian Occupation of Memel .... Vol. 4B
Litwa Srodkowa, Litwy Srodkowej .......... Vol. 2A
Livingston, Ala. .......... 226
Livonia .......... Vol. 5B
Ljubljana .......... Vol. 6B
Llanes .......... Vol. 6A
L McL .......... Vol. 6B
Local .......... Vol. 6B
Local Post .......... Vol. 2A
Lockport, N.Y. .......... 1
Lombardy-Venetia .......... Vol. 1B
Lorraine .......... Vol. 2B
Losen .......... Vol. 6A
Lothringen .......... Vol. 2B
Louisville, Ky. .......... 191
Lourenco Marques, L. Marques ... Vol. 4A
Lower Austria .......... Vol. 1B
L P overprinted on Russian stamps .......... Vol. 4A
LTSR on Lithuania .......... Vol. 4A
Lubeck, Luebeck .......... Vol. 3A
Lubiana .......... Vol. 6B
Lublin .......... Vol. 5B
Luminescence .......... 30
Luxembourg .......... Vol. 4A
Lviv .......... Vol. 6B
Lydenburg .......... Vol. 6B
Lynchburg, Va. .......... 226

**Macao, Macau .......... Vol. 4B**
Macedonia .......... Vol. 4B
Machin Head definitives .......... Vol. 3A
Macon, Ga. .......... 227
Madagascar, Madagasikara ........ Vol. 4B
Madagascar (British) .......... Vol. 4B
Madeira .......... Vol. 4B, Vol. 5B
Madero Issue (Mexico) .......... Vol. 4B
Madison, Ga. .......... 227
Madison Court House, Fla. .......... 227
Madrid .......... Vol. 6A
Madura .......... Vol. 5A
Mafeking .......... Vol. 2A
Magdalena .......... Vol. 2A
Magyar, Magyarorszag .......... Vol. 3B
Magy. Kir. .......... Vol. 3B
Majunga .......... Vol. 4B
Makedonija .......... Vol. 4B
Malacca .......... Vol. 4B
Malaga .......... Vol. 6A
Malagasy Republic .......... Vol. 4B
Malawi .......... Vol. 4B
Malaya .......... Vol. 4B
Malaya (Japanese Occ.) ... Vol. 4B, Vol. 5A
Malaya (Thai Occ.) .......... Vol. 4B
Malaya, Federation of .......... Vol. 4B
Malaysia .......... Vol. 4B
Malay States .......... Vol. 4B
Maldive Islands, Maldives .......... Vol. 4B
Malgache Republique .......... Vol. 4B
Mali .......... Vol. 4B
Malmedy .......... Vol. 3A
Malta .......... Vol. 4B
Maluku Selatan (So. Moluccas) ... Vol. 6A
Man, Isle of .......... Vol. 3A
Manchukuo .......... Vol. 4B
Manchukuo stamps overprinted ... Vol. 2A
Manchuria .......... Vol. 2A
Manizales .......... Vol. 2A
Mapka, Mapok .......... Vol. 2B, Vol. 5B
Mariana Islands, Marianen .......... Vol. 4B
Marienwerder .......... Vol. 4B
Marietta, Ga. .......... 227
Marion, Va. .......... 227
Markka, Markkaa .......... Vol. 2B
Maroc, Marocco, Marokko .......... Vol. 2B, Vol. 3A, Vol. 4B
Marruecos .......... Vol. 4B, Vol. 6A
Mars Bluff, S.C. .......... 227
Marshall Islands, Marschall-Inseln, Marshall-Inseln .......... Vol. 4B
Marshall Islands (G.R.I. surch.) ... Vol. 5A
Martinique .......... Vol. 4B
Martin's City Post .......... 191
Mauritania, Mauritanie .......... Vol. 4B
Mauritania stamps surcharged .... Vol. 2B
Mauritius .......... Vol. 4B
Mayotte .......... Vol. 4B
Mayreau .......... Vol. 5B
M.B.D. overprinted .......... Vol. 3B
McNeel, A.W. .......... 222
Mecca .......... Vol. 6A
Mecklenburg-Schwerin .......... Vol. 3A
Mecklenburg-Strelitz .......... Vol. 3A
Mecklenburg-Vorpomm .......... Vol. 3A
Mecklenburg-Vorpommern .......... Vol. 3A
Medellin .......... Vol. 2A
Medina .......... Vol. 6A
Medio Real .......... Vol. 2B
M.E.F. ovptd on Great Britain ...... Vol. 3A
Mejico .......... Vol. 4B
Melaka .......... Vol. 4B
Melekeor (Palau #686) .......... Vol. 5A
Memel, Memelgebiet .......... Vol. 4B

# INDEX AND IDENTIFIER

|  |  |
|---|---|
| Memphis, Tenn. | 227 |
| Meng Chiang | Vol. 2A |
| Menge | Vol. 4B |
| Mengtsz | Vol. 2B |
| Merida | Vol. 2B |
| Meshed | Vol. 3B |
| Mesopotamia (British Occupation) | Vol. 4B |
| Metelin | Vol. 5B |
| Mexico, Mexicano | Vol. 4B |
| Micanopy, Fla. | 227 |
| Micronesia | Vol. 4B |
| Middle Congo | Vol. 4B |
| Middle East Forces | Vol. 3A |
| Mihon | Vol. 4A |
| Mil | Vol. 4A |
| Militarpost (Milit. Post) | Vol. 1B |
| Millbury, Mass. | 1 |
| Milledgeville, Ga. | 227 |
| Miller, Gen. | Vol. 5B |
| Milliemes surch. on French Off. in Turkey | Vol. 2B |
| Mitau | Vol. 4A |
| Milton, N.C. | 227 |
| M. Kir. | Vol. 3B |
| Mn. | Vol. 4A |
| Mobile, Ala. | 227 |
| Mocambique | Vol. 4B |
| Modena, Modones | Vol. 3A |
| Moheli | Vol. 4B |
| Moldavia | Vol. 4B, Vol. 5B |
| Moldova | Vol. 4B |
| Moluccas | Vol. 5A |
| Monaco | Vol. 4B |
| Monastir | Vol. 6B |
| Mongolia | Vol. 4A |
| Mongtseu, Mongtze | Vol. 2B |
| Monrovia | Vol. 4A |
| Mont Athos | Vol. 5B |
| Montenegro | Vol. 4B |
| Monterrey | Vol. 4B |
| Montevideo | Vol. 6B |
| Montgomery, Ala. | 227 |
| Montserrat | Vol. 4B |
| Moquea, Moquegua | Vol. 5A |
| Morelia | Vol. 4B |
| Moroocco | Vol. 4B |
| Morocco (British Offices) | Vol. 3A |
| Morocco (German Offices) | Vol. 3A |
| Morocco, French | Vol. 2B |
| Morocco, Spanish | Vol. 6A |
| Morvi | Vol. 3B |
| Moschopolis | Vol. 2B |
| Mosul | Vol. 4B |
| Mount Athos (Greece) | Vol. 3A |
| Mount Athos (Turkey) | Vol. 6B |
| Mount Athos, Russian Offices | Vol. 5B |
| Mount Lebanon, La. | 227 |
| Mount Pleasant, NC | 227 |
| Moyen-Congo | Vol. 4B |
| Mozambique | Vol. 4B |
| Mozambique Co. | Vol. 4B |
| MQE ovptd. on French Colonies | Vol. 4B |
| Muscat and Oman | Vol. 5A |
| Mustique | Vol. 5B |
| M.V.iR | Vol. 5B |
| Myanmar (Burma) | Vol. 1B |
| Mytilene | Vol. 3A |
| **Nabha** | **Vol. 3B** |
| Naciones Unidas | 254 |
| Nagyvarad | Vol. 5B |
| Namibia | Vol. 5A, Vol. 6A |
| Nandgaon | Vol. 3B |
| Nanking | Vol. 2A |
| Nanumaga | Vol. 6B |
| Nanumea | Vol. 6B |
| Naples, Napoletana | Vol. 3B |
| Nashville, Tenn. | 221, 227 |
| Natal | Vol. 5A |
| Nations Unies | 254, Vol. 6A |
| Native Feudatory States, India | Vol. 3B |
| Nauru | Vol. 5A |
| Navanagar | Vol. 3B |
| Navarra | Vol. 6A |
| N.C.E. ovptd. on French Colonies | Vol. 5A |
| Neapolitan Provinces | Vol. 3B |
| Ned. (Nederlandse) Antillen | Vol. 5A |
| Ned. (Nederl, Nederlandse) Indie | Vol. 5A |
| Nederland | Vol. 5A |
| Nederlands Nieuw Guinea | Vol. 5A |
| Negeri Sembilan | Vol. 4B |
| Negri Sembilan | Vol. 4B |
| Nejd | Vol. 5A |
| Nejdi Administration of Hejaz | Vol. 6A |
| Nepal | Vol. 5A |
| Netherlands | Vol. 5A |
| Netherlands Antilles | Vol. 5A |

|  |  |
|---|---|
| Netherlands Indies | Vol. 5A |
| Netherlands New Guinea | Vol. 5A |
| Nevis | Vol. 5A |
| New Britain | Vol. 5A |
| New Brunswick | Vol. 2A |
| New Caledonia | Vol. 5A |
| New Caledonia stamps overprinted | Vol. 5A |
| Newfoundland | Vol. 2A |
| New Granada | Vol. 2A |
| New Greece | Vol. 3A |
| New Guinea | Vol. 5A |
| New Guinea, British | Vol. 5A |
| New Guinea, German | Vol. 3A |
| New Haven, Conn. | 1 |
| New Hebrides (British) | Vol. 5A |
| New Hebrides (French) | Vol. 5A |
| New Orleans, La. | 227 |
| New Republic | Vol. 5A |
| New Smyrna, Fla. | 228 |
| New South Wales | 704 |
| New York, N.Y. | 1 |
| New Zealand | Vol. 5A |
| Nezavisna | Vol. 2A |
| N.F. overprinted on Nyasaland Pro. | Vol. 3A |
| Ngaraard (Palau #686) | Vol. 5A |
| Ngardman (Palau #686) | Vol. 5A |
| Ngaremlengui (Palau #686) | Vol. 5A |
| Ngchesar (Palau #686) | Vol. 5A |
| Ngiwal (Palau #686) | Vol. 5A |
| Nicaragua | Vol. 5A |
| Nicaria | Vol. 3A |
| Nieuwe Republiek | Vol. 5A |
| Nieuw Guinea | Vol. 5A |
| Niger | Vol. 5A |
| Niger and Senegambia | Vol. 6A |
| Niger and Upper Senegal | Vol. 6B |
| Niger Coast Protectorate | Vol. 5A |
| Nigeria | Vol. 5A |
| Nikolaevsk | Vol. 6A |
| Ningsia | Vol. 2A |
| Nippon | Vol. 4A |
| Nisiro, Nisiros | Vol. 3B |
| Niuafo'ou | Vol. 6B |
| Niue | Vol. 5A |
| Niutao | Vol. 6B |
| Nllo. Caledonie | Vol. 5A |
| No Hay Estampillas | Vol. 5A |
| N. O. P. O. (Confed. #62XU1) | 228 |
| Norddeutscher Postbezirk | Vol. 3A |
| Noreg (1st stamp #318) | Vol. 5A |
| Norfolk, Va. | 228 |
| Norfolk Island | Vol. 5A |
| Norge | Vol. 5A |
| North Borneo | Vol. 5A |
| North China | Vol. 2A |
| Northeast China | Vol. 2A |
| Northeast Postal Service | Vol. 2A |
| Northeastern Provinces (China) | Vol. 2A |
| North Epirus (Greek Occupation) | Vol. 3A |
| Northern Cook Islands | Vol. 5A |
| Northern Cyprus, Turkish Rep. of | Vol. 6B |
| Northern Ireland | Vol. 3A |
| Northern Kiangsu | Vol. 2A |
| Northern Nigeria | Vol. 5A |
| Northern Poland | Vol. 5B |
| Northern Rhodesia | Vol. 5A |
| Northern Zono, Morocco | Vol. 4B |
| North German Confederation | Vol. 3A |
| North Ingermanland | Vol. 5B |
| North Viet Nam | Vol. 6B |
| Northwest China | Vol. 2A |
| North West (N. W.) Pacific Islands | Vol. 5A |
| Norway | Vol. 5A |
| Nossi-Be | Vol. 5A |
| Notopher | Vol. 5A |
| Nouvelle Caledonie | Vol. 5A |
| Nouvelle Hebrides | Vol. 5A |
| Nova Scotia | Vol. 2A |
| Novocherkassk | Vol. 6A |
| Nowa | Vol. 1B |
| Nowa Bb ovptd. on Bulgaria | Vol. 5B |
| Nowanuggur | Vol. 3B |
| Nowta | Vol. 6A |
| Nowte | Vol. 4B |
| Noyta | Vol. 1B, Vol. 3A, Vol. 4A, Vol. 5B, Vol. 6B |
| NP surcharged on Great Britain | Vol. 5A |
| Nr. 21, Nr. 16 | Vol. 5A |
| N S B ovptd. on French Colonies | Vol. 5A |
| N. Sembilan | Vol. 4B |
| N.S.W. | 704 |
| Nueva Granada | Vol. 2A |
| Nui | Vol. 6B |
| Nukufetau | Vol. 6B |
| Nukulaelae | Vol. 6B |

|  |  |
|---|---|
| Nyasaland (Protectorate) | Vol. 5A |
| Nyasaland and Rhodesia | Vol. 5B |
| Nyasaland, overprinted | Vol. 3A |
| Nyassa | Vol. 5A |
| N.Z. | Vol. 5A |
| **Oakway, S.C.** | **228** |
| Oaxaca | Vol. 4B |
| Obock | Vol. 5A |
| Ob. Ost ovptd. on Germany (Lithuania) | Vol. 5B |
| Occupation Francaise | Vol. 3B |
| Oceania, Oceanie | Vol. 2B |
| Oesterr. Post, Ofterreich | Vol. 1B |
| Offentlig Sak, Off. Sak. | Vol. 5A |
| Oil Rivers | Vol. 5A |
| O K C A (Russia) | Vol. 5B |
| Oldenburg | Vol. 3A |
| Olonets | Vol. 5B |
| Oltre Giuba | Vol. 4B |
| Oman, Sultanate of | Vol. 5A |
| ONU (UN Offices in Geneva #384) | 288 |
| Oradea | Vol. 5B |
| Orange River Colony | Vol. 5A |
| Oranje Vrij Staat | Vol. 5A |
| Orchha, Orcha | Vol. 3B |
| Ore surcharged on Denmark | Vol. 2B |
| Orense | Vol. 6A |
| Organisation Mondiale de la Sante | Vol. 6A |
| Oriental | Vol. 6B |
| Orts-Post | Vol. 6A |
| O.S. | Vol. 5A |
| Osten | Vol. 5B |
| Osterreich | Vol. 1B |
| Ostland | Vol. 5B |
| Ottoman, Ottomanes | Vol. 2B, Vol. 6B |
| Oubangi Chari | Vol. 6B |
| Outer Mongolia | Vol. 4A |
| Oviedo | Vol. 6A |
| O.V.S. | Vol. 5A |
| Oxford, N.C. | 228 |
| O'zbekiston | Vol. 6B |
| **P** | **Vol. 2A, Vol. 2B, Vol. 4A, Vol. 6A** |
| P on Straits Settlements | Vol. 5A |
| Pacchi Postali | Vol. 3B, Vol. 6A |
| Pacific Steam Navigation Co. | Vol. 5A |
| Packhoi, Pakhoi | Vol. 2B |
| Pahang | Vol. 4B |
| Paid (Confed. #35X, etc.) | 225 |
| Paid (US #4X1, 7X1, many Confed.) | 221, 228 |
| Paid 10 (Confed. #76XU, 101XU, 80XU) | 221, 224, 228, 229 |
| Paid 2 Cents (Confed. #2XU) | 222 |
| Paid 3 Cents (Confed. #2AXU) | 222 |
| Paita | Vol. 5A |
| Pakistan | Vol. 5A |
| Pakke-porto | Vol. 3A |
| Palau | Vol. 5A |
| Palestine | Vol. 2B, Vol. 5A |
| Palestine (British Administration) | Vol. 5A |
| Palestine (Jordan Occ.) | Vol. 4A |
| Palestine overprinted | Vol. 4A |
| Palestinian Authority | Vol. 5A |
| Panama | Vol. 5A |
| Panama (Colombian Dom.) | Vol. 2A, Vol. 5A |
| Panama Canal Zone | 231 |
| Papua | Vol. 5A |
| Papua New Guinea | Vol. 5A |
| Para | Vol. 2B, Vol. 6B |
| Para ovptd. on Austria | Vol. 1B |
| Para ovptd. on France | Vol. 2B |
| Para ovptd. on Germany | Vol. 3A |
| Para ovptd. on Italy | Vol. 3B |
| Paraguay | Vol. 5A |
| Paras | Vol. 2B |
| Paras ovpt. on Great Britain | Vol. 3A |
| Paras ovpt. on Romania | Vol. 5B |
| Paras ovpt. on Russia | Vol. 5B |
| Parma, Parm., Parmensi | Vol. 3B |
| Pasco | Vol. 5A |
| Patiala | Vol. 3B |
| Patmo, Patmos | Vol. 3B |
| Patterson, N.C. | 228 |
| Patton, N.B. (Confed. #138XU1) | 228 |
| Patzcuaro | Vol. 4B |
| Paxos | Vol. 2A, Vol. 3A, Vol. 3B |
| PC CP | Vol. 5A |
| PD | Vol. 5B |
| P.E. (Egypt #4, etc.) | Vol. 2B |
| Pechino, Peking | Vol. 3B |
| Peleliu (Palau #686) | Vol. 5A |
| Pen, Penna | Vol. 2B |
| Penang | Vol. 4B |
| Penny Post (US 3LB, 8LB) | 191, 192 |

|  |  |
|---|---|
| Penrhyn Island | Vol. 5A |
| Pensacola, Fla. | 228 |
| Penybnnka Cpncka | Vol. 1B |
| People's Republic of China | Vol. 2A |
| Perak | Vol. 4B |
| Perlis | Vol. 4B |
| Persekutuan Tanah Melayu (Malaya #91) | Vol. 4B |
| Persia (British Occupation) | Vol. 1B |
| Persia, Persanes | Vol. 3B |
| Peru, Peruana | Vol. 5A |
| Pesa ovpt. on Germany | Vol. 3A |
| Petersburg, Va. | 228 |
| Pfennig, Pfg., Pf. | Vol. 2B, Vol. 3A, Vol. 4A |
| P.G.S. (Perak) | Vol. 4B |
| Philadelphia, Pa. | 192 |
| Philippines | Vol. 2A, Vol. 5A |
| Philippines (US Admin.) | 240, Vol. 5A |
| Philippines (Japanese Occ.) | 245, Vol. 5A |
| Piast., Piaster ovptd. on Austria | Vol. 1B |
| Plaster ovptd. on Germany | Vol. 3A |
| Piaster ovptd. on Romania | Vol. 5B |
| Piastre, Piastra ovptd. on Italy | Vol. 3B |
| Piastre | Vol. 2B, Vol. 4B, Vol. 6B |
| Piastre ovptd. on France | Vol. 2B |
| Piastres ovpt. on Great Britain | Vol. 3A |
| Piastres ovpt. on Russia | Vol. 5B |
| Pies | Vol. 2A, Vol. 3B |
| Pietersburg | Vol. 6B |
| Pilgrim Tercentenary (US #548) | 16 |
| Pilipinas | 246, Vol. 5A |
| Pisco | Vol. 5A |
| Piscopi | Vol. 3B |
| Pitcairn Islands | Vol. 5B |
| Pittsylvania C.H., Va. | 228 |
| Piura | Vol. 5A |
| Plains of Dura, Ga. | 228 |
| Pleasant Shade, Va. | 228 |
| Plum Creek, Tex. | 228 |
| P.O. Paid | 192 |
| Pobres (Spain #RA11) | Vol. 6A |
| РОССIЯ, РОССИR | Vol. 5B |
| Poczta, Polska | Vol. 2B, Vol. 5B |
| Pohjois Inkeri | Vol. 5A |
| Pokutia | Vol. 6B |
| Poland | Vol. 5B |
| Poland, exile government in Great Britain | Vol. 5B |
| Polish Levant | Vol. 5B |
| Polish Offices in Danzig | Vol. 5B |
| Polish Offices in Turkish Empire | Vol. 5B |
| Polska | Vol. 5B |
| Polynesia, French (Polynesie) | Vol. 2B |
| Ponce | 247, Vol. 5B |
| Ponta Delgada | Vol. 5B |
| Р.О.П.иТ | Vol. 5B |
| Poonch | Vol. 3B |
| Popayan | Vol. 2A |
| Port Arthur and Dairen | Vol. 2A |
| Porteado | Vol. 5B |
| Porte de Conduccion | Vol. 5A |
| Porte de Mar | Vol. 4B |
| Porte Franco | Vol. 5B |
| Port Gibson, Miss. | 228 |
| Port Gdansk | Vol. 5B |
| Port Hood, Nova Scotia | Vol. 2A |
| Port Lagos | Vol. 2B |
| Port Lavaca, Tex. | 228 |
| Porto | 247, Vol. 1B, Vol. 6B |
| Porto Gazetei | Vol. 5B |
| Porto Pflichtige | Vol. 3A |
| Porto Rico | 247, Vol. 2A, Vol. 5B |
| Port Said, French Offices | Vol. 2B |
| Portugal, Portuguesa | Vol. 5B |
| Portuguese Africa | Vol. 5B |
| Portuguese Congo | Vol. 5B |
| Portuguese East Africa (Mozambique) | Vol. 4B |
| Portuguese Guinea | Vol. 5B |
| Portuguese India | Vol. 5B |
| Portuguese India overprinted | Vol. 6B |
| Posen (Poznan) | Vol. 5B |
| Post | Vol. 3A, Vol. 3B |
| Post (Postage) & Receipt | Vol. 3B |
| Posta | 361, Vol. 5B |
| Postage(s) | 228, 247, Vol. 3A, Vol. 3B, Vol. 4B, Vol. 5B |
| Postage Due | 795, Vol. 3A |
| Postas le hioc | Vol. 3B |
| Poste Locale | Vol. 6A |
| Postes | Vol. 1B, Vol. 2B, Vol. 4A |
| Postes Serbes ovptd. on France | Vol. 6A |
| Postgebiet Ob. Ost. | Vol. 5B |
| Postmarke | Vol. 3A |
| Post Office (US #7X, 9X) | 1 |
| Post Stamp | Vol. 3B |
| Postzegel | Vol. 5A |

806 INDEX AND IDENTIFIER

P.P. ovptd. on French postage dues ..... Vol. 2B
P.P.C. ovptd. on Poland ..... Vol. 5B
Pre ..... Vol. 6B
Prefecture issues ..... Vol. 4A
Preussen ..... Vol. 3A
Priamur ..... Vol. 6A
Prince Edward Island ..... Vol. 2A
Pristina ..... Vol. 6B
Province of Canada ..... Vol. 2A
Providence (Prov.), R.I. ..... 1
Prussia ..... Vol. 3A
PS ..... Vol. 2A, Vol. 3B
P.S.N.C. (Peru) ..... Vol. 5A
Puerto Principe ..... 236, Vol. 2A
Puerto Rico, Pto. Rico ..... 247, Vol. 2A, Vol. 5B
Puerto Rico (US Admin.) ..... 247, Vol. 5B
Pul ..... 319
Pulau Pinang ..... Vol. 4B
Puno ..... Vol. 5A
Puttialla State ..... Vol. 3B

**Qatar ..... Vol. 5B**
Qu'aiti State in Hadhramaut ..... 314
Qu'aiti State of Shihr and Mukalla ..... 313
Queensland ..... 707
Quelimane ..... Vol. 5B

**R (Armenia) ..... 651**
R (Jind, Iran) ..... Vol. 3B
R ovptd. on French Colonies ..... Vol. 2B
Rajasthan ..... Vol. 3B
Rajpeepla, Rajpipla ..... Vol. 3B
Raleigh, N.C. ..... 228
Rappen ..... Vol. 6A
Rarotonga ..... Vol. 2A
Ras al Khaima ..... Vol. 5B, Vol. 6B
R.A.U. ..... Vol. 6A
Rayon ..... Vol. 6A
Recargo ..... Vol. 6A
Redonda (Antigua) ..... 519
Refugee Relief ..... Vol. 3B
Regatul ..... Vol. 3B
Reichspost ..... Vol. 3A
Reis (Portugal) ..... Vol. 5B
Repubblica Sociale Italiana ..... Vol. 3B
Republic of China ..... Vol. 2A
Republique Arab Unie ..... Vol. 6A
Republique Democratique du Congo ..... Vol. 6B
Reseau d'Etat ..... Vol. 2B
Resistance overprinted on Syria ..... Vol. 6A
Rethymnon, Retymno ..... Vol. 2A
Reunion ..... Vol. 2B
R.F. ..... See France or French Colonies
RF - Solidarite Francaise ..... Vol. 2B
R H ..... Vol. 3B
Rheatown, Tenn. ..... 228
Rheinland-Pfalz ..... Vol. 3A
Rhine Palatinate ..... Vol. 3A
Rhodes ..... Vol. 3B
Rhodesia ..... Vol. 5B
Rhodesia (formerly So. Rhodesia) ..... Vol. 5B
Rhodesia and Nyasaland ..... Vol. 5B
Rialtar ..... Vol. 3B
Riau, Riouw Archipelago ..... Vol. 3B
Ricevuta ..... Vol. 3B, Vol. 6A
Richmond, Tex. ..... 228
Rigsbank Skilling ..... Vol. 2B
Ringgold, Ga. ..... 228
Rio de Oro ..... Vol. 5B
Rio Muni ..... Vol. 5B
RIS on Netherlands Indies ..... Vol. 3B
Rizeh ..... Vol. 5B
Rn. ..... Vol. 4A
RNS ..... Vol. 3B
R. O. ovptd. on Turkey ..... Vol. 2B
Robertsport ..... Vol. 4A
Rodi ..... Vol. 3B
Roepiah ..... Vol. 5A
Romagna, Romagne ..... Vol. 3B
Romana ..... Vol. 3B, Vol. 5B
Romania, Roumania ..... Vol. 5B
Romania, Occupation, Offices ..... Vol. 5B
Romanian Occupation of Hungary ..... Vol. 3B
Romanian Occupation of Western Ukraine ..... Vol. 6B
Romania, Offices in the Turkish Empire ..... Vol. 5B
Roman States ..... Vol. 3B
Ross Dependency ..... Vol. 5A
Rossija ..... Vol. 5B
Rostov ..... Vol. 6A
Rouad, Ile ..... Vol. 5B
Roumelie Orientale ..... Vol. 2B
Rpf overprinted on Luxembourg ..... Vol. 4A
RSA ..... Vol. 6A
R S M (San Marino) ..... Vol. 6A
Ruanda ovptd. on Congo ..... Vol. 3A
Ruanda-Urundi ..... Vol. 5B
Ruffifch-Polen ovptd. on Germany ..... Vol. 5B
Rumania, Roumania ..... Vol. 5B
Rumanien on Germany ..... Vol. 5B
Rupee on Great Britain ..... Vol. 5A
Russia ..... Vol. 5B
Russia (Finnish Occupation) ..... Vol. 4A, Vol. 5B
Russia (German Occupation) ..... Vol. 5B
Russian Company of Navigation & Trade ..... Vol. 5B
Russian Dominion of Poland ..... Vol. 5B
Russian Empire, Finland ..... Vol. 2B
Russian Occupation of Crete ..... Vol. 2A
Russian Occupation of Germany ..... Vol. 3A
Russian Occupation of Korea ..... Vol. 4A
Russian Occupation of Latvia ..... Vol. 4A
Russian Occupation of Lithuania ..... Vol. 4A
Russian Offices ..... Vol. 5B
Russian Offices in China ..... Vol. 5B
Russian Offices in Turkish Empire ..... Vol. 5B
Russian stamps surch. or ovptd. ..... 651, Vol. 2B, Vol. 3A, Vol. 4A, Vol. 5B, Vol. 6A
Russian Turkestan ..... Vol. 5B
Rustenburg ..... Vol. 6B
Rutherfordton, N.C. ..... 228
Rwanda, Rwandaise ..... Vol. 5B
Ryukyu Islands ..... 247

**S on Straits Settlements ..... Vol. 4B**
S A, S.A.K. (Saudi Arabia) ..... Vol. 6A
Saar, Saargebiet, Saar Land ..... Vol. 5B
Sabah ..... Vol. 4B
Sachsen ..... Vol. 3A
Sahara Occidental (Espanol) ..... Vol. 6A
St. Christopher ..... Vol. 5B
St. Christopher-Nevis-Anguilla ..... Vol. 5B
Ste. Marie de Madagascar ..... Vol. 5B
St. Georges, Bermuda ..... Vol. 1B
St. Helena ..... Vol. 5B
S. Thome (Tome) E Principe ..... Vol. 5B
St. Kitts ..... Vol. 5B
St. Kitts-Nevis ..... Vol. 5B
St. Louis, Mo. ..... 1
St. Lucia ..... Vol. 5B
St. Martin ..... Vol. 5B
St. Pierre and Miquelon ..... Vol. 5B
St. Thomas and Prince Islands ..... Vol. 5B
St. Vincent ..... Vol. 5B
St. Vincent and the Grenadines ..... Vol. 5B
St. Vincent Grenadines ..... Vol. 5B
Salamanca Province ..... Vol. 6A
Salem, N.C. ..... 228
Salem, Va. ..... 228
Salisbury, N.C. ..... 228
Salonicco, Salonika ..... Vol. 3B
Salonika (Turkish) ..... Vol. 6B
Salonique ..... Vol. 5B, Vol. 6B
Salvador, El ..... Vol. 5B
Salzburg ..... Vol. 1B
Samoa ..... Vol. 5B
Samos ..... Vol. 2B, Vol. 3A
San Antonio, Tex. ..... 228
San Marino ..... Vol. 6A
San Sebastian ..... Vol. 6A
Santa Cruz de Tenerife ..... Vol. 6A
Santa Maura ..... Vol. 3A, Vol. 3B
Santander ..... Vol. 2A
Sao Paulo ..... Vol. 1B
Sao Tome and Principe ..... Vol. 5B
Saorstat ..... Vol. 3B
Sarawak ..... Vol. 4B, Vol. 6A
Sardinia ..... Vol. 3B
Sarre overprinted on Germany and Bavaria ..... Vol. 5B
Saseno ..... Vol. 6A
Saudi Arabia ..... Vol. 6A
Saudi Arabia overprinted ..... Vol. 4A
Saurashtra ..... Vol. 3B
Savannah, Ga. ..... 229
Saxony ..... Vol. 3A
SCADTA ..... Vol. 2A
Scarpanto ..... Vol. 3B
Schleswig ..... Vol. 3A, Vol. 6A
Schleswig-Holstein ..... Vol. 3A
Schweizer Reneke ..... Vol. 6B
Scinde ..... Vol. 3B
Scotland ..... Vol. 3A
Scutari, Italian Offices ..... Vol. 3B
Segel Porto (on Neth. Indies) ..... Vol. 3B
Segnatasse, Segna Tassa ..... Vol. 3B
Seiyun ..... 312
Selangor ..... Vol. 4B
Selma, Ala. ..... 221, 229
Semenov ..... Vol. 2B
Sen, Sn. ..... 247, Vol. 4A, Vol. 5A
Senegal ..... Vol. 6A
Senegal stamps surcharged ..... Vol. 2B
Senegambia and Niger ..... Vol. 6A
Serb Administration of Bosnia, Banja Luca ..... Vol. 1B
Serbia, Serbien ..... Vol. 6A
Serbia & Montenego ..... Vol. 4B, Vol. 6A
Serbian Occupation of Hungary ..... Vol. 3B
Service ..... Vol. 3B, Vol. 5A
Sevastopol ..... Vol. 6A
Seville, Sevilla ..... Vol. 6A
Seychelles ..... Vol. 6A
S.H. ..... Vol. 3A
Shanghai ..... Vol. 2A, Vol. 6A
Shanghai (U.S. Offices) ..... 177
Shanghai and Nanking ..... Vol. 2A
Shansi ..... Vol. 2A
Shantung ..... Vol. 2A
Sharjah ..... Vol. 6A
Shensi ..... Vol. 2A
Shihr and Mukalla ..... 313
Shqipenia, Shqiptare, Shqiperija, Shqiperise (Albania) ..... 360
S.H.S. on Bosnia and Herzegovina ..... Vol. 6B
S.H.S. on Hungary ..... Vol. 6B
Siam (Thailand) ..... Vol. 6B
Siberia ..... Vol. 6A
Siberian stamps overprinted or surcharged ..... Vol. 2B
Sicily, Sicilia ..... Vol. 3B
Siege de la Ligue Arabe (Morocco #44) ..... Vol. 4B
Sierra Leone ..... Vol. 6A
Sikang ..... Vol. 2A
Silesia, Eastern ..... Vol. 2B
Silesia, Upper ..... Vol. 6B
Simi ..... Vol. 3B
Sinaloa ..... Vol. 4B
Singapore ..... Vol. 6A
Sinkiang ..... Vol. 2A
Sint Maarten ..... Vol. 5B
Sirmoor, Sirmur ..... Vol. 3B
Six Cents ..... 192
Sld. ..... Vol. 1B
Slesvig ..... Vol. 6A
Slovakia ..... Vol. 2B, Vol. 6A
Slovene Coast ..... Vol. 6B
Slovenia, Slovenija ..... Vol. 6A
Slovenia, Italian ..... Vol. 6B
Slovensko, Slovenska, Slovensky ..... Vol. 2B, Vol. 6A
S. Marino ..... Vol. 6A
Smirne, Smyrna ..... Vol. 3B
Smyrne ..... Vol. 5B
S O ovptd. on Czechoslovakia, Poland ..... Vol. 2B
Sobreporte ..... Vol. 2A
Sociedad Colombo-Alemana ..... Vol. 2a
Sociedade de Geographia de Lisboa ..... Vol. 5B
Societe des Nations ..... Vol. 6A
Soldi ..... Vol. 1B
Solomon Islands ..... Vol. 6A
Somali, Somalia, Somaliya ..... Vol. 6A
Somalia, B.M.A. ..... Vol. 3A
Somalia, E.A.F. ..... Vol. 3A
Somali Coast (Djibouti) ..... Vol. 6A
Somaliland Protectorate ..... Vol. 6A
Sonora ..... Vol. 4B
Sonsorol (Palau #686) ..... Vol. 5A
Soomaaliya, Sooomaliyeed ..... Vol. 6A
Soruth, Sorath ..... Vol. 3B
Soudan ..... Vol. 2B, Vol. 6A
South Africa ..... Vol. 6A
South African Republic (Transvaal) ..... Vol. 6B
South Arabia ..... Vol. 6A
South Australia ..... 710
South Bulgaria ..... Vol. 2B
South Borneo ..... Vol. 5A
South China ..... Vol. 2A
Southern Nigeria ..... Vol. 6A
Southern Poland ..... Vol. 5B
Southern Rhodesia ..... Vol. 6A
Southern Yemen ..... Vol. 6B
South Georgia ..... Vol. 2B, Vol. 6A
South Georgia and South Sandwich Islands ..... Vol. 6A
South Kasai ..... Vol. 6A
South Korea ..... Vol. 4A
South Lithuania ..... Vol. 4A
South Moluccas ..... Vol. 6A
South Orkneys ..... Vol. 2B
South Russia ..... Vol. 6A
South Russian stamps surcharged ..... Vol. 5B
South Shetlands ..... Vol. 2B
South Sudan ..... Vol. 6A
South Viet Nam ..... Vol. 6B
South West Africa ..... Vol. 6A
Southwest China ..... Vol. 2A
Soviet Union (Russia) ..... Vol. 5B
Sowjetische Besatzungs Zone ..... Vol. 3A
Spain ..... Vol. 6A
Spanish Administration of Andorra ..... 451
Spanish Dominion of Cuba ..... Vol. 2A
Spanish Dominion of Mariana Islands ..... Vol. 4B
Spanish Dominion of Philippines ..... Vol. 5A
Spanish Dominion of Puerto Rico ..... Vol. 5B
Spanish Guinea ..... Vol. 6A
Spanish Morocco ..... Vol. 6A
Spanish Sahara ..... Vol. 6A
Spanish West Africa ..... Vol. 6A
Spanish Western Sahara ..... Vol. 6A
Sparta, Ga. ..... 229
Spartanburg, S.C. ..... 229
SPM ovptd. on French Cols. ..... Vol. 5B
Srbija I Crna Gora ..... Vol. 6A
Sri Lanka ..... Vol. 6A
Srodkowa Litwa ..... Vol. 2A
Stamp (Tibet #O1) ..... Vol. 6B
Stampalia ..... Vol. 3B
Stanyslaviv ..... Vol. 6B
Statesville, N.C. ..... 229
Steinmeyer's City Post ..... 191
Stellaland ..... Vol. 6A
Stempel ..... Vol. 1B
Straits Settlements ..... Vol. 6A
Straits Settlements overprinted ..... Vol. 6A
Strombus gigas Linne (Neth. Antilles #1193) ..... Vol. 5A
STT Vuja, STT Vujna ..... Vol. 6B
Styria ..... Vol. 1B
S.U. on Straits Settlements ..... Vol. 4B
Submarine mail (Correo Submarino) ..... Vol. 6A
Sudan ..... Vol. 6A
Sudan, French ..... Vol. 2B
Suid Afrika ..... Vol. 6A
Suidwes-Afrika ..... Vol. 6A
Suiyuan ..... Vol. 2A
S. Ujong ..... Vol. 4B
Sultanate of Oman ..... Vol. 5A
Sumatra ..... Vol. 3B, Vol. 5A
Sumter, S.C. ..... 229
Sungei Ujong ..... Vol. 4B
Suomi (Finland) ..... Vol. 2B
Supeh ..... Vol. 2A
Surakarta ..... Vol. 3B
Surinam, Suriname, Surinaamse ..... Vol. 6A
Suvalki ..... Vol. 5B
Sverige ..... Vol. 6A
S.W.A. ..... Vol. 6A
Swaziland, Swazieland ..... Vol. 6A
Sweden ..... Vol. 6A
Switzerland ..... Vol. 6A
Switzerland, Administration of Liechtenstein ..... Vol. 4A
Syria, Syrie, Syrienne ..... Vol. 5A, Vol. 6A
Syria (Arabian Government) ..... Vol. 6A
Syrie ..... Vol. 6A
Syrie-Grand Liban ..... Vol. 6A
Szechwan ..... Vol. 2A
Szeged ..... Vol. 3B

**T ..... Vol. 1B, Vol. 2B**
T ovptd. on stamps of Peru ..... Vol. 5A
Tabora ovptd. on Belgian Congo ..... Vol. 3A
Tacna ..... Vol. 5A
Tadjikistan, Tadzikistan ..... Vol. 6A
Tae Han (Korea) ..... Vol. 4A
Tahiti ..... Vol. 6A
Taiwan (Republic of China) ..... Vol. 2A
Taiwan (Formosa) ..... Vol. 2A
Taiwan, Japanese ..... Vol. 2A, Vol. 4A
Tajikistan ..... Vol. 6A
Takca ..... Vol. 1B
Takse ..... 361, 407
Talbotton, Ga. ..... 229
Talca ..... Vol. 2A
Talladega, Ala. ..... 229
Tallinn ..... Vol. 2B
Tanganyika ..... Vol. 6A
Tanganyika and Zanzibar ..... Vol. 6A
Tanganyika (Tanzania), Kenya, Uganda ..... Vol. 4A
Tanger ..... Vol. 2B, Vol. 6A
Tangier, British Offices ..... Vol. 3A
Tangier, French Offices ..... Vol. 2B
Tangier, Spanish Offices ..... Vol. 6A
Tannu Tuva ..... Vol. 6A
Tanzania ..... Vol. 6A
Tanzania-Zanzibar ..... Vol. 6B
Tartu ..... Vol. 2B
Tasmania ..... 712

# INDEX AND IDENTIFIER

|  |  |
|---|---|
| Tassa Gazzette | Vol. 3B |
| Taxa de Guerra | Vol. 4B, Vol. 5B |
| Taxyapom | Vol. 2B |
| Tchad | Vol. 2A |
| Tchongking | Vol. 2B |
| T.C. overprinted on Cochin | Vol. 3B |
| T.C., Postalari | Vol. 6A |
| Te Betalen | Vol. 1B, Vol. 5A, Vol. 6A |
| Tegucigalpa | Vol. 3B |
| Teheran | Vol. 3B |
| Tellico Plains, Tenn. | 229 |
| Temesvar | Vol. 3B |
| Ten Cents | 192 |
| T.E.O. ovptd. on Turkey or France | Vol. 2A, Vol. 6A |
| Terres Australes et Antarctiques Francaises | Vol. 2B |
| Territorio Insular Chileno (Chile #1061) | Vol. 2A |
| Teruel Province | Vol. 6A |
| Tete | Vol. 6A |
| Tetuan | Vol. 6A |
| Thailand, Thai | Vol. 4B |
| Thailand (Occupation of Kedah) | Vol. 4B |
| Thailand (Occupation of Kelantan) | Vol. 4B |
| Thailand (Occupation of Malaya) | Vol. 4B |
| Thailand (Occupation of Perlis) | Vol. 4B |
| Thailand (Occupation of Trengganu) | Vol. 4B |
| Thessaly | Vol. 6B |
| Thomasville, Ga. | 229 |
| Thrace | Vol. 6B |
| Three Cents | 192 |
| Thuringia, Thuringen | Vol. 3A |
| Thurn and Taxis | Vol. 3A |
| Tibet | Vol. 6B |
| Tibet (Chinese province) | Vol. 2A |
| Tibet, Chinese Offices | Vol. 2A |
| Tical | Vol. 6B |
| Tientsin (Chinese) | Vol. 2A |
| Tientsin (German) | Vol. 3A |
| Tientsin (Italian) | Vol. 3B |
| Tiflis | Vol. 3A |
| Timbre ovptd. on France | Vol. 2B |
| Timor | Vol. 6B |
| Timor-Leste | Vol. 6B |
| Timor Lorosae | 310, Vol. 6B |
| Tin Can Island | Vol. 6B |
| Tjedan Solidarnosti (Yugoslavia #RA82) | Vol. 6B |
| Tjenestefrimerke | Vol. 2B, Vol. 5A |
| Tlacotalpan | Vol. 4B |
| Tobago | Vol. 6B |
| Toga | Vol. 2A |
| Togo, Togolaise | Vol. 6B |
| Tokelau Islands | Vol. 6B |
| Tolima | Vol. 2A |
| Tonga | Vol. 6B |
| Tongareva | Vol. 5A |
| Tonk | Vol. 3B |
| To Pay | Vol. 3A |
| Toscano | Vol. 3B |
| Tou | Vol. 3B |
| Touva, Tovva | Vol. 6A |
| Transcaucasian Federated Republics | Vol. 6B |
| Trans-Jordan | Vol. 4A, Vol. 5A |
| Trans-Jordan (Palestine Occ.) | Vol. 4A |
| Transkei | Vol. 6A |
| Transvaal | Vol. 6A |
| Transylvania | Vol. 3B |
| Trasporto Pacchi | Vol. 3B |
| Travancore | Vol. 3B |
| Travancore-Cochin, State of | Vol. 3B |
| Trebizonde | Vol. 5B |
| Trengganu | Vol. 4B |
| Trentino | Vol. 1B |
| Trieste | Vol. 1B, Vol. 3B, Vol. 6B |
| Trinidad | Vol. 6B |
| Trinidad and Tobago | Vol. 6B |
| Trinidad Society (Trinidad & Tobago #B1) | Vol. 6B |
| Tripoli di Barberia (Tripoli) | Vol. 3B |
| Tripoli, Fiera Campionaria | Vol. 4A |
| Tripolitania | Vol. 4A, Vol. 6B |
| Tripolitania (B.M.A.) | Vol. 3A |
| Tristan da Cunha | Vol. 6B |
| Trucial States | Vol. 6B |
| Tsinghai | Vol. 2A |
| Tsingtau | Vol. 2A, Vol. 3A |
| T. Tu. C | Vol. 6B |
| Tullahoma, Tenn. | 229 |
| Tumbes (Peru #129-133) | Vol. 5A |
| Tunisia, Tunisie, Tunis, Tunisienne | Vol. 6B |
| Turkestan, Russian | Vol. 5B |
| Turkey, Turkiye, Turk | Vol. 6B |
| Turkey (Greek Occupation) | Vol. 3A, Vol. 6B |
| Turkey in Asia | Vol. 6B |
| Turk Federe Devleti | Vol. 6B |
| Turkish Empire, Austrian Offices | Vol. 1B |
| Turkish Empire, British Offices | Vol. 3A |
| Turkish Empire, French Offices | Vol. 2B |
| Turkish Empire, Georgian Offices | Vol. 3A |
| Turkish Empire, German Offices | Vol. 3A |
| Turkish Empire, Italian Offices | Vol. 3B |
| Turkish Empire, Polish Offices | Vol. 5B |
| Turkish Empire, Romanian Offices | Vol. 5B |
| Turkish Empire, Russian Offices | Vol. 5B |
| Turkish Occupation of Iran | Vol. 3B |
| Turkish Republic of Northern Cyprus | Vol. 6B |
| Turkish stamps surcharged or overprinted | Vol. 2B, Vol. 3A, Vol. 6A |
| Turkish Suzerainty of Egypt | Vol. 2B |
| Turkmenistan, Turkmenpocta | Vol. 6B |
| Turks and Caicos Islands | Vol. 6B |
| Turks Islands | Vol. 6B |
| Tuscaloosa, Ala. | 229 |
| Tuscany | Vol. 3B |
| Tuscumbia, Ala. | 221, 229 |
| Tuva Autonomous Region | Vol. 6A |
| Tuvalu | Vol. 6B |
| Two Cents (Confed. #53X5) | 227 |
| Two Pence | 704 |
| Two Sicilies | Vol. 3B |
| Tyosen (Korea) | Vol. 4A |
| Tyrol | Vol. 1D |
| UAE ovptd. on Abu Dhabi | Vol. 6B |
| U.A.R. | Vol. 2B, Vol. 6A, Vol. 6B |
| Ubangi, Ubangi-Shari | Vol. 6B |
| Uganda, U.G. | Vol. 6B |
| Uganda, and Kenya | Vol. 4A |
| Uganda, Tanganyika, Kenya | Vol. 4A |
| Ukraine, Ukraina | Vol. 6B |
| Ukraine (German Occupation) | Vol. 5B |
| Ukraine stamps surcharged | Vol. 5B |
| Ukrainian Soviet Socialist Republic | Vol. 6B |
| Ukraine, Western | Vol. 6B |
| Uku Leta | 238 |
| Ultramar | Vol. 2A |
| Umm al Qiwain | Vol. 6B |
| UNEF ovptd. on India | Vol. 3B |
| UNESCO | Vol. 2B |
| U.N. Force in Congo or Gaza (India) | Vol. 3B |
| Union Island, St. Vincent | Vol. 5B |
| Union Islands | Vol. 6B |
| Union of South Africa | Vol. 6A |
| Union of Soviet Socialist Republics | Vol. 5B |
| Uniontown, Ala. | 229 |
| Unionville, S.C. | 229 |
| United Arab Emirates | Vol. 6B |
| United Arab Republic (UAR) | Vol. 2B, Vol. 6A, Vol. 6B |
| United Arab Republic, Egypt | Vol. 2B |
| United Arab Republic Issues for Syria | Vol. 6A |
| United Kingdom | Vol. 6A |
| United Nations | 254 |
| United Nations European Office | 283, Vol. 6A |
| United Nations Offices in Geneva | 283 |
| United Nations Offices in Vienna | 296 |
| United Nations - Kosovo | 310, Vol. 4A |
| United Nations - West New Guinea | 309 |
| United State of Saurashtra | Vol. 3B |
| United States Adm. of Canal Zone | 231 |
| United States Adm. of Cuba | 236, Vol. 2A |
| United States Adm. of Guam | 238 |
| U. S. Adm. of Philippines | 240, Vol. 5A |
| U. S. Adm. of Puerto Rico | 247, Vol. 5B |
| U. S. Military Rule of Korea | Vol. 4A |
| United States of America | 2 |
| United States of Indonesia | Vol. 3B |
| United States of New Granada | Vol. 2A |
| United States, Offices in China | 177 |
| Un Real | Vol. 2B |
| U.S. Zone (Germany) | Vol. 3A |
| Universal Postal Union, Intl. Bureau | Vol. 6A |
| UNTEA ovptd. on Netherlands New Guinea | 309, Vol. 3B |
| UNTEAT | Vol. 6B |
| UPHA ROPA | Vol. 4B |
| Upper Austria | Vol. 1B |
| Upper Senegal and Niger | Vol. 6B |
| Upper Silesia | Vol. 6B |
| Upper Volta | Vol. 1B |
| Urgente | Vol. 6A |
| U.R.I. ovptd. on Yugoslavia | Vol. 6B |
| Uruguay | Vol. 6B |
| Urundi ovptd. on Congo | Vol. 3A |
| Uskub | Vol. 6B |
| U.S. Mail | 192 |
| U.S.P.O. | 192 |
| U.S.P.O. Despatch | 191, 192 |
| U.S.S.R. | Vol. 5B |
| U. S. T.C. overprinted on Cochin | Vol. 3B |
| Uzbekistan | Vol. 6B |
| Vaitupu | Vol. 6B |
| Valdosta, Ga. | 229 |
| Valencia | Vol. 6A |
| Valladolid Province | Vol. 6A |
| Valona | Vol. 3B |
| Valparaiso | Vol. 2A |
| Vancouver Island | Vol. 2A |
| Van Diemen's Land (Tasmania) | 712 |
| Vanuatu | Vol. 6B |
| Varldspost Kongress (Sweden #197) | Vol. 6A |
| Vasa | Vol. 2B |
| Vathy | Vol. 2B |
| Vatican City, Vaticane, Vaticano | Vol. 6B |
| Venda | Vol. 6B |
| Venezia Giulia | Vol. 1B, Vol. 3B |
| Venezia Tridentina | Vol. 1B |
| Venezuela, Veneza., Venezolana | Vol. 6B |
| Venizelist Government | Vol. 3A |
| Vereinte Nationen | 296 |
| Vetekeverria | 361 |
| Victoria | 714 |
| Victoria, Tex. | 229 |
| Victoria Land | Vol. 5A |
| Vienna | 296, Vol. 1B |
| Vienna Issues | Vol. 3B |
| Viet Minh | Vol. 6B |
| Viet Nam | Vol. 6B |
| Viet Nam Buu Chinh | Vol. 6B |
| Viet Nam Buu Dien | Vol. 6B |
| Viet Nam Cong-Hoa | Vol. 6B |
| Viet Nam Dan-Chu Cong-Hoa | Vol. 6B |
| Viet Nam, Democratic Republic | Vol. 6B |
| Viet Nam Doc-Lap | Vol. 6B |
| Viet Nam, (Int. Com., India) | Vol. 3B |
| Viet Nam, North | Vol. 6B |
| Viet Nam, Republic | Vol. 6B |
| Viet Nam, South | Vol. 6B |
| Villa Bella (Brazil #97) | Vol. 1B |
| Vilnius | Vol. 4A, Vol. 5B |
| Vineta | Vol. 3A |
| Virgin Islands | Vol. 6B |
| Vladivostok | Vol. 2B |
| Vojna Uprava | Vol. 6B |
| Volksrust | Vol. 6B |
| Vom Empfanger | Vol. 2B, Vol. 3A |
| Vorarlberg | Vol. 1B |
| V.R. ovptd. on Transvaal | Vol. 2A, Vol. 6A |
| Vryburg | Vol. 2A |
| Vuja-STT, Vujna-STT | Vol. 6B |
| Wadhwan | Vol. 3B |
| Walachia | Vol. 5B |
| Wales & Monmouthshire | Vol. 3A |
| Wallis and Futuna Islands | Vol. 6B |
| Walterborough, S.C. | 229 |
| War Board of Trade | Vol. 6A |
| Warrenton, Ga. | 230 |
| Warsaw, Warszawa | Vol. 5B |
| Washington, Ga. | 230 |
| Watermarks (British Colonies) | See table of contents |
| Weatherford, Tex. | 230 |
| Weihnachten Joos van Cleve-Geburt Christi (Austria 2479) | Vol. 1B |
| Wenden, Wendensche | Vol. 5B |
| Western Army | Vol. 4A |
| Western Australia | 718 |
| Western Samoa | Vol. 5B |
| Western Szechwan | Vol. 2A |
| Western Thrace (Greek Occupation) | Vol. 6B |
| Western Turkey | Vol. 3A |
| Western Ukraine | Vol. 6B |
| West Irian | Vol. 3B |
| West New Guinea | 309, Vol. 3B |
| West Saxony | Vol. 3A |
| Wet and dry printings | 233 |
| Wharton's U.S. P.O. Despatch | 191 |
| White Russia | Vol. 1B |
| Wiederaufbauspende | Vol. 3A |
| Wilayah Persekutuan | Vol. 4B |
| Wilkesboro, N.C. | 230 |
| Williams City Post | 191 |
| Winnsborough, S.C. | 230 |
| Wir sind frei | Vol. 2B |
| Wn. | Vol. 4A |
| Wohnungsbau | Vol. 3A |
| Wolmaransstad | Vol. 6B |
| World Health Organization | Vol. 6A |
| World Intellectual Property Organization | Vol. 6A |
| World Meteorological Organization | Vol. 6A |
| Worldwide | Vol. 3A |
| Wrangel issues | Vol. 5B |
| Wurttemberg | Vol. 3A |
| Wytheville, Va. | 230 |
| Xeimappa | Vol. 2B |
| Yambo | Vol. 6A |
| Y.A.R. | Vol. 6B |
| Yca | Vol. 5A |
| Yemen | Vol. 6B |
| Yemen Arab Republic | Vol. 6B |
| Yemen People's Republic | Vol. 6B |
| Yemen, People's Democratic Rep. | Vol. 6B |
| Yen, Yn. | 247, Vol. 4A |
| Ykp. H.P., Ykpaiha | Vol. 6B |
| Yksi Markka | Vol. 2B |
| Yuan | Vol. 2A |
| Yucatan | Vol. 4B |
| Yudenich, Gen. | Vol. 5B |
| Yugoslavia | Vol. 6B |
| Yugoslavia (German Occupation) | Vol. 6B |
| Yugoslavia (Italian Occupation) | Vol. 6B |
| Yugoslavia (Trieste) | Vol. 6B |
| Yugoslavia (Zone B) | Vol. 6B |
| Yugoslavia Offices Abroad | Vol. 6B |
| Yugoslavia stamps overprinted and surcharged | Vol. 1B |
| Yunnan (China) | Vol. 2A |
| Yunnan Fou, Yunnansen | Vol. 2B |
| Za Crveni Krst (Yugoslavia #RA2) | Vol. 6B |
| Z. Afr. Republiek, Z.A.R. | Vol. 6A |
| Zaire | Vol. 6B |
| Zambezia | Vol. 6B |
| Zambia | Vol. 6B |
| Zante | Vol. 6B |
| Zanzibar | Vol. 6B |
| Zanzibar, French Offices | Vol. 2B |
| Zanzibar (Kenya, Uganda, Tanganyika) | Vol. 4A |
| Zanzibar-Tanzania | Vol. 6B |
| Z.A.R. ovptd. on Cape of Good Hope | Vol. 2A |
| Zelaya | Vol. 5A |
| Zentraler Kurierdienst | Vol. 3A |
| Zil Eloigne Sesel | Vol. 6A |
| Zil Elwagne Sesel | Vol. 6A |
| Zil Elwannyen Sesel | Vol. 6A |
| Zimbabwe | Vol. 6B |
| Zimska Pomoc ovptd. on Italy | Vol. 6B |
| Zone A (Trieste) | Vol. 3B |
| Zone B (Istria) | Vol. 6B |
| Zone B (Trieste) | Vol. 6B |
| Zone Francaise | Vol. 3A |
| Zuid Afrika | Vol. 5A, Vol. 6A |
| Zuidafrikaansche Republiek | Vol. 6B |
| Zuidwest Afrika | Vol. 6A |
| Zululand | Vol. 6B |
| Zurich | Vol. 6A |

# 2025 VOLUME 1A DEALER DIRECTORY YELLOW PAGE LISTINGS

This section of your Scott Catalogue contains advertisements to help you conveniently find what you need, when you need it...!

| | | | |
|---|---|---|---|
| Appraisals......811 | China - PRC......811 | United States......812 | Websites......812 |
| Auctions......811 | Collections......811 | U.S. - Classics/ | Worldwide......812 |
| British Asia......811 | Ducks......811 | Moderns......812 | Worldwide - |
| British | New Issues......811 | U.S. - Collections | Collections......812 |
| Commonwealth......811 | Stamp Stores......811 | Wanted......812 | |
| Buying......811 | Supplies......812 | Wanted Worldwide | |
| Canada......811 | Topicals - Columbus......812 | Collections......812 | |

## INDEX TO ADVERTISERS 2025 VOLUME 1A

| ADVERTISER | PAGE |
|---|---|
| **– A –** | |
| Almaz Co. | Yellow Pages |
| **– B –** | |
| Jim Bardo | 21 |
| **– C –** | |
| Colonial Stamp Co. | Yellow Pages |
| **– G –** | |
| Henry Gitner Philatelists, Inc. | 13 |
| **– H –** | |
| William Henry Stamp Co. | 255 |
| **– J –** | |
| Michael Jaffe | 219 |
| **– K –** | |
| Walter Kasell | 159, 176 |
| Patricia A. Kaufmann | 221 |
| Daniel F. Kelleher Auctions | Inside Front Cover |

| ADVERTISER | PAGE |
|---|---|
| **– M –** | |
| Miller's Stamp Co. | 5 |
| Mystic Stamp Co. | Back Cover |
| **– P –** | |
| Philasearch.com GmbH | 7, 23, 239, 241, 575, 715 |
| **– S –** | |
| Robert A. Siegel Auction Gallery | 3 |
| **– U –** | |
| United Postal Stationery Society | 193 |
| United States Stamp Society (TX) | 19 |
| **– V –** | |
| Vidiforms Company, Inc. | Yellow Pages |
| **– W –** | |
| Laurence Winum | 15 |

## DEALER DIRECTORY AND YELLOW PAGES

### Appraisals

**DR. ROBERT FRIEDMAN & SONS STAMP & COIN BUYING CENTER**
2029 W. 75th St.
Woodridge, IL 60517
PH: 800-588-8100
FAX: 630-985-1588
stampcollections@drbobstamps.com
www.drbobfriedmanstamps.com

### Auctions

**DUTCH COUNTRY AUCTIONS**
The Stamp Center
4115 Concord Pike
Wilmington, DE 19803
PH: 302-478-8740
FAX: 302-478-8779
auctions@dutchcountryauctions.com
www.dutchcountryauctions.com

### British Asia

**THE STAMP ACT**
PO Box 1136
Belmont, CA 94002
PH: 650-703-2342
thestampact@sbcglobal.net

### British Commonwealth

**ARON R. HALBERSTAM PHILATELISTS, LTD.**
PO Box 150168
Van Brunt Station
Brooklyn, NY 11215-0168
PH: 718-788-3978
arh@arhstamps.com
www.arhstamps.com

**ROY'S STAMPS**
PO Box 28001
600 Ontario Street
St. Catharines, ON
CANADA L2N 7P8
Phone: 905-934-8377
Email: roystamp@cogeco.ca
www.roysstamps.com

**THE STAMP ACT**
PO Box 1136
Belmont, CA 94002
PH: 650-703-2342
thestampact@sbcglobal.net

### Buying

**DR. ROBERT FRIEDMAN & SONS STAMP & COIN BUYING CENTER**
2029 W. 75th St.
Woodridge, IL 60517
PH: 800-588-8100
FAX: 630-985-1588
stampcollections@drbobstamps.com
www.drbobfriedmanstamps.com

### Canada

**ROY'S STAMPS**
PO Box 28001
600 Ontario Street
St. Catharines, ON
CANADA L2N 7P8
Phone: 905-934-8377
Email: roystamp@cogeco.ca
www.roysstamps.com

### China - PRC

**THE STAMP ACT**
PO Box 1136
Belmont, CA 94002
PH: 650-703-2342
thestampact@sbcglobal.net

### Collections

**DR. ROBERT FRIEDMAN & SONS STAMP & COIN BUYING CENTER**
2029 W. 75th St.
Woodridge, IL 60517
PH: 800-588-8100
FAX: 630-985-1588
stampcollections@drbobstamps.com
www.drbobfriedmanstamps.com

### Ducks

**MICHAEL JAFFE**
PO Box 61484
Vancouver, WA 98666
PH: 360-695-6161
PH: 800-782-6770
FAX: 360-695-1616
mjaffe@brookmanstamps.com
www.brookmanstamps.com

### New Issues

**DAVIDSON'S STAMP SERVICE**
Personalized Service since 1970
PO Box 36355
Indianapolis, IN 46236-0355
PH: 317-826-2620
ed-davidson@earthlink.net
www.newstampissues.com

### Stamp Stores

### Connecticut

**MILLER'S STAMP COMPANY**
P.O. Box 1011
Niantic, CT 06357
www.millerstamps.com
PH: 860-908-6200

### Stamp Stores

### Delaware

**DUTCH COUNTRY AUCTIONS**
The Stamp Center
4115 Concord Pike
Wilmington, DE 19803
PH: 302-478-8740
FAX: 302-478-8779
auctions@dutchcountryauctions.com
www.dutchcountryauctions.com

### Florida

**DR. ROBERT FRIEDMAN & SONS STAMP & COIN BUYING CENTER**
PH: 800-588-8100
FAX: 630-985-1588
stampcollections@drbobstamps.com
www.drbobfriedmanstamps.com

### Illinois

**DR. ROBERT FRIEDMAN & SONS STAMP & COIN BUYING CENTER**
2029 W. 75th St.
Woodridge, IL 60517
PH: 800-588-8100
FAX: 630-985-1588
stampcollections@drbobstamps.com
www.drbobfriedmanstamps.com

### Stamp Stores

### Indiana

**KNIGHT STAMP & COIN CO.**
237 Main St.
Hobart, IN 46342
PH: 219-942-4341
PH: 800-634-2646
knight@knightcoin.com
www.knightcoin.com

### New Jersey

**TRENTON STAMP & COIN**
Thomas DeLuca
Store: Forest Glen Plaza
1800 Highway #33, Suite 103
Hamilton Square, NJ 08690
Mail: PO Box 8574
Trenton, NJ 08650
PH: 609-584-8100
FAX: 609-587-8664
TOMD4TSC@aol.com
www.trentonstampandcoin.com

### Ohio

**HILLTOP STAMP SERVICE**
Richard A. Peterson
PO Box 626
Wooster, OH 44691
PH: 330-262-8907 (O)
PH: 330-201-1377 (C)
hilltop@bright.net
hilltopstamps@sssnet.com
www.hilltopstamps.com

### Supplies

### British Commonwealth

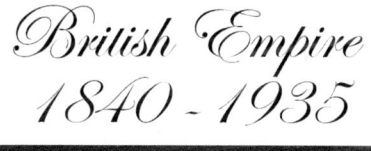

*Aden to Zululand Mint & Used
Most complete stock in North America*

For over 40 years, we have built some of the world's finest collections. Our expert *Want List Services* can do the same for you. Over 50 volumes filled with singles, sets and rare stamps, we are sure we have what you need. We welcome your Want Lists in Scott or Stanley Gibbons numbers.

Put our expertise to work for you today!
You'll be glad you did!

"Rarity and quality are remembered
...long after price is forgotten"

5757 Wilshire Blvd., Penthouse 8
Los Angeles, CA 90036 USA
Tel: +1 (323) 933-9435 Fax: +1 (323) 939-9930

Email: Info@ColonialStamps.com
www.ColonialStamps.com

Ask for your free
Public Auction
Catalogue today!

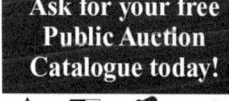

## Supplies

**BROOKLYN GALLERY COIN & STAMP, INC.**
8725 4th Ave.
Brooklyn, NY 11209
PH: 718-745-5701
FAX: 718-745-2775
info@brooklyngallery.com
www.brooklyngallery.com

## Topicals - Columbus

**MR. COLUMBUS**
PO Box 1492
Fennville, MI 49408
PH: 269-543-4755
David@MrColumbus1492.com
www.MrColumbus1492.com

## United States

**ACS STAMP COMPANY**
2914 W 135th Ave
Broomfield, Colorado 80020
303-841-8666
www.ACSStamp.com

**BROOKMAN STAMP CO.**
PO Box 90
Vancouver, WA 98666
PH: 360-695-1391
PH: 800-545-4871
FAX: 360-695-1616
info@brookmanstamps.com
www.brookmanstamps.com

**MILLER'S STAMP COMPANY**
P.O. Box 1011
Niantic, CT 06357
www.millerstamps.com
PH: 860-908-6200

## U.S. Classics/Moderns

**BARDO STAMPS**
PO Box 7437
Buffalo Grove, IL 60089
PH: 847-634-2676
jfb7437@aol.com
www.bardostamps.com

## U.S.-Collections Wanted

**DUTCH COUNTRY AUCTIONS**
The Stamp Center
4115 Concord Pike
Wilmington, DE 19803
PH: 302-478-8740
FAX: 302-478-8779
auctions@dutchcountryauctions.com
www.dutchcountryauctions.com

## U.S.-Collections Wanted

**DR. ROBERT FRIEDMAN & SONS STAMP & COIN BUYING CENTER**
2029 W. 75th St.
Woodridge, IL 60517
PH: 800-588-8100
FAX: 630-985-1588
stampcollections@drbobstamps.com
www.drbobfriedmanstamps.com

## Wanted - Worldwide Collections

**DUTCH COUNTRY AUCTIONS**
The Stamp Center
4115 Concord Pike
Wilmington, DE 19803
PH: 302-478-8740
FAX: 302-478-8779
auctions@dutchcountryauctions.com
www.dutchcountryauctions.com

## Websites

**ACS STAMP COMPANY**
2914 W 135th Ave
Broomfield, Colorado 80020
303-841-8666
www.ACSStamp.com

## Worldwide

**GUILLERMO JALIL**
Maipu 466, local 4
1006 Buenos Aires
Argentina
guillermo@jalilstamps.com
philatino@philatino.com
www.philatino.com (worldwide stamp auctions)
www.jalilstamps.com (direct sale, worldwide stamps)

## Worldwide-Collections

**DR. ROBERT FRIEDMAN & SONS STAMP & COIN BUYING CENTER**
2029 W. 75th St.
Woodridge, IL 60517
PH: 800-588-8100
FAX: 630-985-1588
stampcollections@drbobstamps.com
www.drbobfriedmanstamps.com

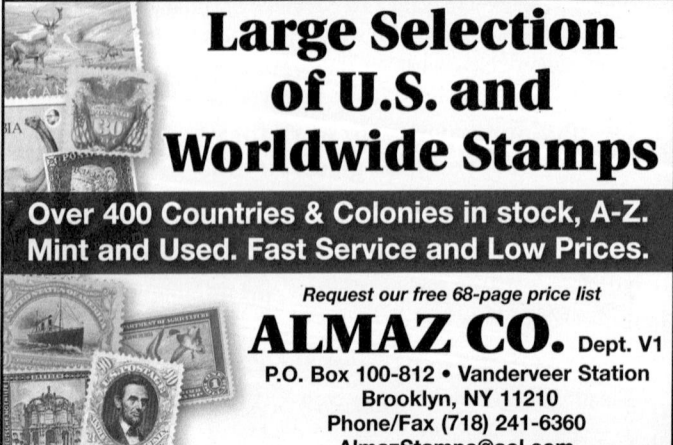

## United States

**Large Selection of U.S. and Worldwide Stamps**

Over 400 Countries & Colonies in stock, A-Z.
Mint and Used. Fast Service and Low Prices.

Request our free 68-page price list

**ALMAZ CO.** Dept. V1
P.O. Box 100-812 • Vanderveer Station
Brooklyn, NY 11210
Phone/Fax (718) 241-6360
AlmazStamps@aol.com